ENCYCLOPEDIA OF
Banking & Finance

# ENCYCLOPEDIA OF Banking & Finance

NINTH EDITION
REVISED AND EXPANDED

GLENN G. MUNN
F. L. GARCIA
CHARLES J. WOELFEL

**BANKERS PUBLISHING COMPANY
PROBUS PUBLISHING COMPANY
Chicago, Illinois
Cambridge, England**

© 1993, Glenn G. Munn, F. L. Garcia, and Charles J. Woelfel

ALL RIGHTS RESERVED. No part of this publication may be reproduced, stored in a retrieval system, or transmitted by any means, electronic, mechanical, photocopying, recording, or otherwise, without the prior written permission of the publisher and the copyright holder.

This publication is designed to provide accurate and authoritative information in regard to the subject matter covered. It is sold with the understanding that the publisher is not engaged in rendering legal, accounting or other professional service.

Authorization to photocopy items for internal or personal use, or the internal or personal use of specific clients, is granted by PROBUS PUBLISHING COMPANY, provided that the US$7.00 per page fee is paid directly to Copyright Clearance Center, 27 Congress Street, Salem MA 01970, USA; Phone: 1-(508) 744-3350. For those organizations that have been granted a photocopy license by CCC, a separate system of payment has been arranged. The fee code for users of the Transactional Reporting Service is: 1-55738-378-2/93/$0.00 + $7.00

ISBN 1-55738-378-2

Printed in the United States of America

BB

1 2 3 4 5 6 7 8 9 0

Publisher's Foreword

The *Encyclopedia of Banking and Finance* has been the preeminent publication of Bankers Publishing Company since 1924. Throughout the encyclopedia's sixty-seven year history it has been recognized as the standard authority in its field. Considered indispensable by librarians, it can be found in most public, university, and special libraries where it is used by business professionals and students at all levels. However, it can also be found as part of the everyday working library of bank officers, institutional investors, corporate treasurers, and other financial executives. In addition to these traditional readers, the recent burgeoning interest in business, economics, and personal finance has resulted in wider use of the encyclopedia among the general public, who are increasingly concerned with money, banking, investments, and the effect that the country's , and even the world's, economy is having on their daily lives. It is for this composite audience that the revised and expanded ninth edition was carefully prepared.

In the period since the last edition was published in 1983, the banking and financial services industry has been faced with tremendous change. technology has dramatically revolutionized operations. Competition for control of the world's assets and a blurring distinction among banks, investment companies, brokerage firms, insurance companies, and retailing giants has resulted in far-reaching and dramatic developments. The savings and loan crisis has focused the attention of every taxpayer on the financial services industry. The need for information on all aspects of the financial world has never been stronger.

The encyclopedia contains almost 4200 entries. In addition to definitions of thousands of basic banking, business, and financial terms, in-depth entries provide a wealth of valuable information such as historical background, analysis of recent trends, illustrative examples, statistical data, and citation of applicable laws and regulations.

Each term was reviewed, recent developments were researched, and the term's entry was updated and expanded as necessary. New terms were added to reflect developments in the field. Bibliographies, tables, and other statistical material were updated with the latest information available in Fall 1990. Then all manuscript copy was given the most thorough independent review in the history of the encyclopedia. Each entry term was edited for clarity and consistency of style. material was reorganized and placed under a new or different entry term whenever this would result in greater convenience for the reader.

Page headings are another feature that make it easier and faster to locate entries. Each left-hand page is headed by the first entry and each right-hand page is headed by the last entry appearing on these pages.

A style of SMALL CAPS is used to indicate a cross-reference. These appear both within the discussion of an entry term and at the end of entries. These frequent cross-references are very helpful in locating further information within the encyclopedia. As an aid to researching information beyond the scope of the encyclopedia, bibliographies have been included at the end of many entries.

In summary, every effort was made to make this edition worthy of its widely admired predecessors. We recognize, as did the original editor Glenn G. Munn in 1924, that "a work of this compass may not be wholly free from error and that it is capable of improvement and elaboration." Work on the next edition will begin shortly and we welcome your criticisms and your participation in the living growth of this fine work.

Preface to the Ninth Edition

The *Encyclopedia of Banking and Finance* has deservedly earned the reputation as the preeminent publication in its field. Under the creative talents of its original editor Glen G. Munn from 1924 to 1947 and later under the editorship of Professor F. L. Garcia, the encyclopedia has been recognized as the standard authority in banking in the United States. The revised and expanded ninth edition is intended to follow in the paths prepared by its predecessors. The ninth edition updates the monumental information base established in prior editions and incorporates banking and financial developments since the 1984 edition.

Since 1984, the banking system has responded to major operating and structural innovations such as electronic banking, deregulation, and Garn-St Germain. In the middle and late 1980s, banking and financial institutions have had to deal with such major issues as regulatory compliances; new products (e.g., CATS, ZEBRAS, PERLS, STAGS, and STRIPS); nonbanking financial intermediaries expansions; the increasing competitiveness of the banking environment; major bank failures; deterioration of the savings and loan industry and bailout efforts; intrastate and interstate banking expansion which encompassed 45 of the United States in 1989; governmental housing scandals; bank mergers; the globalization of banking and investing activities; foreign banking expansion into the United States and U.S. banking expansion abroad; the drastic growth of Japanese banking in size and significance; a major stock market crash and subsequent tremors; and the emerging European Economic Community (1992).

In the 1990s, banking and financial institutions will experience the impact of many of these same issues but will also focus or refocus on questions of mission, goals and objectives; adapting to change; monetary and fiscal policies directions; supervisory and regulatory considerations; risk-based capital adequacy; risk management; marketing financial services; customer and community service; wholesale and retail lending activities; computerization of the industry; accounting rules and regulations; profitability and cost controls; uncertainty, volatility, and vulnerability; a competitive environment; asset/liability management; and continuing professional education and training.

The encyclopedia deals with these issues and many other product, structural, and regulatory developments within the banking and financial industries. The quality of bank management will be the key to how the financial industry will adapt to its evolving environment. Information will be the critical factor in the management equation. This encyclopedia has been designed to assist those individuals and entities facing these problems and opportunities meet their responsibilities.

In Glenn Munn's Preface to First Edition, Munn wrote: "It has been the author's aim to attain three ends: (1) comprehensiveness, (2) accuracy, and (3) convenience." These have also been the overriding objectives of the current editor.

Encyclopedia entries contain a variety of information: examples; statistical data; citations of laws and regulations; and bibliographies (e.g., dictionaries, encyclopedias, basic references, manuals, textbooks, and journal articles). Relevance and timeliness were primary considerations in determining what information to include.

Entry selection for inclusion in the encyclopedia was based primarily on their relationship to banking and financial institutions. While some of the entries are necessarily brief, many others are comprehensive and encyclopedic in nature. Professional judgment determined what the coverage should be. Careful cross-referencing enhances the useability of the encyclopedia. Multiple bibliographies broaden the scope of the work.

The editor communicated with and consulted many individuals and organizations: Federal departments and agencies; regulatory agencies; U.S. Senate and House banking and finance committees; international financial institutions and agencies; regional and national stock exchanges; bankers; and academicians. The editor also conducted extensive library searches, examined scholarly production, reviewed chronicles and public records, archives, periodical indexes, periodicals (newspapers, magazines, journals, newsletters, and looseleaf services), and official publications (expecially accounting and regulatory).

In the writing process, the editor placed emphasis on content, fitness, emphasis (proportion), meaning, and language (grammar, rhetoric, and logic). It is hoped that the style is clear, concise, complete, and appropriate to the task (suitable, fit, and precise). Attention to detail promoted accuracy and thoroughness. Finally, the editor strove mightily to prepare the encyclopedia with a passion for honesty and nonpartisanism. Objectivity was a co-editor throughout the research and writing phases of the project.

The editor has focused on utilizing original sources wherever possible and verifying secondary sources whenever relied upon. The editor has relied heavily on official documents and publications for descriptions of governmental departments, agencies, boards, and committees. The editor is especially grateful to Bank Administration Institute and the following persons for their insightful comments and suggestions: Mr. Willis I. Else, *Senior Vice President*, National City Corporation; Mr. Gerald M. Gunn, *Senior Vice President*, Bank of America; Mr. Charles J.T. Kovacs, *Vice President*, Chase Manhatten Bank, NA; Mr. John W. Spiegel, *Executive Vice President*, SunTrust Banks, Inc.; Mr. Lester J. Stephens, Jr., *Senior Vice President*, Chase Manhatten Bank, NA.

CHARLES J. WOELFEL

Preface to First Edition

In addition to the general encyclopedia, many of the more important branches of knowledge have brought forth special encyclopedias of their own. There have appeared encyclopedias of law, medicine, engineering, economics, literature, accounting, business, and other subjects. In fact, many of these subjects can boast of several specialized encyclopedias. Because of the scope, complexity, and growing importance of banking and finance in the economic life of the nation, it would appear that an encyclopedia of banking and finance is altogether fitting. Accordingly, the publication of this volume marks the advent of the first encyclopedia of American banking and finance.

In a country where there are over 30,000 banking institutions of various types; the total value of securities reaching an aggregate of over one hundred billion dollars; millions of dollars of new securities being offered for sale to the public annually; practically every business having relations with a bank in one or more important respects; over 90 percent of the business transacted by means of credit paper; the check system in practically universal use; banking and currency regulated by law and regulatory bodies more strictly than in most other countries; and interest in wealth, money, credit, finance, foreign exchange and trusts, constantly growing; the need for an authoritative encyclopedia, covering the entire subject-matter of these related branches, should be too obvious to require further emphasis. Certainly, the banking and financial field is entitled to be dignified by placing an encyclopedia at its disposal quite as much as other professions where encyclopedias have already been provided.

There may be some objection to the designation of this book as an encyclopedia. It is true that terms and expressions, as well as financial slang, have been selected without reference to their dignity. The sole test of admissibility has been whether the term finds a place in the actual vocabulary of bankers, investors, financiers, and brokers. Some of these terms and expressions, having been borrowed from other fields, have an entirely distinct and separate connotation in the language of finance.

Many definitions will necessarily appear to be distorted unless they are viewed in their specialized sense—that of finance. But wherever possible, it has been the aim to interpret the several applications of such terms, including the general, but always with particular weight given to the banking or financial approach. While in many cases definitions and explanations are brief, especially where special meanings are denoted, it will be found that on the whole, both as respects the number of terms included and the detail with which the subject-matter is treated, the work is truly of an encyclopedic character. This contention is reinforced by the fact that in the great majority of instances cross references to other terms are cited, and in the case of the more important subjects, biblographies are appended.

While this volume claims to be the first encyclopedia of American banking and finance, there is no intention on the part of the author or publishers to create the impression that this is the first work presenting definitions of terms belonging to this field

In 1919, a very excellent and complete *Dictionary of Banking* dealing exclusively with British practice was published in London with William Thompson as author. Owing to the many differences between American and British banking systems, laws, practice, and nomenclature, however, this book could perform but scant service in the United States.

This encyclopedia of banking and finance has also had its American predecessors. In 1903, Mr. Howard Irving Smith published a Financial Dictionary, which has long since been out of print. This was followed in 1907 by Mr. Montgomery Rollin's *Money and Investments*, primarily intended as a handbook for investors.

In 1911, there appeared *The Financial encyclopedia*, edited by Mr. C. A. Shea. This was a two volume work of somewhat greater pretentiousness, and contained definitions of many business terms. In 1923, the Thomas Y. Crowell Company brought out *Crowell's Dictionary of Business and Finance*, which is chiefly a compendium of business terms.

None of these volumes, although excellent as far as they go, covers the same field or was designed to meet the same purpose as this encyclopedia. The essential function of this volume is to serve the banking, financial, and allied vocations by providing explanations of greater length than has heretofore been attempted—of the subjects that are comprehended within the limits of this department of economic life. It lays no claim to being a business encyclopedia.

In the sense that this book presents subjects with which practically every individual and business necessarily has an interest, its appeal as a reference work should be almost universal. Its most direct appeal, however, is to banks and trust companies, both executives and employees, investment and stock exchange houses, insurance companies, financiers, brokers, investors, speculators, lawyers, and students of banking, finance, and markets. As an aid to university students specializing in courses in applied economomics, this compilation should prove indispensable.

In the preparation of this encyclopedia, which has covered a period of nearly three years, it has been the author's aim to attain three ends: (1) comprehensiveness, (2) accuracy, and (3) convenience.

Comprehensiveness. This book contains some 3,050 terms. These have been gained from the author's seven years' experience in teaching classes in banking, finance, and economics; from first-hand acquaintance with the affairs of the "Street"; and from an extensive search of the bibliography of the field, including the banking and financial magazines, and the reports and publications of the various official organizations concerned with the regulation of banking. As a result, this volume is more than a mere glossary or list of definitions. A full exposition of the most important subjects is presented. There has also been included the text of the principal banking laws, and the forms and phraseology of the principal instruments of banking and finance.

Accuracy. An honest attempt has been made to achieve accuracy. Original sources have been employed wherever possible. The work of the author has been reviewed by six different experts in their own field. Great care has been taken to secure fine distinctions. In many instances, several meanings or applications of the same term have been stated.

Convenience. A tremendous mass of organized information pertaining to money, banking, credit, and finance has been brought within the covers of a single volume. Whatever other advantages this encyclopedia may possess, it should prove a valuable time-saving device for locating desired information quickly, Being alphabetically arranged, it is an automatic index, and should be considered a labor-saving device in a bank or investment house just as much as a telautograph, announciator, or bookkeeping machine. Cross-references have been widely employed. Thus, the reader is given access to all aspects of a subject by bringing his attention to related subjects.

Grateful acknowledgment is made of the cooperation received from the following persons who reviewed separate portions of the encyclopedia, and who made many valuable suggestions and criticisms: Eugene E. Agger, Ph.D., associate professor of economics, Columbia University, reviewed the terms pertaining to money, credit, and banking history and principles; L. H. Langston, M.S., author of *Practical Bank Operation*, and President of the Benjamin Franklin Institute, reviewed the terms pertaining to practical banking and foreign exchange; Harold Dudley Greeley, LL.M., C.P.A., (N.Y.), practicing public accountant, member New York Bar, and Lecturer at Columbia University, reviewed terms pertaining to accounting and auditing; Henry Hazlitt, formerly financial editor of the *New York Evening Mail*, reviewed terms pertaining to speculation, markets, and brokerage; J. E. Brady, LL.B., editor of the *Business Law Journal*, reviewed terms relating to trusts and bank law; and Richard Roelofs, Jr., of Hallgarten & Company, New York City, reviewed terms on investments.

The writer is also indebted to a number of publishing houses and other organizations which have kindly granted permission to quote passages from various authors and books. Further reference to these books and authors is made either in footnotes to the text or in connection with bibliographies at the conclusion of certain terms.

It is clearly recognized that a work of this compass may not be wholly free from error and that it is capable of improvement and elaboration. Suggestions for additional terms, and criticisms relating to included terms, or otherwise, will be welcomed.

GLENN G. MUNN

About the Editors

Mr. Munn was for many years a vice president of the brokerage firm of Paine, Webber, Jackson & Curtis in New York City. Prior to joining this firm he had worked with the Chase National Bank and the Standard & Poors Corporation, both of New York City. Mr. Munn was active in the American Institute of Banking where he taught courses in both the New York City and Hudson County, New Jersey chapters. He was also the author of the book, *Meeting the Bear Market*. Mr. Munn died in September, 1977.

Professor Garcia enjoyed a multifaceted career in banking and finance with exemplary credentials in both the academic and professional worlds. He earned a B.S. cum laude from New York University; an LL.B. and J.D. from Brooklyn Law School; and LL.M. from National University School of Law in Washington, D.C.; and an M.A. in economics from Fordham University.

He also received diplomas from the American Institute of Banking in both commercial banking and investment banking. He was the recipient of a Ford Foundation grant to study at the Graduate School of Business Administration at Harvard University. Professor Garcia taught finance at Southeastern University, Georgetown University, and finally at Fordham University. He served as chairperson of the department of finance at Fordham and was named professor emeritus by Fordham's College of Business Administration after twenty-five years on the faculty. Professor Garcia practiced law in Washington, D.C. and held two positions as a security analyst in New York City. The first of these was with the over-the-counter market firm of Hoit, Rose & Troster and the second was as manager of the analytical department of R.M. Horner & Company. He was a member of the New York Society of Security Analysts, a fellow of the National Federation of Financial Analysts, and a member of the New York bar. He is the author of *How to Analyze a Bank Statement*, also published by Bankers Publishing Company. Mr. Garcia died in 1987.

Dr. Charles Woelfel, Professor of Accounting at the University of North Carolina in Greensboro, North Carolina, is the editor of the *Encyclopedia of Banking & Finance, 9th edition*. He is a graduate of Notre Dame University, has a Doctorate from the University of Texas and has authored numerous books and professional journal articles in the areas of business, finance and accounting. In light of the many recent developments in banking and finance, Dr. Woelfel has updated the *Encyclopedia of Banking & Finance* to meet the demands of government deregulation and compliance issues.

There are also numerous expanded entries in the areas of marketing, insurance and real estate. In addition to editing the encyclopedia, Dr. Woelfel has authored the *Complete Executive's Encyclopedia of Accounting, Finance, Investing, Banking & Economics* and the *Desktop Encyclopedia of Corporate Finance and Accounting*.

Abbreviations

Business Abbreviations

@	At
A	Series "A" Bonds or debentures; class "A" preferred or common stock
a.a.	Always afloat
a.a.r.	Against all risks
ABACUS	American Bankers Association Computer Utilization Computer System
ABS	Automated bond system
ACH	Automated clearinghouse
Al	Highest class; best grade; gilt-edged
A & F	Semiannual payments of interest or dividends in August and February
A & O	Interest payable on August 15 and February 15; likewise for other combinations, e.g., A & O, J & J, etc.
A.&r.	Air and rail
A.C.	Assistant cashier
A.c.	American conditions (insurance)
A/c, A/C	Account, account current
Acc.	Accept, acceptance, account
Acce	Acceptance
Accrd. Int.	Accrued Interest
Acct	Account, accountant
Accum.	Accumulations
ack., ackn.	Acknowedge, acknowledged
Ackgt	Acknowledgment
Acpt.	Acceptance
ACRS	Accelerated cost recovery system
A/cs Pay.	Accounts payable
A/cs Rec.	Accounts receivable
A/D	After date or alternate days
A-D	Advance-Decline line
a.d.	After date
Adj.	Adjustment, adjuster
Adm.	Administration
Admstr.	Administrator
ADR	American Depository Receipts
ADR	Automated dividend reinvested
ADR	Asset Depreciation Range System
Adv.	Advice, Advise, advance
Ad Val., A/V	Ad valorem (according to value)
A.F.B.	Air Freight Bill
AFT	Automated Funds transfer
ag.	Against
Agt	Agent
Ag'y	Agency
A.H.	After-hatch
AICPA	American Institute of Certified Accountants
A.J.O.J.	Quarterly payments of interest or dividends in April, July, October, and January
ALCO	Asset and Liability Management Committee
ALLL	Allowance for Loan and Lease Losses
ALM	Asset and liability management
alt.	Alternate
AMA	Asset management account
Am., Amer.	America, American
AMEX	American Stock Exchange
AMT	Alternative Minimum Tax
amt	Amount
a.n., A.N.	Arrival notice
A.N.F.M.	Quarterly payments of interest or dividends in August, November, February and May
Ann.	Annual, annuity
a/o, A.O., A/O	Account of
AON	All or none
a.p.	Additional premium
A/P	Authority to purchase, authority to pay
APB	Accounting Principles Board
appd	Approved
appin	Application
APR	Annual percentage rate
a.r., a/r, A/R	All rail, all risks or against all risks (marine)
ARB	Accounting Research Bulletin
Arb	Arbitrageur
ARM	Adjustable rate mortgage
arr., arr'd	Arrival, arrived
arrgt	Arrangement
Art.	Article
a.s., a/s, A/S	At sight, after sight, account sales
Asmd	Assumed
Assmet	Assessment, assortment
Assn	Association
assoc., Assoc'n	Associate, associated, association
Asst. Cash.	Assistant cashier
Astd.	Assented
Asstd.	Assorted
A/T	American terms
Atchd.	Attached
Atl.	Atlantic
ATM	Automated teller maching
ATS	Automated Transfer Service
Att.	Attention, attorney, attached
Attn	Attention
Att'y, atty	Attorney
Aud.	Auditor, audit
Avg.	Average
a.w., a/w	All water, actual weight
awb., AWB	Air waybill
B	Series "B" bonds or debentures; class "B" preferred or common stock
BA	Banker's acceptance
BAI	Bank Administration Institute
Bal., Balce	Balance
BAN	Bond amortization note
BBB	Better business bureau
BBI	Bond buyer index
B & L Assn.	Building and loan association
B/C	Bill for collection
B/D	Bills discounted, bank draft
BD	Broker/dealer
Bd	Bond, board
B/E	Bill of exchange
B/E	Break even
b/f, B/F	Brought forward
BIF	Bank Insurance Fund
BIS	Bank for International Settlements
Bk	Bank

ENCYCLOPEDIA OF BANKING AND FINANCE

ABBREVIATIONS

Bkg	Banking
B/L	Bill of lading
B/L Atchd	Bill of lading attached
B.O.	Buyer's option
BO	Branch office
BOM	Beginning of month
BOP	Balance of payments
BOT	Bought
B.M.	Board measure
B/P, B'PAY	Bills payable
B/R, B'REC	Bills receivable
B.S., B/S	Bill of sale, balance sheet
BSA	Bank Secrecy Act
Bt	Bought
BTA	Board of Tax Appeals
B.t.u.	British Thermal unit
B/V	Book Value
¢	Cents in U.S. and Canada
c	Cents, circa, clean
C	Series "C" bonds or debentures; class "C" preferred or common stock; contra
C.A.	Chartered accountant, current assets
C/A	Current assets, capital account, credit account
Cab.	Cables, cabinet (bonds), cabin
C.A.D.	Cash against documents
C.A.F., c.a.f.	Cost, assurance, freight
Canc.	Cancel, cancellation
C & D, c & d	Collection and delivery
C & F, c & f	Cost and freight
C & I, c & i	Cost and insurance
CAMEL	Capital / asset quality / management / earnings / liquidity regulatory ratings
Cap.	Capital, capitalization, capacity
Cap'y	Capacity
Carr. pd., Cge. pd.	Carriage paid
Cash.	Cashier
Cash B/L	Cash against bill of lading
Cash Docs	Cash against documents
CATS	Certificate of accrual on Treasury securities
C/B	Cash book
CBA	Cost-benefit analysis
CBCT	Customer-bank communications terminal
C.B.D.	Cash before delivery
CBOE	Chicago Board of Option Exchange
CCh	Commerce Clearning House
C.C.	Cashier's check, contra credit
C/D, C.D.	Certificate of deposit, cash discount
cd forwd	Carried forward
CEO	Chief executive officer
Cert.	Certify, certified, certification, certificate
C.F.&I, c.f.&i, c.f.	Cost, freight and insurance
CF	Commercial finance
CFA	Chartered Financial Analyst
CFO	Chief financial officer
CFR	Code of Federal Regulations
C.H.	Clearing House, customs house
Chgs	Charges
Ch. ppd.	Charges prepaid
Chq.	Cheque
C/I	Certificate(s) of indebtedness
C.I., c.i.	Cost and insurance
C.I.A., c.i.a.	Cash in advance
C.I.&F., c.i.&f.	Cost, insurance and freight
C,U,F.&C.,	Cost, insurance, freight and commissions (or c.i.f.&c charges)
C.I.F.C.&I.,	Cost, insurance, freight, commisions (or c.i.f.c.&i collection) and interest
C.I.F.&E., c.i.f.&e.	Cost, insurance, freight and exchange
C.I.F.&I.	Cost, insurance, freight and interest
C.I.F.C.E.&I.,	Cost, insurance, freight, commissions (or c.i.f.c.e.&i. collection), exchange and interest
C.I.F.I., c.i.f.i.	Cost, insurance, freight and interest
C.I.F.I.&E., c.i.f.i.&e.	Cost, insurance, freight, interest and exchange
Ck	Check
C.L., c.l.	Carload, current liabilities
C/L	Cash letter, current liabilities
CL	Commercial loan
CLADR	Class life asset depreciation range (tax)
Cl	Class
Cl, B/L	Clean bill of lading
c.l.d.	Cost laid down
Cld.	Cleared
CMO	Collateralized mortgage obligation
CMV	Current market value
coml, com'l, comm'l	Commercial
CN	Consignment note
C/N	Credit note
C.O.	Cash order
CO.	Company
COC	Comtroller of the Currency
C.O.D., c.o.d.	Cash on delivery
Coll.	Collateral, collection
Coll/L	Collection letter
Coll, Tr.	Collateral trust
Com	Common
Com'l Paper	Commercial paper
Comm.	Commission
Comp.	Comparison, compound, composite
Comp't	Comptroller
Conf., conf.	Confirm, confirmation, conference
Cons. Cert.	Consular certificate
Con. cr.	Contra credit
Cons.	Consolidated, consigned, consignment, consul
Consol.	Consolidated
Constr.	Construction
Contra	Against
Conv.	Convertible
Corp.	Corporation, corporate
Corr.	Correspondent, corresponding, correspondence
C/P	Charter party, custom of the port
CP	Commercial paper
C.P.A.	Certified public accountant
CPFF	Cost plus fixed fee
CPI	Consumer price index
CPM	Cost per thousand
CPPC	Cost plus a percentage of cost
Cps.	Coupons
C/R, C.R., c.r.	Current rate, company's risk
CR	Class rate, carrier risk, current rate
CR, cr	Credit, creditor
CRA	Community Reinvestment Act
C.R.M.	Cash by return mail, cash on receipt of merchandise
CRT	Cathode Ray Tube
C.R.S.	Cash by return steamer
c/s	Case(s)
C.S.	Capitol Stock
CSVLI	Cash surrencer value of insurance
CT, C/T	Collateral trust, cable transfer
C.T.L.	Constructive total loss
Ctfs	Certificates
Cts	Cents, centimes
Cum.	Cumulative
Curr.	Current, currency
CUSIP	Communiform security identification procedure
Cv.	Convertible
Cvt.	Convert, Convertible
C.W.O., c.w.o.	Cash with order
CWT, cwt	Hundredweight
Cy	Currency
D	Days, discount, delivery dollar
d	Pence, day, dollar
D/A, d/a	Documents against acceptance, days after acceptance, deposit account, discharge afloat, deductible average
D.A.D.	Documents against discretion (of collecting bank)
D/atchd	Documents attached
D&B	Dun & Bradstreet
D.&J.	Semiannual payments of interest or dividends in

ENCYCLOPEDIA OF BANKING AND FINANCE

ABBREVIATIONS

	December and June
d.b.a.	Doing busines as
DBF	Domestic bought funds
DC	Deep discount issue (bond)
D/C	Deviation clause
D/D, d/d	Delivered docks, demand draft, days after date, delivered
D.D.	Deferred delivery
DDA	Demand deposit account
DDB	Double-declining balance depreciation
Deb., Debs.	Debenture(s)
Decl., decl.	Declaration, declared
Def., def.	Deficit, deferred, definitive, default
Del'y, dely	Delivery
Dem.	Demand, demurrage
Denom.	Denomination
Dep.	Deposit, depositary
Depr.	Depreciation
D.F., d/f	Dead freight
DFT/a, dft/a	Draft attached
DFT/c, dft/c	Clean draft
DIF	Deposit insurance fund
Dir.	Director
Disbs.	Disbursements
Disc.	Discount
Disch.	Discharge(d), Discharging
Div.	Dividend, divisional
DL	Day letter
D/L	Demand Loan
Dls.	Dollars
D.M.J.S.	Quarterly payments of interest or dividends in December, March, June, and September
D/N	Demand note, debit note
D/O, d/o	Delivery order
Docs, docs	Documents
D.O.F., d.o.f.	Delivery (delivered) on field
Dom. Ex.	Domestic exchange
D/P	Documents against payment
DPC	Debt previously contracted
D/R	Deposit receipt
Dr.	Debit, debtor, drawer
D/S, d/s	Days sight, days after sight
D/W	Dead weight, dock warrant
dwt	Penny weight
E.& O.E.	Errors and omissions excepted
EA	Earnings asset
E&O	Errors & omissions
E.c	English conditions (insurance)
ECOA	Equal Credit Opportunity Act
EDD	Estimated delivery date
EDM	End of month
EDP	Electronic data processing
E.E.	Errors excepted
EE	Series EE savings bonds
EFTA	Economic Recovery Tax Act of 1981
EFTS	Electronic Fund Transfer System (Service)
EITF	Emerging Issues Task Force
Encl.	Enclosure, enclosed
End.	Endorsement, endorsed)
End. Guar.	Endorsement guaranteed
E.O.M.	End of month
E.O.S.	End of season
E/P	Earnings/price ratio
EPS	Earnings per share
E.P.T.	Excess profits tax
Eq. Tr.	Equipment trust
ERA	Equal Rights Amendment
ESIRA	Employee Retirement Income Security Act
ESOP	Employee stock option plan
Est., est'd	Estimate(d), establish(ed)
e.t.a.	Estimated time of arrival
Ex	Without, out of
Ex., ex'd	Extension, extended
Exch.	Exchange, Exchequer
Exd.	Examined
Ex D, Ex Div.	Ex dividend, i.e., without dividend
Ex Int.	Ex interest, i.e., without interest
Exmr.	Examiner
Exp.	Expense, expresss, export
Ex R, Ex Rts.	Ex rights, i.e., without rights
Ex Ship	Delivered out of ship
Extd.	Extended
Ex W, Ex Warr.	Ex warrants, i.e., without warrants
Ex Whse.	Delivered out of warehouse
F	Flat, folio
F.A., f.a.	Free alongside, fixed assets
F.A.A., f.a.a.	Free of all average
FAF	Financial Accounting Foundation
F.A.F., f.a.f.	Free at factory or fly away at factory
F.A.M., f.a.m.	Free at mill
F.a.q.	Fair average
FASB	Financial Accounting Standards Board
F.A.S., f.a.s.	Free alongside ship
FAX	Facsimile
F.B., f.b.	Freight bill
F.B.H., f.b.h.	Free on board in harbor
F.C.S., f.c.s.	Free of capture and seizure
F.C.S.R. & C.C.,	Free of capture, seizure, riots, and civil commotion
F/d	Free docks
F. * D.	Freight and demurrage
Fd.	Fund
Fdg.	Funding
FED	Federal Reserve System
FEI	Financial Executives Institute
FF	Federal funds
F.f.a.	Free foreign agency
F.F.A., f.f.a.	Free from alongside
F.G.A., f.g.a.	Free general average, foreign general average
F.I.A., f.i.a.	Full interest admitted
F.I.B., f.i.b.	Free into bunker or barge
FICA	Federal Insurance Contribution Act
Fid.	Fidelity, fiduciary
FIFO	First in, first out
Fin.	Finance, financial
F.I.O., f.i.o.	Free in and out
FIRREA	Financial Institutions Reform, Recovery, and Enforcement Act
F.I.T., f.i.t.	Free in truck
Flt	Flat
F.M.A.N.	Quarterly payments of interest or dividends in February, May, August, and November
FMC	Fair market value
F.O.	Free over side
f.o.	For orders
F.O.B., f.o.b.	Free on board
F.O.C., f.o.c.	Free of charge(s)
F.O.D., f.o.d.	Free of damage(s)
F.O.I., f.o.i	Free of interest
FOIA	Freedom of Information Act
FOK	Fill or kill
Fol.	Folio, following
F.O.R., f.o.r.	Free on rails
Forg.	Forgery
F.O.S., f.o.s.	Free on steamer
F.O.T., f.o.t.	Free on truck
F.O.W., f.o.w.	Free on wagons or water
F.P.A., f.p.a.	Free of particular average
F.P.A.A.C., f.p.a.a.c.	Free of particular average (American conditions)
F.P.A.E.C., f.p.a.e.c.	Free of particular average (English conditions)
F.pd.	Fully paid
F.R.B.	Federal Reserve Bank
Frt.	Freight
FSLIC	Federal Savings and Loan Insurance Corporation
FTP	Funds transfer pricing
FUTA	Federal Unemployment Compensation Act
Fwd.	Forward
F.X., FX	Foreign exchange
Fxd	Fixed
FY	Fiscal year, Future value
Fy pd.	Fully paid

ENCYCLOPEDIA OF BANKING AND FINANCE

ABBREVIATIONS

G.A., G/A	General average	LC	Deferred cable
GAAP	Generally accepted accounting principles	L.c.l.	Less than carload
GASB	Governmental Accounting Standards Board	LDC	Less developed country
G.D.	Good delivery	Ld. Gt.	Land grant
Gen.	General	Led.	Ledger
Gen. Led.	General ledger	L.F.	Ledger folio
Gen. Mtge.	General mortgage	LIBOR	London Interbank Offering Rate
GO	Government obligation bond, General obligation	LIFO	Last in, first out
GPM	Government payment bond	Ln.	Lien
Govt.	Government	Loco.	On the spot
Grs. T.	Gross ton	LPA	Loan Production Office
G.T.C.	Good 'til canceled	L.S.	Locus sigilli (place for seal)
Gtd.	Guaranteed	Lshld	Leasehold
Guar.	Gurantee(d)	L.t.	Long ton
		Ltd.	Limited
HELOC	Home equity line of credit	L. tn.	Long ton
HLT	Highly leveraged transaction	Ltr.	Letter
HMDA	Home Mortgage Disclosure Act		
H.O.	Head or home office	MACRS	Modified accelerated cost recovery system
Hon'd	Honored	M. & N.	Semiannual payments of interest or dividends in May and November
H.R. 10	Keogh plan	M. & S.	Semiannual payments of interest or dividends in March and September
IASC	International Accounting Standards Committee	M.A.N.F.	Quarterly payments of interest or dividends in May, August, November, and February
IBAA	Independent Bankers Association of America		
IBF	International Banking Facility	Marg.	Margin
ICC	Income capital certificate	Mat. or Mat'y	Maturity
Ident.	Identification	MBO	Management by objectives
Indent.	Indenture	M-cats	Municipal certificates of accumulation on tax-exempt securities
Imp.	Improvement, import		
Inc.	Income, incorporated	MCC	Mutual capital certificate
Ind. Led.	Individual ledger	M.D., m.d., m/d	Months' date or months after date
Indm.	Indemnity		
Ins.	Insurance, insured	Mdse.	Merchandise
Inst.	Instant (of the present month), installment, instrument	MFA	Most favored nation (tariff)
		Mfst.	Manifest
Int.	Interest	M.I.P.	Marine insurance policy, monthly investment plan
Intermed.	Interermediate	M.J.S.D.	Quarterly payments of interest or dividends in March, June, September, and December
In trans.	In transit		
Inv.	invoice, investing, investment	Mkt.	Market
I.O.U.	I owe you (debt memorandum)	M/m	Made merchandise
I. P/A	Individual, partnership, and corporation (deposits)	MMC	Money market certificate
IRA	Individual Retirement Account	MMDA	Money market deposit account
IRB	Internal Revenue Bulletins	MMMFTP	Matched maturity marginal fund transfer pricing
IRC	Internal Revenue Code	M.O.	Money order or mail order
IRR	Internal rate of return	M.O.M.	Middle of the month
Irred.	Irredeemable	M/P, M.P.	Months after payment, mail payment
Irrev.	Irrevocable	MSA	Metropolitan statistical area
ITC	Investment tax credit	MS	Margin of safety
J/A, J.A.	Joint account	M/S, M.S., m/s	Months after sight, months' sight
J.A.J.O.	Quarterly payments of interest or dividends in January, April, July, and October	Mtg., Mtge.	Mortgage
J. & D.	Semiannual payments of interest or dividends in June and December	Mty.	Maturity
		Mun.	Municipal
J. & J.	Semiannual payments of interest or dividends in January and July	N/A, n/a, n.a.	No account, nonacceptance
J.O.J.A.	Quarterly payments of interest or dividends in July, October, January, and April	N. & M.	Semiannual payments of interest or dividends in November and May
Jour.	Journal	NASD	National Association of Securities Dealers
Jr.	Junior	Natl.	National
J.S.D.M.	Quarterly payments of interest or dividends in June, September, December, and March	N/B	Nota Bene (note well)
		N.C.	Noncallable
Jt.	Joint	N.D., n.d.	Not dated
Jun.	Junior, June	Neg. Inst.	Negotiable instrument
		N/E	No effects
K	Kilo	n.e.i.	Not elsewhere included or indicated
KD, kd	Knocked down	n.e.m.	Not elsewhere mentioned
KD, l.c.l.	Knocked down in less than carload lots	N.F., N/F, NF	No funds
Kg	Kilogram	N.G.	Not good
Kw	Kilowatt	NIM	Net interest margin
Kwh	Kilowatt hour	NL	Night letter
		NL	No load
L/A	Letter of authority	NOL	Net operating loss
L. & D., l. & d.	Loans and discounts, loss and damage	N/m	No mark
L.b.	Long bill	N/O	No orders
LBO	Leveraged buyout	No.	Number
L/C, l/c	Letter of credit	No a/c	No account

No Adv.	No advice	P.L.	Partial loss
Non-cum	Noncumulative	P.L.	Price list
Non-vtg.	Nonvoting	PLC	Public utility company
n.o.p.	Not otherwise provided	P.M., pm.	Purchase money mortgage, premium
n.o.p.f.	Not otherwise provided for	PMI	Private mortgage insurance
n.o.s.	Not otherwise stated	PN	Promissory note
Not. Pub.	Notary public	POD	Price on delivery
NOW account	Negotiable Order of Withdrawal Account	POL	Port of embarkation, port of entry
N/P, N.P.	Notes payable, notary public	P.O.R.	Payable on receipt
N.P.N.A.	No protest nonacceptance	POS	Point-of-sale electronic transfer payments system
NPV	Net present value	POST	Point-of-sale terminal or transfer
N/R	Notes receivable	P.p.	By proxy
n.s.	Not specified	P.P.I.F.I.A.	Policy proof of interest, full interest admitted
NSE	New York Stock Exchange	Prem.	Premium
N.S.F.	Not sufficient funds	Pres.	Presentation, president
n.s.p.f.	Not specially provided for	Pr. Ln.	Prior lien
Nts.	Notes	Pro.	Protest
NWC	Net worth certificate	Prox.	Proximo
		PSA	Principal supervisory agent
O/A	On account, open account	Pts.	Participating
O.A., o.a.	On acceptance	Pt. Pd.	Part paid
O. & A.	Semiannual payments of interest and dividends in October and April	P.V.	Par value
		PV	Present value
OAPEC	Organization of Arab Petroleum Exporting Countries		
		Q	Quarterly
o. & r.	Ocean and rail	QC	Quality control
OASDI	Old Age, Survivors, and Disability Insurance	Quar., Qtr.	Quarter
O.B.	Ordered back, opening of books		
O. B/L	Order bill of lading	R/A	Refer to acceptor
O/c	Open charter	RAM	Reverse annuity mortgage
Oc.B/L	Ocean bill of lading	RAN	Revenue Anticipation note
O/D, O.D.	On demand, overdraft	RAP	Regulatory account procedures
O.E., o.e.	Omissions excepted	RB	Relationship banking
O.J.A.J.	Quarterly payments of interest or dividends in October, January, April, and July	Rcd.	Received
		Rcpt., rct.	Receipt
O.K.	Correct, approved	R/D	Refer to drawer
OLEM	Other loans especially mentioned	Rdj.	Readjustment
O/N	Order notify	Rec.	Receipt, receivable
On a/c	On account	Recap.	Recapitulation, recapitalization
O/o, o/o	Order of	Redisc.	Rediscount
OPM	Other peoples money	Ref.	Refunding, referee, reference
Opt.	Option, optional	Reg.	Registered, registrar, regular
O/R	Owner's risk	Regs.	Registered tonnage
O.r.b.	Owner's risk of breakage	Reg'd	Registered
Ord.	Ordinary, order	REIT	Real estate investment trust
OREO	Other real estate owned	Rem.	Remit, remittance
O/T	Old terms	REMIC	Real estate mortgage investment conduit
O.T.C.	Over-the-Counter	Res.	Reserve, reserved
Outstdg.	Outstanding	RESPA	Real Estate Settlement Procedures Act
		REO	Real estate owned
p	Per	Rev.	Revocable
p.a., per ann.	Per annum	Rfg.	Refunding
P/A, P.A., p/a	Private account, power of attorney, particular average	R.I.	Reinsurance
		ROA	Return on assets
P. & C.	Puts and calls	ROE	Return on equity
P. & I.	Protection and indemnity	R.O.G.	Receipt of goods
P. & L.	Profit and loss	ROI	Return on investment
P. & S.	Purchase and sale	R/P, R.P.	Reply paid, return of post
PA	Power of attorney, public accountant, purchasing agent	RP	Repurchase agreement
		R.R.	Railroad
Part.	Participating	RRP	Reverse repurchase agreement
Payt.	Payment	RSA	Rate sensitive assets
PC	Participation certificate	RSL	Rate sensitive liabilities
P.C., P/C, P.c.	Percent, price current, petty cash	RSU	Remote service unite
pcs.	Pieces	Rts.	Rights
Pd	Paid	Ry.	Railway
P.D.	Post dated		
P/E	Price/earnings ratio	S.	Signed
Per cap.	Per capita	S.7	Seller's delivery in seven days (N.Y. Stock Exchange)
Per Pro.	Per procuration	S.A., SA	Semiannual
Perp.	Perpetual	SAIF	Savings Association Insurance Fund
Pf. of Pfd.	Preferred	SAVE	System for automatic value exchange
P.f.	Pro forma	S. & L. Assn.	Savings and loan association
PIN	Personal identification number	S. & M.	Semiannual payments of interest or dividends in September and March
PIP	Personal identification project		
PITA	Principal, interest, taxes, and insurance	S&P	Standard & Poor's
Pkgs.	Packages	S/b	Short bill

ABBREVIATIONS

S/D	Sight ddraft, sea dmanage
S.D.B.L.	Sight draft, bill of lading attached
S/D D/P	Sight draft documents against payment
S.D.Co.	Safe deposit company
S.D.M.J.	Quarterly payments of interest or dividends in September, December, March and June
SDR	Special drawing rights
SE	Shareholders equity
SEC	Securities and Exchange Commission
Sec.	Security, secured
SEP	Simplified employee pension plan
Ser.	Series, serial
S.F., SF	Sinking fund
SG&A	Selling, general, and administrative expenses
Sgd.	Signed
Shipt.	Shipment
Shs.	Shares
Sig.	Signature
Sig. Mis.	Signature missing
Sig. Unk.	Signature unknown
Sld.	Sold
SLO	Stop limit order, stop loss order
SMSA	Standard metropolitan statistical area
S/N	Shipping note
SNAFU	Situation normal, all fouled up
S.O., S/O	Seller's option, shipping order
SOP	Standard operating procedure, Statement of Position
S.O.S.	Suspend other service
S.P.	Stop payment, supra protest
S.S., S/S	Steamship
S.S. B/L	Steamship bill of lading
S.T., S. tn	Short ton(s)
STC'S	Stock trust certificates
Stg.	Sterling
Stk.	Stock
Stk. Exch.	Stock exchange
Stpd.	Stamped
STRIPS	Separate trading of registered interest and principal securities
Subs.	Subsidiary
Substn.	Substitution
Sur.	Surplus
S.W.	Sent wrong
S-X	SEC regulations
Synd.	Syndicate
T/A	Trade acceptance
TA	Transfer agent
T.A.N.	Tax anticipation note
T/B	Trial balance
T-bill	Treasury bill
T.C.	U.S. Tax Court
T.C.	Telegram to be repeated
TCM	Tax Court Memorandum Decision
TC's	Trust certificates
T.D.	Treasury decision
TEFRA	Tax Equity and Fiscal Responsibility Act of 1982
TEY	Tax equivalent yield
Term.	Terminal
T.f.	Till forbidden
TIL or TILA	Truth in Lending Act
TIN	Taxpayer indentification number
TM	Trade mark
TN	Treasury note
T/L	Time loan, total loss
T.L.O.	total loss only
T/R, TR, T.R.	Trust receipt, tons register
Tr. Co.	Trust company
Treas.	Treasurer, treasury
Trf.	Transfer
T.T.	Telegraphic transfer
Tx.	Tax(es)
U/a	Underwriting account
UBPR	Uniform bank performance report
UCC	Uniform Commercial Code
UCCC	Uniform Consumer Credit Code
U.K.	United Kingdom
UOP	Unit of production
USC	United States Code
USIT	Unit share investment trust
USTC	U.S. tax cases
Ult.	Ultimo (last)
U. & O.	Use and occupancy
Uif.	Unified, uniform
U/w's	Underwriters
V., vs.	Versus (against)
VAT	Value added tax
Var.	Various, variable
V.P.	Vice-president
V.T.C.'s	Voting trust certificates
Vtg.	Voting
W.A.	With average
Warr.	Warrants
W.B.	Waybill
WHOOPS	Washington Public Power Supply System
W.I., WI	When issued
W/M	Without margin, weight of measurement
W.N.P.	Wire nonpayment
W.O.G.	With other goods
W.P.	Wire payment
W.P.A.	With particular average
W/R	Warehouse receipt
W/S	With stock
W/W, ww	With warrants
W/W	Warehouse warrant
X	No protest
X-C	Ex coupon
X-D	Ex dividend
X-dis	Ex-distribution
X-I	Ex interest
X-Rts.	Ex rights
X-Warr.	Ex warrants
Y/A	York-Antwerp Rules
YLD	Yield
YTC	Yield to call
YTM	Yield to maturity
ZBA	Zero bracket account
ZBB	Zero-based budget
ZCS	Zero coupon security

Government Abbreviations

ABMC	American Battle Monuments Commission
ACDA	Arms Control and Disarmament Agency
ACE	Active Corps of Executives
ACP	Agriculture Conservation Program
ACUS	Administrative Conference of the United States
ACYF	Administration for Children, Youth, and Families
ADAMHA	Alcohol, Drug Abuse, and Mental Health Administration
ADD	Administration on Developmental Disabilities
ADP	Automatic Data Processing
ADTS	Automated Data and Telecommunications Service
AECB	Arms Export Control Board
AFDC	Aid to Families with Dependent Children
AFIX	American Forces Information System
AID	Agency for International Development
AMS	Agricultural Marketing Service
Amtrak	National Railroad Passenger Corporation
ANA	Administration for Native Americans
AOA	Administration on Aging
APHIS	Animal and Plant Health Inspection Service
ARS	Advanced Record System
ASCS	Agricultural Stabilization and Conservation Service
BEA	Bureau of Economic Analysis
BIA	Bureau of Indian Affairs

ENCYCLOPEDIA OF BANKING AND FINANCE

ABBREVIATIONS

BIB	Board for International Broadcasting	FEC	Federal Election Commission
BJS	Bureau of Justice Statistics	FEMA	Federal Emergency Management Agency
BLM	Bureau of Land Management	FFB	Federal Financing Bank
BLS	Bureau of Labor Statistics	FFIEC	Federal Financial Institutions Examination Council
BPA	Bonneville Power Administration	FGIS	Federal Grain Inspection Service
BSC	Business Service Centers	FHA	Federal Housing Administration
		FHLBB	Federal Home Loan Bank Board
CAB	Civil Aeronautics Board	FHLMC	Federal Home Loan Mortgage Corporation
CAP	Civil Air Patrol	FHWA	Federal Highway Administration
CBO	Congressional Budget Office	FIC	Federal Information Centers
CCC	Commodity Credit Corporation	FIP	Forestry Incentive Program
CCR	Commission on Civil Rights	FLETC	Federal Law Enforcement Training Center
CDBG	Community development block grants	FLRA	Federal Labor Relations Authority
CDC	Centers for Disease Control	FMC	Federal Maritime Commission
CEA	Council of Economic Advisers	FMCS	Federal Mediation and Conciliation Service
CENTO	Central Treaty Organization	FmHA	Farmers Home Administration
CEQ	Council on Environmental Quality	FNMA	Federal National Mortgage Association (Referred to as "Fannie Mae.")
CETA	Comprehensive Employment and Training Act		
CFNP	Community Food and Nutrition Programs	FNS	Food and Nutrition Service
CFR	Code of Federal Regulations	FOIA	Freedom of Information Act
CFTC	Commodity Futures Trading Commission	FOMC	Federal Open Market Committee
CIA	Central Intelligence Agency	FPM	Federal Personnel Manual
CNO	Chief of Naval Operations	FPRS	Federal Property Resources Service
Comcens	Federal Communications Centers	FR	Federal Register
Conrail	Consolidated Rail Corporation	FRA	Federal Railroad Administration
CONUS	Continental United States	FRCs	Federal Regional Councils
CPSC	Consumer Products Safety Commission	FRS	Federal Reserve System
CRS	Community Relations Service	FSLAC	Federal Savings and Loan Advisory Committee
CSA	Community Service Administration	FSLIC	Federal Savings and Loan Insurance Corp.
		FSQS	Food Safety and Quality Service
DARPA	Defense Advanced Research Projects Agency	FSS	Federal Supply Service
DAVA	Defense Audiovisual Agency	FTC	Federal Trade Commission
DCA	Defense Communications Agency	FTS	Federal Telecommunications System
DCAA	Defense Contract Audit Agency	FWS	Fish and Wildlife Service
DDIC	Depository Institutions Deregulation Committee		
DEA	Drug Enforcement Administration	GAO	General Accounting Office
DIA	Defense Intelligence Agency	GATT	General Agreement on Tariffs and Trade
DIS	Defense Investigative Service	GNMA	Government National Mortgage Association
DLA	Defense Logistics Agency	GNP	Gross national product
DMA	Defense Mapping Agency	GPO	Government Printing Office
DNA	Defense Nuclear Agency	GSA	General Services Administration
DOD	Department of Defense		
DODDS	Department of Defense Dependents Schools	HCFA	Health Care Financing Administration
DOE	Department of Energy	HDS	Office of Human Development Services
DOT	Department of Transportation	HIRE	Help through Industry Retraining and Employment
DSAA	Defense Security Assistance Agency	HRA	Health Resources Administration
		HSA	Health Services Administration
EDA	Economic Development Administration	HUD	Department of Housing and Urban Dev.
EEC	European Economic Community		
EE"O	Equal Employment Opportunity	IADB	Inter-American Defense Board
EEOC	Equal Employment Opportunity Commission	IAEA	International Atomic Energy Agency
EIA	Energy Information Administration	ICAF	Industrial College of the Armed Forces
EO	Executive office	CAO	International Civil Aviation Organization
EO	Executive order	ICC	Interstate Commerce Commission
EPA	Environmental Protection Agency	ICM	Intergovernmental Committee for Migration
ERA	Economic Regulatory Administration	IDA	International Development Association
ESARS	Employment Service Automated Reporting System	IDCA	United States International Development Cooperation Agency
ETA	Employment and Training Administration		
EXIMBANK	Export-Import Bank of the United States	IFC	International Finance Corporation
		IMF	International Monetary Fund
FAA	Federal Aviation Administration	INS	Immigration and Naturalization Service
FAC	Executive office	INTERPOL	International Criminal Police Organization
FADA	Federal Asset Disposition Association	IRS	Internal Revenue Service
FAIR	Fair Access to Insurance Requirements	ITA	International Trade Administration
FAO	Food and Agriculture Organization of the United Nations	ITU	International Telecommunications Union
FAS	Foreign Agricultural Service	JAG	Judge Advocate General
FBI	Federal Bureau of Investigation	JCS	Joint Chiefs of Staff
FCA	Farm Credit Administration	JFMIP	Joint Financial Management Improvement Program
FCC	Federal Communications Commission	JOBS	Job Opportunities in the Business Sector
FCIA	Foreign Credit Insurance Association		
FCIC	Federal Crop Insurance Corporation	LEAA	Law Enforcement Assistance Administration
FDA	Food and Drug Administration	LMSA	Labor-Management Services Administration
FDAA	Federal Disaster Assistance Administration		
FDIC	Federal Deposit Insurance Corporation	MA	Maritime Administration
FDPC	Federal Data Processing Centers	MAC	Military Airlift Command
FEBs	Federal Executive Boards	MBD	Minority Business Development Agency

ENCYCLOPEDIA OF BANKING AND FINANCE

ABBREVIATIONS

MSC	Military Sealift Command	PBS	Public Buildings Service
MSHA	Mine Safety and Health Administration	PCMR	President's Committee on Mental Retardation
MSPB	Merit Systems Protection Board	PEP	Public Employment Program
MSSD	Model Secondary School for the Deaf	PHS	Public Health Service
MSRB	Municipal Securities Rulemaking Board	PRC	Postal Rate Commission
MTB	Materials Transportation Bureau	PSE	Public Service Employment
		PTO	Patent and Trademark Office
NARS	National Archives and Records Service		
NASA	National Aeronautics and Space Administration	RCWP	Rural Clean Water Program
NATO	North Atlantic Treaty Organization	RDS	Rural Development Service
NIBS	National Bureau of Standards	REA	Rural Electrification Administration
NCCB	National Consumer Cooperative Bank	RIT	Rochester Institute of Technology
NCDC	New Community Development Corporation	RRB	Railroad Retirement Board
NCI	National Cancer Institute	RSA	Rehabilitation Services Administration
NCPC	National Capital Planning Commission	RSVP	Retired Senior Volunteer Program
NSCSL	National Center for Service Learning	RTB	Rural Telephone Bank
NCUA	National Credit Union Administration	RTC	Resolution Trust Corporation
NDU	National Defense University		
NEED	National Environmental Education Dev.	SALT	Strategic arms limitation talks
NFIP	National Flood Insurance Program	SAO	Smithsonian Astrophysical Observatory
NHTSA	National Highway Transportation Safety Administration	SBA	Small Business Administration
		SBIC	Small Business Investment Companies
NIC	National Institute of Corrections	SCS	Soil Conservation Service
NIE	National Institute of Education	SEA	Science and Education Administration
NIH	National Institutes of Health	SEAN	Scientific Event Alert Network
NIJ	National Institute of Justice	SEATO	Southeast Asia Treaty Organization
NLM	National Library of Medicine	SEC	Securities and Exchange Commission
NLRB	National Labor Relations Board	SIPC	Securities Investor Protection Corporation
NOAA	National Oceanic and Atmospheric Admin.	SITES	Smithsonian Inst. Traveling Exhibition Service
NRCX	Nuclear Regulatory Commission	SLS	Saint Lawrence Seaway Development Corp.
NSA	National Security Agency	SPARS	Women's Coast Guard Reserves (from Coast Guard motto "Semper Paratus—Always ready")
NSC	National Security Council		
NSF	National Science Foundation	SSA	Social Security Administration
NTIA	National Telecommunications and Information Administration	SSIE	Smithsonian Science Information Exchange, Inc.
		SSS	Selective Service System
NTID	National Technical Institute for the Deaf	Stat.	United States Statutes at Large
NTIS	National Technical Information Service		
NTSB	National Transportation Safety Board	TPUS	Transportation and Public Utilities Service
NWC	National War College	TRIMIS	Tri-Service Medical Information Service
		TVA	Tennessee Valley Authority
OA	Office of Administration		
OAS	Organization of American States	UCPP	Urban Crime Prevention Program
OCC	Office of The Comptroller of the Currency	UIS	Unemployment Insurance Service
OCED	Office of Comprehensive Employment Development Programs	UMTA	Urban Mass Transporation Administration
		UN	United Nations
OCHAMPUS	Office of Civilian Health and Medical Program of the Uniformed Services	UNESCO	United Nations International Children's Emergency Fund
OCSE	Office of Child Support Enforcement	UNICEF	United Nations International Children's Emergency Fund (now United Nations Children's Fund)
OECD	Organization for Economic Cooperation and Development	USA	United States Army
OFCC	Office of Federal Contract Compliance	USAF	United States Air Force
OFPP	Office of Federal Procurement Policy	U.S.C.	United States Code
OFR	Office of the Federal Register	USCG	United States Coast Guard
OGSM	Office of the General Sales Manager	USDA	United States Department of Agriculture
OICD	Office of International Cooperation and Dev.	USES	United States Employment Service
OJARS	Office of Justice Assistance, Research and Statistics	USFA	United States Fire Administration
OJT	On-the-job Training	USIA	U.S. Information Service
OMB	Office of Management and Budget	USICA	United States International Communication Agency
ONP	Office of National Programs	USTC	United States International Trade Commission
ONR	Office of Naval Research	USMC	United States Marine Corps
OOG	Office of Oil and Gas	USN	United States Navy
OPFI	Office of Programs and Fiscal Integrity	USPS	United States Postal Service
OPIC	Overseas Private Investment Corporation	USTS	United States Travel Service
OSHA	Occupational Safety and Health Administration	UYA	University Year for ACTION
OSHR	Occupational Safety and Heal Review Comm.		
OSM	Office of Surface Mining	VA	Veterans Administration
OSTP	Office of Science and Technology Policy	VES	Veterans Employment Service
OTA	Office of Technology Assessment	VISTA	Volunteers in Service to America
OTS	Office of Thrift Supervision	VOA	Voice of America
OWBA	Office of Women's Business Ownership		
OWRT	Office of Water Research and Technology	WAPA	Western Area Power Administration
		WAVES	Women Accepted for Volunteer Emergency Service
PACE	Professional and Administrative Career Examination	WFAOSB	World Food and Agricultural Outlook and Situation Board
PADC	Pennsylvania Avenue Development Corp.	WHO	World Health Organization
PAHO	Pan American Health Organization	WHS	Washington Headquarters Service
PBGC	Pension Benefit Guaranty Corporation	WIN	Work Incentive Program

ABBREVIATIONS

WMO	World Meteorological Organization
YCC	Youth Conservation Corps

Additional International Abbreviations

ACM	Arab Common Market
ACU	Asian Currency Unit
ADB	Arab Development Bank
AFDB	African Development Bank
AID	Agency for International Development
AMF	Arab Monetary Fund
AMU	Asian Monetary Unit
ANCOM	Andean Common Market
ANZUS	Australia, New Zealand, U.S. (Pacific Council)
AsDB	Asian Development Bank
ASEAN	Association of southeast Asian Nations
BENELUX	Belgium, Netherlands, Luxembourg
BCEA	Banque des Estats de l'Afrique Centrale
BCEAO	Banque Centrale des Estats de l'Afrique de l'Ouest
BIS	Bank for International Settlements
BLEU	Belgium-Luxembourg Economic Union
CABEI	Central American Bank for Economic Integration
CACH	Central American Clearing House
CACUM	Central American Common Market
CARICOM	Caribbean Common Market
CARIFTA	Caribbean Free Trade Association
CBD	Caribbean Development Bank
CEPT	Conference of European Post and Telecomm.
CFA	Communaute Financiere Africaine
CFP	Comptoirs Francais du Pacifique
CIAP	Inter-American Committee on the Alliance for Progress
CIPEC	Council of Copper Exporting Countries
CITES	Convention on International Trade in Endangered Species of Wild Fauna and Flora
CMEA	Council for Mutual Economic Assistance
COMECON	Council of Mutual Economic Assistance
EADB	East African Development Bank
EAEC	East African Economic Community
ECC/EC	European Economic Community
ECE	Economic Commission for Europe
ECLA	Economic Commission for Latin America
ECOSOC	Economic and Social Council (United Nations)
ECU	European Currency Unit
EDSC	European Coal and Steel Community
EDC	European Defense Community
EDF	European Development Fund
EDI	Economic Development Institute (of IBRD)
EFTA	European Free Trade Association
EIB	European Investment Bank
EMA	European Monetary Agreement
EMS	European Monetary Agreement
EPA	European Production Agency
EPU	European Payments Union
ERP	European Recovery Program
EUA	European Unit of Account
EURATOM	European Atomic Energy Community
EUROVISION	European Broadcasting Union
GAB	General Agreements to Borrow (IMF)
GATT	General Agreement on Tariffs and Trade
GCC	Gulf Cooperation Council
IADA	Inter-American Development Bank
IBEC	International Bank for Economic Cooperation
IBRD	International Bank for Reconstruction and Development ("World Bank")
ICO	International Coffee Organization
ICSID	International Centre for Settlement of Investment Disputes
IDA	International Development Association
IDB	Inter-American Development Bank
IFAP	International Frederation of Agricultural Producers
IFC	International Financial Corporation
IGGI	Inter-Governmental Group for Indonesia
IIIA	International Investment Ins. Agency (of IBRD)
ILO	International Labour Org. (United Nations)
IMCO	Inter-Governmental Maritime Consultative Organization (United Nations)
IMF	International Monetary Fund
ITO	International Trade Organization (United Nations)
LAFTA	Latin American Free Trade Association
LAIA	Latin American Integration Association
LIBOR	London Inter-Bank Offering Rate
NATO	North Atlantic Treaty Organization
NORDEK	Nordic Customs Union
OAS	Organization of American States
OAU	Organization of African Unity
OBEC	Organization for Economic Cooperation and Development
OCAM	Common Organization of African, Malagasy, and Mauritian States
OEEC	Organication for European Economic Coop.
OPAS	Operational Assistance Scheme (of UNDP)
OPEC	Organization of Petroleum Exporting Countries
PIA	Preferential Trade Area
SDRs	Special drawing Rights (IMF)
TC	Technical Cooperation
UNDEAC	Central African Customs and Economic Union
UN	United Nations
UNDP	United Nations Development Programme
UNESCO	U.N. Educational, Scientific and Cultural Organization
UNICEF	U.N. Children's Emergency Fund (now U.N. Children's Fund)
UNTA	United Nations Technical Assistance Program
UPU	Universal Postal Union (United Nations)
WHO	World Health Organization

"New Deal" Agency Abbreviations

AAA	Agricultural Adjustment Administration
ACA	Advisory Committee on Allotments
ACAA	Agricultural Conservation and Adjustment Administration
ALB	Automobile Labor Board
AMA	Agricultural Marketing Administration
AOA	Administration of Operation Activities
ARA	Agricultural Research Administration
BAC	Business Advisory Council
BAE	Bureau of Agricultural Economics
BEW	Board of Economic Warfare
BFC	Banks for Cooperatives
BPS	Bonneville Power Administration
BWC	Board of War Communications
CAA	Civil Aeronautics Administration
CAB	Civil Aeronautics Board, Consumers Advisory Board
CAP	Civil Air Patrol
CCC	Civilian Conservation Corps, Commodity Credit Corporation
CEA	Commodity Exchange Administration
CES	Committee on Ecoomic Security
CFB	Combined Food Board
CMB	Combined Munitions Board
COI	Coordinator of Information
CPA	Council of Personnel Administration
CPLO	Crop Production Loan Office
CPRB	Combined Production and Resources Board
CRMB	Combined Raw Materials Board
CSAB	Combined Shipping Adjustment Board
CSB	Central Statistical Board

ENCYCLOPEDIA OF BANKING AND FINANCE

ABBREVIATIONS

CSC	Cotton Stabilization Corporation
CWA	Civil Works Administration
DAI	Division of Applications and Information of the Works Relief Administration
DCADA	District of Columbia Alley Dwelling Authority
DCB	Defense Communications Board
DGIAB	Durable Goods Industries Advisory Board
DHC	Defense Homes Corporation
DLB	Deposits Liquidation Board
DLC	Disaster Loan Corporation
DPC	Defense Plants Corporation
DSC	Defense Supplies Corporation
EC	Executive Council
ECFL	Emergency Crop and Feed Loan
ECNR	Executive Council for National Recovery
ECW	Emergency Conservation Works
EHFA	Electric Home and Farm Authority
EIB	Export-Import Bank
EPOCA	Emergency Price Control Act
FAC	Federal Aviation Commission
FACA	Federal Alcohol Control Administration
FCA	Farm Credit Administration
FCC	Federal Communications Commission
FCIC	Federal Crop Insurance Corporation
FCT	Federal Coordinator of Transportation
FCU	Federal Credit Unions
FCUS	Federal Credit Union System
FDA	Food Distribution Administration
FDIC	Federal Deposit Insurance Corporation
FEA	Foreign Economic Administration
FEHC	Federal Emergency Relief Administration
FESO	Federal Employment Stabilization Office
FFc	Foreign Funds Control
FFMC	Federal Farm Mortgage Corporation
FHA	Federal Housing Administration
FHLB	Federal Home Loan Banks
FHLBB	Federal Home Loan Bank Board
FICB	Federal Intermediate Credit Banks
FISC	Fur Industry Salvage commission
FLA	Federal Loan Agency
FLB	Federal Land Banks
FMC	Federal Mortgage Corporation
FPC	Federal Power Commission
FPHA	Federal Public Housing Authority
FPE	Federal Prison Industries
FREB	Federal Real Estate Board
FSA	Farm Security Admin., Federal Security Agency
FSCC	Federal Surplus Commodity Corporation
FSHC	Federal Subsistence Homesteads Corporation
FSLA	Federal Savings and Loan Associations
FSLIC	Federal Savings and Loan Insurance Corp.
FSRC	Federal Surplus Relief Corporation
FTC	Federal Trade Commission
FTZB	Federal Trade Zones Board
FTSA	Special Adviser to the President on Foreign Trade
FWA	Federal Works Agency
GFA	Grain Futures Administration
GSC	Grain Stabiization Corporation
HIF	Housing Insurance Fund
HLB	Home Loan Bank, Home Loan Board
HOLC	Home Owners' Loan Corporation
IAB	Industrial Advisory Board
ICCP	Interdepartmental Committee on Commercial Policy
IEC	Industrial Emergency Board
JEB	Joint Economic Board
JSLB	Joint Stock Land Banks
LAB	Labor Advisory Board
LBC	Land Bank commissioner
MRC	Metals Reserve Company
NACA	National Advisory Committee for Aeronautics
NBAPC	National Business Advisory and Planning Council
NCB	National Compliance Board
ND	National Defense Advisory Commission
NDMB	National Defense Mediation Board
NEC	National Emergency Council
NHA	National Housing Agency
NIRA	National Industrial Recovery Act
NIRB	National Industrial Recovery Board
NLRB	National Labor Relations Board
NMB	National Mediation Board
NPB	National Planning Board
NPPC	National Power Policy Committee
NRA	National Recovery Administration
NRAB	National Railroad Adjustment Board
NRB	National Resources Board
NRC	National Resources Committee
NRRB	National Recovery Review Board
NRPB	National Resources Planning Board
NRS	National Re-employment Service
NSLRB	National Steel Labor Relations Board
NWLB	National War Labor Board
NYA	National Youth Administration
OADR	Office of Agricultural Defense Relations
OAPC	Office of Alien Property Custodian
OAWR	Office for Agricultural War Relations
OBCCC	Office of Bituminous Coal Consumers Council
OC	Office of Censorship
OCD	Office of Civilian Defense
OCIAA	Office of Coordinator of Inter-American Affairs
OCR	Office of Civilian Requirements
OCS	Office of Civilian Supply
ODN	Office of Dependency Benefits
ODHWS	Office of Defense and Health Welfare Services
ODT	Office of Defense Transportation
OEM	Office of Emergency Management
OES	Office of Economic Stabilization
OFC	Office of Fishery Coordination
OFE	Office of Foreign Economic Coordiation
OFF	Office of Facts and Figures
OFRRO	Office of Foreign Relief and Rehabiitation Operations
OGR	Office of Government Reports
OLLA	Office of Lend-Lease Administration
OOC	Office of Censorship
OPA	Office of Price Administration
OPACS	Office of Price Administration and Civilian Supply
OPCW	Office of Petroleum Coordination for War
OPM	Office of Production Management
OSFCW	Office of Solid Fuels Coordinator for War
OSRD	Office of Scientific Research and Development
OSS	Office of Strategic Services
OWI	Office of War Information
OWM	Office of War Mobilization
PA	Petroleum Administration
PAB	Petroleum Administrative Board
PAW	Petroleum Administration for War
PBA	Public Buildings Administration
PCC	Production Credit Corporation
PCES	President's Committee on Economic Security
PIWC	Petroleum Industry War Council
PRA	Public Roads Administration
PRR	Puerto Rico Reconstruction Administration
PWA	Public Works Administration
PWAP	Public Works Arts Projects
PWEHC	Public Works Emergency Housing Corporation
PWRCB	President's War Relief Control Board
RA	Resettlement Administration
RACC	Regional Agricultural Credit Corporation
REA	Rural Electrification Administration
RFC	Reconstruction Finance Corporation
RRA	Rural Resettlement Authority
RRC	Rubber Reserve Company
RRRB	Railroad Retirement Board

ENCYCLOPEDIA OF BANKING AND FINANCE

ABBREVIATIONS

SA	Sugar Agency
SAB	Science Advisory Board
SAPFT	special Adviser to President on Foreign Trade
SCS	Soil Conservation Service
SEC	Securities and Exchange Commission
SES	Soil Erosion Service
SHD	Subsistence Homesteads Division
SLIC	Savings and Loan Insurance Corporation
SLRB	Steel Labor Relations Board, State Labor Relations Board
SMA	Surplus Marketing Administration
SPAB	Supply Priorities and Allocations Board
SSB	Social Security Board
SSS	Selective Service System
SWPC	Smaller War Plants Corporation
TEC	The Executive Council
TFI	Textile Foundation, Inc.
TVA	Tennessee Valley Authority
TVAC	Tennessee Valley Associated Cooperatives, Inc.
TWAB	Textile Work Assignment Boards
UNRR	United Nations Relief and Rehabilitation Administration
USECC	U.S. Employees Compensation Commission
USES	U.S. Employment Service
USHA	U.S. Housing Authority
USHC	U.S. Housing Corporation
USIS	U.S. Information Service
USMC	U.S. Maritime Commission
USTB	U.S. Travel Bureau
WAB	War Allotment Board
WDC	War Damage Corporation
WEPL	War Emergency Pipe Lines, Inc.
WFA	War Food Administration
WLB	War Labor Board
WC	War Manpower Commission
WMI	War Materials, Inc.
WMPC	War Man Power Commission
WPA	Works Progress Administration
WPB	War Production Board
WRA	War Relocation Authority, Work Relief Admin.
WSA	War Shipping Administration
WSTIB	Woolen and Silk Textiles Industries Board
WWB	Writers War Board

Foreign Currency Abbreviations
Abbreviation with example

Country	Monetary Unit	Currency Abbreviation
Afghanistan	Afghani	AF 45.00
Albania	Lek	AL7
Algeria	Dinar	DA 4.93706
Angola	Kwanza	K 31.50
Argentina	Peso	$a 4.00
Australia	Dollar	$A 125
Austria	Schilling	S 25.80
Bahamas	Dollar	B$ 100
Barbados	Dollar	B$ 100
Belgium-Luxembourg	Franc	BF or Lux F 50
Bhutan	Ngultrum	N 200
Bolivia	Peso	$b 11.875
Botswana	Pula	P 100
Brazil	Cruzeiro	Cr$2,200
Burma	Kyat	K 4.76190
Burundi	Franc	FBu 86.50
Cambodia	Riel	CR 200
Cameroon	CFA Franc	CFAF 246.853
Canada	Dollar	Can$1.08108
Cape Verde	Cape Verde Escudo	C.V. Esc 35
Central African Rep.	CFA Franc	CFAF 246.853
Chad	CFA Franc	CFAF 246.853
Chile	Chilean Peso	Ch$ 33
China, People's Republic of	Yuan	Y 1,000
Columbia	Peso	Col$9-94
Comoros	Comoros Franc	CF 50
Congo (People's Republic of)	CFA Franc	CFAF 277.710
Costa Rica	Costa Rican Colo´n	C 6.62
Cyprus	Pound	£C 1,500
Denmark	Krone	DKr 6.8575
Djibouti	Djibouti Franc	DF 176
Domincan Rep.	Peso	RD$5.00
Ecuador	sucre	S/ 18.00
Egypt	Egyptian Pound	LE 70
El Salvador	Salvadoran Colo´n	C 2.50
Equatorial Guinea	Ekwele (plural: Bipkwele)	Bipk 500
Ethiopa	Birr	Br 2
Fiji	Fiji Dollar	F$ 0.818
Finland	Markka	Fmk 3.20
France	Franc	F 4.93706
Gabon	CFA Franc	CFAF 246.853
Gambia (The	Dalasi	D 4
Germany (Fed. Rep. of)	Deutsche Mark	DM 3.97
Ghana	Ghanaian Cedi	C 2.75
Greece	Drachma	Dr 29.90
Grenada	East Caribbean Dolar	EC$ 3
Guatemala	Quetzal	Q 1.00
Guinea	Guinean Syli	GS 24
Guinea-Bissau	Guinea-Bissau Peso	PG 44
Guyana	Guyana Dollar	G$100,000
Haiti	Gourdew	G 5.00
Honduras	Lempira	L 1.98
Hong Kong	Dollar	HK$5.71429
Iceland	Krona	IKr 43.00
India	Rupee	Rs 7.50
Indonesia	Rupiah	Rp 105
Iran	Rial	Rls 75.00
Iraq	Dinnar	ID 500
Ireland	Pound	Ir£ 100
Israel	Pound	I£ 3.00
Italy	Lira	Lit 620.50
Ivory Coast	CFA Franc	CFAF 246.853
Jamaica	Jamaica Dollar	J$ 1
Japan	Yen	¥ 362.70
Jordan	Dinar	JD 50
Kenya	Kenya Shilling	K Sh 7.144286
Kuwait	Dinar	KD 100
Lao, People's Democratic Rep.	Kip of Liberation	KL 400
Lebanon	Pound	LL 3.0725
Lesotho	Maloti	M 200
Liberia	Dollar	Lib$100
Libyan Arab Republic	Pound	£L100
Malagasy Rep.	Franc	FMC 246.853
Malawi	Kwacha	MK 1.054
Malasia	Ringgit	M$ 2.20
Maldives	Rufiyaa	Rf 7.60
Mali	Franc	MF 246.853
Malta	Malta Pound	£M 1
Mauritania	Ouguiya	UM 46
Mauritius	Mauritian Rupee	Mau Rs 12
Mexico	Peso	Mex$12.51
Morocco	Dirham	DH 5.0159
Nepal	Rupee	NRs 7.619
Netherlands	Guilder	f 3.59 1/4
Netherlands Antilles	Guilder	Ant. f. 1905
New Zealand	New Zealand Dollar	$N 100
Nicaragua	Cordoba	C$7.00
Niger	CFA Franc	CFAF 246.853
Nigeria	Naira	N 150
Norway	Krone	Nkr 7.09
Oman	Rial Omani	RO 50
Pakistan	Rupee	PRs 4.75
Panama	Balboa	B 100
Papua New Guinea	Kina	K 100
Paraguay	Guarani	G 126
Peru	Sol	S/26.82

ENCYCLOPEDIA OF BANKING AND FINANCE

ABBREVIATIONS

Phillipines	Peso	P 3.89
Portugal	Escudo	Esc 28.75
Qatar	Qatar Riyal	QR 5
Romania	Leu	Lei 5
Rwanda	Franc	RF 50
Sao Tome and Principe	Dobra	Db 45
Saudi Arabia	Riyal	SRIs 4.50
Senegal	CFA Franc	CFAF 246.853
Seychelles	Rupee	Sey Rs 13
Sierra Leone	Leone	Le 500
Singapore	Singapore Dollar	S$3.0612
Solomon Islands	Dollar	SI$ 25
Somalia	Somali Shilling	So. Sh. 200
South Africa	Rand	R 199.75
Spain	Peseta	Ptas 60.00
Sri Lanka	Rupee	SL Rs 15.49
Sudan	Pound	LSd 100
Suriname	Guilder	Sur. f. 188585
Swaziland	Lilangeni (plural: \ Emalangeni)	E 500
Sweden	Krona	SKr 5.17321
Switzerland	Franc	Sw F 4.45
Syrian Arab Rep.	Pound	LS 3.80
Taiwan	New Taiwan Dollar	NT$40
Tanzania	Tanzania Shiling	T Sh 7.14286
Thailand	Baht	B 20.84
Togo	CFA Franc	CFAF 246.853
Trinidad and Tobago	Dollar	TT$1.71
Tunisia	Tunisian Dinar	D-O.525
Turkey	Lira	LT 9.08
Uganda	Uganda Shilling	U Sh 7.14286
United Arab Emirates	U.A.E. Dirham	Dh 5
United Kingdom	Pound Sterling	£100
Upper Volta	CFA Franc	CFAF 246.853
Uruguay	New Peso	NUr$100
U.S.S.R.	Ruble	R 1,000
Vanuatu	Vatu	VT 200
Venezuela	Bolivar	Bs 4.40
Viet Nam	Dong	VD 2.66
Yemen Arab Rep.	Yeman Rial	YRls 5.5
Yeman, People's Democratic Rep.	Yemeni Dinar	YD 0.34
Yugoslavia	Dinar	Din 12.50
Zaire	Zaire	Z 1.31
Zambia	Zambian Kwacha	K 1
Zimbabwe	Zimbabwe Dollar	Z$ 50

Currency and Trade Areas

Sterling Area
United Kingdom
Channel Islands
Gibraltar
Isle of Man

U.S. Dollar Area
United States, Puerto Rico, U.S. virgin Islands
Bolivia
Canada
Colombia
Costa Rica
Dominican Republic
Ecuador
El Salvador
Guatemala
Haiti
Honduras
Liberia
Mexico
Micronesia
Nicaragua
Panama
Philippines
Venezuela

Franc—zone France
Andorra
Benin
Burkina Faso
Cameroon
Central African Republic
Chad
Comoros
Congo, Peoples' Republic
Cote d'Ivoire
Gabon
Guadeloupe
Guiana
Mali
Martinique
Mayotte
Monaco
Niger
Polynesia (French)
Reunion
St. Peirre-et-Miquelon
Senegal
Togo
Wallis-et-Futuna

European Economic Community
Belgium/Luxembourg
CFA Area (Associate)
Denmark
France
Germany, West
Greece
Ireland
Italy
Kenya (Associate)
Malta (Associate)
Mauritius (Associate)
Morocco (Associate)
Netherlands
Nigeria (Associate)
Portugal
Spain
Sudan (Associate)
Tanzania (Associate)
Turkey (Associate)
Uganda (Associate)
United Kingdom

European Free Trade Association
Austria Finalnd (Associate)
Iceland
Norway
Portugal
Sweden
Switzerland

Ruble-Yuan Area
Albania
Bulgaria
China, People's Republic
Cuba
Czechoslovakia
Germany, East
Hungary
Korea (North)
Mongolia
Poland
Romania
U.S.S.R.
Viet Nam

Central American Common Market
Costa Rica
El Salvador
Guatemala
Honduras
Nicaragua

Latin American Free Trade Association
Argentina
Bolivia
Brazil
Chile
Colombia
Ecuador
Mexico
Paraguay
Peru
Uruguay
Venezuela

Caribbean Community and Common Market
Anguilla
Antigua & Barbuda
Barbados
Belize
Dominica
Grenada
Guyana
Jamaica
Montserrat
St. Kitts—Nevis
St. Lucia
St. Vincent Grenadines
Trinidad & Tobago

Organization of Petroleum Exporting Countries
Algeria
Ecuador
Gabon
Indonesia
Iran
Iraq
Kuwait
Libya
Nigeria
Qatar
Saudi Arabia
United Arab Emirates

BIBLIOGRAPHY

Abbreviations, Acronyms, Ciphers and Signs. Brewer, Annie M. Gale Research Co., Detroit, MI, 1981.

Abbreviations Dictionary. Desola, Ralph. Elsevier North-Holland, Inc., New York, NY, 1981.

Acronyms, Initialisms, and Abbreviations Dictionary. Gale Research Co., Detroit, MI, 1987. Three volumes.

Business Acronyms. Gale Research Co, Detroit, MI, 1988.

Pugh's Dictionary of Acronyms and Abbreviations: Abbreviations in Management, Technology and Information Science. American Library Association, Chicago, IL, 1987.

World Guide to Abbreviations of Organizations. Gale Research Co., Detroit, MI, 1984.

ENCYCLOPEDIA OF Banking & Finance

ABANDONMENT In law, generally the express or implied relinquishment of title, possession, or claim.

In finance, the term particularly pertains to inactive or dormant deposit accounts (*see* UNCLAIMED BALANCES) and other forms of intangibles (unclaimed dividends and interest, money transfers, cash surrender, or matured values of life insurance policies, etc.). Some 39 states provide for abandoned property, escheat, or custodial laws.

See ESCHEAT.

In industry, the term refers especially to the public service industries, particularly the railroads. The Transportation Act of 1920 forbade the abandonment of "all or any portion of a line of railroad, or the operation thereof, unless and until there shall first have been obtained from the [Interstate Commerce] Commission a certificate that the present or future public convenience and necessity permit of such abandonment." The Interstate Commerce Commission follows the policy of balancing carrier and community interests in passing on the increased number of petitions for abandonments of railroad service by the railroads in recent years.

See RAILROAD INDUSTRY.

ABA TRANSIT NUMBER The code number assigned to a bank pursuant to the numerical transit system devised by the American Bankers Association to facilitate collection of transit items (checks and other items on out-of-town banks).

Use of such a code number eliminates the necessity for detailing the drawee banks' titles and addresses in transit letters, and facilitates sorting of transit items for collection.

The ABA number of a bank is also used as the numerator in the fractional code number of the combined check routing symbol–transit number developed for collection of out-of-town checks through the Federal Reserve banks.

Thus the fractional form of routing symbol–transit number

$$\frac{8\text{-}26}{430}$$

printed on the face of checks near the upper right-hand corner, stands for the following: 8 is the transit code number for the city of Pittsburgh; 26 is the transit code number for the Mellon Bank; 4 stands for the Fourth (Cleveland) Federal Reserve District; 3 is the code for the Pittsburgh branch of the Federal Reserve Bank of Cleveland; and 0 is the code for item receivable for immediate credit.

Encoded Check Routing Symbol–Transit Number. The fractional form of the transit number–routing symbol, of which the above is an example, will continue to appear on encoded checks, printed as heretofore in nonmagnetic ink on the face of checks in the upper right-hand corner, even if checks are encoded for electronic processing, because not all banks either have now or will have electronic equipment for mechanized check handling by electronic means.

On encoded checks, the above combined routing symbol–transit number would appear encoded in magnetic ink, in specially designed type, along the bottom of the face of checks, in the following form, for par banks:

0430-0026

The prefix (8 in the above example) is eliminated. The complete encoded number will always consist of eight digits with a hyphen dividing each four of the digits (nonsignificant zeros being used if no specific numbers apply). The first set of four digits will refer to the Federal Reserve district; the head or branch office of the Federal Reserve bank concerned; and the code number for immediate credit or deferred credit (*see* FEDERAL RESERVE CHECK COLLECTION SYSTEM for detailed explanation). The second set of four digits will consist of the suffix of the transit number of the bank, together with insignificant zeros.

In the case of nonpar banks, the encoded transit number on their checks will indicate that the subject drawee bank is a nonpar bank by the figure 90 preceding the present transit number:

9061-0404

in which 90 is the code for nonpar bank; 61 the code number for the state of Alabama; and 404 (together with nonsignificant zero preceding) stands for the Bank of Columbia of Columbia, Alabama, a nonpar bank.

For details of construction and use of ABA transit numbers, *see* NUMERICAL TRANSIT SYSTEM. *See also* AUTOMATION for description of automation of bank operating procedures, including mechanized check handling.

A-B-C AGREEMENT An applicant's seat on the NEW YORK STOCK EXCHANGE may be purchased by a member firm for his use through funds advanced by the member firm. In such a case, the application must be accompanied by release from the member firm financing the purchase and by the a-b-c agreement signed by the applicant. The agreement in essence provides that should the individual member retire from the member firm or die, he or his representative will (a) retain the membership and pay the member firm funds for the purchase of another seat; or (b) sell the seat and pay over the proceeds to the member firm; or (c) transfer his seat for a nominal value to a designee of the member firm acceptable to the board of governors of the exchange.

See Rule 301 and supplementary materials, NEW YORK STOCK EXCHANGE GUIDE.

ABEYANCE A banking term that refers to a temporary suspension of title to property before the correct owner is established. Claims or shortcomings that interfere with title to real property create a "cloud on title."

ABILITY TO PAY THEORY In taxation, the doctrine that tax burdens should be distributed according to ability to pay, and that rates therefore should be progressive (rates rising as the tax base increases), based on the normative principle of minimizing sacrifice of taxpayers having varied financial circumstances.

Income, the basis for income taxes, is one criterion of ability to pay. But wealth, personal expenditure, and savings have also been advocated as criteria, and there is no agreement as to measurement of subjective sacrifice and as to the degree of progressivity of rates in view of the effects upon incentives and economic growth. The English economist McCulloch wrote that when proportionality in taxation is abandoned "you are at sea without rudder or compass, and there is no amount of injustice and folly you may not commit" (*A Treatise on the Principles and Practical Influence of Taxation and the Funding System*, 1845).

BIBLIOGRAPHY

HEMMING, R. "Income Tax Progressivity and Labour Supply." *Journal of Public Economics*, August 1980.

ENCYCLOPEDIA OF BANKING AND FINANCE

McLure, C. E., Jr. "The Elusive Incidence of the Corporate Income Tax: The State Case." *Public Finance Quarterly*, October 1981.

Yeh, C. "Musgrave's Paradox and Progressive Income Taxation." *Public Finance Quarterly*, vol. 36 (1), 1981.

ABOVE PAR A price quoted above the face value of a security.
See par, premium.

ABRASION The loss of weight in coins occasioned by friction, i.e., ordinary wear and tear of circulation, as distinguished from loss of weight due to mutilation, debasement, clipping, or sweating.

When various U.S. fractional coins in circulation become too worn for further use, or are bent or twisted out of shape, they are withdrawn by Federal Reserve Banks and branches and the Treasurer of the U.S. as uncurrent coins exchanged at face value. The mints melt and recoin uncurrent coins, as provided by law. But mutilated coins (punched, clipped, plugged, fused together, or so defaced as not to be readily and clearly identifiable as to genuineness and denomination) are accepted at the coinage mints only at actual bullion or metal value.

In the case of gold coins, all were legal tender in all payments at full face value when not below the standard weight and limit of tolerance prescribed by law; when below such weight and tolerance, they were legal tender only in proportion to actual weight.

See debasement, light coin, light gold, mutilated currency, sweating, tolerance.

ABSOLUTE ENDORSEMENT See endorsement.

ABSOLUTE PRIORITY RULE The principle that creditors' rights are to be satisfied in full before stockholders' equities in corporate liquidations or reorganizations.

This rule, first enunciated by the U.S. Supreme Court in *Northern Pacific Ry. v. Boyd*, 228 U.S. 482 (1913), was upheld in two later notable cases:

1. *Case v. Los Angeles Lumber Products Co., Ltd.*, 308 U.S. 106 (1939), in which stockholders of the defendant debtor sought recognition for intangible values contributed by them to the reorganization. The Court denied the stockholders' appeal, ruling that absolute priority be accorded to the creditors' position. Stockholders were not entitled to consideration until the creditors' claims had been satisfied, unless they supplied new money. The priority of creditors could not be waived, even by their own voluntary action. Stockholders whose equity had been destroyed by insolvency could not obtain a right to participate in reorganization by contract prior to reorganization proceedings, unless such participation was fair and equitable.
2. This application of the "rigorous standards of the absolute or full priority doctrine" of the *Boyd* case was upheld in *Consolidated Rock Products Co. et al. v. E. Blois du Bois*, 312 U.S. 510 (1941).

In practice, application of the principle in liquidations or reorganizations would call for the satisfaction in full (at book values, including accruals of interest, for allowed proofs of claim) of secured creditors, in their own relative priorities as to each class of secured creditors, against the assets pledged. If such pledged assets are insufficient to cover secured claims in full, then as to any deficiency the secured creditors still have an unsecured claim, to be shared proportionately with other unsecured claims against the unpledged assets. Only should there be a residue, after satisfaction in full of all creditors, would stockholders share, unless they bought such participation by contribution of new money, with preferred stock ranking ahead of common.

The rule has been criticized as to reorganizations, in that it fails to accord value to "going concern" values in a reorganization, in which the value of a firm reorganized and continuing to operate should be worth more than liquidation value; and in such "going concern" values, therefore, there is an element of equity value for which stockholders are entitled to recognition. Thus distribution of the new securities in reorganization should be on the basis of relative priority of all claims, including equities, in the estimated "going concern" value.

Under the Bankruptcy Act of 1978 (P.L. 95-598), codified as Title 11 of the U.S. Code, "Bankruptcy," the absolute priority rule was abolished. It was replaced by a "more than liquidation" standard for creditors.

See bankruptcy.

ABSOLUTE TITLE Unqualified ownership of personal property or ownership of real property in fee simple. Such a title confers on the owner and his heirs, representatives and assigns absolute right to the property in perpetuity.

ABSORB When buying orders are in sufficient volume to counterbalance selling orders without a substantial change in prices, the stock or other market is said to absorb or assimilate offerings, e.g., "the market encountered selling in the last hour but absorbed all offerings without appreciable price changes."

ABSORPTION AND DIRECT COSTING Direct (or variable) costing and absorption costing are two approaches to product costing. With direct costing, ending inventory includes only variable production costs, such as direct materials, direct labor, and variable manufacturing overhead. Fixed overhead costs, which do not change with changes in production levels (such as rent, insurance), are expensed when incurred. With absorption costing, the cost of inventory includes both variable and fixed factory overhead costs. Variable costing is frequently used for decision-making, but is not generally accepted for external financial reporting. The differences between the two methods are due entirely to the treatment of fixed factory overhead.

When production exceeds sales, absorption costing will cause net income to exceed net income under direct costing because some fixed overhead costs are deferred in inventory rather than being written off as a period cost. When sales exceed production, the opposite effects on net income occur because some previously deferred fixed factory costs are included with current fixed overhead costs in cost of goods sold.

Direct costing is useful for controlling current costs, profit planning (sales promotions; special pricing; make-or-buy decisions). When direct costing is used, periodic net income varies directly with sales volume since variable costs are proportional to sales. When absorption costing is used, the volume/profit relationship becomes more difficult to estimate since fixed costs are a component of inventory.

ABSORPTION POINT The saturation point; the point at which a market refuses to accept greater offerings without price concessions.

See digested securities, undigested securities.

ABSTRACTION OF BANK FUNDS The wrongful taking of bank funds for personal use from, e.g., a cash drawer, is included in the restatement in 18 U.S.C. 656, of the former Section 5209, Revised Statutes, as follows: "Whoever, being an officer, director, agent or employee of, or connected in any capacity with any Federal Reserve Bank, member bank, National bank or insured bank, or a receiver of a National bank, or any agent or employee of the receiver, or a Federal Reserve Agent, or an agent or employee of a Federal Reserve Agent or of the Board of Governors of the Federal Reserve System, embezzles, abstracts, purloins or willfully misapplies any of the moneys, funds, or credits of such bank or any moneys, funds, assets or securities entrusted to the custody or care of such bank, or to the custody or care of any such agent, officer, director, employee or receiver, shall be fined not more than $5,000 or imprisoned not more than five years, or both; but if the amount embezzled, abstracted, purloined or misapplied does not exceed $100, he shall be fined not more than $1,000 or imprisoned not more than one year, or both."

As used in this section, the term "National bank" is synonymous with "National banking association"; "member bank" means and includes any national bank, state bank, or bank and trust company that has become a member of one of the Federal Reserve banks; and "insured bank" includes any bank, banking association, trust company, savings bank, or other banking institution, the deposits of which are insured by the Federal Deposit Insurance Corporation.

ABSTRACT OF TITLE A complete historical summary of all recorded documents affecting the title to a particular piece of real property. It shows in chronological order all recorded grants and conveyances and identifies all recorded easements, mortgages, wills, tax liens, judgments, pending lawsuits, marriages, divorces, and similar matters that might affect the title.

Each document listed in an abstract is summarized and the date and source are noted. In the case of a deed, the abstract shows the grantor and the grantee, the type of deed, and any restrictions or conditions listed in the deed. The abstract also shows a description of the property transferred by the deed and the recording date along with the book and page numbers where the deed may be found in the county registrar of deeds office. For a mortgage, the abstract shows the borrower and the lender, a description of the mortgage contents, whether or not the mortgage has been repaid, the book and page numbers where the mortgage release documents are recorded along with the date of release. The abstract also includes a list of the public records searched and those not searched in preparing the abstract.

Abstracts are normally prepared by attorneys or others who may be experts in the field of title search. These persons charge a fee for their services. When a piece of property is sold, this fee is usually paid by the buyer.

An abstract is often given to an attorney when a property is to be sold. The attorney renders his opinion as to the identity of the owner of the property and names anyone else who may have rights or interests in the property. The attorney's opinion when signed and attached to the abstract is known in many states as a certificate of title. In some states, an abstract and certificate of title must be prepared each time a property is sold.

See DEED, TITLE INSURANCE.

ACCELERATED COST RECOVERY SYSTEM (ACRS)

The Accelerated Cost Recovery System (ACRS) is a tax system of recovering the cost of capital expenditures through periodic depreciation deductions that is mandatory for most depreciable types of tangible property placed in service after 1980. Such costs are recovered over specified recovery periods according to statutory percentages that do not require the computation of a useful life.

The Tax Reform Act of 1986 provided a Modified Accelerated Cost Recovery System (MACRS) for tangible property placed in service after December 31, 1986. Eligible personal property is assigned a three year class, a five year class, a seven year class, a ten year class, a fifteen year class, or a twenty year class. The cost of real property is recovered using the straight-line method over 27.5 years for residential rental property and 31.5 years for nonresidential real property.

All the depreciation calculations for income tax purposes are based on the half-year convention; that is, depreciation for half a year is recorded in the year of acquisition and in the last year of the ACRS life. The residual value is not considered when the ACRS is used. The asset is depreciated to a zero value.

ACCELERATION CLAUSE

A clause (in a note, bond, or mortgage) providing for quickening or advancing date of payment of the entire balance due because of breach of some specified condition, such as default in payment of interest or installment of principal when due, insolvency of the debtor, failure to keep mortgaged premises insured, etc.

The acceleration clause allows the lender to speed up the rate at which a loan comes due. It can be employed if the borrower misses payments and for other reasons. A sample acceleration clause could read:

In the event any installment of this note is not paid when due, time being of the essence, and such installment remains unpaid for 30 days, the Holder of this note may, at its option, without notice or demand, declare the entire principal sum then unpaid, together with secured interest and late charges thereon, immediately due and payable. The lender may without further notice or demand invoke the power of sale and any other remedies permitted by applicable law.

ACCELERATION PRINCIPLE

Aftalion's concept that a given fluctuation in consumption, at full operating utilization of capital stock (capital equipment), will induce much greater fluctuation in warranted investment (derived demand for capital goods).

For example, assume fully employed capital stock of 100,000 units, with replacement factor of 10% per annum. If demand for output should increase 10%, new investment of 10,000 units would be warranted, or gross investment of 20,000 units. Thus a 10% increase in consumption could generate a 100% increase in gross investment. But if demand thereafter should remain unchanged, gross investment would decline 45%, consisting merely of the 11,000 units of replacement on the previously enlarged capital stock. The accelerator is the ratio or coefficient between induced consumption and induced investment.

In post-Keynesian economics, Aftalion's acceleration principle has been combined with the Kahn-Keynes MULTIPLIER, to demonstrate the fully cyclical nature of the fluctuation in national income caused by the interaction of the accelerator and the multiplier upon given increments of additional autonomous spending.

BIBLIOGRAPHY

AFTALION, A. *Les crises periodiques de surproduction*, 2 vols., 1913.
BLANCHARD, O. J. "What Is Left of the Multiplier Accelerator?" *American Economic Review*, May, 1981.
SAMUELSON, P. A. "Interaction Between the Multiplier Analysis and the Principle of Acceleration." *Review of Economics and Statistics*, May, 1939.

ACCEPTABILITY

In addition to being technically eligible, a paper presented for rediscount at a Federal Reserve bank must be acceptable, i.e., collectible in the opinion of the Federal Reserve bank. For the purpose of determining acceptability, the member bank listing the customer's paper on the offering sheet to the discount department of the Federal Reserve bank may be required to submit financial statements of the customer and other pertinent data for analysis of acceptability by the credit department of the Federal Reserve bank. Final decision as to acceptability is made by the credit committee of the Federal Reserve bank.

Acceptability as well as eligibility tests apply to paper offered for rediscount as well as paper offered as collateral for advances from the Federal Reserve bank on the borrowing member bank's own collateral note.

See ELIGIBLE PAPER, REDISCOUNT.

ACCEPTANCE

This term has three meanings:

1. One of the essential conditions necessary for a CONTRACT to be legally binding between parties. Offer and acceptance to a contract are essential to its validity.
2. As applied to a time draft or bill of exchange, acceptance is the drawee's signification of intention to pay at maturity. It is the signification by the drawee of his assent to the order of the drawer. Acceptance consists of writing the word "accepted" across the face of the instrument, indicating the date and bank where payable, with the signature of the drawee thereunder. After acceptance, a DRAFT or bill has the same status in law as a promissory note. The acceptor becomes primarily liable and the drawer becomes secondarily liable.
See NEGOTIABLE INSTRUMENTS LAW.
3. Although, technically, acceptance consists of the act of accepting a time DRAFT or bill of exchange by the drawee, the term is more commonly used to designate the accepted bill itself. Acceptances are of two classes: TRADE ACCEPTANCE and bankers acceptance.
See BANK ACCEPTANCE.

ACCEPTANCE CREDIT

One means of financing import and export, as well as domestic, transactions is by arranging an acceptance credit with a bank. Commercial banks, including member banks and foreign banking corporations organized under state laws and the Edge Act (Sec. 25a of the Federal Reserve Act), are authorized to engage in the acceptance business under regulation (Reg. C) of the Board of Governors of the Federal Reserve System.

Acceptance credit may originate in the following situations:

1. Acceptance credit to finance imports. In such a case, the terms of trade between the importer and exporter would require the importer to obtain a commercial LETTER OF CREDIT from his bank, which is addressed to the exporter and authorizes the latter to draw drafts (usually time drafts), usually with shipping documents attached, upon the drawee bank in strict accordance with the letter of credit. The drawee bank's acceptance of the draft drawn upon it gives rise to a BANK ACCEPTANCE, which may be held to maturity or sold in the money market by the drawer (exporter) or, more likely, by the foreign bank which likely discounted the drafts drawn by the exporter and forwarded

them for acceptance. The drawee bank, in turn, will customarily release the shipping documents to the importer, thus allowing him access to the goods for processing and sale, under protection of a TRUST RECEIPT which protects the bank's interest as technical beneficiary. Moreover, the drawee bank's acceptance liability is secured by its customer's (importer) liability, sometimes collateralized, to provide the funds with which to pay the acceptances at maturity.

2. Acceptance credit to finance exports. Commercial letter of credit is requested by the foreign importer, or more customarily by his bank, from a domestic bank, addressed to the domestic exporter and authorizing the latter to draw on the domestic bank in strict accordance with the letter of credit, usually with shipping documents attached. Upon acceptance of the drafts so drawn, bank acceptances would be created, which similarly could be retained to maturity or discounted in the money market.

3. Acceptance credit to finance the domestic shipment of goods. To prevent such acceptance credit from being misused as working capital, the shipping documents conveying or securing title must be attached to the drafts drawn or be in the physical possession of the accepting bank or its agent at the time of acceptance.

4. Acceptance credit to finance the temporary storage in the U.S. or in any foreign country of readily marketable staples. This is of particular help in the orderly marketing of farm crops. The draft or bill of exchange must be secured at the time of acceptance by warehouse receipt or other document conveying or securing title to such staples.

5. Acceptance credit to create dollar exchange. This is a temporary, nontrade arrangement, of particular help to countries exporting commodities having severely seasonal fluctuations. A bank in such a country will, pursuant to agreement, draw clean (nondocumented) drafts on an American bank correspondent and, upon their acceptance, discount such bank acceptances in the money market. Thus dollar exchange balances are created to supply the dollar needs of such foreign bank's customers in the seasonally slack periods in exports. The drawer bank will place the drawee bank in funds in time to meet the maturities, presumably out of dollar proceeds of export sales by customers.

Banks are subject to statutory and administrative regulation of their acceptance activity (*see below*). Customers requesting acceptance credit pay acceptance fees, on the order of a standard 1.5% per annum (which may be higher because of risk), and must reckon with the prevailing discount rates for bank acceptances in the money market. In times of low rates on direct commercial loans, such direct loans might involve lower costs than the total charges involved in acceptance credit. Moreover, acceptance credits, pursuant to statutory and administrative regulation, must be short-term in maturities; this factor might make acceptance credits unsuitable to finance transactions where foreign trade customers require long-term credits.

Limitations on Acceptance Credits. Although banks' liability in connection with their outstanding acceptances is covered by customers' liability in connection with such acceptances, and such customers' liability may be specifically secured, both the aggregate amount of the banks' liability and the maturities and nature of the transactions involved are subject to statutory and administrative regulation.

With respect to the acceptance by member banks of the Federal Reserve System of drafts or bills of exchange, the seventh paragraph of Section 13 of the Federal Reserve Act (12 U.S.C. 372) provides as follows.

Any member bank may accept drafts or bills of exchange drawn upon it having not more than six months' sight to run, exclusive of days of grace, which grow out of transactions involving the importation or exportation of goods; or which grow out of transactions involving the domestic shipment of goods, provided shipping documents conveying or securing title are attached at the time of acceptance; or which are secured at the time of acceptance by a warehouse receipt or other such document conveying or securing title covering readily marketable staples.

No member bank shall accept, whether in a foreign or domestic transaction, for any one person, company, firm, or corporation bills an amount equal at any time in the aggregate to more than 10% of its paid-up and unimpaired capital stock and surplus, unless the bank is secured either by attached documents or by some other actual security growing out of the same transaction as the acceptance; and no bank shall accept such bills to an amount equal at any time in the aggregate to more than one-half of its paid-up and unimpaired capital stock and surplus; provided, however, that the Board of Governors of the Federal Reserve System, under such general regulations as it may prescribe, which shall apply to all banks alike regardless of the amount of capital stock and surplus, may authorize any member bank to accept such bills to an amount not exceeding at any time in the aggregate 100% of its paid-up and unimpaired capital stock and surplus; and provided further that the aggregate of acceptances growing out of domestic transactions shall in no event exceed 50% of such capital stock and surplus.

The authority to accept drafts or bills of exchange is on commercial drafts or bills involving the following:

1. The importation or exportation of goods, i.e., the shipment of goods between the United States and any foreign country, or between the United States and any of its dependencies or insular possessions, or between dependencies or insular possessions and foreign countries, or between foreign countries. A member bank accepting such instruments "will be expected to obtain before acceptance and retain in its files satisfactory evidence," documentary or otherwise, showing the nature of the transactions underlying the credit extended.

2. The shipment of goods within the United States, provided shipping documents conveying or securing title are attached or are in the physical possession of the accepting bank or its agent at the time of acceptance.

3. The storage in the United States or in any foreign country of readily marketable staples, provided that the draft or bill of exchange is secured at the time of acceptance by a warehouse receipt or other such document conveying or securing title covering such readily marketable staples. A "readily marketable staple" is specified to mean an article of commerce, agriculture, or industry, of such uses as to make it the subject of constant dealings in ready markets with such frequent quotations of price as to make the price easily and definitely ascertainable and the staple itself easy to realize upon by sale at any time. Also, Federal Reserve banks may neither discount nor purchase bills arising out of the storage of readily marketable staples unless the acceptor remains secured throughout the life of the bill.

The aggregate limitation of not more than 10% of the bank's unimpaired capital stock and surplus, in acceptances for any one person, does not apply if the bank is and remains secured as to the amount in excess of such 10% limitation by either attached documents or some other actual security growing out of the same transaction as the acceptance. But a trust receipt which permits the customer to have access to or control over the goods will not be considered actual security within the meaning of this limitation.

In connection with the 50% of paid-up and unimpaired capital stock and surplus limitation on aggregate acceptance liability on commercial drafts or bills, and the permissive authority to accept such instruments up to 100% of such base, commercial drafts or bills accepted by another bank, whether domestic or foreign, at the request of a member bank which agrees to put such other bank in funds to meet such acceptances at maturity shall be considered part of the acceptance liabilities of the member bank requesting such acceptances, as well as of such other bank if a member bank, within the meaning of these limitations.

Any member bank desiring authority to accept commercial drafts or bills up to 100% of the capital funds base shall file with the Board of Governors of the Federal Reserve System, through the Federal Reserve bank of its district, an application for permission to exercise such authority. Such application need not be made in any particular form, but shall show the present and anticipated need of the applicant bank for the authority requested. The board of governors may at any time rescind any authority granted by it pursuant to this provision, after not less than 90 days' notice in writing to the bank affected.

With respect to dollar exchange acceptances, the twelfth paragraph of Section 13 of the Federal Reserve Act (12 U.S.C. 373) provides as follows.

Any member bank may accept drafts or bills of exchange drawn upon it having not more than three months' sight to run, exclusive of days of grace, drawn under regulations to be prescribed by the Board of Governors of the Federal Reserve System by banks or bankers in foreign countries or dependencies, or insular possessions of the United States for the purpose of furnishing dollar exchange as required by the usages of trade in the respective countries, dependencies, or insular possessions. Such drafts or bills may be acquired by Federal Reserve banks in such amounts and subject to such regulations, restrictions, and limitations as may be prescribed by the Board of Governors of the Federal Reserve System; provided, however, that no member bank shall accept such drafts or bills of exchange referred to in this paragraph for any one bank to an amount exceeding in the aggregate 10% of the paid-up and unimpaired capital and surplus of the accepting bank unless the draft or bill of exchange is accompanied by documents conveying or securing title or by some other adequate security; and provided further that no member bank shall accept such drafts or bills in an amount exceeding at any time the aggregate of one-half of its paid-up and unimpaired capital and surplus.

Any such dollar exchange draft or bill must be drawn and accepted in good faith for the purpose of furnishing dollar exchange as required by the usages of trade in the country, dependency, or insular possession in which the draft or bill is drawn. Drafts or bills drawn merely because dollar exchange is at a premium in the place where drawn, or for any speculative purpose, or drafts or bills commonly referred to as "finance bills" (i.e., which are not drawn primarily to furnish dollar exchange) will not be deemed to meet the requirements.

The aggregate of drafts or bills of exchange accepted by such member bank for any one foreign bank or banker shall not exceed an amount which the member bank would expect such foreign bank or banker to liquidate within the terms of the agreements under which the drafts or bills were accepted, through the proceeds of export documentary bills or from other sources reasonably available to such foreign bank or banker arising in the normal course of trade.

(Dollar exchange drafts or bills are accepted on the basis of anticipated future dollar exchange earnings from expected future transactions, instead of being based on current transactions, or from other sources reasonably available to the foreign banks or bankers involved in the normal course of trade, particularly trade with marked seasonal variation.)

The limitation on acceptance of dollar exchange drafts and bills, to an aggregate amount not exceeding at any one time 50% of the member bank's paid-up and unimpaired capital and surplus, is separate and distinct from and not included in the limitations prescribed above with respect to acceptances of commercial drafts or bills. Dollar exchange drafts or bills accepted by another bank, whether domestic or foreign, at the request of a member bank which agrees to put such other bank in funds to meet such acceptances at maturity shall be considered as part of the acceptance liabilities of the member bank requesting such acceptances as well as of such other bank if a member bank.

In explaining the general scope of the exceptions from the general limitation of 10% of the national bank's paid-in and unimpaired capital stock and surplus fund as lending limit to any one borrower, the Comptroller of the Currency points out Exception 5 in the statute (12 U.S.C. 84(5)\), consisting of obligations in the form of bankers acceptances of other banks of the kinds described in 12 U.S.C. 372 and 373 (eligible acceptances), shall not be subject under the statute to any limitation of lending limit based upon such capital and surplus. Other kinds of acceptances (ineligible acceptances) made by other banks are included within the purchasing bank's lending limit to each acceptor bank. In Ruling 7.1550, the Comptroller of the Currency explains that obligations described in 12 U.S.C. 372 and 12 U.S.C. 373 which arise out of the acceptance by a national bank itself of drafts eligible for rediscount are subject to the limits contained in Sections 372 and 373, *supra*; said limits are distinct from the Section 84 limit (the general limit, as to any person, of 10% of capital stock and surplus of the national bank). Thus a national bank may accept eligible drafts for a customer up to the amount permitted by Sections 372 and 373, and at the same time that customer may be indebted in other ways to the national bank up to his Section 84 limit.

An ineligible acceptance (a time draft accepted by a national bank which does not meet the requirements for discount with a Federal Reserve bank) may be accepted on behalf of a customer only within the limits of Section 84. All nonexcepted indebtedness of the customer to the accepting bank must be combined with his obligations in regard to ineligible paper, and the total may not exceed the Section 84 lending limit (Ruling 7.1550(c)(2) of the Comptroller of the Currency).

During any period within which a national bank holds its own acceptance, eligible or ineligible, having given value therefor, the amount thereof is included against the Section 84 limit of the customer for whom the acceptance is made (Ruling 7.1550(c)(3) of the Comptroller of the Currency).

In general (Interpretive Ruling 7.7420 of the Comptroller of the Currency), national banks are not limited in the character of acceptances which they may make in financing credit transactions, and bankers acceptances may be used for such purpose, since the making of acceptances is an essential part of banking authorized by 12 U.S.C. 24.

See LETTER OF CREDIT.

ACCEPTANCE FOR HONOR The Uniform Commercial Code omits provision for this procedure as obsolete, because of modern speed of communications and availability of substitute arrangements to protect the credit of the drawer.

The term denoted the acceptance of a draft or bill of exchange by another party when acceptance had been refused by the drawee, and protest for nonacceptance had been made. When the drawee refused to accept a bill, or to pay an acceptance thereof when due, any party could accept or pay it in order to save the honor of the drawer, or of an endorser, by declaring before the notary public executing the protest that he accepted (or paid) the bill *for honor* and *for whose honor*. Acceptance for honor was also called "acceptance supra protest."

See COMMERCIAL CODE, NEGOTIABLE INSTRUMENTS LAW.

ACCEPTANCE LIABILITY The total liability which a bank assumes in accepting bills drawn on it by its customers in the financing of export, import, and domestic transactions. Although banks accept bills drawn by high-grade risks, they are required to keep a record of the aggregate of the liability created by such acceptances in an account entitled "liability on account of acceptances." This account is offset by a corresponding asset entitled "customers' liability on account of acceptances." If the customers fail to deposit funds to meet the acceptances at maturity, the bank has recourse against them.

See ACCEPTANCE CREDIT, ACCEPTANCE LINE, LETTER OF CREDIT.

ACCEPTANCE LIABILITY LEDGER A ledger in which full particulars of bills accepted for each customer are entered under an account bearing his name. The particulars are usually as follows: name and address of customer (drawer), line, date, letter of credit number, acceptance number, expiration date, amount of bill, total amount accepted or expired, and date of payment.

ACCEPTANCE LINE The maximum limit in dollars which a bank commits itself to accept for a single customer. This limit is usually fixed by the credit officers of the bank, acting upon recommendation of the manager of the foreign department in the case of acceptances arising out of import and export transactions. The acceptance line cannot exceed the legal limitation.

See ACCEPTANCE CREDIT.

ACCEPTANCE MATURITY TICKLER A record in which acceptances are journalized according to maturity dates in order that the amount of daily maturities may be determined at a glance. A single page is usually devoted to the maturities for each date.

See TICKLER.

ACCEPTANCE REGISTER A journal in which full particulars of all bills accepted by the bank for its customers are chronologically recorded. These particulars are usually as follows: date of acceptance, bank's acceptance number, name of officer sanctioning, signature of officer signing, customer's number of bill, date, tenor, maturity, drawee, payee, for the account of, list of documents received, whether original or duplicates attached, number, and date of credit.

ACCEPTOR *See* ACCEPTANCE, DRAFT.

ACCESSION In law, the doctrine that the owner of property is entitled to all that is added or united to it, either naturally or by the labor or materials of another. Not to be confused with ACCRETION.

ENCYCLOPEDIA OF BANKING AND FINANCE

ACCESSION RATE The ratio of all permanent and temporary additions to work force during a month, whether new or rehired employees, to the average work force during the month.

The Bureau of Labor Statistics of the U.S. Department of Labor regularly publishes the accession rate for manufacturing, indicating the rate of accessions per 100 employees. This is one of the leading indicators in analysis of business cycles, designated by the National Bureau of Economic Research.

See BUSINESS BAROMETERS.

ACCOMMODATION Supplying with funds when application for credit is made to a bank. Such accommodation is usually arranged beforehand by means of the LINE OF CREDIT.

ACCOMMODATION BILL OF LADING A BILL OF LADING issued by an agent of a common carrier prior to receipt of the merchandise, usually to enable the seller to present his documents to a bank before a specified time limit. This is a dangerous practice because the order bill of lading may be used as a basis for credit, leading to possible fraud if delivery of the goods does not occur. At common law, many courts held that a carrier was not bound by a bill of lading issued by an agent without actual receipt of the goods. The Uniform Bills of Lading Act, however, imposes liability on the carrier to relying holders or consignees on negotiable or nonnegotiable bills of lading issued by an agent whose actual or apparent authority includes their issuance. The Uniform Commercial Code makes similar provision for the carrier's liability (Sec. 7-301(1)).

See COMMERCIAL CODE, NEGOTIABLE INSTRUMENTS LAW.

ACCOMMODATION PAPER A note or bill signed by a party as maker, acceptor, or endorser to accommodate another party whose credit is not strong enough to enable him to borrow on his single name.

Accommodation paper is quite common in personal and business lending. Precautions in handling accommodation paper by lenders include:

1. Check of the credit worthiness of the comaker or accommodation endorser, as to whether it actually strengthens the obligation. In lending to closely held corporations, personal endorsement by the principal officers or stockholders also has psychological value.
2. Check of the wording of the promise to pay in comaker notes, to make clear that the makers are jointly and severally liable, not merely jointly liable, for collection in full from the comaker in case of default.
3. Check of the collateral note form as to whether it provides following or similar continuing scope of collateral as "security for the payment of this note and any other liabilities, contingent or otherwise, of the makers, guarantors, endorsers, and any other parties to this note and each of them, to the holder hereof, now due or to become due or that may be hereafter contracted."
4. Check, in the case of corporate notes, as to the corporation's charter and/or statutory power to become accommodation guarantor or endorser. General rule is that such accommodation by a corporation even if authorized shall be of direct benefit to the corporation in furtherance of its corporate purposes.
5. Check of the authority of officers to sign on behalf of a corporation, as evidenced by resolution of the board of directors or stockholder approval.
6. Check, in the case of partnership notes, for personal endorsements of all partners, so that the obligation may rank as both a business and a personal debt of the individual partners.
7. Check, in states which still provide for dower and curtesy, for endorsement of wife or husband, as appropriate, on loans to married individuals.

Under Paragraph 7.1125, Obligations of Accommodation Parties, of the Interpretive Rulings of the Comptroller of the Currency, the liability of a maker, acceptor, drawer, endorser, or guarantor is an obligation within the meaning of the statute (12 USC 84) when the party has obtained a loan or has sold or discounted the paper, but not otherwise.

See LOAN.

BIBLIOGRAPHY

COMPTROLLER OF THE CURRENCY. *Comptroller's Manual for National Banks.*

ACCOMMODATION PARTY A party to a negotiable instrument who signs a note or bill as maker, acceptor, or endorser, to accommodate another party and enhance the credit worthiness of the paper.

The Uniform Negotiable Instruments Law (Art. II, Sec. 29) specified that an accommodation party is one who thus signed an instrument "without receiving value therefor."

The Uniform Commercial Code (Sec. 3-415(1)) has eliminated such reference to nonreceipt of consideration as the distinguishing feature of an accommodation party. It is no longer determining that he signed gratuitously. The accommodation party is a surety or guarantor whose obligation is supported by any consideration for which the instrument is taken before due. If he signs as accommodation maker or acceptor, the accommodation party is bound without prior resort to his principal. If he signs as accommodation endorser, he is bound only after presentment, notice of dishonor, and protest. But the accommodation party who pays the instrument becomes subrogated to the rights *of the holder* paid, as surety, as to recourse on the instrument.

See ACCOMMODATION PAPER.

ACCORD AND SATISFACTION A settlement of a claim in which the creditor agrees to accept in payment something different from what might be enforced legally.

ACCOUNT A record of financial transactions, whether CONTROL ACCOUNT in the general ledger or individual account in subsidiary ledgers, involving debits and/or credits reflecting increases and decreases in the subject of the account.

Account with a bank or broker is the business relationship, express or implied, arising by agreement with the customer.

See BANK ACCOUNT.

ACCOUNT ANALYSIS A comparison of the cost of service provided to support a checking account and the earnings on the balances in the account during the month or other period. The excess of cost over earnings is assessed as a charge against the account.

ACCOUNT AND RISK All transactions between broker and customer are at the risk of the customer, who is the principal. Rules of the NEW YORK STOCK EXCHANGE provide that under no circumstances may a customer's account be guaranteed against loss. Confirmations of transactions sent in writing by a broker to the customer customarily indicate in printing, "We have bought/sold for your account and risk" (that of the customer).

See CONFIRMATION.

ACCOUNTANT An association of individuals engaged in a vocation or occupation that generally is expected to meet the following criteria:

1. Renders an essential service to society.
2. Depends on a body of specialized knowledge acquired through formal education.
3. Has developed a language of its own.
4. Has requirements for admission to the profession regulated by law.
5. Governed by principles that emphasize the virtues of honesty, probity, and concern for the welfare of those served (the public interest).
6. Has procedures for disciplining those whose conduct violates ethical standards.

Accounting is a profession along with law, medicine, education, the ministry, and others. The accounting profession is typically subdivided into public accountants who function as independent experts and perform services for clients and internal accountants who work for a particular firm or organization. The accounting profession can be further subdivided as follows:

ENCYCLOPEDIA OF BANKING AND FINANCE

Public Accountant	Internal (or private) Accountant
External auditor	Financial or general accountant
Tax specialist	Cost accountant
Management consultant	Internal auditor
	Tax accountant
	Systems analyst

A certified public accountant (CPA) is an accountant who has fulfilled certain requirements (education, qualifying experience, an acceptable score on a national written examination) established by a state law for the practice of public accounting and becomes licensed to practice public accounting in that state. To become a CPA, an accountant must pass a comprehensive examination in accounting theory and practice, auditing, and business law. The examination is being restructured to become effective possibly in 1993-94 as follows: (1) professional responsibilities and business law, (2) auditing, (3) accounting and reporting—B (taxation; managerial; governmental; not-for-profit),and (4) accounting and reporting—A (business enterprises). CPAs are expected to have a high moral character and must conduct their professional practices according to a code of professional conduct. In addition to the CPA examination, other professional examinations have been developed to test the competency level of practitioners. These examinations include the Certificate in Management Accounting (CMA) and the Certified Internal Auditor (CIA). Other countries have professional designations simi-lar to CPA, sometimes referred to as Chartered Accountant.

The largest American accounting firms include (in alphabetical order):

Arthur Andersen & Co.
Coopers & Lybrand
Deloitte and Touche
Ernst & Young
Peat Marwick Main & Co.
Price Waterhouse & Co.

These firms employ approxcimately 12 percent of the 200,000 CPAs in theUnited States. They audit the financial statements of approximately 85 percent of the 2,600 largest corporations.

Positions within public accounting firms and other organizations are shown here:

Public Accounting Firms	Private Accounting
Partner	Major Operating Executive
Manager	Chief Financial Officer, Controller, or Treasurer
Senior Accountant	Senior Accountant
Staff Accountant	Staff Accountant

The American Institute of Certified Public Accountants (AICPA) is the national professional organization of CPAs. The AICPA participates in the development of accounting and auditing principles and standards. The Institutes's Auditing Standards Board formulates generally accepted auditing standards that apply to the manner in which CPAs perform audits. The AICPA publishes a monthly professional *Journal of Accountancy*. The National Association of Accountants (NAA) is the major professional of cost and management accountants. The NAA administers the Certified Management Accountant (CMA) examination and publishes the monthly journal *Management Accounting*. The Institute of Internal Auditor (IIA) is the major association of internal auditors and publishes *The Internal Auditor*. The American Accounting Association (AAA) is the major academic association for accountants and promotes education and research in accounting. The Financial Executives Institute (FEI) is an association of financial executives who function in the financial area. The Institute publishes the *Financial Executive*.

See AUDIT.

ACCOUNT CURRENT In accounting of the FACTOR, the monthly statement prepared by the factor in account with the factor's client.

Credits include the net proceeds from the current month's ACCOUNT OF SALES, which begin drawing interest in advance for the month at the same rate as the interest charged for the value-date period, plus interest credited in advance for the month on the balance carried forward from the preceding month's account current. Debits include withdrawals by the client plus interest on the withdrawals from date of withdrawal to the end of the month (in view of the fact that interest on the credits was credited in advance).

ACCOUNT DAY One of the SETTLEMENT DAYS on the LONDON STOCK EXCHANGE, where settlements are made twice a month. The settlement lasts three days, and the account day, also known as payday, is the third and last of the settlement days, on which delivery and payment are made for the transactions of the preceding half month.

ACCOUNTING An information system that accumulates,processes, and communicates information, primarily financial in nature, about a specific economic entity. Accounting was defined in Accounting Terminology Bulletin No. 2 of the American Institute of Certified Public Accountants as follows:

> Accounting is the art of recording, classifying in a significant manner and in terms of money, transactions and events which are, in part at least, of a financial character, and interpreting results thereof.

This definition emphasizes the work that the accountant does and makes little reference to the users of the information that the accountant provides.

The American Accounting Association defined accounting in a Statement of Basic Theory, 1966, as follows:

> Accounting is the process of identifying, measuring and communicating economic information to permit informed judgments and decisions by users of the information . . . . The objectives of accounting are to provided for the following purposes:
>
> 1. Making decisions concerning the use of limited resources, including crucial decision areas, and determination of goals and objectives
> 2. Effectively directing and controlling an organization's human and material resources.
> 3. Maintaining and reporting on the custodianship of resources.
> 4. *Facilitating social functions and controls.*

This definition identifies the major role of accounting as providing information for those who use the information. The definition specifies three major functions of accounting: identifying, measuring, and communicating economic information.

In 1970, the Accounting principles Board of the American Institute of Certified Public Accountants developed the following definition:

> Accounting is a service activity. Its function is to provide quantitative information, primarily financial in nature, about economic activities that is intended to be useful in making economic decisions—in making reasoned choices among alternative courses of action.

This definition of accounting is goal-oriented rather than process-oriented or function-oriented. It emphasizes economic decision-making activities rather than the functions of accounting as the major objectives of accounting. In a popular sense, accounting has been referred to as the language of business, since it is the basic tool for recording and reporting economic events and transactions that affect business enterprises. Other concepts of accounting view accounting as a historical record, a mirror of current economic reality, a subset of a total business information system, and as a commodity that is the product of economic activity.

See ACCOUNTING ASSUMPTIONS, ACCOUNTING FUNCTIONS, ACCOUNTING POLICIES AND PROCEDURES, ACCOUNTING THEORY, GENERALLY ACCEPTED ACCOUNTING PRINCIPLES, AUDIT.

See also ACCOUNTING.

BIBLIOGRAPHY

Abacus.
Accountancy.
Accountants Digest, 1935-. Quarterly. Accountants' Index, 1920-. Quarterly.
Accounting Historians Journal.
Accounting Horizons.
Accounting Issues.
Accounting, Organizations and Society.
The Accounting Review.
Accounting Today.
Accounting Trends and Techniques. American Institute of Certified Public Accountants, New York, NY. Annual.
———. *AICPA Audit and Accounting Manual.* Latest edition.
———. *AICPA Codification of Statements on Auditing Standards.* Latest edition.
———. *AICPA Codification of Statements on Auditing Standards.* Latest edition.
———. *AICPA Professional Standards, U.S. Auditing Standards, Accounting and Review Services, Ethics, Bylaws, International Accounting, International Auditing Management Advisory Services, Quality Control, and Tax Practice.* Two volumes. Annual.
———.*AICPA Technical Practice Aids.* Latest edition.
———.*Audits of Banks*, 1985.
———.*Audits of Finance Companies*, 1973. Anthony, R. N. *Fundamentals of Management Accounting.* Richard D. Irwin, Inc., Homewood, IL., 1985.
Australian Accountant.
CA Magazine.
Chartered Accountant in Australia.
COMMERCE CLEARING HOUSE. *American Institute of Certified Public Accountants Professional Standards.* Four volumes. Commerce Clearing House, Chicago, IL. Latest edition.
COOPER, W. W., and IJIRI, V., eds. *Kohler's Dictionary for Accountants.* Prentice Hall, Inc., Englewood Cliffs, NJ. Latest edition.
Cost and Management.
The CPA Journal.
ESTES, R.W. *Dictionary of Accounting.* MIT Press, Cambridge, MA, 1985.
Government Accountant's Journal.
International Journal of Accounting Education & Research.
Journal of Accountancy.
Journal of Accounting and Economics.
Journal of Accounting and Public Policy.
Journal of Accounting and Research.
Journal of Accounting, Auditing and Finance.
Journal of Taxation.
KIESO, D. E., and WEYGANDT, J. J. *Intermediate Accounting.* John Wiley and Sons, Inc., New York, NY. Latest edition.
Management Accounting.
MCGLADREY & PULLEN. *Banking Industry Manual.* Minneapolis, MN, 1987.
———. *Procedure Manual*, 1988.
———. *Report Manual*, 1987.
MUNTER, P., and RATCLIFFE, T. A. *Applying GAAP and GAAS.* Matthew Bender & Co., Inc., New York, NY. Two volumes. Latest edition.
National Tax Journal.
NIKOLAI, L. A. *Principles of Accounting.* PWK-Kent Publishing Co., Boston, MA, 1990.
O'MALIA, T. J. *A Banker's Guide to Financial Statements.* Bank Administration Institute, Rolling Meadows, IL, 1989.
The Practical Accountant.
PEAT MARWICK, MAIN & CO. *Principles and Presentation: Banking.* Peat Marwick, Main & Co., New York, NY. Annual.
The Practical Accountant.
Spectrum.
The Tax Advisor.
WELCH, G. A., and SHORT, D. *Fundamentals of Financial Accounting.* Richard D. Irwin, Inc., Homewood, IL, 1987.
Who Audits America. Data Financial Press, Menlo Park, CA. Semi-annual.
WOELFEL, C. J. *Corporate Finance and Accounting.* Probus Publishing Co., Chicago, IL, 1987.
Woman CPA.

ACCOUNTING ASSUMPTIONS Broad concepts that underlie generally accepted accounting principles. The major accounting assumptions include the following: the business entity assumption, the continuity assumption, the periodic and timely reporting assumption, and the monetary unit assumption.

A basic assumption in accounting is that economic activity can be identified with a particular unit (or entity) of accountability. This unit is the one to be accounted for. The business entity assumption determines the nature and scope of the reporting that is required for the unit. The entity for accounting purposes is identified as the economic unit that controls resources, incurs obligations, and otherwise is involved in directing economic activities that relate to a specific accountability unit. Accounting units (or entities) include corporations, partnerships, proprietorships, not-for-profit entities, trusts, and others.

Accounting is based on the assumption that the accounting unit is engaged in continuous and ongoing activities. The accounting unit is assumed to remain in operation into the foreseeable future in pursuit of its goals and objectives. This assumption is referred to as the continuity or going-concern assumption.

The continuous operations of a unit over an extended period of time can be meaningfully segmented into equal time periods, such as a year, quarters, or months. The periodic and timely reporting assumptions require that accounting reporting should be done periodically and on a timely basis so that it is relevant and reliable.

The monetary unit assumption requires that financial information be measured and accounted for in the basic monetary unit of the country in which the enterprise is located. The monetary value of an economic event or transaction, determined at the time it is recorded, is not adjusted for subsequent changes in the purchasing power of the monetary unit (as occurs in periods of inflation or deflation).

See ACCOUNTING, ACCOUNTING FUNCTIONS, ACCOUNTING POLICIES AND PROCEDURES, ACCOUNTING THEORY, GENERALLY ACCEPTED ACCOUNTING PRINCIPLES (GAAP).

ACCOUNTING BASIS Methods for recognizing revenue, expenses, assets and liabilities in accounting statements. Major bases of accounting include the accrual, cash, and modified cash bases. In accrual accounting, revenue and gains are recognized in the period when they are earned. Expenses and losses are recognized in the period when they are incurred. Accrual-basis accounting is concerned with the economic consequences of events and transactions rather than only with cash receipts and cash payments. Under accrual accounting, net income does not necessarily reflect cash receipts and cash payments for a particular time period. Accrual accounting generally provides the most accurate measure of earnings, earning power, managerial performance, cash flows, and stewardship.

Cash-basis accounting recognizes only transactions involving actual cash receipts and disbursements occurring in a given period. Cash-basis accounting recognizes revenues and gains when cash is received and expenses and losses when cash is paid. No attempt is made to record unpaid bills or amounts owed to or by the unit. Cash-basis accounting is generally deficient as an accounting model that attempts to produce a statement of financial position and an income statement. However, cash-basis accounting is widely used for income tax purposes.

Under a modified cash basis of accounting, certain expenditures are capitalized and amortized in the future. For example, under cash-basis accounting, the purchase of equipment for cash is expensed immediately; under a modified cash basis, the purchase is recorded as an asset. A portion of the acquisition cost is later recognized as an expense when the services of the asset are consumed.

Net income from operations computed according to generally accepted accounting principles (accrual basis) can be converted to cash flow from operations according to the following general procedures:

Net income from operations

+   Items reducing income but not using cash, such as depreciation, depletion, and amortization expenses
     Decreases in current assets other than cash
     Increases in current liabilities

−   Increases in current assets other than cash
     Decreases in current liabilities

=   Cash flow from operations

See ACCOUNTING, GENERALLY ACCEPTED ACCOUNTING PRINCIPLES (GAAP).

ACCOUNTING CONTROLS Accounting controls include the plan of organization and the procedures and records dealing with the broad objectives of safeguarding assets and improving the reliability of financial records required for the preparation of financial statements. Accounting controls are concerned primarily with systems of authorization and approval, controls over assets internal auditing procedures, and other financial matters. It is management's responsibility to establish and maintain an appropriate system of internal accounting control.

According to the AICPA's Statements on Auditing Standards No's. 1 and 30, the operative objective of accounting controls is designed to provide reasonable assurance that:

1. Transactions are executed in accordance with management's general or specific authorization.
2. Transactions are recorded as necessary (1) to permit the preparation of financial statements in conformity with generally accepted accounting principles or any other criteria applicable to such statements, and (2) to maintain accountability for assets.
3. Access to assets is permitted only in accordance with management's authorization.
4. The recorded accountability for assets is compared with the existing assets at reasonable intervals and appropriate action is taken with respect to any difference.

Accounting control systems provide reasonable, not absolute, assurance that the accounting control objectives are met. The concept of reasonable assurance recognizes that accounting control systems are subject to cost-benefit constraints.

See ADMINISTRATIVE CONTROLS.

ACCOUNTING CYCLE A sequence of activities that records, summarizes, and reports economic events and transactions. The steps in the accounting cycle include journalizing transactions, posting to a ledger, taking a trial balance, adjusting the accounts, preparing financial statements, closing the accounts, and taking a post-closing trial balance. The accounting cycle is repeated each accounting period. The operations of the cycle can be conceptualized as appended.

See ACCOUNTING, ACCOUNTING SYSTEM.

The Accounting Process (or Cycle)

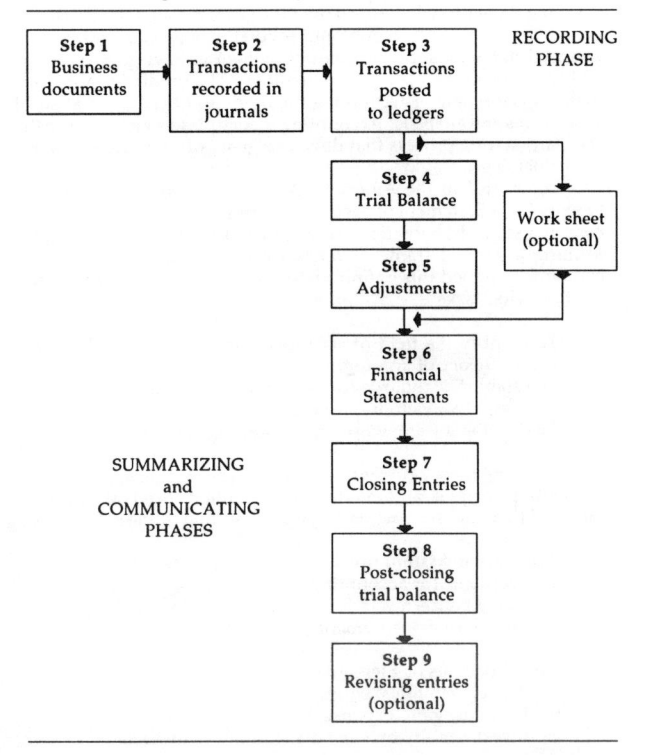

```
Step 1              Step 2           Step 3            RECORDING
Business    →    Transactions   →   Transactions       PHASE
documents        recorded in        posted
                 journals           to ledgers
                                        ↓
                                    Step 4
                                    Trial Balance
                                        ↓              Work sheet
                                    Step 5             (optional)
                                    Adjustments
                                        ↓
                                    Step 6
                                    Financial
                                    Statements
                                        ↓
SUMMARIZING                         Step 7
and                                 Closing Entries
COMMUNICATING                           ↓
PHASES                              Step 8
                                    Post-closing
                                    trial balance
                                        ↓
                                    Step 9
                                    Revising entries
                                    (optional)
```

ACCOUNTING EQUATION The accounting equation expresses the relationship that exists among assets, liabilities, and owners' equity. In its simplest form, the accounting equation can be represented as follows:

Assets – Liabilities = Owners' Equity (or Capital)

The equation states an equality and establishes a relationship among the three major accounting elements. Assets are the economic resources a business or other entity owns that are expected to be of benefit in the future. Liabilities are economic obligations payable to outsiders. Owners' equity is shown as the residual of assets over liabilities. The accounting equation can also be stated in this form:

Assets = Liabilities + Owners' Equity

This formulation of the accounting equation shows that owners and creditors have claims against the assets of the enterprise. The accounting equation can also be expressed in a format that combines liabilities and owners' equity into a single concept referred to as equities (legal and economic claims to the assets):

Assets = Equities

ACCOUNTING FUNCTIONS Accounting deals with numbers and measurable quantities. The accounting system accumulates, measures, and communicates numbers and measurable quantities of economic information about an enterprise. These three functions can be represented as a flow of information from source to destination as follows:

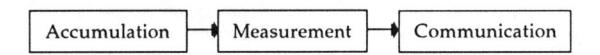

| Accumulation | → | Measurement | → | Communication |

Accumulation refers primarily to recording and classifying data in journals and ledgers. The accounting system accumulates data related primarily to completed transactions and events. Measurement refers to the quantification of business transactions or other economic events that have occurred, or that may occur. Measurement determines how to select the best amounts to recognize in the financial statements. The accounting system communicates relevant and reliable information to investors, creditors, managers, and others for internal and external decision-making.

See ACCOUNTING, ACCOUNTING SYSTEM.

ACCOUNTING PERIOD The time period for which financial statements are prepared. Custom as well as income tax and other legal considerations have focused on annual reporting periods and an annual accounting cycle. If the reporting period begins on January 1 and ends on December 31, it is referred to as a calendar-year accounting period. Any other beginning and ending period of one year is called a fiscal year. The accounting period is identified on the financial statements.

When selecting an annual reporting period, some entities adopt a reporting period that ends when operations (inventories and accounts receivable) are at a low point in order to simplify year-end accounting procedures and to permit more rapid preparation of financial statements. Such an accounting period is referred to as a natural business year since it conforms to the natural annual cycle of the entity.

Some firms use a 52-53-week accounting period for reporting purposes. The yearly reporting period varies from 52 to 53 weeks since it always ends on the same day of the week (for example, the last Friday of the year), either the last one of such days in a calendar month, or the closest one to the last day of a calendar month.

Financial reports for periods shorter than one year, such as quarterly reports, are referred to as interim reports or interim statements.

For income tax purposes, the accounting period is usually a year. Unless a fiscal year is chosen, taxpayers must determine their tax liability by using the calendar year as the period of measurement. A change in the accounting period requires approval of the IRS.

See ACCOUNTING, ACCOUNTING ASSUMPTIONS, ACCOUNTING FUNCTIONS, ANNUAL REPORTS, FINANCIAL STATEMENTS, INTERIM FINANCIAL REPORTS.

ACCOUNTING POLICIES AND PROCEDURES The accounting policies of a reporting entity are the specific accounting principles and the methods of applying those principles that are judged by the management of the enterprise to be the most appropriate in the circumstances to present fairly a financial position, results of operations, and cash flow in accordance with generally accepted accounting principles.

Information about the accounting policies adopted by a reporting enterprise is essential for financial statement users, and should be disclosed adequately. Accounting principles and their methods of application in the following areas are important:

1. A selection from existing alternatives.
2. Areas that are peculiar to a particular industry in which the company operates.
3. Unusual and innovative applications of generally accepted accounting principles.

Examples of commonly required disclosures by a business enterprise include those relating to depreciation methods, inventory pricing, basis of consolidations, and recognition of profit on long-term, construction-type contracts.

The preferred place to disclose accounting policies is under the caption "Summary of Significant Accounting Policies" or as the initial note to the financial statements.

Accounting procedures are those rules and practices associated with the operations of an accounting system. They lead to the development of financial statements. Accounting procedures include the methods, practices, and techniques used to carry out accounting objectives and to implement accounting principles. For example, LIFO, FIFO, and other inventory methods are accounting procedures as are various depreciation methods such as straight-line depreciation and accelerated depreciation methods. An accounting convention is an accounting procedure that does not have official approval by an authoritative body such as the Financial Accounting Standards Board.

Accounting procedures can vary from company to company and from industry to industry. An accounting procedure should be selected in a given circumstance if its use reflects generally accepted accounting principles and if it is appropriate to record, process, and report the event or transaction.

See ACCOUNTING, ACCOUNTING FUNCTIONS, ACCOUNTING SYSTEM, GENERALLY ACCEPTED ACCOUNTING PRINCIPLES (GAAP).

BIBLIOGRAPHY

ACCOUNTING PRINCIPLES BOARD OPINION No. 22, *Disclosure of Accounting Policies*, 1972.
KELLY-NEWTON, LAUREN. *Accounting Policy Formulation*, 1980.

ACCOUNTING PRINCIPLES *See* GENERALLY ACCEPTED ACCOUNTING PRINCIPLES (GAAP).

ACCOUNTING PROFIT In accounting, profit and income are considered net concepts and refer to amounts resulting from the deduction from revenues, or from operating revenue, of cost of goods sold or other expenses and losses. The terms are generally preceded by a qualifying adjective such as "gross," "operating," or "net."

In economics, accounting profit has a unique meaning. Accounting profit is defined, for a given time period, as total revenue minus total costs. In this calculation, total cost includes the firm's explicit costs of operations such as wage payments and interest on capital equipment.

ACCOUNTING SYSTEM An accounting system is a management information system that is responsible for the collection and processing of data to produce information useful to decision-makers in planning and controlling the activities of an organization. An accounting system deals primarily with one category of information, namely, financial information that concerns the flow of financial resources through the organization.

The data processing cycle of an accounting system can be conceptualized as the total structure of records and procedures associated with five activities: collection or recording; classifying; processing, including calculating and summarizing; maintenance or storage; and output or reporting. The processing of data in a typical accounting system can be illustrated as follows:

Source document	Journals	Ledgers	Trial balance	Financial statements
Collection	Classifying, Processing, Maintenance			Output

The development of an accounting information system includes the following stages: analysis, design, implementation, and operations. During the system analysis stage, the analyst determines the information needs of the system, the sources of information, and the strengths and deficiencies of the current system. The design stage typically involves an evaluation of different kinds of data processing equipments, processing methods, and procedures that are suitable to the proposed project. During the design stage, the detailed system design is completed. After the system is designed, the implementation of the system commences. During the implementations stage, the system is installed and made ready to begin functioning. After the system has been implemented, it becomes operational. Modifications of the system may be required as problems arise or as needs or technology develops.

BIBLIOGRAPHY

GELINAS, U. J., ET AL. *Accounting Information Systems*, 1990.
MOSCOVE, S. A., and SIMKIN, M. G. *Accounting Information Systems*, 1984.

ACCOUNTING THEORY Theory is a systematic statement of principles that serve as a foundation and explanation for underlying phenomena. In general, theory should provide an explanation, a basis for predicting outcomes or results, and guidance for practice. Accounting theory consists of a systematic statement of accounting principles and methodology.

Accounting theory has been developed using either a deductive or an inductive approach. The deductive approach involves reasoning from the general to the particular; the inductive approach involves reasoning from the particular to the general. No generally recognized, comprehensive theory of accounting exists at present.

The objective of accounting theory is to establish a framework or reference point to guide and evaluate accounting practice. Accounting theory also provides a basis for inherent logic, consistency, and usefulness of accounting principles and procedures. Much of accounting theory has developed over the years through the process of general acceptance by accountants, regulatory agencies, and users of financial statements. Some accounting theories have gained acceptability based on their predictive qualities. The predictive approach to the development of accounting theory relies heavily on statistical procedures and analysis. Accounting theory plays a major role in the standard-setting process that develops generally accepted accounting principles.

A committee of the American Accounting Association defined "theory" in A Statement of Basic Accounting Theory (ASOBAT) as "a cohesive set of hypothetical, conceptual and pragmatic principles forming a general frame of reference for a field of study." The committee applied this definition to accounting and assigned itself the following tasks:

1. To identify the field of accounting in order to develop a coherent theory of accounting.
2. To establish standards for accounting information.
3. To suggest ways to improve accounting practice.
4. To develop a framework for accounting research.

Accounting theory currently consists of assumptions, concepts or elements, principles, and modifying conventions used in the preparation of financial statements. A general outline of these factors is:

1. Accounting Assumptions
    a. Economic (or accounting) entity
    b. Going concern
    c. Monetary measurement
    d. Periodicity
2. Basic Concepts or Elements
    a. Assets, liabilities, equities
    b. Revenue, gain, expense, loss, comprehensive income
    c. Investment by owners, distribution to owners

3. Broad Principles
   a. Historical (or acquisition) cost
   b. Revenue realization
   c. Revenue recognition
   d. Matching costs and revenues
   e. Accrual accounting
   f. Consistency
   g. Adequate (or full) disclosure
   h. Objectivity
   i. Articulated (or interrelated) financial statements
4. Modifying Conventions
   a. Materiality
   b. Conservatism
   c. Industry practices

See EXPENSES, LIABILITIES

BIBLIOGRAPHY

AMERICAN ACCOUNTING ASSOCIATION. *Statement on Accounting Theory and Theory Acceptance,* 1977.
AMERICAN ACCOUNTING ASSOCIATION. *Accounting and Reporting Standards for Corporate Financial Statements and Preceding Statements and Preceding Statements and Supplements,* 1957.
AMERICAN ACCOUNTING ASSOCIATION. *A Statement of Basic Accounting Theory,* 1966.
AMERICAN INSTITUTE OF CERTIFIED PUBLIC ACCOUNTANTS. *The Basic Postulates of Accounting,* Accounting Research Study No. 1, 1961.
AMERICAN INSTITUTE OF CERTIFIED PUBLIC ACCOUNTANTS. *Basic Concepts and Accounting Principles Underlying Financial Statements of Business Enterprises,* APB Statement No.4, 1970.
AMERICAN INSTITUTE OF CERTIFIED PUBLIC ACCOUNTANTS. *A Tentative Set of Broad Accounting Principles for Business Enterprises,* Accounting Research Study No.3, 1962.
AMERICAN INSTITUTE OF CERTIFIED PUBLIC ACCOUNTANTS. *Inventory of Generally Accepted Accounting Principles for Business Enterprises,* Accounting Research Study No. 7 (AICPA, 1965).
BELKAOUI, A. *Accounting Theory.* Harcourt Brace Jovanovich, Publishers, San Diego, CA, 1985.
KAM, V. *Accounting Theory.* John Wiley and Sons, New York, NY, 1986.
WOLK, H. I. and others. *Accounting Theory: A Conceptual and Institutional Approach* 1984.

ACCOUNT OF SALES A statement submitted by a consignee, broker, or other commission merchant or agent, showing the proceeds of the sale of goods or securities sold for the account of the owner. The statement shows full particulars, viz., selling price, expenses incurred (such as freight, warehousing, insurance, etc.), commission, and, finally, the net proceeds due to the owner.

In operations of the factor, the account of sales indicates the gross sales less all deductions for a given month, prepared on the basis of the copies of invoices sent to the factor by the factor's client. After deduction of the factor's commission, the net balance is assigned a future value-date which is computed on the basis of the average due date of the invoices plus collection time allowance (usually ten days). The period between this value-date and the current date of the account of sales is charged interest by the factor; this represents the last deduction made before the net proceeds thus arrived at of the account of sales are credited to the account current.

ACCOUNTS PAYABLE Accounts due to creditors as shown by the books of a business, but not evidenced by notes, drafts, or acceptances (open book accounts); the aggregate sum due to trade creditors; a control account in the general ledger to indicate the total of balances due to creditors on open book accounts, as shown by the subsidiary (accounts payable, purchases, or creditors) ledger.

Accounts payable are one of the current liabilities if in fact due either on the date of the statement or in twelve months from the date of the statement, pursuant to conventional accounting practice.

ACCOUNTS RECEIVABLE Accounts due from customers as shown by the books of a business, but not evidenced by notes, drafts, or acceptances (open book accounts); the aggregate sum due from trade debtors; a control account in the general ledger to indicate the total of balances due from customers on open book accounts, as shown by the subsidiary (accounts receivable, sales, or customers') ledgers.

Accounts receivable are one of the CURRENT ASSETS if in fact the claims represented are payable as of the date of the statement or payable in 12 months from the date of the statement, pursuant to conventional accounting practice.

BIBLIOGRAPHY

ROBINSON, D. A. *Accounts Receivable and Inventory Lending.* Bankers Publishing Co., Rolling Meadows, IL, 1987.

ACCOUNTS RECEIVABLE FINANCING Accounts receivable represent a promise from customers to pay for goods sold or services rendered. Accounts receivable financing is a form of collateralized lending in which accounts receivable are the collateral. A bank often lends money against an agreed-on percentage of accounts receivable assigned to it, usually in the range of 50 to 90 percent. The borrower usually extends credit and makes collections; customers are not notified of the assignment of their debt to the bank. Collections pay down the loan and new loan funds are often granted as new receivables are generated.

Accounts receivable financing provides the bank with an active loan market. The loan is collateralized and the collateral is generally examined thoroughly and continually to ensure performance and to eliminate unacceptable receivables. Credit is controlled in that lending follows the sales made by the borrower. Repayment of the loan is somewhat automatic as the customer makes collections. Bank credit is usually tailored to the needs of the borrower because financing responds to expanding or contracting sales. The cost of accounts receivable financing is typically higher than that associated with unsecured lending by a qualified borrower.

Accounts receivable financing should not be confused with factoring. In factoring, a bank purchases (versus collateralized lending) selected accounts receivables from its customer at a percentage of their face value.

BIBLIOGRAPHY

ROBINSON, D. A. *Accounts Receivable and Inventory Lending,* Banker's Publishing Co., Rolling Meadows, IL, 1987.

ACCOUNTS RECEIVABLE TURNOVER In analyzing statements as a basis for measuring credit risks, it is important to ascertain how fast the accounts receivable are being turned over, i.e., whether the terms of credit of the concern are being fulfilled as shown by collections. The TURNOVER of accounts receivable is also known among credit people as the sales-to-receivables ratio. It is computed by dividing the annual credit sales by the average amount of accounts receivable standing on the books for the given 12 months' period. This will produce the multiple of turnover, which may then be divided into 12 months (the period represented) to obtain the AVERAGE COLLECTION PERIOD. Alternatively, the average collection period may be obtained by computing average daily volume of annual credit sales, and dividing it into the average amount of accounts receivable standing on the books for the given 12 months' period. What the turnover of accounts receivable and the average collection period should be depends upon the terms of credit offered by the concern in sales to its customers. Where credit sales are fairly constant from month to month, and the terms of credit are 30 days net, in an ideal case, the turnover would be 12 times and thus the average collection period would be one month (30 days). Sales in any given month should be paid pursuant to such terms in the next succeeding month, i.e., the collections of any one month should equal the credit sales of the next preceding month. Consequently, the accounts receivable outstanding one month would be one-twelfth of the total credit sales for the year. If this turnover were 24 to 1, it would be evident that the terms of credit were being anticipated and advantage was being taken of cash discounts offered, with average collection period of one-half month or 15 days. If, on the other hand, the turnover multiple should be a lower one, such as 6 to 1, this would indicate that under these terms of credit collections were lagging, and one or all of five conclusions might be confirmed upon investigation:

1. The credit department has overextended credit and allowed customers to overcommit themselves.

2. A poorer class of customers, who have been unable to pay their bills promptly, has been accommodated.
3. The credit department has been lax in enforcing collections.
4. External conditions are becoming abnormal—money is tight and everybody is experiencing difficulty in paying promptly.
5. Sales are expanding and collections have not yet caught up; or terms of credit have been lengthened.

Other significant turnovers in RATIO ANALYSIS include INVENTORY TURNOVER, turnover of invested capital, and turnover of operating assets.

See CREDIT BAROMETRICS, STATEMENT ANALYSIS.

ACCRA One of the standard growths of cocoa, traded on a spot basis in New York, and also traded in futures contracts, for which it is identified as a standard growth as "Ghana, of the main crop."
See COFFEE, SUGAR & COCOA EXCHANGE, INC.

ACCRETION This term has two meanings:

1. In computing yields and in valuation of bonds bought at discounts below par, accretion is synonymous with ACCUMULATION of the discount on annual straight-line basis to maturity. Accretion is the term officially used by the Board of Governors of the Federal Reserve System in its Regulation F. Securities of Member State Banks (similar regulation by the Federal Deposit Insurance Corporation), governing the preparation of registration statements and periodic financial statements pursuant to the 1964 amendments (78 Stat. 565) to the SECURITIES EXCHANGE ACT OF 1934. Securities accounts, for purposes of both the balance sheet and the income statement, shall reflect cost adjusted for amortization of premium and, at the option of the bank, for accretion of discount. If the reporting bank does not accrete bond discount, the amount that could have been accreted shall be set forth in footnote.
2. In law, the doctrine that an owner's property, and hence the security of any liens or mortgages thereon, is increased by the added land resulting from the *gradual* action of the elements, such as the gradual permanent receding of a stream or lake. Where a sudden and not gradual submersion of an owner's land occurs (avulsion), the doctrine is that the owner does not lose title to any of the land thus submerged.

ACCRUAL BASIS Under the accrual basis of accounting, income and expenses are recorded on the books for the fiscal period in which they are earned or incurred, regardless of whether the income was actually received or expenses actually paid in the period. This contrasts with the cash basis, under which income and expenses are recorded only when actually received or paid out in the period. Consequently, the accrual basis affords a more accurate record of income and outgo for a particular period.

Tax returns must be filed on the cash basis, unless accounts are kept on the accrual basis. Cash basis for tax purposes means not only income actually received in a tax year but also income constructively received. Income is constructively received when it is credited or set aside for a taxpayer and thus may be drawn upon by the taxpayer at any time. Examples: uncashed salary or dividend checks; bank interest credited to depositor's account; matured bond coupons.

Accrual basis is prescribed for bank registration statements and reports by Regulation F of the Board of Governors of the Federal Reserve System (similar regulation by the Federal Deposit Insurance Corporation), issued pursuant to the 1964 amendments to the SECURITIES EXCHANGE ACT OF 1934.

ACCRUED DIVIDEND Dividends on stocks (preferred and/or common) are not accrued from last payment dates in security market practice like interest on bonds and debentures. Dividends are uncertain and do not become payable until and unless declared, whereas interest of the fixed type is an obligation which must be met, whether or not covered by current earnings.

Instead of accruing dividends, security market prices are CUM DIVIDEND (dividend on) until such time after declaration as they are quoted EX DIVIDEND (without dividend). The ex dividend date depends upon the stockholders of record date fixed in the dividend declaration and upon the normal delivery time for security transactions in the security market concerned.
See DIVIDEND.

In special cases, by private agreement between the parties, sales of stocks with accrued dividends might conceivably occur, especially where guaranteed stocks or preferred stocks are involved. In estate accounting, APPORTIONMENT of dividends is not to be confused with accrual of dividends.

ACCRUED INTEREST Interest earned, but not yet due and payable. Interest accrues on promissory notes, commercial paper, and fixed-interest bonds and debentures. On the stock exchanges of the U.S., unless otherwise specified, bonds are quoted and traded at a net price, i.e., a price exclusive of accrued interest. The price quoted is for the principal amount alone, to which must be added accrued interest at the coupon rate from the last interest payment date to the date of delivery.

Interest on $1,000 from 1 Day to 5 Months

Day	3.5%	4.0%	4.5%	5.0%	6.0%	7.0%
1	$ 0.0972	$ 0.1111	$ 0.125	$ 0.1389	$ 0.1667	$ 0.1944
2	0.1944	0.2222	0.250	0.2778	0.3333	0.3889
3	0.2916	0.3333	0.375	0.4167	0.5000	0.5833
4	0.3889	0.4444	0.500	0.5556	0.6667	0.7778
5	0.4861	0.5555	0.625	0.6944	0.8333	0.9722
6	0.5833	0.6667	0.750	0.8333	1.0000	1.1667
7	0.6805	0.7778	0.875	0.9722	1.1667	1.3611
8	0.7778	0.8889	1.000	1.1111	1.3333	1.5555
9	0.8750	1.0000	1.125	1.2500	1.5000	1.7500
10	0.9722	1.1111	1.250	1.3889	1.6667	1.9444
11	1.0694	1.2222	1.375	1.5278	1.8333	2.1389
12	1.1667	1.3333	1.500	1.6667	2.0000	2.3333
13	1.2639	1.4444	1.625	1.8055	2.1667	2.5278
14	1.3611	1.5555	1.750	1.9444	2.3333	2.7222
15	1.4583	1.6667	1.875	2.0833	2.5000	2.9167
16	1.5555	1.7778	2.000	2.2222	2.6667	3.1111
17	1.6528	1.8889	2.125	2.3611	2.8333	3.3055
18	1.7500	2.0000	2.250	2.5000	3.0000	3.5000
19	1.8472	2.1111	2.375	2.6389	3.1667	3.6944
20	1.9444	2.2222	2.500	2.7778	3.3333	3.8889
21	2.0417	2.3333	2.625	2.9167	3.5000	4.0833
22	2.1389	2.4444	2.750	3.0555	3.6667	4.2778
23	2.2361	2.5555	2.875	3.1944	3.8333	4.4722
24	2.3333	2.6667	3.000	3.3333	4.0000	4.6667
25	2.4305	2.7778	3.125	3.4722	4.1667	4.8611
26	2.5278	2.8889	3.250	3.6111	4.3333	5.0555
27	2.6250	3.0000	3.375	3.7500	4.5000	5.2500
28	2.7222	3.1111	3.500	3.8889	4.6667	5.4444
29	2.8194	3.2222	3.625	4.0278	4.8333	5.6389
30	2.9167	3.3333	3.750	4.1667	5.0000	5.8333
1 Month	2.9167	3.3333	3.750	4.1667	5.0000	5.8333
2 Months	5.8333	6.6667	7.500	8.3333	10.0000	11.6667
3 Months	8.7500	10.0000	11.250	12.5000	15.0000	17.5000
4 Months	11.6667	13.3333	15.000	16.6667	20.0000	23.3333
5 Months	14.5833	16.6667	18.750	20.8333	25.0000	29.1667

Bond interest is customarily paid every half year, e.g., March 1 and September 1. If, for example, a $1,000 4% bond is purchased at 85 on April 15 and the semiannual interest dates are March 1 and September 1, it would cost the buyer (exclusive of commission on the transaction) $850 in principal amount plus $5.00 accrued interest (1 month and 15 days' interest accrued for the interval between March 1 and April 15), or a total of $855. On September 1, the new holder of the bond would collect the full semiannual coupon of $20, this representing the $5.00 which was advanced as the accrued interest at the time the bond was purchased and delivered and $15.00 interest accrued between April 15 and September 1.

If specified, bonds may be sold FLAT, meaning that the quoted or agreed price includes any interest which may have accrued since the last coupon date. Income bonds and most adjustment bonds sell flat, just like stocks. In England, the regular method of trading in bonds is flat.

For convenience, bank and brokerage clerks use interest tables in calculating accrued interest such as the table here showing the interest on $1,000 from 1 day to 6 months, at from 3.5% to 7%. By using multiples and fractions, one can compute interest on practically any sum for any period by reference to such a table.

ACCRUED INTEREST PAYABLE In bank accounting, the account in the general ledger of a bank representing the interest owing to depositors upon their balances. It may also include interest on advances from the Federal Reserve bank or other banks. The amount of this item may be ascertained daily or monthly and is determined approximately by multiplying the aggregate of interest-bearing deposit balances by the average rate.

In accounting of business firms, where books are kept on the accrual basis as is the usual case, interest payable should be accrued on outstanding debts, as this item should be included among the CURRENT LIABILITIES for the correct calculation of such concepts as the CURRENT RATIO and WORKING CAPITAL.

ACCRUED INTEREST RECEIVABLE In bank accounting, the account in the general ledger of a bank representing interest accrued upon loans and bond investments, but not yet collectible. It may be accrued upon a daily or monthly basis and determined, approximately, by multiplying the aggregate of loans and bonds held by the average earnings rate.

In accounting of business firms, examples of incomes that accrue are interest, rent, and royalties, but *not* unbilled sales. Such accrued items of income earned but not yet received are to be included among the CURRENT ASSETS, and thus figure in the computation of the CURRENT RATIO and WORKING CAPITAL.

ACCUMULATED DEPRECIATION Depreciation is the process of allocating the cost less the salvage value of a tangible fixed asset over its estimated useful life in a rational and systematic manner. The accounting entry to record depreciation is made as an adjusting entry at the close of each accounting period. The entry recognizes an expense as the portion of the cost less salvage value of the asset that is to be allocated to this particular accounting period. The entry takes the following form:

Dec. 31	Depreciation Expense: Building	50,000	
	Accumulated Depreciation: Building		50,000

Depreciation expense is reported in the income statement. The Accumulated Depreciation account is a contra asset account. It is deducted from the related asset account in the balance sheet:

Building	$600,000	
Less: Accumulated depreciation	− 150,000	= $450,000

In this illustration, the carrying value (book value) of the building is its cost ($600,000) less its accumulated depreciation ($150,000 for three years of $50,000 depreciation). One should not assume that the carrying value of an asset is identical to its fair market value.

ACCUMULATED EARNINGS TAX An additional tax imposed on a corporation (other than those subject to the personal holding company tax) that allows its earnings to accumulate, instead of being distributed, to avoid payment of tax on dividends in high brackets by individual stockholders. As a general rule, a corporation can accumulate up to $250,000 over the years without risk of this special tax. The tax is currently 27.5% on the first $100,000 of accumulated earnings and 38.5% on the remainder.

ACCUMULATION This term has two meanings:

1. The opposite of AMORTIZATION.
2. The assembling of blocks of securities by quiet purchase without unnecessarily bidding up prices, especially when current prices have declined to a point below the normal or intrinsic values represented by underlying assets, potential earning power, and current or prospective interest or dividends. Such buying is undertaken in the anticipation of eventual turnover profits from such a long position when higher prices eventually materialize to full potential of the blocks accumulated. Accumulation usually implies the purchase of securities by well-informed and substantial interests during a CAMPAIGN.

With reference to the SPECULATIVE CYCLE, the period of accumulation begins as the rounding of a bottom of the bear market or price movement develops, when average prices still are at a low level, and lasts until prices have risen high enough to induce distribution.
See BANKING SUPPORT.

ACCUMULATIVE Same as cumulative.
See CUMULATIVE DIVIDENDS, PREFERRED STOCK.

ACCUMULATIVE DIVIDENDS CUMULATIVE DIVIDENDS.
See PREFERRED STOCK.

ACID TEST An expression used among bank credit people in analysis of statements to indicate the ratio of combined cash and trade receivables to total current liabilities. Like the CURRENT RATIO, it is another means of testing the current position or degree of liquidity of a concern. The acid test does not include inventories as part of the liquid funds and compares merely the total of cash (plus any high-grade, readily marketable securities held as secondary reserve for working capital) and trade receivables with the total current liabilities. The trade receivables are subject to adequate deduction for reserve for bad debts and are to include only collectible trade accounts. Thus, the acid test is the ratio of the highest grade and most liquid of the current assets to the total current liabilities. Wherever this ratio is at least 1:1 or better, a favorable liquid position is indicated.

ACKNOWLEDGMENT A declaration, admission, or certificate taken before a notary or other attesting officer stating that the maker of an instrument or document has appeared before him and subscribed it as a voluntary act without duress.

ACQUISITIONS A generic term for the taking over of one company by another. Depository financial institutions were exempt from U.S. antitrust laws until 1961 because they were not involved in interstate commerce. The Sherman Act and the Clayton Act did not apply. In 1966 the Bank Holding Company Act and the Bank Merger Act were amended to include anti-trust language to deal with the concentration of financial capital. This language followed the language in the earlier antitrust legislation. Federal supervisory agencies became responsible for evaluating mergers and consolidations. The Bank Merger Act of 1960 provides that:

"(5) The responsible agency shall not approve (a) Any proposed merger transaction which would result in a monopoly, or which would be furtherance of any combination or conspiracy to monopolize or to attempt to monopolize the business of banking in any part of the United States, or (b) any other proposed merger transaction whose effect in any section of the country may be substantially to lessen competition, or to tend to create a monopoly, or which in any other manner would be in restraint of trade unless it finds that the anticompetitive effects of the proposed transaction are clearly outweighed in the public interest by the probable effect of the transaction in meeting the convenience and needs of the community to be served."

Antitrust evaluations of proposed mergers and consolidations by the Justice Department are concerned primarily with whether the proposed transaction is anticompetitive to actual or, in more recent cases, potential competition between the parties. The basic questions relate to legal concepts of *relevant line of commerce* and the *relevant geographic section of the country*. In 1963, the Supreme Court in deciding the case against the Philadelphia National Bank and the Girard Corn Exchange Bank commented:

"We agree with the District Court that the cluster of products (various kinds of credit and services, such as checking accounts and trust administration) denoted by the term 'commercial banking'... composes a distinct line of commerce. Some commercial banking products or services are so distinctive that they are entirely free of effective competition from products or services of other financial institutions; the checking account is in this category."

An amendment to the Expediting Act in 1975 required bank mergers to proceed through both the district court and the court of appeals before being considered by the Supreme Court. Administrative agencies continue to apply "current antitrust standards" to mergers and consolidations.

The *relevant geographic section of the country* requirement was defined as the area "where, within the area of competitive overlap, the effect of the merger on competition will be direct and immediate." This concept is referred to as the "relevant banking market" or

ENCYCLOPEDIA OF BANKING AND FINANCE

"relevant market area." The banking market is generally determined according to the guidelines of the regulatory authorities and the Department of Justice, but currently tends to consider the broadness of the market when evaluating the adverse impact on competition. The Justice Department typically files a competitive factors report and defines its own banking markets when dealing with mergers and consolidation applications and holding company formations and/or acquisitions as they impact antitrust requirements. In a few cases, factors such as managerial competency, earnings performance, and projected performance, and the needs and convenience of the public have been important.

The Bank Merger Act, as amended, requires that all proposed bank mergers between insured banks receive prior approval from the federal bank regulatory agency under whose jurisdiction the surviving bank falls. The act also requires the responsible authority to obtain reports on competitive factors from the two other banking agencies and from the Department of Justice. Mergers of two bank holding companies are governed by the Federal Reserve. The responsible agency cannot approve any merger that would "substantially lessen" competition or tend to create a monopoly, unless the agency determines that the probable beneficial effect on the convenience and needs of the community overrides the anticompetitive impact of the merger.

The Office of the Comptroller of the Currency has its own guidelines on relevant banking markets. The Federal Deposit Insurance Corporation's guidelines are similar to those of the Justice Department. The Federal Reserve's requirements are within the range of the other regulatory agencies. In the final analysis, the determination of the Justice Department is most basic to the situation.

Standards for competitive impact for a proposed merger, consolidation, or holding company formation/acquisition are procompetitive, neutral, slightly adverse, adverse, substantially adverse, and monopolistic. An adverse rating implies that the transaction on competition is more than slight but warranted by the needs and conveniences to serve the public. A substantially adverse rating indicates a significantly adverse impact on competition that questions whether the transaction should be approved. The Justice Department ordinarily does not become involved unless its determination is substantially adverse.

The Bank Merger Act of 1960, as amended, provides for the emergency merger or consolidation of commercial banks where, in the opinion of the responsible agency, a bank is in such a weak condition that it must be closed. When such cases exist, the state and federal supervisory agencies evaluate potential merger candidates capable of bidding for the bank. Emergency situations are typically processed quickly, and sometimes approval is obtained in one day. Bank holding company acquisitions are also allowed emergency treatment according to the Depository Institutions Deregulation and Monetary Control Act (DIDMCA).

The 1987 "Regulators" Bill, which amended the Depository Institutions Act of 1982, arranged for the emergency interstate acquisition of large failed banks and gave the Federal Deposit Insurance Corporation a wide range of options to deal with bank failures. The bill provided authority for the FDIC to establish "bridge banks" that could serve as vehicles for facilitating the FDIC's disposition of large failing banks. This authority empowered the FDIC to establish an interim organization to stabilize the deteriorating condition of the bank and allow time to arrange an orderly acquisition or merger.

From 1960 through 1979, approximately 3,840 banks in the United States (with an estimated $100 billion in deposits) were acquired by other banks or bank holding companies. An average of 400 mergers were reported from 1980-1985. Research studies indicate that most mergers involve the payment of significant premiums which support the fact that the acquiring bank estimates that significant gains will result from the merger. Methods widely used to value acquisitions include estimating market values of the potential acquisitions and the present value of expected future benefits. The present value method involves three basic variables: the cash inflows and outflows expected from the acquisition, the terminal value of the acquisition, and the acceptable rate of return. A range of values and exchange ratios that compare an acquiring bank and the selling bank include book value, price/earnings, and earnings (past and predicted) comparisons.

The causes of acquisitions and mergers have sometimes been categorized as those resulting from external pressures and internal pressures. Major external causes include:

1. Deregulation of thrift institutions, enabling them to offer traditional banking services.
2. Increase of domestic nonbank competition from security brokers and dealers, insurance companies, and nonfinancial firms such as Sears and J.C. Penney.
3. Advent of interstate banking.
4. Technological change with increased automation and customer self-service, building greater fixed costs into the banking firm.
5. Increase in foreign bank competition that has reduced profit margins, especially on corporate banking services.
6. Economic adversity in selected industries, such as agriculture, oil, and gas, which have been weakened by foreign competition.

Internal pressures stimulating merger activity include:

1. Rise in bank operating costs, especially deposit interest, salaries and wages, and equity capital costs.
2. Credit quality problems, as evidenced by rising loan losses and more classified loans.
3. Increase in risk exposure, particularly interest-rate risk, credit risk from loans, and risk to the long-run survival of the banking institution.
4. Management succession problems, reflecting a shortage of experienced managerial talent in the industry.

The current trend in acquisitions and expansions has tended to increase competition, especially when statewide branching is permitted. It is generally believed that as banking markets expand geographically so that commerce is broadened to include not only banks but also other deposit and nondeposit financial institutions, the adverse anticompetitive impact of such transactions will diminish.

See ANTITRUST LAWS, BUSINESS COMBINATION, CONSOLIDATIONS, MERGERS.

ACQUITTANCE A written document which releases a person from paying a debt or performing contractual or other obligation.

ACTION This term has three meanings:

1. In security markets, the performance by a security with respect to trading volume and price trend.
2. In law, a lawsuit. Causes of action are of two types: *ex contractu*, arising out of contract, and *ex delicto*, arising out of tort (breach of general legal duty), such as negligence.
3. The French term for a share of stock.

ACTIVE ACCOUNT This term has two meanings:

1. In banking, an account in which deposits and withdrawals are frequently made. The expense of handling an account varies directly with its activity because of the chargeable costs (clerical, stationery, use of the bank's space and equipment, etc.). An active account should maintain larger average daily balances than an inactive one, in order to offset the costs involved.
See ANALYSIS DEPARTMENT, BANK COST ACCOUNTING.
2. In securities markets, an account with a broker showing frequent purchases and sales. Such active accounts generate commissions (which are charged on purchases as well as sales), and thus they are usually given preferential treatment in differentials on rate of interest charged, for example, on debit balances.

ACTIVE ASSETS Assets which are employed in the generation of sales or revenues and profits for a business; productive assets; the opposite of dead assets.

Active assets are more comprehensive in coverage than operating assets (see OPERATING ASSETS TURNOVER), as the latter term is concerned only with assets used in operations, such as FIXED ASSETS and CURRENT ASSETS, but excluding such nonoperating assets as investments in and advances to other corporations, and INTANGIBLES.

ACTIVE CAPITAL Capital continuously employed in profit-making pursuits; fully invested funds, as contrasted to funds "on the sidelines" (in cash, uninvested, or cash reserve).

ACTIVE CROWD Also called the free crowd, this was the division of the bond department of the NEW YORK STOCK EXCHANGE

(NYSE) before electronic automation of the bond department, where trading in active bonds (free bonds) occurred. By contrast, the NYSE designated those inactive bonds which were to be dealt in by the use of cabinets cabinet bonds, involving different physical facilities and procedures in the cabinet crowd. Bonds traded in the active crowd were a small minority of the total bonds traded on the NYSE, and were mostly convertible bonds. Traded in the inactive or cabinet crowd were U.S. Government, New York State and City, International Bank for Reconstruction and Development, and foreign bonds, and the greater number of domestic corporate bonds listed.

Bond Room Automation. In January, 1972, the board of governors of the NYSE approved a bond room automation plan, to develop and implement an AUTOMATED BOND SYSTEM, which provides electronic storage, retrieval, and matching of orders in nonconvertible cabinet bonds, and quotations for all bonds traded on the NYSE. The system calls for the entry of orders into a computerized order-matching and quotation system by bond firms using a cathode ray tube terminal and keyboard. When the system went on line, it replaced the cabinets in which orders for most bonds had been manually filed and matched for execution on the bond trading floor.

Yet most bond trading volume in the bond market as a whole occurs over-the-counter, on markets maintained by bond dealers. Rule 396, the "Nine-Bond Rule" of the New York Stock Exchange, provides that unless the prior consent of the Exchange has been obtained, every order for the purchase or sale of bonds, whether on a principal or agency basis, shall be sent to the floor for execution except:

1. When the order calls for the purchase or sale of 10 bonds or more; or
2. After a market on the floor has been diligently sought and it has been ascertained that the order may be executed at a better price elsewhere; or
3. In the case of an agency transaction (including intraoffice cross transactions), when the customer specifically directs that the particular order shall not be executed on the floor; but no member organization shall solicit such instructions before sending the order to the floor and diligently seeking a market there n; or
4. When the order calls for the purchase or sale of securities of the United States, Puerto Rico, the Philippine Islands, or states, territories or municipalities therein, or of bonds which, pursuant to call or otherwise, are to be redeemed within twelve months.

At one time, the New York Stock Exchange provided an active trading market for U.S. Government securities. With expansion in the federal debt and in the volume of trading in "governments," however, trading in government securities has shifted to the over-the-counter dealer market provided by government securities dealers. This shift began during the early 1920s despite policy of the U.S. Treasury at that time of favoring trading in government securities on the New York Stock Exchange. The Treasury has changed this policy since the mid-1920s, and in recent years, despite continued promotion by the exchange, trading volume in government securities on the New York Stock Exchange has been negligible compared with the volume handled by the government securities dealers, which includes open market operations volume with the Federal Reserve Bank of New York on behalf of the system account of the Federal Reserve System.

During the time when the New York Stock Exchange still handled an important volume of trading in government securities, the government crowd designated the group of brokers handling transactions in active government issues. This was an active crowd.

ACTIVE MARKET One in which the volume of trading is large, whether the trend of prices is upward, downward, or horizontal. Another indicator of market activity for a specific security is the spread between the bid and asked prices therefor; the closer such prices are, the closer to meeting of the minds are buyers and sellers, and so frequent transactions are more likely (trading volume).

Market activity may be measured by the absolute totals of shares traded. On this basis, reported stock volume of trading on the New York Stock Exchange (NYSE), has been booming in recent years.

On the other hand, market activity may be judged in relation to the total number of shares listed. What was considered to have been an active market decades ago, when total listings were smaller, might not be so considered in recent years, in the aggregate. Annual turnover of the total shares listed on the NYSE has risen appreciably in recent years to 36%, but this compares with 50% in 1933; and in 1929, turnover was 119%, compared with 132% in 1928.

Ordinarily, markets become more active in an advancing phase rather than in a declining trend, reflecting broadened public (as well as institutional) participation of a speculative and investment nature, attracted by the advance. Under circumstances of severe liquidation, however, this general rule is excepted. For example, in October 1929, a month of severe decline in stock prices, the record for daily volume that stood for many years thereafter was established on October 29, 1929 (16.4 million shares). Also, on May 29, 1962, a day of severe decline in prices considered the worst since 1929, volume totaled 14.7 million shares. On the other hand, advancing prices have marked the most active days of share volume in recent years, which have left the October 29, 1929, previous record well down the list. On January 7, 1981, a record 93 million shares were traded.

Sharply increased institutional participation in the market is reflected in the NYSE's studies of recent years. The latest NYSE Public Transaction Study showed that institutions and intermediaries accounted for a significant percentage of NYSE public volume and most recently, computerized trading has greatly expanded trading volumes, making 100 million share days routine occurrences.

ACTIVE SECURITIES Securities in which there is a continuous market, i.e., in which transactions occur frequently; in which there is a narrow spread between the bid and asked prices; in which sales may be quickly made; and in which there is minimum price fluctuation caused by the effected transaction, whether a purchase or sale. Such securities are said to enjoy a good market and consequently possess an extra type of demand—for trading accounts which favor the issues with high marketability as trading media—and high loan value.

See MARKET LEADERS.

ACTIVE TRUST A TRUST pursuant to whose declaration of trust the trustee has some active functions or duties to perform, in contrast to the passive trust.

ACTIVITY CHARGE The service charge upon a depositor's account. Such charge on conventional checking accounts should be based upon cost analysis of account activity and is of two types, the flat and the measured activity charge. The flat charge is a set charge per item, usually above a maximum number of free items, or a set monthly charge upon the account when the average balance falls below a specified minimum. Measured types of charges range from the simple to the complex in calculation but usually involve determination of average monthly collected balance and cost of activity.

The average monthly collected balance in the account is also called the free or compensating balance. From the average daily ledger balance of the account, the average daily collections are deducted, to obtain the average daily collected funds. After deduction of legal reserve and till money requirement, the net balance is the average daily collected balance available for investment, which is usually credited with the average earnings rate on invested funds as an offset to cost of activity in the account.

Cost of activity includes (1) cost per check drawn on the account, usually over and above a maximum number of free checks per units of specified minimum balance ($100, for example); (2) cost of handling items deposited in the account; and (3) cost of account maintenance and overhead.

In lieu of minimum balance requirements, flat charge of so much per check, plus monthly service charge, have been developed, and are the uniform costing basis for special (popular) checking accounts requiring no minimum balance.

See CHECKING ACCOUNTS, MINIMUM FREE BALANCE, NO MINIMUM BALANCE CHECKING ACCOUNT, REGISTER CHECK SERVICE.

BIBLIOGRAPHY

ZIMMERMAN, J., and MCDONALD, H. B. "Profitability Analysis, Cost Systems, and Pricing Policies." In BAUGHN, W. H., and WALKER, C. E., eds., *The Bankers Handbook,* rev. ed., 1978.

ACT OF BANKRUPTCY See BANKRUPTCY.

ACTUARY An INSURANCE expert in mathematics and statistics. He or she computes risks based upon mortality tables and the law of probabilities and averages, determines annuity rates, premiums upon policies, reserves against death claims, dividends upon participating policies, and other statistical data necessary to determine cash or loan values, amounts of extended and paid-up insurance, etc.

ADDITIONS In the system of accounts for railroads prescribed by the Interstate Commerce Commission, structures, facilities, equipment, and other properties added to those in service at the beginning of operations and not taking the place of any property for the like purpose previously held.

Both additions and betterments are gross additions to Account 211, Investment in Road and Equipment, and are listed separately in Account 211-L, Investment Made During the Year in Additions and Betterments on Leased Lines.

ADD-ON RATES For many types of consumer installment loans, interest charges are quoted in terms of an "add-on" rate. The add-on rate applies to the original loan principal and is charged over the life of the loan. For example, assume that a loan requires an add-on rate of 10% on a $1,000, one-year loan to be repaid in monthly installments. The interest of $100 is added to the amount borrowed; monthly payments are determined by dividing principal plus interest ($1,100) by 12 (monthly payments). The average outstanding loan balance during the year is $500. The effective annual rate will be significantly higher than the add-on rate of 10%.

The more frequent the installments, the higher the effective interest rate. Currently, installment loans must also be quoted in annual percentage rates; the total dollar finance charge must be disclosed according to Regulation Z, which deals with truth-in-lending legislation.

ADJUSTABLE CURRENCY See ELASTIC CURRENCY.

ADJUSTABLE-RATE MORTGAGE A mortgage that allows the interest charges on a loan to increase or decrease automatically with change with a predetermined index. Adjustable-rate mortgages (ARMs), or adjustable-mortgage loans (AMLs), were initially authorized by the Federal Home Loan Bank Board (FHLBB) for federally chartered savings and loan institutions in March 1981. AMLs originated in California and now are recognized nationally. The interest rate on an adjustable-rate mortgage, or adjustable mortgage loan, is tied to some publicly available index of the cost of funds, such as the one-year Treasury bill rate or the FHLBB's national average for all types of lenders. As the cost of funds as measured by the index moves up or down in the national market, the interest rate the lender receives from the borrower rises and falls.

The purpose of ARMs is to relieve mortgage lenders of some of the interest rate risk that lenders traditionally have assumed. Lending institutions have typically borrowed short term by offering deposit accounts to savers and have lent these funds long term to mortgage borrowers. As long as interest rates are stable and the short-term deposit rate is less than the long-term mortgage rate, the arrangement is satisfactory. However, when short-term deposit rates rise, lenders who have invested in long-term, fixed-rate mortgages will experience a profit-margin squeeze. ARMs are designed so that interest payments to lenders will more closely parallel the cost of funds.

To encourage borrowers to accept ARMs, lenders have offered ARMs that carry initial interest rates that are lower than the prevailing rates on fixed-rate mortgages of similar maturities. The advantage to the borrower is that the lower initial payment on an ARM may make the difference between being able to qualify or not qualify for the loan. The borrower assumes extra risk from the possibility of future interest rate increases, resulting in higher loan payments.

The most commonly used index for ARMs is the one-year Treasury bill rate. The ARM borrower normally is required to pay this rate plus a margin of 2 to 3% or higher. This margin is often constant over the life of the loan.

An important element in the ARM contract is the adjustment period, or frequency with which the mortgage rate can be adjusted for interest rate changes. The most common adjustment period is one year, but six-month, three-year, and five-year adjustment periods are also used.

Many lenders offer an interest rate cap, or ceiling, limiting the amount of increase in the rate during any one adjustment period. The cap limits somewhat the borrower's risk of future interest rate changes. Some lenders offer borrowers a lifetime cap, which limits the maximum interest rate adjustment that can be made under the ARM contract. Other ARM contracts provide for a payment cap that limits the actual dollar amount of the increase in the borrower's monthly payment during any one adjustment period.

When the payment cap comes into effect, the difference between the payment required by the change in the index rate and that allowed by the payment cap can be added to the amount owed on the loan. This difference then earns interest for the lender. When this occurs, there is negative amortization (instead of the loan balance falling each month as payments are made, it rises). Most ARM contracts limit the amount of negative amortization that can occur during the life of the mortgage. A limit of 125% of the original loan balance is often used.

BIBLIOGRAPHY

BARNETT, P. M., and McKENZIE, J. A. *Alternative Mortgage Instruments.* Warren Gorham & Lamont, Boston, MA. Supplemented 1985, 1986, 1987.

MORTON, T. *Real Estate Finance: A Practical Approach.* Scott, Foresman & Co., Glenview, IL, 1984.

ADJUSTABLE-RATE MORTGAGE-RATE CAP A limit on how much the interest rate can fluctuate according to an index on ADJUSTABLE-RATE MORTGAGE.

ADJUSTED CAPITAL FUNDS In calculation of capital adequacy ratios of banks, the adjustment in book total of capital funds to reflect truer availability of such capital cushion to risk assets, for computation of the RISK ASSET RATIO. The analytical method, for example, of the Federal Reserve Bank of New York involved the following adjustment of book capital funds: (1) add all capital and bad debt reserves; (2) deduct assets classified as loss and half of assets classified as doubtful in examinations; (3) reflect neither appreciation nor depreciation in investment-grade securities in the total capital funds. The adjusted capital funds resulting are then related to the total capital requirement as follows: (1) 5% against minimum risk assets; (2) 12% against portfolio assets; (3) 20% against substandard assets and assets specially mentioned in examination reports; (4) 50% against workout assets; and (5) 100% against fixed assets. Overall ratio of 100% to 125% would call for supervisory judgment; ratio above 125% would seldom be questioned.

BIBLIOGRAPHY

CROSSE, H., and HEMPEL, G. H. *Management Policies for Commercial Banks,* 3rd ed., 1980.

ADJUSTMENT BONDS Bonds usually issued in connection with corporate reorganizations but which sometimes are issued in an adjustment of several existing issues into one class to provide for a uniform interest rate, thus a form of the consolidated type of refunding issue. Adjustment bonds are practically synonymous with INCOME BONDS in that interest is payable only if earned. Failure to pay the stated rate of interest, when not earned as determined by the provisions of the indenture, does not constitute act of default. Interest upon adjustment bonds or income bonds is a claim on earnings only after payment of interest on all prior fixed interest obligations. Thus it is a claim upon earnings prior to stock issues only.

The adjustment bond is a flexible instrument. As its name implies, it is a device used by reorganization managers to aid in the adjustment of a capital structure that is too large for a company's anticipated earnings. In approving railroad reorganizations under Section 77 of the National Bankruptcy Act, the Interstate Commerce Commission generally approved the issuance of contingent interest-bearing obligations, designated as income bonds, usually with an interest rate of 4.5% and limited cumulative feature, against the substantial probability of earning power to cover income bond interest but whose regular annual continuance could not be counted upon in periods of recession or depression. The term *income bonds* has been used in such modern reorganizations, in lieu of *adjustment bonds,* to designate such contingent interest obligations. To make the capitalization more flexible and to reduce fixed charges, the holders of junior fixed-interest obligations of a reorganizing corporation are asked to accept in part, or perhaps in whole, adjustment bonds or income bonds on which the payment of interest is contingent upon earnings. Their function, therefore, is the substitution of contingent charges for fixed charges. If the reorganized company, under the new capital structure, is successful, interest will be paid on the contingent interest adjustment bonds or income bonds; and if the times-earned-fixed-and-contingent-charges ratio is substantial regularly, such adjustment bonds or income bonds may attain an investment rating. For example, the Atchison, Topeka & Santa Fe Adjustment 4s of 1995, originally issued in 1895, now command an investment rating.

Adjustment or income bonds as basically part of the bonded debt provide a tax advantage for the issuing corporation as compared with the new stock issued for old debt, in view of the tax deductibility of interest. Yet in the event of insufficiency of current earnings to pay contingent interest, the company would not be embarrassed by default as in the case of fixed interest obligations. Moreover, as debt securities, adjustment or income bonds provide leverage for the stocks. Adjustment or income bonds may be more than mere debentures if they are secured by a mortgage, in which case they are secured debt obligations, albeit usually with a junior lien as to assets pledged.

An important feature to note in connection with adjustment bonds or income bonds is the nature of the contingent interest claim: if earned, the interest is mandatorily payable; if not earned, the interest is fully cumulative, limited cumulative, or noncumulative.

Graham and Dodd in their *Security Analysis* (4th ed.), the standard in this field, suggest an analytical adjustment in computing the times-fixed-and-contingent-charges-earned ratio which will reflect the contingent nature of the interest claim as well as the mandatory or discretionary payment by directors: if interest is mandatory if earned, it is suggested that the coupon rate be stepped up by 30% and calculation of the coverage ratio be made by the overall (cumulative deductions) method, before applying the "before tax" standards for fixed-interest bonds of investment grade; if the interest is discretionary, that the step-up factor be 50%. Such an adjustment would give weight to the difference in interest claim and make comparable the application of investment grade standards, although the precise weighting is open to question.

Another structural feature of income bonds that should be noted is whether the definition of "available net income" includes provision for sinking fund and capital fund as deductions.

Accounting-wise, sinking and capital funds are dispositions of funds and not properly speaking income statement charges; and so in judging the higher grade income bonds for investment purposes, Graham and Dodd suggest *not* including such funds as part of fixed and contingent charges. For lower grade income bonds, however, where probability of interest payment is the important factor, Graham and Dodd would include such funds as prior charges. Consistency with regard to such funds as appropriations of surplus, rather than income account charges, and with regard to determination of grade, would seem to call for the same basis for analysis. But note that probability of interest payment is the concern in the case of lower grade income bonds.

Income bonds issued under railroad reorganizations are callable, most of them at no premium. By contrast, the Atchison Adjustment 4s, example of reorganization issue of an earlier day, are noncallable. A number of the railroad income bonds are convertible, most of them into common but a few into preferred stock.

Some income bonds and adjustment bonds have split coupons, a portion fixed and a portion contingent. In analysis, the entire interest (fixed and contingent) should be figured in applying the standards for income bonds generally, according to Graham and Dodd, as in their view the substantial margins of coverage required for investment grade would if met result in payment of both the fixed and contingent portions of interest. It may be argued, however, that the step-up factor in figuring overall times fixed and contingent charges earned should apply only to the contingent interest portion of the coupon rates.

Under New York Stock Exchange's rules, fixed-interest bonds are traded "and interest," i.e., the seller receives accrued interest from last interest payment date on the bonds, in addition to the sale price. Most income and adjustment bonds, however, have traded flat, without such accrued interest to the seller; although where such bonds have achieved a high quality rating, they may sell on an "and interest" basis, like fixed-interest bonds, as in the case of the Atchison, Topeka & Santa Fe Ry. Adjustment 4s.

BIBLIOGRAPHY

GRAHAM, B., DODD, D. I., and COTTLE, S. *Security Analysis, Principles and Technique*, 4th ed., 1962.

ADJUSTMENT PREFERRED STOCK Preferred stock issued in connection with adjustment of claims in a reorganization. The basic feature is that dividends are payable if earned.

In modern times, preferred stocks issued in reorganizations have been income preferred stocks, as exemplified by reorganized railroad preferreds issued under the former Section 77 of the National Bankruptcy Act, having the same contingent dividend feature as the old-styled adjustment preferreds.

ADJUSTMENTS This term has two meanings:

1. The correction of errors in statements of account submitted by banks to their customers due to misposting, omission of deposits, unauthorized payment of checks, overcharges for service charges, failure to credit earnings credit on average collected balances of conventional checking accounts, etc. Adjustments are made by the bookkeeper or AUDITING DEPARTMENT.
2. In analysis of bank income statements, the deductions and charges made from current earnings or from surplus and undivided profits and in some cases from reduction in capital, to charge off losses on loans and discounts, securities or other assets, and to provide additional valuation reserves against such assets. Return flow of funds from such adjustments would be a RECOVERY.

ADMINISTRATION, LETTERS OF See LETTERS OF ADMINISTRATION.

ADMINISTRATIVE CONTROLS Administrative controls include the plan of organization and the procedures and records associated with the decision processes involved in management's authorization of transactions. Administrative controls are designed to facilitate management's responsibility for achieving the objectives of the organization and to improve operational efficiency and compliance with management's policies. Administrative controls are the basis for establishing the accounting control over transactions.

Administrative controls can be contrasted with accounting controls. Examples contracting administrative and accounting controls include:

Accounting Controls	*Administrative Controls*
Cash	
Cash receipts are to be deposited daily; all cash disbursements are to be made by check.	Use cash forecast to determine short-term borrowing requirements.
Inventory	
The perpetual inventory method is to be used to account for inventory.	Inventory modeling techniques are to be used to determine the quantity of inventory to order and the timing of orders.

See ACCOUNTING CONTROLS.

BIBLIOGRAPHY

STATEMENT OF AUDITING STANDARD NO. 30, "Report on Internal Accounting Control."

ADMINISTRATOR A person appointed by the probate or surrogate court, or by the registrar of wills, to settle the estate of an intestate decedent (one who has died without leaving a will). Like an EXECUTOR or trustee, he holds the legal title to property destined for the benefit of others, the equitable owners.

His or her authority to act consists of LETTERS OF ADMINISTRATION, issued by the court of jurisdiction appointing him or her. He or her qualifies by giving bond. Thereafter, he or she follows much the same procedure for settlement of the estate as an executor. He or she assembles and safeguards the assets, pays administration expenses and debts, distributes the net estate, renders an accounting to the court, and, finally (in many states), obtains either releases or a discharge.

Administrators are of the following classes: (1) general administrator, appointed to act where there is no will; (2) administrator *cum testamento annexo* (with the will annexed), who acts when a decedent leaves a will without naming an executor, or when the executor has died, has become incapacitated, or refuses to act; (3) administrator *de bonis non*, who acts when the first administrator has died or has been discharged before the estate has been fully settled; (4) administrator *pendente lite*, who is appointed to take charge of an estate pending the outcome of litigation over a contested will; (5) administrator *durante minori aetate*, who is appointed to act during the minority of an executor; (6) administrator *ad litem*, who acts wherever the deceased has been, or his estate is, a party to a suit, but only for the purpose of such action.

ADMINISTRATRIX The feminine form of ADMINISTRATOR.

ADMITTED ASSETS In the filing of INSURANCE COMPANY STATE-MENTS with the insurance departments of the various states, only admitted assets, i.e., assets which may be included pursuant to state insurance laws and departmental rulings, are reported.

Nonadmitted assets, however, have considerable value. Examples are the value of parent company holdings in affiliates in excess of book value valuation; overdue premiums and other going concern items; salvage on losses paid, especially for surety companies; additional premiums due on worker's compensation and liability business indicated by payroll audits; etc.

AD VALOREM Latin for *according to value.* This term is used in connection with customs duties on imports. There are two bases for levying customs duties: one is based on number or weight, the other on declared value. The first is called a specific duty; the second, an ad valorem duty.

See TARIFF.

ADVANCE This term has four meanings:

1. In general, a loan, although an advance may be on open account as well as being evidenced by a note, with or without collateral. In member bank borrowings from Federal Reserve banks, advances to member banks on their 15-day notes payable, collateralized by U.S. government securities, have consistently topped REDISCOUNTS of customers' ELIGIBLE PAPER as basis for Federal Reserve bank lending to member banks: (1) rediscounting means the giving up of an earning asset; (2) application for rediscount, supported by financial statements of customers whose paper is involved, is required at the discount window; and (3) advances may be flexibly repaid in practice before the end of the 15-day period or may be renewed for additional 15-day periods, bearing in mind that borrowing by member banks at the Fed is a privilege and not a right and that continuous borrowing by member banks is not entertained by Federal Reserve banks.

   For adjustment, extended, and seasonal credit available at the discount window of Federal Reserve banks for depository institutions, *see* FEDERAL RESERVE BOARD REGULATIONS (Regulation A).
2. A payment on account or before a contract is completed or legally due.
3. Advance on wages or salaries refers to the privilege of employees of drawing before actual work performance. Examples are advances during slack seasons to employees on a commission basis, wage advances to employees, and payment of wages before the regular pay day.
4. A rise in price. TECHNICAL MARKET DATA may include the cumulative total of difference between advances and declines in the stock market each day, starting with any arbitrary number. The direction of movement, and not the absolute level of such data, is considered a trustworthy market indicator of trend: (1) used in conjunction with the Dow Jones Industrial Average, if both move in the same direction, the assumption is that the same market trend will continue; (2) if the DJIA continues up after the advances-declines indicator has made a top, then a topping out of the market may be expected; and (3) conversely, if the DJIA continues down after the advances-declines indicator has made a bottom, then a bottoming out of a market decline may be expected. At major tops, the advances-declines indicator has turned down several weeks before the Dow Jones Industrials have done so, which would make such an indicator a leading indicator as to trend, without the lag in confirmation that the DOW THEORY may sometimes incur.

ADVANCEMENT An inter vivos gift made in anticipation of a devise or inheritance from the donor's estate and intended to be deducted from property passing to the donee at the donor's death.

ADVANCES Short-term emergency borrowings at the Federal Reserve discount windows, secured by U.S. Treasury or federal agency securities that are held at the district bank in the Fed's capacity as the coupon clipper for the commercial bank. Advances are usually sought by commercial banks to meet reserve requirements or other emergencies. Advances are often used by banks instead of discounting notes, which is a somewhat more involved process. The advance process is usually carried out by bookkeeping entries.

ADVERSELY CLASSIFIED LOANS Regulatory authorities have established classifications for loan portfolios. The classification reflects to some extent the lending policy and the administration of the entire loan portfolio. Loans that present more immediate risk of nonpayment are classified as adversely classified. Adversely classified loans are further categorized:

1. *Substandard loans*: inadequately protected by the capital and paying capacity of the borrower, or the pledged collateral. Substandard loans will probably result in some loss if deficiencies are not corrected.
2. *Doubtful loans*: loans having the weaknesses of substandard loans but which have deteriorated and have a high probability of substantial loss.
3. *Loss loans*: loans considered uncollectible and of little value.

ADVERSE POSSESSION Possessor of land who is not the owner. An adverse possessor must have open and notorious possession of the property to the extent that the possession would give reasonable notice to the actual owner. The possession is hostile in that it indicates the intention of attaining ownership. Hostile possession is not satisfied if the possessor acknowledges the ownership of the actual owner. Adverse possession also requires the actual and continuous possession of the property consistent with its normal use. Continuous possession need not be constant but as normally used. The adverse possessor must have possession to the exclusion of other parties.

The adverse possessor must hold the property for the statutory period as required by the statute of limitations that varies from state to state. The statutory period begins to run from the taking of possession. The true owner must begin legal action before the statute runs out or the adverse possessor obtains title. The true owner of a future interest in the property is not affected by adverse possession.

ADVICE A form letter sent by a bank to a customer or bank acknowledging the receipt or credit of money, checks, drafts, securities, or other documents, or acknowledging that it has executed the instructions of its customer, such as to make a telegraphic transfer, a payment of money, or a purchase of securities or to issue a letter of credit. A bank also receives advice from correspondent banks, etc.; these are known as incoming or returning advices.

ADVICE BOOK A book or file in which duplicate outgoing and incoming advices are kept.

ADVICE DEPARTMENT The department of a bank which handles advices, receipts, or acknowledgments of deposits, securities, etc., received from customers and which receives and checks incoming and return advices.

See ADVICE.

ADVICE FATE ITEM WIRE FATE ITEM.

AFFIDAVIT Latin for "has pledged his faith." A written statement subscribed and sworn to before a notary public, commissioner, consul, or other officer empowered to administer oaths. The affidavit must contain the affiant's (deponent's) name and address and the signature of the attesting officer.

AFFILIATE A concern whose management is closely connected with that of another concern. An affiliate may be linked with another company by a minority or controlling stock interest, or by means of an interlocking directorate or community of interest. An affiliated company is closely allied to a SUBSIDIARY COMPANY, except that in the latter control is achieved by at least bare majority ownership of the voting securities.

See SECURITY AFFILIATES.

AFFIRMATIVE ACTION A deliberate effort by an employer, educational institution, or other organization to correct past prejudicial practices against specific classes of individuals, such as women or blacks, by providing them temporary preferential treatment until equal opportunity is attained. Affirmative action is a relatively new concept in U.S. law and business practice.

Affirmative action can be either coercive or voluntary. Coercive action is imposed under government contracts or grants under Executive Order 11246 and under the Rehabilitation Act of 1973 that benefits the handicapped. Affirmative action can also be court imposed under Title VII of the Civil Rights Act of 1964. It is generally expected that affirmative action cases will be decreasing in the future.

BIBLIOGRAPHY

BLANCHARD, F. A. and CROSBY, F. J., eds. *Affirmative Action in Perspective*, 1988.
CONRAD, P. J. and MADDEN, R. B. *Guide to Affirmative Action*, 1988.

AFRICAN DEVELOPMENT BANK The African Development Bank (AFDB) was formed in 1963 by 33 independent African countries to contribute, individually and jointly, to the economic and social progress of its regional members. In 1973, non-African countries joined with AFDB to establish the African Development Fund as the concessional lending affiliate of AFDB. The fund loans only to the poorest African countries. (Africa is home to 22 of the world's 30 poorest countries.) Membership in the bank was limited to 50 African nations until 1982, when 26 nonregional countries began to join the institution. The United States became a member of AFDF in 1976 by virtue of the African Development Fund Act (90 Stat. 591; 22 USC 290g note), and in February 1983 the United States became a member of AFDB by virtue of the African Development Bank Act (95 Stat. 741; 22 USC 290i note). The non-African countries hold about one-third of the bank's shares.

The African Development Bank has a capital base of $22 billion with annual lending in excess of $2 billion in 1988, an amount that approaches the lending of the World Bank's financing of the continent. In 1988, the bank continued attempts to consolidate and convert into long-term, low-interest bonds all external debt of African countries. The bank also assisted in developing debt programs for approximately 20 countries. The bank supports lending strategies that relate to the basics of African life and culture as contrasted with proposals of Western planners. The bank also is restructuring itself into an all-purpose research and development institution, especially in imports and exports. The bank committed itself to investing $12.3 billion in Africa during 1987-1991, which exceeds the investing in the previous 22 years combined. The bank can lend for 50 years with an initial 10-year grace period on repayments.

Source: The United States Government Manual.

AFTER ACQUIRED PROPERTY CLAUSE A protective provision in a mortgage whereby the lien of the mortgage will attach to any additional property acquired by the mortgagor subsequent to the date of the mortgage.

Although this provision nominally appears to be a severe restriction upon additional borrowing power of mortgages, it may be bypassed by various methods:

1. Redemption (through exercise of call provision if any) by proceeds of new refunding issue without such clause.
2. Exchange offer sufficiently attractive of new bonds without the clause.
3. Modification offer, to induce bondholders' consent to removal of the clause.
4. Use of purchase money mortgage in acquisition of new assets
5. Financing future acquisitions through subsidiaries.
6. Consolidation (new consolidated company not being subject to such clause).
7. Arrangements such as lease or conditional bill of sale, utilized in railroad equipment trust financing, that avoid taking title to new assets until the new financing has been fully paid for.

AFTER DATE The time expression used in notes, drafts, and bills of exchange measuring the maturity of notes or the time after acceptance of time drafts and bills of exchange, which will fix maturity of acceptances.

Examples:

1. (Note) "90 (Ninety) days after date, we promise to pay to the order of . . . ." This fixes maturity of the note.
2. (Draft) "60 (Sixty) days after date pay to the order of . . . ."
3. (Draft) "60 (Sixty) days after sight pay to the order of . . . ."

The "days after" expression on the above time drafts fixes maturity upon acceptance by the drawee.

By contrast, a sight draft would read as follows: "At sight, pay to the order of . . . ." Such a draft is payable immediately upon presentation to the drawee.

USANCE or TENOR pertains to the length of time specified in the draft for payment.

See ACCEPTANCE, NOTE.

AFTER SIGHT After acceptance, e.g., a draft payable "30 days after sight" is payable 30 days after presentation and acceptance. This term should not be confused with AT SIGHT. The former gives rise to an ACCEPTANCE with 30 days' maturity from date of acceptance, the latter, a demand (sight) draft, calling for payment upon presentation.

AGAINST THE BOX In a SHORT SALE, where the individual selling short actually owns the stock sold short but for some reason does not wish to or cannot deliver the particular stock owned in order to settle the sale transaction with the buyer. Consequently, he or she makes arrangements through his or her broker to borrow the stock, in order to make delivery. The principal reason would be that he or she wished to engage in selling that stock short, believing it would go lower in price, but does not wish to go to the trouble of delivering his or her own stock and then buying back the stock at the expected lower price, as in the case of a regular long sale. Also, the certificates may be inaccessible to him or her, in a safe deposit box or pledged, etc. In such a case, the order must be executed in the same manner as any other order to sell marked "short."

The short seller against the box may cover (complete the short sale by the purchase transaction) by using his or her own stock or buying other stock in the market.

The Securities Exchange Act of 1934 (Sec. 16(c)) prohibits corporate insiders (directors, officers, and beneficial owners of more than 10% of any class of any equity nonexempt security) from both the ordinary speculative short sale and short sale against the box of stock in their corporation. These individuals may not sell the corporation's stock short (1) if they do not own it (ordinary speculative short sale); or (2) if they do own the security but do not deliver it against such a sale within 20 days thereafter or do not deposit it in the mails within five days.

AGENCY A relationship by agreement between two parties whereby one party (agent) agrees to act on behalf of the other party (principal). An agent is subject to the control of the principal and is a fiduciary who must act for the benefit of the principal. The agent's authority is determined by the principal. Agents generally have the authority to perform legal acts for the principal that come under the agency agreement. The agent can bind the principal contractually with third parties. Employees are distinguished in law from an agent.

General agents have broad powers to act for the principal in various transactions. Special agents are appointed for a limited purpose or a specific task. Gratuitous agents agree to act without compensation. Subagents are appointed by an authorized agent to perform for the agent. Also, a rarer type of agent is the universal agent, empowered with the broadest grant of authority to perform every act that the principal can lawfully delegate to an agent. Whatever business a person can transact for himself or herself may be delegated to an agent.

Agents are created by appointment (by agreement between the principal and the agent), representation (principal represents to a third party that another is his/her agent), estoppel (principal causes third party to believe an agency exists), necessity (a matter of public policy requires the relationship), and ratification (approval after the fact of an unauthorized act).

The principal has an obligation to the agent to compensate the agent according to the agreement, reimburse the agent for reasonable expenses, indemnify the agent against loss or liability for duties performed on behalf of the principal, inform the agent of risks, and others. The agent's obligations to the principal require that the agent act in the best interest of the principal and with complete loyalty, carry out the instruction of the principal with reasonable care and skill, account to the principal, indemnify the principal for damages wrongfully caused the principal, provide information to the principal relating to the agency, not to compete or act adversely to the principal, and others.

Principal/agent relationships are terminated by agreement as specified in the original agreement, mutual consent, accomplishment of objective, and by operations of law (death, insanity, bankruptcy, illegality). Third parties who have dealt with an agent or have known of the agency must be given notice if the agency terminated by acts of the party.

See CONTRACTS.

AGENCY FOR INTERNATIONAL DEVELOPMENT
Created as an agency within the Department of State by departmental authority, pursuant to Executive Order 10973 (November 3, 1961) and section 621, Foreign Assistance Act of 1961 (22 U.S.C. 2381), the Agency for International Development (AID) succeeded the International Cooperation Administration, the Foreign Operations Administration, the Mutual Security Agency, and the Economic Cooperation Administration (*see* MUTUAL SECURITY PROGRAM).

The Foreign Assistance Act of 1961, AS AMENDED, AUTHORIZES AID to administer two kinds of foreign economic assistance: development assistance and economic support funds. The agency, in cooperation with the Department of Agriculture and the Department of State, also implements P.L. 480, the Agricultural Trade Development and Assistance Act of 1954, as amended (7 U.S.C. 1691 et seq.), specifically the sale on concessional terms (Title I), the donation of agricultural commodities (Title II), and the provision of food under the Food Development Program (Title III).

AGENT A person who represents or acts for another person called the principal in dealing with third parties. An agent is not to be confused with a servant or independent contractor. An agent differs from a servant and an independent contractor in that he or she brings the principal into new contractual obligations. Normally, an agent is employed to represent the principal in certain business or professional transactions.

Agents are generally of two kinds: (1) special, who are authorized to perform one or more specific acts for the principal and no others, and (2) general, who are authorized to conduct all the business of the principal or business of a certain kind with stipulated limitations. Also, a rarer type of agent is the universal agent, empowered with the broadest grant of authority to perform every act which the principal can lawfully delegate to an agent. Whatever business a per-son can transact for himself or herself may be delegated to an agent.

AGENT DE CHANGE The title given to a member of the Paris Bourse and other bourses of continental Europe.

AGGRESSIVE INVESTING POLICY Relative to INVESTMENT RISKS (financial (also termed business, or credit) risk, interest rate (also termed money) risk, purchasing power (also termed price level) risk, psychological risk, market risk, etc.), the policy of deliberate assumption of higher degrees of risk, with proper timing, in anticipation of relatively larger returns in capital appreciation and yield, than pursuant to defensive investing policy.

The term is necessarily subjective, referring to the investor's ability to tolerate higher degrees of the various types of investing risks. It also implies a varied portfolio for consistently aggressive position with regard to the various types of investing risks, since no single type of security is perfectly aggressive (or defensive) relative to all of the investing risks.

See INVESTMENT, SPECULATION.

BIBLIOGRAPHY

FISCHER, D. E., and JORDAN, R. J. *Security Analysis and Portfolio Management*, 2nd ed., 1979.

AGING OF RECEIVABLES In accounts receivable financing, collectibility analysis of accounts receivable as to number and net amounts outstanding less than 30 days, 30 to 60 days, etc., which maturities may then be compared with credit terms of sale.

Another aggregative method of checking on collectibility of accounts receivable is to calculate the average collection period. This is determined by reducing annual total credit sales to a daily average and then dividing total accounts receivable (sometimes also total notes receivable arising from credit sales) by the daily average credit sales. Comparison may then be made of the resulting average collection period with credit terms extended to customers to determine average collectibility within credit terms. In the alternative, average collection period may be computed by determining turnover of accounts receivable (credit sales divided by accounts receivable) and dividing the twelve months represented by the accounting year involved by the turnover multiple.

In cash budgeting, the average collection experience on accounts receivable (percentages of credit sales collected in month of billing; one month after billing; two, three, etc., months after billing) may be used for computing collections on accounts receivable projected on credit sales each month.

See ACCOUNTS RECEIVABLE TURNOVER.

AGIO The premium which the metallic or other currency of a country may command over legal tender paper money which is its face equivalent. This term is restricted in its use to continental Europe.

AGRICULTURAL ADJUSTMENT ACT
Agricultural Adjustment Act of 1933 (48 Stat. 31). An act approved May 12, 1933, originally intended in its agricultural aspects to be an emergency measure to aid agriculture in adjustment to then prevailing severe market conditions, but also containing omnibus provisions pertaining to farm mortgage aid and the monetary system.

Principal provisions were as follows:

1. To establish a system of production control for basic commodities (originally wheat, cotton, rice, tobacco, field corn, hogs, and milk, but in the next two years extended by amendments to include rye, flax, barley, grain sorghums, cattle, peanuts, sugar, and potatoes). Basic idea was for the secretary of agriculture to pay cooperating farmers rental or benefit payments based on leasing of farm land for withdrawal from production or acreage allotments. Marketing quotas, in addition to acreage restrictions, were applied to cotton and tobacco by amendments shortly after the act was passed. Loan-storage program was initiated later in 1933 when the COMMODITY CREDIT CORPORATION was established by executive order of the President in October, 1933. Rental or benefit payments under the act were chiefly financed by processing taxes levied upon processors of agricultural commodities and were designed to cover the difference between current market prices and parity prices. In the case of cotton and tobacco growers cooperating on marketing quotas, benefits were in the form of certificates exempting them from taxes imposed on cotton ginnings and tobacco sales.

2. To provide for system of marketing agreements, as an alternative to production control, whereby the secretary of agriculture licensed processors, producer associations, etc., in the marketing of agricultural commodities in interstate and foreign commerce. Such marketing agreements, like the NRA codes for industry, would specify elements of unfair practices in marketing, including pricing.
3. To authorize farm mortgage relief by refinancing farm mortgages at 4.5% interest through the issuance of not over $2 billion in government bonds (originally government guaranteed as to interest only, but by later amendment, guaranteed also as to principal).
4. To stimulate prices by deliberately inflating the money supply by as much as $3 billion in Treasury notes not secured by gold but solely by the credit of the U.S. Government ("greenbacks") and authorizing the President (see THOMAS AMENDMENT) to devalue the gold content of the dollar by as much as 50% and, for six months after passage of the act, to accept up to $200 million of silver at prices not exceeding $0.50 an ounce, in payment of war debts due from any foreign government to the U.S.
5. To authorize the RECONSTRUCTION FINANCE CORPORATION (RFC) to make loans in an aggregate not exceeding $50 million to drainage, levee, irrigation, and similar districts.

The production-control provisions of the Agricultural Adjustment Act of 1933, as amended, together with its linked processing tax provisions, were ruled unconstitutional by the U.S. Supreme Court in the case of *U.S.* v. *Butler et al., Receivers of Hoosac Mills Corporation*, 297 U.S. 1 (1936). The production-control and processing tax provisions were held to be regulation of agricultural production and thus an invasion of states' rights. Amendment to the act in 1935 had authorized the secretary of agriculture to institute marketing orders instead of licensing to implement marketing agreements approved, a change necessitated when the National Industrial Recovery Act and its code system for industry were held unconstitutional in the case of *Schechter Poultry Corp.* v. *U.S.*, 295 U.S. 495 (1935). The Hoosac Mills decision did not invalidate this marketing order system or the loan-storage operations of the Commodity Credit Corporation. The omnibus mortgage aid and monetary provisions were also unaffected.

Soil Conservation and Domestic Allotment Act. This legislation, which had been enacted April 27, 1935 (49 Stat. 163) as the "Soil Erosion Act of 1935" establishing the Soil Conservation Service and instituting a system of control and prevention of soil erosion, was expanded by amendment dated February 29, 1936 (49 Stat. 1148) and the entire act renamed the "Soil Conservation and Domestic Allotment Act." In its expanded form, this legislation set up a substitute for the system of production controls through acreage adjustment of the invalidated portions of the 1933 act. Under the objective of agricultural conservation, farmers were now assisted through payments and grants of aid in carrying out approved soil and water conservation measures. Conservation payments included payments for decreasing acreage in soil-depleting crops (the basic crops designated for production-control under the 1933 act) and increasing acreage devoted to soil-conservation crops, and payments for use of methods of soil fertility (such as strip cropping, terracing, etc.). An amendment dated August 7, 1956 (70 Stat. 1115) provided specifically for conservation program in the great plains states. Authority of the secretary of agriculture to carry out the program on a national basis was originally limited by the 1936 act to a period of two years, during which time it was expected that a majority of the states would enact legislation for state plans pursuant to the act. This legislation provided for "soil conserving" and "soil building" payments to cooperating farmers. Soil-building payments were made for shifting acreage from soil-depleting to soil-conserving crops, and the program was extended from time to time on a national basis. Although this legislation made for better land use, it provided inadequate authority for the price and income stabilization operations deemed necessary.

Agricultural Adjustment Act of 1938 (52 Stat. 31). This act, "to provide for the conservation of national soil resources and to provide an adequate and balanced flow of agricultural commodities in interstate and foreign commerce and for other purposes," did the following: (1) strengthened and broadened the Soil Conservation and Domestic Allotment Act, (2) provided for assistance in the marketing of agricultural commodities for domestic consumption and export, (3) provided for price support loans on wheat, corn, cotton, and other agricultural commodities, (4) authorized parity payments for corn, wheat, tobacco, cotton, and rice when funds were appropriated therefore, (5) provided for farm marketing quotas for tobacco, corn, wheat, cotton, and rice, and (6) established the FEDERAL CROP INSURANCE CORPORATION.

This 1938 act has been amended many times, as follows:

1941 Act of April 3, 1941 (55 Stat. 90), providing for loans on peanuts; Act of May 26, 1941, as amended (55 Stat. 203, 55 Stat. 860), providing for loans on basic commodities through the 1946 crops; Section 4 of the act of July 1, 1941, as amended (55 Stat. 498, 56 Stat. 768, the "Steagall Amendment"), providing that if the secretary of agriculture issued an announcement requesting the expansion of production of a nonbasic agricultural commodity, he should provide price support on such commodity for two years after World War II.
1942 Section 8 of the Stabilization Act of 1942, as amended (56 Stat. 767, 58 Stat. 643, 58 Stat. 784), providing for loans on basic commodities for two years after World War II.
1945 Act of July 28, 1945 (59 Stat. 506), providing for loans on tobacco.
1947 Act of August 5, 1947, as amended (61 Stat. 769, 62 Stat. 1248), providing for price support on wool.

Much of the above legislation expired with termination of the wartime emergency and was succeeded by the Agricultural Act of 1948 (62 Stat. 1247). But a year later, the Agricultural Act of 1949 (63 Stat. 1051) superseded or repealed prior legislation effective for the 1950 and subsequent crop years and instituted a sliding scale of price supports ranging from 75% to 90% of parity prices keyed to scales of supply percentages; substantial changes were also made in the marketing quota provisions for cotton and rice.

Agricultural Act of 1954 (68 Stat. 897). Repealed the authority for marketing quotas for corn, but authority for corn acreage allotments was retained.

Agricultural Act of 1956 (70 Stat. 188). Made a number of changes in the marketing quota provisions for several commodities.

Agricultural Act of 1958 (P.L. 85–835, August 28, 1958). Departed importantly from the postwar agricultural policy of high price supports. Principal provisions included the following:

1. Cotton was provided minimum price supports at 80% of parity in 1959, 75% in 1960, 70% in 1961, and 65% thereafter. For 1959 and 1960 cotton planters were given the choice of accepting acreage allotment (minimum of 1958 allotment or 10 acres, whichever smaller) and such price supports or 15-point lower price supports for an increase in acreage, to be set by the secretary of agriculture, of as much as 40%.
2. Corn growers were given the opportunity of voting in referendum as to continuance of existing system of acreage allotments and price supports, or beginning in 1959, minimum price supports of 90% of average market price for the three preceding years or 65% of parity, whichever higher, and discontinuance of acreage allotments. Referendum November 25, 1958 voted for the latter.

TOBACCO price supports, which had remained at fixed 90% of parity since 1950, were revised by P.L. 86–389 (February 20, 1960) for 1961 and subsequent crops to variable levels.

Agricultural Act of 1961 (P.L. 87–128, August 8, 1961). An original bill form proposed a supply management concept substantially extending government controls over production and marketing, for more effective control of supply. Congress did not accept the concept, but did pass the following principal provisions:

1. Wheat program for 1962 imposing a mandatory 10% reduction in acreage allotments and authorizing an additional voluntary reduction of 30% in wheat acreage, both in consideration of cash and in-kind government payments for such acreage diverted to conservation uses.
2. Corn, grain sorghums, and barley program imposing a 20% reduction in acreage for eligibility for price supports, in consideration for cash or in-kind government payments for the acreage diverted to conservation uses and permitting an additional 20% acreage reduction, in return for either in-kind payments or planting the diverted acreage to other specified crops.

Food and Agriculture Act of 1962 (P.L. 87–703, September 27, 1962). Particularly noteworthy for wheat farmers' rejection, in 1963 referendum, of this act's proposed first choice in wheat program offering the following alternatives, effective in 1964:

1. First alternative, a two-price control system, as follows:
   a. Only certificated wheat, limited to government-specified total of bushels grown on acreage allotment, which could be sold for human consumption and export, would be entitled to price supports of 65%–90% of parity, precise support level to be determined by the secretary of agriculture. For 1964, $2 a bushel support price was indicated by the secretary. Overplanting would be severely fined.
   b. Balance of wheat grown on acreage allotment could be sold only for feed, seed, etc., and would be supported at lower price (indicated at $1.30–$1.40 a bushel for 1964).
2. Second alternative, support at only 50% of parity for farmers complying with allotments (indicated by the secretary of agriculture as possibly as low as "$1 wheat," but ten months later Congress passed a voluntary program with total support of $2 a bushel, below).

Agricultural Act of 1964 (P.L. 88–297, April 11, 1964). Provided for a voluntary wheat program for 1964 and 1965, based essentially on the first alternative offered by the 1962 act, but without planting controls:

1. For 1964, cooperating farmers would receive a total of $2.00 a bushel combined price support and value of certificates on wheat for domestic food use, $1.55 a bushel on export wheat, $1.30 a bushel on wheat sold for feed and seed, and diversion payments on mandatory land retirement (maximum of about $0.65 a bushel) and voluntary additional retirement.
2. For 1965, same total payments of $2.00 and $1.55 per bushel on wheat for domestic food use and for export but no payment for mandatory diversion, although voluntary diversion payments would be made to farmers diverting 10% to 20% of 1965 allotments (about $0.625 a bushel).

The 1964 Act also provided a new program for COTTON, including a subsidy to domestic cotton textile mills.

Food and Agriculture Act of 1965 (P.L. 89–32, November 4, 1965). This comprehensive law, considered then the most inclusive legislation since New Deal days, provided four-year commodity programs (1966–1969 crops) for feed grains, wheat, and upland cotton. It continued the payment method for wool. It authorized a Class I milk base plan for the 75 federal milk marketing orders, and a long-term diversion of cropland under a cropland adjustment program. The act basically continued the feed grain diversion and payment programs and the wheat diversion and certificate program with modifications. It also extended the payment and diversion program to cotton. It provided for market support of cotton, feed grains, and wheat prices through price support loans and payments (certificates in the case of wheat).

Extension of Food and Agriculture Act of 1965. The 1965 Act was extended for one year, through December, 1970, by P.L. 90–559, approved October 11, 1968. Previously, P.L. 90–475, approved August 11, 1968, had provided for lower price support loans for extra-long staple cotton, supplemented by price support payments.

Agricultural Act of 1970. This act, approved November 30, 1970, and applicable through 1973, initiated a cropland set-aside approach for participating producers in the wheat, feed grains, and upland cotton programs (1971–1973 crop years) and established a payment limitation of $55,000 annually per crop on payments to producers of upland cotton, wheat, and feed grains, with the limitation to consider all payments made for price support, set-aside, diversion, public access, and wheat marketing certificates. This limitation did not include loans and purchases.

Agriculture and Consumer Protection Act of 1973. This act, amending the Agricultural Act of 1970, was signed into law on August 10, 1973. Its provisions included the following.

The total payments a person could receive under one or more of the wheat, feed grain, and upland cotton programs (combined) for the 1974 through 1977 crops were not to exceed $20,000. This limitation did not apply to Commodity Credit Corporation purchases or commodity loans available to eligible program participants or any part of any payment which represented compensation for resource adjustments or public access for recreation. The feed grains affected were corn, grain sorghum, and, if designated by the secretary of agriculture, barley.

The authority was continued through the 1977 crop years for the secretary of agriculture to establish cropland set-aside (and additional diverted acreage) if he determined that these provisions were deemed necessary for the wheat, feed grain, or upland cotton programs. The secretary suspended for the life of this act the conserving base requirement for participants in the programs.

Established or "target" prices were initiated in the act for wheat, feed grains, and upland cotton, with payments to eligible producers, based on allotted acres, to be made under specified conditions.

1. No payments would be made as long as the average market price received by producers during the first five months of the marketing year, or in the case of upland cotton during the calendar year in which the crop was planted, remained at or above the target level.
2. If the average market price for the stated period dropped below the target level, eligible farmers would receive a payment on the allotment (for cotton, the acreage planted within the allotment) equal to the difference between the target price and the higher of the loan level or the average market price.
3. Target prices for 1974 and 1975 were set in the act at $0.38 per pound for upland cotton, $2.05 per bushel for wheat, and $1.38 per bushel for corn, with reasonable rates to be set for grain sorghum (and barley, if desired) in relation to the rate for corn.
4. Target prices for the 1976 and 1977 crop years would be set by taking an established price for each year and increasing or decreasing it to reflect changes in prices paid by producers, as shown by an index of production costs (production items, interest, taxes, and farm wage rates) published by the Department of Agriculture, and productivity. Productivity was measured by comparing the most recent national three-year average for each crop with the three-year average ending with the preceding year.

The act also authorized "disaster" payments. If an eligible producer of wheat or feed grains was prevented from planting any portion of his or her allotment to wheat, feed grains, or other nonconserving crop or an eligible producer of cotton was prevented from planting any portion of his or her allotment to cotton because of drought, flood, or other natural disaster, or conditions beyond his or her control, the payment rate for that portion would be the larger of the regular calculated rate or one-third of the target price.

Also, if because of the same circumstances, the total quantity of the commodity (or authorized substituted crop) harvested on the farm was substantially less than the "expected production," the payment rate for the deficiency in production below 100% would be the larger of the regular calculated rate or one-third of the target price. ("Expected production" was the farm payment yield multiplied by the farm acreage allotment for the grains and the farm base acreage allotment for cotton.)

Provision was made to establish a disaster reserve of inventories not to exceed 75 million bushels of wheat, feed grains, and soybeans to alleviate distress caused by a natural disaster.

The act increased the minimum dairy support price on manufacturing milk to 80% of parity for the balance of the 1973 marketing year and for the 1974 marketing year, which ended March 31, 1975.

The 1973 act also continued through the marketing year ending December 31, 1977, the support price under the National Wool Act as amended, for shorn wool at $0.72 per pound, grease basis, and the support price for mohair at $0.802 per pound, grease basis. The total amount of payments under the program was limited to 70% of the accumulated totals of duties collected on imports of wool and wool manufactures.

The 1973 act extended basic support programs for wheat, feed grains, cotton, and dairy products for four years.

The Agricultural Act of 1977, signed September 29, 1977. In response to complaints from the agricultural sector that the 1973 act had set target prices too low, below production costs, the 1977 act for the first time set target prices in the light of production costs, and raised them. However, in raising the 1978 target price to $3.00 a bushel for wheat, the act provided that if farmers restricted production of wheat to 1.8 million bushels or less in 1978, the target price would be $3.05 per bushel. In later years, target prices would be based on those for the previous year, adjusted for changes in production costs. Other target prices for 1978 included $2.10 per bushel for corn, with target prices for other feed grains set in relation to the corn price, and oats and barley included in the target price program, and $0.52 a pound for cotton, with future target prices to be set according to production costs but not to fall below $0.51 a pound.

Limits on price support payments on wheat, feed grains, and cotton were set by the act at $40,000 per person for 1978; $45,000 for 1979; and $50,000 for 1980 and 1981.

As a condition for price support payments or loans on wheat, feed grains, and cotton, the set-aside program called for specific amounts of acreage to be set aside. The act further provided that a wheat storage program be established, the wheat thus stored to be continued to be owned by the producers. Normal short-term price support loans, for which the stored crops could be used as collateral, would be extended for three to five years to finance the program.

Emergency Farm Act, May 4, 1978. With pressure mounting from the farm sector for higher target prices and "100% of parity," the bill for this act cleared Congress, in the face of presidential opposition to 100% of parity price supports, as a compromise measure. It authorized the administration to raise target prices for the next four years on grains and cotton. The secretary of agriculture indicated that he would proceed under the new law to raise the 1978 wheat target price to $3.40 a bushel, except that if the 1978 crop should be less than 1.8 billion bushels, the target price would be raised to $4.05 a bushel; the loan level for cotton would be raised to $0.48 a pound from $0.44; authorization was granted to farmers to grow crops on set-aside land for the production of alcohol for gasohol; and the borrowing authority of the Commodity Credit Corporation was increased from $14.5 billion to $25 billion effective October 1, 1978.

The Carter Farm Aid Plan of March 29, 1978, had provided that farmers participating in an existing 20% set-aside would be paid up to $0.50 a bushel for wheat that would have been grown on such set-aside acreage, 40% of which could be used for grazing; the government would purchase up to 220 million bushels of wheat for use as an international wheat reserve; the 35 million ton ceiling on wheat and feed grain reserves held by farmers would be raised to permit the withdrawal of more supplies from the market; and the loan rate on soybeans would be raised to $4.50 a bushel from $3.50 a bushel. In addition, the President on July 28, 1980 ordered a $1 billion increase in price support loan rates in order to "help grain farmers to survive a serious cost-price squeeze."

Agricultural Act of 1980, signed December 3, 1980. Loan rates were raised, and the act authorized a target price for 1981-crop wheat of $3.81 per bushel, compared with $3.63 a bushel if planted within the normal crop acreage for 1980-wheat ($3.08 a bushel if above the normal crop acreage). For the 1981 crop year, there was no set-aside or voluntary paid diversion, and there was no normal crop acreage requirement, although any increase in acreage in 1981 would not be used in determining the normal crop acreage in future years.

Agriculture and Food Act of 1981. This act continued the administration's attempts to reduce the huge crops which had been wreaking havoc with market prices.

1. An acreage reduction program was in effect for the 1982 wheat crop. Participating farmers had to reduce their acreage of wheat planted for harvest by at least 15% from an established wheat base. Generally, the base would be the higher of either the 1981 planted acreage or the average of the 1980–1981 planted acreages. Participation in the program was voluntary, but only farmers who took part would be eligible for target price protection and regular price support or farmer-owned reserve loans. No direct payments would be made for acreage reduction.

    The acreage taken from production had to be devoted to conservation uses and had to be eligible cropland protected from wind and water erosion. Wheat, barley, and oats acreage planted before January 29, 1982, and designed as conservation use acreage could be cut for hay or grazed. Otherwise, acreage designed to meet the conservation requirement could not be mechanically harvested and grazing would not be permitted during the six principal growing months. Farmers owning or operating more than one farm would not be required to participate on all farms in order to obtain program benefits on participating farms. Also, participation in the wheat program was not required to qualify for program benefits on other crops grown on the farm. However, under then prevailing law, such limitations as normal crop acreages, national program acreages, allocation factors, and voluntary reduction provisions were not applicable, since acreage reduction programs would be in effect.

2. Target price for the 1982-crop wheat was set at $4.05 per bushel. If the national weighted average market price received by farmers during the first five months of the marketing year (June through October, 1982), as determined by the secretary of agriculture, as below the target price, deficiency payments would be made to eligible producers. The payment rate would be the difference between the target price and the higher of the five-month weighted national average price received by all farmers or the national loan rate. Deficiency payments would be determined by multiplying the payment rate times the farm program acreages times the farm program yield.

3. National loan rate for wheat would be $3.55 per bushel for average-quality wheat. County loan rates would be established to reflect the national average.

    Loans would be available for wheat from harvest through March 31, 1983. Loans would mature on demand, but no later than the last day of the ninth calendar month following the month that the loan was made. At any time prior to the final maturity date of the loan, producers could repay the loan amount plus any interest that had accrued. If the loan was not repaid by the final loan maturity date, the Commodity Credit Corporation (CCC) would take title to the commodity as full payment of the loan and interest charges. The regular loan rate of interest on 1982-crop commodity loans would be the rate charged the CCC by the U.S. Treasury, adjusted each month.

    Only farmers participating in the acreage reduction program would be eligible for loans on 1982 crops. In addition, loan participants' grain was eligible to enter the farmer-owned reserve unless national average wheat prices were at or above the release trigger level of $4.65 per bushel.

4. Wheat could be purchased by the CCC from eligible producers at the country basic loan rate, adjusted by premiums or discounts for quality. Purchases would be made after the final loan maturity date.

5. 1982-crop wheat was eligible for immediate entry into the farmer-owned reserve program. There would not be a cap on the amount of grain in the reserve, nor would farmers be required to sell their grain when the release trigger level ($4.65 per bushel) was reached. Storage payments would be $0.265 per bushel for wheat. Loan rates for 1982-crop wheat placed in the reserve would be $4.00 per bushel.

The 1981 act gave the secretary of agriculture flexibility to determine when farmers could withdraw their grain from the farmer-owned reserve, and when withdrawals would be encouraged by ending storage payments or increasing interest rates. The secretary had the authority to waive or adjust interest payments on reserve loans. Reserve loan rates were also at the secretary's discretion, except that they could not be lower than rates for regular commodity loans.

To ensure that the U.S. would be able to meet its food aid commitments in times of short supply, a food security wheat reserve of 4 million tons had been established by P.L. 96-494.

Agriculture and Food Act of 1981 (P.L. 97-98, signed December 22, 1981). Termed a "four-year farm bill" by the Reagan administration, the act increased minimum target prices for the four years 1982–1985 as follows:

	1982	1983	1984	1985
Wheat, per bushel	$ 4.05	$ 4.30	$ 4.45	$ 4.65
Corn, per bushel	$ 2.70	$ 2.86	$ 3.03	$ 3.18
Rice, per cwt.	$ 10.85	$ 11.40	$ 11.90	$ 12.40

Cotton: Target prices were set at the higher of 120% of loan level or $0.71 per pound for 1982, $0.76 for 1983, $0.81 for 1984, and $0.86 for 1985. Loans for cotton were to be set by formulas based on market prices, with a minimum of $0.55 per pound.

Dairy: The price support level was continued at $13.10 per cwt. for fiscal year 1982, equivalent to 80% of parity, and at the following levels for subsequent fiscal years: 1983, $13.25; 1984, $14.00; and 1985, $14.60. But, beginning in 1983, the minimum support level for dairy products could be set at either 70% or 75% of parity, "depending on the anticipated amount of Federal purchases of dairy products."

Peanuts: Acreage allotment controls were eliminated, but the poundage quota system was continued, the national poundage quota for 1982 being specified at 1.2 million tons and the price support level for 1982 set at $550 per ton. The 1982 poundage quota, which was approved by referendum of growers in January, 1982, was 17% below 1981.

Sugar: The Agriculture and Food Act of 1981 provided for a new price support program for sugar: the secretary of agriculture was required to support sugar prices "through duties and fees on imported sugar or other means" (since duties on imported sugar are subject to international agreements, the secretary would have limited discretion in this regard), so that the higher market prices domestically which would result "would make Government purchases of sugar unnecessary." Price support levels for domestic cane sugar (support levels for beet sugar to be determined relative to the support levels for cane sugar) were set in the act at the specified levels for crop years as follows: 1982, $0.17 per pound; 1983, $0.175; 1984, $0.1775; and 1985, $0.18. An interim domestic support price of $0.1675 a pound was set for raw cane and $0.1915 for refined beet for the period December 22, 1981, to March 31, 1982.

However, continued decline in world sugar prices caused the existing levels of import duties and fees on sugar to be too low as of early 1982 to result in U.S. sugar producers being willing to sell at the low market prices rather than to the government at the established higher price support levels and then letting the sugar go to the Commodity Credit Corporation on the nonrecourse loan program. Two presidential proclamations, therefore, were issued: (1) the market stabilization price for domestic sugar was raised to $0.1988 a pound, versus the former $0.1908 a pound, for the remainder of the October, 1981–September, 1982, crop year, and a quarterly import fee was imposed for the difference between the market stabilization price level and the domestic (No. 12) market spot price average for 20 trading days, and (2) sugar import quotas were reimposed, after many years (see below), set initially at a total of 220,000 short tons for the balance of the second quarter of 1982. Future import quotas would be announced with a 15-day lead time before the quarter, and the import allocations for the quota system were to be based on average shipments to the U.S. for the period 1975–1981, not counting the highest and lowest years in the period.

Sugar quotas were first imposed by the Jones-Costigan Act of May, 1934, an amendment to the Agricultural Adjustment Act of 1933. When the production control and processing tax provisions of the latter act were declared unconstitutional in 1936, sugar quotas continued in effect, but subsequently were revised and reenacted in the Sugar Act of 1937. The latter act also provided for payments to producers of sugar cane and sugar beets who complied with specified conditions relating to child labor, farm wages, acreage allotments, soil conservation, and for payments to producers who were also processors who paid other producers "fair prices" for sugar beets or sugar cane. The Sugar Act of 1948 (61 Stat. 922) reenacted the Sugar Act of 1937 with changes, most important of which related to the annual estimates of sugar consumption and establishment of annual area sugar quotas, leading to annual scrambles for same by producers. The Sugar Act of 1948, with changes made by amendments in 1951, 1956, 1960, 1962, and 1971, was extended by the last-named amendment through December 31, 1974.

With prices for domestic raw sugar rising as the result of a decline in worldwide raw sugar stocks, the Sugar Act of 1948 expired December 31, 1974. The House of Representatives rejected a bill to extend the Sugar Act for five years on June 5, 1974, but world prices for sugar were so far above the support prices proposed under the bill that Senator Long was quoted as saying that "the Act was not really needed."

In the following years, as sugar stocks were built up, raw sugar prices dropped severely, from a peak of $0.64 per pound on the domestic market in November, 1974, to an average of some $0.105 per pound by the summer of 1977. With prices below the cost of production, an interim price support payment program was initiated under the Agricultural Act of 1949, as amended, to help maintain "a viable domestic sugar industry" until new legislation providing for a support program could be enacted.

The payment program became effective on September 15, 1977, for all 1977-crop sugar marketed or committed for sale through November 7, 1977. Following enactment of the Food and Agriculture Act of 1977, the payment program was terminated, and the loan program was put into effect on November 8, 1977. The act brought sugar cane and sugar beets for the 1977 and 1978 crop years into the price support program at minimum support level of 52.5% of parity, but not less than $0.135 a pound. The domestic support price was raised to $0.15 a pound for 1979, after sugar import fees were raised to $0.0335 a pound for raw sugar and $0.0387 a pound for refined sugar. Another substantial price rise in 1980 (averages for domestic sugar at New York) carried sugar prices to a year's average of $0.306 a pound for 1980, against $0.153 in 1979, including highs in 1980 of $0.372 in September, $0.427 in October, and $0.409 in November, well above support prices. The subsequent drop in market prices necessitated the price support action and restoration of import quotas referred to above.

See SUGAR.

Wool: See WOOL for the support program under the National Wool Act of 1954, as amended to latest years, for wool and mohair.

Innovations in Legislation.

Target price concept: New with the Agriculture and Consumer Protection Act of 1973 was the concept of guaranteed or "target" prices and deficiency payments for wheat, feed grains, and upland cotton. Deficiency payments would not be made as long as the average market price received by farmers during the first five months of the marketing year—or, in the case of cotton, during the calendar year in which the crop was planted—remained above the target price level. But when the average market price dropped below target levels, a farmer's cash price for the commodity would be supplemented on allotment production on the amount that the target price exceeded the larger of the loan rate or the five-month national average price, weighted by the historical quantity of production sold in each month. This arrangement would provide a farmer with a guaranteed return on the portion of the crop produced on his allotment, freeing him to concentrate on all-out production without fear that a market decline would drop grain prices below the level of profitability.

Moreover, an "escalator provision" was included in the act, effective during the 1976 and 1977 crop years, under which the target prices would increase if the cost of production went up more than overall farm productivity.

Disaster payments: Another new provision of the 1973 act was one under which payment at a special rate might be considered when a producer was prevented by natural disaster from planting any portion of his wheat or feed grain allotment to wheat, feed grains, or other nonconserving crops, or if a natural disaster caused total actual production to be less than two-thirds of normal production on allotment acres. Other nonconserving crops could be substituted for wheat and feed grains in evaluation of the two-thirds provision.

Farmer-owned grain reserve: The Food and Agriculture Act of 1977 authorized a reserve policy representing an important departure from previous agricultural policy, the farmer-owned grain reserve (FOR) program, for wheat and feed grains. The program's objective was to encourage producers to store these grains when they are in abundant supply and extend the time period for their orderly marketing. Its function was to stabilize grain prices, not to provide for emergency or disaster needs.

An objective of farm commodity programs from the early 1930s to the early 1970s was to support prices and income through supply management or limitation. During this period, stocks of grain turned over to the government under its price-support program piled up, and at times it maintained large inventories in government-owned storage facilities. These facilities were purchased from 1939 through 1956, and had a peak capacity of 748 million bushels in 1960. The government-owned stocks declined from that time until the last stocks were removed and the storage facilities were sold in 1974. The government-owned grain was sold at various times during the period.

Under the farmer-owned reserve program, any producer owning designated FOR grains is eligible for a three-year FOR loan. To qualify for an FOR loan, a producer generally must have had the grain under a price-support loan or have qualified to have such a loan. The aim of the program is to encourage producers to store wheat and feed grains when they are in abundant supply and extend the time for their orderly marketing. The reserve grain cannot be sold without penalty until predetermined market price levels, known as release and call levels, are reached. At "release," producers may but do not have to remove their grain from the reserve. At "call," producers must repay their loans or forfeit the grain. When the price-support loan expires, one of the producer's options is to extend the loan for three years under the FOR program if the FOR program is still open for that commodity at the time.

As of 1981, the board of directors of the Commodity Credit Corporation had declared wheat, corn, barley, oats, sorghum, and rice as eligible for the FOR. The CCC board has the authority to specify additional commodities. Until April, 1980, producers had to comply with other program requirements, such as set-aside programs (which take land out of production) or "normal crop acreage" (NCA) limitations, when in effect, to qualify for FOR program participation.

A participating producer must provide storage space of permanent construction for the grain, either on the farm or in commercial storage space. In return, the producer receives a storage payment which is paid annually in advance. The producer is responsible for maintaining the grain quantity and quality. To fulfill this responsibility, the producer may, with approval of the Agriculture Department's Agricultural Stabilization and Conservation Service (ASCS), rotate FOR grain with grain of equal quality and quantity. (See "Farmer-Owned Grain Reserve Program Needs Modification to Improve Effectiveness," June 26, 1981, Report to the Congress by the Comptroller General of the U.S., for criticism that the program has not fully met its objectives because it has not: (1) materially increased grain inventories as intended, (2) removed the government from its role as a significant grain storer, or (3) reduced price variability.)

Summary. The agricultural problems of the U.S. seemingly are unceasing, to judge from the stream of legislation enacted over the years. An optimistic note was sounded by Richard E. Lyng, deputy secretary of agriculture, in an address to the 1981 U.S. General Accounting Office Planning Symposium on Food in the Future, as follows:

During the '70s, the foreign production/consumption gap for wheat and coarse grains increased at a pace of 7 million tons a year.

During the '70s, the U.S. accounted for 51 percent of the increases in world wheat exports and for about 89 percent of the increase in coarse grain exports. We are now at a point where we supply a full 43 percent of the world wheat exports, about 71 percent of the coarse grain exports, and 84 percent of the soybean exports.

These are the trends that will accelerate. Even though I am sure of that, I would not predict the exact figures or percentages. I only point out that some U.S. Department of Agriculture analysts argue that, despite any foreign increases in productivity, by 1985 the world outside the U.S. will depend on us for 15 percent of its agricultural products, compared with 2 percent in the early '50s and 11 percent in the late '70s.

Inevitably, then, as supplies tighten, the world will call upon America's comparative advantage in agriculture to prove itself. The administration has signaled that the age of persistent, large U.S. surpluses is over. And while target prices and deficiency payments may have been appropriate to times of considerable surplus, it is our belief that without such payments, market forces will suffice to spur American farmers to greater remunerative productivity.

See PARITY.

BIBLIOGRAPHY

ADAMS, D. W., and GRAHAM, D. H. "A Critique of Traditional Agricultural Credit Projects and Policies." *Journal of Development Economics,* June, 1981.
BOGGESS, W. G., and HEADY, E. O. "A Sector Analysis of Alternative Income Support and Soil Conservation Policies." *American Journal of Agricultural Economics,* November, 1981.
COFFEY, J. D. "The Role of Good in the International Affairs of the United States." *Southern Journal of Agricultural Economics,* July, 1981.
COMPTROLLER GENERAL OF THE UNITED STATES. "Farmer-Owned Grain Reserve Program Needs Modification to Improve Effectiveness." Report to the Congress, Vol. 1, June 26, 1981.
GARDNER, B. "Farmer-Owned Grain Reserve Program Needs Modification to Improve Effectiveness: Consequences of USDA's Farmer-Owned Reserve Program for Grain Stocks and Prices," prepared for the U.S. General Accounting Office. Report to the Congress, Vol. 2, June 26, 1981.
LUTTRELL, C. B. "Grain Export Agreements—No Gains, No Losses." Federal Reserve Bank of St. Louis *Review,* August/September, 1981.
MEYERS, W. W., and RYAN, M. E. "The Farmer-Owned Reserve: How Is the Experiment Working?" *American Journal of Agricultural Economics,* May, 1981.
PORTER, R. B. "The U.S.-U.S.S.R. Grain Agreement: Some Lessons for Policymakers." *Public Policy,* Fall, 1981.
SCHNITTKER, J. A. "A Framework for Food and Agricultural Policy for the 1980s." *American Journal of Agricultural Economics,* May, 1981.
SCHULTZ, F. H. Statement to Subcommittee on Conservation, Credit and Rural Development. House Committee on Agriculture, June 23, 1981. *Federal Reserve Bulletin,* July, 1981.
SECRETARY OF AGRICULTURE. *Annual Report.*
SHARPLES, J. A., and HOLLAND, F. D. "Impact of Farmer-Owned Reserves on Privately Owned Wheat Stocks." *American Journal of Agricultural Economics,* August, 1981.
SPITZE, R. G. F. "Future Agricultural and Food Policy." *Southern Journal of Agricultural Economics,* July, 1981.
U.S. GENERAL ACCOUNTING OFFICE. *Food in the Future: Proceedings of a Planning Symposium,* 1981.

AGRICULTURAL CREDIT Present authority for the activities of the borrower-owned banks and associations that constitute the cooperative farm credit system, which are supervised, examined, and coordinated by the FARM CREDIT ADMINISTRATION, an independent agency of the U.S. government, is vested in the Farm Credit Act of 1971, P.L. 92–181, as amended.

Farm Credit Administration.

1. FEDERAL LAND BANKS and FEDERAL LAND BANK ASSOCIATIONS: long-term first mortgage mortgage loans on farms or ranches as security.
2. FEDERAL INTERMEDIATE CREDIT BANKS: loans to, and discount of agricultural paper for, production credit associations, state and national banks, agricultural credit corporations, livestock loan companies, and similar lending groups; also loans to and discount paper for banks for cooperatives and federal land banks. Maturities of notes discounted or accepted as security ordinarily coincide with the usual time for the marketing of crops or livestock from which liquidation is expected, usually not more than 12 months, although the law permits maximum maturities of 7 years.
3. PRODUCTION CREDIT ASSOCIATION: short-term credit for all types of farm and ranch operations, for general agricultural purposes and other requirements.
4. BANKS FOR COOPERATIVES (12 district banks) and central banks for cooperatives: 12 district banks for cooperatives make commodity, operating capital, and facility loans to farmer cooperatives; the Central Bank for Cooperatives serves the district banks by making direct loans to them and participating in loans that exceed their respective lending limits.

Agencies in the Department of Agriculture Engaged in Credit and Financial Operations.

Under the Under Secretary, International Affairs and Commodity Programs:

1. COMMODITY CREDIT CORPORATION (CCC): financing of price support and production stabilization programs; disposition of commodities acquired under the price support program, through domestic and export sales, transfers to other government agencies, and donations for domestic and foreign welfare use; exchange of surplus agricultural commodities acquired, for strategic and other materials and services produced abroad; activities assigned under P.L. 480, the Agricultural Trade Development and Assistance Act of 1954, as amended (sale of surplus agricultural commodities for foreign currencies, disposition of commodities for famine relief and other foreign assistance, and long-term credit and supply contracts); administration of U.S. operations under the International Wheat Agreement; and provision of storage adequate to carry out storage facilities programs where commercial storage facilities are inadequate. In performing its principal operations, the CCC utilizes personnel and facilities of the Agricultural Stabilization and Conservation Service.
2. AGRICULTURAL STABILIZATION AND CONSERVATION SERVICE: administers (1) pricing support, (2) production adjustment, (3) conservation and land-use adjustment assistance, (4) the inventories of the CCC, (5) disaster relief, and (6) international commodity agreements.

3. FEDERAL CROP INSURANCE CORPORATION: crop insurance for wheat, cotton, tobacco, corn, flax, dry edible beans, soybeans, barley, grain sorghums, oats, rice, citrus fruit, peaches, peanuts, peas, potatoes, raisins, apples, canning cherries, tomatoes, safflower, sugar beets, tung nuts, and the investment in several crops under combined crop protection plan.

Under the Under Secretary, Small Community and Rural Development:

1. FARMERS HOME ADMINISTRATION: provides credit, financial assistance, and management assistance to (1) farmers, to operate, develop, and purchase family farms; (2) farmers and rural residents, to build and improve homes and essential farm buildings; (3) rural groups, to develop recreational facilities and community water supply and waste disposal systems, carry out soil conservation measures, and shift land use to grassland and forestry; (4) local organizations, to help finance watershed projects; (5) individuals and groups, to build housing for domestic farm laborers and rental housing for the elderly; (6) rural families and groups, to raise and maintain income and living standards of low-income families; (7) public agencies in rural areas, for the development, conservation, and utilization of natural resources, and carrying out projects to improve the economy of farm families and residents in the areas; (8) farmers who suffer loss of income and property and crop damage from natural disasters. Applicants must be unable to obtain needed credit elsewhere.
2. RURAL ELECTRIFICATION ADMINISTRATION: loans to finance electric distribution, transmission, and generation facilities for adequate electric service on an area coverage basis to persons in rural areas not having it (pursuant to law, preference in making electrification loans shall be given to public bodies and cooperatives); some short-term rural electrification loans for the financing of electric wiring and electric and plumbing appliances and equipment; loans to finance facilities to furnish and improve telephone service in rural areas on an area coverage basis (pursuant to law, preference in making telephone loans shall be given to persons providing telephone service in rural areas, and to cooperatives): and furnishing technical assistance in engineering, accounting, and operations to borrowers in support of the security of the government loans. REA also assists its borrowers in initiating projects to stimulate economic development in the areas they serve.
3. RURAL TELEPHONE BANK: an agency of the U.S., the Rural Telephone Bank was established in 1971. Bank loans are made, in preference to Rural Electrification Administration (REA) loans, to telephone systems able to meet its requirements. The bank's management is vested in a governor (the REA administrator) and a board of directors, including six who are elected by the bank's stockholders. Bank loans are made for the same purposes as loans made by the REA but bear an interest rate consistent with the bank's cost of money. In addition, loans may be made to purchase stock in the bank required as a condition of obtaining a loan. The bank uses the facilities and services of the REA and other Department of Agriculture agencies.

BIBLIOGRAPHY

SCHULTZ, F. H. (then Vice Chairman, Board of Governors of the Federal Reserve System). Statement to Subcommittee on Conservation, Credit, and Rural Development, House Committee on Agriculture, June 23, 1981. *Federal Reserve Bulletin*, July, 1981.

AGRICULTURAL CREDIT ACT OF 1987

A major farm credit act that marked the beginning of a new era in farm lending. The legislation outlined guidelines for restructuring the Farm Credit System (FCS). A major provision of the act provided federal assistance to the Farm Credit System and specified certain rights for the Farm Credit System and Farmers Home Administration borrowers. The act created the Federal Agricultural Mortgage Corporation (FAMC or Farmer Mac) which created a new secondary market for farm and rural housing mortgages which could change the competitive balance among new and existing farm lenders.

The act provided up to $4 billion in direct financial assistance to the Farm Credit System. The money would be raised by a newly created FCS Financial Assistance Corporation which was authorized to sell uncollateralized bonds backed by the full faith and credit of the U.S. Government. The new corporation would be capitalized by mandatory stock purchased by FCS institutions. Banks and associations of the FCS are required to purchase stock in the amount by which unallocated retained earnings exceed 5% of assets of banks and 13% of the assets of associations. The assessments are similar to those provided for the defunct Farm Credit Capital Corporation. The assistance will be administered by the Farm Credit Assistance Board, consisting of the secretaries of Agriculture and the Treasury and a third member, an agricultural producer appointed by the President. The board has almost unlimited powers in overseeing the financial and business management of FCS units that receive assistance. The law requires that the Federal Land Bank and Federal Intermediate Credit Bank in each Farm Credit District must have merged by June 1988. Within six months of the district-level merger, any Production Credit Association (PCAS) and Federal Land Bank Association (FLBA) serving substantially the same geographic area must submit a plan for merging to stockholder approval. The mergers are expected to allow one-stop servicing of borrowers' long- and short-term credit requirements.

A large scale consolidation of the system units must also be submitted for stockholder approval. An 18-month schedule for considering consolidation of the 12 Farm Credit districts into as few as six districts is contemplated. The act also calls for plans to merge the 12 Banks for Cooperatives and the Central Bank for Cooperatives into a single National Bank for Cooperatives. Such mergers are intended to help reduce the system's overhead costs.

The act contains a "bill of rights" for farmers who borrow from the FCS and FMHa. These rights identify the procedures the FCS and FMHa must follow when dealing with troubled loans. For example, the borrowers must be informed of the terms of their loans, be granted reviews of adverse credit decisions and actions, and be given their due options before lenders can foreclose. Borrowers are given 45 days' notice that their loans may be eligible for restructuring before foreclosures proceed and, generally, loans must be restructured when restructuring would cost less than foreclosure. If foreclosure occurs, the borrower must be given the right of first refusal to lease or purchase the foreclosed property.

The act allows the creation of a secondary market for farm and rural housing mortgages by bringing about the Federal Agricultural Mortgage Corporation, or Farmer Mac. Farmer Mac's role in the new secondary market is similar to that of Ginnie Mae, Fannie Mae, and Freddie Mac, in the secondary residential mortgage market. Farmer Mac guarantees timely payment of principal and interest on securities that represent interests in pools of farm mortgages and are sold to the investing public by loan poolers certified by Farmer Mac. The guarantee is supported by a 10% reserve fund formed by the originators or poolers of each loan pool and ultimately supported by a $1.5 billion line of credit at the U.S. Treasury. Treasury funds cannot be used until the reserve fund is depleted.

Yields on the secondary mortgage market securities are usually between the yields on Aaa-Aa-rated corporate bonds. In recent years prior to 1990, yields on Ginnie Mae mortgage-backed securities have averaged 110 basis points higher than the yield on 10-year Treasury bonds, 24 basis points higher than the yield on Aaa corporate bonds, and 20 basis points less than the yield on Aa bonds. The spread between yields on Farmer Mac securities and Treasury securities is not likely to differ much from the spread between FCS and Treasury securities. Yields on seven-year FCS bonds averaged 44 basis points higher than yields of Treasury securities in 1986 and 1987.

It is anticipated that the secondary farm mortgage market will be far smaller than the secondary residential mortgage markets because the total value of farm real estate assets and debt is comparatively small. The value of U.S. farm real estate totaled $576 billion at the end of 1987. Debt against this real estate totaled only $90 billion, about 4% of the value of all residential mortgages outstanding. Transfers of farmland every year average roughly $20 billion, and about $8 billion in new farm mortgage credit is extended every year. Not all of the new farm credit extended every year will qualify for the new secondary market. Underwriting standards will be used to identify qualifying mortgages.

Source: Barkema, A., Drabenstott, M., and Froere, L. "A New Era in Farm Lending: Who Will Prosper?" *Economic Review*, Federal Reserve Bank of Kansas City, Kansas City, MO., June 1988.

See FARM CREDIT ACTS, FARM CREDIT ADMINISTRATION, FARM CREDIT ADMINISTRATION BOARD, FARM CREDIT BANK, FARM CREDIT SYSTEM, FARM

CREDIT SYSTEM FINANCIAL ASSISTANCE BOARD, FARM CREDIT SYSTEM INSURANCE CORPORATION, FARM LAND BANK, FEDERAL AGRICULTURAL MORTGAGE CORPORATION.

AGRICULTURAL CREDITS ACT An act approved March 4, 1923 (42 Stat. 1454), which created two classes of corporations designed to provide intermediate credit. These two classes of corporations were the Federal Intermediate Credit banks and National Agricultural Credit corporations. The Federal Intermediate Credit banks were brought under the Farm Credit Administration in 1933, which in turn under the Farm Credit Act of 1953 is now an independent executive agency. Functions of National Agricultural Credit corporations are now performed by Production Credit associations (Farm Credit Act of 1933).

The federal land banks, institutions of the Farm Credit System (FCS) and part of the FCS network of cooperatively organized lenders operating under federal charter to meet agriculture's credit needs, have experienced significant capital losses in recent years as a result of the recent agricultural depression. To address their financial problems and to provide debt relief to farm borrowers with problem loans, Congress passed the Agricultural Credit Act of 1987 (P.L. 100-233). This act authorizes a $4 billion financial assistance package for the most undercapitalized FCS lenders, mandates FCS organizational changes, protects the full value of FCS borrower stock when retired, requires the FCS and the federal government's lender of last resort to farmers (FmHA unable to obtain credit elsewhere) to restructure problem farm loans that meet specified criteria, establishes a secondary market for farm real estate loans, and authorizes federal matching funds for state farm loan mediation programs.

See AGRICULTURAL CREDIT.

AGRICULTURAL PAPER Notes, drafts, bills of exchange, and bankers acceptances arising out of agricultural transactions, as distinguished from commercial and industrial transactions.

Banks lend to farmers for a variety of operating and investment purposes, including:

1. *Short-term:* current operating and living expenses; feeder live stock operations.
2. *Intermediate term:* other livestock operations; investment in machinery and equipment; consumer durable goods; improvements in land and buildings.
3. *Long-term:* farm real estate purchase; construction of farm buildings and dwellings.
4. *Financial:* debt repayments and refinancing.

In nonreal estate farm lending, banks face the competition of Production Credit associations, livestock loan companies, agricultural credit corporations, the rediscounting facilities for the preceding of the Federal Intermediate Credit banks, and the Farmers Home Administration as well as miscellaneous lenders. In farm mortgage lending, banks face stiffer competition from Federal Land banks (lending through Federal Land Bank associations), life insurance companies, Farmers Home Administration, and individual and other lenders.

As of the close of 1981, commercial banks were the largest lenders of non–real estate farm credit, accounting for 42.4% of the total such debt then outstanding; the second largest source of such debt, the Production Credit associations, accounted for 27.0%. Largest sources of farm real estate debt were the Federal Land banks (59.0%), with 17.6% for life insurance companies and 11.2% for commercial banks.

Banks having negotiable agricultural paper maturing within nine months from date of advances or discounts may tender such paper to Federal Reserve banks for advances and discounts. Purposes of making such paper eligible include:

1. Paper issued for production and marketing of agricultural products and for the breeding, raising, fattening, and marketing of livestock
2. Paper of marketing cooperatives used for advances by the cooperative to members for agricultural purposes
3. Bankers acceptances drawn for agricultural purposes and secured at time of acceptance by warehouse receipts and similar documents conveying or securing title covering readily marketable staples, provided such acceptances have maturity at time of discount of not more than six months' sight, exclusive of days of grace (Sec. 13, Federal Reserve Act)
4. Construction loans to finance residential or farm buildings, with original maturities of not over six months, and maturing within 90 days of the date of advance or discount.

Regulation A of the Board of Governors of the Federal Reserve System (12 CFR 201), as last revised effective as of September 1, 1980, contains the specifics on the requirements for agricultural and other paper to be eligible for advances and discounts from Federal Reserve banks.

(For the different types of agricultural paper handled by federal institutions, *see* institutions listed under AGRICULTURAL CREDIT.)

AGRICULTURE The art and science of farming. Economic conditions in U.S. agriculture were severely depressed between World War I and World War II. The run-up in prices, incomes, and land values during World War I was followed by more than 20 years of general decline in real farmland values, severe debt repayment problems, and widespread rural bank failures. U.S. agriculture staged a strong, broad recovery in 1987. Farm income hit record highs, farmland values bottomed, and the farm financial crisis faded. After six years of deep recession, the turnaround was welcomed. It is now estimated that grain surpluses are likely to decline, thereby reducing the need to take additional U.S. farm resources out of production. Competitiveness remains a principal concern for the industry as negotiations in General Agreement on Tariffs and Trade (GATT) continue.

In addition to problems with product imbalances, problems also existed with regard to the supply of and demand for capital, especially loanable funds, in agriculture. On the demand side, farming was risky and returns low. The supply of loanable funds was either unreliable, or available only at very high interest rates and at restrictive terms resulting in the undercapitalization of agriculture.

Farm debt is serviced by seven types of lenders: (1) the Farm Credit System, which accounts for approximately 30% of all farm debt outstanding, (2) commercial banks (20%), (3) merchants, dealers, individuals, and other lenders, (4) life insurance companies, (5) Farm Home Administration, (6) the Commodity Credit Corporation, and (7) the Small Business Administration.

The federal government responded by adopting programs to reduce risks and to assure farmers of easier access to credit at more favorable rates and terms. Chief among the institutions to administer these programs were, and are, the Commodity Credit Corporation (CCC), Farmers Home Administration (FmHA) and predecessor agencies, and the banks of the Farm Credit System (FCS). These institutions changed the credit situation so that a technological revolution and capital restructuring of U.S. agriculture between the 1930s and 1970s occurred. In the late 1970s and early 1980s, funds became scarcer, although farmers continued to have easier access to loans than did many others in the economy. This situation contributed to inflated prices of land and other capital goods.

Federal government activities in providing credit assistance can be grouped by four major categories: (1) government-sponsored credit agencies, (2) government-insured loan programs, (3) government-guaranteed loan programs, and (4) direct loans. Government-sponsored credit agencies are federally chartered financial intermediaries performing specific credit functions. The federally-sponsored credit agencies are privately financed after being initially capitalized by the government. Debt securities of these agencies can be held by federally regulated financial institutions. They are exempt from federal and state income taxes.

Under a loan guarantee, the government promises to pay all or part of the principal and interest on loans made by private lenders in the event of default. The guaranteed obligation may also be a security sold in the capital market or to the Federal Financing Bank. Guaranteed loans are made to individuals, businesses, and state, local, and foreign governments under a variety of programs. A loan guarantee transfers some or all of the risk to the government. Interest rates on guaranteed loans are usually lower than what would be available through commercial sources. This has the effect of redirecting economic resources toward those activities for which guaranteed loans are available.

Direct loans are made by federal agencies to channel economic resources to particular uses. Federal agencies provide credit at rates sometimes significantly below commercial rates and often at longer maturities. Agriculture is a major recipient of direct federal lending.

ENCYCLOPEDIA OF BANKING AND FINANCE

AGRICULTURE

The 1985 Farm Bill had two primary goals: the support of farm income and the reduction of domestic government-held grain stocks. The secondary goal was to modify farm credit mechanisms that were having financial problems. Initially these goals were to be met through programs that placed greater reliance on market signals to make agricultural policies effective for the long term. The Food Security Act of 1985 was a mirror of previous farm policy. The bill eliminated the yearly increases in support prices in effect since 1977. It retained the traditional two-tiered price support system and otherwise merely extended production limits, trade incentives, and farm credit programs.

The Agricultural Credit Act of 1987 marked the beginning of a new era in farm lending. The law provided assistance to the largest and most beleaguered commercial lender, the Farm Credit System. Among its major provisions, the act enables the creation of a new secondary market for farm and rural housing mortgages through the Federal Agricultural Mortgage Corporation (FAMC or Farmer Mac). This new market can revolutionize farm lending by changing the competitive balance among new and existing farm lenders. The act outlined guidelines for restructuring the system and specified certain rights for FCS and Farmers Home Administration borrowers.

The deregulation of banking institutions constitutes one of the more significant recent developments affecting the supply of agricultural credit. Elimination of controls on interest can improve efficiency in the flow of funds in local markets and make pricing policies more responsive to national market conditions. Deregulation should mean that agriculture will compete more directly with other sectors of the economy for access to credit.

An article appearing in the Federal Reserve Bank of Richmond, "An overview of Agricultural Policy... Past, Present, and Future," by Raymond E. Owens, provides a major review of agriculture and governmental agriculture policy. The remainder of this entry draws heavily from the Owens article. In the broadest sense, agricultural policy is any government policy that affects the decisions of the agricultural industry regarding investment, production, pricing, or distribution. Historically federal agricultural policy sought to increase farm income by increasing gross farm receipts. Agricultural policies try to boost receipts by limiting output or by guaranteeing farmers a higher price.

The purpose of acreage reduction programs and other output limitations is to reduce supplies and increase prices. Acres taken out of production are often idled, leaving them unavailable for the production of other crops. Because the quantity of farm commodities demanded is relatively insensitive (inelastic) to changes in price, gross farm receipts (price times quantity) will be higher with the restrictions. The farmers' gain is at the expense of consumers who now pay more for less, reflecting a redistribution of income.

The nonrecourse loan program acts as a "floor" to the market price. The government lends to the farmer an amount equal to the value of his crop at the guaranteed loan price. The farmer puts up the crop as collateral. If the market price rises above the loan price, the farmer pays back the loan and keeps the rest. If market price is below the loan price, the farmer forfeits the crop and keeps the loan amount. Under such a program, part of the crop is "sold" to the government. In practice, guaranteed prices are coupled with output reduction programs. If they are effective, they limit the subsidy amount and excess quantity supplied. To the extent that farmers work their remaining land more intensively, some subsidy and surplus production remains.

Crop (commodity) price support programs are intended to supplement farm income and limit the acreage planted in many field crops. Crops covered in price support programs include wheat, corn, sorghum, barley, oats, rye, rice, soybeans, peanuts, cotton, sugar, and tobacco. For most field crops, the programs attempt to limit production by reducing the program participant's "base acreage," which is determined from the number of acres he or she has historically devoted to the production of the crop. The USDA then requires the participant to limit acres planted of the crop to some portion of the base acreage. For peanuts, tobacco, and rice, production control limits a participant's total production. Price supports are most often structured in two tiers. The first is a nonrecourse loan and the second a deficiency payment. At harvest each year, farmers may sell their crop at the market price. Farmers meeting USDA's production limitation requirements have a second option, a nonrecourse loan, available. Those who take the loan must store their crop as collateral, placing the crop in a government-approved storage facility. Borrowers are required to repay the loans plus interest at the maturity date (usually nine months from the date the loan is made) or forfeit the collateral and keep the loan proceeds. No penalty is associated with the nonpayment loans beyond collateral forfeiture. Crop loan prices were sharply reduced in the 1985 Farm Bill. In addition, the Secretary of Agriculture has an option to reduce loan prices further if market conditions dictate, which he or she has exercised.

Total price support compensation is not dictated so much by the loan price as by the target price, which is legislated. When market prices and basic loan prices fall below the target price, eligible farmers receive a deficiency payment equal to the difference between the target price and the market price or between the target price and basic loan price, whichever is less. Payment can be made in either cash or commodity certificates. Commodity certificates may be used to redeem agricultural commodities owned by the government or sold for cash.

Fewer price support programs are available to livestock producers. The dairy industry is the prime example, operating under a marketing order program. Under the program, the government purchases or "removes" excess dairy products at a set price. The government price remains fixed as long as removals remain within a range determined by the dairy program. If the removals exceed the government limit, dairy price supports fall. If removals are below the limit, program provisions are in place to increase support price levels. Beef producers have price support through restrictions on the quantity of imported meat that comes into the United States. Import limits are normally exercised through voluntary agreements among major suppliers. In addition, the federal government adds to domestic demand through beef purchases.

In addition to crop and livestock programs, Congress has established incentives for foreign nations to purchase American farm commodities. These programs are intended to reduce surplus stocks by encouraging additional foreign demand. A primary incentive included in the export programs is providing credit assistance for foreign purchases of American farm products. Stocks of government-held grain and dairy products also are made available to exporters and others to counter "unfair" trade practices, to offset high domestic price supports and unfavorable movements in the exchange value of the dollar, and to expand markets. Public Law 480 is another conduit for exports. The law allows a qualifying nation to receive U.S. food grain stocks and dairy products free or at favorable long-term financing if the recipient qualifies under the law.

Along with export subsidies, the food stamp program is aimed at subsidizing domestic consumption of agricultural products. This program, along with programs such as the school lunch program, has relatively little effect on total domestic demand for agricultural products.

In recent years, Congress has focused attention on such concepts as decoupling, targeting, trade negotiations, and resource conservation. Decoupling refers to the elimination of the linkage between farm income programs and commodity production. Under decoupling, the government would make direct cash payments to farmers to support their incomes, but the payments would be disassociated from production. The market would determine supply and demand of commodities. Surplus stocks should not occur under such a system. Targeting refers to an identification mechanism that would replace production as a means of determining the distribution of government payments to farmers. Under targeting, criteria would be developed to determine the eligibility for and amount of payments to particular farmers. This procedure would allow the government to encourage or discourage specific activities within agriculture. Trade negotiation attempts to dismantle, through international cooperation, protection in the global marketplace. Resource conservation programs would encourage the removal of erodible and dry farmland that has been brought into agricultural production because of high commodity price supports. Farmers would be paid "rent" by the government to remove eligible land over a long-term basis, usually 10 years.

The 1988 drought was one of the worst on record for the central United States. Crop yields fell sharply and large inventories were drawn down to meet market needs. Nevertheless, net cash income to farmers was near the record $57.1 billion of 1987. The federal government's response was coordinated by the Interagency Drought Policy Committee. Federal actions included feed and financial assistance to farmers, fire suppression (5 million acres burned), the dredging of inland waterways, management of water and natural resources affected by the drought, and analyses of weather and climatic conditions.

U.S. agricultural exports in fiscal 1988 reached $35.2 billion in value, up 26% from the previous year. Export volume was up 14%. The U.S. continued to elaborate on its 1987 proposal calling for the elimination of all trade-distorting subsidies and import barriers. An historic United States-Canada Free Trade Agreement was approved by both nations and became effective January 1, 1989. Domestic policy focused on conservation and water quality.

See AGRICULTURAL ADJUSTMENT ACT, AGRICULTURAL CREDIT ACT OF 1987, AGRICULTURAL CREDITS ACT, FEDERAL AGRICULTURAL MORTGAGE CORPORATION.

Source: U.S. Department of Agriculture

BIBLIOGRAPHY

Agricultural Banker.
Agricultural Credit and Related Data. American Bankers Association, Washington, DC. Annual.
Agricultural Finance. American Institute of Banking.
Farm Mortgage Debt. U.S. Department of Agriculture. Annual.
KOHL, D. M. "Administering Agricultural Credit in the New Environment."*Journal of Commercial Bank Lending*, November, 1988.

AGRICULTURE, DEPARTMENT OF

Created by act of Congress on May 15, 1862 (12 Stat. 387; 5 U.S.C. 511, 514, 516) and signed into law by President Lincoln. The Secretary of Agriculture achieved cabinet status in 1889. Work of the department as a whole is directed by the Secretary of Agriculture, assisted by the deputy secretary. Agencies of the department report as follows:

Under the assistant secretary, rural development:

1. FARMERS HOME ADMINISTRATION.
2. RURAL ELECTRIFICATION ADMINISTRATION (REA). The REA finances electric and telephone facilities in rural areas of the United States and its territories. The REA itself does not own or operate rural electric or telephone facilities. Its function is to provide, through self-liquidating loans and technical assistance, adequate and dependable electric and telephone service to rural people under rates and conditions that permit full and productive use of these utility services.

Under the assistant secretary for marketing services:

1. AGRICULTURAL MARKETING SERVICE (AMS), which administers standardization, grading, voluntary and mandatory inspection, market news, marketing orders, regulatory, and related programs.
2. ANIMAL AND PLANT HEALTH INSPECTION SERVICE (APHIS), which was reestablished by the secretary of agriculture March 14, 1977, pursuant to authority contained in 5 U.S.C. 301 and Reorganization Plan 2 of 1953. APHIS was established to conduct regulatory and control programs to protect and improve animal and plant health for the benefit of people and their environment. In cooperation with state governments, the service administers federal laws and regulations pertaining to animal and plant health and quarantine, humane treatment of animals, and the control and eradication of pests and diseases.
3. FEDERAL GRAIN INSPECTION SERVICE (FGIS), established in the Department of Agriculture on November 20, 1976. The primary task of this agency is to carry out the provisions of the U.S. Grain Standards Act (7 U.S.C. 71 et al.), including changes made by the 94th Congress in 1976, to assure integrity in the inspection, weighing, and handling of U.S. grain. An administrator, appointed by the President and subject to Senate confirmation, heads the agency.

Under the assistant secretary for food and consumer services:

1. FOOD AND NUTRITION SERVICE (FNS), established on August 8, 1969, by the secretary of agriculture, under authority of 5 U.S.C. 301 and Reorganization Plan 2 of 1953. It administers the programs to make food assistance available to people, including the food stamp program; child nutrition programs; food distribution; and supplemental food programs (the WIC Program for women, infants, and children).
2. FOOD SAFETY AND QUALITY SERVICE (FSQS), established by the secretary of agriculture on March 14, 1977, pursuant to authority contained in 5 U.S.C. 301 and Reorganization Plan 2 of 1953. It was created to provide assurance to the consumer that foods are safe, wholesome, and nutritious; that they are of good quality; and that they are informatively and honestly labeled; and to provide assistance to the marketing system through purchase of surplus food commodities and those needed in the national food assistance programs.

Under the assistant secretary for international affairs and commodity programs:

1. AGRICULTURAL STABILIZATION AND CONSERVATION SERVICE (ASCS), established June 5, 1961 by the secretary of agriculture under authority of 5 U.S.C. 301 and Reorganization Plan 2 of 1953, as well as all other statutes and prior reorganization plans vesting authority in the secretary of agriculture. ASCS is the agency of the Department of Agriculture that administers specified commodity and related land use programs designed for voluntary production adjustment; resource protection; and price, market, and farm income stabilization.

   Spotted organizationally in conjunction with the ASCS is the COMMODITY CREDIT CORPORATION, the financing arm to stabilize and protect farm income and prices, to assist in maintaining balanced and adequate supplies of agricultural commodities and their products, and to facilitate the orderly distribution of commodities.
2. FEDERAL CROP INSURANCE CORPORATION, dating from 1938, whose scope has been modified from time to time by amendatory legislation, the latest of which was approved July 28, 1972 (7 U.S.C. 1520). It has as its immediate objective continuing development of a sound system of crop insurance and as its ultimate objective making this protection generally available to farmers on the major part of their annual crop investments (it does not ensure profit for the farmer nor cover avoidable losses such as those due to neglect or poor farming practices).
3. FOREIGN AGRICULTURAL SERVICE (FAS), the export promotion and service agency for U.S. agriculture.
4. OFFICE OF THE GENERAL SALES MANAGER (OGSM), established February 29, 1976, by the secretary of agriculture under authority of 5 U.S.C. 301 and Reorganization Plan 2 of 1953, as well as all other statutes and prior reorganization plans vesting authority in the secretary of agriculture. The office was organized to improve the department's ability to develop export policy and assist in orderly export marketing of agricultural commodities. It administers export programs that facilitate exports of commodities in ample supply in the U.S. These programs improve demand for farm products, avoid costly buildup of surpluses in the U.S., and in this way give American farmers the market incentives they need to produce food and fiber abundantly for domestic and export needs. Some of these programs serve the humanitarian objectives of feeding poor and disaster-stricken people in foreign lands. By collecting and publishing current information on export sales made by the private trade, it helps keep farmers and the general public informed on export activity.

Under the assistant secretary for conservation, research and education:

1. SCIENCE AND EDUCATION ADMINISTRATION (SEA), established by the secretary of agriculture on January 24, 1978 (43 FR 3254) to consolidate the former Agricultural Research Service, the Cooperative State Research Service, the Extension Service, and the National Agricultural Library. In addition, SEA was assigned new program responsibilities contained in the National Agricultural Research, Extension, and Teaching Act of 1977 (7 U.S.C. 3101–3316). Its basic mission is to improve the nationwide effectiveness of research, extension, and teaching in the food and agricultural sciences.
2. FOREST SERVICE, created originally in 1905, which transferred the federal forest reserves and the responsibility for their management from the Department of the Interior to the Department of Agriculture. The protection and development of the reserves (which became the national forests in 1907) are governed by the act of June 4, 1897 (16 U.S.C. 473–478), as amended; the Multiple Use–Sustained Yield Act of June 12, 1960 (16 U.S.C. 528–531); the Forest and Rangeland Renewable Resources Planning Act of 1974 (16 U.S.C. 1601–1610); and the National Forest Management Act of 1976 (90 Stat. 2947). The Weeks law of March 1, 1911 (16 U.S.C. 480), as amended, allowed the government to

AIRLINES

purchase and exchange land for national forests. The Forest Service has the federal responsibility for national leadership in forestry.

3. SOIL CONSERVATION SERVICE (SCS), established under authority of the Soil Conservation Act of 1935 (16 U.S.C. 590a–f). It has responsibility for developing and carrying out a national soil and water conservation program in cooperation with landowners, operators, and other land users and developers; community planning agencies and regional resource groups; and other agencies of government—federal, state, and local. The SCS also assists in agricultural pollution control, environmental improvement, and rural community development. The soil and water conservation program is carried on through technical help to locally organized and operated conservation districts and local sponsors of watershed protection projects and resource conservation and development projects, and through consultive assistance to other individuals and groups. About 2,950 conservation districts cover more than 2 billion acres in all the states, Puerto Rico, and the Virgin Islands.

Under the director for economics, policy analysis and budget:

1. WORLD FOOD AND AGRICULTURAL OUTLOOK AND SITUATION BOARD (WFAOSB), which coordinates and reviews all commodity and aggregate agricultural and food data and analyses used to develop outlook and situation material prepared within the Department of Agriculture. The objective is to improve the consistency, objectivity, and reliability of the material being disseminated to the public. In carrying out its responsibilities, the board oversees and clears for consistency of analytical assumptions and results all estimates and analyses which significantly relate to international and domestic commodity supply and demand.

2. ECONOMICS, STATISTICS, AND COOPERATIVES SERVICE, which carries out a national program of economic research and analysis, statistical programs, and other work relating to the production and marketing of farm commodities. It includes evaluations of the organization and performance of major commodity subsectors, costs and returns to farmers and marketers, situation and outlook, commodity projects, price spreads, and analysis of U.S. farm commodity programs. The service deals with the entire agricultural sector and centers around the more aggregate issues cutting across commodity lines.

Current Services Budget Authority by Function and Program (in millions of dollars)

Major missions and programs	1981 Fiscal year actual	1982 Fiscal year estimate	1983 Fiscal year estimate	1984 Fiscal year estimate
Farm income stabilization				
Commodity price support and related programs	$4,036	$6,343	$1,850	$2,215
Crop insurance	1	212	318	431
Agricultural credit	-228	405	698	857
Other programs and unallocated overhead	184	81	60	60
Subtotal: farm income stabilization	$3,993	$7,041	$2,926	$3,564
Agricultural research and services	1,540	1,596	1,572	1,530
Deductions for offsetting receipts	38	-4	—	-4
Total outlays	$5,572	$8,633	$4,494	$5,090
Addendum				
Off-budget federal entity				
Federal financing bank:				
Agricultural credit:				
Budget authority	$6,815	$5,391	$3,071	$4,952
Outlays	5,790	1,066	-394	-443

Source: Budget of the United States Government, Fiscal Year 1983

Summary. The predominance of farm income stabilization in budgeted authority for agriculture is indicated by the comparison of recent fiscal years in the appended table.

BIBLIOGRAPHY

DEPARTMENT OF AGRICULTURE, *Your United States Department of Agriculture.* Latest edition.

NATIONAL ARCHIVES AND RECORDS ADMINISTRATION, *The United States Government Manual.* Latest edition.

AIRLINES Legislation to deregulate the domestic airline passenger industry was enacted in October, 1979 (P.L. 95–504). The legislation allows the forces of competition in the marketplace to determine the price, quality, and variety of air service for the air transportation system. This severe competition has complicated operating problems. The deregulation took place in scheduled phases.

The Civil Aeronautics Board (CAB) was responsible for economic regulation of the commercial air carrier industry-authorizing entry into the industry, selecting intercity routes, and controlling the establishment of cargo rates. Legislation deregulating domestic air cargo operations (P.L. 95–163) was enacted in November, 1977, and as of 1982 the CAB was left with only limited control over the air cargo industry.

Because of the projected increase in traffic and because of aging equipment, the 1980s were extremely trying times for the Federal Aviation Administration (FAA) as it strove to maintain a safe and effective air traffic control system.

Critics of deregulation of passenger service point to such factors as a chaotic and incomprehensible fare pattern in some cases, arbitrary reduction or elimination of service to small cities, drastic layoffs of airline employees, difficulties in obtaining credit for company operations and equipment transactions, and cash flow problems (because of operating losses) and high debt which are expected to lead to further bankruptcies. On the other hand, supporters of deregulation believe that competition will weed out or reduce inefficiencies.

During the 1980s, buyouts of U.S. airlines were a major phenomenon of the industry. In one major buyout effort, the management of United Airlines attempted a management/employee buyout but was frustrated in this attempt as of early 1990. With few exceptions, the air transport industry's performance continued to lag the market in the late 1980s. Fuel costs rose steeply along with other operating costs. Traffic growth was predicted to accelerate in the 1990s and net profits for most carriers were expected to decline in the early 1990s. Fare discounting and special pricing procedures were common during the 1980s and were expected to extend into the 1990s. Frequent Flyers programs were widely used, often confusing, and very popular.

Composite statistics for U.S. air transport industry is appended.

Composite Statistics: Air Transport Industry*

1985	1986	1987	1988	1989	1990		92-94E
34.4	32.1	37.5	44.4	47.1	50.0	Revenues ($bill)	62.5
54.3%	57.7%	59.1%	58.8%	63.0%	61.5%	Load Factor	61.5%
10.9%	11.2%	10.2%	11.0%	8.0%	9.5%	Operating Margin	13.5%
2.29	2.30	2.28	2.60	2.57	2.67	Depreciation ($bill)	3.20
573.6	191.6	d18.6	616.6	190	950	Net Profit ($mill)	2750
42.2%	63.9%	NMF	56.4%	37.0%	37.0%	Income Tax Rate	37.0%
1.6%	0.6%	NMF	1.4%	0.4%	1.9%	Net Profit Margin	4.4%
12.0	12.1	13.5	13.4	12.3	12.9	Long Term Debt($bill)	18.0
9.22	9.91	11.2	9.70	9.9	10.6	Net Worth($bill)	20.0
5.4%	3.1%	2.5%	5.7%	6.5%	9.5%	% Earned Total Cap'l	10.0%
6.2%	1.9%	NMF	5.4%	2.0%	9.0%	% Earned Net Worth	14.0%
4.5%	0.8%	NMF	5.4%	0.5%	7.5%	% Retained to Comm Eq	13.0%
29%	62%	NMF	22%	72%	17%	% All Div'ds to Net Profit	7%
24.2	72.5	–	18.6	Bold figures are Value Line estimates		Avg Ann'l P/E Ratio	10.0
1.96	4.92	–	1.54			Relative P/E Ratio	0.85
0.7%	0.8%	0.7%	0.7%			Avg Ann'l Div'd Yield	0.6%

*Excludes Airborne Freight, Air Express, British Airways, Federal Express and KLM.

ENCYCLOPEDIA OF BANKING AND FINANCE

BIBLIOGRAPHY

AIR TRANSPORT ASSOCIATION OF AMERICA. *Air Transport* (annual).

AIR POCKET A stock market expression used to indicate abrupt and extreme weakness in a specific issue, i.e., a decline out of pro-portion to that in the general list or a decline in the face of general strength. It is caused by a sudden withdrawal of nearby bids. The term is akin to soft spot but is more forceful since it refers to a more violent downturn.

ALDRICH-VREELAND ACT See NATIONAL MONETARY COMMISSION.

ALIEN A person who is not a citizen of the country in which he or she resides. Aliens who are in the U.S. lawfully have the same contractual rights as citizens. They can be sued and use the courts to enforce their contractual rights. An enemy alien is unable to enforce a contract; the contract could be held in abeyance until the termination of the war. The federal immigration laws determine whether or not a person is an alien. Statutory law distinguishes between (1) resident and nonresident aliens and (2) friends and enemies of the United States. The U.S. Constitution provides protection for aliens. Individuals who are not U.S. citizens and who do not qualify as residents may be subject to U.S. income tax. Such persons are referred to as nonresident aliens and are taxed on certain types of income that are received from U.S. sources. These amounts are taxed at a flat rate of 30%.

ALLIANCE FOR PROGRESS A program of economic cooperation between the U.S. and Latin American countries to promote the economic and social development of Latin America, initiated in 1961 pursuant to the Charter of Punta del Este. The U.S. would help in these efforts by providing economic and technical aid. The Latin American countries, in addition to providing an increasing share of their own resources to development, would carry out substantial reform programs. The U.S would assist development activities, particularly in agriculture, education, health, and economic integration. In order to stimulate economic activity in a region, Alliance loan dollars of the AGENCY FOR INTERNATIONAL DEVELOPMENT (*see* MUTUAL SECURITY PROGRAM), previously restricted to U.S. procurement, were made eligible for procurement of goods and services throughout Latin America.

Development aid from the U.S. to Latin American countries has continued, but not under the title "Alliance for Progress." One reason for the change was that the term translates into Spanish as "La Alianza Para El Progreso," which can also be read as "The Alliance Stops Progress," and this alternative translation was seized upon and used for derision of the program by politically antagonistic elements in Latin America. Moreover, in 1975, the Latin American Economic System (SELA) was chartered, with 25 countries in Latin America and the Caribbean as members, but not the U.S. SELA was termed by its supporters as the "antithesis of the Alliance for Progress of the Organization of American States."

On February 24, 1982, President Reagan in a speech to the Organization of American States proposed a new Caribbean aid plan of trade and investment incentives and technical assistance, intended to improve economic conditions and to ensure U.S. military security in the Caribbean Basin and Central America.

ALLOCATION Allocation has a distinct meaning in accounting and economics. From an accounting perspective, allocation is generally considered to be the accounting process of assigning or distributing an amount according to a plan or a formula. Allocation problems arise in many situations that involve accounting, such as:

1. Reducing an amount by periodic payments or write-downs:
   a. Reducing a liability that arose as a result of a cash receipt by recognizing revenue (for example, unearned rent).
   b. Reducing an asset (for example, depreciation, depletion, amortization, including amortization of prepayments and deferrals).
2. Assigning manufacturing costs to production departments and subsequently to units of product to determine product cost.
3. Apportioning the cost of a lump-sum or basket purchase to individual assets on the basis of their relative market value.

Accountants recognize that within the existing framework of conventional accounting principles and methods, allocations are generally arbitrary. The generally recognized minimum criteria of any allocation method include:

1. The method should be unambiguous.
2. The method should be defendable (that is, theoretically justifiable).
3. The method should divide up what is available to be allocated (that is, the allocation should be additive).

From an economic perspective, allocation is the process of choosing. Resources that are limited are referred to in economics as scarce resources. Most resources are scarce. Because scarcity is a fact of life, choosing among alternative resources is a necessity. Economics can be defined as the study of the process of allocating scarce resources among alternative uses.

ALLONGE A slip of paper attached to a bill of exchange or promissory note to provide for additional endorsements because the original instrument does not afford sufficient space.

ALLOTMENT The share or portion of an issue of securities apportioned or assigned by an investment house or syndicate to the subscriber. In an underwriting syndicate, the allotment would be made to syndicate members (participants). An allotment may be less than the amount subscribed, since the offerings of securities are made subject to allotment.

ALLOTMENT NOTICE A letter issued to a subscriber or applicant for bonds or stocks, announcing the quantity allotted or assigned to him or her, the sum and date payable or, if payable in installments, the several payment dates, etc.

ALLOTTEE A person, investment house, or syndicate member to whom securities are allotted in response to a subscription therefor.

ALLOWANCE FOR LOAN LOSSES ACCOUNT A balance sheet account with a net credit balance. The balance in the account represents the estimated uncollectible amount of loans included in the bank's portfolio. The balance in this account is deducted from the total amount of loans on the balance sheet. The resulting balance represents the estimated cash value (net loans) of the bank's loans. The allowance account is both a valuation account and a contra-asset account. As a valuation account, the account reflects the estimated loss or decrease in value of certain loan accounts. As a contra-asset account, the account presents a net credit balance that should be subtracted from a related debit balance-sheet asset account.

The balance in the allowance account is based on management's judgment concerning such factors as the dollar amount and quality of the loan portfolio, problem loans, loss experience, and current economic conditions.

ALLOY In monetary systems, a base metal or metals mixed with gold or silver, the standard monetary metals, to impart greater durability to coins made therefrom, because pure gold and silver are too soft for public circulation durability. Lowest denomination coins traditionally were coined entirely from the base metals, but in recent years coinage systems have been composed purely of base metal coins, as illustrated by the U.S. system.

U.S. Monetary System. Title II of P.L. 91–607, December 31, 1970, provided authorization of completely nonsilver dollars and half-dollars for general circulation, similar in composition to the completely nonsilver quarters and dimes authorized by the Coinage Act of 1965. The former standard silver dollar, consisting of 412.50 grains troy weight (371.25 grains silver (90%) and 41.25 grains of copper, or 10% alloy) was no longer being minted when the Coinage Act of 1965 was passed. The act kept the silver dollar unchanged in composition but did provide that silver dollars would not be minted for five years from the date of that act (July 23, 1965).

The Coinage Act of 1965 provided for the clad half-dollar: (1) cladding of 800 parts of silver and 200 parts of copper; and (2) a core of silver-copper, so that the whole coin weighed 11.5 grams (4.6 grams of silver (40%) and 6.9 grams of copper, or 60% of total weight). P.L. 91–607 (referred to above) authorized any coins minted under its

ENCYCLOPEDIA OF BANKING AND FINANCE

authority, including half-dollars, to be clad coins (an alloy of 75% copper and 25% nickel, weighing not less than 30% of the weight of the nonclad coin, with a core of copper). These completely nonsilver half dollars are 1.205 inches in diameter and weigh 11.34 grams.

The quarters and dimes, as authorized by the Coinage Act of 1965, were continued unaffected by P.L. 91–607. The quarter dollar is 9.955 inches in diameter and weighs 5.67 grams. The dime is 0.705 inch in diameter and weighs 2.268 grams.

Minor coins were unaffected by both the Coinage Act of 1965 and P.L. 91-607. Metallic contents are as follows: nickel ($0.05) 57.87 grains copper and 19.29 grains nickel; and penny ($0.01) 45.60 grains copper, 2.40 grains zinc. Tin was eliminated from the bronze alloy of the penny after September 5, 1962 (31 U.S.C. 317).

P.L. 95-447, dated October 10, 1978, authorized the issuance of the new Susan B. Anthony dollar coin. It further provided that the minting of the Eisenhower circulating dollar coin be discontinued as of December 31, 1978.

The Susan B. Anthony dollar is a copper-nickel clad coin, as are all U.S. coins valued at $0.10 or greater. The Susan B. Anthony dollar costs $0.03 to produce and will last 15 years or more in good condition.

ALL-SAVERS CERTIFICATE A fixed-rate, tax-exempt time deposit authorized in the Economic Recovery Tax Act of 1981 (P.L. 97-34) that became available to individuals by depository institutions between October 1981 and December 1983. ASCs mature in and must be held for exactly 52 weeks. ASCs earned interest at 70 percent of the yield on 52-week U.S. Treasury bills offered near the time of a certificate's issuance. The interest exclusion from federal income taxation was limited to $1,000 for an individual ($2,000 for couples filing a joint return). Issuing institutions were required to invest a percentage of the face amount of ASCs or, alternatively, of net new retail savings and time deposits, in housing-related assets or agricultural loans. Special rules applied to the amount of certificates credit unions could offer. Permission to issue ASCs expired in 1983.

ALPHA STOCKS As the result of adaptation to usage as technical market data of the statistical technique of determination of simple regression and correlation, the glossary of terms current in Wall Street now includes alpha stocks and beta stocks.

Plotted for given time periods on a scatter diagram, the alpha and beta coefficients for a given stock, relative to the general market (as represented by a market average such as the Standard & Poor's index), may be shown. The dependent variable (return on the stock selected) is plotted on the vertical axis of the chart (the y axis). The independent variable (return from the market in general, as represented by the market index) is plotted on the horizontal axis of the chart (the x axis). A series of scatter points, expressing the relationship of the respective returns for the time periods selected, will result. Next, the characteristic or trend line may be plotted, either precisely statistically or approximately by visual inspection, through the field of scatter points, to establish the alpha and beta coefficients.

The alpha coefficient is determinable at the intercept, i.e., where the characteristic line intercepts the vertical axis. At this point, the stock's return is indicated where movement of the market, as indicated by the market average, is zero (stationary). The slope of the characteristic line (vertical movement divided by the horizontal movement) indicates the beta coefficient. If the beta coefficient is higher than unity (over 1), the stock plotted has more volatility than the general market as measured by the plotted market average. If the beta coefficient is less than unity (less than 1), the stock plotted is a slower mover than the general market.

Stocks with beta coefficients of over 1 are termed aggressive stocks. Stocks with beta coefficients of less than 1 are termed defensive stocks, which they may or may not be. Whether a stock is aggressive or defensive should be determined by its characteristics relative to the risks in INVESTMENT.

See INVESTMENT RISKS.

ALTERATION According to the Uniform Commercial Code (UCC) (Sec. 3–407), any change which alters the contract of any party to a negotiable instrument in any respect, including any change in the number or relations of the parties, any change in an incomplete instrument by its completion otherwise than as authorized, or any change in the writing as signed by adding to it or by removing any part of it.

The consequence (as against any person other than a subsequent holder in due course) of alteration by the holder of the instrument, provided such alteration is both fraudulent and material, is discharge of any party whose contract is thereby changed, unless that party assents or is precluded from asserting this personal defense of discharge (e.g., estoppel).

If the alteration is not fraudulent and not made by the holder (e.g., spoilation by a stranger or otherwise unauthorized by the holder), a material alteration does not discharge any party, and the instrument may be enforced according to its original tenor or (with regard to completion of incomplete instruments) according to the authority given to complete.

A subsequent holder in due course may in all cases enforce the instrument according to its original tenor. When an incomplete instrument has been completed, such holder has the option of enforcing it as completed or according to the authority given.

Protection for Banks. The UCC codifies (Sec. 4–401 (2)(a)), aspects of so-called bankers statutes added by the various states in varying provisions in their enacted versions of the Uniform Negotiable Instruments Law (UNIL). The UCC in this section gives banks, as its Section 3–115 does other drawees, the same protection as afforded holders in due course against asserted defense of discharge, because of alteration, by the party liable. If the bank in good faith makes payment of an item to a holder, it may charge its customer's account according to the original tenor of the altered item or according to the tenor of the completed item, even though the bank knows the item has been completed, unless the bank has notice that the completion of the item is improper.

Also codified in the UCC is Section 4–406, imposing duty on the bank's customer to discover any unauthorized signatures or alterations by examining with reasonable care and promptness the statement of account and paid items furnished to him and to promptly notify the bank. Establishment by the bank of the customer's failure to carry out this duty precludes the customer from: (1) asserting against the bank the unauthorized signature or any alteration on the item, if the bank also establishes that it has suffered loss because of such failure; and (2) asserting against the bank unauthorized signatures or alterations by the same wrongdoer on any other items the bank has paid in good faith, after the first items and statement of account were made available to the customer for a reasonable period not exceeding 14 calendar days and before the bank has received notification from the customer of such unauthorized signatures or alterations. But this preclusion of the customer does not apply if the customer establishes lack of ordinary care on the part of the bank in paying the items.

However, this preclusion of the customer will apply, regardless of exercise of ordinary care or lack of such care by either the bank or the customer, if the customer: (1) fails to discover and report to the bank an unauthorized signature or any alteration on the face or back of the item within one year from the date of availability of the statement of account and items to the customer, or (2) fails to discover and report any unauthorized endorsement within three years from such availability.

Check protecting devices help to minimize and prevent fraudulent alteration of checks. Protection against alteration of instruments is a continuing responsibility of both customers and banks. Customers will avoid trouble by: (1) drawing instruments completely and accurately; (2) attesting as to genuineness of alterations made by the drawer by full signature or, better yet, drawing a fresh instrument to avoid possible future difficulties; (3) promptly examining the monthly bank statements and accompanying paid items furnished by the bank for any irregularities and promptly reporting them to the bank. The UCC imposes upon a payor bank the responsibility of knowing its customer's signature (Secs. 3–418 and 4–207) and suffering the loss if the drawer's signature is forged and neither the collecting banks nor the original depositor of the item had knowledge of the FORGERY.

See FORGED INSTRUMENTS.

ALTERNATE DEPOSITS Deposits made in the names of two persons connected by the word *or*, e.g., John or Mary Doe. Such deposits made in the names of two persons, payable to either or payable to either or the survivor, are termed "joint accounts" in banking parlance and are frequently used by husband and wife or by members of a partnership. Because use of the words *and* and *or* might have different legal effects from those intended by the parties, the deposit agreement should specifically state the right of either depositor to withdraw funds from the account and the right of the bank to pay the balance to the survivor, if so intended. In the absence of specific agreement, the laws of the particular state will control.

ALTERNATIVE MINIMUM TAX A tax that applies to individuals, corporations, and estates and trusts if it exceeds the taxpayer's regular tax liability. Alternative minimum taxable income is the taxpayer's taxable income (1) increased by tax preference items and (2) adjusted for income, deductions, and losses that have been recomputed under the alternative minimum tax system. A noncorporate taxpayer is subject to a 21% tax on alternative minimum taxable income in excess of $30,000 ($40,000 on a joint return).

ALTERNATIVE MORTGAGE TRANSACTION PARITY ACT OF 1982 Title VII of Public Law 97-320 that provides for nonfederally chartered lending institutions to offer alternative mortgages in accordance with federal regulations, unless state laws prevent such transactions.

ALTERNATIVE PAYEE If an instrument is payable to the order of two or more persons in the alternative (e.g., to A or B), either of the parties who is in possession of the instrument is a holder and thus may negotiate, enforce, or discharge the instrument. By contrast, an instrument payable to A and B (not in the alternative) is payable to all such payees and may be negotiated, enforced, or discharged only by all of them. If the instrument is payable to A and/or B, it is payable both in the alternative (to A or to B) and to A and B together (not in the alternative), so that it may be negotiated, enforced, or discharged either alternatively or together (Uniform Commercial Code Sec. 3–116, revising Sec. 41 of the Uniform Negotiable Instruments Law).

ALUMINUM One of the chemical elements, a silvery lightweight, easily worked metal that resists corrosion and is found abundantly, but only in combination: symbol, Al; at. wt., 26.97; at. no., 13. It typically requires about two pounds of alumina to produce one pound of aluminum. The price range in the late 1980s was around $250-$275 a ton for this commodity. Alumina supplies were at a low level historically. Capacity was expected to increase, especially in Australia, which is the world's largest producer.

Also susceptible to the business cycle, U.S. aluminum companies were expected to prosper in the 1990s from the food packaging and aerospace sectors of the economy. Similar growth in the building/construction and automotive industries was not expected. Exports were the major force in the aluminum industry in 1989 and were expected to continue. Environmental concerns affected the industry in the 1980s and were expected to continue. Major aluminum companies include Alcoa, Alcan, and Reynolds Metals.

BIBLIOGRAPHY

ALUMINUM ASSOCIATION, *Aluminum Statistical Review* (annual).

AMALGAMATION See BANK MERGERS, COMBINATION, CONSOLIDATION OF BANKS, MERGER.

AMERICAN BANKERS ASSOCIATION (ABA) A national trade association for U.S. commercial banks of all sizes and types. Established in 1875, the ABA enhances the role of commercial banks as the preeminent provider of financial services. This mission is accomplished through federal legislative and regulatory activities, and communications, research, education, and training programs.

ABA's 12,000-plus members account for approximately 95 percent of the industry's assets. The organization derives one-third of its income from member dues and two-thirds from products, services, conferences, and academic programs.

The day-to-day activities of the ABA are carried on by a professional staff at the national headquarters in Washington, D.C. ABA policy is developed through a committee process. The committees are made up of volunteer bankers who donate their time and experience to the association. Proposals for new policies usually originate with one or more of the association's working committees or divisions.

ABA testifies regularly before congressional committees on a wide range of issues. The staff submits draft bills for key legislation, organizes bankers' lobbying efforts on critical industry issues, and maintains liaison relationships with federal bank regulators. ABA also works closely with state banker associations and sponsors annual visits to Washington that bring more than 1,500 bankers from 38 states to the Capitol to lobby Congress and meet with federal regulators. The ABA also collects and disperses significant amounts in BankPac funds per election cycle to candidates running for House and Senate seats.

ABA serves every major banking occupation (16 divisions and three units) and annually operates national schools, specialized newsletters, national and regional conferences, and numerous workshops and seminars. The Stonier Graduate School of Banking is the largest industry-sponsored educational program in the world.

ABA conducts national public relations and advertising programs on behalf of the industry. Member communication programs keep bankers current on industry issues. Publications include the *ABA Bankers Weekly*, and the *ABA Banking Journal*. In addition newsletters and quarterly magazines are published on specialized topics.

ABA also sponsors an insurance program to provide director and officer liability and blanket bond, trust errors and omissions, and other coverage for ABA members.

ABA represents the banking industry on the U.S. Delegation to the United Nations Commission on International Trade Law, serves as Secretariat of the International Monetary Conference, acts as Secretariat of the Financial Institutions Committee for the American National Standards Institute, and functions as the official registrar and number-issuing agent for the International Standards Organization.

AMERICAN DEPOSITARY RECEIPTS Forms for listing of shares of foreign companies on American stock exchanges in an acceptable American bank or trust company, representing the deposit of an equivalent amount of underlying foreign shares. Direct listing of foreign shares is considered only in special cases where the form of the security itself, the facilities for ready transferability in New York, prompt interchangeability with certificates outstanding in the primary foreign market, and arrangements for distributing dividends and other rights and benefits to American holders are equivalent to those provided by the use of American depositary receipts. Form 19 of the Securities and Exchange Commission is required to be filed with the SEC and the stock exchange concerned for the permanent registration of American certificates (either American depositary receipts for foreign shares or American participation certificates in foreign bonds or notes) issued against securities of foreign issuers deposited with an American depositary and of the foreign securities so deposited.

AMERICAN INSTITUTE OF BANKING The educational section of the AMERICAN BANKERS ASSOCIATION. The American Institute of Banking (AIB) provides self-development opportunities for banking men and women through organized programs of education and training. The basic mission is to help bank employees acquire and apply knowledge, and develop attitudes and skills for more successful careers. Courses are offered to bank employees through chapters and study groups in cities and towns throughout the nation and through correspondence study.

Membership in the AIB is the largest in the world for an educational enterprise of its kind. Publications of the AIB include its own textbooks and the AIB *Bulletin*.

AMERICAN PARITY A foreign exchange term to indicate the equivalent in U.S. money of the foreign price of a security traded in internationally.

AMERICAN STOCK EXCHANGE The second largest stock exchange in the U.S. measured by total shares traded as well as dollar value of trading, the American Stock Exchange adopted its present title effective January 5, 1953. Former titles were as follows: 1929–1953, New York Curb Exchange; 1921–1929, New York Curb Market; 1911–1921, New York Curb Market Association; and 1908–1911, New York Curb Agency, the first attempt, by E. E. Mendels (called the "Father of the Curb Exchange") and other brokers, at formal organization of the market. The market moved indoors into a new building in 1921, which was enlarged into its present structure in 1931, at 86 Trinity Place, New York City. The market outdoors, referred to as the Curb, is believed to have begun about 1849, operating at the following outdoor locations in the financial district of New York City: at first, at Wall and Hanover Streets; then on

AMORTISEMENT

William Street, from the Civil War to about the turn of the century; and finally on Broad Street from about 1900, gradually moving southward on Broad Street from the original location just south of Wall and Broad Streets, until it moved indoors in 1921. To old-timers, the exchange is still the Curb, but the title American Stock Exchange (AMEX in familiar shortened reference) was adopted as being more descriptive of its importance as a national and international securities market (it also ranks second in dollar value of trading in Canadian securities on the North American continent).

The American Stock Exchange recorded significant growth, profitability, and resilience in the turbulent 1980s markets. The annual net income in the decade of the 1970s averaged $360,000 per year; the average for the 1980s was $5.5 million. Trading volume, powered by investor interest in attractive and highly capitalized companies that listed in the latter part of the decade, account for the bulk of current trading volume. Equity turnover in 1979 totaled 1.1 billion shares; trading in 1987 reached a high of 3.5 billion and exceeded 3.1 billion shares in 1989. The Amex trades puts and call options on more than 140 listed and over-the-counter stocks, as well as options on U.S. Treasury notes and bills, and on stock indices.

In 1990 close to 800 companies traded on the Amex. They include both domestic and foreign (53 in 1990) companies. Primarily, these are mid-sized companies. Nearly 16% are involved in consumer goods. Some 15% are in the service field. About 14% each are in financial, natural resources, high technology, and capital goods fields.

Option volume, which totaled 16.9 million contracts in 1979, trebled in the next decade, reaching a high of 67.9 million contracts in 1987 and exceeding 48 million contracts as of the end of 1989. The Amex Market Value Index, introduced in 1973 to replace the old price change index, showed a 205.9% gain from the end of 1979 to its 378.00 close for 1989. In terms of listings, the Amex ended the last decade with 1,029 issues of 931 companies; at the end of 1989 the total stood at 1,069 issues of 859 companies. Issues and companies on the exchange during 1988 and 1989 are shown here:

	12/31/89	12/31/88
Total number of stock issues	1,057	1,100
Total number of bond issues	279	310
Total number of companies	859	895

Market value of the Amex list at the end of 1979 totaled $57.8 billion, with 3.1 billion shares outstanding for trading. This number increased to 9.0 billion shares outstanding and a record market value of $132.5 billion at the end of 1989.

Some highlights of the 1980 decade include the following:

- 1981 Exchange expands automation facilities; Amex board increased from 21 to 25 members.
- 1982 Exchange introduces options trading on U.S. Treasury notes and bills and launches American Gold Coin Exchange to trade gold bullion coins.
- 1983 Amex introduces trading in index options to complement put and call options on equities. The Amex adapted touch-screen technology to high-speed order execution.
- 1984 Exchange completes floorwide installation of AUTOPER. AUTOAMOS, the options counterpart to AUTOPER, is introduced.
- 1985 Amex introduces new Institutional Index Option which tracks the performance of stocks most popular with institutional investors.
- 1987 October market turbulence fuels volume surge culminating in all-time record equities and options trading. New highs set in membership prices. Amex Major Market Value Index options begin trading on European Options Exchange in Amsterdam.
- 1988 Amex raises specialist capital requirements and option margins and joins other markets in agreeing to market-wide circuit-breaker rule.
- 1989 Equity Index Participation introduced as new derivative products; EIPs later sidetracked by court challenge to SEC authority. New pricing system for options introduced.

The Exchange requires every listed company to make available to the public information necessary for informed investing and to take reasonable steps to ensure that all who invest in its securities enjoy equal access to such information. The Exchange has adopted six specific policies concerning disclosure:

(a) Immediate Public Disclosure of Material Information.
(b) Thorough Public Dissemination.
(c) Clarification or Confirmation of Rumors and Reports.
(d) Response to Unusual Market Action. The company is required to make inquiry to determine whether the rumors or other conditions requiring corrective action exist, and, if so, to take whatever action is appropriate.
(e) Unwarranted Promotional Disclosure—Such activity includes inappropriately worded news releases, public announcements not justified by actual developments in a company's affairs, exaggerated reports or predictions, flamboyant wording and other forms of overstated or overzealous disclosure activity which may mislead investors and cause unwarranted price movements and activity in a company's securities.
(f) Insider Trading—Insiders should not trade on the basis of material information which is not known to the investing public. Moreover, insiders should refrain from trading, even after material information has been released to the press and other media, for a period sufficient to permit thorough public dissemination and evaluation of the information.

The appended table provided by the American Stock Exchange describes the listing requirements for the American Stock Exchange. The approval of an application for the listing of securities on the American Stock Exchange is a matter solely within the discretion of the Exchange. To assist companies interested in applying for listing, the Exchange has established certain guidelines which are considered in evaluating potential listing applicants. There are other relevant factors that must be considered in evaluating whether or not a company qualifies for listing. Major emphasis is placed on such matters as the nature of a company's business, the market for its products, the reputation of its management, its historical record and pattern of growth, its financial integrity and risk, its demonstrated earning power, and its future outlook.

Also appended are the following tables: Current Amex Membership, 1988-1989; Amex Seat Sales, 1988-1989; Amex Specialists' Personnel, 1989; Annual Amex Stock and Bond Volumes, 1965-1989; Annual Amex Stock and Index Options Volumes, 1975-1989; Amex Market Value Index, 1975-1989; and Most Active Amex Stocks Classes, 1989.

BIBLIOGRAPHY

The American Stock Exchange offers numerous publications describing the Exchange and its activities along with statistical data relating to the Exchange. This material is available from the Exchange's Corporate Communications Division.

AMORTISEMENT AMORTIZATION

AMORTIZATION   This term has two meanings:

1. Literally, "killing off" or wiping out, a term applied to (1) the gradual reduction of a debt by equal periodic payments sufficient to pay current interest and to extinguish the principal completely by final maturity (see AMORTIZED LOANS); (2) the periodic writing off of an asset over a specific term, such as capitalized expenses (deferred charges) and intangibles (such as goodwill, patents, trademarks, and copyrights). Depreciation is a process of regular amortization of the depreciable cost, including accelerated amortization of defense-essential facilities.
2. The process of periodically reducing or writing off the premium on a bond brought above par, in order to bring its investment or basis value into coincidence with par (face amount of denomination of the bond) on the maturity date. The premium paid for a bond at the time of purchase represents a part of the investment which will not be returned at maturity. Consequently, a part of the cash interest paid periodically on the bond should not be regarded as income but as an amount to be applied to the reduction of the premium. This is accomplished by a charge at each bond interest date to the cash interest account and a corresponding credit to the cost basis on the bond or to valuation reserve, amortization of premium.

AMORTIZATION

Listing on the American Stock Exchange

Financial Guidelines

	Regular	Alternative
Pre-Tax Income	$750,000 latest fiscal year or 2 of most recent 3 years	—
Market Value of Public Float	$3,000,000	$15,000,000
Price	$3	—
Operating History	—	3 Years
Stockholders' Equity	$4,000,000	$4,000,000

Distribution Guidelines
(applies to regular and alternative guidelines)

	Alternative 1	Alternative 2	Alternative 3
Public Float	500,000	1,000,000	500,000
Stockholders	800	400	400
Average Daily Volume	—	—	2,000

Regarding Alternative Listing Guidelines
It is recognized that certain financially sound companies are unable to meet fully the Exchange's regular listing criteria because, for example, of the nature of their business, or because of continuing large expenditures of funds for research and development. Such companies may, however, qualify for listing provided they meet the numerical criteria outlined above, have sufficient financial resources to continue operations over an extended period of time, and other otherwise regarded as suitable for Exchange listing.

Initial Public Offerings
In certain circumstances, the Amex may approve an issue for listing "subject to official notice of issuance" immediately prior to effectiveness of the company's initial public offering.
While the Exchange has not adopted special criteria for IPO's, added emphasis is placed on the company's financial strength and its demonstrated earnings history and/or outlook.

Amex Specialists' Personnel

	12/31/89	12/31/88
Number of Units	25	24
Number of Specialists	217	213
Average Number of Specialists Per Unit	8.7	8.9

Current Amex Membership

	12/31/89	12/31/88
Regular Members	661	661
Associate Members	162	167
Options Principal Members	203	203
Limited Trading Permit Holders	36	36

Regular Members—May transact business in equities and options.
Options Principal Members—May execute principal transactions in options only.
Associate Members—Have wire access to the trading floor where orders are executed by regular members.
Limited Trading Permit Holders—In 1987, the Amex expanded its options membership through the offering of these permits to augment market-making activities in non-equity options. These permit holders must do one-third of their trades in Institutional Index options.

Annual Amex Stock and Bond Volumes

Year	Stocks (Shares)	Bonds (Principal Amount)
1989	3,125,107,840	$708,836,000
1988	2,515,025,340	603,882,000
1987	3,505,954,875	686,922,000
1986	2,978,611,984	810,151,000
1985	2,100,815,250	644,882,000
1984	1,545,140,660	371,857,000
1983	2,080,922,014	395,089,000
1982	1,337,725,430	325,145,000
1981	1,343,400,220	301,226,000
1980	1,626,072,625	355,723,000
1979	1,100,263,500	225,892,000
1978	988,559,026	265,514,000
1977	653,128,700	284,696,000
1976	648,297,321	301,054,000
1975	540,934,210	259,395,000
1974	482,173,297	256,865,000
1973	759,840,245	457,940,000
1972	1,117,989,153	728,524,000
1971	1,070,924,002	876,046,000
1970	843,116,260	641,270,000
1969	1,240,742,012	913,940,000
1968	1,435,765,734	970,403,000
1967	1,145,090,300	554,824,000
1966	690,762,585	159,724,000
1965	534,221,999	146,927,000

Amex Seat Sales

	1989 Price	Date Arranged	1988 Price	Date Arranged
Regular Memberships				
High	$215,000	Mar. 31, 1989	$255,000	Feb. 19, 1988
			$255,000	May 17, 1988
Low	$155,000	Nov. 2, 1989	$180,000	Nov. 30, 1988
	$155,000	Nov. 10, 1989		
Last	$160,000	Dec. 21, 1989	$180,000	Nov. 30, 1988
Options Principal Memberships				
High	$175,000	Jan. 30, 1989	$250,000	May 10, 1988
	$175,000	Mar. 23, 1989		
Low	$125,000	Nov. 24, 1989	$175,000	Oct. 28, 1988
Last	$130,000	Nov. 24, 1989	$175,000	Oct. 28, 1988
Limited Trading Permits				
High	$ 7,500	Nov. 14, 1989	$ 59,000	Oct. 4, 1988
Low	$ 7,500	Nov. 14, 1989	$ 40,000	Dec. 6, 1988
Last	$ 7,500	Nov. 14, 1989	$ 40,000	Dec. 6, 1988

ENCYCLOPEDIA OF BANKING AND FINANCE

AMORTIZATION

Annual Amex Stock and Index Options Volume

Year	Puts & Calls Combined (Contracts)	Calls	Puts
1989 [1]	48,397,918	36,418,925	11,978,993
1988	43,606,525	33,212,348	10,394,177
1987	67,981,745	50,992,090	16,989,655
1986 [2]	62,343,990	46,887,638	15,456,352
1985 [3]	46,726,621	33,947,679	12,778,942
1984 [4]	38,924,981	27,879,107	11,045,874
1983 [5]	37,940,048	27,361,952	10,578,096
1982	37,687,768	26,889,731	10,798,037
1981	33,674,212	25,502,860	8,171,352
1980	27,891,451	23,951,708	3,939,743
1979	16,800,914	15,871,514	929,400
1978	14,037,373	13,213,207	824,166
1977 [6]	9,874,984	9,458,462	416,522
1976		8,828,456	
1975 [7]		3,482,258	

1. 1989 volume also included: Options trading on the International Market Index—50 leading foreign stocks actively traded in the United States either directly or in the form of American Depositary Receipts (ADRs)—began May 12, 1989.
2. 1986 volume also included: Options trading on the Institutional Index—75 major stocks most widely held as equity investments by the largest institutions—began October 3, 1986. Options on both the Amex Market Value Index and the Airline Index ceased trading in the year.
3. 1985 volume also included: Options trading on the Airline Index (a replacement for the Transportation Index)—five airline companies—began November 18, 1985.
4. 1984 volume also included: Options trading on the Transportation Index—20 transportation-related companies—began March 28, 1984.
5. 1983 volume also included: Options trading on the Major Market Index—20 blue-chip industrial corporations—began April 29, 1983. Options trading on the Amex Market Value Index—companies listed on the American Stock Exchange—began July 8, 1983. Options trading on the Computer Technology Index—30 computer-related companies—began August 26, 1983. Options trading on the Oil Index (formerly the Oil and Gas Index)—15 oil-related companies—began September 9, 1983, revised and renamed October 22, 1984.
6. Put options began June 3, 1977.
7. Stock options trading began January 13, 1975, with calls only.

Amex Market Value Index

1989 Close:	378.00
1988	306.01
1987	260.35
1986	263.27
1985	246.13
1984	204.26
1983	223.01
1982	170.30
1981	160.32
1980	174.50
1979	123.54
1978	75.28
1977	63.95
1976	54.92
1975	41.74

Most Active Amex Stocks and Options Classes

Stocks	Volume	Year-End Price
B.A.T. Industries plc.	153,710,000	13 5/16
Texas Air Corporation	98,499,200	11 5/8
Wang Laboratories, Inc. (B Com)	98,132,100	5 1/8
Amdahl Corporation	81,987,800	14 3/8
Echo Bay Mines Ltd.	70,520,800	18 3/8
Fruit of the Loom, Inc. (A Com)	66,622,100	14 7/8
DWG Corporation	50,477,700	12 1/8
Energy Service Company, Inc.	46,593,900	4 3/8
Diasonics, Inc.	43,006,500	4 1/8
Hasbro, Inc.	33,637,100	18 3/4

To illustrate the mathematical history of a bond bought at a premium and carried currently on an investment basis, suppose a 6.0% tax-exempt bond, paying interest semiannually March 1 and September 1, with a four-year maturity, is bought March 1, 1978, to yield 4.5%, or a cost of $1,054.40. The appended table (Mathematics of Amortization) shows what portion of the cash interest is to be regarded as net interest income or yield and how much as reduction of the principal of the investment (amortization of the premium).

Mathematics of Amortization

Date	Cash interest (6.0%)	Net income (4.5%)	Reduction of book value of the investment, or amortization	Book Value	Par
1978: 3-1	...	...	...	$1,054.40	$1,000.00
9-1	$ 30.00	$ 23.70	$ 6.30	1,048.10	
1979: 3-1	30.00	23.60	6.40	1,041.70	
9-1	30.00	23.40	6.60	1,035.10	
1980: 3-1	30.00	23.30	6.70	1,028.40	
9-1	30.00	23.10	6.90	1,021.50	
1981: 3-1	30.00	23.00	7.00	1,014.50	
9-1	30.00	22.80	7.20	1,007.30	
1982: 3-1	30.00	22.70	7.30	1,000.00	1,000.00
	$240.00	$185.60	$54.40		

The yield is determined by multiplying the book value, which in the first instance is the purchase price, by the predetermined yield or basis rate, 4.5%. The net income for September 1, 1978, therefore, is determined by multiplying $1,054.40 by 2.25% (the semiannual rate). This is $23.70. The difference between $23.70 (yield or net income) and $30.00 (cash interest) is $6.30, which is the first amortization installment to be applied in the reduction of the book value of the investment. The new book value for September 1, 1978, is the difference between $1,054.40 and $6.30, or $1,048.10. Since the book value is constantly being reduced, the net income for such subsequent interest periods declines. It will be seen that the total of the amortization is equal to the premium and that provision has been made to extinguish it completely.

The entry on the book for the first interest period should be as follows:

Dr. Cash	$30.00
Total	$30.00
Cr. Interest Income	$23.70
Amortization of Bond Premium	6.30
Total	$30.00

Accumulation. Bonds bought at a discount are treated exactly the same way, except that the book value of the investment is constantly being added to instead of being reduced. The amount added to the book value at each interest period is called ACCUMULATION or ACCRETION of the bond discount. The appended table (Mathematics of Accumulation) illustrates the mathematical history of a bond bought at a discount and carried currently on an investment basis, e.g., a 3.0% bond, paying interest semiannually March 1 and September 1, with four-year maturity, bought March 1, 1978 to yield 4.5%, or a cost of $945.60.

The yield is determined by multiplying the book value, which in the first instance is the purchase price, by the predetermined yield, or basis rate, 4.5%. The net income for September 1, 1978, therefore, is determined by multiplying $945.60 by 2.25%. This is $21.30. The difference between $21.30 (yield or net income) and $15.00 (cash interest) is $6.30, which is the first accumulation increment to be applied in accretion of the book value of the investment. The new book value for September 1, 1978, is the summation of $945.60 and $6.30, or $951.90. Since the book value is constantly being increased,

Mathematics of Accumulation

Date	Cash interest (3.0%)	Net income (4.5%)	Increase in book value of the investment, or accumulation	Book Value	Par
1978: 3-1	...	...	...	$945.60	$1,000.00
9-1	$15.00	$21.30	$6.30	951.90	
1979: 3-1	15.00	21.40	6.40	958.30	
9-1	15.00	21.60	6.60	964.90	
1980: 3-1	15.00	21.70	6.70	971.60	
9-1	15.00	21.90	6.90	978.50	
1981: 3-1	15.00	22.00	7.00	985.50	
9-1	15.00	22.20	7.20	992.70	
1982: 3-1	15.00	22.30	7.30	1,000.00	1,000.00
	$120.00	$174.40	$54.40		

the net income for each subsequent interest period rises. It will be noted that the total of the accumulation is equal to the total of the original discount in price of the bond and that provision has been made to accumulate it completely.

The entry on the books for the first interest period should be as follows:

Dr. Cash	$15.00
Accretion of Bond Discount	$6.30
Total	$21.30
Cr. Interest Income	$21.30
Total	$21.30

Bank Accounting Practices. Section 1.11 of Investment Securities Regulation of the Comptroller of the Currency provides that when an investment security is purchased at a premium over par, the bank shall charge off the entire premium at the time of purchase or provide for amortization of the premium so that it shall be entirely extinguished at or before maturity of the security.

Section 1.10 of the Comptroller's regulation provides that when a bank purchases an investment security convertible into stock or with stock purchase warrants attached, the bank shall at time of purchase write down the cost of the security to investment value of the security considered independently of the conversion feature or attached stock purchase warrants. Giving effect to such write-down, if investment value results in a premium still, Section 1.11 of the Investment Securities Regulation then applies, requiring a program of amortization of such remaining portion of the original total premium, so that it shall be entirely extinguished at or before maturity of the security.

The Comptroller's ruling number 7550 explicitly provides that discount (accretion of discount) on any bond, including a public or investment security, whether arising upon original issue or purchase in the market, may be accrued if there is concurrent accrual of income tax on such discount. The Comptroller of the Currency furnishes ""Report of Income and Dividends" forms and instructions for their preparation and filing annually for the 12-month period ending December 31st (Comptroller's Regulations, 12 CFR 4.11(3)).

For state member banks of the Federal Reserve System, and for other state banks insured by the Federal Deposit Insurance Corporation, Regulation F of the Board of Governors of the Federal Reserve System and companion regulation by the Federal Deposit Insurance Corporation specify that securities accounts, for both the statement of condition and income statement, shall reflect cost adjusted for amortization of premium and, at the option of the bank, for accretion of discount. If the reporting bank does not accrete bond discount, the amount that could have been accreted shall be set forth in footnote.

It is the position of the Board of Governors of the Federal Reserve System that a member state bank may not lawfully invest in a convertible security whose price exceeds, by more than an insignificant amount, the investment value of the obligation, considered independently of the conversion feature.

See COMPTROLLER OF THE CURRENCY.

AMORTIZATION LOANS Long-term loans, including farm mortgage loans, as allowed under the FEDERAL FARM LOAN ACT, in which the principal is extinguished or amortized during the period for which the loan is made. Amortization loans are the only kind permitted under the Federal Farm Loan Act. Before the enactment of this law, it was customary for farmers to borrow on farm mortgages as security subject to renewal. Each renewal necessitated the payment of commissions and agent's fees, and in times of financial stringency, farmers sometimes lost their farms because they could not get their loans renewed.

Under the Federal Farm Loan Act, farmers, as members of local cooperative associations now known as Federal Land Bank associations, may take out loans from the Federal Land Bank System for as short a period as five years and for as long a period as 40 years. Payments are made annually or semiannually so as to liquidate the entire indebtedness in the period of the loan.

The original Federal Farm Loan Board, since succeeded by the Farm Credit Administration, encouraged the Federal Land banks in establishing a standard 33-year loan. It did this because this sort of loan was one which simplified the bookkeeping, made the matter of payments and amortization plain to everybody, and gave every borrower the chance to turn himself so far as time was concerned. It spread the privilege of payment over a generation in time, and met every want of almost every borrower.

AMORTIZED LOANS Home mortgages calling for the payment by the borrower of monthly (usually) or quarterly or semiannual payments, in equal amounts. Included in the uniform monthly periodic payment will be the portion allocated to repayment of the principal, the remainder being interest on the remaining unamortized principal amount for the period involved. Besides use in AMORTIZATION LOANS on farm mortgages, the amortized loan has become practically universal on urban real estate mortgage loans, particularly as the result of popularization by the savings and loan associations.

Long-term, high ratio of appraised value, amortized loans were also stimulated by operations of the FEDERAL HOUSING ADMINISTRATION (FHA) under Title II, Section 203 (b) of the National Housing Act of 1934, as amended, in providing insurance of mortgages on one-to four-family homes and by guarantee by the Veterans Administration of a portion of home mortgage loans to veterans under the Servicemen's Readjustment Act of 1944 (GI Bill of Rights).

TERM LOANS to business firms are amortized loans. Pursuant to the term loan agreement, periodic payments provide for amortization of principal as well as current interest, the amortization schedule being fitted to projected cash flow from operations of the borrower firm.

AMORTIZED VALUES In valuation of bonds, the original cost price, minus the AMORTIZATION of premium (on straight-line basis) to maturity of earlier call feature producing lowest amortized value. This is the basis prescribed, for example, by New York State for all insurance companies for 1967 (amortized values on amortizable securities and values on the "convention" basis for other securities).

See CONVENTION VALUES.

Banks in valuing bonds are required to amortize premium and have the option of accreting discount.

See COMPTROLLER'S REGULATION.

ANALYSIS DEPARTMENT An organizational title often found in the organizational structure of banks, investment banking firms, and brokerage firms, generally indicating a staff function concerned with the analysis and study of operational data, particularly budgeting, cost accounting, and operations planning, with the aim of improving methods and performance. The larger the institution, the more likely such a managerial function will be provided organizationally, because of the problem of efficiencies in size, under various titles, such as "operations supervision" under a separate vice-president or managing partner, or under the comptroller or cashier.

ENCYCLOPEDIA OF BANKING AND FINANCE

ANALYTICAL DEPARTMENT

In brokerage firms, the investment analysis, advisory, and research department was often referred to as the "statistical department," a term now generally found replaced by these more descriptive titles.

See BANK COST ACCOUNTING.

ANALYTICAL DEPARTMENT In an investment or brokerage house, a service department to aid salespeople and customers. It is this department that studies and prepares the statistical data that are furnished with prospectuses, bond and stock circulars, and other advertising material. The work of this department often embraces a wide field of investigation with a view of assisting the house and its clients to make intelligent decisions in their investment selections.

See BANK COST ACCOUNTING.

ANCILLARY RECEIVER A RECEIVER appointed for an insolvent corporation, generally a "foreign" corporation (one incorporated in another state), to assist and be subordinate to the foreign receiver in the collection and marshaling of assets of the insolvent corporation.

See RECEIVERSHIP.

AND INTEREST In bond quotations and sales, denotes that ACCURED INTERST is to be added to the price, i.e., the price quoted is exclusive of interest.

ANNUAL PERCENTAGE RATE (APR) The Consumer Credit Protection Act (CCPA) passed in 1986 requires that each creditor disclose both the finance charge and the annual percentage rate (APR) of finance charge in connection with any credit sale or loan to a consumer. The basic objectives of this requirement are to translate the interest rates charged into a common format and to require their disclosure. The law applies not only to lenders but also to parties who arrange the loan for a customer with a bank. Only consumer-credit transactions are covered by the legislation. Credit extended to a natural person for family, personal, household, or agricultural purposes is governed by the act. Real-estate financing and transactions involving personal property are also covered. Transactions other than those involving real-estate mortgages are excluded if the amount financed exceeds $25,000. The Federal Reserve Board has been assigned the authority to prescribe regulations required to accomplish the objectives of the act. The board issued Regulation Z that details the procedures to be followed by lenders to comply with the act. Two types of information must be included in the disclosure statement: the finance charge and the annual percentage rate. The finance charge is defined by the CCPA as "the sum of all charges, payable directly or indirectly by the person to whom the credit is extended, and imposed directly or indirectly by the creditor as an incident to the extension of credit. . . ." The finance charge includes more than interest. The finance charge includes all overhead expenses charged for the money borrowed, including any amount that is payable as a discount, points or loan fees, service or carrying charges, credit-report fees, and credit and other types of insurance premiums charged in connection with the loan, and other charges. Amounts excluded include taxes, recording fees, license fees, default or delinquency charges, and bona fide closing costs (title examination). The finance charge is used to calculate the annual percentage rate. The disclosure statement typically includes the finance charges in dollars, the annual percentage rate, and an interest rate. The amount of each payment and the number of payments must also be disclosed.

ANNUAL REPORT A report prepared for a company's stockholders and others prepared annually following the end of the company's fiscal year. The report typically includes a letter to the shareholders from the chairman of the board, management's discussion of previous financial performance, and financial highlights for the previous period(s). It contains the required comparative FINANCIAL STATEMENTS, including notes thereto for the current and preceding year(s) prepared in accordance with GENERALLY ACCEPTED ACCOUNTING PRINCIPLES on a basis consistent with the preceding year. The report also includes the auditor's report wherein the independent accountants express an opinion as to the fairness of the financial data presented in the financial statements.

See INTERIM FINANCIAL REPORT.

BIBLIOGRAPHY

AREVALO, C. B. *Effective Writing: A Handbook for Accountants.* Prentice Hall, Inc., Englewood Cliffs, NJ, 1989.

Accounting Trends and Techniques in Published Corporate Annual Reports. American Institute of Certified Public Accountants, New York, NY. Annual.

COMPUSTAT. Standard & Poor's. Englewood, CO. Online data base.

DUNSPRINT. Dun and Bradstreet, Inc., New York, NY. Online data base.

SEC Financial Reporting: Annual Reports to Shareholders, Form 10-K, and Quarterly Financial Reporting. Matthew Bender & Co., Inc., New York, NY. Looseleaf.

HAWKINS, D. *Corporate Financial Reporting: Text and Cases.* Richard D. Irwin, Inc., Homewood, IL. Latest edition.

ANNUAL RETURN *See* RETURN, YIELD.

ANNUITANT One who receives an ANNUITY.

ANNUITY Periodic fixed money payments, payable annually, semiannually, quarterly, or monthly, at the beginning or close of the period, received from an insurance company in consideration of payments made to it either in a lump sum or in installments. Classification of annuities may be as to:

1. Methods of purchase: single premium annuity, one purchased with a lump sum; and annual premium annuity, one purchased over a period of time by payment of installments.
2. Method of payments to the annuitant: immediate annuity, one payable beginning in one year, one half year, one quarter year, or one month; and deferred annuity, one that does not begin income payments until after a longer period of time to allow for completion of purchase of the annuity by accumulation of installments.
3. Duration: certain annuity, when income payments are continued for a fixed, certain period; contingent annuity, when income payments are continued for an uncertain period; life annuity, when income payments are continued during a person's lifetime; perpetual annuity, when income payments are continued perpetually; terminable annuity, when income payments cease at a certain time or event.

Single premium annuities, purchasable with a lump sum, are suitable for persons or donors who have already accumulated a large fund. They are, generally speaking, particularly suitable for older people because such persons are of ages at which the return on the annuity is most attractive. On the other hand, deferred annuities are usually suitable for younger people, especially when paid for in installments. In recent years, the acute investment problem of life insurance companies, caused by lower returns on eligible investments resulting from money rates generally, and the accumulation of large funds available for investment have resulted in less interest by insurance companies in offering annuities and a reduction in the number of available annuity contracts offered. Representative of annuity contracts offered currently are the following, offered by a large New York life insurance company:

Immediate Life Annuity. The annuity is payable during the lifetime of the annuitant, either yearly, half yearly, quarterly, or monthly, the first payment being a year, half year, quarter year, or month, respectively, after the date of the contract, according to the contract purchased. No proportionate amount is payable for the fraction of a period from the last periodic payment to date of death. Evidence that the annuitant is living is required when each payment is made. The consideration depends on the age and sex of the annuitant at date of purchase. The consideration must be not less than $500 and the income payments must not be less than $10 each. Evidence of age is required before issuance of contract. No medical examination is necessary. If the applicant is a male under age 50 or a female under age 55, the company will not issue this contract but will issue the life annuity with payments guaranteed ten years at ages 15 and over. The rates for these two types of annuities do not differ materially at lower ages, and the applicant thus secures the guarantee of ten years' payments at the younger ages for practically the same consideration as would be required under the life annuity. Immediate life annuities do not participate in the surplus of the

ANNUITY

Life Annuities—Males and Females

Income payments for life of annuitant. First payment a year, a half year, a quarter year, or a month, respectively, after purchase.

Price of $100 annuity

Age last birthday		$100 each year	$50 each half year	$25 each quarter year	Price of annuity of $10 monthly
Male	Female				
50	55	$2,051.00	$2,078.00	$2,091.00	$2,520.00
51	56	2,002.00	2,029.00	2,042.00	2,461.00
52	57	1,952.00	1,979.00	1,992.00	2,401.00
53	58	1,903.00	1,930.00	1,943.00	2,342.00
54	59	1,854.00	1,881.00	1,894.00	2,284.00
55	60	1,805.00	1,832.00	1,845.00	2,225.00
56	61	1,756.00	1,783.00	1,796.00	2,166.00
57	62	1,707.00	1,734.00	1,747.00	2,107.00
58	63	1,658.00	1,685.00	1,698.00	2,048.00
59	64	1,609.00	1,636.00	1,649.00	1,990.00
60	65	1,560.00	1,587.00	1,600.00	1,931.00
61	66	1,512.00	1,539.00	1,552.00	1,873.00
62	67	1,464.00	1,491.00	1,504.00	1,816.00
63	68	1,417.00	1,444.00	1,457.00	1,759.00
64	69	1,370.00	1,397.00	1,410.00	1,703.00
65	70	1,323.00	1,350.00	1,363.00	1,646.00
66	71	1,277.00	1,304.00	1,317.00	1,591.00
67	72	1,231.00	1,258.00	1,271.00	1,536.00
68	73	1,186.00	1,213.00	1,266.00	1,482.00
69	74	1,141.00	1,168.00	1,181.00	1,428.00
70	75	1,097.00	1,124.00	1,137.00	1,375.00
71	76	1,054.00	1,081.00	1,094.00	1,324.00
72	77	1,011.00	1,038.00	1,051.00	1,272.00
73	78	970.00	997.00	1,010.00	1,223.00
74	79	929.00	956.00	969.00	1,174.00
75	80	888.00	915.00	928.00	1,124.00
76	81	849.00	876.00	889.00	1,078.00
77	82	811.00	838.00	851.00	1,032.00
78	83	773.00	800.00	813.00	986.00
79	84	737.00	764.00	777.00	943.00
80	85	701.00	728.00	741.00	900.00
81		666.00	693.00	706.00	858.00
82		633.00	660.00	673.00	818.00
83		600.00	627.00	640.00	779.00
84		568.00	595.00	608.00	740.00
85		538.00	565.00	578.00	704.00

Life Annuities—Males and Females

Income payments for life of annuitant. First payment a year, a half year, a quarter year, or a month, respectively, after purchase.

Annuity purchased by $1,000

Age last birthday		Amt. of each yearly payment	Amt. of each half-yearly payment	Amt. of each quarterly payment	Amt. of each monthly payment
Male	Female				
50	55	$ 48.76	$ 24.06	$ 11.96	$ 3.97
51	56	49.95	24.64	12.24	4.06
52	57	51.23	25.27	12.55	4.16
53	58	52.55	25.91	12.87	4.27
54	59	53.94	26.58	13.20	4.38
55	60	55.40	27.29	13.55	4.49
56	61	56.95	28.04	13.92	4.62
57	62	58.58	28.84	14.31	4.75
58	63	60.31	29.67	14.72	4.88
59	64	62.15	30.56	15.16	5.03
60	65	64.10	31.51	15.63	5.18
61	66	66.14	32.49	16.11	5.34
62	67	68.31	33.53	16.62	5.51
63	68	70.57	34.63	17.16	5.69
64	69	72.99	35.79	17.73	5.87
65	70	75.59	37.04	18.34	6.08
66	71	78.31	38.34	18.98	6.29
67	72	81.23	39.75	19.67	6.51
68	73	84.32	41.22	20.39	6.75
69	74	87.64	42.81	21.17	7.00
70	75	91.16	44.48	21.99	7.27
71	76	94.88	46.25	22.85	7.55
72	77	98.91	48.17	23.79	7.86
73	78	103.09	50.15	24.75	8.18
74	79	107.64	52.30	25.80	8.52
75	80	112.61	54.64	26.94	8.90
76	81	117.79	57.08	28.12	9.28
77	82	123.30	59.67	29.38	9.69
78	83	129.37	62.50	30.75	10.14
79	84	135.69	65.45	32.18	10.60
80	85	142.65	68.68	33.74	11.11
81		150.15	72.15	35.41	11.66
82		157.98	75.76	37.15	12.22
83		166.67	79.74	39.06	12.84
84		176.06	84.03	41.12	13.51
85		185.87	88.50	43.25	14.20

company, and have no cash or loan values. For example, under latest tables (see samples appended), a minimum consideration of $10 each month payable to a male aged 72 at time of application would cost $1,272.

Life Annuity with Payments Guaranteed Ten Years. This annuity is payable as long as the annuitant lives, with the additional guarantee that if the annuitant dies before ten years' payments have been made, the annuity will be continued to the beneficiary until the end of ten years from the date of the contract. Annuity payments will be made either yearly, half yearly, quarterly, or monthly (first payment being a year, a half year, a quarter year, or a month, respectively after the date of the contract), according to the contract purchased. Evidence that the annuitant is living is required when each payment, due after the end of the first ten years, is made. The consideration depends on the age and sex of the annuitant of date of purchase. Consideration must be not less than $500 and the income payments must be not less than $10 each. Evidence of age is required before issuance of the contract. No medical examination is necessary. There is no participation in the surplus of the company and no cash or loan values.

Joint and Survivor Annuities. These annuities are payable until death of the survivor of two annuitants, either yearly, half yearly, quarterly, or monthly (first payment a year, a half year, a quarter year, or a month, respectively, after the date of the contract). The annuity is not reduced upon the first death. No proportionate amount is payable for the fraction of a period from the last periodic payment to date of death of the survivor. Evidence that at least one of the annuitants is living is required when each payment is made. The consideration depends upon the ages of the two annuitants at date of purchase and upon their sexes. Consideration must be not less than $500 and the income payments must be not less than $10 each. Evidence of age is required for each annuitant before issuance of the contract. No medical examination is necessary. The contract is nonparticipating and has no loan or cash values.

Retirement Income Contract. The income payments commence at the anniversary of the contract nearest age 55, 60, or 65 (maturity date), as selected, and are payable monthly thereafter for the life of the annuitant, with payments for at least ten years certain. Installments for the purchase of the contract (premiums) are payable annually, semiannually, quarterly, or monthly up to maturity date. Minimum monthly income must be $10 and the minimum premium must be $5. Surplus is distributed annually on the anniversary of the contract. Dividends may be drawn in cash, applied in part payment of any premium due, or deposited at compound interest (never less than 2%), as detailed in the contract. In default of other election, dividends are deposited in accordance with last option above. Dividend deposits may be used at maturity date to increase the monthly retirement income. When the income begins, excess interest earnings at such rate as the company declares for each year will be allotted. Cash value is available from the date of the contract and not later than the maturity date. The company may at its option defer paying a cash

ENCYCLOPEDIA OF BANKING AND FINANCE

ANNUITY BONDS

value for not more than six months after it is requested. Loan value is available from the date of the contract and prior to the maturity date. Loan value is the amount which with interest at 5% will be within the limit of the cash value on the next anniversary. The company may at its option defer granting a loan other than to pay premiums subsequent to the first, for not more than six months after it is requested. In the case of lapse, the contract if not surrendered for its cash value will be automatically continued as paid-up nonparticipating retirement income of reduced amount payable on the same terms as the regular income except that where the amount of reduced paid-up life income would be less than $5 a month, the cash value less indebtedness is paid instead and the contract is terminated. Such paid-up contract may be surrendered not later than the maturity date for a cash value.

If the annuitant dies prior to the maturity date, the cash value at that time is payable to the beneficiary. If the annuitant dies after the maturity date and before all of the payments certain have been made, the remaining payments certain will be discounted at 2% interest, compounded annually and paid in a single sum, unless otherwise provided by endorsement.

On or before the maturity date of the retirement income contract, the proceeds arising from a claim by death or from surrender for cash may be settled by any one of the optional modes of settlement generally allowed under policies of insurance, provided such proceeds are at least $1,000 and the guaranteed payment is at least $10.

Other flexible features are the option of change to another maturity date, and the privilege to change to any form, kind, or plan of insurance upon payment of such cost and furnishing of such requirements as are requested by the company.

In furnishing evidence of age, which is required before issuance of the retirement income contract, as well as for the other contracts offered, statements of affidavits as to the date of birth, based on memory, even from relatives, are not sufficient. An official certificate from a record made at or near time of birth of either birth or baptism, giving the date of birth, is the best form of evidence.

Group Annuities. In addition to individual annuity plans offered on both an immediate and a deferred basis, the latter offered on both a participating and nonparticipating basis, group annuities have been offered by life insurance companies in recent years, many such offerings taking the form of tax-sheltered annuities, which are qualified under Section 403(b) of the Internal Revenue Code and also group annuity contracts offered to corporate pension plans qualified under Section 401 of the code. In many cases, the policyholders have the option to allocate their funds to accounts under which principal and minimum interest rates are guaranteed or to separate accounts in which the policyholder assumes the investment risk.

See VARIABLE ANNUITIES.

BIBLIOGRAPHY

AMERICAN COUNCIL OF LIFE INSURANCE. *Life Insurance Fact Book* (annual).
WOELFEL, C.J. *The Desktop Reference to Money, Prime Interest, and Yields,* 1986

ANNUITY BONDS So called because of their payment of interest in fixed amount every year "perpetually" (no maturity date), such bonds were last exemplified in American finance by the Lehigh Valley Railroad 4.5% annuity bonds. The 1949 Debt Adjustment Plan of the Lehigh Valley Railroad eliminated the perpetual, or no maturity and no call date, feature of their annuity bonds—$10 million of 6% and $2.6 million of 4.5% annuity bonds—by setting a maturity date of April 1, 1989, and providing for redemption of the 6s at prices on a scale-down from 120, and of the 4 1/2 s at par.

The former 6% Perpetual Interest Bearing Certificates of the Public Service Corp. of New Jersey were exchanged beginning July 1, 1948, in equal principal amounts for Public Service Electric & Gas Co. Debenture 6s, 1998.

ANTECEDENTS In a credit investigation, the business history of the subject of inquiry. The history is regarded as important in order to show the concern's rate of progress or retrogression, and it is particularly desirable to know the history of the concern's personnel and their record for responsible management. The credit investigator should determine whether the business has been under the control of the present managers for a long or a short period and whether it has frequently changed hands. In case the present personnel are new, it is desirable to ascertain what their previous or antecedent business connections were and with what success their operations were attended.

ANTEDATE To give a date prior to the current date to a check or other instrument. If today is September 1, 1982, a date of July 1, 1982 on an instrument makes it antedated. Negotiability of an instrument is not affected by the fact that it is antedated (or undated, or postdated). Where an instrument is antedated (or postdated), the time when it is payable is determined by the stated date if the instrument is payable on demand or at a fixed period after date (Uniform Commercial Code, Sec. 3–114).

See POSTDATED CHECK.

ANTHRACITE ROADS Those railroads whose tonnage in large part consisted of hard coal (anthracite), a now largely obsolete fuel. Railroads normally reporting the highest proportionate freight revenues derived from shipments of anthracite coal were Reading Company, Delaware & Hudson, Lehigh Valley, Central Railroad of New Jersey, Erie-Lackawanna, and the New York, Susquehanna & Western.

ANTICIPATED ACCEPTANCE A bank or other ACCEPTANCE which is paid before it becomes due.

ANTITRUST LAWS In addition to the basic SHERMAN ANTITRUST ACT and CLAYTON ACT as amended, antitrust laws include the Federal Trade Commission Act and amendments, the Export Trade Act, laws relating to banking corporations authorized to do foreign banking business, and laws relating to price discrimination.

The following summary lists major antitrust legislation enacted since 1933:

Communications Act of 1934 (P.L. 416, June 19, 1934), relating to applicability of anti-trust laws to the wire and radio communication industries and the preservation of competition in interstate and foreign commerce therein.

Patman-Robinson Price Discrimination Chain Store Act (P.L. 692, June 19, 1936), amending Clayton Act to apply to chain store pricing.

Amendment of Patman-Robinson Price Discrimination Chain Store Act (P.L. 650, May 26, 1938).

Miller-Tydings Resale Price Maintenance Act (P.L. 314, August 17, 1937), exempting manufacturer retail price-fixing contracts from the antitrust laws, if state laws so provided.

Wheeler-Lea Act (P.L. 447, March 21, 1938), amending the Federal Trade Commission Act to place advertising of pure food and drugs under the Federal Trade Commission.

Walter-McCarran Act (P.L. 15, March 9, 1945), exempting the insurance business until January 1, 1948 (see later Walter-McCarran Act. P.L. 238, July 25, 1947, for amendment to June 30, 1948) from the anti-trust laws (legislation occasioned by the case of *U.S.* v. *Southeastern Underwriters Association*, 322 U.S. 533, 1944, holding insurance to be commerce).

P.L. 107, June 30, 1945, amending P.L. 740, October 10, 1942, to suspend until June 30, 1946, the running of the statute of limitations applicable to violations of the antitrust laws.

Hobbs Act (P.L. 486, July 3, 1946), amending the Anti-Racketeering Act of June 18, 1934.

Reed-Bulwinkle Act (P.L. 662, June 17, 1948), exempting common carriers with respect to certain agreements between carriers from the Clayton Act, as amendment to the Interstate Commerce Act.

P.L. No. 774, September 8, 1950, construing voluntary agreements of industry and business under the Defense Production Act of 1950 as not within prohibitions of the anti-trust laws and Federal Trade Commission Act.

O'Mahoney, Kefauver-Celler Act (P.L. 899, December 29, 1950), amending the Clayton Act to close loopholes and prohibit competitor corporations from purchasing assets of competing corporations.

Johnson-Preston Act (P.L. 906, January 2, 1951), prohibiting transportation of gambling devices in interstate and foreign commerce, and declaring intent not to interfere with or reduce authority or interpretations of the authority of the Federal Trade Commission under the Federal Trade Commission Act as amended.

Maguire Act (P.L. 542, July 14, 1952), extension of federal fair trade exemption to include "nonsigner" state fair trade laws whereby if one retailer in a state signs a manufacturer's price-fixing agreement, all other retailers in that state must maintain the same price.

Proposed Revision of Antitrust Laws. A 60-person study committee appointed by the attorney general in 1953 submitted its report in March, 1955. Indicative of problem areas, the recommendations included

1. Repeal of the federal fair trade laws (Maguire Act and Miller-Tydings Act)
2. Increase from $5,000 to $10,000 in the penalty for criminal violations of the antitrust laws
3. Repeal of the requirement for mandatory treble damages in private antitrust suits, and granting to trial judges of discretionary power to fix the amount to injured parties
4. Repeal of the penalty of $1,000 and one year's imprisonment for persons found guilty of price discrimination under the Patman-Robinson Act
5. Consolidation of investigative forces of the Department of Justice and Federal Trade Commission, to avoid duplication
6. No leaving unchanged the laws governing corporate mergers
7. Amendment of the Clayton Act to provide a four-year statute of limitations (instead of none) for private suits seeking damages caused by monopolistic practices.

In the light of the above recommendations, it is of interest to note subsequent legislation, as follows:

P.L. 135, July 7, 1955, amending the Sherman Act to increase fine from not exceeding $5,000 to not exceeding $50,000.

P.L. 137, July 7, 1955, amending the Clayton Act to provide for a four-year statute of limitations.

P.L. 1026, August 8, 1956, "to balance the power now heavily weighted in favor of automobile manufacturers, by enabling franchise automobile dealers to sue to recover damages sustained by reason of the failure of automobile manufacturers to act in good faith in complying with the terms of franchises or in terminating or not renewing franchises with their dealers."

Automobile Disclosure Act (P.L. 85–506, July 7, 1958), to require the full and fair disclosure of suggested retail price and other information in connection with the distribution of new automobiles in commerce.

Textile Fiber Products Identification Act (P.L. 85–897, September 2, 1958), to protect producers and consumers against misbranding and false advertising of the fiber content of textile fiber products.

P.L. 86–107, July 23, 1959, to amend the Clayton Act to provide for the more expeditious enforcement of cease and desist orders issued thereunder.

P.L. 87–331, September 30, 1961, to amend the anti-trust laws to authorize leagues of professional football, baseball, basketball, and hockey teams to enter into television contracts.

P.L. 87–664, September 19, 1962, to authorize the attorney general to compel the production of documentary evidence in civil investigations for the enforcement of the antitrust laws, known as the "Antitrust Civil Process Act."

P.L. 89–175, September 9, 1965, to provide for exemptions from the antitrust laws in connection with the Voluntary Restraint Program to safeguard the balance of payments position of the U.S.

P.L. 89–775, November 3, 1966, the "Fair Packaging and Labeling Act," to regulate interstate and foreign commerce by preventing the use of unfair or deceptive methods of packaging or labeling of consumer commodities distributed in such commerce.

P.L. 89–800, November 8, 1966, to provide for extension of tax-exempt status under Section 501 (c)(6) of the Internal Revenue Code of 1954, to expanded professional football leagues.

Hart-Scott-Rodino Antitrust Improvements Act (P.L. 94-435, 15 U.S.C. 18a, 1976), effective February 27, 1977.

For legislation and applicability of the antitrust laws to banks, *see* BANK MERGERS; for applicability to insurance companies, *see* INSURANCE.

The basic antitrust laws which the preceding series of acts have pertained to are the Sherman Antitrust Act (15 U.S.C. 1–7 (1976)), originally enacted in 1890; the Clayton Act (15 U.S.C. 12–27 (1976)), originally enacted in 1914; and the Federal Trade Commission Act (15 U.S.C. 41–45 (1976)), originally enacted in 1914 also. Each shares the objective of protecting and promoting competition in the marketplace. Two agencies have shared responsibility for enforcing the antitrust laws: the Antitrust Division of the Department of Justice through civil and criminal legal proceedings; and the Federal Trade Commission, through adjudication before administrative law judges. Over the years, however, the extent and efficiency of such enforcement by these agencies have varied considerably under different presidential administrations with their varying emphasis on antitrust enforcement.

The "golden age" of antitrust enforcement efforts by the Antitrust Division of the Department of Justice occurred in the years 1937-1942, when the division, headed by Thurman Arnold, filed in a single year more Sherman Act cases than had been brought during the first twenty years of the act. Passage of the Celler-Kefauver Act of 1950 also led to effective efforts against horizontal mergers affecting competition; and while conglomerate merger cases are more difficult, the U.S. Supreme Court under Chief Justice Earl Warren upheld the government in all of the conglomerate merger cases that reached the Court in the late 1960s and early 1970s, until a change in membership of the U.S. Supreme Court in 1973-1974 ended the "pro-antitrust" majority on the Court.

Dr. Willard F. Mueller (University of Wisconsin), in the reference listed in the bibliography below, ascribes the "anti-antitrust" movement, which actually began "two decades ago," to the broader conservative movement that has since spread, and that is reflected in continuation of the lackluster enforcement efforts by the Antitrust Division of the Department of Justice and by the Federal Trade Commission. Both of these agencies in 1982 terminated important cases. The Department of Justice settled the longstanding case against American Telephone & Telegraph Co. and ended the equally longstanding case against International Business Machines, and the Federal Trade Commission ended its case against leading cereal companies.

1982 Antitrust Guidelines. One feature of the new 1982 antitrust guidelines of the Antitrust Division of the Department of Justice is the measurement of high market concentration in the "relevant market" by use of the Herfindahl Index, instead of merely the percentage of a relevant market above 75% for the four largest companies in the market. The Herfindahl Index computes the square root of the market share of each company in a relevant market; if the total of the square roots is more than 1,800, high market concentration is indicated. Thus combinations occurring in that market which would add more than 100 points to the total of the square roots now at 1,800 (high concentration) would likely be challenged; those combinations which added less than 50 points would likely not be challenged. By contrast, any market group of companies with less than 1,000 total on the Herfindahl Index would be considered least concentrated and not likely to arouse challenge if the index still remained at less than 1,000 if mergers occurred thereafter. (It should be noted that this scoring system would apply to horizontal mergers; conglomerate mergers, the type more prevalent in recent years among giant companies, would continue to present more complicated economic and legal problems.)

See MERGER.

The Case Against the Antitrust Laws. Dr. Lester C. Thurow's reasons for regarding "the antitrust approach (as) a failure" (see reference in bibliography below, *The Zero-Sum Society*) include the following:

1. In international trade, the U.S. antitrust laws, if they do anything, serve only to hinder U.S. firms which must observe antitrust restrictions which their foreign competitors can ignore. Instead, U.S. firms should have freedom to compete.
2. The general rise in income tends to greatly increase the relevant market in which monopolistic firms actually must compete. Monopolistic firms face a downsloping demand curve—meaning that they are subject to the law of demand (quantity demanded by consumers varies inversely with price), both for their particular products and for other competing products in interproduct competition for consumer dollars.
3. Monopolistic "rents" (excess profits above "normal" profits) are inherently limited in an economy full of large conglomerate firms. "Excess rates of return attract competitors, and potential competitors have the ability to enter *all* those markets that are not natural monopolies." Thus such power of entry will serve to restrain monopolistic "rents." Moreover, a monopolistic firm will maximize profit by charging not the highest prices that the "traffic will bear," but that price which combined with quantity demanded will result in the maximized profit.
4. Antitrust costs exceed the benefits. For if a one-firm (monopoly) case is successfully broken up into three or four firms, the latter will act not noticeably different from the former monopoly (one firm) as a three- or four-firm industry (oligopoly).

ENCYCLOPEDIA OF BANKING AND FINANCE

APPLICATION

5. The antitrust laws unduly stress absence of price competition, whereas there may be much nonprice competition in an industry, such as advertising, product differentiation and quality, which management may choose as the most efficient ways to compete.

Dr. Thurow nevertheless would not abolish the antitrust laws but would have them serve to prohibit collusive predatory pricing and to prohibit explicit cartels that share either markets or profits. Firms could grow by driving competitors out of business or by absorbing them, but not by agreeing not to compete with each other.

The Case for the Antitrust Laws. Dr. Mueller (see reference in bibliography below) puts the case for the antitrust laws with specific reference to Dr. Thurow's points as follows:

1. In international trade, the allegation that U.S. antitrust laws disadvantage U.S. firms in trying to compete with foreign firms, is not supported by the facts. First, U.S. firms in international trade are considerably bigger than their foreign competitors. Second, U.S. antitrust laws mainly restrict U.S. firms from participation in cartels—and facts indicate that firms outside a cartel have greater sales and profits than the cartel's members.
2. Monopolistic firms are able by relevant market barriers, such as trademarks and huge advertising and promotional outlays, to benefit from interproduct and infraproduct competition and to maintain higher than competitive prices.
3. There is growing evidence that continuing mergers among large conglomerate firms are eliminating more potential competitors, and that conglomerates do not show significant de novo entry into highly concentrated industries, among the important reasons being the fact that entry by conglomerates into other conglomerates' fields might invite hostile retaliation.
4. Breakup of monopolistic firms into smaller units would not continue the monopolistic situation, because the smaller units would be subject to more effective competition and entry would be easier into the deconcentrated industry.
5. Price-fixing should be of important concern in antitrust enforcement, because in recent years hundreds of U.S. corporations have been indicted for price-fixing. In the words of Adam Smith, "people of the same trade seldom meet together, even for merriment and diversion, but the conversation ends in a conspiracy against the public in some contrivance to raise prices"(see LAISSEZ-FAIRE).

Summary. The Mueller-Thurow debate no doubt illustrates the underlying business, economic, and political forces at interest on the subject of the antitrust laws. Both sides, however, do agree on the stand against collusive and predatory price-fixing, and against cartelization.

See ACQUISITIONS

BIBLIOGRAPHY

Antitrust Law Journal.
AREEDA, P. E. *Antitrust Law: An Analysis of Antitrust Principles and Their Application*, Little, Brown & Co., Boston, MA, 1989.
BALDWIN, W. L. *Market Power Competition and Antitrust Policy*, Richard D. Irwin, Inc., Homewood, IL, 1987.
CALVANI, T. and SIEGFRIED, J. J. *Economic Analysis and Antitrust Law*, Little, Brown & Co., Boston, MA, 1988.
COMEGYS, W. B. *Antitrust Compliance Manual: A Guide for Counsel, Management, and Public Officials*, Practicing Law Institute, 1986.
KOWOKA, J. E., JSR., AND WHITE, L., EDS. *The Antitrust Revolution*, Scott, Foresman & Co., Glenview, IL, 1986.
HAYES, W. J. *State Antitrust Laws*, Bureau of National Affairs, Inc., Washington, D.C. 1988.
HOLMES, W. C. *Antitrust Handbook.* Clark Boardman, 1988.
MARKE, J. J., AND SAMIE, N. *Antitrust and Restrictive Business Regulation*, Oceana Pubns., Inc., Dobbs Ferry, NY, 1982.
PARZYCH, K. M. *A Primer in Antitrust and Regulatory Policy*, University Press of America, 1987.
WILLIAMSON, O. *Antitrust Economics*, Basil Blackwell, Cambridge, MA, 1987.

APPLICATION An offer to buy something or to enter into some kind of contract. For instance, applications are made for an allotment of bonds or stocks offered for sale by signing a subscription list or blank. Applications are also made for money orders, letters of credit, cable transfers, bank accounts, loans, participations in loans, etc. It should be understood that an application is merely an offer and not an acceptance of an offer. Prior to acceptance, it does not, therefore, bind either party.

APPORTIONMENT In the administration of estates and trusts, the allocation of receipts and expenses between principal and income. The subject is important enough to have led to formulation of a Revised Uniform Principal and Income Act for the states to legislate for greater uniformity in state laws on the subject.

In general, allocations between principal and income are to be made with due regard to the respective interests of income beneficiaries and remaindermen, and the fiduciary shall refer for guidance first to the terms of the WILL or other instrument, which shall be controlling if they are contrary to the statute; next to the statute; and finally to the test of what is equitable and reasonable.

See TRUST.

APPRAISAL The act of placing a value upon property, either real or personal. Appraisals are made for various purposes, e.g., taxation, adjustment by insurance companies of fire losses, by engineers for property to be offered for sale, by banks for determining collateral value, and by public utility commissions for determining the capital investment in public utility properties as a basis for adjusting rates to yield a reasonable return.

In appraising real estate for sale or mortgage loan purposes, the most important factors to be considered are (1) value of similar adjacent property as established by recent sales; (2) capitalization of current net income from the property; (3) trend of income in the past five years; (4) likelihood of enhancement of deterioration of the property based upon the future of the district in which it is located.

BIBLIOGRAPHY

AMERICAN INSTITUTE OF REAL ESTATE APPRAISERS. *The Dictionary of Real Estate Appraisal*, American Institute of Real Estate Appraisers, 1984.
HARRIS, L.A. *The Real Estate Industry*, ORYX Press, Phoenix, AZ, 1987

APPRAISER A person who makes the APPRAISAL.

In the field of REAL ESTATE, the Society of Real Estate Appraisers, an international professional association of real estate appraisers and specialists in property valuation, is the oldest (organized in 1935) and largest (total membership as of March, 1968, of 321 Senior Real Estate Appraisers, 4,403 Senior Residential Appraisers, and 12,965 Associates) independent association of real estate appraisers in North America. The society's objective is to achieve higher standards of real estate appraising and to establish the qualifications of persons making such appraisals. To qualify for the designation SREA (Senior Real Estate Appraiser, highest designation awarded by the Society), appraisers must already hold the SRA (Senior Residential Appraiser designation), must demonstrate outstanding proficiency and extensive experience of at least eight years in several broad areas of real estate appraising, and must undergo a reevaluation every five years to prove professional growth and performance. The SRA (Senior Residential Appraiser) designation is awarded to appraisers of recognized ability who have the equivalent of at least five years of active appraisal experience in appraising residential property. Members who are Associates, although participating in all the informational and educational activities of the society and its 183 local chapters throughout North America, are not permitted to refer to their affiliation with the society in any way that might imply professional endorsement.

APPRECIATION Increase in the value of any kind of property, through a rise in its market price, appraised value, capitalized value, or other current fair market value basis, excluding any income, e.g., income, dividends, or rents that may have accrued thereon, as compared to cost or other original valuation.

Appreciation may be unrealized or realized (capital gains). In general, write-ups of assets retained instead of sold, creating unrealized increments in value, are not favored in generally accepted accounting principles, except to (1) facilitate a business purpose (e.g., obtaining a loan secured by the particular assets valued at current fair value); (2) adjust asset value in relation to the amount of debt secured thereby; and (3) avoid a materially misleading balance sheet. Institutional investors and investing institutions also create unrealized appreciation when they follow prescribed or voluntary valuation bases to reflect current fair values for their portfolios of securities. In the case of business firms, increase in surplus resulting from unrealized appreciation (properly, on tangible fixed assets, pursuant to independent appraisal), is surplus arising from reevaluation of fixed assets, or unearned increment, to be separately identified as such under stockholders' equity.

APPROPRIATION A fund authorized and set aside by a business for some special use, e.g., advertising, new building.

The term also applies to fiscal legislation. The federal Constitution provides that "no money shall be drawn from the Treasury, but in consequence of appropriations made by law" (Art. I, Sec. 9, cl. 7). This limitation is absolute and prohibits payment even of judicially established government debts unless Congress enacts an appropriation from which such payment may be made. Revenue bills must originate in the House of Representatives (U.S. Constitution, Art. I, Sec. 7, cl. 1), but appropriation bills may originate in the House or Senate, although customarily they originate in the House. The Bureau of the Budget has the duty of preparing budgets for the President to submit to Congress as basis for the making of appropriations. The annual message from the President transmitting the proposed budget to Congress, together with testimony by officials of the various branches of the federal government before the Appropriations Committee, is the basis for the various appropriation bills which are drafted by the House Committee on Appropriations.

New obligational authority (NOA), permitting government agencies to enter into obligations requiring either immediate or future payment of funds, usually takes the form of appropriations and may take the form of contract authorizations, which permit entering into obligations but require an appropriation to liquidate in order to permit expenditures of funds in payment of the obligations. Reappropriations and reauthorizations are congressional authority to continue availability of unused balances which would otherwise expire. NOA may also take the form of authorizations to spend debt receipts, permitting the use of borrowed money to incur obligations and make expenditures. Authority to use Treasury borrowing is an authorization to spend frompublic debt receipts; authority to borrow directly from private enterprise, granted only to certain government corporations, is an authorization to spend from corporate debt receipts.

Most appropriations for current operations are made available for obligation only within the fiscal year (one-year appropriations). Some are for a longer specified longer period (multiple-year appropriations). Some, including most of those for construction, some for research, and nearly all trust fund appropriations, are made available by Congress until expended (no-year appropriations), and remain available for obligation until the objectives have been completed.

See NATIONAL BUDGET.

BIBLIOGRAPHY

The Budget of the United States Government (each fiscal year), U.S. Government Printing Office.

APPROVED BONDS Mutual savings banks are closely regulated in their investments in bonds, by statutes prescribing minimal standards or by such statutes plus lists of specific securities considered legal investments for savings banks pursuant to the statutes ("legal list" states). (*See* SAVINGS BANK INVESTMENTS.) TRUST FUNDS similarly may be subject to prescribing statutes (*see* INVESTMENTS TRUST FUND). Life insurance companies are also subject to statutory specifications of standards.

See LIFE INSURANCE COMPANY INVESTMENTS.

Commercial Banks. Although there is no such thing as a "legal list" of specific bonds eligible for investment by commercial banks, as there is for savings banks in the "legal list" states, the investment securities regulations of the Comptroller of the Currency, effective September 12, 1963, and rulings published by the Comptroller of the Currency on the eligibility of specific issues for bank purchase, do tend to establish certain securities as "bank quality" bonds. The investment securities regulations do not specifically refer to bond quality ratings as such, but bonds rated the top four quality ratings of the rating services (Standard & Poor's, Moody's), namely AAA, AA, A, BBB, or their equivalent, are generally regarded as eligible for bank investment. State member banks are subject, under the provisions of the Federal Reserve Act, to the same limitations and conditions with respect to the purchasing, selling, underwriting and holding of investment securities and stock as are applicable to national banks under Section 5136 of the U.S. Revised Statutes. The investment securities regulations of the Comptroller of the Currency, pursuant to Section 9 of the Federal Reserve Act, are applicable to state member banks as well as to national banks, insofar (as the Board of Governors of the Federal Reserve System in published interpretations emphasizes) as they conform to paragraph seven of Section 5136 of the revised statutes.

See COMPTROLLER'S REGULATION, NATIONAL BANK SECURITIES REGULATIONS, STATE BANK.

ARBITRAGE Buying a specified item—whether FOREIGN EXCHANGE, stocks, bonds, gold or silver bullion, bills of exchange, and less frequently grains and other commodities—or its equivalent in one market and simultaneously selling it or its equivalent in the same market, or in other markets, for the differential or spread prevailing at least temporarily because of conditions particular to each market.

Profits through arbitrage would be impossible if the prices of the currencies, commodities, or securities traded in were adjusted to exact parities. Through the operation of world markets, there is an international price level for the principal commodities, foreign currencies, and international securities. Each local market, however, such as New York or London, is affected by temporary disturbances and conditions, which will result in prices, after allowing for costs of transactions required in arbitrage, out of equivalence or parity. When permitted by exchange restrictions and regulations, therefore, successful arbitrage transactions in foreign exchange consist of buying (or going long) in the weak market and simultaneously selling (technically going short, with delivery from the long position) in the strong market. Besides permissive exchange regulations or complete freedom of exchange transactions, exchange arbitrage also depends upon efficient telegraphic or cable connections between the markets operated in, a knowledge of international price movements, capacity to make rapid computations in order to take advantage of frequently very temporary price conditions, and, finally, a large capital, because arbitrage profits are small in comparison with the amount of money involved. Arbitrage houses in widely separated markets must be in constant communication and keep each other informed on market prices and trends. Arbitrage transactions between two houses are usually conducted on a joint account basis, profits being equally divided between the engaging parties.

Foreign Exchange. Simple two-point arbitrage in foreign exchange may be illustrated by the following example. Suppose that sterling is selling in New York at $2.395, but is available at $2.39 in London. The arbitrage would be effected by selling sterling in New York for $2.395 and having a London bank or foreign exchange firm sell dollars in London for $2.39, to obtain the sterling needed for delivery in New York. The gross profit ($0.05 per pound sterling) would be significant on a substantial transaction. Such arbitrage transactions usually occur on the basis of cable rates, which are spot prices not tying up funds in forward or future funds. The selling in the strong market would tend to lower prices there, and the buying in the weak market would tend to raise prices there, thereby tending to restore equivalence in rates.

Three-point arbitrage may be illustrated by the following. Situation: cable rate on pounds in New York, $2.40; Canadian dollars in New York, $1.00; cable rate on pounds in Toronto, $2.38. Action: sell pounds in New York for $2.40, buy $2.40 of Canadian dollars; then buy pounds in Toronto, costing only $2.38. Net result: $0.02 per pound profit, gross.

Arbitrage in Securities. Security arbitrage may occur in stock rights, convertible securities, exchange offers, reorganizations, mergers, and consolidations, both within one market and in multiple markets. Arbitrage in securities "dually listed" (traded in on more than one registered national securities exchange) may also occur between different domestic exchanges, as well as in international securities markets.

Arbitrage in corporate takeovers, which have been numerous in recent years, typically takes the form of buying the acquiree's stock upon announcement of the definite intention of the acquirer corporation to acquire the acquiree and selling short the stock of the acquirer corporation. Such arbitrage is particularly likely if the acquirer corporation has "sweetened up" the offer for the acquiree above previously prevailing market prices or upon encountering competition for the takeover or regulatory or acquiree demurrer further sweetens up the offer. The risk is that the acquisition might nevertheless fail to occur. The speculation for takeover arbitrage profits in recent years has been so high that in 1981 mere *rumors* of an acquisition offer for an oil company, which did not materialize, led stampeding speculators to run the oil company's stock to excessive levels from which it plummeted with a decline of 37.25 points in one day. Reliable information and prompt action, as well as hedging methods (just in case the acquisition does not go through) to protect the arbitrage itself, such as use of options, are of the essence for professional arbitrageurs.

Arbitrage in the Money Market. The money market may also abound in opportunities for arbitrage, including such situations as yield spreads, yield patterns, and interest rate changes.

From an economic standpoint, the effect of arbitrage dealings is to correct maladjustments in the prices of foreign exchange, or securities, or commodities. It is a force tending to equalize, i.e., establish parities among markets for the same item through competition of arbitrageurs. For instance, when prices in one market tend to sag, arbitrageurs will buy, and as a result of the increased demand, prices advance until the equilibrium is restored. Conversely, when the prices tend to advance out of line, arbitrageurs will offer freely, until prices recede to the level called for by equivalence.

See BACK SPREAD, SPREAD.

BIBLIOGRAPHY

BALLARD, F.L., JR., *ABCs of Arbitrage*, 1988.
WERSWEILLEN, R., ed. *Arbitrage*, 1987.

ARBITRAGE HOUSE A stock exchange house, private banker, investment banker, or foreign exchange dealer that specializes in arbitrage transactions.

ARBITRAGEUR One skilled in ARBITRAGE; an arbitrage dealer. Also spelled arbitrager.

ARBITRATION OF EXCHANGE A calculation based on rates of exchange to determine the difference in value of a given currency in three different places or markets, particularly when made with a view to determining the cheapest way of making a remittance between two countries. The result is called the arbitrated exchange, but this term is gradually being replaced by the term commercial parity. When three places are involved, the calculation is called simple arbitration; when more, compound arbitration.

ARE A measure of surface in the METRIC SYSTEM.

ARM'S-LENGTH TRANSACTION An arm's-length transaction is one in which buyer and seller pursue their own best interest and both are free to act accordingly. Transactions between related parties and affiliated companies are often not arm's-length transactions. In dealings between related parties, the following question should be asked: Would unrelated parties have handled the transaction in the same way? When assets are acquired at a cost, it is assumed that each acquisition results from an arm's-length market transaction by two independent parties who are presumed to be acting rationally in their own self-interest.

Arm's-length transactions are the basis for a fair market value determination used to record the acquisition, or historical cost, of assets. The arm's-length concept is also an important judicial concept relating to tax law.

ARREARS A debt or contingent obligation due but unpaid, such as past due installments or rents and unpaid interest on bonds. Dividends on cumulative preferred stock which have not been paid are also said to be in arrears, but such arrears on preferred stock are not akin to interest on debt, do not themselves become entitled to interest while still unpaid or unsettled for, and are not debt claims in any reorganization or liquidation (instead, they are added to the asset preference of the PREFERRED STOCK ahead of the common stock in sharing in any residual treatment).

ARRIVAL DRAFT A draft with shipping documents attached, payable upon arrival of the shipment against which it is drawn. Arrival drafts are usually forwarded by the shipper to the collecting bank (presumably a correspondent of the shipper's bank) located at the domicile of the consignee, with instructions not to demand payment therefor until the goods for which the draft has been drawn in payment have arrived at the drawee's (consignee's) destination.

An arrival draft is usually drawn and forwarded for collection at the time the goods are shipped, and consequently the draft invariably reaches its destination before the goods. An arrival draft is first presented upon receipt to notify the drawee of its arrival and where it is held for payment, so that when the shipment arrives (the consignee will be notified by an arrival notice from the transportation company) the drawee may take it up. In case the goods arrive before the presentation of the draft for notification, the draft becomes payable immediately.

An arrival draft provides a means of insuring payment for the goods against which it is drawn before delivery. Shippers usually consign goods to their own order and in such cases the bill of lading must bear the shipper's endorsement. Since the transportation company will not release the goods without surrender of the bill of lading, and the collection bank will not surrender the bill of lading until the draft is paid, the shipper protects himself by retaining title until the goods are paid for.

Sometimes the drawee, before paying an arrival draft, will ask permission to inspect or even sample the goods. This is justified if the shipment is of a perishable nature and a delay in transportation has occurred. The right of inspection is conferred by the collection bank only if allowance of inspection or sampling is specified in the bill of lading. Otherwise it is necessary to wire the shipper or consult the shipper's local representative for instructions. If the consignee should reject the shipment, the shipper or the shipper's local representative is notified immediately and the goods are disposed of in accordance with instructions.

ARTICLES OF ASSOCIATION The organizational document, akin to the articles of incorporation (CERTIFICATE OF INCORPORATION) of a business corporation, and the articles of co-partnership for partnerships, of national banking associations (national banks), as well as mutual, mutual benefit, social, charitable, and other nonstock corporations, the term being derived from the signatures of the document by the prescribed minimum number of persons "uniting to form the association."

National Banks. There is no statutory or regulatory requirement that any set of articles of association or bylaws be adopted. Nevertheless, the office of the Comptroller of the Currency makes available latest revised forms of articles of association and bylaws for national banks as sample documents incorporating model provisions, covering all of the rulings issued. The text of the official sample of the articles of association is appended herewith; see BYLAWS for the text of sample bylaws and comment.

Sample Articles of Association

THE _____ NATIONAL BANK
CHARTER NO. _____
ARTICLES OF ASSOCIATION
For the purpose of organizing an association to carry on the business of banking under the laws of the United States, the undersigned do enter into the following Articles of Association:

(The paragraphs marked with an asterisk below are optional. Other provisions not contrary to law may be added.)

FIRST. The title of this association shall be _____

SECOND. The main office of the association shall be in_____

County of _____
State of _____
The general business of the association shall be conducted at its main office and its branches.

THIRD. The board of directors of this association shall consist of not less than five nor more than twenty-five shareholders, the exact number of directors within such minimum and maximum limits to be fixed and determined from time to time by resolution of a majority of the full board of directors or by resolution of the shareholders at any annual or special meeting thereof. Unless otherwise provided by the laws of the United States, any vacancy in the board of directors for any reason, including an increase in the number thereof, may be filled by action of the board of directors.

FOURTH. The annual meeting of the shareholders for the election of directors and the transaction of whatever other business may be brought before said meeting shall be held at the main office or such other place as the board of directors may designate, on the day of each year specified therefore in the Bylaws, but if no election is held on that day, it may be held on any subsequent day according to the provisions of law; and all elections shall be held according to such lawful regulations as may be prescribed by the board of directors.

Nominations for elections to the board of directors may be made by the board of directors or by any stockholder of any outstanding class of capital stock of the bank entitled to vote for election of directors. Nominations, other than those made by or on behalf of the existing management of the bank, shall be made in writing and shall be delivered or mailed to the president of the bank and to the Comptroller of the Currency, Washington, D. C., not less than 14 days nor more than 50 days prior to any meeting of stockholders called for the election of directors, provided, however, that if less than 21 days' notice of the meeting is given to shareholders, such nomination shall be mailed or delivered to the president of the bank and to the Comptroller of the Currency not later than the close of business on the seventh day following the day on which the notice of meeting was mailed. Such notification shall contain the following information to the extent known to the notifying shareholder: (a) the name and address of each proposed nominee; (b) the principal occupation of each proposed nominee; (c) the total number of shares of capital stock of the bank that will be voted for each proposed nominee; (d) the name and residence address of the notifying shareholder; and (e) the number of shares of capital stock of the Bank owned by the notifying shareholder. Nominations not made in accordance herewith may, in his discretion, be disregarded by the chairman of the meeting, and upon his instructions, the vote tellers may disregard all votes cast for each such nominee.*

FIFTH. The authorized amount of capital stock of this association shall be _____ shares of common stock of the par value of _____ dollars ($ ____) each; but said capital stock may be increased or decreased from time to time, in accordance with the provisions of the laws of the United States.

(Instruction: With the prior approval of the comptroller of the currency, the authorized amount of capital stock may include a number of shares to be held by the association as authorized but unissued shares. Authorized but unissued shares may be issued from time to time in the discretion of the Board of Directors, with the prior approval of the Comptroller of the Currency, for any proper consideration.)

(Use one of the following two paragraphs or insert other lawful provisions as to shareholders' preemptive rights.)

If the capital stock is increased by the sale of additional shares thereof, each shareholder shall be entitled to subscribe for such additional shares in proportion to the number of shares of said capital stock owned by him at the time the increase is authorized by the shareholders, unless another time subsequent to the date of the shareholders' meeting is specified in a resolution adopted by the shareholders at the time the increase is authorized. The Board of Directors shall have the power to prescribe a reasonable period of time within which the preemptive rights to subscribe to the new shares of capital stock must be exercised.*

No holder of shares of the capital stock of any class of the corporation shall have an preemptive or preferential right of subscription to any shares of any class of stock of the corporation, whether now or hereafter authorized, or to any obligations convertible into stock of the corporation, issued or sold, nor any right of subscription to any thereof other than such, if any, as the board of directors, in its discretion, may from time to time determine and at such price as the board of directors may from time to time fix.*

The association, at any time and from time to time, may authorize and issue debt obligations, whether or not subordinated, without the approval of the shareholders.*

SIXTH. The board of directors shall appoint one of its members president of this Association, who shall be chairman of the board, unless the board appoints another director to be the chairman. The board of directors shall have the power to appoint one or more vice presidents; and to appoint a cashier and such other officers and employees as may be required to transact the business of this association.

The board of directors shall have the power to define the duties of the officers and employees of the association; to fix the salaries to be paid to them; to dismiss them; to require bonds from them and fix the penalty thereof; to regulate the manner in which any increase of the capital of the association shall be made; to manage and administer the business and affairs of the association; to make all bylaws that it may be lawful for them to make; and generally to do and perform all acts that it may be legal for a board of directors to do and perform.

SEVENTH. The board of directors shall have the powers to change the location of the main office to any other place within the limits of _____ , without the approval of the shareholders but subject to the approval of the Comptroller of the Currency; and shall have the power to establish or change the location of any branch or branches of the association to any other location, without the approval of the shareholders but subject to the approval of the comptroller of the currency.

EIGHTH. The corporate existence of this association shall continue until terminated in accordance with the laws of the United States.

NINTH. The board of directors of this association, or any three or more shareholders owning, in the aggregate, not less than 25 percent of the stock of this association, may call a special meeting of shareholders at any time.

(Instruction: If this language is not used, alternative procedure for the calling of special meetings of shareholders should be provided for.)

Unless otherwise provided by the laws of the United States, a notice of the time, place, and purpose of every annual and special meeting of the shareholders shall be given by first-class mail, postage prepaid, mailed at least ten days prior to the date of such meeting to each shareholder of record at his address as shown upon the books of this Association.

TENTH. Any person, his or her heirs, executors, or administrators, may be indemnified or reimbursed by the Association for reasonable expenses actually incurred in connection with any action, suit, or proceeding, civil or criminal, to which he/she or they shall be made a party by reason of his or her being or having been a director, officer, or employee of the Association or of any firm, corporation, or organization which he or she served in any such capacity at the request of the Associations, provided, however, that no person shall be so indemnified or reimbursed in relation to any matter in such action, suit, or proceeding as to which he or she shall finally be adjudged to have been guilty of or liable for negligence or willful misconduct in the performance of his or her duties to the association, and provided further that no person shall be so indemnified or reimbursed in relation to any matter in such action, suit, or proceeding which has been made the subject of a compromise settlement except with the approval of a court of competent jurisdiction, or the holders of record of a majority of the outstanding shares of the association, or the Board of Directors, acting by vote of directors not parties to the same or substantially the same action, suit, or proceeding, constituting a majority of the whole number of the directors. The foregoing right of indemnification or reimbursement shall be be exclusive of other rights to which such person, his or her heirs, executors, or administrators, may be entitled as a matter of law.*

ELEVENTH. These Articles of Association may be amended at any regular or special meeting of the shareholders by the affirmative vote of the holders of a majority of the stock of this association, unless the vote of the holders of a greater amount of stock is required by law, and in that case by the vote of the holders of such greater amount.

IN WITNESS WHEREOF, we have hereunto set our hands this ____ day of _____ 19 ____ .

(To be signed by not less than five persons uniting to form the association.)
See NATIONAL BANKING SYSTEM, BANK ORGANIZATION.

ASIAN DEVELOPMENT BANK (ADB)

The purpose of the bank is to foster economic growth and contribute to the acceleration of economic development of the developing member countries in Asia, collectively and individually.

The agreement establishing the Asian Development Bank (ADB) came into effect on August 22, 1966, when it was ratified by 15 governments. The bank commenced operations on December 19, 1966. As of 1987, it had a membership of 47 countries, 30 of which are from the Asian region. The U.S. became a member by virtue of the Asian Development Bank Act of March 16, 1966 (80 Stat. 71; 22 U.S.C. 285–285h).

Membership in the ADB is open to members and associate members of the United Nations Economic and Social Commission for Asia and the Pacific and other regional countries and nonregional developed countries which are members of the United Nations or of any of its specialized agencies. The 15 developed nonregional countries include the U.S., Canada, the United Kingdom, and 15 Western European countries as members.

Operations. Bank operations are financed from two main sources: ordinary capital resources and special funds. Ordinary capital resources are obtained through paid-in capital from member countries, borrowings in the world capital markets, and income from investments. Special funds are obtained from contributions from developed member countries, income from special funds loans and investments, and amounts transferred from ordinary capital resources by a special vote of the board of governors of the bank.

ADB's special funds constitute the "soft loan" window at low rates of interest to meet the needs of the smaller and poorer member countries. In 1973, the Bank established the Asian Development Fund to consolidate special fund resources on an organized and regular basis. However, a separate fund is maintained to finance technical assistance operations.

Since its founding, the bank has made loans totaling $19.5 billion (through 1986), contributing to a total investment of over $48 billion. During calendar year 1986, agriculture and agro-industry accounted for the largest share of bank lending (111%), while the increasing importance of energy development was reflected in substantial lending in this sector (19%). Other sectors funded were social infrastructure (19%), and transport and communications (9%).

The bank lends at near-market rates through its ordinary capital window and on highly concessional terms to the region's poorer nations through the Asian Development Fund. The U.S. 1988 appropriation request included contributions to both funds in the amount of $234 million (plus $277 million for callable capital).

BIBLIOGRAPHY

ASIAN DEVELOPMENT BANK, *Annual Reports.*

ASKED PRICE The price at which a security or commodity is quoted or offered for sale, as compared with bid price, the price at which it is quoted or bid for purchase.
See BID AND ASKED QUOTATIONS, BID PRICE, BIDS AND OFFERS, QUOTATIONS.

AS PER ADVICE In a letter or upon a draft or bill of exchange, indicate that notice has been or is to be given to the drawee that the draft has been drawn.

ASSAY A test to determine the percent of pure metal in a specimen of ore or bullion. An assay report indicates that a certain gold ore submitted for analysis will yield, say, $14, $50, or $600 of pure gold per ton, or that certain bullion is 0.985 fine.

ASSAY COMMISSION The Annual Assay Commission is appointed by the President of the United States to examine and test the weights and finenesses of coins in the monetary system of the U.S. This historical trial of the coins is akin to the English TRIAL OF THE PYX. It is required by Section 3547, as amended, of the Revised Statutes of the United States, and is the official test by private citizens to assure the public that coins have been manufactured in accordance with law. A representative sample of coins is selected and tested by the committees on counting, assaying, and weighing. The committees report that the coins meet fully the prescribed legal standards and that the trial is entirely satisfactory.

ASSAY OFFICE A laboratory for testing metals and ores, usually gold and silver. Official assay offices are located at New York, N.Y. and San Francisco, Cal., and are part of the organization of the Bureau of the Mint, which also includes mints at Philadelphia and Denver, the gold bullion depository at Fort Knox, Kentucky, and the silver bullion depository at West Point, N.Y., the last-named being an adjunct of the New York Assay Office. An electrolytic refinery for refining precious metals is located in New York. Each MINT and assay office performs a number of operations relating to the manufacture, distribution, and redemption of domestic coins; the receipt, processing, custody, disbursement, and movement of gold and silver bullion; the manufacture of medals of a national character, including special medals authorized by acts of Congress and medals for other U.S. government agencies; the manufacture of foreign coins; the assays of ores for the public; and other technical services.
See COINAGE.

ASSAY OFFICE BAR A bar of pure or nearly pure gold or silver manufactured at a mint and assayed by an ASSAY OFFICE. Gold issue bars manufactured are in 400-troy ounce size, and silver issue bars manufactured are in 1,000-troy ounce size. Gold and silver commercial bars, however, are manufactured in miscellaneous sizes.

ASSENTED SECURITIES Securities whose owners have agreed to some change in their status, especially in case of reorganization where an assessment is made or the amount of securities is scaled down according to some definite plan. The stock certificates of stockholders who have paid their assessment would be stamped "assessment paid" or "assented."

ASSESSABLE *See* NONASSESSABLE STOCK.

ASSESSED VALUATION For the purpose of levying general property taxes, the valuation placed on real and personal property and recorded on the assessment roll. Standard of valuation for assessed valuations is usually specified in applicable law as value which could ordinarily be obtained for the property at private sale. Ratios of such assessed valuation, for tax purposes, will vary in taxing jurisdictions from full value to fractions of full value, e.g., three-fourths, two-thirds, one-half, etc., of full value, a factor calling for adjustment to comparable basis in comparative analysis of municipal bonds.

Apart from establishing the basis for apportionment of taxes and thus determining specific tax rates, assessed valuations establish in the various states the basis for debt limits, by consitutional or statutory limitations, of municipal units of government, e.g., 2.5% of assessed valuations. Thus in analysis of municipal bonds, the ratio of net debt to total assessed valuation of property is a key ratio, although not a conclusive indication of ability to provide for debt service, since there may be important sources of revenues other than property taxes and since there may be possible manipulation of assessed valuations. Nevertheless, existence of debt limits are a motivation for the rise of municipal financing outside debt limits, such as REVENUE BONDS and financing by special authorities.

ASSESSMENT This term has three meanings:

1. In property taxation, assessment is the procedure involved in determining assessed valuation for tax purposes and the valuation itself thus determined.
2. Assessment liability of stock that is not fully paid and nonassessable (full par value or no par value stock's full subscription price not paid at issuance of the stock) is the liability of the holder thereof to a trustee in bankruptcy of the corporation upon the trustee's levy therefore, for the balance of the par value, or the subscription price of no par value stock, not paid for the stock at its issuance. Such collection is for the benefit of the creditors of the corporation in bankruptcy and is illustrative of the principle in corporate law of the trust fund in full of the capital stock for the benefit of creditors.
3. In the case of bank stocks, in the event of failure of a bank, the receiver could levy an amount, as necessary, up to the par value of each share of stock held by stockholders, on the stockholders of record as of the date of failure. This was defined as DOUBLE LIABILITY; i.e., in addition to losing an investment because of the bank's failure, the stockholder was liable for the additional loss represented by collection of an amount by the bank's receiver, as necessary, up to the par value of the closed bank's stock, to pay depositors and other creditors (in recent times, depositors not fully covered by deposit insurance). Such double liability of bank stock has been generally eliminated by repeal of the pertinent statutes. However, before a bank is closed, the banking authority may call upon the directors to levy and collect each stockholder's share of an existing impairment in capital stock, and thus avoid the closing of the bank. Such

assessment liability of stockholders, to cover impairment of capital and avoid closing of a bank, still continues.

ASSESSOR One who appraises or assesses the value of property, e.g., a tax assessor.

ASSET CURRENCY GENERAL ASSET CURRENCY. *See* BALTIMORE PLAN.

ASSET/LIABILITY MANAGEMENT Asset/liability management (ALM) has been defined as "a planning procedure that accounts for all assets and liabilities of a financial institution by rate, amount, and maturity. Its intent is to quantify and control risk. The focus is on the risk management of the net interest margin for profit." ALM planning impacts directly on the volume, mix, maturity, rate sensitivity, quality, and liquidity of a bank's assets and liabilities. It involves an integrated financial management policy. Emphasis is placed on positioning a bank's portfolio of loans and investments to maximize flexibility and return. In theory, this requires that a bank secure funds at a particular rate of interest and employ those funds at a yield in excess of the cost for a maturity identical with that of the source of funds. To increase earnings, management must maintain a larger spread between the cost and use of funds while maintaining similar maturities. Asset/liability management also utilizes a process involving the mismatching of maturities between rate-sensitive assets and liabilities. For example, if a bank obtains fixed-rate liabilities and uses them in floating rate assets during a period of rising interest rates, earnings increases on the floating rate assets can be obtained.

Typical risks that ALM considers include those related to capital adequacy, liquidity, interest sensitivity, credit risk, foreign exchange risk, capital expenditure (acquisitions, branching), and service production risk (discount brokerage, trust). ALM attempts to produce an acceptable risk/reward ratio for a bank because of increased competition and inflationary pressure on the pricing.

Procedures vary for positioning assets and liabilities in ALM programs. One recommended procedure requires that (1) assets and liabilities be classified as rate-sensitive or nonrate-sensitive according to maturity; (2) determining each asset's and each liability's interest rate yields (costs) and dollar vloume; and (3) using measurement tools for analyzing these data and a format for interpreting the results. This procedure enables management to interpret the impact of interest rate changes on the profitability of its ALM program.

Interest-rate sensitive assets include floating rate loans, loans maturing, investments maturing, and fixed-rate loan amortization/payoffs. Maturing investments include federal funds, money market assets, government securities, and municipal securities that mature during a forecast period and can be reinvested at current market rates. Interest-sensitive liabilities include short-term borrowing, maturing certificates of deposit and money market certificates, and floating rate liabilities. Certain assets and liabilities become interest-rate sensitive as they approach maturity.

Some banks use the following format or matrix, or some variation thereof, for rate-sensitive analysis:

	3 mo.	6 mo.	9 mo.	1 year
Rate-sensitive assets (dollars)				
Rate-sensitive liabilities (dollars)				
Difference (RSA − RSL)				
Ratios:				
RSA/RSL				
RSA/Total assets				
RSL/Total liabilities				

The maturity matching of assets and liabilities can be analyzed using a format similar to the following to analyze any maturity gap and yield spread for a given time period:

Assets (same format for liabilities)

($000) Amount	% of Total	Maturity	Weighted Factor	Yield (cost of funds)	Weighted Factor

A weighted average maturity factor is computed for the assets and the liabilities by taking the proportion of assets and liabilities maturing within each maturity interval and multiplying that percentage by the number of days to maturity. A weighted factor yield (cost of funds) factor can also be computed using the same procedure.

The difference between the weighted average asset maturity and the weighted asset liability maturity indicates a "GAP/maturity mismatch." The difference between the weighted average yield and the weighted average cost of funds indicates any "net interest margin/spread." These ALM procedures can by used by management to develop rate tolerance policies to assist in evaluating and dealing with interest-rate risks. A bank can influence its rate risk by modifying the maturity of its assets or liabilities, the volume of its rate-sensitive assets or profits, the volatility in interest rates, and deregulation have resulted in a renewed interest in ALM. Bank managers can adopt aggressive, defensive, or a middle ground approach to risk management.

It is generally recognized that cash flows, profits, rates, balances, and time constitute the basic elements of any acceptable ALM program. Funds management and liquidity management are essential to a sound ALM. Funds management established a close coordination of all aspects of funds acquisition and disposition. The consolidation of funds management operations facilitates efforts to centralize the management of interest-rate risk. ALM also enables a bank to cultivate and develop direct sources of funds. Liquidity management relates primarily to the ability of a bank to meet maturing liabilities (GAP analysis), and customer demands for cash. A liquidity ratio is sometimes defined as :

(Assets maturing within 90 days + Readily salable assets + Deposit inflows expected in the next 90 days + Unused capacity to borrow − Net loan growth expected in the next 90 days/Earning assets)

Management would usually develop a liquidity ratio tolerance range. The liquidity ratio then would be managed, e.g., by adjusting the maturity of assets and liabilities or by diversifying and broadening sources of funds.

It is generally recognized that pricing (fixed or floating rate) and liquidity (quality and marketability) are key factors in any ALM. The most significant aspects of liability management are generally considered to be the dependability of funding and liabilities, pricing policies and other balance-sheet techniques as well as with financial futures, options, and swaps.

Bank credit risk involves evaluating and managing the growth and diversification of loans and investments and establishing tolerance ranges for credit and investment ratios such as the ratio of loan-loss allowance to total loans.

Many banks centralize the management of rate, credit, and liquidity risks through the use of profit centers in which departments, functions, or operating units "buy" and "sell" funds through a Treasury function. In the final analysis, ALM is more an art than a science at its current developmental stage.

Bankers have developed a variety of analytical tools that are useful in ALM. The major objective of ALM is to optimize net interest income while minimizing liquidity RISK, capital-adequacy risk, and interest-rate risk. These tools include:

1. **Asset allocation.** A method that matches liabilities and capital with assets according to interest rates, volatility, and maturities. Assets and liabilities are assigned to "maturity buckets" and variances are interpreted and dealt with. A funding source is allocated to assets and judgments made concerning its adequacy. The primary focus of ALM is liquidity.
2. **Gap management.** A method that assesses interest rate sensitivity according to maturities. Rate-sensitive assets are associated with rate sensitive liabilities and any resulting gaps are identified. Funding surpluses and deficits are examined in "time buckets." The basic formula is: rate-sensitive assets minus rate-sensitive liabilities equals the interest rate sensitivity gap. The gap can represent either a surplus or a deficit.
3. **Duration analysis.** A method that examines market price (value) changes resulting from interest rate shifts. When interest rates increase, the value of assets goes down. Duration analysis can provide an estimate of the weighted average maturity of an instrument or total portfolio. By matching durations, a bank can protect assets from the market value risk and the reinvestment risk.

4. **Simulation.** A method of applying "what if" observations and previewing the impact of an operation or functions enabling the impact of alternatives to be considered before implementation. Simulation is useful in making forecasts or projections.
5. **Optimization.** A powerful method for making economic decisions that emphasizes the efficient allocation of resources to maximize or minimize an objective, such as maximizing profits ot minimizing costs. The mathematical solution to such problems is optimization. Linear programming is one mathematical tool that is particularly effective in optimizing. Artificial intelligence is a promising method of optimizing.

BIBLIOGRAPHY

BANK ADMINISTRATION INSTITUTE. *The Bank Director's Handbook,* 2nd ed., 1986.
BINDER, B. F., and LINDQUIST, T. W. F. *Asset/Liability and Funds Management at U.S. Commercial Banks.* Bank Administration Institute, Rolling Meadows, IL, 1982.
———. *Asset/Liability Management: A Handbook for Commercial Banks.* Bank Administration Institute, Rolling Meadows, IL, 1982.
KALLBERG, J. G., and PARKINSON, K. L. *Current Asset Management.* John Wiley and Sons, New York, NY, 1984.
MARKOVICH, D. *Effective Asset/Liability Management for the Community Bank.* Bank Administration Institute, Rolling Meadows, IL, 1988.
WILLIAMS, W. *Asset/Liability Management Techniques.* Bank Administration Institute, Rolling Meadows, IL, 1988.
———. *Asset/Liability Measurement Techniques.* Bank Administration Institute, Rolling Meadows, IL, 1987.

ASSETS   Probable future economic benefits obtained or controlled by a particular entity as a result of past transactions or events. Future economic benefits refer to the capacity of an asset to benefit the enterprise by being exchanged for something else of value to the enterprise, by being used to produce something of value to the enterprise, or by being used to settle its liabilities. The future economic benefits of assets usually result in net cash inflows to the enterprise.

To be an asset, a resource other than cash must have three essential characteristics:

1. The resource must, singly or in combination with other resources, contribute directly or indirectly to future net cash inflows.
2. The enterprise must be able to obtain the benefit and to control the access of others to it.
3. The transaction or other event giving rise to the enterprise's right to or control of the benefit must already have occurred.

Assets currently reported in the financial statements are measured by different attributes, including historical or acquisition cost, current (replacement) cost, current market value, net realizable value (selling price of the item less direct costs necessary to convert the asset), and present value of future cash flows, depending on the nature of the item and the relevance and reliability of the attribute measured.

Assets are recognized in the financial statements when the item meets the definition of an asset, when it can be measured with sufficient reliability, when the information about it is capable of making a difference in user decisions, and when the information about the item is reliable (verifiable, neutral, or unbiased, and representionally faithful). Assets need not be recognized in a set of financial statements if the item is not large enough to be material and the aggregate of individual immaterial items is not large enough to be material to those financial statements.

Assets are usually classified on a balance sheet in order of their liquidity (or nearness to cash) as follows:

1. Current assets.
2. Long-term investments.
3. Property, plant, and equipment.
4. Intangible assets.
5. Other assets (including deferred charges and organizational costs).

Current assets are cash and other assets that are reasonably expected to be converted into cash, sold, or consumed within the normal operating cycle of the business or one year, whichever is longer. An operating cycle is the average time required to expend cash for inventory, process and sell the inventory, collect the receivables, and covert them back into cash.

Accounts appearing on the balance sheets of banks include:

Cash and due from banks: Currency and coins held by tellers reserve cash in the vault. Due-from-bank items represent deposits with correspondent banks.
Federal funds sold: Claims to deposits held by the Federal Reserve for member banks that enable them to meet reserve requirements. The purchase and sale of federal funds is sometimes used for short-term adjustments to market and regulatory conditions.
Investments in U.S. Treasury securities: U.S. government marketable obligations, including Treasury bills, notes, or bonds.
Investments in obligations of other U.S. Government agencies and corporations: Debt securities issued by agencies of the federal government such as the Federal Land Bank.
Investments in obligations of states and political subdivisions: Debt securities referred to as municipal bonds and tax-exempt bonds.
Real estate loans: Loans resulting from real-estate purchases and development transactions. The real estate serves as collateral for the loan.
Commercial loans: Loans made for business purposes.
Installment loans: Consumer loans.
Office buildings, equipment, and leasehold improvements: Historical cost of bank property used for banking purposes less accumulated depreciation.

See CURRENT ASSETS, FIXED ASSETS, INTANGIBLES, TANGLIBLE ASSETS.

ASSET VALUE   Applied to book value or equity value of investment companies (so-called investment trusts) and generally expressed on a per share basis.

See EQUITY, LIQUIDATING VALUE.

ASSIGNATS   Paper money authorized to be issued in 1789 by the revolutionary French government. Assignats were noninterest bearing notes, which originally were secured by the confiscated properties of the church and were a typical example of fiat money. Successive issues were authorized and issued in such volume without security that they depreciated rapidly and in the end became valueless.

See INFLATION.

ASSIGNED BOOK ACCOUNTS   Book or open accounts of a business, the title of which has been transferred to a commercial credit company or to a bank as collateral for a loan. This is a type of commercial loan which has been receiving increased attention from commercial banks, as compared with low regard in past years, in view of the satisfactory experience of finance companies with this type of business under proper legal safeguards and operating supervision. Where state banking laws prohibit the actual purchase of accounts receivable, because they are choses in action, and only permit loans on the accounts, such loans can be made secured by the assignment of the accounts, together with agreement for repurchase or substitution of accounts in default, provision for repayment out of collections, and other safeguards, lending either against individual accounts or under revolving loan agreement, either on the notification or non-notification of debtor's basis. The notification type is preferred, as it makes better collateral.

BIBLIOGRAPHY

COMPTROLLER OF THE CURRENCY. *Handbook for National Bank Examiners,* Section 207.1: Accounts Receivable Financing.
LOTT, K. L., and MYERS, R. G. "Secured Lending." In BAUGHN, W. H., and WALKER, C. E., eds., *The Bankers Handbook* (rev. ed.), 1978.

ASSIGNEE   The party to whom an ASSIGNMENT has been executed. Under the common law, the assignee had no right to bring suit in his own name in the event or default or breach, as the suit had to be brought in the name of the ASSIGNOR. This common law rule has been changed in modern times to give the assignee the right to bring suit in his or her own name.

See ASSIGNMENT FOR THE BENEFIT OF CREDITORS, ASSIGNMENT IN BLANK.

ASSIGNMENT An assignment occurs when one party to a contract (a right, claim, or interest) transfers (assigns) his or her rights under the agreement to a third person. The person who transfers the right is called the assignor; the person to whom the right is transferred is called the assignee. The other party to the contract against whom the right can be exercised is the obligor.

Generally, only contractual rights (not contractual duties) can be assigned. Contractual duties can be delegated if they do not require personal services or the personal attention of the obligor. To be enforceable, an assignment must constitute a contract, i.e., a statement indicating an intent to make the assignee the owner of the right, claim, or interest. The assignment can usually be made orally or in writing.

Special rules have been formulated by stock exchanges to govern the assignment of stock.

See ASSIGNMENT IN BLANK, ASSIGNMENT FOR THE BENEFIT OF CREDITORS, GOOD DELIVERY, STOP TRANSFER ORDER.

ASSIGNMENT FOR THE BENEFIT OF CREDITORS

The action by which an individual or company (assignor) transfers legal title to property to a trustee (assignee), who is empowered to administer and liquidate the property and to distribute the proceeds to the creditors.

Such an action is one of the acts of bankruptcy constituting grounds for the involuntary petition in bankruptcy by creditors.

See NATIONAL BANKRUPTCY ACT.

ASSIGNMENT IN BLANK

A formal transfer of title to stock or registered bonds in which the space for the insertion of the name of the new owner is left blank, so that the name may be written in at any subsequent time. An assignment form will be found on the reverse side of certificates of stock or registered bonds. Stock certificates or registered bond assigned in blank become bearer instruments in that title passes by mere delivery; thus they should not be purchased from an unknown person without proper identification and evidence of genuineness of the signatures of the assignor and witnesses. A STREET CERTIFICATE is assigned in blank.

A form of assignment on the reverse side of a stock certificate which has been approved by the Committee on Stock List of the New York Stock Exchange is appended.

Reverse Side Stock Assignment Form

For value received _____

hereby sell, assign and transfer unto _____ shares of the capital stock represented by the within certificate, and do hereby irrevocably constitute and appoint _____ attorney to transfer the said stock on the books of the within named company with full power of substitution in the premises.
Dated _____
(Signature) _____
In the presence of _____

Note: The signature of this assignment must correspond with the name as written on the face of this certificate in every particular without alteration or enlargement or any change whatever.

Such an assignment is a means of transferring title of stocks from a seller to purchaser, assignment being the method of negotiating stocks, whereas endorsement (and delivery) is the method of negotiating checks, drafts, money orders, and other negotiable instruments.

In collateral loan practice, it is customary to pledge any unendorsed certificates plus executed separate assignments in blank with the lender, so that the certificates may be returned and the assignments destroyed upon payment of the loan. For assignment separate from the stock certificate, the following form is approved by the New York Stock Exchange:

Separate Stock Assignment Form

For value received _____ hereby sell, assign and transfer unto _____
(_____) Shares of the _____
Capital Stock of the _____
standing in _____ name
on the books of said _____
represented by Certificate No. _____
herewith and do hereby irrevocably constitute and appoint _____ attorney to transfer the said stock on the books of the within named Company with full Power of Substitution in the premises.
Dated _____
(Signature) _____

For assignment separate from the registered bond, the following form is approved by the New York Stock Exchange:

Separate Bond Assignment Form

For value received _____ hereby sell, assign and transfer unto _____
one bond of the _____
for _____ ($ _____),
No. _____ herewith, standing
in _____ name on the books
of said _____ and do hereby
irrevocably constitute and appoint _____
_____ attorney to transfer the said bond on the books of the within named company, with full Power of Substitution in the premises.
Dated _____
(Signature) _____

ASSIGNMENT OF CLAIMS ACT

Approved Oct. 9, 1940, "to assist in the national defense program by amending Sections 3477 and 3737 of the Revised Statutes to permit the assignment of claims under public contracts" (P.L. 811, 76th Congress). Such assignment of claims allowed manufacturers to assign the contracts as security for borrowings from banks needed for defense plant construction.

Accordingly, a new form of uniform bankable contract was developed by the NATIONAL DEFENSE ADVISORY COMMISSION after consultation with the War and Navy departments and the Comptroller General. This contract had two purposes: to expedite signing of supplies contracts by the Army and Navy by assuring the contractor against loss on construction undertaken for military purposes and to safeguard the government's interest in such facilities on termination or completion of the contract.

The contract provided that the government reimburse the contractor not in additions to the unit price, as previously, but in five equal annual installments covering the amount of his capital expansion costs. Thus, cost of supplies and amortization of construction cost would be kept separate. Prices were held at a minimum, and while the manufacturer was relieved of the risk involved in building fixed assets for the emergency, he still absorbed the risks involved in production. The contract also contained provisions whereby the contractor might by purchase or lease from the government acquire use of the facilities for himself after they had served their emergency needs.

ASSIGNOR

One who makes an assignment to a transferee or ASSIGNEE. The assignee "stands in the shoes" of the assignor as to rights and liabilities per the ASSIGNMENT, and the defense available against the assignor is also available against the assignee.

See ASSIGNMENT FOR THE BENEFIT OF CREDITORS, ASSIGNMENT IN BLANK.

ASSIMILATE

Denotes that the demand for securities is sufficient to ABSORB offerings without appreciable decline in prices.

See DIGESTED SECURITIES.

ASSOCIATION

A body of persons who unite for some special business or other purpose. The association is vested with some, but not complete, corporate rights and powers. For income tax purposes, an association is taxed in the same manner as a corporation.

See TRADE ASSOCIATION

ASSUMABLE MORTGAGE

A MORTGAGE that can be passed on to a new owner at the previous owner's interest rate. Some lenders have been calling in such loans under "due on sale" clauses when buyers and sellers attempt to arrange an assumable mortgage. Such clauses have recently been upheld in court.

ASSUMED BONDS Bonds of one corporation whose liability has been assumed by another. When one corporation purchases another, exchanges its shares for those of another, or gains control of another through lease or ownership of a majority of the stock, it may assume the latter's debts, including its bonds; e.g., a parent company assumes the bonds of its newly acquired subsidiary. In railroad finance, assumed bonds are usually divisional bonds, i.e., the bonds of smaller companies acquired and operated as divisions.

See DIVISIONAL BOND.

Assumed bonds are sometimes improperly called GUARANTEED BONDS. In assumed bonds primary liability is assumed, whereas in guaranteed bonds the original obliger continues to be primarily liable and secondary liability attaches to the guarantor.

ASSURANCE Life coverage provided by contracts of life insur-ance companies, as contrasted with INSURANCE for contracts of fire and casualty insurance companies. Formerly, the term was often used for insurance, especially in maritime law.

AT CALL On call.
See CALL MONEY, CALL MONEY MARKET.

AT MARKET Instructions in a MARKET ORDER in which no price is specified. Such an order is to be executed at once at the best possible market price, regardless of what it may be, by the commission broker's floor member.
See ORDERS.

AT OR BETTER In connection with a brokerage buying order, to purchase at the price specified or under; in selling order, to sell at the price specified or above.

AT SIGHT In drafts and bills of exchange, indicates that payment is due on demand or presentation.

ATTACHMENT A writ authorizing the seizure, or the act of seizure itself, by a sheriff or other levying officer of the law, of property belonging to the defendant in an action at law, and the holding of it or the prevention of holding of it by the defendant, in order to satisfy a claim or judgment that plaintiff hopes to recover. An attachment is a legal means used by a creditor to circumvent loss that might occur by an act of the debtor (e.g., fraud or misrepresentation in obtaining credit, insolvency while goods are in transit, assignment to a third party, actual or contemplated removal of the person or property of the debtor from the jurisdiction of the court), and also as a means of collecting a claim or judgment granted or decreed by a court. It is usual to require the creditor to furnish bond for double the amount involved, should the attachment subsequently be vacated as illegal or improper. By its very nature, a writ of attachment is a provisional remedy for an emergency situation.

ATTESTATION A communicated statement of opinion in which an independent, competent individual expresses an opinion based on evidence. An accountant's OPINION attests to the degree of correspondence of reported financial information with established criteria.
See AUDIT.

AT THE OPENING In reference to an order placed with a broker specifying execution at the opening of the particular security involved. No price limit is specified. If the order is for the purchase or sale of an ODD LOT, however, it must be executed one-fourth of a point above or below the opening price for a full lot, if 40 and over; or one-eighth of point above or below such opening price for the full or round lot.
See ORDERS.

ATTORNEY-CLIENT PRIVILEGE A rule of law that provides that confidential communications between an attorney and client during the period of the professional relationship cannot be revealed without the client's consent. The privilege generally applies to individuals asserting the privilege as a client, or a person seeking to become a client; the attorney is a member of the bar and acts in a professional capacity in receiving the information; or the information is revealed as the client seeks to obtain an opinion in law or for a specific legal proceeding.

ATTORNEY'S OPINION See LEGALITY OF SECURITIES.

AUCTION A special market in which there is one seller and many buyers. An auction sale is conducted by an auctioneer who permits buyers to bid against one another, the goods going to the highest bidder. The public at large is invited to participate, by advance notice and advertisements. In an honest auction, the goods are sold regardless of cost, unless the seller reserves the right to reject all unsatisfactory offers, and the final price is determined by the value of the article to the successful bidder. Auctions are usually conducted for the purpose of selling out the property of the estate of a deceased person or liquidating an insolvent business. Auction terms are usually spot cash for immediate delivery. Auction prices are sometimes referred to as liquidating prices, "forced sales," or "under-the-hammer" (mallet or hammer used by the auctioneer) prices.

An auctioneer is not required to accept a bid. He invites bids from the persons present at the sale, but no bid becomes a binding sale contract until accepted by him or her. The auctioneer does not make an offer; he merely invites them.

Herewith are typical conditions of sale at an advertised auction:

1. The highest bidder is to be the buyer, and if any dispute arises between two or more bidders, the lot so in dispute shall be immediately put up again and resold.
2. Any bid which is not commensurate with the value of the article offered, or which is merely a nominal or fractional advance, may be rejected by the auctioneer if in his or her judgment such bid would be likely to affect the sale injuriously.
3. The purchasers are to give their names and addresses and to pay down a cash deposit, or the whole of the purchase money, if required, in default of which the lot or lots so purchased are to be immediately put up again and resold.
4. The lots are to be taken away at the buyer's expense and risk upon the conclusion of the sale, and the remainder of the purchase money is to be absolutely paid or otherwise settled for to the satisfaction of the auctioneer on or before delivery, in default of which the auctioneers will not hold themselves responsible if the lots are lost, damaged, or destroyed, but they will be left at the sole risk of the purchaser.
5. The lots are to be taken away and paid for, whether genuine or authentic or not, with all faults and errors of description, at the buyer's expense and risk, within two days from the sale, the auctioneers not being responsible for the correct description, genuineness or authenticity of, or any fault or defect in any lot, and making no warranty whatever.
6. Goods will be delivered on presentation of a receipted bill. A receipted bill presented by any person will be recognized and honored as an order by the buyer, directing the delivery to the bearer, of the goods described therein. If a receipted bill is lost before delivery of the property has been taken, the buyer should immediately notify the auction company of such loss.
7. To prevent inaccuracy in delivery and inconvenience in settlement of the purchases, no lot can on any account be removed during the sale.
8. If, for any cause, an article purchased cannot be delivered in as good condition as the same may have been at the time of its sale, or should any article purchased thereafter be stolen or misdelivered or lost, the action company is not to be held liable in any greater amount than the price bid by the purchaser.
9. Upon failure to comply with the above conditions, the money deposited in part payment shall be forfeited; all lots uncleared within the time aforesaid shall be resold by public or private sale, without further notice, and the deficiency, if any, attending such resale shall be made good by the defaulter at this sale, together with all charges attending the same. This condition is without prejudice to the right of the auctioneer to enforce the contract made at this sale, without such resale, if he or she thinks fit.
10. Unless the sale is advertised and announced as absolute and unrestricted, owners reserve the right to bid.
11. All claims must be made within ten days after sale.
12. Shipping, boxing, or wrapping of purchases is a business in which the auction company is in no wise engaged, and will not

be performed by the auction company or purchasers. The auction company, however, will afford to purchasers every facility for employing at current and reasonable rates carriers and packers, doing so, however, without any assumption of responsibility on its part for the acts and charges of the parties engaged for such service.

13. The records of the auctioneers and the auction company are in all cases to be considered final, and the highest bid shall in all cases be accepted by both buyer and seller as the value against which all claims for losses or damages shall lie.
14. In lots where quantities are specified, articles are sold at so much each.

"Auction Market" in Stocks. Orders on stock exchanges are executed on the basis of a "free auction market" in the sense that every transaction involves a double competition—i.e., buyers compete with one another and stock is sold to the highest bidder, and sellers similarly compete with one another and stock is purchased from the lowest offeror.

See Rules 61 through 80, pertaining to the rules and policies administered by the Department of Floor Procedure governing the Auction Market, New York Stock Exchange Constitution and Rules.

BIBLIOGRAPHY

Auction Bulletin.
Auctioneer.
Weekly Auction Bulletin.
Book Auction Records. International publications Service. Annual.

AUCTION-RATE PREFERRED STOCK A type of floating-rate preferred stock whose dividend rate is based on the issuer's current credit rating. This dividend rate is reset periodically.

AUDIT A systematic process of objectively obtaining and evaluating evidence by a competent independent person about a specific entity for determining and reporting on the correspondence between assertions about economic events, actions, and other information and established criteria for reporting these assertions. An audit and the auditor's report provide additional assurance to users of financial statements concerning the information presented in the statements.

Three major types of audits include the financial statements audit, the operational audit, and the compliance audit. A financial statement audit (or attest audit) is a systematic examination of financial statements, records, and related operations to ascertain adherence to generally accepted accounting principles, management policies, and other considerations. Operational auditing is a systematic review of an organization's activities for assessing performance, identifying opportunities for improvement, and developing recommendations for improvement or further action. A compliance audit has as its objective the determination of whether the entity being audited is following procedures or rules established by a higher authority.

The audit committee is a major committee of the board of directors of a corporation. The committee is often composed of outside directors who nominate the independent auditors and react to the auditor's report and findings. Matters that the auditor believes should be brought to the attention of the shareholders should be first brought before the audit committee. The independent auditor performs an examination with the objective of issuing a report containing an opinion on a client's financial statements. The attest function of external auditing refers to the auditor's expressing an opinion on a company's financial statements. Generally, the criteria for judging an auditee's financial statements are generally accepted accounting principles. The typical audit leads to an attestation regarding the fairness and dependability of the statements that is communicated to the officials of the audited entity in the form of a written report accompanying the statements.

The auditing process is based on standards, concepts, procedures, and reporting practices. The auditing process relies on evidence, analysis, convention, and informed professional judgment. Auditing standards imposed by the American Institute of Certified Public Accountants are presented below. The standards for internal auditors are established by the Institute of Internal Auditors. The General Accounting Office establishes audit standards for governmental auditors.

AICPA AUDITING STANDARDS

General Standards

1. The examination is to be performed by a person or persons having adequate technical training and proficiency as an auditor.
2. In all matters relating to the assignment, an independence in mental attitude is to be maintained by the auditor or auditors.
3. Due professional care is to be exercised in the performance of the examination and the preparation of the report.

Standards of Field Work

1. The work is to be adequately planned and assistants, if any, are to be properly supervised.
2. There is to be a proper study and evaluation of the existing internal control as a basis for reliance thereon and for the determination of the resultant extent to which auditing procedures are to be restricted.
3. Sufficient competent evidential matter is to be obtained through inspection, observation, inquiries, and confirmations to afford a reasonable basis for an opinion regarding the financial statements under examination.

Standards of Reporting

1. The report shall state whether the financial statements are presented in accordance with generally accepted accounting principles.
2. The report shall state whether such principles have been consistently observed in the current period in relation to the preceding period.
3. Informative disclosures in the financial statements are to be regarded as reasonably adequate unless otherwise stated in the report.
4. The report shall contain either an expression of opinion regarding the financial statements, taken as a whole, or an assertion to the effect that an opinion cannot be expressed. When an overall opinion cannot be expressed, the reasons therefore should be stated. In all cases where an auditor's name is associated with financial statements the report should contain a clear-cut indication of the character of the auditor's examination, if any, and the degree of responsibility he or she is taking.

The auditor generally proceeds with an audit according to the following process:

1. Plans the audit.
2. Gathers evidence:
   a. Studies, tests, and evaluates the firm's accounting control system.
   b. Performs and evaluates substantive tests including:
      1. Independent tests of account balances and transactions, including compliance tests.
      2. Other general procedures, including analytical tests (ratios and trends) and background information (to understand the client's business, operations, and personnel).
3. Issues a report.

In planning the audit, the auditor develops an audit program that identifies and schedules audit procedures that are to be performed to obtain the evidence supporting the auditor's report. Audit evidence is proof obtained to support the audit's conclusion. Audit procedures include those activities undertaken by the auditor to obtain the evidence. Evidence-gathering procedures include observation, confirmation, calculations, analysis, inquiry, inspection, and comparison. An audit trail is a chronological record of economic events or transactions that have been experienced by an organization. The audit trail enables an auditor to evaluate the strengths and weaknesses of internal controls, system designs, company policies and procedures.

The independent audit report sets forth the independent auditor's opinion regarding the financial statements, that is, that they are fairly presented in conformity with generally accepted accounting principles applied on a basis consistent with that of the preceding year (or in conformity with some other comprehensive basis of accounting that is appropriate for the entity). A fair presentation of financial statements is generally understood by accountants to refer to whether:

1. The accounting principles used in the statements have general acceptability;
2. The accounting principles are appropriate in the circumstances.
3. The financial statements are prepared so as to favorably affect their use, understanding, and interpretation;
4. The information presented in the financial statements is classified and summarized in a reasonable manner; and
5. The financial statements reflect the underlying events and transactions in a way that presents the financial position, results of operations, and cash flows within reasonable and practical limits.

The auditor's standard report identifies the financial statements audited in an introductory paragraph, describes the nature of the audit in a scope paragraph, and expresses the auditor's opinion in a separate opinion paragraph. A typical short-form audit report on financial statements covering a single year is illustrated here.

SAMPLE INDEPENDENT AUDITOR'S REPORT

We have audited the accompanying balance sheet of X Company as of December 31, 19XX, and the related statements of income, retained earnings, and cash flows for the year then ended. These financial statements are the responsibility of the Company's management. Our responsibility is to express an opinion on these financial statements based on our audit.

We conducted our audit in accordance with generally accepted auditing standards. Those standards require that we plan and perform the audit to obtain reasonable assurance about whether the financial statements are free of material misstatement. An audit includes examining, on a test basis, evidence supporting the amounts and disclosures in the financial statements. An audit also includes assessing the accounting principles used and significant estimates made by management, as well as evaluating the overall financial statements presentation. We believe that our audit provides a reasonable basis for our opinion.

In our opinion, the financial statements referred to above present fairly, in all material respects, the financial position of X Company as of (at) December 31, 19XX, and the results of its operations and its cash flows for the year then ended in conformity with generally accepted accounting principles.

Signature
Date

The auditor's standard report identifies the financial statements audited in an introductory paragraph, describes the nature of an audit in the scope paragraph, and expresses the auditor's opinion in a separate opinion paragraph.

Various audit opinions are defined by the American Institute of Certified Public Accountants' Auditing Standards Board as follows:

1. **Unqualified opinion.** An unqualified opinion states that the financial statements present fairly, in all material respects, the finan-cial position, results of operations, and cash flows of the entity in conformity with generally accepted accounting principles.
2. **Explanatory language added to the auditor's standard report.** Circumstances may require that the auditor add an explanatory paragraph (or other explanatory language) to his or her report.
3. **Qualified opinion.** A qualified opinion states that, except for the effects of the matter(s) to which the qualification relates, the fi-nancial statements present fairly, in all material respects, the financial position, results of operations, and cash flows of the entity in conformity with generally accepted accounting principles.
4. **Adverse opinion.** An adverse opinion states that the financial statements do not represent fairly the financial position, results of operations, or cash flows of the entity in conformity with generally accepted accounting principles.
5. **Disclaimer of opinion.** A disclaimer of opinion states that the auditor does not express an opinion on the financial statements.

The fair presentation of financial statements does not mean that the statements are fraud-proof. The independent auditor has the responsibility to search for errors or irregularities within the recognized limitations of the auditing process. An auditor understands that his or her examination based on selective testing is subject to risks that material errors or irregularities, if they exist, will not be detected.

The current audit report will not use the words "subject to" that formerly served in certain situations as a cautionary sign. A "subject to" report was considered a qualified opinion of the financial results, but was removed by the AICPA's Auditing Standards Board, the major audit rule-making body. Investors should now examine the auditor's report for citation of problems such as debt-agreement violations or unresolved lawsuits. "Going concern" references can suggest that the company may not be able to survive as a functioning operation. If an "except for" statement appears in the report, the investor should understand that there are certain problems or departures from generally accepted accounting principles in the statements that question whether the statements present fairly the company's financial position and that will require the company to resolve the problem or somehow make the accounting treatment acceptable.

Auditors sometimes perform social audits and statutory audits. A social audit is an examination of an accounting entity in areas of social and environmental concerns, such as minority relations, waste management, etc. A statutory audit is an audit performed to comply with requirements of a governing body, such as a federal, state, or city government.

Internal auditing is an independent appraisal function established by an organization to examine and evaluate its activities as a service to the organization. Internal auditors are employees of the organizations whose activities they evaluate. The primary focus of internal auditing is the determination of the extent to which the organization adheres to managerial policies, procedures, or requirements.

The legal responsibilities of the auditor are determined primarily by the following:

1. Specific contractual obligations undertaken,
2. Statutes and the common law governing the conduct and responsibilities of public accountants, and
3. Rules and regulations of voluntary professional organizations.

Bank audits may be conducted by professional public accountants, by directors of the bank, or by the staff auditor of the Auditing Department. "Quasi audits" conducted by official bank examiners are known as examinations.

See BANK EXAMINATION, ACCOUNTANT.

BIBLIOGRAPHY

American Institute of Certified Public Accountants Professional Standards. Vol. I: U.S. Auditing Standards, Commerce Clearing House, Chicago, IL.
———. *Audits of Banks*, 1983.
———. *Audits of Finance Companies*, 1973.
———. *Auditing: A Journal of Practice & Theory.*
BANK ADMINISTRATION INSTITUTE. *Anticipatory Auditing Using Key Indicators.* Bank Administration Institute, Rolling Meadows, IL, 1985.
———. *Internal Auditing in the Banking Industry.* Three volumes, 1984.
BAVISHI, V. B., and WYMAN, H. E. *Who Audits the World?* Center for Transactional Accounting and Financial Research, University of Connecticut, Storrs, CT, 1983.
EDWARDS, R. *Control and Audit of EFT.* Bank Administration Institute, Rolling Meadows, IL, 1988.
HARRIS, S. *Who Audits America.* Data Financial, Menlo Park, CA, Latest edition.
HERMANSON, ROGER H., STRAWSER, JERRY R., and STRAWSER, ROBERT H. *Auditing Theory and Practice*, Fifth ed., 1989.
Koltveit, J.M. *Accounting for Banks.* 1986.
McGLADREY & PULLEN. *Banking Industry Manual.* McGladrey & Pullen, Minneapolis, MN, 1987.

MILLER, M. A. *Miller Comprehensive GAAS Guide.* 1982. Troy, MO. Annual.

PEAT MARWICK, MAIN & CO. *Principles and Presentation: Banking.* Peat Marwick, Main & Co., New York, NY. Annual.

AUDITING DEPARTMENT The department of the bank which supervises the bookkeeping, accounting, and auditing functions, usually in the charge of an officer known as an auditor. The purpose of this department is to secure a daily control of all transactions occurring in each department by condensing the department proofs; to secure periodic reconciliations of customers' accounts and to make investigations of errors and exceptions reported; to analyze expenses and earnings; to conduct examinations of the departments having custody over the bank's assets to verify the physical existence of the assets as reported upon the books and to appraise these assets as a safeguard against possible overvaluation; to secure an independent accounting control over each department in order to test the accuracy of its records; and to compile various reports and statements of condition as may be required by the bank's officers, official bank examiners, comptroller of the currency, or State Banking Department. As usually organized, this department combines with auditing the functions of comptrolling.

AUDITOR Broadly, one who conducts an AUDIT. The auditor in a bank is organizationally the officer of the institution charged with responsibility for establishing and maintaining controls, including the continuous types of internal verification; for systematically examining and verifying the banks' accounts and records; and for reporting directly either to the president of the bank or to the board of directors or trustees.

See AUDITING DEPARTMENT, BANK EXAMINERS, CERTIFIED PUBLIC ACCOUNTANT, INTERNAL AUDITING.

AUDITOR'S REPORT A statement made by an independent certified public accountant or accounting firm in which the accountant or the firm expresses an opinion, using standardized terminology, that: (1) the accountant or firm has examined and tested the records upon which a company's financial statements were prepared, and (2) in its OPINION whether the current year's financial statements present fairly the financial position, results of operations, retained earnings, and cash flows for the company in conformity with GENERALLY ACCEPTED ACCOUNTING PRINCIPLES (GAAP) applied on a basis consistent with that of the previous year. If an opinion cannot be issued, the auditor would then issue a qualified opinion, an adverse opinion, or a disclaimer of opinion. The annual report is addressed to the group or individual(s) that requested them—including the stockholders and/or the board of directors. The introductory paragraph identifies the responsibilities of both the client and the auditor regarding the financial statements. The auditor(s) discuss the scope of their examination in what is called the scope paragraph. They express their opinion in the opinion paragraph. The reports are dated as of the date the audit work was completed and is signed by a member of the CPA firm.

See AUDIT.

AUDIT RISK The risk that the auditor may fail to appropriately modify his or her opinion on financial statements that are materially misstated.

AUTARCHY Economic self-sufficiency. Also spelled autarkie and autarchie, this term has European, and especially German, connotations, although it was suggested to von Schmoller by the writings of Aristotle, and the concept is at least as old as the ancient Greeks. A nation has applied the principles of autarchy when it endeavors to provide for all, or as many as possible, of its home needs by means of its domestic raw material resources, technical equipment, and labor. Absolutely applied, it means that a nation would neither export or import, but would become an autonomous economic unit, relying entirely upon itself. Autarchy, however theoretically desirable as a defensive policy, as during a war, is practically impossible to attain completely, since no nation possesses the natural resources and climatic conditions to produce the variety of finished products essential to civilized life. Autarchy is an expression of extreme nationalism, or of nationalistic idealism, and exists more in the breach than in the observance.

AUTHORITY AND AGENCY BONDS Authorities and agencies are created by the federal and state government including their subdivisions to perform specific functions, such as the operation of water, electric systems, bridges, tunnel, schools and highways. The authority or agency often has the authority to levy fees and charges for its services. Authorities and agencies are sometimes authorized to issue bonds to support their activities. Such bonds are usually referred to as authority and agency bonds. When issued by states or their subdivisions, they are tax-exempt securities.

AUTHORITY TO PURCHASE An instrument used as a substitute for the commercial letter of credit. A foreign shipment may be financed by the importer, through either a letter of credit or an authority to purchase. The former instrument vests the exporter with the right to draw drafts upon a bank. On the other hand, an authority to purchase instructs the shipper to draw his draft upon the importer directly, but assures him or her that the draft will be purchased by the notifying bank. Thus, the authority to purchase gives rise to private bills rather than bankers acceptances.

Authorities to purchase apply almost exclusively to far eastern commerce, to facilitate exports from the U.S. to far eastern countries. They are practically always issued in dollars. They follow the same differences as a LETTER OF CREDIT as to tenor of drafts, documents required, form of currency, and privilege of cancellation.

A sample authority to purchase is appended.

Sample Authority to Purchase

No. _____

AUTHORITY TO PURCHASE

The _____ Bank

Hong Kong _____ 19 __

To _____

Dear Sirs:

We hereby authorize you to negotiate to the debit of our account, the drafts drawn by _____ on _____ of _____ at _____ sight, up to the aggregate amount of _____ to _____ Insurance against all risks is to be effected by the shipper, unless otherwise instructed.

Drafts are to be made out in duplicate and to contain the clause "with interest added at the rate of _____ per annum from date hereof to approximate date of receipt of remittance in _____ and to be accompanied by a full set of Bills of Lading, or Parcel Post Receipts, or Insurance Policies (all made out or indorsed to the order of the _____ Bank), and invoices of goods shipped for the amount of such drafts.

Drafts drawn under this Authority to Purchase must also state that they are "Drawn under _____ Bank A/P No. _____ , dated _____ 19 __

This authority remains in force until _____ 19 __ , and is subject to revocation or irrevocable without the consent of the beneficiaries.

AUTHORIZED BONDS The amount of bonds which a corporation, state, or municipality may legally issue. Corporations are not required to issue at one time the entire amount authorized in the indenture. A part of the bonds authorized may be held awaiting the need for additional capital. Power to issue bonds usually is fixed in general by the corporation laws of the home state of incorporation and in specifics by the corporate charter, and usually requires minimum voting consent of the stockholders. In the case of public utility and railroad corporations, bonds cannot be issued without the permission of the administrative agencies concerned (in the case of public utilities, the SEC, FPC, FCC among federal agencies within their jurisdictions and the state utility commissions concerned; and in the case of railroads, the ICC). A state or municipality is usually not permitted to issue bonds in excess of the debt limit specified by law. In the case of municipalities, this limit is usually based upon total assessed valuation of property within the jurisdiction.

See BOND, INDENTURE, CLOSED END MORTGAGE, OPEN MORTGAGE.

ENCYCLOPEDIA OF BANKING AND FINANCE

AUTHORIZED CAPITAL STOCK The amount of CAPITAL STOCK which a corporation is authorized to issue according to its charter or certificate of incorporation. A corporation is not required to issue the entire amount of stock authorized. The difference between the authorized stock and the unissued amount would include the outstanding stock and any treasury stock, the latter technically being issued but not outstanding stock. Stock of business corporations may be issued for cash, services, or property actually received for the use and lawful purposes of the corporation, or distributed as stock dividends; but in order to have the status of fully paid and nonassessable stock (limited liability), it must not be issued for a consideration less than its par value if it has par value, or less than any minimum specified by law, if it has no par value. A corporation may change its authorized capital stock, but only by amendment to its certificate of incorporation.

AUTOMATED BOND SYSTEM Since 1976, the NEW YORK STOCK EXCHANGE has transformed the former nonelectronic bond trading market into the automated bond system (ABS), with computer-based capabilities. This system has done away with the need to manually search the cabinets. With a press of a button of the ABS console in the subscriber's office, the current best bid and offer with sizes is carried on the New York Stock Exchange's Bond Quotation Service.

The quote display provides complete details of an issue, including the bond symbol, yield to maturity, interest rate and maturity date, price and time of opening trade, and tick information along with price and date of the previous last sale, best bid and offer with size, volume figures, news indicators, date of the last interest payment, and interest accrued to settlement.

Coupled with this firm quote information are the data available through the ABC cabinet display, where every order on file for a particular bond is shown, and the ABS terminal order entry and automatic matching capabilities for order entry and order execution.

The NYSE considers that its automated bond system has created a new market for bonds, a market that is based on protecting the best interests of investors while offering an efficient alternative to cumbersome odd-lot alternative dealings. The NYSE is now considered the primary marketplace for odd-lot business, offering competitive prices, depth, and liquidity.

AUTOMATED CLEARING HOUSE An automated clearing house (ACH) processes and delivers electronic debit and credit payments among participating depository institutions.

Electronic debits include preauthorized insurance premiums and mortgage payments, deducted from a customer's account at a depository institution. Electronic credits include preauthorized direct deposit of paychecks and corporate dividends, added to a customer's account at a depository institution.

Participating institutions primarily are commercial banks, savings banks, savings and loan associations, credit unions, and foreign bank branches and agencies in the U.S.

ACHs bear similarity to check clearing houses where checks are exchanged among member institutions. However, at check clearing houses, checks are not sorted, and payment instructions are carried on paper-the check. At an ACH, a sorting operation is performed, and payment instructions are recorded electronically, such as on magnetic tape.

During the past 20 years, the Federal Reserve System has played an active role in promoting the modernization of the nation's payments system. One major step has been to provide automated clearing house services to participating depository institutions. At last count, there were 28 automated clearing houses in the U.S., serving more than 24,000 participating depository institutions. Since 1978, all ACHs have participated in an interregional network that enables an ACH to exchange electronic payments with others throughout the nation. Previously, an ACH only could receive and exchange payments for institutions located in the area it served.

With the exception of the ACH in the Second Federal Reserve District, ACHs are operated by Federal Reserve banks, in cooperation with local ACH associations. The ACH in the Second Federal Reserve District, the New York Automated Clearing House, is operated by the New York Clearing House Association. (The Second Federal Reserve District comprises New York State, the 12 northern and central counties of New Jersey, and Fairfield County, Connecticut.) The Federal Reserve Bank of New York provides support services to the NYACH, such as settlement, interregional transmission of ACH payments data to other ACHs, and delivery of ACH payments date by courier to participating district depository institutions outside New York City.

As a fiscal agent of the U.S., the New York Federal Reserve Bank also provides electronic payments support services for the U.S. Treasury's ACH-based program for direct deposit of federal recurring payments. These include Social Security payments, Veterans Administration benefits, and federal salary payments.

There are at least five participants in an ACH transaction. The first is the customer or employee, who authorizes electronic entries to be applied to an account at a depository institution. For example, a customer may authorize a company to withdraw funds electronically from a bank account on a specified day to pay recurring bills. Alternatively, an employee may authorize a company to deposit checks electronically into the employee's account on paydays.

The second participant is a company which introduces the electronic payment data into the banking system through its depository institution. The company originated the ACH payments data.

The third participant is the originating depository institution, which receives the electronic payment data from the company. The originating depository institution retains the payments to be applied to accounts of its customers and forwards the remaining electronic payments to the ACH.

The fourth component is the ACH, which receives the electronic entries from the originating depository institution and processes and delivers the electronic payments to the appropriate receiving depository institution. Settlement is made on the books of a Federal Reserve Bank. The ACH transmits electronic entries for institutions served by other ACHs to the appropriate ACH. The final participant is the receiving depository institution, which receives the electronic entries from the ACH and posts them to the accounts of its customers.

The ACHs enable speedier payments and reductions in costs for participating institutions. Consumers also benefit by having paychecks or federal recurring payments deposited directly and safely in their depository institutions, or by having recurring bills paid automatically, without having to write a check or deliver cash.

See AUTOMATION, CLEARINGHOUSE, ELECTRONIC FUND TRANSFER ACT.

AUTOMATED CUSTOMER SERVICES The computerized nonbanking transaction, reporting, and recordkeeping functions performed by the bank for customers. The term is also used to describe the automated services that one bank sells to another.

AUTOMATED TELLER MACHINES (ATMs) Devices that can mechanically accept deposits, issue withdrawals, transfer funds between accounts, collect bills, and make small loans. It is estimated that ATMs can perform 90% of a bank's routine operations.

ATMs often function around the clock and may be located either on the premises of the financial institution that owns them or at some remote location off the premises. The exact services offered by ATMs and their location are dictated by the institutions that own them and the restrictions imposed by state law.

The issue of whether an ATM should legally be considered a bank branch has been the subject of controversy. For state chartered banks, this issue is left to the states. For national banks, the issue was decided in 1985 by the U.S. Court of Appeals in the case of *Independent Bankers Association of New York State* vs. *Marine Midland Bank*. The appeals court upheld the view of the Comptroller of the Currency that an ATM owned or rented by a national bank was a branch. Banks are free to join together in ATM networks without violating interstate branching laws.

Many financial institutions have formed regional or national networks of ATMs since the late 1970s. These networks can be used by customers of any one of the participating institutions.

ATMs offer bank customers the convenience of 24-hour operation and easy access at numerous locations. Many ATMs were found not to be cost effective. However, the institutions that have invested heavily in ATMs predict the networks will become more profitable as the cost of human tellers increases and the public becomes more accepting of computerized transaction devices.

BIBLIOGRAPHY

BAKER, D. *The Law of Electronic Fund Transfer Systems*. Warren, Gorham & Lamont, 1986.
PETENERSON, K. *The Automated Teller Machine As a National Bank Under the Federal Law*. W. S. Hein Publisher, 1988.

AUTOMATIC CURRENCY See ELASTIC CURRENCY.

AUTOMATIC STABILIZERS Economic factors which automatically exert countercyclical effects in a depression or inflation. For example:

1. **Unemployment insurance.** In a period of decreased employment, contributions to the system based on payroll taxes would decrease whereas payments to the increased number of unemployed would increase, thereby preventing personal income (which includes such transfer payments) from falling as far as it otherwise would. In an inflationary expansion, unemployment insurance contributions would increase as payrolls expand, whereas payments would decrease because unemployment would decline in such an upturn in the cycle, thus decreasing the inflation in personal income.
2. **Progressive income taxes (with steeply graduated rates).** These would cause sharp increase in tax revenues as taxable incomes rise in an inflation, thus restraining the inflation in disposable personal incomes; and would cause sharp fall in tax revenues as taxable incomes fall in a deflation, thus making disposable personal incomes larger than they would otherwise be.

In the "new economics," the concept of automatic stabilizers is not favored, although it originated in early Keynesian economics, because they create "fiscal drag" in the attainment of growth objectives, creating tax "surpluses" embarrassing to continued expansion; and, unless strongly modified (e.g., by introduction of "negative taxes" or "compulsory saving") they are not considered strong enough to exercise appreciable countercyclical effects. They might also be anathema because of their comfortable implication of automaticity, which might prevent full use of compensatory FISCAL POLICY. Instead of allowing the restraint of high progressive income tax rates to operate, reductions in income tax rates in recent years of record prosperity have been justified in order to attain even higher levels of gross national product, and thus to close the fiscal gap between actual level of GNP and full potential GNP.

(For review and justification of the famous 1964 income tax cuts, both before and after, see Council of Economic Advisers, Annual Reports, 1964 and 1965.)

AUTOMATIC TRANSFER SERVICE A banking service provided by commercial banks that allows a bank to debit savings accounts to cover checks written against checking accounts. This service allows the depositor to earn interest on a transaction balance until the funds are actually spent. The Consumer Checking Account Equity Act of 1980 governs the offering of ATSs.

AUTOMATION In bank operations, the use of electronic equipment. Bank automation has accelerated both extensively, in number of banks automating, and intensively, in types of operations automated within banks. A checkless society is envisioned for the future, with the development of communication links between the computer and bank customers; linkage of consumers to a central system (customer terminal); and development of customer identification and verification systems for use at customer terminals. A corollary is expansion of techniques of operations research into the field of bank management. A further corollary is that electronic technology can be and is increasingly provided by nonbank competition.

Bank Applications. Bank applications currently computerized include bank cost accounting; central information file; charge accounts or credit cards; commercial loans; corporate trust; demand deposits; general ledger; installment credit; lines of credit; mortgage loans; personal trusts; proof and transit; and savings. Example of what one medium-sized bank has computerized includes the following activities:

1. *Proof and transit operations and demand deposit accounting:* "capturing" of on-us items; item count; float information; daily uncollected funds figures (making it impossible to "kite" checks); statistical analyses of account profitability (useful also in considering loan applications); management reports.
2. *Bank expense accounting:* divisional and departmental reports.
3. *Payroll accounting:* automatic deposits to employees' accounts; labor cost distribution; preparation of 941A reports and W-2 forms.
4. *Checking account reconciliation:* relieving commercial depositors of reconciliation problems.
5. *Passbook savings accounts:* computation of monthly interest.
6. Money order operations.
7. *Personal trust accounting:* cash statements; summary of assets; daily cash book; tax work sheet; overdraft reports; excessive balance reports; bond maturity and call reports; fee forecasts; registration reports; updating accounts daily; updating security prices; automatic posting of bond interest.
8. *Bond and investment analysis:* income and expense data; pledge data; market profit or loss information; location and cash flow information for audit control; actual general ledger entries.
9. *Mortgage loan program:* investor information in addition to normal accounting reports; use of magnetic ink character recognition (MICR) encoded turnaround remittances with notices and receipts mailed; improvement in MICR checking account reconciliation; budget accounting program developed and correlated with total expense accounting program.
10. *Installment loans:* use of MICR input and development of "pseudoledger card." including all necessary information for handling late and bad accounts, for collection purposes.
11. *Corporate stock transfer:* all stock transfer and division accounting.
12. *Disk file:* for total management information program.
13. *Integrated security file:* for trusts, safekeeping, commercial loan collateral, and bank's own investment portfolio.
14. *Computer log usage analysis:* monthly evaluation of computer system efficiency and cost analysis by applications.

Operations Research. In addition to enabling banks to maximize efficiencies in performing clerical and recordkeeping operations, computers also facilitate quick mathematical testing of models and quantification of tested models from centralized management information, involved in operations research-essentially the application of a variety of scientific methods, techniques, and tools of analysis to particular problems for optimal or most feasible solutions and methods.

The Checkless Society. If money transfers can be made instantly by electronic communication with computers storing the details and changes of the accounts involved, there is a basis for expecting the development of the "checkless society", an era of electronic payments and credits. "Checkless society" refers to a system for transfer of funds that may largely replace the bulk of check volume, since smaller institutions particularly may quite effectively compete with automated institutions by emphasizing personalized services. For example:

1. Instead of drawing checks, depositors would activate low-cost "input terminals" (e.g., Touch-Tone pushbotton telephones) installed in places of business and in homes, triggered by customer identification cards.

    Such input devices would be connected with the computer storing the details of accounts and activated to make the necessary debits and credits, as well as to respond to requests for current balances in such accounts. Periodic credits to accounts, such as salaries, wages, contractual payments, etc., would be automatically made, with concurrent debits to the paying accounts, by the computer by prearrangement.
2. Instead of current charge account practice, the customer presents his bank card dialer identification card to the store clerk; the clerk inserts it in Touch-Tone telephone connected with the computer, which identifies the customer when the latter taps out his secret identification code on the telephone keyboard; the clerk taps out the amount of the purchase and the departmental code; the computer records the addition to the store's accounts receivable. (Here, if accounts receivable financing is involved, the bank could automatically discount the receivable, crediting net proceeds to the store's deposit account.)

At the end of the month, the store will receive a statement of receivables; the customer will receive a statement along with prepunched bill payment cards bearing the store's account number and distinctive printing, punched and printed with due date and amount due. To pay, the customer inserts the identification card in the card dialer telephone, inserts the bill payment card, and activates the computer to transfer the amount of payment from the customer's account to the store's account on the due date punched on the bill payment card. The card dialer telephone device could be located in a telephone booth, a supermarket or other store, the post office, etc., requiring no coin for operation (the bank could cover the cost by arrangement with the telephone company).

Implications. Those who have thought out the implications of electronic banking foresee a number of possible fundamental changes and impacts upon the financial system:

1. A decrease in the number of banks. Governor Mitchell of the Federal Reserve Board believed such a reduction in number of banks is indicated because smaller banks will find it difficult to compete with the larger banks offering electronic banking services. On the other hand, smaller banks are offered off-premises computer service.
2. Lessened need for extensive systems of branch offices. Branch offices might develop into automated electronic banking stations, where customers activating the equipment could contact central computer headquarters for lines of credit, check on current balances, make deposits, or take withdrawals in cash from activated equipment like a vending machine. Current branch banking restrictions might become academic in an era of telephone banking offered by the larger banks.
3. Greater velocity (turnover) of a smaller necessary volume of demand deposits, which might therefore shift to larger totals of time and savings deposits. Monetary controls would require greater quantitative impact upon bank reserves, to offset higher velocity. Because of their effects upon velocity, time and savings deposits (near money) might require greater controls both intensively and extensively (possibly subjecting noncommercial banks to Federal Reserve controls).
4. Higher fees and activity charges, especially because of interest cost of expanded volume of time and savings deposits and the higher velocity of deposits. Emphasis on marketing of services.
5. Reduced float and quicker availability of credits to accounts.
6. Fiercer competition for consumer credit, for volume-geared electronic banking systems, interbank as well as by private credit card companies and among retailers.
7. Possibility of public utility status for any single bank computer system serving an area, requiring availability to competing institutions such as savings banks and savings and loan associations, and rate regulations.
8. Impersonalized banking service for individuals. Some individuals may prefer present conventional system, with canceled checks as record of payments, opportunity for float and delayed payments, and personalized contacts with local tellers and floor officers.
9. Centralization of account data of borrowers and depositors in computer centers. This would make for easier collection of banking data, tax collections, and credit-checking. Unless controls are assured, some firms and individuals might object to such pooling of confidential data on accounts.
10. Necessary adjustments to antitrust law, banking law, and commercial code, and in training of bank personnel.

Some Common Abbreviations in Bank Automation:

ABACUS	American Bankers Association Computer Utilization System.
ACH	Automated clearinghouse.
ATM	Automated teller machine.
ATS	Automatic transfer service (type of account).
CUSIP	Common uniform security identification procedure.
EDP	Electronic data processing.
EFTS	Electronic fund transfer service.
MICR	Magnetic ink character recognition.
MIS	Management information system.
PIP	Personal identification project.
POS	Point of sale electronic transfer payments system.
SAVE	System for automatic value exchange.

BIBLIOGRAPHY

BAKER, D. *The Law of Electronic Fund Transfer Systems.* Warren, Gorham & Lamont, 1986.

PETENERSON, K. *The Automated Teller Machine As a National Bank under the Federal Law.* W.S. Hein Publisher, 1988.

AUTOMOBILE BACKED Pools of car loans serve as collateral.

AUTOMOBILE LENDING Banks make both direct and indirect loans on new automobiles. They represent one form of consumer credit lending. Such loans typically have a maximum maturity of 48 months, although longer terms are sometimes provided. Direct automobile loans are loans made to the purchaser/consumer for the purchase of an automobile; the automobile secures the loan through a chattel mortgage. Indirect automobile loans are made to automobile dealers. In indirect lending, the purchaser/consumer applies for a loan from the dealer who collects credit information from the customer and conveys this information to the bank. The bank then indicates acceptance or rejection of the loan request. Banks usually acquire indirect loans from dealers in packages. Packages can contain loans that vary in quality and acceptability. Delinquencies on such packages can be expected to be higher than those on direct loans.

Banks also offer floorplan financing to dealers and support dealers' leasing programs. Floor planning finance (trust receipt financing) is a form of inventory financing. In floor planning finance, title of the inventory is temporarily given to the bank. The borrower is given funds to pay for goods obtained from suppliers. The borrower holds the inventory in trust for the bank by issuing a trust receipt to the bank. As the borrower sells the inventory, the borrower sends the proceeds to the bank. Frequently, the borrower also sells its credit sales to the bank that provides a form of continuous financing for the borrower.

It is estimated that the percentage of consumer income allotted to car purchases fell to about 5% in the early 1980s compared with 6.7% in the late 1970s. Automobile loans represent the largest single loan type and account for more than 40% of the total consumer credit market at the end of 1986. The market share held by commercial banks declined from 49.2% at the end of 1983 to 40.4% as of September 1986. This decline is partially attributed to domestic automobile manufacturer interest subvention programs and leasing programs. In subvention programs, the man-ufacturer subsidizes the lender to offer below market rates to the consumer to stimulate car sales. Consumer response to both interest subvention and leasing programs was positive. Banks have sometimes offered longer maturities on automobile loans to remain competitive. Other banks have transferred their lending efforts to other areas of the consumer credit market. Banks have also used a closed-end program with a final balloon payment (residual value financing) that provide some of the features of leasing. The customer has the option of selling the vehicle and using the funds to pay the balloon payment or financing the balance due for an additional term. Balloon payment loans increase the credit risk associated with the loan because the customer does not establish a satisfactory equity interest in the property used as collateral.

AVAILABILITY DATE First read FEDERAL RESERVE CHECK COLLECTION SYSTEM.

The date upon which the proceeds of checks or other items drawn on out-of-town banks, and forwarded by the sending bank for collection through the Federal Reserve check collection system, are received and credited by the Federal Reserve bank to the reserve account of the sending bank. Each Federal Reserve bank publishes a "Schedule Showing When the Proceeds of Items Will Become Available," covering every point in the U.S., so that member or clearing member banks sending checks for collection through a Federal Reserve bank may know on what days such checks will be credited to their reserve accounts.

AVAILABLE FUND(S) This term has two meanings:

1. A fund held by a nonstock savings bank in cash or on deposit with another bank or trust company for the purpose of paying withdrawals in excess of current receipts, meeting current obligations, or awaiting a more favorable opportunity for investment. In New York State this fund is limited to 20% of deposits.
2. Total funds of a bank available at any time for conversion into earning assets or other investment are not only its deposits but its total capital funds and any borrowed money as well.

AVAILS *See* NET AVAILS.

AVERAGE In ocean shipping, the loss or damage sustained by a ship or its cargo, or the amount payable by the owner of the ship and the owners of the cargo to make good such loss or damage.

Average is of two classes—particular and general. A particular average is borne entirely by the owner (or his insurer) of the particular property which is lost or damaged, whether a part of the ship or of its cargo. The loss of or damage to any particular property cannot be assessed among all the cargo owners. A general average, however, is one incurred in the common interests of the ship and cargo and is borne by all the parties interested in the ship and cargo, in proportion to such interests as ascertained by persons known as average adjusters. Jettison (throwing overboard a certain part of the cargo in order to save the rest) is a loss that would be defined as a general average.

See DOW JONES AVERAGES, MARKET AVERAGES, STOCK PRICE AVERAGES.

AVERAGE BALANCE In the case of a borrowing account, the average balance maintained by borrowers against loans or LINE OF CREDIT is a principal determinant of account profitableness for a bank, similar to minimum free balance in the case of conventional checking (nonborrowing) account. Usually banks request borrowers to keep on deposit about 20% of borrowings in order to maintain a relative proportion between credit extended and cash balances, and to provide for cash withdrawal needs of other borrowing customers.

See COMPENSATING BALANCES, TWENTY PERCENT RULE.

AVERAGE COLLECTION PERIOD In RATIO ANALYSIS of financial statements, the average number of days of credit sales represented by average total ACCOUNTS RECEIVABLE. When compared to the terms of sale on credit sales, it affords a test of current collectibility of the accounts receivable.

Calculation may be made directly as follows (assume annual credit sales of $7,200,000 on terms of "$^2/_{10}, ^n/_{30}$" and average accounts receivable of $600,000):

$$\frac{\text{accts. receivable } \$600,000}{\text{credit sales } \$7,200,000} \times 360 = 30 \text{ days}$$

Thus, the average collection period in this case is in line with maximum credit terms; but since it is a dollar average, including accounts that take the cash discount by paying in 10 days, AGING OF RECEIVABLES would indicate dollar amounts of any accounts past due, and how long past due.

See ACCOUNTS RECEIVABLE TURNOVER, CREDIT BAROMETRICS, STATEMENT ANALYSIS.

AVERAGE LOAN AND BALANCE FILE A card file or book customarily kept by banks to show each customer's average daily or monthly loans and deposits over a period of, say, 10 years. The information posted on these cards is obtained from the depositors' ledgers and the loan and bills discounted ledgers. It furnishes a quick and convenient means of obtaining important information concerning depositors' accounts, e.g., (1) amount of average deposits and loans as a measure of profitableness; (2) the average balance as a measure of possible borrowing power when applying for a loan; (3) whether the average balance is in proportion to loans (usually 20% average balance is required to be maintained against loans); and (4) whether the deposit balance is increasing or decreasing.

See CENTRAL FILE.

AVERAGE RESERVE POSITION *See* RESERVE.

AVERAGES *See* DOW JONES AVERAGES, INDEX NUMBERS, MARKET AVERAGES, STOCK PRICE AVERAGES.

AVERAGING A method used by stock market investors and speculators to reduce the cost of purchases. "Averaging down" means to buy more stock of a given issue at a price less than the last purchase successively as the price declines. "Averaging up" means to buy more of a given security at successively higher prices as prices advance. This method is employed out of recognition of the fact that the high and low points of a price movement cannot be exactly predicted. Averaging, therefore, is a method of insurance against altogether missing the market. Where a constant sum is periodically and regularly invested, at whatever prices prevail at the time of such investment, dollar averaging results, basically a defensive technique insofar as the problem of price fluctuation is concerned.

AWARD In general, the decision of a board of arbitrators, commission, investigators, mediators, or broadly even the decision of judges or referees, on the case, question, or matter that has been submitted to them for decision. Technically, the term refers to the decision of a panel of arbitrators.

Also, the acceptance of a competitive bid to buy a block of securities. Bond issues, particularly municipal bonds, are frequently offered for sale to competitive buyers under sealed bids. This term is generally used to indicate the formal acceptance by the proper authorities of the offer to purchase (bid) by the investment banking group which has been the successful bidder.

See COMPETITIVE BIDDING.

B

BABY BONDS Bonds with denominations of $100, and even less ($50, $25, or $10), issued as a means of reaching small investors and thus widening the possible market and permitting increased diversification for small investors. Baby bonds, however, are not a GOOD DELIVERY.

BACK An abbreviated term for BACKWARDATION.

BACKDATING The placing on a document a date prior to the date on which it has been prepared or drawn. Backdating usually has an illegal or unethical purpose.

BACK SPREAD *First read* ARBITRAGE.

In arbitrage transactions in securities, commodities, or foreign exchange when the price of the same thing in different markets is less than the normal difference. Suppose, for example, United States Steel is selling on the New York Stock Exchange at $90 and on the London Stock Exchange at $93. The difference in the quotations represents a permanent difference due to cost of shipment, insurance, exchange rates, loss of interest, etc., making them equivalent or establishing commercial parity. Assuming three points to be the normal difference in quotations for this stock between these two markets, no profit could be made by buying in New York and selling in London or vice versa. If, however, the London quotations should be less than $93, say $91, making the difference less than normal, a profit could be made by buying the stock in London and selling simultaneously in New York. Such a transaction is known as a back spread.

A back spread differs from a SPREAD in that in the latter the difference in price between two markets is greater than the normal difference.

BACK-TO-BACK Operations where a loan is made in one cur-rency in one nation against a loan in another currency in another nation; credit opened by a bank on the strength of another credit. Back-to-back letters of credit are two letters of credit with identical documentary requirements, except for a difference in the price of merchandise as shown by the invoice and the draft.

BACKWARDATION The practice of delaying settlement on the London Stock Exchange. Suppose a speculator who has sold stock for delivery at the next fortnightly settlement wishes to postpone the delivery until the following settlement period because he or she believes that the price of the security will in the meantime decline. Accordingly he or she arranges with his or her broker to postpone delivery. This is secured either through obtaining the consent of the purchaser to delay delivery for a consideration or by borrowing the stock from someone else. The consideration or charge made by the purchaser or lender of the stock for the privilege granted to the seller by extending the time of delivery is called backwardation. Backwardation is paid by the seller, while CONTANGO is paid by the buyer.

See SETTLEMENT DAYS.

BAD DEBT ALLOWANCE An allowance for probable loss on credit accounts in the valuation of ACCOUNTS RECEIVABLE for financial reporting purposes. The allowance is created under the accounting reserve method by entries debiting (increasing) allowance for bad debts (a VALUATION RESERVE), reported as a deduction from gross (ACCOUNTS RECEIVABLE). When a specific account receivable actually proves to be partially or completely uncollectible, the charge-off should be made by debiting (reducing) the allowance for bad debts and crediting (reducing) gross accounts receivable. A periodic review of actual loss experience should indicate whether the rate or method of setting the allowance for bad debts should be changed to reflect more accurately probable losses.

BAD DEBTS In valuation of ACCOUNTS RECEIVABLE, the usually anticipatory allowance for probable loss on accounts. The loss may be matched to the credit sales when they occur by entry debiting bad debts expense (expense item, closed out to the profit and loss statement) and crediting allowance for bad debts (valuation reserve, reported as a deduction from gross accounts receivable). Subsequently when the accounts actually prove to be partially or completely lost, debit to allowance for bad debts and credit to gross accounts receivable would effect the charge-off. Periodically, review of actual loss experience would call for adjustments in the allowance by change in rate or method.

For income tax purposes, bad debts may be charged to taxable income by election of either the reserve method as above (subject to test of reasonableness based on collection experience) or the specific charge-off method (losses taken in year actually sustained).

See BANK BAD DEBT RESERVES.

BAD DELIVERY In the sale and transfer of stock certain conditions are imposed by the rule of stock exchanges. These rules relate to days and hours of delivery, assignment of stock, power of attorney, etc. If deliveries are made without the proper observance of these rules, they are known as bad deliveries.

See GOOD DELIVERY.

BAHIA One of the three standard growths of cocoa.
See COFFEE, SUGAR & COCOA EXCHANGE, INC.

BAILEE One to whom personal property is delivered for some temporary specific purpose, upon completion of which it is to be returned to the owner. The bailee has temporary possession of such goods entrusted to him or her but has only a limited property interest. A railroad company which receives a shipment of goods for transportation under a contract of bailment, called the bill of lading, is a bailee. Warehousepersons who accept property for storage are also bailees, the contract of bailment being a warehouse receipt.

Safe deposit companies which receive the valuables of customers for safekeeping act as bailees, and as such have a lien on the property deposited in case rentals are not paid after a specified time. While the laws in the various states differ, as a rule if the rental on a safe deposit box is not paid for two years, notice may be sent to the renter that, if not paid before, the contents will be sold in 30 days for payment of the rent.

When a bank or trust company acts as custodian of securities, it is a bailee.

BAILEE RECEIPT A receipt given to a bank holding title to goods by a bailee, a customer of the bank who is permitted to sell them for the account of the owning bank. Bailee receipts are often used in lieu of trust receipts given upon release of documents covering imports for the purpose of warehousing, selling, or manufacturing. The TRUST RECEIPT has proved to be inadequate collateral and only as good as the credit standing of the signer. It has often failed the banks in pressing claims against third parties who have purchased goods from the borrower. In releasing shipping documents so that imports may be procured at the steamship terminal and sold in advance of the maturity of the draft drawn against the bank, banks sometimes require customers of doubtful standing to sign a bailee receipt. This instrument is regarded as more stringent than the trust receipt and is supposed to offer the bank greater protection. The opinion has been expressed, however, that a trust receipt is *a priori* a bailee receipt and that legally no difference exists between the two instruments.

A sample bailee receipt form is appended.

Sample Bailee Receipt Form

Received from the _____ Bank, solely for the purpose of selling the same for account of said bank, the following property, marked and numbered as follows:

_____

and _____ hereby undertake to sell said property for account of said bank, and collect the proceeds thereof and deliver the same immediately upon receipt to the said bank in whatever form collected to be applied to the credit of _____ , hereby acknowledging _____

_____ to be bailee of said property for the said bank, and _____ do hereby assign and transfer to the said bank the accounts of the purchasers of said property to the extent of the purchase price thereof, of which fact notice shall be given at the time of delivery of said property by _____ to said purchaser or purchasers, and all invoices therefor shall have printed, written, or stamped thereon the following: "Transferred and payable to the _____ Bank."

If said property is not sold and the proceeds so deposited within ten days from this date, _____ undertake to return all documents at once upon demand or to pay the value of the goods at the bank's option.

The said goods while in our hands shall be fully insured against loss by fire for the benefit of the bank.

The terms of this receipt and agreement shall continue and apply to the merchandise above referred to, whether or not control of the same or any part thereto be at any time restored to the _____ Bank and subsequently delivered to us.

BAILMENT The deposit of personal property by a bailor with the BAILEE for a specific purpose, such as safe custody, transportation, or storage.

BAILOR A party who bails or delivers to another (the BAILEE) for a specific purpose under contract of BAILMENT.

BAILOUT The rescue of a failed bank by a regulatory authority. Supervisory authority over banks is provided by a variety of entities, including the Federal Reserve, the Federal Deposit Insurance Corporation, the Federal Savings and Loan Insurance, the Office of the Comptroller of the Currency, 50 state bank supervisors, the Justice Department, the Securities and Exchange Commission, the Treasury Department, the Federal Home Loan Bank Board, and the National Credit Union Administration. Frequently the role and function of these authorities overlap.

When a bank fails, the FDIC typically has three choices: (1) return insured depositors their money, (2) sell the bank with the assistance of the FDIC; or (3) bail it out, which is to say, prevent it from failing. The FDIC received bailout authority in 1950 and, in less restrictive language, in 1980 and 1982. The 1982 modification provided for the waiving of the prohibition against out-of-state sales for institutions with assets of at least $500 million along with a provision allowing for the providing of assistance to keep a failing bank open if such assistance is less costly than a payoff.

In a bailout, the bank remains open. A capital infusion is required from investors and/or the FDIC to preserve the bank in its present corporate existence. Insured and uninsured depositors are protected. Management is usually replaced and stockholders experience a significant dilution of their equity. Section 13(c)(4)(A) of the FDIC Act gives the FDIC board the sole discretion to bail out banks. To bail out a bank, the board must present a finding that the insured bank is in danger of failing and "is essential to provide adequate banking service in its community."

BAIT MONEY A group of bills separated from usable currency, consisting of fresh $10 or $20 bills. The serial numbers of the bills are recorded separately for use in the identification and conviction of a bank robber.

BALANCE The sum necessary to equalize the debit and credit totals of an account. A debit balance is the excess of debits over credits, and a credit balance is the excess of credits over debits. Balancing is the process of bringing two sets of related figures into agreement, as in balancing a checking account (reconciling the book balance for cash with the bank balance) and proof work (bringing total deposits in agreement with the totals of items composing the deposit).

BALANCED BUDGET AMENDMENT For over a decade there has been strong sentiment among voters to amend the Constitution to require that the federal budget be balanced each fiscal year. While such a balanced budget amendment was approved by the Senate in 1982, it was rejected by the House of Representatives in that same year.

See GRAMM-RUDMAN-HOLLINGS ACT.

BALANCE OF PAYMENTS A record of all of a country's international transactions for goods and services, IOUs, other financial assets, and investments. The balance of payments takes into consideration the spending of money abroad and foreign spending in the domestic nation. Theoretically, the U.S. balance of payments should be zero because every transaction is two-sided, with debits balancing credits. For example, if a U.S. computer company sells $50 million of computers to West Germany on a one-year credit, the U.S. current account shows a trade surplus of $50 million for the computer sale and the U.S. capital account shows a $50 million capital deficit from the IOU. The balance of payments nets to zero.

More generally, in balance-of-payments accounting, the total of all inflows from abroad equals the total of all outflows. This follows from the fact that the following accounting identity must be satisfied:

$$X - M - S - T - I - R = 0$$

where

X = Exports
M = Imports
S = Net service outflows
T = Gifts, transfers, and remittances
I = Net investment outflows
R = Net official reserve inflows

In practice, the balance of payments will not always equal zero. This can be due to, among other things, a country's central bank engaging in transactions that are not counted toward the country's balance of payments, or the lack of available statistical data to record all transactions. A typical balance of payment (in billions of dollars) could appear as follows:

Merchandise trade balance		− 36.3
Exports	+ 211.0	
Imports	− 247.3	
Military transactions, net		+ 0.6
Net investment income		+ 28.7
Receipts	+ 85.9	
Payments	− 57.2	
Net travel and transportation		
expenditures		− 1.3
Other services		+ 8.1
Balance of trade on goods and		
services		− 0.2
Remittances, pensions, and other		
unilateral transfers		− 7.9
Balance on current accounts		− 8.1

Changes in U.S. and Foreign Assets

U.S. assets abroad, net	(−)	− 118.3
U.S. official reserve	− 5.0	

BALANCE OF TRADE

U.S. Government assets		− 5.7	
U.S. private assets		− 107.6	
Foreign assets in U.S., net	(+)		+ 84.5
Foreign official assets		+ 3.0	
Other foreign assets		+ 81.5	
Statistical discrepancy			+ 41.9
			+ 8.1

The balance of payments indicates whether or not a nation will have an inflow or outflow of currency or the purchase or sale of short-term securities. Currently deficits and surpluses are settled through changes and adjustments in U.S. and foreign assets, both government and private. The lower part of the foregoing schedule indicates how the $8.1 billion deficit in the U.S. balance of payments was settled. Apparent deficits are usually settled or eliminated by changes in U.S. and foreign liquid assets and occasionally by the flow of gold.

A surplus or deficit is not as important as the means of settlement. The balance of payments is considered by some economists to be equivalent to a statement of income, showing income or loss, instead of a balance sheet.

BALANCE OF TRADE The difference between the money value of a nation's merchandise exports and imports, as shown by customs' data adjusted for differences in timing and coverage for calculation of a nation's INTERNATIONAL BALANCE OF PAYMENTS, therefore reflecting the visibles.

A more inclusive concept of items related to a nation's gross national product, including invisibles (services) as well as the visibles, is CURRENT ACCOUNT BALANCE.

See FOREIGN EXCHANGE, FOREIGN TRADE, GOLD MOVEMENTS.

BIBLIOGRAPHY

CROOK, C. "America's Next Trade Crisis." *Economist*, September 24, 1988.
DOWD, A. R. "What to Do About Trade Policy." *Fortune*, May 8, 1989.
"Why Worry About Trade Gap?" *Economist*, September 17, 1988.
SENDER, H. "Japan Bets on Its Consumers." *Institutional Investor*, September 17, 1988.

BALANCE SHEET A report that shows the financial position of the enterprise at a specific time, including the firm's economic resources (assets), economic obligations (liabilities), and the residual claims of owners (owners' equity). This financial statement is also referred to as the statement of financial position.

Assets are probable future economic benefits obtained or controlled by a particular entity as a result of past transactions or events. Liabilities are probable future sacrifices of economic benefits arising from present obligations of a particular entity to transfer assets or provide services to other entities in the future as a result of past transactions or events. Equity is the residual interest in the assets of an entity that remains after deducting its liabilities. In a business enterprise, the equity is the ownership interest. Assets are usually shown in the order of the liquidity (nearness to cash) and liabilities in the order of their maturity date.

The balance sheet is usually presented in one of the following formats:

1. Account form: Assets = Liabilities + Owners' equity
2. Report form: Assets − Liabilities = Owners' equity

The balance sheet discloses major classes and amounts of an entity's assets as well as major classes and amounts of its financing structure, including liabilities and equity. Major classifications used in the statement of financial position of business enterprises include:

1. Assets
    a. Current assets (cash, marketable securities, accounts receivable, inventory, prepaid expenses)
    b. Investments
    c. Property, plant, and equipment
    d. Intangible assets (patents, copyrights, goodwill)
    e. Deferred charges or other assets

2. Liabilities
    a. Current liabilities (accounts payable, notes payable, wages payable, accrued liabilities, unearned revenue)
    b. Long-term liabilities
3. Owners' equity (corporation)
    a. Capital stock
    b. Paid-in capital in excess of par or stated value
    c. Retained earnings

Current assets are cash and other assets that are expected to be converted into cash, sold, or consumed either in one year or in the operating cycle, whichever is longer. Current liabilities are the obligations that are reasonably expected to be liquidated either through the use of current assets or the creation of other current liabilities. Working capital is the excess of current assets over current liabilities and can be computed from data shown on the balance sheet. This significant figure is useful in determining the ability of the firm to finance current operations and to meet obligations as they mature. The relationship between current assets and current liabilities is referred to as the current ratio and is a measure of the liquidity of the enterprise.

Assets and liabilities reported on the balance sheet are measured by different attributes (for example, historical cost, current replacement cost, current market value, net realizable value, and present value of future cash flows), depending upon the nature of the item and the relevance and reliability of the attribute measured. Historical cost is the exchange price of the asset when it was acquired. Current cost is the amount of cash or cash equivalent required to obtain the same asset at the balance sheet date. Current market value or exist value is the amount of cash that may be obtained at the balance sheet date from selling the asset in an orderly liquidation. Net realizable value is the amount of cash that can be obtained as a result of a future sale of an asset. Present value is the expected exist value discounted to the balance sheet date.

Balance sheets are usually presented in comparative form. Comparative statements include the current year's statement and statements of one or more of the preceding accounting periods. Comparative statements are useful in evaluating and analyzing trends.

The balance sheet assists external users in assessing the firm's liquidity, financial flexibility, and operating capabilities and in evaluating the earning performance for the period. Liquidity describes the amount of time that is expected to elapse until an asset is realized or otherwise converted into cash or until a liability has to be paid. Financial flexibility is the ability of an enterprise to take effective actions to alter the amounts and timing of cash flows so it can respond to unexpected needs and opportunities.

The balance sheet does not reflect current value because accountants have adopted a historical cost basis in valuing and reporting most assets and liabilities. Historical or acquisition cost has the advantages of being verifiable and objective.

See ACCOUNTING, BANK BOOKKEEPING, BANK STATEMENT.

BIBLIOGRAPHY

HENRY, T. M. "Electronic Spreadsheet: A Versatile 1-2-3 Trial Balance Template." *Computer in Accounting*, April/May 1988.
WOELFEL, C. J. *Financial Statement Analysis*. Probus Publishing Co., Chicago, IL, 1986.

BALANCE SHEET TESTS See STATEMENT ANALYSIS.

BALLOONING The forcing of quotations of a given stock, or of the entire market, to unreasonably high or inflated values, i.e., to levels out of accord with asset values and present or prospective earning power.

BALLOON MATURITY LOANS Single-payment loans ("bullet" loans).

BALTIMORE PLAN Although not enacted, this banker proposal in pre-Federal Reserve days for the conversion of national bank notes into a general reserve currency is of interest in the historical development of currency reform in the U.S.

The plan was presented and approved by the convention of the American Bankers Association at Baltimore in 1894. It was proposed that the requirement in the National Bank Act for the deposit of government bonds with the U.S. Treasurer to secure the circulating notes of national banks be repealed. The proposed substitute plan recommended that the national banks be allowed to issue circulating notes up to half of their paid-up and unimpaired capital, the notes to be subject to an annual tax of 0.5%. Provision was also made for an emergency currency subject to a heavier tax, up to an additional amount of 25%. The proposal recommended that the notes should constitute a first lien on the assets of national banks and should be further secured by a 5% guaranty fund to be held by the U.S. Treasurer.

See NATIONAL BANK NOTES.

BALTIMORE STOCK EXCHANGE   See PHILADELPHIA STOCK EXCHANGE, STOCK EXCHANGES.

BANK
Any organization engaged in any or all of the various functions of banking, i.e., receiving, collecting, transferring, paying, lending, investing, dealing, exchanging, and servicing (safe deposit, custodianship, agency, trusteeship) money and claims to money both domestically and internationally. Under this broad concept, the title bank is found in the American financial system applied to such institutions as *Banks for Cooperatives, Central Bank for Cooperatives, Export-Import Bank, Federal Intermediate Credit banks, Federal Land banks,* industrial banks, investment bankers, and mortgage bankers.

In its more specific sense, however, the term bank refers to institutions providing deposit facilities for the general public. Such institutions may be classified into two broad groups: (1) commercial banks and their central banks; and (2) noncommercial bank institutions. Included in the latter group are such institutions as the savings and loan associations, mutual savings banks, and credit unions. These institutions are often referred to as the thrift institutions, although commercial banks also provide savings and time deposit accounts.

In their specialized heyday, commercial banks were unique in not only being banks of deposit but specifically providing the most important means of payment, checkbook money or demand deposits subject to check, the M1 component of the money supply in addition to currency in public circulation. Demand deposits could be expanded or contracted by commercial banks by their lending and investing. Other financial institutions could also lend and invest in their specialized fields, but such lending and investing was supplied from their available funds (their own deposit accounts at commercial banks, plus their capital funds and borrowings), thereby not increasing or decreasing the money supply in the M1 sense but rather affecting the velocity (turnover) of existing demand deposits.

In recent years, as the result of legislation and regulations, the M1 concept of the money supply, and specifically its demand deposits component, has been broadened to include negotiable order of withdrawal (NOW) accounts and automatic transfer service (ATS) accounts at banks and thrift institutions; credit union share drafts (CUSD) accounts; demand deposits at mutual savings banks; and traveler's checks of nonbank issuers.

The U.S. commercial banking system consists of the following:

1. The FEDERAL RESERVE SYSTEM with its 12 Federal Reserve banks, the central banking system;
2. National banks, federally chartered by the comptroller of the currency, which must belong to the Federal Reserve System and may be licensed by the comptroller of the currency to provide trust services;
3. State banks and state banks and trust companies, chartered by the various states to provide commercial banking or combined commercial banking and trust services, which have the option of belonging to the Federal Reserve System;
4. Trust companies, chartered by the various states with charter powers to provide trust services but most of which have diversified into commercial banking services; and
5. Miscellaneous state institutions of lesser total importance, such as private banks, and industrial banks with bank charters or authorized to receive deposits and maintain special deposit facilities, such as the cooperative exchanges in Arkansas and cash depositaries in South Carolina.

State banking laws generally allow:

1. Unit banking—Bank operates in only one location.
2. Statewide branch banking—Bank can operate branches throughout the state.
3. Limited branch banking—Bank may open branches only within specifically defined geographic areas within a state.
4. In-state multibank holding companies—Ownership or control of a number of banks within the state.
5. Multistate multibank holding companies—Out-of-state bank holding companies.

The largest system of noncommercial bank institutions which engages in deposit banking is the FEDERAL HOME LOAN BANK SYSTEM, created in 1932 to provide a central credit facility for the nation's home financing institutions. The system links mortgage lending institutions to the capital markets by issuing consolidated obligations and discount notes in large denominations. The system serves as a source of secondary liquidity to its members in meeting heavy or unusual withdrawal demands. All federally insured SAVINGS AND LOAN ASSOCIATIONS are required by law to belong to the Federal Home Loan Bank System. Membership is open on a voluntary basis to qualified state chartered mutual and stock savings and loan associations, mutual and stock SAVINGS BANKS, and life insurance companies, which are eligible because of their mortgage lending operations. Federally chartered mutual savings banks are newly authorized types of members of the FHLB System. CREDIT UNIONS, both federally chartered under the National Credit Union Administration and state chartered, are also depository institutions in the thrift group.

Commercial banks, originally specialists in credit to business, have diversified into operations formerly in the field of the "thrifts": savings and time deposits, mortgage lending, and other forms of home financing; consumer loans, including personal loans, originally the specialized field of the finance companies; the securities business, until restricted by the Glass-Steagall Act; and the trust business and other personal financial services. In turn, the "thrifts" have been given a statutory start into diversification in fields of the commercial banks with the following provisions:

1. Up to 20% of the assets of a federal savings and loan association may consist of consumer loans, commercial paper, and corporate debt securities.
2. Federal savings and loan associations may issue credit cards.
3. A federal mutual savings bank may accept demand deposits in connection with commercial, corporate, or business loans.
4. Federal savings and loan associations may exercise trust and fiduciary powers.
5. Federal mutual savings banks may have up to 5% of their assets in commercial, corporate, and business loans (if the loans are made only within the state where the bank is located or within 75 miles of the bank's home office).
6. Federal credit unions may make residential real estate loans on residential cooperatives.
7. Federal savings and loan associations may even invest in shares or certificates of open-end investment companies registered with the Securities and Exchange Commission, if the portfolio of the investment company is restricted to investments that savings and loan associations may invest indirectly.

But broader expansion of powers of the savings and loan associations was urged in proposed legislation sponsored by the Federal Home Loan Bank Board.

Both the commercial banks and the "thrifts" have been affected by the new products and services developed by securities firms, including the MONEY MARKET FUNDS and cash management accounts. Securities firms and retail chains have developed financial services offered nationwide which banks and "thrifts" are not permitted to offer. But in specific instances banks have acquired discount brokerage firms, increased their activity in the private placement markets, and sponsored closed-end investment companies.

Many present-day banks, organized as national banks or state banks and trust companies and located in the larger cities, are already financial "department stores," engaging in many kinds of banking and related services. A complete banking service would comprehend a variety of functions, including any of the following:

1. Receive demand deposits and pay customers' checks drawn against them, and operate automated teller machines (ATMs);
2. Receive time and savings deposits, issue negotiable orders of withdrawal (NOWs), and pay interest thereon, as well as provide automatic transfer service (ATS) for funds from saving accounts to cover checks;

BANK

3. Discount notes, acceptances, and bills of exchange;
4. Supply credit to business firms with or without security, issue letters of credit and accept bills drawn thereunder;
5. Transfer money at home and abroad;
6. Make collections and facilitate exchanges;
7. Issue drafts, cashier's checks, and money orders, and certify checks;
8. Furnish safe deposit vault service;
9. Provide custodianship for securities and other valuables;
10. Provide personal loans and credit card services to individuals, and lend on or discount customer installment receivables of vendors;
11. Act in a fiduciary capacity for individuals, as well as establish common trust funds;
12. Provide corporate trust services (stock transfer agent, registrar, paying agent, escrow agent, and indenture trustee);
13. Act as factors and engage in equipment leasing;
14. Deal in U.S. Government securities and underwrite general obligation state and municipal securities;
15. Invest in government and other debt securities;
16. Act as fiscal agent or depositary for the U.S. Government, states, and subdivisions of states;
17. Provide miscellaneous services such as place orders in securities for customers; act as insurance agent if incidental to banking transactions; serve as finder to bring buyers and sellers together; act as travel agent and issue travelers letters of credit and traveler's checks; provide Christmas Club accounts and other special purpose accounts; act as agent for accepting service of legal process if incidental to normal banking or fiduciary transactions of the bank; act as payroll issuer; establish charitable foundations; invest in small business investment corporations and bank service corporations; deal in foreign exchange; buy and sell gold bullion under license from the Treasury Department, and foreign coin; provide domestic and international correspondent banking services, etc.

Foreign banks are a significant part of the U.S. banking system. Foreign banks operate in the U.S. as branches, agencies, commercial banks, New York State Investment companies, and Edge or Agreement corporations. Edge corporations are chartered by the Federal Reserve Board to engage in international banking. State and federally chartered banks that are subsidiaries of foreign banks are examined and supervised by federal and state banking authorities similar to other state or federally chartered banks. The International Banking Act of 1978 (IBA) provides the framework for foreign banking activity in the U.S.

Government Banking. Federal credit aids (direct loans and insurance or guarantees of private loans) play a major role in government programs for improvement of housing and encouragement of home ownership, development of agricultural and other natural resources, assistance to economic development and military preparedness abroad, promotion of business (especially exports, transportation, and small business generally, redevelopment of communities and regions, and aid to higher education. The Office of Management and Budget (OMB) considers that the best index of the level of federal credit programs over a period of years is provided by the total outstanding direct and guaranteed loans.

Pattern of Banking Regulation. For the first time in U.S. financial history, the Monetary Control Act of 1980 requires all depository institutions (commercial banks, savings and loan associations, savings banks, and credit unions) to maintain directly or indirectly specified ratios of reserve requirements against transaction accounts demand, negotiable order of withdrawal (NOW), share draft, deposits subject to automatic and telephone transfer—and against nonpersonal time deposits with Federal Reserve banks, to facilitate control of the monetary aggregates by the Board of Governors of the Federal Reserve System. The referenced act calls for such reserves to be in the form of balances at Federal Reserve banks, but also, with the consent of the board of governors, in the form of vault cash. Nonmembers of the Federal Reserve System may keep balances with correspondents, a Federal Home Loan bank, or the National Credit Union Administration Central Liquidity Facility, if those institutions maintain balances at Federal Reserve banks.

The Depository Institutions Deregulation Act of 1980 created the Depository Institutions Deregulation Committee (DIDC) having the authority to prescribe rules for payment of interest, and under the act required to exercise its authority to provide for the phase-out and ultimate elimination of interest and dividend rate ceilings paid by depository institutions and for the increase of all such rates to market rates as soon as feasible during the six-year period following March 31, 1980.

Supervising the national banks, member banks of the Federal Reserve System, and other insured banks are the comptroller of the currency, the Board of Governors of the Federal Reserve System, and the Federal Deposit Insurance Corporation, which provides deposit insurance of up to $100,000 per account, involving full insurance coverage for over 99% of all accounts. National banks and state banks that are members of the Federal Reserve System are automatically insured as a corollary of that status, and regulation thereof is primarily through the comptroller of the currency for national banks, and the Board of Governors of the Federal Reserve System for state member banks. The FDIC has regulatory functions, in connection with its insurance of deposit accounts.

Under the jurisdiction of the various state banking departments are the state banks, trust companies, mortgage companies, title insurance companies, savings banks, state-chartered savings and loan associations (or building and loan associations), safe deposit companies, industrial banks, state-chartered credit unions, personal loan companies and brokers, licensed pawnbrokers, and private banks. In addition to the deposit banking types are found such organizations as investment bankers, stock exchange brokers, over-the-counter market dealers and brokers, commercial paper and bankers acceptance dealers, note brokers, foreign exchange brokers, discount houses, and investment companies. "Blue sky laws" may require registration of firms, personnel, and securities offered within the state by some of such types. The federal pattern of regulation in particular aspects of operations in these areas includes the Securities Act of 1933 (securities), Securities Exchange Act of 1934 (securities markets), Investment Company Act of 1940 (investment companies), and the Investment Advisers Act of 1940.

The Federal Savings and Loan Insurance Corporation provides insured savings and loan associations with insurance of accounts up to $100,000 per account, similar to that provided for commercial banks by the Federal Deposit Insurance Corporation.

Mutual savings banks chartered by states can be members of the Federal Reserve System, may be insured by the Federal Deposit Insurance Corporation, and may belong to the Federal Home Loan Bank System. Mutual savings banks in particular states have their own collective organizations. In New York State, savings bank institutions included the savings bank trust company, a central banking organization for mutual savings banks; INSTITUTIONAL SECURITIES CORPORATION, a mortgage banking institution providing mortgage and real estate services; and the Institutional Investors Mutual Fund, Inc., a mutual fund whereby New York mutual savings banks may participate in equity investments of the type and quality eligible for savings bank investment.

Credit unions may be federally chartered (since Act of March 10, 1970, 12 U.S.C. 1752, by the National Credit Union Administration; formerly, by the Bureau of Federal Credit Unions, in the Department of Health, Education and Welfare) or state-chartered. Federal- and state-chartered credit unions have been approved for share insurance by the National Credit Union Administration, comparable to the FDIC and FSLIC insurance programs offered by banks and savings and loan associations.

Structural Changes. Legislation relaxing constraints on the geographic expansion of banks and bank holding companies has come principally from the states. The major recent federal legislation affecting the geographic expansion of banks was the Depository Institutions Amendments of 1982 (the Garn-St Germain Act). This act allowed a limited amount of interstate banking by allowing acquisitions of large failing banks by out-of-state banking organizations. The easing of restrictions on the intrastate expansion of multibank holding companies permitted banking organizations to expand statewide by chartering separate banks under one holding company.

Changes in the structure of the banking industry at the local level historically have been limited by antitrust laws. During the 1980s, the implementation of these laws changed with the passage of legislation that reduced the differences between commercial banks and nonbank financial firms. Legislation allowing nonbank depository institutions to compete more directly with banks has altered the effect of antitrust laws. Congress expanded the investment powers of thrift institutions and also permitted them to offer transactions accounts that are functionally equivalent to demand deposits. Currently savings and loans and savings banks offer many of the products traditionally made available through commercial banks. Federal and state legislation also has reduced the differences between banks and various nondepository financial firms. At the federal level, legislation phased out interest rate ceilings on most bank accounts and permitted interest-bearing transactions accounts nationwide. In 1982, banks were allowed to issue insured money market deposit accounts at rates that were competitive with money market mutual funds.

During the 1980s, legislative and regulatory changes have caused banking organizations to increase significantly their geographic coverage and the range of products they offer. As the size of banking organizations increased, overall asset concentration within the industry rose significantly.

Since the mid-1970s, the U.S. banking system has become significantly more concentrated at the national, regional, and state levels, although not on the local level. Nationally, decreases in the number of banking organizations and dramatic increases in concentration have occurred principally due to the growth of large regional and super regional bank holding companies, often through merger or acquisition. Changes in regional and state concentration vary, with the Northeast and Southeast showing the greatest increases. Four-fifths of the states recorded increases in concentration over the past decade, but the extent of the increase varied widely.

These structural changes can be traced in large part to the relaxation of legal restrictions on the geographic expansion of banking organizations and on the products they can offer. The enactment of interstate banking laws in 45 of the 50 states and increased concentration at the state level helped bring about increases in national and regional concentration. These increases occurred in part because interstate banking laws allowed the development of fast-growing super regional and regional bank holding companies. At the state level, increases in concentration can be tied to more liberal branching laws adopted in the past decade.

While legislative and economic changes have led to increased concentration among banking organizations, they have also allowed increased competition between banks and other financial institutions. Greater competition for banks from thrift institutions and other firms and the lack of any substantial increase in concentration at the local level should mitigate antitrust concerns raised by structural changes.

Banking has been affected by many federal laws. In addition to those already mentioned, other laws having a significant impact on banking include the Truth-in-Lending Act (1968) and the Truth-in-Lending Simplification and Reform Act (1981), The Bank Merger Act of 1960, and the Bank Secrecy Act of 1970. The Truth-in-Lending acts were consumer protection legislation concerned with abuses by creditors. These acts imposed major compliance burdens on banks. The Bank Merger Act was passed as an amendment to the Federal Deposit Insurance Act. It legislated the power of appropriate regulatory agencies to approve or disapprove bank mergers. The Department of Justice was to act in an advisory role to comment on anticompetitive aspects of the mergers. The Bank Secrecy Act of 1970 required banks to maintain financial records and also required reports on unusual financial transactions and currency transfers; such reports were to be used in criminal, tax, or regulatory investigations or proceedings.

The appended tables present significant banking data for commercial banks prepared by the Federal Reserve Board of Governors and the Federal Deposit Insurance Corporation.

See BANKING HISTORY, UNITED STATES; BANKING LAW AND REGULATION, INVESTMENT COMPANY, MUNICIPAL BONDS, NATIONAL BANK, PRIVATE BANKING, STATE BANK.

BIBLIOGRAPHY

Banking Associations:
American Bankers Association.
American Society of Bank Directors.
Association of Bank Holding Companies.
Association of Reserve City Bankers.
Bank Administration Institute.
Bankers Association for Foreign Trade.
Bank Marketing Association.
BANK PAC.
Conference of State Bank Supervisors.
Consumer Bankers Association.
Independent Bankers Association of America.
Mortgage Bankers Association of America.
National Association for Bank Cost and Management Accounting.
National Association of Bank Women.
National Bankers Association.
National Council of Savings Institutions.

Laws and Regulations (selective):
Board of Governors of the Federal Reserve System. *Federal Regulatory Service.*
Comptroller of the Currency. *Comptroller's Manual for National Banks.*
———. *Comptroller's Handbook for National Bank Examiners.*
———. *Annual Report.*
Federal Deposit Insurance Corporation, *Rules and Regulations.*
———. *Annual Report.*
Federal Financial Institutions Examination Council.
———. *Annual Report.*

Indexes:
American Banker Index.
Banking Literature Index.
Business Periodicals Index.
Business Publications Index and Abstracts.
Index to Legal Periodicals. H. W. Wilson Co.
Index to U.S. Government Periodicals.
Legal Contents: The Biweekly Compilation of Tables of Contents from Law Reviews, Journals and Symposia.
Management Contents: The Biweekly Compilation of Tables of Contents from Business Magazines.
PAIS Bulletin.

Periodicals:
ABA Banking Journal.
American Banker.
American Bankers Index.
Arkansas Banker.
Bank Accounting and Finance.
Bank Acquisition Report.
Bank Administration.
Bank Asset/Liability Management Report.
Bank Auditing and Accounting Report.
Bank Automation Newsletter.
Bank Director's Report.
Banker.
Bankers Magazine.
Bankers Monthly.
Bankers New Weekly.
Bankers Research.
Bank Executives Report.
Bank Financial Strategies.
Bank Fraud.
Banking.
Banking Law Journal.
Bank Letter.
Banking World.
Bank Marketing Magazine.
Bank Marketing Report.
Bank Network News; News and Analysis of Shared EFT Networks.
Bank Operations Report.
Bank Personnel Report.
Bank Stock Quarterly.
Bank Systems and Equipment.
Bank Tax Report.
BNA's Banking Report. Bureau of National Affairs, Inc.
Canadian Banker.
Computers in Banking.
Corporate EFT Report.
Digest of Bank Insurance.
EFT Press Alert.
EFT Report.
Export-Import Bank of Washington.
Federal Reserve Banks, Reviews:
  Federal Reserve Bank of Atlanta Economic Review.
  Federal Reserve Bank of Chicago International Letter.

BANK

Earnings and Other Data for All Insured Banks
(in millions of dollars)

Financial Data	1979	1980	1981	1982	1983R	1984R	1985R	1986R	1987	1988
Interest Income	137,364	174,416	228,675	235,121	216,050	245,638	241,819	230,630	236,531	271,345
Interest Expense	87,570	119,758	169,268	168,553	143,210	167,334	155,212	140,489	142,325	164,432
Net Interest Income	49,794	54,658	59,407	66,568	72,840	78,304	86,607	90,141	94,206	106,913
Provision for loan losses	3,764	4,453	5,059	8,291	10,614	13,704	17,504	21,538	36,337	16,577
Miscellaneous income	9,914	12,508	13,538	15,517	17,776	21,953	28,096	34,398	37,423	NA
Service charges	2,517	3,173	3,905	4,573	5,399	6,518	7,333	7,908	8,655	NA
Total Other Income	12,431	15,681	17,443	20,090	23,175	28,471	35,429	42,306	46,078	45,007
Personal expenses	21,465	24,565	27,927	31,218	33,636	36,463	39,467	42,262	44,528	NA
Other optional expenses	19,051	21,898	25,528	29,913	32,761	36,784	42,000	46,532	50,870	NA
Non-interest expenses	40,516	46,463	53,455	61,131	66,397	73,247	81,467	88,794	95,398	100,929
Income before taxes	17,843	19,435	20,149	19,172	18,995	19,824	23,063	22,115	8,548	34,414
Taxes	4,736	5,009	4,611	3,639	4,076	4,660	5,499	5,184	5,304	10,154
Net earnings	12,758	13,933	14,677	14,872	14,919	15,163	17,565	16,931	3,245	24,260
Net securities gains or losses	(350)	(492)	(861)	(661)	(30)	(146)	1,506	3,785	1,394	404
Average total assets (billion $)	1,593	1,768	1,933	2,101	2,245	2,401	2,559	2,753	2,882	3,057
Return on assets	0.80	0.79	0.76	0.71	0.67	0.64	0.70	0.62	0.12	0.79

Source: FDIC.

Breakdown of Reported Assets
As % of Total Assets for All Member Banks
(in billions of dollars)

End of year	Total loans	%	Fed. govt. secur.	%	Other securities	%	Other assets	%	Total assets
1988	1,724	63	333	12	173	6	508	19	2,737
1987 R	1,605	62	313	12	177	7	494	19	2,589
1986	1,530	59	283	11	176	7	584	23	2,573
1985	1,390	ERR	249	ERR	161	ERR	?	ERR	2,302
1984	1,269	60	238	12	133	6	458	22	2,098
1983	1,080	55	248	13	176	9	445	23	1,949
1982	988	55	197	11	168	9	447	25	1,800
1981	919	56	177	11	161	10	382	23	1,639
1980	853	55	170	12	155	10	360	23	1,538
1979	799	59	142	10	142	10	270	21	1,353

Source: Federal Reserve Board.

Sources of Revenue
(Percent of gross revenues—all insured banks)

Year	Net interest income on loans	Net interest income on investments	Commissions, fees & other income
1987	49.7	18.2	32.2
1986	51.1	18.9	30.0
1985	52.7	19.3	28.0
1984	54.2	19.0	26.7
1983	51.6	21.4	27.0
1982	53.6	22.0	24.3
1983	53.9	21.6	24.5
1981	56.4	21.2	22.3
1980	59.4	20.6	20.0
1979	59.6	21.0	19.4

R Revised.
Source: Federal Reserve Board.

Loan Trends, for All Commercial Banks
(Outstanding at end of year, in billions of dollars)

Year	Commercial industrial & agric.†	Real estate	Personal	All Other†	Total
1988	667.7	663.2	353.6	162.2	1,846.5
1987	631.2	588.4	327.8	156.0	1,703.5
1986	618.8	489.0	314.2	161.0	1,583.0
1985	577.5	422.4	291.5	158.2	1,449.7
1984	552.4	376.2	251.5	136.2	1,316.3
1983	483.1	334.6	219.2	94.1	1,131.0
1982	459.7	303.1	191.9	87.3	1,042.0
1981	421.2	285.7	185.1	81.8	973.9
1980	366.7	252.2	179.7	75.2	873.7
1979	329.2	227.7	176.7	72.8	806.3

R Revised.
† Includes financial institutions, and as of 1984, foreign banks.
‡ Includes lease financing, loans for which securities are used as collateral, foreign official institutions, and state and political subdivisions.
Source: Federal Reserve Board.

Rates on Loans and Investments for All Insured Commercial Bank
(In percent)

Year	Gross interest return Loans	Investments†	Gross interest expense	Net charge-offs*	Net interest margin†
1987	10.4	9.1	6.1	0.94	4.04
1986	10.8	10.5	7.0	1.00	4.28
1985	12.1 R	11.5 R	8.3 R	0.86	4.38
1984	13.7	12.2	10.2	0.77	4.35
1983	12.7	12.1	9.5	0.66	4.18
1982	15.2	12.4	12.2	0.55	4.20
1981	16.4	11.7	13.9	0.35	4.10
1980	13.7	11.8	11.1	0.36	4.20
1979	12.0	10.0	9.1	0.28	4.20
1978	10.3	9.3	6.8	0.32	4.20

R Revised.
* As percentage of average loans.
† Taxable equivalent.
Source: Federal Reserve Board.

Federal Reserve Bank of Dallas Economic Review.
Federal Reserve Bank of Kansas City Economic Review.
Federal Reserve Bank of Minneapolis Quarterly Review.
Federal Reserve Bank of New York Quarterly Review.
Federal Reserve Bank of Philadelphia Business Review.
Federal Reserve Bank of Richmond Economic Review.
Federal Reserve Bank of Saint Louis Review.
Federal Reserve Bank of San Francisco Business and Financial Letter.
Federal Reserve Bulletin.
Financial Computing.
Financial Services Week: The Competition Report for Banks and Financial Institutions.
Financier: The Journal of Private Sector Policy.
Independent Banker.
International Financial Law Review.
International Journal of Bank Marketing.
Issues in Bank Regulation.
Journal of Bank Cost and Management Accounting.
Journal of Banking and Finance.
Journal of Banking Strategy.
Journal of Bank Research.
Journal of Commercial Bank Lending.
Journal of Financial Economics.
Journal of Money, Credit, and Banking.
Journal of Retail Banking.
Louisiana Banker.
Magazine of Bank Administration.
Monthly Bank Clearings.
Mortgage Banker.
One Hundred Highest Yields Among Federal-Insured Banks and Savings Institutions.
National Thrift and Mortgage News.
New Jersey Banker.
New York State Banker.
The Ohio Banker.
PMT.
Product, Marketing, and Technology.
Quarterly Journal. Comptroller of the Currency.
Savings Bank Journal.
Savings Institution Banker.
The Southern Banker.
Tarheel Banker.
United States Banker.
See also *Financial Journals and Serials: An Analytical Guide to Accounting, Finance, Insurance, and Investment Periodicals.* Greenwood Press, New York, NY, 1986.

Statistical Sources:
American Banker Yearbook. Gale Research Co., Detroit, MI.
Aggregate Reserves and Member Bank Deposits. Federal Reserve Board, Washington, DC.
Bank Operating Statistics. Federal Deposit Insurance Corporation, Washington, DC.
Debits and Deposit Turnover at Commercial Banks.

Federal Reserve Board:
All-Bank Statistics, United States.
Annual Reports.
Annual Statistical Digest.
Banking and Monetary Statistics.
Federal Reserve Regulatory Service.

Comptroller of the Currency:
Annual Reports.
Comptroller's Manual for National Banks.
Comptroller's Handbook for National Bank Examiners.

Encyclopedia and Dictionaries:
Banking Language: A Running Press Glossary. Running Press Book Publishers, Philadelphia, PA, 1977.
Banking Terminology. ABA, Washington, DC, 1981.
The Complete Executive's Encyclopedia of Accounting, Finance, Investing, Banking, and Economics. LINK, A. N., and WOELFEL, C. J. Probus Publishing Co., Chicago, IL, 1989.
Dictionary of Banking & Financial Services. ROSENBERG, J. M., John Wiley and Sons, New York, NY, 1985.
Elsevier's Banking Dictionary of Six Languages: English / American, French, Italian, Spanish, Dutch, and German. Elsevier Scientific Publishing Co., New York, NY, 1983.
Encyclopedia of Banking. JUD, D., and WOELFEL, C. J., Probus Publishing Co., Chicago, IL, 1988.
Encyclopedia of Banking and Finance. MUNN, G. G., and WOELFEL, C. J., Bank Administration Institute, Rolling Meadows, IL, 1990.
Encyclopedia of Banking and Financial Tables. THORNDIKE, D., Warren, Gorman and Lamont, Inc., New York, NY, 1987.
Encyclopedia of Business Information Systems. Gale Research Co., Detroit, MI.
Glossary of Fiduciary Terms. American Bankers Association, Washington, DC, 1968.
Glossary of Terms. Chartered Accountant in Australia, June, 1988.
Money A to Z: A Consumer's Guide to the Language of Personal Finance. Facts on File, New York, NY, 1984.
Money Encyclopedia. RACHLIN, H., ed. Harper & Row Publishers, Inc., New York, NY, 1984.

Bibliographies:
Banks and Banking. U.S. Government Printing Office, Washington, DC.
Deregulation and Nonbank Banks: A Selected Bibliography. Vance Publications, Monticello, VA.
Economics and Business: An International Annotated Bibliography. Gordon and Breach Science Publishers.
The FED in Print. Federal Reserve Bank of Philadelphia.
Guide to Statistical Sources in Money, Banking, and Finance. Oryx Press, Phoenix, AZ.
Information Sources. Gale Research Co., Detroit, MI.
Money, Banking, and Macroeconomics: A Guide to Moody's Bank and Finance Manual. Moody's Investors Services, New York, NY.
Sources of World Financial and Banking Information. Greenwood Press, Inc., Westport, CT.

Handbooks, Manuals, and Looseleaf Services:
American Banker Yearbook. Gale Research Co., Detroit, MI.
Bank Administration Manual. SEGLIN, J. L., Bank Administration Institute, Rolling Meadows, IL, 1988.
Bank and Finance Manual. Moody's Investors Services, New York, NY.
Bank Director's Handbook. Auburn House Publishing Co., Inc., Dover, MA.
Bankers Almanac. MILLER, R. B., Bankers Publishing Co., Rolling Meadows, IL.
Bankers' Almanac and Yearbook. International Publications Service, New York, NY.
Banker's Handbook. Dow Jones-Irwin, Inc., Homewood, IL.
Banking Law. Matthew Bender & Co., Inc., New York, NY.
Banking Law Manual: Legal Guide to Commercial Banks, Thrift Institutions, and Credit Unions. Matthew Bender & Co., Inc., New York, NY.
Commercial Banking. American Management Association, New York, NY. Looseleaf self-study course.
Control of Banking. Prentice Hall, Inc., Englewood Cliffs, NJ. Looseleaf volumes.
Corporate and Commercial Finance Agreements. TOMCZAK, S. L., Shepherds/McGraw Book Co., Colorado Springs, CO. Looseleaf.
Emerging Trends in Retail Banking. FIND/SVP, New York, NY.
Federal Banking Law Reports. Commerce Clearing House, Inc., Chicago, IL.
Handbook for Bank Strategies. Bank Administration Institute, Rolling Meadows, IL.
Moody's Bank and Finance Manual. Moody's Investors Services, New York, NY.
Responsibilities and Liabilities of Bank and Bank Holding Companies Directors. Commerce Clearing House, Inc. Chicago, IL.
Taxation of Financial Institutions. Matthew Bender & Co., New York, NY.
Value Line Investment Survey. Value Line, Inc., New York, NY.
World Banking Handbook. MURO, V.

Directories:
American Bank Attorneys. Capron Publishing Co.
American Bank Directory. McFadden Business Publications.
American Bankers Association Key to Routing Numbers. Rand McNally and Co.

BANKABLE PAPER

Bank Administration Check Processing Equipment Directory. Bank Administration Institute, Rolling Meadows, IL.
Bank Administration Coin and Currency Processing Directory. Bank Administration Institute, Rolling Meadows, IL.
Bank Administration Microcomputer Directory. Bank Administration Institute, Rolling Meadows, IL.
Bank Administration Retail Delivery Systems Directory. Bank Administration Institute, Rolling Meadows, IL.
Bankers School Directory. American Bankers Association.
Bank Marketing Directory of Bank Marketing Services Issue. Bank Marketing Association.
Bank Systems and Equipment Directory. Gralla Publications.
Branch Directory and Summary of Deposits. Decision Research Sciences, Inc.
Business Organizations, Agencies, and Publications Directory. Gale Research Co., Detroit, MI.
Callahan's Credit Union Directory, 1986. Annual.
Datapro Reports on Banking Automation. Datapro Research Corp.
Deposit History and Projections. Decision Research Sciences.
Directory of American Savings and Loan Associations. T. K. Sanderson Organization, 1955. Annual.
Financial Buyers Guide. Commerce Publishing Co., Chicago, IL.
Financial Services Software Directory. Longman Financial Services Publishing.
Financial Sourcebooks' SOURCES: The Directory of Financial Research, Marketing Surveys and Services. Financial Sourcebooks.
Lawyer's Register by Specialties and Fields of Law, Including a Directory of Corporate Counsel. The Lawyer's Register Publishing Co.
Polk's World Bank Directory, 1985. Semiannual.
Rand McNally Bankers Directory, 1872. Semiannual.
The U.S. Savings & Loan Directory, 1982. Annual.

Government Publications—General:
Bureau of Economic Analyses. *Business Conditions Digest.*
———. *Survey of Current Business.*
———. *Business Statistics.*
Treasury Department. *Treasury Bulletin.*
U.S. Council of Economic Advisers. *Economic Indicators.*

Online Data Bases:
ABI/INFORM. UMI-Data Courier, Inc. Business periodicals.
American Statistics Index: A Comprehensive Guide and Index to the Statistical Publications of the United States Government. Congressional Information Service, Inc.
Banker. Bell & Howell, Wooster, OH.
Economic Literature Index. American Economic Association.
FINIS: Financial Industry Information Service. Bank Marketing Association.
Innerline. Bank Administration Institute.
Legal Resource Index. Information Access Co. Legal periodicals.
LEXIS. Mead Data Central. Indexes of legal cases, statutes, orders, and opinions.
Management Contents. Information Access Co.
NEXIS. Mead Data Central. Periodicals and newspapers.
PTS U.S. Time Series. Predicasts, Inc. Time series data.
Trade & Industry Index. Information Access Co. Business periodicals.
WILSONLINE. H. W. Wilson Co. Periodical indexes.

Key Economic Indicators:
Consumer Price Index (CPI). Bureau of Labor Statistics. Monthly.
GNP. Bureau of Economic Analysis.
Housing Starts. Census Bureau, Commerce Department. Monthly.
Industrial Production Index. Board of Governors of the Federal Reserve System. Monthly.
Leading Indicators. Bureau of Economic Analysis. Monthly.
Personal Income. Bureau of Economic Analysis. Monthly.
Producer Price Index (PPI). Bureau of Labor Statistics. Monthly.
Retail Sales. Bureau of Economic Analysis. Monthly.
Unemployment. Bureau of Labor Statistics. Monthly.

Other References:
AUSTIN, D. V., and others. *Modern Banking: A Practical Guide to Managing Deregulated Institutions.* Bank Administration Institute, Rolling Meadows, IL, 1985.
AUSTIN, D. V., HAKALA, D. R., and SCAMPINI, T. J., *Modern Banking.* Bankers Publishing Co., Rolling Meadows, IL, 1988.

J. BALACHANDRAN, M. *A Guide to Statistical Sources in Money, Banking, and Finance.* Oryx Press, Phoenix, AZ, 1988.
BARNETT, R. E. *Responsibilities and Liabilities of Bank and Bank Holding Company Directors.* Commerce Clearing House, Inc. Chicago, IL. Latest edition.
Economic and Business: An International Annotated Bibliography. Gordon and Breach Science Publishers, Cooper Station, NY. Latest edition.
GARCIA, F. L. *How to Analyze a Bank Statement.* Bankers Publishing Co., Rolling Meadows, IL, 1984.
GOLDFIELD, S. M. *The Economics of Money and Banking.* Harper Row Publishers, Inc., New York, NY, 1985.
HASLEM, J. A. *Commercial Bank Management: Text and Readings,* Prentice Hall, Inc., Englewood Cliffs, NJ, 1985.
HEMPEL, G. H., and others. *Bank Management.* John Wiley and Sons, Inc., New York, NY, 1986.
HUTCHINSON, H. D. *Money, Banking, and the United States Economy.* Prentice Hall, Inc., Englewood Cliffs, NJ, 1988.
JOHNSON, F. P., and JOHNSON, R. D., *Commercial Bank Management.* Dryden Press, Hinsdale, IL, 1985.
JANNOTT, P. F. *Improving Bank Profits; How to Decrease Operating Expenses and Increase Income.* Bank Administration Institute, Rolling Meadows, IL, 1984.
KOCH, T. *Bank Management.* Dryden Press, Hinsdale, IL, 1988.
KUSNET, J., and ANTOPOL, J. T. *Modern Banking Checklists.* Warren, Gorham and Lamont, Inc., Boston, MA. Cumulative supplements.
MARKS, L. A. "Managing Your Bankers." *Corporate Accounting,* Spring, 1988.
MORIARTY, R. T., KIMBALL, R. C., and GAY, J. H. "The Management of Corporate Banking Relationships." *Sloan Management Review,* Spring, 1983.
RACHLINE, H., ed. *The Money Encyclopedia.* Harper & Row, Publishers, New York, NY, 1984.
REED, E. W. *Commercial Banking.* Prentice Hall, Inc., Englewood Cliffs, NJ, 1984.
SEGLIN, J. *Bank Administration Manual.* Bank Administration Institute, Rolling Meadows, IL, 1988.
Statistical Information on the Financial Services Industry. American Bankers Association, Washington, DC. Periodical update.
Strategic Management for Bankers. Planning Forum, Oxford, OH, 1984.

BANKABLE PAPER PAPER, principal debtors or endorsers of which have a sufficiently high credit standing that a bank will readily discount it.

BANK ACCEPTANCE As defined by the board of governors of the Federal Reserve System in its Regulation A (advances and discounts by Federal Reserve Banks), "a draft or bill of exchange, whether payable in the United States or abroad and whether payable in dollars or some other money, accepted by a bank or trust company or a firm, person, company or corporation engaged generally in the business of granting bankers' acceptance credits." A bank acceptance, therefore, is the acceptance obligation of a bank or trust company engaged also in banking; bankers (the apostrophe is usually dropped) acceptance is a broader term including those of other acceptor firms in the business, referred to as discount houses. Bill dealers buy and sell bankers acceptances, which are referred to as bankers bills, or simply bills.
See DISCOUNT CORPORATION.
Federal Reserve Promotion of Bankers Acceptances. The Federal Reserve System has been closely connected with development of bankers acceptances as an important sector of the U.S. money market. The Federal Reserve banks became, beginning in 1916, substantial purchasers and holders of bankers acceptances, posting fixed rates above or below the market, as monetary policy called for, at which the banks stood ready to buy bills. Until 1955 it was the passive policy of the system to buy and never sell, so that while the purchases were technically open market operations, actually Federal Reserve buying of bills resembled more the discounting function, since it was not at the initiative of the Federal Reserve banks. Since 1955, however, bill buying by the Fed has been at its initiative, so that such operations have become full-blown open market operations, including repurchase agreements if appropriate with bill dealers. The Federal Reserve banks adjust their holdings of bills by simply not replacing those paid at maturity.

ENCYCLOPEDIA OF BANKING AND FINANCE

Regulation B of the board of governors of the Federal Reserve System governs open market operations in bills by Federal Reserve banks. This regulation prescribes the following:

1. Any bankers acceptance or bill of exchange which is eligible for discount is eligible for purchase by Federal Reserve banks in the open market, with or without the endorsement of a member bank if: it has been accepted by the drawee prior to purchase; or it is accompanied or secured by shipping documents or by warehouse, terminal, or other similar receipts conveying security title; or it bears a satisfactory bank endorsement.
2. A bankers acceptance growing out of a transaction involving the importation or exportation of goods may be purchased if it has a maturity not in excess of six months, exclusive of days of grace, provided that it conforms in other respects to the eligibility requirements.
3. A bankers acceptance growing out of a transaction involving the storage within the U.S. of goods actually under contract for sale and not yet delivered or paid for may be purchased. On such paper, however, the acceptor must be secured by the pledge of such goods; and the acceptance must conform in other respects to the eligibility requirements.

Unless endorsed by a member, a bill of exchange is not eligible for purchase until a satisfactory statement has been furnished of the financial condition of one or more of the parties thereto. Similarly, unless accepted or endorsed by a member bank, a bankers acceptance is not eligible for purchase until the acceptor has furnished a satisfactory statement of its financial condition in form approved by the Federal Reserve Bank, and has agreed in writing with a Federal Reserve bank to inform it upon request concerning the transaction underlying the acceptance.

Member Bank Discounting of Bills. Any member bank may discount at its Federal Reserve bank bankers acceptances which have the following features of eligibility for discount under Regulation A:

1. Endorsed by a member bank.
2. Growing out of transactions involving the importation or exportation of goods, the shipment of goods within the U.S., or storage of readily marketable staples. In the case of an acceptance growing out of the storage of readily marketable staples, the bill must be secured at the time of acceptance by a warehouse, terminal, or other similar receipt conveying security title to such staples. Such receipt shall be issued by a party independent of the customer or issued by a grain elevator or warehouse company duly bonded, licensed, and regularly inspected by state or federal authorities with whom all receipts for such staples and all transfers thereof are registered and without whose consent no staples may be withdrawn. Moreover, the acceptor must remain secured throughout the life of the acceptance. If the goods are withdrawn from storage before maturity of the acceptance or retirement of the credit, a trust receipt or other similar document covering the goods may be substituted in lieu of the original document, provided that such substitution is conditioned upon a reasonably prompt liquidation of the credit. To this end, it should be required, when the original document is released, either that the proceeds of the goods will be applied within a specified time toward a liquidation of the acceptance credit or that a new document, similar to the original one, will be resubstituted within a specified time.
3. Drawn by a bank or banker in a foreign country, or dependency or insular possession of the United States, for the purpose of furnishing dollar exchange.
4. Having a maturity at the time of discount of not more than 90 days' sight, exclusive of days of grace. Acceptances drawn for agricultural purposes and secured at the time of acceptance by warehouse receipts or other such documents conveying or securing title covering readily marketable staples may be discounted with a maturity at the time of discount of not more than six months' sight, exclusive of days of grace. Nevertheless, no acceptance discounted by a Federal Reserve bank should have a maturity in excess of the usual or customary period of credit required to finance the underlying transaction or of the period reasonably necessary to finance such transaction.

No acceptance growing out of the storage of readily marketable staples should have a maturity in excess of the time ordinarily necessary to effect a reasonably prompt sale, shipment, or distribution into the process of manufacture or consumption.

Acceptances for any one customer in excess of 10% of the capital and surplus of the accepting bank must remain actually secured throughout the life of the acceptance. In the case of acceptances of member banks, this security must consist of shipping documents, warehouse receipts, or other such documents, or some other actual security growing out of the same transaction as the acceptance, such as documentary drafts, trade acceptances, terminal receipts, or trust receipts which have been issued under such circumstances and which cover goods of such a character as to ensure at all times a continuance of an effective and lawful lien in favor of the accepting bank. Other trust receipts are not considered such actual security if they permit the customer to have access to or control over the goods.

Acceptance Powers of Banks. Authority of a member bank to accept drafts or bills of exchange drawn upon it is based on the Federal Reserve Act, particularly the seventh and twelfth paragraphs of Section 13 of the Act, and Regulation C of the FEDERAL RESERVE BOARD REGULATIONS, which governs member bank acceptance of commercial drafts or bills and acceptance of drafts or bills to furnish dollar exchange.

Any member bank may accept drafts or bills of exchange (commercial drafts or bills) drawn upon it which grow out of any of the following transactions:

1. The shipment of goods between the U.S. and any foreign country, or between the U.S. and any of its dependencies or insular possessions and foreign countries, or between foreign countries. A member bank accepting any commercial drafts or bills growing out of such transactions will be expected to obtain before acceptance and retain in its files satisfactory evidence, documentary or otherwise, showing the nature of the transactions underlying the credit extended.
2. The shipment of goods within the U.S., provided shipping documents conveying or securing title are attached or are in the physical possession of the accepting bank or its agent at the time of acceptance.
3. The storage in the U.S. or in any foreign country of readily marketable staples, provided that the draft or bill of exchange is secured at the time of acceptance by a warehouse receipt or other such document conveying or securing title covering such readily marketable staples. A readily marketable staple means an article of commerce, agriculture, or industry used as to make it subject to constant dealings in ready markets with such frequent quotations of price as to make the price easily and definitely ascertainable and the staple itself easy to realize upon by sale at any time. In connection with member bank discounting at the Fed of such bills, the Federal Reserve banks may neither discount nor purchase bills arising out of the storage of readily marketable staples unless the acceptor remains secured throughout the life of the bill.

No member banks shall accept any commercial draft or bill unless at the date of its acceptance such draft or bill has not more than six months to run, exclusive of days of grace.

Limitations on acceptance by member banks of commercial drafts or bills are as follows:

1. *Acceptance for one person.* No member bank shall accept commercial drafts or bills, whether in a foreign or domestic transaction, for any one person, company, firm, or corporation in an amount equal at any time in the aggregate to more than 10% of its paid-up and unimpaired capital stock and surplus, unless the bank be and remain secured as to the amount in excess of such 10% limitation, either by attached documents or by some other actual security growing out of the same transaction as the acceptance. A trust receipt which permits the customer to have access to or control over the goods will not be considered actual security within the meaning of this limitation.
2. *Limitation on aggregate amount.* No member bank shall accept commercial drafts or bills in an amount equal at any time in the aggregate to more than 50% of its paid-up and unimpaired capital stock and surplus (except that, with the permission of

the board of governors of the Federal Reserve System, as provided in the following paragraph 3, any such member bank may accept such drafts or bills in an amount not exceeding at any time in the aggregate 100% of its paid-up and unimpaired capital stock and surplus; but in no event may the aggregate amount of such acceptances growing out of domestic transactions exceed 50% of such capital and surplus). Commercial drafts or bills accepted by another bank, domestic or foreign, at the request of a member bank which agrees to put such other bank in funds to meet such acceptances at maturity shall be considered as part of the acceptance liabilities of the member bank requesting such acceptances as well as of such other bank if it is a member bank.

3. *Authority to accept up to 100%.* Any member bank desiring authority to accept commercial drafts or bills up to 100% shall file with the board of governors, through the Federal Reserve bank of its district, an application for permission to exercise such authority. Such application need not be made in any particular form, but shall show the present and anticipated need of the applicant bank for the authority requested. The board of governors may at any time rescind such authority granted by it after not less than 90 days' notice in writing to the bank affected.

Authority to Accept Drafts or Bills to Furnish Dollar Exchange. Any member bank, after obtaining the permission of the board of governors, may accept drafts or bills of exchange drawn upon it by banks or bankers in foreign countries, dependencies, or insular possessions of the U.S. for the purpose of furnishing dollar exchange (dollar exchange drafts or bills) as required by the usages of trade in the respective countries, dependencies, or insular possessions, subject to the conditions set forth herein. Any member bank desiring to obtain such permission shall file with the board of governors through the Federal Reserve bank of its district an application for such permission. Such application need not be in any particular form but shall show the present and anticipated need for the authority requested. The board of governors may at any time rescind any permission granted by it after not less than 90 days' notice in writing to the bank affected.

Any such foreign country, dependency, or insular possession of the U.S. must be one of those specified in a list published by the board of governors for these purposes, with respect to which the board of governors has found that the usages of trade are such as to justify banks or bankers therein to draw on member banks for the purpose of furnishing dollar exchange. Any member bank desiring to place itself in position to accept drafts or bills of exchange from a country, dependency, or insular possession not specified in such list may request the board of governors through the Federal Reserve bank of its district to add such country, dependency, or insular possession to the list, upon a showing that the furnishing of dollar exchange is required by the usages of trade therein. The board of governors may at any time, after 90 days' published notice, remove from such list the name of any country, dependency, or insular possession contained thereon.

Any such dollar exchange draft or bill must be drawn and accepted in good faith for the purpose of furnishing dollar exchange as required by the usages of trade in the country, dependency, or insular possession in which the draft or bill is drawn. Drafts or bills drawn merely because dollar exchange is at a premium in the place where drawn or for any speculative purpose, or drafts or bills commonly referred to as finance bills (bills not drawn primarily to furnish dollar exchange) will not be deemed to meet these requirements.

The aggregate of drafts or bills accepted by a member bank for any one foreign bank or banker shall not exceed an amount which the member bank would expect such foreign bank or banker to liquidate, within the terms of the agreements under which the drafts or bills were accepted, through the proceeds of export documentary bills or from other sources reasonably available to such foreign bank or banker arising in the normal course of trade.

A member bank shall not accept any dollar exchange draft or bill unless at the date of its acceptance it has not more than three months to run, exclusive of days of grace.

Limitations are as follows:

1. *Acceptances for one bank or banker.* A member bank shall not accept dollar exchange drafts or bills for any one bank or banker in an amount exceeding in the aggregate 10% of the paid-up and unimpaired capital and surplus of the accepting bank, unless it be and remain secured as to the amount in excess of such 10% limitation by documents conveying or securing title or by some other adequate security.

2. *Aggregate amount.* A member bank shall not accept dollar exchange drafts or bills in an amount exceeding at any one time in the aggregate of 50% of its paid-up and unimpaired capital and surplus. This limitation is separate and distinct from and not included in the limitations prescribed above with respect to acceptances of commercial drafts or bills. Dollar exchange drafts or bills accepted by another bank, whether domestic or foreign, at the request of a member bank which agrees to put such other bank in funds to meet such acceptances at maturity shall be considered as part of the acceptance liabilities of the member bank requesting such acceptances as well as of such other bank, if a member bank, within the meaning of these limitations.

Summary. Since the close of World War II, the volume of bankers acceptances outstanding has expanded substantially to new peaks, totaling over $7.9 billion at the close of 1971, compared with $154 million at the close of 1945 and $1,732 million at the close of 1929. Expansion in recent years became pronounced beginning in the late 1950s, reflecting the expansion in world trade, reestablishment of currency convertibility, and increased use of dollar arrangements in international trade. Prime bankers acceptances are those of highly regarded banks and bankers active in acceptance financing.

Yields (discount basis) vary with money rates and may range 50 to 100 basis points higher than those on Treasury bills of similar maturity. Six dealers, all in New York City, maintain markets in bankers acceptances. Most investors who buy normally hold to maturity. For investors other than commercial banks, savings banks, insurance companies, and varied types of nonfinancial corporations, bankers acceptances compete with other money market instruments like Treasury bills, commercial paper, and negotiable time certificates of deposit as to suitable denominations, convenience of maturities, adequacy of supply, and marketability. The Federal Reserve System, as indicated *supra*, has been especially interested in development of the market for bankers acceptances, as evidenced by active open market operations therein, repurchase agreements with nonbank dealers since 1955, and establishment by the New York Federal Reserve Bank of a separate acceptance department in January, 1964.

See ACCEPTANCE CREDIT, LETTER OF CREDIT.

BIBLIOGRAPHY

JENSEN F. H. and PARKINS, M. "Recent Developments in the Bankers Acceptance Market." *Federal Reserve Bulletin*. January, 1986.
STIGUM, M. *The Money Market*. Dow Jones-Irwin Inc., Homewood, IL, 1983.

BANK ACCOUNT Funds deposited in a bank. Types of bank accounts are checking, savings, and time deposit accounts.

Checking account deposits are payable on demand without prior notice of withdrawal.

Savings deposits are evidenced by a passbook, written receipt, or agreement under which the depositor is required, or may at any time be required (requirement customarily waived), by the bank to give prior written notice of intended withdrawal of not less than 30 days. Withdrawals of savings deposits are permitted in two ways: upon presentation of the passbook, through payment to the person presenting the passbook; or without presentation of the passbook, through payment to the depositor himself or herself but not to any other person, whether or not acting for the depositor.

Time deposits include time certificates of deposit, open account time deposits, and international banking facility time deposits. The Board of Governors of the Federal Reserve System has defined these accounts as follows:

1. Time certificates of deposit are deposits evidenced by a negotiable or nonnegotiable instrument which provides on its face that the amount of such deposits is payable to the bearer or to any specified person or to his or her order:
   a. On a certain date, specified in the instrument, not less than 14 days after date of the deposit, or
   b. At the expiration of a certain specified time not less than 14 days after the date of the instrument, or

c. Upon notice in writing which is actually required to be given not less than 14 days before the date of repayment (a deposit with respect to which the bank merely reserves the right to require notice of not less than 14 days before any withdrawal is made is not a time certificate of deposit within the meaning of the definition), and

d. In all cases only upon presentation and surrender of the instrument.

2. Open account time deposits are deposits, other than a time certificate of deposit, with respect to which there is in force a written contract with the depositor that neither the whole nor any part of such deposit may be withdrawn, by check or otherwise, prior to the date of maturity, which shall be not less than 14 days after the date of the deposit, or prior to the expiration of the period of notice which must be given by the depositor in writing not less than 14 days in advance of withdrawal. Deposits, such as Christmas Club accounts and Vacation Club accounts, which are made under written contracts providing that no withdrawal shall be made until a certain number of periodic deposits have been made during a period of not less than three months constitute open account time deposits, even though some of the deposits are made within 14 days from the end of the period. A deposit with respect to which the bank merely reserves the right to require notice of not less than 14 days before any withdrawal is made is not an open account time deposit within the meaning of the above definition.

3. International banking facility time deposit, or IBF time deposit, is a deposit, placement, borrowing, or similar obligation represented by a promissory note, acknowledgment of advance, or similar instrument that is not issued in negotiable or bearer form. An IBF time deposit also has these characteristics:

a. It is payable on a specified date not less than two business days after the date of deposit, upon expiration of a specified period of time not less than two business days after the date of deposit, or upon written notice that actually is required to be given by the depositor not less than two business days prior to the date of withdrawal.

b. It represents funds deposited to the credit of a non-U.S. resident or a foreign branch, office, subsidiary, affiliate, or other foreign establishment (foreign affiliate) controlled by one or more domestic corporations provided that such funds are used only to support the operations outside the U.S. of the depositor or of its affiliates located outside the U.S.

c. It is held under an agreement or arrangement under which no deposit or withdrawal of less than $100,000 is permitted, except that a withdrawal of less than $100,000 is permitted if such withdrawal closes an account.

NOW Accounts. Title III of the DEPOSITORY INSTITUTIONS DEREGULATION AND MONETARY CONTROL ACT OF 1980 (P.L. 96-221, 94 Stat. 146) provided nationwide NOW account authority, effective December 31, 1980, under which all depository institutions are permitted to offer to certain depositors negotiable order of withdrawal (NOW) accounts, on which interest or dividends are paid and through which customers can make third-party payments using negotiable or transferable instruments. Those eligible to hold such NOW accounts are generally the same as those eligible to hold savings accounts. To promote consistency, to reduce confusion, and to eliminate the need to make determinations of eligibility in individual cases, the board of governors of the Federal Reserve System issued an interpretation (found in its Regulation Q) that the following classes of depositors are eligible to hold NOW accounts: (1) individuals, including sole proprietorships; (2) specific types of nonprofit organizations described in the Internal Revenue Code; and (3) governmental units holding funds for the use of medical and educational facilities. The interpretation permanently "grandfathered" NOW accounts opened before September 1, 1981, by those who were no longer eligible because of the Board's interpretation of Regulation Q.

Automatic Transfer Service. Automatic transfer service provides for the transfer of funds from savings to checking accounts. The board of governors of the Federal Reserve System in an interpretation of its Regulation Q cautioned that advertisements and promotional materials should clearly indicate that the automatic transfer service involves two separate accounts—a savings account and a checking account. For example, terms such as "checking-savings plan, "interest/checking plan," and "savings/checking accounts" are acceptable, since use of the hyphen, slash, or other similar sign or the plural "accounts" highlights that the service involves two accounts.

The board cautioned that one should avoid making reference to the automatic transfer service as equivalent to or similar to paying interest on checking accounts. The board believes that statements such as "interest on checking," "interest checking account," "interest-paying checking plan," and "almost like interest on checking" are inappropriate. Such statements do not accurately describe the nature of the service or indicate the existence of two separate accounts and may convey the incorrect impression that depositors will be receiving interest on demand deposits, which as of 1982 was still prohibited by federal law.

Similarly, the board believes it is inappropriate to refer to the automatic transfer service as "checking on savings" or "checkable savings." Such statements are undesirable because they could result in the mistaken belief that checks may be drawn by depositors against their interest-bearing savings accounts (NOW accounts are restricted to certain classes of depositors; see above).

Member banks were also reminded by the board that depositors must be specifically informed at the time of authorization of the automatic transfer service that the bank reserves the right to require a notice period of at least 30 days of intended automatic withdrawals of savings deposits. Written agreements entered into by member banks and their depositors must prominently disclose this reservation. Such withdrawal notice on passbook savings accounts has been as a matter of practice often waived.

Actions on Accounts by the DEPOSITORY INSTITUTIONS DEREGULATION COMMITTEE **(DIDC).** The DIDC was established on March 31, 1980, by the Depository Institutions Deregulation and Monetary Control Act of 1980. The purpose of the DIDC is to provide for the orderly phase-out of interest rate limitations on deposits at all federally insured commercial banks, saving and loan associations, and mutual savings banks over a six-year period. The DIDC's authority was scheduled to terminate on March 31, 1986.

BANK ACCOUNTING Format, classification of accounts, and definitions which would be followed beginning in 1969 by banks in the preparation of CALL REPORT of condition and their annual statement of income and dividends were disseminated by the three federal banking agencies and the National Association of State Supervisors of Banks. The aim was to restore the greatest degree of uniformity in requirements. Also motivating these changes were the disclosure requirements of the Securities Acts Amendments of 1964. In 1974, Section 12(i) of the Securities Exchange Act of 1934 was amended to require the banking agencies to adopt rules and regulations substantially similar to those of the SEC. (*See* particular reports for details.)

Besides the call report of condition, call reports include the following: (1) affiliate reports, when required by the comptroller of the currency with the call report of condition; (2) report of income and dividends, required annually by the comptroller of the currency for the 12-month period ending December 31; (3) trust department reports, to be submitted annually to the comptroller of the currency by each national bank which exercises trust powers; (4) reports of establishment of foreign branches or other international banking offices, report preceding acquisition of controlling interest in a foreign bank or other corporations, and report to the Comptroller within 30 days after relocation of foreign branch or office and after acquisition of noncontrolling interest in a foreign bank or other corporation.

Under current practice, bank call reports are collected by the appropriate federal regulator, each under its own authority. For national banks, the FDIC acts as the Comptroller of the Currency's processing agent for the data. The timing of the call reports is fixed by interagency agreement to coincide with each calendar quarter end, and their content is coordinated in accordance with section 1066(c) of Title X of the FINANCIAL INSTITUTIONS REGULATORY AND INTEREST RATE CONTROL ACT under the auspices of the FEDERAL FINANCIAL INSTITUTIONS EXAMINATION COUNCIL. Under existing statutes, the NATIONAL CREDIT UNION ADMINISTRATION and the FEDERAL HOME LOAN BANK BOARD are also subject to the Council's mandate respecting uniform reporting systems but are not obligated to provide the FDIC with call report data on credit unions and savings and loan associations.

BANK ACCOUNTING

Detailed instructions and filing criteria are published by the Federal Financial Institutions Examination Council in call report instruction booklets designed for small banks, standard banks, and banks with foreign offices.

Sample financial statements of a commercial bank are appended. *See* MEMBER BANK CALL REPORT.

The comptroller of the currency also requires that each national bank submit four times each year a report of the condition of its commercial department. The comptroller may also call for additional reports of condition from all national banks and special reports of condition from any national bank whenever he determines that such reports are necessary for the performance of his supervisory duties.

Federal Reserve member bank reports of condition and, if requested, reports of affiliates are submitted on call of the board of governors and submitted to the district Federal Reserve bank. The board of governors may also require reports from bank holding companies.

FIRST SAMPLE BANK
BALANCE SHEETS
December 31, 19X2 and 19X1

	19X2	19X1
ASSETS		
Cash and due from banks	$ 11,820,189	$ 15,009,846
Investment securities (Approximate market value $50,405,000 and $39,162,000 respectively) (Note 2)	51,172,385	41,284,011
Federal funds sold	2,040,000	5,000,000
Loans, net (Notes 3 and 5)	73,983,971	68,475,492
Direct lease financing (Note 4)	1,897,025	1,113,423
Bank premises and equipment, net (Note 6)	3,663,495	3,565,867
Accrued income receivable	1,378,072	1,121,050
Other real estate owned	95,000	50,000
Prepaid exenses and other assets	180,270	148,200
	$146,230,407	$135,767,889
LIABILITIES AND STOCKHOLDERS' EQUITY		
Liabilities:		
Deposits:		
Demand	$ 35,694,104	$ 36,304,092
NOW Accounts	25,957,283	18,763,947
Savings	29,346,911	29,569,682
Time, $100,000 and over (Note 7)	8,304,600	6,488,800
Other time	28,460,224	27,001,136
	$127,763,122	$118,127,657
Federal funds purchased	1,000,000	1,000,000
Notes payable (Note 7)	5,000,000	5,000,000
Accrued expenses and other liabilities	511,401	728,339
Deferred income tax credits (Note 9)	884,000	726,000
Subordinated debentures (Note 8)	1,196,000	1,196,000
	$136,354,523	$126,777,996
Commitments and contingenies (Note 11)		
Stockholders' equity:		
Capital stock:		
Preferred, no par value; authorized 20,000 shares; issued none	$ —	$ —
Common, $5 par value; authorized and issued 600,000 shares	3,000,000	3,000,000
Surplus	3,000,000	2,000,000
Retained earnings (Notes 7 and 14)	3,875,884	3,989,893
	$ 9,875,884	$ 8,989,893
	$146,230,407	$135,767,889

See Notes to Financial Statements.

For details on the annual and quarterly reports submitted pursuant to the Securities Exchange Act to the comptroller of the currency (12 CFR 11.4) and to the board of governors of the Federal Reserve System (Regulation F).

See ACCOUNTING, BANK BOOKKEEPING, BANK COST ACCOUNTING, BALANCE SHEET, BANK STATEMENT.

BIBLIOGRAPHY

American Institute of Certified Public Accountants. *Audits of Bank.* American Institute of Certified Public Accountants, New York, NY, 1984.

"Accounting for Liquidating Banks and Credit Card Portfolio Transactions." *Journal of Accountancy.* March, 1989.

CANRIGHT, C. "Measuring Product Profitability Requires a Cost Accounting System." *Magazine of Bank Administration*, January, 1989.

CATES, D. C., and DAVIS, H. A. "Risk Management of Off-Balance-Sheet Activated. *Journal of Commercial Bank Lending*, January, 1989.

Comptroller of the Currency. *Comptroller's Manual for National Banks.* Periodic updates.

Federal Reserve Regulatory Service.

FRANKSTON, F. M., and others. *Bank Accounting.* American Bankers Association, Washington, DC, 1984.

TIMEWELL, S. "All the King's Men." *Banker*, December, 1988.

VALENZA, C. G. "Cash Flow Controversy (FASB 95)." *Magazine of Bank Administration*, January, 1989.

WANG, P. "A Colossal Case of Apples and Oranges." *Forbes*, March 20, 1989.

FIRST SAMPLE BANK
STATEMENTS OF INCOME
Years Ended December 31, 19X2 and 19X1

	19X2	19X1
Interest income:		
Interest and fees on loans	$6,182,453	$5,822,016
Lease financing income	125,204	74,599
Interest on investment securities:		
U.S. Treasury	693,253	596,179
U.S. Government agencies and corporations	501,479	451,738
States and political subdivisions	1,157,170	959,094
Other	351,959	355,042
Interest on federal funds sold	382,895	537,412
	$9,394,413	$8,796,080
Interest expense:		
Interest on deposits	$4,381,893	$3,780,690
Interest on securities sold under agreements to repurchase and federal funds purchased	405,992	549,745
Interest on capital notes	89,700	89,700
	$4,877,585	$4,420,135
Net interest income	$4,516,828	$4,375,945
Provision for possible loan losses (Note 5)	89,000	96,000
Net interest income after provision for possible loan losses	$4,427,828	$4,279,945
Other income:		
Trust department income	$ 147,270	$ 236,583
Service fees	410,584	412,110
Other	154,441	115,843
Securities gains (losses)	105,827	(16,998)
	$ 818,122	$ 747,538
Other expenses:		
Salaries and wages	$1,668,093	$1,539,427
Pensions and other employee benefits (Note 10)	291,373	237,997
Occupancy expenses	198,374	166,868
Equipment rentals, depreciation, and maintenance	243,487	301,255
Other operating expenses	954,632	775,333
	$3,355,959	$3,020,880
Income before income taxes	$1,889,991	$2,006,603
Applicable income taxes (Note 9)	332,000	520,500
Net income	$1,557,991	$1,486,103
Net income per share of common stock	$ 2.60	$ 2.48

See Notes to Financial Statements.

BANK ACCOUNTING

FIRST SAMPLE BANK
STATEMENTS OF STOCKHOLDERS' EQUITY
Years Ended December 31, 19X2 and 19X1

	Preferred Stock	Common Stock	Surplus	Retained Earnings	Total
Balance, December 31, 19X0	$—	$3,000,000	$2,000,000	$3,103,790	$8,103,790
Net income	—	—	—	1,486,103	1,486,103
Cash dividends declared	—	—	—	(600,000)	(600,000)
Balance, December 31, 19X1	$—	$3,000,000	$2,000,000	$3,989,893	$8,989,893
Net income	—	—	—	1,557,991	1,557,991
Cash dividends declared	—	—	—	(672,000)	(672,000)
Transfer to surplus	—	—	1,000,000	(1,000,000)	—
Balance, December 31, 19X2	$—	$3,000,000	$3,000,000	$3,875,884	$9,875,884

See accompanying Notes to Financial Statements.

FIRST SAMPLE BANK
STATEMENTS OF CASH FLOWS
Years Ended December 31, 19X2 and 19X1

	19X2	19X1
Cash flows from operating activities:		
Interest received from:		
Loans and leases	$ 6,125,042	$ 6,030,872
Investment securities	2,509,887	2,290,103
Federal funds sold	383,462	537,412
Trust department income	147,270	236,583
Service fees	410,584	412,110
Other income	154,441	115,843
Interest paid to depositors	(4,598,831)	(3,589,933)
Interest paid on federal funds purchased	(405,992)	(549,745)
Interest paid on capital notes	(89,700)	(89,700)
Cash paid to suppliers and employees	(3,193,922)	(2,806,158)
Income taxes paid	(174,000)	(430,500)
Net cash provided by operating activities	$ 1,268,241	$ 2,156,887
Cash flows from investing activities:		
Proceeds from sales of investment securities	$ 10,610,000	$ 9,321,000
Purchase of investment securities	(20,273,547)	(7,996,125)
Federal funds sold, net	2,960,000	(2,150,000)
Principal collected on loans	25,316,540	13,695,098
Loans made to customers	—	(30,959,019)
Purchase of assets to be leased	(1,457,204)	(568,520)
Principal payments received under leases	673,602	278,356
Capital expenditures	(914,041)	(697,315)
Proceeds from sale of capital items	622,306	—
Net cash used in investing activities	$(13,421,363)	$(3,094,540)
Cash flows from financing activities:		
Net increase in demand deposits, NOW accounts and savings accounts	$ 6,360,577	$ 858,770
Proceeds from sales of time deposits	40,218,400	39,857,412
Payments for maturing time deposits	(36,943,512)	(33,942,480)
Dividends paid	(672,000)	(600,000)
Net cash provided by financing activities	$ 8,963,465	$ 6,173,702
Net increase (decrease) in cash and cash equivalents	$ (3,189,657)	$ 5,236,049
Cash and cash equivalents, beginning	15,009,846	9,773,797
Cash and cash equivalents, ending	$ 11,820,189	$15,009,846

ENCYCLOPEDIA OF BANKING AND FINANCE

BANK ADMINISTRATION INSTITUTE Bank Administration Institute (BAI) is a not-for-profit professional organization whose broad goals are to help bank managers achieve high levels of professional effectiveness and to help solve significant banking problems. These goals are pursued through programs of research and development, education, and technical assistance. Founded in 1924, the Institute is today the largest technical banking association in the world. It is governed by a board of directors. Responsibility for the management of the Institute's activities within a framework of policy established by the Board rests with the president, who is assisted by the Institute's staff located in Rolling Meadows, Illinois.

Bank Administration Institute is unique among professional organizations serving banking and financial services. Directly and through its affiliate, Bank Administration Foundation, BAI provides bankers with operational assistance, publications and periodicals, and professional educational development programs, that contribute to superior performance. By enabling managers and professionals at all levels to expand their knowledge and skills, the Institute enhances the effectiveness of financial institutions. Its not-for-profit status allows the Institute to serve bankers objectively as both advisor and analyst.

The Institute blends the policy-level experience of bankers with the specialized expertise of its professional staff. Members who serve on the board of directors, technical commissions, and advisory groups ensure that the Institute meets bankers' changing needs with high quality relevant programs and services. Information is presented across a wide range of banking specialties: operations and technology, security, checking and other payment services; taxation and financial products; financial and strategic planning; human resources; professional development; auditing and accounting.

BANK ADVERTISING *See* PUBLICITY DEPARTMENT.

BANK ANALYSIS The analysis department of a bank is typically concerned with analyzing data that affect budgeting, accounting, and operations. The goal is to improve the bank's performance.

Bank analysis procedures improved in the late 1970s as a result of the improvements in data availability and analytical concepts. Three important events occurred in financial disclosure, which made possible the effective analysis of U.S. banks and bank holding companies:

1. The call report, the statement all U.S.–domiciled banks are required to file regularly with federal regulators, was redesigned to display important new detail on reserves and deposits, among other things.
2. The Federal Reserve Board began to require all bank holding companies to file financial statements according to a standard format.
3. The Securities and Exchange Commission (SEC) published detailed guidelines governing the financial disclosure of publicly held bank holding companies.

See RATIO ANALYSIS, STATEMENT ANALYSIS.

BANK APPLIANCES Mechanical appliances adopted by banking institutions in recent years to shortcut the great volume of clerical detail and to mechanize operations in order to reduce expenses. The principal machines used in modern banking are adding machine, adding typewriter, addressing machine, anunciator, bookkeeping and billing machine, calculating machine, check cancellation machine, check endorsing machine, check protecting and writing machine, computing machines, coupon cutter, dictaphone, automatic cashier, automatic coin counting and wrapping machine, automatic typewriter, endorsing machines, envelope sealing machine, folding machine, letter opener, mailing machine, mimeograph, multigraph, numbering machine, pencil sharpener, photocopier, perforating machine, posting machine, proof machine, receipt machine, Recordak equipment, stamp-affixing machine, tabulating equipment, telautograph, time dating stamp, time lock, time recording machine, transit machine, typewriter.

See BANK EQUIPMENT. For development and bibliography in the field of bank automation, *see* AUTOMATION.

BANK-AT-HOME SERVICES Banking services that allow customers to use the telephone or other communication devices to transfer funds from their account to a merchant's account from their home or office.

BANK AUDITING *See* AUDIT, AUDITING DEPARTMENT, BANK EXAMINATION.

BANK BAD DEBT RESERVES Under the former Treasury Department ruling applicable after December 31, 1964, banks were entitled to tax-deductible build-up of debt reserves, subject to effective annual addition ceiling of 0.8% of loans at year-end, until they amounted to 2.4% of year-end eligible loans. Subsequent tax revisions modified these rulings.

Nothing prevents a bank from building up loss reserves beyond the levels specified, but such additional provision would not be entitled to tax-deductibility. Actually, loss experience of commercial banks since the depression-affected early 1930s had been below the tax guideline.

Reporting Requirements. Banks whose securities are subject to the registration requirements of Section 12(b) or Section 12(g) of the Securities Exchange Act of 1934 are required to submit financial statements, among other registration requirements, with the comptroller of the currency (national banks) and the board of governors of the Federal Reserve System (member state banks). The pertinent regulations are 12 CF 11, Securities Act Disclosure Rules, issued by the comptroller of the currency for national banks and Regulation F of the board of governors of the Federal Reserve System (12 CFR 206, Securities of Member State Banks). For nonmember state banks, the regulations on the subject of the Federal Deposit Insurance Corporation are designated Part 335.

Specification for accounting purposes in these regulations as to provision for loan losses by banks is similar. The following, from the Comptroller's Regulation (12 CFR 11.71), pertains to provision for loan losses (shown as operating expenses) in the bank statement of income:

1. Banks shall include a provision for potential losses in the current loan portfolio based on bank management's evaluation of the loan portfolio in light of all relevant factors.
2. Banks shall furnish in a note to financial statements an expla nation of the basis for determining the loan loss provision.
3. Banks which do not provide for loan losses on a reserve basis shall include the amount of actual net charge-offs (losses less recoveries) for the current year.

Pursuant to the TAX REFORM ACT OF 1986, banks are limited to a year-end bad debt reserve of 0.6% of loans for tax years beginning after 1992 and before 1988. Banks must compute reserves according to their own actual average loss experience for the current and the five preceding taxable years. If the loss reserves are equal to or in excess of 0.65%, they need not be reduced, but any addition thereto will be limited to the greater of either restoring them to their amount at the beginning of the period or restoring them to a percentage ceiling. If the loss reserves are less than 0.6%, the addition thereto will be limited in any one year to not more than 20% of the difference. The excess of the deduction allowed for a reasonable addition to a bad debt reserve over the deduction based on the institution's actual experience is a tax preference item for the alternative minimum tax. To change to the reserve method, a bank must obtain consent from the INTERNAL REVENUE SERVICE.

After 1986, certain large banks were not allowed to deduct for any addi-tion to their bad debt reserves; however, special recapture provisions apply for existing reserves of large and financially troubled banks. Large banks are defined as those with average adjusted bases of all assets exceeding $500 million or as members of a parent-subsidiary controlled group for which all assets exceed $500 million.

See BANK STATEMENT.

BIBLIOGRAPHY

COMPTROLLER OF THE CURRENCY. *Comptroller's Manual for National Banks.* Periodic updates.

BANK BALANCE This term has two meanings:

1. The amount standing to the credit of a depositor's account at a bank, representing the sum he or she is entitled to withdraw.
2. The difference between the total debits and credits, whether

against or in favor, of a bank at the clearinghouse, i.e., a given bank's clearinghouse debit or credit balance.

BANK BALANCE SHEET *See* BANK STATEMENT.

BANK BOOK PASSBOOK.

BANK BOOKKEEPING Bookkeeping which in most respects follows the principles of bookkeeping in other lines of business, but differs in two important particulars: (1) transactions must be recorded as soon after their occurrence as possible; and (2) the bank should be able to determine its exact financial status and results of operations at the close of each day's business.

A bank deals with cash and cash items. Most of its assets are quick or liquid assets which it endeavors to keep liquid so that customers may make withdrawals at their pleasure. A bank is a huge accounting machine, an instrument by which its customers mutually settle their debts. In keeping financial accounts for its customers a bank is an important factor in insuring their solvency. If, through an oversight in the bookkeeping department, a customer's account shows an overdraft when as a matter of fact funds have been received which would create a credit balance, but are not yet posted, the customer's position may be seriously jeopardized. Since a bank must handle a great volume of checks and other cash items affecting many separate accounts, some scheme must be provided for securing the posting of transactions to the ledgers with utmost dispatch and accuracy.

Examination standards call for the daily statement as of the date of the examination to be prepared by the bank from the general ledger as soon as possible after starting the examination. Moreover, reasonably frequent trial balances are one of the internal controls checked by examiners.

Even without this requirement, ordinary prudence would dictate a daily balancing of books. Because of the sheer volume of transactions a bank is called upon to administer, it is essential that each separate department and the bank as a whole prove its work daily, so that in case errors occur they can be ferreted out immediately, before matters become further involved. Furthermore, a proof is essential in determining the bank's condition as to solvency, liquidity, and profits. To protect its customers whose solvency partly depends upon the solvency of their bank, it is necessary for a bank to determine its financial condition at the close of each day's business.

The bookkeeping or accounting system of a bank varies according to its type, size, and kind of service performed, but most of its books and many of its operations are common to all. The bookkeeping work of a bank may be divided into the following tasks:

1. Preparation of the original entry records in the various operating departments;
2. Preparation and sorting of posting mediums for posting to depositors' and general ledgers;
3. Preparation of daily department proofs of original entry records;
4. Keeping the accounts of depositors in the depositors' or individual ledgers;
5. Keeping the general accounts (general ledger and statement book); and
6. Keeping the various departmental subsidiary ledgers, e.g., liability ledger, bond ledger, etc.

A bank's bookkeeping records may be classified in four broad divisions: exclusively corporate records, general accounting records, depositors' or individual ledgers, and department records. The exclusively corporate records consist of the following:

1. Stock journal or stock certificate book from which shares of stock are issued and which shows the evidence of ownership of the shares;
2. Stock transfer journal which is a chronological record of the transfers of shares;
3. Stock ledger which shows the number of shares owned and held by each stockholder;
4. Directors' minute book which contains the minutes of directors' meetings and their resolutions, which often affect the accounting records;
5. Articles of incorporation which contain the authorization for the bank's existence and affect the records with respect to capital stock;
6. Dividend book which contains a record of dividend disbursments and the names and addresses of stockholders entitled to receive dividends.

The general accounting records consist of a general ledger, statement book, and general expense book. The department records consist of various subsidiary ledgers, ticklers, and other facilitating records.

The following is a list of the more important bookkeeping records especially applicable to a commercial bank: acceptance ledger, acceptance liability ledger, acceptance maturity tickler, acceptance register, accounts opened and closed record, advice book, bank note register, bill ledger (book), bill maturity tickler, bill register, bond classification record, bond earnings record, bond journal, bond ledger, bond maturity tickler, branches ledger, cash book, cashier's check register, certificate of deposit register, certified checks register, collection ledger, commission record, coupon check register, coupon ledger, customers' securities control, depositors' ledger, discount ledger, discount maturity tickler, discount register, dividend book, exchange record, expense book, Federal Reserve ledger, Federal Reserve register, general ledger, indexes, individual ledgers, journal, letters of credit register, loan ledger, loan register, minute book, mortgage ledger, mortgage register, note tickler, offerings book, overdue bills book, real estate record, safe deposit register, securities ledger, securities register, security numbers record, signature records, stock certificate book, stock ledger, stock transfer journal, time deposits ledger, time loan maturity tickler, trust general ledger, trust securities register.

See AUDITING DEPARTMENT, BANK STATEMENT, GENERAL BOOKKEEPING DEPARTMENT, GENERAL LEDGER, STATEMENT DEPARTMENT.

See BIBLIOGRAPHY UNDER AUTOMATION.

BANK BRIBERY AMENDMENTS ACT OF 1985 In 1984, the Bank Bribery Act (18 U.S.C. Sec. 215) was amended as part of the Comprehensive Crime Control Act. These amendments made it a felony for employees of federally insured banks to give or receive anything of value in connection with any business of the bank. Interpreted literally this meant that nothing could be accepted that was even remotely connected to a transaction. These changes threatened the way bankers do business. The broadness and vagueness of this statute raised an outcry that led to further amendments.

The Bank Bribery Amendments Act of 1985 was passed to narrow and clarify the law. These amendments added two important conditions to the existing statute. As amended, the statute prohibits the giving or receiving of things of value in connection with the business of the bank only if such things are given or accepted *corruptly* and with the *intent* to influence or be influenced. The penalty provisions established under the old law are not changed. In response to these amendments, many banks established detailed guidelines as to the types of gifts and factors that could be accepted.

Federal statutes applicable to banks and bank employees containing additional ethical ramifications include:

12 U.S.C. Sec 78	Employment in securities businesses prohibited
12 U.S.C. Sec 92(a)(h)	Unlawful loan of trust fund
12 U.S.C. Sec 93(a)(b)	Personal liability of directors and penalties
12 U.S.C. Sec 503	Establishes liability of directors and officers of banks
12 U.S.C. Sec 375(a)(b)	Regulation of credit to insiders and political campaigns
12 U.S.C. Sec 501	Certifying a check drawn on an account in which there are insufficient collected funds
18 U.S.C. Sec. 1004	Falsifying of certified checks
122 U.S.C. Sec. 1972	Prohibition against tying arrangements and regulation of correspondent accounts
15 U.S.C. Sec 78(dd 1,2)	Foreign Corrupt Practices Act
18 U.S.C. Sec. 212	Making loans to bank examiners
18 U.S.C. Sec 215	Bank Bribery Act
18 U.S.C. Sec 656	Theft, embezzlement, misapplication of funds or assets

18 U.S.C. Sec. 1005	Unauthorized issuance of obligations or making false entries
18 U.S.C. Sec. 1344	Bank fraud statute

Source: Bank Administration Institute, *Codes of Conduct in the Financial Services Industry*, 3rd Ed., Rev. 1987.

BANK CAPITAL Major forms of bank capital include subordinated debt, preferred stock, and common equity. Subordinated debt includes interest-bearing obligations that represent a fixed amount of money at some future time, including capital notes and longer term debentures. Regulatory authorities have established rules that debt must meet to qualify as bank capital. Historically, the primary components of bank capital recognized by the three federal regulatory authorities include:

Common Stock
Perpetual preferred stock
Surplus (funds generated internally or externally)
Undivided profits (accumulated earnings less amounts shifted to the surplus account)
Contingency and other capital reserves
Mandatory convertible instruments
Allowance for possible loan and lease losses
Minority interest in equity accounts of consolidated subsidiaries
Less intangible assets and assets classified loss

Secondary components of bank capital include other financial instruments that possess some of the features of capital:

Limited-life preferred stock
Bank subordinated notes and debentures and unsecured long-term debt of the parent company and its nonbank subsidiaries
Add back intangible assets and assets

Secondary components were required to have an original weighted average maturity of at least seven years. Scheduled repayments would be made at least annually once contractual repayment of principal begins. The amount repaid in a given year shall be no less than the amount repaid in the previous year. The aggregate amount of limited-life preferred stock and subordinated debt qualifying as bank capital cannot exceed 50% of the amount of the bank's primary capital. The outstanding balance of the secondary components must be amortized in accordance with regulatory schedules.

The four major functions of bank capital are generally recognized to be the following:

1. To protect the uninsured depositor in the event of insolvency and liquidation.
2. To absorb unanticipated losses with enough margin to inspire continuing confidence to enable the bank, when under stress, to continue as a going concern.
3. To acquire the physical plant and basic necessities required to provide banking services.
4. To serve as a regulatory restraint on unjustified asset expansion.

Member banks of the Federal Reserve System must comply with Section 9 of the Federal Reserve Act and Regulation H of the board of governors. Regulation H specifies that the net capital and surplus of a member bank must be adequate in relation to the character and condition of its assets, deposit liabilities, and corporate responsibilities. Various ratios have been used by regulatory authorities to measure capital adequacy, including the ratio of capital to deposits and the ratio of capital to total assets. A capital-to-risk assets measurement tool was used by the comptroller's office. Risk assets were considered to be total assets less holdings of cash and U.S. Government securities. In the 1970s, the Comptroller's Office, the FDIC, and the Federal Reserve used trends and peer group comparisons of selected ratios to determine capital adequacy. The ratios considered included:

Equity capital/Total assets
Total capital/Total assets
Loans/Total capital
Classified assets/Total capital
Fixed assets/Total capital
Net rate-sensitive assets/Total assets
Reserve for charge-offs/Net charge-offs
Net charge-offs/Loans
Asset growth rate/Capital growth rate

In 1985, the three major federal bank regulatory agencies agreed on the following capital adequacy guidelines: Banks and bank holding companies must have "primary" capital of at least 5.5% of adjusted total assets and "primary and secondary" capital of at least 6% of adjusted total assets. Adjusted total assets refers to total assets plus reserves for loan and lease losses minus intangible assets and assets classified as loss but not charged off.

In 1989, federal banking regulators issued new capital guidelines for commercial banks. These guidelines are discussed under CAPITAL ADEQUACY, TIER ONE CAPITAL, and TIER TWO CAPITAL.

In an economic sense, bank capital refers to the permanent risk capital contributed by the owners. In cases involving a bank holding company, a distinction is made between the capital of the underlying bank(s) owned by the holding company and that of the parent corporation owned by outside shareholders. The economic definition excludes all debt. Some economists would include long-term convertible debt that has been issued by bank holding companies without restrictive covenants or sinking funds and with a small premium for conversion into common stock. Generally, if a security issue is available to absorb losses and shares in the profits, it can be considered capital. This concept of bank capital is somewhat similar to the regulatory concept.

BANK CHARTER *See* ARTICLES OF ASSOCIATION.

BANK CHARTER ACT *See* BANK OF ENGLAND.

BANK CHECK *See* CHECK.

BANK CLEARINGS Exchanges for the clearing house; checks and other items presented for collection through the clearing house by its members. Total bank clearings and balances for the principal cities having clearing house associations are published daily. Recapitulations on a weekly and annual basis are accumulated by various sources, including DUN & BRADSTREET, and the *Commercial and Financial Chronicle*, as a barometer of business activity.

Bank clearings, however, do not provide an inclusive barometer of deposit activity, as there are many transactions which do not clear through the clearing house. Also, as the number of banks is reduced by merger or consolidation, the volume of clearings is necessarily reduced. Accordingly, BANK DEBITS are a superior indicator of business activity as reflected in turnover of deposits and volume of money payments.

See BUSINESS BAROMETERS.

BANK COMMERCIAL PAPER Under Paragraph 7530, Rulings of the Comptroller of the Currency, first issued August 28, 1964, a National bank may issue at par or discount its negotiable or nonnegotiable promissory notes of any maturity. If there is to be a public offering of such notes or series of such notes, the provisions of Regulation 16 of the Comptroller of the Currency (12 CFR 16) as to registration requirements (filing of registration statement and use of offering circular) apply.

Such issuance of its own unsecured promissory notes by a national bank, similar to COMMERCIAL PAPER, was announced by Boston's largest national bank in September, 1964, at a time when Regulation Q of the Federal Reserve Board Regulations imposed a ceiling of 4% on time deposits, including time certificates of deposit, of 90 days or longer maturity. Since such notes would be borrowings rather than deposits, yields offered would not be subject to such ceiling set on time deposits, and the funds would not be subject to legal reserve requirement on deposits. Such notes, however, as borrowings would be subject to the general limitation on borrowings of national banks (100% of capital and 50% of surplus, 12 U.S.C. 82). Offerings would be made directly to investors, either on an interest or discount basis, in minimum denominations of $1 million, in maturities fitted to demand for short-term paper of 90 to 180 days, although any maturity up to limit of three years could be flexibly offered.

Bank commercial paper issues, however, did not at that time become widespread because Regulation Q subsequently raised interest rate ceilings on time certificates of deposit, because borrowing at the statutory limit could be better utilized for long-term capital notes and/or debentures for capital structure, and because in various states (e.g., New York) state-chartered banks were not authorized to issue such short-term, commercial paper type of bank notes. Moreover, the Board of Governors of the Federal Reserve System in its Regulation D, defining deposits subject to legal reserve requirements, included as managed liabilities such member bank short-term commercial paper. Such supplementary legal reserve requirements were imposed in 1979 but became zero in 1980.

See BANK NOTES.

BANK COMMISSIONER A title given in some states to the chief of the STATE BANKING DEPARTMENT. In other states this officer is known as Superintendent of Banks.

BANK COST ACCOUNTING Although first associated with manufacturing, cost accounting has become especially adaptable to banking; in fact, it is essential if proper charges for various services are to be made, and to determine whether given accounts are profitable or unprofitable. While cost accounting in banks is usually taken as synonymous with account analysis, its scope is more extensive. It includes the determination of costs by departments, classes of service, unit services, and deposit accounts. In a well-managed bank, the cost accounting system and budget system will serve as mutual checks on each other.

Various systems or methods of departmental or functional costing are in use, differing in detail and in execution. The following is suggestive of principles followed:

1. The first step is to define the departmental and functional cost classifications to be costed.
2. The next step is to analyze income and allocate it to each of the income-producing classifications. Income should be strictly of the operating type, excluding profits on sale of securities and recoveries. It is derived from two main sources: loans and investments (net, after provision for losses) and miscellaneous services and sources. Income credited is a net overall average rate, on the pooled aggregates of the net available funds: deposits (average balances less "float," legal reserve requirements, and till money requirements) and capital funds (less investment in bank buildings, furniture, and equipment). Once determined, the average earnings rate is then applied to each income-producing function's contribution of available funds, to establish the earnings credit.
3. The next step is the scheduling and breakdown of each type of expense and its inclusion in each category (service departments, indirect expenses, advertising, new business, operating functions, etc.). The respective expenses within each cost classification having been thus accumulated, the cost classifications may then be allocated to each income-producing department and function, either directly if specially traceable or on some suitable distribution formula (e.g., square feet used for building occupancy cost classification; services rendered for service type cost classifications; direct expense allocation for new business, advertising, and other direct expenses). Once each department's total direct and distributed costs have been accumulated, they may then be readily reallocated to each subdivision of that department to establish subcosts. Finally, the comparison of total direct and distributed costs, with the income credit, will indicate the relative profitableness of each income-producing department and function.

Account costs consist of account maintenance costs and costs of transactions handled. Account maintenance costs are those which exist regardless of size of activity of the account, and would include such items as preparation of statements, computations, proofing, file maintenance, etc. By noting by time studies the proportion of time in each department devoted to such work, one can determine the portion of that department's total operating expenses ascribable to account maintenance. Total departmental expenses, minus account maintenance costs, gives the total transaction cost which, divided by total weighted items handled, indicates the costs per unit of work handled. Weighting of items handled is necessary because of the difference in time required to handle each type of item. The weighting system may be devised by defining a standard weight unit (e.g., one minute), and by time studies determining the normal actual time required for a specific item's handling (e.g., an item requiring five minutes to handle is assigned a weight of five). Per item cost may be determined by multiplying the average cost of each unit of work by the weight assigned to that kind of item.

Two generic costing methodologies are used in cost analysis: actual (average item) costing and standard costing. In actual costing, unit costs are determined by dividing the total cost by the related volume.

$$\frac{\text{Estimated total costs for a budget period}}{\text{Average volume}} = \text{Unit costs}$$

Estimating total costs of an activity usually requires analyzing costs into variable and fixed costs. Total variable costs (interest expense, computed paper) change in proportion as the level of activity changes; total fixed costs (usually officers' salaries, depreciation, insurance, rent) remain constants over a relevant range of volume. On a per unit basis variable costs remain relatively constant; fixed costs per unit change with volume (they decrease as volume increases and increase as volume decreases). Variable costs are incurred as a result of activity. If there is no activity, there are no variable costs.

In standard costing, benchmark data are used to determine what the cost should be. Standard costs are used as a basis for comparison. They represent the criterion for what the value of an activity or product should be. Standard costing relies on consistent measurement for work or activity. Bank measurement programs for establishing standards are designed to assist in staffing and costing. Time ladders represent one work measurement technique. Time ladders break an employee's work day into segments (ladders). Time allocated to specific tasks can be identified. The identified tasks are accumulated into activities for costing purposes. These data can then be used for costing products and services.

A 1989 survey of cost accounting in large banks and savings and loan associations ranked goals of cost accounting as follows:

1. Product development and pricing.
2. Achieving cost reductions.
3. Performance evaluation.
4. Industry cost comparison.

The above fundamentals are of general application, but bank cost accounting systems will differ widely, based on local adaptation of principles to specific needs. An essential first step in all cost accounting systems is to know what costs are in sufficient degree of detail. To help in the determination of this, the assistance of professional bank analysts, correspondents, and banking associations is available to supplement the bank's own accounting and auditing staff. Knowing its costs per department, per account, or per item, a bank is then able to apply corrective measures. In analysis of accounts, for example, reduction of any interest paid, increase in average balance requirement, reduction in activity, and, finally, service charges may be necessary steps in bringing account cost into line with applicable earnings.

BIBLIOGRAPHY

CHEATHAM, C. B. *Cost Management for Profit Centers*. Institute for Business Planning, 1981.
COLE., L. P. *Cost Analysis and Control in Banks*. Bankers Publishing Company, Rolling Meadows, IL, 1985.
MOTLEY, L. B. *Pricing Deposit Services*. Bankers Publishing Company, Rolling Meadows, IL, 1983.
National Association of Accountants, New York, NY:
  Accounting for Costs of Capacity.
  Analysis of NonManufacturing Costs for Managerial Decision.
  Applications of Direct Costing.
  Costing Joint Products.
  Direct Costing.
  Separating and Using Costs as Fixed and Variable.

BANK CREDIT The EARNING ASSETS of commercial banks, including the variety of short- and long-term loans made to individuals, partnerships, corporations, other business firms, banks, and governmental units and agencies; the banks' holdings of investments (U.S. Government, state and municipal, and corporate obligations). Expansion of loans and investments creates derivative deposits and thus depends upon the banks' supply of EXCESS RESERVES, or cash resources in excess of legal reserve requirements against deposits. Bank reserves, and specifically excess reserves, are influenced by demand for bank credit, banks' expansion or contraction of earning assets, and MONETARY POLICY of the Board of Governors of the Federal Reserve System.

Federal Reserve credit consists of those Federal Reserve factors which supply (if increased) or reduce (if decreased) member bank reserves, including, for the 12 Federal Reserve banks: holdings of U.S. Government securities and federal agency issues bought outright as the result of OPEN MARKET OPERATIONS or temporarily held as the result of REPURCHASE AGREEMENTS; bills (bankers acceptances) bought outright or under repurchase agreements; discounts and advances to member banks; and "float" (excess of cash items in process of collection over deferred availability items), which measures the credit to member bank reserve balances given on collection items pursuant to deferred availability schedule. Other Federal Reserve assets have also become an important part of Federal Reserve credit because such item, in the consolidated weekly statement, includes Federal Reserve holdings of foreign currencies in connection with foreign exchange operations by the Federal Reserve Bank of New York.

Bank credit, which if expanded results in creation of deposits, is to be distinguished from TRADE CREDIT, also referred to as commercial credit or mercantile credit, which is credit in kind (goods and services) extended by business firms to other business firms, and from the PUBLIC CREDIT or credit standing of governmental units and agencies resorting to borrowing.

See CREDIT, SCHEDULE SHOWING WHEN PROCEEDS OF ITEMS WILL BECOME AVAILABLE.

BANK CREDIT CURRENCY *See* CREDIT CURRENCY.

BANK CREDIT PROXY The total of all member bank deposit liabilities subject to reserve requirements (private demand deposits, U.S. Government demand deposits, and time and savings deposits). There was usually a close correlation, although not necessarily day to day, between changes in bank credit (loans and investments) and changes in such deposits subject to legal reserve requirements, according to the chief of the banking section, Division of Research and Statistics, board of governors of the Federal Reserve System. Thus these deposits could afford an indicator of the direction and relative size of bank credit movements over the short run.

Beginning in May, 1966, directives of the FEDERAL OPEN MARKET COMMITTEE on open market operations included a proviso clause, and the bank credit proxy came to be used to implement instructions in that clause. An example is found in the committee's directive for the September 13, 1966, meeting, which instructed the manager of the system open market account to maintain "firm but orderly conditions in the money market; provided, however, that operations shall be modified in the light of unusual liquidity pressures or of any apparently significant deviations of bank credit from current expectations."

The annual report for 1966 of the board of governors explained the introduction of the proviso clause and its implementation. Such a proviso clause, which had been under discussion by the committee and its staff for several months, was designed to permit the manager to modify day-to-day operations if cumulating evidence of an undesirably rapid expansion of credit developed during the interval between committee meetings. The initial choice of required reserves as the conditioning variable in the proviso was made largely on practical considerations involving the timely availability of data relating to current bank credit and money supply expansion. Later in the year the conditioning variable was shifted to total member bank deposits subject to reserve requirements, the so-called bank credit proxy. The proviso clause was used in one form or another in the directives throughout the rest of the year. It provided a means of responding to unexpectedly or undesirably large movements in the banking aggregates, while still allowing open market operations to facilitate a generally smooth day-to-day functioning of the banking system and the overall payments mechanism in the face of sharply fluctuating flows of reserves and deposits in the short run. Reference to the bank credit proxy continued to be made until mid-1977.

Advantages of the bank credit proxy, from the point of view of the monetary authorities were as follows:

1. With member banks accounting for close to 85% of total deposits of all commercial banks, the proxy gave fairly comprehensive coverage of the commercial banking system as a whole.
2. Such deposit information is readily available. In complying with legal reserve requirements each member bank files with its Federal Reserve bank a weekly report showing daily deposit totals by type of deposit.
3. These daily basic data can be converted to weekly and monthly averages of daily figures, thereby smoothing out erratic day-to-day fluctuations in deposits and providing data amenable to more precise seasonal adjustment. The result is a more reliable measure of current trends than a series based on single-day figures available from the board's end-of-month bank credit series would be.
4. Member bank deposit information is reported promptly after the close of each weekly period, so that nearly final figures for all member banks are available with only a one-week lag. These deposit data are supplemented by data on required reserves collected daily from nearly all large reserve city banks and by data on deposits and reserves collected once in the middle of each reporting week from a sample of small country banks. On this basis, projections of total deposits for the current week can be updated at any time during the week if the additional data suggest a movement significantly different from that projected.

The disadvantages of the bank credit proxy were as follows:

1. Significantly different movements in total deposits and in bank credit can and do occur, both in the very short run and over longer periods. For example, rather large discrepancies developed during 1966 itself as a result of changes in volume of EURODOLLARS that American banks borrowed from their foreign branches to accommodate domestic loan demand, when large city banks were squeezed for funds because of runoffs in time certificates of deposit. Other sources of discrepancies between total deposits and bank credit would include changes in bank capital, borrowings at the Federal Reserve, and changes in cash or fixed assets.
2. Bank credit trends, although traditionally an important guide to monetary policy, are neither the only nor necessarily the most important factor taken into account in current policy formulation and administration. Basic considerations include real factors (developments in industrial production, labor market, business investment, wholesale and retail prices, etc.) and significant financial variables (developments in the international payments position of the U.S., money and capital markets, interest rates, bank reserve positions, aggregate reserve behavior, distribution of reserves among banks, changes in the money supply and in commercial bank time deposits and savings deposits, and flows of funds through other lending institutions).
3. Also, a change in the share of total bank credit of nonmember banks would affect the correlation between the member bank proxy and total bank credit.
4. For the general public, the bank credit proxy data become available in the *Federal Reserve Bulletin* with a month's lag, too slow an availability. Accordingly, the *Morgan Guaranty Survey* suggested a "proxy for the proxy" in the form of total of member bank reserves held against deposits: (1) volume of reserves will change more or less in line with changes in deposits, in the absence of changes in reserve requirements, which can be estimated and allowed for; (2) changes in composition of total deposits, as between demand and time deposits, and as between deposits held by country banks and those held by reserve city banks, will affect reliability of volume of reserves as a guide; but in the short run such changes in composition of deposits may be assumed not to be drastic. Availability for the general public is prompt. Every Thursday, the board of governors publishes daily average total reserves for the week ending the preceding day; and the Federal Reserve Bank of St. Louis adjusts the total reserves both for seasonality and for the estimated effect of any changes in legal reserve requirements (available weekly).

As a second possible "proxy for the proxy" to ensure prompter availability for the general public, the *Morgan Guaranty Survey* suggested use of the weekly "Money Supply and Time Deposits" release of the board of governors (numbered H.6). This release provides a weekly estimate of the daily average demand deposits component of money supply as well as time deposits adjusted for all commercial banks, roughly corresponding to such components of the official proxy. But it does not show the U.S. government demand deposits reported on a seasonally adjusted basis.

Summary. As analysts of the Federal Reserve's staff and the *Morgan Guaranty Survey* pointed out, neither the bank credit proxy nor any other single measure could be perfectly indicative of monetary trends and therefore a guide to monetary policy. But the bank credit proxy was held in high regard by the board's chief of the banking section of the Division of Research and Statistics: "The availability of a sensitive current measure of bank credit trends, which the proxy represents, has contributed significantly to improving the factual foundation for the discussion, formulation, and implementation of monetary policy."

BANK DEBITS Data for bank debits and demand deposit turnover, published in the G.6 statistical release of the Board of Governors of the Federal Reserve System, was revised in 1977. The new series, which began with July, 1977, and is based on reports from a national sample of about 300 member banks, replaced the series for 233 standard metropolitan statistical areas (SMSAs), which was terminated with the June, 1977, data.

The new series provides monthly estimates of debits, deposits, and deposit turnover at all commercial banks for demand deposits, total savings deposits, business savings deposits, and savings deposits of all other customers. For purposes of the new series, demand deposits include deposits of individuals, partnerships, and corporations, and of states and political subdivisions in the U.S. All debits and turnover estimates are expressed as annual rates. Both the aggregate debits to demand deposits and the demand deposit turnover are seasonally adjusted.

Debits to deposit accounts measure the transactions velocity or turnover of the deposits, for "indeed, changes in the rate of money turnover may be as significant in determining policies intended to achieve appropriate levels of spending as the quantity of money itself, however measured" (Garvy and Blyn, *The Velocity of Money*). In recent years, because of electronic funds transfer mechanisms and other improvements in the rapidity of transmission of funds, including automated clearing houses, the effective money supply (total of the money supply as of given dates, times the rate of turnover) has become even more meaningful for monetary policy than merely the totals of the money supply as of given dates. Whether by means of checks drawn or wire transfers of funds resulting in debits to deposit accounts, turnovers have increased both in number and rapidity, reducing "float," shortening the period for availability of deposited funds, and making possible the carrying of smaller cash balances in deposit accounts. Moreover, both demand deposits and savings deposits have been involved in the rise in turnover.

Income velocity of the money supply (net national product times the money supply) has come to be more emphasized than transactions velocity in economic analysis. In the exercise of monetary policy, velocity of both types is the most difficult factor to control. An increase in the money supply might be offset by a decline in velocity, while a decrease in the money supply might similarly be offset by an increase in velocity.

BANK DEPOSIT   See BANK ACCOUNT, DEMAND DEPOSITS, DEPOSITS, TIME DEPOSITS.

BANK DEPOSIT INSURANCE ACT   The act of June 16, 1934, which extended to June 30, 1935, the temporary plan for insurance of bank deposits originally set up by the BANKING ACT OF 1933. Public Resolution of June 28, 1935, further extended the temporary plan for insurance of commercial bank deposits to August 31, 1935. Permanent deposit insurance was provided by the BANKING ACT OF 1935, approved August 23, 1935. On September 21, 1950, the Federal Deposit Insurance Act (64 Stat. 873; 12 U.C.S. 1811-1831) was made a separate independent law, with numerous amendments, representing its withdrawal from Section 12B of the Federal Reserve Act as amended, which previously had carried the bank deposit insurance act and amendments.

BANK DIRECTORS   See DIRECTORS.

BANK DISCOUNT RATE   A method for calculating loan interest based on the amount to be repaid. When this method of calculating the interest charge is used, the amount loaned is equal to the amount to be repaid minus the interest amount. For example, $2,400 is borrowed at 15% and repaid after one year. The interest would be $360 for one year. In the bank discount method, that $360 would be deducted from the $2,400, leaving $2,040 to be used for the year. The effective interest rate is 17.647 % ($360 divided by $2,040). Regulation Z would require the bank to disclose the true annual percentage rate.

BANK DRAFT   A sight or demand draft, drawn by one bank as drawer upon another bank as drawee. Such an instrument is to be distinguished from a CASHIER'S CHECK.

Bank drafts purchasable at small fees by a bank's customers provide a highly acceptable instrument of DOMESTIC EXCHANGE. For example, New York funds would be readily provided by the bank draft of an interior bank, drawn on its New York City correspondent bank, purchased by the interior bank's customer faced with the necessity of payment in New York City, as compared to a local check.

In FOREIGN EXCHANGE, bankers' sight or demand drafts, drawn on balances maintained with foreign bank correspondents, provide a demand form of payment in the foreign currency concerned which may be available at spot rates if the distance involved permits quick airmail arrival of the instruments.

See BANK ACCEPTANCE, DRAFT.

BANK EMPLOYEES   See BANK OCCUPATIONS, PERSONNEL DEPARTMENT.

BANK ENDORSEMENT   See BANK STAMP.

BANK EQUIPMENT   As the result of AUTOMATION of bank operations by use of electronic equipment, equipment in the modernized bank may be classified in two categories, the conventional and the electronic.

Conventional bank equipment includes such manual, semiautomatic, and automatic items as the following: adding machine, adding typewriter, addressing machine, annunciator, automatic typewriter, bookkeeping and billing machine, calculating machine, cash register, check cancellation machine, check endorsing machine, check protecting and writing machine, check signer, check sorters (vertical, flat, and rotating), coin counters, sorters, trays and wrappers, coupon cutter, dictaphone, dictation machine, duplicator, dry copier, endorsing machine, envelope sealing machine, files (elevator, power, rotary, and visible), folding machine, letter opener, mailing machine, microfilm processor, mimeograph, multigraph, numbering machine, paper destroyer, perforating machine, photostat, posting machine, posting tray cabinets, proof machine, receipt machine, Recordak equipment, stamp–affixing machine, tabulating equipment, telautograph, time dating stamp, time lock, time recording machine, transit machine, and typewriters (manual, electric).

Electronic bank equipment includes the following: electronic bookkeeping machines; MICR (magnetic ink character recognition) check equipment, including electronic reader-sorter and computer; automated teller machine (ATM) equipment; electronic data processing equipment, including punched card tabulating equipment, sorting machine, tabulating and printing machine, and computer; TV bank protection units, including TV cameras; TV bank signature verifier; video tape recorder; tape listers; selective tape printers; on-line disk files; electronic accounting computer; and data communication equipment.

Bank equipment, comprehensively, includes all movable furniture and fixtures of the bank. By contrast, bank premises includes vaults, fixed machinery and equipment, after-hours depositories, parking lots owned adjoining or not adjoining the bank premises that are used by customers or employees, and potential building sites. Equipment expenses include normal and recurring depreciation charges; rental costs of office machines and tabulating and data processing equipment, if any; and ordinary repairs to furniture and office machines, including servicing costs. Taxes on equipment should be included as part of equipment expenses. If the bank leases equipment to others, Regulation F of the Board of Governors of the Federal Reserve System calls for netting the income from any such rents received against equipment expenses.

See BIBLIOGRAPHY under AUTOMATION.

ENCYCLOPEDIA OF BANKING AND FINANCE

BANKER A person engaged in the banking business; one who lends funds belonging to others, as distinguished from one who lends his own money (a capitalist). The banking laws of many states reserve the term banker to designate private banks as distinguished from incorporated banks, at the same time restricting the term bank to incorporated banks. The term is often improperly used as the equivalent of the term FINANCIER, to include investment bankers, stock exchange brokers, syndicate managers, etc.

See INDIVIDUAL BANKER, PRIVATE BANKING.

BANKERS ACCEPTANCE See BANK ACCEPTANCE.

BANKERS' ASSOCIATIONS Groups of banks, bankers, trust companies, etc., formed to promote their general welfare and useful information on banking practices and customs and to secure mutual protection against crime. The most important of these associations is the AMERICAN BANKERS ASSOCIATION, which includes a division each for national banks, state banks, stock savings banks, and trust companies. Other bankers' associations of national scope and influence are the Association of Reserve City Bankers, BANK ADMINISTRATION INSTITUTE, INVESTMENT BANKERS ASSOCIATION OF AMERICA, National Association of Mutual Savings Banks, Farm Mortgage Bankers' Association of America, and Morris Plan Bankers' Association.

Besides the bankers' associations of national scope, practically every state has a separate bankers' association, e.g., New York Bankers' Association, Ohio Bankers' Association, Wisconsin Bankers' Association. Many of these statewide associations publish a sectional bank magazine under their auspices. In several states mutual savings banks and investment bankers have organized separate state associations.

See FINANCIAL MAGAZINES.

BANKER'S BANK A bank located in a large city which specializes in transactions with other smaller banks; also a CENTRAL BANK, such as the Federal Reserve banks or the Bank of England.

In the United States, the banker's banks are one of the 12 Federal Reserve District Banks:

Districts	City (Branch or *Facility*)
1	Boston
2	New York (Buffalo)
3	Philadelphia
4	Cleveland (Cincinnati, Pittsburgh)
5	Richmond (Baltimore, Charlotte, *Culpepper*)
6	Atlanta (Birmingham, Jacksonville, Miami, Nashville, New Orleans)
7	Chicago (Detroit)
8	St. Louis (Little Rock, Louisville, Memphis)
9	Minneapolis (Helena)
10	Kansas City (Denver, Oklahoma City, Omaha)
11	Dallas (El Paso, Houston, San Antonio)
12	San Francisco (Los Angeles, Portland, Salt Lake City, Seattle)

BANKER'S BILL A bill of exchange drawn by a bank in one country upon a bank in another country, usually against credit balances and without supporting documents, as distinguished from a commercial bill.

See BILL OF EXCHANGE.

BANKERS BLANKET BOND An insurance contract designed to reimburse the bank for loss due to employee dishonesty, robbery, burglary, theft, forgery, mysterious disappearance, and in some cases, damage and destruction to premises. This contract provides coverage in a combination policy that usually is not available separately.

Most blanket bonds are written with some form of deductible.

Many surety companies regard deductibles as a method of reminding banks that good internal controls will reduce their loss expense.

Notable exclusions contained in most blanket bond forms include losses arising from credit or charge cards; ATMs; safe deposit liability; check kiting operations; and outside agents, especially mortgage servicing or data processing. Several of these areas can be covered through special endorsements to the blanket bond, and some are covered in separate policies. Banks can also cover in separate endorsements coverage for stop-payment liability, special transit cash letter coverage, and securities deposited with correspondents.

Premiums for bankers blanket bonds issued by domestic companies are established through an experience rating plan by the Surety Association of America. Premium costs are based on the actual loss experience of each bank in the various deposit groups.

As a general rule, it is desirable to carry the broadest form of protection available; coverage should apply automatically to new risks of the same character; continuous policies are preferable to term policies; policies should be written for a fixed premium so that a definite amount can be budgeted as the cost of the coverage for the year; insurance policies should have a common premium anniversary date; and coverage should be secured in as few contracts as possible and from as few companies as possible.

BANKER'S DRAFT A check or bill drawn by one bank against balances deposited with another. The term usually applies to domestic transactions.

See DRAFT.

BANKERS' SHARES Introduced with the early American investment trust shares of the fixed type, now largely obsolete, the term designated the certificates of ownership issued by the trustee, usually a trust company, upon deposit by the sponsor of units of the underlying securities. For example, upon deposit with the trustee of the designated fixed unit, say 10 shares each of 25 specific companies, the trustee issued to the sponsor 2,000 certificates of ownership, or bankers' shares, which were sold to investors by the sponsor and distributors. Each certificate of ownership evidenced the holder's 0.0005% interest in the underlying unit. Upon accumulation of 2,000 certificates of ownership the holder usually had the privilege of presenting them for the underlying unit under stated conditions.

The 1929-1932 deflation took a heavy toll of fixed type investment trusts, and none is now being actively offered. Because of termination dates in the future, however, various of these fixed type companies were still in legal existence, slated for complete liquidation upon termination dates.

For full treatment of this subject, see INVESTMENT COMPANY.

BANK EXAMINATION An inspection of the financial condition of a bank, initiated by the bank itself or conducted by legally constituted authorities, to assure the depositors, stockholders, and the public that the affairs of the bank are being conservatively and efficiently managed. Bank examinations may be classified as external and internal. The former are compulsory and are conducted by agencies created by the law for that purpose. The latter are conducted by the bank's own auditing department or by public accountants at the request of the bank.

National banks are subject to at least two examinations a year by national bank examiners, acting under the supervision of the Comptroller of the Currency. State banks are also usually subject to two examinations a year, acting under the supervision of the state banking department. The New York State banking laws also require periodic examinations to be made by the board of directors of a bank, but they are allowed to engage public accountants to conduct the examination in their stead. The purpose of directors' examinations is to place the board on record as having intimate knowledge of the affairs of the institution which they direct. Banks which are members of a clearing house association are often subject to examination by such association. Clearing house examinations are not required by law, but are instituted as a matter of conservative banking practice.

Examiners of the Federal Deposit Insurance Corporation may examine any state nonmember bank which is insured or is making application for insurance. Also, with consent of the Comptroller of the Currency and the Board of Governors of the Federal Reserve System, the Federal Deposit Insurance Corporation may examine any national bank or state member bank; it can also examine any closed insured bank.

Federal Reserve banks are subject to examination by the Federal Reserve Board which maintains a division of examinations and a chief federal reserve examiner. The Federal Reserve Board also has power to examine member banks. The Federal Reserve Act provides that any Federal Reserve bank may, with the approval of the Federal Reserve Board, examine any member bank within its district. In practice, the district Federal Reserve bank usually secures a copy of

BANK EXAMINATION

the examination of the district national bank examiner and thus does not examine further in the case of national banks in the district. The district Federal Reserve bank, however, has power to examine any member bank in the district if improper use of Federal Reserve credit is being made. State member banks are also examined by district Federal Reserve banks, usually at the same time and in cooperation with state examiners. The trust department of a national bank is subject to examination by the banking department of the state in which it is located.

The specific purposes of an external bank examination are to ascertain (1) whether the bank is solvent as shown by a verification of its assets and liabilities; (2) whether the management is conforming to the restrictions imposed by law; and (3) whether the bank, although conforming to the legal restrictions, is adopting policies which may lead to embarrassment or disaster at a future date.

An external bank examination is not a complete AUDIT and is not so intended. They are distinct in their purposes. Bank examiners do not set up a complete financial statement which purports to be a true and correct exhibit of the bank's financial condition. Neither do they certify that no defalcations have occurred.

A bank that may be thoroughly examined in one or two days could not be completely audited in less time than one or two weeks. Every bank in the system should receive a thorough audit at least once a year by qualified accountants not connected with the management of the bank in any way.

It is incumbent upon an examiner, in addition to seeing that the business of the bank is conducted within the provisions and limitations of the banking laws, to satisfy himself that every dollar that has been paid into the institution, as shown by its books, is properly accounted for. But it is the business of an auditor to determine by balancing and verifying each and every account whether the books show correctly every dollar received.

It is no reflection upon an examiner who fails to discover a shortage which is the result of the pernicious practice, which prevails in some of the smaller banks, of permitting the individual ledger bookkeeper to receive deposits and make entries in and balance passbooks or a receiving teller to make entries in the ledgers. A shortage due to the opportunities afforded by this objectionable practice may remain concealed for years unless revealed by accident and can be discovered only by balancing or verifying the passbooks.

After the examination is completed, a comprehensive report is prepared and submitted in writing by the chief bank examiner to the board of directors. The board of directors is required to adopt the recommendations of the bank examiner who may, for example, require writing off all overdue notes or depreciation on investments, and even that more capital be furnished to make good losses sustained, even though a deficit has not occurred. Improvident policies and loose accounting methods are criticized, and recommendations are made for their improvement. The report of a national bank examiner is required to be read at the next succeeding meeting of the board of directors and noted in the minutes.

Internal examinations conducted by a bank's own auditing department may be classified as continuous and spot. The general control of the bookkeeping and accounting routine, summarization of department proofs, and reconcilement of customers' accounts may be regarded as a continuous audit. These functions are performed daily in order to secure protection against theft or defalcation and to prevent clerical errors.

Spot examinations are irregular, the element of surprise being their chief characteristic. The auditors make their appearance in a certain department of the bank and verify the assets under custody without being announced. It is calculated that a spot audit tends to assure constant alertness in the clerical force.

Uniform Agreement on Classification of Assets and Appraisal of Securities Held. Examination procedures established in 1938, revised July 15, 1949, and further revised May 7, 1979, in a joint statement issued by the Board of Governors of the Federal Reserve System, the Office of the Comptroller of the Currency, the Federal Deposit Insurance Corporation, and the Conference of State Bank Supervisors. The joint statement called for the classification of assets and the appraisal of securities held by banks.

1. *Classification of assets in bank examinations.* During the 1980s classification units were designated as substandard, doubtful, and loss. A substandard asset is considered inadequately protected by the current sound worth and paying capacity of the obligor or of the collateral pledged, if any. Assets so classified must have a well-defined weakness or weaknesses that jeopardize liquidation of the debt. They are characterized by the distinct possibility that the bank will sustain some loss if the deficiencies are not corrected. An asset classified doubtful has all the weaknesses inherent in one classified substandard, with the added characteristic that the weaknesses make collection or liquidation in full, on the basis of currently existing facts, conditions, and values, highly questionable and improbable. Assets classified loss are considered uncollectible and of such little value that their continuance as bankable assets is not warranted. This classification does not mean that the asset has absolutely no recovery or salvage value, but rather it is not practical or desirable to defer writing off this basically worthless asset even though partial recovery may be effected in the future. Fifty percent of the total of doubtful and all of loss will be deducted in computing the net sound capital of the bank. Amounts classified loss should be promptly charged off.

2. *Appraisal of securities in bank examinations.* Investment quality securities are marketable obligations in which the investment characteristics are not distinctly or predominantly speculative. This group generally includes investment securities in the four highest rating grades and unrated securities of equivalent quality. Neither market appreciation nor depreciation in these securities will be taken into account in figuring net sound capital of the bank. This policy is intended to apply to recognized sound investment practices of banks and not to those situations where the portfolio requires special treatment by a supervisory agency.

Subinvestment quality securities are those in which the investment characteristics are distinctly or predominantly speculative. This group generally includes securities in grades below the four highest grades and unrated securities of equivalent quality, defaulted securities, and subinvestment quality stocks.

Securities in grades below the four highest rating grades and unrated securities of equivalent value will be valued at market price, and the depreciation will be classified doubtful; remaining book value will be classified substandard. Depreciation in defaulted securities and subinvestment quality stocks will generally be classified loss; remaining book value will be classified substandard.

An exception to the above will be made in the case of municipal general obligations which are backed by the credit and taxing power of the issuer. The entire book value of subinvestment quality municipal general obligations, which are not in default, will be classified substandard. These exceptions will not apply in those instances where the supervisory authorities determine that there is no likelihood that the municipality will be able ultimately to repay or satisfactorily restructure its obligations. In the event of a default of a municipal general obligation, a period of time is usually necessary to permit the market for these defaulted securities to stabilize or for the issuer to put in place budgetary, tax, or other actions that may eliminate the default or otherwise improve the post-default value of the securities. The market for the defaulted securities will be periodically reviewed by the regulatory authorities. Upon a determination that a functioning market has been reestablished, depreciation on defaulted municipal general obligations will be classified as loss. During such interim, the book value of all defaulted municipal general obligation securities will be classified doubtful.

Uniform Interagency Examination Procedures for Country Risk. The examination system for assessing country risk concentrations is administered by a nine-member committee made up chiefly of experienced examiners and supervisory personnel from the three federal bank regulatory agencies. The committee is known as the Interagency Country Exposure Review Committee. Its primary functions are to perform the following tasks:

1. Review economic conditions in countries where loans are made by U.S. banks.
2. Determine the levels of a bank's capital funds at which concentrations should be commented on.
3. Determine when credits should be classified as substandard, doubtful, or loss because of an interruption in payment or when an interruption is imminent.
4. Prepare commentaries on developments in foreign countries for use by examiners.

The May 7, 1979, statement by the referenced committee includes several other important comments. Diversification is particularly relevant to international lending because the assessment of country risk involves great uncertainties and is subject to a considerable margin of error. Determinations of the adequacy of diversification within a bank's portfolio are based primarily on comparisons of individual country risk exposures to a bank's capital funds. Where concentrations are found, examiners separate a bank's loans in a country by type of credit, type of borrower, and loan maturities. The degree of risk involved is assessed in the light of these components as well as internal and external factors that have an impact upon the debt service capacity of public and private borrowers within the country.

With the primary objective of encouraging appropriate diversification in the international lending portfolios of U.S. banks, the country exposure examination procedures attempt to point out special risk situations and, where necessary, secure corrective action. In a special section of the examination report, examiners list all country risk exposures that seem large in relation to the lending bank's capital funds. The examiners also make special comment on concentrations of loans in countries with high debt service requirements or other actual or potential balance of payments weaknesses. Normally these comments will refer to relatively large exposures in such countries and give particular emphasis to situations that include a high proportion of longer-term loans. Lending in any country able to meet its current obligations will not be subject to special comment unless the lending is considered excessive relative to a bank's capital funds. Aggregate credits to a country will be classified substandard, doubtful, or loss due to country risk only when there has been an interruption in debt servicing or when such an interruption is considered imminent.

Another key element of the procedures is an assessment of a bank management's ability to analyze and monitor country risk in its international lending. Examiners are instructed to evaluate a bank's procedures for monitoring and controlling exposure to country risk, the bank's system for establishing limits to lending in a country, and the bank's methods for analyzing country risk. Senior bank management is expected to monitor closely all situations listed or commented on by examiners.

Examinations of Bank Holding Companies. The board of governors from time to time may require reports under oath to keep it informed as to whether the provisions of the Bank Holding Company Act as amended, and regulations and orders issued thereunder, have been complied with. The board of governors may make examinations of each bank holding company and of each subsidiary thereof, the cost of which shall be assessed against and paid by such holding company. The board of governors shall, as far as possible, use the reports of examinations made by the comptroller of the currency, the Federal Deposit Insurance Corporation, or the appropriate state bank supervisory authority.

Confidentiality of Reports of Examination. The Comptroller of the Currency makes available to each national bank, and in some cases to holding companies thereof, a copy of the report of examination of such bank or company. The report of examination is the property of the Comptroller of the Currency (12 CFR 4.18(c)), and is loaned to the bank or holding company for its confidential use only. Under no circumstances shall the bank or holding company or any director, officer, or employee thereof make public or disclose in any manner the report of examination or any portion of the contents thereof to any person or organization not officially connected with the bank as officer, director, employee, attorney, auditor, or independent auditor. Any other disclosure or use of this report except as expressly permitted by the Comptroller of the Currency may be subject to the criminal penalties provided in 18 U.S.C. 641.

The authority to correct problems varies according to federal and state banking regulations. Typically, a *letter of agreement* or an *informal memorandum of understanding* is written to the bank, requesting it to take action against any questionable or illegal practices. Regulatory agencies are also legally empowered to issue *cease-and-desist orders*, especially where there is a finding that an offender is engaging, has engaged, or may engage in unsafe and unsound banking practices. These orders can be enforced with the threat of financial penalties if further violations occur. If a bank examination reveals severe cases of illegal action, the FDIC can deny insurance, or a state or federal banking agency may remove bank officers or directors from the bank. Judicial reviews are provided for under various statutes once the bank examination has been completed. SEC regulations require that any formal *cease-and-desist orders* and corrective actions must be disclosed (for those banks whose securities are registered). Oral presentations on the findings of examinations and inspections to the directors and management of large organizations and relatively troubled organizations are sometimes made by regulatory agencies.

See AUDIT, BANK EXAMINERS, COMPTROLLER OF THE CURRENCY, DIRECTORS' EXAMINATIONS, STATE BANKING DEPARTMENT, VISITORIAL POWERS.

BIBLIOGRAPHY

AMERICAN BANKERS ASSOCIATION. *A Guide to General Examinations for National Banks,* 1977.
COMPTROLLER OF THE CURRENCY. *Comptroller's Handbook for National Bank Examiners.*
FEDERAL RESERVE REGULATORY SERVICE. *Miscellaneous Supervisory Material,* June, 1982.

BANK EXAMINERS Persons appointed pursuant to the national banking laws, the Federal Reserve Act, Federal Deposit Insurance Act, and state banking laws to examine the affairs of banks and banking institutions within each jurisdiction.

National Banks. Field organization of the comptroller of the currency is now headed by regional administrators of national banks, located in each of 14 regions throughout the U.S. Regional administrators are now authorized to deal directly with national bank officials on matters requiring attention in connection with examinations. Formerly, bank officers dealt with the Washington headquarters. Regional administrators do, however, forward the original copy of the report of examination to Washington headquarters, in addition to furnishing a copy to the national bank examined (within 15 calendar days following completion of the examination).

Additional responsibilities delegated to regional administrators include the following:

1. Training newly appointed examiners.
2. Appointing national bank examiners who meet prescribed standards.
3. Transferring personnel within regions.
4. Acting on requests for extension of time in connection with opening of approved branches.
5. Acting on requests for prior approval of contemplated cash dividends (12 U.S.C. 60{b}).
6. Approving investments in banking house (12 U.S.C. 371d).
7. Granting preliminary approvals for the payment of stock dividends and sale of additional common stock.
8. Issuing certificates of final approval of capital increases by stock dividends and sales of additional common stock for cash.
9. Participation in the program of federal executive boards (coordination of federal activities at the local level).

Existing training of bank examiners has been expanding as the complexity of the banking industry increases and new training programs are developed and implemented to meet the new responsibilities. Both existing training and new programs are developed through the Federal Financial Institutions Examination Council for uniform application to all member agencies of the council. The budget of the office of the comptroller of the currency includes costs of sending personnel to council-approved courses and costs associated with using personnel of the comptroller of the currency to develop programs for the council. Education and training costs must take into account the high turnover rate among the bank examiners, who constitute over 75% of the total employment of the OCC. This turnover is of particular concern to the OCC in mid-career examiners (four to five years of experience) and career examiners (ten or more years of experience) because of the many opportunities in the banking industry at salary scales substantially in excess of federal pay ceilings.

The headquarters of each examiner is selected by the regional administrator at a location providing maximum geographic accessibility to banks and economy of operation. The head office of a bank and all branches is examined concurrently, the latter on a rotating basis if personnel limitations dictate.

Additional provisions for untouchability of examiners include the following:

1. Prohibition, under penalty, of the borrowing of money or acceptance of gratuity from national banks (18 U.S.C. 212).

ENCYCLOPEDIA OF BANKING AND FINANCE

BANK EXCHANGES

2. Prohibition of performance of services for any bank or banking or loan association, or for any officer, director, or employee thereof, or for any person connected therewith in any capacity. Except with the approval of the Comptroller of the Currency, examiners are expressly prohibited from accepting outside employment, whether or not for compensation; and no person employed by the Office of the Comptroller of the Currency shall accept a position with a national bank without first obtaining the permission of the Comptroller of the Currency or his authorized representative.

3. Except with the approval of the Comptroller of the Currency, no ownership or acquisition of shares of stock in a national bank, a corporation holding the control of a national bank, or an affiliate of a national bank. This restriction also applies to the spouse and minor children of an examiner.

All information which comes to the attention of examining personnel in the performance of their duties is required to be treated as strictly confidential. Examining personnel shall not, in any manner, disclose or permit disclosure of such confidential information to anyone other than the Comptroller of the Currency or an employee of his office properly entitled to such information for the performance of his official duties. An exception is that examining personnel are authorized to discuss with directors and officers of the bank concerned matters relevant to the performance of an examination. Improper disclosure of information is governed by the penal provisions of 18 U.S.C. 1905 and 1906, and Comptroller's Regulation 4.13(b)(12 CFR 4.13(b)).

Other Banks. The Federal Reserve Board's Division of Examinations examines the 12 Federal Reserve banks and their 24 branches, pursuant to Section 21, Federal Reserve Act. In conjunction with examination of the Federal Reserve Bank of New York, the board's examiners also audit the accounts and holdings of the system open market account and foreign currency operations, and report thereon to the Federal Open Market Committee. Procedures followed by the board's examiners are surveyed and appraised by certified public accountants, pursuant to the policy of having such reviews made on an annual basis. State member banks are subject to examinations made by direction of the Federal Reserve bank of the district in which they are located by examiners selected or approved by the board. Established policy is to conduct at least one regular examination of each state member bank, including its trust department, during each calendar year, with additional examinations if considered desirable. Wherever practicable, joint examinations are made in cooperation with state banking authorities, or alternate independent examinations are made by agreement with state authorities.

Examiners of the Federal Deposit Insurance Corporation, operating out of offices headed by supervising examiners located in regional or field offices throughout the country, regularly examine insured state banks which are not members of the Federal Reserve System, except those located in the District of Columbia, which are under the jurisdiction of the Comptroller of the Currency. Banks examined by the corporation comprise about half of all banks and account for about one-fourth of all bank assets. In over half of the states, these examinations may be made jointly or concurrently with the respective state supervisory authorities. As a rule the corporation itself does not examine national banks or state banks which are members of the Federal Reserve System, but it reviews the reports of examination made by the other federal agencies.

See BANK EXAMINATION.

BANK EXCHANGES EXCHANGES, or EXCHANGES FOR CLEARINGHOUSE.

BANK EXPORT SERVICE ACT OF 1982 Also known as the Export Trading Company Act; an act designed to encourage U.S. exports by permitting bank holding companies and other financial institutions, with the approval of the BOARD OF GOVERNORS OF THE FEDERAL RESERVE SYSTEM, to own and operate an export trading company (Title III) and allowing exporters certain exemptions from antitrust law (Title III). The act also liberalized the Federal Reserve Board's limits governing BANK ACCEPTANCES.

BANK FAILURES Banks closed temporarily or permanently on account of financial difficulties, and including banks whose deposit liabilities were assumed by other banks at the time of closing, with the aid of loans or purchase of assets by the FDIC (thus in effect constituting hidden failures).

The bank failure problem in the U.S., in the magnitude that prevailed during the period 1921-1933, ceased to be serious coincident with the advent of nationwide deposit insurance in 1934. Although stability of depositor confidence engendered by deposit insurance should continue to be of material assistance in keeping the rate of bank failures considerably below the rate of business failures, bank solvency problems, of course, have not been eliminated by deposit insurance and are of continuing concern to supervisory officials, including those of the Federal Deposit Insurance Corporation.

In their pioneer study, *Bank Suspensions in the United States, 1892-1932,* the Federal Reserve System concluded that comprehensive and dependable statistics on bank suspensions are available only beginning with 1921. In their *Banking and Monetary Statistics,* Section 7, "Bank Suspensions," the board of governors of the Federal Reserve System reported suspensions numbering 5,411 banks for the 1921-1929 period (total deposits of $1,623,000,000), and 9,106 banks ($6,858,633,000 in total deposits) for the 1930-1933 period. Since total commercial banks, to which these data refer, numbered 29,788 on June 30, 1921, and 13,949 on June 30, 1933, the net attrition was 15,839 banks, or 53%, for this period. Of this total, 10,555 banks disappeared between June 30, 1929, and June 30, 1933, including 3,853 for the period December 31, 1932, to June 30, 1933, during which came the presidential "bank holiday" proclamation on March 6, 1933; the Emergency Banking Act of March 9, 1933, authorizing the president to permit the reopening of only sound banks; and the President's Executive Order on March 10, 1933, empowering the Secretary of the Treasury to license reopenings through Federal Reserve banks of member banks and authorizing state banking authorities to permit reopenings of nonmember banks. By December 31, 1933, the number of commercial banks was back to 14,440.

The Federal Deposit Insurance Corporation began operations on January 1, 1934. The appended chart gives the number of bank failures because of financial difficulties for the period 1934-1988.

Bank Failures

Number of banks insured by the FDIC closed in each year

Source: Federal Deposit Insurance Corporation

In the event of a deposit payoff, the FDIC immediately makes payment in full to each depositor up to the insurance limit, and when designated as receiver begins liquidating the assets of the failed bank. When a purchase and assumption transaction is arranged, the FDIC takes over for liquidation any assets the acquiring bank may not want. Assets accepted by the FDIC for liquidation may include bad loans and investments, bank buildings and equipment, and security from defaulted loans.

In disposing of assets that the FDIC retains from a purchase and assumption, the FDIC first repays its insurance fund the cash it advanced to facilitate the transaction. It then returns any excess to subordinated debt holders and shareholders. When the FDIC has paid off insured depositors, it shares any liquidation proceeds proportionately with depositors having accounts in excess of the deposit insurance limit and with other general creditors. The FDIC converts the assets of closed banks to cash as early as practicable and strives to realize maximum recovery.

The FDIC reported that managerial weaknesses and illegal

practices, rather than economic conditions, had been primarily responsible for bank failures in prior years. Illegal practices included fraudulent use of unissued stock certificates, fictitious loans, and self-serving financial operations by leading officers of the banks concerned. However, economic conditions and imprudent lending practices by banks began playing a greater role in bank failures.

Recent failures have been somewhat geographically concentrated in farming and energy-producing regions.

The Financial Institutions Supervisory Act of 1966 (P.L. 89–695, October 16, 1966) authorized the FDIC and other bank supervisory authorities concerned to issue temporary and permanent cease-and-desist orders to insured institutions with respect to violations of law, rule, regulation, charter, or written condition or agreement, or with respect to unsafe and unsound practices. In addition, a new remedy was provided by empowering the bank supervisory authorities to take action to suspend or remove officers or directors of insured institutions for violation of law, ruling, regulation, or a final cease-and-desist order, or for engaging or participating in any unsafe or unsound practice where personal dishonesty is involved. Provision also was made for suspension or removal of persons convicted of any criminal offense involving dishonesty or a breach of trust or charged with a felony of that nature. These provisions of the act were to expire on June 30, 1972, but P.L. 91–609, December 31, 1970, made permanent these provisions.

See BAILOUT, FEDERAL DEPOSIT INSURANCE ACT, FEDERAL DEPOSIT INSURANCE CORPORATION.

BIBLIOGRAPHY

CATES, D. C. "Bank Risk and Predicting Bank Failure," *Issues in Bank Regulation*, Autumn 1985.
———. "What's an Adequate Loan Loss Reserve?" *ABA Banking Journal*, March 1985.
COLLINS, S. H. "National Bank Failures Studied in OCC Report." *Journal of Accountancy*, April, 1988.
DINCE, R. R. "Domestic Failure and Bank Examination." *Issues in Bank Regulation*, Summer, 1984.
DOUKAS, J. "Bankers Versus Bankruptcy Prediction Models: An Empirical Investigation." *Applied Economics*, May 1986.
FEDERAL DEPOSIT INSURANCE CORPORATION. *Annual Reports*.
FREER, K. O., and GLANCZ, R. R. "Acquiring D&O Insurance After the Fall." *Magazine of Bank Administration*, November, 1988.
MARGOLIES, D. "Anatomy of a Bank Closing." *Bankers Monthly*, June, 1988.
MOSKOWITZ, M. "Why Banks Fail." *Bankers Monthly*, April, 1988.
PANKAU, E. J. "Beating Bank Fraud." *Security Management*. November, 1988.
PAROUSH, J. "The Domino Effect and the Supervision of the Banking System." *Journal of Finance*, December, 1988.
SPRAGUE, I. H. *Bailout: An Insider's Account of Bank Failures and Rescues*. Harper & Row Publishers, Inc., New York, NY, 1988.

BANK FOR INTERNATIONAL SETTLEMENTS An in-stitution organized as part of the Young plan to effect a revised settlement of the various financial claims among creditor nations arising out of World War I reparations. The Young plan replaced the Dawes plan of reparation payments, and the Bank for International Settlements (BIS) took over the function of the agent general. The bank opened in May, 1930, under Swiss charter, at its headquarters in Basle, Switzerland. Original capital consisted of 200,000 shares, allotted equally to the central banks of the sponsoring nations (Belgium, France, Germany, Italy, Japan, United Kingdom, and the U.S.), which they could purchase or sell to others. The American interest totaled 9.9%, but because the U.S. Government would not permit an American representative to participate officially in the collection of German reparations, a group of private American banks instead joined in the guarantee of capital by the original subscribers. All of the American stock was sold in the U.S. market, with most of it finding its way back to European holders. The Japanese interest similarly was held by a banking group and has been repurchased by founder-nation central banks. The Federal Reserve Bank of New York acts as the American correspondent for the BIS.

The bank received the $300 million proceeds of the first of a series of Young plan loans late in May, 1930, and distributed them to the German and creditor governments. The first monthly statement was published as of June 30, 1930. Although established for the main purpose of collecting and transferring German reparations, the bank engaged in other functions permitted by its charter: protecting currencies, handling deposits and transfers for central banks, and otherwise acting as common agent for them.

During World War II, the bank, because of its primary function and the fact that most of its assets were German claims, necessarily kept close connections with the German financial situation. At the Bretton Woods Conference in 1944, a resolution was adopted recommending liquidation of the BIS in view of the organization of the International Monetary Fund and the International Bank for Reconstruction and Development. Liquidation, however, was avoided, and subsequently the BIS became technical agent under the Agreement on Multilateral Monetary Compensation of the post–World War II multilateral intra-European agreements, drafted November 18, 1947, and subsequently adhered to by practically all countries participating in the European Recovery Program. The bank's work consisted of the technical operation of the compensation arrangements, including the debiting or crediting of payments-agreements accounts for the purpose of compensations, and the collection and analysis of statistics on payments agreements.

Subsequently, at the request of the Organization for European Economic Cooperation (OEEC), the organization in Paris of European countries participating in the ERP, the BIS in 1948 agreed to continue acting as technical agent under the successor Agreement for Intra-European Payments and Compensations. This agreement was signed in Paris on October 16, 1948, by the governments of the 16 countries participating in the ERP and representatives of the Bizone and French Zone of Germany and of the Free Territory of Trieste. This agreement operated through a monthly compensation of balances held under intra-European payments, plus utilization of drawing rights, and was subsequently renewed with modifications through June 1950. The BIS's work in carrying out monthly operations was practically a continuation of its technical functions under the 1948 agreement.

With the expansion in capital, the BIS in the years since, to date, has expanded its diversified activities, as indicated by the following current description provided by the Federal Reserve Bank of New York.

The Bank for International Settlements is a bank for central banks. Almost all European central banks, as well as those of the United States, Canada, Japan, Australia, and South Africa, participate in or are closely associated with the various activities of the BIS. The BIS assists central banks in the investment of monetary reserves, provides a forum for international monetary cooperation, acts as agent or trustee in carrying out international loan agreements, and conducts extensive economic research.

In managing central banks' funds, the BIS engages in traditional types of investment. Funds not required for lending to other central banks are placed in world financial markets. The main forms of investment include deposits with commercial banks and purchases of short-term negotiable paper, including U.S. Treasury bills. These operations currently constitute a major portion of the bank's business.

The BIS also lends to other central banks some of the funds received as deposits from central banks. BIS credit transactions may take the form of swaps against gold, collateralized credits secured by gold or marketable short-term securities, credits against gold or currency deposits of the same amount and for the same duration held with the BIS, unsecured credits in the form of advances or deposits, and standby credits. Combinations of these and other types of credit also are used. In foreign exchange, the BIS is a part of the Federal Reserve's swap network. BIS is not permitted, however, to make advances to governments or to open certain types of accounts in their names. Real estate transactions also are excluded. In conducting banking operations, the BIS is required by its statutes to ensure conformity with the monetary policy of the central banks concerned.

The BIS also organizes periodic meetings of experts to examine economic, monetary, and other questions of interest to central banks. It conducts studies in the field of domestic and external monetary theory and policy. It has responsibility for observation of the international financial markets, the establishment of a data bank for the central banks of the Group of Ten countries and Switzerland, and statistical coverage of international banking. (The Group of Ten is composed of Belgium, Canada, France, Italy, Japan, the Netherlands, Sweden, United Kingdom, U.S., and West Germany. Switzerland also participates.)

The BIS has the legal form of a corporation as provided by its charter as an international organization originating from the 1930

ENCYCLOPEDIA OF BANKING AND FINANCE

Hague Agreement. A board of directors is responsible for the bank's operations. The board of directors is composed of the governors of the central banks of Belgium, France, West Germany, Italy, and the United Kingdom, as well as five representatives of finance, industry, or commerce, appointed one each by the governors of those five central banks. The statutes of the BIS provide that these 10 directors may elect other persons as co-opted directors from among the governors of those member central banks which do not have a representative on the board. The governors of the central banks of the Netherlands, Sweden, and Switzerland are co-opted members and have been on the board of directors for many years. The 13-member board of directors elects the chairman of the bank from among the directors.

As an international organization, the BIS performs several trustee and depository functions for official groups. For example, the BIS provides the secretariat for the Committee of Governors of the *European Community* (EC) central banks and for the Board of Governors of the European Monetary Cooperation Fund, as well as their subcommittees and groups of experts, which prepare documents for the central bank governors. Further, the BIS acts as agent for the EMCF, carrying out the financial operations connected with the settlement of balances on behalf of the EC countries participating in the monetary union. Similarly, it has responsibility for the technical administration of the EC system of reciprocal short-term monetary support and for transfer payments in connection with EC borrowing operations.

Upon formation of the BIS, participating central banks were given the option of subscribing for BIS shares or arranging for their subscription in their own countries. About 15% of BIS shares have not been acquired by central banks and are currently owned by private shareholders. The shares allotted to the U.S. were declined by the Federal Reserve and were subscribed to by several U.S. commercial banks. The shares were purchased during 1930 in the name of the First National Bank of the City of New York (now Citibank N.A.) by a syndicate consisting of J. P. Morgan and Company, First National Bank of Chicago, and the First National Bank of the City of New York. In 1930 the BIS designated the First National Bank of the City of New York to represent and vote by proxy the U.S. shares. Although all shares carry equal rights to participation in the bank's profits, private shareholders do not have voting rights or representation at the BIS general meeting.

BIBLIOGRAPHY

BANK FOR INTERNATIONAL SETTLEMENTS. *Annual Reports.*

BANKHEAD COTTON CONTROL ACT Enacted April 21, 1934, this legislation was auxiliary to the original AGRICULTURAL ADJUSTMENT ACT OF 1933 in behalf of cotton and featured a cotton ginning tax. When the U.S. Supreme Court declared the Agricultural Adjustment Act of 1933 unconstitutional on January 6, 1936, particularly on the grounds of invalidity of the system of processing taxes, Congress on February 10, 1936, by the Cotton-Tobacco-Potato Repeal Act repealed the Bankhead Cotton Control Act in addition to the Kerr Tobacco Act and the Potato Control Act. New Sections 7 to 17 of the Soil Conservation and Domestic Allotment Act were enacted February 29, 1936 (49 Stat. 1148), to replace in part certain provisions of the Agricultural Adjustment Act of 1933 invalidated by the Supreme Court.

BANK HOLDING COMPANY ACT The Bank Holding Company Act of 1956 (May 9, 1956, 70 Stat. 133) for the first time brought holding companies in the banking field under comprehensive regulation.

The BANKING ACT OF 1933 provided for mild federal regulation of bank holding companies owning interest in member banks only. Its definitional test of "holding company" was a company owning a majority interest in one or more banks. Such a holding company was subject to regulation by the Board of Governors of the Federal Reserve System only if it voluntarily applied for a voting permit to vote at elections of directors of subsidiary banks. As a condition for such voting permit, the holding company had to agree to submit itself and its controlled banks to examinations, to establish minimum reserve funds, to dispose of any interest in securities affiliates, and to declare dividends only out of net earnings. After five years from enactment of the Banking Act of 1933, every such holding company was required to possess, during the life of such permit, readily marketable assets other than bank stock of not less than 12% of the aggregate par value of all bank stocks controlled by the holding company. It was also required to increase such assets by annual increments of not less than 2% of the par value of bank stocks held from all net earnings in excess of 6% per annum on the holding company's own book value, until such assets amounted to 25% of the aggregate par value of all bank stocks controlled by the holding company. But there was no limitation on nonbanking interests of the holding company, nor was there any restriction on the holding company's ability to add to its number of controlled banks and thus effect concentration in banking. Holding companies as affiliates of a member bank were subject to the limitation on the amount of loans lendable by the member bank to any of its affiliates (loans to any one affiliate, 10% of capital and surplus limit; the aggregate of all loans, repurchase agreements, investments, etc., in all affiliates, 20% of the bank's capital and surplus limit). But "upstream" loans to the holding company, within these limitations, were permissible.

In 1938, the president in a special message to Congress recommended tighter regulation of bank holding companies. This was not done, however, until the Bank Holding Company Act of 1956 which, with Regulation Y of the Board of Governors of the Federal Reserve System, adds to but does not take the place of provisions of other laws, such as Section 5144 of the Revised Statutes (12 U.S.C. 61, as amended by the banking acts of 1933 and 1935) and the board's Regulation P thereunder, which relate to "holding company affiliates" as distinguished from "bank holding companies."

The principal features of the Bank Holding Company Act of 1956, popularly known as the Spence-Robertson Act, may be summarized as follows:

1. **Definition of holding company.** A bank holding company is defined as any company:
   a. Which directly or indirectly owns, controls, or holds with power to vote, 25% or more of the voting stock of each of two or more banks (not just member banks), or of a company which is or becomes a bank holding company.
   b. Which controls the election of a majority of directors in each of two or more banks.
   c. Which places 25% or more of the voting shares of each of two more banks in trust for the benefit of its shareholders or members.

The definitional requirement of holding in two or more banks automatically exempted thereby some 117 bank holding companies whose holdings were concentrated in one bank. The act specifies five other exemptions: bank shares held in a fiduciary capacity; a company registered under the Investment Company Act of 1940 prior to May 15, 1955; a company holding bank stocks as underwriter for the purpose of resale; a company formed for the sole purpose of soliciting proxies; and any company whose assets are 80% or more agricultural. Government- or state-owned corporations; nonprofit religious, educational, and charitable organizations; and partnerships are also exempt.

2. **Registration.** Bank holding companies subject to the act had 180 days after enactment thereof to register with the Board of Governors of the Federal Reserve System through the Federal Reserve banks. Companies becoming bank holding companies have the same period of time within which to file a registration statement with the board. Both limits may be extended by the board in its discretion upon a satisfactory showing of need.

The Board of Governors of the Federal Reserve System thus becomes the supervisory agency for bank holding companies. Each bank holding company shall furnish the board, on the board's prescribed form, an annual report of its operations and file same in duplicate with the Federal Reserve bank. Additional information, at such times as the board may require, shall be furnished. The board may examine any bank holding company or any of its subsidiaries, the cost of any such examinations being assessed against and paid by the bank holding company. But as far as possible, the board will use reports of examinations made by the Comptroller of the Currency, the Federal Deposit Insurance Corporation, or the appropriate state bank supervisory authority.

3. **Regulation of acquisitions.** Transactions requiring approval of the Board of Governors of the Federal Reserve System include the following:
   a. Any action which will result in a company's becoming a bank holding company.
   b. Any direct or indirect acquisition of ownership or control by a bank holding company of any voting shares of any bank.
   c. Any acquisition of all or substantially all of the assets of a bank by a bank holding company which is not a bank or by a nonbanking subsidiary of a bank holding company.
   d. Any merger or consolidation of a bank holding company with any other bank holding company.

Prior approval of the board of governors, however, is not required as to any of the following transactions:

   a. Any acquisition by a bank holding company of direct or indirect ownership or control of any voting shares of any bank, if, after such acquisition, such company will not directly or indirectly own or control more than 5% of the voting shares of such bank.
   b. Any acquisition by a bank holding company of additional shares in a bank in which such bank holding company already owned or controlled a majority of the voting shares immediately prior to such acquisition.
   c. Any acquisition by a bank, including a bank which is a bank holding company or a subsidiary of a bank holding company, of the voting shares of any bank if: (1) such shares are acquired in good faith in a fiduciary capacity and are not held for the benefit of shareholders of the acquiring bank; or (2) such shares are acquired in the regular course of securing or collecting a debt previously contracted in good faith, provided that such shares shall be disposed of within two years from date of acquisition.

Criteria specified in the act for the board of governors to apply in judging applications for approval of nonexempt transactions are as follows:

   a. The financial history and condition of the company or companies and the banks concerned.
   b. Their prospects.
   c. The character of their management.
   d. The convenience, needs, and welfare of the communities and the area concerned.
   e. Whether or not the effect of such acquisition or merger or consolidation would be to expand the size or extent of the bank holding company system involved beyond limits consistent with adequate and sound banking, the public interest, and the preservation of competition in the field of banking.

The Douglas Amendment (Sec. 3(d) of the act) directs that no application for approval of a nonexempt transaction shall be approved which will permit any bank holding company or subsidiary thereof to acquire, directly or indirectly, any voting shares of, interest in, or all or substantially all of the assets of any additional bank located outside of the state in which such bank holding company maintains its principal office and place of business, or in which it conducts its principal operations, unless such acquisition is specifically authorized by the statute laws of the state in which such bank is located, by language to that effect and not merely by implication.

4. **Procedure on applications.** Applications for approval of nonexempt transactions are filed in triplicate with the Federal Reserve bank of the district at least 60 days before proposed consummation of the transaction, subject to exception as to filing time at the board's discretion. One application is filed for each bank involved. The Federal Reserve bank forwards two copies to the board. The board transmits a copy of the application to the Comptroller of the Currency if a national bank or district bank is involved. If a state bank is involved, the board transmits a copy to the appropriate supervisory authority of the state in which such bank is located. Such agencies have 30 days in which to file written recommendations with the board. If disapproval is recommended, the board so notifies the applicant in writing and, within three days thereafter, gives to all concerned notice of hearing, to be held not less than 10 days nor more than 30 days after date of notification of the applicant of the agencies' disapproval. The board, after the conclusion of such hearing, will by order grant or deny the application on the basis of the record of the hearing. Where neither the Comptroller of the Currency nor the state supervisory agency concerned recommends disapproval, the board will by order grant or deny the application after its receipt of affirmative recommendation from those agencies. If no recommendation at all is received from those agencies, the board will act on the application after the expiration of 30 days from receipt of copy of the application by those agencies. An unfavorable decision of the board of governors may be appealed directly to a U.S. Court of Appeals.

5. **Disposition of nonbanking assets.** Under the act, bank holding companies are forbidden to acquire any stocks other than bank stocks, and are given two years in which to dispose of holdings of stocks other than bank stocks. The board of governors in its discretion, upon "timely request and upon a satisfactory showing of the need therefor," may extend the two-year period. As provided by the act, however, no such extension of time may be approved by the board for more than one year at a time, or for any period beyond a date five years after the date of enactment of the act, or five years after the date as of which the company became a bank holding company, whichever is the later. Moreover, after two years from the date of enactment of the act, no certificate evidencing shares of any bank holding company shall purport to represent shares of any other company except a bank or a bank holding company. The ownership, sale, or transfer of shares of any banking holding company shall not be conditioned in any manner whatsoever upon the ownership, sale, or transfer of shares of any other company except a bank or a bank holding company.

There is embodied in the act, however, a long list of exceptions to these compulsory "spin-off" provisions:

   a. Any company engaged solely in holding or operating properties used wholly or substantially by any bank owned by the bank holding company in its operations or acquired for such future use; or any company engaged solely in conducting a safe deposit business, furnishing services to or performing services for such bank holding company and its banks, or liquidating assets acquired from the bank holding company and its banks.
   b. Any shares acquired by a banking holding company which is a bank, or by any banking subsidiary of a bank holding company, in satisfaction of a debt previously contracted in good faith. But such shares shall be disposed of within two years from date of acquisition or date of enactment of the act, whichever is later.
   c. Any shares acquired by a bank holding company from any of its subsidiaries which in turn have been requested to dispose of such shares by any federal or state examination authority. But such shares shall be disposed of by the bank holding company within two years from date of acquisition or date of enactment of the act, whichever is later.
   d. Any shares held or acquired by a bank holding company which is a bank, or by any banking subsidiary of a bank holding company, in good faith in a fiduciary capacity (except where such shares are held for the benefit of the shareholders of such bank holding company or any of its subsidiaries); or any shares which are of the kinds and amounts eligible for investment by national banks under Section 5136 of the revised statutes (the investment securities section of the national banking laws, authorizing regulation by the Comptroller of the Currency); or any shares "lawfully acquired and owned prior to the date of enactment of this act by a bank which is a bank holding company or by any of its wholly owned subsidiaries" (a "grandfather" clause).
   e. Any shares of any company held or acquired by a bank holding company which do not constitute more than 5% of the outstanding voting securities of such company, and do not have a value greater than 5% of the value of total assets of the bank holding company; or any shares, securities, or

obligations of an investment company which is not a bank holding company and not engaged in any business other than investing in securities, which securities as owned by the bank holding company do not include more than 5% of the outstanding voting securities of any such company and do not constitute a single asset having a value greater than 5% of the value of total assets of the bank holding company.
   f. Shares of any company whose entire activities are of a "financial, fiduciary, or insurance nature"; and which the board, after due notice and hearing and on the basis of the record made of such hearing, by order has determined "to be so closely related to the business of banking or of managing or controlling banks as to be a proper incident thereto."
   g. Any bank holding company which is a labor, agricultural, or horticultural organization and which is exempt from taxation under Section 501 of the Internal Revenue Code of 1954.
   h. Shares held or acquired by a bank holding company in any company which is organized under the laws of a foreign country and which is engaged principally in the banking business outside the U.S.

6. **"Upstream" loans and investments.** From and after the date of enactment of the act, it shall be unlawful for a bank:
   a. To invest any of its funds in the capital stock, bonds, debentures, or other obligations of a bank holding company of which it is a subsidiary, or of any other subsidiary of such bank holding company.
   b. To accept any such collateral security for advances made to any person or company, except as security for debts previously contracted in good faith; but such collateral shall not be held over two years.
   c. To purchase securities, other assets, or obligations under repurchase agreement from a bank holding company of which the subject bank is a subsidiary, or any other subsidiary of such bank holding company.
   d. To make any loan, discount, or extension of credit to a bank holding company of which it is a subsidiary, or to any other subsidiary of such bank holding company.

     Not to be deemed a loan or advance to the bank of deposit, however, would be noninterest-bearing deposits to the credit of a bank; and not to be deemed a loan or advance to the depositing bank would be the giving of immediate credit to the bank upon uncollected items received in the ordinary course of business.

7. **Reservation of rights to the states.** The act declares that the enactment by the Congress of the act shall not be construed as preventing any state "from exercising such powers and jurisdiction which it now has or may hereafter have with respect to banks, bank holding companies, and subsidiaries thereof."

    In perhaps the most important of the decisions by the Board of Governors of the Federal Reserve System under the Bank Holding Company Act of 1956 (denial, 5 to 2, of the application each of the First New York Corporation, First National City Bank of New York, and International Banking Corporation to become bank holding companies, July 10, 1958), the board considered the New York State freeze against any holding company acquiring 25% of the stock of two or more banks unless the banks were located within the same city or New York State banking district, a state statute which would have prohibited consummation of the transactions applied for to the board. The board held that no provision of the Bank Holding Company Act of 1956, including the above reservation of rights to the states, precluded the board from approving these applications, even though the transactions contemplated appeared to be in contravention of the state statute. The reason for this holding was that the act conferred no new powers upon the states over national banks, as evidenced by a Senate committee report on the meaning of the act indicating no intent to permit states to exercise powers and jurisdiction inconsistent with the act.

8. **Tax provisions.** In connection with "spin-offs" required under the act, various alternatives were provided by amendment of the Internal Revenue Code of 1954, so as to minimize unfavorable tax implications of such distributions by affected bank holding companies.

9. **Follow-up reports to Congress.** The Board of Governors of the Federal Reserve System is directed to report to Congress before the expiration of two years from date of enactment of the act, and each year thereafter in the board's annual report to Congress, as to any substantial difficulties encountered in carrying out the purposes of the act and any recommendations as to changes in the law deemed desirable by the board.

1966 Amendments. (P.L. 89-485, July 1, 1966) Sponsored by the Board of Governors of the Federal Reserve System, amendments to the Bank Holding Company Act of 1956 finally enacted by the Congress in 1966 included the following:

1. Extension of the act to cover long-term nonbusiness trusts. The largest trust thus brought under regulation was the Alfred I. DuPont Trust of Florida, established in 1936 under the will of Alfred I. DuPont. The trust organized a bank holding company (Florida National Banks of Florida, Inc.) in its plan to divest itself of holdings in the 30 banks controlled as of 1966, as required by the act. It then exchanged its holdings in the banks for shares in Florida National and subsequently reduced its percentage of ownership in the voting shares of Florida National to less than 25%, the crucial ratio of ownership determinant of quantitative control in the act. The Board of Governors of the Federal Reserve System, however, ruled that the trust had not effectively divested itself of control of the banks held through Florida National, and ordered it to do so with additional time granted to accomplish the divestiture.
2. Repeal of previous exemptions for nonprofit religious, charitable, and educational institutions; certain agricultural companies; and companies registered under the Investment Company Act of 1940 and their affiliates. Repeal of the last-named type of exemption brought under regulation the Financial General Corporation of Washington, D.C., affiliated with the Equity Corporation which was registered under the Investment Company Act of 1940. Financial General controlled 21 banks as of 1966, including 15 banks acquired since enactment of the Bank Holding Compacy Act of 1956, located in several different states.
3. Repeal of the provisions of Section 6 of the Bank Holding Company Act of 1956, which prohibited loans and investments by subsidiary banks involving other companies within the same holding company group ("upstream" and "cross-stream" loans and investments). The board of governors felt that this was too rigid in preventing legitimate and beneficial portfolio adjustments, and that application of Section 23A of the Federal Reserve Act to bank holding companies (below) would effectively limit such intraholding company transactions.
4. Amendment of Section 23A of the Federal Reserve Act, relating to loans and other dealings between member banks and their affiliates, to cover member banks as well as insured nonmember banks. Section 23A prohibits a bank from extending credit (through loans and investments) totaling more than 10% of its capital and surplus to any one affiliate, or more than 20% for all affiliates.
5. Application to proposed acquisitions, mergers, and consolidations under the Bank Holding Company Act of the standards and antitrust procedures applicable to bank mergers under the act of February 21, 1966 (P.L. 89-356), which amended the Bank Merger Act of 1960. This amendment to the Bank Merger Act requires that consideration be given by the bank supervisory authorities, the Department of Justice, and the courts to the effect that a proposed merger might have in creating a monopoly, substantially lessening competition, or restraining trade. But a merger might be approved if the anticompetitive effects were clearly outweighed in the public interest by the probable effect with respect to the convenience and needs of the community to be served. Moreover, the consummation of a merger, in usual circumstances, could not take place until 30 days after approval by the appropriate supervisory authority, in order to give the Department of Justice an opportunity to contest the merger in the courts if it so desired. But if a suit was not filed within that period, the merger could not thereafter be attacked judicially on the ground that it was a violation of an antitrust law other than Section 2 of the Sherman AntiTrust Act.
6. Repeal of the provisions of Section 5144 of the revised statutes and of Section 9 of the Federal Reserve Act that required holding company affiliates to obtain permits to vote the stock of member banks. The Bank Holding Company Act prohibits

formation of a bank holding company without the approval of the board of governors; prohibits existing bank holding companies from acquiring more than 5% of any bank's voting shares without the board's approval; prohibits a bank holding company from engaging in any business other than banking, or acquiring more than 5% of the voting shares of any such business; and requires the holding company to divest itself of any such interests previously acquired.

7. Amendment of Section 25 of the Federal Reserve Act to permit direct investments by member banks in the stocks of foreign banks under regulations of the board of governors.
8. Redefinition of the term "bank" to limit the term to institutions accepting deposits withdrawable on demand, i.e., commercial banks.

However, the Board of Governors of the Federal Reserve System pointed out that for every holding company then registered under the act, there were 10 or more that were exempt, chiefly because of the one-bank exemption. Deposits of banks owned by one-bank holding companies totaled some $15 billion, compared with $26 billion for the subsidiary banks of all registered holding companies at that time. Also, about one-fourth of the one-bank holding companies were located in one-bank towns. The act also continued to exempt individuals and partnerships, in which the board of governors concurred.

In a rush to take advantage of this loophole of exemption of one-bank holding companies, before Congress acted to eliminate it, and in the apparent belief that Congress would grant "grandfather rights" to such formations, many banks throughout the country formed parent holding companies and became subsidiaries thereof. Such one-bank holding companies were free to become conglomerates and assemble interests in nonbanking fields without regulation.

Congress finally acted, and P.L. 91–607 (December 31, 1970), the Bank Holding Company Act Amendments of 1970, expanded the coverage of the Bank Holding Company Act of 1956 to include a holding company that controls only one bank. Other major provisions of the 1970 legislation included the following: (1) a revision of Sec-tion 4(c)(8) of the Holding Company Act, under which bank holding companies may acquire interests in nonbank activities, but subject to specified restrictions and under certain conditions; (2) an expansion in authority of the Board of Governors of the Federal Reserve System to determine that a company controls a bank; (3) a revision of the rules and expansion of the board's authority with respect to foreign activities of domestic-based holding companies and domestic activities of foreign-based holding companies; and (4) a prohibition against any bank extending services to any customer upon certain conditions, commonly described as "tie-in" arrangements.

Between 1971 and 1980, the Board of Governors of the Federal Reserve System, pursuant to the statute and its Regulation Y, approved 1,447 applications by bank holding companies to engage in nonbank activities. Expansion in permitted nonbank activities, particularly in the range of financial services, was an objective of such proposed legislation as S. 2490.

As holding companies grew in number and size, Congress become concerned about the increasing concentration in banking and passed the Bank Holding Company Act of 1956, popularly known as the Spence-Robertson Act. This act granted the FEDERAL RESERVE SYSTEM authority over bank holding companies. They were required to register with the board of governors and to furnish the board with an annual report of their operations. They and any of their subsidiaries were subject to Fed examination, although as far as possible, the board was to use reports of examinations made by the COMPTROLLER OF THE CURRENCY, the FEDERAL DEPOSIT INSURANCE CORPORATION, or the appropriate state bank supervisory authority. The FED was also empowered to approve or exempt holding company acquisitions of additional banks, although this power was limited somewhat by the Douglas amendment, which permitted only those acquisitions that state laws allowed.

Also under the 1956 act, bank holding companies were forbidden to acquire any stocks other than bank stocks and must dispose of any such holdings within two years, except as extended by the board of governors acting within specified time constraints. The act embodied a long list of exceptions to its compulsory "spin-off" provisions, however. Furthermore, the act defined a holding company as one that owns or controls two or more banks, thereby exempting some 117 banks holding companies whose holdings were concentrated in one bank. The act specified several other exempt types of organizations, as well.

As a result of current legislation, multibank holding companies have used several different organizational structures. Some holding companies operate similar to a branching system where each bank has a separate board. The subsidiary boards generally have relatively little power. All banks in the affiliation have the same name and functions. Investment loan rates and deposit rates are set at the holding company level. Other holding companies have retained a decentralization of management. Each banking unit is managed by a board of directors who retain a considerable degree of autonomy and authority in establishing lending and investing policies. Such arrangements usually allow for local citizens and business leaders to become actively involved in the separate banking units. The holding company tends to serve as an informed and advisory stockholder or as a staff organization.

1966 Amendments. (P.L. 89–485, July 1, 1966). Sponsored by the Board of Governors, the 1966 amendments to the Bank Holding Company Act of 1956 (1) expanded the act to cover nonbusiness trusts; (2) repealed previous exemptions for nonprofit institutions, certain agricultural companies, and companies registered under the Investment Company Act of 1940 and their affiliates; (3) permitted subsidiary banks to invest in and make loans to companies within the same holding company group ("upstream" and "cross-stream" loans and investments); (4) amended Section 23A of the Federal Reserve Act, which prohibits a bank from extending credit (through loans and investments) totaling more than 10% of its capital and surplus to any one affiliate, or more than 20% for all affiliates, by extending its coverage to include member banks as well as insured nonmember banks; (5) applied the standards and antitrust procedures for bank mergers under the Bank Merger Act of 1960 to proposed acquisitions, mergers, and consolidations under the Bank Holding Company Act; (6) repealed provisions of Section 5144 of the revised statutes and of Section 9 of the Federal Reserve Act that required holding company affiliates to obtain permits to vote the stock of member banks; (7) permitted direct investments by member banks in the stocks of foreign banks under regulations of the Board of Governors; and (8) redefined the term "bank" to include only commercial banks.

1970 Amendments. In a rush to take advantage of the exemption of one-bank holding companies before Congress acted to eliminate it and in the apparent belief that Congress would grant "grandfather rights" to such formations, many banks throughout the country formed parent holding companies and became subsidiaries thereof. Such one-bank holding companies were free to become conglomerates and assemble interests in nonbanking fields without regulation. Consequently, Congress passed the Bank Holding Company act Amendments of 1970 (P.L. 91–607), which expanded the coverage of the Bank Holding Company Act of 1956 to include a holding company that controls only one bank, thus limiting the permissible activities of those banks to those "closely related to banking." The intent was that holding companies not enter into activities that could threaten the safety of the bank or result in conflicts of interest.

The GARN–ST GERMAIN ACT OF 1982. This act expanded bank holding companies' access to interstate banking and to thrift activities by allowing them to acquire financially troubled commercial banks, mutual savings banks, and savings and loan associations. Preference is still given to intrastate depository institutions of the same type, however, and FDIC assistance is still limited to acquisition of commercial and mutual savings banks with $500 million or more in assets; no acquisition assistance limits exist for savings and loan associations.

The act tightened restrictions on bank holding company insurance activities by prohibiting them from providing insurance as principals, agents, or brokers, but Regulations governing transactions of banks with their affiliates. It significantly expanded the assets eligible to serve as collateral on loans to affiliates, although it still barred the use of substandard loan obligations as collateral.

Garn–St Germain also expanded the powers of banks to form service corporations. Such corporations had been allowed to provide services only to commercial banks. Under the new act, bank-owned service corporations may offer the followings services to depository and nondepository institutions and to the general public: depository institutions services, nondepository institutions services permitted to banks, and other activities the Board of Governors considered closely related and properly incident to commercial banking. Thus, banks are now allowed to provide discount brokerage.

ENCYCLOPEDIA OF BANKING AND FINANCE

The Export Trading Company Act. This act, formally entitled the BANK EXPORT SERVICE ACT OF 1982, permitted bank holding companies and other financial institutions to make equity investments in EXPORT TRADING COMPANIES. These special entities are to engage only in foreign trade. Upon approval of the Office of Export Trading Company affairs of the Department of Commerce, all exporters, including export trading companies, are granted an export trade certificate of review. This certificate grants such exporters protection against antitrust liability for specific export activities.

For detailed statistics on banking offices, assets, and deposits of banks in all holding company groups, see Board of Governors of the Federal Reserve System, *Annual Statistical Digest.*

See HOLDING COMPANY.

BIBLIOGRAPHY

BOARD OF GOVERNORS OF THE FEDERAL RESERVE SYSTEM. *Annual Statistical Report.*
BROWN, D. M. "The Effect of State Banking Laws on Holding Company Banks." *Federal Reserve Bank of St. Louis Review*, August/September 1983.
FISCHEL, D., ROSENFIELD, A., and STILLMAN, R. "The Regulation of Banks and Bank Holding Companies." *Virginia Law Review*, March, 1987.
FRIEDER, L. A. and APILADO, V. P. "Bank Holding Company Expansion: A Refocus on Its Financial Rationale." *Journal of Financial Research*, Spring, 1983.
JEFFRIES, M. H. JR. "Holding Company Advantages." *Southern Banker*, March 1983.

BANK HOLIDAY OF 1933 President Franklin D. Roosevelt issued Presidential Proclamations No. 2039, March 6, 1933, and No. 2040, March 9, 1933, which temporarily suspended banking transactions by member banks of the Federal Reserve System. The suspension of normal banking functions lasted until March 13 when they were resumed, subject to restrictions. Ratifying legislation was passed on March 9, 1933 (12 U.S.C.A., 95b). At present, member banks of the Federal Reserve System are forbidden to transact banking business, except under regulations of the Secretary of the Treasury, during an emergency proclaimed by the President (12 U.S.C.A., 95).

BANK HOLIDAYS There is no such thing as a national holiday in the U.S., as each state by statute or by proclamation of its governor designates the legal holidays. The following holidays are observed by all the states:

New Year's Day	January 1
Independence Day	July 4
Labor Day	First Monday in September
Thanksgiving Day	Fourth Thursday in November
Christmas	December 25

Federal legislation on the subject of holidays applies only to the District of Columbia and to employees of the federal government throughout the U.S. Nevertheless, such federal designation of holidays is followed by many states. Thus the legislation of June 28, 1968, is of broad importance because it provided that beginning January 1, 1971, four major holidays will fall on Mondays every year as follows:

Martin Luther King Day	Third Monday in January
Washington's Birthday	Third Monday in February
Memorial Day	Last Monday in May
Columbus Day	Second Monday in October
Veterans Day	Fourth Monday in October

Although many states follow the federal pattern, others differ as to dates and to inclusion. Some state holidays are unique to state history. Bank practice is to follow state holiday designations and state laws regarding closing. The Board of Governors of the Federal Reserve System, in 1986, adopted the standard (federal) 10-holiday schedule for Federal Reserve banks. Also effective beginning in 1987, a paying bank that closes on a nonstandard holiday must pay for checks made available to it on that day or else reimburse the Federal Reserve bank for the value of the resultant FLOAT.

When a holiday falls on Sunday, the next day is commonly observed as the holiday. State laws regarding closing of banks on Saturdays are generally permissive, but many banks through their collective bankers' associations, especially in the larger cities, provide for all-day Saturday closing.

Under the UNIFORM COMMERCIAL CODE (Sec. 33–503(3)), where any presentment is due on a day which is not a full business day for either the person making presentment or the party to pay or accept, presentment is due on the next following day which is a full business day for both parties. This broader provision, as compared with that in the former Uniform Negotiable Instruments Law, makes allowance for the closing of banks and business firms on Saturdays and other days of the week as well as Sundays.

See NEGOTIABLE INSTRUMENTS LAW.

BANKING See subjects beginning with BANK, also AMERICAN BANKERS ASSOCIATION, BANK, BANK INTEREST, BUILDING AND LOAN ASSOCIATION, CREDIT UNION, FEDERAL LAND BANK ASSOCIATIONS, FEDERAL LAND BANKS, FEDERAL RESERVE BANK, FEDERAL RESERVE SYSTEM, FOREIGN BANKING CORPORATIONS, INVESTMENT COMPANY, LAND BANKS, MORRIS PLAN, MORTGAGE COMPANY, NATIONAL BANK, NATIONAL BANKING SYSTEM, PERSONAL LOAN COMPANY, POSTAL SAVINGS BANK, PRIVATE BANKING, SAFE DEPOSIT COMPANY, SAVINGS BANKS, SAVINGS AND LOAN ASSOCIATIONS, STATE BANK, TITLE INSURANCE COMPANY, TRUST COMPANY.

For a bibliography on banking, see BANK

BANKING ACT OF 1933 Approved June 16, 1933 (48 Stat. 164), the first of the major banking laws enacted by the Roosevelt Administration (the second was the BANKING ACT OF 1935), effecting important changes in the banking laws. It was also known as the Glass Act and Glass-Steagall Act after its Senate and House sponsors.

Among other things, this act accomplished the following:

1. Provided for the coordination of Federal Reserve open market operations, for the prevention of speculative uses of bank credit, for regulation of interbank control, for the insurance of deposits of member banks, for regulation of their operations, for separation of security affiliates from banks, and for extension of branch banking.
2. Created the Federal Open Market Committee (Sec. 12A, Federal Reserve Act), bringing open market operations of the Federal Reserve System formally under a statutory body for the first time (importantly revised and amended by the Banking Act of 1935 and Act of July 7, 1942).
3. Created the Federal Deposit Insurance Corporation and provided for a deposit insurance fund initially consisting of $150 million appropriated by the federal government, plus stock subscriptions.
4. Provided for a Temporary Deposit Insurance Fund, from January 1, 1934, to June 30, 1934, insuring individual deposits up to $2,500.
5. Provided that after July 1, 1934, the Federal Deposit Insurance Corporation should insure the deposits of all member banks on the following scale: deposits under $10,000, 100% coverage; the next $40,000, 75%; over $50,000, 50%. Deposits in nonmember state banks holding class A stock in the Federal Deposit Insurance Corporation were insured until July 1, 1936. Membership in the insurance corporation after July 1, 1936, was to be limited to national banks and members of the Federal Reserve System. Interest on demand deposits was prohibited.
6. Forbade member banks to act as agent in security loans to brokers or dealers, to extend credit to purchase securities under repurchase agreement from any affiliate, to invest in affiliate obligations, or to accept obligations of affiliates as collateral on loans exceeding 10% of capital and surplus.
7. Provided that no executive officer shall borrow from his member bank and that he or she must report to his or her board of directors concerning loans from another member bank.
8. Permitted investment transactions by a bank without recourse for customers' accounts, permitted purchases on own account under comptroller's regulations, and provided that the securities of a single obligor should not exceed 10% of the outstanding single issue.
9. Forbade security affiliates to member banks after one year; securities firms were prohibited from engaging in banking business.
10. Permitted branch banking within a city, with the approval of the comptroller of the currency, to national banks wherever state banks were expressly so authorized; branch banking for national banks within a state was permitted wherever state

statutes specifically permitted. But no branches were permitted beyond the head office city unless unimpaired capital was at least $500,000, or a minimum of $250,000 in states with population under 1,000,000 and cities therein of more than 100,000 population, or a minimum of $100,000 in states with under 500,000 population and no cities exceeding 50,000 population.

Many of these provisions were importantly modified or revised by the BANKING ACT OF 1935.

BANKING ACT OF 1935
Approved August 23, 1935 (49 Stat. 717), the second of the major banking laws of the Roosevelt Administration, amendatory of the BANKING ACT OF 1933, the Federal Reserve Act, and other banking statutes. Title 1 concerned itself with federal deposit insurance; Title II, with amendments to the Federal Reserve Act; and Title III, with technical amendments to the banking laws and with amendments to the Federal Reserve Act, National Bank Act (revised statutes), and miscellaneous laws.

The principal provisions of the Banking Act of 1935 may be summarized as follows:

1. Created an open market committee of seven Federal Reserve board members and five representatives of the 12 regional Federal Reserve banks, with power to control credit fluctuations by the open market purchase and sale of government securities by the Federal Reserve banks.
2. Provided for variation in legal reserve requirements. By a vote of not less than five of the seven members of the Federal Reserve board, the then existing requirements of 7%, 10% and 13% against demand deposits and 3% against time deposits could be doubled, but not lowered below those minima.
3. Allowed Federal Reserve banks to continue to propose changes in rediscount rates, but subject to Federal Reserve board approval, rates to be announced at least every two weeks. The board could veto the proposed rates or change them.
4. Reorganized the Federal Reserve board into a seven-member bipartisan board, all members appointive and all having the title of governor, to serve 14-year terms at $15,000 salaries. The Secretary of the Treasury and the Comptroller of the Currency were removed as ex-officio members. Not more than four of the seven members could be of the same political party. The president would select a chairman and vice chairman from the seven members to serve for four years.
5. Gave the heads of the 12 Federal Reserve banks the title of President instead of governor, so as not to conflict with the new titles of board members. Presidents would be elected for five-year terms by the bank boards, subject to board of governors' approval.
6. Made permanent the temporary law expiring August 31, 1935, fully insuring bank deposits up to $5,000. Provided for annual assessment on banks for insurance fund membership of one-twelfth of 1% of total deposits, assessments to continue until the fund reached $500 million, then to be resumed when that total was impaired 15%. An important revision was that the former Section 12B of the Federal Reserve Act, relating to deposit insurance, was withdrawn and enacted as a separate act by the Act of September 21, 1950 (64 Stat. 873).
7. Required all state banks organized after the enactment of the law to join the Federal Reserve System by July 1, 1937, in order to obtain deposit insurance. The same requirement would be applied to all state banks then in operation with deposits of $1 million or more if they desired to remain insured. (This has been revised.) Although all member banks, national and state-chartered, must participate in deposit insurance, nonmember state banks and mutual savings banks may at their option obtain deposit insurance if approved by the FDIC.
8. Prohibited a banker from serving on the board of directors of more than two banks or as officer or employee thereof, subject to specified exemptions (revision of Sec. 8 of Clayton Act). Service as such with the second bank is subject to approval of the Federal Reserve Board of Governors and their regulation.
9. Permitted national banks to make five-year real estate loans of up to 50% of appraisal value of the property, with aggregate loans not to exceed the capital and surplus of the bank, or 60% of its combined time and savings deposits, whichever is greater. Loans could be made up to 60% if secured by an amortized mortgage providing for repayment of at least half the loan in 10 years.

See FEDERAL DEPOSIT INSURANCE CORPORATION, MORTGAGE LOANS.

BANKING AFFILIATES ACT OF 1982
Public Law 97-320 that amends the Federal Reserve Act designed to prevent abuses of banks' resources related to nonarm's-length transactions, including the extension of credit between a bank and its affiliates not to exceed 10% of the bank's capital and surplus. Terms and conditions of such lending must be consistent with sound banking practices.

BANKING COMMITTEE, U.S. HOUSE OF REPRESENTATIVES
For more than a century, the Committee on Banking, Housing, and Urban Affairs of the U.S. House of Representatives has been responsible for legislation central to a stable monetary and banking system, a productive and competitive economy, and recent housing and living environments for millions of Americans. The committee's efforts are reflected in major legislative measures, many of which have had continuous, far-reaching effects across the nation, including the Currency Act of 1900, the Federal Reserve Act, the Reconstruction Finance Act, the Banking Act of 1933, the Federal Credit Union Act, the Federal Home Loan Bank Act, the Bretton Woods Agreement Act, the Defense Production Act, the Small Business Act, the Truth in Lending Act, and the Housing Acts.

The committee was created in March 1865, when the House amended its rules to provide for the establishment of a Committee on Banking and Currency. Prior to that time, matters and legislation relating to banking and currency were handled by the Ways and Means Committee. Because of the increased importance of banking, it was believed that a separate committee should be formed.

The jurisdiction of the committee is set forth in clause 1(d) of Rule X of the Rules of the House of Representatives as follows:

(d) Committee on Banking, Housing, and Urban Affairs.
  (1) Banks and banking, including deposit insurance and federal monetary policy.
  (2) Money and credit, including currency and the issuance of notes and redemption thereof; gold and silver, including the coinage thereof; valuation and revaluation of the dollar.
  (3) Community development (including metropolitan and nonmetropolitan areas).
  (4) Public and private housing.
  (5) Economic stabilization, defense production, renegotiation, and control of the price of commodities, rents, and services.
  (6) International finance.
  (7) Financial aid to commerce and industry (other than transportation).
  (8) International Financial and Monetary organizations.

An enumeration of some of the specific subjects contained in bills referred to the committee will provide a better understanding of the subject matters coming within the jurisdiction of the committee. Agencies and departments subject to legislative jurisdiction:

Commerce, Department of
Export-Import Bank
Federal Deposit Insurance Corporation
Federal Home Loan Bank Board
Federal Preparedness Agency, GSA
Federal Reserve System
Federal Savings and Loan Insurance Corporation
National Credit Union Administration
Treasury, Department of
  Bureau of the Comptroller of the Currency
  Bureau of Engraving and Printing
  Bureau of the Mint
Banks and Banking
  Bank holding companies
  Branches of national banks
  Chartering, regulation, conservation, and liquidation of national banks

Examination of national banks, insured banks, and
    Federal Reserve member banks
Federal Deposit Insurance Corporation Act
Federal Reserve Act
Foreign branches
Insurance of bank deposits
Interest rate ceilings
Investments by national banks
Mergers, consolidations, and conversions of insured banks
National Bank Act
Reserve requirements of Federal Reserve member banks
Coins and Coinage
Consumer Credit
    Truth in lending
    Extortionate credit transactions
    Garnishments
    Credit reporting and credit bureaus
    Equal credit opportunity
    Debt collection
    Electronic funds transfers
    Creditor remedies and defenses
    Federal aspects of the Uniform Consumer Credit Code
    Credit and debt cards
    Preemption of state usury laws
Credit Controls
    Consumer and installment credit terms
    Real estate and credit terms
Creation of Government Corporations
    Export-Import Bank
    FDIC
    Federal Home Loan Mortgage Corporation
    Federal National Mortgage Association
    Federal Savings and Loan Insurance Corporation
    National Consumer Cooperative Bank
    Government National Mortgage Association
Currency
    Counterfeiting; denominations, value, and design; issue and
        redemption, printing, verification and destruction.
Deposit Insurance
Federal Credit Unions
    Chartering, regulations, examinations, and supervision
Government Lending
    Defense production loans
    Export-Import Bank loans
    Food and catastrophe loans
    Loans for elderly housing
    Loans for community rehabilitation
    Loans to state and local development companies
    Loans to state and local governments
International Finance
    African Development Fund
    Asian Development Bank
    Balance of payments
    Bretton Woods Agreements Act
    Exchange Stabilization Fund
    Foreign Investment in the U.S.
    Foreign exchange
    Inter-American Development Bank
    International Bank for Reconstruction and Development
    International commodity agreements
    International Development Association
    International Finance Corporation
International Monetary Fund
Money and Credit
    Bank reserves
    Credit terms
    Federal credit programs
    Federal guarantees and issuance
    Federal Reserve Board and banks
    Federal reserve rediscounts, rates,
    Federal securities markets
    General price level
    Gold and gold standard
    Gold payments and ownership
    Interest rates
    Issue of, and reserve behind, Federal Reserve notes
    Monetary policy; coordination

Operation of Federal Open Market Committee
Support of U.S. Government bonds
Valuation and revaluation of the dollar
Residential Mortgage Credit, Insurance, and Guarantee
    FHA insurance programs
    Secondary mortgage markets (FNMA, FHLM Corp., and
        GNMA)
    National bank real estate loans
Savings and Loan Associations
    Chartering and supervision of Federal savings and
        loan associations
    Federal Home Loan Bank System
    Federal supervision
    Savings and loan holding companies
Silver:
    Coinage, value and use, and redemption thereof; gold and
        silver, including the coinage thereof.

BIBLIOGRAPHY

UNITED STATES SENATE. *Rules of Procedure and Jurisdiction of the Committee on Banking, Housing, and Urban Affairs.*

BANKING DEPARTMENT　　See STATE BANKING DEPARTMENT.

BANKING HOUSE　　The premises or building in which a bank conducts its business. The banking house, fixtures, and appliances are the only fixed assets a national bank is permitted to own. Other real estate of national banks therefore represents realty taken to avoid or minimize loss on defaulting loans on real estate, and must be disposed of within a reasonable time.

Under the Banking Act of 1933, no national bank, without approval of the Comptroller of the Currency, and no state member bank, without approval of the Board of Governors of the Federal Reserve System, may invest in or lend on bank premises directly or indirectly if the total of such loans and investments will exceed the bank's capital stock.

Very often the banking house is carried on the balance sheet at a nominal value, i.e., at a value much below the market value.

BANKING, HOUSING, AND URBAN AFFAIRS, SENATE COMMITTEE　　The Standing Rules of the Senate, Rule XXV (d)(1), Standing Committees, describes the Senate Committee on Banking, Housing, and Urban Affair's Rules of Procedures and Jurisdiction as follows:

(d) (1) Committee on Banking, Housing and Urban Affairs, to which committee shall be referred all proposed legislation, messages, petitions, memorials, and other matters relating to the following subjects:

1. Banks, banking, and financial institutions.
2. Control of prices of commodities, rents, and services.
3. Deposit insurance.
4. Economic stabilization and defense production.
5. Export and foreign trade promotion.
6. Export controls.
7. Federal monetary policy, including Federal Reserve System.
8. Financial aid to commerce and industry.
9. Issuance and redemption of notes.
10. Money and credit, including currency and coinage.
11. Nursing home construction.
12. Public and private housing (incl. veteran's housing).
13. Renegotiation of Government contracts.
14. Urban development and urban mass transit.

(2) Such committee shall also study and review, on a comprehensive basis, matters relating to international economic policy as it affects United States monetary affairs, credit, and financial institutions; economic growth, urban affairs, and credit, and report thereon from time to time.

BIBLIOGRAPHY

UNITED STATES SENATE, *Rules of Procedure and Jurisdiction of the Committee on Banking, Housing, and Urban Affairs.* Revised periodically.

BANKING MULTIPLIER *See* BANKING POWER.

BANKING POWER The lending or investing power of a bank as measured by its excess reserves, i.e., reserves maintained in excess of legal reserve requirements, which furnish the basis for expansion of loans and investments. For the banking system as a whole, the power to expand loans and investments, and thus transaction account balances, is conventionally expressed as the reciprocal of the average legal reserve requirement. It is important, however, to note that this is the theoretical maximum, based on the assumptions that every bank in the system is individually maximizing and that there is no cost to the system from expansion other than legal reserve requirement against the transaction account balances (no leakages such as increase in money in circulation, exports of currency, shift from demand deposits to time and savings deposits, loss of deposits to other financial institutions, etc.).

Under the DEPOSITORY INSTITUTIONS DEREGULATION AND MONETARY CONTROL ACT OF 1980, effective November 13, 1980, legal reserve requirements of 3% on the first $25 million of net transaction accounts and 12% on the total of same over $25 million were imposed. The act requires that the amount of transaction accounts against which the 3% requirement will apply be modified annually to 80% of the percentage increase in transaction accounts held by all depository institutions on the previous June 30, so that at the beginning of 1982 the first transaction accounts amount interval was increased from $25 million to $26 million.

Transaction accounts include all deposits on which the account holder is permitted to make withdrawals by negotiable or transferable instruments, payment orders of withdrawal, and telephone and preauthorized transfers (in excess of three per month) for the purpose of making payments to third persons or others. Thus transaction account balances, plus currency in public circulation, correspond to the M1 measure of the money supply. By lending and investing, banks and other depository institutions providing transaction accounts will create such transaction balances, derived from the loans and investments.

Granted the heroic assumptions, therefore, as to maximum expansion of loans or investments, and thus transaction account balances, and with the legal reserve requirements against transaction accounts figured at approximately 12%, depository institutions as a whole can expand loans and investments, and thus transaction account balances, by approximately eight and one-third times for every dollar in excess reserves.

The above hypothetical expansion for the system as a whole, without leakages, may be concisely stated as follows:

$$TA = \frac{X}{R}$$

where TA is transaction accounts, X is excess reserve, and R is the legal reserve requirement.

Examples of leakages insofar as transaction accounts are concerned would include the following: Nonpersonal time deposits with maturities of less than three and one-half years are subject to 3% legal reserve requirements; if such maturities are three and one-half years or more, the legal reserve requirement is zero.

1. Nonpersonal time deposits are time deposits, including savings deposits, that are not transaction accounts and in which the beneficial interest is held by depositors who are not natural persons.
2. Personal time deposits (including passbook savings) are not subject to legal reserve requirements under the Monetary Control Act of 1980; the classification "small-denomination time deposits, including retail repurchase agreements (RPs), issued in amounts of less than $100,000" includes such personal time deposits.
3. Eurocurrency liabilities of all types are subject to 3% legal reserve requirement; this classification includes overnight RPs and Eurodollars.
4. Currency in circulation, along with transaction accounts, indicates the M1 total of the money supply, but since it may be considered withdrawals ordinarily from transaction accounts for transaction purposes, it is in effect a leakage as far as transaction account balances are concerned.

Finally, in connection with utilization of excess reserves, there will be depository institutions that will not utilize, either voluntarily or involuntarily, all of their excess reserves in expansion of loans or investments and hence in expansion of transaction account balances.

Accordingly, the following expanded formula gives effect to such leakages in expansion power per dollar of excess reserves:

$$TA = \frac{X}{R + NPT + C + U}$$

where TA is transaction accounts, X is excess reserves, R is the legal reserve requirement on transaction accounts, NPT is nonpersonal time deposits, C is currency in circulation, and U is unutilized excess reserves.

Assuming excess reserves are $300 million, the expansion power at the maximum, without leakages, in transaction accounts would be

$$\$2{,}500 \text{ million} = \frac{\$300 \text{ million}}{0.12}$$

However, giving effect to estimated amounts as of 1982 for the leakages, the expansion power in transaction accounts would be

$$\$500 \text{ million} = \frac{\$300 \text{ million}}{0.12 + (3\%)100\% + 0.40 + 0.05}$$

12% is taken as the legal reserve requirement on transaction accounts; 3% is the legal reserve requirement on nonpersonal time deposits, which in amount are approximately the same size as the total of transaction accounts; 40% is the approximate percentage of total currency in circulation relative to the total of transaction accounts; and 5% is taken as the unutilization ratio of excess reserves.

Of course, since M1 money supply is conventionally defined as transaction accounts plus money in public circulation, the expansion in total money supply in the last example above would be larger than the increase in transaction accounts alone by the amount of the increase in money in public circulation allowed for above.

The calculation of the banking power is complicated by the provision of the GARN–ST. GERMAIN ACT OF 1982 that exempted $2 million of reservable liabilities (transaction accounts, nonpersonal time

Cost in Excess Reserves of Making $1 in Loans

	Individual bank		Banking system	
1. Withdrawals:				
Credit to transaction deposits	$1.00		$1.00	
20% Compensating balance	0.20		1.00*	
Withdrawal costs		$0.80		$0.00
2. Legal reserve cost:				
Increase in transaction deposits	$0.20		$1.00	
Legal reserve	x12%		x12%	
Legal reserve costs		$0.024		$0.12
3. Total costs in excess reserves to make $1 in loans		$0.824		$0.12
Ratio per dollar of excess reserves		1.21:1		8 1/3:1

Assumptions:
1. 12% legal reserve requirement (approximate) for both the individual bank and the banking system.
2. 20% compensating balance requirement by the individual bank.
3. No return flow to the individual bank of funds checked out by borrowers (proceeds of the loan).
4. No leakages for the banking system as a whole.

---

* Under assumption of no leakages for the banking system, checkouts from the individual bank are deposited in other banks of the system, so that the system incurs no withdrawals of the derivative transaction account balance created by the loan.

BANKING SALARIES

deposits, and Eurocurrency liabilities) per institution from reserve requirements and that requires the board of governors to adjust this exemption each year by 80% of the percentage increase in total reservable liabilities of all depository institutions; this exemption stood at $2.9 million at the beginning of 1987.

For the individual bank, however, expansion power per dollar of excess reserves cannot be much more than 1:1, even allowing for the compensating balance limitation upon freedom of borrowers to draw upon deposit proceeds of loans made by the bank. This may be illustrated by the appended table.

See EXCESS RESERVES.

BANKING SALARIES The 1990 Salary Survey conducted by Robert Half International Inc. included current information on compensation trends for banking. This survey, which has been conducted since 1950, uses confidential data available from the job order files of Robert Half offices. Many banks use this data as a guide in determining starting salaries and for compensation reviews. The U.S. Department of Labor uses the Robert Half Salary Survey in their Employment Outlook series. The appended tables present data for the following categories: Money Center/Regional ($1 Billion and Higher Assets), Large ($500MM to $1 Billion Assets); Medium ($100MM to $500MM Assets); Small ($100MM Assets and Lower).

BIBLIOGRAPHY

ROBERT HALF INTERNATIONAL INC. *Salary Survey 1990: Accounting & Finance, Banking, Information Systems*, 1989.

BANKING SUPPORT The purchase of securities by large and influential banking and financial interests in sufficient volume to stabilize the market after a break in prices. Since 1933, with the prohibition of pools and other speculative devices in security markets, the liquidation of security affiliates of banks, the raising of margin requirements, and the increase in capital gains taxes, banking support on declines in security markets has become more fictional than real. The most important source of institutional support has now developed in the INVESTMENT COMPANY.

See SUPPORT.

Banking—Medium ($100MM to $500MM Assets)

Title	1989	1990	% Change vs. 1989
Senior Lender/Head of All Lending	$61,000 - $76,000	$65,000 - $80,000	+5.8
Lending Department Head	57,000 - 72,000	60,000 - 75,000	+4.7
Commercial Lenders 1-3 yrs. exp. (Commercial, Middle Market, ABL)	28,000 - 38,000	30,000 - 40,000	+6.1
Commercial Lenders 3+ yrs. exp. (Commercial Middle Market, ABL)	32,000 - 52,000	35,000 - 55,000	+7.1
Residential Real Estate Mortgage Lenders	28,000 - 38,000	30,000 - 40,000	+6.1
Commercial Real Estate Mortgage Lenders	32,000 - 42,000	33,000 - 43,000	+2.7
Executive/Professional Lenders	28,000 - 40,000	30,000 - 43,000	+7.4
Branch Managers	24,000 - 34,000	25,000 - 35,000	+3.4
Operations Manager	28,000 - 33,000	29,000 - 34,000	+3.3
Consumer Lender	25,000 - 30,000	26,000 - 32,000	+5.5
Trust Officer	30,000 - 38,000	31,500 - 40,000	+5.1

Banking—Small ($100MM Assets and Lower)

Title	1989	1990	% Change vs. 1989
Senior Lender/#2 Person	$38,000 - $63,000	$40,000 - $65,000	+4.0
Commercial Lenders 1-3 yrs. exp.	26,000 - 33,000	29,000 - 35,000	+8.5
Commercial Lenders 3+ yrs. exp.	28,000 - 37,000	30,000 - 40,000	+7.7
Consumer Lender	23,000 - 29,000	24,000 - 30,000	+3.8
Trust Officer	27,000 - 33,000	28,000 - 35,000	+5.0
Branch Manager	22,000 - 33,000	24,000 - 34,000	+5.5

Banking—Large ($500MM to $1 Billion Assets)

Title	1989	1990	% Change vs. 1989
Senior VP/Head of Lending	$75,000 - $87,000	$78,000 - $90,000	+3.7
Lending Division/Head Lender	50,000 - 73,000	53,000 - 75,000	+4.1
Commercial Lenders 1-3 yrs. exp. (Commercial, Middle Market, ABL)	28,000 - 38,000	30,000 - 40,000	+6.1
Commercial Lenders 3+ yrs. exp. (Commercial, Middle Market, ABL)	34,000 - 58,000	36,000 - 60,000	+4.3
Commercial Real Estate Mortgage Lender	32,000 - 53,000	33,000 - 54,000	+2.4
Residential Real Estate Mortgage Lender	24,500 - 35,000	26,000 - 36,000	+4.2
Consumer Loan Officer	24,000 - 34,000	25,000 - 35,000	+3.4
Executive Professional Lender, 1-3 yrs. exp.	28,000 - 38,000	29,000 - 39,000	+3.0
Executive Professional Lender, 3+ yrs. exp.	30,000 - 58,000	32,000 - 60,000	+4.5
Loan Review Officer	25,500 - 37,500	27,000 - 39,000	+4.8
Loan Workout Officer	28,000 - 43,000	30,000 - 45,000	+5.6
Branch Administrator (Multi-Branch Offices)	33,000 - 43,000	35,000 - 45,000	+5.3
Asset-Liability/Investment Manager	36,000 - 43,000	38,000 - 45,000	+5.1
Operations Officer	29,000 - 39,000	30,000 - 40,000	+2.9
Corporate Trust Officer	32,000 - 40,000	33,000 - 42,000	+4.2

Source: Robert Half International Inc.

ENCYCLOPEDIA OF BANKING AND FINANCE

BANKING SYNDICATE Loosely, a group of investment banking firms associated for the purpose of underwriting and public offering of securities, with one firm as manager. Under the BANKING ACT OF 1933, member banks were forbidden to underwrite and trade in securities, except U.S. government direct and guaranteed obligations and general obligation state and municipal issues. The same act required the divorcement of SECURITY AFFILIATES by member banks within one year from June 16, 1933.

See SYNDICATE.

BANK INSOLVENCY As far as the Federal Deposit Insurance Act (Section 11(b)) is concerned, an insured bank shall be deemed to have been closed on account of inability to meet the demands of its depositors in any case in which it has been closed for the purpose of liquidation without adequate provision being made for payment of its depositors. A basic form of insolvency is the inability to pay deposit liabilities.

Section 11(c) of the Federal Deposit Insurance Act states: "Notwithstanding any other provision of law, whenever the Comptroller of the Currency shall appoint a receiver other than a conservator of any insured national bank or insured District bank, or of any noninsured national bank or District bank hereafter closed, he shall appoint the Federal Deposit Insurance Corporation receiver for such closed bank."

References to insolvency by the Comptroller of the Currency in his regulations include the following:

1. **Receivership.** If the Comptroller determines that a national bank is insolvent, he may appoint a receiver for such bank.
2. **Appointment of the Federal Deposit Insurance Corporation as receiver.** In cases in which the Comptroller appoints the FDIC as receiver, the FDIC prescribes the procedures it follows in liquidation of the insolvent bank.
3. **Other receivers.** "In those cases in which the Comptroller of the Currency does not appoint the Federal Deposit Insurance Corporation as receiver, he appoints a receiver of his own choice." The Comptroller prescribes a form of proof of claim. The receiver appointed by the Comptroller issues a certificate of proof of claim to claimants who prove their claims to the satisfaction of the Comptroller or establish their claims by litigation.
4. **Conservatorship.** The Comptroller may appoint a conservator of his own choice for any national bank when he determines that such action is necessary to conserve the assets of the bank for the benefit of its depositors and other creditors. The conservator acts under the direction of the Comptroller and has the powers and duties of a receiver. The procedures followed, since the Comptroller's conservatorship authority is exercised in emergency situations, depend upon the circumstances of each case which dictate the action necessary to conserve the assets of the bank.

A receiver shall be appointed for a national bank, and shall proceed to close up the bank, in the following situations:

1. Whenever a national bank is dissolved and its rights, privileges, and franchises declared forfeited, as prescribed in 12 U.S.C. 93. Statute provides for such forfeiture if the directors of the national bank shall knowingly violate or knowingly permit any of the bank's officers, agents, or servants to violate any provisions of the national banking laws. Such violation, however, shall be determined and adjudged by suit brought in proper federal court for the purpose by the Comptroller of the Currency, in his own name, before the national bank shall be declared dissolved.
2. Whenever any creditor of a national bank shall have obtained a judgment against it in any court of record and made application, accompanied by a certificate from the clerk of the court stating that such judgment has been rendered and has remained unpaid for 30 days.
3. Whenever the Comptroller of the Currency shall become satisfied of the insolvency of a national bank, he may, after due examination of its affairs, in either case, appoint a receiver who shall proceed to close up such bank.

Other situations resulting in receivership for national banks include:

1. Failure to pay up capital stock, and impairment of capital stock by losses or otherwise (12 U.S.C. 55). Under this statute, failure by a national bank, within three months after receiving notice of impairment of capital stock from the Comptroller of the Currency, to pay the deficiency in the capital stock by assessment upon the shareholders pro rata for the amount of capital stock held by each, and refusal to go into liquidation, is subject to appointment of receiver to close up the business of the bank per 12 U.S.C. 192 referenced above. 12 U.S.C. 51b-1 also refers to impairment of capital: (1) if any part of the capital consists of preferred stock, determination of whether or not the capital of the bank is impaired, and the amount of such impairment, shall be based upon the par value of its stock, even though the amount which the holders of the preferred stock are entitled to receive in retirement or liquidation is in excess of par value of such preferred stock; (2) if the bank has outstanding any capital notes or debentures "of the type which the Reconstruction Finance Corporation is authorized to purchase pursuant to the provisions of Section 304 of the Emergency Banking and Bank Conservation Act, approved March 9, 1933," the capital of such bank may be deemed to be unimpaired if the sound value of its assets is not less than its total liabilities, including capital stock, but excluding such capital notes and debentures and any obligations of the bank expressly subordinated thereto. (This section 304 of the Emergency Banking and

Banking—Large ($500MM to $1 Billion Assets)

Title	1989	1990	% Change vs. 1989
Senior VP/Head of Lending	$75,000 - $87,000	$78,000 - $90,000	+3.7
Lending Division/Head Lender	50,000 - 73,000	53,000 - 75,000	+4.1
Commercial Lenders 1-3 yrs. exp. (Commercial, Middle Market, ABL)	28,000 - 38,000	30,000 - 40,000	+6.1
Commercial Lenders 3+ yrs. exp. (Commercial, Middle Market, ABL)	34,000 - 58,000	36,000 - 60,000	+4.3
Commercial Real Estate Mortgage Lender	32,000 - 53,000	33,000 - 54,000	+2.4
Residential Real Estate Mortgage Lender	24,500 - 35,000	26,000 - 36,000	+4.2
Consumer Loan Officer	24,000 - 34,000	25,000 - 35,000	+3.4
Executive Professional Lender, 1-3 yrs. exp.	28,000 - 38,000	29,000 - 39,000	+3.0
Executive Professional Lender, 3+ yrs. exp.	30,000 - 58,000	32,000 - 60,000	+4.5
Loan Review Officer	25,500 - 37,500	27,000 - 39,000	+4.8
Loan Workout Officer	28,000 - 43,000	30,000 - 45,000	+5.6
Branch Administrator (Multi-Branch Offices)	33,000 - 43,000	35,000 - 45,000	+5.3
Asset-Liability/Investment Manager	36,000 - 43,000	38,000 - 45,000	+5.1
Operations Officer	29,000 - 39,000	30,000 - 40,000	+2.9
Corporate Trust Officer	32,000 - 40,000	33,000 - 42,000	+4.2

Source: Robert Half International Inc.

BANK LAW

Bank Conservation Act, however, was repealed by Act of June 30, 1947.)

2. Discontinuance of banking operations for a period of 60 days, without having gone into liquidation by vote of two-thirds of the stock (12 U.S.C. 181) and without having had a receiver already appointed for other lawful cause. In such case, the Comptroller of the Currency, if he deems it advisable, may appoint a receiver for such bank (12 U.S.C. 288).
3. Forfeiture of all rights, privileges, and franchises of the bank granted under the National Bank Act or under the Federal Reserve Act, for failure to comply with any of the provisions of the Federal Reserve Act (12 U.S.C. 501(a)<V>).
4. Violation of limitations on number of directors of a national bank, continued after 30 days' notice from the Comptroller of the Currency, to not less than 5 nor more than 25 directors (12 U.S.C. 71(a)), giving the Comptroller power to appoint a receiver or conservator for the bank.
5. Overcertification of any check in excess of amount on deposit, which check shall be a good and valid obligation against the bank but subject the bank to appointment of receiver by the Comptroller of the Currency (12 U.S.C. 192), and subject the officer, director, agent, or employee of the bank responsible for maximum criminal penalty of $5,000 fine and/or imprisonment for five years (18 U.S.C. 1004).

Before an insured bank is allowed to close, however, the Federal Deposit Insurance Corporation may step in to reduce the risk or avert threatened loss to it on its deposit insurance liability. By loans, purchase of assets, guarantee against loss, etc., the FDIC may facilitate merger or consolidation of the insured bank with another insured bank, or facilitate the purchase of assets and assumption of liabilities by another insured bank.

See BANK DEPOSIT INSURANCE ACT, FEDERAL DEPOSIT INSURANCE CORPORATION, DEPOSIT INSURANCE, INSURED BANK.

BANK LAW A general term to designate the statutes of the U.S. and of the various states under which banking institutions are organized, operated, and regulated. It also refers to the large number of court decisions concerning banking and negotiable instruments, bank forms, documents, etc., and to administrative regulations of the supervisory authorities, including those of the Board of Governors of the Federal Reserve System, Comptroller of the Currency, Federal Deposit Insurance Corporation, Treasury Department, and state banking departments.

BIBLIOGRAPHY

BOARD OF GOVERNORS OF THE FEDERAL RESERVE SYSTEM. *Federal Reserve Regulations Service.* Federal Reserve System, Washington, DC. Annual Reports.
COMPTROLLER OF THE CURRENCY. *Comptroller's Handbook for National Bank Examiners; Comptroller's Manual for National Banks.* Federal Reserve System, Washington, DC. Periodic updates.
FEDERAL DEPOSIT INSURANCE CORPORATION. *Bank Examination Manual: Rules and Regulations.* Federal Reserve System, Washington, DC. Annual Reports.

BANK LOANS See LOAN.

BANK MAGAZINES See FINANCIAL MAGAZINES.

BANK MERGERS Bank mergers became an active legal subject as the result of passage of the Bank Merger Act of 1960 (P.L. 86–463, May 13, 1960); enactment of amendments to the Bank Merger Act of 1960 contained in P.L. 89–356, February 21, 1966 (referred to as the Bank Merger Act of 1966); and an active program of prosecutions by the Department of Justice in this field under the antitrust laws.

As of July, 1982, with issuance by the Board of Governors of the Federal Reserve System of guidelines for permitted acquisitions by bank holding companies of nonvoting stock of banks in states other than their home states, a resurgence of merger activity was considered probable in anticipation of interstate banking acquisitions with voting control.

Bank Merger Act of 1960. Bank mergers before 1960 were presumably not subject to the general antitrust laws, and would be subject thereto only if expressly made so. Approvals by the banking agencies concerned were considered sufficient, and the antitrust division of the Department of Justice did not challenge such approvals. However, in March, 1959, the Department of Justice filed action to enjoin an intended merger that would result from acquisition of bank shares by a holding company, a plan approved by the Board of Governors of the Federal Reserve System. Motion to dismiss, on the grounds of *res judicata* (the approval by the Federal Reserve board), was denied by the trial court, and the U.S. Supreme Court denied *certiorari* (*First-America Corporation* v. *U.S.*, 361 U.S. 928, 1960). This action was subsequently settled, but it was significant in indicating the change in position of the Department of Justice. This change had occurred despite the Kefauver-Celler Act of 1950, which, in extending coverage of Section 7 of the Clayton Act to acquisitions of assets in addition to existing reference therein to acquisitions of stock, specifically limited applicability to corporations subject to jurisdiction of the Federal Trade Commission, which does not include banks.

In 1960, Congress passed the Bank Merger Act of 1960, which confirmed that the banking agencies concerned would have the power to approve or disapprove bank mergers, with the Department of Justice having an advisory role in connection with anticompetitive aspects. The act (12 U.S.C. 1828(c)) amended Section 18(c) of the Federal Deposit Insurance Act in connection with mergers or consolidations of insured banks. It has the following provisions:

1. No insured bank shall merge or consolidate with any other insured bank, or directly or indirectly acquire the assets of or assume the deposits in any other insured bank, unless prior written approval shall have been obtained from the Comptroller of the Currency, where the resulting bank is a national bank; the Board of Governors of the Federal Reserve System, where the resulting bank is a state member bank; or the Federal Deposit Insurance Corporation, where the resulting bank is an insured nonmember bank.
2. Unless it is determined that immediate action is necessary to prevent the probable failure of one of the banks involved, the appropriate approving banking authority shall, prior to deciding upon the application, request the Attorney General and the other approving banking authorities to submit reports on the competitive factors involved in the proposed action.
3. In acting upon an application, the appropriate banking agency is to consider as to each bank involved: its financial history and condition; the adequacy of its capital structure; its future earnings prospects; the general character of its management; the convenience and needs of the community; and whether or not its corporate powers are consistent with the purposes of the act. The appropriate banking agency shall also take into consideration the effect of the transaction on competition, and shall not approve the transaction unless it finds that the transaction will be in the public interest.

The Bank Merger Act of 1960 seemed to settle the issue of the role of the Department of Justice in bank mergers, and during the year 1960 and early 1961 a number of bank mergers were effected or agreed upon with approval of the appropriate approving banking agencies. However, in February, 1961, suit was filed by the Department of Justice to enjoin the merger of the Philadelphia National Bank and Girard Trust Corn Exchange Bank, which had been approved by the Comptroller of the Currency, alleging violation of both Section 1 of the Sherman Act and Section 7 of the Clayton Act. The District Court held that Section 7 of the Clayton Act could not be the basis for action against the merger.

The U.S. Supreme Court, however, in *U.S.* v. *Philadelphia National Bank*, 374 U.S. 321 (1963), held in its majority opinion that:

1. Section 7 of the Clayton Act does apply to bank mergers. The specific text of Section 7, as amended in 1950, was as follows: "That no corporation engaged in commerce shall acquire, directly or indirectly, the whole or any part of the stock or other capital and no corporation subject to the jurisdiction of the Federal Trade Commission shall acquire the whole or any part of the assets of another corporation engaged also in commerce, where in any line of commerce in any section of the country, the effect of such acquisition may be substantially to lessen competition, or to tend to create a monopoly."

The Supreme Court held that Section 7 of the Clayton Act is applicable to all mergers, including bank mergers, as best expressing the broad purpose of Congress, despite lack of reference to mergers as such in text or legislative background

of the Kefauver-Celler Act; and that mergers are neither precisely acquisitions of stock nor acquisitions of assets but rather "lie somewhere between the two ends of the spectrum."
2. The "line of commerce" to which Section 7 of the Clayton Act refers is a cluster of products termed "commercial banking" in the case of banks. Whether the effect of a bank merger "may be substantially to lessen competition"depends on whether it is "a merger which produces a firm controlling an undue percentage share of the relevant market, and results in a significant increase in the concentration of firms in that market . . . ." The Court in this case found that 30% would be an upper limit on the extent of concentration permissible by merger in market structure.
3. The Bank Merger Act of 1960 does not insulate banks from the federal antitrust laws; and regardless of that act's emphasis on public interest vis à vis effect on competition, a bank merger the effect "of which "may be substantially to lessen competition' is not saved because, on some ultimate reckoning of social or economic debits or credits, it may be deemed beneficial."

In a dissenting opinion, Mr. Justice Harlan wrote: "The result is, of course, that the Bank Merger Act is almost completely nullified; its enactment turns out to have been an exorbitant waste of congressional time and energy . . . . This frustration of a manifest congressional design is, in my view, a most unwarranted intrusion upon the legislative domain."
4. Jurisdiction of the Board of Governors of the Federal Reserve System to enforce Section 7 of the Clayton Act, concurrently with the Department of Justice, was found by the Supreme Court to be deemed to have been repealed by implication when the Bank Merger Act of 1960 was enacted.

Bank Merger Act of 1966. This act's main purpose was declared to be the resolution of conflicts in interpretation of the Bank Merger Act of 1960, by providing that the bank supervisory agencies, the Department of Justice, and the courts shall take into account the same set of standards in their actions with respect to bank mergers:

1. The responsible banking agency and any court shall not approve the following:
   a. Any proposed merger transaction which would result in a monopoly, or which would be in furtherance of any combination or conspiracy to monopolize or attempt to monopolize the business of banking in any part of the U.S.
   b. Any other proposed merger transaction whose effect in any section of the country may be substantially to lessen competition, or tend to create a monopoly, or which in any other manner would be in restraint of trade, unless it finds that the anticompetitive effects of the proposed transaction are clearly outweighed in the public interest by the probable effect of the transaction in meeting the convenience and needs of the community to be served.
   c. In every case, the responsible agency shall take into consideration the financial and managerial resources and future prospects of the existing and proposed institutions, and the convenience and needs of the community to be served.
2. The consummation of a merger, in usual circumstances, cannot take place until 30 days after approval by the appropriate supervisory authority, in order to give the Department of Justice an opportunity to contest the merger in the courts, if it so desired. If a suit is not filed within that period, the merger cannot thereafter be attacked judicially on the ground that it is a violation of an antitrust law, other than Section 2 of the Sherman Act (the monopoly section).
3. In any action brought against a bank merger under the antitrust laws, the court shall review *de novo* the issues presented and apply the same standards directed to be applied by the banking agency concerned.
4. Consummation of any bank merger challenged in an antitrust action shall be stayed, unless the court shall otherwise specifically order.
5. Any bank merger consummated before June 17, 1963, the date of the *Philadelphia National Bank* case, shall be exempt from any further antitrust prosecution, except under Section 2 of the Sherman Act.
6. Any bank merger consummated after June 16, 1963, and before February 9, 1966, and against which the Attorney General had not commenced litigation prior to February 9, 1966, shall be exempt from any future antitrust prosecution, except under Section 2 of the Sherman Act.
7. In any case filed after June 16, 1963, against bank mergers by the Attorney General under the antitrust laws, the court shall apply the substantive law contained in the act, whether the case was pending in court on February 9, 1966, or filed later.

The Department of Justice, however, took the following position with regard to the Bank Merger Act of 1966, as contained in a letter to the presiding judge on the *Crocker-Anglo* case by the chief of the antitrust division of the Department of Justice:

> While a purpose of the law is to define uniform standards to be applied by the banking agencies and the courts in judging bank mergers, it is our position that the supposed differences in the standards applied have been overstated. Moreover, insofar as uniformity is concerned, what the new law does is impose on the banking agencies responsibility for giving—not just equal—but paramount consideration to the competition implications of bank mergers. This is what the courts in anti-trust cases, including *Philadelphia*, have always done . . . While the new legislation thus gives emphasis to the new uniformity in the bank merger field, it is our view that it has not resulted in any substantial change in substantive anti-trust law . . .

On this basis, the Department of Justice proceeded with pending cases against bank mergers in San Francisco, Nashville, and St. Louis, and filed new cases under the Clayton Act against mergers approved under the Bank Merger Act of 1966 in Philadelphia, Houston, and Hawaii. Although rebuffed in trial court rulings, the Department of Justice won a complete victory for its position in the U.S. Supreme Court, in appeals from the district courts in *U.S.* v. *First City National Bank of Houston* and *U.S.* v. *Provident National Bank*. These combined bank merger appeals involved Section 7 of the Clayton Act (the Comptroller of the Currency had approved both mergers under the Bank Merger Act of 1966). On March 27, 1967, by unanimous decision the following four points were established:

1. An action challenging a bank merger on the ground of its anticompetitive effects is brought under the antitrust laws by specific provisions of the Bank Merger Act of 1966. Thus, the government's failure to base the actions on or mention the Bank Merger Act of 1966 is not a defect in its complaints. All that the Bank Merger Act of 1966 does is to provide a new defense or justification to the merger's proponents, i.e., "that the anticompetitive effects of the proposed merger are clearly outweighed in the public interest by the probable effect of the transaction in meeting the convenience and needs of the community to be served." This is an additional standard, in addition to innovation in machinery for obtaining the prior approval of the banking agency primarily responsible and preliminary expression of views by the Attorney General and the other banking agencies.
2. Burden of proof of claim of exception to the antitrust laws, on the ground that a given merger is so beneficial to the convenience and needs of the community to be served that it would be in the public interest to permit it is on the defendant banks, not on the Department of Justice.
3. Provision is made in the Bank Merger Act of 1966 that in any judicial proceeding against a bank merger under the antitrust laws the court shall review *de novo* the issues presented. This means that the court should make an independent determination of the issues. It does not mean that the banking agency's decision is in the category of other administrative rulings which are sustained unless clearly unsupported or not supported by substantial evidence, since traditionally in antitrust actions involving regulated industries, the courts have never given presumptive weight to prior agency's decision, and the Bank Merger Act of 1966 does not so provide.
4. To avoid the difficulty of unscrambling two or more banks after their merger, the normal procedure should be maintenance of the status quo until the antitrust litigation has run its course.

Thus this decision restored the situation to that specified in the *Philadelphia National Bank* case, i.e., applicability of the general antitrust laws to banks, with the above modifications.

Statistical Background. For the years 1924–1933, commercial bank mergers averaged 526, compared to averages of 190 for 1934–1937 and 88 for 1938–1951, including a few mutual savings banks (Senate Select Committee on Small Business, Special Staff Report by Board of Governors of Federal Reserve System, *Recent Developments in the Structure of Banking*, 87th Congress, 2nd Session, 1962). For 1950–1959, a total of 1,502 mergers and consolidations, or an average of 150 for the decade, were reported in the *Federal Reserve Bulletin*, including highs for the decade of 207 banks in 1954 and 232 in 1955. For the years 1960–1970, however, the number of consolidations and absorptions slowed to an average of 147, compared with a high of 232 in 1955. By 1971, they were down to 103, the fewest since 1952. Note should be taken, however, of the surge in acquisitions by bank holding companies in recent years; holding company groups as of the end of 1980 included over 33% of all commercial banks, compared with 9% in 1950.

See ACQUISITIONS AND MERGERS, BANK FAILURES, BANK HOLDING COMPANY ACT, BANK INSOLVENCY, BRANCH BANKING, MERGER.

BIBLIOGRAPHY

ALBERTS, W. W. "Have Interstate Acquisitions Been Profitable?" *American Banker*, September 18, 1986.
ADAMS, J. "Making All Systems Go for 'Day One' of a Merger." *American Banker*, May 18, 1986.
Antitrust Law Journal.
BURKE, J. "Antitrust Laws, Justice Department Guidelines, and the Limits of Concentration in Local Banking Markets." Staff Study No. 138, Federal Reserve System, June, 1984.
EASTERBROOK, B. "Workable Antitrust Policy." *Antitrust Law Journal*, 21, 1985
KERWIN, J. S., and ROBISON, R. A. "Charting a Bank's Value: Number Analysis and Beyond." *ABA Banking Journal*, July, 1986.
MCKINSEY & CO., INC. *Bankers' Merger and Acquisition Choices*. Bank Administration Institute, Rolling Meadows, IL, 1985.
NADLER, P. S. "After the Big Merger, Whose Side Are Bank Officers On?" *American Banker*, August 12, 1985.
ROSE, P. S. *Bank Mergers in a Deregulated Environment*. Bank Administration Institute, Rolling Meadows, IL, 1988.
SCRANTON, D. "Management of Credit Risks in a Bank Merger." *Journal of Commercial Bank Lending*, January, 1986.
SULLIVAN, M. P. "Understanding of Cultures Is Critical in Managing Acquisitions." *American Banker*, November, 1986.
WELKEN, D. L. "Thrift Competition: Does It Matter?" *Economic Review*, Federal Reserve Bank of Richmond, Jan.-Feb., 1986.

BANK MONEY ORDER A money order issued and sold by banks, as distinguished from postal and express money orders. They are practically a modified form of cashier's check, and unlike postal money orders may be endorsed any number of times. Their cost on a similarly graduated basis is normally below post office fees for postal money orders. Many banks have also installed the registered check service in lieu of money orders or no minimum balance checking accounts.

See MONEY ORDERS, NO MINIMUM BALANCE CHECKING ACCOUNT, REGISTER CHECK SERVICE.

BANK NOTES A bank's own promise to pay to bearer upon demand, and intended to be used as money. Bank notes are often referred to as circulating notes or circulation. The current emission of note issue in the U.S. is now confined to the Federal Reserve banks, which issue FEDERAL RESERVE NOTES. Power to issue notes still exists in national banks, but no government bonds bearing the circulation privilege are issued or outstanding. So does the power to issue bank notes continue to exist in state banks, but federal 10% tax thereon in the Internal Revenue Code continues to bar issue as a matter of feasibility. Since March, 1935, funds have been on deposit with the Treasurer of the U.S. to cover retirement of all FEDERAL RESERVE BANK NOTES and, since August, 1935, to cover retirement of all outstanding NATIONAL BANK NOTES.

Bank Commercial Paper (Promissory Notes). The question of whether a member bank may issue its own commercial paper in the open market found the Comptroller of the Currency and the Board of Governors of the Federal Reserve System divided.

The Comptroller has ruled that a national bank may do so (Par. 7530, *Rulings*). A national bank may issue at par or discount its negotiable or nonnegotiable promissory notes of any maturity. The provisions of Regulation 16 (12 CFR 16) should be consulted for registration requirements if there is to be a public offering of such notes or a series thereof. In its latest form, however, Par. 7530 of the Comptroller's *Rulings* omits former additional matter as follows: "Such promissory notes, issued in the regular course of business to obtain working funds for use in making loans and the performance of ordinary banking functions, represent liabilities of the nature excepted from the provisions of 12 U.S.C. 82 (note: the general limitation on indebtedness of a national bank to the amount of its capital stock plus 50% of unimpaired surplus fund). Such notes may, therefore, be issued without regard to the limitations or indebtedness contained in that section. Notwithstanding the provisions of Regulations Q and D issued by the Federal Reserve board, it is the position of the Comptroller of the Currency that the proceeds of such notes do not constitute deposits and that the provisions of 12 U.S.C. 461, 462, and 1813 relating to reserves, interest limitations, and deposit insurance are not applicable."

The Board of Governors of the Federal Reserve System disagreed. In their Regulation D, as amended effective January 1, 1967, definitions of deposits subject to legal reserve requirements included "any promissory note, acknowledgment of advance, due bill, or similar instrument that is issued by a member bank principally as a means of obtaining funds to be used in its banking business, except any such instrument (1) that is issued to another bank, (2) that evidences an indebtedness arising from a transfer of assets that the bank is obligated to repurchase, or (3) that has an original maturity of more than 2 years and states expressly that it is subordinated to the claims of depositors" (exempting any instrument issued before June 27, 1966). Similar provision was found in the board's Regulation Q, as amended effective January 1, 1967, relating to regulation of interest on deposits.

See COMMERCIAL PAPER.

BIBLIOGRAPHY

Bank Finance. "A Note on Banknote Characteristics and the Demand for Currency By Denomination. *Journal of Banking and Finance*, September, 1988.
ZWEIG, J. "From Munis to Money." *Forbes*, February 10, 1989.

BANK OCCUPATIONS The principal jobs in a commercial bank are as follows: accountant, adding machine operator, advice clerk, assistant cashier, auditor, bill clerk, bond clerk, bookkeeper, cashier, certifications clerk, check-desk clerk, chief clerk, clearinghouse settlement clerk, collateral clerk, collection clerk, commercial credits clerk, comptroller, computer programmer, coupon clerk, coupon collection clerk, coupon collection teller, coupon teller, credit analyst, credit correspondent, credit investigator, custodianship teller, customers' securities clerk, data processor, dictaphone operator, discount clerk, discount teller, draft clerk, electronic banking clerk, fanfold machine operator, file clerk, foreign currency teller, foreign exchange bookkeeper, foreign exchange clerk, foreign exchange trader, general bookkeeper, guard, junior clerk, ledger clerk, letter of credit clerk, loan clerk, loan officer, mail teller, messenger, money clerk, night watchman, note teller, page, paying teller, personnel officer, secretary, securities clerk, senior clerk, shipping clerk, signature clerk, statement machine clerk, statistician, stenographer, stenotypist, stockroom clerk, stop-payment clerk, substitution clerk, transit clerk, translator, trust officer, typist, vault attendant, voucher clerk.

BIBLIOGRAPHY

BROWN, A. J., JR. *The Effective Branch Manager: Ways to Development Management Skills*, 2nd ed., 1980.
GEORGIA, R. C. "Performance-Oriented Personnel Development Programs." In BAUGHN, W. H., and WALKER, C. E., eds., *The Bankers' Handbook*, rev. ed., 1978.

BANK OF CANADA Established in 1934, the Bank of Canada began operations March 11, 1935, as the central bank and bankers' bank for Canada. It acts as the fiscal agent for the government of Canada. The preamble to the Bank of Canada Act specifies the functions of the bank as being "to regulate credit and currency in the best interests of the economic life of the nation, to control and protect the external value of the national monetary unit and to mitigate by its influence fluctuations in the general level of production, trade, prices, and employment, so far as may be possible within the scope of monetary action, and generally to promote the economic and financial welfare of the Dominion."

As a central bank, the Bank of Canada has the following functions:

1. Acts as fiscal agent for the government of Canada.
2. Has the sole right of note (currency) issuance.
3. Has the following instruments of monetary policy.
   a. Sets the bank rate (the rate at which the Bank of Canada's discount window provides credit, an indicator of monetary policy).
   b. Intervenes into the money market including the market for Treasury bills (open market operations), which in effect really makes the floating bank rate more managed than freely floating.
   c. Administers the Canadian system of legal reserve requirements of the banks.

The new Bank Act established two classes of banks: Schedule A banks, those presently chartered and any incorporated in the future, whose shares are widely held, which shall be subject to maximum ownership of 10% of the voting shares by any one stockholder or group of stockholders; and Schedule B banks, which can be closely held initially upon incorporation and would include subsidiaries of foreign banks which may with permission open branches and call themselves banks. But such subsidiaries of foreign banks are required to obtain licenses, renewable or granted annually for the first five years and for up to three-year periods thereafter. Such incorporation by foreign banks of Canadian subsidiaries is conditioned upon reciprocal incorporation by Canadian banks of subsidiaries in the home countries of the foreign banks. But Schedule B banks and foreign bank subsidiaries cannot have branches outside Canada. Their growth in size individually and in the aggregate is limited to 8% of all banks' domestic assets.

The new Bank Act also established the new Canadian Payments Association to replace the national system of clearing and settlement of checks previously operated by the Canadian Bankers Association. Clearing members now settle directly with the Bank of Canada, which under the new Bank Act has the power to lend to members of the Canadian Payments Association having accounts at the Bank of Canada. Near-banks are permitted direct access to the new Canadian payments system in the clearance and settlement of negotiable instruments drawn on financial institutions of a depository nature.

Monetary Policy. In the implementation of monetary policy seeking to provide for real growth and a stable Canadian dollar both domestically and in foreign exchange markets, the Bank of Canada has basically relied on the targeting of specific growth rates in the money supply (M1 concept).

The government's national energy program, moreover, which seeks at least 50% ownership of domestic oil and gas production by Canadians as against foreign ownership, has led to takeovers and buyouts of foreign holdings, financed liberally by Canadian banks. A program of subsidies and incentives for Canadian firms to bring in new production has been initiated, thus contributing to outflow of funds in the balance of payments and to inflationary effects. In addition, despite a high unemployment rate, Canadian labor has continued to be aggressive in wage demands and in resistance to wage adjustments.

In recent years, the dramatic fall in energy prices created severe problems for Canadian energy companies, many of which had paid for acquisitions at prices reflecting peak petroleum costs. Parts of the country that depended on petroleum as a major source of economic activity were devastated, with far-reaching damage done to real estate and financial institutions. Several smaller banks were merged to protect their depositors, and even the major banks had their earnings and asset quality reduced. The government elected to run counter to its general tendency to open markets to competition and retained a relatively tight control structure for Canada's financial institutions, discouraging the entry of new (and especially foreign) competition.

BANK OF CIRCULATION   BANK OF ISSUE.

BANK OF DEPOSIT
Strictly, any bank that receives deposits, which would include practically every banking type. In ordinary usage, however, it applies to banks which receive deposits subject to check, and therefore to commercial banks and the banking departments of trust companies. These institutions, in addition to receiving such primary deposits, create derivative deposits by their lending and investing functions.

BANK OF DISCOUNT
A bank that discounts notes, acceptances, and bills of exchange and otherwise lends its credit, as distinguished from a savings bank, mortgage company, etc. All commercial banks are banks of discount, including national banks, state banks, and the banking departments of trust companies. Federal Reserve banks also come under this designation.

See BANK.

BANK OF ENGLAND
The central banking institution of England, with its main office in London at Threadneedle Street, E.C. 2, popularly known as the Old Lady of Threadneedle Street. Originally chartered by act of Parliament in 1694, the Bank of England has branches for note issuance and exchange control activities at eight locations (Birmingham, Bristol, Leeds, Liverpool, Manchester, Newcastle upon Tyne, Southampton, and Law Courts (London)). The bank's constitution rests principally on the Bank of England Act of 1946 and the charter granted in the same year, when the bank came into government ownership. The capital, represented by £14,553,000 bank stock, was then transferred to the Treasury Solicitor, who holds it on behalf of H.M. Treasury. Stockholders received 3% government bonds, redeemable at par on and after April 5, 1966, in such amount as would provide gross annual interest equal to the annual dividend of 12% declared during the 20-year period ended March 31, 1945. Thus stockholders received £400 in bonds for each £100 in par value of the bank's stock. The act empowered the government to appoint the "court" of the bank: the governor and deputy governor, appointed for five-year terms but reappointable for any additional number of terms, and the 16 directors (for four-year terms, four retiring each year), of whom four must serve full time. The Treasury was also empowered statutorily to do what could have been done on a *de facto* basis, i.e., give directions to the bank after consultation with and advice by the governor; in turn the bank was empowered, upon authorization from the Treasury, to request information from and give directions to the banks when considered necessary in the public interest.

New Banking Act. The Banking Act of 1979, Britain's first comprehensive banking law, received the royal assent on April 4, 1979, and became effective October 1, 1979. From October 1, 1979, the appointed day, no new deposit-taking institution to which the act would apply could legally be established without prior authorization of the Bank of England. The bank summarized its activities as follows.

Each deposit-taking institution falling within the scope of the act is required to complete an application and submit it to the Bank of England. A common form was devised for all applications, whether for recognition as a bank or for a license to carry on a deposit-taking business.

The grant of either recognition or a license requires an applicant institution to meet criteria set out in Schedule 2 of the act, relating to the quality of management and to the prudent conduct and financial soundness of the business. To assist it in reaching a judgment on whether these criteria are satisfied, the Bank of England asks in every case for information about those responsible for running the business and requires the submission of detailed statistics relating to the business. In addition, in the case of applicant institutions with a principal place of business outside the United Kingdom and carrying on a deposit-taking business through a branch in the United Kingdom, the bank, as empowered by Section 3(5) of the act, seeks assurances from the appropriate overseas supervisory authorities that they are satisfied with respect to the management of the institution and its overall financial soundness. Applicants for recognition as a bank are required to satisfy further criteria relating to high reputation and standing in the financial community and the provision of either a wide range of specified banking services or a highly specialized banking service.

In forming its judgment about the reputation and standing of an institution, the bank obtains market opinion and makes other appropriate inquiries. In forming its judgment about the provision of a wide range of banking services, the bank asks for information about the volume and range of business undertaken, its quality and contribution to earnings, and the staff and other resources devoted to it, so as to assess the nature and scope of each particular service.

The Banking Bill of 1979 called for the establishment of a deposit protection fund with an initial capital of a modest dollar equivalent of $12 million, and financed by levies upon all banks as well as ldt's in proportion to their deposits. Depositors of institutions that failed would be covered on their deposits to the extent of 75% of their first dollar equivalent of $20,000 in deposits, also quite a modest coverage in comparison with the first $100,000 of deposits covered in banks insured by the U.S. FEDERAL DEPOSIT INSURANCE CORPORATION. This feature of the bill, however, was challenged as superfluous in view of the supervisory role of the Bank of England.

New Methods of Monetary Control. As of August 20, 1981, the Bank of England had made a number of innovations in its techniques for achieving the implementation of monetary policy:

1. The minimum lending rate (MLR), which was known as the bank rate before 1971 and posted every Thursday (literally, on a board at the Bank of England and on the trading floor of THE LONDON STOCK EXCHANGE), ceased to be thus announced, as part of the newer methods of monetary control to reduce emphasis on discount window lending and instead emphasize open market operations in eligible bills. The MLR corresponded to the discount rate in Federal Reserve practice in the U.S., whose discontinuance also has been advocated by some U.S. economists as a technique of implementing monetary policy.
2. Instead of providing the MLR, the Bank of England each morning now issues a bulletin indicating its expectations of flow of funds in the money market for that day. This bulletin is followed by a later bulletin that day providing information on the rates and volume on transactions by the bank in the market in bands (maturity categories), e.g., band one, bills up to 14 days; band two, 15- to 33-day bills; band three, 33- to 63-day bills; and band four, 64- to 91-day bills. Bills of a larger list of banks became eligible for discounting at the Bank of England. Banks thus are to judge from this information on rates and volume of transactions by the Bank of England what their appropriate base rates and other rates should be. After the close of business each day, a final bulletin is issued by the bank on its activity. This system is supposed to have the banks determine market interest rates rather than the Bank of England, but it loses the precision and announcement effects of the former MLR as an indicator of monetary policy by the bank.
3. The banks' required reserve asset ratio (minimum reduced in early January, 1981, from 12.5% to 10.0%) was eliminated, and the London clearing banks' agreement to maintain balances at the Bank of England of 1.5% of eligible liabilities was instead changed to require a 0.5% cash ratio of all banks. This action also was an indicator of increased reliance by the Bank of England upon open market operations as the basic technique of its monetary control.

Note Issue. Since 1844, the Bank of England's operations have been departmentalized into two departments, the note issue department and the banking department. The note issue department issues Bank of England notes to the banking department and holds as assets the government securities, gold bullion, and coin held as collateral. Under the Currency and Notes Act of 1928, the Treasury's issuance of notes for circulation was suspended, and since that time the Bank of England has had the sole power of note issue. The bank's issue of notes, beyond the amount covered by gold bullion and coin, was then fixed at £260 million (the fiduciary note issue) and the Treasury was given the power, if requested by the bank, to authorize temporary increases in the amount of the fiduciary issue. Since this act, all profits derived from note issuance have been paid to the Treasury.

The Currency and Bank Notes Act of 1939 fixed the amount of the fiduciary issue at £300 million and required that the assets of the note issue department, including gold, should be valued weekly at current prices.

Under provisions of the Currency and Bank Notes Act of 1954, the amount of the fiduciary note issue was fixed at £1.575 billion, but this total may be altered by direction of the Treasury after representations by the Bank of England. As of February 28, 1981, the fiduciary issue was £10.325 billion, reflecting official increases under the 1954 act. The Radcliffe Report on the working of the English monetary system put it thus: "In effect the authorities may add to or reduce the note issue as they think fit, informing Parliament after the event by laying a Treasury Minute, though so long as the note issue exceeds the maximum fixed by the act (£1.575 billion), the Treasury is obliged to make a statutory order every two years extending the excess, and the order can be prayed against (and therefore debated) in the House of Commons" (p. 118).

The residual gold holding of the issue department, totaling £0.4 million, was sold to the Exchange Equalisation Account on August 6, 1970, and since then the Bank of England's note issue has been entirely backed by holdings of government debt and other securities.

The clearing banks hold part of their cash reserves in the form of balances at the Bank of England, identified on the bank's statement as bankers deposits. These balances facilitate clearing settlements among the banks, both at the "City" and the Bank of England's branch offices. The clearing banks also use the Bank of England as a source of notes and coin, as well as the source to which to return excess notes and coin for credit to reserve balances. Coins are obtained by the Bank of England from the Royal Mint by crediting the Exchequer account.

The Bank of England as the sole bank of note issue in England and Wales does its own printing and engraving. A decimal system of currency was introduced in the United Kingdom on February 15, 1971.

Other Operations. Other activities of the Bank of England include managing the national debt, acting as depository for Treasury funds, administering the foreign exchange regulations (foreign exchange controls were ended in October, 1979), and operating in the foreign exchange markets within the constraints of the new arrangements and policies. The bank also has holdings in the equity share capital of companies.

The Bank and British Industry. The bank attaches great importance to hearing firsthand from those engaged in industry as to how they see their prospects and problems. Accordingly, contact has been maintained with companies around the country and with representatives of trades unions in several regions.

Summary. With entry of the United Kingdom into the enlarged EEC (Common Market) formally on January 1, 1973, a new environment with its constraints and arrangements, economic and political, was entered into by the Bank of England.

The "Old Lady of Threadneedle Street" has adopted many young ideas in central bank operation, which are of interest internationally. It now has increased supervisory responsibility over the English banking system, mixing policy-making with operational functions.

See BANK OF ENGLAND RETURN, BANK RATE, ENGLISH MONEY TABLE.

BIBLIOGRAPHY

MUEHRING, K. "Can the Bank of England Regain Its Clout?" *Institutional Investor*, May, 1987.

BANK OF ENGLAND ACCOUNTS For the first time, the Bank of England published, in its report and accounts for the year ended February 28, 1971, the bank's annual accounts, certified by chartered accountants, consisting of full balance sheet and profit and loss account.

Although the bank's constitution is not governed by the Companies Acts of 1948 to 1980 (comparable to the Securities Act of 1933 in the U.S.), the accounts were prepared so as to comply with the requirements of those acts insofar as "they are material and appropriate."

The fullness of the published balance sheet for the banking department consists of some relocation of specific accounts in the format of the balance sheet, plus explanatory footnotes, as compared to the weekly BANK OF ENGLAND RETURN. It is still, however, a quite condensed balance sheet. Because the Bank of England is concerned in such transactions only as an agent on behalf of the Treasury, commitments in foreign currencies and gold, or on a gold basis, undertaken in the name of the bank for the account of the Treasury in the course of operating the Exchange Equalisation Account are not included in these accounts.

The dichotomy of the banking department and the issue department is continued, and the two departments are not consolidated, pursuant to the Bank Charter Act of 1844, by which the bank is required to keep separate the business of the banking and issue departments, a legislative determination whose banking theory has long been criticized, but which has not been corrected.

The mission of a central bank is not primarily to make a profit from operations, but rather to achieve the desired aggregative and rate effects upon the banking system, regardless of profit or loss, in the interests of general monetary policy.

Summary. Compared with the former content of the Bank of England's annual report, "the meagerness of which," according to the Radcliffe Report, "has become a byword," the new content of the annual report, with the accounts of the bank, shows progress in disclosure which, it is hoped, will continue for full understanding and appreciation of this prestigious prototype of the world's central banks.

BANK OF ENGLAND RETURN

The regularly published statement of the Bank of England is the weekly bank return, originally prescribed by the Bank Charter Act of 1844, as modified since. In addition, the bank beginning with its February 28, 1971, annual report, reports full balance sheet and profit and loss account in its annual report. The return, which reports figures as of each Wednesday, appears Thursday morning of each week and thus provides interim figures.

Since February 28, 1971, the figures in the bank return reflect certain changes in the treatment of reserves in the books of the banking department, in connection with the publication in the Bank of England's annual report of the bank's accounts (full balance sheet and profit and loss account). The main effects of these changes were to increase the figures on the assets side for government securities and for other securities, and on the liabilities side for other accounts because reserves previously earmarked against specific assets were brought together on the liabilities side of the account.

Following publication on July 28, 1971, of the annual report and accounts of the bank for the year ended February 28, 1971, some other minor changes were made in the figures of the banking department published in the weekly bank return. The changes were as follows: on the liabilities side, unallocated profit of the bank formerly described as rest was included in reserves and other accounts, which replaced the item other accounts on the assets side; Treasury bills discounted for customers were included in government securities instead of in discounts and advances, the title of which was changed to advances and other accounts; and the title of other securities was changed to premises, equipment and other securities. Moreover, changes in the figures are shown in comparison with the preceding week only.

The weekly bank return has continued on the above bases ever since. The *Quarterly Bulletin* of the Bank of England reproduces the bank return's figures but not quite on a week-to-week basis.

The *Quarterly Bulletin* of the Bank of England as of June, 1982, introduced an additional concept of the money supply, M2, compiled as one of the measures indicated in the 1981 budget to "improve information" about the measures of the money supply. The objective was "to design a new measure which could be expected to be more directly related to transactions in goods and services than sterling Ms and somewhat less sensitive to relative interest rates than M1."

The new M2 concept includes all noninterest-bearing sight deposits, all deposits against which checks may be drawn, and other deposits of less than £100,000 which can be turned into cash in less than one month. M1 consists of notes and coin in circulation with the public, plus UK private sector sterling sight deposits, which consist mainly of noninterest-bearing such balances, plus interest-bearing such balances. M3 consists of M1 plus UK private sector sterling time deposits and UK public sector sterling deposits, to provide M3 money stock sterling. Adding to that UK residents' deposits in other currencies, including certificates of deposit, provides a broader M3 money stock.

BANK OFFICERS

A national bank has the power, among other corporate powers, to elect or appoint directors, and by its board of directors to appoint a president, vice president, cashier, and other officers, define their duties, require bonds of them and fix the penalty thereof, dismiss such officers or any of them at pleasure, and appoint others to fill their places (12 U.S.C. 24, Par. 5). The president of the bank shall be a member of the board of directors and shall be the chairman thereof, but the board may designate a director in lieu of the president to be chairman of the board, who shall perform such duties as may be designated by the board (12 U.S.C. 76).

The larger the bank, the more likely there will be such additional officers as comptroller, auditor, trust officer, and functional vice presidents in charge of particular divisions, with assistant officers in these categories. Institutions with trust company charters are likely to designate the treasurer, secretary, and assistants to such officers, in addition to the above senior officers.

See AUDITOR, BANK ORGANIZATION, CASHIER, COMPTROLLER, TRUST OFFICER.

BANK OF FRANCE

Originally established in 1800 and formally chartered in 1803, at a time when no other French banks existed, the Bank of France for over a century was the largest commercial bank in France, serving the public directly through a large network of branches and offices besides serving as the nation's central bank. It no longer transacts as large an amount of private banking business, although it still maintains a large system of offices throughout France.

Reorganization of the French Banking System in the 1940s. In France's history, from the royal manufacture of tapestries and porcelain to the concessions for trade and industrial development, the government has long had a hand in the economic activity of the nation. France, however, also built its public sector through government takeovers.

In 1936-1937, the Popular Front government embarked on a nationalization program affecting certain armament and aircraft manufacturers and the remaining railroads. At the end of World War II, among the first acts of the provisional government headed by General de Gaulle was the nationalization of the coal mines (now Charbonnages de France), the Renault automobile company, Moteurs Gnome-et-Rhône (aircraft motors, now SNECMA), Havas (press, travel, and advertising agency), and air transport companies (now Air France).

This was followed in 1945-1946 by nationalization of the central bank (Banque de France), the four leading commercial banks (then representing 55% of deposits), 34 insurance companies (62% of premiums), and the private electric and gas companies (now Electricité de France and Gaz de France). The nationalized companies, with some exceptions, continued to operate as separate entities and remained part of the competitive sector of the French economy.

The 1945 legislation that nationalized the Bank of France as well as the four large deposit banks—Crédit Lyonnais, Société Générale, Banque Nationale pour le Commerce et l'Industrie, and Comptoir National d'Escompte de Paris (the last two of which were merged, in mid-year 1966, as the Banque Nationale de Paris)—also established the National Credit Council.

The National Credit Council consisted of the Minister of Finance (who was president de jure of the council), the governor of the Bank of France (who presided over the council in the absence of the Minister of Finance), and 43 other members, representatives of financial, business, and labor interests in the economy. The council evolved into the policy-making body for monetary policy, although originally intended to be advisory in function. The Bank of France, through its governor, was considered in fact to play the leading role in credit policy. This *de facto* situation, however, did not necessarily mean that the Minister of Finance could not play a more dominant role in the council, nor did it mean that monetary policy in fact played a dominant role in economic policy of the nation. Actually, monetary policy appeared to be subordinated to fiscal policy, to facilitate and implement, insofar as monetary measures were concerned, the objectives of the economic plans and other government programs. Of course the governor of the Bank of France in his coordination with the Minister of Finance was in a position to make recommendations on economic policy.

The Banking Control Commission, established in 1941 as the supervising and examining agency over the regulated banks and nonbank financial institutions, was also headed by the governor of the Bank of France as *ex officio* president.

The National Credit Council was likened to the legislative branch of monetary authority in the French monetary system; the Bank of France, the executive; and the Banking Control Commission, the judicial.

The financial system thus came to consist of the following:

1. The deposit banks, which accept demand and time deposits of not over a two-year term, but which have a low volume of time and savings deposits (less than 10% of deposits) and whose time deposits are mainly business time deposits, often in negotiable certificates of deposit (bons de caisse) with maturities of up to 24 months. The deposit banking sector is dominated by the government-owned deposit banks referenced above. In addition, there were the three then nonnationalized deposit banks (Crédit Commercial de France, Crédit Industriel et Commercial, and Société Centrale de Banque); the Parisian deposit

banks (active in financing of foreign trade, foreign exchange operations, and the gold market), which elected in 1945 to be classified as deposit banks as compared with other Parisian banks which registered as banques d'affaires (investment bankers); the regional banks; and local banks.

The larger deposit banks mix investment banking and securities functions with their commercial banking (originating, underwriting, and distributing securities; holding direct equity investments in nonfinancial firms of up to 10% of such firms' equity capital, subject to an overall limit of 75% of the bank's capital funds, and in other banks and financial institutions deemed necessary for operations; acting as dealers and brokers as members of the Paris Bourse; performing advisory services and depository functions for investment companies; etc.).

2. The banques d'affaires (investment banking firms which in 1945 elected to be regulated and registered as such) which, in addition to investment banking functions (origination, underwriting, and distribution of securities), make permanent investments (participations) in business firms for income and management, and accept short-term deposits from such firms in which the investment bankers hold at least 15% of registered capital. Each of the regulated banques d'affaires has attached to it a government commissioner who can initiate policy recommendations and has the power to veto decisions that are deemed to be in conflict with overall economic policy. This veto is appealable to the National Credit Council. Thus, although not nationalized, the banques d'affaires are subject to close supervision.

3. The public and semipublic financial institutions, each a specialist in its type of financial operations:

   a. The important Caisse des Dépôts et Consignations, originally established in 1816 and serving as a depository for funds of the savings banks, except for vault cash (since 1950, savings banks may upon request manage up to 50% of their deposits by investing in local government securities), plus funds of the Social Security system and other savings funds including those of private insurance companies. About the same size as the four nationalized deposit banks, the Caisse has over half of its assets in medium-term paper financing business, construction, and equipment outlays, most of it originating in the banking system and accepted by a specialized public or semipublic institution and rediscounted with the Caisse. The Caisse in turn may rediscount some of this paper with the Bank of France. Among the important functions of the caisse are making deposits and advances to the Treasury and investing in government securities; investing in debentures of semipublic institutions (Crédit National, Crédit Foncier, and Caisse de Crédit Agricole); trading in Treasury bills and buying long-term government securities from the public at support prices; occasionally serving as a source of day-to-day money to the discount houses in the French money market.

   b. The Crédit National, established in 1919 to finance reconstruction through medium- and long-term credits directly to industry and commerce. It is the most important intermediary for medium-term credits, especially term loans to small- and medium-sized business firms to finance equipment purchases and construction, with maturities of up to five years, which it may discount or endorse, thus making such paper eligible for rediscount at the Caisse des Dépôts (referenced above).

   c. Crédit Foncier, established in 1852, which makes mortgage loans on property and advances to local governments, and through a subsidiary makes available medium-term loans to finance construction work.

   d. The agricultural credit system, consisting of local credit associations organized into regional associations, which in turn are members of the Caisse Nationale de Crédit Agricole, an agricultural central banking institution with rediscount privileges at the Bank of France, providing short-term as well as medium- and long-term agricultural credits.

   e. The banques populaires (urban credit cooperatives), which provide banking services to small local firms and are linked with the mutual guarantee societies and associations serving the fishing and marine industries through the Caisse Central de Crédit Cooperatif.

Monetary Powers. The Bank of France has the usual central banking powers, but their exercise is distinctive in adaptation to the French institutional framework.

Open market operations are of relatively minor importance as a tool of monetary control, except in recent years to smooth supply and demand conditions and to assist the banks with repurchase agreements on a short-term basis. The Caisse des Dépôts and the public and semipublic credit institutions provide demand and support for long-term government securities.

Discounting has always been a primary function of the Bank of France, but it is coupled with qualitative measures, such as rediscount ceilings and discretionary granting of credit, and a system of multiple discount rates including penalty rates applicable to additional rediscounting above the ceilings, to provide for flexibility. Also, changes in the acceptability standards of paper have occurred while the discount rates remained nominally constant.

Reorganization of French Banking System in the 1980s. Central to the electoral program that brought M. Francois Mitterand to the French presidency on May 10, 1981, was the promise that the Socialist government would seek the nationalization of certain additional segments of the nation's industry and financial establishment. On the expanded public sector would rest the weight of France's drive to secure its place among the leaders of the industrialized world.

Mitterand's electoral promise became reality in 1982. On February 11, 1982, final approval was given to the plan for the public takeover of five industrial groups, 39 banks, and two financial organizations. The decision to pursue the nationalization rested on three basic principles of the Mitterand administration. First, certain components of the French economy, because of the nature of their activity, ought to serve the public interest in order to help France surmount the economic crisis. Second, in an era of rapid technological change large businesses should utilize their know-how to produce innovations which can be used for the good of all. Third, a nationalized business could be the showcase of a new relationship between the worker and his or her place of work.

France's new leaders considered that they were now faced with the task of strengthening the economy "not only to withstand the challenges of the modern international marketplace, but also to keep pace with technological change while providing economic and social growth for the nation."

The industries which were nationalized in 1982 reflected the Mitterand government's economic goals. Some were leaders in telecommunications, computer, and aerospace, areas where the technological ability of France, and thus its national independence, was considered by the administration as most threatened. Others, such as the steel and chemical firms, were the first step of the manufacturing process and therefore had repercussions on the entire economic chain. Finally, there were among the new additions to the public sector companies whose activities in areas such as health care products and pharmaceuticals directly affected the well-being of the French people.

The public credit sector was also expanded, because of "the government's belief that it could not embark on a new industrial policy without effective control of France's financial resources. The government hopes that these banks will better serve the nation after changes in their lending habits and strategies."

Title III of the nationalization bill authorized the takeover of two financial organizations, the Compagnie Financiè re de Paris et des Pays-Bas, known as Paribas, and the Compagnie Financiè re de Suez. These two organizations are holding companies which embrace activities in industry, banking, insurance, and real estate. Both were shareholders in most of the five nationalized industrial groups; for example, Suez and its subsidiaries controlled 20.3% of the stock in Saint-Gobain. The famous Saint-Gobain was founded on the order of Louis XIV in 1665 to provide glass for the windows of the royal palace at Versailles. In modern times it had expanded its interests to include a wide range of industrial glass and, through its acquisition of the Pont-à Mousson company in 1968 to become Saint-Gobain-Point-à Mousson, in building and packaging materials. It controlled 51% of the Compagnie des Machines Bull, which itself held 53% of the computer manufacturer C.I.I.-Honeywell-Bull.

The nationalization law provided for government takeover of the parent companies of the mentioned industrial groups and financial institutions via a transfer of their stock from private to government hands. This differed significantly from some previous nationalizations, such as that of the mines, electric and gas utilities, and Renault, where the government took control of physical assets in addition to stock.

"Compensation for stockholders will be legally above reproach and financially equitable," according to Prime Minister Pierre Mauroy, July 8, 1982. The law provided that the compensation payable for the shares of each nationalized company, with the exception of those banks which were not listed on the Bourse as of October 1, 1980, would be the highest average monthly price of the company's shares on the Bourse during the six months from October, 1980, to March, 1981, adjusted to reflect changes in capital during this period, to which was added a dividend for 1981 equal to the dividend paid in 1980 and an increase of 14% to reflect monetary depreciation. For the banks not traded at the Bourse, the date of nationalization was postponed until July 1, 1982.

The aggregate compensation paid for the companies which were traded at the Bourse would exceed substantially the aggregate market value of the shares immediately prior to the May, 1981, elections as well as the aggregate average market values of such shares during the preceding six- and 12-month periods.

The Mitterand administration stated its belief that government involvement in the nationalized companies must be kept to a minimum, and provisions on management in the nationalization law reflect this philosophy. The phrase "Renault-style management" has been used to describe their intention to leave the day-to-day affairs of the company to its executives, in much the same way that the auto manufacturer has been operated since its nationalization. Each company will define its own long-term goals. These contracts, which will be negotiated between the nationalized company and the government, represent the government's desire to realize a cohesive industrial policy. The Minister of Industry outlined the new relationship between the government and the public sector in a letter to the presidents of the nationalized companies.

It is stated officially that the nationalization law in no way affects the rights of foreigners to set up banks in France, as defined in the law of July 10, 1975. Requests to open new foreign banks in France, either in the form of branches or of majority participation in an establishment under French law, will continue to be examined according to the same criteria prevailing in the past, that is, "in a spirit of liberalism that rules out any discrimination on the basis of nationality." The same applies to the conditions under which these banks exercise their activity in France.

BANK OF GERMANY The law establishing the new federal bank of issue (Bundesbank) of the Federal Republic of Germany was passed by the Bundestag on July 4, 1957, and became effective August 1, 1957.

The Bank of Germany (Deutsche Bundesbank) replaced the former central banking system which consisted of the Bank Deutsche Laender, the nine land central banks, and the Berlin Central Bank. Under the consolidation procedure, the latter were merged with the former, which then became the Deutsche Bundesbank.

The new institution is a public law corporation with capital of DM 290 million, entirely owned by the government. The administrative bodies of the Bundesbank are the following:

1. The central bank council (Zentralbankrat), which decides the bank's monetary and credit policy and consists of the members of the board of management and the presidents of the land central banks.
2. The board of management (Direktorium), which is responsible for carrying out the central bank council's decisions and whose members are appointed by the President of the Federal Republic upon the recommendation of the Cabinet after the latter have consulted with the central bank council.
3. The managing committees (Vorstande) of the land central banks.

The former land central banks and Berlin Central Bank became branches of the federal bank, retaining the title of land central bank. The president appoints the land central bank presidents in accordance with recommendations made by the appropriate land authority and submission by the Upper House of Parliament after consultation with the central bank council. In each land, the land office of the Bundesbank, which continues to be called the land central bank, is responsible for operations conducted with the land authorities and with the credit institutions in its territory. Each land central bank has an advisory council, which consults with the bank's president on questions of monetary and credit policy and with the managing committee on matters relating to its functions.

The government, which had no power of appointment of the leading officials of the former Bank Deutscher Laender, now has the power of appointment over the two highest positions in the new Bundesbank, the president and vice president of the board of management. Appointments to the full board of management are normally for eight years. Reflecting the views of proponents of both a federal system and a centralized system, the new Bundesbank is "bound to support within the scope of its task" the general economic policy of the federal government; yet the law expressly stipulates that in the discharge of its duties the bank "shall be independent of instructions" from the government. Legal duties and powers of the bank concern influencing the circulation of money and the supply of credit by:

1. Establishing the interest and discount rates applicable to its transactions.
2. Laying down policies for its credit and open market transactions.
3. Requiring that credit institutions maintain balances on giro accounts with the bank (minimum reserves) representing percentages of liabilities specified in the law as fixed by the bank.
4. Serving as fiscal agent of the federal government and the land governments. The bank may grant cash advances to those authorities within the limits of the various maximum amounts specified in the law, and those authorities are required to deposit their liquid funds on giro accounts with the Bundesbank. The bank may not grant discount credits and advances on securities except to credit institutions in the federal area.

As long as the seat of the federal government is not Berlin, the seat of the Bundesbank will be Frankfort am Main.

Bank Rate. The Bundesbank's discount rate applies to eligible commercial paper within discount quotas set by the bank. Treasury bills may also be discounted, but the German banks usually find it more profitable to sell such bills to the Bundesbank in its open market operations. Outside the discount quotas are such media as money market prime bankers acceptances of not over 45 days' maturity; notes of German exporters issued within the discount line set by the Bundesbank for the Ausfuhrkredit, A.G. to finance medium-term and long-term exports; and advances against securities at a small premium above the discount rate for eligible paper.

German banks mix investment banking, brokerage, and banking functions, as well as the holding of equity investments in German industry. As members of stock exchanges, the banks as brokers account for the bulk of stock transactions, many not executed on exchanges but rather within the banks.

BANK OF INDIA *See* RESERVE BANK OF INDIA.

BANK OF ISSUE A bank empowered with the note issuing privilege. For example, the Bank of England, the Bank of France, and the Federal Reserve banks are banks of issue.
See BANK NOTE, CIRCULATING NOTES.

BANK OF ITALY *See* CENTRAL BANK.

BANK OF JAPAN *See* CENTRAL BANK.

BANK OF NEW YORK The earliest bank in New York City, organized on March 15, 1784, and first opened for business on June 9, 1784.

The bank was strongly capitalized at the start at $500,000, all in specie. Its charter forbade the bank to incur debts in an amount more than three times its capital or to buy stocks or to speculate in real estate. Alexander Hamilton, then but 27 years old, was one of the founders and members of the first board of directors and wrote its constitution. Dividends have been paid in every year since organization except 1837, when the bank was prevented from doing so because of a statewide suspension.

This institution was the only bank in New York City for 15 years, until the Manhattan Company, ostensibly a water company but with banking powers, was chartered by the New York State Legislature in 1799, under the sponsorship of Hamilton's political rival, Aaron Burr, and associates.

The Bank of New York is still in operation under that name in New York City, although several mergers have occurred in its history.

It still holds clearing house number 1 in the New York Clearing House Association.

BANK OF NORTH AMERICA
The earliest bank in the history of the U.S., originally located in Philadelphia and chartered by the Continental Congress on May 26, 1781. It was the only charter granted by that body and was made perpetual. The original capital was fixed at $160,000, but this was shortly thereafter increased. The bank was planned by Robert Morris, Superintendent of Finance of the American revolution, and began operations on January 7, 1782. Because some doubt was raised as to the right of the Continental Congress to charter a bank, it obtained a new but not perpetual charter from the Commonwealth of Pennsylvania in 1784. The bank performed the functions of a commercial bank, made loans to the government, and issued circulating notes redeemable in coin. It was a success, as demonstrated by the fact that after the revolution it paid annual dividends of 14%.

Under the Pennsylvania charter, which was renewed at intervals, the bank continued its operations until it was granted a charter under the National Bank Act. It then continued operation as a national bank, without, by special dispensation, a change in its original title.

As of March 1, 1923, this bank relinquished its national bank charter and its assets were purchased by the Commercial Trust Company of Philadelphia, which on the same date changed its title to Bank of North America & Trust Company under a charter from the Commonwealth of Pennsylvania. In 1929, the Bank of North America & Trust Company was merged by the institution now known as First Pennsylvania Banking & Trust Co.

BANK OF THE UNITED STATES
A bank known as the first Bank of the United States, chartered by Congress in 1791, began operations in December of that year with a capital of $10 million, one-fifth of which was subscribed by the government. The plans of the bank were outlined by Alexander Hamilton, then secretary of the Treasury.

The bank was permitted to establish branches without limit, and eight were actually put into operation. The business of the branches was restricted to receiving deposits and discounting commercial paper. The head office was located in Philadelphia.

The note issue of the bank was limited to the amount of its capital stock, and no indebtedness could be carried in excess of its deposits. It made advances to the government and acted as its fiscal agent. It was dissolved through the expiration of its charter in 1811.

The second Bank of the United States was established in 1816 through the efforts of President Madison with a capital of $35 million, one-fifth of which was subscribed by the government. It was organized and operated along the same lines as the first Bank of the United States, but its operations were not successful until after 1819, when it became a strong institution, provided a sound circulating medium, and furnished the soundest banking system then devised in the U.S. Because of the antagonism of political interests sponsoring the state banking system, the renewal of the charter was refused, and it was dissolved in 1836.

BIBLIOGRAPHY
DEWEY, D. R., and HOLDSWORTH, J. T. *The First and Second Banks of the United States.* National Monetary Commission Studies, 1910.
REMINI, R. V. *Andrew Jackson and the Bank War,* 1987.
TAYLOR, G. R., ed. *Jackson versus Biddle's Bank: Struggle Over the Second Bank of the United States.* 2nd ed., 1972.
WILBURN, J. A. *Biddle's Bank: the Crucial Years.* 1967.

BANK OF UNITED STATES
This New York City institution, chartered under New York laws in 1913, had no connection whatever with the United States or federal banking, and at first it was denied the use of the name on the grounds of public policy. Subsequently, however, permission was granted by the New York State Banking Department. The bank failed on December 11, 1930, with some 60-odd affiliates, mostly holding companies, to which the bank had diverted loans mainly for real estate, insurance, hotel operating, and security trading operations. This bank failure was the greatest in American banking history, with 413,000 depositors and claims totaling $139 million. Claims were subsequently paid a total of about 76%, or $102 million, the final liquidating dividend being paid on May 16, 1944. This liquidation experience was after 100% assessment of the stockholders of the bank, or full par value of $25 per share on the approximately 1 million shares ($25 million capital) under the double liability statute then prevailing. However, because of collection difficulties, only about 42% of stockholder assessments were collected, or approximately $10 million.

BANK ORGANIZATION
The scheme or plan by which the various divisions, departments, sections, operating units, and individual jobs of a bank are coordinated and subordinated, authority defined, functions described, and responsibilities located for each officer and employee, to the end that the banking business may be properly controlled and made to operate smoothly. The modern metropolitan bank performs numerous types of services, quite diverse in their nature, which call for expert supervision. Usually these different branches of bank service are rendered better when administered by specialists. For the convenience of the public and the internal administration, many banks create separate divisions of service for which a separate officer, usually a vice-president, is responsible. To illustrate a suggested line type of organization effective for a bank of large size, a bank organization chart is appended with permission of the Bank Management Commission, American Bankers Association.

A bank is owned by its stockholders, but this body is too large and unwieldy actively to manage its affairs. Control of the policies and management of the bank are therefore vested in the board of directors, elected by the stockholders, usually annually. This body is responsible to the stockholders for successful management and to the government banking officials for the observance of the banking laws. The actual administration of the bank's operation, however, depends upon the officers, who are appointed by the directors. The officers usually consist of a president, who in a small bank may be merely a figurehead who is primarily interested in another line of business; one or more vice presidents; a cashier, who is usually equivalent to the general manager and whose duties are never delegated; in large banks, a number of assistant cashiers; and perhaps a comptroller.

In the largest banks, with local, national, and international operations, the problem of most efficient organizational structure is a more complex matter, involving more variations in the spotting of operating and staff divisions. One giant money center bank has the following structure at the general management level, under the president (the vice chairman of the board of directors is given the operating direction of the legal division, including the office of the secretary of the bank):

1. *Operating divisions (each under executive or senior vice president):* Metropolitan department (local operations of all branches in metropolitan area; operations in the metropolis; electronic customer services; and installment credit); United States department (operations in other geographic districts of the U.S.; and for the aerospace and energy industries); international department (operations in Asia, Oceania, Middle East, and North Africa; Europe and Sub-Saharan Africa; Latin America; and U.S., Canada, and Caribbean; and foreign exchange trading); municipal bond division (municipal sales and trading; and underwriting and syndication); trust department (corporate trust, agency, and custody; pension trusts; and personal trusts).
2. *Staff divisions:* Bank operations (accounting and reports; check processing; corporate trust operations; general services; insurance; international operations; loan services; premises; protection; systems, standards, and information processing; taxes; and trust operations); personnel relations advisory committee (personnel administration, management development, and organization planning); corporate planning and research group (bank forward planning; corporate planning; economic research; international planning development; market research; and operations research); public relations and marketing-advertising group (public relations; marketing-advertising); controller's department (banking audit, domestic branch audit; E.D.P. audit; trust audit; overseas branch audit) (controller's department is directly accountable to the board of directors for all of the bank's internal auditing and control work); credit and loan standards department (financing development and technical services; global credit; loan review; and real estate and mortgage loans); portfolio and investment, bankers group (investment bankers and brokers; correspondent bank and

corporate portfolio advisory; and bank's portfolio); and fiduciary investment department (investment advisory; investment research; personal trust and estate investment; pension trust investment; and research planning and coordination).

Instructions for Organization of a New National Bank (based on revised procedures implemented in 1980 by the Office of the Comptroller of the Currency). After a letter granting preliminary approval to organize a national bank has been received, the following steps should be taken to effect the corporate organization.

1. Articles of association shall be drawn, executed in triplicate, and submitted to the regional administrator. While the articles may contain other provisions not contrary to law, the sample articles should be followed except for the provisions marked optional. The individuals signing the articles, hereinafter referred to as organizers, shall be the same persons who signed the application unless prior approval has been obtained for variance.
2. Simultaneously with the articles, an organization certificate, signed by the organizers and notarized (including the seal of the notary and expiration date where necessary) is submitted in duplicate to the regional administrator. The certificate must show the number of shares subscribed for by each organizer. Organizers who are to be directors must subscribe for at least $1,000 par value of shares. Other organizers must subscribe for at least one share. It is not necessary for the organization certificate to show subscriptions totaling the actual amount of capital stock with which the association will commence business.
3. The articles of association and organization certificate must be received by the regional administrator within thirty days of receipt of the letter granting preliminary approval. If the articles and organization certificate are found to be in proper form, they will be accepted for filing and a letter of advice to that effect will be sent to the agent. One copy of the articles of association will be returned with the letter. The bank's corporate existence for the purpose of entering into contracts and performing all necessary actions other than the business of banking may commence as of the date of the notarization of the organization certificate (see 12 U.S.C. 24). The bank may not commence the business of banking until the charter is issued (see 12 U.S.C. 27).
4. Immediately following notification that the articles of association and organization certificate have been accepted for filing, a meeting of the organizers should be held. The following items of business are accomplished at this meeting:
    a. Approve the articles of association and organization certificate as filed with the Comptroller.
    b. Fix the number of interim directors to serve until the first meeting of shareholders.
    c. Elect as interim directors persons who have been approved by the comptroller.
    d. Approve the location of the bank's main office.
5. Immediately following the first meeting of organizers, the first meeting of interim directors shall be held. The following items of business should be accomplished at this meeting:
    a. Execute oath of director and list of interim directors.
    b Appoint an interim chairperson and interim secretary of the board. Authorize the interim chairperson and secretary to sign checks and other documents.
    c. Adopt a form of stock certificate containing all information required by 12 U.S.C. 52.
    d. Adopt a form of corporate seal.
    e. Designate a bank as depository of stock subscription funds. The depository agreement should provide that funds collected cannot be released until authorization is received from the regional administrator.
    f. Authorize the solicitation of stock subscription, including setting of approved price at which stock is to be sold and authorization for application to the Comptroller of the Currency for approval of an offering circular pursuant to Part 16 of the Regulations of the Comptroller of the Currency (12 CFR 16).
    g. Adopt bylaws.
    h. Authorize the purchase of fidelity bond.
    i. Approve organizational expenses to date.

The interim board should meet on a monthly basis, and minutes of each meeting should be submitted to the regional administrator within five business days of the meeting.

6. Immediately following the first meeting of interim directors, the following documents should be forwarded in duplicate to the regional administrator. All documents should be certified to be true, accurate, and complete by the secretary.
    a. Minutes of the meeting of organizers.
    b. List of interim directors.
    c. Oaths of interim directors.
    d. Minutes of first meeting of interim directors.
    e. Bylaws.
    f. Sample stock certificate.
    g. A copy of the agreement with the depository bank.

Upon receipt of the above documents in proper form, all further correspondence from this office will be directed to the interim chairperson or secretary. The regional administrator should be advised of the name and address of the individual designated to receive all correspondence from this office.

7. If not previously approved, the interim board should now proceed to select a chief executive officer to be submitted to the regional administrator for approval. The individual selected should submit confidential biographical and financial reports in duplicate to the regional administrator and make arrangements for a personal interview in the regional Office.
8. The information requested in the preliminary approval letter relative to the specific location and fixed asset investment should be forwarded to the regional administrator. If any fixed asset will be purchased or leased from individuals associated in any manner with the bank, the following should be provided:
    a. Name and address of owner of property.
    b. Relation to bank.
    c. Property to be acquired.
    d. Date property acquired by current owner.
    e. Cost of property to current owner.
    f. An independent appraisal.
    g. Any other relevant information that demonstrates the proposed transaction is fair, reasonable, and comparable to similar arrangements that could have been made with unrelated parties.
    h. A board resolution approving the specific details of the transaction.
9. Upon receipt of advice that the fixed asset investment and the chief executive officer are acceptable to the regional administrator and that all of the aforementioned documents are in order, the interim directors may proceed to solicit offers to subscribe for stock of the bank. An offering circular complying with the requirements of Part 16 of the Regulations of the Comptroller of the Currency (12 CFR 16) must be used. The circular should be submitted to the regional administrator for approval prior to distribution. A sample offering circular is contained in 12 CFR 16.7. If a broker or dealer will be used to assist in the stock distribution, a draft of the agreement with the broker or dealer should be submitted to the regional administrator for approval prior to execution.

When offers to subscribe for the total capital stock have been received, the following information should be forwarded in duplicate to the regional administrator: a list of subscribers, in alphabetical order, containing the name, home address, relationship of subscriber to any other subscriber, and number of shares subscribed. The interim chairperson will be advised by letter if the proposed list of subscribers is acceptable to this office. When payment of total capital funds has been received, the following items should be submitted, in duplicate, to the regional administrator.

a. Certificate of payment of capital stock.
b. Certification from depository bank that the capital funds have been deposited to the credit of the organizing bank.
c. A final list of shareholders of the bank, containing the same information supplied in the list of subscribers. This shall be certified to be complete, true, and accurate by the secretary of the bank.

BANK ORGANIZATION

No disbursements may be made from the capital funds until the total subscription has been collected and the certificate of payment accepted by the OCC.

10. Upon advice of approval of the foregoing items, notices should be sent of the time and place of the first meeting of shareholders. The form of notice of shareholders meeting, proxy statement, and proxy must be submitted to and approved by the regional office prior to the mailing to shareholders. Stock certificates should be not issued until after the bank opens for business. At the first meeting of the shareholders, the following items of business should be accomplished:
    a. Election of a board of directors to serve for one year and until their successors have been elected and qualified. Approval of the regional administrator is necessary for any directors not previously approved.
    b. Approval of organization expenses and commitments made to be reimbursed or paid from capital funds.
    c. Ratification of the articles of association, organization certificate, and all official acts of the organizers, interim directors and officers since organization of the association.
    d. Such other business as may properly come before the meeting.
11. Following the first meeting of shareholders, an organization meeting of directors shall be held and the following items of business accomplished:
    a. Execute oath of directors and list of directors.
    b. Appointment of officers.
    c. Appointment of standing committees.
    d. Ratification of bylaws.
12. Immediately following the first meeting of shareholders and directors, the following documents should be sent to the regional administrator:
    a. Minutes of shareholders meeting.
    b. Certified list of directors.
    c. Oaths of directors.
    d. Minutes of director's meeting.
13. The board should now select the remainder of the bank's executive staff for submission to the regional administrator for approval. Each proposed executive officer should submit confidential biographical and financial reports and make arrangements for a personal interview in the regional office. All directors and executive officers should complete Form CC-9030-29, with the completed forms placed on file at the bank.
14. If not previously submitted, the board should submit a schedule of fidelity insurance to be in effect on the day the bank opens for business. This information should be presented at least thirty days prior to the anticipated opening date of the bank.
15. When the bank is ready to open for business, a national bank examiner will be assigned to visit the bank to verify that preparations are complete. The examiner will review those items listed in the instructions for preopening review and any other matters considered appropriate. The examiner will meet with management at the completion of the visitation to apprise them of his findings. It will be necessary for any significant deficiencies to be corrected prior to the opening of the bank.
16. Upon advice of the examiner that satisfactory operational procedures and policies have been established and receipt of duplicate copies of the following documents in proper form, the comptroller's certificate of authority to commence the business of banking (charter) will be issued.
    a. Advice from the Federal Reserve Bank that the necessary payment has been made for the bank's subscription to Federal Reserve Bank stock.
    b. A detailed list of all disbursements.
    c. A detailed list of all organization expenses of every type for which the bank is committed and which have not been paid.
    d. Reconcilement of disbursements made from capital funds to the amount then remaining in the depository bank to the credit of the organizing bank, with appropriate notation for outstanding checks.
    e. The definite date fixed for opening the bank and confirmation of the exact address, including postal designation. This information should be furnished not less than two weeks prior to the scheduled opening date.
17. When the bank has opened for business, the following actions should be taken:
    a. Stock certificates should be issued to the stockholders.
    b. The regional office should be advised by telegram of the date the bank opened for business.
    c. A copy of the charter should be published in a newspaper printed in the city or county where the bank is located at least once each week for nine consecutive weeks immediately following the opening of the bank for business. Upon completion of the publication requirement, the affidavit of publication of charter should be executed and forwarded to the Regional Administrator of National Banks.
    d. A report on security devices should be filed with the regional administrator using Form CC-9030-01.

Major accounting firms have developed their form of 'cycle' organization, designed primarily for (a) their review of internal control systems, and (b) performance of their required audit reviews and tests. The appended chart (The "Cycle" Concept of a Banking Organization) illustrates how the "cycle" concept can assist in arriving at the final organizational structure for a bank. The chart is based on (a) the cycles that are now applicable or may be applicable in the future to a specific bank's operations, (b) the assignment of authority and responsibility for each cycle of subelements, and (c) the development and implementation of effective systems of internal control, based on items (a) and (b). The cycle concept is built on five control objectives: authorization, transaction processing, classification, substantiation, and evaluation. The cycle concept is intended to assure that the necessary authority and responsibility have been properly assigned for each bank facility, activity, function, product, service, or organizational entity (e.g., division, department). The concept is also intended to assure that sound internal control systems are in place and functioning.

(Adapted from William T. Thornhill's *Effective Risk Management*, BAI.)

See ARTICLES OF ASSOCIATION, BYLAWS, NATIONAL BANKING SYSTEM.

The "Cycle" Concept of a Banking Organization

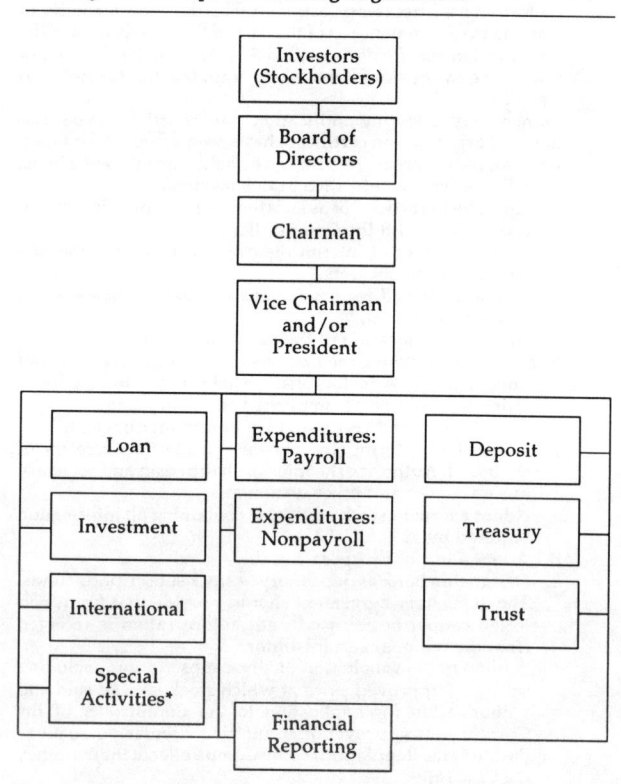

```
          Investors
        (Stockholders)
               |
          Board of
          Directors
               |
          Chairman
               |
        Vice Chairman
           and/or
          President
               |
  ┌────────────┼────────────┐
  Loan    Expenditures:   Deposit
           Payroll
Investment  Expenditures: Treasury
           Nonpayroll
International               Trust
  Special
Activities*
          Financial
          Reporting
```

*Special activites refer to all nonbanking activities allowed by law and/or regulation, such as finance company, brokerage, insurance, or whatever may be authorized.

BANK RATE The rate of discount fixed by the central bank of a country for the rediscounting of eligible paper, and also the rate charged by the central bank on advances on specified collateral to banks; as distinguished from the open market rates or day-to-day money. The term in particular is applied to the lowest or prime rate charged by the central bank where, as is usual, there are multiple central bank rates depending upon the type of paper and maturities involved. The bank rate is especially a term of English origin, and refers to the minimum rate at which the Bank of England stands ready to lend as lender of last resort to the discount houses which have the privilege of access to the discount office of the bank, either by rediscounting bills of approved quality or by lending against the security of such bills or of short-term government securities.

The equivalent to bank rate in the U.S. is the discount rate of each of the 12 Federal Reserve banks, which usually does not differ in the separate Federal Reserve districts.

See REDISCOUNT RATE.

BANK RECORDS Bank records reflect financial transactions and also verify compliance with regulations of the FDIC, the Federal Reserve System, and the Comptroller of the Currency. In addition, they satisfy recordkeeping requirements as corporations, lenders, investors, employers, and taxpayers. The BANK SECRECY ACT is one major example of legislatively imposed record retention requirements. In addition, state statutes have imposed recordkeeping requirements on banks and other enterprises. State laws frequently identify corporate and accounting records that must be retained permanently and what to consider when developing a policy for other bank records. Such laws permit the destruction of records after a retention period expires and allow reproduction of records by microphotographic processes.

Record management concerns organizing information and the way it is recorded, processed, reproduced, filed, stored, retrieved, and destructed. Compliance records satisfy direct legal requirements either at the federal or state level. This entry focuses on record retention policies and practices.

Banks usually classify records as primary or secondary. Primary records establish and support the final position of the bank and account relationships with bank customers. Secondary records contain important information about transactions and accounting. Major record classifications can be conceptualized as follows:

Major Records Classifications

Type	Description
Compliance	Direct statutory requirements for recordkeeping or retention. Internal or external use for regulatory examination, tax reference, summons or subpoena.
Primary	Represents the fiscal position of the bank. Represents account relationships with customers.
Secondary	Directly related to primary records.
Vital	Essential to continuity and resumption of bank operations during an emergency or a disaster. Off-site remote location for these records is desirable.

Records are segmented into two major divisions: (1) those that relate to the administration of the bank as a corporation, and (2) those that relate to the customer account relationship. These divisions can be conceptualized as follows:

Corporation	Deposits, Administrative, Personnel, Security, Tax
Customer Accounts	Accounting, Loans, Investments, Trust

Bank Administration Institute recommends that the following guidelines be used when there is no definitive or legally authoritative reference for record retention:

Corporate Records

General

Minutes	Permanent
Bylaws	Permanent
Annual reports	Permanent
Capital stock ledger	Permanent
Investment ledger	Permanent
Examination reports	Permanent
Call reports	Permanent
General ledger or journal	Permanent
Daily statements of condition	Permanent
Accounts payable ledger	6* years
Audit reports	6* years
Audit workpapers	3* years
Purchase orders	6* years
Invoices	6* years
Charged-off asset records	6* years
Insurance policies, after expiration	6* years

*Or state's statute of limitations.

Administrative

Records of loans to executive officers, directors, and shareholders (Regulation O)	Not specified
Records of indebtedness by executive officers or principal shareholders to banks and correspondents	3 years
Requests for disclosure and disposition of executive officers and shareholders whose indebtedness exceeds a specified amount	2 years
Stock register and shareholder information	Permanent
FDIC assessment and verification statements, after filing or resolution of dispute	5 years
Dividend register for checks paid	Permanent
Charitable contribution records	Not specified

Accounting

Reserve for loan-loss records	Permanent
Travel and expense records	Not specified
Depreciation records	Permanent

Personnel

Pension benefit plans required by ERISA, after filing	6 years
Employment tax records, after payment	4 years
Employee information related to wages, hours, sex, occupation, conditions of employment required by the Fair Labor Standards Act	3 years
Employee records that contain name, address, date of birth, occupation, rate of pay, and weekly compensation required by the Age Discrimination in Employment Act	3 years
Handicapped employee records required by Fair Labor Standards Act	3 years
Employment and earnings records, work schedules and job evaluations required by the Fair Labor Standards Act	2 years
Hiring, promotion, demotion, transfer, layoff, termination, pay rates, or training records, after filing or final disposition of action	6 months

ENCYCLOPEDIA OF BANKING AND FINANCE

BANK REFERENCE

Employee job tests and selection process records	2 years
Job application, promotion, discharge, aptitude tests, and advertisements, after action	1 year
Employee benefit plans, after termination	1 year
Application forms for temporary positions	90 days
Occupation injury and illness records, including annual summary requirement by OSHA, after disclosure	5 years
Security	
Management certification of compliance with security requirements	3 years
Evidence of compliance to standards for installation of security devices (Reg. P)	Not specified
Evaluation of adequacy of security program	Not specified
Inspection records for security devices (Regulation P)	Not specified
Reports of law enforcement officer who advised on the installation, maintenance, and operation of security devices	Not specified
Crime reports of robbery, burglary of nonemployee larceny committed or attempted	Not specified
Evidence of noncompliance with standards for installing security devices	Not specified
Fire protection records under OSHA	Not specified

Tax
Federal tax records must be kept so long as the contents may become material in the administration of any Internal Revenue law. Although some records should be kept indefinitely, general requirements are stated in terms of the following:

1. Records of property subject to gain or loss treatment must be retained until taxable disposition is made.
2. Records supporting items of income, deductions and credits, including gains or losses appearing on a return, should be kept, at a minimum, until the statute of limitations for the return expires.

Source: Adapted from *Bank Record Retention Guide*, Mary J. Williamson, Bank Administration Institute, 1988.

BANK REFERENCE The name of the bank with which a concern has an account, given to another concern as a reference in order that its credit standing may be investigated. Before accepting new accounts banks usually investigate the character, ability, and financial responsibility of their customers, and through constant contact are in a position to give an opinion to others concerning the standing of their customers.

Such interchange of credit information by banks is a function not to be taken lightly, not only so as to assure meaningful credit information but also so as to avoid possible liability for erroneous information. Every bank credit analyst should be thoroughly conversant with the Robert Morris Associates' *Code of Ethics* on credit inquiries, first adopted in 1916 and revised several times since.

BIBLIOGRAPHY

McHugh, H. F. "Credit and Loan Administration." In Baughn, W. H., and Walker, C. E., eds., *The Bankers' Handbook*, rev. ed., 1978.

BANK RESERVE A term having three possible meanings in banking:

1. In connection with resources of a bank, primary reserves are cash availabilities (vault cash, reserve balances at the Federal Reserve bank of the district or other authorized reserve depository in the case of state banks not members of the Federal Reserve System) and due from banks (demand balances with correspondent banks). Checks in the process of collection (exchanges for the local clearinghouse, or in the process of collection (transit items) from out-of-town banks) cannot be included in primary reserves, since they are gross and do not reflect the checks in turn that may be presented upon our bank through the local clearing house, the Federal Reserve bank, or correspondent banks.
2. SECONDARY RESERVES, those highest quality, highly marketable, short-term securities of a bank which are intended to supplement in invested form the primary reserves in providing standby liquidity for deposit withdrawals or availability for expansion in loans.
3. The legally required reserves, based upon percentages of net demand deposits and of time and savings deposits, that national banks, other members of the Federal Reserve System, and nonmember banks may be required to maintain.

In addition to these banking concepts, the term may also be found in banking to refer to the customary accounting meanings of RESERVE, i.e., earmarked portions of retained earnings and undivided profits as equity reserves, or valuation reserves applicable to particular assets.
See LEGAL RESERVES.

BANK RETURN The bank statement (balance sheets for the issue department and banking department) published weekly by the Bank of England, i.e., BANK OF ENGLAND RETURN; in more general references, the weekly release "Factors Affecting Bank Reserves and Condition Statement of Federal Reserve Banks" (Release H.4.1) from the Board of Governors of the Federal Reserve System and the CLEARING HOUSE STATEMENT of local clearing houses.

BANK RUN Rapid withdrawals of deposits from a bank.
Since the cash reserve a bank keeps is only a fraction of the deposit liabilities outstanding, a series of large withdrawals in a relatively short time can deplete available cash and force the bank to shut down and possibly go out of business.

Historically, the United States has seen countless bank runs on small institutions and several widespread bank runs that have shaken the whole industry and economy. The term finds its origin from earlier times when customers would panic on a rumor and run to the bank to close their accounts. Whether or not the rumor was founded, the PANIC would create its own disaster as the customers made the bank illiquid.

Runs on banks were common during the panics of 1837, 1857, 1873, and 1900. The banking panic of 1907 resulted in the establishment of the Federal Reserve System, which became the lender-of-last-resort. The banking panics of the 1930s were responsible for the creation of federal deposit insurance. These eventually culminated in state banking "holidays" and in the nationwide bank suspension declared by President Roosevelt.

Banks become vulnerable to bank runs from the illiquidity of bank assets compared to liabilities. This illiquidity is partially a result of the inherent risk associated with banking. Mob psychology also plays a role. Inadequacies associated with bank management undoubtedly have played a significant role in bank runs. Federal deposit insurance has reduced, to a considerable extent, runs by eliminating depositor risk. However, in so doing, it has also created incentives of excessive risk-taking by banks whereby losses are shifted to insurance.

Recent bank runs have been of two types: corporate runs, in which corporations whose balances exceed the insured maximum remove their funds when rumors of a bank's insolvency surface; or runs created by the withdrawal of interbank deposits. A problem similar to those runs can be created by holders of the commercial paper of bank holding companies refusing to renew when the paper becomes due. In this instance, however, the banks in the system may be solvent.

BANKRUPT Although the title of P.L. 95–598, November 6, 1978, contains the term bankruptcy (Federal Bankruptcy Reform Act of 1978, codifying and enacting the laws relating to bankruptcy as

Title 11 of the U.S. Code, and replacing the former National Bankruptcy Act as amended, effective October 1, 1979), the term bankrupt is replaced by the term debtor, defined as a person or municipality concerning which a case under the new code has been commenced. In a voluntary proceeding under the code, "order for relief" replaces the former term "adjudicated bankrupt" (adjudication); in an involuntary proceeding, the order for relief would similarly be entered if the involuntary petition was objected to by the debtor but he was not paying his debts when due or a custodian (receiver or trustee) was appointed within 120 days prior to filing of the petition to enforce a lien against the debtor's property. Both liquidation and reorganization types of relief continue to be provided in the new code.

See BANKRUPTCY.

BANKRUPTCY The U.S. Constitution (Art. I, Sec. 8) expressly confers upon Congress the power to establish "... uniform laws on the subject of bankruptcies throughout the U.S." There was no lasting federal bankruptcy law for many years, however, as federal legislation in this field at first was temporary, to aid in making the necessary adjustments following depressions. The first bankruptcy law passed by Congress was enacted in 1800 and repealed three years later. It grew out of the business crisis created by English and French restraints on American trade. The second bankruptcy act, passed in 1841, was directly due to the acute distress resulting from the Panic of 1837 and lasted 18 months. The next bankruptcy law was enacted in 1867, and was repealed 11 years later. The NATIONAL BANKRUPTCY ACT (as amended) dated from 1898; unlike its predecessors, it was not repealed when the crisis prompting its enactment had passed. So long as there was no federal bankruptcy law, the states' bankruptcy laws applied; but as the federal law preempts the field, bankruptcy proceedings are federal cases, initiated in the federal district courts. From 1898 until the amendments beginning in 1933, the National Bankruptcy Act provided only for the liquidation in bankruptcy remedy; in the absence of statutory provisions for reorganizations, compositions, and extensions, resort developed to the equity receivership in state courts of equity for such relief. Equity receiverships, however, required ancillary receivers for property in other states. No minimum ratio of consent to a reorganization plan could bind the dissenting creditors, who had to be paid off the cash amount of their claims upon consummation of the plan, usually effected by foreclosure and sale proceeding. The reorganization plan was left to be worked out by the protective committees, as the receiver had no duty and responsibility of formulating a plan. Frequently, such reorganizations were mild, being management-dominated as the result of friendly consent receiverships, usually prearranged with out-of-state creditors to provide the diversity of citizenship ground for bringing the case in the federal district court in the state (which with technical advantages applied the state's doctrine to the case). Equity receiverships are now obsolete because of the advantages of resorting to the reorganization types of relief provided for in the Bankruptcy Reform Act of 1978 and its predecessors beginning in 1933 (including the Chandler Act, 1938).

The nonjudicial, nonstatutory remedies for financial difficulty or failure (extensions, compositions, creditors' committee management, assignment for the benefit of creditors) have the basic advantage of avoiding the expense and delay involved in judicial proceedings, whether statutory or nonstatutory. The nonjudicial, nonstatutory remedies, however, suffer from the necessity for 100% consent of the creditors concerned. Moreover, only in bankruptcy may preferences be set aside, and fraud and concealment of assets be detected and penalized, integrally as part of the case, and the debtor be awarded his order for relief if entitled to it.

Federal Bankruptcy Reform Act of 1978. The Federal Bankruptcy Reform Act of 1978 (P.L. 95-598, November 6, 1978, effective October 1, 1979) repealed the National Bankruptcy Act of 1898 as amended, and codified and enacted the federal bankruptcy law as Title 11 of the U.S. Code, entitled "Bankruptcy." The result of comprehensive studies and reports on the subject, and work by the congressionally created Commission on the Bankruptcy Laws of the United States, the act made fundamental organizational, procedural, and substantive changes in the federal bankruptcy law.

A fundamental organizationl change was the provision for a new bankruptcy court system, creating in each federal judicial district a U.S. bankruptcy court as an adjunct to the federal district court and having exclusive jurisdiction over bankruptcy cases. The act, however, went further in providing that the bankruptcy judges of such bankruptcy courts have jurisdiction to consider and decide issues "arising in or related to" bankruptcy cases. On June 28, 1982, the U.S. Supreme Court ruled to be unconstitutional, effective prospectively after October 4, 1982, such jurisdiction of bankruptcy judges over matters against a bankruptcy party not directly related to the bankruptcy proceeding.

The new act provided procedural and substantive changes in the bankruptcy law, including the following.

Petition for relief: Petitions may seek liquidation (Chapter 7) or reorganization (Chapter 11). Filing of a petition automatically operates as a stay of specified actions against the debtor (the new term used instead of "bankrupt"). A person may be a debtor under Chapter 7 only if such person is not any of the following:

1. A railroad.
2. A domestic insurance company, bank, savings bank, cooperative bank, savings and loan association, building and loan association, homestead association, or credit union.
3. A foreign insurance company, bank, savings bank, cooperative bank, savings and loan association, building and loan association, homestead association, or credit union, engaged in such business in the United States.

Only a person who may be a debtor under Chapter 7, except a stockholder, a commodity broker, or a railroad, may be a debtor under Chapter 11.

An entity may be a debtor under Chapter 9 if and only if such entity meets the following qualifications:

1. Is a municipality.
2. Is generally authorized to be a debtor under such chapter by state law, or by a governmental officer or organization empowered by state law to authorize such an entity to be a debtor under such chapter.
3. Is insolvent or unable to meet such entity's debts as such debts mature.
4. Desires to effect a plan to adjust such debts.
5. a. Has obtained the agreement of creditors holding at least a majority in amount of the claims of each class that such entity intends to impair under a plan in a case under such chapter; or
   b. Has negotiated in good faith with creditors and has failed to obtain the agreement of creditors holding at least a majority in amount of the claims of each class that such entity intends to impair under a plan in a case under such chapter; or
   c. Is unable to negotiate with creditors because such negotiation is impracticable; or
   d. Reasonably believes that a creditor may attempt to obtain a preference.

A debtor under Chapter 13 (Adjustment of Debts of an Individual with Regular Income) can be only an individual with regular income who owes, on the date of the filing of the petition, noncontingent, liquidated, unsecured debts of less than $100,000 and noncontingent, liquidated, secured debts of less than $350,000; or an individual with regular income and such individual's spouse, except a stockbroker or a commodity broker, who owe, on the date of the filing of the petition, noncontingent, liquidated, unsecured debts and similarly noncontingent, liquidated, secured debts of less than the preceding amounts.

A voluntary case under a chapter is commenced by the filing with the bankruptcy court of a petition under such chapter by an entity that may be a debtor under that chapter. An involuntary case may be commenced only under Chapter 7 or Chapter 11, and only against a person, except a farmer or a corporation that is not a moneyed, business, or commercial corporation, who may be a debtor under the chapter. An involuntary case is commenced by the filing with the bankruptcy court of a petition under Chapter 7 or 11:

1. By three or more entities (defined as person, estate, trust, or governmental unit), each of which is either a holder of a claim against such person that is not contingent as to liability or an indenture trustee representing such a holder, if such claims aggregate at least $5,000 more than the value of any lien on property of the debtor securing such claims held by the holders of such claims;
2. Should there be fewer than 12 such holders, excluding any

employee or "insider" of such person and any transferee of a transfer that is voidable under the act (see below), by one or more of such holders that hold in the aggregate at least $5,000 of such claims;
3. If such person is a partnership:
   a. By fewer than all of the general partners in such partnership; or
   b. If relief has been ordered under the act, with respect to all of the general partners in such partnership, by a general partner in such partnership, the trustee of such a general partner, or the holder of claim against such partnership; or
4. By a foreign representative of the estate in a foreign proceeding concerning such person.

Eliminated as a prerequisite to petition, voluntary or involuntary, was any one of the following acts of bankruptcy committed by the debtor within four months immediately preceding the petition, with the petition required to be brought within four months from the commission of the act of bankruptcy:

1. Conveyed, transferred, concealed, or removed, or permitted to be concealed or removed, any part of the debtor's property with intent to hinder, delay, or defraud his creditors. Condition of insolvency was not necessary in this connection.
2. Transferred, while insolvent, any portion of his property to one or more of his creditors with intent to prefer such creditors over his other creditors (see preferences below).
3. Suffered or permitted, while insolvent, any creditor to obtain a lien upon his property through court action and not having vacated or discharged such lien within 30 days from the date thereof, or at least 5 days before the date set for any sale or other disposition of such property.
4. Made a general assignment for the benefit of creditors. Condition of insolvency was not necessary in this connection.
5. While insolvent or unable to pay his debts as they mature, procured, permitted, or suffered voluntarily or involuntarily the appointment of a receiver or trustee to take charge of his property.
6. Admitted in writing his inability to pay his debts as they mature, and his willingness to be adjudged a bankrupt.

Instead of the former prerequisites for involuntary petition as above, the new act provides for an order for relief against an involuntary debtor: (1) if the debtor is generally not paying such debtor's debts as such debts become due; or (2) if within 120 days of the filing of the petition, a custodian (defined as receiver or trustee of any of the property of the debtor, appointed in a case or proceeding not under the act; assignee under a general assignment for the benefit of the debtor's creditors; or trustee, receiver, or agent appointed or authorized to take charge of the property of the debtor for the purpose of enforcing a lien against such property, or for the purpose of general administration of such property for the benefit of the debtor's creditors) has been appointed over all or substantially all property of the debtor.

Preferences: The trustee's power to avoid any transfer of property of the debtor on account of antecedent debt while insolvent, to or for the benefit of a creditor, has been shortened from a four-month period preceding the petition in the former law to 90 days, or between 90 days and one year if such creditor at the time of the transfer was an "insider" and had reasonable cause to believe the debtor was insolvent at the time of such transfer.

Full priority rule: The absolute priority rule of the former Chapter X of the Federal Bankruptcy Act has been replaced by the adequate protection principle of the new bankruptcy code, providing for secured creditors prompt protection for the lien by the trustee by means of cash payments, replacement liens, or other provision as "will result in the realization by such entity of the indubitable equivalent of such entity's interest in such property."

Right of setoff: As in the former Federal Bankruptcy Act, a creditor has the right to offset a mutual debt owing by such creditor to the debtor that arose prior to commencement of the case against a claim of such creditor against the debtor similarly arising before commencement of the case. But such right of setoff would not apply if the claim of such creditor against the debtor was disallowed; or if such claim was transferred to such creditor by an entity other than the debtor (1) after commencement of the case or (2) after 90 days before date of filing of the petition and while the debtor was insolvent; or if the debt owed to the debtor by such creditor was incurred by such creditor after 90 days before date of filing of the petition, while the debtor was insolvent, and for the purpose of obtaining a right of setoff. As in the case of floating liens in inventory and receivables, setoffs are also subject to the "improvement of position" test. If the creditor offsets a debt within 90 days prior to the petition, the creditor must give up to the trustee any improvement in his position. Such an "improvement of position" test did not appear in the former bankruptcy act.

Exemptions: The new code provides for liberalized exemptions for debtors and affords them the choice between such federal exemptions and exemptions provided under their state's laws. But the code also provides that the states may deny their residents the choice of taking the federal exemptions, and such states as Florida, Virginia, and New York have done so and instead have reduced the liberality of exemptions so as to minimize the relative attraction of declaring bankruptcy.

Other provisions: There are many other aspects of the new federal bankruptcy code that in the judgment of its sponsors modernize the bankruptcy law and improve its administration. A briefer summary of principal changes follows.

The bankruptcy judicial system has been strengthened with its provision for bankruptcy courts and bankruptcy judges. Such courts have exclusive civil jurisdiction over all matters related to a bankruptcy case, except for the power to punish for criminal contempt and to enjoin other courts.

Bankruptcy judges are appointed by the President for terms of 14 years.

A five-year experimental program in 18 judicial districts established a governmental administrator to supervise private trustees to determine feasibility of such means of relieving bankruptcy judges of their administrative duties.

Consumers are given the benefit of reaffirmation of their consumer debts, conditioned upon court approval.

Availability of the popular wage-earner plan was expanded in the new code and its provisions were strengthened.

Powers of the trustee were modernized, and the law of preferences was substantially changed.

For the first time, statutory criteria were established to guide the courts in resolving any disputes between secured creditors and the debtor's estate.

See INSOLVENCY.

BIBLIOGRAPHY

AARON, R. I. *Bankruptcy Law Fundamentals*. Clark Boardman Co., Ltd., New York, NY. Looseleaf.

———. *Bankruptcy Law Handbook*. Clark Boardman Co., Ltd., New York, NY, 1988.

ANDERSON, J. C. *Chapter 11 Reorganization*. Shepard/McGraw-Hill Book Co., Inc., Colorado Springs, CO, 1985.

BLINN, J. R., and SUTHERLAND, J. M. *Bankruptcy Strategies for Lenders*. Professional Education Systems, Eau Claire, WI, 1987.

COHEN, A. B. *Bankruptcy, Secured Transactions, and Other Debtor-Creditor Matters*. Michie Co., Charlottesville, VA, 1985.

COMMERCE CLEARING HOUSE. *Bankruptcy Law Reports*. Commerce Clearing House, Chicago, IL. Periodic.

Cowans Bankruptcy Law and Practice, with Forms. West Publishing Co., St. Paul, MN. Periodic supplements.

DRAKE, W. H. *Chapter 13 Practice and Procedure*. Shepard/McGraw-Hill Book Co., Colorado Springs, CO. Looseleaf.

DUGAN, M. T., and ZABVGREN, C. V. "Bankruptcy Prediction Research: A Valuable Instructional Tool." *Issues in Accounting Education*, Spring, 1988.

Economist. "American Bankruptcy: The Uses and Abuses of Chapter 11." March 18, 1989.

ELLINGSEN, J. E. "SAS No. 59: How to Evaluate Going Concern." *Journal of Accountancy*, January, 1989.

Federal Reserve Bulletin. Federal Reserve System, Washington, DC.

FRAWLEY, R. D. "Bankrupt Firms Can Be Attractive Acquisitions." *Journal of Business Strategy*, March/April, 1989.

GAHLON, J. M., and VIGELAND, R. L. "Early Warning Signs of Bankruptcy Using Cash Flow Analysis. *Journal of Commercial Bank Lending*, December, 1988.

HAMBRICK, D. C., and D'AVENI, R. A. "Large Corporate Failures As Downward Spirals." *Administrative Science Quarterly*, March, 1988.

HERZOG, A. S., and KING, L. P. *Collier Bankruptcy Manual.*, Matthew Bender & Co., Inc., New York, NY. Looseleaf.
———. *Collier Bankruptcy Practice Guide.* Matthew Bender & Co., Inc., New York, NY. Looseleaf.
JACKSON, T. *The Logic and Limits of Bankruptcy Law.* Harvard University Press, Cambridge, MA, 1986.
JOHNSON, R. E. "Bankruptcy: An Overview." *Journal of Petroleum Accounting*, Spring 1988.
MORSE, D., and SHAW, W. "Investing in Bankrupt Firms." *Journal of Finance*, December, 1988.
MORRISON, R., *Business Opportunities from Corporate Bankruptcies.* John Wiley and Sons, Inc., New York, NY, 1984.
MURPHY, P. A. *Creditors' Rights in Bankruptcy.* Shepard/McGraw-Hill Book Co., Colorado Springs, CO, 1980.
NEWTON, G. W. *Bankruptcy and Insolvency Accounting: Practice and Procedure.* John Wiley and Sons, Inc., New York, NY, 1985.
NORTON, W. L., JR. *Annual Survey of Bankruptcy Law: 1979-1988.* Callaghan & Co., Deerfield, IL, 1989.
———. *Norton Bankruptcy Law and Practice: 1987-1989.* Callaghan & Co., Deerfield, IL, 1989.
PATCHAN, J., ed. *Federal Rules of Bankruptcy.* Clark Boardman Co., Ltd., New York, NY.
SCRANTON, D. F. "Operating Leases in Bankruptcy." *Journal of Commercial Bank Lending,*" May 1988.
Shepard's Bankruptcy Citations: Cases and Statutes. Shepard/McGraw-Hill Book Co., New York, NY.
WEINTRAUB, B., and RESNICK, A. N. *Bankruptcy Law Manual.* Warren, Gorham and Lamont, Inc., Boston, MA., 1985.
West's Bankruptcy Reporter. West Publishing Co., St. Paul, MN. Multivolume set. Periodic supplements.
WILLIAMS, R. E. *Bankruptcy Practice Handbook.* Callaghan & Co., Deerfield, IL, 1989.
ZAUGREN, C. V., and others. "Association Between Probabilities of Bankruptcy and Market Responses—A Test of Market Anticipation." *Journal of Business Finance and Accounting*, Spring, 1988.

BANKRUPTCY ACT See BANKRUPTCY.

BANK SECRECY ACT This is the common name for the Currency and Foreign Transactions Reporting Act. Passed originally in 1970, the act was amended in 1982 (Money and Finance Act), in 1984, and again in 1986 (Money Laundering Control Act of 1986). Following initial enactment, it was immediately challenged as a violation of Amendment IV, Protection Against Unreasonable Search and Seizure. In 1974, the Supreme Court ruled that the act was constitutional. The Bank Secrecy Act consists of a number of recordkeeping and reporting requirements designed to overcome foreign bank secrecy laws. These records and reports are used in criminal, tax, or regulatory investigations or proceedings associated with illegal or questionable transactions. The movement of large amounts of cash (currency) can involve some kind of criminal activity if it is not associated with legitimate retail business activity.

The law's intent is to deter criminal activity and aid criminal investigations by making it mandatory to report the large cash transactions that are typical in tax evasion, embezzlement, securities violations, drug trafficking, and other illegal activities. Some key provisions of the law are:

1. Financial institutions are required to report to the IRS all currency transactions in excess of $10,000. Included are both domestic and international transactions, in both U.S. and foreign currencies, and multiple transactions in the same day by or for the same person.
2. Citizens and resident aliens are required to report foreign financial accounts that reach $10,000 in a given year in which they have a financial interest or signature authority.
3. Complete identification of the customer must be supplied and verified by the financial institution. The report must be filed within 15 days of the transaction date.
4. All reporting violations are felonies. Structuring transactions to avoid reporting requirements is a crime.

Banks do not have to fill out a Currency Transaction Report (Form 4789) for currency transactions with other domestic banks.

Banks have a general exception to the filing of Form 4789 concerning currency transactions over $10,000 with Federal Reserve Banks, Federal Home Loan Banks, or other domestic banks. The term "bank" includes commercial banks, trust companies, private banks, savings and loan associations, savings banks, industrial banks, thrift institutions, credit unions, and state organizations chartered under state banking laws. There is a requirement that transactions in currency over $10,000 with foreign financial agencies must be reported on Form 4789. Banks are required to maintain a list of the names and addresses of the domestic banks whose transactions are exempted. This is the only recordkeeping requirement concerning bank exceptions.

In other exemptions, the transactions exempted must be in the amounts that the bank may reasonably conclude do not exceed amounts commensurate with the customary conduct of the lawful domestic businesses of the customer. In each situation, the bank must obtain a written statement, signed by the customer, describing the customary conduct of the lawful domestic business of that customer and a detailed statement of reasons why such person is qualified for an exemption. The statement shall include the name, address, taxpayer identification number, and account number of the customer being exempted.

Banks can except from the reporting requirements currency transactions over $10,000 with the following categories of customers involved in the conduct of legitimate business:

Retail business as defined by regulation.
Certain specifically enumerated businesses.
Local and state governments or the United States or any of its agencies or instrumentalities.
Payroll exceptions.

Retail businesses are those businesses engaged primarily in providing goods to ultimate consumers and for which the business is paid in substantial portion by currency. Dealerships that buy or sell motor vehicles, vessels, or aircraft are not included and their transactions are not exempt. The retail business exception is restricted to deposits or withdrawals of currency from an existing account by an established depositor who is a U.S. resident and who operates a retail business in the United States.

Specifically enumerated businesses include sports arenas, bars, racetracks, restaurants, amusement parks, hotels, check-cashing services licensed by state or local governments, vending machine companies, theaters, regularly scheduled passenger carriers, and public utility companies. These exemptions are restricted to deposits with or withdrawals of currency from an existing account by an established depositor who is a U.S. resident and who operates one of the preceding types of businesses in the United States.

Payroll exceptions include withdrawals for payroll purposes if the withdrawals are made from an existing account by an established depositor who is a U.S. resident, and who operates a firm that regularly withdraws more than $10,000 in currency to pay employees.

A record of each of the four situations specified and the reason for it must be made at the time it is granted. The exemptions must be maintained in a centralized list. The record should contain the following information:

The name, address, type of business, taxpayer identification number of each depositor who has engaged in currency transactions that have not been reported because of the exemption.
Whether or not the exemption covers withdrawals, deposits, or both.
The dollar limit of the exemption.

The regulations issued pursuant to the Bank Secrecy Act provide that a bank may apply to the Secretary of the Treasury for additional authority to grant an exemption to the reporting requirements if the bank believes that the circumstances warrant such an exemption.

The exceptions were formulated to avoid putting an undue burden on legitimate commercial transactions. The exceptions allow banks to carry on legitimate commercial business without imposing an unnecessary paperwork burden. The transactions that have to be reported are unusual. They are not the kind of transactions normally associated with everyday legitimate commercial activity. The exceptions are for the benefit of banks, not for their customers. A request by a customer to get on a bank's exempt list should be viewed with suspicion.

Most serious violations of the Bank Secrecy Act's reporting requirements are usually (1) failing to file a Currency Transaction

BANK SECURITIES

Report (CTR) for each transaction over $10,000, unless exempted, (2) granting an exemption to an unqualified entity, and (3) failing to file a CTR for a nonexempt transaction with an exempt entity.

BIBLIOGRAPHY

BYRNE, J. J. "Confused About Compliance?" *ABA Banking Journal*, July 1987.ed. *Security Compliance Guide*. Mosler Anti-Crime Bureau, Hamilton, OH, 1987.
FEDERAL HOME LOAN BANK BOARD. Office of Examinations and Supervision. *Audit Requirements Relating to the Currency and Foreign Transaction Reporting Act*, April 17, 1986..
POWIS, R. *Bank Secrecy Act Compliance*. Bank Administration Institute, Rolling Meadows, IL, 1987.

BANK SECURITIES The types of commercial bank securities now available include the following: (1) convertible or nonconvertible capital debentures; (2) convertible or nonconvertible preferred stock; and (3) common stock.

Capital Debentures. The Comptroller of the Currency issued in December, 1962, a regulation (Sec. 14.5, Capital Debentures, in Part 14, Changes in Capital Structure, found in 12 CFR) indicating that it is the policy of the Comptroller of the Currency to permit the issuance of convertible or nonconvertible capital debentures by national banks, "in accordance with normal business considerations." National banks may, with the approval of the stockholders owning two-thirds of the stock of the bank entitled to vote, or without such approval if authorized by their articles of association, issue convertible or nonconvertible capital debentures in such amounts and under such terms and conditions as shall be approved by the Comptroller. There is no covering statute.

However, the principal amount of capital debentures outstanding at any time, when added to all other outstanding indebtedness of the bank, except those forms of indebtedness exempt from the provisions of 12 U.S.C. 82 (which specifies the debt limitation which follows), shall not exceed an amount equal to 100% of the bank's unimpaired paid-in capital stock plus 50% of the amount of its unimpaired surplus fund.

Most states also authorize their chartered banks to issue capital notes or debentures. In fact, such senior debt securities were authorized by various states when the Emergency Banking and Bank Conservation Act of March 9, 1933, authorized the RECONSTRUCTION FINANCE CORPORATION to invest in national bank preferred stock and in such debt securities of state-chartered banks.

The sharp expansion in commercial bank issues of capital notes and debentures is indicated by the table appended.

Substantial increase in credit demand in recent years has required faster growth in capital funds than that arising from retained earnings alone. But instead of raising the additional capital funds entirely in common stock, banks (especially the larger institutions) have turned to senior securities (largely convertible or nonconvertible capital notes and debentures). As between preferred stock and capital notes or debentures, there has been a marked preference for the latter as the media for senior security financing because, among other factors, of the cheaper cost of funds resulting from the full tax deductibility of interest on the capital notes or debentures. Characteristics of issues of bank capital notes and debentures include the following:

1. Capital notes or debentures as to liability of the parent bank may be direct liability subordinated issues (subordinated to deposits and other specified liabilities). Because of the large relative volume of deposit liabilities alone, the strength of the claim of such subordinated bank capital notes or debentures is, compared to that of subordinated debentures of industrial companies, quite junior. However, protective provisions in such bank subordinated capital notes or debentures may restrict or prohibit additional issues senior to or equal in strength of claim to existing issues, entirely aside from statutory limitation on total bank indebtedness, *supra*. Parent banks may also guarantee principal and interest of debt issues by affiliates, which may also have outstanding unguaranteed issues, in connection with sale and leaseback of the parent bank's building.
2. Typical maturity of capital notes or debentures has been 25 years, with or without sinking fund provision. A large number of the issues have been placed with investors in private placements rather than public offerings. Call provision is typical, many of the issues having deferred call provision. A number of the issues are convertible into common stock, a source of potential dilution for the common stock. The extent of the total capital notes or debentures in proportion to total capital accounts does not appear large in the overall (see table appended), but among the banks issuing capital notes or debentures, capital structure proportions of 25% to 30% represented by such debt securities are not unusual. This may be considered about the limit of prudent capital structure leverage, in view of the susceptibility of earnings to cyclical influences (principal earning assets are normally loans, which unavoidably will reflect the ups and downs of business activity).
3. The larger and thoroughly entrenched banks show ample earning power relative to interest requirements on capital notes or debentures. But an analytical question arises as to total interest requirements in view of subordination of many such issues to deposits and other specified debt. Another analytical question is whether interest coverage should be figured on the basis of above the line earnings (net current operating earnings) or below the line earnings (net income or transferred to undivided profits), referring to the bank accounting issues discussed in BANK ACCOUNTING.

Preferred Stock. Bank financing in preferred stock has been relatively light. From an investing point of view, bank preferred stocks command high coverage of dividends, senior equity position, and, moreover, taxability of only 15% of dividend income to corporate investors. But callability, nonparticipating fixed dividends, and, as high-grade preferreds, susceptibility adversely to rise in interest rates and in yields on high-grade fixed return securities, marketwise, makes bank preferred stocks less satisfactory for long-term investment as bank equities than bank common stocks, unless such preferred stock carries convertibility into common stock of the bank concerned.

Common Stock. Common shares of well-entrenched, well-managed banks, as reflected in high current earning power and long-term growth rate, are entitled to high investment regard for long-term investing purposes. Within given banking markets, management of particular banks may be more aggressive than the group as to mergers, branch banking, and diversification of banking services, resulting in superior earnings and growth rates. Bank common stocks are highly leveraged equities even without the capital structure leverage provided by capital notes, debentures, and/or preferred stock, because of the volume leverage derived from deposits and reflected in earning assets per dollar of capital funds. In given banks, the issuance of capital notes or debentures to as much as 25% to 30% of total capital structure, along with deposits of 10 to 15 times capital funds, magnifies leverage more than ever and will result in greater variation in common stock earnings over cycles of business activity.

Even more leveraged, however, are common shares of bank holding companies, whose own capital structure leverage rests upon that of subsidiary banks and other subsidiaries, and whose own expansion in bank-related or other permitted fields would be greater than that of any one subsidiary bank. Constraints imposed by regulation would serve to temper expansion that otherwise might spill over into speculative nonbanking or bank-related lines under the spur of competition.

Analytically, common shares of a bank holding company, even if such a holding company holds only interests in banks, call for analysis of consolidated and nonconsolidated data to determine the respective sources of earning power and equity of such holding company common stock. Diversification of holdings in banks and bank-related lines available in the bank holding company's common stock should normally be a favorable consideration and justify higher price-earnings multiples.

The massive changes created by the partial deregulation of the financial marketplace have often resulted in intense competition in products banks formerly thought to be secure profit generators. In addition, problems in the energy (both petroleum and nuclear power), international, and real estate sectors have eroded the profitability of many banks. High interest rates during the early eighties severely damaged the fixed-rate lending institutions in the thrift industry. Thus, while the common stock of some banks has maintained a high investment status, the stock of many institutions has assumed a much more speculative character.

See BANK HOLDING COMPANY ACT.

BANKS FOR COOPERATIVES The banks for cooperatives were established to provide a permanent source of credit (commodity loans, operating capital loans, and facility loans) on a sound business basis to farmers' cooperatives. The Central Bank for

Cooperatives (Washington, DC) and the 12 district banks for cooperatives (one in each farm credit district) were organized under the Farm Credit Act of 1933 (48 Stat. 257). The Central Bank for Cooperatives serves the district banks for cooperatives by making direct loans to them and by participating in loans that exceed their respective lending limits.

To be eligible to borrow from a bank for cooperatives, a cooperative must be an association in which farmers act together in marketing farm products, purchasing farm supplies, or furnishing farm business services, and otherwise meet the requirements now specified in the Farm Credit Act of 1971 (85 Stat. 583; 12 U.S.C. 2001 note), approved December 10, 1971, which superseded all previous laws governing the Farm Credit System and the Farm Credit Administration.

Revised authority for the activities of the banks for cooperatives may be found in Title III of the Farm Credit Act of 1971, as amended. All of the capital stock of the 12 district banks for cooperatives is held by borrowing cooperatives. All of the stock of the Central Bank for Cooperatives is held by the district banks. The Central Bank for Cooperatives is controlled by a board of 13 directors. Twelve of these directors are elected, one each, by the district boards. The thirteenth is appointed by the governor of the Farm Credit Administration with the advice and consent of the Federal Farm Credit Board.

Any association of farmers, ranchers, or producers or harvesters of aquatic products or any federation of such associations which operates on a cooperative basis and provides marketing, processing, supply, or business service functions for its members may be eligible to borrow from a bank for cooperatives. However, 80% of the voting control of such associations must be held by bona fide farmers, ranchers, or producers or harvesters of aquatic products, or federations of such associations. The cooperative must also do as much business with or for members as it does with or for nonmembers. Excepted from this requirement is business transacted with the U.S. and services and supplies furnished by the cooperative as a public utility.

The banks for cooperatives make three basic types of loans which are adapted to the particular needs of cooperatives. These are seasonal loans, term loans, and loans secured by commodities. All the banks work together to provide a complete loan service to cooperatives. The Central Bank for Cooperatives participates with the district banks on larger loans.

Interest rates are determined by the boards of directors with the approval of the Farm Credit Administration. Distributions of earnings by the banks to their borrowers have the effect of reducing the rates of interest.

The country was originally divided into 12 farm credit districts. At the same location in each district, there was a federal land bank, a federal intermediate credit bank, and a bank for cooperatives. The Central Bank for Cooperatives was located in Washington, DC, but relocated in Denver, Colorado in August, 1972.

Each of the 12 farm credit districts had a district farm credit board of seven members. These boards set policies and hire management for each of the three banks in their respective districts and also act as district boards setting policies which governed those functions which the three banks carry on jointly.

The federal land bank associations, production credit associations, and cooperatives holding stock in the respective banks in each farm credit district each elected two directors to the district board. The seventh member of the board, the director-at-large, was appointed by the governor of the Farm Credit Administration with the advice and consent of the Federal Farm Credit Board.

The *Agricultural Credit Act of 1987* mandated organizational restructuring of the Farm Credit System institutions. On May 5, 1988, the Farm Credit Board approved a voluntary merger plan for the separate Banks for Cooperatives to form either a National Bank for Cooperatives or a United Bank for Cooperatives. Details of the restructuring are presented in the entry FARM CREDIT ADMINISTRATION.

The Farm Credit Act of 1971 authorized the three branches of the farm credit system (federal land banks, federal intermediate credit banks, and banks for cooperatives) to issue a joint security, obligating each branch for the liability of the others.

The Farm Credit Act of 1971 also authorized the banks which loan funds to cooperatives to issue debentures equivalent to 20 times the net worth of the bank's assets rather than the limit of 8 times the net worth previously in effect.

The Farm Credit Act of 1955 provided for eventual ownership of the banks by farmers' cooperatives and for the retirement of the U.S. Government's investment. This was accomplished on December 31, 1968, when the remainder of the U.S. Government capital was retired.

The law provides that the U.S. Government shall assume no responsibility, direct or indirect, for any bonds, debentures, or other such obligations issued by the federal land banks, federal intermediate credit banks, or banks for cooperatives.

The Farm Credit Act of 1971 provides that the amount of bonds, debentures, or similar obligations issued and outstanding may not exceed 20 times the capital and surplus of all the banks primarily liable on the issue or such lesser amount as the Farm Credit Administration shall establish by regulation.

The law requires that the collateral security for the bonds and debentures of the farm credit banks shall be at least equal in amount to the bonds and debentures issued, and shall consist of notes and other obligations representing loans made under the authority of the Farm Credit Act, obligations of the United States or any agency thereof, other readily marketable securities approved by the Farm Credit Administration, or cash.

Regulation A of the Board of Governors of the Federal Reserve System provides that the bonds and debentures of the farm credit banks may be accepted by Federal Reserve banks as collateral security for advances to member banks under Section 13 of the Federal Reserve Act. They are also eligible for outright purchase and sale by the Federal Reserve System in its open market operations.

National banks and state member banks of the Federal Reserve System may invest in the bonds and debentures of the federal land banks and federal intermediate credit banks without being subject to the statutory limitations and restrictions generally applicable as to dealing in, underwriting, and purchasing investment securities for their own account. In the opinion of the general counsel of the Farm Credit Administration, debentures of the banks for cooperatives are also eligible for investment by state member banks of the Federal Reserve System.

The law provides that the bonds and debentures of the farm credit banks shall be lawful investments for all fiduciary and trust funds under the jurisdiction of the U.S. Government. They are eligible as security for government deposits. They are also legal investments for banks, trust companies, savings banks, and trust funds in various states, subject to such conditions and restrictions as are contained in applicable state statutes and regulations. The bonds and debentures are also lawful investments for federal credit unions and federal savings and loan associations.

Consolidated bonds and debentures of the federal land banks, federal intermediate credit banks, and banks for cooperatives, and the income derived therefrom, are exempt from state, municipal, and local taxation. But interest on such bonds and debentures is not exempt from taxation by the U.S. Government; and neither gain from sale or other disposition of the bonds and debentures nor transfer by inheritance or other means is exempt from federal or state taxation.

Offerings of bonds and debentures are announced publicly by the fiscal agency or dealers or dealer banks belonging to the selling group. There is an active secondary market in outstanding issues of farm credit bonds and debentures.

See FARM CREDIT ADMINISTRATION.

BANK SERVICE CORPORATION ACT An act that provides that an insured bank may invest not more than 10 percentum of paid-in and unimpaired capital and unimpaired surplus in a bank service corporation. No insured bank shall invest more than 5 percentum of its total assets in bank service corporations. The act provides that an insured bank may invest in a bank service corporation that performs and a bank service corporation may perform, the following services only for depository institutions: check and deposit sorting and posting, computation and posting of interest and other credits and charges., preparations and mailing of checks, statements, notices, and similar items, or any other clerical, bookkeeping, accounting, statistical, or similar functions performed for a depository institution. A bank service corporation shall not take deposits (12 U.S.C. 1861).

BANK STAMP The endorsement of a bank placed on the reserve side of a check, note, acceptance, or other negotiable instrument with a rubber stamp or an endorsement machine. Bank endorsement stamps are of two kinds, direct and general. In a direct endorsement the name of the payee bank is specifically stated, whereas a general endorsement bears the words "Pay to the order of any bank or banker." The general endorsement is in more common use since it permits standardization, thus enabling the bank to dispatch large numbers of checks with the minimum of time and labor.

ENCYCLOPEDIA OF BANKING AND FINANCE

BANK STATEMENT The financial statement, statement of condition, or BALANCE SHEET of a bank, presenting the nature and amount of its assets, liabilities, and capital accounts. The term bank statement is also applied to the weekly statement of the *Federal Reserve banks*, individually and on a consolidated basis, as well as to the statistical report "Weekly Condition Report of Large Commercial Banks" (Report H.4.2) of the Board of Governors of the Federal Reserve System. In the days before creation of the Federal Reserve System, the term was also applied to the weekly report of the New York Clearing House banks, otherwise known as the individual bank return, or bank return.

The voluntarily published, usually condensed statements of condition are the type given public distribution by banks. The statutorily required call reports of condition, prepared on forms and per instructions prescribed by the bank supervisory agency concerned, are filed with such agency and published in legal notice form in local newspapers. In addition, the Securities Acts Amendments of 1964 led to promulgation of Regulation F of the Board of Governors of the Federal Reserve System and similar regulation by the Federal Deposit Insurance Corporation for insured state nonmember banks; to regulations of the Comptroller of the Currency (Parts 11 and 18, *Comptroller's Manual for National Banks*) governing registration; and also to statement requirements for national banks. The Comptroller of the Currency summarizes the required reports of national banks as follows:

1. *Commercial department reports.* Each national bank must submit to the Comptroller of the Currency four times each year a report of the condition of its commercial department. The Comptroller may also call for additional reports of condition from all national banks and special reports of condition from any national bank whenever he determines that such reports are necessary for the performance of his supervisory duties. Reports of condition shall be submitted to the Comptroller on such dates and in such form and shall contain such information as may be determined by the Comptroller. National banks are furnished with report of condition forms and instructions for their preparation, filing, and publication to the extent required by law.

2. *Affiliate reports.* When required by the Comptroller of the Currency, each national bank which has one or more affiliates must submit with its report of condition a report of condition of each such affiliate. The Comptroller furnishes affiliate report forms and instructions for their preparation, filing, and publication to the extent required by law.

3. *Reports of income and dividends.* Each national bank must submit annually to the Comptroller of the Currency a report of its income and dividends for the 12-month period ending December 31. The Comptroller furnishes report of income and dividends forms and instructions for their preparation and filing (publication is not required).

4. *Trust department reports.* Each national bank which exercises fiduciary powers must submit annually to the Comptroller of the Currency, on the date specified by him, a report of the condition of its trust department. The Comptroller furnishes trust department annual report forms and instructions for their preparation and filing. If a national bank administers collective investment funds, Regulation 9 of the Comptroller of the Currency applies.

5. *Reports of international operations.* The International Operations Regulation (Part 21, *Comptroller's Manual for National Banks*) requires that a national bank notify the Comptroller before the establishment of a foreign branch or other controlled international banking office and before the acquisition of a direct or indirect controlling interest in a foreign bank or in certain other corporations. The regulation requires that a national bank report to the Comptroller within 30 days after the relocation of such branch or office and after the acquisition of an interest in a foreign bank or other corporation which does not result in control.

6. *Reserve reports of District of Columbia banks.* Each bank or trust company located and doing business in the District of Columbia which is not a national bank and which is not a member of the Federal Reserve System must maintain a reserve on the same basis and subject to the same conditions as prescribed for national banks located in the District of Columbia. Such reserve must be established and maintained with a national bank or a state member bank which is approved for such purpose by the Comptroller of the Currency. Each such District of Columbia bank or trust company must submit to the Comptroller each week a report of net deposits and reserves required. The depository national bank or state member bank must submit to the Comptroller each week a report of reserve held.

The statutes governing the preceding reporting requirements are 12 U.S.C. 161, 481, and 1817(a); and 26 D.C. Code (1961 Ed.) 102, 336.

Reports to Other Federal Banking Agencies. Section 7(a)(3) of the Federal Deposit Insurance Act (12 U.S.C. 1817, *passim*) applies to the Comptroller of the Currency with respect to national banks, as well as the other two federal bank regulatory agencies, in specifying four call reports of condition annually: (1) each insured state nonmember bank (except a District of Columbia bank) shall make a call report to the Federal Deposit Insurance Corporation; (2) each insured national bank and each insured District of Columbia bank shall make call reports to the Comptroller of the Currency; and (3) each insured state member bank shall make a call report to the Federal Reserve bank of which it is a stockholder. These four call reports of condition will be made annually upon dates selected by the Chairman of the Board of Directors of the Federal Deposit Insurance Corporation, the Comptroller of the Currency, and the Chairman of the Board of Governors of the Federal Reserve System, or a majority thereof. The dates selected shall be the same for all insured banks, except that when any of the said reporting dates is a nonbusiness day for any bank, the preceding business day shall be its reporting date.

Two dates shall be selected within the semiannual period of January to June, inclusive. The reports on such dates shall be the basis for the certified statement as to deposit liabilities to be filed in July with the Federal Deposit Insurance Corporation. Two dates shall be selected within the semiannual period of July to December, inclusive, to serve as the basis for the certified statement as to deposits to be filed in January with the Federal Deposit Insurance Corporation.

Each such report of condition shall contain a declaration by the president, a vice president, the cashier, or the treasurer, or by any other officer designated by the board of directors or trustees of the reporting bank to make such declaration, that the report is true and correct to the best of his knowledge and belief. The correctness of such reports of condition shall be attested by the signatures of at least three of the directors or trustees of the reporting bank, other than the officer making such declaration, or by at least two if there are not more than three directors or trustees, with the declaration that the report has been examined by them and to the best of their knowledge and belief is true and correct. Nothing, however, shall preclude any of the foregoing bank supervisory agencies from requiring banks under their jurisdiction to make additional reports of condition at any time.

The above statutory reference to call reports is now part of the National Banking Laws (R.S. 5211(a), 12 U.S.C. 161(a). The provisions of the Federal Reserve Act (Sec. 9, Federal Reserve Act, 12 U.S.C. 324), calling originally for three reports of condition annually, are now obsolete.

Reports of Income and Dividends. Each national bank submits its annual report of income and dividends for the 12-month period ending December 31 per statutory requirement contained in 12 U.S.C. 161(b). The Board of Governors of the Federal Reserve System and the Federal Deposit Insurance Corporation similarly call for one calendar year report of income and dividends, the former pursuant to its general authority to require statements and reports (Sec. 11(a), Federal Reserve Act) and the latter pursuant to 12 U.S.C. 1819 and Sec. 304.2 of its Rules and Regulations. The three agencies coordinate on format and instructions for preparation of such reports of income and dividends, which are submitted by the banks concerned. They are not published individually but instead serve as the basis for aggregative statistical tabulations.

Annual Reports. Informational requirements of stockholders and investors, however, are covered by the requirements for annual and other reports and for filing of registration statements by subject banks.

Although some of the larger American banks were voluntarily publishing annual reports, including management's comments on the economy in general and on the bank's operations in particular, the first formal requirements for annual reports adopted by any bank supervisory agency were issued December 20, 1962, by the

Comptroller of the Currency. These regulations required national banks with total deposits of over $25 million to furnish shareholders and the Office of the Comptroller of the Currency with proxy statements, prescribed annual financial reports, and reports of major changes in ownership. Subsequently, with passage of the Securities Acts Amendments of 1964, these regulations as amended were extended to national banks with 750 or more shareholders (after May 1, 1967, 500 or more shareholders). "Annual Report to Stockholders," Part 10 of Regulations of the Comptroller of the Currency, was amended May 10, 1967, to include, as a minimum, the schedules and related information required by and prepared in accordance with the new Part 18, "Form and Content of Financial Statements," per the Securities Acts Amendments of 1964, which are the subject of Part 11 of the regulations.

Similarly, Regulation F of the Board of Governors of the Federal Reserve System and companion regulation of the Federal Deposit Insurance Corporation (Part 335, Rules and Regulations) prescribe the registration requirements and submission of annual and quarterly reports on securities of state member banks of the Federal Reserve System and of insured state nonmember banks, applicable to banks having assets of $1 million or more and 500 or more stockholders.

Annual reports to stockholders upon specific request may be treated as part of the annual report for registration purposes. The latter requires verified balance sheet as of the close of the fiscal year and verified statement of income for the fiscal year. Consolidated statements shall be filed for the bank and its majority-owned (1) bank premises subsidiaries; (2) subsidiaries operating under the provisions of Section 25 or Section 25(a) of the Federal Reserve Act (agreement corporations and Edge Act corporations; and (3) significant subsidiaries (those accounting directly or indirectly for over 5% of the capital accounts of the bank, or those in which the parent bank's proportion of the subsidiary's gross operating revenues exceeds 5% of the bank's gross operating revenues). Such consolidated statements, reported in the annual report to stockholders and voluntarily published in abbreviated form (just the balance sheet) in bank advertising, were preferable to the call reports, with its purely domestic basis. Although the call report's format has now been revised by the Comptroller of the Currency, the Board of Governors of the Federal Reserve System, and the Federal Deposit Insurance Corporation (Rev. 6-69) to provide for consolidated domestic and foreign basis (for banks engaged in foreign operations) and for consolidated domestic basis (for banks engaged in purely domestic operations), the annual report is still preferable because of its commentary and comprehensiveness, including footnotes to the statements.

Annual reports to stockholders, moreover, may be certified by certified public accountants who are in fact independent. With an increasing number of bank stocks, especially stocks of bank holding companies, being admitted to trading on stock exchanges, such certification has also been adopted in complying with listing requirements, as well as voluntarily. In addition to the independent public accountants' certificate, the certified statements are supported by a number of footnotes covering accounting details. The CPAs, moreover, have their own standards as to generally accepted accounting principles in audits of banks.

See BANK ACCOUNTING, CALL REPORT, CLEARING HOUSE STATEMENT, CONDITION OF MEMBER BANKS, FEDERAL RESERVE STATEMENT.

BIBLIOGRAPHY

Audits of Banks, American Institute of Certified Public Accountants, New York, NY, 1984.
COMPTROLLER OF THE CURRENCY. *Comptroller's Manual for National Banks.* Periodic updates.

BANK STOCK   See BANK SECURITIES.

BANKWIRE   The system for transfer of bank funds available to bank members in the Payment and Administrative Communications Corporation, a cooperative which owns the operating company, the Payment and Telecommunications Services Corporation. The bankwire system is an alternative to the Federal Reserve's wire network.

BARGAIN COUNTER   Stock market securities offered for sale at prices below their INTRINSIC VALUE, especially during a panic, severe decline, or following a period of prolonged liquidation.

BARGAIN HUNTER   A speculator or investor who waits till securities are on the BARGAIN COUNTER before purchasing; one who defers the purchase of securities until he believes prices are at their extreme low range.

BAR GOLD   See GOLD BARS.

BAROMETERS   See BUSINESS BAROMETERS, INVESTMENT BAROMETERS.

BAROMETER STOCKS   Standard, active stocks which lead the movement in other stocks and indicate the general trend of the market; stocks whose movements are followed sympathetically by other stocks. United States Steel common is regarded as a barometer for industrial stocks, and New York Central for railroad stocks.

See BUSINESS BAROMETERS, MARKET LEADERS, SPECULATIVE CYCLE, STEEL, SWINGS.

BARRATRY   Damage, embezzlement, or fraud committed by a vessel's master or crew against the vessel or its cargo resulting in loss to the owners. It is one of the long list of risks for which an ocean carrier is not liable as indicated in an ocean bill of lading. This risk must, therefore, be covered in the MARINE INSURANCE certificate.

BARREN MONEY   Money which does not earn interest or other income.

BAR SILVER   See SILVER BULLION.

BARTER   The direct exchange of commodities without the use of money and without reference to price, e.g., the exchange of four cows for one horse. Barter is a primitive and inconvenient means of trading. In indirect barter, very often a standard commodity, e.g., grains, cattle, tobacco, or jewels, was used as a medium of exchange, or third commodity, to serve as a middle term between other commodities.

BASE COINS   Coins made of metals less valuable than gold or silver, e.g., nickel and copper. In the U.S., new dollars, half dollars, quarters, and dimes under the Coinage Act of 1965 as amended are cupro-nickel. The five-cent piece (nickel) is cupro-nickel. The 1982 cent is zinc-copper.

In England, the term base coins is used to denote counterfeit coins.
See MINOR COINS, UNITED STATES MONEY.

BASE INDEX   The reference point from which index rate changes are measured on a mortgage with a variable rate. The base index rate is known when the mortgage originates; it is the most recently available value of the index series at, or within six months prior to, the date of the closing of the loan. Generally, the maximum rate change from the origination of a mortgage with a variable rate cannot exceed the difference between the current value of the index and the base index value.

BASE PERIOD PRICE   From September, 1933, through December, 1949, the PARITY price of a supported commodity was computed simply by multiplying the average price received for the commodity in a fixed base period by an index of prices paid. The average base period price was not changed once it was established. For about one-third of the commodities concerned, the base price was the average of monthly prices during the five years, August, 1909–July, 1914. For the other two-thirds of the commodities, base prices were averages of season average prices in various periods: 1919–1929 or some portion thereof; 1934–1939; and 1936–1941. These periods were used where price information either was lacking completely or was considered inadequate for all commodities on a 1909–1914 base.

The first action to modernize parity was taken in the Agricultural Act of 1948, which provided for an adjusted base price that would reflect trends in the most recent 10-calendar-year period in the revision of parity price effective January 1, 1950, cushioned by transitional parity, which limited decline in parity price to not more than 5% per year beginning in 1950 for nonbasics and in 1956 for BASIC COMMODITIES.

The method of calculation of modernized parity price, showing how the adjusted base price for a commodity figures in the formula, follows:

1. **Average price received for the commodity.** The calendar year or seasonal average price received by farmers during the 10 preceding years for the commodity for which parity is being determined is calculated in dollars and cents. For 1969, it was the January, 1959–December, 1968 average; for 1970, it would be the January, 1960–December, 1969 average, etc. Where appropriate, the price data include allowance for unredeemed loans and other supplemental payments resulting from price support operations.
2. **Adjusted average or base price for the commodity.** An adjusted base price is then computed. This is done by dividing the 10-year average price received by farmers for the commodity, calculated under (1) above, by the average of the index of prices received by farmers for all commodities (1910–1914 = 100) for the same 10-calendar-year period. Where appropriate, the price data include unredeemed loans and other supplemental payments resulting from price support operations. This adjusted base price is recalculated at the beginning of each year. It is subject to major change only in January, when a new 10-year period is used to obtain the average price for the commodity on which parity is being determined and for all commodities. It is subject to subsequent minor changes prior to the beginning of harvest to reflect more accurate estimates of prices of the preceding year's crop, and also to reflect May revisions in the index of prices received by farmers.
3. **Index of prices paid.** An index of prices paid by farmers, including interest, taxes, and wage rates, is computed; this is the revised index of prices paid.
4. **New parity price.** This is calculated by multiplying the adjusted base price for the commodity by the current index of prices paid by farmers, including interest, taxes, and wage rates (1910–1914 = 100).

Parity prices are computed every month by the Agricultural Marketing Service, U.S. Department of Agriculture, and published in its report called *Agricultural Prices*.
See PARITY INDEX.

BASE RATE LOAN PRICING A method of pricing loans that sets rates at relatively narrow spreads of 25 to 75 basis points over money market rates and below the prime rate. The cost base for money market base rates is the rate on federal funds, CDs, or Eurodollars that approximate the maturity of the loan. The prime rate is also used as a loan rate administered by large money market banks. The trend in banking is away from large, prime-based short-term loans toward pricing on money market base rates.

BASIC COMMODITIES The Agricultural Act of 1949, as amended, made price support mandatory for extra long staple cotton, peanuts, rice, and tobacco; and loans and payments mandatory for corn, upland cotton, and wheat. These are the basic commodities. The 1949 act, as amended, also required price support for designated nonbasic commodities: tung nuts, honey, milk, barley, oats, rye, and grain sorghums. The National Wool Act of 1954 required price support for wool and mohair. Price support for other nonbasic commodities was discretionary. The Secretary of Agriculture was authorized by Congress to announce a commodity program if he deemed it necessary under statutory authority, and under terms and conditions that he determined applicable under legislative provisions. The Sugar Act of 1948 provided for conditional payments to producers of sugarcane and sugarbeets, and as of 1982 has been replaced by restoration of the former quota system for imports and associated domestic supports (*see* SUGAR). The COMMODITY CREDIT CORPORATION also may carry out operations to remove and dispose of surplus agricultural commodities in order to stabilize prices at levels not in excess of those permissible by law.

The Department of Agriculture further explains: except as otherwise provided by statute, the secretary determines or approves the amounts, terms, and conditions of price support operations.

Eight factors set forth in Section 401(b), Title IV, of the Agricultural Act of 1949 were taken into consideration in determining, in the case of any commodity for which price support is discretionary, whether a price support operation is undertaken and the level of support. For many of those commodities for which price support is mandatory, these same factors are considered to determine the level of support above the minimum set forth by law. These factors are as follows:

1. The supply of the commodity in relation to the demand.
2. The price levels at which other commodities are being supported, and, in the case of feed grains, the feed values of each grain in relation to corn.
3. The availability of funds.
4. The perishability of the commodity.
5. The importance of the commodity to agriculture and the national economy.
6. The ability to dispose of stocks acquired through a price support operation.
7. The need to offset temporary losses of export markets.
8. The ability and willingness of producers to keep supplies in line with demand.

Support Level. For many commodities, Congress has established either a specific parity level (*see* PARITY) at which, or a range within which, loan, purchase, and payment rates must be set.

Support Eligibility. In order to be eligible to participate in a program, a producer must comply with the requirements of the applicable legislation and such additional terms and conditions as may be established by the Secretary of Agriculture as a condition of eligibility.

Several of the commodity programs under The Food Security Act of 1985 originated with the Agricultural Adjustment Acts of 1933 and 1938 and with the Agricultural Act of 1949. These acts are commonly referred to as permanent legislation; the 1985 act and other "nonpermanent" legislation mainly adjust program levels. The Food Security Act was amended on February 28, 1986, and again on March 20, 1986. The act mainly adjusts diversion levels and conditions for wheat, and sets new deficiency payment and loan rates for this crop.

See AGRICULTURAL ADJUSTMENT ACT, PARITY, PARITY INDEX, PRICE SUPPORT.

BASIS The rate of yield to maturity on bonds and other debt securities. By extension, yields on preferred stocks and common stocks are often referred to as the basis, representing the annual rate of current return on such equities. The reciprocal of such yields is price, so that the yields are an alternative way of expressing market levels. Basis points refer to hundredths of 1% yield; thus 25 basis points higher yield would mean 0.25% higher yield for the particular issue. U.S. Treasury bills are traded and quoted on a rate basis frequently referred to as yield, but actually U.S. Treasury bills are traded and quoted on a bank discount basis, which should be converted from such 360-day basis to full 365-day basis for comparable investment return or yield basis.

In trading in commodities, basis is the spread (difference) between the spot (cash) price and price of near futures contracts in the particular commodity or distant futures.
See RETURN, YIELD.

BASIS GRADE In the commodity markets, the basic contract grades deliverable on contracts at par, without premium or discount. There may be more than one basis grade; e.g., the grades deliverable on futures contracts in wheat on the Chicago Board of Trade, without premium or discount, are the following:

No. 2 Soft Red (and No. 3 Heavy)*
No. 2 Dark Hard Winter (and No. 3 Heavy)*
No. 2 Hard Winter (and No. 3 Heavy)*
No. 2 Yellow Hard Winter (and No. 3 Heavy)*
No. 2 Dark Northern Spring (and No. 3 Heavy)*
No. 2 Heavy Northern Spring
No. 1 Northern Spring

*All factors equal to No. 2 grade or better except maximum 2% foreign material, maximum 8% total defects, and maximum 10% wheats or other classes.

Seven other grades are deliverable at premiums, and six other grades at discount.
See COMMODITY EXCHANGES, COTTON FUTURES, GRADING, WHEAT.

BASIS POINT One-hundredth of a percentage point (0.01%) of yield on a bond or note. A yield of 8.00% is 800 basis points. Basis points can be used to measure small changes in interest rates.

BASIS SWAP A type of interest rate swap in which the contracting parties exchange obligations to make floating interest rate payments. These payments are tied to various interest rate indexes.

BASIS VALUE The value of a security as an investment and, in the case of bonds, as bearing a series of interest incomes if held to maturity. Bonds are usually bought on a certain basis, or to yield a certain percent. Other things being equal, bond values are compared by the effective interest rate, i.e., basis value or yield.
See INVESTMENT VALUE, YIELD.

BASLE AGREEMENT The agreement on risk-based capital adequacy standards for commercial banks reached by central banking authorities from the United States, Western Europe, and Japan. It was finalized in July 1988, at the Bank for International Settlements in Basle, Switzerland. The Federal Reserve Board's final risk-based capital regulations are based on this agreement. Regulations that have been or will be issued by other U.S. federal banking regulators and by banking regulators in Western Europe and Japan are based on the Basle Agreement.

BASLE CONCORDAT See BASLE AGREEMENT. An agreement made by the Cooke Committee and endorsed by the governors of the world's major central banks in December 1975. The agreement establishes guidelines relating to supervisory responsibilities for banks operating in more than one national jurisdiction, including foreign banks, branches, and subsidiaries.

BATCH SYSTEM See BLOCK SYSTEM.

BEAR Among operators in various markets, a person who be-lieves that security or commodity prices will decline, and who accordingly sells on that expectation, as distinguished from a BULL. Bears are also short sellers, i.e., they sell what they do not possess in anticipation of a decline in price at which they can buy back (cover) at a profit.

Bears are market pessimists who take the view that market or business conditions are growing worse. One may be a bear on a particular security without being bearish on the entire market. The public usually takes the bull side of the market, while the bear side is largely confined to professional operators.
See SHORT SALE.

BEAR ACCOUNT SHORT ACCOUNT.

BEARER The person in possession of an instrument, document of title, or security payable to bearer or endorsed in blank (Uniform Commercial Code, Sec. 1-201); the holder of money or a check, bill, note, or other instrument. Title to valuable papers can be transferred by delivery or by endorsement. If transferable by delivery they are called bearer instruments (e.g., money, coupon bonds, coupons, bearer checks, bearer notes or bills, bearer bonds, etc.); if transferable by endorsement, they are negotiable only by endorsement (e.g., checks, notes, bills of exchange, etc.) plus delivery. The term assignment is usually intended to describe the transfer of a nonnegotiable chose in action, such as stock certificates, registered bonds, and bills of lading, as well as nonnegotiable bills, notes, or checks.

BEARER BONDS COUPON BONDS, which are payable to bearer and carry detachable interest coupons.

BEARER INSTRUMENTS See BEARER, PAY TO BEARER.

BEAR MARKET The stock market when the influence of the bears is predominant and the trend of prices is downward. It is more particularly applied to a market in which the downward tendency has been prolonged or is expected to be prolonged, with minor upward interruptions, over an extended period such as a year or more. In terms of the DOW THEORY, a bear market is one in which the primary trend is downward.
See BULL MARKET, SPECULATIVE CYCLE.

BEAR RAID On the stock market, vigorous short selling by the bears, taking tactical advantage of the technical position of an overbought market to force prices down and thus compel those who are long of stocks to sell at a loss while the bears cover at a profit.

Under Section 9(a) of the Securities Exchange Act of 1934, bear raids involving the use of manipulative and deceptive devices are prohibited, such as the activities of pools (which themselves are prohibited) resorting to organized bear raids seeking to crack confidence in particular stocks by dissemination of false and misleading tips, rumors, and information. It should be noted, however, that a SHORT SALE under controlled procedures and without resort to manipulative and deceptive devices continues to be authorized as a legitimate expression of price opinion in a free market.

BEATING THE GUN Solicitation of orders for a security before the effective date for the offering as filed by amendment to the registration statement for a public offering with the Securities and Exchange Commission. This is prohibited.
See REGISTRATION STATEMENT.

BELOW PAR A price quoted below the face value of a security.
See PAR.

BENEFICIARY One in whose favor a trust operates, or in whose behalf a life insurance policy or other document conferring value is drawn. The beneficiary under a letter of credit is the party in whose favor it is issued and who is entitled under its terms to draw a bill of exchange for acceptance by the issuing bank and for discount by the notifying bank.

BENEFIT-COST ANALYSIS Benefit-cost analysis is one of several methods for evaluating a project or program. Unlike other methods of analysis, benefit-cost analysis includes in the calculations estimates of both primary and secondary costs and benefits. Usually, this decision-making approach is used to evaluate public programs where there are a large number of secondary recipients.

Benefit-cost analysis maximizes benefits for a prescribed level of costs, determines the minimum level of expenditures to achieve a pre-specified level of benefits, or maximizes net benefits. The methodology involves a comparison, in present value, of benefits and cost. Often, if the ratio of benefits to costs is greater than unity, the project will be selected (unless a competing project has a better ratio).

Benefit-cost analysis often has a subjective element, namely, the identification of the secondary recipients of the benefits and the secondary parties incurring costs. For example, if a project were being contemplated to improve the water quality of a recreational lake, the number of individuals currently using the lake could be identified, but projections of those who would use the lake only if it were cleaner are more difficult. Other areas of application relate to pollution in general and employee morale and safety.

BENEFIT PRINCIPLE OF TAXATION Taxes are levied by all levels of government on the basis of two broad principles: the benefit principle and the ability-to-pay principle. The benefit principle of taxation is based on the premise that those consumers who directly receive the benefits from public goods and services should themselves finance these public goods and services. This principle underlies the rationale for every citizen to be taxed to pay for public goods, such as national defense. Also, user taxes, such as gasoline taxes earmarked to finance highway construction and repair, are levied according to this principle.
See ABILITY-TO-PAY THEORY.

BENELUX A group of European countries, including Belgium, the Netherlands, and Luxembourg formed to encourage and develop economic activity among themselves.

BEQUEST A gift or legacy of personal property left by a decedent in his will; a testamentary gift of personalty, as distinguished from a testamentary gift of realty, called a DEVISE.

BETA STOCKS The terms beta stock and alpha stock derive from the coefficients for the linear relationship between an investor's return on a specific investment and the return on the overall market as calculated in the market model and the capital Asset Pricing Model. The relationship can be represented graphically by making a scatter plot of a particular stock's return (vertical axis) against the market return (horizontal axis) and drawing a statistically fitted straight line through the points. The slope of the line is the beta coefficient and the intercept with the vertical axis is the alpha coefficient.

The beta coefficient provides information on how a stock's return changes relative to changes in the market return. A positive beta means the stock tends to move in the same direction as the market; a negative beta stock tends to move against the market. A beta greater than one indicates a stock that tends to move proportionately

ENCYCLOPEDIA OF BANKING AND FINANCE

more than the market. It rises further when the market rises and falls further when the market goes down. A beta of less than one describes a stock that is less volatile than the market.

The alpha coefficient gives the expected return on a stock when stock prices in general are stationary, when the market return is zero. A positive alpha indicates a stock that will tend to earn a positive return when the market return is zero. Other things being equal, higher alpha stocks are preferred to lower alpha stocks.

The alpha and beta coefficients are an aid in portfolio analysis. For example, if the market return is expected to be high, the optimum stock is a high alpha, high beta stock; if it is expected to be low or negative, a high alpha, low beta stock is best. Some risk is still present because these coefficients reflect tendencies only, not certainties, and because their values can change over time. Since rational investors do not take on additional risk without demanding additional returns to compensate for the additional risk, investors who hold high-beta stocks will usually demand above-market returns. Similarly, investors who hold low-beta stocks can usually expect to be compensated with below-average returns.

The beta coefficients for most publicly traded companies are published by Merrill Lynch, Value Line, and other investor advisory services. These values are calculated using actual trading data. Usually, beta is tabulated by estimating a regression line as follows:

$$R = A + B \times RM$$

where
R = Return on the stock
RM = Return on the market
B = Beta coefficient

The estimated slope of this regression line is equal to the beta coefficient for the individual stock.

BETTERMENTS   Betterments (often referred to as improvements) are substitutions of one asset for another. A betterment is the substitution of a better asset for one currently used (a concrete floor for a wooden floor). A replacement is the substitution of a similar asset (a special glass window for a plain glass window). If the expenditure increases the future service potential of the asset, it should be capitalized.

In the system of accounts for railroads prescribed by the Interstate Commerce Commission, physical changes in roadway, structures, facilities or equipment, the object of which is to make the properties affected more useful or of greater capacity than they were at the time of their installation or acquisition.
See ADDITIONS.

BID-AND-ASKED QUOTATIONS   Prices at which securities are wanted and at which they are offered for sale. Bid and asked quotations on stocks listed on the NEW YORK STOCK EXCHANGE are obtainable through member firms, who employ an electronic interrogation device which has instant access to a computer center that receives current market information from the exchange's market data system. A similar system is available on AMERICAN STOCK EXCHANGE issues. In over-the-counter issues, the NASDAQ (NATIONAL ASSOCIATION OF SECURITIES DEALERS AUTOMATED QUOTATIONS SYSTEM) traded the securities of nearly 4,700 companies in 1987.
See QUOTATIONS.

BID PRICE   The price offered for a security or commodity by a prospective buyer; the price at which a security or commodity is wanted, and subject to immediate acceptance, unless otherwise stated, for the amount specified.

BIDS AND OFFERS   Stock exchange rules define the various kinds of bids and offers which may be made. On the New York Stock Exchange, the recognized quotations are public bids and offers in lots of one trading unit or multiples thereof. A unit of trading in stocks is 100 shares, except in the case of certain stocks designated by the exchange to have a unit of trading of a lesser number of shares. A unit of trading in bonds is $1,000 original principal amount. Bids or offers for less than the unit of trading must specify the principal amount of the bonds or number of shares of stock covered by the bid or offer (odd lots). Bids or offers in stocks above $1 per share shall not be made at a variation less than one-eighth of $1 per share; in stocks selling below $1, but above $0.50 per share, in one-sixteenth; and in stocks selling below $0.50 per share, in one-thirty-second. For corporate bonds, similarly, price variation is one-eighth of 1% of the principal amount. Price variation is one-thirty-second of 1% of principal amount for bids and offers in bonds of the U.S. Government, Puerto Rico, and states, territories, and municipalities therein; the bonds of the International Bank for Reconstruction and Development; and securities guaranteed by the U.S. Government as to principal and interest. With reference to delivery and payment, bids and offers may be made according to the recognized TRADING METHODS.

BIG BOARD   Colloquially, the NEW YORK STOCK EXCHANGE.

BIG HIT   A problem-prone circumstance associated with lending practices that can result in substantial loan losses. Big hits can sometimes be avoided by careful selection of large clients and risk-acceptance within tolerable limits. Early-warning systems are often useful in avoiding big hits. Close supervision in lending and monitoring hits is critical to avoiding the big hit.

BIG SIX   A reference to the six largest public accounting partnerships. Mergers in the late 1980s resulted in the reduction of the former Big Eight to what is now currently referred to as the Big Six or the Giant Six. The Big Six include:

Arthur Andersen & Co.
Coopers & Lybrand
Deloitte & Touche
Ernst & Young
KPMG Peat Marwick
Price Waterhouse

See AUDIT.

BILL BOOK   LIABILITY LEDGER.

BILL BROKER   In England, a merchant or firm that negotiates and discounts commercial paper, or buys and sells it in the open market for a profit. English bill brokers correspond to American NOTE BROKERS.

BILL FOR PAYMENT   A draft or bill of exchange drawn and presented for payment, as distinguished from a bill for acceptance.
See PRESENTMENT.

BILL OF CREDIT   This term has two meanings:

1. A written advice requesting the party to whom it is addressed to extend credit to the bearer on the voucher or security of the signer.
2. "Paper issued by the sovereign authority and intending to circulate as money" (John Marshall). The U.S. Constitution empowers Congress to borrow money and to emit bills of credit. The use of this term to denote government paper money is practically obsolete.

BILL OF EXCHANGE   The Uniform Commercial Code (Sec. 3–104) provides that a writing which complies with the requirements of that section for any writing to be a negotiable instrument is a DRAFT (bill of exchange) if it is an order.

The terms bill of exchange and draft are used interchangeably, but the former is usually applied to an order to pay money arising out of a foreign transaction, while the latter term is more often reserved for domestic transactions. Technically, moreover, a bill of exchange is always a negotiable instrument, whereas a draft may be nonnegotiable.

A bill of exchange is a three-party instrument in which the first party (drawer) draws an order for the payment of a sum certain on a second party (drawee) for payment to a third party (payee) at a definite future time. According to the Uniform Commercial Code, a bill of exchange is the same as a draft.

A foreign bill of exchange is drawn in one country upon a person in another country not governed by the same laws. A bill of exchange drawn in one state upon a person residing in another state is considered a foreign bill.
See DRAFT, FOREIGN BILLS OF EXCHANGE.

ENCYCLOPEDIA OF BANKING AND FINANCE

Bill of Exchange

July 15, 1990

On July 15, 1990, pay to Williams Company or bearer $10,000 plus 10% annual interest from June 5, 1990.

To: XYZ Corporation
/S/ Charles W. Waters

Types of drafts include:

1. Trade acceptance in which a seller of goods extends credit to a purchaser by drawing a draft on the purchaser directing him or her to pay the seller a sum of money on a specified date.
   a. Trade acceptances require the signature of the buyer on the face of the instrument.
   b. The seller can usually discount the instrument and receive cash.
   c. The seller is usually both the drawer and the payee.
2. Bankers acceptance is a draft in which the drawee and the drawer are a bank.
3. Sight draft is payable upon presentation to the drawer.
4. Time draft is payable at a specified date or payable a certain period of time after a specified date.
5. Money order is a draft purchased by one party to pay payee in which the third party is usually the post office, a bank, or a company.
6. Check is a draft that is payable on demand and the drawee is a bank.

BILL OF LADING A receipt issued by a carrier, as bailee, certifying that it has received the therein described goods from the within-named consignor, for transportation to a specified destination, to a specified consignee, or to the order of any person. In addition to serving as a receipt of goods and as a contract of transportation, the bill of lading serves the function of identification (complete description of the shipment, parties, route, etc.) and the function of information (a source of data for the preparation of other documents by the carrier).

As a receipt, the bill of lading should describe the goods so that they can be readily identified. It should be free from any disclaimer concerning the unsatisfactory condition of the wrapping of boxes or other containers, and from clauses limiting the carrier's responsibility—"said to contain," "shipper's load and count," etc. In other words, a bill of lading should be "clean."

As a contract of transportation, a bill of lading should be signed by a responsible regularly established carrier or agent, and the points of origin and destination should be set forth.

As a document of title, the various rights under a bill of lading depend upon its type. The Federal Bill of Lading Act distinguishes sharply between a straight and order bill of lading. The first states that the goods are consigned or destined to a specified consignee, and is intended primarily for domestic shipments; the latter consigns the goods to the order of any person, and is intended for both domestic and foreign shipments. A straight bill of lading must be marked, therefore, "nonnegotiable," and duplicates thereof must be similarly marked. Title to the goods rests with the consignee, and while he or she may transfer his or her title by endorsement and delivery, he or she can transfer no better title than he himself or she herself holds. So a lender on a straight bill of lading to a wrongful person has no protection, even though lending in good faith and without knowledge of defect of title. An order bill of lading, however, may be negotiated, and when the bill is properly endorsed, any holder thereof in good faith has title to the goods without question. Thus such an order bill of lading would be good bank collateral.

Legal incidents of bills of lading are controlled by the Federal Bill of Lading Act, passed August 29, 1916, effective January 1, 1917, as amended; the Uniform Bill of Lading Act (enacted in 29 states and Alaska); the Federal Carriage of Goods by Sea Act of 1936; and the Uniform Sales Act (enacted in 34 states, the District of Columbia, and two territories). The Carriage of Goods by Sea Act provided for the paramount clause in ocean bills of lading, i.e., that such bill of lading is subject to the provisions of the Hague Rules (adopted at international convention at The Hague in 1921). The air waybill is the forwarding and carrying agreement between the air carrier and the shipper; when the railway express agency or other express agency handles the shipment, the air waybill is issued by that agency. Contents of the uniform air waybill in foreign commerce were the subject of Section III of the Air Transportation Convention (Warsaw, 1929), which was proclaimed by the President of the U.S. in 1934. On goods moving for export, domestic bills of lading will be issued by a railroad, air carrier, or motor carrier for carriage of the goods to shipping point, where the ocean or steamer bill of lading or transocean air waybill will be exchanged for the domestic bill of lading.

The Uniform Commercial Code, prepared by the Commissioners on Uniform Laws and the American Law Institute and presented for enactment by the states beginning in 1953, restates as a whole and modernizes intrastate rules governing documents of title, including the Warehouse Receipts Act, Bill of Lading Act, and Sales Act. Article 7 of the code, which pertains to warehouse receipts, bills of lading, and other documents of title, settles conflicts in state interpretations of the Uniform Bill of Lading Act, but the federal Bill of Lading Act governs interstate shipments. In order to apply to interstate and foreign shipments, the code would require federal enactment as well.

Uniform commercial bills of lading for interstate shipments by railroads are prescribed by the Interstate Commerce Commission, e.g., the uniform domestic bill of lading, the uniform export bill of lading, and the uniform livestock contract. These forms, conforming to the federal Bill of Lading Act, have in turn influenced state forms used for intrastate shipments. Government bills of lading are prescribed by government standard forms for shipments by commercial concerns to government installations when the government pays the freight charges. Liability of shipping companies under ocean bills of lading for shipments in foreign commerce, but not in domestic commerce, is governed by the Federal Carriage of Goods by Sea Act. To the extent that water carriers come under the jurisdiction of the Interstate Commerce Commission, they are subject to the Carmack Amendment (1906) and the Cummins Amendments (1915 and 1916) to the Interstate Commerce Act affecting carrier liability. In the absence of statutes, common carriers are subject to common law rules of liability, as modified by contractual limitations on liability to the extent upheld by the courts. At the Seventh Congress of the International Chamber of Commerce in 1938, formal rules regarding documentary credits, which are observed by foreign departments of U.S. banks, were adopted by representatives of the U.S. and those of 12 other countries.

These elements of a bill of lading should be scrutinized before it is accepted as collateral: (1) date, which should be sufficiently recent so as to be persuasive that the shipment has not already been delivered (the bill should not be "stale"—a back date should arouse suspicion as to possible fraud); (2) name of issuing carrier, which should be a responsible railroad, steamship company, or air carrier; (3) points of origin and destination; (4) names of consignor and consignee (in an order bill of lading, the names of these parties may be the same, and in such case the consignor must make an endorsement in blank or special endorsement in order to convey title to the holder); (5) description of the merchandise, which should be clear and conform, in the case of ocean bills of lading, to the related documents, e.g., seller's invoice, certificate of origin, consular invoice, certificate of weight and inspection, etc.; (6) issuance in sets, which if designated as such should be complete, whether two, three, or four, as the case may be; (7) carrier's liability, which should be clearly defined therein so as to indicate the limitations on such liability.

The following terms associated with bills of lading are contained in *Black's Law Dictionary*.

Bills in a set. A series of bills of lading each bearing a number and providing that a certain bill is valid only if goods have not been delivered against another bill. U.C.C. Section 7-304.

Clean bill. One which contains nothing in the margin qualifying the words of the bill of lading itself.

Common law. The written evidence of a contract for the carriage and delivery of goods sent by sea for a certain freight. A written memorandum, given by the person in command of a merchant vessel, acknowledging the receipt on board the ship of certain specified goods, in good order or "apparent good order," which he undertakes, in consideration of the payment of freight, to deliver in like good order (dangers of the sea excepted) at a designated place to the consignee therein named or to his assigns.

Foul bill. Bill of lading containing notation that goods received by carrier were defective.

BILL OF SALE

Negotiable bill. One which by its terms calls for goods to be delivered to bearer or to order of named persons, or where recognized in overseas trade, if it runs to named persons or assigns. U.C.C. Section 7-104(2).

Ocean bill. A negotiable bill of lading used in shipment by water.

On board bill. Bill of lading which shows that loading has been completed.

Order bill. One in which it is stated that goods are consigned to order of any person named therein.

Overseas bill. Where the contract contemplates overseas shipment and contains a term C.I.F. or C. & F. or F.O.B. vessel, the seller unless otherwise agreed must obtain a negotiable bill of lading stating that the goods have been loaded on board or, in the case of a term C.I.F. or C. & F., received for shipment. U.C.C. Section 2-323(1).

Straight bill. One in which it is stated that goods are consigned to a specified person.

Through bill. One by which a railroad contracts to transport over its own line for a certain distance carloads of merchandise or stock, there to deliver the same to its connecting lines to be transported to the place of destination at a fixed rate per carload for the whole distance. Embodies undertaking to be performed in part by persons acting as agents for issuer. U.C.C. Section 7-302.

BIBLIOGRAPHY

AMERICAN LAW INSTITUTE. *Uniform Commercial Code*, Articles 2 ad 7.
INTERNATIONAL CHAMBER OF COMMERCE. *Incoterms*, 1980 rev.
———. *Uniform Customs and Practice for Documentary Credits*, Publication No. 290, 1974 rev.

BILL OF SALE A document which conveys title to, or right or interest in, personal property from the seller to the buyer.

BILLS This term has six meanings:

1. BILL OF EXCHANGE.
2. A statement of account or of money due.
3. NOTE.
4. BILL OF LADING.
5. BILL OF SALE.
6. A way bill or written list and description of goods which a railroad accepts for transporting goods.

BILLS DISCOUNTED The aggregate of notes, acceptances, and bills of exchange which a bank has discounted for its customers, as distinguished from loans; the title of an account in the general ledger which controls the BILLS DISCOUNTED LEDGER to indicate the total bills discounted.

BILLS DISCOUNTED LEDGER A subsidiary ledger in which the details of all notes, acceptances, and bills of exchange discounted are classified by customers so that the amount and nature of the liability of each borrower on this class of paper can be readily ascertained; the LIABILITY LEDGER.

BILLS DISCOUNTED OVERDUE The aggregate of notes, acceptances, and bills of exchange which were not paid at maturity and are held separately awaiting collection, legal action, or writing off as a loss. Paper which is not paid at maturity is deducted from the bills discounted account and added to bills discounted overdue, since the former contains only unmatured items. This term is also the title of a controlling account in the general ledger.

See BAD DEBTS.

BILLS DISCOUNTED REGISTER A journal or register in which notes, acceptances, and bills of exchange discounted are entered numerically and chronologically. It contains the first complete record of each note discounted, and is a permanent record. After notes are recorded in this register they are posted in the LIABILITY LEDGER.

BILLS FOR COLLECTION *See* FOREIGN COLLECTIONS.

BILLS IN A SET Bills of exchange and accompanying documents (e.g., bill of lading) are usually issued in duplicate and sometimes in triplicate.

See BILL OF LADING, FIRST OF EXCHANGE.

BILLS PAYABLE Notes or acceptances upon which a business is the principal debtor as shown by its books; aggregate sum due to trade creditors as evidenced by notes or acceptances held by them; a controlling account in the general ledger to indicate the total of notes and acceptances which the business is bound to pay at their maturity.

The term also applies to the sum which a depository institution has borrowed from the Federal Reserve bank of its district or on its own collateral note. The Federal Reserve Act requires all advances at the discount window of district Federal Reserve banks to be secured.

Until March 31, 1980, generally only member commercial banks were eligible to borrow at Federal Reserve banks. As a result of the INTERNATIONAL BANKING ACT OF 1978 (IBA) and the DEPOSITORY INSTITUTIONS DEREGULATION AND MONETARY CONTROL ACT OF 1980 (DIDMCA), all depository institutions, including U.S. branches and agencies of foreign banks, with transaction accounts or nonpersonal time deposits were given the same discount window privileges as member banks. The district Federal Reserve banks administer discount window credit under provisions of the Federal Reserve Act and Regulation A, which was amended effective September, 1980, to reflect changes brought about by the IBA of 1978 and the DIDMCA of 1980.

Starting in September, 1980, four types of credit became available to eligible depository institutions: short-term adjustment credit and three types of extended credit.

The general practice at the Federal Reserve Bank of New York has been to limit maturities on adjustment credit advances to not more than two weeks for smaller banks, to the end of the weekly reserve period for larger banks, and to overnight for the largest banks. Discount window loans may generally be renewed beyond their initial maturity if institutions need the additional time to make adjustments in their assets and liabilities. Interest on adjustment credit generally is at the basic rate, plus any surcharge which might be applied depending on the length and frequency of the borrowing.

Seasonal credit is extended for periods of up to six months to smaller depository institutions which generally lack continuous access to market funds. Advances for seasonal credit also are at the basic interest rate, plus any surcharge.

A second type of extended credit assists institutions that experience special difficulties arising from exceptional circumstances or practices involving only that institution. Assistance in these cases is provided only when funds are not available from other sources.

A third type of extended credit may be granted where more general liquidity strains affect a broad range of institutions, such as thrift institutions that emphasize longer-term, mortgage assets, to which credit may be provided to address the problems of the institutions being affected by the general situation.

In very unusual circumstances, a Federal Reserve bank may, after consultation with the Board of Governors of the Federal Reserve System, advance credit to individuals, partnerships, and corporations that are not depository institutions, if the Federal Reserve bank determines that credit is not available from other sources and failure to obtain that credit would adversely affect the economy.

Rates for extended credit other than seasonal credit may be more than the basic rate, depending upon policy considerations and money market conditions. Emergency credit for individuals, partnerships, and corporations other than depository institutions would be at a rate in excess of the highest discount rate in effect for depository institutions.

If any member bank to which advances have been made shall, during the continuance of such advances and despite official warning from the Federal Reserve bank or of the board of governors, increase its outstanding security loans (loans secured by collateral in the form of stocks, bonds, and other securities other than government securities), such advances shall immediately become due and payable, and such member bank shall be ineligible to be a borrower at the Federal Reserve bank for such period as the Board of Governors of the Federal Reserve System shall determine. Temporary carrying or clearance loans made solely for the purpose of facilitating the purchase or delivery of securities offered for public subscription shall be excluded from consideration as such security loans (Sec. 13, par. 8, Federal Reserve Act).

See REDISCOUNT, REPURCHASE AGREEMENTS.

BILLS RECEIVABLE Notes and acceptances given by customers, usually in payment of merchandise as shown by the books of a business; aggregate sum due from trade debtors evidenced by notes and acceptances upon which they are the principal debtors; a controlling account in the general ledger to indicate the total of notes and acceptances on hand and which the principal debtors thereon are bound to pay at maturity.

BIMETALLISM The free concurrent coinage of two metals, usually gold and silver, without limitation as to quantity at an established coinage or mint ratio into coins of full legal tender power. A distinction is sometimes drawn between bimetallism and the double standard. Bimetallism differs from the double standard in that in bimetallism the government mints are open to free coinage of either metal without limit. Under the double standard, while coins of both metals are endowed with full legal tender powers, only one is freely coined, the other being coined on government account only.

The U.S. was on a bimetallic standard from 1792 to 1862. The Coinage Act of April 2, 1792, established the standard on the recommendation of Alexander Hamilton, first Secretary of the Treasury, and the Act of February 25, 1861, authorized the issuance of GREENBACKS. The Coinage Act of February 12, 1873 ("Crime of '73") failed to provide for coinage of the standard silver dollar, and the Resumption Act of 1875 provided for redemption on or after January 1, 1879, of greenbacks in coin (interpreted by the Treasury to mean in gold). After a period of the LIMPING STANDARD, a gold standard with peglegs of silver, the Currency Act of 1900 (popularly referred to as the Gold Standard Act) unequivocally placed the U.S. on a gold coin standard until 1933.

BINDER A preliminary written agreement that sets forth the most significant items of a contract and gives temporary protection to the holder before the formal contract is drawn up.

BLACK FRIDAY September 24, 1869. At this time the balance of trade was heavily against the United States. Since gold was rapidly flowing out of the country and the U.S. Treasury had discontinued the sale of gold, Jay Gould, then president of the Erie Railroad and bold speculator, attempted to get a corner on the merchantable stock of gold, and to compel those who had sold it short to cover at dictated prices. He organized a pool and the joint venture plan was put into operation. The price was forced from 133 to 162 in about 20 days, the highest price being attained on Black Friday. Thereafter the price quickly receded to normal.

BLACK MONDAY Black Monday refers to October 19, 1987, when the New York Stock Exchange collapsed and triggered similar losses in major financial markets throughout the world. The Dow Jones industrial average fell 508 points, representing a loss of 22.6% of its value. Trading was extremely heavy. The volume of 606 million shares traded was almost double the previous record for volume.

The sharp drop in prices on major U.S. stock markets in October 1987 affected the stability and liquidity of the international financial system. On October 19 and 20, stock prices declined by 21% in the United Kingdom, 18% in the United States, 17% in Japan, 11% in the Federal Republic of Germany, and 10% in France. The Hong Kong market was closed.

On August 24, 1989, the Dow Jones industrial average topped its old record of 2722.42 set August 25, 1987, closing at 2734.64. This marked the market's climb back from the 1987 collapse. The rally was powered by buyout speculation, program trading, and investor enthusiasm, factors which were involved in the 1987 crash.

On October 13, 1989, the market plunged 190-points, setting off fears that another meltdown was coming. Many of the same factors that triggered the 1987 decline were also present in 1989. The market recovered the October decline during the following months.

Although panic selling contributed to the magnitude of the collapse, the collapse itself was seen as a warning that the continuing massive federal and trade deficits in the United States could lead to a more general economic collapse at some future time.

The Brady Commission's study of the October 1987 "market break" determined that the markets for stock, stock index futures, and options were not separate markets but one interrelated marketplace. The commission concluded that there were a few very important intermarket issues that should be coordinated consistently across all the separate marketplaces within the equities market. At the top of the list was a recommendation that clearing and credit mechanisms be strengthened and unified across marketplaces to reduce financial risk. During the market break, pressures caused by heavy selling and rapid changes in stock prices placed great strain on the clearing and credit mechanism.

The commission also emphasized the importance of a game plan for coordinated trading halts—circuit breakers—at times when there was a rapid change in prices. The game plan should be understood ahead of time, so that the participants in the market would know what to expect and be able to interpret what was going on. The trading halts should be coordinated across the market—the New York Stock Exchange, the Chicago Futures, the Options Exchanges, and the other exchanges, including the regional exchanges. In addition, margin requirements should be consistent across marketplaces to control speculation and financial leverage.

The commission also urged that improvements be made in the information systems so that trading could be more easily monitored and interpreted on a real-time basis. Weeks after the meltdown of the stock market, it took a very creative process to piece together what happened in the markets overall.

BLACK TUESDAY October 29, 1929, the date of the Great Crash of stock prices on the New York Stock Exchange, when the volume of trading for that single day, 16,410,000 shares, was twice the volume on any one day recorded during the preceding bull market. The Dow Jones industrial average opened on October 29, 1929, at 252.38 and plunged 40.05 points before reaching that day's low of 212.33 (from which it rebounded upward in the final two hours of trading by nearly 18 points). Actually, the October 29, 1929, low on the DJIA was penetrated November 13, 1929. On October 25, 1929, the *Wall Street Journal* had carried the famous editorial by William P. Hamilton, "A Turn in the Tide," in which he indicated that by their action on October 23, 1929, the industrial and railroad averages (Dow theory) had indicated the end of the six-year bull market and the beginning of a bear market.

See DOW THEORY.

BLAND-ALLISON ACT An act passed February 28, 1878, which required the Treasury Department to purchase at the market price not less than $2 million or more than $4 million of silver bullion a month for immediate coinage into standard silver dollars of 412.5 grains at the mint ratio of 15.988 to 1. The act was a compromise measure between those in favor of the remonetization of silver and those opposed. As first introduced it provided for the FREE COINAGE of silver, but it was later amended to read as stated above. About $25 million in silver dollars were coined annually for the ensuing 12 years, thus adding huge quantities of overvalued silver dollars to the currency. The act provided for the deposit of silver dollars in the U.S. Treasury and the issue of a corresponding amount of silver certificates redeemable in the silver dollars deposited as security. The Bland-Allison Act was repealed in 1890, and superseded by the SHERMAN SILVER-PURCHASE ACT.

The Bland-Allison Act was one of the "peglegs" of silver of the "limping standard" of the U.S. from 1879 to 1900.

See BIMETALLISM.

BLANK ENDORSEMENT An endorsement in blank speci- fies no particular endorsee and may consist of a mere signature. An instrument payable to order and endorsed in blank becomes payable to bearer and may be negotiated by delivery alone until specially endorsed. The holder may convert a blank endorsement into a special endorsement by writing over the signature of the endorser in blank any contract consistent with the character of the endorsement (Sec. 3-204 (2) and (3), Uniform Commercial Code).

See ENDORSEMENT.

BLANKET MORTGAGE A mortgage covering all the property or group of properties of a corporation which is given to secure a single debt. A blanket mortgage has about the same significance as a CLOSED END MORTGAGE.

See AFTER ACQUIRED PROPERTY CLAUSE.

BLANK TRANSFER An assignment or transfer of stock in blank.

See ASSIGNMENT, ASSIGNMENT IN BLANK.

BLIND TRUST Prior to enactment of the "qualified trust" provisions of the Ethics in Government Act of 1978 (P.L. 95-521, as amended), there was no accepted definition of a properly formulated blind trust. However, there was general agreement that the use

BLOCK

of blind trusts frequently could ameliorate potential conflicts of interest. An underlying concept is that if a government official does not know the identity of his or her financial interests, his or her official actions should not be subject to collateral attack by questions of conflict of interest or the appearance of such a conflict. In other words, if the government official does not know what he or she owns, it is impossible for him or her intentionally to take actions to benefit specifically his or her own personal interests.

Therefore, the general public policy goal to be achieved through the use of blind trusts is an actual "blindness" or lack of knowledge by the government official with respect to the holdings held in trust. In unusual cases, this goal may be deemed to have been achieved with respect to an official appointed to a position by the President, by and with the advice and consent of the Senate, where there is a general dispersion of securities held in trust among individual entities and economic sectors under circumstances in which it is unlikely that official actions taken by him or her will affect individual holdings to such a degree that the overall value of the entire portfolio will be materially enhanced. The result of wide diversification under the conditions prescribed is considered tantamount to actual blindness (Sec. 734.401(a)(1), 5 CFR 734, November 20, 1980).

The Office of Government Ethics, Office of Personnel Management (the latter was created as an independent establishment by Reorganization Plan No. 2 of 1978, effective January 1, 1979, pursuant to Executive Order 12107 of December 28, 1978, and to it were transferred many of the functions of the former United States Civil Service Commission) applies the standards of qualified trusts to specific cases as follows.

The individual or institution in charge of a qualified trust, and therefore of investing the assets of the trust, must be independent of the government official in reality and appearance. The trustee must not be subject to control or influence in the administration of the trust by any interested party: the official, spouse, or dependent children. Permissible trustees are limited to members of professional groups with standards of conduct governing their actions as fiduciaries (financial institutions, attorneys, accountants, investment advisers, and brokers). The trustee cannot be a relative, employee, or business partner of the official, spouse, or dependent children.

The trust document must, except for limited exceptions, expressly prohibit communications between the trustee and the government official, and other interested parties, regarding the trust's holdings and activities. The trustee must be empowered to make investment decisions independent of any consultation with or control by the interested parties. Generally, communications about the trust between the interested parties and the trustee must be in writing. Copies of all written communications must be filed with the Office of Government Ethics. The trust document must also provide that the interested parties will not attempt to obtain information about the trust holdings and activities except as specifically provided therein.

In the case of a qualified blind trust, an asset placed in trust by an interested party is considered a financial interest of the government official for the purposes of 18 U.S.C. 208 and any other conflict of interest statutes or regulations of the federal government until the party is notified by the trustee that the asset has been disposed of, or has a value of less than $1,000. Thus the trust is considered blind only as to assets subsequently purchased by the trustee. The interested parties will have no knowledge of the trustee's acquisitions, and thus the government official and the other interested parties will be truly blind with respect to these holdings.

In the case of a qualified diversified trust, the trust's holdings are not deemed financial interests of the government official for purposes of 18 U.S.C. 208 or any other federal conflict-of-interest law. This type of trust may only be utilized by an official appointed by the President, by and with the consent of the Senate. It must be established to the satisfaction of the Director, Office of Government Ethics that the assets of a diversified trust proposed for qualification consist of a well-diversified portfolio of readily marketable securities. None of the assets initially placed in the trust may consist of securities of issuers having substantial activities related to the reporting individual's primary area of responsibility.

Before a trust can be certified, every proposed trust document and proposed trustee must be approved by the Office of Government Ethics. This is essential so that the office can ensure in advance that the proposed trust arrangement satisfies the letter and spirit of the established standards. Model qualified trust instruments are available from the office for attorneys' use in drafting trust agreements to be proposed for qualification.

Under the provisions of Subpart G, 5 CFR 734, November 20, 1980, civil and criminal sanctions are provided for any government official or trustee who violates his or her obligation under a qualified trust. In addition, the Office of Government Ethics has authority under the act to impose appropriate administrative or other sanctions.
See TRUST.

BIBLIOGRAPHY

OFFICE OF PERSONNEL MANAGEMENT. *Executive Personnel Financial Disclosure Requirements; Employees' Responsibilities and Conduct*, 5 CFR Parts 734 and 735, November 20, 1980.

BLOCK This term has two meanings:

1. A large amount of stocks or bonds sold or offered for sale; a multiple of a full lot of stock (e.g., 1,000 shares, 6,000 shares) or of bonds (e.g., $200,000 par value).
2. A lot, batch, or bundle of checks deposited for credit with a bank together with their relative deposit slips for sorting into self-checks, clearinghouse checks, nonclearinghouse or messenger checks, and transit checks and for proving with the relative deposit slips.

See BLOCK SYSTEM.

BLOCKED CURRENCY A currency designated for a special use, as distinguished from a free universal use. A blocked currency arises from the decision of a government to withhold payments from various classes of foreign creditors, and is used as a means of controlling its exchange and trade movements. In the years 1933–1935, Germany represented a prominent example of the use of blocked exchange. In addition to free marks, a number of special types of blocked marks were established to be used only for such purposes as the German financial authorities might designate. Because the blocked marks were restricted, they were cheaper than free marks; this rule is applicable to any blocked currency or exchange. The extent to which a blocked currency is discounted from the free exchange depends upon the degree to which its use is restricted.
See EXCHANGE RESTRICTIONS.

BLOCK SYSTEM A system also known as the batch system, used in the receiving teller's, mail teller's, and clearinghouse (check) departments of a bank for sorting and proving checks against their relative deposit slips. It is a system of preliminary accounting employed in most banks of any importance to save time in proving customers' deposits before the deposit slips are posted to the individual customers' ledger or ledgers.

When deposits are received over the receiving teller's window, the receiving teller usually verifies only the cash. The checks are scrutinized only when the number is small and to note the regularity of endorsements, etc. The verification of the footing of the deposit slip with the checks is performed after the entry is made in the depositor's passbook by a special group of clerks, very often organized into a block department.

A block consists of a group of checks, usually numbering from 100 to 400, together with their relative deposit slips. To prove a block, the checks are first sorted into the divisions required by the conditions in each particular bank, e.g., self-checks, clearinghouse checks, messenger or nonclearinghouse checks, checks drawn on the U.S. Treasury, postal money orders, matured coupons, etc. After this sorting process is finished, an adding machine total of the checks is secured by divisions. Another adding machine total of the deposit slip footings is secured, which, if the block proves, equals the total of the checks.

A block is a relatively small unit of work complete in itself. Blocks can be proved as deposits come in instead of after the receiving teller's window closes for the day. If errors occur they can be discovered comparatively easily, since they are confined to a part of the work instead of all of it. It is necessary to reexamine and prove only the block in which the error exists, instead of reexamining the entire amount of deposits.

A typical form of block proof is appended.

ENCYCLOPEDIA OF BANKING AND FINANCE

Block Proof

In proving deposit tickets, clerks must number the deposit tickets, and sign this proof.		No.		Date		Proved by	

Deposit Tickets

No.	....	....	....	....	Self-checks	....	....	....	....
No.	....	....	....	....	Clearing house	....	....	....	....
No.	....	....	....	....	Messenger	....	....	....	....
No.	....	....	....	....	Transit	....	....	....	....
No.	....	....	....	....	Treasury	....	....	....	....
No.	....	....	....	....	Coupons	....	....	....	....
No.	....	....	....	....	Cash	....	....	....	....
No.	....	....	....	....		....	....	....	....
TOTAL					**TOTAL**				

BLOTTER Among bank and brokerage bookkeepers, an original entry record of transactions, e.g., securities sales blotter, securities withdrawals blotter; a journal or temporary record of transactions which are later posted to a ledger.

BLUE CHIP Taken from poker game terminology, stock issues commanding high prices, particularly in relation to earning power, relative to other stock issues; a stock to which a high degree of popular esteem or preference is attached so that it is relatively high-priced. In the game of poker, where white, red, and blue chips are used, the blue chips represent the highest value. So a blue chip stock is an active, leading, well-known stock with wide appeal, but for which a price premium is exacted by the market because of these qualities. The term in modern times is often applied to the 30 industrials contained in the DOW JONES AVERAGES.

BLUE LIST The *Blue List of Current Municipal Offerings* is a daily financial publication that provides a listing of bonds offered for sale by dealers and banks. It is one of the most complete sources of information on volume and activity in the municipal bond market. The *Blue List* is published by Standard & Poor's. The offerings are arranged by state, by issuer, by specific bond, maturity, coupon, the yield to maturity at which the bonds are being offered for sale, and the broker making the offering. A potential buyer can call the offering broker directly and negotiate a transaction price. The list is merely a way for brokers to advertise offerings of bonds; actual transactions must be negotiated directly. The Kenny wire is an electronic auction of offerings of municipal bonds that identifies the offering and the size of the issue. The Kenny wire operates through a network of teletype terminals in the offices of banks and municipal bond firms. Kenny identifies the highest bid on an offering and calls the original offered to determine whether the bid is acceptable. The Kenny wire is sponsored by the New York broker-dealer J. J. Kenny and Co. The Barban Treasury securities electronic quotation system shows Treasury securities offered at firm prices.

BLUE SKY LAWS The laws enacted by all but one state (Nevada) to provide for the issuance of securities; the flotation or sale of a particular issue or block of securities; and the regulation of the business of dealing in securities. The main purpose of blue sky laws is to prevent fraud in the sale and disposition of stocks, bonds, and other securities, and to protect the investing public, especially the inexperienced, from doubtful, fraudulent, and worthless security promotions. These laws are an outgrowth of recognition of the fact that the principle of *caveat emptor* (let the buyer beware) leaves the improvident and credulous public at the mercy of unscrupulous promoters, tipsters, and stock salespeople who purvey doubtful or worthless securities.

Kansas in 1911 was the first state to enact a blue sky law, and this was amended in 1913. It was followed by similar acts in other states, 22 of which were passed in various states in 1912–1913. The great majority of the blue sky laws are of the preventive type, requiring registration or licensing of personnel and the registration of securities, as contrasted with the punitive or antifraud type of New York, New Jersey, Maryland, and Delaware. Requirements and the details of procedure vary widely. The Federal Securities Act of 1933 does not supplant blue sky laws; consequently, nonexempt securities offerings must comply not only with the federal act but also with each state's varying requirements for nationwide offering. This situation led to formulation and presentation of the Uniform Securities Act in 1956 to the states for adoption, seeking uniformity in all or any of the four parts of the suggested act: (1) fraudulent and other prohibited practices; (2) registration of broker-dealers, agents, and investment advisers; (3) registration of securities; and (4) definitions, exemptions, judicial review, investigative, injunctive, and criminal provisions required by the first three parts.

The proposed Uniform Act, among other provisions, provides for three methods of registration of securities:

1. By notification, intended for offerings of high-quality securities exempt from SEC registration. Unless the state blue sky law administrator enters an order stopping or suspending effectiveness within two days of filing, registration automatically becomes effective.
2. By coordination, intended for issues required to be registered with the SEC. Registration under the uniform blue sky law would automatically become effective on the same date as federal registration provided the state administrator has not previously objected, and provided the registration statement has been on file 10 days, maximum and minimum prices have been filed for at least two days, and final price data are promptly furnished.
3. By qualification, where neither notification nor coordination is permissible, involving the filing by the registrant of data and documents specified.

Not all the states have adopted the Uniform Act. Since each state has its own background and experience with the operation of its blue sky law, it is unlikely that the Uniform Act will achieve complete uniformity, but at least its sponsors hope for relative uniformity within the particular parts and details of the Uniform Act legislated by the states. In particular, some states' blue sky laws go beyond the Federal Securities Act and require compliance with substantive standards (e.g., reasonable underwriters' and sellers' discounts or commissions, promoters' profits, or options).

Following is a summary of registration of personnel and issues in many state blue sky laws.

Registration or licensing of dealers and brokers, mostly annually, is required in most of the states. Information required varies from the brief to the comprehensive, and registration is not effective until receipt of certificate or license in some states, and merely upon filing in others. In a few states, a separate license for the dealer or broker is required for each issue of securities to be sold. In about half of the states requiring registration or licensing, posting of bonds is required with registration, amounts of the bonds ranging between $5,000 and $25,000; in others, merely proof of financial responsibility is sufficient. Some states require that the registrant shall have been regularly doing business within the state for a specified time, a condition

BOARD

which is impossible for many out-of-state brokers and dealers to meet. Out-of-state brokers and dealers are also generally required to assent to designation of a state agency for service of process in case of litigation. Registration or licensing of salespeople and agents is required in a majority of the states, a few of which also require the posting of bonds in amounts ranging between $500 and $5,000 per person.

A majority of the states require registration, either annually or expiring upon completion of offerings, of securities nonexempt from the registration requirement. Registration by notification is confined to securities of specified established and sound companies, and is effective upon filing of the relatively brief information required together with filing fee. Registration by qualification for other issues requires the filing of specified information on the security, which generally may not be sold until the state administrator issues the permit for sale.

See MARTIN ACT.

BIBLIOGRAPHY

Blue Sky Law Reporter. Commerce Clearing House, Chicago, IL. Looseleaf.

BOARD The board in a brokerage office upon which stock market prices and/or quotations are posted; also the stock market itself.

The New York Stock Exchange is sometimes called the Big Board. See BOARD ROOM.

BOARD LOT The unit of trading for securities upon an exchange. On the New York Stock Exchange, the unit of trading in stocks shall be 100 shares, except that in the case of certain stocks designated by the exchange the unit of trading shall be "such lesser number of shares as may be determined by the exchange, with respect to each stock so designated" (in modern times, usually 10 shares). The unit of trading in bonds is $1,000 original principal amount. In the case of rights, except as otherwise designated by the exchange, transactions in rights to subscribe are on the basis of one right accruing to each share of issued stock (New York rights), and the unit of trading in rights is 100 rights. Any order for less than the unit of trading is called an ODD LOT; all bids or offers for less than the unit of trading shall specify the principal amount of the bonds or number of shares of stock involved.

See BABY BONDS.

BOARD OF DIRECTORS See DIRECTORS.

BOARD OF TRADE An organization formed to promote community, industrial, and commercial interests, also known as a chamber of commerce. The title is also sometimes given to a special exchange, e.g., CHICAGO BOARD OF TRADE.

BOARD ROOM The customers' room of a broker's office where quotations from the principal markets, e.g., stock exchange, board of trade, etc., may be seen immediately after the transactions are consummated.

BOB English colloquialism for SHILLING.

BOBTAIL POOL A POOL in which the members acted independently of one another and not through the manager; an informal pool, in which each member closed out his contracts as he pleased, instead of acting as part of a unit.

Pools and other forms of manipulation of security prices are prohibited by the SECURITIES EXCHANGE ACT OF 1934.

BOILER PLATE Routine legal and financial clauses included in a loan contract, motions, wills, real estate closings and others. Boiler plate clauses often are required by federal or state regulatory agencies, or state/federal law. Some financial institutions and borrowers mistakenly considered these clauses to be relatively unimportant.

BONA FIDE Without fraud; in good faith.

BONANZA The Spanish word for prosperity. The word was originally applied in finance to a fortunate discovery of a rich mine, the exploitation of which made the discoverer wealthy. It is now applied colloquially to any enterprise which earns an unusually large return on its invested capital.

BOND An interest-bearing certificate of debt, being one of a series constituting a loan made to, and an obligation of, a government or business corporation; a formal promise by the borrower to pay to the lender a certain sum of money at a fixed future day with or without security, and signed and sealed by the maker (borrower); a promise to pay a principal amount on a stated future date and a series of interest payments, usually semiannually until the stated future date; "all subdivided interest-bearing contracts for the future payment of money that are drawn with formality whether they are secured or unsecured, whether the interest is imperative under all conditions, or not, as in the case of income bonds" (L. Chamberlain, *The Principles of Bond Investment*).

The difference between a bond and promissory note is aptly explained by F. A. Cleveland (*Funds and Their Uses*) as follows:

The only way that a bond is distinguished from an ordinary promissory note is by the fact that it is issued as part of a series of like tenor and amount, and, in most cases, under a common security. By rule of common law the bond is also more formal in its execution. The note is a simple promise (in any form, so long as a definite promise for the payment of money appears upon its face), signed by the party bound, without any formality as to witnesses or seal. The bond, on the other hand, in its old common-law form, required a seal and had to be witnessed in the same manner as a deed or other formal conveyance of property, and though assignable was not negotiable. This is still the rule with many jurisdictions.

A bond differs from an investment note only in the time which it has to run before maturity. Ordinarily the dividing line is five years; if the term of the funded debt exceeds this period, the issue is called bonds; if within this period, notes.

A bond differs from a share of stock in that the former is a contract to pay a certain sum of money with definite stipulations as to amount and maturity of interest payments, maturity of principal, and other recitals as to the rights of the holder in case of default, sinking fund provisions, etc. A stock contains no promise to repay the purchase price or any amount whatsoever. The shareholder is an owner; a bondholder is a creditor. The bondholder has a claim against the assets and earnings of a corporation prior to that of the stockholder, and while the bondholder is an investor, the stockholder speculates on the success of the enterprise. The former's claim is a definite contractual one; the latter's claim is contingent upon earnings.

Numerous classifications of bonds are possible. The following classifications have been selected as the most important and useful:

1. Character of obligor.
    a. Civil bonds. Examples: government bonds, state bonds, municipal bonds.
    b. Corporation bonds. Examples: railroad bonds, public utility bonds, industrial bonds.
2. Purpose of issue. Examples: equipment bonds, improvement bonds, school bonds, terminal bonds, refunding bonds, adjustment bonds.
3. Character of security.
    a. Unsecured. Examples: civil bonds, corporate debentures.
    b. Secured.
        (1) Personal security. Examples: endorsed bonds, guaranteed bonds.
        (2) Lien security. Examples: first mortgage bonds, general mortgage bonds, consolidated mortgage bonds, collateral trust bonds, chattel mortgage bonds.
4. Terms of payment of principal. Examples: straight maturity bonds, callable bonds, perpetual bonds, sinking fund bonds, serial bonds.
5. Terms of payment of interest.
    a. Fixed interest as a fixed charge.
    b. Contingent interest (payable if earned, in income bonds).
    c. Zero-interest bonds (such bonds pay no interest, but provide accretion of discount by being issued at discount but by paying full principal of bond at maturity). The Internal

Revenue Service, however, as of 1982 ruled that the zero-interest bondholder must pay income tax each year on the effective annual yield, a negative tax impact.

6. Evidence of ownership and transfer. Examples: coupon bonds, registered bonds, registered coupon bonds.

Bonds may also be classified according to tax exemption, convertibility, eligibility for investment by savings banks, insurance companies and trust funds, eligibility for securing government deposits, etc.

Bonds may also be classified as domestic or foreign bonds, the latter including Eurobonds and bonds payable as to principal and/or interest in specified choice of foreign currency as well as currency of the country of issuance.

Specific kinds of bonds are described under separate titles, e.g., ADJUSTMENT BONDS, BEARER BONDS, COLLATERAL TRUST BONDS, DEBENTURE BONDS, EXTENDED BOND, FIRST MORTGAGE BONDS, GENERAL MORTGAGE BONDS

For bibliography on bonds, *see* INVESTMENT.

See BOND CIRCULAR, BOND VALUES TABLES, COUPONS, INVESTMENT, INVESTMENT MARKET, INVESTMENT MEDIA, INVESTMENT SECURITIES.

Corporate bonds are usually issued in denominations of $1,000. The amount shown on the bond is the face value, maturity value, or principal of the bond. Bond prices are usually quoted as a percentage of face value. For example, a $1,000 bond priced to sell at $980 would be quoted at 98, which means that the bond is selling at 98% of $1,000.

The nominal or coupon interest rate on a bond is the rate the issuer agrees to pay and is also shown on the bond or in the bond agreement. Interest payments, usually made semiannually, are based on the face value of the bond and not on the issuance price. The effective or market interest rate is the nominal rate adjusted for the premium or discount on the purchase and indicates the actual yield on the bond. Bonds that have a single-fixed maturity date are term bonds. Serial bonds provide for the repayment of principal in a series of periodic installments.

If bonds are sold above face value, they are said to be sold at a premium. If bonds are sold at a premium, the effective interest rate is less than the nominal rate because the issuers received more than the face amount of the bond but are required to pay interest on only the face amount. If bonds are sold below face value, they are said to be sold at a discount. If bonds are sold at a discount, the effective interest rate paid is more than the nominal rate since the issuer received less than the face amount of the bonds but are required to pay interest on the face amount.

Callable bonds are bonds that can be redeemed by the issuer at specific prices, usually at a premium, prior to their maturity. Convertible bonds are bonds that at the option of the bondholder can be exchanged for other securities, usually equity securities of the corporation issuing the bonds during a specific time at a determined or determinable conversion rate. The conversion price is the price at which convertible securities can be converted into common stock. The conversion ratio is the number of shares of common stock or other securities that may be obtained by converting one convertible bond.

Secured bonds are bonds that have a specific claim against assets of the issuing corporation. If the corporation fails to make interest payments or the maturity payment, the pledged assets can be seized by the bondholders or his/her representative. Real estate mortgage bonds have a specific claim against certain real property of the issuer, such as land and building. A chattel mortgage bond has a claim against personal property, such as the securities owned by the bond issuer, such as stocks or bonds. Guaranteed bonds are bonds on which the payment of interest and/or principal is guaranteed by another party. Income bonds are bonds on which interest payments are made only from operating income of the issuing entity. Unsecured bonds, or debentures, are bonds the holder of which has no claim against any specific asset(s) of the issuer or others but relies on the general creditworthiness of the issuer for security.

Senior securities are securities that have claims that must be satisfied before payments can be made against junior securities. Junior securities have a lower-priority claim to asset(s) and income of the issuer than senior securities.

Registered bonds are issued in the name of the owner and are recorded in the owner's name on the records of the issuer. Coupon bonds are bearer bonds that can be transferred from one investor to another by delivery. Interest coupons are attached to the bonds. On interest payment dates, the coupons are detached and submitted for payment to the issuer or an agent. Sinking fund bonds are bonds for which a fund is established into which periodic cash deposits are made for redeeming outstanding bonds.

Bonds may be sold by the issuing company directly to investors or to an investment banker who markets the bonds. The investment banker might underwrite the issue, which guarantees the issuer a specific amount, or sell the bonds on a commission (best efforts basis for the issuer).

The price of bonds can be determined either by a mathematical computation or from a BOND VALUES TABLE. When mathematics is used, the price of a bond can be computed using present value table. The price of a bond is:

1. The present value at the effective rate of a series of interest payments (that is, an annuity) and
2. The present value of the maturity value of the bond.

To determine the price of a $1,000 four-year bond having a 7% nominal interest rate with interest payable semiannual purchased to yield 6%, use the following procedure:

1. Present value of maturity value at effective rate (3%) for 8 periods:

   $1,000 x .7894909 (= present value of 1 at 3% when the number of periods is 8) $789.41

2. Present value of an annuity of 8 interest receipts of $35 each at effective interest rate of 3%:

   $35 x 7.01969 (= present value of an annuity of 1 at 3% for 8 periods)   245.69

   Price of the bond $1,035.10

The carrying value (or book value) of the bond issue at any time is the face value plus any amortized premium or minus any unamortized discount. The periodic write-off of a bond discount or bond premium adjusts the carrying value of the bond toward the bond's face value. Amortization of the discount increases the amount of interest expense while the amortization of a premium decreases the amount of interest expense reported.

Credit rating agencies, such as Standard & Poor's, Moody, and others, report on the quality of corporate and municipal bond issues. The reports of these agencies serve as a basis for evaluating the risks, profitability, and probability of default on bond issues. Bond ratings are based on various factors, including the issuer's existing debt level; the issuer's previous record of payment; the safety of the assets or revenues committed to paying off principal and interest; the mortgage provisions in the bond indenture, the existence of a sinking fund, and others. Symbols such as AAA or Aaa (referred to as triple A) refer to the highest-quality rating. Other symbols are used to refer to high-quality bonds, investment grade bonds, substandard bonds, speculative bonds, and bonds in default.

Once established, the rating on a particular issue of corporate or municipal debt is reviewed periodically by the rating agencies. When rating changes occur, they almost always have a substantial effect on the market price of the securities. Usually, when a company announces a large new public debt issue, the rating agencies review the ratings on all of the company's outstanding securities. To avoid triggering such an overall rating review, companies have sometimes turned to bank financing in the expectation of postponing a rating review until their financial condition improves.

See BOND RATING, BOND VALUES TABLE.

BIBLIOGRAPHY

Bond Buyer.
Bond Guide.
Bond Week. Weekly.
Credit Markets. Weekly.
DARST, D. M. *The Handbook of the Bond and Money Markets.* McGraw-Hill Book Company, New York, NY, 1981.
———. *The Complete Bond Book.* McGraw-Hill Book Company, New York, NY, 1975.
DONOGHUE, W. E. "High-Risk Investments." *Executive Female,* November/December, 1988.

Dow–Jones Investor's Handbook. Dow–Jones Publishing Co., Homewood, IL. Annual.
FABOZZI, F. J., and GARLICKI, T. D. *Advances in Bond Analysis & Portfolio Strategies.* Probus Publishing Co., Chicago, IL, 1987.
HOLT, R. L. *The Complete Book of Bonds: How to Buy and Sell Profitably.* Harper & Row Publishing Co., Inc., New York, NY, 1985.
NEWPORT, J. P., JR. "Junk Bonds Face the Big Unknown." *Fortune,* May 22, 1989.
Moody's Bond Record. 1932. Monthly.
Moody's Bond Survey. 1932. Weekly.
Moody's Municipals and Governments Manual. Periodic.
SCHIFRIN, M. "Zombie Bonds." *Forbes,* April 3, 1989.
STANDARD & POOR'S. *Bond Guide,* 1938. Monthly.
———. *Called Bond Record.* Semimonthly.
———. *Credit Week.* Weekly.
———. *Directory of Bond Agents.* Bimonthly.
———. *Registered Bond Interest Record.* Weekly.
VEALE, S. R. *Bond Yield Analysis.* New York Institute of Finance, New York, NY, 1988.

BOND ACCOUNTS See GENERAL LEDGER, SECURITIES LEDGER.

BOND AMORTIZATION See AMORTIZATION.

BOND CIRCULAR An advertisement issued by a bank, syndicate, or bond house offering bonds for sale, or for the purpose of influencing purchases in bonds. Since the Securities Act of 1933, which requires REGISTRATION STATEMENT and PROSPECTUS to be filed on new offerings of securities, the term bond circular still continues to be applied to descriptive data issued on any EXEMPT SECURITY. Banks, whether or not members of the Federal Reserve System, may still underwrite U.S. Government, state, and municipal securities. A bond circular usually contains a description of the offering in detail. The elements of a well-planned bond circular are title of the bond and brief description of its security; dates of issue, maturity, and interest payments; denomination and form; amount authorized and amount issued; state and federal income taxes; conditions under which additional bonds may be issued; redemption price, if any; name of trustee; whether listed on stock exchange; guaranty, if any; description of properties of corporation issuing; past and current earnings and latest balance sheet; sinking fund specifications; territory of corporate operations; franchises, if any; engineer's and auditor's reports; attorney's opinion; whether legal for savings banks and trust funds; price and yield; reservation as to if, as, and when issued; reservation that orders are subject to prior sale; and general reservation.

BOND CROWD New York Stock Exchange members trading bonds. The bond traders enter their orders directly through terminals in their own offices or on the NYSE bond room trading floor. As of August, 1977, trading information on all listed nonconvertible bonds was almost instantaneously available through a data processing system that had been introduced on a pilot basis in 1976. The AUTOMATED BOND SYSTEM matches orders by computer and provides current quotations, size, volume, interest rates, yields, maturities, last sale, and even late news bulletins concerning bond issuers. Instead of embarking on the former nine-step manual operation and a tedious search through cabinet files, the bond crowd can now push a few buttons and find the full range of bids and offers, with size, for any bond in the system.
See ACTIVE CROWD.

BOND DISCOUNT See AMORTIZATION, DISCOUNT.

BOND DURATION A measure of the weighted average life of a bond. The present values of the cash flows expected from the bond each period are used as weights in calculating the average.
Calculating the bond duration yields a single number that measures the average age of the security in units of time such as months or years. If a security yields only one payment at maturity, for example, a zero-coupon bond, duration is equal to the maturity of the security. For securities that yield periodic payments of interest and principal up until maturity, duration is less than maturity. Duration is useful in measuring the sensitivity of bond value to changes in the market rate of interest.
Knowledge of the bond's duration provides the bondholder with an easy way to measure the interest rate risk associated with the bond. For example, assume the duration of a bond is 5 and that the current rate of interest is 10%. If the market rate were to rise to 11%, the value of the bond would fall by $[5 \times (.01/(1 + .1) = .04555]$ or 4.55%.
Because duration is the weighted average life of a bond, it is not a constant. As a bond ages, its duration changes and must be recalculated.
The concept of duration can be used to help eliminate interest rate risk. If, for example, an investor knows that he or she will need a certain amount of money at a known future date, the investor should invest in bonds of matching duration.
Because duration is an additive concept, it is possible to calculate the average duration of a bond portfolio. The calculation provides a measure of the interest rate risk associated with the portfolio as a whole.
The concept may also be applied to expected cash outflows. Thus, an institution such as a pension fund or an institutional trust may calculate the average expected duration of its liabilities. It is then possible for a portfolio manager to offset the institution's interest rate risk by investing its funds in a portfolio of bonds with an average duration that matches the duration of the liabilities of the institution.

BONDED DEBT FUNDED DEBT; the fixed debt of a government or business corporation represented by bonds.

BOND HOLDER An owner of bonds, whether COUPON BONDS, which are negotiable bonds payable to bearer, or REGISTERED BONDS, which are registered in the name of the owner as to either principal and interest or principal only. The bondholder is a creditor of the issuer.
See BOND.

BOND HOUSE A firm engaged in underwriting, distributing, and dealing in bonds primarily, and generally also other securities.
See INVESTMENT BANKER.

BOND INTEREST PAYMENTS Most bond interest payment dates, particularly of fixed interest bonds, are semiannual, such as January 1 and July 1, February 1 and August 1. Interest on income bonds, particularly those issued in connection with railroad reorganizations, is usually payable once a year, usually in March or April, when allocation of available income of the preceding calendar year is determined in accordance with indenture provisions. A minority of fixed interest bonds have quarterly interest dates.
See COUPON BONDS, QUARTERLY DISBURSEMENTS, REGISTERED BOND.

BOND MARKET Although the various STOCK EXCHANGES list bonds, the principal markets for bonds U.S. Government, federal agency, international and foreign, state and municipal, and corporate are the over-the-counter markets, with markets made and trading carried on by bond houses tending to specialize in trading as well as underwriting in one or more of these sectors. Commercial banks of larger size are also found in this field as bank dealers, underwriting and trading U.S. Government and general obligation state and municipal securities.
The bond market is predominantly institutional, with commercial banks particularly heavy investors in state and local government issues.
The above trends reflect the restriction of savings institutions largely to the bond market by statutes and administrative regulations and, on the other hand, their low motivation because of light taxability to invest in state and municipal issues, which are exempt (as to their interest income) from the federal income tax. Commercial banks, however, are subject to federal income taxes, and thus have found the tax exempts to be attractive in recent years in view of higher volume of time and savings deposits and the higher interest rates paid on such deposits.
By contrast, pension funds, investment companies, and individuals in recent years have shown relatively light increases in ownership of straight bonds, reflecting their investing preferences for convertible bonds and debentures and for common stocks directly.
See BOND, MUNICIPAL BONDS, UNITED STATES GOVERNMENT SECURITIES.

BIBLIOGRAPHY

Corporate Bond Ratings: An Overview. Standard & Poor's Corporation, New York, NY. Periodic updates.

BOND OF INDEMNITY A written instrument in which the signer, the bondsman, guarantees to protect another party against loss. It is usually used in securing a corporation against loss in the case of presentment in the future of a security lost by the owner and reissued by it. It is also used to protect the drawee bank when the drawer issues a stop-payment order against a certified check.

BOND RATINGS Measures or yardsticks of investment quality, i.e., of BUSINESS RISK and FINANCIAL RISK present in bonds. The principal rating agencies publishing ratings on bonds are Moody's (a subsidiary of Dun & Bradstreet, the latter itself specializing in municipal bond ratings) and Standard & Poor's (a subsidiary of McGraw Hill, Inc.).

Corporate Bond Ratings. Standard & Poor's Corporation, Moody's Investors Service, and Fitch Publishing Company provide quality ratings for corporate bonds, expressed in alphabetical letter grades, ranging from the highest quality designation to successively lower levels of investment quality down to speculative and in default. Bond ratings are value judgments as to possibility of default and encompass comprehensive analyses of earning power and financial condition. Although banks, in the Investment Securities Regulation of the Comptroller of the Currency, are no longer to be primarily reliant upon such bond ratings, nevertheless by analogy the four highest ratings are considered to indicate bonds eligible for investment by banks.

U.S. Government bonds are not rated, but are considered as a yardstick against which to measure all other issues. Beyond figures on the company's probable future earning power, its financial resources, its property protection (encumbrance of property by other debt), and the bond's indenture provisions, data for ratings are supplemented by managerial facts obtained from top management (e.g., product planning, research goals, expansion plans, etc.).

Municipal Bond Analysis. Revenue bonds of municipalities, which are not full faith and credit obligations and depend for debt service upon profitability of the facilities involved, are akin to corporate obligations in their dependence upon revenue trends, operating ratios, and earnings coverages of debt service. Although it is still conventional in analysis of general obligations to compute quantitative ratios, rating of municipal bonds is even more of an art than rating of corporate obligations. Quantitative ratios such as net debt to full assessed valuation, net debt per capita, and debt service percentage of operating budget have decreased in relevancy in recent years, especially for the larger municipalities, for the following reasons: (1) the changed composition of sources of revenues, the property tax decreasing in importance while reliance upon federal and state grants-in-aid has been increasing proportionately; (2) the changed composition of urban population, dramatized by the flight to the suburbs of the middle class and the proportionate rise in lower-income and welfare groups placing more strain upon municipal social services and aid; and (3) the operating budgets that provide for such social services and aid rising faster than the debt service, so that this ratio has actually declined in many instances. Instead, qualitative factors have assumed increased importance, such as trends and structural diversification of business and industry, and internal versus external sources of revenues and their relative stability. Overall, the quality of the municipality's administration in facing the numerous social and economic problems is crucial.

See COMPTROLLER'S REGULATION, NATIONAL BANK SECURITIES REGULATIONS.

BIBLIOGRAPHY

Corporate Bond Ratings: An Overview. Standard & Poor's Corporation, New York, NY. Periodic updates.

BOND REGISTER An original entry record kept by a bank or trust company for entering the details of each purchase or sale of bonds belonging to the investment account. From the register or journal, postings are made to the bond or securities ledger. Bond register is also applied to the record kept by a corporation of its bonds sold direct, and to the records of the registrar of bonds, such as a bank or trust company, when acting in that capacity for a corporation which has issued registered bonds.

See SECURITIES LEDGER.

BONDS AS LEGAL INVESTMENTS *See* LEGALITY OF SECURITIES, LIFE INSURANCE COMPANY INVESTMENTS, SAVINGS BANK INVESTMENTS, TRUST FUND INVESTMENTS.

BOND VALUES TABLE Tables of bond yields or bond values which assist in computing bond yields to maturity, or in calculating the price of value of a bond necessary to afford a given yield to a given maturity.

Various types of tables are available. For computing bond yields to maturity, the Rollins tables show the value to the nearest cent of a bond of specified maturity bearing interest rates of 2%, 2.5%, 3%, 3.5%, 4%, 4.5%, 5%, 6%, and 7%, and yielding from 2% to 7%. Appended is a sample from the 20 years' maturity table, interest payable semiannually. It is apparent from the table that a 20-year 4% bond, interest payable semiannually, purchased at 103.50, will yield 3.75% to maturity.

By means of interpolation, or calculation based on proportion of differences, exact yields not directly given by the table may be calculated. For example, the yield to maturity of a 20-year 4% bond, interest payable semiannually, purchased at 104, is not directly given by the table. However, the table does show nearest prices of 104.21, at which yield to maturity is 3.70%, and 103.50, at which yield to maturity is 3.75%. The differences are 0.71 in price and 0.05% in yield. Since the given purchase price, 104, is 0.50 greater than 103.50, it will therefore yield 50/71 of 0.05% less than 3.75% and, conversely, 21/71 of 0.05% more than 3.70%. In either case, the answer is 3.7148% or, rounded out, 3.72%.

Similarly, it may be desired to calculate the price or value of a 20-year 4% bond, interest payable semiannually, necessary to afford a 3.75% yield to maturity. It is apparent from the table that the price is 103.50. Where the exact price is not directly given by the table, it may be calculated by means of interpolation. For example, it may be desired to calculate the price or value of a 20-year 4% bond, interest payable semiannually, necessary to yield 4.85% to maturity. The nearest prices given are 89.79, at which the yield is 4.80%, and 88.90, at which the yield is 4.875%. The difference of 0.075% in yield is equal to the difference of 0.89 in price. Therefore, the difference of 0.05% between 4.80% and the required yield of 4.85% is equal to a difference of 0.593 in price (0.05/0.075 of 0.89 or, expressed in ratio form, 0.075:0.89 as 0.05:0.593). This indicates a price of approximately 89.25 (89.79 less 0.593, or 89.197).

See YIELD.

BONUS A gift; gratuity; something which is given free in addition to what is called for by a contract.

See BONUS BONDS, BONUS STOCK.

BONUS BONDS Bonds issued in payment of, or to raise money for, promoters' services, or bonds issued by a municipality to induce a manufacturing industry to locate in or a railroad to enter the town. The validity of such bonds is questionable. As investments these bonds are to be avoided. This title is sometimes also given to soldiers' bonus bonds, as soldiers' adjusted compensation bonds, issued by various states to raise funds to pay bonuses to veterans of the world wars.

See RAILROAD BONDS.

BONUS STOCK Shares of stock given as a bonus to purchasers thereof; for instance, a certain percentage of common stock is sometimes given with purchases of bonds or the preferred stock of a corporation. This is tantamount to selling bonds or stock at a discount. The laws of some states prohibit the issuance of bonus stock or else make the holder liable for the par value thereof.

See FOUNDERS' SHARES.

BOOK On the stock exchange, the specialist's book which contains the limited orders to buy and sell the stocks in which the specialist specializes. As limited orders are conveyed to the floor for execution at prices away from the prevailing market levels, their quantity and price are entered on the buying or selling side of the book of the specialist who handles the transactions in the

BOOK CREDIT

Bond Values Table:
20 Years' Maturity, Interest Payable Semiannually

Yield to maturity (percent per annum)	Price for bond with coupon of

Yield	3%	3.5%	4%	4.5%	5%	6%	7%
2.900	101.51	109.06	116.60	124.15	131.70	146.80	161.89
3.000	100.00	107.48	114.96	122.44	129.92	144.87	159.83
3.100	98.52	105.93	113.34	120.75	128.16	142.98	157.81
3.125	98.15	105.55	112.94	120.33	127.73	142.52	157.31
3.200	97.06	104.41	111.75	119.09	126.44	141.13	155.82
3.250	96.34	103.66	110.97	118.28	125.59	140.21	154.83
3.300	95.63	102.91	110.19	117.47	124.75	139.30	153.86
3.350	94.93	102.17	109.42	116.66	123.91	138.40	152.89
3.375	94.58	101.81	109.04	116.27	123.49	137.95	152.41
3.400	94.23	101.44	108.66	115.87	123.08	137.51	151.93
3.450	93.54	100.72	107.90	115.08	122.26	136.62	150.98
3.500	92.85	100.00	107.15	114.30	121.45	135.74	150.04
3.550	92.17	99.29	106.41	113.52	120.64	134.87	149.11
3.600	91.50	98.58	105.67	112.75	119.84	134.01	148.18
3.625	91.16	98.23	105.30	112.37	119.44	133.58	147.72
3.650	90.83	97.88	104.94	111.99	119.04	133.15	147.26
3.700	90.17	97.19	104.21	111.24	118.26	132.30	146.35
3.750	89.51	96.50	103.50	110.49	117.48	131.46	145.44
3.800	88.86	95.82	102.78	109.74	116.70	130.63	144.55
3.875	87.90	94.81	101.73	108.64	115.56	129.39	143.22
3.900	87.58	94.48	101.38	108.26	115.18	128.98	142.78
4.000	86.32	93.16	100.00	106.84	113.68	127.36	141.03
4.100	85.09	91.86	98.64	105.42	112.20	125.76	139.32
4.125	84.78	91.54	98.31	105.07	111.84	125.37	138.90
4.200	83.87	90.59	97.31	104.03	110.75	124.19	137.63
4.250	83.27	89.96	96.65	103.35	110.04	123.42	136.80
4.300	82.68	89.34	96.00	102.66	109.33	122.65	135.98
4.375	81.80	88.42	95.04	101.65	108.27	121.51	134.75
4.400	81.51	88.11	94.72	101.32	107.93	121.14	134.35
4.500	80.35	86.90	93.45	100.00	106.55	119.65	132.74
4.600	79.22	85.72	92.21	98.70	105.19	118.18	131.16
4.625	78.94	85.42	91.90	98.38	104.86	117.82	130.77
4.700	78.11	84.55	90.99	97.43	103.86	116.74	129.61
4.750	77.57	83.98	90.39	96.80	103.20	116.02	128.84
4.800	77.02	83.40	89.79	96.17	102.55	115.32	128.08
4.875	76.22	82.56	88.90	95.24	101.59	114.27	126.95
4.900	75.95	82.28	88.61	94.94	101.27	113.92	126.58
5.000	74.90	81.17	87.45	93.72	100.00	112.55	125.10
5.100	73.86	80.09	86.31	92.53	98.76	111.20	123.65
5.125	73.61	79.82	86.03	92.24	98.45	110.87	123.29
5.200	72.85	79.02	85.19	91.36	97.53	109.87	122.22
5.250	72.34	78.49	84.64	90.78	96.93	109.22	121.51
5.300	71.85	77.97	84.09	90.21	96.33	108.57	120.81
5.375	71.11	77.19	83.27	89.36	95.44	107.60	119.77
5.400	70.87	76.94	83.01	89.07	95.14	107.28	119.42
5.500	69.90	75.92	81.94	87.96	93.98	106.02	118.06
5.625	68.72	74.68	80.64	86.59	92.55	104.47	116.39
5.750	67.57	73.46	79.36	85.26	91.15	102.95	114.74
5.875	66.43	72.27	78.11	83.95	89.78	101.46	113.13
6.000	65.33	71.11	76.89	82.66	88.44	100.00	111.56
6.125	64.25	69.97	75.69	81.41	87.13	98.57	110.01
6.250	63.19	68.85	74.51	80.18	85.84	97.17	108.50
6.375	62.15	67.76	73.36	78.97	84.58	95.79	107.01
6.500	61.14	66.69	72.24	77.79	83.34	94.45	105.55
6.625	60.14	65.64	71.14	76.64	82.13	93.13	104.12
6.750	59.17	64.62	70.06	75.50	80.95	91.83	102.72
6.875	58.22	63.61	69.00	74.39	79.78	90.57	101.35
7.00	57.29	62.63	67.97	73.31	78.64	89.32	100.00

issue in question. By reference to the book where orders are arranged in order of price, it is possible to ascertain quickly the number of shares wanted at each level down, and the number offered at each step up.

See SPECIALISTS.

BOOK CREDIT See OPEN ACCOUNT.

BOOK CROWD A section of the bond trading department of the NEW YORK STOCK EXCHANGE, also called the inactive or cabinet crowd, which handles inactive bonds.

See ACTIVE CROWD.

BOOK ENTRY The book-entry program of the Federal Reserve System and U.S. Treasury, the New York Federal Reserve Bank points out, has succeeded in steadily replacing paper U.S. Government and federal agency securities with computer entries at Federal Reserve banks. With the elimination of certificates, government and agency securities are better safeguarded and more rapidly transferred throughout the banking system.

Securities in book-entry form are less vulnerable to theft and loss, cannot be counterfeited, and do not require counting or recording by certificate number. In addition, owners need not cut coupons to obtain interest payments or present certificates to redeem securities at maturity. The New York Fed reports that by the close of 1980, some 94% of the total outstanding marketable government securities, and about 99.5% of total outstanding federal agency securities, were in computerized book-entry form.

The first steps toward modern securities clearance were taken in the 1920s, when Treasury securities became transferable by telegraphic wire within the Federal Reserve System. At that time, all transfers required specific approval by the Treasury's Commissioner of the Public Debt. In time, these telegraphic securities transfers became known as CPDs.

Under the early CPD system, the sender of a security—usually a commercial bank—delivered certificates to the local Federal Reserve office. That office, as fiscal agent of the U.S., retired the securities and sent a telegram to another Reserve office located near the institution receiving the security. The Reserve office receiving the telegram issued identical physical securities to the bank to which they were being transferred or deposited them in that bank's safekeeping account at the Federal Reserve. Thus, the CPD arrangement required individual deliveries of paper securities to and pickups from Federal Reserve offices for each transfer transaction between the Federal Reserve and a financial institution.

The difficulties involved in making "street" deliveries of government securities to and from the Federal Reserve Bank in New York City, and among the banks and dealers in the city, led to the establishment of New York's Government Securities Clearing Arrangement (GSCA) in 1965. At the end of 1977, when the need to settle transactions in physical securities was eliminated, the GSCA was disbanded. Under the GSCA, the Federal Reserve Bank of New York and 12 of the largest New York City banks arranged to make transfers by teletype message, debiting or crediting the bank's securities clearing account on the books of the New York Fed. Using this method, only one delivery of securities to or from each participating bank was necessary at the end of the day and only in the net amount due to or from that bank.

Banks participating in the former GSCA program, as well as 23 other banks in the New York Federal Reserve District, several federal agencies, and two international organizations, now are linked by on-line communications facilities to a computer system at the New York Fed, and through that system to one another. A similar electronic network connects all Federal Reserve banks and branches in the U.S. Thus, each participant in this New York wire network can make transfers for its own account, or for customer accounts, directly from communications terminals on its own premises to any other participant. Also, transfers can be made through the New York Fed and the Reserve System's computer center at Culpeper, Virginia, to any member bank in the U.S. via its local Federal Reserve bank or branch.

In 1968, another major step toward automating the government securities market was taken when federal regulation authorized the first book-entry procedures to eliminate paper representing a government obligation. Under book-entry procedures, securities are entered electronically on the records of a Reserve bank. All marketable government securities held by member banks—whether owned by them or held on behalf of correspondent banks or other customers—are eligible for book-entry conversion and for transfer by wire.

As a result of the International Banking Act of 1978 and the Depository Institutions Deregulation and Monetary Control Act of 1980, U.S. branches and agencies of foreign banks and domestic depository institutions will have access to book-entry conversion and wire transfer services at explicitly set prices. Also, any eligible

ENCYCLOPEDIA OF BANKING AND FINANCE

securities a depository institution purchases, such as weekly Treasury bills, notes, or bonds, can be issued directly in book-entry form when originally sold.

Customers of depository institutions also can use book-entry facilities. For example, if a brokerage firm purchases new Treasury securities at a Federal Reserve bank, it can instruct the Federal Reserve bank to deliver the purchased securities to the firm's commercial bank for its account. No physical securities are issued. If later the brokerage firm needs physical securities for some purpose, it can obtain them. The firm instructs its commercial bank to obtain the paper securities from a Federal Reserve bank. On instructions from the commercial bank, the Federal Reserve bank issues the securities to the commercial bank, which in turn delivers them to or on behalf of the brokerage firm.

As part of the program to expand use of book-entry procedures, the Treasury began in December, 1976, issuing 52-week Treasury bills in book-entry form only. At that time, the Treasury also began to establish direct book-entry accounts for any subscribers who elected not to deal through commercial banks. This service was provided at no cost to subscribers, who could present tenders and payments either through a Federal Reserve bank or directly to the Department of the Treasury in Washington, D.C.

Other bill maturities were phased in during 1977, and by September, 1977, physical bills had been virtually eliminated. Physical securities were issued to a limited class of holders required by law or regulation to hold securities in physical form. That practice ended in December, 1978. The Treasury also planned eventually to cease issuance of physical notes and bonds.

BOOKKEEPING A distinction is made between accounting and bookkeeping. Bookkeeping is usually associated with the mechanical, routine, and repetitive aspects of the accounting process, such as journalizing (recording a transaction in a journal, the book of original entry), posting (transferring of amounts from a journal to a ledger—a book of accounts), and taking a trial balance (list of ledger accounts with their balances). Accounting relates to the theoretical, conceptual, and logical relationships of the entire information system as well as to the practical operations of the system. Accounting is concerned with such matters as the preparation of financial statements, compliance with generally accepted accounting principles, the fairness of the financial statements, system design, transaction analysis, budgeting, income taxes, and cost reports. Accounting includes bookkeeping.

BOOKS *See* BANK BOOKKEEPING.

BOOKS CLOSE The day on which the transfer books of a corporation close in order that the corporation itself (if doing its own work) or its transfer agent may make a correct list of the stockholders who are entitled to receive the dividend declared on the payable date. The term record date refers to either the date for the taking of a record of the holders of a stock (the books need not close for such purpose) or the date for the closing of the transfer books for such stock. Books close does not refer to the EX DIVIDEND date, nor does the record date. The method of delivery regular way normally determines the ex dividend dates on security markets. Most common regular way delivery basis is the five-day delivery basis. Pursuant thereto, the normal generally understood procedure is to allow ex dividend dealings to commence on the stock on the fourth business day prior to the record date, and this procedure is followed whenever possible. Deferment of ex dividend dealings necessitates the use of DUE BILL in dealing in the stock on the security market during the period of deferment and, being a deviation from the normal ex dividend procedure, sometimes results in confusion. Consequently, such deferment is avoided, by the New York Stock Exchange for example, except when required by the public interest, as in the case of a large stock dividend, or in the case where payment of a stock dividend is subject to fulfillment of some requirement or condition which will not or may not be fulfilled before the normal ex dividend date (fourth business day prior to the record date).

Cash transactions made on the ex dividend date and up to and including the record date carry the dividend.

See CLOSING THE BOOKS, DELIVERIES.

BOOKS OPEN The day the transfer books of a corporation are open for the transfer of stocks, after having been closed over an interval for the purpose of determining the stockholders of record who are entitled to receive dividends, to vote, etc.

See BOOKS CLOSE, STOCK TRANSFERS.

BOOK VALUE The value of a business as a whole, or of one of its assets as shown by its accounting records. For instance, the book value of a bond is the amount at which it is carried on the books. Originally it should be entered at cost. Subsequently the amount may be changed to bring it into agreement with its amortized value. Similarly, the book value of a fixed asset is original cost, plus additions and improvements, less reserve for depreciation and less retirements, although frequently fixed assets are arbitrarily marked down below true book values.

The book value of a corporation is its stockholders equity. Where there are various classes of owners, book value is sometimes expressed in terms of dollars per share of its common stock, after deducting the value of the preferred stock at liquidation preference. The surplus, whether free (e.g., available for dividends) or set aside in equity reserves, belongs to the common stockholders. Thus a corporation that has common stock totaling one million dollars (10,000 shares at $100 par value), surplus of $600,000, and an equity type reserve of $200,000 has a book value of $180. The book value of no par common stock is found by dividing the amount of the capital plus retained earnings and reserves by the number of outstanding shares.

The book value of a partnership is equal to the sum of the partners' capital accounts plus undivided profits, if any. The book value of a sole proprietorship is shown by the proprietor's capital account after adjustment for profits or losses, contributions, or withdrawals.

The book value (or carrying value) of a bond issue at any time is the face value plus any unamortized premium or minus any unamortized discount. The periodic write-off of a bond discount or bond premium adjusts the carrying value of the bond toward the bond's face value.

In security analysis, it has been conventional to compute the book value on a tangible basis, i.e., tangible net asset value per share, after deduction completely of goodwill, patents, and any other intangibles carried in the balance sheet. This traditional practice presumably had its origin historically in the often artificial and "watered" asset values assigned to intangible assets. Accounting principle, however, calls today for capitalizing goodwill if purchased; if permanent, goodwill need not necessarily even be written off against retained earnings.

See AMORTIZED VALUES, GOODWILL, INTANGIBLES, ASSET VALUE.

BOOM A movement characterized by industrial and commercial activity, rising prices, and sentimentally by optimism and speculative enthusiasm until unwarranted high levels are reached, culminating in a reaction. Booms are both specific and general. There may be specific booms in land, stocks, bonds, or grain, acting independently of one another. A general boom is one in which the values of all properties, securities, and commodities rise sympathetically.

See BUSINESS CYCLE, INFLATION, PROSPERITY.

BOOT Monetary consideration related to exchanges of property, plant, and equipment (nonmonetary assets); the "other property" received in an exchange which, but for such other property, the transaction would be nontaxable (tax).

BORDERLINE ROAD In analysis of railroad securities, a railroad which is in a marginal position, i.e., has a weak credit position or low earning power as indicated by narrow margin of coverage of fixed charges.

See RAILROAD BONDS.

BORROWED BONDS Bonds are sometimes borrowed by one bank from another with or without commission because of a shortage of bonds eligible to secure government deposits or to serve as collateral for loans with a Federal Reserve bank. An account should be set up in the general ledger to show the liability for borrowed bonds, if any.

Bonds, like stocks, are sometimes borrowed by brokers in order to arrange for delivery when SHORT SALE contracts have been made by customers.

BORROWED STOCK Stock borrowed by brokers in order to make delivery on SHORT SALE contracts executed for customers.

BORROWER A person or concern to which money is loaned. There are as many classes of borrowers as there are classes of loans.
See LOAN.

BORROWING PEAK The period of a business when its borrowings from banks normally stand at the highest figure of the year. Most businesses are seasonal in character and require more capital at some periods than at others. The periodic recurrence of the heaviest demand for working capital is called the seasonal peak. The borrowing peak is reached at this time. Bank credit and loan officers know when the borrowing peak for each class of trade occurs and plan to meet the requirements of their customers accordingly. While the borrowing peak varies among merchants and manufacturers, the borrowing peak for the largest number of enterprises occurs in the fall of the year.

BORROWING POWER The capacity of an individual, firm, or corporation to borrow or to procure accommodation at a bank.
See CREDIT.

BOSTON LEDGER A form of ledger, also known as the progressive ledger, which has been almost universally adopted throughout banking practice. Instead of giving a page to each account, as in the case of a balance ledger, one writes or prints the names of the accounts (usually 20 to 30 on a page) in alphabetical order vertically down the ledger sheet, with occasional spaces allowed for inserting new names. Preferably the names should be printed down the center of the page. The days run horizontally across the width of two pages, the column for each day being divided to provide for debit and credit postings.

The advantages of the Boston ledger are that it provides immediate availability of the balance of each account, which is carried forward each day and can be ascertained at a glance; it allows for quick posting and proving; and it saves space. Since there are about 20 to 30 accounts on a page, it is not necessary to thumb so many pages in order to locate a given account, as in the case of the balance ledger.

Its disadvantage is its inflexibility. It must be renewed frequently, not only because each page provides for a limited number of days, but also to allow for changes in titles of accounts.

BOSTON STOCK EXCHANGE Organized on October 13, 1834, this stock exchange has with a single exception continued its activities uninterruptedly since that date. The exception represented the period from July 30, 1913, to December 10, 1914, when the Boston Stock Exchange, like the New York Stock Exchange and other exchanges, suspended operations temporarily because of the chaotic conditions precipitated by the beginning of World War I.

The original name adopted was the Boston Stock and Exchange Board. It was not until about 1885 that memberships, or seats, were considered to have a transferable value. Since April 11, 1911, the exchange has been located at 53 State Street. On January 18, 1892, a stock exchange clearinghouse was organized, the second of its kind in the country. For the first time in the Boston Stock Exchange's history, an incorporated securities firm was admitted to full membership on June 23, 1941. Thus the Boston Stock Exchange became the first of the larger national securities exchanges to extend full membership to an incorporated firm.

In 1965, the Board of Governors of the Boston Stock Exchange ordered a broad reorganization of the exchange, including the employment of a full-time president and staff to replace the former voluntary committee system of administration of the exchange. The new president began his duties in August, 1965. Effective November, 1965, the Boston Stock Exchange amended its rules, as have several other regional stock exchanges, to permit its members to share commissions with nonmembers. Trading volume rose, prices of seats increased, and membership expanded. To accommodate the increased volume, trading facilities were modernized.

BOTTOM When average prices reach the lowest level in a major swing, the market is said to be touching bottom or dragging bottom. The bottom usually is reached when, or shortly before, a business depression is at its worst, confidence impaired, sales and earnings small, prices low, and buying power limited. It is recognized by a period of dullness and small price fluctuations, following a long consistent downward trend in prices. It is characteristic of the market to make two low dips at either end of the low level before the reverse trend sets in. This is known as the double bottom and is regarded as an indication that the downward price movement has been concluded. Inasmuch as the bottom marks the lowest ebb of business, it also heralds the beginning of the next major swing upward.
See BUSINESS CYCLE, SPECULATIVE CYCLE, SWINGS.

BOTTOM DROPPED OUT A sharp decline in prices occurring when the market is already believed to be well-liquidated, or touching bottom, thereby creating a panicky condition.

BOTTOM PRICE The lowest price; the price at which a single security, or the market average, reaches the lowest point in a single day's trading, or in a major or minor movement.

BOTTOMRY A loan secured by a lien on a vessel.
See BOTTOMRY BOND.

BOTTOMRY BOND A document by which the master of a ship pledges the vessel as collateral for a loan. This may become necessary when a ship is in a foreign port and the master has no other means of raising funds to make certain repairs required to enable the ship to continue its voyage. A master has no authority to bind a shipowner, except in case of necessity, and the lender must use caution to see that the repairs are urgent. Sometimes the master pledges both the vessel and its cargo for a loan. In this case the document is a RESPONDENTIA bond.

BOURSE The stock exchanges in the principal cities of continental Europe. Boerse is the Dutch equivalent, and Bolsa the Spanish equivalent. The word is usually capitalized in order to distinguish it from the French *la bourse*, which means the purse.

Generally, the European Bourses have been active since the 1950s, reflecting Western European economic recovery.
See PARIS BOURSE.

BOURSIERS The accredited members of the PARIS BOURSE.

BRACKET CREEP A reference to the movement of taxpayers into higher tax brackets as their income rises to keep pace with inflation. In 1985, the tax laws were changed to provide for indexing to eliminate bracket creep by raising the tax brackets, personal exemptions, and standard deduction each year to reflect the rising cost of living.

BRANCH BANKING The system of banking in which a banking institution conducts branches or offices at locations other than that of the main or head office, as distinguished from single-office banking. In many foreign countries, notably in Canada, England, France, and Germany, the branch system of banking prevails. In the U.S., by contrast, there is no nationwide branch banking.

Branch banking is to be distinguished from CHAIN BANKING and GROUP BANKING. As defined by the Board of Governors of the Federal Reserve System, branch banking is a type of multiple-office banking under which a bank as a single legal entity operates more than one banking office. Chain banking refers to the type of multiple-office banking in which the operations or policies of at least three independently incorporated banks are controlled by one or more individuals, such chain systems being generally built around a key bank. Group banking is the type of multiple-office banking in which three or more independently incorporated banks are controlled directly or indirectly by a corporation, business trust, association, or similar organization, generally popularly called a bank holding company.
See BANK HOLDING COMPANY ACT.

The branches of a bank are considered separate and distinct. Checks drawn on a particular branch are usually not payable at another branch or at the main office. If deposited for credit at another branch, they are cleared through the clearinghouse in the same manner as a check drawn on a separate institution. Similarly, notes payable at a branch office may not be presented for payment at the head office or any other branch office.

Branch Banking Laws

State authorization of branch banking varies according to the broad categories in the appended table. (Reference to specific state law is necessary for details.) Federal law may be summarized as follows.

Geographic Restrictions on Branch Banking in the States (September 1985)

Statewide branch banking prevalent	Limited branch banking prevalent	Unit banking prevalent
Alabama	Arkansas	Colorado
Alaska	Georgia	Illinois
Arizona	Indiana	Kansas
California	Iowa	Missouri
Connecticut	Kentucky	Montana
Delaware	Louisiana	North Dakota
Florida	Michigan	Texas
Hawaii	Minnesota	Wyoming
Idaho	Mississippi	
Maine	Nebraska	
Maryland	New Hampshire	
Massachusetts	New Mexico	
Nevada	Ohio	
New Jersey	Pennsylvania	
New York	Tennessee	
North Carolina	Virginia	
Oregon	West Virginia	
Rhode Island	Wisconsin	
South Carolina		
South Dakota		
Utah		
Vermont		
Washington		

Source: Conference of State Bank Supervisors, *A Profile of State-Chartered Banking* (Washington, D.C.: Conference of State Supervisors, 1986).

National Banks.
Branches permitted: 12 U.S.C. 36 (R.S. 5155) provides:

(c) A national banking association may, with the approval of the Comptroller of the Currency, establish and operate new branches: (1) Within the limits of the city, town, or village in which said association is situated, if such establishment and operation are at the time expressly authorized to State banks by the law of the State in question; and (2) at any point within the State in which said association is situated, if such establishment and operation are at the time authorized to State banks by the statute law of the State in question by language specifically granting such authority affirmatively and not merely by implication or recognition, and subject to the restrictions as to location imposed by the law of the State on State banks. In any State in which State banks are permitted by statute law to maintain branches within county or greater limits, if no bank is located and doing business in the place where the proposed agency is to be located, any national banking association situated in such State may, with the approval of the Comptroller of the Currency, establish and operate, without regard to the capital requirements of this section, a seasonal agency in any resort community within the limits of the county in which the main office of such association is located, for the purpose of receiving and paying out deposits, issuing and cashing checks and drafts, and doing business incident thereto: *Provided,* That any permit issued under this sentence shall be revoked upon the opening of a State or national bank in such community.

12 U.S.C. 36 (R.S. 5155) further provides:

(a) A national banking association may retain and operate such branch or branches as it may have in lawful operation at the date of the approval of this Act (February 25, 1927), and any national banking association which has continuously maintained and operated not more than one branch for a period of more than twenty-five years immediately preceding the approval of this Act (February 25, 1927) may continue to maintain and operate such branch.

(b) (1) National Bank resulting from the conversion of a State bank may retain and operate as a branch any office which was a branch of the State bank immediately prior to conversion if such office—

(A) might be established under subsection (c) of this section as a new branch of the resulting National Bank, and is approved by the Comptroller of the Currency for continued operation as a branch of the resulting National Bank;

(B) was a branch of any bank on February 25, 1927; or

(C) is approved by the Comptroller of the Currency for continued operation as a branch of the resulting National Bank.

The Comptroller of the Currency may not grant approval under clause (C) of this paragraph if a State bank (in a situation identical to that of the National Bank) resulting from the conversion of a National Bank would be prohibited by the law of such State from retaining and operating as a branch an identically situated office which was a branch of the National Bank immediately prior to conversion.

(2) A National Bank (referred to in this paragraph as the "resulting bank"), resulting from the consolidation of a National Bank (referred to in this paragraph as the "national bank") under whose charter the consolidation is effected with another bank or banks, may retain and operate as a branch any office which, immediately prior to such consolidation, was in operation as—

(A) a main office or branch office of any bank (other than the national bank) participating in the consolidation if, under subsection (c) of this section, it might be established as a new branch of the resulting bank, and if the Comptroller of the Currency approves of its continued operation after the consolidation;

(B) a branch of any bank participating in the consolidation, and which, on February 25, 1927, was in operation as a branch of any bank; or

(C) a branch of the National Bank and which, on February 25, 1927, was not in operation as a branch of any bank, if the Comptroller of the Currency approves of its continued operation after the consolidation.

The Comptroller of the Currency may not grant approval under clause (C) of this paragraph if a State bank (in a situation identical to that of the resulting National Bank) resulting from the consolidation into a State bank of another bank or banks would be prohibited by the law of such State from retaining and operating as a branch an identically situated office which was a branch of the State bank immediately prior to consolidation.

(3) As used in this subsection, the term "consolidation" includes a merger ...

(e) No branch of any national banking association shall be established or moved from one location to another without first obtaining the consent and approval of the Comptroller of the Currency.

(f) The term "branch" as used in this section shall be held to include any branch bank, branch office, branch agency, additional office, or any branch place of business located in any State or Territory of the United States or in the District of Columbia at which deposits are received, or checks paid, or money lent ....

(h) The words "State bank," "State banks," "bank," or "banks," as used in this section, shall be held to include trust companies, savings banks, or other such corporations or institutions carrying on the banking business under the authority of State laws.

Capital required:

(c) ... no such association shall establish a branch outside of the city, town, or village in which it is situated unless it has a combined capital stock and surplus equal to the combined amount of capital stock and surplus, if any, required by the law of the State in which such association is situated for the establishment of such branches by State banks, or, if the law of such State requires only a minimum capital stock for the establishment of such branches by State banks, unless such association has not less than an equal amount of capital stock.

(d) The aggregate capital of every national banking association and its branches shall at no time be less than the aggregate minimum capital required by law for the establishment of an equal number of national banking associations situated in the various places where such association and its branches are situated.

The provisions regarding capital requirements for the establishment of branches do not apply to the establishment of seasonal agencies in resort communities.

State Member Banks.
Branches permitted: Section 9, Paragraph 3 of the Federal Reserve Act provides:

Any such State bank which, at the date of approval of this Act (February 25, 1927), has established and is operating a branch or branches in conformity with the State law, may retain and operate the same while remaining or upon becoming a stock holder of such Federal Reserve bank; but no such State bank may retain or acquire stock in a Federal Reserve bank except upon relinquishment of any branch or branches established after the date of the approval of this Act (February 25, 1927) beyond the limits of the city, town, or village in which the parent bank is situated: *Provided, however,* that nothing herein contained shall prevent any State member bank from establishing and operating branches in the United States or any dependency or insular possession thereof or in any foreign country, on the same terms and conditions and subject to the same limitations and restrictions as are applicable to the establishment of branches by national banks except that approval of the Board of Governors of the Federal Reserve System, instead of the Comptroller of the Currency, shall be obtained before any State member bank may hereafter establish any branch and before any State bank hereafter admitted to membership may retain any branch established after February 25, 1927, beyond the limits of the city, town, or village in which the parent bank is situated. The approval of the Board shall likewise be obtained before any State member bank may establish any new branch within the limits of any such city, town, or village (except within the District of Columbia).

Capital required: Same as for establishment of branches by national banks.
"Bank" defined: Section 1, Paragraph 2 of the Federal Reserve Act states:

Wherever the word "'bank" is used in this Act, the word shall be held to include State bank, banking association, and trust company, except where national banks or Federal Reserve banks are specifically referred to.

Insured State Banks Not Members of Federal Reserve System.
Branches permitted: Section 18(d), Federal Deposit Insurance Act, provides:

No State nonmember insured bank (except a District bank) shall establish and operate any new branch unless it shall have the prior written consent of the Corporation (the F.D.I.C.), and no State nonmember insured bank (except a District bank) shall move its main office or any branch from one location to another without such consent. The factors to be considered in granting or withholding the consent of the Corporation under this subsection shall be ... (the same factors which the F.D.I.C. is required to consider in determining whether a State non-member bank is entitled to the benefits of deposit insurance).

Capital required: No additional capital is required.

Growth of Branch Banking

Banking in the U.S. used to be largely conducted by single-office local institutions owned by local capital, managed by resident officers, and typically medium-sized or small. This characteristically unit type or independent banking dates back to the lack of provision for branch banking in the original National Bank Act of 1863, and to the 10% tax on state bank note circulation effective in 1866, which originally had the effect of driving many state banks into the national banking system. Although under the National Bank Act these converting state banks could keep their existing branches, many chose either to discontinue their branches or to organize their branches into separate unit banks. In 1909, the controversy over the merits of branch banking was again revived with passage of the Branch Banking Act of California, which authorized statewide branch banking and led to development subsequently in that state of the largest state branch banking system in the U.S. today, that of the present Bank of American National Trust & Savings Association. The development of such state branch banking in competition with national banks, and the growth of banking requirements for larger business units, contributed to liberalization of the national banking laws, particularly by the PEPPER-MCFADDEN ACT of 1927, which completely revised Section 5155, Revised Statutes, relating to branch banking powers of national banks, and authorized the establishment of branch banks within the limits of city or town of location if such branches were expressly authorized to state banks in that locality. Later, the BANKING ACT OF 1933 further liberalized branch banking powers by permitting national banks to establish statewide branches if such were affirmatively permitted for state banks, subject to maintenance of minimum capital requirements varying as to population.

In 1927, only 739 of the 25,170 banks operated domestic branches, or 2.9%. In 1933, following the Bank Holiday, bank population declined to 13,221, so that the 584 banks operating branches were 4.4% of the bank population. Since that year, growth in domestic branch banking has been steady, particularly following World War II, when more banks expanded retail banking (personal loans and other consumer credit) and aggressively promoted special checking accounts of the no minimum balance type for the public at large.

Foreign Branches

Besides having powers to establish domestic branches to the extent permitted by state law, national banks possessing capital and surplus of $1,000,000 or more may, under Section 25 of the Federal Reserve Act, establish branches in foreign countries or dependencies or insular possessions of the U.S. in furtherance of foreign commerce; and may invest a maximum of 10% in aggregate of paid-in capital stock and surplus in the stock of one or more banks or corporations organized under federal or state laws and principally engaged in international or foreign banking or banking in a dependency or insular possession of the U.S., either directly or through the agency, ownership, or control of local institutions in foreign countries, or in dependencies or insular possessions of the U.S. Application to and approval of the Board of Governors of the Federal Reserve System are necessary, including agreement to restrict operations or conduct such business under such limitations and restrictions as the board of governors may prescribe for the places where such business is to be conducted.

Any state member bank may establish and operate branches in any dependency or insular possession of the U.S. or in any foreign country, on the same terms and conditions and subject to the same limitations and restrictions as are applicable to national banks.

The larger U.S. banks have expanded substantially in foreign branching in recent years. Edge Act corporations, which may now mix both banking and financing operations, are alternatives to foreign branches as such in engaging in foreign banking, but nevertheless the number of foreign branches of U.S. banks has multiplied.

In reviewing the proposed foreign branches, the board considers the requirements of the governing statute, the condition of the bank, and the bank's experience in international business.

See CANADIAN BANKING SYSTEM, EDGE ACT CORPORATION, FEDERAL RESERVE BRANCH BANKS, FOREIGN AGENCIES, FOREIGN BRANCHES.

BIBLIOGRAPHY

"Banks Consider Innovative Branch Locations." *Magazine of Bank Administration,* June 1988.
COMPTROLLER OF THE CURRENCY. *Comptroller's Manual for National Banks.* Office of the Comptroller of the Currency, Washington, DC.
FEDERAL DEPOSIT INSURANCE CORPORATION. *Annual Reports.*

BREAK A sudden and sharp undermining of prices occurring on a stock or other exchange; an abrupt fall in market quotations.

Such a break may occur after a period of narrow fluctuation and light volume, creating a gap in the chart (downside breakaway gap) accompanied by heavy trading volume, a decisive although not necessarily significant move from a forecasting standpoint, depending on the relative volume before and after the gap.

BIBLIOGRAPHY

EDWARDS, R. D., and MAGEE, J. *Technical Analysis of Stock Trends,* 1964.

BREAK-EVEN To conclude a transaction, purchase, or sale with neither a profit nor a loss.

In managerial literature and accounting analysis, the break-even point is that point at which income of a firm equals costs and expenses. The value to management of determining a break-even point is not only to avoid loss, but also to achieve as much volume as possible above it. The higher the rate of operation above break-even point, the larger will be the net profit margin on sales, as fixed expense will not, by definition, rise with larger volume.

Usually the break-even point is depicted on a chart similar to that illustration, in which case it is that point where the total cost curve (variable costs plus fixed costs) intersects the sales curve. The conventional break-even point chart assumes that fixed expenses and variable expense ratio to sales will not change at various sales levels. Thus if fixed expenses are $150,000 and variable expense ratio to sales is set at 25%, the break-even point is $200,000 (fixed expenses divided by margin of income {75%} available for fixed expenses). At sales volumes up to capacity, the same amount of fixed expenses and the same ratio of variable expense (25%) are assumed.

The margin of safety is the dollar difference between break-even sales revenue and sales revenue at a certain volume level.

Margin of safety can be expressed as a rate:

$$M/S = \frac{\text{Sales at given level} - \text{Break-even sales}}{\text{Sales at given level}}$$

Generally, a high margin of safety indicates a relatively safe business position. The margin of safety rate indicates the percent decline in sales from the current level before reporting a net loss.

If a firm has a relatively large fixed expense, a relatively small variable expense rate, and a low margin of safety, it would usually try to improve its profit position by increasing volume or by reducing fixed expense. If the margin of safety for a firm is relatively small and the unit contribution margin is also small, the firm might consider the advisability of increasing the selling price or reducing the variable expense. Managers should appreciate the fact that, if they operate with a small margin of safety, a small decline in sales is likely to bring net losses.

The principal uses of break-even analysis are summarized here:

1. To understand the relationships between costs, volume, and price.
2. To test the profit impact of a sales forecast.
3. To find the break-even volume of sales in dollars and/or in units of sales.
4. To determine the volume of sales required to attain certain profit goals.
5. To estimate the effect on the break-even point and on profits or changes in the firm's cost and revenue structures.

Break-Even Chart

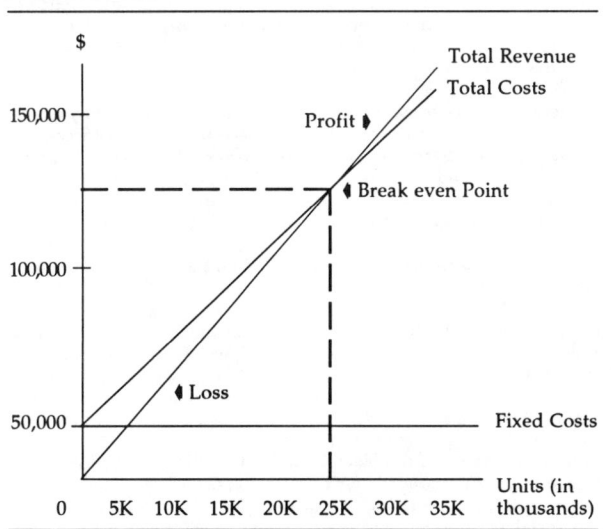

Major assumptions underlying break-even analysis include:

1. All costs can be separated reliably into their variable and fixed components within a relevant range of activity.
2. Fixed costs remain constant in total amount throughout a relevant volume range.
3. Variable costs do not change per unit and fluctuate in total in direct proportion to volume.
4. Selling prices remain constant at any relevant volume, and
5. Production and sales volume will be equal.

BREAK-UP POINT LIQUIDATING VALUE, indicating the actual or estimated market or value of net assets per share applicable to each class of security according to its priority in the capitalization.

BRETTON WOODS AGREEMENT The Articles of Agreement adopted by the international monetary conference of 44 nations which met at Bretton Woods, New Hampshire, July 1–22, 1944. These articles proposed the establishment of two international institutions, the INTERNATIONAL MONETARY FUND (IMF) and the INTERNATIONAL BANK FOR RECONSTRUCTION AND DEVELOPMENT, as part of the economic foundation for a peaceful and prosperous post-war world advocated by the U.S. The proposals were the outgrowth of three years of study by the technical staffs of the Treasury, State Department, Board of Governors of the Federal Reserve System, and other agencies of the U.S. Government. The United States adopted the Articles of Agreement by the Bretton Woods Agreement Act, which became law on July 31, 1945. These original articles of agreement were signed in Washington, D.C., on December 27, 1945, by representatives of nations whose subscriptions to the fund totaled 80% of subscriptions, thus enabling the fund and the bank to come into existence. The function of the fund is to maintain orderly currency practices in international trade, while the function of the bank is to facilitate extension of long-term investments for productive purposes.

Effective April 1, 1978, the Second Amendment to the Articles of Agreement of the IMF became effective, in effect legalizing the exchange arrangements prevailing after abandonment of the par value system, but establishing principles and procedures for surveillance that the IMF is now required to exercise. The First Amendment to the Articles of Agreement 1969 had been created to establish the SPECIAL DRAWING RIGHTS (SDRs) as a legal concept, giving the SDRs the character of a reserve asset because of the obligation of the IMF to designate a transferee, when requested by a participant, whenever the participant wishes to use its holdings of SDRs.

The IMF monitors compliance and assists nations in defending their officially established exchange rates. The IMF was empowered to lend foreign exchange ($U.S. dollars and other convertible currencies) to countries sustaining reserve losses because of downward market pressure on their exchange rates. If a country's foreign exchange problems prove to be more than temporary, the IMF often advises the country to devalue its currency and to undertake domestic monetary and fiscal policy actions designed to stem further declines in the value of its currency.

BRIDGE BANKS Created under the COMPETITIVE EQUALITY BANKING ACT OF 1987, a new method of dealing with bank failures by allowing the FDIC to bridge the gap between a failed bank and a satisfactory takeover that is still incomplete at the time of the target bank's failure. The bridge bank would assume the assets and liabilities and carry on the business of the failed bank for a limited time.

The act requires that the FDIC, before using the bridge bank mechanism, determine that the net cost of the bridge bank would not exceed the net cost of liquidating the failed bank and that operation of the bridge bank is essential to the community or in the best interest of the depositors and the public.

BRIDGE BONDS Bonds issued to finance the construction of bridges, either public, privately owned, or toll bridges, by public bodies, municipalities, railroads, and private bridge corporations.

In municipal issues, if the bridge bonds are secured solely by the revenues of the bridge, such bonds are revenue bonds, not general obligations or full faith and credit bonds of the municipality. In recent years, most bridge projects have been financed on a revenue basis with bonds issued under corporate titles other than that of the municipality or municipalities involved; e.g., the Triborough Bridge and Tunnel Authority (New York City), the Calumet Skyway (Chi-

---

ENCYCLOPEDIA OF BANKING AND FINANCE

cago), the California Toll Bridge Authority (San Francisco–Oakland Bay Bridge), and the Port of New York Authority. Examples of bridge bonds issued by private companies are the International Bridge (Detroit-Windsor) bonds and the San Mateo–Hayward Bridge bonds (San Francisco Bay).

BRIDGE LOAN   A loan made to meet a customer's needs until it can raise additional permanent funds. Bridge (swing) loans are often used in construction loans. Bridge loans can be relatively risky, especially when repayment depends on a firm's ability to sell stock in an uncertain market.

BRING OUT   For an investment house or syndicate, to place a new issue of securities on the market; to make a public offering of a new issue.
See REGISTRATION STATEMENT.

BRITISH BANKING SYSTEM   See BANK OF ENGLAND, JOINT-STOCK BANKS.

BRITISH TREASURY BILLS   British treasury bills are of two types as to channels of issuance: (1) market treasury bills, for which tenders are invited on a discount basis every Friday for bills to be issued in the following week, with maturities usually of 91 days (occasionally 63 days); and (2) tap treasury bills, issued directly to government departments, including the Issue Department, the National Debt Commissioners, and the Exchange Equalisation Account. The discount houses (12 major firms constituting the London Discount Market Association, with another approximately dozen firms also operating in the market) are the dealers in short-term obligations and short-term bonds.
See BANK OF ENGLAND.

BROAD MARKET   A market in which a large proportion of the stocks listed are being traded in. Broadness and activity accompany each other and usually indicate public participation. A broad market, as opposed to a narrow market, also applies to a particular stock, and indicates that frequent bids at close prices exist for that stock, that the sources of demand for it are many and diverse, and that trading in it is comparatively active.

BROKEN LOT   ODD LOT.

BROKER   An intermediary who brings together buyers and sellers of the same security or commodity and executes their orders, receiving a commission or brokerage therefor. A broker is a specialist, and accordingly is well versed in the technique of his or her particular market, knowing the sources of supply and demand and being an expert on prices and price trends. There are brokers in many fields—stock, grain, cotton, produce, note, ship, real estate, mortgage, arbitrage, insurance, discount, money, etc.

The relationship between customer and broker is that of principal and AGENT, and in most cases, such as stock exchange broker, the broker is a special agent. The law of agency, therefore, underlies the customer-broker relationship.

A stock exchange broker is a member of the stock exchange and as such is bound not only by the law of agency but also by the rules of the exchange. The customer-broker relationship starts with the opening of the account by the customer. Under New York Stock Exchange rules, the broker must obtain essential facts about the customer, usually on an information or signature card signed by the customer, giving residence, occupation, employment, age, and one or more references. He or she also must obtain information for proper handling of the account, such as type of account (cash, margin, or commodity account); instructions on notices and statements; account number, etc.

Customers' Accounts.   Cash account transactions are all in cash. No margin purchases or short sales occur in this type of account. General accounts (margin accounts) comprehend cash transactions, margin purchases, and short sales. For the latter type of accounts, the customer signs the margin agreement (also known as the customer's agreement or standard customer's agreement), which contains a series of clauses pertaining to margin transactions: (1) authority to the broker to pledge the customer's securities in collateral loans, either alone or with other customers' securities (security loan consent or hypothecation agreement); (2) authority to the broker at his or her discretion to sell the securities carried on margin and securing the customer's liability for debit balance (amount of credit plus interest), on notice, when in the broker's opinion the customer's margin is inadequate; (3) communication consent authorizing the broker to make all notices and demands upon the customer by mail, telegraph, telephone, or orally; and (4) specification that all transactions shall be subject to rules and customs of the exchange where such transactions are consummated, including reference to arbitration of any differences or controversies. In addition to initial margins prescribed by the Board of Governors of the Federal Reserve System, both initial and maintenance margins are prescribed by New York Stock Exchange rules.

Thereafter, the customer's instructions to the broker will be observed by the latter as agent, including the different types of orders: market, limit, stop, stop and limit orders with respect to price; and day, week, month, and open or good 'til canceled (GTC) orders with respect to time limits. Completely discretionary orders are regulated by Rule 408 of the New York Stock Exchange, which provides that in addition to carrying the customer's written consent, such an order shall be approved and initialed on the day entered by a member, allied member, or a manager designated with written authority by a member or allied member to do so.

Cash or margin accounts will not be accepted for persons under 21 years of age. Parents, however, may buy securities for their own account and transfer them to the minor children upon their reaching 21 or serve as custodians for the minor children on gifts of securities and manage the investment for the children until they reach 21 (other adults may also be designated as custodians), under gifts to minors acts of various states.

Cash or margin accounts of employees of the New York Stock Exchange and employees of member firms must have the prior written consent of the employer. Such prior written consent of the employer is also required for margin accounts of employees of banks, trust companies, insurance companies, or any other broker or dealer in securities in any form, bills of exchange, acceptances, or other forms of commercial paper. Such disabilities (Rule 407 of the New York Stock Exchange) are not considered to apply to independent insurance agents or officers of banks, trust companies, insurance companies, etc.

Besides the basic cash accounts and margin accounts, special types of accounts, for particular kinds of transactions or to allow for particular application of margin rules and regulations, include the following:

1. When issued margin accounts, to cover transactions on a when issued basis.
2. Special subscription accounts.
3. Arbitrage accounts.
4. Specialists' accounts.
5. Omnibus accounts for a number of customers of a securities firm placing the orders through a correspondent firm.
6. Special bond accounts for exempt securities.
7. Memorandum accounts for such miscellaneous activity as collection or exchange of securities, foreign exchange transactions, etc., for customers and miscellaneous transactions for other securities firms. Commodity accounts would encompass activity in commodities for customers.

Customer Relations.   Many stock brokerage houses may act as dealers for their own account in transactions with customers in unlisted securities and as broker for customers in transactions in listed and unlisted securities. Strict rules in many cases prevent a broker from acting as both broker and dealer in the same transaction.

The customer receives from his or her stockbroker the confirmation of execution of the transaction, whether purchase or sale, by mail. The confirmation is usually mailed on the day of the transaction. In addition, member firms of the New York Stock Exchange send monthly statements to all customers with active accounts, showing the transactions affecting the account during the month and indicating by the bring-down on the lower part of the statement the net securities position (inventory) of the customer in the account at the end of the month. The customer has a reasonable time after receipt of this statement, which in legal effect is an account stated, in which to challenge any item thereon.

A member firm of the New York Stock Exchange must immediately notify the exchange in writing as soon as it commences to carry accounts or hold securities for customers. In addition, each member and member firm shall answer financial questionnaires whenever called for by the exchange, and be subject to an audit, by independent public accountants, as of the date of an answer to a financial questionnaire. Moreover, each member firm doing business with the public is required to have an annual surprise audit by independent public accountants. Each member firm shall make available to any customer at his or her request a statement of its financial condition as of the date of its most recent answer to the financial questionnaire of the exchange or as of a date subsequent thereto, which financial statement in the opinion of the firm shall fairly present its financial condition. Each monthly statement sent to a customer by a New York Stock Exchange firm carries a legend reading: "A financial statement of this firm (or corporation) is available for your personal inspection at its offices, or a copy of it will be mailed upon your written request." Moreover, within 35 days of the date after each annual audited financial questionnaire is required to be filed with the exchange, each customer shall be sent either the statement based upon such audit, or a notice with return postcard inviting personal inspection of the statement at the firm's offices or a request for mailing of the statement.

Reports to Exchange. The New York Stock Exchange also requires other financial reports from members, allied members, and member organizations, including the following:

1. Reports on loans obtained where any part of the proceeds is used to supply working capital to the firm. (Note: Net capital of the firm, figured pursuant to rules of the exchange, is required to equal at all times at least $6\,^2/_3$% of total liabilities, including free credit balances of customers.)
2. Periodic reports with respect to the following:
   a. Short positions in listed securities.
   b. Obligations in respect of security underwritings and net positions resulting therefrom.
   c. Total of collateral loans from banks, trust companies, and other lenders in the U.S., excluding borrowings from other members of national securities exchanges.
   d. Customers' debit and credit balances.
   e. Total fail to deliver and fail to receive contracts.

Problem of Fails. Fail contracts originate when the selling broker or dealer in a transaction fails to deliver the securities on the normal settlement date of the trade to the buying broker or dealer. On the books of the selling broker or dealer, the fail to deliver creates a long security position. On the books of the buying broker or dealer, the fail to receive creates a short security position.

Data on fails to deliver securities afford the best single measure of the extent of the brokerage industry's paperwork backlog. Among the consequences of fails are the following: (1) imposition by the exchange of restraints, where firms had not voluntarily done so, on business emanating from such problem areas as over-the-counter transactions, where numerically most of the fails originated; (2) promulgation of the mandatory buy-in rule (NYSE Rule 282) to provide for mandatory buy-ins of securities not delivered 50 calendar days after the due date; (3) inauguration of the fail clearance system, whereby old fails submitted by firms are paired off and intermediate deliveries are eliminated, with money differences settled directly; and (4) addition of a special operations questionnaire required by the exchange on the status of each major area of recordkeeping, including general ledger and customer account postings, dividends and stock record, and information on such related topics as overtime, customer complaints, etc. The log-jam also led to the extraordinary action of a voluntary closing of the markets, per recommendation of the Ad Hoc Committee on Back-Office Procedures, on the New York Stock Exchange, American Stock Exchange, and over-the-counter markets on four separate business days in June and early July, 1968, and extension of closings to include the last four Wednesdays in July, 1968. With computer confusion finally cleared away (but not until various firm casualties had occurred), the Wall Street community resumed a normal situation with regard to fails.

Disagreements between a broker and a client are sometimes submitted to arbitration. A 1987 decision of the U.S. Supreme Court confirmed the binding nature of the arbitration clause, which precluded filing suit in federal court before the arbitration process was complete and limiting the nature of appeals from the arbitration decision.

See AMERICAN STOCK EXCHANGE, DEALERS, BULLION, COMMISSION HOUSE, FLOOR TRADER, NEW YORK STOCK EXCHANGE, NOTE BROKERS, ODD-LOT DEALERS, OUTSIDE BROKER, PRIVILEGE BROKER, SPECIALISTS, STOCK JOBBER, TWO-DOLLAR BROKER.

BROKERAGE OFFICE ORGANIZATION

A complete and well-equipped stock commission house is organized with the following departments:

1. Customers' room containing quotation boards for all active stocks, stock and bond tickers of the various exchanges, bulletin board and news ticker, and representatives to take orders and furnish information.
2. Telephone division for answering inquiries and taking orders for execution by those who cannot visit the customers' room.
3. Correspondence division for taking care of business and inquiries received by mail.
4. Private wire system (for wire houses) to connect home office with branch offices and correspondents, and available for orders, quotations, and news.
5. Statistical department to provide information and figures on all corporations whose stocks or bonds are listed.
6. Order department which transmits orders from the office to the floor of the exchange for execution, giving report of executions, quotations, and open orders monthly.
7. Accounting department which
   a. Figures and posts buying and selling orders as executed and mails notices of such executions.
   b. Records receipts and disbursements of cash.
   c. Records loans from banks with supporting collateral, together with substitutions of collateral and comparisons, and collects and credits dividends and coupons.
   d. Records the receipt, delivery, and transfer of securities purchased and sold through the Stock Clearing Corporation or directly.
   e. Handles customers' ledgers, figures margins, and sends margin notices when additional sums are required to protect the customer's equity.
   f. Renders monthly statements of accounts.

The accounting department is under the supervision of the cashier, who is responsible for cash, loans, and receipts and deliveries of securities.

BROKERED DEPOSITS

Packaged deposits of $100,000 each from many clients of brokerage firms. Because these deposits are insured by the FDIC, they go to the highest rate-payer. Brokered deposits have often been used by fast-growing or high-risk commercial banks as a source of funds. They often reflect a special liquidity risk.

BROKERS' LOAN

Loan made to a broker or dealer in securities by a bank for the purpose of purchasing or carrying securities, and in the aggregate representing the amount required to finance the floating supply of securities and the margin requirements of speculative traders in securities; also called street loans or call loans.

Great public interest in brokers' loans, created by allegations that these loans were syphoning off bank credit to finance market speculation, led to regular publication of brokers' loan statistics by the Federal Reserve Board and the New York Stock Exchange beginning in 1926. At present, although the interest in brokers' loans is not as great as formerly because of high margin requirements and regulations thereof, various statistical series are available regularly on brokers' loans:

1. A Weekly Condition Report of Large Commercial Banks and Domestic Subsidiaries (H.4.2), released Wednesdays and containing data for the Wednesday of one week earlier, is prepared by the Board of Governors of the Federal Reserve System. So is the Condition Report of Large Commercial Banks in New York and Chicago (H.4.3), released Thursdays and containing data from the previous Wednesday. Assets and Liabilities of All Commercial Banks in the United States (H.8), released Wednesdays, contains data for the Wednesday of two weeks earlier. The monthly Assets and Liabilities of All Member Banks by Districts (G.7.1), released about the 14th of the month, contains Wednesday figures for the last Wednesday of the previous month. The semiannual release (in May and November) Assets and Liabilities of All Commercial Banks, by Class of

Bank, contains data for the end of the previous December and June.
2. For call report data on the volume of bank credit extended to brokers and dealers for purchasing or carrying securities, the series "Loans and Investments by Class of Bank," reported monthly in the *Federal Reserve Bulletin* for the call dates, contains a breakdown as to all insured banks, total member banks (separately for New York City, City of Chicago, other reserve city banks, and country banks), and nonmember banks.
3. The New York Stock Exchange reports monthly data on member firm borrowing. Beginning in June, 1970, the NYSE member organizations were required to report monthly their aggregate debits in stock margin, convertible bonds margin, and subscriptions accounts, as well as aggregate free credits in cash and margin accounts. Through Form R-1, the NYSE provides the Federal Reserve with data on all types of margin accounts.
4. The *Federal Reserve Bulletin* reports monthly stock market customer financing (end-of-month data), indicating total margin credit at brokers and banks, other security credit at banks, and free credit balances at brokers. Margin credit includes all credit extended to purchase or carry stocks or related equity instruments and secured at least in part by stock. Other security credit at banks includes loans to purchase or carry margin stock if these are unsecured or secured entirely by unrestricted collateral. Free credit balances are in accounts with no unfulfilled commitments to the brokers and are subject to withdrawal by customers on demand.

Total margin credit is classified and reported as regulated and unregulated. As to regulated margin credit, Regulations T and U of the Board of Governors of the Federal Reserve System permit special loan values for convertible bonds and stock acquired through exercise of subscription rights (subscription accounts), in addition to assigning a current loan value to margin stock generally. As to unregulated margin credit, at banks loans to purchase or carry nonmargin stocks are unregulated; at brokers such stocks have no loan value. Nonmargin stocks are those not listed on a national securities exchange and not included on the list of over-the-counter margin stocks of the Board of Governors of the Federal Reserve System.

Between October, 1928, and October, 1929, total security loans are estimated to have increased from $12.825 billion to $17.115 billion, including an increase from $2.749 billion to $2.824 billion in bank loans to brokers and dealers; an increase from $6.375 billion to $7.875 billion in bank security loans to other customers; and a sharp increase from $3.701 billion to $6.416 billion in loans to brokers and dealers by others, meaning lenders other than banks and thus beyond control of the banking authorities. The pyramiding of this security market credit and its subsequent deflation led to legislation prohibiting banks from lending for the account of others, inaugurating regulation of margin requirements, and granting power to the Board of Governors of the Federal Reserve System to restrict security loans of member banks. The Banking Act of 1933 and the Securities Exchange Act of 1934 prohibited banks from acting as agents for depositors (others) in extending security loans. The Board of Governors of the Federal Reserve System under the Banking Act of 1933 can fix the percentage of a member bank's capital and surplus that may be loaned on securities, as well as limit rediscount privileges of banks that continue to expand security loans after official warning to desist. Pursuant to the Securities Exchange Act of 1934, the Board of Governors of the Federal Reserve System may fix the maximum loan values on registered securities, thus imposing margin requirements. By Regulation T, relating to extension of credit by brokers and dealers and effective October 1, 1934, and Regulation U, relating to loans made by banks for the purpose of purchasing or carrying listed securities and effective May 1, 1936, the Board of Governors of the Federal Reserve System now exercises close control over margin requirements and security loans. Effective March 11, 1968, the Board of Governors of the Federal Reserve System issued Regulation G, extending to other lenders (other than banks and brokers) the same margin requirements and regulation.

Also, effective July 8, 1969, the Board of Governors of the Federal Reserve System revised its regulations governing margin requirements principally to: (1) extend the coverage of margin requirements to credit that banks (Regulation U) and other lenders (Regulation G) may extend for the purpose of purchasing and carrying certain securities traded over-the-counter as distinguished from those traded on registered national securities exchanges; and (2) permit brokers and dealers to extend credit (Regulation T) on such securities.
See CALL MONEY MARKET, FEDERAL RESERVE BOARD REGULATIONS, MARGIN, MARGIN ACCOUNT, MARGIN BUYING, SECURITY LOANS.

BIBLIOGRAPHY

BOARD OF GOVERNORS OF THE FEDERAL RESERVE SYSTEM. *Regulation G, T, and U, Federal Reserve Regulatory Service.*

BRONZE COINS In the U.S. coinage system, one-cent pieces of bronze composition (pennies, or coppers) are the largest in outstanding volume, but the proportions of metals in the bronze alloy have varied a number of times. The alloy used immediately preceding enactment of P.L. 87–643, approved September 5, 1962, was 95% copper and 5% tin and zinc, with tin 0.1%. The referenced legislation authorized the elimination of tin. Thus the bronze one-cent coin is now 95% copper and 5% zinc, which is the same as that coined during 1944, 1945, and 1946. The weight of the individual one-cent coin (48 grains) remained the same.

One-cent coins, along with other MINOR COINS, were legal tender only up to $0.25 in any one payment, until they were made full legal tender in unlimited amounts by the THOMAS AMENDMENT of May 12, 1933, and the GOLD REPEAL JOINT RESOLUTION of June 5, 1933. P.L. 89–81, July 23, 1965, recodified the legal tender provision, now found in 31 U.S.C. 392.

BROOKINGS INSTITUTION The Brookings Institution, founded in 1927, is a "think tank" located in Washington, D.C. It is devoted to nonpartisan research, education, and publication in economics, government, foreign policy, and social sciences generally. Its principal purpose is to promote public understanding of issues of national importance.

BUBBLE ACT Specifically, the English Statute 6 Geo. I. c. 18 (1719), which prohibited the public sale of shares by companies unless they held royal charter. This legislation, urged by the royal-chartered (1710) South Sea Company (governor and company of merchants of Great Britain trading to the South Seas and other parts of America and for the encouragement of fishing), was the basis for dissolution by the government of a large number of unchartered companies (bubble companies) formed in the speculative mania stimulated by the success of the South Sea Company in England and of the Mississippi Company in France. Although the act could not prevent the subsequent collapse in 1720 in English company share prices, with ruinous losses, the act is significant in being considered the forerunner in Anglo-American law of required chartering and of our modern BLUE SKY LAWS.
See MISSISSIPPI BUBBLE.

BIBLIOGRAPHY

LORD ERLEIGH. *The South Sea Bubble,* 1933.

BUCKETEER A stock exchange, grain, cotton, or other broker who does an illegitimate business.
See BUCKET SHOP.

BUCKET SHOP A dishonest and illegitimate brokerage house, which usually operates in stocks, grain, or cotton. The essence of bucket shop operations is either nonexecution of customers' orders or resale of stocks through a house account, or dummy account, so that at the end of the day's business no securities are held. The bucket shop takes a position in the market opposite that of the customer, and since the prevalent attitude of the amateur speculator is that of a BULL, the position of the bucket shop is normally that of a BEAR. Consequently, a falling market is profitable for the bucket shop, while a rising market is apt to precipitate it into bankruptcy. The bucket shop is thus a place where the broker bets against the customer without his consent. It is a place where wagers are made on security quotations, and dealings are in profits and losses rather than in the securities themselves. Whereas the legitimate broker merely acts as agent for his customer and executes his orders accordingly, the bucketeer stakes his judgment against that of the customer.

The success of the bucket shop depends upon misleading customers, accepting inadequate margins, the ability to get stock exchange quotations, and a falling market.

In their original form, bucket shops were merely quotation betting places, since stocks were actually neither bought nor sold. The broker merely made bookkeeping entries and kept accounts with customers as if orders were executed. Dealings of bucket shops, therefore, had no effect in the making of stock prices. This old type of bucket shop had become obsolete by 1916 as a result of the Hughes investigation of 1909 and the stricter legislation that ensued. In the bear market of 1919-1921, bucketeering again flourished under a more subtle and artful guise. The bucketeer actually executed orders to buy and sell stock, but immediately reversed the transaction through various dummy accounts, perhaps names of actual individuals, so that no actual position existed. A rising market began in the autumn of 1921, and in early 1922 many bucket shops came to grief when customers asked for delivery of the securities they had bought upon payment of the debit balance.

Antibucket shop laws have been enacted in most of the states, and the rules of every reputable exchange expressly prohibit the bucketing of orders, violations being punishable by expulsion. In addition, the Securities and Exchange Commission, through its regulations and visitorial powers, and dealer associations, through their self-policing, make the bucket shop a vestige of the past.

BUDGET An orderly and coordinated plan of financial planning and management. Budgeting ia a major tool for planning, motivating, and controlling business operations. The budgeting process requires management to determine its goals and objectives and to develop a coordinated plan for achieving those ends. Budgetary control results from establishing department, center, or unit budgets that relate managerial responsibilities to the requirements of organizational goals and objectives and the continuous comparison of actual results with budgeted proposal to provide a basis for appropriate action. The appended chart provides an overview of the strategic planning process.

The master or comprehensive budget is a relatively complete blueprint of the firm's future operations. The budget period is usually short enough to permit reasonably accurate predictions and long enough to allow time for implementation. The budget period usually coincides with the fiscal period of the business so that actual results of operations can more easily be compared with budgetary estimates. The master budget for a business enterprise is usually prepared in terms of (1) an operating budget, and (2) a financial budget. The operating budget produces an income statement and supporting schedules. The financial budget consists of a budgeted balance sheet indicating how the budget will affect the company's resources and obligations, including supporting schedules showing cash flow, capital expenditures, and similar items affecting the balance sheet. The operating and financial budgets are usually prepared for a year, with supporting schedules in monthly or quarterly terms. A capital expenditure or project budget is usually developed for a longer time period.

The budgeting process usually involves the determination by a budget committee of basic assumptions under which the details of the budget are to be prepared. The board of directors (or other high-level, decision-making group) approves the assumptions set forth by the budget committee. A budget director then begins to prepare the detailed budget. Detailed budgeting usually begins with a forecast of revenue from sales of products or services. After revenues have been estimated, estimates are made of expenses, costs, collections, and payments. Budgeted financial statements are then compiled and examined to determine how the budgeted activities will affect the company, stockholders, creditors, and other external parties. The budget is then implemented.

Compiling a bank's operating budget often is developed during the third quarter of the year so as to consider current trends that can affect the following quarters. Major factors to consider in preparing the budget include anticipated or desired loan and deposit levels,

Overview of the Strategic Planning Process

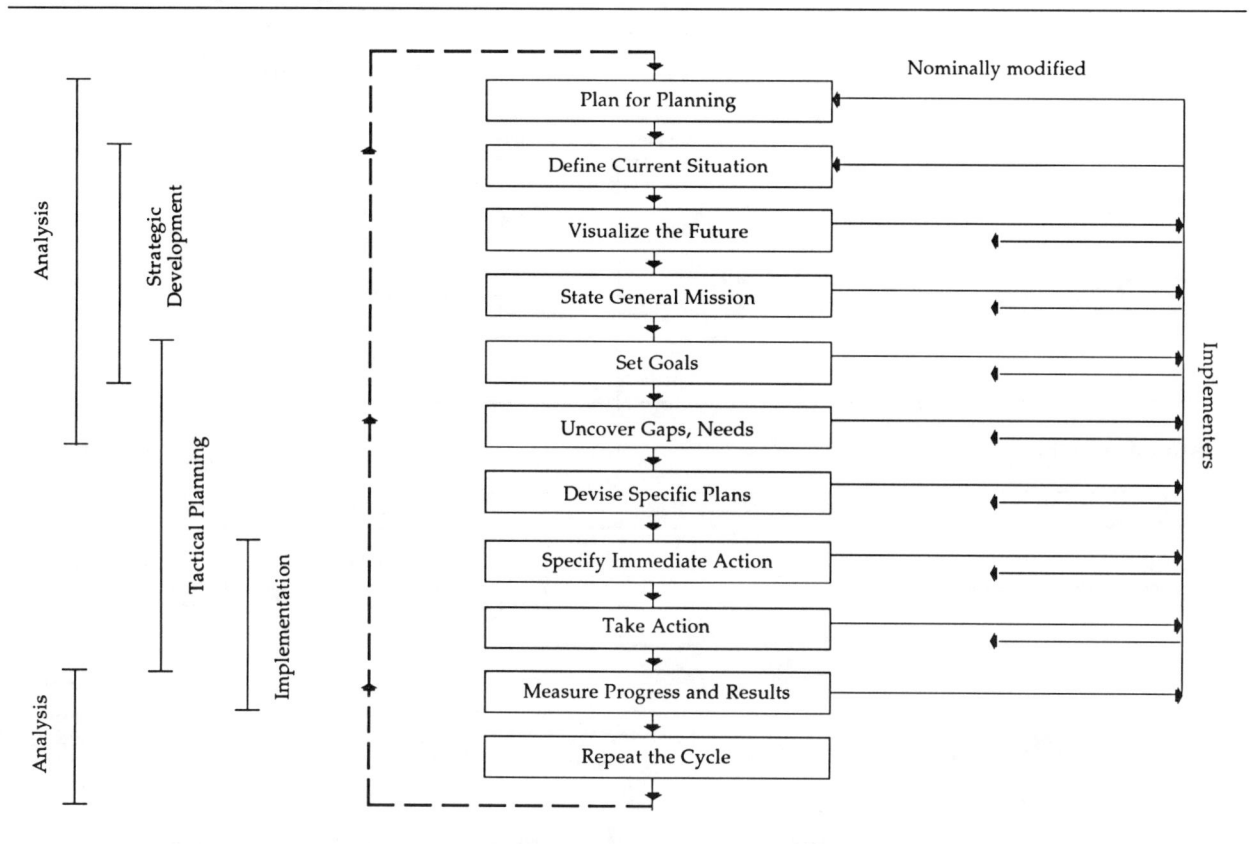

Source: William T. Thornhill. *Effective Risk Management.* Rolling Meadows: IL; Bank Administration Institute, 1989

BUDGET

interest income and expense, fee income, and personnel requirements. The completed budget is usually supported by specific programs designed to accomplish the budget objectives. The completed budget is submitted to management and the board for approval. The budget is used primarily for monitoring results and appraising the quality of management. A chart of a master budget is appended here.

The second phase of the budget control process involves monitoring operations so that operating plans and targets can be attained. Budgetary control relies primarily on the analyses of differences (1) between actual costs and standard costs. Aspects of the control process involve (2) establishing lines of responsibility for performance, communicating plans to those assigned performance responsibilities, (3) evaluating variances between actual results and budgeted estimates, and (4) taking appropriate action.

The master budget is primarily a planning tool. It is often a static or inflexible budget and is usually prepared for one level of activities—the anticipated or normal level of output. A flexible or variable budget is usually used as the tool for controlling costs and evaluating performance. A flexible budget is prepared for a range of activities because costs are affected by changes in the level of activity. Flexible budgets are often expressed in terms of units of output or in standard direct-labor hours allowed for that output.

A capital budget is a plan for acquiring and maintaining long-term assets. The capital budget is also a means of providing the means of financing these activities. Financial theory strongly supports the separation of the investment decision from the financing decision. A capital budget typically includes one or more of the following:

1. New facilities and major additions.
2. Major renovations and repairs to existing facilities.

A variety of methods are currently used for making investment decisions associated with capital budgets. The net present value method or some modification thereof is usually considered the preferred method. The application of the net present value method of capital budgeting involves the following process:

1. Estimate the future cash inflows and outflows from each alternative project under consideration.
2. Discount the future cash flows to the present using the firm's cost of capital as the discount rate.
3. Accept or reject the proposed project according to a decision rule that will maximize the firm's wealth.

Components of the Master Budget

OPERATING BUDGET

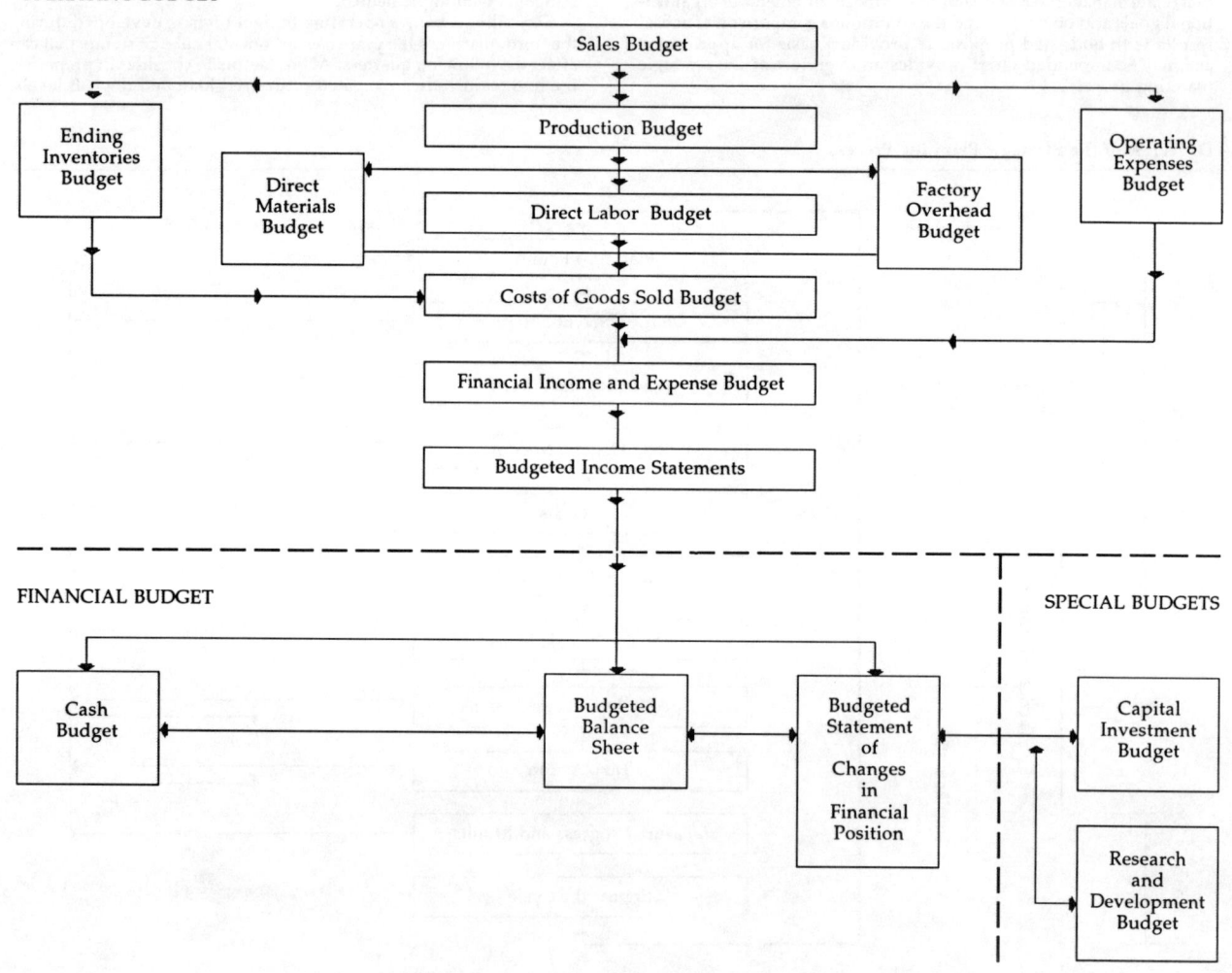

- Sales Budget
- Ending Inventories Budget
- Production Budget
- Direct Materials Budget
- Direct Labor Budget
- Factory Overhead Budget
- Operating Expenses Budget
- Costs of Goods Sold Budget
- Financial Income and Expense Budget
- Budgeted Income Statements

FINANCIAL BUDGET

- Cash Budget
- Budgeted Balance Sheet
- Budgeted Statement of Changes in Financial Position

SPECIAL BUDGETS

- Capital Investment Budget
- Research and Development Budget

ENCYCLOPEDIA OF BANKING AND FINANCE

Conventional wisdom makes the following assertions concerning budgeting:

1. Planning and budgeting should be integrated.
2. Budgeting is a process for estimating priorities.
3. Planning and budgeting should be data based outcome-oriented.
4. Budgeting is a process of resource allocation.
5. Confrontation can result from economic factors, allocation processes, lack of understanding, parochialism, and leadership inadequacies.
6. Budgeting is political in nature and involves the arts of persuasion and compromise.
7. There is a permanent dichotomy between organizational needs and wants and the availability of resources.
8. Financial resources are neither inexhaustible nor self-replenishing.
9. Budgeting is representation in monetary terms of institutional goals and objectives.
10. Budgeting relationships should systematically relate the expenditures of funds to the accomplishment of planned objectives.
11. Budgeting relies on people making optimal choices about economic and noneconomic matters.
12. Resource reallocation is the main source of flexibility when income growth ends.
13. Budgeting decisions are frequently negotiated, often subjectively.
14. Disagreements are often resolved by the use of discretionary power.

Various types of budgets are used in businesses and not-for-profit institutions. Five major types of budget include:

1. Incremental budget (used with object-of-expenditure, or line-item, budgets),
2. Formula budget,
3. Planning, programming, and budgeting systems,
4. Zero-base budgeting, and
5. Performance budgeting.

Incremental budgeting uses an object-of-expenditure approach to budgeting. Incremental budgets show line-item categories of expenditures to be made during the period. Line item refers to objects of expenditures, such as salaries and supplies. In incremental budgeting, either each line item is considered for an increment or it remains unadjusted in the base. Frequently, increments are calculated as uniform percentage adjustments for every line item or group of line items. The basic philosophy is that the current budget is distributed properly among both the functions and objects of expenditures and that little programmatic change needs to occur. Changes in institutional priorities often result through *ad hoc* determination concerning what increase is needed to effect a programmatic change. When resources become scarce, incremental budgeting tends to perpetuate the existing programs regardless of how ineffective or inefficient they may be. Incremental budgeting emphasizes the short run and continuity at the possible expense of the long-run goals of the organization. It encourages spending at the risk of jeopardizing cost control efforts.

Formula budgeting is the technique by which the financial needs or operating requirements of an institution may be determined through the application of a formula. Planning, programming, and budgeting systems (PPBS) is a managerial technique designed to merge the planning process with the allocation of funds by making it difficult to allocate funds without planning. PPBS emphasizes performance, i.e., output and efficiency. Performance budgeting is a budgeting structure that (1) focuses on activities or functions that produce results and from which resources are used, or (2) promotes a budgetary process that links organizational objectives to source utilization. Its principal focus is on improving efficiency by means of activity classifications and cost measurements. In zero-base budgeting, former budgets are not relied upon for making current budgetary estimates. Every activity, function, or program must be justified anew from a zero basis.

The finances of the U.S. Government are controlled by a budget under the supervision of the Director of the Office of Management and Budget. (The former Bureau of the Budget was succeeded by the Office of Management and Budget pursuant to Reorganization Plan 2 of 1970, effective July 1, 1970.)

See BUDGET MANUAL.

BIBLIOGRAPHY

Budget of the United States Government. U.S. Office of Management and the Budget. Washington, DC. Annual.
FALLON, W. K. *AMA Management Handbook*. American Management Association, New York, NY, 1983.
HOLCK, M. *Annual Budgeting: Developing and Using An Annual Budget Effectively*. Augsburg Publishing House, Minneapolis, MN. Annual.
Planning Review. Bimonthly.
WOELFEL, C. J. *Budgeting, Pricing & Cost Controls*. Probus Publishing Co., Chicago, IL, 1987.

BUDGET BUREAU *See* MANAGEMENT AND BUDGET, OFFICE OF.

BUDGET MANUAL The preparation of a budget can be simplified to some extent if a firm has a budget manual that documents the budgeting procedures and provides guidelines to be followed throughout the budgeting process.

The budget manual should be designed with the end users in mind. Participation in the preparation of the budget manual should include major participants in the budgeting process at various management levels. The person or group having authority over the budget should ordinarily draft the budget manual, e.g., the budget director, controller, or budget committee. The budget manual should define budget activities relating to the following:

1. What budget activities should be performed?
   Budget preparation; monitoring operations; operational feedback; performance evaluation.
2. How should budget activities be performed?
   Detailed instructions for completing the budget activities; forms, lists, and schedules to be used.
3. When should budgeting activities occur?
   A timetable for the performance of activities involved in the budgeting process.
4. Who should perform specific budgeting activities?
   The managers and subordinates who are to be assigned specific responsibilities for the performance of budgeting activities.

A survey of the contents of typical budget manuals indicates that the following information is specified in the manuals:

1. Statement of budgeting purpose (goals and objectives).
2. Statement of expected results (links budget to goals and objectives).
3. Budgetary duties of managers and employees (by position); names of persons associated with the position can be listed separately.
4. Preparation of the budget (details and processes).
5. Approval of budget estimates and budget revision (positions/persons responsible for approving estimates and revisions, e.g., budget director, controller, or budget committee).
6. Budget calendar for preparing the budget (realistic and attainable).
7. Sample forms and reports (usually presented in an appendix).
8. Supplemental data (e.g., price lists, cost schedules, personnel charts, and other data requiring frequent revisions; usually reported in an appendix).

The budget manual should be updated periodically to accommodate changes in management goals and objectives, business strategies, forecasts, policies, economic conditions, and other factors.

See BUDGET.

BUILDING AND LOAN ASSOCIATION An early title of the modern savings and loan association. Other early titles for such financial institutions specializing in savings and home financing were building association, homestead association (in Louisiana and other states), and cooperative bank (in New England). The first organization of this type in the U.S., organized in 1831, was the Oxford Provident Building Association. Savings association as a title began to appear toward the latter part of the last century, as the savings function came to be particularly emphasized. The modern savings and loan associations may be chartered either by the state concerned or the Federal Home Loan Bank Board, a dual system suggestive of the same duality in chartering of commercial banks in the U.S.

Earliest organizations of this type were voluntary associations. Later many became corporate in nature by incorporation under general corporation laws of the various states. Modern charters are provided by specific banking incorporation laws.

For details of organization, supervision, and operation, *see* SAVINGS AND LOAN ASSOCIATIONS.

BULGE   A small and sudden, but unsustained, advance in security prices.

BULK FILING   Procedures for storing checks in bundles or groups by date paid within statement cycles. Bulk filing eliminates prefile examination, signature verification of most items, and individual account filing of on-us items. The major objective of bulk filing is to improve productivity by improving the overall use of human and equipment resources. One of the most common types of bulk files is the account range. This method assigns the bulk file accounts into one or more sets of account number ranges. Within the bulk file range(s), the individual cycles would be defined. Many banks use the account number self-checking digit to determine statement cycle. This is a method where the usually unsorted last digit (the check digit) in the account number is used to identify the the statement cycle. For example, in this code 123-456-7, the check digit "7" identifies the statement cycle "7." Another bank might use the two numbers immediately preceding the check digit in the account number (56) to cycle sort the checks. The statement cycle would be 11. This example of cycle 11 would have an approximate correlation with the 11th business day of the month.

BULL   A person who believes that security or commodity prices will rise and who buys on that assumption.

Bulls are market optimists and take a favorable or constructive view of business conditions. On the grain and cotton markets, however, a bull may be one who expects a rise in prices through a blight, flood, drought, frost, or some other unfavorable development that causes higher prices by creating a shortage.

One may be a bull on a particular security without being bullish on the entire market. It is said that some persons are always bulls and some persons are always bears. The successful trader is likely to be neither one nor the other, but one who adjusts his or her attitude, whether it is bullish or bearish, to fundamental conditions.

See BEAR.

BULLION   Metal in the mass; gold or silver in the crude or in the form of bars, lumps, ingots, or nuggets, whether of standard or other fineness, as distinguished from minted coins which are known as specie. Basic weights are 400 troy ounces for gold bars and 1,000 or 1,100 troy ounces for silver bars, with customary trade tolerances above and below these basic weights and assaying specified minimum fineness.

Internationally, official intergovernmental transactions in gold are in bullion, as are those on the free markets, i.e., principal auction markets in London and Zurich. Gold monetary reserves are held in bullion form. Silver spot and futures markets are in silver bullion.

After March 1968, when free world central bankers instituted the two-tier gold price system, the U.S. Treasury stopped selling gold to domestic industrial and artistic users and bullion became obtainable only through private dealers, at prices determined by the international free markets, principally London and Zurich. In 1974, Sections 3 and 4 of the Gold Reserve Act of 1934 (31 U.S.C. 442 and 443) were repealed, and no provisions of any law, rule, regulation, or order in effect on that date may be construed to prohibit any person from purchasing, holding, selling, or otherwise dealing in gold in the United States or abroad. On December 31, 1984, President Ford promulgated Executive Order 11825 (40 FR 1003) revoking prior executive orders and provisions of executive orders insofar as they pertained to the regulation of the acquisition or holding of gold, or other transactions therein. Previously licensed gold bullion dealers thus became free to continue such dealing without licenses.

See BULLION DEALERS, GOLD BARS, SILVER, SILVER BULLION.

BULLION DEALERS   Firms and institutions dealing in gold and silver bullion. After March, 1968, when the two-tier gold price system was instituted by free world central bankers, U.S. Treasury sales of gold to domestic industrial and artistic users were stopped, and thereafter this supply became obtainable only through private dealers, at prices determined by the international free markets, principally London and Zurich.

P.L. 92–110, 87 Stat. 352, and P.L. 93–373, 88 Stat. 445, provided that effective December 31, 1974, Sections 3 and 4 of the Gold Reserve Act of 1934 (31 U.S.C. 442 and 443) were repealed, and no provisions of any law, rule, regulation, or order in effect on that date may be construed to prohibit any person from purchasing, holding, selling, or otherwise dealing in gold in the U.S. or abroad. On December 31, 1974, President Ford promulgated Executive Order 11825 (40 FR 1003) revoking prior executive orders and provisions of executive orders insofar as they pertained to the regulation of the acquisition or holding of gold, or other transactions therein. Previously licensed gold bullion dealers thus became free to continue such dealing without necessity for licenses. The Silver Purchase Act of 1934 was repealed in 1963. Besides spot markets in gold and silver, both metals are traded on commodity exchanges.

See COMMODITY EXCHANGES, GOLD BARS, SILVER, SILVER BULLION.

BULLION VALUE   The commercial or market value of a coin as metal, or commodity value, as distinguished from its monetary face or denominational value.

Gold Bullion Value.   In the U.S., various Treasury orders in 1933 retired gold in any form from monetary circulation and required its delivery to the Federal Reserve banks for payment in other lawful money at the former statutory gold price of $20.67 per troy ounce (23.22 fine grains, troy weight, gold content of the dollar). In turn, the gold in Federal Reserve banks was ordered turned in to the U.S. Treasury pursuant to the Gold Reserve Act of January 30, 1934, again with payment being made in gold certificates, series of 1934, to the Federal Reserve banks at the former statutory gold price of $20.67 per troy ounce. Thus upon Presidential Proclamation January 31, 1934, devaluing the dollar from 23.22 fine grains troy to 13.71 fine grains troy (raising the monetary gold price from $20.67 per troy ounce to $35 per troy ounce), all of the gold profit was reflected on the U.S. Treasury's accounts. Since 1933, pursuant to the Gold Reserve Act of 1934, the monetary gold reserves of the U.S. are carried only in bullion form.

Effective May 8, 1972, a change in par value of the U.S. dollar resulted in a monetary gold price of $38 per troy ounce, thus creating a profit on the U.S. total holdings of monetary gold of $828 million. Including the U.S. reserve position in the International Monetary Fund and the U.S. allocation of special drawing rights, the total of U.S. international reserve assets increased $1.016 billion as the result of the change in the par value of the dollar.

Effective October 18, 1973, a further change in the par value of the U.S. dollar created a new monetary gold price for the U.S. dollar of $42.22 per fine troy ounce, resulting in an increase of $1.436 billion in the U.S. international reserve assets ($1.165 billion in value of the gold stock, $54 million in U.S. reserve position in the International Monetary Fund, and $217 million in special drawing rights).

Beginning in July 1974, the International Monetary Fund (IMF) began valuing the U.S. reserve position in IMF and special drawing rights in terms of a weighted average of exchange rates for 16 currencies; since 1981, it has used five currencies. As a result, these assets are no longer directly valued in gold. As of the end of 1986, the dollar price of gold still stood at $42.22 per ounce, and the total value of the U.S. reserve gold stock was $11.1 billion.

Silver Bullion Value.   Title II of P.L. 91–607, December 31, 1970, eliminated the usage of silver in all U.S. coins for general circulation, including authorization of nonsilver dollar and nonsilver half-dollar coins. Their composition is copper and nickel, similar to that of the quarter and dime coins authorized by the Coinage Act of 1965. Moreover, the Treasury discontinued its offerings of silver at auctions through the General Services Administration on November 10, 1970. However, the Treasury must buy newly mined domestic silver, if tendered, at $1.25 an ounce, pursuant to a provision in the Coinage Act of 1965. The last year in which the average New York price for silver indicated feasibility of such tenders was 1962, when the year's average price was $1.08521. Prior to September 9, 1963, the price of silver was continuously below $1.2930, the price which prevailed until May 18, 1967.

Under the Coinage Act of 1965, the Treasury had the statutory power to prohibit by regulations the melting, treatment, and export of silver coins. Such authority was invoked on May 18, 1965. However, this ban was revoked May 12, 1969, by the Treasury, following such recommendation by the Joint Commission on the Coinage, established in 1967 pursuant to the Coinage Act of 1965.

See GOLD, SILVER, UNITED STATES MONEY.

BULL MARKET A market in which the bulls are in ascendency and optimism and rising prices prevail; to use a term of the DOW THEORY, a market in which the "primary trend" is upward. In such a market, short selling is a negligible factor, sales being confined largely to long stock. While there are always technical reactions in a bull market, due to profit-taking on long stock and short selling for covering on technical reactions, there is always the expectation that the market will move to higher levels; in the terminology of the Dow theory, there is no "reversal of primary trend." The term therefore usually applies to the broad or primary swings of the market.

See BEAR MARKET, SPECULATIVE CYCLE.

BUNCHED This term has two meanings:

1. Consecutive sales of the same security at the same or different prices recorded on the tape of a stock exchange ticker.
2. When brokers combine orders from different customers for execution in a single transaction, they are said to be bunched. Under Rule 372 of the New York Stock Exchange, no member or member organization shall execute bunched orders without charging the required commission. Moreover, a member or member organization shall not combine orders (Rule 411) given by several different customers to buy or sell odd lots of the same stock into a round-lot order without the prior approval of the customers interested.

BUNCO The practice of cheating or swindling by so-called confidence men, who play upon the credulity and avarice of their victims. After winning the confidence of the intended victim, the swindler might impose counterfeit money upon him or induce him to purchase worthless stock or to cash a bogus check.

See SWINDLING.

BUNDLING In the charging of brokerage commissions to the public for the execution of orders on securities, the practice of full service brokerage firms of charging such commissions high enough to cover the costs of all services provided to customers, beyond the "bare bones" service of the actual execution of orders, regardless of the use by customers or provision thereto of other services, such as investment counseling, research, publications, tax assistance reports, etc., without "unbundling" them.

Prior to the passage of the 1975 amendments to the Securities Acts (P.L. 94-29), the SECURITIES AND EXCHANGE COMMISSION adopted its Rule 19b-3 (Securities Exchange Act Release No. 10986, August 27, 1974) eliminating fixed commissions on exchange transactions as of May 1, 1975. Upon passage of the 1975 amendments, the SEC proposed Rule 19b-3 and subsequently adopted it under the statute (Sec. 6(e) of the 1975 amendments). The Commission set forth as its basic reason for the adoption of Rule 19b-3 "the conclusion that, under present circumstances, the free play of competition can provide a level and structure of commission rates which would better serve the interests of the investing public, the securities markets, the securities industry, the national economy and the public interest than any system of price fixing which can reasonably be devised."

The first major New York Stock Exchange member firm to "unbundle" the services included in commission rates, and to provide commission discounts on stock and bond commissions, announced the summary of its "Alpha Account" services and fees effective May 1, 1975. The firm explained that "for many years, New York Stock Exchange member firms were required to charge individual investors according to a uniform schedule of commission rates. For many investors, the services provided under that system were exactly what they required. For some, however, the fit was not as good." Actually this firm was then and still is a full service brokerage firm, but it did lead the way in "unbundling" the services.

In the latter part of 1975, discount brokers began to appear, offering discounts on a "no frills" basis strictly for the execution of orders, without providing any of the other services provided by full service brokers. Then in June, 1976, a specialist firm on the New York Stock Exchange also became a public discount broker, the first NYSE member firm to substantially lower commissions without eliminating the traditional broker-client relationship. A number of other long-established full service brokerage firms have also in recent years offered special plans for reduction in commission charges to small investors, while at the same time providing other services reflected in charges. By July, 1981, various discount brokers were departing from their "no frills" policy and adding to the range of investor services provided.

As the result of development of the discount brokerage business and the unbundling of services, investors have greater choice in the selection of brokerage services desired, from the "bare bones" service of execution of orders to the full service types of brokerage. The entry of major banks into the business, through their parent holding companies, highlights the efforts by banks to overcome the restraints imposed by banking laws and regulations upon their diversification into a full range of services, in meeting the competition of nonbanks in providing a similarly full range of financial services, including bank-like services.

BUOYANCY A rising tendency of stock prices. The term has no technical connotation in security market analysis, but sometimes is found in lay reference to market action that is upward in "primary trend."

See BULL MARKET, DOW THEORY.

BUREAU OF ECONOMIC ANALYSIS A Department of Commerce bureau that has the responsibility for reporting descriptive statistics related to the macroeconomy. These data are reported annually in the Economic Report of the President, among other places.

The goal of BEA is to provide a clear picture of the U.S. economy through the preparation, development, and interpretation of the national income and product accounts, summarized by the gross national product; the wealth accounts, which show the business and other components of national wealth; the input-output accounts, which trace the interrelationship among industrial markets; personal income and related economic series by geographic area; the U.S. balance of payments on accounts and associated foreign investment accounts; and measures relating to environmental change within the framework of the national economic accounts.

The work on the national economic accounts is supplemented by the preparation and analysis of other measures of business activity, including various tools for forecasting economic developments, such as surveys of investment outlays and plans of U.S. business, econometric models of the U.S. economy, and a system of leading, coincident, and lagging economic indicators. The data and analyses prepared by BEA are disseminated mainly through its monthly publications, the *Survey of Current Business*, including periodic supplements to the *Survey*, and *Business Conditions Digest*.

BIBLIOGRAPHY

"A User's Guide to BEA Information: Publications, Computer Tapes, Diskettes, and Other Information Services." *Survey of Current Business*, March, 1989.

RYSCAVAGE, P. "Understanding Real Income Trends: An Analysis of Conflicting Signals." *Business Economics*, January, 1989.

BUREAU OF ENGRAVING AND PRINTING One of the bureaus of the U.S. Treasury Department, headed by a director appointed by the Secretary of the Treasury. Its functions include the designing, engraving, and printing of all major items of a financial character issued by the U.S. Government. It produces paper currency; Treasury bonds, bills, notes, and certificates; postage, revenue, customs, documentary, and savings stamps; and food coupons. In addition, the bureau prints commissions, certificates of awards, permits, and a wide variety of other miscellaneous items.

Operations of the bureau are currently financed by means of a revolving fund established in accordance with the provisions of P.L. 656, which requires the bureau to be reimbursed by customer agencies for all costs of products manufactured and services performed. The bureau is also authorized to assess amounts to acquire capital equipment and provide for working capital needs. During 1987, the bureau delivered 6.5 billion Federal Reserve notes, and projected total deliveries of currency for the 1988 fiscal year were 6.1 billion. Except for a small force of employees engaged in control and accountability at the plant of the distinctive paper manufacturer, all bureau operations are in Washington.

See CURRENCY SHIPMENTS, REDEMPTION OF MONEY.

BUREAU OF LABOR STATISTICS (BLS) A Department of Labor bureau that has the responsibility for reporting descriptive statistics related to aspects of the labor market. For example, the BLS calculates unemployment rates as well as the Consumer Price Index. These data are reported annually in the Economic Report of the President, among other sources.

BUREAU OF THE BUDGET Succeeded by the Office of Management and Budget, which was established in the Executive Office of the President pursuant to Reorganization Plan 2 of 1970.

BUREAU OF THE MINT A bureau of the U.S. Department of the Treasury. The Mint produces domestic and foreign coins, manufactures and sells official medals, and manufactures and sells coin sets for collectors.

BUREAU OF THE PUBLIC DEBT The Bureau of the Public Debt is located in the Department of the Treasury. The Bureau supports the management of the public debt, prepares Department of the Treasury circulars offering public debt securities; directs the handling of subscriptions and making of allotments; formulates instructions and regulations pertaining to security issues; and conducts or directs the conduct of transactions in outstanding securities. The Bureau performs the final audit of retired securities and interest coupons; maintains accounting control over public debt receipts and expenditures, securities, and interest costs; keeps individual accounts of owners of book-entry and registered securities and authorizes the payment of principal and interest; and adjudicates claims on account of lost, stolen, destroyed, or mutilated securities.

Under Bureau supervision, transactions in public debt securities are conducted by the Federal Reserve banks and their branches as fiscal agents of the United States. Most banks and other financial institutions act as issuing and paying agents for U.S. Savings bonds, and as paying agents for U.S. Savings notes.

BUREAU OF TRUSTS One of the bureaus in the former Office of Alien Property Custodian. The functions of the Office of Alien Property Custodian were transferred in 1946 to the Department of Justice. This transfer was made permanent by Reorganization Plan 1, effective July 1, 1947. In the Department of Justice, the Assistant Attorney General in charge of the civil division was also the Director of the Office of Alien Property. That office was terminated as an organizational entity on June 30, 1966 (per Executive Order 11281, May 13, 1966). The foreign funds control functions were transferred to the Office of Foreign Assets Control, Treasury Department, and the remaining functions pertaining to alien property continue to be discharged by the Assistant Attorney General in charge of the civil division, Department of Justice, pursuant to the Trading with the Enemy Act as amended, the International Claims Settlement Act as amended, and other pertinent statutes. Title 8, Chapter II of the Code of Federal Regulations codifies regulations under the Office of Alien Property.

BUSINESS BAROMETERS Trade data; indices of industry and commerce; statistical indicators of business conditions; fundamental and comparative business statistics by which business volume, activity, credit supply, price trends, profit prospects, and investment opportunities may be measured. Like weather barometers which forecast meteorological conditions, business barometers may also be used as data and instruments whereby to forecast business, credit, and investment tendencies.

By P.L. 120, 81st Congress, approved June 23, 1949, the Congress by joint resolution authorized the Joint Economic Committee to issue a monthly publication entitled *Economic Indicators*. This is prepared for the Joint Economic Committee by the Council of Economic Advisers and is available to the public through the Government Printing Office. The economic indicators selected for these purposes are published and explained in *1980 Supplement to Economic Indicators: Historical and Descriptive Background*, prepared for the Joint Economic Committee by the Office of Federal Statistical Policy and Standards, Department of Commerce, the Council of Economic Advisers, and the source agencies. The materials contained in this publication are explained in nontechnical language. In addition they contain judgments and evaluations on use and limitation which are of special interest in connection with particular economic indicators. A discussion of those indicators deserving of coverage follows.

Total Output, Income, and Spending.

Gross national product: Gross national product (GNP) is the total national output of goods and services. It is published in both current and constant dollars, the latter deflated for price change. It measures output in terms of expenditures in final markets. The expenditures encompass four major market categories: (1) personal consumption expenditures, (2) gross private domestic investment, (3) net exports of goods and services, and (4) government purchases of goods and services. The goods and services included in the GNP are for the most part within the framework of money transactions in the market economy. There are some nonmarket items, the most important of which is the imputed rental value of owner-occupied dwellings. The methods used to eliminate seasonal variation differ with the particular series to be adjusted. The GNP is also deflated or expressed in dollars of constant purchasing power. The procedure in general is to divide detailed components of the current dollar GNP by appropriate price indexes, utilizing as fine a product breakdown as possible, and then to sum the components to obtain the constant dollar or real GNP.

The GNP is the most comprehensive measure of trends in the nation's economic activity. It has high value as an analytic tool, since the movements of many sectors of the economy, including the sales of many industries and enterprises, are quite closely related to changes in the level of GNP.

Nonfinancial corporate business—output, costs, and profits: The gross domestic product of nonfinancial corporate business is the output less intermediate purchases of nonfinancial corporations. It is measured from the income side of the accounts and is the sum of the following: (1) capital consumption allowances with capital consumption adjustment; (2) indirect business tax and nontax liability; (3) business transfer payments less subsidies; (4) compensation of employees; (5) net interest; and (6) corporate profits with inventory valuation and capital consumption adjustments. The constant dollar gross domestic product of nonfinancial corporations is the value expressed in 1972 prices. The current dollar cost and profit per unit of output is the current dollar product divided by the constant dollar product.

The nonfinancial corporation group is comparable to the similarly named sector of the flow of funds accounts of the Federal Reserve Board. It is also consistent with the net and gross stocks of reproducible fixed capital and inventories data produced by the Bureau of Economic Analysis (BEA) in the Department of Commerce.

National income: National income is the aggregate of earnings by labor and property which arise in the current production of goods and services by the nation's economy. It is the sum of five major items: (1) compensation of employees; (2) proprietors' income; (3) rental income of persons; (4) net interest; and (5) corporate profits.

The national income is a useful measure of the rate of flow of earnings from current output. By definition it excludes income from the revaluation of past output, e.g., capital gains and losses. The movements of this series correspond with movements in production. However, the value of the national income series lies more in the composition than in the total. It may mean little to know that national income (unadjusted for price changes) has gone up; but it may be very important to know the relative contribution of wages and profits to that increase.

The chief cautions for use result partly from the definitions employed and partly from the nature of the basic data. For example, variations in wages and profits do not necessarily indicate changes in the welfare of workers or in the ability of corporations to provide new capital. For such purposes, these variations must be considered in the light of other factors such as the cost of living and the cost of new plant and equipment. With respect to the basic data—which are particularly applicable to the current data on net interest, proprietors' income, and rental income of persons—it should be recognized that many of the available data permit only fair approximations of the phenomena being measured, and therefore these statistics should not be considered as instruments of precise measurement.

Sources of personal income: Personal income is the current income received by persons from all sources, inclusive of transfers from government and business but exclusive of transfers among persons. Not only individuals (including owners of unincorporated enterprises), but nonprofit institutions, private trust funds, and private health and welfare funds are classified as persons. Personal income is measured on a before-tax basis, as the sum of wage and salary disbursements, other labor income, proprietors' and rental income, interest and dividends, and transfer payments, minus personal contributions for social insurance. Labor income is principally wages and salaries. It excludes employer contributions for social insurance. Proprietors' income and rental income of persons are defined in the section on national income. Dividends are payments in cash or other assets excluding stock by corporations organized for profit to stockholders who are U.S. persons. Personal interest income is the sum of the net interest component of national income, total interest paid by consumers to business, and interest paid by government to persons and business, less interest received by government. Transfer payments include payments not resulting from current production, such as Social Security benefits and military pensions.

The estimates for personal income and components and for disposable income (see next section) measure trends in spending power of individuals. The inclusion of substantial nonmonetary items—imputed rent, interest, food, fuel—should be noted, but the effect of these items should not be overemphasized. They tend to make income estimates more stable, but have little effect on the ability of the estimates to show when a change is occurring and the direction of the shift.

Disposition of personal income: Disposable personal income is equal to personal income less taxes on individuals (including income and other taxes not deductible as business expense) and other general government nontax payments of individuals. Personal outlays are the sum of personal consumption expenditures, interest paid by business to consumers, and personal transfer payments to foreigners (net). Personal consumption expenditures are the sum of monetary and imputed expenditures made by persons (individuals, nonprofit institutions such as hospitals, etc.) for goods and services. The expenditure total covers total purchase cost to persons, including general sales taxes. The full cost of automobiles, refrigerators, furniture, and the like is included in the period when sold—month, quarter, or year—regardless of when payments are made or completed. The purchase of homes is not included as a personal consumption expenditure; instead, the expenditure is included as an investment expenditure, and the estimated rental value to the homeowner is included in personal consumption expenditures, as he occupies the home.

Durable goods are those items which on the average last three years or longer in use. Nondurable goods are tangible commodities with a shorter life. Services include purchases such as housing, telephone, electricity, shoe repair, gas, and water, and also such items as the expense of handling life insurance and banking services furnished without a specific charge.

Personal saving is personal income less the sum of personal outlays and personal tax and nontax payments. It is the current saving of individuals (including proprietors), nonprofit institutions, private noninsured welfare funds, and private trust funds. Personal saving equals the change in the net worth of persons, which may also be viewed as the sum of net acquisition of financial assets (such as cash and deposits, securities, and the net equity of individuals in life insurance and in private noninsured pension funds), and physical assets (housing), less the sum of net borrowing and of capital consumption allowances.

Per capita disposable personal income is the disposable personal income divided by the Census Bureau's estimate of the total population of the United States, including Armed Forces overseas and the institutionalized population, for the middle of the period covered. Per capita disposable personal income in 1972 prices is obtained by dividing the current dollar series by the implicit deflator for personal consumption expenditures on a 1972 base used in the GNP series.

Disposable personal income is often used as a measure of income available for spending or saving. For measuring changes in real terms, i.e., in consumers' buying power, the estimates of disposable personal income in constant prices are to be preferred. The estimates of personal consumption expenditures represent a generally useful, reliable measure of trends in consumer purchases. They may be used to study trends in the ratio of wages, or more generally of income, to expenditure, and to review the division of the national output between consumer demand, business capital formation, and government defense or other expenditures. The estimates of personal saving are residual from two larger estimates. The errors and limitations present in the hundreds of series developed for other purposes, which must be used at present in estimating the national income, may not completely cancel out. To this extent these errors are transmitted into the saving estimate. Quarter-to-quarter changes for recent periods are subject to revision as better data become available.

Farm Income. The farm income accounts treat farming as a business sector within the U.S. economy. Production of farm commodities is essentially viewed as taking place on one large farm in each state. The accounts measure the sector's value-added product and income of farm operators and operator landlords. Returns to nonoperator landlords are not included as farm income. Certain transactions between farms, such as within-state sales of livestock, are not included. Conceptually these cancel within the sector, although the estimated gross receipts and expenses are less than the direct sum of such items for all farms.

Gross farm income consists of cash marketing receipts, the value of physical changes in farm inventories of crops and livestock, direct government payments, other farm cash income, the value of farm products consumed directly in farm households, and an imputed gross rental value of farm dwellings. Farm production expenses are the sum of all current operating expenses and overhead charges including those on farm dwellings. Net farm income, a residual component, represents the return to farm operators for their family labor, management, and capital investment in the farm. It measures the net return from the current year's output. A second net measure—net cash income—is the difference between gross income and expenses that are limited to cash items. This latter series is only available on an annual basis.

The farm income estimates measure the farm sector in the aggregate. As a result, their most appropriate use is in the context of the national income and product accounts. These accounts treat the economy in terms of interactions between and among sectors with respect to product and income flows. While certain types of transactions within the farm sector are not measured, estimated receipts and expenses do serve as meaningful measures of the sector's economic activity. For example, cash receipts estimates by commodity and state have been widely used by businesses which serve agriculture and by public officials to explain changing agricultural conditions among and within states.

One limitation of the net farm income series is that it does not provide a complete picture of the financial condition of farm operators. As a group, farm operator families have significant amounts of income from sources other than farming. And historically investments in farm real estate have had greater nominal returns in the form of capital gains than in current earnings. Therefore, the overall debt, equity, and cash flow situation, in addition to current income, should be included in a broader analysis of the condition of the farm sector.

Corporate Profits. The corporate profits and related series of the BEA pertain to all U.S. corporations organized for profit and to mutual financial institutions. Data are shown for broad industry groups, and estimates are made of the distribution of profits among corporate tax liability, dividends, and undistributed profits.

The national income concept of profit is used in these series. Dividends received by corporations are deducted from profits and dividends to obtain unduplicated totals reflecting income originating in the U.S. corporations. Profits are calculated inclusive of domestic depletion, which is not considered an element of capital consumption or of other expenses in the income and product accounts (depletion allowances are not included in the capital consumption allowance estimates). Capital gains or losses are eliminated from profits because they do not measure gains or losses originating from current production. Bad debt expenses are measured by actual losses, not additions to reserves; and the profit or loss of bankrupt firms includes the gain from unpaid debt. Adjustments for international flows affecting profits are made. In these respects the national income measure of profits differs from those shown in the Internal Revenue Service tabulations of tax returns. The national income profits measure also differs from those commonly shown in company reports and from the financial reports series of the Federal Trade Commission.

The corporate profits series is an important economic indicator, reflecting the state of health of a substantial part of the nation's business community. Certain limitations of the series, however, require that it be used with caution:

1. As its title implies, the series measures only the profits of corporations. It does not therefore portray fully the profit position of all business.

BUSINESS BAROMETERS

2. The corporate profits estimates contained in *Economic Indicators* are rather broad aggregates and need to be supplemented by data pertaining to specific industries for some analytical uses.
3. The quarterly corporate profits estimates are less reliable than the annual estimates, especially the annual estimates for periods more than two years prior to the current year. There are two principal reasons for this:
   a. Quarterly income statements on which the quarterly series are based are inherently less reliable than annual income statements.
   b. Wide gaps in the financial data available quarterly for some industries, such as services, make the underlying basis of the quarterly estimates weaker than that of the annual estimates.

Gross Private Domestic Investment. Gross private domestic investment is one of the major components of gross national product. The series consists of the net acquisitions of fixed capital goods by private business and nonprofit institutions; commissions arising in the sale and purchase of new and existing fixed assets, principally real estate; and the value of the change in the volume of inventories held by business. It covers all private dwellings including those acquired by persons for their own occupancy. Separate statistical series are published for fixed investment, which in turn consists of separate series for nonresidential fixed investment and residential fixed investment, and for change in business inventories. The structures series used in computing gross private domestic investment is based on the private construction component of the new construction series, with the addition of estimates for oil- and gas-well drilling, commissions arising in the sale of new and existing structures, and net purchases of structures from government. Quarterly estimates of producers' durable equipment and change in business inventories are revised annually to reflect more complete data than were available when the initial estimates were made. The revisions in the change in business inventories series have sometimes been quite sizable, and have resulted primarily from revisions in the basic book value of inventory aggregates.

Changes in business investment are a major, if not the major, factor determining business conditions. Unfortunately, there are many shortcomings in the data on which both fixed investment and inventory changes are based, especially for current quarters. The absence of reliable current data on government purchases of producers' durable equipment constitutes a special problem. The limitations of the data on manufacturers' commodity sales and on new plant and equipment expenditures affect the current estimates of investment in producers' durable equipment. The rate of investment in construction is also subject to many data inadequacies, requiring the use of phasing patterns and also synthetic statistical techniques.

The figures on change in business inventories are useful indicators of the physical volume change in inventories during the period under review. A limitation in the series is inherent in the basic method that must be used. The estimates are calculated as the difference between large and possibly volatile inventory totals at two points in time. Even small errors in the estimates of total inventories can lead to large relative errors in the estimates of change in inventories.

Expenditures for New Plant and Equipment. The BEA of the Department of Commerce provides quarterly measures of business expenditures for new plant and equipment for actual outlays and for planned expenditures for two succeeding quarters and the current calendar year. The series measures the expenditures by all private business (except farming, real estate, the professions, and nonprofit and other institutions) for new plant and machinery and equipment for which depreciation accounts are maintained. Expenditures charged off as current expenses are excluded. Estimates of the actual and projected outlays are based on survey data from business firms.

The plant and equipment series is one of the few economic series in which estimates of planned events as well as historical events are made. Planned capital outlays, especially for the coming year, are of great importance in the analysis of business conditions. Planned expenditures for a period differ from actual expenditures for the same period for a number of reasons. Nevertheless, for most periods the planned outlays adjusted for seasonal variations and systematic biases have been a reliable indicator of the overall trend of capital expenditures. The survey has generally reflected the cyclical turning points in the postwar period.

There are two principal deficiencies in the statistical procedures employed in making the estimates of expenditures for new plant and equipment. One of these is the inadequacy of the same of companies surveyed for some industries. This is so despite the fact that a continuing effort is made to add additional firms to the sample. The second deficiency is that the benchmark data are only available with a substantial lag, and in several areas such data are of limited reliability.

Status of the Labor Force. The monthly labor force data provide basic measures of the performance of the economy in human terms. They are used in analyses of the supply of labor in relation to the population, sensitivity of employment trends to changes in industry output, and the relationship of unemployment to inflation. These analyses in turn are used in the formulation of fiscal, monetary, and wage-price policies for the overall management of the economy. In addition to providing input for these macroeconomic policies, detail on the demographic and economic characteristics of the labor force facilitates analyses of structural aspects of job markets for assessing and shaping employment, training, and placement programs for target groups of the population.

Because the household survey is based on a sample, the results may differ from the figures that would be obtained if a universal survey using the same questionnaire and procedures were taken. As in any survey, the results are subject to errors of response and reporting. The standard error is primarily a measure of sampling variability, that is, of the variation that occurs by chance because a sample rather than the entire population is surveyed. The chances are about 68 out of 100 that an estimate from the survey differs from a figure that would be obtained through a complete census by less than the standard error. Approximation of the standard errors for these and many other unemployment and labor force estimates are published monthly in the explanatory notes of *Employment and Earnings*, published by the Bureau of Labor Statistics (BLS) of the Department of Labor. These statistics are derived from the current population survey (CPS), which is a monthly survey of 65,000 households (beginning in 1980) conducted by the Bureau of the Census for the BLS.

Production and Business Activity.

Index of industrial production: The total index of industrial production is probably the most widely used indicator as a coinciding measure of conditions. It is used with related data on employment, inventories, trade, prices, and other economic data in analyzing short- and long-run developments in the economy. The component indexes are used to determine the areas in which important changes accounted for the observed changes in the total index. They may also be used in analysis related to individual industries—for example, studies of a company's output and sales figures in relation to the output movements of the industry. The scope of the index is limited to manufacturing, mining, and electric and gas utilities. It should not be used as a measure of total production, because agriculture, construction activity, transportation, trade, and various other sectors are not included. It should be noted, however, that changes in the output of manufactures, minerals, and utilities are especially significant, because they account for much of the cyclical variation in total economic activity.

Capacity utilization: Several sets of capacity utilization statistics now exist, and they differ as to their arithmetic means, variances, and cyclical variability. The Federal Reserve and the Wharton series, both based on production indexes, conform very closely to each other in terms of cyclical patterns and vary more over the cycle than do rates based solely on company survey responses, such as those published by the BEA of the Department of Commerce. Mean utilization rates from the census survey of plant capacity are much lower than BEA, McGraw-Hill, and Federal Reserve rates, while those from Wharton are much higher, reflecting coverage and methodological differences in the various series.

Capacity utilization rates along with unemployment rates are important indicators of the level of resource use. High utilization rates, in general, are associated with increased levels of investment; high utilization rates in certain industries, particularly those that produce materials, may be indicative of bottlenecks and supply-side inflationary pressures. The estimated capacity indexes appear to be reasonably good measures of production capabilities over time, but they should not be considered to be accurate indicators of short-term changes in capacity. The capacity utilization figures are inherently inexact, combining errors in the measurement of output and capacity. The latter concept is a potentiality rather than a reality and is thus

ENCYCLOPEDIA OF BANKING AND FINANCE

ambiguous and hard to measure. Generally it is prudent to interpret utilization rates in regard to their own past peaks, lows, and means and not solely in terms of their current level. A peak rate of 100% has never been achieved for total manufacturing because of factors such as imbalances of materials used in the manufacturing process that contribute to bottlenecks in the process, lack of skilled labor, and nonsynchronized peak rates.

New construction: The new construction series indicates the current volume of this segment of economic activity. Construction has an important impact on employment in the contract construction and building materials industries, and on additions to capital stocks of structures in the private and public sectors. It is used in short-term cyclical and long-term growth analyses. Since the series does not include maintenance and repair, it cannot be related directly to the total use of construction labor and materials.

New private housing—units authorized by permit places: Units authorized are general indicators of the available inventory of new homes. They can be used as advance indicators of the need for new construction. Building permit data are also presented in considerable geographic detail not available for housing starts, the data thus being helpful to a wider range of users. But the residential construction measurable from building permit records does not reflect construction activity outside of areas subject to local permit requirements.

Business sales and inventories: The monthly wholesale trade series is an important economic indicator which reflects the level of economic activity at an intermediate stage of the distributive process. The wholesale data together with similar data for manufacturing and retail trade provide a consistent aggregate series for total business. The wholesale inventory data are used in developing the inventory change component of the gross national product. The monthly estimates of sales and inventories are based on a sample and are therefore subject to sampling variability. In addition, they are subject to nonsampling errors, such as the failure of respondents to submit reports in time for tabulation, to submit correct figures, or to respond at all. The estimates of sales are more accurate than the estimates of inventories. The statistics on inventories are based on estimates by respondents or imputations due to nonresponse to a greater extent than are sales statistics, reflecting the fact that wholesalers do not keep inventory records on a monthly basis to the same extent that they keep monthly sales records.

The retail sales and inventories are useful indicators of probable future economic activity at the manufacturing and other earlier stages of production and distribution. The series is also used in developing the consumer expenditure and inventory change components of the gross national product. Since the monthly retail sales estimates are based on a probability sample, they are subject to sampling variability, as well as such biases as nonresponse or reporting errors. The monthly sales estimates are compared with census of retail trade data when those statistics become available.

Manufacturers' shipments, inventories, and orders: The shipments series reflects the demand for the goods and services of manufacturers; trends in the inventories and changes in inventories series reflect the difference between production and shipments of manufacturers; the new orders series indicates the probable future course of manufacturers' activity in some industries in the immediate future. The manufacturers' inventory data, together with inventory data for retailers and merchant wholesalers, are the basic data used in computing estimates of the change in business inventories component of the gross national product. In measurement of the change in business inventories, the book value inventory change data are adjusted to remove the effect of changes in replacement costs.

Prices.

Producer prices: Producer price indexes are used for a wide variety of purposes in both the public and the private sector. The Bureau of Labor Statistics features the finished goods price index in its monthly news release as one of the best available measures of inflation at the primary market level. This and other stages of processing indexes are currently used as the principal framework for analyzing the sources and transmission of price changes throughout the U.S. economy. They are thus important for the formulation and evaluation of governmental policies in fiscal and monetary affairs. Analysis of more detailed commodity indexes is also useful for studies of governmental policies targeted for specific industries or products, such as energy or steel.

The usefulness of producer price indexes is limited in a number of ways. For example, commodities and reporting companies have been drawn on a judgment sampling basis, rather than a probability sampling basis. In most cases only volume-selling products produced by major companies have been priced directly. The index may not precisely measure price changes because identical qualities are not always available in successive periods. Statistical measures of accuracy are not possible under the current system. The stages of processing groups, commodity groups, and other structures of producer price indexes do not match the standard industrial classification system, thereby hampering comparisons of price data with data on wages, productivity, and the like. Producer price indexes currently cover only about half of the total value of production in the mining and manufacturing sectors; there is no coverage of such crucial sectors as services, transportation, insurance, communications, and distribution. These and other problems will be addressed during the producer price index revision, which will be phased in during the 1980s.

Consumer prices: The consumer price indexes (CPIs) are compiled monthly by the Bureau of Labor Statistics (BLS) of the Department of Labor. They provide measures of price change for fixed marketbaskets of goods and services purchased by all urban consumers and by urban wage earners and clerical workers. Prior to January, 1978, there existed only the consumer price index for urban wage earners and clerical workers (unrevised CPI-W). Effective with release of data for January, 1978, the BLS introduced: (1) an updated and revised CPI for urban wage earners and clerical workers (CPI-W), and (2) a broader-based CPI for all urban consumers (CPI-U), including salaried workers, the self-employed, the retired, and the unemployed, as well as urban wage earners and clerical workers. Both of these indexes were linked to the unrevised CPI-W; i.e., for the month of December, 1977, all three indexes had the same value.

The indexes are often called cost of living indexes, and they are frequently used as approximate measures of change in the cost of living. The CPI is used by the public and private sectors in wage and salary negotiation, administration, and escalation, and for analyses of the functioning of the economy and the interrelationship of its components. They are also used in commercial negotiations and in formulating business strategy. The indexes are designed to measure only the changes in prices, not expenditures resulting from changes in purchasing habits or standard of living; they do not measure how much consumers actually spend to live. Also, they measure price changes for only their specific population groups. Other qualities of commodities and expenditure weights would have to be used to measure price changes for specific subgroups of the population, such as the poor or the retired, or for other groups, such as farm families. The fixed marketbaskets represent the average quantities bought by all members of the index population and are not necessarily representative of the purchases made by any single family or individual consumer.

Prices received by farmers: This index should not be confused with the farm product component of the producer price index. The index of prices received by farmers measures changes in prices at the point of first sale, and is based on average prices for all grades of a given commodity; the producer price index generally measures prices in selected central markets and is based on prices of specific grades or qualities.

The index is widely used as a measure of changes in average prices received by farmers for farm commodities. It is an approximation of the price component of receipts by farmers from the sale of farm products. It is required for the computation of adjusted base period prices, which are necessary for calculation of commodity parity prices under the formula prescribed by the Agricultural Adjustment Act of 1938, as amended. Livestock commodities not covered in the index account for about 2% of the total cash receipts, and the uncovered crops account for about 7% (major crop items not covered are forest, nursery, and greenhouse products).

Prices paid by farmers: This is a measure of the price component of aggregated expenditures by farmers for living and production costs. The series is used by analysts to determine whether inputs originating in farming have changed more in price than those of nonfarm origin, and in market planning and negotiating marketing contracts. The parity index (1910–1914 = 100) is used to establish commodity parity prices for agricultural price support programs. Pricing points of the prices paid series are generally not the same as those for the CPI and PPI. Prices paid indexes represent sales to farmers or sales to rural areas, not seasonally adjusted or adjusted for quality changes.

One limitation of the index of prices paid by farmers relates to coverage. The index does not contain price data for approximately

10% of total expenditures for services used in farm production. The larger excluded items are machinery repair, veterinary services, and construction of farm buildings. Another problem is that no adjustments are made for quality changes of products priced.

Parity ratio: Parity ratio measures the purchasing power of products sold by farmers in terms of the goods and services they buy, compared to the purchasing power in the base period (1910-1914 = 100). When the index of prices received by farmers is divided by the index of prices paid by farmers, and expressed as a percentage, the result is called the parity ratio. Nonprice income supplements, such as government payments, are not represented in the index of prices received. Because of this, an adjusted parity ratio is also published which adjusts the parity ratio for the nonprice income.

Money, Credit, and Security Markets.

Money stock measures and liquid assets: Money stock data are published weekly by the Board of Governors of the Federal Reserve System, in the H.6 statistical release "Money Stock Measures," and monthly in the *Federal Reserve Bulletin.* The new money stock measures adopted in 1980 are explained in "The Redefined Monetary Aggregates," *Federal Reserve Bulletin,* February, 1980. In the judgment of the Joint Economic Committee, in general "the series are reasonably accurate, but lack of complete reporting by banks and other institutions, changes in accounting practices, and other measurement problems impact on the accuracy and reliability of the series."

Consumer installment credit: The Federal Reserve Board provides monthly estimates of consumer installment credit for new extensions, liquidations (repayments), outstandings, and changes in outstandings. The series covers most short- and intermediate-term credit extended to individuals through regular business channels, usually to finance the purchase of consumer goods and services or to refinance debts incurred for such purposes. Such credit is scheduled to be repaid or with the option of repayment in two or more installments. The series generally excludes mortgage financing, although some credit secured by junior liens on real estate may be reported in the data for certain holders such as finance companies. Also excluded are the following: (1) credit card or other receivables held by a holding company rather than by its subsidiary financing institution; (2) extensions of funds against the cash value of life insurance policies or generally against savings accounts; (3) loans to farmers; and (4) noninstallment credit extended to individuals. Some components of the series include unearned (recomputed) finance charges.

The widespread interest in consumer installment credit is due in part to its importance as a source of consumer purchasing power and especially its importance and significance in the market for consumer goods frequently bought on the installment plan. Also, consumer debt reflects an important aspect of the general financial position of consumers, and is an important element in the demand for funds in the financial community. A relatively small sample size, for some holders of credit, does somewhat impair the accuracy of the data.

Bank loans, investments, and reserves: The series on loans and investments of all commercial banks is a useful indicator for current banking and monetary analysis. In view of the substantial seasonal and cyclical movements in bank credit, a seasonally adjusted series facilitates historical analysis. It also makes it easier to view the current trend in bank credit and its components, and to evaluate the banking system's responses to change in monetary policy.

An increase in total reserves supports a multiple expansion of bank deposits and bank credit, while contraction of reserves has the opposite impact. Thus the rates of growth of the reserve aggregates are used by some analysts as indicators of monetary policy, although actual reserve aggregate measures are not very useful for analytical purposes because of frequent breaks in the series due to change in regulations and the complex reserve requirements currently in effect.

Sources and uses of funds, nonfarm nonfinancial corporate business: The sources and uses of funds data are based on the flow of funds accounts that are published quarterly by the Federal Reserve Board. They provide a comprehensive picture of the financial lending and borrowing transactions of the U.S. economy. The flow of funds data provide the framework for developing projections of capital financing that are both realistic and consistent with projections of gross national product. This type of analysis is one of several factors used by the Federal Reserve in establishing targets for monetary policy associated with overall employment and anti-inflation goals. The data are also used by financial analysts for projecting the probable trend of interest rates.

In the integration of the data with the economic accounts, measured uses of funds (within the household capital account) are typically larger than measured sources of funds; however, for business, the relation is the opposite, with the sources being larger than the uses. These discrepancies reflect inadequacies in the underlying financial and nonfinancial data.

Current assets and liabilities of nonfinancial corporations: The Federal Trade Commission and Federal Reserve Board jointly provide quarterly measures of current assets and current liabilities for nonfinancial corporations. This series on corporate liquidity gives the major components of working capital for a significant segment of U.S. business.

Interest rates and bond yields: These include: three-month Treasury bills, constant maturities Treasury securities, high-grade municipal bonds, corporate Aaa bonds, prime commercial paper, new home mortgage yield (compiled by the Federal Home Loan Bank Board, in cooperation with the Federal Deposit Insurance Corporation, from information received by a sample of major mortgage lenders), Federal Reserve discount rate, and the average prime rate charged by banks. Analysts use these measures of cost or return on short-, intermediate- and long-term funds in judging and projecting money rates in response to monetary policy.

Common stock prices and yields: The Joint Economic Committee selected as economic indicators the New York Stock Exchange indexes of common stock prices, the Dow Jones industrial average, and data prepared by Standard & Poor's (their 500-stock composite index, as well as the dividend-price ratio and earnings-price ratio on the 500 stocks in the composite index).

Federal Finance.

Federal budget receipts, outlays, and debt: The main use for budget receipts and outlays is as a guide to executive and legislative budget and fiscal policy. Budget receipts and outlays data for the current year and the budget year include estimates both under existing law and under changes in laws and programs as proposed by the President. The budget is the vehicle for congressional review and enactment of annual appropriation bills, and also is an important factor in the consideration of changes in tax legislation. Moreover, the relationship between the total of budget receipts and budget outlays usually serves as the major determinant of increases or decreases in the debt held by the public. Finally, since this series is prepared in detail based on the government's financial accounts, it is a basic source of data for various other series on federal financial transactions that are important for economic analysis.

There are two basic areas of limitations on the use of federal budgetary data: (1) since there is no state or local government finance series that is compiled on a basis completely compatible with the federal budget, either the census or the national accounts series is frequently used along with the respective state and local government finance figures to show total government finances for the U.S. or to compare state and local finances with federal finances; and (2) the federal sector national account figures are an integral part of the total national income and product accounts, which constitute the primary system of measuring the size, composition, and changes in the economy. Consequently, the national accounts data are generally preferred by economists to budget data when examining the economic impact of the budget.

Federal budget receipts by source and outlays by function: Budget receipts by major source are available from the Office of Management and Budget for all years from 1940 to the present. Since these data are on a unified budget basis, this supplies a more useful series than the Treasury data for the years 1940–1953, which are on the old administrative budget basis. Budget outlays by major function are available on a comparable basis for each year starting with 1948. In addition, for many categories the data are available back to 1940. Subfunctional data are available for each year starting with 1962.

The distribution of available data on monthly receipts by source is reliable, but the data on monthly outlays by function are less so.

Federal sector, national income accounts basis: The BEA of the Department of Commerce provides quarterly measures of national income and product accounts. The federal sector data are designed to measure the purchases of current output by the federal government and the relationship of federal receipts and other federal expenditures to national, personal, and disposable personal income. The federal sector is recorded in a manner consistent with the conceptual treatment of the personal, business, state and local government, and foreign sectors in the national income and product accounts.

Federal purchases of goods and services are measured, insofar as is possible, on a delivery basis rather than on an obligation, checks-issued, or payments basis. Many receipts are on an accrual basis. For example, corporate profits taxes are included on an accrual basis rather than when collected. There may be a substantial lag between the accrual of a liability and its collection.

International Statistics—Major Industrial Countries.

Industrial production: The industrial production indexes of major industrial countries (United States, Canada, Japan, France, Germany, Italy, and United Kingdom) are designed to show changes in the physical volume or quantity of output of the manufacturing and mining industries and public utilities. As industrial production accounts for a major portion of the gross domestic product of these economies, the indexes serve as useful and timely measures of overall economic activity. The monthly national indexes for the six countries are released from four to seven weeks after the reported month.

Changes in industrial output from country to country as measured by these indexes reflect the differing patterns of production, but are also influenced by variations among the national series in coverage, weighting, and calculation methods. The monthly indexes are typically based on a more limited coverage of national output than those used for the annual indexes. Estimates are usually relied upon to improve the monthly indexes' compatibility with the annual index.

Consumer prices: The consumer price indexes of the major foreign industrial countries are designed to show changes in the cost of goods and services representative of consumption. The indexes are presented in terms of the U.S. base year, 1967, converted from national series with base years varying from 1970 to 1976.

The price movements indicated by these indexes vary considerably from country to country, not only because of real differences in consumer prices but also because the calculations of the national series differ, particularly as to weighting and coverage. In some of the countries, the weights used are revised annually on the basis of family expenditures surveys using large samples. In others, the weights are somewhat out of date and do not necessarily reflect current patterns of consumption. The variety and number of commodities checked also differ substantially, as does the size of the sample of families covered. Generally, the rural population is not covered.

U.S. merchandise exports and imports: Monthly statistics on merchandise exports and imports between the United States and other nations are compiled and published by the Bureau of the Census. These series provide timely indicators of the movement of merchandise exports and imports. As a measure of cyclical or long-term movements, monthly foreign trade data even after seasonal adjustment are erratic. While these data will necessarily be followed by users from month to month, judgments as to trend are more properly based on derived series for longer periods, such as quarterly or four-month moving totals.

Although merchandise trade bulks large among the sources of international payments, the balance of payments can be comprehended only in terms of the full range of merchandise, service, capital, unilateral, and other transactions. Undue importance should not be attached to the trade figures alone or to the surplus or deficit in merchandise trade. Because of the variety of bases on which foreign trade data are presented, the user must be attentive to the precise specifications of particular series, especially when they are to be used with other series. Similarly, when U.S. trade statistics are compared with those of other countries, special attention should be given to the extent to which the series differ as to valuation and coverage.

U.S. international transactions: The balance of payments of the United States is published quarterly by the BEA of the Department of Commerce. It provides a summary of economic transactions between residents of the United States and residents of the rest of the world.

The balance of payments statistics present an integrated summary of international transactions and their relation to the international financial position of the United States. The individual components are presented in an analytically neutral framework, recognizing that no single number can adequately portray the underlying international payments position of the United States.

The double-entry bookkeeping principle is used in constructing the international transactions accounts. Briefly, this means that there are two offsetting entries for each transaction, so that in theory the net of all transactions is zero. The actual collection of data, however, is from a wide variety of sources, with the result that a statistical discrepancy arises. The statistical discrepancy is a residual item, equal to the algebraic sum of all the other lines in the international accounts with the sign reversed. It includes errors and omissions that may have occurred in any of the other accounts due to such factors as statistical errors, reporting deficiencies, and differences in timing in recording both sides (credit and debit) of a single transaction. Its entry secures the equality of credits and debits, i.e., the balance of payments "always balances." What then is a "balance of payments deficit"? Actually, there is no such overall situation; instead, particular portions of the balance of payments statement may indicate surpluses or deficits, such as: balance on merchandise trade (net exports or net imports); balance on goods and services (the basis for and closely related conceptually to the net exports or net imports sector in the national income and product accounts; balance on current account (net exports or net imports of goods and services and unilateral transfers); and international capital transactions, divided into the broad categories of U.S. assets abroad and foreign assets in the United States. U.S. assets abroad are subdivided into official reserve and other government assets, and private assets. Foreign assets in the United States are subdivided into assets of foreign official agencies and other foreign assets. The international accounts also include data on allocations of special drawing rights (SDRs), the statistical discrepancy, and the value of the holdings of U.S. official reserve assets at the end of the period).

Summary. The above sampling of statistical data for the guidance of Congress and the public is indicative of a portion only of the vast amount of statistical data now prepared by government agencies regularly. For a more comprehensive collection, see:

Survey of Current Business (monthly), Department of Commerce.
Business Statistics (biennial), U.S. Department of Commerce.
Historical Statistics of the United States, Colonial Times to 1970, U.S. Bureau of the Census, 1975.

The latter two volumes provide the historical statistics necessary for background in use of current figures, as well as the basic data on construction of each series necessary in order better to understand and utilize the individual series.

Although the U.S. has made important progress in statistical compilations and is probably ahead of any other nation in this regard, from the viewpoint of the barometrician the timeliness and gaps in economic and business data still leave much to be desired. Reference is made to the following studies, published by the Subcommittee on Economic Statistics of the Joint Economic Committee of the U.S. Congress:

Improved Statistics for Economic Growth, March, 1966.
Inflation and the Price Indexes, July, 1966.
Government Price Statistics, July, 1966.

Business barometers when analyzed and interpreted afford a basis for the appraisal and forecasting of business conditions and prospects, which are necessary for proper application of fiscal and monetary policy at the aggregative or governmental level, and for business planning and budgeting at the microeconomic or firm level. Many attempts have been made to evolve accurate methodology in the use of business barometers or forecasting systems, the particular problem being the forecasting of the business cycle. Methods include the following:

1. The historical comparison type, including the variant seeking to isolate particular business barometers or statistical series showing consistent leads or lags relative to overall business and economic activity, exemplified by the cyclical indicators approach based on the leading, roughly coincident, and lagging indicators maintained by the National Bureau of Economic Research, Inc.
2. The econometric model concept, which utilizes historical and mathematical relationships among consumption, private investment, government, and various components of these major aggregates to generate forecasts of gross national product and its composition.

3. The type utilizing anticipations and intentions data based upon surveys or interviews of and with firms and consumers, including the SEC–Department of Commerce surveys of expenditures for new plant and equipment and the surveys on buying plans of consumers by the Survey Research Center of the University of Michigan, and by the Bureau of the Census based on its quarterly household survey.
4. The labor force–productivity approach, which projects gross national product on the bases of estimated employment, average work week, and output per person-hour.

For data on series titles and sources and on cyclical indicators, as well as on additional approaches, see *Business Conditions Digest*, succeeding the former *Business Cycle Developments*, published monthly by the Bureau of the Census, U.S. Department of Commerce, under the general guidance of a government interagency committee established by the Bureau of the Budget (now the Office of Management and Budget).

See BUSINESS CYCLE, BUSINESS FORECASTING SERVICES, FUNDAMENTAL CONDITIONS, INVESTMENT, MARKET SENTIMENT, SPECULATIVE CYCLE.

See bibliography for BUSINESS CYCLE and ECONOMIC INDICATORS.

BUSINESS COMBINATIONS

A business combination occurs when a corporation and one or more incorporated or unincorporated businesses are brought together into one accounting entity. The single entity carries on the activities of the previously separate, independent entities.

Business combinations can be classified structurally into three types: horizontal, vertical, and conglomerate. A horizontal combination is one that involves companies within the same industry that have previously been competitors; a vertical combination involves a company and its suppliers or customers; and a combination resulting in a conglomerate is one involving companies in unrelated industries having few, if any, production or market similarities.

Business combinations can also be classified by method of combination as statutory mergers, statutory consolidations, and stock acquisitions. A statutory merger occurs when one company acquires all of the net assets of one or more other companies. The acquiring company survives; the acquired company or companies cease to exist as a separate legal entity. For example, a merger occurs between corporations A and B if A remains the same legal entity (essentially with the combined assets and liabilities of A and B) and B goes out of existence.

A statutory consolidation requires the formation of a new corporation that acquires two or more other corporations; the acquired corporations then cease to exist as separate legal entities. For example, corporations A and B agree to transfer their assets and liabilities to a new corporation C and then go out of existence, leaving C as the corporation to carry on the activities of A and B.

A stock acquisition occurs when one corporation pays cash or issues stock or debt for more than 50% of the voting stock of another company and the acquired company remains intact as a separate legal entity. The relationship of the acquiring company to the acquired company in a stock acquisition is described as a parent-subsidiary relationship. The acquiring company is referred to as the parent (investor) and the acquired company as a subsidiary. The related companies are called affiliated companies. Each of the affiliated companies continues as a separate legal entity. The parent company carries its interest in a subsidiary as an investment in its accounts. Consolidated financial statements are prepared only when the business combination was carried out as a stock acquisition.

The relationship between mergers, consolidations, and stock acquisitions can be summarized as follows:

	Prior to Combination	Survivor(s)
Statutory Merger	A and B	A or B
Statutory consolidation	A and B	C
Acquisition	A and B	A and B

The accounting concept of a business organization emphasizes the single entity and the independence of the combining companies prior to their combination when business resources and operations come under the control of a single management. Control is established in a business combination in which (1) one or more corporations become subsidiaries, (2) one company transfers its net assets to another, or (3) each company transfers its net assets to a newly formed corporation.

Currently, there are two generally accepted methods of accounting for business combinations—the pooling of interests method and the purchase method. A pooling of interests can occur only when one company uses its common stock to acquire the assets or stock of another company. A business combination that meets the criteria of APB Opinion No. 16 for a pooling of interest must be accounted for under the pooling method. All other business combinations must be accounted for under the purchase method. Currently, about 10% of the business combinations are treated as poolings of interest.

The criteria established for determining whether purchase or pooling accounting is appropriate are divided into three categories:

1. **Attributes of the combining companies.** Each of the combining companies is autonomous and has not been a subsidiary or division of another corporation within two years before the plan of combination is initiated. Each of the combining companies is independent of the other combining companies.
2. **Manner of combining interests.** The combination is effected in a single transaction or is completed in accordance with a specific plan within one year after the plan is initiated. A corporation offers and issues only common stock with rights identical to those of the majority of its outstanding voting common stock in exchange for substantially all of the voting common stock interest of another company at the date the plan of combination is consummated. None of the combining companies changes the equity interest of the voting common stock in contemplation of effecting the combination whether within two years before the plan of combination is initiated or between the dates the combination is initiated and consummated; changes in contemplation of effecting the combination may include distributions to stockholders and additional issuances, exchanges, and retirements of securities. Each of the combining companies reacquired shares of voting common stock only for purposes other than business combinations, and no company reacquires more than a normal number of shares between the dates the plan of combination is initiated and consummated. The ratio of the interest of an individual common stockholder to those of other common stockholders in a combining company remains the same as a result of the exchange of stock to effect the combination. The voting rights to which the common stock ownership interests in the resulting combined corporation are entitled are exercisable by the stockholders; the stockholders are neither deprived of nor restricted in exercising rights for a period. The combination is resolved at the date the plan is consummated, and no provisions of the plan relating to the issue of securities or other consideration are pending.
3. **Absence of planned transactions.** The combined corporation does not agree directly or indirectly to retire or reacquire all or part of the common stock issued to effect the combination. The combined corporation does not enter into other financial arrangements for the benefit of the former stockholders of a combining company, such as a guarantee of loans, secured by stock issued in the combination, which in effect negates the exchange of equity securities. The combined corporation does not intend or plan to dispose of a significant part of the assets of the combining companies within two years after the combination other than disposals in the ordinary course of business of the formerly separate companies and elimination of duplicate facilities or excess capacity.

Under the pooling of interests method, the ownership interests of the combined companies are assumed to be united and continue relatively unchanged in the new accounting entity (i.e., continuity of ownership). No new basis of accountability is established. Assets and liabilities of the combining companies are carried forward to the combined entity at book value. Retained earnings of the combining companies is also carried forward to the pooled entity (subject to certain limitations). Under pooling accounting, the combining companies are treated as if they had always been combined. The combination is treated as if it occurred before the earliest period for which statements are presented.

Under the purchase method, it is assumed that a business combination is a transaction in which one entity acquires the net assets of the other combining companies. The acquiring corporation records the net assets received at their fair value at the time of the combination. Any excess of cost over the fair value of net assets acquired is allocated to goodwill and amortized over a maximum period of 40 years. The purchase method is appropriate for business combinations in which owners of one or more of the companies give up their ownership rights.

Statement of Financial Accounting Standards Mo. 72, *Accounting for Certain Acquisitions of Banking or Thrift Institutions*, applies to the acquisition of a commercial bank, a savings and loan association, a mutual savings bank, a credit union, other depository institutions having assets and liabilities of the same types of those institutions, and branches of such enterprises. In a business combination accounted for by the purchase method involving the acquisition of a banking or thrift institution, intangible assets acquired that can be separately identified shall be assigned a portion of the total cost of the acquired enterprise if the fair values of those assets can be reliably determined. The fair values of such assets that relate to depositor or borrower relationships shall be based on the estimated benefits attributable to the relationships that exist at the date of acquisition without regard to new depositors, or borrowers that may replace them. Those identified intangible assets shall be amortized over the estimated lives of those existing relationships. The intangible assets shall be amortized to expense by the interest method over a period no longer than the discount on the long-term interest-bearing assets acquired is to be recognized as interest income. The Statement also specified that financial assistance granted to an enterprise by a regulatory authority in connection with a business combination shall be accounted for as part of the combination if receipt of the assistance is probable and the amount is reasonably estimable.

Certain business combinations are prohibited by law. Section 7 of the Clayton Act (1914) prohibits any business combination in which "the effect of such acquisition may be substantially to lessen competition or tend to create a monopoly." Federal ANTITRUST LAWS are enforced by the Justice Department and the Federal Trade Commission. These agencies have developed over the years certain precombination notification regulations: A company with assets or sales of at least $10 million that plans to acquire a manufacturing company with assets or sales of at least $10 million must file a detailed 21-page form 30 days before the planned date of consummation. If the target company is not a manufacturing company, notification is required if one company has at least $1090 million in sales or assets and the other company has sales or assets of at least $10 million. These regulations enable the enforcing agents to review proposed business combinations before they occur. The agents are empowered to obtain a preliminary court injunction against the proposed sale and have used this authority.

See CONSOLIDATED FINANCIAL STATEMENTS, EQUITY METHOD OF ACCOUNTING.

BUSINESS CYCLE An interval that embraces alternating periods of business prosperity and depression. It is one of the most significant phenomena of the capitalistic system and appears to be an outgrowth of a system in which production requires considerable capital investment and some lead time before consumption. Business cycles are characterized by a series of phases that are more-or-less predictable in occurrence but not necessarily in timing or intensity. In the United States, since the 1930s, government intervention has been used to try to influence the timing and help dampen the intensity of business cycles. A description of the cyclical phases in the absence of such intervention follows:

1. **Crisis.** This is the turning point or decisive moment that marks the collapse of a period of prosperity, rising prices, increasing shortages, and considerable speculation in the expectation that prices will rise faster. Crisis is likely to be followed by panic, primarily a financial phenomenon characterized by a collapse of the credit structure; a universal demand for money payments; lack of confidence in the ability of debtors to pay debts; and usually a series of important business, brokerage, and banking failures, often brought about by the mounting accumulation of inventories acquired at high prices and financed on credit. Because of the sudden demand for cash, banks are the storm centers of the panic. If important bank failures occur, bank runs, even on sound banks, are likely to ensue, placing a great strain upon the banking system. Interest rates may rise to entice depositors to leave their funds with financial intermediaries.
2. **Emergency liquidation.** Following the crisis (and panic, if one occurs) comes a period emergency liquidation. During the previous period of prosperity and high demand, production boomed, eventually leading to an overall accumulation of high-priced inventories. When the crisis ends the period of high prices, businesses are eager to unload these inventories before prices decline, and they place goods on the market for whatever they will bring. This tendency is exacerbated by high rates of interest, which makes holding inventories expensive in a flat or falling market.
3. **Depression.** This is a period of low prices and drastic curtailment of production, resulting in widespread unemployment, reduction or elimination of profits, overcapacity in production facilities, many business failures, and a general reluctance or inability to use credit or to make new capital investment or spend on consumption. Interest rates drop in nominal terms but may remain high in real terms.
4. **Readjustment.** When the bottom of the price movement has been struck, the period of readjustment begins. It is characterized by an irregular and uneven process of price stabilization and readjustment of supply/demand relationships. Business becomes "leaner and meaner"—inefficient businesses have been eliminated, production costs are lower, and competition is sharper. Survivors tend to accumulate liquidity rather than other assets. Interest rates are low in real terms.
5. **Recuperation or revival.** The period of readjustment blends so imperceptibly into the recuperative phase that the latter is not easy to detect. By this time, the deflation process has been completed, bank reserves are high, and interest rates are low. The combination of easy credit and lower prices begins to stimulate demand, first through revival of consumer spending and eventually through business expansion. Unemployment begins to decline.
6. **Prosperity.** As the demand for goods increases, industrial activity picks up and more labor and capital are employed, resulting in increased purchasing power. This, in turn, stimulates demand. Because inventories are comparatively low, production and deliveries lag orders, and idle labor and productive capacity are pressed into service. This condition leads to increased production costs and rising wages, prices, and profits. With the revival of credit demand, interest rates begin an upward trend.
7. **Overextension and speculation.** Eventually, businesses find existing plant and equipment inadequate to supply the demand. This leads to an expansion of capital spending but at higher cost and at higher interest rates on borrowed money. Although product prices and profits are rising, production costs tend to rise faster as less productive inputs are brought into use. To maintain profit levels, producers raise product prices until they meet buyer resistance, which sets the stage for another crisis.

Many hypotheses have been advanced as to the cause of the business cycle. Haberler (*Prosperity and Depression*, 3rd ed., 1952) has identified the following classification of theories: (1) purely monetary; (2) overinvestment; (3) changes in costs, horizontal maladjustments, and over indebtedness; (4) underconsumption; (5) psychological factors; and (6) the harvest theories (relating agriculture and the business cycle, including the sun spot theories).

The analytical tools found in Keynes *General Theory of Employment, Interest and Money* (1936)—liquidity preference, marginal efficiency of capital, and the consumption function—are compatible with any of the above theories, but Keynes himself seemed to stress the psychological factors, emphasizing the role of expectations in the behavior of both consumers and investors. Followers of Keynes, however, cite underconsumption or oversaving—both consequences of changed expectations—as casual factors.

A monetarist school, led by Milton Friedman and often called the Chicago school because of his position on the faculty of the University of Chicago, has emphasized the importance of changes in the money supply as being more important than interest rates in determining the national economic health. In its simplest form, the approach argues that the central government should ensure modest but regular increase in the real money stock to allow for orderly long-

BUSINESS CYCLE

run growth. This approach found much favor in the early 1980s but proved more difficult to implement than expected.

In recent times, the great debate regarding business cycles is whether government countercyclical measures now preclude the possibility of a serious depression. Since the Great Depression of the 1930s, many measures have evolved that are intended to take the "edge" off of the traditional business cycle. FISCAL POLICY and MONETARY POLICY, acting within a more effective institutional environment, can derail economic developments that once led inexorably to crisis. AUTOMATIC STABILIZERS help prop up or slow down consumer spending that might otherwise exacerbate cyclical lows and highs. Greater regulation of financial institutions and practices helps prevent panic and abuse. Better economic information helps prevent the unanticipated accumulation of inventories.

A counterargument is that private investment is the keystone of cyclical phenomena. Investment responds to changes in sales expectations—that is, it anticipates demand. Government actions can bolster demand but not in time to stimulate investment based on expectations of demand. Automatic stabilizers might slow down but could not prevent a prolonged downtrend in business activity.

Fiscal policy mechanisms are slow and cumbersome, and monetary policy alone cannot actively stimulate business investment if the business community does not anticipate sustained or increased demand for products and services. (It can, however, discourage business investment by raising the cost of credit.) Therefore, com-

U.S. Business Cycles: Reference Dates and Duration

		Duration in months			
Business cycle reference dates		Contraction (trough from previous peak)	Expansion (trough to peak)	Cycle	
Trough	Peak			Trough from previous trough	Peak from previous peak
December 1854	June 1857	....	30	....	....
December 1858	October 1860	18	22	48	40
June 1861	April 1865	8	46	30	54
December 1867	June 1869	32	18	78	50
December 1870	October 1873	18	34	36	52
March 1879	March 1882	65	36	99	101
May 1885	March 1887	38	22	74	60
April 1888	July 1890	13	27	35	40
May 1891	January 1893	10	20	37	30
June 1894	December 1895	17	18	37	35
June 1897	June 1899	18	24	36	42
December 1990	September 1902	18	21	42	39
August 1904	May 1907	23	33	44	56
June 1908	January 1910	13	19	46	32
January 1912	January 1913	24	12	43	36
December 1914	August 1918	23	44	35	67
March 1919	January 1920	7	10	51	17
July 1921	May 1923	18	22	28	40
July 1924	October 1926	14	27	36	41
November 1927	August 1929	13	21	40	34
March 1933	May 1937	43	50	64	93
June 1938	February 1945	13	80	63	93
October 1945	November 1948	8	37	88	45
October 1949	July 1953	11	45	48	56
May 1954	August 1957	10	39	55	49
April 1958	April 1960	8	24	47	32
February 1961	December 1969	10	106	34	116
November 1970	November 1973	11	36	117	47
March 1975	January 1980	16	58	52	74
July 1980	July 1981	6	12	64	18
November 1982		16	....	28	....
Average, all cycles:					
1854-1982 (30 cycles)		18	33	51	51[1]
1854-1919 (16 cycles)		22	27	48	49[2]
1919-1945 (6 cycles)		18	35	53	53
1945-1982 (8 cycles)		11	45	56	55[3]
Average, peacetime cycles:					
1854-1982 (25 cycles)		19	27	46	46[3]
1854-1919 (14 cycles)		22	24	46	47[4]
1919-1945 (5 cycles)		20	26	46	45
1945-1982 (6 cycles)		11	34	46	44

Note: Underscored figures are the wartime expansions (Civil War, World Wars I and II, Korean war, and Vietnam war), the postwar contractions, and the full cycles that include the wartime expansions.

[1] 29 cycles   [2] 15 cycles   [3] 24 cycles   [4] 13 cycles

Source: National Bureau of Economic Research, Inc.

Business Cycle Expansions and Contractions—Months of Duration: 1919 to 1987
(The lower turning point of a cycle is considered a trough, the upper turning point a peak. Business cycle reference dates are determined by the National Bureau of Economic Research, Inc.)

Business Cycle Reference Date		Contraction (trough from previous peak)	Expansion (trough to peak)	Length of Cycle	
Trough	Peak			Trough from previous trough	Peak from previous peak
March 1919	January 1920	7	10	51	17
July 1921	May 1923	18	22	28	40
July 1924	October 1926	14	27	36	41
November 1927	August 1929	13	21	40	34
March 1933	May 1937	43	50	64	93
June 1938	February 1945	13	80	63	93
October 1945	November 1948	8	37	88	45
October 1949	July 1953	11	45	48	56
May 1954	August 1957	10	39	55	49
April 1958	April 1960	8	24	47	32
February 1961	December 1969	10	106	34	116
November 1970	November 1973	11	36	117	47
March 1975	January 1980	16	58	52	74
July 1980	July 1981	6	12	64	18
November 1982	NA	16	NA	28	NA
Average, all cycles:					
1919-1945 (6 cycles)		18	35	53	53
1945-1982 (8 cycles)		11	45	56	55
Average, peacetime cycles:					
1919-1945 (5 cycles)		20	26	46	45
1945-1982 (6 cycles)		11	34	46	44

NA Not applicable. Source: U.S. Bureau of Economic Analysis, *Business Conditions Digest*, January 1988.

petitive markets, rather than government directives, are as a rule the most efficient instruments for organizing production and consumption. The government creates an atmosphere favorable to economic activity when it encourages private initiative, curbs monopolistic tendencies, avoids encroachment on the private sector, and "privatizes" as much as of its own work as is practicable.

In the mid-1970s, partly as a result of the large increases in the price of oil, the economy was confronted with "stagflation," characterized by the coexistence of inflation and stagnant or falling demand. This combination tested many economic theories and in 1974-75 produced the most severe recession since the 1930s. In late 1979, the Federal Reserve Board tightened credit severely to bring inflation under control. This policy dampened the economy during the early 1980s but also set the stage for the long period of prosperity that was still in progress in 1988.

The National Bureau of Economic Research has measured the duration of U.S. business cycles, from turning point to turning point, from 1854 to the current date. These data are shown in the following table. Note that the November 1982 trough is the latest date shown in the table because no peak had yet been reached as of mid-1988.

Major business cycles expansions and contractions from 1919 to 1987 are presented in the appended table.

BIBLIOGRAPHY

See also bibliography for ECONOMIC INDICATORS.

AUERBACH, A. J. "The Index of Leading Indicators: 'Measurement Without Theory,' Thirty-Five Years Later." *The Review of Economics and Statistics*, November, 1982.

Andrews Trading Cycles. Andrews Publishing Co., Morgan Hill, CA. 18 times per year.

BUREAU OF ECONOMIC ANALYSIS, WASHINGTON, DC. Statistical Indicator Computer Tapes available from the Bureau:
  Business Conditions Digest Data File.
  Long-Term Economic Growth, 1860–1970.
  Seasonal Adjustment, Composite Diffusion Indexes, and Time Series Processor Programs.
  X-11 Seasonal Adjustment Program.
  X-11Q Seasonal Adjustment Program.
  Composite-Diffusion Indexes Program.
  Time Series Processor Program.

Cycles. Foundation for the Study of Cycles. Monthly.

GORDON, R. J. *The American Business Cycle: Continuity & Change*. University of Chicago Press, Chicago, IL, 1984.

MITCHELL, W. C. *Business Cycles: The Problem and Its Setting*. University of California Press, Berkeley, CA, 1927.

———. *What Happens During Business Cycles: A Progress Report*. University of California Press, Berkeley, CA, 1951.

———. *Business Cycles and Their Causes*. University of California Press, Berkeley, CA, 1941.

NELSON, C. R. *Investor's Guide to Economic Indicators*. John Wiley and Sons, New York, NY, 1987.

SCHUMPETER, J. A. *Business Cycles: A Theoretical, Historical, and Statistical Analysis of the Capitalist Process*. Porcupine Press, Inc., Philadelphia, PA, 1981.

BUSINESS FAILURES See FAILURES.

BUSINESS FORECASTING SERVICES

If cyclical movements of prices of commodities, securities, and finished goods occur, as explained under the term BUSINESS CYCLE, and business conditions and price movements are subject to analysis and interpretation, as explained under the term BUSINESS BAROMETERS, then the trend of business activity becomes, at least in part, amenable to forecasting. Although most businesspeople recognize the validity of the principles underlying the business cycle and the importance of watching business barometers, few regard themselves as capable of analyzing and interpreting available data without specialized assistance. Business forecasting, therefore, has become a specialized profession.

Various organizations are engaged in the business of furnishing business, speculative, and investment forecasting services. The statistical services, which provide factual descriptive data as well as interpretative services, are primarily Moody's Investors Service and Standard & Poor's.

The interpretative or economic services, in addition to the above, include Alexander Hamilton Institute Service, American Management Association, National Industrial Conference Board, Research Institute of America, United Business Service, and Value Line Service.

Besides the above, there are active a large number of interpretative and economic advisory services such as Baxter, Data Resources,

Evans, Shilling, Sindlinger, University of Michigan, and Wharton. There are also a large number of active securities and commodity market advisory services. The INVESTMENT ADVISERS ACT OF 1940, effective November 1, 1940, requires registration with the Securities and Exchange Commission by individuals, partnerships, corporations, or other forms of organization who for compensation engage in the business of advising others either directly or through publications or writings as to the value of securities or as to the advisability of investing in, buying, or selling securities, or who for compensation and as part of a regular business disseminate analyses or reports concerning securities.

In addition to services available to the public, there are many technical services usually available through professional channels, such as the Argus Research Corporation service on securities; Dun & Bradstreet confidential credit reports available to subscribers; national stock and bond summary service of the National Quotation Bureau on over-the-counter securities; Ward's Automotive Reports; R. L. Polk & Co. statistical services, especially on the automobile industry; F. W. Dodge Corporation statistical research services on the construction industries; Alfred M. Best Co., Spectator Co., and National Underwriter Co. informational services on insurance companies; Roy Wenzlick & Co. and E. H. Boeckh and Associates, Inc. services on real estate and construction, etc.

Government publications, complete catalogs on which are obtainable from the Superintendent of Documents, U.S. Government Printing Office, Washington, D.C. 20402, provide a variety of data for business forecasting. The *Survey of Current Business,* published monthly by the Department of Commerce, regularly carries 40 pages of government and business statistics, together with interpretative and analytical articles on specific subjects. The *Business Conditions Digest,* published monthly by the Department of Commerce and Bureau of the Census, is particularly useful for its specialization in data useful for business analysis and forecasting. The monthly *Federal Reserve Bulletin,* published by the Board of Governors of the Federal Reserve System, regularly publishes "principal statistics of current significance relating to financial and business developments in the United States," as well as international data, together with review and analytical articles. For regional data, the monthly reviews of the 12 Federal Reserve banks are basic, although varying in content and details of data and range of statistical series carried. Bank publications, such as those of the First National City Bank, Morgan Guaranty Trust Company, and Cleveland Trust Company, also provide monthly interpretative and statistical data on selected subjects.

Trade associations (e.g., Air Transport Association of America, Aluminum Association, Automobile Manufacturers Association, Manufacturing Chemists Association, Edison Electric Institute, Electronic Industries Association, American Petroleum Institute, American Iron & Steel Institute, Association of American Railroads, Rubber Manufacturers Association, Institute of Life Insurance), chambers of commerce including the U.S. Chamber of Commerce, and private research organizations are also sources of data and advisory services of value for forecasting purposes. Many of the larger corporations have specialized full-time economic staffs, devoted to preparation of data suitable for general forecasts as well as specialized forecasts and market surveys bearing on the specific company's interest, and frequently part of the company's budgetary procedure.

See FINANCIAL MAGAZINES, FINANCIAL NEWSPAPERS, MANUALS, MERCANTILE AGENCIES, MOODY'S INVESTORS SERVICE, STANDARD & POOR'S CORPORATION, TRADE ASSOCIATION.

BUSINESS INCUBATORS Facilities that nurture new and young enterprises, or tenant firms, by providing affordable space, shared office services, and management assistance. The first contemporary versions of the incubator appeared in the mid-1970s and were primarily financed by private firms. Today, universities and public agencies as well as private firms, are establishing incubators. Job generation is the primary outcome desired from publicly financed incubators. Sponsors of these incubators also aim for economic diversification, tax-base expansion, building rehabilitation and reuse, and the creation of a positive development image. Investors in privately financed incubators are mainly interested in obtaining a high return and increasing the value of commercial and industrial real estate. Sponsors of university incubators share some of the interests of both public sponsors and private investors. The success of the incubator concept is apparent in the survival of its firms.

BUSINESS INDEX *See* INDEX NUMBERS, NEW YORK TIMES BUSINESS INDEX.

BUSINESS INSURANCE Every kind of INSURANCE taken out by business firms, including fire, casualty, and life. In a specific sense, it applies to CREDIT INSURANCE. In a special sense, it also applies to life insurance taken out on the key principals in a business firm to make good the loss to the business or personal estate which would be caused by their premature demise. Life insurance is a potential quick asset, and the funds that become available when the key principal in a business dies, his life having been insured for the benefit of the business, fortify the business against possible impairment of credit availability that might result, at least temporarily. The theory is that the insurance money will tide the firm over the transition period until the successors in the business prove that they can carry on the business as competently as before. In the meantime, before maturity of such policies, the cash surrender value of such life insurance that accumulates can serve as a basis for borrowing by the firm on policy loans, and also can be justifiably carried as a current asset in the financial statement of the firm.

BUSINESSMAN'S INVESTMENT The type of commitment in securities, whether debt or equity securities, which have higher than average business risk and financial risk and therefore is sensitive to fluctuations in business, earnings, and security prices. Such investments are suitable only for aggressive investors, such as businessmen, who can accept the higher than average risk in consideration of higher than average returns possible in such securities on their upswings. Many other persons have financial circumstances or constraints that limit them to defensive securities, i.e., those having minimized investing risks, albeit more modest returns. A businessman's investments are particularly chosen, usually, for their promise of attractive capital gains, which on a long-term basis are taxable at much lower rates than ordinary income. On the other hand, should the anticipations of capital gains go awry and capital losses instead result, the businessman investor usually has substantial ordinary income against which the capital loss can be applied within the allowable limits per year.

See INVESTMENT, SPECULATION.

BUSINESSMAN'S RISK A risk such as is involved in a business or security, the income from which is uncertain, but which promises large returns under favorable management. A risk which a businessman is warranted in taking because of his knowledge of business conditions, the management of the concern in which the investment is made, and his ability to protect himself in case of unfavorable developments. But while a businessman is justified in taking such a risk, it would be an unwise risk for others not familiar with these facts.

See BUSINESS RISK, FINANCIAL RISK.

BUSINESS PAPER That class of COMMERCIAL PAPER which is given in payment of merchandise and discounted by the payee at his or her bank. Trade acceptances may be classified as business paper.

When such customer's paper meets the standards for eligibility for rediscounting at Federal Reserve banks by member banks of the Federal Reserve System, specified in Regulation A of the Board of Governors of the Federal Reserve System, it is ELIGIBLE PAPER.

Commercial paper technically consists also of promissory notes placed in the open money market by business firms and finance companies, the former through commercial paper dealers and the latter directly in recent years. Money market rate quotations on such paper, usually on the basis of four to six months' maturity, prime, refer to such open market commercial paper.

BUSINESS RESERVE Sometimes applied to the reserve for contingencies, a portion of retained earnings (earned surplus) earmarked to cover possible adverse contingencies or eventualities without disturbing the main body of retained earnings. Another motivation for such earmarking is to temper possibly unduly high stockholders' dividend anticipations, since cash dividends are chargeable to retained earnings and the latter is reduced by such provision for reserve. In any event, however, the reserve for contingencies, not specifically allocated for some specific valuation writedown or loss, is properly part of the stockholders' equity. Most firms do not fund the reserve for contingencies (do not earmark funds on the assets side of the balance sheet in equal amount), as this would

tie up funds otherwise usable in working capital for a merely contingent purpose.
See CONTINGENT RESERVE.

BUSINESS RISK That element of a credit risk which depends upon the business ability of the managers of the concern under consideration. The expression is used by credit people in contradistinction to moral risk and property risk. The chief test of this risk is capacity to produce profits over a period of time. In measuring or testing a business risk the credit analyst investigates the following points:

1. Is the business sound, well established, and stable, or relatively new and risky?
2. Is the volume of business declining, advancing, or stationary?
3. Are modern production and sales methods being used?
4. What reputation does the product of the concern enjoy in the trade?
5. What has been the ratio of profits to invested capital for, say, the past five years?
6. What is the
   a. range of fluctuation of gross profits?
   b. percentage of operating expenses to gross profits?
   c. range of fluctuations of this percentage?
   d. margin of profits above operating expenses and its range of fluctuation?

Such questions relate also to the nature of the firm's product line and pattern of demand therefor (i.e., whether the products are well-established consumer nondurables, for example, with relatively inelastic demand), so that relative stability of demand prevails over the BUSINESS CYCLE and profit margins may be maintained in the event of rise in costs.

Business risk as well as FINANCIAL RISK are the basic risks estimated and evaluated by quality ratings for bonds and preferred stocks.

BUSINESS SOLVENCY The financial condition of a firm when liquid resources are adequate in amount and timing to meet debts as they become due. This is solvency in the equity sense. It should also be accompanied by an excess of total assets over total liabilities by at least the total amount of the capital, so that capital is not impaired, and thus SOLVENCY in the BANKRUPTCY sense exists. If solvency in the equity sense exists, it is possible for a firm to continue in operations as long as it manages to keep solvent in the equity sense, despite the absence of solvency in the bankruptcy sense. However, such a condition would be extremely marginal, credit both financial and mercantile would be extremely difficult to obtain, and such a condition would generally reflect unprofitable operations, so that it might only be a question of time before the firm would become insolvent in either or both senses.
See FAILURES, INSOLVENCY.

BUSINESS STATISTICS See BUSINESS BAROMETERS, BUSINESS FORECASTING SERVICES, INDEX NUMBERS, STATISTICS.

BUSINESS TRUST An organizational form of business whereby property is placed in the hands of trustees who manage the business and who deal with it for the use and benefit of beneficiaries.

BUTTER See CHICAGO MERCANTILE EXCHANGE.

BUYDOWN A lending procedure in which a borrower pays the bank a lump sum of money in advance to reduce the monthly interest charges on a mortgage.

BUYER'S OPTION See OPTIONS.

BUY IN This term has two meanings:

1. Buy in to COVER indicates the purchase of securities or commodity contracts previously sold short.
2. Buy in UNDER THE RULE refers to the purchase of a member firm's contracts to buy and sell under New York Stock Exchange rules.
See FAILS.

BUYING BACK Purchasing a security which has previously been sold short; covering short sales. Stock which has been sold short must be bought back, or covered, in order to complete the transaction.
See SHORT SALE.

BUYING ON A SCALE Stock is frequently bought on a scale for the purpose of averaging the purchase price on the principle that the low point of a given market movement cannot be exactly predicted. Buying orders are placed with a broker for execution at prices representing regular intervals downward, e.g., to buy 100 shares of U.S. Steel at 40, 37 $1/2$, 35, 32 $1/2$, etc.
See DOLLAR AVERAGING.

BUYING ON BALANCE Excess of buying activity. While it is true that purchases and sales in the aggregate must balance, any given broker on a single day may execute (in number of shares) more buying orders than selling orders. Commission houses with a branch organization and extensive wire connections throughout the country receive and execute a wide variety of orders during a day's session. If, after the close when the books are balanced, the house determines that their clients purchased more shares than they sold, the house is said to be a buyer on balance. If, on the other hand, executions to sell were in preponderance, the house was a seller on balance.

BUYING ORDER An order given to a broker to purchase securities, commodities, etc., with certain specifications. Among brokerage houses, there are two ordinary classes of round-lot orders as to price limits: market orders and limit or limited orders. Classified as to time limits, orders are day orders (a market order is always a day order), week or month orders, and open or GTC (good 'til canceled) orders. Special types of orders include stop order, stop and limit order, discretionary order, immediate or cancel order, and cancel order (straight cancel order or cancel former order).
See ORDERS.

BUYING OUTRIGHT The purchase of securities for immediate delivery for which full cash payment is made. It is the contrary of buying on margin.

BUYING RATE Among foreign exchange banks and brokers, the rate at which they agree to buy foreign currency, cable transfers, or bills of exchange on foreign countries for stated maturities and amounts, as distinguished from the quoted selling rates, which obviously are higher. Different rates are quoted for cables, checks, and time bills.
See CABLE RATE, CHECK RATE, LONG RATE, SHORT RATE.

BYLAWS As part of the organization procedure for national banks, after the directors are elected but prior to the date of the organization certificate, the directors must take the oath of office, after which they adopt the bylaws. The bylaws must not be inconsistent with the bank's ARTICLES OF ASSOCIATION or with bank law. As in the case of other types of corporations, the bylaws of banks outline the powers and duties of the officers and other details of operation of the bank. The Comptroller of the Currency furnishes a model for the bylaws available as a guide for national banks. After the officers are selected by the directors, a copy of the bylaws and signatures of the officers are forwarded to the Comptroller of the Currency.

Appended are sample bylaws suggested as a guide by the Comptroller of the Currency.
See BANK ORGANIZATION.

Model Bylaws
(Form CC 7029-05) Office Comptroller of the Currency

BYLAWS

ARTICLE I

Meetings of Shareholders

Section 1.1. *Annual Meeting*. The regular annual meeting of the shareholders, for the election of directors and the transaction of

BYLAWS

whatever other business may properly come before the meeting, shall be held at the Main Office of the Association, No. _____ Street, City of _____, or such other place as the Board of Directors may designate, at _____ o'clock, on the _____ of _____ of _____ each year. Notice of such meeting shall be mailed, postage prepaid, at least ten days prior to the date thereof, addressed to each shareholder at his address appearing on the books of the Association. If, from any cause, an election of directors is not made on the said day, the Board of Directors shall order the election to be held on some subsequent day, as soon thereafter as practicable, according to the provisions of law; and notice thereof shall be given in the manner herein provided for the annual meeting.

Section 1.2. *Special Meetings.* Except as otherwise specifically provided by statute, special meetings of the shareholders may be called for any purpose at any time by the Board of Directors or by any three or more shareholders owning, in the aggregate, not less than twenty-five percent of the stock of the Association. Every such special meeting, unless otherwise provided by law, shall be called by mailing, postage prepaid, not less than ten days prior to the date fixed for such meeting, to each shareholder at his address appearing on the books of the Association, a notice stating the purpose of the meeting.*

Section 1.3. *Nominations for Director.* Nominations for election to the Board of Directors may be made by the Board of Directors or by any stockholder of any outstanding class of capital stock of the bank entitled to vote for the election of directors. Nominations, other than those made by or on behalf of the existing management of the bank, shall be made in writing and shall be delivered or mailed to the President of the bank and to the Comptroller of the Currency, Washington, D.C., not less than 14 days nor more than 50 days prior to any meeting of stockholders called for the election of directors, provided however, that if less than 21 days' notice of the meeting is given to shareholders, such nomination shall be mailed or delivered to the President of the bank and to the Comptroller of the Currency not later than the close of business on the seventh day following the day on which the notice of meeting was mailed. Such notification shall contain the following information to the extent known to the notifying shareholder: (a) the name and address of each proposed nominee; (b) the principal occupation of each proposed nominee; (c) the total number of shares of capital stock of the bank that will be voted for each proposed nominee; (d) the name and residence address of the notifying shareholder; and (e) the number of shares of capital stock of the bank owned by the notifying shareholder. Nominations not made in accordance herewith may, in his discretion, be disregarded by the chairman of the meeting, and upon his instructions, the vote tellers may disregard all votes cast for each such nominee.#

Section 1.4. *Judges of Election.* Every election of directors shall be managed by three judges, who shall be appointed from among the shareholders by the Board of Directors. The judges of election shall hold and conduct the election at which they are appointed to serve; and, after the election, they shall file with the Cashier a certificate under their hands, certifying the result thereof and the names of the directors elected. The judges of election, at the request of the Chairman of the meeting, shall act as tellers of any other vote by ballot taken at such meeting, and shall certify the result thereof.*

Section 1.5. *Proxies.* Shareholders may vote at any meeting of the shareholders by proxies duly authorized in writing, but no officer or employee of this Association shall act as proxy. Proxies shall be valid only for one meeting, to be specified therein, and any adjournments of such meeting. Proxies shall be dated and shall be filed with the records of the meeting.

Section 1.6. *Quorum.* A majority of the outstanding capital stock, represented in person or by proxy, shall constitute a quorum at any meeting of shareholders, unless otherwise provided by law; but less than a quorum may adjourn any meeting, from time to time, and the meeting may be held, as adjourned, without further notice. A majority of the votes cast shall decide every question or matter submitted to the shareholders at any meeting, unless otherwise provided by law or by the Articles of Association.

ARTICLE II

Directors

Section 2.1. *Board of Directors.* The Board of Directors (hereinafter referred to as the "Board") shall have power to manage and administer the business and affairs of the Association. Except as expressly limited by law, all corporate powers of the Association shall be vested in and may be exercised by said Board.

Section 2.2. *Number.* The Board shall consist of not less than five nor more than twenty-five shareholders, the exact number within such minimum and maximum limits to be fixed and determined from time to time by resolution of a majority of the full Board or by resolution of the shareholders at any meeting thereof; *provided, however,* that a majority of the full Board of Directors may not increase the number of directors (i) to a number which exceeds by more than two the number of directors last elected by shareholders where such number was fifteen or less; and (ii) to a number which exceeds by more than four the number of directors last elected by shareholders where such number was sixteen or more, but in no event shall the number of directors exceed twenty-five.

Section 2.3. *Organization Meeting.* The Cashier, upon receiving the certificate of the judges, of the result of any election, shall notify the directors-elect of their election and of the time at which they are required to meet at the Main Office of the Association for the purpose of organizing the new Board and electing and appointing officers of the Association for the succeeding year. Such meeting shall be appointed to be held on the day of the election or as soon thereafter as practicable, and, in any event, within thirty days thereof. If, at the time fixed for such meeting, there shall not be a quorum present, the directors present may adjourn the meeting, from time to time, until a quorum is obtained.

Section 2.4. *Regular Meetings.* The Regular Meetings of the Board of Directors shall be held, without notice, on the _____ of each _____ at the Main Office. When any regular meeting of the Board falls upon a holiday, the meeting shall be held on the next banking business day unless the Board shall designate some other day.

Section 2.5. *Special Meetings.* Special meetings of the Board of Directors may be called by the _____ of the Association, or at the request of three (3) or more directors. Each member of the Board of Directors shall be given notice stating the time and place, by telegram, letter, or in person, of each such special meeting.*

Section 2.6. *Quorum.* A majority of the directors shall constitute a quorum at any meeting, except when otherwise provided by law; but a less number may adjourn any meeting, from time to time, and the meeting may be held, as adjourned, without further notice.*

Section 2.7. *Vacancies.* When any vacancy occurs among the directors, the remaining members of the Board, in accordance with the laws of the United States, may appoint a director to fill such vacancy at any regular meeting of the Board, or at a special meeting called for that purpose.

ARTICLE III

Committees of the Board

(Instruction: The Board of Directors has power over and is solely responsible for the management and administration of the Association. The Board of Directors may delegate such of its powers (but not any of its responsibilities) to such persons or Committees as the Board may determine. If it is desired to have a Discount Committee, Examining Committee, or other Committees, the following sections may be used.)

Section 3.1. *Discount Committee.* There shall be a Discount Committee composed of _____ Directors, appointed by the Board annually or more often. The Discount Committee shall have power to discount and purchase bills, notes, and other evidences of debt, to buy and sell bills of exchange, to examine and approve loans and discounts, to exercise authority regarding loans and discounts, and to exercise, when the Board is not in session, all other powers of the Board that may lawfully be delegated. The Discount Committee shall keep minutes of its meetings, and such minutes shall be submitted at the next regular meeting of the Board of Directors at which a quorum is present, and any action taken by the Board with respect thereto shall be entered in the minutes of the Board.

Section 3.2. *Examining Committee.* There shall be an Examining Committee composed of not less than _____ Directors appointed by the Board annually or more often, whose duty it shall be to make an examination every six months into the affairs of the Association, and to report the result of such examination in writing to the Board at the next regular meeting thereafter. Such report shall state whether the Association is in a sound condition, whether adequate internal

ENCYCLOPEDIA OF BANKING AND FINANCE

audit controls and procedures are being maintained and shall recommend to the Board such changes in the manner of doing business or conducting the affairs of the Association as shall be deemed advisable.

Section 3.3. *Other Committees.* The Board of Directors may appoint, from time to time, from its own members, other committees of one or more persons, for such purposes and with such powers as the Board may determine.

ARTICLE IV

Officers and Employees

Section 4.1. *Chairman of the Board.* The Board of Directors shall appoint one of its members to be Chairman of the Board to serve at the pleasure of the Board. He shall preside at all meetings of the Board of Directors. The Chairman of the Board shall supervise the carrying out of the policies adopted or approved by the Board. He shall have general executive powers, as well as the specific powers conferred by these Bylaws. He shall also have and may exercise such further powers and duties as from time to time may be conferred upon, or assigned to, him by the Board of Directors.

Section 4.2. *President.* The Board of Directors shall appoint one of its members to be President of the Association. In the absence of the Chairman, he shall preside at any meeting of the Board. The President shall have general executive powers, and shall have and may exercise any and all other powers and duties pertaining by law, regulation, or practice, to the office of President, or imposed by these Bylaws. He shall also have and may exercise such further powers and duties as from time to time may be conferred upon, or assigned to, him by the Board of Directors.

Section 4.3. *Vice President.* The Board of Directors may appoint one or more Vice Presidents. Each Vice President shall have such powers and duties as may be assigned to him by the Board of Directors. One Vice President shall be designated by the Board of Directors, in the absence of the President, to perform all the duties of the President.

Section 4.4. *Secretary.* The Board of Directors shall appoint a Secretary, Cashier, or other designated officer who shall be Secretary of the Board and of the Association, and shall keep accurate minutes of all meetings. He shall attend to the giving of all notices required by these Bylaws to be given. He shall be custodian of the corporate seal, records, documents and papers of the Association. He shall provide for the keeping of proper records of all transactions of the Association. He shall have and may exercise any and all other powers and duties pertaining by law, regulation or practice, to the office of Cashier, or imposed by these Bylaws. He shall also perform such other duties as may be assigned to him, from time to time, by the Board of Directors.

Section 4.5. *Other Officers.* The Board of Directors may appoint one or more Assistant Vice Presidents, one or more Trust Officers, one or more Assistant Secretaries, one or more Assistant Cashiers, one or more Managers and Assistant Managers of Branches and such other officers and Attorneys-in-fact as from time to time may appear to the Board of Directors to be required or desirable to transact the business of the Association. Such officers shall respectively exercise such powers and perform such duties as pertain to their several offices, or as may be conferred upon, or assigned to, them by the Board of Directors, the Chairman of the Board, or the President.

Section 4.6. *Clerks and Agents.* The Board of Directors may appoint, from time to time, such Paying Tellers, Receiving Tellers, Note Tellers, Vault Custodians, bookkeepers and other clerks, agents and employees as it may deem advisable for the prompt and orderly transaction of the business of the Association, define their duties, fix the salaries to be paid them and dismiss them. Subject to the authority of the Board of Directors, the President, or any other officer of the Association authorized by him, may appoint and dismiss all or any clerks, agents and employees and prescribe their duties and the conditions of their employment, and from time to time fix their compensation.

Section 4.7. *Tenure of Office.* The President shall hold his office for the current year for which the Board of which he shall be a member was elected, unless he shall resign, become disqualified, or be removed, and any vacancy occurring in the office of President shall be filled promptly by the Board of Directors.

ARTICLE V

Trust Department

Section 5.1. *Trust Department.* There shall be a department of the Association known as the Trust Department which shall perform the fiduciary responsibilities of the Association.

(Instruction: The Board of Directors has power and is solely responsible for the management and administration of the Trust Department. The Board of Directors may delegate such of its fiduciary powers (but not any of its fiduciary responsibilities) to such persons or Committees as the Board may determine. It is a requirement of Regulation 9 that there be a Trust Audit Committee. If it is desired to have a Trust Officer or Trust Investment Committee, Sections 5.2 and 5.3 may be used.)

Section 5.2. *Trust Officer.* There shall be a Trust Officer of this Association whose duties shall be to manage, supervise and direct all the activities of the Trust Department. He shall do or cause to be done all things necessary or proper in carrying on the business of the Trust Department in accordance with provisions of law and applicable regulations. He shall act pursuant to opinion of counsel where such opinion is deemed necessary. Opinions of counsel shall be retained on file in connection with all important matters pertaining to fiduciary activities. The Trust Officer shall be responsible for all assets and documents held by the Association in connection with fiduciary matters.

The Board of Directors may appoint such other officers of the Trust Department as it may deem necessary, with such duties as may be assigned.

Section 5.3. *Trust Investment Committee.* There shall be a Trust Investment Committee of this Association composed of ____ members, who shall be capable and experienced officers or directors of the Association. All investments of funds held in a fiduciary capacity shall be made, retained or disposed of only with the approval of the Trust Investment Committee; and the Committee shall keep minutes of all its meetings, showing the disposition of all matters considered and passed upon by it. The Committee shall, promptly after the acceptance of an account for which the bank has investment responsibilities, review the assets thereof, to determine the advisability of retaining or disposing of such assets. The Committee shall conduct a similar review at least once during each calendar year thereafter and within fifteen months of the last such review. A report of all such reviews, together with the action taken as a result thereof, shall be noted in the minutes of the Committee.

Section 5.4. *Trust Audit Committee.* The Board of Directors shall appoint a committee of ____ Directors, exclusive of any active officers of the Association, which shall, at least once during each calendar year and within fifteen months of the last such audit, make suitable audits of the Trust Department or cause suitable audits to be made by auditors responsible only to the Board of Directors, and at such time shall ascertain whether the department has been administered in accordance with law, Regulation 9, and sound fiduciary principles.

Section 5.5. *Trust Department Files.* There shall be maintained in the Trust Department files containing all fiduciary records necessary to assure that its fiduciary responsibilities have been properly undertaken and discharged.

Section 5.6. *Trust Investments.* Funds held in a fiduciary capacity shall be invested in accordance with the instrument establishing the fiduciary relationship and local law. Where such instrument does not specify the character and class of investments to be made and does not vest in the bank a discretion in the matter, funds held pursuant to such instrument shall be invested in investments in which corporate fiduciaries may invest under local law.

ARTICLE VI

Stock and Stock Certificates

Section 6.1. *Transfers.* Shares of stock shall be transferable on the books of the Association, and a transfer book shall be kept in which all transfers of stock shall be recorded. Every person becoming a shareholder by such transfer shall, in proportion to his shares, succeed to all rights and liabilities of the prior holder of such shares.

Section 6.2. *Stock Certificates.* Certificates of stock shall bear the signature of the President (which may be engraved, printed or impressed), and shall be signed manually or by facsimile process by the Secretary, Assistant Secretary, Cashier, Assistant Cashier, or any other officer appointed by the Board of Directors for that purpose, to be known as an Authorized Officer, and the seal of the Association shall be engraved thereon. Each certificate shall recite on its face that the stock represented thereby is transferable only upon the books of the Association properly endorsed.

ARTICLE VII

Corporate Seal

The President, the Cashier, the Secretary or any Assistant Cashier or Assistant Secretary, or other officer thereunto designated by the Board of Directors, shall have authority to affix the corporate seal to any document requiring such seal, and to attest the same. Such seal shall be substantially in the following form:

(Impression)
(of)
(Seal)

ARTICLE VIII

Miscellaneous Provisions

Section 8.1. *Fiscal Year.* The fiscal year of the Association shall be the calendar year.

Section 8.2. *Execution of Instruments.* All agreements, indentures, mortgages, deeds, conveyances, transfers, certificates, declarations, receipts, discharges, releases, satisfactions, settlements, petitions, schedules, accounts, affidavits, bonds, undertakings, proxies and other instruments or documents may be signed, executed, acknowledged, verified, delivered or accepted on behalf of the Association by the Chairman of the Board, or the President, or any Vice President, or the Secretary, or the Cashier, or, if in connection with the exercise of fiduciary powers of the Association, by any of said officers or by any Trust Officer. Any such instruments may also be executed, acknowledged, verified, delivered or accepted in behalf of the Association in such other manner and by such other officers as the Board of Directors may from time to time direct. The provisions of this Section 8.2 are supplementary to any other provision of these Bylaws.

Section 8.3. *Records.* The Articles of Association, the Bylaws and the proceedings of all meetings of the shareholders, the Board of Directors, standing committees of the Board, shall be recorded in appropriate minute books provided for the purpose. The minutes of each meeting shall be signed by the Secretary, Cashier or other officer appointed to act as Secretary of the meeting.

Section 8.4. *Banking Hours.* The Main Office of the Association shall be open for business from _____ o'clock, A.M., to _____ o'clock, P.M., of each day, excepting Saturdays, when the hours shall be from _____ o'clock, A.M., to _____ o'clock, and Sundays and days recognized by the laws of the State of _____ as legal holidays.

ARTICLE IX

Bylaws

Section 9.1. *Inspection.* A copy of the Bylaws, with all amendments thereto, shall at all times be kept in a convenient place at the Head Office of the Association, and shall be open for inspection to all shareholders, during banking hours.

Section 9.2. *Amendments.* The Bylaws may be amended, altered or repealed, at any regular meeting of the Board of Directors, by a vote of a majority of the whole number of the Directors.

I, _____ , CERTIFY that: (1) I am the duly constituted (Secretary) or (Cashier) of _____ and Secretary of its Board of Directors, and as such officer am the official custodian of its records; (2) the foregoing Bylaws are the Bylaws of said Bank, and all of them, as now lawfully in force and effect.

IN TESTIMONY WHEREOF, I have hereunto affixed by official signature and the seal of the said Bank, in the City of _____ , on this ___ day of _____ , 19 ___ .

_____
Secretary (or Cashier)

(Note: The paragraphs marked with an asterisk * are not mandatory. However, the subject covered by such paragraphs should be adequately covered by alternative provisions in a manner consonant with law. The paragraph marked with a # is optional and may be omitted.)

BY-PASS TRUST An irrevocable trust which provides that the principal of the trust shall pass to the beneficiaries without being assessed estate taxes upon the death of the trustor. The by-pass trust gives a surviving spouse or beneficiary a lifetime interest, to avoid estate taxes on a second death.

C

CABINET DISPLAY *See* AUTOMATED BOND SYSTEM.

CABLE RATE The rate quoted for a CABLE TRANSFER as distinguished from the check (demand draft) rate and the rate for 30-, 60-, and 90-day bills of exchange. The cable rate is always higher than the check rate and rate for time bills, because the bank selling the cable transfer does not have use of its funds deposited abroad as long as it would in the case of issuing a check or time draft. In the case of a check, the foreign bank cannot draw against the selling bank nor charge its account until the advice arrives (10 days to six weeks later); in the case of a time draft, until its maturity. In the case of a cable transfer, the selling bank's account is charged by the bank ordered to make the disbursement as soon as the funds are paid to the beneficiary. Thus the cable rate may be regarded as equivalent to the check rate plus interest that is saved while the check is transiting, modified by the market situation in cable funds.

From the standpoint of a purchaser, the higher rate for a cable transfer represents the cost of the privilege of deferring the purchase of funds until actually needed abroad, and leaves him or her in a position to take advantage of any intervening decline in rates. The cable rate does not include the cable charges which are borne by the purchaser.

See CHECK RATE, LONG RATE, SHORT RATE.

CABLES Communications usually in code; particularly orders to pay money, sent abroad over transoceanic cable lines or by wireless.

See CABLE TRANSFER.

CABLE TRANSFER A means by which a bank or foreign exchange dealer enables its customers to remit funds abroad immediately. Suppose "A" in New York wishes to remit one thousand pounds sterling to "B" in London. "A" will apply to a foreign ex-change banker for a cable transfer, ordering payment to be made to "B" in London. The New York bank will cable its correspondent in London and authorize it to pay one thousand pounds to "B" and charge the cabling bank's account for the amount. In practice, customers having accounts with a bank maintaining a foreign exchange department do not pay for the cable transfer until the following day, or the day when the funds are paid abroad. When the cable reaches the London correspondent, it notifies "B" to call for the funds, and upon identification pays him or her.

Cable transfers may be made payable in dollars or in a foreign currency, usually the latter. When in a foreign currency, the rate quoted includes the bank's commission. For dollar cable transfers, a commission is charged in addition to cablegram charges. The principle of the cable transfer is the same as the domestic telegraphic or wire transfer, except that in the latter foreign exchange rates are not involved.

Bankers usually deal in cable transfers in order to take advantage of temporary money market conditions here or abroad, or to provide funds for meeting withdrawals from balances held abroad.

CALL This term has five meanings:

1. A demand for the payment of an installment on the purchase price of bonds or stocks subscribed for, the time of call usually being discretionary with the issuing organization but sometimes according to definite prearranged dates. The subscribed but uncalled capital of a corporation may be called at any time, but only in accordance with the agreement made with subscribers when the stock was first allotted.
2. The exercise of the right of REDEMPTION by a corporation, reserved by the corporation under specific provisions, of bonds, debentures, or preferred stocks. *See* CALLABLE, CALLABLE BONDS, REDEEMABLE.
3. In options trading, a contract whereby the holder is entitled to purchase the standardized size of 100 shares of the specified common stock, at a specified price (striking price) on or before the specified expiration date.

Although both the buyer and seller of the call are represented by their respective brokers on the floor of the Exchange in exchange trading, the Options Clearing Corporation (OCC) performs the intermediary functions of acquiring the call from the seller (the writer) and issuing the call to the buyer. The OCC is a corporation owned by the five stock exchanges that trade in options; it deals only with members of these stock exchanges (clearing members), thus assuring creditworthiness of the option contracts. When the option is exercised, the holder's broker, upon tender of the funds to cover the purchase, notifies the OCC and it designates a broker representing a writer of that call to make delivery to the holder's broker. Should the option not be exercised on or before the expiration date, it will cease to exist as a contractual obligation upon the writer.

Option strike prices are standardized: strike prices for stocks selling below $50 are fixed at intervals of $5; for stocks selling between $50 and $200, at intervals of $10; and for stocks selling over $200, at intervals of $20. Option contracts are also standardized by the cycle of expiration months: June, September, December; July, October, January; and August, November, February.

Besides exercising the call should it be "in the money" on or before the expiration date (its striking price below the actual market price of the stock), the holder of a call may choose to sell it, since its prevailing price will always be greater than or equal to its intrinsic value (difference between its striking price and the prevailing market price of the stock).

A call might be bought for a variety of reasons: to enter the market at a cost lower than a purchase on margin, for leveraged speculation (calls have high sensitivity to the prices of the underlying stock; a 5% or 10% rise in the price of the underlying stock might be reflected in a 30% or 60% rise in the value of the call), or to protect a profit on a short sale. If the stock rises instead of falls, a call assures the short seller of stock coverage of the short sale at a price still affording him a profit on the selected call. If the short sale has just been made, a call will afford protection against a rising market, as the call can be exercised at the specified call price.

For further discussion of options, *see* OPTION, PUT.

4. Comptroller's call, *See* CALL REPORT.
5. MARGIN CALL.

CALLABLE Bonds and preferred stocks that are subject to the right of an obligor or issuer to prepay before maturity in the case of bonds and to retire at any time on specified notice. A penalty is usually attached to such right in the form of a premium over par in the case of bonds and a premium over liquidation preference in the case of preferred stock.

See CALLABLE BONDS.

CALLABLE BONDS Bonds that may be called for redemption before compulsory maturity as a result of the option exercised

ENCYCLOPEDIA OF BANKING AND FINANCE

by the debtor (issuer), recited in the bond indenture and frequently on the face of the bond certificate. Bonds are often issued subject to call, i.e., redemption in whole or in part on any interest date, upon proper notice. Because of the disturbance of the holder's investment holding of the bonds, the issuer exercising the right of redemption is usually obliged, under a redemption provision, to pay a premium upon redemption, i.e., some specified amount above par. This payment compensates the investor for the disadvantage of seeking a new investment medium, perhaps on less favorable terms, and for loss of interest in case notice of redemption escapes his or her notice, since these bonds do not bear interest after the redemption date. Callable bonds are not likely to reach a market price above that at which they are subject to call, unless they enjoy a conversion privilege of conversion into stock, for a buyer at such price above call price might find his or her bond called at the lower call price. In the case of convertible bonds selling above call price as justified by value of the stock into which convertible, the bond, in case of call, could be converted immediately into the stock, within the period of advance notice of the call, usually 30 days.

There are several reasons why an issuer may wish to retain the redemption privilege when issuing its bonds. It is possible that the issue could be refunded at a lower rate for sinking fund purposes or because of a decline in money rates. The issuer might also desire to modify its capital structure or finance an expansion, and therefore might wish to consolidate its bond issues.

Callable bonds are also known as optional bonds or redeemable bonds.

CALL COTTON Cotton bought or sold on call under CALL PURCHASE or CALL SALE contracts.

CALLED BONDS Bonds which have been called for redemption by lot or otherwise.
See CALLABLE BONDS.

CALL LOAN A loan on a demand basis, which either the borrower or lender may terminate at will. Most SECURITY LOANS are made on a call basis; with discontinuance of the Money Desk on the New York Stock Exchange, such loans are made directly by banks to brokers and dealers, under a general loan agreement in which the specific amount of loan is not specified and under which successive loans and repayments may be made from time to time with substitutions of collateral, provided adequate margins and sufficient diversification are maintained. In recent years, call loans have rarely been called by the lending institution, repayment normally being at the initiative of the borrowers; however, the lender has the legal right to call. The call may be either the sharp call (without compunction) or the slow call which has an informal understanding that the loan will not be called except as a last resort. Interest is usually computed daily at the prevailing rate. Call loans to brokers may be secured by government securities collateral and by New York Stock Exchange collateral. Call loans to dealers are secured by government securities.

Government securities dealers and dealers in over-the-counter issues may be more likely to use DAY LOANS and the OVERNIGHT LOAN.

Call loans, if called, are usually not called after 12:15 P.M. to 12:30 P.M., after which the broker has until 2:15 P.M. to make payment. The lending institution, however, could give notice of call as late as 3 P.M. and be entitled to repayment the same day.
See BROKERS' LOAN, CALL MONEY MARKET, DEMAND LOAN, RENEWAL RATE.

CALL LOAN RATE The rate at which money lent at call bears interest. This is subject to change each day if the RENEWAL RATE is changed.
See CALL MONEY MARKET.

CALL MONEY Money lent by banks, usually to stock exchange brokers, which may be called, i.e., demand may be made for payment, at any time. Call money is also known as day-to-day money and demand money.
See CALL LOAN, CALL MONEY MARKET.

CALL MONEY MARKET A particular sector of the money market which provides brokers and dealers with call (demand) funds secured by government securities and stock exchange collateral to meet their money requirements for carrying customers' margin accounts and their own securities inventory. New York is the principal call loan center of the country, and New York banks are the chief suppliers of this form of credit. Sums are also invested in call loans by New York banks for the account of interior bank correspondents. Since 1935, loans for the account of out-of-town banks have been low in volume; the Securities Exchange Act of 1934 prohibits banks from making loans to brokers and dealers for the account of "others'" than banks, so most of the volume of loans to brokers and dealers in New York by New York banks has been for own account.

Until the 1930s, call loans on stock exchange collateral were largely arranged by New York banks through the Money Desk on the New York Stock Exchange and, to a lesser extent, through direct loans to borrowing brokers maintaining accounts directly at banks. Beginning in the 1930s, however, banks began to make the bulk of brokers' call loans on a direct basis to their broker customers. Activity on the Money Desk declined and in about 1946 the Money Desk finally ceased as an outside money market mechanism for bringing together brokers and lending banks.

Now that call loans are arranged by banks on a direct basis, the question of whether they may no longer be classified strictly as outside loans also implies the question of whether banks would feel as free in exercising sharp calls in view of their direct relationship with the broker borrowers. Since call loans can be terminated on short notice by either the bank or the borrowing broker, in theory there should be no question about the right of a bank to make sharp calls. In practice, even if sharp calls are made by a bank, brokers usually maintain accounts in more than one bank. Unless all banks are calling loans, brokers can resort to other banks in order to pay off the calls of particular banks. In recent years, however, the initiative in payment of call loans has been with the broker borrowers. Under ordinary circumstances, the liquidity of call loans and their suitability for bank secondary reserves are not different now than when the outside mechanism of the Money Desk was used.

As an outlet for bank short-term funds for secondary reserve purposes, call loans have taken a decidedly subordinate position in recent years relative to U.S. Government short-term securities. In particular, New York banks adjust their reserve position by resorting to federal funds and Treasury bills. The repetition of the call money panics of the past, when the volume of call loans was substantially larger than in recent years, is considered unlikely, and call loans have ceased to be an important money market instrument.

In October 1987, following a severe drop in the value of the stock market, leading brokerage houses complained that the call money market had dried up, the banks refusing to extend additional credit to the brokers or wanting repayment of outstanding loans. As part of its efforts to contain the crisis, the Federal Reserve System provided direct call loans to brokers needing funds to carry the inventory of securities they had purchased.

BIBLIOGRAPHY

FEDERAL RESERVE BANK OF CLEVELAND. "Call Loans." *Economic Review*, October, 1964.

CALL OF MORE A London Stock Exchange term to denote an option that gives the holder the right to call for an additional amount of stock equal to the amount named in the contract at the same price.

It is "the premium paid for the rate of calling or putting stock at some future date at a stipulated price, and is sometimes included in the price at which a transaction is done, for the same date, in firm stock; thus a 'giver' of option money will buy a certain amount of stock firm for delivery, say two months ahead, at a figure sufficiently over the current market price for that period to carry with it the option of calling a like amount at the same price. This transaction in options is known as buying stock 'call of more'"
(Higgins, *The Put and Call*).

CALL PURCHASE A contract for the purchase of a commodity, commonly used in cotton trading, under which the price is fixed by the seller in the future. This fixing of the price is at the call of the seller and is set within a certain number of points above or below the price of a specified future on the day of fixing the contract price.
See CALL SALE.

CALL REPORT Statement of a bank's condition and income submitted in response to calls by the supervisory authorities:

COMPTROLLER OF THE CURRENCY for national banks, Federal Reserve banks for state member banks, FEDERAL DEPOSIT INSURANCE CORPORATION for insured nonmember banks, and state banking authorities for state banks and trust companies. The call report must be submitted on a specified form in accordance with instructions. These forms are of four types, differing according to whether the bank has foreign offices and according to size; the report for banks with domestic offices only and with total assets of less than $100 million is less detailed than that for other banks, while the report for banks with foreign offices is the most detailed. Normally, these reports are required on a quarterly basis.

Under the FEDERAL FINANCIAL INSTITUTIONS REGULATORY AND INTEREST RATE CONTROL ACT OF 1978, the FEDERAL FINANCIAL INSTITUTIONS EXAMINATION COUNCIL was charged with developing uniform reporting systems for federally supervised financial institutions, their holding companies, and the nonfinancial institutions subsidiaries of such institutions and holding companies. The council, whose membership consists of representatives of the three major bank regulatory agencies plus the Federal Home Loan Bank Board and the National Credit Union Administration, through its Task Force on Reports, is concerned with such reporting systems issues as development and interpretation of reporting instructions, application of accounting standards, monitoring of data quality, publication and distribution of reports, and development of processing standards.

See BANK ACCOUNTING.

BIBLIOGRAPHY

COMPTROLLER OF THE CURRENCY. *Annual Reports.*
———. *Comptroller's Manual for National Banks.* Periodic updates.
FEDERAL DEPOSIT INSURANCE CORPORATION. *Annual Reports.*
FEDERAL FINANCIAL INSTITUTIONS EXAMINATION COUNCIL. *Annual Reports.*

CALL SALE A contract for the sale of a commodity, generally used in cotton trading, under which the price is to be fixed by the buyer in the future. This fixing of the price is at the call of the buyer and is set within a certain number of points above or below the price of a specified future on the day of fixing the contract price. The reverse of the CALL PURCHASE.

CAMBISM CAMBISTRY.

CAMBIST This term has two meanings:

1. A person skilled in the exchange of foreign moneys; one who is able to determine, on the basis of current quotations, the cheapest method of remitting to a foreign country; a dealer or expert in foreign exchange.
2. A table or manual used in computing foreign exchange transactions, prepared by a cambist, in order to save time that would be needed to compute each transaction separately. This manual exhibits the principal currencies of the world and their weight, fineness, and equivalent values.

See CAMBISTRY.

CAMBISTRY The science of exchange of foreign currencies, particularly with reference to determining the cheapest method of remitting to a foreign country. Cambistry involves a knowledge of various countries of the world; weights, measures, and fineness of metals used as a basis of coinage in various countries; methods of dealing in bullion; assaying operations; issuance of bills of exchange, international checks, and postal money orders; commercial parities; and computations in the ARBITRATION OF EXCHANGE.

See FOREIGN EXCHANGE, FOREIGN MONEYS.

BIBLIOGRAPHY

RIEHL, H., and Rodriguez, R. *Foreign Exchange Markets,* 1977.

CAMPAIGN In free markets, prior to the Securities Exchange Act of 1934, a type of organized speculation or demonstration in a security or group of securities, sometimes for the purpose of depressing values, but more frequently for raising values thereby attracting public participation so that stocks could be distributed at the higher levels. A campaign usually implied fictitious activity and fluctuation in a stock in order to draw speculative attention to it and cause the dissemination of news and rumors about it, favorable or unfavorable, according to the purpose of those conducting the campaign.

Under the Securities Exchange Act of 1934, manipulation of security prices, including campaigns as practices of pools, is prohibited.

See POOL.

CAMPS Cumulative auction market preferred stock.
See FINANCIAL INSTRUMENTS: RECENT INNOVATIONS.

CANADA–U.S. FREE TRADE AGREEMENT On January 2, 1988, the United States and Canada entered into a free trade agreement. (H.R. 5090; P.L. 100–449). The Canadian Parliament subsequently approved the agreement. The agreement provides for the elimination of almost all tariffs between the countries within 10 years. It also establishes a special binational dispute settlement mechanism for antidumping and countervailing duty cases. The agreement was generally supported by the U.S. business community, but in Canada it was the subject of an intense public debate.

Additional major provisions of the Canada–U.S. Free Trade Agreement include the following:

1. The agreement provides for a two-track system of safeguard actions. If imports from one party alone are a substantial cause of injury, the other party may suspend duty reductions provided by the agreement for a maximum of three years. Both countries retain their Article XIX rights under the General Agreement on Tariffs and Trade (GATT).
2. Existing quantitative restrictions, with a few exceptions, will be eliminated or phased out according to a timetable.
3. Sectoral trade in agriculture, wine, distilled spirits, and energy will be liberalized. Existing free trade arrangements in automobiles will remain essentially intact.
4. Trade in services will be dealt with in accordance with a set of disciplines based on the principle of national treatment, right of commercial presence, and right of establishment. Financial services will grandfather existing privileges in each other's market and improve access and competition consistent with each country's supervisory and regulatory requirements.
5. The two countries agreed to provide each other's investors with national treatment regarding the establishment of new businesses, and the conduct, operation, and sale of existing businesses.
6. The two countries agreed to expand access to purchases by governments.
7. The agreement establishes a Canada–U.S. Trade Commission to supervise its implementation and administration and to resolve disputes.

CANADIAN BANKERS ASSOCIATION Originally formed as a voluntary association in 1890, this bankers' association is unique in that it was specifically chartered by act of the Canadian Parliament in 1900 (amendment to the Canadian Banking Act) to effect greater cooperation among Canadian banks in the issuance of notes, in credit and control, and in various other aspects of bank activity. Membership is compulsory for all banks to which the Canadian Bank Act, as amended, applies. Although the original functions, such as supervision of note issuance of the chartered banks and central gold reserves, have been since curtailed by the advent of central banking in Canada, the association continues to provide many services for Canadian banks in the interests of uniformity and cooperation. Among these are the educational program for Canadian banks' personnel, analogous to the AMERICAN INSTITUTE OF BANKING in the U.S., and the publication of the *Canadian Banker.*

CANADIAN BANKING SYSTEM In 1792 a group of Montreal businessmen attempted to establish a bank in Canada. The attempt was not successful. In 1817, the Montreal Bank (now the Bank of Montreal) was founded by nine Montreal merchants. This bank is the oldest Canadian bank in existence. By 1867 there were 35 banks in British North America. Banks were originally incorporated by individual provinces. At Confederation in 1867, the new federal government had exclusive jurisdiction over all matters associated with money and banking. The final version of the Bank Act was adopted in 1871. The Bank Act is revised every 10 years.

The Bank Act governs the activities of the chartered banks. The

ENCYCLOPEDIA OF BANKING AND FINANCE

CANADIAN BANKING SYSTEM

Table 1 / Highlights

	Date	Current	Year ago	Percent change
Assets ($ Millions)				
Total Assets	Dec. 31/86	466,703	443,761	5.2
Foreign Currency Assets	Dec. 31/86	207,332	202,010	2.6
As a % of Total Assets	Dec. 31/86	44.4	45.5	—
Business Loans Outstanding	Dec. 31/86	61,868	64,923	-4.7
Under $1 Million	Dec. 31/86	19,625	19,614	0.1
Over $1 Million	Dec. 31/86	42,244	45,310	-6.8
Personal Loans Outstanding	Dec. 31/86	43,370	39,274	10.4
Credit Card Loans Outstanding	Dec. 31/86	5,862	5,180	13.2
Agricultural Loans Outstanding	Dec. 31/86	8,361	10,286	-18.7
Residential Morgage Loans Outstanding *	Dec. 31/86	49,641	40,899	21.4
Investments (Canada)	Dec. 31/86	29,933	27,532	8.7
Deposits ($ Millions)				
Total Canadian $ Deposits	Dec. 31/86	199,627	187,766	6.3
Personal Savings Deposits	Dec. 31/86	129,765	119,063	9.0
Other Notice Deposits	Dec. 31/86	47,693	45,086	5.8
Demand Deposits	Dec. 31/86	20,123	19,267	4.4
Government of Canada	Dec. 31/86	2,045	4,350	-53.0
Other Information (Number)				
Personal Savings Accounts	Apr. 30/86	31,873,409	31,502,586	1.2
Other Deposit Accounts	Apr. 30/86	7,024,145	7,412,327	-5.2
Branches—in Canada	Oct. 31/86	6,966	7,014	-0.7
—Abroad	Oct. 31/86	237	269	-11.9
Employees in Canada	Oct. 31/86	162,667	162,163	0.3

* Includes morgage subsidiaries.
Source: The Canadian Bankers' Association

1980 revision allows for the existence of two types of banks. The eleven that were in business before the revision are known as Schedule A banks. Schedule B banks are either subsidiaries of foreign banks or banks owned by Canadians in which one party holds more than 10% of the outstanding shares. Schedule A banks cannot be closely held banks. As of July 1987, there were eight Schedule A banks and 59 Schedule B banks. The chartered banks' nationwide system of branches consisted of almost 7,000 serving all provinces and territories. Table 1 presents highlights of Canadian banking operations.

The December 1, 1980 Bank Act revision sets forth how a bank can be established, the capital required, qualifications and limitations of directors, their duties and responsibilities, how mergers and amalgamations are carried out, the distribution and transfer of shares, the financial reports that a bank must make to its owners and to government, and details of what banks must and must not do generally. The act links the commercial banking system to the government-owned Bank of Canada for monetary purposes by requiring them to hold primary and secondary reserves. Banks earn no interest on the primary reserves. The Bank of Canada is the "bankers' bank" because it controls the clearing system that the chartered banks and other financial institutions use to settle accounts among themselves. The Minister of Finance regularly monitors the banks.

Each bank has a chief executive officer who is directly responsible to the board of directors. The shares of the Schedule A banks are traded on the major stock exchanges.

The three basic types of deposit accounts are savings accounts, checking accounts, and term deposits. New generations of accounts are also available. Canadian dollar deposits in chartered banks are insured by the Canada Deposit Insurance Corporation, a federal agency, to a maximum of $60,000 per depositor in each bank.

Canadian banks are active in foreign markets. Foreign currency assets in 1986 represented over 45% of total assets. Foreign operations make up a significant portion of the banks' earnings. Canadian banks maintain nearly 300 branches in some 30 countries.

Loans to the agricultural sector by chartered banks totaled $8.4 billion at the end of 1986. Residential mortgage loans exceeded $49.6 billion at the end of 1986. Consumer loans reached over $43 billion at the end of 1986. The banks account for over 65% of the consumer credit market in Canada. Almost $30 billion of chartered banks' Canadian dollar assets are invested in Canadian securities—Government of Canada Treasury bills; direct and guaranteed bonds; and provincial, municipal, and corporate securities. In total, they make up 6.4% of the banks' Canadian dollar assets.

Interest rates are determined by market forces that influence the demand for and the supply of money. The federal government exerts a major influence on rates. The federal government through its agent, the Bank of Canada, established monetary policy in response to international conditions and domestic needs.

Banking is highly regulated in Canada. The Bank Act provides the basis of bank regulation. Other federal statutes that affect banks directly or indirectly include the Bill of Exchange Act, the Canadian Payments Association Act, Canada Labor Standards Act, the Canada Pension Standards Act, the Canada Deposit Insurance Corporations Act, the Canada Mortgage and Housing Corporation Act, The Canada Business Corporations Act, and the Income Tax Act. The Bank of Canada—established as the central bank in 1945—also has major impacts on commercial banking in Canada.

Under the 1980 Bank Act, an annual statement is to be submitted to the shareholders of the bank including:

1. A consolidated statement of assets and liabilities in the form set out in Schedule K to the act.
2. A consolidated statement of income in the form set out in Schedule L to the act.
3. A consolidated statement of appropriations for contingencies in the form set out in Schedule M to the act.
4. A consolidated statement of changes in shareholders' equity in the form set out in Schedule N of the act.

As a result of changes introduced by the 1980 Bank Act, the financial reporting practices of banks have been brought into conformity with generally accepted accounting principles in Canada in all significant respects other than accounting for loan losses and the maintenance of a reserve for contingencies which is excluded from shareholders' equity. Full disclosure of such matters is required.

Relationships with the Bank of Canada. The BANK OF CANADA, Canada's central bank, does not accept deposits from individuals or compete with the chartered banks in the commercial banking field. The provisions of the Bank Act, however, enable the Bank of Canada to determine the total amount of cash reserves available to the chartered banks as a group. Each chartered bank must maintain a stipulated average amount of cash reserves in the form of deposits at the Bank of Canada and holdings of Bank of Canada notes (the Bank of Canada has the sole right to issue paper money for circulation in Canada). In place of a requirement for a 4% reserve against notice deposits and 12% against demand deposits, the new rates approved by the Bank Act were set at 3% and 10%, respectively, with the first $500 million of notice deposits requiring only 2%. The reduction was phased in over a period of three and a half years. Coins would be counted against the requirement. It was estimated that these changes would result in a reduction of about one-fifty in reserve requirements. The reserve requirement for non-encashable deposits having a term of more than one year was removed. Certain other deposits were also exempted, including RRSPs, RHOSPs, deposits of other banks, deposits of nonbank members of the CBA, and Canadian currency deposits of nonresidents. The reserve requirement was extended to wholly-owned foreign subsidiaries and to deposits held by wholly-or partially-owned factoring and leasing corporations.

The Bank of Canada may make loans or advances for a period not exceeding six months to chartered banks on the pledge of certain classes of securities. Loans or advances may be made under certain conditions and for limited periods to the government or any province. The bank rate is the minimum rate at which the Bank of Canada is prepared to make loans or advances.

The Bank of Canada may also require the chartered banks to maintain a secondary reserve which the bank may vary within certain limits. The secondary reserve consists of cash reserves in excess of the statutory requirement, Treasury bills, and day-to-day loans to investment dealers.

Other Canadian Government Financial Institutions. The Farm Credit Corporation was established in 1959 to provide for the extension of long-term mortgage credit to farmers. The Canada Mortgage and Housing Corporation (formerly the Central Mortgage and Housing Corporation) was incorporated in 1945 to insure mortgage loans made by approved lenders and to make direct mortgage loans. The Federal Business Development Bank (FBDB) was established in 1975 to provide financial and advisory management services to small-and medium-sized businesses in Canada. The FBDB is the successor to the Industrial Development Bank, which was established in 1944 as a subsidiary of the Bank of Canada.

International Activity of Canadian Banks. The increasing importance of the international activities of the Canadian banks and the work of the BANK FOR INTERNATIONAL SETTLEMENTS (BIS) Committee of Bank Supervisors is reflected in the following three ways in the 1980 Bank Act in Canada. First, full con-solidation of subsidiaries will be required in the accounts of the banks (this goes beyond the existing law which provided only for consolidation of wholly-owned banking subsidiaries). Second, a bank will be prevented from controlling a Canadian or foreign corporation unless the bank obtains from the board of directors of that corporation a resolution giving the Inspector General of Banks the right of access to the firm's books, minutes, and accounts, subject only in the case of a foreign corporation to the laws of the jurisdiction in which it is incorporated. Finally, the Inspector may, as a special exception to a tight secrecy provision imposed on his office, provide information regarding the affairs of a bank "to senior officials responsible for the supervision of banks in jurisdiction other than Canada, where in the opinion of the Inspector, it is in the interests of Canada to exchange such information and where the officials to whom the information is provided are required by law to maintain secrecy in respect of information so provided." (The office of the Inspector General of Banks in Canada was established in 1924 by amendment of the Bank Act, following the failure in 1923 of the Home Bank, a retail bank whose failure was widely felt.)

Foreign Banks in Canada. The criteria applicable under the 1980 Bank Act to a foreign bank seeking to own foreign bank subsidiaries in Canada will include the following:

1. It must be a foreign bank.
2. It should have sufficient assets, expertise, and earnings to support the Canadian operation.
3. It should usually be widely held.
4. It should be well supervised and in good standing.
5. It must provide evidence of ability to contribute to competitive banking in Canada, and of reciprocity in the home jurisdiction.
6. It must be willing to provide a letter of comfort, that is, a letter indicating its willingness to stand behind the banking subsidiary.

It also should be noted that there is a limitation on the total dominion assets of foreign bank subsidiaries collectively, that being 8% of all banks' domestic assets. Representative offices of foreign banks will be required to register.

The Canadian Bankers' Association has provided much of this information about the chartered banks of Canada.

BIBLIOGRAPHY

Canadian Banker. The Canadian Bankers' Association. *Banking in Canada*, 1983.
―――. *The Chartered Banks of Canada: Their Role and Organization*. 1987.
THE CHARTERED BANKS OF CANADA. *Bank Facts*. 1987.
Review. Bank of Canada.

CANADIAN COMMODITY EXCHANGE An exchange organized in Montreal on October 22, 1934, to deal in silver spot and future contracts, following the nationalization of silver in the United States. The exchange operated until institution of the Foreign Exchange Control Board in accordance with the Exchange Fund Order in 1940. There has since been no free market in silver, all silver transactions being cleared through the Foreign Exchange Control Board at the official rates.

CANCELED CHECKS Checks that the drawee bank has paid and canceled. Checks are canceled by the drawee bank on the day they are paid and charged to the drawer's account. They are usually canceled with the date paid and name and clearing house number of the paying bank. Canceled checks are kept in the records of the bank until the end of the month, when they usually are delivered to, or called for by, the customer, together with the monthly statement.

When a check is paid, it becomes the property of the drawer, but the paying bank is entitled to retain it as a voucher until the statement of account has been submitted to and reconciled by the customer, and agreed to as correct.

Canceled checks furnish the best evidence of the payment of money and should be preserved by the drawer as receipts or vouchers.

See STATEMENT DEPARTMENT, VOUCHER, VOUCHER CHECK.

CANCELLATION An annulment or rendering void or in operative of financial instruments, e.g., bonds, coupons, stocks, and checks, upon their payment and retirement, or transfer; termination of open orders for the purchase or sale of securities.

For the purpose of protecting themselves against fraud and possible presentation of a bond which may have become lost and in the illegal possession of the holder, it is incumbent upon the issuers to exercise reasonable care in the redemption of bonds and in the handling of the accompanying coupons. A customary procedure is to provide a blank book for each issue of bonds, one page being devoted to a single bond, below which spaces are numbered to correspond with each of the originally attached coupons. When coupons have matured and been paid off, they are canceled and pasted in the blank spaces, according to serial number. Likewise when the bond itself has matured and been redeemed, it is pasted in the space provided for it. In this way it is possible for the issuer to furnish evidence that the entire obligation has been extinguished, and that no bonds or coupons are outstanding.

Cancellation of bonds and coupons is sometimes accomplished by cremation.

See CREMATION OF BONDS.

CAPACITY One of the three elements of CREDIT. Among credit analysts, the test of capacity is called the business risk. In weighing a credit risk, one must be satisfied that the management is capable and competent. The most important information for measuring the business risk is the detailed operating statement showing sales, expenses, and profits (or losses) over a period of years. The final criterion of business capacity, and one that can be reduced to a mathematical basis, is whether good profits on a fairly stable basis have been made over a sustained period. On a strictly scientific basis, therefore, the measurement of the business risk can best be determined by a study of the comparative profit and loss statements taken over a period of years. The following particulars should be observed in judging capacity of a business:

ENCYCLOPEDIA OF BANKING AND FINANCE

CAPITAL

1. Pertaining to personnel and methods—managerial ability, one-man business versus group management, modernness of methods, knowledge of financial and credit principles, knowledge of markets and sales promotion principles, use of budget system, degree of cooperation of official personnel, relations with employees.
2. Pertaining to equipment—location of business with reference to raw materials and markets, modernness of plant equipment, cost system installed and utilized, research department.
3. Pertaining to product—stability of demand for products, reputation of products in the trade.
4. Pertaining to results—stability of gross sales, stability of gross and net profits, percent of returns to gross sales, margin of profits over total expenses, percent of uncollectables to net sales, percent of net profits to net sales, percent of net profits to capital invested.

See BUSINESS RISK, CREDIT.

CAPITAL This term has four meanings:

1. In the economic sense, it is equivalent to capital goods, i.e., the store of produced goods (physical quantity rather than money value) saved, or wealth represented by the surplus of production over consumption. In other words, it is a short expression for capital goods or capital value, especially that portion of wealth set aside for the furtherance of productive enterprise.

   Economists distinguish between production goods and consumption goods. The former are instruments of production, or intermediate wealth employed in the manufacture of consumable goods or services. Thus buildings, factories, machinery, equipment, railroads, etc., represent production goods. Consumption goods, on the other hand, comprise goods destined for immediate use, e.g., food, clothing, stocks of merchandise on retailers' shelves, personal service, etc.

   In the U.S., economists are particularly interested in capital expenditures (for new plant and equipment) as the most volatile component of national income. As a result of the unusually high rate of capital expenditures in the post–World War II period, and the additional expansion in capacity following passage of the Defense Production Act in the fall of 1950, induced by accelerated tax amortization of defense-essential business expenditures for plant and equipment, the stock of capital equipment has reached a high level both in the absolute and in productivity. The recognition in the 1954 Internal Revenue Code of the accelerated depreciation methods, which since have been available to business taxpayers, also has tended to stimulate business investment. Another powerful stimulant of investment outlays by business has been the investment tax credit.

   Reflecting the comprehensive revision of new plant and equipment expenditures by the Bureau of Economic Analysis, U.S. Department of Commerce for 1947–1977, which expanded coverage to all nonfarm business, incorporated new source data, and introduced separate estimates by major industry groups. Capital goods prices may be measured by the implicit price deflator for fixed nonresidential investment, in the national income and product accounts. See NATIONAL INCOME.

2. In the accounting sense, capital is synonymous with net assets and is measured by the excess of assets over liabilities. In a sole proprietorship, capital is represented by the account or accounts which indicate the accountability of the business to the owner; in a partnership, by the sum of the partners' accounts; and in a corporation, by the sum of the various capital stock accounts, retained earnings, and or equity reserves, if any. See CAPITAL STOCK.
3. In business, a distinction is made between working capital and fixed capital. WORKING CAPITAL, also known as liquid assets, in the ordinary course of business will be converted into cash, e.g., merchandise, accounts receivable, notes receivable, etc. Fixed capital, on the other hand, corresponds roughly to the economists' concept of production goods and consists of assets which in the ordinary course of business will not be converted into cash, but instead are necessary for carrying on the business. It is locked up or sunk into fixed assets, e.g., land, buildings, machinery, equipment, etc.
4. In credit analysis, the PROPERTY RISK.

BIBLIOGRAPHY

CROWLEY, D. K., and KIRK, J. H. "The Impact of Risk-Based Capital on U.S. Banking." *Magazine of Bank Administration*, November, 1988.
NEVIN, I. H., and BENTON, H. A. "Capital Ideas." *United States Banker*, February, 1989.
PARLIAMENT, T. "Credit Risk Focus in Capital Rule May Alter Asset Mixes." *Savings Institutions*, March, 1989.
"Final Guidelines Issued on Risk-Based Capital Requirements." *Federal Reserve Bulletin*, March, 1989.
"Final Rule—Amendment to Regulations H and Y." *Federal Reserve Bulletin*, March, 1989.
KIM, D., and SANTOMERO, A. M. "Risk in Banking and Capital Regulation." *Journal of Finance*, December, 1988.

CAPITAL ACCOUNT The account that denotes the amount of the owner's investment in a business; it represents net worth. It is known as a proprietorship account in the case of a sole proprietorship, as partners' accounts in the case of a partnership, and as CAPITAL STOCK in the case of a corporation.

See CAPITAL, CAPITAL AND REVENUE EXPENDITURES.

CAPITAL ADEQUACY In 1989 federal banking regulators issued new capital guidelines for commercial banks. The basic purpose of the guidelines is to increase capital levels of commercial banks as their financial structures increase. Capital adequacy is basic to the regulation of safety and soundness.

Under the 1989 guidelines, risk-weighted capital ratios must equal 7.25% by year-end 1990 and 8% by year-end 1992. Transitional rules are in effect during the transitional period beginning January 1, 1990. Most banks will have no problem meeting the new guidelines.

Under the guidelines, capital consists of Tier One (core) and Tier Two (supplementary) capital. The sum of both tiers must equal or exceed 8% of the sum of risk-weighted assets and credit equivalents. Tier One capital consists of equity capital plus disclosed reserves, with two adjustments. Goodwill is deducted from the sum of equity capital and disclosed reserves. Bank holding companies may count both cumulative and noncumulative perpetual preferred stock. Tier Two capital consists of five elements that can serve the loss-absorption function: undisclosed reserves, revaluation reserves, general loan loss provisions, hybrid instruments, and subordinated term debt. Tier Two is limited to the amount of Tier One and cannot include loan reserves in excess of 1.25% of risk-weighted assets. Regulators are required to monitor compliance with the guidelines and can make exceptions or require higher capital levels.

According to the guidelines, assets are classified into one of four categories from the least risky to the most risky: (1) cash and direct debt of the U.S. Government and its agencies—0% weighting, (2) claims on domestic depository institutions, debt conditionally guaranteed by the U.S. Government, and debt of government-sponsored agencies—20% weighting, (3) accruing loans secured by first liens on one- to four-family houses, mortgage-backed securities backed by conventional mortgages, and certain state or local revenue bonds or revenue-backed obligations—50% weighting, and (4) all other assets—100% weighting.

Off-balance-sheet risks such as letters of credit, assets sold with recourse, and formal loan commitments are included in assets through conversion to credit equivalents. To determine a credit equivalent amount, each off-balance-sheet risk is weighted (0%, 20%, 50%, or 100%) and assigned to the appropriate risk category based on the obligor, guarantor, or type of collateral.

The capital ratio is computed as the sum of Tiers One and Two capital divided by the sum of risk-weighted assets and credit equivalents.

The capital guidelines are comprehensive and detailed. It is anticipated that bank auditors will give special attention to the classification of home loans and securities, reporting of off-balance-sheet risks, procedures used to compute loan loss reserves that could be used to minimize specified losses, accounting used to avoid consolidating subsidiaries, underwriting standards for home loans, analyzing competitor banks to determine their risk-based capital positions, pricing off-balance-sheet risks and loan products, computing and applying risk-based capital ratios, and analyzing bond portfolio records to ensure proper classification.

The 1989 guidelines will have a significant impact on commercial banks and their customers. Many banks will undoubtedly attempt

CAPITAL ADEQUACY

to improve their capital leverage. Banks with capital in excess of the requirements may opt for aggressive growth to improve their leverage. Also, because of the requirements of the guidelines, it is possible that home mortgages will become more attractive (qualifying home loans require only half the capital of other loans); as a result, rates for first-mortgage home loans may decrease while rates for personal and commercial loans may increase, other things remaining the same.

An example of applying risk-based capital guidelines is presented in the appended table.

The Basle Agreement signed at the Bank for International Settlement (BIS) in Basle, Switzerland, in July 1988 by central bank representatives from the Group of Ten countries (Belgium, Canada, France, Germany, Italy, Japan, the Netherlands, Sweden, Switzerland, the United Kingdom, and the United States) and from Luxembourg provided the historical setting for the current risk-based capital adequacy standards. Capital and risk were the foundation of the Basle Agreement on risk-based capital.

The Board of Governors of the Federal Reserve System approved the Basle Agreement by a vote of five to one on August 3, 1988. A draft of the Federal Reserve Board's final regulation became available in mid-December 1988. The draft was approved on December 16, 1988, by a unanimous vote. These approved regulations were issued in the January 27, 1989, edition of the *Federal Register*. They took effect on March 15, 1989 (54 Fed. Rg. 4186). The Office of the Comptroller of the Currency also issued regulations pursuant to the Basle Agreement in the *Federal Register* (January 27, 1989). These regulations apply to all nationally chartered banks and are almost identical to the board's regulations. The Federal Deposit Insurance Corporation issued risk-based capital regulations pursuant to the Basle Agreement in the *Federal Register* (March 21, 1989). These apply to state-chartered banks that are not members of the Federal Reserve System and are similar to the board's final regulations.

The Basle Agreement and the 1989 regulations are based to some extent on the assumption that market forces cannot be relied on to bring about an optimal capital ratio and that regulatory-determined capital is necessary. Regulatory-determined capital is designed to absorb losses, particularly unexpected losses, arising from a bank's asset portfolio or its off-balance-sheet activities. It is also maintained that regulatory-determined capital is required to instill public confidence in the banking system.

The risk-weighting system in the Basle Agreement was the credit risk, not interest rate or currency risk. Credit risk is the risk that the obligor (counterparty) will not make good on its obligations. The Basle Agreement established five credit risk categories: 0, 10, 20, 50, and 100%. The 100% category represents the standard risk category.

The Federal Financial Institutions Examination Council Final Regulation approved changes in bank call reports designed to give regulators data on risk-based capital levels and off-balance-sheet activities. The revision includes a simplified test for banks to determine if they meet minimum risk-based capital ratios. Banks with assets under $1 billion meeting this test will not have to answer a number of detailed questions. After December 1990, the reported data will be publicly available.

The following terms associated with capital adequacy were selected from the source referenced:

Example of Applying Risk-based Capital Guidelines
(000's omitted)

	Balance sheet amount	Credit conversion factor	Amount	0%	20%	50%	100%	
Qualifying real estate loans	$1.500	N/A	$1,500			$1,500		
Other loans, net of $50 reserve	1,000	N/A	1,000				$1,000	
U.S. Treasury bonds	500	N/A	500	$500				
Nonguaranteed agency bonds	500	N/A	500		$500			
Other bonds	500	N/A	500				500	
Other assets	330	N/A	330				330	
Total assets	$4,330							
Off-balance-sheet items	$400	50% [1]	200				200	
Category totals				$500	$500	$1,500	$2,030	
Risk-weighted totals				$0	$100	$750	$2,030	$2,880

Capital:	Amount	Tier 1	Tier 2	Total
Shareholder's equity—common	$216	$216		$216
Capital notes	20		$20	20
Loan reserve	50		36	36 [2]
		$216	$56	$272

Capital ratios:

Old guidelines	—Primary	6.07% [3]
	—Total	6.53% [4]
New guidelines	—Tier 1	7.50% [5]
	—Tier 2	1.94% [5]
	—Total	9.44% [5]

[1] Assumed that the off-balance-sheet item involved qualified for the 50% credit conversion factor and the 100% risk weight category.
[2] Limited to 1.25% of total risk-weighted assets ($2,880).
[3] Computed as the sum of common equity ($216) plus the loan reserve ($50) divided by the sum of total assets ($4,330) plus loan reserves ($50).
[4] Primary capital ($266) plus capital notes ($20) divided by the primary capitol ratio denominator ($4,380).
[5] Tier 1 ($216), tier 2 ($56) and total capital ($272) divided by risk-weighted assets ($2,880).

Source: Kelley, J.R. "Risk-Based Capital Guidelines for Banks." *Journal of Accounting*, January 1990. Adapted with permission.

CAPITAL EXPENDITURES

Capital Most generally, the difference between total assets and total liabilities. In the context of banking regulation, those items included in the numerator when the capital/asset ratio is calculated.

Capital/asset ratio The amount of capital maintained, divided by the total assets owned. Also known as a leverage ratio or gearing ratio.

Capital/risk-weighted assets ratio The amount of capital maintained, divided by the sum of (1) the total assets owned, where the value of each asset is assigned a risk weight and (2) the credit equivalent amount of all off-balance-sheet activities, where each credit equivalent amount is assigned a risk weight.

Common stock Shares of ownership in a corporation that entitle the holder to dividend distributions made by the issuer. Common stock counts as Tier One capital.

Core capital Tier One capital.

Counterparty The other or opposite party to a contract.

Credit conversion factor A percentage amount applied to the full face value of off-balance-sheet activities other than interest or foreign exchange rate contracts to determine a credit equivalent amount.

Credit equivalent amount The deemed actual credit exposure arising from an off-balance-sheet activity. A credit conversion factor is applied to the full face value of the activity. A risk weight is then applied to the credit equivalent amount to calculate the risk-weighted value for the activity.

Credit risk The risk of financial loss from a default on an obligation.

Currency risk The risk of financial loss from an adverse foreign exchange rate movement.

Current credit exposure The mark-to-market value of a foreign exchange rate contract or interest rate contract.

Current exposure method The method prescribed in the Basle Agreement to calculate the credit equivalent amount on foreign exchange and interest rate contracts. It involves calculation of the current credit exposure and the potential future credit exposure. The sum of these is the replacement cost, which is taken to be the credit equivalent amount. A risk weight is then applied to this amount.

Disclosed reserves Reserves that are created or increased by appropriations of retained earnings or other surplus disclosed on the balance sheet. Essentially, disclosed reserves consist of retained earnings and paid-in capital in excess of par value (or capital surplus if no-par stock is issued).

Equity capital Under the Basle Agreement, equity capital consists of common stock, noncumulative, preferred stock, and (for bank holding companies) perpetual preferred stock.

Floating-rate preferred stock Preferred stock whose yield varies with a certain index. The index may be a market interest rate, the issuer's credit standing, or the issuer's financial condition. Also called adjustable-rate preferred stock.

General provisions and general loan loss reserves Provisions and reserves that are held against future unidentified losses and are freely available to meet any subsequent losses.

Goodwill An intangible asset reflecting the excess of the purchase price over the fair market value of net assets in an acquisition in which the purchase method of accounting is used.

Hidden reserves See Undisclosed reserves.

Hybrid instruments Financial instruments that combine features of debt and equity. An example is mandatory convertible debt. Hybrid instruments may be included in Tier Two capital.

Interest rate risk The risk of financial loss from an adverse interest rate movement.

Leverage ratio See Capital/asset ratio.

Limited life preferred stock Preferred stock with a stated maturity.

Loan loss provisions See General provisions and general loan loss reserves.

Loss absorption The reduction in a capital account that corresponds with the reduction in an asset account.

Mark-to-market value The current market value of an item.

Netting Treating several transactions between the same counterparties not individually but as a whole. That is, considering the net claim arising from all transactions between the same counterparties rather than the gross claims.

Obligor The party obligated to perform on a contract.

Perpetual preferred stock Preferred stock that has no fixed maturity and cannot be redeemed at the holder's options. Perpetual preferred stock may be noncumulative, which means that dividends do not accrue (if they are not paid, they do not accumulate as arrearages). By contrast, unpaid dividends on cumulative perpetual preferred stock do accrue and must be paid off before any dividends on common stock are paid.

Preferred stock Stock that entitles the holder to a preference in dividend distributions and/or a liquidation distribution over common stockholders.

Replacement cost The cost to the nondefaulting party of replacing the cash flows that it was entitled to under a foreign exchange or interest rate contract but that were lost because of counterparty default.

Revaluation reserves Reserve accounts on the right-hand side of the balance sheet that are increased whenever an asset on the left-hand side is revalued to reflect its market value. A revaluation reserve thus reflects the unrealized appreciation in an asset. The full amount of unrealized appreciation of a fixed asset may be included in Tier Two capital, as may 45% of the unrealized appreciation of common stock. U.S. banks and bank holding companies are not permitted to revalue assets, but banking organizations in some other countries, such as Japan, are permitted to do so.

Risk weight A percentage amount applied to the full value of each on-balance-sheet asset and the credit equivalent amount of each off-balance-sheet activity.

Risk-weighted assets The denominator of the capital/risk-weighted assets ratio. This denominator consists of the sum of (1) the risk-weighted amounts of all on-balance-sheet assets and (2) the risk-weighted credit equivalent amounts of all off-balance-sheet activities.

Subordinated term debt Fixed-term debt obligations that are subordinated in some way to other securities of the issuer. The amount of subordinated term debt that can be included in Tier Two is limited to 50% of the value of Tier One. Further, the amount of any particular subordinated term debt instrument that can be included diminishes as the instrument nears maturity. Specifically, during the final five years of any subordinated term debt instrument's life, a 20% discount is applied.

Supplement capital Tier Two capital.

Tier One capital The sum of equity capital and disclosed reserves, as adjusted. Bank holding companies may include cumulative perpetual preferred stock in Tier One. Also known as core capital.

Tier Two capital The sum of general provisions and general loan loss reserves, hybrid debt/equity instruments, revaluation reserves, subordinated term debt, and undisclosed reserves. Also known as supplementary capital.

Total capital The numerator of the capital/risk-weighted assets ratio. This numerator consists of the sum of Tier One capital, as adjusted, the Tier Two capital, minus investments in certain unconsolidated subsidiaries.

Undisclosed reserves Accumulated after-tax retained profits that are not disclosed on a balance sheet. The Federal Reserve Board does not permit U.S. banks or bank holding companies to maintain undisclosed reserves. Regulators in other countries, such as Japan, do permit all their banking organizations to maintain undisclosed reserves. These may be included in Tier Two. Also known as hidden reserves.

BIBLIOGRAPHY

BHALA, RAJ. *Risk-Based Capital: A Guide to the New Risk-Based Capital Adequacy Rules,* 1989. Published by the Bank Administration Institute, Rolling Meadows, Illinois. This book has an extensive bibliography for those who need more detailed information about capital adequacy guidelines and standards.

CAPITAL EXPENDITURES

Significant costs that benefit two or more accounting periods. They could be the initial costs of acquiring tangible plant assets or costs incurred subsequent to the purchase of plant assets, such as additions, betterments, or extraordinary repairs. Capital expenditures make the plant asset more valuable or extend its useful life. Revenue expenditures are significant costs that benefit only a single accounting period and are made primarily for the purpose of maintaining the asset in satisfactory operating condition. Examples include ordinary repairs, maintenance, or the replacement of minor parts. Revenue expenditures do not increase the serviceability of the asset beyond the original estimated life. They are recognized as expenses of the current accounting period.

CAPITAL AND SURPLUS A term frequently used in the condensed statement of condition of a bank to indicate the bank's financial strength. The two accounts, capital and surplus, are combined because the surplus account of a bank corresponds to capital surplus and, like capital stock, is not available for the payment of dividends. The surplus account should be distinguished from UNDIVIDED PROFIT, which corresponds to the earned surplus account of industrial and mercantile corporations, and which is available for dividends.

The amount of combined capital and surplus is important because the limitation upon loans to one customer is based thereon, in the case of national banks, member banks of the Federal Reserve System (insofar as Federal Reserve rediscount of such paper is concerned), and some of the nonmember state banks. Under the banking laws of some states, e.g., New York, the combined capital and surplus for this purpose includes undivided profits.

See CAPITAL STOCK.

CAPITAL ASSETS *See* FIXED ASSETS.

CAPITAL FLIGHT The acquisition of foreign assets or currency, often in violation of national legislation, motivated by maximizing the return on capital, protecting capital from anticipated adverse exchange movements (usually as an overvalued currency can no longer be maintained), avoiding domestic political or economic risk, or escaping taxation by the home country. The inclusion of "flight" in the description implies a sudden shift in outlook by the capital holders in an economy, who are often willing to take considerable short-term loss to protect capital in the longer term.

When exchange restrictions are used to prevent direct capital flight, gold movements or exports of other assets, as well as shifts in international trade earnings, may be used to accomplish the same end. Capital flight can create a severe problem for a country if the funds would otherwise have been invested in the country's productive base. Assessing the magnitude of these often illegal and unreported money flows is difficult. Four methods used are:

1. **The broad method.** The sum of additions to foreign assets (apart from official reserves) and balance-of-payments errors and omissions.
2. **Private-sector debt.** The sum of additions to total external debt by bank and nonbank institutions and balance-of-payments errors and omissions.
3. **The narrow method.** The sum of short-term capital outflows from the nonbank private sector and balance-of-payments errors and omissions.
4. **The derivative method.** The share of foreign assets not giving rise to a tax return.

The International Monetary Fund estimates that about two-thirds of capital outflows can be viewed as capital flights under the derivative method, representing between $100 billion and $200 billion (U.S.) from 1975-1985 period. The general reason for capital flight from a country is that the expected return on investment is higher abroad. Three motivations are common. First, in an unstable political climate investors may fear a sudden increase in taxes or outright nationalization of assets. Second, unrealistic economic policies can lead to fears of economic collapse. Third, the financial systems of developing countries often make competition with foreign markets difficult. Attempts to aid domestic producers by fixing interest rates can be unproductive if inflation is high, reducing returns on domestic assets and decreasing domestic savings. If rates are increased to encourage domestic savings and attract foreign capital, the central bank may lose control of the money supply.

See CAPITAL MOVEMENTS.

CAPITAL INVESTMENTS Investments of funds in capital or fixed assets, or in nonmarketable securities, as distinguished from funds invested in liquid or short-term assets.

CAPITALISM One type of economic system, usually considered at the opposite end of the spectrum from COMMUNISM. Capitalism is presumed to have originated during the Middle Ages, when the merchants and guilds increasingly took control of the production and distribution of goods, leaving the state to deal with legal and military issues. Three features have often been used to distinguish a capitalistic economic system:

1. Private ownership of property and commodities, especially the means of production.
2. Disaggregation of the economic decision-making process. Individuals, driven by self-interest, choose how they want to allocate their resources between the various production and consumption possibilities. Organized markets act to mediate these decisions and arrive at prices such that the total demand for any given product equals the total supply of that product.
3. Accumulation of wealth in the form of commodities intended for exchange rather than the direct use of the owners.

BIBLIOGRAPHY

BERLE, A. A., and MEANS, G. C. *The Modern Corporation and Private Property*. Commerce Clearing House, Chicago, IL, 1932.
FRIEDMAN, M. *Capitalism & Freedom*. University of Chicago Press, Chicago, IL, 1962.
KEYNES, JOHN MANYARD. *The General Theory of Employment, Interest and Money*, 1936.
LOUCKS, W. N., and HOOT, J. W. *Comparative Economic Systems*. Harper and Brothers, New York, NY. Latest edition.
MARSHALL, JOHN. *Principles of Economics*, 1890.
MILLS, JOHN STUART. *Principles of Political Economy with Some of Their Applications to Social Philosophy*, 1848.
Readings in Economics. Barnes & Noble, Inc., New York, NY. Latest edition.
SMITH, ADAM. *Wealth of Nations*, 1776.
TAWNEY, R. H. *The Acquisitive Society*. Harcourt, Brace, New York, NY, 1920.
VEBLEN, T. *The Engineers and the Price System*. Viking Press, New York, NY, 1933.
———. *Theory of the Leisure Class*, 1899.
WEBB, SIDNEY and BEATRICE. *The Decay of Capitalist Civilization*. Harcourt, Brace, New York, NY, 1923.

CAPITAL ISSUES Corporate or government obligations, the proceeds of which have been invested in fixed or capital assets, or to add to the permanent working capital or available funds. Stocks, bonds, debentures are capital issues, as distinguished from notes and accounts payable, commercial paper outstanding, trade acceptances payable, etc., which are current liabilities and are in reduction of current assets. Capital issues are those that are sold to furnish the permanent or long-term funds needed permanently to carry on business or government undertakings. The amount of stocks and bonds that may be issued is limited by a corporation's charter and bylaws, and indentures.

See BOND, CAPITAL STOCK.

CAPITALIZATION The aggregate of the authorized par value of the stocks and bonds of a corporation, although in some jurisdictions capitalization is legally defined as the total value of the authorized stock. The amount of the capitalization may or may not be represented by an equivalent property value, although the latter often exceeds the capitalization. Surplus forms a part of the capital but is not represented in the capitalization.

Capitalization sometimes applies to the rate-making base or value of property upon which a fair rate of return is calculated.

There are several bases of capitalization: cost of property less depreciation; cost of duplication; cost of replacement on the basis of the present state of the technical arts; capitalization of earning power; and prudent investment theory.

The capitalization of a public utility corporation is usually regulated by the public service commission of the state in which it is located, if intrastate in nature; by the Federal Power Commission, if operations are interstate; and by the Securities and Exchange Commission, if a registered holding company is involved.

CAPITALIZATION OF EARNING POWER One of the bases for determining the proper capitalization or value of a business property. This method implies that a business property may be regarded as an income-producing unit in the same manner as, for example, a bond or stock. Accordingly, the value of a business is equal to the present worth of an indeterminable series of probable incomes discounted at a rate of interest currently earned for properties of the same class. Thus a property which yields an average annual net income of $1,000 is worth $10,000 if capitalized at 10%

($1,000 divided by 0.10); $12,500 if capitalized at 8%; $16,666 if capitalized at 6%; or $20,000 if capitalized at 5%.

CAPITALIZATION OF INTEREST Companies frequently borrow to finance the construction of an asset. Interest charged on such borrowings is usually considered a financing charge and not a part of the cost of an asset. Currently, generally accepted accounting principles require the capitalization of interest costs incurred in financing certain assets that take a period of time to prepare for their intended use, if its effect is material. Qualifying assets include assets that an enterprise constructs for its own use, such as new facilities, and assets intended for sale or lease that are constructed as separate projects, such as ships or real estate developments. The objectives of capitalizing interest are (1) to obtain a measure of acquisition cost that more clearly reflects the enterprise's total investment in the asset and (2) to charge a cost that relates to the acquisition of a resource that will benefit future periods against the revenues of the periods benefited (FASB Statement No. 34).

CAPITALIZATION RATE Rate at which a stream of future cash flows is discounted to find the present value, i.e., the discount rate.

CAPITAL LEASE A noncancelable lease that meets one or more of the following four criteria:

1. The lease transfers ownership of the property to the lessee.
2. The lease contains a bargain purchase option.
3. The lease term is equal to 75% or more of the estimated economic life of the leased property.
4. The present value of the minimum lease payments (excluding executory costs) equals or exceeds 90% of the fair value of the leased property.

Leases that do not meet any of the criteria are classified and accounted for by the lessee as operating leases.

In a capital lease transaction, the lessee is using the lease as a source of financing. The lessor finances the transaction (provides the investment capital) through the leased asset, and the lessee makes rent payments, which are for practical purposes installment payments. The rental payments to the lessor represent a payment of principal plus interest over the life of the property rented.

Under the capital lease method of accounting, the lessee treats the lease as if an asset were purchased on time. The lessee records a capital lease as an asset and a liability.

CAPITAL LIABILITIES The long-term debts of a corporation representing the combined capital stock and bonded debt. Capital liabilities are practically equivalent to capitalization, but differ from fixed liabilities in that the latter include long-term debts due to creditors and not to stockholders.

CAPITAL MOVEMENTS This term has two meanings:

1. In accounting for international payments of a country, the changes in indebtedness (loans and investments, long-term and short-term) and in gold stock, which act as balancing items. Thus the net of factor payments to the U.S. (wages and salaries, interest, dividends, branch profits, etc.), and net purchases from the U.S. (from business, government, and persons), if it results in a net amount due to the U.S. from foreign countries, must be paid for by a net capital movement, either by a net gold movement to the U.S. or by an increase in foreign indebtedness to the U.S. Actually, in most post–World War II years, foreign aid and American business investment abroad, together with expansion in imports to the U.S., have resulted in a net capital outflow from the U.S.
2. The flight of capital, as expressed primarily in shifting of bank funds and credits resulting from international trade, as well as in net GOLD MOVEMENTS, from one country to another. It is the purpose of EXCHANGE RESTRICTIONS, among other objectives, to impede if not prevent altogether the flight of capital to other countries.

See INTERNATIONAL BALANCE OF PAYMENTS.

CAPITAL RATING One of the ratings given by a mercantile agency in appraising the net worth of a business concern. It is intended to show the amount of capital invested in the business, although it is generally understood to indicate the commercial value of the par value of the assets which the firm rated may be considered to have in its business, all things being taken into consideration.

See CREDIT RATING.

CAPITAL/RISK-WEIGHTED ASSETS RATIO The amount of capital maintained, divided by the sum of (1) the total assets owned, where the value of each asset is assigned a risk weight and (2) the credit equivalent amount of all off-balance-sheet activities, where each credit equivalent amount is assigned a risk weight.

CAPITAL STOCK The stock of a corporation issued to its stockholders for money or property, or out of accumulated earnings. The entire capital stock of a corporation is divided into a number of equal parts of shares, usually with a specified par value, the exact amount authorized being fixed by the certificate of incorporation. A corporation is not obliged to issue all the stock authorized. Any amount of the authorized capital stock not issued is known as unissued stock. Issued and outstanding shares of stock are certificates of ownership held by the purchasing stockholders, representing their interest in the corporation; capital stock is the aggregate of these shares.

The capital stock of a corporation represents its nominal value, as distinguished from its actual or property value. It represents the amount of the corporation's accountability to its stockholders, but uncollectible by them through legal procedure, as distinguished from the corporation's liability to outside creditors. It is share capital as distinguished from loan capital.

See AUTHORIZED CAPITAL STOCK, COMMON STOCK, DEFERRED STOCK, FULLY PAID STOCK, PREFERRED STOCK, STOCK CERTIFICATE, STOCKHOLDER.

CAPITAL TURNOVER A credit term used especially among bank credit people to indicate the rapidity with which the capital (net worth) of a business is turned over, e.g., if the sales are $1.5 million and the invested capital $1 million, the capital turnover is 1.5 times. It is a vitality index, and each business has a capital turnover normal to itself. In general, the higher the turnover, the healthier the condition which is disclosed. If comparative balance sheets show a falling ratio, an accumulation of idle capital is indicated. A rising ratio is favorable up to a certain point, beyond which it indicates excessive borrowing, thereby making the RATIO OF DEBT TO NET WORTH unfavorable.

See STATEMENT ANALYSIS.

CARAT This term has two meanings:

1. As a unit of weight (quantitative measurement) the metric carat is equal to 3.086 grains troy, and is used to weigh precious stones, particularly diamonds.
2. As a unit of quality (qualitative measurement) it is used among goldsmiths, jewelers and assayers, to denote the fineness or purity of gold or other metal, being the twenty-fourth part of any weight, e.g., pure or fine gold is 24 carat. A ring which by weight is half gold and half copper is 12 carats fine. The term "18 carat gold" means that the gold is $^{18}/_{24}$ fine, i.e., 18 parts pure gold and 6 parts alloy.

CARDs Certificates of amortizing revolving debts. *See* FINANCIAL INSTRUMENTS: RECENT INNOVATIONS.

CARE OF SECURITIES There are two principal means to provide for the safekeeping of securities: renting a safe deposit vault or box; and placing them under the custodianship of a bank or trust company. In the former arrangement the securities remain under the depositor's exclusive supervision and control, while in the latter they are in a bank or trust company's custody but always immediately available and subject to the orders of the owner. There has been no known instance of loss of securities deposited in a safe deposit vault where the depositor has a covering contract. Modern construction of safe deposit vaults offers too many obstacles for the operations of even the most scientific burglars. For all practical purposes these vaults are fire, water, burglar, and mob proof. No such guarantees are provided by ordinary office safes, some of which even fail to provide for protection against fire.

ENCYCLOPEDIA OF BANKING AND FINANCE

Wherever securities may be kept, the holder should make a detailed descriptive record to include number, denomination, name of issue, date of issue, due date, name of issuing organization, and name of person to whom issued, if any. In case of loss, theft, or destruction by fire or other cause, means are then available whereby the securities may be identified, recovered, or replaced. If securities are deposited in a safe deposit box or held in custody by a bank or trust company, this list will be useful and perhaps save trips to the bank when the depositor wishes to know dividend or interest dates, or numbers in case bonds are called for previous redemption.

Registered bonds offer means of protection against loss since interest and principal are payable only to the person in whose name the bonds are registered on the books of the issuing organization. Notice of loss, however, should be made promptly in order to prevent assignment and transfer. There is no way of protecting the owner of coupon bonds in case of loss, although quick action and cooperation with the Treasury Department or Federal Reserve bank sometimes leads to the recovery of lost government bonds. In case these bonds are lost, the owner should immediately notify the Secretary of the Treasury in Washington and Federal Reserve bank of his or her district, giving a full description. The same notification should be sent in case of loss of registered bonds. Upon satisfactory proof of loss and the filing of an indemnity bond, a duplicate will be issued. Duplicates for coupon or registered bonds destroyed, wholly or in part, or so defaced as to impair their value to the owner, will be issued upon fulfillment of the requirements of the Secretary of the Treasury, including the filing of an indemnity bond.

In case stocks are lost or stolen, notify the issuing corporation and place a STOP TRANSFER ORDER with its transfer agent.

In case of loss of a municipal bond, notify the treasurer of the municipality and the distributing investment banking house. If a corporation bond is lost, notify the treasurer of the corporation. If a real estate mortgage is lost, notify the attorneys who executed it. One purpose of recording acts is to preserve on public file the evidence of real estate conveyances, including mortgages.

See CUSTODIANSHIPS, SAFE DEPOSIT COMPANY, VAULT.

CARLOADINGS Railroads of the U.S. report the number of cars of freight loaded on their lines and received from connecting railroads. The total is reported to the Association of American Railroads (AAR), which compiles the information and releases it publicly. Few barometers of business volume are more accurate, since the figures show the physical volume of goods moving from producers to consumers and from producers to producers. Unlike clearings or bank debits, they need no correction for changes in the price level. Representing deliveries on previous orders, they do not promptly report current business undertakings, but the lag is probably not more than two weeks to one month. Thus railroad carloadings are a good measure of distribution, especially if considered in conjunction with freight tonnage of the MOTOR CARRIERS.

CARRIERS Companies engaged in transportation, e.g., railroad, motor, express, steamship, street railway, subway, etc. In stock market terminology, carriers are particularly railroads.

See COMMON CARRIER.

CARRY This term has three meanings:

1. To hold securities; to be long of stock.
2. To supply funds to a customer especially when it becomes necessary for a bank to renew the notes of its borrowers in order to tide them over a difficult period.
3. When a broker furnishes funds to customers who trade by margin accounts represented in the difference between the purchase price of the securities (or commodities) and the customer's partial payment thereon, the broker is said to carry the securities which he or she holds as collateral for the customers' loans.

CARRYING BROKER The broker or commission house carrying a client's account.

CARRYING CHARGES This term has two meanings:

1. The interest on debit balances charged by brokers for credit extended to customers for the purpose of purchasing or carrying securities on margin; the cost of borrowing from a broker to carry securities purchased on margin. Such interest or service charge is levied whether the broker derives the funds from his or her own funds, proceeds of bank loans, or funds of other customers of the broker with free credit balances. Customarily, the customer's rate is the call money rate plus a service charge; in recent times, a service charge for large accounts and a larger service charge for small accounts has been added to the prevailing call money rate. In classifying the account, brokers take into consideration such factors as size of the debit balance, activity of the account, competitive conditions, type of securities carried, etc. Carrying charges (interest plus service charge) are computed monthly and reported to the customer in his or her monthly statement; subsequent charges will be based on total debit balance including interest and service charges, so that they are compounded.
2. The cost of carrying commodities held in a warehouse for speculation or otherwise, such as charges for storage, insurance, haulage, and loss of interest on the investment.

CARRYING-OVER DAY A London Stock Exchange term meaning contango day, or postponed day of delivery.

See BACKWARDATION, CONTANGO.

CARRY-OVER This term has two meanings:

1. A London Stock Exchange term to signify delay in settlement of a stock exchange contract from one settlement day to the next.
2. Applies to the stock of some staple commodity, e.g., wheat held in elevators, warehouses, or on farms over another year or beyond another harvest.

CARs Certificates of automobile receivables. *See* FINANCIAL INSTRUMENTS: RECENT INNOVATIONS.

CARTEL An agreement of independently-owned business firms within an industry to collude on certain elements of competition. Cartels are generally used to fix prices, to rationalize production and thus maintain prices in a market plagued with excess capacity, and to set market shares. In many parts of the world, cartels have been used to promote exports. The agreement may be binding on member firms, with penalties assessed for violations.

Cartels are illegal in the United States, at least for purposes of price setting, on grounds that they are not conducive to market efficiency. Cartel is the anglicised term for the German term kartell, which is similar, if not identical, to the American industrial combination or trust. Before World War I, the cartel movement grew in Germany with great rapidity. Contrary to the situation in this country, the cartel was encouraged in Germany by favorable legislation. The purpose of encouraging the German cartel movement was to build up the German export trade. By means of developing large-scale, cheap, and efficient production in finished manufactures, the cartels were often able to undersell foreign competitors.

While the cartel was a fairly well-known economic development in Europe before World War I, its vigorous resumption in post-war years, coupled with the equally important tendency toward industrial mergers and consolidations, made it a factor of outstanding economic importance. The American is apt to view the European cartel from the standpoint of its possible effect on American trade. To the European, however, the cartel was first an attempt to reconstruct industry on the continent, and only secondarily an effort to penetrate the foreign markets occupied by others.

The great weakness in European industry was a discrepancy between the productive capacity and consumption. On the whole, industries of Europe were well equipped for their operations, partly because of the stimulus of the war years. An overtaxed and impoverished population, however, did not offer an adequate market. The cartel was an outgrowth of mass production, and its object was to restrict competition. It could do this by three methods: by allocating territories for market purposes; by fixing prices; or by actually restricting production. To be effective, an international cartel requires a high degree of industrial organization within the countries represented. In Europe, therefore, there was a marked tendency toward growth of large monopolistic corporations. For the most part, the industries concerned were involved in production of raw materials or use of patents applied to raw materials (chemicals)—functions that lent themselves readily to close control under consolidated companies.

ENCYCLOPEDIA OF BANKING AND FINANCE

Most of the great corporations in Europe were dominant in one of these two fields—e.g., the Vereinigte Stahlwerke (United Steelworks) of Germany, the second largest steel company in the world and one that controlled 50% of the German output; I. G. Farbenindustrie, one of the largest corporations in the world, with a great range of products chiefly of a chemical nature; Courtaulds, Inc., of Great Britain, in the rayon industry; Imperial Chemicals, Ltd.; and Aluminum Francaise in France. The world aluminum industry was controlled almost entirely by one American company, one British company, one French company, and one German state enterprise. These illustrations are cited merely to indicate that throughout the range of industries of this kind, there are one or two companies which constitute the controlling factor in their country.

With this internal organization as a basis, the cartel agreements between entire industries in different countries were facilitated. It is estimated that when World War II began, over 200 international cartels controlled over 30% of international trade, particularly in rubber, tin, steel, chemicals, and quinine.

Most of these cartels were concerned with the production of a raw material such as steel, or a chemical product involving a patent, such as linoleum and rayon. Germany was a member of practically every one of these cartels, while the United States was a member of various cartels, apparently chiefly motivated by the purpose of developing foreign trade.

The predominant position of Germany in the cartel movement was in keeping with that country's preeminence in industrial development on the continent of Europe, and was related to the trend toward industrial amalgamation previously referred to. In no country in the world was industry so highly organized and so closely controlled as in Germany. France, Belgium, and Switzerland followed Germany's lead, although lacking the same extensive industrial organization. Great Britain also participated in the cartel agreements of continental Europe.

The ORGANIZATION OF PETROLEUM EXPORTING COUNTRIES (OPEC) is a notable current example of a cartel. Many of the major oil-exporting countries participate in OPEC. The cartel attempts to set a common world price for petroleum exports, maintained through export quotas for its members.

Accordingly, it is of interest to note:

1. The 1957 Cartel Law of West Germany, establishing a Cartel Authority to license cartels and control them as to possible abuses, establishing a Cartel Register in the Federal Cartel Office for registration by all cartels except licensed "pure export cartels," and repealing former legislation on cartels, including the Ordinance on Price Control of November 23, 1940, and the decartelization legislation of the occupying powers. Indicating the basic philosophy of the act, the Federal Minister of Economics, regardless of the Cartel Authority, may permit creation of any cartel if limitation of competition becomes necessary for the general welfare based upon overwhelming necessity.
2. The English antitrust laws (Monopolies and Restrictive Practices (Inquiry and Control) Act of 1948, as amended in 1956; and the Restrictive Trade Practices Act of 1956), establishing the Monopolies Commission, with powers of investigation and recommendation for laws upon request from the Board of Trade, and establishing a new court of record, the Restrictive Practices Court, before which the Registrar of Restrictive Trading Agreements may bring proceedings against registered trading agreements pursuant to priorities established by the Board of Trade.

See ORGANIZATION OF PETROLEUM EXPORTING COUNTRIES.

BIBLIOGRAPHY

EVANS, M. *Trusts.* Butterworth Legal Publishers, Butterworth, WA, 1989.
HOBSON, J. A. *Cartels, Trusts & the Economic Power of Bankers.* Institute for Economics and Financial Research, Albuquerque, NM, 1985.

CAR TRUST   See EQUIPMENT TRUST.

CAR TRUST BONDS   See EQUIPMENT TRUST.

CAR TRUST CERTIFICATE   See EQUIPMENT TRUST.

CARTWHEEL   A colloquialism for the United States silver dollar.

CARVEOUT   A part of a stream of cash to be received from future transactions that has been sold in advance or pledged as security for the financing necessary to generate the cash flow.

CASH   This term has four meanings:

1. As a noun, money; circulating medium; coins and paper money that pass freely as currency, i.e., from bearer to bearer without endorsement. Checks, matured coupons, and due bills are frequently counted as cash because they are easily converted into money. Nothing should be regarded as cash, however, which does not constitute immediate purchasing power.
See MONEY.
2. For accounting purposes, cash includes anything that a bank will accept as a deposit. Cash includes coins and currency in hand, deposits in checking and savings accounts, and checks and money orders that have been received but not yet deposited. Postage stamps and postdated checks are not cash.
3. As a verb, to convert a negotiable instrument, such as a check, money order, or matured coupon, into money; to give the holder money for such an instrument.
See CASH ITEMS, FOR CASH.
4. In trading practice on the New York Stock Exchange, one of the TRADING METHODS, calling for delivery on the same day of the transaction, as contrasted to the regular five-day delivery.

BIBLIOGRAPHY

BANK ADMINISTRATION INSTITUTE. *Internal Cash Management for Banks: A Practical Guide.* Bank Administration Institute, Rolling Meadows, IL, 1986.
———. *Cash Management Balance: Reporting Specifications,* Version 2, 1987.
———. *Cash Management Balance Reporting Overview.*
———. *The Profitability of Cash Management Services,* 1985.
BEEHLER, P. J. *Contemporary Cash Management: Principles, Practices, and Perspectives.* John Wiley and Sons, New York, NY, 1983.
ROSS, D., CLARK, I., and TAIYEB, S. *International Treasury Management,* 1988.

CASH ACCOUNT   An account in the ledger which summarizes the cash transactions of a business, the left or debit side representing receipts and the right or credit side, disbursements. The balance represents cash on hand. A cash account with a bank is an account receivable, but is usually shown in a balance sheet as cash.

CASH ASSETS   Assets appearing in a financial statement represented by actual cash on hand (in a safe or petty cash drawer) and the sum of the bank deposits.

CASH BASIS   A method of accounting in which transactions are recorded on the books when cash is actually received or paid out and not necessarily when the transaction takes place. For tax purposes, income on a cash basis also includes income constructively received (such as uncashed salary checks, interest on passbook savings, or matured bond coupons) that is available to the recipient at any time after the initial date payment is due.
See ACCRUAL BASIS.

CASH BOOK   A cash journal; an account book in which cash transactions are chronologically recorded.

CASH BUYING   The purchase of securities or commodities outright, i.e., buying outright, or paying cash in full for immediate delivery.

CASH COMMODITY   Analogous to "spot commodity," denoting a commodity which is available and ready for delivery on the spot.
See SPOT, SPOT PRICE.

CASH CREDIT   In CONSUMER CREDIT, credit made available by banks, personal finance companies, etc., in the form of cash directly to individuals on single payment, conventional, or other types of installment credit. In business credit, credit made available by banks, finance companies, factors, insurance companies, etc., directly to business firms, specifically by deposit proceeds and checks.

See REVOLVING CHECK CREDIT.

CASH DISCOUNT A reduction in price offered by a business selling goods on credit to encourage prompt payment. Cash discounts vary in the different trades, and according to the terms of credit offered. Almost without exception, however, cash discounts are offered where payment is made in advance of the time allowed by the terms of credit. In most trades the terms of credit are normally 30 days but a 2% discount is allowed if bills are paid in 10 days. In some trades a greater cash discount is available upon the payment of spot cash. Cash discounts for anticipation of payment in advance of the credit terms frequently range from 12 to 18% a year. In some lines of business, the margin of net profit may be so slight that profits depend upon taking advantage of all cash discounts offered.

The keen businessperson takes advantage of cash discounts; it is one of the functions of commercial banks to furnish working capital for this purpose. A business whose statement does not show the practice of regularly discounting bills sometimes has difficulty in obtaining loans because it shows itself not to be cognizant of all the commercial advantages open to it, and therefore not a good business risk.

CASH DISCOUNT ACT Public Law 97–25, which amends the Truth in Lending Act and provides that credit card issuers may not prohibit any seller from offering a discount to a cardholder to induce the cardholder to pay with cash, check, or another mechanism instead of a credit card.

CASH DIVIDEND *See* DIVIDEND.

CASH FLOW In November 1987, the FINANCIAL ACCOUNTING STANDARDS BOARD issued its Statement No. 95, "Statement of Cash Flows." This pronouncement requires companies to include a statement of cash flows as part of their audited annual financial statements. The "Statement of Changes in Financial Position," established as a requirement by the ACCOUNTING PRINCIPLES BOARD Opinion No. 19, was abandoned. Statement 95 provided much more specific presentation requirements and limited the flexibility companies formerly had in reporting changes in financial position.

The statement of cash flows is a major financial statement prepared to report the cash provided and used by operating, investing, and financing activities and the aggregate effect of these activities on the cash balance during a period of time. It is important to investors and creditors in identifying the amount and sources of cash receipts and cash payments of an entity during a period of time.

The new format focuses on cash plus cash equivalents—a reconciliation to changes in working capital is no longer allowed. Most investing and financing cash flows must be presented in gross amounts rather than as net changes. Noncash investing and financing transactions (such as using a capital lease to acquire property) are to be delegated to separate disclosures. Rules provide for the recognition of foreign currency cash flows.

Statement 95 provides specific directions on identification of cash transactions as investing and financing categories. Cash flows not qualifying as appropriate for one of these two categories should be classified as operating cash flows. Investing activities include making or collecting loans; acquiring or disposing of loans and debt instruments of other entities; and acquiring or disposing of long-lived productive assets such as property, plant, and equipment. Financing activities include obtaining resources from the owners, repaying the investment, and providing a cash return (such as dividends) on it; borrowing or repaying money; obtaining or repaying funds from creditors on a long-term basis. All other transactions are considered operating activities. Operating activities create revenues and expenses in the entity's major line of business. Cash flows that affect net income (such as interest) generally fall into this category.

The indirect or direct method of reporting operating activities is permitted. The indirect method of reporting operating activities reconciles net income and net cash flows from operations by removing the effect of accruals, deferrals, noncash expenses, and gains or losses on nonoperating transactions. The direct method (preferred by the FASB) represents the major categories of cash receipts and disbursements, the net cash flow from operating being the difference between these receipts and payments. The statement of cash flows reports only those transactions with cash effects. At a minimum, the following items must be specified:

Collections from customers (including lessees and licensees)
Interest and dividends received
Other operating cash received
Cash paid to employees and other suppliers of goods and services
Interest paid
Income taxes paid
Other operating cash payments

A statement of cash flows using the direct method would take the following format:

ABC Company
Statement of Cash Flows
For the Year Ended December 31, 19X2
(amounts in thousands)

Cash flows from operating activities:		
Receipts:		
Collections from customers		$100
Interest received on notes receivable		10
Dividends received on stock investments		20
Total cash receipts		130
Payments:		
To suppliers	$ 20	
To employees	30	
For interest	10	
For income tax	10	
Total cash payments		70
Net cash inflows from operating activities		50
Cash flows from investing activities:		
Acquisition of plant assets	$ (75)	
Loan to another company	(10)	
Proceeds from sale of plant assets	100	
Net cash inflows from investing activities		15
Cash flows from financing activities:		
Proceeds from issuance of common stock	$100	
Proceeds from issuance of long-term debt	50	
Payment of long-term debt	(25)	
Payment of dividends	(10)	
Net cash inflows from financing activities		135
Net increase in cash		$200
Cash balance, December 31, 19X1		15
Cash balance, December 31, 19X2		$215

A company that uses the direct method for reporting operating activities on the cash flow statement must also report the reconciliation of net income to cash flow from operations.

In a statement of cash flows, cash includes not only currency on hand but also demand deposits with banks and other financial institutions, and cash equivalents. Cash equivalents are short-term highly liquid investments that are (1) readily convertible to known amounts of cash and (2) so near their maturity that they present insignificant risk of changes in value because of changes in interest rates. Generally, only investments with original maturities of three months or less to the entity holding the investment qualify as cash equivalents.

In 1989, the Financial Accounting Standards Board issued Statement 104, "Statement of Cash Flows—Net Reporting of Certain Cash Receipts and Cash Payments and Classification of Cash Flows from Hedging Transactions," which amends FASB Statement 95. The amendment affects bank reporting. Bankers requested the reconsideration of how certain gross data required under Statement 95 were to be reported by banks. Bankers maintained that certain gross data required under Statement 95 were of little value and were difficult and costly to accumulate.

The board concluded that for banks, savings institutions, and credit unions, the cost of providing information about certain gross cash receipts and payments generally exceeds the benefit to users of their statements of cash flows. Banks, savings institutions, and credit unions are not required to report gross amounts of cash receipts and cash payments for (1) deposits placed with other financial institutions and withdrawals of deposits, (2) time deposits accepted and repayment of deposits, and (3) loans made to customers and principal collections of loans. When those enterprises constitute part of a consolidated enterprise, net amounts of cash receipts and cash payments for deposit or lending activities of those enterprises shall be reported separate from gross amounts of cash receipts and cash payments for other investing and financing activities of the consolidated enterprise.

The concept in the analysis of financial statements of the cash earnings from operations of a firm, is sometimes conceived to be the net income before DEPRECIATION, although in principle it should be figured before all noncash types of costs and expenses are charged to current earnings.

See STATEMENT ANALYSIS.

BIBLIOGRAPHY

BECHLER, P. J. *Contemporary Cash Management.* John Wiley and Sons, Inc., New York, NY, 1983.
Cash Newsletter. Journal of Cash Management.
HARDING, W., and KREMER, C. "Using Your Microcomputer for Cash Flow Statements." *Journal of Accountancy,* February, 1989.
MAZHIN, R. "A Spreadsheet Template for the Statement of Cash Flows." *Journal of Accountancy,* March, 1989.
TONCRE, E. *Maximizing Cash Flow: Practical Financial Controls for Your Business.* John Wiley and Sons, Inc., New York, NY, 1986.
VALENZA, C. G. "Cash Flow Controversy." *Magazine of Bank Administration.* January, 1989.
———. "FASB No. 95 Compliance: Banks Face Adoption, Reporting Decisions." *Magazine of Bank Administration,* December, 1989.

CASH FLOW ANALYSIS The STATEMENT OF CASH FLOWS pro-vides the basis for evaluating a company's cash flows. The statement shows the impact of operating, financing, and investing activities of cash. Some analysts prefer to take net income and add back depreciation and other expenses not requiring cash outlays. This concept of cash flows is defective in that it does not reflect cash flows where accrued incomes and expenses are involved. Other analysts calculate what is referred to as "free cash flows," which is interpreted to mean net income minus debt payments; discretionary costs (R&D, a percentage of capital expenditures) are also sometimes added on. Negative cash flow for more than one year is a strong sign of potential problems that can affect operations as well as lending and investing activities.

CASH FLOW analysis can provide information about a company's liquidity, flexibility, and ability to generate future cash flows (amounts, timing, and uncertainty). An examination of the relationships between items such as sales and net cash flows from operating activities, or net cash flow from operating activities and increases or decreases in cash, makes it possible to predict future cash flows to some extent.

Cash flow analysis can provide information about an entity's ability to pay dividends and meet its obligations. It can also account for the difference between net income and net cash flow from operating activities. By examining the difference between net income and net cash flows, analysts can assess the reliability of the income amount. Cash flow analysis can also provide information concerning cash and noncash investing and financing transactions during a period. This enables analysts to assess why assets and liabilities increased or decreased during a period.

CASH GRAIN Grain purchased for cash in full for immediate delivery; same as spot grain.
See SPOT.

CASHIER Commonly, a person who receives and disburses money for a business. In banking, an officer who is responsible for the custody of the bank's assets and whose signature is required on all official documents. While other higher officers of a bank may delegate their authority, or act as dummies, a cashier never does so, even in the largest banks. His or her duties vary according to the size of the bank. Usually he or she is the chief administrative officer and has direct charge of the bank's operations, and corresponds to the general manager in a mercantile or industrial establishment. Among large banks the duties of the cashier are so numerous that assistant cashiers are appointed to administer separate assigned functions and have authority to sign instruments in the same manner as the cashier.

CASHIER'S ACCOUNT *See* CASHIER'S CHECK.

CASHIER'S CHECK A bank's own check; a check drawn upon a bank and signed by its cashier, or assistant cashier, being a direct obligation of the bank. Cashier's checks are issued to borrowers when loans are made in lieu of a deposit credit or actual cash, sold to customers for remittance purposes, and issued in payment of the bank's own obligations, money transfers, etc. When a cashier's check is issued, it becomes a credit, and upon its return through the clearinghouse or otherwise, a debit to the cashier's account. Canceled cashier's checks are preserved as vouchers in the bank's files.

CASH ITEMS Checks, drafts, notes, or acceptances deposited with a bank for immediate credit, but which are subject to cancellation of credit if they are not subsequently paid. Items deposited, other than money, over the receiving teller's window are cash items.
See COLLECTION ITEMS.

CASH LETTERS *See* LETTER.

CASH MANAGEMENT ACCOUNT A unified consumer account, offered by a brokerage house in cooperation with a bank, that allows individuals to consolidate the operation of their holdings of cash and securities; their checking, savings, and investment accounts; and their borrowing. A cash management account enables the consumer to use the securities in the investment account as collateral for advances and loans. This type of account was originated and the name registered by Merrill Lynch in partnership with Bank One of Ohio.

CASH MARKET A market in which transactions for purchase and sale of the physical commodity are made under whatever terms are agreeable to the buyer and seller and are legal under the law and the rules of the market organization, where such exist. Cash market can also refer to an organized, self-regulated central market, such as the cash grain sections of commodity exchanges in the livestock industry. It can also refer to an over-the-counter type of market, in which buyers and sellers, and/or dealers, compete in decentralized locations, possibly under rules of an organized association. The term also refers to methods of purchasing and selling the physical commodity that are prevalent in the industries using that commodity.

CASH ON DELIVERY A purchase made with the understanding that the goods will be paid for when delivered.

Such terms of sale are to be distinguished from cash terms, as the latter actually entitle the buyer to a reasonable period of time for acceptance of the goods.
See TERMS OF SALE.

CASH RESERVE Vault cash that is treated as part of banks' legal reserves. Originally, under the FEDERAL RESERVE ACT, national banks and member banks could count cash on hand as part of their required reserves, but this privilege was eliminated by a 1917 amendment to the act. Congress amended the act again in 1959 so as to authorize the BOARD OF GOVERNORS OF THE FEDERAL RESERVE SYSTEM, by regulation, to permit member banks to treat vault cash as part of their legal reserves. Consequently, later in 1959, the board amended Regulation D to permit member banks to count part of their currency and coin for legal reserve purposes. Country banks (banks not classified as reserve city or central reserve city banks) having vault cash in excess of 4% of their net demand deposits were permitted to count the excess as part of their required reserves; reserve city banks (the classification of "central reserve city" was terminated) similarly were permitted to count vault cash in excess of 2% of their net demand deposits as part of their required reserves. These percentages were adjusted several times during the subsequent year, as were the reserve requirements themselves.

The treatment of vault cash as reserves was intended to correct a generally recognized inequity arising because some banks needed larger amounts of vault cash for operating purposes than did other banks. In the board's view, both vault cash holdings and reserve balances at the reserve banks should be counted as reserves because they are interchangeable and both serve the same purpose in influencing the volume of bank credit. Counting vault cash as reserves would also have collateral advantages such as reducing the costs of transporting and handling currency and making larger stocks of currency available over widely dispersed areas for use in a national emergency. In addition, the amendment made the composition of member bank reserves more comparable to that of member banks, which were already permitted by state law to use vault cash as reserves.

CASH SURRENDER VALUE That portion of the annual life insurance premium that will be returned to the policyholder in the event the policy is canceled. The cash surrender value of the policy increases each year as long as the policy is in force. Part of each annual premium represents an investment and part represents insurance expense. The part of the yearly premium that does not increase the cash surrender value of the policy represents insurance expense. Not all insurance policies have a cash surrender value.

CASH TRADE A transaction in securities, grain, real estate, etc., in which cash is paid in full for immediate delivery, possession, and title.
See FOR CASH.

CASUALTY INSURANCE The classification applied to insurance other than life or fire and marine insurance, and including such lines as automobile liability, worker's compensation, and accident and health (the three largest lines for volume) and miscellaneous lines such as automobile property damage, liability other than automobile, automobile collision, fidelity, surety, plate glass, steam boiler, etc.
See INSURANCE.

BIBLIOGRAPHY

Best's Review. Property Casualty Insurance Edition. A. M. Best Co., Oldwick, NJ. Monthly.
Best's Aggregates and Averages: Property Liability. A. M. Best Co., Oldwick, NJ. Annual.
Best's Insurance Management Reports; Property Casualty Edition. A. M. Best Co., Oldwick, NJ. Weekly.
Best's Insurance Reports: Property Casualty. A. M. Best Co., Oldwick, NJ. Annual.
Casualty Actuarial Society Yearbook. Casualty Actuarial Society. Annual.
———. *Insurance Facts.* Insurance Information Institute. Annual.
Insurance Journal. Biweekly.
Insurance Review. Bimonthly.
Journal of American Insurance. Quarterly.
Journal of Risk and Insurance. Quarterly.
National Underwriter, Property and Casualty Edition. National Underwriter Co. Weekly.
Risk Management. Monthly.

CATs CERTIFICATES OF ACCRUAL ON TREASURY CERTIFICATES.
See FINANCIAL INSTRUMENTS: RECENT INNOVATIONS.

CATS AND DOGS Highly speculative securities, particularly non-income-bearing stocks of uncertain or no value; stocks acknowledged to be a gamble because the underlying properties are not yet developed and which are worthless as bank collateral.

CATTLE LOAN COMPANY A company organized for the purpose of lending its credit to cattlemen for the purchase, raising, and marketing of cattle or other livestock, referred to in the Federal Reserve Act as livestock loan companies. They are sometimes separate companies, but in most instances are affiliated with, or owned or controlled by, state or national banks located at or near the large stockyards or in producing centers. In many instances these institutions are connected with banks specializing in the livestock business and use the same building and officers. As affiliates, these companies are excepted from the restrictions contained in Section 23-A of the Federal Reserve Act as to loans and investments to affiliates or collateral loans on their obligations, the ordinary restrictions on loans and investments being applicable.

The function of a cattle loan company is to relieve the commercial banks from the burden of carrying cattle paper, which under normal circumstances amounts to millions of dollars. Very often these companies act as middlemen between cattlemen-borrowers and the ultimate investors, i.e., the banks in the large centers. Some classes of cattle paper are also eligible for rediscount and for market purchases by the Federal Reserve banks.
See CATTLE LOANS.

CATTLE LOANS Loans made for the purpose of financing the cattle industry, which includes the purchase or breeding, feeding, grazing, fattening, and marketing of cattle. They may be divided into three classes: feeder, stocker, and dairy loans. Feeder loans are made on beef steers ready for the last stage of feeding prior to their sale as finished beef. These loans range from three to six months' maturity. Stocker loans are made on cows for breeding purposes and on young calves. They usually have a six months' maturity, subject to three or four renewals, and require about 50% margin. Dairy loans are made for the purchase of high-grade cows and pure-bred sires for the purpose of improving the dairy business. Their usual maturity is six months, subject to four or five renewals.

The procedure in making cattle loans is as follows: application of the borrower; sworn statement of the financial condition of the borrower; inspection of borrower's cattle with reference to location, brands, number, approximate weight per head, etc.; search of records to ascertain whether any liens against the borrower's real or personal property exist; execution of chattel mortgage in which the market value is usually at least 20% above the amount of the loan; and execution of the note.

Under 12 U.S.C. 84(7), which contains limitations on loans by national banks (also applicable to state member banks) to any one person, obligations of any person in the form of negotiable instruments secured by shipping documents or instruments of title covering livestock or giving a lien on livestock, which are secured 115% by such collateral, are entitled to another 15% of capital and surplus in addition to the basic 10% of capital and surplus limitation. P.L. 86–251, enacted September 9, 1959, added a new sentence to this paragraph, similarly permitting national banks (and thus state member banks) to make loans up to 25% of capital and surplus (rather than the 10% general limitation previously applicable) to dealers in *dairy* cattle when the obligations carry a full recourse endorsement or unconditional guaranty of the seller and rise out of the sale of dairy cattle.
See CATTLE LOAN COMPANY.

CAVEAT A warning, caution, or sign of danger. The term is sometimes used in phrases such as *caveat emptor* (let the buyer beware) and *caveat venditor* (let the seller beware).

CEASE AND DESIST ORDER This term has two meanings:

1. An order by a regulatory body or court directing a change in practices.
2. A form of directive issued to a bank and its directors by a regulative authority. Unless the directors agree to the order and to the appropriate implementation, the regulatory authorities have wide latitude in replacing the directors and the management with an administration prepared to take the actions the authorities are requesting. The penalties for violation of a cease and desist order are severe.

CEDULE In Europe, where the warehouse receipt is issued in duplicate, the receipt copy used in transfers or assignments, as compared with the "warrant" or "bulletin" copy used as collateral for loans. In the United States, the warehouse receipt is not issued in duplicate.
See WAREHOUSE RECEIPT.

CEILING PRICES Governmental direct controls on prices and wages for the purpose of preventing or containing INFLATION. Ceiling prices were in effect during World War II and the Korean War in anticipation of price increases caused by shortages in supply of consumer goods. Price control in the Korean War period was characterized by congressional change of prescribed minimums in response to increased production costs, particularly wage costs, and was not particularly successful.

Peacetime Price Controls. In 1971, as part of the Nixon administration's INCOME POLICY to control inflation and stimulate the economy, the United States imposed the country's first peacetime price and wage controls. The Cost of Living Council (CLC), a cabinet-level agency established by executive order, administered the initial controls, which began with a 90-day freeze on prices, rents, wages, and salaries announced by the president on August 15, 1971. The Office of Emergency Preparedness was delegated by the authority to administer, monitor, and enforce the freeze, which was to hold wages, prices, and rents at their July 16, 1971, levels through November 14, 1971.

Phase II of the program was to reduce the rate of inflation to the 2 to 3% range by the end of 1972, about half the prefreeze rate. The general rule was that no price might be increased beyond the ceiling price established for the freeze period, except in accordance with regulations of the Price Commission, a body composed primarily of private sector members. By the end of 1972, the annual rate of price inflation had been reduced to about 3.5%, which compared well with the inflation rate of 6% prevailing in 1969.

In early 1973, Phase II was replaced with Phase III, which relied primarily on voluntary controls, although wage reporting and record-keeping requirements generally remained in effect, the final phase (IV) regulations went into effect in August 1973. These regulations were designed to slow the rate of inflation by postponing some price increases in the expectation that monetary and fiscal policy would slow the rate of growth of demand, thus eliminating the pressure on prices and establishing conditions that would allow a return to a free market economy. In general, Phase I restrictions were stricter than those of Phase II.

Effectiveness of Phase IV controls in 1973 was the poorest yet experienced, in part because of the increase in the prices of certain raw materials resulting from worldwide shortages. There was a 51% increase in the CONSUMER PRICE INDEX during 1973, attributed to farm prices. Another 11% rise in the index was accounted for by the higher price of energy purchased directly by consumers. The large rise in industrial materials prices also contributed to the increase in retail prices.

With the expiration of the Economic Stabilization Act in April 1974, Congress, at the request of President Ford, established the Council on Wage and Price Stability, with authority to conduct several monitoring functions.

Carter Administration Voluntary Standards. At the beginning of 1978, the Carter administration called for a program designed to slow wage and price increases. Individual industries were asked to aim for smaller price and wage increases in 1978 than their own average increases for the previous two years. This program was not generally effective. In October 1978 the administration decided to incorporate explicit, though still voluntary, standards for wage and fringe benefit increases and price deceleration standards for individual firms. The pay standard limited the increase in hourly wages and private fringe benefit payments to a maximum of 7% for each employee group in a company, with some flexibility allowed for individual workers. The price standard required that individual firms limit their cumulative price increases for the next year to one-half of a percentage point below the firm's average annual rate of price increases during 1976-1977, with a ceiling of 9.5%; any increase of 1.5% or less was automatically in compliance.

Sharply higher prices, led by rising world oil prices, caused a substantial reduction in real wages in the first program year. Pressures mounted to relax the standard in ways that would aggravate inflation. In September 1979, the Carter administration and the leadership of the American labor movement began a cooperative effort to reduce inflation equitably through a tripartite (labor, management, public) Pay Advisory Committee. Although the Council of Economic Advisers, in its 1981 economic report, conceded that the Carter approach may have had a moderating effect on inflation, it also stated that "workers and firms no longer appear to be willing to moderate wage and price rises in the expectation that the standards will restrain inflation." The council urged that the voluntary standards program be supplemented by a TAX-BASED INCOME POLICY, featuring tax credits for complying firms and workers.

The voluntary approach to inflation control was generally the victim of stronger upward pressures on prices—rising world oil prices and the growing national budget deficit. With the advent of the Reagan administration, committed to a program of deregulation and reliance on market forces, general controls, particularly monetary policy, became the fundamental approach to the problem of inflation.

BIBLIOGRAPHY

COUNCIL OF ECONOMIC ADVISERS. *Annual Reports*.
FLANAGAN, R. J. "The National Accord as a Social Contract." *Industrial Labor Relations Review*, October, 1980.
HABERLER, G. "Incomes Policy and Inflation: Some Further Reflections." *American Economic Review*, May, 1972.
MITCHELL, D. J. B. "The Rise and Fall of Real Wage Insurance." *Industrial Relations*, Winter, 1980.
PERRY, G. L. "Inflation in Theory and Practice." *Brookings Papers on Economic Activity*, 1980 (1).
REES, A. "New Policies to Fight Inflation: Sources of Skepticism." *Brookings Papers on Economic Activity*, 1978 (2).
SAULNIER, R. J. "The President's Economic Report: A Critique." *Journal of Portfolio Management*, Summer, 1978.
SEIDMAN, L. S. "Tax-Based Incomes Policies." *Brookings Papers on Economic Activity*, 1978 (2).
TREBING, M. E. "The Economic Consequences of Wage-Price Guidelines." Federal Reserve Bank of St. Louis *Review*, December, 1978.

CENT The coin of lowest denomination in the U.S., being equivalent in value to one-hundredth of a dollar. Its composition is 45.6 grains of copper and 2.4 grains of alloy, or 95% copper and 5% alloy. During the 1946 fiscal year, the cent pieces coined were composed of 95% copper and 5% zinc. The bulk of cent coin circulation consists of the bronze cent (95% copper, 4% zinc, and 1% tin). During the World War II years, the copper-zinc cent (copper 70% and zinc 30%) and the zinc-coated steel cent (steel with zinc coating on each side, 0.0005 inch) were temporarily coined as metal conservation measures. Formerly, the cent piece was legal tender up to $0.25 in any one payment, but the Thomas Amendment of 1933 and the Joint Resolution of Congress of June 5, 1933, expressly provided that all coins and currencies of the U.S. shall be full legal tender for all debts (public and private), public charges, taxes, duties, and dues. The one-cent piece now coined in the U.S. is the bronze cent (95% copper, 5% zinc-tin).

A report by a Carter administration task force on money, released September 25, 1979, included a recommendation that the cent be made with a cheaper aluminum alloy "when and if copper costs more than $1.15 a pound." Copper prices then were between $0.93 and $0.95 a pound.

See TOKEN MONEY.

CENTERS Organizations typically are organized in terms of responsibility centers, depending upon the type and extent of authority and responsibility assigned to the center. Four major types of centers frequently established by businesses include profit centers, revenue centers, expense (cost) centers, and investment centers. A profit center is a subunit or segment of an organization that is accountable for planning and controlling both revenues and expenses. A profit center is analogous to an independent business, although certain investment and financing activities are sometimes not delegated. In profit centers, managers are assigned responsibility for both production and sales. Profit measures the ability of managers to create value from resources at their disposal and the input factors they acquire.

In expense (or cost) centers, managers are usually held responsible for the efficiency (relationship between inputs and outputs) and effectiveness (the achievement of desired production at assigned levels of quality and timeliness) with which they are able to meet externally determined demand as long as the demands are within the capacity level of the center. In such cases, managers are not held responsible for underabsorbed overhead due to volume variances. The control of fixed costs is a part of their responsibility. Since managers of cost centers do not determine price, they are not responsible for revenue or profit.

In revenue centers, managers are primarily responsible for organizing revenue-producing activities, especially those relating to marketing activities. Revenue centers usually acquire finished products from a manufacturing division and are responsible for selling and distributing the product. Managers should try to maximize the marginal contribution of products under their control. They should not attempt to increase total sales by excessive spending on advertising and promotion or to promote low-profit products. Such activities might have an adverse effect on total corporate profitability.

An investment center can be conceptualized as a profit center that also has planning and controlling responsibilities for investment decisions associated with capital assets, including working capital and physical assets. These combined responsibilities make managers of investment centers similar to managers of independent businesses. Long-term financing decisions are frequently reserved to the central office or parent corporation. Managers of investment centers are responsible both for the profitability and the return on investment (ROI) of their centers.

CENTRAL BANK A BANKERS' BANK; a bank which holds the main body of bank reserves of a country and which is the ultimate reservoir of credit. These banks are usually characterized by the following functions:

1. Keeping the banking reserves of all or a majority of the commercial banks
2. Rediscounting and loaning against high-grade commercial paper and other collateral for member banks
3. Performing fiscal services for the government
4. Monopolizing bank note issue
5. Controlling the gold reserves or other monetary reserves of the country
6. Assisting in check collection
7. Coordinating credit policy and other governmental policy implementation

Some central banks, however, are not absolutely restricted to dealings solely with banks, especially those which evolved from original status as private banks. Banks may conduct business directly with the public, such as the BANK OF FRANCE and the Commonwealth Bank of Australia, the latter's central banking functions having been segregated into the new Reserve Bank of Australia in January, 1960, along with its rural credits department, after engaging directly in banking operations through its general banking division, mortgage bank, and industrial finance department.

In the post–World War I period, formation of central banks was urged by the League of Nations Conference at Geneva in 1920 as a means of bringing about uniformity and stabilization in national currencies, as well as unified international monetary relations through other central banks. In the post–World War II period, formation of central banks appears to have been motivated by the need for organized banking assistance to national economic development.

Basic models of central banks may be classified as the European type, featuring highly centralized operating and policy powers in the governor, and the Federal Reserve type, featuring detailed statute and decentralization of operations as well as policy making. Table 1 appended herewith lists principal central banks.

BIBLIOGRAPHY

BANK FOR INTERNATIONAL SETTLEMENTS. *Annual Report.*
BANK OF ENGLAND. *Annual Report; Quarterly Bulletin.*
BOARD OF GOVERNORS OF THE FEDERAL RESERVE SYSTEM. *Annual Report. Federal Reserve Bulletin.*
HUMPHREY, T. M., and KELEHER, R. E. "The Lender of Last Resort: A Historical Perspective." *Cato Journal,* Spring/Summer, 1984.

CENTRAL BANK FOR COOPERATIVES See BANKS FOR COOPERATIVES.

CENTRAL FILE A file around which the work of the new business and advertising departments revolves, and in which complete detailed information concerning each of the bank's customers and prospects is recorded. The file cabinet is usually provided with 7 X 10 cards which are ruled and printed on both sides. One card is allotted to each customer or prospect.

The purpose of the central file is to reveal what services and departments each customer utilizes and fails to utilize, what the average monthly deposits and loans are, what the commercial agency and credit department ratings are, and what advertising literature has been sent. Briefly, its intent is to disclose the possible sources of new business. If the cards are kept up to date, they become an almost indispensable adjunct to an aggressive new business policy.

See NEW BUSINESS DEPARTMENT, PUBLICITY DEPARTMENT.

CENTRAL INFORMATION FILE A file listing information on the customers, the services which the customers utilize as to type and volume, and contacts with the customers including new business calls in person or by telephone.

In addition to serving as an internal source of information as to possible additional business from present customers, central information file (CIF) data can be the basis for profitability studies and evaluation of services.

BIBLIOGRAPHY

BATES, C. F. Central Information File, Bankers Publishing Co., Rolling Meadows, IL, 1976.

CENTRALIZATION VERSUS DECENTRALIZATION
Companies ordinarily use multiple factors to evaluate divisional and profit center manager's performance. Such factors include profitability; productivity (ratio of output to input); market position; product leadership; personnel development (ratio of persons promoted to the number considered promotable); employee attitudes (surveys on job satisfaction, pay policies, and promotion opportunities); public responsibility (surveys of suppliers, customers, local community, etc.); and balance between short- and long-range goals and objectives.

CENTRAL RESERVE CITIES Originally, one classification of U.S. banks, based on location, for purposes of setting reserve requirements. Under this system, banks were classified as country, reserve city, or central reserve city banks. Under the NATIONAL BANK ACT and the original FEDERAL RESERVE ACT, New York, Chicago, and St. Louis were designated central reserve cities. This distinction is now obsolete, and banks are presently classified for reserve purposes according to size of deposits. Reserve cities are defined as those having a bank with net demand deposits exceeding $400 million or those cities in which Federal Reserve banks or branches are located.
See RESERVE, RESERVE CITIES.

Table 1 / Central Banks

Argentina	Banco Central de la Republica Argentina
Australia	Reserve Bank of Australia
Austria	Oesterreichische Nationalbank A.G.
Bahamas	Central Bank
Bahrain	Bahrain Monetary Agency
Bangladesh	Bangladesh Bank
Barbados	Central Bank of Barbados
Belgium	Banque Nationale de Belgique
Belize	Central Bank of Belize
Benin	Banque Centrale des Etats de l'Afrique de l'Ouest
Bolivia	Banco Central de Bolivia
Botswana	Bank of Botswana
Brazil	Banco Central do Brasil
Burkina Faso	Banque Centrale des Etats de l'Afrique de l'Ouest
Burma	Union of Burma Bank
Burundi	Banque de la Republique du Burundi
Cameroon	Banque des Etats de l'Afrique Centrale
Canada	Bank of Canada
Cayman Island	Cayman Island Currency Board
Central African Republic	Banque des Etats de l'Afrique Centrale
Chad	Banque des Etats de l'Afrique Centrale
Chile	Banco Central de Chile
Columbia	Banco de la Republica
Comoros	Banque des Etats de l'Afrique Centrale
Congo	Banque des Etats de l'Afrique Centrale
Costa Rica	Banco Central de Costa Rica

CENTRAL RESERVE CITIES

Table 1 / Central Banks (continued)

Cyprus	Central Bank of Cyprus	Niger	Banque Centrale des Etats de l'Afrique de l'Ouest
Denmark	Danmarks Nationalbank	Nigeria	Central Bank of Nigeria
Djibouti	Djibouti Treasury	Norway	Norges Bank
Dominican Republic	Banco Central de la Republica Dominicana	Oman	Central Bank of Oman
Ecuador	Banco Central del Ecuador	Pakistan	State Bank of Pakistan
Egypt	Central Bank of Egypt	Papua New Guinea	Bank of Papua New Guinea
El Salvador	Banco Central de Reserva del Salvador	Paraguay	Banco Central
Ethiopia	National Bank of Ethiopia	Peru	Banco Central de Reserva
Fiji	Central Monetary Authority of Fiji	Philippines	Central Bank of the Philippines
Finalnd	Bank of Finland	Poland	National Bank of Poland
France	Banque de France	Portugal	Banco Central de Portugal
Gabon	Banque des Etats de l'Afrique Centrale	Romania	National Bank of the Socialist Republic of Romania
Gambia	Central Bank of the Gambia	Rwanda	Banque Nationale du Rwanda
Germany, Federal Rep. of	Deutsche Bundesbank	Saudi Arabia	Saudi Arabian Monetary Agency
Ghana	Bank of Ghana	Senegal	Banque Centrale des Etats de'lAfrique de l'Ouest
Greece	Bank of Greece	Seychelles	Seychelles Monetary Authority
Guatemala	Bancode Guatemala	Sierra Leone	Bank of Sierra Leone
Guinea	Central Bank of the Republic of Guinea	Singapore	Monetary Authority of Singapore
Guinea-Bissau	National Bank of Guinea-Bissau	Solomon Islands	Solomon Islands Monetary Authority
Guyana	Bank of Guyana	Somalia	Somali Central Bank
Haiti	Banque Nationale de la Republique d'Haiti	South Africa	South African Reserve Bank
Honduras	Banco Central de Honduras	Spain	Banco de España
Hungary	National Bank of Hungary	Sudan	Bank of Sudan
Iceland	Sedlabanki Islands	Suriname	Centrale Bank van Suriname
India	Reserve Bank of India	Swaziland	Mnetary Authority of Swaziland
Indonesia	Bank Indonesia	Sweden	Riksbanken
Iran	Bank Markazi	Switzerland	Banque Nationale Suisse
Ireland	Central Bank of Ireland	Syrian Arab Republic	Banque Centrale de Syrie
Israel	Bank of Israel	Tanzania	Bank of Tanzania
Italy	Banca d'Italia	Thailand	Bank of Thailand
Ivory Coast	Banque des Etats de l'Afrique de l'Ouest	Togo	Banque Centrale des Etats de l'Afrique de l'Ouest
Jamaica	Bank of Jamaica	Trinidad and Tobago	Central Bank of Trinidad and Tobago
Japan	Bank of Japan	Tunisia	Banque Centrale de Tunisie
Jordan	Bank Markazi	Turkey	Merkez Bankasi
Kenya	Central Bank of Kenya	Uganda	Bank of Uganda
Korea	Bank of Korea	United Arab Emirates	United Arab Emirates Currency Board
Kuwait	Central Bank of Kuwait	United Kingdom	Bank of England
Lesotho	Lesotho Monetary Authority	United States of America	Federal Reserve System
Liberia	National Bank of Liberia	Uruguay	Banco Central
Luxembourg	Monetary association with Belgium	Venezuela	Central de Venezuela
Madagascar	Banque Centrale de la Republique Malagasy	Western Samoa	Monetary Board of Western Samoa
Malawi	Reserve Bank of Malawi	Yemen Arab Republic	Central Bank of Yemen
Malaysia	Bank Negara Malaysia		
Maldives	No central bank (Dept. of Finance)	Yemen Peoples Dem. Republic	Central Bank of Yemen
Mali	Banque Centrale du Mali		
Malta	Central Bank of Malta	Yugoslavia	National Bank of Yugoslavia
Mauritania	Banque Centrale de Mauritanie	Zaire	Banque du Zaire
Mauritius	Bank of Mauritius	Zambia	Bank of Zambia
Mexico	Banco de Mexico	Zimbabue	Reserve Bank of Zimbabue
Morocco	Banque du Maroc		
Nepal	Nepal Rastra Bank		
Netherlands	Netherlands Bank		
Netherlands Antilles	Bank van de Nederlandse Antillen		
New Zealand	Reserve Bank of New Zealand		
Nicaragua	Banco Central de Nicaragua		

Source: International Monetary Fund Government Finance Statistics Yearbook, 1987.

CENTRAL RESERVE CITY BANKS This is no longer a classification of member banks for legal reserve purposes.
See CENTRAL RESERVE CITIES, RESERVE CITIES.

CERTIFICATE See CERTIFICATE OF ANALYSIS, CERTIFICATE OF DEPOSIT, CERTIFICATE OF INCORPORATION, CERTIFICATE OF INDEBTEDNESS, CERTIFICATE OF INSPECTION, CERTIFICATE OF ORIGIN, CLEARINGHOUSE LOAN CERTIFICATES, GOLD CERTIFICATES, HYPOTHECATION CERTIFICATE, RECEIVER'S CERTIFICATES, SILVER CERTIFICATES, STOCK CERTIFICATES.

CERTIFICATED STOCKS Those amounts of a commodity that are stored in warehouses approved by a commodity exchange and that are certified as being deliverable on future contracts.
See FUTURES.

CERTIFICATE OF ACCOUNTS Also known as auditors' certificate, report of independent auditors, report of independent public accountants, opinion of independent accountants, accountants' report, etc. The certification issued by auditors or certified public accountants after examination of the accounts of a firm. The certification attests as to the correctness and verification of the accounts in accordance with accepted accounting principles, noting, if necessary, any departure from accepted principles.

The certification does *not* guarantee solvency of the company concerned, but merely that the statements present fairly the financial position and results of operations and were prepared in accordance with generally accepted accounting principles applied consistently. Note also that the certification directs attention to any material departure from such accepted principles.

The listing rules of the NEW YORK STOCK EXCHANGE, as embodied in the current form of listing agreement, require that all annual financial statements, as submitted to stockholders, be audited by independent accountants qualified under the laws of some state or country and be accompanied by a copy of the certificate made by such independent accounts, with respect to their AUDIT of such statements, showing the scope of such audit and the qualification, if any, with respect thereto. This agreement does not apply to interim financial statements. Banks or insurance companies which have not previously been audited may be granted a transition period of reasonable duration, normally one year, to arrange for the first audit. Exception has been made to this requirement in the case of railroads.

The current form of listing agreement also requires that the NEW YORK STOCK EXCHANGE be given prompt notice of any change in the accounting firm which regularly audits the books and accounts of the company.
See AUDIT.

BIBLIOGRAPHY

See bibliography for AUDIT.

CERTIFICATE OF ACCRUAL ON TREASURY SECURITIES (CATS) One of several securities created by investment bankers in recent years in response to the increased fluctuation in interest rates. Other securities of this type include Treasury investment growth receipts (TIGERS) and separate trading of registered interest and principal securities (STRIPS).

To create CATS and TIGERS, investment bankers purchase a large pool of U.S. Treasury securities and place them with a custodian such as a commercial bank. The investment bankers then sell new securities to the public that represent the legal rights to specific cash flows generated by the Treasury portfolio. The new securities promise investors a single future lump-sum cash payment for a set price. In effect, the new securities are zero-coupon bonds created by "stripping" the cash flows of interest and principal from the Treasury securities that are held by the custodian. Investment banks maintain a secondary market in CATS and TIGERS.

CATS and TIGERS enable investors to avoid the reinvestment risks inherent in Treasury bonds, because they can lock in a certain interest rate for a set period of time and not have to worry about how to invest coupon payments received prior to maturity. Such securities are considered free from default risk and are largely noncallable.

The STRIP program was introduced by the Treasury in 1985. Under this program, selected Treasury securities are maintained in the book-entry system operated by the Federal Reserve in a manner that allows separate ownership and trading of the interest and principal payments. Once the securities have been sold at normal auction by the Treasury, the Federal Reserve facilitates trading in the secondary market by maintaining separate ownership records for specific interest and principal payments. Trading takes place in $1,000 units.

CERTIFICATE OF ANALYSIS One of the documents that an importer may require a foreign seller to send along with the bill of exchange drawn against a shipment as prescribed by the terms of the applicable letter of credit. It is intended to protect the importer by certifying that the merchandise ordered from a foreign seller conforms in all respects to specifications. This is especially important in the purchase of chemicals, drugs, precious metals, jewels, or other merchandise, where the value, quantity, quality, fineness, or chemical constituency must meet exacting requirements.

A certificate of analysis is usually certified by an expert, such as a chemist or assayer, although it may be certified by the shipper. It usually contains a statement as to the quantity, quality, fineness, or other exact details of the shipment and is sometimes sworn to before a notary public.
See LETTER OF CREDIT.

CERTIFICATE OF DEPOSIT A receipt for the deposit of funds in a bank. Certificates of deposit (CDs) are of several types:

1. **Demand CDs.** Demand CDs are noninterest bearing and payable on demand; they are used mainly as a guarantee of payment—for example, as lottery prizes.
2. **Time CDs.** Time CDs are interest bearing and may range in maturity from 30 days to several years; denominations vary from less than $1,000 (individual CDs) to more than $100,000 (institutional CDs); the very large denominations may be negotiable and, properly endorsed, may serve as security for loans. Zero-rate CDs are sometimes used in lieu of compensating balances because of their lower reserve requirements.
3. **Variable-rate CDs.** Variable-rate CDs were instituted in 1973; their interest rate is tied to the 90-day CD rate and is adjusted every 90 days.
4. **Variable interest CDs.** Variable interest plus CDs were discontinued in 1981; their interest rate was tied to the weekly auction of six-month Treasury bills, and they could be used as collateral for short-term loans.

Banks are required to keep reserves against demand and time CDs corresponding to the reserves for demand and time deposits, respectively.

Time certificates of deposit were subject to Regulation Q interest rate ceilings, but in 1970, to curb the outflow of deposits when market interest rates exceeded ceiling rates, the ceiling on CDs of $100,000 or more and of less than 90 days' maturity was removed; in 1973, the ceiling rates on all such large CDs was eliminated; and in 1986, pursuant to the schedule set by the DEPOSITORY INSTITUTIONS DEREGULATION AND MONETARY CONTROL ACT OF 1980, deposit interest rate ceilings on all time and savings deposits expired.

5. **No-penalty CDs.** No-penalty CDs let investors make withdrawals at any time or at set intervals. Federal law no longer requires financial institutions to charge for early withdrawals of principal but are allowed to deduct one to three months' interest on CDs of one year or less, three to six months' interest on longer terms.
6. **Rising-rate CDs.** Rising-rate CDs pay a continually higher rate each time they are rolled over during a specified term, e.g., every six months over a period of three years.
7. **Stock-indexed CDs.** Yields are tied to the stock market. A "bull" version allows the investor to bet on a market rise; a "bear" version allows for a bet on a market decline.
8. **Brokered CDs.** CDs obtained from a stockbroker instead of from a bank or S&L. Brokered CDs are traded on secondary markets, which gives the investor the option to sell without penalty before the CD matures.
9. **Sports/Election-linked CDs.** Sports CDs were marketed by Skokie (Illinois) Federal Savings, which once issued a Super Bowl CD tied to the Chicago Bears. Sports CDs have also been indexed to basketball, football, hockey, and baseball and to professional, college, and high-school teams.

ENCYCLOPEDIA OF BANKING AND FINANCE

CERTIFICATE OF INCORPORATION

BIBLIOGRAPHY

Alton, G. R. "Recent Changes in Handling Bank Failures and Their Effects on the Banking Industry." *Federal Reserve Bank of St. Louis Review*, June/July, 1985.

"CDX—A New Exchange for Fully Insured CDs." *ABA Banking Journal*, February, 1983.

Hung, T. Q. "U.S. Banks Have Resumed Issuing Eurodollar CDs." *Currency 7 Bond Market Trends*, Vol. 1, No. 18. Merrill Lynch Capital Markets, Securities Research Division/International Research, May 6, 1985.

Huertas, T. F., and Strauber, R. L. "Deposit Insurance Overhaul or Tune-Up?" *Issues in Bank Regulation*, Winter, 1986.

Kaufman, G. G. "Measuring and Managing Interest Rate Risk: A Primer." Federal Reserve Bank of Chicago, *Economic Perspectives*, January/February, 1984.

Morrison, Pat. "The ABCs of the New CDs." *Money Magazine*, February-March, 1990.

World Financial Markets. Morgan Guaranty Trust Company of New York, New York, NY.

CERTIFICATE OF INCORPORATION The charter or franchise that the original incorporators of a company receive from the secretary of state of the state of incorporation, legally empowering it to act as a corporation. (See CAPITAL STOCK.)

A certificate of incorporation for each type of bank or trust company must be applied for from the proper authority. Application for a national bank charter is made to the Comptroller of the Currency. Organizing state banks and trust companies apply to the proper state authority known under different titles, e.g., superintendent of banks (New York), commissioner of banking (Massachusetts), auditor (Illinois). A typical certificate of incorporation for all types of banking institutions contains the following information: name of bank; location; capital and number of shares; name, address, financial worth, and number of shares of each stockholder; and acknowledgment that the certificate is made in order to take advantage of either the national or state banking laws. The certificate is executed in duplicate, one copy for the Comptroller of the Currency (or state banking department) and the other for the bank.

See ARTICLES OF ASSOCIATION, ORGANIZATION CERTIFICATE.

CERTIFICATE OF INDEBTEDNESS A short-term note, corporate or issued by a governmental body, representing floating indebtedness (current debt). A corporate certificate of indebtedness is merely an unsecured promissory note, the holder having a general creditor's recourse against the unpledged or general assets. U.S. Treasury certificates of indebtedness were obligations with maturity of not over one year, which were issued in the past with and without coupons. Beginning in 1929 certificates of indebtedness were replaced by Treasury bills as the U.S. Treasury's instruments of short-term finance, and since 1966 none have been outstanding. When outstanding, certificates of indebtedness were acceptable collateral to secure deposits of government moneys. However, they were not acceptable to pay taxes, and income therefrom was subject to all federal income taxes. Certificates of indebtedness were issued in bearer form, in denominations of $1,000, $5,000, $10,000, $100,000, $1,000,000, $100,000,000 and $500,000,000, the latter two denominations available only on certain issues in the past. When available, Treasury certificates of indebtedness were suitable for the secondary reserve portion of investment accounts of commercial banks, as well as for investment of tax reserves and other liquidity needs of corporations and other business units.

See UNITED STATES GOVERNMENT SECURITIES.

CERTIFICATE OF INSPECTION This certificate, or a combined certificate of weight and inspection, is a document which an importer may require the foreign seller to send along with the bill of exchange drawn against the shipment in accordance with the terms of the applicable letter of credit. It is prepared by a trade association or concern authorized to make inspection and tests, and gives a description of the goods shipped by packages, boxes, barrels, weights, contents, markings, etc., but without prices. This instrument is frequently required in the shipment of heavy and bulky materials and differs from a certificate of analysis in that the latter usually applies to goods of high value and small bulk.

See LETTER OF CREDIT.

CERTIFICATE OF ORIGIN A certificate sometimes required by an importer to ensure that merchandise originated in a particular country and is not being relayed from another country. An importer sometimes desires to protect himself against purchasing goods of a belligerent country, which may masquerade as coming from another country. A certificate of origin contains practically the same information as a seller's invoice, gross and net weight stated, but prices omitted.

In peacetime the chief purpose of this certificate is to protect the most favored nation clause in the customs tariff.

See LETTER OF CREDIT.

CERTIFICATE OF PROTEST *See* NOTARIAL PROTEST CERTIFICATE.

CERTIFICATE OF STOCK STOCK CERTIFICATE.

CERTIFICATE OF WEIGHT *See* CERTIFICATE OF INSPECTION.

CERTIFICATION DEPARTMENT The department of a bank which certifies checks. Among small banks, checks are certified at the paying teller's window, but larger banks maintain a separate window or windows, usually adjacent to the paying teller's window, whenever the volume of certification business is sufficiently large to warrant a separation of functions. The certification of checks is a part of the paying teller's functions, because certifying a check is equivalent to paying it.

See CERTIFIED CHECK.

CERTIFICATIONS *See* CERTIFIED CHECK.

CERTIFIED CHECK A check that certifies that the signature of the drawer is genuine and that the depositor has sufficient funds on deposit for its payment. The amount certified is then set aside for the express purpose of paying the check and payment cannot be refused because of insufficient funds. When a bank certifies a check, certification is acceptance, i.e., the check becomes an obligation of the bank, instead of being an order on the bank. It is incorrect, however, to say that the bank guarantees payment of the check.

The Uniform Commercial Code (Sec. 3–411 (2)) now makes specific the point that unless otherwise agreed, a bank has no obligation to certify a check. When a check is presented at the window for certification, the drawer's account in the ledger is first inspected to see that sufficient funds are on deposit to cover the amount which is immediately deducted from the drawer's deposit balance before the check is certified. Certification consists of stamping or writing across the face of the check the word "certified" or "accepted," together with the date, the bank's title, and the signature of the officer authorized to make certification.

Since a certified check becomes an obligation of the bank, when a check is certified, the drawer's account is reduced (charged) and the certified checks account in the general ledger is increased (credited). When certified checks are returned through the clearinghouse or other channels, the certified checks account is reduced (charged). Thus the balance of this account represents the total certified checks outstanding.

Although a bank is not obliged by law to certify checks for its customers, among the banks in the larger cities, especially in New York, certification business forms a very important service, especially for customers who deal in securities. Certified checks are also extensively used in those types of businesses where it is important to receive the equivalent of cash, without at the same time using cash, such as in brokerage and security transactions, payments of loans, and real estate transfers.

A check may be certified at the instance of either the holder or drawer. Where a holder obtains the certification, the drawer and all prior endorsers are discharged (Sec. 3–411 (1), Uniform Commercial Code). On the other hand, certification obtained by the drawer of the check still leaves him or her liable in the event the certifying bank should fail before the check is presented for payment. A bank may certify a check before returning it for lack of proper endorsement, but if it does so, the drawer is discharged (Sec. 3–411 (3), Uniform Commercial Code).

CERTIFIED PUBLIC ACCOUNTANT An ACCOUNTANT to whom a state has given a certificate to the effect that he or she has met its requirements as to age, education, experience, and technical qualifications, as shown by the fact that he or she has passed the prescribed examination. The holder of such a certificate is permitted to use the designation "certified public accountant," or the letters C.P.A., as an abbreviation, within the state of issue.

State requirements for the C.P.A. certification generally require that a candidate be a citizen and of high moral character and have adequate educational prerequisite (some states require a college degree, with major in accounting; others, at the very least, a high-school diploma). The key requirement is to pass a comprehensive examination in accounting, both theory and practice; auditing; business law; and, in some states, economics. The C.P.A. examination is being restructured to become effective possibly in May 1994 as follows: (1) professional responsibilities and business law, (2) auditing, (3) accounting and reporting—B (taxation; managerial; governmental; not-for-profit). Following is an overview of the examination structure.

The New CPA Exam / May 1994

Section	Time period	MC	OOAF	FRE/P
Day 1				
Business Law & Professional Responsibilities	3 hours	50–60%	20–30%	At least 20%
Auditing	4 1/2 hours	50–60%	20–30%	At least 20%
Day 2				
Accounting & Reporting-A (Business Enterprises)	4 1/2 hours	50–60%	20–30%	At least 20%
Accounting & Reporting-B (Taxation; Managerial; and Governmental & Not-For-Profit Organizations	3 1/2 hours	50–60%	40–50%	
Total	15 1/2 hours			

The format consists of: MC = Multiple Choice
OOAF = Other Objective Answer Format
FRE/P = Free Response Essay/Problems

The examination is prepared by the American Institute of Certified Public Accountants. In addition, the candidate is required to have one to five years of experience in the offices of a C.P.A. or the equivalent. Interested parties are referred to the State Board of CPA Examiners (or other appropriate agency) of the state in which they intend to become candidates in order to obtain the specific requirements in the state concerned.

BIBLIOGRAPHY

Accountancy Law Reports. Commerce Clearing House, Inc., Chicago, IL. Looseleaf service.
ALTMAN, M. A., and WEIL, R. I. *Managing Your Accounting and Consulting Practice.* Matthew Bender & Co., New York, NY. Looseleaf.
AMERICAN INSTITUTE OF CERTIFIED PUBLIC ACCOUNTANTS, New York, NY:
Accounting Firms and Practitioners. Biennial.
AICPA Audit and Accounting Manual. Looseleaf service.
AICPA Technical Practice Aids. Looseleaf service.
Careers in Accounting.
Choosing the CPA That's Right for You.
A Post Baccalaureate Education Requirements for the CPA Profession.
What Does a CPA Do?
AICPA Future Issues Committee.
Major Issues for the CPA.
Profession and the AICPA, American Institute of Certified Public Accountants, New York, NY, 1984.
CPA Journal.
CPA Letter.
GLEIM, I. N., and DELANEY, P. R. *CPA Examination Review Set.* John Wiley and Sons, Inc., New York, NY. Semiannual.
GROLLMAN, W. K. *The Accountant as Business Advisor.* John Wiley and Sons, Inc., New York, NY, 1986.
Journal of Accountancy. List of Members. Library Binding Institute, Rochester, NY. Annual.
MCRAE, M. K. "How to Help Small-Business Clients Secure Loans." *Practicing CPA,* June, 1988.
National Public Accountant. Uniform CPA Examination:Questions and Unofficial Answers. American Institute of Certified Public Accountants, New York, NY. Semiannual.
Woman CPA.

CERTIORARI   A writ of certiorari is the form used to appeal a lower court (U.S. Court of Appeals) decision to the Supreme Court. The Supreme Court reviews the writ to determine whether or not it will accept the appeal. Unless a constitutional issue is involved or the lower courts are in conflict, the Supreme Court will generally not accept the appeal. If the Supreme Court does not accept the appeal, the certiorari is denied (cert. den.).

CESTUI QUE TRUST   The beneficiary of a TRUST or the person in whose favor a trust operates. The cestui que trust holds the equitable title to an estate, while the trustee holds the legal title.

CHAIN BANKING   As defined by the Board of Governors of the Federal Reserve System, a type of multiple office banking in which the operations or policies of at least three independently incorporated banks are controlled by one or more individuals. This control may be accomplished through stock ownership, common directors, or any other manner permitted by law. Generally speaking, chain systems are built around a key bank that is considerably larger than the other banks in the chain.

See BRANCH BANKING, GROUP BANKING.

CHAIN STORES   Development of chain stores in the U.S. was a sequential rather than a direct accompaniment of mass production methods. By furnishing many retail outlets, served by central warehouses all under one general control, chain store organization as a form of mass merchandising was the inevitable answer to mass production. Although the movement began in the 1890s, the F. W. Woolworth chain being the oldest of the important systems, a rapid expansion began in the decade 1921–1930; so rapid, in fact, that by 1929 competition among the various chains effected a retardation of sales growth and profit margins. A fresh surge of expansion occurred in the post–World War II period, caused by such factors as the increase in population, the rise in the general standard of living, the shift of population from the cities to suburbia and "exurbia," the rise of shopping centers, and the popularization of the home freezer and giant-sized refrigerator. These factors led particularly to development of the supermarket in the food field, with its emphasis on larger space and larger sales per customer.

In principle, chain stores offer an ideal plan of distribution of standardized nonperishable merchandise, the demand for which is constantly recurring and in which the style factor is unimportant. Chains are particularly adapted to the following lines: variety ("five and tens," although even they have long since abandoned such price limits), groceries, apparel, candy, gasoline stations, luncheonettes, restaurants, sporting goods, radios and TVs, records, household appliances, tobacco, drugs (actually variety stores with pharmaceutical backdrop), and automobile accessories. By eliminating middlemen, credit customers, deliveries (not always), elevator service, and expensive overhead charges, the chain store places merchandise in the hands of the consumer at a minimal markup per unit, on a low-cost, self-service basis. The supermarket in particular has been able to achieve large sales per customer and per store because of self-service, large wheeled market baskets, readily accessible and attractively displayed goods, centralized high-speed checking stations, and loading of customers' cars in the convenient parking space provided.

In the grocery trade especially, the rise of supermarkets, mostly under chain control, and the mergers of small chains with larger chains have led to a continuous rise in the proportion of grocery business done by organizations with 11 or more retail outlets.

Vertical Integration.   The large grocery chains and many of the smaller chains in this field have integrated backwards to the processing stage—operating their own dairies, bakeries, cheese manufacturing plants, coffee roasting plants, meat packing plants, canneries, etc.—leading to heavy volume of their own sponsored brands for distribution in their stores in competition with established national brands. Similarly, the mail-order houses, operating chains of retail outlets, have a large volume in their own sponsored brands of various types of goods. Besides profitable control over pricing and quality characteristics, another advantage of such integration is the bargaining position of such chains in distribution of competing brands and goods.

Public Policy. The rise of the giant interstate and integrated chains has posed problems for chains in regard to the antitrust laws, alleged price discrimination practices, and discriminatory state taxation. Chains have in general adjusted successfully to these reactions against their bigness, although these factors continue to be problems. In particular, the growth of chains has antagonized independent retail merchants. Although the independent cannot hope to compete with the chain in mass buying and mass distribution, there is a definite place for the independent merchant in providing differences in goods carried, service, hours of operation, and locational convenience, even in such a line as groceries which is highly amenable to chain store organization and operation.

Chain Store Management. In no line of merchandising is efficient management more important than in chain store operation. Upon the judgment and experience of the central executive staff depends the success of every store. Standardized operations make it possible to centralize chain store control. The trained staff that would formerly have been needed for a single large store can successfully control the operation of 50 or more chain units. Detailed accounting systems keep the executives informed as to the progress or lack of progress of individual stores. Perpetual inventories keep them in close touch with changes in public demand and store turnover. The following are elements of good management: purchases should be handled so as to assure a high turnover of the goods at attractive prices; stores should be well located and should be leased with cancellation clauses to avoid tying up capital in real estate and to avoid inflexibility in store locations; space should be large and fixtures, including freezer cabinets and self-service meat cabinets, should assure attractive display, so as to maximize sales per store and per customer; financial policy should be sound to ensure the maintenance of good credit, steady expansion, and increasing earnings. Funds are needed for expensive fixtures, inventories, and working capital. These should preferably be financed through self-liquidating bank loans, paid off from cash flow generated by operations, without undue recourse to funded trading on the equity or dilution of equity.

BIBLIOGRAPHY

Chain Store Guide Information Services. Annual.
Current Retail Trade. U.S. Department of Commerce, Washington, DC.
Expenses in Retail Business. NCR Corporate Education—Learning Systems. Annual.
Fairchild's Financial Manual of Retail Stores. Fairchild Publications. Annual.
Financial and Operating Results in Department and Specialty Stores. National Retail Merchants Association. Annual.
Retailing Today. Sales in 100 Department Stores. National Retail Merchants Association. Annual.
Sheldon's Retail Stores. Phelon, Sheldon and Marsar, Inc. Annual.
Stores Magazine.

CHAMBER OF COMMERCE A merchants' forum; a title often adopted by an organization formed to promote industrial and commercial interests of a city or a state. The Chamber of Commerce of the State of New York, for example, is the oldest organization of its kind in the world, formed in 1768. The Chamber of Commerce of the United States, a federation of chambers of commerce and trade associations throughout the U.S. as well as American chambers of commerce abroad, was formed in 1912.

CHANCELLOR OF THE EXCHEQUER See EXCHEQUER.

CHANGE IN THE BANK CONTROL ACT OF 1987
Title VI of the Financial Institutions Regulatory and Interest Rate Control Act of 1978 that gives federal bank supervisory agencies the authority to disapprove changes in control of insured banks and bank holding companies. The Federal Reserve Board is the responsible federal banking agency for changes in control of bank holding companies and state member banks, and the Federal Deposit Insurance Corporation and the Comptroller of the Currency are responsible for insured state nonmember banks respectively. The act specifically exempts holding company acquisitions of banks and bank mergers because these transactions are covered by other statutory and regulatory procedures. The act requires that the federal banking agency consider such factors as the financial condition, competence, experience, and integrity of the acquiring person or group of persons, and the effect of the transaction on competition. The Federal Reserve's objectives in its administration of the act are to enhance and maintain public confidence in the banking system by preventing serious adverse effects from anticompetitive combinations of interests, inadequate financial support, and unsuitable management.

CHAPTER 7 Straight BANKRUPTCY or LIQUIDATION. Most bankruptcy proceedings start under Chapter 7, which applies to business and consumer bankruptcy cases. Chapter 7 involves collecting the debtor's nonexempt property, liquidating or selling of such property, and distributing the proceeds to the creditors by the trustee as provided by the Federal Bankruptcy Code. Chapters 9, 11, and 13 are debtor rehabilitation proceedings. Under these chapters, the debtor looks to rehabilitation and reorganization instead of liquidation. Generally, creditors look to future earnings of the debtor for satisfaction instead of to the debtor's property.

CHAPTER 9 REORGANIZATION under the Federal Bankruptcy Code. Chapter 9 provides a process for municipalities that have financial difficulties to work with creditors to adjust their debts. After adjustment, refinancing, and payment of claims, the court confirms the plan.
See BANKRUPTCY.

CHAPTER 11 REORGANIZATION under the Federal Bankruptcy Code. Chapter 11 is available to businesses and to individuals. The purpose of Chapter 11 filings is to restructure a business' finances to enable it to continue to operate, repay its creditors, and eventually become a profitable operation. In Chapter 11 cases, a plan of reorganization for the debtor is developed and confirmed by the court. The plan establishes the amount and manner in which creditors will be paid and how the business will continue.
See BANKRUPTCY.

CHAPTER 13 Adjustment of debts of an individual with regular income under the Federal Bankruptcy Code. Chapter 13 enables a debtor who is an individual to develop and perform a plan for the repayment of creditors over an extended period. The plan might provide for full or partial repayment. Chapter 13 allows the debtor to retain his or her property, unless he or she agrees otherwise in the plan.
See BANKRUPTCY.

CHARACTER One of the elements of a credit risk and usually regarded as the most important. It is the most difficult element to appraise because it is varied and often elusive and intangible. It is a personal equation and represents the MORAL RISK. Some of the factors investigated in appraising character are as follows:

1. Reputation or standing for business honesty
2. Attitude toward obligations, promptness in paying debts
3. Personality and standing in social community
4. Record in antecedent business connections
5. Reputation of immediate business associates
6. Gambling and speculation tendencies
7. Social and political ambitions
8. Breaches in observance of accepted code of business ethics, such as welching on contracts in adverse markets, engaging in unfair competition or misleading in advertising, circulating false rumors or statements, taking advantage of the uninformed
9. Bankruptcy record
10. Fire record
11. Police record
12. Civil court record

See CREDIT.

CHARGE ACCOUNT BANKING In retail banking, a type of CONSUMER CREDIT utilizing the increasingly popular credit card. The Federal Reserve Bank of Philadelphia summarizes a typical charge account plan as follows.

1. The bank signs up an assortment of retail stores and issues charge cards to selected individuals. Cardholders may charge purchases at any participating store simply by presenting their card and signing the sales slip.
2. The participating retailer turns the slip over to the bank and receives credit for the face amount, less a discount of 5% to 7%.
3. The bank handles all collection matters. At the end of each month it bills the customer for his or her purchases. The customer has the option of paying the entire sum right away or extending the payments over a period of months. Most banks have put a limit on the amount that any one customer may owe.

Charge account banking provides small retailers with a credit plan, at reasonable cost, with which to compete with large merchants and department stores. In turn, the bank profits from the discount and the substantial interest earned on extended payments, and it also obtains prospects for net loan and deposit business. Although individual banks originally offered these services in their own market areas with their own cards, these have been largely supplemented by two international bank credit card systems. VISA grew out of the bank charge card developed by Bank of America, and Master Card was organized as a bank cooperative to compete with the VISA group.

Such charge account plans are to be distinguished from REVOLVING CHECK CREDIT.

CHARGE OFF See WRITE OFF.

CHARGES The sum of expenses involved in the execution of an order or in the shipment of goods, including such items as commission, interest, insurance, cable charges, freight, haulage, warehousing, etc.

See CARRYING CHARGES.

CHARGE TICKET A bank bookkeeping form or posting medium on which the complete details of a transaction leading to a debit entry in a ledger account are described.

CHARTERED ACCOUNTANTS An English title corresponding roughly to CERTIFIED PUBLIC ACCOUNTANT in the U.S. A chartered accountant holds a certificate from the Institute of Chartered Accountants which states that he has passed the examination given by that body and is qualified to practice public accounting.

CHARTERED FINANCIAL ANALYST A designation given to those who have successfully passed a series of examinations administered by the Institute of Chartered Financial Analysts, headquartered in Charlottesville, Virginia, and who have also met the experimental qualifications for being certified as a qualified financial analyst.

CHARTER PARTY A written agreement by which the owners of a vessel or their agents place it at the disposal of a merchant (shipper), the charterer, for the carriage of a full cargo of merchandise. A charter party may hire the services of the vessel and its crew for a single voyage, a number of voyages, or a definite time.

CHARTING A practice of graphically presenting stock price indexes or individual stock prices to present a picture of price behavior over a period of time. Charting is used primarily in technical analysis to provide information about price trends and for forecasting. Examples of charting include simple-line charts, trendline charts, moving-average charts, point-and-figure charts, and many others.

CHARTIST A stock market trader or operator who interprets market action and predicts future action of prices, usually over the short term, from the graphic record of price and volume upon charts. Although chart patterns are often criticized as a guide to trading, because they record and do not project market fluctuation, chartists are confident of their ability to do the latter.

A number of stock market services currently offered base their market advice wholly or in part upon chartist principles. The systems employed vary in complexity, but all have as their objective the forecasting of future market action based on interpretation of charts of prices and volume.

BIBLIOGRAPHY

CHARTCRAFT, INC. *Chartcraft Monthly Chart Book.*
GRANVILLE, J. E. *The Granville Market Letter. Professional Tape Reader* (twice monthly).
RUSSELL, R. *Dow Theory Letters.*
STANDARD & POOR'S CORP. *Trendline* (weekly).
UNITED BUSINESS SERVICE, SECURITIES RESEARCH CO. *Security Charts* (monthly); *Cycli-Graphs* (quarterly).

CHART OF ACCOUNTS A list of a firm's general and subsidiary ledger accounts systematically organized. The chart of accounts is the complete listing of the account titles to be used by the entity. The classification and order of the items in the chart of accounts correspond to the position of the account in the financial statements. Code numbers are usually assigned to each account in the ledger to facilitate posting and to reduce the possibility of errors.

CHATTEL Tangible moving personal property. A legal term to signify any tangible movable article of personal property, as distinguished from fixed or real property. Chattels include movable goods of all kinds capable of transfer by delivery, e.g., portable machinery, furniture, livestock, merchandise, or tangible personal property, as contrasted with CHOSE IN ACTION, which is intangible or representative forms of personalty. Sometimes the distinction between real property and chattels is difficult to make. Uncut forests are real property, while cordwood and growing and harvested crops are chattels.

CHATTEL MORTGAGE A mortgage with chattels instead of real property given as security. Movable goods (personal property) such as railroad equipment, machinery, furniture, automobiles or trucks, livestock, crops, may be the chattels pledged in a chattel mortgage. In form, the chattel mortgage is like the real estate mortgage, constituting a defeasible conveyance of the pledged property as security for the loan, as well as the promissory note evidencing the personal promise to pay the debt. One important similarity of both real property mortgages and chattel mortgages is that ordinarily there can be no substitution of collateral, the mortgage in each case applying to the specific items described therein; thus in chattel mortgages, care should be taken to assure ready identification of the specific items covered because their movability makes them liable to unauthorized substitution. After-acquired-property clauses, however, although upheld in real property mortgages as to additions and betterments to the mortgaged property, are not upheld in chattel mortgages if in fact they are sought to apply to additional items of personal property.

Chattel mortgages nevertheless are preferred by most lenders, in financing personal property transactions, to the conditional bill of sale. In various states, statutes strictly control the terms and procedure of conditional bill of sale transactions and repossessions, whereas the chattel mortgage does not so rigidly control the lender's recourse pursuant to mortgage provisions.

With expansion in consumer credit and other forms of lending on personal property in modern times, chattel mortgages have long since ceased to be regarded as a sign of weakness in a credit risk.

CHEAP MONEY Money procured at low interest rates; EASY MONEY.

CHECK As defined by the Uniform Commercial Code (Sec. 3-104) and by the British Bills of Exchange Act, "a bill of exchange drawn on a bank, payable on demand." Commentators usually treat checks under the general classification of bills of exchange, but checks differ from bills of exchange in that they purport to be drawn against a deposit and are always payable on demand.

As defined by the Board of Governors of the Federal Reserve System (footnote to Regulation J, pertaining to check clearing and collection), "a check is generally defined as a draft or order upon a bank or banking house, purporting to be drawn upon a deposit of funds, for the payment at all events of a certain sum of money to the order of a certain person therein named, or to him or his order, or to bearer, and payable on demand."

Under the Uniform Commercial Code, checks (along with drafts, certificates of deposit, and notes) are COMMERCIAL PAPER, covered specifically by Article 3 of the code, which represents a complete revision and modernization of the Uniform Negotiable Instruments Law. All such commercial paper under Article 3 must have the attributes of negotiability (signed by the maker or drawer; containing an unconditional promise or order to pay a sum certain in money and no other promise, order, obligation, or power given by the maker or drawer except as authorized by this article; payable on demand or at a definite time; and payable to order or to bearer). If it is a draft drawn on a bank and payable on demand, it is a check.

Other definitions of a check are a written order drawn by a depositor upon his or her bank to pay a sum of money to a designated party; an order on a bank (drawee) by a depositor (drawer, maker, or payer) to pay a certain sum of money to a third party (payee); an order upon a bank or banker for the payment of money to a stated party out of funds credited to the account of the drawer. While a check from a legal point of view is an order calling for the payment of money, in actual practice it is an order for transferring bank credit from one account to another, used as a substitute for money.

The essential elements of a check are

1. The words of negotiability—"order" or "bearer"—express or implied (The phrase "pay to the order of" imparts negotiability to the check and makes it an unconditional promise to pay upon demand. The single word ""pay," if used, makes such a check not negotiable, i.e., payable only to the person named as the payee.)
2. Name of payee—person in whose favor the check is drawn (Checks are sometimes made out payable to self, currency, bearer, or cash, which makes them payable to bearer.)
3. Amount payable in figures
4. Amount payable in written words
5. Name and location of drawee bank
6. Signature of drawer or maker (In the case of some corporations, the signature and countersignatures of designated officers are necessary. The signature is the final touch without which the check is valueless.)
7. Endorsement (The check should be endorsed as drawn, either in blank or by a special or other endorsement.)

In cashing checks, the paying teller observes the following points to ensure against irregularities, informalities, or discrepancies which, if unnoticed, might involve the drawee bank in a loss: identification of presenting party; DATE; FILLING; ALTERATION; SIGNATURES (authority to sign and forgery); stop payment; financial responsibility; whether a home debit or drawn on another bank; endorsement.

Checks should not be dated ahead (postdated); otherwise they are, in effect, time bills of exchange. Checks should be presented promptly. In the case of an uncertified check which is drawn and payable within the United States and which is not a draft drawn by a bank, the following are presumed to be reasonable periods within which to present for payment or to initiate bank collection: (1) with respect to the liability of the drawer, 30 days after date or issue whichever is later; and (2) with respect to the liability of an endorser, seven days after his or her endorsement (Sec. 3–503 (2), Uniform Commercial Code). Banks usually refuse to honor checks more than six months old (known as stale checks), since when checks are not presented within a reasonable time after they are drawn there arises a presumption of irregularity. However, the date is not an essential element of a check and an undated check is valid.

The amount written in words should agree with the amount written in figures; when there is a discrepancy between the two, the amount denoted by the words is the sum payable.

A bank is usually responsible to its customer for paying raised or altered checks. A number of mechanical devices have been invented to prevent the fraudulent alteration of checks. See CHECK PROTECTING DEVICES.

A bank is not required to make a partial payment on a check whenever the drawer has insufficient funds to his or her credit to make payment in full. Checks made payable to cash, currency, or self legally require no endorsement when presented by the drawer, but as a matter of practice, paying tellers request endorsement as a type of receipt. In case the drawer himself or herself does not present the check so drawn, the endorsement of the presentor, the drawer's representative, should be requested by the paying teller.

Checks may be classified according to method of collection into five groups: (1) checks drawn on the bank in which they are deposited for credit or cashed over the paying teller's window, known as own checks, self checks, or home debits; (2) checks drawn on banks in the same city and which will be paid through the clearinghouse, known as clearinghouse checks; (3) checks drawn on banks, corporations, and individuals in the same city which are not members of the clearinghouse and which must be presented for payment either through the city collection department of the clearinghouse or directly by messengers; (4) checks drawn on banks located at various out-of-town points which must be collected through the Federal Reserve Clearing System or through correspondents or other collecting agents, known as out-of-town checks, transit checks, or foreign checks; and (5) checks drawn on or issued by a bank located in a foreign country.

See CASHIER'S CHECK, CERTIFIED CHECK, CHECKBOOK, CHECKING ACCOUNTS, COMMERCIAL CODE, CREDIT INSTRUMENTS, CROSSED CHECKS, FORGED INSTRUMENTS, NEGOTIABLE INSTRUMENTS LAW, STALE CHECK, TRAVELERS' CHECKS, VOUCHER CHECK.

BIBLIOGRAPHY

HUMPHREY, D. B. "Economies to Scale in Federal Reserve Check Processing Operations." *Journal of Econometrics*, January, 1981.
KEARNEY, K. J. "The New Payments Technology." *Journal of Bank Research*, Winter, 1981.
KIMBALL, R. C "Wire Transfer and the Demand for Money." *New England Economic Review*, March/April, 1980.
MITCHELL, G. W., AND HODGDON, R. F. "Federal Reserve and the Payments System: Upgrading Electronic Capabilities for the 1980s." *Federal Reserve Bulletin*, February, 1981.
SOLEIL, M. "A New Payment Technique: The Memory Card." *Journal of Bank Research*, Winter, 1981.
STARKE, W. "Payment Methods of the Future." *Journal of Bank Research*, Winter, 1981.

CHECKBOOK A book containing blank checks furnished by banks to depositors who have checking accounts from which funds on deposit may be withdrawn. Checkbooks are usually available in several different styles from which the depositor may select the most convenient for his or her purposes. These styles vary from those suitable for carrying in the pocket to desk checkbooks with three or more checks on a single sheet. Some checkbooks are issued with stubs to enable the depositor to keep account of his or her transactions, i.e., deposits and withdrawals, to determine the balance, and to reconcile the balance as shown by his or her checkbook with the monthly statement as submitted by the bank. The stubs of the checkbook, if they contain a record of all deposits and payments by check, constitute, in effect, a duplicate cashbook.

In providing blank checks as a matter of service to large accounts which draw a large volume of checks, banks usually print the customer's name and business thereon. Such checkbooks and loose blank checks should be safeguarded by depositors to prevent dishonest persons from securing blank checks and forging signatures on them.

CHECK CREDIT See REVOLVING CHECK CREDIT.

CHECK DESK A name sometimes given to the bookkeeping and statement departments of a bank, so called because checks received through the paying and receiving teller's window and through the clearinghouse are posted to the appropriate accounts in the customers' ledgers and statements of account.

CHECKING ACCOUNTS A bank account against which checks may be drawn against credit balances. A checking account is to be distinguished from a savings account in which deposits may be withdrawn only upon presentation of the passbook in which deposit and withdrawal entries are made. From the bank's standpoint, checking accounts represent demand deposits, because they are subject to check and, therefore, to immediate withdrawal. Savings accounts represent time deposits which are not subject to check and for which notice of intention of withdrawal from

30 to 60 days may be required. Checking accounts do not draw interest, since under the Banking Act of 1933 demand deposits do not draw interest.

The advantages of a checking account are

1. Removes risk of losing money and making wrong change
2. Prevents possibility of paying same bill twice (since canceled check is an absolute proof of payment)
3. Prevents possible loss through robbery
4. Provides instantaneous check of financial position
5. Permits an analysis of receipts and expenditures and thereby budgetary control
6. Aids in determining income tax liability
7. Prepares for establishing more important banking relationships e.g., borrowing capacity
8. Wins prestige in business relationships

Checking accounts may be the popular, no minimum balance type, involving a small charge per check plus a monthly service charge, or the conventional type, requiring minimum balance and subject to service charges based on costing of activity, but also entitled to earnings credit on average collected balance.

See BANK COST ACCOUNTING, NO MINIMUM BALANCE CHECKING ACCOUNT.

CHECKING COMMERCIAL PAPER *First read* COMMERCIAL PAPER.

Among banks in the larger cities a considerable amount of commercial paper is bought for investment. Since at least one-half of commercial paper is one-name paper, its strength depends upon the financial responsibility and assets of the maker as disclosed by the financial statement. For this reason the note broker selling commercial paper is required to furnish a current statement of his or her client's business. The credit department of a bank in considering the purchase of commercial paper must conduct an investigation, i.e., "check" the paper.

An investigation leading to a recommendation of purchase must show a favorable condition as disclosed by the analysis of a recent statement; favorable reports from other banks which have had experience with the name in question; favorable reports from the trade, preferably several creditors and debtors and a competitor; and favorable mercantile agency reports.

See NOTE BROKERS, STATEMENT ANALYSIS.

CHECK PROTECTING DEVICES
Mechanical devices designed to prevent check raising and alteration of the payee's name. Several types of machines now on the market have succeeded in minimizing the fraudulent alteration of checks. One type mechanically bruises the portion of the check into which the words and figures are injected in indelible ink into the fiber of the paper. The paper is also bruised over the payee's name to prevent erasure and insertion of a wrongful name. Another device cuts the words and figures into the check by means of small perforations. Another method of protection is to indicate a maximum amount to be paid on the margin of the check, or just above the signature, by imprinting the words, "not over . . . ." Postal money orders are protected on the left-hand margin by a figure which represents the maximum amount payable. These devices are simple and inexpensive methods of guarding against losses arising through the raising of checks, and banks should educate business houses in their use. Checks are also protected by the use of various kinds of "safety" paper designed to expose fraudulent attempts at alteration, whether by acid, knife, or erasure. Such paper is provided with fine ingrained watermark lines and special surfacing which is sensitive to all types of alterations.

CHECK RATE
The basic rate in FOREIGN EXCHANGE transactions from which all other rates are computed. Foreign exchange rates are quoted for cables; checks and time bills of 30, 60, 90 days; and other maturities. The check rate is the rate quoted for checks as distinguished from the others. It is less than the cable rate but more than the rate for time bills, for the reasons explained under CABLE RATE. It is also known as the demand rate.

See GOLD POINTS, LONG RATE, SHORT RATE.

CHECK ROUTING SYMBOL *See* FEDERAL RESERVE CHECK COLLECTION SYSTEM.

CHEQUE Another spelling for CHECK.

CHEQUE RATE CHECK RATE.

CHICAGO BOARD OF TRADE
The most important grain exchange in the United States, incorporated under a special act of the Illinois legislature in 1859 but existing as a voluntary association since 1848. About 90% of the world's grain futures trading is handled on its floor. It is also the largest spot (cash) market for corn

Futures Contracts Traded, Chicago Board of Trade, 1983–87

Commodity	Contract unit	1983	1984	1985	1986	1987
Wheat	5,000 bu	3,886.9	2,974.9	2,128.0	2,090.3	1,929.3
Corn	5,000 bu	11,924.6	9,108.5	6,392.8	6,160.3	7,253.2
Oats	5,000 bu	359.8	155.1	99.0	141.0	291.1
Soybeans	5,000 bu	13,680.3	11,362.7	7,392.1	6,133.7	7,378.8
Soybean Oil	60,000 lb	3,858.6	4,009.5	3,647/4	3,183.0	3,912.4
Soybean Meal	100 tons	3,872.5	3,822.2	3,339.3	3,049.0	3,798.0
Plywood	76,032 sq ft	50.4	4.5			
Silver	5,000 oz	21.5				12.1
Silver	1,000 oz	2,643.2	1,887.3	1,034.8	511.2	510.0
Gold	100 oz	4.1				24.9
Gold	kilo	302.7	302.7	168.5	124.5	159.6
GNMA Mts, CDR	$100,000	1,692.0	862.4	84.4	24.1	7.6
GNMNMA II	$100,000		37.6			
Cash Settle, GNMA	$100,000				7.4	
T-Bonds	$100,000	19,550.5	29,963.3	40,448.4	52,598.8	66,841.5
T-Notes (2 yr)	$100,000	0.6				10.6
T-Notes (6 1/2–10 yr)	$100,000	814.5	1,661.9	2,860.4	4,426.5	
Corp. Bond Index	$1,000 x Index					
Unleaded Reg. Gas	1,000 bbl	51.6				
Crude Oil	1,000 bbl	94.6	0.6			
Heating Oil	1,000 bbl	3.2				
Institutional Index	$500 x Index					0.2
Muni Bond Index	$1,000 x Index			334.7	907.0	1,613.1
Major Mkt Index	$100 x Index		1,514.7	1,062.1	36.3	
MMI Maxi	$250 x Index			422.1	1,738.9	2,630.9
NASDAQ 100	$250 x Index			139.9	3.7	

and soybeans and handles substantial amounts of spot wheat and oats. Agricultural COMMODITY FUTURES traded on the Chicago Board of Trade are for wheat, corn, oats, soybeans, soybean oil, and soybean meal. Trading in petroleum products futures was discontinued by 1984, as was trading in plywood.

The Chicago Board of Trade also has been a market for several types of financial FUTURES and OPTIONS, including U.S. Treasury bonds and bills, GMMA mortgage-backed securities, the Municipal Bond Index, and the AMEX Major Market Index (MMI). Silver and gold futures are also traded in this market.

The volume of futures contracts traded on the Chicago Board of Trade in recent years is presented in the accompanying table.

The Board of Trade is designated as a contract market by the Secretary of Agriculture under the COMMODITY EXCHANGE ACT and thus is subject to regulation by the COMMODITY FUTURES TRADING COMMISSION. The exchange's management is headed by the board of directors, elected annually on a staggered basis. The board includes the chairman, vice-chairman, president, 15 member directors (three of whom must be nonresidents), and three nonmember (public) directors (nominated by the president and approved by the board of directors).

See HEDGING, PIT.

BIBLIOGRAPHY

CHICAGO BOARD OF TRADE. Publications 1981 (variety of printed materials available upon request from the Chicago Board of Trade, Marketing Department, LaSalle at Jackson, Chicago, Illinois 60604).

CHICAGO BOARD OPTIONS EXCHANGE

The Chicago Board Options Exchange, Inc. (CBOE) was formed by the CHICAGO BOARD OF TRADE following a four-year research project. After approval by the SECURITIES AND EXCHANGE COMMISSION, it opened for business on April 2, 1973, in the Chicago Board of Trade's building, specializing in providing facilities for trading in options on specified stocks actively traded on the NEW YORK STOCK EXCHANGE.

In the beginning, the CBOE traded options on 16 stocks and had a membership of 284 members, with representatives of 121 firms, initial membership price having been $10,000. At the beginning of fiscal year 1977, the CBOE had been joined by three other national securities exchanges listing such standardized call options for trading under pilot programs approved by the SEC in prior years. The CBOE had led the way in such trading in April, 1973, followed by the AMERICAN STOCK EXCHANGE (AMEX) in January, 1975, the PHILADELPHIA STOCK EXCHANGE (PHLX) in June, 1975, and the PACIFIC COAST STOCK EXCHANGE (PCSE) in March, 1976. During that period, the CBOE experienced a boom in options trading, growing from the smallest securities exchange in the U.S. to the second largest in trading volume in less than three years. Faced with such explosive expansion and with applications for additional listings, the SEC called for a moratorium on listing of any new options classes for the exchanges pending completion and implementation of the SEC's Special Study of the Options Markets.

Trading in options on U.S. Treasury bonds and notes began in 1982. With the introduction of options on two broad-based market indexes, the Standard & Poor's 100 and 500 (OEX and SPX) in 1983, CBOE solidified its position at the forefront of the options industry. These indexes, which track the Dow in a .97 correction, are two of the most widely traded derivative products in the country. OEX alone holds more than 80% of the index options market.

Also in 1983, narrow-based indexes designed for institutions to hedge industry portfolios were introduced at CBOE and several other exchanges. These products were not successful at any exchange. An over-the-counter stock options index was also introduced at this time, also with no success, although individual over-the-counter stock options continue to trade at CBOE.

Options on six foreign currencies were introduced at CBOE in 1985, followed by a seventh in early 1987. Because of CBOE's late entry in the foreign currency options market, the products were not successful, and the contract was transferred to the Philadelphia Stock Exchange currency market in mid-1987.

In 1986, CBOE affiliated with the Cincinnati Stock Exchange. As of 1987, CBOE traded call and put options on 166 listed equities, nine over-the-counter equities, U.S. Treasury bonds and notes, and the OEX and SPX indexes. The exchange had nearly 2,169 members in three categories: special members, licensed to trade a limited number of CBOE's options; regular members, with full access to all products on CBOE's floor; and CBT exercisers, members of the Chicago Board of Trade with trading privileges on CBOE. These members represent more than 300 firms.

CBOE's trading volume reached 184 million contracts in fiscal 1987, with an average daily trading volume of 725,000 contracts. Included in the 1987 total were 115 million index contracts, which had an annual daily volume of 454,000 contracts. Growth in trading volume on the CBOE is shown in the accompanying table.

Chicago Board Options Exchange Trading Volume
(thousands of contracts)

Year	Calls	Puts	Total
1976	21,501	—	21,501
1977	23,583	1,257	24,840
1978	30,743	3,979	34,722
1979	29,918	5,250	35,168
1980	42,941	9,954	52,895
1981	40,799	16,783	57,582
1982	50,214	25,507	75,722
1983	57,858	24,610	82,469
1984	78,933	44,341	123,274
1985	100,156	48,733	148,889
1986	114,788	65,570	180,358

Source: Securities and Exchange Commission and the Chicago Board Options Exchange.

On March 26, 1980, the moratorium imposed by the SEC was terminated and the SEC began to permit further expansion of the options markets. On May 30, 1980, the SEC approved proposals by the options exchanges incorporating a listing procedure devised jointly by them for the selection of 60 additional call options classes; and based on representations that expansion in puts would not adversely affect exchange surveillance, operational capabilities, or member firms' back office operations, the SEC also approved proposals to enable each options exchange to list puts on any securities underlying that exchange's call option classes.

In 1987, CBOE members voted to enhance the exchange's "pure" market-maker trading system with a modified specialist system for new products. It also formed a link with the Chicago Board of Trade to develop and jointly trade new options and futures products. For the future, CBOE plans to trade options on an interest rate composite.

See OPTIONS for the role of the Options Clearing Corporation in options trading.

CHICAGO MERCANTILE EXCHANGE

The Chicago Mercantile Exchange (the "Merc") was founded in 1919 as a nonprofit organization to provide a national marketplace for trading in spot and FUTURES contracts for commodities.

Trading in frozen pork bellies (bacon in the rough) was pioneered by the Chicago Mercantile Exchange (CME) in 1962. Another exchange innovation (in 1966), the live cattle contract, has provided a means for ranchers, processors, and distributors to hedge what has been a rather volatile market. The exchange has not been successful in developing trading volume in such innovations as onions, scrap iron, frozen shrimp, frozen broilers, hides, and apples. The tom turkey, butter, and egg contracts also failed to develop.

The CME has become a leading exchange for futures trading in financial instruments and foreign currencies. As of 1987, through its International Monetary Market division, it had introduced trading in seven foreign currencies, Eurodollars, and European Currency Units (ECU). It also provided a market for U.S. Treasury bills, stock index futures, certificates of deposit, and gold. Volume of trade on the CME in recent years is appended.

The Chicago Mercantile Exchange is regulated by the COMMODITY FUTURES EXCHANGE COMMISSION. Administration of the exchange is headed by its board of governors, and execution of the exchange's rules and regulations is the responsibility of the business manager and executive vice president. Membership is limited to 500, and members must qualify on the basis of financial, moral, and commercial standing. Members are entitled to appear on the floor of the exchange during trading hours; to vote at all regular and special meetings of the exchange; and to have orders executed and cleared by a clearing-house member at members' rates when such trades are

Futures Contracts Traded, Chicago Mercantile Exchange, 1983–87

Commodity	Contract unit	1983	1984	1985	1986	1987
Live Hogs	30,000#	2,790.7	2,169.0	1,719.9	1,963.9	2,040.5
Pork Bellies, Fzn.	38,000 lb	2,403.3	1,908.0	1,457;.4	1,100.3	1,097.0
Live Cattle	40,000#	4,248.2	3,553.3	4,437.3	4,690.5	5,229.0
Feeder Cattle	42,000 lb	537.2	317.0	455.9	411.4	645.9
Lumber	130,000 bd ft	731.0	753.6	581.5	502.5	437.1
Gold	100 oz	994.1	8.8	0.0		261.6
Leaded Reg. Gas	1,000 bbl		4.0			
No. 2 Fuel Oil	1,000 bbl		4.6			
T-Bills (90 day)	$1,000,000	3,789.9	3,292.8	2,413.3	1,815.2	1,927.0
Dom CD (90 day)	$1,000,000	1,079.6	928.7	84.1	3.1	0.1
Eurodollar (3 mo)	$1,000,000	891.1	4,193.0	8,900.5	10,824.9	20,416.2
Eur. Curr Unit	125,000				43.8	0.3
British Pound	25,000	1,615.0	1,444.5	2,799.0	2,701.3	2,592.2
Canadian Dollar	100,000	558.7	345.9	469.0	734.1	914.6
Deutsche Mark	125,0000	2,423.5	5,508.3	6,449./4	6,582.1	6,037.0
Japanese Yen	12,500,000	3,442.3	2,334.8	2,415.1	3,969.8	5,358.6
Mexican Peso	1,000,000	40.3	15.4	12.7		
Swiss Franc	125,000	3,766.1	4,129.9	4,758.2		
Australian Dollar	100,000				4,998.4	5,2683
Dutch Guilder	125,000	0.2				53.3
French Franc	250,000	26.3	8.4	9.3	2.7	10.4
S & P 500 Index	$500 x Index	8,101.7	12,363.6	15,056.0	19,505.3	19,044.7
S & P 100 Index	$200 x Index	390.9	166.2	1.7	3.5	
S & P OTC	$500 x Index			94.9	5.3	
Total		37,830.0	43,449.7	52,115.2	59,831.2	71,334.1

Source: Futures Industry Association, Inc.

for their personal accounts. Members may be qualified to trade in all commodities if they have been authorized to do so by a firm or corporation that is a clearing member. Clearing members execute all trades on the floor of the exchange, either for customers or for other members.

See COMMODITY FUTURES, HEDGING, PIT.

CHICAGO RICE AND COTTON EXCHANGE (CRCE)

Formerly the New Orleans Cotton Exchange, the second largest cotton exchange in the United States, until it suspended trading on July 9, 1964. Incorporated January 17, 1871, not long after the organization of the New York Cotton Exchange in 1870, the New Orleans Cotton Exchange operated under its charter of May 6, 1873, as amended.

The exchange moved to Chicago in 1983 as a result of an agreement with the MidAmerica Commodity Exchange. In 1986, the CRCE rough rice futures contract began trading on the CBOT trading floor. CRCE contracts are cleared through the Board of Trade Clearing Corporation. The CRCE does about 1% of the total futures market.

CHIEF CLERK
The title given to an executive position in some banks, now generally obsolete, whose function is administration of office clerical routine. The chief clerk was the bank office manager and was responsible for seeing that the work of the bank not directly in the charge of department heads was smoothly and efficiently performed; that all operations moved on schedule; and that proper supplies and equipment were furnished. In some banks, such operations as clearing, collections, mail, and statements were the responsibility of the chief clerk as far as availability of personnel, scheduling, and promptness of performance; thus in such banks functions of the chief clerk included employment, transfer, and training of employees.

The larger the bank, the more likely it was that such functions would be specialized; and because of the importance of semantics, even the old title chief clerk has been replaced by more prestigious titles such as chief administrative officer, assistant cashier, or assistant secretary.

See BANK OCCUPATIONS.

CHIEF FINANCIAL OFFICER (CFO)
A business executive in charge of the financial division or operations. A bank's CFO is responsible for asset/liability management and oversees the activities of the treasurer and controller (or comptroller). The CFO also develops and implements long-term financial plans and policies. In smaller institutions, the CFO is often the treasurer, and possibly the controller.

The bank treasurer manages the institution's investment portfolio and is not involved with the accounting duties of the controller. The treasurer's responsibilities include developing investment policies and maintaining banking and investment broker relationships and investment analysis.

The controller supervises the accounting department and is responsible for the accounting system. The controller also is responsible for the following activities: establishing a classification system for general ledger accounts that complies with regulatory reporting requirements and provides management with information; analyzing individual income and expense items; reviewing and approving bank capital and operating expenditures; establishing and implementing operational and internal control procedures; reviewing management information needs; implementing reporting systems; assisting in developing operation budgets; supervising financial report preparation; directing accounting personnel training; and acting as a liaison between the institution and regulatory authorities for audits and examinations.

A survey prepared by the U.S. League of Savings Institutions in 1989 of compensation paid by savings institutions indicated that chief financial officers earn an average of $60,000; senior auditors, $38,500; staff auditors, $23,800; treasurers, $43,800; controllers, $36,500; assistant controllers; $25,600; staff accountants, $20,700. See COMPTROLLER.

BIBLIOGRAPHY

YINGST, R. A. "Banking Futures." *New Accountant*, March 1990.

CHOSE IN ACTION
A law term which denotes a claim or right to personal property not in one's possession, as distinguished from property actually in one's possession, known as chose in possession. A claim arising out of a breach and which can be collected only by an action at law, e.g., an open account which the debtor refuses to pay.

CHRISTMAS CLUB
A savings account established for the specific purpose of accumulating periodic savings in advance of withdrawal of total accumulation for Christmas expenditures.

Other special purpose accounts, such as vacation clubs, travel clubs, etc., are also promoted by some savings banks and commercial banks with savings departments. The Christmas club type is most popular because of the purpose, as well as advertising and promotion by banks and vendors of Christmas club supplies.

Christmas club accounts in recent years have begun to be paid interest-dividends, but are generally subject to service and penalty rates (e.g., for opening the account, for withdrawing funds before maturity, and for not completing payments). Whether such accounts are profitable for a bank depends upon the adequacy of such charges, the size and frequency of payments, the detail required for handling, and the earnings rate on average funds.

CHURNING   Excessive turnover of an investor's holdings, usually by the brokerage firm or representative, and at its worst motivated by the pressure to create commission income. By extension, the term includes the excessive switching of a customer's holdings from one load or no load investment company's shares to those of another load investment company.

The NATIONAL ASSOCIATION OF SECURITIES DEALERS, INC. (NASD) in an official statement to its member firms has specified that "members are under an obligation to supervise transactions in a manner that will ensure that improper SWITCHING is not taking place within the organization." According to the NASD, suitability of the new investment and fair treatment of the customer are the bases for judging propriety, "rather than on the argument that they result in profits to customers."

See INVESTMENT COMPANY, SPECULATION.

CINCINNATI STOCK EXCHANGE   A registered securities exchange under the Securities Exchange Act of 1934. It was the first stock exchange to be established in Ohio, dating from 1887.

Like other stock exchanges, this regional exchange has as its objectives: to maintain high standards of commercial honor and integrity among members; to promote and inculcate just and equitable principles of trade and business; to furnish rooms and other facilities for the convenient transaction of business.

The Cincinnati Stock Exchange's multiple dealer facility (CSE system) represents an experiment in the use of a fully automated electronic stock market trading system, first approved on an experimental basis by the Securities and Exchange Commission (SEC) on April 18, 1979. The CSE system, as described by the SEC, enables CSE members, through an electronic communications network and without the necessity of maintaining a presence on the floor of the CSE or any other exchange, to participate in a market conducted in accordance with certain auction-type trading principles by entering bids and offers for securities for their own account and as agents for their customers' accounts.

In addition, CSE rules permit a specialist on any national securities exchange, without becoming a member of the CSE, to enter bids and offers in the system as principal or as agent in any security in which that specialist is registered on another exchange. Orders entered into the CSE system are stored in the CSE's computer facilities and queued for execution as follows: priority is governed first by price (i.e., the highest bid and lowest offer); between orders at the same price, priority is governed by time of entry. However, public agency orders, as defined in the CSE's rules, regardless of time of entry, are granted priority over other orders at the same price.

In the SEC's view, both the ITS (Inter-Market Communications Linkage filed jointly by the American Stock Exchange, Boston Stock Exchange, New York Stock Exchange, Pacific Coast Stock Exchange, and the Philadelphia Stock Exchange, which provided for an intermarket linking the various participants) and the CSE system offered opportunities to the SEC and the brokerage community to assess the ability of differing types of market linkage systems to integrate trading in physically separate locations and to observe the effects of these linkage systems on the operation of the markets.

CIPHER CODE   Originally a method of communicating secret written messages unintelligible to third parties—dispatched by mail, telegraph, or cable. The term is now applied to telegraphic or wireless messages transmitted not in longhand, but by a shorthand key or code, primarily to secure condensation and economy rather than secrecy. Most international banking codes are in general use and the keys are accessible to all, so anyone taking the pains can secure a translation. Where secrecy is important, private codes must be employed.

Code messages, making one five-letter word the equivalent of a phrase or sentence, accomplish five purposes: economy; safety (in making payments, a test word is used so that a paying bank may know that the cablegram is authentic); accuracy (the message must prove); simplicity (the message can be boiled down to a few words), and efficiency (time is saved in writing and sending the message). As an example of the economy effected by sending messages in code, an illustration taken from one of the international banking codes is given: "SHANY AYFAX."

SHANY means: "We accept your rate and will pay on next Friday to your correspondent in Christiania for your account."

AYFAX means: "Kroner seventy thousand."

The principal international codes are Lieber's Five-Letter American Telegraphic Code, Western Union Code, Bentley's Complete Phrase Code, Improved Peterson's International Banking Code, and Lloyd's Bank Code. Special private codes are often arranged by banks for exclusive use in transactions with correspondents and branches in foreign countries.

Code messages involving the transfer of funds or other items of value are tested, i.e., supplied with a word or number computed by a complex formula known only to the sender and receiver. They can thus be proved to be authentic.

See CABLE TRANSFER, TEST NUMBER.

CIRCUIT BREAKER   A mechanism that could halt trading in the stock, futures, and options markets when prices fell too far in one trading session. One suggestion by the White House Working Group on Financial Markets presented in May 1988 following BLACK MONDAY, October 19, 1987, would halt trading for one hour whenever the Dow Jones industrial average fell 250 points below its previous day's closing value, and for two hours whenever the Dow fell 400 points. The recommendation was not enthusiastically received by the investing community.

CIRCULAR   See BOND CIRCULAR, PROSPECTUS.

CIRCULAR LETTER OF CREDIT   See TRAVELER'S LETTER OF CREDIT.

CIRCULATING ASSETS   CURRENT ASSETS.

CIRCULATING BANK NOTES   See CIRCULATING NOTES.

CIRCULATING CAPITAL   Capital invested in CURRENT ASSETS.

CIRCULATING MEDIUM   All forms of money which have the quality of currency, i.e., the circulation from bearer to bearer without endorsement. Circulating medium is the proper term for what is ordinarily called currency, which includes coin and paper money.

See MONEY SUPPLY, UNITED STATES MONEY.

CIRCULATING NOTES   FEDERAL RESERVE BANK NOTES and NATIONAL BANK NOTES, also known as "circulation" by bankers, both of which are no longer issued and have been in the process of retirement (although residuals still outstanding are included in the "currency no longer issued" total reported in the Statement of United States Currency and Coin).

See BANK NOTES.

CIRCULATION   Circulating bank notes.
See CIRCULATING NOTES.

CIRCULATION STATEMENT   Published each month by the Fiscal Service of the Bureau of Government Financial Operations, Department of the Treasury, reporting the following data and renamed Monthly Statement of United States Currency and Coin.

1. Amounts outstanding and in circulation (total amounts outstanding, for total currency and coin; for coin (excluding coin sold to collectors at premium prices), as to total, dollars, and fractional coin; and for currency.
2. Currency in circulation by denominations ($1, $2, $5, $10, $20, $50, $100, $500, $1,000, $5,000, and $10,000).

ENCYCLOPEDIA OF BANKING AND FINANCE

3. In addition, for current and past long-term dates, the statement carries the comparative totals of money in circulation ("circulation" in the concept of coin and currency outside of the Treasury and the Federal Reserve banks, as reported in the statement) and the per capita figures on same, based on Bureau of the Census estimates of population.

See MONEY CIRCULATION.

CIRCUS Combined currency and interest rate swap.
See FINANCIAL INSTRUMENTS: RECENT INNOVATIONS.

CITY BONDS See MUNICIPAL BONDS.

CITY COLLECTION DEPARTMENT The department of a bank which receives sight and time drafts, checks, notes, and acceptances over the window from local depositors and from out-of-town correspondents for collection within the city. The city collection department handles collection items only, i.e., those which are credited to depositors' accounts only when and if actually collected.
See COUPON COLLECTION DEPARTMENT.

CITY COLLECTIONS See COLLECTION ITEMS.

CITY ITEMS Used in banking practice to denote checks, drafts, notes, or acceptances drawn on a bank, individual, firm, or corporation located in the same city as the bank where they have been deposited for collection, either through the clearinghouse or by messenger.

CIVIL BONDS Bonds issued by a government or political subdivision thereof, e.g., federal government; states; counties and parishes; municipalities (cities, towns, boroughs, and townships); special districts (school, water, sanitary, road, street improvement, park, drainage, irrigation, and levee districts); and special statutory authorities (port authorities, toll road commissions, bridge authorities, housing authorities, and hospital, canal, dormitory, parking, and electrification, etc., authorities). Where obligations of states and subdivisions thereof are general obligations, they are backed by the full faith and credit of the governmental unit (i.e., the full taxing power, which may be limited or unlimited) as contrasted to limited obligation bonds, such as special assessment and revenue bonds, which are payable solely out of special taxes or funds without pledge of the faith and credit of the governmental unit.
See MUNICIPAL BONDS, UNITED STATES GOVERNMENT SECURITIES.

CIVIL LOANS Loans made by a government or political subdivision thereof.
See CIVIL BONDS.

CLASS BONDS CLASSIFIED BONDS.

CLASSIFIED BONDS Bonds of the same corporation issued in series, e.g., Series A, Series B, Series C, etc., differing as to interest payment or issue or maturity date, but issued under the same open end or limited open end mortgage.

CLASSIFIED FINANCIAL STATEMENTS Financial statements arranged according to categories or classifications. A classified balance sheet arranges the major categories of assets, liabilities, and owners' equity into significant groups and subgroups. Classifying items on the balance sheet provides information concerning the liquidity of the assets and the maturity dates of liabilities. Assets and liabilities are frequently classified as follows on a classified balance sheet:

Assets
   Current assets
   Long-term investments (or Investments)
   Property, plant, and equipment
   Intangible assets
   Deferred charges (or Other assets)
Liabilities
   Current liabilities
   Long-term liabilities

Owners' equity (for a corporation)
   Capital stock
   Additional paid-in capital
   Retained earnings

CLASSIFIED STOCK Stock of the same corporation issued in series, the first in the series having rights prior to the others, e.g., first preferred stock, second preferred stock, third preferred stock, or Class A, Class B, Class C common stock.

CLASS I RAILROADS Railroad companies, including switching and terminal companies, having annual operation revenues (total gross revenues) of $50 million or more, per Interstate Commerce Commission rule effective January 1, 1978.
See RAILROAD EARNINGS.

CLASS II RAILROADS Railroad companies, including switching and terminal companies, having annual operating revenues (total gross revenues) of under $50 million. All railroad companies not classified as Class I are Class II (effective January 1, 1978).
See RAILROAD EARNINGS.

CLAYTON ACT Passed on October 15, 1914, "to supplement existing laws against unlawful restraints and monopolies, and for other purposes" (see ANTITRUST LAWS). Applicability to banks lies in the following areas.

Section 7, as amended, prohibits any corporation from acquiring the stock or assets of other corporations engaged in commerce where, in any line of commerce in any section of the country, the effect may be substantially to lessen competition or tend to create a monopoly. As far as banks are concerned, this section applies only to acquisitions of *stock* and does not cover acquisitions of bank *assets*; it does not apply to bank mergers or consolidations. The latter situations, however, are provided for by the new P.L. 86–463, May 13, 1960 (an amendment to Sec. 18(c) of the Federal Deposit Insurance Act of 1950), which now requires approval of the banking supervisory agencies (Comptroller of the Currency for national banks; Board of Governors of Federal Reserve System for state member banks; and Federal Deposit Insurance Corporation for insured nonmember banks) for bank mergers and consolidations in all cases, regardless of capital diminution resulting. In addition to specifying specific factors bearing on approval, including the effect upon competition, this new law requires each of the supervisory agencies to obtain the views of the other agencies and the attorney general in each case, as to the effect upon competition of each proposed merger or consolidation.
See BANK MERGERS, FEDERAL DEPOSIT INSURANCE ACT.

Section 8, as amended, provides that no director, officer, or employee of any member bank of the Federal Reserve System shall be at the same time a director, officer, or employee of any other bank, national or state, except that the Board of Governors of the Federal Reserve System may by regulation permit such service for not more than one other such bank. This general prohibition, however, does not apply to the following:

1. Banks in which the United States (sic) controls more than 90% of the stock, directly or indirectly.
2. Banks in formal liquidation.
3. Foreign banking corporations organized under Section 25 of the FEDERAL RESERVE ACT.
4. Banks owned over 50% by persons also owning over 50% of the common stock of the subject member bank.
5. Banks located in places not the same as or contiguous and adjacent to the location of the subject bank.
6. Banks not engaged in the same class of business.
7. Mutual savings banks.

The Board of Governors of the Federal Reserve System officially regards the provisions of the first three paragraphs of Section 8 of the Clayton Act (15 U.S.C. 19) to have been supplanted by the revised and more comprehensive prohibitions on management official interlocks between depository organizations in the Depository Institutions Management Interlocks Act (Title II of the Financial Institution Regulatory and Interest Rate Control Act, P.L. 95–630, November 10, 1978). Regulation L of the FEDERAL RESERVE BOARD REGULATIONS, effective May 9, 1980, implements the Interlocks Act, whose purpose is to foster competition by generally prohibiting a management official of a depository institution or depository holding company from also serving as a management official of another depository institution or depository holding company if the two organizations are not affiliated and are very large or are located in the same local area.

CLEAN BILL OF EXCHANGE A bill of exchange not accompanied by shipping documents, such as bill of lading, insurance certificate, etc., and therefore undocumented. Bankers' bills are usually clean.
See BILL OF EXCHANGE.

CLEAN BILL OF LADING One which does not lessen the issuing transportation company's liability by such restricting clauses as "said to contain . . . ," "shipper's load and count," etc., or clauses referring to packages as not being intact.
See BILL OF LADING.

CLEAN BOND A coupon bond that bears no endorsement or marks, as distinguished from a marked bond.
See STAMPED SECURITY.

CLEAN CREDIT A LETTER OF CREDIT issued by a bank against which the designated foreign seller may draw a bill without documentary support. The issuing bank engages to accept a clean bill, if otherwise drawn in accordance with the conditions imposed by the relative letter of credit. A clean credit is granted only to concerns of the highest credit standing.

CLEAR This term has four meanings:

1. Checks are cleared through the CLEARINGHOUSE, i.e., collected or passed through for payment.
2. Active securities are cleared through a stock exchange clearinghouse. *See* STOCK CLEARING CORPORATION.
3. A legal expression meaning free from incumbrance.
4. A vessel clears a port only after notice has been given of its intended departure, and examination and leave by the customs' officials have been given. Clearance papers constitute a certification showing that a vessel bound for a foreign port has fulfilled the requirements of the law and has authority to leave port.

CLEARANCE This term has four meanings:

1. The process of effecting clearings in CLEARINGHOUSE practice.
2. A vessel clearance is the right of a vessel to depart from a port, as evidenced by a certificate obtained from the collector of port, certifying to compliance with customs, health, and other port regulations.
3. The customs entry of goods. Every import of goods into the United States, unless expressly exempted, must be entered by filing the required forms with the customs house, whether or not goods are duty-free.
4. The total volume of commodities shipped out from a port for a particular date.

See CUSTOMS DUTY, CUSTOMS PORTS.

CLEARANCE PAPERS *See* CLEAR.

CLEARING AGREEMENT In international trade, an agreement between countries governing the clearance and offset of claims arising out of trade and international transactions with each other. Such agreements are typically bilateral, are made even by countries having full convertibility, and customarily involve a strong currency country which wishes to continue exports to a weak currency country which has imposed EXCHANGE RESTRICTIONS in order to protect its currency. Clearing agreements involve such points as establishment of control accounts in each country; provision for payments in clearing currency out of the control account usable for specified purposes; periodic clearance (settlement of net surplus or net deficit) in the control accounts; and a stipulated exchange rate between the two countries for the purpose of such clearances. Clearing agreements may cover either just foreign trade (exports and imports of goods) or the entire range of international transactions, thus partially or wholly bypassing the foreign exchange market.

CLEARING CONTRACTS In the operation of clearing contracts traded in on commodity exchanges, the process of substituting principals to transactions, thus facilitating settlement of accounts.
See FUTURES.

CLEARINGHOUSE A voluntary association of banks located in the same city, joined together to facilitate the daily exchange of checks, drafts, and notes among its members instead of separate exchanges of "local items" made individually by each bank with the others. The objects of the New York Clearing House Association, for example (the pioneer American clearinghouse, organized in 1853), are set forth in its constitution as follows. "The effecting at one place, of the daily exchanges between the members thereof and the payment at the same place of the balances resulting from such exchanges, the promotion of the interests of the members and the maintenance of conservative banking through wise and intelligent cooperation." It will be noted that in addition to the basic operational function, the objectives are also promotional and self-regulative—a scope of functions emulated in other clearinghouse associations throughout the U.S.

Origin of Clearinghouses. The New York Clearing House Association states that although the clearinghouse idea as applied to banks originated in London, England, as far back as 1773, it was not until 1853 that the New York Clearing House was formed. This was the first institution of its kind in the U.S., although some 20 years prior thereto, Albert Gallatin, Secretary of the Treasury in the Jefferson and Madison administrations, a prominent banker of his time, and an able economist, had suggested to his banking associates the establishment of a clearinghouse in New York similar to that maintained in London. Between the years 1849 and 1853, the number of banks in New York City increased from 24 to 57, following the increase of business incident to the discovery of gold in California; this increase in the number of local banks made it necessary that some plan be worked out which would bring about a more prompt settlement of balances between banks. At that time, all banks presented checks on each other by hand and for a while settlement had been made in gold and bank notes. From this arrangement, the plan of weekly settlement was developed, but this was not found to be satisfactory or adequate for various reasons.

Ten times in the history of the New York Clearing House the members have pooled their resources to make available to the business public the largest possible supply of credit. This was arranged through the issuance of clearinghouse certificates. The first issue was in 1860 when Abraham Lincoln was elected President, the second was in 1873, and the third was in 1890. Subsequent issues followed in the Panic of 1893, which marked the end of the boom period of railroad and city building in the west; in 1907, when runs on certain New York banks caused withdrawals of deposits on a large scale and the so-called money panic was the result, there being a lack of legal provision for the issuance of currency to meet the unusual demands; and in 1914, at the outbreak of World War I, when the New York Stock Exchange was closed for several weeks. With the establishment of the Federal Reserve System and provision for the issuance of Federal Reserve notes, the currency system has been made very flexible and able to take care of emergency demand for currency which might arise.

Clearinghouse Interbank Payment System. The New York Clearing House Association's computerized communications network, called CHIPS, went on-line with live transactions on April 6, 1970. The CHIPS payments system enables large sums to be transferred between member banks electronically, thus eliminating the use of official checks. The system, which subsequently was expanded to include nonmember as well as member banks, comprises a network of telephone lines extending from a central computer at the New York Clearing House to terminal computers (which can both send and receive messages) located in each participating bank. Payment messages prepared on terminals in sending banks are transmitted over telephone lines into the clearinghouse computer and out over telephone lines to terminal computers in receiving banks. Payment messages are printed on standard forms by a typewriter device which is an integral part of the terminal computer in both sending and receiving banks.

At the close of each business day, each participating bank is furnished a report of all the messages sent and received by it. Another report indicates the dollar amount of items sent by each participant, netted against the amount received by each participant.

Participants are required to settle their balances through the account of any settling participant on the books of the Federal Reserve Bank of New York. To accomplish this, Federal Reserve wire transfers in the net amounts are made directly between debtor and creditor settling participants.

Because of the potential risk inherent in large-dollar transfer networks, the Federal Reserve Board, in March 1986, introduced a policy to control and reduce "daylight overdrafts." Daylight overdrafts occur during the day when an institution has sent more funds over Fedwire than it has in its reserve or clearing account or has sent more funds over CHIPS than it has received, even though the balances are expected by the end of the day. The Fed's policy statement encourages each depository institution that incurs daylight overdrafts to adopt a "cross-system sender net debit cap," the maximum debit it may incur at any one time on all large-dollar wire transfer systems in which it participates. This cap amount is a multiple of the depository institution's adjusted primary capital.

The president of the association is elected yearly from among the persons elected as members of the clearinghouse committee. He can serve two consecutive years. This is an office that is highly regarded in the banking field and one that is considered an honor.

CLEARINGHOUSE AGENT A member of a clearinghouse that clears the checks of another bank that is not.

CLEARINGHOUSE BALANCE The total of the debit and credit balances at a CLEARINGHOUSE each day, as distinguished from the aggregate of checks and other items constituting the exchanges or clearings.

CLEARINGHOUSE BANK RETURN See CLEARINGHOUSE STATEMENT.

CLEARINGHOUSE CERTIFICATES J. G. Cannon, famous banking authority with the old Fourth National Bank of New York, who is believed to have organized the first formal credit department for a U.S. bank, wrote that there were two kinds of clearinghouse certificates—those secured by a deposit of gold coin and those secured by a deposit of collateral securities. The former were employed in ordinary times as a means of settling clearinghouse balances solely as a measure to economize time, labor, and expense by minimizing the risk in handling large sums of money. The latter, properly called CLEARINGHOUSE LOAN CERTIFICATES, were employed in times of financial disturbance or panic. Both were used exclusively for the purpose of settling clearinghouse balances among the members of the clearinghouse association. With inauguration of the Federal Reserve System, both became obsolete as settlement or emergency devices.

CLEARINGHOUSE COMMITTEES The New York Clearing House Association has four standing committees, the members of which are elected annually from among the officers of member clearinghouses. These committees are as follows: clearinghouse committee, conference committee, committee on admissions, nominating committee. The clearinghouse committee is the most important, its duties consist of the following: to appoint the manager and all necessary employees; to collect moneys and supervise expenditures; to establish rules and regulations not provided for in the constitution; to examine the members of the association; to establish rules regarding collections on out-of-town banks and fixing the rates to be charged therefor; to establish a scale of fines for errors, disorderly conduct, and other irregularities.
See CLEARINGHOUSE.

CLEARINGHOUSE EXCHANGE RATES Rates of exchange (usually minimal) established by a CLEARINGHOUSE association, which members thereof were bound to observe, penalties being provided for violations. The original establishment of uniform exchange rates for clearinghouse members in New York City grew out of the severe competition of members for deposits, many banks receiving checks drawn on out-of-town points for deposit at par, ignoring any exchange charge. This arrangement seemed unfair in view of the fact that southern and western banks continued to charge exchange for checks received for deposit and drawn upon New York banks, with the result that the New York banks sustained losses through collection of these checks at par. Accordingly, the New York Clearing House Association, in the interests of conservative banking, in order to discourage circuitous routing of items and to place all members on an even plane of competition, originally prescribed minimum exchange charges. This schedule of rates was established by the clearinghouse committee and was revised from time to time. In this schedule, points in adjoining states were par points and many points further away were discretionary, i.e., the rate of exchange was discretionary with the bank receiving the item for deposit.

The rate of exchange upon items that were collected in out-of-town points depended upon three variables: (1) the kind of item, i.e., whether checks and drafts, bankers acceptances, or other items (bankers acceptances received a preferential rate); (2) whether the bank on which the item was drawn was located in a Federal Reserve bank city (or branch city) or elsewhere (the former being accorded a lower rate); (3) the mail time between the point of deposit and the point of collection.

In July, 1926, the New York Clearing House revised its constitution to abolish exchange charges. As a result of the facilities for the collection and payment of checks at par by the Federal Reserve System, par collection being a condition of membership in the system, the great majority of banks now remit on checks at par.
See DOMESTIC EXCHANGE, PAR LIST.

CLEARINGHOUSE INTERBANK PAYMENTS SYSTEM A computerized network for transfer of international dollar payments, linking about 140 depository institutions which have offices or subsidiaries in New York City. The New York Fed describes the Clearing House Interbank Payments System (CHIPS) as follows.

As of March 1986, some 105,000 interbank transfers valued at $350 billion were being made daily through the network. The transfers represented about 90% of all interbank transfers relating to international dollar payments.

Until late spring of 1970, most international dollar payments were made by official bank checks. At that time, the New York Clearing House Association, a group of the largest New York City banks, organized CHIPS for eight Federal Reserve member commercial banks that also were members of the CLEARINGHOUSE. The system eventually was expanded to include other commercial banks, Edge corporations, U.S. agencies, branches of foreign banks, Article XII investment companies, and private banks. Article XII refers to that article in the New York State Banking Law (Sec. 507–519), and investment companies refers to banking organizations organized as subsidiaries having the power to receive money for transmission and to transmit money between the U.S. and any foreign country and otherwise to engage in foreign banking and investing. They may be agreement corporations, such as state-chartered, Edge Act type of banking subsidiaries (see EDGE ACT).

Until recent years, in the CHIPS arrangement final settlement, or the actual movement of balances at the Federal Reserve, occurred on the morning after the transfers. Next-day settlement was acceptable until volume rose substantially, and New York Clearing House and CHIPS participants became increasingly concerned about overnight and over-weekend risks.

Accordingly, on October 1, 1981, a major change was made, enabling same-day settlement through a special account at the Federal Reserve Bank of New York. Under an agreement signed in August, 1981, the New York Fed established a settlement account for CHIPS-settling participants into which debt settlement payments are sent and from which credit settlement payments are disbursed. Settlement is made at the close of each business day by CHIPS-settling participants sending and receiving Fedwire transfers through the settlement account. (Fedwire is the Federal Reserve System's electronic funds and securities transfer network.)

The New York Federal Reserve Bank is not required to provide financial assistance to ensure completion of the settlement. Settlement is completed when all settling participants owing funds have made payments to the special account and funds have been transferred from the special account to CHIPS-settling participants' due funds.

In a typical transaction, suppose a London bank wants to transfer $1 million from its account at a New York correspondent bank A to an account at another bank outside New York which maintains a correspondent relationship with New York correspondent bank B. Banks A and B are both CHIPS participants.

Bank A receives the London bank's transfer message by telex or through the SWIFT system. (SWIFT, the Society for Worldwide Interbank Financial Telecommunications, is a private electronic message transfer system to which some depository institutions and central banks belong.)

CLEARINGHOUSE LOAN CERTIFICATES

Bank A verifies the London bank's message and enters the message into its CHIPS terminal, providing the identifying codes for the sending and receiving banks, the identity of the account at bank B which will receive the funds, and the amount.

The message is then stored in the CHIPS central computer. As soon as bank A approves and releases the stored transaction, the message is transmitted from the CHIPS computer to bank B. The CHIPS computer also makes a permanent record of the transaction and makes appropriate debits and credits in the CHIPS account of banks A and B. When bank B receives its credit message, it notifies the bank outside New York, which in turn notifies its customer.

Immediately following the closing of the CHIPS network at 4:30 P.M. (Eastern time), the CHIPS computer produces a settlement report showing the net debit or credit position of each participant. A separate settlement report shows the net position of each settling participant. The net position of a nonsettling participant is netted into the position of its correspondent settling participant.

Each settling participant has a set period to determine whether it will settle the net position of its participant respondents. After that time, if no settling participant refuses to settle, the settling participants with net debit positions have until 5:45 P.M. (Eastern time) to transfer their debit amounts through Fedwire to the CHIPS settlement account on the books of the New York Fed.

When this procedure has been accomplished, the New York Clearing House, acting on the New York Fed's behalf, transfers those funds via Fedwire out of the settlement account to those settling participants with net creditor positions. The process usually is completed by 6 P.M. (Eastern time). Fedwire transfers of funds are final and irrevocable when the recipient receives or is advised of the transfer.

Because of the potential risk inherent in large-dollar transfer networks, the Federal Reserve Board, in March 1986, introduced a policy to control and reduce "daylight overdrafts." Daylight overdrafts occur during the day when an institution has sent more funds over Fedwire than it has in its reserve or clearing account or has sent more funds over CHIPS than it has received, even though the balances are expected by the end of the day. The Fed's policy statement encourages each depository institution that incurs daylight overdrafts to adopt a "cross-system sender net debit cap," the maximum debit it may incur at any one time on all large-dollar wire transfer systems in which it participates. This cap amount is a multiple of the depository institution's adjusted primary capital.

See FEDERAL RESERVE COMMUNICATIONS SYSTEM FOR THE EIGHTIES.

BIBLIOGRAPHY

FEDERAL RESERVE BANK OF NEW YORK. *C.H.I.P.S.*, Fedpoints 36, March, 1986.

CLEARINGHOUSE LOAN CERTIFICATES An emergency form of currency for use in settling clearinghouse balances only, issued at times of shortages in currency in the past before organization of the Federal Reserve System. The New York Clearing House reports that 10 times in the history of the New York Clearing House the members have pooled their resources to make available to the business public the largest possible supply of credit. This was arranged through the issuance of clearinghouse certificates; the first issue was in 1860 when Abraham Lincoln was elected President of the United States, the second was in 1873, and the third was in 1890. Subsequent issues followed in the Panic of 1893, denoting the end of the boom period of railroad and city building in the west, and again in 1907 when runs on certain New York banks caused withdrawals of deposits on a large scale and the so-called money panic was the result, there being a lack of legal provisions for the issuance of currency to meet the unusual demands. The next issuance of clearinghouse certificates was in 1914 at the outbreak of the World War, when the stock exchange was closed for several weeks. With the establishment of the Federal Reserve System and the provisions for the issuance of Federal Reserve notes, the currency situation has been made very flexible and thus able to take care of any emergency which might arise.

Under the Federal Reserve System which provides for rediscounts and elastic currency, it is doubtful whether clearinghouse loan certificates will ever again be needed. The real explanation for the necessity to resort to these certificates in the past lay in an organic defect in the national banking system—failure to provide for ELASTIC CURRENCY which expands and contracts with the needs of business.

CLEARINGHOUSE PROOF A proof of each day's clearings at a clearinghouse as determined by the clearinghouse manager as a result of the exchanges of items by members and clearing nonmembers. This proof shows the amount brought to and received from the clearinghouse by each exchanging institution and the credit or debit balance of each. The proof is obtained by securing agreement between the total debits and credits and between the total debit and credit balances.

In the New York Clearing House and other clearinghouses, a certified copy of the clearinghouse proof is used as a journal entry by which the balances due to or from each member may be adjusted through the reserve accounts of the members at the Federal Reserve bank, thus effecting settlements with maximum efficiency.

CLEARINGHOUSE RETURN CLEARINGHOUSE STATEMENT.

CLEARINGHOUSE SETTLEMENT Payment by a bank of its debit balance to, or receipt of its credit balance from, the CLEARINGHOUSE. It is an adjustment by each bank with all other banks involved in the clearings of their mutual claims against one another. The most advanced mode of settlement is through the reserve accounts of clearing members at the Federal Reserve bank.

CLEARINGHOUSE SETTLEMENT SHEET A sheet prepared by each member of a CLEARINGHOUSE association showing the amount of checks that it holds against each other bank of the association, and which will be presented for collection at the next clearing. The total of this sheet, i.e., the aggregate of claims against other members, represents the bank's credit balance at the clearinghouse.

CLEARINGHOUSE STATEMENT A statement issued periodically, usually once a week, by the larger clearinghouse associations, which displays in condensed and detailed form the financial condition (loans, investments, legal reserve, vault cash, demand and time deposits) of the member banks.

The weekly detailed statement of the New York Clearing House Association was discontinued beginning with the week ended March 31, 1928, except information as to deposits, capital, and undivided profits. It had been published regularly since the organization of the New York Clearing House in 1853; the realization that the returns no longer served a useful function led to its discontinuance. Formerly the aggregate position of the New York Clearing House banks was regarded as extremely important information because it reflected the banking strength of the country as a whole, since practically all interior banks maintained deposits in New York. It was, in fact, practically the only display of bank data available weekly.

Since the passage of the Federal Reserve Act, which compels all members to keep their reserves in the Federal Reserve banks, it was the opinion of the clearinghouse officials that the weekly statement of condition of the clearinghouse member banks was only of local interest and useless as a reflection of the financial status of banks on a countrywide basis. It was felt that ample data regarding current banking conditions are now provided by the weekly Federal Reserve statement (combined and individual), condition of member banks in leading cities (weekly) as reported by the Federal Reserve Board of Governors, weekly reports of the Federal Reserve Board of Governors on loans to brokers secured by stocks and bonds, monthly report of brokers' loans issued by the New York Stock Exchange, and weekly reports of Federal Reserve Board of Governors on debits to individual accounts.

CLEARING MEMBER BANK A bank which is not a member of the Federal Reserve System, but which may collect its out-of-town checks through the FEDERAL RESERVE CHECK COLLECTION SYSTEM. Banks can become clearing members by keeping a balance with the Federal Reserve bank of their district against which incoming collections may be charged. A further qualification is that clearing members must agree to accept all checks drawn on, and presented against them, at par.

See PAR CLEARANCES, PAR LIST.

CLEARINGS *See* BANK CLEARINGS.

CLEARING STOCKS This term has two meanings:

1. In centralized clearing of transactions on stock exchanges, those stocks designated for such clearing. At the present time,

the New York Stock Exchange's STOCK CLEARING CORPORATION provides clearing for all stocks listed on the exchange but no bonds. Originally, when the centralized clearing system was inaugurated for New York Stock Exchange issues in May, 1982, only four railroad stocks were cleared.

2. In the New York Clearing House operation, the exchanges of stock certificates to and from representatives of transfer agents and registrars for the purposes of registration. These exchanges for stock certificates have proved to be of great assistance to the registrar and transfer departments of the participating institutions, a large proportion of the deliveries being handled through this channel.

See CLEARINGHOUSE.

CLEOs Collateralized lease equipment obligations.
See FINANCIAL INSTRUMENTS: RECENT INNOVATIONS.

CLIFFORD TRUST A type of *inter vivos* personal trust (one created in the lifetime of the settlor) whereby the parent settlor transfers income-producing assets to a trustee with instructions to pay the income therefrom to specified children. Since such beneficiary children would pay lower income taxes than the parent, a tax-saving motivation is indicated.

At the end of 10 years and a day, the Clifford trust will terminate, and the principal of the trust (the trusteed assets) will be returned to the parent settlor, the objective of providing income for the beneficiary children having been achieved in the time period for such purposes as college education.

See TRUST.

CLIQUE An informal group of persons or financial interests who work for a common end; as applied to stock speculation in former free markets before the SEC, a group organized to manipulate the price of a security or group of securities. In financial reviews, bull cliques and bear cliques were often referred to as groups of individuals interested in forcing prices up or down. A clique differed from a POOL in that there was no formal written agreement and the management of the clique was not in the hands of a particular person. In a clique there was merely an informal understanding that a certain stock was to be exploited, while in a pool there was a written agreement in which the profits or losses were shared by the members. Under the Securities Exchange Act of 1934, manipulation of security markets such as matched orders or wash sales, is prohibited. Short sales, stop-loss orders, price-pegging, and stabilizing are placed under Securities Exchange Commission control and regulation, which thus hits directly at former clique practices.

See MANIPULATION.

CLOCK LOCK *See* TIME LOCK.

CLOCK STAMP A device for imprinting the hour and day of arrival upon all mail and other matter received. Such a stamp is useful for future reference and to test efficiency and speed in filling orders or answering letters.

CLOSE In commodity exchange trading, the short period of time just before the end of the market session, when all trades are officially declared to be executed at or on the close. Also, the last recorded price for a security or commodity, also called the last, for a particular trading session.

See CLOSING PRICE.

CLOSE CORPORATION A corporation, the shares of which are held by a few persons, usually officers, employees, or others close to the management, and are rarely offered to the public.

CLOSED–END MORTGAGE A MORTGAGE that precludes further indebtedness on the property which it pledges as security, i.e., the limit which can be borrowed under the mortgage has already been attained. Such a mortgage, as contrasted to the OPEN-END MORTGAGE, is advantageous to its holder or to bondholders whose security consists therein, in that it is thereby protected against DILUTION without the necessity of protective provisions designed to afford a measure of protection against the latter.

CLOSED–END MUTUAL FUND A mutual fund that does not make a continuous market for its securities. The shares of many closed-end funds are listed on a stock exchange. In recent years, closed-end mutual funds have often been traded at a discount from the market price of the securities they held.

CLOSED OUT Refers to the SELLING OUT of a margin account by a broker, pursuant to the margin agreement entered into by the customer; indicates that a business or account has been disposed of or liquidated.

CLOSE MONEY Money obtained at fairly high interest rates. Close money rates are not as high as TIGHT MONEY rates

CLOSE PRICES Describes the stock market when changes in prices between successive transactions are small fractions, or when the final bid and asked quotations differ by small fractions.

CLOSING In real estate and certain other financial transactions, an arranged meeting of the buyer and seller or their agents at which time an agreed upon transaction occurs, usually a sale.

CLOSING AN ACCOUNT When a bank account is closed as shown by a complete withdrawal of the deposit balance, notice is sent by the bookkeeper (ledger clerk) to the new business department and credit department for their information and records. The reason for closing an account is usually ascertained, if possible, and recorded. Frequently a letter is written or a representative sent to the customer in the interest of ascertaining the reason for withdrawing the account and to attempt to secure a reinstatement thereof.

CLOSING ENTRIES In accounting, the journal entries that for the particular period close the nominal accounts, mainly revenues and expenses, combine their net balances into summary accounts, and close out the summary accounts to account, for final transfer to the capital accounts the retained earnings (for a corporation).

CLOSING PRICE The price at which the last sale of each stock, bond, or commodity is effected daily on a stock or commodity exchange. These prices are quoted in the daily newspapers, usually with the opening (first), high, and low prices of the day. The net change in price of a security as reported from day to day is the difference between the closing prices of successive days.

CLOSING THE BOOKS Refers to the temporary closing of a corporation's stock transfer books on a date fixed by the board of directors at the time dividends are declared, in order to determine the stockholders of record, i.e., those entitled to receive the dividend on the payable date. The last date for transferring stock in order to participate in the dividend distribution is the day the "books close." Closing the books enables the transfer agent to prepare a list of the stockholders so that dividends may be sent to the stockholders of record. This purpose may also be accomplished, however, without closing the books; the announcement of the dividend declaration will indicate whether or not the books will close. Because of the four day regular delivery basis on security markets, stocks will sell EX-DIVIDEND on the third business day preceding the record date.

Closing the books also refers to closing entries that close the revenue, expense, and other temporary capital accounts at the end of an accounting period. The closing process reduces these account balances to a zero balance.

See DELIVERIES, STOCK TRANSFERS.

CLUB ACCOUNTS Deposit accounts of unincorporated organizations, such as clubs, societies, and groups. As in the case of corporation accounts, the bank should obtain and file resolution by the organization specifying the officers who are authorized to sign checks, together with signature card.

See SIGNATURE DEPARTMENT, SIGNATURES.

CMPS Capital market preferred stock.
SEE FINANCIAL MARKETS: RECENT INNOVATIONS.

COALERS Refers to those railroads that derive a large part of their freight traffic from coal loadings.
See RAILROAD INDUSTRY.

COASSIGNEE A joint ASSIGNEE.

ENCYCLOPEDIA OF BANKING AND FINANCE

COBWEB THEOREM A general tendency toward equilibrium is a basic postulate of Marshallian economics. Given pure competition, equilibrium price is determined by the interaction of demand and supply. If actual price is below the equilibrium point, demand exceeds supply, so that price has an upward tendency toward equilibrium. Conversely, if actual price is above equilibrium, supply exceeds demand, and price has a downward tendency toward equilibrium.

However, as pointed out by econometricians (Tinbergen, Schultz, and Ricci), this postulate of a general tendency toward equilibrium is confounded by the tendency of specific commodities to go back and forth between the supply and demand curves, in a cobweb pattern on a diagram. Instead of having a tendency toward equilibrium, the pattern may diverge outwards or be continuous, depending upon the specific shapes of the supply and demand curves (relative elasticity). This is caused by the varying lags in adjustment of supply to price changes, as for example in agricultural commodities. Price may be determined by current supply, but in turn succeeding supply may be determined by preceding price. Only where supply is less elastic than demand would there be a tendency to converge toward equilibrium.

COCOA EXCHANGE See COFFEE, SUGAR & COCOA EXCHANGE, INC.

CODE See CIPHER CODE.

CODE OF CONDUCT OF FINANCIAL PLANNERS
The International Association for Financial Planning's code of ethics prescribes the minimum ethical conduct required of members. The code encourages voluntary compliance with standards that exceed the minimum. The code establishes three kinds of standards:

1. *Canons:* maxims that reflect exemplary professional conduct.
2. *Rules:* specific standards derived from the canons.
3. *Guidelines:* explanatory statements that interpret the canons and rules.

The canons contained in the code of ethics are presented here:

1. Members should endeavor as professionals to place the public interest above their own.
2. Members should seek continually to maintain and improve their professional knowledge, skills, and competence.
3. Members should obey all laws and regulations, and should avoid any conduct or activity that would cause unjust harm to others.
4. Members should be diligent in the performance of their occupational duties.
5. Members should establish and maintain honorable relationships with other professionals, with those whom the members serve in a professional capacity, and with all those who rely upon the members' professional judgments and skills.
6. Members should assist in improving the public understanding of financial planning.
7. Members should use the fact of membership in a manner consistent with the association's rules of professional conduct.
8. Members should assist in maintaining the integrity of the code of professional ethics of the association.

CODES OF CONDUCT OF BANKS Principles, rules, guidelines, and policies of an enterprise, industry, or profession describing and/or prescribing moral (right or wrong) or legal behavior expected of employees and management. Almost all financial institutions have written codes of conduct.

Many banks have adopted codes of conduct for their employees and administrators. These codes are sometimes used as a marketing or publicity tool, a guide to internal operations, a defensive tool relating to legal responsibilities, and an affirmative statement of acceptable conduct. Bank codes generally contain broadly stated principles, comprehensive guidelines for bank or employee activity, and/or rules and interpretations. Codes should contain a corporate creed, ethical guidelines, and a section on compliance and enforcement.

The bank should establish a system to monitor and enforce the code and a procedure for reassessing and revising the code when necessary. Sample code provisions deal with corporate governance; bank business practices (credit policy, lending activities); departmental practices; statutory and regulatory compliance; standards of conduct for directors, officers, and employees; bank relations with employees and the community; and compliance with regulatory and statutory requirements.

Many statutory and regulatory provisions have major ethical implications for banks. For example, the Bank Bribery Act (18 U.S.C. Sec. 215) was amended as part of the Comprehensive Crime Control Act to make it a felony for employees of federally insured banks to give or receive anything of value in connection with any business of the bank. The statute prohibits the giving or receiving of things of value in connection with the business of the bank only if such things are given or accepted corruptly and with the intent to influence or be influenced. Section 10(b) of the Securities and Exchange Act of 1934 and SEC Rule 10b-5 prohibit against insider trading as follows: company insiders may not trade in securities of the firm when in possession of material nonpublic information. Insider trading is a criminal violation. A conviction for insider trading carries a fine of up to $100,000 and a jail term of up to five years. Federal statutes with ethical ramifications applicable to banks and bank employees include the following (the list is not intended to be complete):

12 U.S.C. Sec. 78	Employment in securities business prohibited
12 U.S.C. Sec. 92(a)(b)	Unlawful loan of trust funds
12 U.S.C. Sec. 503 and 93(a)(b)	Personal liability of directors and penalties
12 U.S.C. Sec. 375(a)(b)	Regulation of credit to insiders and political campaigns
12 U.S.C. Sec. 501 18 U.S.C. Sec. 1004	Certifying a check drawn on an account in which there are not sufficient collected funds
12 U.S.C. Sec. 1972	Foreign Corrupt Practices Act
18 U.S.C. Sec. 212	Making loans to bank examiners
18 U.S.C. Sec. 215	Bank Bribery Act
18 U.S.C. Sec. 656	Theft, embezzlement, misapplication of funds or assets
18 U.S.C. Sec. 1344	Bank Fraud Statute

BIBLIOGRAPHY

BANK ADMINISTRATION INSTITUTE. Codes of Conduct in the Financial Services Industry.

CODICIL A written addition to a WILL; a testamentary instrument altering or supplementing an existing will. It is neither necessary nor customary to have the codicil written on the same paper as the will or attached to it, but it must be executed with the same formalities as the will itself, e.g., if the laws of the state require attestation by three witnesses for the will, the codicil requires the same number.

COEXECUTOR One of two or more executors; a person, bank, or trust company appointed to act as EXECUTOR jointly with another.

COFFEE EXCHANGE See COFFEE, SUGAR & COCOA EXCHANGE, INC.

COFFEE, SUGAR & COCOA EXCHANGE, INC.
Formed September 28, 1979, when the New York Coffee & Sugar Exchange, Inc. merged with the New York Cocoa Exchange, Inc. and officially assumed its present title.

The Coffee Exchange of the City of New York was founded in 1882 to trade coffee futures. The exchange added the trading of SUGAR futures in 1914 to replace European raw sugar markets closed by the outbreak of World War I. In 1916, the exchange changed its name to the New York Coffee & Sugar Exchange, Inc. The New York Cocoa Exchange had opened for business on October 1, 1925, establishing the world's first exchange for trading in cocoa beans.

Located in the Commodities Exchange Center at Four World Trade Center, New York City, the current exchange is the world's leading marketplace for futures trading in coffee, sugar, and cocoa. The exchange's membership seats are held by representatives of every segment of the coffee, sugar, and cocoa industries, as well as by floor brokers and futures commission merchants. The exchange is regulated by the federal COMMODITY FUTURES TRADING COMMISSION (CFTC), which was created after Congress amended the Commodity Exchange Act in 1974. With creation of the CFTC, internationally traded commodities were brought under federal regulation for the first time.

Coffee Futures. The coffee "C" contract is the most active coffee futures contract traded on the exchange. The "C" contract deals in washed arabica coffee produced in several Central and South American, Asian, and African countries. Contract size is 37,500 pounds in approximately 250 bags. Delivery months are March, May, July, September, and December. Minimum fluctuations are in units of $0.0001 (a point) per pound, which is equivalent to $3.75 per contract. Daily price fluctuation limit (from previous day's settlement price) is $0.04 (400 points), or $1,500 per contract. In recent years, trading volume has reached record levels.

Sugar Futures. The exchange offers two sugar contracts for trading. The no. 11 (world) contract is the more actively traded. This contract calls for delivery of cane sugar in bulk f.o.b. (free on board) stowed, from any of 27 foreign countries of origin as well as from the United States. Contract size is 50 long tons (112,000 pounds). Delivery months are January, March, May, July, and October. Minimum fluctuations are in units of $0.0001 per pound, which is equivalent to $11.20 per lot. Daily price fluctuation limit (from previous day's settlement price) is $0.005 (50 points), or $560 per lot.

The no. 12 (domestic) contract, which trades less actively than the no. 11 (world) contract, calls for delivery of cane sugar in bulk, c.i.f. (cost, insurance, and freight) duty paid at named Atlantic and Gulf ports. Contract size is 50 long tons (112,000 pounds). Delivery months are January, March, May, July, and November. Minimum fluctuations are in units of $0.0001 per pound, which is equivalent to $11.20 per lot. Daily price fluctuation limit (from previous day's settlement price) is $0.005 (50 points), or $560 per lot. Deliverable growths are cane sugars of the United States, duty free, and of foreign origin, duty paid and delivered in bulk through delivery points at New York, Philadelphia, Baltimore, and New Orleans.

Cocoa Futures. The cocoa contract on the exchange trades in March, May, July, September, and December trading months. Contract size is 10 metric tons, with prices quoted in cents per ton. Minimum price fluctuation is $1.00 per ton (a point), or $10.00 per contract. Daily limit in price fluctuation is $88 (88 points), or $880 per contract.

According to the CSCE, as part of a long-range plan for growth through diversification, the exchange formed the Economic Index Market in 1985 as a division of the CSCE. The consumer price index futures contracts (also known as inflation futures), which provides a way to manage the multiple risks associated with the uncertainty of inflation rates, was the first futures contract of this type to be approved for trading by the Commodity Futures Trading Commission. The unit of trading in the inflation futures is the CPI-U. The value of the contract is $1,000 times the index. Futures contracts are traded for settlement during the months of January, April, July, and October, extending over the period 12 months from the current trading date. The final settlement value of any month's contract is based on the value of the index released in that month. Price increments are multiples of .01 (one one-hundredth) of the index. The minimum price fluctuation is $10. Maximum daily price fluctuation is three points, or $3,000 per contract.

The International Market Index, a broad-based, international stock index with real-time pricing throughout the U.S. trading day, is also traded on the exchange. IMI measures the performance of 50 leading foreign stocks that actively trade in the United States. The index includes stocks from Australia, Denmark, Hong Kong, Italy, Japan, the Netherlands, Norway, Spain, Sweden, the United Kingdom, and 20 industry groups. The index is heavily weighted in Japanese and U.K. stocks. The composition of the index is reviewed quarterly and updated to assure that all component stocks meet the qualifying criteria. The International Market Index is market-value weighted, also called "capitalization weighted", which means the index value corresponds to the sum of the market values of each of the component stocks, divided by the divisor that was set to establish an initial value of the IMI of 200.00 at the close of trading on January 2, 1987. The divisor is adjusted to maintain index continuity. The trading unit is $250 multiplied by the index value. Quotations are in points and hundredths of a point. One point equals $250. Minimum price fluctuation is 0.05 or $12.50 per contract. The contract months include the current calendar month, the immediately following two calendar months, and every March, June, September, and December thereafter in a 14-month period from the current calendar month. Settlement is in cash, based on opening index value on the business day after the last trading day. Daily price limits of 30 points below and 50 points above the previous day's settlement price are imposed.

BIBLIOGRAPHY

The Coffee, Sugar & Cocoa Exchange, Inc. publishes many investor information booklets, including: An Introduction and Strategy Guide—Options on Coffee Futures; An Introduction to Inflation Futures; Annual Reports; CPI Futures Contract: Questions & Answers; *Economic Index Market* (monthly newsletter); *On the Market* (quarterly newsletter); Options Trading Strategies Handbook; Statistical Annual Yearbook; Strategies for Buying and Selling Options on Cocoa Futures; Trading in Cocoa Futures; Trading in Coffee Futures; Trading in Sugar Futures; Understanding Options on Futures; World White Sugar Futures.

See COMMODITIES for commodity futures contracts trading volume.

COINAGE The process of identifying, by stamping a piece of metal intended to be used as money, by a sovereign power, i.e., a national government. When metal was first coined, only the obverse face was stamped with an image of the sovereign, with an indication of the weight. In the process of evolution, the reverse side was also stamped to prevent clipping, and finally the edges were milled to prevent trimming the edges. The purpose of coinage is to avoid inconvenience and delay in each act of exchange. Since coinage is a governmental certification of the weight and fineness of coins, the necessity of testing the weight and fineness of metal, when used as medium of exchange, is obviated. Good coinage involves the following requisites: easy recognition of denomination, easy identification of the issuing government, certification of weight and fineness, difficulty of being counterfeited or altered, difficulty of being abraded.

See ABRASION, FREE COINAGE, GRATUITOUS COINAGE, MILLING, MINT, SEIGNIORAGE, UNITED STATES MONEY.

COINCIDENT ECONOMIC INDICATORS ECONOMIC INDICATORS that move with (as opposed to before or after) the business cycle. These include an index of industrial production, levels of nonagricultural employees, real personal income (less transfer payments), and sales in the manufacturing sector.

COINS Metallic money as distinguished from paper money; metal stamped by a government authority for use as money, as distinguished from bullion (metal in the mass).

U.S. coins have a design, composition, weight, and fineness fixed by statutes (latest major legislation is the Coinage Act of 1965, P.L. 89–91, which changed the metallic content of the three denominations of U.S. fractional coins—the half dollar, quarter dollar, and dime), and are manufactured only by the federal government under the supervision of the director of the MINT.

For details of types, metallic contents, etc., *see* UNITED STATES MONEY.

BIBLIOGRAPHY

Coinage.
Coin Prices.
Coins.
Coins and Medals. U.S. Government Printing Office. Annual.
Coin World. Weekly.
Coin Yearbook.
INTERNATIONAL PUBLICATIONS SERVICE. Philadelphia, PA. Annual.
Collector's Data Service. On-line Data Base. Collector's Data Service, Ltd., Seattle, WA.
Numismatic News. Krause Publications, Inc., Iola, WI. Weekly.

COINSURANCE A sharing of insurance risk between insurer and insured depending on the relation of the amount of the policy and a specified percentage of the actual value of the property insured at time of loss. The coinsurance clause of a fire insurance policy ordinarily provides that in the event of loss, the insurer shall be liable for no greater proportion of the loss than the ratio of the sum of the policy to the specified percentage (usually 80%) of the actual value of the property insured at the time when the loss is incurred. Consequently, it is in the interest of the insured to keep up insurance coverage, as the lower the amount of the policy in relation to the percentage of actual value specified, the greater will be the insured's coinsurance at time of loss.

The coinsurance indemnity is expressed as follows:

ENCYCLOPEDIA OF BANKING AND FINANCE

$$\frac{\text{Face amount of policy}}{\text{Coinsurance percentage x Fair value of property at date of loss}} \times \text{Fair value}$$

To illustrate, assume a company purchases a $20,000 insurance policy on some equipment; the policy has an 80% coinsurance clause. A $6,000 fire loss occurs at a time when the fair value of the equipment is $30,000. The amount recoverable from the insurer is computed as follows:

$$\frac{\$20,000}{(80\%)(\$30,000)} \times \$6,000 = \$5,000$$

The insured can recover the lowest of the face of the policy, the fair value of the loss, or the coinsurance indemnity.
See INSURANCE.

COLLATERAL Security given by a borrower to a lender as a pledge for payment of a LOAN. Such lenders thus become secured creditors; in the event of default, such creditors are entitled to proceed against the collateral and, in the event of its insufficiency in coverage, are entitled to treatment as unsecured creditors to the extent of deficiency judgment obtained on the note evidencing debt obligation of the borrower. Securities collateral is deposited with the lender, along with an assignment in blank, and may be used to satisfy the claim of the lender in the event of failure of the borrower to meet the debt at maturity.

Any kind of property which has a ready and stable market may be employed as collateral, but the collateral value of different kinds of property is subject to wide variation depending upon a number of factors. The principal kinds of collateral are real estate, bonds, stocks, notes, acceptances, certificates of deposit, passbooks, chattels (including grain and livestock), bills of lading covering readily marketable and nonperishable staples, warehouse receipts, assigned book accounts, and trust receipts. Some kinds of property are not suitable to serve as collateral because they have no ready market and their value is unascertainable.

The chief factors bearing upon the value of property as collateral are readiness and steadiness of market, activity of market, ease of transfer of title, degree of fluctuation in market value, and character of the collateral (e.g., in security loans, the securities collateral should be well diversified). The collateral or HYPOTHECARY VALUE of property is the ratio of the amount which can be borrowed to its market value.

In bank credit doctrine, the mere provision of collateral does not indicate a superior credit as compared with the unsecured loan. Nevertheless, the provision of collateral statutorily does add to the basic legal loan limit as to maximum loan to any single borrower on various types of loans (see NATIONAL BANK LOANS). In addition to this motivation, convenience (e.g., shift in status of securities on hand from custody account to collateral account at the Federal Reserve bank) is a factor in collateralized interbank loans, collateral on which does not mean impugning of the credit worthiness of the borrower banks involved.

The amount a lender may advance against most stock pledged as collateral, when the purpose of the loan is to purchase stock, is subject to the margin requirements set by the BOARD OF GOVERNORS OF THE FEDERAL RESERVE SYSTEM through its Regulations T, U, G, and X. These requirements apply to transactions in stock and related instruments such as options, warrants, and bonds convertible to stock. The margin requirements specify the percentage of the purchase price borrowers must supply in cash (and, by implication, the percentage they may borrow). The margin set applies only at the time of the initial transaction; if the price of a stock bought on margin falls, the borrower is not required to put up additional collateral or pay off part of the loan in order to restore the original relationship between the loan and the underlying collateral.
See MARGIN, MARGIN BUYING, SECURITY LOANS.

COLLATERAL HEIR See HEIR.

COLLATERALIZED MORTGAGE OBLIGATION (CMO) A type of pay-through mortgage-backed security that gives the holder a security interest in, but not ownership of, the underlying assets. Returns on a CMO are tied directly to returns on the underlying assets. Each CMO issue is divided into different maturity classes, called tranches.

BIBLIOGRAPHY

PARSEGHIAN, G. "Collateralized Mortgage Obligations: A Primer." *The Journal of International Securities Markets*, Winter, 1987.

COLLATERAL LOAN A short-term loan for which the borrower has deposited with the lender some kind of COLLATERAL security, such as bonds, stocks, documents of title, etc., which may be sold to satisfy the debt, if not paid at maturity.

COLLATERAL MORTGAGE BONDS COLLATERAL TRUST BONDS that are secured by a deposit of mortgage bonds; bonds that are in turn secured by a deposit of mortgage bonds and therefore indirectly secured by a mortgage. The title has sometimes proved to be a misnomer because the security is sometimes stocks or bonds not constituting a direct lien.

COLLATERAL NOTE A NOTE evidencing a loan secured by collateral—generally stocks, bonds, or mortgages.

COLLATERAL SECURITY Property SECURITY as distinguished from PERSONAL SECURITY.
See COLLATERAL.

COLLATERAL TRUST BONDS Bonds secured not by real property but by a deposit in trust of securities, usually bonds and sometimes stocks. A parent company that owns bonds or stocks of its subsidiaries may use them as collateral against an issue of its own bonds. The investment value of collateral trust bonds depends upon the margin of safety or excess value of the collateral above the collateral trust issue, range of fluctuation in the price of the collateral, protection offered by the deed of trust, and the general credit standing of the issuing corporation.

COLLATERAL VALUE Value of collateral relative to the amount of the loan.

Securities qualify for high collateral value on the basis of grade, strength of claim, marketability, and diversification ("mix") of the securities pledged. Emphasis on value of the collateral is indicated by the usual provision in collateral loan agreements for maintenance of a minimum ratio of current market value to amount of the outstanding loan.

Qualities of commodities which influence collateral value are grading, perishability, marketability, and steadiness in demand. Judged by these requirements, many commodities qualify as sound collateral for bank loans. In the leading commodities in which commodity exchanges maintain active markets in futures, an additional protection to the bank is the requirement that the borrower hedge a position in the commodity loaned on by sale of a futures contract in the commodity. How higher ratio of market value to amount of loan increases the legal lending limit on loans to any one borrower on commodities collateral is detailed in NATIONAL BANK LOANS.

COLLECTION AGENT A bank acting as agent or correspondent for another bank located in another city, with which arrangements have been completed for the collection of checks and other items drawn on points in the former's locality and for the conduct of other business.

COLLECTION CHARGES Charges made by a bank for the collection of checks, coupons, drafts, notes, and acceptances drawn upon banks, corporations, or individuals at points outside the city in which the sending bank is located. Local clearinghouse associations usually fix a minimum compulsory collection charge for items drawn on out-of-town points, when cashed or deposited for credit at its member banks. This charge is made to compensate for the loss of interest upon the money while the check is in process of collection, and is based upon the amount and the time necessary to collect the item.

Federal Reserve banks, through their transit departments, collect out-of-town checks for member banks or any bank which agrees to pay checks drawn on it at par (known as clearing member banks), without charge. See FEDERAL RESERVE CHECK COLLECTION SYSTEM.

When out-of-town checks are collected through regularly established collection agents on a prearranged basis of reciprocity or otherwise, the charge for collection is fixed at the discretion of the collecting bank.

See DOMESTIC EXCHANGE, FREE ITEMS.

COLLECTION CLERK A bank clerk responsible for discharging the details in connection with the collection of checks, drafts, and other items drawn on out-of-town points. Where the volume of out-of-town checks is large, a separate department known as a collection or TRANSIT DEPARTMENT is created.

COLLECTION DEPARTMENT The functions of the collection department of a bank are more complicated than those of the clearing and transit departments. Among items handled by the collection department are presentation for payment of coupons, notes, drafts, or acceptances at proper places of presentment; surrendering of documents attached to drafts, notes, etc., upon payment or acceptance; presentment of periodical file collections on installment contracts or notes secured by collateral involving such part payments; handling of any items, such as checks, notes, drafts, and acceptances, that are not collectible by the clearing or transit departments.

Each collection item is given individual care, as mishandling might lead to legal implications. Each collection is given a separate number, which facilitates tracing and reference in correspondence or advices. Items are carefully recorded with complete descriptions. The work of the collection department in large banks is often subdivided into subdivisions as to items or as to local, out-of-town, incoming from other banks, file, and other collections.

BIBLIOGRAPHY

CORNS, M. C. *The Practical Operations and Management of a Bank*, 2nd ed., 1968.
GUSHEE, J. W. H. "Correspondent Bank Services." In BAUGHN, W. H., and WALKER, C. E., *The Bankers' Handbook*, rev. ed., 1978.

COLLECTION ITEMS Checks, drafts, notes, or acceptances deposited with a bank for credit only if and when payment is made, as distinguished from CASH ITEMS, which are credited to the customer's account upon receipt, but which are subject to cancellation in case of nonpayment. Most items deposited are cash items. Collection items are those where some doubt is entertained by the depositor of their eventual payment and they are therefore accorded individual treatment, each item being given a special number for the purpose of identification and a separate deposit slip describing it in detail. Collection items may be divided into four classes: city collections—items drawn on banks, corporations, or individuals within the city; country collections—items drawn on out-of-town banks, corporations, etc.; special collection items, with special documents attached, e.g., bills of lading, mortgages, stocks, and bonds; foreign collections—items drawn on banks, individuals, etc., located in foreign countries.

COLLECTION LEDGER A ledger, also known as float ledger, constituting a part of the bookkeeping records of a bank transit department for the purpose of temporarily holding charges to various banks for checks and other items while in transit or process of collection. Separate ledgers are provided for items forwarded for collection to Federal Reserve banks and those forwarded directly to collecting agents. The collection ledger is usually a Boston or progressive type ledger, with an extra column placed next to the debit column so that the availability date of each posting may be indicated.

By reference to the collection ledger, it is possible to ascertain the amount of items in process of collection through the Federal Reserve check collection system and through country correspondents or collecting agents. These amounts are tied up with the general ledger through the accounts entitled "due from Federal Reserve bank, collections" and "due from banks, collections," respectively. As items are collected, the collection ledger accounts are credited and the Federal Reserve bank or country correspondent is debited.

COLLECTION LETTER A letter of transmittal or deposit slip accompanying a collection item, i.e., one to be credited to the sender's account only if and when collected. Collection items are treated individually, given a separate collection number for identification purposes, and only one is listed on a single collection letter.

Collection letters are usually form letters. Completed, they contain the following information: name of collecting agent, date forwarded for collection, name of sender (owner), sender's collection number, name of maker or drawer, where payable, maturity date if the item is a note or acceptance, whether the item is to be protested or not, amount, special instructions.

COLLECTION NUMBER The number assigned to a collection item in the accompanying COLLECTION LETTER and by which it is identified in subsequent correspondence and the records.

COLLECTION PERIOD In RATIO ANALYSIS of financial statements, the "average" collection period is the number of days that the receivables represent when compared with annual net credit sales. This may be compared with the known credit terms of sale, to judge whether or not the receivables on the average are in line. Although conventionally receivables are said to include accounts and notes receivable, notes receivable should be included when they arise normally out of the credit terms of sale, and relatively few U.S. firms contemplate payment for invoices by the customers' notes. The ratio may be computed by either of two methods: (1) annual credit sales are reduced to daily basis by division by 365 days, and such daily credit sales are then divided into the total of the receivables to compute the number of days of credit sales represented by the receivables; (2) annual credit sales are divided by the receivables to arrive at the turnover rate, e.g., 12 times, which then on a 12 months' basis means an average collection period of one month.

COLLECTIONS See CITY COLLECTION DEPARTMENT, CLEARING-HOUSE, COLLECTION ITEMS, COUPON COLLECTION DEPARTMENT, FEDERAL RESERVE CHECK COLLECTION SYSTEM, FEDERAL RESERVE INTERDISTRICT COLLECTION SYSTEM, MESSENGER, NOTE TELLER, TRANSIT DEPARTMENT.

COLLECTION TELLER A bank teller who supervises the collection of checks and other items deposited for credit only if and when collected.

See CITY COLLECTION DEPARTMENT, COLLECTION CLERK, TRANSIT DEPARTMENT.

COLLECTIVE BARGAINING The process of negotiation between management and unions over a contract. The National Labor Relations Act of 1935, or Wagner Act, mandated that management bargain in good faith with unions. This act established the National Labor Relations Board to oversee the negotiation processes.

COLLUSION Any agreement, explicit or implicit, between firms that adversely affects the competitive process.

COLONIAL BILLS Colonies of the continental European countries usually settled their trade balances in the currency of the mother country, bills of exchange drawn being payable in the mother country's currency. Although no longer colonies, sterling members of the British Commonwealth (and a few other countries having long tradition of linkage with sterling, such as Burma, Iceland, and Iraq) continue trade linkage with the United Kingdom, pegging of currencies to sterling, holding of reserves in sterling, and free access to central gold and dollar reserves held in London.

See STERLING AREA.

COMBINATION This term has two meanings:

1. An association of individuals or corporations for the furtherance of some project.
2. In business relationships, a broad term going beyond mergers and consolidations to include informal methods such as "gentlemen's agreements," pools, association agreements, and cartels; "communities of interest"; interlocking directorates; and purchase and sale contracts, as well as use of the lease, trust, and holding company as combinational devices. The Sherman Antitrust Act of 1890 is directed against "every . . . combination in the form of trust or other-wise . . . " in restraint of trade or commerce among the several states or with foreign nations.

See ANTITRUST LAWS, BUSINESS COMBINATIONS, MERGERS.

ENCYCLOPEDIA OF BANKING AND FINANCE

COMMERCE, DEPARTMENT OF

U.S. Department of Commerce

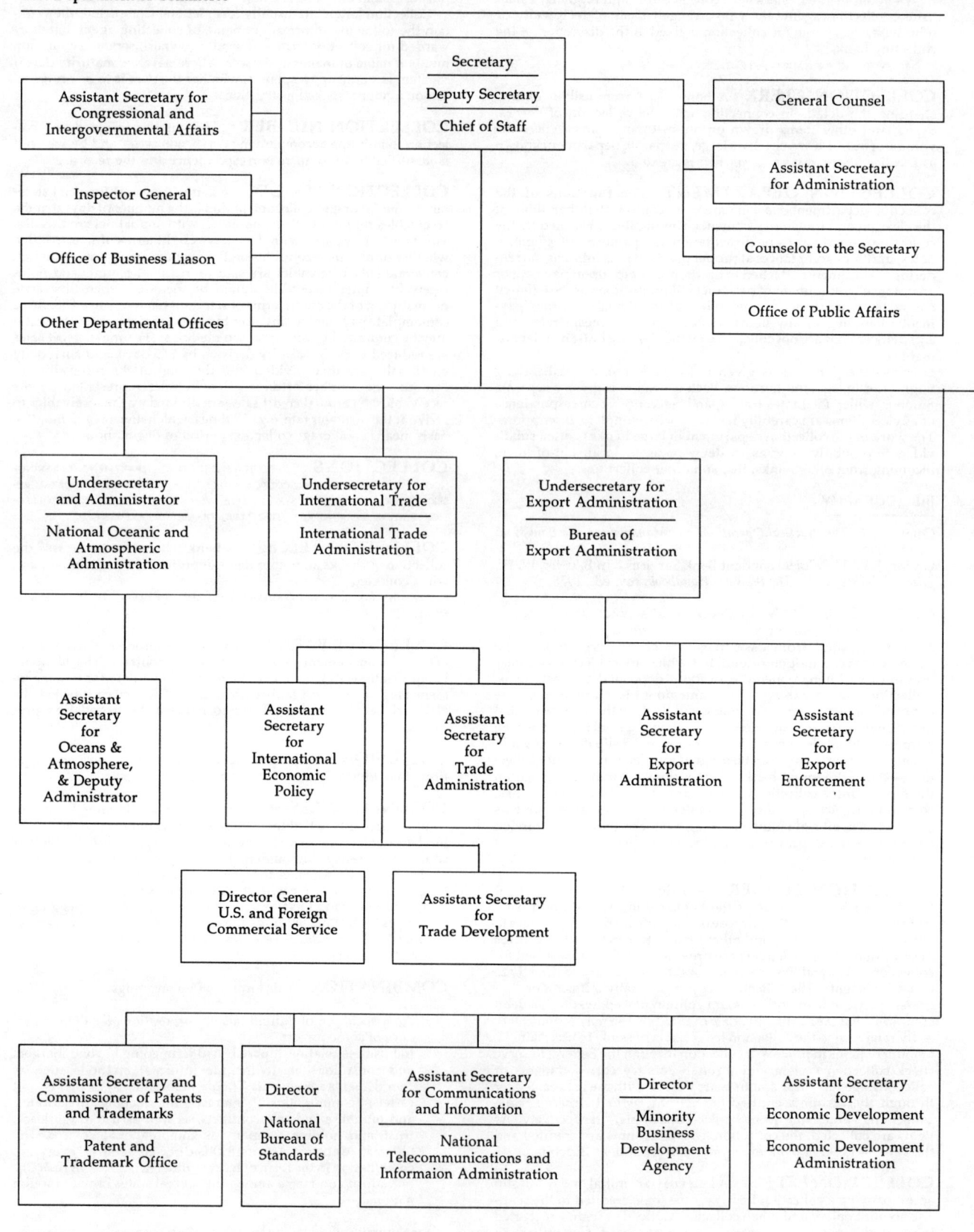

- Secretary / Deputy Secretary / Chief of Staff
  - Assistant Secretary for Congressional and Intergovernmental Affairs
  - Inspector General
  - Office of Business Liason
  - Other Departmental Offices
  - General Counsel
  - Assistant Secretary for Administration
  - Counselor to the Secretary
    - Office of Public Affairs

- Undersecretary and Administrator — National Oceanic and Atmospheric Administration
  - Assistant Secretary for Oceans & Atmosphere, & Deputy Administrator

- Undersecretary for International Trade — International Trade Administration
  - Assistant Secretary for International Economic Policy
  - Assistant Secretary for Trade Administration
    - Director General U.S. and Foreign Commercial Service
    - Assistant Secretary for Trade Development

- Undersecretary for Export Administration — Bureau of Export Administration
  - Assistant Secretary for Export Administration
  - Assistant Secretary for Export Enforcement

- Assistant Secretary and Commissioner of Patents and Trademarks — Patent and Trademark Office
- Director — National Bureau of Standards
- Assistant Secretary for Communications and Information — National Telecommunications and Informaion Administration
- Director — Minority Business Development Agency
- Assistant Secretary for Economic Development — Economic Development Administration

ENCYCLOPEDIA OF BANKING AND FINANCE

U.S. Department of Commerce (continued)

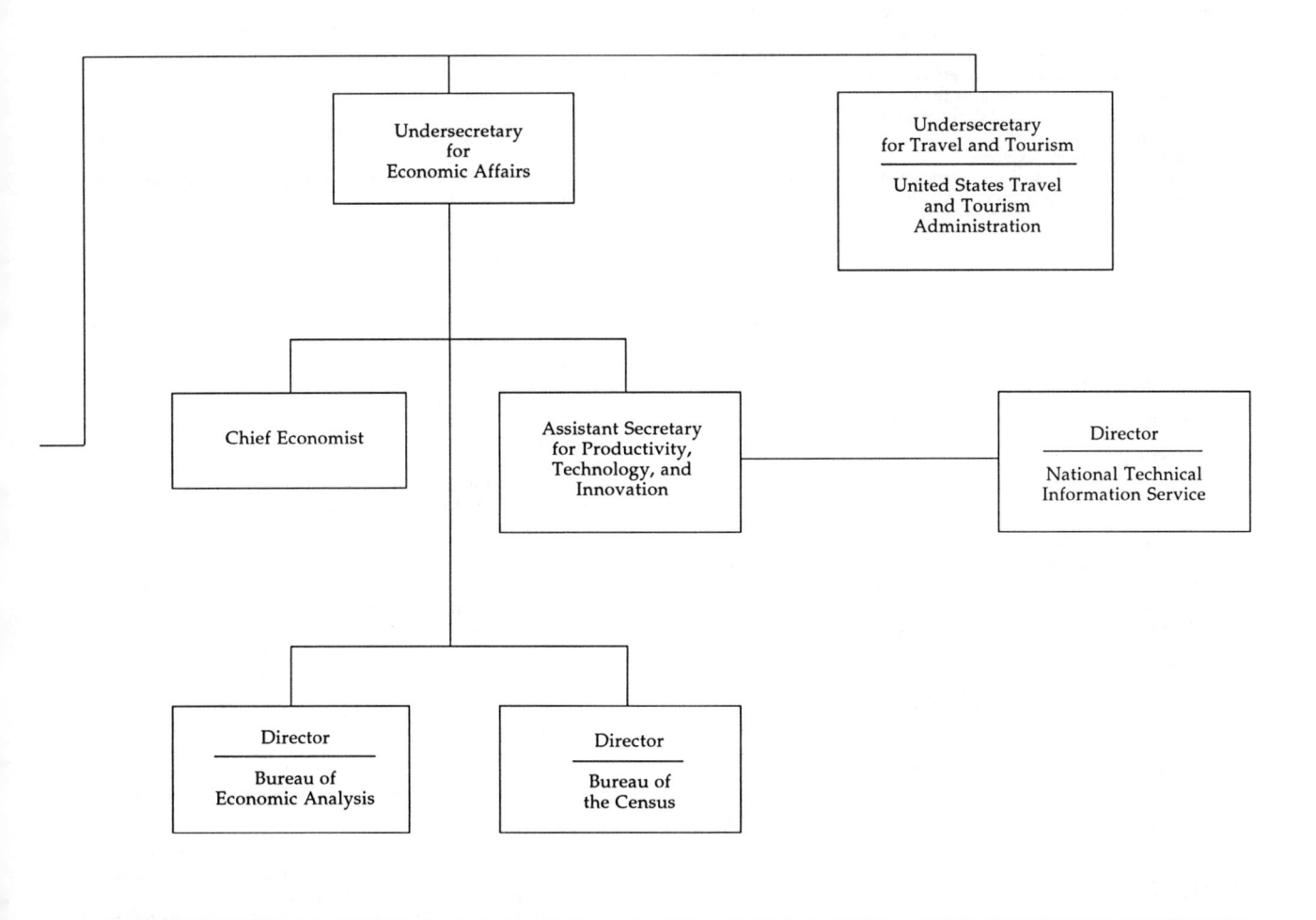

```
                    ┌─────────────────┐              ┌─────────────────┐
                    │  Undersecretary │              │  Undersecretary │
                    │       for       │              │ for Travel and  │
                    │ Economic Affairs│              │     Tourism     │
                    └─────────────────┘              ├─────────────────┤
                             │                       │ United States   │
                             │                       │ Travel and      │
                             │                       │ Tourism         │
                             │                       │ Administration  │
                             │                       └─────────────────┘
            ┌────────────────┼────────────────┐
   ┌────────────────┐  ┌─────────────────────┐                  ┌──────────────────┐
   │ Chief Economist│  │ Assistant Secretary │                  │    Director      │
   └────────────────┘  │ for Productivity,   ├──────────────────┤                  │
                       │ Technology, and     │                  │ National Technical│
                       │ Innovation          │                  │ Information Service│
                       └─────────────────────┘                  └──────────────────┘
            ┌────────────────┬────────────────┐
   ┌────────────────┐                ┌─────────────────┐
   │    Director    │                │    Director     │
   ├────────────────┤                ├─────────────────┤
   │   Bureau of    │                │   Bureau of     │
   │Economic Analysis│               │   the Census    │
   └────────────────┘                └─────────────────┘
```

COMMERCE, DEPARTMENT OF The Department of Commerce was designated as such by an act of March 4, 1913 (37 Stat. 736), which reorganized the Department of Commerce and Labor (created in 1903) by transferring all labor activities into a new and separate Department of Labor. The organizational scheme of the Department of Commerce, as of 1988, is shown in the appended chart.

Under the direct supervision of the Secretary of Commerce are five major subdivisions, each headed by an undersecretary, and a group of smaller agencies, each led by a director or assistant secretary. The functions of the major constituent offices of the Department of Commerce are described below.

The National Oceanic and Atmospheric Administration (NOAA). Formed in 1970 by Reorganization Plan No. 4, NOAA's duties are to explore and chart the oceans and their living resources and to manage those resources; to describe, monitor, and predict conditions in the atmosphere, ocean, sun, and space environments; to issue warnings about impending destructive natural events; to assess the consequences of inadvertent environmental modifications; and to gather and disseminate long-term environmental information. NOAA publishes *The NOAA Magazine* monthly.

The International Trade Administration (ITA). The ITA was established in 1980 to promote world trade and to strengthen the (nonagricultural) international trade and investment position of the United States. The International Economic Policy arm of ITA analyzes foreign commercial barriers and opportunities, counsels U.S. businesses on foreign market conditions, and participates in trade negotiations with other countries; the agency maintains a large number of country desks, with specialists on business practices and opportunities in those countries who are available to the public for advice on trade opportunities. The Trade Administration branch of ITA deals with import and export administration issues and administers U.S. antidumping and countervailing duty laws. The Trade Development Administration Division carries out programs to strengthen U.S. exports through industry analysis and promotion of trade by specific industries; this branch also promotes the formation of export trading companies and issues certificates of review. U.S. and Foreign Commercial Services, through its 50 domestic district officers and overseas posts manages trade fairs, missions, and seminars abroad and assists U.S. businesses and states with export financing. ITA publishes *Business America*, which is mainly concerned with trade developments, and *U.S. Industrial Outlook*, an annual review of conditions and prospects for about 350 U.S. industries.

The Bureau of Export Administration. The newest agency within the Department of Commerce, created in October 1987, this bureau assumed responsibility for export control, particularly the regulation of high-technology exports, a function previously within ITA. Its objectives are to reduce the processing time for export licenses, decontrol the technologies whose export poses no threat to U.S. security, and eliminate unilateral controls on technologies that have widespread foreign availability. It also investigates and enforces export control laws.

COMMERCIAL AGENCIES

Economic Affairs. The principal agencies under this branch of the department are the Bureau of Economic Analysis (BEA) and the Census Bureau. BEA is best known for its preparation, development, and interpretation of the national income and product and balance-of-payments accounts; it also develops and disseminates various business forecasting tools such as the economic indicators. It publishes *Survey of Current Business* and *Business Conditions Digest*. For a description of the Bureau of the Census, *see* CENSUS BUREAU.

U.S. Travel and Tourism Administration. This agency, which has regional offices located in major cities throughout the world, promotes U.S. tourism "exports."

Other major branches of the Department of Commerce include the PATENT AND TRADEMARK OFFICE and the NATIONAL BUREAU OF STANDARDS, each of which is described under its own heading.

BIBLIOGRAPHY

CUTSHAW, K. A. "New Rules on Export of Technical Data Will Be Easier to Use and to Understand." *Business America*, February, 13, 1989.

"How Commerce Helps You Export to Japan." *Nation's Business*, November, 1988.

COMMERCIAL AGENCIES *See* MERCANTILE AGENCIES.

COMMERCIAL BANK A name given to one of the classes of nongovernmental banking institutions under BANK. Commercial banks are designed primarily to finance the production, distribution, and sale of goods, i.e., to lend short-term funds, as distinguished from the service of lending long-term or capital funds. The bulk of deposits of commercial banks consists of demand deposits which are invested in short-term loans. National and state banks are the best examples of commercial banks, although in most states trust companies are also permitted to engage in commercial banking. Private banks are usually commercial banks.

The term full-service banking has been promoted in recent years as a more descriptive term because of the diversification of commercial banks into many operations other than commercial lending, including consumer banking (direct financing of consumers, credit cards, personal loans, consumer receivables financing); mortgage banking; savings banking; commercial sales financing and factoring; international banking and foreign exchange; trust, safe deposit, custody, and investment management functions; underwriting and trading U.S. Government and state and municipal obligations; travel service, travelers checks, money orders, etc.

COMMERCIAL BAR *See* ASSAY OFFICE BAR, EXPORT BAR.

COMMERCIAL BILLS Bills of exchange arising out of commercial transactions as distinguished from clean bankers' bills, travelers' letters of credit, travelers checks, remittance drafts, finance bills, etc.

See FOREIGN BILLS OF EXCHANGE.

COMMERCIAL BORROWERS Merchants (wholesalers and retailers) who borrow on short-term notes largely to finance inventories or who realize on notes and accounts receivable by discounting them.

COMMERCIAL CODE *See* UNIFORM COMMERCIAL CODE.

COMMERCIAL CREDIT This term has two meanings:

1. Used to indicate CREDIT furnished to manufacturers, wholesalers, jobbers, and retailers—those engaged in the manufacture and distribution of commodities. Commercial credit is distinguished from personal, banking, public, agricultural, and investment credit.
2. A transaction involving the use of a commercial letter of credit.

See LETTER OF CREDIT.

COMMERCIAL CREDIT COMPANIES Concerns also sometimes known as credit or finance companies, engaged in the business of lending or buying and collecting on installment contracts and open book accounts from manufacturers and merchants. These companies themselves are often substantial borrowers from banks, although their paper itself is not eligible paper within the meaning of Regulation A of the Board of Governors of the Federal Reserve System.

See ASSIGNED BOOK ACCOUNTS.

COMMERCIAL CREDIT DOCUMENTS A generic term for instruments used in connection with commercial loans, such as bills of lading.

See BILL OF LADING, TRUST RECEIPT, WAREHOUSE RECEIPT.

COMMERCIAL DISCOUNTS This term has two meanings:

1. Notes given to lending banks by mercantile firms upon which interest is paid in advance.
2. Cash discounts offered by a seller to a purchaser to encourage the payment of invoices in advance of the maturity allowed by the terms of credit.

See CASH DISCOUNT.

COMMERCIAL PAPER All classes of short-term negotiable instruments (notes, bills, and acceptances) that arise out of commercial, as distinguished from speculative, investment, real estate, personal, or public transactions; short-term notes, bills of exchange, and acceptances arising out of industrial, agricultural, or commercial transactions, the essential qualities of which are short-term maturity (three to six months), automatic or self-liquidating nature, and nonspeculativeness in origin and purpose of use.

To be eligible for discount at Federal Reserve banks, commercial, agricultural, and industrial paper must have the following characteristics (Regulation A of the Board of Governors of Federal Reserve System):

1. It must be a negotiable note, draft, or bill of exchange bearing the endorsement of a member bank, which has been issued or drawn, or the proceeds of which have been used or are to be used in producing, purchasing, carrying, or marketing goods in one or more of the steps of the process of production, manufacture, or distribution; or in meeting current operating expenses of a commercial, agricultural, or industrial business; or for the purpose of carrying or trading in direct obligations of the United States (i.e., bonds, notes, Treasury bills, or certificates of indebtedness of the United States). (The last purpose referred to is *not* in keeping with the traditional concept of "commercial" paper.)
2. It must not be a note, draft, or bill of exchange, the proceeds of which have been used or are to be used for permanent or fixed investments of any kind, such as land, buildings, or machinery, or for any other fixed capital purpose.
3. It must not be a note, draft, or bill of exchange, the proceeds of which have been used or are to be used for transactions of a purely speculative character, or issued or drawn for the purpose of carrying or trading in stocks, bonds, or other investment securities except direct obligations of the United States.
4. It must have a maturity at the time of discount of not more than 90 days, exclusive of days of grace, except that agricultural paper as defined may have a maturity of not more than nine months, exclusive of days of grace.

In the narrower, technical sense, commercial paper consists of notes maturing in less than one year (usually four to six months) which are the direct obligations of issuing mercantile or industrial corporations or copartnerships, and are sold through the medium of commercial paper dealers and brokers, principally to banks in the larger financial centers and, to a smaller extent, to insurance companies, savings banks, and business corporations. In recent years, however, minimum denomination has become $100,000 generally, and round lots of $1 million are not uncommon. Rates vary according to the credit standing of the issuer and money market conditions. Moody's Investors Service and Standard & Poor's Corporation provide credit ratings for commercial paper borrowers to guide investors buying paper in the commercial paper market; the companies rated are those popular with investors in the money market. Prime paper, of course, is easiest to place with investors.

Commercial paper borrowing may be for the purpose of buying or carrying stocks of merchandise to be quickly resold, and may be regarded as a convenient method of financing inventory requirements at the seasonal peak. Four classes of commercial paper usually appear in the open market: unsecured single name, which accounts

ENCYCLOPEDIA OF BANKING AND FINANCE

for most of the total; two-name paper, including trade paper, i.e., promissory notes given in settlement for goods purchased and endorsed by the seller, and nontrade paper bearing endorsement; collateral notes, which represent a minor portion of the total offered; finance company paper. Besides finance companies, in recent years industrial companies, electric utilities, telephone companies, and bank holding companies have become substantial borrowers in the market. Federal agencies, such as the Export-Import Bank and the Federal National Mortgage Association, have also resorted to this market.

The advantages of issuing commercial paper from the standpoint of the borrower are fivefold.

1. To obtain cash with which to take advantage of cash discounts offered by trade creditors. Credit terms differ among various lines, but almost without exception cash discounts are offered where payment is made in advance of the term allowed for payment of invoices. In the wholesale hardware field, for example, most frequently used terms are 2%/10 days, net 30 days to industrial buyers; and 2%/10 days, net 30 days, E.O.M. (end of month) to jobbers and retailers. In some lines, an even better discount may be allowed for spot cash. Thus discounts and anticipations might range from 12% to 36% or more per year on a rate basis. Since commercial loans even on a 16.5% (1981) basis indicate an important saving on merchandise purchases, cash discounts should be taken, since the cost of failure to take them is high even when resort is had to borrowing for the purpose.
2. To establish national credit. Many enterprises which issue commercial paper are nationally known organizations that have created a national market for their products through interstate selling and advertising. In such cases, the issuance of commercial paper is prima facie evidence of a national credit reputation.
3. To keep a reserve of borrowing power at local banks. Local banking connections may not be able to supply all of a firm's seasonal requirements on open lines of credit or, if able to do so, may not supply the credits at as favorable rates as might be secured through the open market issuance of commercial paper. By issuing commercial paper, a concern may keep its credit lines at its banks in reserve, and meanwhile have recourse to the money market where its commercial paper may be sold at cheaper rates. It is conventional, moreover, for unexhausted lines of credit to cover commercial paper borrowings.
4. To borrow at cheaper rates than is possible at the firm's banks.
5. To establish a broader market for the paper than is possible locally. Commercial paper may be sold anywhere, the function of commercial paper houses and note brokers being to find the most advantageous markets for their paper. Usual "spread" for dealers is 0.125%, but this may rise to 0.25% for smaller issues, or 0.375%. The commercial paper is listed on offering sheets and sold by mail, telephone, and salespersons.

The advantages of commercial paper from the standpoint of buyers are fourfold.

1. The paper is rated prime. In addition to the buyer's own credit check, commercial paper dealers and brokers maintain extensive credit files and the paper that they place is subjected to credit examination. Such middlemen could not long continue in business if commercial paper issuers from whom they purchase could not meet their maturities. Commercial paper dealers and brokers, therefore, in recent decades have raised the standards of their paper through use of audited financial statements, credit investigation, and even influence over the borrowing and operating policies of borrowers, so that losses on commercial paper have been negligible even in years of depression. Commercial paper purchases, therefore, are arranged only with concerns that have a firmly established earning power, open lines of credit to cover outstandings, adequate balances and financial condition, and other satisfactory banking relationships. Insolvency of the Penn Central in June, 1970, with some $82 million in prime rated commercial paper unpaid, was a shock to the commercial paper market and severely affected volume. Confidence gradually returned, however, as evaluation and rating procedures were tightened. As of 1981, a virtual boom in commercial paper outstandings had developed.
2. There is no moral obligation to renew commercial paper, i.e., insistence on payment at maturity and refusal to renew are no reflection on the commercial paper investor. This differs from loans made to a bank's customers, where renewals might be necessary either as protection to the bank or as favor to a temporarily embarrassed borrower.
3. Commercial paper furnishes a good investment medium, either for diversification of the "note pouch" of an investing bank to avoid overlarge proportion of local loans or for paper when the demand for credit over-the-counter has slackened.
4. Commercial paper is attractive on a yield basis, in view of its quality, maturity, and liquidity.

The alleged disadvantage of commercial paper for the buyer is that usually it is single-name paper which does not evidence on its face the purpose for which the proceeds are used. This disadvantage, however, is more apparent than real in view of the credit tests applied to the issuer. Commercial paper is usually purchased on an option running from 10 to 20 days. Within this period, the prospective purchaser retains the right to return any notes that he or she finds to be undesirable, the purpose of the option period being to give the buyer the opportunity to check the credit responsibility of the issuer.

Instead of commercial banks and corporations, as has been the case in past years, chief classes of investors in commercial paper are such nonbank investors as money market funds and other mutual funds, savings banks, insurance companies, private pension funds, and state and municipal retirement funds.

Nonfinancial company commercial paper is issued to meet the needs of public utilities and firms in manufacturing, construction, mining, wholesale and retail trade, and transportation and service industries.

BIBLIOGRAPHY

BANK FOR INTERNATIONAL SETTLEMENTS. *Recent Innovations in International Banking*, Bank for International Settlements, Washington, DC, 1986.

HURLEY, E. "The Commercial Paper Market Since the Mid-Seventies." *Federal Reserve Bulletin*, June, 1982.

SIGUM, M. *The Money Market*. Dow Jones-Irwin, Inc., Homewood, IL, 1983.

COMMERCIAL PAPER FUTURES The commercial paper futures contract on the CHICAGO BOARD OF TRADE calls for delivery of prime commercial paper rated A-1 by Standard & Poor's Corporation and P-1 by Moody's Investors Service, Inc. and approved as deliverable by the Chicago Board of Trade, maturing not more than 90 days from the date of delivery.

The basic unit of trading for commercial paper futures is commercial paper with a stated face value of $1 million (or multiples thereof).

Prices are quoted as an annualized discount. Minimum price fluctuations are 0.01%, also known as one basis point, which is $25 per contract (minimum price fluctuations are calculated on the basis of 0.01% of $1 million – $100; $100 then is divided by four because prices are quoted on a 90-day basis, rather than 360-day).

Normal daily limits on price fluctuations are 0.25% (25 basis points or $625 per contract) above and below the previous day's settlement price. Price limits do not apply to trading in contracts for delivery during a specific month on or after the last business day of the preceding month.

In all other futures contracts traded on the exchange the long is the taker of delivery and the short is the deliverer of the commodity; this is reversed in commercial paper futures. Long is defined as the commitment to deliver paper and short as the commitment to take delivery. In other words, the short commits to deliver the loan; the long commits to pay in commercial paper. This allows the long to make money when the price goes up and the short to make money when the price goes down, just as in other commodity markets.

BIBLIOGRAPHY

ANREDER, S. S. "Ballooning Debt: Month by Month, Commercial Paper Soars to New Highs." *Barron's*, May 28, 1979.

Business Week. "Rush into U.S. Paper." January 26, 1981.
MURRAY, R. F. "Lessons for Financial Analysts." In "Lessons of the Penn Central Debacle," *Journal of Finance,* May, 1971.
PUGLISI, D. J. "Commercial Paper: A Primer." *Federal Home Loan Bank Board Journal,* December, 1980.
SALSBURY, S. *Inside the Penn Central Crisis,* 1980.
WALSH, J. M. "Growing Use of Commercial Paper Market." *Euromoney,* May, 1981.

COMMERCIAL PAPER HOUSE See NOTE BROKERS.

COMMERCIAL PAPER NAMES Among bank credit persons, refers to corporations and partnerships which habitually borrow through the open market by issuing COMMERCIAL PAPER.

COMMERCIAL PARITIES See FOREIGN EXCHANGE.

COMMERCIAL STOCKS Stocks of grain reported at leading grain centers, as reported by the Department of Agriculture. These reports are of interest to the trader in commodities as bearing on the supply and demand situation.

COMMISSION In general, compensation paid by a principal to an agent for services rendered in that capacity. The charge made by brokers or banks for various services rendered to customers. Commissions are charged by broker members of the various stock and commodity exchanges for buying and selling securities, commodities, etc. Commission schedules for executing orders on the various stock and commodity exchanges are the subject of regulation by the exchanges concerned, as to rates for members and nonmem-bers (the public), for different classes of securities (stocks, bonds) and commodities, and for both round and odd or job lots. The 1975 Securities Act Amendments prohibited the imposition of any schedule or fixing of rates of commissions, allowances, discounts, or other fees by a national securities exchange to be charged by its members for effecting exchange transactions. The Securities and Exchange Commission adopted its Rule 19b-3, eliminating fixed commissions on exchange transactions as of May 1, 1975.

Banks charge fees or commissions for acting as custodian, fiscal agent, registrar, or stock transfer agent, and for various trust services, issuing letters of credit, accepting drafts drawn under letters of credit, etc.

Note brokers charge commission for selling commercial paper, and money brokers for placing loans.

COMMISSION CREDIT BUREAU A special mercantile agency, the service of which is confined to release of credit information upon textile and dry goods names, including all branches of these trades.

COMMISSIONER OF BANKING In state regulation of banks and trust companies, a title to designate the official charged with such responsibility; also known as superintendent of banks in some states.

See STATE BANKING DEPARTMENT.

COMMISSION HOUSE A brokerage concern, a member or members of which are also members of a stock or other exchange and execute orders to buy and sell on such exchange or exchanges, as distinguished from exchange members who trade only for their own accounts.

COMMISSION TRADE A transaction in which the legal relationship is that of principal (customer) and agent (broker) and in which the broker is compensated for his or her services by a COMMISSION. No commission is charged in transactions wherein a dealer acts as principal in the transaction with the customer, as in such capacity the firm is not acting as agent but for its own account. Where the commission broker on the floor of the stock exchange enlists the aid of a floor broker in execution of public's orders, the floor broker's commission comes out of the total commission paid by the public customer to the commission broker; no extra commission is charged to the public customer. Odd lot charges of ODD LOT DEALERS, however, are shifted to the public customers placing odd lot orders (buy or sell) through commission brokers.

COMMITMENT A pledge or engagement; a contract involving financial responsibility or a contingent financial obligation to be performed in the future, e.g., an obligation to pay for subscribed stock on call, to take up bonds subscribed or purchased on the delivery date, or orders entrusted to a broker for buying and selling securities.

BIBLIOGRAPHY

BERLIN, M. "Loan Commitments: Insurance Contracts in a Risky World." *Federal Reserve Bank of Philadelphia Business Review,* May/June, 1986.
MELNIK, A., and PLANT, S. E. "The Economics of Loan Commitment Contracts: Credit Pricing and Utilization." *Journal of Banking and Finance,* June, 1986.

COMMITTEE FOR ECONOMIC DEVELOPMENT An independent research and educational organization consisting of business executives and educators. It is nonprofit, nonpartisan, and nonpolitical.

COMMITTEE ON LUNACY A person appointed by a court, usually upon the initiative of relatives, to administer the affairs and protect the state of a person adjudged to be a lunatic. The term is synonymous with CONSERVATOR, the terminology used varying among the states.

COMMITTEE ON UNIFORM SECURITIES IDENTIFICATION PROCEDURES A committee of the American Bankers Association which devised numerical and alphabetical descriptions of securities traded on the exchanges and in the over-the-counter markets, as well as certain others.

The problem is that there is no uniformity in the security identification codes in use within the securities and banking industries. Uniformity in numerical identification is a prerequisite for the optimum use of computers and other machines in processing securities transactions within and between the two industries.

Under the Committee on Uniform Securities Identification Procedures (CUSIP) system, a unique and permanent number, much like an individual's Social Security number, is assigned to each security, both corporate and governmental. More than one million CUSIP numbers have been assigned to specific securities. General agreement has been reached on placement of the CUSIP number on stock certificates; both the New York Stock Exchange and the American Society of Corporate Secretaries specified that it should be in the lower right-hand portion of the "open throat" of the certificate.

COMMODITIES A basic agricultural, mineral, or other basic product traded on a commodity exchange. A commodity exchange is an organization typically owned by its trading members organized to facilitate bringing buyers and sellers of various commodities, or their agents, together to foster spot or futures trading in specified commodities. A spot sale of a commodity is one for cash and current delivery. A commodity futures contract is a contract to purchase or sell a specific amount of a given commodity at a future date.

The Commodity Exchange Act of 1936 regulates trading on the commodity exchanges and strives to reduce fraud and manipulation in commodities and to establish limitations in trading to prevent excessive speculation. The Commodity Exchange Commission, established by the Commodity Exchange Act of 1922, consisted of the U.S. Secretary of Commerce, Secretary of Agriculture and the Attorney General. The Commodity Exchange Commission was succeeded by the Commodity Futures Trading Commission upon passage of the Commodity Futures Trading Commission Act of 1974.

Major commodity exchanges include:

AMEX Commodities Exchange, Inc.	
Chicago Board of Trade	(CBOT)
Chicago Mercantile Exchange	(CME)
Chicago Rice and Cotton Exchange	(CRCE)
Coffee, Sugar & Cocoa Exchange	(CSCE)
Commodity Exchange	(COMEX)
Kansas City Board of Trade	(KCBOT)
MidAmerica Commodity Exchange	(MACE)
Minneapolis Grain Exchange	(MGE)

New York Cotton Exchange	(CTN)
New York Futures Exchange	(NYFE)
New York Mercantile Exchange	(NYME)
Philadelphia Board of Trade	(PBOT)

See CHICAGO BOARD OF TRADE; CHICAGO MERCANTILE EXCHANGE; COFFEE, SUGAR & COCOA EXCHANGE, INC.; COMMODITY EXCHANGE ACT; COMMODITY EXCHANGE COMMISSION; COMMODITY EXCHANGE, INC.; COMMODITY EXCHANGES; COMMODITY FUTURES TRADING COMMISSION; NEW YORK COTTON EXCHANGE; NEW YORK MERCANTILE EXCHANGE.

BIBLIOGRAPHY

BUCKLEY, J., ed., *Guide to World Commodity Markets.* Gale Research Co., Detroit, MI, 1986.
Commodity Futures Trading: A Bibliography. Chicago Board of Trade, Chicago, IL. Annual.
Commodity Year Book. Commodity Research Bureau, Inc., New York, NY. Annual.
TAUCHER, F. A. *The 1990 Commodity Trader's Almanac.* Probus Publishing Co., Chicago, IL, 1989.
TAYLOR, W. T. *Commodity Trading Systems, Software & Databases.* Probus Publishing Co., Chicago, IL, 1986.

COMMODITY CREDIT CORPORATION The Commodity Credit Corporation (CCC) was organized October 17, 1933, pursuant to Executive Order No. 6340. Originally incorporated under the laws of the state of Delaware, this agency was managed by and operated in close affiliation with the RECONSTRUCTION FINANCE CORPORATION up to July 1, 1939, as an agency of the United States. On that date, the CCC was transferred to and made a part of the U.S. Department of Agriculture, pursuant to the President's Reorganization Plan 1. Approval of the Commodity Credit Corporation Charter Act (P.L. 806, 80th Congress) on June 29, 1948, established the CCC, effective July 1, 1948, as an agency of the United States under a permanent federal charter. P.L. 85, 81st Congress, approved June 7, 1949, amended the charter act.

The Commodity Credit Corporation Charter Act, as thus amended, authorizes the CCC to:

1. Support prices of agricultural commodities through loans, purchases, payments, and other operations.
2. Make available materials and facilities required in the production and marketing of agricultural commodities.
3. Procure agricultural commodities for sale to other government agencies, foreign governments, and domestic, foreign, or international relief or rehabilitation agencies, and to meet domestic requirements.
4. Remove and dispose of surplus agricultural commodities.
5. Increase domestic consumption of agricultural commodities through development of new markets, marketing facilities, and uses.
6. Export or cause to be exported, as aid in the development of foreign markets for agricultural commodities.
7. Carry out such other operations as Congress may specifically authorize or provide for.

The CCC is directed to utilize, to the maximum extent practicable, the customary channels, facilities, and arrangements of trade and commerce in carrying on purchasing and selling operations (except sales to other government agencies) and in conducting warehousing, transporting, processing, and handling operations.

The CCC may contract for the use of plants and facilities for the handling, storing, processing, servicing, and transporting of agricultural commodities subject to its control. The CCC has authority to acquire personal property and to rent or lease office space necessary for the conduct of its business. It is prohibited from acquiring real property or any interest therein except for the purposes of protecting its financial interests and for providing adequate storage to carry out its programs effectively and efficiently. No refrigerated cold-storage facilities may be constructed or purchased except with funds specially provided by Congress for that purpose.

To encourage storage of grain on farms, the CCC is directed to make loans available to grain producers for financing the construction or purchase of suitable storage.

The CCC is authorized to accept strategic and critical materials produced abroad in exchange for agricultural commodities it acquires.

Operations of the CCC are administered by the personnel and through the facilities of the Agricultural Stabilization and Conservation Service, an organization set up within the Department of Agriculture on November 2, 1953, which administers CCC programs including price support; disposal, through domestic and foreign sale, barter, transfer, and donation of government-owned surplus farm products; International Wheat Agreement; storage facility loans; transportation, warehousing, and relative service activities; and certain supply and foreign purchase operations.

The commodity loan program and other CCC activities are governed, as of 1987, by the Food Security Act of 1985 (1985 from bill) and the CCC charter. The 1985 farm bill, as amended, extended CCC support of sugar beets and sugarcane and continued the soybean loan support program and quotas for peanuts. The act also continued the target price system to augment commodity loans in supporting farm income and prices.

TARGET PRICES are the basis of "deficiency" payments to producers that participate in wheat, feed grains, cotton, and rice programs. Producers receive CCC deficiency payments equal to the difference between the established target price of a commodity and the higher of actual market or CCC loan value of the commodity. Program participants must conform to specified acreage reduction and soil conservation requirements to be eligible for CCC deficiency payments and other USDA benefits.

Other CCC activities under the 1985 farm bill include: commodity marketing loans to enhance U.S. competitiveness in world markets; rental payments to producers to remove erodible land from production under the conservation reserve program; purchases of dairy products to bolster prices received by dairy producers; and payments to dairy producers to eliminate excess capacity in the dairy industry.

Finances. The capital of the CCC was established at $3 million in 1933. The act of April 10, 1936, increased the capitalization to $100 million, a level at which it has remained ever since. The capital stock is entirely owned by the U.S.

The CCC borrows from the U.S. Treasury to meet its daily cash requirements. It may also borrow from private lenders. As of 1988, CCC has authority to have outstanding borrowings of up to $30 billion at any one time. The corporation is authorized to be reimbursed with U.S. Treasury funds for net realized losses each fiscal year. Net realized gains during a fiscal year are to be deposited in Treasury and credited to miscellaneous receipts. Net realized losses and costs of price support and related operations between October 17, 1933, and September 30, 1987, totaled $166 billion. Net realized losses for the fiscal year ending September 30, 1987, were $26.8 billion; this amount includes $15.1 billion in outstanding loans and $11.7 billion in inventory. Actual total net outlays of the corporation were $22.4 billion in fiscal year 1987.

Management. Management of the CCC is vested in a board of directors, subject to the general supervision and direction of the Secretary of Agriculture, who is an ex officio director and is chairman of the board. The board consists of six members (in addition to the Secretary of Agriculture), who are appointed by the President by and with the advice and consent of the Senate.

The Commodity Credit Corporation Charter Act, as amended, provides for an advisory board consisting of five members appointed by the President. Not more than three of the members shall belong to the same political party. The advisory board is required to meet at the call of the Secretary of Agriculture at least every 90 days. The function of this board, which consists of members having broad agricultural and business experience, is to survey the general policies of the CCC, including those connected with the purchase, storage, and sale of commodities, and the operation of lending and price support programs.

The Secretary of Agriculture is directed to appoint such officers and employees as may be necessary for the conduct of the CCC's business, define their authority and duties, delegate to them such of the powers vested in the CCC as he may determine, require that such of them as he may designate be bonded, and fix penalties therefor.

For details on how the CCC operates in price support of commodities, and the activities related to price support, see PRICE SUPPORT.

COMMODITY EXCHANGE ACT The original act was the Grain Futures Act of 1922. In 1936, the law was amended to include commodities other than grain and its short title was changed

COMMODITY EXCHANGE AUTHORITY

to Commodity Exchange Act (49 Stat. 1491, June 15, 1936). The act was amended various times, the amendments of February, 1968, broadening regulatory powers by giving authority to the COMMODITY EXCHANGE AUTHORITY (CEA) and the Secretary of Agriculture to deny registration to commission merchants and floor brokers for falsification or omission of facts from applications, or other good cause (previously, denial of registration could be made only upon revocation or suspension of a prior registration) and by giving authority to the CEA to set standards of fitness for registrants as futures commission merchants, which the CEA later in 1968 exercised.

The Commodity Exchange Act was succeeded by the Commodity Futures Trading Commission Act of 1974 (88 Stat. 1389; 7 U.S.C. 4a), which established the COMMODITY FUTURES TRADING COMMISSION.

COMMODITY EXCHANGE AUTHORITY The agency of the Department of Agriculture which acted for the Secretary of Agriculture in the administration and enforcement of the COMMODITY EXCHANGE ACT. The Commodity Exchange Authority also acted for the COMMODITY EXCHANGE COMMISSION, consisting of the Secretary of Sgriculture, the Secretary of Commerce, and the Attorney General, which functioned principally in the fixing of limits on speculative trading and violations of law by contract markets.

Both the Commodity Exchange Authority and the Commodity Exchange Commission were succeeded in 1974 by the COMMODITY FUTURES TRADING COMMISSION.

COMMODITY EXCHANGE COMMISSION Established by the Commodity Exchange Act of September 21, 1922 (42 Stat. 998; 7 U.S.C. 2, 8), to initiate complaints, conduct hearings, and issue cease and desist or suspension orders for violations of the act by any board of trade (commodity exchange) designated as a contract market; conduct hearings and fix trading limits in connection with the sale of commodities for future delivery made on or subject to the rules of contract markets; hear and decide complaints of contract markets seeking to exclude from membership therein any cooperative organization or corporation; hear and decide appeals from a refusal by the Secretary of Agriculture of designation of any board of trade as a contract market.

The Commodity Exchange Commission was succeeded by the COMMODITY FUTURES TRADING COMMISSION upon passage of the Commodity Futures Trading Commission Act of 1974.

COMMODITY EXCHANGE, INC. The successor, by merg-er in 1933 during the Great Depression, to four former commodity exchanges:

New York Hide Exchange
National Metal Exchange
National Raw Silk Exchange
New York Rubber Exchange

The exchange, now located in the World Trade Center in New York, started operations by providing facilities for dealing in futures in crude rubber, raw silk, hides, silver, copper, and tin. COMEX is the world's most active metals market and is among the largest commodity futures exchanges in the world. As the dominant exchange for gold futures and options trading, COMEX is a major force in the world gold market. In addition to its prominence in international gold trading, COMEX is the dominant world market for silver and copper futures and options and is the only U.S. exchange to offer trading in aluminum futures. Contracts on U.S. Government securities and foreign currencies were introduced in the mid-1970s. These were joined, in the early 1980s, by futures on stock indexes. Later, options on these products were introduced. Commodity futures trades for recent years are shown in the appended table.

According to the Commodity Exchange, Inc., COMEX provides a centralized market where contracts for the future delivery of various commodities are bought and sold by competitive auction. Each contract for a particular commodity is identical, representing a specific amount and grade of a commodity designated for delivery at a specified date, which may be as far as two years in the future. The contracts are standardized; only the price of the contract is negotiable and is determined on the floor of the exchange. Futures markets serve both hedgers and speculators.

COMEX gold options are available for several different expiration dates and strike prices. Following is a summary of major contract features.

Contract months. COMEX conducts trading in both call and put options on the nearest four of the following COMEX gold futures contract months: February, April, June, August, October, and December.

Strike prices. On the first day of trading for an option contract, there are nine listed strike prices for puts and nine for calls. Additional strike prices are then added in accordance with futures price movements based on a predetermined formula.

Trading hours. Hours of 8:20 A.M. and 2:30 P.M. EST are observed.

Expiration. Gold options expire on the second Friday of the month prior to the expiration of the underlying futures contract.

Exercise. An option can be exercised until 3:00 P.M. on any business day on which the option is listed for trading. On expiration day, the buyer has until 4:00 P.M. to exercise an option.

COMEX silver futures contract calls for delivery of a specified grade of refined silver in standard bars during one of the specified futures months.

Trading months. Trading is conducted for delivery during the current calendar month; the next two calendar months; any January, March, May, July, September, and December falling within a 23-month period beginning with the current month.

Trading hours. Hours of 9:05 A.M. to 2:25 P.M. EST are observed.

Trading unit and grade. In fulfillment of every silver futures contract, the seller must deliver 5,000 troy ounces (6% more or less) of refined silver, assaying not less than 999 fineness, cast bars weighing 1,000 or 1,100 troy ounces each and bearing a serial number and identifying stamp of a refiner approved and listed by COMEX.

Price multiples. Price changes are registered in multiples of one-tenth of one cent ($.001) per troy ounce, equivalent to $5 per contract.

Price fluctuation limits. During any one trading day, price fluctuation for each delivery month is limited to 50 cents per troy ounce above or below the settlement price established at the close of the preceding business day.

COMEX is a not-for-profit membership organization similar to a securities exchange. It's 772 seats are held by individuals and on behalf of firms who meet rigorous financial requirements. COMEX policy is established by an elected governing board representing the three primary groups that trade through the exchange and headed by a member-elected chairman. A voting member of the 25-seat board of governors, the president also serves as chief executive officer of the exchange's administrative staff.

COMEX is regulated by the COMMODITY FUTURES TRADING COMMISSION,

Selective Comex Trading Volume

Commodity	Contract Unit	Contracts traded (000)				
		1983	1984	1985	1986	1987
Copper	25,000 lb	3,186.9	2,506.4	2,444.6	1,872.2	2,569.2
Silver	5,000 oz	6,433.0	6,742.5	4,821.2	3,849.7	5,055.7
Gold	100 oz	10,382.8	9,115.5	7,773.8	8,400.2	10,239.8
Aluminum	40,000 lb	11.9	82.7	77.1	52.6	8.5
Moody's Index		—	—	—	—	11.5
Total		20,014.6	18,447.0	15,116.7	14,174.7	17,884.6

Source: Futures Industry Association, Inc.

an independent government agency established in 1975 to administer the provisions of the Commodity Exchange Act. This act subjects all commodity futures and options trading to federal oversight and restricts trading to futures exchanges designated and licensed by the commission.

The Commodity Exchange, Inc. is governed by a board of 25 governors, elected by the membership, including three nonmember public governors.

BIBLIOGRAPHY

COMMODITY EXCHANGE, INC. *Annual Reports.*
Commodity Exchange, Inc. offers numerous educational services:

Brochures:
Member Firm Directory; Rule Book; Overview of COMEX; Gold Futures, An Introduction; Options on Gold Futures, An Introduction; Silver Futures, An Introduction; Options on COMEX Silver Futures, An Introduction; Copper Futures, An Introduction; Options on Copper Futures, An Introduction; Aluminum Futures, A Guide for Investors; Aluminum Futures, A Guide for Hedgers.

Miscellaneous publications:
COMEX Diary; Precious Metal Options, Strategies for the Investor; COMEX: The Game brochure; Hedgemaster brochure; Gold/Silver Ratio booklet.

Software:
COMEX: The Game (precious metals version; copper version); Hedgemaster (Master; Demonstration).

COMMODITY EXCHANGES
Organized markets for trading in commodities and futures contracts and/or cash (spot) trading.

The term exchange includes only those commodity exchanges which are designated as contract markets and have trading activity. On July 18, 1975, the COMMODITY FUTURES TRADING COMMISSION gave contract market designations to many of the exchanges which traded in previously unregulated commodities. The commission had given provisional contract market designations to these exchanges on April 18, 1975, and had extended such designations on May 5, 1975. The effect of the July 18, 1975 designations was to bring under federal regulation all commodities for which a futures market was actively traded. Previously unregulated commodities contracts, such as the COMEX's mercury and rubber contract, for which no contract market designation was granted on that date, were not permitted to continue futures trading after July 18, 1975.

Newer Commodity Exchanges. The NEW YORK FUTURES EXCHANGE opened for business in August, 1980. The New Orleans Commodity Exchange commenced operations in April, 1981. Near the end of fiscal 1979, the Commodity Futures Trading Commission approved the exchange rules which effected the merger of the New York Cocoa Exchange into the New York Coffee & Sugar Exchange, which is known as the COFFEE, SUGAR & COCOA EXCHANGE, INC. The CHICAGO MERCANTILE EXCHANGE includes commodities traded on the International Monetary Market, which merged with the Chicago Mercantile Exchange in March, 1976.

As of 1987, the following commodity exchanges were in operation and designated as contract markets:

AMEX Commodities Exchange, Inc.
Chicago Board of Trade
Chicago Mercantile Exchange
Chicago Rice & Cotton Exchange
Coffee, Sugar & Cocoa Exchange, Inc.
Commodity Exchange, Inc.
Kansas City Board of Trade
Mid-America Commodity Exchange
Minneapolis Grain Exchange
New Orleans Commodity Exchange
New York Cotton Exchange
New York Futures Exchange
New York Merchantile Exchange
Philadelphia Board of Trade

(The Mid-America Commodity Exchange was previously named the Chicago Open Board of Trade until its name change effective November 22, 1972.)

International Commodity Exchanges. Overseas commodity exchanges as of 1981 included the following:

Australia: Sydney Futures Exchange
Austria: Vienna Commodity Exchange
Bermuda: The International Futures Exchange Ltd. (INTEX)
Brazil: Bolsa de Mercadorias de Sao Paulo
Canada: Eastern Lumber Futures Market; Winnipeg Commodity Exchange
France: International Cocoa Futures Market; International Robusta Coffee Futures Market; International White Sugar Futures Market
Germany: Frankfort Corn and Produce Exchange; Grain and Commodity Exchange Rhein Ruhn Duisburg-Essen; Worms Grain and Produce Exchange
Hong Kong: Chinese Gold and Silver Exchange Society; Hong Kong Commodity Exchange Ltd.
India: Bangalore Coffee Board
Indonesia: Indonesian Commodity Exchange Board
Italy: Borsa Merci di Padova; Commodity Exchange of Bologna
Japan: Hokkaido Grain Exchange; Kobe Rubber Exchange; Maibashi Dried Cocoon Exchange; Osaka Grain Exchange; Osaka Textile Exchange; Tokyo Grain Exchange; Toyohashi Dried Cocoon Exchange
Kenya: East Africa Tea Trade Association
Malaysia: Kuala Lumpur Commodity Exchange; Kuala Lumpur Tin Market
The Netherlands: Porker Terminal Market; Potato Terminal Market
Norway: Oslo Fur Auctions Ltd.
Pakistan: Karachi Cotton Association
Singapore: Rubber Association of Singapore; Singapore International Monetary Exchange (SIMEX)
Switzerland: Grain and Produce Exchange of Berne; Zurich Grain Exchange
United Kingdom: Baltic International Freight Futures Exchange; British Fur Trade Association; Coffee Terminal Market Association of London Ltd.; Federation of Commodity Associations; Federation of Oils, Seeds and Fats Association Ltd.; International Commodities Clearing House; International Petroleum Exchange of London Ltd.; Liverpool Cotton Association; London and New Zealand Futures Association; London Cocoa Terminal Market Association Ltd.; London Commodity Exchange Company Ltd.; London Gold Futures Market Ltd.; London Grain Futures Market; London International Financial Futures Exchange (LIFFE); London Jute Association; London Meat Futures Exchange Ltd.; London Metal Exchange; London Potato Futures Market; London Rubber Terminal Market Association Ltd.; London Soya Bean Meal Futures Market; London Sugar Futures Market; Tea Brokers' Association of London.

See COMMODITIES.

COMMODITY FUTURES
Trading in commodity futures contracts has increased in recent years, both in volume and kind, principally reflecting trading innovations by the various commodity exchanges. In fact, trading in the traditional commodities, except for energy products, has declined absolutely and as a proportion of all futures trading. At the same time, trading in financial futures has more than tripled, and trading in index futures, which is relatively new, has more than doubled. These changes are shown in the following tables.

BIBLIOGRAPHY

Basic Facts About Commodity Futures Trading. U.S. Commodities Futures Trading Commission, Washington, DC.
COMMODITY RESEARCH BUREAU. *CRB Commodity Index Report.* Commodity Research Bureau, New York, NY. Weekly.
———. *CRB Commodity Year Book.*
———. *CRB Guide to Commodity Chart Analysis.*
———. *CRB Futures Chart Service.*
———. *CRB Outlook.*
———. *Economics of Futures Trading.*
———. *Electronic Futures Trend Analyzer.* Daily.
———. *Futures Market Service.* Weekly.

COMMODITY FUTURES TRADING COMMISSION

Table 1 / Commodities Traded on U.S. Futures Exchanges, 1983 and 1987

Commodity	Exchanges Where traded*	Contracts traded (000) 1983	1987
Agricultural:		57,829.2	43,366.5
Cocoa	CSCE	1,162.5	5,784.4
Coffee	CSCE	427.4	964.6
Corn	CBT, MCE	12,554.3	7,564.9
Corn Syrup	MGE	—	6.0
Cotton	CRCE (1983), NYCE	1,551.1	1,396.0
Cattle	CME, MCE	4,873.7	5,919.3
Live hogs	CME, MCE	2,899.4	1,084.9
Lumber plywood	CBT (1983), CME	781.4	437.1
Oats	CBT, MCE	371.6	298.1
Orange juice	MGE	124.3	266.6
Pork Bellies	CME	2,043.3	1,097.0
Potatoes	NYME	33.7	6.2
Rice	CRCE	12.3	31.1
Soybean meal	CBT, MCE (1987)	3,872.5	3,801.2
Soybean oil	CBT	3,858.6	3,912.4
Soybeans	CBT, CRCE (1983), MCE	14,851.8	7,796.4
Sugar	CSCE	3,286.1	3,923.4
Sunflower seeds	MGE	0.0	—
Wheat	CBT, KCBT, MCE	5,163.6	3,090.0
Metals:		25,751.2	20,395.1
Aluminum	COMEX	11.9	8.5
Copper	COMEX, MCE (1987)	3,186.9	2,569.2
Gold	CBT, CME, COMEX, KCBT, MCE	12,032.7	10,703.9
Palladium	NUME	241.2	160.3
Platinum	MCE (1987), NYME	1,053.3	1,361.7
Silver	CBT, COMEX, KCBT, MCE (1987)	9,098.2	5,674.4
Energy Products:		2,776.4	20,952.4
Crude oil	CBT (1983), NYME	417.8	14,581.6
Gasoline	CBT (1983), NYME	458.3	2,056.2
Heating oil	CBT (1983), NYME	1,871.5	4,293.4
Propane	NYCE, NYME	—	57.5
Currencies:		11,910.6	20,537.0
Australia dollar	CME	—	53.3
British pound	CME, MCE	1,615.9	2,603.2
Canadian dollar	CME, MCE	558.9	922.3
Deutschemark	CME, MCE	2,430.1	6,122.0
Dutch guilder	CME	—	0.2
Eur. Currency Unit	CME, NYCE	42.5	—
French franc	CME	26.3	10.4

Commodity	Exchanges Where traded*	Contracts traded (000) 1983	1987
Currencies:			
Japanese yen	CME, MCE	3,453.1	5,417.4
Mexican peso	CME	—	40.3
Swiss franc	CME, MCE	3,785.7	5,365.9
Financial Instruments:		28,123.3	95,487.2
Domestic CDs	CME	1,079.6	0.1
Eurodollars	CME	891.1	20,416.2
GNMA mtgs.	CBT	1,692.0	6.6
T-bills	CME, MCE	3,827.7	1,952.6
T-bonds	CBT, MCE	19,817.8	67,856.9
T-notes	CBT	815.1	5,253.8
Indexes:		12,752.9	27,307.3
Commodity Research Bureau	NYFE	—	136.8
CPI-W	CSC	—	0.0
Dollar	NYCE	—	403.8
Institutional	CBT	—	0.2
Major Market Maxi	CBT	—	2,630.9
Mini Value Line	KCBT	15.1	28.5
Moody's	KCBT	—	11.5
Municipal Bonds	CBT	—	1,613.1
NYSE Composite	NYFE	3,506.4	2,915.9
NYSE Financial	NYFE	3.8	—
Russell 2000	NYFE	—	5.6
Russell 3000	NYFE	—	10.7
S&P 100	CME	390.9	—
S&P 500	CME	8,101.7	19,044.7
Value Line	KCBT	725.0	505.6

Note: — indicates no trading; 0.0 indicates fewer than 100 (rounded) contracts.

* CBT = Chicago Board of Trade
CME = Chicago Mercantile Exchange
CRCE = Chicago Rice & Cotton Exchange
CSCE = Coffee, Sugar & Cocoa Exchange
COMEX = Commodity Exchange
KCBT = Kansas City Board of Trade
MCE = MidAmerica Commodity Exchange
MGE = Minneapolis Grain Exchange
NYCE = New York Cotton Exchange
NYFWE = New York Futures Exchange
NYME = New York Mercantile Exchange

Source: Futures Industry Association, Inc.

Table 2 / Composition of Commodity Futures Trading, by Commodity Group, 1983 and 1987

Commodity group	Contracts traded (% of total) 1983	1987	% change 1983–1987
Total	100.0	100.0	60.7
Agricultural	41.6	19.0	−25.0
Metals	18.5	8.9	−20.8
Energy products	2.0	9.2	654.7
Currencies	8.6	9.0	72.4
Financial instruments	20.2	41.8	239.5
Indexes	9.2	12.0	114.1

Source: Futures Industry Association, Inc.

———. *Modern Commodity Futures Trading.*
———. *Techniques of a Professional Commodity Chart Analyst.*
———. *The Fastest Game in Town.*
———. *Understanding the Futures Market.*
———. *Understanding the Securities Market.*
Guide to World Commodity Markets. Gale Research Co., Detroit, MI, 1986.
Options on Futures: A New Way to Participate in Futures. The Chicago Mercantile Exchange, Chicago, IL.
The Options for the Future. New York Futures Exchange, New York, NY.

COMMODITY FUTURES TRADING COMMISSION

Established as an independent agency by the Commodity Futures Trading Commission Act of 1974 (88 Stat. 1389; 7 U.S.C. 4a).

As the successor to the Commodity Exchange Authority under the Department of Agriculture, the Commodity Futures Trading Commission (CFTC) has been given additional authority and responsibilities under the act which are designed to make possible more effective regulation of the commodity futures markets. The commission regulates all commodity futures, whereas many commodities were not regulated under prior law. The act also requires the registration of additional persons engaged in futures trading who were not previously required to register, such as commodity trading advisers, commodity pool operators, and persons associated with futures commission merchants.

The CFTC is empowered to regulate option transactions in commodities, leverage contracts in silver and gold, foreign currencies, and U.S. government and mortgage securities. The act imposes additional requirements on contract markets, such as a demonstration that the market will not be contrary to the public interest, as well as a requirement that markets provide settlement procedures for customers' claims and grievances. Further, the commission is authorized to impose new sanctions, such as fines and penalties, for violations under the act; to enjoin practices in violation of the act; and to litigate its own cases.

Major purposes of the trading regulations are to prevent price manipulation, market corners, and the dissemination of false and misleading commodity and market information affecting commodity prices. Other responsibilities are to protect market users against cheating, fraud, and abusive practices in commodity transactions and to safeguard the handling of traders' margin money and equities by establishing minimum financial requirements for futures commission merchants and by preventing the misuse of such funds by brokers.

CFTC is based in Washington, D C, and maintains regional offices in Chicago, New York, and other locations. The agency's five commissioners are appointed by the president. They serve staggered, five-year terms, with one designated by the president with the consent of the Senate to serve as chairman. No more than three commissioners at any one time may be from the same political party.

The commission regulates trading on the 11 futures exchanges that offer active futures and options contracts. It also regulates the activities of numerous commodity exchange members, public brokerage houses (futures commission merchants), commission-registered futures industry salespeople and associated persons, commodity trading advisers, and commodity pool operations. The Division of Enforcement investigates and prosecutes alleged violations of the Commodity Exchange Act and commission regulations. Violations may involve trading of commodity futures and option contracts on domestic commodity exchanges or the improper marketing of those and similar commission-regulated commodity investment vehicles. The division takes actions against individuals and firms registered with the commission, others who are engaged in commodity futures and options trading on designated exchanges, and those engaged in the unlawful offer and sale of options and futures contracts that are not traded on exchanges.

BIBLIOGRAPHY

"CFTC Renewal Gets Tougher." *Futures*, March, 1989.
COMMODITY FUTURES TRADING COMMISSION. *Annual Reports*.
———. *Basic Facts About Commodity Futures Trading*.
PIERO, K. "Futures and Fraud: Cleaning Up the Industry." *National Underwriter (Life & Health/Financial Services Edition)*, February, 1989.
ZIGAS, D., and SMART, T. "The CFTC Drops Its Kid Gloves." *Business Week*, May 22, 1989.

COMMODITY OPTIONS Options to buy or to sell commodity futures contracts at a specified price within a specified time, similar to stock options. In mid-1978 the COMMODITY FUTURES TRADING COMMISSION suspended trading in commodity options, and subsequently commodity options were statutorily banned.

On October 16, 1978, however, the commission announced the adoption of an amendment to its option regulations which exempted the sale of options on physical commodities (so-called dealer options) by persons and firms which met specified requirements from the general suspension of commodity option transactions. Subsequent amendments to the rules established reporting requirements for both the grantors of dealer options and the futures commission merchants who offer and sell dealer options to the public. And as of June, 1981, permission to trade commodity options on certain commodities was the subject of public hearings by the commission.

With the commission's mid-1978 suspension of the trading in commodity options and the subsequent statutory ban, the Division of Enforcement of the commission took action against a variety of illegal and often fraud-befogged off-exchange commodity transactions during fiscal 1979.

COMMODITY PAPER As originally defined by the Board of Governors of the Federal Reserve System (Regulation A, Series of 1917), a "note, draft, bill of exchange, or trade acceptance accompanied and secured by shipping documents or by a warehouse terminal, or other similar receipt, covering approved and readily marketable, nonperishable staples properly insured."

In a later revision of Regulation A, the elements of commodity paper are governed by the classification "bills of exchange payable at sight or on demand." A Federal Reserve bank may discount for any of its member banks negotiable bills of exchange payable at sight or on demand that bear the endorsement of a member bank; grow out of the domestic shipment or the exportation of nonperishable, readily marketable staples; and are secured by bills of lading or other shipping documents conveying or securing title to such staples. A readily marketable staple within the meaning of the regulation is an article of commerce, agriculture, or industry of such uses as to make it the subject of constant dealings in ready markets with such frequent quotations of price as to make the price easily and definitely ascertainable and the staple itself easy to realize upon by sale at any time.

See FEDERAL RESERVE BOARD REGULATIONS.

COMMODITY PRICES Prices for commodities are quoted either on a cash (spot) basis or on a future basis, the difference being measured mainly by the carrying charges involved in carrying the commodity for the period of the future delivery.

In computation of monthly parity prices, the adjusted base price represents the average price of the commodity for the 10 preceding years, divided by the average of the index of prices received by farmers for the same 10 years. PARITY prices are then computed by multiplying the adjusted base prices by the current index of prices paid by farmers, including interest, taxes, and wage rates.

Producer Price Index (PPI). The most comprehensive measurement of commodity prices is the producer price index of the Bureau of Labor Statistics, U.S. Department of Labor. All types of commodities, from raw materials to fabricated products, are included in the representative commodities selected for the index. For commodities traded on organized exchanges, such as livestock and grains, the quotations (monthly) are furnished by the exchanges or government agencies, or are taken from published sources. For some standardized commodities, such as certain chemicals and specified constructions of cotton gray goods, quotations are taken from authoritative trade publications. For the majority of fabricated products, prices are reported to the BLS by producers. Prices are quoted at the level of the first significant commercial transaction, and for each commodity the reporter is requested to quote the price which is charged to specific types of purchasers. The prices relate to a particular day of the month, about the middle of the month. Insofar as possible, identical qualities of the commodities are priced from period to period, so that the index will measure only real price changes, not changes due to differences in qualities or terms of sale.

The individual price series are combined into the index (new base period of 1967 = 100, to conform with such base period for other governmental indexes) by multiplying the value weight assigned each item by its current price relative, and summing to obtain the current aggregate. The current aggregates are totaled by product classes, subgroups, groups, and all commodities. The current index for each of these is obtained by dividing the current aggregate by its appropriate value weight in the base period. Each commodity price series in the index, as representative of prices for a group of commodities, is assigned its own direct weight (the value of the shipments for sale of that individual commodity), plus the weight of other commodities it was selected to represent in the index. Weights for commodities not priced in the index are assigned to commodities which are priced on the basis of available information on similarity of manufacturing process and price movements.

Uses and Limitations. The producer price index, caution the Joint Economic Committee's staff and the Office of Statistical Standards of the Office of Management and Budget, is based for the most part on producers' prices; therefore it should not be used as a measure of price change at the wholesale market level; nor are the prices those paid or received by wholesalers, jobbers, or distributors. Also, the PPI and the consumer price index should not be used as a measure of the change in retailers' margins in the specified group of commodities, because of differences in weighting and in lists of commodities used. Moreover, the PPI is not designed to measure changes in manufacturers' average realized prices, which are

COMMODITY RATE

Product Price Indexes for Major Commodity Groups
(Indexes: 1967 = 100)

Year	All commodities	Farm products [1]	Processed foods and feeds	All industrial commodities
1929	49.1	64.1		48.6
1930	44.6	54.2		45.2
1931	37.6	39.7		39.9
1932	33.6	29.5		37.3
1933	34.0	31.4		37.8
1934	38.6	40.0		41.6
1935	41.3	48.1		41.4
1936	41.7	49.5		42.2
1937	44.5	52.9		45.2
1938	40.5	42.0		43.4
1939	39.8	40.0		43.3
1940	40.5	41.4		44.0
1941	45.1	50.3		47.3
1942	50.9	64.8		50.7
1943	53.3	75.0		51.5
1944	53.6	75.5		52.3
1945	54.6	78.5		53.0
1946	62.3	90.9		58.0
1947	76.5	109.4	82.9	70.8
1948	82.8	117.5	88.7	76.9
1949	78.7	101.6	80.6	75.3
1950	81.8	106.7	83.4	78.0
1051	91.1	124.2	92.7	86.1
1952	88.6	117.2	91.6	84.1
1953	87.4	106.2	87.4	84.8
1954	87.6	104.7	88.9	85.0
1955	87.8	98.2	85.0	86.9
1956	90.7	96.9	84.9	90.8
1957	93.3	99.5	87.4	93.3
1958	94.6	103.9	91.8	93.6
1959	94.8	97.5	89.4	95.3
1960	94.9	97.2	89.5	95.3
1961	94.5	96.3	91.0	94.8
1962	94.8	98.0	91.9	94.8
1963	94.5	96.0	92.5	94.7
1964	94.7	94.6	92.3	95.2
1965	96.6	98.7	95.5	96.4
1966	98.8	105.9	101.2	98.5
1967	100.0	100.0	100.0	100.0
1968	102.5	102.5	102.2	102.5
1969	106.5	109.1	107.3	106.0
1970	110.4	111.0	112.0	110.0
1971	113.9	112.9	114.3	114.1
1972	119.1	125.0	120.8	117.9
1973	134.7	176.3	148.1	125.9
1974	160.1	187.7	170.9	153.8
1975	174.9	186.7	182.6	171.5
1976	183.0	191.0	178.0	182.4
1977	194.2	192.5	186.1	195.1
1978	209.3	212.5	202.6	209.4
1979	235.6	241.4	222.5	236.5
1980	268.8	249.4	241.2	274.5
Aug. 1980	273.8	263.8	249.4	278.2
Aug. 1981	296.2	257.8	250.7	307.0
1982 [2]	100.0	100.0	100.0	100.0
1983	101.3	101.8	102.0	101.1
1984	103.7	104.8	105.5	103.8
1985	103.2	104.4	100.7	103.7
1986	100.2	103.2	101.2	100.0
1987	102.8	107.1	103.7	102.6

Source: Bureau of Labor Statistics, *Producer Price Indexes*, monthly and annual.

[1] After 1981 Farm Products are replaced by Metal Products.
[2] After 1981 the Index is 1982=100, prior to 1981, excludes Alaska and Hawaii.

affected by product mix and terms of sale as well as by price movements.

The appended table for the producer price index (1967 = 100) compares principal components of the index since 1929.

See BASE PERIOD PRICE, CEILING PRICES, COST OF LIVING INDEX, PARITY INDEX, PRICES, SPOT PRICE.

BIBLIOGRAPHY

BUREAU OF LABOR STATISTICS, U.S. DEPT. OF LABOR. *Quarterly Review of Productivity, Wages, and Prices.*
———. *Monthly Labor Review.*
Joint Economic Committee.
Economic Indicators (monthly), and *Supplement to Economic Indicators* (biennial).

COMMODITY RATE The rate of interest charged on COMMODITY PAPER.

COMMON CARRIER A company authorized to undertake transportation as a regular business, e.g., railroads, motor carriers, steamship companies, express companies, traction lines. Common carriers are subject to the basic law of public callings and as such must furnish service to all who apply, provide adequate facilities for all, charge reasonable rates, and charge nondiscriminatory rates. This law is also applicable to all public service corporations.

COMMON SIZE STATEMENT The 100% statement; facilitates credit analysis and comparison of statements by reducing all items in assets and liabilities to a percentage of the total assets and total liabilities. This method enables the analyst to compare quickly the current statement with past statements for a single company and to compare the subject company with other companies, large or small, as the common size statement reduces the individual asset or liability dollar figures to a common comparable basis of percentages. Customarily, in common size comparison forms the dollar amounts are shown side by side with the common size percentages, as the dollar amounts have an interest and validity of their own.

See STATEMENT ANALYSIS.

COMMON STOCK That part of the CAPITAL STOCK of a corporation which represents the last claim upon assets and dividends, as distinguished from PREFERRED STOCK. Dividends upon common stock may not be paid until interest upon all bonds, floating indebtedness, and dividends on preferred stock issues have been met. Common stockholders bear the greatest risk, but usually have the greatest control, and are entitled to the largest profits, if earned, since dividends are contingent upon earnings.

The value of common stock usually is subject to wide fluctuations, due to variations in earnings. As a general proposition, common stock must therefore be classified as a speculation rather than an investment, depending upon soundness and seasonability. For the tests of soundness of stocks, *see* INDUSTRIAL STOCKS.

In England shares of common stock are known as ordinary shares. *See* STOCK, STOCK CERTIFICATE.

COMMON TRUST FUNDS A fund maintained by a bank or trust company exclusively for the collective investment of money contributed to the fund by the bank or trust company as trustee, executor, guardian, administrator, or custodian.

Until 1913, national banks were prohibited from engaging in trust activities, although state banks were not. Subsequently, the FEDERAL RESERVE ACT permitted national banks to offer trust services, subject to Federal Reserve Regulation F. In 1962, regulatory jurisdiction over the trust powers of national banks was transferred from the FEDERAL RESERVE SYSTEM to the COMPTROLLER OF THE CURRENCY, who grants and supervises the trust powers of national banks.

Under the Comptroller's Regulation 9, a bank's collective investment fund is to be established and maintained in accordance with a written plan that has been approved by the bank's board of directors and filed with the Comptroller of the Currency. The plan must be consistent with the Comptroller's regulations, including provisions relating to the bank's investment powers and its general investment policy with respect to the fund; the allocation of income, profits, and losses; the admission or withdrawal of participation in the fund; the auditing of the bank's accounts with respect to the fund; the basis and method of valuing assets in the fund, and the minimum frequency for valuation; the basis for termination of the fund; and clear definition of the rights of participants.

Except for trusts exempt from federal income taxation, no one participant may have an interest aggregating more than 10% of the current market value of the fund. Similarly, no investment by the fund in the stocks, bonds, or other obligations of any one person, firm, or corporation may exceed 10% of the market value of the fund, except for direct obligations of the United States or those fully guaranteed by the government. Banks may commingle small trust accounts if that would be to the advantage of participants. They may not, however, provide investment services (under GLASS-STEAGALL ACT prohibitions) but may act in a FIDUCIARY CAPACITY.

Any bank administering a collective investment fund must maintain enough cash and readily marketable investments to provide adequately for the needs of participants and to prevent inequities among them. Also, the bank may not issue public shares in the fund, and it must maintain strict separation of its commercial banking functions from its trust fund operations.

See INVESTMENT COMPANY.

Pursuant to statute enacted September 28, 1962 (76 Stat. 668, 12 U.S.C. 92a), regulatory jurisdiction over the trust powers of national banks was transferred from the Board of Governors of the Federal Reserve System to the Comptroller of the Currency, including the granting and supervision of trust powers exercised by national banks. Immediately upon enactment of this law, the Comptroller issued his Regulation 9, which was essentially the same as the board's Regulation F (the board's former Regulation F, not the present Regulation F pertaining to compliance with the Securities Exchange Act's registration requirements by smaller state-chartered member banks). Revision effective April 5, 1963, contained a number of changes, including one particularly pertaining to collective investment, summarized as follows by the *National Banking Review*.

1. Investment was permitted in a common trust of the funds of "managing agency accounts," whereby agency agreements conferred on the bank, in fact or in effect, a power of attorney and investment discretion, exercised by the bank in deciding whether to invest such funds of a managing agency account in a common trust fund or in any other investment program. (The U.S. Supreme Court, in *Investment Company Institute* v. *Camp*, 401 U.S. 617, decided in 1971 that commingled managing agency funds—offerings involving the combination of individual managing agency accounts and traditional common trust funds—were activities prohibited to banks by Sections 16 and 21 of the GLASS-STEAGALL ACT.)
2. A bank shall be required to publish a summarized annual report of its common trust funds in a form prescribed by the Comptroller of the Currency. (As currently specified in the *Comptroller's Manual for National Banks*, per 12 CFR 9.18 (5)(ii), a bank administering a collective investment fund shall at least once during a period of 12 months prepare a financial report of the fund, which shall be based upon required audit and contain a list of investments in the fund showing the cost and current market value of each investment; a statement for the period since the previous report showing purchases, with cost; sales, with profit or loss and any other investment changes; income and disbursements; and an appropriate notation as to any investments in default. Also the financial report may include a description of the fund's value on previous dates, as well as its income and disbursements during previous accounting periods; no predictions or representations as to future results may be made, and neither the report nor any other publication of the bank shall make reference to the performance of funds other than those administered by the bank. Moreover, the bank shall not advertise or publicize its collective investment fund(s), except to the extent of publicity given solely in connection with promotion of the fiduciary services of the bank, and shall furnish a copy of the financial report to each participating account without charge as well as to prospective customers or to any person for a reasonable charge.)
3. Regulation 9. Each collective investment fund shall be established and maintained in accordance with a written plan which shall be approved by the bank's board of directors and filed with the Comptroller of the Currency. The plan shall contain appropriate provisions not inconsistent with the rules and regulations of the Comptroller of the Currency as to the manner in which the fund is to be operated, including provisions relating to the investment powers and a general statement of the investment policy of the bank with respect to the fund; the allocation of income, profits, and losses; the admission or withdrawal of participations in the fund; the auditing of accounts of the bank with respect to the fund; the basis and method of valuing assets in the fund, including the specific criteria for each type of asset; the minimum frequency for valuation of assets of the fund; the period following each such valuation date during which the valuation may be made (which period should not in usual circumstances exceed 10 business days); the basis upon which the fund may be terminated; and such other matters as may be necessary to define clearly the rights of participants. A copy of the plan shall be available at the principal office of the bank for inspection during all banking hours and, upon request, a copy of the plan shall be furnished to any person.
4. Property held by a bank in its capacity as trustee of retirement, pension, profit sharing, stock bonus, or other trusts which are exempt from federal income taxation under any provisions of the Internal Revenue Code may be invested in the bank's collective investment funds if they qualify for tax exemption under Revenue Ruling 56–267 and subsequent rulings.
5. Where not in contravention of local law, funds held by a national bank as fiduciary may be also invested collectively in a common trust fund maintained by the bank exclusively for the collective investment and reinvestment of moneys contributed thereto by the bank in its capacity as trustee, executor, administrator, guardian, or custodian under a Uniform Gifts to Minors Act; or in a fund consisting solely of assets of retirement, pension, profit sharing, stock bonus, or other trusts which are exempt from federal income taxation under the Internal Revenue Code.
6. Except in the case of collective investment funds of trusts exempt from federal income taxation under the Internal Revenue Code such as retirement, pension, profit sharing, stock bonus, or other trusts, no funds or other property shall be invested in a participation in a collective investment fund if as a result of such investment the participant would have an interest aggregating in excess of 10% of the then market value of the fund.

    No investment for a collective fund shall be made in stocks, bonds, or other obligations of any one person, firm, or corporation if as a result of such investment the total amount invested in stocks, bonds, or other obligations issued or guaranteed by such person, firm, or corporation would aggregate in excess of 10% of the then market value of the fund (this limitation shall not apply to investments in direct obligations of the United States or other obligations fully guaranteed by the United States as to principal and interest).

    Any bank administering a collective investment fund shall have the responsibility of maintaining in cash and readily marketable investments such part of the assets of the fund as shall be deemed to be necessary to provide adequately for the needs of participants and to prevent inequities between such participants. If prior to any admissions or withdrawals from a fund the bank shall determine that after effecting the admissions and withdrawals to be made, less than 40% of the value of the remaining assets of the collective investment funds would be composed of cash and readily marketable investments, no admissions into or withdrawals from the fund shall be permitted as of the valuation date upon which such determination is made (however, ratable distribution upon all participations shall not be so prohibited in any case).
7. In a common trust fund maintained by the bank for the collective investment of cash balances received or held by a bank (in its capacity as trustee, executor, administrator, or guardian) which the bank considers to be individually too small to be invested separately to advantage, total investment must not exceed $100,000. The number of participating accounts is limited to 100, and no participating account may have an interest in the fund in excess of $10,000.
8. A bank may (but shall not be required to) transfer up to 5% of the net income derived by a collective investment fund from mortgages held by such fund during any regular accounting period to a reserve account (but no such transfers shall be made which would cause the amount in such account to exceed 1% of the outstanding principal amount of all mortgages held in the

fund). The amount of such reserve account, if established, shall be deducted from the assets of the fund in determining the fair market value of the fund for the purposes of admissions and withdrawals.

9. No bank administering a collective investment fund shall issue any certificate or other document evidencing a direct or indirect interest in such fund in any form (sic). (This unusual provision apparently is designed to avoid any semblance of similarity to customary practice of investment companies in public offerings of their shares, an activity prohibited to banks under the Glass-Steagall Act.) Yet in addition to the investments permitted, funds or other property received or held by a national bank as a fiduciary may be invested collectively, to the extent permitted by local law, in shares of a mutual trust investment company, organized and operated pursuant to a statute that specifically authorizes the organization of such companies exclusively for the investment of funds held by fiduciaries, commonly referred to as a bank fiduciary fund.

See INVESTMENT COMPANY.

BIBLIOGRAPHY

AMERICAN LAW INSTITUTE. *Proposed Official Draft, Federal Securities Code*, 1978.
COMPTROLLER OF THE CURRENCY. *Regulation 9, Comptroller's Manual for National Banks*.
GREEN, D. S., and SCHUELKE, M. *The Trust Activities of the Banking Industry*. Trustees of the Banking Research Fund, Association of Reserve City Bankers, 1975.
INVESTMENT COMPANY INSTITUTE. "Misadventures in Banking: Bank Promotion of Pooled Investment Funds." Summer, 1979.
WADE, W. A. "Bank Sponsored Collective Investment Funds: An Analysis of Applicable Federal Banking and Securities Laws." *Business Lawyer*, January 1980.

COMMUNISM Literally, common or collective ownership of property; the abolition of private property, individual initiative, and profits. The implements of production, land, mineral deposits, utilities, etc., would be owned by the local or central government and the products distributed on the basis of need. Except on a small scale as a trial utopia, a completely communistic state has never been in practical operation.

In 1989-90, communist economies and governments collapsed throughout Eastern Europe, Nicaragua, and elsewhere. The Soviet Union was critically weakened and near collapse. Democracy and free enterprise (capitalism) helped bring about the restructuring of the communist world.

BIBLIOGRAPHY

ENGELS, F. *The Origin of the Family, Private Property and the State*, 1902.
HOOK, SIDNEY. *Towards the Understanding of Karl Marx*, 1933.
LASKI, H. J. *The Rise of European Liberalism*, 1936.
LENIN, V. I. *The Teachings of Karl Marx*. No date.
MARX, KARL. *Das Kapital*, 1867.

COMMUNITY PROPERTY A concept of ownership of property which regards husband and wife as beneficial coowners of the community estate (all property acquired after marriage, other than separate property acquired by devise, bequest, or from proceeds of noncommunity property). The community estate is dissolved on death of either husband or wife, divorce, or separation of property without divorce. The community property concept is found in the laws of Arizona, California, Hawaii, Idaho, Louisiana, Nevada, New Mexico, Texas, and Washington.

COMMUNITY REINVESTMENT ACT OF 1977 An act passed to further a congressional intent that banks meet the credit needs of their local communities (a form of affirmative action program for neighborhoods or communities) and to encourage investment in the immediate communities served by depository institutions. The concern over "redlining" was a major impetus for the passage of this act. Regulation BB provides the basic compliance requirements for this act. Bank examiners are required to consider the performance of the bank in meeting the needs of its service area, especially low- and moderate-income areas. A local community is considered to be the "contiguous areas surrounding each office or groups of offices."

Regulatory authorities are required to consider this basic need when considering application for new branches or relocation of an existing branch, for mergers and consolidations, for the creation of a bank holding company, for a holding company to acquire another bank or to merge or consolidate with another holding company, and other activities requiring approval.

Banks are required by federal regulations to prepare annually a delineation of the local community or communities that make up the entire community, using maps for that purpose.

COMMUNITY TRUST A form of charitable trust under which gifts and money bequests are received to be applied for public purposes and administered by a bank or trust company in conjunction with an advisory board of citizens. The community trust plan was first developed in Cleveland, Ohio, in 1914.

The community trust makes available a plan combining assurance of the effectual utilization of bequests with adequate flexibility to adapt itself to changes, which history demonstrates are sure to occur. It provides a means of meeting the varying conditions of coming years, conceding to each generation a measure of ability to administer wisely its own affairs rather than attempting what has so often failed, and a way to divine in detail the needs and problems of all the future. It gives new significance and opportunity to the ownership of wealth. It guarantees to donors of funds a proper custody, proper management, and proper distribution of income. It affords a means for the application of an accumulated fortune, in whole or in part, to the permanent service of the community. In short, it makes wealth more respected and respectable by ensuring its usefulness.

See TRUST.

COMPANY See CORPORATION, HOLDING COMPANY, INVESTMENT COMPANY, JOINT-STOCK COMPANY, OPERATING COMPANY, PARENT COMPANY, TRUST COMPANY.

COMPARATIVE STATEMENT FORM Used by bank credit analysts in the process of investigating a credit risk. Such forms are not standardized, although the form approved by the Committee on Credit Systems of the Robert Morris Associates has come to be used by many banks. The purpose of the form is to permit a rearrangement and reclassification of the items appearing on a balance sheet submitted by a prospective borrower in such a way as to indicate what seems to the bank the truest exhibit of the borrower's condition. By comparing one period with another, one can picture the rate of growth or of retrogression and changes in the amounts of the separate assets, liabilities, and equities.

See STATEMENT ANALYSIS.

COMPARATIVE STATEMENTS Financial and income statements for consecutive years used as a basis for noting the progress or regress of a business applying for credit.

See STATEMENT ANALYSIS.

COMPARISONS A periodic, reciprocal statement of purchases and sales occurring between brokers, or between brokers and bankers for collaterals held by a bank against brokers' loans, in order to determine the accuracy of the records of each. Brokerage comparisons are made daily by means of slips exchanged between the transacting brokers. Brokerage comparisons with banks are customarily made monthly by means of a reciprocal statement of collaterals held against a loan.

COMPENSATED DOLLAR See MONEY.

COMPENSATING BALANCES A demand deposit balance maintained by a borrower from a bank or a user of its services to compensate the bank for services rendered. The noninterestbearing amount is available for the bank's use, and, in return, the bank foregoes its fee or part of its interest on the loan. A common way to ensure that the balance is not used for transactions, as well as to minimize the reserve requirements involved, is to open a zero-rate certificate of deposit rather than a demand deposit account.

The practice of requiring compensating balances, once very common, nearly vanished during the mid-1970s, when many regional banks experienced slack loan demands and found that the compensating balances earned less than direct fees.

See AVERAGE LOAN AND BALANCE FILE.

BIBLIOGRAPHY

NADLER, P. "Balances and Buggy Whips in Loan Pricing." *Journal of Commercial Bank Lending.* Bank Administration Institute, Rolling Meadows, IL, 1989.

COMPENSATION Payment for services or goods. In law, the payment of damages to make an injured party whole; the money relief afforded an injured employee under workers' compensation acts.

BIBLIOGRAPHY

BANK ADMINISTRATION INSTITUTE. *The Incentive Compensation Plan: Workbook and disk.*
Compensation and Benefit Plans. Ernst & Young, 1990.

COMPENSATORY FINANCE In fiscal theory, the Keynes-ian principal that government FISCAL POLICY should be so planned and executed as to promote economic stability by counteracting major business fluctuations. Elements to accomplish such an objective are classifiable as follows:

1. Built-in stabilizers, such as a steeply progressive income tax system, which will dampen booms as income expands and lighten tax burden as incomes decline; unemployment insurance system, involving lighter tax receipts and larger benefit payments in depressions, with the reverse true in boom periods; and farm price supports, which cushion farm income when commodity prices decline.
2. Automatic measures, such as preplanned scale of heavy nonincome taxes to create budgetary surpluses in boom periods and a light scale of such taxes to lighten tax burden in depressions, together with heavy governmental expenditures in depressions for both consumption and investment-type outlays. Such preplanned compensatory tax rates would automatically be placed in effect upon signals by objective indicators such as production, income, or employment indices.
3. Managed compensatory measures involving, instead of automatic action, discretionary action by the President and Congress based upon judgment and appraisal of current conditions.

All of the above measures are concerned with the stabilization or stimulation of effective demand in aggregative terms, and their effectiveness would depend upon coordinated planning of all governmental units—federal, state, and local. Such measures would also entail abandonment of the traditional fiscal goal of annually balanced budgets.

BIBLIOGRAPHY

STEIN, H. *The Fiscal Revolution in America,* 1969.

COMPETITIVE BIDDING In securities financing, the procedure of awarding the new issue to the highest bid received (on basis of lowest net cost of money to the issuer), usually from investment banking groups formed in purchase syndicates. Competitive bidding contrasts with financing on a direct negotiated basis through a particular purchase syndicate.

The extent of competitive bidding may be summarized as follows.

1. **Treasury bills.** The Secretary of the Treasury invites tenders under competitive and noncompetitive bidding. Competitive bids must tender prices on the basis of 100, expressed with not over three decimal places. Noncompetitive tenders (generally for $200,000 or less) are usually accepted in full at the average of the prices of accepted competitive bids.
2. **State and municipal obligations.** Competitive bidding has been traditionally required in this field, ostensibly to prevent possible collusion between municipal securities dealers and venal politicians.
3. **Railroad securities.** In 1926, the Interstate Commerce Commission by rule required competitive bidding in the issuance of railroad equipment trust certificates. This was extended to other railroad securities, with minor exceptions, on July 1, 1944.
4. **Public utility securities.** The Securities and Exchange Commission, pursuant to its jurisdiction under the Public Utility Holding Company Act of 1935, first required competitive bidding in 1938 (Rule U-12F-2) in cases where underwriters judged to have affiliations with the issuer received fees of over 5% of total fees paid in financing. Since May 7, 1941, Rule U-50 required competitive bidding for public utilities under the jurisdiction of the SEC; however, the SEC has granted exceptions from the rule. Various state utility and railroad commissions also require compulsory competitive bidding.

Some companies, including industrials, voluntarily have resorted to competitive bidding, but the number of such instances has been minor, in view of the advantages of negotiated underwriting: continuing relationship between the issuer and the investment bankers, advice and counsel on provisions and timing of sale, allocation of expenses.

Chief arguments for competitive bidding are that it breaks up *de facto* monopoly of financing for the issuer by a particular investment banker and its syndicates, thus reducing concentration of financing in a relatively few firms; enables issuer to obtain a better price (assuming the bidding is representative enough); frees the issuer of banker domination. In fact, these motivations for the promotion of competitive bidding, concentration, and monopoly were stressed in the Temporary National Economic Committee (TNEC) hearings on investment banking aspects in 1939 in its "Investigation of Concentration of Economic Power."

During the early 1980s, a number of security types were developed that require the interest rate to be reset periodically as the result of a competitive bid. Institutions not holding the issue are allowed to bid, and those holding it do not have to bid. A variety of methods, including a "Dutch auction" (all pay the lowest marginal price that would clear the entire issue), are used to set the rate. In the event the amount bid falls short of the amount of the security outstanding, the terms of the security provide for the security to remain with the existing holders and for the rate to be set according to a formula. This may result in a high enough rate that one borrower will refinance the issue.

BIBLIOGRAPHY

EDERINGTON, L. H. "Negotiated versus Competitive Underwriting of Corporate Bonds." *Journal of Finance,* March, 1976.

COMPETITIVE EQUALITY BANKING ACT OF 1987
On August 10, 1987, the president signed into law the CEBA. This legislation contains several provisions that are of significance for the FDIC and state nonmember banks. The FDIC prepared a report dealing with this act, which is summarized in this entry.

The Federal Deposit Insurance Act is amended to permit (1) out-of-state holding companies to acquire qualified stock institutions, as well as mutual savings banks, before they fail if they have assets of $500 million or more; (2) a holding company to be sold, in whole or in part, to an out-of-state holding company if the in-state holding company has a bank or banks with aggregate banking assets of $500 million or more in danger of closing and the bank or banks represent 33% or more of the holding company's banking assets; and (3) an out-of-state holding company expansion rights in the state of acquisition through the bank holding company structure. This section also prevents regional compact restrictions from applying to a holding company that makes an acquisition under the emergency authority. The concurrence of the state bank supervisor of the failing bank is required before the interstate acquisition provisions may be used.

CEBA permits the FDIC to establish a bridge bank to assume the deposits and liabilities and purchase the assets of a failed bank if: (1) the cost of establishing a bridge bank does not exceed the cost of a liquidation; (2) the continued operation of the failed bank is essential to provide adequate banking services in the bank's community; or, (3) the continued operation of the failed bank is in the best interest of the depositors and the public. The bridge bank must have a separately chartered national bank, and it must be operated by a five-member board of directors appointed by the FDIC. The bridge bank may operate for up to three years while the FDIC seeks a purchaser.

Agricultural banks may, under certain circumstances, write down

COMPILATION

their losses on agricultural loans over seven years rather than deduct the amount of loss from capital as soon as the loss is recognized. Agricultural banks are defined as banks in economic areas dependent on agriculture, with assets of $100 million or less, which have at least 25% of their loans in agricultural loans.

Because companies that acquire nonbank banks after March 5, 1987, are required to comply with the Bank Holding Company Act or divest their bank subsidiary's, "nonbank banks" are in effect prohibited.

The act authorized a newly established financing corporation funded by the Federal Home Loan banks to raise $10.8 billion for the FSLIC by selling bonds in the capital markets. FSLIC is limited to spending up to $3.75 billion per year in conjunction with failed thrift institutions. The financing corporation is given authority to levy assessments against insured savings and loan institutions.

Provisions of the Glass-Steagall Act that prohibit affiliations and interlocking directors, officers, and employees between banks and securities firms were extended to FDIC-insured nonmember banks (and thrift institutions) until March 1, 1988. Other provisions of CEBA require the FDIC to consider and minimize the adverse economic impact of a liquidation on the local community and to require institutions offering adjustable rate mortgages to include a maximum interest rate that may apply during the term of the loan.

The FDIC and other financial institutions regulatory agencies are exempt from the apportionment provisions of the Anti-Deficiency Act and the sequestration provisions of the Gramm-Rudman-Hollings Act.

COMPILATION A presentation in the form of financial statements that is the representation of management without the expression of any assurance on the statements from certified public accountants. An accountant's compilation report states that a compilation has been performed, describes a compilation, and states that no opinion or other form of assurance is expressed on the statements. A compilation is not an audit or a review.

COMPLIANCE Adherence or to be in conformity with laws, rules, regulations, etc. Compliance has become a major issue in modern banking. Most bank functions come under compliance requirements of one sort or another. Regulatory agencies have imposed extensive regulations that require strict compliance by banks and thrift institutions. Proof of compliance is typically required by regulatory agencies or bank administrators. Banks typically install formal compliance programs to assure that the requirements are satisfied.

A compliance program consists of three major elements: a commitment from management; the authority to operate and enforce the program; and a plan to build the program. Many banks have a compliance officer or function to assure that the bank is in compliance with regulatory and administrative regulations.

Compliance policy, procedures, and actions should ordinarily include the following areas: compliance philosophy, purpose, structure and organization, authority, compliance analysis, compliance procedures, compliance evaluation and control, compliance review, compliance goal, compliance communication, compliance training, compliance reporting, and compliance evaluation.

Major areas of banking compliance requirements include the following:

Fair lending. Equal Credit Opportunity Act (Regulation B); Home Mortgage Disclosure Act (Regulation C); Fair Housing Act; Fair Credit Reporting Act; Fair Credit Billing Act; Consumer Credit Protection Act (1969); Financial Institutions Regulatory and Interest Rate Control Act of 1978; Fair Housing Home Loan Data System; Leasing (Regulation M); Interest on Deposits (Regulation O and 12 CFR 1204).

Consumer. Truth in Lending Act (Regulation Z); 12 U.S.C. 85 and 86a(a)(usury preemption); Fair Debt Collection Practices Act; Flood Disaster Protection Act; 12 CFR 29 (adjustable-rate mortgages); Electronic Fund Transfer Act (Regulation E); Regulation Q and DIDC Rules (interest rates); 12 CFR 590 (mobile home loans); Real Estate Settlement Procedures Act (Regulation X); Regulations Z, Q, DIDC rules, and Fair Lending laws as applicable to advertising.

Community. Community Reinvestment Act (CRA)(12 CFR 25).

Other. Regulation O (Loans to Executive Officers, Directors, and Principal Shareholders); Employee Retirement Income Security Act of 1974 (ERISA); Financial Recordkeeping and Currency and Foreign Transactions Reporting Act (1970); Garn-St Germain Depository Institutions Act of 1982; Interest and Dividend Tax Compliance Act of 1983; Taxpayer Identification Number (TIN); False Claims Act (1982); Kick-Back Law (1986) (U.S. Code: Chapter 41., Section 51-58).

BIBLIOGRAPHY

BANK ADMINISTRATION INSTITUTE. *Bank Compliance Alert.* Published every other week. Bank Administration Institute, Rolling Meadows, IL.
———. *A Banker's Guide to Expedited Funds Availability,* 1988.
———. *A Guide to Bank Secrecy Act Compliance,* 1987.
———. *A Guide to TIN Compliance,* 1988.
———. *Expedited Funds Availability: A Video Training Package.*
———. *Issues in Bank Regulation.* Quarterly.
———. *Legal Availability Schedules Reference Guide,* 1988.
LASH, N. A. *Banking Laws and Regulations.* Prentice Hall, Inc., Englewood Cliffs, NJ, 1987.
POWIS, ROBERT. *Bank Secrecy Act Compliance.* Bank Administration Institute, Rolling Meadows, IL, 1987.
———. *Security Compliance Guide.* Bank Administration Institute, Rolling Meadows, IL, 1987.
STEVENSON, T. R. *Compliance for Community Bankers.* Bank Administration Institute, Rolling Meadows, IL, 1987.

A basic compliance library could include the following references:

A Guide to Bank Secrecy Act Compliance. Bank Administration Institute.
A Guide to TIN Compliance. Bank Administration Institute.
Alternative Mortgage Instruments. Warren, Gorham & Lamont.
Bank Compliance Handbook. Bank Administration Institute.
Bank Compliance Magazine. American Bankers Association.
Banker's Guide to Expedited Funds Availability. Bank Administration Institute.
Bank Records Retention Guidelines. Bank Administration Institute.
Bank Regulatory Reporting Requirements. Bank Administration Institute.
Bank Secrecy Act Compliance. Bank Administration Institute.
Compliance Alert. The Institute for Strategic Development.
Compliance Examination Update. Warren, Gorham & Lamont.
Compliance for Community Bankers. Bank Administration Institute. This book contains an extensive bibliography on compliance with specific and broader references.
Desk Guide to Consumer Regulation Compliance Procedures. Independent Bankers Association of America.
Desktop Reference Manual of Compliance Terms. Bank Administration Institute.
Disaster Recovery for Banks: A Comprehensive Program for Today's Regulatory Climate. Bank Administration Institute.
EFT Compliance E Comprehensive Compliance Manual. American Bankers Association.
Legal Availability Schedules Reference Guide. Bank Administration Institute.
Real Estate Lending Comprehensive Compliance Manual. American Bankers Association.
The Community Reinvestment Act. Bank Administration Institute.
Truth-in-Lending: A Comprehensive Guide. Law & Business, Inc.
Truth-in-Lending for the Community Bank. Bank Administration Institute.

COMPOUND INTEREST See INTEREST.

COMPTROLLER The officer of a bank who supervises the bookkeeping, accounting, auditing, and reporting procedure, and who is responsible for initiating improvements in the accounting and auditing methods. All reports, internal statistics, and data concerning the financial condition should be prepared or approved by him or her; to be most effective he or she should report directly to the president or chairman of the board of directors. He or she should also be responsible for controlling all financial records and for providing a system of internal check that will guard against inaccuracies and fraud.

The comptroller must have a thorough knowledge of bank organization and operations, banking principles and law, accounting, and auditing technique.

See CHIEF FINANCIAL OFFICER, COMPTROLLER OF THE CURRENCY.

COMPTROLLER OF THE CURRENCY The Office of the Comptroller of the Currency was created by act of Congress approved February 25, 1863 (12 Stat. 665), as an integral part of the National Banking System. The Comptroller is required by law to report directly to Congress annually.

The most important functions of the Comptroller of the Currency relate to the organization, operation, and liquidation of national banks. His approval is required by law in connection with the organization of new national banks, the conversion of state-chartered banks into national banks, and consolidations or mergers of national banks with national banks or of state banks with national banks where the continuing institution is a national bank. The establishment of branches by national banks also requires approval by the Comptroller.

The office exercises general supervision over the operations of national banks. Each national bank is required to publish and file reports of condition not less than four times a year. National bank examiners, under the immediate supervision of the regional administrators of national banks, examine each national bank at least three times each two years. Such examinations are for the purpose of determining the financial condition of national banks, the soundness of their operations, and their compliance with the requirements of the National Bank Act and other applicable statutes.

In case of deliberate violation of law by a national bank, suit may be brought in the name of the comptroller for the forfeiture of the bank's charter. If it appears to the comptroller that a national bank is in an insolvent condition, he is empowered to appoint a receiver, which must be the FEDERAL DEPOSIT INSURANCE CORPORATION, to take over its affairs.

The Comptroller of the Currency is an *ex-officio* member of the board of directors of the Federal Deposit Insurance Corporation.

By act of September 28, 1962, jurisdiction over the granting of special permits to national banks to exercise fiduciary powers, and the subsequent examination of trust departments of such banks, was transferred from the Board of Directors of the Federal Reserve System to the Comptroller of the Currency.

In accordance with statutory direction, the Comptroller of the Currency promulgates regulations governing the operations of national banks, contained in the *Comptroller's Manual for National Banks* and the *Comptroller's Manual for Representatives in Trusts*. The office also publishes authoritative compilations of banking statistics, particularly in connection with the Comptroller's annual report to Congress.

Comptroller's Call. Every national bank shall, in accordance with Section 5211 of the Revised Statutes (12 U.S.C. 161), make to the Comptroller of the Currency not less than four reports during each year, according to the form prescribed by the Comptroller. These reports shall be verified by the declaration of the president, vice president, cashier, or any other officer designated by the board of directors of the bank to make such declaration that the report is true and correct to the best of his knowledge and belief. The correctness of the report of condition shall be attested by the signatures of at least three of the directors of the bank other than the officer making such declaration, with the declaration that the report has been examined by them and to the best of their knowledge and belief is true and correct.

Each such call report of condition shall exhibit in detail and under appropriate heads the resources and liabilities of the bank. The chart of accounts and instructions for their preparation are furnished to the reporting banks by the Office of the Comptroller (*see* BANK STATEMENT). Reported condition shall be as of the close of business on any past day specified by the Comptroller in his call (mid-year and year-end calls are in practice as of the calendar dates, for statistical purposes), but the intervening first quarter and third quarter are more likely to involve surprise calls, i.e., as of varying dates. Report shall be transmitted to the Comptroller within 10 days after the receipt of call therefor. In addition, the report of condition in the same form in which it is made to the Comptroller shall be published at the expense of the bank in a newspaper published in the place where the national bank is established, or if there is no newspaper in the place, then in the one published nearest thereto in the same county. Proof of publication shall be furnished to the Comptroller as specified by him.

The Comptroller of the Currency may call for additional reports of condition, in such form and containing such information as he may prescribe, on dates to be fixed by him, and may call for special reports from any particular national bank whenever, in his judgment, the same are necessary for his use in the performance of his supervisory duties. Special reports called for by the Comptroller need contain only such information as is specified by the Comptroller in his request therefor, and the publication of such reports need be made only if directed by the Comptroller.

The same requirements also apply to each of the national bank's affiliates other than member banks, to the end that the Comptroller be enabled to inform himself as to the effect of such affiliates upon the affairs of the national bank. However, reports of affiliates are no longer required of national banks unless specifically requested by the Comptroller.

Any national bank which fails to make and transmit any report required by the above statute shall be subject to a penalty for each day that such failure continues.

Prior to June 21, 1917, state member banks were required to submit their reports to the Comptroller of the Currency, the same as national banks. State member banks now submit their reports to the Federal Reserve bank concerned in each district. Each national bank sends a copy of its call report to the district Federal Reserve bank in addition to the official copy sent to the Comptroller.

Although they serve a legal reportorial purpose, call reports of condition, as published, do not contain the detail for analytical purposes that the now required annual report of national banks contains; nor are they intended to serve in place of the reports of examination (confidential to the Comptroller and the bank) for regulatory purposes.

Major divisions of the Office of the Comptroller of the Currency appear below.

Deputy Comptroller for Industry and Public Affairs
    Director, Communications
    Senior Deputy Comptroller for Bank Supervision
        Chief National Bank Examiner
        Deputy Comptroller, Trust and Securities
        Deputy Comptroller for Multinational Banking
        Deputy Comptroller, International Relations and Financial Evaluations
        Deputy Comptroller for Special Surveillance
        Deputy Comptroller for Supervisory Analysis
    Senior Deputy Comptroller for National Operations
        Deputy Comptroller for Operations
        Deputy Comptroller for Management Resources
    Senior Deputy Comptroller for Policy and Planning
        Deputy Comptroller for Bank Organization and Structure
        Deputy Comptroller for Systems and Financial Management
    Deputy, Economic and Policy Analysis
    Deputy to Director of the FDIC
    Chief Counsel
    Deputy Chief Counsel (Policy)
    Deputy Chief Counsel (Operations)
    Assistant Chief Counsel

A deputy comptroller heads each district and functions as chief executive officer of the district. A district administrator manages day-to-day operations of the district. Each district office has a district counsel, directors for administration, bank supervision, analysis, and field office directors.

See BANK EXAMINATION.

COMPUTER "A device designed to execute mathematical operations or logical operations. These operations are performed automatically according to the sequence in which they are received. Computers are used primarily for high-speed processing of data. Computers are classified in many ways. However, the most important distinction is generally considered to be their processing power. Computers include, as part of their basic design, separate functions: (a) performing arithmetic operations and logical operations on data; (b) controlling the flow of data; (c) moving and storing information; and (d) interfacing with input and output devices."

Computer security is a major concern for banks. Computer security includes "those procedures necessary to protect a computer system, including its related software, from damage, destruction, malfunction, or unauthorized access. System security includes such techniques as: (a) the provision of backup, recovery, and restoration facilities; (b) provision of alternative resources in the event of a disaster; and (c) protection of data through such techniques as

COMPUTER

password protection and encryption. The matter of privacy is a related concern." (Robert A. Edmunds, *The Prentice-Hall Standard Glossary of Computer Terminology*, 1984, p. 86.)

Computer hacks and others present internal and external security risks to computer operations. William T. Thornhill in *Effective Risk Management* identifies some of these risks:

Virus An infection entered into software that can infect the computer system much as a biological virus infects human beings.

Trojan horse Hides instructions within a legitimate program belonging to a legitimate user that grant improper privileges to the perpetrators.

Trap door Use of secret entry point in the operating system left there by developer so they can get in to repair flaws.

French roundoff Credits the fractions of cents of interest calculations to the perpetrator's account.

Logic bomb Hidden instructions that do harmful functions.

Misguided missile Turns the control of the system over to the perpetrator, such as access ability.

Limp Procedure that ties up all computer resources so that the system grinds to a halt or crashes.

Scavenging One user is able to read information left in the computer's main memory by the preceding user.

A pyramid of computer internal controls could assume the following structure:

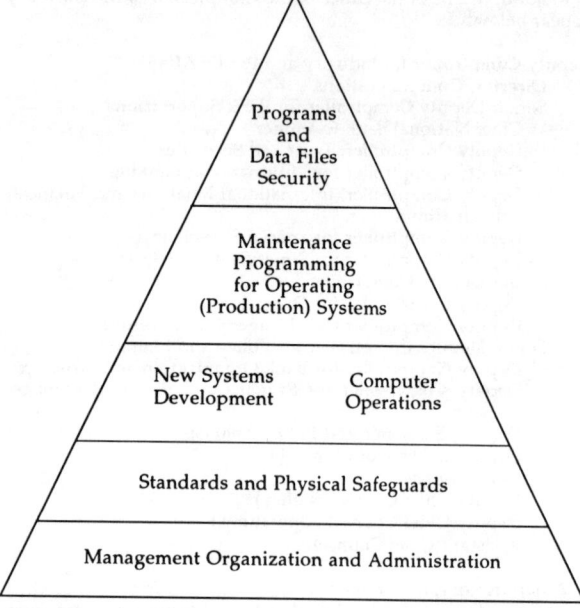

```
                    /\
                   /  \
                  /Programs\
                 /   and    \
                / Data Files \
               /   Security   \
              /----------------\
             /    Maintenance   \
            /    Programming     \
           /    for Operating     \
          /  (Production) Systems  \
         /--------------------------\
        /   New Systems  | Computer  \
       /   Development   |Operations  \
      /------------------------------  \
     /    Standards and Physical Safeguards \
    /----------------------------------------\
   /   Management Organization and Administration \
  /------------------------------------------------\
```

Source: William T. Thornhill, *Effective Risk Management*, Bank Administration Institute, 1988.

An entire dictionary of computer terms has been created since the introduction of the computer. Some of these terms are listed here.

Access Ability to get information or use a computer or program.

Address Designates the location of an item of information stored in a computer's memory.

Alphanumeric Composed of letters and numerals.

Arithmetic logic unit (ALU) The part of the central processing unit that performs arithmetic tasks, comparisons, and data transformation.

Backup file A copy of a current file used if the current file is destroyed.

BASIC Beginner's All-purpose Symbolic Instruction Code. A popular computer language used in personal computer systems.

Batch processing Processing in which a series of similar transactions are collected and processed simultaneously.

Binary A reference to the base-2 number system in which the allowable digits are O and 1.

Bit A binary digit, the smallest storage unit of data in a computer.

Boot To start the computer; booting or bootstrap.

Bug A mistake that occurs in a program or in the electrical system.

Byte The amount of space required to store a single character. A byte generally represents eight binary digits (bits).

Chip An integrated circuit and package that contains coded signals.

COBOL Common business-oriented language. A major programming language for business applications.

Compiler A program that converts (compiles) a program written in a source language into machine language.

Control unit The part of the CPU that controls the other units by retrieving machine language instructions from storage and interprets the instructions. It generates the commands that instruct other units to perform their operations.

CPU Central processing unit. The principal hardware components.

Data base Data stored in an organized format.

Data base system Systems that store data in a central location that enables the data to be shared by several different applications.

Default drive The drive used by the computer to list, save, and retrieve files and perform other functions unless another drive is specified.

Directories Used to organize files on disks; directories contain files.

Disk drive Peripheral equipment that stores information on disks.

Diskette A disk that contains one or more directories.

Document A file.

Documentation User or operator instructions that come with hardware or software and explain how to use the material.

DOS Disk Operating System. Software that directs the flow of information between the computer and disk drives.

Dump A printout of the contents of any file.

Editing Input controls related to the cycle of proofing, correcting, and improving a previous draft of a document.

File A collection of related records arranged sequentially.

Floppy disk A disk used in a disk drive that is used to record and store data.

Font A print style.

Format An arrangement by which information is stored.

Graphics Pictures or illustrations in computer programs.

Hard disk Fixed disk as opposed to a floppy disk.

Hardware The physical components of a computer system, such as the computer, printer, modem, etc.

Kb (Kilobyte) 1,024 bytes of information or storage space.

Language Commands or instructions that are used in computing.

Machine language A language that a computer can execute without translation. Distinguished from source language.

Macro A special file that is capable of remembering a series of keystrokes to be used later.

Master file A file containing relatively permanent data that is updated periodically.

Memory The internal storage of data.

Menu A list of options enabling the user to select a particular function or command.

Merge To insert fields, files, and keyboard input into specific places in a form.

Microcomputer A computer system that is similar to a minicomputer but smaller and with less computing power.

Minicomputer A relatively small, programmable, general-purpose computer.

Modem An acoustic or nonacoustic coupler for transmitting information from one computer to another by telephone or on a direct line.

Monitor (CRT) The screen.

On-line Equipment or devices that are in direct contact with the CPU and usually under its direct control.

Pitch The number of characters per inch. Pica and Elite are 10 and 12 pitch.

Printer An output device that produces printed copy.

Program Coded instructions on how a computer is to perform specific functions.

RAM Random access memory. A form of microchip that can be changed by the user; the data it produces can be stored on tape, disk, or in printed form.

Real–time The processing of transactions as they occur and which provide an immediate response to the user.

ROM Read only memory. A form of microchip that cannot be changed by the user.

Scrolling Moving through a document that is longer or wider than the screen.

Software Programs and routines that facilitate the use of hardware.

Terminal The device through which data are entered using a typewriter keyboard or optical scanner.
Test deck A technique to test programmed procedures and controls.
User-friendly A computer, computer system, or software program that enables users to function readily when using a computer.
Utility program A program that performs routine tasks, such as sorting or merging files.
Word processor A text-editing program or system.

BIBLIOGRAPHY

ACM Guide to Computing Literature.
AMERICAN ASSOCIATION OF INDIVIDUAL INVESTORS, *The Individual's Guide to Computerized Investing*, 1989.
BANK ADMINISTRATION INSTITUTE. *Microcomputers in Banking: A Basic Guide to Their Use and Control*. Bank Administration Institute, Rolling Meadows, IL, 1984.
———. *The 1987 Bank Microcomputer Directory*, 1987.
BELZER, J., and others. *Encyclopedia of Computer Science and Technology*. Dekker Morcel, Inc., New York, NY, 1980. 16 volumes.
CLEWORTH PUBLISHING CO. *Financial Computing.* Bimonthly.
EDMUNDS, R. A. COMPUTERS IN ACCOUNTING. *The Prentice Hall Standard Glossary of Computer Technology*. Prentice Hall, Inc., Englewood Cliffs, NJ, 1984.
FAULKNER COMMUNICATIONS. *Computers in Banking.* Monthly.
FREEDMAN, A. *The Computer Glossary*, 1988.
HOYT, D., and others, eds. *Computer Security Handbook*, 1988.
LOUGHRAN, T. "The Smart Computer That Grades Loans." *Bankers Monthly*, July, 1988.
MORTGAGE BANKERS ASSOCIATION. *Mortgage Banking Software '89.*
TAYLOR, W. T. *Commodity Trading Systems, Software & Databases*, 1986.

CONCESSION This term has three meanings:

1. A shading or decrease in the market price of securities.
2. A reduction in the price of a security offered to a bank or investment house that retails securities by a syndicate wholesaling securities, from the public offering price. The concession below the public offering price represents the profit to the investment dealer.
3. The right granted to a lessee to use property of the lessor for certain purposes for a stipulated period. More broadly, any grant or lease of a property privilege made by a government for political or economic advantage to a foreign corporation or association to enable it to exploit mineral resources, to build canals or railroads, etc.

CONDEMNATION The taking of private property for a pub-lic use by a public authority. The owner of the property is compensated by the public authority for the property taken. A condemnation is an exercise of the power of eminent domain.

CONDENSED STATEMENT OF CONDITION In bank statements of condition, the voluntarily published nonlegal type of statement of condition, in which the individual items of resources, liabilities, and groupings thereof may vary considerably from those specified in the legal or call report.
See BANK STATEMENT, CALL REPORT.

CONDITION As of June, 1982, available data on the condition of member banks of the Federal Reserve System, provided by the Board of Governors of the Federal Reserve System, include those in the appended table.
See BANK STATEMENT.

CONDITIONAL ENDORSEMENT *See* ENDORSEMENT.

CONDITIONAL SALES CONTRACT A contract whereby a seller retains title to goods sold and delivered to a purchaser until full payment has been made.

CONDOMINIUM Legally, an estate in real property defined as a separate specified unit in a multiunit structure which is subject to individual ownership in fee coupled with ownership in common of related parts of structure, site and appurtenances. Such an interest in real property now is statutorily recognized in all 50 states, the Virgin Islands, and Puerto Rico, the last-named having led the way with legislation in 1958.

Condominiums are not to be confused with cooperatives. In condominiums the purchaser takes title to his or her own individual

Condition of Member Banks of the Federal Reserve System

Data	Approximate release date	Date or period referred to
Aggregate reserves of depository institutions and monetary base—(1.20)	Thursday	Week ended previous Wednesday
Assets and liabiities of domestically chartered and foreign related banking institutions—H.8 (510) (1.25)	Monday	Monday, three weeks earlier
Changes in state member banks—K.3 (615)	Tuesday	Week ended previous Saturday
Factors affecting reserves of depository institutions and condition of federal reserve banks—H.4.1 (503) (1.11)	Thursday	Week ended previous Wednesday
Selected borrowings in immediately available funds of large member banks—H.5 (507) (1.13)	Wednesday	Week ended previous Thursday
Weekly consolidated condition report of large commercial banks and domestic subsidiaries—H.4.2 (504) (1.26, 1.28, 1.29, 1.30)	Friday	Wednesday, one week earlier
Changes in status of banks and branches—6.4.5 (404)	1st of each month	Previous month
Consumer installment credit—G.19 (421) (1.55, 1.56)	Mid-month	Second month previous
Debits and turnover at commercial banks—G.6 (406) (1.20)	12th of each month	Previous month
Loan commitments at selected large commercial banks—G.21 (423)	2nd week of each month	Second month previous
Major nondeposit funds of commercial banks—G.10 (411) (1.24)	3rd week of each month	Previous month
Loans and securities at all commercial banks—G.7 (407) (1.23)	3rd week of each month	Previous month
Maturity distribution of outstanding negotiable time certificates of deposit at large commercial banks—G.9 (410)	3rd week of each month	Last Wednesday of previous month
Geographical distribution of assets and liabilities of major foreign branches of U.S. banks—E.11 (121)	15th of Mar., June, Sept., and Dec.	Previous quarter
Survey of terms of bank lending—E.2 (111) (1.34)	Mid-month of Mar., June, Sept., and Dec.	Previous month
Domestic offices, commercial bank assets and liabilities, consolidated report of condition—E.3.4 (113) (1.26, 1.27, 1.28)	March, June, Sept., Dec.	Previous 3 months
Country exposure lending survey—E.16 (126)	Jan., Apr., July, Oct.	Previous 3 months
Aggregate summaries of annual surveys of security credit extension—C.2 (101)	Feb.	End of previous June

ENCYCLOPEDIA OF BANKING AND FINANCE

unit, whereas in cooperatives each member has a stock interest in the entire cooperative property and has the right to live in one of the units.

BIBLIOGRAPHY

The ABCs of Condominiums. Institute of Real Estate, Chicago, IL.
BOYER, R., AND SKLAR, W. *Condominiums, Cooperatives and Cluster Developments.* 2 vols. Butterworth Legal Publishers, Butterworth, WA, 1986.
Current Developments in Cooperative & Condominium Practice. Real Estate Law & Practice Service, 1988.

CONDUIT FINANCING A form of financing in which a governmental entity lends its name to a bond issue although merely acting as a conduit through which funds flow. Conduit financing links the buyer of the bond and the use of the project (a hospital or industrial development) being financed. The bondholder ordinarily looks only to the project for debt financing, and not to the government.

CONDUIT PRINCIPLE In tax law, the provisions that allow specific tax characteristics to be passed through certain entities to the owners of the entity without losing their identity. For example, the short-term capital gains of a partnership would be passed through to the partners and retain their character as short-term capital gains on the tax returns of the partners. This principle applies to partnerships, S corporations, estates, and trusts.

CONFIDENCE INDEX An index of investors' optimism and pessimism; A ratio of yield on Barron's High-Grade Bond Index to the yield on the Dow Jones Composite Bond Average. The index suggests the confidence of experienced investors in medium-grade corporate bonds relative to high-grade bonds. When lower-grade bond issues outperform high-grade bonds, the confidence index rises, which is an optimistic sign for stock prices. Investors are not worrying about safety and are willing to purchase a lower-quality bond. The converse is also true.

CONFIDENCE MEN Professional swindlers.
See BUNCO, SWINDLING.

CONFIRMATION An order or agreement in writing to verify or confirm one previously given orally, by telephone, or by telegraph. Executions of orders to buy or sell securities are confirmed in writing by brokers to their customers.

CONFIRMED CREDIT A LETTER OF CREDIT that cannot be canceled or modified without the consent of both buyer and seller.

CONGENERICS Holding companies and/or mixed holding companies (combining holding company with operating functions) characterized by holdings in other companies and/or operations which are complementary, supplementary, or allied in nature, not necessarily in exactly the same lines of activity. For the nonrelated type of holdings and/or operations of parent companies, *see* CONGLOMERATES.

Holding company structures in the banking field are required to be congeneric in nature, whether one-bank holding companies or those controlling two or more banks, as the result of passage of the Bank Holding Company Act Amendments of 1970 (P.L. 91-607, December 31, 1970), which expanded the coverage of the Bank Holding Company Act of 1956 to include a holding company that controls only one bank. In particular, Section 4(c)(8) of the Holding Company Act was revised, under which bank holding companies may acquire interests in nonbanking activities subject to specified restrictions and upon specified conditions. Among the activities of bank holding companies that have been determined by the Board of Governors of the Federal Reserve System to be permissible, as closely related to banking, are

1. Mortgage company operation.
2. Finance company operation.
3. Credit card company operation.
4. Factoring company operation.
5. Industrial bank operation.
6. Servicing loans.
7. Trust company operation.
8. Furnishing portfolio investment advice.
9. Furnishing general economic information and advice.
10. Leasing of personal property, including industrial equipment.
11. Investing in community welfare projects.
12. Serving as investment adviser to real estate investment trust (REITs) and closed-end investment companies.
13. Furnishing bookkeeping or data processing services.
14. Acting as insurance agent or broker if the insurance is connected with extension of credit (for certain types of insurance, and under certain conditions).

The Board of Governors of the Federal Reserve System has determined that the following activities are not so closely related to banking, managing, or controlling banks as to be a proper incident thereto for bank holding companies:

1. Insurance premium funding (combined sale of mutual funds and insurance).
2. Underwriting life insurance that is not sold in connection with a credit transaction by a bank holding company, or a subsidiary thereof.
3. Real estate brokerage.
4. Land development.
5. Real estate syndication.
6. Management consulting.
7. Property management.
8. Operation of savings and loan associations (but as indicated in its statement announcing this action, this activity may be the subject of further consideration by the board).

Under the GARN-ST. GERMAIN DEPOSITORY INSTITUTIONS ACT OF 1982, bank holding companies can acquire financially troubled mutual savings banks and savings and loan associations, both in and out of state. The COMPETITIVE EQUALITY BANKING ACT OF 1987 imposed a moratorium on regulatory approval of banks' applications to engage in commercial insurance, real estate, or securities underwriting until March 1, 1988, pending permanent legislation governing these activities; as of mid-1988, no such legislation had been enacted, and some banks had received approval to enter these activities.

See BANK HOLDING COMPANY ACT.

CONGLOMERATES Although definitions of the conglomerate company differ, elements of the concept include the following:

1. Diversification of acquisitions to include companies in nonrelated industries, so that a number of different lines of business, classes of products, or services are encompassed within the overall holdings of the parent company.
2. Importantly, emphasis on aggressive policy of acquisitions as a key aspect of growth. Conversely, pursuant to similar emphasis upon maintenance or improvement in growth rates, conglomerates in various instances have resorted to dispositions, spin-offs (entire or partial), and reorganizations of holdings.
3. An organizational arrangement in which the parent company may furnish centralized coordination, supervision, planning, and allocation of resources among the operating subsidiaries, while keeping operational responsibilities with the latter. Thus there may exist joint costs also for such factors as common facilities, personnel and staff services, and financial services.

Conglomerates pose problems for the enforcement of the ANTITRUST LAWS in connection with mergers and acquisitions; for accounting and disclosure standards; and for security analysis (multiindustry holdings and variation in managerial emphasis for particular holdings complicate problems of analysis). Among the accounting requirements affecting conglomerates have been Accounting Principles Board Opinions No. 16 (Accounting for Business Combinations) and No. 17 (Accounting for Intangible Assets), requiring accounting for goodwill that might arise in connection with the purchase of assets method of accounting for business combinations and requiring certified statements for at least a three-year period for firms being acquired. Disclosure requirements include the disclosure to the SEC of the principals proposing to acquire 10% or more (later revised to 5% or more) of a company's stock, the source of their funds, and purposes of the acquisition offer, and disclosure of the figures of product or service divisions contributing 10% or more to total sales and operating revenues.

BIBLIOGRAPHY

Commerce Clearing House. *Financial Accounting Standards, Original Pronouncements.*
Fiflis, T. J. "Accounting for Mergers, Acquisitions and Investments, in a Nutshell: The Interrelationships of, and Criteria for, Purchase or Pooling, the Equity Method and Parent-Company-Only and Consolidated Statements." *Business Lawyer,* November, 1981.

CONGRESSIONAL BUDGET OFFICE A nonpartisan con-gressional support agency charged with analyzing the interaction between the federal budget and the nation's economy and with assessing the fiscal and budgetary consequences of legislative actions. The Congressional Budget Office (CBO) does not make policy recommendations but presents options for the Congress to consider.

The Balanced Budget and Emergency Deficit Control Act of 1985 (gramm-rudman-hollings law) assigned CBO additional statutory tasks of, twice a year in conjunction with the Office of Management and Budget, (1) reporting whether the projected federal deficit exceeds the maximum deficit amount allowed by the law for the fiscal year; (2) calculating the amounts and percentages of budgetary resources that must be sequestered to eliminate any deficit excess; (3) alerting the Congress to a recession in the economy that might warrant the suspension of the deficit targets. The act was amended in 1987 after the Supreme Court found certain provisions were unconstitutional. These amendments, enacted as the Balanced Budget and Emergency Deficit Control Reaffirmation Act of 1987, added to CBO's tasks that of studying, in consultation with the General Accounting Office, and reporting to the Congress on federal credit programs.

Much of CBO's analysis involve economic forecasts, baseline budget projections, bill cost estimates, analysis of the President's budget, program analysis, budget options, and sequestration reports.

CBO is organized into six divisions that are administered by a director and deputy director. The director is appointed for a four-year renewable term by the Speaker of the House of Representatives and the President Pro Tempore of the Senate, acting upon recommendations of both budget committees.

CONSERVATISM A basic accounting convention that requires the reasonable anticipation of potential losses in recorded assets or in the settlement of liabilities at the time when financial statements are prepared. The principle of conservatism is sometimes expressed as follows: "Recognize all losses and anticipate no profit." Conservatism is sometimes justified on the grounds that it compensates for the overoptimism of managers and owners. Another view is that it is preferable to understate net income and net assets rather than overstate them since the consequences of loss or bankruptcy are more serious than those associated with profitable operations.

CONSERVATOR This term has two meanings:

1. The name given in some states to a person appointed by a court to manage the estate of an incompetent or lunatic in much the same way as a guardian administers the affairs of a ward. The conservator is charged with preserving the property and keeping it on a conservative income basis and is required to make frequent statements to the court. The death of the lunatic terminates the conservatorship.
2. Under the Emergency Banking Relief Act, approved March 9, 1933, the Comptroller of the Currency was empowered to appoint conservators for any national bank when this was considered necessary to conserve its assets. The conservator was empowered to allow such withdrawals by existing depositors on a ratable basis as the Comptroller might decide as safe, and to receive new deposits which would be segregated and subject to unrestricted withdrawal. The same act permitted the reorganization of national banks, if necessary, upon approval of the Comptroller and either depositors holding 75% of total deposits or holders of two-thirds of the outstanding stock, or both.

CONSIGNEE One to whom merchandise is forwarded or shipped. In freight shipments, the consignee is notified by an arrival notice from the transportation company. In parcel post and express shipments, delivery is made directly to the consignee.

CONSIGNMENT In a general sense, a shipment of goods from the consignor to consignee, whether the consignor is owner or merely acts as agent in their sale. In a narrower sense, a shipment of goods to a commission merchant who acts as agent for the owner or for the owner and consignor, for the purpose of immediate sale according to the consignor's instructions and for his account.

Under a consignment, the consignor ships merchandise to the consignee (dealer), who acts as agent for the consignor in selling or marketing the merchandise. The consignee accepts the merchandise and agrees to exercise due diligence in caring for and selling it. After deducting a sales commission and any chargeable expenses, the consignor remits cash received from customers to the consignee. The merchandise is carried as the inventory of the consignor until sold by the consignee. The consignee periodically reports to the consignor an account sales that shows the merchandise received and sold, expenses chargeable to the consignment, and the cash remitted. The consignor then recognizes revenue.

Under a consignment, the consignor accepts the risk that the merchandise might not be sold and relieves the consignee of the need to provide working capital for inventory.

See account of sales.

CONSIGNOR A shipper or sender; one who ships merchandise. The consignor takes a bill of lading, express receipt, or parcel post receipt as evidence of his shipment.

CONSISTENCY An accounting principle that encourages conformity from period to period by a firm in the use of accounting policies and procedures. Consistency is essential to improving comparability across accounting periods.

CONSOLIDATED ANNUITIES   consols.

CONSOLIDATED BONDS *See* consolidated mortgage bonds.

CONSOLIDATED FIRST MORTGAGE BONDS Bonds secured by a first mortgage on consolidated property; sometimes a misnomer for consolidated mortgage bonds.

CONSOLIDATED MORTGAGE A mortgage upon an entire unit of real property formed by the consolidation of several smaller parcels. A consolidated mortgage is not necessarily a first mortgage. It may be a first mortgage on some of the parcels entering into the consolidated property and a second or even third mortgage upon other parcels.

CONSOLIDATED MORTGAGE BONDS Bonds secured by a consolidated mortgage. These bonds are frequent among railroad securities and are distinguished from divisional bonds in that the latter are secured by separate railroad properties. Consolidated mortgage bonds are similar to general mortgage bonds and are secured by a first mortgage upon a part of the company's property and a second or other mortgage upon other parts.

CONSOLIDATED STATEMENT Statement of a parent company and its subsidiaries (balance sheet showing condition, income account showing results of operations, and a cash flow statement) presenting the more significant composite situation, as if the companies were a single firm, instead of the statements of the parent company alone, particularly if the latter is strictly a holding company whose assets consist very largely of holdings in subsidiaries. Intercompany items are eliminated in the consolidated statements, such as amounts owed by one affiliated company to another, securities held by one affiliated company in another, and assets purchased by one affiliated company from another, as well as intercompany income account items, so that the underlying operating companies' situation, the basis for the intercompany system, shows through. To the extent there is any minority holding of the voting stock of subsidiaries, such minority interest is Consolidated statements eliminate intercompany items, such as amounts one affiliated company owes another, securities one affiliated company holds in another, and intercompany income account items (intercompany sales and purchases). Any minority interest (stockholders of a subsidiary who are outside the affiliation structure) represents the investment in the consolidated net assets by stockholders outside the affiliation structure. This interest is reported on the consolidated statement as a separate ownership interest, a liability, or as both. Consolidated financial statements are generally considered to be more useful to the stockholders of the parent company than are the separate statements of the members of the affiliation.

Although consolidated statements have the advantage of presenting the network as a single unit, sometimes the separate statements for each of the subsidiaries as well as the holding company itself are especially revealing of intercompany transactions, such as upstream loans to the parent company from subsidiaries and intercompany transfers, which are meaningful for analysis and appraisal of management.

When a parent company owns at least an 80% interest in a domestic subsidiary, the companies may elect to file a consolidated income tax return.

For uniform bank call reports, the consolidation process eliminates the results of all transactions and all outstanding asset/debt relationships between offices. Each subsidiary must consolidate its majority-owned subsidiaries in accordance with the general consolidation rules. Each subsidiary or consolidated subsidiary must be carried upward to the next succeeding level to determine whether consolidation is required.

Minority interest consists of the shares of stock now owned by the reporting bank. Minority interest in the reporting bank's consolidated subsidiaries is shown along with other liabilities. Income associated with a minority interest is shown in the report of income as "other noninterest expense."

CONSOLIDATION OF BANKS Prior to enactment of the National Bank Merger Act of 1950 on August 17, 1950 (P.L. 706, 81st Congress), as amended by P.L. 515, 83d Congress (see 12 U.S.C. Secs. 214, 214a, 214b, 214c, 215, 215a, and 215b), there was no express statutory authorization for national banks to convert into, merge with, or consolidate with state banks. Thus, national banks desiring to convert their charters into state bank charters were obliged to dissolve and liquidate voluntarily, which, in view of the invariable capital gains involved, exposed stockholders to tax liability and thereby set up an important stumbling block to such conversion. On the other hand, various states specifically authorized state banks to convert into, merge with, or consolidate with national banks, thus eliminating the dissolution and liquidation alternative and thereby the tax difficulty.

Under the above-referenced federal legislation, national banks now may leave the National Banking System without the requirement of voluntary liquidation and without the approval of the Comptroller of the Currency, provided that the state concerned does not require approval of conversion, merger, or consolidation of state banks into national banks and permits such conversion, merger, or consolidation under conditions no more restrictive than those contained in the federal legislation. The necessity for dissolution and liquidation is eliminated, and thereby the tax difficulty, because the act specifically provides that the state bank resulting from conversion by a national bank shall be considered the same business and corporate entity as the national banking association (Sec. 3, P.L. 706, 81st Congress).

See BANK MERGERS.

CONSOLIDATION OF BILLS Borrowing a sum for the payment of past-due bills.

CONSOLS A market name for perpetual British government bonds.

The term is derived as a contraction of consolidated annuities and consolidated stock (government bonds commonly being known as stock in England and on the Continent). Consols represent the premier investment of England, just as the government bonds of this country are the highest grade investments here. Their price is regarded as one of the chief barometers of British public credit. Most of the consols are in registered form, although bearer bonds with coupons are obtainable.

See UNITED STATES GOVERNMENT SECURITIES.

CONSTANT-DOLLAR MODEL An accounting model in which the dollar is valued in terms of its purchasing power. Inflation and deflation can distort the purchasing power of the dollar. Adjustment of accounting or financial data for changes in purchasing power so as to reflect "real" value is referred to as constant-dollar accounting, constant purchasing power accounting, or general price-level accounting. The primary objective of constant-dollar accounting is to maintain capital in terms of constant purchasing power as measured by a general index of prices. The more widely used indexes of price changes computed regularly by federal agencies are:

1. The gross national product implicit price deflator (GNP deflator)
2. The consumer price index for all urban consumers (CPI-U)
3. The wholesale price index
4. The composite construction cost index
5. The 22 commodity price index

The CPI-U reflects the average change in the retail prices of a broad "basket" of consumer goods. It is reported monthly and is not revised after its initial publication.

The procedure for restating dollars of varying purchasing power is done by multiplying the amount to be restated by a fraction, the numerator of which is the index for current prices and the denominator of which is the index for prices that prevailed at the date related to the amount being restated. For example, the cost of an asset acquired for $10,000 in 1980 is restated in terms of 1990 dollars as follows:

$$\frac{1990 \text{ index}}{1980 \text{ index}} \times \$10,000 = \text{cost in terms of 1990 dollars.}$$

Holders of money and money equivalents lose general purchasing power during inflation because a given amount of money purchases fewer goods and services as prices rise. Fixed amounts of money payable in the future become less of a burden during inflation because they are payable in dollars of reduced general purchasing power. Such gains and losses resulting from monetary assets and liabilities are described as price-level gains or losses or purchasing power gains or losses.

Data expressed in terms of constant dollars provide an objectively determined quantification of the impact of inflation on business and financial operations. Constant-dollar adjustments eliminate the effects of inflation from financial data and preserve comparability of financial data over time, thereby improving trend analysis. The Financial Accounting Standards Board encourages but does not require companies to prepare information on changing prices.

CONSTANT-DOLLAR PLAN An investment planning technique that keeps a fixed number of dollars in stocks with a fluctuating amount in bonds or other defensive instruments. If stocks rise, some shares are sold and the extra money beyond the previously decided fixed amount is used to buy bonds. If stocks go down, bonds are sold and the money is used to buy shares to bring the dollars in the stocks up to the desired amount.

CONSTANT-RATIO FORMULA An investment plan that keeps a fixed ratio of money in stocks and bonds (for example 50% in each). As the market fluctuates, stocks are sold and bonds are bought, or vice versa, to keep the ratio constant. This plan is supposed to work well in a complete market cycle that includes some wide swings.

CONSTRUCTIVE RECEIPT DOCTRINE The tax principle for entities reporting on a cash basis that cash has been received at the time the recipient first had the opportunity of receiving payment.

CONSTRUCTIVE SIDE OF THE MARKET Denotes the position taken by those who believe that business and financial conditions warrant an advance in security values and who therefore purchase securities to hold for higher prices; the bull side of the market.

Table 1 / Consumer Installment Credit Outstanding, Seasonally Adjusted

		Debt Holder					
Year	Total	Commercial Banks	Finance Companies	Credit Unions	Retailers	Savings Institutions	Gasoline Companies
Billions of Dollars							
1977	230.8	112.4	44.9	37.6	23.5	9.4	3.0
1978	275.6	136.2	54.3	45.9	24.9	11.1	3.2
1979	312.0	154.2	68.3	46.5	28.1	11.1	3.7
1980	313.5	147.0	76.8	44.0	28.4	12.7	4.5
1981	335.7	147.6	89.8	46.0	39.3	16.5	4.4
1982	355.8	152.5	98.7	47.3	32.7	20.6	4.1
1983	396.1	172.0	102.9	53.5	35.9	27.7	4.1
1984	453.6	209.2	96.1	66.5	37.1	40.3	4.4
1985	522.8	242.1	113.1	72.1	38.9	52.4	4.3
1986	577.8	261.6	136.4	77.9	40.6	59.5	3.2
1987	612.1	275.0	143.8	84.4	40.6	64.8	3.5
Percent of Total							
1977	100.0	48.7	19.5	16.3	10.2	4.1	1.3
1980	100.0	46.9	24.5	14.0	9.1	4.5	1.4
1981	100.0	44.0	26.7	13.7	11.7	4.9	1.3
1982	100.0	42.9	27.7	13.2	9.2	5.8	1.1
1983	100.0	43.4	26.0	13.5	9.1	7.0	1.0
1984	100.0	46.1	21.2	14.7	8.2	8.9	1.0
1985	100.0	46.3	21.6	13.8	7.4	10.0	0.8
1986	100.0	45.2	23.6	13.5	7.0	10.3	0.6
1987	100.0	44.9	23.5	13.8	6.6	10.6	0.6

CONSTRUCTIVE TRUST The TRUST relationship imposed upon a wrongdoer by a court of equity whenever necessary to prevent injustice to the innocent party, regardless of the intent of the parties. Thus if A, who is B's agent, fraudulently induces his or her principal B to transfer to him or her property at a fraction of its true value, a court of equity would impose a constructive trust upon A, holding him or her to be trustee of the property for the benefit of B. The constructive trust is to be distinguished from the RESULTING TRUST.

CONSULAR INVOICE A document usually certified in triplicate at the shipping point by a consul of the country of destination of the shipment and forwarded by such consul to the customs officials of the port of destination. The consular invoice contains the information usually given in a seller's invoice—quantity and value. Its purpose is to inform the customs officials of the port of entry of the nature of the imports expected so that they can prevent possible fraud. Imports cannot be released from the port of entry until the consular invoice has arrived unless the importer executes a bond of indemnity.

CONSUMER ADVISORY COUNCIL An advisory group to the Federal Reserve System that represents the interests of the financial industry and consumers. The council usually meets with the Board of Governors four times each year. Academic and legal specialists in consumer matters are represented on the council.

CONSUMER CREDIT As defined by the Board of Governors of the Federal Reserve System who publish monthly statistics thereon, the short- and intermediate-term debt owed by individuals to financial institutions, retailers, and other distributors, for financing consumer purchases of goods and services, but not including real estate mortgages and insurance policy loans.

Truth in Lending Act. Regulation Z of the Board of Governors of the Federal Reserve System, effective July 1, 1969, was issued pursuant to Title I (Truth in Lending Act) and Title V (General Provisions) of the Consumer Credit Protection Act (P.L. 90–321,) enacted May 29, 1968. The purpose of the act is to assure that every customer who has need for consumer credit is given meaningful information with respect to the cost of that credit, which in most cases must be expressed in the dollar amount of the finance charge and as an annual percentage rate computed on the unpaid amount of the amount financed. Other relevant credit information must also be disclosed so that the customer may readily compare the various credit terms available to him or her from different sources and avoid the uninformed use of credit. Regulation Z also implements the provision of the act under which a customer has a right in certain circumstances to cancel a credit transaction which involves a lien on his or her residence. Advertising of consumer credit terms, in addition, must comply with specific requirements and certain credit terms may not be advertised unless the creditor usually and customarily extends such terms. However, neither the act nor Regulation Z is intended to control charges for consumer credit or interfere with credit practices, except to the extent that such practices might be inconsistent with the purposes of the act.

See DEPOSITORY INSTITUTIONS DEREGULATION AND MONETARY CONTROL ACT OF 1980, FEDERAL RESERVE BOARD REGULATIONS.

Table 2 / Commercial Bank Consumer Credit Outstanding, by Type

	Billions of Dollars		% of Bank Consumer Credit		% of Consumer Credit Outstanding	
Type of Credit	1977	1987	1987	1987	1977	1987
Automobile	49.6	106.5	44.1	38.8	59.8	40.7
Revolving	18.4	95.2	16.4	34.6	46.8	65.2
Mobile home	9.1	8.3	8.1	3.0	60.3	32.4
Other	35.3	64.8	31.4	23.6	37.8	36.2

BIBLIOGRAPHY

BOARD OF GOVERNORS OF THE FEDERAL RESERVE SYSTEM. *Annual Reports.*
BRENNAN, M. J. "Vendor Financing." *Journal of Finance*, December, 1988.
KLEIN, R. J. "Want Fair Treatment from Lender? *Money*, December, 1988.
LAMAUNTE, D. "Walking the Tightrope of Serious Debt." *Black Enterprise*, January, 1989.
SILVIA, J. E., and WHALL, B. "Home Equity Loans and the Business Cycle." *Business Economics*, January, 1989.

CONSUMER FINANCE CHARGES

CONSUMER FINANCE CHARGES On May 29, 1968, Congress passed the Consumer Credit Protection Act, Title I of which is cited as the Truth in Lending Act, actually statutorily entitled Consumer Credit Cost Disclosure. It directs that the Board of Governors of the Federal Reserve System shall prescribe regulations to carry out the purposes of the title, which the board of governors has done (Regulation Z, effective July 1, 1969). The act and Regulation Z apply to banks, savings and loan associations, department stores, credit card issuers, credit unions, automobile dealers, consumer finance companies, residential mortgage brokers, craftsmen (e.g., plumbers and electricians), doctors, dentists, other professionals, hospitals, and in fact any individual or organization that extends or arranges credit for which a finance charge is or may be payable or which is repayable in more than four installments. Regulation does not apply to the following types of credit: business and commercial credit, except agricultural credit; credit to federal, state, or local governments, although governmental units extending credit to individuals are affected by the law and regulation; transactions in securities and commodities accounts with a broker dealer registered with the Securities and Exchange Commission; transactions under certain public utility tariffs; credit over $25,000, except that all real estate credit transactions for personal, family, household, or agricultural uses are covered regardless of amount.

Before the effective date of the regulation, finance charges were disclosed to buyers and borrowers in nonuniform ways, including simple interest, add-on interest, interest discounted, monthly interest, etc., while home buyers could find "points'" added to the basic mortgage price. The act and Regulation Z now standardize statement of the dollar amount of costs included in the finance charge (e.g., interest; loan fee; finders fee or similar charge; time price differential; amount paid as a discount; service, transaction, or carrying charge; points; appraisal fee (except in real estate transactions); premium for credit life or other insurance, if such is made a condition for giving credit; and investigation or credit report fee (except in real estate transactions)). However, costs that would be paid if credit were not employed may be excluded, provided they are itemized and shown to the customer, such as taxes, license fees, registration fees, certain title fees and other legal fees, some real estate closing fees, etc.

The annual percentage rate must also be clearly stated (in the sale of dwellings, total dollar finance charge need not be stated, but the annual percentage rate must be). The annual percentage rate must be accurate to the nearest 0.25%. Regulation Z does not fix maximum, minimum, or any charges for credit, but does require showing whatever rate is charged. The method of computation of the annual percentage rate depends on whether the credit is open end or other than open end.

1. Open-end credit, typically covering most credit cards and revolving charge accounts in retail stores, where finance charges are usually imposed on unpaid amounts each month. Finance charge is divided by the unpaid balance to which it applies, giving the rate per month or whatever time period is used. This result is multiplied by 12 or the other number of time periods used per year.

   For example, for a typical charge of 1.5% imposed on unpaid balances per month, the annual percentage rate would be 12 X 1.5%, or 18%. (For other methods of computing annual percentage rate on open-end credit, see Regulation Z (Sec. 226.5 (a) and Sec. 226.7 (b)(6)).
2. Credit other than open end, including both loans and sales credit, in every case for a specified period of time where the total amount, number of payments, and due dates are agreed upon with the customer. Examples are a loan from a finance company to buy an automobile, credit extended by a store to buy a household appliance, and a single payment loan. The following information must be presented to the customer in writing, as applicable, plus additional information relating to the type of credit extended.
   a. Total dollar amount of the finance charge, except in the case of a credit transaction to finance purchase of a dwelling.
   b. Date on which the finance charge begins to apply, if different from the date of the transaction.
   c. Annual percentage rate (an exception is found in Sec. 226.8(b)(2)(i)(ii) of Regulation Z).
   d. Number, amounts, and due dates of payments.
   e. Total payments, except in the case of first mortgages on purchases of dwellings.
   f. Amount charged for any default, delinquency, etc., or method used for calculating that amount.
   g. Description of any security to be held.
   h. Description of any penalty charge for prepayment of principal.
   i. How the unearned part of the finance charge is calculated in the case of prepayment (charges deducted from any rebate or refund must be stated also).

Additional information must be furnished to customers as follows.

1. **Credit sales.** In addition to above information, the following: cash price; down payment, including trade-in; difference between the two; all other charges, itemized, that are included in the amount financed but not part of the finance charge; unpaid balance; amounts deducted as prepaid finance charges or required deposit balances; amount financed; total cash price, finance, and all other charges (this does not apply in the case of sale of a dwelling).
2. **Loans.** In addition to above information, the following: amount of credit to be given to the customer, itemized, including all charges which are part of the amount of credit extended but are not a part of the finance charge; amounts that are deducted as prepaid finance charges and required deposit balances.

The annual percentage rate on loans or credit other than open end must be calculated by the actuarial method—payments are applied first to interest due and any remainder is then applied to reduce principal. (This method is *not* the constant-ratio method, which is relatively simple to use; thus the Board of Governors of the Federal Reserve System has prepared tables showing the annual percentage rate based on the finance charge and the number of weekly or monthly payments to be made. These tables are available from the Board of Governors of the Federal Reserve System and the Federal Reserve banks at nominal cost.)

For example, suppose a bank loan of $100 repayable in equal monthly installments over one year is made, at a 6% add-on finance charge. Thus the borrower would repay $106 over a year, and would only have the use of the full $100 until he or she made his or her first payment, with less and less each month as payments were made. The effect is that the actual annual percentage rate is almost twice the add-on percentage rate (11%).

If the 6% finance charge were discounted in advance, the annual percentage rate would be 11.5%, because the customer would only receive $94 and have to repay $100; thus he or she would have full use of only $94 of the loan up to the time he or she made his or her first payment.

A sample page from a table prepared by the Board of Governors of the Federal Reserve System to simplify calculation of the annual percentage rate by the actuarial method is appended.

Other Requirements. Other requirements of the Truth in Lending Act are concerned mainly with standardized language, timing of disclosure, rules for advertising, and the right to rescind in certain instances a credit arrangement within three business days if the party's residence is used as collateral for credit. The right to cancel or rescind a credit transaction does not apply to a first lien or mortgage to finance the purchase or construction of a home. But if a homeowner wants to borrow to build a swimming pool on his or her home property, which would lead to a creditor taking a lien, mortgage, or other security interest on the home, the homeowner must be informed in writing that he or she has the right to cancel the transaction within three business days.

Penalties under the Truth in Lending Act for failure to make disclosures as required under the act include the customer's right to sue for twice the amount of the finance charge—for a minimum of $100 up to a maximum of $1,000, plus court costs and attorney's fees. Willful or knowing disobedience of the law or of Regulation Z, and conviction therefor, could lead to a fine of up to $5,000, imprisonment for one year, or both.

See FEDERAL RESERVE BOARD REGULATIONS (Regulation Z).

CONSUMER FINANCE CHARGES

Federal Reserve Annual Percentage Rate Tables, Sample Page from Table for Computing Annual Percentage Rate for Level Monthy Payment Plans

Example		Finance charge = $35.00; total amount financed = $200; number of monthly payments = 24.
Solution	Step 1	Divide the finance charge by the total amount financed and multiply by $100. This gives the finance charge per $100 of amount financed. That is, $35.00 ÷ $200 = .1750 x $100 = $17.50.
	Step 2	Follow down the left-hand column of the table to the line for 24 months. Follow across this line until you find the nearest number to $17.50. In this example $17.51 is closest to $17.50. Reading up the column of figures shows an annual percentage rate of 16%.

Number of payments	14.00%	14.25%	14.50%	14.75%	15.00%	15.25%	15.50%	15.75%	16.00%	16.25%	16.50%	16.75%	17.00%	17.25%	17.50%	17.75%
1	1.17	1.19	1.21	1.23	1.25	1.27	1.29	1.31	1.33	1.35	1.37	1.40	1.42	1.44	1.46	1.48
2	1.75	1.78	1.82	1.85	1.88	1.91	1.94	1.97	2.00	2.04	2.07	2.10	2.13	2.16	2.19	2.22
3	2.34	2.38	2.43	2.47	2.51	2.55	2.59	2.64	2.68	2.72	2.76	2.80	2.85	2.89	2.93	2.97
4	2.93	2.99	3.04	3.09	3.14	3.20	3.25	3.30	3.36	3.41	3.46	3.51	3.57	3.62	3.67	3.73
5	3.53	3.59	3.65	3.72	3.78	3.84	3.91	3.97	4.04	4.10	4.16	4.23	4.29	4.35	4.42	4.48
6	4.12	4.20	4.27	4.35	4.42	4.49	4.57	4.64	4.72	4.79	4.87	4.94	5.02	5.09	5.17	5.24
7	4.72	4.81	4.89	4.98	5.06	5.15	5.23	5.32	5.40	5.49	5.58	5.66	5.75	5.83	5.92	6.00
8	5.32	5.42	5.51	5.61	5.71	5.80	5.90	6.00	6.09	6.19	6.29	6.38	6.48	6.58	6.67	6.77
9	5.92	6.03	6.14	6.25	6.35	6.46	6.57	6.68	6.78	6.89	7.00	7.11	7.22	7.32	7.43	7.54
10	6.53	6.65	6.77	6.88	7.00	7.12	7.24	7.36	7.48	7.60	7.72	7.84	7.96	8.08	8.19	8.31
11	7.14	7.27	7.40	7.53	7.66	7.79	7.92	8.05	8.18	8.31	8.44	8.57	8.70	8.83	8.96	9.09
12	7.74	7.89	8.03	8.17	8.31	8.45	8.59	8.74	8.88	9.02	9.16	9.30	9.45	9.59	9.73	9.87
13	8.36	8.51	8.66	8.81	8.97	9.12	9.27	9.43	9.58	9.73	9.89	10.04	10.20	10.35	10.50	10.66
14	8.97	9.13	9.30	9.46	9.63	9.79	9.96	10.12	10.29	10.45	10.62	10.78	10.95	11.11	11.28	11.45
15	9.59	9.76	9.94	10.11	10.29	10.47	10.64	10.82	11.00	11.17	11.35	11.53	11.71	11.88	12.06	12.24
16	10.20	10.39	10.58	10.77	10.95	11.14	11.33	11.52	11.71	11.90	12.09	12.28	12.46	12.65	12.84	13.03
17	10.82	11.02	11.22	11.42	11.62	11.82	12.02	12.22	12.42	12.62	12.83	13.03	13.23	13.43	13.63	13.83
18	11.45	11.66	11.87	12.08	12.29	12.50	12.72	12.93	13.14	13.35	13.57	13.78	13.99	14.21	14.42	14.64
19	12.07	12.30	12.52	12.74	12.97	13.19	13.41	13.64	13.86	14.09	14.31	14.54	14.76	14.99	15.22	15.44
20	12.70	12.93	13.17	13.41	13.64	13.88	14.11	14.35	14.59	14.82	15.06	15.30	15.54	15.77	16.01	16.25
21	13.33	13.58	13.82	14.07	14.32	14.57	14.82	15.06	15.31	15.56	15.81	16.06	16.31	16.56	16.81	17.07
22	13.96	14.22	14.48	14.74	15.00	15.26	15.52	15.78	16.04	16.30	16.57	16.83	17.09	17.36	17.62	17.88
23	14.59	14.87	15.14	15.41	15.68	15.96	16.23	16.50	16.78	17.05	17.32	17.60	17.88	18.15	18.43	18.70
24	15.23	15.51	15.80	16.08	16.37	16.65	16.94	17.22	17.51	17.80	18.09	18.37	18.66	18.95	19.24	19.53
25	15.87	16.17	16.46	16.76	17.06	17.35	17.65	17.95	18.25	18.55	18.85	19.15	19.45	19.75	20.05	20.36
26	16.51	16.82	17.13	17.44	17.75	18.06	18.37	18.68	18.99	19.30	19.62	19.93	20.24	20.56	20.87	21.19
27	17.15	17.47	17.80	18.12	18.44	18.76	19.09	19.41	19.74	20.06	20.39	20.71	21.04	21.37	21.69	22.02
28	17.80	18.13	18.47	18.80	19.14	19.47	19.81	20.15	20.48	20.82	21.16	21.50	21.84	22.18	22.52	22.86
29	18.45	18.79	19.14	19.49	19.83	20.18	20.53	20.88	21.23	21.58	21.94	22.29	22.64	22.99	23.35	23.70
30	19.10	19.45	19.81	20.17	20.54	20.90	21.26	21.62	21.99	22.35	22.72	23.08	23.45	23.81	24.18	24.55
31	19.75	20.12	20.49	20.87	21.24	21.61	21.99	22.37	22.74	23.12	23.50	23.88	24.26	24.64	25.02	25.40
32	20.40	20.79	21.17	21.56	21.95	22.33	22.72	23.11	23.50	23.89	24.28	24.68	25.07	25.46	25.86	26.25
33	21.06	21.46	21.85	22.25	22.65	23.06	23.46	23.86	24.26	24.67	25.07	25.48	25.88	26.29	26.70	27.11
34	21.72	22.13	22.54	22.95	23.37	23.78	24.19	24.61	25.03	25.44	25.86	26.28	26.70	27.12	27.54	27.97
35	22.38	22.80	23.23	23.65	24.08	24.51	24.94	25.36	25.79	26.23	26.66	27.09	27.52	27.96	28.39	28.83
36	23.04	23.48	23.92	24.35	24.80	25.24	25.68	26.12	26.57	27.01	27.46	27.90	28.35	28.80	29.25	29.70
37	23.70	24.16	24.61	25.06	25.51	25.97	26.42	26.88	27.34	27.80	28.26	28.72	29.18	29.64	30.10	30.57
38	24.37	24.84	25.30	25.77	26.24	26.70	27.17	27.64	28.22	28.59	29.06	29.53	30.01	30.49	30.96	31.44
39	25.04	25.52	26.00	26.48	26.96	27.44	27.92	28.41	28.89	29.38	29.87	30.36	30.85	31.34	31.83	32.32
40	25.71	26.20	26.70	27.19	27.69	28.18	28.68	29.18	29.68	30.18	30.68	31.18	31.68	32.19	32.69	33.20
41	26.39	26.89	27.40	27.91	28.41	28.92	29.44	29.95	30.46	30.97	31.49	32.01	32.52	33.04	33.56	34.08
42	27.06	27.58	28.10	28.62	29.15	29.67	30.19	30.72	31.25	31.78	32.31	32.84	33.37	33.90	34.44	34.97
43	27.74	28.27	28.81	29.34	29.88	30.42	30.96	31.50	32.04	32.58	33.13	33.67	34.22	34.76	35.31	35.86
44	28.42	29.97	29.52	30.07	30.62	31.17	31.72	32.28	32.83	33.39	33.95	34.51	35.07	35.63	36.19	36.76
45	29.11	29.67	30.23	30.79	31.36	31.92	32.49	33.06	33.63	34.20	34.77	35.35	35.92	36.50	37.08	37.66
46	29.79	30.36	30.94	31.52	32.10	32.68	33.26	33.84	34.43	35.01	35.60	36.19	36.78	37.37	37.96	38.56
47	30.48	31.07	31.66	32.25	32.84	33.44	34.03	34.63	35.23	35.83	36.43	37.04	37.64	38.25	38.86	39.46
48	31.17	31.77	32.37	32.98	33.59	34.20	34.81	35.42	36.03	36.65	37.27	37.88	38.50	39.13	39.75	40.37
49	31.86	32.48	33.09	33.71	34.34	34.96	35.59	36.21	36.84	37.47	38.10	38.74	39.37	40.01	40.65	41.29
50	32.55	33.18	33.82	34.45	35.09	35.73	36.37	37.01	37.65	38.30	38.94	39.59	40.24	40.89	41.55	42.20
51	33.25	33.89	34.54	35.19	35.84	36.49	37.15	37.81	38.46	39.12	39.79	40.45	41.11	41.78	42.45	43.12
52	33.95	34.61	35.27	35.93	36.60	37.27	37.94	38.61	39.28	39.96	40.63	41.31	41.99	42.67	43.36	44.04
53	34.65	35.32	36.00	36.68	37.36	38.04	38.72	39.41	40.10	40.79	41.48	42.17	42.87	43.57	44.27	44.97
54	35.35	36.04	36.73	37.42	38.12	38.82	39.52	40.22	40.92	41.63	42.33	43.04	43.75	44.47	45.18	45.90
55	36.05	36.76	37.46	38.17	38.88	39.60	40.31	41.03	41.74	42.47	43.19	43.91	44.64	45.37	46.10	46.83
56	36.76	37.48	38.20	38.92	39.65	40.38	41.11	41.84	42.57	43.31	44.05	44.79	45.53	46.27	47.02	47.77
57	37.47	38.20	38.94	39.68	40.42	41.16	41.91	42.65	43.40	44.15	44.91	45.66	46.42	47.18	47.94	48.71
58	38.18	38.93	39.68	40.43	41.19	41.95	42.71	43.47	44.23	45.00	45.77	46.54	47.32	48.09	48.87	49.65
59	38.89	39.66	40.42	41.19	41.96	42.74	43.51	44.29	44.29	45.85	46.64	47.42	48.21	49.01	49.80	50.60
60	39.61	40.39	41.17	41.95	42.74	43.53	44.32	45.11	45.11	46.71	47.51	48.31	49.12	49.92	50.73	51.55

Source: Board of Governors of Federal Reserve System

ENCYCLOPEDIA OF BANKING AND FINANCE

BIBLIOGRAPHY

Board of Governors of the Federal Reserve System. *Annual Percentage Rate Tables* (Regulation Z—Truth in Lending), Vol. I (Regular Transactions), 1969; Vol. II (Irregular Transactions), 1969.

CONSUMER LEASING ACT An act that requires disclosure of information to help consumers compare the cost and terms of one lease of consumer goods with another, and the cost of leasing with that of buying on credit or for cash.

CONSUMER LENDING REGULATIONS Historically, Congress has passed major regulatory legislation designed to protect consumers in their dealings with financial institutions. Major regulations and laws requiring banking compliance include the following:

Regulation AA. Consumer inquiries and complaints. Establishes procedures for investigating and processing complaints when denied credit, especially unfair or deceptive acts or practices.

Regulation B. *Equal Credit Opportunity Act.* Prohibits discrimination against a credit applicant on the basis of race, sex, color, national status, religion, age, receipt of public assistance, or national origin.

Regulation BB. Forbids the arbitrary consideration of geographic factors or redlining in granting credit.

Regulation C. Requires disclosure of geographical data on home mortgages for the purpose of detecting redlining practices.

Regulation CC. Specifies availability of funds and collection of checks.

Regulation E. Limits consumer liability for unauthorized use of lost electronic funds transfer credit or debit cards.

Regulation Z. *Truth in Lending Law.* Requires that consumers be given information on the cost of credit.

Fair Housing Act. Prohibits discrimination in housing and housing credit on the basis of race, color, religion, national origin, or sex.

Fair Credit Reporting Act. Gives consumers access to their credit bureau records.

Real Estate Settlement Procedures Act. Requires detailed statement of settlement costs on real estate transactions and reporting of borrowers' rights in the granting of mortgage credit.

CONSUMER LOANS See CONSUMER CREDIT, CONSUMER FINANCE CHARGES, PERSONAL FINANCE, SMALL LOAN BUSINESS.

CONSUMER PRICE INDEX See COST OF LIVING INDEX.

CONSUMPTION FUNCTION In macroeconomics, the proportionate, although not necessarily stable, relationship between consumption expenditure and total income. This concept is based primarily upon the Keynesian conclusion that consumption is a function of income—that of all the possible motivations for increased consumption, increased income is the active determinant. As income changes in any direction, consumption will change in the same direction, although by a smaller amount. This is the so-called psychological law of Keynes and is based upon a factor of change (change in consumption divided by change in income, or "marginal propensity to consume") of less than one (less than "unity"), and one which is stable in the short-run. Granted these assumptions about the marginal propensity to consume, *average* consumption must decrease as income goes up, even if the marginal propensity to consume remains constant. Thus, given a constant marginal propensity to consume of 0.5 and assuming both consumption and income are $100 billion, if income goes up $10 billion, consumption will go up $5 billion. Now consumption will total $105 billion and income $110 billion, or average consumption of 95%, so that saving has increased from 0 to 5% of income. Inherent in this increase in saving as income goes up is the gist of the Keynesian theory of the business cycle—that as income goes up, saving will increase, and hence increased investment must occur to absorb the savings in order to maintain the higher level of income, since income is the sum of consumption and investment.

The Keynesian exposition had many faults which the post-Keynesians have sought to correct, such as the mixture of static and dynamic concepts in the models; the failure to allow for interaction of the ACCELERATION PRINCIPLE with the MULTIPLIER; the oversimplified conclusion that the marginal propensity to consume can be regarded as stable at less than one invariably in the short-run; etc.

BIBLIOGRAPHY

Blanchard, O. J. "What Is Left of the Multiplier Accelerator?" *American Economic Review*, May, 1981.
Kaliski, S. F. "Inflation, Stagflation and Macroeconomics: Does Received Macro-Theory Explain Our Economic Circumstances?" *Canadian Public Policy*, Supplement, April, 1981.
Meltzer, A. H. "Keynes' *General Theory*: A Different Perspective." *Journal of Economic Literature*, March, 1981.
Stein, J. L. "Monetarist, Keynesian, and New Classical Economics." *American Economic Review*, May, 1981.

CONTANGO The charge made for the accommodation when a speculator who has bought stock desires to postpone delivery. This charge, based on the interest on the amount of the transaction during the period between the settlement days, is made because the seller must wait until the next settlement for his or her money. Contango is the reverse of BACKWARDATION.

CONTANGO DAY The first day of the fortnightly settlement on the London Stock Exchange.

CONTEMPORANEOUS RESERVE ACCOUNTING See RESERVE.

CONTINENTAL BILLS Bills of exchange drawn on banks located in European countries other than Great Britain.

CONTINENTAL CURRENCY The currency of European countries other than Great Britain.

CONTINENTAL RATES Rates quoted for currencies and bills of exchange drawn on banks located in European countries other than Great Britain.

CONTINGENCIES An existing condition, situation, or set of circumstances involving uncertainty as to possible gain or loss to an enterprise that will ultimately be resolved when one or more future events occur or fail to occur (FASB Statement No. 5). The resulting gain or loss is referred to as a "gain contingency" or a "loss contingency." Gain contingencies do not receive accounting recognition because of the principle of conservatism. Loss contingencies are related to the possible incurrence of LIABILITIES or the impairment of assets. Examples of loss CONTINGENCIES include obligations related to product warranties, product defects, and customers' premiums; threat of expropriation; litigation; claims and assessments; and guarantees of indebtedness of others.

Three terms are used to describe the range of possibilities of an event occurring: probable, reasonably possible, and remote. Different accounting is prescribed for contingencies that fall within these ranges:

Term	Definition	Accounting Action
Probable	The future event(s) is likely to occur.	Record the probable event loss in the accounts if the amount can be reasonably estimated. If not estimable, disclose facts in a note to the statements.
Reasonably possible	The chance of the future event(s) occurring is more than remote but less than likely.	Report the contingency in a Note.
Remote	The chance of the future event(s) occurring is slight.	No recording or reporting unless contingency represents a guarantee. Then disclosure is required.

Loss contingencies related to general or unspecified business risks, such as losses related to a strike or recession, are not disclosed in financial statements.

CONTINGENT FUND In general, a fund set aside out of earnings to provide for emergencies (e.g., unexpected operating losses, shrinkage in value of inventories, damage claims) or with which to provide for expansion in plant and equipment when a favorable opportunity arises; a business reverse.

The term contingent fund usually involves a confusion in the use of the terms reserve fund and reserve. The better accounting practice is to consider a fund as "a sum of money or its equivalent employed in, set aside for, or available for a specific or general purpose" (Committee on Terminology of the American Institute of Accountants), and actually covered on the assets side of the statement by a corresponding segregated asset. Therefore, a reserve should denote merely an earmarked portion of retained earnings, without covering segregated asset.

CONTINGENT INTEREST A right to property which depends for vesting or realization upon the happening of some future uncertain event. Thus if A by will leaves property to B for life, then to C if C outlives B, B's interest is vested but C's interest is contingent upon his outliving B. C's interest, by contrast, would also be vested if A instead left the property to B for life, then to C or C's ESTATE. Contingent interests are subject in the various states to the particular state's version of the rule against remoteness of vesting, also known as the rule against perpetuities. For example, all interests must vest not later than 21 years after the end of some designated life or lives in being as of the time a will or trust becomes effective.

CONTINGENT LIABILITIES Potential liabilities; liabilities for which a business may be held, but which it never expected to be compelled to meet; liabilities that depend upon the fulfillment or lack of fulfillment of certain conditions; secondary liabilities.

Contingent liabilities may be classified in two main groups. The first group comprises definite and tangible liabilities discoverable through the accounts and records of a business. The second group is less tangible, such as conditions in the trade, likelihood of a falling market, possibility of cancellation of contracts, return of goods sent on approval or consignment, possibility of supersession of merchandise or of its quality through superior inventions or advance in industrial technology, or of possible costly litigation to protect against infringement of patents.

The first main group may be again divided into three subclassifications.

1. Those of a financial nature such as are usually incurred in the sale, transfer, endorsement, or guarantee of negotiable instruments or other financial obligations. Contingent liabilities of this nature arise as a result of:
   a. Discount, sale, or transfer of notes receivable, trade acceptances, bank acceptances arising under commercial letters of credit, and foreign drafts.
   b. Endorsements of notes for affiliated or subsidiary concerns.
   c. Endorsement of commercial paper as accommodation party.
   d. Selling, pledging, or assigning of accounts receivable where the transfer attaches a contingent liability to the seller, pledgor, or assignor.
   e. Issuing and guaranteeing letters of credit.
   f. Guaranteeing of payment of interest on principal of the bonds of another party.
   g. Accepting suretyships, including those guaranteed for others.
   h. Contracts for purchase of foreign exchange for future delivery.
   i. Liability for unpaid stock subscriptions.
   j. Advances against accounts or bills receivable.
   k. Taking up leases.
2. Liabilities incurred as a result of agreements on contracts concerning the purchase or sale of merchandise or services. This subclassification includes liabilities arising as the result of:
   a. Guarantees of satisfactory performance of services or of merchandise.
   b. Contracts for future delivery of merchandise, plant construction, etc.
   c. Guaranteed merchandise orders not subject to cancellation (including those guaranteed for affiliated or subsidiary concerns).
   d. Provisions for returned merchandise, rebates, trade discounts, etc.
   e. Provisions for allowances for returned containers.
3. Responsibilities incurred in various manners other than by expressed agreement or contract, such as those arising as result of:
   a. Pending lawsuits.
   b. Possibility of litigation, such as alleged infringement of patents.
   c. Pending judgments where suit has been taken on appeal to a higher court.

The credit analysts in the banking and mercantile world recognize that financial statements must completely set forth the contingent liabilities in order to serve as an adequate instrument upon which to judge a credit risk.

See CONTINGENCIES.

CONTINGENT REMAINDER A remainder is a future interest in property dependent upon the termination of the prior estate created at the same time and by the same instrument. Thus, A leaves property to B for life, then to C. C's interest is a remainder. It is a contingent remainder if vesting depends upon A's specification that C outlive B; it is a vested remainder if A's specification is to C or C's heirs.

See CONTINGENT INTEREST.

CONTINGENT RESERVE In accounting practice, an earmarked portion of retained earnings or undivided profits not allocated to any asset or liability items and thus a true equity reserve, free and clear of any actual present needs. Its purpose is to meet any unanticipated needs among assets, involving revaluation or losses, and any unexpected liabilities, such as taxes or interest, not definitely known.

See CONTINGENT FUND, RESERVE, RESERVE FUND.

CONTINUED BONDS Bonds which are not repaid at maturity but which are extended for a further definite or indefinite period with the same security and with the same or different interest rate. They are usually known as extended bonds.

See EXTENDED BOND.

CONTINUING ACCOUNT An open or running book account in which settlements are made at regular intervals, e.g., 30 to 60 days.

CONTINUING AGREEMENT *See* GENERAL LOAN AND COLLATERAL AGREEMENT.

CONTINUING GUARANTY *See* GUARANTY.

CONTINUING RESOLUTION Legislation enacted by Congress providing the required budgetary authority and appropriation to continue specific federal activities at a specified level. It is used when appropriation legislation is expiring and a regular appropriation bill has not yet been approved.

CONTINUOUS COMPOUNDING Compounding interest continuously instead of in discrete time periods.

CONTRACT An agreement involving an arrangement or prom-ise that the law will enforce. Rights are acquired by one party or parties to certain acts or forbearance from acts on the part of another or others. Contracts are a basic business tool in any civilized society. A contract may be written, oral, or implied. Certain agreements must be in writing, especially those covered by the Statute of Frauds. As a general rule, a written contract cannot be changed or contradicted by oral evidence. However, many agreements need not follow any prescribed format to be enforceable. The Uniform Commercial Code rules differ from common law rules in several important ways.

The legal elements of a binding contract include offer and

CONTRACT GRADES

acceptance; consideration, if the law requires it; capacity of the parties to contract; legality of purpose; reality of consent; and the form specified by law.

Offers must be definite and certain as to what will be agreed upon. Offers must be communicated to the offeree by the offeror or his or her agent. Mistakes in transmission of an offer are considered to be offeror's fault (risk). Offers terminate when they are rejected by the offeree or revoked by the offeror. An offer is an offer that is supported by consideration and cannot be revoked before a specified time. An option is a separate contract to keep an offer open. A counteroffer is a rejection coupled with a new offer. Lapse of time or the death or insanity of the offeror terminates an offer. Illegality terminates an offer, as does bankruptcy or insolvency of either offeror or offeree. An offer terminates if it is impossible to perform the contract.

Acceptance may be written or oral. An offer can be accepted only by the person to whom it was directed. The intent to accept is required. Acceptance must be unequivocal and unconditional. Silence is not acceptance unless the offer indicates that silence would constitute acceptance. Acceptance also occurs when the offeree takes benefit of services or goods and exercises control over them when the opportunity to reject them exists.

Consideration is an act, promise, or forbearance that is offered by one party and accepted by another as inducement to enter into the agreement. Courts generally do not look into the amount of an exchange to determine the adequacy of the consideration. However, an exchange of unequal amounts of money or fungible goods is not enforceable. Moral obligation is generally not consideration, but there are exceptions to this rule. Contract modifications require new consideration on both sides to be legally binding.

Legal capacity implies the capacity to contract and is required to keep the contract from becoming void or voidable. For example, a minor may contract, but some such agreements are voidable by minor only.

Contracts are unenforceable if they are illegal or violate public policy. In situations where both parties are guilty, neither will be given relief. Examples of illegal contracts include wagering contracts, usury (contract for greater than legal interest rate), agreements to interfere with justice, illegal restraints of trade, and others.

Mutual assent or reality of consent is essential to every contract. For example, fraud may make a contract void (no contract) or voidable. Mistakes are acts done under an erroneous conviction. Generally, unilateral mistakes are not grounds to rescind a contract. Duress can render a contract voidable. For example, a client threatens to criminally prosecute a supplier unless he signs a contract. Undue influence or mental coercion can render a contract void or voidable.

Contracts are discharged by performance, agreement, release or covenant not to sue, impossibility of performance, breach of contract (failure to carry out terms of the contract), and by other means.

Remedies to breach of contract include rescission (annulment that places the parties in the positions they held before the contract was formed), restitution (return of consideration to the injured party), specific performance (compels performance promised), injunction (compels an act by the party or restrains an act), and damages (payment of money).

See STATUTE OF FRAUDS; STATUTE OF LIMITATIONS.

BIBLIOGRAPHY

Corbin on Contracts. West Publishing Co., St. Paul, MN. Periodic supplements.
Lexis. Online data base. Mead Data Central, Dayton, OH.
Williston on Contracts. Lawyers Co-operative Publishing Co., Rochester, NY. 22 volumes.

CONTRACT GRADES *See* GRADING.

CONTRACT MARKETS Those COMMODITY EXCHANGES or boards of trade designated by the Commodity Futures Trading Commission to trade in futures contracts.
See COMMODITIES, FUTURES.

CONTRACTS OF SALE Technically, agreements of sale or purchase, or agreements to sell or purchase. In commodity exchange trading, instead of awaiting delivery on a purchase and then delivering on a sale, the trader may offset a previous purchase by a sale for the same delivery month.
See DELIVERY DAY.

CONTRARY OPINION Investing action that differs from what the general investing public does at a certain time. Its purpose is to outsmart the market. The underlying idea of this investing theory is that what a majority of investors know is not worth knowing.

CONTRIBUTION MARGIN Sales revenue less variable expenses. Contribution margin can be illustrated as follows:

Sales (50,000 units)	$100,000
Less: Variable expenses	60,000
CONTRIBUTION MARGIN	40,000
Less: Fixed expenses	10,000
Net income	$30,000

Variable expenses are those that change in direct proportion to the change in volume of sales over the relevant range of business activity. Fixed expenses remain constant at any relevant range of volume within the operating capacity of the firm. A company's break-even point (where revenues equal expenses and no profit or loss is made) can be computed using the contribution rate:

$$\text{Sales at B/E point} = \frac{\text{Fixed expense}}{\text{Contribution rate (contribution margin/sales)}}$$

$$= \frac{\$10,000}{.40}$$

$$= \$25,000$$

Proof:	
Sales	$25,000
Deduct:	
Variable expenses (60% x $25,000)	(15,000)
Fixed expenses	(10,000)
	0

CONTROL ACCOUNT In accounting practice, an account in the general ledger to which are posted in totals the debits or credits shown in separate detailed accounts in subsidiary ledgers; controlling account. Examples are the accounts receivable and accounts payable accounts, controlling the customers and creditors subsidiary ledgers carrying separate accounts for each customer or creditor by name. The total or balance of the controlling account is the same as the sum of the balances of the various accounts in the subsidiary ledger controlled.

CONTROLLED ACCOUNT In security or commodity trading, an account in which trading is controlled or directed by a person other than the customer whose account it is. Many firms do not accept discretionary accounts because of the onus and responsibility involved. A registered employee of the New York Stock Exchange may exercise full discretion for an account, but the customer must specifically empower him or her to do so by a power of attorney, and a partner of the firm must approve and initial each discretionary order before it is executed.

CONTROLLED INFLATION *See* INFLATION.

CONTROLLING COMPANY *See* HOLDING COMPANY, PARENT COMPANY.

CONTROLLING INTEREST A person or group of persons who own a sufficient percentage of the common stock of a corporation to control its policy through their majority voting power. Ownership of over 50% of the stock is sufficient for this purpose. Very often a group owning a much smaller percentage of the stock can secure working control by procuring proxies of scattered shares.

CONTROLLING RECORDS Classes of records of a financial nature in a bank which comprise the controlling books or accounts of the bank.
See CONTROL ACCOUNT.

CONVENTION VALUES In insurance company valuation of securities, the valuation procedure approved by the national convention of Insurance Commissioners whereby states authorized use of amortized values for bonds of specified standing and average values for stocks, rather than actual market values, during the abnormal decline in security prices in the early 1930s. While reporting their surplus officially on the convention basis, many companies nevertheless noted the actual market value basis as a footnote to surplus throughout the period of depression.
See INSURANCE COMPANY STATEMENTS.

CONVERSION This term has six meanings:

1. In law, the unauthorized exercise of ownership over personal property belonging to another, resulting in exclusion of the owner's rights or in alteration of the personal property. The wrongful sale of stock held as margin for a trading account by a broker without the consent of the owner-trader is conversion.
2. The exercise of the conversion privilege attached to bonds or stocks. For example, convertible bonds or preferred stocks may be converted into common stock at the option of the holder.
3. In commodity trading, the CONVERSION CONTRACT.
4. In accounting, conversion cost is the comprehensive term covering labor, overhead, and materials outlay involved in processing an article into the desired intermediate or finished form.
5. The exchange of a charter granted by the state for a federal charter and similar exchanges.
6. The exchange of dollars into foreign currencies.

CONVERSION CONTRACT A type of contract in spot trading in which the price is tentatively designated as a futures price but the basis grade left unspecified. Later, in accordance with the time limit agreed on, the price is to be adjusted according to the current grade at time and place of delivery in relation to the basis grade of the futures contract.
See SPOT PRICE.

CONVERTIBILITY In free foreign exchange markets, freedom of exchange of currencies, which necessarily entails freedom of exchange of balances into gold as an international means of payment if premiums for exchange are such as to make shipments of gold profitable.

A currency may be said to be fulfilling its complete exchange function if it is freely convertible into gold both domestically and internationally. Domestically, convertibility into gold ordinarily should not be essential, since people normally are interested in currency for its purchasing power in goods and not for its gold redemption. The ideal of international convertibility, however, conflicts with domestic economic policy if that policy is stability. In the event of adverse balance of payments, free convertibility into gold might result in draining a country of gold reserves and the country would suffer deflation as the price of maintaining convertibility.

Under current world conditions, the ideal of world convertibility is difficult to realize in full because the problem basically involves the international balance of payments of particular countries. Thus, still prevalent EXCHANGE RESTRICTIONS are widely held to be necessary for balance of payments purposes. Insofar as the U.S. is concerned, the problem basically has been a world shortage of dollars and gold for dollar purposes in the post–World War II period; but as the result of shrinkage of favorable trade balance on merchandise account in most recent years and continued outflow of U.S. foreign aid and investment abroad, unfavorable total international balance of payments of the U.S., accompanied by gold exports, would, if resumed, pose in sharp relief the issue of domestic versus international interests and motivations.
See INTERNATIONAL MONETARY FUND.

CONVERTIBLE BONDS Bonds that at the option of the holder are convertible into other securities of the corporation. Such bonds are usually convertible at a certain price into preferred or common stock; if the value of the stock into which they can be converted should rise above the value of the bonds at the conversion price, the owner will find it profitable to exercise his or her option of converting. When bonds are convertible into stock, the stock into which they are convertible must be authorized at the time the bonds are issued. Convertible bonds have a speculative feature and tend to fluctuate in price in accordance with the movement of the stock into which they are convertible.

The advantage of convertible bonds to the issuing corporation is the increased chance of creating a large market for their sale. A corporation is not always able to raise additional capital to advantage by the issue of stock, and its bonds could be sold only at a high interest rate. To the investor, convertible bonds combine both safety of principal and possibility of enhancement in value through the conversion privilege. If the owner elects to convert, the fixed charges of the corporation are to that extent reduced.

Convertible bonds offer the investor the opportunity of combining an investment position with speculative possibilities; that is, they will sell at a level expressing the minimum credit position of the issuer, but at the same time fully reflect any advance in the stock into which the bond is convertible once the conversion price is approached or exceeded. Sometimes the conversion privilege offers a greater speculative flavor than the stock itself, especially where conversion is allowed in a large number of shares. If a convertible bond is convertible into stock at 40, it can be exchanged for 25 shares. If the stock should sell at 50, the the bond should be priced at approximately 125 in order to reflect the value of the conversion feature.

BIBLIOGRAPHY

WOOD, P. "International Convertible Bond Issues." *Journal of International Banking Law*, 1, 1986.

CONVERTIBLE PAPER MONEY PAPER MONEY that according to its terms may be redeemed at par in gold or lawful money. Convertible paper money is distinguished from inconvertible paper money. In recent decades, because of the maldistribution of world stock of gold, convertibility of paper money has been eliminated or restricted, and even the U.S., with the world's largest stock of monetary gold, since 1933 has withdrawn gold coin and gold certificates from circulation in accordance with the executive gold bullion standard adopted.
See IRREDEEMABLE PAPER MONEY.

CONVERTIBLE PREFERRED STOCK PREFERRED STOCK that the holder may exchange at his or her option for common stock at the stipulated conversion price or share exchange ratio. Usually the option cannot be exercised immediately, but only after a certain date or in accordance with certain conditions. Convertible preferred stock may be exchanged par for par or in other proportions as prescribed. This type of stock is attractive because it combines stability with possible enhancement of value through larger earnings. In case of large earnings, the stockholder may derive a larger income by converting into common stock, but at the expense of greater risk.

CONVEYANCE In general law, denotes an assignment, lease, settlement, or covenant to surrender made by a deed, mortgage, or sale. In general usage, however, the term denotes the deed by which real estate is conveyed from the seller to the buyer.

CONVEYANCING The science and act of transferring title to real estate from one person to another. Conveyancing is that part of an attorney's business which relates to the alienation and transmission of property and other rights from one person to another and to the formulation of legal documents intended to create, define, transfer, or extinguish rights. It therefore includes the searching of titles to real estate and the preparation of agreements, wills, articles of association, etc.

COOPERATIVE AGENCIES FOR CREDIT INFORMATION There are in the U.S. a large number of associations which reciprocate credit information through the credit departments of their various members. Practically every trade and manufacturing association maintains a credit organization for the purpose of determining the credit standing of dealers in the trade with the view to preventing credit losses through granting credit to buyers who are financially irresponsible. Not only do various trades maintain credit organizations, but many banks in the larger cities, chambers of commerce, and credit men's associations throughout the country have established cooperative credit exchanges where information is available to members and affiliations.

See CREDIT INFORMATION SOURCES, MERCANTILE AGENCIES.

COOPERATIVE BANKING In Massachusetts, a law was passed authorizing the establishment of cooperative savings fund and loan associations on May 14, 1877. In 1883, they became known as cooperative banks. From this idea sprang building and loan associations. The BUILDING AND LOAN ASSOCIATION, CREDIT UNION, FEDERAL LAND BANK ASSOCIATIONS, LABOR BANK, SAVINGS AND LOAN ASSOCIATIONS, AND SAVINGS BANKS are forms of cooperative banking.

COOPERATIVES The modern cooperative as a form of business enterprise may be said to date from the establishment in 1844 in England of the Rochdale Society of Equitable Pioneers, a consumer cooperative. Previously, in 1830, a producer cooperative had been formed by Rochdale weavers but subsequently failed. The 1844 cooperative, the first successful consumer cooperative, was formed by 28 flannel weavers to sell themselves butter, flour, oatmeal, and sugar at market prices at a single store. The idea caught on, and in five years the original store had 900 members and funds of £7,172. Other friendly societies, industrial societies, and provident societies sprang up. Growth, however, had to await legalization of such powers as patronage dividends (1852); limited liability, retention, and application of profits to educational purposes; power of local societies to form and own district wholesale societies to purchase and operate sources of supply (1862). In modern times, the wholesale cooperative societies in the British Isles supply to local consumer cooperatives such items as food, clothing, and household equipment and such services as laundry, dry cleaning, funerals, consumer credit, and legal services. There are over 1,000 consumer cooperatives serving some 7 million consumers in the British Isles and, through affiliation with wholesale cooperatives, owning and operating farms, plantations, factories, and grain elevators in England and other parts of the world. The cooperative movement spread to Europe, especially Sweden, where consumer cooperatives have over 1 million members and operate over 7,400 stores, and where cooperatives are also important in agriculture and housing; and Denmark, where there are nearly 2,000 affiliated consumer societies including about 480,000 households or 45% of the population, and where farm cooperatives operate over 1,250 dairies, slaughterhouses, and bacon processing plants.

In the U.S., cooperatives first became important in agriculture. The Cooperative Research and Service Division of the Department of Agriculture was authorized by the Cooperative Marketing Act of 1926 to assist and advise farmer cooperatives; its functions are now handled by the Farmer Cooperative Service of the Department of Agriculture. This agency estimates that three out of five American farmers now belong to marketing, farm supply, and related service cooperatives.

The cooperative originally developed in England with a sociological as well as economic motivation; thus John Stuart Mill, the famous English economist, wrote that "we may through the cooperation principle, see our way to a change in society." Such a grandiose goal was a pivotal part of the program of labor unions, including those in the U.S. until the hard-headed Samuel Gompers of the American Federation of Labor took over leadership of the American labor movement later in the nineteenth century. To this day, however, democratic participation in management by members is a fundamental characteristic of cooperatives. A unique feature of the Rochdale type of cooperative is common law voting (one vote per member), no voting by proxy, and voting by mail only on the matters notified in writing. This principle has been departed from under the Capper-Volstead Act of 1922 for American federally chartered cooperatives. Modern cooperatives may be either stock or nonstock in capitalization; limit membership by conditions for membership and withdrawals and by power of the directors to recall the stock of any member for value (as contrasted with the policy of early English cooperatives of encouraging membership without restriction); and limit number of shares and dividends per member.

The cooperative is also important in the U.S. in modern times in banking and credit fields (see COOPERATIVE BANKING), especially the savings and loan associations, credit unions, and farm credit cooperatives.

BIBLIOGRAPHY

Cooperative Accountant.

COPPER One of the most important nonferrous metals in tonnage and value (copper is the heat conducting and exchanging metal, in the view of industry executives, with only silver rivaling it in such uses), with its biggest markets in the construction and electrical machinery industries. Copper is erratic in price behavior, which renders it vulnerable to competition, chiefly from aluminum, and the most international of the nonferrous metals in world interdependence of sources of supply and prices and in world dependence upon political stability for trade flows.

International political tensions and their effects upon world copper are illustrated by the situation in Chile, which in 1971 expropriated the El Teniente mine (49% owned by the U.S.'s Kennecott Copper) and took over mines of the U.S.'s Anaconda Copper and Cerro Corp., whereupon the policy by Kennecott Copper to enjoin copper shipments or the funds in payment therefor identifiable as from the El Teniente mine, in non-Communist ports, aroused the united opposition of the four developing countries referred to, which account for most of the world's export volume of copper.

Market prices in the U.S. are the producers' prices, set by the producers that market their own output, and the custom smelters' prices, those of smelters purchasing ores chiefly from small mines and marketing the refined copper. The latter prices are more sensitive to market conditions. Despite efforts by the major producers to stabilize prices, difficulties in production and distribution control for the industry as a whole have impeded such rationalization. What the big producers do in the interests of stability, without running afoul of the antitrust laws, does have an effect, however, as they control about 75% of domestic mine output. Domestic prices are also affected by prices on the volatile London Metal Exchange Market, the most sensitive of the markets. Futures trading in copper is also provided on the COMMODITY EXCHANGE, INC. in New York.

COPPER A TIP An expression to indicate that one acts contrary to the advice or information received in a TIP.

COPPERS This term has two meanings:

1. A nickname for U.S. one-cent pieces. *See* BRONZE COINS, CENT.
2. An expression used to designate the COPPER stocks. In the U.S., the principal states for mine production of recoverable copper are Arizona and Utah. In Arizona, the Morenci branch of the Phelps Dodge Corporation is the largest copper producer. In Utah, in the West Mountain (Bingham) district, is located the leading copper mine in the U.S., Kennecott's Utah Copper Mine. The open pit mines of Kennecott, especially the Bingham District, and of Phelps Dodge compare favorably in costs with foreign mines having higher grade ores because of lower efficiency of foreign labor, higher transportation costs, and higher taxes.

COPS Covered option securities.
See FINANCIAL INSTRUMENTS: RECENT INNOVATIONS.

CORN This great feed grain of the U.S. finds its way directly into marketing to a comparatively minor extent, accounting along with the other feed grains (oats, barley, and the sorghum grains) for only about 8% of the total cash receipts of farmers. Nevertheless, as crops, the feed grains are the largest of the crops in volume and dollar value. The feed grains mainly reach the market indirectly, in the form of livestock and poultry. Principal corn producers are the North Central States (especially Iowa and Illinois). The principal market for corn is in Chicago, on the CHICAGO BOARD OF TRADE.

BIBLIOGRAPHY

Agricultural Letter. Federal Reserve Bank of Chicago. Weekly.
ALDRICH, S. R., and others. *Modern Corn Production.* A & L Publishers, Champaign, IL, 1986.

Commodity Year Book. Commodity Research Bureau, Inc. Annual.
Daily Market Record. Daily.
Statistical Annual: Grains, Options on Agricultural Futures. Chicago Board of Trade. Annual.
United States Census of Agriculture. Bureau of the Census. Quinquennial. Most recent: 1982.

CORNER "Control or monopoly over a commodity or security to get control of or to dictate prices" (S. S. Pratt, "Work of Wall Street"). Technically, a corner occurs on a stock exchange when shorts cannot borrow stock, i.e., have sold more stock than the floating supply makes available for purchase. Those who have a corner can dominate the situation and dictate price terms to their unfortunate victims—the shorts who are forced to settle at artificially dictated prices, thereby incurring heavy losses. The two important corners in stocks were the Northern Pacific corner (1901) and the Stutz corner (1920).

Corners have been more frequent in grain than in stock speculation and in most cases have proved disastrous for their promoters. The three great corners on the Chicago Board of Trade are known as the Hutchinson corner (1888), the Leiter corner (1898), and the Patten corner (1909). An attempt to corner silver occurred in the 1980s.

A corner has been declared to be illegal by the courts for two reasons: it is a gambling transaction and contracts thereunder are therefore unenforceable, it is in restraint of trade.

Under the COMMODITY EXCHANGE ACT and its successor the Commodity Futures Trading Commission Act of 1974, the Commodity Futures Trading Commission can set limitations both upon the amount of speculative trading done daily by any one individual and upon the speculative net position, long or short, of any speculative account at any one time, and requires the reporting to it of any holdings in excess of certain amounts. Under the Securities Exchange Act of 1934, operations of the stock exchanges and their members, and of security brokers and dealers generally, are subjected to regulation of the Securities and Exchange Commission.

BIBLIOGRAPHY

SARNOFF, P. *Silver Bulls*, 1980.

CORN-HOG RATIO The number of bushels of corn equal in value to 100 pounds of hog, liveweight, which indicates at market prices the relative attractiveness to farmers of selling their corn or feeding it to their hogs for hog marketing.

In addition to the corn-hog ratio, the Department of Agriculture also regularly compiles other local market commodity-feed price ratios, such as the egg-feed ratio (pounds of laying feed equal in value to one dozen eggs), broiler-feed ratio (pounds of broiler grower equal in value to one pound of broiler, liveweight), turkey-feed ratio (pounds of turkey grower equal in value to one pound of turkey, liveweight), and milk-feed ratio (pounds of concentrate ration equal in value to one pound of whole milk).

CORN PIT *See* PIT.

CORPORATE AGENT A person or firm empowered to act for another. Banks serve as corporate agents for a fee in various capacities for corporations, state and local governments, municipalities, and persons, including the following:

1. **Stock transfer agent.** Banks maintain stock transfer books and shareholders' ledger when retained by a corporate client.
2. **Stock registrar.** Banks serve as stock registrars who countersign stock certificates and ensure that each certificate is properly issued.
3. **Coupon and bond paying agent.** Banks and trust companies occasionally pay maturing coupons and principal of corporate clients. Paid coupons and bonds are cremated and either a cremation certificate or the paid coupons and bonds are returned to the principal.
4. **Dividends disbursing agent.** Banks pay dividends to stockholders of record and provide a report to the corporation of such disbursements when retained to do so.
5. **Fiscal agent.** Banks serve as fiscal agent for a government, especially for taxes withheld that are deposited with it for the account of the government.

CORPORATE RECORDS Those records of a CORPORATION required by incorporation laws and pertaining to its corporate character. Among these are the certificate of incorporation, bylaws, book of minutes of the board of directors, stock book, stock transfer book, etc. Section 10 of the New York Stock Corporation Law requires that every stock corporation keep at its office correct books of account of all its business and transactions and a stock book showing the names of all persons, alphabetically arranged, who are stockholders of the corporation, their addresses, number of shares of stock held, the time when they became stockholders, and the amount paid thereon.

CORPORATE STOCK In municipal financing, sometimes used as the title for bonds of long-term maturity, with sinking fund retirement and other characteristics of bonds.
See MUNICIPAL BONDS.

CORPORATE TRUSTS *See* TRUST.

CORPORATION The corporate form of business organization is dominant in the U.S. in manufacturing and wholesale trade both in number of firms and in operating terms (sales, employees). In retail trade and the service industries, corporations are in the minority numerically but account for more sales and employment than unincorporated firms (U.S. Bureau of the Census, U.S. Census of Business). This dominant position of the corporation as to size of operations underscores the major financial and managerial advantages of the corporate form. Financially, the corporate form structurally facilitates more extensive financing for a firm for the following reasons.

1. **Limited liability.** When stockholders become investors in a corporation they can foretell the limits of maximum loss (the extent of the investment), without personal liability for debts of the firm, unlike the case for the proprietorship and the general partnership.
2. **Separability of investor and managerial motivations.** The investor who is not interested in active participation in management may invest in nonvoting stock or, where he invests in voting stock, may by proxy designate persons to vote for him, in his name, place, and stead, in elections of directors and on other corporate matters. In either case, management may be delegated to others (the directors, who in turn appoint the officers). If the stockholder is so motivated, he may participate actively in election of directors or become a member of the board of directors and/or member of the officers to the extent that his voting power and qualifications justify. The corporation's capitalization may be appropriately proportioned as to debt, nonvoting stocks, and voting stocks.
3. **Divisibility and transferability of ownership.** The corporation's total ownership is divisible into an appropriate number of units (shares of stock) by the device of par value (or if no par value stock is issued, by number of shares with suitable stated value per share). Such conveniently sized units of ownership may be sold to a larger number of investors, as contrasted to total lump sum proprietorship interest or proportionate interests of partners. Further, a fundamental right of stockholders is to receive certificates of ownership, which may be readily assigned to new owners and/or transferred, heightening marketability.
4. **The absence of "delectus personae" among stockholders** (the personal right of general partners to choose their associates as partners). Each and every stockholder of a particular class of stock is entitled to all the rights and privileges applicable to all other holders of that class of stock. Existing stockholders cannot refuse to admit new stockholders to full status as such.
5. **Separate legal existence of the corporation as an entity, apart from its owners, creditors, and agents** (directors, officers, employees, etc.). Because the corporation may own, buy, and sell property in its own name; make contracts; sue and be sued in its own name; exercise all its express, implied, and incidental authorized powers, it may continue its separate existence, with its own financial integrity, apart from turnover of such individuals, pursuant to its charter. Such durability of existence facilitates long-term financing.

A *de jure* corporation is one formed in compliance with the provisions of an incorporation statute. A *de facto* corporation is one formed without full compliance with all material, mandatory provisions of an incorporation statute.

Corporations are also classified as public or private. Private corporations may be stock or nonstock corporations. Stock companies normally operate for profit, while nonstock corporations such as certain hospitals and churches usually are not-for-profit organizations. Corporations also can be classified as follows:

1. Public corporations are government-owned entities such as the Federal Deposit Insurance Corporation.
2. Open corporations are private stock corporations whose stock is available to the public and is usually traded on a stock exchange (a listed corporation) or in the over-the-counter market (unlisted).
3. Closed corporations are private corporations whose stock is not offered for sale to the general public but is usually held by a few individuals.
4. Domestic corporations are incorporated in a particular state. Foreign corporations operate in a state other than the one in which they are incorporated.

Managerially, the corporate form, aside from its general advantage of assembling skills, money, and property, especially facilitates use of the line and line and staff types of internal organization for large-scale operations, making possible functionalization and decentralization of operations with centralization of responsibility and accountability maintained.

The rise of the corporation as the most important form of business organization was especially facilitated in the latter part of the last century by enactment of general incorporation statutes among the states, making it possible for any group of incorporators complying with the objective statute's requirements to form corporations freely. By contrast, the previous system of special acts of the legislatures for chartering corporations inhibited new incorporations by making it possible for existing corporate interests to block the new charters by political pressure.

The corporation is a creature of statute, both as to procedure for formation and subsequent exercise of permissible powers, but the corporation is legally protected against arbitrary impairment of charter powers by the sovereign, the state, because the corporate charter is a contract that the state of incorporation may not impair (*Dartmouth College v. Woodward*, 4 Wheat. 518 (1819)). The corporation, although a legal entity, has no freedom of movement, as natural persons have, to do business in any state; as a foreign corporation seeking to do business in other states, it may validly be required to be licensed and designate agent therein for service of process in case of litigation. As a creature of statute, the corporation may be subjected to nonarbitrary or discriminatory regulation, especially in such fields as banking, insurance, and other regulated lines of activity.

Since the corporation is a separate legal entity, it is itself the legitimate object of taxation, both federal and state, both organizational taxes (incorporation fees, annual franchise taxes) and operational taxes (income, property, and excise taxes). This leads to the disadvantage for stockholders of double taxation (the corporation pays taxes and stockholders pay income taxes on dividends declared and distributed). To the extent of properly retained earnings, the corporation may legitimately avoid such double taxation. Intercorporate dividends are taxed only at their tax rate on only 15% of the dollar amount, so that, for example, at a 46% tax bracket for the corporation, the net tax is 6.9%, which constitutes welcome relief from the double taxation. The giant corporation of modern times is likely to be either purely or partly a HOLDING COMPANY, owning interests in other corporations.

The growth of giant corporations led some early observers (e.g., A. A. Berle, Jr., and G. C. Means, *The Modern Corporation and Private Property*, 1933) to view with alarm the concentration of industry in relatively few corporations and, projecting such growth, to conclude that the giant corporation was a threat to government itself. Other observers viewed with misgivings the impersonal nature of the corporation, hiding its principals behind its corporate veil and giving rise to a new professional class—the managers—normally insulated against effective accountability to independent stockholders because of massive proxy voting. The dire projections of concentration, however, have been modified by growth of the economy as a whole. Proxy battles for control indicate the vulnerability of arbitrary managements; the emphasis by giant corporations upon stockholder relations and public relations indicates responsibility as compared with the predatory irresponsibility of the latter part of the nineteenth century. And government, with its proliferations of laws and administrative agencies in regulation of business, has not been taken over by the corporation.

See PARENT COMPANY.

BIBLIOGRAPHY

All You Should Know About Establishing and Operating a Small Corporation. Contemporary Books, Inc., Chicago, IL, 1986.
Corporate Counsel's Annual. Matthew Bender & Co., Inc., New York, NY. Annual.
Corporation Journal.
Corporation Law Guide. Commerce Clearing House, Chicago, IL. Biweekly.
DRUCKER, P. F. *The Concept of the Corporation.* New American Library, New York, NY, 1983.
Encyclopedia of Legal Information Sources. Gale Research Co., Detroit, MI, 1988.
Federal Register. Office of the Federal Register, Washington, DC.
Fletcher Corporation Law Adviser. Callaghan & Co. Monthly.
Legal Resource Index. Information Access Corp, Belmont, CA. Online data base.
Model Business Corporation Act Annotated. American Bar Association, Chicago, IL. Five volumes. Periodic supplements.
MCDONALD, A. L. *Communicating with Legal Databases: Terms and Abbreviations for the Legal Researcher.* Neal Schuman Publishers, Inc., New York, NY, 1987.
Organizing Corporate and Other Business Enterprises. Matthew Bender & Co., Inc., New York, NY. Looseleaf.
Reference Book of Corporate Managements. Dun and Bradstreet, New York, NY.
Securities Law Series. Clark Boardman Co., Washington, DC. Looseleaf.
Securities Regulation and Law Report. Bureau of National Affairs, Inc., Washington, DC. Weekly.

CORPORATION BONDS Obligations of a business corporation as distinguished from civil bonds, obligations of a governmentality (federal, state, or municipal government).

The soundness of corporation bonds depends upon many factors including the character of collateral offered, the character of the issuer, the nature of the industry, and the stability of its earnings. The market value of corporation bonds is primarily influenced by money rates in the case of highest grade obligations, and business activity and conditions in the case of lower grade issues, while civil bonds of fiscally sound public bodies are primarily influenced by the level of money rates.

See BOND, INDUSTRIAL BONDS, INVESTMENT, PUBLIC UTILITY BONDS, RAILROAD BONDS.

CORPORATION FINANCE The division of finance that deals with the promotion, organization, capitalization, financing, reorganization, and financial conduct of business corporations. "Corporation finance aims to explain and illustrate the methods employed in the promotion, capitalization, financial management, consolidation, and reorganization of business corporations" (S. E. Mead, *Corporation Finance*, 1910). The descriptive approach of pioneer texts, emphasizing legal and accounting aspects of the subject, continues to be fundamental in modern works, but added thereto has been more emphasis on theory and decision-making, particularly from case materials, accentuating the managerial approach.

BIBLIOGRAPHY

WOELFEL, C. J. *The Desktop Encyclopedia of Corporate Finance & Accounting.* Probus Publishing Co., Chicago, IL, 1987.

CORPORATION PAPER Notes, acceptances, and bills of exchange issued by corporations, as distinguished from paper issued by individuals and copartnerships.

CORPORATION: TAX FORMULA The computation of the federal income tax liability for a corporation is presented here:

Total income (from whatever sources)
- Exclusions from gross income
= Gross income
- Deductions (most business expenses)
= Taxable income x Applicable tax rates
= Gross tax
- Tax credits and prepayments
= Tax due (or refund)

Related corporations (i.e., affiliated groups) may elect to file a single income tax return called a consolidated tax return. An affiliated group is one or more chains of includible corporations connected through stock ownership with a common parent company, if certain criteria are met:

1. The common parent directly owns stock with at least 80% of the total value of at least one includible corporation.
2. Stock with at least 80% of the total voting power and 80% of the total value of each other corporation included in the affiliated group is owned directly by one or more group members.

The consolidated return includes the income and expenses of each of its members. The two main advantages of filing a consolidated return are that: (1) income of a profitable member of the group can be offset against losses of another member and (2) profits or gains reported on intercompany transactions are generally deferred until a sale outside the group takes place.

CORRELATION Correlation is the relationship between two or more sets of variables. The more closely two (or more) series are related, the higher the degree of correlation. For example, the sales manager of an insurance company might want to know if there is a correlation between the weeks of training a salesperson receives and that person's average daily output.

The value of the coefficient of correlation falls between 0 and 1.00, representing degrees of relationship ranging from no correlation to perfect correlation. When $r = .60$ and $r(2) = .36$, it can be said that 36% of the variance in the y variable is related to variations in the x variable; or 64% of the variance is not related.

Multiple regression analysis takes into account simultaneously the relationship among all the variables when two or more independent variables are used to estimate the dependent variable. For example, a manager may accumulate the following information about a firm's manufacturing operations:

Output per employee in units
Aptitude test scores of employees
Years of experience of employees

Multiple regression analysis can be used to estimate the output of an employee from a knowledge of the person's aptitude test score and years of experience.

Partial correlation is a method of measuring the net correlation or partial correlation between one independent variable and the dependent variable, eliminating the relationship with the other independent variables in the study. This measure of relationship is known as the coefficient of partial correlation.

See STATISTICS.

CORRESPONDENT A bank having direct connection or friendly service relations with another. Most banks, especially country banks, find it convenient to maintain balances with a bank in a larger city or cities, either as a reserve or as a fund against which drafts may be sold and out-of-town checks collected. A Painesville, Ohio bank, for instance, might keep a balance in Cleveland and another in New York. Often mutual collection agreements are arranged which specify each bank's obligations and remuneration. Most of the larger eastern banks have correspondents in foreign countries.

Some of the stock exchange commission houses have out-of-town correspondents, usually local investment security firms, which procure orders which are transmitted by private wire for execution on the New York Stock Exchange, Chicago Board of Trade, etc.

COST An expenditure (a decrease in assets or an increase in liabilities) made to obtain an economic benefit, usually resources that can produce revenue. A cost can also be defined as the sacrifice to acquire a good or service. Used in this sense, a cost represents an asset. An expense is a cost that has been utilized by the company in the process of obtaining revenue. Costs can be classified in many ways, including the following:

1. Direct and indirect costs
   a. Direct costs are outlays that can be identified with a specific product, department or activity (e.g., direct labor and direct material costs).
   b. Indirect costs are outlays that cannot be identified as can direct costs (e.g., taxes, insurance, telephone expense).
2. Product and period costs
   a. Product costs are outlays that can be associated with production.
   b. Period costs are associated not with production, but with the passage of time. The President's salary, advertising expense, and interest expenses are examples of period costs.
3. Fixed, variable, and mixed costs
   a. Fixed costs remain constant in total (not per unit) regardless of the volume of production or sales, over a relevant range of production or sales. Rent and depreciation are typically fixed costs. Total depreciation remains constant; depreciation per unit of output changes with changes in volume or activity.
   b. Variable costs fluctuate in total (not per unit) as the volume of production or sales fluctuates. Direct labor costs, direct material costs used in production, and sales commissions are examples of variable costs. Total commission expense varies with changes in sales volume; commission expense per unit of sales remains constant as sales volume changes.
   c. Mixed costs contain elements of fixed and variable costs. Costs of supervision and inspections are often mixed costs.
4. Controllable and uncontrollable costs
   a. Controllable costs are identified as a responsibility of an individual or department and can be regulated within a given period of time. Office supplies would ordinarily be considered as a controllable cost for an office manager.
   b. Uncontrollable costs cannot be regulated by an individual or department within a given period of time. For example, rent expense is uncontrollable by the factory foreman.
5. Out-of-pocket costs and sunk costs
   a. Out-of-pocket costs require the use of current economic resources, usually cash. Taxes and insurance are usually out-of-pocket costs.
   b. Sunk costs are outlays or commitments that have already been incurred. The cost of equipment already purchased is a sunk cost.
6. Incremental, opportunity, and imputed costs
   a. Incremental (or differential) cost is the difference in total costs between alternatives. Incremental costs can also be considered as the total cost added or subtracted by switching from one level or plan of activity to another.
   b. Opportunity costs are costs that can be associated with an economic event when no exchange transaction has occurred. For example, if a company "rents to itself" a building that it might otherwise have rented to an outside party, the rent for the building is an imputed cost.
7. Relevant cost. A relevant cost is an expected future cost that represents the difference in costs among alternatives. Assume you purchased an airline ticket from New York to London at a cost of $300 and that you have made an nonrefundable $75 down payment on the ticket. The remaining $225 will be paid when you pick up the ticket. The ticket is nontransferable. You later discover that you can purchase a ticket to London on another airline for $200. Everything related to the two tickets is equal. The $75 down payment is not relevant to this decision since it is not a future cost that differs among alternatives. You should buy the new ticket for $200.

See BANK COST ACCOUNTING.

BIBLIOGRAPHY

BRANTLEY, R. L. "Measure Functional Costs to Pinpoint Performance." *Savings Institutions*, June, 1988.
COLE, L. P. *Cost Analysis and Control in Banks*. Bankers Publishing Co., 1985.

WALLACE, J. M. "Case Study: How CBT Reduced Noninterest Expenses by 15%." *Bank Accounting & Finance*, Spring, 1988.

COST ACCOUNTING See BANK COST ACCOUNTING

COST AND FREIGHT Used chiefly in import and export transactions to mean that the price quoted includes the cost of the merchandise and the freight to the point of destination, but does not include insurance. The abbreviation used is c. and f.

COST, INSURANCE, AND FREIGHT The price quoted includes not only the cost of the merchandise but also the freight and insurance charges to the point of destination. The abbreviation used is c.i.f.

COST OF CAPITAL The cost of funds invested in an enterprise. The cost of capital is the weighted average of the cost of each type of debt and equity capital. The weight for each type of capital is the ratio of the market value of the securities representing that particular source of capital to the market value of all securities issued by the company. To illustrate, assume that the market value of a company's common stock is $600,000 and the dividend yield is 10%. The market value of the company's interest-bearing debt is $400,000 with an average after-tax yield of 8%. The average cost of capital for the company can be estimated as follows:

Source	Proportion of	Cost	Weighted Amount
Common stock	0.60	0.10	0.06
Debt	0.40	0.08	0.032
Average cost of capital			0.092

Cost of capital is also used to refer to the discount rate that equates the expected present value of future cash flows to common shareholders with the market value of the common stock at a specific time.

COST OF GOODS SOLD The expense incurred for merchandise (or goods) sold during a particular period. Cost of goods sold can be computed as follows:

Beginning inventory, January 1	$100,000
Add: Purchases (net) during the year	700,000
Goods available for sale during the year	800,000
Less: Ending inventory, December 31	60,000
Cost of goods sold	$740,000

Gross margin is the excess of sales over cost of goods sold:

Sales (net)	$950,000
Less: Cost of goods sold	740,000
Gross margin	$210,000

COST OF LIVING INDEX The popular concept of the consumer price index (CPI), prepared by the Bureau of Labor Statistics of the U.S. Department of Labor. It is not, however, an index of consumers' living costs or of consumer prices, as indicated by the following official explanation of its concepts and calculation.

The consumer price indexes (CPIs) are statistical measures of the average changes in the cost of fixed or constant "market baskets" of consumer goods and services purchased by the index population, either all urban consumers or urban wage earners and clerical workers.

A major revision of the indexes was completed in December, 1977. Effective with release of the January 1978 index, the Bureau of Labor Statistics introduced an updated and revised CPI for urban wage earners and clerical workers (CPI-W) and a broader-based CPI for all urban consumers (CPI-U), including salaried workers, the self-employed, the retired, and the unemployed, as well as wage earners and clerical workers. The revision included an updating of the expenditure weights for the various spending categories such as food, clothing, medical care, etc.; and the area, outlet samples, and item. In addition to the introduction of the CPI-U, which represents about 80% of the population (whereas the CPI-W represents about 40%), other improvements included monthly or bimonthly indexes which are available for 28 major urban areas (compared with monthly or quarterly indexes for 23 areas previously), regional indexes which are available for urban areas of different population-size classes, and some index components which are of a more general character than a very specific item. Less obvious improvements included more accurate reflection of current purchases in the fixed market basket, more representative outlets, increased monthly and bimonthly pricing—largely replacing quarterly pricing, substantially lower measurement errors, and a more modern conceptual basis and statistical methods. Both the new and revised CPI-U and CPI-W were linked to the unrevised CPI-W as of December, 1977, to provide continuous series.

In 1983, BLS changed to an owners' equivalent-rent approach to homeowner costs for the CPI-U, which in 1985 was extended to the CPI-W. The old measure of homeownership costs was based largely on the purchase and financing of an asset, thus failing to distinguish the investment aspect of owning a home from the consumption of housing services. Because the CPI is conceived as a measure of price change of consumption, inclusion of investment purchases was deemed inappropriate. The equivalent-rent index measures the change in the rental cost of housing services provided by owner-occupied housing.

Both the CPI-W and the CPI-U were updated again as of January 1987 to make more current the sample of items included in the market basket and the expenditure weights, to enlarge the sample of urban areas, and to include a more representative selection of outlets priced. These revisions were based on data gathered from the annual Survey of Consumer Expenditures for 1982 to 1984, the 1980 Census of Population, and the ongoing Point-of-Purchase Survey.

The Department of Labor publishes the national average CPI-W in its *Monthly Labor Review*, along with data classified by geographic region and by population size, for each item included in the total index. Also published monthly are data for five major metropolitan areas. An additional 22 metropolitan areas are covered on a bimonthly or semiannual basis.

The appended table compares, for 1977 through 1987, the total indexes and principal components.

Consumer Price Indexes, 1977–1987 (1982 – 84 = 100)

		CPI-U				Percent Change *	
				Commodities			
Year	CPI-W	Total	Food	Less Food	Services	CPI-W	CPI-U
1977	60.9	60.6	65.5	63.8	56.0	6.5	6.5
1978	65.6	65.2	72.0	67.5	60.8	7.7	7.6
1979	73.1	72.6	79.9	75.3	67.5	11.4	11.3
1980	82.9	82.4	86.8	85.7	77.9	13.4	13.5
1981	91.4	90.9	93.6	93.1	88.1	10.3	10.3
1982	96.9	96.5	97.4	96.9	96.0	6.0	6.2
1983	99.8	99.6	99.4	100.0	99.4	3.0	3.2
1984	103.3	103.9	103.2	103.1	104.6	3.5	4.3
1985	106.9	107.6	105.6	105.2	1-9.9	3.5	3.6
1986	108.6	109.6	109.0	101.7	115.4	1.6	1.9
1987	112.5	113.6	113.6	104.3	120.2	3.6	3.6

* Commonly referred to as the inflation rate.
Source: Bureau of Labor Statistics.

Despite its limitations in scope and coverage and the necessity for use of statistical techniques in order to make possible monthly data with small time lags (release on or about the 19th of the month, covering index for the preceding month), the Consumer Price Index is the best statistic available to measure the cost of living (see table appended) at the retail level. For adjustment of the gross national product and its components, however, the U.S. Department of Commerce supplies the price deflator for such data, a more appropriate and comprehensive price index (1958 = 100), for calculation of gross national product level and changes in constant dollars (i.e., adjusting for inflation).

BIBLIOGRAPHY

Blinder, A. S. "The Consumer Price Index and the Measurement of Recent Inflation." *Brookings Papers on Economic Activity*, 1980 (2).

Guthrie, R. S. "The Relationship Between Wholesale and Consumer Prices." *Southern Economic Journal*, April, 1981.

Jones, R. A. "Which Price Index for Escalating Debts?" *Economic Inquiry*, April, 1980.

Layng, W. J. "The Revision of the Consumer Price Index." Reprinted from the *Statistical Reporter*, February, 1978, No. 78-5 (U.S. Department of Commerce).

Mitchell, D. J. B. "Does the CPI Exaggerate or Understate Inflation?" *Monthly Labor Review*, May, 1980.

Norwood, J. L. "Two Consumer Price Index Issues: Weighting and Homeownership." *Monthly Labor Review*, March, 1981.

COST PRINCIPLE An accounting principle that requires that assets, liabilities, owners' equity, and other elements of accounting be initially recorded in the accounting system at the time of exchange and at the price agreed upon by the parties to the exchange. The cost principle is also referred to as the historical (or acquisition) cost principle. The cost principle is based on the assumption that cost represents the fair market value at the date of acquisition. It also provides verifiable and objective data.

COST-PUSH INFLATION Inflation is a continuous increase in the average price level. One explanation for inflation is that increases in the cost of production push up the prices of final goods and services. A key cost element is wages, and it is maintained that excessive union demands for higher wages fuel inflation. Monopoly control over key resource inputs can have the same effect.

COTTON Cotton production in the U.S. involves some 20 states (largest producers: Texas, Mississippi, and Calilfornia). Largest producing regions are the Southwest (Texas, Oklahoma, and Kansas) and the Delta (Missouri, Arkansas, Tennessee, Mississippi, Louisiana, Illinois, and Kentucky), but the highest yields per acre are found in the West (California, Arizona, New Mexico and Nevada). The western states are the largest producers of irrigation cotton which, in comparison with rainfall cotton, generally has longer staple, longer growing season, and better controlled moisture.

COTTON BILL A bill of exchange drawn to finance an export of cotton and secured by the bill of lading.

COTTON CONTROL ACT BANKHEAD COTTON CONTROL ACT, which was repealed on February 10, 1936.

COTTON FUTURES Contracts for future delivery of cotton, traded in on organized commodity exchanges. A cotton futures contract is an agreement, enforcible at law and under the rules of the exchange, to deliver or to accept a definite quantity of cotton during a specified calendar month at a stated price. Most of the terms of the contract are set by the rules of the exchange, the variables being the price and month of delivery. Trading unit (quantity per contract) is standardized under rules of the exchange.

See COTTON FUTURES ACT, FUTURES.

COTTON FUTURES ACT An act which became effective February 18, 1915, the full title of which is United States Cotton Futures Act. The purpose of the act was to standardize the practice in trading in COTTON FUTURES, and to correct the abuses which had previously existed by compelling adoption of uniform prestandard grades as determined by the Department of Agriculture (*see* COTTON GRADES), exclusion from deliveries of cotton of inferior quality or less than seven-eighths of an inch in length of staple, and adjustment of differences in value of the various grades on the basis of commercial differences based on prices actually paid for the different grades at the various cotton markets of the country and not upon fixed differences.

The Commodity Exchange Act, which originally applied to grains only, was amended in 1936 to pertain to other commodities, including cotton. Cotton futures trading is now subject to the regulations imposed by the Commodity Futures Trading Commission Act of 1974 and the COMMODITY FUTURES TRADING COMMISSION which designates the commodity exchanges that may operate contract or FUTURES markets in cotton.

COTTON GRADES Cotton grading depends upon three variables—color, presence of extraneous substances, and length of fiber. Grades are determined by the Department of Agriculture. Cotton is usually graded as follows.

1. White cotton. Full grades: middling fair, good middling, low middling, good ordinary. Half grades: strict middling fair, strict good middling, strict middling, strict low middling, strict good ordinary. Intermediate grades: fully good middling, barely good middling, fully middling, barely middling, full low middling.
2. Tinged cotton: strict good middling tinged, good middling tinged, strict middling tinged, middling tinged, strict low middling tinged, low middling tinged.
3. Stained cotton: middling stained.

Grades in order of value for white cotton are good middling, strict middling, middling, strict low middling, low middling, strict good ordinary, and good ordinary. Split grades (middling plus, strict low middling plus, etc.) fall between all these grades below strict middling. The grade of most U.S. cotton is below strict middling. The seven color groupings indicate the degree of whiteness: white, light spotted, spotted, tinged, stained, light gray, and gray.

Staple length refers to the average length of the fibers in the particular bale, measured in 32nds of an inch. Most U.S. cotton is of the upland type, which for the most part ranges from $^{29}/_{32}$ inch to 1 $^{1}/_{8}$ inches in staple length. Extra long staple, or American-Egyptian cotton, is grown mostly in Arizona and the El Paso area of Texas and New Mexico, and ranges from 1 $^{5}/_{16}$ inches to 1 $^{7}/_{16}$ inches in length.

Both grade and staple length are determined by the individual judgment of cotton classers through comparison with the prepared government standards.

Mike (micronaire) measurement of fiber fineness is also part of the classification system. Cotton of less than 3.5 micronaire readings (the weight in micrograms per inch of fiber) tends to cause both spinning and dyeing difficulties; accordingly such readings are not deliverable on NEW YORK COTTON EXCHANGE futures contracts.

Cotton intended for certification for delivery on futures must be stored in a warehouse licensed by the New York Cotton Exchange. Sampling and weighing are done under the supervision of the exchange. The samples are then sent to a U.S. Board of Cotton Examiners for classification and certification.

COTTONSEED For every pound of cotton ginned, there is produced nearly two pounds of seed, a versatile by-product. Most cottonseed is sold by cotton farmers to the ginner, who in turn sells it directly to cottonseed processors. The Department of Agriculture describes the ensuing process as follows.

At the processing plants, the seed is cleaned, delinted, and hulled, and the resulting flaked "meat"' is separated from the hulls. These processes give two of the four original products obtained from cottonseed: linters (the short fuzz or fibers remaining on the seed coat after ginning) and hulls (the stiff outer coating of the seed). The other two products—oil and cottonseed cake or meal—are obtained from the flaked meat through mechanical or solvent extraction processes.

In mechanical extraction, which accounts for the bulk of cottonseed processed, the meats are rolled into flakes and cooked with or without pressure. The oil is then extracted from the meat by hydraulic or screw presses. The resulting cake is either ground into meal or cracked into smaller pieces; the meal is then often further processed into cubes or pellets.

Solvent extraction is rapidly increasing in importance because it takes less work and gives a greater proportion of oil. In this process, the flaked meats are exposed to chemical solvents, which dissolve out the oil. The oil is separated from the solvent by distillation.

Oil is by far the most valuable of the cottonseed products. After extraction, it is further processed mainly into such edible products as shortening, cooking oils, salad oils, salad dressing, and margarine. The major processing steps are refining, bleaching, winterizing, hydrogenating, and deodorizing. Meal or cake, the second most valuable cottonseed product, and hulls are used primarily as feed for livestock. Linters have a wider variety of uses than any of the other cottonseed products; most important of these uses is as chemical cellulose, for which they are cooked or digested with chemicals, bleached, washed, and dried. The resulting linter pulp, which is practically pure cellulose, is used in the manufacture of many products, mainly rayon, plastics, film, explosives, paper, and lacquers. The longest lengths and highest grades of linters are spun into coarse yarns. Others serve as a filler in bedding, furniture, and automobiles.

As a by-product of cotton, cottonseed cannot adjust to market conditions for oilseed and edible oils. The principal competitor of cottonseed oil is soybean oil, except for such uses as salad oil and shortening for which soybean oil is not entirely satisfactory as a substitute, although improving as the result of better refining. Soybean oil also has wide industrial usage. Cottonseed cannot be held through the season without deteriorating, except by the use of cooling equipment; therefore it is crushed as early as possible. This gives a highly seasonal pattern in crushings and oil output. By contrast, soybeans can be readily stored for longer periods without loss of quality so their volume of crushings is fairly uniform throughout the season. As a result, in most seasons, the price differential between cottonseed oil and soybean oil is small during the fall, when the output of both oils is heavy, but subsequently, cottonseed oil usually works up to a premium over soybean oil as cottonseed oil output tapers off and supplies decline. The bulk of consumption of cottonseed's products is domestic, export volume being minor.

COTTONSEED OIL See COTTONSEED.

COURGs Certificates of government receipts.
See FINANCIAL INSTRUMENTS: RECENT INNOVATIONS.

COULISSE One of the markets for securities on the PARIS BOURSE. The Parquet, on the main floor, is where the seasoned securities are traded. The role of the smaller Coulisse is analogous to the American Stock Exchange's relationship to the New York Stock Exchange. The hors-cote market corresponds to the over-the-counter market.

COUNCIL OF ECONOMIC ADVISERS An agency within the Executive Office of the President that analyzes the national economy and its various segments, advises the President on economic developments, appraises the economic programs and policies of the federal government, recommends policies for economic growth and stability, and assists in the preparation of the annual *Economic Report of the President* to Congress. It also prepares the monthly report, *Economic Indicators*, for the JOINT ECONOMIC COMMITTEE of Congress.

The CEA was established by the Employment Act of 1946. Since 1953, it also has functioned under Reorganization Plan No. 9. The council has three members, appointed by the President with the advice and consent of the Senate. Day-to-day direction of CEA's professional staff is the general responsibility of the two council members other than the chairman. Staff responsibilities are divided informally by assigned subject areas.

BIBLIOGRAPHY

COUNCIL OF ECONOMIC ADVISERS. *Annual Reports.*

COUNTER CASH That part of the money stock of a bank that is entrusted to the paying teller, as distinguished from the reserve cash, i.e., the money that the bank is required by law to maintain as reserve against deposits. The counter cash, also known as till money, is taken into the paying teller's cage during the day and kept in a separate compartment of the vault at other times. It is an amount sufficient to provide for the cashing of checks, as shown by experience.

COUNTER CHECK A special form of check, so marked, available to the depositors at the desks in the lobby of a bank for convenience in case the checkbook has been left at home. A counter check can be cashed only at the paying teller's window and by the drawer thereof in person. Its purpose is to prevent swindlers or forgers from using blank checks fraudulently. A check provided by the bank for the convenience of depositors; can be cashed only by drawer in person.

COUNTERFEIT CURRENCY See COUNTERFEITS.

COUNTERFEITS Fraudulent, spurious, bogus, or imitation money; money manufactured in imitation of genuine money. The government has a monopoly of coinage and any private person who makes coins or paper money is a counterfeiter.

One of the duties of paying tellers, receiving tellers, and money clerks is to detect counterfeit money, and consequently they should be skilled in the art of counterfeit detection. Counterfeits are not easily detected by the visual process. They are more easily caught by the feeling of the weight and texture than by the appearance. The paper furnishing the basis for paper currency is made by a secret process and is difficult to imitate. Generally counterfeit paper is inferior in quality to the paper used by the government and red and blue ink lines are used to imitate the red and blue silk threads in the genuine bills.

There are three principal methods of making counterfeit bills. The first is copying bills by hand, reproducing each finest line and imitating the silk thread in the paper of the genuine issue with delicate pen and ink work. Such work is performed only by experts—probably those who have formerly been engaged in the Bureau of Engraving and Printing. Some of these notes have been so skillfully imitated as to deceive the naked eye of experts.

The second method is to engrave a steel plate from which the counterfeit bills are printed. This process is more remunerative than the first because many bills can be reproduced from the same plate.

The third and most usual process is that of photographic reproduction. The photoengraving process bills are not as accurate as the steel engraved bills and are the easiest of all to detect. The engraving is apt to be less distinct and of lighter color than in the genuine because the plates are made from photographs of the original and something is lost in the process.

There are two principal methods of making counterfeit coins. The first is casting from a mold; the second is stamping with a die and press. In the casting process a mold is made from a new and genuine coin. In the stamping process a die is made and the counterfeit money is struck off with sharp blows of a heavy press. The stamping process produces better results because the impression is more clearly cut, this, in fact, being the method used in manufacturing genuine coins.

No exact formula can be given for the detection of counterfeits. Judgment, experience, knowledge of counterfeiters' technical processes, and familiarity in handling currency are the best guides. The most competent assistance available for discovering counterfeits comes from publications of the Secret Service Division of the U.S. Treasury Department and of the protective divisions of banking associations. Whenever counterfeits are discovered, the account of the customer depositing them should be charged and the Secret Service Division of the U.S. Treasury Department notified.

Counterfeit notes found in remittances from banks are canceled and returned for the purpose of enabling the owner to make reclamation; after such use they must be returned to the Treasurer of the United States for transfer to the Secret Service Division of the Treasury Department.

Counterfeit notes found in remittances from individuals are canceled and sent to the Secret Service Division. The sender is advised of the fact and informed that, if he will communicate with the chief of that division, arrangements may be made to have such note submitted for reclamation.

Counterfeit coins found in remittances to the treasurer are canceled and sent to the Secret Service Division, a receipt for the same being returned to the sender, who may communicate with the chief of that division if he desires to have such coin submitted for reclamation.

Counterfeit coin received at the subtreasuries (now Federal Reserve banks) is retained, to be called for by agents of the Secret Service at certain stated periods. A receipt is issued to the sender or depositor, when desired, to enable him to make reclamation for coin so retained.

BIBLIOGRAPHY

BOARD OF GOVERNORS OF THE FEDERAL RESERVE SYSTEM. *U.S. Currency* (Consumer Education Pamphlet).
U.S. DEPARTMENT OF THE TREASURY. *Facts About United States Money.*
———. Secret Service. *Know Your Money.*

COUNTERMAND To cancel an order which has not yet been executed.

COUNTERPART FUNDS Creation of the control device of counterpart funds was an original feature of the Economic Cooperation Act of 1948 (Marshall Plan), and was continued under subsequent legislation (see FOREIGN AID), particularly P.L. 480 (Titles I and IV of the Agricultural Trade Development and Assistance Act of 1954).

A Title I agreement with the host country specified the appropriate exchange rate and the percentage of the local currency, received in nominal payment for U.S. farm commodities, which would be reserved in the host country for U.S. use and what part for usage for approved purposes by the host country. A Title IV agreement stipulated the payment period, interest rate, and repayment schedule for the dollar long-term credit sales of surplus agricultural commodities.

Country-use currencies could be lent to the recipient country (Sec. 104(g), loans to promote economic development in participating countries) and to private U.S. or foreign firms located in the host country (Sec. 104(e), Cooley loans); granted to the recipient country for economic development; or used to purchase military supplies, facilities, or services.

U.S.-use portions of the currency balances could be used for a variety of expenses of agencies of the U.S. government with operations abroad.

Empirically, about three-fourths of local currencies generated under Title I were designated for use by the recipient country and one-fourth for use by U.S. agencies.

COUNTERSIGNATURE A signature denoting approval or vouching for another signature. For purposes of internal check and to locate responsibility for purchases, many corporations provide that all disbursement checks shall be signed by more than one official. Whenever a check is signed by more than one official, the additional signatures are called countersignatures. A copy of the resolution of the board of directors authorizing certain officials to disburse the company's funds is placed upon file in the records of the bank having the account so that the bank and its paying officers may be apprised of the proper number of signatures that should appear upon a company's checks before it cashes them or receives them for credit.

COUNTRY BANKS The Board of Governors of the Federal Reserve System, by its Rule for Classification of Reserve Cities (found in 12 CFR 204), designated particular member banks in particular RESERVE CITIES to be subject to the higher legal reserve requirements (imposed by the board's Regulation D) than all other member banks, termed country banks (authority of the board of governors to classify or reclassify cities as CENTRAL RESERVE CITIES was terminated effective July 18, 1962). Thus, country banks are those member banks located in UNDESIGNATED CITIES and not in reserve cities.

From the standpoint of collection of country checks through the Federal Reserve par collection system, country banks are those not located in a city where a Federal Reserve bank or branch thereof is established.

COUNTRY CHECKS Out-of-town or transit checks; also checks drawn on banks not located in a city where a Federal Reserve bank or branch is established.

COUNTRY COLLECTIONS See COLLECTION ITEMS.

COUNTRY RISK The risk that most or all economic agents (including the government) in a particular country will for some common reason become unable or unwilling to fulfill international financial obligations. Country risks include those arising from social, political, or economic changes in a foreign country to which domestic banks extend loans that can lead to repudiation of the debt, delayed payments, or controls of funds.

BIBLIOGRAPHY

BARRETT, M., AND IRVINE, L. "The Euromoney Country Risk Ratings." *Euromoney*, September, 1988.
CLARK, E. "An Alternative Ranking [modern portfolio theory applied to country-risk analysis]." *Euromoney*, September, 1988.
MARTINSON, M. G., and HOUPT, J. V. "Transfer Risk in U.S. Banks." *Federal Reserve Bulletin*, April, 1989.

WALTERS, I. "Country Risk and International Bank Lending." *University of Illinois Law Review*, 1982.

COUPON See COUPONS.

COUPON BONDS Negotiable bonds not registered in the name of the owner, as distinguished from registered bonds. Coupon bonds are payable to bearer, title passing by delivery without endorsement. Interest upon coupon bonds is received by clipping the attached COUPONS as they mature and presenting them for payment to the issuer (debtor organization) or the issuer's fiscal agent.

See REGISTERED BOND, REGISTERED COUPON BOND.

COUPON BOOK See COUPON LEDGER.

COUPON CHECK See COUPON PAYMENTS ACCOUNT.

COUPON COLLECTION DEPARTMENT A division of the collection department in large banks or trust companies, especially in financial centers, to receive coupons from individual customers and bank correspondents for presentation to and collection from the various designated paying agents. Coupons are sorted and presented to the advertised paying agents ascertained by reference to various guides and financial services which publish the names and addresses of paying agents for the principal issues of bonds. Announcements of interest payments are also frequently published in the financial newspapers.

Coupons detached from all government bond issues are collected through Federal Reserve banks, and coupons collectible through out-of-town paying agents are forwarded through the mails in the same manner as out-of-town checks.

Matured coupons are accepted both for cash and for collection. If on a cash basis, the proceeds are credited to the depositor's account immediately; if on a collection basis, the proceeds are credited when and if paid.

COUPON COLLECTION TELLER A bank teller who manages the collection of matured coupons deposited on a collection or credit basis by depositors and correspondents. The coupon collection teller is the manager of the COUPON COLLECTION DEPARTMENT.

COUPON LEDGER The ledger in which a bank or trust company, acting as coupon-paying agent, records the receipts of funds with which to pay coupons, disbursements for their redemption when presented for payment, and the numbers of coupons paid. By reference to this ledger it is possible to ascertain the sum received to pay coupons, amount of coupons presented and paid, and amount outstanding, if any.

COUPON PAYING DEPARTMENT A department of a bank or trust company located in a financial center which, because of its special facilities, is appointed paying agent by various debtor organizations (corporations and civil divisions) for the specific purpose of paying matured coupons and bonds. This department is a specialized department for performing this distinct fiscal agent function when the volume of this business is sufficiently large to warrant the organization of a separate department.

By appointing a bank or trust company to pay its coupons, the issuer shifts the burden of making a large number of small disbursements to an institution which has superior facilities for performing the service safely, efficiently, and economically. The debtor organization needs only to authorize its agent and to issue one check, whereas the bank or trust company is called upon to make many small disbursements when matured coupons are presented for payment by their owners or when other banks present them in behalf of their customers.

Coupons are not paid unless the bank or trust company has been officially appointed as fiscal or paying agent or has instructions to pay from the debtor organization or its fiscal agent, and unless funds have been deposited in sufficient amount to redeem in full the maturing bonds or coupons. Usually the institution acting as paying agent has standing instructions to pay maturing coupons at each successive maturity date. The commission for paying bonds and coupons has become standardized and is usually 0.25% for coupons and 0.125% for bonds.

ENCYCLOPEDIA OF BANKING AND FINANCE

COUPON PAYMENTS ACCOUNT A general ledger account which represents the total coupon checks outstanding. Coupons are usually paid by the institution acting as fiscal agent by a special check, marked coupon check, so that coupon redemption payments may be readily distinguished from other checks issued by the bank or trust company. This account is credited when coupon checks are issued and debited when they return through the paying teller's department, clearinghouse, or otherwise.

COUPONS Certificates attached to a (coupon) bond which represent sums of interest due at stated maturities which the bond promises to pay. Coupons are negotiable instruments which state that the debtor organization (issuer and obligor) through its paying agent, usually a bank or trust company, will pay to the bearer at maturity a certain sum of money representing interest due for a stated period upon the bond of a specified issue. A bond is a contract to pay two things^a principal amount on a stated future date and a series of interest payments, usually semiannually but sometimes annually or quarterly, during the life of the bond. The bond itself stands for the principal, and the coupons stand for the series of interest payments due each half year, or other period, and are promises to pay just as the bond itself is. Popularly expressed, coupons are miniature or "baby promises to pay," attached to bonds which are "parent promises to pay."

The essential facts recited on a coupon, which must be identified with its parent bond, are as follows:

1. Name of debtor organization
2. Name of issue
3. Face value of coupon
4. Coupon maturity date
5. Name of paying agent
6. Serial number (numerical order of the interest payment from the first of the series)
7. Number of parent bond.

Coupons are negotiable instruments, title passing by delivery without endorsement, provided ownership certificates prescribed by the Treasury Department are attached, except in the case of bonds of the U.S. government where they are unnecessary. To stop payment upon coupons, the paying agent must, as in the case of a certified check, be protected by a bond of indemnity, from the issuer. Stopping payment on coupons has sometimes been used as a technical excuse for beginning foreclosure proceedings. Without a bond of indemnity, a paying agent has no legal ground for refusing to pay coupons presented except where flagrant irregularities exist.

COUPON STRIPPING The process of producing single-payment (zero-coupon) instruments from existing conventional bonds. It is accomplished either by separating the coupons from the principal or by selling receipts representing the individual coupons and principal on a security held by a trustee.

COUPON TELLER A bank teller who manages the redemption of matured coupons when presented for payment. His or her function is similar to that of the paying teller except that he or she cashes coupons instead of checks. When coupons are presented for payment they are scrutinized to see that they are genuine and regular in all respects. Since a number of fraudulent and worthless coupons are in circulation, the coupon teller must be thoroughly familiar with the general appearance of the coupons of the most important issues in order to avoid paying worthless varieties. Among other points the coupon teller must see that the bank has been authorized as paying agent, that funds have been deposited in sufficient amount to redeem the issue, that the coupons have matured, that no stop–order has been issued against them, that the correlative bonds have not previously been called for redemption, that they bear the bond number, etc. The coupon teller is the manager of the COUPON PAYING DEPARTMENT.

COURT OF CLAIMS A court established on February 25, 1855 (10 Stat. 612; 28 U.S.C. 171), to provide a means to determine the validity of certain kinds of claims against the United States. Formerly, relief in these cases could be obtained only by special act of Congress. The Court of Claims decides suits filed with it against the United States and determines claims referred by Congress and the executive departments.

The court consists of a chief judge and six associate judges. The court hears cases sitting en banc, with all judges present. In addition, it has 16 trial judges, one of whom is designated as chief of the trial division, a clerk, a marshall-bailiff, and staff. Its jurisdiction is set forth in detail in 28 U.S.C. 1491–1506.

COURT TRUSTS Trusts in which the trustee acts under the appointment or order of a court. From this standpoint, trusts are classified as court trusts and private trusts.

COVENANTS IN MORTGAGES Covenants are agreements or stipulations, express or implied, in contracts, deeds, leases, mortgages, etc. In the New York statutory form of mortgage (Section 258, Real Property Law), the mortgagor covenants:

1. That the mortgagor will pay the indebtedness. (This covenant must be express, will not be implied.)
2. That the mortgagor will keep the buildings on the premises insured against loss by fire for the benefit of the mortgagee.
3. That no building on the premises shall be removed or demolished without the consent of the mortgagee.
4. That the whole of the principal sum shall become due after default in the payment of any installment of principal or of interest for specified number of days, or after default in the payment of any tax, water rate, or assessment for specified number of days after notice and demand.
5. That the holder of the mortgage, in any action to foreclose it, shall be entitled to the appointment of a receiver.
6. That the mortgager will pay all taxes, assessments, or water rates, and in default thereof, the mortgagee may pay the same.
7. That the mortgagor within specified number of days upon request in person or within specified number of days upon request by mail will furnish a statement of the amount due on the mortgage.
8. That notice and demand or request may be in writing and may be served in person or by mail.
9. That the mortgagor warrants the title to the premises.

In corporate mortgages of the open type, in which the amount of bonds authorized under the mortgage is unlimited, the usual protective covenants for the benefit of bondholders are that the corporation will not issue any additional bonds beyond a prescribed percentage of new property acquired and that additional bonds will not be issued unless the resulting total charges are earned a specified minimum.

See BOND, OPEN MORTGAGE.

COVER This term has three meanings:

1. Signifies the purchase of stocks by short sellers to complete their contracts. To cover is to buy back stock that has previously been sold short. *See* SHORT SALE.
2. Frequently used instead of the term security. A loan evidenced by a promissory note is said to be covered when secured by bonds, stocks, or other collateral of equal or greater value. It is especially used in connection with the security behind different forms of paper money, e.g., cover behind Federal Reserve notes.
3. The contingencies or risks outlined in an insurance policy for which the insurance company is liable, e.g., a marine insurance policy covers losses due to damage by fire, flood, collision, sinking, but not losses due to riot, rebellion, or capture and seizure by an enemy. A life insurance policy covers the life of the insured.

COVERAGE In financial STATEMENT ANALYSIS, the ratio by which assets cover specific liabilities; in income account analysis, the ratios by which earnings cover charges or dividend requirements.

CRAM-DOWN RULES Rules in bankruptcy proceedings that allow the court to confirm a reorganization plan even when an impaired class has not accepted it. Under these rules, the court may confirm if the plan treats the class in a "fair and equitable" manner. Among the requirements that a plan must meet to be considered fair and equitable are: (1) With respect to a nonaccepting class of secured claims, the holders of those claims must retain their liens on property of the debtor. If the property is sold, their liens will be shifted to

ENCYCLOPEDIA OF BANKING AND FINANCE

the proceeds. (2) With respect to a nonaccepting class of unsecured claims, the claimants must receive the full value of their claim or no claim junior to the claims of the class in question will receive anything.

CREATOR A grantor, settlor, or trustor; one who creates a voluntary *inter vivos* trust, or creates a trust by will (a testamentary trust).

See TRUST.

CREDIT Derived from the Latin word credo, meaning "I believe," and usually defined as the ability to buy with a promise to pay, or the ability to obtain title to and receive goods for enjoyment in the present although payment is deferred to a future date. It therefore consists of an actual transfer and delivery of goods in exchange for a promise to pay in the future.

Modern business to a large extent is conducted on a credit basis. The occasion for credit arises out of the nature of present-day industrial processes in which a series of productive and distributive operations transpires between the beginning of production and ultimate consumption when the account is finally liquidated. Credit is the instrument by which this gap is bridged, i.e., by which each factor in the sequence of productive and distributive processes receives payment for his contribution in moving goods to the consumption point, before consumption actually occurs. Although credit furnishes waiting power, it cannot be considered as identical with CAPITAL, but it makes capital mobile.

Expansion of bank credit is a necessary condition of expansion of business operations. But an overexpansion of credit may so increase the purchasing power of businesspersons that it will merely result in enabling them to bid against one another for limited supplies of goods and materials so as to force prices above what consumers are willing and able to pay. Bank credit often expands so rapidly that it lifts the buying or investment power of businesspersons out of line with the general buying power of the community. Because of their strategic position, the banks have an unusual duty and an exceptional opportunity to give sound information and counsel to businesspersons.

Granting credit depends upon the confidence which the lender places in the debtor (borrower), and is based on three essential factors: character, capacity, and capital. Lending on character is known as the MORAL RISK; on capacity, as the BUSINESS RISK; on capital, as the PROPERTY RISK.

Of these three elements, character should be the most important. The personal equation transcends all others because without character and integrity no person can be trusted regardless of the ability or property he may possess. Character includes integrity of purpose, reputation for honesty, promptness in paying debts and fulfilling contracts, high standard of business ethics, record of past performances and antecedent connections, etc. Capacity involves business ability, reputation of product, and soundness of business methods, particularly as evidenced by profit-making records. The real index for measuring the business risk is the detailed comparative operating statements by which the rate of return to invested capital over a period of time is disclosed. Capital is net worth—the real measure of a borrower's collateral. Property which has a ready market, whether used in the business or not, constitutes the basis of the property risk.

The most satisfactory manner of evaluating this managerial ability or capacity factor is by means of an industrial or commercial survey, a survey which goes behind the balance sheet and income statements and determines the degree to which the fundamentals of sound management have been made effective. The science of industrial engineering and the practical application of economics to business problems have now reached a state of development where, through their intelligence, many of the factors which were formerly considered intangible and impossible to measure can now be subjected to scientific analysis and actual measurement. Such a survey should include an analysis of organization and personnel, managerial ability and stability, financial policies and methods, marketing policies and methods, manufacturing policies and methods, and methods of control.

An ideal borrower or credit risk combines all three of these elements in a high degree, i.e., unimpeachable moral character, unquestioned business ability, and adequate capital. Character stands foremost, ability second, and capital third. It is safe to say that no loans will be granted where the first essential does not exist. Certainly loans will not be granted where business ability has not been proven unless adequate collateral is given. On the other hand, if the first two elements are strong, inadequate capital may not necessarily operate as a deterrent influence.

From the banking standpoint, credit has reference to a person's or concern's power to command funds or to secure deposit credits. Persons or concerns already well known, and having an established credit reputation, are usually granted a LINE OF CREDIT at their banks. This line is the normal limit of accomodation. Such a line of credit is not always definitely fixed but varies from time to time in accordance with the financial standing of the borrower as shown by his financial statement, the bank's loanable resources, and general money and trade conditions.

See CREDIT BALANCE, CREDIT DEPARTMENT, CREDIT FILES, CREDIT INFORMATION SOURCES, CREDIT INSTRUMENTS, CREDIT INSURANCE, MERCANTILE AGENCIES, STATEMENT ANALYSIS.

BIBLIOGRAPHY

ALEXANDER, J. "Missing Link: Understanding the Credit Information Process." *Business Credit*, June, 1988.
BOARD OF GOVERNORS OF THE FEDERAL RESERVE SYSTEM. *Consumer Handbook to Credit Protection Laws*. Federal Reserve System, Washington, DC, 1987.
Credit. Credit Manual of Commercial Laws. National Association of Credit Management. Annual.
Credit Markets. Credit World.
JOHNSON, R. N. "What the New Auditor's Report Means for Bankers." *Journal of Commercial Lending*, January, 1989.
LYNN, D. M., and CAMPBELL, D. *Creditor's Rights Handbook*. Clark Boardman Co., New York, NY. Annual.
PHIFER, E. "Automating the Credit Analysis Function." *Commercial Bank Lending*, June, 1988.
PHILLIPS, A. L., and MOODY, S. M. "The Effect of Defeased Debt on Loan Decisions." *Journal of Commercial Bank Lending*, February, 1989.
SANDLER, R. "Let the Buyer Beware." *Business Credit*, November, 1988.

CREDIT AGENCY See MERCANTILE AGENCIES.

CREDIT BALANCE The excess of credits over debits in an account.

A bank depositor customarily has a credit balance. A debit balance occurs only when an overdraft has been made. The amount of the credit balance represents the depositor's claim against the bank and the bank's debit to the depositor.

Marginal accounts with a broker normally show a debit balance because the customer is borrowing from the broker to carry stocks for which the customer has not fully paid. A credit balance exists in favor of the customer only when there is money due the customer above all claims, such as interests, commissions, taxes, etc.

CREDIT BANKS Sometimes applied to commercial banks, i.e., banking institutions which primarily extend credit to borrowing customers in the form of direct loans or discounts.

See BANK.

CREDIT BAROMETRICS First used by Alexander Wall in the "Banker's Credit Manual," the test ratios applied by credit analysts in the analysis of financial statements submitted as bases for bank loans. The following ratios, discussed under separate headings, are used in credit analysis work: ratio of current assets to current liabilities (*see* CURRENT RATIO), ratio of current assets (excluding inventories) to current liabilities (*see* ACID TEST), RATIO OF CURRENT ASSETS TO TOTAL LIABILITIES, ratio of merchandise to sales (*see* MERCHANDISE TURNOVER), RATIO OF NET PROFITS TO NET WORTH, ratio of receivables to sales (*see* ACCOUNTS RECEIVABLE TURNOVER), RATIO OF DEBT TO NET WORTH, ratio of net worth to fixed assets, ratio of net worth to sales, RATIO OF MERCHANDISE TO RECEIVABLES, ratio of fixed assets to sales.

See RATIO ANALYSIS.

CREDIT CARDS The phenomenon of the universal credit card is an aspect of the easy personal credit of modern times. Actively promoted by such giant firms as Diners Club, Inc. (the pioneer in the universal credit card field, 1950), American Express Company, and Hilton Credit Corporation (both of which entered the field in 1959), universal credit cards are responsible for a dynamic and still growing segment of noninstallment consumer credit. Universal credit

CREDIT CLEARINGHOUSE

cards are an outgrowth of the extensive use of specialized credit cards of particular firms. Beginning in the 1920s but especially proliferating in the post–World War II period, various individual firms, such as oil companies, hotel chains, and automobile rental firms, issued cards entitling the holders to credit at their establishments.

In addition to the T & E (travel and entertainment) cards, the principal system being the American Express cards, bank credit cards have become an even more dynamic part of the industry. Originally introduced by a relatively small but aggressive Long Island (N.Y.) bank in 1951, the bank credit card became increasingly prevalent in the 1960s, as major banks aggressively promoted its use.

Bank credit cards have come to compete successfully with the T & E cards in several respects: lower discount charged to member retailers, quicker availability of credits to member retailer accounts, and no or lower charge to cardholders, who in addition may have the option of converting balances to monthly bank installment credit.

The VISA bank credit card was introduced in 1958 as an all-purpose family credit card under the name BankAmericard. In 1970, the BankAmericard trademarks and service marks were licensed to National BankAmericard, Inc., a Delaware corporation. In March, 1977, National BankAmericard, Inc. changed its name to VISA U.S.A. and VISA International, and began a major expansion program.

The appended table shows data relating to credit cards, including cardholders, number of cards, spending, and debt for the years 1980-1987.

See CONSUMER CREDIT, REVOLVING CHECK CREDIT.

BIBLIOGRAPHY

"Accounting for Liquidating Banks and Credit Card Portfolio Transactions." *Journal of Accountancy*. March, 1989.
"Bank Credit Card Use Expands." *Business Credit*. December, 1988.
BOARD OF GOVERNORS OF THE FEDERAL RESERVE SYSTEM. *Regulation Z*.
LINDLEY, J. T., and others. "Credit Card Possession and Use: Changes Over Time." *Journal of Economics and Business*, May, 1989.

CREDIT CLEARINGHOUSE Applied to credit interchange bureaus, the purpose of which is exchange of credit information among its members, each member thus benefiting from the records and experiences of all members. Handling of inquiries may be direct, by investigation with concerns which have dealt with the subject, whereby ledger experience and opinion are obtained from firms which have had actual dealings with the subject; or indirect, by supplying the inquirer with a list of leads or references.

See CREDIT INTERCHANGE BUREAUS, NATIONAL ASSOCIATION OF CREDIT MANAGEMENT.

CREDIT CONTROL Quantitative and qualitative control exercised by the monetary authorities over the volume and nature of credit and over interest rates. Quantitative control is effective on volume and distribution of excess reserves of the banking system and on levels of interest rates. Qualitative controls in the U.S. generally have not been favored because of the difficulties of administration and the existence of well-developed money markets for effective quantitative controls, but have been exercised to a limited extent through regulation of margin requirements (stock market credit), consumer credit and real estate credit under wartime conditions, and examination procedures.

The three principal powers of the Board of Governors of the Federal Reserve System are aggregative rather than selective in nature—open market operations (buying and selling of government securities, principally Treasury bills in practice, through a group of government securities dealers), variation in Federal Reserve bank discount rates, and changes in legal reserve requirements.

On March 4, 1951, the Board of Governors of the Federal Reserve System and the Treasury issued a joint statement to the effect that they had "reached full accord with respect to debt management and monetary policies to be pursued in furthering their common purpose to assure the successful financing of the government's requirements and, at the same time, to minimize monetization of the public debt." The significance of this accord was that it marked the end of a decade during which monetary policy had been subordinated to debt-management policy, with the Federal Reserve System purchasing large quantities of government securities at pegged prices. As long as such rigid support of the government securities market continued, the three principal powers of the board above could not be used flexibly in the discharge of the board's own responsibility to exercise credit control for promoting economic stability. Hence since that time a revival of monetary policy has occurred, not only because of such greater freedom in exercise of credit controls but also because monetary policy has greater impact at times of high economic activity financed through the banking system.

CREDIT CONVERSION FACTOR A percentage amount (100, 50, 20, or 0%) applied to the full face value of off-balance-sheet activities other than interest or foreign exchange rate contracts to determine a credit equivalent amount.

CREDIT CURRENCY Redeemable paper money which the government promises to pay, but for which there is not a full specie reserve—i.e., money not fully secured by a metallic reserve—such as the United States notes of 1863, also known as legal tenders. Unlike silver certificates, which circulate in lieu of an equal amount of coin, these notes are not intended as substitutes for metallic currency, but for the purpose of expanding the volume of currency. In a gold bullion standard, such as that of the United States, with no domestic circulation of gold coin or gold certificates permitted, credit currency is only generally secured by the gold reserve; in countries with low metallic reserves, the larger portion might be secured only by the general assets and credit of the issuing government. Credit currency is also known as fiduciary currency.

CREDIT DEPARTMENT In mercantile agencies, the department of a company through which all credit orders—i.e., orders for current delivery, but with payment postponed—are passed for

Credit Cards—Holders, Numbers, Spending and Debt: 1980 to 1987

Type of Credit Card	Cardholders (mil.) 1980	1985	1987	Number of Cards (mil.) 1980	1985	1987	Credit Card Spending (bil. dol.) 1980	1985	1987	Credit Card Debt (bil. dol.) 1980	1985	1987
Total	NA	NA	107.2 [1]	NA	NA	841.4 [2]	205.4	322.7	374.8	81.2	128.0	152.5
Bank	63.3	73.3	79.0	110.6	161.4	204.6	52.9	125.9	165.3	25.0	65.6	91.4
Travel and entertainment	10.5	15.5	15.6	10.3	18.8	21.9	21.2	51.0	80.4	2.7	6.4	10.0
Retail store	83.0	91.0	92.8	290.5	341.0	380.8	74.4	90.0	68.8	47.3	50.5	38.4
Oil company marketers	68.5	78.0	59.9	109.6	117.0	118.8	28.9	28.8	24.1	2.2	2.7	3.2
Other [3]	NA	NA	80.0 [4]	NA	NA	80.0 [4]	28.0	27.0	36.2	4.0	2.8	9.5

NA Not available.
[1] Cardholders may hold more than one type of card.
[2] Includes other types not shown separately.
[3] Spending and debt data cover airline and automobile rental cards, telephone company cards and other miscellaneous credit cards.
[4] Telephone cards.

Source: HSN Consultants Inc., Los Angeles, CA, The Nilson Report, monthly. (Copyright used by permission.)

ENCYCLOPEDIA OF BANKING AND FINANCE

acceptance or rejection. The department scrutinizes new applications for credit through various CREDIT INFORMATION SOURCES and checks running or open accounts. It fixes a line of credit for each customer and determines and carries out the collections policies.

In banks, the department of a bank organized primarily to determine and measure credit risks, which leads to a recommendation for action when applications for loans are made. The purpose of the department is to reduce to a minimum, if not absolutely to prevent, losses arising through the failure of concerns to which money is loaned. Credit departments of many banks also exchange credit information with correspondent banks, trade customers, and other affiliations, and for this reason serve as a checking bureau not only for their own organization, but for others as well. The most important type of assistance rendered is that of presenting to the credit officers and the loan and discount committee such facts as are necessary to provide a basis for intelligently granting or rejecting loans, discounts, and renewals thereof, issuing letters of credit, purchasing bills of exchange, and also establishing lines of credit.

The work of the credit department may be broadly divided into three parts, that of gathering credit information (credit investigation), filing and storing credit information (credit files), and utilizing and distributing credit information (credit analysis).

See MERCANTILE AGENCIES, STATEMENT ANALYSIS.

BIBLIOGRAPHY

HOLLAND, R. "Using Business Instincts." *Business Credit*, November, 1988.
OANOS, G. C. "Walking the Line." *Business Credit*, October, 1988.

CREDIT ENHANCEMENTS A generic term for collateral, letters of credit, guarantees, and other contractual mechanisms aimed at reducing credit risk.

CREDIT FILES The part of a bank credit department in which credit information is recorded, classified, filed, and stored. Usually the credit information on each name is recorded in a folder placed in a metal sectional file cabinet. In large banks, credit files become very extensive in the course of time and often contain thousands of names. The files are the backbone of the department since they contain the raw material from which all inquiries concerning the credit standing of the names on record are answered.

See CREDIT FILES REVISION, CREDIT FOLDER.

CREDIT FILES REVISION Information in the credit files must be kept up to date. Information previously gathered is valuable because it affords insight into the history of a concern or individual and these antecedent relations are always important. Yet the character and earning power of a business may change very suddenly, and consequently names upon which no new information has been recorded for one year are usually regarded as out of date and require revision if inquiries are made. Borrowing bank accounts should be revised only every second year. Trade names are revised more frequently, because business concerns are less apt to be stable than banks and their financial status therefore is more apt to fluctuate. Trade names are not usually revised periodically, but whenever conditions seem to warrant. If a report is desired and the standing information is more than nine months old, a revision is usually advisable. Revision of a credit folder follows the same lines as an original investigation: direct investigation of trade and banking connections in and out of town, mercantile agencies, and the note broker, in the case of commercial paper names.

See CREDIT INFORMATION SOURCES, CREDIT INVESTIGATION.

CREDIT FOLDER A binder or cover which contains the complete record of credit information concerning a given name. To distinguish between different classes of names, e.g., banks, trade names, public utilities, commercial paper names, different colored folders are often used. Folders are filed alphabetically according to names in metal filing cabinets.

Information in the credit folder is generally classified according to some logical grouping and separated by guides that help one locate the particular information desired. A typical classification of information in a credit folder is as follows: history sheet, average loans and balances, financial statements, investigation and report inquiries, agency reports, affiliations and subsidiaries, circulars and prospectuses, newspaper clippings, summarization.

CREDIT FONCIER DE FRANCE The oldest mortgage banking institution in France, established in 1852 to make loans on property and later loans to local governments. Capital is privately subscribed, but the bank is government controlled and its sources of funds are largely grants and advances from the government as well as public sale of long-term debentures.

See BANK OF FRANCE.

CREDIT INFORMATION SOURCES Sources of credit information are becoming more varied as the demand for accurate credit information and the desire to eliminate undesirable risks becomes more insistent. The sources open to a bank differ depending upon whether the subject of inquiry is a local, out-of-town, or foreign name.

In the case of local names, a credit investigator usually is sent to interview the subject of inquiry or one of its responsible representatives, i.e., the individual or concern under investigation. The investigator also usually interviews several trade references of the subject of inquiry, including trade creditors, trade debtors and possibly a competitor. Interviews conducted with the banking connection or connections are regarded as especially important. In the case of commercial paper names, the note broker who sells the paper of the concern is interviewed. Written inquiries may be directed to trade and banking references out of town whenever there is reason to believe that better information may be derived from these sources.

Next in importance are the financial statements—balance sheets and the income, and slated inflows statements. Reports from the mercantile agencies are almost always available, but only information of the most general nature can be expected from them.

The records of the bank should contain valuable information on names which are customers of the bank, e.g., size of balances, method of borrowing, lines of credit, securities on deposit, requests for renewals, promptness in meeting maturities, allowing notes to go to protest, etc. An examination of the endorsements on canceled checks will also reveal the purposes for which the concern is spending its money. Public records such as judgment indexes, records of pending suits, and records of mortgages and real estate transfers are always available. Information is often contained in various financial publications, manuals, and services. The officers of the institution usually have intimate personal knowledge of the affairs of many of their customers.

In the case of out-of-town names, the same sources of information are available except that it becomes necessary to omit personal investigation; written inquiries directed to the same sources may be submitted.

The chief credit information sources for foreign names are as follows: the principal New York banks that maintain foreign departments and close relations with correspondent banks abroad; New York import and export houses, which are ready to furnish their clients and banking connections with information regarding names with which they do business; the foreign departments of the principal mercantile agencies; foreign chambers of commerce located in New York City, which are supported by the merchants of the countries they represent for the purpose of promoting trade relations; and various trade associations, such as the National Association of Credit Management.

CREDIT INSTRUMENTS Paper or documents, other than paper money supported by specie, that evidence current or long-term debt. Credit instruments include checks of all kinds, certificates of deposit, drafts, bills of exchange, notes, acceptances, money orders, letters of credit, bonds, stock certificates, certificates of indebtedness, coupons, etc.

From a legal standpoint, credit instruments may be divided into two classes—promises to pay and orders to pay. The chief types of promises to pay are promissory notes, trade acceptances, bank acceptances, bonds, coupons, and certificates of debt. The chief types of orders to pay are checks, drafts, bills of exchange, money orders, telegraphic transfers, cable transfers, and letters of credit.

In the U.S., credit instruments, particularly the check, have largely displaced money as a means of payment. Considering turnover of checking accounts (*see* BANK DEBITS) and estimating turnover of paper and metallic currency, it is estimated that over 90% of transactions in the U.S. are settled by means of checks. The extent of use of credit instruments depends upon banking facilities, individual and business banking habits, and degree of confidence in banks.

See CREDIT.

ENCYCLOPEDIA OF BANKING AND FINANCE

CREDIT INSURANCE Insurance provided against losses from BAD DEBTS arising from the sale of goods on CREDIT. Coverage for uncollectible accounts, though far less common than coverage for fire losses, is equally important, since bad accounts occur more frequently than fires and are as much a loss as destroyed or damaged merchandise.

Credit insurance does not usually indemnify the insured against all credit losses, but only for an amount in excess of the average over a certain period, say four years. Policies also usually subject the insured to certain limitations, e.g., limitations of line of credit to each purchaser, limitation of sales to purchasers having a certain commercial rating or better.

See MERCANTILE AGENCIES.

CREDIT INTERCHANGE BUREAUS Bureaus that engage in the business of supplying credit information on a cooperative basis. In recent years, a number of credit interchange bureaus have come to take a rather prominent place in supplying credit information on trade corporations and partnerships (individuals not included). While these bureaus are organized chiefly for trade creditors, many banks are member-subscribers. Like trade members, banks provide credit information but not to the extent of giving precise figures, since bank credit data are considered more confidential than those of the trades.

The most important credit interchange bureau system is that of the National Association of Credit Management. This system, which embraces a countrywide system of bureaus and districts, is not organized for profit, service charges to members being fixed to cover operating costs only. Each bureau is an independent unit and is conducted under the auspices of the offices of the local association. All the bureaus are under the direct control and supervision of a committee of the National Association of Credit Management, and the manager of the Credit Interchange Bureau Department of the national organization. The purpose of the interchange bureau is to provide a means of exchanging among its members their ledger experiences with common trade creditors and, as stated in the charters of some of the bureaus and restated by T. N. Beckman ("Credits and Collections in Theory and Practice"), "to provide an impartial medium between debtors and creditors and between creditors themselves, to establish a system whereby those who are interested in any accounts may freely and unreservedly interchange the facts contained in their ledgers: (1) without the necessity of direct reference, each to the other; (2) without divulging the information under their own name; (3) and receiving in exchange for data contributed by them, a summary of experiences of all others interested in the account."

CREDIT INVESTIGATION Assembles accurate and complete information and provides an evaluation of a borrower's credit standing. The process may be summarized as fact-gathering (*see* CREDIT CLEARINGHOUSE, CREDIT FILES, CREDIT FILES REVISION, CREDIT INFORMATION SOURCES, CREDIT INTERCHANGE BUREAUS), analysis of data (*see* CREDIT BAROMETRICS, STATEMENT ANALYSIS), and evaluation (*see* CREDIT RATING, CREDIT RISK, MORAL RISK). The elaborateness of a credit investigation as a practical matter depends upon its cost relative to the magnitude of the principal and interest involved and the security. Thus in personal loans procedure of commercial banks and finance companies, the credit investigation is usually streamlined to the point where large volume and the law of averages are depended upon to spread a specific credit risk or moral risk so that a normal reserve for losses, depending on economic conditions prevailing, is counted upon to cover average losses, which may be in effect regarded as part of the cost of the total loan volume.

CREDIT INVESTIGATOR A representative of a bank, mercantile agency, commercial paper house, or business firm whose function it is to procure credit information. In the case of mercantile agencies, he is called a reporter. The process of collecting credit information is an essential part of credit analysis, for evaluation of credit risks can be no better than the facts assembled. Members of the Robert Morris Associates observe their Code of Ethics for the Exchange of Information (*see* Robert Morris Associates, *A Training Guide for the Bank Credit Department, 1958*).

CREDIT LINE *See* CREDIT, LINE OF CREDIT.

CREDITOR A person or firm to whom money or its equivalent is due. Secured creditors are those whose credit is secured by specific collateral; in case of default or liquidation, they are entitled to recourse to the collateral, after compliance with procedural requirements, for primary satisfaction of their secured claims, pursuant to their lien position. In the event of deficiency, such deficiency becomes a general claim, entitled to share proportionately with other unsecured or general claims of other creditors in the proceeds of sale of the unpledged assets in case of liquidation. In REORGANIZATION, secured creditors also take precedence, pursuant to their lien position, over general or unsecured creditors under the absolute priority rule of treatment in reorganization. The specific rights of creditors will vary with the type of transaction involved and the federal or state laws applying.

CREDITOR COUNTRY A country which has a trade balance in its favor, i.e., whose exports are greater than combined visible and invisible imports.

CREDIT RATING The evaluation of the credit worthiness of an individual or of a business concern based on relevant factors indicating ability and willingness to pay obligations (payment record) as well as on net worth. In mercantile or trade credit (credit extended by business firms to other business firms), various credit information agencies have worked out their systems of codes and symbols for credit ratings for easier publication and ratings. DUN & BRADSTREET provide credit ratings whose symbols reflect an evaluation of estimated financial strength and of composite credit appraisal for the approximately 3 million firms listed in the reference book on which sufficient information for such ratings is available.

CREDIT RATIONING Where central bank and commercial bank reserves are low and in turn domestic business working capital is low but demand for bank credit high, the banking system may be obliged to institute rationing of credit as a means of most effective utilization of available reserves. For example, the Reischbank, former central bank of Germany, resorted to credit rationing in connection with scarce reserves of foreign exchange. In the U.S., the VOLUNTARY CREDIT RESTRAINT PROGRAM, which was terminated in May, 1952, may be said to have been an example of voluntary credit rationing. At the commercial bank level, LINE OF CREDIT of a firm may have to be cut back by the bank at a time of tight availability of bank reserves.

CREDIT RISK Applied by bankers and credit analysts to an individual, firm, or corporation to whom money is loaned or to whom merchandise or service is delivered on a credit basis. Wherever credit is extended it is attended with the risk of nonpayment varying from practically zero to a large percentage. The degree of risk involved is determined by the credit department, and when it is too high, credit is refused. By extension, therefore, the term is used to refer to anyone to whom credit is given.

In investment analysis, credit risk, otherwise termed BUSINESS RISK, is the risk that the issuer company might be unable to perform all that it has contracted to do or is reasonably anticipated to do in its specific kinds of securities issued. Credit policy should provide standards on which the bank will extend credit and project total outstanding as part of a long-range strategic plan. The development of a credit policy should take into account projected economic conditions, competition for loans, and needs of the geographic area served. The traditional five "Cs" of credit management include:

1. **Capacity.** The ability of the borrower to repay.
2. **Character.** Competency of management and willingness to repay.
3. **Capital.** Base of equity or wealth of borrower against which credit will be extended.
4. **Collateral.** Nature and marketability of collateral.
5. **Conditions.** Internal operating efficiency, market share or volume of sales, competitive factors, and current and predicted economic conditions.

Basic elements to consider in a bank's credit policy include (1) regulatory requirements, (2) legal considerations (lending limits,

---

ENCYCLOPEDIA OF BANKING AND FINANCE

loan purpose), (3) administrative maximums for loans, (4) loan portfolio mix, (5) delegation of authority and responsibility, (6) pricing (to compensate for cost of funds, costs of extending and administering credit, the credit risk, time risk), (7) market area, (8) quality standards, (9) liquidity of portfolio, and (10) management experience and capabilities.

Adapted from *Effective Risk Management*, William T. Thornhill, BAI.

BIBLIOGRAPHY

MENGLE, D. L., and others. "Intraday Credit: Risk, Value, and Pricing." *American Economic Review*, March, 1986.

CREDIT SCORING SYSTEM A statistical system banks and other credit grantors use to rate credit applicants according to various characteristics that relate to creditworthiness. Such characteristics may not include race, color, religion, national origin, sex, marital status, or age (with certain limitations). Regulation D implements this feature of the Equal Credit Opportunity Act.

CREDIT TESTS In analysis of statements, the ratios or CREDIT BAROMETRICS, which serve as an effective aid in forming judgment on credit risks.

See STATEMENT ANALYSIS.

CREDIT TICKET A posting medium used in banking and brokerage bookkeeping to secure the posting of a transaction occurring in any department to the credit side of the customers' or general ledger. It carries a complete description of the transaction and is preserved for future reference.

CREDIT UNION The Federal Credit Union Act was passed June 26, 1934 "to establish a Federal Credit Union System, to establish a further market for securities of the United States, and to make more available to people of small means credit for provident purposes through a national system of cooperative credit, thereby helping to stabilize the credit structure of the United States." Administration of the act was made the responsibility of the FARM CREDIT ADMINISTRATION. Executive Order 9148 of April 27, 1942, transferred the administration of the act to the FEDERAL DEPOSIT INSURANCE CORPORATION, effective May 16, 1942. Effective July 29, 1948, Congress transferred these functions, powers, and duties to a Bureau of Federal Credit Unions, which was established in the Federal Security Agency (62 Stat. 1091). By department order, this bureau became one of the program bureaus of the Social Security Administration, subject to the direction of the Commissioner of Social Security. With establishment of the National Credit Union Administration by act of March 10, 1970 (12 U.S.C. 1752), as an independent agency of the executive branch, a new era opened up for credit unions.

Official description of the National Credit Union Administration indicates that the mission of the administration is to promote self-help security through privately owned and democratically controlled federal credit unions; stimulate systematic savings to provide capital and cash reserves for credit union members; make available to people of small means credit for provident purposes at reasonable rates through a national system of cooperative thrift and credit; help stabilize the economy of the United States by developing sound thrift, credit, and personal financial management practices; make studies of the personal financial problems of persons of small means to determine how cooperative saving and lending may help and to publish the results of such service; and to administer a program of insuring the member accounts of all federal credit unions and the member accounts of state credit unions which apply and qualify for insurance.

The administration's mission is achieved through four major activities: chartering, supervising, examining federal credit unions, and providing a system of share insurance for federal and state credit unions.

The DEPOSITORY INSTITUTIONS DEREGULATION AND MONETARY CONTROL ACT of 1980 brought all depository institutions, including credit unions, under the jurisdiction of the Board of Governors of the Federal Reserve System for the direct or indirect submission of reports of assets and liabilities and for the maintenance of specified reserves against transaction accounts. Under that act, a new DEPOSITORY INSTITUTIONS DEREGULATION COMMITTEE (DIDC) was created, one of whose voting members is the chairman of the National Credit Union Administration (NCUA) Board, with the mission to provide for the phase-out of limitations on dividend rates and interest paid by depository institutions. Part of the Monetary Control Act of 1980 (the Consumer Checking Account Equity Act) provided for nationwide permission to offer negotiable orders of withdrawal accounts (NOW accounts) at all depository institutions for individuals and specified nonprofit organizations. A federal credit union was authorized thereby to charge up to 15% annually on loans, with the NCUA Board authorized to establish a higher loan interest ceiling for periods not exceeding 18 months. Federally insured credit unions were authorized under the act to offer share draft accounts. Federal deposit insurance at depository institutions, including credit unions, was increased to $100,000 per account.

The credit union idea first began in Germany (1848), promoted by Friedrich Wilhelm Raiffeisen, and then was popularized in Italy. Canadian credit unions first appeared in 1900. In the U.S., state-chartered credit unions were particularly promoted by the Boston merchant Edward A. Filene. Large numbers of credit unions are found among government employees, federal and state, as well as in public utilities. A summary of basic statistics relating to federal and state-chartered credit unions from 1970-1987 is appended. The data show the number of operating credit unions and members, assets, loans outstanding, and savings.

BIBLIOGRAPHY

Credit Union Executive. Quarterly.
Credit Union Guide. Credit Union National Association. Looseleaf.
Credit Union Information Service Newsletter. Biweekly.
Credit Union Magazine. Monthly.
Credit Union Report. Credit Union National Association. Annual.
Credit Union Statistics. Credit Union Administration. Monthly.
Directory of All Federally Insured Credit Unions. National Credit Union Administration, 1988.

Federal and State-Chartered Credit Unions—Summary: 1970 to 1987

(As of December 31, Federal data include District of Columbia, Puerto Rico, Canal Zone, Guam, and Virgin Islands. Beginning 1984, excludes State-insured and non-insured State-chartered credit unions and corporate central credit unions which have mainly other credit unions as members.)

Year	Operating Credit Unions Federal	Operating Credit Unions State	Members (1,000) Federal	Members (1,000) State	Assets (mil. dol.) Federal	Assets (mil. dol.) State	Loans Outstanding (mil. dol.) Federal	Loans Outstanding (mil. dol.) State	Savings (mil. dol.) Federal	Savings (mil. dol.) State
1970	12,977	10,679	11,966	10,853	8,861	9,089	6,969	7,137	7,629	7,857
1975	12,737	9,871	17,066	14,196	20,209	17,804	14,869	13,300	17,530	15,522
1980	12,440	9,025	24,519	19,235	40,092	33,143	26,350	22,633	36,263	29,480
1984	10,548	4,645	28,170	15,205	63,657	29,188	42,132	19,951	57,927	26,327
1985	10,125	4,920	29,576	15,689	78,205	41,525	48,241	26,168	71,616	37,917
1986	9,758	4,935	31,045	17,363	95,484	52,244	55,305	30,834	87,954	48,097
1987	9,401	4,934	32,067	17,999	105,190	56,972	64,104	35,436	96,348	52,083

Source: National Credit Union Administration, Annual Report of the National Credit Union Administration, and unpublished data.

International Credit Union Yearbook. Credit Union National Association.
NATIONAL CREDIT UNION ADMINISTRATION. *Annual Report.*
STATE CHARTERED CREDIT UNIONS. National Credit Union Administration.
UNITED STATES NATIONAL CREDIT UNION ADMINISTRATION. Quarterly.

CREMATION CERTIFICATE A certification that retired securities have been destroyed by burning; a statement signed by certain persons (e.g., trustees, committee), selected or appointed, that they have witnessed the total destruction by fire of the therein-mentioned securities.

CREMATION OF BONDS Destruction of bonds by fire. One method of disposing of bonds that have been redeemed and canceled is to burn them. This is usually the method used when the bonds are secured by a mortgage held by the trustee for the bondholders. After the mortgage has been satisfied of record, the bonds are burned in the presence of the trustee and a CREMATION CERTIFICATE is executed.

CRIME OF '73 A derisive designation applied to the Coinage Act of 1873, which made no provision for coinage of standard silver dollars although it provided for a TRADE DOLLAR of 420 grains silver. This led to a subsequent fight by silver mining interests to restore full silver coinage.

CRIMINAL OFFENSES Under the Bank Protection Act of 1968 (82 Stat. 295), the comptroller of the currency by regulation (12 CFR 21) established minimum standards with which each national bank or District of Columbia bank must comply with respect to installation, maintenance, and operation of security devices; procedures to discourage robberies, burglaries, and larcenies; and assistance in the identification and apprehension of persons who commit such acts.

The comptroller's regulation established time limits within which each subject bank shall comply with the standards and required the submission of reports with respect to the installation, maintenance, and operation of bank security devices and procedures.

The act of June 25, 1948, repealed many criminal provisions of the federal banking laws and recodified them (18 U.S.C.). Any offense punishable by death or imprisonment for a term exceeding 1 year is classified as a felony. Any other offense is a misdemeanor. Any misdemeanor not punishable by imprisonment for over 6 months or fine of over $500, or both, is classified as a petty offense.

A summary of crimes and penalties covered in 18 U.S.C. as currently numbered follows.

Loans or gratuities to bank examiners. Fine of not more than $5,000 or imprisonment of not more than 1 year, or both, plus further fine which may be levied equal to the sum loaned or gratuity given (18 U.S.C. 212).

Acceptance of loans or gratuities by bank examiners. Fine of not more than $5,000 or imprisonment of not more than 1 year, or both, plus further fine which may be levied equal to the sum loaned or gratuity given, and disqualification from holding office as examiner (18 U.S.C. 213).

Receipt of commissions or gifts for procuring loans. Fine of not more than $5,000 or imprisonment of not more than 1 year, or both (18 U.S.C. 215).

Illegal issuance of Federal Reserve notes. Fine of not more than $5,000 or imprisonment for not more than 5 years, or both (18 U.S.C. 334).

Circulation of obligations of expired federal corporations. Fine of not more than $10,000 or imprisonment for not more than 5 years, or both (18 U.S.C. 335).

Political contributions or expenditures by any national bank or any corporation organized by authority of Congress, or by any corporation whatever or any labor organization. Every corporation or labor organization which makes any contribution or expenditure in violation of this section shall be fined not more than $5,000. Every officer or director of any corporation, or officer of any labor organization, and any person who accepts or receives any contribution in violation of this section, shall be fined not more than $1,000 or imprisoned for not more than 1 year, or both. If the violation was willful, such parties shall be fined not more than $10,000 or imprisoned for not more than 2 years, or both. Such contributions or expenditures are in connection with any election at which presidential and vice-presidential electors or a senator or representative in, or a delegate or resident commissioner to, Congress are to be voted for; or in connection with any primary election, political convention, or caucus held to select candidates for any of the foregoing offices. Recipients referred to are any candidate, political committee, or other person (18 U.S.C. 610).

Theft by bank examiners. Fine of not more than $5,000 or imprisonment of not more than 5 years, or both; except if the amount taken or concealed does not exceed $100, fine of not more than $1,000 or imprisonment for not more than 1 year, or both, plus disqualification from holding office as examiner (18 U.S.C. 655).

Theft, embezzlement, or misapplication by bank officer or employee. Fine of not more than $5,000 or imprisonment for not more than five years, or both; except if the amount embezzled, abstracted, purloined, or misapplied does not exceed $100, fine of not more than $1,000 or imprisonment not more than 1 year, or both (18 U.S.C. 656).

False advertising or misuse of names to indicate federal agency. Fine of not more than $1,000 to the corporation, partnership, business trust, association, or other business entity; fine of not more than $1,000 or imprisonment for not more than 1 year, or both, for the officer or member thereof participating or knowingly acquiescing or individual violating (18 U.S.C. 709).

Making extortionate extensions of credit. Fine of not more than $10,000 or imprisonment for not more than 20 years, or both (18 U.S.C. 892).

Financing extortionate extensions of credit. Fine of not more than $10,000 or an amount not exceeding twice the value of the advance, whichever is greater, or imprisonment for not more than 20 years, or both (18 U.S.C. 893).

Collection of extensions of credit by extortionate means. Fine of not more than $10,000 or imprisonment for not more than 20 years, or both (18 U.S.C. 894).

Purchase or sale of obligations in the U.S. of foreign governments or political subdivisions issued after April 13, 1934, or new loans to such while foreign governments or political subdivisions are in default to the U.S. Fine of not more than $10,000 or imprisonment for not more than 5 years, or both. Does not apply to federal corporations or to foreign governments which are members of the INTERNATIONAL MONETARY FUND and the INTERNATIONAL BANK FOR RECONSTRUCTION AND DEVELOPMENT (18 U.S.C. 955).

Illegal certification of checks. Fine of not more than $5,000 or imprisonment for not more than 5 years, or both (18 U.S.C. 1004).

False bank entries, reports and transactions. Fine of not more than $5,000 or imprisonment for not more than 5 years, or both (18 U.S.C. 1005).

False entries, unauthorized issuance of obligations, receipt of benefits. Fine of not more than $10,000 or imprisonment for not more than 5 years, or both (18 U.S.C. 1006).

False representation. Fine of not more than $500 or imprisonment for not more than 1 year, or both (18 U.S.C. 1013).

Participation by financial institutions in lotteries. Fine of not more than $1,000 or imprisonment for not more than 1 year, or both (18 U.S.C. 1306).

Disclosure of information by bank examiner. Fine of not more than $5,000 or imprisonment for not more than 1 year, or both (18 U.S.C. 1906).

Examiner performing other services. Fine of not more than $5,000 or imprisonment for not more than 1 year, or both (18 U.S.C. 1909).

Bank robbery and incidental crimes (18 U.S.C. 2113).
(a) Taking or attempt to take by force and violence or intimidation from a person or presence of another; entry or attempt to enter a bank or building used wholly or partly by a bank or savings and loan association, with intent to commit any felony affecting such bank or savings and loan association and violating any U.S. statute or any larceny. Fine of not more than $5,000 or imprisonment for not more than 20 years, or both.
(b) Taking and carrying away, with intent to steal and purloin, any value exceeding $100 belonging to or in the possession of any bank or savings and loan association. Fine of not more than $5,000 or imprisonment for not more than 10 years, or both. If the value does not exceed $100, fine of not more than $1,000 or imprisonment for not more than 1 year, or both.
(c) "Fence" for any value, knowing same to have been taken from a bank or savings and loan association in violation of (b) above. Same punishment as in (b) above for taker.
(d) Assault of any person or placing life of any person in jeopardy

by use of dangerous weapon or device, in committing or attempts to commit offenses in (a) and (b) above. Fine of not more than $10,000 or imprisonment for not more than 25 years, or both.

(e) Killing of any person or forcing any person to accompany without consent, in committing any offense in entire section, or in avoiding or attempting to avoid apprehension, or in freeing or attempting to free oneself from arrest or confinement. Imprisonment for not less than 10 years, or death penalty if jury verdict shall so direct.

BIBLIOGRAPHY

CLINARD, M. B., and YEAGAR, P. C. *Corporate Crime.* The Free Press, New York, NY. 1983.
GOEHLERT, R. *Crime Prevention: A Selected Bibliography.* Vance Bibliographies, Monticello, IL, 1987.
———. *Criminal Psychology: A Selected Bibliography,* 1987.
———. *Criminal Statistics: A Selected Bibliography,* 1987.
Criminal Law Review. Clark Boardman Co., Washington, DC. Annual.
GREEN, G. *Introduction to Security.* Butterworth Pubs., Stoveham, MA, 1987.
SCHWEITZER, J. *Computer Crime and Business Information.* Elsevier Science Publishing Co., Inc., New York, NY, 1985.

CRISIS The collapse of a period of prosperity, i.e., the termination of a rising price trend, general optimism, inflation, and speculation. It is a turning point or decisive moment at the crest of the business cycle when it becomes clear that the price structure has become topheavy and that the next movement must be downward. It may be precipitated by a sudden realization that prices have gone too high (buyers' strike), by a sudden restriction of or stringency in the supply of credit, by an unexpected bankruptcy of some conspicuous bank or business concern, or by the outbreak of war.

A crisis should not be confused with a PANIC, the latter being a serious financial and credit disturbance into which a crisis may degenerate. A crisis may be followed by a panic and is almost invariably followed by an industrial depression.

See BUSINESS CYCLE.

CROP INSURANCE *See* FEDERAL CROP INSURANCE CORPORATION.

CROPPER A tenant farmer or sharecropper who owns no land, no tools, and no livestock. He cultivates the land of a landlord who provides him with tools, work, stock, and seed, usually with rations for himself and family and with a shack for shelter. When farm land values are high, farm tenancy is a necessitous condition, but the tenant should be granted such rights as will enable him to derive just compensation for maintenance and improvement of the farm property.

See FARMERS HOME ADMINISTRATION.

CROP REPORTING BOARD Crop reporting headquarters in the Department of Agriculture at Washington, D.C. Individual reports of farmers and other producers are collected by trained field agents in each state and forwarded to Washington, where they are assembled, collated, prepared, and published in final form. Reports cover a wide range of subjects and statistics on principal agricultural commodities, including acreage planted, growing conditions, yields, prices, and other factors.

See CROP REPORTS.

CROP REPORTS Periodic reports issued by official government sources and unofficial private sources, showing the condition, acreage, and estimated and actual yields of the important crops. The Department of Agriculture issues monthly reports containing current information on growing crops and crop estimates. These estimates are based upon individual reports of farmers in every county and township in the United States, collected by trained field agents in each state. After being checked, the final estimates are prepared by a crop reporting board in Washington. Information on growing crops and size of acreage on the principal agricultural products, including wheat, corn, oats, rye, barley, soybeans, and many other commodities, is contained in these reports. In addition, the Bureau of Agricultural Economics issues monthly farm and parity prices. The Census Bureau issues ginning reports, a monthly consumption report, a mill stock report, and a monthly spinning activity report on cotton. The large grain brokerage houses and other commodity specialists issue unofficial reports of crop conditions during the growing season in the principal producing states.

Besides reports on acreage planted and estimated yields, reports on weather conditions and crop damage are also available from both official and private sources. Among factors in crop damage is damage from pests, such as the boll weevil for cotton, and plant disease, such as black rust, a fungus disease which attacks spring and winter wheat, and red rust (leaf rust infection), a less damaging variety of leaf rust in wheat. During recent years, rust-resistant varieties of wheat have greatly reduced crop damage from this source.

CROPS *See* CORN, COTTON, CROP REPORTS, MOVEMENT OF CROPS, WHEAT.

CROSS-CURRENCY INTEREST RATE SWAP An exchange of obligations between two parties. The first party agrees to make payments on an obligation incurred by the counterparty, and vice versa. The payments made by each party are in different currencies, and one party's payments are tied to a floating interest rate index while the other party's payments are fixed.

CROSSED CHECKS A form of check not employed in the United States but extensively used in England where it is recognized by law. Crossing is of two kinds—general and special. General crossing consists of drawing two parallel or transverse lines across the face of a check without the addition of any words. The words "and Company" or an abbreviation thereof, with or without the words "not negotiable," may be inserted between the lines but add nothing of significance. If the name of the bank or banker is added in a crossing, however, the check is crossed to the banker named, and is known as a special crossing.

When a check is crossed, generally the bank on which it is drawn may not pay it to any party other than a bank; when it is crossed specially, to no other than the banker specified in the crossing. The purpose of crossing is to prevent payment to wrongful holders and therefore to circumvent losses through forgery, since payment will not be made over the counter but only by a deposit credit through a bank, even though the payee can establish his identity. A bank which pays a crossed check other than as specified is liable to the true owner.

CROSS-HEDGE Hedging a cash market instrument (commodity) with a futures contract whose deliverable instrument is similar but not identical to the cash instrument.

CROSSING TRADES A transaction between brokers, prohibited by the rules of all securities and commodity exchanges, by which a buying order of one is offset by a selling order of the other for the same unit of the same stock or commodity. Instead of the orders being executed on the exchange, the brokers effect a cross trade between themselves. One broker, for instance, might turn over a customer's trade, say a buying order, to a second broker in exchange for a selling order placed with the second broker, instead of both brokers executing these orders in the open market.

The Commodity Futures Trading Commission Act makes it unlawful to enter into any cross trades. This manipulative practice is also prohibited by the Securities Exchange Act of 1934.

In the case of SPECIALISTS on the floor of the New York Stock Exchange, the exchange's rules provide that should the specialist's book have an order to buy and an order to sell the same stock at the same price (e.g., $50 per share), the specialist must first publicly offer the stock in the crowd at least at a tick higher than the bid ($50 $1/8$ per share). If there are no takers, the specialist may then properly cross the orders and be entitled to the usual specialist's commission from both brokers represented by the two orders. The specialist, however, cannot trade for his own account when it is possible to cross orders as above. The specialist may cross for his own account, provided he offers the public stock, at least at a tick higher than his bid; the price is justified by the market; and the broker represented on the specialist's book by such order is notified and accepts the transaction. The specialist, however, may not collect commission in such a case.

CROSS RATES In foreign exchange, the expression of the exchange rate between a foreign currency and the domestic currency determined through comparison of the rates for each in terms of other foreign currencies. Cross rates thus indicate the disparity

ENCYCLOPEDIA OF BANKING AND FINANCE

between a particular country's rate and the rates available in other countries. The latter, however, might be officially established cross rates rather than open market rates, and thus ARBITRAGE to equalize rates would be dependent upon latitude allowed by EXCHANGE RESTRICTIONS.

CROWDING OUT The reduction in private sector borrowing resulting from the government financing its deficit. Because there is a limited amount of credit to loan in the credit market, the presence of the government crowds out some private sector borrowers.

CROWN TRUST A type of *inter vivos* trust ("living trust"), named for the Chicago businessman Henry Crown, which basically serves as an income splitting and therefore tax-saving device in providing for children's education and other needs.

As an example, if $50,000 is invested by a parent to produce 15% in income, the $7,500 income therefrom, assuming a 50% tax bracket for the parent, would net only $3,750 that the parent would realize for a son's college education. Instead, if the parent provides an interest-free demand loan of $50,000 yielding the same income to the son and appoints a trustee (not a blood relative) to invest the loan at the same income return, the beneficiary son would be paying through the trustee only $750 in income taxes (up to $1,000 of income is exempt from income tax for children), and thus net $6,750 for the expenses of college. Moreover, the trust is revocable by the parent, so that the principal of $50,000 is returnable upon revocation. Crown trusts were challenged by the Internal Revenue Service but were upheld in litigation. Subsequent legislation restricted these arrangements to trusts that could hold the assets for ten years plus one day; these were known as Clifford trusts. The TAX REFORM ACT OF 1986 provided that all income of children under 14 should be taxed at their parents' rate and also raised the tax rates on trusts and income not distributed, thus effectively eliminating the advantages of both Crown and Clifford trusts.

See TRUST.

CUM DIVIDEND An English term meaning with the dividend included, as distinguished from ex dividend. The buyer of a stock cum dividend is entitled to receive the pending dividend.

CUM RIGHTS With rights included. The buyer of stock cum rights is entitled to exercise whatever privilege such rights carry.
See RIGHT.

CUMULATIVE DIVIDENDS Dividends on cumulative PREFERRED STOCK; dividends which accumulate if not paid regularly or in full, and if earned must be paid in the future before dividends can be paid on common stock. The interest upon income bonds may also be cumulative to the extent earned.

CUMULATIVE VOTING Section 5144 Revised Statutes (12 U.S.C. 61) provides for compulsory cumulative voting in all elections of directors of national banks, i.e., each shareholder shall have the right to vote the number of shares owned by him for as many persons as there are directors to be elected, or to cumulate such shares and give one candidate as many votes as the number of directors multiplied by the number of his shares shall equal, or to distribute them on the same principle among as many candidates as he shall think fit. In deciding all other questions at meetings of stockholders, each shareholder otherwise entitled thereto shall be entitled to ordinary voting power^one vote on each share of stock held by him.

State incorporation laws for business corporations provide in many states for cumpulsory cumulative voting or permissive cumulative voting. The pioneer state in providing for cumulative voting for stockholders of corporations was Illinois (1870), which to this day provides for it compulsorily in its constitution. Joseph Medill, the Chicago publisher, is credited with having principally promoted its enactment, influenced by John Stuart Mill's advocacy of proportional representation for political minorities.

Cumulative voting enables minority stockholders having the minimum shares required for at least one director under the cumulative formula to have such minimum representation on the board of directors; by contrast, under ordinary statutory voting of one vote per share of voting class of stock, a bare majority holding could elect all the directors. Basically, the total block of cumulative votes is derived by multiplying the total number of directors to be elected by the number of shares held and entitled to vote; e.g., if five directors are to be elected and 100 shares are held, 500 votes may be voted for any single individual as director, or this block of votes may be distributed over as many individuals as desired. For full effectiveness, however, minority holders should know the minimum number of shares necessary to elect the desired number of directors and concentrate the cumulative votes instead of overdistributing them. As long ago as January, 1910, in the *Journal of Accountancy*, Mr. Charles W. Gerstenberg, attorney and pioneer writer on corporation finance, published his formula for determining the minimum number of shares required to be sure under cumulative voting of electing the desired directors.

$$\frac{\text{Total number of shares voting} \times \text{Number of directors desired}}{\text{Total number of directors} + 1} + 1 \text{ (adding any fraction of 1 reading)}$$

To illustrate: If there are five directors to be elected and 500 shares are outstanding and voting for the election of directors, the minimum number of shares necessary to elect one director would be 84 shares. Proof: 84 shares times five directors to be elected equals 420 votes, all cast for one director. Assuming the rest of the stock (416 shares) votes en bloc as the majority, such total of 2,080 votes distributed among five directors would be 416 votes each. Therefore, the individual representing the minority and receiving its 420 votes is sure to get one of the places on the board, the majority getting the other four places. The minority in this example must be sure to vote all of its 420 votes for one director; if it distributed the 420 votes among two, it obviously would not win any places on the board.

Cumulative voting, therefore, does *not* automatically assure the minority of representation on the board; the minority must have the minimum shares necessary for election of the directors desired and, second, must concentrate its cumulative votes properly. A good general rule to remember is Dr. Harry G. Guthmann's generalization: the minority for election of at least one director fraction of the total board must own the next lower fraction plus one share; e.g., on a board of five directors, the minority must have one-sixth of the stock plus one share; six directors, one-seventh of the stock plus one share, etc. Cumulative voting, moreover, requires a majority of the stock to be able to elect a majority of the board; in the above example, to elect three of the five directors, 251 shares are necessary, or a majority of the 500 shares total.

The very purpose of cumulative voting—to enable minority stockholders to have at least minimum representation on the board of directors—is challenged as its disadvantage, on the grounds that such minority director is likely to be an outsider and dissenter on the board. Compulsory cumulative voting for directors of national banks was provided by the BANKING ACT OF 1933. Many bankers were in favor of that part of the Financial Institutions Act proposed in 1957 which would permit cumulative voting only if provided for in the national bank's articles of association (permissive). This part of the proposed legislation, however, did not pass. The Board of Governors of the Federal Reserve System stated in its presentation of its views on the proposed legislation that it feels the principle of cumulative voting is sound and that it "questions whether the proposed change should be made unless Congress is satisfied that cumulative voting has produced undesirable results so great as to outweigh the obvious justice of giving proper representation to minority interests."

In illustrating the practice and procedure under the statute (12 U.S.C. 61, *supra*) applicable to national banks, the rulings of the comptroller of the currency (Ruling 4300) provide the following example. Where a national bank has a board of directors consisting of seven members, one shareholder, owning 150 shares, cumulates his 1,050 votes so as to cast 525 votes each for two of nine candidates. The remaining (majority) shareholders, owning 300 shares, cast 300 votes for each of seven other candidates. The two candidates who received 525 votes would be elected. None of the seven candidates who received 300 votes each would be elected to the remaining five directorships. A second ballot would be held to elect five directors; in his second ballot, the shareholder whose shares were voted for the two directors elected on the first ballot could not vote his shares again. In other words, on the second ballot (and any subsequent ballots which might prove necessary) a stockholder is not entitled to vote shares which he has already fully cumulated and voted in favor of a successful candidate. This rule is based on the fact that to permit such shares to be voted again would result, in some cases, in defeating the proportional representation of all interests which is the purpose of cumulative voting.

BIBLIOGRAPHY

COMPTROLLER OF THE CURRENCY. "Cumulative Voting in Election of Directors." Interpretive Ruling 7.4300, Comptroller's Manual for National Banks.
STURDY, H. F. "Mandatory Cumulative Voting: An Anachronism." *Business Lawyer*, April, 1961.
WHETTEN, L. D. Cumulative Voting for Directors: Its Origin and Significance, 1959.

CURATOR A person, bank, or trust company appointed by a court to care for the estate of an incompetent or insane person under the court's direction.
See CONSERVATOR.

CURB BROKER A broker who transacts business on a CURB MARKET.
See AMERICAN STOCK EXCHANGE.

CURB MARKET A stock market either originally or now carried on in the open street. Curb markets were originally unorganized markets, but most of them are now organized and located indoors. The function of a curb market is to furnish a place for centralized exchange trading in securities that are not listed on the larger stock exchanges because they do not meet the higher re-quirements for listing thereon. In this sense, curb markets are secondary stock exchanges and provide a centralized market where new, unseasoned securities (shares of companies in the promotional, developmental, or early operating period) are bought and sold.

In New York City, the exchange formerly known as the New York Curb Exchange is now known as the AMERICAN STOCK EXCHANGE.

CURRENCY The quality of circulating freely; consequently, any form of money that serves as a medium of exchange and passes from bearer to bearer without endorsement. Currency may consist of coins or paper money. U.S. currency consists of all kinds of metallic and paper money but does not include checks, money orders, drafts, etc.
See ELASTIC CURRENCY, UNITED STATES MONEY.

CURRENCY ACT OF 1900 *See* GOLD STANDARD ACT OF 1900.

CURRENCY AND FOREIGN EXCHANGE TRANSACTIONS REPORTING ACT *See* BANK SECRECY ACT.

CURRENCY BONDS Bonds, the principal and interest on which are by their terms payable in lawful money, i.e., legal tender, of the United States, as formerly distinguished from gold bonds which were payable in gold coin.

CURRENCY DESIGNS The designs which appear upon various kinds and denominations of coins and paper money, each of which is distinctive and intended to serve as a means of ready recognition, and to render counterfeiting difficult. The DENOMINATIONAL PORTRAITS on the various kinds of paper money operate as the only means by which raised bills can be detected, since each denomination of paper money bears a given engraved portrait.

CURRENCY SHIPMENTS One of the functions of Federal Reserve and large city banks is to supply member (or correspondent) banks with suitable kinds and denominations of metallic and paper money. Currency shipments may be classified as paper money, coins, and orders for the transfer of money. Coins and currency are secured from Federal Reserve banks. In fund transfers, currency is shipped to a third bank; the remitting bank reimburses itself by charging the account of the correspondent bank.

Each spring, on the basis of recommendations of the FEDERAL RESERVE AGENT at each of the 12 Federal Reserve banks, printing orders are placed with the COMPTROLLER OF THE CURRENCY. The Comptroller, after reviewing requests passes them on to the Bureau of Engraving and Printing, which produces the appropriate denominations with the seal of the ordering Federal Reserve bank. The uncirculated FEDERAL RESERVE NOTES are shipped under guard to the ordering Federal Reserve bank, where they are held by the reserve agent until requested and collateralized.

The procedures involved in circulating new coin are similar. The supply of coin is governed primarily by demand, as well as facilities available to mint coin. Currently, coins are made in Philadelphia, Denver, and San Francisco under the control of the director of the mint. Like paper currency, coin is shipped to the Federal Reserve banks and through these institutions to member commercial banks and on to the public. Unlike paper currency, coin is bought by Federal Reserve banks from the Treasury at face value. In essence, Federal Reserve banks maintain inventories of coin at levels which permit them to fill orders from banks to meet public demands. Inventory levels are based upon historical demand patterns with additional provision for normal growth in demand. Federal Reserve banks arrange, in advance, for shipments of new coin from the mints for the coming year in amounts and on a time schedule to maintain inventories at required levels. Under this arrangement, the mints can schedule production of coin efficiently, and at the same time the Federal Reserve banks can provide coin as required to meet public demand. Federal Reserve banks are required to adhere to the advance shipping schedules. Except in emergencies, there is no provision for obtaining additional coin.

In addition to providing paper currency and coin to the public, member commercial banks also often distribute currency to non–Federal Reserve member commercial banks and thrift institutions through correspondent arrangements. As a general rule, member commercial banks have as customers nonmember commercial banks and thrift institutions. When nonmember institutions need currency or coin, they contact a correspondent bank which is a member of the Federal Reserve system. The member bank then provides the nonmember with the necessary currency or coin, and charges the correspondent's account.

The DEPOSITORY INSTITUTIONS DEREGULATION AND MONETARY CONTROL ACT OF 1980 specifies that fees are to be set for various Federal Reserve bank services, including currency and coin transportation and coin wrapping.

BIBLIOGRAPHY

FEDERAL RESERVE BANK OF NEW YORK. *How Currency Gets into Circulation* (Fedpoints 1).

CURRENCY SWAP A transaction in which two counterparties exchange specific amounts of two different currencies at the outset and repay over time according to a predetermined rule that reflects interest payments and possibly amortization of principal. The payment flows in currency swaps (in which payments are based on fixed interest rates in each currency) are generally like those of spot and forward currency transactions.

CURRENCY WARRANTS Detachable options included in securities issues giving the holder the right to purchase from the issuer additional securities denominated in a currency different from that of the original issue. The coupon and price of the securities covered by the warrant are fixed at the time of the sale of the original issue. Can also be a currency option in negotiable form.

CURRENT ACCOUNT Open, continuing, and running account; also, specifically, that account in the U. S. INTERNATIONAL TRANSACTIONS ACCOUNTS that includes trade (export and imports) in goods and services plus remittances, pensions, and other unilateral transfers (excluding military transfers).
See CURRENT ACCOUNT BALANCE, OPEN ACCOUNT.

CURRENT ACCOUNT BALANCE The net of merchandise trade (exports and imports), income on investments, rents, royalties, shipping, banking, insurance, and tourism. Sometimes, although not items includable in gross national product because they are unilateral transfers, private remittances and donations may be included in current account if the aim is to show total demand for and supply of foreign exchange on current account.

The net current account balance had been a net credit for the U.S. traceable to the substantial favorable trade balance (excess of exports over imports of merchandise) in recent years. But the increases in the cost of imports, mainly because of the rise in oil prices perpetrated by the Organization of Petroleum Exporting Countries (OPEC), created a net debit (excess of imports over exports of merchandise) in the trade balance carried down to the net current account.

Exports of goods and services are included in GNP because they are produced by the nation's economy. Since imports of goods and services are included in the other components of GNP (consumers, business, and government), they must be deducted from total exports of goods and services to measure the net foreign trade component of GNP.

CURRENT ASSETS Economic resources of an entity that are in the form of cash and those that are reasonably expected to be sold, consumed, or converted into cash during the normal operating cycle of the business or within one year if the operating cycle is shorter than one year. The normal operating cycle of a business is the average time it takes to convert cash into inventory, sell the inventory, and collect the amount due that results from the sale. Typical items included among current assets include cash, temporary investments, accounts and notes receivable, inventory, and prepaid expenses. In the balance sheet, current assets are usually listed in the order of their liquidity—that is, the ease and speed with which they could be converted into cash.

The excess of current assets over current liabilities is referred to as working capital. Adequate working capital is necessary for a business if it is to pay its debts as they come due. Creditors often consider working capital to constitute a margin of safety for paying short-term debts. Current assets are also used in computing the current ratio, which is one measure of the liquidity of a firm. The ratio is computed as follows:

Current assets / Current liabilities

See STATEMENT ANALYSIS.

CURRENT DEBT See CURRENT LIABILITIES.

CURRENT DELIVERY In commodity futures trading, a distant delivery becomes a current delivery on the first delivery day of the designated futures month. The seller must give prior notice of intention to deliver. Rather than take delivery, traders or speculators prefer to sell the maturing futures contract, as they are not interested in carrying the spot commodity.

See DELIVERY NOTICE.

CURRENT EXPOSURE METHOD The method prescribed in the Basle Agreement to calculate the credit equivalent amount on foreign exchange and interest rate contracts (and thus on all swaps). It involves calculation of the current credit exposure (the mark-to-market value of a foreign exchange rate contract or interest rate contract) and the potential future credit exposure. The sum of these is the replacement cost, which is taken to be the credit equivalent amount. A risk weight is then applied to this amount.

CURRENT LIABILITIES An obligation that must be discharged within the normal operating cycle of the business or within one year, whichever is longer. Current liabilities are normally expected to be paid using existing resources properly classified as current assets or by creating other current liabilities. Items commonly included in current liabilities include accounts payable, collections received in advance of delivery of goods or services, and other debts resulting from the normal operations of the enterprise. Current liabilities are usually listed on the balance sheet in the order of their liquidation date and are usually reported as the amount to be paid. Current liabilities are important in computing working capital, which is the excess of current assets over current liabilities.

Current liabilities are commonly classified as either (1) definitely determinable liabilities or (2) estimated liabilities. Current liabilities that can be measured precisely are referred to as definitely determinable liabilities and include obligations that are established by contract or by statute. Estimated liabilities are definite obligations of the enterprise the exact amount of which cannot be determined until a later date. Examples of estimated liabilities include product warranties, vacation pay, income taxes, and property taxes.

CURRENT RATIO The ratio of current assets to current liabilities, which is one of the credit barometrics applied to test a financial statement submitted by a prospective borrower.

Among credit analysts of the old school it has always been a rule-of-thumb formula that the applicant for credit should show at least a two for one ratio between current assets and current liabilities on his financial statement. This excess of current assets is required because the lending bank, for purposes of safety, must regard the prospective borrower not only as a going concern, but also as a liquidated one. In case a business should be forced into liquidation and compelled to realize upon its current assets at forced sale, such assets would almost certainly shrink in value, while the liabilities would remain constant or even increase if contingent liabilities existed and suddenly became primary liabilities. With a two-to-one ratio, current assets could shrink by 50% and still be sufficient to liquidate the current liabilities. This ratio has been used because experience has shown that current assets do not usually shrink by 50% under forced liquidation, and that therefore current assets would normally be more than sufficient to pay off current liabilities, leaving a margin as a factor of safety.

The two-for-one formula, while safe in most cases and practical because of its simplicity, is not scientific because it does not take into consideration other significant relations, such as variation in business types, merchandise turnover, terms of credit, territory served, and seasonal influences. Businesses having a rapid turnover, such as the grocery trade, may have a current ratio considerably less than two for one and still represent a better risk than a furniture dealer having a full two-for-one ratio. In the grocery trade there is a rapid turnover of merchandise for which the demand is universal so that in the event of liquidation the business would not suffer an appreciable loss through decline in value of its inventories. In the furniture business, however, a two-for-one ratio might not be satisfactory, since the turnover is less rapid and the shrinkage in value in the event of liquidation would be more severe. For this reason modern credit analysts recognize that the current ratio standing alone is not satisfactory as a credit test but should be considered in relation to other tests given under the subject CREDIT BAROMETRICS and discussed under the subject STATEMENT ANALYSIS.

CURRENT YIELD Obtained by dividing cash dividends received on a share of stock for one year by current market price. If a purchase has been made, the current yield on the investment is obtained by dividing the current annual cash dividend by original purchase price and subsequently by the prevailing price. Where the stock is not on a regular dividend basis, it is impossible to figure current yield on such regular rate for the coming year. This is more significant for the prospective purchaser of the stock than dividend for the past year. If the stock is not on a regular dividend basis, a projection for the coming year is often made on an indicated basis, based on most recent payments. Dividends in same stock of the declaring corporation itself are considered to afford no true yield, although often a yield is calculated by reference to the distribution rate. Thus, if two shares are distributed for every five shares, the YIELD is a 40% stock dividend.

Current yield on a bond with definite maturity is not a true yield, as it does not reflect the premium or discount involved in holding to maturity. It is obtained by dividing the coupon rate on an annual basis by current market price or original purchase price. Therefore "yield to maturity" is the more relevant yield calculation for bonds or debentures.

CURTESY See DESCENT, LAWS OF.

CUSHION BONDS Often applied to high coupon (high interest rate) bonds of high grade selling at premium levels over par, which, in comparison with otherwise comparable issues, afford a higher YIELD TO MATURITY and to first call date than par bonds (those selling at par, in line with prevailing new issue or estimated going yield rates) or than discount bonds (those selling below par).

Such yield spreads of cushion bonds provide a safety cushion which would in part absorb the decline in market price that would result from a possible rise in market prevailing yields. On the other hand, however, the rise in market prices that would result from a possible fall in market prevailing yields would generally result in best market performance by the discount bonds.

Yield spreads are empirical, varying over time pursuant to general market conditions, specific market conditions for various submarkets in bonds, and investor preferences and expectations. The yield differences resulting between high coupon and low coupon issues, otherwise similar in basic features, have been reported as often being large, and occasionally their market trends have been in opposite directions.

BIBLIOGRAPHY

FINANCIAL PUBLISHING CO. *Directory: Publications and Services*, 1981.
HOMER, S., and LEIBOWITZ, M. L. *Inside the Yield Book*, 1972.

CUSTODIANSHIPS The safekeeping and accounting for, under instructions, of valuable and usually income-bearing personal property, a relatively modern facility offered by the larger banks and trust companies to their customers. Custodianship accounts are also known as safekeeping, agency, and financial secretary accounts.

A custodianship involves keeping the property intact; collecting the income-interest, dividends, rents, etc., and disbursing them in accordance with instructions; redeeming bonds called at or before maturity and disbursing proceeds according to instructions; receiving rights which may accrue on stocks; and transmitting instructions for purchase and sale of securities through a broker.

A custodianship account differs from a safe deposit account in that in the former the customer's property is kept under control of the bank but always subject to the customer's orders, whereas in the latter the property is held entirely under the control of the renter of the safe deposit box. It differs from a voluntary trust in that in a custodianship the bank or trust company acts as agent, whereas in the latter it acts as trustee. As agent, the bank or trust company is responsible for the safekeeping of the property, but as trustee it is responsible for maintaining the value of the property.

The advantages of a custodianship over a safe deposit box are as follows: (1) in addition to protection provided by the vault, the customer has a receipt of the bank or trust company for the property, which clearly sets forth what has been deposited; (2) income is collected promptly, whereas if securities are deposited in a safe deposit box, collection is frequently delayed; (3) orders to buy and sell securities may be left for execution; (4) financial advice is always available and customers are automatically advised of the calling of bonds, the right to convert bonds into stocks and to subscribe to new issues, the privilege of selling to sinking funds; the increasing, reduction, or passing of dividends; the reorganization, recapitalization, or merger plans of the respective companies whose securities are held; and of any fact pertinent to investments.

See CUSTOMERS' SECURITIES DEPARTMENT, SAFE DEPOSIT COMPANY.

CUSTOMER OWNERSHIP The ownership of stock by customers of a corporation. This method of financing was popular with public utilities in the 1920s, chiefly motivated by the aim of promoting better understanding and identification of interests with the communities served. High dividend rate preferred stocks were generally the type of security thus offered and often with the privilege of buying the security on the installment plan. With the decline in security prices which set in during the 1930s, however, this method of financing lost its chief advantages; the decline in open market prices left customers still paying on installment contracts for stock at par and thus created ill will under adverse conditions. Customer ownership, however, is still a method of financing of importance for smaller concerns as a means of assuring themselves of identification with large customers or suppliers.

CUSTOMERS' LIABILITY An account appearing in a bank general ledger or financial statement as an offset to outstanding letters of credit guaranteed but not paid. This account is an asset arising from the fact that recourse may be had against customers who fail to fulfill the obligations which they guarantee to fulfill when letters of credit are issued to them. When a bank issues a letter of credit, the customer pledges to guarantee payment of all drafts drawn thereunder. In case payment is not made at maturity according to such guaranty, the bank has recourse against the customer and has the right to attach any property that he has in the bank, including deposits, securities, or other collateral, and to start an action at law to recover any balance still remaining.

See LETTER OF CREDIT.

CUSTOMERS' MEN REGISTERED REPRESENTATIVES.

CUSTOMERS' ROOM A room in a broker's establishment (i.e. commission house) for the convenience of customers. Its chief feature is a BOARD upon which quotations from various exchanges are posted as soon as they are printed on the tickers.

CUSTOMERS' SECURITIES DEPARTMENT The department of a bank or trust company which assumes custodianship of securities and other valuables belonging to its customers. Institutions undertaking to render these facilities offer to provide the same care in protecting customers' securities as they do in protecting their own. The customers' securities department becomes a bailee and not only assumes custodianship of customers' securities but may receive orders to buy and sell securities in the open market. These are transmitted for execution by a regular broker.

This department also sometimes performs such services as transferring stock, exchanging temporary securities for permanent or definitive securities, and holding securities for safekeeping while awaiting instructions of customers. Matured coupons are detached from bonds and credited to the account of customers or checks are remitted. These services may be rendered gratuitously or for a fee.

See CUSTODIANSHIPS, SAFE DEPOSIT COMPANY.

CUSTOMS DUTY The tax levied and collected by customs officials in accordance with the tariff laws upon imports.

CUSTOMS PORTS Ports where ships carrying import cargoes enter. Among the most active ports handling imports in recent years have been (as to tonnage) Delaware River and tributaries; New York City; Baltimore Harbor and Channels, Maryland; Portland Harbor, Maine; Mobile Harbor, Alabama; San Francisco Bay Area, California; Boston, Massachusetts; New Orleans, Louisiana; Los Angeles Harbor, California; and Norfolk Harbor, Virginia.

See CUSTOMS SERVICE.

CUSTOMS SERVICE Regional offices of the United States Customs Service, designated as such by Treasury Department Order 165-23 of April 4, 1973, following establishment of the Bureau of Customs as a separate agency under the Treasury Department on March 3, 1927, operate in the nine customs regions into which the 50 states, plus the Virgin Islands and Puerto Rico, are divided, containing within these regions 45 subordinate district area offices under which there are approximately 300 ports of entry. In addition, foreign field offices of the United States Customs Service are located in Bankola, Bonn, Brazilia, Brussels, The Hague, Hong Kong, London, Karachi, Mexico City, Ottawa Panama City, Paris, Rome, Riyadh, Seoul, St. Cloud, Tokyo, Vienna. Headquarters of the service is located in Washington, D.C., under the supervision of the commissioner of customs, who is appointed by the Secretary of the Treasury. The United States Customs Service was one of the earliest agencies created in the federal government, originally established by the fifth act of the first Congress passed on July 31, 1789, which established customs districts and authorized customs officers to collect duties on goods, wares, and merchandise imposed by the second act of the first Congress.

The customs service collects the revenue from imports and enforces customs and related laws. The service also administers the Tariff Act of 1930, as amended, and other customs laws. Some of the responsibilities that the United States Customs Service is specifically charged with are properly assessing and collecting customs duties, excise taxes, fees, and penalties due on imported merchandise; interdicting and seizing contraband, including narcotics and illegal drugs; processing persons, carriers, cargo, and mail into and out of the U.S.; administering certain navigation laws; detecting and apprehending persons engaged in fraudulent practices designed to circumvent customs and related laws; protecting U.S. business and labor by enforcing statutes and regulations such as the Anti-Dumping Act; countervailing duties; copyright, patent, and trademark provisions; quotas; and marking requirements for imported merchandise.

The customs service cooperates with and assists numerous government agencies in administering and enforcing over 400 statutory or regulatory requirements relating to international trade. Functions also include the collection and compilation of international trade statistics and protection of the general welfare and security through enforcement of the requirements of other agencies, such as automobile safety and emission control standards required under the National Traffic and Motor Vehicle Safety Act of 1966 and the Clean Air Act and the prohibition on discharge of refuse and oil into or upon coastal and navigable waters of the United States as outlined in the

ENCYCLOPEDIA OF BANKING AND FINANCE

CUTTING A MELON

Oil Pollution Act. These cooperative activities also involve the enforcement of laws and regulations regarding electronic product radiation and radioactive material standards, counterfeit monetary instrument prohibitions, flammable fabric restrictions, animal and plant quarantine requirements, and food, drug, and hazardous substance prohibitions.

Customs has an extensive involvement with outside commercial and policy organizations and trade associations, and with international organizations and foreign customs services. Customs participates in and supports the activities and programs of a wide range of international organizations and agreements, including the GENERAL AGREEMENT ON TARIFFS AND TRADE (GATT), the International Civil Aviation Organization, and the Organization of American States.

CUTTING A MELON See MELON.

CYCLE See BUSINESS CYCLE.

CYCLICAL STOCKS
Stocks of corporations whose earnings fluctuate with the business cycle. Such companies have relatively low earnings per share during recessions and sharply increasing earnings during the recovery phase of the business cycle. Cyclical stocks are generally considered to include basic manufacturing industries such as machinery and automobile manufacturing.

CY PRES DOCTRINE
From the Norman French words meaning "near to it." A doctrine applied to charitable trusts which for one reason or another cannot be carried out in exact accordance with the terms of the trust agreement. In such cases the courts may apply the cy pres doctrine, universally recognized in the common law, and direct that the TRUST be used in such a way as will most nearly carry out the original design of the donor. This doctrine is based on the principle that the state is ultimately the protector of all objects of charity.

D

DAILY ADJUSTABLE TAX-EXEMPT SECURITIES
Long-maturity bonds with coupon rate adjusted daily; the investor has the right to sell the bond back to the issuer.

DAILY BALANCES See AVERAGE LOAN AND BALANCE FILE, INTEREST BALANCE.

DAIRY LOANS See CATTLE LOANS.

DAMAGES A monetary award that may be recovered in the courts by a person who has suffered loss, injury, or detriment to his or her person, rights, or property as a result of another's acts or omissions. Damages may be nominal, punitive, or compensatory. Nominal damages are awards of a trivial amount, usually for the technical breach of the contract resulting in the injured party being placed in a better position as a result of the other party's breach. Compensatory damages compensate the injured party for the actual loss sustained from the contractual breach. Punitive or exemplary damages are assessed against a defendant beyond that amount necessary to compensate the plaintiff for the injuries suffered. The purpose of punitive damages is to establish a precedent example of the defendant to demonstrate that a certain type of behavior will not be tolerated.

Under certain circumstances, parties to a contract can stipulate the specific amount of damages to be paid by a party who might breach the contract. These are referred to as liquidating damages.

DARTS Dutch auction rate transferable securities.
See FINANCIAL INSTRUMENTS: RECENT INNOVATIONS.

DATE The indicated day, month, and year on which an instrument is drawn.

The validity and negotiable character of a check, note, draft, or other negotiable instrument are not affected by the fact that it is not dated. When a time instrument is undated any holder may insert the true date of issue or acceptance. Otherwise, where an instrument is not dated, it is considered to be dated as of the time it was issued.

Postdated checks, i.e., checks dated ahead, are not payable until the due date. A bank has authority to pay a check only when it is dated as of the day of presentation or a date antecedent thereto. Where the date is missing, it may be inserted and paid. Stale checks, i.e., checks more than six months old, usually should not be paid by a bank without consulting the drawer. It is intended that checks be presented for payment within a reasonable time after their issue.

Notes should not be dated on a holiday. According to the NEGOTIABLE INSTRUMENTS LAW, if a note matures on a Sunday or holiday it becomes payable the next succeeding business day. A few states have modified this provision to make such notes payable on the preceding business day.
See UNIFORM COMMERCIAL CODE (Secs. 3-114, 3-502, and 3-503).

DATING See TIME TO RUN.

DAYLIGHT TRADING Transactions for the purchase of a security balanced by transactions for the sale of such security within the course of a single trading session; short sales effected and covered on the same day.

DAY LOANS Loans made to stock exchange brokers without security but only for a day as a means of circumventing overcertification, which is unlawful. Necessity for such day loans has been reduced greatly by operation of clearing facilities (see STOCK CLEARING CORPORATION). In settling in the morning for the previous day's transactions, brokers settled by use of certified checks. Sometimes, however, a broker did not have the necessary balance. Overcertification is forbidden to banks; consequently, in order to service these brokers, it became the practice of banks to extend a temporary day loan to the broker, provided his credit standing was of the highest type, with the understanding that as soon as available collateral resulted during the day's transactions, it would be pledged as security for the loan as in a regular call loan. A day loan is also known as a clearance loan or morning credit.

DAY ORDER An order good for the day only; an order placed with a broker for execution on the day it is given, after which it is automatically canceled.
See ORDERS.

DAYS' DATE See DRAFT.

DAYS OF GRACE A privilege to defer payment of a note, acceptance, draft, or other time instrument after the indicated maturity for a number of days. Three days' grace is allowed in England and was formerly allowed in the U.S. Section 85 of the old Uniform Negotiable Instruments Law (since replaced by the Uniform Commercial Code) states that "every negotiable instrument is payable at the time fixed therein without grace."

Where the instrument is not payable on demand, presentment for payment must be made on the day it falls due. Where it is payable on demand, presentment must be made within a reasonable time after its issue, except that in the case of a bill of exchange, presentment for payment will be sufficient if made within a reasonable time after the last negotiation thereof.
See UNIFORM COMMERCIAL CODE (Sec. 3-503), NEGOTIABLE INSTRUMENTS LAW.

DAY-TO-DAY LOAN An English equivalent for call loan in the United States.

DAY-TO-DAY MONEY CALL MONEY.
See CALL LOAN, CALL MONEY MARKET.

DAY TRADING A trading practice in which all of the investor's positions are completely closed at the end of every day, leaving the investor with an overnight portfolio consisting only of cash.

DEAD ASSETS Unproductive assets; assets which produce no income, e.g., waste or unimproved land, or an industrial plant that is not operated because of obsolete or inefficient layout and facilities.

DEAL This term has two meanings:

1. For the purposes of taxes on the privilege of doing business, denotes regularity and recurrence of transactions, not isolated or occasional trades.
2. An expression sometimes used in finance to indicate a large transaction that involves a change in ownership usually arranged with or without general public knowledge, e.g., a traction deal, railroad deal, or deal in some other property.

ENCYCLOPEDIA OF BANKING AND FINANCE

DEALER In securities transactions, the person who has the legal status of a principal in relations with his customers, as contrasted with the broker's role of agent. Firms in the over-the-counter markets do business as both brokers and dealers (but not in the same transaction), and those using the mails or instrumentalities of interstate commerce must register with the Securities and Exchange Commission, except those doing purely intrastate business or in exclusively exempt securities.

Members of registered national securities exchanges act as brokers in their executions for customers of orders on securities listed on the exchange. Such member firms, however, may have unlisted securities departments in connection with which transactions might be on a brokerage basis or on a dealer basis (where the firm "makes markets" in the unlisted securities and thus trades with the customer as dealer).

The basis, whether as broker or as principal, is reported to the customer in the confirmation of the transaction.

Regulatory actions against members of registered national securities exchanges are reported by the exchanges to the Securities and Exchange Commission. The commission pursuant to authority contained in the SECURITIES EXCHANGE ACT OF 1934 makes reasonable periodic, special, or other examinations of the books and records of over-the-counter brokers and dealers.

See BROKER.

DEAR MONEY Money obtainable only at high interest rates.
See MONEY MARKET.

DEATH DUTIES See ESTATE TAXES.

DEBASEMENT Reduction in the purity of the metal forming the coinage of a country from its original or standard fineness. One of the purposes of government coinage is to ensure maintenance of purity of its coins. Coins might be debased by individuals, but ordinarily the term refers to the historical practice of government in taking a part of the pure metal out of its coins and replacing it with a baser metal, thus reducing the monetary metal content. No civilized commercial country has directly debased its coinage in modern times, knowing that the results of debasement are disastrous upon business by undermining confidence in the money affected, causing high or fluctuating prices, unstable conditions, etc. Debasement is different from DEVALUATION of the standard monetary unit, the former being insidious reduction in the monetary metal content, whereas the latter is public and nonsecretive, keeping the standard fineness usually the same on the reduced monetary metal content.

The ceremony in England known as the TRIAL OF THE PYX is established by law for the purpose of ensuring the maintenance of purity of the standard coin. In the U.S., annual assay commissions meet at the Philadelphia Mint the second Wednesday in February, as required by law, to examine and test the weight and fineness of U.S. coins. In addition to tests of the Annual Assay Commission, the director of the MINT in Washington makes metallurgical and chemical laboratory tests of coinage.

The Coinage Act of 1965 authorized a basic change in the composition of U.S. dimes, quarters, and half dollars. Formerly these coins contained 90% silver. The act eliminated silver from the dime and the quarter, and the silver content of the half dollar was reduced to 40%. In 1970, total elimination of silver from the half dollar was authorized, and the silverless half dollars first appeared in 1971. At the same time, two versions of the Eisenhower dollar were authorized—one silverless and the other containing 40% silver—and both appeared in 1971. The silverless version was intended for general circulation; the 40% silver version was a special numismatic coin sold at a premium. As of 1979, the circulating Eisenhower dollar version was being phased out, replaced by the new Susan B. Anthony dollar which was introduced into circulation July 2, 1979.

All coins currently in circulation in the U.S. are composed of the baser metals—cupronickel composition for the dollar, half dollar, quarter, and dime; cupronickel for the five-cent coin; and zinc-copper for the one-cent coin.

Elimination of silver from the silver coinage was ascribed by the Treasury to the world shortage of silver and the necessity of conserving this metal for industrial and military uses and has been accomplished openly as devaluation rather than debasement.

DEBENTURE A class term for all forms of unsecured, long-term debt, whether for corporate or civil (government, state, or municipal) obligations, although it is usually applied to a certificate of debt issued by a corporation.

In England debentures are often specifically secured by real estate mortgages but in the United States are secured only generally by the assets and the general credit of the obligor. The term is usually used in connection with bonds.

See DEBENTURE BONDS, DEBENTURE STOCK.

DEBENTURE BONDS Bonds without any security other than the general assets and credit of the issuer. Government, state, and municipal bonds, i.e., all civil bonds, are by definition debenture bonds since they are not secured by mortgages or any other specific pledge of assets. Notwithstanding this fact, civil bonds represent the highest class of investments because their payment rests upon the taxing power and general credit.

Debenture bonds issued by corporations are, as a class, not considered high-grade investments, although where the general credit of the issuer is strong, they may command a high position. Their strength depends upon the equity in the general assets, the extent of bond issues having prior liens, range of fluctuation of earnings, and margin of average earnings over prior charges. Debenture bonds are sometimes known as plain debentures.

See SUBORDINATED DEBENTURES.

DEBENTURE INCOME BONDS INCOME BONDS not secured by a mortgage or other specific pledge of assets.

DEBENTURE STOCK Infrequently used in U.S. finance, usually applying to a special type of stock conferring rights superior to those of both preferred and common stock. This stock is in the nature of a prior preference or first preferred stock.

In England debenture stock is equivalent to U.S. debenture bonds.

DEBIT In accounting, refers to the left side of any account; "credit" refers to the right side. Asset and expense accounts normally have debit balances; liability, income, and equity accounts normally have credit balances.

DEBIT BALANCE The excess of debits over credits in an account. In a bank account a debit balance occurs when the account is overdrawn. In a brokerage account a debit balance indicates the net amount due to the broker from the customer, which the customer would have to pay in order to take up his securities. Brokers charge interest on debit balances at comparable rates.

DEBIT CARD A card used to access directly the cash in a holder's account or credit line. Debit cards are used as automated teller machine (ATM) access cards and as point-of-sale (POS) cards to make point-of-purchase transactions with automatic debiting to the customer's account.

DEBIT TICKET A posting medium used in banking and brokerage bookkeeping to secure the posting of a transaction occurring in a certain department to the customers' or general ledger. It carries a complete description of the transaction and is preserved for future reference.

DEBITS TO INDIVIDUAL ACCOUNTS See BANK DEBITS.

DEBT A pecuniary obligation of a debtor; a sum of money one party owes to another as a result of a transaction in which value has passed to the debtor as evidenced by verbal or written contract or agreement. A note or bond is prima facie evidence of a debt, but an open book account can become an account stated only by the debtor's admission of liability, or by the debtor's failure to deny liability or to object to the account rendered.

See GOVERNMENT DEBT, INTERNAL DEBTS, NATIONAL BUDGET, PUBLIC DEBT.

DEBT AGREEMENT Contract between borrower and lender containing specific terms under which a loan is made. Debt agreements usually contain covenants (specific agreements or promises) made to the lender that the borrower will perform as specified. Covenants usually relate to specific events, transactions, or conditions that require compliance over time. The agreement often specifies what can occur on default or failure of the borrower to comply with a covenant. A cross-covenant specifies that a default or event of default under one debt agreement constitutes a default or event of default under another debt agreement. Subjective covenants refer to value requirements that cannot be measured objectively, such as those calling for "no adverse changes" or for "continued favorable earnings." A waiver refers to a document that provides evidence that the lender relinquishes or abandons a right, claim, or privilege.

The SEC, Rule 4-08(c) of Regulation S-X, requires the disclosure of the facts and amounts concerning any default in principal, interest, sinking fund, or redemption provisions, or any breach of covenant of an indenture or agreement, if the default or breach existed at the date of the most recent balance sheet filed and has not been cured.

DEBTEE One to whom money or other value is owing; rarely used term for creditor.

DEBT LIMIT Statutory limitation placed on U.S. federal debt. Sometimes erroneously called the public debt limit. The statutory limit does not apply to all PUBLIC DEBT but does apply to some debt other than public debt.

Until World War I, Congress ordinarily authorized a specific amount of debt for each separate bond issue. Beginning with the Second Liberty Bond Act of 1917, the nature of the limitation was modified in several steps until it developed into a ceiling on the total amount of most federal debt outstanding. This type of limitation has been in effect since 1941 and currently applies to the total of the following categories:

1. Most public debt issued by the Treasury since September 1917, whether held by the public or by the government.
2. Certain participation certificates issued by the FEDERAL NATIONAL MORTGAGE ASSOCIATION and the EXPORT-IMPORT BANK.
3. Other federal agency obligations that are guaranteed as to principal and interest by the United States in the statute authorizing their issuance. Currently, the only outstanding, nonmatured securities of this type are certain FEDERAL HOUSING ADMINISTRATION debentures and negligible outstanding amounts of matured, guaranteed issuances of the FEDERAL MORTGAGE CORPORATION and the HOME OWNERS LOAN CORPORATION.

In addition, the unamortized discount on Treasury ZERO-COUPON BONDS, such as the bonds Treasury sold to Mexico in 1988, is subject to the statutory debt limit. The price of the Mexican bonds was 20% of par value. The difference is counted in the statutory debt in an amount that will diminish with amortization of the bonds.

The largest part of the Treasury debt not subject to the statutory limit is debt issued by the Federal Financing Bank (FFB), an entity within the Treasury Department. The FFB is authorized to have outstanding up to $15 billion of publicly issued debt that is not subject to the statutory limitation. Between 1874 and 1985, the FFB borrowed from the Treasury, because the Treasury can borrow from the public at slightly lower rates than could FFB. Subsequently, in 1985 and 1986, when Treasury securities sales were approaching the debt limit, it issued FFB securities to the Civil Service Retirement and Disability Trust Fund. The amount of FFB securities outstanding as of mid-1988 was $10 billion, which was scheduled to mature in $5 billion increments in 1989 and 1990. The only other Treasury debt not subject to the debt limit consists almost entirely of currencies no longer issued.

Although the major part of agency debt is not subject to the general debt limit, most agency issues have their own separate statutory limits. For example, in 1959 the Tennessee Valley Authority was authorized to issue revenue bonds up to a limit of $750 million outstanding; after several increases by Congress, this limit stood at $30 billion in 1988.

The appended table shows the amounts of federal debt subject to and excluded from statutory debt limits.

Changes in the Debt Limit. Congress has frequently increased the statutory debt limit: thirteen times in the 1960s, eighteen times during the 1970s, and two or four times each year from 1980 to 1987.

Debt Subject to Statutory Limit, 1986–89
(in millions of dollars)

Description	1986	1987	1988[1]	1989[1]
Federal debt held by public	1,746,112	1,897,836	2,025,083	2,152,104
Federal debt held by govt. accounts	383,919	457,444	556,473	673,184
Gross federal debt	2,130,031	2,355,280	2,581,556	2,825,288
Debt not subject to limit:				
Treasury				
Federal Financing Bank	15,000	15,000	10,000	5,000
Other	601	600	599	599
Agencies				
Department of Defense	40	22	10	9
Department of Interior	15	13	8	8
Export–Import Bank	6	—	—	—
Small Business Administration	67	74	74	74
Postal Service	250	250	250	250
FDIC	442	200	703	470
FSLIC	—	920	4,506	6,106
Tennessee Valley Authority	1,625	1,380	1,380	1,380
Participation certificates [2]	1,030	830	—	—
	19,076	19,289	17,530	13,896
Total				
Gross debt subject to limit	2,110,955	2,335,991	2,564,026	2,811,392
Unamortized discount on zero-coupon bonds	—	—	7,904	7,728
Other debt & adjustments	22	23	23	23
Total debt subject to statutory limit	2,110,975	2,336,014	2,571,954	2,819,143

Note: Totals may differ from the sum of constituent items because of rounding.

[1] Estimate.
[2] Certificates of participation in loans issued by the Government National Mortgage Association on behalf of several agencies.

Source: "Special Analyses, Budget of the United States Government, fiscal year 1989," Office of Management and Budget.

The limit for 1989, established in the Balanced Budget and Emergency Deficit Control Reaffirmation Act of 1987, was $2.8 trillion.

The nature of debt limit legislation has also changed several times in recent years. From 1971 to 1983, the statutory limit consisted of a permanent limit of $400 billion plus a temporary increment that was usually scheduled to expire in a year or less and that required legislation to extend each time. On several occasions, Treasury had to suspend all auctions and issuances of new securities, including savings bonds, because the temporary increment expired before new legislation was passed.

In May 1983, Congress combined the permanent limit and the temporary increment into a single, higher limit without an expiration date. Under this system, when the debt limit is reached, Treasury can sell new securities to refund maturing issues rather than using cash to do so, and this system does not raise the amount of debt outstanding. Because the debt limit was usually set at a level expected to be reached in a few months, however, frequent increases were still needed, as well as several temporary increments.

Since 1980, Congress has attempted to relate the process of setting the debt limit more closely to the budget approval process. The debt limit may still be changed by ordinary legislation, but it is subject to the constraints imposed by the GRAMM-RUDMAN ACT (The Balanced Budget and Emergency Deficit Control Act of 1985). Under this act, neither house of Congress may consider a change in the debt limit for a fiscal year until after the congressional budget resolution for that year has been adopted. The act was designed to eliminate the federal budget deficit in a series of steps over several years by setting annual deficit targets and establishing a mechanism to enforce them. The Supreme Court, however, declared a key element of the enforcement mechanism unconstitutional.

In May 1987, with the debt limit set at $2.1 trillion, the current temporary increase to $2.3 trillion expired. In the absence of further legislation, the debt limit reverted to $2.1 trillion on July 18, and Treasury had to suspend the auction of bills and notes, sales of all other securities, and the investment of trust funds and other government accounted. Thus, it had to redeem all maturing bills with cash. Between that date and September 24, Congress enacted extremely short-term debt limit increases, which expired three times, with the limit reverting to $2.1 trillion each time. Finally, it passed the Balanced Budget and Emergency Deficit Control Reaffirmation Act, which raised the debt limit to $2.8 trillion, revised the annual deficit targets established by the Gramm-Rudman Act, and established a new enforcement mechanism. Although the new limit was expected to be sufficiently high to avoid the need for further increases in the debt limit in calendar 1988, a shortfall was anticipated during fiscal year 1989.

The Relationship of the Deficit and the Debt Limit. Changes in the federal debt subject to limit are not principally determined by the size of the federal deficit. This is because the federal trust fund surplus or deficit does not affect the amount of debt subject to limitation.

The budget consists of two major groups of funds: federal funds and trust funds. The former are derived mainly from tax receipts and borrowing and are used for general purposes; the latter comprises certain taxes and other receipts earmarked for special purposes such as Social Security, unemployment insurance, and other "off-budget" expenses.

A deficit in the federal funds generally must be financed by borrowing from the public, even if the trust funds have a surplus. The federal funds deficit can be financed by securities purchased by the trust funds, but then the Treasury must issue that amount in trust and fund debt to keep those funds fully invested. By law, any trust fund surplus must be invested in federal funds securities. Therefore, even if no deficit exists in federal funds, but trust fund surplus does, the debt subject to the statutory limit will rise by the amount of the surplus. The debt held by the public will remain constant; the debt held by government accounts (the trust funds) will increase.

See UNITED STATES GOVERNMENT SECURITIES.

DEBT RESTRUCTURING A situation that occurs when a creditor, for reasons related to the debtor's financial difficulties, grants a concession to the debtor that it would not otherwise consider at a point earlier than the scheduled maturity date. The two principal types of debt restructuring are a transfer of assets or equity interest from a debtor to a creditor in full settlement of a debt and a modification of terms. Modifications of terms include such arrangements as interest rate reductions or maturity date extensions.

Debtors experience gains and creditors recognize losses on troubled debt restructurings.

The accounting procedures for troubled debt restructurings can be summarized for the debtor and creditor as follows:

Form of restructure	Accounting for debtor and creditor
1. Settlement of debt:	
a. Transfer of assets	a. Debtor recognizes gain; creditor recognizes loss on restructure. Debtor recognizes gain or loss on asset transfer.
b. Granting an equity interest.	b. Debtor recognizes gain; creditor recognizes loss on restructure.
2. Modified terms; debt continues:	
a. Carrying amount of debt is less than total future cash flows.	a. No gain or loss is recognized on restructure.
b. Carrying amount of debt is greater than total future cash flows.	b. Gain or loss is recognized on restructure. No interest expense or income is recognized over the remaining life of the debt.

DEBTS OF CITIES *See* MUNICIPAL DEBT.

DEBTOR One who owes money or other value, whether on open account or evidenced by note, bond, or otherwise. Debtors may be classified as individual, corporate, or civil (government, state, county, and municipal).

DEBTOR BANK Indicates a bank that is debtor on net debit balance to the clearinghouse.

DECEDENT A deceased person; used in connection with inheritance, estates, wills, etc. A decedent who has made no will is called an intestate decedent; one who has made a will, a testator.

DECENTRALIZED RESERVE SYSTEM *See* FEDERAL RESERVE SYSTEM.

DECIMAL COINAGE A coinage system in which the denominations of the principal coins are decimals of the monetary unit and the denominations of all coins and paper money are even fractional parts or multiples of the unit of value. In the United States, the dollar is the monetary unit, a dime the tenth part, a cent the hundredth part, and a mill the thousandth part, each being one-tenth of the previous unit in the series.

The advantages of the decimal system are obvious as a convenience in making money calculations. Most of the monetary systems of the world are decimal systems, England having been the only great nation with a nondecimal system. However, in March, 1966, the British government announced its decision to adopt a decimal currency based on the pound as the major unit, subdivided into 100 minor units. This system was introduced in February, 1971.

See ENGLISH MONEY TABLE.

DECIMAL CURRENCY The currency of nations using the DECIMAL COINAGE.

DECLARATION OF DIVIDENDS Dividends on stock cannot be paid unless and until declared. Power to declare dividends rests solely with a corporation's board of directors, which determines the amount and date of the disbursement.

See DIVIDEND.

DECLARATORY JUDGMENT A decision by a judge in civil litigation in favor of either the plaintiff or the defendant based on uncontested facts and an interpretation of the law.

DECLINE Used in connection with securities and commodities to indicate a decrease or lowering of prices. Other terms employed to suggest the same meaning, either with greater or less intensity, are fall, sag, react, soften, slump, weaken, recede, drop, retreat, slip, sell off, shade off, toboggan, and break.

DEED In general, any instrument signed, sealed, and delivered as the act and deed of its maker. In business, however, the term usually refers to a written instrument to convey real property, i.e., to transfer its title from the seller to the buyer. There are two ordinary types of deeds—quit-claim and warranty. The person who gives a quit-claim deed gives up his own claim, rights, and interest in the property conveyed without responsibility as to whether the title is perfect or imperfect; he conveys no better title than he himself possesses. On the other hand, the person who gives a warranty deed guarantees a perfect title, and if subsequent defects appear the purchaser is entitled to recover any loss that he may thereby sustain.
See MORTGAGE.

DEED OF ASSIGNMENT A written instrument that appoints an ASSIGNEE, usually a trust company, to take charge of the affairs of an insolvent business and prescribes the powers and duties of such assignee.

DEED OF TRUST An indenture or mortgage indenture; a written or printed instrument (mortgage) in which the title to the therein described property is conveyed to a trustee, personal or corporate, who holds the property in trust for and on behalf of others, usually holders of bonds secured by the mortgage. It is a contract involving the issuing corporation (grantor and mortgagor), the trustee for the bondholders (mortgagee), and the bondholders themselves.

A deed of trust is a comprehensive and complicated instrument and describes the duties, responsibilities, and compensation of the trustee; the transfer of the title to the mortgaged property to the trustee, subject to defeasance clause; the details of the mortgaged property; the covenants of the mortgagor to pay the principal and interest on the bonds and to maintain the mortgaged property in good condition; and the procedure of the trustee in case of default.

DEEP DISCOUNT BOND Zero-interest debenture bonds sold at a discount that provides the buyer's total interest payoff at maturity.

DEFACED COINS Metallic coins which have been mutilated by clipping, sweating, cutting, punching, or otherwise. Ordinary wear and tear or abrasion is not defacement.
See MUTILATED CURRENCY.

DE FACTO AND DE JURE CORPORATIONS A de fac-to corporation is one that has been formed in fact but has not been formed properly under the law. Such corporations are often defective because of some small error, e.g., no good faith attempt to form the corporation or comply with the incorporation statute. A de jure corporation is a one that has been formed correctly in compliance with the incorporation statute. A corporation by estoppel is one that does not qualify as a de facto or de jure corporation but has held itself out to be a corporation or has been recognized as such.

DEFALCATION The fraudulent appropriation or abstraction of money or property entrusted to a person by reason of his employment, or held in a fiduciary capacity by such person; usually applied to public officials or officers of corporations.
See EMBEZZLEMENT.

DEFAULT Failure to perform an engagement or to meet an obligation, particularly applying to the failure to pay a bond or note at maturity or the interest due thereon at the stipulated interest date. Default in payment of the principal or interest on mortgage bonds, or in setting aside sinking fund installments, gives the bondholders rights and recourse under the terms of the mortgage indenture, such as right to accelerate maturity, right to institute foreclosure proceedings, and, wherever default occurs in any secured or unsecured corporate bonds, right to apply for a receivership. One who fails to meet a contractual obligation to pay money is a defaulter.
See REPUDIATION.

DEFAULTED BONDS No DEFAULT has ever occurred in U.S. government bonds. State and municipal bonds have a very low default percentage. Railroad and public utility bonds have a less enviable default record, but industrial bonds have the highest ratio of default of all classes. Among foreign government bonds, numerous defaults have occurred in principal and interest (see FOREIGN BONDHOLDERS' PROTECTIVE COUNCIL).

DEFAULT RISK The probability that a borrower will be unable to repay a loan. In a corporate setting, default risk is a real phenomenon and should be considered seriously when an investor contemplates purchasing corporate bonds. Moody's and Standard & Poor's are two financial advisory services that rate corporate bonds according to their default risk. Borrowers must compensate lenders for higher default risk by offering them a higher return on their investment.

DEFEASANCE This term has two meanings:

1. The defeasance clause in a MORTGAGE defeats the granting clause of the mortgage upon compliance by the mortgagor with the covenants in the mortgage.
2. Defeasance is the retirement of debt in substance, by not in fact. The term has also come to be applied to the "creative accounting" practice of some companies in recent years of "window dressing" their income statements and balance sheets. Specifically, the practice might involve, for example, the company's depositing government securities with a trustee for the purpose of providing the income with which to cover the interest charges on outstanding debt issue of the company periodically, as well as providing the principal sum to cover payment of the debt at its maturity. Accordingly, the interest charges on the debt involved would no longer be reported on the company's income statement, thus increasing the reported earnings; and the liability for the principal amount of the debt would no longer be reported in the company's balance sheet, thus reducing the debt-equity ratio of the company. The Financial Accounting Standards Board justified the accounting for defeasance on the basis of its definition of liabilities found in SFAC 6, para 35: "Probable future sacrifices of economic benefits arising from present obligations of a particular entity to transfer assets or provide services to other entities in the future as a result of past transactions or events." Because a debtor placed essentially risk-free assets into an irrevocable trust used solely to repay the debt, and because the possibility for future payments on the debt is remote, a transaction has been entered into which effectively satisfies the debtor's obligation.

DEFENSE MATERIALS SYSTEM A limited materials control system succeeding the former full control system, CONTROLLED MATERIALS PLAN, effective July 1, 1953.

The Defense Materials System assured deliveries of enough steel, copper, and aluminum (the three critical metals) during the Korean War defense effort to meet the requirements of the Department of Defense and the Atomic Energy Commission, provided for spreading the impact of military production requirements equitably over affected industries, and furnished a mechanism for lending special assistance wherever necessary to break up production bottlenecks and expedite military and Atomic Energy Commission production and construction.

Under the system, the Atomic Energy Commission and the Department of Defense furnished estimates of the quantities of steel, copper, and aluminum needed each quarter to meet their programs. The National Production Authority then issued setasides and directed the production of specified quantities of types, shapes, and sizes of these three controlled materials. The mills then reserved a suitable portion of their total production for defense orders in accordance with the authority's directives.

DEFENSIVE-INTERVAL RATIO A financial statement ratio computed by dividing defensive assets (cash, marketable securities, and net receivables) by projected daily expenditures from operations. The ratio is a measure of the time a firm can operate on present liquid assets without relying on revenues from next year's sources. Projected daily expenditures are computed by dividing cost of goods sold plus selling and administrative expenses and other ordinary cash expenses (projected daily operating

DEFENSIVE PRODUCTION ACT

expenditures based on past experience minus noncash charges) by 365 days. This ratio, along with the current ratio (current assets/current liabilities) and the acid-test ratio (cash, receivables, and marketable securities/current liabilities), is useful in evaluating the liquidity of the enterprise.

DEFENSE PRODUCTION ACT An act passed September 8, 1950 (64 Stat. 798, 65 Stat. 131; 50 U.S.C. App. 2061-2166), as amended, which provided the legal basis for the controls and incentives associated with the Korean War effort. The direct controls authorized included rationing (never imposed); establishment of price ceilings, rent controls, and stabilization of wages and salaries; priorities and allocations for materials and transportation facilities; special provisions concerned with settlement of labor disputes; and controls over consumer and real estate credit. With the easing of the active phase of the Korean War, these controls progressively expired or were eliminated. Thus, pursuant to the act, the Board of Governors of the Federal Reserve System in September, 1950, issued Regulation W, regulating extension of installment credit; in October, 1950, issued Regulation X, regulating extension of credit for the purchase of new housing; and in March, 1951, instituted the VOLUNTARY CREDIT RESTRAINT PROGRAM. All of these controls have been terminated—Regulation W and the Voluntary Credit Restraint Program were suspended in May, 1952, and Regulation X in September, 1952. Congress in 1952 repealed the act's authority for consumer credit regulation.

DEFENSIVE INVESTING POLICY See INVESTMENT.

DEFERRED ANNUITY An annuity that does not start to produce rents until two or more periods have passed. For example, an annuity of four annual rents deferred three years means that no rents will be paid (or received) during the first three years. The first of the four rents will be payable (or received) at the end of the fourth year.

DEFERRED AVAILABILITY ITEMS The account appearing in the weekly Federal Reserve bank statement that indicates the liability offset to uncollected items listed among the assets. Uncollected items represent the amount of checks in process of collection for member and clearing member banks by the Federal Reserve banks, i.e., checks in transit and in the process of becoming converted into credits to reserve balances. Uncollected items are contingent assets, while the deferred availability items are contingent liabilities. Their difference in amount is FLOAT.
See FEDERAL RESERVE STATEMENT, FEDERAL RESERVE CHECK COLLECTION SYSTEM, SCHEDULE SHOWING WHEN PROCEEDS OF ITEMS WILL BECOME AVAILABLE.

DEFERRED BONDS Bonds upon which the payment of interest is postponed until some condition with respect to earnings has been fulfilled, or upon which the interest periodically increases to a maximum rate, after which it remains uniform.
When the payment of the principal of bonds is deferred without changing the status of its underlying collateral, the issue is said to be extended.
See EXTENDED BOND.

DEFERRED CHARGES In accounting, certain expense outlays actually incurred, but which are properly chargeable to operations over a period of years by capitalizing (setting up as an asset). Examples are unamortized bond discount and expense, development expenses, organizational costs, etc. Deferred charges are to be distinguished from prepaid EXPENSES such as unexpired insurance, unused supplies, etc., which represent actual cash outlays in full, in advance, but which have not been incurred in full, so that only the portion actually applicable for a particular period is charged to operations.

DEFERRED DIVIDENDS Dividends on stock that are postponed until a fixed time has elapsed or until a certain event has occurred.
See DEFERRED STOCK.

DEFERRED INTEREST This term has two meanings:

1. Interest, the payment of which is postponed. When bonds are sold at a discount, the amount of the discount represents what the investing public demands in the way of additional return over the periodic cash or coupon interest to pay for the added risk involved in view of prevailing rates. While from the standpoint of the investor this raises yield in advance, from the standpoint of the issuing organization it represents deferred interest. For instance, if an issue of $100,000 of bonds is sold at 5% discount, the issuing organization receives only $95,000. At maturity, however, the issuing organization must pay the bondholders $100,000. The difference, or $5,000, represents a deferred interest or additional borrowing cost which must be accumulated evenly over the life of the bonds.
See AMORTIZATION.
2. The delay in crediting out-of-town (transit) checks deposited by customers having accounts with interest-bearing balances for interest purposes for the number of days required to collect them.
See INTEREST BALANCE.

DEFERRED PAYMENTS Payments to be made in the future. All credit transactions and time credit instruments involve deferred payments, e.g., bonds and notes. One of the functions of MONEY is to serve as a standard of deferred payments, and as such it should possess stability of value.

DEFERRED REVENUE Unearned income or revenues collected in advance. Deferred revenues are collected during the current period but will not be earned until a later accounting period. Deferred revenues create a liability because cash has been collected but the related revenue has not been earned by the end of the accounting period. There exists a current obligation to render the services or to provide the goods in the future.

DEFERRED STOCK Stock, dividends on which are not payable until the expiration of a fixed time or until some certain event has occurred. In England, deferred stock ranks behind ordinary stock (the English equivalent for U.S. common stock) and occupies the same position with regard to ordinary stock as the latter to preference stock. FOUNDERS' SHARES are a special type of deferred stock.

DEFERRED TAX LIABILITY The amount of deferred tax consequences attributable to existing temporary differences that will result in net taxable amounts (taxable amounts less deductible amounts) in future years. Taxable income in the tax return is computed in accordance with prescribed tax regulations and rules, whereas pretax financial income is measured in accordance with generally accepted accounting principles. Therefore, taxable income and pretax financial income often differ. These differences are identified as temporary or permanent. A temporary difference is the difference between the tax basis of an asset or liability and its reported (carrying or book) amount in the financial statements that will result in taxable amounts (will increase taxable income) or deductible amounts (will decrease taxable income) in future years when the reported amount of the asset is recovered or when the reported amount of the liability is settled. Permanent differences are items that affect financial income but never affect taxable income or vice versa.

DEFICIENT RESERVES See RESERVE.

DEFICIT Excess of liabilities over assets; the reverse of capital or net worth; a debit balance in the retained earnings account. The term is sometimes improperly used as synonymous with "loss," which means an excess of expense over income during a period of time. Deficit should be reserved to refer to a condition at a fixed moment of time. The term also refers to a debit balance in the retained earnings account (accounting).
The national budget deficit consists of the sum of shortfalls in (1) federal funds derived from tax revenues that are used for the general purposes of government and (2) taxes and other receipts that are earmarked for special purposes such as Social Security or unemployment insurance benefits. (See DEBT LIMIT, PUBLIC DEBT).

DEFICIT SPENDING An expansionary fiscal policy initiated either by increasing government purchases, decreasing taxes, or both. Each option increases deficit spending by the federal

ENCYCLOPEDIA OF BANKING AND FINANCE

government. Deficit spending arises when government purchases exceed revenues in an effort to expand economic growth. Deficit spending will result in a higher level of GNP, higher prices, and higher interest rates.

DEFINED BENEFIT PENSION PLAN A pension plan in which the contributions to the plan are calculated on an actuarial basis to provide a sum sufficient to generate the defined benefits to the pensioner (such as a pension equal to 67% of an employee's highest five-year average salary). The contribution level is sensitive to certain assumptions such as the rate the invested contributions will earn. Because the actuarial assumptions are estimates, the funds deposited may not be sufficient to meet the expected obligations. In that case, the employer is usually required to make up the difference to the pensioners. Defined benefit plans are flexible enough to be adjusted for inflation and can be modified to pay benefits on death, disability, or retirement, usually in the form of periodic lifetime payments for participants and their spouses. In such plans, the employer assumes the primary risk that the pension plan will not fall short at the retirement of employees. The employer projects what future benefit payments will be and puts aside funds in an investment fund to cover those costs when the time arrives for payments. If the investment fund falls short, the employer is expected to make up the difference.

Defined benefit plans have historically been the cornerstone of the private pension system. Such plans in 1990 covered 28.9 million participants and held more than $41 billion in assets. The major disadvantage to these plans is that they tend to penalize employees who change jobs frequently. Employees who leave before their pension rights have vested, usually after five years, often receive nothing. Those who leave after vesting do receive benefits, the amount of which is frozen at the time they leave. The payments they ultimately receive can look very small if years of high inflation come before retirement.

If the employer terminates a plan as a result of proven financial distress (a "distress termination"), the PENSION BENEFIT GUARANTY CORPORATION, an agency of the federal government, may become trustee, assume administration of the plan, and make the contractual payments. A pension plan may be terminated voluntarily (a "standard termination") if it has sufficient assets to provide for all benefit liabilities. The employer or plan administrator must purchase annuities for the existing and potential beneficiaries or otherwise arrange to meet the defined benefits. Any excess assets revert to the employer.

Federal legislation, especially the Employee Retirement Income Security Act of 1974, have greatly increased the cost and the legalities for employers sponsoring these traditional plans.

Accounting for pensions is discussed primarily in FASB Statement No. 87, "Employers' Accounting for Pensions," issued in December 1985. Also in December 1985, the Financial Accounting Standards Board issued FASB Statement No. 88, "Employers' Accounting for Settlements and Curtailments of Defined Benefit Pension Plans and for Termination Benefits." Pension expense (net periodic pension cost) recognized by a company includes five components:

1. **Service cost.** The actuarial present value of the benefits attributed by the pension benefit formula to services rendered by the employees during the current period.
2. **Interest cost.** The increase in the projected benefit obligation due to the passage of time.
3. **Actual return on plan assets.** The difference between the fair value of the plan assets at the end of the period and the fair value at the beginning of the period, adjusted for contributions by the company and payments of benefits to retired employees during the period.
4. **Amortization of unrecognized prior service cost.** Amendments to pension plans often include provisions that grant increased retroactive benefits to employees based on services rendered in prior periods. The prior service cost is amortized by assigning an equal amount to each future period of service of each active, participating employee at the date of the amendment who is expected to receive future benefits under the plan.
5. **Gain or loss.** Two elements: (a) amortization of any unrecognized net gain or loss from actuarial assumptions (interest rate, employee turnover, retirement assumptions) from previous periods and (b) the difference between the actual return on plan assets and the expected return.

A liability, unfunded accrued pension cost, is recognized and reported on the company's balance sheet if the net periodic pension expense recognized to date is greater than the amount funded. Alternatively, an asset, prepaid pension cost, is recognized and reported if the net periodic pension expense to date is less than the amount funded.

If the accumulated benefit obligation is greater than the fair value of the plan assets at the end of the period, an additional liability may have to be recognized. The unfunded accumulated benefit obligation is the accumulated benefit obligation minus the fair value of the plan assets, and is the minimum pension liability that the company must recognize. Recognition of this liability is required only if an unfunded accumulated benefit obligation exists and (1) an asset has been recognized as prepaid pension cost, (2) the liability already recognized as unfunded accrued pension cost is less than the unfunded accumulated benefit obligation, or (3) no accrued or prepaid pension cost has been recognized.

The pension liabilities, assets, and stockholders' equity items that may be reported on a company's balance sheet can include the following:

Assets:
  Prepaid pension cost
  Deferred pension cost (intangible asset)
Liabilities:
  Unfunded accrued pension cost
  Additional pension liability
Stockholders' equity:
  Excess of additional pension liability over unrecognized
  prior service cost (negative element)

Companies with a defined benefit pension plan must make the following disclosures:

1. Description of the plan, including employee groups covered, type of benefit formula, funding policy, and types of assets held.
2. The amount of the pension expense showing separately the service cost component, the interest cost component, the actual return on assets for the period, and the net total of other components.
3. A schedule reconciling the funded status of the plan with amounts reported in the company's balance sheet.
4. The weighted average discount rate and rate of compensation increase used to measure the projected benefit obligation and the weighted average expected long-term rate of return on plan assets.
5. The amount and types of securities included in plan assets.
See DEFINED CONTRIBUTION PENSION PLAN.

DEFINED CONTRIBUTION PENSION PLAN A form of pension plan in which the specific contributions to an investment fund over the years, by the employee or the employer or both, of the potential beneficiary are made on some basis other than the expected defined benefit. The formula used in the plan might consider such factors as age, length of service, employer's profits, and compensation level. Only the contribution is defined; no promise is made to be paid out to the employees. What the employee gets at retirement is whatever has accumulated in his or her account: the amount contributed to the plan, the return earned on investments of those contributions, and forfeitures of other participants' benefits that may be allocated to such participant's account. A common measure is a percentage of salary. Each beneficiary's account is run like an individual mutual fund, credited with the individual gains, losses, and contributions. At the time of an employee's retirement, the balance in the account is transformed into some type of annuity, which is paid out for the beneficiary's pension.

The advantage of such a plan is that defined contribution accounts are easily portable from one employer to another. In addition, many such accounts allow preretirement withdrawals for other purposes. This also can be a disadvantage in that the withdrawals reduce the retirement benefits. The main disadvantage of defined contribution plans is that the worker carries all the investment risk and pays some or all of his or her retirement cost.

Defined contribution plans have been increasing in recent years as a percentage of "primary" pension plans—those the Labor Department considers will be the retiree's main pension. This trend can be attributed to the regulatory burden imposed by the federal government on defined benefit plans.

In defined contribution plans, pension expense for the employer and the amount reported on the income statement is the contribution required each period.

See DEFINED BENEFIT PENSION PLAN.

DEFINITIVE BOND A permanent engraved bond given in exchange for a temporary or interim receipt or certificate. On account of the time required to prepare engraved bonds, it is often necessary when bonds are marketed to issue temporary receipts or certificates. Temporary certificates are then exchangeable for permanent engraved bonds when issued and ready for delivery.

See INTERIM CERTIFICATES.

DEFLATE A nominal value is deflated to a real value by dividing the nominal value by the relevant price index. For example, the GNP nominal values are deflated by dividing the GNP by the GNP deflator (divided by 100) where the base year is 1982-100:

Year	GNP ($ billions)	Deflator/100	Real GNP ($ billions)
1940	$ 100.4	0.130	$ 772.31
1980	2,732.0	0.857	3,187.86
1987	4,486.2	1.175	3,818.04

DEFLATION A period or phase of the business cycle characterized by emergency liquidation; abnormal falling prices of securities and representative staple commodities; contraction of bank loans; and decrease in bank clearings, bank deposits, volume of currency, production, and employment. The opposite of inflation.

See BUSINESS CYCLE.

DEFUNCT COMPANY A corporation that has ceased to exist; a corporation that has undergone the process of dissolution, whether nonjudicial (voluntary, upon ratification by vote of a specified (by statute or by certificate of incorporation) number of holders of outstanding shares entitled to vote, e.g., two-thirds) or judicial dissolution.

Under Section 1006 of the New York Business Corporation Law, a dissolved corporation, its directors, officers, and shareholders may continue to function for the purpose of winding up the affairs of the corporation in the same manner as if the dissolution had not taken place, subject to the statute or court order, and the corporation may sue and be sued in its corporate name.

DELAYED DELIVERY ORDERS Orders for securities in which an agreed time for delivery to the buyer, such as seven days, is specified. Specifying delayed delivery (DD) on the order permits sellers located at points distant from New York, for example, the necessary time in which to make delivery and yet take advantage of the New York market for securities.

See TRADING METHODS.

DELIVERIES Deliveries of securities purchased upon stock exchanges must be made in accordance with the rules of the exchange. These in turn vary according to the particular securities and methods of trading involved in transactions.

1. **Bonds, rights, and 100-share-unit stocks.** Bids and offers in securities admitted to dealings on an issued basis, except for U.S. government securities, shall be made only as follows and may be made simultaneously as essentially different propositions, but when made without stated conditions shall be considered to be "regular way."
   a. Cash, i.e., for delivery on the day of the contract.
   b. Regular way, i.e., for delivery on the fifth business day following the day of the contract.
   c. Seller's option, i.e., for delivery within the time specified in the option, which time shall be not less than six business days nor more than sixty days following the day of the contract except that the exchange may provide otherwise in specific issues of securities or classes of securities.

2. **Rights.** In the case of rights to subscribe, on the second, third, fourth, and fifth business days preceding the final day for subscription, bids and offers in rights to subscribe shall be made only "next day," i.e., for delivery on the next business day following the day of the contract, and shall be made only for cash on the day preceding the final day for subscriptions. (See RIGHT.)

   A special situation also arises in connection with rights and the commencement of trading therein. The filing of the last non-delaying amendment to the registration statement (filed with the Securities and Exchange Commission) on a rights offering, containing full details of the subscription (holders of record and expiration dates, subscription price), determines the effective date of the registration statement. Customarily the holders of record date is determined by the effective date of the registration statement, and the New York Stock Exchange will specify that the stock sells "ex rights" on the first business day after the effective date of the registration statement so that the stock will trade on the exchange "cum rights" only for the one day, the effective date of the registration statement. Therefore, a due bill will have to accompany the delivery after the record date on transactions made before the ex-rights date.

3. **Less than 100-share-unit stocks.** Stocks having a unit of trading of less than 100 shares, not assigned by the exchange for dealings by the use of cabinets, shall be dealt in as provided for 100-share-unit stocks (above). Anything contained in the rules to the contrary notwithstanding, the following rule shall apply to deliveries of less than 100-share-unit stocks dealt in pursuant to the rule: unless otherwise directed by the exchange, an ODD LOT of stock sold by an odd-lot dealer for his own account shall be delivered on the fourteenth day following the day of the contract and may be delivered on any business day prior thereto, except that delivery shall not be made before the fifth business day following the day of the transaction, unless otherwise agreed.

4. **U.S. government securities.** Bids and offers in securities of the U.S. government admitted to dealings on an issued basis shall be made only as follows and may be made simultaneously as essentially different propositions, but when made without stated conditions shall be considered to be regular way.
   a. Cash, i.e., for delivery on the day of the contract.
   b. Regular way, i.e., for delivery on the business day following the day of the contract.
   c. Seller's option, i.e., for delivery within the time specified in the option, which time shall be not less than two business days nor more than sixty days following the day of the contract, except that the exchange may provide otherwise in such securities.

(Note: the major market for U.S. government securities is the dealer market maintained by dealers in U.S. government securities, not that on the New York Stock Exchange. Cash, regular way, and delayed delivery transactions involve the same settlement (delivery and payment) details as specified above by the NYSE as analogous practices. Payment in the dealer market is normally in federal funds, and odd-lot transactions are normally on a five-business-day settlement basis.)

Centralized deliveries and clearance as well as settlement therefor are provided on all stocks listed on the New York Stock Exchange by its Stock Clearing Corporation, but not all members of the exchange are clearing members of the latter. In the absence of centralized clearing, deliveries and payment therefor have to be done on an individual firm-to-firm basis.

In the event of failure to deliver, the buying broker serves a buy-in notice on the seller, reciting that with failure to deliver, the buying broker will buy the stock in the open market and make delivery to his customer, holding the defaulting broker liable for any loss. This is buying in UNDER THE RULE.

To constitute a GOOD DELIVERY, the securities must meet certain standards including proper assignment, with the signature of the registered owner, if not in "street name," guaranteed by a member firm.

DELIVERY DAY In trading in commodity futures, usually considered to be the first trading or business day of the month in which the future contract matures. Ordinarily, however, the exchange authorities determine and publish the dates for each month's deliveries. For instance, the dates for December deliveries may begin November 29 and last until December 15, thereby permitting the purchaser to call for delivery of December's contracts at any time within that period. In the case of seller's options, delivery may be made on any business day of the month for which the sale was made.

DELIVERY NOTICE In commodity exchange trading, the notice sent by the seller on "notice day" to the clearinghouse containing the details of the delivery he is prepared to make on the maturing FUTURES contract for a specified commodity. The clearinghouse in turn passes on the notice to the person "long," or buyer. Since most traders in futures do not wish to accept delivery of the actual commodity, instructions in advance to their broker will call for reselling the contract and passing on the notice to the new buyer who will be a person willing to take delivery. Usually, before DELIVERY DAY the trader will have given orders to his broker to transfer his long position to later futures months in the commodity.

DEMAND CURVE A curve that indicates the number of units of a good or service that consumers will buy at various prices at a given time (economics). The demand curve is a graphic representation of how the quantity of a good or service that would be bought varies inversely with price. The typical demand curve moves downward to the right (more will be sold at lower prices).

DEMAND BILLS Sight or presentation bills.
See BILL OF EXCHANGE.

DEMAND DEPOSITS Deposits subject to check and which may be withdrawn by the depositor immediately and without notice of intended withdrawal. The great bulk of demand deposits are commercial DEPOSITS of corporations, partnerships, and individuals.

DEMAND LOAN A loan that is terminable at the option of the borrower or lender, having a fixed rate of interest but with no prescribed maturity. The term is generally used for commercial loans but is sometimes used as the equivalent of CALL LOAN, which properly should apply to brokers' loans.

DEMAND-PULL INFLATION An explanation for inflation that states that increases in demand pull prices upward, thus creating inflationary pressures in the economy. When an economy is near full employment, increases in demand cannot be met, so prices must increase as consumers bid for the limited products.

DEMAND STERLING Sight bills of exchange drawn in pounds, principally on banks in London but also on banks at other points in England.
See STERLING, STERLING EXCHANGE.

DE MINIMIS PUD A planned unit development in which the common area amenities do not affect the market value of each unit.

DEMONETIZATION To take away from a metal the power of acting as monetary standard, i.e., to strip it of free coinage and full legal tender powers; to relegate a coin serving as STANDARD MONEY to serve as token money. In the United States, silver was demonetized by the Act of 1873, known as the CRIME OF '73; i.e., its quality as standard money was discontinued, and although it retained its full legal tender qualities, it was not freely coined. After 1873, silver was coined on government account in large quantities under the BLAND-ALLISON ACT and the SHERMAN SILVER-PURCHASE ACT, both of which were subsequently repealed. While the Act of 1873 practically demonetized silver, the GOLD STANDARD ACT OF 1900 definitely and formally demonetized silver by reducing the silver dollar to the position of token money and making gold the standard money. The GOLD RESERVE ACT OF 1934, approved January 30, 1934, declared the coinage of gold at an end, the metal to be held in bullion form as metallic cover.

DEMONSTRATION A sharp advance or sudden display of activity in a stock or group of stocks. Before the regulation of stock markets, a demonstration was usually fictitious activity and was conducted by some individual trader, clique, or pool for the purpose of attracting speculative attention. Under the Securities Exchange Act of 1934, manipulation of security prices is prohibited, including activity for the purpose of creating a false or misleading appearance of active trading.

DEMONSTRATION LEGACY See LEGACY.

DEMURRAGE Literally a charge for delaying. A charge made for the loss of time caused by detaining or stopping a freight car on a side track or a vessel at a pier for loading or unloading beyond the specified period permitted by the carrier.

DENOMINATION The face value of a bond, note, coupon, coin, paper money, etc. When applied to stocks, it denotes the number of shares per certificate. Bonds usually bear $1,000 denominations, although they may occur in denominations of $500, $100, and $50. Government securities are issued in the following denominations.

1. **Treasury bills.** $5,000 (book-entry). Minimum order $10,000, then multiples of $5,000.
2. **Treasury notes.** $1,000, $5,000, $10,000, $100,000, $1,000,000, and multiple of those amounts.
3. **Treasury bonds.** $1,000, $5,000, $10,000, $100,000, and $1,000,000.

The denominations of coupons vary according to the interest rate of the relative bonds and the interest period.
The denomination of stock certificates is usually 100 shares. When issued in smaller amounts they are known as fractional certificates. The denominations of the various kinds of metallic and paper money are indicated under UNITED STATES MONEY.

DENOMINATIONAL PORTRAITS The portraits that appear upon each denomination of the various kinds of U.S. paper money. Each kind of paper money carries a series of portraits, by reference to which raised bills may be readily detected. Paying tellers, receiving tellers, money clerks, and others whose duty it is to guard against accepting raised bills should have a thorough knowledge of denominational portraits and other features of currency designs.

On July 10, 1929, the Treasury Department first introduced reduced-size paper currency into circulation and began to retire old-size currency. The purpose of the smaller currency was to secure economy in use of paper and printing, to ensure the highest degree of protection against counterfeiting and fraudulent alterations, and to eliminate confusion through simplification of the number of designs compatible with the necessity for distinguishing between the five kinds of paper money. Wholly new designs on a denominational basis were adopted. Whereas the old currency bore different designs (especially portraits) for the same denomination of various kinds of currency, there is now a characteristic design and portrait for each denomination regardless of kind.

A new type of distinctive paper was adopted for the present reduced-size currency. The paper basically is of the type formerly developed but with a higher folding endurance, particularly in the cross direction, than the paper formerly in use. The use of small segments of silk fiber as a distinctive feature has been retained, but the segments are scattered throughout the sheet and not localized in rows as formerly. The reason for the change was that, in a test of genuineness, dependence should not be placed on an outstanding characteristic that in itself inherently affords no protection.

A description of the essential characteristics of the designs of the present small-size currency follows. The size is $6\,5/16 \times 2\,11/16$ inches. The principle of denominational designs has been strictly followed. Along with the introduction of small-size currency notes in 1929, uniform back designs were adopted, many of them including vignettes of buildings or monuments closely associated with the persons pictured on the faces of the notes.

The portraits and back designs on U.S. currency notes being printed as of 1988 are listed in the appended table.

Notes of the $500, $1,000, $5,000, and $10,000 denominations have not been printed for many years, and as they are returned to Federal Reserve banks they are removed from circulation. The portraits selected for these notes were McKinley for the $500, Cleveland for the $1,000, Madison for the $5,000, and Chase for the $10,000.

The Treasury also reissued a new $2 Federal Reserve note in 1976, in conjunction with the bicentennial. One side of the note bears an

DEPARTMENT

Designs of U.S. Currency and Coins

Denomination and class		Portrait	Back design
$1	Federal Reserve Note	Washington	Great Seal of the United States (obverse andreverse)
$5	Federal Reserve Note	Lincoln	Lincoln Memorial
$10	Federal Reserve Note	Hamilton	U.S.Treasury Building
$20	Federal Reserve Note	Jackson	White House
$50	Federal Reserve Note	Grant	U.S. Capitol
$100	Federal Reserve Note	Franklin	Independence Hall
$100	United States Note	Franklin	Independence Hall
	Penny	Lincoln	
	Nickel	Jefferson	
	Dime	Roosevelt	
	Quarter	Washington	
	Half-Dollar	Kennedy	

engraving of the early 1800s portrait of Thomas Jefferson painted by colonial artist Gilbert Stuart. The same portrait appeared on the earlier $2 denomination U.S. note. The other side is a vignette based on John Trumbull's painting "The Signing of the Declaration of Independence." The previous printing of $2 bills was the 1963-1963A series of U.S. notes in 1965. The notes had been discontinued for a time because of lack of public demand for such a denomination.

Star notes: When a note is mutilated in the course of manufacture it has to be replaced. To replace it with a note of exactly the same serial number would require the use of special machinery and would be costly and delaying. In consequence, star notes are substituted. Except that they have their own serial number with a star, these notes are the same as the others and of course are worth only their face value. On U.S. notes, a red star is substituted for the prefix letter; on Federal Reserve notes, a green star is substituted for the prefix letter. A star note is also used for the one-hundred-millionth note in a series, since eight digits are the maximum practicable in the mechanical operation of the numbering machines.

Federal Reserve bank designations: On the face of Federal Reserve notes the issuing Federal Reserve bank is identified by letter of the alphabet in the center of a seal, preceded by the arabic number of the Federal Reserve bank outside the seal, to its left.

The Federal Reserve bank number is repeated in the upper and lower left and right corners of the bill. These numbers are helpful in cases involving claims made by the public for redemption of burned or mutilated notes when only portions of the notes can be identified. The two identical series of numbers, including the prefix and suffix letters or star in the upper right and lower left sections of the notes, are referred to as serial numbers. The letter in the Federal Reserve bank seal and the prefix letter of the serial number are always identical.

See COUNTERFEITS, CURRENCY OF THE UNITED STATES.

DEPARTMENT See AGRICULTURE, DEPARTMENT OF; COMMERCE, DEPARTMENT OF; etc.

DEPLETION The tendency to exhaustion of the assets of an extractive industry, e.g., mining, quarrying, oil, forestry. As coal or ore is taken out of a mine or oil is taken out of a well, the supply is reduced and progressively approaches the exhaustion point. Proper accounting treatment calls for a charge to be made on the books of extractive industries to provide for depletion of the assets so that when the exhaustion point is reached there will be funds on hand sufficient to pay the stockholders or owners in full. This involves an estimate of ore or oil reserves upon which even leading geologists and mining engineers often go astray. Under the Internal Revenue Code, in the case of mines, oil and gas wells, other natural deposits, and timber, a reasonable allowance for depletion is a proper deduction from gross income. Because of the difficulty in estimating these reserves, some businesses make no attempt to provide for depletion, and accordingly no depletion charges are made. Investors or speculators in mining, oil, and coal securities should determine whether accounting provision for depletion has been provided.

Holders of stock, in case depletion charges are not made, should regard dividends upon their stock not only as a return on investment, but also as a partial return of investment. Those companies that pay dividends including depletion usually indicate to the stockholders, for their tax returns, the proportion of dividends that is accountable to depletion and thus is a return of capital rather than ordinary income. Under the Internal Revenue Code, eligible taxpayers may claim a reasonable allowance for depletion as a proper deduction from gross income. The code provides for both cost depletion and percentage depletion and requires taxpayers to use the method that yields the largest deduction. The deductions for depletion and DEPRECIATION, in the aggregate, are expected to return the cost or other basis of the property.

The cost method divides the adjusted basis by the total number of recoverable units and multiplies by the number of units sold (or payment received for, if cash basis) during the year. Adjusted basis is cost less accumulated depletion (but not below zero). The percentage method uses a specified percentage of gross income from the property during the year. The deduction may not exceed 50% of the taxable income (before depletion) from the property; may be taken even after costs have been recovered and there is no basis; may be used for domestic oil and gas wells by an independent producer or royalty owner; cannot be used for timber. The percentage is a statutory amount and generally ranges from 5% to 20% depending on the mineral or other natural resource.

See WASTING ASSETS.

DEPOSITARY This term has two meanings:

1. DEPOSITORY.
2. Under plans of reorganization, escrow agreements, voting trust agreements, etc., a bank or trust company that accepts the deposit of securities and issues certificates of deposit therefor.

DEPOSIT BANKING The part of commercial banking that embraces receiving DEPOSITS, paying them out by check, collecting checks on other banks, and remitting on checks forwarded for collection. In addition to these activities in primary deposits, commercial banks create derivative deposits through their expansion of loans and investments.

See BANK, COMMERCIAL BANK.

DEPOSIT BOOK PASSBOOK.

DEPOSIT CURRENCY Checks and other credit instruments deposited with a bank as the equivalent of cash. Deposit currency describes the character and composition of the major proportion of a bank's deposits, which consists of checks, money orders, drafts, matured acceptances, matured coupons, etc., rather than actual money. It is estimated that normally 90% of the business transactions in the United States are settled by means of deposit currency. It is the only perfectly ELASTIC CURRENCY automatically expanding and contracting with the requirements of business—expanding with business activity and high prices, contracting with inactivity and low prices.

See CIRCULATION, CREDIT INSTRUMENTS.

DEPOSIT INSURANCE Antecedents of nationwide deposit insurance were the various state deposit-guaranty laws which followed the banking panic of 1907, as follows: Oklahoma, 1907; Kansas, Nebraska, and Texas, 1909; Mississippi, 1914; South Dakota, 1915; and North Dakota and Washington, 1917. Although characterized by varying terms and restrictions which inhibited their effectiveness, these state deposit-guaranty plans had the same basic principle—the levying of assessments upon the banks for the purpose of providing guaranty for DEPOSITS. Lack of territorial diversification and financial strength of the guaranty funds led to heavy losses when the number of bank failures increased.

At most depository institutions, deposits are currently insured up to $100,000 by a federal agency. Since all depository institutions are considered to encounter basically the same type of risks, insurance premiums are based upon a percentage of the institution's total deposits as follows:

FDIC	00.08%
FSLIC	0.125% (including a special assessment)
NCUSIF	1.0% of insured shares

If sufficient funds exist to cover failures, a rebate against the FDIC premium at the end of the year is possible.
See FEDERAL DEPOSIT INSURANCE CORPORATION.

DEPOSIT INSURANCE ACT See BANK DEPOSIT INSURANCE ACT.

DEPOSIT INSURANCE CORPORATION See FEDERAL DEPOSIT INSURANCE CORPORATION.

DEPOSIT INTEREST RATES Before March 31, 1980, the Federal Reserve Board, the Federal Deposit Insurance Corporation (FDIC), and the Federal Home Loan Bank Board set the maximum rates that federally insured commercial banks, mutual SAVINGS BANKS, and savings and loan associations could pay on deposits. Title II of the Depository Institutions Deregulation and Monetary Control Act of 1980 transferred this authority of the agencies to the Depository Institutions Deregulation Committee, which was to provide for the orderly phaseout by March 31, 1986, of deposit interest rate ceilings. Accordingly, ceilings for time accounts of more than 31 days were removed on October 1, 1983; for NOW accounts, money market accounts, and the accounts of less than 31 days, on January 1, 1986; and for savings accounts, on April 1, 1986. The only present constraint on payment of interest on deposits is that no interest may be paid on demand deposits.

The BANKING ACT OF 1933 ushered in the year of regulation of deposit interest rates by prohibiting member banks from paying interest on demand deposits and by requiring the Federal Reserve Board (through Regulation Q) to prescribe limitations on the rates of interest member banks could pay on time and savings deposits. THE FEDERAL DEPOSIT INSURANCE CORPORATION, upon its organization in June 1934, adopted the same ceiling for insured nonmember banks.

Because average interest rates actually paid on time and savings deposits were well below the ceilings for the next twenty-some years, the ceilings were academic, and no problems of DISINTERMEDIATION developed. As general interest rates began to rise in 1956, the Federal Reserve Board and the FDIC raised their interest rate ceilings on time and savings deposits five times between 1957 and 1965 to prevent banks from losing deposit funds to more attractive forms of saving and investment, which were not subject to regulation.

The Interest Rate Adjustment Act (September 21, 1966) for the first time granted the FEDERAL HOME LOAN BANK BOARD explicit authority to fix maximum rates insured mutual savings banks could pay on deposits. Also in 1966, a differential first appeared in the rates that commercial banks, savings and loan associations, and the mutual savings banks could pay. In late 1966, mutual savings banks could pay a full 1% more for savings deposits than could commercial banks, while savings and loan associations could pay 0.75% more on such accounts than could commercial banks.

In 1966 and again in 1968, the interest rate ceilings led to liquidity crunches for commercial banks. Corporations shifted substantial amounts of funds from maturing CERTIFICATES OF DEPOSIT in banks into higher-yielding MONEY MARKET MUTUAL FUNDS. Accordingly, elimination of rate ceilings on single-maturity CDs in minimum amounts of $100,000 began in mid-1970.

A law enacted August 16, 1973, permitted depository institutions (except credit unions) in Massachusetts and New Hampshire to offer interest-or dividend-bearing accounts with negotiable order of withdrawal features (NOW ACCOUNTS). In 1980, the Depository Institutions Deregulation and Monetary Control Act extended NOW account privileges to all depository institutions. NOW accounts are technically savings accounts because the depository institution may require prior notice of withdrawal. They do carry checking privileges, however, and thus function as interest-bearing demand deposits. Interest rates on such accounts were subject to Regulation Q ceilings.

Despite liberalization of Regulation Q ceilings on interest rates and other restrictions, during the late 1970s, open market money rates and yields surged to record levels, and depository institutions were faced with serious disintermediation in favor of money market funds offered by investment companies and investments in top-quality money market media. The funds featured high liquidity by offering checking privileges against balances in the funds. By 1982, the assets of these funds had grown to $230 billion. In response, Congress, in the GARN-ST. GERMAIN DEPOSITORY INSTITUTIONS ACT OF 1982, authorized commercial banks and thrift institutions to offer money market deposit accounts (MMDAs), which are insured up to $100,000, have no interest rate ceilings and no minimum balance restrictions, but allow only six transactions a month, only three of which may be by check, draft, or debit card. Authority for MMDAs was to expire on March 31, 1986, but the Federal Reserve Board continued them, and by the end of 1986 they accounted for 19% of all commercial bank deposits.

DEPOSIT LIABILITIES The aggregate liability of a bank to its depositors represented by its combined demand, time, and other deposits, including certificates of deposit. The deposit liabilities of a bank are the largest of all liabilities but normally should not exceed ten to twelve times the combined capital stock, surplus, and undivided profits. However, in recent years of deficit financing and substantial credit expansion (which creates derivative deposits in the banking system), the volume of deposits has expanded to fifteen to twenty times capital funds. Since this high deposit leverage is substantially invested in risk assets (see RISK ASSET RATIO), regulatory concern with banks' CAPITAL adequacy is a continual subject.

DEPOSIT LINE The average balance to the credit of a depositor's account in a bank over a given period; the average balance of deposits. This is useful in determining the profitableness of an account and in fixing the LINE OF CREDIT.
See AVERAGE LOAN AND BALANCE FILE, TWENTY PERCENT RULE.

DEPOSIT LOAN A loan that is created by giving the borrower a credit in his deposit account against which checks may be drawn as required.

DEPOSITOR One who has a bank account; one who has funds deposited to the credit of his account in a bank.
See DEPOSITS.

DEPOSITORY A bank that is designated and authorized to accept deposits of funds belonging to the federal government or other governmentalities (state, county, city, etc.), court funds, trust funds, or funds from other banks which the latter are required by law to maintain as reserve against deposits. If authorized to receive government funds a bank is called a government depository; if authorized to receive state funds, a state depository; if authorized to receive trust funds, a depository for trust funds; etc. A bank authorized to receive the reserve, or portion thereof, of other banks is known as a RESERVE DEPOSITORY.

The Federal Reserve Act confers upon the secretary of the treasury the right to use Federal Reserve banks, or member banks, as government depositories. The twelve Federal Reserve banks were appointed to act as government depositories and fiscal agents of the government by the secretary of the Treasury, effective January 1, 1916. The operations of the subtreasuries of the United States as a part of the fiscal system were required to terminate on June 21, 1921, by an act of Congress. The subtreasuries are now operated as a part of the Federal Reserve banks. Member banks may also be designated as government depositories and to act as government fiscal agents, at the direction of the secretary of the Treasury, to accept deposits made in tax and loan accounts, although most active Treasury funds are deposited with the Federal Reserve banks. Banks holding deposits of the United States and the lesser governmentalities are required to pledge certain required bonds as security therefore.

DEPOSITORY INSTITUTION MANAGEMENT INTERLOCKS ACT Title II of the FINANCIAL INSTITUTIONS REGULATORY AND INTEREST RATE CONTROL ACT OF 1978, approved November 10, 1978 (P.L. 95-630).

This law prohibits management officials of financial institutions, including directors and trustees of savings banks, from serving in a similar capacity with another financial institution located in the same standard metropolitan statistical area, city, town, or village.

Interlocks between a financial institution of more than $1 billion in assets and another institution with more than $500 million in assets are prohibited regardless of geographic location.

However, the law permits a director whose service began before the act was passed and signed to continue in office for ten years, to 1988. The federal regulatory agencies subsequently issued regulations that grant interlock exemptions of up to five years to financial institutions located in low-income areas, to those managed by minority groups or by women, to newly chartered institutions, to institutions in deteriorating condition, and to institutions that sponsor credit unions solely for their employees.

DEPOSITORY INSTITUTIONS

A wide range of financial institutions that accept deposits on account, including banks, savings and loans, mutual savings banks, and credit unions. All depository institutions, even those that are not members of the Federal Reserve System, may borrow at the discount window, although thrift institutions are expected to go first to their industry lenders (such as Federal Home Loan banks).

DEPOSITORY INSTITUTIONS DEREGULATION AND MONETARY CONTROL ACT OF 1980

An act giving the FEDERAL RESERVE SYSTEM increased powers over the full range of depository institutions. This legislation resolved some of the many problems pertaining to the structure of financial institutions and gave the Federal Reserve Board tighter control over monetary policy.

The uneven and inequitable level of reserve requirements applicable to similar accounts in various financial institutions had concerned the Federal Reserve Board for many years (see RESERVE). Universal reserve requirements would also help meet the problem of attrition in Federal Reserve membership and the weakening of the board's monetary reserve base. The board also supported the gradual phaseout of interest rate ceilings on deposits (see DEPOSIT INTEREST RATES) and broader investment privileges for thrift institutions.

The main provisions of the act are described below.

Title I, Monetary Control Act of 1980.

Reserve requirements: Reserve requirements must be uniformly applied to all transaction accounts at all depository institutions; for nonpersonal time deposits, they may vary by the maturity of such deposits. Depository institutions are defined, for purposes of the act, to include COMMERCIAL BANKS, MUTUAL SAVINGS BANKS, SAVINGS BANKS, SAVINGS AND LOAN ASSOCIATIONS, and CREDIT UNIONS, if they are federally insured or eligible for federal insurance. The Federal Reserve Board was also given the authority, upon the affirmative vote of not less than five members, to impose a supplemental reserve requirement on every depository institution of not more than 4% of its total transaction accounts. This supplemental reserve may be imposed only for the purpose of increasing the amount of reserves to a level essential for the conduct of monetary policy; it may not be imposed to reduce the cost burdens resulting from the basic reserve requirements or to increase the balances needed for clearing purposes. Any supplemental reserve must be terminated at the close of the first 90-day period during which the average amount of reserves required is less than the amount of reserves that would have been required if the initial ratios for the basic reserves had been in effect.

The Federal Reserve Board may impose a supplemental reserve requirement only after consultation with the FEDERAL DEPOSIT INSURANCE CORPORATION, the FEDERAL HOME LOAN BANK BOARD, and the NATIONAL CREDIT UNION ADMINISTRATION BOARD. In addition, it must promptly transmit to Congress a report stating the basis for imposing the supplemental reserve. The Federal Reserve banks are to maintain the supplemental reserves in an earnings participation account and to pay interest on that account at a rate not more than the rate earned on the securities portfolio of the Federal Reserve System during the previous calendar quarter.

Depository institutions that are members of the Federal Reserve System are to maintain their required reserves at the FEDERAL RESERVE BANK at which they maintain accounts. Reserves of nonmember institutions may be held at a correspondent depository institution holding required reserves at a Federal Reserve bank, a FEDERAL HOME LOAN BANK, or the National Credit Union Administration Central Liquidity Facility, if such reserves are passed through to a Federal Reserve bank. The board may permit all depository institutions to maintain all or a portion of their required reserves in the form of vault cash. Balances maintained to meet reserve requirements may be used to satisfy liquidity requirements imposed under other provisions of federal or state law.

The act exempted from reserve requirements any financial institution that is organized solely to do business with other financial institutions, does not do business with the general public, and is owned primarily by the financial institutions with which it does business, such as a Federal Reserve bank and various other specified financial institutions.

Any depository institution holding reservable transaction accounts or nonpersonal time deposits became entitled to the same Federal Reserve discount and borrowing privileges as member banks. The Federal Reserve System is required to take into consideration the special needs of savings and other depository institutions for access to discount and borrowing facilities consistent with their long-term asset portfolios and the sensitivity of such institutions to trends in the national money markets.

The act requires all depository institutions, at intervals prescribed by the board, to make such reports of their liabilities and assets as the board determines to be necessary or desirable to enable it to monitor and control monetary and credit aggregates. Member banks and other depository institutions subject to reserve requirements are to report directly to the board. Other depository institutions are to report through the appropriate federal supervisory agency in the case of federally insured institutions and through the state officer or agency designated by the board for other depository institutions.

Pricing of services: By September 1, 1981, the board was to begin putting into effect a schedule of fees for Federal Reserve bank services for;

1. Currency and coin services of a nongovernmental nature
2. Check clearing and collection
3. Wire transfer
4. Automated clearing house
5. Settlement
6. Securities safekeeping
7. Federal Reserve float
8. Any new service offered, including payment services to effectuate the electronic transfer of funds

In determining the fee schedule, the board is to observe the following principles:

1. All services covered by the fee schedule are to be explicitly priced.
2. Federal Reserve bank services covered by the fee schedule are to be made available to nonmember depository institutions at the same fees as to member banks. Nonmembers, however, may be required to hold balances sufficient for clearing purposes and be subject to any other terms that the board may determine applicable to member banks.
3. Over the long run, fees should cover all direct and indirect costs actually incurred in providing services, except that the board must consider competitive factors and provide an adequate level of services nationwide.
4. Interest on items credited prior to collection is to be charged at the current federal funds rate.

Miscellaneous amendments to Title I include:

1. Collateral is no longer required behind Federal Reserve notes held in the vaults of the Federal Reserve banks.
2. The kinds of eligible collateral for Federal Reserve notes were expanded to include obligations of, or fully guaranteed as to principle and interest by, a foreign government or agency of a foreign government, as well as any other assets that may be purchased by Federal Reserve banks.
3. A member bank is permitted to keep on deposit with any depository institution that is authorized to have access to the discount window sums in excess of 10% of its own paid-up capital and surplus.
4. The penalty rate on Federal Reserve advances to depository institutions secured in "ineligible" paper was repealed.

Title II, Depository Institutions Deregulation Act of 1980.

Title II provided for the orderly phaseout and ultimate elimination within six years (that is, by March 31, 1986) of limitations on the maximum rates of interest and dividends that depository institutions may pay on nondemand deposits and accounts. To effect the phaseout, Congress created the DEPOSITORY INSTITUTIONS DEREGULATION COMMITTEE.

Title III, Consumer Checking Account Equity Act of 1980.
This act continued the authority for banks to provide automatic transfer services from savings to checking accounts; for savings and loan associations to establish remote service units to credit and debit saving accounts, credit payments on loans, and carry out related financial transactions; and for federally insured credit unions to offer share draft accounts.

The act also extended nationwide the authority of depository institutions to offer NOW accounts to individuals or nonprofit organizations and increased federal deposit insurance from $40,000 to $100,000.

Among other amendments to the Federal Credit Union Act, Title III increased the loan rate ceiling for federal credit unions from 12% to 15%. The National Credit Union Administration Board was authorized to establish higher interest ceilings for a period not to exceed 18 months, after consultation with the appropriate committees of the Congress, the Department of the Treasury, and the federal regulatory agencies.

The FEDERAL HOME LOAN BANK BOARD was permitted to authorize the Federal Home Loan banks to be drawees of, and to engage in or to be agents for, the collection and settlement of instruments drawn on or issued by members of any Federal Home Loan bank or institutions eligible for membership. A Federal Home Loan bank is to make reasonable charges for clearing services consistent with the principles set forth in the Federal Reserve Act on pricing for services. A Federal Home Loan bank may use the services of, or act as agent for, or be a member of, a Federal Reserve bank, clearing house, or other public or private financial institution or other agency in the exercise of clearing and settlement functions. The National Credit Union Administration Board may authorize the Central Liquidity Facility or its agent members to engage in the same collection and settlement function as that authorized for the Federal Home Loan banks.

Title IV, Powers of Thrift Institutions and Miscellaneous Provisions.
Title IV amended the HOME OWNERS' LOAN ACT to authorize various new investment authorities for federally chartered savings and loan associations. Such associations may invest up to 20% of their assets in consumer loans, commercial paper, and corporate debt securities. They may also invest in shares or certificates of open-end investment companies registered with the Securities and Exchange Commission, if the company's portfolio is restricted to investments that savings and loan associations are permitted to make directly.

The authority to make real estate loans was expanded by removing any geographical lending restriction, providing for a 90% loan-to-value limit in place of the existing $75,000 limit, and removing the first-lien restriction on residential real estate loans. The authority to make acquisition, development, and construction loans was also expanded.

Federally chartered savings and loan associations were given authority to offer credit-card services and to exercise trust and fiduciary powers.

Under regulations of the Federal Home Loan Bank Board, savings and loan associations may issue mutual capital certificates as part of their general reserve and net worth. These mutual capital certificates are to be subordinate to savings accounts, saving certificates, and debt obligations but are entitled to the payment of dividends and may have a fixed or variable dividend rate.

Federal mutual savings banks were authorized to make commercial, corporate, and business loans up to 5% of their assets, but only within their home states or within 75 miles of their home offices. They were also authorized to accept demand deposits in connection with a commercial, corporate, or business loan relationship.

Title V, State Usury Laws.
The federal government preempted the provisions of a state constitution or law limiting the rate or amount of interest, discount points, finance charges, or other charges with respect to loans, mortgages, and credit sales or advances made after March 31, 1980, that are secured by a first lien on residential real property, by a first lien on stock in a residential cooperative housing corporation, or by a first lien on a residential manufactured home if the loan on the residential manufactured home is in compliance with consumer protection regulations of the Federal Home Loan Bank Board. A state was permitted to take action reinstating USURY limitations on mortgage loans if, after April 1, 1980, and before April 1, 1983, it adopted a law or certified that the voters of such state had voted against the federal usury override. State usury ceilings also were preempted to prevent discrimination against state-chartered institutions by permitting insured state banks, branches of foreign banks, insured savings and loan associations, insured credit unions, and small business investment companies to charge interest on loans at a rate of 1% above the basic Federal Reserve discount rate. In addition, Title V eliminated any state restrictions on the rate or amount of interest that depository institutions may pay on deposits and accounts.

Title VI, Truth in Lending Simplification and Reform Act.
The "Simplification Act" reduced the number and detail of truth in lending disclosure requirements and made them more understandable for consumers. It required separation of the disclosures from all other information and required the use of simple English descriptive phrases for key terms, such as "annual percentage rate" and "finance charge." The Federal Reserve Board was to issue model forms and clauses that, if used properly, would insulate creditors from civil liability. A creditor's exposure to civil liability was also reduced because statutory penalties would attach only to certain disclosures and because creditors would have 60 days in which to remedy errors discovered after disclosures are provided. The act also authorized the board and the other enforcement agencies to require reimbursement to consumers when the actual annual percentage rate or finance charge exceeds that shown on the disclosure statement.

Other general highlights of this title include the elimination of agricultural credit from coverage under truth in lending; the requirement that creditors provide consumers with good faith estimates of all required disclosures within three business days of a mortgage application; the elimination of the requirement that lenders itemize the amount financed or the components of the finance charge, although they must provide such itemization upon written request.

The Simplification Act also made some important changes in open-end checking. For example, it simplified the rules for identifying transactions on periodic billing statements. It also permitted creditors to send a summary of billing error rights and obligations once rather than twice a year.

The act extended the right of rescission (the three-day cooling-off period during which a consumer may cancel certain obligations) to transactions in which a security interest is taken in a mobile home, if the mobile home is used as the consumer's principal dwelling. It also eased the rescission requirements (for an experimental three-day period) for open-end credit plans involving advances secured by consumers' principal residences.

Title VII, Amendments to the National Banking Laws.
The comptroller was authorized, upon the request of the Federal Reserve, to assign examiners to examine foreign operations of state member banks.

The BANK HOLDING COMPANY ACT was amended to prohibit the Federal Reserve Board from rejecting an application for the formation of a one-bank holding company solely because the transaction involves a bank stock loan for a period of not more than 25 years; it may, however, reject an application solely because the other financial arrangements are considered unsatisfactory. The board is to consider, on a case-by-case basis, applications to form a one-bank holding company based on bank stock loans having a maturity of 12 years or more but may not approve any transaction in which the board believes the safety or soundness of the bank may be jeopardized.

DEPOSITORY INSTITUTIONS DEREGULATION COMMITTEE
The Depository Institutions Deregulation Committee was established by Title II of the DEPOSITORY INSTITUTIONS DEREGULATION AND MONETARY CONTROL ACT OF 1980.

The committee's membership consists of the secretary of the treasury, the chairman of the Board of Governors of the Federal Reserve System, the chairman of the Board of Directors of the Federal Deposit Insurance Corporation, the chairman of the Federal Home Loan Bank Board, and the chairman of the National Credit Union Administration Board, all as voting members, and the Comptroller of the Currency as a nonvoting member.

The referenced act transfers to the committee all the statutory authority of the Federal Reserve Act, the Federal Deposit Insurance Corporation Act, and the Federal Home Loan Bank Act to prescribe rules governing the payment of interest and dividends and the establishment of classes of deposits or accounts, including limitations on the maximum rate of interest and dividends that may be paid, and the authority in Section 102 of P.L. 94-200 to administer the differential between ceiling rates for thrift institutions and commercial banks on categories of deposits.

Mission. The act directed the committee as rapidly as economic conditions warrant to provide for the orderly phaseout and the ultimate elimination of maximum rates of interest and dividends that may be paid on deposits and accounts. This goal was to be achieved by the gradual increase in limitations applicable to all existing categories of accounts, by the complete elimination of the limitations applicable to particular categories of accounts, by the creation of new categories of accounts not subject to limitations or with limitations set at current market rates, by any combination of those methods, or by any other method. The committee was directed to work toward providing all depositors with a market rate of return on their savings with due regard for the safety and soundness of depository institutions, and also to increase to market rates as soon as feasible all limitations on the maximum rates of interest and dividends that may be paid on deposits and accounts. The committee could not increase such limitations above market rates during the six-year period beginning March 31, 1980.

The act provides targets to assist the committee in meeting these statutory objectives. These targets specify that the committee shall vote no later than March 31, 1983, 1984, 1985, and 1986, on whether to increase the limitations on the maximum rates applicable to all categories of deposits and accounts by at least 0.5%. The committee could adjust ceilings applicable to all categories of deposit to rates that are higher or lower than the specified targets.

With the accomplishment of its objectives, the committee ceased to exist on March 31, 1986.

See DEPOSITS for types of accounts and table summarizing reserve requirements and fixed ceiling interest rates.

DEPOSITORY RECEIPTS

Receipts issued by a trust company or other depository evidencing the deposit of foreign securities and facilitating trading in such interests on U.S. stock exchanges; sometimes applied to a CERTIFICATE OF DEPOSIT issued by protective committees or reorganization committees through a designated depository, usually a trust company.

See AMERICAN DEPOSITARY RECEIPTS.

DEPOSITORY TRUST COMPANY

Developed by the NEW YORK STOCK EXCHANGE (NYSE) as a subsidiary in which the exchange now shares ownership with banks and other organizations.

The New York Stock Exchange reports that while brokers may arrange to have customers' trades cleared and settled anywhere within a national network of stock clearing organizations, most NYSE trades today are cleared and settled through the computer complex operated by the Securities Industry Automation Corporation (SIAC), a joint subsidiary of the New York and American Stock Exchanges, for the National Securities Clearing Corporation in New York. The computers operated by the Depository Trust Company expedite delivery and related cash settlements between clearing brokerage firms and institutions in machine book-entry fashion.

DEPOSITS

Balances due to depositors of a bank; funds credited to the accounts of depositors.

General, Specific, and Special Deposits. General deposits consist of money or DEPOSIT CURRENCY. Wherever deposits are of this character, the relation between the bank and depositor is that of debtor and creditor. The bank becomes the owner of the deposit. The depositor has a claim against the bank for the amount deposited. All deposits are mingled together and become indistinguishable. The bank is not bound to return the identical deposit of cash, inasmuch as it is not a BAILEE as it is in the case of special deposits. Should a national bank fail, the general depositor becomes a general creditor and shares in the liquidating assets available for distribution proportionately with the other general creditors. The same provisions hold good in the case of state banks in most jurisdictions, although in a few states, depositors in state-chartered banks have a claim prior to other creditors.

Specific deposits are those made for a specific purpose in which the bank acts as bailee, e.g., money left to discharge a note, or to purchase securities.

Special deposits consist of property other than money, e.g., bonds, stocks, notes, life insurance policies and other valuable papers, jewelry, silverware, plate, etc., left with a bank as custodian for safekeeping and in which title remains with the depositor. Here the relationship between the bank and depositor is that of bailee and bailor. Special deposits never become the assets of the bank, and in case of failure are not applicable to the payment of liabilities but must be returned intact to depositors. Special deposits are taken under a contract of bailment, and many banks not equipped with safe deposit vaults provide custodianship for the valuables of their depositors, giving them the same care as their own securities but without further liability, either for a compensation or gratuitously.

See CUSTODIANSHIPS, CUSTOMERS' SECURITIES DEPARTMENT, SAFE DEPOSIT COMPANY.

Secured and Unsecured Deposits. Secured deposits are deposits collateralized by the pledge of specified securities, thus making such depositors secured creditors, rather than general creditors as in the case of unsecured deposits. Banks holding deposits of the United States and the lesser governmentalities are required to pledge specified bonds as security therefor.

Demand and Time Deposits. Deposits are also classified as DEMAND DEPOSITS and TIME DEPOSITS, with the following detailed classifications as called for in call reports of condition.

Demand Deposits
    Mutual savings banks
    Individuals, partnerships, and corporations
    U.S. government
    States and political subdivisions
    Foreign governments, central banks, etc.
    Commercial banks in United States
    Banks in Foreign countries
    Certified and officers' checks, etc.

Time Deposits
    Accumulated for personal loan payments
    Mutual savings banks
    Individuals, partnerships, and corporations
    U.S. government
    States and political subdivisions
    Foreign governments, central banks, etc.
    Commercial banks in United States
    Banks in foreign countries

Savings Deposits
    Individuals and nonprofit organizations
    Corporations and other profit organizations
    U.S. government
    States and political subdivisions
    All other

Ownership. Classified as to ownership, deposit accounts may be individual accounts or joint accounts. Joint accounts may be owned in any manner conforming to applicable state law.

    Joint tenants with right of survivorship
    Tenants by the entireties
    Tenants in common
    By husband and wife in community property in states recognizing this type of joint ownership.

Insurance. Classified as to coverage by deposit insurance, all types of deposits received by a bank in its usual course of business are insured, including the following items.

    Checking deposits
    Savings deposits
    Christmas savings and other open-account time deposits
    Time certificates of deposit
    Uninvested trust funds
    Certified checks
    Cashiers' checks
    Officers' checks
    Money orders and drafts
    Letters of credit and travelers checks on which an insured bank is primarily liable

Also insured by the Federal Deposit Insurance Corporation are testamentary accounts such as the following or any similar accounts that evidence an intention that the funds shall pass on the death of the owner to a named beneficiary; all are insured as a form of individual account.

> Revocable trust accounts
> Tentative or "Totten trust" accounts
> Payable-on-death accounts

Accounts held by a person in the following capacities are insured separately from his individual account.

> Executor
> Administrator
> Guardian
> Custodian
> Other similar fiduciary capacity

Uninvested funds of each separate trust estate held by an insured bank in a fiduciary capacity, such as the following, are also insured to the maximum per account.

> Trustee
> Guardian
> Administrator
> Executor
> Agent
> Other fiduciary capacity

An account held by a corporation, partnership, or unincorporated association is insured separately from the individual accounts of the stockholders, partners, or members—if the corporation, partnership, or unincorporated association is engaged in an "independent activity." The term independent activity is defined as any activity other than one directed solely at increasing the deposit insurance coverage.

For reserve requirements initially prescribed under the DEPOSITORY INSTITUTIONS DEREGULATION AND MONETARY CONTROL ACT OF 1980, see Title I, Monetary Control Act of 1980 under that term; for adjustments in interest rate ceilings initially made by the DEPOSITORY INSTITUTIONS DEREGULATION COMMITTEE, see that term. Deposit insurance per account was increased from $40,000 to $100,000 as of March 31, 1980, by the above referenced act, at federally insured banks, savings and loan associations, and credit unions. See FEDERAL DEPOSIT INSURANCE CORPORATION, FEDERAL SAVINGS AND LOAN INSURANCE CORPORATION.

DEPOSIT SLIP A slip upon which the details of a deposit are listed and which accompanies the deposit when handed to the receiving teller. The deposit slip is an original entry record. It is the posting medium through which the amount of the relative deposit is credited to the depositor's account in the bank's ledger. It should be made out by the depositor in each instance; if incorrect, the depositor should be required to submit a correct one to take its place. It is nonnegotiable. If a deposit is made without the passbook, a duplicate deposit slip so stamped may be made out at the same time for the convenience of the depositor.

A deposit slip "is an original entry in the eyes of the law and an important document. It is the bank's record of what the depositor offers for deposit. . . . They often become exceedingly valuable for reference in case differences and misunderstandings occur as to credit dealings with depositors"(W. H. Kniffin, *The Practical Work of a Bank*). Deposit slips should be retained by the bank at least until the next statement is reconciled. Some banks keep them longer, and still others, indefinitely.

DEPOSIT TICKET DEPOSIT SLIP.

DEPRECIATED CURRENCY Currency not accepted at its face or par value because of depreciation in exchange value resulting from unsound fiscal policies, unfavorable balance of payments, and lack of confidence; or, domestically, because of lack of redemption in standard money or suspension of redemption in standard or lawful money. Suspension of redemption in paper money may be the inevitable result of the depletion of the metallic reserves of a country, as illustrated by the case of the currencies of European countries. The depreciation of U.S. notes or "greenbacks" during the Civil War and until 1879 was primarily due to the suspension of specie payment coupled with overissue.

DEPRECIATION An accounting term to denote the shrinkage in value of an asset due to physical deterioration or wear and tear; obsolesence; and passage of time, inadequacy, and action of the elements. Depreciation in accounting practice is reckoned only for fixed assets (except land) of the tangible type, including buildings, tools, delivery equipment, office equipment, and leasehold improvements. The exhaustion of fixed tangible assets of the extractive industry type—mines, quarries, and natural resource deposits such as oil, gas, timber, etc.—is accounted for by DEPLETION. Fixed assets of the intangible type—goodwill, trademarks, patents, copyrights, and franchises—are written off by AMORTIZATION. The periodic depreciation, depletion, and amortization provision is set up in expense accounts, to be charged against current operations. Because such expense provision affects taxable net income of business taxpayers, the Internal Revenue Code regulates methods and allowances.

The Internal Revenue Code of 1954 (Sec. 167(b)\) specifically authorized, for taxable years ending after December 31, 1953, "reasonable allowance" for depreciation computed under any of the following methods: the straight line method; the declining balance method, at twice the straight line rate ("200% declining balance" method); the sum of digits method; and any other consistent method productive of an annual allowance that, when added to all allowances, does not during the first two-thirds of the useful life of the property exceed the total allowance using the 200% declining balance method.

Straight line method. It is the simplest, and perhaps the most widely used, method. Depreciable cost (cost of the asset minus estimated scrap value if any) is divided by estimated years of useful life to determine the depreciation each year. Thus, if an item cost $1,300 and is estimated to have scrap value of $100 and useful life of 5 years, the depreciation each year is $240.

200% declining balance method. Under this method, twice the straight line rate per year (40%) is applied to the declining balance each year, as in appended Table 1.

Table 1 / 200% Declining Balance Method of Depreciation

Year	Balance [1]	Depreciation	New Balance
1	$1,300.00	$520.00	$780.00
2	780.00	312.00	468.00
3	280.80	112.32	168.48
5	168.48	67.39	101.09 [2]

[1] There is no allowance for scrap value in depreciable cost under this method of depreciation (but the asset is not to be depreciated below a reasonable scrap value).
[2] Remaining undepreciated balance, which is to approximate reasonable scrap value and will serve as "basis" cost for computation of gain or loss on final disposition of the asset.

It will be noted that a total of $1,019.20, or 78.4% of original net depreciable cost, is accumulated in depreciation for the first three years of the estimated useful life of 5 years. This "accelerated" depreciation would compare with only $720, or 60%, under the straight line method for the same period. Herein lies the principal advantage of the 200% declining balance method—not that any more depreciation over the entire period is charged off compared to the straight line method, but that most of the depreciation is bunched in the earlier years of estimated useful life. This accelerated effect would be of interest to those firms interested in maximizing cash flow and saving taxes in years of high tax rates. True, the last two years of useful life would involve total remaining depreciation of only 13.8% on original depreciable cost; but having taken the bulk of depreciation, a firm might be induced to replace the asset at the end of the third year (replacement or trade-in may be made at any time, remaining undepreciated balance being the basis for computation of gain or loss on disposition). Accordingly, motivation for authorization of this accelerated method in the code was the possibility thereby of increasing the tempo of business investment.

Sum of digits method. This method also affords an accelerated effect like the 200% declining balance method. For accelerated effect, the number of years of useful life is added up and the depreciation each year is in a decreasing progression, on constant base (original depreciable cost), as in appended Table 2.

It will be noted that in the first three years of the total useful life of 5 years, a total of $960 in depreciation is accumulated, or 80% of the depreciable cost of $1,200.

ENCYCLOPEDIA OF BANKING AND FINANCE

DEPRESSION

Table 2 / Sum of the Digits Method of Depreciation

Year	Rate[1]	Depreciation
1	5/15	$ 400.00
2	4/15	320.00
3	3/15	240.00
4	2/15	160.00
5	1/15	80.00
15	15/15	$1,200.00

(sum of years' digits)

[1] Rate applied to depreciable cost (cost of $1,300 minus $100 scrap value, or $1,200 depreciable cost).

Other methods. There are many other methods of computing depreciation, including the sinking fund, compound interest, annuity, retirement expense, and appraisal methods, as well as the sum-of-years-digits increasing progression variant and the declining balance method with mathematically exact rate that will assure full depreciation taken by end of estimated useful life. Although these methods will result in differing amounts of depreciation each year as compared with constant amounts in the straight line method, all including the straight line method provide depreciation as a "fixed expense," i.e., amount of depreciation is a function of passage of time, rather than a "variable expense," i.e., where depreciation reflects variation in usage or operating rate. Where usage is the most important basis, the production or use method of depreciation will provide depreciation as a variable expense. Under this method, useful life is estimated in so many total units of output or hours of operating life; this number is then divided into the total depreciable cost to give the depreciation rate per unit of output or per hour of operation. Thus, the actual output in units or total hours of operating time in an accounting year, times the depreciation rate, gives the amount of depreciation for the year.

The ECONOMIC RECOVERY TAX ACT OF 1981 (ERTA), signed on August 13, 1981, provided for an Accelerated Cost Recovery System (ACRS) which greatly reduced the effects of inflation on capital expenditures by eliminating the useful-life principle and by providing for accelerated depreciation and hence cost recovery. The act itself provided schedules of accelerated recovery.

The Tax Reform Act (TRA) of 1986 kept the ACCELERATED COST RECOVERY SYSTEM (ACRS) structure that was established by the Economic Recovery Tax Act of 1981. However, the TRA of 1986 changed the way assets are classified and depreciated. Asset classification is based on asset depreciation range (ADR) class lives—the length of time the asset is expected to be used in business. The TRA of 1986 lengthened the ACRS depreciation periods for real property and certain long-life equipment placed in service after 1986. Statutory tables listing depreciation percentages are not provided as they were previously. Salvage value is not considered. The objective of this system is to encourage investments in productive assets by allowing faster write-off. ACRs is not considered to be an acceptable allocation method in accordance with generally accepted accounting principles.

BIBLIOGRAPHY

Depreciation and Investment Credit Manual. Prentice Hall, Inc. Paramus, NJ. Annual.
Depreciation Bibliography. Iowa State University Research Foundation, Ames, Iowa. 1986.
National Automated Accounting Research System. Online data bases. American Institute of Certified Public Accountants, New York, NY.
Statistics of Income: United States Business Tax Returns. U.S. Internal Revenue Service. Annual.

DEPRESSION A protracted period of business dullness when activity is below normal; the phase of a BUSINESS CYCLE that follows a crisis and period of emergency liquidation and is characterized by a drastic curtailment of production, contraction of bank credit, business inactivity, falling or bottom prices and efforts to "feel for the bottom" in the price movement, widespread unemployment, high rate of business failures, general unsettlement, etc.

DEREGULATION *See* FINANCIAL DEREGULATION

DERIVATIVE DEPOSITS Deposits created out of a loan in which no cash of its equivalent, e.g., DEPOSIT CURRENCY, is deposited. Among commercial banks, DEPOSITS are frequently created by lending a customer a sum not in money but by credit to his account against which he may draw checks as he needs it.

DESCENT, LAWS OF Laws, which differ in the several states, defining the rules by which the property of an owner devolves to his descendants and is transferred to them upon his death. Property is transferred upon the death of an owner either by will or, where there is no will, in accordance with the intestate laws of the state of which the owner was a resident. In general, a person by means of a will can devise his real property and bequeath his personal property to whomever he pleases with the following exceptions: the debts of the testator (one who makes a will) are a first charge upon the estate; the widow has a right of dower (and the husband the right of curtesy) in the testator's real property, which in most states is equal to a life interest in one-third of the real property, from which the widow cannot be cut off unless a provision expressly in lieu of dower is made in the will and is assented to by her; and trusts in perpetuity cannot be made.

When a person dies intestate, i.e., without having made a will, the laws of descent and distribution of the state in which the owner is resident govern the inheritance of all real property situated within the state and the succession of personal property wherever situated.

DETROIT STOCK EXCHANGE Founded in 1907 by seven brokers and located in the Penobscot Building, this registered national securities exchange ranked as one of the smaller regional exchanges in trading volume. It ceased operations June 30, 1976.

DEVALUATION The process of reduction in the monetary metal content of the standard money unit of a country, which thereby lowers its par (ratio of monetary metal content relative to that of money units of other countries). Such reduction is effected by appropriate amendment of the monetary statute of the country that defines the standard money unit.

Reciprocally, such a reduction in monetary metal content is an increase in the monetary value of the metal because the remaining monetary metal content of the money unit continues to have the standard money unit value. Under the GOLD RESERVE ACT OF 1934, the President was given the power to devalue the dollar to 50%-60% of its then statutory gold content. Then existing gold content of the dollar was 25.8 grains of gold, 0.9 fine, or 23.22 grains fine, accordingly valued at $20.67 an ounce, as follows.

$$\frac{480 \text{ (total grains in troy ounce)}}{23.22 \text{ grains, fine}} = \$20.67$$

The range of authorized reduction in gold content and the actual devaluation effected by the President's Proclamation of January 31, 1934, were as indicated in the appended table.

Range of Reduction in Gold Content

	Range of reduction		Actual reduction
	50%	60%	40.96%
Metal Content of $1	12.9 gr.	15.48 gr.	15.24 gr.
Fineness	0.9	0.9	0.9
Pure gold	11.61	13.93	13 5/7
Gold value per ounce	$41.34	$34.45	$35.00

Effective August 16, 1971, the U.S. dollar's convertibility (internationally, for official accounts) into gold was suspended. Effective May 8, 1972, such convertibility was restored, upon devaluation of the U.S. dollar, as follows, to 12.63 grains, fine (troy).

$$\frac{480 \text{ (total grains in troy ounce)}}{12.63 \text{ grains, fine dollar content}} = \$38.00$$

Effective October 18, 1973, the gold content of the U.S. dollar was further reduced to 11.37 troy ounces fine, thus raising the monetary value per ounce of gold to $42.22, as follows.

$$\frac{480 \text{ (total grains in troy ounce)}}{11.37 \text{ grains, fine dollar content}} = \$38.00$$

Total U.S. reserve assets, internationally, increased by $1.016 billion resulting from change in the par value of the U.S. dollar May 8, 1972, and by $1.436 billion resulting from change in the par value of the U.S. dollar October 18, 1973. These and all other values of the monetary gold stock of the U.S. have been "monetized" by the U.S. Treasury. The monetization of the gold stock of the U.S. by the U.S. Treasury results in an increase in the gold certificate account of the 12 Federal Reserve banks and a concurrent increase in deposits of the U.S. Treasury, general account, at the Federal Reserve banks.

Devaluation is inflationary in effect, as domestically a "gold profit" resulted from the markup in monetary value of gold stock from $20.67 to $42.22 an ounce, and internationally a realignment of par values and exchange rates relative to the dollar resulted. *See* INTERNATIONAL MONETARY FUND, for a discussion of a new system of managed "floating" exchange rates and issuance of special drawing rights (SDRs).

Devaluation is tantamount to an increase in the price of gold, stated in the subject currency, or in the exchange value of other currencies. In most cases, the intent of devaluation is to shift demand from imports (by raising their domestic price) to domestic goods and to increase demand for exports of domestic goods (which are now cheaper in foreign currencies). Thus, devaluation usually creates inflationary pressures because of increased demand for domestic goods (for export and for home consumption) and higher (domestic) prices for the goods that continue to be imported. The purpose of devaluation is defeated if a large number of countries (or principal trading partners) all devalue, or depreciate, their currencies simultaneously, as happened during the Depression. Since that time, various orderly trade arrangements and international monetary agencies have been developed to try to avoid the use of such "beggar-thy-neighbor" policies.

See EXCHANGE RESTRICTIONS, FOREIGN EXCHANGE, INTERNATIONAL MONETARY FUND, MANAGED CURRENCY, SPECIAL DRAWING RIGHTS.

DEVELOPMENT BANK A bank established to make intermediate- and long-term loans for the purpose of supporting economic development within a country. The bank is usually a governmental agency or one that is privately owned and operated. The Export-Import (Exim) Bank is an independent agency of the U.S. government established in 1934 to facilitate the financing of exports from the United States. The Inter-American Development Bank, founded in 1959 by several Latin American countries along with the United States, makes public and private loans for purposes of improving economic development in the member countries. Other development banks include the Industrial Reorganization Corporation in Britain, Wiederaufbau in West Germany, and the Instituto Mobiliare Italiano (a privately owned bank) in Italy.

DEVELOPMENT LOAN FUND Originally established within the International Cooperation Administration by the Mutual Security Act of 1957 (71 Stat. 355) to assist, on the basis of self-help and mutual cooperation, the efforts of free peoples abroad to develop their economic resources and to increase their productive capacity. Assistance from the Development Loan Fund (DLF) was entirely in the form of loans or guarantees or other financing transactions; no grants of funds were made. Loans could be repaid in the currency of the borrowing country. However, the DLF could extend loans to private business firms abroad. Financing was provided only if unavailable from other free world sources on reasonable terms.

The Mutual Security Act of 1958 (72 Stat. 261) created the DLF as an independent corporate agency. The Foreign Assistance Act of 1961 (75 Stat. 445) abolished the DLF and redelegated authority to the Agency for International Development, pursuant to letter of the President dated September 30, 1961, and Executive Order 10973 of November 3, 1961.

See INTERNATIONAL COOPERATION ADMINISTRATION, MUTUAL SECURITY PROGRAM.

DEVELOPMENT STAGE The beginning or early period in the life of an industry, as when its plant is being erected, or its product has not yet been placed on the market. The securities of a company in this stage are purely speculative, since they represent an enterprise which is unseasoned and has not yet proved to be a success.

For accounting purposes, a development stage enterprise is one that is devoting almost all of its efforts to establishing a new business and either of the following conditions exists:

a. Planned principal operations have not commenced.
b. Planned principal operations have commenced but there have been no significant revenues.

SFAS No. 7 requires that these enterprises prepare their financial statements in accordance with the same generally accepted accounting principles applicable to established companies. Additional disclosures are required.

DEVELOPMENT WORK The initial efforts in establishing a new enterprise.
See DEVELOPMENT STAGE.

DEVISE A gift of real property by will.
See DESCENT, LAWS OF.

DEVISEE A person to whom a gift of real property is made by will.
See DESCENT, LAWS OF.

DEVISEN Derived from the French word *devise*, the strict meaning of which is foreign bills and checks. The work is often loosely used, especialy in Germany, where the form is *devisen*, to mean foreign bills, checks, and foreign balances. International financial circles often use valuta as a synonym for divisen. Valuta is of Italian origin and in its narrowest sense means foreign currency. Thus a purist might say that the devisen (or devises, in the French plural form) were payable in valuta. But for the most part, international banking circles use the words interchangeably to mean foreign short-term assets, whether in the form of bills of exchange, checks, or balances.

DEVISOR One who bequeaths real property to another or others by will.
See DESCENT, LAWS OF.

DEVOLUTION The passing of title of real estate by hereditary sucession. The laws of descent and devolution vary among the states.
See DESCENT, LAWS OF.

DIARY A book or other record kept for the purpose of journalizing the maturity dates of notes, bonds, acceptances, or other time instruments; a TICKLER or maturity index.

DIGESTED SECURITIES Securities sold to persons who intend to keep them for the purpose of deriving an income; securities purchased outright and in the hands of real investors or ultimate owners. When first distributed, an issue of securities is likely to be purchased in part by speculators who intend to dispose of their holdings at the first favorable market opportunity. This situation tends to bring about fluctuating prices. When securities are well "digested," price changes are apt to be less volatile and reflect investment trends.
See UNDIGESTED SECURITIES.

DILUTION The weakening of each share of stock's proportion of earnings or asset value caused by an increase in the number of shares without corresponding increase in total earning power or asset value. Thus per share earnings and asset value decline. Marketwise, such dilution has a dampening effect.

Dilution arises particularly in connection with CONVERSION of convertible securities (bonds, debentures, preferred stock, or convertible classified common) into the junior equity, common stock, which increases the latter's total number of outstanding shares without increase in earning power and asset value, and may add to the "floating supply" of the stock in the market.

ENCYCLOPEDIA OF BANKING AND FINANCE

Temporary earnings dilution occurs in the case of additional financing in common stock, whether by new offerings or by subscription rights. The number of shares sold or subscribed for enlarges the total shares outstanding, but the new money brought in as the result of such financing has not as yet produced increased earnings on the increased number of shares. To adjust for this, some security analysts on a pro forma basis allow an assumed rate of earnings (usually current earnings rate) on the increased funds. As a minimal adjustment, the average number of shares outstanding during the accounting period is computed to determine the per share earnings and asset value.

Where the stock is priced below existing asset value in the case of new financing or subscription privileges exercised, such as options and warrants, dilution in asset value also would occur, since the new stockholders would be paying in less than asset value for their shares, and the per share figure on the enlarged total number of shares would decline. From the standpoint of most efficient financing, where additional common stock cannot be sold because of market conditions at least at net asset value, deferred common stock financing in the form of convertible senior securities (bonds, debentures, preferred stock) would bring in the needed funds, with high conversion ratios appropriately fixed relative to earning power and asset value, for conversion at a subsequent date when higher earning power and asset values would enable the common stock to absorb the dilution better.

APB Opinion No. 15, "Earnings per Share," superseding in some respects APB Opinion No. 9, "Reporting the Results of Operations," both published by the Accounting Principles Board of the American Institute of Certified Public Accountants, provides that if potential dilution (convertible securities outstanding, warrants, options) exists in any of the periods presented in the statement of income or summary of earnings, the dual presentation of primary EARNINGS PER SHARE and fully diluted earnings per share data should be made for all periods presented.

Primary earnings per share is the amount of earnings attributable to each share of common stock outstanding, including common stock equivalents (securities that because of their terms or the circumstances under which they were issued, are substantially equivalent to common stock). Fully diluted earnings per share is the amount of current earnings per share reflecting the maximum dilutions that would have resulted from conversions, exercises, and other contingent issuances that individually would have deceased earnings per share and in the aggregate would have had a dilutive effect. All such issuances are assumed to have taken place at the beginning of the period (or at the time the contingency arose, if later).

DIME The U.S. ten-cent piece. Under the Coinage Act of 1965 (P.L. 89-91), silver is completely eliminated from the dime. The two outer layers of this denomination are composed of a cupronickel alloy of 75% copper and 25% nickel, metallurgically bonded to a center core or inner layer of pure copper. Obverse and reverse sides are white in appearance, and the copper core gives the coin a distinctive copper-colored edge. The "clad" dime weighs 2.268 grams, compared with 2.5 grams for the silver dime formerly issued.

See FRACTIONAL CURRENCY, TOKEN MONEY.

DIMINISHING RETURNS The economic principle that suc-cessive additions of variable factors of production to a fixed factor of production will eventually result in declining marginal returns, even though output is still increasing. The "point of diminishing returns" varies among industries and, within industries, among different levels of production. Until this point is reached, increasing output by adding variable inputs will reduce per-unit costs (because of higher productivity) when diminishing returns set in, productivity declines and per-unit costs rise. Industries that require very large amounts of initial capital equipment, as most utilities do, may enjoy "returns to scale" up to a very high level of output.

DIRECT DEPOSIT An arrangement whereby the recipient of a periodic payment authorizes the paying company or agency to send the payment directly to his or her account at a depository institution. Such deposits may be accomplished electronically without preparing separate checks. The corporation or agency, or its data processing contractor, generates credit entries representing deposits, which are delivered to its bank on or before the due date for payment. The bank extracts the entries for its own customers, crediting their accounts, and sends the remaining entries to the local AUTOMATED CLEARING HOUSE. The clearing house makes settlement between the originating and receiving banks and transmits the entries to the appropriate receiving banks, which then credit the accounts of their customers that are due payment.

The U.S. Treasury Department, the Social Security Administration, the Federal Reserve System, and many other public and private payments issuers are now using and promoting direct deposit on grounds that it reduces the risk of lost, misplaced, or stolen checks; allows interest earnings, if any, to start accumulating sooner; provides immediate availability of funds; and reduces handling costs, both for the payor and the depository institution.

DIRECT EARNINGS Earnings actually reported by a corporation without allowance for a possible equity in the surplus earnings, in excess of dividend payments, of subsidiary and or affiliated companies. This term is in contrast with indirect or EQUITY EARNINGS. Consolidated earnings include both direct earnings of the parent company and equity earnings in undistributed earnings of subsidiaries, after allowance for minority interest.

DIRECT LIABILITY A primary liability as distinguished from a contingent liability; an absolute and certain debt that must be paid on demand or at maturity by the principal debtor. A note is the direct liability of the maker.

DIRECT OBLIGATION See OBLIGATION.

DIRECT PLACEMENT The selling by the borrower of financial obligations such as commercial paper directly to the ultimate purchaser or lender without the assistance of a financial intermediary.

DIRECT REDUCTION MORTGAGE A mortgage that is amortized over a definite period of time and has periodic (usually monthly) payments of a like amount. The payment is applied first to interest and then to principal.

DIRECTORATE The board of directors of a corporation.

DIRECTOR OF THE BUDGET See MANAGEMENT AND BUDGET, OFFICE OF.

DIRECTOR OF THE MINT See MINT.

DIRECTORS The persons in whom the management of a corporation rests.

Directors of a national bank are required to be, during their whole term of service, citizens of the United States; at least two-thirds of the directors must have resided in the state, territory, or district in which the bank is located, or within 100 miles of the location of the head office of the bank, for at least one year immediately preceding their election; and they must be residents of such state or within a 100-mile territory of the location of the bank during their continuance in office.

Every director of a national bank must own in his own shares of the capital stock of the bank of which he is a director, during tenure as a director.

Each director of a national bank, when appointed or elected, must take an oath that he will, so far as the duty devolves upon him, diligently and honestly administer the affairs of such national bank and will not knowingly violate or willingly permit to be violated any of the national banking laws; that he is the owner in good faith, and in his own right, of the number of shares of stock required, *supra*, subscribed by him or standing in his name on the books of the national bank; and that such shares are not hypothecated or in any way pledged as security for any loan or debt. This oath of directors, subscribed by the directors making it and certified by notary public or other officer having an official seal and authorized by the state to administer oaths, shall be immediately transmitted to the Comptroller of the Currency to be filed and preserved in his office for a period of ten years.

Directors of a national bank shall be elected by the shareholders at a meeting to be held at any time before the bank is authorized by the Comptroller of the Currency to commence business, and afterwards at an annual meeting to be held on such day as is specified therefor in the bylaws of the bank. The directors shall hold office for one year, or until their successors are elected and have qualified. Any vacancy in the board shall be filled by appointment by the remaining directors, and any director so appointed shall hold his place until the next election. If, from any cause, an election of directors of a national bank is not held on the day fixed, or in the event of a legal holiday on the next following banking day, an election may be held on any subsequent day within 60 days of the day fixed, to be designated by the board of directors. If the directors fail to fix the day, the day for the election may be fixed by shareholders representing two-thirds of the shares. At least 10 days' notice of such meeting must in all cases be given by first-class mail to the shareholders.

The president of a national bank shall be a member of the board of directors and shall be the chairman thereof; but the board may designate a director in lieu of the president to be chairman of the board, who shall perform such duties as may be designated by the board.

Cumulative voting for directors is compulsory for national banks.

No officer, director, or employee of any incorporated or unincorporated firm and no individual primarily engaged in the issuance, flotation, underwriting, public sale, or distribution (wholesale or retail, or through syndicate participation) of stocks, bonds, or other similar securities shall serve at the same time as an officer, director, or employee of any member bank, except as the Board of Governors of the Federal Reserve System by regulation may permit, when in its judgment such service would not unduly influence the investment policies of the member bank or the advice it gives its customers regarding investments. However, the Fed's Regulation R permits member bank directors, officers, and employees to serve simultaneously as directors, officers, partners, or employees of organizations involved only in government securities transactions. These securities generally include, for example, those of the United States, the International Bank for Reconstruction and Development, and the Tennessee Valley Authority and the general obligations of states and municipalities.

Any member bank may contract for, or purchase from, any of its directors, or from any firm of which one of its directors is a member, any securities or other property, when (and not otherwise) such purchase is made in the regular course of business, upon terms not less favorable to the bank than those offered to others, or when such purchase is authorized by a majority of the board of directors not interested in the sale of such securities or property. Such authority shall be evidenced by the affirmative vote or written assent of such directors. However, when any director, or firm of which any director is a member, acting for or on behalf of others, sells securities or other property to a member bank, the board of governors by regulation may, in any or all cases, require a full disclosure to be made, on forms to be prescribed by it, of all commissions or other considerations received. Also, whenever such director or firm, acting in his or its own behalf, sells securities or other property to the bank, the board of governors by regulation may require a full disclosure of all profit realized from such sale.

Similarly, any member bank may sell securities or other property to any of its directors, or to a firm of which one of its directors is a member, in the regular course of business on terms not more favorable to such director of firm than those offered to others, or when such sale is authorized by a majority of the board of directors of a member bank, to be evidenced by their affirmative vote or written assent.

No member bank shall pay to any director, officer, attorney, or employee a greater rate of interest on the deposits of such director, officer, attorney, or employee than that paid to other depositors on similar deposits with the member bank.

It is unlawful for any national bank to lend any officer, director, or employee any funds held in trust. There is no other specific federal statutory provision bearing on loans to directors of national banks; by contrast, most states statutorily specify on the subject. In the absence of statutory provision on loans to directors of national banks, the common law rule applies. Morse, on banks and banking, states the common law rule to be that loans or discounts to a director are not prohibited, but the director concerned must have his request acted upon by the majority of his fellow directors, strictly exclusive of himself, and he must not vote or officially aid in the board's decision on the request. He must conduct himself strictly like any other outside customer of the bank. The proceeding will be severely scrutinized for rigid enforcement of any applicable law and for any circumstance of impropriety or suspicion of irregularity regarding the application, the manner of making it, or the procuring of its acceptance.

Loans to executive officers. In the case of executive officers (assumed in Regulation O of the Board of Governors of the Federal Reserve System to include the chairman of the board, the president, every vice-president, the cashier, secretary, and treasurer of a member bank, unless by resolution of the board or by the bank's bylaws any such officer is excluded from participation in major policy-making functions, otherwise than in the capacity of a director of the bank, and he does not actually participate therein), permit executive officers to borrow from their own banks to finance the education of the children of the officer within specified limits. Instead of requiring prior approval of such loans by the board of directors of the officer's bank, the law and regulation now require only that the officer report the borrowings to his board of directors. Reports of borrowings from other banks would be required only where they exceed in the aggregate the applicable ceiling on borrowing from his own bank.

New corporate emphasis. Cases such as *Escott* v. *BarChris Construction Corp.*, 283 F. Supp. 643 (1968), and *SEC* v. *Texas Gulf Sulphur Co.*, 401 F. 2d 833 (1968), involving the federal securities acts and SEC rules holding directors to active diligence, and directors, officers, and other "insiders" to a fiduciary standard with regard to inside information vis à vis the public, have generated a wholly new and far-reaching body of federal corporation law.

BIBLIOGRAPHY

BANK ADMINISTRATION INSTITUTE. *The Bankers' Handbook*. Bank Administration Institute, Rolling Meadows, IL, 1988.
BAUGHN, W. H., STORRS, T. I., and WALKER, C. E. *The Bankers' Handbook*. Dow Jones-Irwin, Inc., Homewood, IL, 1988.
BEXLEY, J. B. *The Bank Director*. Bank Administration Institute, Rolling Meadows, IL, 1985.
COMPTROLLER OF THE CURRENCY. *The Director's Book: The Role of a National Bank Director*. Office of the Comptroller of the Currency, Washington, DC, 1987.
COX, E. B., and others, eds. *The Bank Director's Handbook*. Auburn Publishing Company, Dover, MA, 1986.
FOCER, A. "Yes, Virginia, Banks Still Lend Money to Insiders." *Bankers Monthly*, March, 1989.
HAMILTON, J. G. "States Act on Liability Crisis." *ABA Banking Journal*, January, 1989.
HAYS, F. H., and others. "Community Bank Directors: Should Your Bank Have an External Loan Review?" *Journal of Commercial Bank Lending*, April, 1989.
LITTLE, ARTHUR D., INC. *The Bank Director's Handbook*. Bank Administration Institute, Rolling Meadows, IL, 1986.
SEGLIN, J. *Bank Administration Manual*. Bank Administration Institute, Rolling Meadows, IL, 1988.

DIRECTORS' EXAMINATIONS Although neither the statutes nor the Comptroller's Regulations prescribe examinations of a national bank by its board of directors, the Comptroller of the Currency in effect does require such directors' examinations inasmuch as the bylaws of the national bank must contain such provision to obtain the Comptroller's approval, as follows.

Examining Committee. There shall be an Examining Committee composed of not less than . . . Directors appointed by the Board annually or more often, whose duty shall be to make an examination every six months into the affairs of the Bank, and to report the result of such examination in writing to the Board at the next regular meeting thereafter. Such report shall state whether the Bank is in a sound condition, whether adequate internal audit controls and procedures are being maintained, and shall recommend to the Board such changes in the manner of doing business or conducting the affairs of the Bank as shall be deemed advisable.

In national banks lacking adequate audit controls, the Comptroller of the Currency encourages the board of directors to employ outside auditors to make an examination in their behalf. If this is done, however, the Directors' Examining Committee or the board of directors as a whole should participate in such examinations at least to the extent of appraising policies and making a careful review of the audit report with the auditors. Copies of the audit report made either by the Director's Examining Committee or by outside auditors

DISAGIO The term is used chiefly in Continental Europe. The discount that depreciated paper currency suffers from standard or subsidiary coins of like face value; discount upon a coin for loss of weight by abrasion or mutilation. Disagio is the opposite of AGIO.

DISASTER RECOVERY PLAN A comprehensive statement of consistent actions to be taken before, during, and after a disaster. The plan is designed to provide for the continuity of operations and the availability of critical resources should a disaster occur. A disaster recovery plan can also provide a sense of security, minimize delays in setting up and changing operating or processing locations, guarantee the reliability of standby systems, provide a standard for testing the plan, and minimize decision making during a disaster. Factors to consider in determining the probability of a specific disaster include: geographic location; topography of the area; proximity to major sources of power, bodies of water, and airports; accessibility to the institution; history of local utility companies in providing uninterrupted services; history of the area's susceptibility to natural threats.

Disaster management became law under Executive Order 11490, signed on October 30, 1969. Government regulations require financial institutions to prepare emergency plans that address the following matters: assigning responsibility for emergency operations to a specific individual; developing and distributing written emergency preparedness procedures; training personnel periodically in emergency response procedures; developing an effective program for safeguarding and duplicating records; defining plans for succession of senior officers.

The Securities Exchange Act of 1934 was amended by the 1987 Foreign Corrupt Practices Act to require all publicly held companies to keep accurate records and maintain internal control systems to safeguard assets.

The Comptroller of the Currency has issued directives related to disaster recovery planning:

1. **Banking Circular 177.** Provides that contingency planning for a bank's information systems should extend beyond the data center and into key operational areas of the bank.
2. **Banking Circular 187.** Addresses the importance of reviewing the financial status of organizations that provide data processing services to be assured of uninterrupted data processing support.
3. **Banking Circular 226.** Issued jointly by the Federal Financial Institutions Examination Council on risks associated with end-user computing activities.
4. **Banking Bulletin 87-3.** Addresses risks associated with contracting long-term EDP services. The comptroller recommends several considerations for EDP service contracts, including establishing a method to develop and test contingency plans.

The Federal Home Loan Bank Board has also issued several requirements for disaster recovery planning.

1. **Regulation PA-7-1a.** Requires a written contingency plan for response to a wide variety of disasters, including potential disruptive activities in the computer room, loss of computer hardware, and loss of data files. Contingency plans and use of backup hardware should be reviewed and tested periodically.
2. **Memorandum R 67.** Describes guidelines for contingency disaster recovery plans required for insured institutions and service corporations.
3. **Memorandum R67-1.** Deals with risks associated with end-user computing activities. Source: Geoffrey H. Wold and Robert F. Shriver, *Disaster Recovery for Banks*, Bank Administration Institute.

DISBURSEMENT In general, a cash payment or expenditure. It refers particularly to cash outgo representing expenses rather than outgo representing the purchase of assets.

DISC DOMESTIC INTERNATIONAL SALES CORPORATION.

DISCLAIMER A renunciation or repudiation. A transportation company may place in its bill of lading a disclaimer clause refusing responsibility for losses which may arise because the "shipper's load and count" do not tally with actual deliveries made to it.

DISCLOSED RESERVES Reserves that are created or increased by appropriations of retained earnings or other surplus disclosed on the balance sheet. Essentially, disclosed reserves consist of retained earnings and paid-in capital in excess of par value (or capital surplus if no-par stock is issued).

DISCLOSURE An accounting principle that requires full (ade-quate) disclosure of all material (significant) matters affecting the financial statements that would be of interest to a concerned investor or creditor. The accounting policies used in preparing financial statements should be disclosed. Generally, full disclosure is required when alternative policies are available (LIFO, FIFO), principles peculiar to a particular industry, and unusual or innovative application of accounting principles. Examples of important accounting principles and policies include method of consolidation, depreciation method, inventory pricing, and long-term contract accounting.

It is useful if accounting policies are disclosed separately in a Summary of Significant Accounting Policies preceding the notes to the financial statements or as the initial note.

DISCOMFORT INDEX An index composed of the percentage unemployment rate added to the percentage change in the most commonly utilized price change index. The index reflects the impact of inflation rates and unemployment. In the 1960s and early 1970s inflation rates and unemployment levels rose at the same time, resulting in the deterioration in the discomfort index.

DISCONTINUED OPERATIONS Operations of an enterprise that have been sold, abandoned, or otherwise disposed of. The results of continued operations must be reported separately in the income statement from discontinued operations, and any gain or loss from disposal of a segment must be reported along with the operating results of the discontinued segment. A segment of a business is a component whose activities represent a separate major line of business or class of customer. A segment may be a subsidiary, a division, or a department if its assets, results of operations, and activities can be distinguished physically, operationally, and for financial reporting purposes from those of the entity. The presentation of discontinued operations should be reported as follows;

Income from continuing operation		XXX
Discontinued operations:		
Income from operations of discontinued division (less applicable income taxes)	XXX	
Loss (or gain) on disposal of division	XXX	XXX
Net income		XXX

DISCO DOMESTIC INTERNATIONAL SALES CORPORATION.

DISCOUNT This term has six meanings:

1. CASH DISCOUNT.
2. Bank discount. Interest paid in advance or, more accurately, INTEREST paid at the beginning of a loan based upon the sum to be repaid at its maturity. The rate of discount charged by a bank is not the same as the rate of interest paid by the borrower. Interest is retained by the lender at the time a note, acceptance, or bill of exchange is discounted and the proceeds given to the borrower, and not at maturity. The interest so taken is called discount, or bank discount. For illustration, suppose a $10,000 note maturing in six months is discounted at 6%. The discount would be 0.03 of $10,000, which is $300, the proceeds being the balance, or $9,700. Although this is the commercial and bank method of computing discount, it is not mathematically correct, inasmuch as the borrower is paying interest in advance of the use of the funds, and therefore pays interest upon interest. True discount, explained below, is the accurate method of computing interest paid in advance.
See INTEREST TABLES.
3. True discount. This differs from bank discount in that interest is computed on the proceeds or amount borrowed and does not

entail the payment of interest upon interest. In principle it is the same as determining the present worth of a sum of money due on a future date. In the example used in illustrating bank discount, true discount is found by first computing the proceeds. This is ascertained by dividing $10,000 by 1.03 (1 representing the principal and .03 representing the interest on $1.00 for six months at 6%, which gives $9,700.87. The true discount is the difference, or $299.13. From this result it is clear that true discount is slightly more favorable to the borrower than bank discount.

4. Discount on securities. This indicates the percentage amount below par value at which a security sells, being the opposite of premium. A bond of $1,000 par value, selling at 90, is at 10%, or $100, discount. A preferred stock of $25 par value, selling at 24, is at 4%, or $1.00, discount.

To the issuer, bond discount represents DEFERRED INTEREST because the issuing organization must retire the bonds at par, thereby increasing the effective interest rate. The discount upon the issue should logically be accumulated during the life of the bond as an additional cost. This process is called accumulation.

When stock is sold at discount by the issuing corporation, the amount of discount becomes in reality a capital deficit. It is capitalized as the amortizable asset, discount on stock.
See AMORTIZATION.

5. Paper money is at a discount when it does not circulate at par with the standard money or other metallic currency. When more than a dollar of paper money must be given in order to purchase a dollar of standard money, paper money is at a discount.
See DEPRECIATED CURRENCY.

6. Exchange discount.
See DOMESTIC EXCHANGE, FOREIGN EXCHANGE.

DISCOUNT BROKER   A broker who provides execution services for buyers or sellers of securities, as agent, but who does not provide advice to customers.

DISCOUNT CLERK   A bank employee responsible for handling the clerical routine in the discount department, including computations in discounting notes, acceptances, etc. The discount clerk also has charge of all records maintained in connection with bills discounted, e.g., register, ledger, rate book, and maturity tickler.

DISCOUNT CORPORATION   A banking corporation engaged in the purchase and discount of trade and bankers acceptances, bills of exchange and other forms of commercial paper, etc. Such a corporation may be organized under federal authority (EDGE ACT) or under various state jurisdictions. Its function is to supplement the regular banking facilities for discounting trade and bankers acceptances, especially those arising out of export and import transactions.

Discount corporations are more numerous in England because of the greater volume of foreign bills handled in London, the world discount and money market.
See EDGE ACT CORPORATION, FOREIGN BANKING CORPORATIONS.

DISCOUNTING THE MARKET   Market action in anticipation of an event. Discounting the market for a particular security is giving effect to the expected event before it occurs by a rise or decline in prices according to whether the future event is favorable or unfavorable. For example, if it becomes commonly acknowledged by signs of improvement that business activity will greatly increase in the next six months, although prosperity is not now actually existent, speculators will anticipate the improvement by gradually bidding higher prices. Conversely, if business conditions are expected to become depressed in the immediate future, the discounting process will take place in the opposite direction. Coming events cast their shadows before, and intelligent speculation is based upon predicting the future of prices. Not all events can be discounted because not all can be foreseen, e.g., a Supreme Court decision, a sudden declaration of war, an earthquake, labor strikes.

It is possible to both underdiscount and overdiscount a future event. This is what happens in practically every period of boom or depression. The momentum of speculative enthusiasm carries prices beyond the values represented by equities and potential earning power, and the momentum of liquidation carries prices below these values.

The stock market is said to register or discount events from three to nine months ahead, so that by the time an event has occurred, the particular security affected or the entire market has already reflected the changed condition. In this way violent and sudden price fluctuations are prevented or at least mitigated.

DISCOUNT LEDGER   *See* BILLS DISCOUNTED LEDGER, LIABILITY LEDGER.

DISCOUNT MARKET   The open market for acceptances and commercial paper, as contrasted with a bank's discounts for its own customers. As part of the money market, the discount market consists of the Federal Reserve banks, banks, discount houses, commercial paper houses, note dealers, etc., that make up the supply and demand for such paper.

DISCOUNT RATE   The rate of interest at which a bank discounts notes, acceptances, and bills of exchange. It varies according to money market conditions, the borrower and maturity. The best names (prime paper) command a lower rate than other names. This term frequently is used synonymously with bank rate.

Federal Reserve bank discount rate. Discount rate is the term applied, instead of rediscount rate, to refer to the rate at which member banks may borrow funds for short periods directly from district Federal Reserve banks. The Federal Reserve Act requires the board of directors of each district Federal Reserve bank to establish the discount rate every 14 days or more often, subject to the review and determination thereof by the Board of Governors of the Federal Reserve System.

Over the years, the discount rate has come to be uniform for all 12 Federal Reserve banks. The board of governors explains that in the original Federal Reserve Act it was envisioned that each Federal Reserve bank would set a discount rate in accord with its regional banking and credit conditions. In the early years of the system it was assumed that in its review process the board would look particularly to regional banking conditions, but over the years the progressive integration of regional credit markets into a fluid national market gradually produced a national perspective for discount rate determination. Establishment by Congress of national economic goals in the Employment Act of 1946 further enhanced the role of national considerations in proposals for changes in reserve bank rates and in the board's determination with respect to proposed changes.

Because the discount rate establishes the cost to members of reserves borrowed from Federal Reserve banks, it has played a significant role in the decisions that a bank makes about whether to borrow at the Federal Reserve discount window. Although bankers may be reluctant to borrow from the Federal Reserve and may do so only to cover temporary adjustments needs (borrowing from the Fed is privilege, not a right), a low discount rate in relation to other rates on money market claims makes it more likely that a bank will seek funds at the discount window instead of using alternative sources.

For example, if the rate on short-term Treasury bills is high in relation to the discount rate, a member bank may prefer to borrow from the Federal Reserve bank rather than sell Treasury bills from its portfolio. Similarly, if the rate charged for reserves obtained through the federal funds market is high, a bank has an incentive to use the discount window. Or if rates are high on large time certificates of deposit (CDs), which may be sold in some volume and relatively impersonally in the money market, the demand for borrowing from the Federal Reserve is stimulated. Consequently, when spreads in these various market rates over the discount rate make it profitable, and particularly if economic activity is buoyant and credit demands on banks are strong, member banks in need of funds tend to make increasing use of the discount window.

To help control the volume and profitability of borrowing at the discount window, the Federal Reserve adjusts the discount rate from time to time to relate it more closely to other money market rates. On occasion, however, changes in the discount rate may signal Federal Reserve concern over unfolding economic developments and a possible intent to alter current and future policy accordingly. Reactions of the financial community to such signals announcement effects may exert a significant impact on the securities market because market participants will tend to adjust their investment strategies in anticipation of coordinated system actions via other policy instruments. Changes in the discount rate, therefore, must be interpreted in terms of how they complement, or are likely to be complemented by, other policy actions.

In gauging what volume of reserves to supply through open market operations to achieve monetary policy objectives, the Federal Open Market Committee (FOMC) must take into account the extent to which member banks may wish to borrow reserve funds from the Federal Reserve banks, or to repay outstanding borrowings.

Federal Reserve lending and changes in the discount rate, originally conceived as being the heart of the U.S. central banking operation, have long since been displaced in this key role by OPEN MARKET OPERATIONS. For some time, in the view of the board of governors itself, the Federal Reserve discount window has served mainly as a complement to open market operations in the implementation of monetary policy.

Future of discount rate. Under the DEPOSITORY INSTITUTIONS DEREGULATION AND MONETARY CONTROL ACT OF 1980, any depository institution holding reservable transaction accounts or nonpersonal time deposits is entitled to the same discount and borrowing privileges as member banks. This provision became effective on March 31, 1980. In administering the discount and borrowing privileges, the Federal Reserve System is required under that act to take into consideration the special needs of savings and other depository institutions for access to discount and borrowing facilities consistent with their long-term asset portfolios and the sensitivity of such institutions to trends in the national money markets.

For further detail and background on the discount rate and operation of the discount window, for both member and nonmember institutions, *see* REDISCOUNT RATE.

DISCOUNT RATE INVESTMENT YIELD ON TREASURY BILLS
The investment yield to maturity on Treasury bills is computed as follows:

Investment Yield = $(\$100 - p) \times 365/p \times$ days to maturity where p = price of T-bill in dollars per \$100 of face amount.

For example, if an investor purchases a 91-day Treasury bill for \$96.562 per \$100 of face amount, the yield would be .1428 or 14.28%.

BIBLIOGRAPHY

COOK, T., and HAHN, T. "The Information Content of Discount Rate Announcements and Their Effect on Market Interest Rates." *Working Paper 86-5*. Federal Reserve Bank of Richmond, September 1986.

DISCOUNT REGISTER   *See* BILLS DISCOUNTED REGISTER.

DISCOUNT WINDOW
The figurative expression used to refer to the Federal Reserve facility for extending credit directly to member banks and now, under the DEPOSITORY INSTITUTIONS DEREGULATION AND MONETARY CONTROL ACT OF 1980, to any depository institution holding reservable transaction accounts or nonpersonal time deposits. The expression arose from the procedure in earlier years of the Federal Reserve System of having representatives of the borrowing bankers come to a Federal Reserve bank teller window to obtain credit.

See DISCOUNT RATE, REDISCOUNT RATE.

BIBLIOGRAPHY

ALTON, G. R. "Operating Procedures for Conducting Monetary Policy." *Federal Reserve Bank of St. Louis Review*, February, 1985.
GOODFRIEND, M. "Discount Window Borrowing, Monetary Policy, and the Post-October 6, 1979 Federal Reserve Operating Procedure." *Journal of Monetary Economics*, September, 1983.
GORTON, G. "Private Clearinghouses and the Origins of Central Banking." *Federal Reserve Bank of Philadelphia Business Review*, January/February, 1984.
HUMPHREY, T. M., and KELEHER, R. E. "The Lender of Last Resort: A Historical Perspective." *Cato Journal*, Spring/Summer, 1984.
WALLICH, H. C. "Recent Techniques of Monetary Policy." *Federal Reserve Bank of Kansas City Economic Review*, May, 1984.

DISCOVER CARD
A multimerchant credit card sponsored by Sears Roebuck and Company that competes directly with bank cards.

DISCRETIONARY ACCOUNTS
Accounts placed with a broker in which decisions as to the selection of securities and the time and price of their purchase and sale are left with the broker.
See CONTROLLED ACCOUNT.

DISCRETIONARY ORDERS
Authority given to a broker to execute purchases and sales of securities at the latter's selection and option as to price, with the expectation of yielding a profit but at the risk of the customer. Most stock exchange brokers refuse to accept discretionary orders.
See CONTROLLED ACCOUNT.

DISCRIMINANT FUNCTION SYSTEM
The computerized system used by the Internal Revenue Service to indentify and select income tax returns for examination. The system uses secret mathematical formulas to select returns that have a probability of tax errors or evasion.

DISHONOR
Failure or refusal by the maker of a note or acceptor of a bill of exchange to pay the instrument at maturity; also the refusal of a drawee bank to pay its customer's check. This is called dishonor for nonpayment. Failure or refusal to accept a time bill of exchange constitutes dishonor for nonacceptance.

An instrument is dishonored when a necessary or optional presentment is duly made and due acceptance or payment is refused or cannot be obtained within the prescribed time or, in the case of bank collections, the instrument is seasonably returned by the midnight deadline (specified in Sec. 4-301, Uniform Commercial Code); or presentment is excused and the instrument is not duly accepted or paid (Sec. 3-507, Uniform Commercial Code).

Subject to any necessary notice of dishonor and protest, the holder has upon dishonor an immediate right of recourse against the drawers and endorsers (Sec. 3-507, Uniform Commercial Code).

Notice of dishonor may be given in any reasonable manner. It may be oral or written and in any terms that identify the instrument and state that it has been dishonored. Notice of dishonor may be given to any person who may be liable on the instrument by or on behalf of the holder or any party who has himself received notice, or any other party who can be compelled to pay the instrument (Sec. 3-508, Uniform Commercial Code).

Protest of any dishonor, unless excused, is necessary to charge parties secondarily liable on any draft that on its face appears to be drawn or payable outside the states or territories of the U.S. and the District of Columbia. A holder may at his option make protest of any dishonor (Sec. 3-501(3), Uniform Commercial Code). Although protest might not be required, notarized protest will have prima facie evidentiary value in case of action on the instrument.
See NOTARIAL PROTEST CERTIFICATE.

A bank will dishonor a check under the following conditions: when the drawer has issued a stop payment order; when there is some irregularity or informality, e.g., insufficient funds, postdating, etc. (*see* IRREGULARITIES); upon receipt of a garnishee order; upon notice of the drawer's death; and upon notice of bankruptcy of the drawer, in which case the funds are held for the trustee or awaiting court order. Refusal of a bank to certify a check is not an act of dishonor.
See CERTIFIED CHECK.

DISINTERMEDIATION
An excess of withdrawals from a depository institution's interest-bearing accounts over its deposits in such accounts. Disintermediation occurs when the interest rates on such accounts fall below market rates or yields on competing investments. It was a particular problem in the early 1980s when MONEY MARKET FUNDS were offering highly liquid savings vehicles at interest rates that were well above the ceiling rates the Federal Reserve had set under Regulation Q for interest-bearing accounts. Disintermediation is much less likely to occur since the elimination on March 31, 1986, of federally determined interest rate ceilings, leaving rate determination to the marketplace.

DISPOSABLE INCOME
An individual's income after taxes. The term refers to the portion of earnings that an individual can dispose of (spend). At the macroeconomic level, disposable income refers to all individuals' income, less taxes, plus transfer payments. Disposable income at this aggregate level reflects purchasing potential.

DISSOLUTION The winding up and termination of a firm's existence, after the sale of its assets and discharge of its liabilities, first to the preferential creditors (employees for wages, government for taxes), second to the secured creditors, third to the unsecured or general creditors, and last to the owner.

See DEFUNCT COMPANY.

DISTRESS SELLING Imperative or necessitous selling. When stocks owned on margin are sold because declining prices have impaired or exhausted equities, this is referred to as distress selling or forced liquidation.

DISTRESSED LOAN A loan that the borrower does not have the financial capacity to repay according to its terms. A review of banks' and government agencies' policies for dealing with distressed loans reveals that these loans generally have at least one of the following characteristics:

1. The borrower is demonstrating adverse financial and repayment trends.
2. The loan is delinquent or past due under the terms of the loan contract.
3. One or both of these factors, together with inadequate collateralization, presents a high probability of loss to the lender.

The cost of foreclosure includes:

1. The difference between the outstanding balance and the liquidating value of the loan, taking into consideration the borrower's repayment capacity and the net recovery value of the collateral.
2. The estimated cost of maintaining the loan as a nonperforming asset.
3. The estimated cost of administrative and legal actions necessary to foreclose and dispose of the property acquired, including attorneys' fees, court costs, and sales costs.
4. The estimated cost of changes in the value of collateral used to secure the loan during the period beginning on the date of the initiation of an action to foreclose or liquidate the loan and ending on the date of the disposition of the collateral.
5. All other costs incurred as a result of foreclosure or liquidation.

In making the determination of whether to restructure or foreclose, the lender must also consider:

1. The present value of interest income and principal foregone in carrying out the restructuring plan.
2. Reasonable and necessary administrative expenses in working with the borrower to finalize and implement the restructuring plan.
3. Whether the borrower has presented a preliminary restructuring plan and cash flow analysis, showing a reasonable probability that orderly debt retirement will occur as a result of the proposed restructuring.
4. Whether the borrower has furnished or is willing to furnish complete and current financial statements in a form acceptable to the institution.

DISTRIBUTING SYNDICATE See SYNDICATE.

DISTRIBUTION, PERIOD OF The last phase of a speculative cycle which may be divided into three phases occurring in rotation—accumulation, advance, distribution. Distribution is the period that follows the great advance in security prices and during which experienced speculators and large interests, anticipating conditions in advance and knowing that prosperity must again give way to depression, close out their holdings while prices are still high and before the speculative crisis which marks the beginning of a period of liquidation takes place.

See SPECULATIVE CYCLE.

DISTRIBUTION OF ESTATES See DESCENT, LAWS OF.

DISTRIBUTION OF RISK A well-known investment principle popularly expressed in the maxim "don't put all your eggs in one basket." The principle, usually applied by conservative investors and speculators and enforced upon the banks by the banking laws, implies the spreading of investment funds over a number of media instead of a single medium. As an illustration of diversification in investment holdings, a fund of $100,000 might be divided in the following proportions among different classes of investments: $20,000 in U.S. government and/or highest-grade municipals; $20,000 in other bonds (good grade corporates, divided among public utility, railroad, and industrial bonds); $10,000 in good grade preferred stocks, divided among utility, railroad, and industrial preferred stocks; and $50,000 in common stocks, divided among utility, railroad, and industrial issues, and ranging in selection equally from sound, seasoned common stocks to medium-grade and the more attractive of the speculative common stocks. Such a selection affords diversification both as to defensive and aggressive securities and as to industries. The theory of diversifying investment media is to reduce the risk of loss as much as possible without at the same time unduly sacrificing income. One investment medium may prove unprofitable, but it is unlikely that disaster will befall all of them, at least not in the same degree.

Distribution of risk does not preclude specialization in one class of investment media, provided diversification in a single class is obtained. One who decides to invest exclusively in bonds should not purchase railroad bonds only and certainly not the bonds of a single railroad. If bonds are to be the investor's specialty, purchases should be distributed among government, railroad, public utility, and industrial issues. One may, however, specialize in railroad bonds and still secure a distribution of risk, although to a lesser degree, by purchasing bonds of different railroad companies. Neither does the principle preclude the selection of the highest-grade investments in each class of investment media; it simply demands that the investment be spread among several particular possibilities in a given class. Diversification is not any less important as a safeguard against loss in high-grade bonds, because this class is subject to depreciation from rise in money rates; hence diversification as to maturities is important.

A practical application of the use of this principle is exemplified in the case of bank loans and investments. National banks are not permitted to lend more than 15% of their combined capital and surplus to one borrower (with certain exceptions). Good management requires, moreover, that a bank extend loans not only to a large number of businesses and persons but also to borrowers who represent a high diversity of business types. One of the functions of bank examinations is to see that the legal restrictions giving effect to the principle of distribution of risk are not violated, to the end that the depositors' interests may be fully protected.

DISTRIBUTION OF SECURITIES See DISTRIBUTION, PERIOD OF; INVESTMENT MARKET.

DISTRIBUTOR See BROKER, INVESTMENT MARKET, SYNDICATE.

DIVERSIFICATION See DISTRIBUTION OF RISK.

DIVERSIFIED INVESTMENT COMPANY A type of mutual fund with an investment policy specifically directed toward maintaining a portfolio invested in a wide variety of businesses.

DIVIDEND The proportion of the net earnings of a corporation distributed to stockholders, representing their profits in the enterprise. Dividend disbursements are either a percentage of the par value of the stock (customarily in the case of preferred stock) or, in the case of stock of no par value, a certain sum per share. Dividends are usually declared at regular intervals, e.g., monthly, quarterly, semiannually, or annually, but usually quarterly. Dividends do not become payable until declared by the board of directors. At the time of declaration this body also sets the holders of record date and the date of the disbursement.

See BOOKS CLOSE, STOCKHOLDERS OF RECORD.

Dividend disbursements are of four kinds: cash, regular or irregular and extra; scrip, interest-bearing and non-interest-bearing; stock; and property.

Ordinarily, dividends are paid in cash, but sometimes when earnings have been above normal, an extra cash dividend is declared over and above the regular dividend and is so designated. It is a principle of good corporate finance that regular dividends should be paid at a regular rate that presumably can be maintained and that when profits are above normal, extra dividends may be declared, but specified as such.

DIVIDEND BOND

Scrip dividends are those paid in the company's promises to pay, instead of cash. They are paid when either current or past earnings are sufficient to permit cash dividends, but the company desires temporarily to conserve its holdings of cash. Scrip dividends may bear a definite maturity date or the disbursement date may be left to the discretion of the board of directors. Such dividends may be interest-bearing or non-interest-bearing.

A STOCK DIVIDEND is a dividend payable in the company's own stock. The term is also loosely applied sometimes to a dividend in stock of another company held as an asset.

Dividends may also be paid in commodities. In some instances, corporations have distributed dividends in goods from inventory.

Besides dividends representing disbursements of profits, there are dividends representing the liquidation of the assets of a business upon dissolution. Such a dividend is called a liquidating dividend.

Considerable conflict of opinion has occurred among courts and accountants as to what constitutes profits for dividend purposes. It is well understood, of course, that dividends must not be paid out of capita but only out of profits, whether earned currently or in a past accounting period, but various questions—whether dividends can be paid from capital surplus; whether money can be borrowed to pay dividends, provided the dividends have been earned; and whether dividends should be paid out of the proceeds of the sale of fixed assets when the business continues as a going concern—have given rise to conflicting opinions and state laws.

A national bank cannot disburse its entire earnings as dividends until its surplus equals its capital stock. Until this amount has been reached, one-tenth of its net profits at each accounting period must be carried to the surplus account. But R.S. 5199, as amended (12 U.S.C. 60), requires the approval of the Comptroller of the Currency for dividends by national banks "if the total of all dividends declared by such association (bank) in any calendar year shall exceed the total of its net profits of that year combined with its retained net profits of the preceding two years, less any required transfers to surplus or a fund for the retirement of any preferred stock." And R.S. 5204 (12 U.S.C. 56) reads in part: "If losses have at any time been sustained by any such association (bank), equal to or exceeding its undivided profits then on hand, no dividends shall be made; and no dividend shall ever be made by any association (bank), while it continues its banking operations, to an amount greater than its net profits then on hand, deducting therefrom its losses and bad debts." Interpreting this, the Comptroller of the Currency has ruled that the following capital-structure accounts constitute a national bank's profits which are legally available for payment of dividends: the undivided profits account and that portion, if any, of the surplus account which is in excess of the amount of the common capital account.

For guaranteed dividends, see GUARANTEED STOCKS.

BIBLIOGRAPHY

Barron's National Business & Financial Weekly.
Disclosure Database. Online data base. Disclosure, Inc., Bethesda, MD.
Moody's Dividend Record. Semiweekly.
Standard and Poor's Dividend Record. Daily, weekly, or quarterly.
Stock Values and Dividends for Tax Purposes. Commerce Clearing House, Inc., Chicago, IL. Annual.
VENKATESH, P. C. "The Impact of Dividend Initiation on the Information Content of Earnings Announcements and Returns Volatility." *Journal of Business,* April, 1989.
Wall Street Journal. Daily.

DIVIDEND BOND   *See* PARTICIPATING BONDS.

DIVIDEND FORECAST CHART   A chart prepared by the statistical department of a brokerage house that shows the past and present earnings and dividend rates, and the probable future dividend rates based upon current business conditions, for a selected group of representative stocks; a chart showing prospective dividends for leading companies

DIVIDEND IN LIQUIDATION   *See* DIVIDEND.

DIVIDEND PAYER   A stock market expression used to indicate a corporation the stock of which pays dividends.

DIVIDEND/PRICE RATIO   The dividend per share divided by the market price per share and multiplied by 100. This measure is also called the dividend yield when it is quoted in percentage terms.

DIVIDEND WARRANT   An order to pay a dividend to a stockholder.

DIVIDENDS IN ARREARS   The accumulated unpaid dividends on cumulative preferred stock from prior years.

DIVISIONAL BOND   Bond that is the obligation of a division of a railroad as distinguished from the rest of the system. In a loose sense, divisional bonds are branch line bonds. The most usual interpretation of a divisional bond is one that is secured by a mortgage on the property constituting a certain division of a railroad as distinguished from property of the entire system. Divisional bonds may be bonds that were originally obligations of a separate railroad, but have since been taken over and assumed by another. Ordinarily divisional bonds are issued by a railroad corporation, secured by a mortgage on a certain division of its property.

DIVISION OF ISSUE   *See* DIVISION OF REDEMPTION.

DIVISION OF LABOR   An economic principle which holds that there are efficiencies gained in production from specialization of labor. This theory can be traced to Adam Smith in *Wealth of Nations*: "The division of labor, however, so far as it can be introduced, occasions, in every art, a proportionable increase of the productive powers of labor." According to Smith, there are three advantages associated with the division of labor: an "increase of dexterity in every particular workman," a "savings of the time which is commonly lost in passing from one species of work to another," and to the invention of machines that "enable one man to do the work of many."

DIVISION OF REDEMPTION   Among its assigned activities, the Bureau of Government Financial Operations of the U.S. Treasury Department handles claims from the public for the redemption of partially destroyed U.S. currency, determining its value and authorizing payment to claimants. The bureau also audits the operations of Federal Reserve banks in verifying and destroying U.S. currency which is unfit for circulation.

DOCK RECEIPT   A receipt given by a steamship company to the shipper or shipper's agent when goods are delivered on the steamship pier for transportation abroad. It is an interim document, an ocean bill of lading issued before shipment being given in exchange therefor.

DOCUMENTARY ACCEPTANCE BILL   *See* DOCUMENTS AGAINST ACCEPTANCE.

DOCUMENTARY BILLS   A bill of exchange having shipping or other documents attached, e.g., bill of lading, invoice, insurance certificate, securities, insurance policies, bonds and coupons, or other documents having intrinsic value. Documentary bills give prima facie evidence of the transfer of values and therefore of their self-liquidating nature. Where shipping documents are attached there is prima facie evidence that the bill has arisen out of a commercial transaction. Documentary bills are secured by the documents concerned, by the liability of the drawee, and by the liability of the drawer until the bill is accepted or paid by the drawee.

See BILL OF EXCHANGE, FOREIGN BILLS OF EXCHANGE.

DOCUMENTARY COMMERCIAL BILL   Bill of exchange arising out of commercial transactions and supported by a bill of lading and relative papers.

See BILL OF EXCHANGE, DOCUMENTARY BILLS.

DOCUMENTARY PAYMENT BILL   *See* DOCUMENTS AGAINST PAYMENT.

DOCUMENTS   Generally, the relative papers that may accompany a foreign bill of exchange arising out of commercial transactions, including ocean or through bill of lading, marine insurance certificate, seller's invoice, etc. Sometimes the following

ENCYCLOPEDIA OF BANKING AND FINANCE

documents also accompany a bill of exchange: Consular invoice, certificate of analysis, certificate of origin, certificate of inspection, and warehouse receipt. In the strict sense documents are those instruments that convey title to the goods that secure the bill of exchange.

DOCUMENTS AGAINST ACCEPTANCE Domestic or foreign bill of exchange drawn D/A, which is a notification that the supporting documents are not to be released to the drawee until the bill has been accepted. Such bills are known as documentary acceptance bills.

DOCUMENTS AGAINST PAYMENT Domestic or foreign bill of exchange drawn D/P, which is a notification that the supporting documents are not to be released to the drawee until the bill has been paid. Such bills are known as documentary payment bills.

DOLLAR The monetary unit of the U.S. and also of some 14 other countries (see FOREIGN MONEYS).

Although it is the MONETARY UNIT and STANDARD OF VALUE in the U.S., defined in GOLD (11.37 fine troy ounces of gold), the dollar has no domestic circulation in any gold or SILVER form (bullion, coin, or paper) and no domestic redemption in any gold or silver form. Section 5 of the GOLD RESERVE ACT OF 1934 provided that "no gold shall hereafter be coined, and no gold coin shall hereafter be paid out or delivered by the United States: Provided, however, that coinage may continue to be executed by the mints of the United States for foreign countries in accordance with the Act of January 29, 1874 (U.S.C., Title 31, Sec. 367). All gold coin of the United States shall be withdrawn from circulation, and, together with all other gold owned by the United States, shall be formed into bars of such weights and degrees of fineness as the Secretary of the Treasury may direct."

P.L. 94-373, August 14, 1974, provided for an end to all government restrictions on the purchase, sale, or ownership of gold as of December 31, 1974. Persons subject to the jurisdiction of the United States can now freely import, export, and trade in gold and gold coins, within the United States and abroad, except (as of 1980) gold transactions (e.g., imports or exports) involving Cuba, Democratic Kampuchea, North Korea, and Viet Nam. Commercial banks may deal in gold bullion and gold coin, with the same exceptions. Treasury licensing for importers, exporters, producers, refiners, and processors of gold is not required. Producers may sell their gold output in the free market, with the same country exceptions. The U.S. Treasury itself announced on April 18, 1979, that the amount of gold for sale at its monthly auctions would be reduced from 1.5 million ounces to 750,000 ounces; and on October 16, 1979, it announced that its future gold auctions would not follow a regular monthly pattern but instead would be subject to variations in amounts and dates. The monetary gold stock of the U.S., all nationalized since 1934, totaled 264,599,629.1 ounces as of the end of January, 1980, including gold held by the EXCHANGE STABILIZATION FUND, valued at $42.22 per fine troy ounce.

Gold stock of the U.S. was valued at $35 per fine troy ounce until May 8, 1972, when it was revalued at $38 pursuant to the Par Value Modification Act, P.L. 92-268, approved March 31, 1972. The increment amounted to $822 million. On October 18, 1973, monetary gold stock of the U.S. was further revalued at $42.22 pursuant to the amending of Section 2 of the Par Value Modification Act, P.L. 93-110, approved September 21, 1973. This increment amounted to $1,157 million.

All of the gold assets of the U.S. have been monetized into gold liabilities as follows as of the end of January, 1980: gold certificates (Series 1934) issued only to Federal Reserve banks; gold certificates fund, Federal Reserve System; redemption fund for FEDERAL RESERVE NOTES until March 18, 1968, when it was combined with the gold certificates fund pursuant to P.L. 90-269, approved March 18, 1968; and gold reserve against UNITED STATES NOTES, until March 18, 1968, when it was transferred to the public debt also pursuant to P.L. 90-269.

Internationally, the U.S. closed the "gold window" (convertibility of dollars into gold) August 15, 1971. Although the U.S. dollar's position as a key reserve currency has lost ground in recent years, the U.S. dollar is still a principal component of international reserve assets of many nations.

Domestically, the U.S. dollar is a completely fiat currency, with no redemption of any form of circulation into gold or silver, but with full legal tender power in unlimited amounts for all forms of domestic circulation. For details of denominations, see UNITED STATES MONEY. The coinage system is all based on the baser metals, including cupronickel composition for the dollar coin as well as subsidiary coinage (half dollar, quarter, and dime). The active form of paper currency, Federal Reserve notes, is also irredeemable; with the minimum 25% gold certificates reserve requirement eliminated in 1968, their 100% collateral cover in specified assets of issuing Federal Reserve banks remains as the sole brake on issuance (it may be only a question of time before such collateral requirement, too, is eliminated).

See GOLD COINS, MONEY OF ACCOUNT, SILVER CERTIFICATES, SILVER DOLLAR, STANDARD MONEY, TRADE DOLLAR.

DOLLAR ACCEPTANCE See DOLLAR EXCHANGE.

DOLLAR AVERAGING In the process of accumulating a portfolio of securities, the timing of the price of purchases is a problem, for even the best securities may be bought poorly, i.e., at excessively high prices. For example, the 1929 high of American Telephone & Telegraph common stock was 310. One generation later, at the highest price reached by the stock since (1960 high, 96 $1/8$, giving effect to a 3:1 split-up), the market price of this "blue chip" had not yet equaled the 1929 high.

Dollar averaging—or, more correctly, dollar cost averaging—is a method of solving this problem of timing of purchases by simply taking prices at random at regular intervals. The specific mechanics preferably call for the INVESTMENT at regular intervals of a fixed dollar sum, but lesser dollar averaging results may also be obtained by investing irregular sums, or investing just the sum sufficient to purchase a fixed number of shares at regular intervals. The interval may be per month, per quarter, per semiannual period, or even per year, but obviously the more frequent the period, the more average will be the pricing results obtained. The result is an average cost price, based on the number of shares obtained at each of the prices prevailing on the date of purchase. Thus, in the case of American Telephone & Telegraph common, a purchaser on the dollar averaging basis would have bought some at 310 in 1929, but would also have "averaged down" as prices declined subsequently, and thus would have brought down his average cost, accumulating more shares at the lower prices. Although it is unrealistic to assume that all individuals, as contrasted to investing institutions, would have the financial ability to continue the steady investment of fixed sums at steady intervals over the long term, dollar averaging plans followed conscientiously over time should be productive of gains, assuming the stock or stocks chosen justify the confidence and the terminal prices by the cutoff date are high enough to result in an average annual increment that is at least representative.

No dollar averaging plan, however, can guarantee terminal gains on the total accumulation by the target or cutoff date, because the last or closing price is crucial for success. At any intervening interval of decline in prices, also, there might be a loss, and if the stock has changed radically in outlook and quality, continued buying would be "sending good money after bad," with little likelihood of recovery. No dollar averaging plan, therefore, for specific stocks should be so automatically regarded as an unbeatable formula that supervision and review of the selections are forgotten.

Dollar averaging literature often cites examples of buying the averages, but few individual investors buy the average; they buy specific stocks which might vary considerably in results from the averages. However, buying investment company shares, whether open end or closed end, depending on the investing policy of the company and the diversified portfolios involved, would be one means for the small individual investor to "buy the averages," to the extent that such companies have the diversification and the motivation to at least keep up with the averages.

If there is any price fluctuation at all for the stock selected, the average cost of the accumulation of shares in a dollar averaging plan will always be less than the simple average of the prices prevailing at the time of purchases because the average cost is a weighted average, reflecting the increased number of shares bought as prices decline, where constant dollar sum is periodically invested. Whether or not there is a capital gain or loss by the cutoff date, however, depends on the last prevailing market price. This is illustrated in the appended table for three price patterns: the continuous rise pattern; the continuous decline pattern; and the cyclical pattern (first up, then down, or vice versa).

DOLLAR BILLS OF EXCHANGE

Price Patterns of Stock

(1) Continuous Price Rise

Period	Sum invested	Price prevailing[a]	Shares bought
1	$120	$2	60
2	120	4	30
3	120	6	20
4	120	8	15
5	120	10	12
Totals	$600	$6 (Average)	137

Last price	$10.00
Average cost	4.38
Capital gain	$5.62

(2) Continuous Price Decline

Period	Sum invested	Price prevailing[a]	Shares bought
1	$120	$10	12
2	120	8	15
3	120	6	20
4	120	4	30
5	120	2	60
Totals	$600	$6 (Average)	137

Last price	$2.00
Average cost	4.38
Capital loss	$2.62

(3) Cyclical Pattern

Period	Sum invested	Price prevailing[a]	Shares bought
1	$120	$2	12
2	120	4	15
3	120	6	20
4	120	4	30
5	120	2	60
Totals	$600	$3.60 (Average)	137

Last price	$2.00
Average cost	3.00
Capital loss	$1.00

[a] Assuming price reflects also the costs of execution of orders.

Proponents of dollar averaging hold that it eliminates the problem of timing of purchases. Some of these proponents would suggest continuance of a dollar averaging plan that by terminal date shows a loss, in the hope that subsequent price recovery will produce profits; but this again raises the question of timing—how long to continue and when to cut off. Moreover, many investors having a dollar averaging accumulation plan have a target use in mind, such as the purchase of a home, purchase of an interest in a business, financing a college education, retirement, etc., which end use cannot be postponed, so that liquidation of the portfolio for such use at terminal date would show a loss. Critics of dollar averaging say that the problem of timing cannot be avoided by a mechanical formula, that judgment in timing of purchases must be exercised (especially whether or not to continue buying when prices reach fantastically high levels), and that profits are maximized by reasonable success in timing purchases when prices are low. They also point to the danger that the dollar averaging formula might lull the individual investor into forgetting the necessity for constant review and reexamination of selections. Paradoxically, the best results for share leverage in dollar averaging plans are in stocks that show wide range of fluctuation, as more shares are bought when prices decline; yet it is usually such stocks that are most speculative.

See FORMULA PLANS.

BIBLIOGRAPHY

ASCHER, L. W. "Dollar Averaging in Theory and in Practice." *The Financial Analysts Journal*, Sept.-Oct., 1960.
COTTLE, C. C., and WHITMAN, W. T. *Investment Timing: The Formula Plan Approach*, 1953.
DINCE, ROBERT R. "Another View of Formula Planning." *Journal of Finance*, December, 1964.
TOMLINSON, L. *Practical Formulas for Successful Investing*, 1953.

DOLLAR BILLS OF EXCHANGE   See DOLLAR EXCHANGE.

DOLLAR CREDIT   LETTER OF CREDIT providing for drafts to be drawn in dollars.
See DOLLAR EXCHANGE, ACCEPTANCE CREDIT.

DOLLAR EXCHANGE   Bankers acceptances and bills of exchange drawn in a foreign country and payable in the United States or another country in dollars, or drawn in the United States and payable in a foreign country in dollars. Acceptances for the creation of dollar exchange by members of the Federal Reserve System are permitted subject to regulations of the board of governors, and subject to a limit at any time in the aggregate of 150 percent of capital and surplus. Maturity must be not more than three months' sight, exclusive of days of grace.
See ACCEPTANCE CREDIT.

DOLLAR FOREIGN BOND   Bond issued by foreign governments, states, cities, or corporations in foreign countries, with principal and interest payable in dollars in the United States.
See EXTERNAL BOND.

DOLLAR STABILIZATION   See MONEY.

DOLLAR VALUE LIFO   A variation of conventional LIFO (last in, first out) inventory valuation in which layers of inventory are priced in dollars adjusted by price indexes instead of at unit prices. LIFO is applied to pools of inventory items instead of to individual items. The cost of record keeping is less than under unit LIFO. An involuntary liquidation of LIFO is less likely to occur with inventory pools because of the increased number of items in the pool and because the pools can be adjusted for changes in product composition or product mix.

DOMESTIC ACCEPTANCE   An ACCEPTANCE in which both drawer and drawee are located in the United States, and, therefore, payable in this country.
See ACCEPTANCE CREDIT.

DOMESTIC BILL   Bill of exchange in which both drawer and drawee are located in the United States, and, therefore, payable in this country.
See BILL OF EXCHANGE, DRAFT.

DOMESTIC EXCHANGE   Inland exchange; checks, drafts (bank and commercial), and acceptances drawn in one place and payable in another within the United States, as distinguished from checks, bills of exchange, bank drafts, and acceptances drawn in this country and payable abroad, which are known as FOREIGN EXCHANGE.

"Bills, drafts, etc., arising in domestic clearings, payable in any place, are sometimes spoken of as the 'exchange' of that place, although in practice 'exchange' is pretty generally limited to bank drafts. A draft on a New York bank is thus "New York exchange,' on a Chicago bank it would be "Chicago exchange,' and so on. In the main, however, the term "exchange' is confined to drafts on the large centers" (E. E. Agger, *Organized Banking*).

Formerly, before the introduction of PAR CLEARANCES inaugurated by the Federal Reserve banks in 1916, the value of exchange on the various central points in the United States fluctuated in accordance with supply and demand. For example, New York exchange would be quoted in Chicago or San Francisco above or below par in accordance with the relation existing between the supply of and demand for New York funds in those centers. If the supply of New

York funds held as balances in New York banks by Chicago banks was excessive and tending to increase faster than the demand for such funds, then the exchange rate on New York would be quoted at a discount; if demand was relatively heavier than supply, however, New York exchange would command a premium. As in the case of foreign exchange, the limits of fluctuation in exchange rates were fixed by the cost of shipping currency.

Under the Federal Reserve interdistrict check collection system, approximately 85% of the banks of the United States acceded to the plan of accepting and remitting for checks drawn upon themselves and passed through the FEDERAL RESERVE CHECK COLLECTION SYSTEM at par. All members of the Federal Reserve System were required to accept their own checks at par, and any other bank could use the facilities of the Federal Reserve check collection system if it signified its willingness to do the same, thereby becoming a CLEARING MEMBER BANK.

Member banks were no longer obliged to be put to any expense in shipping currency from one point to another in order to create a supply of exchange against which they could sell their drafts. Federal Reserve banks were always prepared to transfer funds for the account of member banks from one part of the country to another without cost. These transfers were effected without actual currency shipments by means of book credits and the wire system, debit and credit balances among the Federal Reserve banks being settled daily through the operation of the INTERDISTRICT SETTLEMENT ACCOUNT.

See CLEARING HOUSE INTERBANK PAYMENTS SYSTEM, ELECTRONIC FUND TRANSFER ACT, ELECTRONIC FUND TRANSFER, FEDERAL RESERVE COMMUNICATIONS SYSTEM FOR THE EIGHTIES, FLOAT, PAR LIST, PAR POINTS.

DOMESTIC INTERNATIONAL SALES CORPORATION Part of the fiscal package proposed for adoption by the Nixon Administration on August 15, 1971, was authorization for a new type of tax-subsidized export organization, the Domestic International Sales Corporation (DISC). Usually organized as a subsidiary of a parent domestic company, the DISC can engage in exporting both as a principal and as commission agent, and provided that at least 95% of its assets are export-related and at least 95% of its income is derived from export sales and rentals, up to 50% of taxable income of the DISC is not currently taxed. The tax deferred income is never taxed to the DISC, but would be taxed to the DISC's shareholders if distributed, if the shareholder sold the stock, and if the DISC no longer qualified as such. While a DISC cannot be included in a consolidated tax return of the parent company, and dividends therefrom would not be entitled to the 85% or 100% exemption from tax as intercorporate dividends for the parent corporation, DISC dividends are considered tax-wise to be from a foreign corporation, so that foreign tax credit to the extent of taxes paid by the DISC to foreign countries could be claimed by the parent U.S. company.

Certain trade partners with the United States argued that this tax preference constituted an illegal export subsidy in violation of the GENERAL AGREEMENT ON TARIFFS AND TRADE (GAAT). In response, the United States set up a new system, FOREIGN TRADE CORPORATIONS, which complied with GATT regulations but still protected U.S. companies from the competitive disadvantage of being taxed on their international income.

DOMESTIC TRAVELER'S LETTER OF CREDIT *See* TRAVELER'S LETTER OF CREDIT.

DOMICILE Literally, residence or home. It has acquired a technical meaning in commerce, especially in connection with negotiable instruments which are said to be domiciled at the place where they are payable, unless a contrary intent of the parties is shown, and will be governed by the laws of that jurisdiction.

In trust business, domicile means residence. However, in law generally, domicile is more than mere residence, and is defined by the Restatement of the Conflict of Laws as "the place with which a person has a settled connection for certain legal purposes, either because his name is there, or because that place is assigned to him by the law."

DONATED STOCK Stock that, having been originally issued and fully paid, has been given bak to a corporation by its promoters or stockholders, representing a part of their holdings, especially when the stock has been issued in payment of services. The purpose of donated stock is to enable a corporation to raise cash for working capital purposes through its sale, at any price, if such stock was originally issued for full par or subscription price if no par, as fully paid and, therefore, nonassessable.

DONOR A giver; also a person who creates a voluntary trust, also known as settler, grantor, and trustor.
See TRUST.

DORMANT ACCOUNT An account that had no activity for a prescribed period of time and where the bank, after using reasonable means of communication, has determined that contact with customer has been lost. An inactive account is one in which the customer has not initiated any transactions but for which the bank has not lost contact with the customer.

DOUBLE BOTTOM *See* BOTTOM.

DOUBLE EAGLE The United States $20 gold piece. It weighed 516 grains and was 0.900 fine. The Gold Reserve Act, approved January 30, 1934, ended coinage of all GOLD COINS until 1976, when the MINT issued 36,000 gold medallions commemorating the U.S. bicentennial; these were not legal tender, having bullion value only. On July 15, 1980, the mint issued a larger number of two commemorative gold coins, a one ounce Grant Wood and a half ounce Marian Anderson, which sold at 2% over the New York spot price for gold; they too have only bullion or collectors' value.
See CURRENCY OF THE UNITED STATES.

DOUBLE-ENTRY SYSTEM A system of accounting that requires that for each transaction or event recorded, the total dollar amount of the debits entered in all the related accounts must equal the total dollar amount of the credits. For example, the journal entry to record the acquisition of equipment with cash and a note payable is shown here:

Equipment (debit)	10,000	
Cash (credit)		2,000
Note payable (credit)		8,000

A single-entry accounting system makes only a record or memorandum entry of a transaction and does not record the dual effect of each transaction.

DOUBLE LIABILITY The liability to creditors of stockholders of a bank in the event of failure, in an amount up to but not in excess of the par value of the stock owned. Liability was double in the sense that the stockholder was subject to such assessment by the receiver in addition to losing his original investment. This additional liability was imposed upon shareholders in national banks by the provisions of Section 5151 of the Revised Statutes and Section 23 of the Federal Reserve Act. If afforded an additional source of funds for payment of deposits and was generally regarded as protection for the depositors. In actual practice, however, collections from stockholders fared poorly, and with the inauguration of nationwide deposit insurance provision was made for elimination of double liability.

The Banking Act of 1933 provided that double liability should not apply with respect to shares in any national bank issued after date of enactment of the act (June 16, 1933). The Banking Act of 1935 further provided that double liability should cease on July 1, 1937, or thereafter with respect to all shares issued by any national bank, provided that not less than six months' notice of such prospective termination of double liability had been given in a newspaper locally published or circulated. If the national bank should fail to give such notice for the original July 1, 1937 termination date, double liability could thereafter be terminated six months after such notice was published.

In accordance with these provisions, national banks generally published the required notice and have terminated double liability, thus removing an objection to investment in bank stocks. State banking laws generally had similar provisions for double liability and were similarly amended.

The assessment liability upon shareholders to cover impairment in capital still continues on all national bank stock, both old and new. Under Section 5205, Revised Statutes (12 U.S.C. 55), every national bank whose capital stock shall have become impaired by losses or otherwise shall, within three months after receiving notice from the Comptroller of the Currency, pay the deficiency in the capital stock by assessment upon the shareholders pro rata for the amount of capital stock held by each. If thereafter the national bank shall fail to pay up its capital stock and shall refuse to go into liquidation for three months after receiving notice from the Comptroller, a receiver may be appointed to close up the business of the bank. If any stockholder neglects or refuses after three months' notice to pay the assessment, it shall be the duty of the board of directors to cause a sufficient amount of the capital stock of such stockholder to be sold at public auction to make good the deficiency pro rata assessed, and the balance if any above the assessment shall be returned to the delinquent stockholder.

DOUBLE NAME PAPER   See TWO-NAME PAPER.

DOUBLE STANDARD   See BIMETALLISM.

DOUGLAS AMENDMENT   An amendment to the Bank Holding Company Act of 1956 that allows a holding company owning a bank chartered in one state to acquire a bank chartered in another state if permitted by the law of the second state.

DOWER   See DESCENT, LAWS OF.

DOW JONES AVERAGES   The stock market averages prepared by Dow Jones & Co. and published daily in the *Wall Street Journal*. The DOW THEORY is based on "confirmation" of change in primary trend as indicated by the Dow Jones industrials and Dow Jones transportation averages.

Industrials average. The Dow Jones industrial average was first published on July 3, 1884 by Charles H. Dow as an index of active stocks. This average of the closing prices of twelve actively traded stocks of major companies:

The First DJIA

American Cotton Oil
American Sugar
American Tobbacco
Chicago Gas
Distilling & Cattle Feeding
General Electric
Laclede Gas
National Lead
North American Co.
Tennessee Iron & Coal
U. S. Leather preferred
U.S. Rubber

Table 1 shows the components of the Dow Jones industrial, transportation, and utility averages.

On September 3, 1928, the Dow reached a high of 381.17, the low was registered on December 15, 1921 at 63.90. On October 28, 1929, the Dow collapsed along with the market. The industrial average plunged almost 40 points and lost another 30 on the 29th, to close at 230.07, down 40% for the year's high. On July 8, 1932, the Dow touched a record low of 41.22. In 1987, the Dow dropped 508 points, or 22.6%, to 1738.74 on October 19, the worst stock market crash in history. It is estimated that investors lost more than $500 billion. Trading volume was 604, 330, 000 shares on the New York Stock Exchange. A tabulation of the DIJA from 1954 to 1988 is shown in Table 2.

Editors of the *Wall Street Journal* select companies for the list. Typically, companies with large market value, extensive ownership by individuals and institutional investors, consistent earnings and dividends and a leading position in an important industry are selected. It is generally held that the index serves as a proxy for the market.

In 1916, the number of stocks was increased to 20, and on October 1, 1928, to 30 stocks. Initially, the average was calculated as the simple arithmetic average of the daily closing prices, with in some cases multiples of prices of stocks split up being used for prices of the individual stocks concerned, in order to keep the average free of distortion. Beginning on September 10, 1928, the constant divisor method of adjustment was adopted, whereby the sum of the closing prices for the stocks is divided not by the total number of the stocks in the average, but by a figure, calculated initially on the basis of September 8, 1928 closing prices, which would give approximately the same average on the new basis as on the old basis for the day just prior to the changeover to the constant divisor method. Thereafter, the constant divisor was changed whenever necessary because of stock split-ups, stock dividends, or substitutions.

Following is a simplified illustration of how the constant divisor method works.

1. Assume the average contains just three stocks, as follows, which close on a specific day at the following prices.

    stock A   30
    stock B   25
    stock C   45

    $3\overline{)100}$ = 33.33, close for average

2. The following day, a 3:1 split-up is effective for stock C, which closes at 20. Stocks A and B close at 35 and 30, respectively. Using the old divisor of 3 would produce a close of 28.33, which would be misleading, because the market actually moved up, not down. Therefore, the divisor must be changed to eliminate the distortion. To derive it, recompute the previous day, above, giving effect only to the split-up in stock C, as follows.

    stock A   30
    stock B   25
    stock C   15   (3:1 split)

    Divided by old average $33.33\overline{)70}$ = 2.10
    new constant divisor

3. Now compute the following day's average, as follows.

    stock A   35
    stock B   30
    stock C   20

    $2.10\overline{)85}$ = 40.48, close for average

    stock A   30
    stock B   25
    stock C   45

    $3\overline{)100}$ = 33.33, close for average

It will be noted that this method penalizes stock C because it now has least price weight in the new average, whereas it had the highest price in the old average; yet stock C presumably is the market leader, as evidenced by its split-up and substantial price rise. If the multiplier method of eliminating the distortion were used, stock C would continue to have most weight, as follows.

    stock A   35
    stock B   30
    stock C   60 (20 times 3, the split multiple)

    $3\overline{)125}$ = 41.67, close for average

The constant divisor is subject to change if stock dividends, split-ups, and substitutions of stocks in the average cause appreciable distortion. No change is made in the divisor if the stock split, stock dividend, or substitution causes a distortion of less than five points in the industrials average, less than two points in the transportation (formerly railroad) average, and less than one point in the utilities average.

Transportation companies. As of January 2, 1970, the Dow Jones average of 20 railroad stocks was modified to include other forms of transportation. The transportation average, as it is now known, is a continuation of the railroad average, except that nine railroad stocks have been deleted and replaced by nine other transportation securities. Thus the number of stocks in the average remains at 20, and the total in the Dow Jones composite average continues unchanged at 65. Transition to the revised average was effected through adjustment of divisors for the transportation average and the 65 stocks average. The additions and deletions created a divisor for the Dow Jones transportation average of 4.084, compared with the old railroad average divisor of 4.721, and changed the divisor for the 6.5 stocks average to 10.141, from 10.568.

As of 1989, the stocks in the transportation average were as shown in appended Table 1.

Dow Jones explained that the change in the railroad average to the transportation average was dictated by the drastically altered pattern of commercial transportation itself. When the railroad average was begun toward the end of the nineteenth century, the railroads were the giant movers of both freight and people. Automobiles, trucks, buses, and airplanes had not even arrived on the scene. As recently as 20 years ago, the railroads still carried 62% of all intercity freight on a ton-mileage basis. By 1969, however, that share had shrunk to 41%. Over the same 20 years, the share carried by commercial truckers nearly doubled, rising from 11% to 21%, the rest being moved by pipelines, water transport, and airplanes. By 1969, the movement by railroads of intercity passengers had shrunk to a thin 1.2% of the total, on a passenger-mile basis, from nearly 10% two decades previously. Private automobiles carried a huge 86% of the intercity passenger load in 1969, airlines had 9.4% of the traffic, and buses 2.5%. Also considered in the revision of the average was the contraction through merger of the number of leading railroads and the diversification of some railroad companies into nontransportation business.

Utilities average. The utilities average was initiated in 1929, with 20 stocks, including Commonwealth & Southern and Niagara Hudson Power, which were not available for all of 1929. Accordingly, the constant divisor method was used in working back the average for all of 1929, based on 18 stocks for the period when these two stocks were not available. On June 2, 1938, the number of stocks was reduced to 15.

As of 1989, the stocks in the utility average were as shown in appended Table 1.

Composite average (65 stock average). The composite average was a simple arithmetical average of the 70 stocks then comprising the Dow Jones industrials, rails, and utilities when it was begun November 9, 1933. The number of issues became 65 when the utilities average was reduced from 20 to 15 on June 2, 1938. Changeover to the constant divisor method occurred on May 10, 1945.

Bond averages. In addition to the stock averages, Dow Jones also prepares and publishes the 20-bond average, representing the combined average of 10 public utilities and 10 industrials issues, which are also computed in their two respective averages; U.S. government bonds price average; 2nd average of municipal bond yields.

Table 1 / Components of Dow Jones Averages

Industrial Average

Allied–Signal	Exxon	Philip Morris
Aluminum Co. of America	General Electric	Pinmenca
American Express	General Motors	Procter & Gamble
AT & T	Goodyear	Sears Roebuck
Bethlehem Steel	IBM	Texaco
Boeing	International Paper	Union Carbide
Chevron	McDonald's	United Technologies
Coca–Cola	Merck	USX Corp.
DuPont	Minn. Mining & Manuf.	Westinghouse
Eastman Kodak	Navistar	Woolworth

Transportation Average

Allegis	Consolidated Freightways	Pan Am
AMR Corp.	Consolidated Rail	Piedmont Aviation
American President	Delta Air Lines	Ryder System
Burlington Northern	Federal Express	Santa Fe Southern Pacific
CSX	NWA	TWA
Canadian Pacific	Norfolk Southern	Union Pacific
Carolina Freight		USAir Group

Utility Average

American Electric Power	Consolidated Natural Gas	Panhandle EPL
Centenor Energy	Detroit Edison	Peoples Energy
Columbia Gas System	Houston Industries	Philadelphia Electric
Commonwealth Edison	Niagara Mohawk Power	Public Service Enterprises
Consolidated Edison	Pacific Gas & Electric	Southern California Edison

BIBLIOGRAPHY

Business Week. "Mixed Notices for the New Dow." July 16, 1979. Dow Jones & Co., Inc.
The Dow Jones Investor's Handbook, Annual.

DOWN-UNDER BONDS Euro-Australia dollar and Euro-New Zealand dollar bond issues.

DOW THEORY A theory of stock price movement based upon interpretation of action of the DOW JONES AVERAGES (industrials and transportation companies) for indication of direction of the "primary trend" (major upward or downward movement). "Secondary movements" (rallies in a primary downtrend or reactions in a primary uptrend) are temporary reversals of the primary trend. The daily fluctuations are considered to be of no value individually, but collectively make up the first two movements. Closings for the industrials and the transportation companies (formerly the railroad average) only are used as basic data. The primary trend is likened to the tide; the secondary movements, to the waves; and the daily fluctuations, to the ripples. The forecasting aim in applying the Dow theory is to determine the direction of the primary trend (tide). The primary movement, once established, continues in the same direction, although interrupted by secondary movements, until there

Table 2 / Dow Jones Industrial Average Since 1954

High		Year	Low		High		Year	Low	
Dec. 31	404.39	1954	Jan. 11	279.87	Dec. 11	1036.27	1972	Jan. 26	889.15
Dec. 30	488.40	1955	Jan. 17	388.20	Jan. 11	1051.70	1973	Dec. 5	788.31
Apr. 8	521.05	1956	Jan. 23	462.35	Mar. 13	891.66	1974	Dec. 6	577.60
July 12	520.77	1957	Oct. 22	419.79	July 15	881.81	1975	Jan. 2	632.04
Dec. 31	583.65	1958	Feb. 25	436.89	Sept. 21	1014.79	1976	Jan. 2	858.71
Dec. 31	679.36	1959	Feb. 9	574.46	Jan. 3	999.75	1977	Nov. 2	800.85
Jan. 5	685.47	1960	Oct. 25	566.05	Sept. 8	907.74	1978	Feb. 28	742.12
Dec. 13	734.91	1961	Jan. 3	610.25	Oct. 5	897.61	1979	Nov. 7	796.67
Jan. 3	926.01	1962	June 26	535.76	Nov. 20	1000.17	1980	Apr. 21	759.13
Dec. 18	767.21	1963	Jan. 2	646.79	Apr. 27	1024.05	1981	Sept. 25	824.01
Nov. 18	891.71	1964	Jan. 2	766.08	Dec. 27	1070.55	1982	Aug. 12	776.92
Dec. 31	969.26	1965	June 28	840.59	Nov. 29	1287.20	1983	Jan. 3	1027.04
Feb. 9	995.15	1966	Oct. 7	744.32	Jan. 6	1286.64	1984	July 24	1086.57
Sept. 25	943.08	1967	Jan. 3	786.41	Dec. 16	1553.10	1985	Jan. 4	1184.96
Dec. 3	985.21	1968	Mar. 21	825.13	Dec. 2	1955.57	1986	Jan. 22	1502.29
May 14	968.85	1969	Dec. 17	769.93	Aug. 25	2722.42	1987	Oct. 19	1738.74
Dec. 29	842.00	1970	May 4	631.16	July 5		1988	Jan. 20	1879.14
Apr. 28	950.82	1971	Nov. 23	797.97					

As of 9/1/88

DRAFT

is a confirmation of change in direction. The industrials must be confirmed by the transportation companies, or vice versa, in the indication of change in primary trend.

Confirmation in Dow theory literature may occur through breakouts by both averages in either direction, up or down, from a narrow band of fluctuation ("line"), or through new highs or lows made on secondary movements by both averages. The latter interpretation is preferred by Dow theorists of modern times. In a bull market, as a secondary rise is followed by a secondary reaction, the rise must exceed the previous secondary peak and the low on the secondary reaction must not fall below the low of the previous secondary reaction. If this happens, the direction on the primary trend continues upward. If, however, both averages fail in their secondary movements to sustain the primary trend (e.g., secondary movement high fails to penetrate previous secondary high, and secondary movement low penetrates below the previous secondary low), a change in direction of the primary trend is confirmed from uptrend (bull market) to downtrend (bear market). The new primary trend will continue in that direction, again interrupted by secondary movements, until a new confirmation is given of change in primary trend. Each average must confirm the other, even if it involves a time lag so that the signal of change in direction of primary trend is late.

The Dow theory evolved from the editorials of Charles H. Dow, founder of the Dow Jones Co., Inc., in the *Wall Street Journal* at the turn of the century. The Dow theory is first found labeled as such in S. A. Nelson's *The ABC of Speculation* (1902). William Peter Hamilton, who succeeded Dow as editor of the *Wall Street Journal*, particularly popularized the Dow theory by editorials therein, particularly his famous editorial "A Turn in the Tide," on October 25, 1929. Although the *Wall Street Journal* no longer promotes the Dow theory by editorials, business articles, etc., the theory still has many practitioners and proponents, notwithstanding mixed results with its signals over the years.

DRAFT A written order drawn by one party (the drawer) ordering a second party (the drawee) to pay a sum of money to a third party (the payee). Often the drawer and payee are the same party, the draft being made payable to "ourselves." In reality, a draft is a BILL OF EXCHANGE, except that in this country the term draft is customarily used in domestic transactions, whereas both terms, draft and bill of exchange, are used in foreign transactions. A draft may be made nonnegotiable, but a bill of exchange cannot. Drafts have all the chief characteristics of bills of exchange.

Drafts are of three kinds: (1) sight, demand, or presentation drafts—payable immediately, at sight, or on demand or presentation; (2) arrival drafts—a modification of a sight draft, payable upon the arrival of goods at the destination of the drawee and for which the draft as been drawn in payment; (3) time drafts—payable at a fixed date, or a certain number of days after date (the latter sometimes being called "days after date" drafts).

A time draft payable 30 days after sight must be presented for acceptance, and at maturity for payment. A 30-day sight draft is payable 30 days after ACCEPTANCE by the drawee, when it becomes an acceptance or obligation.

Upon acceptance the drawee becomes the acceptor and principal debtor and is bound to pay the draft at maturity. The bank at which a draft is payable should be indicated on the face of the instrument by the acceptor.

Drafts usually arise out of commercial transactions in which the buyer and seller are located at different points. A draft differs from a check in that it may be a time instrument drawn on an individual, firm, corporation, or bank, and the initiative for payment of the goods is taken by the seller and not the buyer. Usually previous arrangements have been made between the buyer and seller that permit the seller to draw drafts against the buyer in settlement of all transactions between them. Generally a shipper (seller) sends the draft drawn against the drawee (buyer) to its bank to make a presentation and collection with shipping documents attached. The shipper's bank then forwards the draft with documents to its correspondents in the city for which the goods are destined. Instructions are given to the collecting bank to surrender the bill of lading upon either acceptance of payment of the draft, the documents being referred to as documents against acceptance or documents against payment, respectively.

Some drafts do not arise out of commercial transactions but to secure payment for securities sent from one place to another, the draft being sent to a bank for collection with instructions to release the securities only upon payment. Other drafts, without documents attached, merely operate as "duns" or demands for payment of bills past due.

See ARRIVAL DRAFT, FOREIGN BILLS OF EXCHANGE, TRADE ACCEPTANCE.

DRAWEE The party, whether an individual, firm, corporation, or bank, against which a check or draft is drawn and from which payment is expected.

DRAWER A party, whether an individual, firm, corporation, or bank, which draws (i.e., makes) a check, draft, or bill of exchange. The drawer is also known as the maker. In the case of a check, the drawer is a debtor and therefore the payer, while in the case of a draft and bill of exchange the drawer is the creditor and also often the payee.

DRAWN BONDS Bonds which have been called for redemption by lot.
See CALLED BONDS.

DRIVE An expression to indicate a sudden attack upon security or commodity values by sellers in an effort to force prices down. Section 9 of the Securities and Exchange Act of 1934 prohibits manipulative practices in such activity. See MANIPULATION.

DROP An expression to indicate a fall in security or commodity prices.
See DECLINE.

DUAL BANKING A banking system in which two types of banks exist simultaneously. For example, banks in the United States may be chartered either by the individual states or by the federal government.

DUAL TRADING A trading practice that occurs when brokers trade simultaneously for themselves and customers. The practice is usually considered a trading abuse.

DUE BILL In securities market practice, the written claim upon the seller of a stock for the buyer for the dividend to which the buyer is entitled by reason of having bought the stock ""dividend-on" (before the stock sold EX-DIVIDEND) but having been unable to transfer the stock to his name before the ex-dividend date.

DUE DATE The date upon which a note, draft, acceptance, bond, or other evidence of debt becomes payable; the maturity date.
See TIME TO RUN.

DUE FROM BANKS An asset account appearing in the general ledger and financial statement of a bank to indicate the aggregate amount of balances outstanding with and due from other banks.

DUE FROM BANKS, COLLECTIONS A contingent asset account appearing in the general ledger and financial statements of a bank to indicate the aggregate amount of out-of-town checks in process of collection through the medium of collection agents or correspondent banks, but not yet available as cash. When the items are collected, the amount is added to the account entitled "due from banks," and subtracted from this account.

DUE FROM FEDERAL RESERVE BANK An asset account appearing in the general ledger and financial statement of a member or clearing member bank to indicate the balance due from a Federal Reserve Bank. This amount represents approximately the cash reserve required by law to be kept with the Federal Reserve Bank.

DUE FROM FEDERAL RESERVE BANK, COLLECTIONS A contingent asset account appearing in the general ledger and financial statement of a bank to indicate the aggregate of checks in the process of collection through the agency of the Federal Reserve bank, but not yet available as cash reserve. When these items are collected, the amount is added to the account entitled "due from Federal Reserve bank," and subtracted from this account.

DUE FROM FOREIGN EXCHANGE DEPARTMENT
An asset account appearing in the general ledger or financial statement of a bank to indicate the aggregate funds entrusted with the foreign department for use or investment in foreign exchange operations. The operations of a foreign department are usually considered as distinct from those of the rest of the bank, and its bookkeeping operations are kept separate. This sum represents the accountability of the foreign department to the bank.

DUE-ON-SALE CLAUSE A contractual clause giving the lender the right to require immediate repayment of the balance owed if the property changes hands. For example:

> If all or any part of the Property or an interest therein is sold or transferred by Borrower without Lender's prior written consent....Lender may, at Lender's option, declare all the sums secured by this Mortgage to be immediately due and payable.

DUE TO BANKS A liability account appearing in the general ledger or financial statement of a bank to indicate the aggregate amount deposited by banks, as distinguished from individuals, firms, and corporations other than banking corporations.

DULL Used on a stock or commodity exchange to indicate inactive trading, and that little interest is displayed in the movement of prices.

DUMMY Used in connection with directors, officers, stockholders, etc., to indicate a person who acts for another, but who has no real responsibility or liability. He is merely placed in office to complete the number required by law or for publicity purposes.

DUMP To offer suddenly on the market for sale large blocks of securities for the purpose of disposing of them regardless of the prices offered; to unload large blocks of a security or securities.

In a commercial sense this term is used in connection with international trade. When one nation floods the market of another with large quantities of a certain commodity or commodities at prices lower than those at home or in other foreign countries, the foreign nation is said to be dumping its goods in the other country's market. Commercial dumping is commonly described as either distress dumping, predatory dumping, or persistent dumping. Commercial dumping is commonly described as either distress dumping, predatory dumping, or persistent dumping.

The Trade Agreement Act of 1979 repealed the Antidumping Act of 1921 and amended the Tariff Act of 1930 to assign to the U.S. INTERNATIONAL TRADE COMMISSION responsibilities for investigating industry complaints of injury caused by subsidized imports or imports sold at less than fair value *or dumped* in the United States. If the commission's preliminary investigation finds reasonable indication of material injury or threat of material injury to an existing U.S. industry or of material retardation of the establishment of an industry by imports marketed through unfair trade practices, and if the secretary of commerce confirms this finding, then the commission conducts final investigations of the matter. If the commission finds that the complainant industry is injured or threatened with injury, and if no satisfactory corrective agreement is reached with the country involved, the commission so reports to the president, who may impose countervailing duties or other antidumping measures to curtail the offending imports.

DUN & BRADSTREET The oldest and largest mercantile agency of the United States and of the world, supplying credit information and credit ratings on and for all types of business concerns. The present parent company, Dun & Bradstreet Companies, Inc., represents a reorganization in 1973 whereby the bellwether company, Dun & Bradstreet, Inc., the leading U.S. commercial credit reporting organization, became one of a number of operating subsidiaries.

Lewis Tappan, pioneer credit executive and originator of the idea of centralized credit reporting, was first proprietor of The Mercantile Agency, which he founded in 1841. The succession of proprietorship of the Mercantile Agency was as follows: Lewis Tappan & Co., 1841-1849; Tappan & Douglass, 1849-1854; B. Douglass & Co., 1854-1859; and R. G. Dun & Co., 1859-1933. The J. M. Bradstreet & Son's Improved Mercantile Agency was founded in 1849 and was incorporated in 1876 as The Bradstreet Company, continuing as such until the merger with R. G. Dun & Co. in 1933. John M. Bradstreet was a dry goods merchant and lawyer who had acquired a substantial file of credit information in the process of liquidating a large estate.

Besides Dun & Bradstreet, Inc., other operating subsidiaries of Dun & Bradstreet Companies, Inc. include the Reuben H. Donnelley Corp., founded in 1886 and publisher of the Yellow Pages classified sections of telephone directories; Dun-Donnelley, publisher of trade and professional magazines, official airlines guides, and Funk & Wagnalls encyclopedia; Moody's Investors Service, investment service and publisher of financial manuals; the Fantus Company and William E. Hill & Co., which do management consulting; Technical Publishing Co.; Corinthian Broadcasting, which operates a chain of television stations; and the TVS television network. Also featured is D & B International, which provides a comprehensive, computerized marketing data base, called Duns File, containing information on over one million firms worldwide.

See CREDIT RATING, FAILURES.

BIBLIOGRAPHY

DUN AND BRADSTREET:
Business Failure Record.
Cost of Doing Business: Corporations.
Cost of Doing Business: Partnerships and Proprietorships.
The Pitfalls in Managing a Small Business.

DUOPOLY A market structure in which there are only two firms. Although not observed with any degree of regularity in the real world, this construct is useful in economic theory for illustrating the principles of gaming and competitive behavior.

DUPLICATE BILL OF EXCHANGE *See* FIRST OF EXCHANGE.

DUPLICATE BILLS BILLS IN A SET.
See FIRST OF EXCHANGE.

DUPLICATE DOCUMENTS Documents in a set.
See BILLS IN A SET.

DURATION ANALYSIS A technique of ASSET/LIABILITY MANAGEMENT that involves measuring changes in capital values that follow from given changes in interest rates. The term "duration" was coined by Frederick Macauley in 1938. His question was why changes in interest rates cause price changes in bonds that are not strictly proportional to the bonds' maturities. He determined that a bond's term to maturity is only a partial measure of the length of a debt instrument, because maturity does not take into account the size or timing of intermediate cash flows. Macauley developed a set of formulas to explain, in a purely linear fashion, the relationship between bond prices and changes in interest rates. A key measure was a bond's duration, the weighted average maturity based on the PRESENT VALUE of the cash flows rather than on the actual flows, as in the usual average maturity calculation. This set of concepts is the basis for duration analysis.

Measuring Duration. Every asset is exposed to several types of risk, including credit risk, liquidity risk, foreign exchange risk, and price risk. Cash flows from each asset are also subject to reinvestment risk. A bank's overall portfolio is also subject to interest rate risk.

Duration is a measurement of *interest rate risk* exposure based on *price risk* and *reinvestment risk*. Price risk is the chance that interest rates will rise, reducing the market value of an investment; reinvestment risk is the chance that interest rates will fall, so that cash flows from the original instrument can only be reinvested at a lower rate than they had been earning. Obviously, price risk and reinvestment risk move in opposite directions. The decline in the price of a bond in relation to a change in interest rates can be tied directly to the duration of the bond.

The duration of the bond can be expressed mathematically as

$$D = \frac{E([t \times PV(i)])}{EPV(i)}$$

where t = time period (as distinguished from maturity), and $PV(i)$ = present value of cash flow in period t.

DURATION ANALYSIS

To illustrate, consider the following example:

Principal value of instrument = $1,000
Market value = $1,000
Coupon rate = 10%
Yield to maturity = 10%
Maturity = 5 years
Interest paid annually = $100

Calculating the equation requires four steps:

1. Schedule the periodic cash flows.
2. Calculate the present value of each cash flow.
3. Multiply the present value of each cash flow by its period number.
4. Divide the sum of the results in step 3 by the market value of the instrument.

For the basic, straightforward example given, the calculation would proceed as follows:

	Period 1	2	3	4	5	Total
Interest	100	100	100	100	500	500
Principal	0	0	0	0	1,000	1,000
Present value	91	83	75	68	683	1,000
Period x NPV	91	166	225	272	3,415	4,196

Thus, Duration = $\frac{4,169}{1,000}$ = 4.169

In this example, the five-year bond can be thought of as comprising five annual cash flows plus a balloon payment. The first cash flow can be conceived as a one-year zero-coupon instrument, while the last cash flow can be considered a five-year zero-coupon instrument. Duration is a summary of all five cash flows into a single zero-coupon instrument.

Conceptually, by extension to a portfolio, a duration of 4.169 means that as of 4.169 years, regardless of fluctuations in interest rates, the asset portfolio will have yielded a return of 10%, because any change in reinvestment income during the first 4.169 years will be offset by the opposite change in market value at the 4.169th year, *assuming that movements in and out of the portfolio are possible and practical.* The ability to restructure the portfolio is necessary to maintain a portfolio duration of 4.169 and to correct for duration drift (the tendency of durations to change over time due to changes in cash flow patterns) and interest rate changes (for instance, a change in rates from 10% to 11% changes the duration of the example above to 4.0).

Given a concrete value for duration, what would be the change in market value of the asset portfolio if interest rates were to rise, say, 100 basis points? The equation for calculating the approximate change is:

$$\text{Change in market value} = \frac{-D(r) \times \text{current market value}}{(1+r)}$$

where D = duration of the instrument, r = current interest rate, and r = change in interest rate.

Applied to the present example:

$$\text{Change in market value} = \frac{-4.169\,(.01) \times 1,000}{(1+.10)} = -37.90$$

In other words, if rates increase 1%, the asset portfolio value decreases by about $37.90. The accuracy of this estimate declines as the duration becomes longer and the change in rates becomes larger (the precise figure for the decline in market value is $36.96 in the case above).

Viewed from a different perspective, the duration is the maturity date of a zero-coupon bond having the same yield to maturity as the coupon bond alternative and having the future value at duration of the compounded and discounted cash flows of the coupon bond to the duration date. The following table illustrates the calculation of the zero-coupon bond equivalent:

Year	Coupon bond cash flow	Future value at 4.169th year
1	$ 100	$ 135.27
2	100	122.98
3	100	111.80
4	100	101.63
5	1,100	1,016.32
		$1,488.00

A change in interest rates will affect the present value of these two securities in an identical manner as long as the duration remains the same:

Interest rate	Present value of coupon bond flows ($1,488 at 4.169th year)
9%	$1,039
10	1,000
11	963

Regardless of changes in the interest rate, however, a zero-coupon bond delivers the yield to maturity as of date of purchase not only on the initial investment but also on the reinvested interest. It is not subject to price or reinvestment risk if held to maturity.

An equivalent coupon bond will have the same characteristics, with the price risk at sale (4.169 years, in this example) offsetting whatever reinvestment risk exposure exists before then (assuming the interest rates move in parallel as they change). As cash payments are received from the coupon bond, however, its duration may change from that of the original zero-coupon equivalent, which will require a portfolio adjustment in order to maintain the zero coupon.

Matching Assets and Liabilities. A simplistic approach to asset/liability management is to match fund and asset with a liability of equal maturity at a positive spread, neglecting the periodic cash flows the asset throws off (and its duration). The higher the cash yield on an instrument, the higher its periodic cash flow and the shorter its duration, or period of cost recovery. These cash flows will affect income as they are reinvested at rates above or below that on the original instrument and thus will also affect the actual yield to maturity on the initial investment.

In duration analysis, the durations of asset/liability portfolios are matched rather than the maturities for assets and liabilities. For example, given a portfolio in which the market value of assets is 100, the market value of liabilities is 95, and that of equity (the residual figure) is 5, the durations of the assets and liabilities are calculated to be five years and four years, respectively. Suppose that interest rates increase 200 basis points. Using the equation for change in market value, the new value can be derived as:

Change in market value + Original value = New value

For assets: $\frac{-5(2.0) \times 100}{(1+.10)} = -\$9.09$ 100 $\$91$

For liabilities: $\frac{-4(2.0) \times 95}{(1+.10)} = -\$6.90$ $\$95$ $\$88$

Equity value $\$3$

In this scenario, because the asset value fell by a greater amount than the liability ratio, equity value declined from 5 to 3. The capital ratio, which had been 5%, dropped to 3.3%.

ENCYCLOPEDIA OF BANKING AND FINANCE

Equity value (in dollars) could have been protected from this loss in value if asset and liability durations had been set so that the duration of the equity would be zero—that is, so that equity would be immunized from any change in interest rates. The equation to accomplish this is:

$$(D_a \times V_a) = (D_l \times V_l)$$

where the D terms represent durations and the V terms represent market value. The term representing equity drops out because the duration of equity has been set at zero.

In a healthy bank, the value of assets (V_a) should exceed the value of liabilities (V_l). Thus, to balance, the duration of assets (D_a) must be less than the duration of liabilities (D_l). Assuming the duration and value of the asset portfolio are 5 and 100, respectively, and the value of the liabilities portfolio is 95, as in the example above, the desired value for the duration of liabilities is:

$$5 \times 100 = D_l \times 95$$

$$5.26 = D_l$$

Again, suppose interest rates rise by 200 basis points. The new values are:

Change in market value + Original value = New value

$$\frac{-5(2.0) \times 100}{(1 + .10)} = \$9.10 \qquad \$100 \qquad \$91$$

$$\frac{-5.26(2.0) \times 95}{(1 + .10)} = \$9.08 \qquad \$95 \qquad \$86$$

Equity value $5

The nominal equity has been protected from rate changes, and the capital ratio has now increased to 5.49%. (If the duration of the assets and liabilities had been matched, the value of the equity would have fallen but the equity/capital ratio would have remained 5%.) The durations of asset/liability portfolios will change in response to any change in interest rates, however, so a bank must restructure its portfolios accordingly to offset the changes in durations.

Duration Drift. Even if interest rates did not change, and the asset and liability portfolio durations were equal to begin with, the asset and liability durations would change over time because of differences in intermediate cash flows (timing and amounts) of assets and liabilities. This change is called duration drift.

Duration drift is also caused by the difference in the rate of recovery of assets with intermediate cash flows and the single cash flow of zero-coupon bonds. The duration of an asset with intermediate cash flows will decline in a nonlinear fashion because the present value of the income received in the early years is greater than the present value of income received in later years. The duration of the zero-coupon bond declines in a linear fashion because of its single-payment feature. Although an asset portfolio might contain only zero-coupon bonds, the liability portfolio would not; therefore, the duration responses of the two to an interest rate change will differ and will tend to drift apart.

To keep the durations of its portfolios in balance so that equity duration is zero, a bank must constantly monitor the composition of its assets and liabilities, making appropriate changes in the maturities or coupon rates of assets, liabilities, or both (in opposite directions).

Evolution of Duration Analysis. The model described above is the first generation of duration models, usually known as Macaulay's duration. Underlying this model is the assumption that flat interest rate yield curves respond to random events with parallel shifts in the yield curves. This unrealistic assumption could lead to unrealistic results, however. A portfolio of very short-term and very long-term investments can be designed to have the same duration as a portfolio of medium-term investments. If changes at the ends of the yield curve are not the same as changes in the middle, the performance of the two portfolios can be quite different, as some investment officers have learned at great expense.

Second-generation duration analysis involves discounting the yield curve or relevant spot rates of zero-coupon bonds in each year until maturity. Each cash flow is then discounted by the relevant rate for the year in which the cash flow occurs. Third-generation duration analysis entails adjusting the relevant spot yield curve for zero-coupon bonds for historical average volatilities of rates and projecting these into the future. Fourth-generation duration analysis requires the empirical study of random events that influence the determination of short- and long-term rates and building a forecast of rate volatilities based on this study.

A common limitation of all these models is that, although the basic duration calculation is simple, deriving the proper values to use in the calculation is very complex. A bank must first have adequate portfolio data and use them to schedule cash flows over the term of the investments. Actual cash flows may differ from contractual cash flows, however, because of prepayments and defaults. The bank, therefore, must assess the probabilities of prepayments and defaults in order to estimate cash flows more accurately.

The next step is to discount this expected cash flow, which requires some assumptions about the behavior of yield curves. Several models are available of yield curves that are more complex than the simple flat curve, but no single one can provide error-free duration calculations.

An additional complication is choosing appropriate rates by which to discount cash flows. Events affecting interest rates will have differing repercussions on long- and short-term rates. This difference must be taken into account when calculating the effect of rate changes on the duration of any given portfolio.

Thus, duration analysis can not produce hard numbers, only estimates based on certain assumptions. It is not a panacea, but it can be a very useful tool of asset/liability management.—Adapted from Leonard E. Wyderko, Jr., *A Duration Analysis Primer*, Bank Administration Institute, 1985.

BIBLIOGRAPHY

BANK ADMINISTRATION INSTITUTE. *A Duration Analysis Primer*. Bank Administration Institute, Rolling Meadows, IL, 1985.

———. *A Practical Guide to Duration Analysis*. Bank Administration Institute, Rolling Meadows, IL, 1988.

DUTY   *See* CUSTOMS DUTY, TARIFF.

E

EAGLE The U.S. $10 gold piece. It weighed 258 grains and was 0.900 fine. Coinage was abandoned in 1933. The Gold Reserve Act of January 30, 1934, declared the coinage of gold to be at an end.
See GOLD COINS, UNITED STATES MONEY.

EARMARKING Under Section 14 of the Federal Reserve Act, the Federal Reserve Bank of New York maintains accounts with foreign central banks of issue. As part of the operations of such accounts, gold may be held by the Federal Reserve bank under earmark for the account of the foreign central banks or foreign governments. Earmarked gold is not part of the monetary gold stock, which is all held by the Treasury.

The gold certificate account, listed first in the assets of the district Federal Reserve banks, represents gold certificates and/or gold certificate credits issued since 1934 by the U.S. Treasury to the Federal Reserve banks in the process of monetizing the Treasury's holdings of the nation's monetary gold. These gold certificates do not enter the money circulation of the country, and their present function, since they no longer serve as Federal Reserve banks' minimum gold reserve against their deposits and Federal Reserve notes' "cover," is to serve as reserve assets for inter-Federal Reserve district settlements. Interregional payments involve payments and shifts in deposit accounts of member banks and of the Treasury at individual Federal Reserve banks, and final settlements are accomplished by the transfer of gold certificate credits in the gold certificate account from one Federal Reserve bank to another.

The President of the United States, under authority of the act of October 6, 1917 (12 U.S.C. 95a), as amended March 9, 1933 and December 18, 1941, may prohibit or regulate, by means of licenses or otherwise, any transactions in foreign exchange, transfers of credit between or payments by banking institutions, and the export, hoarding, melting, or earmarking of gold or silver coin, bullion, or currency.
See EMERGENCY BANKING RELIEF ACT, GOLD RESERVE.

EARNING ASSETS Loans, discounts, and investments of a bank, constituting the major source of earning power for a commercial bank. Expansion in earning assets depends upon the availability of EXCESS RESERVES, and results in expansion in deposits of the banking system. Conversely, credit deflation (contraction in earning assets) reduces deposits and adds to excess reserves of the banking system. Despite quantitative and qualitative controls over credit expansion and contraction, such as reserve requirements, open market operations and fixing of bill buying and discount rates, statutory limitations on loans and investments, and examination standards, expansion and contraction in earning assets are largely a matter of individual bank credit policy. As a practical matter, however, individual banks tend to follow the group trend voluntarily, to keep up with competitors during expansion and to protect themselves from being last in liquidation of loans and investments whenever the spiral of deflation is started.
See CREDIT.

EARNING POWER The ability of a business consistently to employ its capital profitably over a period of time. When profits show a reasonable return on invested capital and are sufficient also to provide for a high standard of maintenance of properties and necessary plant extensions, the concern is said to have a demonstrated earning power. Demonstrated earning power is the best test of the BUSINESS RISK in passing upon an application for a loan.

EARNINGS Profits; net income.
See GROSS PROFITS, GROSS REVENUES, NET PROFITS.

EARNINGS PER SHARE For basic measures of company profitability, dollar net income after income taxes can be expressed relatively as percentage on sales, i.e., net profit margin, or as percentage on equity, i.e., ROI or return on investment.

But for more specific valuation per unit of investment (i.e., per share of common stock), net income after income taxes and after dividends on the preferred stock, if any, must be reduced by division by total outstanding shares of the company into earnings per share, the basic data used in publicity on company earnings, in computing earnings growth over a past period, in projecting potential future growth, and appraising relative market valuation by computing the price-earnings ratio (market times earnings, or earnings as a percentage of market price).

Undue emphasis, however, should not be attached to a single net income figure and to earnings per share for a particular year (American Institute of Certified Public Accountants, *Accounting Research Bulletin No. 43*, 1953). Analysis should include the income statement as a whole, including the sources of income and structure of costs, their comparative past record, and the position and outlook for the corporation and its industry.

Computational problems in presenting earnings per share include the following (see APB Opinion No. 15, May, 1969).

1. Primary earnings per share, simple capital structures (only common stock or including no potentially dilutive convertible securities, options, warrants, etc., that could in the aggregate dilute over 3% earnings per common share).
   a. Weighted average number of common shares outstanding during each period presented should be used, excluding reacquired shares from date of acquisition.
   b. Stock dividends, stock splits, or reverse splits (increasing or decreasing number of common shares) should be retroactively reflected for all past periods presented so as to be comparable with present capitalization.
   c. Acquisitions of firms accounted for as purchases and involving issuance of shares should reflect the additional shares only from the acquisition date. Combinations of firms accounted for as poolings of interests should reflect the aggregate of the weighted average outstanding shares of the constituent firms, adjusted to equivalent shares of the surviving firm, for all periods presented.
   d. In computing earnings per share, claims of senior securities on earnings for a period should be deducted from net income and from income before extraordinary (nonrecurring) items if shown in the income statement.
2. Primary earnings per share, including common stock equivalents if capital structure is complex and there is dilutive effect.
   a. A common stock equivalent is a security which is not in form a common stock, but which usually contains provisions to enable its holder to become a common stockholder and which, because of its terms and the circumstances under which it was issued, is in substance equivalent to a common stock. The APB concluded that a common stock equivalent is determined only at the time of issuance and should not be changed as long as the security remains outstanding.

ENCYCLOPEDIA OF BANKING AND FINANCE

3. Fully diluted earnings per share, to show the maximum potential dilution of current earnings per share on a prospective basis.
   a. This concept includes senior stock or debt which is convertible into common shares but is not a common stock equivalent; options or warrants; or agreements for the issuance of common shares upon the satisfaction of certain conditions, such as the attainment of specified higher levels of earnings following a business combination.
   b. The computation should be based on the assumption that all such issued and issuable shares were outstanding from the beginning of the period or from the time the contingency arose, if after the beginning of the period.
   c. Previously reported fully diluted earnings per share amounts should not be retroactively adjusted for subsequent conversions or subsequent changes in the market prices of the common stock.
   d. The rule is "one-way," i.e., fully diluted earnings per share should exclude those securities whose conversion, exercise, or other contingent issuance would have the effect of increasing the earnings per share amount.

Earnings per share data are widely used in judging the operating performance of a business. This ratio frequently appears in financial statements and business publications. It is considered the most significant figure appearing on the income statement because it condenses into a single figure the data reflecting the current net income of the period in relation to the number of shares of stock outstanding. Separate earnings per share data must be shown for income from continuing operations and net income. Earnings per share may be reported for the results from discontinued operations, extraordinary items, or cumulative effects of changes in accounting principles if they are reported on the income statement. Current accounting practice requires that earnings per share be disclosed prominently on the face of the income statement.

BIBLIOGRAPHY

AMERICAN INSTITUTE OF CERTIFIED PUBLIC ACCOUNTANTS, ACCOUNTING PRINCIPLES BOARD, Opinion No. 9, *Reporting the Results of Operations*, December, 1966.
———. Opinion No. 15, *Earnings per Share*, May, 1969.
DUDLEY, L. W. "A Critical Look at EPS." *Journal of Accountancy*, August, 1985.

EARNINGS QUALITY Realistic earnings. Accounting principles, methods, and policies can influence the quality of a company's reported earnings. Such factors should be considered when evaluating the financial statements of companies. Generally, accounting principles, methods, and policies that result in the slowest reporting of income are considered the most conservative. When a firm has conservative accounting procedures, its earnings are of high quality.

A company's accounting policies should be compared with industry standards. If the policies are more liberal, earnings quality is generally considered to be lower. Consider the following generalities when evaluating the quality of a company's earnings:

1. A low price/earnings ratio (market price per share divided by earnings per share) generally means lower-quality earnings.
2. FIFO (first in, first out) inventory procedures match the oldest costs against revenue. FIFO is generally considered to be more liberal than other inventory procedures.
3. The completed contract method (revenue recognized when the contract is completed) of accounting for construction firms that have long-term contracts is generally considered to be more conservative than the percentage of completion method (revenue recognized during the construction period).
4. Accelerated depreciation methods that recognize a large amount of depreciation in the early years of the asset are conservative. These include the sum-of-the-years' digits and the declining balance method. The straight-line method of depreciation is generally considered to be among the least conservative depreciation methods. Also, the shorter the depreciation periods, the lower the income and the more conservative the statements.
5. In accounting for pensions, the higher the assumed discount rate used to compute the actuarial present value of the accumulated benefit obligation and the projected benefit obligation, the lower the present value of the liability and the lower the immediate pension cost will be. If the rate is too low, then the projected benefit obligation is too low and vice versa.

An understanding of nature and scope of generally accepted accounting principles will help in evaluating a firms accounting policies. Major accounting principles and policies are disclosed within the financial statements and presented in the notes to the financial statements. Notes are considered an integral part of financial statements. Many accounting policies used in financial statements are disclosed in a Summary of Accounting Policies, which immediately precedes the first note or is the first note to the statements.

EASEMENT The right one person has to use the land of another for a specific purpose. An easement is distinct from the ownership of the soil underlying the easement. Public utility companies are often given easements under property to place their wires and other equipment.

EASE-OFF A gradual and small decline (fractional to one point) in security or commodity prices, without evidence of selling pressure or of enforced liquidation.

EASY MONEY Money that can be obtained at low interest rates and without difficulty because of the existence of a plentiful supply of EXCESS RESERVES among the banks.
See MONEY MARKET.

ECONOMETRICS A useful statistical technique for testing empirically fundamental topics in economics, finance, and management. The collection and application of these techniques is known as econometrics.

The primary technique used by analysts and researchers is regression analysis. It is a statistical procedure for estimating mathematically the average relationship between a dependent variable and an independent variable or variables. Simple regression involves one independent variable, and multiple regression involves two or more.

ECONOMIC COOPERATION ADMINISTRATION
The original agency administering the foreign aid program of the U.S., established by the Economic Cooperation Act of 1948 (Sec. 104, 62 Stat. 138) to administer the European recovery program. The act approved October 10, 1951 (65 Stat. 373) abolished the agency and transferred its functions to the Mutual Security Agency, effective December 30, 1951, pursuant to Executive Order 10300 of November 1, 1951. The Mutual Security Agency was a predecessor of the present Agency for International Development.
See MUTUAL SECURITY PROGRAM.

ECONOMIC CYCLE *See* BUSINESS CYCLE.

ECONOMIC DEVELOPMENT ADMINISTRATION
A governmental administration established under the Public Works and Economic Development Act of 1965 (79 Stat. 552; 42 U.S.C. 3121) to generate new jobs, to protect existing jobs, and to stimulate commercial and industrial growth in economically distressed areas of the United States. The basic programs of the administration include public works grants to public and private nonprofit organizations to build or expand public facilities essential to industrial and commercial growth; loan guarantees to industrial and commercial firms, local development companies, and Indian-owned businesses; technical assistance and grants to help communities and firms solve problems that stifle economic growth; planning grants to pay for the expertise needed to plan, implement, and coordinate comprehensive economic developments programs; special economic adjustment assistance to help state and local governments solve current and anticipated adjustment problems that lead to abrupt and serious job losses; and to help areas implement strategies to reverse and halt long-term economic deterioration.

ECONOMIC GOOD An economic commodity that is material, useful, scarce, and transferable. Economic services are nonmaterial activities that are useful, scarce, and transferable.

ECONOMIC GROWTH A phenomenon that is usually defined in terms of the annual percentage change in real GNP. Increases

ECONOMIC INDICATORS

in real GNP are interpreted to mean that more goods and services are being produced this year as compared to last year. When this occurs, economic well-being increases.

ECONOMIC INDICATORS
Economic, or cyclical, indicators signal changes in the direction of aggregate economic activity. Defined and analyzed by the National Bureau of Economic Research (NBER) since 1938, there are three types of cyclical indicators: leading, coincident, and lagging. The list of indicators is periodically revised. Unless otherwise stated, all indexes use 1967 as their base of 100 and all dollar-valued series are in 1972 dollars. A complete listing and description of the individual time series and composites can be found in the *Handbook of Cyclical Indicators* or in the monthly listings prepared by the Council of Economic Advisors and the BEA's *Business Condition Digest*.

Leading indicators. The composite index of leading indicators consists of 12 series that measure marginal employment adjustments, capital investment commitments, inventory investment and purchasing, profitability, and money and financial flows. Descriptions of these series follow.

1. Average weekly hours of production or nonsupervisory workers in manufacturing.
2. Average weekly initial claims for state unemployment insurance programs.
3. Manufacturer's new orders.
4. Vendor delivery performance.
5. Index of net business formation.
6. Contracts and orders for plant equipment.
7. Index of new private housing building permits.
8. Change in inventories on hand and on order.
9. Change in sensitive materials prices.
10. Index of stock prices (1941-43 = 10).
11. Real money supply, M2.
12. Change in business and consumer credit outstanding.

The first two series measure labor market adjustments and are negatively related series; as weekly hours/worker increase, new unemployment insurance claims will decrease. The next two measure trade orders and deliveries, which are also negatively related series; as orders increase and delivery systems are strained, delivery performance suffers. Series five, six, and seven measure fixed capital investments, which are a measure of the long-term economic outlook and directly follow economic trends. Series eight accounts for inventory adjustments. Series nine and ten address profitability by assessing the cost of and returns to normal business activity. The last two focus on measures of money and credit availability.

Coincident Indicators. The composite index of coincident indicators consists of four series that track employment, personal income, industrial production, and sales. These series have historically reached peaks and troughs at roughly the same time as the economy. The actual series used are:

1. Employees on nonagricultural payrolls.
2. Personal income minus transfers.
3. Index of industrial production.
4. Manufacturing trade sales. The coincident indicators are clustered in three categories: employment, production and income, and consumption.

Lagging indicators. The composite index of lagging indicators comprises six series that track employment, inventories, profitability, and financial market conditions. These series have historically reached their peaks and troughs later than the corresponding business cycle turn, so they are associated with a degree of inertia or adaptive expectations. The series used are:

1. Average duration of unemployment.
2. Ratio of inventories to sales in manufacturing and trade.
3. Index of labor cost/unit of output in manufacturing.

Long-Term Perspective: January 1969 to May 1989

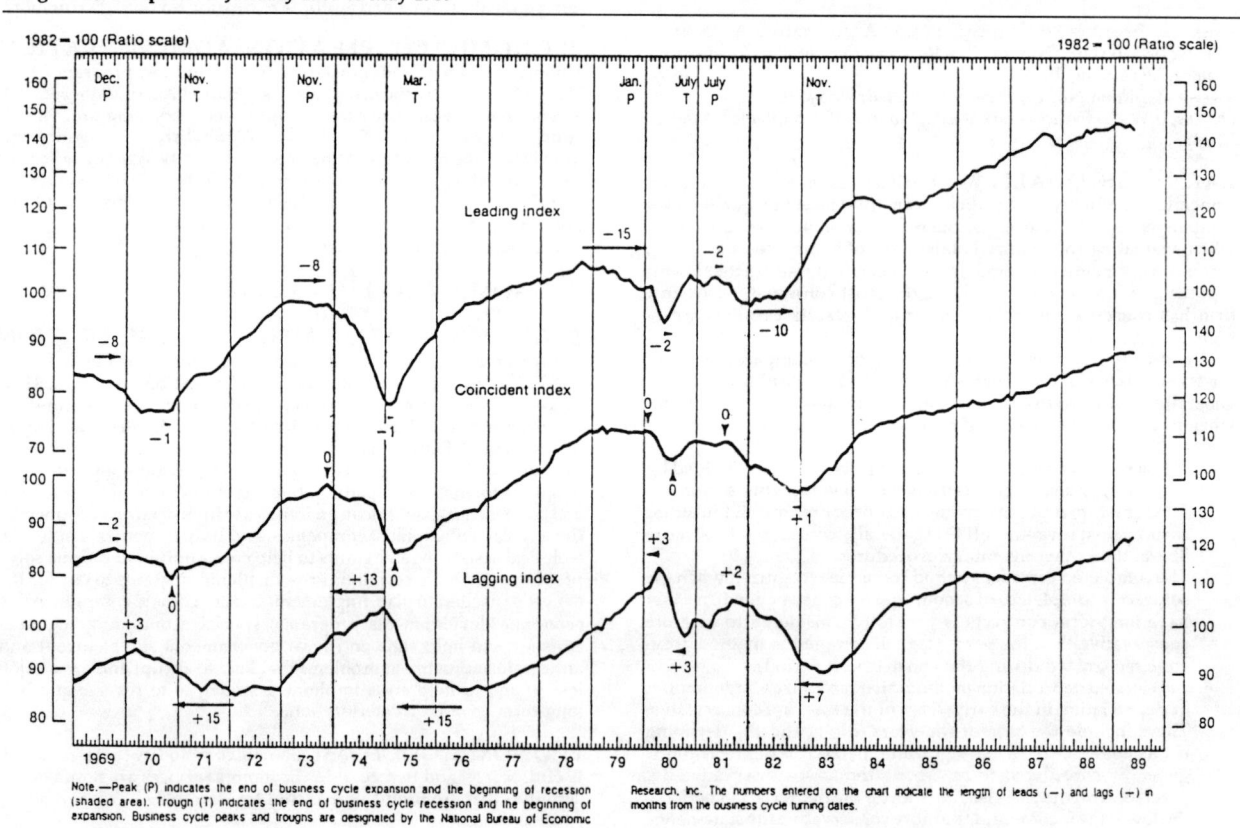

Source: U.S. Department of Commerce, Bureau of Economic Analysis

4. Average prime rate.
5. Commercial and industrial loans outstanding.
6. Ratio of consumer installment credit to personal income.

Except for the employment series, which is countercyclical, these measures directly follow the economic trend with a slight lag. Lagging indicators are used to verify the passing of a peak or trough. If an apparent peak in the coincident indicators is not followed by a subsequent peak in the lagging indicators, then a BUSINESS CYCLE turn will not be established.

The appended table shows the long-term perspective—January 1969 to May 1989—for the leading, coincident, and lagging indexes.

ECONOMIC PROFIT In ECONOMICS, the term profit refers to economic profit. Profit is defined, for a given period of time, as the difference between total revenue and total cost. In the calculation of economic profit, all costs are subtracted, including opportunity costs. Thus, since resources have productive alternative uses, economic profit is less than accounting profit for any particular evaluation.

One of the theoretical conclusions from an economic analysis of a perfectly competitive market is that the firm will earn zero economic profit. When a firm earns zero economic profit, it earns a positive level of accounting profit. Zero economic profit is not bad. It indicates that all resources are being used efficiently and are being paid at a rate equal to their highest valued use.

ECONOMIC RECOVERY TAX ACT A 1981 tax law that provided the largest tax cut bill ever passed. Top individual tax rates decreased from 70% to 50% and the effective tax rates on capital gains were redued from 28% to 20%. Property placed in service after December 31, 1980, became eligible for the accelerated cost recovery system (ACRS); allowable contributions to Keoghs and other retirement systems were increased; two-earner married couples were permitted a deduction to reduce the inequity of the marriage penalty; and the investment credit was extended to include a wide array of investments.

As the title suggests, a major purpose of this legislation was the revitalization of the economy. Its objective was to place more after-tax income in the hands of the taxpayers in the expectation that they would consume more goods and services and thus increase aggregate demand, resulting in economic growth.

Following is a description by the Office of Management and Budget of the principal provisions of the Economic Recovery Tax Act of 1981.

Indexing: Beginning with calendar year 1985, the individual income tax brackets, the zero bracket amount, and the personal exemption adjusted annually for inflation as measured by the consumer price index for all urban households (CPI-U). The adjustment for a given year will be the increase in the CPI-U between fiscal year 1983 and the preceding fiscal year. The 1985 adjustment therefore will be based on the increase in the CPI-U between fiscal years 1983 and 1984.

Taxation of foreign earned income: Under prior law, U.S. taxpayers who had foreign earned income were allowed a variety of deductions and exclusions for expenses incurred abroad. The act replaces these allowances for expenses with a partial exclusion of foreign earned income from tax. Beginning in 1982, each taxpayer may exclude up to $75,000 of foreign earned income from tax. The exclusion will increase by $5,000 annually through 1986, to a maximum exclusion of $95,000. In the case of a married couple, the exclusion is computed separately for each qualifying individual. An exclusion for excess housing costs is also provided.

Capital cost recovery provisions. Taxpayers may claim depreciation deductions for tangible property used in a trade or business. Under prior law, these deductions were determined by the particular "facts and circumstances" of the anticipated use of the property, or according to a system of guidelines known as the asset depreciation range system (ADR). The Economic Recovery Tax Act of 1981 replaces these methods of depreciation with the accelerated cost recovery system (ACRS), which provides for a faster write-off of capital expenditures under simplified and standardized rules.

Corporation income tax rate reductions: ERTA reduced the tax rate on the first $50,000 of taxable corporate income as shown in the appended table.

Corporation Income Tax Rate Reductions in Economic Recovery Tax Act of 1981

	Tax rate		
		Current law	
Taxable corporate income	Prior law	1982	1983 and beyond
First $25,000	17%	16%	15%
Second $25,000	20	19	18
Third $25,000	30	30	30
Fourth $25,000	40	40	40
Over $100,000	46	46	46

Individual retirement accounts (IRAs): Beginning January 1, 1982, eligibility for an IRA was extended by ERTA to all active participants in a tax-qualified employer-sponsored pension plan. In addition, the maximum annual contribution to an IRA established by a working individual for him/herself increased to $2,000 or 100% of compensation, whichever is less. The maximum annual contribution to an IRA established by a worker for him/herself and a nonworking spouse increased to the lesser of $2,250 or 100% of compensation.

Self-employed retirement savings (Keogh plans): The maximum annual contribution to a Keogh plan by a self-employed individual increased from $7,500 to $15,000, effective January 1, 1982.

Estate and Gift Tax Provisions. Several provisions to reduce estate and gift taxes are provided in ERTA.

Marital deduction: Effective January 1, 1982, a surviving spouse was permitted to inherit an unlimited amount without paying tax. Under prior law, the marital deduction was limited to the greater of one-half of the adjusted gross estate or $250,000.

Estate and gift tax credit: The maximum credit against estate and gift taxes was $47,000 under prior law. Since $47,000 is the amount of tax owed on an estate or gift of $175,625, estates or gifts of $175,625 or less were exempt from tax. ERTA increases the credit annually to $192,800 in 1987 and subsequent years, which will exempt from tax all estates of $600,000 or less.

Rate reductions: The maximum tax rate on estates and gifts is reduced by 5 percentage points a year from 70% in 1981 to 50% in 1985 and subsequent years.

Gift tax exclusion: Gift tax annual exclusion is increased from $3,000 to $10,000 per donee, effective January 1, 1982. In addition, an unlimited exclusion is provided amounts paid for certain medical expenses and school tuition.

Corporation Estimated Tax Payments. Corporations are generally required to pay 80% of their income tax liability in estimated payments during the taxable year. The required level of estimated payments has several exceptions, including one that allows corporations to make estimated payments on the basis of the previous year's tax liability. However, under prior law, corporations with taxable income exceeding $1 million in any of the three preceding taxable years were required to make estimated payments equal to at least 60% of their current year's liability, regardless of the previous year's liability. Under ERTA, the required level of estimated payments for such corporations is increased to 65% of the current year's liability in 1982, 75% in 1983, and 80% in 1984 and subsequent years.

See TAX EQUITY AND FISCAL RESPONSIBILITY ACT OF 1982 designed to "improve the fairness of the tax system while preserving the savings and investment incentives necessary for economic recovery" and changing or modifying certain features of ERTA as did subsequent tax legislation.

See also REVENUE ACT.

ECONOMIC RENT The amount that a resource earns above the minimum amount needed to keep it employed in its present use. Because all resources have alternative uses, they will be reallocated if they are paid less than their highest valued alternative use. For example, a firm will not be able to retain an employee who is paid below a fair market salary (where the salary includes an evaluation of the intangible characteristics of the job).

ECONOMIC REPORT OF THE PRESIDENT The Full Employment and Balanced Growth Act of 1978 requires the President's Council of Economic Advisors to prepare an annual report on the state of the economy. This report is called the *Economic*

Report of the President. It is available from the Government Printing Office.

ECONOMICS The study of all phenomena relating to wealth and value. One of the social sciences that deals with economic goods, the creation of wealth through satisfaction of human wants, the explanations of wealth, value, and price, the distribution of income, the mechanism of exchange and markets, etc., of an economy. It is variously defined in a brief way as the "science of wealth"; "science of business"; "science of the development of material resources, and the production, preservation, and distribution of wealth"; "science of production, consumption, value and distribution, and exchange."

Famous definitions of economics include the following.

Aristotle: The function of economic science is "both to found a household and also to make use of it."

Adam Smith: "Political economy, considered as a branch of the science of a statesman or legislator, proposes two distinct objects: first, to provide a plentiful revenue or subsistence for the people, or more properly to enable them to provide such a revenue or subsistence for themselves; and secondly, to supply the State or Commonwealth with a revenue sufficient for the public services."

Marshall: "A study of mankind in the ordinary business of life."

Economics is concerned with choices—how choices are made, why they are made, and what consequences they have. Economists study the choices made by individuals, families, businesses, and nations, as well as the outcomes of these choices.

Objective inquiry is called scientific or positive analysis. In the case of economics, it is called positive economics and it requires economists to sort out fact from opinion. Positive economics is practiced when one predicts that if event A occurs, event B will follow. The distinguishing characteristic of positive economics is that the predictions are testable, if given sufficient information. Thus, positive economic analysis may be either true or false. In contrast, an econ-omist who expresses a personal preference for one outcome over another, is practicing normative economics. Normative economics is not testable; it contains personal value judgments for what ought to be or what is believed to be desirable.

Economics can be divided into two major categories: MICRO-ECONOMICS and MACROECONOMICS. Microeconomics deals with problems and concerns of the individual, firm, and industry. Macroeconomics deals with the aggregates of economics, e.g., total investment and savings, the general price level, full employment, consumer spending, government, the money supply, availability of credit, productivity, INFLATION, foreign trade balances, unemployment rate, and the GROSS NATIONAL PRODUCT.

BIBLIOGRAPHY

Encyclopedias and dictionaries:
American Dictionary of Economics. Facts on File, Inc., New York, NY, 1983.
The Complete Executive's Encyclopedia of Accounting, Finance, Investing, Banking & Economics. Probus Publishing Company, Chicago, IL, 1989.
Dictionary of Business and Economics. Free Press, New York, NY, 1984.
The Dictionary of Modern Economics. MIT Press, Cambridge, MA, 1986.
Encyclopedia of American Economic History. Charles Scribner's Sons, New York, NY, 1980.
Encyclopedia of Economics, McGraw-Hill Book Co., New York, NY, 1982.
The New Palgrave: A Dictionary of Economics. Stockton Press, New York, NY, 1987.

Periodicals (selective):
American Economic Review.
Business Economics.
Business Horizons.
The Economist.
The Economic Review.
Harvard Business Review.
Journal of Business.
Journal of Economics and Business.
Journal of Economic Literature.
Southern Economic Journal.

Econometrics:
Econometrica, The Economic Industry. Northwestern University, Evanston, IL. Bimonthly.
Journal of Applied Econometrics. Quarterly.
Journal of Econometrics. Nine times a year.
Judge, G. G. *An Introduction to the Theory and Practice of Econometrics.* John Wiley and Sons, Inc., New York, NY, 1988.
———. *The Theory and Practice of Econometrics.* John Wiley and Sons, Inc., New York, NY, 1985.
KELEJIAN, H. H., and OATES, W. E. *Introduction to Econometrics: Principles and Applications.* Harper and Row Publishers, Inc., New York, NY, 1981.
WALLACE, T. D., and SILVER, J. W. *Econometrics: An Introduction.* Addison-Wesley Publishing Co., Reading, MA, 1987.

Government Publications—General:
Economic Indicators. U.S. Council of Economic Advisers.
Business Conditions Digest. Bureau of Economic Analyses.
Survey of Current Business. Federal Reserve System.

Other publications:
BARRO, R. J. *Macroeconomics.* John Wiley and Sons, Inc., New York, NY, 1986.
Economic Literature Index. American Economic Association, Nashville, TN, 1979 to date.
Federal Reserve Bulletin.
FLETCHER, J., ed. *Information Sources in Economics,* 1984.
RHYMES, C., and ZIELONKA, DANUTA J. *The American Dream and Other Dangerous Myths: Economic Transition in the 1990s.* International Publishing Co., Chicago, IL, 1989.
SARGENT, T. J. *Dynamic Macroeconomic Theory.* Harvard University Press, Cambridge MA, 1987.
Wharton Econometric Databases. Wharton Econometric Forecasting Associates, Philadelphia, PA.

ECONOMIES OF SCALE In the long run, there are no fixed factors of production; all factors are variable. This means that a firm can expand its output by hiring more of all resources, such as labor and capital. However, there is a limit to how much a firm can expand and still continue to improve its efficiency—that is, to lower its average cost of production.

Larger firms can often operate at a lower average cost of production than smaller ones. One advantage of size is that it allows for specialization of the factors of production. Larger firms can hire specialists to direct various production operations and can use more efficient technical machinery. Average cost will decrease as output expands as a result of the efficiency gains associated with size.

Economies of scale (efficiencies of size) refers to such efficiencies associated with size. Because of economies of scale, a firm's long-run average total cost of production will decrease as output is increased. There is, however, a limit to which such scale efficiencies can be realized. When a firm becomes too large, inefficiencies result and the average cost of production begins to increase. Diseconomies of scale, meaning inefficiencies associated with size, come about when a firm becomes so large that the production process can no longer be supervised properly and the management of the firm can no longer be coordinated effectively. In the diagram below, long-run average total cost increases owing to diseconomies of scale.

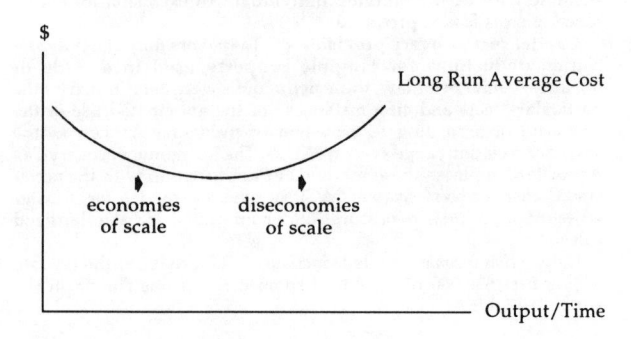

BIBLIOGRAPHY

Baba, Y. "The Dynamics of Continuous Innovation in Scale Intensive Industries." *Strategic Management*, January/February, 1989.

ECONOMIZING The process of applying scarce resources to satisfy unlimited wants.

EDGE ACT An act passed December 24, 1919, as Section 25 (a) of the Federal Reserve Act, with the title "Banking Corporations Authorized to Do Foreign Banking Business." The purpose of this legislation was to permit the establishment under federal jurisdiction of foreign banking corporations to aid in the finance of and to stimulate foreign trade. Such a law had been advocated strongly by the Federal Reserve Board for some years, and represented the latest development in the historical evolution of American banking legislation to procure for U.S. business and financial interests a larger participation in foreign trade and in the profits derived from lending our credit to foreign buyers.

The original Section 25 of the Federal Reserve Act was the first step taken in the interests of building up foreign trade. By this section any national bank with a capital and surplus of $1 million or more was permitted to establish branches in foreign countries and dependencies of the United States with the approval of the Federal Reserve Board. Prior to 1913 practically all the financing of foreign trade had been undertaken by British banks and discount houses, and only a small part of the business was participated in by a few private banks and discount houses in New York.

During World War I the need for further legislation to provide for our growing foreign trade became apparent, and Section 25 of the Federal Reserve Act was amended to permit national banks having legal capital requirements to invest in the capital stock of U.S. banks or corporations already engaged in foreign banking. A few institutions engaging in foreign banking were organized under the banking laws of several of the states, but they were inadequate to provide for all the business.

Other legislation and regulation: Under provisions of Sections 25 and 25(a) of the Federal Reserve Act, and Regulation K of the FEDERAL RESERVE BOARD REGULATIONS, Edge Act or agreement corporations may be established to engage in international banking or foreign financial transactions. These corporations are generally of two types: (1) banking corporations that are located in U.S. commercial centers other than the location of their parent banks and that engage in international banking; and (2) investment corporations that hold foreign investments for their parent banks in such financial institutions as commercial banks, finance companies of various kinds, and leasing companies.

The INTERNATIONAL BANKING ACT OF 1978 amended Section 25(a) of the Federal Reserve Act dealing with Edge Act corporations in several respects:

1. Deletion of the provision that limited an Edge Act corporation's liabilities on account of debentures, bonds, and promissory notes to ten times the corporation's capital and surplus.
2. Removal of the statutory minimum 10% reserve requirement on the deposits of an Edge Act corporation.
3. Permission for foreign banks for the first time to own and control Edge Act corporations.

(Sec. 3(h) of the International Banking Act of 1978 requires the Board of Governors of the Federal Reserve System, as part of its annual report, to assess the effects of these amendments on the capitalization and activities of Edge Act corporations, banks, and the banking system.)

The new Regulation K of the Board of Governors of the Federal Reserve System, issued in 1979 and entitled "International Banking Operations," governs the establishment of foreign branches of member banks, the organization and operation of Edge Act and agreement corporations, and foreign investments by member banks, bank holding companies, and Edge Act and agreement corporations.

Important provisions of the revised Regulation K include the following:

1. Permission for domestic branching of Edge Act corporations.
2. Permission for those corporations to finance the production of goods and services for export.
3. Liberalization of the approval procedures under which foreign investments may be made and foreign branches established.
4. Specification of permissible foreign activities.
5. Permission for foreign ownership of Edge Act corporations.
6. Establishment of a new capital requirement for Edge Act corporations that are engaged in banking activities in the United States—namely, 7% of risk assets.

Revision of Regulation K resulted in part from Section 3 of the International Banking Act of 1978, which was intended to improve the competitiveness and efficiency of Edge Act corporations in providing international banking and financial services. The Congress declared in Section 3 of the International Banking Act of 1978 that Edge Act corporations are to have powers sufficiently broad to enable them to compete with foreign banks in the United States and abroad; to provide all segments of the economy, especially exporters, financing for international trade; and to foster participation by regional and smaller banks in international banking and finance.

On August 14, 1985, the Federal Reserve further revised its Regulation K to expand (on a limited basis) Edge Act banks' domestic activities and to close a loophole in the Edge Act banking statutes that allowed Merrill Lynch, American Express, and Prudential Bache (all nonbank financial services companies) to acquire the charters of existing Edge Act banks and enter the Edge Act banking field in 1984 without the Federal Reserve's prior approval. The revisions took effect in October 1985.

Summary. Edge Act subsidiaries provide various advantages for activities supplementary to international business of their parent banks:

1. Because their charters are federal charters, such Edge Act subsidiaries may operate in various states of the United States without being subject to the particular state's corporation and banking laws, and thus may engage in interstate banking although of a restricted nature.
2. Edge Act corporations may originate and earn on business in low-tax states instead of the high-tax states in which their parent banks are located.
3. Edge Act corporations may serve as the international banking departments of smaller, typically non-New York banks, either for individual banks or for groups of such banks participating in ownership of the Edge Act corporation.
4. With respect to deposits, the International Banking Act of 1978 subjects deposits of foreign banks' branches and subsidiaries, operated outside of the foreign bank's home state in the United States, to equality of limitation, namely, to accepting the types of foreign-source and international banking and finance related deposits permissible for Edge Act corporations operating across state lines in the United States.
5. Permission for foreign banks to own and control Edge Act corporations provides opportunities for expansion of operations and interests.
6. In operations abroad, Edge Act corporations may engage in both conventional banking operations and investment banking and related operations, compared with separation and nonmixture of such operations in conventional banking regulation by the U.S. banking regulatory agencies over U.S. branches abroad.
7. Edge Act corporations provide diversification of operations in the international money markets, in which bankers acceptances especially tend to be bankers acceptances of Edge Act corporations.

EDGE ACT CORPORATION A foreign banking corporation organized under Section 25(a) of the Federal Reserve Act.
See EDGE ACT.

EDUCATION, DEPARTMENT OF Pursuant to the Department of Education Organization Act, passed by the Congress on September 27, 1979, education programs were transferred from the Department of Health, Education, and Welfare to the newly created Department of Education, and were combined with programs of six other federal agencies.

The new Department of Education has cabinet-level status and had a 1980 budget of some $14.2 billion, a sum larger than that of five other departments—Commerce, Energy, Interior, Justice, and State.

EE SAVINGS BONDS U.S. government bonds. Series EE savings bonds are issued in denominations of $50, $75, $100, $200, $500, $1,000, $5,000, and $10,000 at 50% of face amount. Maturity is ten years. A fixed graduated rate increasing from 4.16% after six months to 7.5% after five years is provided. Thereafter, the market-based variable investment yield will be used for determining the redemption value of a bond, unless the minimum investment yield of 7.5% produces a higher value. The bonds can be redeemed any time after six months from issue date. An annual limitation of $15,000 price is set. For tax purposes, interest accrues for federal income, estate, inheritance, and gift taxes. The interest is exempt from state and local income taxes. Federal income tax may be reported as it accrues or in the year the bond matures, is redeemed, or is otherwise disposed of. The bonds are registered in the names of individuals (in single or coownership of beneficiary form) or in names of fiduciaries or organizations (in single ownership). The bonds are not eligible for transfer or pledge as collateral. These bonds can be exchanged for Series HH bonds in multiples of $500; they also offer tax deferral privileges.

It administers over 150 programs and has approximately 19,000 federal employees.

See HEALTH AND HUMAN SERVICES, DEPARTMENT OF.

EFFECTIVE INTEREST METHOD A preferred procedure for amortizing a discount or premium; also called present value amortization. Under the effective interest method, interest expense is based on the increasing (for discounts) or decreasing (for premiums) book value of the bonds. The total interest expense for each interest period is the carrying amount (book value) of the bonds at the start of that period multiplied by the effective interest rate. The amount of amortization of the bond discount or premium is the difference between the total (effective) interest expense for the period and the accrued nominal interest. As the carrying amount changes each period by the amount of amortized discount or premium, interest expense either increases (for discounts) or decreases (for premiums) over the life of the bonds.

A schedule of note discount amortization using the effective interest method for a $10,000, three-year, 10% note discounted at 12% is appended. (The present value of the note is $9,520.)

	Cash Interest 10%	Effective Interest 12%	Discount Amortized	Unamortized Discount Balance	Present Value of Note
Date of issue				$480	$ 9,520
End of year 1	$1,000	$1,142	142	$338	9,662
End of year 2	1,000	1,159	159	179	9,921
End of year 3	1,000	1,179	179	-0-	10,000
Total	$3,000	$3,480	$480		

Cash interest: $10,000 x 10% = $1,000.
Effective interest for year 1: $9,520 x 12% = $1,142
Discount amortization for year 1: $1,142 – $1,000 = $142
Unamortized discount balance for year 1: $480 – $142 = $338
Present value of note year 1: $9,520 + $142 = $9,662

EFFECTIVENESS Effectiveness refers to how a job is performed: Does the work produce the intended results? An organization's effectiveness is evaluated in terms of how what is done relates to goals and objectives. Efficiency is the relationship of outputs per unit of input. Efficiency relates to an activity performed with the lowest consumption of resources.

EFFICIENCY The nonwasteful use of resources. Efficiency im-plies that all resources are being used to their potential. Associated with the efficient use of resources are other concepts in economics, such as the absence of economic rents, zero economic profits in a competitive market, and an economy operating on its production possibility frontier.

See EFFECTIVENESS.

EFFICIENT MARKET HYPOTHESIS The efficient market hypothesis of movements of stock prices in its weak variant stands for the proposition that successive stock prices are mostly unrelated and that prices tend to move in a random manner. The randomness of stock prices is reported to be confirmed by analysis of successive price changes, indicating low serial correlation coefficients, and by simulated charting of random numbers, indicating patterns of price movements similar to actual price movement patterns. On this basis, proponents of the random walk hypothesis dismiss the usefulness of TECHNICAL ANALYSIS, an approach for predicting stock prices based on the price patterns developed by prior price data.

A second variant of the efficient market hypothesis stands for the proposition that: (1) there are many participants in an efficient market; (2) such participants have access to all relevant information affecting stock prices; and (3) such participants compete freely and equally for the stocks, causing, because of such competition and the full information available to the participants, full reflection of the worth of stocks in their prevailing prices. As new information randomly develops and is acted upon and reflected in prices, stock prices in turn behave randomly.

A third variant of the efficient market hypothesis stands for the proposition that prevailing stock prices fully reflect and discount not only publicly available information but also private and expert analyses and information, such as that made available to institutional investors in consideration of routing commission business to particular brokerage firms, and "research boutiques." Since performance of institutional investors such as investment companies is found to be not much different from results of noninstitutional portfolios and from randomly selected portfolios, it is concluded again that prevailing stock prices in responding promptly to randomly developed information, whether publicly or privately available through expert analyses, behave randomly, and that professional money managers do not achieve consistently superior performance because of superior access to superior information.

All three variants of the efficient market hypothesis challenge the validity of fundamentals analysis and technical analysis, and in turn are challenged by adherents of the fundamental and technical approaches.

The efficient markets theory, or what is also called "the new investment technology," is the idea that security markets are efficient and that investment rewards are related to risk.

According to this theory, a market is said to be efficient if it functions in such a way that transaction costs to buyers and sellers in the market are relatively low and information on new developments is quickly disseminated to all parties. Market prices will reflect such new information.

Advocates of the efficient markets theory stress that risk has its rewards, and, on average, investors obtain greater returns for incurring greater risks. They emphasize that if investments are always efficiently priced in the market, the only way for the average investor to obtain returns above the average for the market is to take on more risk.

Over the past several decades, numerous academic studies have examined the question of the relative efficiency of security markets. Most of these studies have found that the money and capital markets are weak-form efficient, and some have reported semistrong-form efficiency. Markets do not appear to be strong-form efficient, so possessors of inside information have a definite advantage over the average investor.

The efficient markets theory suggests that even professional money managers, unless they have access to inside information, cannot consistently obtain returns above the average for the market as a whole unless they are willing to take on an above average level of risk. Some of the most convincing evidence in support of the theory has been amassed by studies that show that the great majority of professional investment managers do not consistently outperform the market averages. Indeed, Burton Malkiel, one of the foremost proponents of the efficient markets theory, claims that "no scientific evidence has yet been assembled to indicate that the investment performance of professionally managed portfolios as a group has been any better than that of randomly selected portfolios."

BIBLIOGRAPHY

GREEN, G. H. "The Effect of Inter-Regional Efficiency on Appraising Single Family Homes." *The Real Estate Appraiser and Analysts*, Winter, 1988.

IPPOLIYO, T. S. "Efficiency With Costly Information: A Study of Mutual Fund Performance, 1965-1984." *The Quarterly Journal of Economics*, February, 1989.

EFFICIENT PORTFOLIO A portfolio that satisfies the following conditions: (1) For a given level of risk there is no portfolio with a higher average return. (2) For a given average return there is no portfolio with a lower level of risk.

EGGS For details of futures trading in eggs, see CHICAGO MERCANTILE EXCHANGE.

EIGHTH STOCKS In the execution of odd-lot orders on the New York Stock Exchange, the odd-lot differential (add-on to the round lot sale of the stock, in case of a purchase; or deduction from the price on the round lot sale of the stock, in case of a sale) was formerly one-eighth ($0.125) per share on stocks selling below 60, and one-quarter ($0.25) per share on stocks selling above 60.

In the current odd-lot system on the New York Stock Exchange, each odd-lot dealer can direct the APARS (automatic pricing and reporting system) to charge or not to charge a differential, which if any was, as of 1979, one-eighth of a point ($0.125) per share.

See ODD LOT.

ELASTIC CURRENCY Money which can be expanded or contracted according to commercial needs. ELASTICITY is one of the essential qualities of a good medium of exchange, and a sound currency system should provide this characteristic. Before the Federal Reserve Act our currency system failed to provide for an elastic currency, but Federal Reserve notes, issued under the authority of the Federal Reserve Act, now supply the elastic element which is lacking in other forms of U.S. currency. Since Federal Reserve notes now represent the largest portion of our circulating medium, elasticity is imparted to the entire circulation. Elasticity is secured by basing the volume of circulating medium upon the volume of credit. Federal Reserve notes expand as business expands, as indicated by increased turnover of member bank deposits and demand for currency to meet withdrawals by drawing on free balances (excess reserves) at the Federal Reserve banks. Likewise when business contracts, the volume of currency in excess of till requirements is turned in, excess reserves are increased, and the excess of Federal Reserve notes is withdrawn from circulation.

See FEDERAL RESERVE NOTES.

ELASTICITY A measure of responsiveness of a good to a change in its price. Several important elasticities are used in economics to quantify the behavioral relationship between variables. These include the advertising elasticity of demand, the cross-price elasticity of demand, the income elasticity of demand, and the price elasticity of demand.

An elasticity measure can be constructed for any variables presumed to be causal; however, economists generally focus on demand-related relationships rather than supply-related relationships for managerial reasons. An elasticity is calculated in terms of percentage changes:

$$\text{Price Elasticity} = \frac{\% \text{ change in quantity}}{\% \text{ change in price}}$$

Elastic demand occurs when the price changes and the quantity changes by a greater percentage. The elasticity is numerically greater than one. It also occurs if price changes and total revenue moves in the opposite direction. Inelastic demand occurs when a relative change in price results in a smaller relative change in quantity sold. Inelastic demand also occurs if price changes and total revenue move in the same direction. An elasticity coefficient of 1.0 is referred to as unitary elasticity and is the point of demarcation between an elastic and an inelastic demand. Characteristics affecting elasticity are summarized here:

Tend toward elastic demand	*Tend toward inelastic demand*
Luxuries	Necessities
Large expenditures	Small expenditures
Durable goods	Perishable goods
Substitute goods	Complementary goods
Multiple uses	Limited uses

ELECTRIC LIGHT AND POWER INDUSTRY See PUBLIC UTILITY INDUSTRY, PUBLIC UTILITY STOCKS.

ELECTRIC POWER OUTPUT Electric output in kilowatt hours is released weekly by the Edison Electric Institute, and is one of the basic business barometers of general business activity.

See PUBLIC UTILITY INDUSTRY.

ELECTROLYTIC COPPER See COPPER

ELECTRONIC DATA PROCESSING A network of computer and software components. The system accepts data, processes the data according to instructions provided by programmers and operators, and prints out or displays the results for those who use the system. Computer facilities have a wide range of capabilities, including speed and storage capacity.

The central processor in a computer data processing system has three major components: the control unit, which directs and coordinates various parts of the computer; the arithmetic/logic unit, which performs the computations and other functions; and the storage (or memory) unit, which retains instructions and other data for later use. Common output devices include printers, card punches, and cathode ray tubes. The appended exhibit illustrates the basic elements in an EDP system and the data processing cycle in accounting.

Basic Components of an Electric Data Processing System

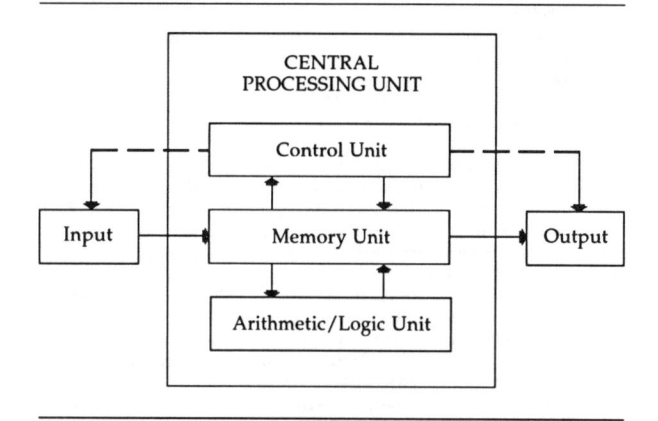

```
                    CENTRAL
                PROCESSING UNIT
              ┌────────────────────┐
              │   Control Unit     │
  ┌───────┐   ├────────────────────┤   ┌────────┐
  │ Input │───│   Memory Unit      │───│ Output │
  └───────┘   ├────────────────────┤   └────────┘
              │ Arithmetic/Logic   │
              │       Unit         │
              └────────────────────┘
```

THE DATA PROCESSING CYCLE IN ACCOUNTING

```
┌─────────┐   ┌────────┐   ┌───────┐   ┌─────────┐   ┌───────────┐
│ Source  │──▶│Journals│──▶│Ledgers│──▶│  Trial  │──▶│ Financial │
│documents│   │        │   │       │   │ balance │   │Statements │
└─────────┘   └────────┘   └───────┘   └─────────┘   └───────────┘
                               │                           │
                           ┌───────┐                  ┌───────────┐
                           │ Files │                  │   Other   │
                           └───────┘                  │ reports and│
                                                      │  analyses │
                                                      └───────────┘
COLLECTION  │       PROCESSING              │         OUTPUT
```

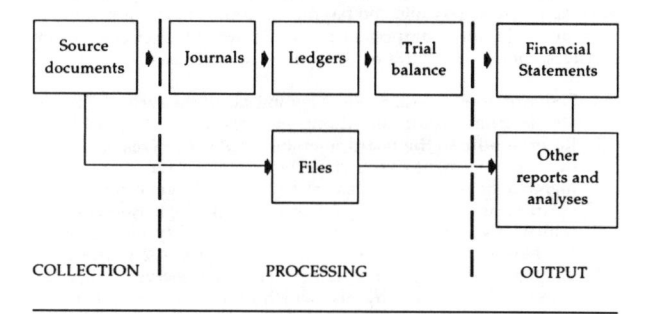

Computer software includes programs, instructions, and routines for using computer hardware.

Systems analysts usually design the data processing system. Programmers develop and write instructions for the computer. Computer operators run the computer system.

ELECTRONIC FILING A method by which qualified electronic filers transmit tax return information directly to an IRS center over telephone lines. Electronic filing reduces IRS processing time, resulting in faster refunds, more accurate returns, and reduced government costs for processing, storage, and retrieval of tax returns.

Any computer can be adapted to file tax returns electronically. The IRS charges a fee for electronic filing.

If the taxpayer chooses, the Treasury Department will directly deposit the refund into the taxpayer's account by electronic transmission. Any federal or state-chartered bank, savings and loan association, mutual savings bank, credit union or similar institution can be designated to receive a direct deposit, provided the taxpayer has an account there.

ELECTRONIC FUND TRANSFER

As defined in the ELECTRONIC FUND TRANSFER ACT, any transfer of funds, other than a transaction that is originated by a paper instrument, that is initiated through an electronic terminal, telephone, or computer or magnetic tape and that orders or authorizes a financial institution to debit or credit an account.

Specifically mentioned in the act are the following:

1. POS (point-of-sale) transfers.
2. Automated teller transactions.
3. Direct deposits electronically of funds, such as deposits of Social Security or salary payments, or payments made electronically from an account, such as for insurance premiums, agreed to by insurance companies.
4. Transfers initiated by telephone pursuant to prearranged plan.

Specifically excluded by the act are the following:

1. Check guarantee and authorization services that do not result directly in debit or credit to an account.
2. Automatic transfers from savings to demand deposit accounts.
3. Wire transfers between banks.
4. Transfers for the purchase or sale of securities.
5. Transfers by telephone not made pursuant to prearranged plan.

Such types of transactions as the preceding, however, would be included in any broad definition of electronic fund transfers, which comprehensively would include all types of transfers and data processing effected by means of electronic equipment and systems, involving both internal transactions within an institution or firm and external transactions with other institutions or firms.

Commercial debits, which arise when an originator firm uses an AUTOMATED CLEARINGHOUSE unit in the automated clearinghouse electronic clearing and settlement system to collect the payments, include consumer payments (such as insurance premiums, mortgages, and utilities) and corporate payments (such as accounts receivable and cash concentration). Commercial credits, which arise when the originator firm uses an automated clearinghouse to make payments, include corporate payments to consumers (such as payroll payments, dividends, and annuities) and corporate payments to other firms (such as accounts payable and payments to credit card merchants).

Included in any comprehensive definition of electronic fund transfers, therefore, would be the following facilities:

1. Fedwire, the Federal Reserve communications system. This is an electronic communications network connecting Federal Reserve offices, the board, member banks, the Treasury, and other government agencies. Fedwire is used for transferring member bank reserve account balances and government securities, as well as for transmission of Federal Reserve administrative, supervisory, and monetary policy information. See FEDERAL RESERVE COMMUNICATIONS SYSTEM FOR THE EIGHTIES.
2. Culpeper switch, a computerized Federal Reserve facility located in Culpeper, Virginia, which serves as a central relay point for messages transmitted electronically between Federal Reserve districts on the Fedwire. Messages moving billions of dollars of funds and securities daily are processed by Culpeper in electronically coded form. They originate in commercial banks, are sent to Reserve banks, and then are transmitted to Culpeper, where they are switched to other Federal Reserve banks and in turn to other commercial banks.
3. BANKWIRE, an electronic communications network similar to Fedwire but owned by an association of banks and used to transfer messages between subscribing banks.

Consumer convenience in retail banking is facilitated by such types of electronic equipment as the following:

1. POS (point-of-sale) systems, which allow for transfer of funds between accounts, authorization for credit, verification of checks, and provision of related services at the time of purchases. POS terminals are located in shopping areas and allow customers of participating financial institutions to effect transactions through the use of machine-readable debit cards.
2. ATM (automated teller machines), which are computer-controlled terminals located on bank premises or elsewhere, through which customers of financial institutions may make deposits, withdrawals, or other transactions as they would through a bank teller.

Summary. For the future, additional volume is projected for both consumer and commercial electronic banking, including expansion in volume of the automated clearinghouse system. In the words of the Senate Banking Committee, "this new generation of financial services offers the public significant new choices in personal banking and has the potential to be of great benefit to consumers."

BIBLIOGRAPHY

Bank Automation Newsletter. Warren, Gorham and Lamont, Inc., Boston, MA. Monthly.
Bank Systems & Equipment. Gralla Publications, New York, NY. Monthly.
EFT Press Alert. Warren, Gorham & Lamont, Inc. Boston, MA. Monthly.
Corporate EFT Report. Biweekly.
The Smart Card. Business Communications, Norwalk, CT, 1986.

ELECTRONIC FUND TRANSFER ACT

Title XX of the FINANCIAL INSTITUTIONS REGULATORY AND INTEREST RATE CONTROL ACT OF 1978, which was signed by the President on November 10, 1978 (P.L. 95-630). It became effective 18 months after enactment except for its provisions on consumer liability and unsolicited card distribution, which became effective 90 days after enactment.

The Board of Governors of the Federal Reserve System summarized the following provisions of the act, among others:

1. Requires disclosure of the terms and conditions of electronic fund transfers (defined to exclude, among other things, wire transfers of funds, telephone transfers not pursuant to an agreement, and transfers made pursuant to an automatic transfer service program) at the time the consumer contracts for an electronic fund transfer (EFT) service.
2. Requires that the consumer be afforded written documentation for each fund transfer made from an electronic terminal, notice as to whether preauthorized transfers were completed, and a periodic statement of account.
3. Requires financial institutions to establish procedures for correcting errors for electronic fund transfers.
4. Provides limitations on the maximum liability of a consumer for unauthorized transfers from his or her account, subject, in part, to whether the consumer reports to the financial institution within prescribed time periods either unauthorized transfers appearing on the periodic account statement or the loss or theft of an electronic fund transfer card. (Note: A consumer who notifies the issuer within two business days of learning that a card has been lost or stolen can be held liable for no more than $50. A consumer who waits longer to notify the institution risks liability of up to $500 for losses that occur after the two business days. But to impose such liability greater than $50, the institution must establish that the subsequent losses could have been prevented if the consumer had given notice within two business days.)
5. Imposes liability on the financial institution under certain circumstances for all damages proximately caused by the institution's failure to make an electronic fund transfer or failure to stop payment of a preauthorized transfer when instructed to do so in accordance with the terms and conditions of the accounts.
6. Permits unsolicited distribution only for unvalidated debit cards.
7. Provides that Title XX does not annul, alter, or affect the laws of any state relating to electronic funds transfers, except to the extent that those laws are inconsistent with Title XX.

ELECTRONIC FUNDS TRANSFER ACT

8. Authorizes the Board of Governors of the Federal Reserve System to exempt from coverage electronic funds transfers within any state that imposes requirements substantially similar to Title XX.
9. In connection with promulgating regulations to carry out the act, requires the Board of Governors of the Federal Reserve System to prepare a statement on economic impact, to issue model clauses to facilitate compliance, and, if necessary, to modify its regulations to ease the compliance burden on small financial institutions.

(*Note:* In the case of an unauthorized EFT that is reflected on a periodic statement, a consumer has 60 days from the institution's transmittal of a statement to examine it and report any unauthorized transfer, and doing so will limit liability of the customer to $50. But failure to report unauthorized transfers may subject the consumer to unlimited liability for related unauthorized transfers occurring after the 60 days have elapsed.

Details of Regulation E. The Board of Governors of the Federal Reserve System on January 31, 1980, announced adoption of additional final rules to complete Regulation E of the FEDERAL RESERVE BOARD REGULATIONS and to implement the Electronic Fund Transfer Act. Sections of Regulation E that were adopted were as follows:

1. On March 7, 1979, effective February 8, 1979: establishing the limitations on customer liability for unauthorized use of an EFT card, and to specify the conditions under which EFT cards may be issued.
2. On June 6, 1979, effective August 1, 1979: absolving consumers of liability for unauthorized transfers if a credit institution has not made the following disclosures, in writing: (1) the extent of a consumer's financial liability for unauthorized use; (2) the institution's telephone number and address for reporting a lost or stolen card; and (3) the institution's normal business days for reporting a lost or stolen card.
3. On August 1, 1979, effective September 10, 1979: limiting the amount for which consumers will be liable if their EFT access card is lost, stolen or otherwise used in a manner unauthorized by the cardholder. As stipulated in the act, a consumer's liability for unauthorized transfers varies according to the time that elapses before the consumer notifies the financial institution of the unauthorized use. Liability rises from $50 to $500 if notification is delayed more than 2 business days from the time the customer learns of the loss or theft of the card. It is unlimited for transfers occurring more than 60 days after transmittal of the statement showing the unauthorized use, if the consumer fails to notify the institution within the 60-day period. Written notice of the loss, theft, or unauthorized use is made effective at the time it is mailed by the consumer rather than upon receipt by the institution.
4. On October 3, 1979, effective November 15, 1979: pertaining to exemptions for certain types of securities or commodities transfers and for intrainstitutional transfers; consumer liability for unauthorized transfers; definitions; and issuance of access devices. The new sections govern special requirements, initial disclosures, changes in terms and error resolution notices, preauthorized transfers, relation to state law, and administrative enforcement. These sections implement the portions of the Electronic Fund Transfer Act that became effective May 10, 1980. (The board decided on January 31, 1980, to take no action at that time on a proposal made in October, 1979, concerning charges made by financial institutions in connection with error resolution. The board said it will monitor industry practice regarding such charges and will take action if consumers appear to need protection in this area.)

Additional final rules were adopted by the Board of Governors of the Federal Reserve System on January 31, 1980, to complete its Regulation E and to implement the Electronic Fund Transfer Act's other provisions which became effective May 10, 1980. The new rules adopted January 31, 1980, as part of Regulation E included the following details:

1. *Documentation of transfers.* The act requires that financial institutions document electronic transfers by making receipts available at automated teller machines or point-of-sale terminals, and by sending consumers of EFT services periodic statements.

Regulation E includes the following requirements: (1) financial institutions must show on periodic statements the date a transfer was debited or credited to the consumer's account; (2) a financial institution may show the location of an automated teller terminal in any of three ways: street address; name of an organization, such as the name of a store; or name of a readily identifiable location where the terminal is situated. (See, below, further amendments to Regulation E adopted on April 10, 1980.)

2. *Preauthorized credits.* The act requires that financial institutions give either positive notice of receipt of preauthorized deposits to a consumer's account (such as sending the consumer notice of receipt of a deposit, for instance, of a direct electronic deposit of Social Security benefits) or negative notice (sending a notice that a scheduled deposit had not been received), unless the payor has given the consumer notice that the transfer has been started (such as notice that an employer has initiated a payroll deposit).

As an alternative, the board provided, as it had suggested in a proposal made in April, 1979, that institutions may provide consumers with a telephone number to be used to verify whether a transfer has or has not been made. Institutions that adopt this alternative are required to provide readily available telephone service and to inform the consumer of the telephone number as an initial disclosure of terms of the institution's EFT service, and also on periodic statements to the consumer.

3. *Availability of funds.* Financial institutions must make electronically deposited funds available to consumers promptly.
4. *Procedures for processing errors.* The act, and Regulation E as adopted, require generally that financial institutions resolve asserted errors in electronic fund transfers within 10 business days of notification by the consumer, either orally or in writing. Alternatively, institutions may take up to 45 calendar days to resolve a complaint, if the account is provisionally recredited within 10 business days for the amount in dispute. Recrediting need not take place unless written confirmation of an oral report of error is received within 10 business days of the oral report by an institution that has advised the consumer that it requires a written report and has provided an address.

When an institution determines that no error has been committed, it must notify the consumer that the account is being debited again for the amount that was credited. It must honor, for the period of investigation and for 5 business days after mailing of a redebiting notice, checks that are payable to third parties up to the amount in dispute.

The institution may limit its investigation to the "four walls" of the institution, when a third party with which the institution has no agreement is involved (including the Social Security Administration).

5. If an EFT card is issued by a financial institution not holding the consumer's account, the institution offering the services is responsible for compliance, with limited exceptions for disclosures having to do with the relationship of the institution holding the consumer's account to that consumer.

Amendments on April 10, 1980, related to rules issued by the board on January 31, 1980, and to proposals made then with respect to sections of the act that became effective May 10, 1980:

1. The board delayed until August 10, 1980, the requirements that a financial institution disclose on periodic statements the name of any third party to or from whom electronic fund transfers were made and the terminal location for transfers initiated at electronic terminals. All other requirements of the regulation went into effect on May 10, 1980, as scheduled.

In taking this action the board made the following statement:

"The Board wishes to insure that consumers enjoy the major protections of the Act and Regulation during the three-month delay. Consequently, a requirement previously stated in the *Federal Register* has been incorporated into the Regulation. When applicable, financial institutions must, upon the consumer's request and without cost, provide the consumer with evidence of proof of payment to another person. The Board reiterates that financial institutions must treat any request for additional information from the consumer as to an incompletely identified transfer as an "error' and comply with the error resolution procedures."

2. The board also permanently "grandfathered" cash dispensers that do not generate a receipt at the time a withdrawal is made, on the condition that the consumer be sent a receipt on the next business day. This exception is available only to terminals that do not perform any electronic transfer function other than dispensing cash. It is also limited to machines that were purchased or ordered by the financial institution before February 6, 1980, the date on which the board's final documentation rules were published. The exception was intended to permit the continuation of a service that is beneficial to consumers, without loss of consumer protection. It would also enable financial institutions to replace these terminals in an orderly and cost-effective manner.
3. The board also adopted an amendment applying to deposits of cash or checks at electronic terminals. In January, 1980, the board had stated the opinion that such deposits are covered by the EFT Act and Regulation E. In response to comments asking that it reconsider the matter, the board reiterated its position, but exempted deposits made at electronic terminals from the requirement that the terminal location be shown on the periodic statement.
4. The board also adopted an amendment relating to the charges that must be disclosed on the periodic statement. Under a rule adopted in January, 1980, institutions were required to disclose separately the total of charges related to electronic transfers, even if the costs were identical for electronic and paper transfers. The amendment now gives institutions the option of disclosing instead the total charges for account maintenance, including any pretransaction charges. This change conforms to the statutory language and was made in response to comments pointing to the operational difficulty in segregating EFT charges, particularly with respect to accounts on which charges are based on minimum balances and may involve rebates. Customers will continue to receive information about specific EFT charges on initial disclosures required by the regulation.

As of 1989, the Fed's network was the only functioning national electronic funds transfer system. However, the linking of regional and statewide electronic funds transfer systems of all major types of depository financial institutions should accelerate, so that as early as 1990, a nationwide and even international EFT network could be operational.

The board's Division of Consumer and Community Affairs points out that Regulation E applies not only to commercial banks but also to SAVINGS AND LOAN ASSOCIATIONS, Credit Unions, and even nonfinancial entities that offer EFT services to consumers.
See CREDIT UNION.

BIBLIOGRAPHY

PHILLIPS PUBLISHING, INC. *Corporate EFT Report.* Biweekly
WARREN, GORHAM & LAMONT, INC. *EFT Press Alert.* Monthly

ELEEMOSYNARY Constituted for the perpetual distribution of alms or bounty of the funders; charitable, as in an eleemosynary institution.

ELEMENTS OF ACCOUNTING The building blocks with which financial statements are constructed; that is, the classes of items that financial statements present. There are currently ten interrelated elements that are directly related to measuring performance and status of a business enterprise, as defined in the FASB's Statement No. 3, "Elements of Financial Statements of Business Enterprises":

Assets are probable future economic benefits obtained or controlled by a particular entity as a result of past transactions or events.
Comprehensive income is the change in equity (net assets) of an entity during a period from transactions and other events and circumstances from nonowner sources. It includes all changes in equity during a period except those resulting from investments by owners and distributions to owners.
Distribution to owners are decreases in net assets of a particular enterprise resulting from transferring assets, rendering services, or incurring liabilities to owners. Distributions to owners decrease ownership interest (or equity) in an enterprise.
Equity is the residual interest in the assets of an entity that remains after deducting its liabilities. In a business entity, the equity is the ownership interest.
Expenses are outflows or other using up of assets or incurrence of liabilities during a period from delivering or producing goods or rendering services, or carrying out other activities that constitute the entity's ongoing major or central operations.
Gains are increases in equity (net assets) from peripheral or incidental transactions of an entity and from all other transactions and other events and circumstances affecting the entity during a period except those that result from revenues or investments by owners.
Investments by owners are increases in net assets of a particular enterprise resulting from transfers to it from other entities of something of value to obtain or increase ownership interests (or equity) in it.
Liabilities are probable future sacrifices of economic benefits arising from present obligations of a particular entity to transfer assets or provide services to other entities in the future as a result of past transactions or events.
Losses are decreases in equity (net assets) from peripheral or incidental transactions of an entity and from all other transactions and other events and circumstances affecting the entity during a period except those that result from expenses or distributions to owners.
Revenues are inflows or other enhancements of assets of an entity or settlement of its liabilities (or a combination of both) during a period from delivering or producing goods, rendering services, or other activities that constitute the entity's ongoing major or central operations.

ELEVATOR RECEIPT A receipt issued by an elevator company to an owner of grain held in storage at an elevator. It is similar in all respects, e.g., legal status, negotiability, and collateral uses, with a WAREHOUSE RECEIPT.

ELIGIBLE ACCEPTANCE See ELIGIBLE PAPER, FEDERAL RESERVE BOARD REGULATIONS (Regulation A).

ELIGIBLE AGRICULTURAL PAPER See ELIGIBLE PAPER, FEDERAL RESERVE BOARD REGULATIONS (Regulation A).

ELIGIBLE BILL OF EXCHANGE See ELIGIBLE PAPER, FEDERAL RESERVE BOARD REGULATIONS (Regulation A).

ELIGIBLE FOR REDISCOUNT See ELIGIBLE PAPER, REDISCOUNT.

ELIGIBLE INVESTMENTS FOR INSURANCE COMPANIES See INSURANCE, INSURANCE COMPANIES, LIFE INSURANCE COMPANY INVESTMENTS.

ELIGIBLE INVESTMENTS FOR SAVINGS BANKS See SAVINGS BANK INVESTMENTS, SAVINGS BANKS.

ELIGIBLE INVESTMENTS FOR TRUST FUNDS See TRUST FUND INVESTMENTS.

ELIGIBLE NOTES See ELIGIBLE PAPER, FEDERAL RESERVE BOARD REGULATIONS (Regulation A).

ELIGIBLE PAPER To be eligible for rediscount at a Federal Reserve bank, a note, bill of exchange, or trade or bank acceptance must possess the following characteristics:

1. It must arise out of a commercial, industrial, or agricultural transaction, i.e., must be issued or drawn, or the proceeds must be used, for the production, purchase, carrying, or marketing of goods (wares, merchandise, or agricultural products including livestock) in one or more steps of the process of production, manufacture, or distribution.(See COMMERCIAL PAPER.)
2. It must not have a maturity exceeding 90 days, except that agricultural paper may have a maturity of nine months.
3. It must bear the member bank's endorsement.
4. Every application for rediscount must contain a certificate of eligibility, executed by the member bank.

The aggregate of notes, drafts, and bills bearing the signature or endorsement of any one borrower, whether person, firm, company, or corporation, rediscounted for any one member bank, whether state or national, must not exceed at any time 10% of the unimpaired capital and surplus of such bank. This restriction does not apply to the discount of bills of exchange drawn in good faith against actually existing values.

The Board of Governors of the Federal Reserve System adopted an interpretation of Regulation A of the FEDERAL RESERVE BOARD REGULATIONS, which specifies the eligibility requirements for extensions of credit by Federal Reserve banks, effective May 10, 1978. It provides that a bankers acceptance secured by a field WAREHOUSE RECEIPT covering a readily marketable staple is eligible for discount by a Federal Reserve bank even though the warehouse manager is a present or former employee of the owner of the goods. This interpretation superseded one that had been adopted by the board in 1933 and took into account the changes in commercial law and business practice over the last 45 years. According to the board, field warehouse receipts are not frequently offered to Federal Reserve banks for discounting; however, by making them eligible for discount, the new interpretation removed the reserve liability that a member bank would have incurred if it sold an acceptance that was not eligible for discount.

The DEPOSITORY INSTITUTIONS DEREGULATION AND MONETARY CONTROL ACT OF 1980 extends access to Federal Reserve bank discount windows, on the same terms and conditions as for member banks, to all depository institutions that hold transaction accounts or nonpersonal time deposits.

See DISCOUNT WINDOW.

EMBEZZLEMENT The fraudulent appropriation by a public officer, or any other person occupying a fiduciary capacity, of the property entrusted to him by virtue of his employment. Embezzlement is not to be confused with larceny or burglary, which implies a wrongful taking away of property belonging to another by trespass or assault. Embezzlement is a misdemeanor or felony, depending upon the value of the property, and is a statutory crime punishable by imprisonment.

See CRIMINAL OFFENSES.

EMERGENCY BANKING RELIEF ACT An act passed March 9, 1933, which confirmed all previous proclamations of President Roosevelt and Secretary of the Treasury Woodin issued during the bank crisis that confronted the inauguration of the new Democratic administration. The act vested in the President and made applicable to peacetime emergencies the World War I powers of regulation over transactions in credit, currency, gold, and silver, including foreign exchange, fixing maximum penalties of $10,000 fine and ten years' imprisonment for violators. It empowered the secretary of the Treasury to require delivery at the Treasury of all gold and gold certificates held by anybody in the country. It author-ized the President, without invoking the war powers, to fix restrictions on the banking business of Federal Reserve members.

It also allowed the Comptroller of the Currency to appoint a conservator for any national bank when considered necessary to conserve its assets. The conservator could set aside for withdrawal by depositors on a ratable basis such amount as the Comptroller decided might be safely used. The Comptroller could allow banks under conservators to receive new deposits, which would be segregated and subject to withdrawal without restriction. National banks could be reorganized upon the approval of the Comptroller and, as the case might be, either of depositors of 75% of total deposits or holders of two-thirds of the outstanding stock, or both.

The act provided for the issuance of preferred stock by national banks, for the purchase of preferred stock of national and state banks, and for loans upon the security of such stock by the RFC when necessary to supply funds for organization or reorganization of such banks.

The act authorized issuance of Federal Reserve Bank notes redeemable in lawful money of the United States, these notes to be issued to the value of 100% of government obligations deposited as security and to the value of 90% of the notes, drafts, bills of exchange, and bankers acceptances deposited as security.

Federal Reserve banks were permitted to make bank note advances to member banks on time limit of March 3, 1935, and were to make 90-day bank note advances to any individual, partnership, or corporation on promissory notes secured by federal obligations.

See NEW DEAL.

EMERGENCY CURRENCY Before the Federal Reserve System was in operation, it was sometimes necessary to resort to the issue of emergency currency in case of a sudden need for money, e.g., a severe panic. Notes issued by national banks under the Aldrich-Vreeland Act of 1908 were of this type. The New York Clearing House banks also, through the New York Clearing House Association, were compelled in six different crises, the last being in 1907, to issue clearinghouse loan certificates. These certificates were used only among the members of the New York Clearing House, but were effective in increasing the supply of money by enabling the banks to settle interbank transactions.

See CLEARINGHOUSE LOAN CERTIFICATES.

EMERGING ISSUES TASK FORCE (EITF) A committee of the FINANCIAL ACCOUNTING STANDARDS BOARD (FASB), organized in 1984 to provide timely guidance on emerging issues in accounting. Members of the task force include representatives of the accounting profession and industry who are knowledgeable in accounting and financial reporting and who are in positions to be aware of emerging problems. The chief accountant of the SEC also participates in task force meetings. The task force identifies significant emerging accounting issues that it considers the FASB should address. The task force also develops consensus positions on implementation issues involving the application of standards. These positions are often viewed as the best available guidance on generally accepted accounting principles. If a consensus is reached within this group (if no more than two members disagree with a position), then no FASB action is required.

The task force has produced a number of guidelines regarding banking and banking-related activities. The following positions were issued between 1984 and 1988.

84-5	Acquisition, development, and construction loans of S&L.
84-9	Deposit float of banks.
84-19	Mortgage loan modifications.
84-20	GNMA dollar rolls.
84-21	Sale of a loan with partial participation retained.
84-22	Prior years EPS after an S&L conversion and pooling.
84-31	Equity certificates of deposit.
85-3	Tax benefits relating to asset dispositions following an acquisition of a financial institution.
85-7	Issuance of Federal Home Loan Mortgage Corporation stock.
85-8	Thrift intangibles amortization.
85-13	Sale of service rights on mortgages owned by others.
85-18	Earnings per share effect of equity commitment notes.
85-20	Recognition of fees for guaranteeing a loan.
85-24	Accounting for distribution fees by distributors of mutual funds that do not have a front-end sales charge.
85-26	Measurement of servicing fee under FASB 65 when loan is sold with servicing retained.
85-31	Comptroller of the Currency's rule on deferred tax debits.
85-33	Disallowance of income tax deduction for care deposit intangibles.
85-41	Accounting for S&L associations under FSLIC management consignment program.
85-42	Amortization of goodwill resulting from recording time savings deposits at fair values.
85-44	Differences between loan loss allowances for GAAP and RAP.
86-21	Acquisition of an operating property and the AICPA's third Notice to Practitioners on ADC transactions.
86-38	Implications of mortgage prepayments on servicing rights.
86-39	Gains from the sale of purchased mortgage loans.
87-5	Interrelationships between Statement 15 and the AICPA savings and loan guide to restructurings.
87-22	Prepayment to the secondary reserve of the FSLIC.
87-34	Sales of servicing rights with subservicing arrangements.

EMINENT DOMAIN The right of the government to take private property for public use upon the payment of reasonable compensation. Quasi-public corporations frequently have the power of eminent domain. For example, an electric company can obtain an easement on private land for the erection of poles; a water company can obtain an easement for the laying of pipe to carry water.

EMPHYTEUTIC LEASE
The name of a contract in the nature of a perpetual lease by which the owner of an uncultivated piece of land granted it to another, either in perpetuity or for a long time, on condition that he should improve it by building on, planting, or cultivating it, and should pay for it in annual rent, with the right to the grantee to alienate it or transmit it by descent to his heirs and under a condition that the grantor should never reenter as long as the rent shall be paid to him by the grantee or his assigns.

EMPLOYEE RETIREMENT INCOME SECURITY ACT
P.L. 93-406, signed on September 2, 1974. Enacted after some seven years of federal legislative activity on the subject, the Employee Retirement Income Security Act (ERISA) was prompted by findings (Sec. 2 of the act) of loss of benefits because of lack of adequate disclosure and information to employees supposedly covered by private pension plans; absence of provisions for vesting (guaranteed right of the covered employee to the specified vested portion of his pension regardless of continued employment for that employer); lack of portability (transfer of pension rights from one employer to another); inadequate funding of pension plans; and terminations of plans.

The U.S. Department of Labor enforces Title I of the act. The Internal Revenue Service of the U.S. Treasury Department and a nonprofit government corporation, the Pension Benefit Guaranty Corporation (PBGC) also carry out the provisions of the law. The PBGC administers the law's plan termination insurance provisions. The provisions of ERISA under the jurisdiction of the IRS and the PBGC are subject to interpretation by those agencies.

Exempt from Title I of ERISA are governmental plans (including Railroad Retirement Act plans and plans of certain international organizations), certain church plans, plans maintained solely to comply with workers' compensation, unemployment compensation or disability insurance laws, plans maintained outside the United States primarily for nonresident aliens, and excess benefit plans (plans maintained solely to provide benefits or contributions in excess of those allowable for tax-qualified plans) which are unfunded.

ERISA applies to two types of private employee benefit plans—pension plans, which provide retirement income to employees or deferral of income by employees for periods extending to or beyond the termination of employment, and employee welfare benefit plans, which provide benefits in the event of sickness, hospitalization, surgery, accident, death, disability, or unemployment. An employee welfare benefit plan may also provide vacation, apprenticeship or other training, day care, scholarship, prepaid legal services, holiday, or severance benefits. Many provisions of ERISA do not apply to employee welfare benefit plans.

The act does not require an employer to have a pension plan, but if the employer does have one, it specifies the following:

1. The employer must submit an annual financial report, both to the covered employees and to the secretary of Labor; and, upon request of a covered employee, a statement of his total and nonforfeitable benefits. Audit or civil action may be taken by the secretary of Labor if subsequent reports are still incomplete after the first has been rejected as such.
2. The employer must provide full vesting by one of three vesting plans: (1) full vesting at the end of 15 years of employment, with at least 25% at the end of 5 years of participation, 5% in each of the following 5 years, followed by 10% in each of the next 5 years; (2) full vesting at the end of 10 years of employment; or (3) vesting of at least 50% for the employee whose age and years of service total 45, with increases thereafter of 10% each year until full vesting is reached. But under the Rule of 45, an employee with 10 years of employment must be 50% vested even though his age and years of service do not total 45.
3. Upon leaving his employment, an employee paid his vested pension benefits must have the option of investing the benefits in an individual retirement account within 60 days of such payment; or, with the consent of the new employer, reinvesting his individual retirement account's assets and earnings from the previous pension plan to the new employer's pension plan.
4. Funding of pension plans by employers must cover funding of full normal costs of administration of plans on a current basis and funding of past service costs on a straight-line basis, over a period of 30 years for plans not in effect on the effective date of the act, but over a period of 40 years for single-employer plans and multi-employer plans (plans maintained by a union and by more than one employer) in effect on the act's effective date. The secretary of Labor, however, could waive the funding requirements and allow an additional 10 years for amortization of past service costs in the case of companies that would encounter financial hardship in meeting the minimum funding requirements. Failure to provide the minimum funding requirements would lead to a 5% excise tax on such employers, which would become 100% (sic) excise tax if the deficiency were not subsequently corrected.
5. Termination insurance provisions (Title IV of the act) included the establishment of the PENSION BENEFIT GUARANTY CORPORATION (PBGC) to guarantee the payment of vested benefits if a plan terminates with insufficient assets to pay its benefit liabilities. The PBGC is financed through (1) premiums collected from pension plans it insures; (2) investment return on PBGC assets, and (3) employer liability payments, which are moneys owed by employers to the PBGC with respect to plans terminated with unfunded guaranteed benefits.

Fiduciary standards. Title I of the act also provided for high fiduciary standards for any person engaged in the control, management, or disposition of a pension fund's assets.

1. No one can become a fiduciary for a pension fund for five years after conviction for a crime or five years after imprisonment, whichever is later.
2. A fiduciary is required to perform his duties pursuant to the "prudent man" rule, "with the care, skill, prudence, and diligence under the circumstances then prevailing that a prudent man acting in a like capacity and familiar with such matters would use in the conduct of an enterprise of a like character and with like aim."
3. A fiduciary is required to act only for the benefit of the participants in the pension plan and their beneficiaries.
    a. A fiduciary is prohibited from dealing with the pension fund for his own account.
    b. A fiduciary is prohibited from taking part in any transactions with parties having interests adverse to those of the pension plan members.
    c. A fiduciary is prohibited from receiving any personal consideration from parties dealing with the pension plan's funds, and from receiving "kickbacks."
    d. A fiduciary is prohibited from transferring property from the plan's funds or acquiring property for it from any part-in-interest, regardless of adequate compensation or payment.
    e. A fiduciary is prohibited from the acquisition or holding of qualified securities of the employer or real property if its value exceeds 10% of the fair market value of the pension plan's assets.
    f. A fiduciary is prohibited from the acquisition of any real property or employer's securities for the plan that are not qualified.
    g. A fiduciary is made liable for any loss to the pension plan occurring because of violation of the fiduciary standards, and, moreover, parties-in-interest who violate a prohibited transaction are made liable for up to 5% of the amount involved.
4. The fiduciaries are also required to diversify the pension fund's investments.

Jurisdiction. The act requires administrators of private pension and welfare plans to file copies of those plans with the U.S. Department of Labor; to provide plan participants with easily understandable summaries of plans; and to report annually on the financial operation of the plans and bonding of persons charged with the handling of plan funds and assets. Such persons must also meet the strict fiduciary responsibility standards administered by the LMSA. Vesting, participation, and funding standards are administered by the Internal Revenue Service.

Insurance Program: The PBGC administers two pension insurance programs: the single-employer program and the multiemployer program.

1. The single-employer insurance program protects approximately 31 million participants in over 110,000 single-employer pension plans. Under this program, a company can voluntarily terminate its plan only if it qualifies for a standard termination or a distress termination. In addition, the PBGC can seek termination of a plan when necessary to protect the interests of the plan participants, the plan, or the PBGC. The PBGC must seek plan termination when a plan cannot pay current benefits.

   In a "standard termination," the plan must have sufficient assets to pay all benefits, both vested and nonvested, promised by the plan and earned by the participants, including benefits guaranteed by the PBGC. A plan that does not have sufficient assets to pay all the benefits can only be voluntarily terminated as a "distress termination." To qualify for a distress termination, the employer must meet one of four tests for financial distress.

2. The multiemployer insurance program protects more than 8 million participants in about 2,300 plans. Multiemployer pension plans are maintained under collectively bargained agreements between employee representatives and two or more unrelated employers. If a PBGC-insured multiemployer plan becomes insolvent, it receives financial assistance from the PBGC, thus enabling the plan to pay participants their guaranteed benefits.

ERISA was amended in 1984 by the Retirement Equity Act (REA) and in 1986 by the Tax Reform Act (TRA). REA provides additional protections for spouses of participants and liberalizes ERISA rules on participation and vesting. The rules are further liberalized by TRA.

A significant cause of the difficulty for many plans had been a shrinking contribution base, caused by industry declines as the result of foreign competition, technological innovations, or other external economic factors. But the PBGC also concluded that prevailing ERISA rules, and the termination insurance program in particular, had done nothing to strengthen financially weak plans and thus had been an incentive to terminations.

ERISA, hailed as the pension reform act when enacted in 1974, has become the target of mounting concern over rising pension costs, inadequate funding of pension plans, and the act's requirements for vesting, funding, fiduciary standards, and the potential lien on employer's net worth to cover benefits paid out by the Pension Benefit Guaranty Corporation on terminated pension plans.

See EMPLOYEE STOCK OWNERSHIP, INDIVIDUAL RETIREMENT ACCOUNTS.

EMPLOYEES' RIGHTS Federal and state laws identifying employees' rights have proliferated both in number and content during recent decades. The following federal statutes are among the more significant:

Equal Pay Act of 1963: Requires that members of one sex be paid at the same rate for the same work and the same job as members of the opposite sex.

Civil Rights Act of 1964: Title VII makes it unlawful to discriminate in employment on the basis of color, religion, race, sex, or national origin. Title VII was a major building block for employees' rights.

Employment Act of 1986: Prohibits age discrimination stating that employers cannot discriminate against people over 40 years of age unless age is a necessary requirement for the job.

Occupation Safety and Health Act of 1970: Requires employers to maintain a safe work environment for employees.

Vietnam Era Veterans' Readjustment Assistance Act of 1972: Requires employers with federal contracts of $10,000 or more to take affirmative action to hire disabled and qualified veterans of the Vietnam War era.

Vocational Rehabilitation Act of 1972: Requires employers with federal contracts of $2,500 or more to take affirmative action to employ and promote qualified handicapped persons.

Employee Retirement Income Security Act of 1974: Requires that employers who provide pensions for their employees must establish and maintain their retirement programs according to minimum standards set by the federal government.

Pregnancy Discrimination Act of 1987: Protects pregnant women from discrimination (provided under Title VII of the Civil Rights Act).

Immigration Reform and Control Act of 1986: Prohibits discrimination against a job applicant on the basis of national origin or citizen status but can give preference to a U.S. citizen over an alien if both are equally qualified.

Employee Polygraph Protection Act of 1988: Prohibits employers from requiring or asking employees or prospective employees to take a polygraph test and from disciplining anyone who refuses to take such a test.

Worker Adjustment and Retraining Act of 1988: Requires employers to give workers 60 days' notification of plant closings and mass layoffs.

Fair Labor Standards Act: Prohibits employers from discriminating or discharging employees for exercising statutory employment rights. Additional protection in this area is provided by other labor legislation.

Civil Rights Act: Title VII requires injured parties in a sexual harassment complaint to file discrimination charges with the equal employment opportunity commission before bringing a suit in a court of law. Lawyers frequently combine sexual harassment claims with common law TORT charges (assault) and thereby bypass Title VII and proceed directly under state statutes.

Right-to-privacy cases have been used by claimants in situations involving drug and alcohol abuse testing, computer monitoring of employees, negligent hiring, defaming employees, and improper use of the common law doctrine of employment at will.

EMPLOYEE STOCK COMPENSATION PLAN Most corporate compensation packages are either cash or stock. Bonuses are a function of both individual performance and corporate profits. Typical bonuses are a fixed percentage of corporate profit or of profits in excess of a specified return on stockholders' equity. Stock awards are assumed to create a positive relationship between the interests of top management and the shareholders. Disadvantages of stock awards include the possibility that top management will focus on short-term profits and exhibit an improper pattern of risk behavior.

Compensation plans for executives have been classified into three major categories:

1. **Market performance plans.** In a market performance plan, the value received by the employee depends solely on the market price, or movements in the market price, of the employer's stock. In the traditional plan, the employee receives the right to purchase a specified number of a company's shares at a specified price over a specified period. In a stock appreciation rights (SAR) plan, an employee is entitled to either cash or corporate stock in an amount equal to the excess of the market value of the company's stock over a predetermined price for a stated number of shares.

2. **Enterprise performance plans.** In an enterprise performance plan, the value ultimately received by the employee depends solely on company performance. In performance unit plans, the employee is awarded performance units, each unit having a specified dollar value based upon specified performance goals during the performance period (typically three to five years). These are cash plans. Book value plans are similar to performance unit plans, but they are related to changes in the book value of a company. Phantom stock plans are awards in units of number of shares of stock. After qualifying for the receipt of the vested units, the executive receives in cash the number of units multiplied by the current market price of the stock.

3. **Combination market-enterprise performance plans.** These are plans in which the value received by the employee depends on both company performance and the market price of the company's stock. These are similar to enterprise performance plans except that the award is in stock instead of cash. Junior stock plans and stock options with performance requirements fall under this category.

Various option pricing models have been proposed for management consideration. The minimum value option pricing method is expressed in a mathematical formula. The equation states that the value of a stock option cannot be negative and must be at least equal to the difference between the market value of the underlying stock and the present value (assuming a risk-free discount rate) of the sum of the exercise price and expected dividends during the exercise period. The minimum value of the stock option increases with:

An increase in the market value of the underlying stock.
A decrease in the exercise price.
A decrease in dividends paid by the company.
An increase in the exercise period.
An increase in the risk-free rate of return.

The Black-Scholes option pricing model is more complex but similar to the minimum value model. The Black-Scholes model takes into consideration probability estimates relating to the future variation of the market price of the underlying stock. According to this model, the riskier the stock, the more valuable the option.

Formula-based plans reduce some of the uncertainty and ambiguity about how performance will be evaluated. However, mechanistic formulas can lead to dysfunctional behavior. As a general rule, a company's incentive program should control for:

1. Increases or decreases in profits caused by accounting conventions rather than operating performance.
2. Increases in profits caused by the failure to adjust for price level changes.
3. Increases in profits resulting from concentrating on short-term rather than long-term performance measures.
4. Actions that maximize divisional performance measures versus overall corporate welfare.

Employee stock options may have tax advantages for their recipients, if the plans meet certain conditions. A stock option purchase plan must be open only to employees owning less than 5% of the stock, and it must be approved by stockholders. The plan must not discriminate in favor of officers or highly compensated personnel, although the amount of optioned stock may be proportionate to salary. The plan must include all employees who have worked with the company for at least two years, except officers, highly compensated personnel, and certain part-time workers. The price of the stock must be at least 95% of its value at the time the option is granted or exercised. No more than $25,000 (valued at time of grant of stock) may accrue for purchase in any one year. The person receiving the option must be an employee of the granting corporation continuously from the grant to three months before the option is exercised. The tax advantage of the qualified stock purchase option lies in the fact that employees realize no income when they receive or exercise an option. Taxation of any gain realized upon sale of the stock varies according to the original option price and the length of time the option was held. If the option price was equal to fair market value at the time the option was granted and the stock was held at least one year after it was acquired and at least two years after the option was granted, the gain is treated as a long-term capital gain. If the option price was less than full market value when granted or exercised and the employee sells it after the required holding period, the gain is treated as ordinary income.

To qualify for special tax treatment, incentive stock options must specify the number of shares to be issued and the employees or class of employees eligible to receive options, and it must be approved by the stockholders. The option must be granted within ten years of the plan's adoption or approval (whichever is earlier), must be exercisable only within ten years of the date of grant, and must not be transferable (other than upon death of the holder). The option price must equal or exceed the stock's fair market value when the option is granted. The employee must not, immediately before the option is granted, own stock representing more than 10% of the voting power of all classes of stock. Since 1987, the per-employee limit on the value of the stock covered by options exercisable in any one year has been $100,000. Like stock purchase plan options, the grant or exercise of incentive options is not considered income for tax purposes, and net income from a sale is taxed as capital gain after the same holding period. If the stock is held for a shorter period, the gain is treated as ordinary income.

See EMPLOYEE RETIREMENT INCOME SECURITY ACT, EMPLOYEE STOCK OWNERSHIP, EMPLOYEE STOCK OWNERSHIP PLAN.

EMPLOYEE STOCK OWNERSHIP
Employee stock ownership programs may include conventional stock purchase plans, STOCK APPRECIATION RIGHTS, stock options, EMPLOYEE STOCK OWNERSHIP plans (ESOPs), and Tax Reform Act Stock Ownership Plans (TRASOPs), under provisions of the Employee Retirement Income Security Act (ERISA) of 1974.

A typical bank employees' stock purchase plan permits all eligible staff members with two years of employment with the parent company or its subsidiaries to purchase shares within a 24-month period, under agreements entered into with such staff members from time to time, at the fair market value or book value per share as of the dates of the agreements. Such stock purchase plans are compensatory in nature, are not qualified for special tax treatment (see below), but appear to be favored by companies over profit-sharing plans in recent years.

Another form of compensatory plan may provide for incentive payments for key staff members, payable at the election of the participants either in cash or in market value of shares of the company's common stock, in three approximately equal installments or on a deferred basis.

Many companies are reported to have adopted stock appreciation rights as a method of incentive compensation. These are rights granted to employees to receive cash, stock, or a combination of cash and stock equal to the excess of the market value of the company's stock as of the date of exercise of the choice, over a value established as of the date of the grant. The company rather than the holder of the right usually determines the form of payment.

Stock options of the compensatory type issued to officers and employees may be the following:

1. Qualified stock options, qualified under the Internal Revenue Code for special tax treatment. The Tax Reform Act of 1976 repealed the provisions for such qualified status, except as to such stock options outstanding under plans adopted prior to that act, which in any event would have had to be exercised prior to May 21, 1981.
2. Unqualified stock options.
3. Restricted stock granted to recipients as a type of deferred bonus, with actual distribution to be made in five years and upon the condition that the recipient remain with the company for such time.

The tax advantage of the qualified stock option lies in the fact that no federal income tax would be charged to the option holder either at the time of receipt of the stock option (price not less than market price of the stock at such time) or upon exercise of the option and obtaining the shares at the option price. Should the shares thus obtained then be held for three years after exercise of the option, any gain or loss would be treated for tax purposes as a long-term capital gain or loss. (The new lower capital gains rates provided by the Tax Reform Act of 1978 would apply.)

The unqualified stock option is granted at a specified price, either at market or below, for exercise within ten years. Upon exercise of the option and obtaining the shares, normal income tax would apply on any gain over the exercise price. Thereafter, should the shares be sold within the ten-year period and after a year of holding, the new lower capital gains rates provided by the Tax Reform Act of 1978 would apply.

An ESOP, employee stock ownership plan, may be established under the Employee Retirement Income Security Act (ERISA) of 1974, popularly known as the Pension Reform Act. An ESOP acquires its assets, which are primarily stock of the sponsoring company, by direct cash contributions from the sponsoring company (tax deductible to the company) which are then used to buy stock of the company at fair market value. In effect, therefore, an ESOP involves a private placement of shares by the company to employee members of the ESOP through the ESOP's investment of the company's contributions which are tax deductible to the company. In turn, if the fair market value of the shares provided by the company is in addition to normal current compensation of employees, the employees may regard the acquisition of the shares as a company-financed arrangement affording them an opportunity for desired ownership that otherwise they might not be able to afford.

TRASOPs, tax reform act stock ownership plans, are tax credit employee stock ownership plans linked to the 10% investment tax credit, which the 1978 Tax Act made permanent. The 1978 Tax Act also provided that an additional 1% investment tax credit, in addition to the usual 10%, could be claimed by sponsoring companies through 1983 for contributions to such plans. Another 0.5% investment tax credit could be claimed by contributing companies if such contributions were matched by employees.

For the cost, liability, and other implications of ERISA *see* EMPLOYEE RETIREMENT INCOME SECURITY ACT.

See EMPLOYEE STOCK OWNERSHIP PLAN

EMPLOYEE STOCK OWNERSHIP PLAN

Authorized under the EMPLOYMENT RETIREMENT INCOME SECURITY ACT of 1974 (ERISA), a trust (the ESOP) formed by a company on behalf of its employees to receive retirement benefit payments and hold securities (primarily of the sponsoring company) until the employees retire or separate from the company. The maximum annual contribution by the sponsoring company (tax deductible) is 25% of the payroll. ESOPs borrow funds backed by the pledge of the ESOP's holdings of the company's stock and by guarantee by the sponsoring company to continue its periodic payments to the plan.

Tax provisions relating to ESOP borrowing have been liberalized since the enactment of ERISA, as shown below:

1974	ERISA	Sanctioned leveraged ESOP; permitted employees to deduct both principal and interest payments on loans to ESOPs.
1984	Deficit Reduction Act	Banks allowed to exclude from taxable income 50% of interest received on loans to ESOPs; permitted a tax-free rollover of proceeds from sale of a large block of stock to an ESOP if proceeds are reinvested in other securities within a year; excluded dividends paid on stock held in ESOPs from corporate taxes.
1986	Tax Reform Act	Excluded 50% of gains on sales of stock to an ESOP by estates; allowed deductions of cash dividends used to repay ESOP loans; required independent appraisal of price paid by ESOP for securities; expanded to mutual funds the 50% income exclusion for financial institutions receiving interest on loans to ESOPs; expanded the 50% exclusion to loans to an employer that are made in conjunction with the employer's contribution of stock to an ESOP; reduced the maximum corporate tax rate from 46% to 34%.

All ESOPs are defined contribution pension programs. Unlike defined benefit pension programs, ESOPs do not provide guaranteed retirement income or annuities. Retirement benefits under an ESOP depend not only on an employee's compensation and length of participation in the program but also on the investment performance of the ESOP trust's securities. When an ESOP is qualified by the Internal Revenue Service, the employer's contributions to the ESOP are tax deductible, including the dividends paid on shares of stock held by the ESOP (provided they are used to repay a loan or are passed through as cash to the participants) and even contributions made in stock instead of cash (in which case, the fair market value of the stock is deductible).

ESOPs differ from other plans, such as pension, profit sharing, stock option, STOCK APPRECIATION RIGHTS, Tax Reform Act Stock Ownership Plans, and stock purchase plans. ESOPs have been exempted from the ERISA provisions that require investment in a diversified portfolio of securities. An ESOP-sponsoring corporation is less likely to extinguish or revert the assets of an ESOP as it could excess pension assets; because an ESOP is not a defined benefit plan, the adequacy of its funding is not relevant, so an ESOP is almost never overfunded or underfunded. ESOPs may or may not be leveraged, as the designers of the plan specify.

Leveraged and unleveraged ESOPs differ in two main respects. First a leveraged ESOP is funded by a loan, while an unleveraged ESOP is funded with annual company contributions of stock or of cash, which is used to purchase stock. Second, an unleveraged ESOP or stock bonus plan can invest in a wider variety of corporate securities, including nonconvertible preferred stock and nonvoting common stock, whereas a leveraged ESOP can invest only in the employer's common stock or stock convertible into common stock. A leveraged ESOP can be used to acquire a large block of stock quickly; an unleveraged ESOP accumulates the stock in smaller increments over time.

In addition, in a leveraged ESOP the portion of the employer's contribution that is used to repay the principal amount of the ESOP debt is tax deductible up to 25% of eligible payroll. Also, that portion of the company contribution that is used to pay interest is deductible without limitation, subject to certain nondiscriminatory tests. For unleveraged ESOPs, the company may deduct its contributions of cash or stock valued at up to 25% of eligible payroll per annum.

When a leveraged ESOP borrows, the debt is normally recorded as a liability on the employer's balance sheet. The offsetting entry is a contra-equity account. As the loan is amortized, the liability and contra accounts are reduced symmetrically. In calculating earnings per share, all shares of the ESOP are treated as outstanding.

Leveraged ESOPs offer unusual potential tax shields. Contributions to the leveraged ESOP are tax deductible, and principal on ESOP loans is repaid in pretax dollars. This advantage is enhanced by making stock rather than cash contributions; the issue of stock is rarely deductible under other circumstances. Half of the interest income from lending to ESOPs is excluded from taxation; this saving is sometimes shared with the borrowing ESOP.

While supplying employee benefits, ESOPs can also influence a firm's financial performance in a number of ways:

1. Changed incentives—Employees have a sense of ownership.
2. Restructure of the equity clientele—Employees can become equity holders of the firm.
3. Strengthening of management control—Stock purchased by a leveraged ESOP initially is held in a suspense account; as the debt is paid off, the shares are allocated among participants' accounts. Trustees, who are usually appointed by management, are allowed to vote unallocated shares and have been used as a takeover defense.
4. Tax shields—ESOPs may increase after-tax cash flows to shareholders by reducing the effective interest rate by substituting lower cost ESOP debt for employer debt. Further, payments to the ESOP are deductible. The Government Accounting Office has estimated (1986) that ESOP tax savings amounted to $12.1 billion to $13.3 billion from 1977 to 1983.
5. Dilution—If an ESOP acquires only previously outstanding shares of the sponsoring firm's stock from other investors, no equity dilution occurs. Only 12% of leveraged ESOPs reported purchasing newly issued or Treasury shares of stock.
6. Benefit substitution—If a newly established leveraged ESOP replaces existing benefit programs, the new debt-service payment is offset by a reduction in the old benefit expenses.
7. Financial guarantee—Banks normally require an employer (or a third party) to guarantee their ESOP's debt, which creates a contingent claim on the value of the firm.

Approximately 5,000 ESOPs had been established by 1986. These included 7 million employees and held $19 billion in assets. About 2% of all participants were covered by leveraged ESOPs, which held about 8% of all ESOP assets.

Specific benefits of leveraged ESOPs include:

1. Buyouts—59% were used to buy out the owners of a private company.
2. Divestitures—37% of leveraged ESOPs were used as divesture vehicles.
3. Rescue operations—8% were used to save a failing company.
4. Tax-free reversions of excess pension assets. Percent not available.
5. Takeover defenses. Percent not available.
6. Source of new capital—11% were used to raise new capital.

Investment banks and large commercial banks are setting up special departments for handling ESOP-related transactions.

See EMPLOYEE STOCK COMPENSATION PLAN, EMPLOYEE STOCK OWNERSHIP.

BIBLIOGRAPHY

Benefits Today.

BLASI, J. R. *Employee Ownership: Revolution or Ripoff?* Ballinger Publishing Co., Cambridge, MA, 1988.

Employee Ownership.

Employee Ownership Plans: How Eight Thousand Companies and Eight Million Employees Invest in Their Futures. Bureau of National Affairs, Inc., Washington, DC, 1987.

ESOPs in the 1980s: The Cutting Edge of Corporate Buyouts. American Management Association, New York, NY, 1988.

Journal of Compensation and Benefits. Bimonthly.

EMPLOYMENT

KALISH, G. I., ed. *The Handbook of Employee Stock-Ownership Plans.* Probus Publishing Co., Chicago, IL, 1989.

The Magic of ESOPs and LBOs: The Definitive Guide to Employee Stock Ownership Plans and Leveraged Buyouts. Longman Financial Services Institute, Inc., Chicago, IL. 1985.

EMPLOYMENT Estimates of the U.S. labor force, total employment, and unemployment are published each month by the Bureau of Labor Statistics of the Department of Labor, based on a sample survey of households conducted by the Bureau of the Census, as part of the various series on labor statistics, which include also data on hours, earnings, and wage rates. These are general-purpose statistics widely used as current economic indicators for analysis of the labor force, for detailed analysis of business conditions, and for measures of progress which can be used by public and private agencies alike in program planning. Related series are also published, such as insured employment and labor turnover. Following is the official description of the estimates of the labor force, total employment, and unemployment.

The estimates are derived from a monthly sample survey of households, which provides the basis for a comprehensive measure of the employment status of persons 16 years of age and over in the civilian noninstitutional population by a number of personal and economic characteristics. The information is collected by trained interviewers from a sample selected by scientific sampling methods. The sample currently covers approximately 59,500 households throughout the country. Beginning in 1955, the figures relate to the activity or status reported for the calendar week (Sunday through Saturday) containing the twelfth day of the month; prior to 1955, the estimates related to the week containing the eighth day of the month.

The original monthly source report, *Employment and Earnings,* provides fully defined concepts, detailed estimating procedures, and specific measures of sampling variability for each category, as well as comparisons with other similar series.

Definitions of the major categories within which the civilian noninstitutional population is classified are given below. Periodic revisions are made to these categories.

The civilian labor force comprises the total of all civilians who are either employed or unemployed, in accordance with the criteria given below. The total labor force also includes the Armed Forces (including those stationed abroad), as obtained from the Department of Defense.

Employed persons comprise those who, during the survey week, were either (1) at work—those who did any work for pay or profit, or worked without pay for 15 hours or more on a family farm or business; or (2) with a job but not at work—those who did not work but had a job or business from which they were temporarily absent because of vacation, illness, labor-management dispute, bad weather, or because they were taking time off for various other reasons (whether or not they received pay for the time off or were seeking other jobs). Each employed person is counted only once; those who hold more than one job are counted in the job at which they worked the greatest number of hours during the survey week.

Unemployed persons comprise (1) those who did not work at all during the survey week, who made specific efforts to find a job within the past four weeks, and who were available for work during the survey week; and (2) those who did not work at all, were available for work, and were waiting to be called back from layoff or were waiting to report to a new wage or salary job within 30 days.

Revised definitions for employed and unemployed persons were adopted beginning with data for 1957 and again beginning with data for 1967. Annual data for 1947-1956 were adjusted to reflect the 1957 changes. Two groups of persons (averaging from 200,000 to 300,000 per month), formerly classified as part of the employed "with a job but not at work" group, were reclassified as unemployed. Effective 1967, changes in the classification of persons as employed or unemployed were made to identify more closely the employed and unemployed as specifically defined above. Prior to 1967, the current availability test was not applied, and the time period for job seeking was ambiguous. Also, prior to 1967, persons may have been counted as unemployed if they were looking for another job while absent from their present job during the survey week because of strikes, bad weather, etc. Other changes were made in definitions, sample, and coverage; figures for persons 14 and 15 years old were now to be excluded. No adjustments to pre-1967 figures could be made for changes in definitions, but, where feasible, data back to 1947 were revised to exclude persons under 16 years of age.

The long-term unemployed group comprises those persons unemployed 15 consecutive weeks or longer. Persons on layoff are included after 15 or more full weeks since the termination of their most recent employment. If a person ceases to look for work for two weeks or more or is employed, the continuity of long-term unemployment is broken. (For unemployment by various other periods of duration, see *Employment and Earnings,* mentioned above.)

Civilians in the noninstitutional population, 16 years of age and over, who are not classified as employed or unemployed are defined as not in the labor force. The group includes those engaged in own home housework, in school, unable to work because of long-term illness, retired, too old, along with seasonal workers for whom the survey week fell in an off season (not reported as unemployed), persons who became discouraged and gave up the search for work, and the voluntarily idle. Also included are those doing only incidental unpaid family work for less than 15 hours during the survey week.

Nonagricultural employment in this series differs in levels and trends from estimates compiled from establishment payrolls. Factors such as definitions, coverage, and sources account for the differences. This series, from the direct household-interview survey, includes domestics and other private household workers, self-employed persons, and unpaid family workers who worked 15 hours or more in the survey week in family-operated enterprises. The payroll or establishment survey covers only employees on payrolls of nonagricultural establishments; persons holding more than one job during the survey week are counted once in the household survey, but multiple jobholders are counted each time (i.e., on each payroll) in the establishment survey; and persons with a job but not at work (i.e., absent because of bad weather, work stoppage, personal reasons, etc.) are included in the household survey but are excluded from the payroll survey if on leave without pay for the entire payroll period.

Other detailed statistics available monthly in *Employment and Earnings* are as follows: employment status of the noninstitutional population by age, sex, and race; civilian labor force participation rates by age, sex, and race; full- and part-time status of the civilian labor force by age, sex, and race; unemployed persons by marital status, by reasons of unemployment, by occupation of last job, by duration of unemployment, and by job search methods; unemployment rates for household heads, for full- and part-time workers, and by industry of last job; employed persons by occupation and by class of workers, such as wage and salary (with detailed data for private household workers, government, etc.), self-employed, and unpaid family workers in both agricultural and nonagricultural industries; persons with a job but not at work by reason; hours of work. Other series include job-losers on layoff; major activity of employed and unemployed persons 16-21 years of age; employed persons cross-classified by major industry and occupational group; labor force status of household heads and for black workers only.

Seasonal adjustment. Effective 1973, the census bureau's X-11 variant of the census method II seasonal adjustment program has been used to adjust the labor force data. (For pre-1967 data, the BLS seasonal factor method was used.) The X-11 method is an adaptation of the ratio-to-moving average method, with allowances for changing seasonal patterns. The procedures used by the BLS incorporate refinements for ascertaining the underlying trend and cyclical fluctuations and for handling irregular values (including sampling errors and short-term fluctuations such as unusual weather, strikes, etc.). A summary of the method, incorporating the latest changes and seasonal factors, appears each year in the February issue of the source publication, *Employment and Earnings.*

The 12 basic component series, which are used in computing the overall unemployment rate, are the four age-sex groups (male and female, 16-19 years and 20 years and over) for unemployment, nonagricultural employment, and agricultural employment. Separate factors are applied to each of these 12 components of the total civilian labor force. Aggregates that are combinations of these groups (such as civilian labor force, total employment, etc.) are derived by combining the seasonally adjusted values of the component groups. The seasonally adjusted rate of unemployment (all civilian workers), for example, is derived by dividing the seasonally adjusted figure for total unemployment (the sum of the four seasonally adjusted age-sex components) by the figure for the seasonally adjusted civilian labor force (the sum of 12 seasonally adjusted age-sex components). Other series are independently adjusted. Beginning in 1976, slight modifications of the procedures were introduced for handling teenage unemployment and a few other unemployment series of which teenagers are the exclusive or major part.

Summary. Present employment data portray the supply side of labor. Many economists, and the Joint Economic Committee, have recommended that the data be complemented by a regular monthly survey of job vacancies, so as to provide information on the demand side of the labor market. The appended table shows major statistical employment data.

Employment

		1970	1980	1985	1986	1987
Civilian labor force, 16 years and over	Mil.	82.8	106.9	115.5	117.8	119.9
Female labor force	Mil.	31.5	45.5	51.1	52.4	53.7
Employed	Mil.	78.7	99.3	107.2	109.6	112.4
Unemployed	Mil.	4.1	7.6	8.3	8.2	7.4
Unemployment rate	Pct.	4.9	7.1	7.2	7.0	6.2
White	Pct.	4.5	6.3	6.2	6.0	5.3
Black	Pct.	9.43	14.3	15.1	14.5	13.0
Labor force participation rate:						
Married men, spouse present	Pct.	86.9	81.2	79.0	78.7	78.8
Married women, spouse present	Pct.	40.8	50.1	54.2	54.6	55.8
With children under 6 years	Pct.	30.3	45.1	53.4	53.8	56.8
Weekly earnings, 1977 dollars	Dol.	187	173	170	171	169
Manufacturing	Dol.	209	212	220	222	220
Services	Dol.	151	140	146	149	149
Retail trade	Dol.	128	108	100	99	97
Index of productivity	1977	88.4	99.3	107.7	110.1	110.0
Index of real compensation per hour	= 100	90.3	96.7	98.8	101.2	101.5

BIBLIOGRAPHY

Affirmative Action News.
CPC Annual. College Placement Council, Bethlehem, MD.
———. *CPC National Directory.* College Placement Council, Bethlehem, PA. Annual.
Dictionary of Occupational Titles. U.S. Department of Labor.
Employment and Earnings. Bureau of Labor Statistics. Annual.
Equal Employment Opportunity Statistics. U.S. Office of Personnel Management. Annual.
Equal Employment Compliance Update. Callaghan & Co., Deerfield, IL. Monthly.
Federal Jobs Digest. Federal Jobs Digest, Washington, DC. Biweekly.
Law of the Workplace: Rights of Employers and Employees. Bureau of National Affairs, Inc., Washington, DC, 1988.
Occupational Outlook Handbook. U.S. Bureau of Labor Statistics. Biennial.
Spotlight on Affirmative Action Programs. U.S. Office of Personnel Management. Bimonthly.

EMPLOYMENT ACT OF 1946 This act (60 Stat; 15 U.S.C. 1023) contains in Section 2 the official statement of economic policy of the U.S.:

"The Congress declares that it is the continuing policy and responsibility of the Federal Government to use all practicable means consistent with its needs and obligations and other essential considerations of national policy, with the assistance and cooperation of industry, agriculture, labor and State and local governments, to coordinate and utilize all its plans, functions, and resources for the purpose of creating and maintaining, in a manner calculated to foster and promote free competitive enterprise and the general welfare, conditions under which they will be afforded useful employment opportunities, including self-employment, for those able, willing, and seeking to work, and to promote maximum employment, production, and purchasing power."

Like most general declarations of policy, the above statement, which came out of the legislative mill in 1946 in the face of a feared post-World War II depression, has language broad enough to satisfy both conservative and liberal viewpoints. Moreover, the language is general enough to allow for administrative variance in interpretation. For example, the phrase "maximum employment, production, and purchasing power" has led to debate and proposed amendments in recent years in connection with alleged federal passivity in the face of economic activity below full employment levels. In addition, two other objectives—reasonable rate of sustainable real (deflated) growth, and international stability—have been the concern of monetary policy and fiscal policy.

The act also provided for submission by the President to Congress of an economic report containing data on economic trends and programs for economic stability and growth; established the COUNCIL OF ECONOMIC ADVISERS; and created the Joint Committee on the Economic Report (now the JOINT ECONOMIC COMMITTEE), consisting of members of the Senate and House of Representatives, to evaluate the President's economic report and programs and to coordinate programs of Congress in the light of objectives of the act.

P.L. 95-523, approved October 27, 1978, popularly known as the HUMPHREY-HAWKINS BILL and officially entitled the Full Employment and Balanced Growth Act, added specifics to national economic policy in the indicated respects.

P.L. 96-10, approved May 10, 1979, amended the Employment Act of 1946 to establish numerical goals for the reduction of the share of the gross national product accounted for by federal outlays in 1981 through 1983, but also provided that such policies and programs shall be designed so as not to impede achievement of goals and timetables for the reduction of unemployment.

ENABLING ACT Legislation which permits communities or districts to organize into an association or district for the purpose of financing and constructing some new public improvement which does not affect any given civil subdivision. Thus districts are organized to provide funds for building schools, sewers, drainage projects, etc., and under enabling acts it is possible for such districts to issue bonds and to levy taxes for their repayment.

The term also supplies to legislation which enables a bank, corporation, association, or community to take advantage of an alternative method of achieving a certain result. Thus many states have enacted laws which permit state banks and trust companies to join the Federal Reserve System and to maintain cash reserves as required by the Federal Reserve Act instead of meeting the requirements of the state banking laws.

ENCUMBRANCE The term has two meanings: (1) a claim or lien on real or personal property, such as a mortgage, which diminishes the owner's equity in the property; (2) a reservation of part of a governmental appropriation that is recognized at the time a commitment is made. The purpose is to ensure that a period's expenditures do not exceed appropriations.

ENDORSE To place one's signature on the back of a document as evidence of its legal transfer and passing of title, such as on a check, note, stock certificate, bill of exchange, bill of lading, etc.
See ENDORSEMENT.

ENDORSED BOND This term has two meanings:

1. A bond endorsed by a person or corporation other than the maker whose direct obligation it is. Endorsed bonds usually arise out of a consolidation in which the parent corporation endorses the bonds of its subsidiary. In order to strengthen their market value, or as collateral for loans, the parent company may endorse them. A guaranty is implied in an endorsed bond, the endorser becoming liable in case of nonpayment, just as in the case of an endorser of a note. The terms of the guaranty are written upon the bonds themselves, or upon a separate document. The underlying security is not changed by the endorsement.

2. A bond with writing or signatures extraneous to the text written thereon. By a rule of the New York Stock Exchange, a coupon bond bearing an endorsement of a definite name of a person, firm, occupation, association, etc., in conjunction with

words of condition, qualification, direction, or restriction not properly pertaining thereto as a security, shall not be a delivery unless sold specifically as an endorsed bond. This rule also applies to bonds with coupons bearing such endorsements.

ENDORSEE One to whom a negotiable instrument payable or endorsed to order is negotiated by endorsement and delivery. If the instrument is payable to bearer on its face, or if it is payable to order on its face and the last endorsement is in blank, the instrument may be negotiated by delivery alone. In the endorsement "Pay to the order of A. B. See, (signed) D. E. Eff," the endorsee is A. B. See. An endorsee is a holder of the instrument and as such may have the rights of a holder in due course (Article 3, Part 3, Uniform Commercial Code).

See ENDORSE, ENDORSEMENT.

ENDORSEMENT The writing on the back of a negotiable or other instrument. The endorsement of a check, bill of exchange, or note consists of words, qualifying or not, followed by the signature of the endorser, who may be the payee, drawee, accommodation endorser, or holder, or simply the signature alone thereof. Endorsement is the means, plus delivery, by which order instruments are negotiated to another person. Negotiation consists of the transfer of title to and rights in an instrument from one person to another so that the transferee becomes the legal holder. If the instrument is payable to bearer, it is negotiable by delivery alone; if payable to order, it is negotiated by the endorsement of the holder completed by delivery.

An endorsement must be written on the instrument itself or upon a paper attached thereto, called an ALLONGE. An endorsement must be an endorsement for the full amount of the instrument, but where the instrument has been paid in part, it may be endorsed as to the remainder. There is no limit to the number of endorsements that may be made on a negotiable instrument, except where negotiability has been destroyed.

There are five kinds of endorsements recognized in the Uniform Commercial Code:

1. Endorsement in blank, also known as general endorsement. If the instrument is payable to A. B. See, the endorsement in blank is his simple signature without additional words, i.e., "A. B. See." It specifies no particular endorsee, and thereafter is payable to bearer and may be negotiated by delivery alone. It is a common form of endorsement, but has the objection that if the instrument is lost or stolen, it may be more easily negotiated by the finder or thief to a holder in due course, the latter as such then having superior rights as against the original owner. The holder may convert an endorsement in blank into a special endorsement.

   An endorsement in blank is an unqualified endorsement, and thus the endorser thereof makes all the warranties to all subsequent holders in due course specified in Section 3-417, Uniform Commercial Code.

2. Special endorsement, also known as direct endorsement and endorsement in full. This endorsement specifies the person to whom or to whose order the instrument is payable, and the endorsement of such endorsee is necessary to the further negotiation of the instrument. If an instrument is payable to A. B. See, the special endorsement is "Pay to Adam Smith, A. B. See" or "Pay to the order of Adam Smith, A. B. See." This is the most proper form of unqualified endorsement and offers the owner the greatest protection from both a legal and a practical standpoint. Without Adam Smith's endorsement, the instrument cannot be negotiated except by forgery, and forgery is a "real" defense against a subsequent holder in due course.

   A special endorsement is an unqualified endorsement, and the endorser thereof makes all the warranties to all subsequent holders in due course detailed in Section 3-417 of the Uniform Commercial Code.

3. Conditional endorsement. This is an infrequent form of endorsement in which the endorser imposes some condition upon the transferee, e.g., "Pay Adam Smith upon the satisfactory performance of his contract, (signed) A. B. See," or "Pay Adam Smith or order if I am elected to the City Council, (signed) A. B. See." Where an endorsement is conditional, a party required to pay the instrument may disregard the condition and make payment to the endorsee or his transferee, whether the condition has been fulfilled or not; but any person to whom an instrument so endorsed is negotiated will hold the same, or the proceeds thereof, subject to the rights of the person endorsing conditionally.

   The conditional endorsement is an unqualified endorsement dependent upon the condition's fulfillment, and the endorser thereof thus makes all the warranties, if the condition is fulfilled, specified in Section 3-417, Uniform Commercial Code. Qualified endorsements are of two types and constitute the endorser a mere assignor of title to the instrument:

4. Qualified endorsement "Without Recourse," or words of similar import. The qualified endorsement "Without recourse, (signed) A. B. See" does not destroy the negotiability of the instrument. The effect of this endorsement is to limit the warranties and engagement to pay; instead the "without recourse" endorser makes the limited warranties found in Section 3-417, Uniform Commercial Code.

5. Restrictive endorsement. A restrictive endorsement is a blank or special endorsement accompanied by words which either (1) prohibit the further negotiation of the instrument; or (2) constitute the endorsee the agent of the endorser; or (3) vest the title in the endorsee in trust for or to the use of some other person. The endorsement "Pay Adam Smith for collection, (signed) A. B. See" constitutes the endorsee the agent of the endorser for the specified purpose. The third type, "Pay Adam Smith in trust for John Jones, (signed) A. B. See," is rare.

A restrictive endorsement confers upon the endorsee the rights to (1) receive payment of the instrument; (2) bring any action thereon that the endorser could bring; (3) transfer his rights as such endorsee, where the form of the endorsement authorizes him to do so. All subsequent endorsees acquire only the title of the first endorsee under the restrictive endorsement.

The restrictive endorser is a qualified endorser, and makes the limited warranties found in Section 3-417, Uniform Commercial Code.

For further details and incidents of endorsements, see Article 3, Part 2 of the Uniform Commercial Code.

ENDORSEMENT IN BLANK The signature of the endorser, without additional words (Sec. 3-204, Uniform Commercial Code). For an example of endorsement in blank, and legal effect thereof, see ENDORSEMENT.

ENDORSEMENT IN FULL An endorsement specifying the person to whom or to whose order the instrument is payable, followed by the signature of the endorser; known as the special endorsement in the Uniform Commercial Code. For an example of an endorsement in full and legal effect thereof, see ENDORSEMENT.

ENDORSER One who transfers his title to an instrument to another party by endorsement.

See ENDORSE, ENDORSEMENT.

ENDOWMENT INSURANCE A form of life insurance which combines INSURANCE with compulsory saving. It differs from ordinary life insurance in that the policy matures and becomes a claim at a fixed time, say 20 or 30 years after the initial premium is paid, after which no further premiums are payable, instead of becoming payable only upon the contingency of death.

The advantage of an endowment policy is that it may be made to mature at an age when the policyholder or beneficiary has passed the income-producing period.

ENERGY The United States and the world learned lessons about energy in the 1970s and 1980s that changed the economic landscape. According to the Department of Energy, the resources of the world are scarce but available. The earth has at least a 200-year supply of coal at current consumption rates. There are between 1 and 2 trillion barrels of recoverable crude oil resources in the world, an amount equal to many decades of global consumption at the current level of about 20 billion barrels per year. There are an estimated 10,000 trillion cubic feet of recoverable natural gas, compared with current world consumption of about 50 trillion cubic feet per year. The life index of the world's crude oil reserves has stayed at about 35 years (plus or minus 5), while the natural gas reserve life index has remained about 50 years (again, plus or minus 5). The world's supply of uranium can sustain converter reactors well into

ENCYCLOPEDIA OF BANKING AND FINANCE

Yearly Supply and Disposition Summary of Total Energy
(Quadrillion Btu per Year)

	\multicolumn{11}{c}{High World Oil Price—Low Growth Case}
Total Supply and Disposition	1970	1975	1980	1985	1986	1987	1988	1989	1990	1995	2000
Production											
Crude Oil and Lease Condensate	20.4	17.7	18.2	19.0	18.7	18.4	18.1	17.5	16.7	14.5	14.6
Natural Gas Plant Liquids	2.5	2.4	2.3	2.2	2.2	2.2	2.4	2.4	2.4	2.3	2.2
Natural Gas [1]	21.7	19.6	20.1	17.1	17.0	16.9	17.7	17.5	17.6	17.4	16.3
Coal [2]	14.6	15.0	18.6	19.3	19.5	20.1	20.7	20.8	21.2	23.9	25.6
Nuclear Power	.2	1.9	2.7	4.2	4.4	4.9	5.4	5.7	6.0	6.4	6.7
Hydropower/Other [3]	2.6	3.2	3.0	3.1	3.2	3.4	3.1	3.1	3.1	3.2	3.2
Total Production	62.1	59.9	64.9	64.9	65.0	66.0	67.4	67.0	67.0	67.8	68.6
Imports											
Crude Oil [4]	2.8	8.7	11.2	6.8	8.6	8.7	7.8	8.3	9.0	10.9	11.5
Petroleum Products [5]	4.7	4.2	3.5	3.8	3.8	4.1	3.6	3.6	3.7	4.1	5.4
Natural Gas [6]	.8	.9	1.0	.9	.7	.9	.8	1.1	1.2	1.8	2.5
Other Imports [7]	.0	.1	.3	.5	.5	.5	.5	.6	.6	.7	.9
Total Imports	8.3	14.0	15.9	12.0	13.6	14.2	12.6	13.4	14.4	17.6	20.3
Exports											
Coal	1.9	1.8	2.4	2.4	2.3	2.3	2.3	2.3	2.3	2.4	2.7
Crude Oil and Petroleum Products	.5	.4	1.2	1.7	1.6	1.6	1.6	1.6	1.6	1.6	1.6
Other [8]	.1	.0	.1	NA	NA	NA	NA	NA	NA	NA	NA
Total Exports	2.5	2.2	3.6	4.1	3.9	3.9	3.9	3.9	3.9	4.0	4.3
Net Stock Withdrawals	−.9	−1.2	−.8	1.0	−.1	.0	−.1	−.1	−.2	−.2	−.2
Adjustments [9]	−.4	.1	−.4	.2	−.4	−1.1	−.1	−.1	−.2	−.1	−.1
Consumption											
Petroleum Products [10]	29.5	32.7	34.2	30.9	31.7	31.4	30.6	30.3	30.4	30.6	32.5
Natural Gas	21.8	19.9	20.4	17.9	17.1	17.4	18.2	18.2	18.3	18.7	18.2
Coal	12.3	12.7	15.4	17.5	17.4	17.8	18.4	18.5	18.9	21.5	23.0
Nuclear Power	.2	1.9	2.7	4.2	4.4	4.9	5.4	5.7	6.0	6.4	6.7
Hydroelectric Power/Other [11]	2.6	3.3	3.2	3.5	3.7	3.8	3.5	3.6	3.6	3.8	3.9
Total Consumption	66.5	70.6	76.0	73.9	74.2	75.3	76.0	76.3	77.3	81.0	84.3

NA - Not available.
[1] Net dry marketed production after removal of nonhydrocarbon gases, plus supplemental natural gas.
[2] Historical coal production includes anthracite, bituminous, and lignite. Projected coal production (1986-2000) includes bituminous and lignite, with anthracite included in bituminous.
[3] Includes hydropower, geothermal power, and wood waste.
[4] Includes imports of crude oil for the Strategic Petroleum Reserve.
[5] Includes imports of unfinished oils and natural gas plant liquids.
[6] Includes dry natural gas imports from Canada and Mexico, and liquefied natural gas imports from Algeria. In both the historical and forecast periods, natural gas imports are net imports.
[7] Includes electricity, coal, and coal coke imports.
[8] Includes electricity and coal coke exports. Gas exports are not included.
[9] Balancing item that includes stock changes, gains, losses, miscellaneous blending components, unaccounted for supply, anthracite shipped overseas to U.S. Armed Forces, and certain secondary stock withdrawals.
[10] Includes natural gas plant liquids and crude oil consumed as a fuel.
[11] Includes industrial generation of hydroelectric power, net electricity imports, and electricity produced from geothermal, wood, waste, wind, photovoltaic, solar thermal sources connected to electric utility distribution systems. Also includes net coke imports.
Note: Totals may not equal sum of components because of independent rounding.
Sources: Historical quantities are from the Energy Information Administration, *Annual Energy Review 1985*, DOE/EIA-0384(85) (Washington, DC, 1986), pp. 5-13, Tables 1, 2, 3, and 5. Historical quantities are through 1985. Projected values are outputs from the Intermediate Future Forecasting System.
Input data file: Historical = D1212861, Projected = IFFSHL.DO107871. Table printed on January 16, 1987.

Source: Energy Information Administration.

the twenty-first century, and breeder technology could turn this fuel into a virtually unlimited supply. University and private researchers have made tentative findings that could revolutionize the energy-producing capabilities of the world.

Energy security in the world depends upon emergency preparedness (i.e., the Strategic Petroleum Reserve and other means), international energy security and cooperation (a hallmark of U.S. policy since the 1970s), basic and applied research, domestic production involving the ability to explore for and develop domestic energy resources, conservation, and efficiency in energy use. The following table summarizes the yearly supply and disposition of total energy projected to the year 2000.

The United States free market economy also encourages innovation and technological change. In 1981, the president challenged the nation to look toward its future with confidence. Not long ago, many believed that the United States was running out of energy and that extreme shortages were inevitable. As a result, the government adopted policies of allocation and price controls on energy. It is widely held that with the right market signals, the right mix of federal cooperation, and the right regulatory climate, the nation can attain energy stability, security, and strength.

See ENERGY INFORMATION ADMINISTRATION.

ENCYCLOPEDIA OF BANKING AND FINANCE

ENERGY, DEPARTMENT OF The Department of Energy was established by the Department of Energy Organization Act, approved August 4, 1977 (42 U.S.C. 7131), and effective October 1, 1977, pursuant to Executive Order 12009 of September 13, 1977. The act consolidated the major federal energy functions into one cabinet level department, transferring to DOE all the responsibilities of the following: Energy Research and Development Administration; Federal Energy Administration; Federal Power Commission; and the Alaska, Bonneville, Southeastern, and Southwestern Power Administrations, formerly components of the Department of the Interior, as well as the power marketing functions of the Department of the Interior's Bureau of Reclamation. Also transferred to DOE were certain functions of the Interstate Commerce Commission and the Departments of Commerce, Housing and Urban Development, the Navy, and the Interior.

Officially, the mission of DOE is described as providing the framework for a comprehensive and balanced national energy plan through the coordination and administration of the energy functions of the federal government. The department is responsible for the research, development, and demonstration of energy technology; the marketing of federal power; energy conservation; the nuclear weapons program; regulation of energy production and use; pricing and allocation; and a central energy data collection and analysis program.

The department's organization includes the Economic Regulatory Administration, the Energy Information Administration, and the Federal Regulatory Commission. The Economic Regulatory Administration (ERA) administers the department's regulatory programs, other than those assigned to the Federal Energy Regulatory Commission. These include the oil pricing, allocation, and import programs designed to ensure price stability and equitable supplies of crude oil, petroleum products, and natural gas liquids among a wide range of domestic users. The Energy Information Administration (EIA) is responsible for the timely and accurate collection, processing, and publication of data on energy reserves, the financial status of energy-producing companies, production, demand, consumption, and other areas. The Federal Energy Regulatory Commission is an independent five-member commission within the Department of Energy which has retained many of the functions of the Federal Power Commission, such as the setting of rates and charges for the transportation and sale of natural gas, the transmission and sale of electricity, and the licensing of hydroelectric power projects. In addition, the FERC has the authority to establish rates or charges for the transportation of oil by pipeline, as well as the valuation of such pipelines, a function assigned to FERC from the Interstate Commerce Commission.

See ENERGY

ENERGY INFORMATION ADMINISTRATION (EIA) A federal administration that collects, analyzes, and evaluates information on energy, sources, reserves, production, consumption, distribution, imports, exports, and related economic and statistical information. This information is published in weekly, monthly, quarterly, annual, triennial, and one-time reports.

BIBLIOGRAPHY

ENERGY INFORMATION ADMINISTRATION, *Energy Information Directory*, Latest edition.

ENGINEER'S CERTIFICATE A statement signed by an engineer, usually with an engineering firm, certifying that he has made an examination of the physical properties of a railroad, public utility, or other business, and that they are in the condition which he thereupon describes. Usually the chief purpose of the engineer's examination and report is to determine whether the properties are adequate for present requirements; to what extent they are adequate for future requirements; and, if not, what expenditures are needed. Such engineering surveys are requisite for proper reorganization of distressed properties.

ENGINEER'S REPORT A report rendered by an engineer concerning the physical condition of a property (usually a railroad or public utility) which he has inspected with particular reference to its needs, improvements, etc., and whether it furnishes an adequate basis as security for further debt.

See ENGINEER'S CERTIFICATE.

ENGLISH BANKING SYSTEM See BANK OF ENGLAND, JOINT-STOCK BANKS.

ENGLISH MONEY TABLE English money denominations prevailing before the adoption of the new decimal currency system (see below) are shown in the appended table.

English Money Denominations Before 1971

Symbol	Name	British value
Copper coins:		
$^1/_4$d.	Farthing (withdrawn)	$^1/_4$ penny
$^1/_2$d.	Halfpenny	$^1/_2$ penny
1d.	Penny	1 penny
3d.	Threepence (rare)	3 pence
Silver coins:		
3d.	Threepence (rare in cities)	3 pence
6d.	Sixpence	6 pence
1s.	Shilling	12 pence
2s.	Florin (rare)	2 shillings
2s. 6d.	Half crown	2 $^1/_2$ shillings
5s.	Crown (rare)	5 shillings
Paper currency:		
10s.	10 shilling note	10 shillings, or $^1/_2$ pound
1£	Pound note	20 shillings
5£	5-pound note	5-pounds

As of March 1, 1966, the Chancellor of the Exchequer announced the government's decision to adopt a decimal currency system in February, 1971. The £ remained the major unit of currency but was divided into 100 minor units instead of into twenty shillings each of twelve pence. Apart from the eventual disappearance of the 10 shilling note, no changes in the denominations, specifications, or designs of bank notes were necessary under the new penny decimal system. The appended table shows the new decimal coins.

Value of New Decimal Coins

New denominations	Old equivalents
$^1/_2$ new penny	1.2d
1 new penny	2.4d
2 new pence	4.8d
5 new pence	1s.
10 new pence	2s.
50 new pence	10s.

The last of the predecimal traditional coins in circulation, the sixpence silver coin known popularly as the "tanner," ceased to be legal tender as of midnight July 1, 1980.

A 20p coin was introduced into circulation in June, 1982, and a £1 coin was introduced in April, 1983. A proclamation dated 28 July 1971 (in effect as of 30 August 1971) had also provided for the following equivalents in the new currency: crown, 25p; double florin, 20p; florin, 10p; and shilling, 5p. The former sixpence was demonetized June 30, 1980.

See FOREIGN MONEYS.

ENTITLEMENTS Payments to which state or local governmental units are entitled, pursuant to an allocation formula determined by the organization providing the monies (usually the federal government). Shared revenues are revenues that are received by one governmental unit (e.g., a state or city) and are shared with other governmental unit(s) or class of governmental units on a predetermined basis.

ENTITY An organization or a section of an organization that is apart from other organizations and individuals as a separate economic unit. For example, a corporation, partnership, proprietorship, city, state, university, and hospital are accounting entities.

ENTREPRENEUR The history of economics holds diverse opinions on the nature and role of the entrepreneur. Contemporary economic theory recognizes entrepreneurship as an independent factor of production on an equal footing with land, labor, and capital. The distinction between manager and entrepreneur is now firmly drawn. However, the ultimate place of risk and uncertainty in the theory of entrepreneurship remains ambiguous. The exact relationship between entrepreneurship and economic development is also a matter of ongoing debate.

Throughout intellectual history, the entrepreneur has worn many faces and played many roles. Twelve distinct themes have been identified in economics literature:

1. The entrepreneur is a person who assumes the risk associated with uncertainty.
2. The entrepreneur is a person who supplies financial capital.
3. The entrepreneur is an innovator.
4. The entrepreneur is a decision maker.
5. The entrepreneur is an industrial leader.
6. The entrepreneur is a manager or superintendent.
7. The entrepreneur is an organizer and coordinator of economic resources.
8. The entrepreneur is the owner of an enterprise.
9. The entrepreneur is an employer of factors of production.
10. The entrepreneur is a contractor.
11. The entrepreneur is an arbitrageur.
12. The entrepreneur is an allocator of resources among alternative uses.

The entrepreneur is a person, not a team, committee or organization. This person has a comparative advantage in decision making and often makes decisions that run counter to the conventional wisdom, either because he or she has better information or a different perception of events. An entrepreneur must have the courage to face the consequences of his or her actions, whether they produce profits or losses. Entrepreneurial actions are performed in all societies by individuals whose judgment differs from the norm. Military and political life provide as much scope for entrepreneurship as economic life, but capitalism is a peculiar set of institutions and property relations that provides the widest berth for entrepreneurship.

BIBLIOGRAPHY

The Pitfalls in Managing a Small Business. Dun and Bradstreet, New York, NY.
Entrepreneurship Theory and Practice. ELLIOTT, B. "A Business of My Own." *Accountancy*, November, 1988.
FINEGAN, J. "Britain's New Generation of Company Builders." *Inc.*, November, 1988.
"The 1990s [special report]." *Venture*, January, 1989.
PRAHALAD, C. K., and PUCIK, V. "Can Entrepreneurs Find a Home In Big Business?" *Business and Society Review*, Winter, 1989.
ZOGHLIN, G. "Departing Executives, Emerging Entrepreneurs." *Personnel Administration*, March, 1989.
Venture.

ENVIRONMENTAL PROTECTION AGENCY An independent agency established in the executive branch pursuant to Reorganization Plan 3 of 1970, effective December 2, 1970.

The Environmental Protection Agency (EPA) was created to permit coordinated and effective governmental action on behalf of the environment. EPA endeavors to abate and control pollution systematically, by integration of a variety of research, monitoring, standard setting, and enforcement activities. As a complement to its other activities, the EPA coordinates and supports research and antipollution activities by state and local governments, private and public groups, individuals, and educational institutions. The EPA also reinforces efforts among other federal agencies with respect to the impact of their operations on the environment. It is specifically charged with publishing its determinations when these hold that a proposal is unsatisfactory from the viewpoint of public health or welfare or environmental quality.

EPA programs include air and waste management programs, water and hazardous materials programs, and toxic substances programs. The air activities include development of national programs, technical policies, and regulations for air pollution control; development of national standards for air quality, emission standards for new stationary sources, and emission standards for hazardous pollutants. Related activities include study, identification, and regulation of noise sources and control methods; technical assistance to states and agencies having radiation protection programs; and national surveillance and inspection programs for measuring radiation levels in the environment.

EPA water quality activities represent a coordinated effort to restore the nation's waters. Functions of this program include development of national programs, technical policies, regulations for water pollution control and water supply; water quality standards and effluent guidelines development; technical direction, support, and evaluation of regional water activities; development of programs for technical assistance and technology transfer; provision for training in the field of water quality; analyses, guidelines, and standards for the land disposal of hazardous wastes; technical assistance in the development, management, and operation of waste management activities; and analyses on the recovery of useful energy from solid waste.

The toxic substances programs include developing national strategies for the control of toxic substances; establishing criteria for assessing chemical substances, standards for test protocols for chemicals, rules and procedures for industry reporting, and regulations for the control of substances deemed to be hazardous to man or the environment; and evaluating and assessing the impact of new chemicals and chemicals with new uses to determine the hazard and, if necessary, appropriate restrictions. It also coordinates activities of other agencies under the Toxic Substances Control Act for the assessment and control of toxic substances. Additional activities include control and regulation of pesticides and reduction in their use to ensure human safety and protection of environmental quality; establishment of tolerance levels for pesticides which occur in or on food; monitoring of pesticide residue levels in food, humans, and nontarget fish and wildlife and their environments; and investigation of pesticide accidents.

Enforcement activities are centered in the EPA's Office of the Assistant Administrator for Enforcement, which provides policy direction to enforcement activities in air, water, toxic substances, solid waste management, radiation, and noise control programs. It plans and coordinates enforcement conferences, public hearings, and other legal proceedings.

The EPA's ten regional offices throughout the U.S. represent the agency's commitment to the development of strong local programs for pollution abatement. The regional administrators are the agency's principal representatives in the regions in contacts with federal, state, interstate, and local agencies; industry; academic institutions; and other public and private groups. They are responsible for accomplishing within their regions the national program objectives established by the agency. They develop, propose, and implement an approved regional program for comprehensive and integrated environmental protection activities.

Related laws. A variety of laws form the statutory background for the EPA activities. They include these statutes:

Refuse Act of 1899. This was the first federal law prohibiting pollution, but was not enforced until 1970, when the Nixon administration had the Department of Justice require a business to have a permit before dumping waste.

Water Resources Planning Act of 1965. This law authorized national air quality and emission standards for both stationary air pollution sources and automotive vehicles, and required each state to submit plans for achieving air quality national standards or have a plan imposed if no acceptable plan was filed. The law basically created a Water Resources Council and river basin commissions.

Solid Waste Disposal Act of 1965. This act authorized a program to develop methods of solid waste disposal, including garbage, paper, and scrap metal, and in addition provided for technical assistance to state and local governments in solid waste disposal programs.

Water Quality Act of 1965. This act gave states the option of setting water quality standards or else having them imposed by the federal government after approval by the U.S. Department of the Interior.

Clean Water Restoration Act of 1966. This act authorized funds for grants to states, cities, and counties to develop improved methods of waste treatment, including water purification, sewer design, and construction of treatment plants.

Air Quality Act of 1967. This act provided for a systematic effort to deal with air pollution on a regional basis. It established coordinated action at various levels of government and segments of industry.

National Environmental Policy Act of 1970. This law required Congress to specify the environmental factors to be considered in land use planning, including zoning, population density, and community size. Developers and builders are required under the act to make and submit environmental impact studies.

Clean Air Amendment of 1970. This act provides for more stringent air quality measures than in any previous legislation. Carbon monoxide and hydrocarbon emission standards for automotive vehicles became applicable in 1975, with the aim of eliminating up to 90% of nitrogen oxides from auto exhausts. Funds amounting to $1.1 billion were provided for research.

Water Quality Improvement Act of 1970. This law strengthened water pollution laws, particularly pollution by oil, and required installation of marine sanitation devices to control sewage from vessels.

Resources Recovery Act of 1970. This law called for an expanded program to improve solid waste disposal. It transferred to the EPA the solid waste program of the Department of Health, Education, and Welfare.

Federal Water Pollution Control Act of 1972. The aim of this law was to promote areawide waste treatment management. Local communities may apply for federal funds to cover 75% to 100% of the cost of dealing with water-waste problems. Any firm that discharges waste into a waterway must apply for a permit and disclose the kind and amount of pollutants.

Recent legislative authority has been granted to the Agency in the following acts: The Comprehensive Environmental Response, Compensation, and Liability Act ("Superfund"), as amended by the Superfund Amendments and Reauthorization Act of 1986; The Resource Conservation and Recovery Act; The Federal Insecticide, Fungicide, and Rodenticide Act; The Toxic Substances Control Act; The Marine Protection, Research, and Sanctuaries Act; and the Noise Control Act. In 1990 Congress considered a major Clean Air Act to clean up air pollution in the United States.

Summary. The Council on Environmental Quality, established by the National Environmental Policy Act of 1969, consists of three members appointed by the President with the advice and consent of the Senate, one of whom is designated by the President as chairman. It is located within the executive office of the President. It administers the environmental impact statement process and provides an ongoing assessment of the nation's energy research and development from an environmental and conservation standpoint. It also assists the President in the preparation of the annual environmental quality report to the Congress. The EPA, by contrast, is headed by an administrator and is the operating agency.

The statutory and administrative basis for environmental control and regulation, therefore, appears to be complete, but in practice the possible conflict between economic and environmental concerns poses problems in prescription and compliance.

EQUAL COVERAGE A protective clause in a corporate indenture providing that in the case of subsequent issues of bonds, the subject bonds shall be entitled to the same security as that of the subsequent issues. Such a clause, in the case of debentures (unsecured obligations), will result in such debentures acquiring a secured status as the result of subsequent issuance of mortgage bonds.

See DEBENTURE BONDS.

EQUAL FULL EMPLOYMENT OPPORTUNITY COMMISSION The Equal Employment Opportunity Commission (EEOC) was created by Title VII of the Civil Rights Act of 1964 (78 Stat. 253; 42 U.S.C. 2000e) and became operational July 2, 1965. The act was amended in 1972 and again in 1978 by the Pregnancy Discrimination Act (92 Stat. 2076; 42 U.S.C. 2000e). The commission seeks to eliminate discrimination based on race, color, religion, sex, national origin, or age in hiring, promoting, firing, wages, testing, training, apprenticeship, and all other terms and conditions of employment. The commission also promotes voluntary action programs by employers, unions, and community organizations to make equal employment opportunity an actuality. EEOC has oversight responsibility for all compliance and enforcement activities relating to equal employment opportunity among federal employees and applicants, including handicap discrimination. The commis-sion operates through a 48-office field structure, which integrates legal and complaint processing functions.

EQUALIZATION FUND See EXCHANGE EQUALIZATION FUND.

EQUATION OF EXCHANGE Changes in the money market affect the level of economic activity in the output market. The relationship between money and aggregate output, or GNP, is related to the concept of velocity. The velocity of money is the number of times money is exchanged for final goods and services within a given year. In other words, velocity refers to the average number of times any given dollar changes hands in transactions for final goods and services in a year.

The equation of exchange relates money (M), velocity (V), and the total output of final goods and services in the economy (Y = GNP) as:

$$M \times V = Y$$

where M refers to M1 money. The equation states that the money supply times the number of times money is used to buy final goods and services is equal to nominal GNP.

EQUILIBRIUM A stable flow of economic activities. A market is said to be in equilibrium when there is no tendency for price or quantity to change. Diagrammatically, an equilibrium occurs where supply equals demand.

EQUIPMENT BONDS See EQUIPMENT TRUST.

EQUIPMENT TRUST A trust created to own and lease railroad equipment. On account of the large amount of fixed assets which a railroad owns and the difficulty of raising capital to purchase equipment outright, locomotives, cars, and all forms of rolling stock are often purchased by mortgaging the equipment and selling securities based upon the mortgage. The mortgage is placed in the hands of a trustee and it, rather than the rolling stock itself, becomes the security for the equipment bonds, notes, or certificates issued thereagainst. Equipment trust securities are considered good investments, provided that the amount of the certificate is not too great a proportion of the cost of the equipment, that there is some provision in the mortgage for the upkeep of the equipment, that the earning power of the equipment will be sufficient to pay off the securities, and that the maturity of the securities is well within the service life of the equipment, their ultimate security.

Under the so-called Philadelphia plan, the rolling stock is leased to the railroad with the provision that stipulated rentals be paid to the trustee for the lessor. Eventually, through a series of rental payments, the principal of the obligation is paid off, and the equipment becomes the property of the railroad.

The Philadelphia plan, under which many equipment trust obligations are currently issued, was introduced originally in Pennsylvania for the circumvention of laws existing in that state declaring conditional sale of railroad equipment illegal, it being considered personal property.

Under this plan of purchasing railroad equipment, the railroad merely leases the property from an appointed trustee, which maintains absolute title throughout the term of contract and until interest and principal of the last outstanding certificate have been extinguished, when title passes to the railroad company. The essence of the plan is that, legally construed, the relationship between the trustee and the railroad company is that of lessor and lessee. Numerous legal decisions have been rendered in Pennsylvania to the effect that where possession of personal property passes under contract of lease, the inclusion of a supplementary agreement that upon the payment of a certain sum title will become vested if transferee does not convert the lease into a conditional sale or invalidate the bailment contract.

Under the conditional sale or New York plan, the title to the equipment purchased with borrowed funds does not pass to the railroad until the last series of the obligation has been retired; that is to say, the equipment is sold by the investors in the equipment trusts to the railroad conditionally. The equipment is used by the railroad, but full legal title is vested in the trustee for the benefit of the trust certificate holders, and the road must comply with the terms of the agreement governing maintenance. In addition the equipment is definitely marked as the property of the trustee, and careful record of each car and locomotive is kept. If the railroad defaults in interest or principal payments, the trustee may take possession of the equipment and sell it to other roads which are constantly in the market, as a means of raising funds with which to retire the equipment obligations.

Differences in the conditional-sale and the Philadelphia plan do not affect greatly the matter of quality, being little more than a legal distinction. Issues in large blocks are constantly offered under both plans. So far as technical provisions of any equipment issue go, there is no intrinsic difference between bonds put out under the two plans. Most equipment trusts run from ten to fifteen years, and mature serially in amounts calculated to reduce the amount outstanding as the properties depreciate in value. Interest is payable twice annually, and sales are made over the counter on a yield basis.

Equipment trust certificates are issued by practically all U.S. railroad companies as the least expensive method of financing equipment purchases. Annual or semiannual installments simplify the matter of meeting maturities. These certificates have a ready market and are a favorite form of investments for institutions because of the good security, serial maturities, and low risk.

EQUIPMENT TRUST CERTIFICATES
See EQUIPMENT TRUST.

EQUITIES The legal and economic claims to the assets of an accounting entity. The concept of equities can be expressed in the accounting equation:

Assets = Equities

where equities include liabilities (debts payable to outsiders) and capital (claims of owners).

Bank equity (capital) consists of three major accounts: capital stock, surplus, and retained earnings (or undivided profits). The surplus account contains elements of additional paid-in capital and retained earnings. The definitions of capital for regulatory purposes differ from those under generally accepted accounting principles. Regulatory authorities have established guidelines for determining CAPITAL ADEQUACY.

EQUITY This term has three meanings:

1. In Anglo-American legal parlance, the administration of justice, not through the inflexible procedures of the law courts, but through the principles of equitable justice developed by Chancery. Thus there are Courts of Law and Courts of Equity and it is possible to bring an action and obtain specific performance or other special relief through a Court of Equity when an adequate remedy is not available in a Court of Law.
2. In accounting and finance, net ownership, i.e., the extent of the owner's right in property above all claims and liens against it expressed in money value. Thus the equity of the stockholders in a railroad corporation is represented by the value of the railroad property in excess of the claims of all creditors, including bond and note holders, secured and unsecured, and all current indebtedness.
3. In margin buying, the customer's equity is the present market value of his securities less the debit balance in his account, i.e., the sum borrowed from the broker to enable the customer to make the purchase.

EQUITY CONVERSION A reverse annuity mortgage (RAM) in which a borrower obtains a loan in the form of monthly payments over an extended period of time, using his or her property as collateral. When the loan comes due, the borrower repays both the principal and interest. A RAM cannot be arranged until the borrower has paid off the original mortgage.

A federal program, named the Home Equity Conversion Mortgage Insurance Demonstration, allows people 62 or older to receive regular payments by borrowing against the equity in their homes. The loans are repaid when the house is sold. The payments are based on life expectancy. The program is sponsored by the Department of Housing and Urban Development, the Federal National Mortgage Association, and the Federal Home Loan Mortgage Corporation. In 1989 federal mortgage agencies began creating a secondary market where lenders can sell the loans after they have been originated. Some lenders have not been overly enthusiastic about the reverse equity program because of the potential losses. The program is designed for homeowners who are "house rich and cash poor." It is estimated that about 1.7 million elderly people own a home worth at least $50,000 but have annual income below $10,000.

EQUITY EARNINGS *First read* DIRECT EARNINGS.

Also called indirect, unreported, or undisclosed earnings, that part of the surplus earnings of a subsidiary company, over and above dividend payments, not reported by the parent company. Most of the large corporations hold or control through full, majority, joint (half, third, quarter, etc.) or minority stock ownership in subsidiary or affiliated companies. Unless the ownership of such subsidiary is a majority interest, the parent company cannot under proper accounting principles consolidate the earnings of a subsidiary or subsidiaries in the income account of the parent company, but only such part of such earnings as may be actually paid to the parent organization as dividends. When earnings of subsidiaries are consolidated in the income account of the parent organization, the proportion of earnings applicable to the minority interest must be deducted.

Under Accounting Principles Board Opinion No. 18, "The Equity Method of Accounting for Investments in Common Stock," the investor company owning a block of voting stock in an investee corporation other than a subsidiary should carry the investment on its books on the equity method (cost basis or market value basis should not be used) if the percentage of ownership is a majority interest or if the percentage of ownership held is not a majority interest but is sufficient in fact to influence the operating or financial decisions of the investee corporation. Under the equity method, the investor corporation records the initial investment in the investee stock at cost, and then adjusts such carrying value, increasing or decreasing it, by the percentage of ownership applied to undistributed earnings of the investee (dividends received from the investee reduce the carrying amount of the investment).

Under the Internal Revenue Code, and subject to regulations, an affiliated group of corporations has the privilege of choosing to be taxed as a single unit by filing a consolidated return rather than separate returns. The code specifically defines an affiliated group to exist when (1) at least 80% of all classes of voting power stock and at least 80% of each class of nonvoting stock of each affiliated corporation (except the common parent corporation) is owned directly by one or more of the other affiliated corporations which may be included; and (2) the common parent corporation owns directly 80% of all classes of the voting stock and at least 80% of each class of nonvoting stock of at least one of the other corporations which may be included. (Stock does not include nonvoting preferred stock.) Consolidated returns are advantageous if some of the affiliated corporations which may be included have losses, which in consolidation will offset profits of the other affiliated corporations. But once a consolidated return is filed, the affiliated group must continue to file consolidated returns unless the IRS concurs in discontinuing such returns.

Even where the parent corporation does not report earnings on a consolidated basis, the security analyst will be interested in total earnings, including equity of the parent in undistributed earnings of subsidiaries. To illustrate the nature of equity earnings, the following example is given.

A parent company owns 800,000 shares of a subsidiary having 1,000,000 shares (its sole capitalization) outstanding. The subsidiary earns $5 million in a given year and pays $3 in dividends, or $3 million. The parent company thereby receives $2.4 million from its subsidiary which is taken up in the parent company's income account and reported accordingly. Such report, however, does not disclose full earnings, since the surplus earnings in excess of the subsidiary's dividend payment are not taken into account. Equity earnings of the parent company for the year in question are equal to its proportionate ownership in the $2 million earned but not disbursed. This proportionate interest or equity earnings is 80% of $2 million, or $1.6 million. Such equity earnings must be added to the actually reported earnings of the parent company to measure its full earning power.

See CONSOLIDATED STATEMENT, HOLDING COMPANY, PARENT COMPANY.

EQUITY FUNDING A combination of mutual fund shares and insurance. Under equity funding plans, the investor buys the mutual fund shares. The shares are then pledged as collateral for a loan whose proceeds are used to defray the cost of the premium on the insurance policy.

See INVESTMENT COMPANY.

Effective September 5, 1972, the Board of Governors of the Federal Reserve System amended its Regulation T (Credit by Brokers and

Dealers) with respect to credit for the combined acquisition of mutual fund shares and insurance. The amendment eliminated the requirement that in order to be eligible for the provisions relating to "special insurance premium funding account," which designation was changed from "special equity funding account," a creditor must be the issuer, or a subsidiary or affiliate of the issuer, of programs that combine the acquisition of mutual fund shares and insurance. Also the amendment clarified that creditors who arrange credit for the acquisition of mutual fund shares and insurance are permitted to sell mutual fund shares without insurance under the provisions of the section relating to special cash accounts.

See MARGIN, MARGIN ACCOUNT, MARGIN BUYING.

EQUITY METHOD OF ACCOUNTING A method of accounting for investments in common stock where the investor owns more than 20% of the outstanding voicing stock of another company and can exercise significant influence. When an investor corporation can exercise significant influence over the operations and financial policies of an investee corporation, generally accepted accounting principles require that the investment in the investee be reported using the equity method. Significant influence can be determined by such factors as representation on the board of directors, participation in policy-making processes, material intercompany transactions, interchange of managerial personnel, and technological dependency. It is presumed that an investor can exercise significant influence if he or she owns 20% to 25% of the outstanding common stock of the investee, unless evidence to the contrary is available.

The equity method of accounting for common stock investments reflects the economic substance rather than the legal form that underlies the investment in common stock of another company. When the equity method of accounting is used, the investor initially records the investment in the stock of an investee at cost. The investment account is then adjusted to recognize the investor's share of the income or losses of the investee after the date of acquisition when it is earned by the investee. Such amounts are included when determining the net income of the investor in the period they are reported by the investee. This procedure reflects accrual-basis accounting in that revenue is recognized when earned and losses when incurred. Dividends received from an investee reduce the carrying amount of the investment and are not reported as dividend income. As a result of applying the equity method, the investment account reflects the investor's equity in the underlying net assets of the investee. As an exception to the general rule of revenue recognition, revenue is recognized without a change in working capital.

In the investor's income statement, the proportionate share of the investee's net income is reported as a single-line item, except where the investee has extraordinary items that would be material in the investor's income statement. In such a case, the extraordinary item would be reported in the investor's income statement as extraordinary. Intercompany profits and losses are eliminated. Any excess of price paid for the shares over the underlying book value of the net assets of the subsidiary purchased must be identified (for example, purchased goodwill) and, where appropriate, amortized or depreciated.

When an investor owns more than 50% of the outstanding common stock of an investee and so can exercise control over the investee's operations, consolidated financial statements for the affiliated group are normally presented.

Investments in unconsolidated subsidiaries are reported in consolidated financial statements by the equity method. In unconsolidated financial statements of a parent company, investments in subsidiaries are reported by the equity method.

See BUSINESS COMBINATIONS, CONSOLIDATED STATEMENTS.

ERISA EMPLOYEE RETIREMENT INCOME SECURITY ACT OF 1974.

ERRATIC The condition of the stock and commodity markets when prices are uncertain, first rising, then falling, or vice versa, in succession without a definite trend.

ERROR ACCOUNT A suspense account in brokers' offices to which errors in executions involving a loss are charged and to which any possible profits are credited.

ERRORS Accounting errors result from mistakes or omissions in the financial accounting process. Typical errors include mathematical mistakes, mistakes in the application of accounting principles, oversight, or misuse of facts. A change from an accounting principle that is unacceptable to a generally acceptable accounting principle is considered a correction of an error (and not a change in accounting principle). The information required for the correction of an error was available during a prior period. The use of newly acquired information or new facts resulting in a change of estimate is not an error. For example, assume that a building was originally estimated to have a 20-year life and was being depreciated over that period. Several years later, an engineering review of the building lowered the estimate to 15 years. Subsequent charges for annual depreciation would take this new information into consideration. Depreciation already recorded in prior years would not be adjusted. This situation is considered a change in estimate and is not an accounting error. The information required to revise the accounting estimate was not available in a prior period when the financial statements were issued.

Correction of an error should be reported as a PRIOR-PERIOD ADJUSTMENT, which requires an adjustment to the beginning retained earnings on the STATEMENT OF RETAINED EARNINGS (and is not reported on the income statement). Disclosure would include the nature of the error, the effect of correcting it on the income before extraordinary items, net income, and related per-share amounts.

ESCHEAT In modern law, the common law doctrine of abandonment of personal property. It is statutorily provided for by the various states in abandoned property laws pertaining to abandonment of personal property. The Uniform Disposition of Unclaimed Property Act (National Conference of Commissioners on Uniform State Laws, Omaha, Nebraska) covers such items as the following: deposits, interest, and contents of safety, agency, or collateral boxes held by banking or financial organizations; funds held by life insurance companies payable under life, endowment, or annuity contracts; deposits and refunds held by public utility companies; corporate cash and stock dividends as well as any interest, payment on principal, profit, distribution, etc.; property of organizations in dissolution; property held by fiduciaries; property held by state courts, public officers, and agencies; and other personal property, tangible or intangible.

Statutes on escheat of bank deposits are based on the doctrine that when deposits remain inactive and lapse of the statutory period has occurred, a presumption arises that the owner has died intestate without heirs. The trend in state legislation is toward comprehensive escheat statutes, a concise example of which is Montana's statute: "Whenever the title to any property fails for want of heirs or next of kin, it reverts to the state. All property within the limits of this state, which does not belong to any person, belongs to the state."

See ABANDONMENT, UNCLAIMED BALANCES.

ESCROW A written agreement, e.g., deed, bond, or other paper, entered into among three parties and deposited for safekeeping with the third party as custodian to be delivered by the latter only upon the performance or fulfillment of some condition. The custodian or depository is obliged to follow strictly the terms of the agreement respecting the other parties.

ESCROW BOND Bond held under an option to purchase or subject to some other condition; bond of an authorized issue, but not yet issued, being held by a trustee until additional funds are needed for improvements or expansion. Such bonds can be released only upon compliance with the terms of the mortgage provisions governing the issuance of additional bonds. Thus escrow bonds are that part of an authorized issue which remains unissued with the trustee until new financing is to be accomplished.

See ESCROW.

ESTATE This term has two meanings:

1. Qualified by the word "real," one's interest in land; substantially identical with REAL PROPERTY. Interests in real property are classified as freehold estates (fee simple and life estates, both of which might be subject to condition precedent or condition subsequent and thus be rendered estates upon condition); estates upon limitation (terminable fees); and leasehold estates. The last-named are also called chattels real (interests in land or other real estate limited as to duration). Chattels personal

consist of either tangible personal property or intangible personal property (choses in action).
2. In popular parlance and for tax purposes, the total market value of all forms of property that a person owns which, after authorized deductions, will lead to the taxable estate subject to estate tax rates in the event of demise.

Real and personal property owned by a person at the time of death are referred to as an estate. Real property is land or anything permanently attached to it. Personal property is all property that is not classified as real property. An estate ceases to exist when the property has been distributed according to a will or the law.

A decedent who leaves a valid will is referred to as the testator or testatrix and is said to have died testate. A person who dies without leaving a will is said to have died intestate. A will is a written instrument, legally executed, by which a person disposes of his or her estate after death. A will is usually executed by the signature of the testator and witnesses. Probate (to prove) refers to the judicial proof of a will. Generally, the validity of a will is determined by an examination of the document and the testimony of the witnesses. Various state courts (probate, surrogate, or orphan's courts) exercise authority over the probate of wills and the administration of estates. Probate is the first step in the orderly passing of assets of a decedent in accordance with a will. If a person dies without leaving a will or without leaving a valid will, his or her estate is nevertheless probated.

When a person dies intestate, real property is distributed according to the laws of descent of the state where the property is located, and personal property is distributed according to the laws of distribution of the decedent's state of domicile. As a general rule, only a spouse or blood relative can receive an intestate distribution. Spouse or blood relative is described as an heir or as next of kin depending on the kind of property distributed. The laws of intestate succession generally favor the surviving spouse, children, and grandchildren and then move to the parents and grandparents and to brothers and sisters.

BIBLIOGRAPHY

CADY, D. F. *Field Guide to Estate Planning, Business Planning and Employee Benefits.* National Underwriters, Cincinnati, OH, 1989.
CCH Estate Planning Guide. Commerce Clearing House, Inc., Chicago, IL. Annual.
Estate Planning. Monthly.
Estate Planning Review. Commerce Clearing House, Inc., Chicago, IL. Monthly.
Estate Planning and Taxation Coordinator. Research Institute of America, Inc., New York, NY. Biweekly.
Estate Planning: Inheritance Taxes. Prentice Hall, Inc. Englewood Cliff, NJ. Looseleaf.
Estate Planning: Wills, Estate and Trusts. Prentice Hall, Inc. Englewood Cliff, NJ. Looseleaf.
Estate Tax Techniques. J. K. Lasser Institute. Matthew Bender & Co., Inc., New York, NY. Looseleaf service.
Federal Estate and Gift Tax Reports. Commerce Clearing House, Inc., Chicago, IL. Annual.
FIORE, E. D., and others. *Modern Estate Planning.* Matthew Bender & Co., Inc., New York, NY. Looseleaf service.
LEIMBERG, S., and others. *Tools and Techniques of Financial Planning.* National Underwriter, Cincinnati, OH, 1986.
How to Save Time and Taxes Preparing Fiduciary Income Tax Returns: Federal and State. Matthew Bender & Co., Inc., New York, NY. Looseleaf service.

ESTATE TAXES Excises upon the right of transfer of property from the decedent to his heirs, legatees, and devisees. Federal estate taxes were first enacted in the act of September 8, 1916, and are imposed upon the entire taxable estate, after authorized deductions, at rates which are progressive according to the size of the taxable estate.

On the other hand, inheritance taxes (succession or legacy taxes) are taxes levied upon the right to receive by beneficiaries, exemptions and rates varying according to the closeness of relationship of the beneficiaries to the decedent, and being progressive in rate structure according to the size of each beneficiary's share. In some states, death taxes are in the form of estate taxes, modeled after the federal estate taxes; while in other states the inheritance tax form prevails.

Florida in 1924 eliminated inheritance taxation, but restored it in 1930 in view of the federal estate tax credit of up to 80% of the federal tax for payment of state inheritance tax. Generally, state estate taxes apply to real property and tangible personal property having a situs in the state of domicile, as well as intangible personal property whether or not located in the state of domicile. Multiple state taxation, therefore, may occur where more than one state claims domicile and also, in the absence of reciprocal exemption provisions in the state's laws, where a state claims the right to tax intangible personalty located within its borders of a decedent domiciled in another state. This has been upheld by the U.S. Supreme Court where the state can show benefits conferred, such as the protection of its laws for a trust of intangible personalty (usually stocks and bonds) set up under its laws.

Estate Tax Formula. A WEALTH transfer tax (an excise tax on the transfer of property upon death). An estate tax return must be filed if the decedent's gross estate exceeds $600,000. Estate taxes currently vary from 18% on small estates to as much as 55% on estates exceeding $3 million. The return must be filed within nine months of decedent's death, unless an extension has been granted. A decedent's estate tax liability can be computed according to the following basic outline:

Gross estate (property owned at death, property that the decedent transfers but for which he/she retains the right to income for life)
− Deductions (expenses and losses)
= Adjusted gross estate
− Deductions (marital deduction; charitable contribution deduction)
= Taxable estate
+ Adjusted taxable gifts (most 1976 taxable gifts)
= Estate tax base
− Post-1976 gift tax
− Unified credit
− State death tax credit
− Credit for pre-1977 gift taxes
− Credit for taxes on prior transfers
− Foreign death tax credit
= Estate tax payable

The gross estate is valued at the date of death or an alternate valuation date. Gifts are valued at the date of gift. The unified credit enables a tax base of a certain size (the exemption equivalent) to be free of transfer taxes. The Tax Reform Act of 1976 combined the gift and estate taxes into a unified transfer tax rate schedule that applies to both life and death transfers. To remove relatively small gifts and estates from the imposition of tax, a unified transfer tax credit of $192,000 is allowed against gift and estate taxes. This is equivalent to exempting the first $600,000 of taxable gifts or taxable estate from the unified transfer tax. The amount of the credit varies depending upon the year of death:

Year of death	Amount of unified credit	Amount of exemption equivalent
1986	$155,800	$400,000
1987 and later	192,800	600,000

The benefit of the unified credit is phased out for tax bases in excess of $10,500,000 if the decedent dies after 1987.

The marital deduction allows for tax-free interspousal transfers other than those for gifts of certain terminable interests. The Internal Revenue Code allows a transfer tax deduction for the amount transferred.

The estate is chargeable for the income taxes due on the decedent's income earned from the beginning of the taxable year to the date of death. In addition, state income taxes must be determined for this fractional period.

Most states have state inheritance taxes based on the right to receive or inherit property. These taxes are imposed on the recipient of the property. Certain exemptions are provided in some states based on the relationship of the heir to the decedent. A large exemption is typically allowed to a surviving spouse.

See INHERITANCE LAWS.

ETHICS

ETHICS A branch of philosophy that is the systematic study of reflective choice, of the standards of right and wrong by which it is to be guided, and of the goods toward which it may ultimately be directed. (Philip Wheelwright, *A Critical Introduction to Ethics*) This definition emphasizes deliberate choice, moral principles, and the consequences of decisions. In a broad sense, ethical behavior is (1) that which produces a good instead of an evil or (2) that which conforms to moral principles.

The most basic requirement of any ethical system is rationality. Rationality implies that what is specified is in conformity with reason, is nondeceiving (honest and authentic), and is attainable. An ethical system must be based on reality at the time and under the existing circumstances, i.e., virtue over vice. The value structure expressed in the system's standards should indicate the means of achieving the results it promises, and allowances should be made for diversity (the exception rule).

The philosophical choice to be ethical requires that one be free and that one accept the responsibilities that freedom bestows. Adhering to a value system provides continuity (consistent behavior) and internal controls (self-discipline and personal responsibility). Major factors influencing ethical behavior include the law, government regulation, social pressure, industry and company ethical codes, and personal standards.

A distinction can be made between ethical, professional, and legal conduct. Ethical conduct implies voluntary behavior or internal dispositions to act for which the individual can be held responsible to a recognized standard of right and wrong. Professional conduct refers to standards of conduct that are normal, expected, or precedented in a particular profession, such as law or accounting. Professional standards prescribe the basis upon which professionals ought to conduct their activities. In addition, professional standards establish the basis by which a profession can be explained, interpreted, and judged. Professional and ethical standards can be distinguished from legal standards, which are established by the rules, laws, and conventions imposed by legislative and administrative authorities. Ethical, professional, and legal standards sometimes overlap.

BIBLIOGRAPHY

ABA/BNA Lawyer's Manual on Professional Conduct. Bureau of National Affairs, Inc., Washington, DC. Looseleaf.
BANK ADMINISTRATION INSTITUTE. *Codes of Conduct in the Financial Services Industry.* Bank Administration Institute, Rolling Meadows, IL, 1987.
CAVANAUGH, G. F. *American Business Values.* Prentice Hall, Inc., Englewood Cliffs, NJ, 1984.
Journal of Business Ethics.
Journal of Ethics.
MARX, T. G. *Business and Society: Economic, Moral, and Political Foundations.* Prentice Hall, Inc., Englewood Cliffs, NJ, 1985.
SEVERINSEN, K. "Executives Stress the Importance of Business Ethics.," *Savings Institutions.*
THOMPSON, T.W. "The Banker Ethic in a Sales Culture." *U. S. Banker*, August, 1987.
URANGA, D. "Navigating the Grey Zone: Ethics in Credit Management." *Business Credit*, June 1988.

ETHICS OF THE ACCOUNTING PROFESSION

The code of professional ethics of the American Institute of Certified Public Accountants is designed to promote higher standards of professional conduct among its members. The code provides guidelines for accounting practitioners. The code also deals with such matters as the independence required of accountants, technical standards, and relationships with clients and colleagues. For example, independence in auditing means that the auditor has an unbiased viewpoint in the performance of the audit both in fact and in appearance. Auditors are also expected to comply with the technical standards of the profession as they relate to generally accepted accounting principles and auditing standards.

A code of ethics for management accountants was prepared by the National Association of Accountants. This statement is referred to as Statement on Management Accounting No. 1C: "Standards of Ethical Conduct for Management Accountants." The statement identifies four major elements of professional conduct for management accountants: competence, confidentiality, integrity, and objectivity. The statement also describes a procedure for resolving conflicts when situations involving ethics arise.

EUROBONDS

Issues floated in European countries payable in a currency foreign to the host countries, e.g., American dollar bonds issued in European countries. By contrast, foreign bonds are offered in a particular country and are payable in the currency of that country.

The bonds are generally denominated in currencies for which there is a market in more than one country, so that the bonds can be sold in more than one national market initially or later on the secondary market. Eurobonds also may be denominated in more than one currency or in a bundle of currencies such as special drawing rights (SDRs).

In an offering of Eurobonds, an international syndicate, consisting of a managing group of four or five leading European banks and/or U.S. investment houses, selects 20 to 50 more financial institutions in various countries to assist in the underwriting. These in turn form selling groups in their own countries to assist in the distribution and placement with investors. Eurobonds are generally exempt from applicable laws and regulations of the country in which they are sold, whereas foreign bonds are subject to all such laws and regulations. All Eurobonds are bearer (unregistered) bonds. Income taxes need not be withheld from interest payments if the borrowing corporation satisfies the regulations of the country in which it is incorporated. Principally in order to avoid tax withholding requirements, many U.S. corporations and some European firms establish separate international financing subsidiaries, usually solely for the purpose of raising funds in the Eurobond market. The parent company generally guarantees bonds sold by the subsidiary.

See FLOATING CAPITAL.

BIBLIOGRAPHY

CREDIT SUISSE FIRST BOSTON EUROBOND INVESTMENT LIBRARY, Boston, MA, 1988:
The CSFB Guide to the UK Government Bond Market.
The CSFB Guide to the Guilder Bond Markets.
The CSFB Guide to Innovations, Structures & Terms of the Eurobond Markets.
The CSFB Guide to the Yen Bond Markets.
FRANK, D. "Take Out Your Tablets." *The Banker*, February, 1989.
LEE, P. "Eurobonds." *Euromoney*, September, 1988.
SCHISSEL, H. "Tell Me How It Works Again." *Euromoney*, September, 1988.
WILSON, N. "Bargain Basement." *The Banker*, January, 1989.

EUROCURRENCY

See EURODOLLARS. The Eurocurrency markets (also termed by Governor Wallich of the Board of Governors of the Federal Reserve System as "Xenocurrency" markets, the "xeno" being the Greek prefix for "foreign") are reported to deal mainly in U.S. dollars.

See Bibliography under EURODOLLARS.

EURODIF

A consortium of five nations—France, Belgium, Spain, Italy and Iran—that built the EURODIF uranium enrichment plant in the Tricastin district of south central France. Each year after 1982, it was planned to make available 10.8 million separative work units. Some 23,000 separative work units are necessary to enrich the 300 tons needed for the first charge of fuel for a 1,000-MW reactor. EURODIF went into operation in 1979.

EURODOLLARS

Dollar deposit claims upon U.S. banks, deposited (transferred) in banks located outside the U.S., including foreign branches of U.S. banks, so that the funds do not physically leave the U.S. banks. These dollar deposit claims in turn may be redeposited in other foreign banks, lent to business enterprises, invested, or retained to improve reserves or overall liquidity, reflecting the acceptability of dollars as a key reserve currency, their availability in Eurodollar form when domestic monetary policies might make money extremely difficult to obtain and/or balance of payments restraints encourage use of Eurodollars, and their competitive rates, as well as freedom from required reserves until recent years.

The Eurodollar market is principally maintained by commercial banks in London, Paris, and other European cities which are willing to accept such U.S. deposit claims as time deposits, or (since 1966) willing to accept them as time certificates of deposit in negotiable form. This market actually includes other currencies, so that it might be more properly referred to as the Eurocurrency market.

Transactions in dollars, however, constitute about three-fourths of the volume of transactions, which take place in wholesale amounts on the order of $1 million to $5 million, with maturities from call basis to one year, although it is reported that maturities of up to five years can be negotiated.

Eurodollar deposits are practically free of regulation by the host country, including U.S. regulatory agencies. For example, they are not subject to reserve requirements and FDIC fees. Regulation D requires that net domestic borrowings from the Eurodollar market be subject to a 3% domestic reserve requirement.

Negotiable Eurodollar CDs were designed by Citibank in London in 1966. They are usually sold in denominations larger than $250,000, although some are sold to smaller investors in certificates of $10,000 or more. Eurodollar CDs are not subject to a 3% reserve requirement and an FDIC fee of about 8 basic points, as are domestic CDs. Eurodollar CDs trade in secondary markets. Default risk and marketability depend on the issuing bank, so the market is usually limited to the largest banks with strong international reputations.

Floating-rate Eurodollar CDs have been introduced in the financial markets. Such CDs can have maturities extending beyond one year. Floating-rate notes have maturities ranging up to approximately 20 years. Floating-rate CDs and notes are priced at a spread off the London interbank offering rate (LIBOR).

Markets also have developed for loans and deposits denominated in other currencies, such as the West German mark, Swiss franc, and Japanese yen, but maintained outside these countries. These markets are referred to collectively as the Eurocurrency market.

Interest rates on Eurodollar deposits are usually higher than the rates paid on deposits in the United States, while Eurodollar market lending rates tend to be somewhat lower. Because Eurobanks operate with lower spreads than banks in the United States, they are able to compete effectively with domestic U.S. banks for loans and deposits. Their lower spread is possible because they do not have the additional costs associated with statutory reserve requirements, deposit insurance fees, and other regulatory constraints imposed on banks in the United States.

The Eurodollar market has grown rapidly since the 1950s, due in part to the U.S. banking regulations (particularly Regulation Q) that have prevented U.S. banks from paying competitive interest rates on savings accounts and have raised the costs of lending. Persistent deficits in the U.S. balance of payments increased the dollar holdings of foreigners, as did the steep rise in petroleum prices that created enormous wealth in the petroleum-exporting countries. These factors, combined with the relative freedom allowed foreign currency banking in many countries, spurred the rapid growth of the market.

Eurodollars are in essence international money, and as such they increase the efficiency of international trade and finance. As money, they provide an internationally accepted store of value, standard of value, and medium of exchange. Because Eurodollars eliminate the costs and risks associated with converting from one currency to another, they allow savers to scan the world more easily for the highest returns and borrowers to search out the lowest cost of funds. They are a worldwide link among various regional capital markets, helping to create a global market for capital. (Eurodollars held by petroleum-exporting countries are sometimes referred to as petrodollars.)

Regulation. Since the origins of the Eurodollar market in the 1950s, the Board of Governors of the Federal Reserve System has shown an active interest in regulating Eurodollar liabilities, borrowings, and loans of U.S. banks. Measures adopted have included the following:

1. Effective October 16, 1969, member banks were required by Regulation M (then pertaining to foreign activities of national banks) to maintain reserves of 10% against balances above a specific base due from domestic offices to their foreign branches. The rate was raised to 20% effective January 7, 1971. Regulation D (Reserves of Member Banks) imposed a similar reserve requirement on borrowings above a specified base from foreign banks by domestic offices of member banks.
Indicative of the Fed's views of the role and impact on monetary policy of Eurodollar activity, as well as its effects upon the U.S. balance of payments, the Fed explained that the raise from 10% to 20% was intended to give banks an added inducement to preserve their reserve-free bases, instead of allowing their bases to be lowered automatically by repaying their Eurodollar borrowings. "A matter of increasing concern was the deleterious effect on the U.S. balance of payments of the repayment by U.S. banks of their Eurodollar borrowings. Such repayments had already assumed heavy proportions, and pressure toward acceleration of that movement seemed certain to intensify if U.S. short-term rates declined further and domestic demands for credit continued to moderate."

2. Effective April 1, 1971, Regulation M was further amended to provide a means by which a member bank could retain its reserve-free base with respect to its Eurodollar borrowings from its foreign branches, by counting within its base the amount of purchases by its foreign branches of a U.S. Treasury offering of certificates of indebtedness to overseas branches of U.S. banks designed to provide an investment outlet in the United States for Eurodollars acquired by the overseas branches. On January 15, 1971, the Board of Governors had made a similar amendment to Regulation M regarding Export-Import Bank securities offered to foreign branches of U.S. banks as part of the effort to strengthen the inducement for such banks to retain their Eurodollar liabilities.

3. By early 1973 the situation had changed to such an extent that the Board of Governors issued an interpretation of Regulation K (Corporations Engaged in Foreign Banking and Financing Under the Federal Reserve Act) and Regulation M, in the form of a statement of policy, whose purpose was "to give guidance to member banks having foreign operations":

(1) The Board of Governors of the Federal Reserve System, as a central bank, is properly concerned with the preservation and promotion of a sound banking system in the United States. The Board of Governors and other Federal banking supervisory authorities have been given specific statutory responsibilities to assure that banking institutions are operated in a safe and prudent manner affording protection to depositors and providing adequate and efficient banking services to the public on a continuing basis. These responsibilities and concerns are shared by central banks and bank supervisors the world over.

(2) Under Sections 25 and 25(a) of the Federal Reserve Act, the Board has particular responsibilities to supervise the international operations of member banks in the public interest. In carrying out these responsibilities, the Board has sought to assure that the international operations of member banks would not only foster the foreign commerce of the United States but that they would also be conducted so as not to encroach on the maintenance of a sound and effective banking structure in the United States. In keeping with the latter consideration, the Board believes it incumbent upon member banks to supervise and administer their foreign branches and subsidiaries in such a manner as to assure that their operations are conducted at all times in accordance with high standards of banking and financial prudence.

(3) Proper administration and supervision of foreign branches and subsidiaries require the use of effective systems of records, controls, and reports that will keep the bank's management informed of the activities and condition of its branches and subsidiaries. At a minimum, such systems should provide the following:

(a) *Risk assets.* To permit assessment of exposure to loss, information furnished or available to head office should be sufficient to permit periodic and systematic appraisals of the quality of loans and other extensions of credit. Coverage should extend to a substantial proportion of the risk assets in the branch or subsidiary, and include the status of all large credit lines and of credits to customers also borrowing from other offices of the bank. Information on credit extensions should include (i) a recent financial statement of the borrower and current information on his financial condition; (ii) credit terms, conditions, and collateral; (iii) data on any guarantors; (iv) payment history; and (v) status of corrective measures employed.

(b) *Liquidity.* To enable assessment of local management's ability to meet its obligations from available resources, reports should identify the general sources and character of the deposits, borrowings, and so forth, employed in the branch or subsidiary with special reference to their terms and volatility. Information should be available on sources of liquidity—cash, balances with

banks, marketable securities, and repayment flows—such as well reveal their accessibility in time and any risk elements involved.
- (c) *Contingencies.* Data on the volume and nature of contingent items such as loan commitments and guaranties or their equivalents that permit analysis of potential risk exposure and liquidity requirements.
- (d) *Controls.* Reports on the internal and external audits of the branch or subsidiary in sufficient detail to permit determination of conformance to auditing guidelines. Such reports should cover (i) verification and identification of entries on financial statements; (ii) income and expense accounts, including descriptions of significant charge-offs and recoveries; (iii) operation of dual-control procedures and other internal controls; (iv) conformance to head-office guidelines on loans, deposits, foreign exchange activities, proper accounting procedures, and discretionary authority of local management; (v) compliance with local laws and regulations; and (vi) compliance with applicable U.S. laws and regulations.

4. By early 1975, the situation had eased, and effective May 22, 1975, the Board of Governors amended its Regulations M and D to reduce from 8% to 4% the reserve requirement on member banks' Eurodollar borrowings and on loans made by member banks' foreign branches to U.S. residents.

5. Effective November 2, 1977, further amendment to Regulation M reduced from 4% to 1% the reserve requirement applicable to funds loaned by foreign branches of U.S. member banks to U.S. borrowers. No change was made in the 4% reserve requirement on borrowings by member banks from their overseas branches or from foreign banks.

6. Amendments of Regulations D and M, effective August 25, 1978, eliminated the 4% reserve requirement that had been imposed on borrowings—primarily Eurodollars—of member banks from their foreign branches or from other foreign banks and on assets held by foreign branches that were acquired from their domestic offices. The board also removed the 1% reserve requirement on loans of foreign branches to U.S. borrowers. These changes were expected to encourage member banks to borrow in the Eurodollar market. The board explained that it took these actions in conjunction with other measures to combat domestic inflation and to counter the disorder that existed in foreign exchange markets.

7. Subsequently, effective November 1, 1978, the board amended Regulation D by establishing a supplemental reserve requirement of 2% on all time deposits of $100,000 or more and on certain other liabilities of member banks, effective with outstanding deposits beginning November 2, 1978, for reserves to be maintained beginning November 16, 1978. This increase in reserve requirements was one of several measures taken jointly by the Federal Reserve and the Treasury Department to improve the position of the dollar on foreign exchange markets and to reduce inflationary pressures. The action was taken to help moderate the expansion of bank credit and to increase the incentive for member banks to borrow abroad, thereby improving the demand for dollar-denominated assets.

8. On February 14, 1979, the board approved technical amendments that removed the provisions governing reserve requirements on foreign deposits from Regulation M and consolidated them within Regulation D. Effective June 8, 1979, the board also approved substantive revisions of the regulations governing the international operations of member banks, Edge Act and agreement corporations, and bank holding companies, and combined them in a new comprehensive Regulation K, International Banking Operations.

9. Effective with the reserve maintenance period beginning October 25, 1979, a marginal reserve requirement of 8% was added to managed liabilities in excess of a base amount, and with the maintenance period beginning April 3, 1980, the requirement was increased to 10%. (Managed liabilities were defined as large time deposits, Eurodollar borrowings, repurchase agreements against U.S. government and federal agency securities, federal funds borrowings from nonmember institutions, and certain other obligations.) In general, the base for the marginal reserve requirement was originally $100 million, or the average amount of the managed liabilities held by a member bank, Edge Act corporation, or family of U.S. branches of a foreign bank for the two statement weeks ending September 26, 1979.

For the computation period beginning March 20, 1980, the base was lowered by (a) 7% or (b) the decrease in an institution's U.S. office gross loans to foreigners and gross balances due from foreign offices of other institutions between the base period (September 13-26, 1979) and the week ending March 12, 1980, whichever was greater. In addition, the base would be reduced further after March 19, 1980, to the extent that such foreign loans and balances continue to decline, the minimum base remaining at $100 million.

10. However, with the domestic economy slipping into recession, the board of governors on May 22, 1980, announced a reduction from 10% to 5% in the reserve requirement imposed on the managed liabilities of member banks and agencies, branches of foreign banks, and large nonmember institutions and also raised by 7.5% the base upon which the reserve requirement was calculated.

This easing of restraints was followed on July 3, 1980, by announcement of elimination by the Fed of the remaining 5% marginal reserve requirement on managed liabilities of the large banks and agencies and branches of foreign banks, beginning July 10, 1980, for reserves required beginning July 24, 1980. In addition, the board eliminated effective the same date the 2% supplementary reserve requirement applicable to member banks on large time deposits, which had been imposed in November, 1978.

Summary. Review of the actions taken by the board of governors with respect to Eurodollar liabilities, borrowings, and loans of U.S. banks and related activities indicates the continued likelihood of frequent changes in regulations imposing restrictions or easing them in accordance with domestic considerations of monetary policy, besides the international aspects of impact upon the balance of payments and position of the dollar in the foreign exchange markets relative to that of other currencies and flows of international funds including "recycling" of oil funds.

BIBLIOGRAPHY

BANK FOR INTERNATIONAL SETTLEMENTS. *Recent Innovations in International Banking.* Bank for International Settlements, Washington, DC, April, 1986.

BOARD OF GOVERNORS OF THE FEDERAL RESERVE SYSTEM. *Federal Reserve Bulletin,* February, 1980.

———. "Money Stock Measures and Liquid Assets." September 11, 1986.

DUFEY, G., and GIDDY, I. H. "Eurocurrency Deposit Risk." *Journal of Banking and Finance,* December, 1984.

SALOMON BROTHERS. *An Analytical Record of Yields and Yield Spreads.* Salomon Brothers, New York, NY, 1986.

STOAKES, C. "Eurodollar Deposits on Trial." *Euromoney,* August, 1985.

EUROPEAN ATOMIC ENERGY COMMUNITY An association of six European nations—Belgium, France, West Germany, Italy, Luxembourg, and the Netherlands—engaged in a joint program to promote the construction of U.S. nuclear power plants in Western Europe, aided by U.S. financing, for peaceful purposes. Research and development were also aided by U.S.

The European Atomic Energy Community (EURATOM) was formed in 1958. Because of the later emphasis on purely national programs in these areas by particular countries, this agency has suffered from sharply reduced budgetary provision for activities.

EUROPEAN COAL AND STEEL COMMUNITY An economic union of European nations' steel and coal. The idea is credited to Jean Monnet, although the proposed pooling was advanced by Robert Schuman, French Foreign Minister, in May 1950, and it became known as the Schuman Plan. Six nations^France, West Germany, Italy, Belgium, Luxembourg, and the Netherlands^ratified the treaty June 16, 1952. The High Authority and Court of Justice of the community assumed their functions August 10, 1952. The High Authority set up a single market for coal, iron ore, and scrap iron on February 10, 1953, among the six members of the community, and a single market for steel on April 1, 1953.

Success of the ECSC led in 1955 to proposals for expansion of the concept to include the total economies of the member nations, which was achieved in 1957 with the signing of the Treaty of Rome establishing the Common Market.

Protectionism trend. The worldwide recession in 1979-1980 and its impact on the world steel industry led to more formal surveillance by the Organization for Economic Cooperation and Development (OECD) through its steel committee, which was established to examine a broad range of government policies on steel. The European Community (EC) initiated a program to regulate prices of domestic and foreign steel. In France, in October, 1978, details of a rescue plan for the ailing steel sector indicated measures far beyond the 1977 measures to shore up the industry. The new plan, which was approved by the National Assembly, had three main goals: (1) to provide the steel companies with new industrial structures; (2) to consolidate and sustain productivity gains in order to make the companies competitive on international markets; and (3) to protect the economic and social equilibrium of the regions directly affected. The state and the state banks would henceforth hold a majority of the capital of the steel companies, so that these companies would come into the public sector without being nationalized. The new boards will actually be running the companies rather than government officials or ministers, and such executives will be acting and setting prices as "they see fit and contending with the risks of the market."

In the U.S., the U.S. Steel Corporation (see STEEL) on March 23, 1980, filed antidumping complaints against steelmakers in seven European countries, alleging injury by the unfair sale of imported steel in the U.S. at prices lower than the foreign steelmakers charge in their home countries. The complaints were directed against steelmakers in France, Belgium, Luxembourg, Italy, Britain, the Netherlands, and West Germany. It was calculated that higher Japanese production costs were offset by currency fluctuations.

See EUROPEAN ECONOMIC COMMUNITY.

EUROPEAN CURRENCY UNIT A "basket" of specified amounts of each European Community currency. Its value is determined by using the current market rate of each member currency. In addition to its functions within the EUROPEAN MONETARY SYSTEM, it is becoming increasingly popular as a private instrument, especially as ECU-denominated traveler's checks, bank deposits, and loans. Businesses are beginning to use the ECU as a currency for invoicing and payment. Significant amounts of ECU-denominated bonds have been placed on international markets. The community in 1984 made the first public offering of such bonds in the United States.

BIBLIOGRAPHY

Currencies of the World. Deusche Bundesbank. Frankfurt, West Germany. Quarterly.
Euromoney. Euromoney Publications, Ltd. London, England. Monthly.
NELSON, J. "New Euromarket Products: RUFs, NIFs, and Eurocommercial Paper," *Commercial Lending Review*, Summer, 1986.
STOAKS, C., and FREEMAN, A., eds. *Managing Global Portfolios*, Euromoney Publications, London, 1989.
SARVER, E. *The Eurocurrency Market Handbook.* New York Institute of Finance, New York, NY, 1987.

EUROPEAN ECONOMIC COMMUNITY Common Market, a single trading unit; as provided for in the Treaty of Rome (March 25, 1957), an economic union setting up a common market among Belgium, Luxembourg, France, West Germany, Italy, and the Netherlands. These original six members of the European Community (EC) had formed the European Coal and Steel Community (ECSC) in 1952, and in 1958 they formed the European Atomic Energy Community (EURATOM). The six nations were joined in 1953 by Denmark, Ireland, and the United Kingdom, which previously had been members of the European Free Trade Association (EFTA). Greece joined as of January 1, 1981 and Spain and Portugal later joined.

On May 9, 1950, Robert Schuman, foreign minister of France, put forward a plan for lifting Europe out of the rubble of World War II. He proposed to pool European coal and steel industries as a first step toward a centuries-old ideal that in the past had been achieved only by force—a united Europe. Plans are now underway to provide for free trade across nations and industrial cooperation by December 31, 1992.

In 1967, the ECSC, EEC, and EURATOM merged their separate executive organs when a single commission and a single council were added to the Parliament and the Court of Justice as EC institutions. The commission, the EC's executive body—headed by 13 commissioners with a staff headquartered in Brussels—administers the EC's operations. The Council of Ministers, composed of 12 ministers from each member nation, is the EC's main decision-making body. The European Parliament, which meets in Luxembourg and Strasbourg, France, has limited budgetary and control powers. Also located in Luxembourg, the Court of Justice, with one judge from each member nation, ensures that policy and implementation conform with community law.

The European Monetary System (EMS) began in March, 1979, with eight members. It is designed to be compatible with the INTERNATIONAL MONETARY FUND and to reduce the short-term fluctuations in the exchange rates of the European currencies. Its European currency unit (ECU), which is based on the values of the member nations' currencies, is used in international currency settlements among the members and incorporates a compulsory intervention mechanism.

The Parliament's first direct elections were held on June 7 and 10, 1979. The 410 parliamentarians, some of them prominent politicians, were expected to push for a greater voice in EC policymaking.

A common agricultural policy (CAP), introduced in 1962, was established to ensure security for food supplies at stable and reasonable prices and to make farming more efficient. It has led to surpluses in certain products and domestic prices well above world market levels. The EC's subsidized agricultural exports have caused frequent U.S. concern.

The EC has framework agreements with many developing nations. In 1975, the EC and more than 50 former colonies in Africa, the Caribbean, and the Pacific entered into the Lome Agreement, providing for duty-free entry into the EC of many products and for other financial and technical assistance. Negotiations for a Lome II Agreement were completed in June, 1979.

The EUROPEAN INVESTMENT BANK, an EC institution, provides loans for public and private investment projects that help the community's poorer regions modernize industry or introduce new technology, support the community's energy policy, improve communications, and protect the environment. The bank is based in Luxembourg.

The EC is striving to further the social dimension of the common market. It has developed policies to improve the living and working conditions of immigrants, the handicapped, and the unemployed. Member states have agreed to try to reduce the differences existing between the various regions. The European Regional Development Fund was created in 1975 to boost investment and create jobs in poorly developed regions. The EC's environmental policy has produced action plans to protect Europe's natural resources. The EC has also developed policies in the areas of health and safety, consumer protection, and culture and sports.

The community has developed a common energy policy whose objectives include breaking the link between economic growth and energy demand, and continued reduction of oil consumption. The community encourages greater use of renewable forms of energy (solar, wind, geothermal, hydroelectric) and provides funds to support their development. The community also provides for a common transport policy, especially regarding road freight, railway and inland waterways, and motor vehicle safety standards. The community's competitive policy is designed to prevent member states from distorting competition by giving favored treatment to certain businesses, and to prevent firms from carving up markets by erecting new barriers to trade. An EC treaty contains provisions on antitrust and state aids; another treaty sets special rules for the coal and steel industries. Community rules prohibit agreements to restrict competition and all forms of abuse of a dominant position on the market—for example, fixing prices or limiting production, markets, or technical development. Treaties also ban or place under the community's supervision national subsidies (state aids) to individual firms or industrial sectors to prevent them from gaining unfair advantage. The community has institutionalized industrial policies by adopting measures to help traditional industries—steel, textiles, and shipbuilding—restructure in the face of increased competition and shrinking demand. It has endeavored to create a dynamic business environment by removing national barriers to the free flow of goods and services and by revitalizing Europe's scientific and technological base.

The community's objective is unity by mutual consent on the basis of a freely accepted body of law. Progress has been slow and laborious. Governments find it difficult to give up their powers, prerogatives, and traditions.

The Community of Twelve has a population of 321 million, about 80 million larger than the United States and 50 million larger than the Soviet Union. It accounts for 22% of world trade. In 1987, the community had more than 60 multilateral agreements and more than 250 bilateral agreements.

Crisis in the common agricultural policy and in the budget threatened to rock the community in 1986. These problems were partially resolved in subsequent years. The European Economic Community holds considerable promise and many problems for the future as it moves along the road towards unity.

The EC commission played a major role in the Tokyo round of multilateral trade negotiations.

The U.S. consistently has supported the goal of European integration. EC representatives and U.S. officials hold formal high-level meetings in Brussels and Washington on such subjects as energy, trade, economic policy, and relations with the developing world. While the U.S. mission to the EC in Brussels and the EC delegation in Washington handle daily business, officials from both sides frequently cross the Atlantic to discuss specific issues. Delegations from the U.S. Congress and from the European Parliament also meet twice a year.

BIBLIOGRAPHY

Barrett, M. "One For All?" *Euromoney*, September, 1988.
Boreman, G. F. "Dropping the Barriers." *Canadian Banker*, November/December, 1988.
Journal of Common Market Studies.
Kay, J. "The Single Market—Myths and Realities." *Accountancy*, November, 1988.
Metzger, A. "Charting a Steady Course." *Transportation and Distribution*, February, 1989.
"1992: Towards a Single Market." *Euromoney*. September, 1988.
Phillips, B. J. "1992: Gearing Up For The New Europe." *Institutional Investor*, July, 1988.
Ramm, U. "The Next Step on the Road To a United Europe [monetary union]." *Euromoney*, September, 1988.
"States Divided Over Tax Plans." *Accountancy*, April, 1989.
Swann, D. *Economics of the Common Market*, 1985.
Rosenbaum, A. "Fortress—Or Facade?" *Industry Week*, February, 1989.

EUROPEAN FREE TRADE ASSOCIATION The agreement forming the European Free Trade Association (EFTA), consisting of Austria, Denmark, Norway, Portugal, Sweden, Switzerland, and the United Kingdom (the "Outer Seven"), was concluded November 20, 1959. Finland joined soon thereafter. European dependencies of these countries, as well as their colonies outside Europe, were eligible for membership. In principle, the agreement provided that any self-governing state could apply to join. The Faroes joined in December, 1968, and Iceland became a member in March, 1970.

The preamble to the agreement emphasized that the EFTA was being established to bring nearer a multilateral association of all the countries of the Organization for European Economic Cooperation (OEEC), including the six members of the European Economic Community (Common Market), according to the rules laid down by the General Agreement on Tariffs and Trade (GATT). Formation of the EFTA, however, was interpreted as a defensive measure vis à vis the Common Market.

The EFTA in its agreement states four main aims: (1) to maintain full employment in the member states; (2) to ensure fair competition between the members; (3) to avoid disparity in the conditions of supply of domestic raw materials between members; and (4) to develop world commerce by reducing trade barriers. However, there was no express intent to establish a customs union or common market.

Continuance of the EFTA was shaken by the United Kingdom's imposition of import restrictions in late 1968, and by her renewed application for membership in the European Common Market in mid-1970. As of January 1, 1973, the United Kingdom and Denmark, along with Ireland, joined the European Common Market.

EUROPEAN FUND See european monetary agreement.

EUROPEAN INVESTMENT BANK Created under Article 130 of the Rome Treaty as one of the institutions of the European Economic Community (Common Market). The bank was set up to take part in financing the development of the less advanced regions of the community and of new industries or projects of common interest to member countries and associated states.

The European Investment Bank (EIB) is an autonomous public institution separate from the european coal and steel community, the european economic community, and the european atomic energy community, with its own governing bodies, sources of revenues, and financial operations. It is solely responsible for its own indebtedness. The EIB is governed by the provisions of the Treaty of Rome and the Statute of the EIB, as amended, which is annexed as a protocol to the Treaty of Rome. The members of the EIB are the nine member states of the EEC, which together have subscribed to the EIB's entire capital. The member states were the following as of 1986:

Belgium
Denmark
Germany
The Hellenic Republic
Spain
France
Ireland
Italy
Luxembourg
Netherland
Portugal
United Kingdom and Northern Ireland

The capital of the bank is twenty-eight thousand eight hundred million ECU, subscribed by the member states. The unit of account is defined as the ECU used by the European Communities. The board of governors consist of ministers designated by the member states. The board of directors, consisting of 22 directors and 12 alternates appointed by the board of governors for five years, has sole power to take decisions in respect of granting loans and guarantees and raising loans; it fixes the interest rates on loans granted and the commission on guarantees. The bank operates on a non-profit-making basis, grants loans, and gives guarantees that facilitate the financing of projects in all sectors of the economy.

Article 22 of the bank's statute enables the bank to grant loans or guarantees only where, (1) in the case of projects carried out by undertakings in the production sector, interest and amortization payments are covered out of operating profits or, in other cases, either by a commitment entered into by the state in which the project is carried out, or by some other means; and (2) where the execution of the project contributes to economic productivity and the attainment of the common market. The bank may neither acquire an interest in any undertaking nor assume any responsibility in its management unless this is reburied to safeguard the rights of the bank in ensuring recovery of funds lent. Applications for loans or guarantees may be made to the bank either through the commission or through the member state in whose territory the project will be carried out.

The bank may borrow on the international capital markets the funds necessary for the performance of its tasks. A reserve fund of up to 10% of the subscribed capital is built up progressively.

EUROPEAN MONETARY AGREEMENT Successor to the european payments union, effective December 27, 1958. This agreement was prepared in 1955, within the framework of the Organization for European Economic Cooperation (OEEC), as an instrument for monetary cooperation to be set up when countries representing more than 50% of the EPU quotas had declared their intention to introduce nonresident convertibility for their currencies.

The agreement provided for the establishment of a multilateral system for settlements and a European fund. The principal role of the multilateral system of settlements was to give each member country's central bank the assurance of obtaining settlement in dollars, at an exchange rate known in advance, of any balance in another member's currency acquired by it. This exchange guaranteed results from the undertaking by each member country to keep the fluctuations of its currency within moderate and stable margins, and for this purpose to declare buying and selling rates designated as limits to the market quotations for its currency. Each country undertook under the agreement, if it should change its rates, to settle any outstanding official balance in its currency at the previous lower limit, except in the case of a continental member's sterling balances and United Kingdom's holdings of continental currencies, for which there were limits to the amounts that might be brought into any one settlement.

Credits from the European Fund were granted in gold. They were available for a maximum period of three years, with the possibility of an additional two-year period for repayment. The decision to grant credit was, as a rule, taken by the council of the OECD, upon recommendation by the board of management. However, credits up to the equivalent of $50 million and with a maximum duration of one year could be decided upon by the board of management itself.

Capital of the fund, expressed in the equivalent of U.S. dollars at $35 per fine ounce of gold, amounted to $607.5 million, consisting of $271.6 million of the former EPU capital and $355.9 million of contributions callable from member countries.

Execution of the agreement was supervised by the board of management of the EMA, which consisted of a group of eight financial experts nominated by member countries and appointed by the council of the OECD. The fiscal agent was the BANK FOR INTERNATIONAL SETTLEMENTS at Basle, with head office in Paris.

New monetary arrangements involving some or all of the members of the OECD went into effect January 1, 1973. These new arrangements replaced the European Monetary Agreement of 1958 and liquidated the EMA's European fund. Reimbursement to the U.S. of its contribution to the fund, amounting to $355.5 million in capital and accrued interest, was made following termination.

EUROPEAN MONETARY SYSTEM The latest in the series of monetary arrangements over the years in the European Community (EC). The European monetary system (EMS) officially came into effect on March 13, 1979. The participating European countries were the following:

Belgium
Denmark
France
Federal Republic of Germany
Greece
Ireland
Italy
Luxembourg
The Netherlands
United Kingdom

(The United Kingdom is a member of the EMS, but does not participate in the intervention arrangements.)

The aim of the agreement creating the EMS was to foster "closer monetary cooperation leading to a zone of monetary stability in Europe."

The agreement consists principally in an intervention requirement on the part of each participant to limit exchange rate fluctuations, by the creation of the ECU (European currency unit, a "basket" of all ten EC currencies) as the center of the system, and by the enlargement of credit facilities already established in the EC.

The intervention mechanism requires that the member nations intervene in the foreign exchange markets to prevent movements greater than 2.25% around parity in bilateral rates between participants. Participating countries whose rates were previously floating against other participants' currencies are permitted to have movements in their bilateral rates of up to 6% around parity. Italy decided to make use of this option.

There exists also a presumption that a participating country will take action when the value of its currency in terms of the ECU diverges from its central rate by more than a uniform percentage, the precise percentage for each country being adjusted to take account of the weight of its currency in the "basket."

Unlimited very short-term credit for intervention purposes continued in the same form as in the original snake arrangement, except that such credit can be extended for a somewhat longer period than before. An initial supply of ECUs was issued by the European Monetary Cooperation Fund against deposits of 20% of both the gold and dollar reserves of participating countries. These ECUs were to be used for the settlement of such intervention debts in accordance with agreed rules. The short-term and medium-term facilities of the EC were substantially enlarged, and credit under the short-term facility can now also be granted over longer periods. It is envisaged that ultimately all the credit facilities under the EMS will be consolidated in a European monetary fund (not to be confused with the erstwhile European fund of the EUROPEAN MONETARY AGREEMENT).

In addition to contributing to increased integration within the EC area, the principal objective of the EMS is to promote internal financial stability. Participating countries in the earlier European common market arrangement, particularly those with small, open economies, have argued that the exchange rate stability gained through that arrangement has assisted their domestic economic policies and strengthened their foreign sectors. The economies of those countries that previously allowed their rates to float but are now joining the arrangement have in the past followed a different path from those of the "snake" countries in response to differing circumstances and policies. It is expected by the participants that the greater exchange rate stability gained by more concerted intervention policies will facilitate the task of harmonizing financial policies.

In view of the International Monetary Fund, these initiatives raise the question of what would be the requirements for a system in which exchange rate fluctuations were reduced and the rate changes that did occur were more consistently in line with long-term underlying trends. Such a system requires orderly underlying economic and financial conditions in member countries. Such conditions imply, inter alia, a closer approximation to reasonable price stability in member countries and a strong commitment by member governments to avoid future departures from price stability. In an environment of this kind expectations could be stabilizing rather than destabilizing. "The world is clearly still a long way from a system of this kind," in the judgment of the IMF, "but the wider recognition that inflation not only leads to instability but also over the longer run adversely affects growth and employment opportunities constitutes an important first step on the road to a more stable international monetary system."

In June 1985, the European Council, composed of the heads of state and government of the EC countries, proposed certain reforms that included a specific timetable for the progressive liberalization of capital movements within the EC with a view to furthering convergence of economic policies within the EMS. According to this proposal, all capital transactions will be liberalized by 1992.

See FOREIGN EXCHANGE.

EUROPEAN PAYMENTS UNION An intra-European payments union centralizing periodic settlement for imports and exports and providing for a pool of credits and gold to be granted to and received from members under a quota system. The EPU was terminated effective December 27, 1958, and succeeded by the European Monetary Agreement.

The EPU came into being July 1, 1950, by agreement of the country members of the Organization for European Economic Cooperation (OEEC). The latter had replaced the original Committee of European Economic Cooperation (CEEC), in April, 1948, and is an organization of European recipients of U.S. economic assistance. The EPU was intended to be a temporary system, designed to assist European countries "until they are fully able to take their place in a world-wide system." The EPU set up the ideal of trade equilibrium among members and removal of trade discriminations.

Although limited progress was made toward these objectives, the EPU as a multilateral settlement scheme was regarded as successful. Member countries paid in original quota contributions generally equal to 15% of all visible and invisible transactions during 1949 with other members of the OEEC and the sterling area. The Economic Cooperation Administration (ECA) of the U.S. made an initial contribution of $350 million as initial operating capital and in addition gave assistance to member structural debtors. At the final accounting, 7 of the 16 member nations showed a cumulative net surplus, the largest creditor, West Germany, accounting alone for $1,026.8 million surplus of total surpluses of net creditor members of $1,314.9 million. Other creditor countries at final accounting were Belgium-Luxembourg, the Netherlands, Italy, Austria, and Sweden. The largest net debtor members were France ($484.8 million) and the United Kingdom ($378.9 million), compared to total deficits of $1,117.4 million for the debtor countries. Other debtor countries were Iceland, Switzerland, Greece, Turkey, Portugal, Denmark, and Norway. The accounting was kept on the basis of a unit equivalent to the U.S. dollar.

EUROPEAN RECOVERY PROGRAM On April 12, 1948, the Foreign Assistance Act of 1948 became law, setting up the Economic Cooperation Administration with a slated term to January 30, 1952, to carry out the European Recovery Program or Marshall Plan, named after Secretary of State Marshall. After Secretary Marshall in June, 1947, made a proposal of substantial U.S. economic aid to Europe for recovery and reconstruction, 16 European nations met in

Paris and drew up the "Sixteen Nations Report of the Paris Conference," which outlined their requirements as $20.4 billion for the years 1948-1951. As enacted in the Foreign Assistance Act, total authorized aid initially was $5.3 billion for a 12-month program, consisting of an authorized appropriation of $4.3 billion and a $1 billion lending authorization for aid to the 16 European nations and West Germany.

To administer the program, the Economic Cooperation Administration (ECA) was set up by the act (Sec. 104, 62 Stat. 138; 22 U.S.C. 1503) as an agency of the U.S. government. The ECA was brought to an administrative end on December 31, 1950, pursuant to the act approved October 10, 1951 (Mutual Security Act), 65 Stat. 373; U.S.C. Sup. 1651 note. The ECA had administered the spending of some $12 billion since inception.

ECA was succeeded by the Mutual Security Agency, established by Executive Order 10300 of November 1, 1951, and under the act, to which were transferred all functions. The program of foreign aid was continued as the Mutual Security Program, with an expiration date of June 30, 1954, and an expanded jurisdiction to cover European recovery and other economic cooperation programs as well as the Point 4 Program for technical assistance to underdeveloped areas, and the mutual defense assistance programs furnishing military aid.

When the Mutual Security Agency expired, it was succeeded by the Foreign Operations Administration (FOA), established by Reorganization Plan 7, effective August 1, 1953, which transferred the functions of the Office of Director of Mutual Security, the Mutual Security Agency, the Technical Cooperation Administration, the Institute of Inter-American affairs, and several other foreign assistance activities to the FOA. The FOA was abolished by Executive Order 10610 (May 9, 1955) pursuant to authority contained in Sections 521 and 525 of the Mutual Security Act of 1954 (68 Stat. 832; 22 U.S.C. 1751), and its functions and offices were transferred to the Department of State (as the International Cooperation Administration) and to the Department of Defense, effective June 30, 1955. The latter agency functioned as a semiautonomous agency within the Department of State, operating aid programs classified as follows:

1. Defense support, consisting of economic assistance in order to secure specific contribution to the common defense by other countries in which U.S. military aid supports significant military forces.
2. Technical cooperation, consisting largely of advice, teaching, training, and the exchange of information with less developed countries.
3. Special assistance, designed to achieve a variety of political, economic or other objectives which the U.S. may have in any country where the U.S. is not providing assistance in support of significant military forces, and where the assistance rendered cannot appropriately be provided either as technical assistance or from the Development Loan Fund, with the aim of "maintenance or promotion of political or economic stability."

In turn, the ICA was abolished by the Foreign Assistance Act of 1961 (75 Stat. 446), and its functions were redelegated to the AGENCY FOR INTERNATIONAL DEVELOPMENT (AID), pursuant to the President's letter of September 30, 1961, and Executive Order 10973 dated November 3, 1961.

See MUTUAL SECURITY PROGRAM.

EVENING UP   The process which occurs when, to cover their contracts, holders of long stock sell and short sellers purchase simultaneously, so that the demand and supply of stocks is about equal and price changes are without significance. Financial reviewers often refer to the "usual week-end evening-up process," indicating that operators have disposed of their holdings or covered their contracts, not desiring to commit themselves over the weekend.

EVEN LOTS   Board lots; full lots. Lots or number of shares of stock sold in the usual trading unit of 100 shares, or a multiple thereof, e.g., 100, 200, 300, etc.

EVENTS AND TRANSACTIONS   Events, transactions, exchanges, and circumstances affecting an entity describe the sources or causes of revenue, expense, gains, and losses as well as changes in assets, liabilities, and equity. Events, exchanges, transactions, and circumstances affect the underlying assets, liabilities, and equity of an enterprise. Consequently, they determine the contents of an enterprise's financial statements and have economic consequences. Events, transactions, and exchanges can be outlined as follows:

1. **Event.** An occurrence that has economic consequences to an entity. Economic events may be external or internal to the entity.
   a. *Internal event.* One that occurs within an entity, such as the use of raw material in the production process.
   b. *External event.* One that requires an interaction between an entity and its environment, such as the sale or purchase of a product.
2. **Transaction.** A particular kind of external event that requires accounting recognition. A transaction involves the transfer of something of value between two or more entities. An investment purchased from a stockbroker is a transaction. Transactions are classified as either an exchange or a nonreciprocal transfer.
   a. *Exchange*. In an exchange, each participant receives and sacrifices something of value, such as the acquisition of inventory for cash.
   b. *Nonreciprocal transfer.* The transfer of assets in one direction. Transfers can occur between the enterprise and its owners and between the enterprise and other entities than its owners. The acquisition and disposition of assets by donation or gifts and property dividends are examples of nonreciprocal transfers.

See ACCOUNTING.

EVERGREENS   A form of accounts receivable home equity financing. Evergreen loans are an open-end, revolving credit product that gives the consumer/borrower considerable control over credit usage and loan repayment. The credit plan provides for a constant in-and-out arrangement where a complete payoff is not required. Accounts receivable financing often relies on borrowing certificates for advances.

EX   Out of; in finance, without, e.g., EX-DIVIDEND.

EX-ALL   Without all rights and privileges. Stocks sold ex-all reserve all privileges, such as pending dividends, the right to subscribe for additional stock, or other advantages to the seller.

EXACT-DAY INTEREST   Interest computed on the basis of a 365- or 366-day year. Interest is charged for the exact number of days.

EXAMINATION PROCEDURE   The Office of the Comptroller of the Currency (OCC) considers the bank examination process to be the OCC's fact-finding arm in discharging its responsibility for promoting and assuring the soundness of the country's system of national banks. The *Comptroller's Handbook for National Bank Examiners* goes on to specify the three essential objectives of an examination to be the following:

1. To provide an objective evaluation of a bank's soundness.
2. To permit the OCC to appraise the quality of management and directors.
3. To identify those areas where corrective action is required to strengthen the bank, to improve the quality of its performance, and to enable it to comply with applicable laws, rulings, and regulations.

Among the procedures utilized to accomplish these objectives are the evaluation of the prudency of practices, adherence to laws and regulations, adequacy of liquidity and capital, quality of assets and earnings, nature of operations, and adequacy of internal control and internal audit.

Compromises with the examination mandate were necessary. The statute itself provides that the Comptroller, in the exercise of his discretion, may waive one examination (or cause such examinations to be made more frequently if considered necessary), but the waiver of one such examination shall not be exercised more frequently than once during any two-year period. In addition, data produced by the computer-based National Bank Surveillance System (NBSS) supplement the examination process by detecting each quarter, based on data both from call reports and from examination reports, those banks which need priority examination. Other banks may be examined by the short form of examination (reportedly, currently used in two of every three examinations) since, according to the data and the last examination, they did not have any significant problems.

During recent years, national bank examiners have devoted less of their time to detailed audit or verification procedures. There has been an increase in both the volume of activity and the variety of services offered by banks, and in the quality of internal control and the program of internal audit of many banks. The examiners handbook further issues this warning:

"Proper internal control . . . is a day-to-day proposition and cannot be satisfactorily accomplished by an outside examination or audit. The boards of directors should assume responsibility for adequate internal controls that should promote, in them, a better understanding and knowledge of the institution and give them a greater involvement in the protection of the interests of the bank's depositors and stockholders."

Classified as to scope of the examination, the OCC's national bank examinations fall into three categories:

1. General examination, which will consist of the standard examination procedures and ordinarily will occur once in a two-year period. The procedures are comprehensive and embrace every phase of activity.
2. Special supervisory examination, which will be performed when the OCC determines that a bank's condition necessitates an examination or supervisory visitation more than twice in one calendar year. Such examinations have no minimum scope requirements, and instead consist of selected procedures specifically designed to fit the circumstances of each case.
3. Specialized examination, which will be performed periodically during the examination cycle and will complement the general examination, taking into account reliance upon the NBSS to identify changing situations in the banking industry and in individual banks. In addition, the OCC recognizes the benefits of periodic examinations of trust departments, electronic data processing (EDP) departments, international departments, and consumer affairs in developing the minimum scope of specialized examinations.

The examiner in charge of a specialized examination will be responsible for selecting the necessary additional procedures to be employed in a particular situation, requiring the preparation of supplemental programs or modification of existing examination or verification programs, considering the following circumstances:

1. Results of the most recent general examinations.
2. Level of risk attributable to the policies and practices employed by the bank.
3. Evaluation of the quality of management and the board of directors.
4. The nature of and risk attributable to transactions with and investments in related organizations.
5. Evaluation of the internal audit function.
6. Scope of the most recent audit, if any, conducted by external auditors and its results.
7. Anticipated impact of local and national economic factors.
8. Significant adverse changes in risk assets, earnings, liquidity, or other significant matters which came to the examiners' attention during performance of the minimum procedures.

For example, the investment securities examination program might be included if the examiner finds that the investment officer has been replaced since the prior examination, if the bank has no written guidelines for investment policy, and/or if the portfolio has undergone significant change through numerous sales and purchases. Some or all of the procedures in the real estate loan program might be included if there has been significant increase in the bank's real estate loans, if the bank does not have an acceptable internal loan review program, and/or if the local real estate market appears to be entering a period of decline.

Regulatory examinations focus on the quality of the bank's assets, capital adequacy, and bank management, especially the formalization of policies for operational areas and compliance with laws and regulations. Financial statement audits of banks emphasize direct verification of assets and compliance with generally accepted accounting principles.

BIBLIOGRAPHY

COMPTROLLER OF THE CURRENCY. *Comptroller's Handbook for National Bank Examiners.*

EXAMINER *See* BANK EXAMINERS.

EXCESS LOANS Loans made by a bank to one customer in excess of the legal maximum amount. Directors of national banks who make or assent to the making of loans in excess of the legal limits specified in 12 U.S.C. 84 have been held by court decisions to be personally liable for losses that may result to a bank as a consequence of making loans to one customer in excess of the legal limit.
See NATIONAL BANK LOANS.

EXCESS PROFITS TAX In November, 1950, the President in a message to Congress urged immediate restoration of an excess profits tax on corporations, effective July 1, 1950, to raise $4 billion annual revenue as a means of taxing Korean war-inflated corporate profits. As enacted on January 3, 1951, the Excess Profits Tax Act of 1950 imposed a tax of 30% on corporation profits in excess of 85% of the average three highest base-period years 1946-1949, to be effective for a period of three years, July, 1950, to June 30, 1953. The law provided an alternative exemption based on invested capital and growth, and automatic relief provisions based on industry rates of return.

The Revenue Act of 1951, effective July 1, 1951, modified the excess profits tax by lowering the 85% exemption to 83%, but allowing special hardship exemptions for newer corporations whose earnings in the base period were low. The sum of normal tax, surtax, and excess profits taxes was limited to a maximum effective rate of 52% for the calendar year 1950 and 62% for 1951 and subsequent years. Maximum excess profits tax rate for the calendar year 1951 was 17.25% of the excess profits net income, and for taxable years beginning after March 31, 1951, maximum of 18%.

The Excess Profits Tax Act, as thus amended, was extended in 1953 to December 31, 1953, when it expired.

An excess profits tax act is aimed to recapture abnormal wartime profits; but masquerading as such because of high exemptions, it may reach nonwar profits. It is difficult to apply fairly, especially to small-income corporations. Its administration is costly, and consequently its net yield is usually less than anticipated.

EXCESS RESERVES The portion of a bank's reserves against deposits in excess of the amount required by law, whether deposited with a Federal Reserve bank in its reserve balance account or in its own vaults.

The volume and distribution of excess reserves is the primary determinant of money rates, as banks are principal factors in the money market and their excess reserves constitute their supply of funds available for conversion into earning assets, including money market items. Mere volume of excess reserves, however, will not induce banks to keep fully invested, as confidence and stability of conditions must exist concurrently with the available reserves. Normally, however, when banks have excess reserves, they like to keep well invested. Consequently the manipulation of the volume and distribution of excess reserves has been one of the principal activities of the Board of Governors of the Federal Reserve System in implementing monetary policy.

For the banking system as a whole, the maximum expansion of loans and investments, granted optimum conditions of maximized expansion by every bank on its available reserves, no increase in domestic money circulation, and no export of funds, is measured by the reciprocal of the average legal reserve requirements. Thus, with reserve requirements averaging about 15% for the Federal Reserve System, the member banks as a whole would have the optimum power to expand loans and investments about six and two-thirds times for every dollar of excess reserves, bearing in mind that expansion in earning assets creates deposits.

Such expansion, however, is influenced not only by the availability of excess reserves, but also by the methods of deriving those reserves. Ideally, banks prefer excess reserves derived from the inflow of primary deposits as compared with excess reserves created

EXCHANGE

by member bank borrowing (from Federal Reserve banks, other banks, or the purchase of federal funds). Moreover, any one individual bank cannot possibly have the multiple expansion power of the banking system as a whole. For every dollar of expansion in loans or investments, the individual bank must reckon not only with cost in excess reserves of legal reserve required against any increase in its deposits thus generated, but also withdrawals of funds from the individual bank in connection with such lending (checkouts of loan proceeds by borrowers, the recipients of such funds redepositing in other banks) and investing (redeposit in other banks of the bank's cashier's checks to securities dealers in payment for security purchases).

In order to show the factors which influence the increase or decrease in the supply and use of member bank reserves, the Board of Governors of the Federal Reserve System and the Federal Reserve banks developed the table "Factors Affecting Bank Reserves" (Release H.4.1), which is released Thursdays and published every Friday in various newspapers, based on figures as of the preceding Wednesday.

Factors which increase member bank reserve balances are increases in Federal Reserve bank credit, gold stock, SDRs certificate account, and Treasury currency, and decreases in currency in circulation, Treasury cash, Treasury deposits with Federal Reserve banks, foreign and nonmember deposits, and other Federal Reserve accounts. Factors which decrease member bank reserve balances are the opposite of the above: reduction in Federal Reserve credit, gold stock, SDRs certificate account, and Treasury currency, and increased circulation, Treasury cash and deposits, foreign and nonmember deposits, and other Federal Reserve accounts. At any one time, the increases or decreases are various, but each item's fluctuation has a positive or negative effect on member bank reserve balances.

The supply or sources of member bank reserve balances are Federal Reserve bank credit, gold stock, SDRs certificate account, and Treasury currency. The uses are currency in circulation, Treasury cash and deposits, foreign and nonmember deposits, and other Federal Reserve accounts. Thus, an equation is implied, the Federal Reserve bank credit, gold stock, SDRs certificate account, and Treasury currency equaling the currency in circulation, Treasury cash and deposits, foreign and nonmember deposits, and other Federal Reserve accounts, plus the total of member bank reserve balances.

The credit and money market policies of the Board of Governors of the Federal Reserve System and the Treasury, insofar as they are concerned with member bank reserve balances, are actively indicated by certain of the factors affecting bank reserves. The powers of the board of governors over member bank reserve balances may be summarized as follows:

1. The most important and actively used power, the power to engage in open market operations (in practice, normally in Treasury bills through the reporting government securities dealers), consisting of the buying or selling on balance for system account on directives from the Open Market Committee by the New York Federal Reserve bank agent for the system account.
2. The power to raise or lower legal reserve requirements within the range of variation permitted by the Federal Reserve Act, as amended, upon determination by the board of governors by regulation.
3. Although borrowing and/or discounting at Federal Reserve banks is at the initiative of the member banks, the power to raise or lower discount rates on such borrowings or discounts. The discount rates are announced at least every 14 days by the Federal Reserve banks and reviewed and determined by the board of governors.
4. Although activity in acceptances is minor, the power to adjust buying rates for such bills. Since 1955, Federal Reserve policy has not been passive in regard to open market operations in bills, mainly by holdings under repurchase agreements.

The Treasury too may importantly affect member bank reserve balances by the following actions:

1. Shifts in its deposit balances (tax and loan accounts) maintained with banks, which are demand balances but in practice are given prior notice of withdrawal.
2. Treasury borrowing and spending operations, which affect the volume and distribution of reserve balances of banks. Adjustments in Treasury balances, cash balances, and deposits with Federal Reserve banks will affect reserve balances in this connection.

Since fiscal policy insofar as the Treasury is concerned is coordinated with Federal Reserve policy, the noncontrollable factors affecting reserve balances are these: currency in circulation, changes in gold stock and special drawing rights certificate account, foreign and nonmember bank adjustments in balances, and float (the amount of net credit depending on the vagaries of check collection relative to schedules in the deferred availability schedules of the Federal Reserve banks). The Federal Reserve System uses open market operations to smooth out fluctuations in reserve balances caused by the most important of these factors.

See RESERVE.

EXCHANGE See COMMODITY EXCHANGES, DOMESTIC EXCHANGE, FOREIGN EXCHANGE, PRODUCE EXCHANGES, STOCK EXCHANGES.

EXCHANGE EQUALIZATION FUND Established originally in April, 1932, and operated by the Bank of England as a means of stabilizing the exchange value of sterling by preventing excessive depreciation or appreciation. The British exchange equalization account at the outset of World War II departed from stabilization functions under the Currency (Defence) Act of 1939 and the Defence (Finance) Regulations to use its resources in "... securing the defence of the realm and the efficient prosecution of any war," including the mobilization by purchase from private U.K. residents of a substantial part of their holdings of U.S. and Canadian dollar securities, and becoming the ultimate buyer and seller of foreign currencies in providing the exchange required for prosecution of the war.

After World War II, under the system of fixed exchange rates of the INTERNATIONAL MONETARY FUND, the Finance Act of 1946 widened the account's role to include "... the conservation or disposition in the national interest of the means of making payments abroad," and in particular the dealing with volatile movements of speculative funds with restoration of convertibility. However, the account in postwar years has "never managed ... to accumulate sufficient foreign exchange resources to cope with the United Kingdom's much enlarged short-term external liabilities," so that international credit facilities have been increasingly resorted to in order to counterfinance balance-of-payments trends in trade account and capital flows.

See BANK OF ENGLAND.

EXCHANGE OF MONEY See MONEY, REDEMPTION OF MONEY.

EXCHANGE RATE The price at which one country's currency can be exchanged for another. The value of the exchange rate, like any other price, is determined by the interaction of supply and demand in the foreign exchange market. Changes in the economic activity of any one country will affect that country's exchange rate with all other currencies.

Country	Currency	Currency per $1
Argentina	Austral	11.96
Australia	Dollar	1.2243
Austria	Schilling	13.23
Britain	Pound	0.593
Canada	Dollar	1.2333
China	Yuan	3.722
France	Franc	6.3825
India	Rupee	14.35
Israel	Shekel	1.646
Japan	Yen	133.7
Mexico	Peso	2270.0
Sweden	Krona	6.4725
Switzerland	Franc	1.584
West Germany	Deutsche mark	1.879

Source: *Wall Street Journal*, August 24, 1988.

Exchange rates can be expressed in terms of foreign currency per

U.S. dollars, or in terms of U.S. dollars per unit of foreign exchange. One expression is simply the reciprocal of the other. Listed in the table below are selected foreign exchange rates. Current rates are published daily in the *Wall Street Journal* and are often posted in major financial institutions.

See CLEARINGHOUSE EXCHANGE RATES, FOREIGN EXCHANGE, FOREIGN MONEYS.

BIBLIOGRAPHY

PICK, P. *World Currency Yearbook.* Annual.

EXCHANGE RESTRICTIONS Official intervention in the FOREIGN EXCHANGE markets, partially or wholly displacing free foreign exchange markets. The following forms of intervention are used.

1. The voluntary suspension of the gold standard and depreciation in exchange value of a currency under a MANAGED CURRENCY program may be classified as a primary form of exchange restriction. In 1931, this policy was inaugurated by the United Kingdom and the STERLING AREA as a means of reversing the deflationary effects of gold outflows and promoting lower export prices of goods to stimulate a more favorable INTERNATIONAL BALANCE OF PAYMENTS. The EXCHANGE EQUALIZATION FUND was established in 1932 as a means of assuring desired levels in the exchange value of the pound sterling. Such stabilization funds, established by other countries subsequently, did not supplant the foreign exchange markets, but operated in them as manipulative forces.
2. In lieu of exchange depreciation, controls over specific items in the balance of payments causing exchange fluctuation are another form of direct exchange control. This necessitated bringing all foreign exchange transactions under official regulation by a centralized official control agency, usually the central bank. Exports of currency and gold were prohibited. All exporters were required to sell their exchange to the control agency at official rates. Purchases of foreign exchange at official rates were permitted for approved transactions only, excluding capital export purposes. Exchange rationing involved making available only a part of needed foreign exchange where particular foreign exchange resources were low.
3. BLOCKED CURRENCY practices would concurrently tie up foreign balances in a country. The foreign balances were blocked even in the purchase of goods for export, in the most extreme version, lest such foreign funds use that device as a means of leaving the country. Negotiation with holders of blocked foreign funds would result in reductions in interest rates, extensions of maturities, and even reductions in principal as consideration for partial unblocking. See STANDSTILL CREDITS.
4. Bilateral agreements between two countries were evolved as a means of agreed operation of exchange controls to mutual advantage. Clearing arrangements and payments agreements were the result of such agreements. (*See* CLEARING AGREEMENT.) Payments agreements would involve the setting of an agreed ratio of exports and imports between two countries, so as to assure the ability of the debtor country to meet service on obligations due the creditor country. Payments would be made in foreign exchange, so that the foreign exchange markets were not bypassed, as in the case of clearing agreements. The foreign exchange derived from exports to the creditor country would be carefully nursed so as to have the exchange available to meet payments for imports and for debt service to the creditor country and withdrawals permitted from blocked accounts.
5. Multilateral agreements arose where three or more countries were parties to exchange control agreements. Before establishment of the International Monetary Fund, the Tripartite Agreement of 1936 brought together the U.S., Great Britain, and France, and later Belgium, Switzerland, and the Netherlands, in a multilateral agreement to avert competitive exchange depreciation.
6. Trade discrimination, or the preference given to particular goods imported from particular countries, also arose as a corollary to exchange controls. Quotas were established officially on the maximum amount of commodities of each kind that could be imported. High tariffs discriminated against particular countries.
7. Multiple exchange rates, involving different rates for different commodities imported or exported to particular countries, were developed both as a means of control and as a device for discrimination in lieu of tariffs and quotas. Favored trade with favored countries would be granted virtual subsidies by favorable rates and retention of exchange quotas granted to traders.

The outbreak of World War II led to imposition of tight licensing of imports and exports, exchange control regulations, freezing of enemy exchange, funds, and property, and requisitioning of private security holdings abroad. With the end of the war, exchange restrictions continued because of balance of payments difficulties. Multiple exchange rates, licensing of imports and exports, exchange controls, and trade discrimination continued in varying degrees despite the efforts of such agencies as the International Monetary Fund and the General Agreement on Tariffs and Trade (GATT). The primary problem of dollar shortage led to the 30.5% devaluation of the pound sterling by the United Kingdom on September 18, 1949, followed in quick succession by devaluation by some 28 other countries in 1949. However, by the close of 1958, nonresident convertibility for their respective currencies was established by the United Kingdom, Austria, Belgium, Denmark, Finland, France, West Germany, Italy, Luxembourg, the Netherlands, Norway, and Sweden.

Most recently, amendment to the articles of agreement of the International Monetary Fund to provide for special drawing rights (SDRs) made it "possible for the international community deliberately to supplement existing reserve assets by the creation of special drawing rights, in order to bring the stock and rate of growth of reserves up to whatever level is deemed desirable and prudent."

BIBLIOGRAPHY

INTERNATIONAL MONETARY FUND. *Annual Report on Exchange Restrictions.*

EXCHANGES This term has two meanings:

1. In banking practice, checks, drafts, matured acceptances, notes, etc., presented for collection through a clearinghouse.
2. The English term for the market for foreign currencies and bills of exchange. What is known in the United States as foreign exchange is known in England as foreign exchanges.

EXCHANGES FOR CLEARINGHOUSE An account appearing in a bank's general ledger and financial statement representing the amount of checks drawn upon clearinghouse banks and collectible on the following business day through the clearinghouse.

EXCHANGE STABILIZATION FUND The Exchange Stabilization Fund (ESF) of the U.S. was established by Section 10 of the Gold Reserve Act of 1934 (enacted January 30, 1934). Presidential proclamation on the following day, pursuant to the act, devalued the dollar from 25.8 grains of gold 0.9 fine, to 15 grains of gold 0.9 fine or, reciprocally, raised the monetary price for gold to $35 an ounce, aginst $20.67 previously. A total "paper profit" of $2,808,512,060 was thus created for the Treasury, which pursuant to the act became the sole legal owner of all monetary gold in the U.S.

A total of $2 billion of this increment was transferred by entry on the Treasury books from "gold in general fund" to "Exchange Stabilization Fund (Special No. 1)." In turn, the $2 billion was split into two parts, the inactive portion of $1.8 billion continuing to be included in total gold stock and the balance of $200 million being set up as the capital of the fund.

The secretary of the Treasury is authorized by the Gold Reserve Act to deal in gold and FOREIGN EXCHANGE for the account of the Exchange Stabilization Fund in order to stabilize the exchange value of the dollar. Originally created as a dollar defense fund in an era of competitive exchange rate depreciation, the fund in the post-World War II world of the INTERNATIONAL MONETARY FUND (IMF) has been mainly devoted to cooperation in exchange agreements to assist various foreign currencies. It no longer is active in foreign exchange dealings. The $1.8 billion inactive portion of the "gold profit" was subsequently used to help defray the cost of U.S. subscription to the IMF, pursuant to the Bretton Woods Agreements Act of 1945. Under that act, the par value of the dollar may not be changed except by Congress (the secretary of the Treasury, otherwise, by paying premium prices for gold, could in effect administratively devalue the dollar). Moreover, as a member of the IMF, the U.S. agreed under its articles to buy and sell gold freely for international transactions at prices that may not vary by more than a specified margin. But on August 15, 1971, at the direction of the President, the secretary of the Treasury suspended the convertibility of the dollar by foreign monetary authorities into gold or other reserve assets of the U.S. Specifically, the secretary of the Treasury notified the International Monetary Fund that, effective immediately, the U.S. would no longer freely buy and sell gold for the settlement of international transactions.

In the era before advent of the International Monetary Fund, when competitive exchange rate depreciation and other restrictive exchange rate and trade practices were rife, the major purpose of the U.S. stabilization fund was to keep the U.S. dollar at desired levels relative to those of other currencies. With the advent of the IMF, the major purpose of the stabilization fund became that of supplementary stabilization activities (gold, specific currencies, etc.).

Beginning in March, 1961, the U.S. Treasury, through its stabilization fund and with the Federal Reserve Bank of New York acting as agent, engaged in foreign exchange operations as part of a cooperative effort by treasuries and central banks on both sides of the Atlantic to create a first line of defense against disorderly speculation in the foreign exchange markets. For several months prior to the meeting of the FEDERAL OPEN MARKET COMMITTEE on January 23, 1962, the FOMC has been studying the question of desirability of instituting a program of Federal Reserve operations in foreign currencies, which would be supplemental to and in collaboration with the activities of the stabilization fund. At the FOMC meeting on January 23, 1962, a motion was approved favoring in principle the initiation of such a program on an experimental basis. That motion also authorized representatives of the FOMC to consult with the Treasury for the purpose of exploring guidelines for such operations, in the light of Treasury experience, and developing plans for effective working relations in this field between the Treasury and the Federal Reserve. At the February 13, 1962, meeting of the FOMC, results of these discussions were reported, and the FOMC approved, effective immediately, a statement of guidelines for Federal Reserve System foreign currency operations and a continuing authority directive on the system's foreign currency operations.

Accordingly, the Federal Reserve System has since engaged in foreign currency transactions, such transactions being designed, from the Federal Reserve System's standpoint, to cushion short-run disturbances in the foreign exchange markets, and not intended to be a substitute for basic measures to reduce the deficit in the U.S. balance of payments. In these operations, the Federal Reserve has made use of the network of reciprocal currency or "swap" arrangements with foreign central banks that it had begun to set up in early 1962. Such swap arrangements add to the sums potentially available or actually being used for the defense of the dollar.

Periodic reports by the senior officer in charge of the foreign function of the Federal Reserve Bank of New York and the special manager of the System Open Market Account covering Treasury and Federal Reserve foreign exchange operations are published in the Federal Reserve Bank of New York *Quarterly Review*. The Federal Reserve Bank of New York acts as agent for both the Treasury and the Federal Reserve System in the conduct of foreign exchange operations.

Such foreign exchange operations assumed greater importance following August 15, 1971, when the U.S. announced a major new program of domestic and international measures, including a 10% temporary surcharge on dutiable imports into the U.S. and suspension of convertibility of the dollar into gold and other reserve assets. The exchange rate structure that emerged after August 15, 1971, was largely the product of controlled rather than free floating rates. Many central banks continued to intervene on an ad hoc basis, according to one of the periodic reports of the Federal Reserve Bank of New York, while the market was further strongly influenced by a proliferation of new exchange controls, the U.S. import surcharge, and sharply conflicting official appraisals of an appropriate alignment of parities.

These international uncertainties temporarily ended on December 18, 1971, with the SMITHSONIAN AGREEMENT of the "Group of Ten" countries, which specified an exchange rate alignment based on an increase in the U.S. official gold price from $35 to $38 per ounce, or an 8.57% devaluation of the dollar. Subsequently, as of October 18, 1973, the U.S. official gold price was raised from $38 to $42.22 per ounce, or a further devaluation of 11.11% of the dollar.

Since the move to floating exchange rates by the major countries in 1973, the Federal Reserve and other central banks have made use of SWAP NETWORK arrangements on numerous occasions to finance exchange market intervention. The objective of these interventions has been to counter disorderly trading conditions.

When the U.S. accepted the revised Articles of Agreement of the International Monetary Fund, the U.S. Congress amended the 1934 Gold Act's references to "exchange stabilization" as being the objective of the Exchange Stabilization Fund. Instead, it was specified that the ESF was to be utilized as the secretary of the Treasury "may deem necessary, consistent with U.S. obligations in the IMF regarding orderly exchange arrangements and a stable system of exchange rates." In addition, the ESF has been utilized in recent years by the U.S. Treasury to finance exchange-related, short-term credit arrangements with foreign governments.

Operations of the ESF normally are conducted through the Federal Reserve Bank of New York, fiscal agent for the government and international arm of the Federal Reserve. Actions on behalf of the Treasury are made at the direction of the secretary of the Treasury, and those for the Federal Reserve System at the direction of the Federal Open Market Committee, the top policy-making unit of the Federal Reserve System. Through continuing consultations at many levels, Treasury and Federal Reserve positions are closely coordinated and often have been conducted jointly. The Federal Reserve Bank of New York is reimbursed by the Treasury for expenses incurred in carrying out Treasury actions.

Although the ESF is also used to finance certain credit arrangements with foreign governments, it is not used to provide foreign aid, to finance any specific trade transactions, or to support any fixed value of a currency.

In addition to carrying out exchange market operations and providing short-term credit needs, the stabilization fund is used for holding and administering SPECIAL DRAWING RIGHTS (SDRs), allocated by the IMF or acquired by the U.S., and to pay for certain ESF-related administrative costs.

The ESF was funded by a U.S. congressional appropriation resulting from funds derived through the devaluation of the dollar. Currently, it obtains funds from gains on operations and from interest earned on U.S. Treasury securities in which it temporarily invests idle balances. Like those of the Federal Reserve System in administering MONETARY POLICY, operations of the stabilization fund are not intended primarily to make profits.

See EXCHANGE EQUALIZATION FUND, EXCHANGE RESTRICTIONS, FOREIGN MONEYS, OPEN MARKET OPERATIONS.

EXCHEQUER The official title of the account of the Chancellor of the Exchequer of the United Kingdom with the Bank of England. Its statutory title is Her Majesty's Exchequer. It is a central account and not directly in contact with the detailed revenue and expenditure accounts. It corresponds in the United States to our Treasury Department accounts with the Federal Reserve banks. It is the account into which gross revenues of the country are paid and from which expenditures are drawn.

EXCHEQUER BILLS The name formerly given to the promissory notes of the British government. They were first issued in 1696 and constituted the chief floating debt of England. They have since been superseded by TREASURY BILLS.

EXCHEQUER BONDS In English terminology, the securities issued by Her Majesty's government, or by nationalized industries and guaranteed by Her Majesty's government, that are dealt in on the London Stock Exchange. Treasury bills are separately identified as such. Short bonds ("shorts") are gilt-edged securities which have less than five years to run to final maturity.

The national debt comprises the total liabilities of the national loans fund, together with nationalized industries' stocks guaranteed by the government. As contingent liabilities of the government these are not strictly part of the national debt, but the markets and the sources used do not generally distinguish them from government stocks, while the authorities carry out transactions in them in the same way as in government stocks.

BIBLIOGRAPHY

BANK OF ENGLAND. *Quarterly Bulletin*.

EXCISES Indirect taxes levied upon rights or privileges, such as the right to conduct business, franchises, licenses, etc. In accordance with Article I, Section 8, Clause 1 of the U.S. Constitution, federal excises shall be uniform throughout the United States. Because they are measured by the money value of sales or commodities involved, excises are frequently considered to be levied on the sales or commodities, but it is the intangible right or privilege which is taxed. Excises are not direct taxes, which under the U.S. Constitution must be apportioned.

Excise taxes are levied on specific products such as gasoline, alcohol, and tobacco. Excise taxes are either a fixed dollar amount per unit consumed or a fixed percentage of the sale price. The excise tax on gasoline may reflect the benefit principle of taxation because such taxes are earmarked for highway expenditures. In general, excise taxes raise tax revenues while making the taxed goods more expensive in order to limit their consumption.

BIBLIOGRAPHY

Excise Tax Guide. Commerce Clearing House, Inc. Chicago, IL. Annual.
Excise Taxes. Prentice Hall, Inc. Englewood Cliffs, NJ, Looseleaf.
Journal of Taxation.

EX-COUPON Without the next maturing interest coupon attached. Bonds sold ex-coupon have the next maturing coupon already detached.

EX-DIVIDEND Without dividend. Under the five-day delivery plan, unless an exchange directs otherwise, stocks sell ex-dividend on the fourth full business day preceding the stockholders of record date. When the record date is a holiday or a Saturday, stocks sell ex-dividend on the fifth preceding full business day. Transactions made on the cash basis on the ex-dividend date and up to and including the stockholders of record date carry the dividend.

For example, under the five-day delivery plan, where the stockholders of record date is a Monday, stocks sell ex-dividend on the preceding Tuesday; Tuesday, on the preceding Wednesday; Wednesday, on the preceding Thursday; Thursday, on the preceding Friday; and Friday, on the preceding Monday. The NEW YORK STOCK EXCHANGE and the majority of other stock exchanges operate on the five-day delivery basis on regular way transactions, i.e., stocks go ex-dividend on the fourth business day preceding the record date as fixed by the corporation, or the day of the closing of the transfer books therefor, except transactions therein made specifically for cash, or transactions for which a special ruling is made.

The AMERICAN STOCK EXCHANGE operates under the five-day delivery plan, but with appropriate adjustment of ex-dividend dates on stocks which transfer outside the New York City metropolitan area. Transactions in stocks shall not be ex-dividend or ex-rights until announcement to that effect is made by the exchange.

See DELIVERIES.

EXECUTION The carrying into effect of an order; the manner in which an order to buy or sell securities is handled. If, in selling securities at the market, a broker offers them down unduly in order to find a taker, he is said to have given a bad execution. If, on the other hand, the broker is able to obtain a good price in view of market conditions, he is said to have given a good execution.

EXECUTOR An individual or trust company appointed in a will by the TESTATOR to carry out, after the death of the testator, the expressed instructions for the disposal of his property as provided in the WILL. When a person dies intestate, i.e., without leaving a will, his property is distributed in accordance with the laws of descent and distribution of the state in which the intestate is a resident. Settlement of the estate of an intestate is conducted by an ADMINISTRATOR who is appointed by the court. Duties of the executor and administrator are similar, i.e., to settle the affairs of the deceased and distribute the real and personal property to the rightful heirs.

The following is a summary of the duties of an executor:

1. Offer the will for probate in the probate (surrogate) court, prove its execution, and defend the will if contested.
2. Secure letters testamentary (the document giving the executor the right to act).
3. Take possession of the property, review all the assets, examine books of account, ascertain bank balances, and locate and check insurance policies.
4. Notify interested parties in the estate, i.e., legatees, devisees, and heirs.
5. Make a complete inventory of all assets.
6. Have the property appraised and protected by insurance.
7. Advertise for the presentation of claims and, after verification, pay them off in the order prescribed by law.
8. Collect claims due to the deceased.
9. If there is a going business, manage it until such time as it can be sold or liquidated.
10. If the deceased was a member of a partnership, collect such interest.
11. If the deceased had a large or controlling interest in a corporation, give attention to its affairs by contact with officers and directors until the stock can be disposed of.
12. Keep accurate records of stocks, bonds, mortgages, and notes, and watch investments for bond calls, interest default, and stock rights.
13. Collect dividends, rents, interest, and insurance claims.
14. Pay legacies and secure releases.
15. Pay inheritance taxes due to the federal government and the state of the decedent's residence, and taxes due to any other state in which the deceased left taxable property.
16. Verify trust clauses of the will, if any, and proceed accordingly.
17. After collecting all assets and paying all debts and expenses of the executorship, liquidate the residue of the estate, unless otherwise directed, and distribute to the persons entitled thereto.
18. Make final accounting to the court and obtain judicial discharge.

Executors are responsible for turning the proceeds of estates over to beneficiaries in the most advantageous condition. The law gives creditors of the estate a certain time within which to file claims. Executors perform their work under the will, letters testamentary, instructions from the court, and the statutes governing descent and distribution of property. The proceedings are technical and usually require advisory services of an attorney. In a large estate, conferences will be held with beneficiaries, creditors, debtors, bankers, brokers, investment houses, tax experts, insurance agents, mortgagors, landlords, tenants, etc.

See DESCENT, LAWS OF; TRUST; WILL.

EXECUTORY CONTRACT A contract in which something remains to be done by either party.

EXECUTRIX The feminine form of EXECUTOR.

EXEMPT SECURITY A security that is exempt by Section 3 of the SECURITIES ACT OF 1933 from all requirements of the act, except the fraud provisions of Section 17.

As specified in the act, the following are exempt securities:

1. Any security issued or guaranteed by the United States or any territory thereof, or by the District of Columbia, or by any state of the United States, or by any political subdivision of a state or territory, or by any public instrumentality of one or more states or territories exercising an essential governmental function, including industrial development bonds.
2. Any security issued or guaranteed by any corporation created and controlled or supervised by and acting as an instrumentality of the government of the United States, pursuant to authority granted by the Congress of the United States.
3. Any security issued or guaranteed by any national bank, or by any banking institution organized under the laws of any state or territory, the business of which is substantially confined to banking and is supervised by the state or territorial banking commission or similar official.

However, the preceding exemption from registration requirements of the Securities Act of 1933 for "any security issued or guaranteed by bank" does not include any interest or participation in any collective trust fund maintained by a bank (meaning any national bank, District of Columbia bank, or any banking institution organized under the laws of any state or territory). But the exemption does apply to any interest or participation in any common trust fund or similar fund maintained by a bank exclusively for the collective investment and reinvestment of assets contributed thereto by such bank in its capacity as trustee, executor, administrator, or guardian. The preceding notwithstanding, the term "bank" in the case of a collective trust fund or common trust fund or similar fund has the same meaning as in the Investment Company Act of 1940 (see INVESTMENT COMPANY).

Moreover, the preceding numbered exemption from registration requirements of the Securities Act of 1933 does not apply to bank holding companies with 500 or more stockholders. Pursuant to the Securities Act Amendments of 1975, banks with 500 or more stockholders are subject to "SEC-like" registration of public offerings with the Comptroller of the Currency in the case of national banks and banks operating in the District of Columbia.

4. Any security issued by or representing an interest in or a direct obligation of a Federal Reserve bank.
5. Any note, draft, bill of exchange, or bankers acceptance which arises out of a current transaction or the proceeds of which have been or are to be used for current transactions, and which has a maturity at time of issuance of not exceeding nine months, exclusive of days of grace, or any renewal thereof the maturity of which is likewise limited.
6. Securities issued by nonprofit organizations.
7. Securities issued by savings and loan, building and loan, or similar organizations, provided the withdrawal fee at or before maturity is not in excess of 3%.
8. Securities issued by motor carriers subject to the Interstate Commerce Act, or any interest in a railroad equipment trust.
9. Certificates issued by a receiver or by a trustee in bankruptcy with court approval.
10. Insurance policies and annuity contracts issued by corporations subject to supervision of state insurance or banking commissioners.
11. Securities exchanged by an issuer with existing security holders exclusively, with no commission or other remuneration involved for soliciting the exchange.
12. Securities sold solely to residents of the state in which the issuer is incorporated and doing business.

The SECURITIES AND EXCHANGE COMMISSION may from time to time by its rules and regulations, and subject to such terms and conditions as may be therein prescribed, add any class of securities to the securities exempted (15 U.S.C. 77c(b)). It can do this if it finds that the enforcement of the registration requirement with respect to such securities is not necessary in the public interest and for the protection of investors because of the small amount involved or the limited character of the public offering, except where the aggregate amount at which such issue is offered to the public exceeds $500,000 (Regulation A general exemption for U.S. and Canadian issues up to that amount). The commission has adopted the following additional exemptions:

1. Regulation B exemption for fractional undivided interests in oil or gas rights up to $250,000.
2. Regulation E exemption for securities of a small business investment company up to $500,000.
3. Regulation F exemption for assessments on assessable stock and for assessable stock offered or sold to realize the amount of assessment up to $300,000.
4. Rules 234-237 and 240 exemptions of first lien notes, securities of cooperative housing corporations, shares offered in connection with certain transactions, certain securities owned for five years, and certain limited offers and sales of small dollar amounts of securities by closely held issuers.

EXHAUST PRICE *First read* MARGIN.
One who carries securities on margin has only an equity or partial interest in the securities he is carrying. In case of a fall in prices which threatens to wipe out the owner's equity or margin, the exhaust price is approached. In other words, the exhaust price is the price at which these securities would have to be sold entirely to obliterate the margin, or the price at which the broker would have to sell in order to protect himself from loss. Brokers compel their customers to furnish additional margin before the exhaust price is reached, or to enter a STOP LOSS ORDER which may be placed several points above the exhaust price.

EX-INTEREST Without interest, meaning that the next maturing coupon has been detached. The term is particularly reserved to use in reference to registered bonds.

EXPANSION A period of business growth, i.e., of increased production and consumption, necessitating an increase in the quantity and rapidity of circulation of money and in the volume of credits, and usually higher prices. If unduly prolonged, expansion may lead to INFLATION.
See BUSINESS CYCLE.

EXPECTATIONS THEORY OF INTEREST RATES
A theory that purports to explain the shape of the yield curve, or the term structure of interest rates. The forces that determine the shape of the yield curve have been widely debated among academic economists for a number of years. The American economist Irving Fisher advanced the expectations theory of interest rates to explain the shape of the curve. According to this theory, longer-term rates are determined by investor expectations of future short-term rates.

In mathematical terms, the theory suggests that:

$$(1 + R_2)^2 = (1 + R_1) \times (1 + E(R_1))$$

where

R_2 = the rate on two-year securities,
R_1 = the rate on one-year securities,
$E(R_1)$ = the rate expected on one-year securities one year from now.

The left side of this equation is the amount per dollar invested that the investor would have after two years if he invested in two-year securities. The right side shows the amount he can expect to have after two years if he invests in one-year obligations. Competition is assumed to make the left side equal to the right side.

The theory is easily generalized to cover any number of maturity classes. And however many maturity classes there may be, the theory always explains the existence of longer-term rates in terms of expected future shorter-term rates.

The expectations theory of interest rates provides the theoretical basis for the use of the yield curve as an analytical tool by economic and financial analysts. For example, an upward-sloping yield curve is explained as an indication that the market expects rising short-term rates in the future. Since rising rates normally occur during economic expansions, an upward-sloping yield curve is a sign that the market expects continued expansion in the level of economic activity.

Financial analysts sometimes use this equation to obtain a market-related forecast of future interest rates. It can be rewritten as follows:

$$E(R_1) = [(1 + R_2)^2 / (1 + R_1)] - 1$$

The equation suggests that the short-term rate expected by the market next period can be obtained from knowledge of rates today.

EXPECTED VALUE The probability weighted value of a variable is the expected value of that variable. If a firm's decision makers think, for example, that there is a 10% probability that next year's profits will be $100,000; a 55% probability that they will be $200,000; and a 35% probability that they will be $300,000, then the expected value of profits is:

E [profits] = 0.10 x ($100,000) + 0.55 x ($200,000) + 0.35 x ($300,000)
= $10,000 + $110,000 + $105,000
= $225,000.

EXPENSE FUND A fund which the law requires to be created by the organizers of a nonstock or mutual savings bank to provide for current expenses until the bank operates upon a profitable basis and to meet current interest charges upon deposits. The expense fund represents the savings bank's working capital when it begins operations.

See GUARANTY FUND.

EXPENSES Outflows or other using up of assets or incurrence of liabilities (or a combination of both) during a period from delivering or producing goods, rendering services, or carrying out other activities that constitute the entity's ongoing major or central operations.

Expenses represent actual or expected cash outflows that have occurred or will eventually occur as a result of the enterprise's ongoing major or central operations during a period. The MATCHING PRINCIPLE of accounting requires that expenses be matched with revenues whenever it is reasonable and practicable. Three major expense recognition principles have been established for determining the accounting period in which expenses are recognized and reported:

1. **Associating cause and effect.** Some costs are recognized as expenses on the basis of a presumed direct association with specific revenues. For example, a sale of a product involves both sales revenue and cost of goods sold. The cost of the goods sold would be recognized in the accounting period that the sales revenue was recognized.
2. **Systematic and rational allocation.** Where there is no cause and effect relationship, an attempt is made to associate costs in a systematic and rational manner with the products of the periods affected. Costs that are associated with periods in a systematic way include depreciation and amortization expenses.
3. **Immediate recognition.** Costs that cannot be related to revenues either by associating cause and effect or by systematic and rational allocation are recognized as expenses of the current period. Such costs could include auditor's fee, research and development costs, and officers' salaries.

Expenses never include such items as dividend payments, repayment of loan principal, and expenditures to acquire items having future value (assets) to an enterprise.

The term cost should not be used to refer to expense. An expense is an expired cost. A cost can refer to an item that has service potential (an asset). An expense would arise when the cost no longer has service potential.

See ELEMENTS OF ACCOUNTING.

EXPIRATION DATE The date upon which the validity or privilege which may be exercised under a contract or document terminates. This term is usually employed in connection with a letter of credit, option, etc.

EXPIRY DATE *See* EXPIRATION DATE.

EXPORT The goods and services sold by the United States to foreign households, businesses, and governments. The net export component of GNP is the value of U.S. exports less the value of U.S. imports over a specified time period. Net exports are negative when the United States buys more goods and services from foreign countries than it sells to these nations. Net exports are positive when the United States is selling more goods and services to foreign countries than it is purchasing.

Listed below are data on U.S. exports and U.S. net exports:

Year	Exports ($billions)	Net Exports ($billions)
1950	14.5	2.2
1960	29.9	5.9
1970	68.9	8.5
1980	351.0	32.1
1981	382.8	33.9
1982	361.9	26.3
1983	352.5	−6.1
1984	383.5	−58.9
1985	369.9	−79.2
1986	376.2	−105.5
1987	426.7	−119.9

Economic Report of the President, 1988.

BIBLIOGRAPHY

BANKS, H. "The Political Realities of Trade." *Forbes*, May 15, 1989.
"Beyond Trade Finance." *Global Trade*, March, 1989.
BRICK, T. G. "How to Succeed in Exporting." *Industry Week*, November 7, 1988.
The Chase Manhattan Bank, New York, NY:
The Chase World Guide for Exporters.
The Chase Guide to Government Export Credit Agencies.
Dynamics of Trade Finance, 1984.
Custom House Guide. North American Publishing Co., Philadelphia, PA. Annual.
Exporters' Encyclopedia. Dun and Bradstreet, Inc. New York, NY. Annual.
FREDERICK, P. G. "Europe: 1992: The Blueprint For Change." *Marketing Communications*, March, 1989.
"Glossary of Terms." *Accountancy*, April, 1989.
GOLOB, S. "Making Trade Freer, Fairer." *Transportation and Distribution*, October, 1988.
KINGMAN-BRUNDAGE, J., and SCHULZ, S. A. *The Fundamentals of Trade Finance*, 1986.
"Legal Aspects of Doing Business Overseas." *Business America.* March, 1989.
"Legislation Update [Omnibus Trade and Competitiveness Act of 1988]." *Business America*, December, 1988.
PILCHER, R. "Managing Exports Effectively." *Accountancy.* April, 1989.
REFERENCE BOOK FOR WORLD TRADERS. Croner Publications, Inc., Jamaica, NY. Looseleaf.
U.S. IMPORT TRADE REGULATIONS. Bureau of National Affairs, Inc. Washington, DC, 1985.
———. *U.S. International Trade Laws.* Bureau of National Affairs, Inc., Washington, DC, 1985.
VENEDIKIAN, H. M., and WARFIELD, G. *Export-Import Financing.* John Wiley and Sons, Inc., New york, NY. Latest edition.
WILLIAMS, K. "Investigating the Export Market." *Management Accounting*, January, 1989.

EXPORT BAR Bar or ingot of pure gold, customarily used in making gold shipments for settlement of international balances.

See GOLD BARS.

EXPORT CONTROLS The primary authority for controlling U.S. exports is the Export Administration Act of 1979. This act was amended by the omnibus Trade and Competitiveness Act of 1988 (P.L. 100-418). The act provided a one-year extension of that act until September 30, 1990.

Export controls have been used to further U.S. national security, foreign policy objectives, and domestic economic goals such as to prevent domestic shortages and inflation. There has been considerable concern about how the Administration would administer export controls without doing harm to U.S. competitiveness in the international markets.

During the post-World War II era, export controls have also been used to restrict Soviet bloc access to dual-use technologies. The U.S. has controlled exports through LICENSING systems. Export controls have been applied unilaterally and in coordination with allies.

The Omnibus Trade and Competitiveness Act of 1988 enhanced multilateral controls over technology exports; to ease controls over exports to the People's Republic of China; to clarify the foreign availability provisions of the Export Administration Act; to simplify the licensing requirements and reduce license processing times; to reduce the size of the control list; and to define the roles of the various U.S. government agencies within the control powers.

EXPORT CREDIT *See* LETTER OF CREDIT.

EXPORT-IMPORT BANK The life of the key federal international banking organization, the Export-Import Bank of the United States (Eximbank), was continued by act of March 13, 1968 (82 Stat. 47). The Export Expansion Finance Act of 1971 (12 U.S.C. 635 note) removed the receipts and disbursements of the bank from the budget of the U.S. government and increased its overall lending authority. The Export-Import Bank of Washington was originally authorized in 1934 as a banking corporation organized under the laws of the District of Columbia (per Executive Order 6581, February 2, 1934). The bank was continued as an agency of the United States by acts of Congress in 1935, 1937, 1939, and 1940. It was made an independent agency of the federal government by the Export-Import Bank Act of 1945 (12 U.S.C. 635), which was subsequently amended in 1947 to reincorporate the bank under federal charter. The official description continues as follows.

The Export-Import Bank Act, as amended, provides for a five-person board of directors, consisting of the president of the Export-Import Bank who serves as chairman, the first vice president who serves as vice chairman, and three additional directors appointed by the President of the United States by and with the advice and consent of the Senate. Of the five members of the board, not more than three may be members of any one political party.

The purposes of the bank are to aid in financing and to facilitate exports and imports and the exchange of commodities between the U.S. or any of its territories or insular possessions and any foreign country or the agencies or nationals thereof. The Export-Import Bank Act of 1945, as amended, expresses the policy of the Congress that the bank should supplement and encourage, not compete with, private capital; that loans should generally be for specific purposes and at rates based upon the average cost of money to the bank as well as the bank's mandate to provide competitive financing and offer reasonable assurance of repayment; that the financing provided for U.S. exports should be competitive with the financing provided by the U.S.'s principal foreign competitors; and that in authorization of loans and guarantees account should be taken of human rights considerations and any serious adverse effects upon the competitive position of U.S. industry, the availability of materials which are in short supply in the United States, and employment in the United States.

The bank is authorized to have outstanding at any one time dollar loans, guarantees, and insurance in an aggregate amount not in excess of $40 billion. The bank is also authorized to have a capital stock of $1 billion and to borrow from the U.S. Treasury on its own obligations up to not more than $6 billion outstanding at any one time.

The recognition that export credit availability is as important a competitive tool as price, quality, or service has resulted in programs designed to meet specific exporter needs and to broaden significantly the horizon of export opportunity for U.S. industry.

Among the programs that Eximbank offers are those relating to direct credits to borrowers outside the United States, export credit insurance, and export credit guarantees. Long-term direct credits to foreign borrowers are usually extended in connection with sales abroad of capital goods. Eximbank will finance a portion of the U.S. costs, with the balance of the financing provided from the borrowers' own resources and private sources. Eximbank may guarantee part or all of the private financing.

The facilities of the Foreign Credit Insurance Association (FCIA), an association of commercial insurance companies formed by Eximbank and the insurance industry in 1961 to provide credit protection for U.S. exporters, are used by businesses of all sizes. Policies issued by the FCIA insure repayment in the event of default by a foreign buyer and may be used as collateral for bank loans to U.S. exporters. FCIA policies cover both short-term and medium-term transactions.

Under a similar program, the Eximbank guarantees repayment to commercial banks which finance medium-term transactions for exporters. It is also issuing guarantees to exporters covering service contracts, leases, and other special situations.

The appended table shows various Export-Import Bank programs.

Important changes inaugurated in fiscal year 1987 make it easier for the bank's programs to support U.S. exports. For example, Eximbank now has essentially one loan program and one guarantee program for both medium- and long-term exporter transactions. Both programs provide up to 85% financing, operate on the basis of preliminary commitments, and are open to any responsible party. Eximbank loans also carry the minimum interest rate allowed by the Organization for Economic Cooperation and Development. Other changes, including a restructuring of the fee schedule based on risk, should help make Eximbank programs more accessible to financial institutions and exporters.

Other Eximbank programs include the Working Capital Guarantee Program, a loan guarantee program designed to provide eligible exporters with access to working capital loans from commercial lenders, and the Engineering Multiplier Program, which provides financing in support of project-related design services or feasibility studies with potential for generating further procurement of U.S. exports.

Short Term (Up to 180 days)	
Product Examples	Appropriate Eximbank FCIA Program
Consumables Small manufactured items Spare parts Raw materials	FCIA policies only

Medium Term (181 days-5 years)	
Capital goods	FCIA policies Commercial bank guarantees Cooperative Financing Facility Discount loans Bank-to-bank guaranteed lines

Long Term (5 years and longer)	
Commercial jet aircraft or other very expensive heavy capital goods	Participation financing: Commercial bank loans combined with direct Eximbank loan Financial guarantee to bank by Eximbank where needed

BIBLIOGRAPHY

EXPORT-IMPORT BANK OF THE UNITED STATES. *Annual Reports*.
———. Export-Import Bank of the United States (current).

EXPORT LETTER OF CREDIT   See LETTER OF CREDIT.

EXPORT SPECIE POINT   See GOLD POINTS.

EXPORT TRADE ACT   See WEBB-POMERENE ACT.

EXPORT TRADING COMPANY   A person, partnership, association, or similar organization established and operated primarily for the purpose of exporting (versus producing) goods and services produced in the United States by persons affiliated with it, or facilitating the exportation of U.S. goods and services produced by unaffiliated persons by providing them with export trade services. Services provided by an export trading company include consulting, advertising, marketing, insurance, research, legal assistance, transportation, communication and processing of foreign orders, warehousing, foreign exchange, financing, and others. The U.S. Department of Commerce is authorized to issue a certificate of review, which makes an export trading company exempt from criminal or civil antitrust action regarding its specified activities.

EXPORT TRADING COMPANY ACT   An act to promote U.S. exports. The Export Trading Company Act of 1982 assists exporters by eliminating antitrust disincentives to individual exporting companies, facilitating the flow of information to exporters concerning export trade service, and improving the availability of trade financing. The Office of Export Trading Company Affairs within the Commerce Department is primarily responsible for implementing policies to achieve these objectives.

The Export Trading Company Act of 1982 contains four basic titles. Title I established the Office of Export Trading Company Affairs (OETCA) within the Commerce Department to administer the antitrust export trade certificate of review program, promote the formation of U.S. Export Trading Companies (ETCs), and facilitate contact between producers of goods and services and export intermediaries. Title IV identified the jurisdictional authorization of the Sherman and FTC acts to export trade.

Title III established antitrust protection to exporters. Procedures for exporters were established which apply to export trade certificate of review. This certificate provides protection against antitrust liability for specific export activities. Exporters no longer need to create a new corporate entity to obtain the protection available under the act. Any exporter can apply for the certificate. Business activities that have been given antitrust protection include: price fixing, exclusive dealing arrangements, customer and territorial allocations, and the exchange of business information.

Title II of the act permits bank holding companies and other financial institutions to make equity investments in ETCs, subject to the approval of the Federal Reserve Board. A bank-affiliated ETC must be exclusively engaged in activities related to international trade and must derive more than 50% of its revenues from exporting.

From October 1983 through October 1987, the Commerce Department issued 892 certificates of review providing antitrust protection to 684 firms and individuals. As of September 1, 1987, $553 million in export sales had been reported by certificate holders in their annual reports.

EXPRESS COMPANY MONEY ORDER See MONEY ORDERS.

EX-RIGHTS First read RIGHT.

Without rights. When stock is sold ex-rights, all privileges are retained by or reserved to the seller.

EX-STOCK DIVIDEND Without the stock dividend. When stock is sold ex-stock dividend, the pending stock dividend is retained as the property of the seller.

See STOCK DIVIDEND.

EXTENDED BOND A bond on which the payment of the principal is postponed. When the repayment of bonds cannot conveniently be met at maturity in cash, the bondholders may be offered new bonds to take their place or the old bonds may be extended. In the latter case, when the security behind them is not changed, the bonds are said to be extended or continued. An extended bond is not to be confused with an EXTENSION BOND.

See CONTINUED BONDS.

EXTENSION BOND A bond similar to a DIVISONAL BOND, but the underlying mortgage of which does not necessarily coincide with the divisions of the issuing organization. Extension bonds usually are covered by railroad property which is a continuation or extension of the existing system. They are frequently secured not only by the extension property, but also by a junior lien upon other portions of the property.

The strength of extension bonds as an investment depends on whether the extended property is a main line and essential to the handling of through traffic.

An extension bond should not be confused with an EXTENDED BOND.

EXTERNAL BOND When a government borrows money by floating a bond issue in a foreign country, it is said to float an external loan, and its bonds are external bonds. The principal and interest of such bonds are issued and payable in the currency of the country in which the bonds are marketed and have the advantage of eliminating the risks of exchange fluctuations for the nationals of the country whose currency is used. Such loans are to be distinguished from INTERNAL BONDS which the government sells to investors within the country.

See FOREIGN GOVERNMENT BONDS.

EXTERNAL LOAN See EXTERNAL BOND.

EXTINGUISHMENT FUND See SINKING FUND.

EXTRA DIVIDEND An additional cash dividend paid out of earnings which are above the normal rate. Whenever dividends are paid out of profits earned at an extraordinary rate, the dividends should be earmarked as extra, so that the stockholders will understand that the additional dividend disbursement is not necessarily to be maintained and therefore not to be regularly expected. It is a good rule of corporation finance that a regular dividend should not be increased unless there is reason to believe that it can be maintained.

See DIVIDEND.

EXTRAORDINARY ITEM A material event or transaction that is both unusual in nature and infrequent in occurrence. To be unusual in nature, the underlying event or transaction must have a high degree of abnormality and be clearly unrelated to, or only incidentally related to, the ordinary and typical activities of the entity, taking into account the environment in which the entity operates. Infrequency of occurrence relates to the requirement that the underlying event or transaction should be of a type that would not reasonably be expected to recur in the foreseeable future, taking into account the environment in which the entity operates. The material effect of individual events or transactions is considered separately and not aggregated unless the effects result from a single identifiable transaction or event that meets the definition of an extraordinary item.

Extraordinary items could result if gains or losses were the direct result of any of the following events or circumstances:

1. A major casualty, such as an earthquake.
2. An expropriation of property by a foreign government.
3. A prohibition under a newly enacted law or regulation.

The INCOME STATEMENT should disclose captions and amounts for individual extraordinary events or transactions on the face of the statement. Income taxes applicable to the extraordinary item should be disclosed. Extraordinary items can be reported as follows:

Income before extraordinary items	$XXX
Extraordinary items (less applicable income taxes of $XXX)	$XXX
Net income	$XXX

A material event or transaction that is unusual in nature or occurs infrequently is reported as a separate element of income from continuing operations and is not classified as an extraordinary item.

F

FACE VALUE The principal or nominal VALUE appearing on a bond, note, coupon, piece of money, or other instrument, PAR VALUE. The face value of a bond is the amount at which the issuing organization contracts to repay it at maturity and is the basis upon which the cash interest rate is computed. While it is ordinarily the plan of an issuing organization to float bonds at a rate of interest attractive enough to justify their sale at approximately par, or at a slight discount, when placed on the market they fluctuate in accordance with money rates and in accordance with general business conditions and earnings. Whether a bond commands a premium or sells at a discount, the nearer it approaches maturity, the nearer the market value approximates its par value, until at the date of maturity, the two values should precisely coincide. Face value is not to be confused with market value, book value, intrinsic value, investment value, or trading value.

FACTOR An accounts receivable financing institution. The essence of factoring in the financial sense is the discounting of acceptable accounts receivable on a nonrecourse, notification basis. Accounts receivable are sold outright to the factor, who assumes the full risk of collection and credit losses, without recourse to the firms discounting the receivables in the event of loss. Customers are notified to remit directly to the factor. Thus firms using a factoring service avoid the tying up of working capital cash in accounts receivable for the full credit period and in addition eliminate the necessity for credit and collection departments. Firms using a factoring service have the privilege of drawing on the net cash proceeds of discounting of the accounts receivable, before the average due date thereof, in which case interest is paid (usually 2% to 3% above the New York bank prime rate), or at the average due date, in which case no interest is charged (instead the factor will pay interest at an agreed rate, usually 2% below the New York bank prime rate). See appended table.

Typical Factoring Arrangement

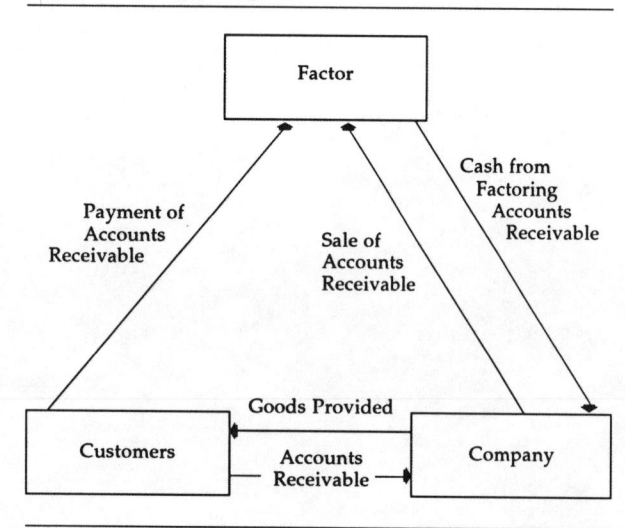

Factors, however, are usually more than merely receivables financing institutions. Other credit extended may include loans on inventories, fixed assets, and other forms of security, as well as unsecured credit. Moreover, factors are uniquely qualified to render valuable advisory services to clients by reason of their long identification with and knowledge of the lines they finance, including advice on budgeting, planning, operations, styling and merchandising, and purchasing.

In addition to charging interest on cash availability before average due date of receivables discounted, factors charge a commission, ranging from less than 1% to 1.5% of the gross amount of invoices.

Factors particularly have been identified with the development of the textile industry, but factoring services in recent years have been extended to a variety of other lines.

BIBLIOGRAPHY

MALTY, T. D. "Export Factoring Moves into the Spotlight." *Global Trade*, July, 1989.
NICHOLS, D. "Factors That Let the Cash Flow." *Venture*, June-July, 1989.

FACTOR OF PRODUCTION Land, labor, capital, and ENTREPRENEURSHIP. A firm uses many factors to assist in the production process. If the output of a firm is viewed in terms of the number of units produced, then there are four important factors. These factors include capital, labor, land, and raw materials. In economics, the output from production is often measured as value added, the value that is added to the final product in the last stage of production. Therefore, the relevant inputs are reduced to only capital and labor. Thus, it is common to see in introductory economics texts a production function written as $Q - f(K,L)$, meaning that value added is derived in the final stage of production from only the contribution of capital and labor. More and more economists are incorporating technology as an input into their theoretical models. The empirical application of these models is limited by the availability of useful measurement of technology inputs.

FACTOR OF SAFETY See MARGIN OF SAFETY.

FAILS In security markets, a fail-to-deliver arises when the selling broker or dealer fails to deliver securities as contracted. On the position book of the selling broker or dealer, a fail-to-deliver increases the long security position; on the money books of account, it gives rise to a debit balance (due from the purchasing broker or dealer upon delivery).

A fail-to-receive arises when the purchasing broker or dealer fails to receive securities as contracted. On the position book of the purchasing broker or dealer, a fail-to-receive increases the short security position; on the money books of account, it gives rise to a credit balance (due the selling broker or dealer upon receipt of the securities.)

One of the important measures undertaken to improve deliveries has been inauguration of Central Certificate Service (CCS), an electronic method for delivering stock between brokers.

Establishment of the DEPOSITORY TRUST COMPANY, new procedures for settlement and clearing, and the growing size of the average trade were also credited by the NEW YORK STOCK EXCHANGE with reducing total fails to normal levels.

Bankruptcy Petitions Filed, By Type and Chapter: 1975 to 1987
(For years ending June 30)

Item	1975	1979	1980 [1]	1981	1982	1983	1984	1985	1986	1987
Total	254,484	226,476	277,880 [2]	360,329	367,866	374,734	344,275	364,536	477,856	561,278
Business	30,130	29,500	36,449	47,415	56,423	69,818	62,170	66,651	76,281	88,278
Non-business	224,354	196,976	241,431	312,914	311,443	304,916	282,105	297,885	401,575	473,000
Voluntary	253,198	225,549	276,691	358,997	366,331	373,064	342,828	362,939	476,214	559,658
Involuntary	1,286	927	1,189	1,332	1,535	1,670	1,447	1,597	1,642	1,620
Chapter 7 [3]	209,330	183,259	214,357	265,721	255,098	251,322	232,994	244,650	332,679	397,551
Chapter 9 [4]	—	1	—	1	4	3	4	3	7	10
Chapter 11 [5]	3,506	3,042	5,302	7,828	14,059	21,207	19,913	21,425	24,443	22,566
Chapter 13 [6]	41,178	39,442	58,216	86,778	98,705	102,201	91,358	98,452	120,726	136,300
Chapter 304 [7]	X	X	5	1	—	1	6	6	1	27

— Represents zero.
X Not applicable.
[1] For the first three months of 1980 the judiciary operated under the Bankruptcy Act and for the last nine months under the new Bankruptcy Reform Act of 1978. Includes only those petitions filed under the new bankruptcy code.
[2] Includes five Section 304 cases filed under the Reform Act in 1980 and 1 in 1981 which are not included in the subcategories of voluntary/involuntary.
[3] Chapter 7, liquidation of non-exempt assets of businesses or individuals.
[4] Chapter 9, adjustment of debts of a municipality.
[5] Chapter 11, individual or business reorganization.
[6] Chapter 13, adjustment of debts of an individual with regular income.
[7] 11 U.S.C., Section 304, cases ancillary to foreign proceedings.

Source: *Survey of Current Business*, U.S. Department of Commerce, Bureau of Economic Analysis.

FAILURES Business failures are the mortality of business firms. Failures are regarded as an important business barometer, although fundamentally they are results and effects of underlying business trends, rather than motivating causes. As may be expected, the number of failures and their total liabilities tend to vary directly with the business cycle.

Economic failure: A business firm which is unable to earn the representative or "going" rate of profit for its line of business, to justify continuance of the invested capital in the firm, may be said to be an economic failure. Indeed, in economics (microeconomics, or that branch of the subject which is concerned with economic theory of the firm), it is customary to include as part of costs of the firm the representative or "going" rate of profit for its line of business.

Failure in the equity sense: A business firm may be technically insolvent, or unable to pay its debts in the amounts and times when due, even though its assets exceed its total liabilities and therefore it has a positive net worth.

Failure in the bankruptcy sense: A business firm may be bankrupt, and hence a failure in that its liabilities exceed its assets and therefore there is no net worth. See appended table.

Business failures of firms both in the equity and in the bankruptcy sense may be accorded relief under the Federal Bankruptcy Code of 1978, codifying and enacting the laws relating to bankruptcy as Title II of the U.S. Code, and replacing the former National Bankruptcy Act as amended, effective October 1, 1979. The term bankrupt is replaced by the term debtor.

Statistics on business failures are prepared and published regularly by DUN & BRADSTREET (D&B) which firm reports failures by divisions of industry and trade, by size of liabilities, by industry groups, in large cities, by Federal Reserve Districts, by geographic regions and states (U.S.), and Canadian failures (by provinces). The Dun's Failure Index is also compiled and published regularly.

For the D&B series, "Business Failures" include those businesses that ceased operations following assignment or bankruptcy; ceased with loss to creditors after such actions as execution, foreclosure, or attachment; voluntarily withdrew leaving unpaid obligations; were involved in court actions such as receivership, reorganization, or arrangement; or voluntarily compromised with creditors out of court. Liabilities, as tabulated in the failure record, include all accounts and notes payable and all obligations, whether in secured form or not, known to be held by banks, officers, affiliated companies, supplying companies, or the government. They do not include long-term, publicly held obligations, and offsetting assets are not taken into account. But all industrial and commercial failures that are petitioned into the federal bankruptcy courts are included in the failure count.

The U.S. Department of Commerce carries the D&B statistics on Industrial and Commercial Failures, both as to numbers and as to total current liabilities, and the Failure Annual Rate (number per 10,000 concerns listed in D&B's Reference Book), in its monthly *Survey of Current Business* and its *Business Statistics*, the biennial supplement to the *Survey of Current Business*.

See BANK FAILURES, BANK INSOLVENCY, NATIONAL BANKRUPTCY ACT.

FAIR CREDIT BILLING ACT An act that establishes procedures for the prompt correction of errors on a revolving credit account and prevents damage to credit ratings while a dispute is being settled. The Fair Credit Billing Act (15 U.S.C. 1666) and the Consumer Leasing Act (15 U.S.C. 1667) were added by act of October 28, 1974, to the Consumer Credit Protection Act, enacted on May 29, 1968, and effective June 1, 1969, which included the Truth-in-Lending Act (15 U.S.C. 1601). With the exception of the Consumer Leasing Act, whose provisions are now implemented by Regulation M of the FEDERAL RESERVE BOARD REGULATIONS pursuant to the Truth-in-Lending Simplification and Reform Act (Title VI of the Depository Institutions Deregulation and Monetary Control Act of 1980), the referenced acts were implemented by amendments to Regulation Z of the Federal Reserve Board Regulations. Administrative enforcement, as for other specific consumer protection laws, is shared by the Federal Reserve System with other federal agencies depending on the type of credit involved.

Regulation Z simplifies billing-error procedures. The statute requires that creditors provide consumers with an annual reminder of their billing rights. As explained by the Board of Governors of the Federal Reserve System, under the regulation, the creditor can do this in one of two ways. First, a complete or long form of the billing rights statement may be sent annually to those consumers entitled to a periodic statement in the cycle in which the billing rights statement is sent. If the creditor uses this alternative, account holders who do not receive a periodic statement in that cycle would not receive the annual notice. For the long form, there is an additional option: it can be sent to all consumers once a year, and more than one billing cycle can be used to complete the mailing.

The creditor's second way to comply is to send a billing rights summary, rather than the full text, with each periodic statement. The summary information need not be part of the periodic statement that the consumer may retain. Although creditors are not required to use the sample notice, all notices must be substantially similar to the sample provided in Regulation Z (appendices G-3 and G-4). The "substantially similar" requirement should provide creditors with sufficient flexibility to adapt their model forms to applicable state "plain-English" laws.

The Fair Credit Billing Act generally applies only to "open end" credit accounts. Open end accounts include credit cards, revolving charge accounts (such as department store accounts), and overdraft checking. The periodic bills or billing statements a customer receives (usually monthly for such accounts) are covered by the FCBA. The act does not apply to a loan or credit sale which

FAIR CREDIT BILLING ACT

is paid according to a fixed schedule until the entire amount is paid back.

The FCBA settlement procedure applies only to disputes over "billing errors" on periodic statements, such as the following:

Charges not made by you or anyone authorized to use your account.

Charges which are incorrectly identified or for which the wrong amount or date is shown.

Charges for goods or services you did not accept or which were not delivered as agreed.

Computational or similar errors.

Failure to properly reflect payments or other credits, such as returns.

Not mailing or delivering bills to your current address provided you give a change of address at least 20 days before the billing period ends).

Charges for which you request an explanation or written proof of purchase.

To be protected under the law, the customer must send a separate written billing error notice to the creditor. The notice must reach the creditor within 60 days after the first bill containing the error was mailed and to the address provided on the bill for billing error notices. The letter must contain the following information: name and account number; statement that the customer believes the bill contains a billing error and the dollar amount involved; the reasons why the customer believes there is a mistake. The customer is advised to send it by certified mail, with a return receipt requested.

The letter claiming a billing error must be acknowledged by the creditor in writing within 30 days after it is received, unless the problem is resolved within that period. Within two billing cycles (but not more than 90 days), the creditor must conduct a reasonable investigation and either correct the mistake or explain why the bill is believed to be correct. The customer may withhold payment of the amount in dispute until the dispute is resolved. While the FCBA dispute settlement procedure is going on, the creditor may not take any legal or other action to collect the amount in dispute. The account may not be closed or restricted in any way, except that the disputed amount may be applied against the customer's credit limit. While the bill is being disputed, the creditor may not threaten to damage the customer's credit rating or report the customer as delinquent to anyone. The creditor is allowed to report that the customer is disputing the bill, but one cannot be denied credit merely for disputing a bill (Equal Credit Opportunity Act).

If the creditor makes a mistake, the creditor must write explaining the corrections to be made on the account. The creditor must also remove all finance charges, late fees, or other charges relating to that amount. If the creditor concludes that the customer owes part of the disputed amount, this must be explained in writing. The customer also has the right to request copies of documents proving he or she owes the money. If the bill is correct, the customer must be told promptly in writing how much is owed and why. The customer can ask for copies of relevant documents. At this point, the customer will owe the disputed amount, plus any finance charges that accumulated while it was disputed. If the customer still disagrees, the customer is encouraged to write the creditor within 10 days after receiving the explanation stating that he or she still refuses to pay the disputed amount. At this point, the creditor may begin collection procedures. If the creditor reports someone to a credit bureau as delinquent, the creditor must also state that the customer does not think he or she owes the money. Also, the customer must be told who receives such reports.

If the creditor does not follow the FCBA dispute settlement procedures, the creditor may not collect the amount in dispute, or any finance charges on it, up to $50, even if the bill turns out to be correct. The customer also has the right to sue a creditor for any violation of the FCBA.

Disputes about quality of goods and services are not necessarily "billing errors." However, the FCBA allows the customer to take the same legal actions against the credit card issuer as one could take under state law against the seller. Before legal action is taken, the customer must give the seller a chance to remedy the problem. Also, unless the seller is also the card issuer, the customer must have bought the item in the creditor's home state or within 100 miles of the sellers, current mailing address, and the amount charged must have been more than $50.

The FCBA also requires "open end" creditors to do the following for their customers:

1. Give written notice when a customer opens a new account, and at other specified times, describing the right to dispute billing errors.
2. Provide a statement for each billing period in which that customer owes more than $1.
3. Mail or deliver the bill to the customer at least 14 days before the payment is due. The customers are given a time period within which to pay the bill without incurring additional finance or other charges.
4. Credit all payments to the customer's account as of the date they are received, unless not doing so would not result in extra charges.
5. Promptly credit or refund overpayments.

A customer can sue a creditor who violates any FCBA provisions. If the customer wins, he or she may be awarded damages resulting from the violation, plus twice the amount of any finance charge (not less than $100 or more than $1,000). The court may also order the creditor to pay attorney's fees and costs.

The FEDERAL TRADE COMMISSION enforces the FCBA for almost all creditors except banks. While the commission does not represent individuals in private disputes, questions or complaints can be addressed to the nearest Federal Trade Commission regional office or to the Federal Trade Commission, Fair Credit Billing, Washington, D.C. 20580.

Rights of consumers under the Fair Credit Billing Act are summarized by the Federal Trade Commission as follows:

1. To be told the name and address of the consumer reporting agency responsible for preparing a consumer report that was used to deny the consumer credit, insurance, or employment, or to increase the cost of credit or insurance;
2. At any time and for any reason, to be told the nature, substance, and sources (except investigative-type sources) of the information (except medical) collected on the consumer by a consumer reporting agency;
3. To take anyone of the consumer's choosing with him when he visits the consumer reporting agency;
4. To obtain the information free of charge when the consumer has been denied credit, insurance, or employment within 30 days of such interview (otherwise, the reporting agency is permitted to charge a reasonable fee for making the disclosure);
5. To be told who has received a consumer report on the consumer within the preceding six months (or within the preceding two years if the report was furnished for employment purposes);
6. In most instances, to have incomplete or incorrect information reinvestigated and, if the information is found to be inaccurate or cannot be verified, to have such information removed from the file;
7. To have the agency notify those the consumer names (at no cost to the consumer) who have previously received the incorrect or incomplete information that the information has been deleted;
8. When a dispute between the consumer and the reporting agency cannot be resolved, to have the consumer's version of the dispute placed in the file and included in subsequent consumer reports;
9. To request the agency to send the consumer's version of the dispute to certain businesses for a reasonable fee;
10. To have a consumer report withheld from anyone who under the law does not have a legitimate business need for the information;
11. To sue a company for damages if it willfully or negligently violates the law and, if successful, to collect attorney's fees and court costs;
12. To have most adverse information not reported after seven years (one major exception is bankruptcy, which may be reported for 10 years). Information reported because of an application for a job with a salary of more than $20,000 has no time limitation. Information reported because of an application for more than $50,000 worth of credit or life insurance has no time limitation. Information concerning a lawsuit or judgment against an individual can be reported for seven years or until the statute of limitations runs out, whichever is longer.

13. To be notified of the fact that a company is seeking information, which would constitute an investigative consumer report;
14. To request from a company that ordered an investigative report further information as to the nature and scope of the investigation;
15. To discover the nature and substance (but not the sources) of the information that was collected for an investigative consumer report.

The Fair Credit Billing Act, however, does *not*:

1. Give the consumer the right to request a report on himself from the consumer reporting agency;
2. Give the consumer the right, when he visits the agency, to receive a copy of or to physically handle his file;
3. Compel anyone to do business with an individual consumer;
4. Apply when the consumer applies for commercial (as distinguished from consumer) credit or business insurance;
5. Authorize any federal agency to intervene on behalf of the individual consumer.

Administrative enforcement of the Fair Credit Billing Act is vested in the Federal Trade Commission and, to the extent specified in the act, in respect to consumer reporting agencies and persons who use consumer reports from such agencies, in the banking agencies (Comptroller of the Currency, for national banks; Federal Reserve board, for member banks of the Federal Reserve System other than national banks; Board of Directors of the Federal Deposit Insurance Corporation, for banks insured by that agency other than members of the Federal Reserve System); in the Federal Home Loan Bank Board (acting directly or through the Federal Savings and Loan Insurance Corporation), in the case of any institution subject to any of the act's provisions; in the administrator of the National Credit Union Administration, with respect to any federal credit union; in the Interstate Commerce Commission, with respect to any common carrier subject to the acts to regulate commerce; in the Civil Aeronautics Board, with respect to any air carrier or foreign air carrier subject to the Federal Aviation Act of 1958; and in the secretary of agriculture, with respect to any activities subject to the Packers and Stockyards Act of 1921.

Financial institutions are likely to be subject to the act as credit grantors, purchasers of dealer paper, issuers of credit cards, and employers. In some instances, a financial institution may also be a consumer reporting agency under the act, as a result of the type of information about consumers that it may provide to others. As noted above, the act does not apply to commercial transactions.

BIBLIOGRAPHY

BOARD OF GOVERNORS OF THE FEDERAL RESERVE SYSTEM. *Federal Reserve Regulatory Service.*

FAIR CREDIT REPORTING ACT The Fair Credit Reporting Act, passed in 1970 and effective April 25, 1971, was designed to "insure fair and accurate reporting of information regarding consumers." When banks use a consumer report obtained from another agency, they must certify that the report is being used for a proper purpose. If a report is used to deny credit, raise the cost of credit, or deny employment, the bank must notify the consumer why the denial was made and give the name of the credit reporting agency from which the bank received the information. The act gives the consumer the right to request information concerning his or her credit file from a credit reporting agency. The credit reporting agency can also be required to disclose who has received information furnished for the previous two years. The consumer has the right under certain circumstances to place rebutting information in the file.

FAIR DEBT COLLECTION PRACTICE ACT An act that specifies debt collectors' responsibilities associated with their practice and outlines the requirements and prohibitions involved in the collection of debts. The act does not directly apply to banks, unless they offer collection services for other creditors.

FAIR MARKET VALUE The amount which a willing buyer would pay a willing seller in an ARM'S LENGTH TRANSACTION.

FAIR RETURN Used principally in connection with earnings of railroad and public utility corporations. It developed out of the notion that such public service corporations, by serving the public interest and in many cases being granted monopolistic franchises, should be allowed to charge only such rates for their services as would yield a reasonable return on the fair value of the assets devoted to providing the service. A fair return, therefore, involves two variables: (1) fair valuation of the property required for the services, and (2) fair rate of return thereon.

For years, the 1898 case of *Smyth* v. *Ames* (169 U.S. 466) was the leading case in valuation cases involving the necessary elements in fair value. The comprehensive rule of that case read as follows: "And in order to ascertain that value, the original cost of construction, the amount expended in permanent improvements, the amount and market value of its bonds and stocks, the present as compared with the original cost of construction, the probable earning capacity of the property under particular rates prescribed by statute, and the sum required to meet operating expenses, are all matters for consideration, and are to be given such weight as may be just and right in each case. We do not say that there may not be other matters to be regarded in estimating the value of the property."

Both the original cost and reproduction cost bases for fair valuation were recognized in the above, as well as capitalization and market value thereof. The Supreme Court, however, did not indicate the basis to be used, or even combination of bases, and as a result the courts became involved in a series of valuation cases over the years. By 1933, the Supreme Court was ready to leave the determination of fair valuation and fair rates to the administrative agency concerned, "so long as constitutional limitations are not transgressed" (*Los Angeles Gas & Electric Corp.* v. *Railroad Commission of California*, 289 U.S. 287). Emphasis on any single formula or combination of formulas was finally abandoned in the landmark case of *Federal Power Commission* v. *Hope Natural Gas Co.*, 320 U.S. 591 (1944), in which the doctrine of end result was enunciated, as follows: "Under the statutory standard of "just and reasonable" it is the result reached not the method employed which is controlling. It is not theory but the impact of the rate order which counts. If the total effect of the rate order cannot be said to be unjust and unreasonable, judicial inquiry under the Act is at an end. The fact that the method employed to reach that result may contain infirmities is not then important."

Thus emphasis has shifted from the valuation formula to the earnings result of rates allowed. The *Hope* case indicated that fair rates would be those "which enable the company to operate successfully, to maintain its financial integrity, to attract capital, and to compensate its investors for the risks assumed...." At the federal level, the Federal Power Commission used to standardize rates of return as 6% for all electric companies and 6.5% for all natural gas companies under its jurisdiction, but in recent years it has abandoned such generalization and passes on rates on an individual basis. The Federal Communications Commission prescribes just and reasonable rates for interstate or foreign communications companies. State regulatory commissions operate under varying statutory conditions, some states providing no rate regulatory powers at all over specified types of utilities.

In the case of railroads, the VALUATION ACT OF 1913 provided for valuation of all railroad properties in the U.S. The Interstate Commerce Commission (ICC) finally completed practically all of the work by mid-1934. Then the TRANSPORTATION ACT OF 1920 enacted among other things the concept of fair return on fair value of the railway property providing the service, setting up the recapture clause. If net railway operating income exceeded 6% of the value of the railway property held for and used by the railroad in the service of transportation, one-half of the excess was to be placed in a reserve fund by the railroad, and the remaining half was to be paid into a general railroad contingent fund, to be maintained for the benefit of railroads generally by the ICC. Many railroads opposed this provision as unconstitutional, many not paying and others paying under protest, but the issue was never upset in a test case. Finally, it was repealed by the Transportation Act of 1933. The ICC therefore follows no precise formulas in deciding on just and reasonable rates for all common carriers (railroad, highway, water, and pipeline) and reasonable minimum rates for contract water and highway carriers.

FALSE CLAIMS ACT A 1982 act that provides severe penalties for submission of false claims relative to work performed for the U.S. government (U.S. Code: Chapter 31., Section 3729-31).

FALSE REPORTS Whoever makes any false entry in any book, report, or tatement of any Federal Reserve bank, member bank, national bank, or insured bank, with intent to injure or defraud such bank, or any other company, body politic or corporate, or any individual person, or to deceive any officer of such bank, or the Comptroller of the Currency, or the Federal Deposit Insurance Corporation, or any agent or examiner appointed to examine the affairs of such bank, or the Board of Governors of the Federal Reserve System, shall be fined not more than $5,000 or imprisoned not more than five years, or both (18 U.S.C. 1005).

See CRIMINAL OFFENSES.

Under court decisions (*Thomas* v. *Taylor*, 224 U.S. 73; *Chesbrough et al.* v. *Woodworth*, 195 Fed. Rep. 875), directors are liable in damages to persons relying thereon for making and publishing false reports of condition. The reports required of a national bank by the Comptroller of the Currency are intended not only for his information, but for that of the public. One who buys bank stock out of reliance upon a published false statement and as a consequence sustains loss, has a right of action against the directors or officers who knowingly authorized the publication of such a report (*Chesbrough et al.* v. *Woodworth*, supra).

FALSE STATEMENT ACTS Impose penalties upon any person who misrepresents true condition in a statement for the purpose of securing in any form whatsoever either the delivery of personal property; the payment of cash; the making of a loan or credit; the extension of credit; the discount of an account receivable; the execution, making, or delivery by any person, firm, or corporation of any bond or undertaking; or the making, acceptance, discount, sale or endorsement of a bill of exchange, or promissory note, for the benefit of either himself or of such person, firm, or corporation.

In modern times, the credit practice of banks that prospective borrowers submit recent financial statement or series of statements as a basis for extension of credit or establishment of a line of credit has become widely adopted as proper credit department procedure. The process of granting credit has become more scientific and this requirement has grown out of a recognition that financial statement analysis will lead to better lending. The financial statements should be accurate and free from willfully false valuations and should show the condition actually prevailing. Accordingly, nearly all states have enacted false statement acts. Although such legislation should deter unscrupulous persons from misrepresenting the facts concerning financial condition or means or ability to pay, pitfalls in statement analysis still abound so as to justify insistence upon audited statements with auditor's certificates of reputable accounting firms, and even then, analysis of the data may indicate inclusion of items or accounting treatment which might call for adjustment of the statements and posting the adjustments before the data are considered satisfactory bases for the credit decision.

BIBLIOGRAPHY

NATIONAL ASSOCIATION OF CREDIT MANAGEMENT. *Credit Manual of Commercial Law*.

FAMILY FARMER BANKRUPTCY ACT OF 1986 See FARM BANKRUPTCY ACT.

FANGS Financial instruments issued by subsidiaries (federal agencies) of the United States government. Federal agency securities are not always guaranteed by the Treasury; hence the slang terminology of "FANGs" (Federal Agency Nonguaranteeds) is sometimes used to refer to such securities. Such securities range from 14 to 20 years in maturities. They are issued in minimum denominations of $1,000 are sold with coupons, and are bearer instruments, negotiable and marketable except for specific issues. FANGs carry a favorable rate differential to U.S. Treasury securities of the same maturity and are attractive to depository financial institutions. No federal security has ever defaulted. In recent years, special funding has been required for the Farm Credit Administration and the Federal Savings and Loan Insurance Corporation. Many of the issues are listed regularly in the financial pages.

FARM BANKRUPTCY ACT Provided for compositions or extensions of time for farmers to pay their debts; expired on March 1, 1949. Under the act (the Frazier-Lemke Act, which in 1933 added Sec. 75 A-R to Chapter VIII of the NATIONAL BANKRUPTCY ACT, as amended, on an emergency basis, subject to extensions) conciliation commissioners would be appointed to arrange voluntary compositions between the debtor-farmers and their creditors, with the aim of effecting fair settlement of farmers' debts, based on fair appraised value of the properties involved and fair rental values of the farms. The legislation, enacted in the midst of the severe agricultural depression of the mid-1930s, was administered by such conciliation commissioners generally in a sympathetic manner insofar as farmer-debtors were concerned. Only when such commissioner voluntary compositions failed, would the farmer then have the recourse of bankruptcy under Section 75-S of the old National Bankruptcy Act. Under the new 1979 Bankruptcy Code (Title 11 of the U.S. Code), farmers, although eligible for voluntary relief, cannot be proceeded against involuntarily.

The Bankruptcy Judges, United States Trustees, and Family Farmer Bankruptcy Act of 1986 included a bankruptcy section—Chapter 12—that established special rules for troubled family farm borrowers. The act applies to farm debtors who can meet specified criteria:

1. Debtor and spouse must operate a farming operation with aggregate debts of no more than $1.5 million. Not less than 80 percent of the debtor's debt can arise from the farming operations, with the exception of a home mortgage. More than 50% of the debtor's income must come from farming.
2. More than 50% of a corporation's or partnership's equity must be held by one family (including relatives). If the family or relatives operate the farm, none of the stock can be publicly traded.

Major provisions of the act include the following:

1. A farmer has up to 90 days to file a reorganization plan following the petition for bankruptcy relief (versus 15 days under Chapter 13 of the Bankruptcy Reform Act of 1978). Creditors cannot form a creditors' committee or submit their own repayment plan.
2. A farm debtor is allowed to sell off property that is not required to reorganize before the debtor's plan is approved.
3. A confirmation hearing must be completed within 45 days of the plan's filing. A plan will not be confirmed unless it allows for unsecured creditors to receive, at minimum, what they would get if the debt was liquidated under Chapter 7 of the bankruptcy act.
4. A bankruptcy filing automatically stops creditors from attempting collections. To remove the automatic stay, a secured creditor must be able to show that his interests are not sufficiently protected. Farmers must pay a "reasonable market rent' for use of farmland collateral.
5. The act imposed no limits on the duration of a plan for secured debts; unsecured debts are covered by a three- to five-year limit.
6. Family farmers can request court permission to convert from Chapter 11 or Chapter 13 to Chapter 12.
7. The 1986 act provided for the appointment of 52 new bankruptcy judges and for experimentation with electronic case management.

FARM COOPERATIVES BANKS FOR COOPERATIVES serve marketing, supply, and business service cooperatives whose headquarters are located within their respective districts. To qualify for a loan, at least 80% of the cooperative's voting control must be vested with farmers, ranchers, producers, or harvesters of aquatic products, or federations of cooperatives. For rural electric, telephone, or public utility cooperatives, 70% of the voting control must be held as indicated above. The cooperative must also do 50% of its business with its members. Excepted from this requirement is business done with the federal government and services or supplies furnished by the cooperative as a public utility. Banks for cooperatives provide complete credit service to cooperatives to fulfill their specialized needs. The Central Bank for Cooperatives participates with the other banks for cooperatives in loans that exceed their individual lending limits.

Banks for cooperatives require borrowers at the time of the loan to own at least one share of $100 par value voting stock. Also, borrowers must purchase additional voting or nonvoting stock up to 10% of the loan amount. The amount of capital stock of each bank is determined by the board of directors and approved by the FARM CREDIT ADMINISTRATION.

See COOPERATIVES.

FARM CREDIT ACTS General and permanent laws enacted by Congress which have particular reference to the FARM CREDIT ADMINISTRATION or the corporations under its supervision (i.e., the Federal Land banks and Federal Land Bank associations, the Federal Intermediate Credit banks and Production Credit associations, the Banks for Cooperatives, and the Federal Farm Mortgage Corporation) will be found in the U.S. Code, 1952 Edition and Supplement IV thereto (Title 12, Ch. 7, except Subch. VIII; and certain sections in Title 18).

The acts include but are not limited to:

1. Federal Farm Loan Act (act of July 17, 1916, Ch. 245, 39 Stat. 360), as amended by act of March 4, 1923 (Ch. 252, 42 Stat. 1454): established the Federal Land banks, Joint Stock Land banks (now liquidated), National Farm Loan associations, and Federal Intermediate Credit banks.
2. Agricultural Marketing Act (June 15, 1929, Ch. 24, 46 Stat. 11), as amended: established the Federal Farm Board to promote the "effective merchandising of agricultural commodities in interstate and foreign commerce, and to place agriculture on a basis of economic equality with other industries." All powers and duties of the Federal Farm Board under the act were transferred to the governor of the Farm Credit Administration by Executive Order No. 6084, March 27, 1933, which also abolished certain functions. Activities under the act were greatly curtailed as a result of amendments made by the Farm Credit Act of 1933, below. All loans made from the Agricultural Marketing Act Revolving Fund (12 U.S.C. 1141d) have been liquidated. The revolving fund is now used to capitalize the Banks for Cooperatives, which are authorized to make loans to cooperative associations as defined in the Agricultural Marketing Act as amended, and for the purposes and subject to the conditions and limitations set forth in the act as amended.
3. Emergency Farm Mortgage Act of 1933 (May 12, 1933, Ch. 25, 48 Stat. 51): authorized loans to farmers made by the Federal Land Bank commissioner on behalf of the Federal Farm Mortgage Corporation.
4. Federal Farm Mortgage Corporation Act (January 31, 1934, Ch. 7, 48 Stat. 344): established the Federal Farm Mortgage Corporation, transferred to the Farm Credit Administration, along with its functions and activities, to be administered therein under general direction and supervision, by the Farm Credit Act of 1953.
5. Farm Credit Act of 1933 (June 16, 1933, Ch. 98, 48 Stat. 273): established Production Credit associations and Banks for Cooperatives.
6. Farm Credit Act of 1937 (August 19, 1937, Ch. 704, 50 Stat. 704): created District Farm Credit boards in each Farm Credit district.
7. Farm Credit Act of 1953 (August 6, 1953, Ch. 335, 67 Stat. 390): reestablished the Farm Credit Administration (FCA) as an independent agency in the executive branch of the federal government. After original establishment as an independent agency by Executive Order No. 6084, effective May 27, 1933, the FCA was transferred to the Department of Agriculture by 1939 Reorganization Plan I, effective July 1, 1939. By the Farm Credit Act of 1953, effective December 4, 1953, the FCA was reconstituted under the direction, supervision, and control of the Federal Farm Credit Board therein provided for and was reestablished as an independent agency in the executive branch.
8. Farm Credit Act of 1955 (August 11, 1955, Ch. 785, 69 Stat. 662): provided for the gradual retirement of government capital in the Banks for Cooperatives and for such banks to be privately owned and operated on a cooperative basis.
9. Farm Credit Act of 1956 (July 26, 1956, Ch. 741, 70 Stat. 659): merged the Production Credit Corporation of each district in the Federal Intermediate Credit bank of each district and provided for the government capital in such banks to be retired, with the Production Credit associations eventually to achieve complete ownership of such credit banks.
10. Farm Credit Act of 1959 (August 18, 1959, P.L. 86 = 168, 73 Stat. 384): amended the Federal Farm Loan Act to transfer responsibility for making appraisals from the Farm Credit Administration to the Federal Land banks.
11. The Food and Agriculture Act of 1977, as amended by the acts of May 15, 1978, September 30, 1978, and March 18, 1980, was applicable to the 1978-1981 feed grain crop years. The 1977 act amended the Agriculture and Consumer Protection Act of 1973, as amended, and prior legislation. The referenced 1977 act amended sections in the Agricultural Adjustment Act of 1938, as amended, and the Agricultural Act of 1949, as amended, relating to acreage adjustment, loans and purchases, payments, allotments, and COMMODITY CREDIT CORPORATION sales policy.
12. Amendments to the Housing Act, enacted on November 30, 1983, provided for changes in the single-family and multifamily housing programs to give priority to serving very-low-income households and making its housing assistance more affordable to low-income persons in rural areas.
13. The Emergency Agricultural Credit Act of 1984 significantly changed FnHA's farm operating and emergency (disaster) loan programs.
14. The Housing and Community Development Technical Amendments Act of 1984 clarified quotas of lending to very-low and low-income families for homeownership under a supplemental appropriations bill and the Amendment Act of 1984.
15. A 1984 Farm Credit Initiative program provided the basis for a debt restructuring plan designed to assist farmers who were good managers, but experiencing severe financial difficulty, to remain in business and develop sound financial footing.
16. The Food Security Act of 1985 made major changes in farm loan eligibility and provided additional protection for borrowers undergoing serious financial difficulty.
17. The Agricultural Credit Act of 1987 made substantial changes in the way the government services its farmer program loans. The law added a provision to permit program loans to be written down to the recovery value of the collateral if the borrower has a feasible plan to continue the farming operations.
18. The Farm Credit Amendments Act of 1987 established a three-member, full-time board of directors for the Farm Credit System and gave additional authority to the board.
19. Based on requirements of the Omnibus Budget Reconciliation Act of 1986 and the Continuing Resolution of 1987, Farmers Home sold portions of its rural housing and community programs loan portfolios to the public. The loans were sold on a nonrecourse, taxable basis.
20. The Agricultural Credit Act of 1987 authorized the Farmers Home Administration to set aside funds for farm ownership loans to eligible members of socially disadvantaged groups who will operate family-size farms. A socially disadvantaged group is one whose members have been subjected to racial or ethnic prejudice because of their identity as members of a group without regard to their individual qualities. These groups are blacks, American Indians or Alaskan Natives, Hispanics, and Asians or Pacific Islanders.
21. In 1988, the government offered water and waste disposal and community facilities loans to borrowers under the Discount Purchase program. Sales generated $975 million, exceeding the agency's goal of $588 million for the year.

Farm Credit Act of 1987. Congress approved various legislation in the 1980s to assist financially troubled Farm Credit System institutions and their distressed borrowers. The authorities for providing that assistance are contained in the Agricultural Credit Act of 1987. An earlier effort came with the Farm Credit Amendment Act of 1985, which was intended to cause financially strong system institutions to aid those that were weak and, if necessary, provide a mechanism for federal assistance. This was to be accomplished by providing funds to the Farm Credit System Capital Corporation, which was established by the amendment. The corporation would use those funds to buy the nonperforming loans and acquired properties of troubled institutions. It would then attempt to dispose of the acquired properties in an orderly fashion. Those efforts, however, were obstructed by certain system institutions through legal actions challenging the assessment provisions of the law and its implementing regulation.

The deficit reduction bill (HR 5300—PL 39-509) of 1986 contained provisions easing the accounting requirements for Farm Credit

FARM CREDIT ACTS

System banks as an alternative to a direct federal cash bailout. (In 1985 Congress passed legislation (Pl 99-205) specifically authorizing an infusion of funds to keep the Farm Credit System afloat.) System officials devised new accounting rules that allowed banks to defer losses in anticipation that they could pay off the losses in a healthy agricultural economy in the future. The new accounting procedures would let the credit system stretch out over the next two decades the losses system banks expected to incur over two and one-half years. HR 5300 allows the system's federal land banks to retire high-cost debt and provisions for loan losses. This permitted some institutions to operate at capital levels that would have otherwise required the FAC to liquidate them. These practices were intended to be temporary measures until permanent solutions to the system's problems could be found. Originally due to expire December 31, 1988, the authority for system institutions to use Regulatory Accounting Practices has been extended until December 31, 1992, by the Agricultural Credit Act of 1987.

The 1987 act is intended to strengthen the Farm Credit System, provide credit assistance to farmers, and facilitate the establishment of a secondary market for farm loans. Intermediate credit banks and banks for cooperatives were authorized to set loan interest rates for farmers without those rates being subject to Farm Credit Administration approval. The 1987 act also allowed banks, subject to FCA approval, to write off losses that exceeded $1/2$ of 1 percent of the loans outstanding and permitted banks to amortize that amount over 20 years. These losses would be repaid from earnings in future years. The act included a nonbinding "policy and objectives" statement that farmers and ranchers were better served by system banks offering competitive interest rates and that system banks should give farmer-borrowers the greatest benefit practicable from savings derived through the new accounting procedures.

Major provisions of Agricultural Credit Act of 1987 (PL 100-233) signed into law January 6, 1988, required the Farm Credit System to establish a new Farm Credit System Assistance Board, replacing the Capital Corporation that was created by Congress in 1985, to take over bad loans and supervise financial assistance to system banks. The board would be overseen by a three-member board of directors; the secretaries of Agriculture and Treasury, and an agricultural producer with experience in financial matters appointed by the president. The board's authority would expire December 31, 1992. The act empowered the board to authorize financial assistance for troubled system institutions. If certified, an institution would issue preferred stock, which would be purchased by another new entity, the Farm Credit System Assistance Corporation. The act allowed the assistance board to impose conditions on institutions receiving assistance, giving it power over debt issuances, interest rates on loans, and business and investment plans. The act established the financial assistance corporation as a part of the Federal Farm Credit Banks Funding Corporation, which raised money for the system in the financial markets. The new corporation would create a revolving fund by issuing up to $4 billion in 15-year, uncollateralized bond obligations, with the principal and interest guaranteed by the U.S. Treasury. In addition, the corporation would set up a trust fund to assist banks repay the bonds, using the proceeds of a one-time assessment on system institutions. The assessments would be set at the amount by which each institution's surplus exceeded either 5% of assets (for district banks) or 13% of assets (for local associations).

In addition to financial assistance provisions, the act provided procedures for dealing with borrower stock guarantees, loan restructuring, system reorganization, capitalization, bond insurance, and the creation of a secondary market for agricultural real estate and certain rural housing loans (Federal Agricultural Mortgage Corporation ("Farmer Mac") within the Farm Credit System.

Details of the Agricultural Credit Act of 1987 provided for financial assistance to certain troubled Farm Credit System institutions through the sale of up to $4 billion in 15-year uncollateralized bonds guaranteed by the U.S. Treasury. The law established the Farm Credit System Assistance Corporation, which may issue the bond and use the funds to buy preferred stock in the troubled institutions. It is authorized to issue up to $2.8 billion in bonds during the period March 8, 1988, through September 30, 1992. Provisions for issuing additional bonds were included in the legislation. The assistance corporation will pay all interest costs on the bonds for the first five years. In the next five years, the interest costs will be shared equally by the Treasury and the system, except the system will pay more as earnings permit. The system will pay all the interest costs during the last five years. Eventual repayments of all obligations will come from funds of system institutions or by refinancing the debt.

To administer financial assistance to Farm Credit System institutions, the law establishes a Farm Credit System Assistance Board, composed of the secretary of the Treasury, the secretary of Agriculture, and an agricultural producer experienced in financial matter, who will be appointed by the president with the advice and consent of the Senate. When the assistance board is chartered, the charter of the Farm Credit System Capital Corporation will be revoked, and the assistance board will assume its assets and liabilities. The powers of the board do not include the management, administration, or purchase or disposition of any loans or other assets owned by system institutions. The purpose of financial assistance is to protect the stock of borrowers, assist in restoring system institutions to economic viability, and permit the system's banks and associations to provide credit at reasonable and competitive terms.

An institution may apply to the assistance board for certification to issue preferred stock and receive financial assistance when the book value of its stock is less than par under generally accepted accounting principles. An institution must, however, apply for assistance if the book value of its stock falls below 75% of par.

The 1987 act requires each system institution to adopt capitalization bylaws, which must be approved by a majority of its stockholders present and voting in person or by proxy at a duly authorized stockholders meeting. It also requires that the Farm Credit Administration issue regulations establishing capital adequacy standards for system institutions based on generally accepted accounting principles. The 1987 act prohibits an institution from reducing capital through patronage refunds or dividends or from retiring stock or allocated equities if such action would prevent the institution from meeting minimum capital adequacy standards.

The 1987 act provides greater flexibility for system institutions to determine their capital structures and classes and types of stock. However, when the loan is made each borrower must acquire voting stock of $1,000 or 2% of the loan, whichever is less. Each institution has the authority to define other classes of stock, including nonvoting stock, and issue stock to persons other than borrowers. Except for the minimum stock purchase, institutions do not have to require stock purchases based on a proportion of the loan.

Financial Condition. The Farm Credit System worked reasonably well for seven decades. The network of banks and lending associations provided relatively cheap loans to family farmers who were the owners and directors of their own lending cooperatives. However, the system reported its first loss since the Depression in 1985. The Farm Credit System reported a net loss of $17 million for 1987, compared to a loss of $1.9 billion in 1986. The decrease was chiefly the result of a substantial reversal in its allowance for loan losses. On December 31, 1987, the system had net loans outstanding of $49.5 billion, compared to $54.6 outstanding of $54.6 billion a year earlier. Of its total loan portfolio at the end of 1987, $5.2 billion was classified nonaccrual and $4.3 billion was classified high risk.

The 12 Federal Land banks had net loans outstanding of $33.3 billion on December 31, 1987, a decline of 13.2% from the $38.3 billion outstanding a year earlier. Nonaccrual loans decreased 25.4%, from $5.9 billion at the end of 1986 to $4.4 billion at the end of 1987. High-risk loans declined from $4.5 billion at the end of 1986 to $3.0 billion at the end of 1987. The combined gross income of the Federal Land Banks for the year ended December 31, 1987, was $3.8 billion, 21.2 % less than their gross income of $4.9 billion the previous year. On December 31, 1987, the Federal Land banks of Louisville, Jackson, St. Paul, Omaha, Sacramento, and Spokane reported deficits, which resulted in the book value of their capital stock being less than its par value. The Federal Land bank of Jackson reported total negative capital on that date, which means its capital stock had no value at all.

The Federal Land Bank associations had combined gross income of $235.6 million in 1987, compared to $227.6 million the previous year. Net gain from operations of $17.6 million in 1987, compared to an operating loss of $52.2 million in 1986.

The 12 Federal Intermediate Credit banks had net loans outstanding of $9.1 billion on December 31, 1987, a decrease of 16% from the $10.9 billion in net loans outstanding a year earlier; $4.2 billion were classified as high risk, $934.0 million had been formally restructured, and $145.6 million were nonaccrual. The banks had net income of $89.3 million in 1987 and $12.1 million in 1986.

Net loans outstanding of the Production Credit Associations stood at $9.1 billion on December 31, 1987, a decline of nearly 15 % from the $10.7 billion a year earlier. Of total loans outstanding at the end of 1987, $765.6 were nonaccrual and $645.4 million were high risk. PCAs had net earnings of $101.0 million for the year ended December 31, 1987, and a net loss of $280.8 million a year earlier.

The 13 banks for cooperatives had net loans outstanding of $8.2 billion on December 31, 1987, an increase of 11.5% over the $7.4 billion outstanding a year earlier. $71.8 million were classified high risk, $67.3 million had been formally restructured, $14.7 million had been otherwise restructured or given reduced interest rates, and $10.8 million were in nonaccrual status. The banks had net gain from operations of $88.0 million in 1986 and $77.9 million in 1987.

With years of loss and little prospect for the future, system officials decided to go to Congress for $6 billion, the third time in three years that assistance was sought. Congress agreed on $4 billion through a bond scheme designed to minimize federal budget outlays. The legislation also restructured the system, created a new secondary market for agricultural loans, and included procedures to protect farmers from foreclosure.

Funding. System institutions obtain the vast majority of their loan funds through the sale of securities to investors in the money and capital markets. These securities, which are the joint and several obligations of all 37 banks, are sold through the Federal Farm Credit Banks Funding Corporation. The funding corporation is owned by the 37 banks and subject to regulation and examination by the Farm Credit Administration.

Other nonlending institutions of the system are the Farm Credit Corporation of America, which provides leadership, coordination, and planning for the system as approved by district board, the Farm Credit Leasing Services Corporation, which leases or arranges leases for cooperatives and their producers, and the Farm Credit System Capital Corporation, which is intended to provide technical and financial assistance to troubled institutions and their borrowers.

System Restructuring. The AGRICULTURAL CREDIT ACT OF 1987 mandated some organizational restructuring among Farm Credit System institutions and permits additional voluntary restructuring. Within six months after the date of enactment, the Federal Land bank and the Federal Intermediate Credit bank in each Farm Credit district are required to merge. The resulting Farm Credit Bank will be a federally chartered instrumentality of the United States with corporate powers similar to those formerly held by the Federal Land Bank and the Federal Intermediate Credit bank. Each Farm Credit Bank will elect a board of directors in accordance with its bylaws. At least one member of the board will be elected by the other directors and shall not be a director, officer, employee, or stockholder of any system institution.

The law also established a process over an 18-month period for the development and consideration of a plan to merge the existing 12 Farm Credit districts into no fewer than six. The plan will be submitted to the stockholders of each affected Farm Credit Bank no later than July 1989.

The law also provided for a special committee to develop a proposal for the voluntary merger of the 12 district banks for cooperatives and the Central Bank for Cooperatives.

FARM CREDIT ADMINISTRATION BOARD
The Farm Credit Administration (FCA) is an independent federal agency in the executive branch of the U.S. government. It has regulatory, examination, and supervisory responsibilities for the banks, associations, and related institutions chartered under the Farm Credit act of 1971, as amended, which collectively comprise what is known as the Farm Credit system.

Before restructuring in the late 1980s (described later), the country was divided into 12 Farm Credit districts. At the same location in each district there was a Federal Land bank, a Federal Intermediate credit bank, and a bank for cooperatives. There was also a Central Bank for Cooperatives. Each of the 12 Farm Credit districts had a district Farm Credit board. The Farm Credit Administration was composed of Federal Land banks and Federal Land Bank associations, Federal Intermediate Credit banks and Production Credit associations, and banks for cooperatives. Originally capitalized by the federal government, the entire system became owned by its users. Offices for the 12 Farm Credit districts were located at Springfield (Mass.), Baltimore, Columbia (S.C.), Louisville, New Orleans, St. Louis, St. Paul, Omaha, Wichita, Houston, Sacramento, and Spokane.

System Restructuring. The Agricultural Credit Act of 1987 mandated some organizational restructuring among Farm Credit System institutions and permits additional voluntary restructuring. Within six months after the date of enactment, the Federal Land bank and the Federal Intermediate Credit Bank in each Farm Credit district are required to merge. The resulting FARM CREDIT BANK will be a federally chartered instrumentality of the United States with corporate powers similar to those formerly held by the Federal Land bank and the Federal Intermediate Credit bank. Each Farm Credit bank will elect a board of directors in accordance with its bylaws. At least one member of the board will be elected by the other directors and shall not be a director, officer, employee, or stockholder of any system institution.

The law also established a process over an 18-month period for the development and consideration of a plan to merge the existing 12 Farm Credit districts into no fewer than six. The plan will be submitted to the stockholders of each affected Farm Credit bank no later than July 1989.

The law also provided for a special committee to develop a proposal for the voluntary merger of the 12 district banks for Cooperatives and the Central Bank for cooperatives. The restructured Farm Credit Administration is directed by a three-member bipartisan board appointed by the president with the advice and consent of the Senate. The board is responsible for Farm Credit Administration policy, the promulgation of regulations, enforcement activities, and general oversight of operations. The board's specific responsibilities include:

1. Approving rules and regulations to implement the Farm Credit act of 1971, as amended.
2. Providing for the examination of the condition and general regulation of the performance of the powers, functions, and duties vested in each institution of the Farm Credit System.
3. Providing for the performance of the power, functions, and duties vested in the Farm Credit Administration.
4. Requiring such reports as it deems necessary from the institutions of the Farm Credit System.

The enforcement authorities of the FCA include the power to issue cease and desist orders, levy civil money penalties, remove officers and directors of system institutions, and place such institutions into conservatorship or receivership. Through its regulatory activity, the FCA also protects the rights of loan applicants and borrowers, and requires full financial disclosure by system institutions to stockholders and investors. The statute mandates the examination of each system institution. The agency exercises its enforcement powers to promote safety and soundness and to protect the public interest.

Farm Credit System Financial Assistance Corporation. On January 12, 1989, the FCA board approved the charter and articles of incorporation for the FARM CREDIT SYSTEM FINANCIAL ASSISTANCE CORPORATION. The assistance corporation was created by Congress to provide capital to Farm Credit System institutions experiencing financial difficulty and is authorized to issue up to $4 billion in 15-year uncollateralized bond obligations guaranteed by the U.S. Treasury.

Farm Credit System Assistance Board. At its January 12, 1988, regular meeting, the FCA board chartered the Farm Credit System Assistance Board, which was created by Congress in 1987 to certify Farm Credit System institutions for financial assistance when their borrower stock falls below its par value, to assist in restoring such institutions to financial viability, and permit them to provide credit at reasonable and competitive rates. The assistance board is comprised of the secretary of Agriculture, the secretary of the Treasury, and one agricultural producer who is appointed by the president. In conjunction with the chartering of the assistance board, the FCA board revoked the charter of the Farm Credit System Capital Corporation.

Capital Adequacy. The AGRICULTURAL ACT OF 1987 significantly altered the capital structure of Farm Credit System banks and associations had relied primarily on borrower-owned stock for their capital base. The 1987 act gave the banks and associations greater flexibility to determine their capital structure and developed sources of at-risk capital. On September 28, 1988, the FCA board adopted final regulations governing the capitalization of Farm Credit System banks and associations. These regulations establish minimum permanent capital standards and require the institutions to adopt capital adequacy plans to meet these standards as required by the Agricultural Credit Act of 1987. Major provisions of these regulations follows.

FARM CREDIT ADMINISTRATION BOARD

1. Each institution must establish a minimum ratio of permanent capital to risk-weighted assets of 7% to be achieved by 1993.
2. Double counting of capital is eliminated between the direct lender and the Farm Credit Bank by making the elimination at the association level rather than at the bank. This allocation requires the counting of such capital at the institution in which there are tangible earning assets equal to capital. Between participating institutions, double-counted capital is eliminated at the originator level. Federal Land Bank associations that are not direct lenders are considered originators for this purpose.
3. During the first five years of the phase-in, the FARM CREDIT BANK and its direct lending associations will be permitted to allocate double-counted capital for the purpose of computing the permanent capital ratios as they determine.
4. A forbearance plan is provided to assure institutions that the FAC will not take an enforcement action solely for failure to meet the interim capital standards if specified forbearance criteria indicating progress toward achieving the minimum capital requirements are met.
5. Provisions are made for FARM CREDIT BANKS and Federal Land Bank associations that are not direct lenders but have loss-sharing agreements with the bank to allocate the assets between them in the same proportion as they have agreed to share losses. These provisions are for the purpose of computing the capital ratio only.
6. Assets are weighted on the basis of credit risk inherent in the type of instrument and the nature of the obligor. Off-balance-sheet items are converted to a balance-sheet equivalent and the risk is weighted on the same basis as other assets.

Borrower Rights. The Agricultural Credit Act of 1987 amended the Farm Credit Act of 1971 by expanding the rights of farm borrowers from Farm Credit System institutions. The FCA board held a public hearing on this subject on June 8, 1988, to aid in it considering the revision of regulations to comply with the 1987 amendments to the Act. On September 6, 1988, the FCA board adopted final regulations implementing expanded borrower rights provisions of the 1987 Act. Major provisions of those regulations follow.

1. Qualified lenders must provide notice that a distressed loan may be a candidate for restructuring and must restructure distressed loans when the cost of restructuring is equal to or less than the cost of foreclosure.
2. Qualified lenders must disclose the effective interest rate, which includes the effect of loan origination fees.
3. Qualified lenders must disclose that borrower stock is at risk, with the exception of eligible borrower stock under section 4.9A of the act.
4. Qualified lenders must give the right of first refusal to certain borrowers to repurchase or lease their former property acquired through foreclosure or voluntary conveyance.

Restructuring Farm Credit System Institutions. During 1988 the FCA board took actions regarding the mandatory and voluntary restructuring of Farm Credit System institutions. The board chartered 11 new Farm Credit banks, which were created by the legislatively mandated merger of the Federal Land bank and Federal Intermediate Credit bank in each Farm Credit district. The two banks in the Jackson district did not merge because the Federal Land Bank of Jackson was in receivership. The board also approved final regulations implementing section 412 of the Agricultural Credit Act of 1987, which provided for the creation of a committee to develop a proposal to reduce the number of these banks to no fewer than six.

On May 5, 1988, the FCA board approved a voluntary merger plan for the 13 banks for cooperatives to form either a National Bank for Cooperatives, if the stockholders of eight or more voted to merge, or a United Bank for Cooperatives, if fewer then eight so voted. Based on the stockholder vote, the FCA chartered the National Bank for Cooperatives on December 27, 1988.

The FCA also approved final regulations implementing the new organization authorities of system institutions and on the election of their boards of directors. In addition, final regulations were adopted governing the required stockholder votes on the merger of Federal Land Bank associations and Production Credit associations that share substantially the same chartered territory.

In 1988 there was also considerable voluntary merger activity among Federal Land Bank associations (FLBAs) and Production Credit associations (PCAs). On January 1, 1987, there were 233 FLBAs and 155 PCAs. During the year stockholders in a number of these associations voted for mergers that reduced the number of associations to 154 FLBAs and 94 PCAs. Although the stockholders of the associations voted to approve these mergers in 1988, the mergers did not become effective until January 1, 1989. In addition, stockholders of 38 FLBAs and 38 PCAs serving substantially the same territories voted for mergers that formed 33 Agricultural Credit Associations.

Lending Authority. On December 31, 1988, there were 11 Farm Credit banks. These banks are authorized to make loans of from 5 to 40 years secured by first mortgages on farm or rural real estate through Federal Land Bank associations or provide the funds for such loans to Agricultural Credit associations which are the direct lenders. Loans may be made to farmers, ranchers, rural homeowners, commercial fishermen, and certain farm-related businesses. Loans may not exceed 85% of the appraised market value of the real estate security or 97% if the loan is guaranteed by a governmental agency. Though the statutory authority exists for Federal Land Bank associations to become direct agricultural and rural real estate mortgage lenders, no such authority had been transferred as of December 31, 1988. Transfer of authority requires the approval of the Farm Credit Administration, the boards of directors of the Farm Credit Bank and the Federal Land Bank Association, and a majority vote of the stockholders of both institutions.

The Farm Credit banks are also authorized to provide short-and intermediate-term loan funds to Production Credit associations, Agricultural Credit associations, and other financing institutions serving eligible borrowers. Generally speaking, PCAs may make loans with terms of up to 20 years (15 years if the loan is made to commercial fishermen for major capital expenditures. PCAs are authorized to make loans to farmers, ranchers, rural homeowners, commercial fishermen, and certain farm-related businesses. ACAs are authorized to operate as direct lenders. ACAs have both short- and long-term lending authority.

A number of Farm Cadit banks, federal Land Bank associations and Production Credit association under common management, and Agricultural Credit associations do business as Farm Credit Service or Farm Credit Services.

As provided in the statute, a special committee has been named to develope a proposal by which the number of Farm Credit districts, and hence Farm Credit banks will be reduced to no fewer than six.

Stockholders of 10 of the 12 district banks for cooperatives and stockholders of the Central Bank for Cooperatives voted to merge their institutions into a National Bank for Cooperatives effective January 1, 1989. The bank will be headquartered in Denver, Colorado, with regional offices in the locations of its constituent banks. Stockholders of the Springfield (Mass.) Bank for Cooperatives and the St. Paul (Minnesota) Bank for Cooperatives voted to remain independent. Each of the three banks for cooperatives is authorized to make loans of all kinds to eligible agricultural, aquatic, and public utility cooperatives in all 50 states and Puerto Rico.

Funding. The Farm Credit banks, which for funding purposes include the banks for cooperatives, obtain the majority of their loan funds through the sale of securities through the Federal Farm Credit Banks Funding Corporation. The securities are Federal Farm Cadit Banks Consolidated Systemwide Bonds and Federal Farm Credit Banks Consolidated Systemwide Notes.

Through the end of 1988, the newly formed Farm Credit banks participated in issues of $8.1 billion in six-month bonds, $12.2 billion in six-month bonds, and $6.3 billion in new term bonds with maturities of one to three years. During 1988, the banks for cooperatives participated in issues of $2.2 billion in 3-month bonds, $2.6 billion in six-month bonds, and $1.2 billion in term bonds with maturities of one and two years.

Farm credit institutions have expanded their use of variable-rate loans, interest rate swaps, and other specialized funding and financing mechanisms to alter the effective repricing characteristics of their funding sources. Also, the institutions have attempted to improve their net interest income while limiting exposure to interest rate risk by adjusting the interest rate and maturity mix of their assets and liabilities. Among the programs used in 1988 were internal debt transfers, interest rate swaps, direct placements, debt reopening, debt repurchases, and floating-rate notes. The specialized funding programs were eliminated to better meet the funding needs of the institutions with respect to maturities and interest rate structures, to achieve a better match between assets and liabilities with respect to interest rate sensitivity, and to provide protection against changing interest rates for future debt issues.

Regulatory Accounting Practices. The FCA board approved final regulations for the use of regulatory accounting practices (RAP) by system institutions. The Agricultural Credit Act of 1987 extended the authorized period of time that system institutions could use RAP to defer and capitalize certain expenses from 1988 to 1992. Other provisions of the 1987 act have the effect of restricting the use of RAP. These provisions require system institutions to retire eligible borrower stock at par value regardless of the stock's book value under generally accepted accounting principles and require institutions to issue permanent capital that must be considered an at-risk investment. The final RAP regulations reflect these requirements.

The regulations continue to allow system institutions to use RAP— among other factors, to evaluate interest rates charged on loans. Those other factors include the institution's cost of funds, overhead, expected losses, margin to provide for adequate capital, and return to stockholders. In no case, however, may an institution use RAP to charge rates below the competition.

Source: FARM CREDIT ADMINISTRATION.

See FEDERAL FARM MORTGAGE CORPORATION.

FARM CREDIT BANK The AGRICULTURAL CREDIT ACT OF 1987 (Public Law 100-233) mandated the merger of FEDERAL LAND BANK and the FEDERAL INTERMEDIATE CREDIT BANK in each of the Farm Credit districts. The resulting Farm Credit bank in each district is a federally chartered instrumentality of the United States with corporate powers similar to the previous Federal Land Bank and Federal Intermediate Credit Bank. Each Farm Credit bank elects a board of directors, subject to terms of the bank's bylaws. At least one member of the bank's board must be elected by the other directors and shall not be a director, officer, employee, or stockholder of a Federal Farm System institution. The initial board of each bank will be the current members of the district board. The district board is dissolved upon the creation of the Farm Credit bank.

FARM CREDIT SYSTEM See FARM CREDIT ADMINISTRATION.

FARM CREDIT SYSTEM FINANCIAL ASSISTANCE BOARD The AGRICULTURAL CREDIT ACT OF 1987 (Public Law 100-233) established the Farm Credit System Financial Assistance Board to provide financial assistance to FARMCREDIT SYSTEM institutions when their stock falls below par, and to assist in restoring system institutions to economic viability. The board's authority was to expire December 31, 1992. The board would supervise financial assistance to System banks and take over the bad loans of the Capital Corporation (1985), which would then cease to exist.

The board was authorized to issue up to $4 billion in 15-year uncollateralized bond obligations guaranteed by the U.S. Treasury. The U.S. Treasury pays all interest costs on each bond for the first five years. In the next five years, the interest costs are shared equally by the Treasury and the system. Each system institution is required to pay a proportional share of the cost based on its volume of performing loans. The system is required to pay all of the interest costs during the last five years. The system will repay the interest payments that were previously made by the Treasury. The act provides for a one-time stock purchase of Assistance Corporation stock by each system institution in an amount equal to its unallocated retained earnings in excess of 5% of its assets as of December 31, 1986; for each association, the amount is equal to its unallocated retained earnings over 13% of its assets. These funds will be placed in the Financial Assistance Corporation Trust Fund and be made available to make payments of principal and interest on assistance corporation obligations if the individual institution that is liable for such payments defaults on its interest payments or is unable to redeem the preferred stock it issued to the assistance corporation. (Adapted from materials provided by the Farm Credit Administration.)

The board consists of the secretaries of Agriculture and Treasury and one agricultural producer experienced in financial matters. This person is appointed by the president with the advice and consent of the Senate. The board appoints a chief executive officer who serves at the board's pleasure and is responsible for the daily operations of the assistance board. According to the Farm Credit Administration, when an institution's stock falls below par it may apply for support from the assistance board. If the stock is impaired by less than 25%, the institution may elect to apply to the board for certification to issue "preferred" stock and receive financial assistance. If stock value is below 75% of par under generally accepted accounting principles (GAAP), the institution must apply for assistance. If the board determines that other actions will be less costly and better serve the credit needs of the area, it can make specific requests to the Farm Credit Administration (FCA). These include the request that the FCA approve merging of the institution with another system institution or appointing a receiver. Mergers must be approved by the stockholders of the institutions involved. The FCA must ensure credit service in these districts.

Under the law, the assistance board may impose terms and provisions on certified institutions designed to improve their financial conditions and service to agricultural borrowers, and to ensure efficient use of assistance funds. The board has access to FCA examination reports and supervisory documents to carry out its functions.

When the assistance board was chartered, the charter of the Farm Credit System Capital Corporation was revoked. All assets and liabilities as well as existing contractual obligations, security and title instruments of the Capital Corporation were transferred to the assistance board on that date.

FARM CREDIT SYSTEM INSURANCE CORPORATION In 1987 Congress established a Farm Credit System Insurance Corporation and a Farm Credit Insurance Fund to insure the timely payment of principal and interest on notes, bonds, debentures, and other obligations of Farm Credit System institutions. The corporation is managed by a board of directors, whose members are members of the Farm Credit Administration. The insurance fund is capitalized by a revolving fund under the jurisdiction of the FARM CREDIT ADMINISTRATION Beginning January 1989, each system bank became insured for purposes of paying insurance premiums subject to the law governing the insurance corporation. System institutions' premium payments are based on the loan volume of each bank. In the first year, the annual insurance premiums will be equal to .0015% of its accruing and .0025% of its nonaccruing loan volume. The insurance corporation is authorized to set appropriate premiums when the fund reaches 2 percent of the aggregate outstanding insured obligations of all insured system institutions (the secure base amount). The fund begins to insure obligation January 5, 1993, following the expiration of the authority of the Farm Credit System Assistance Board to provide assistance. Joint and several liability for system debt obligations continues.

FARMERS HOME ADMINISTRATION Originally established under the Farmers Home Administration Act of 1946 (7 U.S.C. 1001, note), this agency now operates under three principal statutes: Consolidated Farmers Home Administration Act of 1961 (7 U.S.C. 1921), Title V of the Housing Act of 1949 (42 U.S.C. 1471), and Part A, Title III of the Economic Opportunity Act of 1964 (42 U.S.C. 2851). Organizationally, it is spotted in the Department of Agriculture, under the assistant secretary for rural development and conservation. Official description follows.

Functions. The Farmers Home Administration, along with other agencies of the Department of Agriculture, operating through state, area, and county rural development committees, assists other federal, state, and local agencies to make their services known and effective in local rural areas. Applications for loans are made at the agency's local county offices, generally located in county-seat towns. A county or area committee of three individuals, at least two of whom are farmers, certifies or recommends as to eligibility of individual applicants and amounts of loans and reviews borrowers' progress. Each loan is based on a plan that should provide enough income to raise family living standards and to meet payments on the borrower's debt.

Funds for loans and grants made by the Farmers Home Administration come from two sources: (1) annual appropriations by Congress, and (2) private lenders who supply funds for loans which are insured by the agency. Most of the loans are now made on an insured basis.

The Farmers Home Administration provides financial and management assistance through the following types of loans:

Operating loans: Operating loans enable operators of farms not larger than family farms, who cannot get the credit they need from conventional sources, to acquire needed resources, to make improved use of their land and labor resources and make adjustments necessary for successful farming, recreation, and nonfarm enterprises. Funds may be advanced to pay for equipment, livestock, feed,

FARM INCOME

seed, fertilizer, other farm and home operating needs; to refinance chattel debts; to provide operating credit to fish farmers; to carry out forestry purposes; and to develop income-producing recreation and other nonfarm enterprises.

The interest rate is determined each fiscal year by the secretary of the Treasury. Operating loan borrowers are expected to refinance their operating loans and return to conventional sources of credit as soon as they are able to do so.

Farm ownership, individual soil and water conservation, and recreation loans: Farm ownership loans enable farmers and ranchers to buy farms and owners of inadequate or underimproved farms to enlarge or develop farms. Loans are limited to farms which are not larger than family size. Loans may include funds to construct or repair farm homes and service buildings and facilities; to improve land; to develop water, forestry, and fish farming resources; to establish recreation and other nonfarm enterprises to supplement farm income; and to refinance debts.

Individual soil and water conservation loans: Loans are made to owners or operators of farms and ranches including farming partnerships and domestic corporations to assist them in developing, conserving, and making proper use of their land and other resources.

Recreation loans: Recreation loans enable farmers and ranchers to convert all or a portion of the farms or ranches owned or leased by them to outdoor income-producing recreational enterprises.

Loans to Indian tribes: Loans to Indian tribes and tribal corporations are made for the acquisition of lands including interests therein within the reservation or community.

Loans to associations: Loans are made to eligible groups of farmers and ranchers to develop irrigation systems, drain farmland, and carry out soil conservation measures. Loans may also be made to develop grazing areas and forest lands and for other shifts in land use.

Rural housing loans: Loans are made to families of low and moderate income for housing located in open country and small rural communities with populations of not more than 10,000 and in rural towns of 10,000 to 20,000 where there is a lack of housing mortgage credit. Loans are made to build, buy, and repair needed homes and essential farm buildings, and buy building sites.

The maximum term is 33 years. The basic interest rate is determined each fiscal year. Interest credits may be arranged to afford lower interest rates for low-income applicants whose family income will not enable them to pay the basic rate. Also, cosigners on promissory notes are permitted in the case of applicants who are deficient in repayment ability.

Builders may obtain from the agency conditional commitments which signify that houses they propose to build will meet requirements for Farmers Home Administration loan financing.

An owner-occupant who cannot qualify for a regular rural housing loan may obtain a loan (or, in the case of senior citizens, a grant) to make repairs and improvements to remove hazards to the health and safety of the family. These loans are available only to very low-income families.

Loans to individuals, corporations, and partnerships to provide rental or cooperative housing for persons of low or moderate income or elderly persons in rural areas may not exceed $750,000. The maximum term is 50 years. For such loans to nonprofit corporations and cooperatives, rental assistance may be given to help defray rent paid by low-income families.

Loans are also made to individual farmers, groups of farmers, nonprofit organizations, and nonfederal public agencies to finance housing facilities for domestic farm labor.

Grants may be made to public bodies or broadly based nonprofit organizations to help finance part of the cost of housing facilities for domestic farm labor.

The agency is authorized to pay expenses incurred by nonprofit organizations to assist in developing or administering technical and supervisory assistance for low-income persons and families to participate in mutual or self-help housing programs.

Loans are authorized to nonprofit organizations to purchase and develop land for resale as homesites for persons of low to moderate income.

Emergency loans: Emergency loans enable eligible farmers in areas hit by natural disasters such as floods and droughts to obtain credit to finance costs necessary to resume normal farming operations.

Loans offsetting actual losses bear interest at a rate of 4.5%. Loans are limited to $500,00 or 80 percent of actual losses. The secretary of Agriculture determines the interest rates for operating and other nonfarm purposes based on those prevailing in the private market. The loans are repaid from crop or livestock income as it is received.

Watershed protection and flood prevention loans: These loans enable local organizations to help finance projects that protect and develop land and water resources in small watersheds.

Loans may be repaid over 40 years, at an interest rate based on the average rate paid by the Treasury on obligations of similar maturity.

Resource conservation and development loans: Loans are available for natural resource conservation and development in designated areas.

Community facility loans: Loans are authorized to public and semipublic bodies and nonprofit associations and to certain Indian tribes for essential community facilities, such as water and waste disposal systems and other facilities useful to the entire community. Necessary related equipment may also be purchased. The interest rate is set periodically and is based on yields of municipal bonds, and the projects may serve residents of open country and rural towns of not more than 10,000 population.

Emergency livestock loan guarantees: The Farmers Home Administration is authorized to guarantee loans made by legally organized lenders to farmers and ranchers permitting them to maintain their operations during temporary adverse periods. The total amount of loans guaranteed for any one borrower cannot exceed the statutory ceiling of $350,000. FmHA can guarantee up to 90% of principal and interest owed on loans made by acceptable lending institutions. The interest rate is that agreed upon by lender and borrower, not to exceed the legal rate for the state. Maximum repayment terms for these loans is seven years, with possible renewal for up to three additional years.

Rural industrialization loans: The Farmers Home Administration is authorized to make or guarantee loans to public, private, or cooperative associations organized for profit or nonprofit, to certain Indian tribes or tribal groups, or to individuals, for the purpose of improving the economic and environmental climate in rural communities. Grants also may be made for projects to improve water, waste disposal, and industrial site facilities. The purpose is to develop business enterprises in rural areas and cities of up to 50,000 population, with priority to applications for projects in open country, rural communities, and towns of 25,000 and smaller.

Private lenders initiate, process, close, service, and supervise such guaranteed loans. The Farmers Home Administration guarantees a lender against loss on up to 90% of principal and interest. Interest rates are determined between borrower and lender.

Rural development planning and coordination: The planning of rural development program goals and coordination of supportive programs administered by various agencies is managed in the Farmers Home Administration by its Office of Rural Development Policy Coordination and Planning. This unit previously functioned as the Rural Development Service (RDS), a separate agency of the U.S. Department of Agriculture established by secretarial order in 1973. RDS was merged with the FmHA by secretarial order in 1978. The work of planning and coordination is mandated in Section 603 of the Consolidated Farm and Rural Development Act of 1972.

Summary. As indicated, the credits and grants directly made or insured by the Farmers Home Administration are of the marginal type, intended to improve the quality of life and operation in marginal agriculture and rural regions.

FARM INCOME The farm problem of the U.S. is a problem of economics and, specifically, a problem of income. While gross farm income has fluctuated in recent years, production expenses have risen, resulting in a shrinkage of profit margins and in fluctuating net farm income.

Realized gross farm income consists of cash receipts from farm marketings, government payments to farms, imputed home consumption of farm products, and imputed rental value of farm dwellings. Farm operators' total net farm income consists of gross realized farm income less production expenses and includes net change in inventories.

The appended table compares shows income of farmers from all sources, 1940 and 1945-86.

FARM LOAN BOARD   FEDERAL FARM LOAN BOARD.

ENCYCLOPEDIA OF BANKING AND FINANCE

FARM LOAN BOARD

Income of Farmers and Farm People From All Sources: 1940 and 1945-86
(Updated data provided from 1976 onward. In billions—unless otherwise noted.)

Year	Cash receipts from marketings	Government payments to farmers	Gross cash income	Other income from farming [1]	Gross cash income before inventory adjustment [2]	Gross farm after inventory adjustment	Off-farm income [3,7]	Total gross income all sources	Total production expenses	Net farm income before inventory adjustment [4]	Net farm income after inventory adjustment	Total for family personal spending and investment [5,7]	Number farms (millions)
1940	$ 8.4	$ 0.7	$ 9.1	$ 2.2	$ 11.1	$ 11.3		$ 14.8	$ 6.9	$ 4.2	$ 4.5		6.35
1945	21.7	0.74	22.4	3.0	25.8	25.4		31.4	13.1	12.8	12.3		5.97
1946	24.8	0.77	25.6	4.0	29.5	29.6		35.9	14.5	15.0	15.1		5.93
1947	29.6	0.31	29.9	2.5	34.1	32.4		39.6	17.0	17.1	15.4		5.87
1948	30.2	0.26	30.5	6.0	34.7	36.5		44.3	18.8	16.0	17.7		5.80
1949	27.8	0.19	28.0	2.8	31.6	30.8		38.7	18.0	13.6	12.8		5.72
1950	28.5	0.28	28.7	4.4	32.3	33.1		41.1	19.5	12.8	13.6		5.65
1951	32.9	0.29	33.1	5.1	37.1	38.3		46.7	22.3	14.8	15.9		5.43
1952	32.5	0.27	32.8	4.9	36.8	37.8		46.5	22.8	14.0	15.0		5.20
1953	31.0	0.21	31.2	3.2	35.1	34.4		42.6	21.5	13.6	13.0		4.98
1954	29.8	0.26	30.1	4.1	33.7	34.2		41.6	21.8	11.9	12.4		4.80
1955	29.5	0.23	29.7	3.8	33.3	33.5		41.2	22.2	11.1	11.3		4.65
1956	30.4	0.55	31.0	3.0	34.4	34.0		42.0	22.7	11.7	11.3		4.51
1957	29.7	1.02	30.7	4.1	34.2	34.8		42.8	23.7	10.5	11.1		4.37
1958	33.5	1.09	34.5	4.4	38.1	39.0		47.0	25.8	12.3	13.2		4.23
1959	33.6	0.68	34.3	3.6	37.9	37.9		46.3	27.2	10.7	10.7		4.10
1960	34.0	0.70	34.7	3.9	38.2	38.6	8.5	47.1	27.4	10.8	11.2	19.7	3.96
1961	35.2	1.49	36.7	3.9	40.2	40.5	9.2	49.7	28.6	11.6	12.0	21.1	3.83
1962	36.5	1.75	38.2	4.1	41.7	42.3	9.9	52.2	30.3	11.4	12.1	22.0	3.69
1963	37.5	1.70	39.2	4.2	42.7	43.4	11.0	54.4	31.6	11.1	11.8	22.8	3.57
1964	37.3	2.18	39.5	2.8	43.1	42.3	11.6	54.0	31.8	11.3	10.5	22.1	3.46
1965	39.4	2.46	41.8	4.7	45.5	46.5	12.7	59.3	33.7	11.9	12.9	25.6	3.36
1966	43.4	3.28	46.7	3.8	50.6	13.9	64.4	36.5	14.0	14.0	27.8	3.26	
1967	42.8	3.08	45.9	4.6	49.9	50.5	14.5	65.0	38.2	11.7	12.3	26.8	3.16
1968	44.2	3.46	47.6	4.2	51.7	51.8	15.5	67.3	39.5	12.2	12.3	27.8	3.07
1969	48.2	3.79	52.0	4.4	56.3	56.4	16.6	73.0	42.1	14.2	14.3	30.9	3.00
1970	50.5	3.72	54.2	4.6	58.8	58.8	17.6	76.4	44.5	14.4	14.4	32.0	2.95
1971	52.7	3.14	55.9	6.3	60.8	62.1	19.1	81.2	47.1	13.6	15.0	34.2	2.90
1972	61.1	3.96	65.1	6.1	70.3	71.2	21.3	92.5	51.7	18.6	19.5	40.8	2.86
1973	86.9	2.61	89.5	9.5	95.6	99.0	24.7	123.7	64.6	31.0	34.4	59.1	2.82
1974	92.4	.053	92.9	5.4	99.9	98.3	28.1	126.4	71.0	28.9	27.3	55.4	2.80
1975	88.9	0.81	89.7	10.9	97.2	100.6	23.9	124.5	75.0	22.2	25.6	49.5	2.52
1976	95.3	.7	97.2	8.4	97.2	102.9	26.7	129.6	82.7	21.7	20.2	46.9	2.50
1977	96.3	1.8	99.3	9.6	99.3	108.8	26.1	134.9	88.9	18.8	19.9	46.0	2.46
1978	112.4	3.0	117.3	11.2	117.3	128.4	29.7	159.1	103.2	23.3	25.2	54.9	2.44
1979	131.6	1.4	135.1	12.8	135.1	150.7	33.8	184.5	123.3	22.4	27.4	61.2	2.43
1980	139.7	1.3	143.3	14.6	143.3	149.3	34.7	184.0	133.1	22.4	16.1	50.8	2.43
1981	141.7	1.9	146.0	16.2	146.0	166.3	35.8	199.3	139.4	24.5	26.9	62.6	2.43
1982	142.6	3.5	150.6	18.6	150.6	163.5	36.4	199.9	140.0	23.9	23.5	59.9	2.40
1983	136.5	9.3	150.4	17.6	150.4	153.1	37.0	190.1	140.4	23.8	12.7	49.9	2.37
1984	142.2	8.4	155.1	17.6	155.1	174.7	38.3	213.0	142.7	26.4	32.0	70.3	2.33
1985	142.1	7.7	156.9	17.9	156.9	166.0	42.5	208.5	133.1	31.6	32.3	74.8	2.28
1986	144.2	11.8	152.0	17.5	152.0	159.5	44.7	204.2	122.1	34.2	37.5	82.2	2.18

[1] Predominantly noncash income from net change in value of farm inventories, gross value of farm products used on the farm, and a rental value for farm dwellings; also cash income from recreation, machine hire and custom work and forest product sales.
[2] Gross income from farming before adjustments for changes in value of farm inventory of crops and livestock. The next column does allow for an increase or decrease in value of inventories.
[3] Includes nonfarm wages, salaries, interest, dividends, rental property, unemployment compensation, social security, etc., but does not include capital gains income from off-farm sources.
[4] Includes gross income from farming after inventory adjustment plus off-farm income of farm operator families.
[5] Net income from farming after change in value of farm inventory, plus off-farm income of farm operator families.
[6] Per farm numbers based on new farm definition beginning in 1977.
[7] Series began with 1960.
Source: U.S. Department of Agriculture.

FARM LOAN BONDS See FEDERAL FARM LOAN SYSTEM, FEDERAL FARM MORTGAGE CORPORATION, FEDERAL LAND BANKS, JOINT-STOCK LAND BANK BONDS.

FARM LOAN DISTRICTS The 12 Farm Credit districts. See FARM CREDIT ADMINISTRATION.

FARM LOANS See FARM CREDIT ADMINISTRATION, FARMERS HOME ADMINISTRATION.

FARM LOAN SYSTEM See FARM CREDIT ADMINISTRATION, FARMERS HOME ADMINISTRATION.

FARM MORTGAGE COMPANIES Private companies engaged in (1) direct lending on mortgages secured by farm property, financed in some cases by the public sale of obligations secured by the underlying FARM MORTGAGES, including certificates representing fractional interests in the specific mortgages; and (2) serving as middlemen in the placement and servicing of farm mortgages with life insurance companies and other investors located at a distance from the location of borrowers. Although such companies continue to be factors in farm lending, their number and importance have declined over the years, as the lending activities of the federal farm credit system have expanded since 1933 especially and as various large life insurance companies have opened their own offices in farm areas to solicit and service their own mortgages.

FARM MORTGAGE CORPORATION FEDERAL FARM MORTGAGE CORPORATION.

FARM MORTGAGE FORECLOSURE ACT An act approved June 12, 1934, which amended Section 32 of the Emergency Farm Mortgage Act of 1933. This amendment enlarged the lending authority of the land bank commissioner under the Emergency Farm Mortgage Act of 1933 to permit him to make loans to farmers for the purpose, among others, of enabling them to redeem and repurchase farm property owned by them prior to foreclosure, irrespective of the time when such foreclosure took place.

See LAND BANK COMMISSIONER LOAN.

FARM MORTGAGE REFINANCING ACT An act, passed January 31, 1934, which created the FEDERAL FARM MORTGAGE CORPORATION, with a capital of $200 million, to aid in the refinancing of farm debts; which authorized the corporation, with the approval of the secretary of the Treasury, to issue and have outstanding at any one time bonds in an aggregate not exceeding $2 billion guaranteed both as to interest and principal by the U.S.; which granted the corporation permission to exchange such bonds, upon application of any Federal Land bank, for consolidated farm loan bonds of equal face value issued under the amended Federal Farm Loan Act and to exchange such consolidated farm loan bonds held by it for bonds of the corporation of equal face value; which provided that the corporation might purchase, for cash, such consolidated farm loan bonds, make loans to Federal Land banks on the security of such consolidated bonds, and invest its funds in mortgage loans under Section 32 of the Emergency Farm Mortgage Act of 1933; and which granted authority to the Land Bank commissioner, until February 1, 1936, to make loans up to $600 million on behalf of the Federal Farm Mortgage Corporation, either in cash or in bonds of the corporation.

The act made available a revolving fund of $40 million to the governor of the Farm Credit Administration.

FARM MORTGAGES Mortgages upon farm real estate. Borrowing with a farm mortgage as security is the chief means used by farmers to raise capital for the purpose of financing acquisition and operation of farm property.

Farm mortgage loan practice was importantly affected by inauguration of the Federal Land Bank system in 1916. As in the case of urban mortgages, most farm mortgages were straight mortgages (lump sum maturities, nonamortized), running for three to five years. The FEDERAL LAND BANKS introduced the amortized farm mortgage, running for not less than 5 years nor more than 40, payable annually or semiannually. The land banks have also been influencing rates.

All Federal Land banks now have variable interest rate plans in which interest rates may be raised or lowered in relation to the cost of money. These plans have the effect of spreading money costs evenly among all borrowers.

Other practices of the Federal Land banks in connection with farm mortgage loans include the following:

1. A farmer may repay his loan ahead of time if he is able and wishes to do so. The land banks also will accept payments to be set aside and applied to future installments at the direction of the farmer-borrower. The borrower receives interest on these future payments at the same rate as that charged on his indebtedness.
2. The applicant is required to furnish satisfactory evidence of title and pay recording charges. Other costs, if any, are low.
3. A property, to be acceptable for a land bank loan, must be desirable and under typical operation capable of producing during the term of the loan sufficient agricultural earnings to pay operating expenses including taxes and other fixed charges, to maintain the property, and to meet installments on a loan that would be proper to a typical owner of the property. In addition, the property should ordinarily produce enough to cover the family living expenses.
4. Permissible purposes for land bank mortgage loans include: to provide for the purchase of land for agricultural use; to provide for the purchase of equipment, fertilizers, and livestock necessary for the proper operation of the mortgaged farm; to provide buildings and for the improvement of farm lands; to pay indebtedness of the borrower incurred for agricultural purposes, or incurred at least two years prior to the date of the application of the loan; and to provide the farmer with funds for general agricultural uses.

The table appended compares the aggregate balance sheet of agriculture in the U.S. as of recent years.

See FARM CREDIT ADMINISTRATION, FARMERS HOME ADMINISTRATION.

FARM RELIEF ACT OF 1933 The AAA Farm Relief and Inflation Act of May 12, 1933, which provided for farm mortgage relief by authorizing the refinancing of farm mortgages at 4.5% through the issuance of a maximum of $2 billion in government bonds which would be guaranteed as to interest by the government. The act also provided for direct agricultural relief by authorizing the secretary of Agriculture to force increased farm prices through allocation of production or withdrawal of land from production by leasing it. To pay the cost of this program, the secretary of Agriculture was authorized to license and tax processors of agricultural products.

See AGRICULTURAL ADJUSTMENT ACT.

Farmers' Assets, Debts, and Equity, 1940, 1950, 1960, 1970, 1980, and 1985 [1]
(In billions of dollars.)

Item	1940	1950	1960	1970	1980	1985
Assets:						
Real estate	34.0	88.9	139.9	223.8	850.8	606.8
Physical assets other than real estate [2]	15.0	48.0	53.1	77.0	212.4	189.5
Financial	4.7	16.0	17.9	23.2	39.1	50.2
Total	53.7	152.9	210.9	324.0	1,102.3	846.5
Debts:						
Real estate [3]	6.5	6.2	12.8	30.5	97.5	105.8
Nonreal estate [4]	3.3	6.1	12.0	22.3	81.2	82.2
Total	9.8	12.3	24.8	52.8	178.7	188.0
Equity	43.8	140.7	186.1	271.2	923.6	658.5

[1] As of December 31, includes farm households.
[2] Crop inventory value is value of non-CCC crops held on farms plus value above loan rate for crops held under CCC.
[3] Includes storage and drying facilities loans.
[4] Excludes value of CCC crop loans.

ENCYCLOPEDIA OF BANKING AND FINANCE

FARM SECURITY ADMINISTRATION An agency created September 1, 1937, to replace the Resettlement Administration. It made loans and offered guidance in farm and home management to low-income farmers who were unable to obtain credit to meet their needs on reasonable terms from other sources.

By the Farmers Home Administration Act of 1946, approved August 14, 1946, the FARMERS HOME ADMINISTRATION took over the functions of the Farm Security Administration as of November 1, 1946.

FARTHING An English copper coin with the smallest denomination and having the value of one-fourth of a penny. In 1960 the farthing was officially withdrawn from circulation because of its extremely low value.

See ENGLISH MONEY TABLE.

FASCISM The governmental form initiated in 1922 and best exemplified by Italy under the leadership of Benito Mussolini, the first premier under the Fascist regime and chief originator of its principles. Italy was followed into fascism by Germany (under Hitler), Austria, Hungary, Poland (under Gen. Pilsudski), and, on a lesser scale, other central European and Balkan nations. Many of these imitations made no pretense of following fascistic political theory and were bald military dictatorships. Defeat of the Axis nations in World War II doomed the political power of fascism, so that the following is now merely of academic interest.

Fascism held that democracy and representative government, however glorious in the past, were no longer tenable under modern economic and political conditions. To prevent internal political strife and clash of varying shades of political opinion, parliamentary government was abolished and only one party recognized. In Italy, the affairs of state were administered by a dictator—the titular head of the state party—under the supervision of the Grand Fascist Council which delegated authority over various governmental functions.

Fascism contended that the trend was toward new forms in civilization, both in politics and in economics. The state was resuming its right and its prestige as the sole and supreme interpreter of life in all its major aspects. In this sense, modern fascism suggested the kameralistic and mercantilistic doctrines of the sixteenth, seventeenth, and eighteenth centuries. Fascism sought to unify or bind the citizenship by common ties to work for the good of the state under the shibboleths "Everything within the state—nothing without the state—everything for the state." In a corporative, or authoritarian, state, citizens were welded together into a system of organization based on the individual's utility to the state. Thus, the state's organization was based largely upon occupational categories or work guilds in the leading industries, presided over by a cabinet department called the Ministry of Corporations.

The system of occupational unions (*sindacati*) and producers' guilds (*corporazioni*) provided the means for implementing the fascist guild state, i.e., a state in which all national activities (political, economic, social, cultural) were brought within the framework of the state.

The 22 guilds set up in accordance with the resolutions adopted by the Central Guild Committee at its meeting of May 9, 1934, were presided over by the minister of guilds; the vice president of each guild was selected from the executive ranks of the National Fascist Party, and three members of that party, representing the public, sat on each of the respective guild boards. Subject to these general provisions, the breakdown of the boards was as follows:

Cereal guild
Fruit, vegetable, and flower guild
Viticulture and wine guild
Beet and sugar guild
Edible oil guild
Animal husbandry and fisheries guild
Forestry, lumber, and wood guild
Textile fibers and products guild
Metal and engineering guild
Chemical trades guild
Clothing trades guild
Paper and publishing guild
Building trades guild
Water, gas, and electricity guild
Mining and quarrying guild
Glass and pottery guild
Credit and insurance guild
Arts and professions guild
Sea and air transports guild
Inland communications guild
Public entertainments guild
Public hospitality guild

It is apparent that fundamental and tremendous changes in the economic system of Italy were wrought by the fascists in order to solidify their control.

BIBLIOGRAPHY

SCHNEIDER, H. W. *The Fascist Government of Italy*, 1936.

FAVORABLE BALANCE OF TRADE See BALANCE OF TRADE.

FAVORABLE CONDITIONS In financial writing, those forces conducive to higher security or commodity values. Favorable conditions may be divided broadly into two groups: political (U.S. and abroad) and economic (business and financial).

Under favorable political conditions may be classed election of a presidential candidate favored by business interests, a favorable Supreme Court decision, or the passing of legislation directly or indirectly helpful to business (e.g., a tariff, railroad aid, etc.). A favorable political condition may also be international in its effect, such as the settling of an international dispute.

Under favorable financial conditions may be included low money rates, high ratio of cash reserves to deposit liabilities as shown by bank statements, etc.

Under favorable business conditions may be included activity in production and distribution, large bank clearings, good crops, few idle cars, large earnings, few commercial failures, stable or rising prices, etc.

FEDERAL ADVISORY COUNCIL The original Federal Reserve Act created a Federal Advisory Council, to consist of as many members as there are Federal Reserve districts (12). Each Federal Reserve bank by its board of directors is directed by the act to select annually from its own Federal Reserve district one member for this council, who shall receive such compensation and allowances as may be fixed by said board of directors, subject to the approval of the Board of Governors of the Federal Reserve System.

Meetings of the council shall be held in Washington, D.C., at least four times each year, and more often if called by the board of governors. The council may, in addition to the minimum meetings provided, hold such other meetings in Washington or elsewhere as it may deem necessary. It may select its own officers (two of the members are designated as president and vice president, and two nonmembers are designated as secretary and assistant secretary) and adopt its own methods of procedure, with a majority of its members constituting a quorum for the transaction of business. Vacancies in the council are filled by the respective Federal Reserve banks, and members selected to fill vacancies shall serve for the unexpired term.

The council has power, by itself through its officers: (1) to confer directly with the Board of Governors of the FEDERAL RESERVE SYSTEM on general business conditions, (2) to make oral or written representations concerning matters within the jurisdiction of the board, (3) to call for information and to make recommendations in regard to discount rates, rediscount business, note issues, reserve conditions in the various districts, the purchase and sale of gold or securities by Reserve banks, open market operations, and the general affairs of the Federal Reserve System. Thus, although its functions are purely advisory and consultative, the council serves as an important point of contact between the banking community, as represented by the bankers of the council, and the board of governors, and as a sounding board for banking viewpoint on policies and operations of the Federal Reserve System.

FEDERAL AGRICULTURAL MORTGAGE CORPORATION (FAMC or Farmer Mac). A corporation created by the Agricultural Credit Act of 1987 to assist the Farm Credit System (FCS) in meeting its primary goal by providing up to $4 billion in direct financial assistance. FAMC is a federally chartered instrumentality of the United States and an Institution of the Farm Credit System. Its purpose is to facilitate the development of a secondary market for agricultrual real estate loans by providing guarantees on securities that represent either interests in pools of such loans or are collateralized by pools of such loans. FMAC is commonly referred to as Farmer Mac. It is owned jointly by Farm Credit System institutions and non-Farm Credit System institutions.

The money required for FAMC would be raised by having the corporation sell uncollateralized bonds backed by the full faith and credit of the U.S. government. The corporation would be capitalized by mandatory stock purchases by Farm Credit System institutions. Banks and associations of the FCS must buy stock in the amount by which the unallocated retained earnings exceed 5% of assets of banks and 13% of the assets of association. This capital assessment on healthy FCS units is similar to the assessments tried earlier by the now defunct Farm Credit Capital Corporation.

The act creating FAMC provides for an initial $20 million of voting common stock to be offered to commercial banks, insurance companies, system institutions, and other financial entities. Additional voting stock may also be issued, but only to loan originators and poolers. Freely transferable nonvoting common stock and preferred stock may also be issued.

Initially, the FAMC will have a nine-member interim board of directors appointed by the president. Three members will come from the Farm Credit System and three from commercial banks and other financial institutions. The remaining three will consist of two who will be farmers or ranchers and one who will represent the general public, and none will have had experience as a director or officer of any financial institution or entity. The chairman is named by the president. Once the $20 million of common stock is subscribed, the interim board is to arrange for the election of five permanent directors each by holders of the two classes of common stock and for the appointment of five members by the president, subject to confirmation by the U.S. Senate. Ten of the 15 members are to be elected annually, five by Farm Credit System holders of FAMC stock and five by other FAMC stockholders.

Farm Credit Assistance Board, consisting of the secretaries of Agriculture and the Treasury and a third member, an agricultural producer appointed by the president, has almost unlimited powers in overseeing the financial and business management of FCS units that receive assistance.

The objectives of financial assistance are to protect FCS borrower stock, help make FCS institutions financially viable again, and allow units to provide credit on reasonable and competitive terms. In exchange for financial assistance to the FCS, the law calls for the restructuring of system units.

The law provides for the creation of a secondary market for farm and rural housing mortgages by creating a role for the corporation in the new secondary market similar to Ginnie Mae, Fannie Mae, and Freddie Mac in the secondary residential mortgage market. Farmer Mac guarantees timely payment of principal and interest on securi-ties that represent interests in pools of farm mortgages and are sold to the investing public by loan poolers certified by Farmer Mac. FAMC also sets the underwriting, security appraisal, and repay-ment standards in consultation with originators and determines the eligibility of poolers to be certified. The guarantee is supported by a 10% reserve fund formed by the originators or poolers of each loan pool and ultimately supported by a $1.5 billion line of credit at the U.S. Treasury. When a guarantee is issued, the pooler will be assessed a fee of no more than $1/2$ of 1%of the principal amount of the loans in the pool. Each guaranteed pool must have at least 50 qualified loans of varying principal amounts spread among various commodities and over a wide geographic area. A qualified agricultrual loan is one that meets statutory and FAMC standards.

The secondary farm mortgage market will be considerably smaller than the secondary residential mortgage market. The value of U.S. farm real estate totaled $576 billion at the end of 1987. Debt against this real estate totaled only $90 billion, about 4% of the value of all residential mortgages outstanding. Transfers of farmland every year average roughly $20 billion, and about $8 billion in new farm mortgage credit is extended every year. The spread between yields on Farmer Mac securities and Treasury securities is not likely to differ much from the spread between FCS and Treasury securities. Yields on seven-year FCS bonds averaged 44 basis points higher than yields of Treasury securities in 1986 and 1987.

Source: Federal Reserve Bank of Kansas City.

FEDERAL APPROPRIATIONS See NATIONAL BUDGET.

FEDERAL BILL OF LADING ACT See BILL OF LADING.

FEDERAL CREDIT UNIONS
A credit union is a financial cooperative that aids it members by encouraging thrift and by providing members with a source of credit for provident purposes at reasonable rates of interest. Federal credit unions serve occupational, associational, and residential groups.

Pursuant to the act of March 10, 1970 (12 U.S.C. 1752), federal credit unions are under the chartering, supervising, and examining jurisdiction of the National Credit Union Administration, an independent agency of the executive branch, as reorganized by act of November 10, 1978 (12 U.S.C. 226). The referenced 1970 act (in 12 U.S.C. 1752 note) authorized the NCUA to insure share accounts to $20,000 and to charge a premium of $1/12$ of 1% of share accounts; this was raised to $40,000 in 1974 by amendment to the 1970 act (12 U.S.C. 1781 *et seq.*), and to $100,000 by similar amendment contained in the DEPOSITORY INSTITUTIONS DEREGULATION AND MONETARY CONTROL ACT OF 1980, enacted March 31, 1980. The last-named legislation also contained the following provisions of impact upon federal credit unions:

1. Permanent share draft authority was granted to all federally insured credit unions. This replaced the 90-day share draft authority granted on December 31, 1979 for all federal credit unions.
2. Reserve requirements were imposed on transaction accounts.
3. Federal Reserve System services were required to be priced.
4. The Depository Institutions Deregulation Committee (DIDC) was established for the purpose of phasing out savings rate controls within a 6-year period.
5. Authority was granted to federal credit unions to make loans onindividual cooperative units.
6. Increase was authorized in the federal credit union rate ceiling on loans to 15%, with authority for the NCUA Board to further increase this ceiling for periods of 18 months.
7. Overriding of certain state usury laws was provided.
8. Truth-in-Lending (see Regulation Z of the Board of Governors of theFederal Reserve System) was simplified.

The following provisions of the GARN-ST. GERMAIN DEPOSITORY INSTITUTIONS ACT OF 1982 affect all federally insured credit unions.

Reserve requirements: The act's amendment to Section 22(h) of the Federal Reserve Act exempts from reserve requirements the first $2,000,000 of reservable liabilities of each depository institution. Thus unless the credit union has more than $2,000,000 in share drafts and other reservable accounts, it will no longer be subject to reserve requirements.

Due on sale: The act added a new section to the United States Code overturning state laws prohibiting the exercise of a due on sale clause on a real property loan. However, such state prohibitions will continue to have limited application to so-called window period loans. Specifically, for a loan made or assumed between the date that the state established its prohibition and the date of enactment of this federal override, the due on sale clause may be exercised only with respect to assumptions made three or more years after enactment of the federal override.

Share drafts for public units: The act amended Section 205(f)(2) of the Federal Credit Union Act to authorize federally insured credit unions to receive deposits of public funds in share draft accounts.

Alternative mortgages: The act added a new section to the United States Code authorizing state-chartered institutions to make alternative mortgage loans. Thus state-chartered credit unions were authorized to make alternative mortgage loans in accordance with the NCUA's regulations for federal credit unions.

Emergency merger and conservator authority: The act amended Section 205 of the Federal Credit Union Act authorizing the NCUA to merge a failing federally insured credit union without regard to geographic area and field of membership, where other reasonable alternatives do not exist. The act also amended Section 206 of the Federal Credit Union Act authorizing the NCUA to appoint itself as conservator of a federally insured credit union when necessary to protect the assets of the credit union, the interests of its members, or the NCUSIF (National Credit Union Share Insurance Fund). In the case of conservatorship of a federally insured state-chartered credit union, a process was set forth for consulting with and attempting to obtain the state regulator's approval.

Insurance assessments: The act amended Section 202(h) of the Federal Credit Union Act providing that deposits exceeding the

$100,000 insurance limit will not be counted when insurance premiums are assessed by the NCUSIF if the deposit was made by a federally insured or state-insured credit union. Previously, only deposits by federally insured credit unions were excluded. The act also amended Section 202(c)(3) and (6) of the Federal Credit Union Act deleting the statutory requirement that each new credit union be assessed a partial premium during the year in which it is chartered and that each insured credit union that is liquidated receive a rebate on premiums paid.

Study of optional insurance: The act added a new section to the U.S. Code directing the NCUA and the deposit insurance agencies to study various issues including the feasibility of consolidating the insurance funds.

The following provisions of the act affect federal credit unions only.

Par Value, Optional Credit Committee and Titles of Officers. Three important provisions of the act would require federal credit union bylaw changes. These changes provide federal credit unions the options of (1) increasing the par value of shares above $5; (2) having an elected credit committee, a board-appointed credit committee or no credit committee; and (3) designating their own titles for officers of the board of directors. These standard amendments of the bylaws may be adopted by action of the Board of Directors.

Directors' compensation. The act directed the NCUA Board to report to Congress on the feasibility and desirability of permitting federal credit unions to compensate members of their boards of directors.

Corporate credit unions. The act amended Section 120(a) of the Federal Credit Union Act authorizing the NCUA Board to differentiate its regulatory treatment of corporate credit unions versus natural person credit unions. This would authorize the NCUA Board to modify or remove limitations on corporate credit unions that would otherwise exist under the Federal Credit Union Act.

The following amendments of the Federal Credit Union Act by the Garn–St. Germain Depository Institutions Act of 1982 affected daily operation of federal credit unions.

Median sales price: The act amended Section 107(A)(i) of the Federal Credit Union Act to permit federal credit unions to make first mortgage loans of greater than 12 years in maturity without the restriction that the sales price of the home must be not more than 150% of the median sales price of residential (real) property situated in the geographical area in which the property is located.

Refinancing of mortgage loans: The act amended Section 107(5)(A)(i) of the Federal Credit Union Act to delete the requirement that a first mortgage loan be made to finance the acquisition of a one-to-four family dwelling. This would permit a federal credit union to allow borrowers to refinance a first mortgage or permit the federal credit union to take back a first mortgage on property already acquired by the borrower with the loan proceeds being used for purposes unrelated to the acquisition of the property.

Second mortgage loans: The act amended Section 107(5)(A)(ii) of the Federal Credit Union Act to permit all second mortgage loans to have maturities up to 15 years, rather than just those loans characterized as "home improvement" loans.

Advance commitment: The act amended Section 107(5)(A)(iii) of the Federal Credit Union Act to permit a federal credit union to make any loan it may not otherwise be able to make as long as it has an advance commitment to purchase the loan by a government agency that has agreed to the loan terms.

Loans to officials: The act amended Sections 107(5)(A)(iv) and (v) of the Federal Credit Union Act to increase the amount that can be lent to an official without board of directors' approval from $5,000 to $10,000.

Partial prepayments: The act amended Section 107(5)(A)(viii) of the Federal Credit Union Act to permit federal credit unions, on first and second mortgage loans, to require that partial prepayments be made on the date monthly installments are due, and that they be in the amount of that part of one or more monthly installments that would be applicable to principal. This change permitted treatment of mortgage loan prepayments in a manner consistent with the requirements of secondary mortgage market investors, particularly the FEDERAL NATIONAL MORTGAGE ASSOCIATION (FNMA) and FEDERAL HOME LOAN MORTGAGE CORPORATION (FHLMC).

State and local obligations: The act amended Section 107(7) of the Federal Credit Union Act to permit federal credit unions to invest in state and local government obligations, such as municipal bonds, with a limit of 10% of unimpaired capital and surplus as to any one issuer.

Agency obligations: The act amended Section 107(7)(E) of the Federal Credit Union Act to permit federal credit unions to invest in the obligations of any agency of the United States.

Deposits in insured banks: The act amended Section 107(8) of the Federal Credit Union Act to permit federal credit unions to make deposits in any federally insured bank and not just in those in the state in which the credit union does business.

Money transfer services: The act amended Section 107(12) of the Federal Credit Union Act to permit, in addition to the sale of travelers checks and money orders already permitted in this section, federal credit unions to sell similar services and instruments, such as wire transfers. The fees for all such sales no longer would need to be limited to the costs of providing the services.

Annual meetings: The act amended Section 110 of the Federal Credit Union Act to permit federal credit unions to hold annual meetings at any time during the year.

Expulsion: The act amended Section 118 of the Federal Credit Union Act to permit boards of federal credit unions to adopt a policy to expel members who fail to vote in annual elections or who fail to purchase shares or obtain loans.

Conversion of charter: The act amended Section 125(a)(1) of the Federal Credit Union Act to clarify that a conversion from federal to state charter must be approved by a majority of those members voting, rather than a majority of all members.

Custodial accounts: The act amended Section 101(5) of the Federal Credit Union Act to permit the NCUA to insure escrow or custodial accounts held by federal credit unions for loans they have sold, thus permitting federal credit unions to participate more effectively in the secondary market when the account is for a non-member and an institutional investor requires that the servicer place funds in insured accounts.

Space and facilities: The act amended Section 124 of the Federal CreditUnion Act defining the services that can be available, either free or at payment of costs, in federal buildings to federal credit unions serving primarily federal employees. Services include telephone and security devices.

Central Liquidity Facility. The National Credit Union Administration Central Liquidity Facility was established by P.L. 95-630 and began operations on October 1, 1979. The facility is a "mixed ownership Government corporation" within the National Credit Union Administration. It is owned by its member credit unions and managed by the NCUA's board.

The purpose of the facility is to improve general financial stability by meeting the liquidity needs of credit unions and thereby encourage savings, support consumer and mortgage lending, and provide basic financial resources to all segments of the economy. The facility functions as a lender of last resort for credit unions, providing a reliable source of credit to meet liquidity needs when funds are not available from other sources.

Membership in the facility is voluntary and is open to all credit unions, whether federal or state-chartered, insured or noninsured (state-chartered credit unions may be accepted for insurance by the NCUA). Credit unions can gain access to facility loans either directly, as regular members, or indirectly, through an "agent member." Agent membership is available only to corporate credit unions, and when such a corporate credit union becomes an agent, all its member credit unions gain access to the facility through the agent.

The facility is entirely self-supporting. Its capital is supplied by its regular and agent members, who are required to purchase facility capital stock in order to become members. The facility's policy has been to invest all capital.

Funding for the facility's lending activities comes from borrowing, and the borrowed funds are then relent at a spread. The law that established the facility permits it to borrow from any source up to 12 times its subscribed capital and surplus. In fiscal year 1980, Congress limited the facility's borrowing authority to $300 million, but increased that limit to $600 million for fiscal year 1981.

In addition to its regular borrowing authority, the facility is authorized to borrow up to $500 million from the secretary of the Treasury in emergency circumstances. Prior authorization from Congress in the form of an appropriation to the Treasury is required, however; no portion of this emergency line of credit was appropriated for fiscal year 1980 or 1981.

Funds to cover the facility's operating expenses are derived from its earnings on loans and investments. Income in excess of expenses is returned to members in the form of dividends on capital stock.

Facility's lending: The facility's primary activity is providing loans to credit unions to meet liquidity needs. The facility was established to supplement, rather than compete with, private sector sources of funds, and therefore its function is that of a lender of last resort. This role is enforced by setting rates on facility loans slightly above those posted by traditional private sector credit union sources of funds.

Three forms of liquidity assistance are available to credit unions from the facility:

1. *Short-term adjustment credit* (30–90 days), to assist in meeting temporary requirements for funds and to cushion more persistent outflows of funds pending an orderly adjustment of a credit union's assets and liabilities.
2. *Seasonal credit* (90–270 days), to meet liquidity needs arising from annually recurring patterns of movement of loans and shares
3. *Protracted adjustment credit* (1–4 years), to meet liquidity needs in the event of unusual or emergency circumstances that are expected to be of an extended duration. The liquidity problems must result from national, regional, or local difficulties.

The facility also has authority to lend to state credit union share insurance funds.

Special Assistance to Avoid Liquidation. To qualify for special assistance, a credit union must have been in danger of liquidation, must have corrected the problems causing the need for assistance including management changes, must have used all available resources (including statutory reserves and available earnings to reduce the amount of special assistance), and must be able to amortize or repay the special assistance in a reasonable period of time.

Operational Features of Federal Credit Unions. The NCUA *Rules and Regulations*, and specifically the lending regulations, were extensively deregulated in 1980, leading to greater flexibility in the establishment of interest rates on loans and the authorization of prerequisites for and types of loans.

Organization Features of Federal Credit Unions.

Membership: Limited to persons elected by the board of directors from among applicants who are included in the field of membership defined in the charter. Each member present at annual or special meetings has one vote, irrespective of the number of shares held by him. Only members may borrow from the credit union, just as only members may deposit savings.

Directors: The members elect a board of directors of not less than five members at their annual meeting. They also elect a Credit Committee and a Supervisory (or Examining) Committee of three members each. The directors have general management of the credit union, set its policies, approve all applications for membership, set the interest rate within the authorizations permitted by the NCUA on loans, and declare the dividends. They elect a president, vice-president, treasurer and clerk (or secretary). The treasurer's and clerk's office may be held by the same person. Officers and directors meet at least once a month, and hold additional meetings if necessary.

Under the 1968 amendments to the Federal Credit Union Act, the board was allowed to delegate its borrowing authority to the Executive Committee. This removed the previous requirement for the board to convene special meetings in order to authorize the borrowing of funds by the credit union. Delegations would be in the same manner as delegations for the investment of funds, so that policymaking responsibility remains with the board, and Executive Committee actions are subject to board review and evaluation. The 1968 amendments also provided that the audit report to members may be a summary of the report to the directors.

Credit committee: Supervises all loans to members. The Credit Committee meets regularly as often as necessary to approve loans, and not less frequently than once a month. No loans to a director, officer, or member of a committee shall exceed the amount of his holdings in the credit union as represented by shares. No director, officer, or committee member shall endorse for borrowers. Applications for loans shall be made in writing, and must tell the purpose of the loan, security offered, etc.

Supervisory committee: Is the "watchdog" of the credit union, keeping an eye on the operations by audits. Under the 1968 amendments to the Federal Credit Union Act, the Supervisory Committee shall make or cause to be made semi-annual audits, one of which (upon decision by the committee) shall be the comprehensive annual audit, and the other, a less comprehensive audit. Federal credit union examiners will review the reports of such audits as well as work papers, and discuss the audit activities of the Supervisory Committee with committee members during each examination. The law permits the Supervisory Committee to conduct additional audits, and it gives the directors the power to order additional audits. By unanimous vote, the Supervisory Committee has the power to suspend any officer, member of the Credit Committee or board of directors, until the next members' meeting, which shall be called within 7 days of such suspension, to act on same.

Supervisory activities are carried out through examiner contacts and through periodic policy and regulatory releases from the administration. The administration also maintains an early warning system designed to identify emerging problems as well as to monitor operations between examinations. The administration conducts annual examinations of federal credit unions to determine their solvency and compliance with laws and regulations, and to assist credit union management and operations.

Treasurer: Is the active manager of the credit union, keeping the books, making the financial reports (including financial reports to the Director of the Bureau of Federal Credit Unions at least annually), and being in charge of the receipt and disbursement of funds. Before the treasurer enters upon his duties, he is required to give bond with good and sufficient surety, in amount and character to be determined from time to time by the board of directors in compliance with regulations. The treasurer alone, because of his active duties, is entitled to salary, other members of the board and committeemen volunteering their services. Among the powers of the credit union which the treasurer administers is the deposit in national banks and in state banks, trust companies, and mutual savings banks operating under the laws of the state in which the federal credit union does business, of funds of the organization.

Sources of funds are (1) sale of shares to members, par value $5 each or such other par value as the directors may establish by amendment of the bylaws; savings of members; interest charges on loans to members and fines levied on members for failure to pay their obligations promptly; (2) earnings from other permissible earning assets (U.S. government securities, direct or fully guaranteed; loans to other credit unions; and shares or accounts of federal savings and loan associations or any other institutions whose accounts are insured by the Federal Savings and Loan Insurance Corporation); and (3) authority to borrow.

BIBLIOGRAPHY

NATIONAL CREDIT UNION ADMINISTRATION, *Annual Reports*.
———. *Chartering and Organizing Manual for Federal Credit Unions*, 1980.

FEDERAL CROP INSURANCE CORPORATION

Created within the Department of Agriculture under Title V of the Agricultural Adjustment Act of 1938, cited as the Federal Crop Insurance Act, approved February 16, 1938 (7 U.S.C. 1501). The scope of the corporation's functions has been modified from time to time by amendments to the act, the latest of which was approved July 28, 1972. The official description follows.

The basic purpose of the Federal Crop Insurance Program is to promote the general welfare by providing crop insurance against loss from unavoidable causes, such as weather, insects, and disease. The Federal Crop Insurance Act, as amended, authorizes the corporation to insure crops against unavoidable losses and to develop the most practical plan, terms, and conditions of insurance for agricultural commodities. The immediate objective is to continue the development of a sound system of crop insurance, and the ultimate objective is to make this protection generally available to farmers on the major part of their annual crop investments.

The Federal Crop Insurance Corporation does not insure profit for the farmer or cover avoidable losses such as those due to neglect or poor farming practices. Legislation limits the maximum level of coverage to 75% of the average yield but not more than the cost of producing the crop in the areas.

The number of counties in which crop insurance on one or more crops is offered has been gradually expanded since 1946 to over half of the nation's agricultural counties. As of 1988, the corporation insured 50 crops in over 3,000 counties in 49 states. Crops covered include wheat, cotton, tobacco, corn, flax, dry beans, soybeans, barley, grain sorghums, oats, rice, citrus fruit, peaches, peanuts, peas, raisins, apples, tomatoes, sugarbeets, sugarcane, grapes, forage, potatoes, sunflowers, and sweet corn, as well as investment in several crops under a combined crop protection plan.

The corporation was directed to develop this insurance so that the premiums paid by the farmers cover indemnities paid to the policyholders and build a reasonable premium reserve. Administrative costs are financed by annual appropriations which may also authorize the use of specified amounts of premium income for such costs. However, the legislation does not permit including administrative costs in the premium rates. Legislation limits the appropriation for administration to $12 million.

Premium rates are varied through the nation and even within counties, to reflect differences in productivity and risk of loss. As insurance experience is obtained, it is reflected in the rate structure. In recent crop years, over $2 billion in crop investments has been insured.

Management of the Federal Crop Insurance Corporation is vested in the board of directors, subject to the general supervision of the secretary of Agriculture. A manager is charged with running the day-to-day operations.

The corporation is provided in the original act with an authorized capital of $200 million, of which $150 million has been issued. All of the capital stock of the corporation is owned by the U.S. government.

The program delivery system has been shifted largely to the private sector to comply with the mandate in the Federal Crop Insurance Act of 1980, especially through licensed agents and brokers. The corporation now offers insurance through two basic delivery systems: sales and service agencies (master marketers and private insurance companies that it reinsures. Compensation rates are different under each sales agreement because the amount of risk assumed and service provided under each delivery system are different. Master marketers provide management, supervision of at least 25 or more agents, and contract servicing, with the exception of loss adjustment. All loss adjustments and claims functions on policies sold by Master Marketers are carried out by FCIC.

Reinsurance companies offer crop insurance under their own brand names and provide marketing, distribution, servicing, training, quality control, premium collection, and loss adjustment functions. The corporation reinsures these companies against extraordinary operational and actuarial losses.

The flexibility of crop insurance policies offers choices of guaranteed yield amounts and prices to be paid on each bushel or pound of loss. The cost of insurance depends on the level of protection selected. Crop insurance is now more specifically tailored to the individual farmer's needs by the Actual Production History Program. APH allows yield guarantees based upon the individual's verifiable production history. The Federal Crop Insurance Act of 1980 directs the corporation to develop an actuarially sound system of insurance so that the premiums will cover indemnities paid and build a reasonable premium reserve.

FEDERAL DEPOSIT INSURANCE ACT The act approved September 21, 1950 (12 U.S.C. 1811-1831), by which Section 12B of the Federal Reserve Act as amended was withdrawn as part of the Federal Reserve Act and made a separate independent law known as the Federal Deposit Insurance Act. Section 12B of the Federal Reserve Act, in turn, was originally added to the Federal Reserve Act as an entire section by the Banking Act of 1933, passed June 16, 1933 (48 Stat. 168, ch. 89); later amended by the act of June 16, 1934 (48 Stat. 969, 970, ch. 546), which extended the original temporary plan for insurance of deposits to June 30, 1935; Public Resolution of June 28, 1935 (Pub. Res. No. 38, 74th Cong.), which further extended the temporary plan to August 31, 1935; and finally by the Banking Act of 1935, approved August 23, 1935 (Pub. No. 305, 74th Cong.), which established the permanent plan for nationwide insurance of bank deposits.

The Federal Deposit Insurance Act approved September 21, 1950, made various fundamental amendments of the former Federal Deposit Insurance provisions as contained in Section 12B of the Federal Reserve Act, including the following changes:

1. Deposit insurance coverage was increased from $5,000 to $10,000 per account. The principle of limitation of deposit insurance was designed to cover fully depositors with small accounts. The $5,000 original insurance limit, provided effective July 1, 1934, continued at that level until it was increased to $10,000 effective September 21, 1950, under the permanent plan. Insurance per account under the stop-gap temporary plan, from January 1, 1934, to July 1, 1934, was $2,500. As the result of the increase in average size of deposits, the proportion of accounts fully insured had slowly fallen to about 96% in 1950.
2. Rebate of assessments upon insured banks for deposit insurance was provided, although the assessment rate was left unchanged at $1/12$ of 1% annually, payable semiannually on average collected total deposits. Beginning December 31, 1950, and as of December 31 of each calendar year thereafter, the corporation transferred 40% of its net assessment income (after deduction of operating expenses and additions to reserves for insurance losses) to its capital account, and the balance of the net assessment income was credited pro-rata to the insured banks, based upon the assessments of each bank coming due during the said calendar year. Each year, such credit was applied by the corporation toward the payment of the total assessment coming due for the semiannual assessment period beginning the next July 1, and any excess credit was applied upon the assessment next becoming due.
3. Authority of the corporation was clarified to make loans to, or purchase assets from, insured banks in order to facilitate mergers or consolidations, and to reduce risks or avert threatened loss to the corporation, and to prevent the closing of an insured bank when the corporation considers the continued operation of such bank essential to provide adequate banking services in the community.

P.L. 86-463. P.L. 86-463, 86th Congress, approved May 13, 1960, further importantly amended the Federal Deposit Insurance Act (Sec. 18(c) to require federal approval for mergers and consolidations of insured banks. Gist of the amendment is as follows:

1. Any insured bank merging or consolidating with any other insured bank or either directly or indirectly acquiring the assets of or assuming the deposit liability of any other insured bank shall first obtain the prior written consent of the following supervisory authority:
   a. the Comptroller of the Currency if the acquiring, assuming, or resulting bank is to be a national bank or a District of Columbia bank;
   b. the Board of Governors of the Federal Reserve System if the acquiring, assuming, or resulting bank is to be a state member bank (except a District of Columbia bank);
   c. the FEDERAL DEPOSIT INSURANCE CORPORATION if the acquiring, assuming, or resulting bank is to be a nonmember bank (except a District of Columbia bank).
2. Prior notice of such proposed merger, consolidation, acquisition, or assumption, in the form approved by the above authorities, is required by publication in a newspaper of general circulation.
3. In granting or withholding approval, the supervisory authorities referred to shall consider:
   a. the financial history and condition of each of the banks involved;
   b. the adequacy of its capital structure;
   c. its future earnings prospects;
   d. the general character of its management;
   e. the convenience and needs of the community to be served;
   f. whether or not its corporate powers are consistent with the purposes of the act;
   g. the effect of the transaction on competition (including any tendency toward monopoly).
   Approval of the transaction shall not be made unless, after considering all such factors, the authority concerned finds the transaction to be in the public interest.
4. Before acting on the proposed transaction, and in the interest of uniform standards, the supervisory authority concerned shall request a report on the competitive factors involved from the attorney general and the other two banking agencies referred to above (unless it finds that it must act immediately in order to prevent the probable failure of one of the banks involved). This report shall be furnished within 30 calendar days of the date on which it is requested or within 10 calendar days of such date if the requesting agency advises that an emergency exists requiring expeditious action.
5. Each of the supervisory agencies referred to shall include in its annual report to Congress a description of each such

transaction approved by it during the period covered by the report, including the following additional information:
   a. name and total resources of each bank involved;
   b. whether a report has been submitted by the attorney general thereon and, if so, a summary by the attorney general of the substance of such report;
   c. a statement of the basis for approval.

P.L. 86-671. Because of the administrative and technical complications involved in making the deductions and exclusions from the assessment base permissible under the assessment rebate procedure, a procedure costly both to the corporation and to the insured banks, S.2609 was introduced in the 86th Congress on August 27, 1959. This bill became law (P.L. 86-671) on July 14, 1960. This law simplified the procedure and reduced the annual assessments upon the insured banks. Under it, assessments are now based on the average of deposits shown in two reports of condition in each semiannual assessment period, with authorized deductions of $16^2/3$% of demand deposits and 1% of time and savings deposits. The basic annual assessment rate of $1/12$ of 1% remains unchanged. The credit to insured banks is now computed at $66^2/3$% of the net assessment income instead of the former 60%. These changes in the manner of computing deposit insurance assessments upon insured banks became effective with the certified statements submitted in July, 1961. The change in the ratio of net assessment income to be credited to insured banks became effective with the credit for the calendar year 1961, to be made to insured banks for application toward the payment of their assessments due in July 1962. About 99.5% of the insured banks would have paid a lesser net annual assessment for the period 1951-1958 under the new law.

P.L. 91-151. The act approved December 23, 1969 (P.L. 91-151), increased from $15,000 to $20,000 the insurance coverage of deposits insured by the Federal Deposit Insurance Corporation (FDIC).

P.L. 93-495. Effective November 27, 1974, this law amended the Federal Deposit Insurance Act to double deposit insurance coverage from $20,000 to $40,000, and to increase coverage for most public funds, including state and local government time and savings deposits (except deposits held in out-of-state banks) and federal deposits, fivefold to $100,000.

Depository Institutions Deregulation and Monetary Control Act of 1980. One feature of this omnibus banking legislation, signed March 31, 1980, increased federal deposit insurance to $100,000 from $40,000 per depositor and revised the insurance assessment credit formula. Although insured banks continue to be assessed for deposit insurance coverage on total deposits, credits against this assessment reduce their insurance costs. The basis for determining these credits was revised by the act. The assessment was set by law at $1/12$ of 1% of banks' total assessable deposits. The credit is computed after deducting the FDIC's administrative and operating expenses, nonrecoverable insurance expenses, and additions to reserves for losses. The 1980 act changed the basis for the credit to 60% from $66^2/3$% of net assessment income, and authorized the FDIC's board of directors to make adjustments to the credit to maintain the insurance fund within a range of 1.25% to 1.40% of estimated insured deposits and mandated adjustments to keep the fund no lower than 1.10% and no higher than 1.40% of insured deposits.

Insurance of Deposits of U.S. Branches of Foreign Banks. Part 346 of the FDIC's regulations authorizes and in some cases requires insurance coverage of deposits in U.S. branches of foreign banks. A state branch of a foreign bank which accepts initial deposits of less than $100,000 must become insured if it is located in a state that requires state banks to have deposit insurance. A branch may be exempted from this requirement if the acceptance of initial deposits of less than $100,000 is limited to one or more exempt categories. Such a branch of a foreign bank which is exempt from the insurance requirement must notify its depositors that deposits in the branch are not insured by the FDIC.

FEDERAL DEPOSIT INSURANCE CORPORATION

An independent executive agency, originally established by the BANKING ACT OF 1933 to insure the deposits of all banks entitled to federal deposit insurance under Section 12B of the Federal Reserve Act; and under the FEDERAL DEPOSIT INSURANCE ACT, approved September 21, 1950, since the latter date.

The FDIC, as it is referred to, administers the system of nationwide deposit insurance (or, more properly, mutual guaranty of deposits) for U.S. banks, established for the first time in the nation's history effective January 1, 1934. Its functions are more than merely ministerial, however, and it has important supervisory and examination powers which make it the third federal banking supervisory agency, along with the Comptroller of the Currency and the Board of Governors of the Federal Reserve System.

Organization. Management of the FDIC is vested in a board of directors of three members. The President appoints two members for terms of six years, by and with the advice and consent of the Senate. The third member is the Comptroller of the Currency. One of the appointive members is designated chairman of the board of directors. Under the law, not more than two members of the board shall belong to the same political party.

Principal office of the corporation is in Washington, D.C., where the executive offices are maintained and where about one-fourth of the corporation's total number of employees are stationed. District offices are maintained in Atlanta, Boston, Chicago, Columbus, Dallas, Kansas City, Madison, Memphis, Minneapolis, New York, Philadelphia, Richmond, St. Louis, and San Francisco, which service the districts involved. Largest division in terms of personnel is the Division of Examination, over 90% of whose employees, who account for about three-fourths of the corporation's total employment, are assigned to the district offices.

The corporation is entirely self-sustaining. No appropriations are made by Congress for it, its entire net income consisting of:

1. Assessments on insured banks. Assessments are earned by the corporation at the statutory rate of $1/12$ of 1% of total assessable deposits of insured banks. Legislation enacted in 1950 provided that a portion of the assessments earned each year, after allowance for the corporation's insurance losses and operating expenses, be returned to insured banks as a credit against future assessments.
2. Income from investments, which are U.S. government securities. The insured banks do not participate in the corporation's income from investments.

All certified statements submitted by the banks, showing the computation of assessments due, are reviewed by the Washington office for clerical accuracy and for general reasonableness of the figures reported. Field audits of the assessment records of the banks are made by the Audit Division.

Deposit Insurance Fund. This represents the corporation's accumulated net income since inception (i.e., surplus). The fund is available to meet future deposit insurance claims and related losses. Its adequacy to meet these future requirements is dependent upon the soundness of financial condition of insured banks and their ability to maintain solvency despite adverse factors such as unfavorable economic conditions generally and individual bank difficulties specifically. Thus the size of the fund is not a measure of the deposit insurance risk.

The corporation is authorized to borrow up to $3 billion from the U.S. Treasury when in the judgment of the board of directors such funds are required for insurance purposes. This borrowing authority has never been used. There is no outstanding borrowed money.

Originally, the corporation was helped to start operations by the subscription of $150 million in stock by the U.S. Treasury and another $140 million total stock subscribed for by each Federal Reserve bank, in an amount equal to half of the surplus of each Reserve bank as of January 1, 1933. All of this capital was repaid in 1947 and 1948, and interest on the capital was repaid to the U.S. Treasury in 1951.

Powers. The FDIC, aside from its power to collect the deposit insurance assessments from the insured banks (all national banks in the continental U.S. and all state banks that are members of the Federal Reserve System are required to be insured; all nonmember national and state banks may become insured upon applications to the FDIC and compliance with statutory requirements), has the following powers with respect to insured banks:

1. To examine insured banks not members of the Federal Reserve System and to make special examination of any state member bank and any national bank or District of Columbia bank whenever the board of directors deems such special examination necessary to determine the condition of any such bank for insurance purposes.
2. To terminate the insured status of a bank which continues, after notice and hearing, to engage in unsafe and unsound practices.
3. To pass upon conversions, mergers, or consolidations and

FEDERAL DEPOSIT INSURANCE CORPORATION

assumption of deposit liability transactions between insured banks and noninsured banks or institutions, and to prevent capital and surplus diminution in such transactions where the resulting, continuing, or assuming bank is an insured nonmember state bank.

See FEDERAL DEPOSIT INSURANCE ACT for details of power of approval of such transactions from the competitive standpoint.

4. To act as receiver for all national banks placed in receivership and for state banks placed in receivership, when so appointed by state authorities.
5. In protecting depositors, to make loans to or purchase assets from insured banks in order to facilitate mergers or consolidations, and to reduce risks or avert threatened loss to the corporation, and to prevent the closing of an insured bank or to reopen a closed insured bank when the corporation considers the continued operation of such bank essential to provide adequate banking services in the community.
6. To approve or disapprove a proposal to reduce or retire the capital of an insured bank not a member of the Federal Reserve System, except a District of Columbia bank.
7. To approve or disapprove a proposal by an insured bank not a member of the Federal Reserve System, except a district bank, to establish and operate a new branch, or move its main office or any branch from one location to another.
8. To prescribe rules and regulations relating to advertising which banks must use to enable the public to know that they are insured.
9. To require insurance protection against burglary, defalcation, and other similar insurable losses.
10. To publish notice of the termination of the insured status of a bank and to regulate the manner in which the bank shall give the required notice of such termination to depositors.
11. To prohibit the payment of interest on demand deposits of insured banks not members of the Federal Reserve System.
12. To limit rates of interest on time and savings deposits of insured banks not members of the Federal Reserve System and to prescribe different rates for deposits received under different specified conditions. (The chairman of the FDIC is a member of the DEPOSITORY INSTITUTIONS DEREGULATION COMMITTEE {DIDC}, formed pursuant to Title II of the Depository Institutions Deregulation and Monetary Control Act of 1980 to oversee the orderly phaseout of interest rate ceilings for commercial banks and mutual savings banks (as well as savings and loan associations and credit unions). The DIDC's charter includes regulatory authority over all matters relating to interest rates during the phaseout period.)
13. To prohibit, before maturity, the payment of time deposits of insured banks not members of the Federal Reserve System or the waiver of any requirement of notice before payment of any savings deposit, except as to all savings deposits having the same requirement.
14. For the purpose of any hearing under the Federal Deposit Insurance Act, to subpoena any officer or employee, or any books, records, or other papers of the insured bank which are relevant or material to the hearing.

Activities of the FDIC in 1987 and 1988 include the following:

1. **Bank Secrecy Act.** Issued a rule requiring banks to establish and maintain procedures to assure and monitor compliance with the Bank Secrecy Act and the implementing regulations promulgated thereunder.
2. **Capital requirements.** Amended its capital regulations to (a) clarify and revise certain definitions, (b) reserve the authority of the FDIC with respect to the definitions of "primary capital" and "secondary capital," (c) specified that the terms and conditions to which capital instruments are subject must be consistent with safe and sound banking practices, and (d) limited the circumstances in which the FDIC would not approve a proposed merger transaction when the resulting entity will not meet the FDIC's minimum capital requirements.
3. **Foreign bank branches—loan limits.** Specified that exposure in loans to entities or individuals outside the U.S. by insured branches of foreign banks operating as such on November 19, 1984, must be within prescribed limits.
4. **Privacy Act of 1974.** Amended its regulations so that appeals of adverse agency determinations on requests for access to or amendment of records will be considered by the FDIC's general counsel.

Operation of Deposit Insurance. The insurance covers deposits of every kind, including regular commercial deposits, time deposits, savings deposits, and trust funds awaiting investment. No distinction is made between public and private deposits, and the insurance applies even though security, such as depository bonds or collateral, may have been furnished by the bank for the repayment of such deposits. For insurance purposes, the official custodian of public funds is considered to be the depositor, not the public unit; he is entitled to insurance upon such funds deposited in an insured bank and maintained in the same right and capacity to the maximum of $100,000. If the deposited public funds are maintained in different rights and capacities, such official custodian is entitled to the maximum insurance of $100,000 upon funds maintained in each different right and capacity. If the official custodian holds the funds of several public units, the insurance protection will be as above stated with respect to the funds of each public unit.

Similarly, individual accounts in the *same* bank, in different rights and capacities, are entitled each to the $100,000 deposit insurance coverage; and the same right or capacity of an account, in *different* insured banks, is entitled to the maximum deposit insurance coverage in each insured bank. This has had some tendency to distribute deposits among insured banks, as to those individuals who are deposit-insurance conscious.

Procedure in Protection of Depositors. A bank in difficulty may be placed in receivership only by the supervisory authority concerned—the Comptroller of the Currency if a national bank, and the state authority if a state bank. The corporation must be appointed as receiver for all national banks placed in receivership and must accept appointment as receiver for any insured state bank in receivership if tendered by the state supervisory authority. As receiver, the corporation has the rights and obligations provided for by the National Bank Act in the case of a national bank or the applicable state law in the case of a state bank.

Upon the placing of a bank in receivership, the corporation examines the closed bank's records in order to establish the amount of the insured deposit liability. The amount of each depositor's insured deposit—the lesser of the total amount of the deposit or $100,000—is paid upon presentation of a bona fide claim and subrogation of the claim against the receivership. The subrogated claims entitle the corporation to share in receiver's dividends prorata with the depositors having claims in excess of $100,000.

A bank in difficulty may, with the approval of the supervisory authority and of the corporation, be merged with or contract to have its deposit liabilities assumed by another insured bank instead of being placed in receivership. In such cases, the receiving bank (1) assumes all recorded deposit liabilities of the closed bank, and (2) receives those assets of the closed bank that are acceptable and funds equal to the difference between the assumed deposit liabilities and the acceptable assets, which funds are advanced to the closed bank by the corporation. The corporation receives the unacceptable assets from the closed bank in accordance with (1) a loan agreement under which the assets are considered collateral, or (2) a purchase agreement under which the assets are sold to the corporation and may, in some cases, be reacquired by the closed bank.

The corporation liquidates the unacceptable assets and retains the proceeds in reimbursement of the amount advanced to the closed bank, in reimbursement of expenses incurred in connection with the maintenance and liquidation of the assets, and in payment of interest or allowable return on the unliquidated advances and accumulated expenses. In the loan agreement cases, the corporation completes the liquidation of the remaining assets and returns all proceeds in excess of the recoverable amounts to the closed bank, unless the bank elects to reacquire the assets and complete the liquidation. See appended table of FDIC banks closed or assisted due to financial difficulties, and problem banks: 1971-1987. Also see appended Federal Insurance Commercial Banks—Assets and Liabilites: 1975-1987.

The Competitive Equality Banking Act of 1987 contained several major provisions that were particularly significant for the FDIC. The act provided for financial institutions emergency acquisitions. (1)Out-of-state holding companies were permitted to acquire qualified stock institutions, as well as mutual savings banks, before they fail if they have assets of $500 million or more; (2) a holding company to be sold, in whole or in part, to an out-of-state holding company if the in-state holding company has a bank or bank with aggregate

FEDERAL DEPOSIT INSURANCE CORPORATION

banking assets of $500 million or more in danger of closing and the bank or banks represent 33% or more of the holding company's banking assets; and (3) an out-of-state holding company expansion rights in the state of acquisition through the bank holding company structure.

The act also permits the FDIC to establish a bridge bank to assume the deposits and liabilities and purchase the assets of a failed bank under specified conditions. The bridge bank must be a separately chartered national bank and it must be operated by a five-member board of directors appointed by the FDIC.

The FDIC and other financial institutions regulatory agencies are exempt from the apportionment provisions of the Anti-Deficiency Act (Gramm-Rudman-Hollings Act and the Anti-Deficiency Act).

Agricultural banks may, under certain circumstances, write down their losses on agricultural loans over seven years rather than deduct the amount of loss from capital as soon as the loss is recognized.

Nonbank banks are prohibited by requiring companies which acquired a nonbank bank after March 5, 1987, to comply with the Bank Holding Company act or divest their bank subsidiary.

The act authorized a newly established financing corporation funded by the Federal Home Loan banks to raise $10.6 billion for the FSLIC by selling bonds in the capital markets. FSLIC is limited to spending up to $3.75 billion per year in conjunction with failed thrift institutions.

A moratorium was imposed on insured banks with respect to certain securities, insurance, and real estate activities.

Provisions of the Glass-Steagall Act that prohibit affiliations and interlocking directors, officers, and employees between banks and securities firms were extended to FDIC-insured nonmember banks and thrift institutions until March 1, 1988.

Other provisions of the act require the FDIC to consider and minimize the adverse economic impact of a liquidation on the local community and require institutions offering adjustable-rate mortgages to include a maximum interest rate that may apply during the term of the loan.

In 1987, the five federal bank regulatory agencies issued a rule requiring banks to establish and maintain procedures to assure and monitor compliance with the Bank Secrecy Act and the implementing regulations promulgated thereunder by the Department of the Treasury. The FDIC in 1987 amended its capital regulations to (1) clarify and revise certain definitions, (2) reserve the authority of the FDIC with respect to the definitions of "primary capital" and "secondary capital," (3) specify that the terms and conditions to which capital instruments are subject must be consistent with safe and sound banking practices, and (4) limit, on the basis of insurance status, the circumstances in which the FDIC will not approve a proposed merger transaction when the resulting entity will not meet the FDIC's minimum capital requirements.

Appended are (1) FDIC Organization Chart, (2) Insured Deposits and the Deposit Insurance Fund, 1934-1987 (in millions), (3) FDIC Problem Banks, 1983-1987, (4) Failed Banks by State, 1985-1987, (5) Uninsured Deposits of Failed Banks, 1987, (6) Statistical Highlights, 1987, (7) Ten Large Bank Failures (by asset size), (8) FDIC-Insured Banks Closed or Assisted Due to Financial Difficulties, and Problem Banks: 1971 to 1987, and (9) Insured Commercial Banks—Assets and Liabilities 1975 to 1987.

In 1989 the FDIC advised its bank examiners to be especially alert to bank officer, director, or principal stockholder involvement in real estate projects, loans, or other business activities that pose or could pose a conflict of interest with their fiduciary duties of care and loyalty to the bank. The examiners are asked to routinely inquire of senior bank management, through incorporation in the "first day" letter (a letter presented to bank officers by the examiners that requests answers to a series of questions), regarding any situation involving loans or other transactions in which such persons hold a beneficial interest, either direct or indirect. Examiners are reminded to inquire into bank policies and procedures designed to bring conflicts of interest to the attention of the board of directors when they are asked to approve loans or other transactions in which officers, directors, or principal stockholders may be involved. If deficiencies are noted, the bank should be strongly encouraged to remedy the deficiency in which an officer, director, or principal stockholder of the bank holds a beneficial interest; in which an office or principal stockholder of another depository institution holds a beneficial interest; at any other depository instituition, in which a bank officer, director, or principal stockholder holds a beneficial interest.

FDIC Organization Chart

- BOARD OF DIRECTORS
  - Chairman
  - Director
  - Comptroller of the Currency
- OFFICE OF THE CHAIRMAN
  - Division of Bank Supervision
    - Office of Executive Secretary
    - Office of Corporate Communications
    - Office of Legislative Affairs
    - Office of Research and Strategic Planning
  - Division of Liquidation
  - Legal Division
    - Office of Budget and Planning
    - Office of Consumer Affairs
    - Office of Corporate Audits and Internal Investigations
    - Office of Personnel Management
  - Division of Accounting and Corporate Services
    - Office of Equal Employment Opportunity

ENCYCLOPEDIA OF BANKING AND FINANCE

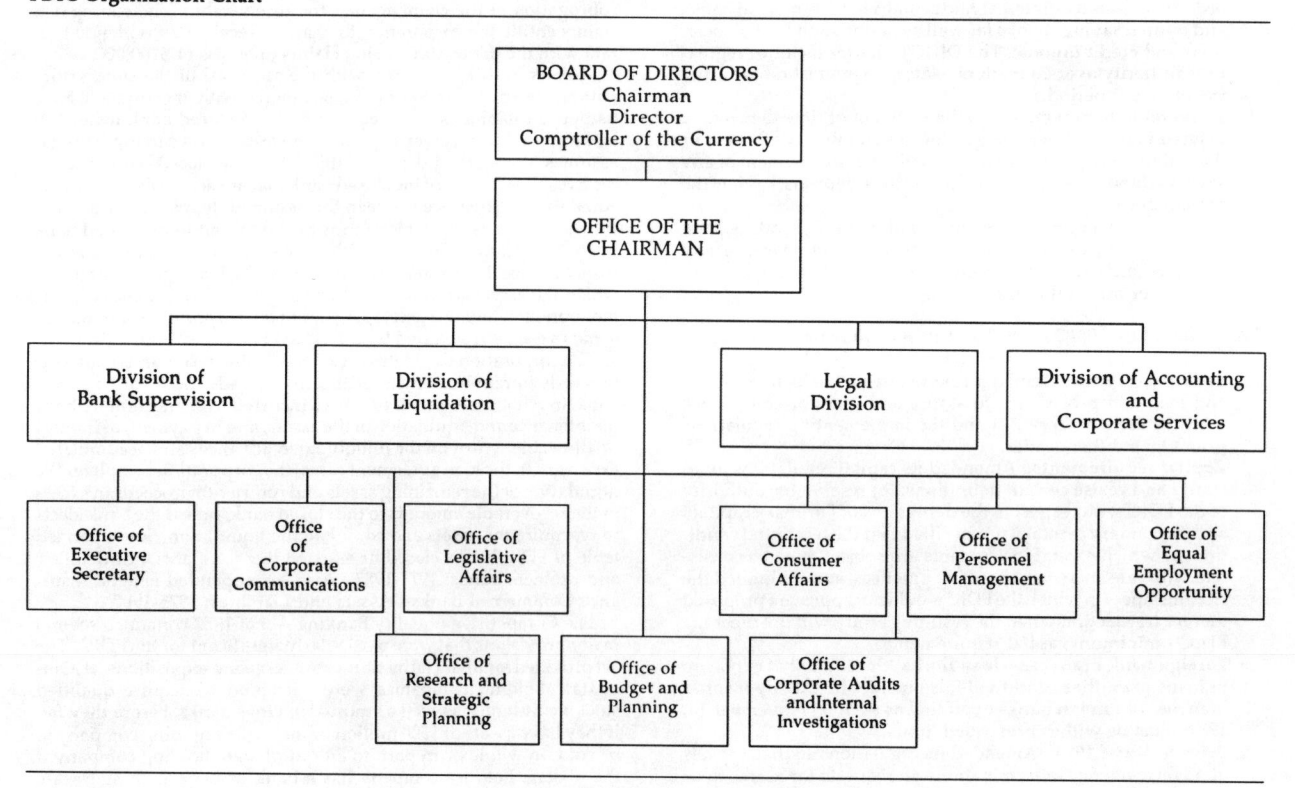

FEDERAL DEPOSIT INSURANCE CORPORATION

Insured Deposits and the Deposit Insurance Fund, 1934-1987 (In millions)

Year (December 31)	Insurance coverage	Deposits in insured banks [1] Total	Percentage of insured deposits	Insured	Deposit insurance fund	Ratio of deposit insurance fund to— Total deposits	Insured deposits
1987	100,000	2,201,549	76.9	1,658,802	18,301.8	.83	1.10
1986	100,000	2,167,596	75.4	1,634,302	18,253.3	.84	1.12
1985	100,000	1,974,512	76.1	1,503,393	17,956.9	.91	1.19
1984	100,000	1,806,520	76.9	1,389,874	16,529.4	.92	1.19
1983	100,000	1,690,576	75.0	1,268,332	15,429.1	.91	1.22
1982	100,000	1,544,697	73.4	1,134,221	13,770.9	.89	1.21
1981	100,000	1,409,322	70.2	988,898	12,246.1	.87	1.24
1980	100,000	1,324,463	71.6	948,717	11,019.5	.83	1.16
1979	40,000	1,226,943	65.9	808,555	9,792.7	.80	1.21
1978	40,000 [6]	1,145,835	66.4	760,706	8,796.0	.77	1.16
1977	40,000 [5]	1,050,435	65.9	692,533	7,992.8	.76	1.15
1976	40,000	941,923	66.7	628,263	7,268.8	.77	1.16
1975	40,000	875,985	65.0	569,101	6,716.0	.77	1.18
1974	40,000	833,277	62.5	520,309	6,124.2	.73	1.18
1973	20,000	766,509	60.7	465,600	5,615.3	.73	1.21
1972	20,000	697,480	60.2	419,756	5,158.7	.74	1.23
1971	20,000	610,685	61.3	374,568	4,739.9	.78	1.27
1970	20,000	545,198	64.1	349,581	4,379.6	.80	1.25
1969	20,000	495,858	63.1	313,085	4,051.1	.82	1.29
1968	15,000	491,513	60.2	296,701	3,749.2	.76	1.26
1967	15,000	448,709	58.2	261,149	3,485.5	.78	1.33
1966	15,000	401,096	58.4	234,150	3,252.0	.81	1.39
1965	10,000	377,400	55.6	209,690	3,063.3	.80	1.45
1964	10,000	348,981	55.0	191,787	2,844.7	.82	1.48
1963	10,000	313,304 [2]	56.6	177,381	2,667.9	.85	1.50
1962	10,000	297,548 [3]	57.2	170,210	2,502.0	.84	1.47
1961	10,000	281,304	57.0	160,309	2,353.8	.84	1.47
1960	10,000	260,495	57.5	149,684	2,222.2	.85	1.48
1959	10,000	247,589	57.4	142,131	2,089.8	.84	1.47
1958	10,000	242,445	56.8	137,698	1,965.4	.81	1.43
1957	10,000	225,507	56.3	127,055	1,850.5	.82	1.46
1956	10,000	219,393	55.2	121,008	1,742.1	.79	1.44
1955	10,000	212,226	54.8	116,380	1,639.6	.77	1.41
1954	10,000	203,195	54.6	110,973	1,542.7	.76	1.39
1953	10,000	193,466	54.6	105,610	1,450.7	.75	1.37
1952	10,000	188,142	54.1	101,841	1,363.5	.72	1.34
1951	10,000	178,540	54.2	96,713	1,282.2	.72	1.33
1950	10,000	167,818	54.4	91,359	1,243.9	.74	1.36
1949	5,000	156,786	48.8	76,589	1,203.9	.77	1.57
1948	5,000	153,454	49.1	75,320	1,065.9	.69	1.42
1947	5,000	154,096	49.5	76,254	1,006.1	.65	1.32
1946	5,000	148,458	49.7	73,759	1,058.5	.71	1.44
1945	5,000	157,174	42.4	67,021	929.2	.59	1.39
1944	5,000	134,662	41.9	56,398	804.3	.60	1.43
1943	5,000	111,650	43.4	48,440	703.1	.63	1.45
1942	5,000	89,869	36.5	32,837	616.9	.69	1.88
1941	5,000	71,209	39.7	28,249	553.5	.78	1.96
1940	5,000	65,288	40.8	26,638	496.0	.76	1.86
1939	5,000	57,485	42.9	24,650	452.7	.79	1.84
1938	5,000	50,791	45.5	23,121	420.5	.83	1.82
1937	5,000	48,228	46.8	22,557	383.1	.79	1.70
1936	5,000	50,281	44.4	22,330	343.4	.68	1.54
1935	5,000	45,125	44.7	20,158	306.0	.68	1.52
1934	5,000 [4]	40,060	45.1	18,075	291.7	.73	1.61

[1] Deposits in foreign branches are omitted from totals because they are not insured. Insured deposits are estimated by applying to deposits at the regular Call dates the percentages as determined from the June Call Report submitted by insured banks.
[2] December 20, 1963.
[3] December 28, 1962.
[4] Initial coverage was $2,500 from January 1 to June 30, 1934.
[5] $100,000 for time and savings deposits of in-state governmental units provided in 1974.
[6] $100,000 for Individual Retirement accounts and Keogh accounts provided in 1978.

ENCYCLOPEDIA OF BANKING AND FINANCE

FEDERAL DEPOSIT INSURANCE CORPORATION

DOL Statistical Highlights, 1987

	Total Failed Banks	Total Assets of Failed Banks* (billions)	Total Collections** (billions)	Estimated Book Value of Assets in Liquidation (billions)	Operating Expenses** (millions)	Number of Employees
1987	184	$ 6.9	$ 2.415	$11.0	$ 264.4 [1]	4,400
1986	138	7.0	1.749	10.9	230.9 [1]	4,706
1985	116	2.8	1.282	9.6	249.3 [2]	3,318
1984	78	2.8	1.538	10.0	232.5 [2]	2,158
1983	48	4.1	1.008	4.1	119.8 [2]	1,153

* Excludes open bank assistance transactions and net worth certificates provided to mutual savings banks.
** Collection and DOL operating expense data exlude Continental Illinois National Bank and First National Bank and Trust Company of Oklahoma City, Oklahoma, where asset servicing agreements are in place.
[1] DOL only.
[2] FDIC-wide expenses.

Failed Banks by State, 1985-1987

	Failed Banks 1987	1986	1985	Purchase and Assumptions (P&As) 1987	1986	1985	Payoffs 1987	1986	1985	Insured Deposit Transfers 1987	1986	1985
Alabama	2	1	1	2	1	1	0	0	0	0	0	0
Alaska	2	1	0	1	1	0	0	0	0	1	0	0
Arkansas	0	0	1	0	0	1	0	0	0	0	0	0
California	8	8	7	6	5	6	1	0	1	1	3	0
Colorado	13	7	6	10	3	5	0	2	1	3	2	0
Florida	3	3	2	2	2	2	0	1	0	1	0	0
Idaho	0	1	0	0	1	0	0	0	0	0	0	0
Illinois	2	1	2	2	1	2	0	0	0	0	0	0
Indiana	3	1	1	2	1	1	0	0	0	1	0	0
Iowa	6	10	11	6	9	11	0	1	0	0	0	0
Kansas	8	14	13	4	11	8	2	3	5	2	0	0
Kentucky	1	2	0	1	1	0	0	0	0	0	1	0
Lousiana	14*	8	0	14*	8	0	0	0	0	0	0	0
Massachusetts	2	0	0	0	0	0	0	0	0	2	0	0
Minnesota	10	5	6	5	4	4	0	0	0	5	1	2
Mississppi	1	0	0	1	0	0	0	0	0	0	0	0
Missouri	4	9	9	2	6	8	2	2	1	0	1	0
Montana	3	1	0	3	1	0	0	0	0	0	0	0
Nebraska	6	6	13	6	6	6	0	0	7	0	0	0
New Mexico	0	2	3	0	2	3	0	0	0	0	0	0
New York	1	0	2	0	0	0	1	0	0	0	0	2
North Dakota	2	0	0	1	0	0	0	0	0	1	0	0
Ohio	1	0	0	1	0	0	0	0	0	0	0	0
Oklahoma	31	16	13	22	7	10	0	4	3	9	5	0
Oregon	1	1	2	1	1	2	0	0	0	0	0	0
Pennsylvania	1	0	0	1	0	0	0	0	0	0	0	0
South Dakota	2	1	0	1	1	0	0	0	0	1	0	0
Tennessee	0	2	5	0	1	4	0	0	0	0	1	1
Texas	50	26	12	37	19	9	5	4	2	8	3	1
Utah	3	3	1	2	3	1	0	0	0	1	0	0
Wisconsin	0	1	1	0	0	0	0	0	0	0	1	1
Wyoming	4	7	5	0	2	3	0	4	2	4	1	0
Puerto Rico	0	1	0	0	2	0	0	0	0	0	0	0
Total	184	138	116	133	98	87	11	21	22	40	19	7

* Includes one failure handled as a bridge bank

FDIC Problem Banks, 1983-1987

	1987	1986	1985	1984	1983
Total Insured Banks	14,289	14,837	14,906	14,825	14,759
Problem Banks	1,575	1,484	1,140	848	642
% Increase in Number of Problem Banks	6.1	30.2	34.4	32.1	74.0
% of Total Insured Banks	11.0	10.0	7.6	5.7	4.4

Uninsured Deposits of Failed Banks, 1987
($000 omitted)

	Assistance Transactions	Purchase & Assumption Transactions	Insured Deposit Transfers	Payoffs
Total Deposits ($)	2,118,000	4,020,700	1,929,400	331,400
Number of Accounts	358,700	695,500	221,000	42,000
Uninsured Deposits ($)	N/A	N/A	63,972	16,593

N/A - Not applicable because all depositors are protected in this type of transaction.

Ten Largest Bank Failures
(By Asset Size)

	Assets	Deposits	Date
Franklin National Bank New York, New York	$3,655,662,000	$1,444,981,606	October 8, 1974
First National Bank and Trust Company, Oklahoma City, Oklahoma	1,419,445,375	1,006,657,507	July 14, 1986
The First National Bank of Midland, Midland, Texas	1,404,092,000	1,076,217,000	October 14, 1983
United States National Bank San Diego, California	1,265,868,099	931,954,458	October 18, 1973
United American Bank in Knoxville, Knoxville, Tennessee	778,434,000	584,619,000	Februrary 14, 1983
Banco Credito y Ahorro Poncero, Ponce, Puerto Rico	712,540,000	607,610,000	March 31, 1978
Park Bank of Florida St. Petersburg, Florida	592,900,000	543,900,000	February 14, 1986
Yankee Bank for Finance and Savings, FSB, Boston, Massachusetts	521,700,000	474,800,000	October 16, 1987
Penn Square Bank, N.A. Oklahoma City, Oklahoma	516,799,000	470,445,000	July 6, 1982
The Hamilton National Bank of Chattanooga, Chattanooga, Tennessee	412,107,000	336,292,000	February 16, 1974

BIBLIOGRAPHY

FEDERAL DEPOSIT INSURANCE CORPORATION. *Annual Report.*
Federal Deposit Insurance Corporation. Vols. I and II. Prentice Hall, Inc., Englewood Cliffs, NJ. Latest edition.
LAPIDUS, L., et al. *State and Federal Regulation of Commercial Banks* (2 vols.). Federal Deposit Insurance Corporation, 1980.
SPRAGUE, I. H. *Bailout: An Insider's Account of Bank Failures and Rescues.* Basic Books, Inc., New York, NY, 1986.

FEDERAL FARM BOARD An agency established by the Agricultural Marketing Act of 1929 (46 Stat. 11; 12 U.S.C. 1141-j), with a revolving fund of $500 million, to attack the problem of farm surpluses by extending aid in organizing farm cooperatives and stabilization corporations and lending them funds to finance withholding of surpluses from the market, and by purchases in the open market. The board had no powers to enforce restriction of production, although it encouraged output reduction and methods of expansion in farm distribution and sales. With commodity prices declining in the 1929-1932 deflation, its accumulated stocks piled up losses.

By 1932, active operations had been practically abandoned. Executive Order 6084 of March 27, 1933, effective May 27, 1933, changed the title of the board to FARM CREDIT ADMINISTRATION (FCA). Functions of the board were abolished, including the offices of the appointed members of the board except for its chairman, whose title was changed to governor of the Farm Credit Administration and who thus assumed that top executive post in the new FCA.

FEDERAL FARM CREDIT BANKS CONSOLIDATED SYSTEMWIDE SECURITIES The joint and several obligations of all 37 Farm Credit banks, sold through a nationwide selling group managed by the banks' fiscal agency in New York. The selling group consists of both commercial bank and nonbank securities dealers. The securities are in the form of discount notes (5 to 270 days), six- and nine-month bonds, and longer-term bonds.

These securities were introduced to the securities markets by the Farm Credit banks in August, 1977, as such. Prior to 1933, debt financing instruments of farm credit institutions were issued individually, but the last remaining issues of the individual institutions were called for payment in 1939, and were succeeded by Consolidated Federal Farm Loan bonds.

FEDERAL FARM CREDIT BANKS CONSOLIDATED SYSTEMWIDE SECURITIES

FDIC-Insured Banks Closed or Assisted Due to Financial Difficulties, and Problem Banks: 1971 to 1987
(Banks are closed either permanently or temporarily by order of supervisory authorities or by directors of banks.
FDIC = Federal Deposit Insurance Corporation.)

Item	Unit	1971-1980	1978	1979	1980	1981	1982	1983	1984	1985	1986	1987
Total banks closed or assisted	Number	84	7	10	11	10	42	48	80	120	145	203
Agricultural banks [1]	Number	NA	NA	NA	NA	1	7	7	31	62	59	57
Deposits, closed and assisted banks	Mil. dol.	10,851	854	111	5,216	3,826	9,908	5,442	29,883	8,059	6,597	8,568
Agricultural banks [1]	Mil. dol.	NA	NA	NA	NA	7	112	114	421	866	1,408	906
Problem banks [2]	Number	X	342	287	217	223	369	642	848	1,140	1,484	1,515

NA — Not available.
X — Not applicable.
[1] Banks with at least 25 pecent of their portfolios devoted to farm loans.
[2] FDIC-insured commercial and savings banks considered to be problem banks by the supervisory authorities, end-of-period.

Source: U.S. Federal Deposit Insurance Corporation, *Annual Report*, and unpublished data.

Insured Commercial Banks—Assets and Liabilities: 1975 to 1987
(In billions of dollars, except number of banks. As of Dec. 31, includes outlying areas. Excludes noninsured banks and nondeposit trust companies. 1975 includes American branches of foreign banks. Except as noted, includes foreign branches of U.S. banks.)

Item	1975	1980	1981	1982	1983	1984	1985	1986	1987
Number of banks	14,384	14,434	14,414	14,452	14,465	14,481	14,404	14,200	13,699
Assets	1,095.4	1,855.7	2,029.1	2,194.3	2,342.1	2,508.6	2,731.0	2,941.1	3,000.9
Securities, total [1]	231.5	334.4	352.1	386.0	441.3	385.8	439.6	485.0	520.7
U.S. Treasury, direct obligations	81.0	104.5	103.7	118.7	168.1	108.2	118.3	127.2	178.2
Obligations of States and subdivisions [2]	100.9	146.3	151.5	155.2	158.4	120.9	160.6	140.4	120.8
Federal funds sold and securities purchased [3]	37.0	70.3	91.2	103.9	93.5	110.8	133.2	139.3	130.6
Net loans and leases [4]	590.1	1,006.4	1,120.2	1,211.6	1,301.3	1,489.7	1,607.8	1,727.8	1,779.8
Commercial and industrial loans	NA	391.0	454.6	504.4	524.8	565.0	577.7	600.9	589.7
Real estate loans	NA	269.1	291.4	308.0	336.8	385.6	438.5	515.3	599.9
Loans to depository institutions [4]	NA	81.2	94.7	106.9	109.2	72.3	68.0	70.3	64.3
Loans to farmers (excluding real estate)	NA	32.3	33.7	37.0	39.9	40.7	36.1	31.7	29.4
Other loans to individuals	NA	187.4	193.0	199.2	224.6	266.9	309.0	335.7	351.2
All other loans [2]	NA	62.6	69.4	73.1	83.6	176.6	195.1	191.9	210.0
Lease financing receivables	NA	14.0	15.9	16.7	17.1	20.2	24.3	27.5	31.0
Cash balances with banks, etc.	189.4	331.9	327.4	334.3	341.9	323.5	340.6	379.2	358.2
Other	47.4	112.8	138.2	158.5	164.2	198.9	209.8	209.8	211.6
Liabilities and Equity Capital	1,095.4 [5]	1,855.7	2,029.1	2,194.3	2,342.1	2,508.6	2,731.0	2,941.1	3,000.9
Deposits	915.9	1,481.2	1,588.8	1,706.5	1,842.5	1,962.6	2,117.9	2,283.5	2,334.9
Demand [7,8]	NA	415.1	369.2	354.2	370.6	421.6	450.9	510.8	455.6
Time and savings [7,9]	NA	755.6	885.1	1,028.1	1,140.9	1,223.4	1,345.2	1,458.9	1,537.7
Deposits in foreign offices	NA	NA	NA	NA	NA	317.6	321.8	313.8	341.6
Individuals, partnerships, and corporations [7]	NA	1,007.8	1,103.9	1,214.9	1,353.6	1,466.8	1,617.1	1,751.9	1,797.2
Government [7]	NA	84.2	85.3	90.0	86.7	96.5	107.5	110.2	111.7
Domestic interbank, foreign government, and other banks in foreign countries [7,10]	NA	77.7	64.2	77.5	70.8	55.6	64.0	77.1	84.4
Miscellaneous liabilities	101.6	260.4	315.4	351.5	352.0	381.4	414.9	458.4	466.9
Subordinated notes and debentures	4.4	6.5	6.5	7.3	7.1	10.2	14.7	16.9	17.6
Limited-life preferred stock	NA	NA	NA	NA	NA	NA	14.0	.1	.1
Equity capital	64.3	107.6	118.3	128.9	140.5	154.3	169.5	182.3	181.4

NA — Not available.
[1] Book value. Includes other categories not shown separately.
[2] Beginning 1984, nonrated industrial development and other obligations of States and political subdivisions are included under all other loans.
[3] Under agreements to resell.
[4] Excludes allowance for loan and lease losses and unearned income.
[5] Includes loans to foreign banks.
[6] Includes reserves on loans and securities, not shown separately.
[7] Represents deposits in domestic offices only.
[8] Beginning 1984, noninterest bearing deposits.
[9] Beginning 1984, interest bearing deposits.
[10] Includes official institutions in foreign countries.

Source: U.S. Federal Deposit Insurance Corporation, *Assets and Liabilities: Commercial and Mutual Savings Banks*, semiannual; beginning 1980, *Annual Report*; and unpublished data.

ENCYCLOPEDIA OF BANKING AND FINANCE

Securities of the Farm Credit banks are not obligations of nor are they guaranteed by the U.S. government. The Farm Credit banks are federally chartered and are supervised and examined regularly by the Farm Credit Administration, an independent agency of the federal government.

Income derived from interest on farm credit securities is exempt from state, municipal, and local taxes. The interest income, however, is subject to federal income taxes. Gain from sale or transfer by gift or inheritance of these securities is subject to both federal and state taxes.

Farm credit securities are legal investment for many public bodies subject to the regulations and restrictions of the individual states. They are accepted as security for fiduciary, trust, and public funds under the control of the U.S. government and are eligible as collateral for Treasury tax and loan accounts and for advances by Federal Reserve banks to member commercial banks.

Interest rates on new issues are set at the time they are sold, consistent with current yields on comparable securities. Offering notices of new issues and pricing announcements appear in financial publications and major newspapers. Farm credit securities have an active secondary market (trading market) supported by those dealers who distribute the original issues.

Denominations. Federal Farm Credit Banks Consolidated Systemwide bonds are issued only in book entry form. Bonds with original maturities of 13 months or longer are in denominations of $1,000. Bonds with original maturities of less than 13 months are in denominations of $5,000. Federal Farm Credit Banks Consolidated Systemwide notes (discount notes) are issued only in definitive form in denominations of $50,000, $100,000, $500,000, $1,000,000, and $5,000,000.

Book-Entry Delivery. Farm credit bonds are now issued in book-entry form only. Investors in book-entry securities do not receive physical certificates. They are not registered but rather are assigned to an investor's account. Federal Reserve banks and branches maintain computerized records of book-entry securities in the names of member banks. These member banks keep separate accounts for securities they own and for those they maintain for investors and other financial institutions. Investors may choose as custodian any bank or other financial institution that maintains book-entry accounts with a member of the Federal Reserve System. The bank or nonbank dealer will issue a custody receipt as evidence of the investor's ownership of the securities. Payment of interest and principal at maturity of book-entry securities is credited to the investor's account and does not require presentation of a coupon or certificate. Investors may be charged a fee for this service.

Farm credit securities are considered to meet the needs of a wide variety of investors, such as commercial banks, insurance companies, state and local governments, fiduciary accounts, thrift institutions, and individuals. The Farm Credit banks offer bonds with short-, intermediate-, and long-term maturities. Discount notes are sold on a daily basis and carry maturities from 5 to 270 days. Every month, the Farm Credit banks issue bonds with six- and nine-month maturities. Intermediate- and long-term issues are offered periodically throughout the calendar year—January, April, July, and October, and as the needs of the banks dictate. Thus the investor is provided with flexibility of issue date and maturity selection.

The Farm Credit System. The banks and associations of the Farm Credit System rank first among institutional lenders to agriculture in the U.S. Farm Credit System loans are made through:

1. The 12 FEDERAL LAND BANKS which provide mortgage credit of up to 40 years through the 520 local offices of the FEDERAL LAND BANK ASSOCIATIONS.
2. The 12 FEDERAL INTERMEDIATE CREDIT BANKS which provide short- and intermediate-term loan funds to farmers and ranchers through 427 local PRODUCTION CREDIT ASSOCIATION offices.
3. The 13 BANKS FOR COOPERATIVES which make loans of all kinds to agricultural marketing, supply, and business service cooperatives.

BIBLIOGRAPHY

FISCAL AGENCY FOR THE FARM CREDIT BANKS. *An Investor's Guide to Farm Credit Securities,* 1981.

FEDERAL FARM LOAN ACT The first major effort on the part of the federal government to provide long-term credit facilities for agriculture. The purposes of the act (39 Stat. 360; 12 U.S.C. 641), which became law on July 17, 1916, were "to provide capital for agricultural development, to create standard forms of investment based upon farm loans, to furnish a market for United States bonds, to create Government depositaries and financial agents for the United States, and for other purposes." The act provided for:

1. The Federal Farm Loan Board, consisting of seven members, including the secretary of the Treasury as chairman ex officio and six members appointed by the President by and with the advice and consent of the Senate. Not more than three of these appointees were to be appointed from one political party, and all six were to devote their entire time to the business of the board.
2. Twelve Federal Land banks, located in cities throughout the U.S. designated by the first Federal Farm Loan Board, which cities were required to be other than those in which the Federal Reserve banks are located.
3. National Farm Loan associations (now known as Federal Land Bank associations), organized and controlled by at least ten or more borrowing farmers, through whom Land Bank credit would be extended.
4. Joint-Stock Land banks, which were privately owned and operated long-term agricultural credit institutions (subsequently liquidated).

The act has been amended many times since. In 1923, the Agricultural Credits Act by amendment created 12 new institutions called Federal Intermediate Credit banks, located in the same cities as the Federal Land banks and operating under the jurisdiction of the Federal Farm Loan Board. The function of the Federal Intermediate Credit banks was to provide intermediate-term credit to agriculture of not less than six months or more than three years by rediscounting.

In 1933, a major revision of the act occurred (Farm Credit Act of 1933), expanding the credit system to include the Central Bank for Cooperatives and Banks for Cooperatives in the farm credit districts, as well as the Production Credit corporations and Production Credit associations. The Farm Credit Act of 1935 also effected an important amendment.

See FARM CREDIT ACTS.

FEDERAL FARM LOAN BOARD With the passage of the Farm Credit Act of 1933, this board was superseded by the FARM CREDIT ADMINISTRATION.

For the purpose of the historical record the following description is given.

The general supervision of the FEDERAL FARM LOAN SYSTEM rested with the Federal Farm Loan Board. It was composed of the secretary of the Treasury (ex officio) and four other members appointed by the President. The powers and duties of the Federal Farm Loan Board in relation to the Federal Farm Loan System were analogous to those of the Federal Reserve Board in the supervision of the Federal Reserve System. The board supervised the operations of the Federal Land banks, Farm Loan associations, and Joint-Stock Land banks, regulated interest rates and charges on farm mortgage loans, supervised the issue of farm loan bonds, conducted examinations of the banks under its jurisdiction, issued regulations for the guidance of the Federal Land banks and Farm Loan associations, and issued reports showing the condition of the banks and of agricultural credit.

FEDERAL FARM LOAN BONDS *See* FEDERAL FARM CREDIT BANKS CONSOLIDATED SYSTEMWIDE SECURITIES.

FEDERAL FARM LOAN SYSTEM The Farm Credit System, operating under the FARM CREDIT ADMINISTRATION, providing long-term and short-term credit to farmers and their cooperative marketing, purchasing, and business service organizations.

Types of credit and the institutions furnishing same are officially summarized as follows.

Long-term Credit. Federal Land Bank loans may be made to persons who are or become members of FEDERAL LAND BANK ASSOCIATIONS and who are bona fide farmers or ranchers, who furnish farmers or ranchers services directly related to on-farm operating needs, or who are owners of rural homes.

Federal Land Bank loans are secured by first liens on the real-estate security. Additional security may be required to supplement the real estate security, and credit factors other than the ratio between the amount of the loan and the security value are given due consideration. In no case can the loan amount exceed 85% of the appraised value of the security.

Loans may be made to farmers and ranchers for any agricultural purpose or other needs of the applicant. Loans may also be made to rural residents for the purpose of financing housing. However, rural housing financing shall be for single-family, moderate-priced dwellings in towns and villages where the population does not exceed 2,500 persons. A Federal Land bank is limited to rural housing loans totaling 15% of the total amount of its loans outstanding.

All FEDERAL LAND BANKS have variable interest rate plans in which interest rates may be raised or lowered in relation to the cost of money. These plans have the effect of spreading money costs evenly among all borrowers.

Authority for the activities of the Federal Land banks and the Federal Land Bank associations may be found in Title 1 of the Farm Credit Act of 1971. All the stock of the 232 Federal Land Bank associations (as of 1988) is owned by their member-borrowers, and all the stock of the 12 Federal Land banks is owned by the associations. Federal Land bank loans may be obtained only with the endorsement of the associations. When a loan is granted, the borrower purchases stock in the association equal to 5% of his loan. The association in turn purchases a like amount of stock in the Federal Land bank. When the loan is repaid, the stock in the bank and in the association is retired.

Each Federal Land Bank association is controlled by a board of directors elected by and from the membership. Each association member is entitled to one vote in the election of directors and in other matters concerning the association.

Loan funds are obtained primarily through the sale of Consolidated Federal Farm Loan Bonds to investors. These bonds are not guaranteed by the government as to either principal or interest. The Federal Land banks use the notes and mortgages of their borrowers and other assets as collateral for the bonds.

Short-term Production Credit. The PRODUCTION CREDIT ASSOCIATION may make loans to bona fide farmers or ranchers, producers or harvesters of aquatic products, persons engaged in performing on-the-farm services to farmers, and rural residents. Loans may be made for periods of up to seven years. Production Credit associations may also participate in loans with other associations or with commercial banks.

Loans may be made for any agricultural purpose or other requirements of eligible borrowers. However, loans made for the purchase, repair, or maintenance of rural homes or the purchase of mobile homes may not exceed 15% of the total loans outstanding for all associations in a district. Such loans cannot be made in towns or villages where the population exceeds 2,500 persons.

Production Credit associations provide credit to members at the lowest possible cost consistent with sound business practice. The rate is dependent, in part, on the rates charged by the respective FEDERAL INTERMEDIATE CREDIT BANKS under rate programs approved by the Farm Credit Administration. Dividends on stock and patronage distributions to members which may be paid by the associations could have the effect of lowering the net rate of interest charged.

Authority for the activities of the Production Credit associations may be found in Title II of the Farm Credit Act of 1971. All the voting stock in the 427 (as of 1981) Production Credit associations is owned by their borrowers. However, two of the Federal Intermediate Credit banks had invested in the capital stock of two Production Credit associations.

When a loan is granted, the borrower invests 5% of the amount of his loan in the capital stock of the association. When the loan is repaid, he may either list the stock for sale back to the association or convert it into nonvoting stock.

Each Production Credit association is controlled by a board of directors elected by and from its active borrowers. Each association member is entitled to one vote in these elections and on other matters affecting the association regardless of the amount of stock owned.

The Production Credit associations obtain most of their funds for loans from the Federal Intermediate Credit banks.

Authority for the activities of the Federal Intermediate Credit banks may be found in Title II of the Farm Credit Act of 1971. All of the capital stock of the 12 Federal Intermediate Credit banks is owned by farmers through their local Production Credit associations. Other financing institutions which discount the notes of farmers with the banks provide some of the necessary capital by holding participation certificates issued to them by the banks.

The Federal Intermediate Credit banks make loans to and discount agricultural paper for the Production Credit associations, state and national banks, livestock loan companies, agricultural credit corporations, and similar organizations. They may also make loans to and discount paper for BANKS FOR COOPERATIVES and Federal Land banks.

The Federal Intermediate Credit banks do not generally lend directly to individuals or conduct a general banking business. However, they may participate in loans with Production Credit associations. They also may invest in the capital stock or surplus of Production Credit associations.

The discount or interest rate charged by a Federal Intermediate Credit bank is determined by the board of directors of the bank, with the approval of the FARM CREDIT ADMINISTRATION.

The banks obtain the funds they use in their lending operations primarily from sales to investors of Federal Farm Credit Banks Consolidated Systemwide securities, which are the joint and several obligations of all Farm Credit banks. These debentures are not guaranteed by the government as to either principal or interest.

Credit for Cooperatives. Authority for the activities of the Banks for Cooperatives may be found in Title III of the Farm Credit Act of 1971.

The Banks for Cooperatives make three basic types of loans which are adapted to the particular needs of cooperatives. These are seasonal loans, term loans, and loans secured by commodities. All the banks work together to provide a complete loan service to cooperatives. The Central Bank for Cooperatives participates with the district banks on larger loans.

Any association of farmers, ranchers, or producers or harvesters of aquatic products, or any federation of such associations which operates on a cooperative basis and provides marketing, processing, supply, or business service functions for its members, may be eligible to borrow from a bank for Cooperatives.

However, 80% of the voting control of such associations must be held by bona fide farmers, ranchers, or producers or harvesters of aquatic products, or federations of such associations. The cooperative must also do as much business with or for members as it does with or for nonmembers. Excepted from this requirement is business transacted with the U.S. government and services and supplies furnished by the cooperative as a public utility.

All of the capital stock of the district Banks for Cooperatives is held by borrowing cooperatives. All of the stock of the Central Bank for Cooperatives is held by the district banks.

The Central Bank for Cooperatives is controlled by a board of 13 directors. Twelve of these directors are elected, one each by the district boards. The thirteenth is appointed by the governor of the Farm Credit Administration with the advice and consent of the Federal Farm Credit board.

Other Farm Credit. In addition to the above cooperative Farm Credit System, various types of credit are made available to farmers by the FARMERS HOME ADMINISTRATION, and the RURAL ELECTRIFICATION ADMINISTRATION, in the jurisdiction of the Department of Agriculture.

Historical Development. Prior to 1916, farmers in the U.S. had no long-term mortgage credit system specifically designed or adapted to meet their needs. The usual term of loans was five years or less on long-term credit, nonamortized, so that at maturity, renewal or refinancing usually involved additional charges. Interest rates and commissions paid by farmers in 1915, for example, in some areas averaged as high as 10% or more. The Federal Farm Loan Act of 1916, creating the Federal Land banks, represented the result of intensive study, including that of special commissions which reported on European agricultural credit systems.

The severe commodity price deflation of 1920-1923, which caused many rural banks to call farm loans and resulted in losses to borrowers obliged to sell crops and livestock at depressed prices, stimulated creation in 1923 of the Federal Intermediate Credit banks as rediscounting institutions.

Finally, in 1933, Production Credit associations were created and Banks for Cooperatives established, making available operating credit as well as credit for marketing, purchasing, and service farmer cooperatives. In 1946, the Farmers Home Administration was established to provide farm credit for marginal borrowers unable to finance elsewhere "at reasonable rates and charges."

As a result, U.S. agriculture may be said to be amply provided with public as well as private credit institutions from which to obtain varied types of credit, well adapted to needs.

See AMORTIZATION LOANS, FEDERAL FARM MORTGAGE CORPORATION.

FEDERAL FARM MORTGAGE CORPORATION

Established by the Federal Farm Mortgage Corporation Act, approved January 31, 1934, to aid in financing lending operations of the FEDERAL LAND BANKS and the LAND BANK COMMISSIONER.

The corporation had an authorized capital stock of $200 million, which was subscribed by the then governor of the Farm Credit Administration on behalf of the U.S. For the purpose of such capital subscription, the funds and proceeds made available to the land bank commissioner under Section 32 of the Emergency Farm Mortgage Act of 1933, and the mortgages taken by the commissioner and the credit instruments secured thereby were transferred to the corporation. The corporation, with the approval of the secretary of the Treasury, could issue and have outstanding at any one time bonds in an aggregate amount not exceeding $2 billion. These bonds, known as Federal Farm Mortgage Corporation bonds, were fully and unconditionally guaranteed both as to principal and interest by the U.S.

Effective July 1, 1939, Reorganization Plan 1, Part 4, Section 401, transferred the corporation to the Department of Agriculture, to operate under the supervision of the Farm Credit Administration. The corporation's authority to make land bank commissioner loans was not extended by Congress beyond July 1, 1947. P.L. 98, June 30, 1945, authorized the corporation to sell its loans and contracts eligible under the act to the Federal Land banks. Finally, the corporation was abolished by act of October 4, 1961 (75 Stat. 773), and its assets were transferred to the secretary of the Treasury.

FEDERAL FINANCIAL INSTITUTIONS EXAMINATION COUNCIL

An interagency body of regulatory agencies responsible for U.S. depository institutions that establishes principles, standards, and reporting forms for the federal examination and supervision of insured depository institutions, bank holding companies, and savings and loan holding companies. The council consists of the Comptroller of the Currency, the chairman of the Federal Deposit Insurance Corporation, a member of the Board of Governors of the Federal Reserve System, the chairman of the Federal Home Loan Bank Board, and the chairman of the National Credit Union Administration.

The five federal financial institutions regulatory agencies represented on the council have primary federal supervisory jurisdiction over more than 32,000 domestically chartered banks and thrift institutions, which, on June 30, 1987, held total assets of almost $5 trillion. The Federal Reserve Board and the Federal Home Loan Bank also have primary federal supervisory responsibility for commercial bank holding companies and for savings and loan holding companies, respectively.

In addition, the three banking agencies have authority to oversee the operations of U.S. branches and agencies of foreign banks. The International Banking Act of 1978 authorizes the Office of the Comptroller of the Currency (OCC) to license federal branches and agencies of foreign banks and permits U.S. branches to apply for insurance with the FDIC. It also subjects those U.S. offices to many provisions of the Federal Reserve and Bank Holding Company Acts. The act gives primary examining authority to the OCC, the FDIC, and the various state authorities for the offices within their juirisdictions and gives residual examining authority over all U.S. banking operations of foreign banks to the Board of Governors of the Federal Reserve System.

The council was given additional statutory responsibilities under the Housing and Community Development Act of 1980 (section 340 of Public Law 96-399, October 8, 1980). Among the assignments are the implementation of a system to facilitate public access to data that depository institutions are requiredto disclose under the Home Mortgage Disclosure Act (HMDA) of 1975, and the aggregation of annual HMDA data, by census tract, for each metropolitan statistical area.

FEDERAL FINANCIAL INSTITUTIONS EXAMINATION COUNSEL STANDARDIZED CALL REPORT SCHEDULE RC–N.

See FINANCIAL DISCLOSURE REQUIREMENTS.

FEDERAL FINANCING BANK

Created on December 29, 1973, to assure the coordination of federal and federally assisted borrowing from the public and to assure that such borrowings are financed in a manner least disruptive of private financial markets and institutions.

The Federal Financing Bank (FFB) has become the vehicle through which most federal agencies finance their programs involving the sale or placement of credit market instruments, including agency securities; guaranteed obligations; participation agreements; and the sale of assets. The major exceptions as of 1982 are Title XI Ship Mortgage Bonds and GOVERNMENT NATIONAL MORTGAGE ASSOCIATION asset sales.

In addition, some programs which formerly used the FFB will now sell their securities in the market. These include the Central Liquidity Facility of the National Credit Union Administration and the STUDENT LOAN MARKETING ASSOCIATION.

See FEDERAL CREDIT UNIONS.

At the first meeting of the Board of Directors of the Federal Financing Bank on May 23, 1974, the board approved a policy of borrowing from the Treasury Department on an interim basis. These borrowings were to be periodically repaid by the sale of FFB securities in the market. On July 23, 1974, the FFB auctioned $1.5 billion of 244-day Federal Financing Bank Bills dated July 30, 1974, which matured on March 31, 1975. In a later meeting on June 5, 1975, the board of directors decided that the bank would borrow all funds from the Treasury Department, matching the terms and conditions of its borrowings from the Treasury with the terms and conditions of its loans.

FFB purchases of federal agencies' debt are not reflected in the totals of the U.S. budget because borrowing and the repayment of borrowings between federal agencies and the Treasury are not budgetary transactions. These transactions are reflected in the accounts of the particular agencies. The use of the FFB permits these agencies to borrow at lower rates than if the agencies went to the market. This was a major reason for the creation of the bank. The transactions are financed by an equal amount of borrowings from the Treasury, which are in addition to the borrowings recorded in the statement of financial condition.

In addition to being able to finance its operations by issuing obligations to the Treasury (the FFB can require that the secretary of the Treasury purchase up to $5 billion of its obligations, although the secretary of the Treasury is authorized to purchase any amounts at his discretion), the FFB can finance by issuing obligations to the public. FFB obligations are general obligations of the United States, identical in this respect to Treasury obligations. In turn, the FFB has followed a policy of purchasing only obligations fully guaranteed as to principal and interest by a federal agency, although it is authorized to purchase partially guaranteed obligations.

The secretary of the Treasury is the chairman of the FFB's board of five directors, the other directors being Treasury officials appointed by the President of the United States. The FFB is under the general supervision of the secretary of the Treasury, and it is managed and staffed by Treasury employees.

FEDERAL FUNDS

Literally, "funds at the Fed," i.e., immediately available funds at a Federal Reserve bank. Sources of federal funds include excess reserves (reserve balances at a Federal Reserve bank in excess of legal reserve requirements) of member banks, checks on the U.S. Treasury's or foreign balances at a Federal Reserve bank, and checks drawn in payment for purchases by the Fed of U.S. government securities.

The principal sources of demand for federal funds are member banks deficient in required reserves (see LEGAL RESERVES) and using federal funds as a fine very short-term (as short as one day) adjustment in reserve position, and other member banks (e.g., a major New York City member bank which announced the policy in 1964) which deliberately use federal funds as a source of additional reserves for earning rates, a situation feasible at times of tight money but high money rates. Nonbank demand for federal funds is principally from U.S. government securities dealers to finance their inventories; there is also participation by foreign banks and their agencies and domestic noncommercial bank financial institutions.

Intermediaries in the market for federal funds, bringing together buyers and sellers of federal funds, consist of some banks and brokers in New York City, correspondent banks, and similar interbank contacts. In addition, there is direct contact between buyers and sellers of federal funds.

The standard unit of trading in federal funds among the larger banks is $1 million, and among the smaller banks, $200,000. The straight one-day transaction in federal funds is unsecured and involves the accounting shift of reserve balances on the books of the Federal Reserve bank, the selling bank's reserve balance being debited and the buying bank's reserve balance being credited. These entries are reversed on the following day, the interest involved being

ENCYCLOPEDIA OF BANKING AND FINANCE

FEDERAL FUNDS MARKET

Average Effective Federal Funds Rate: Monthly Averages of Daily Rates[a]
(percent per annum)

Year	12-month average	Jan.	Feb.	Mar.	Apr.	May	Jun.	Jul.	Aug.	Sep.	Oct.	Nov.	Dec.
1972	4.44	3.50	3.29	3.83	4.17	4.27	4.46	4.55	4.80	4.87	5.04	5.06	5.33
1973	8.74	5.94	6.58	7.09	7.12	7.84	8.49	10.40	10.50	10.78	10.01	10.03	9.95
1974	10.51	9.65	8.97	9.35	10.51	11.31	11.93	12.92	12.01	11.34	10.06	9.45	8.53
1975	5.82	7.13	6.24	5.54	5.49	5.22	5.55	6.10	6.14	6.24	5.82	5.22	5.20
1976	5.05	4.87	4.77	4.84	4.82	5.29	5.48	5.31	5.29	5.25	5.03	4.95	4.65
1977	5.54	4.61	4.68	6.94	4.73	5.35	5.39	5.42	5.90	6.14	6.47	6.51	6.56
1978	7.93	6.70	6.78	6.79	6.89	7.36	7.60	7.81	8.04	8.45	8.96	9.76	10.03
1979	11.19	10.07	10.06	10.09	10.01	10.24	10.29	10.47	10.94	11.43	13.77	13.18	13.78
1980	13.36	13.82	14.13	17.19	17.61	10.98	9.47	9.03	9.61	10.87	12.81	15.59	18.90
1981	16.38	19.08	15.93	14.70	15.72	18.52	19.10	19.04	17.82	15.87	15.08	13.31	12.37
1982	12.26	13.22	14.78	14.64	14.94	14.45	14.85	12.59	10.42	10.31	9.71	9.20	8.95
1983	9.09	8.68	8.51	8.77	8.81	8.63	8.98	9.37	9.56	9.45	9.48	9.34	9.47
1984	12.22	9.56	9.59	9.91	10.19	10.32	11.06	11.23	11.69	11.30	9.99	9.43	8.38
1985	8.4	8.15	8.50	8.58	8.27	7.97	7.53	7.88	7.90	7.92	7.99	8.05	8.27
1986		8.15	9.18	7.48	6.99	6.85	6.92	6.56	6.17	5.89	5.85	6.04	6.91
1987		6.43	6.10	6.13	6.37								

Source: Federal Reserve Bulletin.
[a] Averages of daily effective rates (average of the rates on a given date weighted by the volume of transactions at those rates).

---

paid by separate entry. Secured transactions in federal funds, secured by U.S. government securities, are often found among the smaller banks, in lieu of repurchase agreements. Purchases of federal funds by national banks are not indebtedness subject to the general limitation on a national bank's borrowing (not over capital stock unimpaired plus 50% of unimpaired surplus fund), pursuant to Comptroller of the Currency's Ruling 7518. Nor is such a purchase of federal funds subject to the general 10% limit on loans to any one single borrower (10% of the bank's capital and surplus), pursuant to the Comptroller of the Currency's Ruling 1130.

Federal Funds Rates. Since member banks have recourse to borrowing from the Federal Reserve banks, it would be supposed that the discount rate would serve as a ceiling on federal funds rates. Rates on federal funds, however, may go above discount rates of Federal Reserve banks because in periods of tight money and deficiencies in reserves member banks may already have borrowed from the Fed or may wish to avoid doing so, and also because some banks may use borrowed federal funds as a source of funds for earning asset expansion. Federal funds rates as guides to monetary policy:

The table appended herewith gives the ranges of market rates on federal funds in recent years.

BIBLIOGRAPHY

Board of Governors of the Federal Reserve System. *Annual Report.*
Federal Reserve Bulletin. Various issues.
GOODFRIEND, M. "A Model of Money Stock Determination with Loan Demand and a Banking System Balance Sheet Constraint." *Federal Reserve Bank of Richmond Economic Review,* January/February, 1982.
GOODFRIEND, M., and HARGRAVES, M. "A Historical Assessment of the Rationales and Functions of Reserve Requirements." *Federal Reserve Bank of Richmond Economic Review,* March/April, 1983.
HUMPHREY, T. M., and KELEHER, R. E. "The Lender of Last Resort: A Historical Perspective." *Cato Journal,* Spring/Summer, 1984.
RINGSMUTH, D. "Custodial Arrangements and Other Contractual Considerations." *Federal Reserve Bank of Atlanta Economic Review,* September, 1985.

FEDERAL FUNDS MARKET A market for unsecured loans between depository institutions in the United States in immediately available funds, primarily reserves held at Federal Reserve banks. Typically most activity is for next-day maturity. Term federal funds refers to longer maturities up to several weeks or months.

FEDERAL HOME LOAN BANK ACT Approved July 22, 1932 (47 Stat. 725; 12 U.S.C. 1421, et seq.), established for the first time a reserve system for home financing institutions, analogous to the Federal Reserve System for commercial banks.

It established the FEDERAL HOME LOAN BANK BOARD to provide a permanent credit reservoir for thrift and home-financing institutions through the creation of regional Federal Home Loan banks.

It is of interest to note that this legislation was the result of the calling as early as December, 1931, of the Conference on Home Building and Home Ownership by President Hoover, who recommended the establishment of the system. The Roosevelt administration expanded and enlarged the concept, by passage of the Home Owners' Loan Act of 1933, approved June 13, 1933 which gave authority to the board to charter and supervise locally owned and managed mutual institutions to be known as federal savings and loan associations, to serve as a means of encouraging local thrift and home financing, and Title IV of the National Housing Act, approved June 27, 1934, which provided for the creation of the FEDERAL SAVINGS AND LOAN INSURANCE CORPORATION and placed it under the direction and management of the Federal Home Loan Bank Board.

FEDERAL HOME LOAN BANK ADMINISTRATION
The constituent of the National Housing Agency (which senior agency was created by executive order of the President on February 24, 1942) charged with centralizing nonfarm housing activities; the administration supervising the Federal Home Loan Bank System, the Federal Savings and Loan Insurance Corporation, and liquidation of the Home Owners' Loan Corporation.

Under Reorganization Plan No. 3 of the President, the National Housing Agency was succeeded by the Housing and Home Finance Agency on July 27, 1947, and the Federal Home Loan Bank Administration was renamed the Home Loan Bank Board. The board continued to be in the Housing and Home Finance Agency until enactment of the Housing Amendments of 1955, approved August 11, 1955, which reestablished the Federal Home Loan Bank Board as an independent agency.

FEDERAL HOME LOAN BANK BOARD Originally established by the FEDERAL HOME LOAN BANK ACT in 1932; given the authority to charter and supervise federal savings and loan associations by the Home Owners' Loan Act, approved June 13, 1933; assigned the direction and management of the Federal Savings and Loan Insurance Corporation by Title IV of the National Housing Act, approved June 27, 1934. From 1932 to April 25, 1939, the board functioned as an independent executive agency. After an interim period of nonindependent organizational allocation (April 25, 1939-February 24, 1942, to the Federal Loan Agency; February 24, 1942-July 27, 1947, to the National Housing Agency; and July 27, 1947-August 11, 1955, to the Housing and Home Finance Agency), the Federal Home Loan Bank Board regained its independent agency status under the Housing Amendments of 1955. Official description follows.

Organization. The Federal Home Loan Bank Board is directed by a bipartisan three-person board. The three members are appointed

FEDERAL HOME LOAN BANK BOARD

by the President by and with the advice and consent of the Senate for four-year terms. The chairman is designated by the President.

The name Federal Home Loan Bank Board refers both to the three-member panel, which determines policy, and to the federal agency, which carries out that policy.

Functions. Basic functions of the board are to establish policies, issue regulations, and supervise the operations of the Federal Home Loan Bank System; to charter and supervise federal savings and loan associations; and to supervise the operation of the Federal Savings and Loan Insurance Corporation.

Included among the activities and responsibilities of the board are the periodic examinations of the 12 Federal Home Loan banks (by action on December 31, 1963, the board established a twelfth Federal Home Loan bank located in Spokane to serve states previously in the San Francisco district) and the annual reporting to Congress on their operations. The board appoints four members to the board of directors of each of the banks for four-year terms (public interest members) and conducts the election by the member institutions of the banks of the remaining directors for two-year terms. In addition, it approves the purchase and sale by the banks of certain investment securities, and issues consolidated obligations which are the joint and several obligations of the banks. The board also approves all dividend declarations of the banks, election of officers and counsel, the operating budget of each bank, and other aspects of operations of the banks.

The board acts on applications for membership in the Federal Home Loan Bank System and for insurance of accounts. It issues charters for federal savings and loan associations and approves their branches. It also acts on applications for conversion from state to federal charter.

The board is responsible for the examination and supervision of all federal savings and loan associations and prescribes regulations relating to their dividend rates, lending, and other aspects of operations. In 1966, Congress enacted legislation giving the Federal Home Loan Bank Board explicit power to set the maximum rate that may be paid on different types of savings accounts. Until that time association rates had been unregulated, although commercial bank rates had been controlled since 1933. The law and regulations by the board had the effect of preventing rate wars that could have put some institutions into an unsound financial position. However, the board points out that unfortunately the regulations also raised the specter of DISINTERMEDIATION (people withdrawing their funds from financial intermediaries to make direct market investments, such as government securities, money market funds, etc., whenever general interest rates rose above savings account ceilings).

To help stem such periodic outflows, as the U.S. League of Savings Associations points out, the board authorized a variety of certificate accounts, on which the institution could pay a higher rate for a specified minimum amount of funds that remained on deposit for a specified term. At first, the rate ceilings for associations were set 0.5% higher than for banks. This reflected historical experience^an association typically paid savers more than a bank did, according to the U.S. League of Savings Associations. The rate differential also helped to assure a steady supply of funds for housing; that is, it let associations compete effectively with banks for savings dollars, since banks were able to offer the consumer a much broader range of financial services.

In mid-1973, the interest rate differential was reduced to 0.25%, partly as a result of the gradual regulatory implementation of significant new asset and liability powers that had been granted to associations by the 1968 Housing Act. At the same time, all ceilings and most other restrictions were removed from deposits of $100,000 or more (jumbo certificates of deposits).

In the DEPOSITORY INSTITUTIONS DEREGULATION AND MONETARY CONTROL ACT OF 1980, Congress extended the board's rate ceiling authority and the 0.25% differential for six years, in combination with the plan (through the DEPOSITORY INSTITUTIONS DEREGULATION COMMITTEE, of which the chairman of the Federal Home Loan Bank Board is a voting member) to phase out rate controls entirely over a six-year period.

The Depository Institutions Deregulation and Monetary Control Act of 1980 increased federal deposit insurance to $100,000 per account, an increase from $40,000 per account, insured by the Federal Savings and Loan Insurance Corporation (FSLIC). The board prescribes the regulations applicable to insurance of accounts for all institutions insured by the Federal Savings and Loan Insurance Corporation. In addition, the board examines, or jointly examines with state authorities, all state-chartered associations insured by the FSLIC.

The Savings and Loan Holding Company Amendments of 1967, effective on February 14, 1968, amended Section 408 of the National Housing Act to provide closer regulation of holding companies in this field. It required savings and loan holding companies to register with the board, to file periodic reports on their financial condition and operations, and to submit to regular examinations. A holding company or its subsidiaries that are not savings and loan associations cannot engage in activities on behalf of its savings and loan subsidiaries that would evade any law or regulation applicable to such subsidiaries, nor can a holding company that controls more than one association engage in certain activities unrelated to the savings and loan business. The act also prohibits certain transactions between the subsidiary insured association and its holding company affiliates. It authorizes the board to pass on other affiliated transactions. It requires prior written approval by the board for any acquisition by a holding company of an additional insured association, whether by purchase of stock or assets or by merger. Prior written approval by the board also is necessary before any company not a savings and loan holding company can acquire one or more insured associations. The act authorizes the board, furthermore, to control the incurrence of debt by a holding company, other than a diversified savings and loan holding company, in excess of 15% of its consolidated net worth. A diversified savings and loan holding company, under the statute, is one in which that segment of its business embracing savings and loan and related activities represents less than 50% of its consolidated net worth and 50% of its consolidated net earnings. Such a company is exempt from the debt control provisions of the law.

In acting on applications by holding companies for approval of acquisitions of savings and loan associations, the board considers the financial and managerial resources and future prospects of the company and institution involved. Where the acquiring company already controls at least one savings and loan association, the board also considers the convenience and needs of the community to be served and possible anticompetitive aspects. In evaluating anticompetitive aspects of the acquisition, the board must consider opinions rendered by the attorney general.

The Change in Savings and Loan Control Act of 1978, Title VII of the Financial Institutions Regulatory and Interest Rate Control Act of 1978 (P.L. 95-630), was signed into law on November 10, 1978, effective March 10, 1979. The act was adopted as a companion to the Change in Bank Control Act of 1978 (Title VI of the total act), both designed to fill a gap in the federal regulatory structure to cover transfers of control of existing, federally insured, stock financial institutions and holding companies primarily to individuals or groups of individuals. See FEDERAL SAVINGS AND LOAN INSURANCE CORPORATION for FSLIC administration of the act.

The policy of the board with regard to applications for branch offices is to "further the competitive position of (the) industry by approving branches, including mobile facilities, wherever new branches will not constitute an undue burden on profitability and thus the accumulation of reserves."

The board's objective in the management area of liquidity is a "more truly 'liquid' industry, one in which management decisions to vary holdings of Governments and agencies are not stopped by the need to deal with substantial portfolio losses." The board regards its power to raise and lower required liquidity percentages as having "great potential in stabilizing mortgage credit flows." New liquidity regulations and regulatory accounting regulations have been drawn to complement other new board policies in the credit area. By the end of 1980, the bank board had extensively revised its regulations, in compliance with the Depository Institutions Deregulation and Monetary Control Act of 1980, as outlined by the U.S. League of Savings Associations:

1. *Preemption of state usury laws.* Effective April 1, 1980, FSLIC members may make residential real estate and certain other loans without regard to state usury laws.
2. *Renegotiable rate mortgages.* Effective April 3, 1980, federal associations may make loans with terms of 3, 4, or 5 years, secured by a mortgage of up to 30 years, and observing specified consumer safeguards.
3. *Borrowing limits.* Effective May 30, 1980, FSLIC members may borrow up to 50% of assets (the limit was 50% of savings),

although only 25% of assets may be pledged to secure outside borrowings; may accept more liabilities maturing within a 3-month period; and may otherwise borrow under more liberal rules than formerly.

4. *Interest rates and early withdrawal penalties.* Effective July 9, 1980, Federal Home Loan Bank (FHLB) members may issue money market certificates under a variety of different ceilings, depending on the Treasury bill rate, but never at a ceiling below 7.75%; may issue 30-month certificates at the Treasury composite $2^1/_2$-year rate, but never with the ceiling less than 9.5% or more than 12%; and must charge a penalty of 3 months' simple interest for early withdrawal of certificate deposits with maturities of 1 year or less, 6 months' interest on deposits with longer maturities.

5. *Credit card operations.* Effective July 10, 1980, federal associations and their subsidiaries may issue credit cards, with overdraft privileges not subject to the 20% of assets limit on consumer lending; may offer third-party payment (bill-payment) accounts and travelers' convenience withdrawals under liberalized rules.

6. *Reserve requirements.* Effective July 31, 1980, FSLIC members no longer must maintain a separate federal insurance reserve; may take up to 3 years to convert reserve calculations from a fiscal year to a calendar year basis; and may take up to 30 years, with supervisory permission, to meet the one-time net worth requirement for new institutions.

7. *Loan application registers.* Effective August 1, 1980, FHLB members must maintain three special-purpose registers that include fair lending data at those offices where loan decisions are made; and must submit semiannually summary data reports on loan applications.

8. *Service corporation investment.* Effective August 22, 1980, federal associations may invest up to 3% (the limit was 1%) of assets in service corporations, provided that one-half of the investment exceeding 1% is allocated to investments that serve primarily community or inner-city development purposes.

9. *Large certificates and brokered funds.* Effective November 7, 1980, FSLIC members may issue $100,000-minimum marketable certificates under liberalized regulations; may sell nonmarketable certificates of deposit at a discount to a minimum of $100,000; and may obtain savings deposits from brokers without limit (the limit was 5% of savings).

10. *Net worth requirements.* Effective November 17, 1980, FSLIC members may compute net worth requirements at 4% of all liabilities excluding net worth (the rule was 5% of insurable accounts plus certain borrowings); may reduce the requirements by up to 10% in proportion to holdings of certain long-term debt, flexible-yield mortgages and short-term liquidity; may receive limited exemption from the requirements by selling residential mortgages carrying interest rates of 7.5% or less; and may compute the statutory reserve requirement at 4% (the rule was 5%) of insured accounts.

11. *Real estate lending.* Effective November 17, 1980, FSLIC members may make real estate loans without regard to the geographic location of the security property and may make loans in excess of 90% of value on one- to four-family properties. Also effective November 17, 1980, federal associations may make real estate and property improvement loans without dollar limit (except to one borrower), need not require a first lien on mortgage loans, may make home loans for up to 40 years (was 30), and may make most other loans on more liberal terms and conditions than formerly.

12. *Consumer loans, commercial paper, and corporate securities.* Also effective November 17, 1980, federal associations may make secured and unsecured consumer loans and may buy, sell, and hold commercial paper and corporate debt securities as defined and approved by the bank board, all subject to a combined 20% of assets limitation.

13. *Large certificates and public unit accounts.* Effective November 19, 1980, FHLB members may issue $100,000-minimum certificates and public unit accounts with minimum terms of 14 days (the limit was 30 days).

14. *Mutual capital certificates.* Federal associations with a mutual charter may issue mutual capital certificates that may be used to satisfy reserve and net worth requirements without a percentage-of-assets limitation. Such certificates are subordinated to all other claims against the institution; are not FSLIC-insured; may pay fixed, variable, cumulative, or participatory dividends, or a combination; and are redeemable in limited situations.

15. *NOW accounts.* Effective December 31, 1980, federal associations nationwide may issue negotiable order of withdrawal (NOW) accounts, including overdraft privileges, paying up to 5.25% interest.

16. *Trust powers.* Effective January 1, 1981, federal associations may offer trust services under regulations comparable to those for national banks.

See FEDERAL HOME LOAN BANK SYSTEM for further details of the Federal Home Loan Bank Board's supervisory and regulatory functions.

Broadened Powers and the Gathering Storm. The crisis in the thrift industry brought about significant thrift legislation, the Garn-St. Germain Depository Institutions Act of 1982, signed into law by President Ronald Reagan. With the passage of this legislation, the savings and loan industry was authorized to offer checking accounts for individuals, commercial loans, consumer credit, and loans on nonresidential real estate. Garn-St. Germain also contained three landmark provisions, giving thrifts new business opportunities to help them survive financial storms; granting the Bank Board and the FSLIC new powers to deal with financially troubled associations; and authorizing an emergency rescue program to assist savings institutions that were troubled, but basically sound. Garn-St. Germain deregulated rather than regulated. The act set out to adjust the imbalance in the strict regulation of how thrifts could invest their assets (which limited return on assets) and the more liberal regulation of deposit interest rates (which increased thrifts' cost of funds). The legislation mandated the phase-out of the interest rate differential by January 1984, and had two other deregulatory aspects. It authorized thrifts and banks to issue a new type of account—the money market deposit account—that bore no interest limit and which could compete directly with money market mutual funds. It also gave savings institutions limited authority to expand into additional business areas, such as commercial lending, traditionally reserved for banks. Garn-St. Germain realigned the industry's thrifts industry structure. It made it easier for savings and loan associations to become savings banks and vice versa, and it allowed existing in-stitutions to select either the stock or the mutual form of ownership.

Garn-St. Germain authorized a new capital assistance program for troubled thrift institutions. Under the Net Worth Certificate Program, qualifying associations with less than 3% net worth were permitted to secure promissory notes from the FSLIC in exchange for instruments, issued by thrifts, called net worth certificates. Because the FSLIC's promissory notes guaranteed the notes' face amounts, thrifts could use them to raise their net worth to the required minimum, and thereby hold off a FSLIC takeover. As institutions regained financial health, they would trade back the promissory notes for the net worth certificates, and the obligations eventually would be canceled out, with no cash ever changing hands.

In the second half of 1982, interest rates began declining, and associations were again earning more interest than they were paying out. Still, 35% of all FSLIC-insured thrifts were losing money by the end of 1983. During 1984, the thrift industry continued to grow rapidly. Deposits increased by 17% and assets grew by 19%. By 1985, the new Bank Board regulations slowed the pace of deposit growth sharply, to about half that of 1984. FSLICs reserves continued to drop. The level of thrift failures remained high. The 1984 and 1985 failures resulted primarily from poor assets —loans and investments in default. The 1981 and 1982 failures resulted primarily from high interest rates, as noted earlier. To deal with asset-related failures, the Bank Board adopted regulations that linked net worth requirements to growth rates. The regulations also required thrift to get supervisory approval before undertaking potentially risky ventures—specifically, before investing more than 10% of their assets in equity securities, real estate, or subsidiary service corporations. In 1985, market interest rates fell and insured firms achieved their highest aggregate return on assets since 1979. A significant minority of the industry, some 15%, continued to experience operating losses, many because of unsound lending and investment practices.

The remaining story of the FSLICs problems is told in the entry THRIFT CRISIS which describes the later years and the passage of the Financial Institutions Reform Recovery and Enforcement Act of 1989.

ENCYCLOPEDIA OF BANKING AND FINANCE

In August 1989 the Federal Home Loan Bank Board allowed the nation's eight-largest savings and loan to become a commercial bank and to leave the insolvent Federal Savings and Loan Insurance Corporation. The savings and loan would be allowed to join the Federal Deposit Insurance Corporation that charges its members less for the same federal insurance of $100,000 per account. The decision reduced the revenue to the beleaguered FS&LIC.

In 1989, the Federal Home Loan Bank Board issued a statement of policy which establishes its position on the need for an institution to document prudent investment portfolio policy and strategies. Under the policy statement, an institution must document its overall investment policy for the institution as a whole and its investment strategies for each different type of security portfolio. Policies and strategies must consider adequate LIQUIDITY, protection from INTEREST VRATE RISK, desired rate of return (ROI), asset/liability position, CAPITAL ADEQUACY, and management capabilities of an institution. The investment policy and strategies must distinguish between those securities actively undertaken for investment, for sale, and for trading. The investment policy must be reviewed and approved periodically (but no less than annually) by the institution's board of directors and no less than quarterly by the board of directors or an investment committee, thereof, to ensure that securities activities are consistent with the overall policies and strategies of the institution. Securities activities must be conducted in a safe and sound manner and by competent personnel.

BIBLIOGRAPHY

"Compliance Guide Simplifies Consumer Protection Laws." *Savings Institutions*, October, 1988.

Liscio, J. "Anatomy of a Mess: The True Villains Behind the S&L Crisis." *Barrons*, February 27, 1989.

"The New Acquirers: What Can the Business Expect To See?" *Savings Institutions*, February, 1989.

"Regulators, Lawmakers Step Up Scrutiny of Lending Practices." *Savings Institutions*, March, 1989.

"Risk-Based Capital Rules Would Favor Mortgage Lenders." *Savings Institutions*, December, 1988.

FEDERAL HOME LOAN BANK SYSTEM Established in 1932 to provide a permanent system of reserve credit banks for savings banks, eligible thrift institutions of the savings and loan type, and insurance companies engaged in long-term home mortgage financing. The originating act, the Federal Home Loan Bank Act of July 22, 1932, required the FEDERAL HOME LOAN BANK BOARD to establish regional Federal Home Loan banks and the districts they would serve. Originally 12 districts and banks were established, but the number was later reduced to 11. Their number was restored to 12 by action of the Federal Home Loan Bank Board on December 31, 1963. The act (Sec. 3) specifies not less than 8 nor more than 12 districts, in each of which there shall be established a Federal Home Loan bank at such city as may be designated by the board.

Membership. To be eligible for membership in the Federal Home Loan Bank System, an applicant shall be duly organized under the laws of any state or of the U.S., be subject to examination and regulation by any state or by the U.S., and make long-term home mortgage loans. Each applicant shall also be, in the judgment of the board, in sound financial condition, and the character of its management and its home financing policy shall be consistent with sound and economical home financing.

The banks also developed full NOW (negotiable orders of withdrawal) processing services, "one of the most challenging tasks for the Bank System during 1980"; after studying member needs, ten of the banks developed NOW services and also provided member associations with an efficient alternative for NOW account processing. The banks anticipate that all costs will be recovered over a period of five years through established service fees.

In order to bolster earnings of member institutions, the bank system initiated a special dividend/targeted advances program with the following features: (1) beginning with the second quarter of 1980, maximum bank dividends were permitted to member institutions on a quarterly basis, (2) a $50 million dividend was channeled through the bank system to member associations by the FHLMC, and (3) a targeted advance program (TAP) was established for associations most in need of assistance.

Under the revised dividend policy, several previous restrictions were removed: the cost of funds to members was eliminated as an upper limit on the dividend rate, and the ratio of average advances to undivided profits was abolished as a dividend limitation.

In addition, the banks were authorized to pay dividends out of prior years' earnings. Under the revised policy, the bank system paid out $157.9 million from prior years' earnings and dividend stabilization reserves. In addition, the FHLMC dividend increased the amount available for dividends by $40 million after transfer of 20% of the FHLMC dividend to the banks' legal reserves.

Credit Activity. The banks provide funds to member associations in the form of advances for savings withdrawals, seasonal and expansionary needs, and special purposes such as community development.

Sources of funds. Funds to meet the unprecedented volume of advances were provided from borrowing through bonds and discount notes, member deposits and capital stock, and retained earnings. The banks offer a wide variety of deposit programs with maturities up to one year.

In December, 1979, Congress amended the Federal Home Loan Bank Act to increase the maximum advances-to-capital stock ratio of borrowing member institutions from 12:1 to 20:1. This resulted in reduced stock requirements for some institutions, and the effect was not fully offset by increased stock resulting from the requirement that members purchase capital stock equal to 1% of residential mortgages.

In addition to providing funds for advances, retained earnings (composed of undivided profits, the dividend stabilization reserve, and legal reserves) combined to reduce the overall cost of the banks' funds and permitted the banks to offer advances at lower rates.

The secretary of the Treasury is empowered to purchase up to $4 billion of Federal Home Loan Bank Board obligations whenever the ability of the system to aid thrift and home financing is substantially impaired by monetary stringency or rapidly rising interest rates.

Organization. The Federal Home Loan Bank System is governed and regulated by the Federal Home Loan Bank Board, which is an independent federal agency in the executive branch of the federal government. The bank board is the chartering and regulatory authority for federal savings and loan associations and federal mutual savings banks. The bank board governs the Federal Home Loan Mortgage Corporation (FHLMC), which is a secondary mortgage market facility. The principal function of the FHLMC, which is owned by the Federal Home Loan banks, is to promote the flow of capital into the housing markets by establishing an active secondary market in residential mortgages. The bank board also governs the insurance of accounts in SAVINGS AND LOAN ASSOCIATIONS and federal mutual savings banks through the Federal Savings and Loan Insurance Corporation (FSLIC). The bank board's expenses are met through assessments to the Federal Home Loan banks and the FSLIC and assessments to member institutions for examinations.

Consolidated Federal Home Loan Bank Board obligations are the joint and several obligations of all 12 Federal Home Loan (FHL) banks. Regulation requires that the FHL banks maintain in the aggregate unpledged qualifying assets in an amount equal to the consolidated obligations outstanding. Qualifying assets are defined as cash, obligations of or fully guaranteed by the U.S., secured advances, and federally insured or guaranteed mortgages.

The capital stock of the FHL banks has a par value of $100 per share. Capital stock held by members in excess of their statutory requirement can be redeemed at par value by the FHL banks or sold to other bank members at par value, provided the resulting stock transfer is recorded on the books of the FHL banks.

Dividends on the capital stock of FHL banks may be paid out of current year earnings, undivided profits, and the dividend stabilization reserve.

FHL banks dividends may be paid in the form of capital stock if authorized by the board of directors. The FHL banks must transfer 20% of their net income to the legal reserve semiannually until the reserve equals the capital stock amount; thereafter 5% of the FHL banks' net income must be allocated for this purpose.

Insurance of accounts. Operations of the Federal Savings and Loan Insurance Corporation come under the supervision of the Federal Home Loan Bank Board.

Chartering authority. Unlike the Board of Governors of the Federal Reserve System, the Federal Home Loan Bank Board has the additional operational responsibilities of chartering and supervising federal savings and loan associations, which may be either new institutions or converted from state-chartered institutions upon application.

The required reserves against deposits imposed by the Federal Reserve, pursuant to the Depository Institutions Deregulation and Monetary Control Act of 1980 (DIDMC Act), are authorized by the act to be passed through by the Federal Home Loan banks to the Federal Reserve.

Access to Fed's Discount Window. The Board of Governors of the Federal Reserve System on August 20, 1981, can establish a borrowing rate for extended credit to banks and thrift institutions "that are under sustained liquidity pressures."

The extended credit program was available to commercial banks and thrift institutions alike, including member institutions of the Federal Home Loan Bank System. In the view of the chairman of the Federal Home Loan Bank Board, "it (was) now desirable and prudent for the Federal Home Loan Bank System to encourage the Federal Reserve to supplement its own efforts in funding members' liquidity needs."

The extended credit is available for traditional short-term adjustment purposes and, as circumstances warrant, to meet longer-term needs in the interest of assuring the sound functioning of depository institutions at time of strains on liquidity. *See* Regulation A of the FEDERAL RESERVE BOARD REGULATIONS, September, 1980, revision, for detail on these programs. Such advances may be outstanding for up to 9 to 12 months, and, if necessary, credit may be extended beyond that period. However, as borrowing is more extended, "more rigorous or definite measures to assure ultimate repayment of the loan would be required." The credit would be fully collateralized, with collateral valued at 90% of its estimated market price.

Legislative Milestones. The Federal Home Loan Bank System has identified major federal laws that have impacted the system.

1932 Federal Home Loan Bank Act Established the Federal Home Loan Bank System—the Bank Board and DISTRICT BANKS to serve as a reserve credit system for member savings and loan associations, savings banks, and life insurance companies.

1933 Home Owners' Loan Act Permitted granting of federal charters to savings and loan associations; established the Home Owners' Loan Corporation, allowing lending institutions to exchange delinquent mortgages for Home Owners' Loan Corporation bonds.

1934 National Housing Act Established the FSLIC to insure savings accounts and to prevent default of insured institutions.

1964 Housing Act Permitted federally chartered associations to offer unsecured loans for educational expenses; expanded the area in which an institution could lend from a radius of 50 miles to 100 miles from the main office.

1966 Interest Rate Adjustment Act Allowed the Bank Board to establish ceilings on interest rates paid by member institutions on savings accounts.

1966 Financial Institutions Supervisory Act Required compliance by thrift institutions with cease and desist orders issued by the Bank Board to correct unsafe or unsound practices of the institutions. The act also authorized the Bank Board to remove officers and directors of associations which engage in such practices, or which violate law or federal regulation.

1968 Consumer Credit Protection Act (Truth in Lending(Regulation Z). Required lenders to disclose to borrowers all terms of credit arrangements, including the cost of financing over the life of a loan.

1968 Housing Act Amended the charter of the Federal National Mortgage Association to turn the former government agency into a private organization to purchase mortgages in the secondary market. The act transferred FNMA's housing subsidy function to the newly formed government-owned Government National Mortgage Association.

1969 Housing and Urban Development Act Gave federally chartered associations the authority to invest in mobile home and home equipment loans. The act also permitted federal associations to issue a wide variety of savings plans, notes, bonds, and debentures.

1970 Emergency Home Finance Act Created the Federal Home Loan Mortgage Corporation to increase the supply of funds for housing. The corporation established a secondary market for conventional mortgages and permitted federally chartered savings and loans to make loans anywhere in their home states.

1974 Real Estate Settlement Procedures Act As amended in 1976, the act required lenders to inform loan customers in advance of the total estimated charges to be assessed in granting mortgages.

1975 Home Mortgage Disclosure Act Required most depository institutions to disclose to the public the number and dollar amount of mortgage loans they originate or buy in each census tract.

1977 Community Reinvestment Act Required financial institutions to meet the credit needs of all segments of their communities, including low- and moderate-income neighborhoods.

1978 Financial Institutions Regulatory and Interest Rate Control Act Gave the FSLIC authorization to contribute financial assistance in arranging the merger or acquisition of a failed institution by a strong institution.

1978 Housing and Community Development Act Created the Neighborhood Reinvestment Corporation which institutionalized the development of Neighborhood Housing Services programs begun by the Urban Reinvestment Task Force to revitalize decaying neighborhoods.

1980 Depository Institutions Deregulation and Monetary Control Act Created the Depository Institutions Deregulation Committee made up of the heads of the federal financial regulatory agencies. The committee was charged with phasing out ceilings on all interest rates offered by financial institutions, by 1986.

1982 Garn-St. Germain Depository Institutions Act Gave the FSLIC new power to deal with financially troubled institutions, including the authority to overrule state authorities in seizing insolvent, state-chartered, FSLIC-insured institutions, and if necessary, to merge them with out-of-state institutions. Authorized an emergency federal assistance program to help qualifying FSLIC-insured institutions survive a period of severe economic pressure. Removed all differences between savings and loan associations and savings banks in the kinds of business activities in which they may engage. Permitted thrift institutions to offer checking accounts, business, agriculture, and consumer loans, and a money market deposit account with a floating market rate of interest to attract savings. Ended the interest rate differential under which thrift institutions had been authorized since 1966 to pay a slightly higher interest rate than commercial banks.

The late 1980s thrift crisis which involved the Federal Home Loan Bank System is treated in detail under FEDERAL HOME LOAN BANK BOARD and THIFT CRISIS.

BIBLIOGRAPHY

FEDERAL HOME LOAN BANK BOARD. *Annual Report.*
———. *Journal* (monthly).

FEDERAL HOME LOAN DISTRICT BANKS The thrift industry's bankers. The district banks link the Bank System's other two key elements—the FEDERAL HOME LOAN BANK BOARD and the more than 3,000 federally chartered and state-chartered savings and loan associations and savings banks throughout the country. The majority of savings and loan associations and savings banks turn to one of the twelve federal home loan banks for financial and technical assistance. The district banks opened for business in October 1932, at the lowest point of the Great Depression. They were created under the Federal Home Loan Bank Act, which authorized eight to twelve district banks. The Bank Board created twelve district banks, now located in Boston, New York, Pittsburgh, Atlanta, Cincinnati, Indianapolis, Chicago, Des Moines, Dallas, Topeka, San Francisco, and Seattle.

The district banks' primary mission is to channel money into the housing finance industry by making loans to individual thrift institutions, which use the funds to make loans to home buyers or to meet demands for deposit withdrawals. The district banks normally make advances available at interest rates that are lower than those of the commercial markets, particularly on longer-term funds. This helps member savings institutions manage the interest rate gaps between the rates the institutions pay on the funds they borrow and the rates they earn on the funds they lend. The district banks also provided thrifts with such services as check clearing, safekeeping of securities, demand and time deposit accounts, technical assistance, economic analysis, and access to the federal funds markets. The district banks are profit-making intermediaries, which provide earnings that can return dividends to the banks' stockholders. By examining and supervising their member institutions, the district banks attempt to ensure that thrifts comply with federal law and Bank Board regulations.

The district banks are wholly owned by their members—savings and loan associations, savings banks, and insurance companies—but ultimately controlled by the federal government. Every federally chartered thrift institution must become a member of a district bank. A thrift institution becomes a member of a district bank by purchasing the district bank's stock. The stock can only be sold to member institutions; member institutions can only sell the district stock back to the district bank. Each institution that belongs to the Bank System must purchase stock in its district bank. Since the first issue in 1932, the price of the stock has remained $100 per share. The amount of stock a thrift is required to purchase is based on the amount of its investments in residential real estate financing and the amount of its borrowing from its district bank. The stock held by a member institution must equal at least 1% of the unpaid principal of loans the institution has made to finance residential real estate (including mortgages and mortgage-backed securities), calculated on the basis of an institution's portfolio at the end of each year.

Each district bank is governed by a board of at least fourteen directors, two of whom are designated by the Bank Board each year to serve as the district banks's chairman and vice chairman. The district bank's member institutions elect eight of the directors, and the Bank Board in Washington appoints six.

The federal home loan banks obtain funds from three principal sources: the sale of the federal home loan banks' own obligations (bonds and discount notes); member institutions' deposits; the sale of district bank stock to member institutions. Additional sources of fund included retained earnings; the interest earned on money lent to members institutions, other district banks, and other borrowers; and fees for various services provided to members. Under unusual circumstances, the district banks could also obtain funds from the U.S. Treasury or the Federal Reserve System.

The Federal Home Loan Bank Board sets the overall policy governing advances. Within these guidelines, each district bank's board of directors is free to determine loan policies for its district. Thrifts may use advances for a variety of purposes, such as to meet unexpected savings withdrawals, to make more mortgage loans than local savings can fund, or to obtain longer-term funds than are available from deposits. The current advances policy has two principal goals: preserving the district banks' long-term viability by maintaining adequate net worth and sufficient liquidity to meet the needs of member thrifts; and providing member thrifts with as broad a range of advance programs as is prudent, profitable, and practical. District banks are to price advances to reflect actual conditions in the credit markets. Thrifts may borrow as much as is permitted by federal and state law and they may borrow for up to 20 years. Early in 1983, the Bank Board authorized the district banks to make collateralized advances to the FEDERAL SAVINGS AND LOAN INSURANCE CORPORATION. The Bank Board also authorized the FSLIC to guarantee district bank advances to member thrifts experiencing financial difficulties. District banks are also authorized to make commitments to advance specific amounts of money to member thrifts on specific future dates or within ranges of dates. The district banks are also authorized to offer member institutions interest rate swap programs. These swaps are used as asset-liability management tools, mechanisms to reduce interest rate risk. (Adapted from Federal Home Loan Bank System sources.)

FEDERAL HOME LOAN MORTGAGE CORPORATION
Established July 24, 1970, pursuant to Title III (Federal Home Loan Mortgage Corporation Act) of the Emergency Home Finance Act of 1970 (12 U.S.C. 1430, note). Also known as Freddie Mac. This new agency was established for the purpose of strengthening the existing secondary markets in residential mortgages insured by the FEDERAL HOUSING ADMINISTRATION or guaranteed by the Veterans Administration, and assisting in the further development of secondary markets for non-federally insured or guaranteed residential mortgages. The agency is authorized to purchase residential mortgages and interests in mortgages from members of the FEDERAL HOME LOAN BANK SYSTEM and from other financial institutions whose deposits or accounts are insured by agencies of the U.S. government, as well as from the Federal Home Loan banks and the FEDERAL SAVINGS AND LOAN INSURANCE CORPORATION. The Federal Home Loan Mortgage Corporation (FHLMC) is further authorized to hold, to deal with, and to sell or otherwise dispose of such mortgages or interests therein. Official description continues as follows.

Capitalization. The capital stock of the Federal Home Loan Mortgage Corporation consists solely of nonvoting common stock, issuable only to the 12 Federal Home Loan banks. The board of directors of the FHLMC is composed of the three members of the FEDERAL HOME LOAN BANK BOARD, whose chairman is chairman of the board of the FHLMC.

The FHLMC may raise funds to purchase residential mortgages through issuance of securities in the capital market. As indicated by the president of the FHLMC, when Congress created the FHLMC in 1970, the new quasi-private corporation was mandated to develop a viable secondary market for conventional residential mortgages. Such a market existed at that time only for government-insured or guaranteed mortgages, and it was expected that encouraging the growth of a secondary market for conventional mortgages would increase the effective supply of residential mortgage financing and make mortgage investments more attractive.

The new organization began by developing and introducing a standardized home loan application and single-family appraisal report, as well as uniform documents for conventional mortgages in each state, the District of Columbia, and the territories. It also developed and introduced a conventional residential mortgage passthrough security, the mortgage participation certificates (PC).

In 1972, the FHLMC also developed and introduced a computerized matrix to assist in underwriting single-family conventional mortgages. In 1975, the corporation introduced the guaranteeed mortgage certificate (GMC).

By 1977, the secondary market for conventional residential mortgages had matured, with increased uniformity and acceptance of conventional mortgages and growing sales of mortgage passthrough securities to investors outside the thrift industry. Adding to its original mission, the Mortgage Corporation obtained in 1978 congressional approval to begin developing a purchase program for home improvement loans, such as to finance a room addition, the rehabilitation or improvement of an older home, or the installation of features that would make a home more energy efficient and help conserve the nation's energy resources.

As the secondary market has grown, the Mortgage Corporation's seller/servicers have become more diverse. Savings and loan institutions have been the corporation's principal sellers, but purchases from other kinds of lenders are growing.

Other programs have been (1) the development of a renegotiable rate mortgage purchase program (creating a secondary market for mortgages whose interest rates can change periodically in line with market rates), and (2) the development of a purchase program for the pledged account mortgage (PAM).

Participation Certificates. PCs are in registered form only, with original principal balances of $100,000, $200,000, $500,000, $1,000,000, and $5,000,000. The FHLMC itself acts as registrar and cotransfer agent, the PCs being freely transferable. The FHLMC sells the PCs through a group of securities dealers as well as through the corporation's own marketing department. Each PC holder receives every month the pass-through of a pro rata share of principal payments collected on the pooled mortgages, including prepayments, and interest. The FHLMC guarantees punctual payment of interest at the rate specified on the PC, as well as full payment of principal. Based on anticipated prepayments, the average weighted life of each PC is figured at about 12 years, although the final payment date is specified as 30 years. There is no specific exemption from state or local income taxes on principal or interest.

Guaranteed Mortgage Certificates. These certificates represent undivided interests in conventional (non-FHA-insured and non-VA-guaranteed) residential mortgages, which are most of the holdings purchased by the FHLMC. GMCs pay interest semiannually, as well as principal once a year in guaranteed minimum amounts. Any certificate holder at his option may call upon the FHLMC to repurchase the GMC at par in 15, 20, or 25 years after the original date of issuance, depending upon the specific issue, although normal final payment date is 30 years from date of issuance.

The GMCs are issued in fully registered form, with original principal amounts of $100,000, $500,000, and $1,000,000. The Federal Reserve Bank of New York is registrar and transfer agent. GMCs of the FHLMC are sold through a selected group of securities dealers.

FHLMC swap transactions: The FHLMC as of 1981 had a program of swap transactions designed to enhance the liquidity position of FSLIC-insured savings and loan associations by replacing mortgage loans with guaranteed FHLMC mortgage participation certificates (PCs). These guaranteed PCs would be eligible collateral for borrowings, including repurchase agreements, and thus represent a more liquid type of holding. The program would operate as follows.

A single institution (individual seller swap transaction) or a group of institutions (multiple seller swap transactions) would sell mortgage loans to the FHLMC with an aggregate outstanding principal balance sufficient to meet the FHLMC's pool formation requirement of $100 million. The FHLMC would sell PCs to these institutions backed by the same mortgages. The association(s) would

FEDERAL HOUSING ACT

continue to service the mortgage loans and pay a guarantee fee to the FHLMC. The PC rate would be keyed to the lowest coupon rate of the pooled mortgages, and monthly interest earned in excess of the FHLMC-required net yield would be interest income.

The following criteria would have to be met, in accordance with supervisory requirements:

1. In all such transactions, both the sale of the mortgage loans and the sale of the PCs must be at par.
2. After establishing the original pool of mortgage loans, neither the mortgage loan sellers nor the FHLMC, unless exercising its rights under its warranty requirements, may make any substitution for loans constituting the original pool.
3. When purchasing a pool of mortgages from a group of institutions, i.e., a multiple seller swap transaction, a minimum of 80% of the loans constituting the pool must bear interest rates with a range no greater than 200 basis points between the lowest rate and the highest rate in the pool.

Gains or losses on the subsequent sale, purchase, or exchange of PCs emanating from these swap transactions would have to be accounted for on the books of the insured institution.

The Federal Home Loan Bank Board (HLBB) had late in 1980 amended its regulations to provide a limited exemption of the net worth and reserve requirements for SAVINGS AND LOAN ASSOCIATIONS that sell residential mortgages carrying interest rate of 7.5% or less in the secondary mortgage market. These provisions were intended to serve as incentives to associations to restructure their loan portfolios so as to achieve better matching of asset and liability maturities.

Although the Federal Home Loan Mortgage Corporation is a corporate instrumentality of the United States, it is not considered a federal agency. As a governmental instrumentality, it historically had been exempt from all federal, state, and local taxation. Legislation signed into law on January 18, 1984, repealed Freddie Mac's exemption from federal income tax, effective January 1, 1985. The securities Freddie Mac sells continue to be subject to federal and state taxes.

The Federal Home Loan Mortgage Corporation, like other units in the Federal Home Loan Bank System, has felt the impact of the liquidity crises and lack of profitability resulting in problems of maintenance of net worth that developed for the savings and loan industry (and other thrift institutions) following the record rise in interest rates and aggravated disintermediation that began in October, 1979.

See FEDERAL SAVINGS AND LOAN ASSOCIATIONS.

FEDERAL HOUSING ACT See NATIONAL HOUSING ACT.

FEDERAL HOUSING ADMINISTRATION Established under the provisions of the National Housing Act, approved June 27, 1934 (48 Stat. 1246; 12 U.S.C. 1702), as amended. It has traveled organizationally since as follows: (1) effective July 1, 1939, it was grouped with other agencies to form the Federal Loan Agency (Reorganization Plan I); (2) by Executive Order 9070 of February 24, 1942, its functions were transferred to the Federal Housing Administration (FHA) under the National Housing Agency; (3) effective July 27, 1947, it was transferred to the Housing and Home Finance Agency (Reorganization Plan 3); and (4) the act approved September 9, 1965 (79 Stat. 667), transferred functions, powers and duties to the Department of Housing and Urban Development (HUD), where it is spotted under the assistant secretary for Housing-Federal Housing Commissioner.

See Department of HOUSING AND URBAN DEVELOPMENT.

An important factor affecting FHA-insured volume has been the development of state and local government programs of tax-exempt financing to provide mortgage funds at below-market interest rates.

BIBLIOGRAPHY

DEPARTMENT OF HOUSING AND URBAN DEVELOPMENT. *Mortgagees Guide: Home Mortgage Insurance Fiscal Instructions* (HUD Handbook).
———. *Annual Report.*

FEDERAL INSURANCE CONTRIBUTION ACT Social security legislation that requires employers to withhold a tax (F.I.C.A) from the wages of each employee under certain conditions. Employers must match the tax of the employee and pay the sum of both taxes to the Internal Revenue Service along with the income taxes withheld. The current congressional projected 1989 F.I.C.A. tax rate is 15.02%, one half of which—7.51%—is paid by the employee; the other half is carried by the employer. The projected tax rates on both the employee and the employer are 7.65% for both 1990 and 1991. The annual salary per employee subject to tax changes depending upon the cost-of-living benefit increases for retirees in the preceding calendar year. The base starts with the 1986 amount of $42,000. The projected estimated taxable wage base for 1989 is $47,000 paid to each employee during the calendar year.

FEDERAL INTERMEDIATE CREDIT BANKS The 12 Federal Intermediate Credit banks were established in 1923 under Title II of the Federal Farm Loan Act, as amended. They were intended to discount or purchase short- and intermediate-term notes of farmers and ranchers held by commercial banks and other financing institutions. These organizations, however, did not fully use the services available to them, nor, it was held, did they adequately provide for the production credit needs of agricultural producers. Consequently, in 1933 the Congress passed the Farm Credit Act of 1933, which authorized farmers to organize local credit cooperatives, called Production Credit associations, which could discount farmers' notes with the Federal Intermediate Credit banks.

The capital stock of the Federal Intermediate Credit banks (FICBS) is owned by the Production Credit associations (PCAs). The stock of the associations is owned by farmers and ranchers.

The Farm Credit Act of 1971, enacted in December, 1971, consolidated and updated the various acts under which the units of the Farm Credit System operate.

Lending Operations. The Federal Intermediate Credit banks provide funds for financing bona fide farmers and ranchers, producers or harvesters of aquatic products, rural residents, and persons furnishing to farmers and ranchers services directly related to their on-farm operating needs. They make loans to and discount paper (maturing in not more than seven years) for various types of financing institutions, including Production Credit associations, national and state banks, agricultural credit corporations, incorporated livestock loan companies, and other similar institutions, with their endorsement. The Federal Intermediate Credit banks may also participate as primary lenders with the 135 Production Credit associations and other Federal Intermediate Credit banks in making loans.

In addition to their operations in discounting agricultural paper, the Federal Intermediate Credit banks supervise and assist the Production Credit associations in making sound credit available in rural areas. The Federal Intermediate Credit banks have compiled an outstanding operating record—no loss has been sustained on any loan made since 1933, and no loss has ever resulted from a loan to a Production Credit association. FICBs derive their funds through issues of stock (only PCAs may hold voting stock) and sale of participation certificates. A large portion of their loans are made for production purposes and mature within a year. Farm and rural home loans, however, may have terms of up to 10 years, and loans to producers and harvesters of aquatic products may be made for up to 15 years.

Production Credit Associations. The Production Credit associations are primary lenders which provide borrowers with short- and intermediate-term credit for operating, capital, and other needs. Loans from Production Credit associations may vary from a few months in maturity up to seven years. Production Credit associations may participate with commercial banks in making loans to farmers.

A Production Credit association must obtain prior approval from its district Federal Intermediate Credit bank for any loan it intends to discount if the loan exceeds 15% of the capital structure of the association. In turn, any loan that exceeds 35% of the associa-tion's capital structure must be approved by the Farm Credit Administration.

As primary lenders, Production Credit associations must sustain all losses to the extent of available resources. In their years of operations, losses have amounted to only a fraction of 1% of cash advanced. In all Farm Credit districts, the associations have adopted either mutual loss sharing or participating loan plans or both. These agreements, which have been in existence for several years, have the effect of putting the net worth of the Production Credit associations more directly behind the net worth of the Federal Intermediate Credit banks and their outstanding debentures.

Production Credit associations are controlled by their borrowers through elected boards of directors. Borrowers are required to invest in the capital stock of the associations in an amount equal to 5% of their loans. The associations, in turn, invest equal amounts in the capital stock of their district Federal Intermediate Credit bank.

Participation by Commercial Banks. It is reported that more banks are resorting to PCAs as a source of credit, but that many banks are hesitant to participate with PCAs in loans for two reasons. First, PCAs are competitors for such loans. Second, commercial banks wishing to participate with PCAs in loans must comply with one of the following terms: (1) at least 50% of the loan must be retained, (2) at least 10% of each loan must be retained as long as the ratio of agricultural loans to total loans is not materially reduced, or (3) the maximum amount of the participated loan permitted to which the bank is subject is retained.

Farm Credit System Financing. Securities serving as financing media for the Farm Credit System are consolidated systemwide notes and bonds, the joint and several obligations of all 37 Farm Credit banks. All of the issues are backed by collateral requirements equal to the amount of securities outstanding, which consist of the following types: discount notes of 5- to 270-day maturities sold daily in denominations of $50,000, $100,000, and $1,000,000; six- to nine-month bonds sold each month; and longer-term bonds sold in January, April, July, and October, and as system's needs require. Bonds are issued in book-entry form, with denominations of $1,000 for maturities of over 13 months and $5,000 for shorter maturities. The Farm Credit banks are authorized to issue bonds and notes to a maximum of 20 times the capital and surplus of the banks. The bonds are eligible investments for national banks and state member banks of the Federal Reserve System as well as federal savings and loan associations and federal credit unions, lawful investments for fiduciary and trust funds of the U.S. government, and eligible as security for all public deposits. Taxwise, the bonds and interest therefrom are exempt from state, municipal, and local income taxes, but subject to federal taxation.

Commercial banks are reportedly the largest single group of investors in Farm Credit System securities.

Restructuring. The AGRICULTURAL ACT OF 1987 mandated a restructuring of the Farm Credit System which required the FEDERAL LAND BANK and the FEDERAL INTERMEDIATE CREDIT BANK in each Farm Credit district to merge. The resulting FARMCREDIT BANK will be a federally chartered instrumentality of the United States with corporate powers similar to those formerly held by the FLB and the FICB. Each Farm Credit bank will elect a board of directors in accordance with its bylaws. At least one member of the board will be elected by the other directors and shall not be a director, officers, employee, or stockholder of any system institutions.

See FARM CREDIT ADMINISTRATION, FEDERAL FARM LOAN SYSTEM, FEDERAL LAND BANK ASSOCIATIONS, FEDERAL LAND BANKS.

FEDERAL LAND BANK ASSOCIATIONS

The local cooperative units for the Federal Land Bank System, provided for by the Federal Farm Loan Act of 1916. During the system's first 20 years of operation, about 5,000 associations were granted charters. This resulted in considerable overlapping and duplication of territory served by the associations, a situation which was corrected through consolidations and reorganizations. The number as of 1988 had been reduced to a total of 232 Federal Land Bank associations serving the U.S., including Puerto Rico.

Each association is a separately chartered organization of member-borrowers operating under its own bylaws. Each has its own board of directors elected by and from its members. The board of directors selects the officers and employees and is responsible for the operations of the association. Each is served through an office or offices staffed and equipped for its operation.

The essential purpose of the Federal Land Bank associations is to provide farmers local availability and servicing of Federal Land Bank loans. One of their principal duties is to consider and recommend to the bank only those applications they are satisfied will result in safe, sound loans serviceable to the applicants.

Member-ownership, a first principle of cooperative business organizations, characterizes Federal Land Bank associations. Each member of a Federal Land Bank association purchases stock in the association; the association in turn purchases stock in the Federal Land Bank. This enables farmer-members to become owners of the Federal Land bank in each Farm Credit district. U.S. farmers borrowing from their Federal Land banks now own the largest cooperative farm mortgage credit system in the world.

The member's stock in the association is his personal property. He pledges it with the association as additional collateral for his loan. The associations have considerable amounts in accumulated reserves and surplus funds which protect the members' investments. When a Federal Land bank loan is paid in full, the stock in the bank is retired in full. The association then retires the member's stock in the same manner. In this way the ownership of the system is confined to its users.

In keeping with cooperative principles, the FEDERAL LAND BANKS, after providing for reserves as required by law and good business practice, distribute savings in the form of dividends to Federal Land Bank associations. Since the stock is owned in proportion to the amount of the original loan, these dividends serve essentially as patronage refunds to association members. The associations pass on to their members a substantial portion of the dividends received from the banks, thereby lowering the members' loan costs. The remainder of the dividends received from the banks by the associations and not used for necessary expenses are retained to establish appropriate reserves and maintain satisfactory net worth positions.

Each association operates under a set of bylaws which regulate both the manner in which directors and officers are elected and how the general business of the association is conducted. They provide for annual stockholders' meetings and set up other guides for the operation of the association.

The directors of a Federal Land Bank association are the elected representatives of the membership. Election is by the usual democratic practice of one person/one vote used by cooperatives. The board of an association consists of not less than five nor more than seven members who are elected by the stockholders to serve for terms of three years. Usually the terms are staggered so as to preserve a continuity of experience on the board. The members of the board must be stockholders of the association and residents of its territory.

Under the general supervision of the Farm Credit Administration, the board has control and direction of association affairs. It supervises and directs the association business within the limitations of the act under which it is chartered, the regulations of the Farm Credit Administration, applicable policies of its Federal Land bank, and the rules of its own bylaws. Functions of the board of directors include electing officers and authorizing the employment of qualified personnel to carry on the business of the association, and determining that the operations are carried on in an efficient manner and in accordance with the board's policies and the laws under which the association operates.

Other responsibilities of a board include choosing a loan committee capable of properly considering the qualifications of applicants for loans and electing applicants to membership in the association. The board also has the responsibility of determining that all loans to members are impartially and properly serviced.

The manager is an employee of the association, selected by the directors, and has responsibility for conducting the work of the association under the general direction of the board. He is the principal representative of the association in direct contact with applicants, borrowers, and the public. He is familiar with agricultural conditions in the area and the credit needs of farmers. Generally, his duties are those of executive officer of the association and cover the whole range of association activities.

Each Federal Land Bank association has a loan committee of three or more members. Whenever an application for a mortgage loan is received, this committee is required to make or to have made an investigation of the applicant and the property. A written report must be made by the committee or its investigator as to the character and solvency of the applicant. The committee in approving a loan also must have a report on the value of the security by a qualified appraiser. No loan can be made unless the committee gives a favorable written report. If an application is approved, the committee must recommend the amount and terms of the loan that should be offered to the applicant. The association recommendation is given full weight by the bank when it takes final loan action.

Loans are made through the 232 Federal Land Bank associations, most of which have branch offices. The loans have terms of from 5 to 40 years and may be made in amounts of up to 85% of the appraised value of the real estate security and of up to 97% if the loan is guaranteed by a government agency.

FEDERAL LAND BANK BONDS

Each Federal Land Bank association must hold an annual meeting at which directors are elected and certain other formal decisions are reached. At these meetings reports are made on the business affairs of the association to give members pertinent information about the operations of the association. Members exercise their control in the association through their votes in electing directors. Associations encourage members to keep farmers in their communities informed about the services of the association, and many associations have active new-business committees with members selected from various communities in the area. First responsibility of a member is to meet all payments on or before the due date and see that the condition of his farm and home is adequately maintained.

The income of the association necessary for salaries of employees, office quarters, travel, and other items required to provide a convenient credit service comes largely from two kinds of payments by the Federal Land bank. One is dividends, and the other is payment for servicing loans. Interest on investments and a few other items add varying amounts to the association's income. Associations must maintain adequate reserves to meet their endorsement liability on members' loans.

Restructuring. The Agricultural Act of 1987 mandates some organizational restructuring among Farm Credit System institutions. The Federal Land bank and the Federal Intermediate Credit Bank in each Farm Credit district were required to merge. The resulting Farm Credit bank will be a federally chartered instrumentality of the United States with corporate powers similar to those formerly held by the FLB and FICB. Each Farm Credit bank will elect a board of directors in accordance with its bylaws.

Within six months of the mergers of the FLBs and FICBs, the board of directors of each FLBA and PCA that share substantially the same geographic territory must submit a plan to their stockholders for merging the two associations. The plan must first be approved by the district Farm Credit bank and the Farm Credit Administration. If the plan is approved and adopted by the stockholders, the resulting association will be a direct lender and obtain its loan funds from the Farm Credit Bank in the same manner as PCAs now obtain loan funds from the FICBs. The boards of directors of associations, whether merged or not, will be elected from among their stockholders, except that at least one member will be elected by the other directors and shall not be a director, officer, employee, or stockholder of any system institution.

See FARM MORTGAGES.

FEDERAL LAND BANK BONDS See FEDERAL FARM LOAN SYSTEM.

FEDERAL LAND BANK DISTRICTS
Originally, under the Federal Farm Loan Act of 1916, the 12 districts into which the continental U.S. was divided by the Federal Farm Loan Board (predecessor of the Farm Credit Administration for location therein of the Federal Land banks.

With the creation of additional farm credit institutions, particularly in 1923 and 1933, the Farm Credit Act of 1937 (Sec. 5) renamed the Federal Land Bank districts, providing that there shall be 12 districts in the U.S., including Alaska, Puerto Rico, and Hawaii, which shall be known as Farm Credit districts. The boundaries of the 12 Federal Land Bank districts existing as of August 19, 1937, were by this statute designated as the boundaries of the respective Farm Credit districts.

See FARM CREDIT ADMINISTRATION for a map of Farm Credit districts.

FEDERAL LAND BANKS
The 12 Federal Land banks were organized pursuant to the passage by Congress of the Federal Farm Loan Act of 1916, principally to provide long-term farm mortgage loans at reasonable rates of interest. The act also provided for the establishment of local farmer borrowing associations subsequently termed FEDERAL LAND BANK ASSOCIATIONS, through which the banks make loans. The capital stock of the Federal Land banks is owned by the Federal Land Bank associations. Stock of the associations in turn is owned by farmers and ranchers who were members of the associations and borrowers from the banks.

The Farm Credit Act of 1971, passed by Congress in December, 1971, consolidated and updated the various acts under which the various units of the Farm Credit System, including the Federal Land banks and their Federal Land Bank associations, operate. In addition, this act expanded somewhat the lending authority of the various units to meet the changing credit needs of rural areas.

Business. Business of the Federal Land banks is to make mortgage loans on rural properties within their respective districts. Loans may be made to bona fide farmers and ranchers, producers or harvesters of aquatic products, rural residents, and persons furnishing to farmers and ranchers services directly related to their on-farm operating needs under rules and regulations of the FARM CREDIT ADMINISTRATION.

Each loan must be based on a favorable appraisal report on the real estate offered as security and may not exceed 85% of the value of the property as determined by the appraisal plus the amount loaned to the applicant to purchase required stock in the local Federal Land Bank association. It is the general practice of the Federal Land banks to make loans on amortized plans of repayment. In exceptional circumstances, however, they may make loans with maturities of not less than 5 nor more than 40 years. The largest portion of loans made have maturities of 20 years. Payment of loans in whole or in part is accepted at any time.

As of 1989, the loans have terms of from 5 to 40 years and may be made in amounts of up to 85% of the appraised value of the real estate security and of up to 97% if the loan is guaranteed by a government agency.

All of the Federal Land banks write new loans on variable rate interest plans which enable them to offer loans at the lowest overall cost to borrowers and to adjust their income more readily to fluctuations in the cost of borrowed funds.

Each loan made by a Federal Land bank is closed through and has the endorsement of the local Federal Land Bank association operating in the area in which the property is located. Each borrower is required to purchase stock in the local association in an amount equal to 5% of his loan. The association in turn is required to purchase an equal amount of stock in the Federal Land bank of the district. The borrower's stock is pledged with the association as collateral security for the payment of the loan, and the association's stock in the Federal Land bank is similarly pledged as security for the association's endorsement liability. The bank and association stock must be retired when the loan is paid in full.

The law provides that the U.S. government shall assume no responsibility, direct or indirect, for any bonds or debentures or other such obligations issued by the Federal Land banks, Federal Intermediate Credit banks, or Banks for Cooperatives (the last two being the other types of financing institutions in the Farm Credit System).

The amount and maturity of each issue of bonds or debentures, the rate of interest it is to bear, and the participations by individual banks are determined by the finance committee of the banks, or by its subcommittee, operating through their fiscal agency and subject to the approval of the Farm Credit Administration. The finance committees consist of the presidents of all 12 or 13 banks in each lending system. Between regular meetings, the committees are represented by their respective subcommittees composed of three members each.

The law also provides that the amount of bonds, debentures, or similar obligations issued and outstanding may not exceed 20 times the capital and surplus of all the banks primarily liable on the issue or such lesser amount as the Farm Credit Administration shall establish by regulation.

Collateral security for the bonds and debentures of the Farm Credit banks shall be at least equal in amount to the bonds and debentures issued and shall consist of notes and other obligations representing loans made under the authority of the Farm Credit Act, obligations of the United States or any agency thereof, other readily marketable securities approved by the Farm Credit Administration, or cash.

Investment eligibilities. Regulation A of the Board of Governors of the Federal Reserve System provides that the bonds and debentures of the Farm Credit banks may be accepted by Federal Reserve banks as collateral security for advances to member banks under Section 13 of the Federal Reserve Act. They are also eligible for outright purchase and sale by the Federal Reserve System in its OPEN MARKET OPERATIONS.

National banks and state member banks of the Federal Reserve System may invest in the bonds and debentures of the Federal Land banks (and Federal Intermediate Credit banks), and in so doing they are not subject to the statutory limitations and restrictions generally applicable as to dealing in, underwriting, and purchasing for their own account investment securities. In particular, the limitation that such banks shall not invest more than 10% of their capital stock and surplus fund in the securities of one obligor does not apply to Farm Credit bonds and debentures. (In the opinion of general counsel of the Farm Credit Administration, debentures of the Banks for Cooperatives are also eligible for investment by state member banks of the Federal Reserve System so far as the Investment Securities Regulation of the Comptroller of the Currency is concerned.)

The law provides that the bonds and debentures of the Farm Credit banks shall be lawful investments for all fiduciary and trust funds under the jurisdiction of the U.S. government. They are eligible as security for government deposits. They are also legal investments for banks, trust companies, savings banks, and trust funds in various states, subject to such conditions and restrictions as are contained in applicable state statutes and regulations. The bonds and debentures are lawful investments also for FEDERAL CREDIT UNIONS and FEDERAL SAVINGS AND LOAN ASSOCIATIONS.

Tax status. Consolidated bonds and debentures of the Federal Land banks, Federal Intermediate Credit banks, and Banks for Cooperatives, and the income derived therefrom, are exempt from state, municipal, and local taxation. Interest on such bonds and debentures, however, is not exempt from taxation by the U.S. government, and neither gain from sale or other disposition of the bonds and debentures nor their transfer by inheritance, gift, etc., is exempt from federal or state taxation.

Offerings through dealers. Public offerings of bonds and debentures are made by the 12 Federal Land banks through their fiscal agency (along with the other Farm Credit institutions), with the assistance of a nationwide selling group of bank and nonbank dealers.

FEDERAL LAND BANK SYSTEM
See FARM CREDIT ADMINISTRATION, FARM MORTGAGES, FEDERAL LAND BANKS.

FEDERAL LOAN AGENCY
An administrative agency created by Reorganization Plan I, of April 25, 1939, pursuant to the Reorganization Act of 1939. Grouped under it were various agencies established from time to time to stimulate and stabilize financial, commercial, and industrial activity, including the RECONSTRUCTION FINANCE CORPORATION and its component corporations, the FEDERAL HOME LOAN BANK BOARD (together with the Home Owners' Loan Corporation and Federal Savings and Loan Insurance Corporation), the FEDERAL HOUSING ADMINISTRATION, the Electric Home and Farm Authority (an agency aiding in the distribution, sale, and installation of electric and gas equipment and appliances), and the EXPORT-IMPORT BANK of Washington.

Executive Order 9070, February 24, 1942, transferred to the National Housing Agency the Federal Home Loan Bank Board, the Federal Savings and Loan Insurance Corporation, the Home Owners' Loan Corporation, the Federal Housing Administration, and the Defense Homes Corporation (a unit of the RFC). All other units of the Federal Loan Agency were transferred by Executive Order 9071, February 24, 1942, to the Department of Commerce.

The act of Congress approved February 24, 1945 (59 Stat. 5; 12 U.S.C. 1801) returned to the Federal Loan Agency the RFC and its units. On June 30, 1947, however, an act of Congress (Sec. 204, 61 Stat. 202; 12 U.S.C. 1801) abolished the Federal Loan Agency and transferred all property and records to the Reconstruction Finance Corporation, which was finally abolished by Reorganization Plan 1 of 1957.

FEDERAL NATIONAL MORTGAGE ASSOCIATION
This organization originally was organized on February 10, 1938, by the Reconstruction Finance Corporation (RFC) with capital stock of $10 million, all owned by the RFC, and a surplus of $1 million as the National Mortgage Association, pursuant to Title III of the National Housing Act (48 Stat. 1246). After several organizational transfers, it was rechartered under the Housing Act of 1954 (68 Stat. 590) and made a constituent agency of the Housing and Home Finance Agency. An act approved September 9, 1965 (79 Stat. 667) transferred the association with functions, powers, and duties of the Housing and Home Finance Agency to the Department of Housing and Urban Development. Title VIII of the Housing and Urban Development Act of 1968 (82 Stat. 536), effective September 1, 1968, converted the Federal National Mortgage Association (FNMA) into a government-sponsored private corporation, as to its secondary market operations for home mortgages. Under the same legislation and as of the same date, the GOVERNMENT NATIONAL MORTGAGE ASSOCIATION was established to carry on other functions (special assistance functions, management and liquidating functions, guarantees of mortgage-backed securities, participation sales) as a government corporation operated under the supervision of the secretary of Housing and Urban Development.

The newly emerged Federal National Mortgage Corporation retained the assets and capital structure related to the secondary market operations. These operations were intended from their inception to be carried out on a profitable basis. "The Congress believed that enough experience had been gained to permit this type of business operation to be carried out by a privately owned and managed entity," according to the FNMA's management. As of September 1, 1968, the capital of FNMA represented by privately held common stock amounted to about $140 billion and the preferred stock held by the secretary of the Treasury amounted to about $160 million. On September 30, 1968, FNMA retired its preferred stock with proceeds from the sale of subordinated capital debentures, so that its entire equity interest became privately owned. Nevertheless federal control was retained in that a majority of its then nine-member board of directors continued temporarily to be appointed by the secretary of Housing and Urban Development.

The 1968 act had provided that FNMA would assume responsibility for its own management after a transitional period, which could end at any time on or after May 1, 1970, if the board of directors found, with the concurrence of the secretary of Housing and Urban Development, that at least one-third of FNMA's common stock was owned by persons or institutions in the mortgage lending, home building, real estate, or related businesses. The board of directors made this finding as of February, 1970, and obtained the concurrence of the secretary of Housing and Urban Development at the annual meeting of stockholders on May 21, 1970. Accordingly, the transitional period was declared to be at an end.

Yet the FNMA may be said to continue to be a government-sponsored corporation in that its charter accords certain advantages to the corporation and also makes it subject to several possible forms of federal supervision, including regulations applicable to the FNMA that have been issued by the Department of Housing and Urban Development. Advantages accorded to FNMA that are not normally accorded to business corporations include the following:

1. The secretary of the Treasury has the authority, which is entirely discretionary, to purchase obligations of FNMA up to a specified amount outstanding at any one time. Each such purchase would be at a yield determined by the secretary of the Treasury after taking into account the current average return on outstanding marketable federal obligations. (This authority, which has come to be known as the "Treasury backstop authority," has not been used since FNMA achieved its present status in 1970.) The corporation's management states that it intends to conduct its affairs in such a way that it will not become necessary to use the backstop authority. It also points out that the significance of this authority has become greatly diluted since 1957, when the $2.25 billion authority was established. At that time, FNMA's total debt was less than 63% of the backstop authority, but since then the debt has increased so much that the backstop authority is less than 5.5% of the debt.
2. The corporation's common stock and its other securities are exempt from registration requirements and other laws administered by the Securities and Exchange Commission to the same extent as securities issued or guaranteed by the U.S. government. However, in issuing stock and subordinated capital debentures to the public and in soliciting proxies, the FNMA voluntarily discloses the types of information that other corporations disclose under SEC regulations.
3. Although the FNMA pays full federal corporate income taxes, it is exempt from paying any taxes to any state or local taxing authority except for real property taxes.
4. The corporation's obligations are issuable and payable through the facilities of the Federal Reserve banks, which are paid by FNMA for their services. The corporation's obligations are legal investments for federally supervised institutions.

Thus the FNMA is one of a very limited number of privately owned corporations whose obligations—along with obligations of federally owned corporations—are classified as federal agency securities. The financial markets have tended to give favorable consideration to this class of borrowings. It should be noted, however, that the FNMA's notes and debentures are not federal government obligations nor are they federally guaranteed by an agency of the U.S.

FEDERAL NATIONAL MORTGAGE ASSOCIATION

government. They are general obligations solely of the FNMA. (The only FNMA obligations guaranteed by an agency of the U.S. government, and having the full faith and credit of the United States behind them, are mortgage-backed bonds issued by the FNMA and guaranteed by the Government National Mortgage Association (see below).)

Federal supervision of FNMA, as provided in its charter, may take the following forms:

1. The secretary of Housing and Urban Development has general regulatory power over FNMA to make "such rules and regulations as shall be necessary and proper to insure that the purposes" of its charter act are accomplished. The charter section relating to those purposes reads in pertinent part as follows: "The Congress hereby declares that the purposes of this title are to establish secondary market facilities for home mortgages, to provide that the operations thereof shall be financed by private capital to maximum extent feasible, and to authorize such facilities to ... provide supplementary assistance to the secondary market for home mortgages by providing a degree of liquidity for mortgage investments, thereby improving the distribution of investment capital available for home mortgage financing ... " (Sec. 301 of the charter act).
2. The secretary of Housing and Urban Development has specific authority to require that a reasonable portion of the corporation's mortgage purchases be related to the national goal of providing adequate housing for low- and moderate-income families but with reasonable economic return to the corporation.
3. The corporation's issuance of various forms of debt securities and their maturities and rates of interest are subject to approval by the secretary of the Treasury. (Since the U.S. Treasury is the nation's largest borrower and in some years the FNMA is the second largest, their borrowing activities need to be coordinated to avoid overburdening the financial market, which would unduly increase the borrowing costs of both.)
4. Issuance of stock, obligations, and other securities by the FNMA requires the prior approval of the secretary of Housing and Urban Development. (See below for details of capital structure.)
5. FNMA may require, within statutory limits, that sellers of mortgages to the corporation shall buy its stock. This requirement is subject to the approval of the secretary of Housing and Urban Development. The corporation's requirement that its mortgage servicers shall hold certain minimum amounts of stock in the corporation is also subject to the approval of the secretary of Housing and Urban Development.
6. FNMA's board of directors, at its discretion, determines the amount of dividends paid to stockholders. But the secretary of Housing and Urban Development may from time to time determine what would be a fair rate of return, after consideration of the current earnings and capital condition of the corporation. Cash dividends paid in any one year may not exceed any rate so determined.
7. The secretary of Housing and Urban Development may approve a maximum ratio of the corporation's debt to its capital greater than the 15 to 1 ratio otherwise applicable under its charter. (It has been set at 25 to 1 since 1969.)
8. The authority of FNMA to buy or otherwise deal in conventional mortgages (those which are not federally insured or guaranteed) was made subject to the approval of the secretary of Housing and Urban Development.
9. The secretary of Housing and Urban Development may examine and audit the books and financial transactions of the corporation and may require the corporation to make such reports on its activities as the secretary of Housing and Urban Development deems advisable.

HUD Regulations. Regulations issued by the secretary of Housing and Urban Development regarding FNMA were substantially revised in 1978 (Part 81 of Title 24 of the Code of Federal Regulations). The revision was designed to: (1) codify the statutory approval functions concerning the operations of FNMA which the charter act vested in the secretary; (2) establish standards and goals with respect to the conduct of FNMA's secondary market operations; (3) assure that FNMA is complying with nondiscrimination standards; (4) require from FNMA, on a regular basis, reports which are necessary to enable the secretary to discharge the oversight responsibilities placed on her by the charter act; (5) provide for annual audits of FNMA's books and financial transactions; and (6) make minor technical changes to the existing regulations.

Major provisions established goals for FNMA's purchases of conventional mortgages on properties in the central cities of standard metropolitan statistical areas and of conventional mortgages on housing for low- and moderate-income families (Secs. 81.16 and 81.17 of the regulations). Under these provisions, on March 1 of each year the secretary of Housing and Urban Development may establish a goal for that year for FNMA purchases of either of these two classes of conventional mortgages if the corporation's purchases of that class during the preceding calendar year was less than 30% of all its conventional mortgage purchases.

The regulation contains follow-up provisions for the low- and moderate-income housing mortgage purchase goal but not for the central-city mortgage purchase goal. In any year for which a goal has been established for FNMA purchases of conventional mortgages on housing for low- and moderate-income persons, the secretary shall determine, on the basis of reports from FNMA concerning its purchases during the first half of the year, whether the number of purchases will fall below the established goal. If a determination is made that they will fall below the goal, the secretary shall require FNMA to provide, within 30 working days, either a statement of reasons why the goal for that year should be modified or suspended, or its plan to take special actions to increase its purchases of this class of mortgages. Within 15 days after receipt of FNMA's reply, the secretary shall either modify or suspend the goal for that year or approve, reject, or seek modifications of the FNMA plan for special actions.

If the secretary rejects FNMA's request to change the original goal or rejects the special actions proposed by FNMA for attaining the goal, the secretary may (1) require FNMA to conduct a separate auction or auctions of commitments to purchase conventional low- and moderate-income mortgages, or (2) require FNMA to hold open a public offer to purchase such mortgages that were newly originated, or (3) condition the approval of any further increase in FNMA's borrowing authority upon the use of a designated amount of the increased borrowing authority for the purchase of conventional low- and moderate-income mortgages. FNMA shall not, however, be required to forgo a reasonable rate of return or to make commitments to purchase conventional mortgages which: (1) fail to meet the corporation's underwriting standards, or (2) are not deemed by the corporation to be of such quality and type as to meet generally the purchase standards of private institutional mortgage investors, or (3) cannot be purchased within the range of market prices for the class of mortgages involved, as determined by the corporation. If FNMA implements the foregoing requirements and is nevertheless unable to meet the announced annual purchase goal, the requirements shall be deemed to be satisfied for that calendar year.

Fannie Mae has created a relatively small $100-million fund to provide a way for senior citizens to keep their own homes on favorable terms. The programs were created in 1989 on an experimental basis. The housing arrangement programs are available to persons over 62. Lending standards have been relaxed so that mortgages are easier to obtain.

Loans are made by banks, S&Ls, and mortgage companies who sell the loans to Fannie Mae. These senior citizen housing programs include:

1. **Accessory apartments.** An older person can add a self-contained apartment to his or her house that can be rented out. The program allows an adult child to use this program to build an apartment in his or her home for an elderly parent.
2. **Free-standing units.** A homeowner can install a mobile home on the property to house an elderly relative, assuming zoning regulations permit.
3. **Home-sharing.** An elderly homeowner can purchase a house with another older person, or buy a house to share with a companion who pays some rent and does some housekeeping. Also, a senior citizen housing agency can purchase a house intended to be shared by two or more rent-paying older people.
4. **Sale-leaseback.** An investor is able to purchase the senior citizen's house and lease it back to the original owner who pays rent. Under this program, the senior citizen can cash in on the equity in the home without moving. The investor can be a public or nonprofit agency or others experienced in senior citizen housing.

Senior citizens are advised to enter into these programs only after thorough investigations, counseling, and legal advice.

BIBLIOGRAPHY

Federal National Mortgage Association. *Annual Report; Quarterly Report.*

FEDERAL OPEN MARKET COMMITTEE The Federal Open Market Committee (FOMC) was created by Section 12-A of the Federal Reserve Act, as added by the BANKING ACT OF 1933, completely revised by the BANKING ACT OF 1935, and amended by the Act of July 7, 1942 (56 Stat. 647). The FOMC is composed of the seven members of the board of governors and five Federal Reserve bank officials, usually presidents. The chairman of the Federal Reserve Board of Governors also serves as chairman of the FOMC. Because of the New York Fed's special role in managing the system open market account, the bank's representative is a permanent voting member of the FOMC and, by tradition, the committee's vice-chairman. The other Reserve bank presidents serve on a one-year rotating basis beginning March 1.

Each year, one president or first vice-president is eligible to be elected to the committee by one of the boards of directors of one of the Reserve banks in each of four groups of Reserve banks. Group one consists of Boston, Philadelphia, and Richmond; group two, Cleveland and Chicago; group three, Atlanta, St. Louis, and Dallas; and group four, Minneapolis, Kansas City, and San Francisco. The Reserve bank presidents who are not voting members of the FOMC also attend the meetings to offer their views on economic conditions and policy approaches. The meetings occur about 10 times a year. Should one of the voting presidents be unable to attend a meeting, an alternate president of a Reserve bank, designated each March from the remaining seven, may cast a vote in the place of the absent president. If the New York president is absent, the first vice-president of the New York Fed attends the meeting and votes. Traditionally, the New York Fed first vice-president is the only such officer designated as an alternate. Voting alternates must be from the same group as the presidents they replace.

On a daily basis, the securities portfolio is directed by the manager of the system open market account for domestic operations. The manager is appointed by the FOMC and customarily is a senior officer of the New York Fed. The account manager attends the FOMC meetings to report on domestic operations, as well as to be fully informed of the discussions leading to adoption of the committee's directives to him. In addition, the manager participates daily in a telephone conference call with a designated Reserve bank president and the senior staff of the board of governors. The account manager proposes a plan for the day and receives comment from the president on the call. Each day the board's staff sends a telegram to the voting and nonvoting members of the FOMC covering the discussion of the call.

The Federal Reserve System's open market account is composed of the Federal Reserve System's portfolio of U.S. Treasury and federal agency securities, and bankers acceptances, acquired in open market operations.

Open market operations involve the buying and selling of securities in the marketplace. The open market operations serve as one of the three basic tools the Federal Reserve uses to conduct MONETARY POLICY—which influences the cost and availability of money and credit. Other things remaining equal, a purchase of government securities in the market by the system account adds RESERVES to the commercial banking system, enabling banks to expand their lending and investment activities. A sale of securities by the system account withdraws reserves from the banking system, limiting the ability of commercial banks to make loans and investments.

(The other major tools of Monetary Policy are changes in the DISCOUNT RATE and RESERVE REQUIREMENTS. The discount rate is the interest charge that depository institutions (*see* DEPOSITORY INSTITUTIONS DEREGULATION AND MONETARY CONTROL ACT OF 1980) must pay when they borrow from the Federal Reserve banks. Reserve requirements are the reserves that the various depository institutions must keep in their vault or on deposit directly or indirectly in their reserve account at the Federal Reserve bank, based on a percentage of demand, time, and savings deposits of the institution.

A specified portion of the system's outright holdings in the system account's portfolio is allocated to each of the 12 Federal Reserve banks, but is held by the New York Fed. The securities trading desk of the system account at the New York Fed is the control center of the system's market activities, which are directed by the FOMC. The percentage allotments of the portfolio are adjusted annually to reflect movements of deposits among Federal Reserve banks.

The power to buy and sell government securities was granted to each Federal Reserve bank by the Federal Reserve Act. However, not until the 1920s was the monetary policy impact of changes in the portfolio generally understood. The structure of the FOMC itself, moreover, was not established in its present form until passage of the Banking Act of 1935.

The composition and value of the system account's portfolio fluctuates daily in response to the system account's operations. The interest received by the Federal Reserve on its system account's portfolio holdings constitutes virtually all of the system's earnings. However, unlike individual or private institutions, the Federal Reserve acquires or sells securities purely to implement monetary policy and not in pursuit of profit. The interest earned on the holdings is apportioned to the individual Federal Reserve banks according to the percentages of the portfolio that each Federal Reserve bank owns. A portion of the earnings is used for the salaries and other operating expenses of the Federal Reserve banks, with an amount set aside in a surplus account. In recent years these expenses have amounted to about 8.4% of the annual earnings on the portfolio of the Federal Reserve banks. After additions to surplus and dividends on Federal Reserve bank stock (owned by the member banks), the remaining earnings are paid to the U.S. Treasury on a weekly basis, as interest payments on FEDERAL RESERVE NOTES at a rate established by the Board of Governors of the Federal Reserve System.

The FOMC concentrates on controlling the supply of reserves through the government securities trading desk at the Federal Reserve Bank of New York. The New York Fed conducts open market operations on behalf of the Federal Reserve, pursuant to directives of the FOMC. The FOMC establishes operating guides for the trading desk by choosing growth objectives for various measures of money, the funds available to the public for transaction purposes, and liquid savings. The staff of the board of governors uses the monetary growth objectives as the basis for constructing growth paths for total and nonborrowed reserves which are consistent with the desired money growth.

Total reserves are assets that depository institutions may count to meet the reserve requirements. Most depository institutions must directly or indirectly maintain reserves with the Federal Reserve bank of the district. Nonborrowed reserves represent total reserves less borrowings at the district Federal Reserve bank (the discount window).

Initially, the staff decides how to divide the FOMC's two- or three-month growth objectives into monthly paths. The monthly pattern for money growth is then translated into nonseasonally adjusted weekly levels. Application of the appropriate required reserve ratios to the different categories of deposits results in an estimate of required reserves for the period between FOMC meetings, about once every four to six weeks. Addition of estimated excess reserves results in an estimate of total reserves for the period. Excess reserves are the difference between total reserves and required reserves. Deduction of the borrowing level indicated by the FOMC at its meeting produces the nonborrowed reserve average that the trading desk is expected to achieve.

Each week the trading desk has an objective for such nonborrowed reserves. The reserve objectives for the intermeeting period are reviewed by senior FOMC and trading desk staff, typically each Friday morning. The objectives may be revised to account for factors such as changes in the mix of currency and member and nonmember bank deposits in the money supply and other liabilities.

The path for nonborrowed reserves may also be revised to help speed the adjustment process if demand for total reserves is running well above or below the desired level. The nonborrowed path may be lowered if total reserves are running strong and raised if total reserves are running weak.

Comparison of the projected demand for total reserves with the nonborrowed reserve path for the interval indicates the amount of borrowing consistent with achieving the path. Borrowing needed in subsequent weeks to achieve the average is then deducted from the weekly estimates of the demand for total reserves to give the nonborrowed reserves objective consistent with attaining the desired average for the interval.

Given the week's nonborrowed reserve objective, along with an awareness of the excess and borrowed reserve expectations, the trading desk devises an operating strategy. Each day, the desk receives projections of the supply of nonborrowed reserves for the statement week, prepared by staff at the New York Fed and at the board of governors.

The projected nonborrowed reserve supply is compared with the objective to see whether reserves will need to be added or absorbed. Some factors, such as Federal Reserve FLOAT, are particularly hard to predict and often cause large projection errors. Given this uncertainty about reserves, the trading desk may also draw information about actual reserve availability from the behavior of the market for reserves. For example, a sharp rise in the federal funds rate may suggest reserves are in shorter supply than the projections indicate; a sharp decline may suggest the reverse. Pursuit of reserve objectives involves a daily judgment of when, and how much, to intervene with open market operations to achieve the weekly reserve objective.

System transactions on an outright basis typically occur through an auction process in which dealers are requested to submit bids or offers for securities of the type and maturity that the manager has elected to sell or buy that day. Once dealer tenders have been received, they are arrayed according to price. The manager then accepts amounts bid or offered in sequence, taking the highest prices bid for sales and the lowest prices offered for purchases, until the desired size of the whole transaction is reached. Not all outright transactions occur through the dealer market. Approximately three dozen dealers make up the active market in U.S. government and federal agency securities. These dealers have trading relationships with the trading desk which enables the desk to normally complete large orders promptly. Most of the system's outright transactions, whether in the dealer market or directly, take place in Treasury bills. The Federal Reserve acts as agent for a number of official agencies, such as foreign central bank, in making dollar investments.

In situations that call only for temporary additions to bank reserves, the manager engages in short-term repurchase agreements (RPs) with dealers who agree to repurchase them by a specified date at a specified price. Because the added reserves will automatically be extinguished when the RPs mature, the arrangement is a way of injecting reserves on a short-term basis. Repurchase agreements for the system account may be dated to terminate in one to fifteen business days. Most mature within seven days, and dealers usually have the option to terminate agreements before maturity. Whenever the manager arranges RPs with dealers, the distribution among dealers is determined by auction.

When the manager for domestic operations faces a temporary need to absorb rather than provide bank reserves, matched sale-purchase transactions with dealers are employed. These transactions involve a contract for immediate sale to, and a matching contract for subsequent purchase from, each participating dealer; the maturities of such arrangements usually do not exceed seven days. The initial sale causes surplus reserve to be drained from the banking system; later, when the system purchase is implemented, the flow of reserves is reversed. Such arrangements are usually in Treasury bills.

After each of its meetings, the Federal Open Market Committee issues a directive to the Federal Reserve Bank of New York to guide open market operations in the period before the next meeting. The directive adopted by the FOMC at a given meeting is made public shortly after the next meeting of the committee. It is released along with the policy record summarizing the committee's assessment of the country's economic and financial position at the time of the meeting and the discussion by the members of the appropriate course for policy during the period ahead. The votes of individual members are recorded; if any members dissent, a statement of the reasons for that dissent is also included.

In general, no one approach to the implementation of open market operations is likely to be satisfactory under all of the economic and financial circumstances that monetary policy may face. The approach to policy implementation has been adapted in light of such factors as the need to combat inflation, efforts to encourage sustainable economic growth, uncertainties related to institutional change, and evident shifts in the public's attitudes toward, and use of, money. The more that economic and financial conditions warrant emphasis on a monetary aggregate objective that is closely related to the reserve base, such as M1, the greater is the emphasis that may be placed on guiding open market operations by relatively strict targeting of reserve aggregates. In other circumstances, a more flexible approach to reserve management is required.

Open market operations have their initial impact on the reserves base of the depository system—and directly on nonborrowed reserves. The major objectives for monetary policy are translated into reserve guidelines to form a basis for day-to-day decision making. Various measures of reserves are provided here:

1. Reserve assets. Assets that by statute can be used to satisfy reserve requirements. The Federal Reserve Act specifies only two cash assets: vault cash—the currency and coin held by depositoy institutions in their cash drawers and vaults; and reserve balances with Federal Reserve banks—(other than required clearing balances institutions hold that are related to services provided by the Federal Reserve). Reserves must be posted over a 14-day maintenance period (which runs from a Thursday to the second Wednesday).
2. Total reserves are measured as the sum of reserve balances with Reserve banks plus the part of vault cash holdings actually used to meet reserve requirements. Total reserves can be apportioned into two components, required reserves and excess reserves. Required reserves is the minimum amount of total reserves that a depository institution must hold. This minimum amount is determined by the application of reserve ratios, specified percentages of certain liabilities of depository institutions called reservable liabilities. To determine required reserves, reservable liabilities are averaged over a fourteen-day interval called a computation period (which runs from a Tuesday to the second Monday). The fourteen-day computation period for transaction deposits ends two days before the end of the associated reserve maintenance period. Excess reserves is the second component of total reserves and is the amount by which total reserves exceed required reserves. If required reserves exceed total reserves, the difference is called deficient reserves. Deficiencies not offset by surpluses in surrounding maintenance periods (within allowable limits) are subject to a penalty.
3. Total reserves are provided in two forms: nonborrowed reserves and borrowed reserves. Nonborrowed reserves are reserves that the depository system can obtain only from the Federal Reserve System through open market operations (or through a variety of "technical" factors affecting the Federal Reserve's balance sheet). Borrowed reserves are loans to depository institutions by Federal Reserve banks credited to the institutions' reserve balances with the Reserve banks. These loans are sometimes called discounts and advances, or borrowings from the "discount window."
4. Monetary base is measured as the sum of reserve balances with Federal Reserve banks plus service-related balances plus currency in circulation (currency circulating outside the Federal Reserve and the Treasury). The monetary base is the total reserves plus service-related balances plus the surplus of vault cash holdings over required reserves of institutions satisfying requirements wholly through vault cash plus currency in the hands of the nonbank public (the currency component of the money supply). The nonborrowed monetary base is the monetary base less borrowed reserves.

Open Market Operations in Foreign Exchange. Foreign exchange operations are also conducted by the New York Federal Reserve Bank for the system and the U.S. Treasury, in accordance with the foreign exchange portion of the directives from the FOMC. Like the manager for domestic open market operations, the manager for foreign operations is a senior officer of the New York Federal Reserve Bank; both are appointed to the manager posts annually by the FOMC, and both attend the FOMC meetings to report on operations and to receive the FOMC's directives.

Federal Reserve Act. The Federal Reserve Act provides that no Federal Reserve bank shall engage or decline to engage in open market operations except in accordance with the direction of and regulations adopted by the committee; and that the committee shall consider, adopt, and transmit to the several Federal Reserve banks regulations relating to open market transactions.

The act also provides that the time, character, and volume of all purchases and sales of paper described in Section 14 of the Federal Reserve Act as media for open market operations shall be governed with a view to accommodating commerce and business and with regard to their bearing upon the general credit situation of the country. The board of governors is further directed by the act to keep a complete record of the actions taken by the open market committee upon all questions of policy relating to open market operations, including a record of votes taken in deciding policies and the reasons underlying the actions of the committee in each instance. This record is published periodically in the *Federal Reserve Bulletin*, and is included in the annual report of the board of governors to Congress.

BIBLIOGRAPHY

FEDERAL RESERVE SYSTEM, *Purposes & Functions*.

FEDERAL PUBLIC HOUSING AUTHORITY Created by Executive Order 9070 of February 24, 1942, to administer public housing programs, the authority took over public housing functions performed by the Federal Works Agency and its constituent agencies, the War Department and Navy Department (except housing located on military or naval posts or bases), the Farm Security Administration (nonfarm housing), and the Defense Homes Corporation (administered by the commissioner of the Federal Public Housing Authority).

Functions of this agency were transferred to the Public Housing Administration, established as a major unit of the Housing and Home Finance Agency by Reorganization Plan 3 of 1947, effective July 27, 1947.

Finally, functions, powers, and duties of the PHA were transferred to the Department of Housing and Urban Development by act approved September 9, 1965 (79 Stat. 667), and the PHA lapsed.

FEDERAL REGULATION Regulation of business by the federal government, particularly under an expanded concept of the interstate commerce power especially exemplified by the introduction of the New Deal (Roosevelt administration) in 1933. It continues to be the most controversial type of PUBLIC REGULATION of business because of the danger of overcentralization of such regulation in the federal government, contrary to the federal principle of federal, state, and local government.

See NEW DEAL AGENCIES.

FEDERAL RESERVE ACT Created the FEDERAL RESERVE SYSTEM (38 Stat. 251, ch. 6), approved December 23, 1913, as the new Demo-cratic administration's "Christmas gift to the nation."

The text of the Federal Reserve Act, as amended through December, 1976, with an appendix containing the provisions of certain other statutes affecting the Federal Reserve System, is obtainable from the Board of Governors of the Federal Reserve System. Also available are regulations of the Board of Governors of the Federal Reserve System and published interpretations of the Board of Governors of the Federal Reserve System.

See BANKING ACT OF 1933, BANKING ACT OF 1935.

FEDERAL RESERVE ADVISORY COUNCIL *See* FEDERAL ADVISORY COUNCIL.

FEDERAL RESERVE AGENT The chairman of the board of directors of each Federal Reserve bank, who is also designated as Federal Reserve agent for the district in which the bank is located. He is one of the three Class C directors, all of whom are appointed by the Board of Governors of the Federal Reserve System, and is the official representative of the Federal Reserve Board of Governors with each Federal Reserve bank. His chief function as Federal Reserve agent is to receive applications for the issue of Federal Reserve notes and to secure the approval of the Federal Reserve Board of Governors for their ultimate issue. The collateral for Federal Reserve notes is held under his custody, and he is required to give bond to the Federal Reserve board for the faithful performance of his duties.

As chairmen of the Federal Reserve banks, Federal Reserve agents are organized into a Conference of Chairmen that meets from time to time to consider matters of common interest and to consult with and advise the Board of Governors of the Federal Reserve System.

FEDERAL RESERVE BANK Any one of the 12 Federal Reserve banks created under the FEDERAL RESERVE ACT and operating in one of the 12 FEDERAL RESERVE DISTRICTS. Federal Reserve banks are also known as "central," "reserve," and "regional" banks.

Section 4 of the Federal Reserve Act outlines the organization, corporate powers, and directorate of the Federal Reserve banks. The Banking Act of 1935 made an important organizational change.

Under the original act, the board of directors of the Federal Reserve bank had the power to appoint "such officers and employees as are not otherwise provided for in this act, to define their duties, require bonds for them and fix the penalty thereof, and to dismiss at pleasure such officers or employees." The designation of "governor," which Federal Reserve banks adopted for their chief executive officer, was not provided for in the act.

Under the Banking Act of 1935, and effective March 1, 1936, the board of directors of the Federal Reserve bank has the power to appoint a president, vice-presidents, and such officers and employees as are not otherwise provided for in the act, to define their duties, require bonds for them and fix the penalty thereof, and to dismiss at pleasure such officers or employees. The title "governor" is reserved for members of the Board of Governors of the Federal Reserve System. The president of the bank shall be the chief executive officer of the bank and shall be appointed by the board of directors, with the approval of the Board of Governors of the Federal Reserve System, for a term of five years. The first vice-president of the bank shall be appointed in the same manner and for the same term as the president and in the absence or disability of the president, or during a vacancy in the office of president, shall serve as chief executive officer of the bank. No change was made in the number, classes, or qualifications of the board of directors.

See FEDERAL RESERVE CITIES, FEDERAL RESERVE SYSTEM.

FEDERAL RESERVE BANK ACCOUNT An account which every member bank and clearing member bank is required to maintain with the Federal Reserve bank of its district. This account represents the cash balance due from the Federal Reserve bank and for member banks must be sufficient in amount to provide for legal reserve against deposits.

See BANK RESERVE, LEGAL RESERVES, RESERVE.

FEDERAL RESERVE BANK COLLECTIONS ACCOUNT An account appearing in the general ledger and financial statement of a bank which represents the amount of out-of-town checks sent for collection through the FEDERAL RESERVE CHECK COLLECTION SYSTEM that are in the process of collection and not yet available as reserve. It also represents the total of the balances in the Federal Reserve collection ledger in the transit department. When checks sent for collection in this manner become available, they are added to the Federal Reserve bank account and subtracted from the Federal Reserve bank collections account.

FEDERAL RESERVE BANK EARNINGS Federal Reserve banks are not operated primarily for profit, the profit motive being secondary to the proper exercise of monetary policy.

Division of earnings of Federal Reserve banks is specified by Section 7 of the Federal Reserve Act. Under the original act, Federal Reserve banks were allowed to retain one-half of surplus earnings until surplus was built up to 50% of the paid-in capital. In 1919, this was amended to provide for retention of surplus earnings to build up surplus of 100% of the subscribed capital (which would be 200% of actually paid-in capital); once surplus reached that level, disposition of surplus earnings was to be 90% to the government as a franchise tax and 10% to be retained in surplus.

Section 7 of the act governing disposition of earnings, enacted by Section 4 of the Banking Act of 1933, approved June 16, 1933, provides that after all necessary expenses and 6% cumulative dividend on the paid-in capital stock, the net earnings shall all be retained in surplus of the Federal Reserve banks.

In connection, however, with establishment of the Federal Deposit Insurance Corporation, each Federal Reserve bank was required by the Banking Act of 1933 to pay one-half of its surplus on January 1, 1933, as subscription to the capital stock of the Federal Deposit Insurance Corporation. By the close of 1932, the Federal Reserve banks had accumulated surplus of $278 million, compared with subscribed capital of $302 million. Subscriptions to the FDIC amounted to $139 million, therefore, and reduced surplus to $139 million, well below the subscribed capital. Thus, elimination of the franchise tax by the Banking Act of 1933 was designed to allow the Federal Reserve banks to rebuild their surplus accounts, which in view of the lean earnings at the time appeared to be a slow process. By the close of 1944, surplus accounts had been built up to less than 75% of subscribed capital.

For 1945 and 1946, open market operations of the system resulted in substantial additions to earning assets of Federal Reserve banks,

ENCYCLOPEDIA OF BANKING AND FINANCE

FEDERAL RESERVE BANK EARNINGS

Income and Expenses of Federal Reserve Banks, 1914-87
(Dollars)

Period, or Federal Reserve Bank	Current income	Net expenses	Net additions or deductions (−)	Assessments by Board of Governors — Board expenditures	Costs of currency
1970	3,877,218,444	276,571,876	11,441,829	21,227,800	23,573,710
1971	3,723,369,921	319,608,270	94,266,075	32,634,002	24,942,528
1972	3,792,334,523	347,917,112	(49,615,790)	35,234,499	31,454,740
1973	5,016,769,328	416,879,377	(80,653,488)	44,411,700	33,826,299
1974	6,280,090,965	476,234,586	(78,487,237)	41,116,600	30,190,288
1975	6,257,936,784	514,358,633	(202,369,615)	33,577,201	37,130,081
1976	6,623,220,383	558,128,811	7,310,500	41,827,700	48,819,453
1977	6,891,317,498	568,851,419	(177,033,463)	47,366,100	55,008,163
1978	8,455,390,401	592,557,841	(633,123,486)	53,321,700	60,059,365
1979	10,310,148,406	625,168,261	(151,148,220)	50,529,700	68,391,270
1980	12,802,319,335	718,032,836	(115,385,855)	62,230,800	73,124,423
1981	15,508,349,653	814,190,392	(372,879,185)	63,162,700	82,924,013
1982	16,517,385,129	926,033,957	(68,833,150)	61,813,400	98,441,027
1983	16,068,362,117	1,023,678,474	(400,365,922)	71,551,000	152,135,488
1984	18,068,820,742	1,102,444,454	(412,943,156)	82,115,700	162,606,410
1985	18,131,982,786	1,127,744,490	1,301,624,294	77,377,700	173,738,745
1986	17,464,528,361	1,156,867,714	1,975,893,356	97,337,500	180,779,673
1987	17,633,011,623	1,146,910,699	1,796,593,917 [2]	81,869,800	170,674,979
Total, 1914-87	218,984,053,284	16,535,876,088	2,516,133,525	1,186,604,208	1,803,266,357
Aggregate for each Bank, 1914-87					
Boston	10,848,879,304	1,090,535,395	72,101,026	42,930,786	105,229,233
New York	62,995,337,192	3,359,021,096	666,841,844	306,465,986	438,485,583
Philadelphia	9,265,221,643	873,121,912	112,696,756	58,146,218	86,154,009
Cleveland	15,166,380,180	1,121,951,990	95,960,801	93,502,590	114,293,705
Richmond	17,275,843,408	1,293,376,966	121,317,542	61,444,776	172,331,506
Atlanta	8,964,178,239	1,403,345,106	228,582,698	87,321,760	113,863,060
Chicago	32,269,158,745	2,175,707,020	292,710,361	169,599,672	251,920,841
St. Louis	7,613,054,013	889,177,640	60,001,912	37,308,072	69,851,972
Minneapolis	4,000,971,259	750,880,296	83,389,153	35,230,315	31,957,029
Kansas City	9,598,113,136	1,040,095,559	108,909,533	50,878,009	88,484,537
Dallas	12,505,804,676	929,860,216	254,088,197	75,535,473	107,121,445
San Francisco	28,481,111,490	1,658,005,380	419,533,698	168,240,551	223,573,437
Total	218,984,053,284	16,535,876,088	2,516,133,525	1,186,604,208	1,803,266,357

[1] Details may not add to totals because of rounding.
[2] For 1987 and subsequent years, includes the cost of services provided to the Treasury by Federal Reserve Banks for which reimbursement was not received.
[3] The $2,175,758,899 transferred to surplus was reduced by direct charges of $500,000 for charge-off on Bank premises (1927), $139,299,557 for contributions to capital of the Federal Deposit Insurance Corporation (1934), and $3,657 net upon elimination of sec. 13b surplus (1958); and was increased by transfer of $11,131,013 from reserves for contingencies (1945), leaving a balance of $2,047,086,698 on Dec. 31, 1987.

principally in government securities. By the close of 1946, surplus of Federal Reserve banks totaled over $439 million, compared with subscribed capital of $373 million, and each Federal Reserve bank reported surplus at least equal to subscribed capital. Surplus earnings for 1947 were estimated at $60 million. Accordingly, the Board of Governors of the FEDERAL RESERVE SYSTEM decided to invoke the authority, under Section 16 of the Federal Reserve Act, to levy an interest charge on Federal Reserve notes issued by the Federal Reserve banks. This was the first time that this interest charge on Federal Reserve notes had been invoked, which is levied on the amount of the outstanding notes less the amount of gold certificates or gold certificate credits held by the Federal Reserve agent as collateral security. The board of governors established such rates of interest as made it possible to pay to the Treasury approximately 90% of the net earnings after dividends of Federal Reserve banks. Invoking this authority to charge Federal Reserve notes, the board of governors pointed out, had the same effect as the eliminated franchise tax.

In addition, the board of governors proposed that Congress authorize the repayment of $139 million of capital furnished by the Federal Reserve banks to the FDIC into the Treasury rather than back to the Federal Reserve banks, when the FDIC canceled its capital stock. Accordingly, when the act of August 5, 1947, provided for payment and cancellation of the capital stock of the Federal Deposit Insurance Corporation, the portion of the capital stock subscribed to by the Federal Reserve banks was all paid into the Treasury, along with the Treasury's own original subscription.

1959 Change. This procedure of payment to the Treasury of approximately 90% of the net earnings of Federal Reserve banks, after dividends and after such provisions as might be necessary to bring surplus up to subscribed capital, began in 1947 and continued through 1958.

In 1959, net earnings of the Federal Reserve banks, before dividends and before payments to the U.S. Treasury, amounted to $840 million. Statutory dividends to member banks amounted to $23 million. Payments to the U.S. Treasury, however, as interest on Federal Reserve notes amounted to $911 million in 1959. These payments consisted of (1) all net earnings ($815 million), after the dividends of $23 million and after provision of $2 million for raising surplus to the level of subscribed capital at the two banks where surplus was below that amount; and (2) the amount (totaling $96 million) by which the surplus at the other ten banks exceeded subscribed capital.

Income and Expenses of Federal Reserve Banks, 1914-87 (continued)

Dividends paid	Payments to U.S. Treasury — Franchise tax	Payments to U.S. Treasury — Undersection 13b	Interest on Federal Reserve notes	Transferred to surplus (section 13b)	Transferred to (section 7)
41,136,551	...	...	3,493,570,636	...	32,579,700
43,488,074	...	...	3,356,559,873	...	40,403,250
46,183,719	...	...	3,231,267,663	...	50,661,000
49,139,682	...	...	4,340,680,482	...	51,178,300
52,579,643	...	...	5,549,999,411	...	51,483,200
54,609,555	...	...	5,382,064,098	...	33,827,600
57,351,487	...	...	5,870,463,382	...	53,940,050
60,182,278	...	...	5,937,148,425	...	45,727,650
63,280,312	...	...	7,005,779,497	...	47,268,200
67,193,615	...	...	9,278,576,140	...	69,141,200
				...	
70,354,516	...	...	11,706,369,955	...	56,820,950
74,573,806	...	...	14,023,722,907	...	76,896,650
79,352,304	...	...	15,204,590,947	...	78,320,350
85,151,835	...	...	14,228,816,297	...	106,663,100
92,620,451	...	...	16,054,094,674	...	161,995,900
103,028,905	...	...	17,796,464,292	...	155,252,950
109,587,968	...	...	17,803,894,710	...	91,954,150
117,499,115	...	...	17,738,879,542	...	173,771,400
2,034,414,472	149,138,300	2,188,893	197,612,943,251	(3,657)	2,175,758,899 [3]
84,619,472	7,111,395	280,843	9,511,775,570	135,411	78,362,225
552,984,048	68,006,262	369,116	58,408,180,374	(433,412)	578,302,471
110,896,688	5,558,901	722,406	8,131,451,583	290,661	111,576,022
168,965,677	4,842,447	82,930	13,632,784,356	(9,906)	125,927,193
101,792,775	6,200,189	172,493	15,642,114,052	(71,517)	119,799,708
136,084,434	8,950,561	79,264	7,257,055,223	5,491	186,056,040
282,238,913	25,313,526	151,045	29,380,294,602	11,682	276,631,804
65,237,538	2,755,629	7,464	6,545,604,652	(26,515)	63,139,478
56,820,217	5,202,900	55,615	3,137,667,303	64,874	66,481,863
84,874,737	6,939,100	64,213	8,346,753,737	(8,674)	88,941,450
121,480,077	560,049	102,083	11,345,575,961	55,337	179,602,228
268,419,895	7,697,341	101,421	26,273,685,838	(17,089)	300,938,417
2,034,414,472	149,138,300	2,188,893	197,612,943,251	(3,657)	2,175,758,899

These 1959 payments to the Treasury reflect a conclusion reached by the board of governors, after consultation with the Federal Reserve banks, that the maintenance of surplus at the level of subscribed capital (which is twice the paid-in capital) would be appropriate in the light of present circumstances. The surplus accounts of the Federal Reserve banks had been building up substantially over the years and at a number of the banks already exceeded subscribed capital by substantial amounts. It was therefore decided to discontinue the practice followed in the years 1947-1958 of adding 10% of the annual net earnings of the Federal Reserve banks to the surplus accounts and to pay to the Treasury the amounts by which the surplus accounts exceeded the level of subscribed capital.

The appended table summarizes the earnings, expenses, net earnings, dividends and other disposition of surplus earnings of Federal Reserve banks since 1914.

FEDERAL RESERVE BANK NOTES Circulating notes issued by the various Federal Reserve banks under approximately the same conditions as NATIONAL BANK NOTES issued by national banks. Federal Reserve Bank notes were expected to replace national bank notes eventually, but like national bank notes are now in process of retirement.

Authority for the issuance of Federal Reserve Bank notes against any direct obligations of the United States not bearing the circulation privilege or against eligible commercial paper was repealed by the act of June 12, 1945. No interest-bearing government securities bearing the circulation privilege have been outstanding since August 1, 1935. Lawful money has been deposited for the retirement of Federal Reserve Bank notes, and thus they are being retired from circulation as soon as returned to the Treasury unfit for use.

Originally authorized in the Federal Reserve Act, Federal Reserve Bank notes were issued in small amounts in 1916 and 1917; in 1918-1920, about $250 million were issued in accordance with the PITTMAN ACT. The next large issuance occurred in the banking crisis of 1933, when it was feared that the shortage of collateral for Federal Reserve notes might create an inadequate circulation. Only about $200 million, however, of Federal Reserve Bank notes were actually issued, so that in 1942, in order to utilize the unissued stock of about $660 million of printed Federal Reserve Bank notes, the board of governors authorized the Federal Reserve banks to issue them concurrently with deposit credits to the Treasurer of the United States for equal amount, thus canceling the liability of the Federal Reserve banks for the issued Federal Reserve Bank notes.

See MONEY, UNITED STATES MONEY.

FEDERAL RESERVE BANK STATEMENT See EXCESS RESERVES, FEDERAL RESERVE STATEMENT.

FEDERAL RESERVE BANK STOCK See FEDERAL RESERVE SYSTEM.

FEDERAL RESERVE BOARD OF GOVERNORS The body upon whom the general supervision and coordination of the FEDERAL RESERVE SYSTEM rests. Designated as the board of governors since the Banking Act of 1935, it was known prior thereto as the Federal Reserve Board.

In accordance with Section 10 of the Federal Reserve Act, as amended by the Banking Act of 1935, the board of governors consists of seven members, appointed by the President of the United States, with the advice and consent of the Senate, for a term of 14 years, so rotated as to provide for the expiration of the term of not more than one member in any 2-year period. The Banking Act of 1935 eliminated the Comptroller of the Currency and the secretary of the Treasury as ex-officio members. One of the members appointed shall be designated by the President as chairman and one as vice-chairman of the board, to serve as such for a term of 4 years. Since the Banking Act of 1935, each member of the board shall not be eligible for reappointment after he shall have served a full term of 14 years. Not more than one of the members of the board shall be selected from any one Federal Reserve district. In selecting the members of the board, each of whom shall devote his entire time to the business of the board, the President shall have due regard to a fair representation of the financial, agricultural, industrial, and commercial interests, and geographical divisions of the country, and he may remove any member for cause.

To further ensure the independence of the board, no member may be an officer or director of any banking institution or hold stock in any such institution. Before entering into his duties as a member of the board, each appointee must certify under oath that he has complied with this requirement. Members of the board shall be ineligible during the time they are in office and for two years thereafter to hold any office, position, or employment in any member bank, except that this restriction shall not apply to a member who has served the full term for which he was appointed.

People who served as Chairmen of the Board of Governors of the Federal Reserve System from 1913 are shown in the appended table.

Organization of the board of governors includes six offices (Office of Board Members, Office of Staff Director for Monetary and Financial Policy, Office of Staff Director for Federal Reserve Bank Activities, Office of Staff Director for Management, Office of the Secretary, and Office of the Controller) and nine divisions (Legal, Research and Statistics, International Finance, Federal Reserve Bank Operations, Banking Supervision and Regulation, Consumer and Community Affairs, Data Processing, Personnel, and Support Services).

Official description of functions of most of the preceding organizational units follows.

The Office of Board Members consists of the members of the board, assistants, and special assistants to the board assigned to public affairs and congressional liaison.

Chairmen of the Board of Governors of the Federal Reserve System, 1913 to date

Name	Term
Chairmen[a]	
Charles S. Hamlin	Aug. 10, 1914-Aug. 9, 1916
W. P. G. Harding	Aug. 10, 1916-Aug. 9, 1922
Daniel R. Crissinger	May 1, 1923-Sept. 15, 1927
Roy A. Young	Oct. 4, 1927-Aug. 31, 1930
Eugene Meyer	Sept. 16, 1930-May 10, 1933
Eugene R. Black	May 19, 1933-Aug. 15, 1934
Marriner S. Eccles	Nov. 15, 1934-Jan. 31, 1948
Thomas B. McCabe	Apr. 15, 1948-Mar. 31, 1951
Wm. McC. Martin, Jr.	Apr. 2, 1951-Jan. 31,1978
G. William Miller	Mar. 8, 1978-Aug. 6, 1979
Paul A. Volker	Aug. 6, 1979-
Alan Greenspan	–

[a] Chairman and Vice Chairman were designated Governor and Vice Governor before Aug. 23, 1935

The Office of Staff Director for Monetary and Financial Policy is responsible for preparation of position papers and other documents on monetary policy issues, including issues relating to open market operations, discount, and reserve requirements policy; performance of secretarial functions for the Federal Open Market Committee; coordination of regulatory and statistical issues closely related to monetary policy; liaison with the trading desk at the Federal Reserve Bank of New York in connection with open market operations; liaison with Treasury or other agencies in the domestic financial area; coordination with the system account manager and with the U.S. Treasury on foreign exchange market operations; decision-making with regard to eurodollar and international banking policy issues; coordination of analysis and development of options for the board's consideration with regard to foreign exchange policies and the international payments mechanism; and appropriate staff coordination with other agencies in these areas. The office also reviews and coordinates statistical and regulatory reports required by the board of banks and bank holding companies and performs secretarial functions for the Depository Institutions Deregulation Committee.

The Office of Staff Director for Federal Reserve Bank Activities is responsible for overseeing the Division of Federal Reserve Bank Operations (see below), assisting the board's Committee on Federal Reserve Bank Activities, and coordinating the functions of other board divisions that relate to Federal Reserve Bank matters. The responsibilities of this office also include all Federal Reserve bank director matters, coordination of the annual evaluation program for Federal Reserve banks, the Federal Reserve System's emergency preparedness program, and representing the board in activities pertaining to bank operational matters in meetings with foreign central banks and other U.S. government agencies.

The Office of Staff Director for Management is responsible for the planning and coordination of staff operations and organization, resource management, and supervision of the following functions: board building administration and operations, board budget and accounting activities, data processing, personnel-related activities, equal employment opportunity matters, and contingency planning operations.

The Office of the Secretary, headed by the board's secretary, coordinates and handles items requiring board action, including actions under delegated authority; prepares the agenda for board meetings; implements actions taken at board meetings; prepares, circulates, and indexes minutes of the board; has responsibilities for the board's Regulatory Improvement Project; provides liaison at the staff level with the Federal Advisory Council and ad hoc groups of the Reserve banks; makes arrangements for individuals and groups visiting the board; maintains custody of and provides reference service to official records of the board; handles correspondence and public information requests; secures passports and visas for official foreign travel of system personnel; and provides relief secretarial and stenographic services.

Headed by the board's general counsel, the Legal Division advises the board in carrying out its statutory and regulatory responsibilities by the preparation of board decisions, regulations, rules, instructions, and legal interpretations of statutes and regulations administered by the board; represents the board in civil litigation and administrative proceedings; assists other divisions in fulfilling their responsibilities in such areas as contracting, fiscal agency activities, Federal Reserve bank matters, labor law, personnel, and supervisory enforcement matters; and prepares testimony or comments on proposed legislation.

Headed by a director, the Division of Research and Statistics provides the board and the Federal Open Market Committee with the economic analyses and information needed for current operations, for the formulation of monetary and credit policies, and for the exercise of responsibilities with regard to bank regulation; prepares, publishes, and interprets a variety of statistical series in the financial and nonfinancial fields; and conducts basic research relating to the effects of monetary policy on economic activity and prices and to the effects of financial regulation on the structure and functioning of financial markets.

Headed by a director, the Division of International Finance provides the board and the Federal Open Market Committee with information and economic analyses on international questions affecting U.S. monetary policy and the exercise of regulatory responsibilities; conducts research in these areas; provides staff work in connection with the supervision of foreign operations of the Federal

Reserve System, the membership of the chairman of the board on the National Advisory Council on International Monetary and Financial Policies, and the role of the chairman of the board as U.S. alternate governor to the International Monetary Fund.

Headed by a director, the Division of Federal Reserve Bank Operations advises and assists the board with respect to matters concerning the planning and programs for operations of the Federal Reserve banks. It provides an appraisal of Reserve bank building programs; provides analyses and recommendations for board policy in the payments mechanism areas; provides an appraisal of Reserve bank communication and automation plans and proposals; and maintains liaison with various interested parties on payments mechanism matters. The division is responsible for financial examinations and operational reviews of Federal Reserve bank functions including protection, fiscal agency, open market, check processing, data processing, communications, coin and currency, audit, and various staff functions. The division administers an expense control and budgeting system for collection and analysis of budget and expense data; prescribes accounting principles, standards, and related requirements to be followed by the Reserve banks; and provides certain centralized financial accounting services. The division also maintains liaison with the U.S. Treasury and other government agencies and with various interested parties on matters related to Reserve bank operation within its area of responsibility. The division also coordinates the printing and distribution of Federal Reserve notes and is jointly responsible with the Bureau of the Mint for the production and distribution of coin.

Headed by a director, the Division of Banking Supervision and Regulation coordinates the bank supervisory functions of the system and evaluates the examination procedures of the Reserve banks; exercises general supervision of the commercial and fiduciary activities of state member banks; administers the supervisory features of laws and regulations relating to affiliates and bank holding companies; supervises various foreign banking activities of member banks and foreign banking and financing corporations; administers the public disclosure provisions of the Securities Exchange Act of 1934, as amended, in their application to state member banks, and the provisions of that act giving responsibility to the board for regulating security credit transactions; administers the pertinent provisions of the Financial Institutions Supervisory Act of 1966 and amendments contained in the Financial Institutions Regulatory and Interest Rate Control Act of 1978 in their application to state member banks, bank holding companies, nonbank subsidiaries, Edge Act corporations, foreign banks with domestic operations, and persons related to such institutions; monitors the Currency and Foreign Transactions Reporting Act in its application to state member banks; processes and presents to the board applications filed pursuant to the Banking Holding Company Act of 1956, as amended, and the Bank Merger Act and various other applications submitted under the provisions of the Federal Reserve Act or related statutes; and advises the board regarding developments in banking and bank supervisory policies and procedures.

Headed by a director, the Division of Consumer and Community Affairs implements consumer affairs legislation for which the board has responsibility. Its functions include drafting regulations and interpretations pursuant to the Truth-in-Lending Act, as amended, the Federal Trade Commission Improvements Act, the Equal Credit Opportunity Act, as amended, the Home Mortgage Disclosure Act, the Fair Credit Billing Act, the Consumer Leasing Act, and the Electronic Funds Transfer Act for financial institutions and other firms engaged in consumer credit and leasing activities. The division also administers the board's consumer complaint handling system and monitors enforcement activities with regard to state member banks. The legislation enforced includes the acts mentioned above, as well as the Community Reinvestment, Fair Credit Reporting, Fair Debt Collection Practices, Fair Housing, Flood Disaster Protection, and Real Estate Settlement Procedures acts, and Regulation Q (the board's regulation on interest on deposits).

Headed by a director, the Division of Data Processing supports the board's organization through the development, operation, and maintenance of information processing systems. Activities include systems and mathematical statistical analysis, computer programming, equipment operation, data and production control, and advanced planning and implementation of computer systems and communication networks. The division develops, collects, and processes statistical information on banking developments and on the condition of Federal Reserve banks and member banks, and designs and produces graphics used in economic analysis and information presentation.

Delegations of Authority. The board does not delegate any of its functions relating to rule making or pertaining principally to monetary or credit policies or involving any questions of general policy. However, the board does delegate certain of its supervisory and other functions prescribed by statute or regulations of the board to its members or employees or to the Federal Reserve banks as provided in its *Rules Regarding Delegation of Authority* (12 CFR 265). In addition, the board delegates to the Federal Reserve banks certain functions not provided for by statute or regulations of the board, including the authority to extend the time within which certain transactions may be consummated.

Headquarters: The board sits at Washington, D.C., in its own headquarters building. Meetings are irregular, depending upon need for action. At meetings, the chairman shall preside, and in his absence the vice-chairman shall preside; in the absence of the chairman and the vice-chairman, the board shall elect a member to act as chairman pro tempore. The board has the power to levy semiannually upon the Federal Reserve banks, in proportion to their capital stock and surplus, assessments sufficient to pay its estimated expenses and the salaries of its members and employees. Funds derived from such assessments shall not be construed to be government funds or appropriated moneys.

The Monetary Control Act of 1980 brought all commercial banks under the Fed's prescription of reserve requirements, but reserve balances at district Federal Reserve banks still do not earn any return, although the average reserve requirements have been lowered. Moreover, reserve requirements have been made universal by the act—all depository institutions holding transactional deposits (checking accounts, NOW accounts, share draft accounts at credit unions, and other accounts defined to be transactional in purpose) and deposits in commercial or nonpersonal savings accounts also are subject to the reserve requirements.

The Fed has placed a variety of its services formerly provided free of charge to member banks on a fee basis to using depository institutions, pursuant to the act, which requires that "over the long run fees shall be established on the basis of all direct and indirect costs actually incurred in providing Federal Reserve services priced," taking into account imputed taxes and financing costs that would have been incurred had system services been provided by a private firm (e.g., for such major services as check processing and wire transfers). This suggests that private firms might enter into competition with the Fed in providing certain of such services.

The Monetary Control Act of 1980 also requires that the discount window be available at the Fed to all depository institutions besides member commercial banks, which places additional burdens upon the Fed's function of providing loans and advances, especially of the needy liquidity type for thrift institutions in critical need.

Finally, the rise of giant conglomerates in the financial services field, providing depository services as well as checking privileges in effective competition with banking institutions and beyond the direct control of the Fed, indicates that the era of "universal" monetary control by the Fed will require additional legislation if it is to be truly achieved.

Monetary Powers of the Board of Governors. The monetary instruments of control available to the Board of Governors of the Federal Reserve System may be summarized as follows:

1. *Power to influence credit conditions.* The board still has the power, within narrower limitations and in order to prevent injurious credit expansion or contraction, to change the legal reserve requirements to be maintained by depository institutions against deposits. Another even more important instrument of credit control is open market operations, administered by the Federal Open Market Committee which consists of the entire board of governors plus five additional voting members elected annually by the board of directors of Federal Reserve banks. The board of governors reviews and determines the discount rates charged by the Federal Reserve banks on their discounts and advances. For the purpose of preventing excessive use of credit for the purchase or carrying of securities on margin, the board is authorized to regulate the amount of credit that may be initially extended and subsequently maintained on any security, with specified exceptions (*see* MARGIN BUYING). In addition, the board of governors may exercise "moral suasion" as a general technique of credit control, i.e., direct pressure on

FEDERAL RESERVE BOARD REGULATIONS

member banks through examination emphases, general circular letters to member banks anent desired action, maintenance of credit standards, etc. The foregoing are the principal powers of the board whereby credit conditions (availability of credit, money rates) may be influenced. The board is directed by the act to keep complete record of the actions taken by the board and by the Federal Open Market Committee upon all questions of policy relating to open market operations and reasons therefor and votes taken in connection therewith and to include in the board's annual report to the Congress a full account of the actions so taken during the preceding year. Under the Federal Open Market Committee's new rules relating to the quicker availability of information to the public, the policy record for each meeting is released approximately one month following the date of the meeting and is subsequently published in the *Federal Reserve Bulletin* as well as in the board's annual report.

2. *Supervision of Federal Reserve banks.* The board is authorized to examine the Federal Reserve banks, to require statements and reports from such banks, to supervise the issuance and retirement of Federal Reserve notes, to require the establishment or discontinuance of branches of Federal Reserve banks, and to exercise supervision over all relationships and transactions of Federal Reserve banks with foreign banks or bankers. The board of governors reviews and follows the examination and supervisory activities of the Federal Reserve banks with a view to furthering coordination of policies and practices.

3. *Supervision of member banks.* The board has jurisdiction over the admission of state banks and trust companies to membership in the Federal Reserve System, the termination of membership of such banks, the establishment of branches by such banks (latter two functions delegated by the board of governors to the district Federal Reserve banks), and the approval of bank mergers and consolidations where the resulting institution will be a state member bank. It receives copies of condition reports submitted by member banks to the Federal Reserve banks. It has power to examine all member banks and the affiliates of member banks, and to require condition reports from them. Until passage of the Depository Institutions Deregulation and Monetary Control Act of 1980, it had the power to limit by regulation the rates of interest that could be paid by member banks on their time and savings deposits. It has authority to require periodic and other public disclosure of information with respect to an equity security of a member state bank having over $1 million in assets that is held by 500 or more persons. It establishes minimum standards with respect to the installation, maintenance, and operation of security devices and procedures by state member banks. It has authority to issue cease-and-desist orders in connection with violations of law or unsafe or unsound banking practices by member state banks and to remove directors or officers of such banks in certain circumstances; and it may, at its discretion, suspend member banks from the use of the credit facilities of the Federal Reserve System for making undue use of bank credit for speculative purposes or for any other purpose inconsistent with the maintenance of sound credit conditions.

The board may grant authority to member banks to establish branches in foreign countries or dependencies or insular possessions of the United States, to invest in the stocks of banks or corporations engaged in international or foreign banking, or to invest in foreign banks. It also charters, regulates, and supervises corporations that engage in foreign or international banking and financial activities.

The board is authorized to issue general regulations permitting interlocking relationships in certain circumstances between member banks and organizations dealing in securities or, under the Clayton Anti-Trust Act, between member banks and other banks.

4. *Other functions.* Under the Bank Holding Company Act of 1956, as amended in 1970, the board is required to pass upon certain acquisitions of bank stock or assets by bank holding companies and to make determinations relating to the retention of nonbank stock by bank holding companies. Under the President's program to reduce the deficit of the U.S. balance of payments, the board administered a foreign credit restraint program (terminated in January 1974) for the nation's privately owned financial institutions. As indicated above in the description of the divisions and offices of the board, the board of governors is charged with responsibilities under a number of acts pertaining to consumer protection, including the Truth-in-Lending Act.

Pursuant to the provisions of the Defense Production Act of 1950 and Executive Order 10480 of August 14, 1953, as amended, the board prescribes regulations under which the Federal Reserve banks act as fiscal agents of certain government departments and agencies in guaranteeing loans made by banks and other private financing institutions to finance contracts for the procurement of materials or services which the guaranteeing agencies consider necessary for the national defense.

Summary. The Board of Governors of the Federal Reserve System occupies the position of an independent agency, charged primarily with the responsibility for establishing and implementing monetary policy of the commercial banking system of the United States. Although created by and reporting to the Congress, it must necessarily coordinate with executive department agencies, especially the Treasury, so that monetary policy and fiscal policy may as far as possible be in agreement, and yet keep its independence from pressures from both the Congress and the executive in the interests of objective monetary policy. For a discussion of the efficacy of monetary policy in recent years and the monetarist and fiscalist points of view, *see* MONETARY POLICY.

See FEDERAL RESERVE BOARD REGULATIONS.

BIBLIOGRAPHY

COCHJEO, S. "From Regulated to Regulator." *ABA Banking Journal*, February, 1989.

DYKES, S. E., and WHITEHOUSE, M. A. "The Establishment and Evolution of the Federal Reserve Board: 1913-23." *Federal Reserve Bulletin*, April, 1989.

FEDERAL RESERVE BOARD OF GOVERNORS. *Annual Report*.

——. *Monetary Policy and Reserve Requirements*. Handbook.

FEDERAL RESERVE BOARD REGULATIONS The federal government regulates depository institutions that it charters, or which have obligations insured by it, through five federal agencies. These laws and regulations establish a framework for bank behavior that fosters the maintenance of a safe and sound banking system and the fair and efficient delivery of services to bank customers. The Board of Governors of the Federal Reserve System is empowered to set regulations to ensure the smooth functioning of the central bank and its relationships to financial institutions, commercial banks, bank holding companies and consumer credit. These regulations are the bylaws by which the Federal Reserve System fulfills Congressional policies, defined in various banking legislation since 1913, which have been assigned to the Federal Reserve System for enforcement.

Regulations of the Board of Governors of the Federal Reserve System are published in the Federal Register. In addition, they may be obtained, individually with amendments, from the Board. As of mid-year 1988, twenty-seven regulations were in effect. Interpretations of the regulations are published by the board in the Federal Reserve Bulletin and the Federal Register. Proposed regulations and amendments to existing regulations are circulated in these publications for comment prior to final promulgation.

Summaries of the various regulations follow. These regulations can be and have been amended. To obtain a copy of specific regulations, write to: Publication Service, Board of Governors of the Federal Reserve System, Washington, DC 20551.

Regulations	Subject
A, BB, I, J, N, V	Federal Reserve Banks
K, M, N	Foreign Banking
L, R	Interlocking directorates
F, H, O, P, Q, U	Other member bank requirements
B, C, E, M, Z, AA	Consumer protection
A, D, Q	Monetary policy
G, T, U, X	Securities credit
S	Financial privacy
Y	Bank holding companies
AA, B, BB, C, E, Z	Consumer lending

FEDERAL RESERVE BOARD REGULATIONS

Regulation A: **Loans to Depository Institutions.** Regulation A governs the discount and borrowing privileges of depository institutions. The Monetary Control Act of 1980 opened the discount facilities of the Federal Reserve System to any depository institution that maintains transactions accounts or nonpersonal time deposits. The regulation provides for lending under two basic programs: adjustment credit and extended credit.

Short-term adjustment credit is the primary type of Federal Reserve credit. This type of credit is offered to help borrowers meet short-term needs for funds when their usual sources are not reasonably available. Borrowing to take advantage of a favorable spread between the discount rate and other market rates is not permissible. Interest on adjustment credit will generally be charged at the basic discount rate. However, the Federal Reserve retains the right to impose a surcharge in addition to the basic rate. This surcharge may apply to all, or only selected, borrowers at the Federal Reserve's discretion.

Extended credit is designed to assist depository institutions meet longer-term needs for funds. This category includes seasonal credit regularly given to smaller institutions that lack ready access to national money markets. Under the seasonal credit program, advances are usually made at the basic discount rate, but as with adjustment credit, the Federal Reserve maintains the option to impose a surcharge.

Extended credit also includes assistance to individual depository institutions that experience special difficulties arising from exceptional circumstances and assistance to address liquidity strains affecting a broad range of depository institutions. Such credits are given if the assistance is in the public interest and the needed funds are not available from other sources. Surcharges are not normally applied to extended credit of this type and repayment schedules are usually more lenient than with seasonal credit.

Although the discount facilities of the Federal Reserve are not intended to supplant other reasonably available sources of funds, in unusual circumstances, emergency credit may be advanced to entities other than depository institutions where failure to obtain credit would adversely affect the economy. However such credit is only available after all other sources have been tapped, including other federal agencies.

Regulation AA: **Consumer Complaint Procedures.** Regulation AA provides for the investigation of alleged unfair or deceptive acts by state member banks, or an alleged violation of law or regulations, given the proper filing of a complaint. The regulation also prohibits a bank from including or enforcing any of the following provisions in a consumer credit obligation: a confession of judgment clause; a waiver of exemption; a certain type of wage assignment; and a nonpossessory, nonpurchase money security interest in household goods. In addition, the regulation prohibits pyramiding (a late charge practice) and provides protection for cosigners in consumer credit transactions.

Complaints received by the Board of Governors or a Federal Reserve Bank regarding an act or practice of an institution other than a state member bank will be forwarded to the federal agency having jurisdiction over that institution.

Regulation B: **Equal Credit Opportunity.** Regulation B prohibits discrimination in any credit transaction based on age, race, color, religion, national origin, sex, marital status, or receipt of income from public assistance programs. As a general rule, creditors may not ask the aforementioned characteristics of applicants, but exceptions apply in the case of residential mortgage applications. In addition, creditors may not discriminate from applicants who exercise their rights under the federal consumer credit laws. To facilitate compliance, model credit application forms are provided in the regulation.

The regulation also requires creditors to give applicants a written notice of rejection of an application, a statement of the applicant's rights under the Equal Credit Opportunity Act, and a statement either of the reasons for the rejection or the applicant's right to request the reasons. Creditors who furnish credit information, when reporting information on married borrowers, must report information in the names of each spouse.

To prevent discrimination, the Board of Governors of the Federal Reserve characterized Regulation B as imposing a delicate balance on the credit system, in recognition of the bank's need to know as much as possible about a prospective borrower and the borrower's right not to disclose information that is irrelevant to the transaction. The regulation deals with taking, evaluating, and acting on the application and with furnishing and maintaining credit information. Regulation B does *not* (the Fed's emphasis) prevent a creditor from determining any pertinent information necessary to evaluate the creditworthiness of an applicant.

Regulation BB: **Community Reinvestment.** Regulation BB requires state-chartered banks that are members of the Federal Reserve System to adopt a Community Reinvestment Act (CRA) statement for each local community served. The CRA is designed to encourage banks to help meet the credit needs of their communities. Under this regulation, each bank office must make available a statement for public inspection indicating, on a map, the communities served by that office and the type of credit the bank is prepared to extend within the community. The regulation contains the text of the notice that a bank is required to provide the public in all full-service domestic branches.

The regulation requires each bank to maintain a file of public comments relating to its CRA statement. The Federal Reserve Board, in examining a bank, must assess its record in meeting the credit needs of the entire community, including low- and moderate-income neighborhoods, and must take account of the record in considering certain bank applications.

Regulation C: **Home Mortgage Disclosure.** Regulation C requires banks to disclose mortgage lending information to verify if the housing credit needs of their communities are being met. The regulation carries out the Home Mortgage Disclosure Act of 1975, providing citizens and public officials with information to determine whether depository institutions are meeting the housing credit needs of their local communities.

The regulation applies to commercial banks, savings banks, savings and loan associations, building and loan associations, homestead associations, and credit unions that make federally related mortgage loans. Institutions with assets of $10 million or less and institutions that do not have an office in a metropolitan statistical area or a primary metropolitan statistical area are exempt. Institutions covered by the regulation must disclose, annually, the number and total dollar amount of residential mortgage loans originated or purchased during the most recent calendar year, itemized by census tract in which the property is located. Institutions complying with a similar state or municipal law or regulations which have adequate provision for enforcement may be exempted from this regulation.

Regulation D: **Reserve Requirements.** Regulation D defines the term deposit, specifies the amount of reserves that must be maintained against transaction accounts, establishes the method for computing reserve requirements, and imposes penalties for reserve deficiencies. The Depository Institutions and Monetary Control Act of 1980 contains major amendments to the Federal Reserve Act which affect, and simplify, Regulation D. The changes to this regulation were phased in over a period of eight years, affecting both member and nonmember banks.

Transaction accounts are defined to include checking accounts, NOW accounts, share draft accounts, savings accounts that allow automated transfers or third party payments by automated teller machines and accounts that permit more than a limited number of telephone or preauthorized payments or transfers each month. Reserves must be held equal to 3% of the first $25 million (adjusted annually since 1980 by an amount equal to .8 x percentage change in the level of deposits) and between 8% and 14%, currently 12%, of deposits above $25 million (similarly adjusted since 1980).

Time deposits are deposits or certificates with original maturities of at least 7 days, and savings accounts that allow the institution to require at least 7 days notice by the depositor before a withdrawal is made. Nonpersonal and transferable time deposits with a maturity of less than $1^1/_2$ years are subject to a 3% reserve requirement. Personal and nontransferable short-term time deposits, as well as all long-term (over $1^1/_2$ years) time deposits, possess 0% reserve requirements.

Exceptions to these requirements are frequent. In order to relieve small depository institutions from the burden of reserve requirements, each depository institution need not back the first $2 million (again, an adjusted figure since 1982) of its reservable liabilities. At the discretion of the Board of Governors, the reserve requirements may be temporarily raised for all depository institutions. Such supplemental reserves can only be imposed if essential for the conduct of monetary policy or the smooth working of the money markets. Also, the board may, under extraordinary circumstances, temporarily impose reserve requirements beyond the specified limits at specific institutions due to circumstances particular to that institution.

ENCYCLOPEDIA OF BANKING AND FINANCE

FEDERAL RESERVE BOARD REGULATIONS

Generally, reserves are maintained in the form of vault cash or a noninterest bearing balance held with a Federal Reserve Bank on a direct or indirect basis. Any bank maintaining full federal reserves will be permitted access to all Federal Reserve services. Furthermore, reserves may also be required on the deposit liabilities of foreign branches, subsidiaries and international banking facilities of both member and nonmember banks, but such reserve requirements are at the discretion of the board.

Regulation E: **Electronic Fund Transfers.** Regulation E establishes the rights, liabilities, and responsibilities of parties in electronic fund transfers (EFT) and protects consumers using EFT systems. The major provisions of Regulation E are separated into the consumer's right to know and the issuing institution's need to disclose certain information. For the consumer's protection, Regulation E prescribes rules for the solicitation and issuance of EFT cards and governs consumer's liability for unauthorized electronic fund transfers. With regard to the issuing institution's responsibilities, the regulations requires issuing institutions to disclose certain terms and conditions of EFT services and to provide for documentation of electronic transfers. The regulation also sets up a resolution procedure for errors on EFTs and covers notice of crediting and stoppage of preauthorized payments from a customer's account.

Regulation F: **Disclosure Requirements of Publicly Held Member Banks.** Regulation F requires state-chartered banks with more than 500 stockholders and over $1 million in assets or whose securities are registered on a national securities exchange to periodically file financial statements. Regulations issued by the Board of Governors in this area are substantially similar to those issued by the Securities and Exchange Commission. The Board of Governors states that the principal aim of this regulation is to ensure that investors have sufficient information to make informed investment decisions and intelligently exercise their voting rights as stockholders.

In general, state-chartered member banks must file registration statements, periodic financial statements, proxy statements, statements of election contests, and various other disclosures of interest to investors. Officers, directors, and principal stockholders must file reports on their holdings in the bank. The regulation also prohibits tender offers for the stock of a bank subject to the regulation unless certain information is simultaneously filed with the board.

Regulation G: **Margin Credit Extended by Parties Other than Banks, Brokers and Dealers.** Regulation G is one of four regulations regarding credit extended to finance securities transactions (see Regulations T, U and X). This regulation applies to lenders, other than brokers, dealers, and banks, who are required to register with the Board of Governors. Registration is required by any party who extends credit (secured directly or indirectly by margin stock) in an amount of $200,000 or more in a calendar quarter or who has outstanding credit in excess of $500,000. Once a lender is required to be registered, the regulation applies to all outstanding loans which are secured by margin stock. An exception to this general rule applies to lenders who extend credit via an eligible employee stock option plan which will be used to purchase margin stock of the employer.

Margin stock includes any equity security listed on or having unlisted trading privileges on a national stock exchange, any debt security convertible into such a security, most mutual funds, and any security included on the board's list of over-the-counter margin stocks.

Regulation H: **Membership Requirements for State-Chartered Banks.** Regulation H defines the eligibility requirements of a state bank that wishes to become a member of the Federal Reserve System. This regulation also describes membership privileges and conditions imposed on these banks, explains financial reporting requirements, and sets out procedures for requesting approval to establish branches and for requesting voluntary withdrawal from membership. State-chartered member banks are prohibited from engaging in practices that are unsafe or unsound or that result in violation of law, rule, or regulation. The regulation also imposes specific restrictions on the conduct of some banking practices such as the issuance of letters of credit, acceptances, and lending on the security of improved real estate.

To be eligible for membership, a state bank must possess capital stock and surplus that are considered adequate in relation to the character and condition of its assets and deposit liabilities, both present and future. A mutual savings bank's eligibility is determined by whether its surplus and undivided profits are equal to the capital requirements. The decision to become a member or to withdraw from membership has become less important since the Monetary Control Act of 1980 brought all depository institutions under the jurisdiction of the Board of Governors for the imposition of legal reserve requirements and has opened other Reserve System services to any depository institution that maintains transactions accounts or nonpersonal time deposits.

Regulation I: **Member Stock in Federal Reserve Banks.** Regulation I requires each bank joining the Federal Reserve System to subscribe to the stock of its District Reserve Bank in an amount equal to 6% of the member bank's capital and surplus. Half the total must be paid on approval, while the remainder is subject to call by the Board of Governors. A 6% dividend is paid on backed portions of Reserve Bank stock. The stock is not transferable and cannot be used as collateral. At all times, the 6% ratio of stock to capital must be maintained with all payments directed through the member bank's reserve account.

A member bank's ownership of Federal Reserve stock is subject to cancellation on discontinuance of operations, insolvency or voluntary liquidation, conversion to nonmember status through merger or acquisition, or voluntary or involuntary termination of membership.

Regulation J: **Check Collection and Funds Transfer.** Regulation J establishes procedures, duties, and responsibilities among Federal Reserve banks, the senders and payors of checks and other cash and noncash items, and the originators and recipients of transfers of funds. Regulation J provides a legal framework for depository institutions to collect checks and other cash items and to settle balances through the Federal Reserve System. It specifies terms and conditions under which Reserve banks will receive items for collection from and present items to depository institutions and establishes rules under which depository institutions return unpaid items. The regulation also specifies terms and conditions under which Reserve banks will receive and deliver transfers of funds from and to depository institutions. In accordance with this function, each Federal Reserve Bank shall issue an operating circular governing the details of its funds transfer operations and other matters deemed appropriate.

Regulation K: **International Banking Operations.** Regulation K governs the international banking activities of domestic banks and the domestic banking activities of foreign banks. Regulation K was promulgated in substantially its present form in June 1979. Prior to that date, overseas activities subject to board jurisdiction were covered in several separate regulations. However, the International Banking Act of 1978 provided the motivation for the consolidation of these regulations. The purpose of the current regulation is to grant Edge Act corporations powers sufficiently broad to enable them to compete with foreign banks in the United States as well as abroad and to provide all segments of the U.S. economy with a means of financing international trade, particularly exports.

The activities that may be engaged in overseas under Regulation K must generally be of a financial nature. Member banks' direct overseas investments in foreign companies are limited to foreign banks. Bank holding companies and Edge Act corporations, on the other hand, can directly invest in foreign companies engaged in certain nonbank activities, as well as in foreign banks. Member banks can only invest in foreign nonbank companies by doing so indirectly through Edge Act corporations. As to foreign bank operations in the United States, the regulation reflects limitations on interstate banking and specific exemptions from nonbanking prohibitions. With respect to loans by domestic banking organizations to foreign borrowers, the regulation provides for the establishment of special reserves against certain international rules for accounting for fees on international loans.

Regulation L: **Interlocking Bank Relationships.** Regulation L tries to ensure competition in the banking industry by restricting the interlocking relationships that a management official may have with other depository organizations. The regulation prohibits a management official of a state member bank or bank holding company from serving simultaneously as a management official of another depository organization if both organizations are not affiliated, or are very large, or are located in the same local area.

The regulation included a grandfather clause, providing a 10-year transition period which ended in 1988, for certain interlocks and provided exceptions for interlocks involving depository institutions in low-income or economically depressed areas, organizations owned by women or minority groups, newly chartered organizations, and organizations facing disruptive management loss or conditions endangering safety and soundness.

ENCYCLOPEDIA OF BANKING AND FINANCE

Regulation M: **Consumer Leasing.** Regulation M implements the consumer leasing provisions of the Truth in Lending Act. The purpose of this regulation is to assure that lessees of personal property are given meaningful disclosures of lease terms. The disclosures required under this act must be made before the consummation of the lease agreement. Property subject to this regulation includes personal property leased for personal, family or household use for a minimum of four months.

Regulation M requires leasing companies to disclose in writing the cost of a lease, including any security deposit, monthly payments, license, registration, taxes and maintenance fees and, in the case of an open end lease, whether a "balloon payment" may be applied. It also requires written disclosure of the terms of a lease, including insurance, guarantees, responsibility for servicing property, standards for wear and tear, and any option to buy.

Regulation N: **Relationships with Foreign Banks.** The purpose of Regulation N is to give the Board of Governors the responsibility for approving in advance any negotiations or agreements by Federal Reserve banks with foreign banks, bankers or governments. The regulation recognizes a Reserve Bank's authority to engage in foreign open market operations, however, Reserve banks must keep the Board fully advised of all foreign relationships, transactions and agreements.

Under the direction of the Federal Open Market Committee, a Reserve Bank maintaining accounts with a foreign bank may undertake negotiations, agreements, or contracts to facilitate open market transactions. The Board of Governors has reserved the right to be represented at any meeting concerning such negotiations and agreements, but in any case must be advised of such meetings. In addition, on a quarterly basis, Reserve banks must report to the Board on accounts they maintain with foreign banks.

Regulation O: **Loans to Executive Officers of Member Banks.** Regulation O prohibits member banks from extending credit to their own executive officers and prohibits insured banks that maintain correspondent accounts with each other from extending credit to one another's executive officers on preferential terms. In addition, banks whose officers, directors, or principal stockholders who have received preferential extensions of credit from other banks are prohibited from opening correspondent relationships with those banks.

Each executive officer and principal shareholder of an insured bank is to report annually, to the bank's board of directors, the amount of his indebtedness, and that of "related interests," to each of the insured bank's correspondent banks. The disclosure must include the terms and conditions of the loan. A "related interest" is a company managed by political or campaign committees controlled by or benefiting bank officials and shareholders

Each insured bank is required to include with its quarterly report of condition the aggregate extensions of credit by the bank to its executive officers and principal shareholders, together with the number of these individuals whose extensions of credit from the bank are 5% or more of the bank's equity capital or $500,000, whichever is less. Upon request, the names of such individuals must be publicly disclosed.

Regulation P: **Member Bank Protection Standards.** Regulation P sets minimum standards for security devices and procedures state member banks must establish to discourage robberies, burglaries, and larcenies and to assist in identifying and apprehending persons who commit such acts. A member bank must appoint a security officer to develop and administer a security program at least equal to the requirements of the regulation. The program must be in writing and approved by the bank's directors. Annually, each state-chartered member bank must certify its compliance with the regulation by filing a signed statement with its District Reserve Bank. The regulation also defines the prescribed penalties imposed each day a member bank is found in violation of security standards.

Regulation Q: **Interest of Deposits.** Regulation Q governs the payment of interest on deposits held by banks that are members of the Federal Reserve System as well as U.S. branches and offices of foreign banks. This regulation defines interest for purposes of regulation and deposit categories. In addition, regulation Q includes rules governing the advertising of deposits by member banks.

The Depository Institutions Deregulation Act of 1980 established the phaseout of interest rate ceiling on time and savings deposits which concluded in April 1987. The removal of interest rate ceilings is intended to enable all depositors, including holders of time and savings deposits, to receive a market rate of return on their deposits.

The authority of the Board of Governors to prescribe rules governing member banks' payment of interest and establishment of classes of deposits was transferred to the Depository Institutions Deregulation Committee in 1980.

Regulation R: **Interlocking Relationships Between Securities Dealers and Member Banks.** Regulation R aims at avoiding any potential conflict of interest, collusion or undue influence on member bank investment policies or investment advice to customers due to interlocking relationships between the personnel of securities dealers and member banks. This regulation restates the prohibition in the Glass-Steagall Act that prohibits individuals involved in various phases of securities activities from serving as a director, officer, or employee of a member bank.

While national banks may not underwrite securities, they may purchase investment securities for their own purposes as long as the total amount of these securities does not exceed 10% of their capital stock or unimpaired surplus fund. The regulation does provide an exemption for individuals in government securities transactions. These securities generally include those of the United States, the International Bank for Reconstruction and Development, the Tennessee Valley Authority, and the general obligations of states and municipalities. The aforementioned restrictions do not apply to any government obligation.

Regulation S: **Reimbursement for Providing Financial Records.** Regulation S prescribes the rates and conditions for reimbursement of necessary costs directly incurred by financial institutions in providing customer's financial records to government authorities. Regulation S implements a section of the Right to Financial Privacy Act requiring government authorities to pay a reasonable fee to financial institutions for providing financial records of individuals and small partnerships to federal agencies.

Cost of searching for, reproducing and transporting requested data is covered with certain exceptions. Search time accounts for the personnel costs of complying with the regulation and is paid on a set man/hour wage rate regardless of the actual wage of the employee conducting the search. Reproduction costs are also reimbursed on such a predetermined scale, although, actual transportation costs are returned.

Regulation T: **Margin Credit Extended by Brokers and Dealers.** Regulation T governs credit extensions, made in the course of business, by securities brokers and dealers, including all members of national securities exchanges. This is one of three regulations governing the extension of credit for securities. This one examines the broker-dealer relationship and assures that no preferential credit treatment is afforded brokers nor dealers. In general, such entities may not extend credit to their customers unless the loan is secured by "margin securities" nor may they arrange for credit to be extended by others on terms better than they themselves are permitted to extend.

The maximum credit that may be extended is set by the board as a percentage of the current market value of the securities. When securities on which credit has been extended are withdrawn from an account, cash or securities of an equivalent loan value must be deposited or a portion of the account liquidated so as to maintain the prescribed loan value of the account.

The regulation also prescribes rules governing cash transactions among brokers, dealers and their customers. It also limits the sources from which borrowing brokers and dealers may secure funds in the ordinary course of their business.

Regulation U: **Margin Credit Extended by Banks.** Regulation U is the third regulation governing margin credit. In this regulation, credit issued by banks for the purchasing or carrying of securities on margin is limited if the credit is secured directly or indirectly by stock. Any time a loan is made in which a margin stock serves as collateral, the bank must have the customer execute a purpose statement, Form U-1. If the purpose is to purchase or carry any margin stock, the loan is a purpose credit. Generally, if the purpose credit is stock-secured, it is subject to credit limitations and other restrictions of regulation. For example, the amount of the loan may not exceed the maximum loan value of the securing stock prescribed by the board.

Margin stocks include any equity security listed on or having unlisted trading privileges on a national security exchange, any debt security convertible into such a security, most mutual funds, and any security included on the board's list of over-the-counter margin stock.

FEDERAL RESERVE BOARD SETTLEMENT

Regulation V: **Guarantee on Loans for National Defense Work.** Regulation V facilitates and expedites the financing of contractors, subcontractors, and others involved in national defense work. In addition, this regulation sets forth the procedures and standards that Federal Reserve banks must observe in fulfilling their responsibilities as fiscal agents for those government departments and agencies authorized to guarantee loans for national defense purposes.

The regulation sets forth the maximum rate of interest, guarantee fees, and commitment fees that may be charged for a guaranteed loan. By adopting a maximum interest rate equal to the rate it charges its most creditworthy business customers, a financing institution will be able to adjust the interest rate to market conditions. Nevertheless, the guaranteeing agencies have discretionary authority to set the ceiling rate of interest. If the agency exercises this authority, it cannot discriminate among loan applicants in imposing a higher charge.

Regulation W (revoked): **Extensions of Consumer Credit.** Regulation W prescribed minimum downpayments, maximum maturities, and other terms applicable to extensions of consumer credit during World War II. Regulation W was revoked in 1952.

Regulation X: **Borrowers Who Obtain Margin Credit.** Regulation X extends the provisions of Regulations G, T and U to certain borrowers and to certain types of credit extensions not specifically covered by those regulations. Regulation X applies to borrowers who, for the purpose of purchasing or carrying securities, obtain credit in the United States and to borrowers who act on behalf of United States persons. This regulation requires that the subject borrowers obtaining credit within the U.S. comply with the margin credit regulation that applies, but if the credit is obtained outside the U.S., the subject borrowers must comply as if the foreign lender were subject to Regulation G, T, or U. In general, whenever the regulation applies, the borrower is responsible for ensuring that the credit conforms to one of the three margin regulations. The determination as to which one applies is dependent upon the nature of the lender and is specified in the regulation.

The following borrowers are exempt from the regulation and the controlling statue: (1) any borrower who obtains purpose credit within the United States unless the borrower willfully causes the credit to be extended in contravention of Regulation G, T, or U and (2) any borrower whose permanent residence is outside the United States who has obtained or has outstanding during any calendar year no more than $100,000 in purpose credit obtained outside the United States.

Regulation Y: **Bank Holding Companies.** Regulation Y relates to the bank and nonbank expansion of bank holding companies and to the divestiture of impermissible nonbank interests. Regulation Y also governs the acquisition of a bank by individuals. Any organization that owns a bank is a bank holding company and thus is subject to this regulation. However, unless an organization takes demand deposits and offers commercial loans it is not considered a bank and thus is not affected by this regulation. In the early 1980s, entry of nonbank banks was rampant as these businesses tried to avoid regulation.

The regulation contains the presumptions and procedures the board uses to determine whether a company controls a bank and is thus a bank holding company. The regulation also explains the procedures for obtaining board approval to become a bank holding company and procedures to be followed by bank holding companies acquiring voting shares of banks or nonbank companies. In addition, the board has specified in the regulation those nonbank activities that are closely related to banking and therefore permissible for bank holding companies. Foreign activities of domestic bank holding companies and permissible activities of foreign bank holding companies are dealt with separately within the regulation.

Regulation Z: **Truth in Lending.** Regulation Z prescribes uniform methods of computing the cost of credit, disclosure of credit terms, and procedures for resolving errors on certain credit accounts. Consumer credit is generally defined as credit offered or extended to individuals for personal, family, or household purposes, where the credit is repayable in more than four installments or for which a finance charge is imposed. The purpose of the Truth in Lending Act is to ensure that credit and leasing terms are disclosed so that customers are able to compare alternative terms intelligently.

The major provisions of the regulation require lenders to (1) provide borrowers with meaningful, written information on essential credit terms, including the cost of credit expressed as an annual percentage rate; (2) respond to consumer complaints of billing errors on certain credit accounts within a specific period; (3) identify credit transactions on periodic statements of open end credit accounts; (4) provide certain rights regarding credit cards; (5) informs consumers of the right to rescind certain credit transactions that are secured by a consumer's principal dwelling within a specified period; and (6) comply with special requirements when advertising credit.

BIBLIOGRAPHY

BOARD OF GOVERNORS OF THE FEDERAL RESERVE SYSTEM. *Federal Reserve Bulletin*.
———. *Federal Reserve Regulatory Service*.
———. *The Federal Reserve System: Purposes and Functions*.

FEDERAL RESERVE BOARD SETTLEMENT Settlement of balances arising among Federal Reserve banks as the result of interdistrict collections.
See INTERDISTRICT SETTLEMENT ACCOUNT.

FEDERAL RESERVE BRANCH BANKS Banks operating as branches of a Federal Reserve bank. The Federal Reserve Act authorizes Federal Reserve banks to establish branches, without limit as to number, under regulations approved by the Federal Reserve Board of Governors, but each branch must be within the boundaries of the Federal Reserve district of the Reserve bank which establishes it.

The appended table gives the locations of the branch offices.

For the boundaries of the Federal Reserve districts and the areas served by the branch banks, see the map under FEDERAL RESERVE SYSTEM.

FEDERAL RESERVE BULLETIN The official organ of the Board of Governors of the Federal Reserve System. It is issued monthly under the direction of the staff Editorial Committee, which is responsible for opinions expressed, except in official statements and signed articles. A copy of the *Federal Reserve Bulletin* is sent to each member bank without charge. Member banks desiring additional copies may secure them at a special annual rate.

FEDERAL RESERVE CHECK COLLECTION SYSTEM The Federal Reserve Act authorizes the Board of Governors of the Federal Reserve System to require each Federal Reserve bank to "exercise the functions of a clearing house for its member banks." Although the Federal Reserve System began operations in 1914, the check collection system was not established until July, 1916.

The purpose of the Federal Reserve check collection system was to correct the defects of the methods previously employed, and particularly the following abuses: (1) circuitous routing of checks which grew out of the efforts of banks to avoid exchange charges and which resulted in great delay in the presentation of items, (2) inequitable distribution of exchange charges between eastern metropolitan banks and rural banks, and (3) excessive exchange charges.

RCPCs. In 1971, the Federal Reserve's Board of Governors recommended establishing REGIONAL CHECK PROCESSING CENTERS (RCPCs) to help improve the nation's payments mechanism. The following

Location of Branch Federal Reserve Banks

District	Branches
1st District, Boston	None
2nd District, New York	Buffalo
3rd District, Philadelphia	None
4th District, Cleveland	Cincinnati, Pittsburgh
5th District, Richmond	Baltimore, Charlotte
6th District, Atlanta	Birmingham, Jacksonville, Miami, Nashville, New Orleans
7th District, Chicago	Detroit
8th District, St. Louis	Little Rock, Louisville, Memphis
9th District, Minneapolis	Helena
10th District, Kansas City	Denver, Oklahoma City, Omaha
11th District, Dallas	El Paso, Houston, San Antonio
12th District, San Francisco	Los Angeles, Portland, Salt Lake City, Seattle

year, the first center—the Baltimore-Washington RCPC of the Federal Reserve Bank of Richmond—became fully operational after a one-year pilot test.

RCPCs are operated by Federal Reserve banks to expedite check collection. The centers clear checks and sort them according to the depository institution upon which the checks are drawn. This complements regional clearing arrangements established by depository institutions in the same locality to exchange checks and settle net balances.

RCPCs serve depository institutions within areas not necessarily confined to Federal Reserve district or state lines. Since the function of the centers is to accelerate nationwide check collection, RCPC boundaries are determined by check flows.

RCPCs routinely receive checks drawn on participating institutions from various sources: other participating member banks, other RCPCs, Federal Reserve banks and their branches, and direct-sending member banks. A direct-sending member bank is one authorized by its Federal Reserve bank to send checks drawn on banks in other Federal Reserve districts directly to the appropriate Federal Reserve bank, branch, or RCPC. The direct-sending bank gets credit for those checks in its reserve account at its own Federal Reserve bank. See appended table.

As a result of the International Banking Act of 1978 and the DEPOSITORY INSTITUTIONS DEREGULATION AND MONETARY CONTROL ACT OF 1980, all depository institutions in the U.S., except for certain agencies, have been granted limited deposit access to local facilities. Depository institutions include member and nonmember commercial banks, savings banks, savings and loan associations, and credit unions.

Prior to the preceding two acts, RCPCs also accepted checks deposited by local participating banks that were not members of the Federal Reserve System, providing the checks were drawn on other banks in the same RCPC area.

Processing procedure: The primary objective of RCPCs is to collect checks overnight. To accomplish this, RCPCs sort, clear, and deliver checks rapidly by eliminating various handling stages.

Personal and corporate checks comprise the bulk of items deposited at RCPCs. These checks are generally delivered to the RCPC by private carriers hired by the participating banks. Other cash items deposited at RCPCs include checks drawn on the U.S. Treasury, postal money orders, and redeemed food coupons. These items are deposited by participating depository institutions. RCPCs do not handle cash or securities.

Finally, in addition to providing for speedy clearance, the processing of checks at an RCPC results in quicker identification of fraudulent and other invalid items.

Deferred Availability Items. When a member bank transmits out-of-town checks to a Federal Reserve bank to be collected from another member or clearing nonmember bank, the sending bank is immediately credited in the collection or float account of the Federal Reserve bank. That is to say, the amount of the checks so sent does not become available as reserve credit until the checks are credited as collected pursuant to the automatic timing provided by the SCHEDULE SHOWING WHEN PROCEEDS OF ITEMS WILL BECOME AVAILABLE (deferred availability schedule) of each Federal Reserve bank. In this schedule, the United States is divided geographically as to items payable at specified Federal Reserve bank or branch cities, and those payable at banks on the par list in localities outside of such bank or branch cities. One or two days (depending on the cities where the items are payable) after receipt, the deferred credit ripens automatically to credit to the reserve account of the member bank at its Federal Reserve bank. The same procedure applies to items received on out-of-town points forwarded by nonmember clearing banks, their account at the Federal Reserve Bank being a clearing account rather than reserve account.

Federal Reserve check routing symbol system: Expeditious collection of out-of-town checks, prepared in packages with accompanying listing of amounts of individual checks (cash letters), is aided by the check routing symbol system, a numerical code indicating basic information needed in collections which was developed by the Bank Management Commission of the American Bankers Association and the Committee on Collections of the Federal Reserve System. The routing symbol for Federal Reserve bank purposes is the denominator of a fraction, the numerator being the ABA TRANSIT NUMBER assigned to the drawee bank. The combined symbol is printed on the upper right-hand corner of checks in uniform type. The routing symbol (denominator of the fraction) is composed of not less than three nor more than four consecutive digits printed close together. The code value for handling of collections may be summarized as follows:

In the case of a three-digit routing symbol, the first digit indicates the particular Federal Reserve district. The digits run from 1 to 9 as follows:

Elements of the Check Clearing System

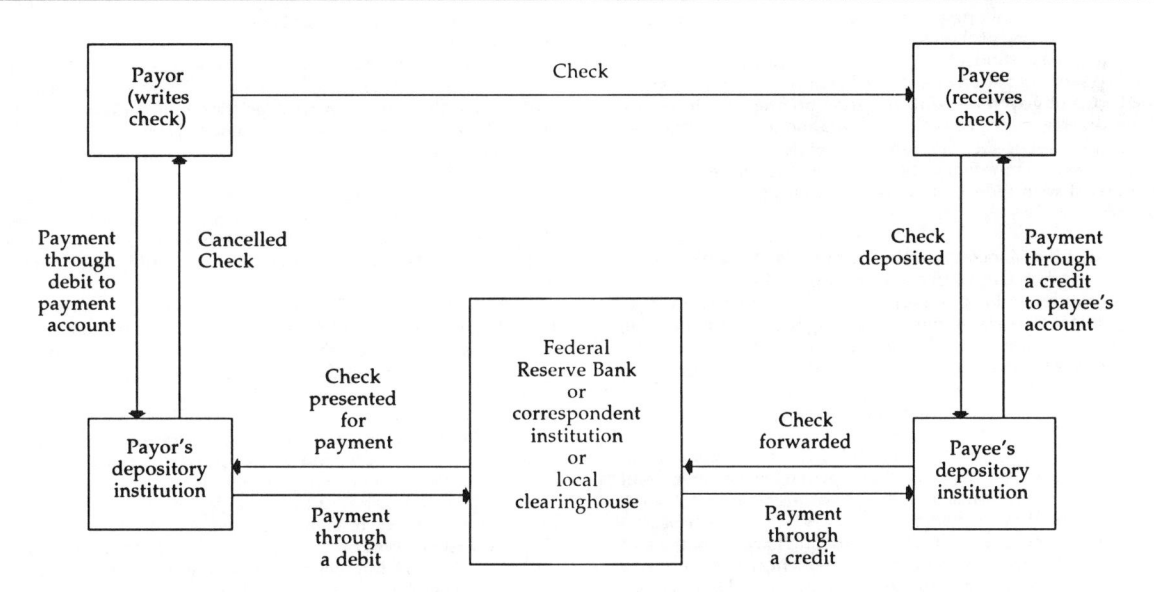

Transactions are settled at the Federal Reserve or a correspondent institution by crediting the deposit account of the payee's depository institution and debiting the deposit account of the payor's depository institution.

ENCYCLOPEDIA OF BANKING AND FINANCE

FEDERAL RESERVE CIRCULATION

Boston	1
New York	2
Philadelphia	3
Cleveland	4
Richmond	5
Atlanta	6
Chicago	7
St. Louis	8
Minneapolis	9

The second digit in a three-digit routing symbol indicates the head office of the Federal Reserve bank or of the branch serving the territory in which the drawee bank is located. Head office is indicated by the digit 1. Branches, if any, arranged alphabetically are indicated by the figures 2 to 5. Figures 6 to 9 are reserved to indicate special collection arrangements.

The third digit in a three-digit routing symbol indicates whether the item is receivable for immediate credit or for deferred credit without regard to the standard days of deferred availability, and the state in which the drawee bank is located. The figure 0 indicates items receivable for immediate credit, if received in time to be cleared the current day. All other figures, 1 to 9, indicate items receivable for deferred credit and also designate the state (arranged alphabetically) in which the drawee bank is located, parts of states, or certain cities.

The 1988 Expedited Funds Availability Act sets forth schedules within which depository institutions must make funds deposited in customer transaction accounts available for withdrawal and requires institutions to disclose to their customers their policies on such availability. In December 1988 the board issued for public comment a series of proposals to implement the act, including ways to improve the return of unpaid checks to the bank of first deposit.

Currently, the Federal Reserve does not explicitly price returned checks; instead, the costs of handling returns are incorporated in the Reserve banks' forward collection fees. The board proposed to price returns explicitly, imposing fees for returned checks on the paying or the returning checks that deposits returns with the Federal Reserve.

Legislative history of the referenced act indicated, according to the Fed, that Congress had two objectives in establishing the requirement that the Federal Reserve price the services it provides:

1. To encourage competition in order to assure provision of the services at the lowest cost. While intending to stimulate competition, Congress did not desire to precipitate the reemergence of undesirable banking practices, such as nonpar banking or circuitous routing of checks, which the Federal Reserve System was designed to eliminate. Also, it desired to ensure an adequate level of services nationwide. Consequently, Congress charged the board of governors with adopting pricing principles that "give due regard to competitive factors and the provision of an adequate level of such services nationwide."
2. To generate revenue that would partially offset the revenue loss associated with reduced required reserves also mandated by the act.

As a result of the Monetary Control Act of 1980, Federal Reserve banks' services covered by the fee schedules, including currency and coin transportation and coin wrapping, check clearing and collection, wire transfer of funds, automated clearinghouse, net settlement, securities services, noncash collection, Federal Reserve float, and any new services that the Federal Reserve System offers, are made available to all depository institutions.

The Federal Reserve began charging explicit fees for services in 1981, including those for check clearing and collection. All such services are priced at the same fee schedule for nonmember depository institutions as for member banks, except that nonmembers shall be subject to any other terms, including a requirement that reserve balances maintained in the district Federal Reserve banks or passed through correspondents be sufficient in size for charging of the fees for services in addition to covering the requirement against deposits.

If reserve balances are small or nonexistent, it may be necessary for the institution to maintain a clearing balance in order to directly obtain Fed services. Clearing balances will accrue earnings credits to offset costs of Federal Reserve services, such earnings credits to be based on the three-month Treasury bills rate but usable only to offset the cost of Reserve bank services. Thus explicit interest is not earned.

Unused earnings credits may be applied up to 12 months after a given maintenance period. Clearing balance deficiencies, however, are subject to the same penalty as reserve deficiencies.

Par and Nonpar Banks. Member banks and nonmember banks clearing through the Federal Reserve banks must agree to remit collection items at par. Charges made by remitting collection items at less than par have been termed *exchange charges*. The annual report for 1980 of the Board of Governors of the Federal Reserve System reported that there were no nonpar banking offices as of December 31, 1980.

It should be noted that neither the Federal Reserve Act, as amended, nor CLEARINGHOUSE rules prohibit depository institutions from charging service fees (which are customary in properly costed accounts and are termed *collection charges*) to customers placing items for collection.

See AUTOMATION, FEDERAL RESERVE INTERDISTRICT COLLECTION SYSTEM, INTERDISTRICT SETTLEMENT ACCOUNT.

FEDERAL RESERVE CIRCULATION See FEDERAL RESERVE NOTES.

FEDERAL RESERVE CITIES The cities in which the 12 Federal Reserve banks are located. Each Federal Reserve bank has a number corresponding to the district in which it operates. The 12 Federal Reserve cities, together with the districts in which they are located, are

1. Boston
2. New York
3. Philadelphia
4. Cleveland
5. Richmond
6. Atlanta
7. Chicago
8. St. Louis
9. Minneapolis
10. Kansas City
11. Dallas
12. San Francisco

See FEDERAL RESERVE BRANCH BANKS, FEDERAL RESERVE DISTRICTS.

FEDERAL RESERVE COMMUNICATIONS SYSTEM FOR THE EIGHTIES A general-purpose data communications network consolidating the functions of previous separate communications networks into a single system capable of accommodating present and future needs. On June 28, 1982, the Federal Reserve System began operations of its new Federal Reserve Communications System for the Eighties, also known as FRCS-80. This system, which had been in the development stage for a number of years, replaces the Fedwire network which was used throughout the previous decade. The Federal Reserve Bank of Dallas describes the FRCS-80 as follows.

The FRCS-80 functions with a minimum capacity of three times the Fed's 1980 peak hour demand and can handle the Federal Reserve's internal communications requirements as well as its communication of statistical data to the Treasury and other government agencies.

In addition, the FRCS-80 will meet the Fed's requirements for providing services to on-line financial institutions, especially those services associated with the anticipated increased volume of electronic payments during the next decade. In 1981, for example, the Federal Reserve completed over 50 million funds transfers with a dollar value of almost $100 trillion. The FRCS-80 is also used to process other services, such as securities transfers and automated clearinghouse messages, and will improve the reliability and efficiency of these types of communications.

The FRCS-80 does not utilize a single central switching site such as the former switch in Culpeper, Virginia, used for the previous network. Instead, the computer power of the FRCS-80 is distributed initially among 14 interconnected communications processors, or nodes. These nodes are now located at the 12 Federal Reserve bank head offices, at the Treasury in Washington, and at Culpeper. Each node can read a message's destination and send it in the proper direction so that a message will travel through no more than two nodes in moving from one Fed to another. The Culpeper site has been transformed into the network management center for the new

ENCYCLOPEDIA OF BANKING AND FINANCE

system. Future expansion of the system and additional nodes are possible.

The FRCS-80 incorporates a new technology known as multipath packet-switching. Packet-switching describes the way in which messages are broken down into small sets of data, or packets, and are then combined with other message fragments in transit in order to maximize the efficiency of transmissions through communications lines. The messages are reassembled into their original form at the receiving point.

Institutions which were on-line with the former network are automatically connected with the new system and do not notice any operational changes resulting from the implementation. The Dallas Fed was offering as of 1982 three levels of on-line service to financial institutions through its Response network, ranging from personal computers linked with the system through telephone communications lines to direct computer-to-computer links with the Fed's system.

FEDERAL RESERVE CREDIT Total volume of Federal Reserve credit outstanding is the supply which the Federal Reserve banks have contributed to member bank reserves and consists principally of earning assets of the Federal Reserve banks: (1) bills discounted, (2) bills bought, either outright or on repurchase agreement, (3) advances to member banks, (4) discounts for member banks, (5) holdings of U.S. government securities, either outright or under repurchase agreements, and (6) all other Federal Reserve bank credit. Included in the miscellaneous forms of Federal Reserve banks' credit is the float, or the difference between items at Federal Reserve banks in process of collection and the total of deferred availability credits, such difference representing credits to accounts of clearing member and nonmember banks before charge to drawee banks upon actual collection.

Also included in the miscellaneous forms of Federal Reserve credit is the catch-all classification "other Federal Reserve assets," which in recent years includes an important international item, holdings of foreign currencies, reflecting swap foreign exchange arrangements with foreign central banks and other operations in foreign exchange, International Monetary Fund gold deposits, as well as Federal Reserve banks' investments in bank premises and other assets.

Such "other Federal Reserve assets" are now reported gross, instead of net after deduction of capital accounts (capital paid in, surplus, and other capital accounts), other liabilities, and accrued dividends. The total of these latter items is now shown gross by itself as "other Federal Reserve liabilities and capital," representing a use instead of a source of member bank reserves.

Federal Reserve credit is the medium through which the Federal Reserve System affects the volume of member bank reserve balances; an increase therein increases member bank reserve balances, a decrease reduces them. For fuller discussion of the factors affecting supply and use of member bank reserves, see EXCESS RESERVES.

FEDERAL RESERVE DISTRICTS The boundaries of the 12 Federal Reserve districts and the location of the Federal Reserve banks and branches, are shown in the map under FEDERAL RESERVE SYSTEM.

FEDERAL RESERVE INTERDISTRICT COLLECTION SYSTEM Out-of-town items may be collected within the same or in another Federal Reserve district through Federal Reserve banks. The former are known as intradistrict collections; the latter, as interdistrict collections. In intradistrict collections, the Federal Reserve bank or branch expeditiously clears such items, pursuant to the deferred availability schedules, by simply adjusting the reserve balances of the member banks and clearing accounts of the nonmember banks concerned. In interdistrict collections, inter-Federal Reserve bank accounting is involved.

For example, suppose a member bank in New York City forwards checks to the Federal Reserve Bank of New York drawn upon banks in Chicago. The New York Federal Reserve Bank forwards them to the Chicago Federal Reserve Bank, which collects them through the Chicago clearinghouse. Between the two Federal Reserve banks, a credit in favor of the New York Federal Reserve Bank arises on the books of the Chicago Federal Reserve Bank. In turn, the Chicago Federal Reserve Bank may have similar credits on the books of the New York Federal Reserve Bank. A net settlement, therefore, may be arranged for the net difference.

At the close of each day, each Federal Reserve bank by leased wire system will notify the settlement fund in Washington of the amounts owed to it by other Federal Reserve banks. The net amounts will then be adjusted, after accumulation of the debits and credits, by the settlement fund for all 12 Federal Reserve banks. This eliminates the necessity for interdistrict settlements individually among the 12 Federal Reserve banks. This system makes it possible to give availability to credits on the day they arise. Clearing among the Federal Reserve banks involves only a change of ownership of balances by book entries, i.e., debits and credits to the interdistrict settlement fund.

Until April 30, 1975, Federal Reserve banks used gold certificate credits daily to settle amounts due to one another from the interdistrict movements of checks and wire transfers of securities and funds. To make settlements, a pool of gold certificate credits was established which was not available to collateralize Federal Reserve notes issued. When the practice ended, the gold certificate credits in the pool became available for pledging as collateral against Federal Reserve notes (but not on a compulsory basis, in view of the termination of the gold cover against Federal Reserve notes [see FEDERAL RESERVE NOTES]).

Federal Reserve banks have since settled amounts due to one another with debit and credit asset entries. Each Reserve bank's statement of condition shows, in separate "interdistrict settlement account" items, the net balances due to or due from other Reserve banks. The items appear directly below "other assets" in the separate (unconsolidated) condition statements, but do not appear on the consolidated condition statement because the net of the "due to" and "due from" balances of the 12 Federal Reserve banks must be zero.

As transactions are made among Reserve banks, each bank's interdistrict settlement account is increased (debited with a "due from" entry) or reduced (credited with a "due to" entry) daily. "Due to" and "due from" settlements are netted. This asset therefore is reported as a negative number when "due to" balances exceed "due from" balances.

When necessary to bring the settlement account balances into alignment, the interdistrict account is settled by reallocating ownership of the U.S. government securities and/or federal agency securities held in the system's open market account. Reserve banks with "due to" balances pay by reducing their portfolio holdings in favor of those Reserve banks with "due from" balances.

See FEDERAL RESERVE CHECK COLLECTION SYSTEM.

FEDERAL RESERVE NOTES Circulating notes issued by the Federal Reserve banks, as authorized by Section 16 of the Federal Reserve Act. They furnish approximately a major position of the currency in circulation in the U.S. and represent the principal liabilities of the Federal Reserve banks.

Any Federal Reserve bank may make application to its Federal Reserve agent (who happens to be also the chairman of its board of directors, one of the three Class C directors all appointed by the Board of Governors of the Federal Reserve System) for such amount of Federal Reserve notes as it may require to meet the demand of member banks for currency. Application is accompanied by tender to the Federal Reserve agent of collateral authorized under the act in an amount equal to the sum of the Federal Reserve notes applied for.

An act of Congress approved March 18, 1968 (P.L. 90-269) eliminated the provision of Section 16 of the Federal Reserve Act under which the Federal Reserve banks were required to maintain reserves in gold certificates of not less than 25% against Federal Reserve notes. The collateral therefor offered was to consist of the following:

1. **Eligible paper.** Notes, drafts, bills of exchange, or acceptances acquired under Section 13 of the Federal Reserve Act, or bills of exchange endorsed by member banks of any Federal Reserve district and purchased under Section 14 of the act (open market operations, or bankers acceptances purchased under Sec. 14 of the act); and/or
2. **Direct obligations of the United States.** Use of government securities as cover for Federal Reserve notes was made permanent by the act of June 12, 1945 (59 Stat. 237). Previously (since 1932) government securities had been authorized for use as cover under temporary authorizations.

P.L. 90-269 also repealed the provision in Section 16 of the Federal Reserve Act that required each Federal Reserve bank to maintain on deposit in the Treasury of the United States a sum in gold certificates sufficient in the judgment of the secretary of the Treasury for the redemption of the Federal Reserve notes issued to such bank but in no event less than 5% of the total amount of notes issued, less the amount of gold certificates held by the Federal Reserve agent as collateral security; such deposit of gold certificates was counted and included as part of the 25% reserve in gold certificates repealed.

However, the Federal Reserve Act as amended continues to require the maintenance of collateral behind net Federal Reserve notes outstanding equal to the face amount of such Federal Reserve notes outstanding. This collateral may be gold certificates credits or special drawing rights credits, U.S. government securities, federal agency securities, or secured discount window borrowings (loans and advances by Federal Reserve banks). As a result of the DEPOSITORY INSTITUTIONS DEREGULATION AND MONETARY CONTROL ACT OF 1980, other collateral became eligible to collateralize Federal Reserve notes, such as foreign government or agency securities acquired by Federal Reserve banks. Each Federal Reserve bank receives a share of the total gold certificates and special drawing rights credits equal to the percentage of total Federal Reserve notes the individual bank has outstanding. If necessary, credits are redistributed to reflect changes in the percentages of notes issued by individual Federal Reserve banks during the previous year.

The Federal Reserve agent is the representative of the Board of Governors of the Federal Reserve System at each Federal Reserve bank. Assistant agents also are stationed at the board of governors and represent the agents at each Federal Reserve bank. To release unissued notes from its vault, the Federal Reserve bank is required to pledge collateral at least equal to the amount of notes it wishes to issue. The Washington-based agent issues the currency to the requesting Federal Reserve bank. The Federal Reserve Act (Sec. 4) requires the board of governors to designate one of the three Class C directors (those appointed by the board of governors) of each Federal Reserve bank as chairman of the board of directors of the Federal Reserve bank and as Federal Reserve agent.

The Federal Reserve agent shall each day notify the board of governors of all issues and withdrawals of Federal Reserve notes of the Federal Reserve bank to which he is accredited. The board of governors may at any time call upon a Federal Reserve bank for additional security to protect the Federal Reserve notes issued to it.

Any Federal Reserve bank may retire any of its Federal Reserve notes by depositing them with the Federal Reserve agent or with the Treasurer of the United States and thus receive back the collateral deposited with the Federal Reserve agent for the security of such notes. Also, any Federal Reserve bank may at any time reduce its liability for outstanding Federal Reserve notes by depositing with the Federal Reserve agent its Federal Reserve notes, gold certificates, or lawful money of the United States. In addition, any Federal Reserve bank may at its discretion substitute other collateral of equal amount with the approval of the Federal Reserve agent.

The act of July 19, 1954 (68 Stat. 495) repealed that portion of Section 16 of the Federal Reserve Act which prohibited one Federal Reserve bank from paying out notes issued by any other Federal Reserve bank, under penalty of a 10% tax, upon the face value of the notes so paid out.

In addition to being secured by the direct pledge of the collateral, Federal Reserve notes are a direct obligation of the issuing Federal Reserve bank and represent a first lien on all the assets of the bank. They are also a direct obligation of the U.S. government. Like all other forms of currency, Federal Reserve notes are full legal tender for all public and private debts.

An act of Congress approved June 4, 1963 (P.L. 88-36), in addition to repealing the Silver Purchase Acts and the related tax on transfers of silver bullion, amended Section 16 of the Federal Reserve Act so as to authorize the issuance of $1 and $2 Federal Reserve notes. The purpose of this legislation was to make monetary silver available for coinage by substituting Federal Reserve notes for silver certificates. Before this amendment, the law limited the issuance of Federal Reserve notes to denominations of $5 and up. Accordingly, Federal Reserve notes in the $1 denomination were first issued in November, 1963. The $2 denomination was included so that Federal Reserve notes would be authorized in all denominations of paper money, i.e., $1, $2, $5, $10, $20, $50, $100, $500, $1,000, $5,000, and $10,000. The $2 Federal Reserve note, replacing the $2 denomination of UNITED STATES NOTES which was discontinued in 1966, was introduced on April 13, 1976. The denominations of $500, $1,000, $5,000, and $10,000 were discontinued by action of the Board of Governors of the Federal Reserve System on December 27, 1945, and on July 14, 1969, their issuance was finally terminated. Notes bear upon their faces a distinctive letter and serial number which are assigned by the Board of Governors of the Federal Reserve System to each Federal Reserve bank.

The original Federal Reserve Act contemplated that Federal Reserve notes would be 100% secured by ELIGIBLE PAPER, which would thus make them truly ideal ELASTIC CURRENCY, expanding and contracting with the supply of such business paper, although the act did permit Federal Reserve banks to reduce their liability for Federal Reserve notes by depositing gold or lawful money with the Federal Reserve agents. This ideal has been gradually relaxed since: in 1916, by authorizing bills bought in the open market as collateral for notes; in 1917, by authorizing gold, gold certificates, and member bank promissory notes as collateral; and beginning in 1932 and made permanent in 1945, by authorizing the use of U.S. government securities as collateral. Nevertheless, the elastic characteristic of Federal Reserve note circulation continues as the volume of circulation fluctuates in line with needs of business and the public for currency.

Federal Reserve notes should not be confused with FEDERAL RESERVE BANK NOTES, which have been in the process of retirement.

See MONEY CIRCULATION for long-term fluctuation in total circulation of Federal Reserve notes compared with other forms of currency.

FEDERAL RESERVE RATIO The ratio of the prescribed assets to the specified liabilities of Federal Reserve banks, the actually prevailing proportion being reported in the weekly *Federal Reserve Statement.* Paragraph 3 of Section 16 of the Federal Reserve Act was amended June 12, 1945, so as to reduce the minimum reserve requirements of the Federal Reserve banks from 40% of their Federal Reserve notes outstanding and 35% of their deposits to 25% of both their notes and deposits. Where the former requirements, however, had permitted lawful money as an alternative to gold certificates as the required assets for the 35% reserve against deposits and reserves in gold certificates for the 40% against Federal Reserve notes in actual circulation, the new requirement permitted only gold certificates or gold certificate credits as the reserve.

Ratio of gold certificates to deposits and Federal Reserve note liabilities, combined, of the Federal Reserve banks had dipped to 41.7% as of December 31, 1945, compared with 90.8% at the close of 1940. Under Section 11(c) of the Federal Reserve Act, when the gold (certificates) reserve held against Federal Reserve notes fell below 40%, the Board of Governors of the Federal Reserve System was to establish a graduated tax of not more than 1% per annum upon such deficiency until the reserves fell to 32.5%; and when the reserve fell below 32.5%, a tax at the rate of not less than 1.5% per annum, upon each 2.5% or fraction thereof that such reserve fell below 32.5% per annum, was to be paid by the Federal Reserve bank concerned, but the bank was to add the amount of the tax to the discount rate.

Under the June 12, 1945, amendment (59 Stat. 237), when the reserve held against Federal Reserve notes fell below 25%, the Board of Governors of the Federal Reserve System was to establish a graduated tax of not more than 1% upon such deficiency until the reserves fell to 20%; and when the reserve fell below 20%, a tax at the rate of not less than 1.5%, upon each 2.5% or fraction thereof that the reserve fell below 20%, was to be paid by the Federal Reserve bank concerned, but the bank was to add the amount of the tax to the discount rate.

By act of Congress approved March 3, 1965 (P.L. 89-3), this reserve requirement contained in Section 16 of the Federal Reserve Act for the maintenance of gold certificates of not less than 25% against Federal Reserve bank deposit liabilities was eliminated. Ratio of gold certificates to Federal Reserve notes outstanding and deposit liabilities, combined, had dipped to 27.5% as of December 31, 1964. Based on the new required coverage of only Federal Reserve notes outstanding, the ratio would have been 42.7% as of December 31, 1964.

By the end of 1967, the ratio of gold certificates to Federal Reserve notes outstanding was down to 27.1%. By act of Congress approved March 18, 1968 (P.L. 90-269), the revised provision of Section 16 of the Federal Reserve Act, under which the Federal Reserve banks were required to maintain reserves in gold certificates of not less than 25% against Federal Reserve notes (the so-called gold cover against the notes) was finally eliminated altogether.

See FEDERAL RESERVE STATEMENT, RESERVE RATIO.

FEDERAL RESERVE REDISCOUNT RATE See REDISCOUNT, REDISCOUNT RATE.

FEDERAL RESERVE ROUTING SYMBOLS See FEDERAL CHECK COLLECTION SYSTEM.

FEDERAL RESERVE STATEMENT In accordance with Section 11 of the Federal Reserve Act, the Board of Governors of the Federal Reserve System shall publish once each week a statement showing the condition of each Federal Reserve bank and a consolidated statement for all Federal Reserve banks. These statements shall show in detail the assets and liabilities of the Federal Reserve banks, singly and combined, and shall furnish full information regarding the character of the money held as reserve and the amount, nature, and maturities of the paper and other investments owned or held by Federal Reserve banks. Pursuant to this requirement, the Consolidated Statement of Condition of All Federal Reserve Banks, published weekly on Fridays based on figures as of the close of business the preceding Wednesdays, includes comparative figures on the 12 Federal Reserve banks combined, as well as data on individual Federal Reserve banks, and also includes a maturity distribution of loans and securities for the 12 banks combined.

In the same weekly release of the board of governors (H.4.1) containing the Consolidated Statement of Condition of All Federal Reserve Banks, the board also publishes Factors Affecting Reserves of Depository Institutions. These data afford an indication of the level of and factors affecting reserves of depository institutions, Federal Reserve bank credit, and related items, including estimates of the board as to required reserves and EXCESS RESERVES at Federal Reserve banks.

The consolidated balance sheet of the Federal Reserve Bank provides an accounting summary of all phases of Federal Reserve Bank operations. This balance sheet, also known as the statement of condition of the Federal Reserve banks, is appended in a condensed form.

Major asset accounts in the consolidated balance sheet includes the following:

1. **Gold certificate account.** This account represents warehouse receipts issued to the Reserve banks by the Treasury against its gold holdings. Ins return the Reserve banks issue an equal value of credits to the Treasury deposit account. This amount represents the nation's entire official gold stock. New gold certificates credits may be issued only if the Treasury acquires additional gold or if the statutory price of gold is increased.
2. **Special drawing rights certificate account.** This account reflects amounts created by the International Monetary Fund to serve as a supplement to the international monetary reserves of the members of the fund. From time to time ESF monetizes SDRs by issuing SDR certificate credits to the Reserve banks.
3. **Coin.** Coin represents only the amount of coins issued by the Treasury that the Reserve banks hold. The public obtains coin from depository institutions.
4. **Loans.** The amount of discount window credit extended by Federal Reserve banks to depository institutions. The proceeds of such loans are credited to the accounts of depository institutions at the Federal Reserve.
5. **Securities.** This account comprises mainly U.S. government securities (Treasury bills, notes, and bonds) and obligations of federal agencies, acquired originally through open market operations.
6. **Cash items in process of collection.** Checks and other cash items that have been deposited with the Reserve banks for collection on behalf of an institution having an account.
7. **Other assets.** This account consists of the value of Federal Reserve Bank premises, interest accrued, Federal Reserve holdings of foreign currency, and other items of minor importance.

Major liability accounts represented in the consolidated balance sheet include the following:

1. **Federal Reserve notes.** The principal type of U.S. currency in circulation.
2. **Deposits of depository institutions.** Reserve balances and service-related balances of depository institutions. Deposits of the U.S. Treasury represent amounts the Treasury draws on these accounts to make payments by check or direct deposit for all major types of federal spending. Deposits of foreign central banks and governments are deposit liabilities at the banks maintained with the Federal Reserve Bank of New York. All the Reserve banks share in the deposit liability. These deposits represent working balances held by foreign authorities for purposes of international settlement. Other deposit liabilities include deposit to some U.S. government agencies and of international organization of which the U.S. is a member, as well as miscellaneous deposits.
3. **Deferred availability cash items.** Such items arise because Reserve banks do not give immediate credit to the account of a depositing institution for all checks presented to the Reserve banks for collection. The difference between the cash items in process of collection account and the deferred availability cash items account is referred to as Federal Reserve "float" and represents checks and other items that although not yet collected by the Reserve banks, have already been credited to the reserve balances of the institutions that deposited them. Float measures the amount of Federal Reserve credit granted to the deposits of depository institutions that is generated by the Federal Reserve's involvement in the national process of check collection.
5. **Other liabilities and accrued dividends.** This item consists of unearned discounts, discounts on securities, and miscellaneous accounts payable.

Capital accounts represented in the consolidated balance sheet include the following:

1. **Capital paid in.** A bank that is a member of the Federal Reserve System must subscribe to the capital stock of the Reserve Bank of its district. The total amount of the subscription is equal to 6% of the bank's current capital stock and surplus. Of this amount 3% is "capital paid in," and 3% is subject to call by the Board of Governors. These shares do not carry voting power to control the policies of the Reserve banks. Member institutions are entitled by statute to a cumulative dividend of 6% per annum on the value of their paid-in stock. Ownership of the stock many not be transferred, nor may the shares be used as collateral for loans.

Consolidated Statement of Condition of All Federal Reserve Banks
Millions of dollars

Account

Assets
1. Gold certificate account
2. Special Drawing rights certificate account
3. Coin
4. Loans
5. Securities
   a. Bought outright
   b. Held under repurchase agreement
6. Cash items in process of collection
7. Other assets
   Total assets

Liabilities
8. Federal Reserve notes
9. Deposits
   a. Depository institutions
   b. U.S. Treasury, general account
   c. Foreign official accounts
   d. Other
10. Deferred availability cash items
11. Other liabilities and accrued dividends
    Total liabilities

Capital accounts
12. Capital paid-in
13. Surplus
14. Other capital accounts
    Total liabilities and capital accounts

2. **Surplus account.** This account represents retained net earnings of the Reserve banks.
3. **Other capital accounts.** This item reflects the unallocated net earnings for the current year up to the date of the statement. The Reserve banks may draw on their surplus to meet deficits and to pay dividends in years when operations result in loss. Virtually all net earnings of Federal Reserve Banks over the years have been paid to the U.S. Treasury. Source: Federal Reserve System.

See RESERVE RATIO.

FEDERAL RESERVE SYSTEM The central banking system of the United States, created by the FEDERAL RESERVE ACT, approved December 23, 1913. It subsequently developed into one of the world's strongest banking systems, combining eclectically the leading features of the principal European central banking systems adapted to American requirements and with American innovations.

The basic system includes the 12 Federal Reserve banks and their 25 branches, 37 automated clearinghouses, 46 regional check processing centers, and the Culpeper Communications and Records Center; national banks, which are required to be stockholding members of the Federal Reserve bank of their district; state-chartered banks and trust companies which elected to become members of the system by meeting the qualifications and requirements for membership; and all other depository institutions—other commercial banks, savings banks, savings and loan associations, and credit unions—brought under the jurisdiction of the Board of Governors of the Federal Reserve System for reporting and reserve maintenance purposes against transaction deposits and commercial or nonpersonal savings accounts pursuant to the DEPOSITORY INSTITUTIONS DEREGULATION AND MONETARY CONTROL ACT OF 1980. As of the close of 1979 (the Monetary Control Act of 1980 was enacted March 31, 1980), the proportion of all commercial banks that were members of the Federal Reserve System had declined to a new low of 38% of all commercial banks, although accounting for 72% of all deposits of commercial banks. Steady erosion had occurred in Federal Reserve membership over the years; at the end of 1941, for example, member commercial banks accounted for 46% of all commercial banks and 87% of all commercial bank deposits. An outline of the Federal Reserve System is structure is appended.

Before passage of the Federal Reserve Act, the banking system of the United States was an atomistic structure, pyramided in reserves toward the money centers, particularly New York. National banks were instituted by the NATIONAL BANK ACT of 1863 and its subsequent amendments, while state-chartered banks and trust companies, numerically again in the majority after a period of decline following passage of the National Bank Act, organized and operated under state laws and regulation of varying degree, dating from early American history. The Federal Reserve Act was enacted as a result of the realization of the glaring instabilities of the atomistic system, dramatically illustrated by the Money Panic of 1907.

Development. The Federal Reserve Act grew out of the defects and insufficiencies of the former decentralized national-state system, especially in the following particulars:

1. There was no provision for directly elastic currency. National bank notes were perversely elastic in behavior because of the operation of circulation accounts by national banks for profit. Circulation would be expanded shortly after business activity turned downward, when government bonds bearing the circulation privilege were still selling at discounts and could be pledged at par to secure circulation; at such time of decline in the cycle, increased circulation was not needed. Subsequently, shortly after the cycle turned upward, when bond prices were still at premiums, circulation would be reduced and profits taken on the government bonds thus released from circulation pledge, at a time when increased business activity needed additional circulation. National bank notes (state bank notes were nonexistent by such time because of a 10% federal tax) were rigid in amount, based upon the bonded debt of the United States, rather than flexible in amount, contracting and expanding directly with the needs of business. This currency system was a panic breeder. At various critical times in the preceding century and into the twentieth century, the banking system had broken down because it was unable to furnish an adequate supply of flexible and sound circulation meriting public confidence.
2. There was no provision for rediscount facilities as a means of furnishing elastic credit, i.e., there was no assured source for the REDISCOUNT of sound business paper held by banks.
3. Reserves were not centralized. Instead, the partial redeposit of reserves by country and reserve city banks at interest in central reserve city banks (particularly in New York City) made the RESERVE structure pyramided and unreliable. Reserves of interior banks were not available when needed in times of stress, when money market banks suspended or became tight because of financial stringency.
4. The system of collection of out-of-town checks was circuitous, inefficient, and uneconomical.
5. There was no rational control over the money market.

Steps toward removing these defects were actively begun as an aftermath of the panic of 1907, when public attention was again centered on the problem of banking reform. Accordingly, in 1908 the Congress created the NATIONAL MONETARY COMMISSION to determine what modifications might be necessary to remove the weaknesses in the prevailing banking system. After four years of investigation, this body reported its recommendations to Congress in full in a plan which later became known as the Aldrich plan. After undergoing numerous modifications and revisions, this scheme was finally submitted for the approval of Congress but defeated in 1912. It provided for a National Reserve Association, capitalized at $300 million subscribed to by member banks and having a branch in each of 15 districts in the country, holding deposits of members (at no interest), issuing notes against gold and commercial paper cover, engaging in open market operations in government bonds, and generally serving as fiscal agent for the government. When the Wilson administration took office in 1913, one of its first major pieces of legislation was the Federal Reserve Act, passed December 23, 1913, "as a Christmas present" to the nation.

Ownership and Earnings. The Federal Reserve banks are primarily banks for banks. Except as to open market operations, and direct loans to individuals, partnerships, or corporations secured by government securities (Sec. 13) in "unusual and exigent circumstances," their dealings are restricted to banks and the government. There are no individual stockholders. The stock is all owned by member banks, which are required to subscribe to the stock of the Federal Reserve bank of their district in an amount equal to 6% of the member bank's capital and surplus. Only one-half of this subscription, i.e., 3%, is called and paid in. The stock has a par value of $100, is of one class, cannot be transferred or hypothecated, and pays a fixed cumulative dividend at the rate of 6%. So long as it is a member of the system, a member bank may retain the stock, and its holdings are increased or decreased to correspond with changes in its capital stock and surplus (any member bank which holds capital stock of a Federal Reserve bank in excess of the amount required on the basis of 6% of its paid-up capital stock and surplus shall surrender such excess stock).

After payment of all necessary expenses and the fixed 6% dividends on the paid-in capital stock, the residual earnings, after surplus is built up to 100% of subscribed capital, are paid into the U.S. Treasury. Prior to 1933, the Federal Reserve Act required payment of a franchise tax to the Treasury of 90% of earnings after each Federal Reserve bank has accumulated a surplus equal to subscribed capital. Such franchise tax was eliminated by the Banking Act of 1933.

The Board of Governors of the Federal Reserve System on April 23, 1947, reinstituted payments to the government by invoking, under the authority of Section 16 of the act, such rates of interest on outstanding Federal Reserve notes not covered by gold certificates collateral as would transfer about 90% of residual earnings, after expenses and dividends and maintenance of surplus at 100% of subscribed capital, to the Treasury. In 1959, the board of governors instituted payments to the Treasury "as interest on Federal Reserve notes" of all net earnings after dividends and after maintenance of surplus at 100% of subscribed capital. In addition, there was paid in 1959 to the Treasury the amounts by which surplus at any Federal Reserve banks exceeded subscribed capital.

Federal Reserve banks, including the capital stock and surplus therein and the income derived therefrom, are exempt from federal, state, and local taxation, except taxes on real estate.

Federal Reserve System

The basic function of the Federal Reserve System is to make possible a flow of credit and money that will foster orderly economic growth and a stable dollar, encourage business and employment, and facilitate long-run balance in our international payments. The System was created by the Federal Reserve Act which became law on December 23, 1913. The statute provides for a Board of Governors in Washington, the 12 Federal Reserve Banks and their branches, the Federal Open Market Committee, the Federal Advisory Council, and the member banks. The relationships of those groups are indicated below. Solid lines indicate statutory relationships; broken lines, an informal relationship.

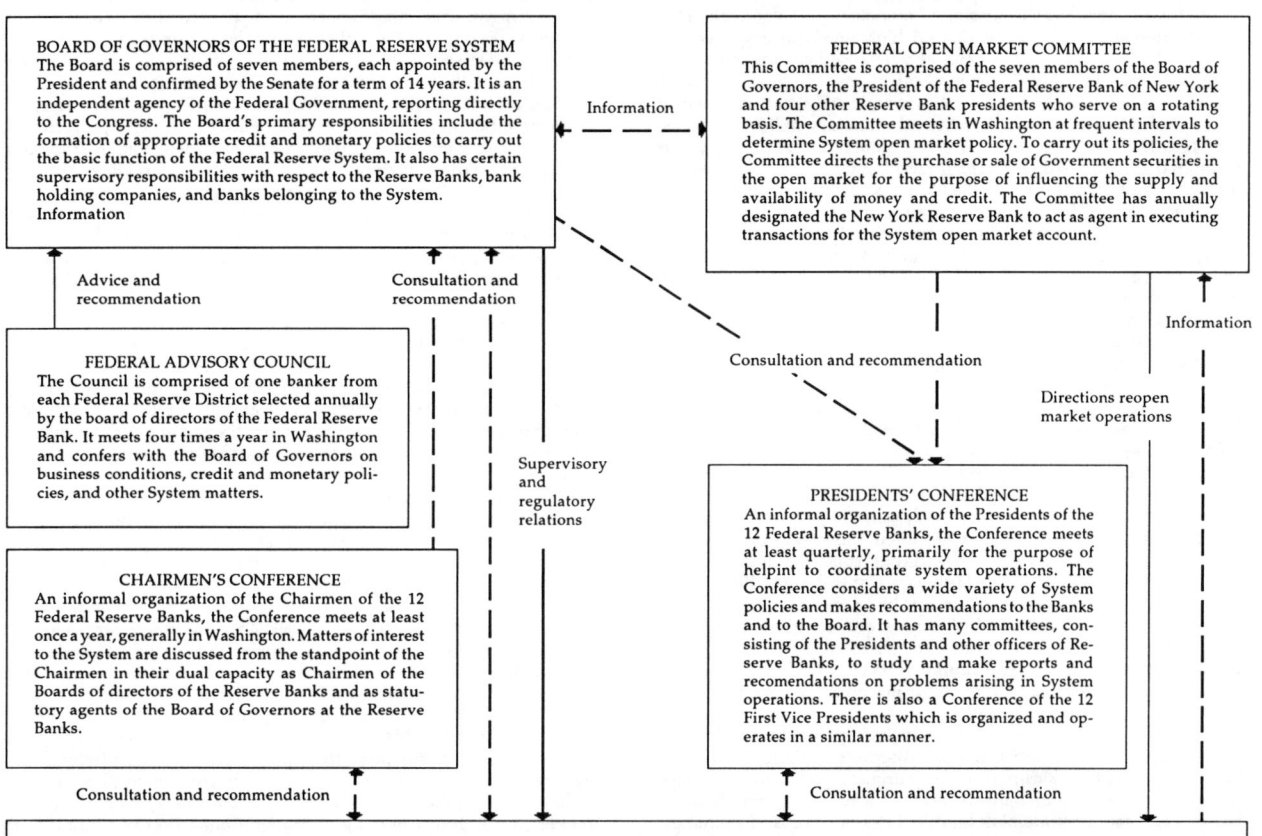

BOARD OF GOVERNORS OF THE FEDERAL RESERVE SYSTEM

The Board is comprised of seven members, each appointed by the President and confirmed by the Senate for a term of 14 years. It is an independent agency of the Federal Government, reporting directly to the Congress. The Board's primary responsibilities include the formation of appropriate credit and monetary policies to carry out the basic function of the Federal Reserve System. It also has certain supervisory responsibilities with respect to the Reserve Banks, bank holding companies, and banks belonging to the System.
Information

FEDERAL OPEN MARKET COMMITTEE

This Committee is comprised of the seven members of the Board of Governors, the President of the Federal Reserve Bank of New York and four other Reserve Bank presidents who serve on a rotating basis. The Committee meets in Washington at frequent intervals to determine System open market policy. To carry out its policies, the Committee directs the purchase or sale of Government securities in the open market for the purpose of influencing the supply and availability of money and credit. The Committee has annually designated the New York Reserve Bank to act as agent in executing transactions for the System open market account.

FEDERAL ADVISORY COUNCIL

The Council is comprised of one banker from each Federal Reserve District selected annually by the board of directors of the Federal Reserve Bank. It meets four times a year in Washington and confers with the Board of Governors on business conditions, credit and monetary policies, and other System matters.

CHAIRMEN'S CONFERENCE

An informal organization of the Chairmen of the 12 Federal Reserve Banks, the Conference meets at least once a year, generally in Washington. Matters of interest to the System are discussed from the standpoint of the Chairmen in their dual capacity as Chairmen of the Boards of directors of the Reserve Banks and as statutory agents of the Board of Governors at the Reserve Banks.

PRESIDENTS' CONFERENCE

An informal organization of the Presidents of the 12 Federal Reserve Banks, the Conference meets at least quarterly, primarily for the purpose of helpint to coordinate system operations. The Conference considers a wide variety of System policies and makes recommendations to the Banks and to the Board. It has many committees, consisting of the Presidents and other officers of Reserve Banks, to study and make reports and recomendations on problems arising in System operations. There is also a Conference of the 12 First Vice Presidents which is organized and operates in a similar manner.

THE TWELVE FEDERAL RESERVE BANKS

For the purpose of administering the Federal Reserve System, the United States has been divided into 12 Federal Reserve Districts with one Reserve Bank in each District. The Reserve Banks differ from commercial banks in that profits are not the objective of their operations; and their stockholders, which are the member banks of the Federal Reserve System, do not have the powers and privileges that customarily belong to stockholders of private corporations.

Each bank is under the immediate supervision and control of a board of nine directors. Under law, three Class A directors, who represent the member banks, and three Class B directors, who are engaged in pursuits other than lending, are elected by the member banks in each District. The three Class C directors are appointed by the Board of Governors; one is designated chairman and another deputy chairman. The chief executive officer of each Bank is its President. He and the First Vice President are each appointed by the board of directors, with approval of the Board of Governors, for a term of five years.

The Reserve Banks are the principal medium through which the monetary and credit policies and general supervisory powers of the System are executed. They perform many of the services which depository institutions perform for the public. In addition, they are fiscal agents, depositaries, and custodians for the United States Treasury and certain other Government agencies.

The Reserve Banks maintain 25 branches and 9 additional offices for check processing in principal cities of the United States. the branches perform for their territories most of the functions performed at the head office. Subject to the regulations of the Board of Governors and general supervision by its parent Reserve Bank, each branch is under the immediate supervision of a board of either five or seven directors, a majority being appointed by the Reserve Bank and the remainder by the Board of governors.

MEMBER BANKS

All national banks are required by law to be members of the System. Banks with State charters may voluntarily join the System if qualified for membership, upon approval by the Board of Governors. Somewhat less than half of all banks in the United States belong to the System but these banks hold about 71 per cent of the country's total bank deposits.

Each member bank is required to hold stock in its Federal Reserve Bank in an amount equal to 3 per cent of the member's capital and surplus. Under the Monetary Control Act of 1980, member banks are subject to a uniform structure of reserve requirements applicable also to nonmember depository institutions. Access to Federal Reserve credit facilites and to Federal Reserve services for which an explicit fee schedule is established including check clearance and transfers of funds is accorded to both member and nonmember depository institutions.

The locations of the twelve Federal Reserve Banks are: Boston, New York, Philadelphia, Cleveland, Richmond, Atlanta, Chicago, St. Louis, Minneapolis, Kansas City, Dallas, and San Francisco.

Source: Federal Reserve Board of Governors.

FEDERAL RESERVE SYSTEM

Components of the Federal Reserve System. The system consists of four organizational layers: (1) the board of governors, the Federal Open Market Committee, and the Federal Advisory Council, the top echelon for determination of policy and achievement of coordination; (2) the 12 Federal Reserve Banks; (3) the member banks; and (4) all other depository institutions, brought under Federal Reserve jurisdiction by the Monetary Control Act of 1980.

Board of Governors of the Federal Reserve System: See FEDERAL RESERVE BOARD OF GOVERNORS for organizational details. The board's functions are to determine monetary policy, exercise supervision over the system, and perform certain operations.

The board considers the mission of monetary policy to seek in the public interest to facilitate sustained high levels of employment, relative stability of average prices, and balanced economic growth. In the opinion of retired Chairman Martin, monetary policy had to assume too much of the burden of economic stabilization in recent years. Both fiscal policy and credit and monetary policy are necessary to influence the level of effective demand. Fiscal policy acts through the relationship between government receipts and expenditures and thus affects directly the after-tax incomes of business and consumers. Initial impact of credit and monetary policy is on expenditures with borrowed funds, particularly those obtained directly or indirectly from commercial banks. Monetary policy also has an effect on expenditures other than with borrowed funds, as liquidity, capitalized values, and profit expectations respond. Both fiscal policy and credit and monetary policy have additional derived effects as higher or lower money incomes lead to increased or reduced expenditures and as changes in consumption demand lead to changes in investment.

The tools of monetary policy of the general type are open market operations (the board participating as members of the Federal Open Market Committee in the establishment of policy and issuance of specific directives), which affect the volume of bank reserves and deposits; review and determination of discount rates of Federal Reserve banks; and prescription of specific legal reserve requirements against deposits of member banks and other depository institutions, within the ranges of variation specified in the Federal Reserve Act as amended by the Monetary Control Act of 1980, which affects level of excess reserves. In applying these tools, guides or indicators have included "feel of the market" (judgment based on such factors as the federal funds rate, Treasury bill rates, current trends in money markets and capital markets, etc); level of interest rates; intensity of demand for credit; net borrowed reserves, free reserves, etc.; and money supply.

Supervisory powers of the board include prescribing rules and regulations governing advances and discounts by Federal Reserve banks to member banks; open market purchases of bills of exchange, trade acceptances, and bankers acceptances by Federal Reserve banks; acceptance by member banks of drafts or bills of exchange; legal reserve requirements of member and nonmember banks and other depository institutions; purchase of warrants by Federal Reserve banks; accounting and disclosure requirements for equity securities of state member banks; extension of securities credit by lenders other than banks, brokers, or dealers; eligibility requirements and conditions for membership in the Federal Reserve System by state-chartered banking institutions; issuance and cancellation of stock of Federal Reserve banks; collection of checks and other items by Federal Reserve banks; regulation of corporations engaged in foreign banking and financing; regulation of interlocking bank relationships under the Clayton Act; regulation of foreign branches of national banks; relationships with foreign banks and bankers; loans to executive officers of member banks; prescription of minimum security devices and procedures for Federal Reserve banks and state member banks; regulation of interest on time and savings deposits; relationships with dealers in securities; bank service arrangements; extension of securities credit by brokers and dealers and by banks for the purpose of purchasing or carrying securities on margin; loan guarantees for defense production; regulation of bank holding companies; and prescription of disclosure and computational requirements on consumer credit charges (the Truth-in-Lending Act), as well as a variety of other functions under other consumer-oriented legislation.

Other supervisory tasks are to pass upon mergers, consolidations, or acquisitions of stock or assets by state member banks in coordination with the Comptroller of the Currency, the *Federal Deposit Insurance Corporation*, and the attorney general; to fix, upon affirmative vote of not less than six of its members, for each Federal Reserve district the percentage of individual bank capital and surplus which may be represented by security loans; to direct any member bank to refrain from further increases in loans secured by stock and bond collateral for any period up to one year, under penalty of suspension of all rediscount privileges; to suspend, at its discretion, but after reasonable notice and hearing, any member bank from use of Federal Reserve credit facilities when in the board's judgment such member bank is making undue use of such credit; to declare immediately due and payable any advance by Federal Reserve banks to member banks when such member banks, after official warning from the board or Federal Reserve bank, increases its loans on stocks and bonds or investments other than U.S. government securities; to remove any officer or director of a member bank who continues to violate any law relating to such bank or continues unsafe and unsound practices in conducting the bank's business, after warning by the Comptroller of the Currency (national and D.C. banks) or Federal Reserve agent (state member banks); to suspend or remove any officer, director, or employee of Federal Reserve banks for cause; to suspend (for violation of any section of the Federal Reserve Act) any Federal Reserve bank, to operate it, and, if necessary, to reorganize it.

Still further supervisory responsibilities are to establish and oversee the implementation of the international credit guidelines under the Voluntary Credit Restraint Program; to permit, or on affirmative vote of five members to require, Federal Reserve banks to rediscount paper for one another at rates approved by the board; to permit Federal Reserve banks to make four-month advances to member banks "secured to the satisfaction of such Federal Reserve Bank"; upon affirmative vote of five members, to permit Federal Reserve banks to make loans to groups of five or more member banks which have inadequate amounts of assets eligible or acceptable under conventional borrowing; and to require the writing off of worthless assets from the books of Federal Reserve banks.

Operational or semioperational powers of the board include operating the Interdistrict Settlement Fund; examining Federal Reserve banks and member banks; reporting the condition of the Federal Reserve banks weekly; adding to or reclassifying RESERVE CITIES (P.L. 86-114, July 28, 1959, terminated the central reserve city classification three years from the date of enactment; and the board suspended its triennial review of reserve city classifications on February 10, 1960); suspending reserve requirements for periods of 15 days (subject to renewal) and imposing graduated taxes as penalties for deficiencies in legal reserves of member banks; supervising through the Comptroller of the Currency the issuance and retirement of Federal Reserve notes and regulating such issuance and retirement; and appointing the three Class C directors of each Federal Reserve bank, as well as designating the chairman of the board (who is also Federal Reserve agent) and vice-chairman from such directors.

In summary, the board of governors now has a diversification of powers, both policy-making and operational, that provide it with more effective means for achieving a unified and coordinated Federal Reserve System. Most of these increased powers and controls were created by the Banking Act of 1933 and 1935. The Monetary Control Act of 1980 added universal and uniform reserve requirements power over all depository institutions. See appended exhibit on the Federal Reserve System: Relationship to Credit Policy Instruments.

Federal Open Market Committee: See FEDERAL OPEN MARKET COMMITTEE for organizational details. This committee has centralized direction and control of open market operations, generally considered the most flexible tool of monetary policy.

The committee was statutorily organized, pursuant to the BANKING ACT OF 1935, on March 1, 1936. Each Federal Reserve bank is required to participate in the committee's operations and may not engage in open market operations for itself without the committee's approval. The BANKING ACT OF 1933 made a start toward such unified direction and control of open market operations by providing that individual Federal Reserve bank open market operations for own account would have to be approved by the Federal Reserve Board except in the case of emergencies. Prior thereto, open market operations were in the hands of committees of Federal Reserve banks which, although nominally under the Federal Reserve Board, could not compel any Federal Reserve bank to participate in unified system operations.

Policy directives of the Federal Open Market Committee, reflecting current monetary policy, are issued to the Federal Reserve Bank of New York as the bank selected by the committee to execute transactions for the system open market account. In the area of domestic open market operations, the Federal Reserve Bank of New

York operates under two separate directives from the Open Market Committee: a continuing authority directive, and a current economic policy directive. The committee follows the practice of reviewing all of its continuing authorizations and directives at the first meeting of the committee following the election of new members from the Federal Reserve banks to serve for the year beginning March 1.

The U.S. Treasury, through its Exchange Stabilization Fund and with the Federal Reserve Bank of New York acting as agent, had been conducting operations in foreign exchange since March, 1961, as part of a cooperative effort by treasuries and central banks to create a first line of defense against speculation in foreign exchange markets. On January 23, 1962, the Federal Open Market Committee (with two dissenting governors) approved the initiation of a program of open market operations in foreign currencies. Until June 7, 1966, the Federal Reserve Bank of New York operated for the committee under three directives: (1) an authorization regarding open market transactions in foreign currencies, (2) a statement of guidelines for system foreign currency operations, and (3) a continuing authority directive on system foreign currency operations. These were replaced on June 7, 1966, with two new directives: (1) an authorization for system foreign currency operations, and (2) a foreign currency directive, which contained the substantive change authorizing the special manager of the system open market account for foreign currency operations to engage in operations on his own initiative to meet a threat of disorderly conditions in the foreign exchange markets, with the requirement that he consult as soon as practicable with the committee or in an emergency with members of a designated subcommittee.

The Federal Reserve banks are authorized under existing law to engage in open market transactions in foreign exchange, subject to the direction and regulation of the Federal Open Market Committee, and for this purpose to open and maintain accounts with foreign banks subject to the consent and regulations (Regulation N, as amended) of the Board of Governors of the Federal Reserve System.

Federal Advisory Council: This body, statutorily provided for in the Federal Reserve Act, has purely advisory and consultative functions. It is composed of 12 members, one from each of the Federal Reserve districts, elected annually by the board of directors of each Federal Reserve bank. The council is required to meet at least four times a year, in Washington, D.C. Being composed entirely of private bankers, the council assists the Board of Governors of the Federal Reserve System by conferring and advising and making recommendations with regard to matters pertaining to business and financial conditions in the respective Federal Reserve districts.

Twelve Federal Reserve Banks: Each Federal Reserve bank has its own distinct organization and serves its own district, so it is sometimes known as a regional bank. The minimum capital for each bank is $4 million (subscribed capital), but the majority of them have capital considerably in excess of this amount.

Each Federal Reserve bank is under the direction of its own board of directors, consisting of nine directors divided into three classes of three directors each. These classes are known as Class A, Class B, and Class C. Class A and B directors are elected by the member banks of the district, and Class C directors are appointed by the Federal Reserve Board of Governors. The three Class A directors are representative of the member commercial banks in the district and are usually bankers; the three Class B directors and three Class C directors are selected to represent the public, with particular consideration being given to the interests of agriculture, commerce, industry, services, labor, and consumers. Thus both the providers and users of banking services in the district are represented on the bank's board. Directors cannot be members of Congress; Class B and C directors cannot be officers, directors, or employees of any bank; and Class C directors cannot own stock in any bank. Additionally, since a Reserve bank directorship is considered to be a form of public service, directors are asked to limit other activities. All directors are expected to avoid participation in partisan political activities.

One of the Class C directors, who shall be a person of tested banking experience, is designated by the board of governors as chairman of the board of directors of the Federal Reserve bank and as Federal reserve agent. Another of the Class C directors shall be appointed by the board of governors as vice-chairman; and in case of the absence of the chairman and vice-chairman, the third Class C director shall preside at meetings of the bank's board of directors. Subject to the approval of the board of governors, the Federal Reserve agent may appoint one or more assistants, who shall be persons of tested banking experience, to assist the Federal Reserve agent in the performance of his duties and to act in his name and stead during the latter's absence or disability.

All directors of a Federal Reserve bank are elected for three-year terms, on a staggered basis (three places on the board to be filled each year). The president and first vice-president the board appoints must be approved by the board of governors.

Class A and B directors are elected by mail by the member banks of the district. For this purpose, the member banks of the district are divided by the board of governors into three groups, each group consisting as nearly as possible of banks of similar capitalization. Within each such size group, each member bank may nominate to the Federal Reserve bank chairman of the board Class A candidates and Class B candidates as first, second, or other choices. Any candidate having a majority of all votes cast as first choice shall be declared elected; recourse is had to addition of the second or other choices to the number of first choices, if necessary, in order to establish the candidates having a majority of all choice votes.

Although member banks are sole stockholders and elect two-thirds of the directors of each Federal Reserve bank, it is apparent that control of policy rests with the board of governors: (1) no Federal Reserve bank may refuse to participate in open market operations pursuant to directives of the Federal Open Market Committee, which consists of all seven board of governors and five senior officers (who vote) from Federal Reserve banks; (2) discount rates set by each bank's directors are subject to review and determination by the board of governors; (3) the board of governors still has the power to change legal reserve requirements within the narrower range of variation prescribed by the Monetary Control Act of 1980, as well as to impose supplemental reserve requirements; and (4) the board of governors controls a variety of operational subjects by its regulations (*see* FEDERAL RESERVE BOARD REGULATIONS).

Federal Reserve banks perform a variety of central banking functions, which may be summarized as follows:

1. To serve as a depository for reserve and clearing balances of depository institutions. The following reserve requirements applied effective November 13, 1980 (but for existing nonmember banks and thrift institutions the phase-in period would end September 3, 1987; for existing member banks the phase-in period was about three years, depending on whether their new reserve requirements were greater or less than the old requirements; and for existing agencies and branches of foreign banks, the phase-in period ended August 12, 1982):

   on net transaction accounts, in amounts from zero to $25 million, 3%; in amounts over $25 million, 12%;
   on nonpersonal time deposits, with maturities of less than four years, 3%; but with maturities of four years or more, zero;
   on eurocurrency liabilities of all types, 3%.

   These required reserves must be held in the form of deposits with Federal Reserve banks or vault cash of the institutions concerned. Since implementation of the Monetary Control Act of 1980, nonmembers of the Federal Reserve System may maintain reserves on a passthrough basis with certain approved institutions.
   See RESERVE.

   Reserve accounts of depository institutions constitute most of the deposits of the district Federal Reserve banks. In addition, however, deposits of the district Federal Reserve banks include deposits of the U.S. Treasury (general account—U.S. Treasurer, one at each of the 12 district Federal Reserve banks); deposits of foreign central banks and governments, maintained for international settlement and foreign monetary reserve purposes; and other deposits (clearing balances of depository institutions and balances of certain government agencies and international organizations). P.L. 89-3, approved March 3, 1965, eliminated the requirement for maintenance of reserves in gold certificates of not less than 25% against Federal Reserve bank deposits.

2. To furnish an elastic currency and credit. A depository institution requiring additional reserves may obtain them from the district Federal Reserve bank by offering ELIGIBLE PAPER for rediscount or by borrowing therefrom on its own notes payable secured by eligible paper or by government securities. The depository institution may elect to receive the proceeds in FEDERAL RESERVE NOTES or other forms of currency, if needed to

meet deposit withdrawals, or as a credit to its reserve account, on which excess reserves (in excess of legal reserve requirements) it may draw or on the basis of which it may expand its loans and investments and thus its deposits. Similarly, a depository institution may return redundant currency, including Federal Reserve notes, to its Federal Reserve bank for credit to its reserve account, and pay off its advances from the Federal Reserve bank by charges to its reserve account. Thus, each Federal Reserve bank affords interconvertibility of excess reserves and currency to its depository institutions.

In turn, each Federal Reserve bank has to meet its collateral requirements for Federal Reserve notes. These notes must be fully secured by gold certificates, special drawing rights, eligible paper, and/or U.S. government direct obligations, tendered to the Federal Reserve agent in the particular issuing district Federal Reserve bank. P.L. 90-269, approved March 18, 1968, eliminated the provision of Section 16 of the Federal Reserve Act under which the Federal Reserve banks were required to maintain reserves in gold certificates (which were included also as part of the gold certificates cover) of not less than 25% against Federal Reserve notes.

3. To provide an efficient system of collecting out-of-town cash items. The Federal Reserve Act empowers each Federal Reserve bank to exercise the functions of a regional clearinghouse for the depository institutions of its district. In turn, through management of the INTERDISTRICT SETTLEMENT ACCOUNT, the board of governors itself serves as national manager for clearing debit and credit balances arising among the various Federal Reserve banks as the result of their clearing operations for depository institutions and transfers for the Treasury and for account of depository institutions.

See FEDERAL RESERVE CHECK COLLECTION SYSTEM, FEDERAL RESERVE INTERDISTRICT COLLECTION SYSTEM.

4. To engage in open market operations; to deal in gold; and to establish foreign correspondents and agencies. Statutory powers of each Federal Reserve bank include the purchase and sale in the open market, at home or abroad, either from or to domestic or foreign banks, firms, corporations, or individuals, of cable transfers and bankers acceptances and bills of exchange eligible for rediscount; the purchase from depository institutions of bills of exchange arising out of commercial transactions and sale thereof, with or without endorsement of the Federal Reserve bank; the purchase and sale of obligations of the United States and of federal agencies, six-month tax anticipation obligations of states and their subdivisions, and acceptances of Federal Intermediate Credit banks (whenever the board of governors shall declare the public interest so requires).

These powers are subject, however, to rules and regulations of the board of governors, which exercises special supervision over all relationships and transactions of any kind of a Federal Reserve bank with any foreign banks or bankers. Freedom of action in open market operations is restricted further by direction of and regulations adopted by the Federal Open Market Committee.

5. To serve as depository and fiscal agent for the Treasury and to carry on subtreasury operations. Each Federal Reserve bank carries an account for the U.S. Treasurer and effects transfers of such Treasury balances without charge, handles issuance and redemption of U.S. government obligations, and performs other fiscal functions for the federal government. With the abandonment of the subtreasury system in 1921, the Federal Reserve banks supply depository institutions with Treasury currency and issue new currency in exchange for worn and mutilated bills and coins.

6. To develop and maintain the U.S. money market. The Federal Reserve banks, subject to regulations of the board of governors and Federal Open Market Committee, assist in the activity of the money market by open market dealings in bankers acceptances and through the system account, in Treasury bills normally in the government securities market. In addition, by their services to depository institutions in rediscounts and advances, they influence money market conditions, since depository institutions are major participants in the money market.

Major Changes. The Depository Institutions Deregulation and Monetary Control Act of 1980 (DIDMCA) constituted the third major legislation affecting the U.S. financial system to be enacted, following the Banking Acts of 1933 and 1935. The two early acts were specifically aimed at changes in the Federal Reserve System affecting commercial banks, whereas the DIDMCA effected depository institutions in general.

Act of May 13, 1960 (12 U.S.C. 1828(c)) amended Section 18(c) of the Federal Deposit Insurance Act, which as far as the Board of Governors of the Federal Reserve System is concerned provides that the board must pass upon each merger, consolidation, purchase of assets, or assumption of liabilities in which the active or resulting bank is to be a state member bank.

The Community Reinvestment Act, Title VIII of P.L. 95-128, October 12, 1977, the Housing and Community Development Act, required federal financial supervisory agencies among other things:

1. To require each appropiate federal financial supervisory agency to use its authority when examining financial institutions and to encourage such institutions to help meet the credit needs of the local communities in which they are chartered consistent with the safe and sound operations of such institutions.
2. To assess, in examining federal insured financial institutions, each lending institution's record in meeting the credit needs of its entire community, including low- and moderate-income neighborhoods, consistent with safe and sound operations, and to take such records into account in its evaluation of an institution that applies for a federal charter, or to relocate a home office or a branch office, or for merger, or for approval of a holding company acquisition.
3. To promulgate regulations implementing this act to take effect 390 days following its enactment.
4. To report annually to the Congress on actions taken to carry out its responsibilities under this act.

P.L. 95-188, November 16, 1977, the Federal Reserve Reform Act, among other things:

1. Extended the authority for flexible interest rate control (Regulation Q) for one year, until December 15, 1978.
2. Required the board of governors and the Federal Open Market Committee to maintain long-run monetary and credit aggregates commensurate with the economy's long-run potential to increase production so as to promote effectively goals of maximum employment, stable prices, and moderate long-term interest rates.
3. Required the board to appear quarterly, alternately before the House and Senate banking committees, and to testify concerning the ranges of monetary and credit aggregates for the upcoming 12 months.
4. Prohibited discrimination on the basis of race, creed, color, sex, or national origin in the selection of Federal Reserve bank directors.
5. Modified qualifications for selection of Class B and Class C Federal Reserve bank directors by providing that such directors shall represent the public and shall be chosen with due but not exclusive consideration given to the interests of agriculture, commerce, industry, services, labor, and consumers.
6. Required Senate confirmation of the chairman and vice-chairman of the board of governors.
7. Applied federal criminal conflict-of-interest provisions for federal employees to Federal Reserve bank directors, officers, and employees.
8. Amended Sections 2(a)(5)(D), 3(a), and 4(c)(2) of the Bank Holding Company Act to authorize the board of governors to extend up to a maximum of five years the period for disposition of shares acquired by a bank or bank holding company in the course of securing or collecting a debt previously contracted in good faith, if such an extension of time would not be detrimental to the public interest.
9. Amended Section 3(b) of the Bank Holding Company Act to provide for expedited board approval of bank and bank holding company acquisitions, consolidations, and mergers in emergency situations or when immediate action is necessary in order to prevent the probable failure of the bank or bank holding company involved in the transaction.
10. Amended Section 11(b) of the Bank Holding Company Act to shorten the usual 30-day lag between the date of board approval of a transaction and the earliest date on which the approved transaction may be consummated, by providing for

immediate consummation in the case of a failing bank or bank holding company, and by providing a 5-day lag between approval and consummation in emergency situations. In all cases, the time periods set the outside limits within which suits may be brought to challenge the board's action as violative of the antitrust laws (except for violations alleged under Sec. 2 of the Sherman Antitrust Act, 15 U.S.C. 2).

P.L. 95-320, July 21, 1978, the Federal Banking Agency Audit Act, provided for General Accounting Office audit of the Federal Reserve Board, the Federal Reserve banks and their branches and facilities, the Federal Deposit Insurance Corporation, and the Office of the Comptroller of the Currency.

P.L. 95-351, August 20, 1978, established the NATIONAL CONSUMER COOPERATIVE BANK.

P.L. 95-369, September 17, 1978, the INTERNATIONAL BANKING ACT OF 1978, contained the following provisions:

1. Authorized the Comptroller of the Currency to waive the requirement that all of the directors of a national bank be U.S. citizens.
2. Removed the requirement in the Edge Act (Section 25(a) of the Federal Reserve Act) that all of the directors of an Edge Act corporation be U.S. citizens. Similarly, the Edge Act was amended to permit one or more foreign banks to own 50% or more of the shares of an Edge Act corporation with the prior approval of the board of governors. Previously, the Edge Act required, without exception, that a majority of the shares of an Edge Act corporation be owned by U.S. citizens.
3. Required the board of governors to revise its regulation dealing with Edge Act corporations within 270 days of enactment of this act. In doing so, the board of governors was required to implement several congressional purposes for Edge Act corporations, including affording Edge Act corporations powers sufficiently broad to enable them to compete in the United States and abroad with similar foreign-owned institutions. Edge Act corporations are also to serve as a means of financing international trade, particularly exports. The minimum of 10% reserve requirement on the U.S. deposits of Edge Act corporations was eliminated, and the board of governors was authorized to impose the same reserve requirements on the corporations as on member banks. The act removed the statutory limitation on the issuance by Edge Act corporations of debentures, bonds, and promissory notes. The board of governors was required to report to the Congress the effects of these amendments on the capitalization and activities of Edge Act corporations, banks, and the banking system.
(This report is contained in the 1978 *Annual Report* of the Board of Governors of the Federal Reserve System.)
4. Authorized the Comptroller of the Currency to license and supervise one or more federal branches or agencies of a foreign bank in states that do not prohibit the establishment of branches or agencies by foreign banks.
5. Prohibited a foreign bank from establishing and operating branches outside its "home" state unless the foreign bank enters into an agreement or undertaking with the board of governors that it will receive only such deposits at the out-of-state offices as are permissible for an Edge Act corporation. Offices of foreign banks that were established, or for which an application had been filed prior to June 27, 1978, were exempt from this prohibition.
6. Required federal deposit insurance for branches of foreign banks that receive deposits of less than $100,000. Required federal deposit insurance for federal branches wherever located and for state branches in states that require deposit insurance for state-chartered banks.
7. Authorized the federal banking agencies to examine U.S. offices of foreign banks and in appropriate circumstances to institute cease-and-desist proceedings against them.
8. Imposed reserve requirements and interest rate limitations on federal branches and agencies of large foreign banks in the same manner and to the same extent as on member banks. The board of governors was authorized to impose the same requirements and limitations on state branches and state agencies after consultation and in cooperation with state bank supervisory authorities. Subject to regulations of the board of governors, branches and agencies that maintain reserves would have access to system facilities.
9. Subjected a foreign bank that had a branch, agency, or commercial lending company in the United States to most provisions of the Bank Holding Company Act in the same manner and to the same extent as bank holding companies. Nonbanking activities engaged in or applied for by July 26, 1978, were exempt under a grandfather clause. Otherwise, a foreign bank may not engage directly or indirectly in nonbanking activities in the United States other than those permissible to bank holding companies.
10. Required that joint studies and reports be undertaken by the President with respect to the PEPPER-MCFADDEN ACT, the secretary of the Treasury with respect to the treatment of U.S. banks abroad, and the board of governors with respect to Edge Act corporations becoming members of the Federal Reserve System.

P.L. 95-405, September 30, 1978, the Futures Trading Act, amended the Commodity Exchange Act to require the Commodity Futures Trading Commission to do the following, among other things:

1. Keep the Treasury, the Board of Governors of the Federal Reserve System, and the Securities and Exchange Commission fully informed of commission activities relating to the responsibilities of those agencies, in order to seek their views on such activities, and to consider the relationships between the volume and nature of investment and trading in commodity futures and in securities and financial instruments under the jurisdiction of those agencies.
2. Deliver to the Treasury and the board of governors a copy of any application by a board of trade to be designated as a contract market involving transactions for future delivery of any security issued or guaranteed by the United States or any of its agencies with a 45-day opportunity for comment; consider all comments it receives from the Treasury and the board of governors; and consider the effect that any such designation, suspension, revocation, or emergency action may have on the debt financing requirements of the U.S. government and the continued efficiency and integrity of the underlying market for government securities.

P.L. 96-592, December 24, 1980, revised and expanded the lending authority of the Farm Credit System, and included the following provisions:

1. The governor of the Farm Credit Administration is to consult regularly with the Board of Governors of the Federal Reserve System in connection with the effect of the Farm Credit System's lending activities on national monetary policy.
2. The Farm Credit Administration is to consult closely on a continuous basis with the board of governors to ensure that the regulations carrying out the export-and-import-loan and related authority of the Banks for Cooperatives conform to national banking policies, objectives, and limitations. Any regulation that poses unresolved differences between the Farm Credit Administration and the board of governors about conformance must be submitted to Congress and is subject to a legislative veto by both houses of the Congress.

Recent Additional Responsibilities. P.L. 95-630, the FINANCIAL INSTITUTIONS REGULATORY AND INTEREST RATE CONTROL ACT OF 1987, gave the federal bank supervisory agencies the authority to disapprove changes in control of insured banks and bank holding companies. The act requires that the federal banking agency consider such factors as the financial condition, competence, experience, and integrity of the acquiring person or group of persons, and the effect of the transaction on competition. The Federal Reserve's objectives in its administration of the act are to enhance and maintain public confidence in the banking system by preventing serious adverse effects from anticompetitive combinations of interests, inadequate financial support, and unsuitable management.

The Federal Reserve also has responsibilities for writing rules or enforcing a number of major laws that offer consumers protection in their financial dealing. The more important of these laws are mentioned here. The Truth In Lending Act requires disclosure of the "finance charge" and the "annual percentage rate"—and certain

FEDERAL RESERVE SYSTEM

Board of Governors of the Federal Reserve System

Balance Sheets

	As of December 31	
	1987	1986
Assets		
Current assets:		
Cash	$ 7,705,996	$ 8,646,210
Accounts receivable	908,883	2,045,873
Stockroom and cafeteria inventories, at cost	244,963	285,843
Prepaid expenses and other assets	760,903	627,054
Total current assets	9,620,745	11,604,980
Property, buildings, and equipment, net (Note 3)	63,356,924	64,827,375
Other assets	429,357	1,708,506
Total assets	$73,407,026	$78,140,861
Liabilities and Fund Balance		
Current liabilities:		
Accounts payable	$ 4,593,746	$ 4,655,794
Accrued payroll and related taxes	2,547,172	2,861,053
Accrued annual leave	4,185,226	3,896,398
Other liabilities	237,951	478,716
Total current liabilities	11,564,095	11,891,961
Commitments and contingencies (Note 5)		
Fund balance	61,842,931	66,248,900
Total liabilities and fund balance	$73,407,026	$78,140,861

The accompanying notes are an integral part of these statements.

Board of Governors of the Federal Reserve System

Statements of Revenues and Expenses and Fund Balance

	For the years ended December 31	
	1987	1986
Board operating revenues:		
Assessments levied on Federal Reserve Banks for Board operating expenses and capital expenditures	$ 81,869,800	$ 97,337,500
Other revenues (Note 4)	3,645,891	3,169,567
Total operating revenues	85,515,691	100,507,067
Board operating expenses:		
Salaries	53,811,021	53,259,376
Retirement and insurance contributions	6,245,296	5,401,797
Depreciation and losses (gains) on disposals	7,530,325	6,156,450
Postage and supplies	3,218,518	3,490,423
Utilities	3,195,502	2,970,714
Travel	2,834,715	2,537,670
Software	2,764,635	1,957,564
Repairs and maintenance	2,731,026	2,083,894
Contractual services and professional fees	2,235,129	2,127,597
	1,398,787	2,598,055
Equipment and facility rentals	1,867,291	2,022,535
Printing and binding	2,089,415	2,150,807
Other (Note 4)		
Total operating expenses	89,921,660	86,756,882
Board operating revenues (under) over expenses	(4,405,969)	13,750,185
Issuance and redemption of Federal Reserve notes:		
Assessments levied on Federal Reserve Banks for currency costs	170,700,082	180,779,673
Expenses for currency printing, issuance, retirement, shipping, and research costs	170,700,082	181,219,573
Currency assessments (under) expenses	—	(439,900)
Total revenues (under) over expenses	(4,405,969)	13,310,285
Fund balance, beginning of year	66,248,900	52,938,615
Fund balance, end of year	$ 61,842,931	$ 66,248,900

The accompanying notes are an integral part of these statements.

other costs and terms of credit—so that consumers can compare the price of credit from different sources. This act also limits liability on lost or stolen credit cards. The Fair Credit Billing Act sets up a procedure for the prompt correction of errors on a revolving credit account and prevents damage to credit ratings while a dispute is being settled. The Equal Credit Opportunity act prohibits discrimination in the granting of credit on the basis of sex, marital status, race, color, religion, national origin, age, receipt of public assistance, or the exercise of rights made under the Consumer Credit Protection Act. The Federal Reserve regulation provides for notice to applicants who have been denied credit of the reason for the denial. It also gives married individuals with jointly held credit accounts the right to have credit histories maintained in the names of both spouses.

The Fair Credit Reporting Act sets up a procedure for correcting mistakes on credit records and requires that the records be used only for legitimate business purposes.

The Consumer Leasing Act requires disclosure of information to help consumers compare the cost and terms of one lease of consumer goods with another, and the cost of leasing with that of buying on credit or for cash.

The Real Estate Settlement Procedures Act requires disclosure of information about the services and costs involved at "settlement," when real property is transferred from seller to buyer.

The Electronic Fund Transfer Act provides a basic framework regarding the rights, liabilities, and responsibilities of consumers who use electronic transfer services and of the financial institutions that offer the services.

The Federal Trade Commission Improvement Act authorizes the Board to identify unfair or deceptive acts or practices on the part of banks and to issue regulations to prohibit them.

The Home Mortgage Disclosure Act requires depository institutions to disclose the geographic distribution of their mortgage and home improvement loans. The purpose of the act is to provide to depositors and others information that will enable them to make informed decisions about whether institutions in metropolitan areas are meeting the housing credit needs of the communities.

Summary. The following achievements may be ascribed to the Federal Reserve System:

FEDERAL RESERVE SYSTEM

Map of the Federal Reserve Districts and Their Branch Territories

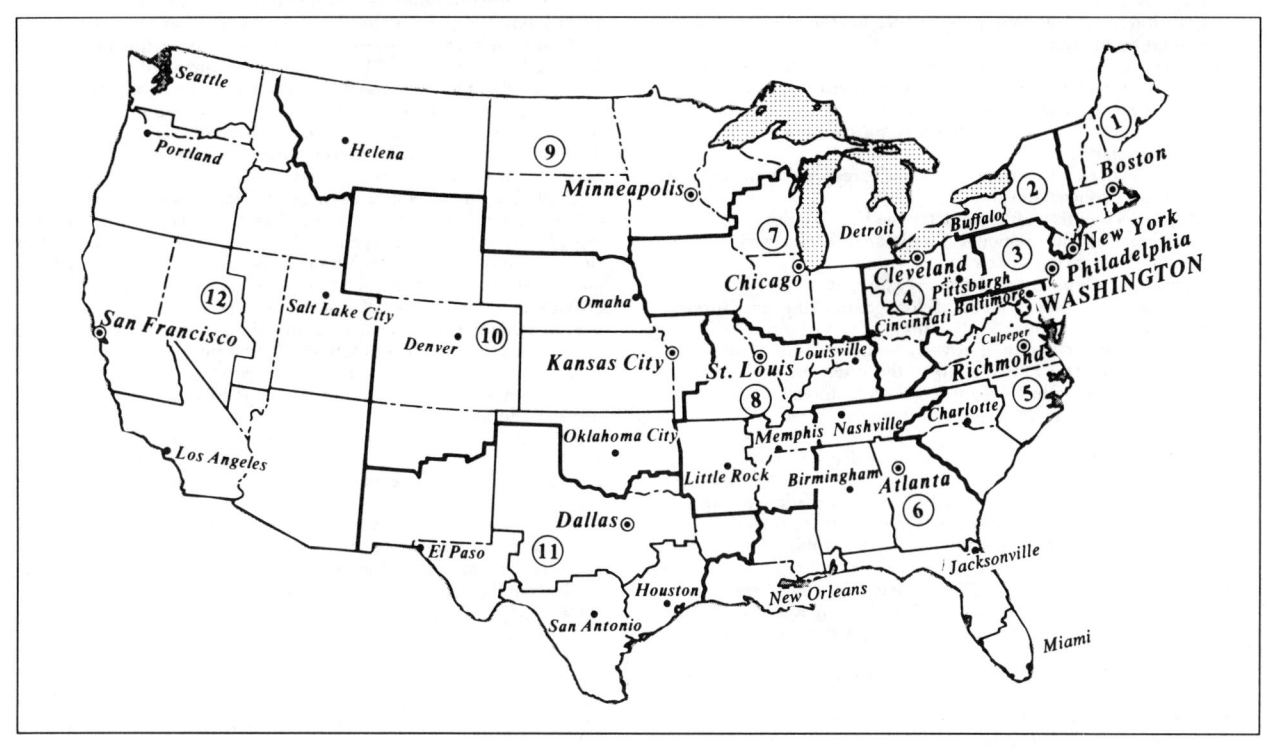

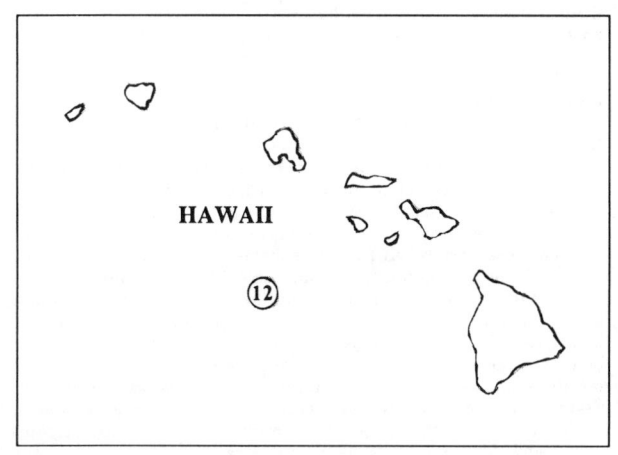

LEGEND

— Boundaries of Federal Reserve Districts

— Boundaries of Federal Reserve Branch Territories

★ Board of Governors of the Federal Reserve System

◉ Federal Reserve Bank Cities

• Federal Reserve Branch Cities

· Federal Reserve Bank Facility

ENCYCLOPEDIA OF BANKING AND FINANCE

FEDERAL RESERVE SYSTEM ADVISORY COMMITTEE

1. Effective concentration of reserves in 12 central bank reservoirs, thereby creating a base for central banking services for depository institutions
2. Creation of central banking structure for the effective implementation of credit and monetary policy
3. Enhancement of the ability of depository institutions to accommodate commerce and business with credit, consistent with prevailing credit and monetary policy
4. Mitigation of business fluctuations by countercyclical credit and monetary policy
5. Provision of elastic currency and credit, responsive to business needs and contraction
6. More effective fiscal functions for the U.S. Treasury
7. Creation of efficient regional and national check-clearing facilities for the banking system
8. Further development of the money market
9. Assistance in development of foreign banking and foreign banking relationships of U.S. banking
10. Effective reconciliation of government regulation with financial interests and needs, so that the intensive and detailed former has come to be regarded with confidence as conventional in the interests of a sound financial system.

As indicated by the foregoing review of legislation pertaining directly or indirectly to the Federal Reserve System, the functions and responsibilities of the system have been broadened and expanded in the financial field as well as in consumer protection. The system's responsibilities in the financial field as the 1980s opened became the greatest ever as the Depository Institutions Deregulation and Monetary Control Act of 1980 ushered in a new era for the Federal Reserve. Also appended: The Federal Reserve System Balance Sheet and Statement of Revenues and Expenses and Fund Balance.

The appended map indicates the boundaries of Federal Reserve districts and their branch territories.

See FEDERAL ADVISORY COUNCIL, FEDERAL RESERVE BOARD OF GOVERNORS, FEDERAL RESERVE CITIES, FEDERAL RESERVE STATEMENT, NAKED RESERVE, REDISCOUNT RATE.

BIBLIOGRAPHY

BAGHESTANI, H., and MOTT, T. "The Money Supply Process Under Alternative Federal Reserve Procedures: An Empirical Examination." *Southern Economic Journal*, October, 1988.
BOARD OF GOVERNORS OF THE FEDERAL RESERVE SYSTEM. *Federal Reserve Board Rules and Regulations*. Federal Reserve System, Washington, DC.
———. *Annual Report*.
———. *Organization of the Federal Reserve System*.
FEDERAL RESERVE BANK OF BOSTON. *Historical Beginnings: The Federal Reserve System*. Reprinted periodically.
JONES, D. M. *Fed Watching and Interest Rate Projections*. New York Institute of Finance, New York, NY, 1986.
"U.S. Treasury and Fed Encourage Automated Funds Transfer," *Business Credit*, December, 1988.

FEDERAL RESERVE SYSTEM ADVISORY COMMITTEE
Several significant advisory committees help the Federal Reserve Board of Governors carry out their responsibilities. Included among these are:

1. The Consumer Advisory Council, established in 1976 by Congress, consists of 30 members who represent consumer and creditor interests. They advise the Board on responsibilities under the Consumer Credit Protection Act and on other issues.
2. The Federal Advisory Council, established under the Federal Reserve Act, is composed of one member from each Federal Reserve district who is elected each year by each of the 12 Federal Reserve banks' boards of directors. The council advises the Board on business and financial conditions and makes recommendations.
3. The Thrift Institutions Advisory Council, established after the Monetary Control Act of 1980, consists of representatives from mutual savings banks, savings and loan associations, and credit unions. The council provides input on the special needs and problems of thrifts.

FEDERAL SAVINGS AND LOAN ASSOCIATIONS
Under Section 5(a) of the Home Owners' Loan Act of 1933, federal charters were provided for federal savings and loan associations, to be chartered and regulated by the FEDERAL HOME LOAN BANK BOARD (FHLBB). Thus a new type of financial institution in the urban home-lending field came upon the scene, accounting as of year-end 1980 for over 55% of total assets of all SAVINGS AND LOAN ASSOCIATIONS in the U.S. As of year-end 1980, there were 1,985 federally chartered savings and loan associations, compared to 2,628 total state-chartered associations (of which 2,017 associations were insured by the FEDERAL SAVINGS AND LOAN INSURANCE CORPORATION).

Organization. Federal savings and loan associations may be established either by the granting of new charters to local organizing groups or by the conversion of existing state-chartered institutions of the savings and loan type. Pursuant to FHLBB regulations, state-chartered stock associations may convert to federal stock charter and state-chartered stock or mutual associations may convert to federal mutual charter under simplified procedures. From 1974 through 1980, 204 mutuals applied for permission to convert to stock associations, and a total of 99 received the permission to convert; in 1980 alone, 51 mutuals applied and 46 received permission. Following conversion, stock associations are required to register their common stock, pursuant to the Securities Exchange Act of 1934, with the Federal Home Loan Bank Board, and as of December 31, 1980, the number of stock associations thus registered totaled 102.

Application for permission to organize a federal association shall be in the form prescribed by the Federal Home Loan Bank Board, the chartering authority, and shall be executed by at least seven persons residing in the community to be served by the proposed association. Information to be furnished in support of the application shall be designed to show that (1) the applicants are citizens of the United States of good character and responsibility, (2) there is a necessity for the proposed association in the community to be served by it, (3) there is a reasonable probability of usefulness and success of the proposed association, and (4) the proposed association can be established without undue injury to properly conducted existing local thrift and home-financing institutions. The application shall include an estimate of the annual income and expenses of the proposed association and of the annual volume of business to be transacted by it and a statement of the personnel and office facilities to be provided for the operation of the association.

Charters K (revised) and N, the types of charters still held by most federal associations, are of the mutual form (nonstock).

Processing of applications for permission to organize a federal association is performed by the board's supervisory agent (the president of the Federal Home Loan bank of the district in which the proposed association is to be located or any other officer or employee of such bank designated by the board as agent), including public notice of filing of application, communications including briefs in favor or in protest, oral argument on the merits of any application based on written filed information, and recommendations to the board, decisions on all applications to organize being made by the board. If the board approves the application, it will specify the requirements as to: (1) minimum number of subscribers (savers in savings accounts) to the association's capital (savings accounts, since most federal charters are of the mutual type—although technically, such savers in savings accounts are shareholders and the savings accounts are savings capital), (2) minimum amount of capital to be paid into the association's savings accounts upon issuance of charter to it, and (3) any other requirements deemed necessary or desirable.

Any member of a Federal Home Loan bank may convert itself into a federal association upon the terms and conditions specified by the board and upon vote of not less than 51% of the votes cast at a meeting called to consider such action, which shall be in compliance with all laws in the jurisdiction which expressly provide for such conversion. In addition to filing the prescribed application for conversion, the applicant shall submit required financial statements and a plan of conversion, which shall expressly provide for: (1) appropriate reserves and surplus for the federal association, (2) satisfaction in full or assumption by the federal association of all creditor obligations of the applicant, (3) issuance by the federal association of its savings accounts to the holders of withdrawable accounts of the applicant in an amount equivalent to the value of their accounts, including the present value of any preferences to which holders are entitled, and (4) issuance by the federal association of its savings

ENCYCLOPEDIA OF BANKING AND FINANCE

accounts to all holders of guarantee, permanent, reserve fund, or other nonwithdrawable capital stock of the applicant in an amount equivalent to the value of such stock.

(*Note:* Each holder of a savings account in a mutual-type federal association is entitled to one vote for each $100 or fraction thereof of the withdrawable value of his account, and each borrower is permitted, as a borrower, one vote. No member, however, shall cast more than 50 votes. Voting may be by proxy.)

The process of conversion from the mutual form to the federal stock type begins with the development of the conversion plan. The FHLBB's regulations require that the plan be approved by two-thirds of the association's board of directors. After informing its members, the association files a conversion application, including the plan, with the Federal Home Loan Bank Board. If the board approves the conversion application, notice of approval is published in the *Federal Register*. The association then issues proxy statements, and any petition to the court for review must be filed within 30 days. A special meeting is called to obtain the approval of association members to convert. If approval is granted, preliminary stock offering, approved by the board, is offered to eligible subscribers. If the offering is not fully subscribed, all remaining stock must be sold to the public. The process is completed when the association issues the stock and the board issues a stock charter. The board has advocated conversions to stock charter as a means of enabling savings and loan associations to attract new capital and strengthen their net worth position.

Federal savings and loan associations are required to be insured by the FEDERAL SAVINGS AND LOAN INSURANCE CORPORATION (FSLIC).

Like the commercial banking system, the savings and loan system has a dual system of chartering and supervision, federal and state. State associations are chartered under state statutes and are supervised and examined by their respective banking or savings and loan departments. Federal associations are chartered under the provisions of the Home Owners' Loan Act of 1933 as amended and are subject to the supervision of the Federal Home Loan Bank Board.

Branches. A significant trend in recent years has been the expansion in number of branch offices of savings and loan associations.

Liberalization of Operations. Legislation and regulations at the federal level have broadened and liberalized operating powers and limits for savings and loan associations. A summary by the United States League of Savings Associations of pertinent legislation in recent years includes the following:

The 1968 Housing and Urban Development Act gave federal associations the authority to invest in mobile home and home equipment loans and expanded their authority to issue a wide variety of savings plans, notes, bonds and debentures.

(*Note:* Until recent years, only state-chartered associations in particular states operated under the stock form of organization; the FHLBB has since authorized a number of conversions of federal associations, formerly exclusively of the mutual (nonstock) type, to stock form.)

The 1970 Emergency Home Finance Act created the Federal Home Loan Mortgage Corporation, under the FHLBB, to provide a secondary market for conventional loans as well as FHA-insured and VA-guaranteed mortgages. Extended from 20 to 30 years the period allowed for associations to accumulate FSLIC-required reserves. (*Note:* Year-end net worth excluding certain items must equal 4% of insured account balances at the start of the year.)

The 1974 Housing and Community Development Act raised single-family and home improvement loan limits for federal associations; granted line-of-credit authority for construction lending; and created a 5%-of-assets category for loans an institution may not otherwise make.

The 1974 Depository Institutions Act increased FSLIC insurance of association savings accounts to $40,000 for private funds, $100,000 for public funds, and delegated Securities and Exchange Commission (SEC) enforcement authority for stock associations to the FHLBB (reporting requirements).

In 1975, Regulation Q and the Home Mortgage Disclosure Act prohibited the elimination or reduction of the interest rate differential on existing types of savings accounts (between the rate ceilings on commercial banks and on thrift institutions for such accounts) without prior congressional approval, and required most financial institutions to disclose the number and dollar amount of mortgage loans made by geographical area.

The 1976 Tax Reform Act reduced certain allowable federal income tax deductions for associations and increased the minimum tax rate.

It also liberalized individual retirement account (IRA) and Keogh account provisions.

The 1977 Housing and Community Development Act raised the ceiling on single-family loan amounts for associations' lending, federal agency purchases, Federal Housing Administration (FHA) insurance, and security for FHLB advances; liberalized the treatment of single-family and multifamily loans that exceed applicable ceilings; raised ceilings on conventional and FHA home improvement loans; and required regulatory agencies to take into account an institution's record of serving the credit needs of its community when evaluating applications for new facilities, mergers, and other matters.

The 1978 Financial Institutions Regulatory and Interest Rate Control Act increased FSLIC insurance limits for IRA and Keogh accounts from $40,000 to $100,000; strengthened FHLBB's regulatory powers over association officers, directors, and related organizations; prohibited top management or director interlocks among depository institutions; created the interagency Federal Bank Examination Council to encourage uniformity in financial institution supervision; authorized Federal Home Loan Mortgage Corporation (FHLMC) purchase of secured home improvement loan packages; and amended the Consumer Credit Protection Act to establish rights and responsibilities for electronic funds transfer.

The 1979 Housing and Community Development Act amendments increased one-family home loan limits for federal associations; reduced the stockholding-to-advances ratio for FHLB System members; raised FHA loan limits and expanded the FHA's Graduated Payments Mortgage program; raised FNMA and FHLMC loan ceilings; and exempted FHA loans from state usury ceilings.

In 1980, the Depository Institutions Deregulation and Monetary Control Act was passed. For all depository institutions, it extended savings interest rate control and the thrift institutions' rate differential for six years; shifted rate-setting authority from individual agencies to the Deregulation Committee, with targeted but not mandatory rate ceiling increases over the committee's six-year life; increased FSLIC and Federal Deposit Insurance Corporation (FDIC) insurance for individually owned savings accounts from $40,000 to $100,000; granted permanent authority for remote service units, automatic funds transfers, and share drafts; extended the federal override of state usury ceilings on certain mortgage and other loans; simplified truth-in-lending standards and reimbursement procedures; created standards and review procedures for simplification of new and existing regulations; and authorized nationwide negotiable-orders-of-withdrawal (NOW) accounts effective at year-end 1980 and established levels of cash reserves that must be held against NOW balances. For federal associations, it authorized investment of up to 20% of assets in consumer loans, corporate debt securities, and commercial paper; eased or removed lending restrictions, including geographical limitations, loan-to-value ratios, and treatment of one-family loans exceeding specified dollar amounts; expanded authority to invest in service corporations; granted authority to invest in mutual funds, to issue credit cards, and to engage in trust operations; and granted authority to issue mututal capital certificates which can be counted toward federal insurance reserve requirements. For FSLIC-insured institutions, it gave regulatory authorities the power to vary the reserve requirement between 3% and 6% (formerly 5%).

The 1980 Housing and Community Development Act permitted negotiated interest rates on certain FHA loans; created a new FHA rental subsidy program for middle-income families; created a secondary market for FNMA property improvement and mobile home loans; extended the provisions of the Home Mortgage Disclosure Act until October 1, 1985; and permitted corporate bonds and commercial paper to be counted toward FHLBB-required liquidity.

The 1982 Garn-St. Germain Depository Institutions Act gave the FSLIC authority to deal with financially troubled institutions, including the authority to overrule state authorities in seizing insolvent, state-chartered, FSLIC-insured institutions, and to merge them with out-of-state institutions. The act also removed all differences between savings and loan associations and savings banks in the kinds of business activities in which they may engage, and ended the interest rate differential under which thrift institutions had been authorized since 1966 to pay a slightly higher interest rate than commercial banks.

The Thrift Institutions Restructuring Act passed in 1981 (Powers Bill) provided for the FSLIC's power to authorize savings and loan holding companies to own institutions in more than one state. Several major acquisitions by sound savings and loan associations of marginal associations occurred in 1981 across state lines, based on regulatory authorization, and the possibility loomed that the Board of Governors of the Federal Reserve System, beyond making available adjustment credit at Federal Reserve banks' discount windows to savings and loan associations (pursuant to the Monetary Control Act of 1980), might permit bank holding companies if not individual commercial banks to acquire savings and loan associations intra- as well as interstate.

Summary. The basic cause of the crisis in the savings and loan industry and other thrift institutions in 1980 and 1981, resulting in outflows of deposits (disintermediation) to higher yielding money market funds and other media, operating losses and shrunken net worths as thrifts defensively offered better yielding but higher cost certificates, and market discounts on low fixed-rate mortgages still constituting the bulk of mortgage portfolios, was the rise in interest rates stimulated by the antiinflation stance of the MONETARY POLICY, mismanagement and outright fraud the Federal Home Loan Bank Board and the Federal Savings and Loan Insurance Corporation are having massive problems attempting to repair the damage.

See FEDERAL HOME LOAN BANK SYSTEM; THRIFT CRISIS.

BIBLIOGRAPHY

"An ABA Banking Journal Roundtable; Life After FSLIC?" *ABA Banking Journal*, January, 1989.
"Banks Cautious About Future." *Journal of Accountancy*, January, 1989.
CROCKETT, J. H. "The Good Bank/Bad Bank Restructuring of Financial Institutions." *The Bankers Magazine*, November/December, 1988.
EDGERTON, J. "You Owe Us $100 Billion." *Money*, March, 1989.
FEDERAL SAVINGS AND LOAN INSURANCE CORPORATION. *Annual Report.*
"Financial Statements For FSLIC-Assisted Acquisitions." *Journal of Accountancy*, February, 1989.
JACOBE, D. "Institution Problems Stem from Government Policies, Say Top Economists [Council of Economic Advisers Economic Report]." *Institutional Investor*, September, 1989.
LARY, B. K. "Insolvent Thrifts: A National Crisis." *Management Review.* March, 1989.
NADLER, P. S. "Will the S&L Crisis Rub Off on Banks?" *Bankers Monthly*, March, 1989

FEDERAL SAVINGS AND LOAN INSURANCE CORPORATION
Established June 27, 1934, by Title IV of the National Housing Act, the Federal Savings and Loan Insurance Corporation (FSLIC) insures the savings accounts in insured SAVINGS AND LOAN ASSOCIATIONS up to $100,000, effective April 1, 1980. Insurance is compulsory for all FEDERAL SAVINGS AND LOAN ASSOCIATIONS. State-chartered associations may obtain insurance upon application and approval by the corporation. The insurance afforded may be provided through the prevention of default or the payment of insurance to savings account holders in the event of liquidation. The former course of action, which results in complete protection to each saver regardless of the amount in his account, is accomplished by making cash grants, or by purchasing all or a part of the association's assets, or by arranging the merger of a problem institution into one financially and managerially strong, which is the rescue technique most frequently used. The corporation is also authorized to make loans to institutions in financial difficulty. Wherever possible, preventive measures are taken to eliminate the necessity of liquidation. In the event that liquidation is necessary, the corporation acts as receiver or coreceiver upon request of state authority in cases involving state-chartered institutions. In addition, the corporation, upon determination by the FEDERAL HOME LOAN BANK BOARD, is empowered to act even retroactively as sole receiver in cases involving state-chartered institutions, under P.L. 90-389 (July 7, 1968); and the board has the authority to appoint the corporation as receiver for federals.

Operations. The corporation functions under the direction of the Federal Home Loan Bank Board, which provides certain administrative services and conducts the examination and supervision of the insured institutions. The expenses of the board and its staff offices are paid from assessments made on the corporation and the district Federal Home Loan banks.

The corporation is entirely self-supporting and in no one year have its operating expenses exceeded its income. Revenues and other receipts have been sufficient to cover all insurance losses and operating expenses, to increase the corporation's primary reserve (cumulative net income), and to establish the corporation's "allowance for estimated losses for contribution agreements."

The original capital of $100 million was completely repaid to the U.S. Treasury, together with an additional $43 million for the use of the funds. The corporation has continuing authority to borrow from the Treasury for insurance purposes, with a limitation of $750 million outstanding at any one time, and can call upon its members for deposits equal to 1% of their total savings. No borrowings or calls under these authorizations have ever been made. The corporation has additional authority to assess against each insured institution as follows:

1. Under Section 404(b) of the National Housing Act, as amended, each insured institution is required to pay a basic insurance premium in an amount equal to $^1/_{12}$th of 1% of its savings accounts.
2. The corporation also may levy an additional premium up to the full amount of all its losses and expenses. Through 1980, the FSLIC had never charged its member associations any additional premiums.
3. For a period of time beginning in 1962, members were required to prepay regular premiums into a secondary reserve of the corporation in order to build up total reserves more rapidly than regular payments alone could do. In 1973, such prepayments were discontinued permanently, and in 1974 Congress enacted legislation providing for the gradual phaseout of the secondary reserve (the refund from the secondary reserve for calendar year 1980 was $119.5 million, compared to $110.2 million in calendar year 1979; the secondary reserve still totaled $792.2 million as of December 31, 1980).

Recent Operations of the FSLIC. Because of the adverse economic conditions affecting the savings and loan industry throughout the 1980s, including record high interest rates, the Federal Savings and Loan Insurance Corporation experienced record cash outlays in protecting the depositors of insured institutions. The major portion of the outlays was for the purchase of Government National Mortgage Association (GNMA) securities by the FSLIC to take up the commitments made by certain savings and loan associations to purchase the GNMA securities.

As authorized by the National Housing Act, a variety of techniques are employed to avoid default of an insured institution, or to effect a transfer of deposits and other liabilities and assets in the event of default. Default is defined in the act as the appointment of a receiver or other legal custodian for the purpose of liquidation. The authority to prevent default or effect a transfer permits the FSLIC to make loans, grant contributions, or purchase assets, or use any combination thereof, as long as the estimated cost of the action does not exceed the expense of liquidating the institution accompanied by the payment of insurance upon its accounts. See appended exhibit.

The FINANCIAL INSTITUTIONS REGULATORY AND INTEREST RATE CONTROL ACT OF 1978 expanded the authority of the FSLIC to provide financial assistance after default. This authorization allows the FSLIC to facilitate a merger (intra-or interstate) of the defaulting institution with a strong insured institution. This authority also allows the FSLIC to enter into purchase and assumption transactions whereby the savings deposits (and generally a portion of the assets) of a defaulting association are transferred to another insured institution, with the remaining assets being acquired by the FSLIC. The FSLIC's policy is to avoid the acquisition of assets whenever possible. Nevertheless, when asset acquisition is the only solution for a problem association and is less costly than a payout of insured accounts, it is given consideration.

The Competitive Equality Banking Act of 1987 provided a $10.8 billion bailout for the Federal Savings and Loan Insurance Corporation after auditors had found the FSLIC had a $6.6 billion deficit in 1986. For all practical purposes, the fund was insolvent and could not repay all the depositors in bankrupt or near-bankrupt thrifts, especially in states hit by farm and energy problems. The new funding was to be repaid by the thrift industry.

The FINANCIAL INSTITUTIONS REFORM, RECOVERY, AND ENFORCEMENT ACT OF 1989, which became law in August, was the most significant financial industry legislation since the Bank Holding Company Act of 1956. This thrift rescue bill affected the entire structure of deposit insurance, supervision, and financial industry competition. THe purposed of the act include:

The Federal Home Loan Bank System

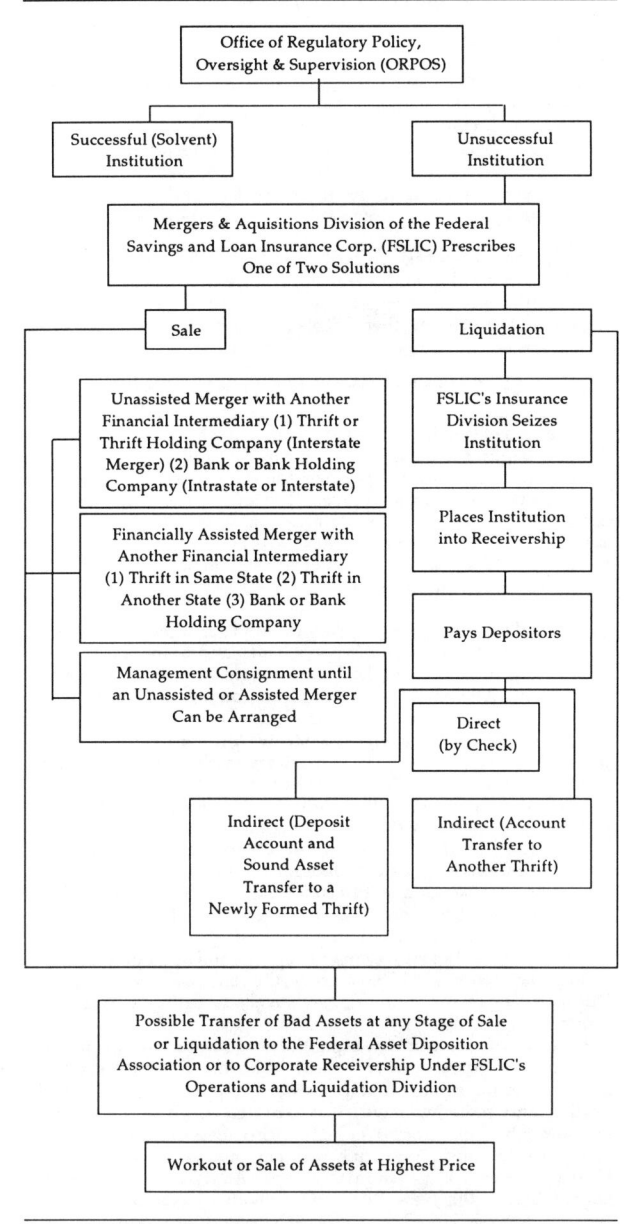

```
Office of Regulatory Policy,
Oversight & Supervision (ORPOS)
         |
    -----+-----
    |         |
Successful  Unsuccessful
(Solvent)   Institution
Institution
                |
   Mergers & Aquisitions Division of the Federal
   Savings and Loan Insurance Corp. (FSLIC) Prescribes
   One of Two Solutions
                |
        --------+--------
        |               |
      Sale           Liquidation
        |               |
        |         FSLIC's Insurance
        |         Division Seizes
        |         Institution
        |               |
Unassisted Merger with Another
Financial Intermediary (1) Thrift or
Thrift Holding Company (Interstate
Merger) (2) Bank or Bank Holding
Company (Intrastate or Interstate)
        |         Places Institution
        |         into Receivership
Financially Assisted Merger with       |
Another Financial Intermediary         |
(1) Thrift in Same State (2) Thrift in
Another State (3) Bank or Bank
Holding Company
        |         Pays Depositors
        |               |
Management Consignment until           |
an Unassisted or Assisted Merger   Direct
Can be Arranged                   (by Check)
        |
Indirect (Deposit        Indirect (Account
Account and              Transfer to
Sound Asset              Another Thrift)
Transfer to a
Newly Formed Thrift)

Possible Transfer of Bad Assets at any Stage of Sale
or Liquidation to the Federal Asset Diposition
Association or to Corporate Receivership Under FSLIC's
Operations and Liquidation Division

Workout or Sale of Assets at Highest Price
```

Source: A Guide to the Federal Home Loan Bank System. Federal Home Loan Bank.

1. Promoting a safe and stable system of affordable housing finance through legislation.
2. improving supervision by strengthening enforcement powers.
3. strengthening capital, accounting, and other supervisory standards.
4. Placing the federal deposit insurance system an a sound basis.

For detail surrounding the late 1980s financial institutions emergency, see THRIFT CRISIS and FINANCIAL INSTITUTIONS REFORM, RECOVERY, AND ENFORCEMENT ACT OF 1989.

BIBLIOGRAPHY

"An ABA Banking Journal Roundtable; Life after FSLIC?" *ABA Banking Journal*, January, 1989.
"Banks Cautious About Future." *Journal of Accountancy*, January, 1989.
CROCKETT, J.H. "The Good Bank/Bad Bank Restructuring of Financial Institutions." *The Bankers Magazine*, November/December, 1988.
EDGERTON, J. "YOU OWE US $100 BILLION." *MONEY*, March, 1989.
FEDERAL SAVINGS AND LOAN INSURANCE CORPORATION. *Annual Report*. "Financial Statements For FSLIC-Assisted Acquisitions." *Journal*.

FEDERAL-STATE UNEMPLOYMENT COMPENSATION PROGRAM The basic program of income support for the nation's unemployed workers. With limited federal intervention, UNEMPLOYMENT COMPENSATION benefits are payable under laws of individual States. The Federal Unemployment Insurance Service (UIS) provides leadership and policy guidance to state employment security agencies for the development, improvement, and operation of the federal-state unemployment insurance system and of related wage-loss, worker dislocation, and adjustment assistance compensation programs, including to ex-service personnel and federal civilian workers, and supplemental or extended benefits programs. The UIS reviews state unemployment insurance laws and their administration by the states to determine whether they are in conformity with federal requirements and oversees the actuarial soundness of the level and relationship of state expenditures, revenues, and reserves of federal appropriations for payment of benefits.

Source: Department of Labor.

FEDERAL TRADE COMMISSION The "watchdog of competition," established as an independent administrative agency in 1915, pursuant to the Federal Trade Commission Act of 1914 (38 Stat. 717; 15 U.S.C. 41-51). The commission was the outgrowth of crystallization of sentiment in favor of regulation of big business and superseded the old Bureau of Corporations. About one month later the Clayton Anti-trust Act vested additional duties upon the commission. Through the years, related duties were delegated to the Federal Trade Commission (FTC) by the Wheeler-Lea Act, the Trans-Alaska Pipeline Authorization Act, the Export Trade Act, the Wool Products Labeling Act, the Fur Products Labeling Act, the Textile Fiber Products Identification Act, the Fair Packaging and Labeling Act, the Lanham Trade-Mark Act of 1946, the Truth-in-Lending Act, the Fair Credit Reporting Act, the Robinson-Patman Act, the Hobby Protection Act, the Magnuson-Moss Warranty-Federal Trade Commission Improvement Act, and the Federal Trade Commission Improvements Act of 1980.

Section 5 of the original Federal Trade Commission Act, which provides regulatory authority for the commission in the prohibition of "unfair methods of competition," was amended in 1938 by the Wheeler-Lea Act, which is designed to protect the consumer against "unfair or deceptive acts or practices in commerce" and prohibits false and misleading advertising of foods, drugs, curative devices, and cosmetics. The Oleomargarine Act of 1950 amended the Wheeler-Lea Act to include misleading advertisements for oleomargarine. Technically, therefore, this aspect of the FTC's jurisdiction is not antitrust in nature, being concerned primarily with unfair methods of competition and deceptive practices.

The commission derives antitrust jurisdiction from Section 2 of the Clayton Anti-trust Act, which as amended by the Robinson-Patman Act of 1936 is concerned with price discrimination, declaring unlawful both the granting and the receipt of such discrimination, and from Section 3 of the Clayton Act, which forbids exclusive-dealing arrangements and tie-in contracts. Both of these sections are concerned with these practices where the effect may be "to substantially lessen competition or tend to create a monopoly in any line of commerce." The Clayton Act also gives the FTC jurisdiction in Section 7, concerned with mergers or consolidations where the effect may be to substantially lessen competition (as amended in 1950 to include acquisitions of assets as well as stock), and Section 8, as amended in 1935, which is concerned with elimination of competition as the result of any interlocking directors between industrial corporations, any one of which has capital, surplus, and undivided profits of more than $1 million.

Organization. The commission consists of five members, each appointed by the President by and with the advice and consent of the Senate for a term of seven years. Not more than three of the commissioners may be members of the same political party. Administrative management of the commission is vested in a chairman, who is appointed by the President. The executive director, who is appointed by the chairman with the consent of the commission, exercises general supervision over the staff of the commission.

FEDERAL TRADE COMMISION IMPROVEMENT ACT

Functions. The commission's principal functions are described officially as follows:

To promote free and fair competition in interstate commerce in the interest of the public through prevention of price-fixing agreements, boycotts, combinations in restraint of trade, other unfair methods of competition, and unfair or deceptive practices.

To safeguard the consuming public by preventing the dissemination of false or deceptive advertisements of consumer products generally and food, drugs, cosmetics, and therapeutic devices, and by preventing other unfair or deceptive practices in interstate commerce.

To prevent discriminations in price, exclusive-dealing and tying arrangements, corporate mergers, and interlocking directorates when the effect of such practices or arrangements may be substantial lessening of competition or a tendency toward monopoly; to prevent the payment or receipt of illegal brokerage; and to prevent discrimination among competing customers in the furnishing of or payment for advertising or promotional services or facilities used to promote the resale of a product.

To enforce truthful labeling of textile and fur products.

To prevent the interstate marketing of dangerously flammable materials intended or sold for use in wearing apparel.

To regulate packaging and labeling of certain consumer commodities so as to prevent consumer deception and facilitate value comparisons.

To supervise the registration and operation of associations of U.S. exporters engaged solely in export trade.

To petition for the cancellation of the registration of trademarks which were illegally registered or which have been used for purposes contrary to the intent of the Trade-Mark Act of 1946.

To achieve true credit cost disclosure by consumer creditors (retailers, finance companies, nonfederal credit unions, and other creditors not specifically regulated by another government agency) as called for in the Truth in Lending Act; to assure a meaningful basis for informed credit decisions; and to regulate the issuance and liability of credit cards so as to prohibit their fraudulent use in or affecting commerce.

To protect consumers against circulation of inaccurate or obsolete credit reports and to ensure that consumer reporting agencies exercise their responsibilities in a manner that is fair and equitable and in conformity with the Fair Credit Reporting Act.

To gather and make available to the Congress, the President, and the public factual data concerning economic and business conditions.

Enforcement functions: As an administrative agency, acting quasi-judicially and quasi-legislatively, the commission deals with trade practices on a continuing and corrective basis. It has no authority to punish. Its function is to prevent, through cease-and-desist orders and other means, the practices encompassed in the laws on federal trade regulation. The commission's law enforcement work falls into two general categories: (1) enforcement through formal litigation leading to mandatory orders against offenders, and (2) law observance achieved by action of a voluntary and cooperative nature.

The formal litigation cases are conducted by proceedings similar to those used in courts. Cases are instituted by issuance of formal complaint charging a person, partnership, or corporation with violation of one or more of the statutes administered by the commission. If the charges are not contested, or if in a contested case the charges are found after hearings to be true, an order may be issued requiring discontinuance of the unlawful practices. Law observance through voluntary and cooperative action may be obtained by way of the trade conference procedure, through individual stipulation-agreements, or through informal administrative correction of minor infractions.

In carrying out the statutory directive to prevent the use in commerce of unfair practices, the commission makes extensive use of voluntary and cooperative procedures. Through these procedures "business and industry may obtain authoritative guidance and a substantial measure of certainty as to what they may do under the laws administered by the Commission." Whenever it is practicable to do so, the commission will furnish an advisory opinion as to whether a proposed course of conduct, if pursued, would be likely to result in further action by the commission. Such opinions are binding on the commission, "but are subject to the right of the Commission to reconsider and rescind the opinion should the public interest require." Information submitted will not be used as the basis for a proceeding against the requesting party, however, without prior notice and opportunity to discontinue the course of action pursued in good faith in reliance upon the commission's advice.

BIBLIOGRAPHY

"AICPA and FTC Reach Compromise on Contingency Fees." *CA Magazine*, November, 1988.
FEDERAL TRADE COMMISSION. *Annual Report*.
KOEPPEL, D. "Mood in Washington Indicates a Trend Toward Regulation." *AdWeek's Marketing Week*, March 6, 1989.
"US Agrees Commissions [contingency fees and commissions to non-audit clients]." *Accountancy*. October, 1988.

FEDERAL TRADE COMMISSION IMPROVEMENT ACT
An act that authorizes Federal Reserve Board to identify unfair or deceptive acts or practices on the part of banks and to issue regulations to prohibit them. This act is one of several consumer protection laws.

FEDERAL UNEMPLOYMENT INSURANCE TAXES
A social security tax (FUTA) that provides unemployment insurance for a limited period of time to individuals who become unemployed. The tax requires a maximum rate of 6.2% to be levied wholly on employers of one or more persons, but the rate applies to only the first $7,000 paid to each employee. The law also provides that 5.4% of the 6.2% be payable to the state, assuming that the state levies an approved unemployment tax. Most state laws allow for a reduction of the typical 5.4% tax through merit-rating plans for those employers who maintain steady employment.

FEDWIRE
The Federal Reserve's funds and securities transfer service. It connects Federal Reserve banks and branches, U.S. government agencies such as the Treasury, and some 8,000 depository institutions. All Fedwire transfers are completed on the day they are initiated, usually in a matter of minutes. They are guaranteed final by the central bank when the receiving institution is notified of the credit to its account. The Depository Institutions Deregulation and Monetary Control Act of 1980 required pricing of funds and securities transfers as well as other Fed services and gave nonmember depository institutions direct access to Fedwire. Fedwire may be used by depository institutions to move funds resulting from the purchase or sale of federal funds, to move balances to correspondent banks and to send funds to other institutions on behalf of their customers. Transfers on behalf of bank customers include funds associated with the purchase or sale of securities, the replenishment of business demand deposits and other time-sensitive or large payments. The U.S. Treasury, the Federal Reserve, and other federal agencies use Fedwire extensively to disburse and collect funds.

Because of potential risk on the large-dollar funds transfer networks, the Board of Governors of the Federal Reserve introduced a risk-reduction policy in March 1986. The policy is aimed at controlling and reducing daylight overdrafts which occur when an institution has sent funds over Fedwire in excess of the balance in its reserve or clearing account, or has sent more funds over the Clearing House Interbank Payment System. As fiscal agent of the United States, the New York Fed provides electronic payments services for the U.S. Treasury's ACH-based program for direct deposit of federal recurring payments. These payments include Social Security, Veterans Administration benefits and federal salary payments.

Source: Adapted from *Fedwire*, Federal Reserve Bank of New York.

FEE
This term has two meanings:

1. A commission; charge for services. This term now is rarely used in finance, being supplanted by the term COMMISSION. It is primary used in connection with court costs in referring to witnesses fees, jurors' fees, and lawyers' fees.
2. FEE SIMPLE.

FEEDER
A branch line or short railroad which originates freight and passenger traffic for a main line or longer railroad. A feeder gathers traffic in territory where business is light and delivers it at a through traffic terminal to a line serving a richer territory.

FEEDER LOAN
See CATTLE LOANS.

FEE SIMPLE The fee simple absolute is the greatest estate in land and is characterized by infinite duration, full possession and enjoyment, free alienation, and descendability and devisability to the heirs of the owner. The fee simple defeasible is a fee which will come to an end automatically at the time specified in the instrument creating it, no reentry by the grantor or his heirs being necessary to terminate it. The fee simple subject to condition subsequent is a fee which will terminate upon the breach of a condition subsequent attached thereto *and* reentry by the grantor or his heirs.

FEVERISH An expression used to describe the stock and commodity markets when prices are hesitating, changeable, and uncertain, especially at a time when fundamental conditions are unsettled.

FIAT MONEY Inconvertible or irredeemable MONEY which a government declares shall be accepted as legal tender in payment of debts, but which is not covered by an available specie reserve. It consists either of government promises to pay the quantity of which is regulated or of undervalued metallic coins (silver, nickel, or copper) coined only on government account, but in no event is there expectation of redeeming either variety in the standard metal.

Fiat money was issued in large quantities during our colonial, revolutionary, and Civil War periods, each time with the same disastrous results—driving full value coins out of circulation or subjecting them to a premium, inflating prices, and in the end causing the fiat money to become worthless, except in the case of the Civil War greenbacks, which became redeemable money by the Specie Resumption Act of 1875.

Since no forms of U.S. paper money are redeemable currently into the standard money of redemption (gold), no gold coins circulate, and the coins in circulation are TOKEN MONEY, the U.S. money system is a fiat money system.

It is of interest to note that transition to the *de facto* fiat money system of modern times was successfully accomplished without sharp discrimination against and discounting of forms of fiat money issued and in circulation, unlike the discounts that prevailed after and during the Civil War for issues of UNITED STATES NOTES until that form of paper money was provided a gold reserve, albeit in partial amount. *See* FORCED CIRCULATION.

FICTITIOUS PAYEE Although the Uniform Commercial Code's Section 3-405(1)(b), which succeeded the Uniform Negotiable Instruments Law's Section 9(3), no longer contains the reference to "fictitious or nonexistent person," if in fact the maker or drawer of a negotiable instrument does make it payable to a fictitious or nonexistent payee and such fact is known to such maker or drawer, the situation is one indicating no intention that such payee shall have any interest in the instrument. Accordingly, in such a situation an endorsement by any person in the name of the indicated payee will be effective, pursuant to Section 3-405(1)(b), Uniform Commercial Code, since the person signing as or on behalf of a maker or drawer intends the indicated payee to have no interest in the instrument.

FIDELITY INSURANCE Insurance provided to indemnify employers against loss by reason of the dishonesty of employees or on account of the nonperformance of contracts. In fidelity insurance contracts, the insurance company undertakes a suretyship issuing fidelity insurance bonds as a guaranty against loss arising from default or dishonesty of the insured person. The beneficiary under this form of insurance may be a private employer, a state, county, or municipality, or the United States government. Fidelity insurance companies require each applicant for a bond for which insurance is to be provided to fill out a form. In considering the application one looks at the reputation and past history of the individual, the opportunity or temptation for theft or dishonesty which his position offers, and the value of the property in his possession by virtue of his employment. In the investigation of his reputation the criminal and civil court records are consulted. Where the risk has a criminal record, the application is usually rejected. Fidelity bonds are issued for three classes of risk: larceny or embezzlement, culpable negligence, and the unfaithful discharge of duty.

FIDUCIARY A person or corporation (bank or trust company) in whom certain property of the principal (settler) is entrusted for some purpose specified in the trust instrument. In a technical trust, the fiduciary is known as the trustee. Other fiduciaries in nontechnical trusts are executors, administrators, guardians, assignees, receivers, committees of estates of lunatics, etc.

More specifically, the Comptroller of the Currency in his *Comptroller's Manual for National Banks* defines fiduciary to mean a bank undertaking to act alone or jointly with others primarily for the benefit of another in all matters connected with its undertaking, and includes trustee, executor, administrator, registrar of stocks and bonds, guardian of estates, assignee, receiver, committee of estates of lunatics, managing agent and any other similar capacity. The Comptroller of the Currency further defines "trust department" of a national bank to mean that group or groups of officers and employees organized under the supervision of officers or employees to whom are designated by the board of directors the performance of the fiduciary responsibilities of the bank, whether or not the group or groups are so named. A national bank desiring to exercise fiduciary powers shall file an application with the Comptroller of the Currency pursuant to 12 CFR 4.7b.

Financial reporting places considerable emphasis on the fiduciary or stewardship function of the management of an enterprise. Managers are accountable not only for the custody and safekeeping of an enterprise's resources but also for the efficient and effective use of those resources, including protecting the enterprise from the unfavorable impact of inflation, deflations, technological and social change, and similar environmental factors. In a larger sense, society may impose stewardship functions on enterprises and their managements. Statements of financial position and income statements are basic references for evaluation of how managers have performed their stewardship function, especially to owners.

Assessing management's stewardship function for nonbusiness organizations is especially important. Information about such organizations' performance should ordinarily be the focus for assessing the stewardship or accountability of managers. Uses of financial statements of nonbusiness organizations require assurance that managers have utilized available resources in a manner that corresponds to those specified by resource providers.

In governmental accounting, fiduciary funds are used to account for assets held in a trust or agency capacity. Fiduciary funds include expendable and nonexpendable trust funds (funds where the corpus may or may not be spent), pension trust funds, and agency funds. The fiduciary responsibility is to operate the fund according to the agreement with the contributor of the principal or corpus.

FIDUCIARY CAPACITY Generally speaking, any relationship of confidence and trust involving the highest degree of good faith and loyalty to the interests of another person. Thus, the term is not restricted to technical trusts, but includes such relationships as attorney and client, broker and principal, corporation director and stockholders, agent and principal, etc. The term more specifically refers to formal fiduciary relationships such as trustee in technical trusts, executor, administrator, conservator, guardian, committee in lunacy, receiver, assignee, etc., for the benefit of beneficiary, distributee, ward, lunatic, debtor, principal, etc. A trustee capacity differs from an agency in that a trustee holds legal title to the property for his beneficiary and in that the agency is usually a personal relationship dependent upon the will and continued existence of the parties, whereas the trust is impersonal in nature.

National banks are permitted to act in fiduciary capacities—trustee, executor, administrator, registrar of stocks and bonds, guardian of estates, assignee, receiver, committee of estates of lunatics, etc.—when not in contravention of state or local laws, under grant of a special permit from the Comptroller of the Currency pursuant to the Comptroller's Regulation 9 and Section 1(j) of the act of September 28, 1962 (76 Stat. 668). In addition to authorizing the organization of trust companies expressly organized with such powers, most states have passed laws enabling state banks to act in fiduciary capacities. *See* TRUST.

FIDUCIARY CURRENCY Credit money; money no part of which is supported by redemption in metallic reserve. Paper money issued on the credit of a bank or government is fiduciary currency. Theoretically, all currency is fiduciary currency in the United States since no currency is domestically redeemable into the standard monetary metal (gold).

The Bank of England's note issue as provided by the Bank Act of 1844 was a partially fiduciary issue, consisting of a limited authorized amount covered by government securities with any note

FIDUCIARY TAXATION

issue in excess thereof fully covered by gold. Since September, 1939, when all gold in the Bank of England's Issue Department was transferred to the exchange equalization account, the Bank of England's note issue has been covered practically entirely by government securities. Thus in English terminology, the note issue is largely fiduciary issue.
See BANK OF ENGLAND.

FIDUCIARY TAXATION Income taxes on estates and trusts. Estates and trusts are referred to as fiduciaries, and their taxation as fiduciary taxation. Estates and trusts are two special tax entities. Income generated by property owned by an estate or a trust is reported on an income tax return for that entity. Generally, the tax rules governing estates and trusts are identical, although there are some exceptions.

The basic tax formula for establishing a fiduciary's (estates and trusts) taxable income and tax liability is similar to that available to individuals. A brief outline of the tax formula is illustrated here:

Gross income (same rules as for individuals)
- Deductions for expenses (e.g., interest, taxes, depreciation and charitable contributions)
- Distribution deduction (income taxes to the beneficiary)
- Exemption deduction ($600 for estate; $300 for simple trust requiring distribution of its income currently; $100 for complex trusts)
= Taxable income x
x Tax on taxable income
- Credits
= Net taxable liability

An estate or trust must file U.S. Fiduciary Income Tax Return, Form 1041, if it has gross income of $600 or more. The return is due by the 15th day of the fourth month following the close of the estate or trust's taxable year. Beginning in 1988, estates and trusts are taxed as follows:

a. First $5,000 of taxable income is taxed at 15%
b. Taxable income in excess of $5,000 is taxed at 28%
c. The 15% bracket is phased out by adding an additional 5% tax on taxable income between $13,000 and $26,000

If estate or trust income is not distributed to beneficiaries, the income is taxable to the estate or trust. If the income is distributed to beneficiaries, the estate or trust received a deduction for the distribution, and the income is taxable to beneficiaries for their table year in which the estate or trust taxable year ends.

Although estates and trusts are separate taxable entities, they will not pay an income tax if they distribute all of their income to beneficiaries.

BIBLIOGRAPHY

Commerce Clearing House Citator.
Prentice Hall Citator.

FIELD BANKING A banking network for which concentration services are used. Field banking networks consist of a number of local depository accounts into which company personnel make deposits.

FIELD WAREHOUSE RECEIPT LOANS Loans made against inventory that is located on the borrower's premises in contrast to a terminal warehouse receipt loan when the goods are located in a public warehouse. A field warehousing company sets off a designated storage area on the borrower's premises for the inventory pledged as collateral for a loan. The warehousing company has sole access to this storage area and maintains strict control over it. The warehousing company issues a warehouse receipt; the lender extends a loan based upon the collateral value of the inventory.

FIFTEEN-YEAR MORTGAGE A variation of the FIXED RATE MORTGAGE that has an interest rate and monthly payments that are constant throughout the loan; the loan is fully paid off in only fifteen years, usually available at a slightly lower interest rate than a longer-term loan. Higher payments are required. A smaller proportion of each monthly payments goes to interest.

FILES See AVERAGE LOAN AND BALANCE FILE, CREDIT FILES.

FILLING The part of a check which contains the amount written both in words and figures. The words and figures should agree, but the Uniform Commercial Code (Section 3-118(c)) follows the rule of construction of the former Section 17, Negotiable Instruments Law, in providing that words control figures except that if the words are ambiguous, the figures control.

FINANCE This term has three meanings:

1. To raise money necessary to organize, reorganize, or extend an enterprise, whether by the sale of stocks, bonds, or notes or otherwise.
2. The theory and practice of monetary credit, banking, and promotion operations in the most comprehensive sense. It includes money, credit, banking, securities, investment, speculation, foreign exchange, promotion, reorganization, underwriting, brokerage, trusts, etc.
3. Originally, the raising of money by taxes or bond issues and the administration of revenues and expenditures by a government. This is now known as PUBLIC FINANCE.

Finance is the science of managing money and is closely related to both economics and accounting. Economics provides an understanding of the institutional structures in which money and credit flow (macroeconomics) and the profit maximization guidelines associated with the theory of the firm (microeconomics). Accounting provides the source of financial and other data for financial management.

Financial theory deals primarily with the accumulation and allocation of economic resources in relation to time and under varied states of the world. Finance also attempts to explain how money and capital markets facilitate the allocation of resources. Finance is concerned with the valuation of the firm as a going concern and investment opportunities and with factors that can change these values. It deals with the acquisition and use of funds, including their impact on the profitability and growth of the firm. Financial theory is applicable to nonprofit entities as well as for-profit enterprises.

The functions of a financial manager are financial analysis and planning, the management of the firm's asset structure, and the management of its financial structure. A firm's asset structure refers to both the mix and type of assets reported on the firm's balance sheet. Financial structure refers to the appropriate mix of short-term and long-term financing, including both debt and equity financing. The goal of financial management is to achieve the objectives of the firm's owners, which is sometimes considered to be the maximization of profit or wealth. The maximization of profit and wealth requires financial managers to consider the owner's realizable return on the investment, a short-run and a long-run viewpoint, the timing of benefits, risks, and the distribution of returns.
See CORPORATION FINANCE.

BIBLIOGRAPHY

PRINGLE, J. AND HARRIS, R. J. *Essentials of Managerial Finance*, 1984.

Finance periodicals:
Barron's.
Business Week.
Digest of Financial Planning Ideas.
Dow Theory Letters.
Financial Analysts Journal.
Financial Executive.
Financial Planning Magazine.
Forbes.
Fortune.
Harvard Business Review.
The Insiders.
Insiders' Chronicle.
Journal of Finance.
Money.
OTC Review.
Professional Tape Reader.
SEC Today.
Speculator.

ENCYCLOPEDIA OF BANKING AND FINANCE

Standard & Poor's.
Street Smart Investing.
Value Line.
The Wall Street Journal.
Weekly Insider Report.

Handbooks and Manuals:
ALTMAN, E. I. *Financial Handbook.* John Wiley and Sons, New York, NY, 1987. DOWNES, J., and GOODMAN, J. E. *Barron's Finance and Investment Handbook.* Barron's Educational Services, Inc., Woodbury, NY, 1987.
FABOZZI, F. J., and ZARB, F. G. *Handbook of Financial Market-Securities Options, Futures.* Dow Jones-Irwin, Inc., Homewood, IL, 1987.
RAO, D. *Handbook of Business, Finance, and Capital Sources*, AMACOM, New York, 1985.

Journals:
See also BANK and ECONOMICS.
Commercial Finance Journal.
Corporate Financing Week.
Credit.
Credit and Financial Management.
Financial Management.
Financial World.
Fortune.
Journal of Finance.
Journal of Financial and Quantitative Analysis.
Journal of Financial Economics.
Journal of Money, Credit and Banking.

Other publications:
BEL AIR, R. *How To Borrow Only Money From A Banker.* AMACOM, New York, NY, 1988.
BREALEY, R., and MYSERS, S. *Principles of Corporate Finance*, McGraw-Hill Book Co., Inc., New York, NY, 1988.
BRIGHAM, E., and GAPENSKI, L. *Intermediate Financial Management*, Dryden Press, Hinsdale, IL, 1985.
BUTLER, R. E., and RAPPAPORT, D. *A Complete Guide to Money and Your Business.* Prentice Hall, Inc., Englewood Cliffs, NJ, 1986.
FAMA, E. "Banking in a Theory of Finance." *Journal of Monetary Economics*, January, 1980.
———. "What's Different About Banks?" *Journal of Monetary Economics*, January, 1985.
GUERARD, J. and VAUGHT, H. T. *The Handbook of Financial Modeling.* Probus Publishing Co., New York, NY, 1989.
WOELFEL, C. J. *The Desktop Encyclopedia of Corporate Finance and Accounting.* Probus Publishing Co., Chicago, IL, 1987.

FINANCE BILL A clean bill of exchange, usually of 60 days' tenor or over, drawn by a bank or banker in one country on a bank or banker in another for the purpose of raising funds and especially when the interest rates in the country on which the bill is drawn are lower than in the country where the bill is drawn. Finance bills are not drawn against the shipment of goods; they are bankers' bills as distinguished from COMMERCIAL BILLS. They are sometimes drawn against balances maintained with the drawee bank but more often are not, being in the nature of an advance from a bank in one country to a bank in another. Finance bills are usually unsecured (up to a maximum limit), but sometimes bonds, stocks, or other collateral is pledged as security. The drawee bank accepts a finance bill for a fixed commission, but only of course when the drawing bank enjoys a high credit rating. Thus a finance bill is drawn for the purpose of raising funds to establish additional balances at home or abroad.

FINANCE COMMITTEE In larger boards of directors, the by-laws or the board by resolution may provide for a finance committee, consisting of those directors who are specialists in finance, who shall have power to supervise the financial affairs of the corporation and shall report to the board of directors from time to time or whenever it shall be called upon to do so.

FINANCE COMMITTEE, U.S. SENATE A Committee of the United States Senate. The Committee currently has 20 members. The Committee has jurisdiction over major areas affecting individuals and businesses including the following:

1. **Tax matters.** The Committee has the responsibility for all revenue used to finance the Federal Government, including the terms and conditions under which the Government borrows money.
2. **Social security.** The social security program provides retirement, survivorship, and disability benefits for workers and their families.
3. **Medicare.** The medicare program provides health insurance for aged and disabled social security beneficiaries.
4. **Supplemental security income.** The supplemental security income program assures all aged, blind, and disabled persons a minimum level of income.
5. **Family welfare programs.** The welfare program provides Federal, State and local aid to families needing assistance.
6. **Social services.** Federal financing provided to assist States in operating programs of social services, child welfare services, adoption assistance, foster care, and related training.
7. **Medicaid.** Federal, State and local medical assistance is provided for needy persons under the medicaid program.
8. **Unemployment compensation.** The Federal and State governments operate compensation programs for unemployed persons for limited periods.
9. **Maternal and child health.** The maternal and child health programs are authorized in the Social Security act.
10. **Tariff and trade legislation.** The Committee has the responsibility for all legislation affecting tariffs and import trade.

The Committee's responsibilities extend to the bonded debt of the United States (except as provided in the Congressional Budget Act of 1974); custom, collection districts, and ports of entry and delivery; deposit of public moneys; general revenue sharing; national social security; reciprocal trade agreements and transportation of dutiable goods.

In addition to its legislative responsibilities, the committee considered presidential nominations and marking recommendations to the Senate whether the nominee should be confirmed. Nominations referred to the Finance Committee include:

Secretary, deputy secretary, under secretaries, assistant secretaries, and general counsel of the treasury department.
Secretary, Under Secretary, most Assistant Secretaries, General Counsel, and Inspector General of the Department of Health and Human Services.
United States Trade Representative and Deputy United States Trade Representatives;
Under Secretary of Commerce for International Trade and certain Assistant Secretaries of Commerce;
Commissioner of Social Security;
Chief of the Children's Bureau;
Commissioner and Chief Counsel of the Internal Revenue Service;
Treasurer of the United States;
Judges of the U.S. Tax Court; and
Commissioners of the International Trade Commission.

FINANCE COMPANY This term has several meanings:

1. SALES FINANCE COMPANIES, which discount installment sales paper of vendors, as well as discount or lend on the pledge of installment or other accounts receivable. Various sales finance companies have diversified operations to include the services of the FACTOR.
2. Personal finance companies, or small loan companies, which specialize in personal loans under small loan laws of the various states.
3. A HOLDING COMPANY where the services of the holding company are particularly financial for subsidiaries.

See appended table of domestic finance companies.

FINANCIAL ACCOUNTING Financial accounting is a subset of financial reporting that is concerned primarily with measuring and reporting financial information in a set of basic general purpose financial statements. Financial accounting is designed to meet the needs of external users of the financial statements of an enterprise. General purpose financial statements are statements designed to meet the needs of most users, primarily investors and creditors. Standards for financial accounting are reflected in GENERALLY ACCEPTED ACCOUNTING PROCEDURES (GAAP). Managerial accounting is as subset of financial reporting that is concerned primarily with

FINANCIAL ACCOUNTING FOUNDATION

Domestic Finance Companies; Business Credit Outstanding and Net Change[1]
(Millions of dollars, seasonally adjusted)

Type	1985	1986	1987	1988 Nov.	1988 Dec.	1988 Jan.	1989 Feb.	1989 Mar.	1989 Apr.
1. Total	156,297	172,060	205,810	233,699	234,529	235,969	237,378	240,186	244,882
Retail financing of installment sales									
2. Automotive	20,660	26,015	35,782	36,444	36,548	37,041	37,301	37,696	38,415
3. Equipment	22,483	23,112	25,170	28,214	28,298	28,429	28,385	28,207	28,790
4. Pools of securitized assets [1]	NA	NA	NA	NA	NA	724	682	855	817
Wholesale									
5. Automotive	23,988	23,010	30,507	32,201	33,300	33,664	34,386	33,528	34,383
6. Equipment	4,568	5,348	5,600	5,980	5,983	6,183	6,193	6,088	6,153
7. All other	6,809	7,033	8,342	9,037	9,341	9,493	9,569	9,682	9,852
8. Pools of securitized assets [1]	NA	NA	NA	NA	NA	0	0	0	0
Leasing									
9. Automotive	16,275	19,827	21,952	24,621	24,673	24,558	24,847	25,584	25,544
10. Equipment	34,768	38,179	43,335	56,973	57,455	58,354	58,045	59,484	60,246
11. Pools of securitized assets [1]	NA	NA	NA	NA	NA	721	699	756	733
12. Loans on commercial accounts receivable and factored commercial accounts receivable	15,765	15,978	18,078	19,407	17,796	16,688	17,404	17,794	18,677
13. All other business credit	10,981	13,557	17,043	20,822	21,134	20,114	19,867	20,512	21,272
Net change									
14. Total	19,607	15,763	33,750	2,396	829	−4	1,409	2,808	4,696
Retail financing of installment sales									
15. Automotive	5,067	5,355	9,767	−235	105	493	260	394	720
16. Equipment	−363	629	2,058	371	84	131	−43	−178	583
17. Pools of securitized assets [1]	NA	NA	NA	NA	NA	NA	−42	173	−38
Wholesale									
18. Automotive	5,423	−978	7,497	−15	1,099	364	722	−858	856
19. Equipment	−867	780	252	104	3	200	10	−105	65
20. All other	1,069	224	1,309	146	303	152	76	114	170
21. Pools of securitized assets [1]	NA	NA	NA	NA	NA	NA	0	0	0
Leasing									
22. Automotive	3,896	3,552	2,125	346	52	−115	289	736	−40
23. Equipment	2,685	3,411	5,156	699	482	−506	−310	1,439	762
24. Pools of securitized assets [1]	NA	NA	NA	NA	NA	NA	−22	57	−23
25. Loans on commercial accounts receivable and commercial accounts receivable	2,161	213	2,100	480	−1,611	−1,108	716	390	883
26. All other business credit	536	2,576	3,486	501	312	385	−247	645	760

[1] Data on pools of securitized assets are not seasonally adjusted.

internal reporting. It relates essentially to planning, controlling, evaluating performance, and product costing for income valuation and income determination. There is some overlap between financial accounting and managerial accounting.

BIBLIOGRAPHY

Kieso, D. E., and Weygandt, J. J. *Intermediate Accounting*. Latest edition.

Nikolai, L. A., and Bazlery, J. D. *Intermediate Accounting*, Latest edition.

FINANCIAL ACCOUNTING FOUNDATION

The Financial Accounting Foundation is an independent, nongovernmental entity whose board of 16 trustees oversees the basic structure of the accounting standard-setting process. Of the 16 trustees, 13 are elected to their positions by eight so-called Electors, who are the official members of the corporation. These individuals are selected by the governing boards of eight sponsoring organizations. The 13 trustees are appointed by representatives of the following organizations: the American Accounting Association (1), AICPA (4), National Association of Accountants (1), Financial Executives Institute (2), Financial Analysts Federation (1), various governmental accounting groups (3), and Securities Industry Association (1). Two of the remaining positions are filled by persons elected by the other trustees. One of these is to come from the commercial banking industry, and the other from the business community. The sixteenth trustee is the senior elected official of the AICPA. The 15 elected trustees can serve no more than two terms of three years each. The trustees appoint members to the FASB (7 members) and to the FASB's advisory council (between 35 and 40 members) as well as seek funds for the FASB's operations.

The Financial Accounting Standards Board is an independent body consisting of seven members appointed by the Financial Accounting Foundation's trustees. The FASB is composed of accountants and non-accountants. Members are expected to have the following qualifications: knowledge of financial accounting and reporting; high level of intellect applied with integrity and discipline; judicial temperament. FASB members serve full-time and are fully remunerated. Members are not required to be CPAs. An affirmative vote of five of the seven FASB members is needed to approve a pronouncement. The Board's deliberations are open to the public. The Board is directed toward achieving three basic tasks: serving as the focal point for research; communicating with constituents; resolving financial accounting issues.

In 1984 a Governmental Accounting Standards Board (GASB) was established to deal with state and local governmental reporting issues. GASB is authorized to establish accounting standards for activities and transactions of state and local governments. Its authoritative pronouncements are issued as *Statements, Interpretations,* and *Technical Bulletins.* GASB *Statement No. 1,* "Authoritative Status of NCGA Pronouncements and AICPA Industry Audit Guide," issued in 1984, recognized the then effective National Council of Government Accountants pronouncements and certain accounting and reporting guidance in the AICPA state and local government audit guide as authoritative—stating that they are "continued in force until altered, amended, supplemented, revoked, or superseded by subsequent GASB pronouncements." These documents were integrated into *Codification of Governmental Accounting and Financial Reporting Standards.* The GASB codification is revised biannually. GASB is financed and overseen by the Financial Accounting Foundation. GASB has five members. The chairman serves full time, while the vice chairman and three other members serve part time. GASB has an advisory council, technical staff, and task forces.

The FASB-GASB jurisdiction policy requires that (1) GASB will establish standards for activities and transactions of state and local governmental entities, and (2) FASB will establish standards for activities and transactions of other entities. The AICPA affirmed this arrangement under Rule 203 of the AICPA Code of Professional Conduct.

The organizational structure of the Financial Accounting Foundation is appended.

BIBLIOGRAPHY

MILLER, P. B. W. "The Conceptual Framework: Myths and Realities," *Journal of Accountancy,* March 1985.
MILLER, P. B. W. and REDDING, R. *The FASB: The People, the Process, & the Politics,* 1986.
PRACTER, PAUL A. "The FASB After Ten Years: History and Emerging Trends," *Financial Accounting Theory,* 1985.
THOMSON, R. C. "How Do You View the FASB?" *Financial Executive,* May, 1984.

FINANCIAL ACCOUNTING STANDARDS BOARD

The Financial Accounting Standards Board (FASB) is the authoritative US standard setter for GENERALLY ACCEPTED ACCOUNTING PRINCIPLES (GAAP) established in 1973 as the successor to the Accounting Principles Board. FASB is a nongovernmental entity.

Since 1973 the Financial Accounting Standards Board has been the designated organization in the private sector for establishing standards of financial accounting and reporting. These standards are essentially rules governing the preparation of financial reports. The FASB standards are officially recognized as authoritative by the Securities and Exchange Commission and the American Institute of Certified Public Accountants (AICPA).

FASB succeeded the Accounting Principles Board (APB) in 1973 as the standard setter for generally accepted accounting principles. When the Accounting Principles Board came under increasing criticism, the American Institute of Certified Public Accountants established a Study Group on Establishment of Accounting Principles (commonly called the Wheat Committee) to examine the organization and operation of the APB. The Study Group recommended the creation of the FASB. This recommendation was implemented by early 1973.

The seven members of FASB are appointed by the trustees of the FINANCIAL ACCOUNTING FOUNDATION. The seven members are fully remunerated and serve full time. They are not required to be CPAs. An affirmative vote of five FASB members is required to approve a pronouncement. FASB issues three major types of pronouncements:

1. *Statements of Financial Accounting Standards (SFASs).* These statements establish new or amend existing generally accepted accounting principles.
2. *Interpretations.* Interpretations clarify, explain, or elaborate on SFASs, APB Opinions, or ARBs. Interpretations are considered a part of generally accepted accounting principles.
3. *Statements of Financial Accounting Concepts (SFACs).* These statements set down objectives and concepts that the FASB uses as the basis for establishing and improving generally accepted accounting principles. SFACs do not establish GAAPs.

Organizational Structure for Establishing Accounting Standards

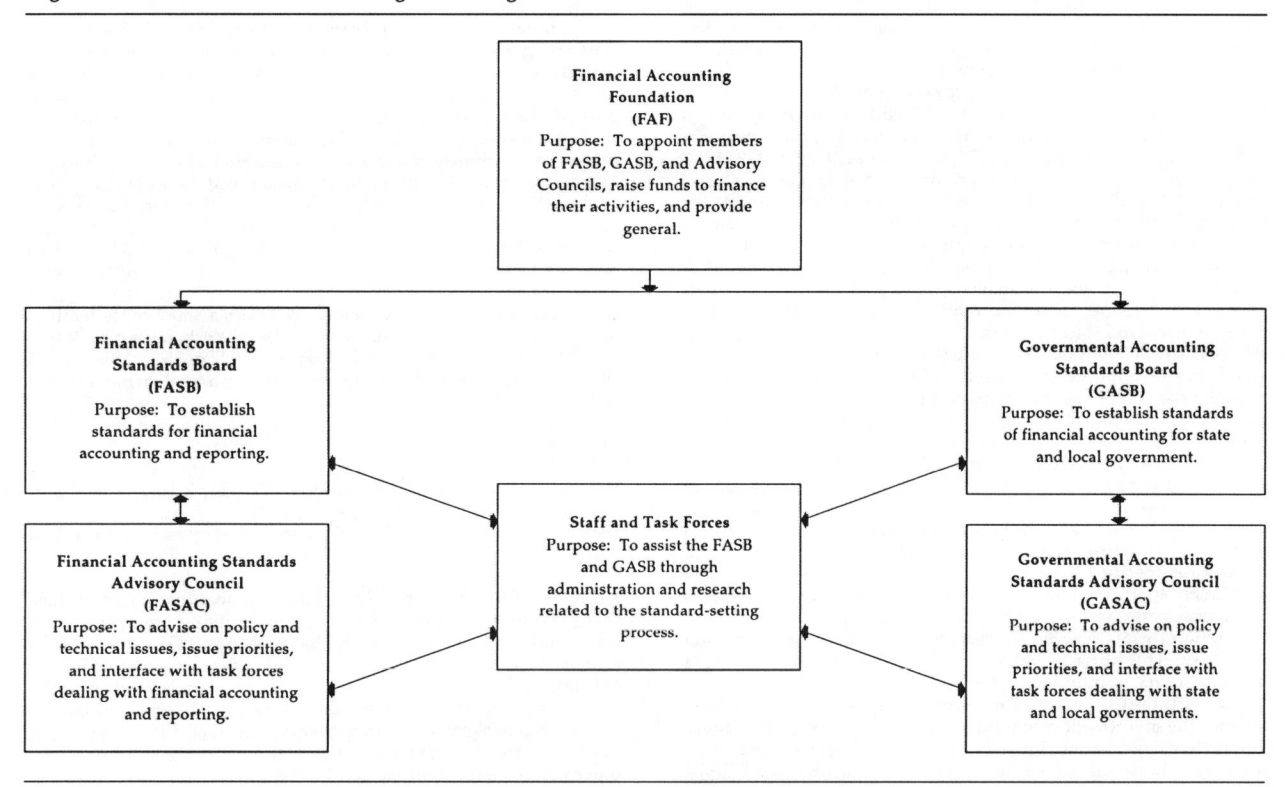

Financial Accounting Foundation (FAF)
Purpose: To appoint members of FASB, GASB, and Advisory Councils, raise funds to finance their activities, and provide general.

Financial Accounting Standards Board (FASB)
Purpose: To establish standards for financial accounting and reporting.

Financial Accounting Standards Advisory Council (FASAC)
Purpose: To advise on policy and technical issues, issue priorities, and interface with task forces dealing with financial accounting and reporting.

Staff and Task Forces
Purpose: To assist the FASB and GASB through administration and research related to the standard-setting process.

Governmental Accounting Standards Board (GASB)
Purpose: To establish standards of financial accounting for state and local government.

Governmental Accounting Standards Advisory Council (GASAC)
Purpose: To advise on policy and technical issues, issue priorities, and interface with task forces dealing with state and local governments.

The FASB staff issues *Technical Bulletins* that are designed to provide guidance on various financial accounting and reporting problems on a timely basis. Bulletins deal with matters relating to the implementation of existing standards in practice.

In 1984, FASB established an EMERGING ISSUES TASK FORCE to attempt to resolve accounting problems on a timely basis, especially with new types of products and transactions. The Task Force is composed of approximately 18 persons who represent CPA firms, major companies, the FASB, and the SEC.

FASB follows due process procedures involving the following major steps: identifies an accounting problem; conducts extensive research on the problem; issues a *Discussion Memorandum* which summarizes the major issues and suggests possible solutions which serves as a basis for public comment; conducts a public hearing; issues an *Exposure Draft* which is a proposed SFAS that is distributed for public comment; the Board issues an SFAS after deliberation.

A Financial Accounting Standards Advisory Council assists FASB in setting priorities and establishing ad hoc task forces. It provides council to FASB.

BIBLIOGRAPHY

BAILEY, L. P. "GASB's Future Role." *Management Accounting*, March, 1989.
BERESFORD, D. R. "How Well Does the FASB Consider the Consequences of Its Work?" *Financial Executive*, March/April, 1989.
———. "Internationalization of Accounting Standards: The Role of the Financial Accounting Standards Board." *CPA Journal*, January, 1989.
"Financial Reporting Issues: Authoritative Voices at FEI Conference." *Financial Executive*. March/April, 1989.
JACOBSEN, J. C., and IHLANFELDT, W. J. "The Rule-Making Process: A Time for Change?" *Financial Executive*, March/April, 1989.
KRIPKE, H. "Reflections on the FASB's Conceptual Framework for Accounting and on Auditing." *Journal of Accounting, Auditing, and Finance*, Winter, 1989.
MILLER, S. H. "Five-Year Review of GASB and FASB." *Journal of Accountancy*, April, 1989.

FINANCIAL ANALYSTS FEDERATION

An international nonprofit professional organization whose members are financial analyst societies located in major cities of the U.S. and Canada; organized in 1947. The total membership of these societies consists of financial analysts engaged in the profession of security analysis and investment management.

The federation is administered by an 18-member board of directors elected by and responsible to the constituent societies through appointed delegates. A national headquarters with a permanent staff is maintained at P.O. Box 3726, Charlottesville, VA 22903.

The objectives of the federation are defined in the articles of incorporation: "The purposes of the Corporation are to provide the member societies, the members of such societies and the general public with information, knowledge and understanding of sound and trustworthy principles, practices and conduct with regard to investments and financial management; to promote good relations between the general public and the members of the profession; to encourage and aid the education of persons engaged in the profession of financial analysis; to provide the member societies and their members with opportunity for exchanging ideas and information; to promote the welfare of the profession of financial analysis and its members; to develop, promulgate and enforce a Code of Ethics and Standards for persons practicing in the profession of financial analysis; and to carry on, sponsor, aid and encourage research, and educational and informational activities in furtherance of the above stated purposes."

The federation holds an annual conference with sessions on subjects ranging from accounting and economics to the investment outlook for specific industries. Seminars and workshops on timely investment topics are also sponsored, including industry seminars. Member societies sponsor more than 1,000 meetings a year at which corporate officials discuss developments in their companies and industries. The press is invited to these meetings, which are a primary source of information for investors.

Each year the Corporate Information Committee of the federation reviews the investment communications of some 600 corporations. The review covers annual reports, quarterly reports, other written communications, and access to corporate officials by professional investors. Awards are given to companies judged as having done an excellent job of reporting to investors, and conferences are held with companies that are considered to be deficient. In 1986-1987, subcommittees evaluated companies in 32 industry categories, citing helpful reporting and calling attention to industry and company weaknesses.

The Federation conducts three annual extended study programs—the Financial Analysts Seminar, a concentrated study of security and economic analysis; the Investment Management Workshop at Princeton University for senior portfolio managers and executives; and the Canadian Investment Seminar devoted to economic, political, and investment topics from the viewpoint of Canadian investors.

The federation publishes a bimonthly magazine, *The Financial Analysts Journal*, for professional investors. Articles cover international monetary problems, the structure of the securities industry, fiscal and monetary policy, portfolio selection, securities evaluation, securities law and regulation, pension fund management, and accounting.

A companion organization, the Institute of Chartered Financial Analysts, was founded in 1959 to establish standards of professional competence in the field of financial analysis, to conduct tests of competence, and to award the professional designation of "Chartered Financial Analyst" (CFA) to those passing the requirements of three rigorous examinations. As of 1987, there were 10,500 Chartered Financial Analysts. Regular members of the constituent societies must either pass the CFA Level I examination and have 3 years experience in financial analysis, or have 6 years experience in financial analysis and have successfully completed a self-administered ethics exam, as well as other membership requirements.

The federation adopted a program of private self-regulation in 1974. This program was designed to unify and professionalize the membership by providing standards of practice which would apply uniformly to analysts included in the membership. Analysts, their employers, and the public are encouraged to inform the federation of possible unethical practices.

The FAF's code of ethics requires that analysts conduct themselves with integrity and dignity and encourage such conduct by others in the profession, act with competence and strive to maintain and improve their competence and that of others in the profession, and use proper care and exercise independent professional judgment.

The Investment Analysis Standards Board of the FAF maintains continuing review of the federation's code of ethics and standards of professional conduct. The Professional Conduct committee is responsible for enforcing professional conduct through an established disciplinary process. Both of these committees may include public representatives. The board of directors of the FAF retains sole authority to impose disciplinary sanctions. Penalties can range from private censure to expulsion. But as a general philosophy, the FAF believes that it is vastly better for the nation's business to be carried on by the private sector. Its Government Relations Committee communicates with regulatory and legislative bodies when subjects relevant to investors and the investing community arise.

The Federation has grown since 1947 from a small confederation of four independent analysts' societies (New York, Boston, Chicago, and Philadelphia) to an organization as of 1987 of 55 societies, and 3 chapters in the U.S. and Canada, representing a total membership of 16,000 analysts.

BIBLIOGRAPHY

FEINBERG, P. "FAF Committee Proposes Standards [investment performance]." *Pension World*, April, 1989.
HENRIQUES, D. "Analysts, Unite! A Merger Proposal Divides Wall Street." *Barrons*, April 24, 1989.

FINANCIAL BROKERS

Financial institutions or entities that perform the brokerage function by bringing together parties who need funds with those who have savings. They perform the economic function of assisting in matching the demand and supply of funds. Investment bankers often serve as financial brokers in the sale of corporate stocks and bonds. Mortgage bankers also function as financial brokers when they become involved in acquiring and placing mortgages. The mortgage banker locates institutional and other investors for mortgages.

FINANCIAL DISCLOSURE REQUIREMENTS

Beginning March 31, 1988, depository financial institutions were required to make financial disclosure to the public, customers, and others interested in the basic condition of the institution in a manner similar to the Call Report and the Statement of Income and Dividends. Disclosures must be made available in the lobby of the institution. The disclosures include the amount and trend of nonperforming assets, nonaccrual assets, other real estate owned, and substandard classified assets. Federal Financial Institutions Examination Counsel Standardized Call Report Schedule RC-N, called past-due and nonaccrual loans and leases is now publicly available. The format for this schedule is appended.

FINANCIAL FORECASTING

In the forecasting of the financial position of an individual firm, the cash budget projects the cash receipts, disbursements, and opening and closing balances, usually monthly. A customary precautionary minimum projected closing cash balance as a desired margin of safety for each month would also serve to satisfy any requirement for compensating balances under commercial bank line of credit arranged in order to strengthen cash position in low months indicated.

Econometric models, linking a number of relevant independent variables with the dependent variable in multiple regression analyses, have become computationally easier to construct for financial forecasting as the result of the increased use of computers, which suitably programmed make short work of formerly formidable computations.

A financial forecast for an enterprise is an estimate of the most probable financial position, results of operations and changes in financial position for one or more future periods. Most probable means that the forecast is based on management's judgment of the most likely set of conditions and its most likely course of action. A financial projection is an estimate of financial results based on assumptions which are not necessarily the most likely (SOP 75-4). A financial projection is sometimes used to present hypothetical courses of action for evaluation. A feasibility study is an analysis of a proposed investment or course of action (SOP 75-4).

A financial forecast presents a prediction of an entity's expected financial position, results of operations, and changes in financial position. A forecast is based on assumptions about expected conditions and expected courses of action, prepared to the best of the preparer's knowledge and belief. A financial projection differs from a financial forecast in that a projection depends upon one or more hypothetical assumptions. A projection responds to the question: "What might happen if . . . ?" Multiple projections consist of two or more projections based on a range of hypothetical assumptions.

Public accountants are primarily associated with forecasts and projects to lend their credibility to them. A client typically initiates the request that the accountant compile or review prospective financial information. In a review engagement, the accountant performs some procedures to achieve a level of assurance on which he/she bases an opinion. The accountant must perform inquiry and analytical procedures to achieve a reasonable basis for expressing limited assurance that there are no material modifications that should be made to the statements in order for them to be in conformity with generally accepted accounting principles or, if applicable, with another comprehensive basis of accounting. In a compilation service, the accountant performs few, if any, procedures; the accountant merely assists the client to "write-up" the financial information. Accountants are expected to render a report on compiled or reviewed prospective financial statements. The compilation report contains a disclaimer and offers no conclusions or any form of assurance. The review report gives the accountant's conclusions about proper presentation and about the reasonableness of the assumptions. The reports are either unqualified, adverse, or disclaimers resulting form scope limitations.

AICPA Rule of Conduct 201(e) prohibits an accountant from being associated with a forecast or projection which may lead readers to believe that the accountant vouches for the authenticity of the forecast or projection.

See BUSINESS BAROMETERS.

BIBLIOGRAPHY

AUDITING STANDARDS BOARD, *Statement on Standards for Accountants' Services on Prospective Financial Information—Financial Forecasts and Projections*, American Institute of Certified Public Accountants, 1986.

FINANCIAL FUTURES *See* FUTURES.

FINANCIAL INDICATORS

Measures of performance that are widely used by professionals to make forecasts and evaluations. The financial indicators which are presented here are not meant to be all inclusive but merely represent widely used indicators.

Interest
    Prime rates charged by large commercial banks
    Discount rate of the Federal Reserve bank
    Federal funds rate
    U.S. Treasury Bills yield
    Treasury bonds and notes yield
    Municipal bonds yield
    Long-term corporate AAA bonds
    Commercial paper rates
    GNMA (Government National Mortgage Association) interest rate
    Average annual yield on savings deposits in savings associations
    Foreign short-term interest rates

Stock market
    The Dow Jones Averages
    Over-the-counter market (NASDAQ) indexes
    Standard & Poor's 500 stock index
    New York Stock Exchange Composite Stock Index
    American Stock Exchange Total Index
    Price/earnings ratios for common stocks
    Common stock yields
    Preferred stock yields
    Corporate profits
    International stock indexes

Economic indicators
    Cyclical economic indicators (U.S. Bureau of Economic Analysis, *Business Conditions Digest*)
        Leading indicators:
            New business formation
            New building permits
            Stock prices
            Initial state unemployment insurance claims
            Change in sensitive materials prices
            Change in credit outstanding
            Vendor performance
            Average work week hours
            Change in inventories
            Contracts and orders for plant and equipment
            New orders for consumer goods and materials
            Money supply (M2)
        Coincident indicators:
            Industrial production
            Employees on nonagricultural payrolls
            Personal income
            Manufacturing and trade sales
        Lagging indicators:
            Labor costs (%)
            Ratio of consumer installment credit to personal income
            Average prime rate charged by banks
            Average duration of employment (weeks)
            Ratio of inventories to sales
            Commercial and industrial loans outstanding
    Gross National Product
    Money supply
    Federal budget deficit or surplus
    Foreign exchange rates
    U.S. trade balance (imports and exports)
    Producer price indexes for major commodity groups (PPI)
    Consumer price index for urban consumers (CPI)
    Unemployment rate (civilian labor force)
    Personal income per capita (by region and state)
    Income by households
    Average weekly hours of work
    Average weekly earnings
    U.S. gold prices
    U.S. silver prices
    Price at well of crude petroleum
    Price of regular gasoline

Real estate
    New home mortgage yields

FINANCIAL INSTITUTIONS REFORM, RECOVERY, AND ENFORCEMENT ACT OF 1989 (FIRREA)

FHA and VA maximum interest rates on home mortgages
Regional housing prices
Sales price of existing single-family homes
Medium sales price of existing single-family homes
Construction permits
Top 10 cities for construction permits
Housing starts
Index of construction costs
Consumer price indexes of residential rents
National rental and homeowner vacancy rates
Quoted office rental rates

The federal government is a major source of financial information. The Department of Commerce, Bureau of Labor Statistics, Bureau of the Census, *Monthly Labor Review*, the Federal Trade Commission, Federal Reserve System (*Economic Indicators*; *Federal Reserve Bulletin*), Federal Deposit Insurance Corporation, U.S. Bureau of Economic Analysis (*Business Conditions Digest* and *Survey of Current Business*), Treasury Department, *The Economic Report of the President*, *The Statistical Abstract of the United States*, the Organization for Economic Development and Co-operation, and the International Monetary Fund. Other sources include Dun and Bradstreet, Robert Morris Associates, Standard & Poor's Corporation, Dow Jones Investor's Handbook, Mortgage Bankers Association of America, U.S. League of Savings Institutions, National Association of Realtors, and *The World Almanac*.

FINANCIAL INSTITUTIONS REFORM, RECOVERY, AND ENFORCEMENT ACT OF 1989 (FIRREA)

Federal legislation resulting from the thrift crisis of the late 1980s that revised the structure of the deposit-insurance system, creating a new Bank Insurance Fund (BIF) and a Savings Association Insurance Fund (SAIF) under the management of the FDIC. The stated purposes of the Act are as follows: To reform, recapitalize, and consolidate the Federal deposit insurance system, to enhance the regulatory and enforcement powers of Federal Financial institutions regulatory agencies, and for other purposes.

The Senate passed S. 774 on April 19 by a vote of 94-2. The House Banking Committee approved its version 49-2 on May 2. FIRREA (P. L. 101-73), which became effective August 9, 1989, is considered by many to be the most important banking legislation since the Bank Holding Company Act of 1956. The appended table presents the Table of Contents of the Act.

The Act dismantled the independent Federal Home Loan Bank System and its regulatory apparatus. The new law divides the Federal Home Loan Bank System into three parts: the Office of Thrift Supervision (OTS), under the general oversight of the Secretary of the Treasury; the Saving Association Insurance Fund, an agency of the FDIC; and the Federal Housing Finance Board, which oversees the credit-advance activities of the 12 district Home Loan banks. A separate FDIC fund, the FSLIC Resolution Fund, was authorized to assume the assets and liabilities of the Federal Savings and Loan Insurance Corporation, except those transferred to the Resolution Trust Corporation. The bill anticipates raising $125 billion from the thrift industry and taxpayers to finance liquidations and capitalize the new insurance fund. The more significant features of the twelve Titles of the Act are summarized in the following sections.

TITLE I
PURPOSES

The purposes of this legislation are stated in Title I—Purposes of the Act as follows (SEC. 101):

1. To promote, through regulatory reform, a safe and stable system of affordable housing finance.
2. To improve the supervision of savings associations by strengthening capital, accounting, and other supervisory standards.
3. To curtail investments and other activities of savings associations that pose unacceptable risks to the Federal Deposit insurance funds.
4. To promote the independence of the Federal Deposit Insurance Corporation from the institutions the deposits of which it insures, by providing an independent board of directors, adequate funding, and appropriate powers.
5. To put the Federal deposit insurance funds on a sound financial footing.

Public Law 101-73
101st Congress
An Act

To reform, recapitalize, and consolidate the Federal deposit insurance system, to enhance the regulatory and enforcement powers of Federal financial institutions regulatory agencies, and for other purposes.

Be it enacted by the Senate and House of Representatives of the United States of America in Congress assembled,
SECTION 1. SHORT TITLE; TABLE OF CONTENTS.
  (a) Short Title.—This Act may be cited as the "Financial Institutions Reform, Recovery, and Enforcement Act of 1989".
  (b) Table of Contents.—

TITLE I—PURPOSES
Sec. 101. Purposes.
TITLE II—FEDERAL DEPOSIT INSURANCE CORPORATION
Sec. 201. Depository institutions.
Sec. 202. Duties of Federal Deposit Insurance Corporation.
Sec. 203. FDIC Board members.
Sec. 204. Definitions.
Sec. 205. Insured savings associations.
Sec. 206. Application process; insurance fees.
Sec. 207. Insurability factors.
Sec. 208. Assessments.
Sec. 209. Corporate powers of the FDIC.
Sec. 210. Administration of Corporation.
Sec. 211. Insurance funds.
Sec. 212. Conservatorship and receivership powers of the Corporation.
Sec. 213. New banks.
Sec. 214. Bridge banks.
Sec. 215. FSLIC Resolution Fund.
Sec. 216. Amendments to section 12.
Sec. 217. Amendments to section 13.
Sec. 218. FDIC borrowing authority.
Sec. 219. Exemption from taxation; limitation on borrowing.
Sec. 220. Reports.
Sec. 221. Regulations governing insured depository institutions.
Sec. 222. Activities of savings associations.
Sec. 223. Nondiscrimination.
Sec. 224. Brokered deposits.
Sec. 225. Contracts between depository institutions and persons providing goods, products, or services.
Sec. 226. Savings Association insurance fund industry advisory committee established.

Aug. 9, 1989
[H.R. 1278]

Financial Institutions Reform, Recovery, and Enforcement Act of 1989.
12 USC 1811 note.

TITLE III—SAVINGS ASSOCIATIONS
Sec. 301. Amendment to Home Owner's Loan Act of 1933.
Sec. 302. Savings provisions.
Sec. 303. Qualified thrift lender test.
Sec. 304. Transitional rule for certain transactions with affliates.
Sec. 305. Transitional rules regarding certain loans and effective dates.
Sec. 306. Amendment of additional powers of Director.
Sec. 307. Amendment to title 31, United States Code.
Sec. 308. Preserving minority financial institutions.
TITLE IV—TRANSFER OF FUNCTIONS, PERSONNEL, AND PROPERTY
Sec. 401. FSLIC and Federal Home Loan Bank Board abolished.
Sec. 402. Continuation and coordination of certain regulations.
Sec. 403. Determination of transferred functions and employees.
Sec. 404. Rights of employees of abolished agencies.
Sec. 405. Division of property and facilities.
Sec. 406. Report.
Sec. 407. Repeals.
TITLE V—FINANCING FOR THRIFT RESOLUTIONS
Subtitle A—Oversight Board and Resolution Trust Corporation
Sec. 501. Oversight Board and Resolution Trust Corporation established.
Subtitle B—Resolution Funding Corporation
Sec. 511. Resolution Funding Corporation established.
Sec. 512. Financing Corporation.
TITLE VI—FEDERAL HOME LOAN BANK SYSTEM REFORMS
Subtitle A—Federal Home Loan Bank Act Amendments
Sec. 701. Definitions.
Sec. 702. Federal Housing Finance Board established.
Sec. 703. Termination of the Federal Home Loan Bank Board.
Sec. 704. Eligibility for membership.
Sec. 705. Repeal of provision relating to rate of interest on deposits.
Sec. 706. Capital stock.
Sec. 707. Election of Bank directors.
Sec. 708. Repeal of provision relating to certain powers of the Federal Home Loan Bank Board.
Sec. 709. Powers and duties of Banks.
Sec. 710. Eligibility of borrowers to secure advances.
Sec. 711. Administrative expenses.
Sec. 712. Nonadministrative expenses.
Sec. 713. Federal Savings and Loan Insurance Corporation Industry Advisory Committee.

Sec. 714.	Advances.
Sec. 715.	Amendments relating to withdrawal from Federal Home Loan Bank membership.
Sec. 716.	Repeal of provisions relating to lawful contract rate.
Sec. 717.	Bank stock and obligations.
Sec. 718.	Thrift Advisory Council.
Sec. 719.	Examination of members.
Sec. 720.	Liquidity.
Sec. 721.	Affordable housing.
Sec. 722.	Transferred employees of Federal Home Loan Banks and joint offices.
Sec. 723.	Transitional provisions.
Sec. 724.	Federal Home Loan Bank reserves.
Sec. 725.	Special account.

Subtitle B—Federal Home Loan Mortgage Corporation
Sec. 731. Federal Home Loan Mortgage Corporation.

Subtitle C—Technical and Conforming Amendments
Sec. 741. Repeal of limitation of obligation for administrative expenses.
Sec. 742. Amendment of title 5, United States Code.
Sec. 743. Amendment of Balanced Budget and Emergency Deficit Control Act provisions.
Sec. 744. Conforming amendments to financial institution related Acts.

TITLE VIII—BANK CONSERVATION ACT AMENDMENTS
Sec. 801. Definitions.
Sec. 802. Appointment of conservator.
Sec. 803. Examinations.
Sec. 804. Termination of conservatorship.
Sec. 805. Conservator; powers and duties.
Sec. 806. Liability protection.
Sec. 807. Rules and regulations.
Sec. 808. Repeals.

TITLE IX—REGULATORY ENFORCEMENT AUTHORITY AND CRIMINAL ENHANCEMENTS
Subtitle A—Expanded Enforcement Powers, Increased Penalties, and Improved Accountability
Sec. 901. Institution-affilated parties of a depository institution subject to administrative enforcement orders; substitution of "depository institution" for "bank" in enforcement provisions.
Sec. 902. Amendments to cease and desist authority with respect to restitution, restrictions on specific activities, grounds for issuance of a temporary order, and incomplete or inaccurate records.
Sec. 903. Merger of removal and prohibition authority.
Sec. 904. Industrywide application of removal, suspension, and prohibition orders.
Sec. 905. Enforcement proceedings allowed after separation from service.
Sec. 906. Expansion of removal powers for state criminal proceedings.
Sec. 907. Amendments to expand and increase civil money penalties.
Sec. 908. Clarification of criminal penalty provisions for violation of certain orders.
Sec. 909. Supervisory records.
Sec. 910. Increased penalty for participation by convicted individuals.
Sec. 911. Amendments to various provisions of law relating to reports.
Sec. 912. Authority of the FDIC to take enforcement action against savings associations.
Sec. 913. Public disclosure of enforcement actions required.
Sec. 914. Agency disapproval of directors and senior executive officers of certain depository institutions.
Sec. 915. Clarification of NCUA's authority to conduct compliance investigations.
Sec. 916. Improved administrative hearings and procedures.
Sec. 917. Task force study of delegation of enforcement actions.
Sec. 918. Annual report to Congress.
Sec. 919. Credit union audit requirements.
Sec. 920. Technical amendments relating to administrative and judicial review.

Subtitle B—Termination of Deposit Insurance
Sec. 926. Revision of procedures for termination of FDIC deposit insurance.

Subtitle C—Improving Early Detection of Misconduct and Encouraging Informants.
Sec. 931. Information required to be made available to outside auditors.
Sec. 932. Depository institution employee protection remedy.
Sec. 933. Reward for information leading to recoveries or civil penalties.

Subtitle D—Right to Financial Privacy Act Amendments
Sec. 941. Definitions.
Sec. 942. Additional exceptions.
Sec. 943. Prohibition.
Sec. 944. Miscellaneous provisions.

Subtitle E—Civil Penalties for Violations Involving Financial Institutions.
Sec. 951. Civil penalties.

Subtitle F—Criminal Law and Procedure
Sec. 961. Increased criminal penalties for certain financial institutions offenses.
Sec. 962. Miscellaneous revisions to title 18.
Sec. 963. Civil and criminal offenses.
Sec. 964. Grand jury secrecy.
Sec. 965. Criminal Division Fraud Section regional office.
Sec. 966. Department of Justice appropriation for the judiciary.
Sec. 967. Authorization of additional appropriations for the judiciary.
Sec. 968. Racketeer influences and corrupt organizations.

TITLE X—STUDIES OF FEDERAL DEPOSIT INSURANCE, BANKING SERVICES, AND THE SAFETY AND SOUNDNESS OF GOVERNMENT-SPONSORED ENTERPRISES
Sec. 1001. Study of Federal deposit insurance system.
Sec. 1002. Survey of bank fees and services.
Sec. 1003. General Accounting Office study.
Sec. 1004. Study regarding capital requirements for government-sponsored enterprises.

TITLE XI—REAL ESTATE APPRAISAL REFORM AMENDMENTS
Sec. 1101. Purpose.
Sec. 1102. Establishment of Appraisal Subcommittee of the Federal Financial Institutions Examination Council.
Sec. 1103. Functions of Appraisal Subcommittee.
Sec. 1104. Chairperson of Appraisal Subcommittees; term of Chairperson; meetings.
Sec. 1105. Officers and staff.
Sec. 1106. Powers of Appraisal Subcommittee.
Sec. 1107. Procedures for establishing appraisal standards and requiring the use of certified and licensed appraisers.
Sec. 1108. Startup funding.
Sec. 1109. Roster of State certified or licensed; authority to collect and transmit fees.
Sec. 1110. Functions of the Federal financial institutions regulatory agencies relating to appraisal standards.
Sec. 1111. Time for proposal and adoption of standards.
Sec. 1112. Functions of the Federal financia insitutions regulatory agencies relating to appraiser qualifications.
Sec. 1113. Transactions requiring the services of a State certified appraiser.
Sec. 1114. Transactions requiring the services of a State licensed appraiser.
Sec. 1115. Time for proposal and adoption of rules.
Sec. 1116. Certification and licensing requirements.
Sec. 1117. Establishment of State appraiser certifying and licensing agencies.
Sec. 1118. Monitoring of State appraiser certifying and licensing agencies.
Sec. 1119. Recognition of State certified and licensed appraisers for purposes of this title.
Sec. 1120. Violations in obtaining and performing appraisals in federally related transactions.
Sec. 1121. Definitions.
Sec. 1122. Miscellaneous provisions.

TITLE XII—MISCELLANEOUS PROVISIONS
Sec. 1201. GAO study of credit union system.
Sec. 1202. OCC employment provision.
Sec. 1203. NCUA employment provisions.
Sec. 1204. Expansion of use of underutilized minority banks, women's banks, and low-income credit unions.
Sec. 1205. Credit standards advisory committee.
Sec. 1206. Comparability in compensation schedules.
Sec. 1207. Study by Secretary of the Treasury.
Sec. 1208. Expenditure of taxpayer money only for deposit insurance purposes.
Sec. 1209. Amendment to section 5373 of title 5, United States Code.
Sec. 1210. Farm Credit Administration and Farm Credit System Insurance Corporation employment provision.
Sec. 1211. Fair lending oversight and enforcement.
Sec. 1212. Amendment to the Community Reinvestment Act of 1977.
Sec. 1213. Comptroller General audit and access to records.
Sec. 1214. Amendment related to the Hart-Scott-Rodino Act.
Sec. 1215. Capital accounting standards.
Sec. 1216. Equal opportunity.
Sec. 1217. NCUA powers as liquiding agent and conservator.
Sec. 1218. Risk management training.
Sec. 1219. Cross-marketing restrictions.
Sec. 1220. Report on loan discrimination.
Sec. 1221. Separability of provisions.

TITLE XIII—PARTICIPATION BY STATE HOUSING FINANCE AUTHORITIES AND NONPROFIT ENTITIES
Sec. 1301. Definitions.
Sec. 1302. Authorization for State housing finance agencies and nonprofit entities to purchase mortgage-related assets.

TITLE XIV—TAX PROVISIONS
Sec. 1401. Early termination of special reorganization rules for financial institutions.
Sec. 1402. Tax exemption for Resolution Trust Corporation and Resolution Funding Corporation.
Sec. 1403. Annual reports on transactions in which Federal financial assis tance provided.
Sec. 1404. Studies of relationship between public debt and activities of Government-sponsored enterprises.

FINANCIAL INSTITUTIONS REFORM, RECOVERY, AND ENFORCEMENT ACT OF 1969 (FIRREA)

6. To establish an Office of Thrift Supervision in the Department of the Treasury, under the general oversight of the Secretary of the Treasury.
7. To establish a new corporation, to be known as the Resolution Trust Corporation, to contain, manage, and resolve failed savings associations.
8. To provide funds from public and private sources to deal expeditiously with failed depository institutions.
9. To strengthen the enforcement powers of Federal Regulators of depository institutions.
10. To strengthen the civil sanctions and criminal penalties for defrauding or otherwise damaging depository institutions and their depositors.

TITLE II
FEDERAL DEPOSIT INSURANCE CORPORATION

Title II of the Act contains the major changes to the deposit insurance system by amending the enabling statute of the FDIC to:

1. Restructure the FDIC Board of Directors;
2. Establish two insurance funds, the Bank Insurance Fund, and the Savings Association Insurance Fund, both managed separately by the FDIC;
3. Impose a five-year ban on conversions (a moratorium) from one insurance fund to another and from thrift to banks;
4. Establish cross-guarantee liability on commonly controlled institutions.
5. Increase the insurance assessments banks and thrift must pay to the government;
6. Update and expand conservatorship and receivership powers of the FDIC;
7. Subject thrift to the Change in Bank Control Act and Bank Merger Act;
8. Limit claims against the FDIC by failed institutions;
9. Subject thrift to the FDIC's emergency acquisition powers;
10. Create a new insurance logo for SAIF members which may be displayed by all insured banks and thrift;
11. Subject state-chartered thrift to certain FDIC controls;
12. Restrict acceptance of brokered deposits by banks and thrift; and
13. Require that junk bonds held by thrift be divested by August 9, 1989 (excludes securities issued by FNMA, FHLMC, GNMA, and other government-sponsored entities).

Section 203 of Title II revises the structure of the FDIC Board. Two new members are added to the three-member board. It now consists of the Comptroller of the Currency, the Director of the Office of Thrift Supervision, and three other presidential appointees confirmed by the Senate. Members have six-year terms. The Chairman and the Vice Chairman of FDIC are to be designated by the President from among the appointed members. No more than three members can be from the same political party. Section 204 of Title II defines *Savings Associations* as "Any federal or state savings association and any corporation (other than a bank) that the Board of Directors of the FDIC and the Director of the OTS determine to be operating in substantially the same manner as a savings association. *Insured Depository Institutions* are defined as "Any bank or savings association whose deposits are insured by the FDIC."

Section 205 of Title II provides that all savings associations insured by the FSLIC before passage of the Act will be insured by the FDIC without application, approval, or entrance fees.

Section 206 permits a new state-chartered savings association to apply to the FDIC for insurance coverage if it presents a certificate from the Director of the OTS which indicates that the association meets the FDIC's insurability factors amended in Section 207. The amendment adds to the factor list the "fitness" of management and "the risk presented" to the BIF and SAIF. Section 206 revises the factors the FDIC may consider when approving insurance for the branch of a foreign bank.

Section 206 also provides that no bank or thrift may engage in a "conversion transaction" without the prior approval of the FDIC. A conversation transaction is defined as: a) a change in insured status from BIF to SAIF membership, or the reverse; b) the merger or consolidation of a BIF member with a SAIF member; c) the assumption of any liability by a BIF member to pay the deposits of a SAIF member, or the reverse; or d) the transfer of a BIF member's assets to a SAIF member in consideration of the assumption of the liability for any portion of the deposits to the BIF membership, or the reverse. Important exceptions include a conversion transaction which affects only an "insubstantial portion" of an institution's deposits; supervisory acquisitions; and thrift subsidiaries of bank holding companies; a bank's acquisition of a thrift in default or in danger of default, if the benefits to the insurance fund or the FTC equal or exceed the assessment income that will be lost during the moratorium. Bank holding companies can acquire healthy thrifts immediately and merge their assets and liabilities into any subsidiary bank. The converted thrift must continue to pay insurance premiums to the Savings Association Insurance Fund for five years.

After a five-year period moratorium, an insured depository institution can switch insurance funds, but must pay an exit fee to the old fund and an entrance fee to the new fund. The FDIC is authorized to establish those fees sufficiently high to ensure that the ratio of fund reserves to total deposits shall not be diminished.

Section 206 also establish cross-guarantee liability on commonly controlled institutions. Should a bank or thrift default or fail, the FDIC is empowered to collect damages from commonly controlled institutions (institutions owned by another or if both are owned by the same holding company). The FDIC's claim is subordinated to the following obligations and liabilities: a) deposits; b) secured obligations (other than as noted above); c) other general or senior liabilities; and d) obligations subordinated to depositors or other general creditors.

Section 206 also adds a liability on commonly controlled depository institutions for any losses incurred by the FDIC as a result of the default of an affiliated institution or FDIC assistance to an affiliated institution. The FDIC's claim is superior to the following obligations and liabilities: a) shareholder obligations; and b) any obligation or liability owed to any affiliate of the institution other than any secured obligation which was secured as of May 1, 1989.

Section 208 significantly revises upward the assessment rates for insured banks and thrifts. The assessment schedule for Bank Insurance Fund members is: until December 31, 1989, 1/12 of 1% (about 0.8%); from January 1, 1990, to December 31, 1990, 0.12%; on and after January 1, 1991, 0.15%; or any other rate determined by the FDIC not exceeding 0.325%, provided the increase in any one year does not exceed 0.075%. Other rates may be established to achieve the "designated reserve ratio" for the BIF which is 1.25% of insured deposits, or up to 1.50% of insured deposits if the FDIC concludes that the BIF faces substantial future losses. Premium rebates are provided for once the funds are replenished. Savings Association Insurance Fund rates were scheduled to increase from 20.8 cents in 1989 to 23 cents in 1991, and to fall to 18 cents in 1994 and 15 cents in 1998.

After 1995, the FDIC is empowered to increase rates for either fund above the scheduled levels to a maximum of 32.5 cents per $100 of deposits if required to bring the fund up to the target ratio of reserves to deposits within a reasonable period of time. The maximum annual increase cannot exceed 7.5 cents per $100 of deposits.

The targets for the two insurance funds is 1.25%, or $1.25 of reserves for each $100 of deposits. The target level can be increased to 1.5% if the insurer concludes, on a year-by-year basis, that there is a significant risk of substantial future losses to the fund. Funds collected in excess of 1.25% would be held in a secondary reserve. Institutions will receive investment income on the reserve.

Section 211 provides for the establishment of the Bank Insurance Fund and the Savings Association Insurance Fund. The funds in the current Permanent Insurance Fund maintained by the FDIC are to be transferred to the BIF. The funding for the SAIF will come from the Treasury department (up to 2 million annually), the FSLIC Resolution Fund, assessments, and, if necessary, the Resolution Trust Corporation. The FDIC may also borrow for SAIF from the Federal home loan banks.

Section 212 gives the FDIC greater authority to override federal and state law in arranging conservatorship and receiverships for banks and thrifts. The FDIC is authorized to act as conservator for institutions in danger of default or as receiver for banks and thrifts. The Resolution Trust Corporation must be appointed the receiver of any savings association closed in the three years between August 9, 1989, and August 9, 1992. As a conservator or receiver, the FDIC is given the express authority to repudiate any contract or lease which a failed bank or thrift may have entered into within a "reasonable period" of time after the FDIC becomes the conservator or receiver. The FDIC has the authority to enforce contracts entered into by a failed bank or thrift before failure, with certain exceptions. The FDIC can hold directors and officers personally liable for monetary damages for gross negligence or conduct that demonstrates a greater disregard for the "duty of care" than gross negligence, including intentional misconduct.

Section 213 is a recodification of the FDIC's authority to organize a new bank, chartered as a national bank, to assure the deposits of a failed institution. An FDIC-owned national bank may exist for no longer than two years.

Section 214 is a recodification and revision of the FDIC's power to organize bridge banks to purchase the assets and assume the deposits and liabilities of failed or failing banks and thrifts.

Section 215 of Title II creates the FSLIC Resolution Fund. The FSLIC Resolution Fund is separate and distinct from the BIF or SAIF and is authorized to assume all of the assets and liabilities of the FSLIC. Its funding is to come from income earned on its assets, liquidations and claims on assets, borrowing from FICO, assessments against SAIF members and, if necessary, the Treasury department. The FSLIC Resolution Fund will dissolve when all debts and liabilities are satisfied and all assets sold.

Section 217 revises the FDIC's authority to engage in assisted bank transactions. This section expands the FDIC's emergency acquisition authority to include not just banks but also thrifts. Bidding priorities which favored same-charter and in-state institutions are eliminated; the FDIC may override the objection of state regulators to an interstate acquisition by a three-fourths vote of the Board; the FDIC is directed to give priority to seeking minority-owned thrifts as acquirors of failing minority-owned thrifts; a bank holding company which acquires a failing thrift is permitted to retain and operate any existing branch or branches of the thrift, and, if the thrift is maintained as a separate subsidiary of the bank holding company, new branches may be established according to branching standards applicable to thrifts not affiliated with bank holding companies.

Section 218 of Title II enables the FDIC to borrow $5 billion from the Treasury department. The previous limit was $3 billion.

Section 219 exempts FDIC from state and local taxes when it acts as a receiver. This section also limits the authority of the FDIC to issue any note or guarantee under certain circumstances. Nevertheless, the agency may issue up to $5 billion in additional liabilities, provided its borrowing authority from the Treasury is reduced by the same amount. The full faith and credit of the U.S. Government is placed behind the principal and interest of obligations issued by the FDIC after FIRREA's enactment, provided the principal and maturity are stated in the obligations.

Section 220 of Title II requires the FDIC to prepare several reports: 1) annual reports on the BIF, SAIF, and FSLIC Resolution Fund must be submitted to Congress; 2) Treasury is to receive quarterly reports on the planning, forecasts, and condition of the FDIC; 3) while the Office of Management and Budget may continue to require reports from FDIC on its operations, it is not given any new authority over the FDIC. Before January 1, 1991, the FDIC must report to Congress on the advisability of assessing premiums on the basis of risk. By February 10, 1990, the FDIC must report on the pass-through of deposit insurance to investors in bank investment contracts. The FDIC, the Treasury, and the Attorney General are directed to report, within six months of enactment of FIRREA, on D&O liability insurance. The Genal Accounting Office is directed to audit the BIF, SAIF, and FSLIC Resolution Fund annually.

Section 221 provides for a common sticker which may be displayed by all insured banks and thrifts. All thrifts must display an insurance sign that states the institution's deposits are backed by the U.S. Government and are insured up to $100,000. The sign will carry the symbol of an eagle, but no reference to any government agency. FDIC-insured banks may display the existing FDIC insurance logo or the insurance logo applicable to thrift institutions.

Section 221 also gives the FDIC authority to approve mergers involving savings banks supervised by the OTS. This section also amends the Bank Merger Act to cover thrifts. Section 221 requires thrifts to notify the FDIC and the Director of the OTS within 30 days of establishing or acquiring a subsidiary. The Director then has the authority to regulate the subsidiary. The FDIC is also authorized to regulate the direct investment activities of federal and state savings association. State thrifts are prohibited from engaging in any activities, as principals, that are not permissible for federal thrifts.

Section 224 of Title II provides that any bank or thrift which does not meet its capital standards ("troubled") may not accept brokered deposits. Such institutions are prohibited from offering rates of interest significantly higher than prevailing rates by similar institutions in the same market area. The FDIC is given authority to waive the brokered deposits prohibition on a case-by-case basis upon a finding that the acceptance of a brokered deposit does not constitute an unsafe or unsound practice.

Direct equity investments in real estate or securities are prohibited for state-chartered savings and loans, except to the extent allowed for federal S&Ls. After January 1, 1990, a state savings association cannot engage, as a principal, in activities not permitted for federally chartered S&Ls, unless the FDIC determines that the activity will not result in a significant risk of loss to the insurance fund and if the fully phased-in capital standards are met.

Section 226 of Title II establishes an 18 member Savings Association Insurance Fund Industry Advisory Committee. Twelve thrift executives are elected by the FHLB banks and six public members appointed by the FDIC. Members serve for one year. The Committee is empowered to "confer" with the FDIC on general and specific business and regulatory issues and to make recommendations to the FDIC on matters within the FDIC's control. The Committee will cease to exist on August 10, 1999.

TITLE III
SAVINGS ASSOCIATIONS

Title III abolishes the Federal Home Loan Bank Board. The bank board is replaced by the Office of Thrift Supervision, headed by a director. The director's office is under the supervision of the Secretary of Treasury. The office is responsible for examining and supervising all savings and loans.

Title III establisheD three separate capital requirements for savings associations by December 7, 1989. The Office of Thrift Supervision is required to promulgate capital requirements no less severe than those for national banks, including a risk-based measure. The second standard is a core capital-to-assets ratio of 3%. Thrifts with supervisory goodwill can use the intangible to meet half of the requirement (phased out by January 1, 1995). Thrifts can also include intangibles allowed national banks. The third standard is a 1.5% tangible capital requirement:

1. Tangible capital of 1.5%, consisting generally of common stock plus retained earnings but excluding most intangible assets such as goodwill.
2. Core capital of 3%, consisting of tangible capital plus supervisory goodwill (the premium paid by an investor who purchased a troubled thrift). Until January 1, 1992, thrifts can count supervisory goodwill for up to half of their core capital requirement.
3. Risk-based capital, consisting of 6.4% of the value of risk-weighted assets. The risk-based rule includes off-balance-sheet risks as well as those that are reported on the institution's financial statements. The capital requirement will increase to a full 8% on December 31, 1992.

The minimum capital for the credit risk component (the risk of a loan not being repaid) is calculated by multiplying the value of each asset (including off-balance-sheet commitments) by one of five risk factors, and holding 8% of the result as the minimum required capital. The five risk categories range from 0% for cash to 200% for certain delinquent loans and repossessed property. For example, a typical home mortgage has a risk factor of 50%. The minimum required capital for a $100,000 home mortgage loan would be $4,000 ($100,000 x 50% x 8%).

Thrifts not meeting the standards by the prescribed dates will have immediate growth restrictions imposed on them by the Office of Thrift Supervisors. Such institutions will also be required to develop acceptable capital restoration plans that show the steps they must take to meet the new standards as quickly as possible. Restoration plans must be submitted by February 5, 1990.

The qualified-thrift-lender test, which requires thrifts to invest 60% of their assets in real-estate related loans, remains in effect until July 1, 1991. After that date, a 70% standard applies. Penalties for noncompliance are substantial. Thrifts that fail the test will be converted into commercial banks and denied branching rights, thrift powers, and access to Federal Home Loan Bank advances. The institution will be required to continue to pay assessments to the Savings Association Insurance Fund until December 31, 1993, and

FINANCIAL INSTITUTIONS REFORM, RECOVERY, AND ENFORCEMENT ACT OF 1969 (FIRREA)

will be assessed entrance exit and fees upon joining the Bank Insurance Fund. Limited, temporary exemptions from the qualified-thrift-lender test can be granted by the director of the Office of Thrift Supervision. Thrifts are also prohibited from making loans to a single individual or institution in excess of 15% of capital, a restriction similar to limits imposed on national banks.

TITLE IV
TRANSFER OF FUNCTIONS, PERSONNEL AND PROPERTY

Title IV abolishes the Federal Home Loan Bank Board and the position of chairman 60 days after enactment. Employees of the Bank Board, the Federal Savings and Loan Insurance Corporation, and the Federal Home Loan banks will be assigned to the FDIC, the RTC, the Office of Thrift Supervision, and the Federal Housing Finance Board by the heads of those agencies. Employees are guaranteed positions having the same status, tenure, and pay for a period of one year.

TITLE V

Title U establishes the Oversight Board along with powers and authorities to oversee and be accountable for the Resolution Trust Corporation.

Title V states that the primary purpose of the Resolution Trust Corporation is to liquidate or dispose of institutions that were insured by the FSLIC and placed in conservatorship or receivership in the three-year period beginning January 1, 1989, and to liquidate the Federal Asset Disposition Association within 180 days. The RTC is required to develop and submit to Congress a strategic plan setting forth its goals and methods. The Resolution Trust Corporation is scheduled to cease to exist on December 31, 1996.

Title V provided the five-member oversight board with policymaking powers. Operating activities were left with the FDIC. The FDIC is required to establish a real estate asset division to assist in the sale of assets and to identify properties of significant natural, cultural, recreational or scientific value. The board was required to establish national and regional advisory boards.

Fifty billion dollars was made available to the RTC. Thirty billion would be raised by the Resolution Funding Corporation (Refcorp), a quasi-private agency. The first twenty billion would be borrowed by Treasury. Refcorp would sell $30 billion in 30-year bonds during fiscal 1990 and 1991. Zero coupon Treasury bonds would be purchased with reserves from the Federal Home loan banks to provide $30 billion at maturity. The district Home Loan banks would contribute $300 million annually to the repayment of interest. The Treasury would provide the remaining financing. The district banks would also be required to contribute an amount that would have been adequate to purchase zero coupon bonds for the first $20 billion that now would be contributed by Treasury.

TITLE VI
THRIFT ACQUISITIONS ENHANCEMENT PROVISIONS

Title VI enables bank holding companies to start acquiring healthy thrifts. The acquired entities can be operated in tandem with their acquirors.

TITLE VII
FEDERAL HOME LOAN BANK SYSTEM REFORMS

Title VII established a five-member Federal Housing Financing Board. The board consists of the secretary of the Department of Housing and Urban Development and four other members appointed by the President with the advice and consent of the Senate. The Board oversees the 12 district Home Loan banks. The major purpose of the board is to oversee credit allocation by the district banks to members in the form of advances. Title VII abolishes the Federal Home Loan Bank Board and its chairman.

Membership in the Federal Home Loan Bank System include federally insured banks and credit unions that hold 10% of their assets in residential mortgage loans and who are willing to make mortgage loans. At least two directors of each district bank must be selected from organizations with at least a two-year history of representing consumer or community needs.

Advances from district banks must be fully secured with low-risk assets, including first mortgages on residential properties or securities backed by such loans; marketable federal agency securities, deposits at Federal Home Loan banks, and certain other real estate loans.

Commercial banks were also allowed to receive advances from district banks for the purpose of making housing-related loans. Only 30% of a district bank's total advances can be made to nonmember institutions with an exception to the limit provided for savings banks. District banks are also authorized to make advances to troubled but solvent thrifts.

When an institution withdraws from membership in a Federal Home Loan bank, the institution is prohibited from rejoining for ten years.

Title VII requires that each district bank must designate a community investment officer to implement a community lending and affordable-housing program. Community-oriented lending refers to loans to home buyers whose incomes do not exceed 115% of the area median income and loans for commercial and economic development activities that benefit low- and moderate-income families.

Each bank is also required to establish a program to provide advances to member thrifts that make subsidized loans to families with incomes at or below 89% of the median for their area.

Each bank is required to appoint an advisory council of 7 to 15 persons from community and nonprofit organizations actively involved in promoting low-income housing projects.

Title VII also gives the Federal Home Loan Mortgage Corporation (Freddie Mac) an independent board of directors. The board has five members appointed annually by the President and 13 others by member institutions. Fannie and Freddie are given the purpose of providing secondary-market support for low- and moderate-income mortgage loans. These two agencies are authorized to operate without restriction to state statutes, including Blue Sky laws.

TITLE VIII

Comptroller of the Currency is the authority to appoint the FDIC as conservator for an institution if certain specified conditions indicate potential insolvency.

TITLE IX
REGULATORY EXFORCEMENT AUGHTORITY AND CRIMINAL ENHANCEMENTS

Title IX increases the enforcement authority including penalties of federal financial-institution regulatory agencies. This act also extends new sanctions and penalties to a broader class of persons than was previously subject to enforcement actions. In addition to insiders, attorneys, accountants, consultants, controlling shareholders, vendors and other parties who deal with depository institutions may now be subject to enforcement actions or to a regulatory ban on further affiliation or relations with any insured institution or its holding company.

The Act also provides for public disclosure of all enforcement actions. This title also adds Title 18 offense of bank fraud (18 USC 1344) to the list of predicate offenses under the Racketeer Influenced and Corrupt Organizations Act. If convicted under the RICO statute, they could be labeled a "racketeer" and be subject to triple damages.

The authority of regulators to order restitution or reimbursement in a cease-and-desist order is clarified and strengthened. Temporary orders can be issued when regulators perceive a significant (versus substantial) dissipation of assets. Regulators can take enforcement actions against institution-affiliated parties for up to six years after they leave the institution. It applies retroactively.

Title IX expands the circumstances under which a civil money penalty could be assessed and increases its maximum. Section 907 establishes a three-tier penalty structure. Tier One provides a civil money penalty of up to $5,000 per day for violations of any law or regulation, final cease-and-desist order, temporary cease-and-desist order, suspension and removal order, any condition relation to an application imposed in writing by the regulator, or a written agreement. Tier Two provides a penalty of up to $25,000 per day for activities that result in unsafe and unsound practices resulting from recklessness or breaches of fiduciary duties. Second-tier penalties may be assessed only if such activities are part of a pattern of misconduct, cause "more than minimal loss" to the institution, or result in any pecuniary gain or other benefit to the party. Tier Three provides that an institution-affiliated party may be assessed a penalty up to $1 million per day if he or she "knowingly" engages in unsafe and unsound practices, breaches a fiduciary duty, and "knowingly or recklessly causes a substantial loss to the institution or a substantial pecuniary gain or other benefit to the party." Mitigating circumstances include: the financial resources and good faith if the institution or institution-affiliated person, the gravity of the violation, the history of previous violations, and such other matters as justice may require. The three tier-penalty structure applies to violations of the Federal Reserve Act, the anti-tying provisions of the Bank Holding Company Act and the Savings and Loan Holding Company Act, the National Bank Act, Section 20 of the Banking Act of 1933 (the Glass-Steagall prohibitions on banks engaging in securities activities); and the Change in Bank Control Act.

Section 911 establishes a separate three-tier civil-penalty structure for failure to file required reports of condition (Call Reports) with the appropriate regulator.

Under Section 916, federal financial-institution regulators must establish their own pool of administrative law judges and develop uniform rules and procedures for administrative hearings.

Under Section 926, the FDIC may start to terminate an institution's insurance if it finds that the institution or its management is operating in an unsafe and unsound manner or has violated any applicable law, rule, regulation, final order, written agreement, or written condition related to an application.

Title IX also authorizes the FDIC to suspend temporarily the deposit insurance of any insured institution if it has no tangible capital that qualities as Tier-one capital. Section 931 requires any insured financial institution audited by an independent auditor in the past two years to provide the auditor with copies of its most recent Call Report and examination report. The independent auditor must be given a copy of any formal or informal supervisory action taken against the institution by a state or federal banking agency.

Section 932 prohibits a financial institution from discharging, or in any other way discriminating against, an employee who provides information to any financial institution regulator or to the Attorney General about a possible violation of law or regulation by the institution or any institution-affiliated party.

Section 933 authorizes regulators to pay a reward to persons who provide information (whistle-blowers) leading to the recovery, restitution, or a penalty of over $50,000 for violations of Title 18 of the U.S. Code. The reward may not exceed the lesser of $100,000 or 25% of the recovered fine or penalty.

Section 941 amends the Right to Financial Privacy Act by permitting disclosure or examination of any financial records by any supervisory agency. This section also prohibits financial institutions from notifying anyone of a grand jury subpoena for violations of Title 18 bank-related crimes.

Section 964 increases the fines and prison terms for convictions of federal financial-institution-related crimes, such as bank bribery, embezzlement, misapplication of funds, false entries, false statements, and bank fraud. The maximum criminal penalty has been increased to $1 million and the maximum imprisonment, to 20 years.

Section 962 prohibits any officer, director, partner, or employee of a financial institution from directly or indirectly, with the intent to obstruct justice, notifying a customer of a grand jury subpoena for records of that institution relating to possible violations of certain laws. Section 964 relaxes the secrecy rules regarding grand jury information about banking-law violations. A court may order disclosure of grand jury information to regulators. Government attorneys may disclose grand jury information to another attorney working for the government, for use in civil actions, investigations of federal banking-related crimes, or in forfeiture proceedings.

Section 965 requires the Department of Justice to create a regional office of the Fraud Section of the Criminal Division in Northern Texas.

TITLE X
STUDIES OF FEDERAL DEPOSIT INSURANCE, BANKING SERVICES, AND THE SAFETY AND SOUNDNESS OF GOVERNMENT-SPONSORED ENTERPRISES

Title X specifies that certain studies be submitted to Congress within 18 months, including a major study of the deposit insurance system, a survey of bank fees and services, a study of the general accounting office, and a study regarding capital requirements for government-sponsored enterprises.

TITLE XI
REAL ESTATE APPRAISAL REFORM AMENDMENTS

Title XI requires the each federal financial institutions' regulatory agency must establish appraisal standards that meet the minimum requirements established by the Appraisal Foundation (a nonprofit institution). Appraisals associated with federally related transactions must be performed by state-certified appraisers who have passed a test established by the Appraisal Foundation. An appraisal subcommittee of the Federal Financial Institutions Examination Council is established to monitor state licensing standards and federal agency requirements.

TITLE XII
MISCELLANEOUS PROVISIONS

Title XII requires the Comptroller General to conduct a comprehensive study of the Nation's credit union system and submit a report to specified Senate and House banking committees. Title XII authorizes the Office of the Comptroller of the Currency to hire employees and fix compensation and benefits. Federal banking agencies must consult in fixing compensation and benefit packages.

Title XII amends the Home Mortgage Disclosure Act of 1979 to provide for reporting of data on mortgage applications by race, gender, and income level to assist regulators in identifying discriminatory lending practices.

The Community Reinvestment Act of 1977 is amended to provide for public disclosure of CRA ratings. The disclosure includes a four-tier descriptive rating and a written evaluation of each institution's performance.

Federal banking agencies are required to establish uniform capital and accounting standards within one year. Grandfathered nonbank banks are prohibited from cross-marketing products and services with their parent firms, with certain exceptions.

TITLE XIII
PARTICIPATION BY STATE HOUSING FINANCE AUTHORITIES AND NONPROFIT ENTITIES

Title XIII clarifies that state housing finance agencies are authorized to purchase mortgage-related assets from the RTC or a financial institution for which the FDIC is conservator.

TITLE XIV
TAX PROVISIONS

Title XIV repealed special rules adopted in 1981 which removed the tax-exemption for assistance payments to financially troubled institutions.

Source: Compliance Alert published by the Bank Administration Institute and the Institute for Strategy Development.

FINANCIAL INSTITUTIONS REGULATORY AND INTEREST RATE CONTROL ACT OF 1978
P.L. 95-630, signed by the President November 10, 1978. This act was omnibus legislation, including in its 20 titles a variety of provisions that made it the most comprehensive act prior to the Depository Institutions Deregulation and Monetary Control Act of 1980. As summarized by the Board of Governors of the Federal Reserve System, the Financial Institutions Regulatory and Interest Rate Control Act provided for the following.

Title I, Supervisory authority over depository institutions: Effective 120 days after enactment, it provides for the following, among other things:

1. Civil penalties for violations of Section 22 (loans to executive officers and transactions with directors) and Section 23A (loans to affiliates) of the Federal Reserve Act to be assessed by the Board of Governors of the Federal Reserve System or the Comptroller of the Currency; for violations of Section 19 of the Federal Reserve Act (reserve requirements and interest rate ceilings) to be assessed by the board of governors; and for violations of the National Bank Act to be assessed by the Comptroller of the Currency.
2. Amendment of Section 22 of the Federal Reserve Act to limit loans to executive officers, or to 10%-owning stockholders or their controlled entities (18%-owning stockholders or their

entities in towns of less than 30,000 population), to 10% of capital and surplus. Loans to any executive officer, director, or 10%-owning stockholder must be made on substantially the same terms as those prevailing for comparable transactions with others and be without more than normal risk; if the aggregate of such loans to any such person and his controlled entities is more than $25,000, advance approval of a majority of the directors, with the interested party abstaining, is required.
3. Prohibition of the payment of an overdraft on the account of an executive officer or director.
4. Authorization for the board to require a holding company to divest a nonbank subsidiary or terminate a nonbank activity if there is reasonable cause to believe that continuation of such activity or control constitutes a serious risk to the financial safety, soundness, or stability of a subsidiary bank.
5. Imposition of civil penalties for violation of the Bank Holding Company Act to be assessed by the board and authorization for the board to issue subpoenas and exercise other procedural authority in connection with hearings or investigations under the Bank Holding Company Act.
6. Provision for cease-and-desist actions directly against directors, officers, employees, agents, or other persons participating in the affairs of a bank and not merely against the bank itself, and against any bank holding company or subsidiary of a bank holding company and against Edge Act and agreement corporations; however, only the board of governors may initiate such proceedings against bank holding companies.
7. Authorization for the federal banking agencies to remove an officer, director, or other person participating in the affairs of a bank in the case of a violation that involves personal dishonesty or a willful or continuing disregard for the bank's safety and soundness.
8. Provision for civil penalties for violation of cease-and-desist orders to be assessed by the federal banking agencies.
9. Amendment of Section 22(g) of the Federal Reserve Act to double the dollar limitation on loans that may be made to executive officers, and thus permit a loan of $60,000 for the purchase of a home, $20,000 to finance the education of children, and $10,000 for any other purpose.
10. Provision for a standard for suspension or removal of an officer, director, or other person participating in the affairs of a bank because of his indictment for or conviction of a felony involving dishonesty or breach of trust.
11. Repeal of the Bank Holding Company Act exemption for labor, agricultural, or horticultural organizations, but inclusion of a grandfather clause for those in existence on January 4, 1977.
12. Authorization of obligations that are fully guaranteed as to principal and interest by the United States or any of its agencies to be eligible collateral for Federal Reserve notes.

Title II, Depository Institution Management Interlocks Act: Effective 120 days after enactment, it contains the following provisions, among others:

1. Prohibits interlocks between management officials of nonaffiliated depositor institutions (banks, thrift institutions, industrial banks, and credit unions) or holding companies in the same standard metropolitan statistical area (SMSA) or in the same or a contiguous or adjacent city, town, or village, except that in the case of depository institutions with less than $20 million in assets, the SMSA test does not apply.
2. Prohibits interlocks of this kind between an institution with more than $1 billion in assets and another with more than $500 million in assets without geographic limit.
3. Excludes from coverage as affiliates holding companies and their subsidiaries, corporations with 50% or more common ownership, insured state banks that are engaged primarily in providing banking services for other banks and not the public whose voting securities are held by other banks or officers of banks, and interlocks between mutual savings banks and existing trust companies owned by mutual savings banks.
4. Exempts a number of organizations, including Edge Act and agreement corporations, credit unions being served by a management official of another credit union, and organizations that do no business in the United States except incidentally to their foreign activities, state-chartered savings and loan guaranty corporations, and Federal Home Loan banks or other banks organized specifically to serve depository institutions.
5. Applies a grandfather clause for a ten-year period to existing interlocks not in violation of Section 8 of the Clayton Act.
6. Divides administrative enforcement, regulatory, and rule-making authority among the five federal supervisory agencies for depository institutions.

Title III, Foreign branching: Effective 120 days after enactment, it provides the following, among other things:

1. Provides that state nonmember insured banks must have the written consent of the Federal Deposit Insurance Corporation to establish foreign branches or to invest in foreign banks.
2. Reduces from three to two the number of directors needed to attest to the correctness of reports of condition.
3. Makes it a federal offense to kill an employee of the federal financial regulatory agencies (including the Federal Reserve banks) when he is in pursuit of his official duties.
4. Amends the International Banking Act of 1978 to apply the federal and state nondiscrimination laws applicable to national or state banks to operations in the United States of foreign banks, branches, and controlled lending companies, and requires that nondiscrimination be agreed to in any federal or state branch or agency application.

Title IV, American Arts Gold Medallions: Effective October 1, 1979, it directs the U.S. Treasury to strike and sell to the general public each year, over a five-year period, gold medallions containing in the aggregate not less than 1 million troy ounces of fine gold and commemorating outstanding individuals in the American arts.

Title V, Credit union restructuring: Effective on the effective date of the act, it establishes a National Credit Union Administration as an independent agency in the executive branch to be managed by a new three-member National Credit Union Administration Board, appointed by the President for a six-year term, with the advice and consent of the Senate.

Title VI, Change in Bank Control Act: Effective 120 days after enactment, it makes the following changes, among others:

1. Provides that no person shall acquire control of any insured bank unless the appropriate federal banking agency has been given 60 days' prior written notice and does not disapprove within that time period or any authorized extension.
2. Except as otherwise provided by regulation, requires the applicant to furnish the agency with a personal history; information on business background; pending legal or administrative proceedings, criminal indictments or convictions; financial statements; the terms and conditions of the proposed acquisition; the source of funds; and any plans to liquidate, sell, or merge the bank or make major changes in its business or management.
3. Authorizes federal banking agencies to disapprove applicants on anticompetitive grounds; because the financial condition of the acquiring person might jeopardize the financial stability of the bank; because the competence, experience, or integrity of an acquiring person or proposed management personnel indicates that the acquisition would be contrary to the interest of the bank; or because any acquiring person fails to furnish all information required.
4. Requires an insured bank to report all loans that it makes that are secured by 25% or more of the stock of another insured bank.
5. Requires the acquired bank to report any changes in its chief executive officer or any director during the year following acquisition.
6. Provides for civil penalties for violations.

Title VII, Change in Savings and Loan Control Act: Effective 120 days after the date of enactment, it provides that no person shall acquire control of any insured savings and loan association (or any savings and loan holding company) unless the Federal Savings and Loan Insurance Corporation has been given 60 days' prior written notice and does not disapprove of the proposed acquisition within that time period or any authorized extension. Other provisions, including criteria for disapproval, are virtually identical to those applicable to insured banks under Title VI, above.

Title VIII, Correspondent accounts: Effective 120 days after the date of enactment, it provides the following, among other things:

1. Prohibits a correspondent bank from extending credit to an executive officer, director, or 10%-owning stockholder of a respondent bank, or from opening a correspondent account for another bank while it has outstanding an extension of credit to an officer, director, or 10%-owning stockholder of that bank, unless that credit is granted on substantially the same terms as those prevailing for comparable transactions with other persons and does not involve more than normal risks.
2. Establishes the same prohibitions for similar transactions initiated by a respondent bank with respect to correspondent banks.
3. Requires each executive officer or 10%-owning stockholder of record to make a written report to the board of directors of that bank for any year during which he has outstanding an extension of credit from a correspondent bank; such reports are to be compiled and forwarded to the appropriate federal banking agency.
4. Requires each insured bank to file a report listing by name the executive officers or 10%-owning stockholders of record who file such reports, together with the aggregate amount of all extensions of credit by correspondent banks to such officers, directors, and their controlled entities.
5. Provides for civil penalties for violations.

Title IX, Disclosure of Material Facts: Effective 120 days after the date of enactment, among other things it requires an insured bank to file an annual report with the appropriate federal banking agency listing each executive officer or 10%-owning stockholder of record of the bank and listing the aggregate amount of all extensions of credit by the bank during the preceding calendar year to them or their controlled entities.

Title X, Federal Financial Institutions Examination Council Act of 1978: Effective 120 days after enactment, it provides the following, among other things:

1. Establishes a Federal Financial Institutions Examination Council consisting of the Comptroller of the Currency, the chairman of the Federal Deposit Insurance Corporation, a governor of the Federal Reserve Board to be designated by the chairman of the board, the chairman of the Federal Home Loan Bank Board, and the chairman of the National Credit Union Administration.
2. Provides that the council shall establish uniform principles and standards and report forms for the examination of financial institutions to be applied by the agencies; make recommendations for uniformity on other matters, such as classifying loans subject to country risk, identifying institutions in need of special supervisory attention, and evaluating large loans shared by two or more institutions; make recommendations regarding the adequacy of supervisory tools for determining the impact of holding company operations on subsidiary financial institutions; and consider the ability of supervisory agencies to discover possible fraud or questionable and illegal payments and practices of financial institutions or their holding companies.
3. Provides that when a recommendation of the council is unacceptable to an agency, the agency shall submit to the council a written statement of its reasons.
4. Provides that the council shall conduct schools for examiners to be open to employees of state supervisory agencies.
5. Establishes a liaison committee composed of five representatives of state supervisory agencies to encourage the application of uniform examination principles and standards by state and federal agencies.
6. Subjects the council to audit by the General Accounting Office.

Title XI, Right to Financial Privacy Act of 1978: Effective 120 days after enactment, except where otherwise provided, it provides the following:

1. Prohibits a government authority from having access to, information from, or copies of a financial institution's customer records, unless obtained pursuant to written consent of the customer, administrative subpoena or summons, search warrant, judicial subpoena, or formal written request (procedures and requirements for each method of obtaining information are specified in detail).
2. Prohibits financial institutions from providing any government authority access to, information from, or copies of any customer's financial records until the government authority certifies in writing that it has complied with the provisions of Title XI.
3. Requires financial institutions promptly to notify all of their customers of their financial privacy rights, provides that the Board of Governors of the Federal Reserve System shall prepare a statement of customers' rights, and provides that any financial institution that provides its customers a statement of customers' rights as prepared by the board shall be deemed to be in compliance with the customer notice requirement. (On March 7, 1979, this section of the act was repealed.)
4. Exempts from the provisions of Title XI examination by or disclosure to any supervisory agency of financial records or information in the exercise of its supervisory, regulatory, or monetary functions with respect to a financial institution, in accordance with procedures authorized by the Internal Revenue Code, when disclosure is required by federal statute or regulation, in connection with criminal or civil litigation to which the government and the customer are parties, and in connection with an official proceeding, investigation, examination, or inspection directed at the financial institution itself.
5. Provides exemption for the Secret Service or a government authority authorized to conduct foreign intelligence activities and exempts the Securities and Exchange Commission for two years.
6. Effective October 1, 1979, generally requires a government authority to reimburse the financial institution for the cost incurred due to its request, subject to regulations of the board of governors establishing the rate and conditions of reimbursement.
7. Provides for civil penalties for violations by a federal agency or department or a financial institution.
8. Provides that financial institutions making disclosure in good-faith reliance on a certificate of a government agency are not liable to the customer for such disclosure.
9. Establishes certain reporting requirements for the administrative office of the U.S. courts and each government authority requesting financial institution records during the year.

Title XII, Charters for Thrift Institutions: Effective 120 days after enactment, it does the following, among other things:

1. Authorizes the Federal Home Loan Bank Board to establish rules and regulations for the organization, examination, and operation of federal mutual savings banks (state mutual savings banks that have converted from state charters where conversion is not prohibited by state law).
2. Prohibits conversion from the state mutual to the stock form of ownership.
3. Subjects state mutuals converting to federal charters to the branching limitations of state law, except as to any numerical limits and except that the Federal Home Loan Bank Board may permit branches in the converted bank's standard metropolitan statistical area or county or within 35 miles of its home office, but only in its state of domicile.
4. Provides that the Federal Savings and Loan Insurance Corporation shall insure the accounts of federal mutual savings banks.

Title XIII, Negotiable-orders-of-withdrawal (NOW) accounts: Effective on the date of enactment, it adds New York to the states that are authorized to issue NOW accounts.

Title XIV, Insurance of individual retirement accounts (IRA) and Keogh accounts: Effective on the date of enactment, it increases federal deposit insurance for IRA and Keogh accounts to $100,000 per account at insured banks, savings and loan associations, and credit unions.

Title XV, Miscellaneous provisions: Effective upon enactment, it provides the following:

1. Extends until February 27, 1981, the prohibition on the imposition of surcharges for use of a credit card and restrictions of cash discounts by credit-card issuers.

FINANCIAL INSTRUMENTS: RECENT INNOVATION

2. For purposes of the Community Reinvestment Act, permits a financial institution serving predominantly military personnel to define its entire community to include its entire customer base without regard to geographic location.
3. Exempts graduated-payment mortgages insured by the Department of Housing and Urban Development from state requirements for a minimum amortization of principal.
4. Enables the Comptroller of the Currency to charter a national bank whose powers are limited to trust activities.

Title XVI, Interest rate control: Effective upon the date of enactment, it extends the authority to set flexible deposit interest rates (Regulation Q) to December 15, 1980, and eliminates the differential for interest rate ceilings on automatic transfer accounts offered by thrift institutions. The maximum rate on such accounts is the commercial bank rate.

Title XVII, Federal Savings and Loan Investment Authority: Effective on enactment, it amends the investment authority of savings and loan associations in the following ways:

1. Permits investment in community development areas.
2. Increases the authority to invest in loans for property alteration, repair, or improvements.
3. Expands the authority to invest in obligations issued by state or local governments for the purpose of rehabilitation, financing, or construction of residential real property.
4. Places in the unlimited-investment category the authority to invest in or lend to state housing corporations, provided that the obligations are secured by real estate insured by the Federal Housing Administration.

Title XVIII, the National Credit Union Central Liquidity Facility Act: Effective October 1, 1979, it does the following, among other things:

1. Establishes a central liquidity facility, with voluntary membership, within the National Credit Union Administration (NCUA). The purpose of the facility is to improve the general financial stability of credit unions by meeting their liquidity needs, defined to include seasonal, short-term adjustment, and longer-term emergency or unusual credit requirements.
2. Prohibits the facility from extending credit to expand credit union portfolios.
3. Authorizes the NCUA, acting in the interest of the facility, to borrow from any source, provided that the total value of these obligations does not exceed 12 times the subscribed capital stock and surplus of the facility; to borrow from the National Credit Union Share Insurance Fund up to $500,000 to defray initial organizational and operating expenses; and to borrow from the Treasury up to $500 million in the event that the NCUA certifies that the facility does not have sufficient funds to meet the liquidity needs of credit unions.

Title XIX: *See* EXPORT-IMPORT BANK Act amendments.

Title XX, Electronic Fund Transfer Act: Effective 18 months after enactment (except for the provision on consumer liability and unsolicited-card distribution, effective 90 days after enactment), it provides for the following, among other things:

1. Requires disclosure of the terms and conditions of electronic funds transfers (defined to exclude, among other things, wire transfers of funds, telephone transfers not pursuant to an agreement, and transfers made pursuant to an automatic transfer service program) at the time the consumer contracts for an electronic funds transfer service.
2. Requires that the consumer be afforded written documentation for each funds transfer made from an electronic terminal, notice as to whether preauthorized transfers were completed, and a periodic statement of account.
3. Requires financial institutions to establish procedures for correcting errors for electronic funds transfers.
4. Provides limitations on the maximum liability of a consumer for unauthorized transfers from his or her account, subject in part to whether the consumer reports to the financial institution within prescribed time periods either unauthorized transfers appearing on the periodic account statement or the loss or theft of an electronic funds transfer card.
5. Imposes liability on the financial institution under certain circumstances for all damages proximately caused by the institution's failure to make an electronic funds transfer or failure to stop payment of a preauthorized transfer when instructed to do so in accordance with the terms and conditions of the accounts.
6. Permits unsolicited distribution only for unvalidated debit cards.
7. Provides that Title XX does not annul, alter, or affect the laws of any state relating to electronic funds transfers, except to the extent that those laws are inconsistent with Title XX.
8. Authorizes the board to exempt from coverage electronic funds transfers within any state that imposes requirements substantially similar to Title XX.
9. In connection with promulgating regulations to carry out the act, requires the board to prepare a statement on economic impact, to issue model clauses to facilitate compliance, and if necessary to modify its regulations to ease the compliance burden on small financial institutions.

Summary. The Financial Institutions Regulatory and Interest Rate Control Act of 1978 was enacted in a year of prosperity for thrift institutions and essentially improved and liberalized the existing financial order. Only one year later, however, in October, 1979, monetary policy was used to pursue a deadly antiinflation program resulting in record highs in interest rates, disintermediation, operating losses, shrunken net worths, and emergency mergers for thrift institutions, complicated by economic recession. And only a few months later, on March 31, 1980, the Depository Institutions Deregulation and Monetary Control Act was enacted, the "most sweeping piece of financial legislation in U.S. history," which would throw the thrifts into a future of no-holds-barred competition with banks and nonbanks for commercial and personal services and markets, calculated to eliminate specialization and segmentation and posing for many institutions the problem of survival in such an environment.

BIBLIOGRAPHY

BOARD OF GOVERNORS OF THE FEDERAL RESERVE SYSTEM. *Annual Report,* 1978.

FINANCIAL INSTRUMENTS: RECENT INNOVATION

Wall Street has developed numerous innovative financial instruments in recent years. These new financial instruments are difficult to classify according to traditional categories: debt, equity, and hedging instruments. Frequently they are hybrid instruments. The following "Glossary of Selected Financial Instruments" has been published in the *Journal of Accountancy*, November 1989, using the following categories: Debt instuments; Asset-backed securities; equity instruments; hedging instruments.

Debt instruments:

Commercial paper: Unsecured short-term (up to 270 days) obligations issued through brokers or directly. The interest is usually discounted. Universal commercial paper: Foreign currency denominated commercial paper that trades and settles in the United States.

Convertible bonds: Debt securities that are convertible into the stock of the issuer at a specified price at the option of the holder.

Carrot and stick bonds: Carrots have a low conversion premium to encourage early conversion, and sticks allow the issuer to call the bond at a specified premium if the common stock is trading at a specified percentage above the strike price.

Convertible bonds with a premium put: Convertible bonds issued at face value with a put entitling the bondholder to redeem the bonds for more than their face value.

Debt with equity warrants: Bonds issued with warrants for the purchase of shares. The warrants are separately tradeable.

Dual-currency bonds: Bonds that are denominated and pay interest in one currency and are redeemable in another currency - thus allowing interest rate arbitrage between two markets.

COPS (covered option securities): Short-term debt that gives the issuer an option to repay the principal and interest in U.S. dollars or a mutually acceptable foreign currency.

ECU bonds (European currency unit bonds): A Eurobond denominated in a basket of currencies of the 10 countries that constitute the

European Community. The bonds pay interest and principal in ECUs or in any of the 10 currencies at the option of the holder.

ICONs (indexed currency option notes): A bond denominated and paying interest and principal in dollars but with principal payments linked to the exchange rate of another currency.

PERLS (principal exchange-rate-linked securities): Securities paying interest and principal in dollars but with principal payments linked to the exchange rate between the dollar and a second currency.

Flip-flop notes: An instrument that allows investors to switch between two types of securities - for example, to switch from a long-term bond to a short-term fixed-rate note.

FRNs (floating rate notes): Debt instruments that feature periodic interest rate adjustments.

Capped floater: An FRN with an interest rate ceiling.

Convertible FRNs: The issuer can convert the FRNs into long_term fixed rate bonds.

Drop-lock FRNs: The FRNs automatically convert to fixed-rate bonds when short-term interest rates fall below a specified level.

Minimax FRNs: FRNs with upper and lower interest limits - that is, a ceiling and a floor.

Indexed debt instruments: Instruments with guaranteed and contingent payments, the latter being linked to an index or prices of certain commodities (oil or gold, for example).

Bull and bear bonds: Bonds linked to upward and downward movements in a designated index. Bulls yield more in a rising market; bears yield more in a falling market.

SPINs (Standard and Poor's indexed notes): A debt instrument featuring interest payments linked to the performance of the Standard and Poor's stock indexes.

Put bonds: Bonds that the investor can put (or tender) back to issuer after a specified period.

Stripped government securities: A type of zero coupon bond, these securities represent long-term Treasury bonds "stripped" of semiannual interest coupons by an investment banker who resells these coupons and an interest in the principal payments. Investment banks market these stripped securities under such registered acronyms as

CATs: certificates of accrual on Treasury certificates.
COUGRs: certificates of government receipts.
STAGs: sterling transferrable accruing government securities.
STRIPs: separate trading of registered interest and principal of securities.
TIGRs: Treasury investment growth certificates
ZEBRAs: zero coupon eurosterling bearer or registered accruing certificates.

Zero-coupon bonds: A bond that's sold at a deep discount from its face value. It carries no interest coupon, but investors receive the gradual appreciate to face value.

LYONs: (liquid yield option notes): Zero-coupon bonds that are convertible into the issuer's common stock.

Asset-Backed Securities:

CMOs: (collateralized mortgage obligations): Debt obligations that are backed by a pool of whole mortgages or mortgage_backed securities such as Ginnie Maes.

Mortgage backed Securities: A participation in an organized pool of residential mortgages, including Ginnie Maes (Government National Mortgage Association), Fannie Maes (Federal National Mortgage Association) and Freddie Macs (Federal Home Loan Mortgage Corporation).

Securitized receivables: Debt securities collateralized by a pool of receivables.

CARDs: (certificates of amortizing revolving debts) backed by credit card debt.

CARs: (Certificates of automobile receivables) backed by automobile loans.

CLEOs: (collateralized lease equipment obligations) backed by leasing receivables.

FRENDS: (floating rate enhanced debt securities) backed by LBO loan participations.

Equity Instruments:

MMP: (money market preferred stock or dutch auction preferred stock): Preferred stock featuring dividends that are reset at a dutch auction - that is, an action in which the securities are sold at the lowest yield necessary to sell the entire issue. Several investment banks have issued these instruments under such registered names as *CAMPS*: cumulative auction market preferred stock.

CMPS: Capital market preferred stock. Convertible MMP stock: MMPs that can be converted into common stock.
DARTS: dutch-auction rate transferable securities.
FRAPS: fixed rate auction preferred stock.
MAPS: market auction preferred stock.
STARS: short-term auction rate cumulative preferred stock.
STRAPS: stated rate auction preferred stock.
PIK (pay in kind) preferred stock: Dividends are paid in additional shares of preferred stock
Exchangeable PIK preferred stock: The issuer can convert the PIK stock into debt.

Hedging Instruments:

Butterfly spread: Options strategy involving two calls and two puts in the same or different markets, with several maturity dates.

Calendar spread: Options strategy that involves buying and selling options on the same security with different maturities.

Cancelable forward exchange contracts: The holder has the unilateral right to cancel the contract at maturity.

CIRCUS: Combined currency and interest rate swap.

Convertible option contracts: A foreign currency option that converts to a forward contract if the forward exchange rate falls below a trigger price.

Cross-hedging: Hedging one exposure with an instrument pegged to another market or index.

Cylinder options: A combined call option and put option on currency.

Range Forwards: A forward exchange contract specifying a range of exchange rates within which currencies will be exchanged at maturity.

ZCRO (zero cost ratio option): A cylinder option with a put written in an amount offsetting the call premiums.

OPOSSMS: Options to purchase or sell specified mortgage-backed securities.

Perpendicular spread: Options strategy using options with the same maturities but different strike prices.

Swaption: An option to enter or be forced to enter a swap.

Synthetic instruments: Two or more transactions that have the effect of a financial instrument. For example, a fixed-rate bond combined with an interest rate swap can result in a synthetic floating rate instrument.

Zero-coupon swap: A swap of zero-coupon debt into floating rate debt.

FINANCIAL INTERMEDIARY The exchange of money between borrowers and lenders in the credit market is accomplished either from a direct exchange of credit between borrowers and lenders or from an indirect exchange through a financial institution. When lenders lend their money directly to borrowers by purchasing an IOU from a borrower in exchange for money, direct borrowing occurs. When lenders deposit their money in or purchase an IOU from a financial institution, and thereby allow the financial institution to lend the money to borrowers, indirect borrowing occurs. With indirect borrowing the ultimate source of the money is not the financial institution, but rather the lender who deposited their money in the financial institution.

These financial institutions are also called financial intermediaries because the institution intermediates (comes between) in the exchange process by bringing together the borrower and the lender. Financial intermediaries include banks; savings and loan institutions; credit unions; money market mutual funds; and mutual savings banks that accept deposits, make loans, and provide other financial services. The appended table shows the total assets of financial intermediaries for periods from 1960-1985.

Financial intermediaries that do not accept deposits but do provide services include financial companies which make loans and insurance companies which provide financial services such as insurance against the loss of life and property.

FINANCIAL LEVERAGE Ratio of debt to equity or ratio of -fixed financial charges to operating profit before fixed charges. See LEVERAGE.

ENCYCLOPEDIA OF BANKING AND FINANCE

FINANCIAL MAGAZINES

Total Assets of Financial Intermediaries at Year-End
(Billions of Dollars)

Financial intermediary	1960	1965	1970	1975	1980	1985*
Commercial banks	$257.6	$377.3	$576.2	$964.9	$1,703.7	$2,460.3
Savings institutions:						
Savings associations	71.5	129.6	176.2	338.2	630.7	952.2
Savings banks	40.6	58.2	79.0	121.1	171.6	325.7
Total	112.1	187.8	255.2	459.3	802.3	1,277.9
Life insurance companies	119.6	158.9	207.3	289.3	479.2	812.0
Private pension funds	38.1	73.6	110.4	186.6	412.5	655.2
State and local pension funds	19.7	34.1	60.3	104.8	198.1	397.2
Finance companies	27.6	44.7	64.0	98.8	191.3	331.7
Money market funds	...	...	...	3.7	74.4	207.5
Investment companies	17.0	35.2	47.6	42.2	58.4	251.5
Credit unions	6.3	11.0	18.0	36.9	71.6	135.3
Total	$598.0	$922.6	$1,339.0	$2,186.5	$3,991.5	$6,528.6

*Preliminary.

Sources: CUNA International, Inc., Federal Home Loan Bank Board, Federal Reserve Board, Institute of Life Insurance, Investment Company Institute, National Council of Saving's Institutions, United States League of Savings Institutions.

FINANCIAL MAGAZINES Banking and financial magazines published in the United States include the following:

Arkansas Banker
Bank and Quotation Record
Bank Stock Quarterly
Bankers Magazine
Bankers Monthly
Bankers News Weekly
Banking
Banking Law Journal
Barron's
Bond Buyer
Bondweek
Burroughs Clearing House
Business Week
Chase Economic Observer
Coast Banker
Columbia Journal of World Business
Commercial and Financial Chronicle
Credit and Financial Management
Dun's Review
Federal Home Loan Bank Board Journal
Federal Reserve Bank Review
Federal Reserve Bulletin
Finance
Finance and Development
Financial Analysts Journal
Financial Executive
Financial Planning Magazine
Financial World
Forbes Magazine
Fortune
Great Lakes Banker
Harvard Business Review
Inc. (magazine)
Institutional Investor
Investing Magazine
Investment Dealers Digest
Journal of Accountancy
Journal of Bank Research
Journal of Commercial Bank Lending
Kansas Banker
Kentucky Banker
MidAmerican Outlook
Mid-Continent Banker
Mid-Western Banker
Mississippi Banker
Money (magazine)
Month's Work (National Association of Mutual Savings Banks)
Morgan Guaranty Trust Company (N.Y.) Survey
Mountain States Banker
National Thrift News (weekly)
Nation's Business
New Jersey Banker
Northwestern Banker
Ohio Banker
Pensions & Investments
Pension World
Practical Banker (quarterly)
Robert Morris Associates Bulletin Savings and Loan News (U.S. Savings and Loan League)
Savings Bank Journal
Southern Banker
Soloman Bros. Bank Stock Weekly
Survey of Current Business
Tarheel Banker
Texas Bankers Record
Trusts and Estates
Wall Street Transcript

For current indexes and guides to periodical literature, see the *Business Periodicals Index* and other guides of the H. W. Wilson Company, New York, N.Y.

FINANCIAL MARKETS A financial market brings together borrowers and lenders (or investors) and establishes and communicates the prices at which they are willing to make transactions. Financial markets assume many shapes and forms.

The appended exhibit describes in general terms the American financial system as it relates to the credit and capital markets. The appended diagram illustrates the flows in the U.S. financial system.

Credit and capital market instruments are sometimes classified as follows: U.S. government securities, state and local government obligations, corporate and foreign bonds, mortgages, consumer credit, bank loans, and other loans (open-market paper, commercial paper, bankers' acceptances, Federal funds and security repurchase agreements, finance company loans to business, U.S. government loans, sponsored credit agency loans, and loans on insurance policies).

Federal and state governments and the securities industry attempt to protect investors through detailed regulations and supervision. Every state has blue sky laws that set forth requirements relating to licensing of securities representatives as well as registration and disclosure procedures for products offered for sale.

BIBLIOGRAPHY

BANK ADMINISTRATION INSTITUTE. *Interest Rates, the Markets, and the New Financial World*, Bank Administration Institute, Chicago, IL, 1986.
BOWDEN, E. V., and HOLBERT, J. L. *Revolution in Banking*. Prentice Hall, Inc., Englewood Cliffs, NJ, 1984.

Diagram of Flows in U.S. Financial System

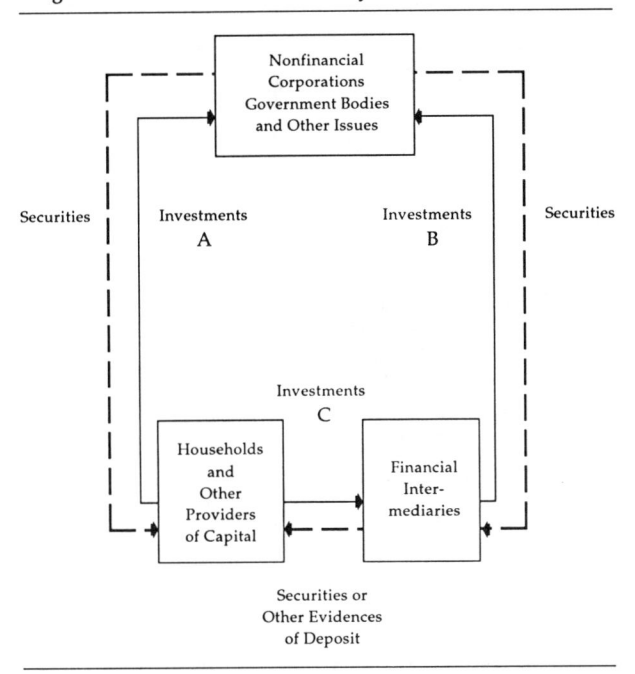

```
                    ┌─────────────────┐
                    │  Nonfinancial   │
                    │  Corporations   │
                    │ Government Bodies│
                    │ and Other Issues│
                    └─────────────────┘
                    Investments   Investments
Securities              A             B         Securities

                    Investments
                         C
        ┌──────────┐              ┌──────────┐
        │Households│              │ Financial│
        │   and    │              │  Inter-  │
        │  Other   │              │ mediaries│
        │Providers │              │          │
        │of Capital│              │          │
        └──────────┘              └──────────┘
                    Securities or
                    Other Evidences
                      of Deposit
```

Source: The Handbook of the Bond and Money Markets. David M. Darst. McGraw-Hill Book Co., New York, N.Y. 1981.

CORRIGAN, E. G. "Financial Market Structure: A Longer View." Federal Reserve Bank of New York. *Annual Report*, February, 1987.
MAYER, M. *The Money Bazaars*, 1984.

FINANCIAL NEWS Dow Jones News Service. In 1882, the Financial News Agency was founded by Charles H. Dow and Edward D. Jones, providing financial news by means of handwritten messages delivered by messenger boys in the financial district of New York. The present-day Dow Jones News Service has subscribers in over 1,000 communities through the U.S. and is also available in Canada as Canadian Dow Jones, Ltd. In January, 1967, the Dow Jones News Service joined with the Associated Press to begin the AP-Dow Jones Economic Report, providing a worldwide business and financial news service, and the two organizations also jointly operate the AP-Dow Jones Financial Wire, a service for businesspeople, bankers, and brokers in Western Europe. In 1968, the Dow Jones Broadcast Service began providing business news for radio and television stations.

See FINANCIAL MAGAZINES, FINANCIAL NEWSPAPERS, MARKET INFLUENCES, TICKER.

FINANCIAL NEWSPAPERS The principal daily financial newspapers exclusively devoted to financial subjects and published in the U.S. are

American Banker
Daily News Record
Financial Times
Journal of Commerce (New York)
Wall Street Journal

In addition to the above specialized publications, which also cover news of general interest, the newspapers of general circulation also carry financial news in varying degrees of completeness of coverage. An outstanding example of a newspaper of general circulation with depth of coverage of financial news and interpretative articles thereon is the *New York Times*, which does not restrict its financial section arbitrarily to one or two pages, as is the case with many other such newspapers; as a newspaper of record on financial items it is superior in various respects to even the specialized financial newspapers.

FINANCIAL PLANNING Personal financial planning involves the evaluation of a person's current financial position and financial goals leading to a presentation of a plan to achieve those goals. A typical financial plan includes the following:

1. A balance sheet analysis
2. Projection of cash flow
3. Long-term accumulation plans for retirement, education, etc.
4. Statement of individual's goals
5. Insurance analysis
6. Estate and tax planning
7. Projection of income taxes
8. Overview of weaknesses and strengths in the individual's financial outlook
9. Recommendations for implementing the plan

Financial planners charge clients in one of three major ways: a fee-only basis, a fee-and-commission basis, or on a commission basis.

Currently two professional organizations accredit planners after they have completed certain educational and professional requirements: The College for Financial Planning confers the Certified Financial Planner (CFP) and the American College confers the Chartered Financial Consultant (ChFC) designation. Two major professional organizations are associated with financial planning: the International Association for Financial Planning and the Institute of Certified Financial Planners.

See PERSONAL FINANCIAL PLANNING

FINANCIAL REPORTING Financial reporting includes not only financial statements but also other means of communicating information that relates, directly or indirectly, to the information provided by the accounting system. Financial reporting is intended primarily to provide information that is useful in making business and economic decisions.

Financial reporting is a broad concept encompassing financial statements, notes to financial statements (and parenthetical disclosures), supplementary information (such as changing prices disclosures and oil and gas reserves information), and other means of financial reporting (such as management discussion and analysis, and letters to stockholders). Financial reporting is but one source of information needed by those who make economic decisions about business enterprises. The appended table illustrates the relationship of financial reporting to other information useful for investment, credit, and similar decisions.

The primary focus of financial reporting is information about earnings and its components. Information about earnings based on accrual accounting usually provides a better indication of an enterprise's present and continuing ability to generate positive cash flows than that provided by cash receipts and payments.

BIBLIOGRAPHY

FINANCIAL ACCOUNTING STANDARDS BOARD. *Accounting Standards*: *Statements of Financial Accounting Concepts*, 1987.

FINANCIAL RESPONSIBILITY The ability of a borrower or prospective borrower to pay his debts based on his wealth or property; a term used among bank credit people to indicate the financial worth (i.e., the conservatively appraised net assets) of a credit risk. Financial responsibility is measured by the PROPERTY RISK.

See CREDIT.

FINANCIAL RISK The risk that the issuer may not be able to perform and comply with all requirements and expectations in issues of debt and equity securities. In investments, financial risk, money risk (interest rate risk, the risk that current interest rates may rise and thus adversely affect current market prices of high grade fixed return securities selling primarily on a yield basis), and PURCHASING POWER RISK (INFLATION risk, the risk of erosion in purchasing power of the fixed return types of securities) are the classifications usually given for the principal risks associated with investing.

In managerial finance, financial risk is often considered synonymous with BUSINESS RISK, but a distinction may be made that purely financial risk relates to the risks of unfavorable or negative LEVERAGE and of higher costs of money or even threats to solvency associated with use of leverage beyond the optimum level of capital structure proportions.

FINANCIAL SERVICE CORPORATIONS

Relationship of Financial Reporting to Other Information Services

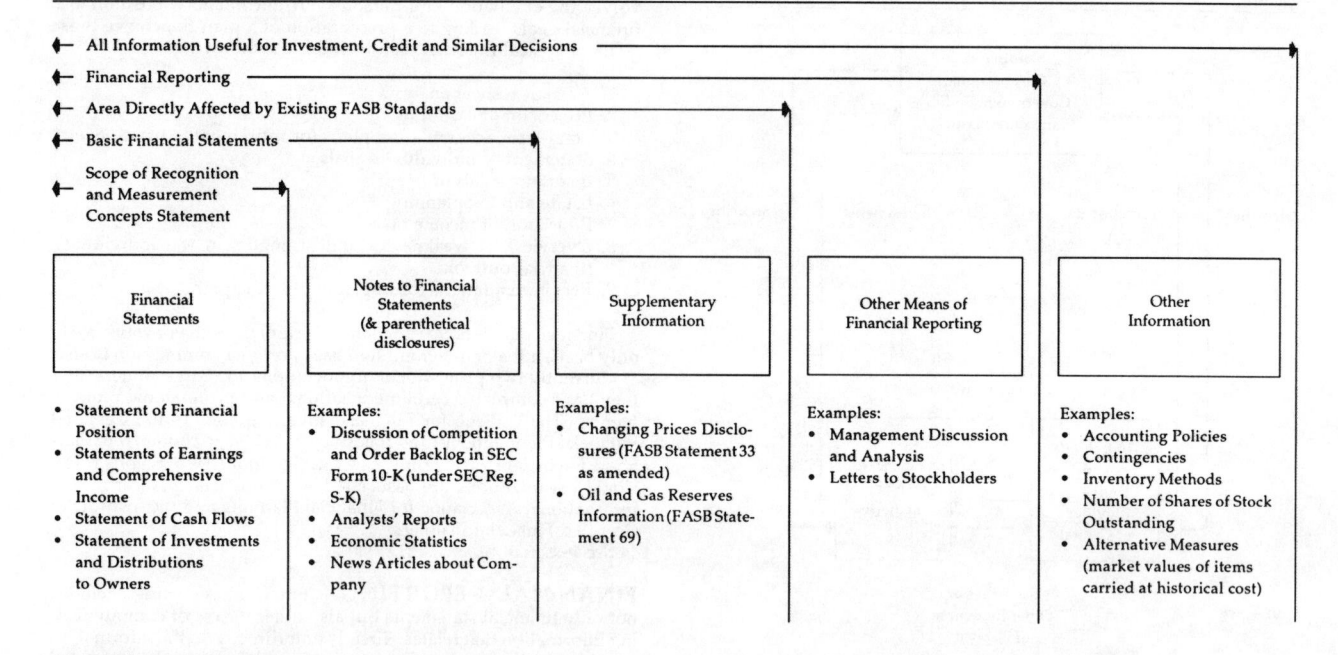

- All Information Useful for Investment, Credit and Similar Decisions
- Financial Reporting
- Area Directly Affected by Existing FASB Standards
- Basic Financial Statements
- Scope of Recognition and Measurement Concepts Statement

Financial Statements	Notes to Financial Statements (& parenthetical disclosures)	Supplementary Information	Other Means of Financial Reporting	Other Information
• Statement of Financial Position • Statements of Earnings and Comprehensive Income • Statement of Cash Flows • Statement of Investments and Distributions to Owners	Examples: • Discussion of Competition and Order Backlog in SEC Form 10-K (under SEC Reg. S-K) • Analysts' Reports • Economic Statistics • News Articles about Company	Examples: • Changing Prices Disclosures (FASB Statement 33 as amended) • Oil and Gas Reserves Information (FASB Statement 69)	Examples: • Management Discussion and Analysis • Letters to Stockholders	Examples: • Accounting Policies • Contingencies • Inventory Methods • Number of Shares of Stock Outstanding • Alternative Measures (market values of items carried at historical cost)

Financial risk in managerial finance can be measured by the ratio of total debt (current liabilities as well as long-term debt) to total assets. But more specifically, because of the usual viewpoint of common equity and the impact of leverage thereon, the denominator used is common equity (usually computed as tangible common equity, excluding the intangible assets). An alternative way of measuring financial risk is to note the permanent capitalization, consisting of long-term debt and equity, and its proportions.

See INVESTMENT.

FINANCIAL SERVICE CORPORATIONS A financial institution that provides a variety of financial services in a financial package to the wholesale or retail customer. For example, Sears Roebuck and Company includes a savings and loan holding company in California, a commercial bank in Delaware, a mortgage banking firm, a full-line insurance company (Allstate), and a brokerage firm (Dean Witter). American Express and Prudential Insurance Company are other examples.

FINANCIAL SOLVENCY The normal condition of a business when current assets are in excess of current liabilities as disclosed by a true and correct financial statement, showing cash and other liquid assets available for payment of liabilities when due. Financial solvency is to be distinguished from BUSINESS SOLVENCY.

See SOLVENCY.

FINANCIAL STATEMENTS Financial statements are the most widely used and the most comprehensive way of communicating financial information to users of the information provided on the reports. Different users of financial statements have different informational needs. General purpose financial statements have been developed to meet the needs of the users of financial statements, primarily the needs of investors and creditors.

The information provided by financial statements is primarily financial in nature quantified and expressed in units of money. The information presented pertains to individual business enterprises, government entities, and other accounting entities, and not to industries or to members of society as consumers. The information provided on the statements is often approximations, rather than exact, measures. The measures involve estimates, classifications, summarizations, judgments, and allocations. The information provided generally reflects the financial effects of transactions and events that have already happened. The information provided involves a cost to provide and use; generally the benefits of information provided should be expected to at least equal the cost involved.

The basic output of the financial accounting process is presented in the following interrelated general purpose financial statements:

1. A balance sheet (or statement of financial position) summarizes the financial position of an accounting entity at a particular point in time.
2. An income statement summarizes the results of operations for a given period of time.
3. A statement of cash flows summarizes the impact of an enterprise's cash flows on its operating, financing, and investing activities over a given period of time.
4. A statement of retained earnings shows the increases and decreases in earnings retained by the company over a given period of time. The statement is sometimes combined with the income statement. The statement of retained earnings is sometimes expanded into a statement of stockholders' equity that discloses changes in other stockholders' equity accounts in addition to retained earnings.

Notes to financial statements are considered an integral part of a complete set of financial statements.

The major financial statements are interrelated (or articulate) with each other. The income statement and the statement of changes in financial position can be viewed as connecting links between the beginning and ending statements of financial position. The income statement basically describes the changes in the statement of financial position accounts that result from operations. The statement of cash flows explains changes in cash between two points in time.

The aggregate condition and income data of FDIC-insured Commercial banks for 1988 and 1989 is appended.

Bank financial statements present a comprehensive report on the financial condition and results of operations. A discussion of these activities is usually presented in management's discussion and analysis of financial condition and results of operations along with other information contained in the annual report. For most banks, two significant purposes of funds management are to provide adequate liquidity and to maintain a reasonable relationship between the repricing of sources and uses of funds or interest sensitive assets and liabilities. This is accomplished through maintaining a

FINANCIAL STATEMENTS

Aggregate Condition and Income Data, FDIC-Insured Commercial Banks
(Dollar figures in millions)

	Preliminary 1st Qtr 1989	4th Qtr 1988	1st Qtr 1988	% Change 88:1 - 89:1
Number of banks reporting	13,001	13,121	13,541	-4.0
Total employees (full-time equivalent)	1,526,079	1,527,048	1,530,746	-0.3

Condition data

Total assets	$3,150,670	$3,130,750	$3,017,506	4.4
Real estate loans	695,024	676,612	615,588	12.9
Commercial & industrial loans	604,297	598,755	595,872	1.4
Loans to individuals	371,483	377,828	350,831	6.2
Farm loans	28,729	30,222	28,607	1.2
Other loans and leases	247,434	248,891	257,854	-4.0
Total loans and leases	1,946,967	1,932,308	1,848,752	5.3
LESS: Reserve for losses	45,871	46,650	50,304	-8.8
Net loans and leases	1,901,096	1,885,658	1,798,448	5.7
Temporay investments	484,316	465,811	472,296	2.5
Securities over 1 year	386,516	382,777	392,794	-1.6
All other assets	378,761	396,504	353,969	7.0
Total liabilities and capital	$3,150,670	$3,130,750	$3,017,506	4.4
Noninterest-bearing deposits	440,208	479,429	438,900	0.3
Interest-bearing deposits	1,988,409	1,952,142	1,880,154	5.8
Other borrowed funds	399,327	380,684	394,079	1.3
Subordinated debt	17,349	17,309	17,505	-0.9
All other liabilities	103,404	104,464	103,834	-0.4
Equity capital	201,972	196,721	183,035	10.3
Primary capital	251,696	246,812	237,180	6.1
Nonperforming assets	69,991	67,065	74,872	-6.5
Loan commitments and letters of credit	835,284	839,393	802,356	4.1
Domestic office assets	2,735,437	2,726,123	2,584,376	5.8
Foreign office assets	415,233	404,627	433,130	-4.1
Domestic office deposits	2,103,765	2,116,492	1,985,327	6.0
Foreign office deposits	324,852	315,079	333,727	-2.7
Earning assets	2,771,909	2,734,246	2,663,537	4.1
Volatile liabilities	1,116,070	1,073,656	1,077,553	3.6

	Full Year 1988	Full Year 1987	% Change	Preliminary 1st Qtr 1989	1st Qtr 1988	% Change
Income data						
Total interest income	$272,279	$244,837	11.2	$75,528	$64,103	17.8
Total interest expense	165,013	144,949	13.8	47,504	38,615	23.0
Net interest income	107,266	99,888	7.4	28,024	25,487	9.9
Provisions for loan losses	16,965	37,505	-54.8	3,592	4,715	-23.8
Total noninterest income	44,932	41,468	8.3	11,735	11,056	6.1
Total noninterest expense	101,280	97,303	4.1	25,929	25,035	3.6
Applicable income taxes	10,012	5,417	84.8	2,993	2,369	26.3
Net operating income	23,942	1,130	2018.3	7,245	4,426	63.7
Securities gains, net	286	1,427	-80.0	52	390	-86.7
Extraordinary gains, net	832	204	308.5	30	132	-77.7
Net income	25,060	2,761	807.5	7,327	4,948	48.1
Net charge-offs	18,468	16,430	12.4	3,489	4,045	-13.8
Net additions to capital stock	3,181	2,613	21.7	197	156	26.6
Cash dividends on capital stock	13,210	10,666	23.8	3,175	3,199	-0.7

Source: U.S. Federal Deposit Insurance Corporation.

combination of sufficient core deposit growth, liquid assets and unused capacity to purchase funds in the money markets. The more stable consumer core deposits are supplemented with large denomination certificates of deposit and purchased federal funds and other sources. Major banks also have access to the Eurodollar market primarily as a source of funding foreign office loans and discretionary placements. It is important that a bank has the ability to support healthy secular asset growth and cyclical peaks in customer loan demand. The core demand and time deposit accounts should be supported with a strong capital base to produce a balance sheet which is asset sensitive (having more assets than liabilities sensitive to changes in market rates).

An objective of asset and liability management is to increase the level of variable rate assets (floating rate consumer and commercial loans, adjustable rate mortgages and shorter maturity investments) to balance increases in market-sensitive liabilities. The long-term strategies of a bank coupled with its short-term tactics must be astutely employed to react to the dynamic effects of money market developments, regulatory changes, competition, customer demand, and other external forces.

The financial condition of a bank can usually be evaluated by reviewing the changes, trends, and relationship in the sources and uses of funds. Deposits are the primary source of funds for most banks. The major use of funds is for interest-earning assets, primarily loans and investment securities. The components of assets, liabilities, and capital should be reviewed (Primary capital: share-

ENCYCLOPEDIA OF BANKING AND FINANCE

holders' equity; allowance for loan losses; long-term debt qualifying as primary capital; minority interest) along with capital ratios (shareholders' equity to total assets; primary capital to total assets; total capital to total assets).

The results of operations are impacted by loan demand and interest rates structures as well as by the marketplace. Earnings performance as reflected in a bank's net interest income and selected average balances (loans; investment securities; interest-bearing bank balances; Federal funds sold and securities purchased under resale agreements; trading account assets); interest expense and selected average balances (savings and interest-bearing demand); money market checking and savings; saving certificates large denomination certificates; time denomination certificates; time deposits in foreign offices; short-term borrowed funds; long-term debt); net interest rate yield (net interest income as a percentage of average earning assets loans; investment securities; interest-bearing bank balances; Federal funds sold and securities purchased under resale agreements; trading account balances); net income per share fully diluted can provide basic information about a bank's performance; taxable equivalent rate/volume variance analysis; nonperforming assets and provision and allowance for loan losses; foreign country exposure; and noninterest income and noninterest expense. Total average assets in relation to equity capital provides are useful in relating a bank with guidelines of federal regulators. Net loan losses as a percentage of loans for a period of years is important in estimating the quality of a bank's loans.

While FINANCIAL STATEMENT ANALYSIS is basic when evaluating a bank, factors above and beyond the financial statements often are as significant in evaluating a bank as are the results of financial reporting: capable people, an understanding of purpose or mission, responsive policies and objectives, competitive services, modern technology, attractive markets, sources of funding, strong and stable capital, sound loans, and sufficient reserves.

For illustrations of financial statements of banks, see the entry GENERAL LEDGER.

See BANK STATEMENT.

BIBLIOGRAPHY

HYLTON, D. P. "On the Usefulness of Consolidated Financial Statements." *CPA Journal*, October, 1988.
WANG, P. "What's Off, What's On? [accounting rules for consolidations]." *Forbes*, February 20, 1989.

FINANCIAL STATEMENT ANALYSIS The purpose of financial statement analysis is to examine past and current financial data so that a company's performance and financial position can be evaluated and future risks and potential can be estimated. Financial statement analysis can yield valuable information about trends and relationships, the quality of a company's earnings, and the strengths and weaknesses of its financial position.

Financial statement analysis begins with establishing the objective(s) of the analysis. For example, is the analysis undertaken to provide a basis for granting credit or making an investment? After the objective of the analysis is established, the data is accumulated from the financial statements and from other sources. The results of the analysis are summarized and interpreted. Conclusions are reached and a report is made to the person(s) for whom the analysis was undertaken.

To evaluate financial statements, a person must:

1. be acquainted with business practices,
2. understand the purpose, nature, and limitations of accounting,
3. be familiar with the terminology of business and accounting, and
4. be acquainted with the tools of financial statement analysis.

Financial analysis of a company should include an examination of the financial statements of the company, including notes to the financial statements, and the auditor's report. The auditor's report will state whether the financial statements have been audited in accordance with generally accepted auditing standards. The report also indicates whether the statements fairly present the company's financial position, results of operations, and changes in financial position in accordance with generally accepted accounting principles. Notes to the financial statement are often more meaningful than the data found within the body of the statements. The notes explain the accounting policies of the company and usually provide detailed explanations of how those policies were applied along with supporting details. Analysts often compare the financial statements of one company with other companies in the same industry and with the industry in which the company operates as well as with prior year statements of the company being analyzed.

Comparative financial statements provide analysts with significant information about trends and relationships over two or more years. Comparative statements are more significant for evaluating a company than are single-year statements. Financial statement RATIOS are additional tools for analyzing financial statements. Financial ratios establish relationships between various items appearing on financial statements. Ratios can be classified as follows:

1. **Liquidity ratios.** Measure the ability of the enterprise to pay its debts as they mature.
2. **Activity (or turnover) ratios.** Measure how effectively the enterprise is using its assets.
3. **Profitability ratios.** Measure management's success in generating returns for those who provide capital to the enterprise.
4. **Coverage ratios.** Measure the protection for long-term creditors and investors.

Horizontal analysis and vertical analysis of financial statements are additional techniques that can be used effectively when evaluating a company. Horizontal analysis spotlights trends and establishes relationships between items that appear on the same row of a comparative statement thereby disclosing changes on items in financial statements over time. Vertical analysis involves the conversion of items appearing in statement columns into terms of percentages of a base figure to show the relative significance of the items and to facilitate comparisons. For example, individual items appearing on the income statement can be expressed as percentages of sales. On the balance sheet, individual assets can be expressed as a percentage of total assets. Liabilities and owners' equity accounts can be expressed in terms of their relationship to total liabilities and owners' equity.

Financial statement analysis has its limitations. Statements represent the past and do not necessarily predict the future. However, financial statement analysis can provide clues or suggest a need for further investigation. What is found on financial statements is the product of accounting conventions and procedures (LIFO or FIFO inventory; straight-line or accelerated depreciation) that sometimes distort the economic reality or substance of the underlying situation. Financial statements say little directly about changes in markets, the business cycle, technological developments, laws and regulations, management personnel, price-level changes, and other critical analytical concerns.

Selected sources of information for financial analysis is appended. Also appended are selected measures of financial condition 1975 to 1987 for FDIC-insured commercial banks.

BIBLIOGRAPHY

Accounting Trends and Techniques. American Istitute of Certified Public Accountants, New York, NY. Latest edition.
BERNSTEIN, L. A. *Financial Statement Analysis.* Richard D. Irwin, Inc., Homewood, IL. Latest edition.
FOSTER, G. *Financial Statement Analysis.* Prentice Hall, Inc., Englewood Cliffs, NJ. Latest edition.
GARCIA, F. L. *How To Analyze A Bank Statement.* Bankers Publishing Co., Boston, MA, 1985.
GIBSON, C. H. *Financial Statement Analysis,* 1986.
O'MALIA, T. J. *A Banker's Guide to Financial Statements,* 1989.
WOELFEL, C. J. *Financial Statement Analysis.* Probus Publishing Co., Chicago, IL, 1988.

FINANCIER One skilled in FINANCE; particularly one engaged in promoting and underwriting.

FINE The degree of purity or FINENESS of a metal expressed in terms of parts, percentages, or carats. Fine gold is 100% pure, or unalloyed gold, which is 24 carats.

See CARAT.

Insured Commercial Banks—Selected Measures of Financial Condition: 1975 to 1987
As of December 31. Capital figures exclude reserves for possible loan losses.)

Item	Unit	1975	1980	1981	1982	1983	1984	1985	1986	1987
Number of banks	Number	14,384	14,434	14,414	14,452	14,465	14,481	14,404	14,200	13,699
Equity and debt capital [1]	Bil. dol.	70.3	114.1	124.8	136.2	147.6	164.5	198.2	199.3	199.1
Equity capital to total assets	Percent	6.1	5.8	5.8	5.9	6.0	6.2	6.2	6.2	6.0
Equity capital to total deposits	Percent	8.5	7.3	7.4	7.6	7.6	7.9	8.0	8.0	7.8
Debt capital to total capital [1]	Percent	6.3	5.7	5.2	5.4	4.8	6.2	14.5	8.5	8.9
Total capital to total assets	Percent	6.5	6.2	6.2	6.2	6.3	6.6	6.7	6.8	6.6
Total capital to total liabilities	Percent	6.9	6.6	6.6	6.6	6.7	7.0	7.2	7.3	7.1
Total capital to risk assets [2]	Percent	9.0	8.4	8.2	8.2	8.4	8.5	9.1	8.7	8.5
Total loans, excluding Federal funds [3]	Bil. dol.	579.4	1,002.5	1,131.3	1,224.4	1,316.9	1,508.3	1,630.8	1,756.6	1,829.3
Total loans to deposits	Percent	63.4	67.7	71.2	71.7	71.5	76.9	77.0	76.9	78.3
Net loan charge-offs to average total loans	Percent	.61	.38	.36	.56	.68	.76	.84	.98	.93
Aggregate net operating income	Mil. dol.	7,146	14,484	15,600	15,587	14,907	15,540	16,267	13,314	1,953
Aggregate net income to average equity capital	Percent	11.7	13.7	13.1	12.1	11.1	10.7	11.3	10.0	2.0
Aggregate net income to average assets	Percent	.78	.78	.77	.72	.66	.65	.70	.63	.12

[1] Beginning 1985 includes limited life preferred stock as debt capital.
[2] Risk assets are total assets less cash, U.S. Government securities, and Federal funds sold.
[3] Beginning in 1984, some assets previously classified as securities are included among loans.

Source: U.S. Federal Deposit Insurance Corporation, *The Condition of the Financial System,* May 1980, and unpublished data.

Selected Sources of Information for Financial Analysis

		Institution Type					Information Type				
		Holding Company	Bank	S&L	MSB	CU	Balance Sheet	Income Statement	Deposits	Ratios	Other
Private Sources:	*Bank Administration Institute* Index of Bank Performance		X								X
	Decision Research Sciences, Inc. Branch Directory and Summary of deposits with Market indicators	X	X	X	X	X			X		X
	Rand McNally International Bank Directory	X	X				X		X		X
	R. L. Polik World Bank Directory	X	X				X		X		X
	Sheshunoff & Associates Bank Operations Statistics		X				X	X	X	X	
	Bank Holding Company Performance	X	X				X	X	X	X	
	Management Profiles	X	X	X			X	X	X	X	
Public Sources:	*Primary Regulators* Reports of Condition		X	X	X		X		X		
	Income & Dividend Reports	X					X	X			
	Comptroller of Currency Member Bank Operating Ratios		X				X	X	X		
	Small Bank Surveillance System (SBSS)		X				X	X	X	X	
	Federal Deposit Insurance Corp. Assets & Liabilities—Commercial & Mutual Savings Banks		X		X		X		X		
	FDIC-Bank Operating Statistics		X		X		X	X	X		
	Federal Financial Institutions Examination Council Uniform Bank Performance Report		X				X	X	X	X	
	Federal Reserve System- Member Bank Operating Ratios		X				X	X	X	X	
	Functional Cost Analysis		X				X	X	X	X	X

FINE GOLD See FINE, FINENESS.

FINENESS The amount of pure metal in a bar, ingot, or coin; the degree of purity of a metal as expressed in terms of parts, percentages, or carats.

Pursuant to the Coinage Act of 1965, the half-dollar clad U.S. coin containing silver had a fineness of 40% (gross weight 11.5 grams, of which 4.6 grams were silver). By contrast, the previous standard silver dollar weighed 12.5 grams, of which 11.25 grams (90% fineness) were silver. Former gold coins of the U.S. (nationalized in 1933 and pursuant to Gold Reserve Act of 1934) were in their last authorized coinages 0.900 FINE. Commercial silver bullion held by the Treasury is 0.999 fine and miscellaneous silver bullion is 0.830 to 0.998 fine, while coinage silver, as noted above, was 0.400 fine.

See COINAGE, MINT FINE BARS, PRESENT STANDARD OF WEIGHT AND FINENESS, STANDARD BULLION.

FINE TUNE A phrase used in economics to describe what monetary and fiscal policies are not intended to do. Monetary and fiscal policies are useful in dampening large fluctuations in economic activity—business cycles. However, the economy is so complex and the time lags associated with such policies are imprecise that these policies should not be used to attempt to remove (fine tune) all economic fluctuations.

FINGERPRINT IDENTIFICATION A method adopted by a number of savings banks as a means of certain identification, especially of foreign-born and illiterate depositors. Many savings banks located in districts serving a foreign population have experienced difficulty and suffered losses by reason of withdrawals from savings accounts by wrongful parties. Test questions in connection with withdrawals from savings accounts by illiterate depositors have been used for many years, but they have not always proved satisfactory, especially where the depositors are unable to speak English.

Fingerprint identification is based upon the persistence of the skin patterns of the fingers, which do not change during the life of the individual and which are different for each individual. Scratching and laceration do not ordinarily obliterate these patterns. The fingerprint is taken at the time an account is opened upon the signature card, which contains the usual additional information, e.g., residence, references, occupation, etc. At each withdrawal a fingerprint impression is taken and compared with the original without inconvenience to the depositor.

Fingerprints were probably first used extensively for identification purposes in India by the British, who applied the system as early as 1899 to the native Hindus. Fingerprints have been taken from the same people during childhood and again during early adulthood and in other cases during early adulthood and middle ages. These records have proven that fingerprints do not change materially during the whole course of life, although the patterns become larger and more pronounced as the fingers and hands grow in size. The whole system of fingerprint identification depends upon the unchangeable character of these ridges. By spreading ink on the undersurface of the fingers and then impressing them upon paper or some other white surface one obtains a fingerprint either as a record or for comparison with a previous print. By carefully comparing patterns according to well-established standards it is possible to show whether or not the impressions were made by the same person. Although at first the patterns made by fingerprints appear very complicated and difficult to recognize, closer study will show that variations in them can be detected with comparative ease. This is accomplished by classifying the various forms of fingerprints into certain types. The first requirement for a person who uses the fingerprint system of identification is to familiarize himself with these various types of prints. Studies of the fingerprints of thousands of persons by those who are constantly working with the system have led to the establishment of four general types of patterns, although combinations or variations are sometimes found. These four types are called arches, loops, whorls, and composites.

The fingerprint system of identification removes the chief objection of savings banks to accepting accounts with illiterates.

FINITE LIFE REAL ESTATE INVESTMENT TRUST (FREIT) A financial trust designed to sell off its invested holdings within a specific period of time. When the time has elapsed, investors receive the sale price and report a capital gain on the investment. FREITs are a variation of the Real Estate Investment Trust (REIT) in that the investor has the option of waiting a finite period of time until the portfolio is sold and cash is distributed.

FIRE INSURANCE See INSURANCE.

FIREWORKS A stock market expression which denotes the soaring of prices in a single security or group of securities; rapid advance in prices.

FIRM This term has two meanings:

1. A PARTNERSHIP; a business or professional association of two or more persons as distinguished from an incorporated company.
2. An expression which denotes steadiness in security or commodity quotations. Prices are firm when they are stable and resist decline, tending upward rather than downward. Somewhat illogically in view of its derivation, a firm market usually implies one in which prices are fractionally higher; it is midway between a strong market when prices are rising and a steady market when prices are stationary.

Money is firm when interest rates hold stationary.

FIRM BID See OFFERED FIRM.

FIRST AND CONSOLIDATED MORTGAGE BONDS Bonds secured by a first mortgage on a part or parts of such properties (usually of railroads) as have been consolidated and by a second or even third mortgage upon the rest. These bonds are practically the same as GENERAL MORTGAGE BONDS.

FIRST AND GENERAL MORTGAGE BONDS Bonds secured by a first mortgage on a part of the property of the issuing corporation (usually a railroad) and by general mortgage on the rest. Such bonds are sometimes issued by a railroad in financing a new extension. A first mortgage is placed upon the new property, and if the previous mortgages upon the old property are of the open type, the remaining equity in the previously mortgaged property is used as further security. These bonds are also known as general and first mortgage bonds.

FIRST AND REFUNDING MORTGAGE BOND A bond secured by a first mortgage on a part of the property of the issuing corporation (usually a railroad) but constituting a junior lien upon other parts, the debt upon which is being refunded. These bonds are practically synonymous with first and consolidated mortgage bonds except that the latter issue is not a refunding issue.

See REFUNDING BONDS.

FIRST BANK OF THE UNITED STATES See BANK OF THE UNITED STATES.

FIRST BOARD On exchanges which deal in futures, the delivery dates for the various positions are designated in advance by the exchange authorities. The first call for cotton, grain, or sugar is often known as the first board.

The term is also used to indicate the first printed sales for particular issues occurring on the New York Stock Exchange, i.e., those between 10 A.M. and noon.

FIRST-CLASS PAPER Gilt-edged or prime paper made or endorsed by concerns which enjoy a nationwide reputation for their products, financial responsibility, and credit standing, as distinguished from second- and third-class paper endorsed by companies not so well known and with less financial responsibility. This term is used primarily in connection with commercial paper marketed by commercial paper dealers.

FIRST CONSOLIDATED MORTGAGE BONDS The first (in point of time) consolidated mortgage bonds issued by a corporation (usually a railroad). Such bonds do not necessarily represent a first lien upon the mortgaged property, since in most cases only a part of the pledged property is secured by a first mortgage. They are practically synonymous with first and consolidated mortgage bonds, but should not be confused with CONSOLIDATED FIRST MORTGAGE BONDS.

FIRST GENERAL MORTGAGE BONDS Literally, the first (in point of time) general mortgage bonds issued by a corporation (usually a railroad). They are in no sense bonds secured by a first mortgage. Since GENERAL MORTGAGE BONDS represent in part a second or even lesser claim upon the mortgaged property, it is not likely that an issue of second general mortgage bonds would ever be floated. First general mortgage bond is, therefore, an equivocal title.

FIRST LEASEHOLD BONDS Bonds secured by a mortgage on the estate in realty held under a lease, or leasehold, rather than on the property itself. This type of bond was popular in real estate financing in the late 1920s, but subsequently proved vulnerable to shrinkage in earning power, as interest on the bonds is really junior to the payment of rental on the lease. Leaseholds as security also proved to be unsatisfactory for bond financing, as payment of rentals was also impaired by shrinkage in earning power.
See REAL ESTATE BONDS.

FIRST LIEN The first claim or right against property. A first mortgage bond represents the first claim to the assets and earnings of a corporation, after the preferential claims (taxes, wages, etc.) have been satisfied.
See LIEN.

FIRST LIEN AND GENERAL MORTGAGE BONDS Bonds which constitute a first lien (or are a first mortgage) on a part (usually a small part) of the property of the issuing corporation and a general mortgage upon the rest. These bonds are the same as FIRST GENERAL MORTGAGE BONDS.

FIRST MORTGAGE BONDS Bonds secured by a first mortgage upon all or part of the property, as well as earnings, of the issuing corporation. While first mortgage bonds are secured by property (usually real estate but sometimes chattels and current assets), they are not necessarily always first-class investments. A second or even third mortgage bond of one corporation may be entitled to a higher investment rating than a first mortgage bond of another. A first mortgage security on a given property, however, is superior to any other security on the same property. The soundness of a first mortgage bond as an investment depends upon the value of the property serving as security in excess of the total par value of the bonds issued, the range of fluctuation of earnings, the margin of average earnings over the combined operating expenses and fixed charges, and the probability of current retirement of the bond at maturity. While foreclosure proceedings may be instituted upon default in payment of either interest or principal of a mortgage bond, there is always danger of loss because of the possible shrinkage in value of the property upon sale and the delay and costs incident to legal action.
See SECOND MORTGAGE BONDS.

FIRST MORTGAGE TRUST BONDS Bonds which are secured by a deposit of other bonds which in themselves are secured by a first mortgage. In other words these bonds are collateral trust bonds, the collateral for which consists of first mortgage bonds.

FIRST OF EXCHANGE Foreign bills of exchange and checks are usually issued in duplicate sets and sometimes in triplicate sets. The purpose of this practice is to insure the ultimate arrival of the bill of exchange at the foreign point where it is payable.
Duplicate bills with duplicate documents attached are transmitted on separate steamers to avoid inconvenience in case one ship is delayed and as a form of marine insurance (since it is not likely that both steamships will meet with a marine disaster). The first bill presented is paid, whether original, duplicate, or triplicate; i.e., any of the set is payable if the others are unpaid. When one of the set is paid, a stop is automatically placed on the others. The duplicate bills are referred to as first of exchange and second of exchange, or as original and duplicate. When only one bill of exchange is issued, it is called SOLA, sole, or solus.
See BILLS IN A SET.

FIRST PREFERRED STOCK See PREFERRED STOCK.

FIRST REFUNDING MORTGAGE BONDS The first (in point of time) refunding bonds issued by a corporation (usually a railroad or public utility). This title is misleading; it does not mean that the bonds are secured by a first mortgage, as does the title REFUNDING FIRST MORTGAGE BONDS.

FIRST TELLER A title sometimes given to the PAYING TELLER for the reason that he assumes greater responsibility and usually receives a higher salary than any of the other tellers.

FISCAL AGENT Financial agent. A bank or trust company may be appointed to take general or special charge of the finances of a corporation client in accordance with any agreement which may be made between them. Acting as treasurer, a bank or trust company may perform such disbursing functions as paying bonds and coupons at maturity, paying bonds which have been called for redemption, paying dividends, paying interest on registered bonds, paying rents, etc. It may also receive sinking fund installments. The fiscal agent function is one of the corporate trust functions.

FISCAL DRAG A budget surplus that can have a dampening effect on the economy.

FISCAL POLICY The coordinated policy of a government with respect to taxation, the public debt, public expenditures, and fiscal management, with an objective, for example, of attempting to stabilize national income of the economy. This concept of the role of fiscal policy regards government revenues and expenditures as balance-wheels vis a vis the economy, to be deployed from the standpoint of COMPENSATORY FINANCE in a counter-cyclical manner so as to achieve the objective of stability. Fundamental to such a fiscal policy would be the adjustment of budgetary deficits or surpluses to conform with the objective of stabilization against either undue inflation or deflation, with allowance for normal growth.
In the U.S., the policy objective of stability consistent with normal growth is specified by Congress in the Employment Act of 1946, which states: "It is the continuing policy and responsibility of the federal government to use all practicable means consistent with its needs and obligations and other essential considerations of national policy, with the assistance and cooperation of industry, agriculture, labor, and state and local governments, to coordinate and utilize all its plans, functions, and resources for the purpose of creating and maintaining, in a manner calculated to foster and promote free competitive enterprise and the general welfare, conditions under which there will be afforded useful employment opportunities, including self-employment, for those able, willing, and seeking to work, and to promote maximum employment, production, and purchasing power." It will be noted that the objective of stability is stated in terms of full employment. The nation's economic budget is required by the act to be reported in the President's annual economic report to Congress, analyzing the aggregate effects of the four sectors (consumers, business, government, and international) in accounting for the gross national product in the past and in guiding policy for the future. See NATION'S ECONOMIC ACCOUNTS. The Employment Act of 1946 has been credited by the Council of Economic Advisers with making possible, through its required coordination and stimulation of systematic and interrelated economic programming, a consistent federal fiscal policy in the post-World War II period, which assisted in preventing a postwar depression and in maintaining a high degree of prosperity. As to the efficacy of fiscal policy in general in preventing extreme booms or depressions, however, there is a difference of opinion.
There are two major types of demand management policies: fiscal policy and monetary policy. Fiscal policy is formulated and implemented by Congress and the President by changing deficit expenditures and the tax system. Monetary policy is formulated and implemented by the Federal Reserve board by changing the money supply.
Fiscal policy is implemented either through a change in government spending or through a change in federal tax rates. Expansionary fiscal policy takes one of two forms: a decrease in tax rates that increase expenditures in the private sector or an increase in government expenditures. In either case, the result is an increase in deficit spending by the government. Contractionary fiscal policy is implemented by a decrease in deficit spending resulting from either an increase in taxes that decreases private sector expenditures or by a decrease in government expenditures.
Household consumption is positively related to disposable income (after-tax income). Thus, a reduction in personal taxes increases disposable income and consumption, which in turn increases

aggregate demand. The Economic Recovery and Tax Act of 1981 lowered individual income marginal tax rates by 23 percent over a three year period in a effort to stimulate the economy. These tax cuts increased the size of the federal deficit and contributed to fiscal policy being expansionary between 1982 and 1985.

Aggregate demand also increases whenever government expenditures increase. Whether the government increases the purchase of goods and services or increases transfer payments to private individuals allowing them to increase their consumption expenditures, aggregate demand increases. For example, the expansion of the military budget and the overall level of government expenditures under President Ronald Reagan's administration represented expansionary fiscal policies. Thus, the simultaneous tax decrease and expenditure increase during Reagan's terms resulted in an expansionary fiscal policy and economic growth.

See BUSINESS CYCLE.

BIBLIOGRAPHY

BOSKIN, M. J. "Consumption, Saving, and Fiscal Policy." *American Economic Review*, May, 1988.
KOTLIKOFF, L. J. "Consumption, Computation Mistakes, and Fiscal Policy." *American Economic Review*, May, 1988.
POTERBA, J. M. "Are Consumers Forward Looking? Evidence From Fiscal Experiments." *American Economic Review*, May, 1988.
TANZI, V. "Issues in Coordination of Fiscal Policies." *Finance and Development*, December, 1988.
WNG, S. Q. "The Cyclically Adjusted Federal Budget and Policy Effectiveness." *The Review of Business and Economic Research*, Fall, 1988.

FISCAL YEAR A term used to indicate the accounting year as distinguished from the calendar year, with which it may or may not coincide. The fiscal year is any annual period which a business or government or subdivision thereof may select as a basis for closing its books in order to determine the results of operations and financial condition. Although most business enterprises close their books and take a physical inventory only at the close of the fiscal year, financial statements are often prepared monthly or quarterly without involving a closing of the books.

The fiscal year of the United States Government shifted beginning with the fiscal year 1977, under provisions of the Congressional Budget Act of 1974. Through fiscal year 1976, the fiscal year was on a July 1-June 30 basis. Beginning October 1976 (fiscal year 1977), the fiscal year has been on an October 1-September 30 basis. The period July 1, 1976, through September 30, 1976, is a separate fiscal period known as the "Transition Quarter." With most businesses the fiscal year corresponds with the calendar year.

FITCH INVESTORS SERVICE, INC. One of three nationally recognized full-service securities rating agencies. Founded in 1913 as the Fitch Publishing Company, it became the largest rater of corporate bonds. In September, 1960, it sold to Standard & Poor's Corporation several publications, its printing operation and the right to use the Fitch-designed bond rating symbols.

In 1961, Fitch Investors Service, Inc. initiated the rating of bonds issued by banks, bank holding companies, and hospitals. The company established the use of (+) and (−) signs to modify a credit within a particular rating category and the use of a "rating comment" in its written reports.

Fitch Investors Service, Inc. published individual reports on issuers and for specific bond and preferred stock issues.

See MANUALS

FIXED ASSETS Property, plant, and equipment acquired for use in normal operations and not for resale, long-term in nature and usually subject to depreciation (land is an exception), that possess physical substance; also referred to as plant assets or property, plant and equipment. Such assets include land, building structures (offices, factories, warehouses), and equipment (machinery, furniture, tools). Historical cost is the usual basis for valuing property, plant, and equipment. Historical cost is measured by the cash or cash equivalent price of obtaining the asset and bringing it to the location and condition necessary for its intended use.

FIXED ASSET TEST One of the general tests applied in analyzing the investment position of securities. The depreciated value of fixed assets (land, buildings, equipment, etc.) should normally be substantially in excess of the funded debt outstanding. Even the railroads, which are allegedly overcapitalized, compare favorably on this test. Net unmatured funded debt of railroads totals about 30% of investment in road and equipment, which means there is over $3.30 invested in road and equipment for every dollar of funded debt.

This test is also computed on the basis of total capitalization (funded debt and capital stock) to the net depreciated value of fixed assets.

See RATIO OF DEBT TO NET WORTH, RATIO OF FIXED ASSETS TO NET WORTH.

FIXED CAPITAL CAPITAL invested in fixed, as distinguished from current, assets; the investment in physical facilities and capacity. Fixed capital is that usually furnished by the stockholders and bondholders, while working capital required for investment in current assets in part may be furnished by banks or through the commercial paper market on short-term paper. Fixed capital is regarded as tied up or locked up and consequently must be furnished permanently or for a long period of time. It is for this reason that stockholders and bondholders contribute fixed capital to a business.

FIXED CHARGES In accounting, those financial expenses which must be paid as they fall due. In railroad accounting, fixed charges include rent for leased roads (usually guaranteed interest or dividends), rent for leased properties, interest on funded debt, interest on short-term or unfunded debt, and amortization of discount on funded debt. Sinking fund appropriations and insurance are sometimes regarded as fixed charges, but since sinking fund charges really are a means of extinguishing debt, it appears more logical to segregate this item as a disposition of surplus, and insurance is generally regarded as an administrative expense.

Fixed charges are sometimes confused with fixed costs, those costs made up of overhead or burden (indirect material, indirect labor, and general administrative costs) which continue regardless of the rate of operation, as compared with variable costs, as set up in cost systems of accounting.

FIXED COST Fixed costs are incurred in the short run (the long run being defined as a period of time long enough for all costs to be variable). Fixed costs are those costs that are invariant to changes in the level of output. For a firm, such costs include rent and payments on capital equipment. Capital, as opposed to labor, is generally considered that fixed factor of production in the short run.

Total fixed cost (TFC) represents all payments to factors of production that are invariant to changes in output. Average fixed cost (AFC) equals total fixed cost divided by output. As output increases, average fixed cost will continually decrease. The figure below illustrates these concepts.

Total Fixed and Average Fixed Cost Relationships

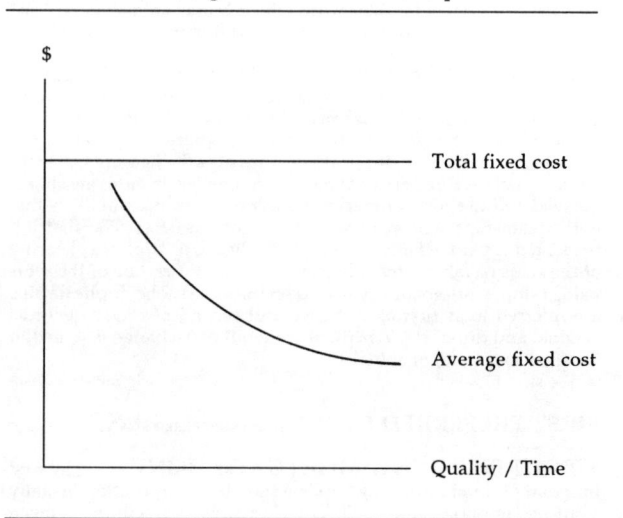

FIXED INCOME Income which does not fluctuate in accordance with the general price level. Those whose income is wholly dependent upon the return from bonds, annuities, or pensions are said to have a fixed income. While business incomes and wages tend to rise and fall with the general price level, fixed incomes do not. The fixed-income class also includes workers whose salaries tend to resist adjustment to changes in the general price level. A period of low prices is beneficial and a period of high prices disadvantageous to those having a fixed income.

FIXED LIABILITIES Long-term debt consisting of probably future sacrifices of economic benefits arising from present obligations that are not payable within the operating cycle of the business, or within a year if there are several operating cycles within one year. Examples of fixed liabilities, or long-term liabilities, include bonds payable, long-term notes payable, mortgages payable, pension obligations, and lease obligations. Long-term debt represents a somewhat permanent method of financing growth and is often used to increase earnings whenever a larger rate of return can be earned on the borrowed funds than is paid out of after-tax interest (leverage). Typically, long-term creditors have no vote in management matters and receive a stated rate of interest. A distinction is usually made between long-term debt and equity financing. A debt instrument typically has a maturity date for the face value (principal amount) to be repaid to the lender.

Long-term debt is often subject to covenants or restrictions for the protection of lenders. Bond indentures and note agreements are often used to reflect these covenants or restrictions.

FIXED TRUST See INVESTMENT TRUST.

FIXTURES Any chattels which have been so affixed or annexed to the realty as to become a part thereof and lose their character as personality. Annexation may be actual or constructive. Examples of fixtures are fences, gas pipes and electric wiring in the walls of a building; mirrors set into the walls of a house so as to become a permanent feature of interior ornamentation; engines or electric motors so affixed to a plant as to become a part thereof, etc. The tests usually applied to determine whether a chattel is a fixture are (1) suitability of the annexed chattel for the purposes of the land or other real property, (2) intention on the part of the annexor to make the affixed chattel a permanent feature of the land, (3) impossibility of severance from the land or other realty without injury to the realty.

In accounting usage, the term fixtures refers to the mechanical equipment, cages, grill work, etc., found in a bank. Safe deposit vaults are often set up separately. Both items are distinguished from furniture. These items are written off usually as rapidly as the tax-allowed depreciation permits and thus usually are carried well below resale values.

FLAGSHIP BANK The largest (lead) bank in a multi-bank holding company.

FLAT In bond transactions, denotes that the price includes any interest accrued since the last interest date. Bonds are usually sold at a price exclusive of ACCRUED INTEREST, the accrued interest at the coupon rate being added. Stocks are usually sold flat, i.e., exclusive of any accrued dividend. Adjustment and income bonds (ordinarily), and bonds in default as to interest, principal, or both, also sell flat.

FLAXSEED One of the important oilseed crops, from which linseed oil is made (a major drying oil, used in paints, varnishes, printing inks, synthetic resins, linoleum, etc.); has been a nonbasic commodity for government price support purposes.

FLEECE A stock market expression of unfavorable connotation meaning to take advantage of the innocent amateur in speculation who "goes it blindly" and is either uninformed or misinformed.
See LAMB.

FLETCHER-RAYBURN ACT SECURITIES EXCHANGE ACT OF 1934.

FLIER A plunge in stocks; a reckless commitment in stocks. A flier is a purchase or sale of a highly speculative security with the hope of making a large profit, but with the full understanding that a correspondingly large loss is equally possible. Such a stock market commitment is undertaken with full realization of its speculative nature out of a spirit of gambling and with a gambler's chance of winning.

FLOAT This term has two meanings:

1. To market securities; to offer for sale an issue of bonds or stock to investors for the purpose of raising capital. Securities may be floated by an underwriting syndicate or securities company or by the issuing organization directly, i.e., over the counter. U.S. government issues are floated through the agency of the Federal Reserve banks.
   See SYNDICATE, UNDERWRITING.
2. An account (also known as floating account) which holds the out-of-town checks outstanding in the process of collection. Banks forward out-of-town checks for collection through either correspondent banks or Federal Reserve banks as collecting agents. While such checks are in transit, i.e., in the process of becoming collected and converted into cash, they are known as the float and represent contingent rather than actual assets. They cannot be counted as reserve and must be segregated from cash balances. The float or aggregate of out-of-town items in process of collection is held in two general ledger accounts entitled "due from banks, collections" and "Federal Reserve bank, collections." The Federal Reserve banks also have a float account consisting of the aggregate of out-of-town items which are in the process of collection for member banks. Before the FEDERAL RESERVE CHECK COLLECTION SYSTEM was in operation, the float for the country as a whole amounted to a very large figure, because checks were often out a month or more before presented for final payment. The Federal Reserve check collection system has greatly reduced the outstanding float and accelerated the collection of checks by ensuring prompt presentation and because of the quick availability made possible by settlement through the two-day deferred availability schedule and the INTERDISTRICT SETTLEMENT ACCOUNT. The Federal Reserve check collection system has also reduced the loss in the use of funds and consequently secured greater economy in the employment of bank funds for exchange purposes, which has been reflected in lower exchange rates.

Federal Reserve pricing for float: The Monetary Control Act of 1980 specified that fees will be set for the types of services provided by Federal Reserve banks, which include Federal Reserve float. The Federal Reserve's August, 1980, pricing proposal suggested a three-phase effort to reduce and/or price Federal Reserve float. Phase I would reduce float through operational improvements which would speed up the collection process and thus debit payor banks more promptly, phase II would adjust availability schedules for depositing banks to reflect actual collection time more closely, and phase III would price any remaining float and incorporate this charge into the price of the service creating the float.

See DUE FROM BANKS, COLLECTIONS; FEDERAL RESERVE BANK COLLECTIONS ACCOUNT; TRANSIT DEPARTMENT.

BIBLIOGRAPHY

The BASI Survey of the Check Collection System. Bank Administration Institute, Rolling Meadows, IL, 1987.
"The Tug-of-War Over 'Float.'" *The Morgan Guaranty Survey*, December, 1983.
YOUNG, J. E. "The Rise and Fall of Federal Reserve Float." *Economic Review*, February, 1986.
———. "The Rise and Fall of Federal Reserve Float." *Federal Reserve Bank of Kansas City Economic Review*, 1986.

FLOATING ASSETS CURRENT ASSETS.

FLOATING CAPITAL Capital invested in current, as distinguished from fixed, assets. Economists refer to floating and circulating capital as that which is constantly being turned over by sale, i.e., capital used for trading purposes. John Stuart Mill wrote that floating capital "does its work not by being kept, but by changing hands." Floating capital is also known as circulating capital and is equivalent to WORKING CAPITAL.

FLOATING CHARGE Used chiefly in England to denote an unsecured debt, e.g., debenture bonds.

FLOATING DEBT

FLOATING DEBT The aggregate of current indebtedness, whether accounts or notes payable, or other current accruals of various current maturities, as distinguished from funded debt, unfunded debt, or current liabilities maturing within the current year. The term is used for the short-term indebtedness of a business corporation or of a government, state, or municipality.

FLOATING DISCOUNT RATE A central bank's DISCOUNT RATE which instead of being fixed at a particular level by the central bank in accordance with its prevailing MONETARY POLICY, as one of the tools of control of such policy, varies pursuant to the changes in a key MONEY MARKET rate, such as that on offerings of Treasury bills. The discount rate of the BANK OF CANADA from 1956 to 1962 floated 0.25% above the Treasury bill rate. An alleged advantage of a floating discount rate of the central bank is the fact that it keeps in line with prevailing money rates, instead of being either above or below the market.

FLOATING EXCHANGE RATES See FOREIGN EXCHANGE.

FLOATING PRIME RATE Under a suggestion advanced by the Secretary of the Treasury in 1982, the PRIME RATE, conventionally defined as the rate which commercial banks charge their highest rated and largest firms for business loans, would float, linked to the rate for COMMERCIAL PAPER.

The suggestion was stimulated by criticism of the prime rate as an indicator of the interest cost of short-term business loans. A study by the Federal Reserve in May, 1982, had shown that 78.6% of short-term business loans made by large commercial banks were below the prime rate, and of course firms considered to be less creditworthy were paying varying premiums above the posted prime rate. Commercial paper rates are the reported market rates for prime-rated commercial paper, whereas the prime rate is an administered rate which is usually changed, on the initiative of one or two of the major banks, with other banks falling in line with the initiated changes.

Changes in the prime rate are usually in response to credit conditions and to developments in the money market and Federal Reserve actions to implement monetary policy, such as fluctuations in the FEDERAL FUNDS effective rate and Federal Reserve DISCOUNT RATE reflecting the direction of OPEN MARKET OPERATIONS and the resulting "tightness" or "ease" in available funds of banks. Actually, the idea of linking the prime rate as a floating rate with commercial paper rates is not new; one of the major banks used to base its prime rate on a moving average of commercial paper rates. The secretary of the Treasury's suggestion was for the "watch rate" to be the commercial paper rate plus half a percentage point.

Prime Rate Futures. On December 14, 1981, the CHICAGO BOARD OF TRADE submitted a proposal for prime rate futures contracts (based on a "benchmark" average of prime rates) to the COMMODITY FUTURES TRADING COMMISSION for approval. The proposal in turn was announced by the CFTC with request for public comments; as of late in 1982, the proposal was still pending.

Contract trading unit under the CBT proposal would be 1-month $3,000,000 floating prime rate loans or multiples thereof. Beginning with the current contract month, trading months would be set in a 42-month cycle. Settlement would be in cash, with settlement prices based on a prime rate index calculated by the CBT from prime rates of 10 representative banks selected by the CBT. At the end of each month, the CBT would calculate the median of the prime rates prevailing each day, and subtract that median from 100 to determine the settlement price for delivery yields.

Because of the volatile behavior of the prime rate in recent years, with many and frequent changes, prime rate futures trading would have appeal, it was felt, for firms borrowing at commercial banks. However, because of the subjective administered nature of each of the 10 prime rates of the banks, the median used in calculation, and the question of whether a particular borrowing firm would be entitled to points below the prime rate or pay above it, hedges would necessarily be imperfect.

FLOATING RATE INSTRUMENTS Debt, preferred stock, and mortgage instruments whose periodic interest or dividend rates are indexed to some financial index such as a Treasury security or the London Interbank Offer Rate. These instruments give a variable rate characteristic that allows both issuer and investor to share the risk inherent in changing interest rates. The volatility of interest rates in recent years led to the creation of these innovative instruments designed to protect players in the fixed income securities markets.

BIBLIOGRAPHY

FABOZZI, F. J. *Floating Rate Instruments*, 1986.

FLOATING RATE NOTES In commercial bank long-term public offerings of debt securities, unsecured notes paying interest at rates varying with the yield from time to time on a selected MONEY MARKET indicator, such as Treasury bills.

For example, the floating rate notes due in 1989 of Citicorp, the bank holding company, are unsecured obligations which pay interest semiannually at 1% above the interest yield equivalent of the average of the weekly per annum discount rates for three-month U.S. Treasury bills (as reported by the Federal Reserve Bank of New York during the 21 days immediately preceding May 20 or November 20, as the case may be) prior to the semiannual period for which the interest rate is being determined. The notes are repayable on any June 1 or December 1 at the option of the holders at the principal amount plus accrued interest. In turn, Citicorp at its option may redeem the notes at their principal amount plus accrued interest beginning June 1, 1984.

Another issue of floating rate notes due in 1986, issued by two Citibank subsidiaries and guaranteed by Citicorp, is denominated in French francs and translated into U.S. dollars at exchange rates current as of December 20.

Although intended to appeal to investors on a yield basis, the floating rate notes of 1989 have been redeemed in substantial amounts by the holders, posing a refinancing problem. Also, although not an immediate or primary factor, the indenture under which these notes were issued prohibits Citicorp, under certain conditions, from paying dividends in shares of capital stock of Citibank and from creating encumbrances on such shares. Moreover, as Treasury bill yields rose, the interest cost on such financing kept pace at the defined formula.

See SUBORDINATED DEBENTURES.

BIBLIOGRAPHY

FABOZZI, F. J. *Floating Rate Instruments*. Probus Publishing Co., Chicago, IL, 1986.

FLOATING RATE PREFERRED STOCK Preferred stock whose yield varies with an index. The index may be a market interest rate, the issuer's credit standing, or the issuer's financial position. Also called adjustable-rate preferred stock.

FLOATING SUPPLY OF SECURITIES The portion of the listed stocks or bonds of a corporation which is available for trading and speculation, i.e., in the hands of brokers and speculators, as distinguished from investors. A large part of the securities, and especially stocks, of large corporations is never purchased outright by investors, but is carried on margin. Whatever amount is so carried by brokers on margin for the account of customers and in the hands of traders and speculators constitutes the floating supply. Stocks owned outright, retained in safe deposit boxes, and not placed on the market or subject to speculative commitment do not constitute floating supply.

The floating supply of some securities is small. This is true of the securities of the investment class or those which for some other reasons are closely held. The floating supply sometimes is so small that a premium may be charged for borrowing. This occurs when short selling has been excessive and brokers find it difficult to borrow stock with which to make delivery from ordinary sources.

FLOAT LEDGER See COLLECTION LEDGER.

FLOOR The facility of an exchange where brokers engage in trading. Only members of the exchange and necessary clerks and other employees are admitted to the floor.

FLOOR BROKER TWO-DOLLAR BROKER.

FLOOR TRADER Floor professionals on the trading floor of the NEW YORK STOCK EXCHANGE include the following:

ENCYCLOPEDIA OF BANKING AND FINANCE

1. Commission brokers, employed by member firms to represent their customers' orders on the trading floor.
2. Floor brokers, primarily individual entrepreneurs, who act as independent commission brokers for a variety of clients.
3. Registered competitive market makers (RCMM), who have specific obligations to trade for their own or their firms' accounts when called upon by an exchange official by making a bid or offer that will narrow the existing quote spread or improve the depth of an existing quote. An RCMM may also be asked to assist a commission broker or a floor broker in executing a customer's otherwise unexecutable order.
4. Competitive traders, who trade for their own accounts, under stringent exchange rules designed to assure that their activities contribute to market liquidity. On January 19, 1977, the SECURITIES AND EXCHANGE COMMISSION (SEC) approved this new designation of "competitive traders" for those members who contribute to liquidity and continuity on the floor by trading for their own account and also approved new minimum access requirements for this category of membership.
5. Stock specialists, key exchange members who are responsible for the maintenance of fair and orderly markets in exchange-listed stocks assigned to them by acting as agent and principal in such stocks, in accordance with close SEC and New York Stock Exchange rules and policies.

FLOOR PLANNING FINANCE A form of inventory financing involving the use of trust receipts; also known as trust receipt financing. Under floor planning financing, the borrower borrows funds with which to pay for goods purchased. The borrower holds the goods in trust for the bank by issuing the bank a trust receipt. As the borrower sells the goods, the borrower forwards the proceeds to the bank.

FLOOR TRADING In 1964, the SECURITIES AND EXCHANGE COMMISSION (SEC) proposed and subsequently adopted its Rule 11a-1 under the SECURITIES EXCHANGE ACT OF 1934, which provides, with specified exceptions, that no member of a national securities exchange, while on the floor of such exchange, may initiate any transaction in any security admitted to trading on the exchange for an account in which such member has an interest. The rule provided exemptions for registered SPECIALISTS (and then ODD-LOT DEALERS), stabilizing activities pursuant to Rule 10b-7 under the Securities Exchange Act of 1934, bona fide arbitrage, transactions approved for the purpose of maintaining a fair and orderly market, and transactions made to offset errors. The rule also permitted floor trading transactions effected in conformity with rules adopted by an exchange and approved by the SEC, which are designed to eliminate floor trading activities not beneficial to the market.

Acting under this latter exemption, the NEW YORK STOCK EXCHANGE filed a plan with the SEC which eventually received the SEC's approval (the American Stock Exchange also filed a plan for the regulation of floor trading on that exchange, and other exchanges requested exemption from Rule 11a-1 under Sec. 11(c) of the act), and floor trading avoided outright prohibition.

Earlier drafts of the original Securities Exchange Act of 1934 contemplated complete prohibition of floor trading, based on the special advantages enjoyed by floor traders because of their presence on the floor, their tendency to trade with the trend, and the conflicts of interest involved in acting as both floor trader and commission broker. On the other hand, in defense of floor trading, it was argued that it contributed to the maintenance of more continuous and more liquid markets. The act (Sec. 11(a)) merely vested responsibility in the SEC to regulate or to prohibit floor trading.

In 1935, the SEC suggested that the exchanges adopt certain rules to regulate floor trading. In 1936, the SEC evaluated the functioning of floor trading and concluded that despite the existence of exchange rules, the undesirable characteristics of floor trading persisted. It was determined, however, not to abolish floor trading but to strengthen its regulation by additional rules. One of these proposals (Report on the Feasibility and Advisability of the Complete Segregation of the Functions of Dealer and Broker, 1936) would have required a complete segregation of floor trading from the floor brokerage function. This proposal was not carried into effect.

Next, after a comprehensive study, the Division of Trading and Exchanges of the SEC filed with the commission a report made public on January 16, 1945, which found that the evils of floor trading persisted, that floor traders enjoyed a formidable advantage over the general public, that floor trading distracted brokers from their duties to the public, and that floor traders traded with the trend and were a destabilizing influence. The report also concluded that the existing exchange rules were ineffective in meeting the problem and that the only adequate solution was complete prohibition of floor trading. The SEC tentatively determined to abolish floor trading in August, 1945, but after considering the matter and holding conferences with the exchange, it determined not to abolish floor trading in light of repeated assurances that the exchanges would develop effective self-regulation of this activity.

Between 1945 and 1961, various commission staff studies continued to report critically upon floor trading practice. A special study (Report of Special Study of Securities Markets of the Securities and Exchange Commission, 1963) recommended that floor trading be prohibited by commission rule and that the feasibility of utilizing floor traders as auxiliary specialists be explored. The commission in a letter to Congress dated July 23, 1963, commented on the special study's recommendation as follows:

"In light of the very serious and basic problems presented by the continuation of floor trading, as brought out by the Report of the Special Study and as evidenced by prior studies, and of the lengthy and apparently unsuccessful efforts to resolve them, the Commission agrees that a rule proposal abolishing floor trading on the New York and American Stock Exchange should be developed, unless those exchanges demonstrate that its continuance would be consistent with the public interest."

The New York Stock Exchange acted by retaining the firm of Cresap, McCormick & Paget, a management consultant firm, to make a study of floor trading and appointed a special committee of governors of the exchange to consider the subject. On March 4, 1964, the special committee presented its proposals to the SEC. The commission rejected the exchange's proposals, but instead of proceeding to abolish floor trading, it had its staff consult with the exchange during March, 1964, in several meetings and develop the gist of Rule 11a-1 as a means of preserving the benefits of floor trading while controlling and limiting its alleged harmful effects.

FLOWER BONDS The popular Wall Street expression for those U.S. government bonds which, when owned by a decedent and part of his estate, are redeemable at par and accrued interest if the secretary of the Treasury is instructed to apply the proceeds to federal estate taxes. If brought at discounts, such bonds are especially attractive for such purpose.

See UNITED STATES GOVERNMENT SECURITIES.

FLOW OF FUNDS ACCOUNTS A national statistical system developed by the Federal Reserve Board and published regularly since 1947. The Flow of Funds Accounts is constructed to show the financial activities of the United States economy in a manner that enables financial activities to be related to the nonfinancial activities of the U.S. economic functions that turn out income, savings, and goods and services. The Flow of Funds Accounts reports the various amounts of debt and equities held by investors and marketed by issuers in a manner that enables analysis in relation to each other and to the types of credit instruments involved. The accounts describe in broad categories practically every investor group and every major type of financial transaction (transactions the result from cash payments or extensions of credit) in the economy (financial assets and liabilities). This system is broader than the GNP account since the flow of funds arise from the transfer of existing assets as well as the sale and purchase of currently produced goods and services.

FLUCTUATING PRINCIPLE The principle of selection of securities (bonds or stocks) on the basis of their range of fluctuation in market prices over a full business cycle. The extent of such fluctuation determines the suitability of specific securities for defensive purposes (for greatest stability), as compared with suitability for aggressive purposes (properly timed commitments for profit from a wide range of fluctuation). The chief factor determining fluctuation for high-grade bond prices is the level of interest rates, and for stocks it is general business conditions affecting earnings and dividends. Gradations in susceptibility to a wider range of fluctuation occur in line with quality variations; for example, which lower-grade bonds, typically sell at discounts and are influenced not by interest rates primarily but the effect of business conditions on earnings coverage of charges of the issuing corporations, typically experience a wider range of fluctuation than do high-grade bonds.

FLUCTUATION

The fluctuating principle may be similarly applied to stocks of corporations in the stablest, as compared to the most susceptible, lines vis a vis the business cycle.

A defensive portfolio, i.e., one requiring greatest stability of market value of principal, would consist of issues with the lowest ranges of fluctuation over a business cycle. On the other hand, an aggressive portfolio, with little or no requirement of stability of principal, would deliberately consist of issues, properly timed as to purchase, with the widest ranges and instability, in the expectation of substantial capital gains as a quid pro quo for the higher risks assumed. The same principle may be applied to income requirements.

Precise data on the range of fluctuation in market price of categories of issues depend upon the period chosen. Thus, in connection with the 1932 major depression, the Standard & Poor's averages of high-grade preferred stocks declined 30% from the October, 1931, high to the June, 1932, low; the averages of 500 common stocks declined 85% from the September, 1929, high to the June, 1932, low. By contrast, high-grade corporate bonds declined only 11% from 1931 to 1932. On the other hand, in recent years of recession, common stocks, depending on the sensitivity of sales and earnings to recession, declined, but so did high-grade bonds because of the rise in interest rates and bond yields above the cash interest rates paid by the bonds. Thus the inverse market action or at least more defensive market performance normally expected from highest-grade bonds in comparison with common stocks may not empirically be shown (rise in interest rates in the period covered was reflected in declines to discount levels in the prices of high-grade bonds). It is suggested that: (1) stability of principal and income required be first established, and (2) the permissible maximum range of fluctuation also be determined subjectively. Then specific issues should be tested on their actual record (conservatively by their worst decline over a complete cycle, and aggressively by their maximum recovery over a cycle).

See INVESTMENT.

FLUCTUATION The variation of prices up and down. A chart of daily fluctuations will reveal the trend in prices over time, whether an intermediate (temporary interruptions up or down to the major trend) or major trend. In DOW THEORY terminology, the two are termed secondary movements and primary trend, respectively.

In security markets, the minimum variation in price for most stocks and corporate bonds is $^1/_8$ of a point ($0.125 per share for stocks, $1.25 for bonds). In the case of government securities, Treasury notes and bond issues are usually quoted in thirty-seconds of a point, e.g., a bid of 104.8 is 104 $^8/_{32}$ points. For each $1,000 of face value, the standard denomination, a full point equals $10 and a thirty-second equals $0.3125. Thus, a quotation of 104.8 means a dollar price on a $1,000 security of $1,042.50, or 104 X $10 + (8 X $0.3125) = $1,042.50. Denominations other than $1,000 are quoted in multiples of such a price.

FLUID ASSETS See CURRENT ASSETS.

FLUID CAPITAL See FLOATING CAPITAL.

FLURRY A commotion in prices; a sudden and sharp advance or decline of prices on a stock market or commodity exchange due to temporary alarm or enthusiasm, e.g., a sharp advance in money rates, a favorable political event, etc. A flurry is of short duration, without effect on fundamental market conditions, and produces no lasting effect.

FLUSH OUT PROVISION In a STOCK PURCHASE WARRANT, the provision that the issuing company may in its discretion reduce the specified exercise price of the warrant for the purchase of the common stock of the particular company at various times and for varying periods during the life of the warrants.

In July, 1969, the AMERICAN STOCK EXCHANGE amended its listing requirements to provide for refusal to list warrants containing flush out provisions unless the issuing company agrees to refrain from invoking such provisions while the warrants are listed. If the company agrees as a prerequisite to listing not to exercise a flush out period while its warrants are listed on the American Stock Exchange, the company is required to inform warrant holders of such agreement.

FLUSH PRODUCTION Unsettled production; applied to an oil well or to the oil properties of a company to indicate that the period of time which it will last and the rate of output are uncertain.

FLY-BY-NIGHT CORPORATION A stigmatic term used with reference to a business organized to exploit a highly speculative, unsound, or temporary venture and controlled by officers who have little or no moral or financial responsibility; a corporation having shady personnel and which is not likely to succeed and therefore likely to be of short duration. The term is especially used among bank credit analysts to refer to a corporation of doubtful or worthless credit standing, without any of the elements necessary to make a good credit risk and therefore not entitled to credit.

FOOD SECURITY ACT OF 1985 Legislation which set U.S. farm policy through 1990. The Act was designed to improve the market orientation of U.S. farm policy. Major provisions of the act include the following:

1. Continue target prices, but they are scheduled to decline over the life of the act.
2. Specifies acreage reduction programs when stocks exceed certain levels.
3. Attempts to control erosion and prevent farm production on erodible croplands and wetlands.
4. Gives the Secretary of Agriculture wide latitude in implementing commodity programs.

FOOD STAMP PROGRAM The Food and Nutrition Service (FNS) is the agency of the Department of Agriculture that administers the programs to make food assistance available to people who need it. These programs are operated in cooperation with States and local governments. FNS administers the family nutrition program, the special nutrition programs, the food distribution program, and the supplemental food programs. The Family nutrition program provides food coupons to needy persons to increase their food purchasing power so they can feed their families adequately. The coupons are used by program participants to purchase food in any retail store that has been approved by FNS to accept and redeem the food coupons.

FOR A TURN An expression used to describe a speculative purchase or sale for the purpose of making a small but quick gain.

FOR CASH Refers to securities or commodities purchased outright for transfer and delivery immediately, for which cash is paid in full. Deliveries of securities purchased for cash must be made by seller to buyer on the day of the sale.

FORCED CIRCULATION FIAT MONEY; money which is not supported by a specific reserve, but which is decreed to be legal tender in payment of all debts and forced into circulation.

In modern times, the money system of the United States has become a fiat money system, since coins are composed of cupronickel and zinc-copper, and no form of paper money is redeemable into the ultimate money of redemption, the nominal standard money gold. But the changeover was publicly accomplished without being forced, in contrast to the discounts against UNITED STATES NOTES that prevailed during and after the Civil War until that form of paper money was provided a partial gold reserve.

FORCED LIQUIDATION Urgent selling; when owners of securities or commodities are obliged to see their holdings for cash (1) to obtain funds necessary for other purposes, (2) because carrying charges (usually interest rates) have advanced so that it is no longer profitable to hold them, (3) to prevent the complete exhaustion of margins in case of a falling market, or (4) to stop further loss.

FORCED SALE A sale of property or assets under certain circumstances, e.g., sale of mortgaged property in default as a result of foreclosure, for the purpose of satisfying mortgages; voluntary sale of a debtor's property to satisfy creditors; and sale of merchandise to avoid moving it to another site in the case of expiration of a lease. Forced sales may be accomplished by means of an auction, closing out sales, etc., it being generally understood that the owner must make some sacrifice in order to realize sales quickly.

See FORCED LIQUIDATION.

ENCYCLOPEDIA OF BANKING AND FINANCE

FORECASTING See BUSINESS BAROMETERS, BUSINESS CYCLE, BUSINESS FORECASTING SERVICES, FINANCIAL FORECASTING.

BIBLIOGRAPHY

ARMSTRONG, J. S. *Long-Range Forecasting: From Crystal Ball to Computers.* John Wiley and Sons, NY, 1985.
GROSS, C. W., and PETERSON, R. T. *Business Forecasting.* Houghton Miffin Co., Boston, MA, 1982.
Journal of Business Forecasting Methods and Systems.
PINDYCK, R. S., and RUBINFIELD, D. L. *Econometric Models and Economic Forecasts.* McGraw-Hill Book Co., New York, NY, 1980.
RYAN, M. R. *Computerized Financial Forecasting and Performance Reporting.* Prentice Hall, Inc., Englewood Cliffs, NJ, 1980.
WHEELWRIGHT, S. C., and MAKRIDAKIS, S. *Forecasting Methods for Management.* Johyn Wiley and Sons, Inc., New York, NY, 1985.

FORECASTING FINANCIAL REQUIREMENTS

Forecasting is a statistical technique that has wide applicability in business activities. Forecasting involves making judgments about future events based on an analysis of past events and factors that might affect those events in the future.

The role of forecasting in business is simple. Accurate forecasts of future events can assist managers make better decisions in the present. For example, forecasting is important for marketing, production and financial matters, among others.

The simplest method to forecast is to extrapolate in to the future based on information from the past. Fitting a trend line is one method to do this, and is perhaps the most common quantitative method used in corporations. More sophisticated empirical techniques are available and involve what is known as time series analysis. Basically, time series analysis attempts to decompose historical data on the event to be forecast into secular, seasonal, cyclical and irregular components. Once these components are known, and assuming that the economic environment in the future is similar to what it has been in the past, accurate projections can be made.

Working capital is the basis for forecasting financial requirements. A percentage of sales approach, using financial ratios, can be used to forecast financial requirements.

To illustrate forecasting financial requirements, assume that the financial statement data appended is available. The company wants to know what amount of additional financing is required if sales are expected to reach the $600,000 level (a 20 percent increase). The percentage of sales approach will be used to provide the answer.

Hypothetical Data for Financial Forecasting

	Assets		Liabilities and Owners Equity
Cash	$10,000	Accounts payable	$ 50,000
Receivables	30,000	Notes payable	150,000
Inventory	60,000	Common stock	100,000
Plant and equipment	400,000	Retained earnings	200,000
Total assets	$500,000	Total	$500,000

Additional data:
Sales	$ 500,000
Net income	50,000
Profit margin on sales	10%
Plant capacity utilized	100%
Dividend payout rate	25% of net income (earnings retention rate is 75%)

Step 1. What balance sheet items vary directly with sales?
Assume that the assets and accounts payable vary directly with sales.

Step 2. Express the balance sheet items that vary directly with sales as a percentage of sales ($500,000).

Cash	2.0	Accounts payable	10.0
Receivables	6.0		
Inventory	12.0		
Plant and equipment	80.0		
Total	100.0		10.0

Assets as a percent of sales	100.0
Less: available credit from suppliers	10.0
Percentage of additional sales dollar to be financed	90.0

For each $1.00 of sales, assets will increase $1.00. This increase must be financed. Accounts payable are assumed to be financed by suppliers who make credit available and so provide 10 percent of new funds. The firm must find additional financing from internal or external sources for 90 percent of each sales dollar.

If sales are to increase from $500,000 to $600,000, then $90,000 (= $100,000 increase in sales x 90%) in new funds are required.

Step 3. How much of the financing required ($90,000) can be financed internally from operations?
Since the sales revenue will be $600,000 and the profit margin is 10 percent, profit will be $60,000. Of this amount, $15,000 is required for dividends ($60,000 x 25% dividend payout). This leaves $45,000 of net income available to finance some of the additional sales.

Step 4. How much of the financing requirement must be financed externally?
If $45,000 of the $90,000 total requirement is provided internally, then $45,000 must be obtained from external sources.

The relationships reflected in this illustration can be summarized in the following formula:

External funds needed = (A/TR)(S)-(B/TR)(S-bm(Q)
where

A/TR = assets that increase spontaneously with total revenues or sales as a percentage of total revenues or sales.
B/TR = those liabilities that increase spontaneously with total revenues or sales as a percent of total revenue or sales
S = change in total revenue or sales
m = profit margin on sales
b = earnings retention ratio
Q = total revenues projected for the year

External funds required = ($500,000) (–$100,000)
($500,000
($50,000) (–$100,000)
(75%)(10%)($600,000)

= $45,000 (same as computed in the discussion)

To summarize, the relationship between sales and assets is the key question in forecasting financing requirements. The formula used in this illustration can be used in different ways by changing the assumptions.

FORECLOSURE The process of law by which a mortgagee or anyone having interest in a MORTGAGE (such as a mortgage bondholder), when the conditions of the mortgage have been violated, may compel the mortgagor to redeem the pledge or to forfeit his right of redemption. It is a privilege given to the mortgagee upon default in the payment of interest or principal of a mortgage to enforce payment of the debt by terminating the right to redeem the property which it secures. In a few states the property covering the mortgage may be sold under a power contained in the mortgage itself, but in most states the mortgagee must apply to equity courts to foreclose and to sell the pledged property at public auction to pay off the debt. The proceeds of sale or mortgaged property are applied first to the indebtedness secured by the mortgage and the foreclosure expenses, and the balances is paid to the mortgagor.

Strict foreclosure involves the lender's petitioning the court of equity to terminate the mortgagor's right of redemption; if the petition is granted, the mortgagor forfeits all interest in the property to the mortgagee after a period of time granted by the court to the mortgagor in which to pay the debt. There is no judicial foreclosure sale of the property.

Judicial foreclosure, found in most states, involves the lender's petitioning the court of equity to foreclose (cut off) the mortgagor's right of redemption and to sell the pledged property at public foreclosure sale.

It is not always possible in a foreclosure sale to realize a sufficient sum to satisfy the mortgagee in full. In this event the mortgagee generally has a claim against the mortgagor for the deficiency based on the latter's personal liability on the bond (promissory note). Such deficiency judgments have been eliminated in a few states.

Other foreclosure processes include (1) by advertisement, (2) by entry and possession, and (3) by writ of entry. When the foreclosure is by advertisement, the mortgagee -notifies the mortgagor of default and advertises that the property will be sold at public auction. The purchaser at the auction receives an ownership certificate instead of legal possession of the property. The purchaser than brings an action for ejectment which dispossesses a defaulted borrower from the premises after a court hearing. When the foreclosure is by entry and possession (Maine, Massachusetts, New Hampshire, and Rhode Island), the mortgagee petitions the court for the right to take physical possession of the pledged collateral on a defaulted loan. The entry must be peaceable, made before witnesses, and attested to by filling a certificate with the court. The mortgagee obtains full legal ownership after a period of time during which the mortgagor may redeem the property by repaying the mortgage lien plus costs. In a foreclosure by writ of entry (Maine, Massachusetts, and New Hampshire), a mortgagee begins a court action to obtain a writ of entry. If the debt is not paid within the time allowed in the writ, the mortgagee receives full legal title to the property.

Obtaining mortgage insurance at the time a mortgage loan is originated is routine for most banks when making high loan-to-value ratio mortgage loans. Before a residential insured loan risk turns into a loss covered by mortgage insurance, the borrower must default in the periodic payments; the borrower surrenders title to the property securing the mortgage through foreclosure or by deed in lieu of foreclosure; and the value of the property, or the proceeds realized from the foreclosure sale, must be insufficient to offset fully the lender's investment in the property. Once these conditions are met, a valid claim can be submitted to the mortgage insurance company.

See DEED OF TRUST, FIRST MORTGAGE BONDS.

BIBLIOGRAPHY

OXENHAM, L. *The Modern Mortgage Banking Guide*, 1988.

FOREIGN AGENCIES Agencies, as distinguished from branches, established by domestic banks in foreign countries for specific purposes but not to conduct a general banking business. In doing their banking in foreign countries, U.S. banks have resorted to correspondent banks abroad, appointing representatives abroad, operating foreign branches, establishing and/or buying into banks abroad, and organizing EDGE ACT corporations. Edge Act corporations themselves may establish branches or agencies abroad (Sec. 25a, Federal Reserve Act), subject to prior approval of the Board of Governors of the Federal Reserve System for the first branch or agency in a particular foreign country.

Federal Reserve banks, with the approval of the Board of Governors of the Federal Reserve System or upon the latter's order and direction and subject to the board's regulation, may open and maintain accounts in foreign countries, appoint correspondents, and establish agencies in such countries wheresoever it may be deemed best for their operations in bills of exchange or acceptances. With the consent of the board of governors, Federal Reserve banks may open and maintain banking accounts for such foreign correspondents or agencies or for foreign banks or bankers or for foreign states. The Banking Act of 1933 added Section 14(g) to the Federal Reserve Act, providing that the board of governors shall exercise special supervision over all relationships and transactions of any kind entered into by any Federal Reserve bank with any foreign bank or banker or with any group of foreign banks or bankers, and all such relationships and transactions are subject to regulations of the board of governors.

International Banking Facilities (IBFs) of U.S. Depository Institutions. Formally proposed in July, 1978, to the Federal Reserve Board of Governors by the New York Clearing House Association, establishment of the IBF was approved on June 18, 1981, by the board of governors. An effective date of December 3, 1981, was established to give state legislatures time to revise tax and banking laws accordingly.

Under Federal Reserve regulations, an IBF can be operated in any state. The revised New York State laws exempt from state and local taxes net income, over a base, derived from an IBF. However, those earnings are subject to federal taxes. IBFs enable depository institutions in the United States to offer deposit and loan services to foreign residents and institutions free of Federal Reserve System reserve requirements and interest-rate regulations and to offer the short-term deposit maturities which are widely employed in foreign markets. IBFs may also offer foreign nonbank residents large-denomination time deposits subject to a minimum notice of two business days before withdrawal. Foreign banking firms and official institutions may place overnight funds with an IBF. Time deposits are governed by a minimum deposit or withdrawal requirement of $100,000. IBFs may also extend credit to foreign residents, other IBFs, or the U.S. offices of the IBF's parent—subject to eurodollar reserve requirements—and may transact business in foreign currency.

Actually, despite the use of such terms as "international banking facilities," "international banking zones," "international banking branches," and the "Yankee dollar market," which convey a meaning of special offices in separate locations, the activities of an IBF can be conducted by institutions from existing quarters. However, IBF transactions must be maintained on a separate set of books of the institution. Moreover, foreign corporations which are subsidiaries of U.S. companies must acknowledge in writing the Federal Reserve Board's policy that funds deposited in or borrowed from an IBF must be used only to support non-U.S. operations.

Among depository institutions which may establish an IBF are U.S. commercial banks, Edge Act corporations, foreign commercial banks through branches and agencies in the U.S., and mutual savings banks. IBFs permit U.S. banks to use heir domestic U.S. offices to offer foreign customers deposit and loan services which formerly could be provided competitively only from foreign offices. Thus, the IBFs are expected to enable institutions operating in the U.S. to compete more effectively for foreign-source deposit and loan business in the eurocurrency markets abroad.

See FEDERAL RESERVE BOARD REGULATIONS.

BIBLIOGRAPHY

BOARD OF GOVERNORS OF THE FEDERAL RESERVE SYSTEM. *Federal Reserve Regulatory Service*, 2 vols., 1981.

FOREIGN BANKING CORPORATIONS Corporations organized under the EDGE ACT (EDGE ACT CORPORATION) and those organized under state laws which enter into agreement with the Board and Governors of the Federal Reserve System as to their type of activities and manner of operations (agreement corporations). Agreement corporations by agreement are limited to the banking type of international banking. Beginning with the September, 1963, revision and continuing with the June, 1979, revision, Regulation K of the Board of Governors of the Federal Reserve System no longer requires an Edge Act corporation to operate either as a banking corporation or as a financing corporation (the latter formerly were not permitted to accept deposits or to invest in foreign concerns engaged in banking, and the former previously were not permitted to engage in equity-type financing and investing). Nevertheless, if an Edge Act corporation does have aggregate demand deposits and acceptance liabilities in excess of its capital and surplus and is thus engaged in banking, the corporation's commitments to any one person are limited to the banking limitation of 10% of its capital and surplus; and its capital and surplus shall be not less than 7% of risk assets. Risk assets shall be deemed to be all assets on a consolidated basis other than cash, amounts due from banking institutions in the U.S., U.S. government securities, and federal funds sold.

In recent years, reflecting the expansion in international trade and investment, there has been substantial expansion in the number of such foreign banking corporations of U.S. banks. These corporations, which are usually subsidiaries of member banks, provide their owner organizations with additional power in two areas: (1) they may conduct a deposit and loan business in states other than that of the parent, provided that the business is strictly related to international transactions, and (2) they have somewhat broader foreign investment powers than member banks, being able to invest in foreign financial organizations such as finance companies and leasing companies, as well as in foreign banks.

The INTERNATIONAL BANKING ACT OF 1978 (IBA) removed the statutory limit on liabilities of an Edge Act corporation under which the corporation's debentures, bonds, and promissory notes could not exceed ten times the corporation's capital and surplus. The 7%

standard for capital and surplus relative to risk assets, *supra*, did in fact lead to some added leveraging by Edge Act corporations.

Foreign banking corporations organized under the laws of other nations with branches or agencies established in the U.S. must comply with the laws of the state in which such offices are located.

The number of foreign loans, agencies, and offices, and Branches is appended. A second table shows foreign branches of U.S. Banks.

BIBLIOGRAPHY

BOARD OF GOVERNORS OF THE FEDERAL RESERVE SYSTEM. *Federal Reserve Regulatory Service.*

FOREIGN BANKING SYSTEMS   See BANK OF CANADA, BANK OF ENGLAND, BANK OF FRANCE, BANK OF GERMANY, CANADIAN BANKING SYSTEM, CENTRAL BANK.

FOREIGN BILL   See INLAND BILL.

FOREIGN BILLS OF EXCHANGE   First read BILL OF EXCHANGE.

Bills of exchange drawn on a foreign drawee and payable in a foreign country. They are the chief means by which settlements are made in international trade. Foreign bills of exchange are classified in many different ways, giving rise to much confusion among laypeople because these classifications are not mutually exclusive but, in fact, overlap.

Five important classification schemes follow:

1. As to class of maker.
   a. Government or official bills.
   b. Bankers' bills (including traveler's checks).
   c. COMMERCIAL BILLS.
   d. Express company drafts.
   e. Shipping bills.
   f. Postal money orders.
2. As to maker's purpose and types of transactions out of which bills arise.
   a. Drawn against funds, balances, or accounts.
      (1) Cables.
      (2) Checks.
      (3) Commercial bills.
   b. Drawn for borrowing purposes.
      (1) FINANCE BILL.
      (2) Reimbursement bills.
   c. Drawn against merchandise.
      (1) Cotton bills.
      (2) Steel bills.
      (3) GRAIN BILLS.
      (4) Breadstuffs bills.
      (5) Machinery bills, etc.
   d. Drawn against services.
      (1) Ocean freight bills.
      (2) Marine insurance bills.
      (3) Bankers' commissions bills.
      (4) Merchants' commissions bills.
      (5) Masters' drafts.
   e. Drawn against securities.
      (1) Purchase and sale of stocks and bonds.
      (2) Dividend and interest remittances.
3. As to security.
   a. Clean bills.
   b. DOCUMENTARY BILLS (shipping documents attached).
   c. Bills with securities or other valuable documents attached (including insurance policies, matured coupons, bonds, mortgages, etc.).
4. As to maturity (time of payment).
   a. Cables.
   b. Sight, demand, or presentation bills (checks).
   c. Arrival bills (shipping documents attached).
   d. Time bills.
      (1) Short bills (less than 30 days after sight or date).
      (2) Long bills (30 days or more after sight or date).
      (3) Days after date bills.
5. As to domicile (place of payment).
   a. Domestic bills in foreign currency.
   b. Foreign bills payable in:
      (1) Dollars.
      (2) Sterling.
      (3) European decimal currencies.
      (4) Other countries.

None of the above classifications is mutually exclusive; it is possible, for instance, to have a 60-day sight bill, drawn in sterling on a commercial house, supported by documents growing out of a shipment of cotton, and payable in London. This may be referred to as a foreign bill, sterling bill, commercial bill, documentary bill, long bill, time bill, or cotton bill. It is each and all at the same time.

The following is a general classification of foreign bills:

1. Commercial bills.
   a. Documentary bills.
      (1) Short (demand or within 30 days sight):
         (a) Documents against acceptance bills:
            (i) Discountable abroad.
            (ii) Held abroad until maturity without discount.
            (iii) Not discountable abroad because not in native currency.
         (b) Documents against payment bills—not discount able abroad.
         (c) Documents on arrival—not discountable abroad on account of indefinite maturity.
      (2) Long (30 days sight or more):
         (a) Documents against acceptance bills:
            (i) Discountable abroad.
            (ii) Held abroad until maturity without discount.
            (iii) Not discountable abroad because not in native currency.
         (b) Documents against payment—rarely over 90 days.
         (c) Days after date bills:
            (i) Discountable abroad.
            (ii) Held abroad until maturity without discount.
            (iii) Not discountable abroad because not in native currency.
   b. Clean bills.
      (1) Cables.
      (2) Checks.
      (3) Sight, demand, or presentation bills.
      (4) Time bills:
         (a) Discountable abroad.
         (b) Held abroad until maturity without discount.
         (c) Not discountable abroad because not in native currency.
2. Banker's bills.
   a. Tenor (term).
      (1) Cables.
      (2) Checks.
      (3) Short bills (within 30 days sight).
      (4) Long bills (30 days sight or more).
   b. Purpose.
      (1) Against current balances.
      (2) Against open credits—finance bills.

See BANKER'S BILL, CLEAN BILL OF EXCHANGE, DOCUMENTARY COMMERCIAL BILL, DOMICILE; FOREIGN EXCHANGE, STERLING BILLS.

FOREIGN BONDHOLDERS ACT OF 1933   Under Title II of the Securities Act of 1933, provision was made for the creation of a Corporation of Foreign Security Holders, to be effective when the President of the United States "finds that its taking effect is in the public interest, and by proclamation so declares." It was contemplated that the activities of the new corporation would be similar to those of the British Corporation of Foreign Bondholders, which has an official status in negotiating with foreign issuers.

The act states that the corporation shall be created "for the purpose of protecting, conserving and advancing the interests of the holders of foreign securities in default."

The secretary of State, however, advised the President that some of the foreign nations whose bonds were in default would regard the creation of such an official corporation as an unfriendly act. In fact, Title II was not contained in the original administration draft of the Securities Act and was added on the floor of the Senate at the insistence of the late Senator Hiram Johnson of California, who had

FOREIGN BONDHOLDERS' PROTECTIVE COUNCIL, INC.

been responsible for the Senate Finance Committee's investigation of sale of foreign bonds in the United States.

Instead of the official corporation provided by the act, the unofficial FOREIGN BONDHOLDERS' PROTECTIVE COUNCIL, INC. was organized in 1933.

FOREIGN BONDHOLDERS' PROTECTIVE COUNCIL, INC.
Organized in December, 1933, as a nonprofit membership corporation to represent U.S. holders of foreign bonds in default in a nonofficial capacity and without benefit of diplomatic sanctions. The council was organized instead of the Corporation of Foreign Security Holders provided for by Title II of the Securities Act of 1933 and having official status.

The council has been the sole nationally accredited bargaining agency to represent U.S. holders of foreign securities. Although the council keeps in close coordination with the U.S. State Department and the Securities and Exchange Commission, there is no official responsibility of any U.S. agency of government for the decisions or recommendations of the council. In turn, the council has been recognized by foreign governments as an appropriate representative of American bondholders.

The council in its work has sought to prevent default by foreign governments, but where defaults have occurred, it has worked to develop offers or proposals providing for fair and equitable treatment of bondholders. It has financed itself primarily by inclusion of provision in settlement offers of fees for its work of 0.25% or less of principal amount of each bond ($2.50 per $1,000 bond or less) from first payment made to assenting bondholders. The council's annual financial statements are made public, and detailed statements of its finances are furnished to the government for its information.

The council's function is solely to recommend action on proposals or offers made by foreign governments to U.S. bondholders or other suitable action on their part. It does not take deposits of bonds or act as agent for bondholders. Much of its work involved the development of adjustment plans for South American bond issues.

FOREIGN BONDS
See EXTERNAL BOND, FOREIGN CORPORATE BONDS, FOREIGN GOVERNMENT BONDS, FOREIGN MUNICIPAL BONDS, INSULAR BONDS, INTERNAL BONDS.

FOREIGN BRANCHES
Branches of domestic banks located in foreign countries or branches of foreign banks located in the U.S.

National banks possessing a capital and surplus of $1 million or more may file application under Section 25 of the Federal Reserve Act with the Board of Governors of the Federal Reserve System for permission to establish branches in foreign countries or dependencies or insular possessions of the United States for the furtherance of the foreign commerce of the United States and to act if required to do so as fiscal agent of the United States. State member banks (Sec. 9 of the act) may establish and operate branches in foreign countries or any dependency or insular possession of the United States on the same terms and conditions and subject to the same limitations and restrictions as are applicable to the establishment of branches by national banks.

Following passage of the Federal Reserve Act, in the period 1914-1920, the number of foreign branches of U.S. banks increased sharply from 26 to 181, but thereafter the number declined steadily, so that at the close of 1945, 7 member banks were reported by the board of governors to be operating 72 branches in 20 foreign countries and dependencies or possessions of the United States. More recently, however, the interest of U.S. banks in foreign branches has increased. In 1986, three branches were approved by the Federal Reserve Board to bring the total to 952 branches of 158 banks. Under provisions of the Federal Reserve Act and the board's Regulation K, member banks may establish branches in foreign countries subject in most cases to the board's prior approval. In reviewing proposed foreign branches, the board considers the requirements of the governing statute, the condition of the bank, and the bank's experience in international business.

FOREIGN COLLECTION ITEMS
See FOREIGN COLLECTIONS.

FOREIGN COLLECTIONS
Includes two classes of items: (1) bills of exchange payable abroad and taken by a bank

Foreign Banks, Agencies and Offices, and Branches

	Banks	Agencies & offices	Branches
1982	201	466	229
1983	226	490	269
1984	251	473	310
1985	256	503	309
1986	263	524	325
1987	266	543	340

Source: American Banker, various issues.

Foreign Branches of U.S. Banks

End of year	U.S. banks operating foreign branches – Number	Percent change from preceding year	Foreign branches of U.S. banks – Number	Percent change from preceding year	Total assets of foreign branches of U.S. banks – Billions of dollars	Percent change from preceding year
1965	13		211		$ 8.9	
1966	13	0%	244	+16%	12.4	+39%
1967	15	+15	295	+21	15.3	+23
1968	26	+73	373	+26	22.8	+49
1969	53	+104	460	+23	35.3	+55
1970	79	+49	532	+16	46.5	+32
1971	91	+15	577	+8	59.8	+29
1972	107	+18	627	+9	78.2	+31
1973	125	+17	699	+11	121.9	+56
1974	125	0	732	+5	151.9	+25
1975	126	+1	762	+4	176.5	+16
1976	126	0	731	−4	219.2	+24
1977	130	+3	738	+1	258.9	+18
1978	138	+5	761	+3	306.8	+19
1979	139	+1	779	+2	364.2	+19
1980	178	+28	—	—	322.7	−11
1981	192	+8	—	—	347.9	+7
1982	198	+3	—	—	325.5	−6
1983	197	−1	—	—	314.5	−3
1984	266	+35	—	—	400.1	+27
1985	272	+2	—	—	405.5	+1
1986	263	−3	—	—	408.2	+1

Source: Federal Reserve Board; FDIC, Statistics on Banking, various issues.

for collection only, i.e., for credit (or payment) to the account of the customer only when and if paid abroad, and (2) bills of exchange payable in the United States taken from foreign correspondents for credit (or payment) to their accounts only when and if paid. The former are sometimes called outgoing or export collections; the latter, incoming or import collections.

Foreign collection items consist of commercial bills of exchange with and without documents attached, money orders, matured bond coupons, matured bonds and bonds called for redemption, traveler's checks, etc. Commercial bills taken for collection arise through the fact that the drawer has not established a line of credit, is unable to give adequate guarantees, and therefore cannot sell his bills, or that the goods against which the bill is drawn have been sold on a C.O.D. basis, or that the maker or endorser of the bill desires to earn interest on the bill that would have been surrendered through its sale or discount. Frequently interest is added to the face of time bills taken for collection for the time elapsing between presentation to the drawee and the approximate due date of the arrival of the return remittance to the collecting bank in this country.

FOREIGN CORPORATION A CORPORATION existing under laws of a state other than the one under which it was organized; for income tax purposes, a corporation which is not organized under U.S. laws (a domestic corporation).

FOREIGN CORPORATION BONDS Bonds of business corporations of foreign countries. Various securities dealers in New York City specialize in these issues, maintaining or quoting markets for them in U.S. funds. As the result of post-World War II economic revival in various countries and easing of foreign exchange restrictions, a markedly increased interest in such issues has developed, with advances in market levels. Foreign corporate dollar bonds have been included in debt adjustment plans of various countries effected with U.S. bondholders, including high cash settlements in various cases, thus reestablishing credit standing in conjunction with economic revival and contributing to the increased interest in such extended issues as well as internal corporate bonds.

Flow of funds data of the Board of Governors of the Federal Reserve System indicate that net domestic purchases of foreign bonds were (in billions of dollars) 4.0 in 1978, 3.7 in 1979, 1.2 in 1980, 5.5 in 1981, 6.6 in 1982, 3.1 in 1983, 3.8 in 1984, 3.8 in 1985, 2.6 in l986, and 6.3 in 1987.

BIBLIOGRAPHY

BOARD OF GOVERNORS OF THE FEDERAL RESERVE SYSTEM. *Flow of Funds Accounts,* Annual Revisions.

FOREIGN CORRESPONDENT A bank in a foreign country selected to act as agent for a domestic bank and in which balances are maintained.
See CORRESPONDENT.

FOREIGN CORRUPT PRACTICES ACT Congress passed the Foreign Corrupt Practices Act (FCPA) in 1977. The FCPA established a legal requirement that publicly held companies must maintain internal accounting controls sufficient to provide reasonable assurances as to the achievement of the accuracy of accounting records. Two major provisions of the act are:

1. It is a criminal offense to offer a bribe to a foreign official, foreign political party, party official, or candidate for foreign political office for the purpose of obtaining, retaining, or directing business to any person.
2. Every public company must devise, document, and maintain a system of internal accounting records to ascertain that the objectives of internal control are attained.

The law specifically prohibits any U.S. company (or any officer, director, employee, and others) from using "the mails or any means or instrumentality of interstate commerce corruptly in furtherance of an offer, payment, promise to pay, or authorization of the payment of any money, or offer, gift, promise to give, or authorization of the giving of anything of value to..."(1) a foreign official, (2) a foreign political party, (3) an official of a foreign political party, (4) a candidate for foreign political office, or (5) any person who will in turn give the money to one of the same individuals or entities for purposes of influencing a decision or act to assist in obtaining or retaining business or directing business to a person. The act provides for fines and/or imprisonment upon conviction.

The law amends the Securities Exchange Act of 1934 by requiring public companies to devise and maintain a system of internal accounting control sufficient to provide reasonable assurance that

(i) transactions are executed in accordance with management's general or specific authorization;

(ii) transactions are recorded as necessary (1) to permit preparation of financial statements in conformity with generally accepted accounting principles or any other criteria applicable to such statements, and (II) to maintain accountability for assets;

(iii) access to assets is permitted only in accordance with management's general or specific authorization; and

(iv) the recorded accountability for assets is compared with the existing assets at reasonable intervals and appropriate action is taken with respect to any differences.

FOREIGN CREDIT INSURANCE ASSOCIATION
A voluntary association comprised of stock and mutual insurance companies throughout the United States. Insurance coverages provide primarily for credit losses and losses resulting from political upheaval. Typically, insurance can cover up to 90% of the credit risk and 95% of the risk from adverse political developments. Insurance rates from FCIA insurance approximates comparable rates obtainable from private insurers.

FOREIGN CROWD Although at one time the volume of trading in active foreign bonds justified a separate designation of bond traders on the New York Stock Exchange (NYSE) as the foreign crowd, trading in bonds on that exchange in recent years has been carried on in the new electronic facilities which supplanted the former cabinet system of listings for trading purposes.

Of the 3,057 bond issues listed on the New York Stock Exchange at the end of 1980 with total par value of $601,527 million, bonds of foreign companies numbered 23, with aggregate par value of $1,440 million; and bond issues of foreign governments (41 issuers) numbered 127, with total par value of $7,897 million and year-end market value of $4,315 million. Both measures were the largest in these categories and were principally of European issuers.

The issuance of EUROBONDS, which began in the mid-1960s, continued to have a major influence. An NYSE listing of such issues is invariably sought to improve marketability. As in the case of other bonds, however, most trading volume in foreign bonds is transacted off the board in the over-the-counter market, particularly by firms making a specialty of trading in foreign issues.

FOREIGN CURRENCIES *See* FOREIGN MONEYS.

FOREIGN CURRENCY BONDS Bonds of foreign countries issued and payable (both interest and principal) in the currency of that country but sometimes traded in outside the country of issue. Such bonds are normally intended for purchase by investors in the country of issue and are to be distinguished from FOREIGN DOLLAR BONDS. They are also sometimes known as INTERNAL BONDS. When bonds are bought outside the country of issue, the purchaser takes the risk of exchange fluctuations, the price of the bonds being adjusted to changes in the exchange rate of the currency in which they are issued.

See FOREIGN CORPORATE BONDS, FOREIGN GOVERNMENT BONDS, INSULAR BONDS.

FOREIGN DEPARTMENT The department of a bank or trust company which handles that part of the business which originates in or is destined to a foreign country. A completely equipped foreign department is prepared to perform practically all the banking operations that a domestic banking department performs except in smaller volume, and its scope is therefore as broad as the banking business itself.

The chief functions of a foreign department are (1) to discount and make advances against clean and documentary bills of exchange drawn against banks, corporations, firms, and individuals in foreign countries, (2) to issue commercial and travelers' letters of credit, (3) to accept bills of exchange drawn under letters of credit, (4) to buy and sell gold bullion and to buy and sell foreign coin and currency, (5) to sell checks, mail payments, money orders, and cables on

FOREIGN DEPOSITS

foreign banks, and (6) to collect bills of exchange, checks, foreign bonds and coupons, money orders, etc.

The chief desks or sections of a foreign department are exchange bought, exchange sold, commercial sight credits, commercial acceptance credits, travelers' checks and letters of credit, foreign collections, and foreign coin and currency.

The foreign department is usually operated as if it were a bank in itself. The bank places a certain sum for investment in foreign operations, e.g., balances abroad, discounting bills of exchange, etc., for which the manager of the foreign department is accountable. A separate set of books and general ledger are maintained, which must at all times tie up with the books of the general bookkeeping department.

See FOREIGN EXCHANGE.

Formerly clearinghouse associations had foreign departments which collected checks for its members over a wider territory than the city in which it was located, e.g., the foreign department of the Boston Clearing House, which before the inauguration of the Federal Reserve check collection system in July, 1916, collected all New England checks. Other clearinghouse associations also formerly maintained foreign departments, but those have been superseded by the FEDERAL RESERVE CHECK COLLECTION SYSTEM.

FOREIGN DEPOSITS Deposits payable only at an office of a bank located outside of the United States, the District of Columbia, Puerto Rico, Guam, and the Virgin Islands shall not be a deposit for any of the purposes of the Federal Deposit Insurance Act or be included as part of total deposits or of an insured deposit (Sec. 3(1)(5), Federal Deposit Insurance Act).

In computations of net demand deposits subject to reserve requirements, net demand deposits were defined by the Banking Act of 1935 as the excess of all demand deposits, including deposits due to other banks and the U.S. government, over demand balances due from other domestic banks (except Federal Reserve banks, foreign banks or branches thereof, FOREIGN BRANCHES of domestic banks or branches thereof, and private banks) and cash items in process of collection.

The prohibition of interest on demand deposits contained in the Banking Act of 1933 has not applied to any deposit which is payable only at an office of the bank located outside of the states of the United States and the District of Columbia.

One of the motives for authorizing International Banking Facilities (IBFs) at New York has been the intention to popularize those IBFs, rather than the offshore Bahamas-Cayman Islands locations.

See EDGE ACT, EDGE ACT CORPORATION.

FOREIGN DIRECT INVESTMENT CONTROL Part of the U.S. program of recent years to strengthen the U.S. balance of payments position by restricting private capital outflows. Other aspects of the program included the VOLUNTARY FOREIGN CREDIT RESTRAINT PROGRAM, administered by the Board of Governors of the Federal Reserve System, and the INTEREST EQUALIZATION TAX (IET), introduced in mid-1963. The Foreign Direct Investment Control, administered by the U.S. Department of Commerce, applied to nonfinancial firms.

The foreign direct investment controls were terminated in January, 1974, after the U.S. balance of payments had turned quite favorable, including a positive trade balance, positive balance on goods and services, positive balance on current account, and, *mirabile dictu*, even a favorable balance on capital flows, all in the fourth quarter of 1973 after a long series of negative balances. The controls were aimed to restrain the growth in U.S. outflow of capital for investment abroad, which aggravated the U.S. balance of payments (BoP) deficits. But such restraint on capital outflows also meant a slowdown in the favorable net investment income for the BoP of the U.S., and the Council of Economic Advisers had "affirmed the case for free international investment, free from capital controls." The euphorias caused by the fourth quarter of 1973 BoP figures were soon to vanish, as the run-up in oil prices on imports from the Organization of Petroleum Exporting Countries (OPEC) was not long in beginning.

FOREIGN DOLLAR BONDS Bonds issued by foreign governments, foreign municipalities, and/or business corporations of foreign countries, payable as to both principal and interest in U.S. dollars (thus constituting external dollar debt).

The Foreign Bondholders Protective Council estimated that in the period 1920-1931, some $10.5 billion of foreign government dollar bonds were publicly issued in the New York market, and that by October, 1933, of the $5.5 billion of such issues then still outstanding, some $2.5 billion were in partial or complete default. Much of this volume of foreign dollar bonds issued in the U.S. consisted of issues of South American governments which carried relatively high interest rates compared with then prevailing rates on domestic bonds and found a market even with institutions, including smaller commercial banks, in the late 1920s, before the depression hit primary commodity prices and impaired export earnings of the issuer countries. The Foreign Bondholders Protective Council, Inc. was active in the 1930s in work on adjustment plans which scaled down principal and interest and extended maturities in various cases.

In addition to specific international monetary conditions and economic fluctuations, a special influence affecting investment flows above has been the interest equalization tax of the U.S., as well as the U.S. voluntary program (later made mandatory) to restrict capital outflows. Both of these measures were terminated early in 1974.

See INTERNATIONAL BALANCE OF PAYMENTS.

BIBLIOGRAPHY

BOARD OF GOVERNORS OF THE FEDERAL RESERVE SYSTEM. *Flow of Funds Accounts, Annual Revisions,* August, 1981.
SECURITIES AND EXCHANGE COMMISSION. *SEC Monthly Statistical Review.*

FOREIGN EXCHANGE The mechanism by which commercial, investment, and other transactions between countries are settled.

Although the term foreign exchange is usually defined as comprehending all those transactions that are concerned with the purchase and sale of the money of foreign countries, it is more accurately described as the transferring by individuals or corporations in one country of credits or debits through their banks by obtaining credits or debits on the books of banks in other countries that are correspondents or branches of the banks through which transmission is arranged.

Transmission of foreign exchange may take the form of a CABLE TRANSFER, commercial or bankers' bills of exchange (*see* FOREIGN BILLS OF EXCHANGE), international postal money orders (*see money orders*), MAIL PAYMENT, TRAVELERS' CHECKS, and TRAVELER'S LETTERS OF CREDIT. While foreign exchange, and not foreign money, is normally used in the settlement of international transactions, each foreign exchange instrument mentioned above is convertible into the currency of the country in which it is made payable.

Thus, foreign exchange is a method of effecting payments in a foreign country without the actual shipment of currency or gold. Gold shipments, however, were confined under the post-World War II system of international payments created by the INTERNATIONAL MONETARY FUND (IMF), following the SMITHSONIAN AGREEMENT, to official (intergovernmental) transactions, with the foreign exchange market ranging between a ceiling and floor of 1% above and 1% below the official par value for the currency for private transactions. But since August, 1971, the gold window has been closed, and foreign exchange rates since then have floated (see below).

Foreign exchange is closely akin to domestic exchange and is arranged through the maintenance of reciprocal balances by banks engaging in the business. For example, leading New York and London banks maintain accounts with each other, just as many rural banks in the United States keep balances with a New York correspondent. The difference is that the New York bank keeps a balance with its London correspondent in pounds sterling, and the London bank keeps a balance with its New York correspondent in dollars. By this arrangement, it is possible for the New York bank to sell its customers who owe money in London—importers, for example—bills of exchange drawn in favor of London exporters. When the London exporter receives the bill of exchange, he presents it for payment or credit to his account, whereupon the London bank reduces the balance maintained with it by the New York correspondent. Should the sum total of bills which a New York bank sells against its balance in London equal the sum total bought for building up its London account, then no settlement is required. But if the New York bank sells more bills on London than it buys, then it will deplete the balance to its credit with the London bank. This can be replenished by buying or depositing London exchange or by borrowing in London.

Foreign exchange differs from domestic exchange in another

ENCYCLOPEDIA OF BANKING AND FINANCE

important respect. It is impossible for an individual or corporation in the United States, for instance, to settle a foreign obligation by drawing a check on a local bank in favor of the foreign seller. This is true because (1) the check is payable only in the currency of the United States, and (2) the credit of the individual is not sufficiently well known. Bank credit, especially of the larger institutions of the East, however, is established internationally, so that the exchange facilities of these banks must be called upon to execute transfers of credits and debits abroad.

Exchange is accumulated, i.e., banks in the United States may establish and increase their credit balances with correspondent banks abroad, in the following ways: (1) by purchasing bills of exchange arising out of exports and forwarding them abroad for collection and credit, (2) by purchasing bills of exchange arising out of U.S. securities abroad, subject to any restrictions as to convertibility and thus availability of such security exchange, and (3) by borrowing from foreign banks.

Exchange is sold, whereby balances maintained by banks in the United States abroad are reduced, in response to the following sources of demand: (1) importation of merchandise, (2) purchase of foreign securities by U.S. investors, (3) lending of funds in the foreign markets, (4) payment of various INVISIBLE IMPORTS, (5) payment for services, e.g, ocean freight and marine insurance charges, (6) immigrants' remittances.

Characteristics of the U.S. foreign exchange markets: The interbank market among banks dealing in foreign exchange consists of transactions between market-making banks (i.e., dealer banks ready to buy and sell specific currencies) or through foreign exchange brokers. In direct dealing between banks, each bank agrees to make a market (stand ready to buy and sell the currency at specific bid and offer quotations at the specific time of the inquiry, provided the other bank reciprocally provides ready-to-trade quotations upon inquiry also). The inquiring bank does not indicate, when it inquires for the bid and offer quotations, either the size of its interest or whether the interest is to buy or to sell, but the quoting bank may sense which side of the market, buying or selling, the inquiring bank is on and may widen the spread between the bid and offer (lowering the bid or raising the offered quotation) accordingly, in the light of the estimated risk, for example, of being hit on the bid.

Nearly all large New York City banks engage in foreign exchange trading, both in home offices and abroad through branches, subsidiaries, or correspondents; and the larger banks in other major cities in the U.S. may also trade foreign exchange at home offices or branches, affiliates, or correspondent banks in New York City and abroad.

Foreign exchange brokers in New York City serve as intermediaries for banks making inquiry as to bid-offered quotations and size on both sides of the quotations, but wishing to remain anonymous until the broker in the inquiring bank's behalf contacts other dealer banks (which are not under any obligation to make a market) and locates actual interest for the inquiring bank; or the broker might already have in hand two-way quotations and size left with the broker by other banks (good until canceled) which the broker will immediately make available to the inquiring bank. (Electronics pose a threat to the foreign exchange brokers' existence, since dealer banks subscribing to the Telerate service, for example, may both supply quotations to the computer terminal and tap the computer by operating the desk console for available quotations.)

Quotations and transactions system: SPOT quotations and transactions occur principally in the interbank market. Settlement date for such transactions, called the value date, may be either next day value date, or two-day value date, or same day value date (called cash transactions) which are rare because of time differences.

Forward Exchange transactions involve value dates more than two days into the future, ranging from a few more days than that to weeks, months, or even (rare) years. The forward transaction only fixes the rate for the currency concerned at the time the transaction is effected; no money settlement occurs until the value date specified. If the forward rate specified is above the then prevailing spot rate, the forward rate is at a premium; if below, at a discount; if the same (rare), the forward rate is flat. Outright forward rates are quoted in dollars and cents or per the number of units of the foreign currency per unit of the subject currency (U.S. terms or European terms, respectively), as is the practice for spot rates. Or the premium or discount on forward exchange, relative to spot rate, may be expressed in terms of percent per annum.

Swap transactions arise out of agreements by dealer banks with other dealer banks or nonbanks, enabling each of the two parties to the transaction to buy and sell simultaneously a given amount of a foreign currency on two different value dates, e.g., buy or sell between the two-day value date for spot and sell or buy the same currency for the forward transaction's value date, at specified rates. Swaps are particularly preferred by dealer banks, because they contract to pay and to receive the same amount of the currency at specified rates, and hence there is no foreign exchange risk; they enable a bank to accommodate the outright forward transactions with customers, to bridge gaps in the maturity structure of outstanding spot and forward roles, and to obtain currency needed at a particular time for a currency not needed at such a time (Kubarych, *Foreign Exchange Markets in the United States*).

Swaps are also used by the Federal Reserve Bank of New York, acting for the Federal Reserve System and the U.S. Treasury, to exchange dollars for the currencies of 14 foreign nations through their central banks up to previously agreed amounts and to reverse the transactions three months later. Objective of such swaps has been to counter unfavorable trading conditions in the foreign exchange markets (*see* SWAP NETWORK).

Floating rates. Under the International Monetary Fund's former system of pars of exchange with limited ceiling and floor rates around such pars, post-World War II international trade and financial flows were helped by resulting relative currency rate stability, thus removing as an active factor of uncertainty wide fluctuation in currency rates possible in the absence of such pegs to market rates, which it might be impossible to hedge against because of unavailability of forward exchange contracts. However, maintenance of given pars of exchange might involve a mix of fiscal and monetary policies which would call for domestic deflation and adjustment, so that in effect the economy would have to adjust while the par of exchange remained constant, an example of the tail wagging the dog.

Advocates of floating rates called for fully flexible fluctuating foreign exchange rates, or wider bands of fluctuation around pars, so that the adjustment should occur in the rates and not exclusively in the domestic economy. It was argued that forward exchange contracts would protect traders and investors against the uncertainty of future fluctuation in rates; such availability of forward exchange for widely fluctuating currencies, however, would be a question of fact.

Advocates of continuation of the IMF's system of pars of exchange and narrow band of permitted market fluctuation pointed out that such pars could be changed and were not rigidly set; that fundamental disequilibrium in international position of a member nation could be justification for and occasion concurrence by the IMF in major revision of pars of exchange; and that such major revisions had occurred since the IMF was established. Creation of the supplementary SPECIAL DRAWING RIGHTS (SDRs) system of the International Monetary Fund was cited as conducive to strengthening of the ability of international balance of payments debtors to overcome temporary balance of payments disequilibria and to maintain current pars of exchange.

See ARBITRAGE, BUYING RATE, CABLE RATE, CHECK RATE, FIRST OF EXCHANGE, FOREIGN COLLECTIONS, FOREIGN EXCHANGE MARKET, FOREIGN GOVERNMENT BONDS, FOREIGN MONEYS, LETTER OF CREDIT, LONG RATE, MARINE INSURANCE, POSITION SHEET, SHORT RATE.

BIBLIOGRAPHY

"Attractive, Safe and Offshore." *Accountancy*, January, 1989.
COWITT, P. P., ed. *World Currency Yearbook*. International Currency Analysis, Inc., Brooklyn, NY, 1955. Annual.
DILWORTH, R. H., and others. "U.S. Tax Treatment of Financial Transactions Involving Foreign Currency." *Taxes*, December, 1988.
FLICK, H. "Determining Functional Currency and Qualified Business Units." *CPA Journal*, November, 1988.
JONES, E., and JONES, D. *Hedging Foreign Exchange*, 1987.
KHOURY, S., and CHAN, K. "Hedging Foreign Exchange Risk: Selecting the Optimal Tool." *Midland Corporate Finance*, Winter, 1988.
LAURIE, S., "Putting the Customer First." *Banker*, June, 1988.
LEE, P., "The Corporate Dealer Is The Star." *Euromoney*, May, 1988.
MURPHY, P. "The Silent Approach." *The Banker*, March, 1989.
ROSS, D. "Managing Foreign Exchange: Borderline Cases." *Accountancy*, October, 1988.

FOREIGN EXCHANGE BROKERS In the New York foreign exchange markets, firms (nonbanks) which service banks dealing in foreign exchange by receiving bids and offers from banks, communicating them (without disclosing names of the quoting banks) to other banks, and assisting in arranging transactions by bringing the interested banks together (at which time the banks of course would disclose their identities).

FOREIGN EXCHANGE INTERVENTION Central banks operate in the foreign exchange market for government transactions, as well as on behalf of other central banks and international organizations. Central banks also intervene to influence market conditions or exchange rate movements. All intervention in the foreign exchange market for the United States is conducted by the foreign trading desk at the Federal Reserve Bank of New York. The Federal Reserve acts in close cooperation with the Treasury. The foreign trading desk follows a broad foreign currency directive issued by the Federal Open Market Committee. The directive is reviewed annually and published in the Federal Reserve Board's annual report.

In assessing the need to intervene in the foreign exchange markets, Fed traders continually monitor market developments, review conditions in the world financing markets and consult with market participants. All transactions in foreign currencies are executed at prevailing market rates.

Since 1973, U.S. intervention in the foreign currency market has been directed at countering disorderly market conditions and influencing the value of the dollar.

Various intervention techniques are employed depending on market conditions and the monetary authorities' objectives. Much of the intervention is conducted to conceal the Fed's activity from general view. The trading desk may also intervene by dealing directly with commercial banks if it desires to have the operation highly visible. The desk usually buys or sells dollars for spot delivery, normally two working days after the transaction date. The United States does not publicly announce when it is intervening in the foreign exchange market. It does report periodically on all operations.

The Federal Reserve and other central banks have made use of swap lines on numerous occasions to finance temporarily their exchange market intervention activity. The swap network (a network of reciprocal currency arrangements) arranges short-term credit to the Federal Reserve or to the other participating foreign central banks and the Bank for International Settlements on a reciprocal basis.

Foreign exchange intervention involving dollars is sterilized (the supply of reserves available in the United States banking system is not altered).

FOREIGN EXCHANGE MARKET There is no formal market or exchange where foreign exchange is traded. The market consists of the large New York banks and other banks of the United States and the rest of the world which are in direct communication with one another and foreign exchange brokers and dealers. In New York City, the foreign exchange brokers in effect service the dealer banks by checking with other dealer banks as to quotations and trading interest.

FOREIGN EXCHANGE QUOTATIONS An exchange rate is the ratio between a unit of one currency and the amount of another currency for which that unit can be converted (exchanged) at a particular time. For example, if $1.50 can be exchanged for one British pound, the exchange rate can be computed directly or indirectly:

Direct quotation (rate expressed in U.S. dollar):

$$\frac{\$150}{1} = \$1.50 \text{ per British pound}$$

Indirect quotation (rate expressed in foreign currency):

$$\frac{1}{\$1.50} = .6667 \text{ British pounds per } \$1$$

The Foreign Exchange section of the Wall Street Journal shows both direct and indirect exchange rates on a daily basis.

A cross rate can be obtained to reflect the exchange rate between two currencies based on the prices of each currency in terms of a third currency. For example, to compute the price of deutsche marks in terms of British pounds where

$$\frac{\text{Deutsche marks } 3.80}{\text{U.S.\$}}$$

$$\frac{\text{British pound } 0.90}{\text{U.S.\$}}$$

solve

$$\frac{3.80}{\text{U.S.\$}} = \frac{\text{Deutsche marks } 4.22}{\text{U.S.\$}}$$

$$\frac{0.90}{\text{U.S.\$}}$$

Forward exchange rates are quoted in terms of swap rates or forward discount or premium. Swap rates are quoted in terms of the points of discount or premium from the spot rate. The forward discount or premium is expressed as a percent per annum when the forward price is lower or higher, respectively, than the spot price. The forward discount (or premium) can be computed as follows:

$$\text{Forward discount (or premium)} =$$

$$\frac{\text{Forward} - \text{Spot}}{\text{Spot}} \times \frac{12}{\text{Number of months forward}}$$

$$= \text{percent per annum discount (premium)}$$

Until 1976, the International Monetary Fund supervised a system of fixed exchange rates in which each country's currency had a specified value for international exchange. Exchange rates have genererally been permitted to fluctuate in response to supply and demand factors. Generally, an excess of supply of a currency increases the demand for it and the relative value of other currencies, other things remaining unchanged. The converse is also generally true.

The appended table shows selected foreign exchange rates for recent years (1986-1989).

FOREIGN EXCHANGE RATE CONTRACTS The generic term in the Basle Agreement for cross-currency interest rate swaps, forward foreign exchange contracts, currency futures, currency options, and similar instruments. Exchange rate contracts with an original maturity of 14 days or less are excluded.

FOREIGN EXCHANGE RATES *See* FOREIGN EXCHANGE, FOREIGN MONEYS.

BIBLIOGRAPHY

FRANKEL, J. "Flexible Exchange Rates: Experience Versus Theory." *Journal of Portfolio Management*, Winter, 1988.

FOREIGN EXCHANGES The English equivalent for FOREIGN EXCHANGE.
See EXCHANGES.

FOREIGN EXCHANGE RISK The financial risk associated with changing international currency values when international transactions are denominated (to be settled) in a currency other than that of the domestic currency (U.S. dollars for a U.S. company). For example, if a U.S. company sells goods to a British company and the transaction is to be settled by the British company paying in British pounds, the U.S. company has a foreign exchange risk that the pound may decrease in value relative to the dollar. Transactions denominated in a third nation's currency potentially exposes both importer and exporter to foreign exchange risk.

FOREIGN EXCHANGE STRATEGIES

Foreign Exchange Rates [1]
(Currency units per dollar)

					1989					
Country/currency		1986	1987	1988	Jan.	Feb.	Mar.	Apr.	May	June
1	Australia/dollar [2]	67.093	70.136	78.408	87.05	85.64	81.69	80.35	77.36	75.61
2	Austria/schilling	15.260	12.649	12.357	12.904	13.022	13.148	13.161	13.691	13.912
3	Belgium/franc	44.662	37.357	36.783	38.441	38.792	39.136	39.148	40.723	41.414
4	Canada /dollar	1.3896	1.3259	1.2306	1.1913	1.1891	1.1954	1.1888	1.1925	1.1986
5	China, P.R./yuan	3.4615	3.7314	3.7314	3.7314	3.7314	3.7314	3.7314	3.7314	3.7314
6	Denmark/krone	8.0954	6.8477	6.7411	7.1143	7.2094	7.2912	7.2803	7.5820	7.7087
7	Finland/markka	5.0721	4.4036	4.1933	4.2553	4.3006	4.2994	4.1961	4.3409	4.4302
8	France/franc	6.9256	6.0121	5.9594	6.2538	6.3004	6.3321	6.3223	6.5815	6.7135
9	Germany/deutsche mark	2.1704	1.7981	1.7569	1.8356	1.8505	1.8686	1.8697	1.9461	1.9789
10	Greece/drachma	139.93	135.47	142.00	152.25	154.72	157.34	159.23	165.41	170.42
11	Hong Kong/dollar	7.8037	7.7985	7.8071	7.8047	7.8009	7.7969	7.7828	7.7799	7.7934
12	India/rupee	12.597	12.943	13.899	15.092	15.240	15.467	15.718	16.102	16.420
13	Ireland/punt [2]	134.14	148.79	152.49	145.82	144.10	142.84	142.67	137.39	134.92
14	Italy/lira	1491.16	1297.03	1302.39	1345.12	1355.28	1372.50	1371.80	1415.83	1434.40
15	Japan/yen	168.35	144.60	128.17	127.36	127.74	130.55	132.04	137.86	143.98
16	Malaysia/ringgit	2.5830	2.5185	2.6189	2.7221	2.7307	2.7535	2.7211	2.6967	2.7086
17	Netherlands/guilder	2.4484	2.0263	1.9778	2.0723	2.0895	2.1085	2.1098	2.1938	2.2292
18	New Zealand/dollar [2]	52.456	59.327	65.558	62.412	61.629	61.547	61.167	60.718	57.376
19	Norway/krone	7.3984	6.7408	6.5242	6.6808	6.7254	6.8059	6.7964	7.0337	7.1852
20	Portugal/escudo	149.80	141.20	144.26	150.74	152.10	154.05	154.54	160.71	164.92
21	Singapore/dollar	2.1782	2.1059	2.0132	1.9404	1.9285	1.9407	1.9497	1.9575	1.9572
22	South Africa/rand	2.2918	2.0385	2.1900	2.3847	2.4570	2.5393	2.5480	2.6710	2.7828
23	South Korea/won	884.61	825.93	734.51	685.28	680.28	675.68	672.10	669.25	669.43
24	Spain/peseta	140.04	123.54	116.52	114.78	115.67	116.40	116.146	121.39	126.55
25	Sri Lanka/rupee	27.933	29.471	31.847	33.132	33.115	33.416	34.021	34.145	33.475
26	Sweden/krona	7.1272	6.3468	6.1369	6.2725	6.3238	6.3933	6.3689	6.5756	6.6872
27	Switzerland/franc	1.7979	1.4918	1.4642	1.5619	1.5740	1.6110	1.6469	1.7290	1.7089
28	Taiwan/dollar	37.837	31.756	28.636	27.821	27.716	27.591	26.998	25.788	26.023
29	Thailand/baht	26.314	25.774	25.312	25.322	25.386	25.542	25.524	25.757	25.909
30	United Kingdom/pound [2]	146.77	163.98	178.13	177.37	175.34	171.34	170.08	163.07	155.30
	Memo									
31	United States/dollar [3]		96.94	92.72	95.12	95.77	96.99	97.24	100.81	103.9

[1] Averages of certified noon buying rates in New York for cable transfers. Data in this table also appear in the Board's G.5 (405) release.
[2] Value in U.S. cents.
[3] Index of weighted-average exchange value of U.S. dollar against the currencies of 10 industrial countries. The weight for each of the 10 countries is the 1972-76 average world trade of that country divided by the average world trade of all 10 countries combined. Series revised as of August 1978 (see *Federal Reserve Bulletin*, vol. 64, August 1978, p. 700).

Firms can usually avoid gains and losses on foreign exchange transactions by immediate settlement of the accounts denominated in a foreign currency or by hedging operations. Forward contracts are often used in hedging operations to avoid the risks of exchange rate fluctuations. The forward market offers contracts to sell or to buy a foreign currency at some future date at a guaranteed rate of exchange.

The exposure to exchange translation losses (losses from translating the financial statements of a foreign subsidiary or branch into U.S. dollars in order to consolidate or combine the statements with those of the parent company or home office) is not usually the same as the economic exposure to exchange losses. Economic exposure is due to many factors including rates of inflation, regulation, interest rate changes, and other factors. Translation exposure is related to what accounts have to be translated at current exchange rates. A company's exposed position represent the net balance of all accounts translated at current exchange rates. Accounts translated at historical rates are not exposed to translation adjustments because the same conversion rate is used each year. The net translation exposure position of a firm can be explained as follows:

Items contributing to exposure:

a. Current assets (not including prepaid expenses).
b. Investments denominated in fixed amounts of local currency (German marks; English pounds).
c. Long-term receivables (net of allowances).

Items lessening exposure:

a. Inventories
b. U.S. dollar assets included in a, b, and c above.
c. Local currency liabilities.

The algebraic sum of the items listed represents the company's net exposure to risk of loss (or exposure to gain) through exchange fluctuations. An exposed position can usually be managed by controlling the company's position in listed securities and by the use of forward exchange contracts with the same economic exposure to exchange losses.

FOREIGN EXCHANGE STRATEGIES The drastic expansion of foreign trade and transactions along with the growth of multinational companies have required companies to adjust their financial goals, policies, and techniques. A manager should realize that from the point of view of a home country, a foreign currency is a commodity that fluctuates in price as does the price of potatoes, rice, and hamburger. Like any other commodity, a country's currency is ordinarily fixed because of economic factors affecting the supply of and the demand for a nation's currency. For example, if a country is in an inflationary period, the purchasing power of its currency will decrease. This reduction in the value of a currency is reflected by a decrease in the positioning of the country's currency relative to other nations' currencies. Additional factors affecting

FOREIGN EXCHANGE STRATEGIES

exchange rate fluctuations are a nation's balance of payments, changes in the country's interest rate and investment levels, and the stability of governance. For example, if interest rates in the United States are higher than in France, international investors would seek to invest in the U.S., thereby increasing the demand for U.S. dollars relative to the franc. Exchange rates are established daily and are published in financial journals, including The Wall Street Journal. To begin to understand the complexities of foreign exchange rate transactions, it is necessary to become acquainted with several basic terms:

Exchange rate—the ratio between a unit of one currency and the amount of another currency into which that unit can be converted at a given time.

Free rate of exchange—an exchange rate established by supply and demand in the marketplace.

Governmental rate of exchange—an exchange rate set by a government. A government may establish a preferential rate of exchange to stimulate imports; a penalty rate of exchange to discourage certain transactions (e.g., the import of luxury merchandise); a dividend rate of exchange for the payment of dividends to nonresident shareholders.

Black-market rates of exchange—an exchange rate set by unauthorized foreign exchange dealers in violation of government regulations.

Blocked accounts—bank accounts in a foreign country which the foreign government imposes laws that restrict the bank accounts of nonresidents to use only within the country.

Direct exchange quotation—an exchange rate quotation in which one unit of foreign currency is stated in terms of its domestic equivalent. For example, if $0.40 can be exchanged for one West German mark, the quotation is direct.

$$\frac{.40 \text{ domestic currency}}{1 \text{ foreign currency}} = \$0.40$$

Indirect exchange quotation—an exchange rate quotation in which one unit of domestic currency is stated in terms of its foreign equivalent. The indirect exchange rate is the reciprocal of the direct exchange rate and represents the number of foreign currency units that can be obtained for 1 local currency unit. Using the example given in the direct exchange quotation, the indirect exchange rate is 2.50 marks for 1 U.S. dollar:

$$\frac{1 \text{ mark}}{\$0.40} = 2.50 \text{ marks}$$

Spot rate—a rate quoted for immediately delivery.

Forward rate of exchange—a rate quoted for the delivery of the exchanged (in 30, 60, or 180 days).

Forward exchange contract—an agreement to exchange currencies of different countries at a specified future date and at an exchange rate agreed upon in advance.

Premium on the forward exchange contract—a difference that arises when the forward rate is greater than the spot rate; that is, the foreign currency is selling at a premium in the forward market.

Discount on the forward exchange contract—a difference that arises when the spot rate is greater than the forward rate; that is, the foreign currency is selling at a discount in the forward market.

Denominated—Assets and liabilities are denominated in one currency if their amount is fixed in terms of that currency. When a transaction is to be settled by the receipt of payment of a fixed amount of a specified currency, the receivable or payable is denominated in that currency.

Translation—the conversion of the assets, liabilities, and operating accounts of a foreign branch or subsidiary from stated amounts of foreign currency into U.S. dollars. The purpose of translation is to enable such accounts into the financial statements of the U.S. home office or consolidated financial statements.

Financial managers have many occasions to develop strategies relating to transactions involving foreign exchange in which foreign exchange rates change. Basically, the strategies involve (1) holding monetary assets in strong currencies and (2) incurring debt in weak currencies. If inflation appears likely, it may be preferable to hold more nonmonetary assets and to use debt financing.

The typical relationship among currencies, imports, and exports can be summarized as follows:

U.S. Dollar Relative to Foreign currency	Direct Exchange Rates	Imports into U.S.	Exports from U.S.
Dollar strengthens	Decreases	Less expensive	More expensive
Dollar increases	Increases	More expensive	Less expensive

Note that if the direct exchange rate increases, it takes more U.S. dollars to acquire one unit of foreign currency. If the direct exchange rate decreases, it takes fewer U.S. dollars to acquire one unit of foreign currency.

Financial managerial policy will be illustrated for hedging operations, debt policy and investment policy where foreign transactions are involved.

Case 1. *Hedging.* Managers can use hedging operations when sales are made to foreign customers on the basis of their currency (transaction denominated in the foreign currency) with the intention of collecting the claim at a later date and converting to domestic currency. For example, if a U.S. company makes sales to a customer in a foreign country and bills the customer 1,000,000 units of the foreign currency (Y). At the time of the sale, 50 units of currency Y were equal to $1 U.S. currency. The U.S. company will eventually collect 1,000,000 units of Y convert to $20,000 units of U.S. currency:

$$\frac{1,000,000}{50} = \$20,000$$

When the receivable is collected, the exchange rate is 60 units of X for $1. The company will collect $16,667, losing $3,333 because the foreign currency weakened relative to the U.S. dollar:

$$\frac{1,000,000}{60} = 16,667$$

The U.S. company could protect itself from changes in the rate of exchange by purchasing a futures contract at the time of the sale at approximately 50 foreign currency units to $1 (allowing the U.S. company to sell 1,000,000 units of the foreign currency at 50 foreign currency units at $1).

1. Collection from customer at a later date: 1,000,000 units
2. Pay 1,000,000 units of foreign currency in exchange for $20,000.

If the U.S. company could have arranged with the foreign company to have the transaction settled by sending $20,000 U.S. dollars, the U.S. company would have avoided the risk associated with changes in the exchange rate.

Case 2. *Debt policy.* Debt a company could also develop a debt strategy to deal with the possibility of changes in foreign exchange rates. If it is known that the foreign currency is a weak currency, the U.S. company could borrow in that currency, when the exchange rate is 50 to 1 ($20,000 purchasing power). If the exchange rate is 60 to 1 when the loan is repaid, the loan can be repaid with $16,667:

$$\frac{1,000,000}{60} = 16,667$$

Case 3. *Investment policy.* As a general rule, bank balances and investments in bonds should be held in strong currencies. For example, assume that $100,000 is deposited in a country having a strong currency. At the time of the transaction, the foreign currency is quoted at 50 U.S. cents. The deposit in terms of the foreign currency is

$$\frac{\$100,000}{.50} = 200,000 \text{ units of foreign currency}$$

Should the foreign currency later trade at $0.60 U.S. dollars, the 200,000 units of foreign currency is worth $120,000:

$$200,000 \times \$0.60 = \$120,000$$

FOREIGN FUNDS AND ASSETS CONTROL

Instituted by the Secretary of the Treasury under authority of Executive Order of April 10, 1940, following the invasion of Denmark and Norway by Germany. In accordance with this authority, the Treasury issued regulations governing the declaration, freezing, and licensing of transfers of assets of the nationals of the invaded countries. Subsequently, foreign funds control was extended to assets of nationals of Germany and Japan in June and July, 1941.

World War II Controls. Foreign assets controls were first instituted by the Secretary of the Treasury under the authority of Executive Order 8389 of April 10, 1940, and the Trading With the Enemy Act. Used initially to block assets of Denmark and Norway after those countries were invaded by Germany, the Treasury restrictions were gradually expanded to the Axis Powers and to other Axis-occupied countries. In addition, restrictions were added which resulted in a complete ban on economic transactions and trade relations, direct or indirect, with enemy countries or enemy-occupied countries.

At the conclusion of hostilities, steps were taken promptly by the U.S. Treasury to unblock financial assets in which there was no enemy interest, based upon certification of non-enemy interest by the countries concerned. In 1948, Treasury made a comprehensive survey of assets still blocked, and supplied information thereon to the pertinent countries participating in the European Recovery Program. Assets which were not unblocked by the end of September, 1948, were transferred to the jurisdiction of the Office of Alien Property of the Department of Justice for vesting. Once vested, such property was administered, liquidated, or sold in accordance with the Trading With the Enemy Act, which authorized the payment of debt claims of U.S. citizens or residents out of the vested property of their debtors. Return of vested property to non-enemies and to certain classes of technically non-hostile enemies was also authorized. The net proceeds of such property, after liquidation and the payment of taxes and expenses, were covered into the Treasury for payment into the War Claims Fund and were thereafter devoted to the payment of certain war claims of U.S. citizens as provided by the War Claims Act of 1948, as amended.

The Office of the Alien Property Custodian was established within the Office for Emergency Management by Executive Order 9095 dated March 11, 1942, under the authority of the Trading With the Enemy Act, to direct, manage, supervise, control, vest, administer, sell and otherwise deal with foreign-owned property in the interests of and for the benefit of the United States. This office was terminated by Executive Order 9788 dated October 14, 1946, and its functions transferred to the Department of Justice effective October 15, 1946; this transfer was made permanent by Reorganization Plan 1 effective July 1, 1947.

The Office of Alien Property (Justice) was transferred to the Civil Division (Justice) by Attorney General Order 249-61 dated September 1, 1961. The office was abolished by Executive Order 11281 dated May 13, 1966, effective June 30, 1966, and foreign funds control functions were transferred to the Office of Foreign Assets Control, Treasury Department. Remaining functions were continued by the Civil Division, Department of Justice. Among the current activities of the latter division are alien property cases and administrative functions in connection with all suits in federal courts and administrative claims resulting from seizure and vesting of alien property during World War II, and the management and liquidation of all vested assets. The assistant attorney general in charge of the Civil Division, Department of Justice, is also responsible for the remaining functions of the Office of Alien Property pursuant to the Trading With the Enemy Act, as amended, the International Claims Settlement Act, as amended, and other pertinent statutes. The Office of Alien Property was terminated as a separate organizational entity on June 30, 1966.

The War Claims Commission, created by the War Claims Act of 1948, was abolished by Reorganization Plan 1, and its functions were transferred to the Foreign Claims Settlement Commission of the United States, effective July 1, 1954. The Foreign Claims Settlement Commission of the United States, created by Reorganization Plan No. 1 of 1954 (68 Stat. 1279) effective July 1, 1954, was transferred to the Department of Justice as a separate agency within that Department effective March 14, 1980 by P.L. 96-209 (22 U.S.C. 1622a). The commission's duties and authority were defined in the International Claims Settlement Act of 1949, as amended (22 U.S.C. 1621-1645), and the War Claims Act of 1948 (50 U.S.C. 2001-2017). On February 26, 1981, the Commission began a Vietnam Claims Program pursuant to Title VII of the International Claims Settlement Act of 1949, as amended (22 U.S.C. 1645), to consider claims of U.S. nationals for losses of property as a result of nationalizations or other takings in Vietnam. As of 1982, the Commission was authorized to receive, determine, and provide for the payment of claims of ex-prisoners of war of the Vietnam conflict and civilian American citizens who were captured and interned by hostile forces in Southeast Asia during the Vietnam conflict (50 U.S.C. App. 2004, 2005).

The Commission was authorized by Act of December 29, 1981 (95 Stat. 1675) to receive and determine the validity and amounts of claims by U.S. nationals against the government of the Czechoslovak Socialist Republic for losses arising after August 8, 1958, out of the nationalization or other taking of property located in the Czechoslovak Socialist Republic. The program had a deadline for completion of October 31, 1984.

The Commission also has the responsibility of performing liquidating functions, as they become applicable, pertaining to 18 programs against the governments of Yugoslavia, Panama, Poland, Bulgaria, Hungary, Romania, Italy, the Soviet Union, Czechoslovakia, Cuba, the German Democratic Republic and the People's Republic of China, all of which are to be administered under the International Claims Settlement Act of 1949, as amended. These liquidation functions also involved 18 programs administered under the War Claims Act of 1948 as amended, the Micronesian Claims Act of 1971, and other statutory authority.

Foreign Asset Control Regulations. Upon the entry of the People's Republic of China into the Korean War, the Secretary of the Treasury, pursuant to section 5(b) of the Trading With the Enemy Act, issued effective December 17, 1950, the Foreign Assets Control Regulations blocking all property in the U.S. in which any interest of the People's Republic of China, North Korea, or their nationals existed, and prohibiting all trade or other financial transactions with those countries or their nationals. The Office of Foreign Assets Control, in the Treasury Department, was made responsible for administering the regulations. Restrictions under the Foreign Assets Control Regulations were extended to North Vietnam effective May 5, 1964, to Cambodia effective April 16, 1975, and to South Vietnam on April 30, 1975. Controls are still maintained on North Korea, Cambodia, and Vietnam but have been lifted as to China, as discussed below.

Subsequent Status of Foreign Assets Control with Respect to People's Republic of China. On May 11, 1979, an agreement on the settlement of mutual claims was reached between the United States and the People's Republic of China. The agreement covered claims of U.S. nationals against the People's Republic of China arising from certain measures taken by that government on or after October 1, 1949; and claims of nationals of the People's Republic of China against the United States arising from the blocking of assets by the U.S. Government on or after December 17, 1950. The government of the People's Republic of China agreed to pay to the U.S. Government US$30 million on October 1, 1979, and US$50.5 million in five equal annual installments starting on October 1, 1980, in full and final settlement of such claims. The U.S. Government agreed to unblock Chinese assets effective January 31, 1980.

On January 25, 1980, Congress approved a resolution granting the People's Republic of China most-favored-nation status in international trade. On February 1, 1980, a bilateral trade agreement of the U.S. with the People's Republic of China came into force.

Cuban Assets Control Regulations. Effective July 8, 1963, the Secretary of the Treasury issued the Cuban Assets Control Regulations under the authority of section 5(b) of the Trading With the Enemy Act. The regulations incorporated and expanded upon a series of economic sanctions imposed against Cuba beginning in 1960. These regulations are substantially similar to the Foreign Assets Control Regulations, which currently apply to North Korea, Vietnam, and Cambodia.

Iranian Assets Control. On November 12, 1979, by presidential proclamation, the import of crude oil from Iran, and of products originating from such oil, was prohibited. This was followed on November 14, 1979, by a prohibition imposed pursuant to the International Emergency Economic Powers Act, 50 U.S.C. 1701-1706, on certain payments and transfers by persons subject to U.S. jurisdiction involving the government of Iran, its instrumentalities, and controlled entities. This action blocked all Iranian government assets in the United States.

On April 7, 1980, certain trade and financial sanctions were applied to transactions involving private Iranian nationals. On

FOREIGN GOVERNMENT BONDS

April 17, 1980, the President imposed further sanctions prohibiting any importation of Iranian products, as well as transactions incident to travel to Iran by U.S. nationals.

Virtually all of the restrictions on current transactions with Iran were lifted effective January 19, 1981, pursuant to the agreements (known as the Algiers Accords) by which U.S. hostages in Iran were released and the U.S.-Iran Claims Tribunal established to adjudicate claims between the two countries arising from the hostage crisis. Most of the frozen Iranian government assets were transferred pursuant to the Accords, and a total of one billion dollars was put into a security account at the Tribunal to be used in paying awards.

Nicaraguan Trade Control Regulations. Effective May 7, 1985, the President imposed certain limited trade and transportation sanctions against Nicaragua pursuant to the International Emergency Economic Powers Act. The sanctions against Nicaragua, administered pursuant to the Nicaraguan Trade Control Regulations, do not involve a freeze of assets or other financial sanctions. They do include a ban on the exportation of goods to Nicaragua, including technical data in tangible form; the importation of goods and services from Nicaragua; the entry of Nicaraguan-registry vessels into U.S. ports; and the provision by Nicaraguan air carriers of air transportation to or from points in the U.S.

Libyan Sanctions Regulations. Under the International Emergency Economic Powers Act, Libyan government assets in the United States were frozen as of January 8, 1986. Comprehensive trade and financial sanctions were imposed effective January 7 and February 1, 1986. These sanctions amount to a comprehensive economic embargo similar to that formerly in effect with respect to Iran.

South African Sanctions Regulations. The Office of Foreign Assets Control of the Treasury Department also administers selected sanctions imposed against South Africa by Congress pursuant to the Comprehensive Anti-Apartheid Act of 1986. Treasury is responsible for administering a ban on loans to the South African Government, a ban on U.S. depository institutions' holding South African Government bank accounts, and a ban on new investment that includes loans to the private sector. Treasury also administers prohibitions on the importation of certain South African goods. South African governmental assets were not frozen under the Comprehensive Anti-Apartheid Act. Agencies other than Treasury have responsibility for other types of sanctions under the Act, such as export restrictions.

Transaction Control Regulations. The Office of Foreign Assets Control administers regulations which prohibit persons in the U.S. from purchasing, selling, or arranging the purchase or sale of strategic commodities outside the U.S. for ultimate shipment to the Soviet bloc and certain allied countries. These regulations supplement the export control laws administered by the Department of Commerce.

BIBLIOGRAPHY

FOREIGN CLAIMS SETTLEMENT COMMISSION. *Annual Report.*

FOREIGN GOVERNMENT BONDS Bonds which are a direct obligation of a foreign government. These bonds are of two classes: (1) external bonds, those marketed and intended for investment by investors in another country and payable as to both principal and interest in the currency of that country, and (2) INTERNAL BONDS, those marketed primarily in the country of issue and payable in the currency of that country. The external bonds of foreign countries which have been marketed in the United States are also known as dollar bonds. A few foreign government issues are payable in several currencies and are known as MULTIPLE CURRENCY BONDS. In addition to foreign (national) government bonds, many foreign municipal issues have been floated in the U.S. market. *See* EXTERNAL BOND.

As to security, foreign government bonds may be divided into two classes: (1) promises to pay or certificates of indebtedness without collateral, and (2) those secured by pledge of specific assets. Most issues are of the former type. The latter type was exemplified by the old borrowings, such as the secured debt of Mexico (examples, the Cons. 5s, 1899, and Gold 4s, 1910), secured by specific revenues.

As investments, the value of these bonds depends upon the same factors as the value of U.S. bonds, i.e., upon the good faith, honor, political stability, degree of industrial advancement, and commercial ability of the issuing government. Motivations for interest by U.S. investors in foreign government bonds include (1) higher income (ordinarily), (2) capital gains in foreign government bonds from depressed discount levels as market prices reflect economic recovery of the countries concerned in recent years, (3) diversification. Extra risk in investing in such issues, however, may include such factors as (1) exchange restrictions, (2) currency instability, (3) governmental instability, and (4) risk of repudiation with change in administrations or governments.

The record of foreign government bonds sold in the United States in modern times is not an enviable one. In the world collapse of 1929-1933, bonds were defaulted by a number of South American countries, and subsequently World War II conditions compelled default on European issues of various nations. As the result of debt adjustment plans and validation arrangements, many of these countries resumed service on their dollar debt with adjusted interest and/or sinking fund payments and extended maturities. (*See* FOREIGN BONDHOLDERS' PROTECTIVE COUNCIL, INC.)

See FOREIGN CORPORATE BONDS, FOREIGN DOLLAR BONDS.

FOREIGN INVESTMENT Foreign ownership of assets in the United States is rapidly growing. Congress and the general public is increasingly concerned over the impact of foreign investment on the industrial and real estate structure and employment as well as regional economies. These inflows of capital reflect the interaction of national economies and complicate U.S. economic policies. State governments are also heavily involved in attracting foreign investments.

The U.S. currently places few restrictions on foreign direct investment. This provides an attractive investment climate for such investments by allowing the relatively free international flow of capital. Restrictions on such investments generally relate to keeping public services or services which impact on national security from coming under foreign control.

In the 1970s, Congress passed legislation that provided for increased collection of data and additional disclosure for foreign owners of U.S. assets.

Since 1970 there has been a sharp rise and dramatic decline in the rate of U.S. foreign direct investment (see appended table). U.S. foreign investment grew at a compound annual rate of 10.4% in the 1970-1974 period and at 12.0% in the 1975-1979 period. The growth was due to the increasing development of petroleum resources and the stagnating U.S. economy. From 1980-1985, the rate declined to 3.6%. This decline was attributed in part to the wide differential in interest rates favoring capital markets in the U.S. In 1970 developed countries received 69% of U.S. foreign investment; less developed countries received 25%, At the end of the 1985 U.S. investment was proportioned with 74% in developed countries and 23% in less developed countries.

In 1989 the Commerce reported that U.S. debt to the rest of the world rose sharply to $532.5 billion which made the U.S. the world's largest debtor. The debt at the end of 1988 was 40% greater than the $378.3 billion reported for 1987. Foreigners' assets in the U.S. increased 15.4% to $1.786 trillion while U.S. assets overseas grew onlly 7.2% to $1.254 trillion. The U.S. began the 1980s as a large creditor but became a debtor nation in 1985. A deficiency of U.S. savings forced the U.S. to borrow from abroad to finance investments. Bush administration economists insist that the flow of foreign capital to the U.S. reflects continued confidence in the U.S. economy.

Foreign direct investment in factories and companies in the U.S. reached a record $57.1 billion, representing a 21% increase for 1988. Britain and Japan accounted for approximately three-fourths of the increase.

Foreign holdings of Treasury securities increased almost 19% to $96.6 billion in 1988. The Commerce Department reported that borrowing by U.S. banks from foreign offices to meet strong domestic loan demand pushed up bank liabilities to foreigners by 11.3% to $609.5 billion.

Approximately three quarters of U.S. direct investment abroad is in developed countries. In 1988, Britain and Japan reflected the largest increase in direct investment with $48 billion and $16.9 billion, respectively.

BIBLIOGRAPHY

Foreign Investments. U.S. Superintendent of Documents (Subject bibl., 275).

ENCYCLOPEDIA OF BANKING AND FINANCE

FOREIGN ITEMS Checks, drafts, bills of exchange, etc., which are payable in a foreign country. This term is also quite generally employed in banking practice to apply to checks, notes, drafts, etc., which are drawn and payable within the United States, but payable at a point outside the place where they are deposited. In other words, this term is often used synonymously with transit items and out-of-town items.

FOREIGN LIQUIDATION The selling of U.S. securities by foreign holders or speculators. Such climactic selling caused the New York Stock Exchange to close August 1, 1914, and remain closed until December 12, 1914, in connection with the outbreak of World War I.

During World War II, however, the requisitioning of U.S. security holdings of foreign citizens by their governments had centralized such holdings, enabling the requisitioning authorities to prevent dumping of such securities at lower prices and provide orderly liquidation from time to time. As a result, the New York Stock Exchange did not suspend operations as in 1914. Potential liquidation on such a basis, however, constituted a market factor for the security markets.

The New York Federal Reserve Bank, in its monthly bulletin for September, 1947, estimated the market value of foreign holdings of U.S. securities at $3.5 billion, as compared with a $2.7 billion value found by the U.S. Treasury's census of foreign-owned assets as of June 14, 1941. The increase, estimated the bank, was entirely caused by the rise in market value, as aggregate net sales had been small, with securities worth $234 million (at market prices) having been sold in the first year after V-E Day and $223 million in the following year. Such liquidation largely represented the sale of British and Canadian holdings, with some liquidation also by Dutch and Latin American sources.

Data relating to capital movements between the United States and foreign countries have been collected since 1935 under Treasury regulations pursuant to Executive Orders 6560 of January 15, 1934, and 10033 of February 8, 1949, and the International Investment Survey Act of 1976. Reports are filed with Federal Reserve banks by banks, bank holding companies, securities brokers and dealers, and nonbanking enterprises in the United States. Statistics on the principal types of data are then consolidated and are published in the monthly *Treasury Bulletin*.

Foreign purchases and sales of long-term foreign securities by types is shown in the appended table.

FOREIGN MONEYS When the second amendment to the articles of agreement of the INTERNATIONAL MONETARY FUND (IMF) became effective on April 1, 1978, all member countries were required to notify the fund of the exchange arrangements that they intended to apply thereafter. They were also required to notify the fund promptly of any changes in their exchange arrangements in the new era of abandonment of maintenance of the value of a currency in terms of gold. At the same time, each country undertook under Article IV of the articles of agreement "to collaborate with the Fund and other members to assure orderly exchange arrangements and to promote a stable system of exchange rates," and the fund in turn was required to engage in "firm surveillance" over members' exchange rate policies to ensure consistency with that broad objective.

Accordingly many countries have revised their exchange rate systems. Several industrial countries have altered their intervention policies (managed floating rates), and another group formed the currency area of the EUROPEAN MONETARY SYSTEM. Some adjustments in exchange arrangements and policies also took place in many developing countries. Like most developing countries, the oil-exporting countries have generally chosen to peg their currencies at fixed nominal exchange rates to a major foreign currency or a basket of currencies. The stability of exchange rates for their currencies thus tends to depend chiefly on the stability of rates among the major currencies or the selected basket of currencies.

Three principles for the guidance of members' exchange rate policies, adopted by the fund in April, 1977, were as follows:

1. A member shall avoid manipulating exchange rates or the international monetary system in order to prevent effective balance of payments adjustment or to gain an unfair competitive advantage over other members.
2. A member should intervene in the exchange market if necessary to counter disorderly conditions which may be characterized *inter alia* by disruptive short-term movements in the exchange value of its currency.
3. Members should take into account in their intervention policies the interests of other members, including those of the countries in whose currencies they intervene.

Exchange rate fluctuations in nominal weighted terms have been sizable since the par system was terminated and the exchange rates of many countries were allowed to react to market pressures. These fluctuations have been significant in a number of currencies but

Foreign Purchases and Sales of Long-Term Foreign Securities by Type
(In millions of dollars; negative figures indicate net sales by foreigners or a net outflow of capital from the United States.)

Calendar year or month	Net foreign purchases of foreign securities (1)	Foreign bonds — Net foreign purchases (2)	Foreign bonds — Gross foreign purchases (3)	Foreign bonds — Gross foreign sales (4)	Foreign stocks — Net foreign purchases (5)	Foreign stocks — Gross foreign purchases (6)	Foreign stocks — Gross foreign sales (7)
1984	−5,031	−3,930	56,017	59,948	−1,101	14,816	15,917
1985	−7,940	−3,999	81,216	85,214	−3,941	20,861	24,803
1986 r	−5,538	−3,685	166,992	170,677	−1,853	49,149	51,002
1987 r	−6,474	−7,601	199,121	206,722	1,127	95,208	94,082
1988 — Jan-Mar	−4,759	−3,877	45,234	49,111	−882	17,391	18,274
1987 — Mar	−1,455	−665	16,657	17,322	−790	7,124	7,914
Apr	−2,032	−776	19,057	19,833	−1,256	7,189	8,445
May	−624	−1,232	20,156	21,389	608	8,080	7,471
June	1,970	2,251	25,839	23,588	−281	8,852	9,133
July	−651	−617	16,380	16,996	−34	8,712	8,746
Aug	−680	−279	12,350	12,628	−401	8,770	9,171
Sept	−155	−638	13,031	13,669	483	8,816	8,333
Oct	−477	−2,566	18,119	20,684	2,089	12,974	10,885
Nov	−1,225	−1,929	17,753	19,682	704	7,592	6,889
Dec	−538	−1,379	12,433	13,812	841	4,897	4,055
	−807	−1,324	12,812	14,136	517	4,989	4,472
1988 — Jan	−2,111	−1,433	15,858	17,291	−678	5,717	6,395
Feb	−1,841	−1,120	16,564	17,684	−721	6,685	7,406
Mar							

Source: U.S. Federal Reserve Board.

ENCYCLOPEDIA OF BANKING AND FINANCE

FOREIGN MONEYS

Exchange Rate Arrangements
(As of September 30, 1987)[1]

	Currency pegged to				Flexibility limited in terms of a single currency or group of currencies		More flexible		
US Dollar	French Franc	Other currency	SDR	Other composite[2]	Single currency[3]	Cooperative arrangements[4]	Adjusted according to a set of indicators[5]	Other managed floating	Independently floating
Afghanistan	Benin	Bhutan (Indian Rupee)	Burma	Algeria	Bahrain	Belgium	Brazil	Argentina	Australia
Antigua & Barbuda	Burkina Faso	Kiribati (Australian Dollar)	Burundi	Austria	Qatar	Denmark	Chile	China, P.R.	Bolivia
Bahamas, The	Cameroon	Lesotho (South African Rand)	Iran, I.R. of	Bangladesh	Saudi Arabia	France	Colombia	Costa Rica	Canada
Barbados	C. African Rep.	Swaziland (South African Rand)	Jordan	Botswana	United Arab Emirates	Germany	Madagascar	Dominican Rep.	Gambia, The
Belize	Chad	Tonga (Australian Dollar)	Kenya	Cape Verde		Ireland	Portugal	Ecuador	Ghana
Djibouti	Comoros		Libya	Cyprus		Italy		Egypt	Guinea
Dominica	Congo		Rwanda	Fiji		Luxembourg		Greece	Japan
El Salvador	Côte d'Ivoire		Seychelles	Finland		Netherlands		Guinea-Bissau	Lebanon
Ethiopia	Equatorial Guinea		Vanuata	Hungary				Iceland	Maidives
Grenada	Gabon			Israel				India	New Zealand
Guatemala	Mali			Kuwait				Indonesia	Nigeria
Guyana	Niger			Malawi				Jamaica	Philippines
Haiti	Senegal			Malaysia				Korea	Sierra Leone
Honduras	Togo			Malta				Mauritania	Somalia
Iraq				Mauritius				Mexico	South Africa
Lao P.D. Rep.				Nepal				Morocco	United Kingdom
Liberia				Norway				Pakistan	United States
Mozambique				Papua New Guinea				Spain	Uruguay
Nicaragua				Poland				Sri Lanka	Zaire
Oman				Romania				Turkey	
Panama				Sao Tome & Principe				Western Samoa	
Paraguay				Singapore				Yugoslavia	
Peru				Solomon Islands					
St. Kitts & Nevis				Sudan					
St. Lucia				Sweden					
St. Vincent				Tanzania					
Suriname				Thailand					
Syrian Arab Rep.				Tunisia					
Trinidad and Tobago				Zimbabwe					
Uganda									
Venezuela									
Viet-Nam									
Yemen Arab Rep.									
Yemen, P.D. Rep.									
Zambia									

[1] Excluding the currency of Democratic Kampuchea, for which no current information is available. For members with dual or multiple exchange markets, the arrangement shown is that in the major market.
[2] Comprises currencies which are pegged to various "baskets" of currencies of the members' own choice as distinct from the SDR basket.
[3] Exchange rates of all currencies have shown limited flexibility in terms of the U.S. dollar.
[4] Refers to the cooperative arrangement maintained under the European Monetary System.
[5] Includes exchange arrangements under which the exchange rate is adjusted at relatively frequent intervals, on the basis of indicators determined by the respective member countries.

Source: International Monetary Fund, *International Financial Statistics.*

particularly in the case of the U.S. dollar, which by reason of its use as a reserve currency, as a medium of trade, and in other international transactions has a profound effect on the relative values of other currencies. After appreciating dramatically during the first half of the 1980s, the dollar peaked in February 1985 and then began a precipitous decline, depreciating both in nominal and in real effective terms between and the end of 1987 by about 40 percent. Over the same period the deutsche mark appreciated by about 25 percent and the Japanese yen by about 35 percent. In reaction to these events, the finance ministers of the major industrial nations reached an agreement in February 1987 (the Louvre Accord) that exchange rates had been brought within ranges broadly consistent with underlying economic fundamentals and that further substantial exchange rate shifts among their currencies could damage growth and adjustment prospects. Despite subsequent government intervention to steady the dollar, the U.S. currency continued to fall throughout the reminder of 1987. The dollar strengthened in 1988 but continued to fluctuate broadly.

Summary. The appended table lists the exchange rate arrangements of the 151 member countries of the International Monetary Fund. Thirty-five countries pegged their currency to the U.S. dollar, 14 to the French franc, 5 to other currencies, and 37 to some sort of currency composite. Four countries limited the flexibility of their currency in terms of the U.S. dollar, and members of the European

Monetary System kept their currencies within predetermined ranges of each other. Five countries used as a criterion a set of indicators of economic performance, while 42 countries allowed their currencies to float more or less freely.

See FOREIGN EXCHANGE.

BIBLIOGRAPHY

INTERNATIONAL MONETARY FUND. *Annual Report.*
———. *Annual Report on Exchange Restrictions.*
———. *International Financial Statistics* (monthly).
PICK, F. *Pick's World Currency Report.*
———. *Pick's Currency Yearbook.*

FOREIGN MUNICIPAL BONDS Bonds of political subdivisions and cities of foreign countries. Generally, the foreign governments added their guarantees to add to the marketability of foreign municipal dollar bonds in the United States.

See FOREIGN GOVERNMENT BONDS.

FOREIGN SALES CORPORATIONS A corporation that provides U.S. businesses which export with tax benefits. Exporters can establish a Foreign Sales Corporation (FSCs) in a specially designated foreign country, or one of several designated U.S. possessions. The statute providing for the establishment of FSCs was part of the Deficit Reduction Act of 1984.

FOREIGN POSTAL MONEY ORDER See MONEY ORDERS.

FOREIGN TAX TREATIES Tax conventions or agreements between the United States and the government of another country that provide the rules governing the taxation of residents or one country by another. Tax treaties have the same authority as laws contained in the Internal Revenue Code. Treaty provisions usually take precedence over those contained in the Code (Section 7852(d)).

FOREIGN TRADE Trade among nations is a common occurrence and normally benefits both the exporter and the importer. In many countries international trade accounts for more than 20 percent of their national incomes.

Foreign trade can usually be justified on the principle of comparative advantage. According to this economic principle, it is economically profitable for a country to specialize in the production of that commodity in which the producer country has the greater comparative advantage and to allow the other country to produce that commodity in which it has the lesser comparative disadvantage. For example, a doctor should practice medicine in which he specialized instead of performing office typing tasks because the doctor has a greater comparative advantage over a typist in this situation; the typist should perform that service in which she has the lesser comparative disadvantage (typing).

Economists generally maintain that the risks of foreign trade increase as a company moves from exporting to direct foreign investment and when its activities are directed to less developed countries rather than to developed countries.

Major obstacles to international trade include tariffs imposed upon imports. A tariff is a duty or tax levied on foreign imports. Tariffs are usually specific tariffs ($30 per pound of a commodity) or ad valorem tariffs (15 percent of the value of the imported commodity). Tariffs are usually imposed to provide revenue or to protect a home industry. These two objectives are normally incompatible. Arguments suggested to support free (or freer) trade include the following: tariffs deny individuals and nations the benefits of greater productivity and a higher standard of living; tariffs eliminate or reduce the advantages of specialization and exchange among nations and prevent the best use of scare world resources.

Basic arguments for tariffs are grouped as follows:

1. Protect infant industries.
2. Equalize costs of production between domestic and foreign producers.
3. Protect U.S. jobs.
4. Protect high W.S. wages.
5. Keep money at home.
6. Develop and protect defense industries.

Import quotas are also used to set the maximum absolute amount of a particular commodity that can be imported. Export subsidies are used to encourage exportation of certain goods or to prevent discrimination against U.S. exporters who sell in a foreign market at a world price lower than the domestic price. Exchange controls are also used to control the flow of international trade. Some controls are used to ration a country's scarce foreign exchange. Some countries use different exchange rates for different commodities to encourage or discourage imports. The United States has granted tariff concessions on thousands of commodities (automobiles, steel, chemicals) to promote world trade as well as economic and political harmony. The Trade Act of 1974 gave the President a wide range of measures that could be used to open trade doors around the world. This Act also allowed the president to extend most-favored-nation treatment to various nations.

The United States and other nations have organized international financial institutions to provide various forms of foreign aid. The International Bank for Reconstruction and Development (the World Bank) is intended "to supplement private investments in foreign countries by nations and individuals having capital to lend." The World Bank issues and sells bonds and uses the proceeds for loans to "any business, industrial, or agricultural enterprise in the territory of a member," and guarantees loans by private investors. The major purpose of the World Bank is to stimulate world production, trade, and investment. The International Finance Corporation (IFC) is affiliated with the World Bank. The IFC attempts to stimulate economic development by encouraging the growth of private productive enterprises, especially in lesser developed areas. It can invest in private enterprises but without government guarantees of repayment. The International Development Administration, also affiliated with the World Bank, was organized to allow underdeveloped nations to borrow funds. The Inter-American Development Bank was organized to stimulate the economic development of the Latin American nations. The United States makes major contributions to these international organizations.

Foreign financing sources for international trade transactions include commercial bank loans within the host country and loans from international lending agencies. Foreign banks can also be used to discount trade bills to finance short term financing. Eurodollar financing is another method for providing foreign financing. A Eurodollar is a dollar deposit held in a bank outside the United States. An active market exists for these deposits. Banks use Eurodollars to make dollar loans to borrowers; the interest rate is usually in excess of the deposit rate. Such loans are usually in very large amounts, are short-term working-capital loans, and are unsecured. U.S. firms frequently arrange for lines of credit and revolving credits from Eurodollar banks. No compensating balances are usually required.

The Eurobond market is widely used for long-term funds for multinational U.S. companies. A Eurobond is a long-term security issued by an internationally recognized borrower in several countries simultaneously. The bonds are denominated in a single currency. Such bonds are usually fixed-income bonds or floating-rate bonds; some bonds are convertible into common stock.

Many countries have organized development banks that provide intermediate- and long-term loans to private enterprises. Such loans are made to provide economic development within a country. The Export-Import Bank (Exim Bank) is an independent agency of the U.S. government organized to facilitate the financing of exports from the United States. It makes long-term loans to foreigners, enabling such parties to purchase U.S. goods and services. The bank often participates with private lenders in extending credit and guarantees payment of medium-term financing incurred in the export of U.S. goods and services.

International trade procedures differ in some respects from those used in domestic trade. Three key documents include the trade draft (an order to pay); a bill of lading (a shipping document used in transporting goods from the exporter to the importer); and a letter of credit (issued by a bank on behalf of the importer to guarantee the creditworthiness of the purchaser). The trade draft, or bill of exchange, is a written statement (an unconditional order) by the exporter ordering the importer to pay a specific amount of money at a specific time. A sight draft is payable on presentation to the party to whom the draft is addressed (the drawee). A time draft is payable a certain number of days after presentation to the drawee. If the draft is accepted by the drawee, it represents a trade acceptance. If a bank accepts the draft, it is referred to as a bankers' acceptance;

FOREIGN TRADE

such instruments are highly marketable. The bill of lading gives the holder title to the goods. The bill of lading accompanies the draft.

U.S. citizens, resident aliens, and domestic corporations generally receive the same tax treatment for the income they earn. U.S. citizens who work in foreign countries for extended periods of time are provided a special exception. Currently, such individuals can exclude up to $70,000 of income earned from performing personal services in foreign countries. A U.S. citizen satisfied the bona fide resident test if the individual (1) has been a resident of a foreign country for an uninterrupted period which includes an entire tax year and (2) has maintained a tax home in a foreign country during the period of residence. Generally, nonresident aliens and foreign corporations are taxed only on their U.S. investment income. However, if such parties conduct a trade or business in the United States at some time during the year, the parties are taxed on both their U.S. investment income and their income that is attributable to the conduct of the U.S. trade or business.

A foreign tax credit permits U.S. taxpayers to avoid double taxation by crediting income taxes paid or accrued to (1) a foreign country or (2) a U.S. possession against the U.S. tax liability. Certain conditions and limitations are imposed.

Appended is a table showing the top 10 U.S. trading partners in manufactured goods in 1986. A second appended table shows foreign trade of the United States (in million of dollars).

Since 1970 there has been a sharp rise and dramatic decline in the rate of U.S. foreign direct investment (see appended table). U.S. foreign investment grew at a compound annual rate of 10.4% in the 1970-1974 period and at 12.0% in the 1975-1979 period. The growth was due to the increasing development of petroleum resources and the stagnating U.S. economy. From 1980-1985, the rate declined to 3.6%. This decline was attributed in part to the wide differential in interest rates favoring capital markets in the U.S. In 1970 developed countries received 69% of U.S. foreign investment; less developed countries received 25%. At the end of 1985, U.S. investment was proportioned with 74% in developed countries and 23% in less developed countries.

In 1989 the Commerce Department reported that U.S. debt to the rest of the world rose sharply to $532.5 billion which made the U.S. the world's largest debtor. The debt at the end of 1988 was 40% greater than the $378.3 billion reported for 1987. Foreigners' assets in the U.S. increased 15.4% to $1.786 trillion while U.S. assets overseas grew onlly 7.2% to $1.254 trillion. The U.S. began the 1980s as a large creditor but became a debtor nation in 1985. A deficiency of U.S. savings forced the U.S. to borrow from abroad to finance investments.

Foreign direct investment in factories and companies in the U.S. reached a record $57.1 billion, representing a 21% increase for the year. Britain and Japan accounted for approximately three-fourths of the increase.

Foreign holdings of Treasury securities increased almost 19% to $96.6 billion in 1988. The Commerce Department reported that borrowing by U.S. banks from foreign offices to meet strong domestic loan demand pushed up bank liabilities to foreigners by 11.3% to $609.5 billion.

Approximately three quarters of U.S. direct investment abroad is in developed countries. In 1988, Britain and Japan reflected the largest increase in direct investment with $48 billion and $16.9 billion, respectively.

For full comparison of all receipts of the U.S. and payments in international trade and capital movements, see INTERNATIONAL BALANCE OF PAYMENTS. General imports include merchandise entered immediately upon arrival into merchandising or consumption channels, plus commodities entered into bonded customs warehouses for storage.

BIBLIOGRAPHY

Foreign Trade & Tariff. U.S. Superintendent of Documents (Subject bibl., 123).
KINGMAN-BRUNDAGE, J., and SCHULZ, S. A. *The Fundamentals of Trade Finance*, 1986.
INTERNATIONAL CHAMBER OF COMMERCE, Publication No. 400. *Uniform Customs and Practices for Documentary Credits*, 1983.

Top 10 U.S. Trading Partners in Manufactured Goods in 1986*
(millions of dollars)

	1980	1981	1982	1983	1984	1985	1986
Leading Purchasers							
Canada	29,582	33,721	28,499	33,067	40,849	42,434	40,820
Japan	8,947	10,080	9,984	10,815	12,110	12,345	16,876
Mexico	11,681	14,421	9,189	6,496	9,082	10,946	10,424
United Kingdom	10,787	10,725	8,992	9,050	10,655	10,071	10,122
West Germany	8,000	7,623	7,050	6,489	7,322	7,461	8,782
France	5,925	5,826	5,562	4,911	4,992	5,186	6,234
Australia	3,754	4,861	4,187	3,580	4,386	5,063	5,171
Netherlands	4,219	3,969	3,966	4,163	4,303	4,317	4,855
South Korea	2,232	2,409	3,040	3,315	3,460	3,571	4,028
Belgium/Luxembourg	4,550	3,751	3,199	3,259	3,524	3,461	3,822
Taiwan	2,856	2,714	2,849	2,932	2,867	2,940	3,583
Italy	3,301	3,095	2,515	2,308	2,702	3,046	3,180
Singapore	2,780	2,613	2,763	3,108	3,350	3,026	3,065
Saudi Arabia	5,221	6,661	8,363	7,268	4,892	3,940	2,892
Brazil	3,301	2,816	2,539	1,774	1,764	2,217	2,859
Leading Suppliers							
Japan	32,527	39,501	39,520	43,065	59,737	71,657	84,736
Canada	27,652	31,543	31,952	36,200	48,738	50,626	53,041
West Germany	11,857	11,373	11,923	12,561	17,042	20,356	25,253
Taiwan	7,106	8,384	9,256	11,764	15,639	17,293	20,709
South Korea	4,294	5,293	5,813	7,495	9,854	10,463	13,237
United Kingdom	7,358	7,303	7,182	7,780	9,664	11,268	12,963
Mexico	4,407	5,293	5,331	6,328	8,246	9,163	10,625
Italy	4,045	4,780	4,794	4,976	7,289	8,868	9,966
Hong Kong	4,944	5,661	5,815	6,763	8,794	8,885	9,348
France	4,772	5,291	4,991	5,375	7,384	8,636	9,256
Switzerland	2,790	2,438	2,314	2,450	3,081	3,460	5,231
Brazil	1,1469	1,982	1,977	2,732	4,535	4,661	4,567
Singapore	1,790	1,954	2,096	2,719	3,771	6,846	4,522
Sweden	1,652	1,741	2,010	2,388	3,226	4,166	4,427
China	791	1,262	1,569	1,759	2,425	2,838	4,171

*Manufactured goods include commodity section 5-9; domestic and foreign merchandise, f.a.s.; general imports c.i.f.

———. Publication 322 *Uniform Rules for Collections.*
———. Publication 325 *Uniform Rules for Contract Guarantees.*
———. Publication 365 *Introduction to I.C.C. Rules on International Contracts.*
———. Publication 417 *Key Words in International Trade.*

FOREIGN TRANSACTIONS AND OPERATIONS ACCOUNTING

When business transactions are undertaken abroad, accounting for these transactions by a U.S. company is done in U.S. dollars—the unit of measurement in the United States. The accountant normally becomes involved in foreign transactions and operations in one of two ways:

1. Foreign currency transactions—transactions that require settlement in a foreign currency, including buying and selling, borrowing or lending, and investing.
2. Translation of financial statements of a foreign subsidiary or branch office whose statements are denominated in foreign currency.

Foreign currency transactions are accounted for as follows according FASB No. 52:

1. Receivables, payable, revenues, and expenses are translated and recorded in dollars at the spot rate existing on the transaction date. An exchange rate that indicates the price of foreign currencies on a particular date for immediate delivery is called a spot rate.
2. At the balance-sheet date, receivables and payable are adjusted to the spot rate.
3. Exchange gains and losses resulting from changes in the spot rate from one point in time to another are usually recognized in the current period's income statement.

Accounting required for forward exchange contracts depends upon management's intent when entering into the contract. A summary of accounting for forward exchange contracts is shown here.

Type of forward contract	Accounting for exchange gain or loss	Accounting for forward contract premium or discount
1. Hedge of an exposed position	Generally no net exchange gain or loss	Amortized against operating income over term of contract
2. Hedge of an identifiable foreign currency commitment	Deferred to transaction date; then adjustment of dollar basis of	May be deferred to transactin date as with exchange gain or loss
3. Speculation	Included currently in income statement	No separate accounting recognition

Accounting principles for purposes of consolidation, combination, or reporting on the equity method for foreign operations (branches, subsidiaries) can be summarized in broad terms as follows:

1. Foreign currency financial statements must be in conformity with generally accepted accounting principles before they are translated.
2. The FUNCTIONAL CURRENCY of an entity is the currency of the primary economic environment in which the foreign entity operates. The functional currency may be the currency of the country in which the foreign entity is located, the U.S. dollar, or the currency of another foreign country. If the foreign entity's operations are self-contained and integrated in a particular country and are not dependent on the economic environment of the parent company, the functional currency is the foreign currency. The functional currency of a foreign company would be the U.S. dollar if the foreign operation is an integral component or extension of the parent company's operations. The daily operations and cash flows of the foreign operation of the foreign entity are dependent on the economic environment of the parent company.
3. If the functional currency is the local currency of the foreign entity, the current rate method is used to translate foreign currency financial statements into U.S. dollars. All assets and liabilities are translated by using the current exchange rate at the balance sheet dates. This method provides that all financial relationship remain the same in both local currency and U.S. dollars. Owners' equity is translated by using historical rates; revenues and gains and expenses and losses are translated at the rates in existence during the period when the transactions occurred. The translation adjustment which result from the application of these rules are reported as a separate component in owners' equity of the U.S. company's consolidated balance sheet (or parent-only balance sheet if consolidation was not deemed appropriate.)
4. If the functional currency is the reporting currency (the U.S. dollar), the foreign currency financial statements are remeasured into U.S. dollars using the temporal method. All foreign currency balances are restated to U.S. dollars using both historical and current exchange rates. Foreign currency balances which show prices from past transactions are translated by using historical rates; foreign currency balances which show prices from current transactions are translated by using the current exchange rate. Translation gains or losses that result from the remeasurement process are reported on the U.S. company's consolidated income statement.

Proponents of the current rate method maintain that the use of this method will reflect most clearly the true economic facts since presenting all revenue and expense items at current rates reflects the actual earnings (those that can be remitted to the home country) of a foreign operation at that time. Also, stating all items at the current rate retains the operating relationships after the translating intact with those that existed before the translation. Critics of the current rate method claim that since fixed assets are translated at the current rate and not at the rate that existed when they were acquired, the translated amounts do not represent historical costs and are not consistent with generally accepted accounting principles.

Since the temporal method states monetary assets at the current rate, proponents of this method claim that this reflects the foreign currency's ability to obtain U.S. dollars. Since historical rates are used for long-term assets and liabilities, the historical cost principle is maintained. However, the use of the temporal method distorts financial statement relationships that exist before and after remeasurement.

The appended exhibits illustrate the temporal method and the current rate method. The temporal method illustration assumes that the functional currency of a Canadian subsidiary is the U.S. dollar. The current rate method assumes that the functional currency of the Canadian subsidiary is the Canadian dollar. The Canadian subsidiary was established at the beginning of the year. The current rate of exchange is $.80; the historical rate used for the building and common stock is $.90; the average rate for the year is $.85. The computation of the exchange loss for the year is shown in an accompanying schedule. The temporal method's $10,406 exchange loss occurred because the subsidiary held net monetary assets denominated in Canadian dollars when the Canadian dollar decreased in value relative to the U.S. dollar. The current rate method's translation adjustment for the year which results from the impact of rate changes on the net monetary position during the year is also shown in a separate schedule.

The exposure to exchange translation losses is not usually the same as the economic exposure to exchange losses. Economic exposure is due to many factors including rates of inflation, regulation, interest rate changes, and other factors. Translation exposure is related to what accounts have to be translated at current exchange rates. A company's exposed position represent the net balance of all accounts translated at current exchange rates. Accounts translated at historical rates are not exposed to translation adjustments because the same conversion rate is used each year. The net translation exposure position of a firm can be explained as follows:

Items contributing to exposure:

FORFAITING

Temporal Method—Remeasurement Under FASB Statement No. 52

	Canadian dollars	Exchange rate	U.S. dollars
Balance Sheet:			
Assets:			
Cash	C$ 77,555	.80	US$ 62,044
Rent receivable	25,000	.80	20,000
Building (net)	475,000	.90	427,500
	C$577,555		US$509,544
Liabilities and equity:			
Accounts payable	C$ 6,000	.80	US$ 4,800
Salaries payable	4,000	.80	3,200
Common stock	555,555	.90	500,000
Retained earnings	12,000	See below	1,544
	C$577,555		US$509,544
Income Statement:			
Rent revenue	C$125,000		US$106,250
Operating expenses	(28,000)	.85	(23,800)
Depreciation expense	(25,000)	.85	(22,500)
Translation exchange loss	—	.90	(10,406)
Net income	C$ 72,000		US$ 49,544
Retained Earnings Statement:			
Balance, January 1, Year 1	C$ —		US$ —
Net income	72,000	See above	49,544
Dividends	(60,000)		(48,000)
Balance, December 31, Year 1	C$ 12,000	.80	US$ 1,544

Computation of Translation Exchange Loss for S for Year 1

	Canadian dollars	Exchange rate	U.S. dollars
Net monetary position, January 1, Year 1	C$ —		US$ —
Plus:			
Cash invested by P	555,555	.90	500,000
Cash and receivable from rents	125,000	.85	106,250
Less:			
Cash disbursed for building	(500,000)	.90	(450,000)
Cash disbursed and liabilities incurred for operating expenses	(28,000)	.85	(23,800)
Cash disbursed for dividends	(60,000)	.80	(48,000)
Subtotal			84,450
Net monetary position, December 31, Year 1	C$ 92,555	.80	74,044
Translation exchange loss			US$ 10,406

Source: Belcher, Finley E., and Stickney, Clyde P., *Business Combinations and Consolidated Financial Statements,* Richard D. Irwin, Homewood, IL.

a. Current assets (not including prepaid expenses).
b. Investments denominated in fixed amounts of local currency (German marks; English pounds).
c. Long-term receivables (net of allowances).

Items lessening exposure:

a. Inventories
b. U.S. dollar assets included in a, b, and c above.
c. Local currency liabilities.

The algebraic sum of the items listed represents the company's

Translation of Foreign Financial Statements—All-Current Methodology

	Canadian dollars	Exchange rate	U.S. dollars
Balance Sheet:			
Assets:			
Cash	C$ 77,555	.80	US$ 62,044
Rent receivable	25,000	.80	20,000
Building (net)	475,000	.80	462,044
	C$ 577,555		US$ 509,544
Liabilities and equity:			
Accounts payable	C$ 6,000	.80	US$ 4,800
Salaries payable	4,000	.80	3,200
Common stock	555,555	.90	500,000
Translation adjustment			(59,156)
Retained earnings	12,000	See below	13,200
	C$ 577,555		US$ 462,044
Income Statement:			
Rent revenue	C$125,000		US$ 106,250
Operating expenses	(28,000)	.85	(23,800)
Depreciation expense	(25,000)	.85	(21,500)
Net income	C$ 72,000	.90	US$ 61,200
Retained Earnings Statement:			
Balance, January 1, Year 1	C$ —		US$ —
Net income	72,000	See above	61,200
Dividends	(60,000)		(48,000)
Balance, December 31, Year 1	C$ 12,000	.80	US$ 13,200

Computation of Translation Adjustment for S for Year 1

	Canadian dollars	Exchange rate	U.S. dollars
Net asset position, January 1, Year 1	C$ —	.90	US$ —
Plus:			
Cash invested by P	555,555	.85	500,000
Net income	72,000	.80	61,200
Less:			
Dividends	(60,000)		(48,000)
Subtotal			513,200
Net asset position, December 31, Year 1	C$567,555	.80	454,044
Translation adjustment			US$ 59,156

Source: Belcher, Finley E., and Stickney, Clyde P., *Business Combinations and Consolidated Financial Statements,* Richard D. Irwin, Homewood, IL.

net exposure to risk of loss (or exposure to gain) through exchange fluctuations. An exposed position can usually be managed by controlling the company's position in listed securities and by the use of forward exchange contracts.

See FOREIGN EXCHANGE RISK; FOREIGN EXCHANGE STRATEGIES.

FORFAITING A nonrecourse financing of receivables similar to factoring; called "forfaitierung" in Austria and Germany. While a factor normally purchases a company's short-term receivables, a forfait bank purchases notes that are long-term receivables with maximum maturities of eight years. The forfaiting bank has no recourse to the seller of the goods, but gets the notes at a substantial discount for cash.

The Comptroller of the Currency has reported that an increasing number of U.S. banks active in international financing have in recent years been financing receivables from Eastern European and developing countries by forfaiting. The centers of forfaiting are Zurich and Vienna, where many large banks, including U.S. banks, provide forfaiting through either their branches or specialized subsidiaries.

Forfaiting is used when government export credits or credit guarantees are not available or when a seller does not extend long-term credits to areas such as Eastern Europe. Forfaiting also is an important method of financing for small or medium-sized companies because it enables them to negotiate transactions that would normally exceed their financial capabilities. By using forfaiting, small or medium-sized firms can immediately sell their long-term receivables without recourse.

The *Handbook for National Bank Examiners* of the Comptroller of the Currency calls for the examiner to review the bank's forfaiting activities carefully, to determine whether long-term receivables have been purchased from firms in countries prone to frequent political changes and fluctuations in exchange rates. Also, the other risks peculiar to factoring are also present in forfaiting, along with the risks associated with the long-term nature of the receivables purchased.

FORFEITURE The loss or relinquishment of money deposited to secure or bind a contract or part payment of a purchase, as a penalty for nonperformance or noncompliance. In the sale of stock by subscription on the installment basis, default in payments due under the subscription agreement in various states would result in forfeiture of the amounts paid.

Forfeiture of bank charter would occur for a variety of reasons specified in banking statutes, including in the case of national banks for such violations as prohibited affiliation with securities dealers; false certification of checks by directors, officers, or employees; refusal to furnish information for and permit examinations of affiliates; and disregard of the permitted number of bank directors. Basic forfeiture would occur if a national bank's directors knowingly violated or permitted any officers, agents, or employees of the bank to violate any of the national banking laws; such forfeiture is effected through court action by the Comptroller of the Currency (12 U.S.C. 93).

FORGED INSTRUMENTS Checks, drafts, bills of exchange, notes, bonds, stock certificates, and paper money with false signatures or false denominations; false instruments with genuine signatures; or COUNTERFEITS. To minimize losses due to forged stock and bond certificates, the New York Stock Exchange requires all certificates of stocks and bonds listed to be engraved with quality and standards satisfactory to the Department of Stock List. Further, the exchange requires the company applying for listing to maintain a separate and independent transfer agent or office and registry office or registrar in the financial district, the function of the registrar being to authenticate certificates issued and check against overissuance of authorized amounts. Also, all certificates (stocks and registered bonds) must carry signatures, guaranteed by a member, member firm, or commercial bank or trust company having principal office in the financial district of New York City.

The Uniform Commercial Code specifies that the bank's customer, upon receipt of the usual monthly bank statement accompanied by canceled checks or other honored items, shall within a reasonable time examine the items to discover whether any of the customer's signatures are forgeries or unauthorized or whether any of the items have been altered. If the customer fails to do so, the bank cannot be charged for honoring such a challenged item as to unauthorized signature or any alteration if the bank also establishes that it suffered a loss by reason of such failure. Moreover, if the customer fails to discover and report the unauthorized signature or alteration after the first item and statement were available to the customer for a reasonable period not exceeding 14 calendar days, the bank cannot be held liable for any further payments made to the wrongdoer before the bank is notified by the customer. The foregoing protection for the bank does not apply if the customer establishes lack of ordinary care on the bank's part in paying the items. But regardless of care or lack of care of either the bank or the customer, failure by the customer to discover and report unauthorized signature or alterations one year from the time the statement and items are made available or failure within three years to discover and report any unauthorized endorsement will preclude action against the bank (Sec. 4-406, Uniform Commercial Code).

Since paying a forged check is one of the chief risks with which a bank is confronted, banks should educate their depositors to protect their blank checks as a means of combatting this risk. Depositors should keep blank checkbooks under control and be able to account for each of the series. Checks should not be signed in blank nor should blank checks be given away to strangers.

See ALTERATION, FORGERY, SIGNATURE DEPARTMENT.

FORGERY In its broadest interpretation, "making or altering any document with the intention of prejudicing another person."

A statutory definition of forgery considers it to include false making, counterfeiting, and the alteration, erasure, or obliteration of a genuine instrument, in whole or in part, the false making or counterfeiting of the signature of a party or witness, and the placing or connecting together with intent to defraud different parts of several genuine instruments.

Thus placing a false signature on a check, raising the amount, or changing the payee's name or the number of the check with intention to defraud constitutes forgery. The alteration of a passbook entry likewise is forgery. Forgery is a statutory crime and is punishable by imprisonment. The following precautions against check forgeries should be taken:

1. Never cash a check for a stranger until he is identified by you through someone you know and upon whom you can rely.
2. Never accept a check just because it looks businesslike. Criminals frequently counterfeit checks of well-known concerns.
3. Always verify bank certifications through the certifying bank. Certifications are frequently counterfeited by criminals.
4. Never do what a stranger suggests in order to identify him, unless the suggestion leads to identification through someone you know and upon whom you can rely. He may have arranged with an accomplice to give you misinformation.
5. Never sign a check in blank or make it out payable to cash or bearer unless absolutely necessary.
6. Never leave your checkbook or canceled vouchers where anyone else can get hold of them.
7. Always write your checks carefully with good ink, typewriter, or checkwriter which will indent the paper. Begin each line at the left-hand side and leave no spaces between your words.
8. Be sure to have a safe place for delivery of your business mail. Do not depend on the type of box that can be easily opened by a criminal.
9. If possible never let anyone else check your bank book with paid and canceled checks returned from the bank. This is the one thing that every businessperson should do monthly and personally whenever possible.

See ALTERATION, COUNTERFEITS, FORGED INSTRUMENTS, RAISED BILLS.

FORMULA PLANS Plans calling automatically for initial purchases and subsequent changes in investment holdings according to prescribed formulas which seek to avoid errors or fallible judgment by substituting therefor a set of allegedly objective signals indicating when to buy, when to sell, and the proportions of classifications of securities to maintain in the portofolio—defensive and aggressive—acting inversely to each other.

Leffler (*The Stock Market*) classifies formula plans as follows:

1. Nonnormal value formula plans.
   a. Dollar averaging.
   b. Constant dollar plan.
   c. Constant ratio plan.
   d. Ten percent plan.
2. Normal value formula plans with variable ratios.
   a. Plans based on price.
      (1) Moving average plans.
      (2) Trend plans.
   b. Plans based on intrinsic values.
      (1) Yield plan.
      (2) Price-earnings plan.
      (3) Two-signal plan.
      (4) Earnings-yield plan.
      (5) Price-dividend plan.

1. **Dollar averaging.** *See* the discussion of this technique under DOLLAR AVERAGING. Although sometimes classified as a formula plan, dollar averaging does not involve a basic technique

FORMULA PLANS

characteristic of formula plans, the division of the portfolio into defensive and aggressive proportions acting inversely to each other. It is a simple technique for accumulation, by investing a constant sum regularly or a sufficient sum to accumulate a fixed number of shares regularly, ignoring the problem of pricing, taking prices at random as of the date of purchase.

2. **Constant dollar plan.** This idea involves keeping a constant dollar sum invested in the stock (aggressive) proportion, the rest of the portfolio being in high-grade defensive securities (such as high-grade bonds and preferred stocks). An initial problem is definition of the starting proportions of such aggressive (stock) and defensive (high-grade fixed return) securities, whether it shall be 50/50, 60/40, 70/30, etc. Unless accurate relative to market conditions, these normal proportions might be conducive to poor results, as they might thereby carry a built-in distortion. Judgment, therefore, cannot be avoided in the definition of the starting proportions of defensive and aggressive securities.

Assuming the starting proportions are 50/50 and $10,000 each is invested in aggressive and defensive portions of the portfolio, a further necessary decision is when to trim the current market values to the starting constant sum for stocks: at regular intervals, whenever a designated stock average changes by a prescribed percentage, or whenever the stock portion of the portfolio rises by a prescribed percentage. Assume it is decided that the original value of $10,000 for the stocks is to be restored when it rises 50%. If such a rise occurs, it is assumed that the defensive portion of the portfolio would have declined by approximately some smaller percentage, as the aggressive and defensive proportions are supposed to act inversely to each other. Thus, with the stocks worth $15,000 and the bonds worth $9,000, $5,000 of the stocks would be sold and the proceeds reinvested in the bonds. It would be unrealistic to assume that the bond portfolio would remain absolutely stable at the original starting amount, $10,000, in the event of a 50% rise in stocks, as such a stock rise is usually accompanied by attraction of funds from the bond markets if not a rise in interest rates incidental to increased bank credit financing the rise in business activity implied. Either factor would influence high-grade bond market prices downward.

This change causes the ratio of respective stocks and bonds to be higher for bonds, but the important principle of this plan is to restore the original amount invested in stocks, the defensive portion acting as a foil for the stock change. The advantage is that profits will be taken on stocks as they rise above the starting amount and the proceeds reinvested in bonds at their lower prices and higher yields. Subsequently, should stocks' value decline 50%, to 5,000, accompanied by some rise in bonds (say to $15,000), $5,000 of the bonds would be sold and the proceeds reinvested in the stocks to restore the stock amount to $10,000. The advantage in so doing is the taking of profits on the bonds and the reinvesting in the stocks at their lower prices and higher yields. Thus, whether the stock market is going up or down, capital gains in either stocks or bonds would be taken, and yields during the period of holding would increase.

Stated thus aggregatively the plan sounds unbeatable, but the problems in practice include: (1) actual selection of the individual issues to serve for aggressive and defensive portions presents a problem of judgment in itself to assure representative action; (2) changes in amount would be across the board proportionately on all issues held, but unfortunately specific issues rarely act in perfect symmetry; thus, when their category (aggressive or defensive) has risen in value, any issues that might have actually declined would be adjusted actually by a higher percentage individually than the category's average; (3) after a period of time, a number of odd lots are bound to result from across-the-board adjustment. Then too, like all formula plans which involve taking profits as they occur according to the formula, during a period of sustained rise in stock prices, for example, the stock portion might already have been substantially sold at lower prices.

3. **Constant ratio plan.** This is a variant of the constant dollar plan, involving the maintenance of the normal ratios between the aggressive (stock) and defensive (high-grade bond) portions of the portfolio. Thus, with starting ratios of 50/50 ($10,000 each in stocks and bonds), if stocks rise to $15,000 and bonds decline to $9,000, the total portfolio is adjusted to $12,000 each in stocks and bonds ($15,000 plus $9,000 divided by 2, to achieve the 50/50 starting ratios).

4. **Ten percent plan.** Under Drew's description of this plan (Garfield A. Drew, *New Methods for Profit in the Stock Market*), the value of a stock portfolio picked as trading media is calculated weekly and the weekly values averaged on a monthly basis. Stocks are then sold if the monthly average declines 10% from the previous highest level; no purchases are resumed until the monthly average again rises 10% above the lowest level reached after the sales.

This is a trading plan, getting out on a downward trend, ostensibly signaled by the 10% decline, and getting aboard on an upward trend. In a sustained primary uptrend (using Dow theory terminology), interrupted by secondary reactions of such size, such a plan entails a built-in delay.

5. **Moving average plans.** These plans compute the central or core moving average of a suitable index, such as the Dow Jones (DJ) industrials average, for a long term, say 120 months. The portfolio is divided into aggressive (stock) and defensive (high-grade bonds) portions, say 50-50 at normal. As the DJ industrials rise 10% above the 120-month central value, stocks are sold so as to reduce the proportions to 40% stocks, 60% bonds, 30/70, 20/80, 10/90, and finally 0/100, with each successive 10% rise. Proceeds of the stock sales are reinvested in the defensive portion of the portfolio, which presumably would be declining as the stocks rose and thus creating attractive purchases in the light of expected subsequent turnaround. No sales of stocks would be made except on rise in the average above the normal or central value. Conversely, no purchases of stocks would be made except on drop in the average below the normal or central value. In the E. I. du Pont & Co. version of this plan, a built-in delay of one month is observed, no changes being made unless the core value of the DJ industrials moves in the same direction two months in a row. (Actually, since daily prices for a month must be averaged for a full month, there is even greater delay.)

6. **Trend plans.** These plans plot the trend of the indicator, such as the Dow Jones industrials average, over the long term. For example, the Keystone Custodian Funds, Inc. version plotted the trend for the Dow Jones average from 1897 to 1940, allowing for secular growth of 3% per year. A central zone around this trend line, 15 percentage points wide, was normal, at which level the proportion of aggressive (e.g., stock funds of the Keystone organization) and defensive (e.g., high-grade funds of the Keystone organization) would be held 50/50 in dollar amounts. Three more zones of equal width were plotted above and three more zones of similar width below the normal or Zone 4. As the DJ average penetrates Zones 5, 6, and 7, the proportion of aggressive securities is reduced to 40%, 30%, 20%, and finally 10%, the proceeds being reinvested in the defensive securities to increase their proportions to 60%, 70%, 80%, and finally 90%; and vice versa if the DJ average declines and penetrates the zones below.

The Vassar College variation similarly was based on the normal long-term trend of the Dow Jones industrials average, plotted from 1897 to 1947, eliminating abnormal levels of 1929 and 1932. As the DJ average rose above normal, changes would be made (sale of the stock aggressive portion) on every 15-point rise in the average, to the extreme position of zero stocks, 100% bonds, and vice versa.

The Yale plan variant was begun 1938, starting with a ratio of 70% in high-grade bonds and preferred stocks, and 30% common stocks (defensive and aggressive portions). Whenever the market value of the aggressive portion rose to a ratio of 40%, it was reduced by sales back to 35%. Whenever the market value of the aggressive portion fell to 20% of total portfolio, purchases of aggressive stocks would be made to restore the aggressive portion to 25%.

The long, sustained bull market rise of 1953-1956 found these formula plans with liquidated aggressive portions and the bull market continuing.

7. **Intrinsic value plans.** Instead of taking a stock average or market values as the indicator of normal, these plans take long-term (say 120-month) earnings and/or yields' moving average. Graham's formula to take average earnings of the Dow Jones industrials for ten years and capitalize them on the basis of twice the yield on high-grade bonds prevailing, to give the normal intrinsic value level for the Dow Jones industrials.

ENCYCLOPEDIA OF BANKING AND FINANCE

Stocks would be sold when the DJ average reached 120% of this intrinsic level and bought when at 80% thereof. The Genstein variant would take average of the Dow Jones industrials for ten years; divide this by the average dividends of the DJ industrials for the same ten years; and multiply the result by current dividends of the DJ industrials to arrive at normal intrinsic value level. Stocks would be sold when the DJ industrials average reached 125% of this normal and bought when it dipped to 80% thereof.

The same principle could be applied to normal price-earnings ratios. Leffler's "two-signal plan" is to establish normal yield and price-earnings ratios and subjectively define a very high level and a very low level for each of these two indicators. Stocks would be sold when the DJ industrials, the basis for the two indicators, reached the very high signal of one of the indicators and this was confirmed by the other indicator, and vice versa.

Summary. Formula plans are attempts to substitute for subjective judgment the automatic signals of the formula. Definition of the formula itself, however, involves judgment. Moreover, even if the formula is initiated with the best of judgment, some formulas above have been rendered obsolete by unusual action of the security markets. Thus many investors who simply dollar averaged in the long, sustained bull market of 1953-1956 wound up with better results than under the formulas, as did many who simply bought and held. The aggressive view is that formulas calling for taking of profits as soon as stocks begin rising reduce profits and that there is no substitute for proper timing.

See INVESTMENT.

BIBLIOGRAPHY

Although the popularity of formula plans has diminished in recent years, primary works on the subject in its heyday are still applicable for reference.

CARPENTER, H. G. *Investment Timing by Formula Plans*, 1943.
COTTLE, C. C., and WHITMAN, W. T. *Investment Timing: The Formula Plan Approach*, 1953.
DINCE, R. R. "Another View of Formula Planning." *Journal of Finance*, December, 1964.
———. "Portfolio Income: A Test of a Formula Plan." *Journal of Financial and Quantitative Analysis*, September, 1966.
DREW, G. A. *New Methods for Profit in the Stock Market*, 1954.
GENSTEIN, E. S. *Stock Market Profit Without Forecasting*, 1954.
LEFFLER, G. L., and FARWELL, L. C. *The Stock Market*, 3rd ed., 1963.
PERSONS, R. H., Jr. *Handbook of Formula Plans in the Stock Market*, 1967.
TOMLINSON, L. *Practical Formulas for Successful Investing*, 1955.
ZUKOSKI, C. F., Jr. "Ten Years of Investment Under Formula Plans." *Commercial and Financial Chronicle*, February 14, 1952.

FORTNIGHTLY SETTLEMENT See SETTLEMENT DAYS.

FORWARD BUYING OR SELLING In commodity trading, the purchase or sale of a spot commodity for deferred delivery instead of immediate delivery.

See SPOT PRICE.

FORWARDING AGENT A person or concern engaged in the business of collecting, transferring, warehousing, and delivering goods.

Part IV of the Interstate Commerce Act, added by an act approved May 16, 1942 (56 Stat. 284, 4. U.S.C. Ch. 13), subjected freight forwarders to regulation of the statute and of the Interstate Commerce Commission. A freight forwarder is any person other than a carrier holding out to the general public to transport or to provide transportation of property for compensation in interstate commerce and in the ordinary and usual course of the activity: (1) assembling and consolidating shipments of property and performing break-bulk and distributing operations with respect to consolidated shipments, (2) assuming responsibility for the transportation of such property from point of receipt to point of destination, and (3) utilizing, for the whole or any part of the transportation of such shipments, the services of carriers. Freight forwarders in foreign commerce are under the jurisdiction of the Federal Maritime Commission.

FORWARD CONTRACT A cash contract by which two parties agree to the exchange of an asset (for example, foreign exchange) to be delivered by the seller to the buyer at some specified future date.

Forward contracts are especially important in the foreign exchange markets because they allow individuals and firms to protect themselves against foreign exchange risk. Suppose a company is going to import electronic parts from a French manufacturer in three months time at a price fixed in terms of francs. If the company waits for three months to buy the francs that it knows it is going to need, it assumes foreign exchange risk: the dollar price of the franc may appreciate, raising the dollar price of the electronic parts. Instead of assuming this risk, the company may choose to purchase a forward contract today for the delivery of francs three months from now. Then even if the price of francs appreciates, the company has guaranteed that it will be able to purchase the electronic parts at a price in dollars that it is willing to pay.

In the foreign exchange market, the forward price and the spot price are linked by the interest parity condition. This condition says that the percentage difference between the forward rate (F) and the spot rate (S), called the forward premium, will equal the difference between the real (inflation adjusted) foreign interest rate (i_f) and the real domestic interest rate (i_d):

$$\frac{(F - S)}{S} = i_f - i_d$$

If, for example, the real foreign interest rate is 10 percent and the real domestic rate is 8 percent, the interest parity condition implies that the forward rate will be 2 percentage points higher than the spot rate.

This condition holds because rational investors who need foreign currency in the future always have the option of buying the currency now on the spot market and investing it in an interest-earning foreign bank account until needed or buying a forward contract for the future purchase and delivery of the foreign currency and investing the funds in an interest-earning domestic bank account until the foreign currency is delivered. The normal operations of efficient markets and rational investors insures that the expected cost of these two alternatives will always be equal; therefore, the difference between the spot rate and the forward rate reflects differences in real interest rates.

A forward contract is very similar to a futures contract, but there are two important differences. First, forward contracts are negotiated between two parties so that they may reflect individualized terms and conditions. In contrast, a futures contract is traded on an exchange. The exchange sets all of the terms of the contract except price, including size of the contract, delivery date, grade of commodity, etc. Second, forward contracts are not marked to market each day by an exchange as is the case with futures contracts. As a result, gains and losses on forward contracts are recognized only when the contract matures, while holders of future contracts must recognize the rise or fall in the value of their contracts as they are marked to market by the exchange.

FORWARD MOVEMENT A market expression which refers to a general rise in the price level of securities or commodities in which all listings participate. The expression may refer to a rising price tendency for the day or for a period of time.

FOUNDATIONS As defined by The Foundation Center, nonprofit, nongovernmental organizations set up as corporations or trusts usually under state laws to receive funds (but not normally to solicit contributions from the public) and to distribute funds for the advancement of human welfare.

The number of foundations in the U.S. organized for nonprofit charitable, educational, and scientific purposes increased during the past three decades from a few to relatively large numbers with substantial financial worth as the result of rise in security values. Stimulus for this growth had been provided by beneficent tax treatment, which provided for tax exemption under certain requirements. Motivations for foundations have included realizing substantial tax savings in the settlement of large estates and perpetuating particular concentrations of holdings, as well as bona fide interest in the eleemosynary purposes.

Of the nearly 26,000 foundations nationwide in the 1980s, ranging

FOUNDERS' SHARES

in size from under $10,000 to over $4.8 billion (the Ford Foundation), more than 90% are known as independent or "family" foundations. Other types of foundations include operating foundations, whose primary purpose is to carry out their own charitable works; company-sponsored or corporate foundations; and community foundations, which derive their funds from many donors and are generally classified as public charities under the tax laws. There are less than 300 of this type.

The growth of foundations accelerated after the imposition of federal income taxes and reached a peak in the 1950s. As security values rose, relatively modest foundations grew in size to substantial financial worth. Growth was encouraged by favorable tax treatment, which not only exempted charities from income tax but also permitted deductions from income, gift, and estate taxes. While tax incentives provided an additional stimulus, the primary motivation for creating a foundation was more deeply rooted in the personal philosophy of the wealthy and a desire to establish a vehicle for systematic giving.

The Tax Reform Act of 1969 imposed tighter restrictions upon foundations, resulting in a drop in new formation in the early 1970s. After modification, most recently in 1985, current regulations include: (1) a 2% excise tax on net investment income; (2) an annual minimum payout rate of 5% of the market value of net investment assets; and (3) a variety of tax penalties for such acts as self dealing, excessive business holding, jeopardy investments, and improper grant activities or taxable expenditures. Federal law also requires private foundations to file an annual information return (990-PF) that is publicly available.

Recent Trends: After a decade long decline that started in 1972 attributed to inflation, poor investment strategies, and a higher payout requirement under the Tax Reform Act of 1969, foundation assets began to show real growth after 1981. The easing of inflation in the mid-1980s allowed for solid gains in the constant dollar value of both assets and grants.

BIBLIOGRAPHY

EDIE, JOHN A. *First Steps in Starting a Foundation.* Council on Foundations, 1987.

FREEMAN, DAVID F. *The Handbook on Private Foundations.* Council on Foundations, 1981.

ODENDAHL, TERESA, Ed, et al. *America's Wealthy and the Future of Foundations.* The Foundation Center, 1987.

FOUNDATION CENTER. *National Data Book,* 1984-1987, Editions 98-12.

FOUNDERS' SHARES A special form of stock issued to the founders or promoters of a company in remuneration of the promoters' services, as distinguished from common or ordinary stock. Founders' stock is a term primarily used in English finance and corresponds approximately with PROMOTERS' STOCK in the United States. It is known as management or DEFERRED STOCK.

401(K) PLANS A tax sheltered retirement plan; also called cash or deferred arrangements (CODAs). Funds placed in this plan are not taxable to the employee and is deductible by the company; contributions and earnings increase tax-free until they are withdrawn. Lump-sum distributions from the plan currently qualify for ten-year averaging when paid out. Deferred salaries can be distributed only upon retirement, separation from service, death, disability, the employee's reaching the age of 59 $^1/_2$, or for hardship reasons (e.g., to meet down payments on principal residence and college tuition). A 10 percent excise tax is imposed on early withdrawals unless used for deductible medical expenses (in excess of the 7.5 percent of adjusted gross income limitation). An individual must start withdrawing 401(k) money by age 70 $^1/_2$. Employees can take a lump-sum distribution, but many plans also provide for the purchase of annuity or installment payments.

401(k) plans must be designed to benefit all employees and comply with nondiscrimination rules and participation standards based on the the percentage of income deferred by both the highly paid and lower-paid employees. The percentage deferred by the highest paid one-third must not be more than 150% of the percentage of salary deferred by other employees, or 250% of the percentage of salary deferred by other employees (but only if that percentage is not more than 3% greater than the salary deferred by other employees.) The plan must provide for immediate vesting.

Employee contributions are limited to $7,627 in 1989. Total contributions are limited to the lesser of 15 percent of compensation or $30,000.

401(k) plans are similar to an IRA. However, in a 401(k), the employee can borrow from the plan the lesser of $50,000 or one-half of his or her account balance. If the balance is less than $20,000, the employee can borrow up to $10,000. Generally, such loans must be repaid within five years and a reasonable interest rate must be charged. Also, 401(k) investment options are limited to options the company selects. There is also no employer matching contribution with an IRA.

A 401(k) can be transferred if an employee leaves his or her present position and transfers to another company if the company accepts rollovers. The balance can also be moved into an IRA, or in many cases it can be left at your former employer until you are ready to use it.

FRACTIONAL CURRENCY Coins having a denomination of less than one dollar. The Coinage Act of 1965 authorized a basic change in the composition of dimes, quarters, and half dollars. Formerly, these coins contained 90% silver. Because of a growing worldwide shortage of silver, it became necessary for the United States to reduce the silver content of its coins. In 1965, silver was eliminated from the dime and the quarter, and the silver content of the half dollar was reduced to 40%. In 1970, total elimination of silver from the half dollar was authorized by P.L. 91-607 (December 31, 1970), and the silverless half dollars first appeared in 1971.

Minor coins, consisting of the cupronickel five-cent coins, and the copper-zinc one-cent coins, complete the fractional currency system. The one-cent coin's composition was changed in 1982 from former 95% copper and 5% zinc, to 97.5% zinc with a 2.5% copper coating.

See MINOR COINS, SUBSIDIARY COINAGE, TOKEN MONEY.

FRACTIONAL LOTS *See* ODD LOT.

FRACTIONAL RESERVE BANK Although the Fed can directly change the monetary base, the total change in the money supply resulting from an open market operation requires assistance from the entire banking system. The U.S. banking system, like banking systems in every nation, is based on fractional reserve requirements. Under a fractional reserve banking system a portion (fraction) of every deposit is held in reserve. The purpose of these reserves is to ensure that banks are able to meet their obligations to customers.

FRANCHISE A privilege conferred by a governmentality, usually a municipality, by which a corporation is vested with powers to engage in a public utility enterprise usually under quasi-monopolistic conditions. A franchise is a grant of power given to the grantee corporation to engage in a business which involves the exercise of the right of eminent domain. This includes all public service businesses (gas, water, electricity, street railway, bus, telephone companies, etc.). Public utility corporations are subject to the conditions imposed by the franchise and a violation of its provisions results in its FORFEITURE. Most states provide for the regulation of their public utilities through a PUBLIC SERVICE COMMISSION.

The principal features covered by a franchise are

1. Duration, which may be fixed (limited), perpetual, or indeterminate (during good behavior)
2. Compensation, which may be a sum of money or performance of certain services
3. Rates
4. Service
5. Improvements, which in most cases revert to the grantor upon the expiration of the franchise
6. Labor conditions and strikes
7. Capitalization
8. Reversion to grantor.

The conditions imposed in a franchise are important in judging public utility investments, the chief points to be considered being that the bonds of these companies should mature within the life of the franchise and should not exceed the replacement value of the company's fixed property.

Business franchising: In the business franchise, the franchisee (buyer of the franchise) for an initial franchise fee is granted the usually exclusive right to use the brand names, trademarks, patents,

ENCYCLOPEDIA OF BANKING AND FINANCE

etc., and to engage in the manufacture and/or sale or provision of product or service originated by the grantor of the franchise (franchisor), usually in a specified area (the area franchise). Thereafter, the franchisor, in consideration of an operational fee based on the franchisee's revenue or of profit on the supply of materials, products, and/or operational services and aids to the franchisee, will have a continuing managerial and operational relationship with the franchisee. From the standpoint of the franchisee, franchising provides an opportunity to start business under the sponsorship of an already established firm, using its business goodwill and operating ideas and methods.

In the late 1960s, a boom in business franchising developed, including newly established franchisors utilizing the names of well-known figures in sports for goodwill attraction, especially in the fast food field (e.g., fried chicken). Stocks of such promotions enjoyed a brief boom, followed by drastic deflation in profits and popularity. Importantly responsible for the decline in profits as the franchisor's sales of new franchises declined was the accounting practice of various franchisors of including entire franchise fees in income when granting franchises, rather than including such income as the franchisee units began operations and subjecting such income to realistic provision for losses on uncollectible notes.

FASB Statement No. 49 specifies the accounting principles to be used by the franchisor. Initial franchise fees are recognized as revenue when all material services have been substantially performed by the franchisor. Substantial performance means that there is no obligation or intent to refund any cash received or forgive any unpaid notes receivables. In effect, substantially all the initial services required by the franchise agreement have been performed. The commencement of operations is generally presumed to be the earliest point at which substantial performance has occurred, unless earlier performance can be demonstrated. At this time, revenue can be recognized under the accrual method of accounting. Continuing franchise fees are recognized as revenue by the franchisor as the fees are earned and receivable from the franchisee.

According to Technomic Inc., the (1) top 10 U.S. fast-food franchisers ranked by numbers of units (1988) and (2) top 10 U.S. fast-food franchisers ranked by average sales per unit (1988) are shown here:

Ranked by Number of Units		*Ranked by Average Sales Per Unit*	
1. McDonald's	7,907	McDonald's	$1,600,000
2. Pizza Hut	5,707	Burger King	984,000
3. Burger King	5,212	Hardee's	920,000
4. Kentucky Fried Chicken	4,899	Wendy's	759,000
5. Domino's Pizza	4,595	Arby's	610,000
6. Dairy Queen	4,556	Kentucky Fried Chicken	597,000
7. Wendy's	3,521	Taco Bell	589,000
8. Hardee's	3,076	Pizza Hut	520,000
9. Taco Bell	2,878	Domino's Pizza	485,000
10. Subway Sandwiches	2,858	Dairy Queen	408,000

See PUBLIC UTILITY STOCKS.

BIBLIOGRAPHY

Business Franchise Guide. Commerce Clearing House, Inc., Chicago, IL. Looseleaf.
CHAPLIN, D., and WILLAND, S. "Sleeping Giant." *Banker*, May, 1988.
Continential Franchise Review. Biweekly.
Franchise.
Franchise Opportunities Handbook. U.S. Department of Commerce.
Franchising in the Economy. U.S. Department of Commerce.
Franchising World.
LIPPER, A. *Financing and Investing in Private Companies*. 1987.
KOTOW, J. M. "Financing a Franchise." *Journal of Commercial Bank Lending*, April, 1988.
RAAB, S. S., and MATUSKY, G. *Blueprint for Franchising a Business*. John Wiley and Sons, Inc., New York, NY, 1987.

SELTZ, D. D. *The Compete Handbook of Franchising*, Addison-Wesley Publishing Co., Inc., Reading, MA, 1981.

FRAPS Fixed rate auction preferred stock. *See* FINANCIAL INSTRRUMENTS: RECENT INNOVATIONS.

FRAUD Fraud is a legal concept that requires a conscious knowledge of the falsity with deliberate intent to deceive. Fraud includes intentional deception, misappropriation of an enterprise's assets, and the manipulation of financial data to benefit the perpetrator (management or employee). Constructive fraud is a deceit that involves a false representation of a material fact without reasonable ground for belief that is relied on by another and results in his damage.

Major deterrents to fraudulent activities are fear of detection and punishment and the moral effect of unethical actions on the perpetrator. The fear factor is associated with the threat and effect of detection and punishment.

A reliable fraud deterrence program should be built around these barriers to fraudulent acts:

1. a well-designed organizational structure
2. sound and comprehensive internal control policies and procedures
3. competent, responsible, and alert management and supervision
4. aware and concerned corporate directors, audit committees, and corporate officers
5. competent, creative, and aggressive audit surveillance
6. comprehensive policies and procedures for dealing with fraud
7. high moral and ethical standards of officers, employees, and auditors

The discovery of fraud can be approached logically from a search for the perpetrator's:

1. *motive:* reason or incentive that moves a person to action;
2. *method:* plan, procedure, process; and
3. *opportunity:* circumstances favorable for the purpose.

The Commission on Auditors' Responsibilities addressed the question of an auditor's responsibility to a client for fraud of client personnel as follows:

Under generally accepted auditing standards the independent auditor has the responsibility, within the inherent limitations of the auditing process . . . to plan his examination . . . to search for errors or irregularities that would have a material effect on the financial statements, and to exercise due skill and care in the conduct of the examination. The auditor's search for material errors or irregularities ordinarily is accomplished by the performance of those auditing procedures that in his judgment are appropriate in the circumstances to form an opinion on the financial statements; extended auditing procedures are required if the auditor's examination indicates that material errors or irregularities may exist. . . . An independent auditor's standard report implicitly indicates his belief that the financial statements taken as a whole are not materially misstated as a result of errors or irregularities.

In tax law, tax fraud falls into two categories: civil and criminal. For civil fraud, the Internal Revenue Service can impose as a penalty an amount equal to 50 percent of the underpayment. For criminal tax fraud, finds and/or imprisonment is prescribed for conviction of various types of fraud. Conviction of civil and criminal fraud requires a specific intent on the part of the taxpayer to evade the tax. Negligence alone is not sufficient. Criminal fraud also requires willfulness (deliberately and with evil purpose). The IRS has the burden of proving fraud. Civil fraud has a penalty of 75 percent of the underpayment. Criminal fraud requires a larger degree of willful intent to evade tax.

See FOREIGN CORRUPT PRACTICES ACT; RACKETEER INFLUENCED AND CORRUPT ORGANIZATION.

BIBLIOGRAPHY

BANK ADMINISTRATION INSTITUTE. *Bank Fraud*. Bank Administration Institute, Rolling Meadows, IL. Monthly.
———. *Check Cashing Fraud Prevention Guide*, 1981.
———. *A Guide to Conducting Bank Investigations*, 1986.

Bilek, A. J. "Developing a Computer Fraud Protection Plan." *Magazine of Bank Administration*, May, 1988.
Business Crime: Criminal Liability of the Business Community. Matthew Bender & Co., Inc., New York, NY. Six looseleaf volumes.
Sherman, M. C. "Forging Ahead in the Battle Against Forgery and Fraud." *Bankers Monthly*, June, 1988.
Tax Fraud: Audits, Investigations, Prosecutions. Matthew Bender & Co., Inc., New York, NY. Two looseleaf volumes.

FRAUDULENT FINANCIAL REPORTING The National Commission on Fraudulent Financial Reporting, chaired by James C. Treadway, Jr.) was organized to identify causal factors which can lead to fraudulent financial reporting and to make recommendation to reduce the incidence of such reporting. This Treadway Commission prepared an important document in 1987: Report of the National Commission on Fraudulent Financial Reporting. Significant conclusions from this document relating to fraudulent financial reporting are summarized in this entry.

Fraudulent financial reporting refers to the intentional or reckless conduct, whether act or omission, that results in materially misleading financial statements. The report noted that fraudulent reporting can involve gross and deliberate distortion of corporate records (such as inventory count tags), or misapplication of accounting principles (failure to disclose material transactions). Fraudulent financial reporting often occurs because of conditions in the internal or external environment. The internal environment refers to poor systems of internal control, management's attitude toward ethics, and similar factors. External environment refers to industry conditions, legal and regulatory considerations, and similar factors. The cause of fraudulent financial reporting are often associated with the following factors:

Incentives:

Desire to obtain higher price from stock or debt offering.
Desire to meet the expectations of investors.
Desire to postpone dealing with financial difficulties
Personal gain, additional compensation, promotion or escape a penalty for poor performance.

Pressures:

Sudden decreases in revenue or market share.
Unrealistic budget pressures.
Financial pressure from bonus plans based on short-term economic performance.

Opportunities:

Absence of board of directors or audit committee that oversees process.
Weak or nonexistent internal accounting controls.
Unusual or complex transactions.
Accounting estimates requiring significant subjective judgment by management.
Ineffective internal audit staffs.

Effect sought: smooth earnings or overstate company assets.

Auditors assess the overall level of risk of an engagement as it relates to irregularities and illegal acts. Various factors are considered when evaluating the risk level including the following:

	Lower Risk	Higher Risk
Management oversight of financial reporting	Group	Person
Management turnover	Nominal	High
Emphasis on meeting earnings projections	Little	Very high
Reputation in business community	Honest	Improper
Profitability relative to industry	Adequate Consistent	Inadequate Inconsistent
Rate of change in industry	Stable	Rapid
Status of industry	Healthy	Distressed
Organization of operations	Centralized	Decentralized
Going-concern problems	Small	Substantial
Contentious accounting issues	None	Many
Difficult-to-audit transactions	Few	Many
Misstatements detected in prior audit	Few	Many
Relationship	Return audit	New audit

Source: D.R. Carmichael, "The Auditor's New Guide To Errors, Irregularities and Illegal Acts," *Journal of Accountancy*, September 1988.

Among the many recommendations made by the commission, emphasis was placed upon improving the tone of the top management of the company to discharge its obligation to oversee the financial reporting process. This requires that companies should maintain effective internal controls that provide reasonable assurance that fraudulent financial reporting will be prevented or detected. Written codes of corporate conduct were highly recommended as techniques for improving financial reporting. The commission also approved the establishment of mandatory independent audit committees. All public companies would be required to include in their annual reports to stockholders management reports signed by the chief executive officer and the chief accounting officer and/or the chief financial officers. The report should acknowledge management's responsibilities for the financial statements and internal control, discuss how these responsibilities were fulfilled, and provide management's assessment of the effectiveness of the company's internal controls. The chairman of the audit committee should be required to have included in the annual reports to the stockholders a letter describing the committee's responsibilities and activities during the year.

Independent public accountants should recognize their responsibility for detecting fraudulent financial reporting, especially by taking affirmative steps in each audit to assess the potential for fraudulent financial reporting and to design tests to provide reasonable assurance of detection.

The committee recommended that the SEC be given additional enforcement remedies, such as to impose civil money penalties in administrative proceedings and to seek civil money penalties from a court directly in an injunctive proceeding. The SEC should pursue criminal prosecution of fraudulent financial reporting cases and should conduct an affirmative program to promote increased criminal prosecution of fraudulent financial reporting cases by educating and assisting government officials with criminal prosecution powers.

Educators were advised to incorporate throughout the curricula knowledge and understanding of the factors that can cause fraudulent financial reporting and the strategies that can lead to a reduction in its incidence.

FREDDIE MAC A nickname for the FEDERAL HOME LOAN MORTGAGE COMPANY.

FRAZIER-LEMKE-LONG ACT FARM BANKRUPTCY ACT.

FREE BALANCE The minimum free balance for checking or nonborrowing accounts corresponds to the average balance for borrowing accounts and is the minimum amount in the account which the bank requires the depositor to maintain. In calculating service charges for checking accounts, the cost systems of most banks allow a service allowance, say of $0.10 a month for each $100 of minimum monthly balance, representing a credit for investment of demand deposits at current rates.

See TWENTY PERCENT RULE.

FREE BONDS Unpledged or unhypothecated bonds; bonds available for immediate disposal.

FREE COINAGE COINAGE of a metal into standard coins without limitation as to quantity, with full legal tender powers, for private persons. Gold was the only metal that enjoyed free coinage in the United States and in all gold standard countries. Since 1933 and the Gold Reserve Act of January 30, 1934, however, coinage of gold in the United States has been at an end, and it has been similarly ended, except for coinage intended for investment and numismatic

demand, throughout the world. Free coinage should be distinguished from GRATUITOUS COINAGE. In recent years, with activation of the Gold Commission in the U.S. to study the feasibility of restoring the gold standard, gold coinage has been one area of consideration.
See FREE SILVER.

FREE CROWD   *See* AUTOMATED BOND SYSTEM for the new electronic system of trading in bonds on the New York Stock Exchange.

FREE ENTERPRISE SYSTEM   In the United States, the free (or private) enterprise system is the basic economic system. In a free enterprise system:

1. Private citizens are free to own and operate a business.
2. The means of production (land, factories, equipment) are privately owned, although government does own and operate some enterprises such as the postal system.
3. Incentive for investors and business is the profit motive, and
4. Competition is a characteristic of the marketplace.

The terms CAPITALISM and free enterprise are often used interchangeably. Accounting serves the free enterprise economic system by providing financial data that can be used to make the economic choices that an enterprise or person must make, especially as these choices relate to the allocation of an enterprise's or investor's economic resources. Accounting also serves other economic systems.

BIBLIOGRAPHY

SMITH, A. *An Inquiry into the Nature and Causes of the Wealth of Nations.*

FREE GOLD   Under former requirement of Section 16 of the Federal Reserve Act, as amended, Federal Reserve banks were required to maintain reserves in gold certificates of not less than 25% against Federal Reserve notes. The excess of gold certificates or gold certificate credits held by Federal Reserve banks, and thus of the underlying gold stock, was "free", i.e., not tied down by such requirement. P.L. 90-269, approved March 18, 1968, eliminated this requirement completely, and thus the Federal Reserve banks became totally exempt from reserve requirements. P.L. 89-3, March 3, 1965, had eliminated the requirement of maintenance in gold certificates of not less than 25% against Federal Reserve banks' deposit liabilities.

The excess of gold stock of the U.S. over that held against gold certificates issued to Federal Reserve banks was termed "Treasury cash," but in recent years all of the U.S. holding of monetary gold has been fully monetized (reflected fully in gold certificates authorized to Federal Reserve banks by the Treasury).

See GOLD RESERVE for a discussion of the net gold position of the U.S.

FREEHOLD   An estate in land of uncertain duration; usually a life estate or fee.

FREE ITEMS   Checks, matured notes, and bankers acceptances, etc., drawn on out-of-town points which are cashed or received for deposit by a bank at par without deduction for exchange or collection charges. Local clearinghouse associations usually determine those items which may be received by members for deposit at par and those upon which exchange must be charged.
See DOMESTIC EXCHANGE.

FREE MARKET   Generally, the open market where prices are determined by free and open competition between buyers and sellers, where volume and prices are free to express truly the prevailing conditions. In the U.S., security exchanges are truly free and competitive markets, free of any trading limits as to price fluctuation or as to positions of traders, long or short. Commodity exchanges, however, are subject to daily price fluctuation limits and, for certain commodities, limits on positions of traders imposed by the COMMODITY EXCHANGE AUTHORITY. All forms of manipulation, by statute and administrative regulation, are forbidden on both stock and commodity exchanges.

In FOREIGN EXCHANGE, where exchange controls are imposed by various countries, floating market rates for exchange transactions relative to specified currencies may be actually floating rates "managed" by governmental intervention, forward premiums and discounts being left to the interplay of market forces in the foreign exchange markets.

FREE OF DUTY   Commodities entering a country free of duty are free from imposition of any duties, whether protective or for revenue purposes. *See* TARIFF.

FREE SILVER   A term used to denote the use of SILVER as a standard money, singly or with gold (as in BIMETALLISM). Free silver refers to the coinage of silver with full legal tender powers for private account at the mint at prescribed mint ratio, without limitation as to amount and without profit to the government. The free silver agitation was rampant in the early 1890s and was a campaign issue in 1896.
See BLAND-ALLISON ACT, FREE COINAGE.

FREE TRADE   Trade among countries without policy restrictions, as opposed to PROTECTIONISM. The January/February 1988 issue of the Federal Reserve Bank of St. Louis's *Review* contained a desription of the economics of free trade and is quoted here:

The most famous demonstration of the gains from trade appeared in 1817 in David Ricardo's "Principles of Political Economy and Taxation." We use his example involving trade between England and Portugal to demonstrate how both countries can gain from trade. The two countries produce the same two goods, wine and cloth, and the only production costs are labor costs. The figures below list the amount of labor (e.g., worker-days) required in each country to produce one bottle of wine or one bolt of cloth.

	Wine	*Cloth*
England	3	7
Portugal	1	5

Since both goods are more costly to produce in England than in Portugal, England is absolutely less efficient at producing both goods than its prospective trading partner. Portugal has an absolute advantage in both wine and cloth. At first glance, this appears to rule out mutual gains from trade; however, as we demonstrate below absolute advantage is irrelevant in discerning whether trade can benefit both countries.

The ratio of the production costs for the two goods is different in the two countries. In England, a bottle of wine will exchange for $3/7$ of a bolt of cloth because the labor content of the wine is $3/7$ of that for cloth. In Portugal, a bottle of wine will exchange for $1/5$ of a bolt of cloth. Thus, wine is relatively cheaper in Portugal than in England and, conversely, cloth is relatively cheaper in England than in Portugal. The example indicates that Portugal has a comparative advantage in wine production and England has a comparative advantage in cloth production.

The different relative prices provide the basis for both countries to gain from international trade. The gains arise from both exchange and specialization.

The gains from exchange can be highlighted in the following manner. If a Portuguese wine producer sells five bottles of wine at home, he receives one bolt of cloth. If he trades in England, he receives more than two bolts of cloth. Hence, he can gain by exporting his wine to England. English cloth-producers are willing to trade in Portugal; for every $3/7$ of a bolt of cloth they sell there, they recive just over two bottles of wine. The English gain from exporting cloth to (and importing wine from) Portugal, and the Portuguese gain from exporting wine to (and importing cloth from) England. Each country gains by exporting the good in which it has a comparative advantage and by importing the good in which it has a comparative disadvantage.

Gains from specialization can be demonstrated in the following manner. Initially, each country is producing some of both goods. Suppose that, as a result of trade, 21 units of labor are shifted from wine to cloth production in England, while, in Portugal, 10 units of labor are shifted from cloth to wine production. This reallocation of labor does not alter the total amount of labor used in the two countries; however, it causes the production changes listed below.

	Bottles of Wine	*Bolts of Cloth*
England	7	+3
Portugal	+10	2
Net	+ 3	+1

The shift of 21 units of labor to the English cloth industry raises cloth production by three bolts, while reducing wine production by seven bottles. In Portugal, the shift of 10 units of labor from cloth to wine raises wine production by 10 bottles, while reducing cloth production by two bolts. This reallocation of labor increases the total production of both goods: wine by three bottles and cloth by one bolt. This increased output will be shared by the two countries. Thus, the consumption of both goods and the wealth of both countries are increased by the specialization brought about by trade based on comparative advantage.

(Adapted from "Protectionist Trade Policies: A survey of Theory, Evidence and Rationale," *Review*, Federal Reserve Bank of St. Louis, January/February 1988.)

FREE TRADE ZONE A port designated by the government of a country for duty-free entry of any nonprohibited goods. In the zone, merchandise can be stored, displayed, and used for manufacturing within the zone and reexported without duties being paid. Duties are imposed on the merchandise when the goods pass from the zone into an area of the country subject to the customs authority.

FREE WORKING CAPITAL The margin or excess of current or quick assets over CURRENT LIABILITIES; also known as net current assets, or just WORKING CAPITAL. The amount in the aggregate of the free working capital is not as valuable an indicator of liquidity of a business as the CURRENT RATIO, or ratio of CURRENT ASSETS to current liabilities. For example, a concern with current assets of $1,000,000 and current liabilities of $500,000 has the same aggregate free working capital as a concern with $1,500,000 in current assets and $1,000,000 in current liabilities, but the first concern is obviously the stronger in liquidity, in view of its 2:1 current ratio, as compared with 1.5:1 for the second concern.

FRENDS Floating rate enhanced debt securities. *See* FINANCIAL INSTRUMENTS: RECENT INNOVATIONS.

FRICTIONAL UNEMPLOYMENT It is unrealistic to believe that the unemployment rate will be zero even in a full-employment economy. At any given time, there are a number of individuals who are literally in between jobs, and are classified as frictionally unemployed. This group includes those searching for a job as a result of leaving an old job, or entering or reentering the labor force.

FRINGE BENEFITS Health maintenance programs, group life insurance, accident/travel insurance and profit-sharing/pension plans that are made available to employees in addition to or as a supplement to wages and salaries. Such benefits are in addition to the mandatory FICA (social security) payments and unemployment and workman's compensation benefits. In 1989, fringe benefits represented between 25% to 35% of the total wages and salaries paid by depository financial institutions.

FRNs Floating rate notes.
See FINANCIAL INSTRUMENTS: RECENT INNOVATIONS.

FROZEN ACCOUNT An account that has been suspended in payment until a court order or legal process once again makes the account available for withdrawal. Generally, the account of a deceased person is frozen, pending the court order that grants disbursement authority to lawful owners or administrators of the account. An account is frozen to protect and preserve existing assets until lawful owners can be identified.

FROZEN CREDITS Coined during the post-World War I credit deflation period to denote bank loans which could not be liquidated without financially embarrassing the borrowers and which were accordingly extended to prevent bankruptcy; loans renewed or extended as a matter of accommodation to customers on account of a precipitate fall in the price of supporting collateral below the amount of the loan, with the hope of future price betterment and ultimate liquidation of the loan without loss to the lenders.
See STANDSTILL CREDITS.

FROZEN LOANS *See* FROZEN CREDITS.

FROZEN OUT This term has three meanings:

1. The condition of a speculator whose account has been closed out by a broker due to the exhaustion of his margin.
   See EXHAUST PRICE.
2. The forcing out of small stockholders by those in control. This is accomplished by frightening them into selling their holdings by circulating reports of distress, or by temporarily depressing the price of the security, or otherwise.
3. An officer or director of a corporation may be frozen out or forced out of office by a concerted plan of the stockholders or others in control.

FULL DISCLOSURE Full or adequate disclosure is an accounting concept which requires that information provided in financial accounting reports be sufficiently complete to avoid misleading users of the reports by omitting significant facts or information. The disclosure concept also refers to revealing information that would be useful in the decision-making processes of informed users. Full disclosure is required for the fair presentation of financial statements. Examples of items usually included in financial statements include accounting policies, depreciation and inventory methods, contingencies, related-party transactions, and lease and pension details.

The Accounting Principles Board in APB Statement No. 4 stated that fair presentation is met when a proper balance has been achieved between the conflicting needs to disclose important aspects of financial positions and results of operations in accordance with conventional aspects and to summarize the voluminous underlying data into a limited number of financial statement captions and supporting notes.

Many disclosures are made in the body of the financial statements and in notes (footnotes), schedules, and supplementary statements. Significant accounting policies are usually disclosed in the first note to the financial statements or in a summary of significant policies preceding the first note. Notes to the financial statements are considered an integral part of the statements.

FULL EMPLOYMENT Congress passed the Employment Act of 1946 in response to the high unemployment rates that occurred during and following the Great Depression. This legislation stated that the government has the responsibility "to promote maximum employment, production, and purchasing power." This charge translates into maintaining full employment in the economy, but there remains controversy as to what the level of full employment actually is.

In the 1960s, full employment was defined as 4 percent unemployment. Full employment was redefined to be near 6 percent by the late 1970s as economists believed that the structure of the economy had changed over the intermittent years. To contrast, the Full Employment and Balanced Growth Act of 1978 set a goal of 4 percent unemployment by 1983 (which was not achieved).

The issue of what defined full employment is not settled, and may never be.

FULL EMPLOYMENT AND BALANCED GROWTH ACT The Full Employment and Balanced Growth Act of 1978, which is frequently referred to as the Humphrey-Hawkins Act, sets forth two goals. The first goal is to be achieved by 1983: a 4 percent rate of unemployment and a 3 percent rate of inflation. The second goal, which is to be achieved by 1988, is a 4 percent rate of unemployment and a zero rate of inflation. The first goal was not achieved. Unemployment was 9.6 percent in 1983 and inflation was 3.8 percent. The economy is close to the 4 percent unemployment rate in 1988, but inflation is near 5 percent.

The act also required improved coordination of macroeconomic policies among the president, and the Federal Reserve board. The Congressional Budget Office was established in 1975 to help in the analysis of tax and expenditure policy being considered by Congress. The act mandated that the Fed report its targets for monetary and credit growth to Congress in February and July of each year. The act also required that the council of Economic Advisers, created by the Employment Act of 1978, formulate policies necessary to achieve the goals set forth in the act.

FULL LOT The standard unit of trading for specified stocks and bonds on a securities exchange; also known as a round lot or board lot.

A round lot for most active stocks on the New York Stock Exchange is 100 shares; any number of shares from 1 to 99, therefore, would be an ODD LOT, subject to an extra charge for the public customer called the odd-lot differential. The round lot on some stocks is 10 shares; therefore, the odd lot on such stocks would be any number of shares from 1 to 9. The standard unit of trading in bonds is $1,000 original principal amount.

In commodity exchange trading, the contract for futures trading specifies the standard unit of quantity for each contract; in certain commodities, the exchange may provide also for job lots, i.e., specified standard quantity for units of trading smaller than the full contract unit.

See CHICAGO BOARD OF TRADE, JOB-LOTS.

FULLY PAID STOCK Stock fully paid for, i.e., upon which no further subscription installments are due. To be entitled to fully paid and nonassessable status, stock shall have been fully paid at least up to the par value thereof for business corporations; such fully paid stock is entitled to limited liability, freedom from any assessments to pay the corporation's debts in the event of the corporation's failure (with minor exceptions in various states). This is the trust fund doctrine or discount rule for par value stock—the legal principle that creditors are entitled at least to the unimpaired capital of the corporation as equity backing for their claims. It may be avoided, however, by: (1) sale of stock for property or services as well as cash; although grossly overstated valuations for property or services would be subject to challenge by creditors through a trustee in bankruptcy, it would ordinarily be difficult to challenge valuations with color of reasonableness; and (2) issuance of no-par-value stock, as authorized in many states, which is flexible in permitting allocation by directors of stock subscription proceeds of any determined proportion to stated capital balance to surplus. Even in the latter case, however, stockholders would be liable for payment of any unpaid portion of subscription liability; in a minority of states, no-par-value stock must be sold at minimum amount; and in any event, creditors are entitled to whatever stated capital was allocated, unimpaired by directors' actions.

In some states, issuance of certificates marked "partly paid" is permissible, in which event buyers from original stockholders take with notice of liability for balance, either by call from the directors or upon claim of creditors. Directors who approve issue of fully paid and nonassessable certificates that in fact are not fully paid are liable to creditors, as buyers from original stockholders of such certificates in good faith without knowledge would not in equity be held liable. Some states (e.g., Delaware), however, provide for a statute of limitations, requiring that, e.g., any claim for discount must be made six years from the date of certificate.

FUNCTIONAL CURRENCY The currency of the primary environment in which an entity operates. Typically, a foreign entity's functional currency is the currency in which it generates and expends cash, but other factors may be considered when the functional currency is not obvious from cash flows.

FUNDAMENTAL CONDITIONS In market letters and financial reviews, the underlying economic factors upon which the state of business, whether active or inactive, moderate or dull, prosperous or depressed, is ascertained. Fundamental conditions at any given time are determined by referring to comparative business statistics, to various business, banking, investment, and credit barometers, and to principles of economics.

See BUSINESS BAROMETERS, FAVORABLE CONDITIONS.

FUNDAMENTALISTS VIEW ON INVESTMENT ANALYSIS *See* TECHNICAL ANALYSIS.

FUNDED DEBT Bonded debt and other long-term indebtedness of a business corporation, or government or political subdivision thereof, as distinguished from the unfunded floating, or current debt. The Interstate Commerce Commission defined this term as comprising all bonds or other certificates of indebtedness not maturing for a year or more.

FUNDING The process of converting the floating indebtedness of a government or political subdivision thereof, or a business corporation, into long-term debt. Funding may be accomplished by converting a series of short-term note issues into long-term bonds when interest rates are low or, in corporate finance, by selling stock and paying off short-term debts with the proceeds. In this way stockholders virtually buy out the interest of the creditors. Funding by means of the sale of additional stock is usually undertaken when the equity market is favorable.

FUNDS Cash or its equivalent, e.g., checks, drafts, money orders. The term may be used to include securities which have a ready market and can be quickly liquidated. It is common to hear the expression liquid funds, meaning cash, and tied-up funds, meaning money invested in income-bearing assets.

Funds also refers to assets in special funds for specific purposes, some of which are unavailable for normal operations because of indenture or other contractual arrangements. Current funds include petty cash fund, payroll funds, and others. Long-term funds are used to retire long-term liabilities (sinking funds), preferred stock (stock redemption funds), and to purchase long-term assets (plant expansion funds). Long-term funds are reported as investments on the balance sheet. A fund actually sets aside cash and other assets to achieve specific objectives. An appropriation of retained earnings is not a fund but merely discloses managerial policy or legal or contractual restrictions. An appropriation of retained earnings does not provide cash.

FUNGIBLE GOODS Goods of a given class, any unit of which is as acceptable as another and will satisfy an obligation expressed in terms of the class. For example, bushels of wheat of a particular grade are fungible goods, as each unit of wheat of the same quality does not differ individually in value from the other units; any may be accepted or tendered without necessity of segregation or selection of particular bushels of wheat.

Much of the grain business of the country is conducted through the medium of grain elevators and warehouses, wherein grain is stored in a common receptacle and treated as common property. The depositor is entitled to grain in the same kind and quantity upon demand.

FUNNY MONEY Using securities that have common stock characteristics—such as warrants—that do not affect earnings per share statistics prior to their issuance.

FUTURE AMOUNT Value at a later date of a given sum that is invested at compound interest.

(a) **Future amount of 1 (or amount of a given sum).** The future value of $1.00 (or a single given sum), a, at the end of n periods at i compound interest rate.

Period	10%	12%
5	1.61051	1.76234
10	2.59374	3.10585

(b) **Future amount of an annuity.** The future value of a series of rents invested at compound interest; the accumulated total that results from a series of equal deposits at regular intervals invested at compound interest. Deposits and interest increase the accumulation.

(1) **Future amount of an ordinary annuity.** The future value on the date of the last rend.

Period	10%	12%
5	6.10510	6.35285
10	15.93743	17.54874

(2) **Future amount of an annuity due.** The future value one period after the date of the last rent. When an annuity due table is not available, use the following formula:

Amount of annuity due of 1 for n rents =
Amount of ordinary annuity for (n + 1 rent) - 1.

FUTURE INTEREST A legal term that includes reversions, remainders, and other interests which are limited to commence in use, possession, or enjoyment at some future date or time.

FUTURES Contracts with standardized provisions, leaving variable only price and delivery month, dealt in on the contract markets, COMMODITY EXCHANGES licensed by the COMMODITY FUTURES TRADING COMMISSION(CFTC) pursuant to the Commodity Futures Trading Commision Act of 1974 to conduct trading in COMMODITIES for future delivery, and other commodity exchanges not so regulated. By such contracts, the seller agrees to deliver the standard unit quantity of the specific commodity, operating under definitions of the exchange as to basis grade, delivery points, deliverable grades at premiums or discounts relative to basis grade, method of adjustment of premiums and discounts, settlement and delivery procedure, etc.

While most futures contracts are settled by offset prior to delivery, it is the right of a person long to stand for delivery of the physical commodity and of a person short to make such delivery if he so elects. The delivery procedure includes the issuance of a delivery notice, which is a document prepared by the seller notifying the buyer that he intends to deliver on a specified day the commodity specified in the futures contract. The original or a copy of each delivery notice tendered by a clearing member of a contract market is furnished to the Commodity Futures Trading Commission. From these notices and from reports of deliveries made by clearing members data on deliveries are compiled by the commission.

A futures contract is said to be open when it has been entered into and not yet liquidated by an offsetting transaction nor fulfilled by delivery. The amount of open contracts for each commodity and contract market is obtained each day by the Commodity Futures Trading Commission by a tabulation of reports made by exchange clearing members. The aggregate of all long open contracts reported by clearing members equals the aggregate of all short open contracts reported. The daily report of the CFTC, however, shows the figures for one side only, not the long and short sides combined.

Licensed contract markets are subject to limits on traders' position. Any trader whose position in one future of any commodity reaches a specified amount is required to report daily to the CFTC all his trades and positions in that commodity. In making this report, the trader also reports the classification of his position as speculative (including spreading or straddling) or hedging. Use of the futures contract for hedging purposes, described in HEDGING, is *not* speculation. As explained by Boyle (*Speculation and the Chicago Board of Trade*):

"Futures trading is of two kinds, speculative and hedging. A part of futures trading is known as 'hedging' and is a form of insurance. A part of futures trading is purely speculative. It is really dealing in grain contracts, rather than in grain. Some members of the Board of Trade devote their energies wholly to speculation, and are known as 'professionals'. Again, there is a sub-class of speculators who are called 'scalpers', or 'pit scalpers', since they buy and sell on each slight drop or rise in the market, trying to scalp a little profit off each fluctuation for themselves. They do not risk carrying any trades overnight, but aim to be even at the close of each day. The "professional speculator,' however, deals for the longer swings of the market, over a period of days, or even weeks."

Besides futures trading, most futures markets also provide separate facilities for spot (cash) trading in commodities. Although the primary function of commodity exchanges is to register existing values for commodities (whether on a spot or futures basis) as the result of interaction of buyers and sellers (whether speculators or hedgers), the notable economic function consists in furnishing manufacturers, processors, and merchants handling the commodity a mechanism for insuring themselves against losses through price fluctuations during the period when their holding of the raw commodity is in the process of fabrication and sale to the ultimate consumer. That is, the commodity exchange is a means by which cash holdings may be hedged against by sale of futures, or vice versa.

After long years of struggle against uninformed hostility and prejudice, futures trading in staple commodities has come into public acceptance and recognition of its functions. For years, the commodity exchanges had to fight a continual battle for existence against disgruntled farmers and businesspeople only too willing, after a sharp commodity price deflation such as in 1920-1921, to blame the commodity exchanges and operations they did not fully understand for the decline in prices. In modern times, futures contract markets have come to be recognized as essential cogs in the distribution system for commodities, and farmers and businesspeople have come to look upon them as organizations to be used rather than abused.

This is particularly true since the Grain Futures Act and most recently the Commodity Futures Trading Commission Act of 1974 placed all futures trading in designated commodity exchanges under statutory and administrative regulation and control by the Commodity Futures Trading Commission. Principal protective features of regulation include the abolition of manipulative practices such as wash sales, cross trades, puts and calls, etc.; prevention of excessive speculation, both by setting daily trading limits as to price and by imposing limitations on the daily amount of speculative trading and net long or net short position of any one speculative account; segregation of customers' funds from commission merchant's funds; registration of all commission merchants and floor brokers; prevention of any cheating or defrauding of the public; etc.

Bankers have long looked with favor upon borrowers who hedge inventory positions, where the commodity involved is required in large amounts by the borrowers, as in such cases even mild price decline in the commodity might mean substantial inventory losses, unless appropriately hedged through futures contracts.

Financial Futures. The most dynamically growing sector of the futures markets have been the financial futures, including interest-rate futures and currency futures. Among the financial instruments futures actively traded are Government National Mortgage Association (GNMAs) (Chicago Board of Trade); Treasury bonds (Chicago Board of Trade); Treasury bonds (New York Futures Exchange); Treasury bills (International Monetary Market); and bank CDs, both on the Chicago Board of Trade and the International Monetary Market as well as the New York Futures Exchange. Submitted for approval to the COMMODITY FUTURES TRADING COMMISSION were proposals to trade in Treasury note futures, prime rate futures, and options on treasury bond futures. Among the active foreign currency futures traded on the International Monetary Exchange are British pounds, Canadian dollars, Japanese yen, Swiss francs, West German marks, and eurodollar time deposit futures.

Futures can also be traded on markets such as the Chicago Mercantile Exchange, the AMEX, NYSE, and COMEX. Not all financial instruments are handled on each market.

Option volume for exchanges is appended.

Standardized futures contracts are shown in the appended table.

See COMMODITY EXCHANGE ACT, COMMODITY EXCHANGE AUTHORITY.

BIBLIOGRAPHY

BERNSTEIN, J. *Facts on Futures*. Probus Publishing, Co., Chicago, IL, 1989.

———. *Jake Bernstein's Facts on Futures*. Probus Publishing Co., Chicago, IL, 1987.

BROWN, P. J. *The Financial Futures Function and Its Implementation*. Bank Administration Institute, Rolling Meadows, IL, 1982.

CHICAGO BOARD OF TRADE. *Commodity Futures Trading: Bibliography*. Chicago Board of Trade, Chicago, IL.

———. COMMODITY TRADING MANUAL, 1985.

Commodity Journal.

Consensus.

Financial Futures and Options in the U.S. Economy. Staff of the Federal Reserve System. Federal Reserve System, Washington, DC, 1985.

FINK, R. E., and FEDUNIAK, R. B. *Futures Trading*. New York Institute of Finance, New York, NY, 1987.

Futures.

Futures: The Magazine of Commodities & Options.

GOULD, B. G. *The Dow Jones-Irwin Guide to Commodities Trades*. Dow Jones-Irwin, Inc., Homewood, IL, 1981.

Journal of Futures Markets.

LABUSZEWSKI, J. W., and NYHOFF, J. E. *Trading Financial Futures: Markets, Methods, Strategies, and Tactics*. John Wiley and Sons, Inc., New York, NY, 1988.

LOFTON, TODD *Getting Started in Futures*, 1989.

Standardized Futures Contracts

Contract	Exchange	Contract size	Min. fluctuation
Aluminum	COMEX	40,000 lbs.	.05¢/lb. = $20.00
Cocoa	CSCE	10 metric tons	$1/ton = $10.00
Coffee "C"	CSCE	37,500 lbs.	.01¢/lb. = $3.75
Copper	COMEX	25,000 lbs.	.05¢/lb. = $12.50
Corn	CBOT	5,000 bu.	$1/4$¢/bu. = $12.50
Cotton	CTN	50,000 lbs.	.01¢/lb. = $5.00
Crude Oil	NYME	1,000 barrels	1¢/barrel = $10.00
DMark	CME	125,000 DM	.01¢/DM = $12.50
DMark	MACE	62,500 DM	.01¢/DM = $6.25
Eurodollars	CME	$1,000,000	.01 = $25.00
Gold	COMEX	100 troy ozs.	10¢/oz. = $10.00
Gold	CBOT	1 kilo	10¢/troy oz. = $3.22
Live Cattle	CME	40,000 lbs.	2.5¢/cwt. = $10.00
Live Hogs	CME	30,000 lbs.	2.5¢/cwt. = $7.50
Lumber	CME	130,000 bd. ft.	10¢/1000 bd ft = $13.00
MMI	CBOT	$250 × index	.05 = $12.50
NYSE Compos.	NYFE	$500 × index	.05 = $25.00
Orange Juice	CTN	15,000 lbs.	.05¢/lb. = $7.50
Rice, Rough	CRCE	2,000 cwt.	.5¢/cwt. = $10.00
S&P 500	CME	$500 × index	.05 = $25.00
Silver	COMEX	5,000 troy ozs.	.1¢/troy oz. = $5.00
Silver	CBOT	1,000 troy ozs.	.1¢/troy oz. = $1.00
Soybeans	CBOT	5,000 bu.	$1/4$¢/bu. = $12.50
Sugar #11	CSCE	112,000 lbs.	.01¢/lb. = $11.20
Swiss Franc	CME	125,000 SF	.01¢/SF = $12.50
Swiss Franc	PBOT	125,000 SF	.01¢/SF = $12.50
T-Bills	CME	$1,000,000	.01 = $25.00
T-Bonds	CBOT	$100,000	$1/32$ = $31.25
Unleaded Gas	NYME	42,000 gals.	.01¢/gal. = $4.20
Value Line	KCBOT	$500 × index	.05 = $25.00
Wheat, Spring	MGE	5,000 bu.	$1/8$¢/bu. = $6.25
Wheat	CBOT	5,000 bu.	$1/4$¢/bu. = $12.50
Wheat	KCBOT	5,000 bu.	$1/4$¢/bu. = $12.50

———. *Trading Options on Futures: Markets, Methods, Strategies, and Tactics.* John Wiley and Sons, New York, NY, 1988.
MELTON, C. R., and PUKULA, T. V. *Financial Futures.* Prentice Hall, Inc., Englewoods Cliffs, NY, 1984.
MURPHY, J. J. *Technical Analysis of the Futures Markets,* 1987.
———. *Study Guide for Technical Analysis of the Futures Markets,* 1987.
NICHOLAS, D. *Commodities Futures Trading: A Guide to Information Sources and Computerized Services.* Mansell, Bronx, NY, 1985.
POWER, M., and VOGEL, D. *Inside the Financial Futures Markets,* John Wiley and Sons, Inc., New York, NY, 1984.
Technical Analysis of Stocks & Commodities: The Trader's Magazine. Technical Analysis, Inc., Seattle, WA. Monthly.
Timing Commodity and Financial Advisory Service. Weekly.

FUTURES COMMISSION MERCHANTS According to the Commodity Futures Trading Commission Act, individuals, associations, partnerships, corporations, and trusts that engage in soliciting or in accepting orders for the purchase or sale of any commodity for future delivery on or subject to the rules of any contract market and that, in or in connection with such solicitation or acceptance of orders, accept any money, securities, or property (or extend credit in lieu thereof) to margin, guarantee, or secure any trades or contracts that result or may result therefrom.

Futures commission merchants are required to be registered with the COMMODITY FUTURES TRADING COMMISSION under the Commodity Futures Trading Commission Act.
See FUTURES.

FUTURES EXCHANGE Any commodity exchange which provides facilities for futures trading. Some COMMODITY EXCHANGES are only spot (cash trades) markets. Major exchanges, however, are futures contract markets, providing in addition facilities for spot trading. Most of the futures contract markets have been designated as such under the Commodity Futures Trading Commission Act and subjected to regulation under that act and the Commodity Futures Trading Commission.

In FOREIGN EXCHANGE, future exchange or forward exchange is the rate for a currency for delivery at a specified future date, either fixed or optional. Foreign currency futures contracts are traded on commodity exchanges (*see* FUTURES).

In 1983 there were 11 commodity futures exchanges registered with the Commodity Futures Trading Commission: Chicago Board of Trade, Chicago Mercantile Exchange, New York Futures Exchange, Kansas City Board of Trade, Commodity Exchange (New York), Coffee, Sugar and Cocoa Exchange (New York), New York Cotton Exchange, MidAmerica Commodity Exchange (Chicago), Minneapolis Grain Exchange, New Orleans Commodity Exchange, and New York Mercantile Exchange. Of these, the Chicago Board of Trade and the Chicago Mercantile Exchange (the International Monetary Market Division) are of major interest to financial institutions because they are significant traders in financial instruments contracts.

FUTURES MARKET A market that enables buyers and sellers to exchange contracts for the future delivery of commodities or financial instruments. If a commodity producer wishes to sell a commodity in the future, he can assure his ability to do so by selling a futures contract today. Alternatively, if a commodity user needs to buy a commodity in the future, he or she can make certain that he may do so by buying a futures contract today. Futures markets, therefore, make it possible for producers and consumers to act today to make sure that they will be able to do what they want to do in the future. Futures markets arose from the need to reduce price risk in commodity trading.

In the early part of the last century, it was common in the United States for farmers to bring their products to market at a set time of the year. Often this resulted in a glut during market season, and farmers found prices very depressed when they came to sell their products. At other times, prices could be very high because of shortages. Some farmers and merchants began to make contracts for future delivery, assuring the farmers at least a minimum price for their crops.

After the Civil War, there evolved the formal practice of futures trading at commodity exchanges like the Chicago Board of Trade and elsewhere, as traders began to exchange contracts for future delivery that were standardized as to grade, size, and time of delivery. Standardization was important to the growth of futures trading because it made on futures contract for a specific commodity identical and thus interchangeable with other contracts for delivery of the same commodity during the same time period.

It is contract standardization that distinguishes a futures contract from a forward contract. A forward contract is tailored to the needs of the individual buyer and seller, and is an agreement between the two of them directly. A futures contract is a standardized agreement that takes place under rules prescribed by the futures exchange on which the contract is traded. Each buyer or seller deals through the exchange clearing house, and each is insured against default by the exchange itself.

Today organized futures markets for the exchange of standardized contracts for future delivery exist for a large number of items, including grains and feeds (wheat, corn, soybeans), livestock (cattle, hogs, porkbellies), metals (copper, silver, gold), lumber, and financial assets (foreign currencies, stocks, and debt instruments). The prices of futures contracts for these items are published daily in the *Wall Street Journal* and elsewhere. The appended table shows a set of quotations for futures contracts traded during a typical day. The exchange where the contracts are traded is shown in parentheses next to the name of the commodity or financial instrument. Each row of price quotes reflects the day's trading in a particular futures contract. The delivery date of the contracts is listed as the first item on each row. For example, July corn traded on the Chicago Board of Trade (CBT) or gold for delivery in August sold on the Commodity Exchange in New York (CMX).

The open price is that of the first transaction during the day. The high and low are the highest and lowest prices during the day. And the settlement price is an average of the high and low prices during the "closing period" as defined by the exchange, usually the last two minutes of trading.

The open interest reflects the number of outstanding contracts at the end of the previous day's trading. For each commodity or financial instrument, the *Journal* also reports the total volume of trading (number of contracts exchanged) on the day in question and on the previous trading day.

Holders of outstanding contracts must ultimately settle their

FUTURES TRADING TERMS: GLOSSARY

Futures Prices

Source: Wall Street Journal, 1990.

positions either by liquidation through offsetting purchases or sales, or by receiving or delivering the physical commodity against the contract. The great majority of futures contracts are settled by offset. Only 3% of all contracts result in delivery of the actual goods.

Interest rate futures are based on long and short-term, fixed-income financial debt instruments with prices that vary inversely to their interest rates. The term "interest rate futures" refers to specific contracts for interest sensitive financial instruments. Stock index futures are based on the performance of a group of stocks; these futures allow investors to protect a portfolio of stock from a decline in value. Stock index futures contracts are based on cash settlement, rather than delivery of a commodity or financial instrument.

The use of futures markets by financial institutions is regulated by the guidelines of regulatory agencies. The guidelines vary across regulators. The Comptroller of the Currency, which regulates national banks, allows the use of financial futures for activities deemed to be "incidental to banking." The Comptroller's policy allows hedging to reduce a bank's overall interest rate exposure. The Federal Home Loan Bank Board, regulator of federal savings and loan associations, allows associations to hedge when the hedging is used to reduce overall interest rate exposure.

The FINANCIAL ACCOUNTING STANDARDS BOARD (FASB) provides guidelines for accounting for futures contract in Statement of Financial Accounting Standards No. 80, *Accounting for futures contracts*, Statement of Financial Accounting Standards, August 1984. The rules allow the use of deferral accounting for futures transactions that meet the following hedge criteria. First, the asset or liability to be hedged exposes the institution to price or interest rate risk. Second, the futures contract selected reduces the interest rate exposure of the institution, is specifically designated as a hedge, and its price is highly correlated with the cash item being hedged. Futures transactions not meeting these criteria will be accounted for by marking-to-market.

BIBLIOGRAPHY

TEWELES, R. J., and JONES, FRANK J. *The Futures Game*, 1987.
This book has an extensive bibliography covering the following areas:
Futures trading and commodity exchanges
History and evolution of futures trading
Economic theory and evidence
Traders: behavior and returns
Individual commodity studies
Regulation of futures trading
Price behavior
Price forecasting
Money management and risk control
Prices and related statistical data
Spreads and options

HERBST, A. F. *Commodity Futures: Markets, Methods of Analysis and Management of Risk*, 1986.

FUTURES TRADING TERMS: GLOSSARY
A glossary of the Commodity Futures Trading Corporation contains a glossary of trading terms complied from generally accepted trade sources. Major terms explained in this glossary are reproduced here.

Abandon: The act of an option holder in electing not to exercise or offset an option.

Actuals: The physical or cash commodity.

Aggregation: The principle under which all futures positions owned or controlled by one trader (or group of traders acting in concert) are combined to determine reporting status and speculative limit compliance.

Arbitrage: Simultaneous purchase of cash commodities or futures in one market against the sale of cash commodities or futures in the same or a different market to profit from a discrepancy in prices.

At-the-market: An order to buy or sell a futures contract at whatever price is obtainable when the order reaches the trading floor. Also called a Market Order.

At-the-money: When an options's exercise price is the same as the current trading price of the under-lying commodity.

Backpricing: Fixing the price of a commodity for which the commitment to purchase has been made in advance.

Backwardation: Market situation in which futures prices are progressively lower in the distant delivery months.

Basis: The difference between the spot or cash price of a commodity and the price of the nearest futures contract for the same or a related commodity. Basis is usually computed in relation to the near futures contract and may reflect different time periods, product forms, qualities, or locations.

FUTURES TRADING TERMS: GLOSSARY

Basic grade: The grade of a commodity used as the standard or par grade of a futures contract.

Basis risk: The risk associated with an unexpected widening or narrowing of basis between the time a hedging position is established and the time that it is lifted.

Bid: An offer to buy a specific quantity of a commodity at a stated price.

Blackboard trading: The practice of selling commodities from a blackboard on a wall of a commodity exchange.

Black-Scholes (Option Pricing) Model: An option pricing formula initially derived by F. Black and M. Scholes for securities options and later refined by Black for options on futures.

Board of trade: Any exchange or association, whether incorporated or unincorporated, of persons who are engaged in the business of buying or selling any commodity or receiving the same for sale on consignment.

Boiler room: An enterprise which often is operated out of inexpensive low-rent quarters (hence the term "boiler room") that uses high pressure sales tactics (generally over the telephone) and possibly false or misleading information in an attempt to get unsophisticated investors to invest in questionable commodity or stock transactions.

Box transaction: An option position in which the holder has established a long call and a short put at one strike price and a short call and a long put at another strike price, all of which are in the same contract month in the same commodity.

Bucketing: Directly or indirectly taking the opposite side of a customer's order into the broker's own account or into an account in which the broker has an interest, without execution of the order on an exchange.

Bulge: A rapid advance in prices.

Bull spread: The simultaneous purchase and sale of two futures contracts in the same or related commodities with the intention of profiting from a rise in prices but at the same time limiting the potential loss if this expectation is wrong.

Buoyant: A market in which prices have a tendency to rise easily with a considerable show of strength.

Butterfly spread: A three-legged spread in futures or options. In the options spread, the options have the same expiration date but differ in strike prices.

Buy (or sell) on close: To buy (or sell) at the end of the trading session within the closing price range.

Buy (or sell) on opening: To buy (or sell) at the beginning of a trading session within the opening price range.

Call: (1) A period at the opening and the close of some futures markets in which the price for each futures contract is established by auction; (2) buyer's call generally applied to cotton, also called "call sale."

Called: Another term for "exercised" when the option is a call. The writer of a call must deliver the indicated underlying commodity when the option is exercised or called.

Call option: A contract that entitles the buyer/taker to buy a fixed quantity of a commodity at a stipulated basis of striking price at any time up to the expiration of the option. The buyer pays a premium to the seller/grantor for this contract. A call option is bought with the expectation of a rise in prices.

Call rule: An exchange regulation under which an official bid price for a cash commodity is competitively established at the close of each day's trading. It holds until the next opening of the exchange.

Cash commodity: The physical or actual commodity as distinguished from the futures contract, e.g., actuals.

Cash market: The market for the cash commodity.

CFO: Cancel Former Order.

Certified or Certified stocks: Stocks of a commodity that have been duly inspected and found to be of a quality deliverable against futures contracts, stored at the delivery points designated as regular or acceptable for delivery by the commodity exchange.

Churning: Excessive trading which permits a broker who controls an account to earn excessive commissions while disregarding the best interests of the customer.

Class (of options): Options of the same type covering the same underlying futures contract or physical commodity.

Clearing house: An agency associated with an exchange which guarantees all trades, assuring contract delivery and/or financial settlement. The clearinghouse becomes the buyer for every seller, and the seller for every buyer.

Closing-out: Liquidating an existing long or short futures or option position with an equal and opposite transaction. An offset.

Combination: Puts and calls held either long or short with different strike prices and expirations.

Commodity Credit Corporation: A government-owned corporation established in 1933 to assist American agriculture. Major operations include price support programs, foreign sales, and export credit programs for agricultural commodities.

Commodity Exchange Authority: A regulatory agency of the U.S. Department of Agriculture established to administer the Commodity Exchange Act prior to 1975; the forerunner of the Commodity Futures Trading Commission.

Commodity Futures Trading Commission: The Federal regulatory agency established by the CFTC Act of 1974 to administer the Commodity Exchange Act.

Commodity Price Index: Index or average, which may be weighted, of selected commodity prices, intended to be representative of the markets in general or a specific subset of commodities.

Contango: Market situation in which prices in succeeding delivery months are progressively higher than the nearest delivery month.

Contract: A term of reference describing a unit of trading for a commodity future or option: an agreement to buy or sell a specified commodity.

Contract month: The month in which futures contracts may be satisfied by making or taking delivery.

Convergence: The tendency of prices of physical and futures to approach one another, usually during the delivery month.

Conversion: When trading options on futures contracts, a position created by selling a call option, buying a put option, and buying the underlying futures contract, where the options have the same strike price and the same expiration.

Corner: To corner is to secure such relative control of a commodity or security that its price can be manipulated.

Cover: Purchasing futures to offset a short position. To have in hand the physical commodity when a short futures or leverage sale is made, or to acquire the commodity that might be deliverable on a short sale.

Covered option: A short call or put option position which is covered by the sale or purchase of the underlying futures contract or physical commodities.

Cox-Ross-Rubinstein Options Pricing Model: An option-pricing logarithm developed by J. Cox, S. Ross and M. Rubinstein which can be adopted to include effects not included in the Black-Scholes model.

Cross trading: Offsetting or noncompetitive match of the buy order of one customer against the sell order of another, a practice that is permissible only when executed as required by the Commodity Exchange Act, CFTC regulations, and rules of the contract market.

Curb trading: The dealing that takes place after the official market has closed.

Day order: An order that expires automatically at the end of each day's trading session.

Day traders: Commodity traders who take positions in commodities and then offset them prior to the close of trading on the same trading day.

Default: Failure to perform on a futures contract as required by exchange rules.

Delivery: The tender and receipt of the actual commodity, the cash value of the commodity, or of a delivery instrument covering the commodity.

Delivery notice: The written notice given by the seller of his intention to make delivery against an open short futures position on a particular date.

Delivery price: The price fixed by the clearing house at which deliveries on futures are invoiced.

Diagonal spread: A spread between two call options on two put options with different strike prices and different expiation dates.

Differentials: The discounts (premiums) allowed for grades or locations of a commodity lower (higher) than the par or basis grade or location specified in the futures contract.

Discount basis: Method of quoting securities where the price is expressed as an annualized discount from maturity value.

Discretionary account: An arrangement by which the holder of an

---

ENCYCLOPEDIA OF BANKING AND FINANCE

FUTURES TRADING TERMS: GLOSSARY

account gives written power of attorney to someone else, often a broker, to buy and sell without price approval of the holder.

Dominant future: The future having the largest number of open contracts.

Elliot Wave: A theory named after Ralph Elliot, who contended that the stock market tends to move in discernible and predictable patterns reflecting the basis harmony of nature; in technical analysis, a charting method based on the belief that all prices act as waves rising and falling rhythmically.

Exercise: To elect to buy or sell, taking advantage of the right conferred by an option contract.

Exercise (or Strike) price: The price specified in the option contract at which the buyer of a call can purchase the commodity during the life of the option, and the price specified in the option contract at which the buyer of a put can sell the commodity during the life of the option.

Expiration date: The date on which an option contract automatically expires.

Fictitious trading: Wash trading, bucketing, cross trading, or other schemes which give the appearance of trading when no bona fide, competitive trade has occurred.

Financial instruments: Currency, securities and indices of their value.

Floor broker: A person eligible to execute a customer order on the trading floor in a futures contract market.

Forced liquidation: The situation in which a customer's account is liquidated by the brokerage firm holding the account or, in the case of leveraged accounts, by the leverage transaction merchant, usually after notification, because the account is undercapitalized.

Force Majeure: A clause in a supply contract which permits either party not to fulfill the contractual commitments due to events beyond their control. These events may range from stikes to export delays in producing countries.

Foreign exchange: Foreign currency.

Forward: In the future.

Forward contracting: A cash transaction common in many industries, including commodity merchandising, in which the buyer and seller agree upon delivery of a specified quality and quantity of goods at a specified future date.

Forward market: An informal trading of commodities to be delivered at a future date.

Frontrunning: Taking an options position based upon non-public information regarding an impending large transaction in the underlying commodity in order to obtain a profit when the options market adjusts to the price at which the transaction occurs.

Futures contract: An agreement to purchase or sell a commodity for delivery in the future.

Grades: Various qualities of a commodity. Hedge ratio: Ratio of the value of futures contracts purchased or sold to the value of the cash commodity being hedged, a computation necessary to minimize basis risk.

Hedging: Taking a position in a futures market opposite to a position held in the cash market to minimize the risk of financial loss from an adverse price change; a purchase or sale of futures as a temporary substitute for a cash transaction that will occur later.

Index arbitrage: The simultaneous purchase (sale of stock index futures and the sale (purchase) of some or all of the component stocks which make up the particular stock index to profit from sufficiently large intermarket spreads between the futures contact and the index itself.

Interest rate futures: Futures contracts traded on fixed income securities.

In-the-money: A term used to describe an option contract that has a positive value if exercised.

Intrinsic value: A measure of the value of an option or a warrant if immediately exercised. The amount by which the current futures price for a commodity is above the strike price of a call option or below the strike price of a put option for the commodity.

Inverted market: A futures market in which near-month contracts are selling at prices that are higher than those of more distant months. An invested market is characteristic of a near-term supply shortage.

Leverage contract: A contract, standardized as to terms and conditions, for the long-term (ten years or longer) purchase (long leverage contract) or sale (short leverage contract) by a leverage customer of a leverage commodity which provides for participation by the leverage transaction merchant as a principal in each leverage transaction; initial and maintenance margin payments by the leverage customer; periodic payment by the leverage customer or accrual by the leverage transaction merchant to the leverage customer of a variable carrying charge or fee on the initial value of the contract plus any margin deposits made by the leverage customer in connection with a short leverage contract; delivery of a commodity in the amount and form which can be readily purchased and sold in normal commercial or retail channels; delivery of the leverage commodity after satisfaction of the balance due on the contract; and determination of the contract purchase and repurchase, or sale and resale, prices by the leverage transaction merchant.

Limit: The maximum price advance or decline from the previous day's settlement price permitted during one trading session as fixed by the rules of an exchange.

Limit order: An order in which the customer specifies a price limit or other condition, such as time of an order, as contrasted with a market order which implies that the order should be filled as soon as possible.

Liquidation: The closing out of a long position.

Liquid market: A market in which selling and buying can be accomplished with minimal price change.

Long: One who has bought a futures contract to establish a market position; a market position which obligates the holder to take delivery; one who owns an inventory of commodities.

Margin: The amount of money or collateral deposited by a customer with his broker, by a broker with a clearing member, or by a clearing member with the clearinghouse, for the purpose of insuring the broker or clearinghouse against loss on open futures contracts. The margin is not partial payment on a purchase.

Margin call: A request from a brokerage firm to a customer to bring margin deposits up to the original level; a request by the clearinghouse to a clearing member to bring clearing margins back to minimum levels required by the clearinghouse rules.

Market correction: A small reversal in prices following a significant trending period.

Market maker: A professional securities dealer who stands ready to buy when there is an excess of sell orders and to sell when there is an excess of buy orders.

Market order: an order to buy or sell a futures contract at whatever price is obtainable at the time it is entered in the reign or pit.

Mark-to-market: Daily cash flow system used by U.S. futures exchanges to maintain minimum level of margin equity for a given futures or option contract position by calculating the gain or loss in each contract position resulting from changes in the price of the futures or option contracts at the end of each trading day.

Maturity: Period within which a futures contract can be settled by delivery of the actual commodity.

Momentum: In technical analysis, the relative change in price over a specific time interval.

Naked option: the sale of a call or put option without holding an offsetting position in the underlying commodity.

Net position: The difference between the open long contracts and the open short contracts held by a trader in any one commodity.

Offer: An indication of willingness to sell at a given price; opposite of bid.

Open interest: the total number of futures contracts long or short in a delivery month or market that has been entered into and not year liquidated by an offsetting transaction or fulfilled by delivery.

Option: A commodity option is a unilateral contract which gives the buyer the right to buy or sell a specified quantity of a commodity at a specific price within a specified period of time, regardless of the market price of that commodity; a term sometimes erroneously applied to a futures contract.

Out-of-the-money: A term used to describe an option that has no intrinsic value.

Paper profit or loss: The profit or loss that would be realized if the open contracts were liquidated as of a certain time or at a certain price.

Pegged price: The price at which a commodity has been fixed by agreement.

Pit: A specially constructed arena on the trading floor of some exchanges where trading in a futures contract is conducted.

Pork bellies: One of the major cuts of the hog carcass that, when cured, becomes bacon.

Portfolio insurance: A trading strategy which attempts to alter the nature of price changes in a portfolio to substantially reduce the likelihood of returns below some predetermined level for an established period of time. This can be achieved by moving assets against stocks, cash and fixed-income securities or, with the advent of stock index futures contracts, by hedging a stock-only portfolio by selling stock index futures in a declining market or purchasing futures in a rising market. The objective is to create an exposure similar to that of a stock portfolio with a protective purchased put option.

Position: An interest in the market in the form of one or more open contracts.

Price discovery: the process of determining the price level for a commodity based on supply and demand factors.

Price manipulation: Any planned operation, transaction or practice calculated to cause or maintain an artificial price.

Program trading: The purchase (or sale) of a large number of stocks contained in or comprising a portfolio.

Put option: An option to sell a specified amount of a commodity at an agreed price and time at any time until the expiation of the option. A put option is purchased to protect against a fall in price.

Pyramiding: The use of profits on existing positions as margin to increase the size of the position, normally in successively smaller increments.

Random walk: An economic theory that price movements in the commodity futures markets and in the securities markets are completely random in character (i.e., past prices are not a reliable indicator of future prices).

Ratio hedge: The number of options compared to the number of futures contracts taken in a position necessary to be a hedge; that is, risk neutral.

Resistance: A price area where new selling will emerge to dampen a continued rise.

Retracement: A reversal within a major price trend.

Reversal: A change of direction in prices.

Risk/reward ratio: The relationship between the profitability of loss and that of profit. This ratio is often used as a basis for trade selection or comparison.

Roll-over: A trading procedure involving the shift of one month of a straddle into another future month while holding the other contract month.

Scalper: A speculator on the trading floor of an exchange who buys and sells rapidly, with small profits or losses, holding his positions for only a short time during a trading session.

Settlement: The act of fulfilling the delivery requirements of a futures contract.

Sharpe Ratio: A measurement of trading performance calculated as the average return divided by the variance of those returns; named after W. P. Sharpe.

Short: The selling side of an open futures contract; a trader whose net position in the futures market shows an excess of open sales over open purchases.

Short selling: Selling a contract with the idea of delivering or of buying to offset it at a later date.

Soft: A description of a price which is gradually weakening.

Speculator: An individual who does not hedge, but who trades in commodity futures with the objective of achieving profits through the successful anticipation of price movements.

Spot: Market of immediate delivery of the product and immediate payment.

Spot price: The price at which a physical commodity for immediate delivery is selling at a given time and place.

Spread (or straddle): The purchase of one futures delivery month against the sale of another futures delivery month of the same commodity; the purchase of one delivery month of one commodity against the sale of that same delivery month of a different commodity; or the purchase of one commodity in one market against the sale of the commodity in another market, to take advantage of and profit from a change in price relationships. The term spread is also used to refer to the difference between the price of one futures month and the price of another month of the same commodity. A spread can also apply to options.

Squeeze: A market situation in which the lack of supplies tends to force shorts to cover their positions by offset at higher prices.

Stop limit order: An order that goes into force as soon as there is a trade at the specified price. The order can only be filled at the stop limit price or better.

Stop order: An order that becomes a market order when a particular price level is reached. A sell stop is placed below the market; a stop is placed above the market. Sometimes referred to as Stop Loss Order.

Striking price (exercise or contract price): The price, specified in the option contract, at which the underlying futures contract or commodity will move from seller to buyer.

Swap: The exchange of one asset or liability for a similar asset or liability for the purpose of lengthening or shortening maturities, or raising or lowering coupon rates, to maximize revenue or minimize financing costs

Switch: Offsetting a position in one delivery month of a commodity and simultaneous initiation of a similar position in another delivery month of the same commodity, a tactic referred to as "rolling forward."

Systematic risk: Market risk due to price fluctuations which cannot be eliminated by diversification.

Tender: To give notice to the clearing house of the intention to initiate delivery of the physical commodity in satisfaction of the futures contract.

Tick: Refers to a minimum change in price up or down.

Time of day order: This is an order which is to be executed at a given minute in the session.

Trader: A merchant involved in cash commodities; a professional speculator who trades for his own account.

Trendline: In charting, a line drawn across the bottom or top of a price chart indicating the direction or trend of price movement. If up, the trendline is called bullish; if down, it is called bearish.

Volume of trade: The number of contracts traded during a specified period of time.

Wash sale: A fictitious transaction usually made so it will appear that there are or have been trades, but without actually taking a position in the market. Such sales are prohibited by the Commodity Exchange Act.

Writer: The issuer, grantor, or maker of an option contract.

Yield curve: A graphic representation of the market yield for a fixed income security plotted against the maturity of the security.

FUTURE VALUE The future value (amount) of a single sum at compound interest is the original amount plus the compound interest thereon, stated as of a specific future date. Selections from a future value of one table is presented here:

Period	10%	14%
1	1.1999	1.1400
4	1.4641	1.6890

For example, what will be the amount in a savings account on December 31, 1990, if $10,000 is invested at 14 percent interest on December 31, 1986? Using a Future Amount of 1 Table for i = 14 percent and n = 4, the future amount can be computed as follows:

$10,000 x 1.68896 = $16,889.60.

ENCYCLOPEDIA OF BANKING AND FINANCE

G

GAINS Increases in equity (net assets) from peripheral or incidental transactions of an entity and from all other transactions, events, and circumstances affecting the entity during a period except those that result from revenues or investments by owners. Gains often arise from events and circumstances that may be beyond the control of an enterprise or its managements. Gains result from such activities as sales of investments in marketable securities, dispositions of used equipment, the settlement of liabilities at other than their carrying amounts, or the winning of a lawsuit.

GAMBLE Used in speculative circles to mean "play the market" blindly. It consists of making speculative commitments without having a knowledge of business conditions, the technical position of the market, cyclical price movements, or the value of the securities traded in from the standpoint of equities and earnings, especially stocks of corporations that have not yet reached the producing stage and the success of which is uncertain. To gamble in stocks is to deal in highly speculative stocks, to deal in stocks without previous knowledge of the risks involved, to trade on thin margins, to load up heavily on one security issue, or merely to bet on the rise or fall of quotations—the practice of the BUC-KET SHOP. In general a gambler is one who takes heavy and un-necessary risks, e.g., one who casts too much on a single throw of the dice.

From a strict economic standpoint, the well-considered purchase of stocks is not gambling, since a real contribution to production is made, i.e., that of furnishing capital for speculative enterprises, whereas in gambling no end is finally achieved. Gambling, moreover, involves the assumption of a needless or artificial risk (often created for the occasion), while speculative trading involves a necessary economic risk. SPECULATION is an existing and inherent risk that cannot be escaped if business is to be carried on. The risk of fluctuating prices is inherent in the economic scheme. In gambling, a risk is created for the sole purpose of assuming it. Wagers on a horse race are deliberately created.

See HEDGING, LAMB.

GAME THEORY Jon von Neumann, a mathematician, and Oskar Morgenstern, an economist, introduced the concept of game theory in the early 1940s. In essence, game theory is an alternative approach to understanding managerial decision making in an industry where there are a few major participants (oligopoly) and where the actions of one firm are interdependent on the actions of another firm.

In a game theory context, the decision maker is uncertain as to the actions of the competitor. The decision maker can adopt a maximum criterion and select the strategy that maximizes the minimum of all possible outcomes given possible responses by the competitor. Alternatively, the decision maker can adopt a minimax criterion and select the strategy that minimizes the maximum of all possible outcomes given possible responses by the competitor.

GAMMA The sensitivity of an option's delta to small unit changes in the price of the underlying instrument. Some option traders attempt to construct "gamma-neutral" positions in options (long and short) so that the delta of the overall position remains unchanged for small changes in the price of the underlying instrument. Using this method writers can produce a fairly constant delta and avoid the transactions costs involved in purchasing and selling the underlying instrument as its price changes.

GAP ANALYSIS A procedure by which a banker matches maturities of an asset/liability portfolio at a positive spread for a guaranteed profit over the life of the investment by measuring interest rate sensitivity; an integrated financial management policy and asset/liability management procedure. Gap refers to a specific time interval, such a a 30-day gap, which is the extent or degree to which assets maturing within 30 days exceed or fall short of liabilities maturing in 30 days. Its objective is to effectively position an institution's portfolio to maximize flexibility and profitability by identifying assets and liabilities that are interest sensitive. GAP analysis is typically short-term oriented and generally does not consider the reinvestment risk of the intermediate cash flows and long-term profitability.

See DURATION ANALYSIS.

GARNISHEE The person upon whom a GARNISHMENT is served.

GARNISHMENT The legal process, notice, or writ that directs a third party who owes money or other property to the defendant, in a case in which the plaintiff is suing to collect a debt, not to deliver such money or property into the defendant's hands, but to appear in court and answer the plaintiff's suit. Garnishment proceedings are instituted in order to secure to the plaintiff a claim due by a third person to such debtor, against whom suit has been brought.

GARN-ST. GERMAIN DEPOSITORY INSTITUTIONS ACT OF 1982 An act that authorizes money market accounts; requires the end of the interest rate differential favoring thrifts; gives assistance to S&Ls and thrift institutions. This was a piece of omnibus financial industry legislation that gave most financial institutions major powers and opportunities for competitive innovations.

The Garn-St. Germain Act sought to provide the Federal Deposit Insurance Corporation and the Federal Savings and Loan Insurance Corporation with the flexibility required to deal with financially distressed depository institutions. Congress authorized these agencies to provide direct assistance to failing or troubled institutions, or to assist in their merger. Congress sought to enhance the competitiveness of all types of depository institutions, to strengthen the financial system, and to retard the further deterioration of institutions weakened by institutional constraints and economic conditions.

Congress also sought to revitalize the housing industry by strengthening the financial stability of home mortgage lending institutions and by insuring the availability of home mortgage loans. Several provisions were included to expand the real estate lending authority of mortgage lending institutions and to remove impediments to such lending activity. The act was intended to streamline the financial services industry and to accelerate the process of banking begun by the Depository Institutions and Monetary Control Act of 1980.

The Garn-St. Germain Act contains eight titles:

Title I—The Deposit Insurance Flexibility Act. Title I expanded FDIC and FSLIC powers to assist failing or troubled depository institutions and, when appropriate, to arrange interstate and cross-industry acquisitions and mergers of such institutions of any size and failing commercial banks with assets or $500 million or higher. It also broadened the authority of the National Credit Union Administration to merge financially distressed credit unions and authorized savings banks to convert from state to federal charters yet continue to be FDIC insured.

Title II—The Net Worth Certificate Act. Title II established a program whereby an insured institution may exchange capital notes with the FDIC and the FSLIC to shore up the qualifying institution's net worth. Qualifying rules include: capital of less than 3% of assets, above 20% of the loan portfolio in mortgages or mortgage-backed securities, and losses in the two previous quarters.

Title III—The Thrift Institutions Restructing Act. Title III broadened the lending and investment powers of federal thrift associations and facilitated the conversion of an association from a state to a federal charter and from a mutual to a stock form. Title III also included several provisions of interest to banks:

1. Directing the Depository Institutions Deregulation Committee to adopt within 60 days of the legislation's enactment a new deposit instrument directly equivalent to and competitive with money market mutual funds. The instrument will have the following characteristics: no minimum maturity; no interest rate ceiling; a minimum denomination of $2,500; only three preauthorized or automatic withdrawals and three drafts permitted in any month and reserve requirements of 0% for individual accounts and 3% for corporate accounts; all types of depositors eligible, and insurance up to $200,000 by the FSLIC or FDIC. These depository instruments were issued starting December 14, 1982.
2. Eliminating all interest rate differentials on deposits by January 1, 1984.
3. Preempting prohibitions against enforcing DUE-ON-SALE CLAUSES in mortgage contracts.
4. Permitting mutual savings banks and savings and loan associations to have more commercial and consumer loans (up to 10% and 30%, respectively, of assets by 1984) and to offer, with restrictions, demand deposits to commercial and agricultural customers.

Title IV—Provisions Relating to National and Member Banks. Title IV amended various statutory provisions primarily affecting commercial banks. The title amended the National Banking Act to revise outdated lending and borrowing limits and to modify the real estate lending authority of national banks. Legal lending limit was raised to 15% and 25% of capital for unsecured or secured borrowers, respectively. Title IV provisions also permitted federal chartering of bankers' banks, liberalized and reformed banking affiliate statutes, and exempted small depository institutions from reserve requirements. The title made minor modifications to the Financial Institutions Regulatory Act of 1978.

Title V—Federal Credit Union Act Amendments. Title V amended the Federal Credit Union Act to simplify the organization process for credit unions, broaden their mortgage lending powers, and make technical modifications to several provisions of that act.

Title VI—Property, Casualty, and Life Insurance Activities of Bank Holding Companies. Title VI restricts bank holding companies and their subsidiaries from providing insurance except as allowed in specific exceptions. Those exceptions are:

1. Grandfathered insurance activities that were engaged in or authorized as of May 1, 1982.
2. Permitted bank holding companies to engage in credit life, disability, and involuntary unemployment insurance activities.
3. Permitted bank holding companies to engage in general insurance agency activities in towns of fewer than 5,000 people or where there is inadequate insurance agency activity.
4. Permitted approximately 2,800 bank holding companies with assets of less than $50 million to engage in insurance agency activities.
5. Contained other provisions (a) involving the insurance activities of finance company subsidiaries, (b) permitting bank holding companies to act as managing general agents, and (c) permitting bank holding companies to continue certain previously approved activities.

Title VII—Miscellaneous Provisions. Title VII contained a series of miscellaneous provisions, including amendments:

Exempting certain student loan transactions from the Truth-in-Lending Act.
Removing disclosure requirements for arrangers of credit.
Making industrial banks eligible for FDIC insurance.
Amending the International Banking Act of 1987.
Modifying statutory provisions concerning the issuance of preferred stock and subordinated obligations of the federal National Mortgage Association.
Establishing a phase-in of reserve requirements for banks that withdrew from the Federal Reserve System between July 1, 1987, and March 31, 1980.
Amending the Bank Service Corporation Act, particularly concerning the ability of banks to invest in such corporations and the permissive activities of such corporations.
Concerning a federal deposits insurance study, the Neighborhood Reinvestment Corporation, and other miscellaneous amendments.

Title VIII—Alternative Mortgage Transaction Parity Act. Title VIII created parity between federally chartered and nonfederally chartered housing creditors by authorizing nonfederally chartered housing creditors to engage in alternative mortgage transactions, and preempting state provisions inhibiting or impeding such transactions, to the extent that the nonfederally chartered housing creditors make loans in compliance with applicable federal regulations.

Summary. The Depository Institutions Deregulation and Monetary Control Act discarded much of the financial regulation dating back to the 1930s. The act directed the gradual removal of Regulation Q ceilings by April 1986 and authorized the continuation of NOW accounts. It preempted state usury ceilings on interest rates and made uniform and reduced reserve requirements, while imposing them on nonmember as well as member banks. Nonmember banks became eligible for Federal Reserve services. The deregulation on deposit interest rates did not stop disintermediation. A rapid transfer of funds from thrifts into money market funds occurred.

The Garn-St. Germain Act of 1982 required the Depository Institution Deregulation Committee, established by the DIDMCA, to permit banks and thrifts to establish two new types of deposits that were free from interest rate ceilings: (1) Money market deposit accounts paying interest rates and offering limited transactions services, insured by the FDIC or FSLIC; (2) Super NOW accounts that were free from Regulation Q ceilings and paid competitive interest rates.

On April 1, 1986, the remaining interest ceilings and minimum deposit requirements on NOW and super-NOW accounts were removed. The result was that the financial services industry became relatively competitive and responsive to interest rate patterns on a wide range of financial instruments. The character of the monetary system began to evolve.

BIBLIOGRAPHY

CHAMNESS, ROBERT P. *The Garn-St. Germain in Depository Institutions Act of 1982: A Complete Reference for Bankers*, Rolling Meadows, IL, Bank Administration Institute, 1983.

GATT See GENERAL AGREEMENT ON TARIFFS AND TRADE.

GENERAL ACCOUNTING OFFICE An independent nonpolitical agency of the federal government established in 1921 to audit and review federal financial transactions and statements and to examine the expenditures of appropriations by federal units. The GAO is directly responsible to the U.S. Congress.

GENERAL ACCOUNTS Accounts that appear in a bank's GENERAL LEDGER; all accounts other than accounts with depositors and depositories, i.e., accounts representing balances due to and due from customers.

GENERAL AGENT See AGENT.

GENERAL AGREEMENT ON TARIFFS AND TRADE (GATT) An international organization, associated with the United Nations, that has as its purpose the reduction of tariffs and other barriers to international trade. The General Agreement on Tariffs and Trade (GATT) has conducted eight rounds of multilateral trade negotiations: Geneva, 1947; Annecy (France), 1949; Torquay (United Kingdom), 1951; Geneva, 1956; Geneva (Dillon round), 1960-61; Geneva (Kennedy round), 1964-67; Tokyo/Geneva (Tokyo round), 1973-79; and Punta del Este (Uruguay round; recent meetings held in Montreal), 1987-. Recent rounds are scheduled as four-year arrangements. GATT has its headquarters in Geneva, and GATT contracts affect more than 90 nations.

GENERAL AGREEMENT ON TARIFFS AND TRADE (GATT)

The Session of Contracting Parties is the basic policy-making body of GATT and meets annually. Member nations have one vote. Majority voting is adhered to except to allow a deviation from specific obligations arising under GATT, when a two-thirds vote is required. Panels of conciliation are established to resolve trade disputes.

Originally negotiated in 1947 and effective beginning January 1, 1948, the General Agreement on Tariffs and Trade (GATT) has been renewed from time to time with amendments. It is a multilateral trade treaty embodying four fundamental principles: (1) nondiscrimination in world trade (the contracting parties are bound by the most-favored-nation clause which requires nondiscriminatory treatment of all imports regardless of origin), (2) protection afforded to domestic industries exclusively through customs tariffs and not through other commercial measures such as import quotas, (3) emphasis on consultation so as to avoid damage to the trading interests of the contracting parties, and (4) provision of a framework for negotiations for the reduction of tariffs and other barriers to trade, and embodiment of the results of such negotiations in a legal instrument.

The GATT was originally intended to be a provisional international trade and tariffs agreement along multilateral lines, pending ratification by nations of the Havana Charter of the INTERNATIONAL TRADE ORGANIZATION for a permanent basis. When the U.S. Senate failed to ratify the ITO Charter in 1950, further work on ratification of that charter was discontinued, and instead the GATT became effective as an international code of trade and tariff rules. The U.S. signed the first GATT as an executive agreement and also signed the March 21, 1955 revised agreement on that basis and not as a treaty requiring Senate ratification.

The 1955 GATT provided for a revival of a proposed permanent organization to administer the GATT, called the Organization for Trade Cooperation; its protocol was signed by representatives of the U.S. State Department on March 21, 1955, conditional upon congressional approval. The OTC protocol was submitted by the President to Congress April 14, 1955, for approval, although legal technicians did not regard it as a treaty requiring congressional approval. The OTC organization would have consisted of a secretariat, an executive committee of 17 members, and an assembly of all the nations signing the GATT. This permanent administrative body would have had the power to deal with trade disputes or complaints for violations of the agreement in an executive and judicial capacity. The OTC protocol was not ratified by the Congress.

Ever since the beginning of GATT in 1947, participation by the U.S. has been financed through general contingency funds rather than through specific appropriations.

Functions. The "Kennedy Round" of tariff reductions, the sixth multilateral trade negotiations undertaken by GATT, began May, 1964, and was concluded June 30, 1967. These comprehensive negotiations were named after President Kennedy, who sponsored the Trade Expansion Act of 1962, enabling the U.S. for the first time to participate in across-the-board tariff reductions. The negotiations resulted in agreement covering tariff concessions of about $40 billion of world trade, including U.S. concessions on about $8.5 billion of imports and concessions by other participating nations covering the same amount in U.S. exports. Tariff reductions of 50% were applied to numerous manufactured products, and significant but smaller reductions were applied to many others. For the four largest participants—the U.S., the members of the European Economic Community (Common Market), the United Kingdom, and Japan—the weighted average reduction of tariffs on manufactured products was about 35%. The U.S. tariff reductions were generally to take effect in five equal annual installments, the first of which became effective January 1, 1968. The Council of Economic Advisers (1968 Report) put the advantages of the Kennedy Round's tariff reductions as follows.

1. The amount of the existing trade covered by the tariff cuts did not reflect the potential expansion of trade, considered "one of the key benefits" of the tariff reductions.
2. New U.S. export opportunities would be created.
3. U.S. producers would experience lower costs as a result of reduced tariffs on many inputs.
4. The welfare of U.S. consumers would be enhanced by lower prices of goods of both domestic and foreign origin.

On the other hand, the Council of Economic Advisers conceded that there could be some adverse effects as well; the increases in imports resulting from reduced U.S. tariffs could cause adjustment difficulties for certain U.S. industries.

However, when the Trade Expansion Act of 1962 expired in June, 1967, the President ceased to have the authority of that act, which generally authorized him to reduce any tariff by not more than 50% of the rate existing as of July 1, 1962, and to eliminate the tariff on any items subject to duty of 5% or less. In addition to such general tariff-reducing authority, the act gave the President special authority to negotiate with the EEC as to reduction to zero of tariff on any article in any overall statistical category in which the U.S. and the EEC together supplied at least 80% of total free world exports in any representative period, reduction or elimination of tariffs and other import restrictions on tropical agricultural and forestry products not produced in significant quantities in the U.S., and reduction or elimination of the tariff on any agricultural article if the President should determine that such reduction or elimination would tend to expand U.S. agricultural exports. The act also provided for government assistance to enable firms and workers injured by increased imports to adjust into other lines of production and employment.

The Trade Bill of 1969, as submitted by the President to Congress in November, 1969, would have continued the movement toward freer trade, and it also explicitly recognized the importance of ensuring that U.S. producers had fair access to foreign markets. Specifically, the bill would have restored presidential power to make limited tariff reductions. It envisioned the elimination of the American selling price (ASP) system, in which certain important duties are based on the domestic selling price of competing American products rather than on the normal basis of actual export price. It would have broadened the authority to act against countries that treated U.S. products unfairly and would have provided new authority to act against those countries that granted export subsidies which resulted in unfair competition against U.S. exports in third markets. At the same time, it would have significantly improved the procedure by which business and workers injured by imports could receive government assistance.

Additional features were subsequently added to the President's 1969 proposal, some of which, including an amendment to allow the DOMESTIC INTERNATIONAL SALES CORPORATION (DISC) that would provide tax deferrals to U.S. exporting firms and the addition of textile quota provisions designed to assist in the conclusion of international agreements on textiles, were supported by the administration. Other amendments, however, many of which were unacceptable to the administration, were eventually included in a bill passed by the House of Representatives. Protectionism particularly appeared in a provision to impose increased restrictions on imports of products which met quantitative criteria in cases where the Tariff Commission (name changed to International Trade Commission) found injury. "This and several other amendments would have threatened to reverse the progress achieved in liberalizing our trade policy," in the judgment of the COUNCIL OF ECONOMIC ADVISERS (February, 1971, *Economic Report*), "and opened the prospect of retaliation by other countries against U.S. exports (as well as) "weakened the fight against domestic inflation." Clearly, concluded the CEA, U.S. trade policy reached a critical juncture in 1970, as although Congress did not adopt protectionist trade legislation, the pressures for greater import restrictions remained strong at the beginning of 1971.

These retaliatory provisions appeared to be designed to mollify considerably increased protectionist sentiment in Congress, reflected in the introduction of many bills proposing imposition of quantitative restrictions on imports.

Tariff Preferences for "LDCs.". In 1968, the United Nations Conference on Trade and Development (UNCTAD) recommended that the more prosperous nations provide preferential tariff rates on the exports of less developed countries (LDCs). The Organization for Economic Cooperation and Development (OECD) appointed a working group to formulate a plan for generalized tariff preferences, and the U.S. submitted a proposal thereto. This departure from the most-favored-nation principle of GATT was, in the view of the administration (1970 Report, Council of Economic Advisers), justified by the stimulation of essential manufacturing development in the LDCs and the expectation that a liberal system of general preferences, replacing specialized regional preferences, would create additional world trade and might reduce existing distortions in trade patterns.

Seventh Round of GATT Negotiations. The seventh round of GATT negotiations, concluded in April, 1979, resulted in the signing in December, 1979, of the agreements reached at said negotiations, the Tokyo Round of the multilateral trade negotiations. The Tokyo Round agreements included significant reductions in tariff and nontariff barriers to trade, and they introduced through a series of codes a set of procedures designed to limit nontariff distortion of trade patterns. The Council of Economic Advisers (January, 1980, Report) reported that the United States and its trading partners made reciprocal tariff cuts. The U.S. reductions averaged about 30%; those of Japan, 22%; and those of the EUROPEAN ECONOMIC COMMUNITY, 27%. Five major codes were agreed upon in the Tokyo Round: (1) the government procurement code, significantly improving the opportunities for suppliers to compete equally for government orders; (2) the agreement on standards, speeding the certification of foreign products; (3) the agreements on subsidies and countervailing duties, and (4) the agreement on antidumping actions, restricting the use of subsidies and clarifying the circumstances in which countervailing and antidumping duties may be imposed; and (5) the agreement on customs valuation, ensuring more consistent practices and thus reducing the scope for offsetting tariff concessions by changes in valuation rules.

The Council of Economic Advisers judged that these agreements themselves do not guarantee success in resolving difficult and detailed nontariff issues, and that only when they are applied in individual circumstances would the procedures specified in the agreements reveal their adequacy. This pragmatic approach has been justified by subsequent events; in its 1981 Report, the Council of Economic Advisers found three specific challenges to open trade: heightened pressures to use trade barriers to save domestic jobs; the increased use of direct and indirect subsidies to promote exports; and the emerging reliance on market-sharing arrangements to ease adjustment.

Eighth Round of GATT Negotiations. The agenda of the 1987 Uruguay round included negotiating freer trade in the services sector (e.g., licensing and investing); lowering tariffs and protecting access barriers for tropical products from Third World countries; establishing a more efficient procedure for settling disputes; and implementing tighter surveillance of countries' trade policies. Other areas scheduled for discussion include agriculture, intellectual properties, textiles, and safeguards (rules that govern emergency measures against imports). The overriding impact was towards developing a better world trade system.

For additional discussion of the relationship of the GATT to the tariff-trade policy of the U.S. See INTERNATIONAL TRADE COMMISSION.

BIBLIOGRAPHY

"The Antidumping Dodge." *Economist*, September, 1988.
BANKS, H. "GATT—Almost Back On Track." *Forbes*, March, 20, 1989.
"GATT and 1992." THE BANKER. January, 1989.
"GATT and the Uruguay Round: The King's Horses to the Rescue." *Economist*, February 11, 1989.
"GATT in the Doldrums." *Economist*, November 26, 1988.
"GATT: Uruguay Round Update." *Business America*, May 22, 1989.
WILSON, J. "Peace Moves Ahead, But Trade Talks Hit a Snag." *Futures*, January, 1989.

GENERAL AND ADMINISTRATIVE COSTS Overhead costs that relate to companywide activities such as institutional advertising, executive salaries, and regulatory reporting costs.

GENERAL AND FIRST MORTGAGE BONDS
See FIRST AND GENERAL MORTGAGE BONDS.

GENERAL ASSET CURRENCY Bank notes that are not secured by a specific pledge of collateral, e.g., specie, bonds, or commercial paper, but that are supported only by the general assets of the issuing bank. The notes of the Bank of France are examples of general asset currency. There are no examples of general asset currency in the United States; FEDERAL RESERVE NOTES, the principal circulating medium, are specifically secured.

GENERAL AVERAGE See AVERAGE.

GENERAL BOOKKEEPER One who has charge of the gen-eral ledger and the GENERAL BOOKKEEPING DEPARTMENT.

GENERAL BOOKKEEPING DEPARTMENT The department of a bank that records all transactions affecting the general accounts as distinguished from customers' accounts. The function of the general bookkeeping department is to summarize the transactions of each of the operating departments of the bank before they are added to or subtracted from the assets, liabilities, or undivided profits accounts. In order that the financial condition of a bank may be visualized, this department becomes the central accounting department where all the transactions of the bank are gathered, condensed, and recorded. The general bookkeeping department maintains a GENERAL LEDGER, statement book, and expense book.

GENERAL DEPOSITS See DEPOSITS.

GENERAL ENDORSEMENT ENDORSEMENT in blank.

GENERAL FIRST MORTGAGE BONDS In most cases, GENERAL MORTGAGE BONDS; although sometimes the bonds constitute a first lien on a part of the mortgaged property. The title is misleading because a general mortgage cannot be a first mortgage. The proper title for this class of bonds is FIRST AND GENERAL MORTGAGE BONDS, or FIRST LIEN AND GENERAL MORTGAGE BONDS.

GENERALIZED SYSTEM OF PREFERENCES A nonreciprocal trade concession given to certain less developed countries (LDC), referred to as beneficiaries, for products exported to industrial nations. The generalized system of preferences (GSP) allows duty-free entry into industrial countries of manufactured and agricultual product of LDC. The basic purpose of GSP is to increase exports from LDCs to promote econoic growth in the LDCs. The United Nations Conference on Trade and Development directs the activities of GSP.

The United States grants duty exemptions under GSP programs from duty on approximately half the products listed in the tariff schedules of the United States when products originate in a LDC country. A product that is entitled to exemption is defined as any article within the five-digit product code in the tariff schedules. The GSP exemption is not the same as that provided under the most favored nation clause.

U.S. law denies duty-free treatment to products from a country where the appraised value of the product to the United States during the calendar year exceeds 50% of the total U.S. imports of that product, or where the appraised value of the shipments of the product to the United States during the calendar year exceeds a fixed amount. This restriction is referred to as the "competitive needs limitations." The restriction can be removed if a country's shipment of the product falls below the 50% or dollar-value level. The president can waive the 50% limitation under certain circumstances.

Duty-free entry under a GSP program requires that the product be included in the U.S. GSP approval list and be imported into the United States directly from the beneficiary. The product must originate in a beneficiary country. An importer is required to request GSP treatment for the product. The GSP program applies to about 2 % of U.S. imports. Additions and deletions of products listed for duty-free entry are implemented by presidential executive order, upon recommendation of the U.S. trade representative.

GENERAL LEDGER The most important accounting record of a bank, containing a summary of all transactions of the institution including general accounts and controlling accounts for the customers' ledgers. Every transaction that occurs in any of the operating departments eventually affects some account in the general ledger and in the ordinary routine reaches the general bookkeeping department for posting to the general ledger. Each general ledger account (e.g., time loans) represents the aggregate of such loans held by the bank and the total represented by the subsidiary loan ledger. Whereas one hundred time loans may be made during the day and as many entries recorded in the subsidiary loan ledger, only one posting is made for the total (one hundred loans) to the debit of the time loans account in the general ledger.

Usually the general ledger is of the Boston or progressive type. Where the number of accounts is large, two separate volumes are frequently used, one each for assets and liabilities. Postings are made to the general ledger from various posting media routed to the general bookkeeping department from the various operating departments. The postings usually are made early in the day after

GENERAL LEDGER

which the ledger is proved. The balances of each customers' ledger must prove with the corresponding controlling account in the general ledger.

The general ledger reveals the cross section of the business each day, and the daily proofs thereof are virtually a series of instantaneous photographs or moving pictures of the bank's financial condition and financial progress.

Each day summary entries may be posted to the general ledger accounts from the journals, registers, and other subsidiary records covering transactions involving the assets, liabilities, and capital accounts, as well as income and expense accounts. The latter are closed each month, following the preparation of adjusting entries to reflect the accrual basis of accounting except for small items covered on a cash basis. The chart of accounts in the general ledger for a national bank specified by the Code of Federal Regulations (12 CFR 11) for reports under the Securities Exchange Act to the Comptroller of the Currency is as follows.

BALANCE SHEET

Assets
1. Cash and due from banks
2. Interest-bearing balances with banks
3. Investment securities:
   a. U.S. Treasury securities
   b. Obligations of other U.S. government agencies and corporations
   c. Obligations of states and political subdivisions
   d. Other bonds, notes, and debentures
   e. Federal Reserve and corporate stock
4. Trading account securities
5. Federal funds sold and securities purchased under agreements to resell
6. Loans, less:
   a. Unearned income on loans
   b. Reserve for possible loan losses
7. Direct lease financing
8. Bank premises, equipment, furniture, and fixtures
9. Real estate owned other than bank premises
10. Investment in unconsolidated subsidiaries and associated companies
11. Customer's liability on acceptances outstanding
12. Other assets
13. Total assets

Liabilities and Capital
14. Deposits in domestic offices:
    a. Demand
    b. Savings
    c. Time
15. Deposits in foreign offices
16. Federal funds purchased and securities sold under agreements to repurchase
17. Liabilities for borrowed money
18. Mortgages payable
19. Bank acceptances outstanding
20. Other liabilities
21. Total liabilities excluding subordinated notes and debentures
22. Subordinated notes and debentures
23. Equity capital:
    a. Capital stock:
       (1) Preferred stock (shares outstanding ; _____ par value $ _____)
       (2) Common stock:
          a. Shares authorized _____
          b. Shares outstanding ; _____ par value $ _____
    b. Surplus
    c. Undivided profits
    d. Reserve for contingencies and other capital reserves
24. Total equity capital
25. Total liabilities, subordinated notes and debentures, and equity capital

Changes in the undivided profit account shall also be reported, furnished insofar as practicable in the following detail as of the end of the latest fiscal quarter.

Undivided Profits
1. Balance at beginning of current fiscal year
2. Net income to date
3. Dividends declared
   a. Common stock:
      Cash
      Stock (percent)
   b. Preferred stock:
      Cash ($ _____ per share)
4. Prior period adjustments (list and describe all credits and charges separately)
5. Other credits and charges (list and describe all these items separately)
6. Balance at end of interim period

Form F-4, Quarterly Report, of the Comptroller of the Currency calls for the following income statement information for the latest quarter and for the fiscal year to date, both also shown for the corresponding prior year.

Summarized Financial Information
1. Operating income:
   a. Interest and fees on loans
   b. Interest on balances with banks
   c. Income on federal funds sold and securities purchased under agreements to resell
   d. Interest and dividends on investments:
      (1) U.S. Treasury securities
      (2) Obligations of other U.S. government agencies and corporations
      (3) Obligations of states and political subdivisions
      (4) Interest on other bonds, notes, and debentures
      (5) Dividends on stock
   e. Income from direct lease financing
   f. Income from fiduciary activities
   g. Service charges on deposit accounts
   h. Other service charges, collection and exchange charges, commissions and fees
   i. Other operating income
   j. Total operating income
2. Operating expenses:
   a. Salaries, wages, and other employee benefits
   b. Interest on time certificates of deposits of $100,000 or more
   c. Interest on deposits in foreign offices
   d. Interest on other deposits
   e. Expense of federal funds purchased and securities sold under agreements to repurchase
   f. Interest on borrowed money
   g. Interest on subordinated notes and debentures
   h. Occupancy expense of bank premises, net (gross occupancy less rental income)
   i. Furniture and equipment expense (including depreciation of $ _____)
   j. Provision for possible loan losses
   k. Other expenses
   l. Total operating expenses
3. Income (loss) before income taxes and securities gains (losses)
4. Applicable income taxes
5. Income (loss) before securities gains (losses)
6. Net securities gains (losses), less related tax effect ($ _____)
7. Net income (loss) or income (loss) before extraordinary items
8. Extraordinary items, less related income tax effect ($ _____)
9. Net income (loss)
10. Earnings (loss) per common share: [a]
    a. Income before securities gains (losses)
    b. Net income (loss)

[a] The per share amount of securities gains (losses) may be stated separately. If extraordinary items are reported, the per share amount of income before extraordinary items and the per share amount of extraordinary items shall be stated separately. When the reporting bank is a wholly owned subsidiary (except for directors' qualifying shares) of a bank holding company, per share data shall be deleted.

A statement of cash flows shall be reported as follows, for the fiscal year to date.

ENCYCLOPEDIA OF BANKING AND FINANCE

Changes in Cash Flows [a]

Cash flows from operating activities:
  Net income
  Adjustments to reconcile net income to cash provided by operations:
    Provision for loan losses
    Depreciation of premises and equipment
    Amortization of intangible assets
    Deferred income taxes
    Gain on sale of investment securities
    Loss on sale of noninterest-earning assets
    Amortization of investment security discount
    Increase in accrued income taxes
    Increase in accrued interest receivable
    Increase in accrued interest payable
    Net change in other accrued and deferred income and expense
    Net trading account activities
      Net cash provided by operations

Cash flows from investing activities:
  Purchases of interest-bearing bank balances
  Maturities of interest-bearing bank balances
  Net increase in federal funds sold and securities purchased under resale agreements
  Purchases of investment securities
  Sales and maturities of investment securities
  Net increase in credit card and other short-term loans
  Longer term loans made to customers
  Principal collected on longer term loans
  Capital expenditures
  Proceeds from sales of premises and equipment
  Net decrease in other assets
  Business combinations
    Net cash used by investing activities

Cash flows from financing activities:
  Net increase in demand, savings and money market accounts
  Proceeds from sales of certificates of deposit
  Payments for maturing certificates of deposit
  Net increase in federal funds purchased and securities sold under repurchase agreements
  Net increase in commercial paper
  Net increase in other short-term borrowings
  Proceeds from issuance of long-term debt
  Payments on long-term debt
  Common stock issued
  Dividend payments
  Treasury stock purchased
  Other equity transactions
  Net decrease in other liabilities
    Net cash provided by financing activities

Increase in cash and cash equivalents
Cash and cash equivalents at beginning of year
Cash and cash equivalents at end of year

Noncash investing and financing activities:
  Addition to premises and equipment financed by long-term debt
  Common stock issued upon conversion of long-term debt
  Common stock issued in bank acquisitions
  Transfer of other real estate assets

---

[a] Historically, this statement has been prepared primarily from a comparison of period-end balances. The bank may, at its option, prepare this statement using average daily balances for changes in asset and liability accounts. If the use of the average daily balance method results in the presentation of data which materially differ from those which would have been shown if the period-end method had been used, such differences shall be disclosed in a note to the financial statements.

[b] Sources and applications of funds shall be shown separately by amounts when they exceed 5% of the average of total funds provided during the reported periods.

Pursuant to the requirements of the Securities Exchange Act of 1934, the bank will duly cause this quarterly report to be signed on its behalf with the name and title of a duly authorized signing officer.

For examples of the Call Report of Condition, *see* CALL REPORT. *See also* BANK BOOKKEEPING.

GENERAL LEGACY *See* LEGACY.

GENERAL LOAN AND COLLATERAL AGREEMENT

Brokers' loans, i.e., stock exchange loans, are not usually evidenced by notes. Instead, brokers borrowing on stock exchange collateral are required to sign a loan contract known as a general loan and collateral agreement, or continuing agreement. Brokers' loans are usually demand loans, and the machinery of the call loan market is such as to require a contract which can operate as a continuing obligation. This contract remains on file with the lending bank and obviates the necessity of preparing a separate note for each loan. Because of its flexibility it is more advantageous both to the borrower and to the bank. In a collateral loan, the collateral is recited, but in the general loan and collateral agreement, no specific loans or collateral are mentioned. The agreement gives the bank, however, the right to sell any collateral securing a loan upon default in payment when called, or upon failure to respond to a call for additional margin. It also gives the bank the right to assign or transfer all or any part of the loan made, or to rehypothecate any government bonds in the collateral against loans from the Federal Reserve Bank. From the viewpoint of the customer, it prevents the inconvenience of signing a note each time a loan is made. The following is a typical form of general loan and collateral agreement.

General Loan and Collateral Agreement

WHEREAS, the undersigned expect, from time to time, to borrow money from the Blank Bank of New York (hereinafter called the Bank) and to pledge with the Bank property of various kinds as collateral security for the payment of such loan or loans to be hereafter made by the Bank; Now, therefore,

IT IS AGREED by the undersigned with the Bank that all property thus pledged with it may be held by it as collateral security for the payment of such loan or loans as well as for the payment of any other obligation or liability, direct or contingent, of the undersigned, or any of them, to the Bank, due or to become due, whether now existing or hereafter arising; and the undersigned agree to deliver to the Bank additional securities, or to make payments on account to its satisfaction, should the market value of said securities, as a whole, suffer any decline. The undersigned hereby give to the bank a lien for the amount of all such obligations and liabilities upon all the property or securities now or at any time hereafter given unto or left in the possession of the Bank, by the undersigned, whether for the express purpose of being used by the Bank as collateral security or for any other or different purpose, and also upon any balance of the deposit account of the undersigned, or any of them, with the Bank.

On the nonperformance of this promise, or upon the nonpayment of any of the obligations or liabilities above mentioned, or upon the failure of the undersigned, forthwith, with or without notice, to furnish satisfactory additional securities, or to make payments on account, in case of decline, as aforesaid, or in case of insolvency, bankruptcy, or failure in business of the undersigned, or any of them, then and in any such case, all obligations and liabilities, direct or contingent, of the undersigned and each of them, shall forthwith become due and payable without demand or notice; full power and authority are hereby given to the Bank to sell, assign, and deliver the whole of the said securities, or any part thereof, or any substitutes therefor, or any additions thereto, or any other securities or property given unto or left in the possession of the Bank, by the undersigned, whether for the express purpose of being used by the Bank as collateral security or for any other or different purpose, or in transit to or from the Bank, by mail or carrier, for any of the said purposes, at any broker's board, or at public or private sale, at the option of the Bank, without either demand, advertisement, or notice of any kind, all of which are hereby expressly waived. At any such sale, the Bank may itself purchase the whole or any part of the property sold, free from any right of redemption on the part of the undersigned, which is hereby waived and released. In case of any sale or other disposition of any of the property aforesaid, after deducting all costs or expenses of every kind for collection, sale, or delivery, the Bank may apply the residue of the proceeds of the sale or sales so made to pay one or more or all of the said obligations or liabilities to it, whether then due or not due, making proper rebate for interest on obligations or liabilities not then due and returning the overplus, if any, to the undersigned, who agree to be and remain liable, jointly and severally, to the Bank for any deficiency arising upon such sale or sales. The undersigned do hereby authorize and empower the Bank, at its option, at any time, to appropriate and apply to the payment and extinguishment of any of the obligations or liabilities hereinbefore referred to, whether now existing or hereafter contracted and whether then due or not due, any and all moneys now or hereafter in the hands of the Bank, on deposit, or otherwise to the credit of or belonging to the undersigned, or any of them.

The Bank may assign or transfer this instrument and may deliver the said collateral security or any part thereof to the transferee or transferees, who shall thereupon become vested with all the powers and rights above given to the Bank, in respect thereto; and the Bank shall thereafter be forever relieved and fully discharged from any liability or responsibility in the matter. No delay on the part of the holder thereof in exercising any rights hereunder shall operate as a waiver of such rights.

See CALL MONEY MARKET

GENERALLY ACCEPTED ACCOUNTING PRINCIPLES (GAAP)
The conventions, rules, and procedures necessary to define accepted accounting practice at a particular time. The Accounting Principles Board stated:

> Generally accepted accounting principles therefore is a technical term in financial accounting . . . . The standards of "generally accepted accounting principles" includes not only broad guidelines of general application, but also detailed practices and procedures.

The responsibility for developing generally accepted accounting principles in the United States prior to 1973 rested to a great degree with the American Institute of Certified Public Accountants (AICPA). In 1938 the AICPA began issuing authoritative statements through its Committee on Accounting Procedure (CAP). This committee was authorized to issue pronouncements on accounting procedures and practices. It published a series of accounting research bulletins.

CAP was replaced in 1959 by another committee of the AICPA called the Accounting Principles Board (APB). The APB was formed to counteract criticism of CAP and to create a policy-making body whose rules would be binding rather than optional. The APB issued a series of statements and opinions. The APB was replaced in 1973 by a new entity—the FINANCIAL ACCOUNTING STANDARDS BOARD (FASB).

FASB currently has the responsibility for setting accounting standards. The FASB is a separate entity from the AICPA. The Financial Accounting Foundation oversees the basic structure of the standard-setting process. The trustees are appointed by representatives of the following organizations: The American Accounting Association (1), American Institute of Certified Public Accountants (AIDPC) (4), National Association of Accountants (1), Financial Executives Institute (2), Financial Analysts Federation (1), Securities Industry Association (1), and various governmental accounting groups (3). The remaining positions are elected by other trustees. One of these comes from the commercial banking industry and the other from the business community. The sixteenth trustee is the senior elected official of the AICPA. The trustees of the Financial Accounting Foundation appoint members to FASB and to FASB's advisory council.

FASB is an independent body consisting of seven members, both accountants and nonaccountants. FASB members serve full time and are fully remunerated. An affirmative vote of four of the seven FASB members currently is needed to approve pronouncements. The board's deliberations are open to the public, and FASB follows due process procedures. FASB's Advisory Council is a diversified group of individuals from various areas of business. The council assists FASB in setting priorities and in establishing ad hoc task forces. It also provides feedback to FASB on proposed pronouncements. The FASB's authoritative pronouncements are issued in the form of *Statements of Financial Accounting Standards and Interpretations*. The FASB also issues *Statements of Financial Accounting Concepts*. Concept statements do not create generally accepted accounting principles. They establish a theoretical foundation upon which to base financial accounting and reporting standards. The FASB also publishes technical bulletins that provide guidance on accounting and reporting problems related to Statements of Standards or Interpretations. FASB established the Emerging Issues Task Force (EITF) in 1984 to identify new accounting and reporting issues that arise from new and different types of transactions. If members of the EITF reach a consensus that there is a single preferred treatment, the chief accountant of the SEC has stated that he will accept the consensus as authoritative support for practices to be used for SEC reporting. FASB has not sanctioned the EITF as an authoritative standard-setting body.

The GOVERNMENTAL ACCOUNTING STANDARDS BOARD (GASB) was established in 1984 to determine generally accepted accounting principles for state and local governmental entities. The General Accounting Office (GAO) and the Comptroller General develop accounting principles for agencies of the federal government. GASB is financed and overseen by the Financial Accounting Foundation, as is FASB. GASB has five members. The chairman serves full time; the vice-chairman and three other members serve part time. The board is assisted by a full-time professional staff and meets in open session. GASB sanctioned NCGA pronouncements and the AICPA *Industry Audit Guide: Audits of State and Local Governmental Units* as authoritative. Authoritative pronouncements of GASB include statements, interpretations, and technical bulletins.

In Statement on Auditing Standards 43, on the meaning of the term "present fairly in conformity with GAAP," the following levels and sources (ranked from highest downward) of accounting principles for business enterprises were identified:

1. Pronouncements of an authoritative body designated by the AICPA council to establish accounting principles, pursuant to Rule 203 (ET section 203.01) of the AICPA Code of Professional Ethics. Includes FASB standards and interpretations and nonsuperseded sections of accounting research bulletins and APB opinions. If the first category does not specify the accounting treatment in particular circumstances, then the second category is applicable.
2. Pronouncements of bodies composed of expert accountants that follow a due process procedure, including broad distribution of proposed accounting principles for public comment, for the intended purpose of establishing accounting principles or describing existing practices that are generally accepted. Includes AICPA *Industry Audit* and accounting guides, statements of position issued by the AICPA, and FASB technical bulletins.
3. Practices or pronouncements that are widely recognized as being generally accepted because they represent prevalent practice in a particular industry or the knowledgeable application to specific circumstances of pronouncements that are generally accepted. Includes AICPA interpretations and prevalent industry practices.
4. Other accounting literature. Includes FASB concept statements, AICPA issue papers, and APB statements.

The Securities and Exchange Commission has played a role in dealing with generally accepted accounting principles for financial institutions. The SEC maintains that financial statements filed with the commission will be presumed misleading unless prepared in accordance with GENERALLY ACCEPTED ACCOUNTING PRINCIPLES. Audited financial statements are the basis of financial disclosures to investors under the commission's disclosure system.

Regulators' accounting requirements may differ from GAAP for specific transactions or filings. Bank regulators do not require that all bank financial statements be audited by independent public accountants. The Federal Reserve Board requires bank holding company financial statements filed with it to conform fully with GAAP.

The vast majority of securities accounting requirements call for GAAP accounting rather than regulatory accounting principles (RAP). The U.S. General Accounting Office (GAO) has identified the federal agencies with authority to establish and enforce auditing and accounting standards affecting private sector companies. The GAO has identified the following differences in GAAP/RAP requirements with respect to the bank regulators:

1. The maximum amortization periods for goodwill permitted by the FDIC and the FRB are shorter than those permitted under GAAP.
2. FDIC and FRB require sales of receivables with recourse to be accounted for as financing, rather than sales as generally required under GAAP.
3. The Garn-St. Germain Depository Institutions Act of 1982 requires the FDIC to treat net worth certificates as part of the

capital accounts of a savings bank; under GAAP, net worth certificates do not increase assets or equity.
4. FDIC and FRB require that in-substance defeasance remain as a liability, whereas GAAP treats the debt as extinguished in certain circumstances.

Other differences relate solely to savings and loan associations regulated by the FHLBB.

Statement of Financial Accounting Standards No. 5, "Accounting for CONTINGENCIES" (1975), governs the general issue of loan loss recognition for GAAP purposes. It requires that loan losses be recognized when it is probable that a loss has been incurred and the amount of loss can be reasonably estimated. Financial institutions generally maintain an allowance for loan losses, which represents the estimated amount of loan losses in the loan portfolio.

Statement of Financial Accounting Standards No. 15, "Accounting by Debtors and Creditors for TROUBLED DEBT RESTRUCTURINGS" (1977), establishes standards for accounting by debtors and creditors solely for troubled debt restructuring.

BIBLIOGRAPHY

AICPA Professional Standards. Commerce Clearing House, Chicago, IL. Latest edition.
DELANEY, P. R., and others. *GAAP: Interpretation and Application*. John Wiley and Sons, Inc., NY, 1989.
FASB Accounting Standards—Current Text. MCGRAW-HILL BOOK CO., New York, NY, 1982. Annual.
FINANCIAL ACCOUNTING STANDARDS BOARD. *Accounting Standards—Current Tests*. Latest edition.
FINANCIAL ACCOUNTING STANDARDS BOARD. *Statements of Financial Accounting Concepts*, 1987/88 edition. Richard D. Irwin, Inc., Homewood, IL, 1988.
GLEIM, I. N., and DELANEY, P. R. *CPA Examination Review*, Volume 1. John Wiley and Sons, Inc., New York, NY. Annual.
GOVERNMENTAL ACCOUNTING STANDARDS BOARD, *Codificaton of Governmental Accounting and Financial Reporting Standards as of November 1, 1987*, 1987. Periodically updated.
KIESO, D. E., and WEYGANDT, J. J. *Intermediate Accounting*. Latest edition.
NIKOLAI, L. A., and BAZLEY, J. D. *Intermediate Accounting*. Latest edition.

GENERAL MORTGAGE BONDS
Bonds secured by a blanket mortgage upon all the property already subject in whole or in part to prior mortgages. These bonds are common among railroad corporations, being issued as a means of raising funds for improvements upon property which has enhanced in value since the issue of the underlying mortgage. Many mortgages have an "after acquired" property clause which places all the property actually owned at the time the bonds are issued, as well as all the property that may subsequently be acquired, under the lien and subject to the mortgage. The after acquired property may be that which is obtained through the proceeds of the sale of the bonds, or it may apply to all property acquired after the date of the mortgage.

General mortgage bonds frequently are issued in sufficient amount not only to raise additional capital but also to provide for the retirement of the original mortgage bonds when they mature. When this is the case, general mortgage bonds eventually become first mortgage bonds.

GENERAL OBLIGATION   See OBLIGATION.

GENERAL OBLIGATION BONDS
Bonds backed by the ability of the municipality, city, or state to levy ad valorem taxes on all taxable real property. General obligation bonds are repayable from the general revenues provided from such taxes and from other available revenues. Such bonds are backed by the full faith and credit and taxing power of the issuer.

GENERAL PURPOSE FINANCIAL STATEMENTS
Financial statements that are expected to present fairly the economic facts of the operationg, investing, and financing activities of an entity for investors, creditors, and other users of the statements.

GEOGRAPHIC RISK
A risk associated with economic, political, and currency transfer policy of a country or region. It is sometimes referred to as the COUNTRY RISK.

GI BILL OF RIGHTS
The Servicemen's Readjustment Act. See VETERANS' BENEFITS.

GIFT CAUSA MORTIS
A gift made in the expectation of imminent death on condition that the donor die. Should the owner die, the title to the property vests in the surviving donee.

GIFT INTER VIVOS
A gift between the living; the gift becomes absolute during the life of the donor and donee.

GI LOANS   See VA LOANS

GIFT TAX
The federal gift tax is an excise tax, levied upon the privilege of giving. The first federal gift tax was effective from June 2, 1924, to December 31, 1926, when it was repealed. A new federal gift tax law was passed June 6, 1932. Thus, any gift made prior to June 6, 1932, and after December 31, 1926, was not subject to federal gift tax.

The Revenue Act of 1948, effective April 3, 1948, created the marital deduction, applicable also on gifts from one spouse to another and allowed in an amount equal to one-half of the gift to the spouse if the amount of the gift was included in the total taxable gifts. Other deductions included the $3,000 statutory exclusion from gifts taxable during any calendar year; the lifetime exemption of $30,000 for a donor; and exemptions as to gifts to charitable institutions and other types of public gifts.

The gift tax was computed cumulatively, and was the difference between two figures: (1) the computation of gift tax on all gifts made between June 6, 1932, and the end of the current calendar year; and (2) the computation of gift tax on all gifts up to the beginning of the current calendar year, excluding gifts for the current calendar year. This cumulative feature of computation made it different from calculation of the income tax, for example, which is generally calculated for the current year, without reference to any previous years (no averaging).

The Federal Tax Reform Act of 1976 completely changed the basis for taxation of gifts by providing for a unified credit on combined estate and gift taxes and subjecting the resulting net estate minus allowable deductions, plus taxable gifts made after 1976 (gift taxes paid are subtracted from the net tax due), to a unified estate and gift tax schedule having graduated rates. In place of the former $60,000 specific exemption on the estate tax and $30,000 lifetime gifts exemption, the new law provided for unified total credit increasing the equivalent of exemption from $120,660 in 1977 to $175,625 in 1981, on estates of decedents dying in the following specified years, based on unified credit of $30,000 for decedents dying in 1977; $34,000 in 1978; $38,000 in 1979; $42,500 in 1980; and $42,500 in 1981 and thereafter.

Economic Recovery Tax Act (ERTA) of 1981. The ERTA of 1981 increased the annual gift tax exclusion from $3,000 ($6,000 for donor and spouse) to $10,000 ($20,000 for donor and spouse) for gifts made after December 31, 1981. Moreover, ERTA provided that, contrary to prior law, gifts made within three years of death can be excluded in computing the taxable estate of the decedents (except gifts of life insurance effected within three years of death).

Additionally, ERTA substantially increased the unified amount of estate and gift tax credit, and hence the amounts of estate transfers or gifts exempted from tax, *for husband and wife each*, as shown in the appended table.

The Tax Reform Act of 1976 combined the gift tax and the estate tax into a unified transfer tax rate schedule that applies to both life (gifts) and death (estates) transfers. To remove relatively small gifts and estates from the imposition of tax, a unified transfer tax credit of $192,800 is allowed against gift and estate taxes. This is equivalent to exempting the first $600,000 of taxable gifts or taxable estate from the unified transfer tax. The following outline illustrates the computation of the gift tax.

  Total amount of individual's gifts for current year
 − One-half of gifts to third parties if gift splitting is elected
 + One-half of spouse's gifts to third parties if gift splitting is elected

GILT EDGED

- Amount exclusions of $10,000 per donee
- Marital deduction (unlimited amount) for gifts made to spouse
- Charitable contribution deduction (unlimited amount)
= Taxable gifts for current period
+ Taxable gifts for all prior periods
= Cumulative taxable gifts
x Tax at current rate on cumulative taxable gifts
- Tax at current rates on taxable gifts of prior periods
= Tax on taxable gifts of current period
- Unified credit for the period, reduced by unified credit used in previous period
= Tax payable for current period

Gross gifts include any transfer for less than an adequate and full consideration. As a general rule, all gifts are valued at their fair market value as of the date of the gift, i.e., the date the transfer becomes complete. The gift-splitting provisions allow spouses to treat a gift that is actually made by one of them to a third party as if each spouse had made one-half of the gift.

An annual exclusion of up to $10,000 per donee is allowed for gifts of present interest (not future interests). Charitable gifts are deductible without limitation. A marital deduction is allowed without limitation for gifts to a donor's spouse.

A gift tax must be filed on a calendar-year basis, with the return due and tax paid on or before April 15 of the following year.

Estate Taxation under ERTA

Year of death or gift	Amount of estate and gift tax credit	Estate transfers or gifts exempted from tax[a]
1982	$ 62,800	$225,000
1983	79,300	275,000
1984	96,300	325,000
1985	121,800	400,000
1986	155,800	500,000
1987 and thereafter	192,800	600,000

[a]For husband and wife each, e.g., for 1982 a husband and wife could give $450,000 tax free to beneficiaries

BIBLIOGRAPHY

"Charitable Lead and Remainder Trust Rules Explained." *Journal of Taxation*, February, 1989.
DEE, R. L. "Section 2036(c): The Monster That Ate Estate Planning and Installment Sales, Buy-sells, Options, Employment Contracts and Leases." *Taxes*, December, 1988.
LASSILA, D. R. "Joint Tenancy Ownership—Advantages and Pitfalls." *CPA Journal*, February, 1989.
McKIE, A. B. "Oh Wid Some Power the Giftie Gie Us." *Canadian Banker*, May/June, 1989.

GILT EDGED Denotes best quality, superior merit, first class, or highest grade. It is used in connection with bonds, notes, acceptances, commercial paper, or other prime investments.

GINNERS' REPORT The Bureau of the Census reports cumulative ginnings of COTTON in "running bales" (average weight of bales as they come from the gin) for 12 specified dates during the cotton year: August 1, August 16, September 1, September 16, October 1, October 18, November 1, November 14, December 1, December 13, January 16, and total ginnings (preliminary figures) on March 20. A final report on total ginnings from the crop grown in the preceding year is issued in May. Total ginnings for the season are given in both running bales and equivalent 500-pound bales (gross weight), the latter figures derived from the reported ginnings in running bales.

The Consolidated Cotton Report (issued by the Bureau of the Census and the Agricultural Marketing Service of the U.S. Department of Agriculture), August to December inclusive, gives estimated total production in 500-pound gross bales.

GINNIE MAE See GOVERNMENT NATIONAL MORTGAGE ASSOCIATION.

GIRO SYSTEM As developed in the banking system of Germany and emulated by other European countries, giro accounts facilitate transfer of funds from accounts of debtors to accounts of creditors upon receipt of orders from the debtors directly to the bank. Thus payment in currency or use of checks, given directly by the debtor to the creditor, is eliminated. In the days of the Reichsbank, banks as well as the public at large maintained such giro or clearing accounts with the Reichsbank, which had some 500 branches throughout the country and in addition cleared with the "Reichspost" giro system of the postal service. In West Germany's modern banking system, the giro service is facilitated through central giro institutions.

GIVE UP In trading in securities or commodities, applied to an order executed by one broker for another broker's customer that the client directs be "given up" to the latter broker.
See TRADING METHODS.

GLASS-STEAGALL ACT OF 1932 An act approved February 27, 1932, which temporarily liberalized the nature of collateral against rediscountable paper and which permitted the temporary use of obligations of the United States as collateral for Federal Reserve notes, by amendment of Section 16 of the Federal Reserve Act. The Act required separation of investment actualities and commercial banking.

Banks that generate numerous asset-backed securities have been proscribed from underwriting such activities by the Glass Steagall Act of 1933. Banks, especially money center banks, have challenged this prohibition vigorously; the investment industry has strongly supported the prohibition. In 1987, the Federal Reserve interpreted a section of Glass-Steagall to allow underwriting activities if they were conducted through a securities subsidiary "not principally engaged" in underwriting. This has been interpreted to mean derived less than 5% of revenues therefrom. The 5% rule is expected to be increased in the future. A small number of banks have been granted the opportunity to underwrite commercial paper, municipal revenue bonds, and asset-backed securities. It is expected the equity securities underwriting will eventually be authorized. Other provisions of the Glass-Steagall Act have also been opposed by the commercial banking community, and its eventual repeal is expected by some.

The title Glass-Steagall Act is more widely known as that used to designate the BANKING ACT OF 1933.

GNP DEFLATOR Real GNP is calculated by dividing nominal GNP by an average price level, thereby correcting for changes in the average price of all goods and services in the economy. Economists use the word deflate for this conversion of a nominal value to a real value. The aggregate price level is based on a price index called the GNP deflator.

The GNP deflator is always referenced to a base year, which is now 1982. By definition, the GNP deflator is defined to equal 100 in the base year. The average price level for any year is calculated by dividing that year's deflator by 100; thus, the average price level for the base year is 1.0. Based on the values of the GNP delator below, the average price level for 1986 was 1.141, meaning that prices in 1986 were 14.1% higher than their 1982 level.

Year	GNP Deflator (1982 = 100)
1950	23.9
1960	30.9
1970	42.0
1980	85.7
1981	94.0
1982	100.0
1983	103.9
1984	107.7
1985	111.2
1986	114.1
1987	117.5

Economic Report of the President, 1988.

GOING CONCERN In accounting, going concern is a basic assumption or postulate. The going concern assumption requires the auditor to assume that unless there is evidence to the contrary, the business will continue to operate for an indefinite period. As a result, liquidation values for assets and equities are not considered; rather, historical costs are usually represented in the financial statements. The assumption is sometimes referred to as the continuity assumption.

A business property in operation as distinguished from one that temporarily has closed down, is defunct, or is being liquidated. The term is frequently used in connection with valuation, the property of a going concern being more valuable than that of one undergoing liquidation. This is particularly true of a manufacturing industry or public utility, the property of which consists largely of fixed assets, real estate, buildings, machinery, equipment, etc. Since most machinery is highly specialized in character and can be used for a single purpose, it naturally suffers a great shrinkage in value when sold for purposes of liquidation. The value of a public utility as a going concern and as a liquidating property would obviously be very different.

BIBLIOGRAPHY

CRUMBLEY, D. L. "Financial Difficulties of Governmental Units." *CPA Journal*, October, 1988.
ELLINGSEN, J. E. "SAS No. 59: How To Evaluate Going Concern." *Journal of Accountancy*, January, 1989.

GOING SHORT Selling short.
See SHORT SALE.

GOLD
A precious metal. Gold is used by industry (electronics, dentistry, space, and defense) and in jewelry because of its special properties: electrical conductivity, durability, luster, and malleability. It has been used throughout history as a medium of exchange (money), as a store of value, and for hoarding. Gold is measured in karats. Pure gold is twenty-four karat.

In 1965 and in 1968, the gold reserve requirements were eliminated for U.S. member bank reserves and U.S. Federal Reserve notes, respectively. On August 15, 1971, the Smithsonian Agreement ended the $35-per-ounce price of gold. Gold prices were allowed to float and be determined more or less by the free international market for gold. Starting in 1974, private U.S. citizens could hold gold legally. In 1974, gold futures contracts began trading on several commodity exchanges: Comex, the Chicago Board of Trade, the International Monetary Market (of the Chicago Mercantile Exchange), and the MidAmerica Exchange. Gold futures markets also exist in Tokyo, Hong Kong, London, Sydney, Singapore, and Winnipeg.

Gold prices reached a high of $850 per ounce in 1980 and dropped below $300 in 1985.

South Africa and the Soviet Union are major producers of gold. South Africa produces and markets the Krugerrand, which is highly prized for hoarding. Canada and the United States follow behind the two leaders in production.

The appended table provides major statistics relating to gold.

See GOLD BARS, GOLD BULLION STANDARD, GOLD CERTIFICATES, GOLD CLAUSE CASES, GOLD COINS, GOLD CONSUMPTION, GOLD EXCHANGE STANDARD, GOLD IMPORTS, GOLD POINTS, GOLD PRODUCTION, GOLD RESERVE, GOLD RESERVE ACT OF 1934, GOLD STANDARD, GOLD STANDARD ACT OF 1900.

BIBLIOGRAPHY

BRUSCA, R. "Good as Gold." *Financial World*. November 1, 1989.
BURNS, J. "Gold Shares." *Futures*, November, 1988.
JACKSON, R. S. *North American Gold Stocks*. Probus Publishing Co., Chicago, IL, 1988.
"Japan's Gold Warehouse." *Economist*, October 1, 1988.
RITER, L. S., AND URICH, T. J. *The Role of God in Consumer Investment Portfolios*, 1984.
SHERMAN, E. J. *Gold Investment*, 1986.
STEIN, J. "Gold, Silver, Economic Weather Vane or Tumbleweed?" *Futures*, November, 1988.
———. "Bob Fink: Institutionalized Trader in the Gold Ring." *Futures*, November, 1988.
WELLING, M. "Will the Glitter Return." *Barrons*, May 8, 1989.

GOLD BARS
Gold ingots. In accordance with the Gold Reserve Act of 1934 and Presidential Proclamation of January 31, 1934, pursuant thereto, the entire monetary gold stock of the U.S. was vested in the Treasury of the United States, including some $3.5 billion held by the Federal Reserve banks. Monetary gold, therefore, has been nationalized since that time.

Until March, 1968, when the two-tier price system for gold was internationally agreed to by the seven active member nations of the Gold Pool (Belgium, West Germany, Italy, the Netherlands, Switzerland, United Kingdom, and the U.S.), private buyers in the U.S. (for industry and the arts) could obtain their gold from the U.S. Treasury at the monetary price of $35 per ounce (plus 0.33% and regular MINT charges). After March, 1968, such supply by the U.S. Treasury and by the other referenced nations to the private gold markets ceased, and nonmonetary uses were filled through the free gold markets (London and Zurich) and licensed dealers (there were some 1,400 firms licensed by the U.S. Treasury to deal in gold).

Public Law 93-373 ended the ban on private ownership of gold by U.S. citizens as of December 31, 1974. Previously, Congress had amended the Gold Reserve Act of 1934 by P.L. 93-110, September 21, 1973, which permitted private citizens to hold gold when the President found that the elimination of regulations on private ownership of gold would not adversely affect the U.S. international monetary position.

Gold—Summary: 1970 to 1987
(See Historical Statistics, Colonial Times to 1970, series M 268-269, for mine production)

Item	Unit	1970	1980	1981	1982	1983	1984	1985	1986	1987
										xxx
Gold										
Ore produced [1]	1,000 sh. ton	3,687	9,893	12,729	17,918	24,142	30,497	35,909	60,682	83,xxx
Production, U.S.	1,000 fine oz.	1,743	970	1,379	1,466	2,003	2,085	2,427	3,739	4,xxx
Value	Mil. dol.	63	594	634	551	849	752	771	1,377	2,xxx
World production	1,000 fine oz.	47,522	39,179	41,250	43,105	45,096	46,827	49,184	51,620	52,xxx
Industrial consumption										
U.S., net	1,000 fine oz.	5,973	3,215	3,276	3,423	3,226	3,350	3,247	3,126	3,xxx
Imports [2]	Mil. dol.	237	2,750	2,157	1,894	1,977	2,947	2,696	5,694	1,xxx
Canada	Mil. dol.	152	1,234	1,314	1,124	987	1,554	1,555	2,444	xxx
Soviet Union	Mil. dol.	—	88	22	4	—	—	—	154	xxx
South Africa	Mil. dol.	(Z)	33	188	38	16	8	—	79	xxx
Exports	Mil. dol.	38	3,648	3,072	1,089	1,326	1,813	1,254	1,819	1,7xx
Price per fine oz. [3]	Dollars	36.4	612.6	459.6	375.9	424.0	360.7	317.7	368.2	4,xxx
Production:										
Nevada	1,000 fine oz.	480	278	525	757	961	1,021	1,276	2,099	2,xxx
South Dakota	1,000 fine oz.	579	268	278	185	310	311	356	(D)	xxx
Utah	1,000 fine oz.	408	180	228	175	238	(D)	135		xxx

Source: U.S. Treasury Department.

GOLD BASIS

In connection with P.L. 93-373, the Board of Governors of the Federal Reserve System authorized the presidents of the district Federal Reserve banks to send a letter to their member state banks regarding banking prudence in gold-related transactions. Text of the letter, as authorized December 4, 1974, was as follows.

Public Law 93-373 provides that on December 31, 1974, the ban on private ownership of gold will end. After that, United States citizens may own gold and trade in it as they might any other commodity. National banks possess statutory authority to buy and sell "exchange, coin, and bullion," and some state laws contain similar provisions with respect to state-chartered banks. The Office of the Comptroller of the Currency has determined that gold will not be acceptable as bullion unless it has a fineness of 0.900 or better.

For the past 41 years, United States citizens have been able to hold gold only under U.S. Treasury license. During this period, private individuals and banks have had negligible experience with gold. Gold is not legal tender. Rather, it is a highly speculative commodity, subject to widely fluctuating prices. In the light of these circumstances, state member banks will wish to proceed cautiously, should they decide to provide gold-related services to customers.

The Federal Reserve System believes that the following information will be useful to state member banks in the event that they decide to participate in gold transactions. Similar information is being issued by other federal banking agencies with respect to banks under their jurisdiction.

If a bank does decide to engage in gold-related activities, it ordinarily would be preferable for it to act only on a consignment basis or otherwise as agent.

The risk inherent in gold transactions is such that any state member bank considering acting as principal with respect to gold transactions should give advance notice to the Federal Reserve bank of its district. The advance notice should contain information relative to experience of personnel, services to be provided, anticipated inventories and positions, safekeeping facilities, insurance coverages, audit procedures, and anticipated impact on earnings.

Banks should not engage in the business of issuing receipts for gold without considering the implications of securities laws; and any gold for which a bank issues any form of receipt must be physically held on hand at all times and under strict safeguards. Moreover, obligations payable in gold or its equivalent are still unenforceable (Public Resolution of June 5, 1933, 31 U.S.C. 463).

As with any commodity loan, it is anticipated that banks will carefully consider such matters as adequacy of margins on loans collateralized by gold, precautions to assure authenticity and safe custody of gold held as collateral and total risk exposure from gold-related loans. Moreover, gold-related loans should be considered nonproductive credits unless extended for commercial or industrial purposes.

If a bank should decide to offer gold for sale, it should carefully avoid excessive or misleading promotions which could lead to unrealized expectations by bank clients and adversely affect public confidence in a particular bank or the banking system.

Examiners will pay strict attention to the relevant accounting practices of banks and recordkeeping for accounts of customers. Any gold owned should be shown on financial statements under "other assets," and any hedging futures contracts should be shown as a memorandum item. It would be anticipated that a bank would revalue accounts at least monthly to reflect current market values.

During examinations of state member banks, examiners will review closely a bank's total involvement in gold-related transactions to assure that individual banks and the banking system are not exposed to undue risk. Among other considerations, examiners will be concerned with management's expertise in this area, risk undertaken in relation to the bank's equity capital, and the needs of customers. An undue concentration of gold loans, as with any imprudent involvement in gold transactions, could constitute an unsafe or unsound banking practice subject to action under the cease-and-desist provisions of the Financial Institutions Supervisory Act of 1966. Our examiners are instructed to be vigorous in countering any manifestations of bank speculation in gold.

At the same time, the Board of Governors of the Federal Reserve System made available to member banks a statement, in the form of a series of questions and answers, regarding the treatment of gold by the Federal Reserve banks. The statement indicated that gold may not be used to satisfy reserve requirements because the Federal Reserve Act provides that only vault cash—consisting of U.S. currency and coin—and Reserve bank balances may be so counted. In addition, it indicated that the Reserve banks will neither perform services related to gold transactions by member banks nor accept gold as collateral for advances to such banks.

As of 1981, the *Comptroller's Handbook for National Bank Examiners* (Sec. 403.1) pointed out that although P.L. 93-373 removed the ban on private ownership of gold by United States citizens, the statute did not provide for a total elimination of prior law on gold transactions. The National Bank Act provides that national banks may exercise their powers "by buying and selling exchange, coin and bullion." Consequently, banks may deal only in gold that qualifies as coin or bullion. The term "coin" means coins minted by a government or exact restrikes, minted at a later date by or under the authority of the issuing government. The term "bullion" refers only to gold and silver. Platinum, or any other precious metal, is not considered bullion. Bullion is also limited to gold that has been refined to a high degree of purity. The Office of the Comptroller of the Currency has determined that, for national banks, gold of 0.900 fineness or better is acceptable as bullion. In most cases banks handle gold of 0.995 or 0.9995 purity, and any gold of less than 0.900 purity will be considered an alloy in which national banks will not be permitted to deal. National banks should have available, for inspection by national bank examiners, evidence of the purity of the bullion they have in inventory.

Even though U.S. citizens have been permitted to own gold since December 31, 1974, they still are bound by the Joint Resolution of June 5, 1933 (31 U.S.C. 463). That resolution declares that contract clauses under which obligations are payable only in gold or in an amount of money measured by the value of gold are against public policy and are unenforceable. The restrictions contained in the BANKING ACT OF 1933 that prohibit investment in or underwriting of securities also are applicable to securities of companies involved with gold.

Pursuant to the Gold Reserve Act of 1934, monetary gold reserves of the U.S. shall be maintained in bullion form, the standard monetary size being 400 ounces (troy). Gold bars, however, come in a variety of commercial sizes, including the kilogram size (used by the jewelry trades) and 1,200-ounce (troy) size poured at the mine.

See ASSAY OFFICE, COINAGE, MINT FINE BARS, STANDARD BULLION.

GOLD BASIS See GOLD CLAUSE CASES, GOLD RESERVE ACT OF 1934, GOLD STANDARD ACT OF 1900, MONETARY UNIT, STANDARD MONEY, STANDARD OF VALUE.

GOLD BLOC Those European countries that, during the world-wide wave of gold suspensions in 1931-1932, steadfastly clung to the gold standard. Specifically, the term was applied to the seven countries—France (assuming the leadership), Switzerland, the Netherlands, Belgium, Luxembourg, Poland, and Italy—that during the World Economic Conference at London in June and July, 1933, pleaded for a return to the gold standard by the some 35 countries that had abandoned it, as a prerequisite to discussions on alleviation and removal of existing barriers to foreign trade.

After devaluation of the U.S. dollar in January, 1934, the gold bloc stood almost alone on the old parities and lost gold heavily to the U.S. in the "flight of capital" to the dollar. During World War II, however, foreign countries ceased to lose gold to the U.S., as the result of Lend-Lease and other military expenditures abroad by the U.S. The INTERNATIONAL MONETARY FUND, established with signing of the Bretton Woods Agreement on December 27, 1945, and initiated in March, 1946, entrenched gold as the common international denominator of members' par values of currencies pursuant to the "pegged" gold content pars of exchange.

With their initiation in 1970, SPECIAL DRAWING RIGHTS (SDRs) have replaced the U.S. dollar as the unit of account of the International Monetary Fund, valued no longer in terms of gold but in terms of a weighted average of major currencies.

See GOLD MOVEMENTS.

GOLD BONDS Bonds that by their terms were payable in gold coin "of the present standard of weight and fineness," if demanded, as distinguished from "currency" or "legal money" bonds. Bonds were also payable in currency, i.e., any money that was legal tender, but bonds payable in silver were unknown in this country.

These distinctions were obviated by passage of the Joint Resolution of Congress of June 5, 1933, which declared that "every provision contained in or made with respect to any obligation which purports to give the obligee a right to require payment in gold or a particular kind of coin or currency, or in an amount in money of the United States measured thereby" is against public policy, and further provided that "every obligation, heretofore or hereafter incurred, whether or not any such provision is contained therein or made with respect thereto, shall be discharged upon payment, dollar for dollar, in any coin or currency which at the time of payment is legal tender for public and private debts." The resolution went on to declare all coins and currencies of the United States (including Federal Reserve notes and circulating notes of Federal Reserve banks and national banking associations) heretofore or hereafter coined or issued to be legal tender for all debts, public and private, public charges, taxes, duties, and dues.

Validity of the Joint Resolution of June 5, 1933, was upheld in the GOLD CLAUSE CASES by the U.S. Supreme Court.

GOLD BRICK A stigmatic term used for securities or business ventures that are unsound, worthless, or actually fraudulent, but which have, nevertheless, the appearance of soundness and attractiveness.

GOLD BULLION STANDARD A gold standard without redemption of currency in gold coin. The gold bullion standard has the advantage of economizing in the use of gold by keeping it from domestic circulation without preventing its free international movement.

From 1934 to 1971, the U.S. had a restricted international gold bullion standard, with domestic currency irredeemable in gold, but the dollar convertible internationally into gold on an official accounts basis until closing of the "gold window" by the U.S. in August, 1971.

See MONETARY STANDARDS.

GOLD CERTIFICATES Gold certificates of the type authorized for public circulation by the acts of March 14, 1900, March 4, 1907, and March 2, 1911 are no longer permitted in circulation. Under the Emergency Banking Act of March 9, 1933, the secretary of the Treasury was authorized, whenever at his discretion he deemed it necessary to protect the currency system of the United States, to require the delivery to the Treasurer of the United States any or all gold bullion, gold coin, and gold certificates, upon payment therefor of an equivalent amount of any other form of currency coined or issued by the United States. Any person failing to comply with any requirement of the secretary of the Treasury in this connection was subject to a penalty equal to twice the value of the gold or gold certificates involved.

Acting under this authority, the secretary of the Treasury issued orders dated December 28, 1933, and January 15, 1934, the latter requiring all gold coin, gold bullion, and gold certificates to be delivered to the Treasurer of the United States on or before January 17, 1934.

A new type of gold certificate, series of 1934, in denominations of $100, $1,000, $10,000, and $100,000, was issued only to Federal Reserve banks against certain credits established with the Treasurer of the United States. These certificates are not paid out by Federal Reserve banks and do not appear in circulation. They bear on their face the wording: "This is to certify that there is on deposit in the Treasury of the United States of America dollars in gold, payable to bearer on demand as authorized by law." Gold certificates, however, have not been printed since January, 1935. Under the Gold Reserve Act of January 30, 1934, all gold held by the Federal Reserve banks was transferred to the U.S. Treasury, in accordance with Presidential Proclamation of January 31, 1934, the former receiving the gold certificate credits on the books of the Treasury at the former statutory price for gold of $20.67 per ounce. Gold assets were valued at $35 per fine troy ounce, giving effect to the devaluation January 31, 1934, until May 8, 1972, when they were revalued at $38 pursuant to the Par Value Modification Act, P.L. 92-268, approved March 31, 1972. The increment amounted to $822 million. Gold assets were subsequently revalued at $42.22 pursuant to the amendment of Section 2 of the Par Value Modification Act, P.L. 93-110, approved September 21, 1973. This increment amounted to $1,157 million. All of the U.S. Treasury's monetary gold stock valuation, including the preceding revaluation increments, has been monetized by the U.S. Treasury by the issuance to the Federal Reserve banks of $11,160,104,000 for their gold certificate account (total as of close of 1980). In addition, the U.S. Treasury monetized $2,518 million (as of close of 1980) of the U.S. special drawing rights by issuance to the Federal Reserve banks for their special drawing rights certificate account.

On the books of the Federal Reserve banks, neither the gold certificate account nor the special drawing rights certificate account plays any restrictive role in Federal Reserve banks' operations. With the U.S. losing monetary gold in recent years of balance-of-payments deficits, causing decline in gold certificates (credits), two restraints were eliminated: P.L. 89-3, March 3, 1965, eliminated the requirement contained in Section 16 of the Federal Reserve Act for the maintenance of reserves in gold certificates by Federal Reserve banks of not less than 25% against Federal Reserve bank deposit liabilities; and P.L. 90-269, March 18, 1968, eliminated the remaining provision in Section 16 of the Federal Reserve Act under which the Federal Reserve banks were required to maintain reserves in gold certificates of not less than 25% against Federal Reserve notes. Gold certificates (credits) held by the individual 12 Federal Reserve banks, therefore, merely reflect the total of monetary gold held by the U.S. and also the individual Federal Reserve bank holdings of gold certificates (credits) to their credit on the books of the INTERDISTRICT SETTLEMENT ACCOUNT. Nevertheless, both the gold certificate account and special drawing rights account at Federal Reserve banks were utilized as eligible assets to serve as part of the 100% collateral pledged with the Federal Reserve agent at each Federal Reserve bank for issues of Federal Reserve notes. (The DEPOSITORY INSTITUTIONS DEREGULATION AND MONETARY CONTROL ACT OF 1980 removed the collateral requirements for Federal Reserve notes held in the vaults of Federal Reserve banks.)

The following history of the pre-1934 type of gold certificates authorized for public circulation is presented for historical purposes.

The gold certificate was a form of United States paper money which in effect read like a warehouse receipt certifying that full value in gold coin had been deposited in the U.S. Treasury for each dollar represented by the certificate. But under one of the GOLD CLAUSE CASES, the U.S. Supreme Court ruled that gold certificates were currency and, constituting legal tender, were not to be regarded as warehouse receipts. Gold certificates circulated in lieu of the equivalent amount of actual gold, in which coin they were redeemable at the U.S. Treasury. They were therefore secured by 100% gold reserve.

Gold certificates were first circulated in 1863. The Act of March 3, 1863, authorized the secretary of the Treasury to receive deposits of gold coin and bullion in sums not less than $20 and to issue certificates therefor in denominations not less than $20, said certificates to be receivable for duties on imports. Under this act, deposits of gold were received and certificates issued until January, 1879, when the practice was discontinued by order of the secretary of the Treasury. The purpose of the order was to prevent the holders of UNITED STATES NOTES from presenting them for redemption in gold and redepositing the gold in exchange for gold certificates. No certificates were issued after January 1, 1879, until the passage of the Bank Act of July 12, 1882, which authorized and directed the secretary of the Treasury to receive gold coin and issue certificates, and made them receivable for customs, taxes, and all public dues.

This act, however, provided that "the secretary of the Treasury shall suspend the issue of gold certificates whenever the amount of gold coin and gold bullion in the Treasury, reserved for the redemption of United States notes, falls below one hundred millions of dollars." The Act of March 14, 1900, reenacted this provision and further provided that the secretary could, at his discretion, suspend such issue whenever and so long as the aggregate amount of United States notes and silver certificates exceeded $60 million. It provided further that of the amount of such certificates outstanding, one-fourth at least should be in denominations of $50 or less, and authorized the issue of certificates in $10,000 denomination, payable to order.

The Act of March 4, 1907, provided for the receipt of deposits of gold coin in sums of not less than $20 and the issue of gold certificates therefor in denominations of not less than $10; the Act of March 2, 1911, authorized the issue of certificates against the deposits of gold bullion or foreign coin, the latter at its bullion value, although the amount of gold bullion and foreign coin so held would be limited thereunder to one-third of the total amount of gold certificates outstanding (changed to two-thirds by Act of June 12, 1916). Act of December 24, 1919, made gold certificates, at long last, legal tender for all debts, public and private.

Gold certificates, pre-1934, were issued in denominations of $10, $20, $50, $100, $500, $1,000, $5,000, and $10,000. These certificates had largely disappeared from public circulation in the decade preceding 1933, as they were eligible to secure Federal Reserve notes and were largely held by the Federal Reserve banks as collateral therefor.

See EMERGENCY BANKING RELIEF ACT, GOLD RESERVE ACT OF 1934.

GOLD CLAUSE CASES The gold clause formerly contained in all public obligations (e.g., government bonds) and in many private long-term obligations (bonds, mortgage notes, and leases) called for payment in gold coin of, or equal to, the "present standard of weight and fineness." For example, the text of a typical gold clause bond, the U.S. Treasury 4.25% bonds of 1947/52, read: "The principal and interest hereof are payable in United States gold coin of the present standard of value." The particular standard referred to was the gold dollar of 25.8 grains 0.9 fine.

A gold clause was first included in the laws of the United States in 1869. As part of the effort to restore the credit of the government after Civil War greenbacks had depreciated in value, Congress enacted a law which pledged the payment of coin or its equivalent for greenbacks and also for interest-bearing obligations.

The Act of February 4, 1910, provided that "any bonds and certificates of indebtedness of the United States hereafter issued shall be payable, principal and interest, in the United States gold coin of the present standard of value." The second liberty bond act authorizing the issuance of bonds provided that "the principal and interest hereof shall be payable in United States gold of the present standard of value."

By the GOLD REPEAL JOINT RESOLUTION of Congress, approved June 5, 1933, "to assure uniform value to the coins and currencies of the United States," the gold clause in all federal and other public obligations as well as private obligations was canceled and eliminated, applicable both to outstanding securities and to those issued thereafter, and providing for payment in legal tender money. Specifically, the resolution accomplishes the following purposes: (1) it declares that the clauses in public and private obligations stating that they are payable in gold or a specific coin or currency are contrary to public policy; (2) it provides that obligations, public and private, expressed to be payable in gold or in a specific coin or currency, may be discharged dollar for dollar in legal tender (inclusion of a clause for payment of future obligations, public or private, in gold or in a specific coin or currency is prohibited); and (3) it clarifies a provision of the Thomas inflation amendment to the Agricultural Adjustment Act which stipulates that coins and currencies issued by the United States shall be legal tender for all debts, public and private.

The constitutionality of the Gold Repeal Joint Resolution was challenged in the U.S. Supreme Court in the gold clause cases, decided February 18, 1935: (1) *Norman v. The Baltimore & Ohio Railroad Co.*, a suit brought upon a coupon of the railroad's issue of February 1, 1930, of 4 1/2s due February 1, 1960; and two cases entitled *United States of America, Reconstruction Finance Corporation et al. v. Bankers Trust Co. and William H. Bixby, Trustees*, involving the gold clause in an issue of bonds of the St. Louis, Iron Mountain & Southern Railway Co. dated May 1, 1903, and due May 1, 1933 (these cases were decided together); (2) *Nortz v. United States*, concerning the gold clause in gold certificates, series of 1928; and (3) *Perry v. United States*, involving the gold clause in liberty bonds issued under the Act of September 24, 1917.

In all of these cases, the U.S. Supreme Court upheld the constitutionality of the Gold Repeal Joint Resolution as a valid exercise of the power of Congress over the monetary system expressly delegated to it by the U.S. Constitution.

GOLD CLEARANCE FUND INTERDISTRICT SETTLEMENT ACCOUNT.

GOLD COINS The Gold Reserve Act of January 30, 1934, declared the coinage of gold at an end. For historical purposes the following information is given.

The table appended herewith tabulates the denominations and weight and fineness of the U.S. gold coins formerly in circulation.

While the gold dollar was the monetary unit and standard of value, the actual coinage of the $1 piece was discontinued under

United States Gold Coins No Longer Coined
(old basis of $20.67 an ounce of gold)

Denominations	Fine gold grains	Alloy grains	Weight grains	Fineness
One dollar ($1)	23.22	2.58	25.80	0.900
Quarter eagle ($2.50)	58.05	6.45	64.50	0.900
Half eagle ($5)	116.10	12.90	129.00	0.900
Eagle ($10)	232.20	25.80	258.00	0.900
Double eagle	464.40	51.60	516.00	0.900

authority of the Act of September 26, 1890. Up to January 30, 1934, gold was coined in denominations of $5, $10, and $20, called, respectively, half eagles, eagles, and double eagles.

Total gold coinage in circulation outside the Treasury and Federal Reserve banks in February, 1933, reached $284 million, compared with $65 million in April, 1931, and $192 million the previous month, January, 1933. Legislative and presidential action to reclaim hoarded gold from circulation began in March, 1933, and on March 9, 1933, the Emergency Banking Act was passed, empowering the secretary of the Treasury to require delivery of all gold and gold certificates held by anybody in the country. Gold certificates had reached a total of $649 million in circulation February, 1933, compared with $591 million in January, 1933.

Under the order of the secretary of the Treasury on December 28, 1933, as amended and supplemented on January 11, 1934, and January 15, 1934, all gold coin domestically owned (with minor exceptions) was required to be delivered for the account of the Treasurer of the United States. The Gold Reserve Act of 1934, passed January 30, 1934, required gold coin to be withdrawn from circulation and formed into bars as backing for paper currency. In January, 1934, when the figure for gold coin was discontinued in the monthly circulation statement issued by the Treasury, $287 million of gold coin was reported as still in circulation. This amount, the board of governors reported, was believed to have been largely lost or melted down, or otherwise to have disappeared from circulation over the years. In 1914, gold coin and gold certificates totaled over 44% of total currency in circulation, but by February, 1933, despite the increase ascribed to hoarding, gold coin and gold certificates totaled only 15% of total circulation and the bulk of circulation was FEDERAL RESERVE NOTES.

United States gold coins were legal tender in all payments at their nominal value when not below the standard weight and limit of tolerance provided by law for a single piece and, when reduced in weight below such standard and tolerance, were legal tender in valuation in proportion to their actual weight. Since gold coins were subject to abrasion, their weight was subject to reduction (*See* TOLERANCE). The public did not generally concern itself about abrasion as long as the impression upon the coin was discernible.

See UNITED STATES MONEY.

GOLD CONSUMPTION Gold consumption in the U.S. has been nonmonetary since 1933, when Executive Order 6102 of April 5, 1933, prohibited the manufacture of gold coins, the hoarding of gold, and the use of gold in any form (bullion, coin, or gold certificates) as money. The GOLD RESERVE ACT OF 1934, enacted January 30, 1934, declared the coinage of gold to be at an end and provided for the nation's monetary gold to be held in bullion form.

In recent years, nonmonetary consumption of gold in the U.S. has compared as shown in the appended table.

Public Law 93-373, enacted August 14, 1974, provided for an end to all government restrictions on the purchase, sale, or ownership of gold on December 31, 1974. Persons subject to the jurisdiction of the U.S. may now freely import, export, and trade in gold and gold coins within the U.S. and abroad. An earlier policy of the U.S. Treasury providing for sales of gold for industrial use and purchases from the private market was terminated on March 18, 1968. Subsequent policy of the U.S. Treasury, begun with the enactment of P.L. 93-373, called for resumption of sales in January, 1975, to the private market from the Treasury's holdings, which amounted to approximately 276 million ounces, with an initial offering of 2 million ounces and additional sales in amounts and on dates to be determined.

Private market sources in the U.S. for gold include Engelhard Industries and Handy & Harman.

See GOLD PRODUCTION.

U.S. Consumption of Gold,[1] by End-use Sector [2]
(Thousand troy ounces)

End-use		1983 R	1984 R	1985 R	1986 R	1987
Jewelry and the arts:						
Karat gold		1,414	1,420	1,398	1,412	1,589
Fine gold for electroplating		21	23	24	86	89
Gold-filled and other		230	216	216	218	216
	Total [3]	1,665	1,658	1,638	1,716	1,894
Dental		325	305	299	255	223
Industrial:						
Karat gold		42	39	39	39	40
Fine gold for electroplating		370	453	381	369	394
Gold-filled and other		673	675	731	741	673
	Total [3]	1,085	1,167	1,151	1,149	1,108
Small items for investment [4]		3	8	7	6	3
	Grand total [3]	3,078	3,140	3,097	3,126	3,228

R Revised.
[1] Gold consumed in fabricated products only; does not include monetary bullion.
[2] Data may include estimates.
[3] Data may not add to totals shown because of independent rounding.
[4] Fabricated bars, medallions, coins, etc.

Source: U.S. Treasury Department.

GOLD DOLLAR The U.S. dollar was a gold dollar from the GOLD STANDARD ACT OF 1900 to Executive Order 6102 of April 5, 1933, which terminated domestic circulation and redemption into gold, and to the GOLD RESERVE ACT OF 1934, which nationalized the nation's gold, as follows.

1. The dollar was statutorily defined to contain a specific unit quantity of gold, 23.22 fine troy grains, making $20.67 per fine ounce the official monetary price for gold.
2. Gold circulated freely in coin and in the form of gold certificates, and coinage of bullion into gold was available at the Mint.
3. Gold certificates and other forms of domestic circulation were redeemable into gold at the $20.67 per ounce official price.
4. Gold and gold certificates played the role of "golden brake" by serving as the minimum reserve requirement specified for Federal Reserve notes and deposit liabilities.
5. Dollars were freely convertible into gold internationally, both for official and for private account, at the official monetary price.

See GOLD COINS, GOLD STANDARD, MONETARY UNIT.

GOLD EXCHANGE STANDARD A system whereby a country keeps its money on a gold basis by keeping it at a substantial parity with the money of a country maintaining a full gold standard. Countries having a gold exchange standard rely upon some form of token money for circulation purposes. Through operations in the foreign exchange market, the domestic money is maintained at a value between the normal gold points. If the money that is used as the standard goes up to the gold export point in terms of the domestic money, the gold exchange standard country (through the maintenance of balances in the country whose money serves as the standard) sells bills on such country until the exchange rate is pushed below the export point. Funds obtained from the sale of exchange are then sequestered until bills on the standard country are offered for it when the exchange rate drops to what would in turn be the gold import point. In this way the domestic money is kept at a normal gold value in the international market. The great advantage of the gold exchange standard is its economy, since no large investment in gold is necessary.

Since currencies of member nations of the INTERNATIONAL MONETARY FUND (IMF) fixed the pars and band of permitted market fluctuation above and below the pars not directly in terms of gold but in terms of the "key reserve currency"—the U.S. gold dollar with full international convertibility of dollars into gold on official accounts—the IMF currency system was a gold exchange standard until the "gold window" was shut down by the Nixon administration in August, 1971.

GOLD EXPORT POINT *See* GOLD POINTS.

GOLD EXPORTS *See* GOLD IMPORTS, GOLD MOVEMENTS.

GOLD FUTURES Principal markets in the U.S. for gold futures are the COMMODITY EXCHANGE, INC. of New York (Comex) and the International Monetary Market of the CHICAGO MERCANTILE EXCHANGE.

Comex Gold Futures Contract. A Comex gold futures contract calls for delivery of a specific grade of refined gold in standard bars during one of the specified future months. The contract's price is established through the meeting of bids and offers by open outcry among brokers trading in the gold ring on the floor of the exchange.

In fulfillment of every contract of gold, the seller must deliver 100 troy ounces (5% more or less) of refined gold, assaying not less than 0.995 fineness, cast either in one bar or in three one-kilogram bars and bearing a serial number and identifying stamp of a refiner approved and listed by Comex.

Trading is conducted for delivery during the current calendar month; the next two calendar months; and any February, April, June, August, October, and December falling within a 23-month period beginning with the current month. Limiting the number of delivery months concentrates and therefore increases trading activity in these months, thereby improving market liquidity and preventing price distortions.

Deliveries of gold bullion against futures contracts traded on Comex are made at the seller's option during any business day within the month specified in the contract. Bullion must be made available to the buyer at one of the vaults licensed by Comex. Licensed depositories are vaults judged by Comex to be safe and sufficiently well guarded to deter theft. Periodic random examinations by independent auditors are conducted at these vaults to ascertain the accuracy of the depository receipts.

Price changes are registered in multiples of $.10 per troy ounce (equivalent to $10 per contract). A fluctuation of $1 is therefore equivalent to $100 per contract.

During any one market day, price fluctuations for each delivery month are limited to $25 per troy ounce above or below the settlement price established at the close of the preceding business day. If the change in the settlement price for any contract month (not necessarily the same month) equals the daily price fluctuation limit on two consecutive days, a system of expanded price limits becomes effective automatically. Price limitations do not apply to prices for the current delivery month.

GOLD HOLDINGS

Commissions are charged by brokerage houses for handling a futures contract trade. Since March 6, 1978, all fixed commission rates have been eliminated and are fully negotiable.

Original margin requirements for Comex trading are designed to maintain the financial integrity of each futures contract. Margin levels are determined by the Comex board of governors and reflect the price volatility of a commodity. A trader must add to his original margin, on a predetermined schedule, whenever the market prices go against the contract he holds. Conversely, a trader may withdraw excess equity as the market moves in his favor.

The largest segment of futures trading on Comex consists of hedging and speculating interests which normally offset their positions before their contracts mature to avoid having to accept or make delivery of physicals. However, Comex points out that it is also a viable physical supply market, with purchases and sales of physicals forming a significant part of Comex trading. Buyers of gold futures contracts who elect an exchange for physical (EFP) will arrange for specific delivery of physicals with a gold supplier while simultaneously offsetting the gold futures contracts previously purchased by selling futures contracts to that supplier. Using an EFP, the supplier will have the advantage of not having to split his delivery into standard 100-ounce or three-kilogram bar lots, and although he will charge delivery costs to the buyer, he will avoid the expenses of transportation, handling, and weighing in the Comex warehouse. EFPs can be arranged by, and handled through, qualified brokers or other Comex member firms who determine various costs and/or savings involved through open negotiation. First delivery notice day is the next to the last business day of the month prior to a maturing delivery month. Last delivery notice day is the second to the last business day of a maturing delivery month (the day after the last trading day). The last trading day is the third to the last business day of a maturing delivery month.

Gold Futures Trading on Other Exchanges. Gold futures in 100-ounce contracts also trade on the CHICAGO BOARD OF TRADE and the International Monetary Market Division of the Chicago Mercantile Exchange. A third Chicago futures market for gold futures, the Mid-America Commodity Exchange, trades in "minicontracts" which are one-third (33.2 ounces) of the standard contract size of 100 troy ounces in gold futures.

Trading Volume. The appended table compares the annual volume of trading in gold futures in recent years.

GOLD HOLDINGS See GOLD RESERVE.

GOLD IMPORT POINT See GOLD POINTS.

GOLD IMPORTS Imports of gold into the U.S. since 1969 have compared with exports of gold and increases in gold under "earmark" as indicated in the appended table. An increase in earmarked gold is the equivalent in effect upon the gold stock of the U.S. of net export; a decrease is the equivalent of net import. Technically, however, earmarked gold is still physically within the country and thus is not included in exports unless actually shipped.

GOLD INFLATION A condition said to exist in a country when it possesses abnormally large holdings of gold, which are available as a basis of credit expansion. According to the exponents of the "quantity theory" of money, gold inflation is one of the causes of high prices. It is a condition that automatically tends to correct itself since high prices discourage foreign buying and encourage importing. This is likely to lead to an excess of imports over exports.

Since an excess of imports usually is paid for in gold, a reduction in gold holdings is thereby effected.

See GOLD RESERVE.

GOLD MOVEMENTS Following the devaluation of the U.S. dollar in January, 1934, and increase in the monetary price of gold from $20.67 to $35 per ounce, a large inflow of gold began to the U.S. This flow was not interrupted until well along into World War II, when Lend Lease and military expenditures abroad were chiefly instrumental in reversing the flow in 1944 and 1945. After resumption of net imports for 1946-1949 inclusive, there ensued an almost steady yearly decline in the U.S. Treasury's gold stock, so that from a post-World War II high of $24,427 million at year-end 1949 (at official valuation of $35 per fine troy ounce), the U.S.'s gold stock declined to $10,732 million at year-end 1970 and $10,332 million at end of July, 1971. By comparison, the U.S. dollar liabilities to official institutions still totaled $32,952 million at the end of July, 1971, and pursuant to the Articles of Agreement of the INTERNATIONAL MONETARY FUND, such dollar liabilities were convertible into U.S. gold stock at the monetary price of $35 per ounce for such official accounts. In the background of this situation was the succession of yearly deficits in the U.S.'s balance of payments, caused principally by substantial capital outflows and the development of a "dollar glut" in foreign holdings of U.S. dollars, aggravated by a fall in interest rates in the U.S. as monetary policy eased to offset the recession in 1970. From the beginning of 1971 to mid-August, 1971, the U.S. Treasury paid out over $3 billion in reserve

Table 1 / U.S. exports of gold, by country[1]

	Total[3]	
Year and country	Quantity (troy ounces)	Value (thousands)
1983	3,139,033	$1,326,434
1984	4,981,090	1,813,002
1985	3,966,678	1,253,764
1986	r4,995,091	r1,819,023
1987:		
Belgium-Luxembourg	41,272	19,278
Brazil	6,658	896
Canada	1,465,970	627,670
France	411,624	183,489
Germany, Federal Republic of	98,846	42,984
Hong Kong	28,670	13,017
Japan	11,575	3,289
Mexico	7,828	3,001
Peru	55,781	25,045
Sweden	39,272	16,794
Switzerland	238,812	100,155
Taiwan	1,182,105	562,064
United Kingdom	238,573	103,237
Other	19,212	7,929
Total[3]	3,846,198	1,708,844

Source: U.S. Treasury Department

Volume of U.S. gold futures trading
(Millions troy ounces)

Exchange	Location	1983	1984	1985	1986	1987
Chicago Board of Trade	Chicago	10.15	9.73	5.42	4.00	8.074
Commodity Exchange Inc	New York	1,038.28	911.55	788.40	842.96	1,029.31
International Monetary Market[1]	Chicago	99.40	.88	([2])	([2])	26.16
MidAmerica Commodity Exchange	do	11.59	2.02	1.04	.70	.65
Total		1,159.42	924.18	794.86	847.66	1,064.19

[1]A division of the Chicago Mercantile Exchange.
[2]Less than 1,000 ounces traded. Trading ceased July 10, 1985 and resumed June 16, 1987.

Source: U.S. Treasury Department

ENCYCLOPEDIA OF BANKING AND FINANCE

Table 2 / U.S. imports for consumption of gold, by country[1]

Year and country	Total[3] Quantity (troy ounces)	Value (thousands)
1983	4,592,956	$1,977,118
1984	7,868,602	2,946,914
1985	8,225,999	2,696,478
1986	15,749,447	5,693,896
1987:		
Australia	14,546	6,391
Bolivia	184,622	71,576
Brazil	5,272	2,262
Canada	1,972,877	867,405
Costa Rica	18,655	7,648
Chile	259,623	114,331
Columbia	4,971	1,919
Dominican Republic	296,864	118,683
Ecuador	12,889	4,107
Finland	11,931	2,904
Germany, Federal Republic of	10,602	4,465
Guyana	20,501	7,521
Honduras	4,604	1,707
Ivory Coast	4,854	2,144
Japan	6,077	2,303
Mexico	43,230	16,426
Panama	7,973	3,336
Switzerland	59,670	27,444
Togo	13,197	5,171
United Kingdom	425,374	170,392
Uruguay	325,177	140,045
Venezuela	54,486	18,634
Yugoslavia	60,087	26,206
Other	25,171	9,944
Total[3]	3,843,253	1,632,966

Source: U.S. Treasury Department

assets, chiefly gold stock, about 40% of this total in early August as the drain accelerated.

On August 15, 1971, the U.S. closed the "gold window" and suspended convertibility of the dollar into gold. The value of the U.S. dollar in terms of several major currencies started to float. An additional tax of 10% on goods imported into the U.S. was imposed. A 10% cut in foreign aid supplied by the U.S. was ordered by the President.

The gold window has remained closed since. The U.S. monetary gold was revalued from $35 per fine troy ounce to $38 per fine troy ounce on May 8, 1972, pursuant to the Par Value Modification Act, P.L. 92-268, approved March 31, 1972, which revaluation created an increment amounting to $822 million. The U.S. monetary gold was further revalued from $38 per fine troy ounce to $42.22 per fine troy ounce on October 18, 1973, pursuant to the amending of Section 2 of the Par Value Modification Act, P.L. 93-110, approved September 21, 1973, which further revaluation created an additional increment of $1,157 million.

In the "managed float" that has ensued in the foreign exchange markets for the U.S. dollar as well as other currencies, the U.S. authorities (Treasury in coordination with the foreign operations of the Federal Reserve System's open market account) have intervened in the FOREIGN EXCHANGE markets either defensively, aggressively, or not at all, according to the dollar's situation relative to economic considerations.

With the U.S. dollar inconvertible into gold, international movement of gold is in private channels. See the appended table under GOLD IMPORTS for recent years' imports, exports, changes in earmarked gold, and the U.S. gold stock.

GOLD NOTES Notes payable in gold coin of the present standard of weight and fineness, if demanded, in the same manner as GOLD BONDS.

The Joint Resolution of Congress of June 5, 1933 (*see* GOLD REPEAL JOINT RESOLUTION), which was upheld by the U.S. Supreme Court in the GOLD CLAUSE CASES, declared it to be against public policy for any obligation to give the obligee the right to require payment in gold or a particular kind of coin or currency. All obligations were thereby made dischargeable by payment in legal tender, which this Joint Resolution and the Emergency Banking Act of 1933 provided should be "all coins and currencies of the United States."

Public Law 89-81 (the Coinage Act of 1965), approved July 23, 1965, repealed the provisions of law formerly contained in Section 43(b)(1) of the Act of May 12, 1933 as amended (31 U.S.C. 462), popularly known as the AAA Farm Relief and Inflation Act (*see* THOMAS AMENDMENT), with respect to the legal tender status of coins and currencies of the U.S., including Federal Reserve notes, but added a new provision of law to the same effect, codified in 31 U.S.C. 392.

GOLD POINTS The gold export and gold import points that, before nationalization and the advent of the international gold exchange standard supervised by the INTERNATIONAL MONETARY FUND (IMF), fixed respectively the upper and lower limits to the range of open FOREIGN EXCHANGE markets for a particular currency in terms of another currency. Gold then could be bought for the account of private banks and firms as compared with movements of gold under the IMF system for official accounts only (governments and government official agencies). Consequently, whenever the market rate of exchange rose to a point where it would be cheaper for importers to export gold than to buy exchange, the gold export point was reached. Under ordinary conditions, the gold export point on a foreign currency represented that premium over the par of exchange at which it was cheaper to ship gold than to pay the premium for the foreign exchange.

On the other hand, when the rate of exchange declined to a point where it was cheaper for foreign importers to buy and ship gold than to remit in exchange at the low rate per unit of their currency, the gold import point was reached.

In practice, international banks handled the movements of gold whenever they occurred for private accounts, but since the gold points marked the limits of fluctuation in rates in the foreign exchange market, there would under ordinary circumstances be little nonspeculative reason to ship gold, except on occasions of capital flights from unstable currencies.

GOLD POOL An informal arrangement or "gentlemen's agreement" established in the autumn of 1961 among the U.S. and the seven major industrial nations of Western Europe (Belgium, France, West Germany, Italy, the Netherlands, Switzerland, and the United Kingdom) that provided for the central banks of these nations to share the burden of intervention in the London gold market in order to keep price fluctuations within a reasonable range. The Bank of England was appointed operating agent with authority to draw on the pool of gold contributed according to agreed quotas, the U.S. taking a 50% share in the consortium.

As characterized by the U.S. Treasury, the Gold Pool was one of the first of many cooperative multilateral arrangements to be worked out during the 1960s to deal with speculative attacks on the markets involving gold and currencies. The pool continued to operate in the markets from late 1961 until mid-March of 1968. Until the devaluation of sterling in November, 1967, it is considered to have successfully carried out its objectives of smoothing out market movements and providing an orderly way for residual supplies of newly mined gold to enter the monetary system.

In March, 1968, the pool supplied another $1.5 billion to the gold market in efforts to cool off the "gold fever," but this was not effective in restoring stability. Therefore, with the new special drawing rights of the international monetary fund close to agreement, the central bank governors of the seven active member nations of the then existing Gold Pool agreed on the two-tier system of gold transactions, under which the central banks involved generally have neither bought nor sold gold in private gold markets. By the close of 1969, the London market price for gold was back to about the official level ($35 per ounce), reflecting observance of the two-tier agreement by central banks, and resolution of the remaining question of handling of newly mined South African gold and reserves within the two-tier system.

GOLD PRODUCTION The principal gold-producing countries in the world in the approximate order of the size of their output in recent years are South Africa, U.S.S.R. (conjectural), Canada, U.S., Rhodesia, Australia, Philippines, Ghana, Colombia, and Mexico.

Before 1840, practically all gold came from Russia. Gold-producing countries are normally gold-exporting countries, but in recent years sales to the private market have declined, whereas additions to monetary stocks of governments and their central banks, as well as international institutions, have increased.

History of Production. From 1860 to 1890, annual world production of gold was relatively stable, with only moderate annual fluctuations. The U.S. produced only small quantities of gold until the discovery of gold in California in 1848. From 1850 to 1886, as a result of gold mining in California, the U.S. produced over one-third of the world's gold, but gradually the American contribution to world production has declined, and in recent years has been only 2% to 3%. Rich gold deposits were also found in Australia about 1850. Gold discoveries in California and Australia accounted for the sudden expansion in world production from 1840 to 1860.

Beginning about 1891, world gold production began another expansion due to the discovery of the Yukon and South African fields and to improvements in methods of extraction (hydraulic and cyanide processes). Recovery of gold from known ore reserves became a technical industrial process. The Yukon mines have declined in importance, but the South African mines have proved to be the most prolific in history.

Gold production reached a then peak level in 1915 for the world and the U.S., and then began a declining trend that lasted seven years, to 1922. Since that year, it increased steadily in the world. Under the old $20.67 per ounce statutory price for the U.S., world production reached a then peak of $525.1 million in 1933.

A new era in gold production opened with the increase in the U.S. statutory price for gold from $20.67 to $35 an ounce. Measured in fine ounces, world production reached a new peak of 42.27 million ounces (Bureau of Mines estimate) in 1940, 66% above the old 1933 peak of 25.367 million ounces. Since 1940, the world total receded, particularly during World War II years, when shortages in equipment and manpower affected production. The rise in the cost of mining also affected production, so that many gold mining companies were obliged to diversify into other ores and extractive industries. Nevertheless, beginning in 1946, an expansion occurred, led by the African mines, which slowed down in the later 1970s.

Gold Stocks. Estimates of total gold holdings for the world and for individual nations would have to include both official and private holdings. Statistics of the INTERNATIONAL MONETARY FUND, which do not include totals for holdings of the People's Republic of China and of the U.S.S.R. and its associated countries, indicated official holdings of 937.94 million troy ounces as of the close of 1980, compared to 930.23 million troy ounces at the close of 1979, and 1,022.04 million ounces at the close of 1978, in turn comparing with a post-World War II high of 1,186.52 million ounces at year-end 1965. The largest of such official holdings reported at the close of 1980 were those of the U.S., 264.32 million ounces, compared to West Germany's 95.18 million ounces, Switzerland's 83.28 million ounces, France's 81.85 million ounces, Italy's 66.67 million ounces, the Netherlands' 43.94 million ounces, and Belgium's 34.18 million ounces. The largest world producer of gold, South Africa, was reported to have 12.15 million ounces in official holdings at the close of 1980. The EUROPEAN MONETARY SYSTEM (EMS) backs its currency unit, the ecu, with 20% of each member nation's gold and dollar reserves, the gold being valued at the average market price of the preceding six months.

The oil exporting countries had a total of 39.94 million ounces of gold at year-end 1980; the largest total was that of Venezuela, 11.46 million ounces, compared with 4.57 million ounces for Saudi Arabia, the largest oil producer. But Saudi Arabia had the largest total reserves (gold, special drawing rights (SDRs), reserve position in the IMF, and foreign exchange holdings) in the oil exporting group, 18,536 million SDRs, compared to 5,579 million SDRs for Venezuela and 21,480 million SDRs for the U.S. in such total reserves.

The appended table compares gold production of the U.S.

GOLD REPEAL JOINT RESOLUTION The following is the text of the Gold Repeal Joint Resolution, approved June 5, 1933, and otherwise known as Uniform Value of Coins and Currencies Resolution.

(Public Resolution—No. 10—73d Congress)
(H.J. Res. 192)

JOINT RESOLUTION

To assure uniform value to the coins and currencies of the United States by states.

Whereas the holding of and dealing in gold affect the public interest, and are therefore subject to proper regulation and restriction; and

Whereas the existing emergency has disclosed that provisions of obligations which purport to give the obligee a right to require payment in gold or a particular kind of coin or currency of the United States, or in an amount in money of the United States measured thereby, obstruct the power of Congress to regulate the value of the money of the United States, and are inconsistent with the declared policy of the Congress to maintain at all times the equal power of every dollar, coined or issued by the United States, in the markets and in the payment of debts. Now, therefore, be it

Resolved by the Senate and House of Representatives of the United States of America in Congress assembled, That (a) every

Mine production of gold in the United States, by State
(Troy ounces)

State	1983	1984	1985	1986	1987
Alaska[1]	39,523	19,433	44,733	48,271	86,548
Arizona	61,991	54,897	52,053	W	95,240
California	38,443	85,858	187,813	425,617	602,605
Colorado	63,063	60,010	43,301	120,347	178,795
Idaho	W	W	44,306	70,440	97,773
Michigan	--	--	W	W	W
Montana	161,436	181,190	160,262	W	234,365
Nevada	960,657	1,020,546	1,276,114	ʳ2,098,980	2,679,470
New Mexico	W	W	45,045	39,856	W
North Carolina	--	--	--	12	--
Oregon	322	310,527	W	W	W
South Carolina	--	W	W	W	W
South Dakota	309,784	--	356,103	W	W
Utah	238,459	W	135,489	W	W
Washington	W	--	W	W	W
Total	2,002,526	2,084,615	2,427,232	ʳ3,739,015	4,966,382

ʳ Revised.
W Withheld to avoid disclosing company proprietary data; included in "Total."
[1] These figures, reported to the Bureau of Mines, probably understate production. Data collected by the State indicate production to have been as follows, in troy ounces: 1983—169,000; 1984—175,000; 1985—190,000; 1986—160,000; and 1987—230,000.
Source: U.S. Treasury Department

provision contained in or made with respect to any obligation which purports to give the obligee a right to require payment in gold or a particular kind of coin or currency, or in an amount in money of the United States measured thereby, is declared to be against public policy; and no such provision shall be contained in or made with respect to any obligation hereafter incurred. Every obligation, heretofore or hereafter incurred, whether or not any such provision is contained therein or made with respect thereto, shall be discharged upon payment, dollar for dollar, in any coin or currency which at the time of payment is legal tender for public and private debts. Any such provision contained in any law authorizing obligations to be issued by or under authority of the United States, is hereby repealed, but the repeal of any such provision shall not invalidate any other provision or authority contained in such law.

(b) As used in this resolution, the term "obligation" means an obligation (including every obligation of and to the United States, excepting currency) payable in money of the United States; and the term "coin or currency" means coin or currency of the United States, including Federal Reserve notes and circulating notes of Federal Reserve banks and national banking associations.

Section 2. The last sentence of paragraph (1) of sub-section (b) of Section 43 of the Act entitled "An Act to relieve the existing national economic emergency by increasing agricultural purchasing power, to raise revenue for extraordinary expenses incurred by reason of such emergency, to provide emergency relief with respect to agricultural indebtedness, to provide for the orderly liquidation of joint-stock land banks, and for other purposes," approved May 12, 1933, is amended to read as follows:

"All coins and currencies of the United States (including Federal Reserve notes and circulating notes of Federal Reserve banks and national banking associations) heretofore or hereafter coined or issued, shall be legal tender for all debts, public and private, public charges, taxes, duties, and dues, except that gold coins, when below the standard weight and limit of tolerance provided by law for the single piece, shall be legal tender only at valuation in proportion to their actual weight."

Approved, June 5, 1933, 4:40 P.M.

Validity of the Gold Repeal Joint Resolution was upheld by the U.S. Supreme Court in the GOLD CLAUSE CASES.

GOLD RESERVE The gold held by central banks and governments that is available for reserve basis for domestic credit expansion of the banking system; gold cover, if any, for domestic money in circulation; and international balance of payments. In connection with balance of payments, "adequate" monetary reserves serve to absorb temporary payment deficits, thus preventing such drastic measures as currency devaluation, trade or exchange restrictions, and domestic deflation. Growth in monetary reserves also facilitates a return to complete or partial degrees of CONVERTIBILITY of the currency internationally, if not domestically, into gold. Since the U.S. dollar was convertible internationally by official accounts, foreign governments and their official institutions could purchase gold from the U.S. Treasury at the monetary price; thus demand deposit balances and short-term investments in the U.S., in addition to direct gold holdings or holdings under earmark at the Federal Reserve Bank of New York, were a more inclusive measure of gold reserves for such foreign governments (member nations of the INTERNATIONAL MONETARY FUND).

In the U.S., as a result of the 1933 nationalization of gold and domestic vesting of monetary gold reserves in the U.S. Treasury under the GOLD RESERVE ACT OF 1934, the Federal Reserve banks received credits redeemable in gold certificates which served as the legal reserve required equal to at least 40% of Federal Reserve notes in circulation (reserves comprising gold certificates or lawful money equal to at least 35% of deposits at Federal Reserve banks were also required), until 1945. Act of June 12, 1945 (59 Stat. 237) reduced this reserve to a uniform 25%; Act of March 3, 1965 (P.L. 89-3) eliminated the 25% gold certificate requirement against Federal Reserve banks' deposit liabilities; and Act of March 18, 1968 (P.L. 90-269) eliminated the 25% gold certificate requirement against Federal Reserve notes in circulation.

In addition to the gold stock held in its general fund, the Treasury kept a relatively small amount in the working balance of the EXCHANGE STABILIZATION FUND. At the close of December, 1970, this totaled $340 million. When the monetary price of gold was raised from $20.67 to $35 an ounce on January 31, 1934, by Presidential Proclamation, the gold "profit" of $2.8 billion thereby created was largely ($2 billion) credited to the Exchange Stabilization Fund, of which $1.8 billion was kept inactive. Most of this profit not credited to the stabilization fund was later used indirectly to retire NATIONAL BANK NOTES. In 1947, $688 million of the $1.8 billion in the inactive portion of the Exchange Stabilization Fund went to pay the gold subscription of the U.S. to the International Monetary Fund (IMF), the balance being added to the general fund of the Treasury or used to cover issuance of gold certificates to the Federal Reserve banks. In 1953, the Treasury issued $500 million in gold certificates against gold in the general fund to redeem government securities held by the Federal Reserve System. Transactions with the IMF in 1956 and 1957 involved the purchase for dollars of $200 million and $600 million of gold, respectively; and in June, 1959, the U.S. paid $344 million in gold into the IMF (25% ratio applicable to all members' 50% increase in quotas, which meant an increase in subscription of the U.S. of a total of $1,375 million; the balance of the U.S. subscription was paid in non-interest bearing special notes, due June 23, 1964, in the amount of $1,031 million). The concurrent subscription to additional shares of stock in the International Bank for Reconstruction and Development did not involve any cash payment; instead, it increased by $3,175 million the U.S. guaranty behind obligations to be issued by the bank to investors in the U.S.

Since gold was nationalized in the U.S., all gold newly produced domestically or imported was automatically bought by the Treasury ($35 an ounce, less 0.25% handling charge), by check on the Treasury's account in each Federal Reserve bank. To replenish this reduction in its accounts at the Fed, the Treasury issued an equivalent amount of gold certificates to the Federal Reserve bank involved, against the increase in gold. Thus, gold stock of the Treasury, gold certificates of the Federal Reserve banks, reserve balances of the member banks, and bank deposits of the sellers of the gold were all increased. Contrary to lay impression, therefore, the gold stock of the U.S. was not simply buried at Fort Knox, serving no useful purpose, but on the contrary importantly entered the credit system. If the sellers of the gold imported were foreign governments or central banks, the U.S. bank deposits and reserves were not increased, as the initial credits were usually to deposits of these foreign authorities at the Federal Reserve bank, until such time as such additional deposits were drawn on for settlements in the domestic U.S. markets.

When gold was sold by the Treasury for earmark or actual export (under general Treasury license) by foreign monetary authorities, the payment therefor could be from such foreign deposits at the Federal Reserve bank or from deposits in member banks. The

Table 1 / Official Holdings of Gold Reserves

	1982	1983	1984	1985	1986	1987	1988
All countries:							
Million of ounces	949.2	947.8	946.8	949.4	949.1	944.5	946.2
Valuation at London	393.1	345.4	297.8	282.6	303.3	322.2	311.6
Industrial countries:							
Million of ounces	787.3	786.6	786.0	786.5	785.7	782.4	783.6
Valuation at London	326.1	286.6	247.2	234.1	251.1	266.6	258.1
Developing countries:							
Million of ounces	161.8	161.2	160.8	162.9	163.4	163.1	162.6
Valuation at London	67.0	58.7	50.6	48.5	52.2	55.7	53.5

Source: International Monetary Fund.

Federal Reserve bank concerned turned over an equivalent amount of gold certificates in payment to the Treasury for the gold, charging the deposit account of the foreign authority or reserve balance of the member bank concerned. In turn, the member bank, if involved, charged the deposit account of the foreign authority concerned. Gold outflow, therefore, reduced gold stock of the Treasury, gold certificate holdings of the Federal Reserve banks, and perhaps reserve balances and deposits of the member banks if the latter handled transactions.

Table 1 indicates the official gold holdings of all countries, industrial countries, and developing countries.

GOLD RESERVE ACT OF 1934 Passed January 30, 1934, authorizing the President to revalue the dollar at 50 to 60% of its existing statutory gold equivalent. On January 31, 1934, the dollar's gold weight was reduced from 25 8/10 grains to 15 5/21 grains, 0.9 fine, by proclamation of the President. This made the dollar's gold value 59.04+% of the par fixed by the GOLD STANDARD ACT OF 1900 and resulted in a gold "profit" or increment of some $2,806 million. It should be noted that the emergency power of the President to alter the weight of the gold dollar expired July 1, 1943, although his power to alter the weight of silver and other coins to the same extent of change in weight of the gold dollar continued.

The act created a $2 billion stabilization fund with the money accruing as a result of devaluation of the dollar, placing it in the sole charge of the secretary of the Treasury and vesting him with authority to expend it in virtually any transactions he might deem necessary for stabilizing the dollar abroad.

The coinage of gold was declared at an end, the metal to be held in bullion form by the Treasury.

The title to all the nation's monetary gold stocks, including $3.5 billion held by the Federal Reserve banks, was vested in the Treasury of the United States.

Several then existing restrictions upon the issuance of government securities were removed, provided that any type of government obligation might be purchased with any other type and that securities might be sold privately; the issuance of $2.5 billion in additional Treasury notes was authorized.

The President (in the Pittman silver amendment) was authorized to pay for newly mined silver in certificates instead of in silver dollars, to issue certificates against the silver bullion which the Treasury would be thus amassing, to issue certificates against all free silver held in the vaults of the Treasury, to reduce the weight of the silver dollar in such amounts as might be necessary to maintain parity with the gold dollar under the new revaluation policy, and to increase the seigniorage, or mint fee, for coinage of foreign silver or silver not produced in the United States or its dependencies.

GOLD SETTLEMENT FUND *See* INTERDISTRICT SETTLEMENT ACCOUNT.

GOLD SHIPMENT POINT *See* GOLD POINTS.

GOLD STANDARD Among monetary standards, that system in which the standard unit of money is defined in terms of gold. Variants of gold standards are the gold coin standard, in which gold coinage is unrestricted, at no charge except "brassage" (mint charge to cover cost of coinage); GOLD BULLION STANDARD, in which use of gold is "economized" to the extent that there is no coinage but in which the types of money in circulation are kept at parity in terms of gold and are redeemable freely in gold bullion bars only; and GOLD EXCHANGE STANDARD, which economizes use of gold the most, by providing that types of money in circulation are redeemable only in a foreign currency, itself on the gold standard.

Currencies on an unrestricted gold standard are freely convertible into gold at the fixed price defined, usually by statute, by the monetary authority, and thus gold may flow internationally as a means of payment or medium for movement of capital. In unrestricted international exchange, this availability of gold at a fixed price establishes the upper and lower limits of fluctuation in exchange rates, called the GOLD POINTS. Thus, for U.S. debtors on foreign claims, purchase and shipment of gold at its total cost (purchase price, drayage, shipment, insurance, loss of interest, etc.) would establish the premium above gold par value of the currency that its exchange rate might go to; at any higher rate, it would be cheaper to buy and ship the gold rather than pay a higher price for exchange, i.e., gold export point. On the other hand, foreign debtors on U.S. claims would find it more productive of dollars to buy gold and ship it if the discount for the U.S. dollar below its gold par value should be more than the cost of purchase and shipment of gold itself, i.e., gold import point.

A freely functioning gold standard, without restrictions on convertibility, would provide an automatic mechanism for adjustment of international balance of payments. Should a country have a balance of payments deficit, and gold leave the country in settlement thereof, the deflationary effect on the economy, tending to stimulate exports and reduce imports, in time would be effective in reversing the gold outflow. On the other hand, should gold inflow develop, the inflationary effect on the economy, tending to reduce exports and stimulate imports, in time would effect a reversal of the gold inflow. This automaticity is postulated on the existence of diversified foreign trade for a country, free of substantial restrictions on trade that would impede such adjustment; countries with chronic balance of payments deficits, reflecting unbalanced structure of exports and imports, would be unable to gain gold on trade account and would have to depend upon inflow of foreign capital to offset the trade deficits. Thus elements of management, such as setting of central bank discount rates at appropriate levels, stimulants to investment, and level of interest rates, as well as trade development programs, would be necessary. Trade creditor nations, in turn, should be interested in investment in trade debtor nations to avoid a breakdown in the gold mechanisms, for any international monetary system in equilibrium must depend upon underlying equilibrium in real trade and investment factors.

Beginnings of the Gold Standard. In terms of world history, the gold standard is a comparatively modern device. The monometallic standard on a gold basis, making gold the single monetary metal and relegating silver to subsidiary coinage, may be said formally to date from 1816 in England. England's law of 1774 (providing that silver coin should not be legal tender for more than 25 pounds in one payment, except at its bullion value) practically accomplished adoption of the single (gold) standard, although its significance was not fully understood at the time. The Bank of England suspended gold redemption of its notes in 1797, but by 1821, when the bank resumed, England was consciously on the gold standard in the sense now known.

Table 2 / U.S. Reserve Assets: 1970 to 1988
(In billions of dollars. As of end of year, except as indicated)

Type	1970	1975	1978	1979	1980	1981	1982	1983	1984	1985	1986	1987	1988, June
Total	14.5	16.2	18.7	19.0	26.8	30.1	34.0	33.7	34.9	43.2	48.5	45.7	41.0
Gold stock [1]	11.1	11.6	11.7	11.2	11.2	11.2	11.1	11.1	11.1	11.1	11.1	11.1	11.1
Special drawing rights	.9	2.3	1.6	2.7	2.6	4.1	5.3	5.0	5.6	7.3	8.4	10.3	9.2
Foreign currencies	.6	.1	4.4	3.8	10.1	9.8	10.2	6.3	6.7	12.9	17.3	13.1	10.8
Reserve position in IMF [2]	1.9	2.2	1.0	1.3	2.9	5.1	7.3	11.3	11.5	11.9	11.7	11.3	10.0

[1] Includes gold in Exchange Stabilization Fund; excludes gold held under earmark at Federal Reserve banks for foreign and international accounts. Beginning 1975, gold assets were valued at $42.22 pursuant to the amending of Section 2 of the Par Value Modification Act, PL-93-110, approved September 21, 1973.
[2] International Monetary Fund.

Source: Board of Governors of the Federal Reserve System, *Federal Reserve Bulletin*, monthly; and Department of the Treasury, *Treasury Bulletin*, monthly.

The U.S. began on an ostensible bimetallic standard (gold and silver on fixed mint ratios), but because of the fluctuation in open market prices for gold and silver bullion and the free recourse in either metal to the mint at fixed ratios, the "bimetallic" standard in practice was actually largely gold or silver, depending upon which metal was overvalued, relative to open market prices, at the Mint. After change in the Mint ratios, retreat from the bimetallic standard may be said to have begun with the Act of 1853, which reduced the weight of subsidiary silver coin; been furthered by the "Crime of '73" (Specie Resumption Act of 1873), which omitted provision for coinage of silver dollars; and been confirmed at last by the GOLD STANDARD ACT OF 1900.

In the "golden age" of the unrestricted gold standard (1900-1914), most financially important nations were on the gold standard: Great Britain; the U.S.; Germany (adopted 1871); Belgium, France, Italy, and Switzerland (1874); the Netherlands (1875); Austria (1892); Russia (1898); Japan (1897); Sweden (1873); and others.

Suspension and Revaluation. During World War I, practically all European nations were unable to maintain the unrestricted gold standard. Embargoes on gold shipments in effect suspended the gold standard. Internally, the monetary standard became a reduced gold basis or paper currency. In the decade following World War I, various currencies became demoralized because of inflation, and the efforts to attain stabilization by means of repudiation, revaluation, or restoration resulted in the following changes in rate of conversion of European currencies into the U.S. dollar (from the Board of Governors of the Federal Reserve System).

Austria: 1923-1924, 1 gold krone, $0.2026; 1925, 1 schilling, $0.1407.
Belgium: 1913-1925, 1 franc, $0.1930; 1926, 1 belga, $0.1390.
Bulgaria: 1913-1926, 1 lev, $0.1930; 1927, 1 lev, $0.0072.
Estonia: 1921-1922, 1 Estonian mark, $0.00238; 1924-1927, 1 Estonian mark, $0.00268; 1928, 1 kroon, $0.2680.
Finland: 1913-1925, 1 markka, $0.1930; 1925, 1 markka, $0.0252.
France: 1913-1928, 1 franc, $0.1930; 1928, 1 franc, $0.0392.
Germany: 1913-1923, 1 mark, $0.2382; 1924, following conversion of the currency at rate of 1 Reichsmark for 1 trillion marks, 1 Reichsmark, $0.2382.
Greece: 1913-1928, 1 drachma, $0.1930; 1928, 1 drachma, $0.0130.
Hungary: 1924, 1 korona, $0.2026; 1925, 1 pengo, $0.1749.
Italy: 1913-1926, 1 lira $0.1930; 1927, 1 lira $0.0526.
Poland: 1913-1923, 1 Polish mark, $0.2382; 1924-1926, 1 zloty, $0.1930; 1927, 1 zloty, $0.1122.
Rumania: 1913-1929, 1 leu, $0.1930; 1929, 1 leu, $0.0060.
Russia: 1913-1917, 1 ruble $0.5146; 1922, 1 chervonetz, $5.1460.

By the close of 1928, the gold standard had been restored by most financially important countries, but its adopted variants differed from the pre-World War I version of the gold standard in being largely gold bullion or gold exchange standards, with restricted redemption; in being to a considerably greater extent managed by intervention of such devices as central banking and fiscal policies; and in being hampered in their operation by tariffs, trade restrictions, and the unbalancing factors of reparations, war debts, and uneven flow of international investment.

Gold Suspensions, 1931-1932. Although a few countries abandoned the gold standard in 1929 and 1930, general abandonment occurred in 1931. After having maintained its pre-World War I gold parity throughout the stress of the decade following World War I, England took the lead in suspending gold in 1931. Following suspension of gold payments by England on September 21, 1931, a great wave of abandonments of the gold standard immediately followed throughout the world during the remainder of 1931 and first half of 1932. Altogether, more than 40 nations deserted the gold standard, either directly and officially or by applying stringent regulations or controls over gold exports and foreign exchange during this period. The "gold bloc" nations became the only important nations to maintain the gold standard; the U.S. suspended gold payments as an act of deliberate recovery policy, and not as a necessitous act, in 1933.

Most countries outside the gold bloc (the latter consisting of France, Switzerland, the Netherlands, and Belgium) became involved in exchange depreciation races or exchange control, and thus there ensued a flight of gold to the gold bloc countries which continued until 1934, when the basically strongest currency of all, the American dollar, was finally devalued and stabilized, and the gold bloc found themselves practically alone on the old gold parities. Then ensued a flight of gold to the U.S., which during the period February, 1934, to December, 1940, gained a total of $15 billion in gold, compared with a $5 billion decline in gold reserve of foreign countries. This flight of gold was induced not only by the increasingly insecure position of some members of the gold bloc, but also by the deepening developments of World War II. The increase in the U.S. monetary price for gold from $20.67 to $35 per fine ounce helped foreign countries considerably in meeting the flight of gold to the U.S. During World War II, the tremendous Lend Lease and military expenditures of the U.S. in foreign countries stopped the flow of gold to the U.S. and, on balance, foreign countries ceased to lose gold.

Post-World War II Period. Basically helpful for post-World War II rationalization of international monetary relations was the stimulation prior to World War II of gold production, as well as the upward valuation in gold reserves through the mark-ups in the monetary price of gold in line with the revaluation in the U.S. gold price in 1933 and 1934. Carryover from pre-World War II imbalances in trade, trade restrictions, exchange restrictions, competitive exchange rate depreciation, etc., as well as the distortions and economic dislocations caused by the war, faced the INTERNATIONAL MONETARY FUND (IMF) when it began operations in 1946 with the objectives of seeking reduction and elimination of restrictive financial and trade practices, exchange instability, and avoidance of competitive exchange depreciation. Par values in terms of gold content for respective currencies would be agreed to with the IMF, with the commitment by the member nation concerned to intervene into the foreign exchange market to keep market rates from going above the ceiling (1% above par) and from going below the floor (1% below par). Such "pegged" rates would provide relative exchange rate stability conducive to reduction of currency risks in international trading and investing; the pars around which they would revolve could be changed in the event of "fundamental disequilibrium" and concurrence by the IMF in par changes of over 10%. On the other hand, to tide over member nations' temporary short-run exchange disequilibria, the IMF would provide drawing rights from the pool of gold, gold currencies, and other currencies paid in as quota subscriptions by the member nations, subject to maxima in such drawing rights and requirements as to repayments. Thus was created a restricted gold exchange standard, with the U.S. dollar as a key currency being added to gold in world monetary reserves.

Under this system, the volume of world trade and investment expanded substantially after the end of World War II. That very success, however, created problems and imbalances that affected and modified the system: ratio of reserves to imports deteriorated for most member nations, and particularly for the U.S. because of its higher balance-of-payments deficits and expanded imports; the U.S. dollar's strength as a reserve currency was affected by the U.S. shrinkage in gold reserves and the abundance of foreign holdings of dollars created by U.S. balance-of-payments deficits; and amendments to the fund's Articles of Agreement provided for several increases in quotas and ultimately for the creation of supplementary drawing rights, the SPECIAL DRAWING RIGHTS of the IMF. Moreover, imbalances and instabilities were magnified by the substantial expansion in movement of "hot" short-term funds from currency to currency, stimulated by yield differentials and expectations regarding changes in exchange rates. Major par value changes included the 30.5% devaluation of the pound sterling in 1949; the 14.3% devaluation of the pound sterling in November, 1967; the creation of the French new franc on January 1, 1960, equal to 100 old francs, and its 11.1% devaluation in August, 1969; and the decision to allow the exchange rate of the West German Deutsche mark to "float" (freed from the ceiling limit specified in the fund's Articles) in May, 1971, following its 9.3% upward revaluation in October, 1969. As the decade of the 1970s opened, the principal internationally disequilibrating factors were the U.S. balance-of-payments deficits and West Germany's balance-of-payments surpluses.

New International Monetary System. With suspension by the U.S. of international gold convertibility for the dollar announced by the President of the U.S. August 15, 1971, as part of his new incomes policy, the U.S. dollar was left to float in the foreign exchange markets, and it ceased to be a key currency that could be held in official reserves in view of former convertibility on demand into gold.

Following the closing of the "gold window" by the U.S. on August 15, 1971, as well as imposition of an additional tax of 10% on imports of goods and a 10% cut in foreign aid ordered by the President, the U.S. dollar began to float in the foreign exchange markets and major currencies moved upward relative to the previous parities against the U.S. dollar. Such relative depreciation in the dollar was welcomed by the U.S. authorities, who figured that the U.S. needed an improvement of about $13 billion in its "basic balance" in the balance of payments (current account balance combined with the balance on long-term capital account, plus government grants), to achieve a stable equilibrium. Market-determined exchange rates, however, were opposed by other nations, whose central banks intervened in foreign exchange markets, at first to hold rates within limits set by the previous parities and later to restrict the pace of the appreciation of their currencies relative to the U.S. dollar.

In the ensuing negotiations between the U.S. and its principal trading partners, the U.S. agreed to consider a new pattern of exchange rates involving an average adjustment that would not fully meet the referenced objective of a $13 billion turnaround, and the negotiations were completed at a meeting of the Group of Ten nations held at the Smithsonian Institution in Washington, D.C. (the SMITHSONIAN AGREEMENT) on December 17-18, 1971. Key elements in the agreement were a new set of exchange rates and provisions for a wider band of permitted market fluctuation around the parities, within which market rates would be free to move up to 2.25% above or below the new central rates. As part of the agreement, the U.S. eliminated the temporary 10% surcharge on imports which had been imposed on August 15, 1971, and the agreement became formally complete when Congress authorized devaluation of the dollar against gold (accomplished by P.L. 92-268, May 8, 1972, the Par Value Modification Act, which reduced the defined gold content of the dollar from 13.71 grains of fine gold ($35 per ounce of fine gold) to 12.63 grains ($38 per ounce of fine gold)). The U.S. did not resume convertibility of the dollar into its gold, but indicated willingness to undertake appropriate convertibility obligations in the context of a suitably reformed international monetary system, provided that the U.S.'s balance-of-payments and reserve positions improved sufficiently to make such an undertaking viable.

The COUNCIL OF ECONOMIC ADVISERS reported that in the ensuing negotiations on reform in 1972, with a Committee of Twenty of the IMF appointed to prepare a draft outline of the main reform proposals in time for the 1973 annual meeting of the IMF, the U.S. proposed an increase in the importance of special drawing rights (agreed upon in principle at the 1967 Rio de Janeiro meeting of the IMF, and introduced in 1970 by the IMF) for international liquidity as a reserve asset; emphasis on disproportionate changes in a nation's reserves in either direction as indication of need for measures to eliminate payments imbalances; and gradual diminution of the role played by gold in the international monetary system. Holdings for reserve assets of foreign currency reserves would be neither banned nor encouraged, but in the U.S. view would be expected to become a smaller proportion of total international reserve assets.

The year 1973 began, however, with a shaky stability which soon gave way to abandonment of the Smithsonian version of fixed exchange rates. On January 22, 1973, Switzerland (the "epitome of financial orthodoxy") decided to allow its franc to float because of heavy inflows of funds from abroad which intensified an already high rate of inflation. Italy allowed the lira to float, as the result of acceleration of capital flight from Italy to Switzerland. Expectations that other exchange rate adjustments were inevitable, particularly for Japan and Germany, led to heavy purchases of marks and yen for dollars, reaching a peak in the first week of February and forcing the closing of foreign exchange markets on February 10. A hurried multilateral adjustment of exchange rate patterns by agreement of the 14 major industrial nations included a further 10% devaluation of the U.S. dollar in terms of SDRs (effective October 18, 1973, pursuant to amendment of Section 2 of the Par Value Modification Act, by P.L. 93-110, approved September 21, 1973). Raising the monetary price for gold in terms of U.S. dollars from $38 per fine troy ounce to $42.22 per ounce accomplished the formal devaluation of the U.S. dollar; and the Japanese yen was allowed to float upward.

But this hurried multilateral adjustment did not restore market confidence, in particular in the rate for the German mark, and large-scale flows of speculative funds out of dollars into marks and some other currencies continued until the foreign exchange markets again were closed on March 2, 1973, not to reopen officially until March 19, 1973, although private trading of currencies continued. On March 19, 1973, five of the European Community (EC) countries—Belgium, Denmark, France, Germany, and the Netherlands—allowed their currencies to float jointly relative to the dollar and other currencies, and as before, these countries decided to keep the exchange rates between any two of their currencies within 2.25% of an agreed relationship (the European "snake"). In addition, Norway and Sweden subsequently decided to peg their currencies to the jointly floating EC currencies.

During the second quarter of the already chaotic year of 1973, the U.S. dollar incurred further substantial depreciation against most European currencies, including declines of 11% in terms of most of the EC currencies floating jointly and as much as 15% relative to the German mark, which was revalued by 5.5% relative to the other EC currencies floating jointly. The rapid drop of the dollar carried it significantly below what many considered its longer-term value and created widespread uncertainty regarding future foreign exchange market trends, and it became increasingly difficult for traders to obtain coverage by forward contracts. (One basic argument in support of freely floating exchange rates is that currency risk can be eliminated by recourse to forward exchange.) Nevertheless, the Council of Economic Advisers reports, foreign exchange markets remained open throughout the period, and "normal international trade and investment transactions continued without major disruption. Fears by many that floating exchange rates would disrupt international trade proved to be without foundation."

By the third quarter of 1973, the emergence of a sizable surplus in U.S. trade of goods and services and announcement on July 18, 1973, that the U.S. foreign exchange authorities would intervene in the foreign exchange market "in order to maintain orderly market conditions," combined with the prevailing opinion that the U.S. dollar had become undervalued, reversed the decline of the U.S. dollar. By the end of 1973, the U.S. dollar was approximately back to its February post-devaluation level.

When the Committee of Twenty met during the IMF annual meetings in September, 1973, it set July 31, 1974, as its target date for agreement on comprehensive monetary reform. But the oil price increases by the OPEC countries announced in October and December, 1973, the acceleration of worldwide inflation, and the spread of floating exchange rates led to further study and adaptation of proposals for amendment of the Articles of Agreement of the IMF, which finally were agreed to by the Interim Committee of the IMF in January, 1976, for submission to the member nations for approval (Kingston, Jamaica meetings, hence the term Jamaica Agreement). Features of the amended articles included the following.

1. Choice to member nations among exchange arrangements, including maintenance by a member of a value for its currency in terms of the SDR or another denominator other than gold; or cooperative arrangements by which members maintain the value of their currencies in relation to the value of the currency or currencies of other members; or other exchange arrangements of a member's choice. But the amended articles would authorize the IMF, upon approval by an 85% majority vote, to establish a system of exchange arrangements based on "stable but adjustable par values when international economic conditions are appropriate."
2. Phasing out of gold with regard to fund transactions. Gold would no longer be a medium of settlement in IMF transactions; one-sixth of the gold holdings of the IMF would be restituted to members (distributed to members in proportion to their quotas); one-sixth of the gold holdings of the IMF would be sold at auction over a period of four years to finance a trust fund for the benefit of the poorer members of the IMF; agreement by the ten largest industrial nations, to be reviewed after a two-year period, would bar any action to peg the price of gold and provide that the total stock of gold held by the fund and the monetary authorities of the participating countries would not be increased.
3. Increase of 33.6% in the fund's resources to 39 billion SDRs, as decided in the sixth quota review. (A second set of allocations of SDRs was provided for 1979-1981, to remedy maldistribution of reserve assets of members.)

The original creation of the SDR, at the Rio de Janeiro meetings in 1968, constituted the First Amendment to the Articles of Agreement of the IMF; hence the above amendment constituted the Second Amendment to the Articles of Agreement, and entered into force on April 1, 1978.

It will be noted that the Second Amendment of the Articles of Agreement gives fund members freedom to choose their exchange arrangements, except for a prohibition against maintenance of the value of a currency in terms of gold. At the same time, each member nation undertakes, under Article IV of the Articles of Agreement, "to collaborate with the fund and other members to assure orderly exchange arrangements and to promote a stable system of exchange rates," and the fund is required to engage in "firm surveillance" over members' exchange rate policies to assure that they are consistent with this broad objective. In order to perform this function, the fund adopted in April, 1977, a set of principles for the guidance of members' exchange rate policies, as well as principles and procedures for the fund's surveillance over these policies. Three principles for the guidance of members' exchange rate policies were devised as a means of assuring that each member country follows exchange rate policies compatible with its general obligations under Article IV.

1. A member shall avoid manipulating exchange rates or the international monetary system in order to prevent effective balance-of-payments adjustment or to gain an unfair competitive advantage over other members.
2. A member should intervene in the exchange market if necessary to counter disorderly conditions which may be characterized inter alia by disruptive short-term movements in the exchange value of its currency.
3. Members should take into account in their intervention policies the interests of other members, including those of the countries in whose currencies they intervene.

Since April, 1978, "many countries have revised their views about what constitutes an appropriate exchange rate regime," and effective January 1, 1979, the EUROPEAN MONETARY SYSTEM (EMS) was established, which was declared to be and "will remain" fully compatible with the fund's Articles of Agreement (since March, 1979, the member nations of the EMS have deposited 20% of their official holdings of gold and U.S. dollars with the European Monetary Cooperation Fund, which issued european currency units (ecus) equivalent to some 20 billion SDRs against the deposits of that portion of EMS members' gold holdings).

Summary. The New International Monetary System no longer requires the mandatory fixed exchange rates (with band of permitted open market fluctuation above and below the fixed rates) based on pars determined by relative gold contents of members' currencies. Gold has been replaced by the SDR as the "numeraire" of the IMF, but it is still part of the total reserve assets of countries in addition to the allocations of SDRs, reserve position in the IMF, and holdings of currencies. Foreign exchange rates are ostensibly floating, but the float is "managed float" consistent with the IMF's guidelines for intervention. The IMF is no longer the strict exchange rate overseer it was under the Bretton Woods system, and its role of surveillance depends upon the cooperation and consensus of members.

See GOLD PRODUCTION, GOLD RESERVE, GOLD RESERVE ACT OF 1934.

BIBLIOGRAPHY

"Floating Rate Sinks: The World Economy Needs a Fixed Standard of Value." *Barrons*, October 2, 1989.

GOLD STANDARD ACT OF 1900 Although a de facto single gold standard was established by statute in 1873, gold did not become the single standard until the resumption of gold redemption in 1879. The Act of March 14, 1900, in providing that the gold dollar of 25.8 grains of gold 0.9 fine be the standard of value of the United States, merely reaffirmed the Act of 1873. This act provided that all forms of money issued or coined by the United States should be maintained at par with gold, and that it should be the duty of the secretary of the Treasury to maintain such parity. The act, however, did not provide adequate machinery for the maintenance of this parity and placed a burden upon the secretary of the Treasury which, if it came to actual test, would have been difficult to fulfill. Nevertheless it did correct the chief defect of the old system by providing a means of maintaining the parity of United States notes (or greenbacks). Other forms of paper money were variously secured—national bank notes by government bonds, gold certificates by gold, and silver certificates by silver.

This act provided for the redemption of United States notes in gold on demand, and for this purpose a reserve of $150 million to be kept in the Treasury was provided. If this fund fell below $100 million, the secretary of the Treasury was required to restore it to $150 million by the sale of bonds. The gold in this reserve could not be used to meet a deficit in revenue and United States notes once redeemed could not be reissued, except in exchange for gold.

The Federal Reserve Act (Sec. 26) specifically reaffirmed the parity provisions of the Act of 1900 and made due provision for enforcement by providing that the secretary of the Treasury, in order to maintain such parity and to strengthen the gold reserve, could borrow by selling bonds authorized under the Act of 1900 or by selling one-year gold notes, or obtain gold by offering these bonds as security therefor.

See GOLD CLAUSE CASES, GOLD REPEAL JOINT RESOLUTION, GOLD RESERVE ACT OF 1934.

GOLD STOCKS *See* GOLD RESERVE.

GOLD SUPPLY *See* GOLD PRODUCTION, GOLD RESERVE.

GOLD SUSPENSION *See* GOLD STANDARD (Gold Suspensions, 1931-1932).

GOOD DELIVERY When securities are deposited with a bank or broker as collateral, or for purposes of sale, they must constitute good delivery. A good delivery of securities implies that they are physically genuine; that title is vested in the owner and properly conveyed by him; that they are in negotiable form so that if it becomes necessary to sell them, either through default or failure to respond to a margin call, the bank or broker possesses good title for purposes of sale.

A good delivery in the technical sense for securities is determined by the rules of the clearing agencies of the securities markets as well as legal requirements. Section 3(a)(23) of the SECURITIES EXCHANGE ACT OF 1934 defines the term "clearing agency" to include clearing corporations and depositaries. Clearing corporations generally clear and settle transactions between participating brokers and dealers (i.e., process the trade data received from participating brokers and dealers and determine the amounts of securities and money that should be exchanged among them). Depositaries hold securities certificates and effect delivery between participants by book entry.

Section 17A (b) of the Securities Exchange Act, which became effective on December 1, 1975, requires a clearing agency to register with the SECURITIES AND EXCHANGE COMMISSION if it performs any clearing agency functions for any security other than an exempted security. The SEC must publish notice of filing of applications for registration so that interested persons may comment on them and, within specified periods, must either grant registration by order or institute proceedings to determine whether registration should be denied. Among the entities that filed applications for registration as clearing agencies was the National Securities Clearing Corporation (NSCC), which was formed in 1976 to combine the clearing operations conducted by the three registered clearing agencies in New York City—the Stock Clearing Corporation, the American Stock Exchange Clearing Corporation, and the National Clearing Corporation—effective January 1, 1977.

The SEC viewed the registration of the NSCC as a key step in achieving a national clearance and settlement system. Thus it welcomed the decision of the U.S. Circuit Court of Appeals for the District of Columbia Circuit (*Bradford National Clearing Corporation* v. *Securities and Exchange Commission*, 590 F.2d 1085, 1978), affirming the commission's decision granting the application of the NSCC for registration as a clearing agency. The court remanded the case for further consideration by the SEC of two issues, both of which were subsequently affirmed by the SEC: the NSCC's selection of the Securities Industry Automation Corporation (SIAC) as the facilities manager of its consolidated system without competitive bidding and the NSCC's use of geographic price mutualization (GPM—the practice of charging all participants the same fee regardless of whether the participants deal with the clearing agency at its main facility or through a branch office).

In its 1981 *Annual Report*, the SEC also reported its approval of a proposed rule change submitted by the NSCC that would establish automated comparison and clearance systems for municipal securities. The approved system (1) enables municipal securities brokers and dealers to compare transactions through a central entity rather than having to relate directly to each broker and dealer with whom they execute transactions, (2) increases standardization in the processing of transactions in municipal securities, and (3) provides the settlement and financial benefits that accrue from the netting of transactions in the same security.

Transfer Agent Rules. Section 17A(c) of the Securities Exchange Act, adopted as part of the 1975 amendments to the Securities Acts, requires a transfer agent to register with its appropriate regulatory agency if it acts as a transfer agent for any security registered under Section 12 of the Securities Exchange Act or for any security which would be registered but for the exemptions from registration for securities of registered investment companies (Sec. 12 (g)(2)(B)) and for securities issued by insurance companies (Sec. 12(g)(2)(G)). After evaluating the comments received as to proposed revised rules, on June 16, 1977, the SEC adopted Securities Exchange Act Rules 17Ad-1 through 17Ad-7. These rules, the first substantive rules in the transfer agent regulatory program, provide a comprehensive structure for the transfer of securities from one record owner to another.

Rule 17Ad-2 treats most requests for the transfer of securities as routine items and requires registered transfer agents to cancel 90% of the old certificates presented and to issue new certificates within three business days. The remaining 10% must be transferred promptly thereafter. (This is to cover certain requests for transfer that cannot be treated as routine, and instead require special review, additional documentation from the person making the request, or an opinion of counsel before the securities can be transferred.)

Good delivery in the particular case would require "proper papers for transfer filed by assignor." For some of the details of such requirements, see NATIONAL SECURITIES CLEARING CORPORATION.

GOOD FAITH Freedom from or absence of knowledge or circumstances that would put another on notice to make further inquiry.

GOOD 'TIL CANCELED ORDERS Buying or selling ORDERS placed with a broker that are valid until executed, canceled, or countermanded. They are also known as open orders, and are usually indicated by the abbreviation G.T.C.

GOODWILL One of the group of intangible assets set up on a balance sheet, e.g., patents, copyrights, trademarks, secret processes, and goodwill, representing a nonphysical value over and above the physical assets. It can never exist in a new company except by purchase, but is established as a result. It is the earning power of a business. Goodwill, like other intangible assets, is subject to the suspicion of being valued at arbitrary value and, as a general rule, should be amortized. Often, for display purposes, goodwill is left with a balance sheet value of $1. Goodwill, like other intangible assets, should be deducted from net worth in computing net tangible equity. It can exist only among competitive businesses and may be defined as the money value of the superior earnings, or the premium set upon a going concern in excess of the tangible or perhaps book value of the assets.

Goodwill was first recognized by the English courts in 1743, and is accepted in England more than in the United States as a growth through untiring efforts of a management. Following are other definitions: "Goodwill is nothing more than the probability that the old customers will resort to the old place" (Lord Eldon). "The value of business connections, the value of the probability that present customers will continue to buy in spite of the allurements of competing dealers" (Hatfield). "The element of an established business which makes the business as a going concern worth more than its book value, that is, its net worth as shown by the books" (Walton). "It is the influence that the proprietor or his organization has upon the purchasing public through which he is enabled to attract and retain patronage" (Wildman). A more scientific definition is that goodwill is a capitalization of excess profits over and above the normal rate of return on the physical investment, discounted at some rate in excess of the current rate of interest.

Goodwill recorded in a business combination accounted for on the purchase method shall be amortized in accordance with the provisions of paragraphs 27 to 31 of Accounting Principles Board Opinion No. 17, "Intangible Assets," which specify among other things that the period of amortization should not exceed 40 years and, moreover, that amortization should be carried out by systematic charges to income over the periods estimated to be benefited, on a straight-line basis (equal annual amounts), unless a company demonstrates that another systematic method is more appropriate.

There are several ways to compute goodwill. One method compares the value of the net tangible and identifiable intangible assets with the bargained purchase price of the acquired business. The difference is considered goodwill. In this sense, goodwill is the residual or the excess of the cost over the fair value of the identifiable net assets acquired.

A second method of computing goodwill determines the earnings in excess of those that normally could be earned by the tangible and identifiable intangible assets. Conceptually, the value of any asset is the discounted value of the net cash flows it produces in the future. Hence, the present value of excess future earnings represents the value of unrecorded unidentifiable assets (goodwill).

Negative goodwill, or bargain purchase, arises when the fair market value of the net assets of a business acquired is higher than the purchase price of the net assets. APB Opinion No. 16, "Business Combinations," requires that an excess of fair value over purchase price should be allocated to reduce proportionately the values assigned to noncurrent assets in determining their fair values. If the allocation reduces the noncurrent assets to zero value, the remainder of the excess over cost should be classified as a deferred credit and should be systematically amortized to revenue over the period estimated to be benefited but not in excess of 40 years.

BIBLIOGRAPHY

ACCOUNTING PRINCIPLES BOARD, American Institute of Certified Public Accountants. *"Intangible Assets,"* APB Opinion No. 17, 1970.

GOVERNMENTAL ACCOUNTING Governmental entities are established primarily to provide services to citizens. Governmental entities differ from profit-oriented entities in a number of significant ways: lack of profit motive, dependence on legislative authorities, responsibilities to citizens, taxes as a major source of revenue, and types of restrictions and controls.

In 1984 the Governmental Accounting Standards Board (GASB) was established as the authoritative body that sets governmental accounting standards. From the 1930s through 1983, governmental accounting standards were established by the National Council on Governmental Accounting (NCGA). The NCGA's official governmental accounting standards pronouncement was "Governmental Accounting, Auditing, and Financial Reporting" (GAAFR). This document was revised in 1979 with the publication of NCGA Statement 1, "Governmental Financial Accounting and Reporting Principles." The GASB specifies that all NCGA statements and interpretations remain in effect until modified by the GASB.

In governmental accounting, funds are established for major activities. Accounting and reporting for these self-balancing sets of accounts are the primary activity of governmental accounting. A fund is defined as "a fiscal and accounting entity with a self-balancing set of accounts recording cash and other financial resources, together with all related liabilities and residual equities and balances, and changes therein, which are segregated for the purpose of carrying on specific activities or attaining certain objectives in accordance with special regulations, restrictions, or limitations" (National Council on Governmental Accounting).

Governmental entities use the accrual, cash, and modified accrual basis of accounting. They also use both budgetary accounts and proprietary accounts. Budgetary accounts are nominal accounts used to record budgetary estimates of revenues and expenditures. Proprietary accounts are used to record actual revenues, expenditures, and other transactions affecting the fund.

Financial statements necessary to fairly present financial position and operating results in conformity with generally accepted accounting principles are referred to as basic statements. It is acceptable for governmental units to present combined financial statements that consist of a balance sheet and a statement of revenues and expenditures, with a separate column for each of the eight fund types and two account groups.

Federal government accounting is similar to that of state and local governments. Accounting serves as a basic mechanism of fund and appropriation control at both the central government and agency levels. The agency or department is generally viewed as the primary accounting entity. Complete financial data are maintained for each agency in the system. Financial reports are prepared by the agency. The Bureau of Financial Operations of the Treasury Department compiles financial reports for the government as a whole. The General Accounting Office prescribes principles and standards for federal agency accounting systems through its *Policy and Procedures*

```
                        CITIZENS
                         of the
                  United States of America
Executive Branch                              Legislative Branch
        │                                              │
┌───────────────────┐                        ┌───────────────────┐
│  THE PRESIDENT    │                        │     CONGRESS      │
│ Overall ultimate  │                        │ Appropriations;   │
│ responsibility    │                        │ general oversight │
│ for Federal       │                        │ over Executive    │
│ financial         │                        │ branch; conduct   │
│ management;       │                        │ investigations    │
│ submit Executive  │                        │ and hearings, etc.│
│ budget annually   │                        └───────────────────┘
│ to Congress       │
└───────────────────┘

┌───────────────────┐      ┌───────────────────┐
│ OFFICE OF         │      │   SECRETARY       │
│ MANAGEMENT        │      │ OF THE TREASURY*  │
│ AND BUDGET (OMB)* │      │ Cash receipts/    │
│ General oversight │      │ disbursements;    │
│ over the          │      │ central accounting│
│ Executive         │      │ and reporting;    │
│ agencies; budget  │      │ debt management.  │
│ preparation;      │      └───────────────────┘
│ apportionment of  │
│ appropriations    │
└───────────────────┘

┌──────────────┐ ┌──────────────┐ ┌──────────────┐ ┌──────────────┐
│ GENERAL      │ │ OTHER FEDERAL│ │ U.S. GENERAL │ │ CONGRESSIONAL│
│ SERVICES     │ │ AGENCIES     │ │ ACCOUNTING   │ │ BUDGET OFFICE│
│ ADMINISTRA-  │ │ Manage agency│ │ AFFICE (GAO)*│ │ Assist       │
│ TION         │ │ resources;   │ │ Assist       │ │ Congress;    │
│ Policy and   │ │ maintain     │ │ Congress;    │ │ recommend    │
│ agency       │ │ adequate     │ │ audit the    │ │ proper levels│
│ support;     │ │ accounting   │ │ Executive    │ │ of Federal   │
│ financial    │ │ systems;     │ │ branch;      │ │ revenues and │
│ management,  │ │ prepare      │ │ prescribe    │ │ expenditures;│
│ procurement, │ │ budgets and  │ │ accounting   │ │ establish    │
│ etc.         │ │ financial and│ │ principles   │ │ national     │
│              │ │ other reports│ │ and standards│ │ budget       │
│              │ │              │ │ approve      │ │ priorities.  │
│              │ │              │ │ agency       │ │              │
│              │ │              │ │ accounting   │ │              │
│              │ │              │ │ systems      │ │              │
│              │ │              │ │ designs.     │ │              │
└──────────────┘ └──────────────┘ └──────────────┘ └──────────────┘
```

*Members, with the Director, Office of Personnel Management, of the Joint Financial Management Improvement Program Steering Committee

---

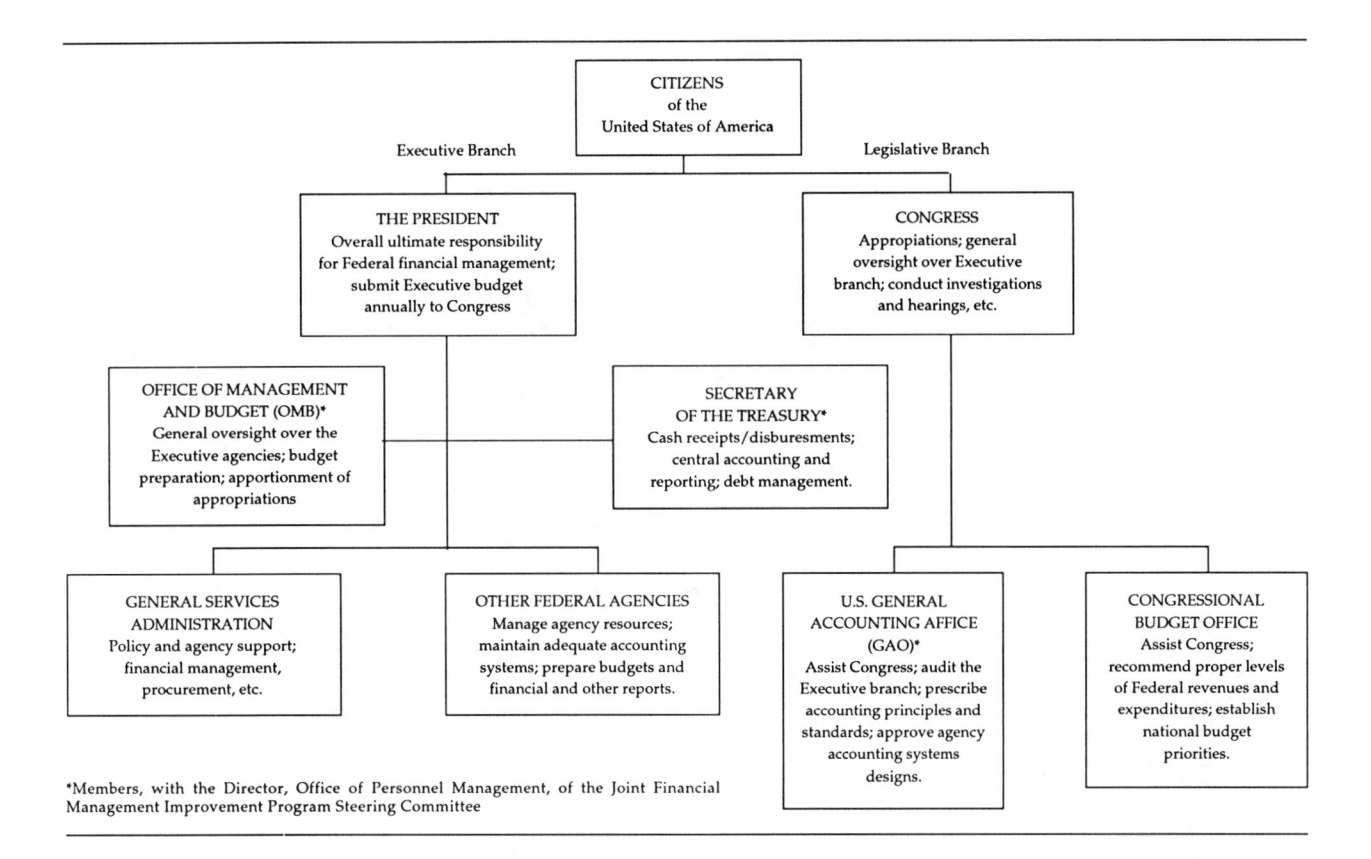

Manual For Guidance of Federal Agencies. Major financial management roles and responsibilities are summarized in the appended exhibit.

Following is a glossary of major federal budgetary and financial accounting terminology:

Appropriations Budgetary authority granted by Congress to incur obligations requiring either current or future disbursements from one or more of the government's funds. Most appropriations for current operations provide obligational authority only within the year for which they are granted, i.e., one-year or annual appropriations. Multiple-year appropriations grant valid obligational authority for several years. No-year appropriations grant obligational authority "until spent or exhausted." Continuing resolutions permit an agency to continue its operations and obligations at the level of its prior-year appropriation pending enactment of the current-year appropriation. Permanent appropriations grant obligational authority to an agency on a continuing or permanent basis to a limited extent.

Apportionment The amount of appropriation or other obliga-tional authority released to an agency by the Office of Management and Budget after reserves are established.

Allotment Amount of obligational authority released to program or field office managers by agency top management, usually monthly or quarterly installments, after administrative reserve of apportioned appropriations are established.

Contract authorizations Authority granted by Congress to enter into contracts that obligate the U.S. government. An appropriation is required before such obligations can be liquidated.

Cost (or applied cost) The amount of resources used or consumed by an agency in conducting its activities or functions during an accounting period.

Disbursements Amount of cash disbursed in payment of agency liabilities.

Expended Appropriations The amount by which obligational authority is used and for which the government is liable for goods received, resources provided, or grant provisions fulfilled.

Financial statements The financial statements required of all federal agencies include statement of assets and liabilities, statement of changes in the investment of the United States government, statement of expenses, and statement of sources and applications of funds.

Funds Fiscal accounting entity with a self-balancing set of accounts recording cash and other financial resources together with all related liabilities and residual equities or balances, and changes therein, which are segregated for the purpose of carrying on specific activities or attaining certain objectives in accordance with special regulations, restrictions, or limitations. Federal agencies imply six major types of funds:

Federal funds	Trust or custodian funds
General fund	Trust funds
Special funds	Deposit funds
Revolving funds	
Management funds	

Fund balance with U.S. Treasury The amount of cash that the agency can order disbursed to liquidate its liabilities.

Obligation The amount by which obligational authority is committed upon placing an order for goods or services.

Obligations incurred The total of expended appropriation during a period plus the unliquidated obligations at period end.

Reimbursements to appropriations Amounts accruing to an agency through billings for services are restored to its appropriations and are available for use without further congressional action.

See FINANCIAL ACCOUNTING FOUNDATION.

GOVERNING COMMITTEE The governing body of the NEW YORK STOCK EXCHANGE, vested with both legislative and judicial powers over members of the exchange, is the board of governors. Standing committees of the board of governors that formerly handled administrative functions such as public relations, stock list, member firms, etc., were discontinued in the last reorganization, and these functions are now handled by administrative departments.

GOVERNMENT ASSAY OFFICE See ASSAY OFFICE.

GOVERNMENT BONDS

Gross Public Debt of U.S. Treasury: Types and Ownership
(Billions of dollars, end of period)

	1985	1986	1987	1988	1988 Q2	1988 Q3	1988 Q4	1989 Q1
Type and Holder	1,945.9	2,214.8	2,431.7	2,684.4	2,547.7	2,602.2	2,684.4	2,740.9
1 Total gross public debt								
By type								
2 Interest-bearing debt	1,943.4	2,212.0	2,428.9	2,663.1	2,545.0	2,599.9	2,663.1	2,738.3
3 Marketable	1,437.7	1,619.0	1,724.7	1,821.3	1,769.9	1,802.9	1,821.3	1,871.7
4 Bills	399.9	426.7	389.5	414.0	382.3	398.5	414.0	417.0
5 Notes	812.5	927.5	1,037.9	1,083.6	1,072.7	1,089.6	1,083.6	1,121.4
6 Bonds	211.1	249.8	282.5	308.9	299.9	299.9	308.9	318.4
7 Nonmarketable [1]	505.7	593.1	704.2	841.8	775.1	797.0	841.8	866.6
8 State and local government series	87.5	110.5	139.3	151.5	146.9	147.6	151.5	154.4
9 Foreign issues [2]	7.5	4.7	4.0	6.6	5.7	6.3	6.6	6.7
10 Government	7.5	4.7	4.0	6.6	5.7	6.3	6.6	6.7
11 Public	.0	.0	.0	.0	.0	.0	.0	.0
12 Savings bonds and notes	78.1	90.6	99.2	107.6	104.5	106.2	107.6	110.4
13 Government account series [3]	332.2	386.9	461.3	575.6	517.5	536.5	575.6	594.7
14 Non-interest-bearing debt	2.5	2.8	2.8	21.3	2.7	2.3	21.3	2.6
By holder [4]								
15 U.S. government agencies and trust funds	348.9	403.1	477.6	589.2	534.2	550.4	589.2	607.5
16 Federal Reserve Banks	181.3	211.3	222.6	238.4	227.6	229.2	238.4	228.6
17 Private investors	1,417.2	1,602.0	1,745.2	1,852.8	1,784.9	1,819.0	1,852.8	1,900.2
18 Commercial banks	198.2	203.5	201.2	195.0	202.5	203.0	195.0	NA
19 Money market funds	25.1	28.0	14.3	18.8	13.1	10.8	18.8	NA
20 Insurance companies	78.5	105.6	120.6	NA	132.2	135.0	NA	NA
21 Other companies	59.0	68.8	84.6	86.1	86.5	86.0	86.1	NA
22 State and local Treasurys	226.7	262.8	282.6	NA	286.3	287.0	NA	NA
Individuals								
23 Savings bonds	79.8	92.3	101.1	109.6	106.2	107.8	109.6	112.2
24 Other securities	75.0	70.5	72.3	77.8	73.9	76.7	77.8	NA
25 Foreign and international [5]	212.5	251.6	287.3	349.3	333.8	334.3	349.3	363.1
26 Other miscellaneous investors [6]			581.2	NA				NA

[1] Includes (not shown separately): Securities listed to the Rural Electrification Administration; depository bonds, retirement plan bonds, and individual retirement bonds.
[2] Nonmarketable dollar-denominated and foreign currency-denominated series held by foreigners.
[3] Held almost entirely by U.S. Treasury agencies and trust funds.
[4] Data for Federal Reserve Banks and U.S. Treasury agencies and trust funds are actual holdings; data for other groups are Treasury estimates.
[5] Consists of investments of foreign and international accounts. Excludes non-interest-bearing notes issued to the International Monetary Fund.
[6] Includes savings and loan associations, nonprofit institutions, credit unions, mutual savings banks, corporate pension trust funds, dealers and brokers, certain U.S. Treasury deposit accounts, and federally-sponsored agencies.

Sources: Data by type of security, U.S. Treasury Department, *Monthly Statement of the Public Debt of the United States*. Data by holder, *Treasury Bulletin*.

GOVERNMENT BONDS   See FOREIGN GOVERNMENT BONDS, STATE BONDS, UNITED STATES GOVERNMENT SECURITIES.

BIBLIOGRAPHY

Bond Buyer. THE BOND BUYER, INC., New York, NY. Daily.
Money Markets. Online data base. Money Market Services, San Francisco, CA.
Moody's Bond Survey. Moody's Investors Service, New York, NY. Weekly.
Moody's Municipals and Governments Manual. Moody's Investors Service, New York, NY.
Weekly Bond Buyer. The Bond Buyer, New York, NY. Weekly.

GOVERNMENT DEBT   Expansion in the federal debt has been principally associated with wars and maintenance of national defense. Debt of the states and local governments, on the other hand, has expanded sharply in recent years to finance needed capital improvements such as school construction, highway building, hospitals, etc.

The appended table compares the growth in federal and in state and local governmental debt since 1949, as reported by the Board of Governors of the Federal Reserve System in its *Flow of Funds Accounts, Assets and Liabilities Outstanding.*

For statistics on the federal debt, see NATIONAL BUDGET, NATIONAL DEBT.

GOVERNMENT DEPOSITARY   A bank designated to receive deposits of government funds. The Federal Reserve banks under the original Federal Reserve Act were designated as depositaries and fiscal agents of the United States. Under the Act of May 29, 1920, which discontinued the subtreasury system, the Federal Reserve banks were also designated to perform any or all of the duties and functions of assistant treasurers and subtreasuries as the secretary of the Treasury should direct.

In addition, the Treasury is authorized to designate commercial banks as depositaries: national banks; state-chartered members of the Federal Reserve System; other domestic banks insured by the Federal Deposit Insurance Corporation; and depositaries in foreign countries, territories, and insular possessions (U.S. financial institutions to be given preference if safe and able to render the service required). Thus implementing the Treasurer's accounts at Federal Reserve banks is a nationwide network of deposit accounts in commercial banks. All government deposits in banks must be secured by a pledge of collateral security, such collateral usually being in the form of U.S. government securities.

In the Second Liberty Bond Act of 1917, Congress provided for the establishment of treasury war loan accounts to take care of the financing of the liberty loans. These accounts were originally established to enable the banks to retain, until called by the Treasury through the district Federal Reserve bank, the proceeds arising from the sale of liberty bonds to such banks or their customers. Later authority for use of these accounts was extended to the sale of other government securities, including U.S. savings bonds and Treasury savings notes. Under the Current Tax Payment Act of 1943 and later legislation, withheld income taxes, certain quarterly income and profit tax payments, Social Security taxes, and excise taxes are deposited in these accounts, which have become known as tax and loan accounts. Subscriptions by commercial banks to U.S. government securities, if so authorized by the Treasury as indicated in announcements of issues, may be made by crediting the Treasury with increase in U.S. government deposits in the bank concerned for the amount o the subscription, the so-called book credit method of subscript on to U.S. government securities, in these tax and loan accounts.

Under authority of P.L. 95-147, the Treasury implemented a program on November 2, 1978, to invest a portion of its operating cash in obligations of depositaries maintaining tax and loan accounts. Under the Treasury tax and loan investment program, depositary financial institutions select the manner in which they will participate in the program. Depositaries that wish to retain funds deposited in their tax and loan accounts in interest-bearing obligations participate under the note option; depositaries that wish to remit the funds to the Treasury's account at Federal Reserve banks participate under the remittance option.

Deposits to tax and loan accounts occur in the normal course of business under a uniform procedure applicable to all financial institutions, whereby customers of financial institutions deposit with them tax payments and funds for the purchase of government securities. In most cases the transaction involves merely the transfer of funds from a customer's account to the tax and loan account in the same financial institution. On occasions, to the extent authorized by the Treasury, financial institutions are permitted to deposit in these accounts proceeds from subscriptions to public debt securities entered for their own account as well as for the accounts of their customers.

The tax and loan system permits the Treasury to collect funds through financial institutions and to leave the funds in note option depositaries and in the financial communities in which they arise until such time as the Treasury needs the funds for its operations. In this way the Treasury is able to neutralize the effect of its fluctuating operations on note option financial institution reserves and the economy.

See DEPOSITORY.

GOVERNMENT DEPOSITS Funds of the U.S. government and postal savings deposits deposited with legal depositaries. Any GOVERNMENT DEPOSITARY is required by the secretary of the Treasury to qualify for receiving government deposits by pledging as collateral for such deposits such securities as are from time to time published as eligible. The amount and rates are also indicated in the published list of eligible collateral, which consists broadly of obligations of the U.S. government and its territorial and insular possessions, state bonds, municipal bonds, and other approved bonds. Under the Banking Act of 1935, reserves are required against U.S. government deposits, although in April, 1943, "war loan" deposit accounts were exempted from reserve requirements until six months after cessation of World War II hostilities.

GOVERNMENT ESTIMATES OF CROPS See CROP REPORTS.

GOVERNMENT EXPENDITURE MULTIPLIER The multiplier concept in economics asserts that changes in one category of aggregate spending will have a multiplied effect on the economy, that is, on GNP. For the most simple representation of the economy, the government expenditure multiplier equals:

$$\frac{1}{(1 - mpc)}$$

where *mpc* (marginal propensity to consume) is the portion of an additional dollar that goes to consumption, on average, in the economy. For the economy as a whole, the mpc is near 90%, making the simple government expenditure multiplier equal to 10 (1 divided by .10). However, the simple multiplier formula, which is taught in all introductory economics courses, is overly simplistic and yields a multiplier that is unrealistically high. When taxes, price level changes resulting from a change in government expenditures, and interest level changes also resulting from changes in government expenditures are taken into account, the government expenditure multiplier is slightly less than 2. This means that, over time, GNP will increase by nearly $2 for every $1 increase in government expenditures.

GOVERNMENT NATIONAL MORTGAGE ASSOCIATION Effective September 1, 1968, the FEDERAL NATIONAL MORTGAGE ASSOCIATION (originally chartered under Title III of the National Housing Act in February, 1938, as the National Mortgage Association of Washington, and name changed in April, 1938) was partitioned into two corporations: the Government National Mortgage Association (GNMA, or popularly "Ginny Mae") and the Federal National Mortgage Association (the new FNMA, popularly still referred to as "Fanny Mae").

GNMA is a corporate instrumentality of the U.S. within the Department of Housing and Urban Development, having no capital stock and with no board of directors. It operates under the supervision of the secretary of the Department of Housing and Urban Development, who exercises the powers normally exercised by a board of directors. GNMA carries out the following programs of the department in accordance with the general policies of the secretary and Title III of the National Housing Act.

1. Special assistance in the financing of eligible types of federally underwritten mortgages under Section 305 of the act, or as authorized by the President of the United States. Practically all of such special assistance to the mortgage market, funds for which are mostly borrowed from the U.S. Treasury, has taken the form in recent years of the tandem plan, whereby the GNMA buys the mortgages from private lenders at prices better than the market, and in turn sells the mortgages to private investors at market prices.
2. Management and liquidation of the portfolio of mortgages acquired by GNMA when it was chartered in 1968 per Section 306 of the act. Although authorized to acquire obligations from the secretary of Housing and Urban Development as well as mortgages or loans from any federal instrumentality for management and liquidation, the GNMA has made no new acquisitions for this function since.
3. Management of the Government Mortgage Liquidation Trust, Small Business Obligations Trust, Federal Assets Liquidation Trust, and Federal Assets Financing Trust, under Section 302(c) of the act. As trustee, GNMA issued participation certificates (PCs), i.e., certificates of beneficial interest in future payments of principal and interest from the pool of mortgages selected from the portfolios of the above trusts. Outstanding at year-end 1979 were a total of $3,004 million of participation certificates, consisting of $289 million PCs of the Government Mortgage Liquidation Trust; $750 million PCs of the Federal Assets Liquidation Trust; and $1,965 million of the Federal Assets Financing Trust. Participation certificates had maturities of 1 to 20 years, and represented beneficial interests in future payments of principal and interest on the pool of mortgages trusteed with the GNMA; proceeds from sales of the PCs by the GNMA were applied by the trustors to reduce their borrowings and other use of government funds.
4. Guaranty of the timely payment of principal and interest on such trust certificates or other securities issued by the Federal National Mortgage Corporation (FNMA) or other institutions approved for this purpose and backed by a trust or pool composed of mortgages insured by the FEDERAL HOUSING ADMINISTRATION (FHA) or guaranteed by the Veterans Administration (VA), under Section 306 of the act. GNMA has issued various types of GNMA-guaranteed mortgage-backed securities.
   a. Mortgage-backed bonds issued by the FNMA and the FEDERAL HOME LOAN MORTGAGE CORPORATION (FHLMC). As of year-end 1979, the totals of such guarantees by GNMA of mortgage-backed bonds were $1,434 million issued by the FNMA and $2,109 million issued by the FHLMC, including in these combined totals $1,229 million of such guaranteed mortgage-backed bonds placed privately. Issues have included maturities of 1 to 25 years.
   b. Passthrough securities, guaranteed by the GNMA and issued by private mortgage lenders against specified pools of FHA, FARMERS HOME ADMINISTRATION (FmHA), or VA-guaranteed mortgages. The GNMA guarantees timely payments of

principal and interest on such securities, such guaranties representing commitment of the full faith and credit of the United States. As principal and interest payments are collected on the mortgages in the specified pools, the payments are "passed through" to holders of GNMA-guaranteed certificates after deduction of servicing and guaranty fees.

Trading Activity. In the wake of substantial volume of trading in GNMA mortgage-backed securities including forward transactions, increased speculation in such options to buy in the future, counting on the hope of increase in value in the event of decline in interest rates, led to formation of a self-regulatory trade group among dealers to regulate trading in mortgage-backed securities and guaranteed loans. It should be emphasized, however, that GNMA securities themselves are considered conservative investments.

Development of GNMA mortgage interest rate futures trading on organized exchanges has added to the activity in GNMA securities.

See GOVERNMENT NATIONAL MORTGAGE ASSOCIATION (GNMA) FUTURES; HOUSING AND URBAN DEVELOPMENT, DEPARTMENT OF; PARTICIPATION LOANS.

GOVERNMENT OBLIGATIONS

The major marketable securities issued by the United States Treasury are Treasury bills, certificates of indebtedness, notes, and bonds. These securities have several important characteristics: They are actively traded, they are considered very safe as to payment of interest and return of principal, and they are excellent collateral for loans. Marketable securities are subject to interest rate risks. If the general level of interest rates rises, the prices of securities held by investors decline. Government obligations are also subject to risks associated with a decline in purchasing power of the dollars in which interest and principal are payable (inflation).

Treasury bills are non-interest-bearing obligations sold and quoted on a discount basis. Bills are issued with maturities of 90 and 180 days and one year. Certificates of indebtedness have maturities of from one to five years. Treasury bonds have maturities of more than five years. Treasury bonds are usually callable by the Treasury at par at an option date several years prior to their maturity.

Treasury bills are auctioned each Monday, one issue maturing in 13 weeks and another in 26 weeks. Allotments are made to the highest bidders down to the price at which sufficient subscriptions have been received to sell the bills offered by the Treasury. Coupon obligations, including certificates of indebtedness, notes, and bonds, are offered through a Treasury announcement at auction. The Treasury offers the holders of maturing issues the right to exchange their securities for new issues. Various opportunities for advance refundings are made available to holders of government securities (for example, prerefundings in which holders of Treasury issues with a maturity of under one year are given the right to exchange their holdings for issues with a longer maturity, from one to five years).

Federal agencies also issue securities. The Federal Landbanks, Federal Intermediate Credit banks, Federal Home Loan banks, the Federal National Mortgage Association, the Bank for Cooperatives, and the Tennessee Valley Authority issue securities. However, these securities are not guaranteed by the Treasury. They are generally considered to be of high quality, are readily marketable, and have relatively attractive yields.

United States savings bonds are designed primarily for individual investors. These bonds are not transferable and cannot serve as collateral for bank loans. They are considered very safe investments and have a moderately attractive rate of return if held to maturity. Series E bonds mature in seven years, nine months, pay income at maturity or earlier redemption. The bonds are redeemable on demand according to a fixed schedule of prices. Owners may extend the maturity date of the bonds for an additional ten years. Series H bonds mature in ten years, are purchased at par, and bear interest paid semi annually by the Treasury to the registered owner. The bonds are redeemable on demand at par.

Interest on most government obligations, including all marketable securities issued since March 1, 1941, and all savings bonds and notes currently issued, are fully taxable under federal tax law. All government securities are exempt from state and local taxes, except estate, inheritance, gift, and excise taxes. The increment on Series E bonds from year to year is taxable as interest either from year to year or at maturity or prior redemption.

Municipal bonds are issued by counties, cities, towns, villages, special tax districts, and authorities. They are usually classified as general obligation bonds, supported with the full faith and credit of the municipality pledged, and limited obligations, which are special assessment and revenue bonds. The quality of municipal bonds is affected by the economics of the municipality, its population, wealth, income, and financial administration.

The process of marketing state and local government issues is described by a publication of the National Bureau of Economic Research as follows:

> Once a state or local governmental unit has completed the necessary legal steps that authorize it to borrow money, the marketing process follows a fairly standardized pattern. If, as is usual, the issue is to be sold by competitive bidding, the interest to borrow is announced formally (informal news has already been circulated in most cases and bids are invited). In the somewhat rarer case of a negotiated offering, a investment banking house acts as the adviser, it may also organize the underwriting syndicate. This dual role, however, is frowned on by some critics. In the more common case of a competitive sale, the second phase is that of the organization of groups for the purpose of bidding on the issue. The third stage, which almost always follows hard upon the award of the bid to the group offering the lowest borrowing cost, is the reoffering of the securities by the successful bidders to ultimate investors.

Municipal bonds are sold primarily in the over-the-counter market. Commercial banks and dealers specialized in making a market in these securities are directly involved in the marketing process. Major investors in state and local obligations include commercial banks, fire and casualty companies, life insurance companies, mutual savings banks, state and local retirement funds, and nonfinancial corporations.

Municipal bonds are repaid by either through a sinking fund or by serial (single issue divided into a number of different maturities) or installment repayments. In certain cases, payment is made from current municipal revenues or by refunding through the sale of a new issue.

The CHICAGO BOARD OF TRADE introduced GNMA futures for trading on October 20, 1975, in GNMA collateralized depositary receipts (CDRs), followed by introduction of trading in GNMA certificate delivery (CDs) on September 12, 1978. The difference between these two types of futures contracts lies in their delivery method. The GNMA CDRs call for the delivery of a collateralized depositary receipt, which is executed by the authorized bank as depositary, evidencing in safekeeping the basic trading unit of $100,000 principal of GNMA 8% coupon or equivalent obtainable upon surrender of the receipt (GNMAs with rates other than 8% are exchangeable for CDRs by use of a factor which will afford the same yield for the GNMA as a GNMA 8% issue when priced at par assumed to be a 30-year certificate prepaid in the twelfth year, based on the FHA's actuarial experience over a 20-year period). The GNMA CDs, on the other hand, call for delivery of the actual GNMA certificate ($100,000 principal) also at yield equivalent of 8% at settlement price of the assumption of a 30-year certificate prepaid in the twelfth year. Price quotations on both types of contracts are in $^1/_{32}$ nds of a point, or $31.25 per contract; both have a daily price limit of fluctuation of $^{64}/_{32}$ nds above and below the previous day's settlement price.

Uses for GNMA Futures. Like other futures, GNMA futures may be used in hedging operations or for speculative purposes. Prices of GNMA futures, like those of Treasury bills, Treasury bonds, and high-grade corporate bonds, vary inversely relative to movements in interest rates. Thus an institutional investor anticipating it will have funds to invest in mortgages or other interest-sensitive commitments might buy GNMA futures with delivery month near the date when the funds for investment would become available and, at such time, sell the GNMA futures contract while at the same time buying the mortgages in the cash market. If interest rates rose during the period, the loss on the sale of the futures would be approximately offset by the reduced price of the mortgages in the cash market. If interest rates declined during the period, the profit on the sale of the futures would be approximately offset by the higher price paid for the mortgages in the cash market.

GNMA Futures Trading on Other Exchange. Amex Commodities Exchange (on the floor of the AMERICAN STOCK EXCHANGE) began trading in GNMA futures (GNMA CDs) on September 12, 1978. The Amex contract called for delivery of $100,000 principal in GNMA certificates. As of the same date, the Chicago Board of Trade opened trading in its new GNMA CD contract, in head-to-head competition with the Amex contract containing similar features.

On November 13, 1979, the COMMODITY EXCHANGE, INC. of New York (Comex) began trading in GNMA CD futures with similar features. Comex explained that the contract was initiated during a turbulent period in the housing and mortgage markets which resulted in, among other things, a sharp decline in the amount of GNMA mortgages being originated and a contraction in secondary market activity for GNMA certificates. Comex, however, believed that its GNMA futures contract had been tailored to meet the needs of mortgage market participants, and predicted that activity in GNMA futures would accelerate as cash market conditions improved.

GOVERNMENT PURCHASES Government purchases include military equipment; the employment of the armed forces and other government workers; and the provision of roads, bridges, and other public goods and services by the local, state, and federal governments. State and local government purchases represent approximately 60% of total government purchases.

There is an important distinction between government purchases and government expenditures. Government expenditures exceed government purchases by the amount spent on both benefit payments (such as Social Security and Medicare) and the interest expense on government debt. These expenditures are not included in the government purchases component of GNP because they represent the transfer of income back to households and firms rather than the purchase of goods and services by the government.

Listed below are total government purchases for selected years:

Year	Government Purchases ($billions)
1950	$ 38.8
1960	100.6
1970	218.2
1980	530.3
1985	816.6
1986	869.7
1987	923.8

Source: Economic Report of the President, 1988.

GOVERNMENT REGULATION The regulatory trend throughout U.S. history has been toward both social and economic regulation. Social regulators include the Environmental Protection Agency, the Occupational Safety and Health Administration, the Consumer Product Safety Commission, and others. Economic regulators include the Federal Trade Commission, Civil Aeronautics Board, Federal Communications Commission, the Interstate Commerce Commission, and others. Public policy issues related to regulation cluster around antitrust policies, equality of economic opportunity, equality of employment opportunity, occupational safety and health, consumerism, and the physical environment.

The State Governmental Affairs Committee described a federal regulatory office as "one which (1) has decision-making authority, (2) establishes standards or guidelines conferring benefits and imposing restrictions on business conduct, (3) operates principally in the sphere of domestic business activity, (4) has its head and/or members appointed by the president . . . . and (5) has its legal procedures generally governed by the Administrative Procedures Act."

Congress has passed major antitrust laws designed to maintain competition and prevent restraint of trade. This legislation also restricts unfair competitive practices.

The Sherman Antitrust Act declared that "every contract, combination . . . or conspiracy in restraint of trade or commerce among the several states is hereby declared to be illegal"; and "every person who shall monopolize, or . . . combine or conspire to monopolize any part of the trade or commerce among the several states . . . shall be deemed guilty of a misdemeanor . . . ." Courts have generally held that the restraint must be "undue" and "unreasonable" before it is considered to be illegal. The courts have held that bigness in and of itself is not proof of violation. The "principle of reason" has to be applied to such cases. Specifically, the Sherman Act prohibited price discrimination when it tends to lessen competition in any line of commerce. The act also forbids sellers from requiring buyers to refrain from buying the goods of their rivals when such a policy tends to create a monopoly (for example, certain tying arrangements and exclusive dealing arrangements).

The Clayton Act, passed in 1914, was directed at the tendency toward corporate combinations that restrained trade or commerce. As it relates to antitrust matters, the Clayton Act states that "unfair methods of competition in or affecting commerce, and unfair or deceptive acts or practices in or affecting commerce are hereby declared unlawful." Specifically, the act prohibits price discriminations that would result in a lessening of competition or tend to create monopoly; tying clauses in contracts that required buyers of products not to use the product of a competitor of the seller; the acquisition of the stock of one corporation by a competing corporation for the purpose of lessening competition; and interlocking directorates. Recent developments in 1977 in antitrust legislation raised the penalty for violations from misdemeanors to a felony punishable by fines not exceeding $1 million for a corporation or $100,000 for an individual and imprisonment not exceeding three years.

The Clayton Act was amended in 1936 when the Robinson-Patman Act was passed. The Robinson-Patman Act was designed to prevent "unfair" competition in trade by giving or receiving discounts or services when such acts amounted to discrimination and in a substantial reduction of competition. Price discrimination can occur when a supplier sells the same product to two different competitive wholesales at different prices, when the effect may be to injure competition. The act also makes it illegal for a buyer to knowingly induce or receive a discriminatory, lower price. Price differentials can be legal if they do not injure competition, they result from cost differences in selling to different customers, they are used to sell obsolete products, they are offered in good faith to meet a competitor's price, and they are offered to noncompeting customers. The act also prohibits sellers from offering various types of advertising or promotional allowances unless they offer them to all customers "on proportionately equal terms."

The Robinson-Patman Act was amended in 1950 by the Anti-Merger Act, or the Celler-Kefauver Amendment, which makes it illegal for one corporation to acquire the assets of another company where the acquisition would substantially lessen competition, restrain commerce, or tend to create a monopoly.

The Federal Trade Commission Act of 1914 declares "that unfair methods of competition in commerce are hereby declared unlawful. The commission is hereby empowered and directed to prevent persons, partnerships, corporations, except banks, and common carriers subject to the acts which regulate commerce, from using unfair methods in commerce." The Wheeler-Lea Act of 1938 empowered the commission to restrain business practices that it considers harmful to the public interest, especially false advertising and the adulteration of manufactured products.

Alternatives to government regulation would include greater freedom in allowing businesses to attain social objectives, increased cooperation between business and government in establishing realistic performance standards, a willingness on the part of business to acknowledge the legitimacy of social objectives and to let the marketplace bring about desired changes in business behavior.

A functional analysis of existing federal bank regulation included in the 1984 *Bush Report* is appended.

GOVERNMENT SECURITIES DEALERS AND BROKERS Dealers purchase and sell government securities for their own accounts as well as arrange transactions with customers and other dealers. Dealers work closely with the Federal Reserve System and the Treasury. They are authorized to purchase debt directly from the Treasury for resale. Primary dealers can purchase government securities directly from the Federal Reserve System in return for maintaining markets in Treasury debt. Generally, dealers must maintain average customer trading volume in government securities of at least 3/4 of 1% of total primary dealer customer volume. Dealers do not charge commission on their own trades, but strive to sell securities at prices above the cost of the securities. There is a broad secondary market for U.S. Treasury securities.

Brokers specialize in bringing together (matching) buyers and sellers among the dealers in the government securities market. Most of the trading is done by phone since there is no centralized marketplace.

GOVERNMENT SPONSORED ENTERPRISES (GSE)

Functional Analysis of Existing Federal Bank Regulation

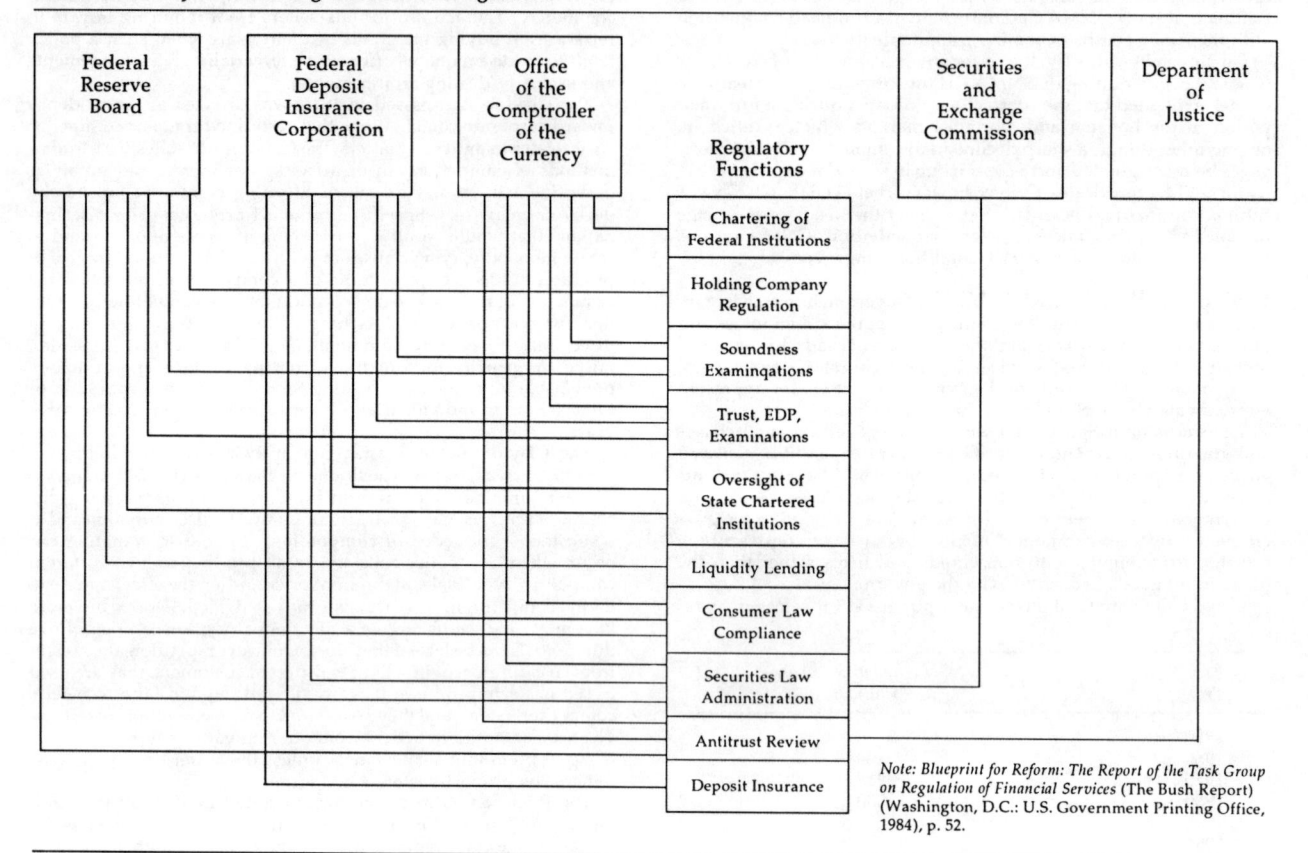

Federal Reserve Board	Federal Deposit Insurance Corporation	Office of the Comptroller of the Currency	Regulatory Functions	Securities and Exchange Commission	Department of Justice
			Chartering of Federal Institutions		
			Holding Company Regulation		
			Soundness Examinations		
			Trust, EDP, Examinations		
			Oversight of State Chartered Institutions		
			Liquidity Lending		
			Consumer Law Compliance		
			Securities Law Administration		
			Antitrust Review		
			Deposit Insurance		

Note: *Blueprint for Reform: The Report of the Task Group on Regulation of Financial Services* (The Bush Report) (Washington, D.C.: U.S. Government Printing Office, 1984), p. 52.

Transactions often involve large amounts. Differences between bid and ask prices are often as low as 1 basis point ($25 per $1 million face value on a 90-day bill). Interest rate expectations and the state of the market usually determine the spread. The Treasury market is the largest securities market in the world, with more than five times the dollar volume of the New York Stock Exchange. Interdealer trading is highly organized. Electronic brokerage screens are commonly used to provide immediate bids and offerings on active issues traded.

Government securities are generally considered to be riskless assets. However, market prices can change rapidly and frequently, resulting in the possibility of trading risks. Interest rate risks remain because government securities are sensitive to changes in interest rates.

GOVERNMENT-SPONSORED ENTERPRISES (GSE)

Off-budget corporations chartered by the federal government. GSEs can borrow funds in capital markets and lend them to selective sectors at favorable rates. GSEs are widely perceived as having implicit government guarantee of their debt. GSEs also have a line of credit at Treasury, exemption from certain taxes, and favorable classifications by the Federal Reserve System. Such entities could cost the taxpayers significant and increasing (up over 150% in the last five years) amount if the government is required to rescue the corporations. Major GSEs include the following:

Farm Credit System. Established in 1917, consisting of Farm Credit banks and banks for cooperative capable of providing loans directly to farms and farmer-owned cooperatives, respectively.

Federal Home Loan Bank System (FHLSB). Established in 1932 to provide short-term liquidity and longer-term credit to the thrift industry.

Federal Home Loan Mortgage Corporation (FHLMC, Freddie Mac). Established in 1970 to create a national secondary market for mortgages.

Federal National Mortgage Association (FNMA, Fannie Mae). Established in 1938 as a government agency to provide a secondary market for FHA and VA-guaranteed mortgages. Became a private corporation in 1968.

Student Loan Mortgage Association (SLMA, Sallie Mae). Established in 1972 to create a secondary market for students.

College Construction Loan Insurance Association (CCLIA, Connie Lee). Established in 1987 to guarantee loans for college construction; owned by the Department of Education and Sallie Mae.

Federal Agricultural Mortgage Corporation (FAMC, Farmer Mac). Established in 1988 to provide a secondary market for farm mortgages as part of the effort to bail out the FCS.

Financial Assistance Corporation (FAC). Established in 1988 to help bail out FSLIC.

Resolution Funding Corporation (REFCO). Proposed in 1989 to help bail out FSLIC.

It is estimated that since 1970, GSEs' loans outstanding have grown at an annual rate of 17%, compared to total debt at an 11% rate. GSEs typically hold non diversified portfolios of loans. Congress bailed out the Farm Credit System after it lost $4.6 billion in 1985 and 1986 when the farm economy weakened. Other bailouts are on the horizon.

The more recently established GSEs were organized to evade Gramm-Rudman deficit limits; their spending does not show up in the federal budget. Their borrowing is not counted against the debt ceiling limits. GSEs have borrowed three-quarters of a trillion dollars on Wall Street as of 1989.

GRACE *See* DAYS OF GRACE.

GRADING Standardization of the differences in quality of staple commodities so that they may be readily recognized for the purpose of facilitating trade. Leading commodities are classified in many grades, representative of recognized and accepted standards in the trade. The Grain Standards Act of 1916 vested in the secretary of Agriculture authority to investigate the handling, grading, and transportation of grain to fix and establish standards of quality and condition for various grains as in his judgment the usages of the trade may warrant and permit. Such standards are known as the official grain standards of the United States. Under the act, original inspections are made by inspectors employed by the grain inspection departments of the state or the grain exchange, or by inspectors who operate independently on a fee basis. All inspectors must be licensed by the secretary of Agriculture; they are not allowed to trade in grain or be employed by grain merchants. Federal grain inspection supervisors at the various markets work with the licensed inspectors to keep them informed as to inspection methods and the correct interpretation and application of grading factors. Federal supervisors also take samples of a cross section of grain tendered for inspection under the act to determine whether the inspections by licensees are made properly.

Each grain exchange also defines its grain standards, which are maintained by the federal and state inspectors and those engaged by the grain exchange. The Commodity Exchange Act also requires that all contracts of sale of any commodity for future delivery on "contract markets" (futures markets) shall provide for the delivery thereunder of commodities conforming to standards of the United States, if such standards have been officially promulgated.

Basic contract grades on the CHICAGO BOARD OF TRADE include the following.

No. 2 Hard Winter Wheat
No. 2 Red Winter Wheat
No. 2 Yellow Hard Winter Wheat
No. 1 Northern Spring Wheat
No. 2 Yellow Corn
No. 2 Heavy White Oats
Nos. 1 and 2 Barley, Class 1 or Malting
No. 2 Rye
No. 2 Yellow Soybeans

Other grades are deliverable at specified premiums and discounts from the basic grades.

Eggs and Poultry. Grading and inspection services cover the grading of live poultry and shell eggs, the certification of dressed poultry produced under Department of Agriculture sanitary standards, inspection for wholesomeness of dressed poultry and dressed domestic rabbits, the grading of dressed poultry and ready-to-cook poultry, inspection of poultry for canning, and the inspection of frozen and dried eggs as to sanitary regulations. The service is elective and is supported by fees, being conducted on the basis of cooperative agreements between the Department of Agriculture and state agencies.

Livestock and Meats. Federal grades form the basis for marketing of livestock and meats, but only part of the meat and none of the livestock is officially graded by the Department of Agriculture. Meat grading in this connection is not the same as the inspection for sanitation and freedom from disease, which is carried on by employees of the Department of Agriculture under the Meat Inspection Act of 1906. Except for times when price controls on meat were in effect and federal meat grading was made compulsory by government order or was required by state or municipal regulations, the meat grading service has been strictly voluntary and performed only on request, being operated on a fee basis.

Cotton. Approximately two-thirds of the cotton crop is classed for farmers under the Smith-Doxey Act. The Department of Agriculture also classes all the cotton tendered on futures and maintains a classing service for the general public. The department maintains more than 30 boards of cotton examiners besides an appeal board of review examiners. Classification or determination of the grade and staple length of cotton is done manually by comparison of samples with the official cotton standards.

Tobacco. Under the Tobacco Inspection Act, inspection of tobacco is available on auction markets if growers vote for it (two-thirds vote), whereupon the secretary of Agriculture designates a market or a group of markets for inspection. The act also provides for permissive inspection, which is reimbursable. Grades are established by division and subdivision of a given type or class of tobacco, each subdivision being called a grade.

Dairy Products. The dairy products grading service of the Department of Agriculture was authorized by act of Congress and inaugurated in 1919. Actual grading and inspection are performed by federal employees except in states where the cooperating state agency provides qualified employees from its staff, who are licensed by the Department of Agriculture.

Fresh and Processed Fruit and Vegetables. Federal grades were authorized under the Food Production Act of 1917. Approximately 140 grades for fresh fruits and vegetables and more than 100 grades for processed fruits and vegetables and their allied products have been developed and promulgated. Operations are conducted on both a federal and cooperative federal-state basis, with fees set at levels designed to make the service as nearly self-sustaining as possible.

See BASIS GRADE.

GRADUATED EQUITY MORTGAGE (GEM)
A mortgage that provides for increased payments on the principal to decrease the loan's maturity. GEMs build equity and shorten the loan's maturity.

GRADUATED PAYMENT MORTGAGE
A fixed interest rate MORTGAGE; payments rise gradually for the first few years, then level off for the duration of the loan. Such loans are designed for home buyers who expect to be able to make larger monthly payments in the near future. The loans are structured to rise at a set rate over a set period, say five or ten years. Then they remain constant for the duration of the loan.

There are five major GPM plans:

Plan	Years to maturity	Years that payments rise	% Increase per year
I	30	5	2.5%
II	30	5	5.0
III	30	5	7.5
IV	30	10	2.0
V	30	10	3.0

The number of years in which payments rise under each plan is called the graduation period. At the end of the graduation period, payments remain constant until maturity. For some of the plans, the difference between the initial payment level in the first year and that at the end of the graduation period is substantial. Appended is a comparison of the beginning and ending payments levels under the five plans, assuming a 30-year, 10% mortgage for $50,000.

Type of loan	Initial payment	Final payment	Percent difference
Conventional	$438.79	$438.79	0.0%
Plan I	400.29	452.88	13.1
Plan II	365.29	466.22	27.6
Plan III	333.29	475.43	43.7
Plan IV	390.02	475.43	21.9
Plan V	367.29	493.60	34.4

The Federal Housing Administration (FHA), which has insured GPMs since 1976, requires that down payments on GPMs be larger than those required under traditional level-payment mortgages because of NEGATIVE AMORTIZATION. The FHA stipulates that mortgage balance outstanding, including deferred interest, cannot exceed 97% of the appraised value of the property at any time over the life of the loan.

GPMs have been eligible for pooling into GNMA pass-through securities since 1979. Since that time, they have come to represent a substantial portion of all FHA-insured mortgages.

A variation of the graduated payment mortgage is the adjustable-rate mortgage. In this mortgage, the loan has graduated payments early in the loan, but the interest rate is tied to changes in an agreed-upon index. If interest rates climb quickly, larger negative amortization occurs during the period when payments

are low. Should rates continue to climb after that initial period, the payments will also climb. This increases the risk for the purchaser.
See MORTGAGE LOANS.

GRADUATE SCHOOL OF BANKING The Stonier Graduate School of Banking, sponsored by the American Bankers Association, was established in 1935. It offers a three-year course for bankers at the policy-making level, providing advanced education in the history, theory, and economics of banking to assist bank officers in making policy and administrative decisions.

To qualify for graduation, each student must complete three summer sessions at the school, which meets for annual two-week summer sessions on the campus of Rutgers University, plus two years of extension study at home. The student must also write a thesis based on original research on some phase of finance. The thesis requirement is designed to train "S.G.S.B." graduates in organized thinking and expression of ideas, and also to afford continuing exploration into the field of banking. Three major subjects are offered: commercial banking, trusts, and savings management and real estate financing. During the day sessions, students concentrate on their selected major; evening sessions are devoted to courses required of all students.
See AMERICAN BANKERS ASSOCIATION.

GRADUATE SECURITIES Sometimes applied to securities that are listed for the first time on the New York Stock Exchange, particularly after a period of "seasoning" either in the over-the-counter market or on other exchanges such as the American Stock Exchange in New York.

GRAIN As defined in the COMMODITY EXCHANGE ACT, wheat, corn, oats, barley, rye, flaxseed, grain sorghums, and soybeans. Trading in grain futures is normally most active in wheat, with corn, oats, rye, and barley following in that order.

GRAIN BILLS Bills of exchange drawn against shipments of grain.
See BILL OF EXCHANGE.

GRAIN EXCHANGES Principal COMMODITY EXCHANGES where grain futures are traded are as follows: corn, Chicago Board of Trade and Kansas City Board of Trade; oats, Chicago Board of Trade and Minneapolis Grain Exchange; rye, Chicago Board of Trade and Minneapolis Grain Exchange; wheat, Chicago Board of Trade, Minneapolis Grain Exchange, and Kansas City Board of Trade.

GRAIN FUTURES See CHICAGO BOARD OF TRADE, COMMODITY EXCHANGES, FUTURES, HEDGING.

GRAIN FUTURES ACT Originally passed in 1921, this act, together with the Act of June 15, 1936, which amended it, constitutes the COMMODITY EXCHANGE ACT, the basic legislation for regulation and supervision of the commodity futures exchanges.

GRAIN PIT The structure (called a PIT) built upon the trading floor of a grain exchange where traders and brokers gather to trade in grain futures. There is one for each of the principal grains traded.

GRAIN SPREADER See SPREADING.

GRAMM-RUDMAN-HOLLINGS ACT Legislation that provides for automatic, across-the-board spending cuts if Congress fails to meet specified deficit targets. The act provides for deficit reductions without requiring Congress to record votes on individual programs that could have strong constituency support. The original act established deficit targets for each fiscal year beginning FY 86. The courts struck down the arrangement for forcing Congress to achieve the deficit targets on the grounds that the act vested executive power in a legislative branch officer (the comptroller general).

In 1987, Congress enacted procedures designed to overcome the constitutional objections. The Balanced Budget and Emergency Deficit Control Reaffirmation Act liberalized the budget targets by extending the deficit reduction timetable. The revision restored the automatic procedure for sequestration by vesting the trigger with the director of the Office of Management and Budget (OMB, who, as an executive officer, issues a sequestration report). Some restrictions were placed on the discretion of OMB and the office must give due regard to an advisory report issued earlier by the director of the Congressional Budget Office (CBO). As amended, the Act extends the process two years, calling for a balanced budget in FY 93 rather than FY 91. Corresponding changes in the deficit targets for each year were also provided: FY 89, from $72 billion to $136 billion; FY 90, from $36 billion to $100 billion; and FY 91, from $0 to $64 billion and for FY 93, $0. The amendment caps the required deficit reduction amount for FY 88 at $23 billion and for FY 89, $36 billion. Sequestration occurs if the estimated deficit exceeds a $10 billion margin of error. As of the summer of 1990 there have been two sequestrations.

GRANGERS The principal grain-carrying railroads.
See RAILROAD INDUSTRY.

GRANTOR A donor; one who bestows a benefit. Also, one who creates a trust; the seller of real property, i.e., the grantor in a deed who gives up title.
See TRUST.

GRANTOR RETAINED INCOME TRUST (GRIT) An irrevocable trust, established by an individual, which has a set period of existence; the trust income is paid to the grantor for a period of years specified in the trust instrument. If the grantor outlives the term of the trust, the trust terminates and the trust assets are distributed to named beneficiaries. If the grantor dies before the term expires, the trust terminates and the trust assets revert back to the grantor's estate. The term of the trust normally runs three years or more.

When the GRIT is established, the grantor makes a gift of the remainder interest to the beneficiaries. The transfer is subject to gift tax. The value of the gift and any gift tax payable is determined on the date the property is transferred to the GRIT. The gift tax value is determined as follows: The fair market value of the property at the time of the gift is reduced by both the value of the retained income interest and the value of the potential reversionary interest held by the grantor were he or she to die before the term expires.

The major advantage to a GRIT is the amount of leverage it gives in valuing property for a fraction of its value at the time of the gift. The gift tax value can be significantly reduced depending on the term in years of the trust and the age of the grantor at the date of the gift. The longer the grantor retains an income interest, the lower the gift tax value. If the GRIT is funded with appreciating assets, all future appreciation will be taken out of the grantor's estate, if he survives the income interest term. Beneficiaries will receive the property with the same income tax basis as the taxpayer had at the time of the gift.

During the income interest term, the grantor is treated as the owner of the trust property; income derived from the property will be taxed directly to him or her. The property used to fund the GRIT should be property that yields an adequate annual income (the IRS table rate generally); otherwise, the IRS may attack the validity of the trust.

If the grantor dies before the termination of the income interest, the assets in the trust will be included in his or her taxable estate. No additional tax liabilities will result from establishing a GRIT.

GRATUITOUS COINAGE COINAGE of the standard metal without charge by the mints; coinage without brassage or SEIGNIORAGE. Gratuitous coinage is to be distinguished from FREE COINAGE.

GRATUITY A gift, donation, or benefit. No member bank, or officer, director, or employee thereof, is permitted to give any gratuity to a bank examiner; nor is a bank examiner permitted to accept such a gratuity. To do so is a misdemeanor, and an offender is subject to fine or imprisonment.

GREENBACKS Also known as "legal tenders," inconvertible notes authorized by three acts of Congress, the first of which was that of February 25, 1862, to a maximum amount of $450 million. They represent the Civil War inflation episode and were the result of wartime needs rather than excursion into inflation by virtue of popular demand. Greenbacks were legal tender for all debts, public and private, except duties on imports and interest on the public debt.

Specie payments had been suspended on December 30, 1861, about a year after the outbreak of hostilities. The premium on gold was only 4% by May, 1862, although early in 1862 it was sufficiently noticeable that brokers had begun to deal in gold coin. A gold exchange was organized in the autumn of 1862. With 100 expressing par for gold, the highest price quoted for gold during the war was 285, or 185% premium. This was in July, 1864 (battle of Gettysburg), when greenbacks were at the corresponding highest discount—namely, worth $0.38 to $0.39. When the war ended in May, 1865, gold dropped to a premium of 30%, at which rate greenbacks were worth $0.77. Thus, public credit reached its lowest ebb in July, 1864, but improved at the conclusion of the war.

The greenback inflation of the Civil War was held in check by the fact that the issues were limited and fluctuated according to the fortunes of the combatants. If the issue had been increased, as might have been necessary if hostilities had been prolonged, the inflation would have been more serious. Issuance of greenbacks inevitably increased the cost of the war by raising the price of war material. The cost of living also advanced. Prices rose from 100 in 1862 to 216 in January, 1865, and then dropped 58 points in five months when the war ended. Real wages fell fully 20%.

The Civil War greenback inflation, however, had an agreeable ending. The Specie Resumption Act, passed December 22, 1874, provided that the secretary of the Treasury on and after January 1, 1879, should redeem in gold the United States legal tender notes outstanding on their presentation for redemption at the office of the assistant treasurer of the United States.

For further particulars on this subject, *See* INFLATION and UNITED STATES NOTES.

GRESHAM'S LAW A monetary principle named after Sir Thomas Gresham, Master of the English Mint under Queen Elizabeth, who while not the first to recognize it, was the first clearly to enunciate it and give it official standing. This principle is that an overvalued money of equal legal tender power tends to displace an undervalued money; that bad money (mutilated or debased money) drives good money out of circulation; or that cheaper money supplants dearer money.

It has long been recognized that two kinds of money of equal legal tender power and nominally of equal value, but in reality of unequal value, cannot be kept in concurrent circulation. The cheaper money becomes a standard of value because people will pay their debts in the cheaper money and hoard, melt, or export the dearer money, or the dearer money commands a premium over the cheaper money. It is the operation of Gresham's Law that makes it desirable for a government to provide for redemption of its overvalued metallic coins and paper money in standard money.

GROSS DEBT Total debt, without adjustments for deductions. Deductions usually include sinking funds and reacquired debt not yet retired.

In municipal bond analysis, deductions from gross debt are sinking funds as well as that portion of the debt which is revenue producing, such as that incurred to finance city-operated facilities (water supply, rapid transit, etc.). The net debt figure resulting is the base for calculating debt per capita and net debt percentage of assessed value of taxable property.

See MUNICIPAL BONDS.

GROSS DEPOSITS Aggregate deposits, without any exclusions or deductions. Included in gross deposits are all types of demand and time deposits, including deposits due to banks and U.S. government deposits.

Gross demand deposits less interbank and U.S. government deposits and less cash items in process of collection (so-called float) appear as "demand deposits adjusted" in memorandum form to the member bank call report. This is a statistical measure designed by the Board of Governors of the Federal Reserve System to indicate aggregate net balances in checking accounts of individuals, partnerships, corporations, and state and local government bodies, after allowing for checks outstanding against these accounts.

Both gross deposits and demand deposits adjusted are to be distinguished from net demand deposits, or deposits subject to reserve requirements according to the definition of "net demand deposits" by the Board of Governors of the Federal Reserve System in accordance with banking law. In accordance with the Banking Act of 1935, net demand deposits are the excess of all demand deposits, including deposits due to other banks and the United States government, over demand balances due from other domestic banks (except Federal Reserve banks, foreign banks or branches thereof, foreign branches of domestic banks, and private banks), and cash items in process of collection.

See DEMAND DEPOSITS.

GROSS EARNINGS Total receipts of income; GROSS REVENUES. In trading or manufacturing concerns, gross receipts are usually sales of merchandise or products shown net after returns and allowances. Any sources of gross receipts other than sales should be shown separately—for example, rental income where products such as machines are leased rather than sold.

GROSS NATIONAL PRODUCT (GNP) The nominal value of all goods and services produced in the economy in a given year. There are two ways to calculate GNP: the expenditure approach and the income approach.

The expenditure approach for measuring GNP focuses on the various categories of consumers who purchase final goods and services in the output market of the economy. There are four major components of GNP (Y) expenditures: consumption (C), investment (I), government purchases (G), and net exports (NX). GNP equals consumption plus investment plus government purchases plus net exports. Approximately 65% of GNP is consumption expenditures. This definition leads to the frequently seen relationship:

$$Y = C + I + G + NX.$$

The expenditure approach to the calculation of GNP is equivalent to adding the values of all expenditures on final goods and services in the output market.

The income approach for measuring GNP focuses on payments to factors of production in the input market. This approach to measuring GNP adds together the total incomes received by all owners of resources.

Employee compensation, which includes the payments of wages and fringe benefits to workers for their labor services and the payment of taxes on labor, accounts for 60% of GNP. Rental income represents payments to the owners of capital goods for the use of their resources. Proprietory income is the payment to the owners of firms for their time, ideas, risk taking, and skills. Corporate profit is the income earned by the shareholders of businesses. Interest is payment received in return for lending financial resources. The last two categories of income are depreciation and indirect business taxes.

GNP will change in value from year to year for two reasons. First, the price of some goods and services may change. Second, the equilibrium quantity of output in some or all markets may change. Ideally, GNP should measure only changes in production, not changes in prices. Real GNP holds prices constant from year to year; therefore, real GNP is called the constant dollar measure of GNP. It is calculated by dividing nominal GNP by an average price level, thereby correcting for changes in the average price of all final goods and services in the economy. This average price level is based on a price index called the GNP deflator.

Values for nominal GNP (referred to simply as GNP) and real GNP (in 1982 dollars) for recent years are reported in the table below.

Table 1 / Nominal vs. Real GNP

Year	GNP ($billions)	Real GNP (billions of 1982$)
1950	$ 288.3	$1,203.7
1960	513.3	1,665.3
1970	1,015.5	2,416.2
1980	2,732.0	3,187.1
1985	4,010.3	3,607.5
1986	4,235.0	3,713.3
1987	4,486.2	3,819.6

Source: Economic Report of the President, 1988.

The gross domestic product of selected countries as percent of United States—1970 to 1986—is appended.

Table 2 / Gross Domestic Product of Selected Countries as Percent of United States: 1970 to 1986
(Comparisons are based on constant (1980) price data converted to U.S. dollars using 1980 exchange rates).

Country	Gross Domestic Product								Per Capita Gross Domestic Product							
	1970	1975	1980	1982	1983	1984	1985	1986	1970	1975	1980	1982	1983	1984	1985	1986
United States	100	100	100	100	100	100	100	100	100	100	100	100	100	100	100	100
Canada	8	9	10	10	10	10	10	10	79	90	93	92	91	90	91	91
France	23	25	25	25	25	23	23	23	92	101	104	108	105	100	99	99
Italy	16	17	17	17	16	16	16	16	63	64	68	70	68	66	66	67
Japan	33	36	39	42	41	40	41	41	65	70	77	82	81	80	81	81
United Kingdom	22	22	20	20	20	19	19	19	80	83	80	81	81	78	79	80
West Germany	30	30	30	30	29	28	28	28	103	105	112	112	111	108	109	109

Source: U.S. Bureau of Economic Analysis. Adapted from *Long Term Economic Growth, 1860-1970,* using data from the Organization for Economic Cooperation and Development.

BIBLIOGRAPHY

Econ Base: Timeseries and Forecasts. Online data base. DWEFA Group, Bala Cynwyd, PA.

IEA Charts. Institute for Economic Analysis, Silver Spring, MD. Monthly.

Long Term Economic Growth. Department of Commerce, Washington, DC.

National Income and Product Accounts of the United States. Bureau of Economic Analysis, Washington, DC.

PTS U.S. Time Series. Online data base. Predicasts, Inc., Cleveland, OH.

Weekly Economic Survey. Online data base. Money Market Services, San Francisco, CA.

GROSS PROFITS Profits on goods sold without deduction of selling and general administrative expenses. Gross profits are determined by subtracting the cost of goods sold from the amount received from their sale. The term gross profits is used because selling and administrative expenses must be deducted in order to determine NET PROFITS. Gross profits measure gross margin, or "contribution" to coverage of selling and administrative expenses.

Gross margin represents the dollar amount of financial resources produced by the basic selling activity of the firm. On an income statement, gross margin appears as follows:

	1991	1990	Change
Sales	$225,000	$100,000	$125,000
Cost of goods sold	90,000	50,000	40,000
GROSS MARGIN	135,000	50,000	85,000
Operating expenses	90,000	35,000	55,000
Net income	$ 45,000	$ 15,000	$ 30,000

Changes in gross margin from period to period may be due to any one or any combination of the following variables:

1. Change in sales caused by:
   a. change in selling price (sales-price variance)
   b. change in volume of goods sold (sales-volume variance)
2. Change in cost of goods sold caused by:
   a. change in unit cost (cost-price variance)
   b. change in volume of goods sold (cost-volume variance)

The four gross margin variances can be computed for year-to-year data using the following formulas and the following data that relate to the income statement shown earlier. The analysis that results from interpreting these variances is referred to as gross margin analysis.

	1991	1990
Number of units sold	$150,000	$100,000
Sales price per unit	1.50	1.00
Cost per unit	0.60	0.50

1. Sales-price variance = Current year's units sold
   x Change in sales price per unit
   = 150,000 x $0.50
   = $75,000 favorable variance
2. Sales-volume variance = Change in units sold
   x Last year's prices
   = 50,000 units x $1.00
   = $50,000 favorable variance
3. Cost-price variance = Current year's units sold
   x Change in cost per unit
   = 150,000 x $0.10
   = $15,000 unfavorable variance
4. Cost-volume variance = Change in units sold
   x Last year's cost
   = 50,000 units x $0.50
   = $25,000 unfavorable variance

When the four variances are combined, the $85,000 change in gross profit from 1990 to 1991 is identified:

Sales-price variance	$75,000
Sales-volume variance	50,000
Cost-price variance	(15,000)
Cost-volume variance	(25,000)
Change in gross margin	$85,000

For a multiproduct firm, a sales-mix variance is usually computed. This variance identifies the change in gross margin attributable to shifts in the sales mix for the company. This approximates the effect of changing the sales mix at a constant volume. This variance can be computed using the following formula:

Sales-mix variance = Current year's sales
   x Change in gross margin rate
   = $225,000 x (.60 - .50)
   = $22,500 favorable variance

GROSS REVENUES In railroad and public utility accounting, the total receipts from operations or operating revenues, corresponding to sales in an industrial or mercantile business.

Railway operating revenues of railroads are classified in accordance with the Uniform System of Accounts for Steam Railway Corporations in annual reports to the Interstate Commerce Commission, and include rail-line transportation revenue, water-line transportation revenue, incidental operating revenues, and joint facility operating revenue, so distributed as to group those assignable to freight, those assignable to passenger and allied services, or those common to both services. Summary reports of operating revenues usually subdivide into freight, passenger, mail, express, and other.

Public utility companies using a uniform system of accounts or a form for annual report prescribed by federal or state authorities follow the segregation of revenues prescribed, generally calling for residential, commercial, and industrial subdivisions applicable.

GROUND FLOOR   Used in finance to designate an especially low price of a security, representing an opportunity for subsequent capital gains as the security rises to more normal levels. The public offering price of a new issue in great demand may represent the ground floor as a premium above the offering price subsequently develops. In such cases, sound underwriting calls for minimizing "free riders" solely interested in profiting from the premium above public offering price.

GROUP BANKING   The form of multiple banking control that, although similar to branch and chain banking, differs in that a holding company controls the group of banks. By contrast, chain banking involves the control of two or more banks by a person or persons through stock ownership and interlocking directors. The function of the holding company is to supervise and to coordinate the banks in the group, but each bank has its own officers and board of directors on whom the responsibility for the affairs of the bank rests.

See HOLDING COMPANY.

GROWING EQUITY MORTGAGE   A rapid-payoff MORTGAGE. Such mortgages combine a fixed interest rate with a changing monthly payment. The interest rate is usually a few percentage points below market. The mortgage term may run for 30 years; however, the loans are frequently paid off over a shorter period because payment increases are applied entirely to the principal. Monthly payment changes are based on an agreed-upon schedule of increases or an index. The borrower's income should be able to keep pace with increased payments.

GROWTH STOCKS   First used in a report of National Investors Corporation in the mid-1930s, in time the term became a popular designation for common stocks in companies experiencing substantial growth well above the average for common stocks in general, reflected in substantially higher per share earnings, dividends, asset values, and market values.

A growth company is one experiencing expansion as the result of either or both of the following factors: (1) higher than average expansion of the industry of which it is a part, and (2) particular company policies, such as emphasis on research and development, aggressive marketing, and acquisitive expansion, which yield superior results for the particular company in comparison with other companies in the same growth industry.

A particular characteristic of growth stocks over time is their share multiplication—stock split-ups and stock dividends—which parlay an original INVESTMENT of the investor into a substantial number of shares, yielding large dividend income on original investment and creating large capital gains. Such share multiplication is resorted to by these companies when their aggregate earnings and dividends, as well as market prices for their shares, rise to such high levels that increase in number of shares by such methods is justified in order to bring down per share earnings, dividends, and market prices to more popular levels. Usually, such adjustment in market prices as the result of splits and stock dividends itself creates a premium over equivalent price for the new stock, as the more popular price attracts additional demand from investors anticipating a continuance of superior growth. Thus growth stocks as a rule sell at very high price-earnings ratios and quite low dividend yields, representing substantial premiums as compared with average stocks.

Therein lies one danger in investing in growth stocks—the danger that current price paid may be so high that it would take years for the purchase to be justified, i.e., that current prices may be discounting earnings and dividends far into the future. High growth and market appreciation of the past are not to be projected simply by extrapolation far into the future, for a superior growth stock in the recent past might not be one in the future, if only because industries and companies are bound to reach a point of full development and maturity.

Ideally, the best time to purchase growth stocks is before they are recognized generally by the market as such and rise to premiums in price accordingly. At such an early stage, however, even if an industry is a superior growth industry, individual companies at such a stage may be quite speculative as selections, falling eventually by the wayside as the survivors prove to be the leaders in the industry. Bellemore therefore suggests waiting until an industry has passed through its initial competitive crisis, and then attempting to select the strongest company that has emerged from the melee. Regrettably, however, by such a time shares in such companies are already commanding fancy premium prices. The problem of projecting estimated future growth that will justify such high prices is not an easy one.

Some formulas for estimating the reasonableness of current prices for growth stocks, relative to future growth, are quite fantastic. Here is the gist of one, as an example. A stock has doubled its annual profit over the past four years, for a compounded annual rate of growth of 19.2%. Assume the chances for a similar doubling over the next four years are pretty good. Therefore, multiply the latest $15 per share annual earnings by two, obtaining $30 per share; capitalize same at the current price-earnings ratio of 25 times, obtaining $750 as a projected price for the stock four years hence. Discount this price by a discount factor of 12% ($1 four years hence would be worth $0.636 today). Presto, the current fair price of $477 justifies investment at the current actual price of $373. This is simple extrapolation. A doubling of earnings in the future, as in the past, is, as a simple statistical matter, a very difficult achievement for an already well-established company. As Benjamin Graham says, "Some of the best-educated guesses, derived from the most painstaking research, have turned out to be abysmally wrong."

A solution for investing in growth stocks, so easy to state in the abstract but so difficult to implement by actual selections, is first of all to block out industries that are fairly new and have high growth potential. Second, make a diversified selection of those companies whose managements are considered within the industry as superior. With this procedure, even if some companies turn out to be disappointments, the chances are favorable that the selection will include some outstanding successes that will produce results substantially in excess of the losses on the disappointments. Research and development by companies in already well-established industries, resulting in outstandingly successful products, may make such companies the growth leaders of the future. For this approach, a knowledge of and constant contact with industries and companies are necessary, something which the ordinary investor is in no position to do himself, but which investing institutions such as investment companies can and should do.

GUARANTEE   See GUARANTY.

GUARANTEED BANK DEPOSITS   See GUARANTY OF BANK DEPOSITS.

GUARANTEED BONDS   Bonds, the payment of the principal, interest, or both of which has been guaranteed by a party other than the original debtor. Railroad and industrial corporations sometimes guarantee the bonds and notes of leased or controlled companies, subsidiaries, or companies in which they are financially interested in order to strengthen their credit or to elevate their investment position.

While the market value of bonds guaranteed by another party is undoubtedly enhanced by such guaranty, investors should not purchase this class of bonds because of the guaranty alone. Such bonds should be intrinsically sound in themselves without the guaranty, since it may be difficult to enforce the guaranty against the guarantors in case of default of the principal debtors in an action at law. Guaranteed bonds should be supported by sufficient security to meet the principal and interest, and the guaranty should be in such form as to compel the guarantor to m et any deficiency on the part of the principal debtor.

When bonds are guaranteed after their issue, the guaranty appears in a separate instrument, and the fact of guaranty is not recited on the face of the bond at all. When bonds are guaranteed by endorsement, the fact of guaranty is stated on the face of each bond which contains the signature of the guarantor company.

Guaranteed bonds are similar to ASSUMED BONDS and endorsed bonds.

See ENDORSED BOND.

GUARANTEED INVESTMENT CONTRACTS Public bonds that typically promise a fixed rate of return for relatively short periods, often two to ten years. Such third-party guaranteed bonds are collateralized issues secured by assets whose value exceeds the outstanding face value of the bond issue. Housing or mortgage issues backed by bank CDs or insurance company-guaranteed investment contracts (GICs) possess interest and principal payments that match debt service requirements on the bonds they secure.

GUARANTEED LETTER OF CREDIT See LETTER OF CREDIT.

GUARANTEED MORTGAGE CERTIFICATES There are two types of GNMA-guaranteed mortgage-backed securities: mortgage-backed bonds, issued by the FEDERAL NATIONAL MORTGAGE ASSOCIATION and the Federal Home Loan Mortgage Corporation, and passthrough securities, guaranteed by the GNMA and issued by private mortgage lenders against specified pools of FEDERAL HOUSING ADMINISTRATION, FARMERS HOME ADMINISTRATION, or VA-guaranteed mortgages. See GOVERNMENT NATIONAL MORTGAGE ASSOCIATION for details of these securities.

Also, see FEDERAL HOME LOAN MORTGAGE CORPORATION for details of its two types of guarantees: guaranteed mortgage certificates (GMCs) and mortgage participation certificates (PCs).

GUARANTEED RAILROAD STOCKS See GUARANTEED STOCKS.

GUARANTEED STOCKS Shares of stock, preferred or common, the payment or dividends on which have been guaranteed by a corporation other than the issuer. Guaranteed stocks arise under much the same circumstances as GUARANTEED BONDS, but they are particularly found in railroad finance, although occasionally they occur among public utilities.

Guaranteed RAILROAD STOCKS arise by reason of one railroad company's lease of its property to another, under the terms of which the lessee railroad guarantees the payment of dividends at a stipulated rate on the stock of the lessor corporation. In default of payment of dividends or disaffirmance of the lease, the lessor may take back its property, in addition to having claim for the default upon the lessee. Leased line stocks particularly arose during the era of expansion of U.S. railroads when the major trunk lines found it necessary to resort to leases for the acquisition of divisional or branch mileage, such leases running for very long terms.

Dividends on guaranteed stocks are part of the fixed charges of the lessee company operating the property, and thus such dividends are a charge on the gross income of the operating or lessee company ranking with the interest on the operating company's own bonds. Consequently they are a charge ranking prior to the operating company's own dividends. Failure to pay the guaranteed rate abrogates the lease. In the final analysis, the importance and essentiality of the leased line to the lessee are determining factors in continued interest of the lessee in the leased line. In some railroad reorganizations of the late 1930s, reduction in fixed charges of railroad debtors involved disaffirmance of some leases on lines whose importance and essentiality to the system had declined over the long term.

Thus railroad guaranteed stocks are rated, among other factors, on the essentiality of the leased line to the lessee in modern times. The seasoned and better quality guaranteed railroad stocks sell on a yield basis comparable to the higher-grade railroad bonds of the lessee systems, with which they are comparable because of the fixed nature of the lease obligation.

Erroneously, preferred stocks having no connection with guaranteed dividends are sometimes referred to as guaranteed stocks, although preferred dividends, even if cumulative, are in no sense guaranteed by the issuer in the absence of specific guarantee.

GUARANTOR A surety; one who guarantees payment. A person, firm, or corporation may agree to guarantee a note for another party and become liable by endorsement to pay the obligations of another in case of failure or default by the original maker (principal debtor). The principal and/or interest on bonds and dividends on stocks are sometimes guaranteed.

See GUARANTEED BONDS, GUARANTEED STOCKS, GUARANTY.

GUARANTY A contract or undertaking in which the signor, i.e., guarantor, engages that the promise of another shall be performed, usually the payment of a debt or the performance of a contract. A guaranty is a contract in which a third party, the guarantor, intervenes in an agreement between two persons by becoming responsible to one for the default of the other, the person for whom the guaranty is made being known as the guarantee. For example, if Railroad No. 1 guarantees the bonds of Railroad No. 2, the former is a guarantor and promises the payment in case the latter, the gurantee, fails to fulfill its obligations.

See GUARANTEED BONDS.

There are two kinds of guaranties of debt—guaranty of payment and guaranty of collection. In the first case, the guarantor is in default the moment the debt is due and unpaid; in the second, the guarantor is in default only after the principal debtor has been sued and the creditor (guarantee) has employed every expedient to enforce payment.

When a bank issues a commercial letter of credit, it requires the person for whom it is issued to sign a guaranty to pay all drafts issued thereunder, and to be responsible for the validity, correctness, and genuineness of the supporting document. A typical form of letter of credit guaranty is the following.

Letter of Credit Guaranty

In consideration of the issuing by the Blank Bank of New York of their commercial letter of credit, _____
No. _____ for account of _____ in favor of _____ amounting to _____ available by _____ sight drafts, we hereby guarantee unconditionally the payment of all drafts issued under and in compliance with the terms of said commercial credit, at their maturity.

It is understood that neither you nor your agents here or abroad will be responsible for the validity, correctness, and/or genuineness of the documents purporting to relate to aforesaid credit, nor for the quality, quantity, and/or arrival of the merchandise described in such documents.

You are to receive a commission of percent together with all expenses incurred by you in connection with arranging the credit and the execution thereof. At least day(s) prior to the maturity of any draft or drafts, the undersigned is to place you in New York funds sufficient to pay each acceptance with interest, if any, and all other charges relating thereto.

Two forms of guaranty agreements are used in connection with bank loans—a continuing guaranty and a specific guaranty. In the former the guarantor is responsible for the default of the debtor for whom the guaranty is made, up to a certain limit so long as the agreement is in force, and may therefore cover all the loans of the debtor. In the latter, the guarantor holds himself responsible only for a particular described loan.

The following are typical forms of guaranty agreements.

Continuing Guaranty

The undersigned, in consideration of One Dollar, receipt whereof is hereby acknowledged, and the credits, discounts, purchases, or loans given or made as hereinafter mentioned, do hereby unconditionally guarantee to the Blank Bank of New York City (hereinafter called the Bank), its successors and assigns, that if before written notice from the undersigned, or any of them, not to give further accommodation hereunder, the Bank shall give any credit to _____ (hereinafter called the Debtor) or discount, or purchase, or make any loan on, any commercial paper made or endorsed by the Debtor, all sums payable upon all such credits, loans, discounts, and commercial paper shall be paid in full when respectively due, and, in case of extension of payment of any thereof, in whole or in part, all sums payable thereon shall be paid when due according to such extension; and also so agree to indemnify and save harmless the Bank, its successors and assigns, for all costs and expenses, including counsel and attorneys' fees of enforcing the obligation of the undersigned hereunder, and/or collecting any item whose payment is hereby guaranteed.

This shall be a continuing guaranty, but the liability of the undersigned hereunder shall not exceed _____ Dollars ($ _____), exclusive of any liability on account of said costs and expenses.

Presentment or demand of payment from maker and notice of receipt or acceptance hereof, or of intention to act, or of acting hereupon, or of nonpayment, or of protest, or of sale of securities, are hereby waived by the undersigned.

Consent is hereby given by the undersigned that, from time to time, without notice to the undersigned, payment of any sum or sums payable upon any items whose payment is guaranteed hereunder, or any security for the payment thereof, may be extended in whole or in part, and any such security may be exchanged or surrendered.

Specific Guaranty

In consideration of One Dollar, receipt whereof is hereby acknowledged, and of the discount or purchase of, or credit, loan, or extension of time given or made on, the following described instruments: _____

_____

by the Blank Bank of New York City (hereinafter called the Bank), _____ hereby unconditionally guarantee to the Bank, its successors and assigns, the genuineness of said instruments, including endorsements thereon, and payment thereof when respectively due, and, in case of extension of payment of any thereof, in whole or in part, payment of all sums due thereunder when due according to such extension or extensions; and hereby consent that, from time to time, without notice to the undersigned, payment of any of said instruments or of any securities therefor may be extended in whole or in part, or any of the securities may be exchanged or surrendered; and hereby waive presentment, demand of payment from the maker, protest and notice of nonpayment or protest, or of sale of securities, or of acceptance hereof or of intention to act or of acting hereupon; and agree to indemnify and save harmless the Bank, its successors and assigns, from all costs and expenses, including counsel and attorneys' fees, of enforcing the obligation of the undersigned hereunder and/or collecting any of said instruments.

If the undersigned be more than one person, whether individual or corporate, their obligations hereunder shall be joint and several.

GUARANTY FUND By amendment to the New York State Banking Law in 1938, the aggregate of the guaranty fund and expense fund of a savings bank in New York State shall constitute the surplus fund. Such fund may be created or increased by contributions made by the incorporators, by transfers from undivided profits, or by transfers from earnings. The surplus fund up to 10% of the amount due depositors shall not be available for the payment of dividends or to pay expenses, except that the part of the fund in excess of 5% of the amount due depositors shall be available without approval of the superintendent of banks for the purpose of absorbing losses.

The incorporators of a savings bank in New York shall not transact business until they shall have deposited to the credit of the savings bank in cash as an initial surplus fund at least $10,000, and, if the superintendent of banks shall so require, shall have entered into an agreement or undertaking with the superintendent to make such further contributions in cash to the surplus fund as in the opinion of the superintendent may be necessary to maintain the savings bank in safe condition, and shall have filed with the superintendent a surety bond securing such agreement or undertaking.

The surplus fund up to 10% of the amount due depositors shall be built up periodically from current earnings. If at the close of any accounting period, the surplus fund of any savings bank in New York State is less than 10% of the amount due depositors, one-tenth of the net earnings for such period shall be credited to the surplus fund, or so much less than one-tenth as will make the surplus fund equal to 10% of the amount due to depositors.

Decline in Net Worth Ratio of Savings Banks. As of the early 1980s, reflecting the impact of higher interest rates prevailing in the money market upon market values of lower-rate mortgages and bonds in their portfolios, and operating losses caused by shift in deposits from passbook savings accounts to the higher yielding savings instruments offered by savings banks to depositors (such as six-month money market certificates geared to the higher rates paid by the U.S. Treasury on its six-month bills), the ratio of net worth to deposits of many savings banks (and other thrift institutions), including the giant savings banks in New York City, declined below 10%, and in some cases below 5%. The New York State Banking Law provides that except with the permission of the superintendent of banks, no dividends (interest) shall be paid on deposits when the ratio of net worth to deposits is less than 5%. As of 1981, such permission had been granted in every case.

See SAVINGS BANKS.

GUARANTY OF BANK DEPOSITS State guaranty of the payment of deposits to depositors in banks that became insolvent through bad management, embezzlement, or otherwise. These state guaranty systems were the predecessors of the present federal system of DEPOSIT INSURANCE in the United States. While banks of issue in Europe and the United States for many years guarded their note issues so strictly as to practically preclude the possibility of loss, the policy of protecting deposits was a new development in U.S. banking, deriving its original impetus from the panic of 1907.

GUARDIAN A person who has the legal power to control the person and/or estate of a minor. The Board of Governors of the Federal Reserve System has the power to grant by special permit to national banks applying therefor, when not in contravention of state or local law, the right to act as guardian of estates, or in any other fiduciary capacity in which state banks, trust companies, or other corporations that come into competition with national banks are permitted to act under the laws of the state in which the national bank is located.

Guardianships are governed by statute in detail, and are of various types, as follows:

1. Guardianship by nature or by birth. The natural parents are natural guardians of the person of the child as soon as the child is born. In New York, the father and mother are joint guardians of the person only of the child.
2. Guardianship by socage, arising where a minor child acquires real property during minority and no general guardian has been appointed. This guardianship exends only to real property and such personal property as is incidental to real property. The natural parents are joint guardians in socage for the minor in New York, unless they are separated or divorced.
3. Testamentary guardianship, arising where a deceased spouse by will appoints a guardian for the minor child. In New York, a testamentary guardian prevails over the surviving spouse if such is in the best interests of the child, although a child over 14 years of age may generally have the right to decide whether to stay with the natural surviving parent or the testamentary guardian. The testamentary guardian has custody over the person as well as both real and personal property of the ward, and thus is required to post bond, file annual accounts and inventory, and be removed for any misconduct in office.
4. Guardianship by deed, a written instrument executed in the lifetime of the grantor, to take effect on his death, and thus of the same effect as the testamentary guardianship.
5. The general guardianship, which in New York is one created by order of the supreme court or surrogate's court after filing of petition therefor, filing of consents, and holding of hearings. The general guardian may have custody over the person, the property, or both of the minor, and must be a person having no interest adverse to that of the minor. The general guardian is held to the highest degree of fiduciary obligation, being required to invest only in legal investments, to file annual inventory and accountings, to post bond if the property is over $10,000, to obtain court orders for the payment of money, to take an oath of office, to be removed for failure to file full and satisfactory accounts of if guilty of incompetence or misconduct, etc.

Guardianships terminate when the ward becomes of age or dies, or if the guardian's authority has terminated. Guardianship over the person of a female ward terminates upon her marriage. When the ward reaches majority (21 years of age), a general accounting is required to discharge the guardian and the estate is delivered to the ward under order of the court.

Other types of guardianships are the GUARDIAN AD LITEM for actions in law and the special guardian for actions in equity.

GUARDIAN AD LITEM A person appointed by a court to represent the interests of a minor in a lawsuit.

ENCYCLOPEDIA OF BANKING AND FINANCE

H

HALF CROWN An English silver coin with a value of 2.5 shillings, and hence also known as a "two and six." It was first coined in 1551.

On February 15, 1971, the decimal currency became the United Kingdom's official currency. No provision was made in the new system for the half crown piece.

See ENGLISH MONEY TABLE.

HALF DIME A former silver coin of the United States, not coined since 1873. It was the first coin minted by the U.S. Mint and was legal tender in amounts up to $10.

See UNITED STATES MONEY.

HALF-DOLLAR A unit of U.S. "subsidiary coinage."

Under the Coinage Act of 1965 (P.L. 89-81, July 23, 1965), the half-dollar authorized by act of February 12, 1873, composed of 192.9 grains, 0.9 fine (173.61 grains of fine silver and 19.29 grains of copper), was replaced by the new clad half-dollar containing only 40% silver. Its total weight is 11.5 grams (4.6 grams of silver, 6.9 grams of copper), compared with the former coin's total weight of 12.5 grams (11.25 grams silver, 1.25 grams copper). Despite its sharply lower silver content, the new half-dollar became scarce in circulation upon issuance.

In 1970, total elimination of silver from the half dollar was authorized, and the silverless half dollars appeared in 1971. The strip used for the silverless clad coins consists of a copper core, faced or "clad" by layers of the same alloy that is used for nickels—75% copper and 25% nickel.

See UNITED STATES MONEY.

HALF EAGLE A former U.S. gold coin with a value of $5. Its composition was the same as, and its weight one-half of, that of the EAGLE. It is no longer in circulation, in accordance with the nationalization of gold in any form pursuant to Executive Order of April 5, 1933 (authorized by Emergency Banking Act of March 9, 1933), which required all persons to deliver to a Federal Reserve bank, or agent thereof, all GOLD COINS (as well as gold bullion and gold certificates) owned by them, for all forms of lawful money, and the Gold Reserve Act of 1934, which required all Federal Reserve banks in turn to relinquish all forms of gold to the U.S. Treasury for gold certificates, series of 1934, and declared the coinage of gold at an end.

HALFPENNY An English bronze coin. The February 15, 1971, conversion of the English coinage system to the decimal system involved the replacement of the former halfpenny (87.5 grains weight, or 5.6699 grams) by a new, smaller halfpenny (1.782 grams weight) having a higher £s.d. equivalent value (1.2d) than the old half penny (0.5).

See ENGLISH MONEY TABLE.

HALF SOVEREIGN An English gold coin (10 shillings) that is no longer in circulation, having been replaced by the 10 shilling note, which itself was replaced in the February 15, 1971 conversion to the decimal system by the new 50 pence coin, having an equivalent £s.d value of 10 shillings.

See ENGLISH MONEY TABLE.

HALF STOCK An obsolete stock exchange term denoting shares of stock of $50 par value, so-called because most shares were of $100 par value. Quotations for half stocks on the New York Stock Exchange were formerly on the basis of two shares. Thus the shares of the Pennsylvania and Lehigh Valley Railroad companies, each having $50 par value, were quoted at a price for two shares, representing $100 par value.

HAMMERING THE MARKET Denotes the heavy and persistent selling of stocks by professional speculators operating on the "short" side, actuated by the belief that prices are inflated and that a period of liquidation is imminent.

HAMMOND'S TIME Formerly the official time for trading sessions of the NEW YORK STOCK EXCHANGE, by which its opening, closing, and closing of the recognized settlement period were regulated.

HARD CASH Denotes metallic money as distinguished from paper money. It is also more loosely used to denote cash assets (whether actual currency or bank balances) as distinguished from other quick assets, e.g., notes and accounts receivable, inventories, and readily marketable securities.

HARD COALERS *See* ANTHRACITE ROADS.

HARDEN A stock exchange expression indicating a stiffening or strengthening of prices throughout the list due to increased buying, especially following an interval of price declines.

HARD SPOT A stock exchange expression to denote any single stock that stands out prominently in the day's quotations because of its firmness or strength when the rest of the list is soft, i.e., tends to decline.

HARDWARE The mechanical components of a computer system, including central circuitry and peripheral equipment such as modems, printers, and monitors.

HARTER ACT An act approved by Congress on February 13, 1893, which set forth the liabilities of shipowners in the carriage of goods at sea, and indicated the contents of the limiting clauses that an ocean carrier may place in its BILL OF LADING.

HAZARD INSURANCE Insurance related to real estate that includes protection against various hazards including loss from fire, certain natural causes, malicious mischief, and vandalism.

HEALTH AND HUMAN SERVICES, DEPARTMENT OF The new title given by 1979 legislation to the federal cabinet-level Department of Health, Education, and Welfare (HEW), originally created by Reorganization Plan No. 1, effective April 11, 1953, pursuant to the Reorganization Act of 1949.

Besides renaming the Department of Health, Education, and Welfare, the 1979 legislation (Department of Education Organization Act, passed by the Congress on September 27, 1979, based on recommended conference report of Senate and House versions) transferred most of HEW's education programs to the newly created federal cabinet-level Department of Education (*See* EDUCATION, DEPARTMENT OF).

The Department of Health and Human Services includes the following among its components.

ENCYCLOPEDIA OF BANKING AND FINANCE

1. Office of Human Development Services, "administering a broad range of social and rehabilitation services and human development programs designed to deal with the problems of specific populations, including the elderly, children of low-income families, persons with mental or physical handicaps, runaway youth, and Native Americans."
2. Public Health Service, including the Food and Drug Administration, National Institutes of Health, Center for Disease Control, Health Resources Administration, Health Services Administration, and the Alcohol, Drug Abuse, and Mental Health Administration.
3. Social Security Administration.
4. Health Care Financing Administration, including the Medicare and Medicaid Bureaus, Health Standards and Quality Bureau, Office of Program Integrity, and Office of Reimbursement Practices.
5. Family Support Administration provides leadership in the planning, development, management, and coordination of the department's Child Support Enforcement and family programs and activities authorized and directed by Title IV-D of the Social Security Act and other pertinent legislation.

See SOCIAL SECURITY.

HEALTH, EDUCATION, AND WELFARE DEPARTMENT
See EDUCATION, DEPARTMENT OF; HEALTH AND HUMAN SERVICES, DEPARTMENT OF. The name of the Department of Health, Education, and Welfare (HEW) was changed to Department of Health and Human Services by the Department of Education Organization Act, passed on September 27, 1979, which created the new federal cabinet-level Department of Education and transferred most of HEW's education programs to the new department.

HEAVY MARKET
A stock or commodity exchange expression used to denote a drop in prices due especially to selling of long stock (or commodity contracts) by holders who are taking profits. It is a condition that exists in a market when supporting bids are not in sufficient volume or high enough to absorb offerings without price concessions, so that the prevailing price level declines. A heavy market is to be distinguished from a weak market, which is a liquidating market, and also from a sagging market in which price declines on the average are merely fractional.

HECTARE
See METRIC SYSTEM.

HEDGING
Reduced to its simplest terms, a form of insurance used among traders or dealers in grain, cotton, foreign exchange, or securities, to prevent loss through price fluctuations. It is not speculation, but the avoidance of speculation. Hedging is the process of protecting one transaction by means of another, and in the commodity markets takes the form of selling a FUTURES contract in an amount equivalent to necessary cash purchases. The process of hedging is based on the theory that the spread between a cash commodity and its futures is constantly uniform—that is, futures prices should be higher than cash prices by an amount representing the cost of storage, insurance, etc., from the time of the transaction until the arrival of the futures month. Hedging in grain is commonly practiced by elevator companies, millers, and exporters. Foreign exchange bankers, brokers, and dealers also practice hedging—the selling by one who is "long" and the buying by one who is "short" of an equal amount of the item dealt in. Thus a person who hedges is in a neutral position: he is committed to both "long" and "short" contracts for an equal amount.

A typical illustration of hedging is that practiced by a flour mill. Suppose a miller has contracts to deliver to customers 4,000 barrels of flour a week for the next six months at a stipulated price. This output will require approximately 470,000 bushels of wheat, more than even the largest miller can carry in stock. It represents a value, moreover, that if purchased at, say, $4.50 a bushel, means an investment of $2,115,000. Should the wheat decline only $0.01 a bushel, a loss of $47,000 is involved. This risk is so great that millers as a class cannot afford to take it. Millers are not speculators but are in the business of milling and derive their profits from milling operations, not through price fluctuations. To avoid assuming this risk, therefore, the miller sells in the futures market an equal amount of wheat, distributing his futures sales contracts to mature at times when he will need to buy cash wheat to fill his flour contracts. In other words, as fast as he buys cash wheat from samples that meet his milling requirements, he sells an equal amount of futures contracts at a stipulated price. Instead of actually making delivery on the futures contracts, however, millers usually sell their futures contracts to professional speculators or others who may want wheat at the delivery time on the futures. In case the price of wheat goes up, the miller has made a profit on his holdings of cash wheat. This profit, however, is offset by the necessity of having to pay a higher price when he covers his contract on delivery date. What he gains in the cash transaction is lost in the futures transaction. On the other hand, if the price declines, the loss on his holdings of cash wheat is offset by having to pay a lesser price when he covers his contract on the delivery date. Thus, whether the price rises or falls, the hedger gains (or loses) as much on his cash contracts as he loses (or gains) on his futures contracts.

A person who is "long" in stocks may also hedge. The hedging short sale, for example, may be used for this purpose. Suppose one owns 100 share of U.S. Steel purchased at 25. The price has declined to, say, 24, and the outlook indicates a still greater decline. By selling 100 shares short, with the intention of subsequently buying ("covering") at lower price, one hedges. Thus if the stock declines to 20, the hedger covers at a 4-point profit, thus offsetting most of the loss on his original purchase. If the stock should instead rise, to, say, 30, the hedger can cover his short sale by delivering his original purchase without loss of the transaction. Or, similarly, a hedge against a possible market decline, may be accomplished by the purchase of a put, entitling the holder to sell 100 shares of U.S. Steel at 25 to the maker of such put for a specified period of time. Should the decline eventuate as expected, to, say, 20, the put may be exercised within its duration at the put price of 25.

Contrary to popular impression, hedging, therefore, whether in commodities, foreign exchange, or securities, is the very opposite of speculation, as it is undertaken for the purpose of protecting against risk of price change.

Banks use interest rate futures to hedge a portfolio security. If interest rates rise, the price of the security falls. The loss will be offset by delivering the security at the price specified in the futures contract or by purchasing back the future at a lower price prior to the specified delivery date. Fixed-rate liabilities can be hedged by buying futures. A six-month CD can be turned into a three-month CD by buying a three-month CD future. Financial futures hedging strategies can protect against unfavorable interest rate movements by locking in a certain position. This strategy also prevents the bank from benefiting from favorable movements in interest rates. Regulatory approval is not required before a bank enters into futures transactions; approval of the bank's board of directors is usually sufficient. The board would normally be interested in having problems or opportunities identified, financial risks quantified, alternative courses of actions and their consequences identified, and operating, control, and record-keeping procedures for financial futures explained for purposes of review.

See CALL.

BIBLIOGRAPHY

ANDERSEN, T. J. *Currency and Interest-Rate Hedging.* New York Institute of Finance, New York, NY, 1987.
BARKER, B. "Hedging Techniques for Interest Rate and Currency Risks." *Banking and Finance Law Review,* October 1988.
KRAMER, S. L., and others. *Options Hedging Handbook.* Center for Futures Education, Spring Mill, PA, 1985.
MCKINZIE, J. L., and SCHAP, K. *Hedging Financial Instruments.* Probus Publishing Co., Chicago, IL, 1988.
NODDINGS, T. *Superhedging.* Probus Publishing Co., Chicago, IL, 1986.

HEIR
In a strict technical sense, a person, also known as an heir-at-law, who is entitled to the real property, or a proportionate share thereof, left by a deceased person who made no will, i.e., a person who succeeds to an intestate estate. In civil law the term has a broader meaning, and includes any person who is created successor of an estate by the operation of law or by will. In the first case (of intestacy) he is the next of kin and is called the heir-at-law, or heir by intestacy; in the second case, the testamentary heir. No person can be an heir of a living person but may be an heir apparent.

A direct heir is a lineal descendant, or one in the direct line of decedent, e.g., son, daughter, father, mother, grandson, granddaughter. A collateral heir is one not in the direct line of decedent, e.g., brother, sister, uncle, aunt, nephew, niece.

HEIR-AT-LAW See HEIR.

HERFINDAHL INDEX The Herfindahl Index is one measure of industry concentration. It is calculated as the sum of the squares of the market shares of all firms in an industry. For n firms in an industry, the index, H, equals:

$$H = S\ S_i^2$$

where S_i is the market share of the ith firm in the industry. When there is only one seller, $S = 1$, and therefore $H = 1$. When then are n sellers of equal size then $H = 1/n$. In recent years the Department of Justice has made increasing use of Herfindahl indexes to guide decisions related to the possible anticompetitive effects of horizontal mergers.

HH SERIES SAVING BONDS U.S. government bonds. Series HH saving bonds are issued at face amounts in denominations of $500, $1,000, $5,000, and $10,000, and have 10-year maturities. Their yield curve is 7.5% for new issues; if held for less than ten years, bonds that were sold for cash will have an interest penalty applied against redemption value. The bonds can be redeemed any time after six months from issue. No limitations are placed on the amount of bonds purchased. Interest on HH series bonds is subject to federal income tax in year interest is paid; the bonds are exempt from state and local income taxes. The bonds are subject to federal and state estate, inheritance, and gift taxes. The bonds are registered in the name of individuals (in single, coownership of beneficiary form); in names of fiduciaries or organizations (in single ownership). Under coownership, either owner may redeem the bond; both owners must join in a reissue request. In coownership of beneficiary form, only the owner can redeem during lifetime; consent of beneficiary to reissue is not required. The bonds are not eligible for transfer or pledge as collateral. The exchange privilege on these bonds allows an exchange for Series E, EE, and savings notes in multiples of $500; continued tax deferral privilege is provided.

HIDDEN RESERVE A so-called reserve or surplus, created by undervaluing assets or overstating liabilities, which is not apparent from an examination of the financial statements. The use of hidden reserves is an inappropriate accounting procedure.

HIDDEN UNEMPLOYMENT During a recession, for example, some people may become discouraged and quit looking for the few jobs that exist. They represent hidden unemployment because they would like to work but have given up looking for work and therefore are not counted in the unemployment statistics.

HIDE EXCHANGE Trading in hide futures on the COMMODITY EXCHANGE, INC. was discontinued on October 16, 1970, because of inactivity. For the fiscal year 1969, trading volume had declined to 680 contracts, compared with 3,023 contracts for the 1968 fiscal year.

Prices quoted on the exchange for hide futures were in respect to domestic standard packer native cow and/or steer hides (No. 1 selection) with delivery from one of the warehouses licensed by the exchange in the city of Chicago or in the city of East St. Louis, or any other designated delivery point. Futures months were January, April, July, and October, with trading conducted in any one of these months within a 15-month period.

Cash (spot) trading in hides (light native cows) is provided in Chicago. Hides are the beef packers' most important byproduct.

HIGH DOLLAR GROUP SORT A Federal Reserve check collecting program with late deposit deadlines for specific noncity financial institutions designated by the Federal Reserve to be receivers of large check presentments. Such institutions generally offer controlled disbursement services.

HIGH FINANCE This term has three meanings:

1. The unwarranted or speculative use of funds belonging to others. Thus the officers of a company who use the company's money for financing an unsound venture, or for buying speculative securities for the purpose of making speculative profits, are guilty of high finance.
2. Any situation in which the money of other people is used by a person or concern in a speculative manner.
3. The practice of borrowing to the utmost limit on one's assets, i.e., trading on a thin equity.

HIGHER EDUCATION ACT OF 1965 Legislation that established the Student Loan Marketing Association (Sallie Mae). The association (corporation) provides liquidity for various types of student loans in a manner similar to FNMA and the FHLMC in the mortgage markets. Sallie Mae purchases loans and warehousing advances and issues letters of credit to support student loan revenue bond issues (municipals). The association can help finance student loans when there is a shortage of funds available from other sources.

During the 1974 to 1982 period, Sallie Mae used debt securities issued to the Federal Financing Bank primarily to finance its activities. The interest rate was set at .125% above 91-day T-bills. After 1981, Sallie Mae used the capital market through the revenue of nonguaranteed discount notes issued in minimum denominations of $100,000. In 1984, the association turned to short-term floating-rate notes with maturities ranging from three years upward.

The secretary of the treasury is authorized to acquire Sallie Mae obligations up to an aggregate amount of $1 billion. Securities issued by the association are considered lawful investments and can be accepted as security for judiciary trust and public funds under control of the United States, but they are not guaranteed by the United States government. They also can be used as collateral for the Federal Reserve discount window. Banks are permitted to deal in, underwrite, and purchase Sallie Mae securities for their own account. The association's securities are exempt from state and local taxes.

HIGH-GRADE INVESTMENTS Investments of superior merit, i.e., of low financial risk (risk of nonpayment if obligations, and risk of lack of earnings and nonpayment of dividends if equities).

Most obligations of governmental units and such bonds of seasoned corporations as are protected by well-established and adequate earning power, in addition to being secured by underlying mortgages if secured obligations, belong to this class. In general, the securities of the federal government, the states, and political subdivisions therof, as well as the senior bonds of seasoned railroad, public utility, and industrial corporations, will be found assigned the highest investment rating, but variations in such quality will be found among the "municipals."In their respective groups, the strongest preferred and common stocks may be characterized as high-grade.

To furnish a quick and convenient measure of quality, the statistical rating services—Moody's, Standard & Poor's, and Fitch-have developed BOND RATINGS to indicate quality; Standard & Poor's has developed quality ratings for stocks, both preferred and common.
See INVESTMENT RISKS.

HIGHLY-LEVERAGED TRANSACTION A transaction in which credit is extended in connection with LBOs, mergers and acquisitions, or corporate restructuring, and where the credit results in an organization that has a total debt/asset ratio exceeding 75%. FDIC recommends how bank examiners are to assess bank policy on portfolio analysis, distribution and participation in HLTs, internal credit reviews, equity investments, mezzanine financing, and loan-valuation reserves. The guidelines also outline approaches to evaluating concentrations of credit and individual highly-leveraged transaction credits. The guidelines are primarily aimed at bank financing of corporate leveraged buyouts, and are in part a response to political pressure related to the risks banks may assume when financing LBOs. FDIC examiners are encouraged to use the 75% figure as a benchmark and to make industry-specific determinations of the significance of debt/asset ratios.

To assess the bank's full exposure to an HLT borrower, the guidelines suggest that the examiner review all loans, extensions of credit, acquisition-related debt and equity securities, standby letters of credit, legally binding contractual commitments, and other financial guarantees. Under the guidelines, an examiner should analyze relevant bank policies, credit concentration, and individual credits.

ENCYCLOPEDIA OF BANKING AND FINANCE

BIBLIOGRAPHY

Highly-Leveraged Transactions (HLTs). Office of the Director of the Division of Bank Supervision, BL-21-89, May 10, 1989.

HIGH-YIELD BONDS or JUNK BONDS; Low grade, speculative bonds below investment grade, given S&P credit ratings of BB, B, CCC, or CC. High-yield bonds are frequently used in corporate takeovers and leveraged buyouts. These bonds have a long history in the financial market but emerged as an important type of debt in the 1980s. The investment banking firm of Drexel Burnham Lambert was a leading underwriter and marketer of these bonds. Defaults on high-yield bonds have been considerably higher than those on investment-grade bonds. In 1986, the default rate was around 3% (the year of the LTV bankruptcy). In 1985 and 1986, junk bonds issued amounted to $22.1 and $29.8 billion, respectively. Insider trading scandals were associated with the issuance of junk bonds in the 1980s.

HISTORICAL COST PRINCIPLE A major accounting principle that states that assets and liabilities are recorded in the financial statements at the exchange price of a transaction at the time the transaction occurs. The exchange price (the historical cost) is typically retained in the accounting system as the value of an item until the item is consumed, sold, or liquidated and removed from the records. The recognition of gains and losses resulting from value changes of assets or liabilities is generally deferred until another exchange has taken place. Historical, or acquisition, costs are considered to be objective and verifiable. A major limitation of this principle is that historical costs do not reflect current value, which many consider more useful for decision making. GENERALLY ACCEPTED ACCOUNTING PRINCIPLES do allow many exceptions to this principle. Inventories and marketable equity securities may be reported at lower of cost or market; certain long-term investments can be reported under the EQUITY METHOD. If market information indicates a permanent and material decline in value, the economic loss should be recognized immediately.

HOARDING Storing money in a secret place. Ordinarily current funds received by individuals or concerns are deposited in banks or used in trading transactions, thus being kept in circulation. Hoarded money is money that is withdrawn from circulation, for which use it was intended.

Hoarding may result from three causes: during a panic, bank depositors may start a "run" on a bank by withdrawing their cash for fear that they will not be able to do so later; illiterates and immigrants, skeptical of the safety of banks or ignorant of their advantages, sometimes keep actual money savings in a hidden place; when paper money is not maintained on a parity with metallic money, the latter may be hoarded or sold at a premium.

HOKEYS A nickname given to HOME OWNERS' LOAN CORPORATION BONDS.

HOLD A banking procedure used to note that an amount of a customer's balance is retained intact until an item has been collected, a check or debit comes through for posting, or there are no existing liens or holds on or against deposits and accounts.

HOLDBACKS Retainages on certain real estate construction loans. Statutes in a number of states require a financial institution to retain or hold back a portion of the draw request. Many lenders hold back 5% to 10% of each advance to the borrower. The purpose of the holdback is to ensure that contractors complete the job as required under the contract.

HOLDER The bearer in possession of an instrument; the payee or endorsee of a bill exchange, check, or note; the person who holds the equitable title to an instrument.
See HOLDER IN DUE COURSE.

HOLDER IN DUE COURSE According to Section 3-302 of the Uniform Commercial Code (UCC), a holder who takes the instrument for value, in good faith, and without notice that it is overdue or has been dishonored or of any defense against it or claim to it on the part of any person. The UCC further provides that a payee may be a holder in due course if in fact he meets the requirements for such status.

The advantages of being a holder in due course (Sec. 3-305 of the UCC) are that, to the extent a holder is a holder in due course, he takes the instrument free from: (1) all claims to it on the part of any person; (2) all defenses of any party to the instrument with whom the holder has not dealt, except infancy (to the extent that it is a defense to a simple contract); such other incapacity, duress, or illegality of the transaction as renders the obligation of the party a nullity; such misrepresentation as has induced the party to sign the instrument with neither knowledge nor reasonable opportunity to obtain knowledge of its character or essential terms; discharge in insolvency proceedings; and any other discharge of which the holder has notice when he takes the instrument. These defenses that are exceptions are called "real defenses" as contrasted to "personal defenses" (e.g., failure of consideration, fraud in the inducement, and breach of warranty).

Holder in Due Course Doctrine in Consumer Credit. Effective May 14, 1976, the FEDERAL TRADE COMMISSION added a new Section 433 to its Trade Regulation Rules, which has become known as the FTC's Holder in Due Course Rule I. In essence the rule provided that it is an unfair or deceptive act or practice, pursuant to Section 5 of the Federal Trade Commission Act, for a seller involved directly or indirectly in the sale or lease of goods or services to consumers to: (1) take or receive a consumer credit contract, or (2) accept in full or partial payment for such sale or lease the proceeds of any purchase money loan made in connection with any consumer credit contract, if the consumer credit contract in either case failed to contain the following notice printed in at least 10-point boldface type:

NOTICE

ANY HOLDER OF THIS CONSUMER CREDIT CONTRACT IS SUBJECT TO ALL CLAIMS AND DEFENSES WHICH THE DEBTOR COULD ASSERT AGAINST THE SELLER OF GOODS OR SERVICES OBTAINED PURSUANT HERETO OR WITH THE PROCEEDS HEREOF. RECOVERY HEREUNDER BY THE DEBTOR SHALL NOT EXCEED AMOUNTS PAID BY THE DEBTOR HERE UNDER.

Although the FTC's Holder in Due Course Rule I did not specifically purport to abolish the doctrine of holder in due course in connection with negotiable instruments (Sec. 3-305, Uniform Commercial Code), it did in connection with consumer credit transactions place subsequent acquirers of the promissory instrument involved on notice as above, and thus in the position of mere assignees subject as such to "all claims and defenses" which the buyer on consumer credit could assert against the vendor of the goods and services.
See UNIFORM COMMERICAL CODE.

HOLDING COMPANY A parent corporation that owns all or the majority of the stock of its constituent subsidiaries, or a corporation whose lesser holding of stock in other corporations is based on control and/or investment motives. The power to hold stock in other corporations is not an inherent power of a corporation and must be specifically authorized either by special legislation or, as is the case today, by general authorization in the general corporation law of a state (New Jersey led the way in 1888, and most states have followed suit), plus express inclusion of such power in the drafting of the certificate of incorporation of the corporation. A holding company may be a "pure holding company," i.e., one confining its functions to holding interests in other corporations, or a "mixed" holding company, such as a parent company engaging in operations of its own but in addition having holdings in other corporations including subsidiaries. Holdings may be assembled by the exchange of the holding company's own securities for the securities of other corporations, or through the purchase of such holdings in subsidiary companies or other corporations from the proceeds of sale of its own securities.

The advantages of the holding company may be classified as financial and managerial. Financially it is a favorite device, with the use of the "trading on the equity" principle, for concentrating control of large properties with a minimum of investment required. In addition to have recourse to senior nonvoting capital for subsidiaries' requirements (bonds, debentures, preferred stock), leaving the common stock for the parent holding company, the latter itself may usually resort to additional leverage by financing its holdings by senior capital (collateral trust bonds, preferred stock) in addition to the common stock. By consolidating the financing for the system as a whole, the holding company may achieve efficiencies in financing costs and terms.

Managerially, the system of a parent holding company and individual subsidiaries makes it possible to decentralize operations with full responsibility and accountability, each subsidiary's management being accountable for implementation of policies and for success of operations on a profit and loss basis. The advatages of goodwill value of subsidiaries' titles and trade names are preserved. Liability is limited as to investment by the parent company in each subsidiary. "Pruning" of holdings in any subsidiaries may readily be made without necessity for managerial reorganization, as in the case of divisions. Specialized staff services for the system as a whole may be maintained by the holding company for the benefit of any of the subsidiaries, such as engineering, merchandising, legal, and financial/accounting staff services.

Public Utility Holding Companies. Because of the large amounts of capital necessary for investment in the industry, holding companies are found particularly in the public utility industry. Prior to passage of the PUBLIC UTILITY HOLDING COMPANY ACT OF 1935, there were two general types of public utility holding companies: those companies whose subsidiaries operated in different parts of the country, furnishing either electric, electric railway, gas, or water service, and "finance companies," which were organized to acquire and to finance subsidiaries. It was not unusual to pyramid the use of the holding company, so that such intermediate layers of holding companies would be subsidiaries themselves of parent holding companies until, finally, the super-holding company was at the top of the pyramid.

Under the Public Utility Holding Company Act of 1935, interstate public utility holding companies (defines as any company owning 10% or more interest in utility companies) were required to register with the Securities and Exchange Commission and be subject to regulation of the commission under that act. Among the requirements of the act carried out by the SEC were integration of properties, simplification of corporate and capital structures, and elimination of holding companies beyond the "second degree" (maximum of two layers of holding companies in addition to the operating companies). The upheaval in the public utility industry caused thereby may be judged by the following. During the 19-year period from December 1, 1935, to June 30, 1954, registered holding companies divested themselves of 829 subsidiaries with aggregate assets of over $11,768 million. The 829 divested companies included 259 public utility companies with assets of $9,201 million, 158 gas utility companies with assets of $874 million, and 412 nonutility companies with assets of over $1,693 million.

Railroad Holding Companies. The INTERSTATE COMMERCE COMMISSION (ICC) was empowered by the Emergency Transportation Act of 1933 (Sec. 202) to exercise jurisdiction over the acquisition by any person of control of railroads. This statutory power, however, applied only after June 16, 1933, so that it did not apply to acquisitions by such railroad holding companies as the Alleghany Corp., formed in the 1920s after the Transportation Act of 1920 had narrowly given the ICC jurisdiction over stock purchases by one railroad into another. During the decade of the 1960s, the ICC again found itself without clear statutory authority over the activities of railroad "conglomerate" holding companies which, in addition to holdings in particular controlled railroads, also acquired mixed industrial and real estate holdings in attempts by railroad managements to diversify into nonrailroad lines of actiity. This issue came to be highlighted by the failure in 1970 of the Penn Central Transportation Co., railroad sub-sidiary of the Penn Central Co., top holding company in the structure consisting of the railroad and nonrailroad holdings (the latter especially in real estate lines), the failure's proximate cause being drained liquidity and inability to meet short-term maturities. Pursuant to provision of the Railroad Revitalization and Regulatory Reform Act of 1976, the Interstate Commerce Commission has been investigating the business interrelationships and transactions of 15 of the nation's major railroads and their holding companies; one purpose of the investigation is to determine "what effects, if any, such diverse structures have had on effective transportation, intermodal competition, revenue levels, and on such other aspects of national rail transportation as may be found relevant."

Banks and Savings and Loan Associations. Holding companies in the commercial banking field were first regulated by the BANKING ACT OF 1933, and later by THE BANK HOLDING COMPANY ACT of 1956, which broadened the regulation but exempted therefrom holding companies owning no more than one bank. In the late 1960s this proved to be a loophole, as many of the larger banks stampeded to form one-bank holding companies, engaging as well in related and nonbank-related lines in a "conglomerate" manner. This loophole was closed by the Bank Holding Company Act Amendments of 1970 (P.L. 91-607, approved December 31, 1970), which expanded coverage to include such one-bank holding companies under regulation of the Board of Governors of the Federal Reserve System. Among other things, the Financial Institutions Regulatory and Interest Rate Control Act of 1978 (P.L. 95-630, signed November 10, 1978) authorized the Board of Governors of the Federal Reserve System to require a holding company to divest itself of a nonbank subsidiary or terminate a nonbank activity if there was reasonable cause to believe that continuation of such activity or control constituted a serious risk to the financial safety, soundness, or stability of a subsidiary bank. Table 1 shows the growth in bank holding companies in terms of offices, assets, and deposits. Table 2 ranks the 20 largest domestic bank holding companies.

Previously, under the Antitrust Improvement Act (P.L. 94-435, signed September 30, 1976), which provided among other things for premerger notification of the federal government (Justice Department and Federal Trade Commission) of planned mergers, bank mergers and bank holding company acquisitions were exempt from the prenotification provisions. However, in the case of acquisitions under Section 4 of the Bank Holding Company Act, a duplicate of the complete application filed with the Board of Governors of the Federal Reserve System must also be filed with the Justice Department and the Federal Trade Commission at least 30 days before the transaction is consummated.

The Federal Reserve Reform Act (P.L. 95-188, approved November 16, 1977) amended Sections 3(b) and 11(b) of the Bank Holding Company Act to provide for expedited board approval of bank and bank holding company acquisitions, consolidations, and mergers in emergency situations or when immediate action is necessary in order to prevent the probable failure of the bank or bank holding company involved in the transaction.

Permissible activities for bank holding companies are listed in the accompanying table.

Table 1 / Bank Holding Companies—Offices, Assets, and Deposits: 1970 to 1987
(As of December 31)

Item	1970	1975	1980	1981	1982	1983	1984	1985	1986	1987
Number of companies	121	1,821	2,905	3,500	4,285	5,399	5,702	5,946	6,467	6,503
Banking offices	4,155	22,056	29,924	33,733	37,068	41,349	44,670	47,106	48,935	50,678
Banks	895	3,674	4,954	5,689	6,731	7,835	8,840	9,156	9,404	9,316
Branches	3,260	18,382	24,970	28,044	30,337	33,514	35,830	37,950	39,531	41,362
Assets (bil. dol.)	92.9	661.3	1,134.4	1,296.7	1,531.0	1,734.9	1,891.5	2,151.5	2,344.0	2,371.5
Percent of all commercial banks	16.1	68.5	74.1	77.3	82.6	86.0	89.4	90.2	90.9	91.1
Deposits (bil. dol.)	78.1	527.5	840.6	938.7	1,108.5	1,279.4	1,411.6	1,595.2	1,757.5	1,785.4

Source: Board of Governors of the Federal Reserve System, *Banking and Monetary Statistics, 1941-1970; Annual Statistical Digest;* and unpublished data.

Table 2 / 20 Largest Domestic Bank Holding Companies
(Ranked by Size of Primary Capital 12/31/87)

Rank 1987	Bank Holding Company	Primary Capital ($000) 12/31/87	Primary Capital ($000) 12/31/86	Rank 1986	Ratio: Primary Capital to Total Assets (%) 1987	Ratio: Primary Capital to Total Assets (%) 1986	Total Capital ($000) 12/31/87	Total Capital ($000) 12/31/86	Total Assets ($000) 12/31/87	Total Assets ($000) 12/31/86
1	Citicorp, New York	16,771,000	13,490,000	1	8.24	6.88	24,462,000	21,531,000	203,607,000	196,124,000
2	BankAmerica Corp., San Francisco	8,040,000	7,361,423	2	8.66	7.07	9,328,000	8,606,402	92,833,000	104,189,297
3	The Chase Manhattan Corp., New York	7,648,000	6,661,000	3	7.71	7.03	10,323,000	8,882,000	99,133,396	94,765,815
4	J.P. Morgan & Co., Inc., New York	7,336,000	6,407,000	4	9.73	8.43	8,806,000	7,728,000	75,414,000	76,039,000
5	Manufacturers Hanover Corp., New York	6,138,253	5,396,266	5	8.37	7.25	9,622,256	8,729,589	73,348,117	74,397,389
6	Chemical New York Corp.	6,081,000	4,407,000	6	7.78	7.28	7,084,000	5,192,000	78,189,000	60,564,123
7	Security Pacific Corp., Los Angeles	5,712,000	4,081,000	7	7.84	6.52	7,212,000	5,132,000	72,838,000	62,606,000
8	Bankers Trust NY Corp.	4,983,721	3,713,000	8	8.82	6.58	5,751,552	4,600,000	56,520,593	56,419,945
9	Wells Fargo & Company, San Franciso	4,046,100	3,551,200	9	9.16	7.97	6,369,500	6,094,700	44,183,300	44,577,100
10	First Chicago Corp.	3,848,396	3,311,832	11	8.70	8.46	4,527,124	3,873,948	44,209,268	39,147,996
11	First Interstate Bancorp, Los Angeles	3,726,231	3,435,564	10	7.32	6.20	4,783,275	4,769,781	50,926,582	55,421,736
12	Bank of Boston Corp.	2,782,811	2,335,406	14	8.16	6.86	3,505,920	3,135,381	34,116,638	34,045,409
13	Mellon Bank Corp., Pittsburgh	2,686,000	2,530,840	12	8.80	7.34	3,191,000	3,030,304	30,525,000	34,499,370
14	First Republic Bank Corp., Dallas	2,510,612	1,528,670	24	7.56	7.30	3,240,650	1,970,468	33,210,686	20,944,300
15	Continental Illinois Corp., Chicago	2,502,000	2,493,423	13	7.72	7.60	2,969,000	3,148,423	32,391,000	32,808,986
16	PNC Financial Corp., Pittsburgh	2,380,824	1,665,886	22	7.57	7.50	2,695,557	1,960,268	31,432,569	22,198,930
17	Marine Midland Banks, Inc., Buffalo, NY	2,301,181	1,837,230	17	9.04	7.41	2,850,449	2,383,243	25,453,332	24,789,596
18	First Union Corp., Charlotte, NC	2,249,547	1,912,026	16	8.14	7.13	2,643,314	2,315,094	27,629,481	26,820,240
19	Bank of New England Corp., Boston	2,184,460	1,404,410	29	7.41	6.25	2,408,696	1,649,223	29,474,763	22,472,935
20	Fleet/Norstar Fin'l. Grp., Inc., Prov., R.I.	2,171,802	—	—	8.85	—	2,626,531	—	24,530,611	—

Source: The American Banker.

Savings and loan holding companies holding interests in SAVINGS AND LOAN ASSOCIATIONS of the stock type (all federal charters are of the nonstock or "mutual" type) were brought under closer regulation of the FEDERAL HOME LOAN BANK BOARD (through the FEDERAL SAVINGS AND LOAN INSURANCE CORPORATION) by the Savings & Loan Holding Company Amendments of 1967, effective February 14, 1968. This legislation amended Section 408 of the National Housing Act (known as the Spence Act), which had provided inadequate regulatory powers. The Financial Institutions Regulatory and Interest Rate Control Act of 1978 authorized cease-and-desist orders against savings and loan association holding companies, their subsidiaries, and service corporations; it also expanded criteria for removal of a director or officer.

Insurance Companies. The holding company also has revolutionized the structure of the INSURANCE industries (life, fire, and casualty insurance companies). Varius leading companies have formed their own holding companies to hold control, for defensive purposes, against the noninsurance conglomerates that especially in recent years have moved into the insurance fields, as well as for aggressive conglomerate acquisitions of their own.

The process of forming a bank holding company involves (1) obtaining a corporate charter (if incorporation is proposed), (2) getting the approval of the Federal Reserve Board, (3) allowing for a Justice Department's 30-day period review of the application as it relates to anticompetitive impacts, and (4) complying with SEC filing requirements.

A bank holding comany must be an association, trust, partnership, or corporation. The corporate form is by far the most common method chosen. Minimum capital requirements must be met. Before a bank holding company can acquire control of a bank, it must obtain prior Federal Reserve Board approval. The Federal Bank Holding Company Act defines control as ownership of 25% or more of a bank's voting stock. Application for prior approval is filed on form FRY-1, which prescribes the required information. The application is usually approved or denied within 90 days. A bank holding company typically has up to 90 days from the date of approval to consummate the transaction. Where financial statements are required by the SEC, the statements must be prepared in accordance with generally accepted accounting principles for the latest fiscal year.

See HOLDING COMPANY, RAILROAD INDUSTRY.

HOLDING COSTS Costs or expenses incurred in the process of holding real estate owned for sale, including, but not limited to, (1) real estate taxes and similar assessments, (2) insurance, (3) maintenance and upkeep, and (4) cost of money, representing an allocation of interest expense.

HOLDING GAIN AND LOSSES Gains and losses resulting from holding assets over time as their prices change. Holding gains and losses are either realized or unrealized. A realized holding gain or loss is the difference between the current cost and historical cost values charged against income. An unrealized holding gain or loss is in total the difference between the current cost and historical cost of the book value of the asset on the balance sheet. Current cost net income measures the total income of an enterprise for a period and takes into account both realized and unrealized holding gains and losses. Many accountants and investors consider this concept of net income to be more appropriate than that provided when the HISTORICAL COST PRINCIPLE is used.

HOLDING THE MARKET Supporting the market.
See SUPPORT.

HOLDOVERS In bank clearings and collections, checks and other items that because of errors or irregularities, e.g., missing bank stamp, postdating, etc., cannot be collected on the day of receipt and are held over as cash until the following day, or until the irregularity can be adjusted.

HOLIDAYS *See* BANK HOLIDAYS.

HOLOGRAPHIC WILL A signed and dated will written entirely in the testator's own handwriting. Approximately half of the states accept holographic wills as legal documents.

HOME *See* HOME OWNERSHIP MADE EASIER.

HOME BANKING The use of electronic payment systems, electronic funds transfer systems, videotex, or other computer-related systems by the consumer to access bank accounts, credit lines, or other bank services. Home banking has the potential for substantially reducing the costs associated with paper transactions.

HOME BANKING

Table 3 / Permissible Activities for Bank Holding Companies

Nonbanking activities permitted under Section 4(c)8 of regulation	*Activities permitted by order of governors of the Federal Reserve System*	*Activities denied by the board*
1. Making and servicing loans and extensions of credit[2]; Mortgage banking; Finance companies; Credit cards; Factoring assets	1. Issuance and sale of travelers checks[2,6]	1. Insurance premium funding (combined sales of mutual funds and insurance)
2. Industrial bank, Morris Plan banks, industrial loan company	2. Buring and selling gold and silver bullion and silver coin[2,4]	2. Underwriting life insurance not related to credit extension
3. Trust company functions[2]	3. Issuing money orders and general purpose variable denominated payment instruments[1,2,4]	3. Sale of level-term credit life
4. Investment or financial advising	4. Futures commission merchant to cover gold and silver bullion and coins[1,2]	4. Real estate brokerage (residential)
5. Full-payout leasing of personal or real property[2]	5. Underwriting certain federal, state, and municipal securities[1,2]	5. Land development
6. Investment in community welfare projects[2]	6. Check verification[1,2,4]	6. Real estate syndication
7. Providing bookkeeping or data processing services[2]	7. Financial advice to consumers[1,2]	7. General management consulting
8. Insurance Agency and underwriting	8. Issuance of small denomination debt instruments[1]	8. Property management
9. Underwriting credit life, accident, and health insurance	9. Arranging equity financing of real estate	9. Computer output
10. Providing courier services[2]	10. Acting as future commissions merchant	10. Underwriting mortgage guaranty insurance[3]
11. Management consulting to depository institutions	11. Discount brokerage	11. Operating a savings and loan association[1,5]
12. Sale at retail of money orders with a face value of not more than $1,000, travelers checks, and savings bonds [1,2,7]	12. Operating a distressed savings and loan association	12. Operating a travel agency[1,2]
13. Performing appraisals of real estate	13. Operating an Article XII Investment Company	13. Underwriting property and casualty insurance1
14. Arranging commercial real estate equity financing	14. Executing foreign banking unsolicited purchases and sales of securities	14. Underwriting home loan life mortgage insurance1
15. Securities brokerage	15. Engaging in commercial banking activities abroad through a limited purpose Delaware bank	15. Investment not issue with transactional characteristics
16. Underwriting and dealing in government obligations and money market instruments	16. Performing apraisal of real estate and real estate advisor and real estate brokerage on non-residential properties	16. Real estate advisory services
17. Foreign exchange advisory and transactional services	17. Operating on Pool Reserve Plan for loss reserves of banks for loans to small businesses	17. Acquisition of an insurance agency[9]
18. Acting as futures commission merchant	18. Operating a thrift institution in Rhode Island	
19. Commodity trading advisory services[8]	19. Operating a guarantee savings bank in New Hampshire	
20. Consumer financial consulting[8]	20. Offering informational advice and transactional services for foreign exchange and services	
21. Armored car services	21. Execution and clearance on major commodity exchanges, of futures contracts on options, municipal band indexes, and stock indexes[10]	
22. Tax preparation and planning[8]	22. Issuance of variably denominated payment instruments payable in foreign currencies with unlimited face values[10]	
23. Operating a collection agency and credit bureau[8]	23. Community development advisory and related services[10]	
24. Appraisals of personal property[8]	24. Employee benefits consulting services[10]	
25. Check guaranty services[8] policy	25. Acquisition of a data processing company[10]	
	26. Automated trading system for options on U.S. Government securities[10]	
	27. Purchase of certain assets and assumption of certain liabilities of a savings and loan association	
	28. Asset based credit facilities for commercial borrowers[10]	

[1] Added to list since January 1, 1975
[2] Activities permissible to national banks
[3] Board orders found these activities closely related to banking but denied proposed aquisitions as part of its "go slow" policy
[4] To be decided on a case-by-case basis
[5] Operating a thrift institution has been permitted by order in Rhode Island, Ohio, New Hampshire, and California
[6] Subsequently permitted by regulation
[7] The amount subsequently was ghanged to $10,00
[8] Effective December 15, 1986
[9] Effective April 16, 1987
[10] Added to the list June, 1988

Source: Regulation Y, Federal Reserve Board.

ENCYCLOPEDIA OF BANKING AND FINANCE

To date, legal and regulatory requirements have dealt primarily with terminal deployment, terminal sharing, security/privacy liability, and antitrust actions.

HOME DEBIT A SELF-CHECK; used among bank employees to designate checks deposited for credit or presented for payment at the bank on which they are drawn.

HOME EQUITY LOAN A loan that allows the borrower to use the equity in his or her home as collateral for a line of credit or for revolving credit. The borrower may then obtain cash advances with a credit card or write checks up to some predetermined limit. Home equity loan interest ranges from the prime rate to one or two points above the prime, and generally fluctuates with it. Some fixed-rate lines are available, but the interest charge is usually higher than on adjustable-rate lines taken out at the same time. Home equity loans are made by many types of financial institutions, including commercial banks, savings and loans, credit unions, and others.

The Tax Reform Act of 1986 has increased the popularity of home equity loans because it phases out the deductibility of interest on unsecured loans, but allows taxpayers to deduct interest on debts secured by their homes under certain circumstances, usually tax-deductible on borrowings of up to $100,000. The conditions under which the interest on a home equity loan may be deducted for tax purposes depends on circumstances specific to each individual taxpayer; for example, when the loan was made, how the credit is used, and if the debt is less than the purchase price of the home plus improvements.

For many consumers, home equity loans are a convenient way to borrow and to access funds. Most financial institutions have made application for a home equity loan easy and inexpensive. The terms and repayment schedule of the loan can be tailored easily to meet the specific needs of the borrower, and interest rates on most loans are variable rate.

On the negative side, however, a home equity loan involves considerable risk because a borrower who cannot meet the repayment terms of the loan may lose his or her home. There is also interest rate risk because most home equity loans are variable-rate arrangements under which the rate is tied to some index of the cost of money such as the three-month rate on certificates of deposit or the prime rate. Some financial institutions include a number of one-time charges, such as loan origination fees, appraisal fees, and other expenses in the cost of processing a home equity loan. Finally, for many households, their home equity traditionally has been a principal savings vehicle and a primary store of wealth. Because home equity loans make it easy for consumers to tap this source of wealth, they may tempt some to buy on impulse and overspend their budgets.

In 1989 the Federal Reserve Board adopted an extensive new disclosure rule governing home equity loans as required by the Home Equity Loan Consumer Protection Act of 1988 (P.O. 100-709). The disclosure rule specifies the truth in lending disclosures for depository institutions that must be incorporated in advertising, marketing programs, applications, and loan approval procedures. The rule imposes extensive compliance requirements.

Home equity loans typically take one of two forms. A traditional home equity loan is a closed-end loan extended for a specified period of time and usually requiring repayment of interest and principal in equal monthly installments. The second form of home equity loan is the more recent "home equity line of credit," a revolving account secured by residential equity. Such accounts permit borrowing from time to time at the account holder's discretion up to the amount of the credit line and have more flexible repayment schedules.

Families with home equity credit lines typically have higher incomes and have built up substantially more equity in their homes than homeowners in general or those with a first mortgage only, reflecting a strong correlation between the use of home equity for loan collateral and levels of family income and equity. In 1987, families with credit line accounts had median incomes of $51,000, and holders of traditional home equity loans had median incomes of $43,000. The median income for those with a first mortgage was $38,000. Median amounts of home equity were $83,000 for credit line holders, $43,000 for those with traditional home equity loans, and $35,000 for those with first mortgage only.

As of 1989, consumer use of home equity lines of credit has been moderate. The amounts that consumers owe are typically well below the maximum amounts allowed under their plans. The median credit line available in one survey was $31,250. Of those, nearly 85% had never used their account; the remaining 15% had paid off a previous obligation and currently carried no balance. Consumers have used traditional home equity loans primarily to repay other debts and to finance home improvements.

The Competitive Equality Banking Act of 1987 (CEBA) and the Home Equity Loan Consumer Protection Act of 1988 (HELCPA) added new truth in lending requirements regarding credit linked to home equity. In 1988, the Federal Reserve adopted new capital adequacy guidelines that makes regulatory capital requirements more sensitive to differences in credit risk profiles among banking organizations.

BIBLIOGRAPHY

MOEBS, MICHAEL. *The Home Equity Survival Guide*, Longman Press. Coauthored.

HOME EQUITY LOAN CONSUMER PROTECTION ACT Legislation that establishes broad standards of disclosure in lending contracts designed to provide adequate disclosure to consumers, effective November 6, 1989. The act prevents lenders from changing the terms of their written agreements unilaterally, unless the changes are to the benefit of the consumer. "Bait and switch" advertising is restricted. Advertisements that describe a favorable part of a loan's price must also disclose other key costs and terms. On credit lines opened after November 6, fees on existing lines and methods of interest calculation cannot be changed, nor can credit lines be cancelled at the discretion of the lender. Disclosure relating to the range of variable interest rate, how payments can rise and fall, what fees are owed, whether the minimum monthly payment is enough to repay the loan during the life of the credit line and "balloon" payment at the end of the loan if one exists, are required.

HOME IMPROVEMENT LOANS Consumer loans or real estate loans normally secured by a second mortgage on the related properties and financed either conventionally or by a government-oriented subsidy or guarantee plan. Home improvement loans are typically financed on the annual percentage rate basis and often carry a higher rate of interest than do mortgage loans. Loans up to ten years are not uncommon. Bankers generally maintain that home improvements retain or increase the value of a property, thereby adding additional security to a first mortgage loan as well as maintaining the neighborhood.

HOME LOAN BANK ACT *See* FEDERAL HOME LOAN BANK ACT.

HOME LOAN BANK BOARD *See* FEDERAL HOME LOAN BANK BOARD.

HOME LOAN BANK SYSTEM *See* FEDERAL HOME LOAN BANK SYSTEM.

HOME MORTGAGE DISCLOSURE ACT Legislation requiring depository institutions to disclose the geographic distribution of their mortgage and home improvement loans and to disclose information about their home mortgage activities to the public and to government officials (12 U.S.C. 2801). The purpose of the legislation is to provide depositors and others information that will enable them to determine whether institutions in metropolitan areas are meeting the housing credit needs of their communities.

The HMDA requires all financial institutions to keep records on the total number and dollar volume of residential mortgage and home improvement loans purchased or originated in each calendar year. Data are to include race and income levels of applicants and borrowers, compiled for each metropolitan statistical area (MSA) or primary metropolitan statistical area (PMSA) in which the financial institution has a home or branch office. A financial institution is exempted from HMDA reporting requirements if its total assets are $10 million or less.

In 1989 the Federal Financial Institutions Examination Council (FFIEC) issued a statement on HMDA reemphasizing the institutions' responsibility to provide federal regulators with accurate and timely HMDA data by March 31 each year. This statement reflected a concern about the frequency of reporting errors and late filings. The statement encouraged institutions to develop policies and procedures to ensure full compliance and warned institutions that failure to comply could result in supervisory or enforcement actions, including cease and desist orders.

HOME OWNER'S LOAN ACT
An act approved June 13, 1933 (48 Stat. 128; 12 U.S.C. 1461-68), as amended by the Home Owners' Loan Act of 1934 (April 27, 1934), which provided for the creation of the HOME OWNERS' LOAN CORPORATION, with $200 million of capital to be provided by the RECONSTRUCTION FINANCE CORPORATION (RFC), and authorization to issue up to $2 billion in bonds to exchange for mortgages. Principal 1933 provisions:

1. Stipulated that the maximum aid to be given to a home owner by the corporation through exchange of bonds for mortgages would be the equivalent of 80% of the value of the mortgaged property, not exceeding $14,000; the corporation, in this refinancing, to exchange its bonds up to the permitted maximum for mortgages and the bonds to bear government-guaranteed interest of 4%.
2. Authorized the corporation, after making such an arrangement, to collect from the home owners interest at 5% on the refinanced mortgages, the home owners to amortize the refinanced loans within 15 years.
3. Provided that home owners unable to benefit by this procedure, because of the reluctance of mortgage holders, might borrow up to 40% of the value of their properties for the purpose of reducing to that extent their indebtedness, these loans in no event to exceed 6% annually.
4. Authorized cash loans up to 50% of the value of homes where comparatively small debts were held against such properties.
5. Provided for limited loans to recover homes for original owners who might lost them by foreclosure or forced sale in the two years preceding the act.

The Home Owners' Loan Act of 1934 authorized the issuance of $2 billion of bonds by the Home Owners' Loan Corporation that might be sold or exchanged for mortgages. Other provisions:

1. Provided that the bonds would be guaranteed as to principal as well as interest by the United States.
2. Provided that the secretary of the Treasury might buy and sell these bonds substantially as other government bonds.
3. Stipulated that the corporation should have power to refund home mortgages only in cases where the home owner was involuntarily in default at the time the Home Owner's Loan Act of 1933 took effect, and was now unable to refinance his home mortgage indebtedness.
4. Permitted the corporation to advance cash in an aggregate not exceeding $200 million, not only to make necessary repairs but also for rehabilitation, modernization, rebuilding, and enlargement of homes.
5. Authorized the corporation to grant an extension of principal or interest to a home owner where justified, but eliminated the three-year compulsory moratorium in the 1933 act.
6. Provided for the redemption of homes lost by the owner subsequent to January 1, 1930, instead of limiting such redemption cases to homes lost within two years prior to the refunding by the corporation.
7. Authorized the Home Owners' Loan Corporation to buy bonds and debentures of Federal Home Loan banks and to make advances to such banks, but provided that not exceeding $50 million be invested or advanced in this manner.
8. Amended the Federal Farm Mortgage Corporation Act of 1934 to provide that the bonds of such corporation should not be issued in excess of its assets.

See HOME OWNERS' LOAN CORPORATION BONDS.

HOME OWNERS' LOAN CORPORATION
An emergency agency created by the Home Owners' Loan Act of 1933, approved June 13, 1933, and amendments, under the supervision and direction of the FEDERAL HOME LOAN BANK BOARD. The general purpose of the corporation was to refinance mortgages on homes on a long-term basis at low interest rates for those who were in urgent need of funds for the protection, preservation, or recovery of their homes and who were unable to procure the needed financing through normal channels.

Mortgages on more than one million homes were thus refinanced, involving a total of $3.5 billion in loans to home owners, advances to borrowers, and other disbursements. A total of 198,000 houses were acquired by the corporation following loans and advances.

Beginning in 1936, the corporation was placed in liquidation. As the recovery in real estate conditions broadened, it was able to achieve a high ratio of collection or liquidation of the original investment in loans and advances. The corporation was finally dissolved by order of the secretary of the Home Loan Bank Board, effective February 3, 1954, pursuant to act approved June 30, 1953 (67 Stat. 121; 12 U.S.C. 1463 note).

HOME OWNERS' LOAN CORPORATION BONDS
The HOME OWNERS' LOAN ACT of 1934 authorized the issuance by the HOME OWNERS' LOAN CORPORATION of $2 billion of bonds that could be sold or exchanged for mortgages. These bonds were dates August 1, 1934, bearing interest at the rate of 2.75% per annum, and matured on August 1, 1949, callable at the option of the Home Owners' Loan Corporation on and after August 1, 1939, at par and accrued interest on two months' notice. Principal and interest on these bonds were guaranteed by the U.S. government. The bonds have all been called.

HOME OWNERSHIP MADE EASIER (HOME)
A savings and equity program designed to give first-time buyers affordable housing. The HOME plan was proposed by the Chicago-based National People's Action, a national lower-income consumer-advocacy group, and developed with the Mortgage Insurance Companies of America, a national mortgage underwriters association. The plan requires that homebuyers contribute savings into a participating bank, thrift, or other lending institution that would be matched by the federal government. For example, homebuyers with 101% to 120% of the median income would get $1.50 in federal deposits for each dollar saved in the account. Individuals with over 120% of the area median income could not participate in the plan. The savings funds would accumulate for a minimum of three years to vest. Withdrawals before three years to purchase a home would give percentage of the federal government's contributions into the savings account. Savers would have to use the funds to purchase a home within seven years or lose the federal contribution and receive 5% interest on their own contributions. The same procedure would be applied to savers who withdrew from the program without purchasing a house.

The federal matching funds used in purchasing a house would be converted into a second mortgage or deed of trust. The house purchaser would pay back the government's deposit at an interest rate of either 3% or 9%, depending on level of income. The federal government would disposed of the second mortgages by selling those with 9% rates to investors.

HOMESTEAD EXEMPTION
A sum of money or other as-sets given or made available to the debtor from the proceeds of the sale of one's residence if it is sold by creditors in order to satisfy a debt. The amount of the exemption varies widely from state to state.

In bankruptcies, the homestead exemption refers to property exempt under the bankruptcy code. The exemption includes up to $7,500 equity in real or personal property used by the debtor as a residence, or in a burial plot. The exemption applies to leaseholds, mobile homes, and beneficial interests in land trusts. A husband and wife filing a joint petition and both choosing the federal exemption can save up to $15,000 equity in jointly owned property used as a residence. The maximum amount of unused homestead exemption that can be used to save other property is reduced to $3,750 as a result of a 1984 amendment to the bankruptcy code.

HOMOGENEOUS PRODUCTION FUNCTION
A functional relationship between inputs and output. For the general production function written as:

$$Q = f(K, L)$$

where output (Q) is a function of capital (K) and labor (L), if

$$f(kK, kL) = k^n f(K, L)$$

then the production function is homogeneous of degree n. In economics, linearly homogeneous production function ($n = 1$) are analyzed to a great extent.

A linearly homogeneous production function exhibits constant returns to scale, meaning that if input doubles then output doubles, etc. If n is greater than 1, the production function exhibits increasing returns to scale, meaning that if input doubles then output more than doubles. And, if n is less than 1, the production function exhibits decreasing returns to scale, meaning that if inputs double then output less than doubles.

HONOR To pay a check or demand draft when it is presented to the drawee for payment; to accept a time draft or other time instrument when it is presented at maturity. A bank honors a check when it pays it.

See ACCEPTANCE FOR HONOR, DISHONOR, PAYMENT FOR HONOR.

HORIZONTAL ANALYSIS A procedure used in FINANCIAL STATEMENT ANALYSIS that indicates the absolute or proportionate change over a period of time. Horizontal analysis is useful in evaluating a trend:

	1991	1990	Difference	% Change
Sales	$1,000,000	$850,000	$150,000	17.6

HORIZONTAL MERGER One method of increasing profit is for a firm to expand its share of the market. This can be accomplished by merging with a firm producing a similar product. This is called a horizontal merger. These types of mergers were most common in the early history of our industrial economy. Most mergers over the so-called first wave, 1887 to 1904, were horizontal mergers. Today, such mergers are closely scrutinized because they may impede competition.

HOUSE BILLS Bill of exchange drawn by a bank or other institution on its branch, agency, or subsidiary abroad. House bills are usually single-name bills.

HOUSING ACT See NATIONAL HOUSING ACT.

HOUSING ADMINISTRATION The Federal Housing Administration, established in June, 1934, by the NATIONAL HOUSING ACT, became a constituent operating agency of the HOUSING AND HOME FINANCE AGENCY.

HOUSING AND HOME FINANCE AGENCY Originally established by Reorganization Plan 3 of 1947, effective July 27, 1947, to be responsible for the principal housing programs and functions of the federal government.

Functions, powers, and duties of the Housing and Home Finance Agency (HHFA) were transferred to the Department of Housing and Urban Development by act approved September 9, 1965 (79 Stat. 667; 5 U.S.C. 624 note), and the HHFA lapsed. See HOUSING AND URBAN DEVELOPMENT, DEPARTMENT OF.

HOUSING AND URBAN DEVELOPMENT, DEPARTMENT OF Established by the Department of Housing and Urban Development Act of September 9, 1965, effective November 9, 1965 (42 U.S.C. 3531-3537).

The Department of Housing and Urban Development is the federal agency principally responsible for programs concerned with the nation's housing needs, the development and preservation of the nation's communities, and the provision of equal housing opportunity for every individual. In carrying out its responsibilities, the department administers a wide variety of programs, including Federal Housing Administration mortgage insurance programs that help families become homeowners and facilitate the construction and rehabilitation of rental units; rental assistance programs for lower-income families who otherwise could not afford decent housing; the Government National Mortgage Association mortgage-backed securities program that helps ensure an adequate supply of mortgage credit; programs to combat housing discrimination and to further fair housing; programs that aid community and neighborhood development and preservation; and programs to protect the homebuyer in the marketplace. The department also encourages a strong, private sector housing industry that can produce affordable housing, and to stimulate private sector initiatives, public/private sector partnerships, and public entrepreneurship.

The department assists the president in achieving maximum coordination of the various federal activities that have a major effect upon community preservation and development; encourages the solution of problems of housing and community development through states and localities; encourages the maximum contribution that may be made by vigorous private homebuilding and mortgage lending industries, both primary and secondary, to housing, community development, and the national economy; and provides for full and appropriate consideration, at the national level, of the needs and interests of the nation's communities and of the people who live and work in them.

The secretary administers the department and is responsible for the administration of all programs, functions, and authorities of the department. The secretary advises the president on federal policy, programs, and activities relating to housing and community development and formulates recommendations for basic housing and community development policies for purposes such as the department's legislative program, the state of the union message, and the president's budget.

The Community Development Block Grant Program was established by Title I of the Housing and Community Development Act of 1974 to meet a wide variety of community development needs with its primary objective being to develop viable urban communities by providing decent housing and a suitable living environment and expanding economic opportunities principally for persons of low and moderate income.

Section 108 loan guarantees to communities are available to finance the acquisition of real property and the rehabilitation of publicly owned real property. To secure the loan guarantee, the community is required to pledge any grant approved or any grant that the community becomes eligible for under Title I of the act of 1974. Obligations guaranteed under Section 108 are sold to an underwriting group of investment bankers for resale through periodic public offerings.

Under Title I of the act, a fund is reserved for secretarial discretion in making community development grants to insular areas and indian tribes for special project grants.

Urban Development action grants are authorized by Title I and are designed to encourage new or increased private investment in cities and urban counties that are experiencing severe economic distress. Action grant funds are available to carry out projects in support of a wide variety of economic recovery activities that involve partnerships with the private sector.

Relocation and acquisition can be arranged under policies and requirements of the department to ensure the fair and equitable treatment of owners of property acquired for a federally assisted project and for persons displaced as a result of such acquisitions.

Department environmental activities include the development of standards, policies, and procedures for environmental assessments and impact statements, and compliance with laws and executive orders on archaeology, historic preservation, floodplain, wetlands, aquifers, endangered species, and other resources.

Departmental energy-related responsibilities call for concerted action with state and local governments to address the economic and social hardships associated with increasing energy costs. Activities include building energy retrofit and installation of solar equipment, production of renewable resources, aid for the assessment and design of district heating and cooling systems and resource recovery projects, provision of technical assistance, and the preparation of comprehensive energy-use strategies.

Section 312 rehabilitation loans are low-interest loans for rehabilitation of residential and nonresidential properties made in conjunction with other federal programs that aid neighborhood revitalization, such as the Community Development Block Grant Program and Urban Homesteading. Urban Homesteading involves transfers, without payment, to states, units of local government or their designated public agencies, secretary-owned, unoccupied, unrepaired, one-to-four-family residences for use in a HUD-approved urban homesteading program. An urban homesteading program must provide for the conditional conveyance of property to homesteaders who agree to repair it, maintain it, and live in it as their principal residence for a minimum of five years in exchange for full legal title.

Rental Rehabilitation Grant Program provides formula grant allocations to make the rehabilitation of rental properties feasible. Direct allocations are made to state and local governments with populations over 50,000 and to urban counties that receive at least a minimum allocation amount established by HUD. Program grant funds can be used only to finance the rehabilitation of privately owned, primarily residential rental properties. Grants are generally limited to 50% of the cost of rehabilitation, not to exceed $5,000 per unit adjusted for high-cost areas. Department policies require that 70% to 100% of each grantee's funds must be spent on rehabilitated properties initially occupied by lower-income tenants.

Neighborhood Development Demonstration Program provides for programs to determine the feasibility of supporting eligible neighborhood development activities by providing federal matching funds to eligible neighborhood development organizations.

The department is authorized to provide loans to private, nonprofit borrowers to develop sound housing projects for the elderly or handicapped. Interest-free loans are authorized under Section 106 to cover up to 80% of the preconstruction costs incurred by nonprofit sponsors in planning a federally assisted Section 202 housing project. Section 8 provides housing assistance payments to participating private owners and public housing agencies to provide decent, safe and sanitary, rehabilitated or existing housing for low-income families and elderly persons at affordable rents. Under the housing development grant program, HUD provides grants to cities, urban counties, and states acting on behalf of local governments to support the development of rental housing in areas with severe rental housing shortages. Grantees use the HUD funds to provide capital grants or loans, interest-reduction payments, rental subsidies, or other types of assistance to facilitate the construction or substantial rehabilitation of rental projects by private owners.

HUD-insured and government-held mortgages are managed and serviced for all mortgage insurance programs under the National Housing Act, as amended, including nursing homes and intermediate-care facilities, manufactured homes and manufactured home parks, hospitals and group practice facilities, and land development.

In accordance with Title III of the National Housing Act, the Government National Mortgage Association (GNMA) carries out the following programs: the GNMA mortgage-backed securities program that provides secondary market financing for most FHA and VA home loans; the management and liquidation of the portfolio of mortgages held by GNMA; and the management of three federal asset trusts.

In the 1980s, government-sponsored housing practically dried up. The demand for government-subsidized housing for low-income households increased an average of 43% in 1988. Long waiting lists caused many cities to stop accepting applications for assisted-housing programs. A table showing eligible households that receive assistance and the average wait for government-assisted housing is presented here for selected cities:

	Eligible households that receive assistance	*Average wait (in months)*
Boston	43%	12-72
Chicago	45	36
Detroit	14	2-3
Los Angeles	Not accepting applications	60+
New Orleans	12	4
Philadelphia	10	36
San Francisco	Not accepting applications	36
Average	29	21

Source: The U.S. Conference of Mayors, 1989.

In the 1980s, HUD was overwhelmed with scandals related to its operations and personnel. It was reported that senior HUD officials at the highest level, including the secretary, were warned repeatedly during the Reagan administration that HUD's multibillion-dollar government insurance program would incur overwhelming losses because of inadequate safeguards on underwriting, inadequate management procedures, misrepresentations, and outright fraud in its multifamily housing and rent-subsidy programs. It appeared that HUD officials approved insurance on many apartment projects despite objections from local and regional HUD housing officials. Appraisal values of housing units applying for insurance were often materially overstated. Major abuses in the use of consultants and political and personal favoritism were a direct cause of much of the problem. Losses of over $1 billion that would eventually be absorbed by the U.S. taxpayer were estimated. The situation became so severe in 1989 that Housing Secretary Jack Kemp halted the elderly-housing program that had lost more than $120 million on projects that government analysts reported were either unnecessary or too large.

BIBLIOGRAPHY

DEPARTMENT OF HOUSING AND URBAN DEVELOPMENT. *Annual Report.*
DAWSON, J. C. "The Battle for President Bush's Housing Soul." *Mortgage Banker,* December, 1988.
HOFMANN, J. L. "Productivity and Privatization." *Bureaucrat,* Winter, 1988-89.
HEINLY, D. "Quarterback Jack Takes Over at HUD [J. Kemp]." *Professional Builder,* February, 1989.

HOUSING BONDS   Revenue bonds secured by mortgage repayments on homes and rental buildings issued by state and local housing authorities. A first mortgage on the property or federal subsidies for lower-income families, including FHA insurance, VA guarantees, as well as private insurance, have been used to provide additional protection. Public Housing Authority bonds (PHABS) were formerly used to provide the services currently provided by housing bonds. PHABS are backed by the full faith and credit of the U.S. government and are traded in the secondary market.

HUMAN CAPITAL   Just as a firm invests in productivity-increasing capital equipment, individuals also invest in themselves through increased education, job training, and other similar productivity-enhancing activities. Economists refer to such investments as investments in human capital.

Just as firms calculate an expected rate of return on a capital investment to assist them in their decision making, many economists believe that individuals follow a similar analysis when contemplating investments in themselves. For example, those attending college perceive that there will be a positive return on their investment of funds, time, and foregone income.

BIBLIOGRAPHY

ARAHOOD, D. *Human Resources Policy Manual,* 1988. Bank Administration Institute.
Human Resources Management for Banks. Bank Administration Institute, Rolling Meadows, IL, 1987.
Human Resource Management.
Human Resource Planning.
TRACEY, W. R. *Human Resources Management and Development.* AMACO, New York, NY, 1985.

HUMPHREY-HAWKINS ACT   Reaffirmed and enlarged upon the commitment of the Employment Act of 1946 by declaring that it is a national objective to provide full oportunities for useful employment to all Americans willing and able to work. The Humphrey-Hawkings Act legislated for the first time a national committment to reduce the rate of inflation. The act also recognized the need for better coordination of monetary and fiscal policies, and to that end established new procedures and requirements for the President, the Congress, and the Federal Reserve System.

The new act requires that the President each year set forth in the *Economic Report of the President* numerical goals for employment, unemployment, production, real income, productivity, and prices during the next five years. Short-term goals for these key indicators of the economy's health are to be established for two years, and medium-term goals for the subsequent three years.

The Humphrey-Hawkings Act sets forth specific numerical goals for unemployment and inflation for the five-year period ahead. The act stated that the goal for unemployment in 1983 should be 4% overall and 3% for workers aged 20 and over. For inflation, the act sets a goal of 3% by 1983 and, after that goal is achieved, 0% by 1988.

The Council of Economic Advisors recommends to the President a wide range of policies that might serve to attack the problems of unemployment and inflation. The act does not require the President to pursue any specific policies nor does it authorize spending on any new programs. If the President wishes to adopt policies mentioned in the act, he must seek congressional authorization to fund the new programs.

The act authorizes the President, beginning with the second *Economic Report of the President* published after passage of the act, to recommend goals for unemployment and inflation 1983 that differ from those provided for in the act, if economic circumstances make such changes necessary. The act provided, however, for continued commitment by the Congress and the President to the objective of reducing unemployment to 4% as soon as feasible.

Each year, the President is required by the new act to present budget recommendations for the two years immediately ahead that are consistent with the short-term goals set forth in his economic report. He is also required to present projections for the budget in the subsequent three years that are consistent with the medium-term goals set out in the *Economic Report of the President*. Similarly, the act calls upon the Congress, in its consideration of the budget, to take into account the economic goals recommended by the President. Every year, when debate on the First Concurrent Budget Resolution is begun in each House of Congress, up to four hours of debate is to be reserved for discussion of the economic situation and its implications for budgetary policy.

The act requires the Federal Reserve board to review the President's budget and economic report and to report to the Congress regarding the President's recommendations and the manner in which monetary policies are related to his goals. The Congress, in its yearly deliberations on the budget, is to take into account not only the President's program but the views and policies of the Federal Reserve board as well. Through this process, the act aims to promote a better coordination of the nation's economic policies.

Congress has been required to modify and adjust various requirements of the act from time to time.

HUNG UP Describes the condition of an investor or speculator who has purchased securities that are now selling below the original purchase prices and that, therefore, cannot be disposed of without loss; to be loaded up with undesirable securities that are tying up one's capital and preventing one from making other commitments at favorable opportunities.

HYDROELECTRIC COMPANY BONDS Bonds of companies producing and selling electrical energy generated by means of hydroelectric plants for power, light and heat. Because of the unpredictability of rainfall and water level, standby steam plants are essential for hydroelectric companies, thus diluting the advantage of low cost of normal hydroelectric plant operation.
See PUBLIC UTILITY BONDS.

HYPERINFLATION Hyperinflation refers to a period of time when the inflation rate is excessive, on the order of 50% or more per month. During such periods the monetary system of the economy usually fails and exchanges become based on barter. Notable was the hyperinflation in several European countries after World War I and the hyperinflation in Argentina during the 1970s. Many economists believe that these periods are caused by consumer and producer expectations that the government will not adopt fiscal or monetary policies to curb the trend in prices, and as a result, price increases snowball.

BIBLIOGRAPHY

SARGENT, T. J., *Rational Expectations and Inflation*, 1986.

HYPOTHECARY VALUE Loan value; COLLATERAL value; the value of securities or other collateral, e.g. notes, acceptances, etc., when placed on deposit with the lender as a pledge for the payment of a loan. Good bonds may have a hypothecary value equal to from 75 to 90% of their market value on "nonpurpose" loans.
See HYPOTHECATION, MARGIN.

HYPOTHECATION The deposit of securities or other COLLATERAL, e.g., notes, acceptances, bills of lading, warehouse receipts, etc., as a pledge for the payment of a loan. Securities must be in negotiable form before they are acceptable as collateral.

HYPOTHECATION CERTIFICATE A certificate attached to a bill of exchange drawn against a shipment of goods, which describes the nature of the shipment and authorizes the banker buying the bill to dispose of the goods in case payment or acceptance of the bill is refused. The hypothecation certificate, also known as a letter of hypothecation, is given by the seller of the bill together with the bill of lading, insurance certificate, and other documents, as further security to the buying bank.

Habitual drawers of bills of exchange sometimes execute a general hypothecation power which is applicable to all the bills which they may sell to their bankers. This is held by the purchasing bank.
See ACCEPTANCE CREDIT, BANK ACCEPTANCE, LETTER OF CREDIT.

I

IBANCO Name changed in 1977 to VISA International Service Association.

ICONs Indexed currency option notes. *See* FINANCIAL INSTRUMENTS: RECENT INNOVATIONS.

IDENTIFICATION A bank is liable to a customer for paying a check to an unauthorized payee; therefore, a bank must use great care in paying out its funds. When an account is opened the identity of the principals should be established immediately and their signatures placed on file.

Checks or other instruments should not be cashed for persons who are unknown. If a check is presented by a stranger, it should not be cashed until the endorsement or guarantee of one of the bank's customers can be secured. This is the best identification. In the case of small items or checks drawn under letters of credit, personal letters, passports, or an identification book may be accepted as identification media.

Very often a concern's payroll clerk, or persons other than the principal of the account, present payroll checks, and authority may be given by the principals for this purpose. The identity of the person receiving the funds should always be established, however, by requiring him to endorse the check. Paying tellers are not usually permitted to cash checks drawn on other banks without approval from an officer.

See FINGERPRINT IDENTIFICATION, SIGNATURE DEPARTMENT, SIGNATURES.

IDLE MONEY Loose funds not being employed; money awaiting investment; free capital.

This term is also often applied to EXCESS RESERVES of the banking system.

IF ISSUED *See* WHEN ISSUED.

ILLIQUID Not readily convertible into cash; the opposite of liquid. Illiquid assets are those that can be realized upon only with difficulty, or at a sacrifice in value. Fixed assets are illiquid assets.

IMMEDIATE CREDIT ACCOUNT In the late 1920s, when banks competed actively for deposits and interest was payable on demand deposits, banks sometimes agreed to credit for interest purposes all local items deposited by a customer immediately upon receipt, and out-of-town items immediately upon collection. These accounts were called immediate credit accounts. Payment of the extra interest amounted to a premium for the accounts.

The motive for this competitive practice of paying extra interest was eliminated by the Banking Act of 1933, which prohibited payment of interest on demand deposits.

IMPAIRED CAPITAL Under the Revised Statutes (Sec. 5205; 12 U.S.C. 55), every national bank that fails to pay up its capital stock, and every national bank whose capital stock becomes impaired by losses or otherwise, is required to pay the deficiency in the capital stock within three months after receiving notice from the Comptroller of the Currency, by assessment upon the stockholders pro rata for the amount of capital stock held by each.

If any such national bank fails to pay up its capital stock and refuses to go into liquidation for three months after receiving the notice from the Comptroller, a receiver may be appointed to close up the business of the national bank.

State member banks are subject to compliance with the same requirements imposed on national banks.

IMPAIRED CREDIT Weakened or diminished credit, especially as expressed in the reduction or total withdrawal of CREDIT usually extended to a concern by its banking connections. Impaired credit may be the result of a breakdown in any one of the essential elements of a credit risk^moral risk, business risk, or property risk.
See LINE OF CREDIT.

IMPERIAL BANK OF INDIA Formerly the outstanding commercial bank of India, founded in 1921 under the Imperial Bank Act of 1920 as the amalgamation of the three presidency banks—the Bank of Bengal, founded in 1806; the Bank of Bombay, founded in 1840; and the Bank of Madras, founded in 1843. In addition to its commercial banking activities, the Imperial Bank was invested with a quasi-public character, performing many fiscal functions for the government, acting as a bankers' bank, operating a large system of branches throughout the country, and stimulating banking development in India. It was originally intended that the Imperial Bank would eventually become the central bank for India, but in 1926 the Hilton Young Currency Commission recommended the creation of a separate bank, the RESERVE BANK OF INDIA, to perform central banking functions, thus leaving the Imperial Bank free to continue its commercial banking activities. The Reserve Bank of India was incorporated under the Reserve Bank of India Act in 1934 and commenced operations on April 1, 1935.

Effective July 1, 1955, the Imperial Bank of India was nationalized by act of the Indian Parliament and its functions were transferred to a new STATE BANK OF INDIA (not to be confused with the central bank of India, the Reserve Bank of India). All shares of the Imperial Bank were transferred to the Reserve Bank of India for payment of the average market value over the 12 months prior to December 20, 1954.

IMPERIAL BANKS *See* JOINT-STOCK BANKS.

IMPLICIT COST *See* IMPUTED AND IMPLICIT COSTS.

IMPORT CREDIT *See* LETTER OF CREDIT.

IMPORT DUTY *See* CUSTOMS DUTY, TARIFF.

IMPORT QUOTA One of the quantitative types of restrictions upon foreign trade which sprang up as a result of balance-of-payments difficulties among trading nations in the early 1930s. To conserve scarce resources in foreign exchange and to keep imports down to the level of exports, nations resorted to direct or indirect restrictions upon imports. Quotas were one of the direct types of restrictions.
See EXCHANGE RESTRICTIONS.

IMPORT LETTER OF CREDIT *See* LETTER OF CREDIT.

IMPORTS U.S. imports are foreign goods and services purchased by consumers, firms, and governments in the United States. As the data in the table below indicate, the U.S. has been importing more goods and services in recent years than it has been exporting; thus, the U.S. has been experiencing a trade deficit (the value of imports is greater than the value of exports).

The United States imports many products for which it does not have a comparative advantage, such as crude petroleum, compact automobiles, tropical fruits, shoes, and many other labor-intensive products.

Imports and EXPORTS for selected years are appended.

Year	Imports ($billion)	Net exports (billions)
1950	$ 12.3	$ 2.2
1960	24.0	5.9
1970	60.5	8.5
1980	318.9	32.1
1981	348.9	33.9
1982	335.6	26.3
1983	358.7	-6.1
1984	442.4	-58.9
1985	449.2	-79.2
1986	481.7	-105.5
1987	546.7	-119.9

Source: *Economic Report of the President*, 1988.

IMPORT SPECIE POINT See GOLD POINTS.

IMPOUND ACCOUNT An escrow account established to provide funds to maintain payment of taxes and insurance, often on a residential mortgage that exceeds 80% of the property value.

IMPROVEMENT BONDS A subclassification of municipal bonds consisting of bonds issued by a municipality or district for the erection of public works or other improvements, usually with more specific titles, e.g., public improvement bonds, or street improvement bonds. They are sometimes SPECIAL ASSESSMENT BONDS. Improvement bonds are municipal debentures and are not to be confused with IMPROVEMENT MORTGAGE BONDS.

IMPROVEMENT MORTGAGE BONDS Bonds secured by a junior mortgage (usually on a railroad or public utility property) to provide for improvements or additions. These bonds are practically equivalent to general mortgage bonds and refunding bonds and, like general mortgage bonds, are customarily authorized and issued in sufficient quantity not only to provide for future betterments, but also to retire the underlying mortgage bonds as they mature. When first issued they represent a second or perhaps third lien, but upon the retirement of the prior or underlying issues they may eventually become a first lien.

They are to be distinguished from extension bonds, which are secured by additional real property or right-of-way, and from IMPROVEMENT BONDS, which are municipal or quasi-municipal issues.

See EXTENSION BOND.

IMPUTED AND IMPLICIT COSTS Expenditures that are attributable to the use of one's own factor of production, such as the use of one's own capital, are imputed costs. In accounting, imputed costs are often ignored when recording transactions.

Interest imputation is the process that estimates the interest rate to be used in finding the cash price of an asset. An imputed interest rate is similar to an implicit interest rate in that it equates the present value of payments on a note with the face of the note, but it can also be established by factors not associated with the note transaction or underlying contract. The imputed rate approximates a negotiated rate (a fair market interest rate) between independent borrowers and lenders. The imputed rate takes into consideration the term of the note, the credit standing of the issuer, collateral, and other factors. For example, an investor is considering the purchase of a large tract of undeveloped land. The offering price is $450,000 in the form of a non-interest-bearing note that is to be paid in three yearly installments of $150,000. There is no market for the note or the property. When the investor considered the current prime rate, his credit standing, the collateral, other terms of the note, and rates available for similar borrowings, a 12 % interest rate is imputed.

Implicit interest is interest implied in a contract. It is neither paid nor received. The implicit interest rate equates the present value of payments on a note with the face of the note. The implicit rate is determined by factors directly related to the note transaction. For example, assume that a dealer offers to sell a machine for $100,000 cash or $16,275 per year for ten years. By dividing the cash price by the annual payments (an annuity), a factor of 6.144 is computed ($100,000/$16,275). By referring to a present value of an annuity of 1 in Arrears table, 6.144 appears in the 10 % interest column when ten payments are involved. Therefore, the implicit interest rate in this offer is 10 %.

INACTIVE ACCOUNT A bank account that shows a stationary or declining balance and against which both deposits and withdrawals are infrequent; or a broker's account which shows few transactions, either purchases or sales. Inactive bank accounts, also called dormant accounts, are usually transferred to an inactive accounts ledger. State statutes usually provide for escheat or forfeiture to the state of inactive or dormant accounts after a specified number of years of inactivity.

See ACTIVE ACCOUNT.

INACTIVE MARKET A market in which the volume of sales for the day or other period is small in comparison with average transactions. In an inactive stock market, the number of securities dealt in and number of shares per transaction are small because of lack of public participation. An inactive market is usually one in which trading is largely confined to professionals. See NEW YORK STOCK EXCHANGE for volume of transactions.

See ACTIVE MARKET.

INACTIVE POST The post on the floor of the New York Stock Exchange at which transactions in inactive stocks take place. The unit of trade for inactive stocks is 10 shares instead of 100 shares. Inactive stocks are those in which trading interest is scant, and frequently embrace those, including preferred stocks, whose capitalizations are small. An inactive stock may be transferred to an active if conditions justify, or vice versa.

INACTIVE SECURITIES Stocks or bonds not frequently traded, whether listed on stock exchanges or unlisted. There are degrees of activity and inactivity. Many securities are not traded daily, some not being quoted more than once a month. One of the objectives of stock exchange listing requirements is to require prerequisites of sufficient distribution of stock ownership in order to tend to create turnover and trading activity. In the course of time, changes causing inactivity in originally qualified listed issues would relegate the issues to the INACTIVE POST on the New York Stock Exchange.

From the standpoint of collateral (loan) value, any security that is traded every day may be regarded as active, although varied trading volume reflects degrees of activity. From a broker's standpoint, however, a security may not be considered relatively active unless, say, 50,000 shares per day are traded; an inactive security might be one in which, say, 500 shares or less are traded.

See ACTIVE SECURITIES.

IN AND OUT Used among speculators to denote a transaction quickly turned over. One who buys and sells (or vice versa) a security on the same day, or within a brief period, is in and out of the market.

INCIDENCE OF TAX The point at which the burden of the tax ultimately rests. The burden of a tax is typically shifted forward to the ultimate purchaser. For example, the incidence of the gasoline, cigarette, and liquor taxes is on the consumer. The effect of a tax is its economic consequence. For example, the imposition of a gasoline tax may increase the price of gasoline and decrease its demand. The impact of a tax is the financial burden related to the payment of the tax.

INCOME Income for accounting purposes has been defined in various ways according to authoritative sources:

1. "Income and profit . . . refer to amounts resulting from the deduction from revenues, or from operating revenues, of cost of goods sold, other expenses, and losses . . ." (Committee on Terminology, 1955).
2. "Net income (net loss)—the excess (deficit) of revenue over expenses for an accounting period . . ." (Accounting Principles Board, 1970).

INCOME

3. "Comprehensive income is the change in equity (net assets) of an entity during a period of transactions and other events and circumstances from nonowner sources" (Financial Accounting Standards Board, 1980).

The measuring and reporting of income and its components are among the most significant accounting problems. Income as reported on the income statement can be conceptualized as follows:

Revenues − Expenses + Gains − Losses = Net income

Income determination is based upon the matching of efforts (expenses and losses) and accomplishments (revenues and gains). Two approaches are used to compute net income: the net assets approach and the transaction approach. Under the net assets approach, the net assets (total assets − total liabilities) of an enterprise are compared at the beginning and ending of a period. If there have been no investments or withdrawals of assets by owners during the period, the increase in net assets represents net income. A decrease represents a net loss. The net assets approach to computing net income can be conceptualized as follows:

Net income = Ending net assets − Beginning net assets + Asset withdrawals − Asset investments.

For example, assume that a company's net assets at the beginning of a period were $100,000 and at the ending, $150,000. Owners invested $10,000 and withdrew $5,000 during the period. Net income is computed as follows:

Ending net assets	$150,000
Deduct: Beginning net assets	100,000
Change in net assets during the period	50,000
Add: Asset withdrawals	5,000
	55,000
Deduct: Asset investments	10,000
Net income for the period	$ 45,000

The transaction approach to measuring income measures and reports revenues and expenses relating to the enterprise that result in net income. This information is especially useful for decision making. For example, the accounting records could provide the following information:

Revenues	$150,000
Deduct: Expenses	105,000
Net income	$ 45,000

The term profit is generally used to refer to an enterprise's successful performance during a period. Profit has no technical meaning in accounting and is not displayed in financial statements. The term has no significant relationship to income or comprehensive income. The term gross profit is sometimes used to indicate the excess of sales over cost of goods sold.

In income tax accounting, moneys received by a taxpayer from all sources; gross income. Section 61 of the Internal Revenue Code defines "gross income" as all income, from whatever source derived, including (but not limited to) the following: compensation for services, including fees, commissions, and similar items; gross income derived from business; gains derived from dealings in property; interest; rents, royalties; dividends; alimony and separate maintenance payments; annuities; income from life insurance and endowment contracts; pensions; income from discharge of indebtedness; distributive share of partnership gross income; income in respect of a decedent; and income from an interest in an estate or trust. The code itemizes the types of income excluded from gross income so as to arrive at "taxable income" in conjunction with exemptions. Exclusions and exemptions are not as of right, but are acts of grace on the part of the sovereignty (federal government) and are subject to change or amendment by Congress.

In the narrower investment sense, the term income refers to the periodic (usually expressed annually) accrual or receipt of income from investments (interest, dividends, or rentals) from income-producing assets, e.g., stocks, bonds, mortgages, notes, real estate, etc., as distinguished from income for services, e.g., salaries, commissions, etc. A particular objective of investing policy might be to emphasize capital gains on turnover of such assets because of differential in taxation rate of such gains, as compared with normal income tax rates, which may be higher for the taxpayer on his investment income. Capital gains, however, do not produce profits unless actually realized, whereas investment income is recurrent without necessity of sale.

For tax purposes, the Sixteenth Amendment states that income arise "from whatever source derived." In economics, income is the gain obtained from capital, labor, or both. In accounting, the term income is not used alone but is referred to as gross income, net income, marginal income, income after taxes, taxable income, and others.

Classification of various kinds of income may be made as in the appended table.

Money income is derived from the production of goods and services in that the factors of production are compensated for their productive contribution in dollars. Real income is the total value of the goods and services produced over a period of time, usually a year.

Kinds of Income

		Income
Property:	1. Land, buildings	Rents, imputed income, and/or capital gains
	2. Negotiable instruments (promissory notes, acceptances)	Interest and/or capital gains
	3. Bonds, stocks, and instruments pertaining thereto	Interest and dividends and/or capital gains
	4. Annuity, life insurance and endowment contracts, matured policies	Income and/or principle distributions
	5. Deposit accounts	Interest and/or interest-dividends
	6. Chattels	Rentals, imputed use income, and/or capital gains
	7. Beneficial interests (pensions, shares in estates or trusts, etc.)	Income and/or capital distributions
	8. Loans	Interest or discount, principal repayments
Personal services:	1. Wages 2. Salaries 3. Commissions and fees	Compensation
Business:	1. Proprietorship interest 2. Distributive share of partnership interest	Profits and/or capital distributions

See NATIONAL INCOME for the macroeconomic (aggregative) concept of income.

BIBLIOGRAPHY

BELKAOUI, A. *Accounting Theory.* Harcourt Brace Jovanovich, San Diego, CA, 1985.

Consumer Income. Bureau of the Census, Washington, DC. Irregular.

KAM, V. *Accounting Theory,* John Wiley and Sons, Inc., New York, NY, 1986.

Review of Income and Wealth. International Association for Research In Income and Wealth. New Haven, CT. Quarterly.

WOLK, H. I. and others. *Accounting Theory.* PWS-Kent Publishing Co., Boston, MA, 1989.

INCOME ACCOUNTS Bank transactions that affect income are classified in income and gain or expense and loss accounts. Income accounts are typically classified into three categories:

1. Interest and dividends
   a. Loans
   b. Investment securities
2. Commissions, fees, and service charges
   a. EDP income
   b. International banking income
   c. Safe deposit rentals
   d. Service charges on deposits
   e. Trading account securities income
   f. Trust department income
3. Gains on investment securities

INCOME APPROACH An approach to measuring GNP that focuses on payments to factors of production. The income method adds together the total incomes received by all resource owners. The seven categories of income used in this method of calculating GNP for 1986 are listed below.

Category of income	% of GNP
Employee compensation	59.0%
Rents	0.5
Corporate profits	6.8
Depreciation	10.7
Proprietary income	7.3
Interest	7.5
Indirect business taxes	8.2
	100.0%

Source: Economic Report of the President, 1988.

See EXPENDITURE APPROACH.

INCOME BASIS *See* BASIS, INCOME RETURN, YIELD.

INCOME BONDS Bonds on which the payment of interest is contingent upon earnings. Income bonds usually grow out of railroad reorganizations in which holders of defaulted mortgage bonds are required to accept income bonds. The principal of income bonds may be secured by a mortgage, but one that constitutes only a junior lien, or they may be collateral trust bonds or plain debentures. Interest on income bonds does not constitute a fixed charge and is payable out of earnings only after all fixed charges have been met. Failure to pay interest on income bonds, except when earned, does not entitle the bondholders to the right to sue. Interest is not paid if earnings are insufficient, but if the entire interest requirements for the issue are not earned, usually such portion as is earned may be declared payable. Income bonds are cumulative or noncumulative, interest being dependent on declaration by the board of directors, as in the case of stocks.

Generally, income bonds are not high-grade investments and are the least desirable of all the bonds of a given corporation. They usually rank just above the preferred stock.

See ADJUSTMENT BONDS.

INCOME CAPITAL CERTIFICATE A Federal Home Loan Bank Board certificate that is an agreement to pay back a corporation's loan, plus interest, when and if an institution in financial difficulty improves its position. Payments are installments and are always less than the institution's net income.

INCOME EFFECT The law of demand states that price and quantity demanded are inversely related, all other factors remaining constant. Graphically, the law of demand is illustrated as a downward sloping demand curve. There are two reasons for this inverse relationship between price and quantity demanded. The first reason is known as the substitution effect and the second is known as the income effect.

When the price of a product decreases, it is as if the consumer's purchasing power increases because less total income is needed than before the price decrease to purchase the same quantity of products. Consumers will use this additional income to purchase more of all normal goods and services, including the product whose price decreased. When the price of a product increases, the reverse is true.

INCOME ENGINEERING A coined phrase synonymous with budgeting.
See BUDGET.

INCOME REDISTRIBUTION The government performs five major functions that affect the allocation of resources and the distribution of goods and services. These functions include administering the legal system, regulating market activities, providing public goods and services, redistributing income, and stabilizing the economy.

The redistribution of income through expenditure and tax policy is based upon an equity argument that greater equality of wealth and income is beneficial to society. Income is redistributed by the government either through in-kind transfers or by direct cash payments. Cash payments are provided to individuals through social insurance programs. These payments are based either on the amount of one's contributions to the programs or on one's need. For example, Social Security, which accounts for over 20% of all federal government expenditures, and unemployment compensation payments are related to the recipients' prior contributions to these programs. Other cash payment programs, such as aid to families with dependent children, supplemental security income, and earned income tax credits also use individuals' earned income as the payment criterion.

INCOME RETURN The money accruing or earned upon an investment per year.

The income return upon stock is found by dividing the amount of annual dividends by the purchase price; thus, if U.S. Steel common is purchased at 30 and pays $1.60 in annual dividends, the income return is 5.33%. The income return on bonds may mean two things—the annual return upon purchase price or the yield if held to maturity. The former is ascertained in the same way as the income return from stock, i.e, by dividing the annual amount of interest by the purchase price. For the return if held to maturity, see YIELD.

INCOMES POLICY In general, the supplementation of MONETARY POLICY and FISCAL POLICY with specific controls on prices and wages and with income and employment stimulants in order to provide price stability consistent with higher employment in the economy.

An incomes policy is an antiinflationary policy that does not affect aggregate demand. Changes in aggregate demand are positively related to changes in prices. From a demand management perspective, a decrease in demand is needed to reduce inflation. Temporary price controls can temper inflation by affecting aggregate demand, but this would not be a lasting solution. Graphically, the solution is a policy that increases aggregate supply. Some call this alternative "supply-side economics."

The Economic Stabilization Program of 1971-1974 in the U.S. is notable for its having been the first and so far the only system of mandatory controls imposed upon the economy during peacetime. In the following review, origins and details of the mandatory controls are indicated, together with a recapitulation of price and wage changes during and after the program.

The Economic Stabilization Program was based on a broad grant of authority originally given to the President ("although not requested by him") when Congress passed the Economic Stabilization Act in August of 1970.

"If we are to restore price stability with high employment in our economy, I see no immediate alternative to a cogent incomes policy" (Arthur F. Burns, Chairman of the Board of Governors of the Federal Reserve System, Statement before the Subcommittee on Foreign Economic Policy and the Subcommittee on International Exchange and Payments, Joint Economic Committee, June 30, 1971).

On August 15, 1971, the President of the U.S. announced new economic policies intended to stimulate employment, stabilize prices, and establish new international monetary arrangements. A précis of the economic program was officially provided as follows.

1. A 90-day freeze of all prices and wages. This freeze would be monitored by the Office of Emergency Preparedness under the policy direction of a newly established cabinet-level Cost of

INCOMES POLICY

Living Council chaired by the secretary of the Treasury.
2. A second stage of price-wage stabilization in which transition would be accomplished from the temporary freeze to the restoration of free markets without inflation. (See below for reference to this Phase II of the program.)
3. "Temporary" suspension of full convertibility of dollars into gold for foreign treasuries and central banks, and the start of international consultation and negotiations to achieve reform in international monetary arrangements. In the process, changes in the exchange rate for the dollar and other currencies ("but not the official dollar price of gold") could be anticipated. This would be expected to end excessive speculation and uncertainty about the future value of the dollar and other currencies and strengthen the international trading and financial position of the U.S.
4. Imposition of a temporary surcharge on imports into the U.S., generally at a rate of 10%. This surcharge was imposed under the authority of the Trade Expansion Act of 1962. Its purpose was to strengthen the U.S. balance of trade and payments during a period when more fundamental measures were coming into effect.
5. Recommendation that Congress establish, effective August 15, 1971, a job development credit (an accelerated investment tax credit) at the rate of 10% for one year, to be followed by a permanent credit at the rate of 5%.
6. Recommendation that Congress repeal the excise tax on automobiles, effective August 15, 1971. The tax rate was 7% of the manufacturer's price, so that the average tax per car would be $200. "It will be insisted" that automobile manufacturers pass the reduction on to customers in lower prices.
7. Recommendation that Congress advance to January 1, 1972, the increase in personal income tax exemptions scheduled by then current law to take effect on January 1, 1973. This would be in addition to the exemption increase then currently scheduled to take effect on January 1, 1972. The additional exemption would be $50 per person.
8. Reduction of federal expenditures in the fiscal year 1972 by $4.7 billion. The main items in this total would be a 5% cut in federal employment, a freeze for six months of the federal pay increase scheduled for January 1, 1972, and the deferral for three months of the effective date of general revenue sharing, and of one year for welfare reform. These expenditure reductions, plus the revenue from the temporary import surcharge, would exceed the revenue loss in fiscal year 1972 from the recommended tax reduction.

The effects of the program on the fiscal year 1972 were estimated to be as indicated in Table 1.

Phase II. The postfreeze continuation of the economic stabilization program was announced October 7, 1971. Basic characteristics of this Phase II program were officially announced as follows.

1. The Cost of Living Council would propose an interim goal of a 2% to 3% inflation rate by the end of 1972, about half of the prefreeze rate, which would be "a great step toward price stability but not so rigid as to preclude adjustments needed for equity and efficiency."
2. Major decision-making responsibilities would be exercised through a tripartite Pay Board and a public-members Price Commission, but overall supervision of the program, on behalf of the President, would be maintained by the cabinet-level Cost of Living Council.
(*Note:* The Pay Board would include five representatives of labor, five representatives of management, and five members representing the public. All members would be appointed by the President. A public member would be designated chairman of the Pay Board, and serve on a fulltime basis. The Price Commission would consist of seven public members appointed by the President with the one designated by the President as chairman serving on a fulltime basis.)
3. Reliance would be placed basically on voluntary compliance, but legal remedies would be available where necessary.
4. The program would cover the economy comprehensively, but closest surveillance would be confined to a "limited, critical part" of the economy.
5. Organization and staff would be sufficient to maintain adequate control of the program, and the staff would be drawn

Table 1 / Effect of Economic Stabilization Program, Phase 1, Fiscal Year 1972 (billions)

Revenue Reduction	
Accelerated investment tax credit	$3.0
Accelerated increase of personal exemptions	1.0
Elimination of auto excises	2.3
Total	$6.3
Revenue increase	
Import surcharge	$2.1
Net revenue reduction	$4.2
Expenditure reductions	
Freeze of federal pay increases	$1.3
Deferral of general revenue sharing	1.1
Reduction of federal employment	0.5
Deferrals of some special revenue sharing	0.7
Deferral of welfare reform and others	1.1
Total	$4.7
Excess of expenditure reductions over revenue reductions	$0.5

almost entirely from other agencies.
6. Effective restraint of interest rates, dividends, and windfall profits would be provided "for the sake of equity, but with sufficient flexibility to avoid serious impairment of economic growth."

Legal basis for the postfreeze program was the Economic Stabilization Act of 1970, the legislation upon which Phase I also rested. This act granted authority to the President to issue and enforce regulations over prices, wages, and rents to control inflation. At the time of announcement of Phase II, the then current act would have expired on April 30, 1972; accordingly, the President asked the Congress to extend the act for one year to April 30, 1973, and to include a standby authority to control interest rates and dividends.

Phase III. The Council of Economic Advisers reported that as 1973 began, economic conditions seemed propitious for a substantial modification in the Phase II system of controls. The rate of inflation had been moderate in 1972. The consumer price index (CPI) rose 3.4% during the year. Wage increases had moderated from their very high rates of early 1971, a sign that expectations of future price increases had diminished. Industrial price increases had slowed to a 2.9% annual rate in the last half of 1972. Thus, in the judgment of the council, fiscal and monetary policy supplemented by the controls had approximately achieved their interim goals by the end of 1972. But with excess capacity declining at the end of 1972, there was a clear possibility that continuation of the Phase II controls program would interfere increasingly with production, productivity, and investment decisions and raise administrative costs, especially if the economy continued to expand as expected.

Against this background it was decided to modify the price and wage controls program to make it more consistent with the further reduction in excess capacity foreseen at this time, and also to move toward the administration's goal of eventually ending the controls. The new system of controls, known as Phase III, involved basic changes in the regulations. To reduce the mounting delays and costs involved in submitting requests for price increases, having them reviewed, and seeking detailed interpretations of increasingly complex rules, the basic principles of regulation developed during Phase II were to be self-administered in Phase III. The prenotification requirement was dropped in most sectors of the economy. Reportfiling requirements were maintained only for the largest economic units. The Price Commission (delegated by the Cost of Living Council, to whom the President had delegated his authority under the act) and the Pay Board (delegated by the Cost of Living Council), having the authority to prescribe standards of permissible prices and of employee compensation, respectively, were absorbed into the staff of the Cost of Living Council; that staff, along with the Internal Revenue Service (IRS) enforcement staff, was reduced. The Cost of Living Council retained authority, and subsequently used it, to impose specific, mandatory regulations where restraint seemed lacking. But in most sectors of the economy, the system was not mandatory without further action by the Cost of Living Council, the interagency committee at cabinet level, chaired by the secretary of the Treasury, to whom the President had delegated his authority under the act.

The need for flexibility in administering the standards for price and wage behavior was given as an important reason for the change to a self-administered program. Phase II had in fact provided important instances of flexibility, but the "changed economic conditions suggested that even more was needed." On February 26, 1973, the newly formed Labor-Management Advisory Committee to the Cost of Living Council issued the pronouncement that no single standard or wage settlement could be expected to apply throughout the economy at any one time.

Also modified in Phase III were the profit margin regulations. The basis for calculating the profit margin limitation was changed to increase the number of fiscal years from which a firm could choose the two years it used in calculating its base. To permit firms to benefit from productivity increases if they practiced price restraint, the profit margin limit was waived if a firm's average price increase was no more than 1.5% in a year. A third change was to permit price increases "necessary for efficient allocation of resources or to maintain adequate levels of supply." Price changes were thus allowed in instances where economic growth led to exceptional demand pressures in particular markets and the alternative was shortages.

Phase III lasted from January 11, 1973, to June 13, 1973. By the first few months of Phase III, increases in the consumer price index and wholesale price index showed that inflation was accelerating for some important raw commodities. Retail meat prices rose 5.4% a month in February and March as a result of a 39% increase in livestock prices from November, 1972, to March 1973; shortages of crude oil pushed up retail fuel oil prices 7.4% during the winter; and a rise of 16% in prices of lumber and wood products was reflected in prices of new houses and indirectly influenced the prices of existing houses. As a result of the acceleration of inflation, pressures mounted to tighten controls. Phase III controls were therefore tightened selectively in an attempt to hold down prices of consumer goods derived almost directly from crude commodities, despite recognition that controls on such goods were unlikely to be effective. On March 6, 1973, cost justification was required of major producers of crude oil and petroleum products who sought price increases yielding more than a 1% yearly addition to their revenues; for increases yielding more than 1.5%, prenotification was required. On March 29, 1973, meat prices at all levels of processing and distribution were subjected to ceilings limiting prices to the highest price level that had prevailed in the preceding 30 days for at least 10% of the sales of each meat item. Farm prices of livestock were not controlled directly, but it was expected that beyond some limit livestock price increases would squeeze margins of processors and retailers and thereby constrain what they could pay for livestock.

Moreover, prices of industrial commodities, which had been increasing by about 0.33% per month in 1972, began in the late winter and spring in 1973 to rise by more than 1% per month. This development signaled the building up of cost pressures, particularly for purchasers of industrial materials, which in turn accelerated a rise in finished goods prices. To slow down the passthrough of these cost pressures, prenotification requirements were reinstated on May 2, 1973, for large firms that proposed weighted average price increases 1.5% above price levels either authorized or in effect on January 10, 1973.

Second Freeze (June 13, 1973-August 12, 1973). With few signs that the inflation would slow significantly in the second half of the year, and with Congress and the administration being urged to take stronger actions to contain inflation, it was deemed necessary to establish a more stringent controls system than Phase III, but one flexible enough to respond to economic developments.

Accordingly, on June 13, 1973, the President announced a freeze on prices, to be followed by a new set of Phase IV controls. The freeze was to last no more than 60 days, ending just as soon as new controls could be put in place. Most prices, but not wages, were prevented from rising above their June 1-8, 1973, levels. Dividends and interest rates remained subject to voluntary controls. Rents and raw agricultural products at the first sale were also excluded from the action.

Phase IV (August 12, 1973-April 30, 1974). In general, standards of Phase IV limited price increases in most manufacturing and service industries to the dollar-for-dollar passthrough of allowable cost increases incurred since the last fiscal quarter ending prior to January 11, 1973. Profit margin limitations related to base-year averages remained in effect for the most part. Prenotification of price increases was required of firms with annual sales exceeding $100 million; implementation after 30 days unless the council ruled otherwise. Firms with annual sales of more than $50 million were required to file quarterly reports with the council. The dollar-for-dollar passthrough and limitation of cost reach-back to late 1972 made price regulations in Phase IV more restrictive than those of earlier phases that had permitted maintenance of profit margins. However, Phase IV was designed to be more flexible through a program of regulation "more closely adapted to conditions in each sector," and through progressive decontrol of industries.

For employees, the general standard of an annual 5.5% increase for wages and an additional 0.7% for qualified fringe benefits, adopted in Phase II and put on a self-administered basis in Phase III, remained in effect. But after the beginning of 1973, the operating philosophy of the wage control program had been to achieve a moderation of wage rate increases entailing less disruption of industrial peace or interference with the collective bargaining process than would result from uniform application of a "mechanical standard." Emphasis was therefore placed on restraining settlements that might have had major "ripple effects" on the wage structure through their influence on bargaining situations in related industries, areas, and occupations, rather than on rigid adherence to a "simple standard." The Labor-Management Advisory Committee had recommended this policy to the Cost of Living Council on February 26, 1973, in one of its first pronouncements.

Termination. Price and wage controls were administered by the Cost of Living Council under authority of the Economic Stabilization Act until April 30, 1974, when the act expired. The existence of the Cost of Living Council was extended to June 30, 1974, by Executive Order 11781, to permit orderly termination of the stabilization programs, including monitoring of voluntary commitments made by companies prior to decontrol. After June 30, 1974, the remaining legal activities and records of the stabilization program were transferred to a small staff in the Office of Economic Stabilization, Department of the Treasury. This organization in turn was terminated at the end of 1974.

The administration did not propose that authority for mandatory controls be extended (except in the construction and health sectors), nor was there substantial support in the Congress for extension. At the request of President Ford, legislation was passed in August, 1974, establishing the Council on Wage and Price Stability with authority to conduct several monitoring functions.

The process of decontrol had begun in 1973, when Phase IV of the mandatory controls was put in place, and the process was accelerated toward the end of 1973 and into 1974. Two approaches to decontrol that were considered were sector-by-sector decontrol and decontrol through a gradual easing of Phase IV rules. The sector-by-sector approach was adopted on a flexible basis related both to the particular conditions in each sector and to voluntary company commitments to restrain prices for specified periods after decontrol, or in some cases to expand production capacity. Both wages and prices were usually decontrolled simultaneously in each sector, but many sectors had been exempted from controls prior to Phase IV^less than half the value of items included in the consumer price index and of wages and salaries were subject to Phase IV on September 10, 1973. On the other hand, 69% of the wholesale price index was covered, with farm products the major exemption.

The progressive decontrol program was designed to spread the possible postcontrol bulge of price increases in two ways. Price increases that were likely to be bunched just after that date were instead phased over the preceding several months, and in exchange for earlier decontrol, commitments were obtained from some companies to restrict price increases to specified amounts at the time of decontrol, with no further price increases to be implemented for various periods extending beyond April 30, 1974. The Cost of Living Council thus sought to defer further into the future some of the postcontrol price increases.

Evaluation of the Mandatory Controls Program. Table 2 measures price and wage changes during and after the Economic Stabilization Program.

The Council of Economic Advisers reasons that the final judgment on the effects of the mandatory price and wage controls imposed under authority of the Economic Stabilization Act beginning in August, 1971, and continuing for more than 32 months "will be long debated and may never be resolved," primarily because there is no

INCOMES POLICY

Table 2 / Measures of Price and Wage Change During and After the Economic Stabilization Program
(percent change; seasonally adjusted annual rates)

Price or wage measure	Freeze and Phase II: Aug. 1971 to Jan. 1973	Phase III: Jan. 1973 to June 1973	Second freeze and Phase IV: June 1973 to Apr. 1974	Phase IV: Dec. 1973 to Apr. 1974	1974 Apr. to Aug.	1974 Aug. to Dec.
PRICES						
Consumer price index						
All items	3.4	8.3	10.7	12.2	12.7	11.8
Food	5.9	20.2	16.2	12.8	7.0	17.0
All items less food	2.7	5.0	8.7	11.8	15.3	9.7
Commodities less food	2.2	4.8	9.2	14.9	16.4	8.6
Services[a]	3.5	4.3	8.6	8.8	13.3	11.7
Personal consumption expenditures deflator[b]	2.8	6.7	10.8	13.9	11.8	11.4
Wholesale price index:[c]						
All commodities	5.9	22.2	15.2	21.9	31.8	10.2
Farm products and processed foods and feeds	13.4	48.9	6.3	0.4	24.5	9.5
Industrial commodities[d]	2.9	12.3	19.6	33.9	35.5	9.4
Finished goods, consumer and producer[e]	1.9	7.2	13.4	23.4	25.8	14.6
Crude and intermediate materials[e]	3.6	12.1	23.33	39.1	40.9	7.1
WAGES[f]						
Average hourly earnings, private nonfarm economy:[g]						
Monthly series	6.2	6.3	6.9	6.5	11.9	9.3
Quarterly series[b]	6.4	5.9	7.0	6.3	10.3	9.7
Average hourly compensation:						
Total private economy[b]	5.8	8.9	7.0	7.0	11.2	9.0
Nonfarm[b]	5.9	8.8	7.5	7.9	10.7	9.3

[a] Not seasonally adjusted.
[b] Percent changes based on quarterly data: 1971-III to 1972-IV (col. 1), 1972-IV to 1973-II (col. 2), 1973-II to 1974-I (col. 3), 1973-IV to 1974-I (col. 4), 1974-I to 1974-III (col. 5), 1974-III to 1974-IV (col. 6).
[c] Seasonally adjusted percentage changes in components of the WPI do not necessarily average to the seasonally adjusted percentage change in the total index because adjustment of the components and the total are calculated separately.
[d] Includes a small number of items not shown separately.
[e] Excludes foods but includes a small number of items not in the industrial commodity index.
[f] Average hourly earnings are for production workers or nonsupervisory employees; average hourly compensation is for all employees.
[g] Adjusted for overtime (in manufacturing only) and interindustry shifts.

Source: Economic Report of the President, Appendix A, February, 1975.

way of "accurately simulating the course of events which would have evolved in the absence of controls." The CEA further points out that " . . . regardless of the overall effect of the program, whatever contribution it may have made was probably concentrated in its first 16 months, when the economy was operating well below its potential. As various industrial sectors reached capacity operations in 1973 under the stimulus of a booming domestic and world economy, the controls system began to obstruct normal supplier-purchaser relationships, and in some cases the controls became quite unworkable. The sharply rising costs of basic materials, often reflecting world market influences and dollar devaluation, were largely uncontrolled; and when passed through to consumers, they resulted in accelerating inflation. Thus, the net benefit of the controls system, however evaluated, had become extremely small by the beginning of 1974, and legal termination of controls only ratified the inevitable process of dismantling them in response to public and market pressures."

"In the current economic environment direct controls cannot be of much benefit in curbing inflation. In fact, comprehensive and relatively inflexible controls over wages and prices would probably do more harm than good because they would prolong the distortions in production and distribution that have become a major problem during the past year. I believe, therefore, that it would be unwise to extend the authority under the Economic Stabilization Act for another year. A more selective approach is needed" (Arthur F. Burns, Chairman of the Board of Governors of the Federal Reserve System, Statement before the Subcommittee on Production and Stabilization of the Committee on Banking, Housing and Urban Affairs, U.S. Senate, February 6, 1974).

Post-Mandatory Controls Developments. The Council on Wage and Price Stability was established within the Executive Office of the President by act of August 24, 1974 (88 Stat. 750; 12 U.S.C. 1904 note) to "identify and monitor economic factors contributing to inflation, including the effects on inflation of industrial, wage, and productivity performance and federal policies, programs, and activities."

Act of Congress approved August 9, 1975 (P.L. 94-78) among other things extended the Council on Wage and Price Stability Act from August 15, 1975, to September 30, 1977. It also authorized the council to require periodic reports for the submission of information maintained in the ordinary course of business and, with respect to businesses having annual gross revenues exceeding $5 million, to issue subpoenas for witnesses or documents relating to wages, costs, productivity, prices, sales, profits, imports, and exports, provided that information obtained from a single firm would not be disclosed to the public.

Act of Congress aproved October 6, 1977 (P.L. 95-121) among other things extended the termination date of the Council on Wage and Price Stability from September 30, 1977, to September 30,

1979. It also required the council, in its hearings, to emphasize the purpose of controlling inflation and to focus on the need for full employment.

At the beginning of 1978, the administration called for a slowing of wage and price increases. Each company was asked to hold its 1978 price and wage increases below the average of the prior two years. Although some individuals and groups did make an effort to meet the standard, the program was not generally effective because, according to the Council of Economic Advisers, the deceleration standard was not specific enough to provide a clear guide for wage and price decisions.

The administration therefore incorporated more explicit standards into the anti-inflation program announced in late October, 1978. The voluntary program now included an explicit numerical ceiling for wage and fringe benefit increases as well as a price deceleration standard for individual firms. The potential effectiveness of the program was heightened by expanded monitoring, by relating federal procurement actions to the standards, and by an innovative program of "real wage insurance" designed to encourage compliance. The pay and price standards were published in preliminary form on November 7, 1978, followed by a 30-day period for public comments. On the basis of the comments offered, and after consultation with business and labor groups, some modifications in the detailed specifications were announced on December 13, 1978. The final standards were published in the *Federal Register* on December 28, 1978.

The pay standard limited the increase in hourly wages and private fringe benefit payments to a maximum of 7% for each employee group in a company. Employee groups subject to the pay standard were individual groups covered by major collective bargaining agreements, other nonmanagement personnel, and management personnel. This grouping took account of the different institutional arrangements for setting wage rates and sought to prevent an inequitable distribution of wage moderation. It also permitted considerable flexibility in distributing wage changes among individuals within a group in resonse to economic circumstances, equity, and other factors, so long as the average increase for the employee group met the standard.

In collective bargaining situations, a newly negotiated contract in which wage and fringe benefit increases averaged no more than 7% annually over the life of the contract was consistent with the pay standard, provided that the increase was no greater than 8% in any year of a multiyear agreement. In determination of compliance with the pay standard, provisions for cost-of-living adjustments would be cost out on the assumption of a 6% annual rate of inflation in the consumer price index over the life of the contract. The standard therefore left room for flexibility in allocating the pay increase between the wage and fringe benefits, and between fixed increases and cost-of-living adjustments. Formal collective bargaining agreements signed before the announcement of the anti-inflation program and (for nonunion employee groups) annual pay plans in operation by October 1, 1978, were not subject to the pay standard.

In determination of compliance with the pay standard, employers' contributions that were required to maintain the existing level of health and pension benefits were distinguished from contributions made to improve the level of benefits. Increases above 7% in the cost of maintaining existing health benefits were not counted in judging compliance. Special provisions also applied to pension plans that paid specific benefits at retirement. Changes in employers' costs resulting from changes in funding methods, amortization periods, actuarial assumptions, and plan experience were not included as pay-rate changes, but changes in employers' costs resulting from plan amendments, changes in the benefit structure, or the effect of wage and salary changes on benefit levels were included. Further details on the application of the pay standard to various pay plans can be found in the regulations issued by the Council on Wage and Price Stability on December 28, 1978.

In the interest of equity and improved productivity, some exemptions from the pay standard were allowed. First, workers who earned an hourly wage below $4.00 on October 1, 1978, were exempt from the standard. Second, wage increases in excess of the standard were acceptable if they were offset by explicit changes in work rules and practices that demonstrably improved productivity to a matching or greater degree. Third, wage increases above the standard were justifiable to preserve a historically close tandem relationship with another employee group. Finally, where several explicit and tightly defined criteria showed that pay rate increases above the pay standard were necessary to attract or retain employees in a particular job category because of an acute labor shortage, the amount of the excess could be exempted from the standard.

In the view of the Council of Economic Advisers, the administration's approach to the deceleration of inflation avoided the pitfalls of failure to recognize inherent variability in rates of productivity growth and relative importance of nonlabor costs and, on the other hand, a simple passthrough of costs. The price standard required that individual firms limit their cumulative price increases over the following ye™ar to 0.5% below the firm's average annual rate of price increase during 1976-1977. Some industries had abnormally high or low rates of price increase during that base period. These extremes were taken into account by limiting the price increase for an individual firm to no more than 9.5% and by regarding any increases of 1.5% or less as complying with the standard. If increases in hourly labor costs within a firm decelerated by more than 0.5% relative to the 1976-1977 rate of increase, the deceleration of prices had to be commensurately greater to be in compliance with the standard. Certain categories of goods and services specified in the price standard regulations issued by the Council on Wage and Price Stability were excluded from the calculation of a company's average price change.

A company that was unable to comply with the price deceleration standard because its average price change could not be calculated, or because of uncontrollable price increases in the goods and services it bought, was asked to satisfy a two-part profit limitation. The company's profit margin could not exceed the average profit margin for two of the company's last three fiscal years prior to October 2, 1978. Besides this, however, program-year profit could not exceed base-year profit by more than 6.5% plus any positive percentage growth in physical volume from the base year to the program year.

Finally, a percentage margin standard was available to companies in the wholesale and retail trade and in food manufacturing and processing industries as an alternative to the price standard.

Real Wage Insurance. Under the real wage insurance proposal to Congress by the administration, employee groups that met the 7% pay limitation would receive a tax credit if the consumer price index increased by more than 7% over the year. The rate of the tax credit would be equal to the difference between the actual increase in the consumer price index and 7%, up to a limit of three percentage points (10% inflation). This rate would be applied to each employee's wages up to a maximum of $20,000 per job. Employee groups that were exempt from the pay standard (low-wage workers and those under existing collective bargaining contracts) would qualify for real wage insurance if their average pay rate increase was 7% or less during the program year.

Second Program Year Revisions. Public Law 96-10 (May 10, 1979) extended the life of the council to September 30, 1980. For the second year of the voluntary controls, beginning October 1, 1979, revisions were made in both the price and pay guidelines: (1) a new two-year price limitation, holding price increases during the two years ending September 30, 1980, to the rate of increase during 1976-1977, which would average out to a 6.75% price increase for the program year beginning October 1, 1979; (2) an intermediate price limitation, holding price change for the 18 months and 21 months to 3/4 and 7/8, respectively, of the two-year price limitation; (3) an alternative profit margin limitation now limiting profit margin to the best two of the last three years prior to October 2, 1978, in any event not to exceed 13.5% in addition to any positive percentage growth in physical volume from the base year to the second program year; (4) relaxation of the pay standard to an annual range of 7.5% to 9.5% for the second program year, compared with 7% for the first program year. Exceptions to the price standard would be granted to companies with higher costs because of the higher pay standard, and it was indicated that the administration would consider the price and pay standards to be in line for whatever standards were adopted for the third program year.

As an important example of exceptions, the council in a 1980 ruling permitted a firm with "uncontrollable" cost increases caused by a labor union contract to have a special price limitation, not disclosed because of "proprietary reasons."

Revival of Demands for Mandatory Controls. Early in 1980, as the consumer price index rose at an 18% annual rate in January following a 13% rise for 1979, and as the outlook indicated further inflation in energy, food, housing, and health costs, demands revived for restoration of mandatory price and wage controls, despite the opposition to them by the Carter administration and many analysts. Among proponents of mandatory controls were various members of Congress and the former administrator of the Carter administration's voluntary controls for the years 1977-1979.

Instead, the President invoked under the terms of the Credit Control Act of 1969 a broad program of fiscal, energy, credit, and other measures designed to moderate and reduce inflationary pressures without restoring mandatory price and wage controls as such. Imposed in March, 1980, eased in May, 1980, and phased out by the end of July, 1980, these measures proved to be unexpectedly severe in impact upon consumer borrowing and demand. After about five years of expansion, economic activity in the first half of 1980 turned down substantially, with industrial production down 7.5%, real gross national product down at an annual rate of 9.1% in the second quarter, housing starts down to near-record postwar lows, employment off about 1.25 million, with the unemployment rate up 1.5 percentage points. Although interest rates and the pace of inflation in prices moderated to lower levels in the latter part of the first half of 1980, inflation was still considered to have strong momentum, fueled by a rise in the federal budgetary deficit, and monetary policy continued to be restrictive in basic stance, consistent with a return to price stability. But the Board of Governors of the Federal Reserve System, in its Monetary Policy Report to Congress submitted July 22, 1980, itself indicated the limitations of sole reliance on monetary policy for inflation control. "But it is clear that if inflation is to be restrained without undue disruption of economic activity, we cannot rely solely on monetary policies. For example, fiscal discipline is essential to ensure that excessive pressure is not placed on the financial and real resources of the economy. The structure of our tax system should be examined with an eye to the incentives it provides for productivity-expanding research and capital formation. And the full range of governmental policies should be reviewed to ensure that they do not add needlessly to costs and do not stunt innovation and competition."

BIBLIOGRAPHY

For experiences with and details of wartime controls in the U.S. see:

ADAMS, G. P. *Wartime Price Control*, 1942 (World War I controls).
MANSFIELD, H. C. *A Short History of OPA*, 1949 (World War II controls).
ROSS, A. M. *The Lessons of Price and Wage Controls*, 1953 (Korean War controls).

For experience with and details of peacetime (mandatory and voluntary) controls see:

AMES, E. "The Consumer and Wage-Price Controls." *Journal of Economics and Business*, Fall, 1977.
BLOUGH, R. M. "Minimizing the Effect of Controls." *Monthly Labor Review*, March, 1974.
BOSWORTH, B. "The Inflation Problem During Phase III." *American Economic Review*, May, 1974.
COUNCIL OF ECONOMIC ADVISERS. *Annual Report*.
FORTUNE, P. "An Evaluation of Anti-Inflation Policies in the United States." *New England Economic Review*, January-February, 1974.
GHALI, M. A. "The Effect of Controls on Wages, Prices, and Strike Activity." *Journal of Economics and Business*, Fall, 1977.
GORDON, R. J. "The Response of Wages and Prices to the First Two Years of Controls." *Brookings Reports on Economic Activity*, 1973.
HAMILTON, M. T. "Price Controls in 1973: Strategies and Problems." *American Economic Review*, May, 1974.
LANZILOTTI, R. F. and ROBERTS, B. "The Legacy of Phase II Controls." *American Economic Review*, May, 1974.
LEKACHMAN, R. "Managing Inflation in a Full Employment Society." *Annals of American Academy of Political Science*, March, 1975.
MILLS, D. Q. "Problems in Formulating a General Pay Standard." *Monthly Labor Review*, March, 1974.
MITCHELL, D. J., and WEBER, A. R. "Wages and the Pay Board." *American Economic Review*, May, 1974.
POOLE, W. "Reflections on U.S. Macroeconomic Policy." *Brookings Papers on Economic Activity*, 1974.
ROBINSON, D. "Wage-Price Controls and Incomes Policies." *Monthly Labor Review*, March, 1974.
SCHUETTINGER, R. L. "Four Thousand Years of Wage and Price Controls." *Policy Review*, Summer, 1978.
TREBING, M. E. "The Economic Consequences of Wage-Price Guidelines." Federal Reserve Bank of St. Louis *Review*, December, 1978.

INCOME STATEMENTS Statements of profit and loss for a particular period. Source of items for the income statement is the temporary income summary account, profit and loss, which is set up in connection with the adjusting and closing entries for the period in order to close out the nominal accounts of income and expense.

The form and content of income statements vary according to the nature of the business, public regulation, and managerial requirements for accounting detail. Regulation S-X of the Securities and Exchange Commission, relating generally to the form and content of financial statements of registrants under the Securities Act of 1933, Securities Exchange Act of 1934, and the Investment Company Act of 1940, has been a standardizing factor in accounting practices and detail of profit and loss or income statements.

In the accounting profession, opinions of the Accounting Principles Board, Financial Accounting Standards Board, and Accounting Research Studies of the American Institute of Certified Public Accountants have laid down postulates and generally accepted accounting principles to be followed in the preparation of income statements.

An income statement presents the results of operations for a reporting period. The income statement provides information concerning return on investment, risk, financial flexibility, and operating capabilities. Return on investment is a measure of a firm's overall performance. Risk is the uncertainty associated with the future of the enterprise. Financial flexibility is the firm's ability to adapt to problems and opportunities. Operating capability relates to the firm's ability to maintain a given level of operations.

The current official view expressed by the Accounting Principles Board and adopted by the Financial Accounting Standards Board is that income "should reflect all items of profit and loss recognized during the period," except for a few items that would go directly to retained earnings, notably prior period adjustments. The following summary illustrates the income statement currently considered to represent generally accepted accounting principles:

Revenues	$ XXX
Deduct: Expenses	XXX
Gains and losses that are not extraordinary	XXX
Income from continuing operations	XXX
Discontinued operations	XXX
Extraordinary gains and losses	XXX
Cumulative effect of change in accounting principle	XXX
Net income	$ XXX

Generally accepted accounting principles require disclosing earnings per share amounts on the income statement of all public reporting entities. Earnings per share data provide a measure of the enterprise's management and past performance and enable users of financial statements to evaluate future prospects of the enterprise and assess dividend distributions to shareholders. Disclosure of earnings per share effects of discontinued operations and extraordinary items is optional but is required for income from continuing operations, income before extraordinary items, the cumulative effect of a change in accounting principle, and net income.

BIBLIOGRAPHY

AMERICAN INSTITUTE OF CERTIFIED PUBLIC ACCOUNTANTS. *Accounting Research Bulletins*.
FINANCIAL ACCOUNTING STANDARDS BOARD. *Financial Accounting Standards*.

INCOME TAX ALLOCATION The process of accruing income taxes during the period the related income occurs. The objectives of financial accounting and the Internal Revenue Code are different. The objective of generally accepted accounting principles for financial reporting is to provide useful information to decision makers about a business. The objective of the Internal Revenue Code is to obtain revenue in an equitable manner to operate the federal government. As a result, differences can arise between taxable income and financial income reported on the income statement. For example, a company may use an accelerated depreciation method for tax purposes and the straight-line method for accounting purposes.

The FINANCIAL ACCOUNTING STANDARDS BOARD indicated that the objective of accounting for income taxes on an accrual basis is to recognize the tax consequences of a transaction in the same year that transaction is recognized in the financial statements. To achieve this objective:

1. A current (or deferred) tax liability is recognized for the current (or deferred) tax consequences of all transactions that have occurred at the date of the financial statements.
2. The current (or deferred) tax consequences of a transaction are measured based on provisions of the tax law to determine the amount of taxes payable or refundable currently (or in future years).
3. Recognition and measurement of a deferred tax liability or asset does not anticipate the tax consequences of earning income or incurring losses or expenses in future years.

Interperiod tax allocation is applied to all temporary differences between taxable income and pretax book income, regardless of the period in which the taxes are paid.

The Financial Accounting Board's Statement of Financial Position (SFAS) No. 96, "Accounting for Income Taxes", supersedes APB Opinion No. 11. SFAS 96 establishes financial accounting and reporting standards for the effects of income taxes that result from an enterprise's activities during the current and preceding years. SFAS No. 96 states:

> The objective in accounting for income taxes on an accrual basis is to recognize the amount of current and deferred taxes payable or refundable at the date of the financial statements (a) as a result of all events that have been recognized in the financial statements and (b) as measured by the provisions of enacted tax laws.

SFAS 96 uses the term *temporary differences* instead of APBO 11's *timing differences*. Temporary differences can arise when tax laws differ from the recognition and measurement requirements of financial accounting standards. Such differences can result when (1) the amount of taxable and pretax financial income for a year differ, or (2) the tax bases of assets or liabilities and their reported amounts in financial statements differ. A deferred tax liability or asset represents the deferred tax consequences of temporary differences, i.e., the amount of taxes payable or refundable in future years as a result of temporary differences at the end of the current year. SFAS 96 lists nine categories of temporary differences. *Permanent differences* are items that (1) enter into accounting income but never into taxable income, e.g., interest received on state and municipal obligations and amortization of goodwill, or (2) enter into taxable income but never into accounting income, e.g., the 80% deduction for dividends received from U.S. corporations. Interperiod tax allocation is not appropriate for permanent differences.

Deferred assets and liabilities are classified as current or noncurrent in the current year's balance sheet. Current deferred tax assets are offset against current deferred tax liabilities; noncurrent deferred tax assets are offset against non current deferred tax liabilities. As a general rule, *current* deferred tax assets and liabilities arise from temporary differences that result in net taxable or tax-deductible amounts in the following year. An exception is made for companies with operating cycles in excess of one year. All other temporary differences should be classified as noncurrent.

Income tax expense must also be allocated within an accounting period (intraperiod income tax allocation) between continuing operations and other components of net income and occasionally to the statement of retained earnings or statement of changes in stockholders' equity (e.g., discontinued operations, extraordinary items). The rationale behind intraperiod tax allocation is contained in the matching concept. Income tax expense is matched against the major components of pretax income to give a fair presentation of the after-tax impact of these items on net income.

BIBLIOGRAPHY

FINANCIAL ACCOUNTING STANDARDS BOARD, "Accounting for Income Taxes," *Statement of Financial Accounting Standards No. 96*, December 1987.

INCOME TAX APPEAL PROCEDURE A taxpayer has the right to information and assistance in complying with the tax laws. The Internal Revenue Service makes available many taxpayer publications and free services. The IRS also provides walk-in tax assistance at many IRS offices, recorded telephone information on many topics (though the IRS Tele-Tax system), informational videotapes that can be borrowed, educational programs for specific groups of taxpayers such as those for small businesses, and other services.

If a taxpayer needs a copy of his/her tax return for an earlier year, the copy can be obtained by filling out Form 4506, Request for Copy of Tax Form, and paying a small fee. If a taxpayer needs certain specific information—such as the amount of taxable income, the number of exemptions, and the tax reported on the return—this information can usually be obtained by writing or visiting an IRS office.

The taxpayer has the right under law to have his/her tax case kept confidential. Under the law, the IRS may share tax information with state tax agencies with which they have information exchange agreements, the Department of Justice and certain other federal agencies under strict legal guidelines, and certain foreign governments under tax treaty provisions.

The IRS's collection process involves a series of steps illustrated in the accompanying outline. To stop the process at any stage, the taxpayer should pay the tax in full or discuss possible ways to pay the tax with the IRS immediately.

The Collection Process

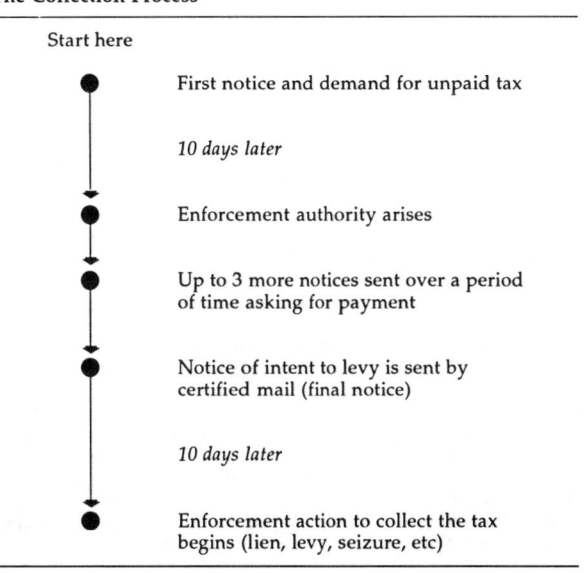

Start here
- First notice and demand for unpaid tax
- *10 days later*
- Enforcement authority arises
- Up to 3 more notices sent over a period of time asking for payment
- Notice of intent to levy is sent by certified mail (final notice)
- *10 days later*
- Enforcement action to collect the tax begins (lien, levy, seizure, etc)

Source: Internal Revenue Service

Most taxpayers' returns are accepted as filed. However, a number of returns are selected by sampling procedures for examination or by other means. Many IRS examinations are handled entirely by mail. If the examination is to be conducted through a face-to-face interview, or the taxpayer requests such an interview, the taxpayer has the right to ask that the examination take place at a reasonable time and place. Throughout the examination, the taxpayer may represent him/herself, have someone else accompany the taxpayer, or, with written authorization, have someone represent the taxpayer in his/her absence. The taxpayer may make a sound recording of the examination.

If a taxpayer does not agree with the examiner's report, the taxpayer may meet with the examiner's supervisor to discuss the case. If no agreement is reached, the taxpayer has the right to appeal. The taxpayer can appeal the findings through the IRS Appeals Office. If the issue in appeals is not settled, the taxpayer can take the case to court. Depending on whether the disputed tax is first paid, the taxpayer can take the case to the U.S. Tax Court, the U.S. Claims Court, or the U.S. District Court. These courts are independent of the IRS.

A taxpayer who disagrees about whether an additional tax is owed, generally has the right to take the case to the Tax Court if the tax has not yet been paid. If the taxpayer has already paid the

Income Tax Appeal Procedure

At any stage

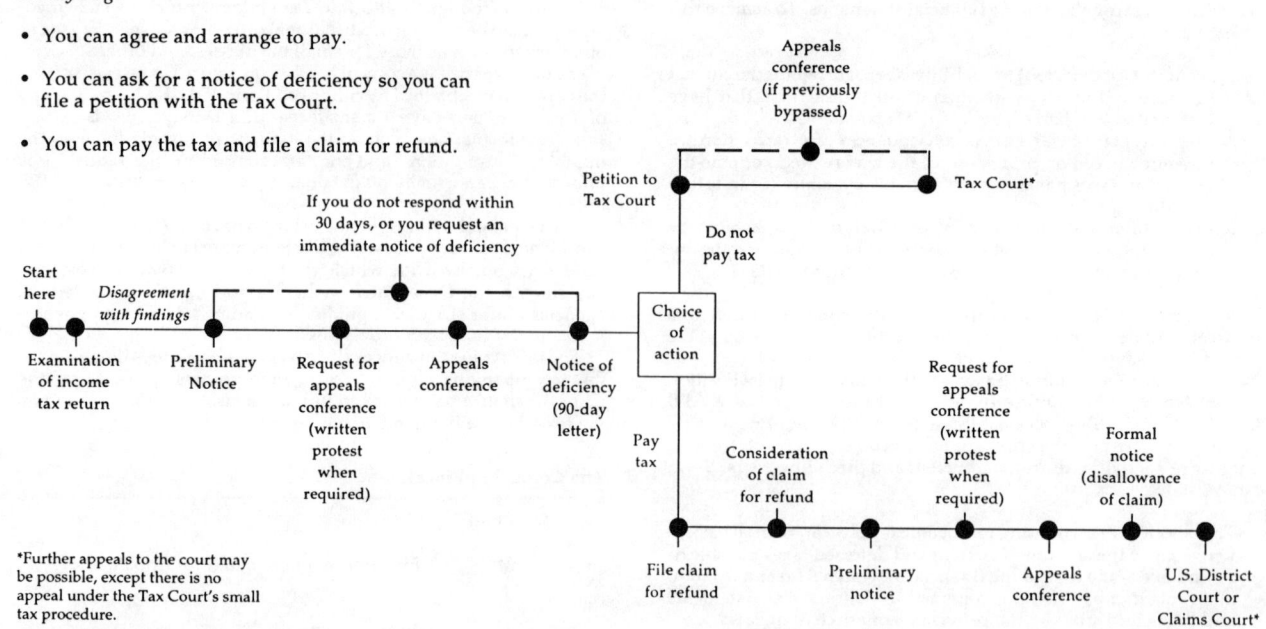

- You can agree and arrange to pay.
- You can ask for a notice of deficiency so you can file a petition with the Tax Court.
- You can pay the tax and file a claim for refund.

[Flowchart: Start here → Examination of income tax return → *Disagreement with findings* → Preliminary Notice → Request for appeals conference (written protest when required) → Appeals conference → Notice of deficiency (90-day letter) → Choice of action. If you do not respond within 30 days, or you request an immediate notice of deficiency, branches to Notice of deficiency. From Choice of action: (Do not pay tax) → Petition to Tax Court → Appeals conference (if previously bypassed) → Tax Court*. (Pay tax) → File claim for refund → Consideration of claim for refund → Preliminary notice → Request for appeals conference (written protest when required) → Appeals conference → Formal notice (disallowance of claim) → U.S. District Court or Claims Court*.]

*Further appeals to the court may be possible, except there is no appeal under the Tax Court's small tax procedure.

Source: Internal Revenue Service

disputed tax in full and filed a claim for refund for it that the IRS has disallowed (or on which the IRS did not take action within six months), the taxpayer can take the case to the U.S. District Court or the U.S. Claims Court. The accompanying outline shows the income tax appeal procedure.

Enforcement collection action includes the filing of a Notice of Federal Tax Lien, the serving of a Notice of Levy, and/or the seizure and sale of the taxpayer's property (person and/or business). The IRS ordinarily does not need a court order for a collection employee to seize a taxpayer's property. However, court authorization is required if the collection employee is to have access to the taxpayer's private premises, including the taxpayer's home or the nonpublic areas of the business.

The appended table shows tax returns filed—examination coverage: 1970 to 1987.

INCOME TAXES Federal income taxes have been continuously levied in the United States since March 1, 1913. In October, 1913, the first federal income tax law was passed, following ratification by the states of the Sixteenth Amendment to the Constitution of the United States the previous February. That amendment added nothing to the taxing powers of the federal government, but merely provided that Congress shall have the power to lay and collect taxes on income without apportionment, and without regard to any census or enumeration. Thus, Congress did have the power to lay taxes on income before March 1, 1913, but under the decision of the U.S. Supreme Court (*Pollock* v. *Farmers Loan & Trust Company*, 157 U.S. 429; rehearing, 158 U.S. 601) in 1895 that income taxes are direct taxes, income taxes before ratification of the Sixteenth Amendment would have had to be apportioned, in accordance with such constitutional requirement for direct taxes.

The United States had a federal income tax enacted during the Civil War (enacted 1861, amended six times, and allowed to expire in 1872). When it was enacted, six states already had income tax laws, so that it was not a purely federal innovation. In 1894, Congress enacted another income tax law, but this was declared unconstitutional by the Pollock case. Congress in 1909 proposed the Sixteenth Amendment to the states, and such amendment was declared ratified by proclamation on February 25, 1913.

The first state to enact modern income taxes was Wisconsin, in 1911. As of the beginning of 1980, 44 states and the District of Columbia had income taxes, in varying degrees of severity.

Following the passage of the Revenue Act of 1913, which approved the concepts of normal tax, surtax, and personal exemptions, the following important changes occurred:

1916	The Revenue Act of 1916 established the estate tax.
1917	Charitable contributions were given tax-deductible status, and personal exemptions allowed.
1924	Gift tax enacted to prevent avoidance of the estate tax.
1935	Federal Social Security Act enacted.
1939	Internal Revenue Code of 1939 codified separately the internal revenue laws.
1943	Current Tax Payment Act adopted the pay-as-you-go system.
1950	Self-employment tax enacted.
1954	Internal Revenue Code of 1954 completely overhauled federal income tax laws.
1964	The Revenue Act of 1964 was designed to stimulate sagging economy. Provided large corporate and individual tax rate reductions.
1974	Employee Retirement Income Security Act of 1974 (ERISA) provided for major changes in the private pension system.
1977	The Tax Reduction and Simplification Act of 1977 simplified the tax system. Established zero-bracket amount exemption deductions.
1978	The Revenue Act of 1978 revised corporate rate structure. Provided for taking the first $100,000 of income on a graduated scale, ranging form 17% to 40%, and at a 46% rate on all taxable income over $100,000.
1978	The Energy Tax Act of 1978 provided a tax credit for residential energy savings.
1980	The Windfall Profit Tax Act provided for an excise tax on domestic oil.
1981	Economic Recovery Tax Act (ERTA) decreased top individual tax rates from 70% to 50%. Provided for Accelerated Cost Recovery System (ACRS). Increased allowable contributions to Keogh and other retirement systems.
1983	Social Security Act Amendments of 1983 provided for bailing out the Social Security System.
1984	Deficit Reduction Act of 1984 reformed the tax law and designed reductions in federal spending.

Tax Returns Filed—Examination Coverage: 1970 to 1987
(In thousands, except as indicated.)

Year and Item	Returns filed [1]	Returns examined Total	Percent of returns filed	By— Revenue agents	By— Tax auditors	By— Service centers	Avg tax/penalty Revenue agents	Avg tax/penalty Tax auditors	Avg tax/penalty Service centers
Individual Returns									
1970	76,431.0	1,672.0	2.2	NA	NA	—	NA	NA	—
1975	81,272.0	1,838.6	2.3	355.2	1,483.4	—	2,609	219	—
1980	90,727.0	1,833.9	2.0	292.5	1,346.3	195.1	1,335	602	39
1981	93,052.0	1,644.1	1.8	289.5	1,193.1	161.5	6,374	579	223
1982	94,013.0	1,455.3	1.6	285.5	1,066.6	103.2	7,505	751	364
1983	95,419.0	1,427.7	1.5	277.9	1,001.9	147.9	10,248	990	316
1984	95,541.3	1,215.9	1.3	276.2	859.4	80.4	11,584	1,314	692
1985	96,496.9	1,265.6	1.3	332.6	810.9	122.1	10,854	1,539	496
1986	99,529.0	1,090.9	1.1	298.9	732.5	59.6	14,052	1,945	862
1987, total	101,750.8	1,109.2	1.1	317.5	610.4	181.3	12,235	2,107	4,084
1040A, total income under $10,000	19,904.9	105.9	.5	11.0	45.2	49.7	10,843	1,335	3,501
Non 1040A, total income: [2]									
Under $10,000	9,904.0	42.0	.4	8.7	24.7	8.6	5,567	1,033	892
$10,000–$24,999, simple	21,285.6	135.8	.6	25.1	86.6	24.1	2,368	9.9	662
$10,000–$24,999, complex	9,897.3	128.7	1.3	29.4	73.9	25.4	2,362	1,015	649
$25,000–$49,999	24,588.3	343.9	1.4	75.9	235.2	32.7	3,107	1,280	1,490
$50,000 and over	10,029.1	224.4	2.2	95.4	95.6	33.4	20,254	5,817	12,030
Schedule C—TGR: [3]									
Under $25,000	1,903.0	26.8	1.4	11.4	14.5	.9	5,834	1,746	1,529
$25,000–$99,999	2,125.0	42.7	2.0	22.4	18.3	2.0	7,277	3,380	9,147
$100,000 and over	1,198.0	46.2	3.9	32.4	11.1	2.6	29,399	8,015	15,835
Schedule F—TGR: [3]									
Under $25,000	240.0	2.2	.9	.7	1.3	.1	4,463	789	1,195
$25,000–$99,999	436.5	4.9	1.1	1.9	2.2	.7	4,436	1,158	569
$100,000 and over	238.6	5.6	2.3	3.2	1.6	.7	70,391	4,766	18,236
1986—Other Returns									
Fiduciary	2,276.2	5.1	.2	5.1	—	—	15,425	—	—
Partnerships	1,713.6	19.8	1.2	19.8	—	—	—	—	—
Corporations, total	3,647.6	55.1	19.5	55.1	—	—	676,232	—	—
Corporations except DISC and S corporations [4]	2,827.5	44.7	1.6	44.7	—	—	236,613	—	—
S corporations [4]	812.0	9.1	1.1	9.1	—	—	438,962	—	—
Form 1120 DISC [5]	8.1	1.3	16.8	1.3	—	—	657	—	—
Estate, total	67.6	15.1	22.4	15.1	—	—	63,697	—	—
Gross estate:									
Under $1 million	51.7	8.8	16.9	8.7	—	—	18,121	—	—
$1 million–$4.999 million	14.6	5.5	38.0	5.5	—	—	50,172	—	—
$5 million and over	1.3	.8	62.9	.8	—	—	643,718	—	—
Gift	101.3	1.7	1.7	1.7	—	—	135,913	—	—
Excise	1,035.5	38.9	3.8	38.9	—	—	4,074	—	—
Employment	27,812.2	46.3	.2	45.2	1.1	—	7,730	528	—
Windfall profit	10.3	4.4	42.4	1.5	—	2.8	701,123	—	2,156
Miscellaneous	—	.1	—	.1	—	—	18,383	—	—
Service center corrections	—	503.3	—	—	—	503.3	—	—	—

— Represents zero.
NA - Not available.
[1] Returns filed in previous calendar year.
[2] Income is that from positive sources only.
[3] Total gross receipts.
[4] Small business corporations. Represents corporations with no more than 35 shareholders (10 prior to 1983), most of which are individuals, electing to be taxed at the shareholder level.
[5] Domestic international sales corporation.

Source: U.S. Internal Revenue Service. *Annual Report of the Commissioner and Chief Counsel of the Internal Revenue Service.*

INCOME TAXES

1986   The Tax Reform Act of 1986 was the most significant and far reaching revision in the history of tax legislation. The tax code was redesignated the Internal Revenue Code of 1986.

1987   Revenue Act of 1987 made significant changes on business tax rules, including accounting for long-term contracts, limitations on the use of the installment method, applied corporate tax rates to master limited partnership, and many other changes.

Before the 1932 depression and subsequent revisions of the income tax laws, both federal and state, personal exemptions were quite high, with the result that the incidence of income taxation among the low-income groups was light, and many evaded payment because of the absence of withholding collection. It is estimated that prior to the 1932 depression, only one out of every nine families paid federal income taxes. Since 1932, however, exemptions have been lowered, rates increased, and the incidence of the income tax broadened considerably.

The individual income tax is by far the largest source of federal revenues. Revenues from individual income taxes are about three times those from the corporation income tax; together, the two income taxes account for 60% of federal tax collections in latest fiscal years. From the standpoint of counter-cyclical fiscal policy, income taxes are said to be an "automatic stabilizer" in that they are high in yield at times of expansion in incomes and profits, thus restraining inflationary tendencies, and lower in yield at times of recession in incomes and profits, thereby lightening the tax load as a recovery factor. Moreover, income tax rates and exemptions may be varied appropriately vis à vis the business cycle as a quicker and more flexible counter-cyclical measure than adjustments in expenditures. Among the states, general sales and gross receipts taxes and motor vehicle fuel sales taxes top individual and corporate income taxes as principal sources of revenue.

To reduce the manual manipulation of tax payments, including the individual and corporation income tax, tax withholders and certain taxpayers are supplied with partial punched hollerith cards (computer readable) which they forward to their banks with their tax payments. The cards are then routed to Federal Reserve banks which complete the punching and forward the cards to the office of the secretary of the Treasury in Washington. The Treasurer's Office enters the data from the cards on magnetic computer tapes which are furnished to the Internal Revenue Service for reconciliation with taxpayers' returns. This procedure obviates the need for normal handling of tax remittances in the department and expedites the crediting of tax payments in the Treasurer's account. This process can utilize electronic processing. The appended table shows federal receipts, by source, and outlays for selected years.

Evaluation of the Income Tax. No other tax in the internal revenue system of the U.S. arouses so much controversy as the income tax. A particular point of contention is the so-called progressivity of rates (steeply higher in the higher brackets of income). Karl Marx in his "Communist Manifesto" advocated "a heavy progressive or graduated income tax" as the second of ten measures whereby the proletariat could begin to erode the old social order by leveling inequalities in distribution of wealth. (The U.S.S.R. had relatively low rates of income tax, relying chiefly on the "turnover" tax, a differentiated sales tax.) Liberal economists defend progressivity as best effectuating the principle of ability to pay and as tending to enlarge markets for mass production. Conservatives, on the other hand, consider that high rates seriously interfere with economic growth by weakening work and risk-taking incentives. Other criticisms of the income tax include vertical and horizontal inequities; stimulation of avoidance by resort to tax-exempt securities, capital gains, expense accounts, and deferred compensation arrangements; and complexities of return and high costs of administration. From the standpoint of yields, the sensitivity of the income tax to the business cycle makes it a highly unstable revenue producer for governments, although this characteristic is considered an advantage as a counter-cyclical factor.

BIBLIOGRAPHY

COMMERCE CLEARING HOUSE. *CCH Federal Taxation: Basic Principles.* Latest edition.
———. *CCH Federal Taxation Advanced Topics.* Latest edition.
INTERNAL REVENUE SERVICE. *Your Federal Income Tax.* Latest edition.
PRENTICE-HALL PUBLISHING CO. *Federal Income Tax.* Latest edition.

Federal Receipts, by Source, and Outlay: 1970 to 1988

(In billions of dollars. For fiscal years ending in year shown; see text, section 9. Receipts reflect collections; outlays stated in terms of checks issued or cash payments. Covers both Federal funds and trust funds (see text, section 10). Excludes government-sponsored but privately-owned corporations, Federal Reserve System, District of Columbia government, and money held in suspense as deposit funds. See *Historical Statistics, Colonial Times to 1970*, series Y 335-338, Y 343-351, and Y 472-487 for related data.)

Source or Function	1970	1975	1980	1982	1983	1984	1985	1986	1987	1988, est.	Percent distribution 1980	Percent distribution 1988
Surplus or deficit (–)	–2.8	–53.2	–73.8	–127.9	–207.8	–185.3	–212.3	–221.2	–150.4	–146.7	X	X
By Source												
Total receipts [1]	192.8	279.1	517.1	617.8	600.6	666.5	734.1	769.1	854.1	909.2	100.00	100.00
Individual income taxes	90.4	122.4	244.1	297.7	288.9	298.4	334.5	349.0	392.6	393.4	47.20	43.27
Corporation income taxes	32.8	40.6	64.6	49.2	37.0	56.9	61.3	63.1	83.9	105.6	12.49	11.61
Social insurance taxes and contributions	44.4	84.5	157.8	201.5	209.0	239.4	265.2	283.9	303.3	331.5	30.52	36.46
Employment taxes and contributions	39.1	75.2	138.7	180.7	185.8	209.7	234.6	255.1	273.0	303.1	26.83	33.33
Unemployment insurance	3.5	6.8	15.3	16.6	18.8	25.1	25.8	24.1	25.6	23.7	2.97	2.61
Contributions for other insurance and retirement	1.8	2.6	3.7	4.2	4.4	4.6	4.8	4.7	4.7	4.7	.72	.52
Excise taxes	15.7	16.6	24.3	36.3	35.3	37.4	36.0	32.9	32.5	35.3	4.70	3.89
Estate and gift taxes	3.6	4.6	6.4	8.0	6.1	6.0	6.4	7.0	7.5	7.6	1.24	.83
Customs duties	2.4	3.7	7.2	8.9	8.7	11.4	12.1	13.3	15.1	16.4	1.39	1.80
Miscellaneous receipts	3.4	6.7	12.7	16.2	15.6	17.0	18.5	19.9	19.3	19.4	2.47	2.13
Federal Reserve earning deposits	3.3	5.8	11.8	15.2	14.5	15.7	17.1	18.4	16.8	16.1	2.28	1.77
By Function												
Total outlays [1]	195.6	332.3	590.9	745.7	808.3	851.8	946.3	990.3	1,004.6	1,055.9	100.00	100.00

INCOME TAXES: INDIVIDUAL There are three types of entities subject to tax under the Federal income tax: individuals, corporations, and estates and trusts. Several other entities are tax exempt or are treated as conduits: partnerships and corporations that elect special treatment under Subchapter S of the code are treated as conduits for tax purposes; governments, churches, eductional institutions, and other not-for-profit entities are exempt from U.S. income taxation.

Taxable income for the individual taxpayer is computed using either the cash method or the accrual method, or a combination of the two basic methods. The cash method requires that income be reported when it is received and deductions taken when the expense is paid. The accrual method requires that income be reported when all events necessary to establish the right to receive payment have occurred and there is reasonable certainty concerning the amount. Deductions are taken in the year in which all events that establish the liability have occurred and the amount of the liability is reasonably determinable. The method used to calculate the tax liabiity is as follows:

- Gross income (all income from whatever source unless specifically excluded)
- Deductions for adjusted gross income (deductions specifically allowed by law, mostly business expenses)
= Adjusted gross income
- Itemized deductions (expenses of a personal nature allowed) or Standard deduction (based on filing status of the taxpayer, including additional standard deduction for age and blindness; beginning in 1989, the deduction is adjusted for inflation)
- Personal exemptions
x Tax rate
= Tax liability
- Tax credits and prepayments (major tax credits include earned income credit, credit for elderly, general business credit, dependent care credit, and foreign tax credit; prepayments include amounts withheld on income and by estimated payments made during the year)
= Net tax due or refund

INCOME TAXES: THE LEGISLATIVE PROCESS
The legislative process can be illustrated as a sequence of events starting with a tax bill being introduced before the House Ways and Means Committee to its becoming law.

INCOME TAX REPORTING Congress has the power to levy and collect taxes on incomes. Because the purposes and policies of tax accounting (for example, related to revenue-producing activities) and financial accounting (for example, related to investment and credit needs) frequently differ, accounting practices also differ. As a general rule, the Internal Revenue Service accepts any accounting method that clearly reflects income as long as the tax statutes and regulations are followed.

Sole proprietors are not separate taxable entities. The owner of the business reports business transactions on his or her individual income tax return. Partnerships are not subject to the income tax. The results of partnership operations flow through to the individual partners. Estates and trusts are similar to partnerships in that income is taxed only once. However, the tax may be imposed on the estate or trust. Whether the income of an estate or trust is taxed to the estate or trust or to the beneficiary generally depends on whether the income is retained by the entity or distributed to the beneficiary. The corporation is taxed as a separate taxpaying entity. Corporate income is taxed again to the shareholder when distributed as dividends, subject to certain limitations. Subchapter S corporations are usually treated as partnerships and so frequently can avoid taxes at the corporate level.

Corporations can select a calendar year or a fiscal year for reporting purposes, as can individuals. A change in accounting period generally requires the approval of the IRS. Corporations can use a variety of accounting methods depending upon the surrounding circumstances: the cash or accrual method, the installment method, or the percentage of completion and the completed contract method when long-term contracts are involved. Corporations that are members of a parent-subsidiary group can file a consolidated income tax return for a taxable year. The affiliated group is considered to constitute a single taxable entity, although the members of the group are legally separate entities.

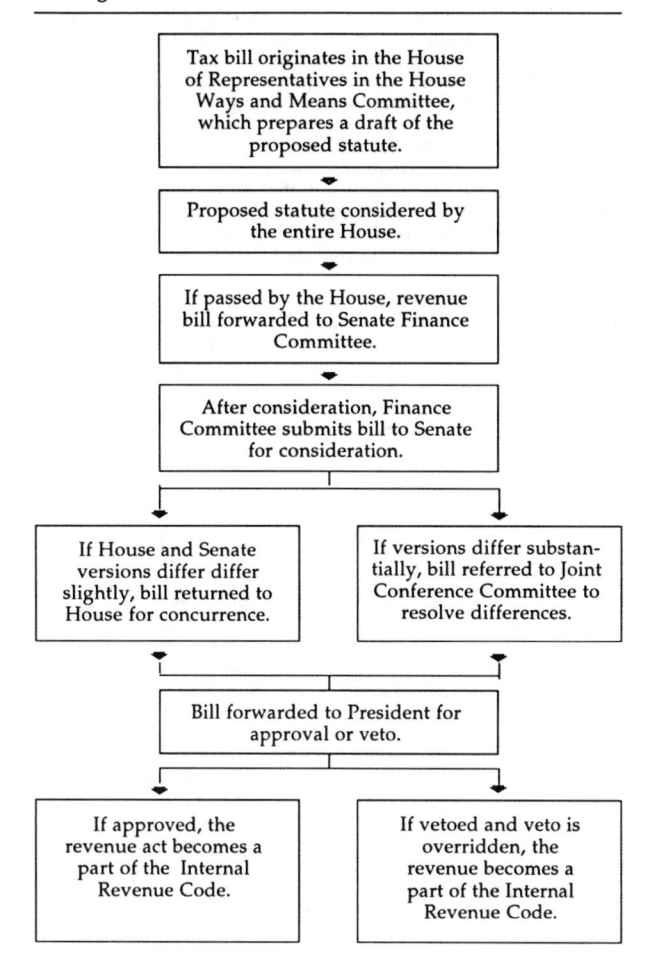

The Legislative Process

```
Tax bill originates in the House
of Representatives in the House
Ways and Means Committee,
which prepares a draft of the
proposed statute.
          ↓
Proposed statute considered by
the entire House.
          ↓
If passed by the House, revenue
bill forwarded to Senate Finance
Committee.
          ↓
After consideration, Finance
Committee submits bill to Senate
for consideration.
       ↙        ↘
If House and Senate    If versions differ substan-
versions differ differ tially, bill referred to Joint
slightly, bill returned to  Conference Committee to
House for concurrence. resolve differences.
       ↘        ↙
Bill forwarded to President for
approval or veto.
       ↙        ↘
If approved, the       If vetoed and veto is
revenue act becomes a  overridden, the
part of the Internal   revenue becomes a
Revenue Code.          part of the Internal
                       Revenue Code.
```

INCOMING EXCHANGES In the exchange of checks at the clearinghouse, each bank is presented by other member banks with the checks drawn against it that other banks previously have taken for credit. Income exchanges are the checks that each bank receives at the CLEARINGHOUSE from other members, as distinguished from the checks that each bank presents against the other member banks. Income exchanges represent debits to the receiving bank's depositors' accounts.

INCONVERTIBLE PAPER MONEY See FIAT MONEY, IRREDEEMABLE PAPER MONEY.

INCORPORATED TRUSTEE A trust company or a commercial bank authorized by law and/or regulation to act in a fid.-ciary capacity, as distinguished from an individual TRUSTEE.

Under the Trust Indenture Act of 1939 (P.L. 253, 76th Congress, August 3, 1939), issuers of obligational securities required to be registered for public offering under the Securities Act of 1933 must qualify indentures for such securities with the Securities and Exchange Commission. The INDENTUREto be qualified shall require that there shall be at all times one or more trustees thereunder, at least one of whom shall at all times be a corporation organized and doing business under the laws of the United States or of any state or territory or the District of Columbia, i.e., an "institutional" or corporate trustee, that is authorized to exercise corporate trust powers and is subject to supervision or examination by federal, state, territorial, or District of Columbia authority.

Such an institutional trustee shall have at all times a combined capital and surplus of not less than $150,000. No trustee shall have any "conflicting interest," i.e., interests in or connections with the issuer or the underwriters. The trustee shall notify bondholders by annual report of such matters as substitutions of collateral it permitted; advances to the issuer or funds of the issuer in its possession; additional bonds authenticated; etc. It shall notify bondholders of any default within 90 days of its occurrence. Upon the occurrence of defaults, the trustee is charged with the "prudent man" rule in the exercise of its powers and duties under the indenture. Lists of bondholders shall be furnished to the trustee by the issuer, and the former shall make such lists available to individual bondholders upon request.

INDEMNITY BOND A written instrument under seal whereby the signer, usually with his or her surety or bondsman, guarantees to protect another's loss by guaranteeing completion of the terms of the contract. Indemnity bonds are an acknowledgment of an obligation to make good the performance by another of some act, duty, or responsibility. Indemnity bonds are usually issued by companies that assume risk of performance by a bonded party for a fee. Performance of the act, duty, or responsibility by the bonded party discharges the obligation. The bonding company retains right of subrogation against the bonded party. Fidelity bonds protect an employer against losses sustained by dishonest employees by guaranteeing faithful performance of duties by employees. Performance bonds such as construction bonds guarantee a builder's obligation to complete construction. In such a contract, the bonding company can be held liable for damages but not for specific performance.

INDENTURE A deed or agreement under seal between two or more parties, so called because originally a deed was indented or zigzagged along one of the margins. Since it was issued in duplicate, proof of genuineness or falsity of the documents was secured by comparing the indentations on the original with those on the duplicate. If the documents were genuine the indentations would coincide.

Under the Trust Indenture Act of 1939, an indenture means any mortgage, deed of trust, trust, or other similar instrument or agreement under which securities are outstanding or are to be issued, whether or not any property, real or personal, is or is to be pledged, mortgaged, assigned, or conveyed thereunder. Indentures of securities offered for public sale and subject to the registration requirements of the Securities Act of 1933 must be qualified by the issuers with the Securities and Exchange Commission. In addition to such content as details of the issue; description of the property pledged as security (if any), protective provisions, etc., indentures must contain the provisions specifically directed by the Trust Indenture Act of 1939 to be contained therein. That act is particularly concerned with the powers and duties of the indenture trustee(s). For example, the indenture to be qualified shall not contain any provisions relieving the indenture trustee from liability for its own negligent action, its own negligent failure to act, or its own willful misconduct ("exculpatory clauses"), except that:

1. The indenture may contain provision that prior to default, the indenture trustee shall not be liable except for the performance of such duties as are specifically set out in the indenture.
2. The indenture may contain provision that the indenture trustee may conclusively rely upon certificates or opinions conforming to the requirements of the indenture as to the truth of the statements and the correctness of the opinions expressed therein, in the absence of bad faith on the part of the trustee (but the indenture shall contain provisions requiring the trustee to examine the evidence furnished to it to determine whether or not such evidence conforms to the requirements of the indenture).
3. The indenture may contain provision protecting the indenture trustee from liability for any error of judgment made in good faith by a responsible officer or officers of the trustee, unless it shall be proved that such trustee was negligent in ascertaining the pertinent facts.
4. The indenture may contain provisions protecting the indenture trustee with respect to any action taken or omitted by it in good faith in accordance with the direction of the holders of not less than a majority in principal amount of the indenture securities at the time outstanding, relating to the time, method, and place of conducting any proceeding for any remedy available to such trustee, or exercising any trust or power conferred upon the trustee under the indenture.

For indentures to be qualified the act requires that they contain provisions requiring the indenture trustee to give to the indenture security holders notice of all defaults known to the trustee within 90 days after their occurrence. However, the indenture may provide, except in the case of default in payment of principal or interest or any sinking or purchase fund installment, that the trustee shall be protected in withholding such notice if and so long as the board of directors, the executive committee, or a trust committee of directors and/or responsible officers of the trustee in good faith determines that the withholding of such notice is in the interests of the indenture security holders.

For trustees, perhaps the most significant required content of indentures under the Trust Indenture Act of 1939 is provision requiring the indenture trustee to exercise in case of default (as such is defined in the indenture) the rights and powers vested in the trustee by the indenture, and to use the same degree of care and skill in their exercise as a "prudent man" would exercise or use under the circumstances in the conduct of his own affairs. Such adoption of the prudent man rule with respect to the trustee's duties after default was in line with the act's objective of making more effective representation and enforcement of indenture security holders' rights.

See INCORPORATED TRUSTEE.

INDEPENDENT BANKERS ASSOCIATION OF AMERICA A commercial bankers association organized in May, 1930. Through its national headquarters in Sauk Centre, Minnesota, the association has been "serving America's Main Street bankers from America's original "Main Street'," the Main Street made famous by Nobel Prize novelist Sinclair Lewis. The Washington, D.C. office is located at 815 15th Street, N.W.

The objective of the Independent Bankers Association of America (IBAA) is to ensure continuation of the independent bank in America because it believes that such an institution is vitally needed in the nation's economy. The association serves primarily the banks in medium-size and smaller communities, and it is active in legislative, education, and research efforts to accomplish its mission. The association's main interest is the bank that is "of, by, and for" the community of its charter, and it strives to help that bank serve its community better and to grow in an environment of free enterprise and fair competition.

When originally organized in 1930, the association was defensively aimed at halting the "predatory acquisition" of small banks throughout Minnesota by two Twin Cities-based holding companies. Within a few years, the association had members in neighboring states, and the association had grown into national scope.

The association's publications include its monthly magazine, the *Independent Banker;* a periodic IBAA newsletter; and occasional books and pamphlets keyed to the needs and interest of members. Conventions of the asociation, attracting some 2,000 participants, are held each March.

INDEPENDENT BANKING SYSTEM A banking system in which banking is conducted by separate local institutions, owned in the community in which they are established, locally managed, and having either a single office or branch offices confined to the same city. Independent banking is one of the features of the U.S. banking structure as distinguished from the BRANCH BANKING of Canada and many of the European countries, where banks are permitted to establish branches without limitation as to number or location.

The advantages claimed for independent banking are that it prevents the development of centralized control and the concentration of banking power in the hands of a few individuals. It is also said to permit sounder banking operations, especially in providing credit, since each banking unit is in closer contact with the local situation, which is more likely to be understood by resident managers than by officials operated from a central office.

INDEPENDENT TREASURY SYSTEM A system established in 1846 under which government funds were taken out of the banks and placed in the Treasury and subtreasuries. Between 1833, three years before the expiration of the charter of the Second Bank of the United States, and 1837, government funds were maintained in state-chartered banks exclusively. It was largely due to the charge of favoritism in the selection of state banks as depositories and their widespread suspensions that the independent Treasury System was finally adopted in 1846. Prior to 1833, government funds were kept in the First and Second Banks of the United States.

In the period from 1846 to 1863, government funds were exclusively in the Treasury and subtreasuries; no banks were used as depositories of government funds until after the National Banking System was established in 1863. After the establishment of this system, national banks to some extent served as government depositories, thereby supplementing the treasuries as custodians of government funds. With the establishment of the Federal Reserve System, the Federal Reserve banks became the chief depositories for government funds, although member banks are still eligible for this purpose and large amounts are still kept on deposit with them.

The disadvantage of the independent Treasury system was that it was likely to disturb the economy by irregular collections and expenditures in specie, "impounding" such "hard money" when it was needed and paying it out when it was not. If irregular deposits and withdrawals happened to occur when money was tight—especially at the crop moving period—the result was likely to be harmful. On the other hand, the Independent Treasury System was of aid in time of a crisis or panic with its payments in specie. Subtreasuries were abandoned in 1921, their functions being taken over by the Federal Reserve banks.

See BANK OF THE UNITED STATES, DEPOSITORY, SUBTREASURY, TREASURY DEPARTMENT, TREASURY STATEMENT.

INDETERMINATE BONDS Bonds that have no fixed maturity date but that are callable at the option of the issuer, usually after a specified date.

See PERPETUAL BOND.

INDEXING The tying of payment increases to some economic index. For example, certain wage contracts are written in such a way that workers will receive an agreed-upon amount per hour plus an additional amount for each point increase in the consumer price index. This type of wage arrangement is often called an escalator clause. Social Security payments are also indexed. This indexing assures that recipients' real incomes will not fall with inflation.

INDEX NUMBERS Numbers that provide a statistical method for measurement of changes in any variable data, such as prices, wages, employment, output, sales, inventories, income, costs, etc. Index numbers may be "relatives" (percentages based on indicated base period); aggregates of absolute values of a defined content of items; or relatives of the values of the second type, expressed as percentages of the indicated base period. They may be weighted or unweighted actual or relative values.

H. G. Moulton defined a price index number as follows: "An index number of any given article at any given date is the percentage which the price of that article at that date is of the price of the same article at a date or period which has been selected as base or standard. The method of computing index numbers may be illustrated as follows: The average price of each commodity for the year 1913 is considered as 100. Then every month the prices of the various commodities are turned into relatives on that scale. Thus if wheat sold in 1913 at $1.00 a bushel and in May, 1918, at $2.26 a bushel, the relative price of wheat is then 226. If, on the other hand, the price of any commodity should drop from 50 cents to 40 cents, the relative price would be 80. To ascertain the change that has occurred from month to month in the general level of prices it is only necessary to strike an average of those prices" (*Financial Organization of Society*).

The problems in construction of an aggregative index number may be summarized as follows: "Making an index number involves several distinct operations: (1) defining the purpose for which the final results are to be used; (2) deciding the number and kinds of commodities to be included; (3) determining whether these commodities shall be weighted according to their relative importance; (4) collecting the actual prices of the commodities chosen, and, in case a weighted series is to be made, collecting also data regarding their relative importance; (5) deciding whether to measure the average variations of prices or the variations of a sum of actual prices; (6) in case average variations are to be measured, choosing the base upon which relative prices shall be computed; and (7) settling upon the form of average to be struck.

"At each one of these successive steps, choice must be made among alternatives that range in number from two to thousands. The possible combinations among the alternatives chosen are indefinitely numerous. Hence there is no assignable limit to the possible varieties of index numbers, and in practice no two of the known series are exactly alike in construction" (W. C. Mitchell, *The Making and Using of Index Numbers*).

In Irving Fisher's *The Making of Index Numbers*, over 150 formulas for the construction of index numbers are given.

Consumer Price Index. Perhaps the most famous of the federal government's regularly published indexes is the consumer price index (monthly index), prepared and published by the Bureau of Labor Statistics, U.S. Department of Labor. *See* COST OF LIVING INDEX. *See* appended table of consumer price indexes, by major groups from 1960 to 1987.

Producer Price Indexes. The Bureau of Labor Statistics (BLS) also prepares and regularly publishes the producer price indexes (these data were previously presented as the wholesale price indexes). These indexes measure average changes in prices received in primary markets of the United States by producers of commodities in all stages of processing. The name producer price indexes (PPI) is now being used to reflect more accurately the coverage of the data. The sample used for calculating these indexes continues to contain nearly 2,800 commodities and about 10,000 quotations selected to represent the movement of prices of all commodities produced in the manufacturing, agriculture, forestry, fishing, mining, gas and electricity, and public utilities sectors. The universe includes all commodities produced or imported for sale in commercial transactions in primary markets in the United States. The BLS further advises as follows.

Producer price indexes can be organized by stage of processing or by commodity. The stage of processing structure organizes products by degree of fabrication (i.e., finished goods, intermediate or semifinished goods, and crude materials). The commodity structure organizes products by similarity of end-use or material composition.

Finished goods are commodities that will not undergo further processing and are ready for sale to the ultimate user, either an individual consumer or a business firm. Capital equipment (formerly called producer finished goods) includes commodities such as motor trucks, farm equipment, and machine tools. Finished consumer goods include foods and other types of goods eventually purchased by retailers and used by consumers. Consumer foods include unprocessed foods such as eggs and fresh vegetables, as well as processed foods such as bakery products and meats. Other finished consumer goods include durables such as automobiles, household furniture, and jewelry and nondurables such as apparel and gasoline.

Intermediate materials, supplies, and components are commodities that have been processed but require further processing before they become finished goods. Examples of such semifinished goods include flour, cotton yarns, steel mill products, belts and belting, lumber, liquefied petroleum gas, paper boxes, and motor vehicle parts.

Crude materials for further processing include products entering the market for the first time that have not been manufactured or fabricated but will be processed before becoming finished goods. Scrap materials are also included. Crude foodstuffs and feedstuffs include items such as grains and livestock. Examples of crude nonfood materials include raw cotton, crude petroleum, natural gas, hides and skins, and iron and steel scrap.

For analysis of general price trends, stage of processing indexes are more useful than commodity grouping indexes. This is because commodity grouping indexes sometimes produce exaggerated or misleading signals of price changes by reflecting the same price movement through various stages of processing. For example, suppose that a price rise for steel scrap results in an increase in the price of steel sheet and then an advance in prices of automobiles produced from that steel. The all commodities producer price index and the industrial commodities price index would reflect the same price movement three times—once for the steel scrap, once for the steel sheet, and once for the automobiles. This multiple counting occurs because the weighting structure for the all commodities PPI uses the total shipment values for all commodities at all stages of processing. On the other hand, the finished goods price index would reflect the change in automobile prices, the intermediate materials price index

INDEX NUMBERS

Consumer Price Indexes, by Major Groups: 1960 to 1987
(1982:–84 = 100. Represents annual averages of monthly figures. Reflects buying patterns of all urban consumers.)

Year	All items	Energy	Food	Shelter	Apparel and upkeep	Transportation	Medical care	Fuel oil	Electricity	Utility (piped) gas	Telephone services	All commodities
1960	29.6	22.4	30.0	25.2	45.7	29.8	22.3	13.5	29.9	17.6	58.3	33.6
1961	29.9	22.5	30.4	25.4	46.1	30.1	22.9	14.0	29.9	17.9	58.5	33.8
1962	30.2	22.6	30.6	25.8	46.3	30.8	23.5	14.0	29.9	17.9	58.5	34.1
1963	30.6	22.6	31.1	26.1	46.9	30.9	24.1	14.3	29.9	17.9	58.6	34.4
1964	31.0	22.5	31.5	26.5	47.3	31.4	24.6	14.0	29.8	17.9	58.6	34.8
1965	31.5	22.9	32.2	27.0	47.8	31.9	25.2	14.3	29.7	18.0	57.7	35.2
1966	32.4	23.3	33.8	27.8	49.0	32.3	26.3	14.7	29.7	18.1	56.5	36.1
1967	33.4	23.8	34.1	28.8	51.0	33.3	28.2	15.1	29.9	18.1	57.3	36.8
1968	34.8	24.2	35.3	30.1	53.7	34.3	29.9	15.6	30.2	18.2	57.3	38.1
1969	36.7	24.8	37.1	32.6	56.8	35.7	31.9	15.9	30.8	18.6	58.0	39.9
1970	38.8	25.5	39.2	35.5	59.2	37.5	34.0	16.5	31.8	19.6	58.7	41.7
1971	40.5	26.5	40.4	37.0	61.1	39.5	36.1	17.6	33.9	21.0	61.6	43.2
1972	41.8	27.2	42.1	38.7	62.3	39.9	37.3	17.6	35.6	22.1	65.0	44.5
1973	44.4	29.4	48.2	40.5	64.6	41.2	38.8	20.4	37.4	23.1	66.7	47.8
1974	49.3	38.1	55.1	44.4	69.4	45.8	42.4	32.2	44.1	26.0	69.5	53.5
1975	53.8	42.1	59.8	48.8	72.5	50.1	47.5	34.9	50.0	31.1	71.7	58.2
1976	56.9	45.1	61.6	51.5	75.2	55.1	52.0	37.4	53.1	36.3	74.3	60.7
1977	60.6	49.4	65.5	54.9	78.6	59.0	57.0	42.4	56.6	43.2	75.2	64.2
1978	65.2	52.5	72.0	60.5	81.4	61.7	61.8	44.9	60.9	47.5	76.0	68.8
1979	72.6	65.7	79.9	68.9	84.9	70.5	67.5	63.1	65.6	55.1	75.8	76.6
1980	82.4	86.0	86.8	81.0	90.9	83.1	74.9	87.7	75.8	65.7	77.7	86.0
1981	90.9	97.7	93.6	90.5	95.3	93.2	82.9	107.3	87.2	74.9	84.6	93.2
1982	96.5	99.2	97.4	96.9	97.8	97.0	92.5	105.0	95.8	89.8	93.2	97.0
1983	99.6	99.9	99.4	99.1	100.2	99.3	100.6	96.5	98.9	104.7	99.2	99.8
1984	103.9	100.9	103.2	104.0	102.1	103.7	106.8	98.5	105.3	105.5	107.5	103.2
1985	107.6	101.6	105.6	109.8	105.0	106.4	113.5	94.6	108.9	104.8	111.7	105.4
1986	109.6	88.2	109.0	115.8	105.9	102.3	122.0	74.1	110.4	99.7	117.2	104.4
1987	113.6	88.6	113.5	121.3	110.6	105.4	130.1	75.8		95.1	116.5	107.7

Source: U.S. Bureau of Labor Statistics, *Monthly Labor Review* and *Handbook of Labor Statistics*, periodic.

would reflect the steel sheet price change, and the crude materials price index would reflect the rise in the price of steel scrap.

To the extent possible, prices used in calculating producer price indexes apply to the first significant commercial transaction in the United States, from the production or central marketing point. Price data are generally collected monthly, primarily by mail questionnaire. Respondents are asked to provide net prices or to provide all applicable discounts. BLS attempts to base producer price indexes on actual transaction prices; however, list or book prices are used if transaction prices are not available. Most prices are obtained directly from producing companies on a voluntary and confidential basis, but some prices are taken from trade publications or from other government agencies. Prices generally are reported for the Tuesday of the week containing the thirteenth day of the month.

In calculation of producer price indexes, price changes for the various commodities are averaged together with weights representing their importance in the total net selling value of all commodities as of 1972. The detailed data are aggregated to obtain indexes for stage of processing groupings, commodity groups, durability of product groupings, and a number of special composite groupings. Each index measures price changes from a reference period which equals 100.0 (usually 1967, as designated by the Office of Management and Budget). An increase of 85% from the reference period in the finished goods price index, for example, is shown as 185.0. This change can also be expressed in dollars, as follows: "The price of a representative sample of finished goods sold in primary markets in the United States has risen from $100 in 1967 to $185."

A note about calculating index changes: Movements of price indexes from one month to another are usually expressed as percent changes rather than index point changes because the index point changes are affected by the level of the index in relation to its base period, while percent changes are not. The following example illustrates the computation of index point and percent changes.

Percent changes for 3-month and 6-month periods are expressed

Index point change	
Finished goods price index	185.5
Less previous index	184.5
Equals index point change	1.0
Index percent change	
Index point change	1.0
Divided by the previous index	184.5
Equals	0.005
Result multiplied by 100	0.005 × 100
Equals index percent change	0.5%

as annual rates that are computed according to the standard formula for compound growth rates. These data indicate what the percent change would be if the current rate were maintained for a 12-month period.

A note on seasonally adjusted data: Because price data are used for different purposes by different groups, the BLS publishes seasonally adjusted as well as unadjusted changes each month.

For analyzing general price trends in the economy, seasonally adjusted data are preferred because they eliminate the effect of changes that normally occur at about the same time and in about the same magnitude every year, such as price movements resulting from normal weather patterns, regular production and marketing cycles, model changeovers, seasonal discounts, and holidays. For this reason, seasonally adjusted data are more clearly revealing of the underlying cyclical trends. Seasonally adjusted data are subject to revision when seasonal factors are revised each year.

The unadjusted data are of interest primarily to users who need information that can be related to the actual dollar values of transactions. Individuals requiring this information include marketing specialists, purchasing agents, budget and cost analysts, contract specialists, and commodity traders. Unadjusted data generally are used in escalating contracts, such as purchase agreements or real estate leases.

New base period: Beginning with data for 1971, the producer (formerly wholesale) price indexes were converted from a 1957-1959 to a 1967 reference base period. The Office of Management and Budget established the new reference base, 1967 = 100, for use by all government statistical agencies in line with the longstanding policy that index bases should be updated periodically, and with the belief that a more current reference base would facilitate comparisons of movements for recent periods both within and among index series. The indexes were rebased by multiplying each monthly and annual index on a 1957-1959 reference base by the appropriate rebasing factor. This factor is the reciprocal of the 1967 annual average on a 1957-1959 base (calculated to eight places after the decimal point and rounded to seven places). For seasonal items where data for each month were not available, the rebasing factor was derived from the average of those months for which actual prices were reported. To summarize, indexes on the 1957-1959 base can be converted to a 1967 base by multiplying the previously published index by the appropriate rebasing factor; indexes on the 1967 base can be converted to the 1957-1959 base by dividing the 1967-based index by the appropriate rebasing factor for the series.

Example 1: The index for farm products for January, 1970, on the 1957-1959 base was 112.5. To convert this index to the 1967 base, multiply by the factor 1.0030090. Thus, 112.5 multiplied by 1.0030090 equals 112.8 (1967 = 100).

Example 2: The index for farm products for January, 1971, was 108.9 on the new 1967 base. To convert this figure to the 1957-1959 reference base, divide by 1.0030090. Thus, 108.9 divided by 1.0030090 equals 108.6 (1957-1959 = 100).

Rebasing an index does not alter the percentage change between index figures over time, except for rounding differences. For example, the percentage change in the wholesale price index between November, 1965, and November, 1970, is the same under the 1957-1959 = 100 base and the 1967 = 100 base, as indicated by the following.

	Nov. 1965 index	Nov. 1970 index	Increase in index points	Percent increase
1957-1959 base	103.5	117.7	14.2	13.7%
1967 base	97.5	110.9	13.4	13.7%

Table 1 ahow the producer price index changes and some of its major groups from 1970 through 1987. Table 2 shows producer and consumer price indexes for selected years.

In addition to the monthly producer price indexes, the BLS also publishes indexes of spot market prices representing monthly averages of the Tuesday indexes of prices on commodity markets and organized exchanges. This Tuesday index is a measure of the price movement of 22 sensitive basic commodities whose markets are presumed to be among the first to be influenced by actual or anticipated changes in economic conditions. The commodities included in the index are either raw materials or products close to the initial production stage that are traded through organized markets or through other markets whose activities are recorded in trade or government publications. Of the 22 commodities, 9 are foodstuffs (butter, cocoa beans, corn, cottonseed oil, hogs, lard, steers, sugar, and wheat) and 13 are raw industrials (burlap, copper scrap, cotton, hides, lead scrap, print cloth, rosin, rubber, steel scrap, tallow, tin, wooltops, and zinc). This Tuesday index of spot market prices is not an abbreviated form of the comprehensive producer price indexes, as it differs from the producer price indexes in method of construction and weighting as well as in coverage.

Implicit Price Index ("GNP Deflator"). This index has been termed the most comprehensive measurement of the general price level (*Economic Report of the President*, January, 1966) since it deflates gross national product (GNP) and its principal components, GNP being the market value of all final goods and services produced in the entire economy for a given annual period. In fact, however, it is not independently calculated but rather is derived principally by dividing specific components of the seasonally adjusted current dollar GNP by appropriate price indexes prepared by private and government agencies, such as the consumer price index, index of prices paid by farmers, producers price index, construction cost indexes, etc., and indexes of unit values of merchandise exports and imports "in as fine a breakdown as practicable." About 100 product groups are deflated separately, and price indexes drawn from existing current series are combined on a 1972 base (1972 = 100) to deflate the current dollar totals. The combined overall deflator is "implicit" in that it may be obtained by dividing gross national product reported in current dollars by the gross national product thus assembled in constant dollars, and multiplying by 100.

U.S. Import and Export Price Indexes. Price data for both indexes are collected for approximately 13,000 products from over 3,300 companies, mostly by mail questionnaire. Respondents are requested to supply the net transaction price for the pricing month. The index series reflect prices for the months shown. Those series with values prior to March, 1974, refer to June of each year; beginning March, 1974, all index values are on a quarterly frequency. Prices are collected on a voluntary and confidential basis. Where possible, indexes

Table 1 / Producer Price Indexes—Average Annual Percent Change in Selected Major Commodity Groups: 1970 to 1987
(Minus sign (–) indicates decrease.)

Commodity Group	1970-75	1975-80	1980-81	1981-82	1982-83	1983-84	1984-85	1985-86	1986-87
All commodities	8.9	9.0	9.1	2.0	1.3	2.4	–.5	2.9	2.6
Farm products	11.0	6.0	2.2	–4.9	2.4	3.0	–9.9	–2.3	2.8
Processed foods, feeds	10.2	5.7	3.1	1.1	1.8	3.5	–1.8	1.8	2.4
Textile products, apparel	5.2	5.9	8.8	2.5	.3	2.4	.2	.3	1.8
Hides, skins, leather, related products	6.1	10.9	4.9	.7	3.2	5.6	–.1	3.8	6.5
Fuels, related products, power	18.3	18.5	21.0	–.2	–4.1	–1.1	–3.6	–23.6	.6
Chemicals and allied products	12.1	7.5	10.6	1.6	.3	2.6	.8	–1.1	3.7
Rubber and plastic products	6.7	7.7	7.0	3.7	.8	1.5	–.4	—	1.1
Lumber and wood products	9.3	10.3	1.3	–2.7	7.9	.1	–1.3	.6	5.2
Pulp, paper, and allied products	9.5	7.9	9.8	5.5	3.3	6.8	2.7	2.5	4.9
Metals and metal products	9.7	9.1	4.8	.4	1.8	2.9	–.4	–1.1	3.8
Machinery and equipment	7.7	8.2	9.8	5.9	2.7	2.3	2.0	1.5	1.5
Furniture and household durables	5.4	6.1	5.7	4.3	3.4	2.2	1.3	1.0	1.6
Nonmetallic mineral products	9.0	10.2	9.4	3.4	1.6	3.7	3.0	1.3	—
Transportation equipment	6.2	7.9	13.8	6.0	2.8	2.3	2.6	2.4	1.8

— Represents zero.
Source: U.S. Bureau of Labor Statistics, *Producer Price Indexes*, monthly and annual.

INDEX OPTION

Table 2 / Summary: Producer and Consumer Price Indices

Prices	Unit	1970	1980	1985	1986	1987
Producer price index:						
Crude materials		35.2	95.3	95.8	87.7	93.7
Fuels, related products and power	1982 = 100	15.3	82.8	91.4	69.8	70.2
Intermediate materials		35.4	90.3	102.7	99.1	101.5
Finished goods		39.3	88.0	104.7	103.2	105.4
Consumer price index, all items		38.8	82.4	107.6	109.6	113.6
Shelter		35.5	81.0	109.8	115.8	121.3
Household fuel and other utilities	1982 - 84 = 100	29.1	75.4	106.5	104.1	103.0
Gas and electricity		25.4	71.4	107.1	105.7	103.8
Transportation		37.5	83.1	106.4	102.3	105.4
Food		39.2	86.8	105.6	109.0	113.5

Source: U.S Department of Labor, Bureau of Labor Statistics.

are rebased to 1967 to conform to standards established by the Office of Federal Statistical Policy and Standards.

The index categories are based on the nomenclature of the Standard International Trade Classification System of the United Nations, revised 1963, except where noted. The individual export price indexes are weighted by 1975 export values according to the Schedule B classification system of the U.S. Bureau of the Census. The prices used in these indexes are collected from a sample of U.S. manufacturers of exports and are "free on board" (f.o.b.) factory transaction prices except where noted. Prices used in the aggregate index for machinery and transportation equipment, which includes price data for categories not shown separately, are also f.o.b. factory prices with the exception of detailed categories as noted. For the import price indexes, products have been classified and weighted by the 1975 Tariff Schedule of the United States Annotated (TSUSA), a schedule for describing and reporting the product composition and value of U.S. imports. Import prices are based on U.S. dollar prices paid by the U.S. importer. The prices are "free on board" (f.o.b.) foreign port, or "cost, insurance, and freight" (c.i.f.) U.S. port transaction prices as indicated. Prices used in the aggregate indexes for food and intermediate manufactured products are generally c.i.f., although some f.o.b. prices are included.

Historical index series may be obtained from the Office of Prices and Living Conditions, Division of International Prices, Bureau of Labor Statistics, Washington, D.C. 20212.

Other Indexes. Agricultural price indexes in great variety are prepared by the U.S. Department of Agriculture, the other principal price collecting and compiling agency of the federal government. Most basic of the indexes prepared and published that figure in the official calculation of price support levels are the index of prices received by farmers and the index of prices paid by farmers (all items, interest, taxes, and wage rates index is the PARITY INDEX); the former divided by the latter determines the parity ratio.

Most famous of the indexes prepared by the board of governors of the Federal Reserve System is the index of industrial production (*see* PRODUCTION INDEX), which measures changes in the physical volume of output.

The U.S. Department of Commerce in its monthly *Survey of Current Business* assembles a great variety of government and private indexes on various data. Various private and unofficial sources in the U.S. compile and publish indexes regularly, providing important types of data that were unavailable as recently as the 1920s. Internationally, the United Nations, the International Monetary Fund, and the Organization for Economic Cooperation and Development are among the sources for international indexes of economic activity, prices, and production.

Summary. For an evaluation and critique of U.S. price statistics, see *Government Price Statistics*, a Report of the Subcommittee on Economic Statistics of the Joint Economic Committee, July, 1966, summarizing findings and containing recommendations based on hearings on the subject held May 25-27, 1966.

BIBLIOGRAPHY

U.S. DEPARTMENT OF LABOR, BUREAU OF LABOR STATISTICS. *Handbook of Methods.* Latest edition.

INDEX OPTION An OPTION that represents the right to buy or sell a specific value of an index at a set price by a specific date. Index options are regulated by the SECURITIES AND EXCHANGE COMMISSION. An index is a measure of the value of a group of stock, debt securities, foreign currencies, or other interests. Indexes are compiled and published by various sources, including securities markets. An index may be based on the prices of all or only a sample of the underlying securities. Indexes are ordinarily expressed in relation to a base period when the index originated. The base may be adjusted to reflect capitalization changes or to preserve continuity when items are added to (another stock becomes more representative) or dropped (result of mergers and liquidations) from the index group. The indexes propose to reflect the result of price changes during trading. Indexes on which options are traded are updated continually during the day, and values are disseminated at frequent intervals. When an index option is exercised, it is settled in cash, usually based on the closing prices of the constituent stocks of the index.

The options markets in the United States strives to provide continuously competitive and orderly market environments for the purchase and sale of standardized option. Their major functions include the selection of options for trading and the establishment of trading rules. Standardized options are issued by OCC, a clearing agency regulated by the Securities and Exchange Commission. The option buyer looks to OCC and not to any particular option writer for performance. Option writers' obligations are owed to OCC and not to any particular buyer. The obligations of writers are guaranteed by a group of brokerage firms—clearing members—that carry the accounts of writers or their brokers.

Most stock brokerage firms, securities exchanges, and the Options Clearing Corporation have educational publications for investors.

INDICATED YIELD Sometimes used to refer to yields on bonds (either current return or yields to maturity) and stocks, especially when yield is determined by reference to YIELD tables. CROP REPORTS also list indicated yields of crops.

Where common stocks are not on a REGULAR DIVIDEND basis, the indicated yield may be figured on DIVIDEND payments "indicated" by current announcements concerning future dividends or by total paid in the last twelve months.

INDICATORS See ECONOMIC INDICATORS.

INDIFFERENCE CURVE An indifference curve represents graphically alternative combinations of two products toward which a consumer is indifferent. In the diagram below, the individual would be indifferent between the combination of goods X and Y denoted by point A and that denoted by point B. The individual would prefer any combination of these goods that is to the right of the indifference curve, and would not choose to be to the left of the indifference curve.

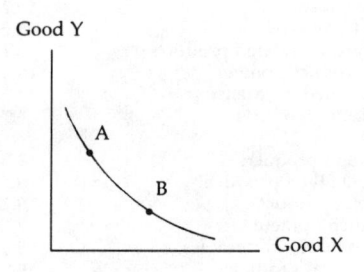

An indifference curve is a theoretical construct used in economics to illustrate certain theoretical propositions, such as the law of demand.

ENCYCLOPEDIA OF BANKING AND FINANCE

INDIRECT EARNINGS EQUITY EARNINGS.

INDIRECT EXCHANGE See ARBITRAGE, ARBITRATION OF EXCHANGE.

INDIRECT TAXES Use taxes levied on the use of certain goods and services. Sales taxes and property taxes are examples of indirect taxes.

INDIVIDUAL BANK DEBITS See BANK DEBITS.

INDIVIDUAL BANK RETURN See BANK RETURN.

INDIVIDUAL BANKER A private bank; an individual partnership or unincorporated association engaged in the banking business and subject to the jurisdiction of the state banking department, as distinguished from an incorporated bank. In most states, the banking function of receiving deposits from the public is restricted to banks incorporated under federal or state law.

INDIVIDUAL DEPOSITS Funds deposited with a bank by individuals, partnerships, firms, and business corporations (other than banking corporations), as distinguished from deposits of banks, trust companies, and other moneyed corporations. The Board of Governors of the Federal Reserve System prepares estimates of individual, partnership, and corporation deposits for its studies on ownership of deposits. Demand deposits, excluding interbank and government deposits, are used in connection with bank debits and calculation of deposit turnover by the board of governors.

INDIVIDUAL RETIREMENT ACCOUNT (IRA)
The Tax Act Reform Act of 1976 authorized a qualified retirement plan for individuals. Currently, a taxpayer with earned income can establish an IRA with a commercial bank, a savings bank, credit union, loan association, and other entities. The annual contribution to an IRA is $2,000 or 100% of compensation, whichever is less. If a taxpayer with earned income has a spouse with minimal or no earned income, the taxpayer may establish a spousal IRA. The total contribution into both IRAs is limited to $2,250 or 100% of compensation, with no more than $2,000 paid into either IRA. The Tax Reform Act of 1986 enacted certain limitations on the deductibility of contributions to an IRA. Once the excess adjusted gross income exceeds $10,000, no portion of a contribution to an IRA is deductible. If the excess is less than $10,000, the deductible portion of an IRA contribution shall not be reduced below $200. The applicable dollar amounts are $40,000 for married taxpayers filing jointly, $25,000 for single taxpayers, and $0 for married taxpayers filing separately. A 6% penalty tax is imposed on any excess contribution left in an IRA after the close of the taxable year.

Income earned in an IRA is tax-exempt, regardless of the deductibility of the contributions to the IRA.

A taxpayer may roll over a lump-sum distribution from a qualified retirement plan rather than paying tax on the distribution (within 60 days of receipt) and defer taxability until a future date.

Except for death or disability, a 10% tax is imposed on any amounts withdrawn before the contributor has attained 59 1/2 years of age. Distributions must start by April in the year after the participant reaches age 70 1/2 to avoid penalties, but can be spread out over the participant's life expectancy.

See KEOGH RETIREMENT PLANS.

INDIVIDUAL TRUSTS See TRUST.

INDUSTRIAL BONDS Bonds issued by industrial corporations (a comprehensive term, encompassing in its conventional use all business corporations other than railroad, public utility, financial, and real estate corporations) including manufacturing, merchandising, service, and extractive industry corporations. The term is so comprehensive as to be virtually a miscellaneous catchall classification and too nonhomogeneous for meaningful analysis. Nevertheless, giving full weight to the differences in operating asset turnover, fluctuation in earnings coverage of charges, and net asset coverages of bonded debt, it is still customary to speak of analysis of industrial bonds in security analysis of various lines of industrial activity.

Industrial bonds, as compared to public utility bonds, are conventionally expected to show higher average earnings coverage of fixed charges in order to command high-grade investment ratings. This reflects the underlying assumption, confirmed empirically in most cases, that earnings available for fixed charges of industrials are likely to be much more susceptible to fluctuation because of the business cycle. Thus industrial bonds, in order to command investment rating, are expected to average earnings (after income taxes) of three times fixed charges. This amounts to requiring earnings available for fixed charges of seven times the fixed charges. Assuming $1 in fixed charges, the net earnings after income taxes would under this test have to be $3.24. With a top corporate income tax bracket of 46%, this means $6 in earnings before income taxes, which, before the $1 in fixed charges, indicates $7 in earnings available for fixed charges. By contrast, investment-grade public utility bonds are expected to show earnings available for fixed charges (before income taxes) of three times. Actually, instead of relying on average earnings coverage ratios, the more conservative approach would be to note the coverage of fixed charges at their worst (usually at the bottom of the business cycle); if a bond can show earnings coverage of charges of two times or better under such conditions, there is relative earnings assurance of interest payments.

As to asset coverage of bonded debt, industrial bonds in the past have been expected to show net fixed assets of at least twice the amount of the bonds. If, in turn, current assets are half the fixed assets and the issuer has a 2:1 current ratio, this would mean net current assets coverage equal to the amount of the bonds. To illustrate, if an industrial corporation has $4 million in net fixed assets, the current assets would be $2 million and a 2:1 current ratio would indicate current liabilities of $1 million; total bonded debt of $2 million would therefore be covered 2 times by net fixed assets and 1:1 by net current assets. Actually, the security device of pledge of fixed assets on bonded debt is more meaningful for its giving secured bondholders the priority of secured creditors over unsecured creditors in the event of reorganization or liquidation. Because most industrial fixed assets are "special purpose" property in nature, and attempted sale in liquidation would usually be in hard times when buyers are even scarcer, fixed assets usually undergo considerable shrinkage in a liquidation that might readily impair even a 2:1 book value ratio to bonded debt. Bondholders would be well advised to normally support, if feasible, a reorganization, as their full claim at book value would be accorded absolute priority in reorganization practice.

Most bonds of this kind are of the revenue (limited liability) type, meaning that the full faith and credit of the issuer is not pledged (if it were, they would be general obligation bonds). Rather, the bonds are dependent upon the rental payments from the lessee to cover interest and principal payments.

After the sharp expansion in volume of new issues of such industrial revenue bonds in the late 1960s, amendment in 1968 to the Internal Revenue Code eliminated the exemption from federal income taxes (which municipal bonds otherwise enjoy) for subsequent issues of industrial revenue bonds of over $5 million.

INDUSTRIAL COLLATERAL Stocks of industrial corporations actively traded on the New York Stock Exchange; one of the two classes of stock exchange COLLATERAL. Brokers who borrow in the CALL MONEY MARKET may present to the lending bank either industrial or regular (also called mixed) collateral.

INDUSTRIAL ORGANIZATION A research and teaching area in economics. According to F. M. Scherer, "The name [industrial organization] is a curious one, distinctive mainly in its inability to communicate to outsiders what the subject is all about." The subject is not the organization of industrial enterprises, but how the organization of industries affects the interactions between consumers and producers.

INDUSTRIAL POLICY In the late 1970s and early 1980s, there were calls for the United States to adopt an industrial policy that would select certain industries for preferential treatment (tax policies and protectionist policies) in order to stimulate their competitiveness in world markets. This notion was patterned after the Japanese strategy of government subsidation to selected industries, such as semiconductors.

Robert Lawrence describes the argument for an industrial policy as: "There are fundamental deficiencies in the U.S. industrial system .... Managers are myopic .... Workers lack discipline .... Trade protection, granted unconditionally, has slowed adjustments to international competition .... The government has failed to plan and coordinate its industrial evolution. It ought to have policies that promote industries with potential and assist those in decline." Advocates for an industrial policy suggested there be a central agency to formulate the policy, operating with advice from industry and from labor. Arguments against having an industrial policy point to the need for the government to strengthen instead the natural forces for increased productivity within the economy by alleviating excessive governmental controls and regulations.

BIBLIOGRAPHY

Economic Report of the President, 1984.
LAWRENCE, R. Z. *Can America Compete?*, 1984.

INDUSTRIAL REVENUE BONDS A special classification of MUNICIPAL BONDS, also called lease rental bonds, typically issued by a municipality to provide funds, for example, for the building of a plant to the specifications of a particular private company, that is granted a long-term lease to the plant at rental designed to be adequate for interest and principal payments on the bonds by the municipality. Motivation for such issues has been to attract desirable industry to particular locations for economic development, and thus another term for such type of bonds has been Industrial Development Bonds, or IDBs.

After the state of Mississippi led the way in 1936, with its "Balance Agriculture with Industry" state legislation authorizing such issues for municipalities, issues of this type were relatively rare until the 1960s, when volume substantially increased to a reported 1968 total of 10% of all long-term tax-exempt state and municipal bond issues. By that time, over 40 states were reported to have passed legislation authorizing such issues; as of 1982, all 50 states and the District of Columbia had enacted laws pertaining to Industrial Revenue Bonds and Small Issue Industrial Development Bonds.

Faced with the rising volume of such IDBs, then exempt from federal income taxes in any amount, the Treasury Department in 1967 issued a ruling making IDBs subject to taxes in any amount, outstanding. The Revenue and Expenditure Control Act of 1968, as amended in 1978, has replaced the Treasury ruling, but has provided tax exemption for specified "small issues" of Industrial Development Bonds in outstanding maximums issued by the municipality of either $1 million or $10 million. The act further specified that substantially all of the proceeds from the small issues must be used to acquire, construct, or improve depreciable property. Besides the "small issue" IDB exemption, the act provided federal tax exemption for issues in any amount for any amount of total capital expenditures on projects of specific types, privately owned, if they satisfy the public-use test, and involve what may be considered traditional municipal functions (sewage or solid-waste disposal facilities, pollution control, water, electricity and gas of a local nature, airports, docks, wharves, sports or convention facilities, mass commuting facilities, industrial parks, etc.). But nontraditional functions also became common.

Tax-exempt bonds were also used to finance residential mortgages, to such an increasing volume in 1979-1980 that the Mortgage Subsidy Bond Tax Act of 1980 was passed prohibiting the issuance of any such bonds to subsidize single-family mortgages after December 31, 1983.

Most IDBs are of the "revenue" (limited liability) type, meaning that the full faith and credit and general taxing power of the issuer are not pledged, which would make them general obligation bonds subject to debt limits, if any, on the issuer. Instead, these issues are dependent upon the receipt of revenue from the private parties financed, to cover interest and principal payments.

See MUNICIPAL BONDS.

INDUSTRIALS See INDUSTRIAL BONDS, INDUSTRIAL STOCKS.

INDUSTRIAL STOCKS Preferred and common stocks of corporations in the "industrial" category (manufacturing, merchandising, service, and extractive industries), as distinguished from railroad, public utility, financial (bank, insurance, finance company, and investment company), and real estate company stocks.

The magnitude of the industrial classification makes it advisable for meaningful analysis to introduce more detailed categories. A current classification, based on nature of industry, is Standard & Poor's breakdown of industrials by subgroups for its group stock indexes, as follows.

Aerospace, air freight, aluminum, automobile, auto parts (after market), auto parts (original equipment), auto trucks and parts, beverages (brewers), beverages (distillers), beverages (soft drinks), building materials (air conditioning), building materials (cement), building materials (heating and plumbing), building materials (roofing and wallboard), chemicals, coal (bituminous), conglomerates, containers (metal and glass), containers (paper), copper, cosmetics, drugs, electrical equipment, electrical-electronics major companies, electrical household appliances, electronics (instrumentation), electronics (semiconductors/components), entertainment, fertilizers, foods, forest products, gaming companies, gold mining, home furnishings, homebuilding, hospital management, hospital supplies, hotel/motel, leisure time, machine tools, machinery (agricultural), machinery (construction and materials handling), machinery (industrial/specialty), metal fabricating, metals (miscellaneous), miscellaneous, mobile homes, office and business equipment, offshore drilling, oil (crude producers), oil (integrated-domestic), oil (integrated-international), Canadian oil and gas exploration, oil well equipment and services, paper, pollution control, publishing, publishing (newspapers), radio-TV broadcasters, railroad equipment, restaurants, retail stores (department stores), retail stores (discount stores), retail stores (drug), retail stores (food chains), retail stores (general merchandise chains), shoes, soaps, steel, sugar refiners, textiles (apparel manufacturers), textile products, textiles (synthetic fibers), tires and rubber goods, tobacco, toys, vending and food service.

The chief characteristics of industrial stocks are the great variety of lines of business they represent; lack of uniformity in methods of operation, accounting, and managerial skill; lack of stability in sales and production and hence in earning power over the business cycle, reflecting the type and demand characteristics of products; and, on the whole, less resort than public utilities and railroads to "trading on the equity" by recourse to bonded debt in capitalization. The last-named characteristic is favorable from the standpoint of earnings stability, for leverage in capitalizations magnifies the swings in earnings on equities over the cycle.

The rise of CONGLOMERATES, especially among industrials, has led to much interindustry diversification. A single parent company thereby has interests in a number of industries with varying characteristics of instability of sales and earning power over the business cycle, financial structure, and growth and expansion possibilities. In addition to analyzing the component parts of such conglomerates, analysis would call for evaluating overall performance of the whole of such combinations.

Industrial equities run the full gamut and range of quality ratings. Among preferred stocks, the highest investment rating is accorded to relatively few industrial preferreds, reflecting the vulnerability of industrial companies' earning power to cyclical fluctuation, in most cases. Many industrials, however, have been successfully financed with convertible preferreds, the conversion feature into common stock imparting common stock appeal to the preferreds in the expectation that the common stock would rise well above the conversion rate from the preferred into the common.

To command high investment rating, an industrial preferred stock should show overall earnings coverage of fixed charges and preferred dividends of at least two times on the average, and few issues substantially exceed this minimum. From the equity standpoint, an industrial preferred stock ideally should be backed at least dollar for dollar by junior common equity, and few issues substantially exceed such minimum.

It is among the industrial common stocks that the outstanding performers in recent years' "bull markets" are found. It is among the industrial common stocks that the premium-priced GROWTH STOCKS have commanded particular attention.

Because common stocks, as the "low men on the totem pole," bear the greatest impact of adverse fluctuation in earnings over the business cycle, and because most industrial companies are vulnerable to the cycle, only a select group of industrial common stocks command the "high grade" rating, which is based on highest numerical rating resulting from combined earnings and dividend stability and growth scores.

In the original financing of many industrial corporations, the preferred stock was often used for the purpose of wholly or partly raising the working capital needed, after bonded debt had financed acquisition of the fixed assets. The common stock often represented "capitalization" of future earning power. Many industrial companies have since built up substantial equity values for their common as well as preferred stock by reinvestment of a portion of annual earnings; with conservatively low dividend pay-out ratios, the bulk of current earnings has been ploughed back into the business for such self-financing purposes as additional working capital, expansion, and payment of debt—a process of internal growth.

Because many industrial common stocks are cyclical in earnings and dividends, and hence in market value, they offer many aggressive investing opportunities when purchase is timed correctly before their major upswings. Growth stocks among the industrials are considered particularly suitable for long-term dollar averaging plans because although such stocks are not immune from considerable cyclical fluctuation, their subsequent recoveries should be to new high levels of earnings, dividends, and market value, in reflection of their superior growth potential. Usually the higher-grade industrial common stocks will also be rated highly as to growth potential, making them suitable for accumulation even during cyclical letdowns. The common stock theory of investment, emphasizing investment in growth equities for superior investing results, particularly relies on selected industrial common stocks for empirical justification. It is also among the industrial common stocks that the so-called hedges against inflation are particularly found, namely equities able to adjust successfully to inflation by showing even faster growth in dollar earnings, dividends, and market value than rise in the price level. Finally, aggressive investors interested in low-priced speculative equities with possibilities of material improvement in a general economic upswing often find these characteristics among industrial common stocks.

See INDUSTRIAL BONDS.

INDUSTRY A collection of all firms producing closely substitutable products. Because there is no operational definition of what closely substitutable means, the government has established for reporting purposes some standard industrial groupings. For example, in the manufacturing sector of the economy there are 20 standard industrial groupings.

BIBLIOGRAPHY

Across the Board. The Conference Board, Inc., New York, NY. Monthly.
American Industry.
AMERICA'S CORPORATE FAMILIES: THE BILLION DOLLAR DIRECTORY. Dun and Bradstreet, Inc., New York, NY. Annual.
Census of Manufacturers. U.S. Bureau of the Census.
DUN'S CENSUS OF AMERICAN BUSINESS. Dun and Bradstreet, Inc. New York, NY. Annual.
Fortune.
FORTUNE 500 DIRECTORY. Time, Inc., New York, NY. Annual.
MILLION DOLLAR DIRECTORY. Dun and Bradstreet, Inc., New York, NY. Annual.
Sources of Information for Industry Analysis. Harvard Business School, Boston, MA. Annual.
Standard and Poor's Register of Corporations, Directors and Executives. Standard and Poor's Corp., New York, NY. Annual.
Thomas Register of American Manufacturers and Thomas Register Catalog File. Thomas Publishing Co., New York, NY. Annual.
United States Industrial Directory. Cahners Publishing Co., Newton, MA. Annual.
Who's Who in Finance and Industry. Marquis Who's Who., Wilmette, IL. Biennial.

INFERIOR GOOD Any good or service whose quantity demanded decreases as income increases. For some consumers, hamburger may be an inferior good. As their income increases, they substitute out of hamburger into a more expensive cut of meat. As a result, the quantity of hamburger demanded falls.

IN-FILE SYSTEM A system for filing checks into separate account files for safekeeping and processing. It provides the basis for the preparation of customers' bank statements.

INFLATION An economic condition characterized by a rise in prices that causes their reciprocal, the purchasing power of money, to fall correspondingly. In this general sense, inflation is the exact opposite of deflation—namely, a decline in the price level, causing the purchasing power of money to rise. In the more specific sense, inflation is a general rise in prices not accompanied by a rise in production of goods and services.

Most concepts of inflation are based on the demand-pull type, i.e., the monetary type in which the supply of money increases without an accompanying increase in the supply of goods and services, so that prices rise (see QUANTITY THEORY OF MONEY). Herewith are several definitions based on this concept.

"I define inflation as a condition brought about when the means of payment in the hands of those who will spend them increase faster than goods can be produced. In other words, the volume and velocity of money must be related to the volume of actual and potential production of real wealth. I asked the question: How is it possible to have inflation when men are idle and plants are idle? There can be speculative excesses when surplus funds bid up stocks or real estate, but inflation in the generally accepted sense can only come about by increasing the means of payment in the hands of people who are willing to spend faster than we can increase production" (Marriner S. Eccles, the chairman of the Board of Governors of the Federal Reserve System, November 22, 1935).

"Inflation exists in a country whenever the supply of money and of bank deposits circulating through checks, so-called deposit currency, increases relatively to the demand for media of exchange in such a way as to bring about a rise in the general price level" (Dr. Edwin W. Kemmerer).

"An increase in the general level of prices growing out of an increase in expenditures while goods available for purchase are not correspondingly increased in amount" (Dr. James Harvey Rogers).

The above demand-pull concept of inflation stresses aggregate excess monetary demand as the causal factor. According to this view, inflation can be controlled by applying conventional monetary and fiscal restraints on the money supply; even if business activity should be dampened in the process, the result will be relative stability in real terms. Such control of the money supply, in this view, will be effective whether the proximate cause of inflation is excessive money supply or cost-induced rise in prices, as the latter also must be "financed" by money supply. A variant of demand-pull theories is the Keynesian view that spending decisions, not the money supply per se, are the primarily causative factors of demand-pull inflation.

A second major concept of inflation in recent years in the United States is the cost-push view of inflation. According to this view, prices have risen persistently in recent years (creeping inflation) in the face of a relatively stable money supply because of "autonomous" upward advances in wages, beyond labor productivity, especially in labor union-dominated industries, and higher costs for other factors of production. (On the other hand, organized labor's view is that the "new" inflation is caused by deliberate increases in "administered" prices by management, unjustified by increases in wages or other costs.)

One group of cost-push theorists believes that cost-push inflation can be restrained by severely restrictive monetary and fiscal policies causing business recession and substantial unemployment, but that this is too high a price to pay for stability. Hence, as the late Dr. Sumner H. Slichter proposed, we should adjust to creeping inflation as inevitable and counteract it by policies designed to maintain maximum output, productivity, and full employment. Another group's remedy for cost-push inflation would be to seek flexibility in prices and wages by rigorous application of the antitrust laws to business and even labor, in an effort to break up "administered" pricing and wage fixing, an approach deemed unrealistic by the Slichterian group in view of the "political facts of life."

Still another concept of the nature of creeping inflation in the United States is factor price inflation. This kind of inflation can occur without either an excess aggregate demand or an autonomous cost push (Dr. Charles L. Schultze, *Recent Inflation in the United States*, 1959). This "originates in excess demand in particular sectors of the economy and spreads via cost increases to other sectors in which demands are not excessive, and indeed to those in which there is unused capacity and unemployment." The boom in business investment and the substitution of fixed costs for variable labor costs have raised fixed costs and breakeven points, so that even at lower

ENCYCLOPEDIA OF BANKING AND FINANCE

operating rates, price increases attempt to recapture the higher fixed costs in particular sectors of industry. In this view, conventional aggregative monetary and fiscal policies, by restricting already low aggregate demand in these sectors, would worsen the situation; instead, selective monetary and fiscal measures aimed at particular sectors where demand for factors is excessive would be necessary to control this type of selective inflation.

Incomes Policy. During the 1960s, the U.S. experienced both a demand-pull and a subsequent cost-push inflation. In 1965, the full employment economic policy of the early 1960s led the economy to a full utilization of its resources. This led to price increases. In effect the economy was becoming overheated with labor shortages in key industries. In an attempt to prevent wages from rising at a faster rate than productivity, the Johnson administration reemphasized the wage guideposts originated in 1962. The purpose of the guideposts for wages was to keep the annual rate of increase of total employee compensation per manhour worked equal to the national trend rate of increase in output per manhour. Wage increases, however, outstripped rise in productivity throughout the latter half of the 1960s, leading to a serious rise in the pace of cost-push inflation. The GNP price deflator began to rise soon after unemployment fell below 4% at the end of 1965. Demand kept rising rapidly after the end of 1965, reducing the unemployment rate below 4% and pushing the pace of inflation still higher. Under those circumstances, "the proper course of policy was clear" (Council of Economic Advisers, *Annual Report*, 1971)^restrictive policy to restrain inflation, which would carry little if any cost in the form of rise in unemployment. But by early 1970, rising unemployment rates began to accompany rising inflation rates. The dilemma of policy as of early 1971 was concisely stated by the Council of Economic Advisers as follows. Confining the economic expansion to a pace that would keep unemployment in the neighborhood of 5.5% to 6% would permit a significant decline in the rate of inflation during 1971 and 1972, but allowing so high an unemployment rate to persist for so long a time would be inconsistent with the Employment Act of 1946 and "undesirable even if there were no act." On the other hand, trying to restore full employment (a 4% unemployment rate) would entail risks on the inflation side.

The Council of Economic Advisers in its 1971 *Annual Report* reported widespread public support for direct price and wage controls, "even if the full consequences that these controls would have in distortions and black markets" were not perceived. But the council concluded that "short of an emergency of a kind which does not exist, mandatory comprehensive price and wage controls are undesirable, unnecessary, and probably unworkable."

On August 15, 1971, the President of the U.S. announced a 90-day price-wage freeze, which was extended October 7, 1971, into the subsequent three phases of compulsory price and wage controls, the first in the peacetime history of the U.S., details of which are given in INCOMES POLICY.

Reflation. This term is more aptly descriptive of credit expansion and a general rise in trade and prices on a real basis that occurs during a period of revival or recovery following a condition of recession or depression. The condition of inflation should be reserved for that final phase of expansion when the economy reaches full employment of resources and prices continue upward in speculative excesses of bidding for goods and services, commodities, stock prices, etc., or "pure inflation," in a splurge of aggregate demand relative to given available supplies of factors, output, and inventories.

Stagflation occurs when the economy has slowed down but inflation persists. The U.S. economy has experienced stagflation several times in recent decades.

The terms "currency inflation" and "credit inflation" refer to the nature of the expansion in money supply creating a condition of pure inflation. Credit inflation is a condition of excessive expansion of commercial bank credit, resulting in excessive volume of bank deposits relative to supply of factors, output, and inventories. Currency inflation is a more primitive type of inflation of the money supply caused by deliberate increase in the currency supply or tinkering with the money unit. Modern inflations have been credit inflations, i.e., expansions in the volume and velocity of bank credit and bank deposits, constituting the bulk of the effective money supply of modern credit systems. Both types of inflations may be effectively controlled by conservative monetary and fiscal policies; the "revival of monetary policy" in recent years, for example, refers to the greater effectiveness of restrictive monetary policy when bank credit is deeply involved in financing an inflation.

Currency manipulation undertaken deliberately by the federal government, as an artificial means of coercing spending, was last tried in the U.S. in the early years of the Franklin D. Roosevelt administration in an extraordinary attempt to stimulate recovery from the severe 1932 depression. This manipulation was intended to raise commodity prices, ease the burden of public and private debt, decrease the claims of creditors in terms of commodity prices considered abnormally low in comparison with prices at the time the credits were extended, prevent further bankruptcies and permit unfreezing of frozen bank assets, protect gold (or other metallic) reserves, and stimulate demand for the nation's products (by lowering the exchange rates of the currency) in world markets. The general objective was to force up the general price level by deliberate alteration of the money side of the equation of exchange, either by increasing the quantity of money, impairing its quality (denying its redeemability, lowering the standard monetary metallic content of the unit, and introducing fiat money or greenbacks), coercing an increase in velocity of circulation, or all three. The grave calculated risk involved was loss of general confidence in the dollar. That a rampant flight from the dollar and a raging currency inflation did not occur was due to the fact that the Roosevelt administration was more conservative monetarily than its actions bespoke; for example, the gold profit of $2 billion resulting from devaluation of the dollar was not fed to the credit system, the $3 billion authority to issue greenbacks under the Thomas Amendment of 1933 was never used, and the monetary nationalization of silver was subsequently repealed.

In the era before the modern credit systems developed, the common form of currency manipulation was debasement of the coinage. A sovereign, hard pressed for funds and not willing or able to impose heavier taxes, had only to substitute baser coins for those outstanding or reduce their metallic content. The assignat inflation of the French Revolution, usually regarded along with the German currency inflation culminating in 1924 as the most disastrous in history, was a deliberate paper money inflation.

Types of Currency Manipulation. Changes in the currency unit designed to produce inflationary consequences include the following.

1. Suspension of redemption in basic monetary metal (gold). This may also mean an embargo on gold exports. Usually, suspension of gold payments involves loss of both rights. It does not, however, necessarily prevent the maintenance of a free gold market in the country that suspends gold payments. It does mean that gold will command a higher price in terms of the currency no longer redeemable in gold, such higher price depending on the intensity of the demand for gold as a means of flight from the currency and on the market's judgment of the basic worth of that currency in terms of gold.
2. Devaluation, i.e., lowering of the gold (or other standard metal) content of the monetary unit and seizure by the government of the resulting "write-up" or profit on gold stocks.
3. Introduction into the monetary system of other monetary metals, such as silver, through BIMETALLISM (without a definite ratio of coinage with the previously monometallic standard metal) or through SYMMETALLISM.
4. Issuance of fiat or irredeemable paper money having only legal tender power as its element of value, usually without limitation as to size of issue.

Suspension of gold payments is an extraordinary procedure for protecting gold reserves or temporarily stimulating export trade, and may be initiated as a defensive measure without inflationary intent. England's suspension of gold payments on September 21, 1931, was designed in furtherance of these ends. Another major purpose of England's suspension of gold payments was to experiment with MANAGED CURRENCY, a policy of releasing the currency unit from the anchor of a fixed gold price, and allowing the currency unit to seek lower levels in the foreign exchange markets, protected against sharp or sudden fluctuations by operations of the EXCHANGE EQUALIZATION FUND.

Strictly speaking, therefore, the mere suspension of gold payments, without other changes in monetary practice, is not, ipso facto, an inflationary step. It may or may not lead to inflation, and it may or may not lead, after a period of trial and de facto stabilization, to a revaluation of the monetary unit at a new but lower gold par value. Experience with managed currency in the 1930s, however, indicated that any temporary advantage derived thereby internationally by a nation is soon vitiated by defensive measures by other countries of the same type, leading in turn to countermeasures and further retaliation, establishment of EXCHANGE RESTRICTIONS, trade barriers, etc., so that the end result is reduced international trade and financial relations. A basic aim of the INTERNATIONAL MONETARY FUND for the post-World War II world was the stimulation of such relations by establishment of par values for currency units, removal of exchange and trade restrictions, and an ending of manipulative paraphernalia of managed currency in its international aspects. Domestically, any exercise of monetary and fiscal policy is management, but this is conventional and expected in modern credit systems.

Devaluation, like suspension of gold payments, does not per se assure a price rise automatically. Devaluation is the statutory adoption of a new monetary unit of less metallic weight (and value) than that which preceded it. France, Belgium, and Italy are examples of countries that devalued their units in the years 1924-1928 by from 75% to 80%, after being off gold a number of years. The inflation in these countries occurred previous to devaluation so that actual devaluation was intended to stabilize prices at the higher levels. Led by the 30.5% devaluation of the pound sterling, 28 countries by October 18, 1949, had devalued their currencies, including most Western European nations, countries in the sterling area, and Finland, Canada, Argentina, and Uruguay. The immediate reason for this devaluation of the pound sterling was the heavy loss in monetary reserves of the United Kingdom. In contrast to the previous wave of devaluations in the 1930s, this series of devaluations was motivated primarily by the dollar balance-of-payments problem, and most countries devalued to approximately the same extent as the United Kingdom, thus maintaining exchange values relative to the pound sterling, but like the UK assuming new positions relative to the dollar. The devaluations were accompanied by adoption of policies designed to control inflation in the devaluing countries but at the same time maintain the competitive advantage in selling to dollar markets. Devaluation provides new pars in foreign exchange, affords the government an opportunity to utilize the gold profit, and provides a basis for controlled credit expansion.

The crudest and most direct method of achieving inflation, whether voluntarily by intent or involuntarily through inability to meet obligations, is by the issuance of fiat or irredeemable paper money. Issuance of irredeemable paper is considered the grossest form of debasement of the currency, a deliberate injection of additional claims for goods or services of the economy without justification of commensurate increase in supply of goods and services. The deliberate expansion in the money supply that will be accompanied by discrimination against the fiat currency will cause prices to rise and purchasing power to decline. If the issue of fiat paper money continues, the rise in prices and depreciation in purchasing power will be aggravated, leading to the necessity for additional issue, causing further inflation, and so on in a spiral that will result ultimately in utter worthlessness of the currency. This will ruin the creditor classes, owning claims to fixed sums of money that will now be worthless, and will rob the wage earners and salaried persons paid for their services in fast depreciating fiat currency, as well as the pensioners, annuitants, insurance policy owners, bank depositors, and all holders of claims in currency units. The continental currency of our preconstitutional government, the inflation in France in the years 1790-1796, and the German paper money inflation of 1920-1924 are the frequently cited examples of paper money hyperinflation that developed to the ultimate extreme of worthlessness. Our Civil War greenback history furnished an example of a paper money inflation that was limited and controlled.

For Civil War paper money inflation, *see* GREENBACKS.

Continental Currency Inflation. The American Revolutionary War was financed largely by the printing of continental dollars on the authorization of the Continental Congress, with the "faith of the Continent" as the only backing. The Continental Congress had no power to tax and could only lay levies upon the states for revenues that were progressively more difficult to collect; thus the Congress was obliged to resort to additional issues of continentals for payment of federal expenses. Over a five year period, 1775-1779, 40 issues aggregating $241,552,780 were resorted to by the Congress. Redemption of the continentals was placed by the Continental Congress upon the states, but instead of honoring redemption of the continentals, the states issued paper money of their own, aggregating $209,424,776 in the period 1775-1789, including additional issues after the continentals became worthless in 1781.

One of the early histories tells the story in these words. "During the summer of 1780 this wretched Continental currency fell into contempt. As Washington said, it took a wagon load of money to buy a wagon load of provisions. At the end of the year 1778, the paper dollar was worth 16 cents in the northern states and 12 cents in the south. Early in 1780 its value had fallen to two cents, and before the end of the year it took ten paper dollars to make a cent.

"In October, Indian corn sold wholesale in Boston for $150 a bushel, butter was $12 a pound, tea $90, sugar $10, beef $8, coffee $12, and a barrel of flour cost $1,575. Samuel Adams paid $2,000 for a hat and a suit of clothes. The money soon ceased to circulate, debts could not be collected, and there was a general prostration of credit."

The final result of this inflation is best summed up in the old saying, "not worth a continental," which has come down to even modern times as an expression of worthlessness.

French Assignat Inflation. The French assignats that were issued between 1790 and 1796 are an outstanding example of deliberate inflation. The French revolutionary government was confronted with the problem of both raising revenue and overcoming a condition of business depression. In response to the demands of the inflationists, the Constituent Assembly in April, 1790, authorized the issuance of assignats to the amount of 400 million livres, to be legal tender and to bear interest at 3%. The currency was to be secured by church lands recently seized.

At the beginning, the effect was to relieve the Treasury of some of its burdens and to stimulate trade. As soon as the assignats began to circulate, however, they depreciated to the extent of about 5%. The 400 million livres of paper were soon exhausted, and there was an immediate agitation for the issuance of additional currency. It was even claimed that the first issue had been a success. Mirabeau, a leading inflationist of the day, advocated that currency be issued equal to the amount of the whole national debt and insisted that such action would bring prosperity to the nation. The Assembly in September, 1790, by a vote of 508 to 423, approved the issuance of additional assignats up to a total of 1.2 billion livres. This issue bore no interest and was payable to bearer but provided that as fast as the assignats were paid in for land they should be burned.

In the latter stages of the issuance of assignats, the printing presses were run at the will of the executive authority, blanket authorization being given for the reissuance of such amounts as might be needed. Within a year, the discount on assignats ran from 18% to 20%, and within two years it amounted to 44%. About that time there was a temporary rise in their value, but in 1795 a rapid depreciation commenced. By February, 1796, it required 288 paper francs to equal one gold franc. Prices of various necessities soared, that of sugar rising 69 times and soap 44 times. Finally the populace joined in a public burning of the printing press machinery on which the assignats had been printed.

In October, 1795, a new government was established, the Directory. It tried to restore order out of the currency chaos by issuing in February, 1796, a new kind of paper money called mandats, secured only by choice public lands. One mandat was made worth 30 assignats. The mandats immediately depreciated to 30% of face value, then fell to 15%, and finally to 5%. On July 16, 1796, the inevitable happened; the Directory decreed that all paper could be accepted at its real value, which meant at nothing. The people ceased even to compute the depreciation after that. When Bonaparte took the consulship, the largest loan available in the land would not meet the government's expenses for a single day.

Unable to do business in such rapidly depreciating money, the market women of Paris had marched on the Assembly and made an appeal, famous among economists, that "laws should be passed making paper as good as gold." The Assembly's actions included the following: in April 1793, a forced loan of 1 billion livres was levied upon the rich; in July of that year, the estates of the nobility were confiscated, and these lands, estimated at 3 billion livres, were also pledged behind the paper money to make it more valuable.

In 1793, 6 years in prison was made the penalty for selling gold at more than its nominal value in paper. Six months later, selling assignats at less than face value was made worth 20 years in prison. Two years later, the guillotine was provided for any Frenchman who made investments in a foreign country.

Napoleon Bonaparte saw enough of paper money inflation in the years 1790-1796 to convince him of its fallacious and dangerous nature. When he took the consulship, conditions were appalling. The government was bankrupt, the troops were unpaid, the further collection of taxes appeared impossible. Nevertheless, when asked at his first cabinet meeting what he intended to do, Napoleon replied: "I will pay cash or nothing!" ("cash" meaning specie), and he carried out that promise to the letter. "While I live," he declared, when he was hard pressed on another occasion, "I will never resort to irredeemable paper."

German Post-World War I Inflation. Germany was involved in budgetary difficulties after World War I. Its national expenditures had increased fivefold during the war period, and its national debt, sixfold. The paper money in circulation had increased from less than 3 billion marks at the beginning of the war to 29 billion at the end of November, 1918. Wholesale prices in Germany more than doubled during the war period. Considering the large expansion of currency, the rise in prices up to the time of the Armistice was moderate.

The German government had borrowed from the Reichsbank during the war by the process of discounting Treasury bills. This was done to an increased extent as it became necessary to meet deficits in the postwar period. By the time the stage of hyperinflation was reached toward the end of 1923, the volume of Treasury bills held by the Reichsbank totaled nearly 200 quintillion marks.

What happened during 1922 and 1923 was unlike anything that had ever occurred in the world's monetary history. Paper marks depreciated more rapidly than the continental currency of the U.S. in Revolutionary War days, or the assignats of France, also in the latter part of the eighteenth century. The expenditures of the German government increased from 145 billion marks for the year ending March 31, 1921, to more than 8 trillion marks two years later, and to 49 quadrillion marks the next year. It was impossible to keep up with expenditures by levying more taxes. Currency in circulaton, which amounted to 252 billion marks in August, 1922, increased to 2 trillion marks in January, 1923, to 28 quadrillion marks in September, 1923, and finally reached a total of 497 quintillion marks at the end of 1923.

By November 20, 1923, one gold mark was regarded as equal to 1 billion paper marks. New Rentenbank notes that were issued at about that time as an intermediate step toward stabilization were exchanged at the rate of one for 1 billion paper marks. Subsequently, when the Reichsbank was reorganized in October, 1924, it issued new gold reichsmarks, one of which was equivalent to 1 trillion old paper marks.

During the inflationary period, the gold value of the mark as quoted in foreign exchange dropped from an original par of 23.82 cents to about one-half cent in December, 1921; one-hundredth of a cent in December, 1922; and three-trillionths of a cent in December, 1923.

The business of accumulating and investing capital in Germany was completely demoralized by the inflation. No one wanted to keep money in the banks. In 1922, all savings in Germany amounted to only 3 billion gold marks, against 20 billion reported by the savings banks alone two years earlier. Speculation was rampant, resulting in excesses in various fields. How much of this capital was remunerative may be judged from the fact that dividend payments in 1922, measured in their gold value, were only one-fiftieth of what they had been before the war.

Russian Post-World War I Inflation. Russia was plunged into currency inflation by efforts to finance governmental deficits through the issuance of fiat money. Early in World War I, the Russian Treasury was allowed to discount its short-term obligations at the state bank to any extent desired, previous restrictions being removed. The currency was on an irredeemable paper basis. As early as 1916, there was only paper money in circulation. The government obtained enormous amounts from the bank. Between January 1, 1917, and January 1, 1923, the quantity of money in circulation increased two hundred thousand times, while prices rose ten million times. The depreciation was more rapid than the rate of issuance of currency. A new Soviet state bank issued notes to meet deficits of the Treasury during 1922 and 1923. Finally in 1924, a new ruble was issued in exchange for 50 billion of the old depreciated rubles.

Types of Price Changes. There are two basic types of price changes:

1. *Specific price levels:* price changes of a specific commodity or item, such as a car or house; and
2. *General price level:* price changes of a group of goods and services.

In a technical sense, inflation refers to changes in the general price level. When the general price level increases, the dollar loses purchasing power—the ability to purchase goods or services. The opposite situation is referred to as deflation. Holding monetary assets and liabilities during periods of inflation or deflation results in purchasing power gains or losses. Monetary items are assets and liabilities that are fixed in terms of current dollars and cannot fluctuate to compensate for the change in the general price level. Monetary assets include cash, receivables, and liabilities.

Changes in the general price level can affect, adversely or otherwise, almost every business decision. Changes in the general price level can affect organizational planning, controlling, and evaluating functions:

1. Is any of the budgeted or reported net income due to inflation?
2. Did the company lose or gain purchasing power from inflation due to holding monetary assets and liabilities?
3. How did inflation affect the financial statements during the period?
4. Were changes in the general price level tgaken into consideration when budgets were prepared? When dividend policy was determined? When analyzing financial statements? When evaluating performance of investment centers? When selecting a source or method of financing?

A price index is used to measure changes in price levels. A price index is a series of numbers, one for each period, representing an average price of a group of goods and services, relative to the average price of the same group of goods and services at a base period. The consumer price index for all urban consumers, published by the Bureau of Labor statistics of the Department of Labor in the *Monthly Labor Review*, is perhaps the most widely used price index. Current cost information is needed to deal with changes in specific prices. Replacement costs are commonly used in current cost systems and for decisions involving specific prices.

The appended table shows the purchasing power of the dollar: 1950 to 1987, for producer and consumer prices.

Summary. These examples of currency hyperinflation are not intended to be alarmist, but their lesson is plain, particularly illustrated by the experience of Germany, a financially most advanced nation with a modern credit system: the problem originates with budgetary deficits of the government; an easy solution therefor is financing the Treasury deficits through the central bank directly, instead of forcing the Treasury to finance in the open market. Although there were extenuating circumstances in the German post-World War I situation, direct financing of Treasury deficits through the central bank makes the latter an engine of inflation. In the U.S., direct financing by the Treasury through the Federal Reserve banks is authorized by Congress only for renewable periods and with limits on such direct financing. In practice, the Treasury resorts to such financing to tide it over low tax collection periods. But even though conventionally financed, persistent federal budget deficits monetize the debt and add to inflationary pressures by increasing the money supply through the banking system.

See GOLD STANDARD, INCOMES POLICY.

BIBLIOGRAPHY

CAPAS, P. and LIPSEY, R. E. "The Financial Effects of Inflation." *National Bureau of Economic Research.*

INFLATIONARY EXPECTATIONS The expectation of inflation in the future has an important impact on certain economic phenomena. For example, nominal interest rates are a combination of two components—a real rate of interest that compensates lenders for their risk and an inflationary expectations component that reflects the fact that the value of the paid-back money is less than the loaned money owing to inflation.

The expectation of inflation may also increase current demand in anticipation of higher prices in the future. This, in turn, puts real upward pressure on prices, which then translates into actual inflation. When inflation is observed, consumers' expectations of inflation are reinforced and the demand-push inflationary spiral continues.

INFORMATION SYSTEMS A process that organizes and communicates relevant information on a timely basis to enable man-agement to perform its functions properly. The term system

Purchasing Power of the Dollar: 1950 to 1987

[Indexes: PPI, 1982 = $1.00; CPI, 1982-84 = $1.00. Producer prices prior to 1961, and consumer prices prior to 1964, exclude Alaska and Hawaii. Producer prices based on finished goods index. Obtained by dividing the average price index for the 1982 = 100, PPI; 1982-84 = 100, CPI base periods (100.0) by the price index for a given period and expressing the result in dollars and cents. Annual figures are based on average of monthly data]

Year	Annual Average as Measured by	
	Producer prices	Consumer prices
1950	$3.546	$4.151
1951	3.247	3.846
1952	3.268	3.765
1953	3.300	3.735
1954	3.289	3.717
1955	3.279	3.732
1956	3.195	3.678
1957	3.077	3.549
1958	3.012	3.457
1959	3.021	3.427
1960	2.994	3.373
1961	2.994	3.340
1962	2.985	3.304
1963	2.994	3.265
1964	2.985	3.220
1965	2.933	3.166
1966	2.841	3.080
1967	2.809	2.993
1968	2.732	2.873
1969	2.632	2.726
1970	2.545	2.574
1971	2.469	2.466
1972	2.392	2.391
1973	2.193	2.251
1974	1.901	2.029
1975	1.718	1.859
1976	1.645	1.757
1977	1.546	1.649
1978	1.433	1.532
1979	1.289	1.380
1980	1.136	1.215
1981	1.041	1.098
1982	1.000	1.035
1983	.984	1.003
1984	.964	.961
1985	.955	.928
1986	.969	.913
1987	.949	.880

Source: U.S. Bureau of Labor Statistics. Monthly data in U.S. Bureau of Economic Analysis, *Survey of Current Business.*

refers to the components or subsystems that interact and interrelate to accomplish a goal or objective.

The activities of an information system include collection, processing, and communication of information. A management information system includes the means by which information is provided to decision makers so that they may attain the organization's goals and objectives. The major attributes of an MIS include the: relevance, accuracy, timeliness, completeness, conciseness, economy, and flexibility. Subsystems of a typical business organization include: personnel subsystems, purchasing subsystems, production subsystems, marketing subsystems, order-processing subsystems, and financial subsystems. A primary subsystem is one that impacts the entire structure of an organization. A secondary subsystem is one that is limited to a single functional part of an organization.

Developing an MIS involves the following steps:

1. Establish the goals of the system.
2. Identify the information needed to attain the goal.
3. Design the system.
4. Test the system.
5. Implement the system.
6. Monitor and control the system.

These steps can be expanded in terms of a feasibility assessment and system design:

1. *Feasibility assessment:* preliminary analysis of current system; identification of reporting needs; requirements in terms of people, equipment, and forms; preliminary assessment of costs and benefits.
2. *System design:* complete description of the system; testing design to ensure that it can accomplish what it is supposed to accomplish.

A management accounting system should be designed to provide timely and accurate information to help management develop product costs, control costs, improve productivity, increase efficiency and effectiveness, and motivate and evaluate performance. The system should serve as a communications channel between various levels of management, especially as they relate to (1) organizational goals and objectives and (2) product performance and production efficiencies. Sophisticated electronic technology is available to develop reporting and control systems that are accurate, timely, and effective.

BIBLIOGRAPHY

Advances in Information Systems Science. Plenum Publishing Corp. New York, NY. Annual.
AMERICAN MANAGEMENT ASSOCIATION. *How to Audit MIS.* American Management Association, New York, NY.
BANK ADMINISTRATION INSTITUTE. *A Financial Information System for Community Banks* (an eight-volume set). Bank Administration Institute, Rolling Meadows, IL, 1984.
BARROW, C., "Executive Information Systems: Automating the CFO Function." *Magazine of Bank Administration*, May, 1988.
EDP Performance Management Handbook. Applied Computer Research, Inc., Phoenix, AZ. Looseleaf.
Encyclopedia of Information Systems and Services. Gale Research,Inc., Detroit, MI, 1989.
FRIEDMAN, J. P. "Information Technology: The Path to Competitive Advantage." *Magazine of Bank Administration*, 62:1, 1986.
REBSGAWM, W, W. "How Profitable Are Your Cash Management Services?" *Magazine of Bank Administration*, May, 1988.
RODGERS, W., and HOUSEL, T. J. "Effects of Information and Cogitative Processes on Decision Making." *Accounting and Business Research*, Winter, 1987.
VIOLANTO, M. "Friendly Software for the Bank CEO." *Bankers Monthly*, May, 1988.

INGOT A bar of metal cast from a mold, such as gold, silver, copper, tin, lead, zinc, etc.

The 400-ounce gold bar is good delivery in international gold movements. Commercial silver bars are 1,000-ounce bars.

See GOLD BARS, SILVER BULLION.

INHERITANCE In popular usage, any property obtained through devise or bequest (by WILL) or through descent and distribution (by laws of intestacy). In the technical sense, inheritance at common law refers to the estate in real property descending to heirs. In New York, all distinctions in intestacy between persons taking as heirs or heirs at law and next of kin were abolished August 31, 1930, and the descent or distribution of real property or personal property now applies to a uniform class of takers called distributees, including a surviving spouse.

See DESCENT, LAWS OF; TESTATOR.

INHERITANCE LAWS Taxes imposed by practically every state in the United States upon the right to receive property by inheritance or succession. They are collected but once—at the time of the transfer of the inheritance to the beneficiaries—unlike other taxes, which are collected periodically.

Inheritance taxes are to be distinguished from the federal ESTATE TAXES that are imposed on the privilege of transferring property at death. Inheritance taxes are of two kinds—direct and collateral. The first applies to property directly descending to the next of kin, e.g., son, daughter, father, mother. The administration and rate of the tax differs among the different jurisdictions. Most inheritance taxes are progressive, the percentage increasing with the size of the estate or individual shares, and with the remoteness of kinship. In England, inheritance taxes are called "death duties."

IN-KIND TRANSFERS Subsidies to individuals that reduce the cost of specific goods and services such as education, food stamps and nutritional programs, housing, medical care, energy assistance, and child care. In-kind transfers are government programs that seek to increase the consumption of the subsidized goods and services.

INLAND BILL As defined by the former Negotiable Instruments Law, a bill of exchange that was or on its face purported to be both drawn and payable within the state (Sec. 129, Uniform Negotiable Instruments Law). Any other bill was a foreign bill. The term was frequently used, however, as synonymous with domestic bill. A foreign bill was required to be protested in case of dishonor, but an inland bill did not have to be (Sec. 152, Uniform Negotiable Instruments Law), although it frequently was because of the evidentiary value of the notarial certificate of protest.

The Uniform Commercial Code (UCC) has eliminated the requirement of protest, except where the instrument is drawn or payable outside the United States and its territories, dependencies, and possessions, and the District of Columbia, and the Commonwealth of Puerto Rico, in which cases it is necessary in order to charge the drawer and endorsers of the instrument unless excused (Sec. 3-511). However, the UCC provides that the holder may at his option make protest of any dishonor of any other instrument and, in the case of a foreign draft, may on insolvency of the acceptor before maturity make protest for better security (Sec. 3-501(3)).

INPUT-OUTPUT ANALYSIS In economics, applies to the input-output money flow system of aggregative national income accounting, and analysis of demand for input—factors in production—for a given output.

1. The input-output money flow methodology provides a system of accounts that include all the allocations made by major sectors of the economy (or every industry) in connection with current production. Each sector or industry is counted twice—for its output and for its input. For example, an industry's total output of $200 billion might have gone $100 billion to manufacturing and $100 billion to households for consumption, and so output is distributed under the latter headings. As to input, the $200 billion might have consisted of $125 billion outlay for labor and $75 billion for industrial materials, and so be listed under household labor and manufacturing. This technique was developed by Dr. Wassily Leontief, the Harvard mathematician.
2. The marginal productivity theory is applied in economics to analysis of production and income distribution (shares in the final product for the productive factors). Based on the rational principle of maximizing aggregate profits, the firm will utilize the most profitable combination of fixed and variable factors of production, at prevailing prices, to the point where net revenue yield from the last or marginal unit is equal to its marginal factor cost. In business practice, breakeven points are figured, based on prevailing variable and fixed expenses, and management seeks to keep sales volume as high past the breakeven point and as close to capacity as possible in order to maximize profit. This may be done on an aggregative dollar basis or on a per unit basis, but only rarely do cost accountants resort to marginal analysis, although the underlying reasoning may be essentially the same.

INPUT-OUTPUT TABLE The Department of Commerce publishes input-output tables for the U.S. economy about every five years. The most recent table describes the 1982 economy and is published in the Survey of Current Business. The data in these tables relate the distribution of inputs in various industries to these uses in other industries. Among other things, these tables illustrate the extent to which industries are interrelated.

INSCRIBED STOCK Stocks or bonds that in English practice exclusively are registered in the name of the holder on the books of the issuing organization and for which no actual certificates (in the U.S. sense) are issued. The owner of inscribed stocks, besides being registered on the company's books as owning a certain number of shares, is given a memorandum of ownership. This memorandum does not prove title nor constitute ownership, and it is nonnegotiable. It cannot be sold or assigned as a stock certificate in America. In order to transfer inscribed stock, the holder must personally attend to the transfer by presenting his memorandum of ownership and signing the inscribed stock register. The original certificate of ownership is then destroyed and a new one issued in its place in the name of the transferee or buyer.

Inscribed stock differs from registered stock in that in the former no actual certificates of ownership are issued, the memorandum of ownership not constituting proof of title.

As a rule, only British government or municipal loans are issued as inscribed stock, British CONSOLS being an example. Most of the securities on the London Stock Exchange are in registered rather than inscribed form. Dividends or interest upon inscribed stock are remitted by check.

INSIDER A person who, because of his employment or business connections, has intimate knowledge of the financial affairs of a concern before such information is published and is available to the public. He is therefore in a peculiarly advantageous position for capitalizing on this information by speculating, i.e., making commitments in the securities of the concern in accordance with this knowledge, in advance of the public.

Under Section 16 of the SECURITIES EXCHANGE ACT OF 1934, every person who is directly or indirectly the beneficial owner of more than 10% of any class of an equity security (except exempted securities) registered on a national securities exchange, or who is a director or officer, is required to file at the time of registration of the security, or within ten days after becoming such owner, director, or officer, a statement with the exchange and with the Securities and Exchange Commission of the amount of all equity securities of the issuing company of which he is the owner. Thereafter, within ten days after the close of each calendar month, he is required to file with the exchange and the commission a statement, if there has been any change in ownership during the month, indicating his ownership at the close of the calendar month and such changes in his ownership as have occurred during the month.

Similar provisions applicable to insiders of registered public utility holding companies and registered closed-end investment companies are contained in the PUBLIC UTILITY HOLDING COMPANY ACT OF 1935 and the Investment Company Act.

The Securities Exchange Act goes on to provide that for the purpose of preventing the unfair use of information which may have been obtained by such beneficial owner, director, or officer by reason of his relationship to the issuer, any profit realized by him from any purchase and sale, or any sale and purchase, of any equity security of the issuing company (other than an exempted security) within any period of less than six months shall inure to and be recoverable by the issuing company, unless such security was acquired in good faith in connection with a debt previously contracted. This recovery shall be irrespective of any intention on the part of such beneficial owner, director, or officer in entering into the transaction of holding the security purchased or of not repurchasing the security sold for a period exceeding six months.

Suit to recover such profit may be instituted at law or in equity in any court of competent jurisdiction by the issuing company, or by the owner of any security of the issuer in the name and in behalf of the issuing company if the latter fails or refuses to bring suit within 60 days after request or fails diligently to prosecute the suit thereafter. However, no such suit shall be brought more than two years after the date such profit was realized.

In connection with insider securities transactions under Section 16 of the Securities Exchange Act, the Securities and Exchange Commission has adopted various amendments to Rules 16B-3 and 16a-6(c) under the act for the purpose of including specified transactions in STOCK APPRECIATION RIGHTS within the exemptions provided by those rules. The amendments exempt from the reporting requirements of Section 16(a) and the shortswing profit recovery provisions of Section 16(b) cash settlement of stock appreciation rights by insiders, provided certain conditions are met. Included among those conditions are requirements relative to the issuer, the rights, and the administration of the plan under which the rights are granted. In addition, the amendments clarify the conditions for the availability of the exemption provided by Rule 16b-3 and make clear the circumstances under which amendments to existing plans must be submitted to an issuer's security holders for approval.

In addition, Section 16 of the Securities Exchange Act of 1934 provides that it shall be unlawful for any such beneficial owner, director, or officer either directly or indirectly to sell any equity security of the issuing company (other than an exempted security) if the person selling the security or his principal does not own the security sold or, if owning the security, does not deliver it against such sale within five days after such sale by depositing it in the mails or using other usual channels of transportation. This provision does not apply in the case of inability to make delivery or deposit within the deadline despite exercise of good faith, or where undue inconvenience or expense is involved.

See INSIDER TRADING SANCTIONS ACT OF 1984.

INSIDER TRADING Trading in securities of a company by one who has special information not available to the general public or stockholders concerning the company because of his or her position with the company or with a person who holds such a position. Many serious violations of insider trading rules during the 1980s discredited major investment houses and traders.

The SEC requires that officers, directors, and stockholders owning more than 10% of a corporation whose securities are listed on a national securities exchange must file monthly reports with the commission.

BIBLIOGRAPHY

A Year of Insider Trades. Staff of *The Insider's Chronicle*, 1984.

INSIDER TRADING AND SECURITIES FRAUD ENFORCEMENT ACT OF 1988 Federal legislation designed to discourage and punish insider trading in securities and securities fraud. One provision of the act authorizes the SEC to award bounties to individuals who provide insider trading information. The bounties are paid out of monies recovered as penalties under the act (instead of directly to the Treasury). Bounties that can be paid from a civil penalty may not exceed 10% of that penalty.

INSIDER TRADING SANCTIONS ACT OF 1984 An act that increased the penalties against persons who profit from illegal use of insider information. The act allows the SEC to seek fines of up to three times the profits gained or losses avoided by those insiders who improperly use material nonpublic information. The act also increases from $10,000 to $100,000 the criminal penalties for market manipulation, securities fraud, and certain other violations. The act does not define "material inside information" or limit its prohibitions to corporate insiders. Anyone who helps another person to violate the insider trading rules can be held liable.

INSOLVENCY The condition of a debtor unable to pay debts. Insolvency in the BANKRUPTCY sense means the excess of liabilities over assets. As defined by the National Bankruptcy Act (Sec. 1), "a person shall be deemed insolvent within the provisions of this Act whenever the aggregate of his property, exclusive of any property which he may have conveyed, transferred, concealed, removed, or permitted to be concealed or removed, with intent to defraud, hinder, or delay his creditors, shall not, at a fair valuation, be sufficient in amount to pay his debts." Whether the debtor is meeting current liabilities is irrelevant in determining solvency in bankruptcy proceedings.

Insolvency in the sense that has been defined by equity courts means the inability of a person to meet debts as they mature. Thus, a person whose assets might not cover all liabilities may nevertheless be solvent in the equity sense because of ability to marshal assets to meet debts as they mature. Both types of insolvency are entitled to relief afforded debtors by the NATIONAL BANKRUPTCY ACT.

Insolvency is to be distinguished from bankruptcy in that the former is an accounting term independent of statute, whereas the latter is a legal term, indicating that the debtor is subject, voluntarily or involuntarily, to the provisions of the National Bankruptcy Act.

See FAILURES.

INSOLVENT An individual or concern that is unable to meet debts as they mature, or whose liabilities exceed assets; the adjective applied to such a financial condition.

See INSOLVENCY.

INSTALLMENT BONDS *See* SERIAL BONDS.

INSTALLMENT A part payment on the purchase price of an article that is sold under agreement that the remaining payments shall be due on specified future dates. The term is especially used in connection with the purchase of consumer goods where a certain percentage is paid initially as a down payment, the balance being payable in a number of payments following at stipulated intervals until the full amount is paid. Such payments are called installments.

The term is also applied to a part payment on a debt, e.g., a note or tax assessment.

See INSTALLMENT SALES.

INSTALLMENT SALES Sales of goods and equipment on a definite plan of payments, involving a specified cash payment as down payment with the balance payable in periodic installments until the debt is extinguished. Prior to 1922, installment sales were confined to comparatively few retail businesses, usually those distributing cheaper grades of merchandise to wage earners. Installment selling gained impetus particularly in the later 1920s, after it had been proved successful in the automobile trade under promotion of the sales finance companies. In recent years, automobile installment credit has continued to provide the largest volume of installment credit.

Documentary basis for installment sales could be either the conditional sales contract, under which title remains with the seller until final payment, or the chattel mortgage, under which title vests in the buyer subject to the chattel mortgage lien. Because various states have detailed restrictions statutorily imposed on conditional sales, most sellers prefer the chattel mortgage as the documentary basis for installment sales. In chattel mortgage practice, the buyer signs a promissory note or a series of notes, secured by the mortgage, that constitute the personal promise to pay. The mortgage contains the usual acceleration clause as well as the power of sale clause (power to repossess the goods and sell same at public sale in the event of default). Buyers on the installment basis would be well advised to avoid such practices as the "balloon" installment arrangement (relatively small preceding installments followed by a very large final installment), which invariably leads to costly refinancing, and the "open end" type of chattel mortgage, under which additional purchases on the installment basis may be made, but the seller retains the chattel mortgage lien on *all* of the purchased goods, whether fully paid up or still owed, so that default on a recently purchased item entitles the seller to repossession of *all* the goods sold under the contract. Buyers should also read the full provisions carefully to avoid any "hidden clauses" including goods or accessories not contemplated for purchase. Financing charges can also be quite high.

See CONSUMER CREDIT.

In post-World War II years, installment selling has become thoroughly established, as commercial banks have joined the sales finance companies in financing dealers' paper. Such financing is essential to dealers selling on the installment plan, as self-financing by carrying the paper to final maturity is out of the question for most dealers. The appended Table shows installment credit—finance rates on selected types of credit for commercial banks and finance companies from 1975 to 1987.

Installment credit controls were authorized by Section 601 of the defense production act of 1950, and effective on September 18, 1950, the Board of Governors of the Federal Reserve System reinstituted Regulation W, prescribing minimum down payments and maximum maturities on consumer installment credit. The regulation was amended October 16, 1950, and July 31, 1951. On May 7, 1952, the board suspended Regulation W "following a review of developments in the economy generally and in the markets directly affected by the regulation." Congress on June 30, 1952, repealed Section 601 of the Act, thus eliminating the statutory authority for installment credit controls. From October 16, 1950, to July 31, 1951, prescribed minimum down payments were the severest—33.3% on automobiles, 25% on major appliances, 15% on furniture and floor coverings, and 10% on home improvement materials, articles, and services, with maximum maturities of 15 months on the first three groups and 30 months on the last group.

Because of the rapid expansion in installment credit, which began to reach substantial proportions in the early 1950s, the increasing number of national banks engaged in this type of lending, and the need for better information as to lending practices and experience, a

INSTALLMENT SALES

Installment Credit—Finance Rates on Selected Types of Credit for Commercial Banks and Finance Companies: 1975 to 1987
(In percent. Annual averages. Commercial bank rates are "most common" rates for direct loans with specified maturities; finance company rates are weighted averages for purchased contracts.)

Type	1975	1977	1978	1979	1980	1981	1982	1983	1984	1985	1986	1987
Commercial banks:												
New automobiles (48 months) [1]	11.36	10.92	11.02	12.02	14.30	16.54	16.83	13.92	13.71	12.91	11.33	10.46
Mobile homes (120 months) [1]	11.82	11.84	12.09	12.77	14.99	17.45	18.05	15.91	15.58	14.96	13.99	13.38
Other consumer goods (24 months)	13.08	12.97	13.19	13.85	15.47	18.09	18.65	16.68	16.47	15.94	14.82	14.23
Credit-card plans	17.16	16.89	17.03	17.03	17.31	17.78	18.51	18.78	18.77	18.69	18.26	17.93
Finance companies:												
New automobiles	13.12	13.14	13.15	13.51	14.82	16.17	16.15	12.58	14.62	11.98	9.44	10.73
Used automobiles	17.63	17.62	17.67	17.98	19.10	20.00	20.75	18.74	17.85	17.59	15.95	14.61

[1] For 1975-1982, maturities were 36 months for new car loans and 84 months for mobile home loans.
Source: Board of Governors of the Federal Reserve System, *Federal Reserve Bulletin*, monthly; *Annual Statistical Digest*; and unpublished data.

special section dealing with installment credit was added to the report of examination of the Comptroller of the Currency in August, 1955. In that year, both the Comptroller and the Board of Governors of the Federal Reserve System circularized national banks and state member banks, cautioning against any loosening of credit standards in installment credit.

1980 Credit Restraint Program. On March 14, 1980, the Carter administration announced an antiinflation program which included among its five proposals the specific empowering by the president of the Board of Governors of the Federal Reserve System to institute direct controls over credit under the Credit Control Act of 1969. Acting under such authority, the board of governors announced the following.

1. A voluntary special credit restraint program, applicable to all domestic commercial banks, bank holding companies, finance companies, and credit extended to U.S. residents by U.S. agencies and branches of foreign banks.
2. A program of restraint on specified types of consumer credit, including credit cards, check credit overdraft plans, unsecured personal loans, and secured credit where the proceeds are not used to finance the collateral. Specifically, the board established a special deposit requirement of 15% for all lenders' increases in covered types of consumer credit for lenders with more than $2 million in such credit outstanding; such special deposit requirement applied to all banks, finance companies, retailers, and anyone extending these types of credit.
3. An increase in the marginal reserve requirement on managed liabilities of member banks from 8% to 10% and a 7% decrease in the base amount on which these percentages applied.
4. A special 10% deposit requirement on managed liabilities of nonmember banks.
5. A special 15% deposit requirement on any increase in the assets of MONEY MARKET FUNDS over the March 14, 1980, base period.
6. A surcharge on "frequent" discount borrowings by large member banks. (See 12 CFR Part 229, Credit Restraint, adopted March 14, 1980, and subsequently amended.)

Reaction of consumer credit to these measures was substantial. Consumer installment credit outstanding contracted at an average annual rate of 10.5% in the April-May, 1980, period, according to the *Federal Reserve Bulletin*, the first drop since May, 1975, and the largest reduction in the postwar era. Substantial decreases in both closed-end and revolving consumer credit occurred as consumers curtailed expenditures and credit use in the face of declining real incomes and worsening employment prospects. But credit-tightening measures by lenders after imposition of the March, 1980, credit control measures by the Board of Governors of the Federal Reserve System contributed to the reduction in credit use. The contraction in consumer credit was most pronounced at commercial banks and credit unions.

Accordingly, by May, 1980, the board of governors began to phase out the special and extraordinary credit control measures imposed in March, 1980, while stressing that such phasing out did not represent any change in basic monetary policy.

Legislative Developments. Although consumer credit controls of the type of World War II and Korean War controls have not been revived even on a standby basis, important federal legislation has been enacted in recent years.

1. Consumer Credit Protection Act, enacted May 29, 1968, became effective immediately except for the following portions: Title 1, called the Truth-in-Lending Act, providing for consumer credit cost disclosure, became effective July 1, 1969; and Title III, containing restrictions on garnishment, became effective July 1, 1970. Title II contained penalties for extortionate credit transactions, and Title IV provided for the creation of a bipartisan National Commission on Consumer Finance to report and recommend to Congress on consumer credit topics specified in the statute.
2. P.L. 91-508, October 26, 1970, added Title V to the Consumer Credit Protection Act, containing provisions relating to the issuance of credit cards, liability of holders of credit cards, and fraudulent use of credit cards. Title VI, containing provisions relating to credit information and statutory rights provided for persons finding themselves the subjects of credit reports, including the right to confront the preparers of the credit reports and to correct any misstatements of fact therein contained, protection against unwarranted disclosure of credit files, elimination of stale information from credit files, and protection against other credit reporting practices deemed unfair. Title VI is referred to as the Fair Credit Reporting Act.
3. Fair Credit Billing Act (an amendment to the Truth-in-Lending Act), P.L. 93-495, October 28, 1974, provided that consumers should have fair methods available to get billing errors corrected.
4. Equal Credit Opportunity Act, enacted by P.L. 93-495, October 28, 1974, provided that consumers seeking credit should not be discriminated against on grounds of sex or marital status.
5. Real Estate Settlement Procedures Act (P.L. 93-533, December 22, 1974) required among other things that a standard real estate settlement form be developed in compliance with the Truth-in-Lending Act requirements for nationwide use in all transactions that involve federally related mortgage loans. This form was to include clear and conspicuous itemizing of all settlement charges imposed upon the buyer and upon the seller and greater disclosure of the nature and costs of real estate settlement services.
6. Home Mortgage Disclosure Act of 1975 (contained in P.L. 94-200, December 31, 1975) required that mortgage lending be free of discriminatory bias and required that depository institutions with offices in standard metropolitan statistical areas and with assets of over $10 million identify the geographic distribution of their home mortgage loans (including home improvement loans). The Home Mortgage Disclosure Act was extended for an additional period of five years (to October 1, 1985) by P.L. 96-399, approved October 8, 1980 (the Housing and Community Development and Home Mortgage Disclosure Act).
7. Consumer Leasing Act of 1976 (P.L. 94-240), an amendment to the Truth-in-Lending Act, required that consumers be provided with full information regarding the terms of their leases of personal property, including open-end and closed-end vehicle and furniture leases.
8. The Fair Debt Collection Practices Act of 1978 made abusive and deceptive debt collection practices illegal for those the act

defined as debt collectors, generally anyone who regularly tries, directly or indirectly, to collect consumer debt for someone else.

9. Truth-in-Lending Simplification and Reform Act (Title VI of the Depository Institutions Deregulation and Monetary Control Act, P.L. 96-221, March 31, 1980), becoming fully effective April 1, 1982, provided that exemption be given for all extensions of credit for agricultural purposes from the disclosure requirements of the Truth-in-Lending Act; eliminated disclosure requirements calling for periodic statements from lenders in connection with closed-end credit transactions (such as mortgage and personal loans); and adopted, in effect, the rule in Regulation Z of the Federal Reserve Board regulations allowed an exception for the "cooling off" period for consumers who pledge their homes as collateral in open-end credit arrangements.

10. The Installment Sale Revision Act of 1980 liberalized the rules for postponing tax on property that is sold on the deferred payment basis. Unless the taxpayer otherwise elects out of installment sale reporting, the installment sale method is mandatory, requiring the taxpayer to report the gain from the sale over the period of time in which he or she will receive the proceeds from the sale. The installment method cannot be used for revolving credit plan sales, for sales of certain publicly traded property (e.g., stock or securities traded on an established securities market), by dealers in personal and real property (other than farm property, timeshares, and residential lots) after 1987.

Summary. Whether the record volume of installment credit and automobile paper in particular is a potential danger to the credit structure is disputed by spokespeople for the sales finance companies, who argue that the public regulation of terms is not needed, in view of maintenance of credit standards by lenders.

INSTALLMENT SALES METHOD A method of accounting that recognizes revenue when cash is collected from receivables over an extended period of time in periodic installments, rather than at the time of sale. The installment sales method of recognizing revenue is a modification of the cash collection method in that it delays the recognition of revenue (and net revenue) until collections from customers are received.

The installment sales method should be used only when there is a significant uncertainty concerning the ultimate collection of the sales proceeds. In such situations, revenue recognition is postponed. For example, a company sold for $100,000 land that cost $60,000. The rate of gross profit on this transaction is 40% ($40,000/$100,000). It is assumed that there is considerable uncertainty concerning the collectibility of the receivable resulting from the transaction. During the first year, the company collected $20,000. Income (gross profit) in the amount of $8,000 ($20,000 x 40%) is recognized. As can be noted, payments are prorated between recovery of the cost of the property and profit to be recognized on the sale.

INSTINET A fully automated communications system provided by the Institutional Networks Corporation, whereby a computer terminal is installed in the trading department of subscribers, almost all of which are institutional investors, connected by a private leased telephone circuit to a centralized computer. Each subscriber's terminal has a compact unit that prints confirmations and records of orders instantaneously, as sent or received.

Subscribers enter their bids or offers into the system, showing the name and amount of the stock, the desired price, and any time limit set on the bid or offer. The subscriber may indicate a desire to have the information broadcast to appear on the computer terminal screens of other subscribers, or to have the order entered only in the "book," to be available to any subscribers specifically interrogating the centralized computer as to the particular security. Any subscriber entering an order which matches another order already in the book will instantly receive a confirmation of the purchase or sale involved. If the subscriber's order is not matched in the book, it may attract another bid or offer which can then be the basis for negotiation of a trade leading to instant confirmation.

The system also simultaneously generates all the information necessary for the prompt settlement of the transaction through an escrow bank, and all negotiating information leading to the final trade is preserved in the system.

Summary. Instinet, therefore, facilitates the "fourth market," i.e., the market whereby institutional investors particularly may communicate with each other, eliminating the dealer in the "third market."

INSTITUTIONAL INVESTORS MUTUAL FUND, INC. An innovation by the New York State mutual savings banks in connection with the legalization of investment in common stocks by savings banks in that state (see SAVINGS BANK INVESTMENTS). Incorporated in New York State on October 29, 1952, this open-end management investment company enables individual savings banks to exchange their common stock holdings for shares of the fund. Ownership of the fund's stock is restricted to savings banks organized under New York State laws. The "load" in offering price is 0.5% above net asset value.

Investments are made in a portfolio of common stocks legal for investment by savings banks in New York State. Up to 10% of total resources may be invested and maintained in short-term Treasury and federal agency obligations. Stock of any company purchased shall not exceed 5% of outstanding shares. The fund may not borrow money without approval of the New York State Superintendent of Banks. The investment adviser is the Savings Bank Trust Company.

INSTITUTIONAL SECURITIES CORPORATION An early example of active self-help by New York State SAVINGS BANKS; one of the two institutions organized in 1933 to impart liquidity as needed to mortgage holdings (the other institution being the Savings Bank Trust Company), by creating a market for mortgages, mortgage loans, and obligations secured by mortgages held by mutual savings banks. The corporation did mortgage servicing also, and in 1942 entered the fields of financing, building, and managing defense housing and investing funds in mortgages insured by the FEDERAL HOUSING ADMINISTRATION (FHA). In 1946, the corporation also was authorized to invest in veterans' loans guaranteed by the Veterans Administration (VA). (See VETERANS' BENEFITS.)

In addition to providing facilities for the acquisition and administration of conventional as well as FHA-insured and VA-guaranteed mortgages via participations, debentures, and trusts, other services included direct servicing of mortgages, nationwide appraisals and inspections of real estate, examinations and ratings of mortgage servicers, and electronic data mortgage accounting. The International Securities Corporation (ISC) is an FHA-approved mortgagee and is a qualified seller of both FHA-insured and VA-guaranteed mortgages to both the FEDERAL NATIONAL MORTGAGE ASSOCIATION (FNMA) and the GOVERNMENT NATIONAL MORTGAGE ASSOCIATION (GNMA).

The ISC management consists of a board of directors elected by the 120 member mutual savings banks in New York State. Pursuant to the bylaws, the board of directors includes representation for all geographical areas of New York State. The president of the Savings Bank Association of New York State is also a member of the board. Two other members of the board have to be members of the New York State Banking Board, so as to maintain liaison between the corporation and the New York State Banking Department, which supervises and regulates the corporation.

In 1957, the Institutional Securities Corporation organized Instlcorp, Inc., a wholly-owned subsidiary. It provides a facility for the investment in mortgages by savings banks and other institutional and pension fund investors through the sale of its collateral trust notes. Instlcorp, Inc. is supervised and under the examination of the New York State Banking Department. It also is an FHA-approved mortgagee and a qualified seller of FHA-insured and VA-guaranteed mortgages, both to the FNMA and to the GNMA. Instlcorp, Inc. is authorized to issue FHA- and VA-backed obligations guaranteed by the GNMA.

INSTLCORP, INC. See INSTITUTIONAL SECURITIES CORPORATION.

INSTRUMENT Any kind of document in writing by which some right is conferred or contract is expressed. Practically all documents used in finance, e.g., check, draft, note, bond, coupon, stock certificate, bill of lading, trust deed, trust receipt, etc., are instruments.

See CREDIT INSTRUMENTS, NEGOTIABLE INSTRUMENTS.

INSTRUMENTALITY Literally, an agency. Corporations organized under act of Congress are exempt from federal income taxes if such corporations are instrumentalities of the United States and if Congress has specifically provided for such exemption under such act. Examples are project notes issued under Section 11(b) of the United States Housing Act of 1937, as amended, and Section 102(g) of the Housing Act of 1949, as amended. Obligations of federal instrumentalities are not automatically guaranteed as to principal and interest by the United States. One example of such a guarantee is that provided for FHA debenture obligations.

INSUFFICIENT FUNDS A term used in banking practice when checks are returned not payable because the drawer does not have sufficient monies in his account. When a check for which the drawer has insufficient funds is presented for collection through the clearinghouse or otherwise, the drawee bank returns it to the presenting bank for credit (by messenger or otherwise) with a memorandum slip attached on which the words "insufficient funds," or "not sufficient funds," are printed.

When a check is presented for payment and a doubt exists, the paying teller examines the account of the drawer to see that sufficient funds are on hand.

INSULAR BONDS Bonds issued by the Philippines, Hawaii, Alaska, and Puerto Rico while these issuers still had territorial status; also known as territorial bonds.

Insular bonds were not direct obligations of the United States, but inasmuch as the bonds were issued by authority of the American Congress and under the supervision of the U.S. Treasury, and since in the opinion of the attorney general of the U.S. the U.S. could compel payment in the event of default, insular bonds were generally considered to be indirect obligations of the U.S. In approving in 1921 the issue of the Philippine Islands $5\,^1/_2$s, due 1941, the attorney general of the U.S. wrote in part as follows.

"This issue and sale of bonds is authorized explicitly by the National Power, and while in the strict and legal sense the faith of the United States of America is not pledged as a guaranty for the payment of the loan or for the due use of the proceeds or the observance of the sinking fund requirements, the entire transaction is to be negotiated under the auspices of the United States of America and by its recognition and aid. There can be no doubt, therefore, that the National Power will take the necessary steps in all contingencies to protect the purchasers in good faith of these securities."

Present status of these bonds may be summarized as follows.

Philippines. Under the provisions of the Philippine Independence Act of 1934, as amended, the Philippine government set aside, in a special account with the U.S. Treasury, the proceeds of certain levies and sinking fund reserves for the specific purpose of providing for payment of Philippine dollar bonds issued prior to May 1, 1934.

All Philippine bonds issued after March 24, 1934, are fully subject to U.S. taxes; dollar Philippine bonds issued prior to March 24, 1934, were tax exempt.

Hawaii. The state of Hawaii assumed all obligations of the territory of Hawaii. General obligation bonds of the territory so assumed totaled $116,679,000. On August 21, 1959, following all necessary procedures and legislation, Hawaii became the fiftieth state by proclamation of the President of the U.S.

State of Hawaii bonds are exempt from federal income taxes, although they may be taxed by other states. Bonds issued by or on behalf of the territory of Hawaii are exempt from federal taxes and, in addition, are immune from taxation by other states (*Farmers and Mechanics Savings Bank of Minneapolis v. State of Minnesota*, 232 U.S. 516).

Alaska. Bonds issued by the territory under a 1956 federal authorization became valid general obligations of the state of Alaska, payable out of the general fund or any monies not otherwise appropriated, when statehood became effective January 3, 1959.

As issued, territorial bonds of Alaska were exempt from federal and state income taxes, and remain so under assumption by the state of Alaska.

Puerto Rico. Bonds of the Commonwealth of Puerto Rico and its municipalities, agencies, and authorities are exempt, as are other MUNICIPAL BONDS, from federal income taxes. In addition, however, by P.L. 600, 81st Congress of the U.S., all bonds issued by Puerto Rican public bodies are further exempt from taxes levied by any state or subdivision thereof, as follows.

"All bonds issued by the government of Puerto Rico, or by its authority, shall be exempt from taxation by the government of the United States, or by the government of Puerto Rico or of any political or municipal subdivision thereof, or by any state, territory, or possession or by any country, municipality, or other municipal subdivision of any state, territory, or possession of the United States, or by the District of Columbia.

The debt-paying record of Puerto Rico is reported clear of default or delinquency; there has never been any forced or managed refunding to avoid default. A similar debt record is also reported for all municipalities and instrumentalities of Puerto Rico.

The two major political parties contending for the governorship of Puerto Rico differ on the issue of whether Puerto Rico should become a state of the United States or continue its current commonwealth political status.

Should Puerto Rico become the fifty-first state of the Union, the question arises as to whether its obligations issued before statehood will remain exempt from all taxes—federal, state, local, and commonwealth.

According to the Economic Development Administration of the commonwealth, legal opinions sought on this question over the past twenty years affirm that Puerto Rico obligations issued prior to statehood would remain tax-exempt, in view of the Puerto Rico Federal Relations Act, the experience with bonds of Alaska and Hawaii when they became states, and that of the Philippines when it gained independence. In all cases, the bonds issued prior to the new status retained their federal tax-exemption features.

The fact that the state of New York made Alaska and Hawaii bonds taxable when the latter became states has cast some doubt about continued tax exemption of Puerto Rico bonds at the state level, should the commonwealth change its status to statehood. Current legal opinion is reported to hold that, the New York State decision notwithstanding, the differences between the Organic Act governing Puerto Rico and the legal status that governed Alaska and Hawaii would preclude New York from taxing Puerto Rico bonds in the event of statehood. For one thing, the Organic Acts of Alaska and Hawaii made no specific tax-exemption provision, as does the Organic Act governing Puerto Rico.

Section 3 of the Federal Relations Act, moreover, which governs Puerto Rico, reads in part as follows: " . . . all bonds issued by the Government of Puerto Rico, or by its authority, shall be exempt from taxation by the Government of the United States, or by the Government of Puerto Rico or by any political or municipal subdivision thereof, or by any State, Territory or Possession, or by any county, municipality, or other municipal subdivision of any State, Territory, or Possession of the United States, or by the District of Columbia . . . . "

INSURABLE INTEREST A relationship between the assured/insured and the risk covered, that if specified events occur, the assured will suffer some substantial loss or injury. Regarding fire or property insurance, insurable interest requires that there be a legally recognized interest and the possibility of a pecuniary loss in the event the property is damaged or destroyed. Legal interest includes ownership and possessory interests (such as future interests, interests of secured creditors, including mortgagees). Generally, the insured must have an insurable interest at the time of issuance and at the time the loss is incurred.

INSURANCE Elimination of or protection against risks amenable to actuarial calculation; voidance or reduction of losses occurring through various misfortunes, such as death, fire, accident, tornado, shipwreck, etc., through the cooperative sharing of such losses, i.e., through contributions made to a single fund by a large group of persons for the purpose of indemnifying losses sustained by such of the group as may be affected.

Insurance is a contract between an insurer and the insured whereby the insurer indemnifies the insured against loss due to specific risks, such as from fire, storm, and death. Insurance contracts require an agreement, consideration, capacity, legality, compliance with the Statute of Frauds, and delivery. Insurance is an integral part of most enterprises' risk management program.

Whether insurance is provided by established "old line" companies, that compute underwriting risks scientifically through the aid of loss experience tables, or by assessment associations, its function is to spread the risk of calculable losses. The essential principle of insurance is cooperation or pooling of the risks of loss that might occur to a large enough group of persons, but that actually through the law of averages will happen only to a small number in such group. For instance, it may be computed actuarially that 3 out of every 1,000 houses in a given locality will burn down each year, but it is not known which of those three houses will be destroyed. The loss to the owners of the 3 houses would be crushing, but if distributed among 1,000 owners, each paying a small premium against the risk that the loss might be his, the actual loss becomes readily bearable.

Insurance does not prevent losses; rather, it substitutes a small certain loss (premium) for a possible or contingent large loss. The insured is indemnified for the amount of the loss, for the insured amount, or for the face of his policy, in return for payment of periodic premiums. It is thus the reverse of gambling, which involves the assumption of the odds against actual loss by a particular person. Insurance seeks to cushion the impact of chance, while gambling seeks to accept chance in full. Thus, paying $25 a year as protection against the contingent loss by fire of a house worth $15,000 is insurance; not doing so, by assuming the risk of loss of $15,000, is gambling.

The principal kinds of insurance are the following.

1. Life—term, ordinary, endowment, limited payment, group, industrial (participating or nonparticipating), and annuities, with a variety of combinations of the first four basic forms, including innovations such as the family plan policy, accident and health addenda, graduation of premiums by size of contract, and guaranteed insurability.
2. Fire and marine—fire, ocean marine, motor vehicle, inland navigation and transportation (with comprehensive coverage), tornado and windstorm, sprinkler leakage, earthquake, riot and civil commotion, explosion, rain, hail, flood, aircraft, etc.
3. Casualty and surety—automobile liability, liability other than automobile, workers' compensation, fidelity and surety, burglary and theft, automobile property damage, accident and health, steam boiler, machinery, plate glass, etc.

Insurance on property greatly exceeds life insurance. Based on aggregate insurance in force, fire and marine heads the list, followed by life and casualty forms of insurance.

Fire insurance is written by stock companies, mutual companies, or associations of individual underwriters, e.g., Lloyd's of London. Until recent years, a feature of the U.S. system of chartering insurance companies was the segregation of companies into life and fire and casualty companies, and the absence of multiple-line companies authorized to write all kinds of insurance, as in the case of European companies. In recent years, however, all states have statutorily authorized multiple-line underwriting for fire and casualty companies; as a result, the "group" or "fleet" organization of companies, with a parent company heading a cluster of companies in the various fields, is no longer necessary as a means of diversification in basic lines. Instead, various fire and casualty companies have organized or acquired life insurance companies in recent years and consolidations have shrunk previously extensive fleets.

Life Insurance Companies. Life insurance companies are of stock and mutual form, the larger companies being mainly the latter, and are usually classified according to the plan of premium payments into "old line" level premium plan companies and assessment associations (mutually assessing members for losses sustained). The old line companies, with their full level premium plan building up reserves and surpluses in accordance with mortality experience tables and expense loading, are structurally stronger as compared with the pay-as-you-go assessment companies. In comparison to fire and casualty companies, life insurance companies are more closely regulated by the various states as to eligible investment media, the regulation reflecting the personal nature of the insurance, the long-term contracts involved, and the necessity for conservative investment of the accumulations of policy reserves.

Basic forms of the level premium plan are the ordinary life plan, in which the premium payments at a fixed sum continue throughout the life of the insured (the policy automatically becoming an endowment at an advanced age, such as 96); the limited payment plan, in which the fixed sum premiums are limited to 10, 15, or 20 or more years, when the policy then becomes paid up (no further premiums payable, the coverage continuing); and the term plan, in which insurance is provided for a term of years, automatically renewable at the same or an advanced rate of premium, with or without medical reexamination. The term type of life insurance is cheapest because the premium charge is basically for insurance only plus expense loading, there being no savings element in the premium collection to be compounded at the allowed earnings rate, and hence no cash surrender value. Endowment is a combination of insurance and the highest savings element, in which the policy matures in a certain number of years after it is issued or, in the case of "family" variations, upon the death of the insured prior to nominal maturity. An endowment policy affords a method of compulsory saving in addition to providing insurance protection.

All mutual and legal reserve life insurance companies provide for a participation in dividends by all policyholders. In this way, the cost of the insurance to the insured is reduced. Legal reserve companies organized as stock companies write life insurance on both participating and nonparticipating bases (mainly the latter), but their initial premiums charged the insured may be lower than those of mutual companies. If the premium payments of a company plus the income from investments exceed mortality claims and expenses, a surplus arises. This may be because actual mortality losses are lower than those allowed for under the given mortality experience tables used to compute premiums, because the investment return is higher than the assumed earnings rate, or because expenses are actually lower than the expense loading. Out of such surplus, participating policies may be allocated dividends based upon the amount of annual premium and the type of policy. Such dividends can usually be taken in a number of alternative ways: as cash payment; as a reduction of premium; to purchase additional paid-up insurance; to accelerate the payment of the total premiums due, i.e., to hasten the time when the policy will be paid up; or to credit a premium deposit fund.

When a policy matures, there also are several optional methods of settlement: (1) payment in cash in one sum; (2) payment of interest on the principal amount of the policy (the principal being left with the company) during the lifetime of the payee and payment of the principal sum with any accrued and unpaid interest thereon on the death of the payee to his or her executors, administrators, or assigns; (3) payment of a specified number of equal installments, whether the payee lives or dies (the first payment beginning immediately), the amount of each installment to be in conformity with the company's prepared tables; (4) payment of equal annual installments (the first installment payable immediately), for 10 or 20 years certain (whether the payee lives or dies) and as many years thereafter as the payee shall live, the amount of each installment to be in conformity with the company's prepared tables; and (5) payment of an annuity during the lifetime of the annuitant (first payment payable immediately), the amount of each payment again, to be in conformity with the company's prepared annuity tables.

The motives for carrying life insurance may be as follows:

1. To provide funds to pay debts and cover funeral expenses
2. To provide an estate for the benefit of spouse and children, the income from which will be sufficient to provide for their material wants (the ideal situation)
3. To provide a monthly income for the spouse and children
4. To provide paid-up insurance for old age, when the insured retires or his earning power declines materially
5. To provide for education of children
6. To provide protection for business associates (business insurance)
7. To provide bequests
8. To provide cash with which to pay estate taxes
9. To pay mortgage on home of the insured
10. To provide an income during periods of sickness or disability
11. To provide current liquidity and basis for borrowing (cash surrender values).

Holding companies appeared increasingly in the life insurance field, formation of which was stimulated by such motivations as defensive structural strategy against acquisition by noninsurance conglomerates, which were attracted by the money flows in insurance operations; alternatives to group or fleet operations; and vehicles for congeneric diversification of operations. Innovations in life insurance "products" in recent years have included promotion of pension plans, separate accounts, variable annuities, and mutual funds.

Life insurance sales have had to contend with competing alternatives for individual savings, including the stock market in general and mutual funds in particular, money market funds, direct investment in money market instruments, pension funds, dividend

INSURANCE

Table 1 / Life Insurance in Force in the U.S.—Summary: 1970 to 1987
(As of December 31 or calendar year, as applicable. Covers life insurance with life insurance companies only. Represents all life insurance in force on lives of U.S. residents whether issued by U.S. or foreign companies. For definition of household, see text, section 1. See also *Historical Statistics, Colonial Times to 1970*, series X 879-889.)

Year	Number of policies, total (mil.)	Life insurance in force Value (bil. dol.)					Average size policy in force (dollars)					Average amount ($1,000)		Disposable personal income per household ($1,000)
		Total	Ordinary	Group	Industrial	Credit[1]	Ordinary	Group	Industrial	Credit[1]	Per household	Per insured household	
1970	355	1,402	731	545	38.6	87.9	6,110	6,910	500	1,000	22.1	26.6	11.3
1974	380	1,985	1,009	827	39.4	109.6	7,690	8,840	550	1,310	28.4	34.2	14.9
1975	380	2,140	1,083	905	39.4	112.0	8,090	9,360	570	1,410	30.1	36.2	16.1
1976	382	2,343	1,178	1,003	39.2	123.6	8,610	10,010	580	1,580	32.2	38.7	17.2
1977	390	2,583	1,289	1,115	39.0	139.4	9,240	10,550	590	1,760	34.8	42.0	18.6
1978	401	2,870	1,425	1,244	38.1	163.1	10,010	11,260	600	1,950	37.8	45.5	20.4
1979	407	3,222	1,586	1,419	37.8	179.3	10,890	12,350	610	2,120	41.7	50.8	22.4
1980	402	3,541	1,761	1,579	36.0	165.2	11,920	13,410	620	2,110	43.8	53.5	23.7
1981	400	4,064	1,978	1,889	34.5	162.4	13,310	15,400	630	2,220	49.3	60.2	25.8
1982	390	4,477	2,217	2,066	32.8	161.1	15,140	16,630	630	2,410	53.6	66.2	27.1
1983	387	4,966	2,544	2,220	31.4	170.7	17,380	17,530	630	2,650	59.2	73.1	28.9
1984	385	5,500	2,888	2,392	30.1	190.0	19,970	18,780	630	2,880	64.5	79.6	31.3
1985	386	6,053	3,247	2,562	28.2	216.0	22,780	19,720	640	3,100	69.7	86.1	32.7
1986	391	6,720	3,658	2,801	27.2	233.9	25,540	20,720	650	3,310	76.0	93.8	34.2
1987	395	7,452	4,139	3,043	26.6	243.0	28,510	22,380	650	3,330	82.8	102.2	35.3

1. Insures borrower to cover consumer loan in case of death.

Source: American Council of Life Insurance, Washington, DC, *Life Insurance Fact Book*, biennial.

Table 2 / Property and Liability Insurance: 1970 to 1987
(In millions of dollars. Premiums written represent total premiums on all insurance policies written by companies, with inception dates in years shown. Minus sign (–) indicates loss. See also *Historical Statistics, Colonial Times to 1970*, series X 918, 923, 928, 933, and 940.)

Item	1970	1975	1980	1982	1983	1984	1985	1986	1987
Premiums written [1]	32,867	49,967	95,509	103,968	108,983	118,166	144,186	176,552	193,246
Auto liability	8,958	13,315	23,319	26,226	28,080	30,217	36,087	44,081	49,205
Physical damage, auto	4,824	7,623	15,833	18,005	19,748	21,766	25,247	29,306	31,995
Liability, other than auto	2,140	3,981	7,692	7,159	7,247	8,254	14,313	22,857	24,878
Medical malpractice	NA	895	1,276	1,490	1,568	1,775	2,769	3,492	4,004
Fire [2]	3,147	3,691	4,784	4,836	4,608	4,853	6,173	6,933	7,656
Homeowners multiple peril	2,565	4,729	9,821	11,747	12,512	13,213	14,066	15,222	16,653
Commercial multiple peril	1,331	3,176	6,886	7,009	7,293	8,287	12,097	16,190	17,231
Workers' compensation	3,492	6,186	14,239	13,945	14,005	15,108	17,048	20,431	23,429
Inland marine	812	1,266	2,291	2,510	2,649	3,017	3,672	3,899	4,120
Ocean marine	465	861	1,065	1,101	1,096	1,155	1,177	1,225	1,355
Surety and fidelity [3]	562	789	1,248	1,454	1,649	1,997	2,853	2,116	2,450
Financial guaranty [3]	NA	NA	NA	NA	NA	NA	NA	575	582
Burglary and theft	135	120	136	115	106	109	122	121	127
Crop—hail	125	312	417	532	444	509	447	379	351
Boiler and machinery	115	173	293	293	356	439	618	531	596
Glass	40	32	32	29	27	28	25	27	25
Statutory underwriting gain/loss	77	–3,594	–1,712	–8,303	–11,088	–19,379	–22,597	–13,748	–7,078
Policyholders' dividends	504	633	1,622	1,987	2,234	2,098	2,196	2,165	2,546
Net underwriting gain/loss	–426	–4,227	–3,334	–10,290	–13,322	–21,477	–24,794	–15,913	–9,625
Net investment income	2,005	4,150	11,063	14,907	15,973	17,660	19,508	21,924	23,960
Net income/loss before taxes	1,579	–77	7,730	4,617	2,651	–3,817	–5,286	6,012	14,336
Assets	58,594	94,118	197,661	231,693	249,121	264,734	311,365	374,088	426,711
Policyholders' surplus	18,520	25,303	52,196	60,395	65,606	63,809	75,511	94,288	103,996

NA — Not available.

[1] Total includes all property, liability, and allied lines; other data are for principal lines only.
[2] Includes extended coverage and allied lines.
[3] Prior to 1986, financial guaranty was included in surety.

Source: Insurance Information Institute, New York, NY, *Insurance Facts*, annual. Data from A. M. Best Company, Oldwick, NJ.

reinvestment plans, other stock purchase plans, etc. The appended Table shows life insurance in June in the U.S. from 1970 to 1987.

Investment Results. Major determinants of overall operating effects upon "policyholders' surplus" (capital and surplus accounts) are investing results (net interest and dividend income from invested assets, net realized gains or losses, and unrealized gains or losses resulting from posting year-end portfolio values in accordance with association values).

Life insurance companies have benefited from the steady year-to-year rise in their net rate of investment income (primarily interest income on bonds owned and loans made, dividends on stock holdings, and rents on real estate owned; capital gains and losses are treated as direct changes in surplus and are not considered as investment income as such). The invested assets base includes the special "separate accounts" which various companies maintain for various life insurance-investing plans and retirement plans. About 50% of the investments of such special accounts, according to the American Council of Life Insurance, have been common stocks, reflecting the primary investing objective of capital appreciation rather than dividend income.

Invested assets of life insurance companies are largely fixed income-producing obligations.

Property insurance companies, enjoy wider regulatory latitude in investing their funds, than do life insurance companies, so that turnover of portfolio securities and unrealized appreciation in posting portfolios to association values have been larger albeit more volatile in recent years, reflecting larger proportionate holdings of diversified common stocks. Casualty insurance companies, however, are characterized by generally higher proportionate holdings in cash and bonds than are property insurance companies. See appended table showing property and liability insurance 1970 to 1987.

Conglomerate and Congeneric Turmoil. Like that of life insurance companies, the structure of the property and casualty insurance industry has been materially affected by conglomerate and congeneric acquisitions of control of companies.

Accounting Changes. Following the adoption by the American Institute of Certified Public Accountants in December, 1972, of its "Audits of Stock Life Insurance Companies," to be effective with 1973 reports, the Securities and Exchange Commission announced in September, 1973, proposals to require the application of "generally accepted accounting principles" (GAAP) by stock life insurance companies for financial statements filed with the commission, as indicated by the following introductory explanation by the SEC.

"The proposed revision in the accounting requirements for (stock) life insurance companies is effected by a complete revision of Article 7A and related schedules in Article 12 of Regulation S-X (the accounting regulation of the SEC). The proposed revision reflects developments in accounting practice during the past ten years, including the recent publication of an Audit Guide for life insurance companies by the American Institute of Certified Public Accountants. The Audit Guide establishes guidelines for the preparation of life insurance company financial statements which are in accordance with generally accepted accounting principles (GAAP). The proposed revision represents a significant departure from the present Article 7A, which specifies that life insurance company financials generally follow the statutory accounting requirements prescribed for Annual Statements filed by these companies with state insurance commissions."

On balance, the statutory accounting requirements prescribed by state insurance departments are considered ultraconservative, in comparison with GAAP, on such matters as exclusion of "nonadmitted assets," accounting for acquisition costs, assumptions used in the calculation of policy reserves, and accounting for income taxes.

Amendments to Articles 7 (fire and casualty insurance companies) and 7A (life insurance companies) of Regulation S-X, issued June 3, 1976, by the Securities and Exchange Commission and on which the comment period ended July 30, 1976, were finally adopted October 21, 1981.

A short glossary of basic life insurance terms provided by the American Council of Life Insurance is presented here:

Accidental death benefit A benefit in addition to the face amount of a life insurance policy, payable if the insured dies as the result of an accident. Sometimes referred to as "double indemnity."

Act of God An unexplained happening attributed to a natural force that is unpredictable and without human involvement.

Actuarial science Techniques by which mathematics is used to establish insurance rates. Factors considered include loss history, interest rates, and various costs projected over time.

Actuary A person professionally trained in the technical aspects of insurance and related fields, particularly in the mathematics of insurance—such as the calculation of premiums, reserves, and other values.

Adjustable life insurance A type of insurance that allows the policyholder to change the plan of insurance, raise or lower the face amount of the policy, increase or decrease the premium and lengthen or shorten the protection period.

Administrative law Governmental regulatory decisions outside the judicial process made by authorized officials.

Agent A sales and service representative or an insurance company. Life insurance agents may also be called life underwriters or field underwriters.

Annuitant The person during whose life an annuity is payable, usually the person to receive the annuity.

Annuity A contract that provides a periodic income at regular intervals for a specified period of time, such as for a number of years, regardless for life.

Annuity certain A contract that provides an income for a specified number or years regardless of life or death.

Annuity consideration The payment, or one of the regular periodic payments, an annuitant makes for an annuity.

Application A statement of information made by a person applying for life insurance. It helps the life insurance company assess the acceptablility of risk.

Arbitration A procedure for resolving disputes between contractual parties.

Assignment The legal transfer of one person's interest in an insurance policy to another person.

Associates at Lloyd's Individuals or firms that perform defined services for members and subscribers at Lloyd's, London. Associates include actuaries, attorneys, and adjusters.

Beneficiary The person named in the policy to receive the insurance proceeds at the death of the insured.

Binder An agreement that provides immediate insurance coverage.

Blanket coverage Insurance coverage using a single face amount of insurance for several locations, insuring clauses, or coverage.

Blue Cross/Blue Shield Plans Insurance service plans established in various states under enabling legislation that provide health care converges. Blue Cross plans were originated by hospitals and Blue Shield plans by physicians. These organizations are not-for-profit associations.

Business interruption insurance Insurance that provides coverage for the loss of profit which occurs as a result of loss to the building or contents; also referred to as prospective earnings insurance or use and occupancy insurance.

Broker A sales and service representative who handles insurance for clients, generally selling insurance of various kinds and or several companies.

Business life insurance Life insurance purchased by a business enterprise on the life of a member of the firm. It is often bought by partnerships to protect the surviving partners against loss caused by the death of a partner, or by a corporation to reimburse it for loss caused by the death of a key employee.

Cash surrender value The amount available in cash upon voluntary termination of a policy by its owner before it becomes payable by death or maturity.

Certificate A statement issued to individuals insured under a group policy, setting forth the essential provisions relating to their coverage.

Claim Notification to an insurance company that payment of an amount is due under the terms of a policy.

Coinsurance clause A clause in an insurance policy that causes the insured to purchase insurance of a specified percentage of value or to participate in a loss (the insured becomes a coinsurer) if the required amount of insurance is not in force at the time of loss. The coinsurance clause usually specifies 80% or more.

Coinsurance formula The amount of insurance carried divided by the amount required multiplied by the amount of loss. The payment cannot exceed the face amount of the policy.

INSURANCE

Convertible term insurance Term insurance that can be exchanged, at the option of the policyholder and without evidence of insurability, for another plan of insurance. Credit life insurance. Term life insurance issued through a lender or lending agency to cover payment of a loan, installment purchase, or other obligation, in case of death.

Declination The rejection by a life insurance company of an application for life insurance, usually for reasons of the health or occupation of the applicant.

Deductible clause A clause in an insurance contract that describes the terms and conditions of any deductible. A deductible is used to reduce the policy premium because the insured is required to absorb specified losses.

Deferred annuity An annuity providing for the income payments to begin at some future date.

Deferred group annuity A type of group annuity providing for the purchase each year of a paid-up deferred annuity for each member of the group, the total amount received by the member at retirement being the sum of these deferred annuities.

Deposit administration group annuity A type of group annuity providing for the accumulation of contributions in an undivided fund out of which annuities are purchased as the individual members of the group retire.

Deposit term insurance A form of term insurance, not really involving a "deposit," in which the first-year premium is larger than subsequent premiums. Typically, a partial endowment is paid at the end of the term period. In many cases the partial endowment can be applied toward the purchase of a new term policy or, perhaps, a whole life policy.

Disability benefit A feature added to some life insurance policies providing for waiver of premium, and sometimes payment of monthly income, if the policyholder becomes totally and permanently disabled.

Dividend A return of part of the premium on participating insurance to reflect the difference between the premium charged and the combination of actual mortality, expense and investment experience. Such premiums are calculated to provide some margin over the anticipated cost of the insurance protection.

Dividend addition An amount of paid-up insurance purchased with a policy dividend and added to the face amount of the policy.

Endowment Life insurance payable to the policyholder if living, on the maturity date stated in the policy, or to a beneficiary if the insured dies prior to that date.

Endorsement An attachment to an insurance policy used to extend or restrict coverage associated with perils, locations, insureds, or exposures. In life and health policies, it is referred to as a rider.

Exclusion A provision in an insurance contract that limits or restricts coverage.

Expectation of life (See: LIFE EXPECTANCY.)

Extended term insurance A form of insurance available as a nonforfeiture option. It provides the original amount of insurance for a limited period of time.

Face amount The amount stated on the face of the policy that will be paid in case of death or at the maturity of the policy. It does not include additional amounts payable under accidental death or other special provisions, or acquired through the application of policy dividends.

Family policy A life insurance policy providing insurance on all or several family members in one contract, generally whole life insurance on the principal breadwinner and small amounts of term insurance on the other spouse and children, including those born after the policy is issued.

Fidelity bond A bond obtained by an employer to protect against the economic loss (of money or property) of dishonest acts of employees.

Fiduciary bond A judicial or surety bond that provides for protection associated with executorship, guardianship, or trusteeship guaranteeing his or her performance as directed by the court.

Flexible premium policy or annuity A life insurance policy or annuity under which the policyholder or contractholder may vary the amounts or timing of premium payments.

Flexible premium variable life insurance A life insurance policy that combines the premium flexibility feature of universal life insurance with the equity-based benefit feature of variable life insurance.

Floater A policy that provides coverage for goods for which it is difficult to establish a specific location, subject to a territorial limit.

Fraternal life insurance Life insurance provided by fraternal orders or societies to their members.

Geographic divisions (in the United States)

NORTHEAST
  New England: Connecticut, Maine, Massachusetts, New Hampshire, Rhode Island, Vermont
  Middle Atlantic: New Jersey, New York, Pennsylvania

MIDWEST
  East North Central: Illinois, Indiana, Michigan, Ohio, Wisconsin
  West North Central: Iowa, Kansas, Minnesota, Missouri, Nebraska, North Dakota, South Dakota

SOUTH
  South Atlantic: Delaware, District of Columbia, Florida, Georgia, Maryland, North Carolina, South Carolina, Virginia, West Virginia
  East South Central: Alabama, Kentucky, Mississippi, Tennessee
  West South Central: Arkansas, Louisiana, Oklahoma, Texas

WEST
  Mountain: Arizona, Colorado, Idaho, Montana, Nevada, New Mexico, Utah, Wyoming
  Pacific: Alaska, California, Hawaii, Oregon, Washington.

Grace period A period (usually 30 or 31 days) following the premium due date, during which an overdue premium may be paid without penalty. The policy remains in force throughout this period.

Group annuity A pension plan providing annuities at retirement to a group of people under a master contract. It is usually issued to an employer for the benefit of employees. The individual members of the group hold certificates as evidence of their annuities.

Group life insurance Life insurance usually without medical examination, on a group of people under a master policy. It is typically issued to an employer for the benefit of employees, or to members of an association, for example a professional membership group. The individual members of the group hold certificates as evidence of their insurance.

Individual policy pension trust A type of pension plan, frequently used for small groups, administered by trustees who are authorized to purchase individual level premium policies or annuity contracts for each member of the plan. The policies usually provide both life insurance and retirement benefits.

Industrial life insurance Life insurance issued in small amounts, usually less that $1,000, with premiums payable on a weekly or monthly basis. The premiums are generally collected at the home by an agent of the company. Sometimes referred to as debit insurance.

Insurability Acceptability to the company of an applicant for insurance.

Insurable interest A doctrine requiring individuals or organizations to be in a position to suffer economic loss before they can insure another person, object, or activity against loss or damage. The insurable interest must exist when the policy is issued and at the time of loss or damage. In life policies, it need exist only at the time the contract is issued.

Insurable value The dollar value of property at risk. Insurable value may be replacement cost or the actual cash value which includes a reduction for depreciation.

Insurance company An organization established to conduct a business to insure persons or firms. The company may be for profit or not for profit. For-profit companies are incorporated (stock companies) or unincorporated (Lloyd's of London). There are also various forms of government insurers, consumer cooperatives, and mutual companies. Producers' cooperatives include prepaid plans (Blue Cross/Blue Shield) and other underwriter associations.

Insurance examiner The representative of a state insurance department assigned to participate in the official audit and examination of the affairs of an insurance company.

Insured or insured life The person on whose life the policy is issued.

Key employee insurance Insurance providing coverage for the loss to a business resulting from the death, injury, or sickness of a key employee. The premium is paid by the firm which is the owner and beneficiary of the policy.

Lapsed policy A policy terminated for nonpayment of premiums. The term is sometimes limited to a termination occurring before the policy has a cash or other surrender value.

Law of large numbers A mathematical concept that states that as the number of exposures increases the more likely the results expected for the event or happening will more closely approach the actual results.

Legal reserve life insurance company A life insurance company operating under state insurance laws specifying the minimum basis for the reserves the company must maintain on its policies.

Level premium life insurance Life insurance for which the premium remains the same from year to year. The premium is more than the actual cost of protection during the earlier years of the policy and less than the actual cost in the later years. The building of a reserve is a natural result of level premiums. The overpayments in the early years, together with the interest that is to be earned, serve to balance out the underpayments of the later years.

Liability insurance Insurance that provides coverage for one or more liability loss exposures (persons, business, professional, automobile-related, and employers' related).

Life annuity A contract that provides an income for life.

Life expectancy The average number of years of life remaining for a group of persons of a given age according to a particular mortality table.

Life insurance Insurance providing coverage associated with the death of the insured. Life policies can be classified as whole life, term life, and endowment. Life policies can be written for individuals or for groups.

Life insurance in force The sum of the face amounts, plus dividend additions, of life insurance policies outstanding at a given time. Additional amounts payable under accidental death or other special provisions are not included.

Life insurance reserves Reserves used to guarantee the performance of future obligation of a life insurer for policies it issues. Reserves are usually held in the form of cash or cash equivalents, fixed assets, and equity.

Limited payment life insurance Whole life insurance on which premiums are payable for a specified number of years or until death if death occurs before the end of th especified period.

Lloyd's, London An insurance exchange involving syndicates of individuals who insure large and unusual risks. Lloyd's began by writing marine insurance.

Loss reserves Reserves established by property or liability insurers. The reserves represent the total estimated amount required to pay the claims reported (adjusted but not paid, received but not adjusted) and those incurred but not reported. Reserves are calculated by the individual case estimate method, statistical or average value method, or loss ratio method.

Master policy A policy that is issued to an employer or trustee, establishing a group insurance plan for designated members of an eligible group.

Mortality table A statistical table showing the death rate at each age, usally expressed as so many per thousand.

Mutual life insurance company A life insurance company without stockholders whose management is directed bya board elected by the policyholders. Mutual companies, in general, issue participating insurance.

No-fault automobile insurance Insurance coverage that eliminates tort liability from automobile losses. The owner or operator accepts responsibility for injuries to passenger(s) in their vehicles in exchange for immunity from tort liability claims by the injured.

Nonforfeiture option One of the choices available if the policyholder discontinues premium payments on a policy with a cash value. This, if any, may be taken in cash, as extended term insurance or as reduced paid-up insurance.

Nonmedical limit The maximum face value of a policy that a given company will issue without the applicant taking a medical examination.

Nonparticipating policy A life insurance policy in which the company does not distribute to policyholders any part of its surplus. Note should be taken that premiums for nonparticipating policies are usually lower than for comparable participating policies. Note should also be taken that some nonparticipating policies have both a maximum premium and current lower premium. The current premium reflects anticipated experience that is more favorable than the company is willing to guarantee, and it may be changed from time to time for the entire block of business to which the policy belongs. (*See also:* PARTICIPATING POLICY)

Ordinary life insurance Life insurance usually issued in amounts of $1,000 or more with premiums payable on an annual, semiannual, quarterly or monthly basis.

Paid-up insurance Insurance on which all required premiums have been paid. The term is frequently used to mean the reduced paid-up insurance available as a nonforfeiture option.

Participating policy A life insurance policy under which the company agrees to distribute to policyholders the part of its surplus which its Board of Directors determines is not needed at the end of the business year. Such a distribution serves to reduce the premium the policyholder had paid. (*See also:* POLICY DIVIDEND; NONPARTICIPATING POLICY)

Permanent life insurance A phrase used to cover any form of life insurance except term; generally insurance that accrues cash value, such as whole life or endowment.

Policy The printed leagal document stating the terms of the insurance contract that is issued to the policyholder by the company.

Policy dividend A refund of part of the premium on a participating life insurance policy reflecting the difference between the premium charged and actual experience.

Policy loan A loan made by a life insurance company from its general funds to a policyholder on the security of the cash value of a policy.

Policy reserves The measure of the funds that a life insurance company hods specifically for fulfillment of its policy obligations. Reserves are required by law to be so calculated that, together with future premium payments and anticipated interest earnings, they will enable the company to pay all future claims.

Policyholder The person who owns a life insurance policy. This is usually the insured person, but it may also be a relative of the insured, a partnership or a corporation.

Premium The payment, or one of the periodic payments, a policyholder agrees to make for an insurance policy.

Premium loan A policy loan made for the purpose of paying premiums.

Profits insurance Insurance providing coverage for economic loss of future earnings by the insured if a loss occurs to finished goods or inventory before it is sold.

Rated policy Sometimes called an "extra-risk" policy, an insurance policy issued at a higher-than-standard premium rate to cover the extra risk where, for example, an insured has impaired health or a hazardous occupation.

Reduced paid-up insurance A form of insurance available as a nonforfeiture option. It provides for continuation of the original insurance plan, but for a reduced amount.

Reinsurance A procedure used by insurance companies to transfer part or all of their liability for an insurance contract to another insurance company (a reinsurer).

Renewable term insurance Term insurance which can be renewed at the end of the term, at the option of the policyholder and without evidence of insurability, for a limited number of successive terms. The rates increase at each renewal as the age of the insured increases.

Replacement cost insurance Insurance that provides that insured property will be replaced without any deduction for depreciation.

Reserve The amount required to be carried as a liability in the financial statement of an insurer, to provide for future commitments under policies outstanding.

Rider A special policy provision or group of provisions that may be added to a policy to expand or limit the benefits otherwise payable.

Risk classification The process by which a company decides how its premium rates for life insurance should differ according to the risk characteristics of individuals insured (e.g., age, occupation, sex, state of health) and then applies the resulting rules to individual applications. (*See:* UNDERWRITING)

Self-insurance A program for protection from loss that requires an individual or organization to set aside funds to pay losses that might occur at a later date. Self-insurance is a form of risk management. Self-insurance can be effective if risk exposure groups are sufficient to allow the laws of probability of loss to apply.

Separate account An asset account established by a life insurance company separate from other funds, used primarily for pension plans and variable life products. This arrangement permits wider latitude in the choice of investments, particularly in equities.

Settlement options The several ways, other than immediate payment in cash, which a policyholder or beneficiary may choose to have policy benefits paid. (See also: *Supplementary contract*)

Stock life insurance company A life insurance company owned by stockholders who elect a board to direct the company's management. Stock companies, in general, issue nonparticipating insurance, but may also issue participating insurance.

Straight life insurance Whole life insurance on which premiums are payable for life.

Subrogation The contractual right of an insured to attempt to recover amounts paid to the insured for damage caused by an at-fault third party. The subrogation clause is typically a condition of property and casualty policies.

Supplementary contract An aggreement between a life insurance company and a policyholder or beneficiary by which the company retains the cash sum payable under an insurance policy and makes payments in accordance with the settlement option chosen.

Suretyship An agreement in a credit arrangement that requires that one party (surety) will answer for the acts or omissions of a second party (principal) in some fashion for a third party (obligee).

Term insurance Life insurance payable to a beneficiary only when an insured dies within a specified period.

Umbrella liability policy An insurance contract that provides bodily injury and property damage liability insurance in excess of the limits of liability of specified liability policies.

Underwiriting The process by which a life insurance company determines whether or not it can accept an application for life insurance, and if so, on what basis.

Universal life insurance A flexible premium life insurance policy under which the policyholder may change the death benefit from time to time (with satisfactory evidence of insurability for increases) and vary the amount or timing of premium payments. Premiums (less expense charges) are credited to a policy account from which mortality charges are deducted and to which interest is credited at rates which may change from time to time.

Variable annuity An annuity contract in which the amount of each periodic income payment may fluctuate. The fluctuation may be related to securities market values, a cost of living index, or some other variable factor.

Variable life insurance Life insurance under which the benefits relate to the value of assets behind the contract at the time the benefit is paid. The amount of death benefit payable would, under variable life policies that have been proposed, never be less than the initial death benefit payable under the policy.

Waiver The voluntary giving up by a party of a right or advantage.

Waiver of premium A provision that under certain conditions an insurance policy will be kept in full force by the company without further payment of premiums. It is used most often in the event of total and permanent disability.

Whole life insurance Life insurance payable to a beneficiary at the death of the insured whenever that occurs. Premiums may be payable for a specified number of years (limited payment life) or for life (straight life).

The appended Table shows U.S. life insurance companies—summary 1970 to 1987.

BIBLIOGRAPHY

AMERICAN COUNCIL OF LIFE INSURANCE. *Life Insurance Fact Book*. Latest edition.

BALDWIN, B. G. *The Complete Book of Insurance*, 1989.

Best, A. M., Co. *Life, Property and Casualty Reports*. Annual.

Best's Review (Life/health insurance edition), 1976. Annual.

Best's Review (Property/casualty insurance edition), 1976. Annual.

Business Insurance.

BROSTOFF, S. "Prop. 103 May Spread, Nader Warns." *National Underwriters* (Property & Casualty/Employee Benefits Edition), December 12, 1988.

DAILY, G. S. *The Individual Investor's Guide to Low-Load Insurance Products*. International Publishing Corp, Chicago, IL, 1989.

DAVIDS, L. E. *Dictionary of Insurance*. Rowman & Allanheld, Totowa, NJ, 1983.

GREENWALD, J. "Congress Probes Insurer Insolvencies." *Business Insurance*, November 14, 1988.

HARKAVY, J., and others. "California Referendum Strikes a National Chord." *Risk Management*. January, 1989.

Journal of Risk and Insurance.

Moody's Investors Service. *Moody's Bank and Finance Manual*, 1900 Moody's Investors Service, New York, NY. Annual.

PEAT MARWICK MAIN. "Insurers Annual Reports Reveal Concerns." *National Underwriter* (Property & Casualty/Employee Benefits Edition), November 21, 1988.

INSURANCE: COINSURANCE AND CONTRIBUTION CLAUSES

Insurance policies sometimes contain a deductible clause that excludes a fixed amount of the loss from recovery. Casualty insurance policies frequently contain a coinsurance clause in the contract. A coinsurance clause provides that the insurance company shall be liable for only a portion of any loss sustained by the insured unless the insured carries insurance that totals a certain percent, frequently 80-90% of the fair value of the asset. In the event of a loss, the insured recovers from the insurance company that portion of the loss which the face of the insurance policy bears to the amount of insurance that should be carried as required by the coinsurance clause.

The coinsurance indemnity is expressed as follows:

$$\frac{\text{Face amount of policy}}{\text{Coinsurance percentage} \times \text{Fair value of property at date of loss}} \times \text{Fair Value}$$

To illustrate, assume a company purchases a $20,000 insurance policy on some equipment; the policy has an 80% coinsurance clause. A fire loss occurs at a time when the fair value of the equipment was $30,000. The amount of the loss was $6,000:

$$\frac{\$20,000}{(80\%)(\$30,000)} \times \$6,000 = \$5,000 \text{ recoverable from insurer}$$

The insured can recover the lowest of the face of the policy, the fair value of the loss, or the coinsurance indemnity.

A contribution clause provides that when more than one policy is carried recovery of a loss is limited to the ratio of the face value of the policy to the total insurance carried. If the policies have different coinsurance requirements, the amount recoverable is computed as follows:

$$\text{Amount} = \text{Fair market value of asset destroyed} \times \frac{\text{Face value of individual policy}}{\text{(Higher of total face value of all policies or coinsurance requirement of individual policy)}}$$

INSURANCE COMPANIES

As a result of formation of holding companies in the INSURANCE field in the late 1960s, and acquisitions of insurance companies by noninsurance operating and holding companies, insurance companies with shares available for

INSURANCE COMPANIES

Table 3 / U.S. Life Insurance Companies—Summary: 1970 to 1987
(As of December 31 or calendar year, as applicable. Covers domestic and foreign business of U.S. companies.
See also *Historical Statistics, Colonial Times to 1970*, series X 879 and X 890-917.)

Item	Unit	1970	1975	1980	1981	1982	1983	1984	1985	1986	1987
U.S. companies	Number	1,780	1,746	1,958	1,991	2,060	2,117	2,193	2,261	2,254	2,265
Sales[1]	Bil. dol.	207	317	655	1,139	920	1,279	1,390	1,530	1,578	1,656
Ordinary	Bil. dol.	135	207	462	700	661	972	1,074	1,187	1,178	1,267
Group[1]	Bil. dol.	65	103	190	436	257	306	315	342	400	388
Industrial	Bil. dol.	7	7	4	3	2	2	1	1	Z	Z
Income	Bil. dol.	49.1	78.0	130.9	151.9	170.0	176.0	206.1	234.0	282.3	314.3
Life insurance premiums	Bil. dol.	21.7	29.3	40.8	46.3	50.8	50.3	51.3	60.1	66.2	76.7
Percent of total	Percent	44.2	37.6	31.2	30.5	29.9	28.6	24.9	25.7	23.5	24.4
Annuity considerations	Bil. dol.	3.7	10.2	22.4	27.6	34.6	30.5	42.8	53.9	83.7	88.7
Health insurance premiums	Bil. dol.	11.4	19.1	29.4	31.8	35.0	38.2	40.7	41.8	44.2	47.6
Investment and other	Bil. dol.	12.3	19.4	38.3	46.2	49.6	57.0	71.3	78.2	88.2	101.3
Disbursements	Bil. dol.	39.0	58.2	88.2	101.8	113.3	123.5	138.5	151.8	186.5	202.3
Payments to policyholders[2,3]	Bil. dol.	25.6	38.1	59.0	65.1	71.2	80.9	89.8	95.7	131.4	144.4
Percent of total	Percent	65.6	65.5	66.9	63.9	62.8	65.5	64.8	63.0	70.5	71.4
Death payments	Bil. dol.	7.2	9.3	12.9	13.6	14.5	16.8	17.6	18.5	19.6	20.7
Matured endowments	Bil. dol.	1.0	1.0	.8	.7	.6	.6	.7	.8	.8	.8
Annuity payments	Bil. dol.	1.7	3.2	7.4	9.6	10.3	12.7	18.0	19.7	17.8	20.3
Policy dividends	Bil. dol.	3.8	5.1	8.1	9.3	9.6	10.8	11.4	12.4	12.4	13.0
Surrender values[3]	Bil. dol.	2.9	3.8	6.4	7.1	9.8	12.5	14.5	15.9	49.6	53.7
Disability benefits	Bil. dol.	.2	.4	.5	.6	.5	.5	.4	.5	.5	.5
Commissions, expenses, etc.[3]	Bil. dol.	12.9	19.4	27.8	35.1	40.3	40.7	46.0	53.1	51.4	54.7
Dividends to stockholders	Bil. dol.	.5	.7	1.4	1.6	1.8	1.9	2.7	3.0	3.7	3.2
Balance Sheet											
Assets	Bil. dol.	207.3	289.3	479.2	525.8	588.2	654.9	723.0	825.9	937.6	1,044.5
Government securities	Bil. dol.	11.1	15.2	33.0	39.5	55.5	76.6	99.8	124.6	144.6	151.4
Corporate securities	Bil. dol.	88.5	133.9	227.0	241.5	268.5	297.0	322.5	374.3	432.9	502.2
Percent of total assets	Percent	42.7	46.3	47.4	45.9	45.7	45.3	44.6	45.3	46.2	48.1
Bonds	Bil. dol.	73.1	105.8	179.6	193.8	212.8	232.1	259.1	296.8	342.0	405.7
Stocks	Bil. dol.	15.4	28.1	47.4	47.7	55.7	64.9	63.4	77.5	90.9	96.5
Mortgages	Bil. dol.	74.4	89.2	131.1	137.7	142.0	151.0	156.7	171.8	193.8	213.5
Real estate	Bil. dol.	6.3	9.6	15.0	18.3	20.6	22.2	25.7	28.8	31.6	34.2
Policy loans	Bil. dol.	16.1	24.5	41.4	48.7	53.0	54.1	54.5	54.4	54.1	53.6
Other	Bil. dol.	10.9	16.9	31.7	40.1	48.6	54.0	63.8	72.0	80.6	89.6
Interest earned on assets[4]	Percent	5.30	6.36	8.02	8.57	8.91	8.96	9.45	9.63	9.35	9.09
Liabilities[2,5]	Bil. dol.	189.9	268.7	444.8	488.4	546.7	608.5	672.6	769.1	873.4	977.1
Policy reserves[2]	Bil. dol.	167.8	237.1	390.4	428.0	479.4	532.4	584.2	665.3	761.9	862.1
Annuities	Bil. dol.	48.9	80.8	181.5	209.1	252.4	296.5	341.7	410.6	488.6	561.7
Group	Bil. dol.	34.0	59.9	140.4	161.0	191.9	221.7	254.6	303.0	355.8	392.5
Individual[6]	Bil. dol.	14.9	20.9	41.0	48.1	60.5	74.8	87.1	107.6	132.8	169.2
Life insurance	Bil. dol.	115.4	150.1	197.9	207.0	213.8	221.0	225.9	235.9	252.0	276.4
Health insurance	Bil. dol.	3.5	6.3	11.0	11.9	13.2	15.0	16.6	18.8	21.3	24.0
Capital and surplus[2]	Bil. dol.	17.3	20.6	34.4	37.4	41.5	46.4	50.4	56.8	64.1	67.4

Z — Less than $500 million.
[1] Includes Servicemen's Group Life Insurance: $16.8 billion in 1970, $1.7 billion in 1975, $44.5 billion in 1981, and $50.8 billion in 1986; as well as Federal Employees' Group Life Insurance: $81.5 billion in 1981 and $10.8 billion in 1986.
[2] Includes operations of accident and health departments of life insurance companies.
[3] Beginning 1986, data not comparable to prior years due to change in accounting method.
[4] Net rate.
[5] Includes other obligations not shown separately.
[6] Includes reserves for supplementary contracts with and without life contingencies.

Source: American Council of Life Insurance, Washington, DC, *Life Insurance Fact Book*, biennial, and unpublished data.

public investment, directly or indirectly through investment in parent company shares, have become a motley group.

Insurance companies are usually organized as stock companies or mutual companies. A stock company is a corporation that is operated for profit and is owned and controlled by its stockholders. Generally the stockholders are not liable in cases of bankruptcy or for an impairment of capital. A mutual company is owned and controlled by its existing policyholders. If it is liquidated, its net assets are distributed to its policyholders after liabilities are settled. Some states provide for the assessment of policies for limited amounts in cases of bankruptcy or impairment of minimum capital requirements. Fraternal benefit societies exist and are organized for the benefit of their members. They operate much like mutual companies.

Insurance companies are regulated by state and federal agencies. State statutes develop and enforce policies that promote solvency, fair dealings with policyholders, and uniform financial reporting. State statutes usually restrict companies to certain types of securities, require minimum levels of capital surplus and policy reserves, and prescribe the methods to be used in valuing securities and other assets. State statutes also provide for various standard provisions in insurance policies and for the review and approval of the policy forms. Licensing of agents, brokers, and salespersons is also a typical state regulatory activity. Insurance companies are required to file annual financial statements in a prescribed form with the state insurance agencies. The Securities and Exchange Commission (SEC) has been assigned jurisdiction over stock insurance companies that

INSURANCE COMPANY INVESTMENTS

have not been specifically exempted and that offered their shares for sale through a national securities exchange.

The 20 leading property-casualty companies and groups ranked by net premiums as of December 31, 1986, include the following according to the American Council of Life Insurance:

20 Leading Property-Casualty Companies & Groups

State Farm Mutual Auto
Allstate
Aetna Life & Casualty
Nationwide Mutual
Liberty Mutual
Travelers
Farmers Insurance
Hartford Fire
American International
CIGNA
CNA
Continental Insurance
SFS&G
Fireman's Fund
Crum & Forster
Chubb
Kemper
St. Paul
General Re
Royal Insurance

The 20 largest life insurance companies ranked by admitted assets as of December 31, 1986, according to the American Council of Life Insurance include:

Prudential Insurance Co. of America
Metropolitan Life Insurance Co.
Equitable Life Assurance Society of the U.S.
Aetna Life Insurance Co.
New York Life Insurance Co.
Teachers Ins. & Annuity Ass. of America
John Hancock Mutual Life Insurance Co.
Travelers Insurance Co.
Connecticut General Life Insurance Co.
Northwestern Mutual Life Insurance Co.
Massachusetts Mutual Life Insurance Co.
Manufacturers Life Insurance Co.
Principal Mutual Life Insurance
Sun Life Assurance Co. of Canada
New England Mutual Life Insurance Co.
Great-West Life Assurance Co.
Mutual Life Insurance Co. of New York
Executive Life Insurance Co.
Mutual Benefit Life Insurance Co.
Connecticut Mutual Life Insurance Co.

Through parent company and/or holding company grouping, or through fleet grouping, all types of insurance (life, property and casualty coverages) are often provided, including in some cases the offering of VARIABLE ANNUITIES and mutual fund shares.

INSURANCE COMPANY INVESTMENTS See LIFE INSURANCE COMPANY INVESTMENTS.

INSURANCE COMPANY STATEMENTS Financial statements of INSURANCEcompanies, submitted in detail annually to the state superintendents or commissioners of insurance, reflect the dual nature of their operations as underwriting and investing institutions.

In general, the largest underwriting and investing insurance companies as a group are the life insurance companies because of both the large volume of new business and the long-term nature of policy contracts which involve the long-term accumulation and investment of reserves. Underwriting operations of all types of companies are regulated in detail by the home state in which the company is domiciled as well as by the states in which the company is admitted to do business, from the approval of types of policy contracts to prescribed accounting. Investing activities of life insurance companies are also regulated in various states in detail—particularly in New York State where, as the result of the Armstrong investigation of life insurance companies in 1906, the Insurance Law prohibits domestic companies from investing in or lending upon any stocks or shares of any corporation or institution except prescribed quality of preferred and guaranteed stocks and common stocks under quantitative limits, or life insurance company stock acquired for the purpose of mutualization. The Insurance Law also empowers the superintendent of insurance to refuse a new or renewal license to any nondomiciled company if he finds that its investments do not comply in substance with the investment requirements and limitations imposed upon domestic companies.

The majority of the large life insurance companies are mutualized, having no capital stock and thus in effect owned by the policyholders (who as general creditors would be entitled to sharing in the residual equity). The stock form of organization is most prevalent in the property and casualty fields, although the mutual companies have grown substantially in these fields.

Income accounts for life insurance companies (income and disbursements, gain and loss exhibit) are mere reports of income, disposition of income, and reconciliation of surplus, rather than statements of true earnings for any particular period. Calculation of true earnings for a specified period would involve determination of a variety of hidden earnings and equities inherent in outstanding policy contracts not reflected in these statements.

In December, 1972, the American Institute of Certified Public Accountants adopted its "Audits of Stock Life Insurance Companies," calling for generally accepted accounting principles (GAAP) in financial statements of stock life insurance companies.

Among property and casualty companies, income accounts (underwriting exhibit, investment exhibit) come closer to reflecting current earnings, except that the reported ("statutory") underwriting results, reported in the statutorily prescribed form, are distorted by fluctuations in the unearned premiums reserve and its influence on the earned premiums credit to underwriting account. In accordance with the Insurance Law, all premiums paid in advance must be credited to the unearned premiums reserve, but the expenses of writing the business are charged immediately to the underwriting account, so that the underwriting profit or loss does not reflect the premiums until they are fully earned by the passage of time.

Another characteristic of insurance company statements has been the use of "association" (formerly "convention") valuations for investment holdings. The National Convention of Insurance Commissioners, which is now known as the National Association of Insurance Commissioners, first authorized the use of convention values for the December 31, 1931, statements, permitting valuation of securities at June 30, 1931, prices as a means of permitting marginal companies to report higher book surpluses at that year-end. The practice of authorizing some modification of "all market" values for year-end statements has been continued in every year since, although the original motive and necessity no longer apply, and the particular valuation formulas may vary among the states. Association values for recent years' statements have called for amortized values for eligible bonds, which shall be current as to payments of principal and interest and shall meet specified minimal quality ratings and analytical standards, and for market values for stocks and bonds ineligible for amortized values. In addition, since 1951 the commissioners have prescribed a mandatory securities valuation reserve for life insurance companies and fraternal benefit societies; for recent years, it was to build up to a maximum accumulation of 2% (of aggregate values at date of statement) to 10% for eligible bonds and 20% for all other bonds; maximum accumulation of 5% for preferred stocks prescribed in "good standing" to 20% for all other preferred stocks; and maximum accumulation of 20% of shares of subsidiary, controlled, or affiliated companies plus 33.3% of all other common stocks and stock purchase warrants or options. Net realized and unrealized capital gains, under the commissioners' treatment, would be credited to the Common Stock Reserve Component as long as such component was below its prescribed maximum accumulation; when it was at maximum accumulation, such capital gains could at the company's option be credited to the bond and preferred stock reserve component so long as the latter component was below its own maximum accumulation. Net realized and unrealized capital losses would be charged to the common stock reserve component after the temporary excess reserve component had been exhausted. The latter arose as a result of the residual allocation of the December 31, 1964, mandatory securities valuation reserve among the above reserve components. These reserves were intended to

---

ENCYCLOPEDIA OF BANKING AND FINANCE

provide a first line of defense against fluctuation in and losses on security holdings. The AICPA's Audit Guide, "Audits of Stock Life Insurance Companies," called for elimination of such mandatory securities valuation reserve.

Book values (net asset values) per share for life insurance companies and for property and casualty insurance companies do not fully reflect full equity values, as they are merely based on policyholders' surplus at market values (capital and surplus and voluntary equity reserves) and do not reflect the additional equities referred to above in discussion of adjustment of life and property and casualty insurance company earnings. In analysis of insurance holding company or parent company equities, full computation of net asset value should include such additional equities beyond the policyholders' surplus totals. Analytically, however, insurance stocks (whether of operating companies or of insurance holding companies) should primarily emphasize earning power (adjusted operating earnings), which in turn is principally determined by investing operations (net investment income and turnover of securities) and fundamentally influenced by the leverage ratio of invested assets to net assets as well as available returns and turnover profits or losses. In fact, insurance companies might be likened to institutional investors with underwriting operations providing cash flows for investing leverage.

See LIFE INSURANCE COMPANY INVESTMENTS.

BIBLIOGRAPHY

AMERICAN INSTITUTE OF CERTIFIED PUBLIC ACCOUNTANTS. *Audits of Stock Life Insurance Companies.* Latest edition.
SECURITIES AND EXCHANGE COMMISSION. *Regulation S-X* (Article 7, Fire and Casualty Insurance Companies, and Article 7A, Life Insurance Companies).

INSURANCE DEPARTMENT The department of a state that supervises the organization, management, and examination of insurance companies, title and mortgage companies, and so on, doing business or having a corporate existence in that state. In three states, the regulation of banking, insurance, mortgage, and title companies is combined in one department known as the Department of Banking and Insurance, headed by the commissioner of banking and insurance. In other states, the head of the department is variously known as the superintendent of insurance, commissioner of insurance, insurance commissioner, director of insurance, etc.

INSURANCE RISK The insurance risk of a property-casualty insurance company is measured by the following ratio:

$$\text{Insurance risk} = \frac{\text{Annual premium income}}{\text{Total capital and surplus}}$$

The Investment risk of a property-casualty insurance company is measured as follows:

$$\text{Investment risk} = \frac{\text{Total common stock holdings}}{\text{Total capital and surplus}}$$

A high insurance risk indicates that the company may be subject to high claims and may seek to maintain higher levels of liquidity, safety, and predictability in its investment portfolio. A high growth rate in premium income may indicate a quantitative increase in the insurance risk ratio. This could result in a weakening in underwriting quality standards to generate business.

INSURANCE: SELF Some companies, governmental institutions, and other entities decide not to purchase insurance. If the decison is not to insure, the entity may decide to periodically set aside funds to provide for potential losses. Such programs are referred to as "self-insurance." They are in effect no insurance programs. Self-insurance should ordinarily not be relied upon unless one's assets are geographically scattered in such a manner that they are not subject to the same area risks.

INSURANCE TRUST A TRUST created by a life insurance policyholder which directs that the funds represented by such policies, when they become a claim against the insurance company or companies, shall be paid to the trustee of the insurance trust agreement and administered according to its terms rather than by direct payment to the estate or to the beneficiaries. Insurance trusts can be established through trust companies or the trust departments of such banks as are eligible to engage in trust business. Insurance trusts are classified as funded if the settlor transfers funds to the trustee out of the income from which the expense of premiums on the policy may be met, or unfunded if he does not. Insurance trusts wherein the beneficiaries are relatives of the insured-settlor are called personal insurance trusts; if the beneficiaries are connected with partnerships or corporations, the trusts are called business insurance trusts.

The principal purpose of an insurance trust is to prevent the impairment or loss of principal of insurance funds paid to beneficiaries through bad management, inexperience in making investments, deliberate swindling by stock promotors, or other ways. Large sums of money are lost to beneficiaries who lack experience in handling large sums, and the insurance trust is a device that may be used for the protection of dependents against their own misjudgment or mismanagement.

The insurance company by means of settlement options often gives the insured choices for final settlement of the policy other than lump sum payment, such settlement options being of three types: holding the proceeds and paying the interest to the beneficiary for life or for a stated number of years, with principal sum payable at the end of the period; paying the proceeds, including interest earnings, in equal installments for a stated number of years, at the end of which period the original principal will have been entirely distributed; and paying the proceeds as a life income to the beneficiary and, in the event the beneficiary dies before the entire proceeds shall have been paid, paying the balance to some other named beneficiary until the entire amount has been distributed. Although the language "holding the proceeds in trust" is often loosely used in this connection, these settlement options do not give rise to legal trusts since the insurance company's liability is really contractual.

Particular advantages of the insurance trust are that the spouse, children, and other dependents are protected against the unwise use of large proceeds; it is not necessary to probate the insurance trust; and insurance payable to beneficiaries other than the executor or administrator of the estate of the insured is not subject to the debts of the insured (N.Y. Insurance Law, Sec. 55a). Until Section 811(g) of the Internal Revenue Code was completely revised in 1942, there was also the advantage of some freedom from estate taxes on the estate of the insured (to the extent of the first $40,000 of the amount receivable by beneficiaries other than the executor or administrator).

INSURED BANK A bank covered by the benefits of federal deposit insurance under the provisions of the Federal Deposit Insurance Act of September 21, 1950 (64 Stat. 873; 12 U.S.C. 1811-1831), formerly Section 12B of the Federal Reserve Act enacted June 16, 1933.

Banks eligible for deposit insurance and/or required to be insured are as follows.

1. All national banks (except those in the territories of the United States, Puerto Rico, Guam, and the Virgin Islands) are required to be insured banks.
2. All state banks that are members of the Federal Reserve System are required to be insured banks.
3. All state banks and national banks that are not members of the Federal Reserve System may become insured banks upon application to the FEDERAL DEPOSIT INSURANCE CORPORATION (FDIC) and compliance with statutory requirements.

Before approving any such application, the corporation's board of directors shall give consideration to the following factors: the financial history and condition of the bank; the adequacy of its capital structure; its future earnings prospects; the general character of its management; the convenience and needs of the community served by the bank; and whether or not its corporate powers are consistent with the purposes of the Federal Deposit Insurance Act. In addition to considering these factors, the corporation's board of directors shall determine upon the basis of a thorough examination of the applying bank that its assets in excess of its capital requirements are adequate to enable it to meet all its liabilities to depositors and other creditors as shown by the bank's books.

State nonmember banks and national nonmember banks may terminate their status as insured banks and still continue to operate, but a state bank cannot continue as a member of the Federal Reserve System, and a national member bank cannot continue to operate, if its insurance is voluntarily or involuntarily terminated.

Number. Since 1934, the number of commercial banks in the United States has remained approximately stable, reflecting mergers and consolidations as well as relatively well controlled granting of new charters, but the number of their branches have expanded over time. In 1934, there were approximately 15,000 banks and 3,000 branches in operation, with about 90% of these banks insured by the Federal Deposit Insurance Corporation. As of December 31, 1985, the 14,936 commercial banks had 41,909 branch offices, of which 98% of all commercial banks were insured by the Federal Deposit Insurance Corporation. In addition, 324 mutual savings banks with 2,516 branches were insured by the Federal Depsosit Insurance Corporation, of the total of 463 mutual savings banks and their 2,865 branches.

INTANGIBLE ASSETS

Special rights, grants, privileges, and advantages possessed by a business that can benefit future operations by contributing to the enterprise's earning power. Intangible assets do not possess physical substance. Intangible assets include patents, copyrights, trademarks, trade names, franchises, licenses, royalties, formulas, processes, organization costs, leasehold and leasehold improvements, and goodwill.

Intangible assets may be acquired from other enterprises or individuals or developed by a company. They can be classified as unidentifiable and identifiable assets. An unidentifiable intangible is one that cannot exist independent of the business as a whole. Goodwill and organization costs are unidentifiable intangible assets. Identifiable intangibles have a separate identity and existence of their own independent of the business as a whole. Patents, copyrights, and medical patient charts are examples of identifiable intangible assets. If acquired by purchase, the intangible item is recognized as an asset. If developed by the enterprise, the research and development costs are expenses when incurred.

The life of an intangible asset may be determinable if fixed by law, regulation, agreement, contract, or by the nature of the asset. The cost of an intangible asset having a determinable life should be amortized in a rational and systematic manner over the term of its existence, but not to exceed 40 years. If the life of the intangible asset is indeterminate, as might be the case for goodwill and trade names, the cost of the assets should be written off over a period of years established by management, but not to exceed 40 years. The straight-line method of amortization should be used to write off the cost of intangible assets over future periods to be benefited by the assets unless another systematic method is considered more relevant and reliable.

A patent has a legal life of 17 years. Copyrights are granted for a period of years covering the life of the creator of the copyright plus an additional 50 years. Franchises may be granted for a limited or unlimited period. Organization costs are incurred during the formation of a corporation and prior to income-producing operations. Such costs include expenditures relating to promoters, attorneys, accountants, underwriters' charges as well as registration and listing fees and printing costs associated with the issuance of securities. Such costs should be written off over a period of time not to exceed 40 years. Leasehold improvements should be written off over the term of the lease.

INTEGRATION

Under the PUBLIC UTILITY HOLDING COMPANY ACT OF 1935, the Securities and Exchange Commission was directed to take action to limit system operation to companies that are "integrated," both geographically and as to nature of operations. An integrated system is defined as one capable of economic operation as a single coordinated system confined to a single area or region in one or more states, and not so large as to impair the advantages of localized management, efficient operation, and effectiveness of regulation. Previously, many large holding company systems were composed of companies operating in many widely separated states.

In expansion and combination of business corporations, integration refers to the direction of such acquisitions by a dominant company. For example, a manufacturing company acquiring units assuring it of owned sources of raw materials would be said to be integrating "backwards," i.e., to the raw material supply; in acquiring sales outlets, it would be said to be integrating "forward," i.e., to direct contact with consumers. Such a manufacturing company, having completed such expansion and/or acquisitions, would be said to be a fully integrated company, i.e., vertically integrated from the sources of raw material to the manufacturing stage and the distribution stage. Horizontal integration would occur if the manufacturing company acquired other manufacturing companies in the same line of industry. Integration is one of the motivations for a MERGER.

INTER-AMERICAN DEVELOPMENT BANK

As of 1987, the subscribed ordinary and interregional capital totaled $34 billion, of which $2.6 billion was paid-in and the balance of $31.4 billion was callable. The U.S. had subscribed to the ordinary capital in the amounts of $920 million paid-in and $11 billion callable.

Besides its capital funds, the IADB had as of 1987 outstanding funded debt of $12.1 billion consisting of the following payable portions: in U.S. dollars, $3.1 billion; in dollar equivalents, $3 billion in Japanese yen, $2.2 billion in Swiss francs, $2.2 billion in German marks, $848 million in Netherlands guilders, $600 million in pounds sterling, $107 million in European currency units, $63 million in Austrian schillings, and $5 million in Trinidad and Tobago dollars.

A draft of the agreement establishing this development institution was approved April 8, 1959, by a specialized committee of the Organization of American States (OAS) in which representatives from the 20 Latin American countries and the U.S. participated. The agreement became effective in December, 1959, when it was accepted by 19 Latin American republics and the U.S., and the first organizational meeting was held February 3-10, 1960. Operations commenced on October 1, 1960. The U.S. became a member by virtue of the Inter-American Development Bank Act (73 Stat. 299; 22 U.S.C. 283 note).

The Inter-American Development Bank (IADB) is owned by the governments of 26 regional and 15 nonregional countries. Nonregional countries admitted to membership since 1976 have included Austria, Belgium, Denmark, Finland, France, West Germany, Israel, Italy, Japan, Norway, the Netherlands, Portugal, Spain, Sweden, Switzerland, the United Kingdom, and Yugoslavia.

The purpose of the institution is "to contribute to the acceleration of the process of economic development of the member countries, individually and collectively." In carrying out its functions, the bank cooperates with national and international institutions and with private sources supplying investment capital. Two kinds of loans are made: "hard" loans, that must be repaid in dollars and carry commercial terms and "soft" loans that may be made from the fund for special operations, repayable in nondollar currencies and carrying low interest rates. The bank may make loans to either governmental or private entities. Loans generally are made for specific projects but also may be granted to development banks and institutions in member countries for relending for projects not large enough to warrant direct credits from the bank. Loans to private borrowers are made with an appropriate guarantee. The bank provides technical advice and assistance in preparing, financing, and executing development plans and projects, including the consideration of priorities and the formulation of loan proposals on specific national or regional development projects.

Proceeds of the outstanding funded debt are included in the ordinary and interregional capital resources available for lending. The bank's policy is not to borrow in excess of 80% of the amount of the uncalled subscription to the callable shares, and such subscriptions are callable only when required to meet the bank's obligations arising from borrowing funds for the bank's ordinary capital or from guarantees chargeable to such resources.

The bank separately administers a fund for special operations, which totaled the equivalent of $8.4 billion as of the close of 1986. In addition, the bank administers funds entrusted to it by various member and nonmember countries. Among such funds are the social progress trust fund, whose resources of $525 million from the U.S. have been committed in loans; the Venezuelan trust fund, $500 million, established in 1975 under agreement between the bank and the Venezuelan Investment Fund to help finance projects in less developed countries, those with limited markets, and those of intermediate development; and other funds established by Argentina, Canada, West Germany, Norway, Sweden, Switzerland, the United Kingdom, the Vatican, and the Intergovernmental Committee for European Migration to help foster the economic and social development of the bank's member countries in Latin America.

Lending Activity. As of the close of 1986, the IADB had extended loans from all of its sources of funds, aggregating $35.4 billion.

Membership. Original members, pursuant to the agreement establishing the Inter-American Development Bank, which came into effect in December, 1959, were 19 Latin American republics and the U.S. Trinidad and Tobago became members in 1967, Barbados and Jamaica in 1969, Canada in 1972, Guyana in 1976, the Bahamas in 1977, and SULINAME in 1980.

Following the Declaration of Madrid, signed on December 17, 1974, the bank completed action to amend its Articles of Agreement on June 1, 1976, enabling the admission of nonregional countries. Belgium, Denmark, Germany, Israel, Japan, Spain, Switzerland, the United Kingdom, and Yugoslavia became members in 1976; Austria, the Netherlands, France, Italy, Finland, and Sweden joined the bank in 1977, Portugal in 1980, and Norway in 1986.

BIBLIOGRAPHY

Dell, S. S. *The Inter-American Development Bank: A Study in Development Banking*, 1972.
Inter-American Development Bank. *Annual Report*.

INTERCHANGEABLE BONDS *First read* coupon bonds, re-gistered bond.

Bonds that may be converted from coupon to registered form (or vice versa) and back again to coupon (or registered) form. Most bonds that have once been converted from coupon to registered form cannot be changed back to coupon form. Registered bonds do not enjoy as ready a market or command as high a price as coupon bonds; for this reason, the option of conversion is valuable.

INTERDISTRICT SETTLEMENT ACCOUNT A gold certificate fund held by the United States Treasurer for the account of and subject to the order of the Board of Governors of the Federal Reserve System but belonging to the 12 Federal Reserve banks, the purpose of which is to effect with as little delay and cost as possible the settlement of inter-Federal Reserve bank transactions. The fund is a part of the machinery of the federal reserve interdistrict collection system provided for in Section 16 of the Federal Reserve Act. By means of this system, domestic exchange has been greatly facilitated and the necessity for frequent currency shipments from one part of the country to another has been practically eliminated.

In this function, the Board of Governors of the Federal Reserve System acts as a clearinghouse for the Federal Reserve banks, which in turn act as a nationwide clearinghouse for their member banks and for such nonmember banks as maintain clearing accounts with the Federal Reserve banks. Originally, the board of governors directed each Federal Reserve bank to forward to the Treasury or to the nearest subtreasury $1 million in gold and, in addition, an amount at least equal to its net indebtedness to all other Federal Reserve banks so that the first weekly settlement might take place May 27, 1915. Since July 1, 1918, settlements have been made daily. Each Federal Reserve bank wires the net credits due to other Federal Reserve banks and their branches to the board of governors daily through the system of private or leased wires connecting practically all Federal Reserve banks and branches and the board. Adjustments are made by book entries to the respective portions of the account of each Federal Reserve bank affected. In this way, the clearances are made and the ownership of each Federal Reserve bank in the account is constantly fluctuating, although the total of the account continues intact.

Items cleared through the account include check collections, transfers of funds for member banks and the Treasury, Federal Reserve bank investment items, and other interdistrict business. Direct forwarding of checks and settlement of interdistrict checks through the Interdistrict Settlement account have reduced materially the average time formerly required to collect out-of-town checks. Wire transfers of funds by member banks through their local Federal Reserve banks may be made at no charge if the transfers are for multiples of $1,000, and at a charge for the cost of telegrams when such transfers are made for designated customers. These transfers are made by wire from the sending to the receiving Federal Reserve bank, and settlements therefor are accomplished through the Interdistrict Settlement Account.

See par clearances, par list.

INTEREST The price of money; rental payment upon money; a charge made to the borrower by the lender for the use of money. Interest is expressed in terms of an annual rate of percentage upon the principal. Thus, if $6.00 is paid for the annual use of $100, the rate is 6%; the (annual) rate is also 6% if $0.50 is paid for one month's use of $100. Interest is often payable at intervals shorter than one year but rarely at longer intervals. Interest on modern amortized mortgages, for example, is paid in monthly installments including as a portion thereof amortization payment on principal. Interest on bonds is usually paid semiannually. Interest on commercial loans may be paid quarterly, while the charge for federal funds (*See* money market) is computed on an actual day basis (360-day year).

Simple interest is that computed upon the principal without reference to the interest period, on the assumption (for exact simple interest) that $1/365$ th of a year's interest accrues each day. It is equivalent to compounding at the day of calculation; if the interest period is less than one year, the nominal simple interest rate is greater than the true interest rate compounded annually. Practically, however, this difference is disregarded.

Ordinary simple interest is based on the assumption that each day is $1/360$ th of a year. Ordinary interest for one day is slightly more than exact interest for one day.

Compound interest is computed upon the principal plus the interest that has accrued and is payable on the agreed interest date. Interest is usually compounded monthly, quarterly, semiannually, or annually.

When interest is compounded more frequently than once a year, it produces an "effective" rate in excess of the nominal or quoted rate. For example, if the nominal interest rate on a $1,000 bond is 4% payable annually, the effective interest rate is the same, i.e., 4%; if payable semiannually, it is 4.04%; if payable quarterly, it is 4.0604%; if payable monthly, it is 4.0742%; and if payable daily, it is 4.0811%. The interest on a $1,000 4% bond compounded annually is therefore $40; $40.40 if compounded semiannually; $40.604 if compounded quarterly; $40.742 if compounded monthly; and $40.811 if compounded daily. Effective savings, therefore, are obtainable by compounding annually instead of more frequently.

In corporate bond practice, there is no compounding of interest. A $1,000 corporate bond bearing 4% interest, payable semiannually, will pay $20 interest on the semiannual interest payment dates specified. The interest on registered bonds is paid by check to the registered owners; in the case of coupon bonds, it is paid upon presentation of properly dated coupons to the payment agent. There is no interest on interest; if coupons are not presented promptly for payment, there will not be any interest on the interest since the specified payment date.

See deposit interest rates, discount, interest balance, interest rate ceiling, interest tables, legal rate of interest, usury.

BIBLIOGRAPHY

Babbel, D. F. "Interest Rate Dynamics and the Term Structure." *Bank Finance*, September, 1988.
"Caps and Floors." *The Banker*, February, 1989.
Degler, W. "How You Can Collar Your Interest Rate Exposure." *Futures*, February, 1989.
Hegde, S. P. "An Empirical Analysis of Implicit Delivery Options in the Treasury Bond Futures Contract." *Journal of Banking and Finance*, September, 1988.
Jamshidian, F. "An Exact Bond Option Formula." *Journal of Finance*, March, 1989.
Lamy, R. E., and Thompson, G. R. "Risk Premia and the Pricing of Primary Issue Bonds." *Journal of Banking and Finance*, December, 1988.
"Risk-Based Capital Rules Would Favor Mortgage Lenders." *Savings Institutions*, December, 1988.
Simonson, D. G. "Asset/Liability Software." *United States Banker*, March, 1989.
Strauss, M. J. "Who Call the Shots on A/L Management?" *Bankers Monthly*, February, 1989.
Titman, S., and Warga, A. "Stock Returns as Predictors of Interest Rates and Inflation." *Journal of Financial and Quantitative Analysis*, March, 1989.
Wright, G. B., and others. "Risk Assessment in Savings and Loan Institutions and the Internal Auditor." *Internal Auditor*, February, 1989.

INTEREST ACCRUED *See* accrued interest.

INTEREST ADDED *See* accrued interest.

INTEREST ADJUSTMENT ACT OF 1966 An act that broadened interest ceilings to cover savings and loan associations and several types of thrift institutions not previously affected by the Banking Act of 1933 (through Federal Reserve Regulation Q). Savings and loan associations could pay a slight interest rate premium over that offered by commercial banks. Several major revisions were made in Regulation Q ceiling rates on savings and small time deposits in 1970, 1973, and 1987. Interest ceilings were eventually phased out on savings account interest rates.

INTEREST AND DIVIDEND TAX COMPLIANCE ACT OF 1983 An act that repealed mandatory withholding on interest and dividend payments as provided in the Tax Equity and Fiscal Responsibility Act of 1982 (TEFRA). The act increased penalties on payor institutions that failed to provide IRS with correct information.

INTEREST BALANCE Prior to passage of the Banking Act of 1933 which prohibited interest on demand deposits, the interest balance of an account was the amount upon which interest for the day was computed. This amount did not necessarily agree with the total credit balance in the account because of deposit of checks and other items not available until cleared or collected.

In modern account analysis, average collected balances, after deducting reverse requirements, are the basis for allowance of the earnings credit to the account, usually based on the current rate or return on earning assets. Against this, the cost of handling items deposited or drawn is charged.

See BANK COST ACCOUNTING.

INTEREST-BEARING SECURITIES Bonds, notes, mortgages, debentures, certificates of indebtedness, equipment trust certificates, and other evidences of debt, that yield interest, as contrasted with equity securities, such as preferred stocks, common stocks, and other evidences of ownership, that yield dividends and other distributions. Interest and dividends differ in their strength of claim, interest being a fixed charge which if not paid entitles the creditors to legal recourse in event of default; whereas dividends are not fixed charges, being dependent upon availability of funds therefor as well as decision by the management of the entity whether or not to pay dividends. Omission of dividends, therefore, does not give the equity owners the power to enforce any claim for dividends; even in the case of *cumulative* preferred stocks, omission of dividends does not give holders of such preferred stocks legal recourse for payment but merely the entitlement to such omitted dividends (on which no interest is paid) plus regular dividends before the common stock shall receive dividends; and in the event of liquidation, entitlement of such omitted dividends plus the asset preferences for the preferred stocks, before the common stock receives any distributions. See BOND, PREFERRED STOCK.

INTEREST COVERAGE RATIO The ratio of earnings before interest and taxes for a particular reporting period to the amount of interest charges for the period. The ratio is one measure of the ability of a company to service its debts in relation to its financial charges. The ratio is a rough measure of financial risk, depending upon the payment schedule of the debt and the average interest rate. The assessment of financial risk can be improved when the coverage ratio is considered in connection with the cash flow ability of the firm to service debt. Investment services companies make extensive use of interest coverage ratios.

INTEREST EQUALIZATION TAX Because of overall deficits in its balance of payments in the 1960s, the U.S. instituted the interest equalization tax in 1963, along with the VOLUNTARY FOREIGN CREDIT RESTRAINT (VFCR) PROGRAM in 1965, and restraints on direct investment (beginning in 1965 on a voluntary basis, but converted into the mandatory Foreign Direct Investment Program in 1968). The tax was extended in 1965, 1967, 1969, and again in 1971 by virtue of P.L. 92-9, extending the tax through March 31, 1973.

On January 29, 1974, the Board of Governors of the Federal Reserve System announced the termination of its VFCR guidelines. The program based on these guidelines had been designed to restrain foreign lending and foreign investment by banks and other financial institutions in order to protect with U.S. balance of payments. The VFCR was ended in conjunction with actions taken by the U.S. Treasury Department to reduce the interest equalization tax to zero, and by the Department of Commerce to terminate its foreign direct investment restrictions.

The tax was in essence an excise tax, applicable to securities sold in U.S. capital markets by developed countries (except new Canadian issues) and long-term bank loans (with similar exemptions). The 1969 extension exempted financing transactions in connection with U.S. exports from the tax. The original 1963 tax imposed a flat rate, equivalent to 1% annual interest, on U.S. purchases of foreign stocks and bonds with maturities of 28.5 years or longer, graduated downwards for bonds with shorter maturities. The 1967 extension raised the effective annual interest rate equivalent to 1.5%; the 1969 extension gave the President the flexible authority to vary the tax from zero to the 1.5% interest equivalent and to reduce the tax on new issues of foreign securities while leaving the existing tax on outstanding foreign issues unchanged.

The interest equalization tax was criticized as not having helped the U.S. balance of payments, although it apparently reduced purchases by U.S. investors of securities of other developed countries. But the tax was only part of the total program of restraints on capital outflows, and of course a variety of other factors also played their part in the U.S. balance-of-payments difficulties.

INTEREST RATE CEILING

Interest Rate Ceiling on U.S. Bonds. P.L. 92-13, signed May 14, 1971, authorized the U.S. Treasury to sell $10 billion in bonds (marketable obligations with maturities of over seven years) without being subject to the interest rate ceiling of 4.25% on such issues first enacted in 1917, in Section 1 of the Second Liberty Loan Act as amended (31 U.S.C. 752). There is no statutory maximum on the interest rate that can be paid for marketable issues of seven years or less (bills, certificates, and notes).

The Treasury had asked for complete elimination of the interest rate ceiling on U.S. bonds because of its inability since mid-1965 to issue marketable securities maturing in over seven years at par, owing to market yields prevailing above the 4.25% ceiling. As a result, the average maturity of the Treasury's marketable debt declined from about 5.5 years in mid-1965 to an average of 3 years, 3 months for the fiscal year 1971, raising the amount of maturing debt to be refunded each year to over $100 billion a year.

The ostensible limit of 4.25% on the interest rate for U.S. bonds has been repeatedly exempted by Congress for specified total amounts of issue in recent years. As of February 1987, the U.S. Treasury was authorized to issue up to $270 billion of publicly held U.S. bonds exempt from any interest rate limit. With prevailing market interest rates for financing in bonds continuing in recent years well above the 4.25% statutory interest rate ceiling, indications pointed to continued additional authorized exemptions from the ceiling so that the Treasury may finance some portion of its requirements in long-term bonds.

Besides increasing flexibility, arguments for total removal of the interest rate ceiling include the following: any such ceiling prevents the lengthening of the average maturity of the federal debt by financing via long-term bonds at times of feasible rates; such an interest rate ceiling is unrealistic and contrary to the principle that the Treasury should pay open market rates of interest determined by the supply and demand for prime money, as reflected in the prices and yields of outstanding issues established competitively in the government securities market, or else be disciplined in its financing plans by such open market rates. On the other hand, arguments for retention are as follows: the interest rate ceiling prevents the funding of debt into long-term maturities at high interest costs; if the Treasury so desires, it can issue new Treasury bonds at yields higher than 4.25% by offering bonds at a discount, rather than by paying interest rates higher than the ceiling.

See UNITED STATES GOVERNMENT SECURITIES.

Interest Rate Ceilings on Deposits. The Board of Governors of the Federal Reserve System, by Subsection (j) of Section 19 of the Federal Reserve Act, is empowered, after consulting with the Board of Directors of the Federal Deposit Insurance Corporation and the Federal Home Loan Bank Board, to limit by regulation (the Board's Regulation Q) the rates of interest that may be paid by member banks on time and savings deposits.

See DEPOSIT INTEREST RATES.

Title II, Depository Institutions Deregulation Act of 1980, of the DEPOSITORY INSTITUTIONS DEREGULATION AND MONETARY CONTROL ACT OF 1980, P.L. 96-221, March 31, 1980, provided for the phasing out over six years of maximum interest rates that financial institutions could pay on deposits. The act directed the Deregulation Committee "as rapidly as economic conditions warrant" to provide for the orderly phaseout and ultimate elimination of maximum rates of interest and dividends that may be paid on deposits and accounts. The committee is directed to work toward providing all depositors with a market rate or return on their savings with due regard for the safety and soundness of depository institutions, and also to increase to market rates "as soon as feasible" all limitations on the maximum rates of interest and dividends that may be paid on deposits and accounts. Collectively, ceilings set by the various regulatory agencies have been referred to as Regulation Q ceilings, although that regulation strictly speaking is that of the Board of Governors of the Federal Reserve System.

The Depository Institutions Deregulation Committee (DIDC) as of July 8, 1981, released the final rules concerning the phaseout of interest rate ceilings on all time deposits at commercial banks, savings and loan associations, and mutual savings banks. (See 12 CFR, Chapter XII, Part 1204.)

The phaseout plan adopted by the DIDC was as follows:

Step 1 (August 1, 1981)

1. Eliminate all rate ceilings on all new time deposits with an original maturity of 4 years or more.
2. Index rate ceilings for new time deposits with an original maturity of 2.5 years to 4 years to the average 2.5-year yield on U.S. Treasury securities and retain the 25 basis point differential between commercial banks and thrift institutions. The interest rate ceiling for thrifts would be the average Treasury yield, and the rate ceiling for commercial banks would be the average Treasury yield less 25 basis points.

Step 2 (August 1, 1982)

1. Eliminate rate ceilings on all new time deposits with an original maturity of 3 years or more.
2. Index rate ceilings for new 2- to 3-year time deposits to the average 2-year yield on U.S. Treasury securities and retain the differential, as described in Step 1 above.

Step 3 (August 1, 1983)

1. Eliminate rate ceilings on all new time deposits with an original maturity of 2 years or more.
2. Index rate ceilings for new 1- to 2-year time deposits to the rate for 1-year Treasury securities without a differential between commercial banks and thrift institutions.

Step 4 (August 1, 1984)

1. Eliminate rate ceilings on all new time deposits with an original maturity of 1 year or more.
2. Index rate ceilings for new time deposits with a maturity of less than 1 year to the rate for 13-week Treasury securities without a differential between commercial banks and thrift institutions.

Step 5 (August 1, 1985)

1. Eliminate rate ceilings on all time deposits.

The new rules apply only to new time deposits issued on or after each of the relevant dates; the rates payable on existing time and savings deposits would be unaffected by the new rules. Moreover, ceiling rates for new time deposits with maturities other than those specified in the phaseout schedule on each of the relevant implementation dates would remain unchanged unless specifically acted upon in the future by the Committee.

Money Market Accounts. Authorized by the GARN-ST. GERMAIN DEPOSITORY INSTITUTIONS ACT OF 1982 (P.L. 97-320, October 15, 1982), such money market accounts are intended to compete with high-yielding MONEY MARKET FUNDS. Specific terms of these new money market accounts, which are federally insured accounts, were set at the November, 1982, meeting of the DIDC, and offered by the depository institutions to the public commencing December 14, 1982.

The DIDC agreed to permit the financial institutions to decide what interest rate would be paid on the money market accounts, without ceiling. However, institutions will not be allowed to guarantee a fixed rate on the MMAs for more than 30 days at a time.

The DIDC also set a $2,500 required minimum balance on the new MMAs. Depositors may make unlimited withdrawals from such accounts, but if the average monthly balance falls below $2,500, the interest rate will be reduced to the ceiling rate applicable to regular negotiable orders of withdrawal (NOW) accounts (not the "Super-NOW" accounts, see below). Congress had suggested that the minimum deposit be no more than $5,000 but left the final determination to the DIDC.

As in the case of money market funds, depositors in the new money market accounts may write checks on such accounts. But depository institutions are authorized to allow three third-party transactions per month on each account and overall a total of just six transfers per month per account (three checks, and three other transactions such as telephone transfers, etc.). Any more than six transfers per month would cause the money market account to be classified as a transaction account, and therefore subject to the legal reserve requirement of banks on transaction accounts. If the referenced limit of six transfers is observed, a money market account held by natural persons is classified as a personal nontransaction account, and hence not subject to any legal reserve requirement as of 1984. Money market accounts held by parties other than natural persons, such as corporations, are subject to the legal reserve requirements on nonpersonal time deposits if the limit of six transfers per month is observed; any transfers over such limit would subject such accounts to the legal reserve requirements on transaction accounts. (See RESERVE.)

The new money market accounts of financial institutions have been called the most important banking innovation in recent times.

New "Super-NOW" Accounts. Also authorized by the DIDC to financial institutions, for offering to the public beginning January 5, 1983, were the new "Super-NOW" accounts, so called because although regular NOW accounts are subject to interest rate ceilings (5.5% for thrift institutions, and 5.25% for commercial banks), the interest rate that may be offered by the financial institutions on the new "Super-NOW" accounts may be set by them without ceilings.

Minimum balance for "Super-NOW" accounts was set at $2,500, the same minimum as for the new money market accounts, and similarly if the minimum balance fell below $2,500, the interest rate would be reduced to the ceiling rates above referred to, for regular NOW accounts. "Super-NOW" accounts would be subject to legal reserve requirements, unlike the new money market accounts; but cash withdrawals, checks drawn, and other transaction transfers would be unlimited. "Super-Now" accounts, like the new money market accounts, would be federally insured.

Indications as of early 1983 were that financial institutions would offer lower interest rates on the new "Super-Now" accounts than on the new money market accounts. In effect, the new "Super-Now" accounts would be checking accounts that would pay higher interest rates than the ceiling limits on the regular NOW accounts, provided the minimum balance requirement is observed by the depositor.

Rates on U.S. Savings Bonds. Pursuant to congressional authority given to the President to raise rates on United States savings bonds by as much as one percentage point during a six-month period, the secretary of the Treasury announced April 29, 1981, a new 1% rise in the interest rate for United States savings bonds and savings notes, effective May 1, 1981.

The interest rate on Series EE bonds purchased beginning May 1, 1981, was increased from 8% to 9%, compounded semiannually, when the bonds are held to maturity. The term to maturity was shortened from 9 to 8 years.

The interest rate on Series HH savings bonds purchased beginning May 1, 1981, was increased from 7.5% to 8.5% to their original maturity, which remained at 10 years. Interest on these bonds is paid semiannually by check.

The increase in yields also raised the yields to maturity on outstanding savings bonds as well as savings notes (Freedom Shares) by 1%.

Floating Rate Savings Bonds. By further legislation included in the legislation increasing the federal debt limit, Congress authorized the Treasury's new formula for determining the interest paid on savings bonds effective July 1, 1982 (P.L. 97-204, June 28, 1982, authorized both the increase in the debt limit and the new "floating rate" formula for interest paid on the savings bonds).

The floating rate formula was concisely stated as follows:

INTEREST RATE FUTURES

1. Note the average yield on 5-year U.S. Treasury marketable securities.
2. Compute this yield daily for six months.
3. Reduce this six-month average by 85%.
4. The resulting figure would be the rate of interest to be paid on savings bonds for the next six months.

However, for the first five years of holding of the EE bonds, interest would accrue at the fixed increasing scale year. On the fifth year, the interest would accrue at 85% of the average yield on outstanding 5-year Treasury marketable securities for the entire period. Every six months thereafter, the Treasury will compute the average market yield on 5-year Treasury marketable securities during the previous half-year. Minimum guaranteed yield would be 7.5%.

Similarly, outstanding E bonds, EE bonds, and savings notes held five years from November 1, 1982, will receive the market-based yield or the guaranteed minimum, according to the new formula, of 7.5%.

Other features not prevailing on outstanding issues will continue, including exemption from state and local taxes of the accrued interest (but not from federal income tax, which may be paid currently or at cashing or final maturity); replacement of bonds lost, stolen, or destroyed; etc.

The new floating rate formula's rates will be announced by the Treasury at the appropriate times.

See UNITED STATES SAVINGS BONDS.

INTEREST RATE FUTURES Interest rate futures "represent a mechanism that permits professional money managers to hedge interest rate risk by transferring that risk to investors willing to accep it in quest of profit opportunities." As interest rates have ri sen and become more volatile in recent years, the risk of unantic pated rate fluctuations has increased substantially.

The interest rate futures market was introduced in October, 1975, by the CHICAGO BOARD OF TRADE, which first offered futures contracts in passthrough mortgage-backed certificates guaranteed by the GOVERNMENT NATIONAL MORTGAGE ASSOCIATION (GNMA); shortly thereafter the CHICAGO MERCANTILE EXCHANGE through its International Monetary Market (IMM) division offered futures contracts in 3-month U.S. Treasury bills. Since that time, the Chicago Board of Trade has added futures trading in long-term Treasury bonds, 90-day commercial paper, certificate delivery GNMAs, 30-day commercial paper, and 4- to 6-year U.S. Treasury notes; the International Monetary Market division of the ChicagoMercantile Exchange has added futures trading in 1-year U.S. Treasury bills. In New York City, the COMMODITY EXCHANGE, INC. since 1979 has introduced futures trading in 90-day U.S. Treasury bills and 2-year U.S. Treasury notes, as well as in GNMA certificates; the NEW YORK FUTURES EXCHANGE, a division of the NEW YORK STOCK EXCHANGE, began trading in August, 1980, in 90-day U.S.

Treasury bills and 20-year U.S. Treasury bonds futures contracts. (See the respective markets for details of the contracts.)

Banks. Banks may utilize interest rate futures contracts in their trading account activities or investment account activities. For its trading account, a bank may utilize futures contracts as a separate trading instrument, taking positions to trade for its own account, or it may use futures contracts as a hedge or arbitrage against other trading positions. In a hedging activity, a futures contract is entered into as a temporary substitute for the purchase or sale of an actual security (cash) position. Consequently, a hedge can be either a long (buying) hedge or a short (selling) hedge. In a long hedge, the trader would purchase a futures contract to protect against the effect of falling interest rates and the resulting rising prices on short positions in the trading portfolio. On the other hand, a short hedge, or the selling of a futures contract, would be entered into to protect a long position against rising interest rates that would result in falling prices.

A perfect hedge would be one where the market risks associated with a cash position were completely neutralized by the risks inherent in the futures contract, i.e., any gain on one position would offset a loss on the other position. This situation would occur when a trader hedged a security that was the same as the security deliverable on the futures contract, e.g., if a bank owned $1 million of T-bills due June 23 and sold short one March T-bill futures contract. Because T-bills owned (the long position) could be used to make delivery on the short futures position, the prices of the two should converge to the same amount on March 23, the date the futures contract settles. Thus in this situation the gain on one position would offset the loss on the other, and therefore any unrealized profit or loss on the position on the date the hedge was entered into would be locked in. However, in a normal business environment, a perfect hedge seldom is possible because futures contracts are limited in contract size, specific delivery dates, and deliverable securities. As a result, in a trading account environment, a hedge can typically be used only to minimize the risk of interest rate movements on identified trading account positions, not to eliminate such risk.

Similar to hedging but with a slightly different intent is utilizing interest rate futures contracts as part of an arbitrage transaction. For example, if a trader perceives a market price disparity between two positions, he may arbitrage the two positions. In this situation, the trader will "go long" on one instrument and "go short" on the other. Once the prices move to their normal relationship, the positions will be closed out. If the trader was correct, the gain on one position should more than offset the loss, if any, on the other position. Futures contracts can be used to arbitrage against a cash position, a forward position, or another futures contract position.

For investment account activities, a bank may utilize futures contracts in two ways.

1. Long hedge: protects purchase commitments against a decrease in yield, i.e., locks in a yield on a future investment security.
2. Short hedge: increases liquidity by mitigating the effects of rising interest rates and declining prices on portfolio securities.

The purpose of a long hedge in the investment account differs from a similar hedge in the trading account. While the purpose of a long hedge in a trading account is to protect the value of short security positions, the purpose of a long hedge in the investment area is to minimize the effect of falling interest rates on anticipated future portfolio purchases. Thus futures contracts are purchased as a temporary substitute for the purchase of an actual security. Ultimately, either the bank will take delivery on the contract, if the deliverable security is the one the bank desires to purchase, or it will close out the futures contract and purchase the desired security itself. The intent is to lock in a desired yield on an anticipated security purchase. For example, an investment account manager who has been instructed to lengthen the maturity structure of the investment account in accordance with current bank objectives might plan to buy $5 million of long-term securities in June when available funds are expected. To protect against falling interest rates, the manager can buy 50 June GNMA futures contracts. That is, the bank can purchase futures contracts to hedge the purchase commitments by either locking in an interest rate if delivery is to be taken or minimizing the effect of changing interest rates if the futures contract is to be closed out and a security purchased directly.

With a short hedge (the selling of futures contracts), a bank attempts to minimize the effect of declining market prices on its portfolio and the resultant impact on bank liquidity.

For example, an investment account manager may desire to invest in long-term, higher-yielding securities but be hesitant to do so because if interest rates rise and a need arises to sell the securities, the bank will realize a loss. Therefore, the investment account manager may decide to minimize the risk by buying shorter-term securities. However, this strategy does have a cost associated with it; under a normal yield curve, the short-term securities yield lower rates than longer-term securities. This cost may be avoided if the investment account manager hedges the longer-term securities by selling the appropriate futures contract short (i.e., a short hedge).

As an example, assume that on January 1 the investment account manager purchased $5 million 7.875% U.S. Treasury bonds due February, 1995, at 98.20, for a total purchase price of $4,931,250. To protect the liquidity of this long-term investment, the investment account manager sells short 50 December Treasury bond futures contracts at 98.24. At the end of June, the market value of the bonds has fallen to $4,771,875 with a book value of $4,933,250 ($2,000 increase due to discount accretion), and therefore there is now an unrealized loss since January 1 of $161,375. However, during this period, the price of the bond futures has also fallen to 95.15 for a gain of approximately $164,000. In this situation, the investment account manager's perception of the market was correct, and as a result of the short hedge, the $161,375 decline in the security was more than offset by the $164,000 gain on the interest rate futures contracts.

It should be noted that if the prices in February and January in the preceding example had been reversed, the unrealized gain on the portfolio cash position should have been more than offset by the loss on the futures contracts. The objective of minimizing the risk of interest rate movements on the investment account would still have been achieved.

Other Uses by Banks of Interest Rate Futures Contracts. The Chicago Board of Trade and the IMM Division of the Chicago Mercantile Exchange, as sponsors of a study by the accounting firm of Arthur Andersen & Co., also indicate the following additional uses by banks and others.

Debt issuance: Futures contracts may be utilized as a tool to protect against rising interest rates. Banks or bank affiliates that actively issue commercial paper or other debt securities may seek to hedge this activity, i.e., minimize the risk of interest rate movements on scheduled debt offerings.

Asset-liability management: Perhaps bankers will find that the most important potential for futures contracts lies in their use as an integral part of a total asset-liability management strategy. This strategy relates to a bank's achieving overall control over the balancing of bank assets and liabilities in an attempt to maximize the differential between interest earned on assets and interest incurred on liabilities, while simultaneously achieving liability maturity objectives consistent with the maturity schedule of its assets. This balancing considers predictions of asset demand, availability of funds, and interest rate movements. Futures contracts may be used as an important tool in this balancing strategy.

Trust department: Futures contracts might be used by trust accounts that have funds invested in securities sensitive to interest rate movements.

Bank Regulatory Policy Statements. The three federal bank regulatory agencies (Federal Reserve Board, Comptroller of the Currency, and the Federal Deposit Insurance Corporation) on November 15, 1979, issued a joint policy statement setting forth precautionary rules and specific guidelines for commercial banks that engage in futures contracts (as well as forward and standby contracts) in U.S. government and agency securities. The policy statement was effective January 1, 1980, for contracts outstanding at that time and for those to be entered into subsequently. However, the agencies invited comment on the policy statement through December 15, 1979.

The agencies noted the following background to the general guidance they gave to commercial banks engaging in interest rate futures (as well as forward and standby contracts). A recent Treasury-Federal Reserve study indicated that banks can effectively use financial futures contracts to hedge their risk of losses due to changes in interest rates, but noted that improper use of interest rate futures contracts increases, rather than decreases, the risk of loss due to changes in interest rates. The study also cited the experience of participants in financial futures markets who have been approached by salespersons who suggested speculative rather than hedging transactions, and indicated that some banks and other financial institutions have issued standby obligations for delivery of securities at predetermined prices in contracts that were so large they exposed the institutions to losses that could, and in some cases did, affect their financial condition.

(*Note:* Outright long or short positions, unhedged, are purely speculative.)

The agencies' policy statement provided the following precautionary rules.

1. Banks that engage in futures, forward, or standby contract transactions should do so only in accordance with safe and sound banking practices.
2. Such transactions should be of a size reasonably related to the bank's business needs and to its capacity to fulfill obligations incurred.
3. The positions banks take in futures, forward, and standby contracts should be such as to reduce the bank's exposure to loss through interest rate changes affecting securities in the bank's investment portfolio.
4. Policy objectives should be formulated in light of the bank's entire mix of assets and liabilities.
5. Standby contracts calling for settlement in excess of 150 days should not be issued by banks except in special circumstances, and ordinarily such long-term standby contracts would be viewed by the agencies as being inappropriate.

The policy statement also provided a ten-point set of guidelines that should be followed by banks authorized to participate in these markets. The guidelines included directives on the role of banks' boards of directors; recordkeeping; monitoring of activities; valuation of contracts; treatment of fee income in connection with a standby contract; disclosures of activity by a bank in futures, forward, and standby contracts; monitoring of credit risk exposure; and internal controls at banks.

The agencies said that they would closely monitor bank transactions in financial futures, forward, and standby contracts and that, depending on what this monitoring disclosed, they might find it necessary to establish position limits or take other supervisory precautions against unsafe or unsound practices. The agencies also said that they might issue a similar policy statement for bank trust departments and trust companies later.

Later Policy Statement. The three federal bank regulatory agencies on March 14, 1980, announced a number of revisions in their guidelines for banks that engage in futures, forward, and standby contracts on U.S. Government and Agency securities.

The Federal Deposit Insurance Corporation (FDIC) and the Federal Reserve Board incorporated the guidelines in a policy statement. The Comptroller of the Currency's guidelines were continued in an operating circular.

In one change adopted by the FDIC and the Federal Reserve, futures and forward contracts executed by state-chartered banks before January 1, 1980, were exempted from the accounting procedures specified in the guidelines. The Comptroller of the Currency retained the January 1 effective date for all contracts entered into by national banks, as the Comptroller had had similar accounting provisions in effect since 1977.

Other principal changes in the guidelines adopted in the light of substantial comment received since publication of the guidelines in November, 1979, included the following.

1. Banks may exercise the option of carrying futures and forward positions on a market or on a lower of adjusted cost or market basis.
2. Futures and forward contract activities associated with bona fide hedging of a mortgage banking operation are exempted from the accounting treatment otherwise prescribed for such contracts.

A number of other technical changes were made, including relaxation of the requirement that a bank's board of directors review contracts at least monthly.

Savings and Loan Regulatory Policy Statement. The regulations issued by the Federal Home Loan Bank Board (FHLBB) effective June 1, 1979 (Sec. 563.17-3 of the Insurance Regulations) were aimed at curbing the speculation by a number of associations in mortgage-backed securities. The specific problems found were attributed to committing in excess of funding capacity, the attractiveness of fees that could be taken into income immediately, arrangements with brokers/dealers such as the extension or fee trade, the lack of good recordkeeping and control, and the absence of a properly informed board of directors. The regulations issued dealt with each of the above problem areas as follows.

1. Associations were authorized to make forward commitments on a safe and sound basis only. The regulations specified that making commitments with an inability to fund them when due is not a safe and sound practice. The associations were required to maintain documentation of ability to fund all outstanding forward commitments when due. In addition, associations' outstanding commitments were limited to either 10 or 15% of assets, depending on their net worth position.
2. Accounting for commitment fees was changed so that associations could no longer take large amounts of fees into current income.
3. Any sale of a forward commitment under agreement to repurchase had to be done at market prices. Also, all profit or loss associated with a disposal or modification of a forward commitment had to be recognized at the time of the disposal or modification. Essentially, this required "marking to market" at the time of any modification of the commitment.
4. A detailed register was required to be maintained on all outstanding forward commitments.

5. The regulations required the minutes of the directors' meetings to include the names, duties, and limits of authority of association personnel authorized to engage in forward commitment activity; the names of authorized brokerage firms; and the dollar limit on transactions with each firm.

In the judgment of the FHLBB, these rules would not eliminate speculation, but they shoud remove some of the incentives for speculative activity in forward commitments, as well as curb the worst abuses. Nonetheless, associations were not to assume that if they were operating within the regulations, they were not engaged in speculation and protected from losses. However, the FHLBB considered that both the firm commitment and the mortgage-backed security itself "clearly have their place in a prudently managed mortgage portfolio," although associations may want to limit the amount of their firm commitments which extend beyond six months. In addition, associations concerned about excessive interest rate risk in their forward commitments might want to offset part of this risk by hedging in the futures market.

Summary. Under conditions of continued volatile swings in interest rates, proponents of participation in the interest rate futures markets view their prudent use by financial institutions as an operational necessity, albeit fraught with risk even with recourse to hedging, requiring expertise in judging interest rate trends and in taking appropriate action.

INTEREST RATE PARITY A theory that is an extension of one price: In free international capital markets with flexible exchange rates, real interest rates will be identical across all currencies. When nominal differences in interest rates reflect differences in expected inflation and changes in relative exchange rates, investors or speculators cannot gain by borrowing in low-rate countries and investing in countries with higher rates. Opportunities exist only when the nominal differences in interest rates do not fully mirror differences in expected inflation. To the extent that profitable opportunities are identified, they can be expected to close quickly as international capital moves to exploit any differences that exist.

INTEREST RATE RISK MONEY RISK. In investing, the risk of open market depreciation in the prices of high-grade bonds and debentures, which move with interest rates, should interest rates rise and thus entail higher yields to maturity for such high-grade obligations. Since the interest that such high-grade issues pay remains constant, being fixed at original issuance, the impact of the adjustment upward in yield to maturity must fall upon price, modified by the annual accretion of discount that results when price goes further below par. The longer the maturity, the greater will be the impact upon price of an upward movement in interest rates.

See SPACED MATURITIES, YIELD TO MATURITY.

INTEREST RATES A percent of the principal of an amount borrowed or lent. The interest rate is the ratio of the amount of interest paid or earned, during a certain period of time, to the amount of principal.

The TRUTH IN LENDING ACT requires that interest rates on consumer loans be stated in annual percentage rate terms. The annual percentage interest rate measures the cost of funds on a yearly basis—what the rate would be if the funds were used for one year. The law also requires that the lender disclose to the borrower any finance charges or other fees connected with the loan.

Interest rate risk arises when one reinvests funds at lower rates of interest than those at which the funds could have been employed if they had been either held to maturity or invested in other alternative investments or loans at the time of the original lending or investing. As the market rate rises, prices of long-term bonds and certain other assets decrease so that investors can receive the market rate of return.

The interest rate is a critical element in banking in that it is associated with risk and return, lending and investing policies, asset valuation, asset/liability management, bank capital financing, deregulation, expense control, loan pricing, term structure, yield curves, and many other banking concerns.

The appended table of interest rates shows the interest rate averages, percent per year, on various money market rates and capital market rates.

See DEPOSIT INTEREST RATES, DISCOUNT, LEGAL RATE OF INTEREST, MONEY MARKET, MONEY RATES, REDISCOUNT RATE.

BIBLIOGRAPHY

BARRO, R. J. "Interest Rate Smoothing." University of Rochester, February, 1987.
BARSKY, R., and others. "The Worldwide Change in the Behavior of Interest Rates and Prices in 1914." University of Michigan, May, 1987.
CLARK, L. "Interest Rate Seasonal and the Federal Reserve." *Journal of Political Economy*, Feb. 1986.
DERAVIL, L., and others. "Deficit Financing Announcements and Asset Prices." *Journal of Economics and Business*, May, 1989.
GOODFRIEND, M. "Interest Rate Smoothing and Price Level Trend-Stationarity." *Journal of Monetary Economics*, 19, May, 1987.
KAUFMAN, H. *Interest Rates, the Markets, and the New Financial World*, 1986.
KASMAN, B., and PIGOTT, C. "Interest Rate Divergences Among the Major Industrial Nations." *Federal Reserve Bank of New York Quarterly Review*, August, 1988.
ROSE, A. K. "Is the Real Interest Rate Stable?" *Journal of Finance*, December, 1988.
WACHTEL, P. *Crises in the Economic and Financial Structure*, 1982.
WOELFEL, C. J. *The Desktop Guide to Money, Time, Interest, and Yields*. Probus Publishing Co., Chicago, IL, 1986.
WOJNILOWER, A. M. "The Central Role of Credit Crunches in Recent Financial History." *Brookings Papers on Economic Activity*. No. 2, 1980.

INTEREST RATE SWAP An agreement between two parties to exchange a series of interest payments based on an agreed principal amount (often termed the "notional" amount). Because the parties exchange only the interest payments without exchanging the underlying debt, interest rate swaps do not appear on the balance sheets of the participants, although the inflows and outflows from swap transactions show up on the income statement.

Early interest rate swaps became popular in the Euromarkets starting around 1981. The typical swap transaction involved a firm with a high credit rating with a desire for short-term funds and a lower-rated company needing longer-term fixed-rate funds. The better-rated company normally had a comparative advantage in raising longer-term funds because investors tend to require a higher-risk premium for securities with longer maturities. The major risk to either party in the transaction is that the other will default.

The largest market for interest rate swaps is denominated in U.S. dollars. Many swaps are now arranged through commercial or investment banks acting as intermediaries for a fee.

The size of the market in swaps has grown dramatically from an estimated $3 billion in 1982 to more than $200 billion by 1986. It is reported that over 50% of the volume of new Eurobond issues is now swap related. It has become common for companies to use the swap market to transform floating-rate debt into fixed-rate obligations, especially for savings and loans associations that traditionally have substantial gaps between the duration of their assets and that of their liabilities. Other companies are able to use swaps to "unlock" high coupon debt by swapping it for lower variable-rate debt.

INTEREST TABLES Tables constructed to show the amount of INTEREST that will accrue on a given convenient (round number) sum, e.g., $1, $100, or $1,000, at different rates of interest for various intervals of time, rendering unnecessary separate and independent computations for each interest transaction.

Interest tables are prepared in many different forms with varying degrees of detail and refinement in decimal places, interest rates, and time intervals, to meet a wide variety of uses. The following list, illustrated by appended tables, includes the more important types of interest tables.

1. Simple interest computed on a given principal. The formula for computing annual simple interest is

$$I = Pr$$

where P = principal and r = rate of interest per year. For example, if principal of $1,000 is invested at a 5% annual rate of interest, the dollar interest per year (assuming that the interest is not reinvested) is

$$I = 1,000(0.05)$$
$$I = 50$$

INTEREST TABLES

Interest Rates Money and Capital Markets
(Averages, percent per year; weekly, monthly, and annual figures are averages of business day data unless otherwise noted.)

	Instrument	1986	1987	1988	1989 Feb.	1989 Mar.	1989 Apr.	1989 May	1989 week ending Apr.28	May 5	May 12	May 19	May 26
	Money Market Rates												
1	Federal funds [1,2]	6.80	6.66	7.57	9.36	9.85	9.84	9.81	9.86	9.88	9.86	9.75	9.74
2	Discount window borrowing [1,2,3]	6.32	5.66	6.20	6.59	7.00	7.00	7.00	7.00	7.00	7.00	7.00	7.00
	Commercial paper [4,5]												
3	1-month	6.61	6.74	7.58	9.29	9.88	9.77	9.58	9.72	9.70	9.66	9.50	9.47
4	3-month	6.49	6.82	7.66	9.37	9.95	9.81	9.47	9.72	9.69	9.59	9.37	9.29
5	6-month	6.39	6.85	7.68	9.35	9.97	9.78	9.29	9.65	9.59	9.46	9.16	9.06
	Finance paper, directly placed [4,5]												
6	1-month	6.57	6.61	7.44	9.21	9.77	9.70	9.48	9.64	9.62	9.58	9.40	9.37
7	3-month	6.38	6.54	7.38	9.11	9.70	9.70	9.27	9.63	9.56	9.41	9.15	9.04
8	6-month	6.31	6.37	7.14	8.65	9.17	9.29	8.97	9.23	9.20	9.19	8.81	8.76
	Bankers acceptances [5,6]												
9	3-month	6.38	6.75	7.56	9.27	9.83	9.68	9.35	9.60	9.57	9.45	9.26	9.18
10	6-month	6.28	6.78	7.60	9.26	9.87	9.63	9.15	9.50	9.43	9.27	9.03	8.95
	Certificates of deposit, secondary market [7]												
11	1-month	6.61	6.75	7.59	9.33	9.91	9.81	9.61	9.75	9.76	9.69	9.52	9.49
12	3-month	6.51	6.87	7.73	9.51	10.09	9.94	9.59	9.84	9.83	9.72	9.49	9.41
13	6-month	6.50	7.01	7.91	9.71	10.40	10.13	9.60	9.96	9.89	9.75	9.48	9.38
14	Eurodollar deposits 3-month [8]	6.71	7.06	7.85	9.61	10.18	10.04	9.66	9.98	9.89	9.85	9.64	9.46
	U.S. Treasury bills [5]												
	Secondary market [9]												
15	3-month	5.97	5.78	6.67	8.53	8.82	8.65	8.43	8.53	8.54	8.43	8.30	8.41
16	6-month	6.02	6.03	6.91	8.55	8.85	8.65	8.41	8.59	8.52	8.42	8.33	8.39
17	1-year	6.07	6.33	7.13	8.55	8.82	8.64	8.31	8.52	8.47	8.36	8.23	8.21
	Auction average [10]												
18	3-month	5.98	5.82	6.68	8.48	8.83	8.70	8.40	8.66	8.64	8.41	8.21	8.32
19	6-month	6.03	6.05	6.92	8.49	8.87	8.73	8.39	8.72	8.64	8.39	8.19	8.33
20	1-year	6.18	6.33	7.17	8.59	8.68	8.75	8.44	NA	NA	8.44	NA	NA
	Capital Market Rates												
	U.S. Treasury notes and bonds [11]												
	Constant maturities [12]												
21	1-year	6.45	6.77	7.65	9.25	9.57	9.36	8.98	9.22	9.16	9.05	8.89	8.86
22	2-year	6.86	7.42	8.10	9.37	9.68	9.45	9.02	9.33	9.22	9.11	8.95	8.86
23	3-year	7.06	7.68	8.26	9.32	9.61	9.40	8.98	9.26	9.18	9.08	8.90	8.82
24	5-year	7.30	7.94	8.47	9.27	9.51	9.30	8.91	9.16	9.09	9.06	8.86	8.73
25	7-year	7.54	8.23	8.71	9.23	9.43	9.24	8.88	9.13	9.07	9.06	8.81	8.67
26	10-year	7.67	8.39	8.85	9.17	9.36	9.18	8.86	9.09	9.07	9.05	8.79	8.63
27	20-year	7.84	NA	NA	NA	NA	NA	NA	NA	NA	NA	NA	NA
28	30-year	7.78	8.59	8.96	9.01	9.17	9.03	8.83	8.95	8.97	9.02	8.80	8.63
	Composite [13]												
29	Over 10 years (long-term)	8.14	8.64	8.98	9.16	9.33	9.18	8.95	9.10	9.11	9.14	8.90	8.74
	State and local notes and bonds												
	Moody's series [14]												
30	Aaa	6.95	7.14	7.36	7.23	7.40	7.37	7.22	7.28	7.28	7.25	7.21	7.13
31	Baa	7.76	8.17	7.83	7.59	7.78	7.82	7.66	7.80	7.75	7.70	7.62	7.58
32	*Bond Buyer* series [15]	7.32	7.63	7.68	7.44	7.59	7.49	7.25	7.40	7.36	7.36	7.18	7.11
	Corporate bonds												
	Seasoned issues [16]												
33	All industries	9.71	9.91	10.18	10.05	10.18	10.14	9.97	10.11	10.08	10.05	9.93	9.80
34	Aaa	9.02	9.38	9.71	9.64	9.80	9.79	9.59	9.75	9.73	9.69	9.54	9.41
35	Aa	9.47	9.68	NA	9.83	9.98	9.94	9.77	9.92	9.88	9.85	9.73	9.63
36	A	9.95	9.99	10.24	10.13	10.26	10.20	10.01	10.16	10.14	10.08	9.98	9.85
37	Baa	10.39	10.58	10.83	10.61	10.67	10.61	10.48	10.59	10.57	10.57	10.46	10.32
38	A-rated, recently offered utility bonds [17]	9.61	9.95	NA	10.25	10.37	10.33	NA	10.22	10.26	10.13	10.03	9.94
	Memo: Dividend/price ratio [18]												
39	Preferred stocks	8.76	8.37	9.23	9.31	9.43	9.50	9.32	9.48	9.46	9.39	9.32	9.19
40	Common stocks	3.48	3.08	3.64	3.59	3.68	3.59	3.52	3.56	3.56	3.60	3.49	3.48

1. Weekly, monthly, and annual figures are averages of all calendar days, where the rate for a weekend or holiday is taken to be the rate prevailing on the preceding business day. The daily rate is the average of the rates on a given day weighted by the volume of transactions at these rates.
2. Weekly figures are averages for statement week ending Wednesday.
3. Rate for the Federal Reserve Bank of New York.
4. Unweighted average of offering rates quoted by at least five dealers (in the case of commercial paper), or finance companies (in the case of finance paper). Before November 1979, maturities for data shown are 30-59 days, 90-119 days, and 120-179 days for commecial paper; and 30-59 days, 90-119 days, and 150-179 days for finance paper.
5. Yields are quoted on a bank-discount basis, rather than in an investment yield basis (which would give a higher figure).
6. Dealer closing offered rates for top-rated banks. Most representative rate (which may be, but need not be, the average of the rates quoted by the dealers).
7. Unweighted average of offered rates quoted by at least five dealers early in the day.
8. Calendar week average. For indication purposes only.
9. Unweighted average of closing bid rates quoted by at least five dealers.
10. Rates are recorded in the week in which bills are issued. Beginning with the Treasury bill auction held on Apr. 18, 1983, bidders were required to state the percentage yield (on a bank discount basis) that they would accept to two decimal places. Thus, average issuing rates in bill auctions will be reported using two rather than three decimal places.
11. Yields are based on closing bid prices quoted by at least five dealers.
12. Yields adjusted to constant maturities by the U.S. Treasury. That is, yields are read from a yield curve at fixed maturities. Based on only recently issued, actively traded securities.
13. Averages (to maturity or call) for all outstanding bonds neither due nor callable in less than 10 years, including one very low yielding "flower" bond.
14. General obligations based on Thursday figures: Moody's Investors Service.
15. General obligations only, with 20 years to maturity, issued by 20 state and local governmental units of mixed quality. Based on figures for Thursday.
16. Daily figures from Moody's Investors Service. Based on yields to maturity on selected long-term bonds.
17. Compilation of the Federal Reserve. This series is an estimate of the yield on recently-offered A-rated utility bonds with a 30-year maturity and 5 years of call protection. Weekly data are based on Friday quotations.
18. Standard and Poor's corporate series. Preferred stock ratio based on a sample of ten issues: four public utilities, four Industrials, one financial, and one transportation. Common stock ratios on the 500 stocks in the price index.
Note: These data also appear in the Board's H.15(519) and G.13(415) releases.

INTEREST TABLES

Table 1/ Ordinary Simple Interest Table, 30 Days to the Month

Day	3.75% $	4% $	4.25% $	4.50% $	4.75% $	5% $	5.25% $	5.50% $	5.75% $	6% $	6.50% $	7% $	7.50% $	8% $
1	0.1042	0.1111	0.1181	0.1250	0.1319	0.1389	0.1458	0.1528	0.1597	0.1667	0.1806	0.1944	0.2083	0.2222
2	0.2083	0.2222	0.2361	0.2500	0.2639	0.2778	0.2917	0.3056	0.3194	0.3333	0.3611	0.3889	0.4167	0.4444
3	0.3125	0.3333	0.3542	0.3750	0.3958	0.4167	0.4375	0.4583	0.4792	0.5000	0.5417	0.5833	0.6250	0.6666
4	0.4167	0.4444	0.4722	0.5000	0.5278	0.5556	0.5833	0.6111	0.6389	0.6667	0.7222	0.7778	0.8333	0.8888
5	0.5208	0.5555	0.5903	0.6250	0.6597	0.6944	0.7292	0.7639	0.7986	0.8333	0.9028	0.9722	1.0417	1.1111
6	0.6250	0.6667	0.7083	0.7500	0.7917	0.8333	0.8750	0.9167	0.9583	1.0000	1.0833	1.1667	1.2500	1.3333
7	0.7292	0.7778	0.8264	0.8750	0.9236	0.9722	1.0208	1.0694	1.1181	1.1667	1.2639	1.3611	1.4583	1.5555
8	0.8333	0.8889	0.9444	1.0000	1.0556	1.1111	1.1667	1.2222	1.2778	1.3333	1.4444	1.5556	1.6667	1.7777
9	0.9375	1.0000	1.0625	1.1250	1.1875	1.2500	1.3125	1.3750	1.4375	1.5000	1.6250	1.7500	1.8750	2.0000
10	1.0417	1.1111	1.1806	1.2500	1.3194	1.3889	1.4583	1.5278	1.5972	1.6667	1.8056	1.9444	2.0833	2.2222
11	1.1458	1.2222	1.2986	1.3750	1.4514	1.5278	1.6042	1.6806	1.7569	1.8333	1.9861	2.1389	2.2917	2.4444
12	1.2500	1.3333	1.4167	1.5000	1.5833	1.6667	1.7500	1.8333	1.9167	2.0000	2.1667	2.3333	2.5000	2.6666
13	1.3542	1.4444	1.5347	1.6250	1.7153	1.8056	1.8958	1.9861	2.0764	2.4667	2.3472	2.5278	2.7083	2.8888
14	1.4583	1.5556	1.6528	1.7500	1.8472	1.9444	2.0417	2.1389	2.2361	2.3333	2.5278	2.7222	2.9167	3.1111
15	1.5625	1.6667	1.7708	1.8750	1.9792	2.0833	2.1875	2.2917	2.3958	2.5000	2.7083	2.9167	3.1250	3.3333
16	1.6667	1.7778	1.8889	2.0000	2.1111	2.2222	2.3333	2.4444	2.5556	2.6667	2.8889	3.1111	3.3333	3.5555
17	1.7708	1.8889	2.0069	2.1250	2.2431	2.3611	2.4792	2.5972	2.7153	2.8333	3.0694	3.3055	3.5417	3.7777
18	1.8750	2.0000	2.1250	2.2500	2.3750	2.5000	2.6250	2.7500	2.8750	3.0000	3.2500	3.5000	3.7500	4.0000
19	1.9792	2.1111	2.2431	2.3750	2.5069	2.6389	2.7708	2.9028	3.0347	3.1667	3.4306	3.6944	3.9583	4.2222
20	2.0833	2.2222	2.3611	2.5000	2.6389	2.7778	2.9167	3.0556	3.1944	3.3333	3.6111	3.8889	4.1667	4.4444
21	2.1875	2.3333	2.4792	2.6250	2.7708	2.9167	3.0625	3.2083	3.3542	3.5000	3.7917	4.0833	4.3750	4.6666
22	2.2917	2.4444	2.5972	2.7500	2.9028	3.0556	3.2083	3.3611	3.5139	3.6667	3.9722	4.2778	4.5833	4.8889
23	2.3958	2.5556	2.7153	2.8750	3.0347	3.1944	3.3542	3.5139	3.6736	3.8333	4.1528	4.4722	4.7917	5.1111
24	2.5000	2.6667	2.8333	3.0000	3.1667	3.3333	3.5000	3.6667	3.8333	4.0000	4.3333	4.6667	5.0000	5.3333
25	2.6042	2.7778	2.9514	3.1250	3.2986	3.4722	3.6458	3.8194	3.9931	4.1667	4.5139	4.8611	5.2083	5.5555
26	2.7083	2.8889	3.0694	3.2500	3.4306	3.6111	3.7917	3.9722	4.1528	4.3333	4.6944	5.0555	5.4167	5.7777
27	2.8125	3.0000	3.1875	3.3750	3.5625	3.7500	3.9375	4.1250	4.3125	4.5000	4.8750	5.2500	5.6250	6.0000
28	2.9167	3.1111	3.3056	3.5000	3.6944	3.8889	4.0833	4.2778	4.4722	4.6667	5.0556	5.4444	5.8333	6.2222
29	3.0208	3.2222	3.4236	3.6250	3.8264	4.0278	4.2292	4.4306	4.6319	4.8333	5.2361	5.6389	6.0417	6.4444
30	3.1250	3.3333	3.5417	3.7500	3.9583	4.1667	4.3750	4.5833	4.7917	5.0000	5.4167	5.8333	6.2500	6.6666

Courtesy of Financial Publishing

Table 2 / Exact Simple Interest Table, 31 Days to the Month

Day	3.75% $	4% $	4.25% $	4.50% $	4.75% $	5% $	5.25% $	5.50% $	5.75% $	6% $	6.50% $	7% $	7.50% $	8% $
1	0.1027	0.1096	0.1164	0.1233	0.1301	0.1370	0.1438	0.1507	0.1575	0.1644	0.1781	0.1918	0.2055	0.2192
2	0.2055	0.2192	0.2329	0.2466	0.2603	0.2740	0.2877	0.3014	0.3151	0.3288	0.3562	0.3836	0.4110	0.4384
3	0.3082	0.3288	0.3493	0.3699	0.3904	0.4110	0.4315	0.4521	0.4726	0.4932	0.5342	0.5753	0.6164	0.6575
4	0.4110	0.4384	0.4658	0.4932	0.5205	0.5479	0.5753	0.6027	0.6301	0.6575	0.7123	0.7671	0.8219	0.8767
5	0.5137	0.5479	0.5822	0.6164	0.6507	0.6849	0.7192	0.7534	0.7877	0.8219	0.8904	0.9589	1.0274	1.0959
6	0.6164	0.6575	0.6986	0.7397	0.7808	0.8219	0.8630	0.9041	0.9452	0.9863	1.0685	1.1507	1.2329	1.3151
7	0.7192	0.7671	0.8151	0.8630	0.9110	0.9589	1.0068	1.0548	1.1027	1.1507	1.2466	1.3425	1.4384	1.5342
8	0.8219	0.8767	0.9315	0.9863	1.0411	1.0959	1.1507	1.2055	1.2603	1.3151	1.4247	1.5342	1.6438	1.7534
9	0.9247	0.9863	1.0479	1.1096	1.1712	1.2329	1.2945	1.3562	1.4178	1.4795	1.6027	1.7260	1.8493	1.9726
10	1.0274	1.0959	1.1644	1.2329	1.3014	1.3699	1.4384	1.5068	1.5753	1.6439	1.7808	1.9178	2.0548	2.1918
11	1.1301	1.2055	1.2808	1.3562	1.4315	1.5068	1.5822	1.6575	1.7329	1.8082	1.9589	2.1096	2.2603	2.4110
12	1.2329	1.3151	1.3973	1.4795	1.5616	1.6438	1.7260	1.8082	1.8904	1.9726	2.1370	2.3014	2.4658	2.6301
13	1.3356	1.4247	1.5137	1.6027	1.6918	1.7808	1.8699	1.9589	2.0479	2.1370	2.3151	2.4932	2.6712	2.8493
14	1.4384	1.5342	1.6301	1.7260	1.8219	1.9178	2.0137	2.1096	2.2055	2.3014	2.4931	2.6849	2.8767	3.0685
15	1.5411	1.6438	1.7466	1.8493	1.9521	2.0548	2.1575	2.2603	2.3630	2.4658	2.6712	2.8767	30822	3.2877
16	1.6438	1.7534	1.8630	1.9726	2.0822	2.1918	2.3014	2.4110	2.5205	2.6301	2.8493	3.0685	3.2877	3.5068
17	1.7466	1.8630	1.9795	2.0959	2.2123	2.3288	2.4452	2.5616	2.6781	2.7945	3.0274	3.2603	3.4931	3.7260
18	1.8493	1.9726	2.0959	2.2192	2.3425	2.4658	2.5890	2.7123	2.8356	2.9589	3.2055	3.4521	3.6986	3.9452
19	1.9521	2.0822	2.2123	2.3425	2.4726	2.6027	2.7329	2.8630	2.9931	3.1233	3.3836	3.6438	3.9041	4.1644
20	2.0548	2.1918	2.3288	2.4658	2.6027	2.7397	2.8767	3.0137	3.1507	3.2877	3.5616	3.8356	4.1096	4.3836
21	2.1575	2.3014	2.4452	2.5890	2.7329	2.8767	3.0205	3.1644	3.3082	3.4521	3.7397	4.0274	4.3151	4.6027
22	2.2603	2.4110	2.5616	2.7123	2.8630	3.0137	3.1644	3.3151	3.4658	3.6164	3.9178	4.2192	4.5205	4.8219
23	2.3630	2.5205	2.6781	2.8356	2.9931	3.1507	3.3082	3.4658	3.6233	3.7808	4.0959	4.4100	4.7260	5.0411
24	2.4658	2.6301	2.7945	2.9589	3.1233	3.2877	3.4521	3.6164	3.7808	3.9452	4.2740	4.6027	4.9315	5.2603
25	2.5685	2.7397	2.9110	3.0822	3.2534	3.4247	3.5959	3.7671	3.9384	4.1096	4.4521	4.7945	5.1370	5.4795
26	2.6712	2.8493	3.0274	3.2055	3.3836	3.5616	3.7397	3.9178	4.0959	4.2740	4.6301	4.9863	5.3425	5.6986
27	2.7740	2.9589	3.1438	3.3288	3.5137	3.6986	3.8836	4.0685	4.2534	4.4384	4.8082	5.1781	5.5479	5.9178
28	2.8767	3.0685	3.2603	3.4521	3.6438	3.8356	4.0274	4.2192	4.4110	4.6027	4.9863	5.3699	5.7534	6.1370
29	2.9795	3.1781	3.3767	3.5753	3.7740	3.9726	4.1712	4.3699	4.5685	4.7671	5.1644	5.5616	5.9589	6.3562
30	3.0822	3.2877	3.4931	3.6986	3.9041	4.1096	4.3151	4.5205	4.7260	4.9315	5.3425	5.7534	6.1644	6.5753
31	3.1849	3.3973	3.6096	3.8219	4.0342	4.2466	4.4589	4.6712	4.8836	5.0959	5.4205	5.9452	6.3699	6.7945

Courtesy of Financial Publishing

ENCYCLOPEDIA OF BANKING AND FINANCE

INTEREST TABLES

Ordinary simple interest is computed on the basis of a 360-day year (see Table 1), while exact simple interest is computed on the basis of a 365-day year (366 days in leap years). To determine the dollar amount of interest for principal invested for less than one year (using exact interest basis of 365-day year), the formula is

$$I = (Pr)(D/365)$$

where D = the number of days for which the principal is invested. For example, if principal of $1,000 is invested for 31 days at an annual rate of interest of 5%, the dollar interest for the 31-day period is

$$I = 1.000(0.05)(31/365)$$
$$= 50(0.0849315)$$
$$= 4.2466 \quad \text{(see Table 2)}$$

By contrast, to determine the dollar amount of interest for principal invested for less than one year (using ordinary interest basis of 360-day year), the formula is

$$I = (Pr \text{ V})(D/360)$$

so that

$$I = 1.000(0.05)(31/360)$$
$$= 50(0.0861111)$$
$$= 4.3056 \text{ (see Table 1, 4.1667 for 30 days plus 0.1389 for 1 day)}$$

Thus the 360-day year basis, although simpler to calculate, results in higher interest. Simplicity of calculation is illustrated by the 60-day, 6% method:

$1,000 for 60 days @ 6% annually equals
$10.00 (simply point off two decimal places)
-8.8333 ($1/_6$th less, or 1%/6%, for 5% rate)

4.1667 for 30 days at 5%

or $1/_{12}$th (30/360) of the $50 interest for one year (1,000 X 0.05) equals $4.1667 for the 30 days.

Table 3 / Compound Interest (r = interest rate per period; n = number of interest periods)

	1%	2%	3%	4%	5%	6%	7%	8%	9%	10%	11%	12%	13%
1	1.0100	1.0200	1.0300	1.0400	1.0500	1.600	1.0700	1.0800	1.0900	1.1000	1.1100	1.1200	1.1300
2	1.0201	1.0404	1.0609	1.816	1.1025	1.1236	1.1449	1.1664	1.1881	1.2100	1.2321	1.2544	1.2769
3	1.0303	1.0612	1.0927	1.1249	1.1573	1.1910	1.2250	1.2597	1.2950	1.3310	1.3676	1.4049	1.4429
4	1.0406	1.0824	1.1255	1.1699	1.2155	1.2425	1.3108	1.3605	1.4116	1.4641	1.5181	1.5735	1.6305
5	1.0510	1.1041	1.1593	1.2167	1.2763	1.3382	1.4026	1.4693	1.5386	1.6105	1.6851	1.7623	1.8424
6	1.0615	1.1262	1.1941	1.2653	1.3401	1.4185	1.5007	1.5869	1.6771	1.7716	1.8704	1.9738	2.0820
7	1.0721	1.1487	1.2299	1.3159	1.4081	1.5036	1.6058	1.7138	1.8280	1.9487	2.0762	2.2107	2.3526
8	1.0829	1.1717	1.2668	1.3686	1.4885	1.5938	1.7182	1.8509	1.9926	2.1436	2.3045	2.4760	2.6584
9	1.0937	1.1951	1.3048	1.4233	1.5513	1.6895	1.8385	1.9990	2.1719	2.3579	2.5580	2.7731	3.0040
10	1.1046	1.2190	1.3439	1.4802	1.6289	1.7908	1.9671	2.1589	2.3674	2.5937	2.8394	3.1059	3.3946
11	1.1157	1.2434	1.3852	1.5395	1.7103	1.8983	2.1049	2.3316	2.5804	2.8531	3.1518	3.4786	3.8359
12	1.1268	1.2682	1.4258	1.6010	1.7929	2.0122	2.2522	2.5182	2.8127	3.1384	3.4984	3.8960	4.3345
13	1.1381	1.2936	1.4685	1.6651	1.8856	2.1329	2.4098	2.7196	3.0658	3.4523	3.8833	4.3635	4.8980
14	1.1495	1.3195	1.5126	1.7317	1.9799	2.2609	2.5785	2.9372	3.3417	3.7975	4.3104	4.8871	5.5348
15	1.1610	1.3659	1.5580	1.8009	2.0789	2.3966	2.7590	3.1722	3.6425	4.1772	4.7846	5.4736	6.2543
16	1.1726	1.3728	1.6047	1.8730	2.1829	2.5403	2.9522	3.4259	3.9703	4.5950	5.3109	6.1304	7.0673
17	1.1843	1.4002	1.6528	1.9479	2.2920	2.6928	3.1588	3.7000	4.3276	5.0545	5.8951	6.8661	7.9861
18	1.1961	1.4282	1.7024	2.0258	2.4066	2.8543	3.3799	3.9960	4.7171	5.5599	6.5435	7.6900	9.0243
19	1.2081	1.4568	1.7535	2.1068	2.5269	3.0256	3.6165	4.3157	5.1417	6.1159	7.2633	8.6128	10.1974
20	1.2202	1.4859	1.8061	2.1911	2.6533	3.2071	3.8697	4.6609	5.6044	6.7275	8.0623	9.6463	11.5231
21	1.2324	1.5157	1.8603	2.2788	2.7860	3.3996	4.1406	5.0338	6.1088	7.4002	8.9491	10.8039	13.0211
22	1.2447	1.5460	1.9161	2.3699	2.9263	3.6035	4.4304	5.4365	6.6586	8.1403	9.9336	12.1003	14.7139
23	1.2572	1.5769	1.9736	2.4647	3.0715	3.8497	4.7405	5.8714	7.2579	8.9543	11.0262	13.5524	16.6267
24	1.2697	1.6084	2.0328	2.5633	3.2251	4.0489	5.0724	6.3412	7.9111	9.8497	12.2391	15.1787	18.7881
25	1.2824	1.6406	2.0938	2.6658	3.3864	4.2919	5.4274	6.8485	8.6231	10.8347	13.5854	17.0001	21.2306
26	1.2953	1.6734	2.1566	2.7725	3.5557	4.5494	5.8073	7.3963	9.3991	11.9181	15.0798	19.0401	23.9906
27	1.3082	1.7069	2.2213	2.8834	3.7335	4.8223	6.2139	7.9880	10.2451	13.1100	16.7386	21.3249	27.1094
28	1.3213	1.7410	2.2879	2.9987	3.9201	5.1117	6.6488	8.6271	11.1671	14.4210	18.5798	23.8839	30.6336
29	1.3345	1.7758	2.3566	3.1186	4.1161	5.4184	7.1142	9.3172	12.1722	15.8631	20.6236	26.7500	34.6159
30	1.3478	1.8114	2.4273	3.2434	4.3219	5.7435	7.6122	10.0626	13.2677	17.4494	22.8922	29.9600	39.1160
31	1.3613	1.8476	2.5001	3.3731	4.5380	6.0881	8.1451	10.8676	14.4617	19.1943	25.4104	33.5552	44.2011
32	1.3749	1.8845	2.5751	3.5081	4.7649	6.4534	8.7152	11.7370	15.7633	21.1137	28.2055	37.5818	49.9473
33	1.3887	1.9222	2.6523	3.6484	5.0032	6.8400	9.3253	12.6760	17.1820	23.2251	31.3081	42.0917	56.4404
34	1.4026	1.9607	2.7319	3.7943	5.2533	7.2510	9.9781	13.6901	18.7284	25.5476	34.7520	47.1427	63.7777
35	1.4166	1.9999	2.8139	3.9467	5.5160	7.6861	10.6765	14.7853	20.4139	28.1023	38.5747	52.7998	72.0688
36	1.4308	2.0399	2.8983	4.1039	5.7918	8.1472	11.4239	15.9681	22.2512	30.9126	42.8179	59.1358	81.4377
37	1.4451	2.0807	2.9852	4.2681	6.0814	8.6361	12.2236	17.2456	24.2538	34.0038	47.5279	66.2321	92.0246
38	1.4595	201223	3.0748	4.4388	6.3855	9.1542	13.0792	18.6252	26.4366	37.4042	52.7560	74.1799	103.9880
39	1.4741	2.1647	3.1670	4.6164	6.7047	9.7035	13.9948	20.1152	28.8159	41.1446	58.5591	83.0815	117.5060
40	1.4889	2.2080	3.2620	4.8010	7.0400	10.2857	14.9744	21.7244	31.4094	45.2591	65.0006	93.0513	132.7820
41	1.5038	2.2522	3.3599	4.9931	7.3920	10.9028	16.0226	23.4624	34.2362	49.7850	72.1507	104.2170	150.0440
42	1.5188	2.2972	3.4607	5.1928	7.7616	11.5570	17.1442	25.3394	37.3175	54.7635	80.0872	116.7240	169.5490
43	1.5340	2.3432	3.5645	5.4005	8.1497	12.2504	18.3443	27.3665	40.6760	60.2398	88.8968	130.7300	191.5910
44	1.5493	2.3901	3.6715	5.6165	8.5571	12.9854	19.6284	29.5558	44.3369	66.2638	98.6754	146.4180	216.4980
45	1.5648	2.4379	3.7816	5.8412	8.9820	13.7646	21.0024	31.9203	48.3272	72.8902	109.5300	163.9880	244.6420
46	1.5805	2.4866	3.8950	6.0748	9.4642	14.5904	22.4725	34.4739	52.6766	80.1792	121.5780	183.6670	276.4460
47	1.5963	2.5363	4.0119	6.3178	9.9060	15.4658	24.0456	37.2318	57.4175	88.1971	134.9520	205.7070	312.3840
48	1.6122	2.5871	4.1323	6.5705	10.4013	16.3938	25.7288	40.2104	62.5851	97.0168	149.7960	230.3920	352.9940
49	1.6283	2.6388	4.2562	6.8333	10.9213	17.3774	27.5298	43.4272	68.2177	106.7190	166.2740	258.0390	398.8830
50	1.6446	2.6916	4.3839	7.1067	11.4674	18.4201	29.4569	46.9014	74.3573	117.3900	184.5640	289.0030	450.7380

ENCYCLOPEDIA OF BANKING AND FINANCE

INTEREST TABLES

2. Compound interest—the amount of interest that a given principal will accumulate if invested at specified rate, compounded at specified frequency for specified total number of periods, if the interest generated is reinvested at the same rate. The formula for the compound interest as such is

$$(1 + r V)^n = 1$$

or the compound amount of $1 invested at rate r per interest period for a specified number of interest periods n minus the principal of $1.

As indicated by Table 3, the compound amount of $1 invested at 5%, compounded annually for 10 years, is as follows:

$$(1 + .05)^{10} = 1.6289$$

so that deducting the $1 of principal implied, the amount of compound interest is

$$1.6289 - 1 = 0.6289$$

The compound amount of $1,000 invested at 5%, compounded annually for 10 years, therefore is as follows:

$$\begin{aligned} C &= P(1 + r)n \\ &= 1000(1 + 0.05)10 \\ &= 1000(1.6289) \\ &= 1,628.90 \end{aligned}$$

where C = compound amount of principal.

To adjust for a specified frequency of compounding, divide the annual rate of interest by the frequency of compounding per year to obtain the interest rate per period; multiply the specified number of years by the frequency of compounding to obtain the total number of interest periods. For example, if the 5% rate above is compounded quarterly, rate of interest per interest period is

$$\frac{0.05 \text{ (annual rate of interest)}}{4 \text{ (frequency of compounding)}} = 0.0125 \text{ (1.25\%)}$$

Table 4 / Future Value of an Annuity of $1 for n Periods at r Rate of Interest

	1%	2%	3%	4%	5%	6%	7%	8%	9%	10%	11%	12%	13%
1	1.0000	1.0000	1.0000	1.0000	1.0000	1.0000	1.0000	1.0000	1.0000	1.0000	1.0000	1.0000	1.0000
2	2.0100	2.0200	2.0300	2.0400	2.0500	2.0600	2.0700	2.0800	2.0900	2.1000	2.1100	2.1200	2.1300
3	3.0301	3.0604	3.0909	3.1216	3.1525	3.1836	3.2149	3.2464	3.2781	3.3100	3.3421	3.3744	3.4069
4	4.0604	4.1216	4.1836	4.2465	4.3101	4.3746	4.4399	4.5061	4.5731	4.6410	4.7097	4.7793	4.8498
5	5.1010	5.2040	4.3091	5.4163	5.5256	5.6371	5.7507	5.8666	4.9847	6.1051	6.2278	6.3528	6.4803
6	6.1520	6.3081	6.4684	6.6330	6.8019	6.9753	7.1533	7.3359	7.5233	7.7156	7.9129	8.1152	8.3227
7	7.2135	7.4343	7.6625	7.8983	8.1420	8.3938	8.6540	8.9228	9.2004	9.4872	9.7833	10.0890	10.4047
8	8.2857	8.5830	8.8923	9.2142	9.5491	9.8975	10.2598	10.6366	11.0285	11.4359	11.8594	12.2997	12.7573
9	9.3685	9.7546	10.1591	10.5828	11.0266	11.4913	11.9780	12.4876	13.0210	13.5795	14.1640	14.7757	15.4157
10	10.4622	10.9497	11.4639	12.0061	12.5779	13.1808	13.8164	14.4866	15.1929	15.9374	16.7220	17.5487	18.4197
11	11.5668	12.1687	12.8078	13.4864	14.2068	14.9716	15.7836	16.6455	17.5603	18.5312	19.5614	20.6546	21.8143
12	12.6825	13.4121	14.1920	15.0258	15.9171	16.8699	17.8885	18.9771	20.1407	21.3843	22.7132	24.1331	25.6502
13	13.8093	14.6803	15.6178	16.6268	17.7130	18.8821	20.1406	21.4953	22.9535	24.5227	26.2116	28.0291	29.9847
14	14.9474	15.9739	17.0863	18.2919	19.5986	21.0151	22.5505	24.2149	26.0192	27.9750	30.0949	32.3926	34.8827
15	16.0969	17.2934	18.5989	20.0236	21.5786	23.2760	25.1290	27.1521	29.3609	31.7725	34.4054	37.2797	40.4175
16	17.2579	18.6393	20.1569	21.8245	23.6575	25.6725	27.8880	30.3243	33.0034	35.9497	39.1899	42.7533	46.6717
17	18.4304	20.0121	21.7616	23.6975	25.8404	28.2129	30.8402	33.7502	36.9737	40.5447	44.5008	48.8837	53.7391
18	19.6147	21.4123	23.4114	25.6454	28.1324	30.9057	33.9990	37.4502	41.3013	45.5992	50.3959	55.7497	61.7251
19	20.8109	22.8406	25.1169	27.6712	30.5390	33.7600	37.3790	41.4463	46.0185	51.1591	56.9395	63.4397	70.7494
20	22.0190	24.2974	26.8704	29.7781	33.0660	36.7856	40.9955	45.7620	51.1601	57.2750	64.2028	72.0524	80.9468
21	23.2392	25.7833	28.6765	31.9692	35.7193	39.9927	44.9652	50.4229	56.7645	64.0025	72.2651	81.6987	92.4699
22	24.4716	27.2990	30.5368	34.2480	38.5052	43.3923	49.0057	55.4568	62.8733	71.4027	81.2143	92.5026	105.4910
23	25.7163	28.8450	32.4529	36.6179	41.4305	46.9958	53.4361	60.8933	69.5319	79.5430	91.1479	104.6029	120.2048
24	26.9735	30.4219	34.4265	39.0826	44.5020	50.8156	58.1767	66.7648	76.7898	88.4973	102.1742	118.1552	136.8315
25	28.2432	32.0303	36.4593	41.6459	47.7271	54.8645	63.2490	73.1059	84.7009	98.3471	114.4133	133.3339	155.6196
26	29.5256	33.6709	38.5530	44.3117	51.1135	59.1564	68.6765	79.9544	93.3240	109.1818	127.9988	150.3339	176.8501
27	30.8209	35.3443	40.7096	47.0842	54.6691	63.9058	74.4838	87.3508	102.7231	121.0999	143.0786	169.3740	200.8406
28	32.1291	37.0512	42.9309	49.9676	58.4026	68.5281	80.6977	95.3388	112.9682	134.2099	159.8173	190.6989	227.9499
29	33.4504	38.7922	45.2189	52.9663	62.3227	73.6398	87.3465	103.9659	124.1354	148.6309	178.3972	214.5828	258.5834
30	34.7849	40.5681	47.5754	56.0849	66.4388	79.0582	94.4608	113.2832	136.3075	164.4940	199.0209	241.3327	293.1992
31	36.1327	42.3794	50.0027	59.3283	70.7608	84.8017	103.0730	123.3459	149.5752	181.9434	221.9132	271.2926	332.3151
32	37.4941	44.2270	52.5028	62.7015	75.2988	90.8898	110.2182	134.2135	164.0370	201.1378	247.3236	304.8477	376.5161
33	38.8690	46.1116	55.0778	66.2095	80.0638	97.3432	118.9334	145.9506	179.8003	222.2515	275.5292	342.4294	426.4632
34	40.2577	48.0338	57.7302	69.8579	85.0670	104.1838	128.2588	158.6267	196.9823	245.4767	306.8374	384.5210	482.9034
35	41.6603	49.9945	60.4621	73.6522	90.3203	111.4348	138.2369	172.3168	215.7108	271.0244	341.5896	431.6635	546.6808
36	43.0769	51.9944	63.2759	77.5983	95.8363	119.1209	148.9135	187.1021	236.1247	299.1268	380.1644	484.4631	618.7493
37	44.5076	54.0343	66.1742	81.7022	101.6281	127.2681	160.3374	203.0703	258.3759	330.0395	422.9825	543.5987	700.1868
38	45.9527	56.1149	69.1594	85.9703	107.7095	135.9042	172.5610	220.3159	282.6298	364.0434	470.5106	609.8305	792.2110
39	47.4123	58.2372	72.2342	90.4092	114.0950	145.0585	185.6403	238.9412	309.0665	401.4478	523.2667	684.0102	896.1985
40	48.8864	60.4020	75.4013	95.0255	120.7998	154.7620	199.6351	259.0565	337.8824	442.5926	581.8261	767.0914	1013.7043
41	50.3752	62.6100	78.6633	99.8265	127.8398	165.0477	214.6096	280.7810	369.2919	487.8518	646.8269	860.1424	1146.4858
42	51.8790	64.8622	82.0232	104.8196	135.2318	175.9505	230.6322	304.2435	403.5281	537.6370	718.9779	964.3595	1296.5290
43	53.3978	67.1595	85.4839	110.0124	142.9933	187.5076	247.7765	329.5830	440.8457	592.4007	799.0655	1081.0826	1466.0777
44	54.9318	69.5027	89.0484	115.4129	151.1430	199.7580	266.1209	356.9496	481.5218	652.6408	887.9627	1211.8125	1657.6679
45	56.4811	71.8927	92.7199	121.0294	159.7002	212.7435	285.7493	386.5056	525.8587	718.9048	986.6386	1358.2300	1874.1649
46	58.0459	74.3306	96.5015	126.8706	168.6852	226.5081	306.7518	418.4261	574.1860	791.7953	1096.1688	1522.2176	2118.8061
47	59.6263	76.8172	100.3965	132.9454	178.1194	241.0986	329.2244	452.9002	626.8628	871.9748	1217.7474	1705.8838	2395.2509
48	61.2226	79.3535	104.4084	139.2632	188.0254	256.5645	353.2701	490.1322	684.2804	960.1723	1352.6996	1911.5898	2707.6335
49	62.8348	81.9406	108.5406	145.8337	198.4267	272.9584	378.9990	530.3427	746.8656	1057.1893	1502.4966	2141.9806	3060.6259
50	64.4632	84.5794	112.7969	152.6671	209.3480	290.3359	406.5289	573.7702	815.0835	1163.7712	1668.7712	2400.0182	3459.5072

ENCYCLOPEDIA OF BANKING AND FINANCE

INTEREST TABLES

and the number of interest periods is

$$10 \times 4 = 40$$

so that the compound amount of principal and the amount of compound interest may be determined as above, based on this adjusted interest rate and adjusted number of interest periods.

3. Future value of a series of payments—the amount to which a series of payments at the end of each period will accumulate at compound interest. The basic formula is

$$S = P_1(1+r)^{n-1} + P_2(1+r)^{n-2} + \ldots + P_n(1+r)^0$$

where S = future value, $P_1, P_2, \ldots, P_n$ = the payment at end of each period, r = interest rate, and n = number of periods. The value of $(1+r)^{n-1}$ can be derived from Table 3. For example, the future value at the end of two years of payments of $1,000 and $2,000 at the end of the first and second years, respectively, invested at 5%, will be

$$S = 1000(1 + 0.05)^1 + 2000(1 + 0.05)^0$$
$$= 1000(1.05) + 2000$$
$$= 1050 < + 2000$$
$$= 3050$$

4. Future value of an annuity. This is a special case of the future value formula above. It is the future value of a series of equal future payments for a given number of periods, at specified interest rate. Applying the future value formula, the future value of an annuity is

$$S = P(1+r)^{n-1} + P(1+r)^{n-2} + \ldots + P(1+r)^0$$

where S = future value, P = periodic payment, r = interest rate, and n = number of periods. Since P, the payment for each period, is equal, the formula can be simplified to

$$S = P\{(1+r)^{n-1}\}/r$$

The value of $\{(1+r)^{n-1}\}/r$ can be found in Table 4, for the specified interest rate r and the number of periods n over which

Table 5/ Federal Farm Loan Interest Table

		Amount required to cancel a $1,000 loan on					
			The simple interest plan				
Time in years	The amortization plan	5%	5.5%	6%	6.5%	7%
---	---	---	---	---	---	---
5	$1,243.99	$1,250.00	$1,275.00	$1,300.00	$1,325.00	$1,350.00
6	1,291.03	1,300.00	1,330.00	1,360.00	1,390.00	1,420.00
7	1,337.41	1,350.00	1,385.00	1,420.00	1,455.00	1,490.00
8	1,383.10	1,400.00	1,440.00	1,480.00	1,520.00	1,560.00
9	1,472.28	1,450.00	1,495.00	1,540.00	1,585.00	1,630.00
10	1,515.69	1,500.00	1,550.00	1,600.00	1,650.00	1,700.00
11	1,558.26	1,550.00	1,605.00	1,660.00	1,715.00	1,770.00
12	1,599.95	1,600.00	1,660.00	1,720.00	1,780.00	1,840.00
13	1,680.49	1,650.00	1,715.00	1,780.00	1,845.00	1,910.00
14	1,719.25	1,700.00	1,770.00	1,840.00	1,910.00	1,980.00
15	1,756.94	1,750.00	1,825.00	1,900.00	1,975.00	2,050.00
16	1,793.49	1,800.00	1,880.00	1,960.00	2,040.00	2,120.00
17	1,828.86	1,850.00	1,935.00	2,020.00	2,105.00	2,190.00
18	1,862.99	1,900.00	1,990.00	2,080.00	2,170.00	2,260.00
19	1,895.80	1,950.00	2,045.00	2,140.00	2,235.00	2,330.00
20	1,927.24	2,000.00	2,100.00	2,200.00	2,300.00	2,400.00
21	1,927.23	2,050.00	2,155.00	2,260.00	2,365.00	2,470.00
22	1,957.23	2,100.00	2,210.00	2,320.00	2,430.00	2,540.00
23	1,985.70	2,150.00	2,265.00	2,380.00	2,495.00	2,610.00
24	2,012.58	2,200.00	2,320.00	2,440.00	2,560.00	2,680.00
25	2,102.04	2,250.00	2,375.00	2,500.00	2,625.00	2,750.00
26	2,037.78	2,300.00	2,430.00	2,560.00	2,690.00	2,820.00
27	2,061.21	2,350.00	2,485.00	2,620.00	2,755.00	2,890.00
28	2,082.80	2,400.00	2,540.00	2,680.00	2,820.00	2,960.00
29	2,102.44	2,450.00	2,595.00	2,740.00	2,855.00	3,030.00
30	2,120.04	2,500.00	2,650.00	2,800.00	2,950.00	3,100.00
31	2,135.49	2,550.00	2,705.00	2,860.00	3,015.00	3,170.00
32	2,148.69	2,600.00	2,760.00	2,920.00	3,080.00	3,240.00
33	2,159.52	2,650.00	2,815.00	2,980.00	3,145.00	3,310.00
34	2,167.86	2,700.00	2,870.00	3,040.00	3,210.00	3,380.00
35	2,173.58	2,750.00	2,925.00	3,100.00	3,275.00	3,450.00
36	2,176.56	2,800.00	2,980.00	3,160.00	3,340.00	3,520.00

Table 6 / Sinking Fund or Annuity Which, Invested at the End of Each Month, Will Amount to $100.00

Period							
	1	$100.0000	$100.0000	$100.0000	$100.0000	$100.0000	$100.0000
	2	49.2611	49.1400	49.0196	48.8998	48.7805	48.5437
	3	32.3530	32.1934	32.0349	31.8773	31.7209	31.4110
	4	23.9027	23.7251	23.5490	23.3744	23.2012	22.8591
	5	18.8355	18.6481	18.4627	18.2892	18.0975	17.7396
	6	15.4597	15.2668	15.0762	14.8878	14.7017	14.3363
	7	13.0506	12.8544	12.6610	12.4701	12.2820	11.9135
	8	11.2456	11.0477	10.8528	10.6610	10.4722	10.1036
	9	9.8434	9.6446	9.4493	9.2574	9.0690	8.7022
	10	8.7231	8.5241	8.8291	8.1379	7.9505	7.5868

ENCYCLOPEDIA OF BANKING AND FINANCE

INTEREST TABLES

the annuity will extend. For example, the value at the end of 10 years of an annuity of $1,000 invested at a 10% interest rate will be

$$= 1000\{(1 + 0.10)^{10} - 1\}/r$$
$$= 1000(15.9374)$$
$$= 15,937.40$$

5. Sinking fund accumulations—the amount of installments to be set aside periodically (annually, semiannually, or quarterly) that at a specified rate of compound interest will accumulate to a total sinking fund sufficient at specified maturity to retire the principal of a given amount of funds. To determine the periodic payments, the formula for calculating the future value of an annuity may be used, as follows:

$$S = P\{(1 + r)^n - 1\}/r$$

In the above formula, the periodic payment is known, but the sum of the payments at the end of the total period at specified interest rate is unknown. For the sinking fund accumulation, the sum is known, but the periodic payment is unknown. Therefore the annuity formula must be solved for P, the periodic payment, rather than S, the sum of the accumulation. Therefore, the formula is

$$P = S/\{(1 + r)^n - 1\}/r$$

For example, to determine the amount to be set aside yearly at a 6% annual rate of interest that will accumulate to $1 million at the end of 10 years, Table 4 provides the value of $\{(1 + r)^n - 1\}/r$, with r at 6% and n at 10, as equal to 13.1808. Therefore:

$$P = 1,000,000/13.1808$$
$$= 75,867.93$$

Examples of sinking fund accumulations are shown in appended Tables 5 and 6.

6. Present value of one or a series of payments to be received (or paid out) in the future, discounted at specified discount rate. The formula for computing present value is

Table 7 / Present Value of $1 Discounted at Discount Rate k, for n Years

	1%	2%	3%	4%	5%	6%	7%	8%	9%	10%	11%	12%	13%	14%	15%
1	.9901	.9804	9709	.9615	.9524	.9434	.9346	.9259	.914	.9091	.9009	.8929	.8850	.8772	.8696
2	.9803	.9612	.9426	.9246	.9070	.8900	.8734	.8573	.8417	.8264	.8116	.7972	.7831	.7695	.8561
3	.9706	.9423	.9151	.8890	.8638	.8396	.8163	.7938	.7722	.7513	.7312	.7118	.6931	.6750	.6575
4	.9610	.9239	.8885	.8549	.8227	.7921	.7629	.7350	.7084	.6830	.6589	.6355	.6133	.5921	.5718
5	.9515	.9057	.8626	.8219	.7835	.7473	.7130	.6806	.6499	.6209	.5923	.5674	.5428	.5194	.4972
6	.9420	.8880	.8375	.7903	.7462	.7050	.6663	.6302	.5963	.5645	.5346	.5066	.4803	.4556	.4323
7	.9327	.8706	.8131	.7599	.7107	.6651	.6228	.5835	.5470	.5132	.4817	.4524	.4251	.3996	.3759
8	.9235	.8535	.7894	.7307	.6768	.6274	.5720	.5403	.5019	.4665	.4339	.4039	.3762	.3506	.3269
9	.9143	.8368	.7664	.7026	.6446	.5919	.5439	.5002	.4604	.4241	.3909	.3606	.3329	.3075	.2843
10	.9053	.8204	.7441	.6756	.6139	.5584	.5084	.4632	.4224	.3855	.3522	.3220	.2946	.2697	.2472
11	.8963	.8043	.7224	.6496	.5847	.5268	.4751	.4289	.3875	.3505	.3173	.2875	.2607	.2366	.2149
12	.8874	.7885	.7014	.6256	.5568	.4970	.4440	.3971	.3555	.3186	.2858	.2567	.2307	.2076	.1869
13	.8787	.7730	.6810	.6006	.6303	.4688	.4150	.3677	.3262	.2897	.2575	.2292	.2042	.1821	.1625
14	.8700	.7579	.6611	.5775	.5051	.4423	.3878	.3405	.2993	.2633	.2320	.2046	.1807	.1597	.1413
15	.8614	.7430	.6419	.5553	.4810	.4173	.3625	.3152	.2745	.2394	.2090	.1827	.1599	.1401	.1229
16	.8528	.7284	.6232	.5339	.4581	.3936	.3387	.2912	.2519	.2176	.1883	.1631	.1415	.1229	.1069
17	.8444	.7142	.6050	.5134	.4363	.3714	.3166	.2703	.2311	.1978	.1696	.1456.	.1252	.1078	.0929
18	.8360	.7002	.5874	.4936	.4155	.3503	.2959	.2502	.2120	.1799	.1528	1300	.1108	.0946	.0808
19	.8277	.6864	.5703	.4846	.3957	.3305	.2765	.2317	.1945	.1635	.1377	.1161	.0981	.0829	.0703
20	.8195	.6730	.5537	.4564	.3769	.3118	.2584	.2145	.1784	.1486	.1240	.1037	.0868	.0728	.0611
21	.8114	.6598	.5375	.4388	.3589	.2942	.2415	.1987	.1637	.1351	.1117	.0926	.0768	.0638	.0531
22	.8034	.6468	.5219	.4220	.3418	.2775	.2257	.1839	.1502	.1229	.1007	.0826	.0680	.0560	.0462
23	.7956	.6342	.5067	.4057	.3256	.2618	.2109	.1703	.1378	.1117	.0907	.0738	.0601	.0491	.0402
24	.7876	.6217	.4919	.3901	.3101	.2470	.1971	.1577	.1264	.1015	.0817	.0659	.0532	.0431	.0349
25	.7798	.6095	.4776	.3750	.2953	.2330	.1842	.1460	.1160	.0923	.0736	.0588	.0471	.0378	.0304
26	.7721	.5976	.4637	.3607	.2812	.2198	.1722	.1352	.1064	.0839	.0663	.0525	.0417	.0332	.0264
27	.7644	.5859	.4502	.3468	.2678	.2074	.1609	.1252	.0976	.0763	.0597	.0469	.0369	.0291	.0230
28	.7568	.5744	.4371	.3335	.2551	.1956	.1504	.1159	.0896	.0693	.0538	.0419	.0326	.0255	.0200
29	.7493	.5631	.4244	.3206	.2429	.1846	.1406	.1073	.0821	.0630	.0485	.0374	.0289	.0224	.0174
30	.7419	.5521	.4120	.3083	.2314	.1741	.1314	.0994	.0754	.0573	.0437	.0334	.0256	.0196	.0151
31	.7346	.5412	.4000	.2965	.2204	.1643	.1228	.0920	.0692	.0521	.0394	.0298	.0226	.0172	.0131
32	.7273	.5306	.3883	.2851	.2099	.1550	.1147	.0852	.0634	.0474	.0354	.0266	.0200	.0151	.0114
33	.7201	.5202	.3770	.2741	.1999	.1462	.1072	.0789	.0582	.0431	.0319	.0238	.0177	.0133	.0099
34	.7130	.5100	.3660	.2635	.1903	.1379	.1002	.0731	.0534	.0391	.0288	.0212	.0157	.0116	.0086
35	.7059	.5000	.3554	.2534	.1813	.1301	.0937	.0676	.0490	.0356	.0259	.0189	.0139	.0102	.0075
36	.6989	.4902	.3450	.2437	.1727	.1227	.0875	.0626	.0449	.0324	.0234	.0169	.0123	.0089	.0065
37	.6920	.4806	.3350	.2343	.1644	.1158	.0818	.0580	.0412	.0294	.0210	.0151	.0109	.0078	.0057
38	.6852	.4712	.3252	.2253	.1566	.1092	.0765	.0537	.0378	.0267	.0190	.0135	.0096	.0069	.0049
39	.6784	.4620	.3158	.2166	.1492	.1031	.0715	.0497	.0347	.0243	.0171	.0120	.0085	.0060	.0043
40	.6717	.4529	.3066	.2083	.1420	.0972	.0668	.0460	.0318	.0221	.0154	.0107	.0075	.0053	.0037
41	.6650	.4440	.2976	.2003	.1343	.0917	.0624	.0426	.0292	.0201	.0139	.0096	.0067	.0046	.0033
42	.6584	.4353	.2890	.1926	.1288	.0865	.0583	.0395	.0268	.0183	.0125	.0086	.0059	.0041	.0028
43	.6519	.4268	.2805	.2852	.1227	.0816	.0545	.0365	.0246	.0166	.0113	.0077	.0052	.0036	.0025
44	.6454	.4184	.2724	.1781	.1169	.0770	.0509	.0338	.0226	.0151	.0101	.0068	.0046	.0031	.0021
45	.6391	.4102	.2644	.1712	.1113	.0727	.0476	.0313	.0207	.0137	.0091	.0061	.0041	.0027	.0019
46	.6327	.4021	.2567	.1646	.1060	.0685	.0445	.0290	.0190	.0125	.0082	.0054	.0036	.0024	.0016
47	.6265	.3943	.2493	.1583	.1010	.0647	.0416	.0269	.0174	.0113	.0074	.0049	.0032	.0031	.0014
48	.6203	.3865	.2420	.1522	.0961	.0610	.0389	.0249	.0160	.0103	.0067	.0043	.0028	.0019	.0012
49	.6141	.3790	.2350	.1463	.0916	.0575	.0363	.0230	.0147	.0094	.0060	.0039	.0025	.0016	.0011
50	.6080	.3715	.2281	.1407	.0872	.0543	.0340	.0213	.0135	.0085	.0054	.0035	.0022	.0014	.0009

INTEREST TABLES

Table 8 / Present Value of an Annuity of $1 for *n* Years, Discounted at Rate *k*

	1%	2%	3%	4%	5%	6%	7%	8%	9%	10%	11%	12%	13%	14%	15%
1	.9901	.9804	.9709	.9615	.9524	.9434	.9346	.9259	.9174	.9091	.9009	.8929	.8850	.8772	.8696
2	1.9704	1.9416	1.9135	1.8861	1.8594	1.8334	1.8080	1.7833	1.7591	1.7355	1.7125	1.6901	1.6681	1.6467	1.6257
3	2.9410	2.8839	2.8286	2.7751	2.7232	2.6730	2.6243	2.5771	2.5313	2.4869	2.4437	2.4018	2.3612	2.3216	2.2832
4	3.9020	3.8077	3.7171	3.6299	3.5459	3.4651	3.3872	3.3121	3.2397	3.1699	3.1024	3.0374	2.9745	2.9137	2.8550
5	4.8534	4.7135	4.5797	4.4518	4.3295	4.2124	4.1002	3.9927	3.8897	3.7908	3.6959	3.6048	3.5172	3.4331	3.3522
6	5.7955	5.6014	5.4172	5.2421	5.0757	4.9173	4.7666	4.6229	4.4859	4.3553	4.2305	4.1114	3.9976	3.8887	3.7845
7	6.7282	6.4720	6.2303	6.0021	5.7864	5.5824	5.3893	5.2064	5.0030	4.8684	4.7122	4.5338	4.4226	4.2883	4.1604
8	7.6517	7.3255	7.0197	6.7328	6.4632	6.2098	5.9713	5.7466	5.5348	5.3349	5.1461	4.9676	4.7988	4.6389	4.4873
9	8.4660	8.1622	7.7861	7.4353	7.1089	6.8017	6.5152	6.2459	5.9953	5.8590	5.5371	5.3282	5.1317	4.9474	4.7716
10	9.4713	8.9826	8.5302	8.1109	7.7217	7.3601	7.0236	6.7101	6.4177	6.1446	5.8892	5.6502	5.4262	5.2161	5.0188
11	10.3676	8.9826	9.2526	8.7605	8.3064	7.8869	7.4987	7.1390	6.8052	6.7951	6.2065	5.9377	5.6869	6.4527	5.2337
12	11.2551	9.7868	9.9540	9.3851	8.8633	8.3839	7.9427	7.5361	7.1607	6.8137	6.4924	6.1944	5.9177	5.6603	5.4206
13	12.1338	10.5753	10.6349	9.9540	9.3936	8.8527	8.3577	7.9038	7.4869	7.1034	6.7499	6.4235	6.1218	5.8424	5.5832
14	13.0037	11.3484	11.2961	10.6349	9.8986	9.2950	8.7455	8.2442	7.7862	7.3667	6.9816	6.6282	5.3025	6.0021	5.7245
15	13.8651	12.1062	11.9379	11.1184	10.3797	9.7123	9.1079	8.5595	8.0607	7.6061	7.1909	6.8109	6.4625	6.1422	5.8474
16	14.7179	12.8492	12.5611	11.6523	10.8378	10.1059	9.4467	8.8514	8.3126	7.8237	7.3792	6.9740	6.6039	6.2651	5.9542
17	15.5623	13.5888	13.1661	12.1657	11.2741	10.4773	9.7632	9.1216	8.5436	8.0216	7.5488	7.1196	6.7291	6.3729	6.0472
18	16.3983	14.2919	13.7535	12.6593	11.6896	10.8276	10.0591	9.3719	8.7556	8.2014	7.7016	7.2497	6.8399	6.4674	6.1280
19	17.2260	14.9920	14.3238	13.1339	12.0853	11.1581	10.3356	9.6036	8.9501	8.3649	7.8393	7.3658	6.9380	6.5504	6.1982
20	18.0456	15.6785	14.8775	13.5903	12.4622	11.4699	10.5940	9.8181	9.1285	8.5136	7.9633	7.4694	7.0248	6.6231	6.2593
21	18.8570	16.3514	15.4150	14.0292	12.8212	11.7641	10.8355	10.0168	9.2922	8.6487	8.0751	7.5620	7.1016	6.6870	6.3125
22	19.6604	17.0112	16.9369	14.4511	13.1630	12.0416	11.0612	10.2007	9.4424	8.7715	8.1757	7.6446	7.1695	6.7430	6.3587
23	20.4558	17.6580	16.4436	14.8569	13.4886	12.3034	11.2722	10.3711	9.5802	8.8832	8.2664	7.7184	7.2297	6.7921	6.3988
24	21.2434	18.2922	16.9355	15.2470	13.7987	12.5504	11.4693	10.5288	9.7066	8.9847	8.3481	7.7843	7.2829	6.8352	6.4338
25	22.0232	18.9139	17.4132	15.6221	14.0940	12.7834	11.6536	10.6748	9.8226	9.0770	8.4217	7.8431	7.3300	6.8729	6.4641
26	22.7952	19.5234	17.8768	15.9828	14.3852	13.0032	11.8258	10.8100	9.4424	9.1610	8.4880	7.8956	7.3717	6.9061	6.4906
27	23.5596	20.1210	18.3280	16.3296	14.6430	13.2106	11.9867	10.9352	9.5802	9.2372	8.5478	7.9425	7.4086	6.9352	6.5135
28	24.3165	20.7069	18.7641	16.6631	14.8981	13.4062	12.1371	11.0511	10.1161	9.3066	8.6016	7.9844	7.4412	6.9607	6.5335
29	25.0658	21.2813	19.1885	16.9837	15.1411	13.5905	12.2777	11.1584	10.1983	9.3696	8.6501	8.0218	7.4701	6.9831	6.5509
30	25.8077	21.8444	19.6005	17.2920	15.3725	13.7649	12.4091	11.2578	10.2838	9.4269	8.6938	8.0552	7.4957	7.0027	6.5660
31	26.5423	22.3964	20.0005	17.5885	15.5928	13.9291	12.5318	11.3498	10.3428	9.4790	8.7331	8.0850	7.5183	7.0199	6.5791
32	27.2696	22.9377	30.3888	17.8736	15.8027	14.0841	12.6466	11.4350	10.4062	9.5264	8.7686	8.1116	7.5383	7.0350	6.5905
33	27.9897	23.4683	20.7658	18.1477	16.0026	14.2303	12.7558	11.5139	10.4644	9.5694	8.8005	8.1353	7.5560	7.0483	6.6005
34	28.7027	23.9885	21.1319	18.4112	16.1929	14.3682	12.8540	11.5870	10.5189	9.6086	8.8293	8.1565	7.5717	7.0599	6.6091
35	29.4086	24.4986	21.4872	18.6646	16.3742	14.4953	12.9477	11.6546	10.5669	9.6442	8.8552	8.1755	7.5856	7.0701	6.6166
36	30.1075	25.4888	21.8323	18.9083	16.5469	14.6211	13.0352	11.7172	10.6118	9.6765	8.8786	8.1924	7.5979	7.0790	6.6231
37	30.7995	25.9694	22.1673	19.1426	16.7113	14.7368	13.1170	11.7752	10.6530	9.7059	8.8996	8.2075	7.6087	7.0868	6.6288
38	31.4847	26.4406	22.4925	19.3679	16.8679	14.8461	13.1935	11.8289	10.6908	9.7327	8.9186	8.2210	7.6183	7.0937	6.6338
39	32.1631	26.9159	22.8082	19.5845	17.0171	14.9491	13.2650	11.8786	10.7255	9.7570	8.9356	8.2330	7.6269	7.0998	6.6380
40	32.8347	27.3555	23.1148	19.7928	17.1591	15.0464	13.3317	11.9246	10.7574	9.7791	8.9510	8.2438	7.6344	7.1051	6.6418
41	33.4997	27.7995	23.4124	19.9931	17.2944	15.1381	13.3941	11.9672	10.7866	9.7991	8.9649	8.2534	7.6410	7.1097	6.6450
42	34.1581	28.2348	23.7014	20.1857	17.4232	15.2246	13.4525	12.0067	10.8134	9.8174	8.9774	8.2619	7.6469	7.1138	6.6478
43	34.8100	28.6615	23.9819	20.3708	17.5459	15.3062	13.5070	12.0432	10.8380	9.8340	8.9886	8.2696	7.6522	7.1173	6.6503
44	35.4555	29.0799	24.2543	20.5489	17.6628	15.3833	13.5579	12.0771	10.8605	9.8491	8.9988	8.2764	7.6568	7.1205	6.6524
45	36.0945	29.4901	24.5187	20.7201	17.7741	15.4559	13.6055	12.1084	10.8812	9.8628	9.0079	8.2825	7.6609	7.1232	6.6543
46	3637273	29.8923	24.7755	20.8847	17.8801	15.5244	13.6500	12.1374	10.9002	9.8753	9.0161	8.2880	7.6645	7.1256	6.6559
47	37.3537	30.2866	25.0247	21.0430	17.9810	15.5891	13.6916	12.1643	10.9176	9.8866	9.0235	8.2928	7.6677	7.1277	6.6573
48	37.9740	30.6731	25.2667	21.1952	18.0772	15.6501	13.7305	12.1891	10.9336	9.8969	9.0302	8.2972	7.6705	7.1296	6.6585
49	38.5881	31.0521	25.5017	21.3415	18.1687	15.7077	13.7668	12.2122	10.9482	9.9063	9.0362	8.3010	7.6730	7.1312	6.6596
50	39.1961	32.4236	25.7298	21.4822	18.2559	15.7619	13.8008	12.2335	10.9617	9.9148	9.0416	8.3045	7.6753	7.1327	6.6605

Table 9 / Years in Which a Given Amount Will Double at Several Rates of Interest

		At compound interest					At compound interest		
Rate	At simple interest	Compounded yearly	Compounded semi-annually	Compounded quarterly	Rate	At simple interest	Compounded yearly	Compounded semi-annually	Compounded quarterly
1.0	100 years	69.660	69.487	69.237	6.0	6.67	11.896	11.725	11.639
1.5	66.66	46.556	46.382	46.297	6.5	15.38	11.007	10.836	10.750
2.0	50.00	35.003	34.830	34.743	7.0	14.29	10.245	10.074	9.966
2.5	40.00	28.071	27.899	27.748	7.5	13.33	9.584	9.414	9.328
3.0	33.33	23.450	23.278	23.191	8.0	12.50	9.006	8.837	8.751
3.5	28.57	20.149	19.977	19.890	8.5	11.76	8.497	8.327	8.241
4.0	25.00	17.673	17.501	17.415	9.0	11.11	8.043	7.874	7.788
4.5	22.22	15.747	15.576	15.490	9.5	10.52	7.638	7.468	7.383
5.0	20.00	14.207	14.035	13.949	10.0	10.00	7.273	7.103	7.018
5.5	18.18	12.942	12.775	12.689	12.0	8.34	6.116	5.948	5.862

ENCYCLOPEDIA OF BANKING AND FINANCE

INTEREST TABLES

$$PV = \frac{1}{(1+k)} + \frac{1}{(1+k)^2} + \ldots + \frac{1}{(1+k)^n}$$

where PV = present value, n = year of last payment received (or paid out), and k = discount rate. For example, the present value of $1 to be received at the end of the first and second years from the present time, discounted at 5%, is as follows:

$$PV = \frac{1}{(1+0.05)} + \frac{1}{(1+0.05)^2}$$

$$= \frac{\$1}{1.05} + \frac{\$1}{1.1025}$$

$$= 0.9524 + 0.9070$$

$$= 1.8594$$

Table 7 provides the present value of $1, received in 1 to 30 years, discounted at the rate of 1% to 50%. Rather than divide each numerator by the denominator in the above equations, multiply the numerator by the present value of $1 discounted at the specified rate for the specified time period, found in Table 7. For example, to determine the present value of a $100 inflow at the end of year one, $200 inflow at the end of year two, and $50 outflow at the end of year three, we may multiply these flows by the present value of $1 indicated in Table 7 for the respective years, as follows, at 5% discount rate.

$$PV = 100(0.9524) + 200(0.9070) - 50(0.8638)$$
$$= 95.24 + 181.40 - 43.19$$
$$= 233.45$$

In capital budgeting, one technique of analysis of feasibility of investing in specific investment proposals is the net present value technique: cash flows each year anticipated from net income plus depreciation for the full useful life of the proposed investment in plant and equipment are discounted at a selected

Table 10 / How Much to Save Each Month at Your Age to Reach Your Goal, with Interest at 4% Compounded Semiannually

Amt. you want at age m	20	22	24	26	28	30	32	34	36	37	40	45	50
$ 5,000	$ 3.33	$ 3.66	$ 4.04	$ 4.46	$ 4.94	$ 5.49	$ 6.11	$ 6.82	$ 7.64	$ 8.60	$ 9.73	$ 13.63	$ 20.30
10,000	6.66	7.33	8.09	8.93	9.89	10.98	12.22	13.65	15.29	17.21	19.47	27.27	40.60
15,000	10.00	11.00	12.13	13.40	14.84	16.47	18.33	20.47	22.94	25.82	29.21	40.91	60.91
20,000	13.33	14.67	16.18	17.87	19.79	21.96	24.45	27.30	30.59	34.43	38.95	54.54	81.21
25,000	16.66	18.34	20.22	22.34	24.74	27.46	30.56	34.12	38.24	43.04	48.69	68.18	101.52
30,000	20.00	22.01	24.27	26.81	29.69	32.95	36.67	40.95	45.89	51.65	58.43	81.82	121.82
40,000	26.66	29.34	32.36	35.75	39.58	43.93	48.90	54.60	61.19	68.87	77.91	109.09	162.43
50,000	33.33	36.68	40.45	44.69	49.48	54.92	61.13	68.25	76.49	86.09	97.39	136.37	203.04

Table 11/ Bond Interest on $1000 from 1 day to 6 months

Days	3.50%	3.75%	4%	4.25%	4.50%	4.75%	5%	6%
1	$ 0.0972	$ 0.1041	$ 0.1111	$ 0.1180	$ 0.125	$ 0.1319	$ 0.1389	$ 0.1667
2	0.1944	0.2083	0.2222	0.2361	0.250	0.2638	0.2778	0.3333
3	0.2916	0.3125	0.3333	0.3541	0.375	0.3958	0.4167	0.5000
4	0.3889	0.4166	0.4444	0.4722	0.500	0.5277	0.5556	0.6667
5	0.4861	0.5208	0.5555	0.5903	0.625	0.6597	0.944	0.8333
6	0.5833	0.6250	0.6667	0.7083	0.750	0.7916	0.8333	1.0000
7	0.6805	0.7291	0.7778	0.8264	0.875	0.9236	0.9722	1.1667
8	0.7778	0.8333	0.8889	0.9444	1.000	1.0555	1.1111	1.3333
9	0.8750	0.9375	1.0000	1.0625	1.125	1.1875	1.2500	1.5000
10	0.9722	1.0416	1.1111	1.1805	1.250	1.3194	1.3889	1.6667
11	1.0894	1.1458	1.2222	1.2986	1.375	1.4513	1.5278	1.8333
12	1.1667	1.2500	1.3333	1.4166	1.500	1.5833	1.6667	2.0000
13	1.2639	1.3541	1.4444	1.5347	1.625	1.7152	11.8055	2.1667
14	1.3611	1.4583	1.5555	1.6527	1.750	1.8472	1.9444	2.3333
15	1.4583	1.5625	1.6667	1.7708	1.875	1.9791	2.0833	2.5000
16	1.5555	1.6666	1.7778	1.8888	2.000	2.1111	2.2222	2.6667
17	1.6528	1.7708	1.8889	2.0069	2.125	2.2430	2.3611	2.8333
18	1.7500	1.8750	2.0000	2.1250	2.250	2.3750	2.5000	3.0000
19	1.8472	1.9791	2.1111	2.2430	2.375	2.5069	2.6389	3.1667
20	1.9444	2.0833	2.2222	2.3610	2.500	2.6388	2.7778	3.3333
21	2.0417	2.0833	2.3333	2.3791	2.625	2.7708	2.9167	3.5000
22	2.1389	2.2916	2.4444	2.5972	2.750	2.9027	3.0555	3.6667
23	2.2361	2.3958	2.5555	2.7153	2.875	3.0347	3.1944	3.8333
24	2.3333	2.5000	2.6667	2.8333	3.000	3.1666	3.3333	4.0000
25	2.4205	2.6041	2.7778	2.9514	3.125	3.2986	3.4722	4.1667
26	2.5278	2.7083	2.8889	3.0694	3.250	3.4305	3.6111	4.3333
27	2.6250	2.8125	3.0000	3.1875	3.375	3.5625	3.7500	4.5000
28	2.7222	2.9166	3.1111	3.3055	3.500	3.6944	3.8889	4.6667
29	2.8194	3.0208	3.2222	3.4236	3.625	3.8263	4.0278	4.8333
30	2.9167	3.1250	3.3333	3.5416	3.750	3.9583	4.1667	5.0000
1 Mo.	2.9167	3.1250	3.3333	3.5416	3.750	3.9583	4.1667	5.0000
2 Mo.	5.8333	6.2500	6.6667	7.0833	7.500	7.9166	8.3333	10.0000
3 Mo.	8.7500	9.3750	10.0000	10.6250	11.250	11.8749	12.5000	15.0000
4 Mo.	11.6667	12.5000	13.3333	14.1666	15.000	15.8332	16.6667	20.0000
5 Mo.	14.5833	15.6250	16.6667	17.7083	18.750	19.7915	20.8333	25.0000

ENCYCLOPEDIA OF BANKING AND FINANCE

discount rate; the sum of such discounted present values is then compared with present investment outlay to show net excess of sum of discounted present values over the investment outlay.

7. Present value of an ANNUITY. A special case of the present value formula above is the present value of a sum of either equal inflows or equal outflows for a given number of periods, discounted at specified rate. Adapting the present value formula in 6 above, since the numerator ($1) is the same for each period, the formula can be simplified to

$$PV = 1\{1 - (1 + k)^{-n}\}/k$$

the value of which can be found in Table 8 at the specified discount rate k and the number of periods n over which the annuity will extend. For example, the present value of an annuity of $1,000 received at the end of each year for 10 years, discounted at 10%, may be determined by multiplying the $1,000 by the factor 6.1446, shown in Table 8.

$$PV = 1000(6.1446) = 6144.60$$

8. Doubling of principal. Given the interest rate, Table 9 will indicate the number of years it will take a given principal to double in amount. For example, at 6% compounded annually, it will take 11.896 years to double the principal.

The formula for determining the number of years in which a given sum will double at different interest rates may be derived from the compound interest formula (above), except that the equation is solved for the number of periods rather than the sum to which the principal will grow. Thus, the compound interest formula is

$$S = P(1 + r)^n$$

but S, the sum, is specified as equal to twice the principal ($S = 2P$), so that substituting for S,

$$2P = P(1 + r)^n$$

which may be simplified to

$$2 = (1 + r)^n$$

which by the use of logarithms becomes

$$n \log (1 + r) = \log 2$$

$$n = \frac{\log 2}{\log (1 + 0.06)}$$

$$= \frac{0.301030}{0.025306}$$

$$= 11.896$$

9. Monthly savings to attain a specified estate. See appended Table 10 for the amount to be saved per month, with interest compounded at 4% semiannually, to accumulate a specified sum at age 65.
10. Bond interest table. See appended Table 11 for the amount of accrued interest on a $1,000 bond for 1 day to 6 months at coupon rates for every 0.25% from 3.5% to 5%, and 6%. The interest on a $1,000 bond at 4.5% for 4 months and 23 days would be $15.00 for 4 months and $2.875 for 23 days; total, $17.875.
11. Income from dividend stocks. See appended Table 12 for the approximate current return, or YIELD, from dividend-paying stocks at prices from 20 to 200, having a cash rate from $2 to $10 annually.

Simple interest tables for computing interest on short-term loans are based on a 360-day and 365-day year. Commercial banks customarily use the 360-day tables, but the Federal Reserve banks compute their transactions on the 365-day table. There are a number of published tables showing the amount of interest on a given sum at various interest rates from 1 to 365 days.

See AMORTIZATION LOANS, BOND VALUES TABLE, DISCOUNT.

Table 12 / Approximate Income from Dividend-Paying Stocks

Price	2%	3%	4%	5%	6%	7%	8%	Price	4%	5%	6%	7%	8%	9%	10%
20	10.0	15.0	20.0	25.0	30.0	35.0	40.0	78	5.1	6.4	7.7	9.0	10.3	11.5	12.8
22	9.1	13.6	18.2	22.7	27.3	31.8	36.4	80	5.0	6.3	7.5	8.8	10.0	11.3	12.5
24	8.3	12.5	16.7	20.8	25.0	29.2	33.3	82	4.9	6.1	7.3	8.5	9.8	11.0	12.3
26	7.7	11.5	15.4	19.2	23.1	26.9	30.8	84	4.8	6.0	7.1	8.3	9.5	10.7	11.9
28	7.1	10.7	14.3	17.9	21.4	25.0	28.6	86	4.7	5.8	7.0	8.1	9.3	10.5	11.6
30	6.7	10.0	13.3	16.7	20.0	23.3	26.7	88	4.6	5.7	6.8	8.0	9.1	10.2	11.4
32	6.3	9.4	12.5	15.6	18.8	21.9	25.0	90	4.4	5.6	6.7	7.8	8.9	10.0	11.1
34	5.9	8.8	11.8	14.7	17.7	20.6	23.5	92	4.4	5.4	6.5	7.6	8.7	9.8	10.9
36	5.6	8.3	11.8	14.7	17.7	20.6	23.5	94	4.3	5.3	6.4	7.5	8.5	9.6	10.6
38	5.3	7.9	10.5	13.2	15.8	18.4	21.1	96	4.2	5.2	6.3	7.3	8.3	9.4	10.4
40	5.0	7.5	10.0	12.5	15.0	17.5	20.0	98	4.1	5.1	6.1	7.1	8.2	9.2	10.2
42	4.8	7.1	9.5	11.9	14.3	16.7	19.1	100	4.0	5.0	6.0	7.0	8.0	9.0	10.0
44	4.6	6.8	9.1	11.4	13.6	15.9	18.2	102	3.9	4.9	5.9	6.9	7.9	8.8	9.8
46	4.4	6.5	8.7	10.9	13.0	15.2	17.4	104	3.9	4.8	5.8	6.7	7.7	8.7	9.6
48	4.2	6.3	8.3	10.4	12.5	14.6	16.7	106	3.8	4.7	5.7	6.6	7.6	8.5	9.4
50	4.0	6.0	8.0	10.0	12.0	14.0	16.0	108	3.7	4.6	5.6	6.5	7.4	8.3	9.3
52	3.9	5.8	7.7	9.6	11.5	13.5	15.4	110	3.6	4.6	5.5	6.4	7.3	8.2	9.1
54	3.7	5.6	7.4	9.3	11.1	13.0	14.8	112	3.6	4.5	5.4	6.3	7.1	8.0	8.9
56	3.6	5.4	7.1	8.9	10.7	12.5	14.3	114	3.5	4.4	5.3	6.1	7.0	7.9	8.8
58	3.5	5.2	6.9	8.6	10.3	12.1	13.8	116	3.5	4.3	5.2	6.0	6.9	7.8	8.6
60	3.3	5.0	6.7	8.3	10.0	11.7	13.3	118	3.4	4.2	5.1	5.9	6.8	7.6	8.5
62	3.2	4.8	6.5	8.1	9.7	11.3	12.9	120	3.3	4.2	5.0	5.8	6.7	7.5	8.3
64	3.1	4.7	6.3	7.8	9.4	10.9	12.5	130	3.1	3.9	4.6	5.4	6.2	6.9	7.7
66	3.0	4.6	6.1	7.6	9.1	10.6	12.1	140	2.9	3.6	4.3	5.0	5.7	6.4	7.1
68	2.9	4.4	5.9	7.4	8.8	10.3	11.8	150	2.7	3.3	4.0	4.7	5.3	6.0	6.7
70	2.9	4.3	5.7	7.1	8.6	10.0	11.4	160	2.5	3.1	3.8	4.4	5.0	5.6	6.3
72	2.8	4.2	5.6	6.9	8.3	9.7	11.1	170	2.4	2.9	3.5	4.1	4.7	5.3	5.9
74	2.7	4.1	5.4	6.8	8.1	9.5	10.8	180	2.2	2.8	3.3	3.9	4.4	5.0	5.6
76	2.6	3.9	5.2	6.6	7.9	9.2	10.5	200	2.0	2.5	3.0	3.5	4.0	4.5	5.0

INTEREST WARRANT

BIBLIOGRAPHY

BOGEN, J. L., and SHIPMAN, S. S. *Financial Handbook*. Latest edition.
FINANCIAL PUBLISHING Co. *Comprehensive Bond Value Tables*.
THORNDIKE *Encyclopedia of Banking and Financial Tables* (including annual Yearbooks).
WOELFEL, C. J. *Money, Time, Interest, and Yield*, 1988.

INTEREST WARRANT An order by a corporation for the payment of interest due on its bonds, notes, etc.—especially an order drawn on a paying agent calling for payment of interest on registered bonds.

See WARRANT.

INTERIM CERTIFICATES Temporary printed certificates; provisional bonds or stocks issued to purchasers of a new issue until the final or permanently engraved securities can be issued to take their place. Final stock certificates or bonds are known as definitive or permanent securities. Since the preparation of the definitive bond and stock certificates involves time and purchasers require some sort of documentary proof of ownership, interim certificates are provided to fill the gap. Interim certificates may be issued by the debtor corporation or by the syndicate managers of the syndicate floating the issue. They are also known as receipts or syndicate managers' receipts.

INTERIM DIVIDEND A dividend paid in anticipation of the usual periodic dividend. Some corporations make a practice of paying an interim dividend at a small nominal rate, usually each quarter, in anticipation of the disbursement of the year-end or full dividend declared at the close of the fiscal year.

INTERIM FINANCIAL REPORTS Reports that cover periods of less than one year. In general, the results for each interim period should be based on the generally accepted accounting principles and reporting practices used in the last annual reporting period, although certain modifications of accounting principles and practices are allowed when applied to interim reports. Interim reports are considered an integral part of the annual reporting period and are not viewed as a discrete time period. Interim reports are essential in providing investors, creditors, and others with timely information as to the financial position and operating results of an enterprise. The usefulness of interim reports depends to a great extent upon how they relate to the annual reports. Major uses and objectives of interim reporting include:

1. To estimate annual earnings.
2. To make projections and predictions.
3. To identify turning points in operations and financial position.
4. To evaluate management performance.
5. To supplement information presented in the annual report.

Publicly traded companies usually report the following summarized financial information at interim dates:

1. Gross revenues, provision for income taxes, extraordinary items, effects of accounting changes, and net income.
2. Primary and fully diluted earnings-per-share data.
3. Material seasonal variations of revenues, costs, and expenses.
4. Contingent items and effects of the disposal of a segment of a business.
5. Material changes in financial position.

Revenues are recognized just as they are for fiscal periods. Procedures for determining product costs and other expenses are similar to those used for the fiscal period, with some exceptions for inventory valuation, income taxes, and other items.

INTERIM RECEIPTS *See* INTERIM CERTIFICATES.

INTERIOR BANKS Banks located outside of New York City, other than Federal Reserve banks, Federal Land banks, etc. Practically all banks not located in New York find it convenient to maintain banking connections and to carry balances with some New York bank. The purpose of these balances is to enable banks outside of New York City to sell drafts on New York, to invest in the money market and security markets, to deal in foreign exchange, to issue letters of credit, etc., the New York correspondent being the instrumentality by which these transactions are consummated. For this reason, New York is treated throughout the country as a financial center.

INTERLOCKING DIRECTORS Directors of one corporation who are at the same time directors of one or more other corporations in the same or similar line of business. By this means, a community of interest is established between or among the corporations concerned, which could be conducive to the lessening or elimination of competition if the corporations concerned are competitors. Interlocking directors as a combinational device was the subject of Section 8 of the Clayton Act, enacted October 15, 1914, as one of the basic antitrust laws, and applying to banks as completely revised by the Banking Act of 1935, as follows.

No private banker, or director, officer, or employee of any member bank of the Federal Reserve System or any branch thereof, shall be at the same time a director, officer, or employee of any other bank, banking association, savings bank, or trust company organized under the National Bank Act or under the laws of any state or of the District of Columbia, or any branch thereof.

However, the Board of Governors of the Federal Reserve System may by regulation permit such service as a director, officer, or employee of not more than one other such institution or branch thereof. The Board of Governors promulgated Regulation L in this connection.

Section 8 of the Clayton Act provides the following statutory exceptions.

1. A bank, banking association, savings bank, or trust company, more than 90% of the stock of which is owned directly or indirectly by the United States, or by any corporation of which the United States directly or indirectly owns more than 90% of the stock.
2. A bank, banking association, savings bank, or trust company that has been placed formally in liquidation or that is in the hands of a receiver, conservator, or other official exercising similar functions.
3. A corporation principally engaged in international or foreign banking, or banking in a dependency or insular possession of the United States, that has entered into an agreement with the Board of Governors of the Federal Reserve System pursuant to Section 25 of the Federal Reserve Act.
(The Board of Governors of the Federal Reserve System regards the provisions of the first three paragraphs of Section 8 of the Clayton Act (15 U.S.C. 19) to have been supplanted by the revised and more comprehensive prohibitions on management official interlocks between depository organizations in the DEPOSITORY INSTITUTION MANAGEMENT INTERLOCKS ACT.)
4. A bank, banking association, savings bank, or trust company, more than 50% of the common stock of which is owned directly or indirectly by persons who own directly or indirectly more than 50% of the common stock of such member bank.
5. A bank, banking association, savings bank, or trust company not located and having no branch in the same city, town, or village as that in which such member bank or any branch thereof is located, or in any city, town, or village contiguous or adjacent thereto.
6. A bank, banking association, savings bank, or trust company not engaged in a class or classes of business in which such member bank is engaged.
7. A mutual savings bank having no capital stock.

Section 32 of the Banking Act of 1933, as amended by the Banking Act of 1935 effective January 1, 1936, provides that no officer, director, or employee of any corporation or unincorporated association; no partner or employee of any partnership; and no individual primarily engaged in the issue, flotation, underwriting, public sale, or distribution, at wholesale, retail, or through syndicate participation, of stocks, bonds, or other similar securities shall serve at the same time as an officer, director, or employee of any member bank. However, in "limited classes of cases," the Board of Governors of the Federal Reserve System may allow such service by general regulations when in the judgment of the board of governors it would not unduly influence the investment policies of such member bank or the advice it gives its customers regarding investments. The board of governors by Regulation R permits such interlocking service by such persons associated with underwriters and distributors of U.S. government securities, direct and fully guaranteed; Federal Intermediate Credit Bank debentures; Federal Land Bank bonds; and general obligations of territories, dependencies and insular possessions of the United States.

Section 10(c) of the Investment Company Act of 1940 provides that after the effective date of that act (August 22, 1940), no registered investment company shall have a majority of its board of directors consisting of persons who are officers or directors of any one bank. A "grandfather" proviso, however, provided that if on March 15, 1940, any registered company did have a majority of its board consisting of such persons, it could continue to have the same percentage of its board consist of such persons.

Section 17(c) of the Public Utility Act of 1935 provides that after one year from the date of enactment (August 26, 1935), no registered holding company or any subsidiary company thereof shall have, as an officer or director thereof, any executive officer, director, partner, appointee, or representative of any bank, trust company, investment banker, or banking association or firm; or any such person of any corporation a majority of whose stock, having the unrestricted right to vote for the election of directors, is owned by any bank, trust company, investment banker, or banking association or firm. However, exception is provided in such cases as rules and regulations of the Securities and Exchange Commission may permit as "not adversely affecting the public interest or the interest of investors or consumers." The SEC specifies the allowable instances in Rule 70, General Rules and Regulations under the Public Utility Holding Company Act of 1935.

Section 305(b) of the Federal Power Act provides that after six months from effective date (August 26, 1935), it shall be unlawful for any person to hold the position of officer or director of a public utility subject to that act and the position of officer or director of any bank, trust company, banking association, or underwriter or distributor of securities of a public utility, unless the holding of such positions shall have been authorized by order of the Federal Power Commission, upon due showing in form and manner prescribed by the commission that neither public nor private interests will be adversely affected thereby.

See CLAYTON ACT, FEDERAL RESERVE BOARD REGULATIONS.

INTERLOCKS ACT   See DEPOSITORY INSTITUTION MANAGEMENT INTERLOCKS ACT.

INTERMARKET TRADING SYSTEM (ITS)   An electronic communications network that links the New York, American, Boston, Cincinnati, Midwest, Pacific and Philadelphia stock exchanges and the NASD. Brokers as well as specialists and market markers trading for their own account can interact with their counterparts in other markets whenever the nationwide Composite Quotation System shows a better price. ITS was started in 1978 with the New York and Philadelphia exchanges trading 11 stocks. At the end of 1987, the 1,537 issues eligible for trading on ITS represented most of the stocks traded on more than one exchange. Of these stock, 1,335 are listed on the NYSE and 202 on the AMEX. In 1987, volume increased 19.2%, representing a peak of 22 billion shares and an 11.2% increase in trades over the previous year.

INTERMEDIATE CREDIT BANKS   See FEDERAL INTERMEDIATE CREDIT BANKS.

INTERMEDIATE GOODS   Goods purchased for use in the production of final products. For example, lumber is an intermediate good in the production of furniture; crude oil is an intermediate good in the production of gasoline; and steel is an intermediate good in the production of automobiles.

INTERNAL AUDITING   The Institute of Internal Auditors, Inc. (IIA) defines internal auditing in its *Standards for the Professional Practice of Internal Auditing* as follows:

> Internal auditing is an independent appraisal function established within an organization to examine and evaluate its activities as a service to the organization. The objectives of internal auditing is to assist members of the organization in the effective discharge of their responsibilities. To this end, internal auditing furnishes them with analyses, appraisals, recommendations, counsel, and information concerning the activities reviewed.

The internal auditor evaluates and reports on the adequacy and effectiveness of the organization's control structure and provides information concerning the quality of the organization's performance. This information is usually acquired through an operational audit.

See AUDIT.

BIBLIOGRAPHY

BANK ADMINISTRATION INSTITUTE. *Internal Auditing in the Banking Industry.* Bank Administration Institute, Rolling Meadows, IL, 1984.
Three volumes:
Vol. 1. *Audit Principles and Methods.*
Vol. 2. *Auditing Basic Bank Functions—Assets.*
Vol. 3. *Auditing Basic Bank Functions—Liabilities and Other Specialized Services.*
———. *An Internal Control and Audit for the Community Bank.*
———. *Statement of Principle and Standards for Internal Auditing in the Banking Industry*, 1977.
HOAR, T. "Examiner's Perspective on Loan Problems." *Journal of Commercial Bank Lending*, May, 1988.
The Internal Auditor.
ROTH, J. J., and CERNICH, M. S. "Using Automated Spreadsheet for Internal Auditing." *Journal of Accountancy*, May, 1988.
Standards for the Professional Practice of Internal Auditing, The Institute of Internal Auditors, Inc., 1987.

INTERNAL BONDS   Bonds issued by a government in its own currency for purchase by domestic investors. Such bonds are to be distinguished from external bonds which the government sells in a foreign market and in the currency of that market.

See EXTERNAL BOND.

INTERNAL CONTROL   The systems, procedures, and policies employed by an enterprise to assure that transactions are properly authorized, executed, and recorded. Internal control applies to both administrative controls and accounting controls. Administrative (operating) controls include a plan of organization, procedures, and records that lead up to management's authorization of transactions. Accounting (financial) controls deal with the plans, procedures, and records required for safeguarding assets and producing reliable financial records.

Auditing standards require that accounting controls be designed to provide reasonable assurance that:

1. Transactions are executed in accordance with management's general or specific authorization.
2. Transactions are recorded as necessary to permit preparation of financial statements in conformity with generally accepted accounting principles or any other criteria applicable to such statements and to maintain accountability for assets.
3. Access to assets is permitted only in accordance with management's authorization.
4. The recorded accountability for assets is compared with the existing assets at reasonable intervals and appropriate action is taken with respect to any difference.

Broad categories of control procedures that apply to both financial and administrative controls include the following:

1. Organizational
   a. Separation of duties
   b. Clear lines of authority and responsibility
   c Formal policies
2. Procedures
   a. Accounting checks
   b. Proper documents and records
   c. Error detection and correction procedures
   d. Physical control over assets and records
3. Competent, trustworthy personnel (bonded where appropriate).

4. Performance goals and objectives
   a. Periodic reviews of performance
   b. Comparisons of recorded accountability with assets
5. Independent review of the system

The FOREIGN CORRUPT PRACTICES ACT passed in 1977 had a major impact on internal control applications in that it requires public companies to maintain reasonably complete and accurate financial records and a sufficient system of internal accounting controls. This legislation was enacted because Congress believed that public companies had inadequate controls to detect bribes and improper payments.

A review of internal accounting controls is essential to an audit of financial statements. A study of internal accounting controls enables the auditor to determine the reliability of the records and the nature, extent, and timing of various tests of the accounting data that the system has produced. Internal controls for banks are numerous and detailed. They involve handling cash (should be segregated), authorizing transactions, opening new accounts, approving adjustments to accounts, assigning account numbers, performing teller duties, opening mail, pinpointing improper recording, guarding against improper access to assets, monitoring reconciliation failures by tellers, handling depositor complaints, selling traveler's checks and savings bonds, serving as custodian for vault cash, and posting ledgers.

Policies for authorizing cash transaction should be established. Such policies could include: the amount of cash available to individual tellers, cashing checks not drawn on the bank, independent checks on performance, paying funds from dormant accounts, large dollar withdrawals, and embezzlement safeguards.

Internal control policies should be established for supervision and review of the cash area: journal entries originating with tellers, the cashing of checks drawn on other banks, documentation of transactions, actions related to missing or misdirected items, unposted debits and credits, and access to electronic data processing equipment.

BIBLIOGRAPHY

AMERICAN INSTITUTE OF CERTIFIED PUBLIC ACCOUNTANTS, *Statement on Auditing Standards No. 55*, "Consideration of the Internal Control Structure in a Financial Statement Audit," 1988.
AMERICAN INSTITUTE OF CERTIFIED PUBLIC ACCOUNTANTS, *Statement on Auditing Standards No. 60*, "Communication of Internal Control Structure Related Matters Noted in an Audit," 1988.
AMERICAN INSTITUTE OF CERTIFIED PUBLIC ACCOUNTANTS, *Statement on Auditing Standards No. 53*, "The Independent Auditor's Responsibility to Detect Errors or Irregularities," 1988.
HERMANSON, R. H., STRAWSER, J. R., and STRAWSER, R. H. *Auditing Theory and Practice*, 1989.
KUONG, J. F. *Computer Auditing, Security & Internal Control Manual.* Prentice Hall, Inc., Englewood Cliffs, NJ, 1987.

INTERNAL DEBTS The domestic indebtedness of a nation, public and private. Comprehensive annual data on net public and private debt are compiled by the U.S. Department of Commerce (Bureau of the Census and Office of Business Economics).

Net public and private debt outstanding is defined as the comprehensive aggregate of the indebtedness of borrowers after elimination of duplicating governmental and corporate debt. The net debt concepts for each of the four classifications reported are summarized as follows.

1. Federal government net debt is that owed to all other sectors of the economy, excepting the federal government proper, its agencies and corporations.
2. State and local government net debt is that owed to all other economic entities except to state and local governments.
3. Corporate net debt is that owed to all other entities (including corporations) except to corporate members of an affiliated system.
4. Private noncorporate debt, net or gross, is the summation of all forms of legal indebtedness with adjustments for duplications.

See FARM MORTGAGES, GOVERNMENT DEBT, MUNICIPAL DEBT, PUBLIC DEBT.

INTERNAL RATE OF RETURN The rate of interest at which the present value of expected net cash flows from a project equals its initial cash outlays; a measure of the rate of profit per dollar of investment. In evaluating a proposed investment, the internal rate of return is computed to the minimum desired rate of return to determine whether a project should be accepted or rejected. If the internal rate of return is equal to or greater than the minimum desired rate of return, the project is desirable. If not, the project is not desirable.

INTERNAL REVENUE Revenue collected by the federal government from domestic (i.e., home) sources, such as corporate and personal INCOME TAXES, excise taxes, estate and gift taxes, etc. Customs duties are the chief source of noninternal federal revenue.

The largest source of internal revenue for the federal government is income taxes, corporate and individual. This heavy dependence upon income taxes makes the federal revenue structure highly unstable, as income tax yields are highly vulnerable to fluctuations in the state of the economy.

Other sources of federal internal revenue, in approximate order of

Internal Revenue Gross Collections, by Source: 1970 to 1987

Source of Revenue	Collections (bil. dol.)								Percent of total			
	1970	1975	1980	1983	1984	1985	1986	1987	1970	1980	1985	1987
All taxes	195.8	293.8	519.4	627.2	680.5	742.9	782.3	886.3	100.0	100.0	100.0	100.0
Individual income taxes	103.7	156.4	287.5	349.6	362.9	396.7	416.9	465.4	53.0	54.9	53.4	52.5
Withheld by employers	77.4	122.1	223.8	266.0	279.0	299.0	314.8	322.5	39.5	43.1	40.2	36.4
Employment taxes [1]	37.4	70.1	128.3	173.8	199.2	225.2	243.9	277.0	19.1	24.7	30.2	31.3
Old age and disability insurance	35.7	67.1	122.5	166.4	189.5	215.6	234.9	266.6	18.2	23.6	29.0	30.1
Unemployment insurance	.8	1.4	3.3	4.3	6.0	5.7	5.3	6.2	.4	.6	.8	.7
Corporation income taxes	35.0	45.7	72.4	61.8	74.2	77.4	80.4	102.8	17.9	13.9	10.4	11.6
Estate and gift taxes	3.7	4.7	6.5	6.2	6.2	6.6	7.2	7.7	1.9	1.3	.9	.9
Excise taxes	15.9	16.8	24.6	35.8	38.0	37.0	33.7	33.3	8.1	4.7	5.0	3.8
Alcohol	4.7	5.4	5.7	5.6	5.4	5.4	5.6 } 11.1		2.4	1.1	.7 } 1.3	
Tobacco	2.1	2.3	2.4	4.1	4.7	4.5	4.6		1.1	.5	.6	
Manufacturers	6.7	5.5	6.5	6.4	10.1	10.0	9.9	10.2	3.4	1.3	1.3	1.2
Windfall profits tax	NA	NA	3.1	15.7	8.1	5.1	8.9	Z	NA	.6	.7	Z
Other	2.4	3.7	6.9	4.0	9.7	12.0	4.7	12.0	1.2	1.3	1.6	1.4

NA — Not applicable.
Z — Less than $50 million or .05 percent.
[1] Includes railroad retirement, not shown separately.

Source: U.S. Internal Revenue Service, *Annual Report of the Commissioner and Chief Counsel of the Internal Revenue Service.*

productivity, are employment taxes, manufacturers' excise taxes, alcohol taxes, estate and gift taxes, and tobacco taxes (highest return among the latter from taxes on cigarettes).

The appended Table shows internal revenue gross collections, by source: 1970 to 1987.

The Internal Revenue Service administers the internal revenue laws embodied in the Internal Revenue Code (Title 26 U.S.C.) and certain other statutes, including the Federal Alcohol Administration Act (27 U.S.C. 201-212), the Liquor Enforcement Act of 1936 (18 U.S.C. 1261, 1262, 3615), the Gun Control Act of 1968 (18 U.S.C., Chapter 44), and Title VII of the Omnibus Crime Control and Safe Street Act of 1968 (18 U.S.C. 1201-1203).

To reduce the manual processing of tax payments^withheld income taxes, Social Security taxes, corporation income taxes, excise taxes, and similar federal taxes^the Internal Revenue Service supplies certain groups of tax withholders and taxpayers with partially punched cards (computer readable) which the taxholders and taxpayers forward to their banks with their tax payments. The cards are then forwarded to Federal Reserve banks which complete the punching and forward the cards to the office of the secretary of the Treasury in Washington. The Treasurer's Office enters the data from the cards on magnetic computer tapes which are furnished to the Internal Revenue Service for reconciliation with taxpayers' returns. This procedure obviates the need for the manual handling of tax remittances in the department and expedites the crediting of tax payments in the Treasurer's account. Electronic transfers are now available.

INTERNAL REVENUE SERVICE (IRS)
The Office of the Commissioner of Internal Revenue was established by act of July 1, 1962. The Internal Revenue Service is a division of the Department of the Treasury. The IRS is responsible for administering and enforcing the internal revenue laws and related statutes, except those relating to alcohol, tobacco, firearms, and explosives. The IRS mission is to collect the proper amount of tax revenue at the least cost to the public, and in a manner that warrants the highest degree of public confidence in the Service's integrity, efficiency, and fairness. To achieve that purpose, IRS will:

Encourage and achieve the highest possible degree of voluntary compliance in accordance with the tax laws and regulations.

Advise the public of their rights and responsibilities.
Determine the extent of compliance and the causes of noncompliance.
Do all things required for the proper administration and enforcement of the tax laws.
Continually search for and implement new, more efficient ways of accomplishing its mission.
Basic IRS activities include:
Ensuring satisfactory resolution of taxpayer complaints; providing taxpayer services and education.
Determining, assessing, and collecting internal revenue taxes.
Determining pension plan qualifications and exempt organization status.
Preparing and issuing rulings and regulations to supplement the provisions of the Internal Revenue Code.

Most revenues collected come from the individual income tax and the social insurance and retirement taxes, with other major sources being the corporation income, excise, estate, and gift taxes. Congress first received authority to levy taxes on the income of individuals and corporations in 1913, pursuant to the Sixteenth Amendment to the Constitution.

The IRS is organized for maximum decentralization, consistent with the need for uniform interpretation of the tax laws and efficient utilization of resources. There are three organizational levels: the national office, the regional office, and the district offices and service centers. Districts may have local offices, the number and location of which are determined by taxpayer and IRS needs.

The national office, located in Washington, DC, develops nationwide policies and programs for the administration of the Internal Revenue laws and provides overall direction to the field organization. The National Computer Center in Martinsburg, WV, and the Data Center in Detroit, MI, also are assigned to the national office. Most of the IRS personnel and activities are assigned to field installations.

There are seven regional offices, each headed by a regional commissioner, which supervise and evaluate the operations of district offices and service centers.

There are 62 Internal Revenue districts, each administered by a district director. Districts may encompass an entire state, or a certain number of counties within a state, depending on population. Programs of the district include taxpayer service, examination, collection, criminal investigation, resource management and, in some districts, pension plans and exempt organizations. Functions performed are: assistance and service to taxpayers, determination of tax liability by examination of tax returns, determination of pension plan qualification, collection of delinquent returns and taxes, and investigation of criminal and civil violations of Internal Revenue laws, with a few exceptions. Directors are responsible for the deposit of taxes collected by the district and for initial processing of original applications for admission to practice before IRS and renewal issuances for those practitioners already enrolled. Local offices may be established to meet taxpayer needs and IRS workload requirements.

Source: Internal Revenue Service, Department of the Treasury.

INTERNATIONAL ALPHABETICAL AGENCIES
Primarily as the result of the formation of the United Nations and international defense and recovery programs sponsored by the U.S., a number of international agencies have been created which are often referred to by their abbreviations.

See ABBREVIATIONS for these and other alphabetical references.

INTERNATIONAL ASSISTANCE
U.S. overseas loans, grants, and assistance from international organizations is extensive. The Foreign Assistance Act and antecedent legislation provide much of the basis for U.S. involvement. U.S. program categories include:

1. Economic assistance
   a. A.I.D.
   b. Food for Peace
   c. Peace Corps
   d. Contributions to international lending organizations
   e. Other economic programs
2. Military Assistance
   a. MAP grants
   b. FMS credit financing
   c. Transfers from excess defense stocks
   d. International military education and training programs
   e. Other military programs
3. Other U.S. Government Loans
   a. Export-Import bank loans
   b. CCC export sales programs
   c. OPIC direct loans
   d. P.L. 480 Title 1 private trade agreements

Assistance from the following international organizations is also available to many countries:

International Bank for Reconstruction and & Development
International Finance Corporation
International Development Association
Inter-American Development Bank
Asian Development Bank
African Development Bank
African Development Fund
United Nations Development Program
Other United Nations Programs
European Economic Community

The appended table provides a summary of U.S. overseas loans and grants—obligations and loan authorizations—for all countries for selected periods and years.

BIBLIOGRAPHY

U.S. Overseas Loans and Grants, Office of Planning and Budgeting, Bureau for Program and Policy Coordination, Agency for International Development.

INTERNATIONAL BALANCE OF PAYMENTS
Broader than the BALANCE OF TRADE concept, a concept including all items involving receipts or payments from or to foreign sources. Although merchandise transactions (exports and imports) are

INTERNATIONAL BALANCE OF PAYMENTS

Summary for All Countries (U.S. Fiscal Years - Millions of Dollars)
U.S. Overseas Loans and Grants—Obligations and Loan Authorizations

Program	Post-war Relief Period 1946-48	Marshall Plan Period 1949-52	Mutual Security Act Period 1953-1961	Foreign Assistance Act Period 1962-84	1985	1986	1987	1988	Total FAA Period 1962-1988	Total Loans and Grants 1946-88 **	Principal Repayments 1946-88	Outstanding Loan Balances 1946-88 **
I. Econ. assist.-total	12,482	18,634	24,053	123,207	12,327	10,786	9,386	8,769	164,455	212,480	21,636	33,555
loans	5,967	2,551	5,850	61,226	1,579	1,216	1,138	852	46,012	55,188	21,636	33,555
grants	6,515	16,083	18,203	81,981	10,748	9,570	8,248	7,897	118,443	157,292	-	-
A. Aid and predecessor	-	14,506	16,885	69,568	8,132	7,446	6,355	5,705	97,206	124,555	8,199	19,951
Loans**	-	1,577	3,266	23,947	686	326	247	159	25,275	28,145	8,199	19,951
Grants	-	12,929	13,619	45,621	7,537	7,120	6,108	5,546	71,931	96,390		
(sec.supp.assist.)	(-)	(348)	(8,853)	(30,672)	(5,247)	(4,913)	(3,912)	(3,021)	(47,766)	(55,584)		
B. Food for peace	-	83	6,416	30,155	2,052	1,649	1,442	1,192	36,490	39,715	7,289	11,647
Loans	-	-	2,526	16,220	984	890	889	689	19,672	18,936	7,289	11,647
Grants	-	83	3,890	13,935	1,068	759	553	503	16,818	20,779		
Title i-total	-	-	3,867	18,622	984	890	889	689	22,074	22,378	7,289	11647
Repay. in $-loans	-	-	-	12,642	984	890	889	689	16,094	15,234	3,903	11,333
Pay. in for. curr.	-	-	3,867	5,980	-	-	-	-	5,980	7,442	3,386	314
Title ii-total	-	83	2,549	11,533	1,068	759	663	503	14,416	18,037		
E. Relief, ec. dev & wfp.	-	-	754	4,630	319	172	210	215	5,546	6,286		
Vol.relief agency	-	83	1,795	6,903	749	587	343	288	8,870	10,751	-	-
C. Other econ. assist	12,482	4,045	752	23,484	2,143	1,691	1,589	1,852	30,759	48,230	6,148	1,957
Loans	5,967	974	58	1,059	*	-	2	4	1,065	8,107	6,148	1,957
Grants	6,515	3,071	694	22,425	2,143	1,691	1,287	1,848	29,294	40,123		
Contr. to ifi	635	-	189	16,095	1,548	1,131	949	1,206	20,929	21,753	-	-
Peace Corps	-	-	-	2,082	130	124	131	152	2,619	2,614	-	-
Narcotics	-	-	-	407	50	60	118	99	734	795	-	-
Other	5,880	3,071	505	3,841	415	376	389	391	5,400	14,961		
II. Mtl. assist.-total	481	10,064	19,302	77,319	5,801	5,839	5,102	4,831	98,892	130,905	15,358	24,364
Loans	-	-	161	31,212	2,365	1,980	953	763	37,273	39,719	15,358	24,364
Grants	481	10,064	19,141	46,107	3,436	3,859	4,149	4,068	61,619	91,186		
A. Map grants	-	9,154	16,547	29,603	805	798	951	703	32,960	58,725		
B. Credit financing	-	-	161	31,212	2,365	1,980	953	763	37,273	39,719	15,358	24,364
C. Intl mtl. ed. trng	-	107	717	1,323	56	52	56	47	1,535	2,349		
D. Tran-excess stock	-	479	1,322	4,847	-	-	-	-	4,847	6,374	-	-
E. Other grants	481	324	555	10,334	2,575	3,009	3,142	3,318	22,377	23,738		
III. Total econ. & mil	12,963	28,698	43,355	200,526	18,128	16,625	14,488	13,580	263,347	343,385	36,994	57,919
Loans	5,967	2,551	6,011	72,438	3,944	3,196	2,091	1,615	83,285	94,907	36,994	57,919
Grants	6,996	26,147	37,344	128,088	14,184	13,429	12,397	11,965	180,062	248,478	-	-
Other U.S. Loans	2,091	900	3,653	50,019	351	875	480	595	52,319	55,632	44,566	10,972
Ex-im bank loans	2,091	900	3,653	42,752	320	377	320	468	44,237	47,446	37,521	9,922
All other	-	-	-	7,267	31	498	160	127	8,082	8,186	7,045	1,050

* Less than $50,000.
** Values in these columns are net of deobligations.
*** Includes capitalized interest on prior year loans.

normally the largest category, capital movements can exercise a major influence on the international balance of payments, and have done so for the U.S. in the post-World War II years.

Since the international balance-of-payments statement is constructed on accounting principles, the receipts (credits) always equal the payments (debits). The concept of a deficit in the international balance of payments of a country, or of a surplus therein, arises when the financing or settlement items are pulled from the balanced debits and credits.

Concepts of the measurement of improvement or deterioration in the international balance-of-payments position of a country include the following, as reviewed by the Council of Economic Advisers in its 1970 and 1971 annual reports.

1. Liquidity balance, equal to the change in the country's holdings of international reserve assets less the change in the country's liquid liabilities to all foreigners, both official (governmental) and private. This is the most commonly used measurement of the U.S. international balance-of-payments position, and was

U.S. International Transaction Balances: 1970 to 1987
(Billions of dollars)

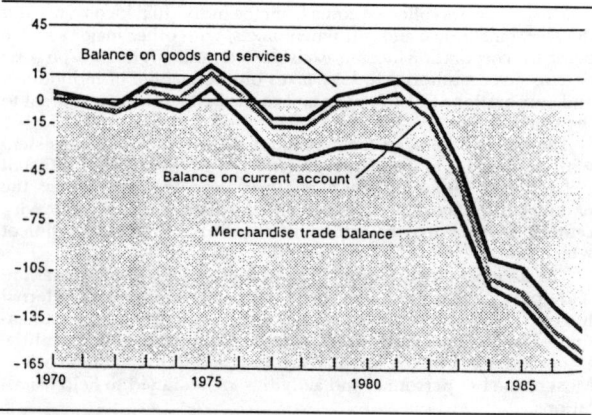

Source: Chart prepared by U.S. Bureau of the Census.

ENCYCLOPEDIA OF BANKING AND FINANCE

originally intended to be a measure of changes in the country's ability to maintain conversions of dollars into gold at a fixed price ratio. The council pointed out that some liquidity deficit will normally arise when a reserve country acts as an international banking center. Foreigners tend to accumulate short-term claims on such a country, and in turn the country may build up a growing net investment in foreign countries at longer term. At the same time, a continuing liquidity deficit means that the ratio of reserves to liquid foreign claims is being lowered. In the judgment of the council, variations in the volume of U.S. liquid liabilities relative to their reserve backing are not the primary determinant of the desirability of the dollar as a reserve asset since the situation resulted partly from the growth of world liquidity, augmented by holdings of dollars, which was necessary to accommodate the expansion of world trade and investment, i.e., the successes of the international economy. Nevertheless, it should be pointed out that the continued heavy deficits in the U.S. international balance of payments in recent years and the drain upon the country's international reserve assets were contributing factors to the August 15, 1971, suspension of gold convertibility by the U.S. and the imposition of a 10% surcharge upon imports.

The liquidity balance concept, however, was considered less significant in recent years, as the U.S. responsibility under the Articles of Agreement of the International Monetary Fund for converting foreign liquid claims into other reserve assets was limited to the dollar holdings of foreign official institutions; with the adoption in March, 1968, of the two-tier gold system, the possibility of flows of monetary gold from the U.S. reserve holdings through foreign official institutions into private hands had apparently been eliminated.

2. Official reserve transactions balance, equal to the change in U.S. holdings of international reserve assets less the change in liquid and certain nonliquid claims on the U.S. by foreign official monetary institutions.

The council points out that this concept has received increasing attention, as this balance with appropriate adjustments measures the quantity of claims on the U.S. that foreign authorities have acquired or given up in the process of maintaining the exchange value of their currencies within the prescribed ceilings and floors around par values. However, there are considerable difficulties in reading the signals given by the official reserve transactions balance. First, it has been volatile, showing wide swings from year to year. Second, a movement of dollars from foreign private accounts to foreign official accounts will increase the official reserve transactions deficit, while movement in the other direction will decrease it. The council comments that such movements may in some cases signal shifts in the degree of foreign confidence in the dollar relative to other currencies; in other cases, they may simply be due to changes in monetary conditions and interest rates which alter the attractiveness of dollar assets to foreign private holders, apart from speculative considerations; and in still other cases, shifts of dollar holdings between the central bank and commercial banks may represent the deliberate exercise of selective measures designed to reduce or enlarge published reserves.

3. Balance on current account (balance on goods, services, and unilateral transfers, both governmental and private), which indicates the extent to which the country is currently earning the foreign exchange it needs to carry out its international lending and investment expenditures. Adjusted for earnings reinvested abroad, for errors and omissions, and for changes in the valuation of domestic and foreign assets, the balance on current account also indicates changes in the country's net international investment position, or "net worth," which may well be considered more meaningful than any other measure of

Table 1 / U.S. International Transactions—Summary: 1960 to 1988
(In billions of dollars. Reserve assets are for end of period. Minus sign (−) indicates debits.)

Year	Merchandise trade balance[1]	Net investment income	Net military transactions	Net travel and transportation receipts	Other services, net	Balance on goods and services	Unilateral transfers[1]	Balance on current account	Net foreign assets in U.S.	Net U.S. assets abroad	Net U.S. official reserve assets
1960	4.9	3.4	−2.8	−1.0	.6	5.2	−2.4	2.8	2.3	−4.1	19.4
1965	5.0	5.3	−2.1	−1.3	1.5	8.4	−2.9	5.4	.7	−5.7	15.5
1966	3.8	5.0	−2.9	−1.3	1.5	6.1	−3.1	3.0	3.7	−7.3	14.9
1967	3.8	5.3	−3.2	−1.8	1.7	5.8	−3.3	2.6	7.4	−9.8	14.8
1968	.6	6.0	−3.1	−1.5	1.8	3.7	−3.1	.6	9.9	−11.0	15.7
1969	.6	6.0	−3.3	−1.8	2.0	3.5	−3.1	.4	12.7	−11.6	17.0
1970	2.6	6.2	−3.4	−2.0	2.3	5.8	−3.4	2.3	6.4	−9.3	14.5
1971	−2.3	7.3	−2.9	−2.3	2.6	2.4	−3.9	−1.4	23.0	−12.5	12.2
1972	−6.4	8.2	−3.4	−3.1	3.0	−1.7	−4.1	−5.8	21.5	−14.5	13.2
1973	.9	12.2	−2.1	−3.2	3.4	11.2	−4.1	7.1	18.4	−22.9	14.4
1974	−5.5	15.5	−1.7	−3.2	4.2	9.4	−7.4	2.0	34.2	−34.7	15.9
1975	8.9	12.8	−.7	−2.8	4.9	23.0	−4.9	18.1	15.7	−39.7	16.2
1976	−9.5	16.0	.6	−2.6	5.0	9.5	−5.3	4.2	36.5	−51.3	18.7
1977	−31.1	18.0	1.5	−3.6	5.7	−9.5	−5.0	−14.5	51.3	−34.8	19.3
1978	−33.9	20.6	.6	−3.6	6.5	−9.9	−5.6	−15.4	64.0	−61.1	18.7
1979	−27.5	31.2	−1.8	−2.9	6.2	5.1	−6.1	−1.0	38.8	−64.3	19.0
1980	−25.5	30.4	−2.2	−1.0	7.8	9.5	−7.6	1.9	58.1	−86.1	26.8
1981	−28.0	34.1	−1.2	.1	9.3	14.3	−7.5	6.9	83.0	−111.0	30.1
1982	−36.4	28.7	−.3	−1.0	9.3	.3	−9.0	−8.7	93.7	−121.2	34.0
1983	−67.1	24.9	−.2	−4.2	9.9	−36.8	−9.5	−46.2	84.9	−49.8	33.7
1984	−112.5	18.5	−2.1	−8.6	9.8	−95.0	−12.1	−107.1	102.6	−22.3	34.9
1985	−122.1	25.9	−3.4	−10.0	9.6	−100.1	−15.0	−115.1	129.9	−32.6	43.2
1986	−144.5	23.1	−4.4	−9.3	11.6	−123.5	−15.3	−138.8	221.3	−98.0	48.5
1987	−160.3	20.4	−2.4	−10.3	12.0	−140.5	−13.4	−154.0	211.5	−76.0	45.8
1988, 1st quarter	−35.2	1.2	−1.0	−2.1	3.4	−33.8	−3.1	−36.9	26.1	6.6	43.2
2nd quarter	−29.9	−1.7	−.9	−1.4	3.5	−30.4	−2.9	−33.3	62.3	−13.3	41.0

[1] Excludes military grants.

Source: U.S. Council of Economic Advisers. *Economic Indicators*, monthly; and *Economic Report of the President*, annual. Data from U.S. Bureau of Economic Analysis and U.S. Dept. of the Treasury.

changes in the basic strength or weakness of our international financial position.

4. Balance on current account and long-term capital (nonliquid or nonvolatile capital transactions), also called the 'basic balance," treating changes in private liquid assets and liabilities as "financing" items. The aim underlying the basic balance is to group together those balance-of-payments items that best reflect broad, persistent forces or underlying trends, treating more volatile classes of transactions among the financing items.

Summary. Since no single balance concept can comprehensively represent the underlying balance-of-payments position of the U.S., the Interagency Committee on Balance-of-Payments Statistics recommended in 1970 that three balances be presented in the regular quarterly balance-of-payments reports prepared by the U.S. Department of Commerce: balance on goods, services, and unilateral transfers; two "central balances," the net liquidity balance and the balance on current account and long-term capital; and the official reserve transactions balance. In June, 1971, the U.S. Department of Commerce commenced the presentation of the balance-of-payments data according to the three group balances.

U.S. International transactions 1960 to 1988 and U.S. balances on international transactions 1985 to 1987 are appended. A chart showing U.S. intersale transactions balances 1970 to 1987 is appended.

See FOREIGN EXCHANGE, FOREIGN LIQUIDATION, GOLD MOVEMENTS, SPECIAL DRAWING RIGHTS.

BIBLIOGRAPHY

HAFER, R. W. "Does Dollar Depreciation Cause Inflation." Federal Reserve Bank St. Louis Review, July-August, 1989..
"Japanese Capital Flows: Ditching the Dollar." *Economist*, November 5, 1988.

INTERNATIONAL BANK FOR RECONSTRUCTION AND DEVELOPMENT The "World Bank," a post-World War II institution, founded at the Economic Conference held at Bretton Woods in July, 1944. The International Bank for Reconstruction and Development (IBRD) began operations in June, 1946. In 1986, the bank had 148 member states. Action is currently pending on several monthly applications. The reconstruction phase of the bank's operations ended a few years after its organization, and since that time it has devoted its loans entirely to economic development, in which field it has expanded activities as a mobilizer and supplier of international long-term capital. Previous emphases upon project lending and upon growth of output have yielded to "program loans" (nonproject lending) as well. "After considerable discussion, the executive directors accepted that program lending was appropriate in special circumstances" (1971 *Annual Report*) and broadened lending for education from an original (1963) policy of concentration on vocational and technical education to emphasis on "the entire learning process as it applies to developing countries." They also broadened lending for population control, urban water supply and sewerage improvements, pollution control projects, and other types of lending aimed at improving the quality of life rather than merely quantitatively increasing the country's output. (See Table 1.) This was a new image for the IBRD under the administration of Robert S. McNamara, who became its president in April, 1968.

Organization. All powers of the IBRD are vested in a board of governors, consisting of one governor appointed by each of the member countries. The board of governors in turn has delegated most of its powers to the 21 executive directors, of whom 5 are appointed by the 6 largest stockholders (U.S., United Kingdom, West Germany, France, and Japan) and the rest are elected by the other member nations. Voting power is approximately proportionate to capital subscriptions of the member nations.

Capital. Subscriptions to capital are based on the economic and financial weight of each member country and are proportional to

Table 2 / U.S. Balances on International Transactions, by Area and Selected Country: 1985 to 1987
(In millions of dollars. Minus sign (-) indicates debits.)

	1985, Balance on—			1986, Balance on—			1987, Balance on—		
Area or Country	Merchandise trade [1]	Goods and services	Current account	Merchandise trade [1]	Goods and services	Current account	Merchandise trade [1]	Goods and services	Current account
All areas	-122,148	-100,093	-115,103	-144,547	-123,520	-138,828	-160,280	-140,519	-153,964
Western Europe	-21,439	-27,654	-28,276	-28,409	-33,649	-34,039	-27,457	-34,162	-34,112
European Economic Community [2]	-17,400	-22,502	-22,283	-22,149	-26,692	-26,427	-21,867	-26,188	-25,623
United Kingdom	-3,388	-5,381	-5,171	-3,881	-12,365	-12,089	-3,418	-12,490	-12,181
Belgium-Luxembourg	1,536	2,858	2,844	1,521	3,752	3,725	1,917	4,008	3,978
France	-2,810	-1,878	-1,948	-2,380	-773	-853	-2,491	-257	-337
West Germany	-10,596	-16,458	-15,971	-14,052	-18,244	-17,493	-15,404	-19,493	-18,561
Italy	-4,798	-4,492	-4,705	-5,599	-3,227	-3,463	-5,567	-4,204	-4,445
Netherlands	3,130	2,810	2,792	3,151	4,096	4,077	3,252	3,774	3,755
Other Western Europe	-4,039	-5,151	-5,993	-6,260	-6,957	-7,612	-5,590	-7,974	-8,489
Eastern Europe	1,411	1,606	1,402	65	605	446	319	253	94
Canada	-15,004	-5,322	-5,565	-13,020	-2,290	-2,567	-12,555	-65	-361
Latin America, other Western Hemisphere	-15,321	-6,929	-9,723	-11,177	-4,080	-6,736	-12,273	-10,319	-13,350
Mexico	-5,718	-4,131	-4,622	-5,343	-4,990	-5,480	-5,740	-5,633	-6,189
Venezuela	-3,458	-2,502	-2,520	-1,709	-1,133	-1,151	-2,094	-1,351	-1,381
Australia	2,363	3,614	3,573	2,494	3,608	3,562	2,339	4,254	4,206
South Africa [3]	-725	-334	-348	-1,327	-723	-546	176	888	874
Japan [4]	-43,508	-45,140	-45,208	-54,422	-56,042	-56,109	-56,944	-58,476	-58,544
Other Asia and Africa	-29,845	-21,604	-31,363	-38,751	-31,881	-42,600	-53,419	-44,395	-53,328
Int'l. and unallocated	192	1,817	577	—	932	-23	—	2,063	1,154

— Represents zero.
[1] Adjusted to balance of payments basis: excludes exports under U.S. military sales contracts and imports under direct defense expenditures..
[2] Includes Denmark, Greece, Ireland, European Atomic Energy Community, European Coal and Steel Community, and European Investment Bank, not shown separately. Beginning in 1986, also includes Spain and Portugal, not shown separately.
[3] Includes New Zealand.
[4] Includes Ryukyu Islands.

Source: U.S. Bureau of Economic Analysis, *Survey of Current Business*, June 1988.

Table 3 / International Investment Position, 1960 to 1987, and by Selected Areas, 1987
(In billions of dollars. Estimates for end of year, subject to considerable error due to nature of basic data. Direct investments at book value; other types at market or face values. See *Historical Statistics, Colonial Times to 1970*, series U 26-39, for similar data.)

Type of investment	1960	1965	1970	1975	1977	1978	1979	1980	1981
U.S. net international investment position	44.7	61.6	58.5	74.2	72.7	76.1	94.5	106.3	141.1
U.S. assets abroad	85.6	120.4	165.4	295.1	379.1	447.8	510.6	607.1	719.8
U.S. official reserve assets	19.4	15.5	14.5	16.2	19.3	18.6	19.0	26.8	30.1
U.S. Government assets, other	17.0	23.5	32.1	41.8	49.5	54.2	58.4	63.8	68.7
U.S. private assets	49.2	81.4	118.8	237.1	310.2	375.0	433.2	516.6	621.1
Foreign assets in U.S.	40.9	58.8	106.9	220.9	306.4	371.7	416.1	500.8	578.7
Foreign official assets	[1]12.4	[1]16.8	26.1	86.9	140.9	173.1	159.9	176.1	180.4
Other foreign assets	28.5	42.0	80.8	134.0	165.5	198.7	256.3	324.8	398.3

						1987				
Type of investment	1982	1983	1984	1985	1986	Total [2]	Western Europe	Canada	Latin America [3]	Japan
U.S. net international investment position	136.9	89.4	3.5	−110.7	−269.2	−368.2	−378.2	50.7	22.4	−80.7
U.S. assets abroad	824.9	873.9	896.1	950.3	1,071.4	1,167.8	407.0	147.0	294.5	113.3
U.S. official reserve assets	34.0	33.7	34.9	43.2	48.5	45.8	12.1	Z	Z	1.0
U.S. Government assets, other	74.6	79.5	84.8	87.6	89.5	88.4	9.9	.4	18.3	Z
U.S. credits and other long-term assets	72.9	77.8	82.9	85.8	88.7	87.6	9.9	.4	18.0	Z
U.S. foreign currency holdings and short-term assets	1.7	1.7	2.0	1.8	.8	.8	Z	Z	.3	Z
U.S. private assets	716.4	760.7	776.3	819.5	933.4	1,033.6	385.0	146.7	276.1	112.3
Direct investments abroad	207.8	207.2	211.5	230.3	259.6	308.9	149.0	56.9	42.3	14.3
Foreign securities	75.5	83.8	89.1	112.8	133.2	146.7	83.3	55.4	1.2	.5
U.S. claims on unaffiliated foreigners [4]	28.6	35.1	30.1	29.1	33.3	30.1	12.9	3.7	8.8	1.6
U.S. claims reported by U.S. banks [5]	404.6	434.5	445.6	447.4	507.3	547.9	139.9	30.6	223.8	95.9
Foreign assets in the U.S.	688.1	784.5	892.6	1,061.0	1,340.7	1,536.0	785.2	96.3	272.0	194.0
Foreign official assets in the U.S.	189.1	194.5	199.3	202.6	241.7	283.1	128.1	5.3	8.8	([6])
U.S. Government securities	132.6	137.0	143.0	143.4	177.3	219.1	([7])	([7])	([7])	([6])
Other U.S. Government liabilities	13.6	14.2	15.0	15.7	17.8	15.0	4.4	.3	.6	1.4
U.S. liabilities reported by U.S. banks [6]	25.0	25.5	26.1	26.7	27.9	31.8	([7])	([7])	([7])	([6])
Other foreign official assets	17.9	17.7	15.2	16.7	18.8	17.3	([7])	([7])	([7])	([6])
Other foreign assets in the U.S.	498.9	590.0	693.3	858.4	1,098.9	1,252.9	657.1	91.1	263.3	(6)
Direct investments	124.7	137.1	164.6	184.6	220.4	261.9	178.0	21.7	15.3	33.4
U.S. securities [8]	93.0	113.8	127.3	206.2	308.8	344.4	239.9	32.2	20.1	37.9
U.S. liabilities to unaffiliated foreigners [4]	27.5	26.9	31.0	29.5	26.6	28.8	14.0	1.8	1.9	4.7
U.S. liabilities reported by U.S. banks [5]	228.0	278.3	312.2	354.5	451.6	539.4	([9])	([9])	([9])	([6])
U.S. Treasury securities	25.8	33.8	58.2	83.6	91.5	78.4	([9])	([9])	([9])	([6])

Z — Less than $50 million.
[1] Includes holdings of international and regional organizations that were shifted to "other foreign assets" in subsequent periods.
[2] Includes other countries, international organizations, or unallocated, not shown separately.
[3] Includes other Western Hemisphere.
[4] Reported by U.S. nonbanking concerns.
[5] Not included elsewhere.
[6] Data included in "Foreign assets in the U.S."
[7] Data included in "Foreign official assets in the U.S."
[8] Excludes U.S. Treasury securities.
[9] Data included in "Other foreign assets in the U.S."

Source: U.S. Bureau of Economic Analysis, *Survey of Current Business*, June 1988, and earlier issues.

their participation in the International Monetary Fund. The authorized capital is broken down into "paid capital" (8.75%) and "capital subject to call," which acts as a guarantee for the borrowing that the bank places on the international capital markets. In recent years, the board of governors has increased the capital on several occasions. In 1980, the capital was increased by 331,500 shares (or approximately U.S. $4 billion), of which 7.5% was to be paid up. The capital was increased by 11,500 shares in 1981, which brought the total capital to 716,500 shares. The payment is one-tenth in gold or U.S. dollars, with the balance in the national currency of each country, which cannot be loaned by the bank without the consent of the countries.

Borrowed funds. Borrowing in international capital markets provides a major portion of the funds necessary for the continued growth of the IBRD's lending operations. The IBRD sells its securities through direct placement with government agencies and central banks or in the public markets where securities are offered through investment-banking firms, merchant banks, or commercial banks. The bank borrows in the various currencies of the member states, but essentially in hard currencies at rates offered to those borrowers with the highest credit rating on the market in question. Since July 1982, the bank has used short term and variable-rate instruments. It sells discount notes in U.S. dollars on the U.S. money market. The bank is also increasingly using swap.

Earnings. Earnings of the preceding year are either allocated to the general reserve (75% to 80%) or attributed in the form of grants to the IDA.

Cofinancing operations. The IBRD uses both parallel cofinancing and joint cofinancing. In parallel cofinancing, each lender finances separately the different parts of a project on its own terms. In joint cofinancing, all the lenders finance the same project at the same time up to the limit of their individual share. In 1983, the IBRD introduced new instruments that allow banks to add to the funds that they have directly loaned for a project situation by participating in a commercial loan. To add to funds directly loaned, the bank will participate in a commercial loan up to 15% to 20% which will considerably extend the maturity of the loan in comparison to a normal loan offered on the market. The borrower will begin by repaying the commercial banks. After their part of the loan is completely repaid, it will repay the World Bank. The bank will sell its part to commercial lenders as the loan is amortized. The bank may also provide contingent participation by the bank in the later maturities of a commercial loan initially financed entirely by commercial banks. The bank may also guarantee the later maturities of a private loan by the World Bank without direct participation.

Financing. The bank uses the following types of financing:

1. Ordinary loans (first window)(at the going market rate).
2. Global loans to development finance institutions.
3. Grants and subsidies.
4. Guarantee extended.

The bank does not participate in special loans (done by the International Development Association), equity investment (done by the International Finance Corporation), venture capital (done by the IFC), leasing, or interest subsidy.

Terms of financing vary.

Amounts by project: minimum-U.S. $2 to 3 million; maximum—indeterminate.

IBRD share: minimum—U.S. $1 to 2 million; maximum—none according to charter, but actually U.S. $200 million.

Average: U.S. $50 to 70 million (or one-third of the project cost).

Maturity period: 15 to 20 years, including a four- to five-year grace period.

Interest rate: as of July 1, 1985, the interest rate was 9.07%, including the front-end fee, which is 0.25% as of that date. Borrowers have the option of capitalizing the front-end fee to spread this additional cost over the life of the loan. A commitment fee is 0.75% on the undisbursed amount. A guarantee is required from the government of the borrowing country. Other agreements involve repayment of the capital by identical semiannual installments; repayment of interest semiannually; and advance repayments allowed with a penalty. The loans are denominated in U.S. dollars, but repayment is in the currencies actually loaned. To limit the borrower's risk, the bank has set up a currency pool for borrowers and accepts payment of interest in one currency whatever the currency of the loan. Participation of the borrower involves 10% to 60% of the project's cost. All nationals and companies of member states are eligible for financing.

IBRD provides technical assistance in financing arrangements. It is always included within the framework of loans to finance supervisory services and performance and development studies of projects.

Project and program distribution. At least 90% of financing must go to projects (creation or development of self-sustaining productive installations) and a maximum of 10% to programs (i.e., import of capital equipment and raw material linked to national development programs).

Distribution based on per capita income. Distribution based on per capita income is determined by the graduation of the bank's borrowers, by the decrease in the IDA's resources, and finally by the accent placed on the reduction of poverty.

The principal criterion for a loan is to grant it where it will have the most effect in terms of the bank's loan program and in consultation with its borrowers. In the 1980s, there was a decrease in the agricultural and rural development sector and an increase in the energy sector. Non-project loans (structural adjustment problems) have also decreased. In 1983, the board of executive directors approved the development of a special assistance program whose goal is to help developing countries maintain their development efforts despite the international economic crisis.

Beneficiaries of bank financing. The following entities may benefit from IBRD loans:

1. Developing member states and their political subdivisions.
2. The public institutions of these developing countries with the state's guarantee.
3. Public or private companies of these developing member states with the state's guarantee.
4. National development banks that relend those resources to finance small projects according to the bank's conditions.

Loans are adapted to a project. Each project must fulfill the same requirements from its inception to its evaluation. This is known as the project cycle, which can stretch over ten to eleven years and usually includes six stages: identification; preparation (or definition); evaluation; the presentation of the project, its negotiation, and the decision by the board of executive directors; project performance and oversight; and a retrospective evaluation.

Source: Investment Financing by International Development Banks, BAI.

Valuation in terms of the SDR: On April 30, 1976, the Board of Governors of the International Monetary Fund approved proposed amendments to the fund's Articles of Agreement (the Second Amendment) which entered into force on April 1, 1978. Under such Second Amendment, currencies no longer have par values, gold is abolished as a common denominator of the international monetary system, and all calculations for the purposes of the fund's articles are made on the basis of the special drawing right (SDR).

When the SDR was introduced into the fund's articles in 1969, it was expressed in terms of a specified weight of gold equal to the gold content of the 1944 dollar. Since July 1, 1974, the value of the SDR in terms of United States dollars has been based on the weighted relative values of a number of major currencies (the "basket," see SPECIAL DRAWING RIGHTS), including the United States dollar. The value of the SDR on July 1, 1974, expressed in terms of United States dollars, was $1.20635, which was the equivalent of one 1944 dollar. On March 31, 1978, the fund made certain changes in the basket of currencies effective July 1, 1978, such that the value of the revised basket in terms of any currency was exactly the same at June 30, 1978, under the revised valuation as under the then existing valuation. On April 25, 1980, the Interim Committee of the board of governors of the fund announced that it favored simplifying the SDR by reducing the number of currencies in the basket and asked the fund's executive board (which has the power to revise the basket) to examine the matter further and to take the necessary action.

As a result of the Second Amendment to the IMF's Articles of Agreement and the simultaneous repeal of Section 2 of the Par Value Modification Act of the U.S. Congress (31 U.S.C. 449), the provisions of United States law defining the par value of the United States dollar in terms of the SDR and gold, the preexisting basis for translating the term "United States dollars of the weight and fineness in effect on July 1, 1944" into current United States dollars or into any other currency no longer exists.

The general counsel of the bank has rendered a legal opinion concluding in substance that upon the entry into force of the Second Amendment to the fund's Articles of Agreement, references in the bank's Articles of Agreement to the 1944 dollar should be read as referring to the SDR, as determined from time to time by the fund, and the mutual obligations of each member and the bank, with respect to maintenance of value of certain currency holdings, will be measured by the value of the currency in question in terms of the SDR at any given time.

The general counsel has, however, also stated that in the exercise of their statutory power under Article IX of the bank's articles, the executive directors could conclude that the 1944 dollar would be taken to mean 1.20635 current dollars, with the consequence that maintenance of value would be measured by that standard.

Restricted Currencies. The portion of capital subscriptions paid into the bank is divided into two parts: $399,589,000 ($374,293,000; 1979) initially paid in gold or United States dollars and $3,596,304,000 ($3,368,632,000; 1979) paid in the currencies of the respective members. Of this latter portion an amount of $147,349,000 ($143,647,000; 1979) was subsequently converted by members into United States dollars, subject to the right of the bank or the members to reverse the transactions. The amounts paid in gold or United States dollars or subsequently converted by members into United States dollars are freely usable by the bank in any of its operations; however, the remaining amounts paid in the currencies of the members, hereinafter called restricted currencies, are usable by the bank in its lending operations only with the consent of the respective members. The equivalent of $2,289,419,000 ($2,200,146,000; 1979) has been used with such consent.

Article II, Section 9 of the Articles of Agreement provides for maintenance of value, as of the time of subscription, of such restricted currencies, requiring the member to make additional payments to the bank in the event that the par value of its currency is reduced or the foreign exchange value of its currency has, in the opinion of the bank, depreciated to a significant extent in its territories. Also, the bank is required to reimburse the member in the event that the par value of its currency is increased. Following the establishment of central rates by several members in lieu of existing par values in March, 1973, the executive directors decided that for all members that established central rates for their respective currencies, pending the establishment of new par values, maintenance of value obligations would be settled on the basis of those central rates. These obligations of the members and of the bank become effective immediately upon the happening of those events with respect to holdings of restricted currencies represented by currency balances and demand obligations. With respect to restricted currencies out on loan, these obligations become effective only as and when such currencies are recovered by the bank, except that in several cases the bank and the members concerned have agreed to make provisional settlements of such obligations by means of one or more payments over periods not exceeding five years. At June 30, 1980, $1,280,000 ($1,655,000; 1979) was receivable and $2,517,000 ($3,262,000; 1979) was payable by the bank on such provisional settlements. These amounts are included in the bank's statement of condition in amounts required to maintain value of currency holdings under the headings "receivable on account of subscribed capital" and "liabilities," respectively.

Prior to April 1, 1978, where market rates of exchange were not related to par values or central rates, as in the cases of a majority of members, and where there were differences between market rates of exchange and the rates at which capital subscriptions of members had been paid or were payable, such differences were shown as translation adjustments on capital subscriptions under the heading "other assets." These amounts represented notional receivables and payables that would become maintenance of value obligations if and when the provisions of Article II, Section 9 of the Articles of Agreement or the decision of the executive directors described above could be applied. According to the legal opinion of the bank's general counsel referred to earlier, maintenance of value pursuant to Article II, Section 9 of the Articles of Agreement would be determined on the basis of the SDR, and would be treated in the financial statements on this basis. Since the bank is still considering the implications of the Second Amendment, and in view of the questions referred to above, the timing of any establishment and settlement of these notional maintenance of value items $513,417,000 ($460,399,000; 1979) receivable and $150,998,000 ($142,271,000; 1979) payable are uncertain. Accordingly, they are included in "other assets," and "liabilities," as notional maintenance of value obligations.

Currency pooling: Agreement was reached in fiscal year 1979 on the adoption of a currency pooling scheme designed to equalize exchange rate risks among the bank's borrowers. The need to devise some system to achieve borrower equity arose from recent significant changes in exchange rates among the various currencies that the bank borrows and lends. It was also agreed in fiscal 1979 to alter the bank's disbursement procedures with development finance companies (DFCs). Because many DFC subborrowers are unprotected by a sort of "natural pooling" that shelters large and frequent bank borrowers, they were reluctant to take on an uncertain foreign exchange liability that may bear no relationship to the source of procurement or to their foreign exchange earnings. To this end it was decided that, on an interim basis, disbursements to DFCs would be made half in U.S. dollars and half in one of three currencies^Deutsche marks, Swiss francs, and Japanese yen. This interim measure was known as the "DFC currency basket scheme."

In fiscal 1980, agreement was reached on the treatment of loans committed before the currency pool began operation (July 1, 1980) and of loans to DFCs. As regards the former, it was decided that the undisbursed portions of existing loans could be included in the currency pool at the option of the borrower, but that portions already disbursed would be excluded. As far as loans to DFCs were concerned, it was decided to include all new loans to DFCs^both those that were protected against exchange risk by governments and those that passed it through to subborrowers^in the pool. With the currency pooling system about to begin operations, there was no need to continue the DFC currency basket scheme; like other borrowers, the DFCs would have the option of transferring the undisbursed balances on existing loans to the pool.

Position of IBRD Bonds. The bank's vice-president and treasurer view the appeal of the bank's bonds to institutions as follows:

1. The bank is a premier AAA borrower.
2. It has never had a default or suffered a loss on a loan, and it does not reschedule loans.
3. The bank's debt is long-term, with the total cost of all funds, debt plus equity, less than 6% (as of 1980).
4. Its callable capital from member governments, which in effect provides a guarantee for bondholders can never be used for any other purpose.

Summary. The World Bank is not, strictly speaking, a bank in the usual meaning of the term, creating derivative deposits for borrowers as the result of its loans. If the bank cannot borrow or does not borrow, it cannot lend. It resorts to the financial markets as vehicles to finance the loans it makes to developing countries.

BIBLIOGRAPHY

WORLD BANK. *Annual Report.*
———. *World Development Report.*

INTERNATIONAL BANKING Encompasses a variety of services and operations facilitating international trade, money flows for investment and payments, and loans to governments and official institutions as well as to the private sector.

U.S. banks are relative newcomers to international banking, and their volume in these markets is relatively concentrated in a few of the larger banks. The extent of participation in international operations by U.S. banks has expanded in volume well beyond an elementary level of servicing domestic firms and individuals with such home office "international division" services as issuance and confirmation of letters of credit, creation of acceptance credits, supply of foreign exchange "spot" and forward contracts, and facilitation of remittances and foreign travel. For such operations carried on at home offices in the U.S., American banks could rely on foreign bank correspondents.

Authorization for national banks to establish foreign branches had appeared in the Federal Reserve Act (Sec. 25) as amended in 1916; and in 1919, U.S. member banks were authorized to organize Edge Act foreign banking corporations (Sec. 25(a), Federal Reserve Act) on approval of the Board of Governors of the Federal Reserve System, with powers to engage in both banking and financing operations abroad (originally an Edge Act subsidiary could not combine both types of operations, but later amendment permits an Edge Act subsidiary to combine both types of operations).

Despite expansion in the preceding types of operations abroad following the end of World War II, U.S. banks' presence abroad continued to be relatively minor compared with domestic operations. What led to subsequent major expansion is explained from two viewpoints.

One view, that of a senior officer in a major international American bank, is that starting with the U.S.-led postwar rehabilitation effort, facilitated by the monetary stability provided by establishment of the INTERNATIONAL MONETARY FUND at Bretton Woods and sustained by the activity generated by the Korean and Vietnam wars, the "global economy" was a functioning reality by the early 1960s. "The instrument that actually forged an integrated global economy out of various conditions and components, however, was the multinational corporation with its supporting financial institutions." By a rapid acceleration of direct investments in overseas markets, the multinational corporations and their banks created global systems of production, distribution, and finance which "literally stretched the perimeter of the marketplace around the entire world." What now exists is a financial network that readily handles the world's international requirements for payments and settlements, securities trading, credit and credit accomodation of all kinds, placement of insurance risks, liquidity movements across borders and continents, and an active and expanding foreign exchange market. This international system created and uses a new marketplace—the Eurocurrency market—which depends on links and flows from domestic financial markets.

Another view is that until early in 1965 when the Board of Governors of the Federal Reserve System issued its Voluntary

Foreign Credit Restraint Program (VFCR) as part of the federal government's overall effort to protect the U.S. international balance of payments by limiting capital outflows, U.S. banks' operations abroad were relatively minor. Under the VFCR, which was terminated effective January 29, 1974, U.S. banks and nonbank institutions were requested to limit both their lending to foreigners and their investments in foreign countries other than Canada. In this view, promulgation of the VFCR program provided the impetus for U.S. banks to expand their presence abroad in order to continue to participate directly in the many opportunities for banking and financing volume and earnings in host countries as well as cross-border operations from locations abroad, including those in "shell" branches in offshore locations providing "tax havens."

In 1979 the Board of Governors of the Federal Reserve System issued a new Regulation K entitled "International Banking Operations." The revised regulation governs the establishment of foreign branches of member banks, the organization and operation of Edge Act and agreement corporations, and foreign investments by member banks, bank holding companies, and Edge Act and agreement corporations.

The revision of Regulation K resulted in part from Section 3 of the INTERNATIONAL BANKING ACT OF 1978, which was intended to improve the competitiveness and efficiency of Edge Act corporations in providing international banking and financial services. The Congress declared in Section 3 of the referenced act that Edge Act corporations are to have powers sufficiently broad to enable them to compete with foreign banks in the United States and abroad; to provide all segments of the economy, especially exporters, financing for international trade; and to foster participation by regional and smaller banks in international banking and finance. Important new provisions of the revised Regulation K permit domestic branching of Edge Act corporations, permit those corporations to finance the production of goods and services for export, liberalize the approval procedures under which foreign investments may be made and foreign branches established, specify permissible foreign activities, and permit foreign ownership of Edge Act corporations.

International Activities of U.S. Banking Organizations. The board of governors has three principal statutory responsibilities in connection with the supervision of the international operations of U.S. banking organizations: (1) to issue licenses for foreign branches of member banks and regulate the scope of their activities; (2) to charter and regulate Edge Act corporations; and (3) to authorize and regulate overseas investments by member banks, Edge Act corporations, and bank holding companies.

Under provisions of the Federal Reserve Act and Regulation K, member banks may establish branches in foreign countries, subject in most cases to the board's prior approval. In reviewing proposed foreign branches, the board considers the requirements of the governing statute, the condition of the bank, and the bank's experience in international business. In 1981, the board approved the opening of 21 foreign branches. By the end of 1981, 156 member banks were operating 800 branches in foreign countries and overseas areas of the United States, a net increase of 11 for the year. A total of 121 national banks were operating 674 of these branches, while 35 state member banks were operating the remaining 126 branches.

International Banking Facilities (IBFs). Effective December 3, 1981, the Board of Governors of the Federal Reserve System amended its Regulations D and Q to permit the establishment of international banking facilities (IBFs) in the United States. IBFs may be established, subject to conditions specified by the board, by U.S. depository institutions, and by Edge Act and agreement corporations. These facilities may also be set up by U.S. branches and agencies of foreign banks.

An IBF is essentially a set of asset and liability accounts that is segregated from other accounts of the establishing office. In general, deposits from and credit extended to foreign resident or other IBFs can be booked at these facilities free from domestic reserve requirements and limitations on interest rates.

IBFs will be examined along with other parts of the establishing office, and their activities will be reflected in the supervisory reports submitted to the bank regulatory agencies by that office. By year-end 1981, 270 offices had established IBFs.

Edge Act and Agreement Corporations. Under Sections 25 and 25(a) of the Federal Reserve Act, Edge Act and agreement corporations may engage in international banking and foreign financial transactions. These corporations, which are usually subsidiaries of member banks, provide their owner organizations with additional powers in two areas: (1) they may conduct a deposit and loan business in states other than that of the parent, provided that the business is strictly related to international transactions; and (2) they have somewhat broader foreign investment powers than member banks, being able to invest in foreign financial organizations, such as finance companies and leasing companies, as well as in foreign banks. In 1981, the board approved the establishment of 19 Edge Act corporations and 1 agreement corporation and the operation of 47 branches by established Edge Act corporations.

Capitalization and Activities of Edge Act Corporations. The International Banking Act (IBA) removed the statutory limit on liabilities of an Edge Act corporation under which the corporation's debentures, bonds, and promissory notes could not exceed ten times the corporation's capital and surplus. The board established a new capital requirement of 7% of risk assets for Edge Act corporations engaging in international banking in the United States, to permit these corporations to compete more effectively with other international organizations that are more highly leveraged. Effective July 29, 1981, the board amended its regulation dealing with Edge Act corporations to provide that, with board approval, subordinated capital notes or debentures, in an amount not to exceed 50% of nondebt capital, may be included for determining capital adequacy in the same manner as for a member bank.

Two other important changes arising from the IBA permitted Edge Act corporations (1) to be owned by foreign banks; and (2) to establish branches within the United States.

Summary. Rapid expansion in international lending to LDCs by the small indicated group of major U.S. banks, both to governments and to the private sector, was fostered by higher interest rates and the expectation that simultaneous default by a number of such countries could not conceivably occur except in worldwide depression. Such international lending includes purely domestic lending in host countries where U.S. banks have branch offices and subsidiaries. The danger to developing countries, in the view of the World Bank staff, is not that banks will stop lending to LDCs but rather that lending growth will slow because individual banks or banking groups have to restrain their lending.

Assets of foreign offices of U.S. banks grew from less than $5 billion in 1960 to more than $500 billion at the end of 1987. However, it is estimated that international lending and the expansion of foreign offices by U.S. banks have slowed, partly because of excessive foreign debt of many nations. The assets of U.S. banking offices of foreign banks and foreign nonbank investors have also increased rapidly, but the growth shows little sign of slowing. From less than $30 billion in 1970, these assets have increased to $229 billion within a decade and to more than $6,500 billion by the end of 1987. The share of all domestic banking assets controlled by foreigners grew from 3.6% in 1972 to almost 20% in 1987.

Foreign banks have not penetrated the domestic consumer market to any considerable extent. Branching is the preferred form of market entry for both U.S. and foreign banks. Legal and regulatory restrictions, tax laws, and market practicalities must be dealt with to make international banking successful.

The trend in international banking laws, regulations, supervisory policies of the United States and its banking agencies, market practices and structures have generally been to grant U.S. banks slightly broader powers to compete abroad with institutions that can offer a wider range of financial services. The most significant U.S. legislation directed toward foreign banks has limited their authority to operate in the United States by reducing earlier advantages they held over domestic banks.

See FOREIGN BANKING CORPORATIONS, FOREIGN EXCHANGE, INTERNATIONAL BANK FOR RECONSTRUCTION AND DEVELOPMENT.

BIBLIOGRAPHY

BANK ADMINISTRATION INSTITUTE. *International Bank Operations.* Bank Administration Institute, Rolling Meadows, IL, 1983.
KHOURY, S. J., and GHOSH, A. *Recent Developments in International Banking and Finance.* Lexington Books, Lexington, MA, 1988.
MARINE MIDLAND BANK. *International Banking Services.* Seafirst Bank, Settle, WA, 1988.

INTERNATIONAL BANKING ACT OF 1978

P.L. 95-369, approved September 17, 1978. The International Banking Act of 1978 (IBA) contained the following provisions as summarized by the Board of Governors of the Federal Reserve System.

1. Authorized the Comptroller of the Currency to waive the requirements that all the directors of a national bank be U.S. citizens.
2. Removed the requirement in the Edge Act (Sec. 25(a) of the Federal Reserve Act) that all of the directors of an Edge Act corporation be U.S. citizens. Similarly, the Edge Act was amended to permit one or more foreign banks to own 50% or more of the shares of an Edge Act corporation with the prior approval of the Board of Governors of the Federal Reserve System. Previously, the Edge Act required without exception that a majority of the shares of an Edge Act corporation be owned by U.S. citizens.
3. Required the Board of Governors of the Federal Reserve System to revise its regulation dealing with Edge Act corporations within 270 days of enactment of the IBA. In doing so, the board of governors was required to implement several congressional purposes for Edge Act corporations including affording the Edge Act corporations powers sufficiently broad to enable them to compete in the United States and abroad with similar foreign-owned institutions. Edge Act corporations are also to serve as a means of financing international trade, particularly exports. The minimum 10% reserve requirement then in effect on the U.S. deposits of Edge Act corporations was eliminated, and the board of governors was authorized to impose the same level of reserve requirements on the Edge Act corporations as on member banks. The IBA removed the statutory limitation on the issuance by Edge Act corporations of debentures, bonds, and promissory notes. The board of governors was required to report to the Congress the effects of these amendments on the capitalization and activities of Edge Act corporations, banks, and the banking system.
4. Authorized the Comptroller of the Currency to license and supervise one or more federal branches or agencies of a foreign bank in states that do not prohibit the establishment of branches or agencies by foreign banks.
5. Prohibited a foreign bank from establishing and operating branches outside its "home" state unless the foreign bank enters into an agreement or undertaking with the board of governors that it will receive only such deposits at the out-of-state offices as are permissible for an Edge Act corporation. Offices of foreign banks that were established, or for which an application had been filed, prior to June 27, 1978, were exempted from this prohibition.
6. Required federal deposit insurance for branches of foreign banks that receive deposits of less than $100,000. Required federal deposit insurance for federal branches wherever located and for state branches in states that require deposit insurance for state-chartered banks.
7. Authorized the federal banking agencies to examine U.S. offices of foreign banks and in appropriate circumstances to institute cease-and-desist proceedings against them.
8. Imposed reserve requirements and interest rate limitations on federal branches and agencies of large foreign banks in the same manner and to the same extent as on member banks. The board of governors was authorized to impose the same requirements and limitations on state branches and state agencies after consultation and in cooperation with state bank supervisory authorities. Subject to the regulations of the board of governors, branches and agencies that maintain reserves would have access to system facilities.
9. Subjected a foreign bank that has a branch, agency, or commercial lending company in the United States to most provisions of the BANK HOLDING COMPANY ACT in the same manner and to the same extent as bank holding companies. Nonbanking activities engaged in or applied for by July 26, 1978, were exempted under a grandfather clause. Otherwise, a foreign bank may not engage directly or indirectly in nonbanking activities in the United States other than those permissible to bank holding companies.
10. Required that joint studies and reports be undertaken by the President, with respect to the PEPPER-MCFADDEN ACT; the secretary of the Treasury, with respect to the treatment of U.S. banks abroad; and the Board of Governors of the Federal Reserve System, with respect to Edge Act corporations becoming members of the Federal Reserve System.

See EDGE ACT, FEDERAL RESERVE BOARD REGULATIONS (Regulation K).

INTERNATIONAL BANKING ACT OF 1987 Legislation that provided for federal regulation of U.S. operations of foreign banks and established Federal Reserve responsibilities for the supervision and regulation of such operations. The act created a federal regulatory and supervisory structure for such operations similar to that applied to U.S. banks ("national treatment"). The Federal Reserve has statutory authority to examine the assets and liabilities of all branches and agencies on-site but relies extensively on examinations performed by state and other federal banking authorities. The act limited the expansion of interstate deposit accumulation and domestic nonbanking activities of foreign banks, required the option of either state or federal licensing for agencies and branches of foreign banks, and required FDIC insurance for branches that engage in retail deposit accumulation.

The ILSA also required U.S. bank regulators to establish minimum capital ratios for U.S. banking institutions that could deal with the differences between capital ratios for U.S. banking institutions and foreign banks. The Federal Reserve maintained that competitive equity require that, in general, foreign banks seeking to establish or acquire banking operations in the United States should meet the same general standards of strength, experience, and reputation as are required of domestic banking organizations and should be able to serve on a continuing basis as a source of strength to their banking operations in the United States.

INTERNATIONAL BANKING DEPARTMENT The international banking department of a bank is primarily responsible for financing foreign customers or domestic clients involved in foreign dealings. The operations typically handled by a bank's international department include:

1. Exchange operations.
2. Opening of documentary credits of importation, as well as providing notices and confirmation of export documentary credits.
3. Remittance to correspondents of documents for collection and handling of collections received from them.
4. Issuing bond guaranties on foreign countries or issuing bonds or guaranties for the account of foreign banks or firms in favor of local firms.
5. Handling foreign currency assets of the bank.
6. Granting lines of credit to banks or firms abroad and securing and handling lines of credit granted to the bank by its correspondents.
7. Maintaining public relations to assure permanent contact, directly or indirectly, with customers within the country or abroad.
8. Maintaining close supervision of relations with correspondent banks worldwide, which, aside from credit and service aspects, also means permanent control over reciprocity received or given.
9. Compiling statistical data to evaluate the evolution of bank operations in the international sector.

The services most frequently found in foreign departments of banks include documentary credit service, collection service, bond guaranty service, and foreign exchange service. The international banking department can subdivide its service structure in a variety of ways. Some banks provide a service designated as "goods" or "merchandise" regardless of whether they are covered by documentary credits or are handled as collections. Others divide services into "import service" and "export service," each which handles documentary credits and collections related to goods entering or leaving the country. Others have created a "documentary credit service" that handles all transactions covered by this instrument and a "collection service" that handles all transactions relating to import or export documents either sent or received for collection.

The foreign exchange service is responsible for receiving and processing transactions with which it is entrusted by customers, foreign banks, or the foreign exchange desk. The principal function of this service is to determine the buy and sell exchange rates of different currencies under which the bank operates. The foreign exchange desk is also responsible for monitoring the bank's foreign exchange position. Typical duties of the chief deal or foreign exchange desk include:

1. Execute and supervise the bank's purchases and sales of foreign currencies.
2. Provide all agencies and branches with daily buying and selling rates of different currencies with which the bank normally deals.
3. Provide current quotes for those same currencies for all operations about which the dealer or desk has been consulted.
4. Modify rates previously transmitted as well as suspend any authorization given to branches and agencies to operate freely up to certain limited amounts.
5. Maintain contact with principal bank customers about foreign exchange matters.
6. Participate with customer service officers and with managers of branches and agencies in promotion activities.
7. Review operations daily.
8. Watch for irregularities.
9. Monitor the foreign exchange position.
10. Keep current regarding the foreign exchange market.
11. Provide monthly statistics about operations activities and profits earned.
12. Supervise the foreign currency cash assets that the bank holds in its correspondent banks abroad.
13. Carry out transfers or coverage transactions so that accounts abroad have the least number of overdrafts, thereby avoiding unnecessary interest charges.

Source: Seglin, Jeffrey L., *Bank Administration Manual: A Comprehensive Reference Guide,* BAI.

INTERNATIONAL CENTER FOR SETTLEMENT OF INVESTMENT DISPUTED (ICSID)
An autonomous institution, created in 1965 by the Convention on the Settlement of Investment Disputes Between States and Nationals of Other States, to provide facilities of conciliation and arbitration of investment disputed between contracting states and nationals with provisions of the convention. Currently there are 87 contracting states.

INTERNATIONAL CHECKS   TRAVELERS' CHECKS.

INTERNATIONAL CLEARINGHOUSE
There is no physical clearinghouse where foreign bills of exchange and other instruments are used in the settlement of foreign transactions. In effect, however, the market for foreign exchange constitutes an international clearinghouse.

INTERNATIONAL CODE   See CIPHER CODE.

INTERNATIONAL COMMERCIAL EXCHANGE, INC.
Formerly a subsidiary of the New York Produce Exchange, designated as a contract market on April 8, 1970, and formed both to supersede the commodity trading of the New York Produce Exchange and to establish a currency futures trading market. Members of the International Commercial Exchange, Inc. consisted of members of the New York Produce Exchange and associate members.

On January 23, 1973, a vote by members of the New York Produce Exchange approved its conversion to a realty trust by issuance of stock and cash to the 473 members. The transfer of commodity operations to another exchange was announced January 24, 1973.
See PRODUCE EXCHANGES.

INTERNATIONAL COOPERATION ADMINISTRATION
From 1955 to 1961, this agency had responsibility for the conduct of the MUTUAL SECURITY PROGRAM, except those parts providing military assistance, those concerning refugees and escapees, and those involving contributions to international organizations; the agency also had responsibilities under the Agricultural Trade Development and Assistance Act of 1954, as amended. It was established by State Department Delegation of Authority 85, June 30, 1955, pursuant to Executive Order 10610 of May 9, 1955, under authority of the Mutual Security Act of 1954 (68 Stat. 832; 22 U.S.C. 1751).

The agency was abolished by the Foreign Assistance Act of 1961 (75 Stat. 446; 22 U.S.C. 2382), and its functions were redelegated to the Agency for International Development (AID), pursuant to the President's letter of September 30, 1961, and Executive Order 10973 of November 3, 1961.

In the latest game of organizational musical chairs, the INTERNATIONAL DEVELOPMENT COOPERATION AGENCY (IDCA) was created in October, 1979, by Presidential Executive Order with full responsibility over the AGENCY FOR INTERNATIONAL DEVELOPMENT (AID).

INTERNATIONAL CREDIT INSURERS UNION
An international association of export credit insurance institutions (Berne Union) founded in 1934 as the Insurers Union for Control of International Credit. The association is composed of both private and government-owned institutions. Its charter now allows membership of insurance institutions who deal exclusively in investment insurance and underwrite investment risks. United States members of the union include the Export-Import Bank, the Foreign Credit Insurance Association, and the Overseas Private Investment Corporation. The Union's purposes are (1) the international acceptance of sound principles of export credit insurance and the establishment and maintenance of discipline in the terms of credit for international trade; and (2) international cooperation in fostering a favorable investment climate and in developing and maintaining sound principles of foreign investment insurance.

INTERNATIONAL DEBT PROBLEM
During the 1980s many Third World countries, especially in Latin America, were unable to service their international debt. The United States and other creditor countries adopted a case-by-case strategy for dealing with the problem. Debtors often received financing from the International Monetary Fund and from commercial banks. Economic austerity programs were imposed and implemented to help resolve the problem. Such programs slowed economic growth in the debtor nations, resulting in cutback of imports and expansion of exports by the debtor nations, which contributed to the deterioration of the international trade balance of the U.S.

The U.S. proposed a program for sustained growth (the Baker Plan) that focused on allowing debtor nations to grow out of their debt problem with financial backing of $20 billion to be provided by commercial banks and $9 billion by multilateral development banks. Unfortunately, debt and net outflow of financial resources from debtor nations continued. The proposed funds were not provided in the amounts projected.

In 1986, proposals were introduced in Congress to deal with the debt problem. Such proposals were usually based on debt relief instead of new financing to avoid an increase in the debt levels of the debtor nations. The Bradley proposal suggested a 3% cut in interest rates and a 3% decrease in principal for each of three years. The Obey/Sarbanes proposal proposed the establishment of a debt facility that would purchase Third World debt at a discount and pass the discount on to the debtors. The Schumer proposal proposed limiting interest payments by the debtor to 2% of a country's annual export earnings, limiting a country's debt service to its ability to pay. The Kerry proposal suggested the debt relief be related directly to a debtor's trade balance; countries having a trade surplus would receive less debt relief than those having a trade deficit. No write-offs were proposed for commercial banks.

In 1989, President Bush cancelled the debt of sub-Saharan African countries to the United States. Africa south of the Sahara Desert refers to all of Africa except South Africa and the North African countries on the Mediterranean—Egypt, Libya, Tunisia, Algeria, and Morocco. The State Department put the total of U.S. loans to sub-Saharan Africa at $4.3 billion, including $743 million in development loans, $1.5 billion from the U.S. government's Export-Import Bank and $1.2 billion in U.S. government loans to buy surplus American farm products.

INTERNATIONAL DEVELOPMENT ASSOCIATION (IDA)
An intergovernmental institution administered by the International Bank for Reconstruction and Development but legally and financially distinct from the bank. The IDA began operations in 1960. All member countries of the International Bank for Reconstruction and Development may be members of IDA. Members are divided into two categories according to their wealth: Part I includes industrialized countries plus Kuwait and United Arab Emirates. Part II includes developing countries. The objectives of the association are the same as the International Bank for Reconstruction and Development, but its aid is essentially for the poorest countries and granted under more liberal conditions. Its aid is for productive ends and to stimulate the economic growth of the developing member countries.

The association's resources come from five sources: capital subscriptions and member contributions (U.S. $30 billion); transfers of a part of the net income of the IBRD (U.S. $1.6 billion); repayments of IDA credits and its net revenue (U.S. $280 million); Swiss loans (U.S. $51 million); cofinancing operations.

Capital contributions represent over 90% of the total resources and come from 33 countries, which are for the most part industrialized. Part I members pay all subscriptions and supplementary resources provided to the association in nonconvertible currencies. Part II members pay 10% of their initial subscriptions in freely convertible currencies, and the remaining 90% of their initial subscriptions and all additional subscriptions and any supplementary resources provided in their own currencies.

IDA loans are called "credits" to distinguish them from IBRD loans. Financing usually takes the form of long-term loans with or without cofinancing. Loans have been for 50 years with a 10-year grace period. Redemption terms are 1% per year during the following years and 3% during the last 30 years. There is no interest rate but there is a 0.75% service charge per year on the dispersed amounts. Since 1982, a 0.50% commitment charge has been added for the undrawn balance.

Distribution is on the basis of per capita income and by sector of activity.

Summary. IDA credits require highly concessional financing of very long maturity. In light of the principal goals of development, identified by the retiring fifth president of the World Bank as acceleration of economic growth and eradication of absolute poverty, the IDA sixth replenishment "while it is generous" will fall far short of meeting the greatly increased needs of the low-income countries.

Source: Investment Financing by International Development Banks, BAI.

INTERNATIONAL DEVELOPMENT COOPERATION AGENCY (IDCA)

A federal agency which has limited responsibilities for coordinating and preparing budget documents for organizations in charge of management and distribution of nonmilitary U.S. aid to development. The IDCA coordinates the following organizations: Agency for International Development, Overseas Private Investment Corporation, Board of International Food and Agricultural Development, Trade and Development Program, and the Development Coordination Committee. IDCA coordinated jointly U.S. Food for Peace Program with the Department of Agriculture, U.S. Participation in Multilateral Development Banks with the Department of the Treasury, and U.S. Participation in International Organizations and Programs with the State Department. The agency is financed primarily by budget allocations.

This agency began operations on October 1, 1979, pursuant to Reorganization Plan No. 2 of the Carter administration to provide a diluted version of Senator Hubert H. Humphrey's idea of creating one superagency for nearly all foreign aid programs. As finally enacted, the reorganization provides that the director of the International Development Cooperation Agency (IDCA) is directly responsible for the policies and budgets of the AGENCY FOR INTERNATIONAL DEVELOPMENT (AID), the Overseas Private Investment Corporation, voluntary contributions to international organizations and programs, the trade and development program, and U.S. contributions to the International Fund for Agricultural Development, which is a multilateral lending organization. But the director of the IDCA shares responsibility with the secretary of the Treasury for developmental aspects of U.S. participation in the multilateral development banks, and with the secretary of Agriculture and other officials for the Public Law 480 food aid program.

Coordination provided by the IDCA is credited with having increased the effectiveness of economic assistance programs. However, with its emphasis on reductions in federal expenditures, the Reagan administration proposed to reduce the Carter administration's 1982 total foreign aid budgetary request 26%, with substantially heavier reductions through 1986, as indicated in the appended table. Such substantial proposed reductions might well lead to further revamping of the organizational layers concerned.

See INTERNATIONAL COOPERATION ADMINISTRATION.

INTERNATIONAL ENERGY AGENCY

Established in 1974, with a membership as of 1980 of 21 industrialized oil-importing nations including the U.S., the International Energy Agency (IEA) had as one of its principal purposes assistance to its members in meeting possible future OIL supply interruptions and/or drastic price increases.

The U.S. urged the establishment of the IEA on members of the ORGANIZATION FOR ECONOMIC COOPERATION AND DEVELOPMENT (OECD), and this advocacy resulted in the Agreement on an International Energy Program that organized the IEA in Paris in November, 1974, under the aegis of the OECD, to develop and administer the agreement's formula for emergency allocation of oil among member countries, to institute an information-gathering system on international oil operations, to set a framework for consultations with individual oil companies, to provide the vehicle for long-term cooperation among member banks on conservation and new energy sources, and to promote cooperative relations with oil-producing and Third World countries.

As a cooperative and consultative body, the IEA lacks the power of sanctions in the event of oil supply interruptions and/or drastic increases in prices for oil imports.

See ORGANIZATION OF PETROLEUM EXPORTING COUNTRIES.

INTERNATIONAL EQUITY

Shares traded away from their country of origin. Capital markets in which equity securities are traded. Many companies currently issue new shares globally much like they issue Eurobonds through a syndicate of international banks (the primary equity market). Since regulations and settlement procedures differ in various countries, a truly international share market is difficult to develop.

Equity (share) markets have traditionally been national: the Paris Bourse, the Zurich Stock Exchange, and others. In the secondary market, international stock can be traded either internationally or on their domestic markets. International equities are traded in London in the "over-the-counter-market." The American Securities Industry Association estimated that in 1985 the gross transaction volume of American equity trading (sales and purchases) in London amounted to $38 billion. This is approximately half the comparable volume of equity trading on the London Stock Exchange. When international trading of non-American stock in London is added, the volume would approximate the London Stock Exchange. Pension funds, insurance companies, and mutual funds are major investors.

International securities (1987 NASDAQ, AMEX fact books, 1988 NYSE fact book) data are appended:

NYSE (1987)	Issuers	Issues	Market Value (10 of million)
Bonds	40	89	9,942
Stocks	67	70	84,153
Total		159	94,095
AMEX (1986)			
Total		55	23,184
Canadian		40	22,488
NASDAQ (1986)			
Total	244	266	N.A.

INTERNATIONAL EXCHANGE   FOREIGN EXCHANGE.

INTERNATIONAL FINANCE CORPORATION

Historical Background. The objective of the IFC's establishment was to help the IBRD fulfill the purpose expressed in Article I (ii) of its own Articles of Agreement. This required the bank to seek to promote private foreign investment by participating in private loans and other investments and, when private capital was not available on reasonable terms, by supplementing private investment from its own resources.

In its first decade, the IBRD, by means of loans to finance public works projects and otherwise, provided developing countries with the infrastructure to support and expand industrial growth; but experience soon showed that, although the bank's founders had recognized the importance of private capital in this task, the bank's own ability to promote private enterprise was limited. This was because IBRD loans had to be made to or guaranteed by the government of the country where the project to be financed was located, and because the IBRD made only fixed-interest loans and could not provide venture capital. In some cases the bank attempted to meet

INTERNATIONAL FINANCE CORPORATION

this situation by providing credits to private enterprise through a local development bank or banking consortium, but this was found to be only a partial answer to the problem. Following a report prepared by the staff of the IBRD in 1952, pointing out the need for increased investment in the less developed areas and proposing the creation of an International Finance Corporation as an affiliate of the bank, the IFC came into being in 1956.

There have been three distinct stages in the IFC's first 15 years. The first projects offered to the IFC covered a wide variety of activities. Financing was sought for enterprises in every important less developed area of the world, although mainly in Latin America. Many inquiries were based on misunderstandings; for example, it was not always realized that the IFC did not finance export credits or installment sales. The IFC concentrated its first operations (as it has done since) in the fields of manufacture and processing, since these most readily attract private capital and provide the greatest economic multiplier through the transfer of technology, management skills, employment, and training. At the end of its first year, the IFC had made four commitments totaling $5.3 million, all in Latin America. By the end of its fourth financial year, in 1960, the IFC had 59 member countries and had made 33 commitments in 17 countries with a total cost of $42 million. These figures showed relatively slow growth, a reflection of a basic restriction under which the IFC had been obliged to work. The original proposal for the creation of the IFC had envisaged an institution able to make loans without government guarantees and to make equity investments. The new IFC, however, was expressly forbidden to make equity investments, based on objection to a public institution's holding capital stock in private enterprises. It had been hoped that this restriction would not unduly limit the IFC's activities. However, four years of operation had shown that the IFC's effectiveness was hampered by the fact that it could function only as a lender and not as an investment banker. The restriction against investment in equities was a serious handicap to the growth of the IFC and to its ability to mobilize private capital for foreign investment. The IFC had tried to meet the problem by making investments that included some characteristics of equity such as profit-sharing participations or options on share capital, but in doing so it was forced into patterns of financing that in the context of developing countries often appeared complicated and unusual, and that were themselves obstacles to the attraction of other private investment.

Accordingly, in 1961 the member governments of the IFC changed the IFC's Articles of Agreement to enable the corporation to invest in equities. This change began the second stage in the IFC's life. The IFC was now able to play a full part in providing and mobilizing risk capital for investment in the less developed countries. It was able to promote projects itself and to reinforce projects in which it invested. It was able to work with sponsors in shaping and setting up investments in a way that would render them attractive to other private investors. It also became possible for the IFC, through underwriting or standby commitments, to help in spreading share ownership in the developing countries. In 1962, the IFC for the first time joined in underwriting a share issue, consisting of capital shares of the largest private steel company in Mexico. Another result of the IFC's ability to invest in equities was that the way was opened for the IFC to support private enterprise through local development finance institutions. The IFC was created to do on an international scale what these institutions were established to do on a local scale. Their activities have thus been complementary, and there has been a constant interchange of information, with the IFC passing to the local institutions projects too small for it to handle economically and they in turn passing to the IFC projects beyond their scope.

By the time the IFC had reached its tenth anniversary in 1966, this new breadth of activity was clearly reflected in the IFC's record. The total number of its investments had reached 124, more than three times as many as five years before, with a total cost of $172 million, more than three times the figure for 1961, while others had invested $890 million in the same enterprises. The increased activity was paralleled by a greater geographical spread in the IFC's operations, which had become virtually worldwide. In 1966, Latin America, with 69 commitments out of a total of 124, was still predominant, but now Asia and Africa together accounted for 36 commitments.

The increase in the IFC's equity operations created a new problem in that there was a demand for loan capital not guaranteed by member governments in larger amounts than the IFC could supply. The problem was met by an amendment to the IFC's Articles of Agreement and to those of the IBRD that enabled the IFC to borrow from the IBRD up to a limit of four times its own unimpaired subscribed capital and surplus. The result of these amendments was to provide the IFC with additional resources for its own loans and to release the IFC's entire share capital and reserves for equity investments.

Availability of these new resources marked the start of the third stage in the IFC's life and led to a new upsurge in its activities. These activities were now diversified still further, for example, into tourism and utilities, and there was a more substantial involvement in pulp and paper and in fertilizers. The IFC was also able to invest larger sums in projects of greater size and complexity.

This upward progression continued in the next three years. In this period there was a marked increase in the IFC's investments in Asia and Africa; in 1967, more than half of the year's new investments were made in Asia and the Middle East. In 1968, more than half were made in Africa alone; these included the year's two largest investments—$20 million in a copper mine in Mauritania and $9 million in a sugar plantation and mill in Ethiopia. The year was also notable for the IFC's largest underwriting through fiscal 1971, a guarantee of half an issue of $14 million in shares of the same Mexican steel concern that the IFC had supported in 1962 in its first underwriting operation. The year 1969 also saw the IFC's largest investment through fiscal 1971—$22 million to a cement project in Thailand.

Organization. Membership in the IFC is reserved for IBRD members. There were 127 members as of June 30, 1985. Of these 106 were developing countries. Each member country has 250 votes plus one additional vote for each share of stock held. The U.S., which has subscribed to about one-third of the total subscriptions, also has about one-third of the voting power, followed by Great Britain, West Germany, Japan, and France, who combined hold over 50% of votes.

The IFC is legally and financially separate from the World Bank but with same board of executive directors and the same president.

Objectives. The IFC participates in the economic development of developing countries by promoting the growth of the private sector of their economies by mobilizing capital to this end either in the country itself or abroad. Its sole purpose is financing private productive projects in developing countries and promoting their financial markets.

Resources. Resources available to the corporation come from four sources: capital endowment; borrowing from the IBRD; borrowing from third parties; loans, redemptions, and undistributed profits.

Financing. The IFC intervenes directly as a supplier of risk capital and indirectly by the encouragement it provides. Sources of risk capital include participations in capital, long-term loans, convertible loans, and the underwriting of public and private bond issues.

The IFC's share of a project may not exceed 25% of the cost and rarely falls below U.S. $1 million except in the least developed countries where it can limit itself to between U.S. $300,000 and $400,000. The investor must supply a minimum of 35 to 40% of the capital stock and a project cost is therefore on the average a minimum of U.S. $3 to $4 million. An average loan maturity is seven to twelve years but can be longer with a grace period of two or more years. A variable interest rate prevails, based on the cost of resources which are essentially borrowings of the IBRD. There is no guarantee by the project country government except for the free transfer of capital, receipts, and other income. Specific guarantees are required with subrogation in commercialization contracts. Repayment terms are by equal semesters for the principal and by quarter for interest. Early repayment is possible without penalties. IFC loans have been almost exclusively denominated in U.S. dollars, with the exchange risk borne by the borrower.

Equity participation of the IFC may not exceed 25% of capital and in principle the IFC must not be the principal shareholder. The minimum and maximum amounts for projects are the same as for loans. The IFC investment usually combines equity participation and a loan.

The IFC intervenes only in developing member countries. It has considerably more projects in Latin American than in Africa, Asia, or in the rest of the world. In recent years, special attention has been reserved for Africa. The IFC finances profitable production units in the industrial, agri-business, tourism, and transport sectors.

Summary. The aggregates of activity of the IFC understandably will not impress those who expect an international financial organization to operate in billions, but it should be remembered that the areas of operations are the less developed countries, and that IFC commitments should be seminal in effects upon development of local capital markets.

BIBLIOGRAPHY

INTERNATIONAL FINANCE CORPORATION. *Annual Report.*

INTERNATIONAL GOLD MOVEMENTS See FOREIGN EXCHANGE, GOLD MOVEMENTS, GOLD RESERVE.

INTERNATIONAL GRAINS ARRANGEMENT
Established at negotiating conference in Rome, July 12-August 18, 1967, called pursuant to Article 36 of the INTERNATIONAL WHEAT AGREEMENT (IWA), in which all members of the United Nations or its specialized agencies were invited to participate on an equal basis.

The International Grains Arrangement (IGA) consisted of two legal instruments: the Wheat Trade Convention and the Food Aid Convention. Each required separate signature and ratification. All member nations of the United Nations or its specialized agencies could participate in one or both conventions. Signatory governments of the Memorandum of Agreement, concluded in May, 1967, of the GENERAL AGREEMENT ON TARIFFS AND TRADE, (GATT), which set forth terms of the settlement on cereals and agreement to negotiate a grains arrangement containing the provisions of the memorandum on as wide a basis as possible, were required to participate in both instruments.

The Wheat Trade Convention and the Food Aid Convention entered into force on July 1, 1968, for a duration of three years.

Wheat Trade Convention. The Wheat Trade Convention as a stabilizing instrument for international trade used the basic approach of the 1962 International Wheat Agreement, with modifications. The stabilization of prices within a prescribed price range remained a central objective of the convention, but greater precision was given by the establishment of minimum and maximum prices for 14 different wheats, rather than only one as in the former IWA. The importing countries were committed to import not less than a stated percentage of their commercial purchases from members of the convention. Exporters in association with one another were obligated to make available quantities of WHEAT sufficient to satisfy the commercial requirements of the importing countries. However, when world prices were at or above the maximum price, the collective supply obligation was subject to an annually adjusted quantitative limit referred to as a "datum quantity."

INTERNATIONAL LABOR ORGANIZATION
A specialized agency associated with the United Nations, originally created by the Treaty of Versailles in 1919 as a part of the League of Nations. The U.S. joined the International Labor Organization (ILO) agency in 1934 but withdrew from it in November, 1977, for several reasons, including "the erosion of the tripartite principle, the ILO's selective concern for human rights, its growing disregard for due process, and the increasing politicization of the organization." (The ""tripartite principle," unique among international organizations, called for representatives of workers, employers, and government all to participate on an equal basis.)

The U.S. rejoined the ILO on February 18, 1980. "Although the ILO had not fully resolved all the issues that led the U.S. to withdraw, it had made significant progress on each" (U.S. Department of State).

1. *Tripartism:* The ILO passed several resolutions strengthening its tripartite decision-making system. For example, a new ILO general conference secret ballot procedure, vigorously resisted by the U.S.S.R., permitted employer and worker delegates to vote their consciences on sensitive issues without fear of government recrimination.
2. *Human rights:* The ILO applied its human rights procedures to Eastern Europe. In November, 1978, the ILO governing body censured Czechoslovakia for illegally firing dissidents from their jobs, and examined worker complaints against the U.S.S.R. and Poland for violating trade union rights.
3. *Due process:* In 1978, the general conference defeated an Arab resolution seeking to extend a 1974 resolution that condemned Israel without any investigation of the facts. A new mechanism to eliminate resolutions representing such violations of due process was negotiated by Western and Third World governments.
4. *Politicization:* ILO meetings became far less politicized, and there was a major turnaround on Middle East issues. When Arab representatives walked out during the speech of the Egyptian labor minister in the 1979 conference, only Communist delegates joined the walkout. The ILO also sent two missions to investigate working conditions of Palestinians in the Israeli-occupied territories. The mission's reports were accepted by both Arabs and Israelis at the 1978 and 1979 general conferences. As a result, no political resolutions were offered on this subject.

Benefits of U.S. Membership. In the view of the U.S. Department of State, membership in the ILO offers the U.S. the following advantages:

1. The opportunity to participate in and influence the formation of international labor standards, which directly affect labor codes in developing countries
2. The opportunity to participate in and influence voluntary agreements such as codes of conduct for multinational enterprises, the ILO version of which is regarded by U.S. labor and business as the most constructive yet developed
3. A framework in which the U.S. labor movement and business community can be in contact with their counterpart organizations throughout the world
4. Influence over ILO execution of UN Development Program projects, totaling about $47 million for 1986
5. An important forum in which the U.S. can carry on discussions with the Third World
6. Participation in the UN system's most effective mechanism for promoting the human rights of workers
7. Participation in the ILO's studies of development, which pioneered the basic human needs approach to development and directly influenced programs of the IBRD and AGENCY FOR INTERNATIONAL DEVELOPMENT (AID).

Membership Costs for the U.S. The U.S. contribution to the ILO was about $30.5 million in 1985.

Organization. The structure of the ILO consists of the following organizational elements.

1. *International Labor Conference:* The conference, which meets annually, serves as an international forum on social questions. It also develops international labor standards called conventions and recommendations. These standards, which are guides for countries to follow, form an international labor code that covers such questions as employment, freedom of association, hours of work, migration for employment, the protection of women and young workers, prevention of industrial accidents, workers' compensation, colonial labor problems, conditions of seamen, and social security. The only obligation on any country is to consider these standards, no country being obligated to adopt, accept, or ratify them.
2. *Governing body:* The executive council of the ILO, elected by the conference, is composed of 28 government, 14 management, and 14 labor representatives who meet quarterly. It supervises the work of the various industrial committees and commissions and the work of the International Labor Office. Ten governments held permanent seats on the governing body because of their industrial importance—Brazil, Canada, People's Republic of China, Federal Republic of Germany, France, India, Italy, Japan, U.S.S.R., and the United Kingdom—before the U.S. rejoined the ILO in 1980 and resumed its place in the organization.
3. *International Labor Office:* The office is the secretariat of the ILO and serves as a world information center and publishing house. In addition it operates the ILO's program of technical assistance in which hundreds of experts in such fields as vocational training, productivity, and handicrafts are assisting countries all over the world in their economic development efforts.

The ILO as of 1986 had a membership of 151 countries. Its headquarters in Geneva, Switzerland. The International Labor Office maintains three regional departments, one each in Africa (Addis Ababa), Asia and the Pacific (Bangkok), and Latin America and the Caribbean (Lima). Each regional department, in turn, maintains a network of area offices throughout its region. In addition there are other offices in 40 cities throughout the world, including Washington, Moscow, London, Bonn, Rome, and Tokyo.

INTERNATIONAL MONETARY FUND

BIBLIOGRAPHY

INTERNATIONAL LABOR ORGANIZATION. *ILO Information* (U.S. Edition). Published five times a year.

INTERNATIONAL MONETARY FUND Established concurrently with its companion institution, the INTERNATIONAL BANK FOR RECONSTRUCTION AND DEVELOPMENT, the International Monetary Fund (IMF) is closely identified with the IBRD in the Articles of Agreement, as membership in the fund is a prerequisite to membership in the IBRD. The Articles of Agreement of the IMF were formulated at the United Nations Monetary and Financial Conference held in Bretton Woods, New Hampshire, July 1-22, 1944, and came into force on December 27, 1945. An organizational meeting of the Board of Directors of the IMF was held March 8, 1946; the executive directors first met on May 6, 1946; and on December 18, 1946, the IMF announced its agreement to the establishment of par values in gold and U.S. dollars for the currencies of 32 of its members. On March 1, 1947, the fund announced readiness to commence exchange transactions.

Industrial countries who are members include:

Australia	Japan
Austria	Luxembourg
Belgium	Netherlands
Canada	New Zealand
Denmark	Norway
Finland	Spain
France	Sweden
Germany, Fed. Rep.	Switzerland
Iceland	United Kingdom
Ireland	United States
Italy	

The seven largest countries in this group in terms of GNP—Canada, the United States, Japan, France, the Federal Republic of Germany, Italy, and the United Kingdom—are collectively referred to as the major industrial countries.

The developing countries include all other fund members, together with certain essentially autonomous dependent territories for which adequate statistics are available.

Iceland
Ireland
Italy

Purposes. Its articles of agreement, state the following as the purposes of the IMF:

1. To promote international monetary cooperation through a permanent institution that provides the machinery for consultation and collaboration on international monetary problems
2. To facilitate the expansion and balanced growth of international trade, and to contribute thereby to the promotion and maintenance of high levels of employment and real income and to the development of the productive resources of all members as primary objectives of economic policy
3. To promote exchange stability, to maintain orderly exchange arrangements among members, and to avoid competitive exchange depreciation
4. To assist in the establishment of a multilateral system of payments in respect to current transactions between members and in the elimination of foreign exchange restrictions which hamper the growth of world trade
5. To give confidence to members by making the general resources of the IMF temporarily available to them under adequate s feguards, thus providing them with the opportunity to correct maladjustments in their balance of payments without resorting to measures destructive of national or international prosperity
6. In accordance with the above, to shorten the duration and lessen the degree of disequilibrium in the international balances of payments of members.

The International Monetary Fund is an organization of countries that seeks to promote international monetary cooperation and to facilitate the expansion of trade, thus contributing to increased employment and improved economic conditions in all member countries.

To achieve its purposes, the fund has a code of economic behavior for its members, makes financing available to members in balance-of-payments difficulties, and provides them with technical assistance to improve their economic management. As of 1987, the fund had 151 member countries, accounting for about four-fifths of total world production and 90% of world trade.

Member countries undertake to collaborate with the fund and with one another to assure orderly exchange arrangements and a stable system of exchange rates, together with a multilateral system of payments that is free from restrictions and thus promotes balance in the payments among countries. Members are free to choose the form of exchange arrangements that they intend to apply, subject to their obligations to the fund and to its surveillance of their exchange rate policies.

The fund maintains a large pool of financial resources that it makes available to member countries—temporarily and subject to conditions—to enable them to carry out programs to remedy their payments deficits without resorting to restrictive measures that would adversely affect national or international prosperity. Members make repayments to the fund so that its resources are used on a revolving basis and are continuously available to countries facing payments difficulties. The policy adjustments that countries make in connection with the use of fund resources support their creditworthiness and thus facilitate their access to credit from other official sources and from private financial markets.

Both the regulatory and the financing features of the fund's policies contribute to the promotion of adjustment of imbalances in members' international payments. These policies evolve in response to changing world economic conditions and the needs of fund members. They apply equally to all member countries, whether industrial or developing, whether their payments are in deficit or surplus, and regardless of their economic system.

To enable the fund to carry out its policies, member countries continuously supply it with a broad range of economic and financial information, and the fund consults regularly with each member country on its economic situation. The fund is therefore in a position to assist members in devising corrective steps when, or preferably before, problems arise in their balance of payments.

Having responsibilities for the international payments system, the fund is particularly concerned with global liquidity^that is, the level and composition of the reserves that members have available for meeting their trade and payments requirements. In 1969, the fund was given the responsibility for creating and allocating special drawing rights (SDRs), the only worldwide reserve asset established by international agreement.

The fund helps members coordinate their national economic policies internationally. In effect, it provides a permanent international monetary forum. The focus of the fund is not only on the problems of individual countries but also on the structure of the international monetary system and on the development of policies and strategies through which its members can work together to ensure a stable world financial system and sustainable economic growth.

Structure. The fund is based on an international treaty—its Articles of Agreement—that was drafted initially at a conference of 44 nations in 1944.

Membership in the fund is a prerequisite to membership in the World Bank (International Bank for Reconstruction and Development) and close working relationships exist between the two organizations, as well as between the fund and the GENERAL AGREEMENT ON TARIFFS AND TRADE (GATT) and the BANK FOR INTERNATIONAL SETTLEMENTS (BIS). The fund is a specialized agency within the United Nations system, cooperating with the UN on matters of mutual interest.

The work of the fund is carried out through a board of governors, an executive board, a managing director, and a staff. Each member country is represented by a governor and an alternate governor on the board of governors, the fund's highest authority, which meets annually and may cast ballots by mail or cable between meetings. A member country's voting power primarily reflects its contribution to the fund's financial resources, which in turn is related to its relative size in the world economy. The largest member, the U.S., has approximately 20% of the total voting power, and the smallest member countries each have considerably less than 1%.

The daily business of the fund is conducted by an executive board of 22 executive directors, chaired by the managing director, at its

ENCYCLOPEDIA OF BANKING AND FINANCE

headquarters in Washington, D.C. Among other duties, the executive board acts on requests by members for financial assistance, conducts consultations with members, takes decisions on general fund policies, and makes recommendations to the board of governors on matters requiring a vote of the governors, such as the admission of new members and increases in the fund's resources.

The five members having the largest voting power^the U.S., the United Kingdom, the Federal Republic of Germany, France, and Japan—each appoint an executive director. In addition, the fund's two largest creditor members may appoint an executive director if they are not among the five members having the largest voting power; as of 1987, Saudi Arabia appointed an executive director on this basis. Sixteen executive directors are elected for two-year terms by groups of other member countries. The elections take place in alternate years at the time of the annual meeting.

Since the early 1970s, the international monetary system has undergone major changes. During this period, the board of governors has been advised by special committees of its members. The first such group, the Committee on Reform of the International Monetary System and Related Issues (the "Committee of 20"), negotiated for two years without achieving a plan for comprehensive reform of the system, but in 1974 it recommended a series of immediate steps in a process of evolutionary reform. Further negotiation in a successor body, the Interim Committee on the International Monetary System, led to the Second Amendment of the Articles of Agreement, which entered into force April 1, 1978.

The interim committee, a 22-member ministerial-level group with a structure paralleling that of the executive board, meets two or three times a year, keeping under review world economic conditions, the international monetary system, and the role of the fund.

The executive board appoints the fund's managing director, who serves both as its chairman and as chief of the operating staff of the fund, with a five-year term of office.

The professional and administrative staff of the fund is composed of international civil servants, appointed by and owing their duty exclusively to the fund. The fund's professional staff consists primarily of economists, but there are among others accountants and legal experts. They are recruited on a wide geographical basis from the fund's member countries. The staff numbers about 1,800, located mainly at the Washington, D.C. headquarters.

The staff is organized in five area departments (for Africa, Asia, Europe, the Middle East, and the Western Hemisphere) and a number of other departments (administration, central banking, exchange and trade relations, external relations, fiscal affairs, IMF institute, legal, research, secretary's, and treasurer's). In addition, there is a Bureau of Language Services a Bureau of Statistics and a Bureau of Computing Services. The fund also maintains small permanent offices in Paris and Geneva and at the United Nations in New York.

Surveillance of Exchange Policies. The fund has the responsibility to ensure the effective operation of the international monetary system. To that end, it oversees the compliance of members with their obligations to collaborate with the fund and with one another to ensure orderly exchange arrangements and to promote a stable system of exchange rates. Members must direct their policies toward orderly economic growth with reasonable price stability and foster orderly underlying conditions for economic and financial stability.

In order to carry out its responsibility, the fund exercises surveillance over the exchange rate policies of members. For this purpose the fund has adopted principles for the guidance of members' exchange policies and has established procedures by which it exercises surveillance. These principles and procedures are designed to identify and encourage the correction of inappropriate exchange rate policies.

In choosing the form of exchange arrangements that they wish to apply, member countries may allow the exchange rate of their currency to fluctuate or they may adopt arrangements that keep the exchange rate fixed in terms of other currencies. Such arrangements include pegging the exchange rate of a currency to the rate of another currency, to the SDR (special drawing right)—which is valued in terms of a basket of 5 currencies—or to some other basket of currencies. Yet another type of exchange arrangement is that of the EUROPEAN MONETARY SYSTEM, under which a group of countries observe fixed margins for the currencies within the group and allow the rates for these currencies to fluctuate with respect to currencies outside the group.

Consultation. The fund conducts a consultation with the member countries—in principle, annually—to appraise the members' economic and financial situations and policies. Consultations are a primary means through which the fund fulfills its obligation to exercise surveillance of members' exchange rate policies. They also help to keep the fund in a position to deal promptly with members' requests to use fund resources and with proposed changes in exchange practices that are subject to approval by the fund. Members also provide the fund with a steady flow of information on their economies, some of which is disseminated to the public in the fund's publications.

Consultations begin with meetings in the member country between fund staff and representatives of the member government. On the basis of these discussions, the staff prepares a report for the executive board. Consultations end with a conclusion formulated by the managing director, expressing the views of the fund on the member's economic situation and policies, and this conclusion is transmitted to the member government by the fund.

Recent years have been marked by unusually severe problems of international indebtedness resulting from persistent high rates of inflation and low utilization of productive capacity in many member countries. These global problems increasingly have required that members seek to coordinate their domestic economic policies at the international level. In order to contribute to this effort, the fund staff conducts special consultations from time to time with members whose policies are of major importance to the world economy. This is done in preparation for the frequent reviews of the world economic outlook by the executive board and the discussions of the world economy at the meetings of the interim committee and the board of governors.

The reviews of the world economic outlook are a principal means by which the executive board monitors developments in the international monetary system and the consequences for the world economy that arise from economic policies of major countries and groups of countries. These reviews, published annually under the title *World Economic Outlook* also help to ensure a better functioning of the international monetary system by bringing into focus the need for coordinating the policies of members, as well as by providing the means for coordination.

Quotas and Resources. The fund's system of quotas is one of its central features. Quotas are used to determine the voting power of members, their contribution to the fund's resources, their access to these resources, and their share in allocations of SDRs. A member's quota reflects its economic size in relation to the total membership of the fund. Each member pays a subscription to the fund equivalent to its quota, and the board of governors decides on the proportion to be paid in SDRs or in the member's currency.

Quotas of all fund members are reviewed at intervals of not more than five years. Several general increases have been agreed on in the past to bring fund quotas into line with the growth of the world economy and the need for additional international liquidity, while special increases from time to time have been agreed on to adjust for differing rates of growth among members and for changes in their relative economic positions. Increases in the total of fund quotas include the addition of quotas of new members, as well as general and special increases. The next review is scheduled for completion in 1988.

As a result of members' payments of subscriptions, the fund holds substantial resources in members' currencies and SDRs, which are available to meet member countries' temporary balance-of-payments needs. As of 1988, these subscriptions amounted to the equivalent of SDR 90 billion (about U.S. $117 billion, based on the average rate for 1987 of SDR 1 = U.S. $1.30). Under previous arrangements, the fund received gold from its members, chiefly in payment of subscriptions. Nearly 50 million ounces of the fund's gold has been sold in 1976-1980 under a program reflecting agreement to reduce the monetary role of gold; about 100 million ounces remained as of 1987.

The fund may supplement its resources by borrowing. As of 1987, the fund has a number of borrowing agreements in effect in order to meet members' supplementary financing needs that could not be met from the fund's own resources. In addition, under the general arrangements to borrow, ten industrial member countries—with Switzerland, a nonmember of the fund and, through a special arrangement, Saudi Arabia included—stand ready to lend to the fund to meet the balance-of-payments requirements of any one of them. These arrangements have been used when needed and extended periodically since they were first agreed to in 1962, and they permit a maximum credit to the

INTERNATIONAL MONETARY FUND

fund equivalent to about SDR 6.5 billion (about U.S. $8.5 billion) in lenders' currencies.

Financial Facilities. The financial resources of the fund are available under a variety of permanent and temporary facilities to help members meet balance-of-payments needs.

When a member uses the fund's resources under any of these facilities, the mechanics of the transaction are as follows. The member uses its own currency to purchase from the fund an equivalent amount of the currencies of other members, or SDRs. The currencies or SDRs drawn from the fund are used to finance the drawing member's balance-of-payments deficit. After a member has made a drawing, the fund holds more of the member's currency and less of the currency drawn or of the SDRs.

Within a specified period, or earlier if the member's balance of payments and reserve position improve, the member must repurchase from the fund its own currency that it paid to make the drawing. In repurchasing, the member uses SDRs or the currencies of other members specified by the fund.

When a member country's currency is used by other members, the fund's holdings of the currency may fall below the amount of the member's quota. This results in the member's having a reserve position in the fund that is termed the reserve tranche. This amount is highly liquid, and if it is drawn upon the drawings need not be repurchased. If the fund's holdings of the member's currency fall below a specified level, the fund pays remuneration to the member for the use of its currency. The rate of remuneration is related to short-term money market interest rates and is reviewed quarterly by the fund.

Basic credit and extended facilities: Under the fund's basic facility, the credit tranches, a member may normally draw up to the amount of its quota, thus raising the fund's holdings of its currency from the equivalent of its quota up to 200% of this amount. When a member country suffers from structural imbalances in production, trade, or prices, so that adjustment requires a longer period and larger resources than are normally permitted under basic credit policies, the member may make use of the extended facility, under which it may purchase up to 110% of its quota.

Drawings are generally made under lines of credit called standby or extended arrangements, depending on whether the basic or extended facility is used. Under a standby arrangement, drawings normally take place over a period of one year but may also be made over a period of up to three years; under the extended facility, drawings are usually made over a period of three years. Under the basic facility, repurchases must begin three years after the drawings and be completed within five years after drawings are made; under the extended facility, repurchases begin after four years and end no later than ten years after the drawings.

Drawings under all permanent facilities, except for reserve positions, are subject to a one-time service charge of 0.5%, plus a charge at an annual rate that rises with the length of time during which the drawing is not repaid. These charges are maintained at lower levels than market interest rates, in keeping with the fund's policies under which members cooperate to promote balance-of-payments adjustment.

The income that the fund receives from charges on drawings under its permanent facilities is used to pay remuneration to creditor countries for the use of their currencies and to meet the fund's operating costs. Any surplus may be used to increase remuneration or reduce charges, or it may be added to the fund's regular resources or distributed to its members in proportion to their quotas. If there is a deficit in any six-month period, the fund is required to review all aspects of its financial position, including the rate of remuneration and its charges.

When a member receives financial assistance under the basic and extended facilities, it must adopt a program to overcome its payments imbalance. This aspect of fund policies is known as conditionality. As a minimum, a member is expected to show the fund that it is making a reasonable effort to overcome its difficulties. If a member's balance-of-payments need grows larger in relation to the size of its quota, a greater adjustment effort is likely to be required to remedy the imbalance, and the program that the member agrees on with the fund therefore requires more substantial justification. Under such circumstances, the fund's financial assistance is disbursed in installments according to performance under the program. Performance is measured by broad economic and financial criteria such as the member's policies regarding credit, government financing, external borrowing, and trade and payments restrictions.

The fund encourages members developing payments problems to promptly adopt corrective measures that can be supported by fund resources. Early action is emphasized because as a country's economic and financial imbalances become widespread and deep-seated, it must usually take more basic, and therefore more difficult, steps to correct them. In helping members to devise adjustment programs, the fund pays due regard to their domestic, social, and political objectives, economic priorities, and circumstances.

Special facilities: The fund makes resources available under two permanent special-purpose arrangements—the compensatory and the buffer stock financing facilities—and under a temporary supplementary financing facility.

Compensatory financing is available to members facing payments difficulties resulting from temporary shortfalls in their export earnings that are largely due to conditions beyond their control, such as falling commodity prices and natural disasters, including bad weather. Buffer stock financing assists members having payments difficulties to finance their contributions to international buffer stocks that are maintained to stabilize world markets for commodities such as tin, and rubber. Charges for drawings under these two permanent facilities follow the same schedule as those for basic credit facility drawings.

To meet particular needs, temporary facilities have sometimes been established. For example, members drew SDR 6.9 billion (about U.S. $9 billion) under temporary oil facilities set up to help meet balance-of-payments needs resulting from higher oil prices in 1974 and 1975. During 1979-1984, the fund made further resources available under its supplementary financing facility to assist members facing payments imbalances that were large in relation to their quotas. Resources under this facility are provided in conjunction with drawings under the basic credit and extended facilities.

Special drawing rights: The SDR is an international reserve asset created by the fund in light of the global need to supplement existing reserve assets. SDRs were created in 1969 under the First Amendment of the Articles of Agreement, in response to widespread concern over the adequacy of the growth of international liquidity. It is the declared intention of member countries that the SDR should eventually become the principal reserve asset in the international monetary system.

Allocations of SDRs are made in proportion to their quotas to member countries that are participants in the special drawing rights department. The first allocations of SDRs, totaling SDR 9.3 billion, were made in the years 1970 to 1972. Allocations of SDRs were resumed with the creation of SDR 4 billion on January 1, 1979. A further SDR 4 billion was allocated on January 1, 1980. After another allocation of SDR 4 billion on January 1, 1981, SDRs in existence totaled SDR 21.3 billion, about 4% of prevailing international reserves, excluding gold.

The method of valuation of the SDR is determined by the fund. The SDR has been valued on the basis of market exchange rates for a basket of currencies. As of 1982, the basket consisted of the currencies of the 5 members with the largest share in world exports. Each business day, the fund publishes the exchange rates of a wide range of currencies in terms of the SDR, and these are reported by a number of daily newspapers and wire services as well as in the fund's twice-monthly *IMF Survey* and in *International Financial Statistics*, its monthly statistical publication.

A participant may use SDRs without limitation, in a wide and increasing variety of ways by agreement with another participant—for example, to obtain currency in a spot transaction, for the settlement of a financial obligation, as a loan, as security for a loan, as a swap against currency, or in a forward exchange operation. In addition, if a participant has a balance-of-payments need, it can use its SDRs to obtain usable currency from another participant designated by the fund. A participant may also use SDRs to make payments to the fund, such as repurchases, and the fund itself may transfer SDRs to a participant for various purposes, including transferring SDRs instead of currency to a member using the fund's resources.

A participant with holdings of SDRs in excess of its allocations earns net interest on the excess, and a participant with holdings below its allocations pays charges at the same rate on its net use of SDRs. The interest rate on the SDR is related to the short-term money market interest rates and is calculated weekly.

The SDR is the unit of account for all purposes of the fund. Outside the fund it is widely used as a unit of account in private contracts, such as SDR-denominated deposits with commercial banks, as well as in international and regional organizations including the African

INTERNATIONAL MONETARY FUND

Development Bank, the ASIAN DEVELOPMENT BANK, the Arab Monetary Fund, the Asian Clearing Union, the Economic Community of West African States, the Islamic Development Bank, and the Nordic Investment Bank.

A number of the fund's member countries have decided to peg their currency to the SDR. The value of the currency is fixed in terms of the SDR, then set in terms of other currencies by reference to their SDR values as calculated daily by the fund.

Gold Sales and Trust Fund. Efforts in recent years to reform the international monetary system have included steps to gradually reduce the monetary role of gold. These measures included abolishing the official price of gold and any requirement that members make payments to the fund in gold. In addition, the sale of 50 million ounces of gold^one-third of the fund's gold holdings at the time the agreement was reached on August 31, 1975^was undertaken in a four-year program through May, 1980.

Half of the gold (25 million ounces) was sold directly at the former official price of SDR 35 an ounce to the countries that were members of the fund at the time of the agreement. These sales were completed in early 1980.

The other 25 million ounces were being sold for the benefit of developing countries in public auctions from June, 1976, through May, 1980. Each of the 104 eligible developing countries received part of the profits from these gold sales directly, according to the ratio of its quota to total fund quotas as of August 31, 1975. The remaining profits financed concessionary loans from a trust fund, which was established to provide additional balance-of-payments assistance to developing countries that were eligible because of their low per capita income and qualified for assistance on the basis of adjustment programs agreed to with the fund.

The appended table shows the currency units per SDR as of March and April 1989.

Technical Assistance. Member countries of the fund in various stages of development make use of its technical assistance on many subjects related to improving the management of their economies. Experts sent to member countries by the fund advise on central and general banking; fiscal, monetary, and balance-of-payments policies and statistics; accounting, exchange, and trade systems; and operational aspects of fund transactions and policies.

The fund has provided technical services at the request of members since its earliest years, and at present technical assistance is provided through consultations, special technical assistance missions, resident representatives from the fund staff, and experts recruited from outside the fund. The Central Banking Department, the Fiscal Affairs Department, and the IMF Institute were established in 1964 to broaden and coordinate the increasing technical assistance given by the fund; the Central Banking Department and the Fiscal Affairs Department participate in a wide range of other fund activities.

The IMF Institute is a department of the fund whose purpose is to improve the expertise of officials from member countries in the use of modern tools of economic analysis, in the management of economies, and in fund procedures and policies. Training courses on financial analysis and policy, balance-of-payments methodology, and public finance are conducted at the fund's headquarters in Arabic, English, French, and Spanish. Some 5,000 officials from nearly every member country have completed such courses since the founding of the IMF Institute, which also provides assistance in its areas of competence to regional and national training centers.

Publications. The fund has an active publications program that includes regular and special reports, statistical bulletins, books, periodicals, and pamphlets. The purpose of the program is to further the fund's work and to carry out its obligation to act as a center for the collection and exchange of information on monetary and financial problems.

The *Annual Report* of the executive board to the board of governors, published in September for use at the annual meeting, reviews the fund's activities and presents an up-to-date analysis of developments in the world economy and in the international monetary system.

The *Annual Report on Exchange Arrangements and Exchange Restrictions*, published in August, reviews developments in exchange restrictions and trade practices having direct implications for the balance of payments of member countries. It includes country-by-country descriptions of the exchange systems of most countries of the world.

The fund is a principal source of internationally comparable

International Monetary Fund Members and Quotas, June 1987
(In millions of SDRs)

Afghanistan	86.7
Algeria	623.1
Antigua and Barbuda	5.0
Argentina	1,113.0
Australia	1,619.2
Austria	775.6
Bahamas, The	66.4
Bahrain	48.9
Bangladesh	287.5
Barbados	34.1
Belgium	2,080.4
Belize	9.5
Benin	31.3
Bhutan	2.5
Bolivia	90.7
Botswana	22.1
Brazil	1,461.3
Burkina Faso	31.6
Burma	137.0
Burundi	42.7
Cameroon	92.7
Canada	2,941.0
Cape Verde	4.5
Central African Republic	30.4
Chad	30.6
Chile	440.5
China	2,390.9
Colombia	394.2
Comoros	4.5
Congo	37.3
Costa Rica	84.1
Cote d'Ivoire	165.5
Cyprus	69.7
Denmark	711.0
Djibouti	8.0
Dominica	4.0
Dominican Republic	112.1
Ecuador	150.7
Egypt	463.4
El Salvador	89.0
Equatorial Guinea	18.4
Ethiopia	70.6
Fiji	36.5
Finland	574.9
France	4,482.8
Gabon	73.1
Gambia, The	17.1
Germany	5,403.7
Ghana	204.5
Greece	399.9
Grenada	6.0
Guatemala	108.0
Guinea	57.9
Guinea-Bissau	7.5
Guyana	49.2
Haiti	44.1
Honduras	67.8
Hungary	530.7
Iceland	59.6
India	2,207.7
Indonesia	1,009.0
Iran, Islamic Republic of	660.0
Iraq	504.0
Ireland	343.4
Israel	446.6
Italy	2,909.1
Jamaica	145.5
Japan	4,223.3
Jordan	73.9
Kampuchea, Democratic	25.0
Kenya	142.0
Kiribati	2.5
Korea	462.8
Kuwait	635.3

INTERNATIONAL MONETARY FUND

Lebanon	78.7
Lesotho	15.1
Liberia	71.3
Libya	515.7
Luxembourg	77.0
Madagascar	66.4
Malawi	37.2
Malaysia	550.6
Maldives	2.0
Mali	50.8
Malta	45.1
Mauritania	33.9
mauritius	53.6
Mexico	1,165.5
Morocco	306.6
Mozambique, People's Republic of	61.0
Nepal	37.3
Netherlands	2,264.8
New Zealands	461.6
Nicaragua	68.2
Niger	33.7
Nigeria	849.5
Norway	699.0
Oman	63.1
Pakistan	546.3
Panama	102.2
Papua New Guinea	65.9
Paraguay	48.4
Peru	330.9
Philippines	440.4
Poland	680.0
Portugal	376.6
Qatar	114.9
Romania	523.4
Rwanda	43.8
St. Christopher and Nevis	4.5
St. Lucia	7.5
St. Vincent	4.0
Saudi Arabia	3,202.4
Senegal	85.1
Seychelles	3.0
Singapore	92.4
Solomon Islands	5.0
Somalia	44.2
South Africa	915.7
Spain	1,286.0
Sri Lanka	223.0
Sudan	169.7
Surinam	49.3
Swaziland	24.7
Sweden	1,064.3
Syrian Arab Republic	139.1
Tanzania	107.0
Thailand	386.6
Togo	38.4
Tonga	3.25
Trinidad and Tobago	170.1
Tunisia	138.2
Turkey	429.1
Uganda	99.6
United Arab Emirates	202.6
United Kingdom	6,194.0
United States	17,918.3
Uruguay	163.8
Vannuatu	9.0
Venezuela	1,371.5
Viet Nam	176.8
Western Samoa	6.0
Yemen Arab Republic	43.3
Yugoslavia	613.0
Zaïre	291.0
Zambia	270.3
Zimbabwe	191.0
TOTAL	**89,987.55**

Source: International Monetary Fund.

statistics on national economies, including financial and economic data that are relevant to the analysis of countries' monetary and payments problems. Consequently, statistical publications form a major part of the fund's publications program. In addition to each country's transactions and operations with the fund, the statistics published include data on exchange rates, international reserves, money and banking, prices, production, external trade, wages and employment, balance of payments, government finance, and national accounts. These areas are all covered in the monthly and annual issues of *International Financial Statistics,* which is published in English, French, and Spanish. The *Balance of Payments Manual* (fourth edition, 1977) specifies the methodology to be used by member countries in computing and reporting balance-of-payments data; the detailed data collected by the fund are given in the monthly and annual issues of the *Balance of Payments Yearbook.* Detailed data on government finance statistics are given in the *Government Finance Statistics Yearbook,* and data on external trade are included in the monthly and annual issues of *Directions of Trade.* Computer tape subscriptions to each of these statistical publications are available.

By having a repository of knowledge on economic and financial matters and maintaining close relations with its members, the fund is well placed to carry out a program of research into economic and financial problems. The results of some of these studies are published in *Staff Papers,* the quarterly economic journal of the fund.

The *IMF Survey,* published twice a month in English, French, and Spanish, reports developments in the fund and the international monetary system in the broader context of world economic and financial news, including changes in countries' policies. A quarterly magazine, *Finance and Development,* published jointly by the fund and the World Bank, carries articles on topics related to the interests of the two institutions.

Recent developments. The 1970s and 1980s provided the most demanding economic challenges of the fund's 40-year history. The collapse of the Bretton Woods par value system and the dramatic rise in oil prices during the 1970s and 1980s brought a reasonably successful response from the IMF. The international debt crisis of the 1980s that resulted when a number of heavily indebted developing countries were unable to repay what they owed to commercial banks and to governments of member countries was equally difficult to deal with. The fund provided loans on an unprecedented scale to support the economic reorganization of such countries by acting as intermediary between debtor countries and their creditors and by participating in efforts to restructure the debt. The fund was able to stabilize the international monetary system. The fund continued its involvement in the debt crisis throughout the 1980s, during which period it began a program of lending at highly concessional interest rates, in conjunction with the World Bank and other lenders, to member countries undertaking comprehensive restructuring of their economies to eliminate protracted difficulties in meeting international payments. Low rates of interest and long payback periods have made this structural adjustment facility attractive. As a result, the fund has enlarged the scope of the program by soliciting additional financing—about $12 billion—from the fund's better-off members.

In the 1980s, the International Monetary Fund has exerted major efforts in dealing with the international debt problem. The IMF has made available SDR 30 billion of its resources in supporting its adjustment programs in 70 member countries and has arranged financial packages for debtor countries from governments, commercial banks, and other financial institutions. In 1985, U.S. Secretary of the Treasury James Baker made a proposal to coordinate international efforts to deal with the debt problems of developing countries. In June 1987, the leaders of seven major industrial nations at the periodic Economic Summit in Venice agreed to improve structures for coordinating their country's policies and to provide further financial assistance to debt-ridden developing countries.

Summary. After the original Bretton Woods par value system broke down in 1971, following the discontinuance in August, 1971, of the gold window by the U.S. for convertibility into gold of foreign official dollar holdings and the subsequent attempt in the Smithsonian Agreement to revive the par value system with a widened band of permitted fluctuation around the pars (December, 1971), the ensuing period of increased exchange rate fluctuation and the beginning in 1973 of free-floating and managed-floating exchange rates led to fears of a return to competitive rate depreciation and other beggar-thy-neighbor practices that would have adversely affected international trade and capital flows as in pre-World War II years.

As long as it lasted, the par value system on the Bretton Woods model unquestionably fostered a substantial expansion in international trade and investment by providing the necessary international environment of relative exchange rate stability, minimization of trade barriers and restrictive practices, and a source of liquidity to help overcome short-term balance-of-payments imbalances. These advantages deserved preservation if possible. Thus when the new Article IV of the Articles of Agreement of the IMF concerning exchange rate arrangements was adopted, allowing members to select a wide variety of exchange rate systems, including free-floating and managed-floating exchange rates, and continuing the role of the IMF in providing conditional and unconditional liquidity, the continuance of the International Monetary Fund as one of the cornerstones of the international monetary system was assured.

Publications. The IMF publishes many authoritative reports, papers, books, and other publications.

Reports and other documents (free)
   Annual report of the executive board for the financial year
   Annual report on exchange arrangements and exchange restrictions
   Bylaws, rules and regulations
   Selected decisions of the international monetary fund and selected documents
   Summary proceedings of the annual meeting of the board of governors.
Subscription publications
   Balance of payment statistics
   Direction of trade statistics
   Government finance statistics yearbook
   International financial statistics
   Staff papers
Occasional papers
World economic and financial surveys

See GOLD STANDARD, INCOMES POLICY, INTERNATIONAL BALANCE OF PAYMENTS.

BIBLIOGRAPHY

CELARIER, M. "Debt Relief Gains Ground." *United States Banker*, December, 1988.
EVANS, J., and TOBIN, M. "Bad Debt and Bad Blood." *Euromoney*, September, 1988.
"Japan Takes Over the IMF." *Euromoney*, September, 1988.
POWNALL, R., and STUART, B. "The IMF's Compensatory and Contingency Financing Facility." *Finance and Development*, December, 1988.
INTERNATIONAL MONETARY FUND, *The Role and Function of the International Monetary Fund*, (Washington: International Monetary Fund, 1985)
"The Dollar's Berlin Wall." *Economist*, October 1, 1988.
"Wither the Fund?" *Economist*, September 24, 1988.

INTERNATIONAL MONEY ORDERS *See* MONEY ORDERS.

INTERNATIONAL SECURITIES
Bonds or stocks that enjoy a ready market on the principal securities exchanges of various nations, known as "internationals." The term also refers to bonds and stocks whose interest or dividend is payable in the financial centers of two or more countries.

By means of the arrangements making possible AMERICAN DEPOSITARY RECEIPTS, American shares, and New York shares, an increased number of foreign equities are traded on the New York Stock Exchange, American Stock Exchange, and the over-the-counter markets in the U.S., in addition to regularly listed shares of foreign companies. Also on the NYSE bond list, but not classified as foreign, are Eurodollar bonds, which are obligations of foreign subsidiaries of American corporations sold abroad but guaranteed by the parent company.

The American Stock Exchange has an even larger number of foreign stocks traded, particularly a large number of Canadian issues.

Where exchange restrictions do not interfere, "internationals" traded on more than one market may be subjected to arbitrage transactions, allowing for foreign exchange, commissions, and other applicable charges where price differentials justify. Such trading, however, is highly specialized and requires intimate knowledge of the markets concerned and their practices.

INTERNATIONAL TRADE *See* FOREIGN TRADE.

BIBLIOGRAPHY

BAIR, F. E. *International Marketing Handbook*, Three volumes. Gale Research Co., Detroit, MI, 1985.
International Tax Planner's Manual. Commerce Clearing House, Inc., New York, NY. Annual.
WALTER, I., and MURRAY, W. *Handbook of International Business.* John Wiley and Sons, Inc., New York, NY, 1982.

INTERNATIONAL TRADE ADMINISTRATION
Established January 2, 1980, in connection with a major overhaul of the federal government's international trade functions. The reorganization sought to expand exports, improve enforcement of U.S. trade laws, and upgrade government trade activities in line with the Multilateral Trade Negotiations (MTN) agreements signed by the U.S. in 1979.

The Department of Commerce already had major responsibilities in export promotion, trade adjustment assistance, and export control. Under the reorganization, the department assumed responsibility for all nonagricultural trade policy implementation.

As a result of the realignment of responsibilities, the former Industry and Trade Administration was abolished and its functions redistributed. Supervision of the new International Trade Administration (ITA) was vested in a deputy secretary and under-secretary for international trade. The agency's role in export promotion was strengthened by assigning it the responsibility for U.S. commercial attachés in most major countries. Commercial attachés had formerly been responsible to the State Department. The secretary of Commerce was designated an ex officio nonvoting member of the board of the EXPORT-IMPORT BANK. In addition the Commerce Department was assigned responsibility for implementation of trade agreements.

The department's analytical capability was increased, and import remedy responsibilities such as antidumping investigations, imposition of countervailing duties and embargoes, and national security trade investigations were assigned to the department. Most of these responsibilities had formerly been in the Treasury Department.

The ITA's activities are divided into three principal areas, each directed by an assistant secretary.

The international economic policy section is concerned with research, analysis, and development of departmental programs on international trade, investment, and services. It provides direction and coordination for the department's international economic policy. It has primary responsibility for monitoring and implementing the *Multilateral Trade Negotiations* that were concluded in 1979.

The trade administration section deals with import and export administration issues, including export licensing and enforcement. It monitors certain critical items and imposes export controls on them if supplies are threatened. Offices within the trade administration section formulate and implement antidumping and countervailing duty policy and regulate bilateral import agreements that support the economic well-being of domestic industry.

The trade development section develops programs to expand exports. Programs include direct assistance to U.S. firms and promotional projects such as trade missions to foreign countries and development of trade centers. These activities are carried out by the U.S. and foreign commercial services. The Office of Export Development provides the commercial services, local trade promotion entities, and individual businesses with technical and analytical support. The U.S. Commercial Service, through its district offices, furnishes information, technical assistance, and counseling to the local business community.

In addition, the Commerce Department manages the Foreign Commercial Service, which assists U.S. traders in countries around the world and gathers information on foreign commercial and industrial trends for the benefit of the U.S. business community.

See COMMERCE, DEPARTMENT OF; GENERAL AGREEMENT ON TARIFFS AND TRADE; UNITED STATES INTERNATIONAL TRADE COMMISSION.

INTERNATIONAL TRADE COMMISSION *See* UNITED STATES INTERNATIONAL TRADE COMMISSION.

INTERNATIONAL TRADE ORGANIZATION The charter for this international specialized agency affiliated with the United Nations was drawn up at the United Nations conference on trade and employment in Havana, Cuba, held November 21, 1947-March 24, 1948, and hence it is known as the Havana Charter. Pending ratification by nations of the Havana Charter, a provisional international trade and tariffs agreement along multilateral lines, the GENERAL AGREEMENT ON TARIFFS AND TRADE (GATT) was negotiated in 1947. Membership by the U.S. was considered vital for the International Trade Organization (ITO) Charter; thus its rejection by the U.S. Senate in 1950 and a decision by the U.S. not to press further for its ratification led to its abandonment. Instead, the GATT became effective as an international code of trade and TARIFF rules without a formal permanent organization and secretariat.

In 1955, the GATT signatories again revived the proposal to provide a permanent organization to administer the GATT, to be called the Organization for Trade Cooperation (OTC). The OTC organization was to consist of a secretariat, an executive committee of 17 members, and an assembly of all the nations signing the GATT. This permanent administrative body would have had the power to deal with trade disputes or complaints for violations of the GATT in an executive and judicial capacity. The ITO protocol was signed by a representative of the U.S. State Department on March 21, 1955, conditional upon congressional ratification, which, as in the case of the ITO Charter, was never obtained, although the protocol was submitted to the Congress with presidential recommendation April 14, 1955. Accordingly, the GATT has continued as the active instrument of international multilateral tariff concessions and elimination of trade restrictions.

INTERNATIONAL WHEAT AGREEMENT First effected on August 1, 1949, and subsequently revised, renewed, or extended in 1953, 1956, 1959, 1962, 1965, 1966, 1967, 1968, 1971, 1974, 1975, and 1976. Fifty-four nations plus the European Economic Community were members of the Wheat Trade Convention, while seventeen governments plus the European Economic Community were members of the Food Aid Convention.

The International Wheat Agreement was composed of two conventions, the Wheat Trade Convention and the Food Aid Convention. Fifty-four nations plus the European Economic Community are members of the Wheat Trade Convention, while 17 governments plus the European Economic Community are members of the Food Aid Convention.

The Wheat Trade Convention contained no economic provisions on maximum or minimum prices, or purchase and supply obligations, because of disagreement (culminating in the termination of negotiations in February, 1979) among developing countries as to the proposed wheat prices and the size of wheat stocks. Consequently, as renewed, the Wheat Trade Convention was purely consultative in nature, with its main function being to continue the operation of the INTERNATIONAL WHEAT COUNCIL (IWC). The IWC is an administrative body that conducts annual reviews of the world wheat situation and provides statistical information to member governments.

The Food Aid Convention, on the other hand, provided for pledges of minimum annual levels of food aid to developing countries, including the U.S. pledge of 1.8 million metric tons (well below the 4.7 million metric tons provided by the U.S. through its P.L. 480 and other bilateral programs) and the European Economic Community's pledge of 1.287 million metric tons.

Renewal of the 1971 International Wheat Agreement to June, 1983, again on a purely consultative basis, occurred at meeting of the International Wheat Council on June 29-July 2, 1981, when an agreement on minimum food aid for developing countries was also reached as part of the extension.

INTERPOLATION In investment practice, the method of obtaining a desired intermediate YIELD or price from a given series of yields or values in bond yield tables. The ordinary method of interpolation, called the straight line method, calculates the desired intermediate figure by simple proportion from its relation to the next nearest upper and lower given figures, known as the bracketing figures.

For example, a 10-year 5% bond is bought at 93 5/8 (93.63 rounded). The bond yield table shows a 5.80% yield at a price of 93.99, and a 5.90% yield at a price of 93.27. What is the yield at a price of 93.63?

Price	% Yield
93.99	5.80
93.63	?
93.27	5.90

According to the bond yield table, for the decrease of 0.72 in price, there is an increase of 0.10% in yield; thus the proportional difference in the yield x is computed as follows.

$$0.72 : 0.10 + 0.36 : x$$

$$x = \frac{0.10 \times 0.36}{0.72} = 0.05$$

Therefore 5.80% + 0.05% = 5.85%, or 5.90% − 0.05% = 5.85%. *See* BOND VALUES TABLE.

INTERSTATE COMMERCE ACT The statutory basis for regulation by the INTERSTATE COMMERCE COMMISSION of U.S. transportation (railroads, motor carriers, water carriers, express companies, sleeping-car companies, and freight forwarders). It was originally enacted to regulate railroads as the Act to Regulate Commerce of February 4, 1887 (24 Stat. 379, 383; 49 U.S.C. 1-22), which established the Interstate Commerce Commission as the pioneer federal administrative agency.

The original act consisted of less than ten pages. It was confined to the regulation of interstate commerce by railroad, or partly by railroad and partly by water. The main objective was to remove discrimination, preference, and prejudice in localities, services, rates, fares, and charges. Since that 1887 original act, there have been the following major amendments to the Interstate Commerce Act.

The Elkins Act, 1903, dealt with discrimination and with deviation from published tariffs of carriers' rates and charges.

The Mann-Elkins Act, 1910, authorized the commission to suspend and investigate new rate proposals. It also established the Commerce Court, which had exclusive original jurisdiction to review commission orders and from which appeal could be taken directly to the U.S. Supreme Court. The court failed to operate successfully and was abolished in 1913.

The Panama Canal Act, 1912, prohibited railroads from continuing ownership or operation of water lines when competition would thereby be lessened. It also authorized the commission to establish routes and rates for combination rail-water movements.

The Esch Car Service Act, 1917, authorized the commission to determine the reasonableness of freight car service rules, prescribe rules in place of those found unreasonable, and in time of emergency suspend the car service rules and direct the car supply to fit the circumstances.

The TRANSPORTATION ACT OF 1920 ended the federal government's control of the railroads in World War I. It gave the commission authority to fix minimum as well as maximum rates, broadened its authority to prescribe intrastate rates when necessary to remove discrimination against interstate commerce, authorized the ICC to regulate the amount and terms of capital security issues of railroads, and provided that railroads must obtain ICC approval for the construction and operation of new lines and for the abandonment of existing lines. The act directed the ICC to devise a program for merging the nation's railroads, but the plan that was developed was never carried out. Finally, it established the number of commissioners at eleven, the number in effect currently being five.

The Motor Carrier Act of 1935 brought motor carriers of property and passengers under the commission's jurisdiction. It became Part II of the Interstate Commerce Act.

The Transportation Acts of 1940 and 1942 brought coastal, intercoastal, and inland water carriers and freight forwarders under ICC jurisdiction, as Part III and Part IV of the act.

The Reed-Bulwinkle Act, 1948, which added Section 5a to the Interstate Commerce Act, permitted common carriers by rail, motor, and water, and freight forwarders subject to the act to join in collective rate-making practices under agreements approved by the commission. Parties to approved agreements are relieved from operation of the ANTITRUST LAWS.

The Transportation Act of 1958 authorized the guaranty of commercial loans to railroads (for a limited period), amended the rule of rate-making, removed the "exempt" status from certain commodities transported by motor carriers, and authorized the ICC to rule upon discontinuance of rail passenger service.

The Department of Transportation Act, effective April 1, 1967, created the U.S. Department of Transportation and transferred to it the jurisdiction over carrier safety practices previously vested in the ICC.

The Rail Passenger Act of 1970 gave the commission the responsibility for establishing and enforcing standards of adequate service by railroads operating intercity passenger trains.

The Regional Rail Reorganization Act of 1973 established a government directed and funded plan for reorganizing a number of bankrupt railroads operating in the northeast quarter of the United States. It created within the commission the Rail Services Planning Office and gave to it a leading role in the reorganization planning. Most importantly, the new office was charged with assuring that there would be the fullest possible public participation in the development of the restructured railroad system in the Northeast.

The Railroad Revitalization and Regulatory Reform Act of 1976 made significant changes in the way the commission regulates railroad transportation. For the first time since the creation of the commission, the Congress enacted legislation reducing somewhat the degree of regulation imposed by the Interstate Commerce Act rather than increasing it. Among the features of the 1976 act were provisions giving railroad management more flexibility to raise and lower individual freight rates, imposing strict time limits upon the commission for the processing and disposition of railroad-related proceedings, establishing an Office of Rail Public Counsel in the ICC to assure that public interest considerations would be fully explored in the course of the commission's decision-making process, and establishing on a permanent basis the Rail Services Planning Office with responsibilities to assist the commission in engaging in long-range planning for the improvement of transportation regulation.

The Motor Carrier Act of 1980 reflected concern by such industry sources as the American Trucking Association and the Teamsters Union about the potential adverse impact of deregulation by phasing in regulatory changes and providing for formal review of the impacts of deregulation. The ICC continued to exercise substantial, although limited, regulatory authority over the trucking industry. Nevertheless, traditional ICC controls over entry into the business, routes served, and commodities carried were largely eliminated by the act.

The Staggers Rail Act of 1980, signed October 14, 1980, while short of wholesale deregulation, nevertheless substantially eased the regulatory burden on the railroad industry by providing significant changes in rules governing rate-making, car control, and other areas of railroading including cost accounting, entry, abandonments, financial assistance, and other technical changes in the Interstate Commerce Act.

See RAILROAD INDUSTRY, RAILROAD TRANSPORTATION (EMERGENCY) ACT OF 1933.

INTERSTATE COMMERCE COMMISSION The senior administrative agency of the federal government, originally created under the Interstate Commerce Act of 1887, which functions under that act as amended many times since (see INTERSTATE COMMERCE ACT) and under other federal statutes in regulating, in the public interest, carriers subject to the Interstate Commerce Act that are engaged in transportation, in interstate commerce, and in foreign commerce to the extent that it takes place within the U.S. Surface transportation under the jurisdiction of the Interstate Commerce Commission (ICC) includes railroads, trucking companies, bus lines, freight forwarders, water carriers, coal slurry pipelines, and transportation brokers.

The agency's activities are directed by five commissioners, each appointed by the President of the United States and confirmed by the Senate. The commissioners serve staggered five-year terms so that no more than two terms expire in any year, and only three may be from the same political party. Commissioners may be reappointed, and a commissioner may continue to serve after his or her term expires, until his or her replacement has been qualified. The President designates the chairman of the commission from its members.

The ICC does not regulate all U.S. transportation. Its area of authority involves interstate commerce performed by surface and carriers. Air transportation is regulated by the Civil Aeronautics Board. Ships in foreign trade are regulated by the Federal Maritime Commission. Oil pipelines and pipelines carrying natural gas are regulated by the Federal Energy Regulatory Commission. Transportation within a single state is usually regulated by the state.

There are various exemptions from ICC regulation authorized by law. Only about one-third of interstate trucking operations are regulated by the ICC. The remainder are exempt, consisting of trucks carrying unprocessed farm products and private companies moving their own products in their own trucks. Other exempt interstate highway transportation includes school buses, taxicabs, hotel buses, national park buses, cooperative associations' vehicles, and vehicles used in newspaper distribution and in movement incidental to air transportation. Most transportation of a local character also is exempt. Only about one-tenth of the water carrier operations are regulated by the ICC. The remainder are exempt, generally because products are in bulk.

Regulation of carrier service by the ICC does not mean absolute control over it. Carrier managements have the initiative to make plans to expand their services and to decide whether to merge with or acquire control of other carriers. But these plans are subject to ICC approval "to assure continued service to the public and to guard against destructive competition as well as to protect employees and stockholders." Regulation of carrier service, rather than control, means that once a carrier obtains ICC certification to perform service, it may operate whatever equipment it finds to be the most efficient (subject to safety requirements), employ persons it chooses, enter into contracts with labor unions, modernize its facilities, and expand the amount of service provided within the scope of its authority without limit. The ICC is concerned with a carrier's safety performance in relation to its fitness to serve the public, but safety authority is vested in the Department of Transportation. The ICC does not have jurisdiction over interstate highway construction, which falls under the Federal Highway Administration in the Department of Transportation.

ICC Controls over Railroads and Commercial Motor Carriers. Criticism of ICC regulations was directed primarily at ICC controls over railroads and commercial motor carriers. The railroads were particularly concerned about their inability to competitively adjust freight rates without obtaining ICC approval and the slowness of the ICC's proceedings to set new freight rates or to approve corporate mergers. The Staggers Rail Act of 1980 (see RAILROAD LEGISLATION) has given the railroads greater pricing flexibility and substantially reduced ICC regulatory controls over them, such as elimination of railroad collective rate-making, resulting in increased competition. The Motor Carrier Act of 1980 also substantially reduced ICC controls over the trucking industry but has not resulted in total deregulation. The traditional ICC controls over entry into the business, routes served, and commodities carried have been eliminated to a large extent by the new legislation, but the potentially adverse impacts of deregulation are minimized by phasing in regulatory changes and by providing for a formal review of the impacts of deregulation.

ICC Procedure. ICC hearings are conducted sometimes by the commissioners, at other times by administrative law judges. They receive the evidence, rule on procedural questions that arise during the direct examination or cross-examination of witnesses, and are responsible for the development of a proper record (the accumulated records of ICC hearings and determinations are volumes long). In certain types of cases, hearings may also be conducted by joint boards which include representatives from state regulatory bodies. ICC hearings are open to the public. Public hearings on matters before the commission may be held at any point throughout the country, but final decisions are made at the Washington, D.C. headquarters in all formal proceedings. The public can protest changes in carriers' proposed rates and fares by writing the commission's secretary, attention of the Suspension and Fourth Section Board, letters to be received by the commission not later than 12 days before the effective date.

Summary. In the maneuvering that went on organizationally in the creation of the Department of Transportation by the act of October 15, 1966, inchoate proposals that did not come to fruition envisaged the creation of a railroad regulatory agency having comprehensive jurisdiction. As finally enacted, the act provided for the Federal Railroad Administration of the Department of Transportation to take jurisdiction over railroad safety, federal assistance to certain railroads, research and development in support of intercity ground transportation, and future requirements for rail transportation, "consolidate government support of rail transportation activities, provide a unified and unifying national rail transportation policy," and thus seemingly become the primary agency concerned with transportation by rail. The ICC retained most of its traditional regulatory functions, which, in a future of deregulation, the policy-making agency may well assume.

See RAILROAD INDUSTRY; RAILROAD TRANSPORTATION (EMERGENCY) ACT OF 1933; TRANSPORTATION, DEPARTMENT OF; TRANSPORTATION ACT OF 1920.

BIBLIOGRAPHY

Interstate Commerce Commission. *Annual Report.*

INTERURBAN BONDS See STREET RAILWAY BONDS.

INTERVENTION The purchase and sale of foreign exchange by the central bank of a country to influence the foreign exchange rate of a country's currency. The Federal Reserve has engaged in foreign currency operations since 1962, in addition to the transactions that it has executed for customers since the 1950s. In the period of flexible exchange rates, the main aim of Federal Reserve foreign currency operations (as provided for in the Foreign Currency Directive) has been to counter disorderly conditions in exchange markets through intervention operations, carried out primarily in the New York foreign exchange market. During some periods of downward pressure on the dollar, the Federal Reserve has purchased dollars (sold foreign currency), thereby absorbing some of the selling pressure on the market value of the dollar. Sales of dollars (purchases of foreign currency) have at times been undertaken to counter upward pressure on the dollar's foreign exchange value. The Federal Reserve's intervention is "sterilized" in that it does not lead to a change in the domestic reserve base. Source: Federal Reserve System.

INTESTACY When a person dies without leaving a will he is known as an intestate decedent and his estate is an intestacy. An intestacy is terminated by an ADMINISTRATOR appointed by a probate (or surrogate) court.

See DESCENT, LAWS OF; LETTERS OF ADMINISTRATION.

INTRINSIC VALUE Literally, the actual value that a thing possesses in itself. This concept is somewhat nebulous and philosophical, but among economists implies value-in-use or utility as distinguished from market value.

In referring to metallic money, intrinsic value denotes the bullion value of the metal comprising the coin. Paper money is sometimes said to have no intrinsic value, meaning that the paper upon which it is printed is worthless. There is a certain amount of quibbling in stressing this point of view, since everyone recognizes that the value of paper money or any credit instrument depends upon the collateral behind it or the credit standing and financial responsibility of the issuer.

In referring to securities, intrinsic value denotes the value of a stock or bond as an investment, i.e., conservatively, its worst as shown by its underlying equities, security, and past and potential earning power of the issuing organization, as distinguished from the ruling market value, which because of depression or speculative enthusiasm may be either below or above intrinsic value.

See INVESTMENT.

INVENTION/INNOVATION Invention is the creation of something new. An invention becomes an innovation when it is put into use. Innovations are diffused throughout the population of potential adopters. An alternative distinction between these two concepts is that an invention is something new brought into being, whereas an innovation is something new brought into use.

BIBLIOGRAPHY

BOZEMAN, BARRY, and LINK, ALBERT N., Investments in Technology: Corporate Strategies and Public Policy Alternatives (New York: Praeger, 1984).

INVENTORY A schedule or listing of property owned by an individual or concern and generally applied to the itemization of a single kind of property^the quantity, unit price, and total value being indicated for each item. Thus a merchandise inventory in a department store would consist of an itemized schedule of each kind of merchandise—shoes, carpets, men's suits, hosiery, etc.—showing the quantity on hand in one column, the unit price in a second column, and the total value (by extension) in a third.

Physical inventories of merchandise, raw materials, goods in process, and finished stocks should be taken at least annually in connection with preparation of the adjusting and closing entries required to close the books and prepare the profit and loss statement and balance sheet for the accounting year. Many firms maintain a perpetual inventory system (records of day-to-day additions, requisitions, and balances on hand), which should be checked at least once a year by the physical inventory. The perpetual inventory system may be expanded into a managerial instrument of control by prescribing for each category of items maximum stock, minimum stock, and reorder points (the latter never at zero, but at a level at least sufficient to allow for normal rate of usage until deliveries on reorders are received).

Inventories are credited with being a "current asset," but as such they and receivables are the riskiest from the standpoints of liquidity and turnover and should be subjected to close review as to both these counts and valuation. Current sales budget inventory requirements, plus managerially determined and desired closing inventory for a period, less the opening inventory, will determine the production or purchase requirements for the period. Valuation of inventories is crucial in determining cost of goods sold for a period and thus the gross profit, as closing inventory is a deduction from cost of goods available (opening inventory, plus purchases or production, equals cost of total goods available, minus closing inventory, equals cost of goods sold). In manufacturing concerns, the reasonableness of the valuation placed on inventory of "work in process" should be especially checked, as in the absence of adequate costing methods such valuation may be arbitrary or a window-dressing guess, and being neither raw nor finished, such in process inventories are the least liquid of the inventories. Inclusion of obsolete items in inventories is another pitfall that analysts of financial statements should be on guard against.

BIBLIOGRAPHY

DAVIS, H. Z. "History of LIFO." *Journal of Accountancy*, May, 1983.
GRANOF, M. H., and SHORT, D. G. "Why Do Companies Reject LIFO?" *Journal of Accounting, Auditing, and Finance*, Summer, 1984.
KIESO, D. E., and WEYGANDT, J. J. *Intermediate Accounting.* John Wiley and Sons, New York, NY, 1987.
MORSE, D. and RICHARDSON, G. "The LIFO/FIFO Decision." *Journal of Accounting Research*, Spring, 1983.
ROBINSON, D. A. *Accounts Receivable and Inventory Lending*, Bankers Publishing Co., Boston, MA, 1987.
SCHIFF, A. I. "The Other Side of LIFO," *Journal of Accountancy*, May, 1983.
WILLIAMS, J. R., and others. *Intermediate Accounting.* Harcourt Brace Jovanovich, San Diego, CA, 1989.

INVENTORY CONCEPTS Basic inventory concepts accepted by the accounting profession include the following AICPA statements, which are quoted here

Statement 1. The term inventory is used herein to designate the aggregate of those items of tangible personal property that (1) are held for sale in the ordinary course of business, (2) are in process of production for such sale, or (3) are to be currently consumed in the production of goods or services to be available for sale.
Statement 2. A major objective of accounting for inventories is the proper determination of income through the process of matching appropriate costs against revenues.
Statement 3. The primary basis of accounting for inventories is cost, which has been defined generally as the price paid or consideration given to acquire an asset.
Statement 4. Cost for inventory purposes may be determined under any one of several assumptions as to the flow of cost factors (such as first-in first-out, average, and last-in first-out); the major objective in selecting a method should be to choose the one which, under the circumstances, most clearly reflects periodic income.
Statement 5. A departure from the cost basis of pricing the inventory is required when the utility of the goods is no longer as great as its cost. Where there is evidence that the utility of goods, in their disposal in the ordinary course of business, will be less than cost, whether due to physical deterioration, obsolescence, changes in

price levels, or other causes, the difference should be recognized as a loss of the current period. This is generally accomplished by stating such goods at a lower level commonly designated as market.

Statement 6. As used in the phrase lower of cost or market, the term market means current replacement cost (by purchase or by reproduction, as the case may be) except that (1) market should not exceed the net realizable value (i.e., estimated selling price in the ordinary course of business less reasonably predictable costs of completion and disposal); and (2) market should not be less than net realizable value reduced by an allowance for an approximately normal profit margin.

Statement 7. Depending on the character and composition of the inventory, the rule of cost or market, whichever is lower may properly be applied either directly to each item or to the total of the inventory (or, in some cases, to the total of the components of each major category). The method should be that which most clearly reflects periodic income.

Statement 8. The basis of stating inventories must be consistently applied and should be disclosed in the financial statements; whenever a significant change is made therein, there should be disclosure of the nature of the change and, if material, the effect on income.

Statement 9. Only in exceptional cases may inventories properly be stated above cost.

Statement 10. Accrued net losses on firm purchase commitments for goods held for inventory, measured in the same way as are inventory losses, should, if material, be recognized in the accounts and the amounts thereof separately disclosed in the income statement.

INVENTORY COST FLOW ASSUMPTIONS Inventory is a term used to identify material or merchandise owned by the enterprise that eventually will be sold to customers or used in the process of production. Merchandise inventory is a term used for goods held for sale by retail or wholesale firms. Goods held for resale by manufacturing firms are referred to as finished goods. Manufacturing firms may also have work-in-process inventories which represent partially completed products still in the production process. Manufacturing firms may also have raw materials inventories which consist of materials which will become part of goods to be manufactured.

The more common methods of assigning cost to inventory include the following:

1. **Specific identification method.** Each item in inventory is individually identified, and a record is kept of its actual cost. The actual flow of goods is monitored and recorded exactly. Each item in the ending inventory can be identified, and its cost is assigned to the item.
2. **First-in, first-out method (FIFO).** The flow of goods is assumed to be such that the oldest items in the inventory are sold or used first. Inventory items on hand at the end of the period are assumed to have been acquired in the most recent purchases.
3. **Last-in, first-out method (LIFO).** The flow of goods is assumed to be such that the items most recently purchased are sold or used first. The ending inventory is assumed to have come from the earliest purchases.
4. **Weighted average method.** The flow of goods is assumed to be such that all items available for sale during the period are intermingled randomly, and items sold or used are picked randomly from this intermingled inventory. The weighted average cost per unit is computed according to this formula:

$$\frac{\text{Beginning inventory} + \text{Purchases}}{\text{Units in beginning inventory} + \text{Units purchased}} = \frac{\text{Average cost per unit}}{}$$

5. **Moving average method.** The flow of goods is assumed to be such that the items in the inventory are intermingled randomly after each addition to the inventory; items sold or used are picked randomly from those items in the inventory at the time. Under this method, an average cost per unit for the items in the inventory is computed after each purchase according to this formula:

$$\frac{\text{Total cost of inventory on hand after each purchase}}{\text{Total number of units in the inventory on hand after each purchase}} = \frac{\text{Average cost per unit}}{}$$

A pooled LIFO method has been developed to reduce recordkeeping costs associated with the single goods LIFO approach.

Under dollar-value LIFO, increases in inventory quantities from period to period form inventory layers. These layers are measured in terms of total dollar value (not physical quantities).

Inventories are frequently reported at the lower of cost or market (market referring to the cost to replace or reproduce). Market cannot be higher than net realizable value (sales price less cost to complete or dispose) nor less than net realizable value less a normal profit margin. Lower of cost or market is a departure from historical cost and is justified on the basis of conservatism (resulting from a loss of future utility, which should be recognized in the period incurred).

The gross profit method is a method of estimating cost of inventory on hand using a gross margin on sales percentage. The gross profit method is unacceptable for annual financial reporting.

The retail inventory method reduces the ending inventory at retail price to approximate the lower of cost or market by applying the cost to retail ratio. The conventional retail method requires that the net markups be included and net markdown excluded when computing the cost to retail ratio. The LIFO retail method can be used to achieve a LIFO cost flow assumption.

The advantages of LIFO are that it matches current costs against current revenues, defers income taxes as price levels increase, improves cash flow by deferring income taxes, and improves the quality of net income by making it less vulnerable to price declines. LIFO disadvantages are related to the fact that earnings tend to be reduced in periods of increasing prices, inventory becomes understated, the physical flow is rarely approximated (although this is not a major accounting concern), and the liquidation of the base inventory can distort net income and result in higher taxes and reduced cash flows. FIFO tends to present a better balance sheet valuation for inventory since the inventory is reported at more current prices. Earnings tend to be larger under FIFO because earlier costs are reported as cost of goods sold (which does not provide a good matching of earlier costs with current sales revenue).

INVENTORY MODEL The control of inventory involves two major considerations:

1. What is the optimal size for a purchase order?
2. When should the order be placed?

When considering the optimal order size, a manager knows that:

1. Certain expenses tend to increase with an increase in order size (for example, storage space cost, insurance, taxes, risk of spoilage or theft, interest on money invested to finance the inventory, etc.).
2. Other expenses tend to decrease with an increase in order size (for example, cost of clerical work associated with purchasing and receiving and paying bills, freight expense, etc.).

As order size increases, the cost of ordering inventory decreases, while the cost of carrying inventory increases. The appended chart illustrates the relationship between order size and inventory-handling costs. The optimal order size is the size at which the ordering cost and carrying cost curves intersect. This relationship can be expressed in the following formula:

$$\text{Economic order size} = \sqrt{2AP/S}$$

where A = annual quantity used in units; P = cost of placing an order; and S = annual cost of carrying one unit in stock for one year. To illustrate this concept, assume that a company uses 3,600 units of inventory each year. The cost of placing an order is $8, and the cost to carry one unit in inventory for one year is $1:

$$\begin{aligned}\text{Economic order size} &= \sqrt{(2)(8)(3{,}600)/\$1} \\ &= 240 \text{ units.}\end{aligned}$$

INVENTORY PROFIT

Economic Order Model for Inventory

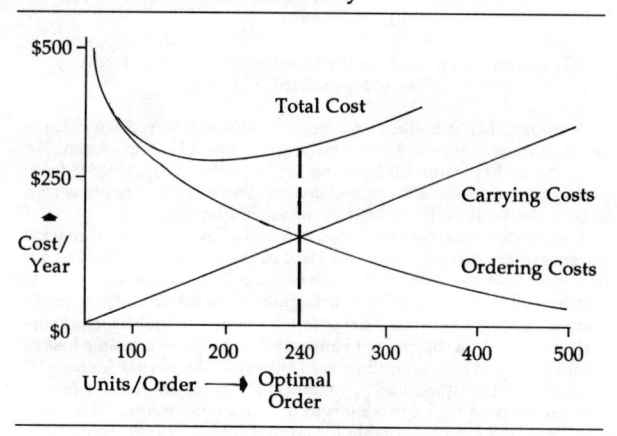

[Chart showing Total Cost, Carrying Costs, and Ordering Costs curves plotted against Units/Order from 0 to 500, with Cost/Year on vertical axis from $0 to $500. The optimal order point is marked at 240 units/order.]

The next issue to consider is when should inventory be ordered. If the lead time (the time between placing an order and receiving delivery), the economic order size, and the average usage are known, the time issue can be resolved. In the illustration, the demand is 3,600 units per year, or approximately 10 units per day. One order of 240 units will last for about 24 days. The time between orders will have to be about 24 days. The order should be placed so that the new order will arrive just as the last one is used up. If it takes 14 days from the time an order is placed until the goods arrive, each order should be placed 10 days after the last one has arrived so that the new goods will arrive on the 24th day after the arrival of the previous order.

INVENTORY PROFIT The Securities and Exchange Commission recommends that publicly owned companies disclose the amount of profit included in the income statement that will not recur due to increased replacement cost of inventories caused by inflation. Such profits are normally referred to as inventory profits (paper profits). The SEC supported this recommendation with the following arguments:

> The most significant and immediate impact of price fluctuations on financial statements is normally felt in cost of goods sold in the income statement. In periods of rising prices, historical cost methods result in the inclusion of "inventory profits" in reported earnings. "Inventory profits" result from holding inventories during a period of rising inventory costs and is measured by the difference between the historical cost of an item and its replacement cost at the time it is sold. Different methods of accounting for inventories can affect the degree to which "inventory profit" are included and identifiable in current income, but no method based upon historical cost eliminates or discloses this "profit" explicitly. Such "profits" do not reflect an increase in the economic earning power of a business and they are not normally repeatable in the absence of continued price level increase. Accordingly, where such "profit" are material in income statements presented, disclosure of their impact on reported earnings and the trend of reported earnings is important information for investors assessing the quality of earnings.

Inventory profit comes from holding inventory in periods of rising prices rather than from selling inventory. The reported net income under FIFO during periods of rising prices is usually larger than under LIFO because LIFO charges the latest, higher cost of inventory to cost of goods sold. The excess of FIFO's net income attributable to this factor over LIFO's net income represents inventory profit. The cost of goods sold under LIFO approximates the replacement cost of the inventory sold and thus minimizes inventory profit. Inventory profit arises primarily when old, low inventory costs (FIFO costs) are matched against current selling prices. It is the difference between the old, low inventory costs and current replacement costs that creates inventory profit.

INVENTORY TURNOVER One of the basic ratios utilized in analysis of financial statements, testing the average saleability of either aggregate inventories or specified categories of inventories, especially when compared with sales of past periods or comparable firms in the same line of activity.

Sales for a period (conventionally a year) at cost (cost of goods sold should be used instead of full sales value because the latter's inclusion of gross profit margin will inflate the ratio), divided by average inventories during the period, will determine the multiple of turnover. Thus, if the cost of goods sold in a year is $100,000, and average inventories were $50,000, the multiple of turnover for the year is two times, so that on the average, the dollar volume of inventories turned over every six months. If comparison with similar firms indicates a slower turnover rate, the disparity is a signal for investigation. A low turnover of inventories may be traceable to low sales volume and high inventories; managerially, the remedies available could be an increase in sales efforts (off-season sales, promotional pricing, more advertising, etc.) or a reduction in normal inventory levels established by management (high inventories may be traceable to inventory speculation, i.e., abnormal advance buying beyond operating needs).

Turnover ratios for specified lines of inventories may be used by management as guidelines for adjusting the production or carrying of lines. Thus minimum turnover ratios may be established for particular products, patterns, designs, sizes, etc.; if such fail to achieve the minimum turnover, an inventory control committee could decide whether to continue the item or eliminate it in order to avoid an accumulation of slowly moving lines.

INVESTING Committing capital with the expectation of profit. The expected profit may be in the form of dividends, interest, or capital appreciation. Speculation refers to an attempt to make profit from short-term changes in the price of an asset.

Investments are classified in financial terms as fixed-income and equity investments. Fixed-income investments include bonds, real estate mortgages, and preferred stock. Equity investments include common stock and real estate. The major classifications of stocks include industrial, financial, public utility, and railroad stocks. The major classes of bonds are U.S. government, state and municipal government, and corporate obligations.

In a broad sense, the investment decision takes into consideration the investor's situation and the characteristics of possible investments. The investor's situation typically involves such matters as their expectations, motives, income, cash requirements, capital, time horizon (short, intermediate, or long-term), safety and other considerations as well as from a proper evaluation of the risks they are willing to assume.

The basic matters to consider when evaluating different investments are yield, risk, duration, liquidity, and tax impact. Yield is required to compensate the investor for the impact of inflation and for risk-taking. The total yield on an investment is the increase in the value of the investment, usually stated as a percent of invested capital per year. When inflation is taken into consideration, the yield is referred to as the real yield. Risk is the probability that the investment will be worth less in real dollars than when it was made, taking into consideration the investment's cumulative yields. Beta is a measure of the risk of an individual stock relative to the stock market as a whole. Risks associated with bonds are typically based on the probability of default on principal or interest. As a general rule, the higher the yield, the higher the risk, and vice versa. Risk can sometimes be avoided through diversification of investments. Risks can also be avoided in some situations by taking into consideration the duration of the investment. Certain stocks are extremely risky over a period of time shorter than the economic cycle which is considered to be three to five years and less risky in the long run. Liquidity of an investment refers to whether the investor can withdraw the invested funds on demand. The degree of required liquidity will affect the type of investment an investor should consider.

Investment instruments are usually either equity or debt, or a combination thereof. Equity, or ownership, entitles the investor to a share in the profit and capital appreciation. Debt instruments provide a return in the form of interest and capital appreciation. Preferred stock is legally an equity interest but has some of the characteristics of a bond with an infinite term. Convertible bonds, convertible preferred stock, and participating preferred stock also contain elements of equity and debt.

Characteristics of various types of investments are summarized in the appended exhibit.

Characteristics of Selected Investments

Type	Purpose	Characteristics
Annuity	Provide income for life or for a determinable number of years. Available at life insurance companies.	Annuities are relatively safe investments and usually have a guaranteed rate of return. Variable annuities often provide a higher rate of return than do regular annuities. Many annuities carry a lower rate of interest than do other available investment opportunities with similar risks.
Asset Management Accounts	Provide a financial service that accumulates into a single account a variety of investment and transaction services, e.g., brokerage services, a money-market fund, and a credit card. Available at commercial banks, brokerage houses, insurance companies, and mutual funds.	Coordinates investment and banking activities, simplifies record-keeping, provides market rates of return on cash balances, makes available margin loans at competitive rates, etc. Many asset management accounts require a relatively large initial investment. The account may not be federally insured. Annual fees can be substantial.
Bankers Acceptances	Negotialble time drafts drawn typically to finance the import, export, transport, or storage of products. Available from banks and brokerage firms.	Relatively safe, short-term investments backed by the credit of the borrowing company. Penalties often imposed for early demand for funds.
Certificate of Deposit	Instrument represents a sum of money left at a bank for a period of time; at the end of the period, the bank pays the deposit plus interest. Available at banks, brokerage firms, savings and loan associations, and credit unions.	Depositor can "lock-in" yield for a specified time. Higher rate of return than on a savings account. Little risk to principal. Penalty often imposed for early withdrawal.
Common Stock	An ownership interest in a corporation. Available at brokerage firms, some banks and savings and loan associations, and financial-services companies.	Equity investments with potenial for relatively high returns and capital appreciation. Some participation in management through right to vote for board of directors. Exposure to market risk. Broker's commissions when buying and selling.
Corporate Bonds	Debt typically issued by large corporations. Available at brokerage firms, investment bankers, and corporations.	Pays a fixed investment return over a relatively long period of time. Relatively safe if held to maturity. Less safe than government bonds of similar maturity. Some can be called before maturity.
Futures	Goods, articles, rights, services, and interests in which contracts for future delivery may be traded. Available on a registered exchange.	Potential to accumulate many contracts on a relatively small investment. Very speculative.
Individual Retirement Accounts (IRA)	Long-term, tax deferred account that enables a person to accumulate retirement funds. Available at mutual-fund companies, banks, brokerage firms and insurance companies.	No taxes paid until withdrawals, typically after retirement when investor is in a lower tax bracket. Withdrawals made prematurely can be penalized.
Keogh Plan	A retirement plan for self-employed persons and their employees. Earnings of plan and new funds deposited are exempt from income taxes until withdrawn, subject to certain specified limits. Available at mutual funds, banks, brokerage firms, credit unions, and insurance companies.	Plan deposits and earnings are available for growth; untaxed until withdrawal. Restrictions are present; withdrawals made prematurely can be penalized.
Money-market Mutual Fund	Pooled money of many investors in a variety of short-term money market securities issued by the federal government, "blue-chip" corporations, and banks. Available at mutual-fund companies, brokerage firms, and financial service companies.	High, short-term interest rates available. Professional management. Diversification of investment. Initial minimum investments may be required. Usually not insured.
Municipal Bond	A contractual obligation between an authorized political subdivision (e.g., state, country, city, school district) and an investor. Available at banks and brokerage firms.	Interest is exempt from federal taxation: frequently exempt from state and local taxes in the state of orgin. Good safety record. Many issues available. Subject to interest-rate risks, e.g., as rates change so does the principal value of outstanding bond. Market risks related to changes in credit rating exist. Prices respond negatively to inflation.
General Obligation Bonds	Bonds of political subdivisions that are to be repaired from taxes on property in the particular subdivision. Available at banks and brokerage firms.	Backed by taxing power of the political subdivision. Yields are relatively lower than yields on revenue bonds of similar rating and maturity.

ENCYCLOPEDIA OF BANKING AND FINANCE

INVESTING

Characteristics of Selected Investments (continued)

Type	Purpose	Characteristics
GNMA-Mortgage backed government securities (Ginnie Maes)	A GNMA investment is made up of a pool of FHA and VA residential mortgages. After the Government National Mortgage Association gives its approval to the mortgages, a GNMA mortgage-backed certificate is issued. GNMA securities are available through brokerage firms, commercial banks and unit investment trusts.	GNMA securities provide monthly principal and interest payments, guaranteed by the U.S. government. Yields are competitive with government and federal agency securities and high grade corporate bonds. The value of the security can fluctuate with changes in interest rates. The securities are very liquid.
Revenue Bonds	Bonds the interest and principal of which is to be paid from a specific source, e.g., tolls, electric or water revenues, etc. Available at banks and brokerage firms.	Relatively high yields as compared with general obligation bonds. Narrow revenue base can increase risks.
Mutual Funds	Pooled resources of many investors; funds invest in a variety of securities, e.g., stocks, bonds, and money-market securities. Available at mutual-fund companies, brokerage firms, financial-services companies and insurance companies.	Provide for diversification of portfolio at a relatively low cost, thereby reducing risk. Professional management. "Switching" privilege from one type of fund to another is typically available. Wide selection of funds. Minimum initial investment. Not federally insured. Subject to market and credit risks. Management fees and sales charges are typical.
NOW Accounts	A savings account that allows checking activity. Available at banks and savings and loan associations.	Deposits earn interest and can be withdrawn readily. Record-keeping reduced for investor. Interest is earned on funds in the account, assuming a minimum balance is maintained.
Options (puts/call, straddles, etc.)	The right to buy (call) or sell (put) a fixed amount of a given stock at a specified price within a limited period of time. Available at brokerage firms.	Provide leverage for investment. Risk limited to amount invested in the option. Speculative. Entire investment can be lost.
Preferred Stock	Corporate stock with a fixed dividend and a priority claim over common stock if the company is liquidated. Available at brokerage firms, banks, savings and loan associations, and financial-service companies.	Preference over common stock in distribution of dividends and assets, if the corporation is liquidated. Usually lower return than for common stock of the same company. Risk/yield usually not as attractive as bonds.
Real Estate Investment Trusts (REITS)	A business trust or corporation that operates by acquiring or financing real estate projects. Available at brokers, banks and financial planners.	Provide for capital appreciation and liquidity. Centralized management. Limited liability. Typical risks associated with investment in real estate.
Repurchase Agreement ("repo")	An interest in a security at a specified price with the agreement that the seller will repurchase the interest in the security at a specified time and price plus interest. Availble at banks and brokerage firms.	Provide short-term investment opportunities with "locked-in," relatively high interest return. Agreements often provide that investment will be replaced in a day or two at a predetermined rate. Typically requires an established relationship with a bank or dealer. Relatively complex. Large dollar amounts.
Treasury Bills, treasury bonds and treasury notes	Bills have maturities of 13, 26 and 52 weeks. Sold in a minimum amounts of $10,000 and in multiples of $5,000 above the minimum. Treasury bills have maturities of more than 10 years; $1,000 minimum. Notes are medium term securities; minimum usually $5,000. Available at Federal Reserve Banks and branches, Bureau of Public Debt, U.S. Treasury Department, banks and brokerage firms.	U.S. Treasury securities are backed by the full faith and credit of the U.S. government. Very liquid. Exempt from state and local taxes. Risks associated with interest-rate fluctuations exist.
Unit Investment Trust	Fixed portfolio of securities accumulated by a sponsor and offered in units to the investor. Available through the sponsor, brokerage firms and banks.	Provide for diversification and professional selection. Sponsor typically quotes bid prices on a daily basis.
Unit Investment Trusts	A unit investment trust is a fixed portfolio of securities designed to attain specific investment goals, principally monthly income and preservation of capital through diversification. Unit investments trusts are assembled and administered by professionals. The portfolio is held in trust on behalf of the investors by a bank trustee. Ownership interests in the trust can be purchased through brokerage firms and commercial banks.	These securities offer diversification, monthly income, high current returns, professional selection, reinvestment options and liquidity.

ENCYCLOPEDIA OF BANKING AND FINANCE

The purpose of bond analysis is to evaluate the ability of the debtor to pay interest and principal as they fall due. The purpose of common stock analysis is to determine the probable future value of a share of stock. Many factors are involved in determining the value of common stock, especially earnings per share and the price/earnings ratio at which the shares sell. Factors affecting investment evaluations include the trend of earning per share, the quality of reported earnings and corporate assets, dividend policy, demand for the stock, and the quality and performance of management. Major factors affecting the quality of earnings include depreciation practices, research and development expenditures, and inventory policies.

A glossary of major terms related to securities trading on exchanges is presented here.

Glossary of Securities Trading on Exchanges

Account Record of client's transactions and credit/debit balances of cash and/or securities with a firm.

Arbitrage The simultaneous purchase and sale of the same or equivalent money, commodity, or security, to take advantage of a price discrepancy. Place arbitrage attempts to take advantage of price discrepancies in different markets (for example, New York and London). Time arbitrage attempts to take advantage of price discrepancies between intermediate delivery or spot prices and future delivery or future quotations. Kind arbitrage seeks to take advantage of discrepancies in price between securities and other instruments that will become equivalent, such as convertible securities or split-up shares.

Asked price Lowest price at which a dealer is willing to sell a security.

Basis point .01% of yield on a fixed-income security. For example, if a bond yield to maturity changed from 9.10 to 10.45, there was a 130 basis points change.

Bid Price at which someone is willing to purchase a security.

Block trading Most of the shares traded on exchanges and over the counter are for large institutions (insurance companies, financial institutions, corporations) instead of for individuals. Such transactions, which involve more than 10,000 shares, are referred to as block trades. If the firm handling the block trade is a member of the NYSE or Amex, the trade must "cross" on the floor of the exchange; the specialist collects a commission for the block and processes the trade through the exchange's computer system so that it appears on the tape and electronic ticker. Non-members can also trade "off the floor." Such off-floor trading of listed securities is referred to as the "third market" as distinct from the primary and secondary markets.

Blue-chip stocks Common stock representing ownership of a major company with a long history of profitability and constant or increasing dividends. Blue-chip stocks are considered to be financially strong and capable of surviving severe economic downturns without significantly affecting their dominant position in the industry, profitability, or dividend-paying ability.

Charting A practice of graphically presenting stock price indexes or individual stock prices to present a picture of price behavior over a period of time. Charting is used primarily to provide information about price trends and for forecasting.

Clearing The settlement of security transactions. The clearing process offsets transactions so that the actual delivery of securities and money can be reduced. The Stock Clearing Corporation is organized to conduct the clearing process for the New York Stock Exchange. Transactions in stocks, rights, and warrants are cleared through the corporation. Odd lots and bonds are delivered by the Central Delivery Department.

Cyclical stocks Stocks of corporations whose earnings fluctuate with the business cycle. Such companies have relatively low earnings per share during periods of recession and sharply increasing earnings during the recovery phase of the business cycle. Cyclical stocks are generally considered to include basic manufacturing industries, such as machinery and automobile manufacturing.

Dollar averaging An investment strategy in which an investor purchases a fixed dollar amount of a particular common stock periodically. The investor hopes to accumulate a large number of shares when the price of the stock is low and a smaller number of shares when the price is high. Hopefully, the average price for all the shares will be substantially lower than the average price the investor would pay if he purchased a constant number of shares periodically.

Dow Jones averages Market indicators published by the financial publishing house of Dow, Jones & Co. Stock averages are computed for 30 industrial, 20 rails, and 15 utility common stocks, and a composite of the three groups. All stocks included in the averages are listed on the New York Stock Exchange. The averages are widely issued to reflect the trend of common stock prices over short or long periods of time.

Dow theory An interpretation of the primary market trend which holds that there is no primary market trend (upward or downward for a year of more) unless there is simultaneous correlation between the movement of the Dow industrial, transportation, and utility averages.

Efficient market A market in which it is assumed that all known information about a security is fully reflected in its price (that is, a price-efficient market). In an efficient market, mispriced securities do not exist. The market price of a security equals its fair intrinsic value. The investor trades only because he has excess cash, needs cash, or wants to attain a tax advantage.

Ex-dividend A stock is purchased ex-dividend when the purchaser acquires the shares without the right to receive a recently declared dividend. An investor who purchases a share of stock on or after the ex-dividend date is not entitled to receive the scheduled dividend. The ex-dividend date is four days prior to the date of record. The date of record is a date established when dividends are declared and is used to obtain a record of all stockholders of record as of the record date, which is usually several weeks prior to the payment date. A transfer of stock ownership prior to the ex-dividend date is said to be "cum dividends" or "dividends on" because the new owner of the shares will receive the dividend payment.

Form 10-K A report filed annually with the Securities and Exchange Commission by a company that issues a separate annual report to shareholders. The company must report the following information in the report: financial statements, supplementary financial information, selected financial data for five years, management's discussion and analysis of financial condition and results of operations, market for the registrant's common stock and related security holder matters, a brief description of the business of the company and its subsidiaries, information for three years relating to industry segments, classes of similar products or services, foreign and domestic operations and export sales, identity of company's directors and officers, their principal occupation or employment, the name and financial business of their employer, and an offer in the annual report or proxy statement to provide without charge a copy of the Form 10-K and the name and address of the person to write to for this material.

Growth stocks Stocks of corporations whose earnings have demonstrated rapid growth in comparison with the the economy and which are expected to grow at above-average rates in the future.

Income stocks Stocks of corporations with relatively constant earnings and dividends along with a high dividend yield in comparison with other stocks. Stocks of utility companies are often considered income stocks.

Junk bonds Speculative bonds with a credit rating of BB or lower; such bonds usually have a high risk and high yield.

Margin trading In margin transactions, the investor purchases securities and pays only a percentage of their cost; the balance is paid by the broker and is treated as a loan to the investor. For example, an investor purchases on margin 100 shares of stock at a price of 90. The investor might be asked to maintain a 60% margin—that is, he must pay 60% of the cost, or $5,400. This amount is his equity in the stock. The broker pays the remaining $3,600 as a loan to the investor, keeping the stock as collateral. The investor is thus able to purchase stock worth $9,000 while putting down only $5,400 of his own funds. The broker charges a commission on the full $9,000 purchase price, and also collects monthly interest on the loan. The investor expects the price of the stock to

INVESTING

rise. Buying stock on the margin provides the investor with considerable leverage.

Odd-lot trading Buying or selling in other than the established unit or round lot. In an odd-lot transaction, one-eighth of a point is added to (or deducted from) the price of each share purchased (or sold).

Options Privileges acquired to buy or sell a security at a specified price within a specified period of time. Options include puts, calls, straddles, spreads, straps, and strips. A put is a contract giving the holder the privilege to deliver a given number of shares of a specific stock to the maker within a certain time and at a certain price. The holder expects to make a profit from a decline in the stock. A call is a contract whereby the holder obtains the privilege of purchasing stock. The purchaser expects to profit from an increase in the price of the shares. Straddles and spreads are combinations of one put and one call. In a straddle, the put and call are at the market when the options are written. When prices are points below the market for the put and above the market for a call, the result is a spread. A strap is a combination of two calls with one put; a strip is two puts with one call. The option price is at the market when the options are written. Put and call brokers publish lists of prices on options from time to time.

Orders An order describes the terms and conditions relating to the execution of an order by a broker for a customer. Market orders to buy and sell at the market are the major type of orders used in securities trading. Limit orders are orders placed by customers to place a limit on the order as to price. A limit buying order must be executed at the limit price or less. A selling order limited to a specific price must be executed at that price or more. Day orders are automatically cancelled if not executed on the same day the order is placed. Open, or GTC (good till canceled), orders are good until executed or specifically cancelled by the customer. Stop-loss orders can be placed to limit losses. Stop-loss orders become market orders when the price of the stock reaches a specified quotation.

Over-the-counter markets The over-the-counter markets are composed of security trading outside organized securities exchanges. These markets bring buyers and sellers together and increase the marketability for the large number of securities not traded on the organized exchanges. Unlisted stocks, government, municipal, and corporate bonds, and new issues are usually traded in the over-the-counter markets. Dealers in this market typically communicate by telephone with other dealers when negotiating (versus auctioning) transactions. The National Quotation Bureau, Inc. collects quotations and distributes a list to subscribers—pink stock sheets and yellow bond sheets divided geographically, Eastern, Central, and Pacific.

Point Market prices are listed in points. A point is equal to a market price of $1 per share. Listings normally are given to the nearest one-eighth of a point.

Round lot Trading on the New York Stock Exchange is done in standard numbers of shares, called round lots. A round lot is usually 100 shares or multiples thereof. For bonds, the standard unit is one $1,000 bond. Lots smaller than round lots are called odd lots.

Securities Exchange Act of 1934 An act designed to make available more reliable information to the public, to prevent and provide remedies for fraud, manipulations and other abuses in security trading, to ensure fair and orderly markets, to regulate the securities markets and brokers and dealers to see that just and equitable principles of trading are observed, to regulate the use of credit in securities trading, and to regulate trading by insiders.

Settlement Settlement refers to when and how a transaction on the exchange must be settled. Except for specific agreements, every transaction must be settled by 12:30 P.M., delivery time, of the fourth following full business day. A cash settlement involves delivery of securities and payment of money on the same day.

Short selling The practice of selling securities that are not owned by the seller. A short sale can occur where the seller does not possess the securities sold; a sale against the box occurs if the seller owns the securities sold but does not intend to deliver them at the time of the sale. A short seller expects the price of the security sold short to decline and to be able to buy back or cover the short sale at a lower price at a future date.

Stock purchase warrants Instruments attached to other securities that entitle the holder to purchase shares of common stock at a specified price per share within a given period or for an indefinite time. Warrants can be issued separately or attached to other securities. Also called option warrants.

Transfer taxes An excise tax levied by the State of New York on all transfers of beneficial ownership of securities within the state. The federal government also levies an excise tax based on the market value of stocks, rights, or warrants sold.

When-issued or when-distributed basis New securities issues are traded on a when-issued basis before the delivery of the securities can be made.

BIBLIOGRAPHY

AAII Journal.
ABERTH, J. "Searching for an Investment Strategy." *ABA Bank Journal*, July, 1988.
AMERICAN ASSOCIATION OF INDIVIDUAL INVESTORS. *The Individuial Investor's Guide to Computerized Investing*, 1989.
BALDWIN, E. *Mortgage-Backed Securities: A Reference Guide for Lenders and Issuers.* Mortgage Bankers, Washington, DC, 1989.
Bank and Quotation Record.
Barron's National Business and Financial Weekly.
Babson's Report.
BURGAUER, J. *Do-it-yourself Investment Analysis: A Practical Guide to Life Cycle, Fundamental and Technical Analyses*, Probus Publishing Co., Chicago, IL, 1989.
CHAPMAN, K. J. *Investment Statistics Locator.* Oryx Publishing Co., Phoenix, AZ, 1988.
COCHRAN, J. S. *Personal Investment Portfolios.* International Publishing Co., Chicago, IL, 1989.
COLER, M., and RATNER, E., eds. *Financial Services.* Prentice- Hall, Inc., New York, NY, 1987.
Commercial and Financial Chronicle.
CURRIER, C. *The Investor's Encyclopedia.* Franklin Watts, Inc., New York, NY, 1987.
FABOZZI, R. J. *Readings in Investment Management.* Probus Publishing, Co., Chicago, IL. 1983.
Financial Analysts Journal.
FINANCIAL STOCK GUIDE SERVICE. *Directory of Obsolete Securities*, 1927. Annual.
Financial World.
Forbes.
Fortune.
HARPER, V. L. *Handbook of Investment Products and Services.* New York Institute of Finance, New York, NY, 1986.
HEERWAGEN, P. F. *Investing for Total Return.* Probus Publishing Co., Chicago, IL, 1988.
HIRT, G., BLOCK, S., and JURY, F. *Investor's Desktop Portfolio Planner.* Probus Publishing Co., Chicago, IL, 1988.
Institutional Investor.
Investor's Daily.
Journal of Portfolio Management.
LEVINE, S. N. *Dow Jones-Irwin Business and Investment Almanac*, 1977. Annual.
MILLER, R. B. *Tax Haven Investing.* Probus Publishing Co., Chicago, IL, 1989.
Moody's Industry Review. Weekly update.
Moody's OTC Investor's Manual, 1970. Twice weekly.
Moody's Municipal & Government Manual, 1955. Supplemented twice weekly.
Moody's Public Utility Manual, 1954. Annual. Supplemented twice weekly.
Moody's Transportation Manual, 1959. Annual. Supplemented weekly.
Moody's Industrial Manual, 1959. Annual. Updated.
Moody's International Manual, 1981. Annual. Updated semiweekly.
MORGAN, J., and OGILVIE, N. "Industry Analysis: A Tool to Diversify Loan Portfolios and Manage Risk Concentration." *Commercial Bank Lending*, June, 1988.
NEW YORK INSTITUTE OF FINANCE. *New York Institute of Finance Guide to Investing.* New York Institute of Finance, New York, NY, 1987.
Personal Wealth Reporter.
PIERCE, P., ed. *The Dow Jones Averages, 1885-1985.* Dow Jones- Irwin, Inc., Homewood, IL, 1986.

———. *The Securities Industry Glossary*. Prentice Hall, Inc., Englewood Cliffs, NJ, 1985.
RESENBERG, J. M. *The Investor's Dictionary*, 1986.
———. *More Words of Wall Street*. Dow Jones-Irwin, Inc., Homewood, IL, 1986.
Smart Money.
Standard & Poor's. *Industry Survey*, 1973. Weekly updating.
———. *Analyst's Handbook*, 1964. Annual. Monthly updates.
———. *Statistical Service*, 1978. Monthly.
———. *Stock Reports*, 1973. Weekly updates.
Value Line Investment Survey, 1936–. Weekly.
Wall Street Transcript.
Weiss Research. *Timing the Market: How to Profit in Bull and Bear Markets with Technical Analysis*. Probus Publishing Co., Chicago, 1986.
———. *After the Trade Is Made*, 1986.
Wall Street Journal.

INVESTMENT In a general sense, any employment of capital in expectation of gain, whether in a business, farm, urban real estate, bonds, stocks, merchandise, education, etc. In its more specific use in the field of securities (bonds, stocks), investment is contrasted to speculation in that investment is primarily for income, whereas speculation is primarily for capital gains; investment is for holding, whereas speculation is for turnover; investment is for the long term, whereas speculation is for the short term.

These distinctions, however, are not fundamental. Investment may be motivated by both types of gain-income and capital gain. Investment rationally should involve turnover whenever the objectives of an investing program have changed or particular selections have reached their full potential or are no longer suitable for particular investing requirements. Speculation may involve long terms of holding, e.g., cyclical or secular speculation.

The basic distinction between investment and speculation has been pointed out by Sauvain. It is in the degree of assumption of investing risks. An investment is a commitment in which the investing risks are minimized, whereas speculation is the aggressive assumption of risks in anticipation of substantial profits in consideration therefor. The crucial problem in investing, however, is that no one type of investment is perfect relative to all the basic risks in investing. Thus when an outstanding security analyst writes that "savings bonds are the safest investment, he is referring to the fact that such bonds are unquestionably highest quality from the standpoint of financial risk (the risk that the obligor might not pay) and interest rate risk (since savings bonds are nontransferable, i.e., nonmarketable, they are immune from the risk of open market depreciation in the event interest rates and yields on high-grade bonds should rise). Savings bonds, however, like other fixed-income and fixed-principal investments, are vulnerable to purchasing power risk (the risk of shrinkage in purchasing power should the price level and cost of living rise). Highest-grade marketable bonds are safest investments from the standpoint of financial risk, but are vulnerable to interest rate risk and purchasing power risk, i.e., speculative from the latter standpoints. Common stocks are varying speculations from the standpoint of financial risk but are defensive from the standpoints of interest risk and purchasing power risk (assuming successful selection as price inflation hedges).

A highest-grade bond, an investment from the standpoint of financial risk, may be successful speculation in interest rate and purchasing power if timed properly, e.g., bought before a drop in interest rates from high levels or before a period of general price deflation. Instead of dropping, however, interest rates might continue rising; instead of price deflation, further price inflation might ensue. These are the risks that the speculator would assume in anticipation that the hoped for trends would develop.

For maximum minimization of investing risks, an investment program must be a diversified selection. The usual solution for a sufficiently large principal is to cover income requirements by a layer of most defensive securities (highest quality from the standpoint of financial risk), which would usually be highest-grade bonds; then add a layer of highest-quality common stocks (from the standpoints of interest rate risk and purchasing power risk). A speculation, by contrast, may ignore diversification and concentrate aggressively in a particular category of securities. Thus an all-common stock portfolio is speculative in varying degrees from the standpoint of financial risk, and an investor with such a portfolio must be prepared to stand the risk of adverse fluctuation in earning power, dividends, and market value for particular common stock selections. On the average, common stocks will normally fluctuate in a wider amplitude relative to financial risk than high-grade bonds will relative to interest rate risk. A purely defensive investor, requiring highest stability of investment income and/or value of principal, would not find such a portfolio appropriate.

The determination of requirements for the particular circumstances of the investor concerned places the emphasis properly on the subjective in investment analysis. Each investor, whether individual or institutional, will have varying circumstances as to supply of funds available for investment, requirements for stability of principal and/or investment income, and objectives for the investment program. A first step in analysis should be to diagnose such requirements. Prognosis of a suitable investment program should then logically follow. Without such analysis, investors would be investing blindly and at random. Individuals particularly have been prone to such random investing without proper planning, flitting from one investing fad to another without consideration of whether particular media are suitable for circumstances and objectives. Educational programs of such sources as the New York Stock Exchange are educating individual investors to increase rationality in investing decisions. By placing emphasis on the prerequisites to investing in securities—adequate personal savings, cash reserves for emergencies, adequate insurance, and normal provision for home ownership—and stressing the importance of defining investing objectives—fund for education of children, to purchase an interest in a business, for estate building, for retirement, etc.—such programs bring about more rational investing and investment results.

FORMULA PLANS and DOLLAR AVERAGING have been particularly promoted as devices to circumvent the problem of price timing and fluctuation and to profit with a minimum of overextended exposure to price risk. There is no unbeatable formula, however, eliminating the necessity for exercise of judgment in initial selection and subsequent timing of changes.

Some Investing Guides. The following general rules are considered to have wide applicability.

1. Have an investing plan adapted to your circumstances and requirements. Do not invest blindly. Have some objective in mind or outlined in writing.

    An ideal investing plan is one closely correlated to available excess income over living expenses, tax bracket, and family reserves. In general, three investing preferences are prevalent: emphasis on stability of principal, with least exposure to the basic investing risks; emphasis on income, consistent with reasonable stability of principal; and emphasis on capital appreciation, with income secondary and capital gains stressed as most important in consideration of increased risks assumed (so-called businessmen's investments).

    Diversification should be a guiding principle in all well-constructed defensive investing plans relative to the basic investing risks. Intensive, nondiversified investment is riskier but often deliberately characteristic of aggressive plans emphasizing capital appreciation. Diversification may be executed as to total commitment in defensive securities as against aggressive securities relative to the basic investing risks; total commitment in any one industry; or total commitment in any one security.
    See DISTRIBUTION OF RISK.

2. Review and revise your holdings periodically. No investment, even the most defensive, is absolutely safe relative to the basic investing risks. There is no bond or share of stock in existence which should be "locked up and forgotten."

3. Devote attention to your investments. If you do not have either the time or qualifications to do so, place your investing affairs in the hands of a competent investment adviser. If your portfolio is not large enough to justify this expense, instead of selecting individual securities yourself, invest in INVESTMENT COMPANY shares, which is a means of delegating the problems of selection, turnover, and diversification to professional management. There are pros and cons to open end (mutual fund) shares and closed end investment company shares.
   See INVESTMENT MARKET, INVESTMENT MEDIA, INVESTMENT SECURITIES.

INVESTMENT ADVISERS ACT An act passed in 1940 (Title II of P.L. 768, 76th Congress) that brought, by means of registration, persons and firms engaged in investment advisory work within regulation of the SECURITIES AND EXCHANGE COMMISSION (SEC). Basis for the act was the investigation and report by the SEC called for by Section 30 of the Public Utility Holding Company Act of 1935.

Under the act, investment advisory contracts that provide for compensation of the investment adviser on the basis of a share of capital gains or capital appreciation of the funds of the client, or that fail to provide for consent of the client to any assignment of the contract or notification of the client of any change in a partnership advisory firm, are not permitted. Prohibited transactions include any devices to defraud clients, operating as a fraud or deceit upon clients, or wherein the adviser acts as principal for his own account without disclosure to and consent of the client. Advisers subject to registration are those engaged in interstate advisory work in registered securities, whose clients number over 15, who hold themselves out generally to the public as investment advisers, and whose clients are not solely investment companies and insurance companies. Advisers are liable to cancellation of their registration if within ten years of issuance of order by the SEC they or controlling persons have been convicted of any felony or misdemeanor involving the purchase or sale of any security or practice in the securities field as investment adviser, underwriter, broker, or dealer.

The act by amendments in 1960 empowered the SEC to inspect periodically the books and records of an investment adviser.

Recent Legislation. The Mutual Fund Bill (P.L. 91-547, December 14, 1970) amended the Investment Advisers Act in various respects, including the following.

1. Effective December 14, 1971, the act was amended to apply the prohibition of compensation based on sharing in realized or unrealized gains to contracts of investment advisers with investment companies.
2. But, effective the same date, the amendment permits advisory contracts with registered investment companies or $1 million or more accounts of any other person (except trust funds or separate accounts, which are accorded exemption under other sections of the Investment Company Act) that provide for compensation increasing or decreasing proportionately with "investment performance" of the investment company or account relative to the performance of an appropriate index of security prices.
3. The Investment Advisers Act was also amended to provide for extension of the disciplinary powers of the Securities and Exchange Commission to cover investment advisers and associates conforming to such powers the SEC possesses over broker-dealers and other persons under the Securities Exchange Act of 1934.

Before the amendment by P.L. 91-547, which eliminated the exemption, investment advisers whose only clients were investment companies had been exempt from provisions of the Investment Advisers Act.

Under the American Law Institute's proposed Federal Securities Code (Prof. Louis Loss, its reporter), all of the seven basic acts that constitute the federal securities laws would be centralized. Section 703(e) of the proposed code would give the Securities and Exchange Commission the authority to prescribe qualifications and operational capability standards for investment advisers. Although federal enactment of the ALI's proposed Federal Securities Code appeared as of 1982 to be far off, the SEC itself in its 1981 *Annual Report* indicated its continuance of a comprehensive review of the Investment Advisers Act and the rules, regulations and administrative practices under it, with the aim of determining whether the existing regulatory structure was adequate. In addition, in August, 1981, the SEC published the views of its staff regarding the applicability of the Investment Advisers Act to financial planners, pension consultants, and other persons who provide investment advisory services to others for compensation as an integral component of other financially related services. Similar provision in legislation was introduced in the Congress in 1976, but was not enacted.

INVESTMENT BANKER A firm engaged in investment banking, i.e., financing the capital requirements of business through the investment markets as distinguished from seasonal or current requirements normally financed by means of bank or finance company credit.

The investment banker is the middleman between issuers of securities requiring capital (public bodies as well as private business firms) and the ultimate investors, institutional and individual, who have money to invest. They facilitate the conversion of available savings into investment and thus perform the important economic function of improving the flow of needed capital. New and expanding enterprises; reorganized, merged, or consolidated firms; and governmental units look to the investment banker for the financing of their capital requirements. The two basic types of UNDERWRITING are negotiated underwriting, in which the business is handled through a particular investment banking firm (the "originator"), and competitive bidding, in which the issuer specifies bidding specifications and invites competing investment banking groups of firms to bid, the business being awarded to the qualified bidders who submit the lowest net cost of money bid (in the case of bonds, net of premium or discount on principal plus interest cost; in the case of stocks, highest net bid). Rule U-50 of the Securities and Exchange Commission requires competitive bidding for public utility securities issued under the jurisdiction of the commission. The Interstate Commerce Commission requires competitive bidding for railroad securities. State and municipal obligations also are subject to competitive bidding, as are new issues of Treasury bills of the U.S. government.

The purchase agreement, between the issuer and the purchase group of investment banking firms formed by the originating firm to share the liability assumed, may involve one of three basic arrangements as to liability to the issuer: firm underwriting, in which the purchase group purchases the issue from the issuer and is accountable for net proceeds to the issuer on the settlement date in full; "best efforts" basis, in which there is no assumption of liability by the investment banking group, the distribution being on an agency basis for the account and risk of the issuer; and standby basis, in connection with offerings of rights to stockholders by issuers, in which the investment banking group assumes full liability for any securities unsubscribed by the stockholders by exercise of the rights. Competitive bidding involves firm assumption of liability by the winning bidders. The purchase group agreement (agreement among the underwriters) specifies the participation by each member of the purchase group in the liability to the issuer by reference to the purchase agreement in which such participation is detailed. Such groups or syndicates of firms (joint ventures for the purposes of the deal concerned) are usually headed by the originating firm, which names the SYNDICATE manager.

Resort to a syndicate of firms is also practiced for maximum distribution power in the formation of the selling group agreement (offering to selected dealers) by the syndicate manager on behalf of the purchase group. Selling group members are specified "concession" from the public offering price (sharing in the underwriting "spread" between net price to the issuer and public offering price), and they in turn are permitted to offer a reallowance to other dealers, not members of the selling group, to further add to distribution power.

Investment banking practice was importantly modified by the requirements for registration of public offerings with the Securities and Exchange Commission, pursuant to the SECURITIES ACT OF 1933, involving a waiting period (normally 20 days but in practice usually longer) between filing and the effective date for public sale.

Antitrust Suit Against Investment Bankers. The antitrust suit brought under the Sherman Act by the Justice Department against 17 leading investment bankers, initiated October 30, 1947, in the Federal District Court in the Southern District of New York, was dismissed September 23, 1953, after a trial lasting from November 28, 1950, to May 19, 1953. The case is of interest for its bearing on conventional relationships among investment banking firms.

The government alleged a conspiracy and combination formed about 1915 and in continuous operation thereafter whereby the defendants as a group developed a system to eliminate competition and monopolize the "cream of the business" of investment banking. Bases for this charge were the alleged respecting by the defendant firms of the entitlement of a defendant firm that first managed an underwriting for an issuer to manage all future security issues of that issuer; the understanding among the defendant firms that a defendant firm once participating as a member of a purchase group for an issue is thereafter entitled to continue such participation in all future issues of an issuer; and a reciprocity agreement among the defendant firms to exchange participations with one another in purchase groups managed. As a means of assuring issuer control, the defendant firms were alleged to have obtained control over the financial and business affairs of issuers by giving free financial advice to issuers, by "infiltrating" the boards of directors of issuers, by selecting friendly officers, and by utilizing their influence with commercial banks handling business of issuers.

The court rejected motions to amend the complaint so as to charge that syndicate price fixing^the agreement of associated underwriters not to sell the offered security at any price except the fixed public offering price during the distribution period—is illegal and proof of a restraint of trade conspiracy. The complaint was dismissed on a finding that no combination, conspiracy, or agreement was shown to exist. Since amendment of the complaint as to price-fixing was not permitted, the court's decision commenting that the fixed price of public offerings gives no offense to the Sherman Act was merely obiter dicta.

BIBLIOGRAPHY

BLOCK, E. *Inside Investment Banking*, 1988.
CONNER, D. R., and FIMAN, B. G. "Making the Cultural Transition to Investment Banking." *Bankers Magazine*, January/February, 1988.
ECCLES, R. G. and CRANE, D. B. *Doing Deals: Investment Banks at Work*.
EPSTEIN, R. *Investment Banking*, 1987.
HOWE, J. T. *Junk Bonds: Analysis and Portfolio Strategies*, 1987.

INVESTMENT BANKERS ASSOCIATION OF AMERICA
Originally organized in 1912, the Investment Bankers Association of America (IBA) combined with the Association of Stock Exchange Firms in 1972 to form the present Securities Industry Association.

INVESTMENT BANKS
A classification of banking institutions sometimes used to indicate those institutions that supply long-term and intermediate credit to borrowers. The term "bank," however, is loosely used in such a sense. The Board of Governors of the Federal Reserve System defines a bank as a financial institution that accepts money from the general public for deposit in a common fund, subject to withdrawal or to transfer by check on demand or on short notice, and makes loans to the general public. This definition therefore includes national banks and state-chartered commercial banks, trust companies, mutual and stock savings banks, and industrial banks (private banks and bankers). It therefore excludes building and savings and loan associations, personal loan and other small-loan companies, credit unions, mortgage companies, sales finance companies, insurance companies, and the various credit agencies owned in whole or in part by the federal government.

Prior to the Banking Act of 1933, which divorced security-selling affiliates of member banks, many banks operated departments for the purchase and sale of securities through their security affiliates, thus coming close to the European concept of investment banks, which not only accept deposits from the public of the savings and commercial type, but also underwrite, purchase, and sell securities in addition to transacting savings and commercial banking.

In recent years, certain of the more aggressive commercial banks have aroused the opposition of the Securities Industry Association and its investment banking members as well as the INVESTMENT COMPANY INSTITUTE, based on the prohibitions to commercial banks contained in the BANKING ACT OF 1933. This opposition is to attempts to authorize commercial banks to underwrite REVENUE BONDS (*see* MUNICIPAL BONDS), to organize and to sell publicly COMMERCIAL BANK-ORGANIZED INVESTMENT COMPANY shares, and to become active as COMMERCIAL PAPER dealers. On the other hand, commercial bankers c mplain of the encroachments upon their banking functions by aggressive investment bankers, as exemplified by organization and sale of money market funds with checking privileges and by the offering to the public of money management accounts involving the acceptance of deposit-like funds from the public. The future is likely to witness increased pressures from both sides in the competition for such financial services.

See INVESTMENT BANKER.

INVESTMENT BAROMETERS
Statistical indicators that have a particular bearing on the trends in security prices. High-grade bonds, for example, are primarily influenced by the trend of interest rates; thus all data pertaining to factors affecting interest rates, both on the supply and demand side for funds as well as on Federal Reserve policy, would be relevant for analysis of the "real" factors having a causal connection. The fundamental approach to forecasting of stock prices concentrates on aggregative and particular data having a bearing on stock earnings. The technical approach concentrates on data developed by security markets themselves, such as price patterns and volume of trading; short interest; proportion of stocks advancing, declining, or making new highs or lows; behavior of odd-lot buyers and sellers (volume of odd-lot buying and selling, orders, and net buying or selling on balance), etc. Techniques or systems for interpretation of the data have abounded, ranging from fundamental to technical in nature.

See DOW THEORY as an example of a technical technique for determining primary trends of stock prices based on interpretation of price trends of industrial and railroad stock averages.

BIBLIOGRAPHY

JOINT ECONOMIC COMMITTEE (U.S. CONGRESS). *Economic Indicators*, Monthly.
U.S. DEPARTMENT OF COMMERCE. *Handbook of Cyclical Indicators*, 1984.

INVESTMENT COMPANY
As defined in the Investment Company Act of 1940, any issuer that:

1. Is or holds itself out as being engaged primarily, or proposes to engage primarily, in the business of investing, reinvesting, or trading in securities
2. Is engaged or proposes to engage in the business of issuing face amount certificates of the installment type, or has been engaged in such business and has any such certificates outstanding
3. Is engaged or proposes to engage in the business of investing, reinvesting, owning, holding, or trading in securities, and owns or proposes to acquire investment securities having a value exceeding 40% of the value of such issuer's total assets (exclusive of government securities and cash items) on an unconsolidated basis.

Face amount certificates of the installment type are defined as obligations to pay on stated or determinable dates, more than 24 months after date of issuance, in consideration of periodic payments similarly ascertained. "Securities," as used in the definition do not include government issues, those of employees' securities companies, or those of majority-owned subsidiaries that are not investment companies.

Money Market Funds Phenomenon. In recent years of record and near-record short-term money rates, the rise in yields and rates of return in money market short-term instruments, occasioned by the Federal Reserve's implementation of an anti-inflation monetary policy, has provided the stimulative background for the phenomenal rise of a new type of open-end fund. The money market fund, so-called because of its specialization in holdings of short-term money market investments, affords investors returns considerably in excess of rates paid on passbook savings accounts by thrift institutions (commercial banks' saving departments, mutual savings banks, and savings and loan associations) and also in excess of returns afforded by such thrift institutions on their savings certificates restricted as to freedom of withdrawals before specified maturity.

Besides the advantage in yields, the following are usually included among the features afforded to investors by money market funds.

1. Lower minimum initial investment (e.g., from $1,000 to $2,500) compared to the usual minimum $10,000 initial investment in thrift institutions' savings certificates, including the six-month money market certificate.
2. Privilege of checkwriting without checking charges, provided minimum holding is maintained (e.g., $500), with yield continuing until the check clears. No penalties for withdrawals.
3. No sales charges to open a money market fund account.

On the other hand, the yield on money market fund shares will fluctuate daily as money market rates vary as a function of portfolio quality and maturities, as well as expenses of the fund.

The money market account is not insured as is the savings account (passbook savings or savings certificates) in commercial banks, mutual savings banks, savings and loan associations, and credit unions.

The spectacular rise of money market funds has been the source of disintermediation (outflow of funds from intermediary thrift institutions) which has proven to be a serious problem for many such institutions, along with the internal shift of deposit funds in such

INVESTMENT COMPANY

institutions from lower-paying passbook savings accounts to the higher-paying savings certificates. Faced with such outflow of funds and higher cost of retained funds on one hand, the thrift institutions on the other hand have been restricted to interest rate ceilings that may be paid on deposits, lack of authority to invest more broadly in higher yielding earning assets (in the case of thrifts other than commercial banks), and low earning rates on mortgage portfolios.

In March, 1980, the Federal Reserve imposed a 15% reserve requirement on new asset growth of existing money market funds, which led sponsors of such funds to organize new "clones" not technically subject to the reserve requirement. Although this restriction on growth and yields was rescinded (see FEDERAL RESERVE BOARD OF GOVERNORS) a few months later in 1980, the idea of imposing a legal reserve requirement was being re-urged as of 1981, based on the checking privileges afforded by the money market funds. Under the DEPOSITORY INSTITUTIONS DEREGULATION AND MONETARY CONTROL ACT OF 1980, interest rate ceilings will be gradually phased out.

Investment companies rank today among the largest investing institutions, and constitute a potent market factor and money pool for investment. The following paragraphs trace the history and development of investment companies, from their early humble beginnings in the U.S., influenced by British investment company practice, to their mushroom growth in the late 1920s, subsequent shakeout caused by the great depression, subjection to federal regulation beginning in 1940, and their present important position.

British Investment Trusts. Although the first investment "trust" (the modern American designation for these investing institutions is "investment company") is said to have been authorized by King William of the Netherlands in Brussels in 1822, and an investment trust was started in Switzerland in 1849, the prototype that still serves as a model for modern investment companies of the general management type first assumed importance in England and Scotland. The first was called the Foreign and Colonial Government Trust and was organized in 1865. There were also the London Financial Association and the International Financial Society. Many of these early investment trusts invested heavily in American securities and those of the colonies of Great Britain. The purpose of the early British investment trusts was to procure the highest yield compatible with safety through the principle of diversification and the substitution of expert investment knowledge for guesswork. The prospectus of the Foreign and Colonial Government Trust stated: "The object of this trust is to give the investor of moderate means the same advantage as the large capitalist in diminishing the risk of investing in foreign and colonial government stocks and reserving a portion of the extra interest as a sinking fund to pay off the original capital. A capitalist who at any time within the last 20 or 30 years had invested, say £1,000,000, in ten or twelve such stocks selected with ordinary prudence, would on the above plan not only have received a high rate of interest, but by this time received back his original capital by the action of the drawings and sinking fund, and held the greater part of his stocks for nothing." (Shades of modern investment company promotional literature!)

British investment trusts went through a baptism of fire caused by the crisis generated by the Baring Brothers failure in 1893. Out of that experience, the surviving companies emerged with sounder accounting practices, such as the crediting of turnover profits to reserves as protection against future market depreciation and losses.

The British investment trust is managed by a board of directors, or trustee-managers. Certain limitations on complete freedom of action have been characteristic, but the trustees nevertheless are vested with wide discretionary powers. Under the specified restrictions imposed by the articles (or memorandum) of association, the directors may, among other things:

1. Issue and allot shares of stocks and debentures
2. Purchase and sell securities and other investments
3. Act as transfer agents for the registration of the company's securities
4. Appoint and fix salaries of officers and clerks
5. Institute, defend, compromise, or settle any legal action on behalf of the company
6. Set aside a portion of the company's earnings as a reserve
7. Determine the profits of the company
8. Negotiate and effect a combination of the interests of the company with those of any other company.

There is usually some provision for limiting the expenses of administering the trust.

Over a period of about a century, British investment trust practice has become fairly well standardized and has assumed the following characteristics: limitation of the amount of capital that may be invested in a single undertaking, which is usually from 5% to 10%; limitation of the amount of debentures and preferred stock to that of the total common stock outstanding ("trading on the equity"); payment of dividends from earnings without reference to possible impairment of the original capital, but the building up of reserves from capital gains; absence of desire to control or operate any enterprise; vesting of control in common or deferred shares, or in founders' shares.

The pattern of capitalization of British investment trusts is also fairly well defined. There are three general classes of securites which are issued—ordinary or common shares, preference or preferred shares, and debentures. A common provision of the declaration of trust is one limiting the issue of debentures outstanding at any one time to the aggregate amount of ordinary and preference shares.

U.S. Investment Companies. U.S. investment companies are of comparatively recent origin, and did not become generally popular before 1923. One of the oldest U.S. investment companies was the Railway & Light Securities Co., which dated through its predecessor, Railway & Light Securities Co., a Maine corporation, from 1904. In the 1920s, the American concept of investment company was broadened to include not only companies or funds operating like the British (the British models being the general management type), but also certain other types of investment participation. In this country in the era of the 1920s five types of investment companies developed, i.e., general management, specialized management, fixed or limited management, holding and financial companies, and trading corporations. What were known as fixed and limited management investment companies in this country became popular for a time in the early 1930s, after disappointment with the results of the general management companies following the 1929 break in security prices, and generally involved the issue of certificates carrying pro rata participation in a group of specified common stocks. The composition of each group, "block," or "unit" was prescribed in the indenture, under whose terms a trust company, acting as trustee, held the underlying securities and issued the participating certificates. The rigidly fixed type of trust indenture provided that no changes were to be made in the units of deposited securities. Other indentures, under which participations were sold to investors, provided for some element of management by defining a large list of eligible securities out of which the specific selection for the units could be made by the "depositor" (the sponsor selling organization creating the fixed trust by agreement with the trust company functioning as trustee under the indenture).

With the deepening of the 1929-1932 depression, weaknesses in investment companies organized during the late 1920s became glaringly pronounced and were fatal to many companies, especially those that had sold large amounts of senior capital (debentures and preferred stocks) at high interest and dividend rates, thus providing for high fixed charges and leverage, and had invested the proceeds in securities at boomtime prices. Under pressure of the collapse in security prices, abuses in management crept in; some investment companies organized by investment firms had become in effect dumping grounds for sticky underwritings; their holdings had been "churned" to generate commission business for the brokerage firm sponsors; and self-serving fees and contracts had served to milk the companies. The financial and holding company type, which with the trading type had been popular in the late 1920s, practically disappeared, and many general management types also passed out of existence, were absorbed, or were reorganized. Popularity of the fixed type of companies sharply waned as the list of stocks rigidly prescribed in the indenture incurred severe depreciation, suspended dividends, and loss of their original investment standing. Many of these indentures, however, continued in existence, as they originally had prescribed 15 and 20 years or longer in term of the trust, so that although such fixed type shares were no longer offered actively, termination and liquidation of the underlying units remained to be accomplished in the future. Beginning about 1932, the open-end (or Boston type) investment company began to rise as a solution for the disadvantages of the fixed type, and today such open-end investment companies are the most numerous and dynamic in growth. Although the mortality rate in investment companies was high, various companies of the closed-end general management type with conservative management weathered the depression safely.

Federal Regulation. In 1935, pursuant to the Public Utility Holding Company Act, the Securities and Exchange Commission (SEC) embarked upon an exhaustive study of investment companies in the U.S. which is the definitive work on U.S. investment company experience prior to federal regulation. This study led to passage of the Investment Company Act of 1940, representing the first federal regulation of investment companies and marking a new stage in their history and development. Besides being remedial in nature by aiming at abuses uncovered by the SEC study, the act is positive in character by prescribing new standards and procedures. The act divided investment companies into three general classes.

1. Face amount certificate companies (those engaged in issuing such participations or having any outstanding).
2. Unit investment trusts, organized under a trust indenture or similar instrument, not having boards of directors, and issuing only redeemable securities that represent undivided interests in units of specified securities (the so-called fixed trust-type).
3. Management companies, which are further subdivided into open-end companies and closed-end companies. These companies are additionally subdivided into diversified and non-diversified companies.

An open-end company is one that offers for sale or has outstanding any redeemable security of which it is the issuer. Shares are continuously offered, hence the open-end capitalization. This is the Boston type, known semantically today as a mutual fund, the most common and most dynamically growing classification of companies. One of the earliest was the Eaton & Howard Management Fund A-1 (now known as Eaton & Howard Balanced Fund), organized under a trust indenture March 23, 1932, felicitous timing (near the depth of the depression) for formation. The closed-end type do not continuously offer their shares, directly or through distributor, and do not redeem their shares upon demand by the holders thereof. A diversified company is one that has at least 75% of the value of its total assets represented by cash and receivables, government securities, and those of other investment companies, and other securities are limited for this purpose in respect to any one issuer to an amount not greater in value than 5% of the investment company's total assets, and to not more than 10% of the outstanding voting securities of the issuer.

Salient regulatory features of the act included the following.

1. **Registration.** Every investment company with more than 100 security holders must register with the SEC.
2. **Adequacy of capital.** Section 14 of the act sets forth three conditions, compliance with one of which is a necessary prerequisite to a public offering; (a) net worth of the issuing company must be at least $100,000; (b) the issuer must have previously made a public offering and at the time thereof have had a similar net worth minimum; (c) provision must be made, as a condition for registration of public offerings under the Securities Act of 1933, to adequately insure (in the SEC's opinion): (1) that after the effective date of the registration, the company will not issue any security, or receive the proceeds of any subscription, until agreements have been made by not more than 25 responsible persons to purchase securities to be issued by the company for an amount that in addition to the net worth of the company will equal at least $100,000; (2) that the agreed payments will be made before any subscriptions are accepted from any persons in excess of 25; and (3) that arrangements will be made for refund without deduction upon demand of any proceeds paid in, should the company not realize a net worth of $100,000 within 90 days after the registration becomes effective. These provisions are aimed to prevent unduly low ""shoestring" capital.
3. **Conservatism of capital structures.** To limit "trading on the equity," closed-end companies are required to have assets of at least three times funded debt or bank loans at time of issuance, and preferred stock must be covered by at least two times by assets. Open-end companies are limited to solely one class of security outstanding, although bank loans are permitted to a limited extent. These requirements as to capitalization applied to capital structures after 1940, and did not disturb capitalizations built up prior thereto.
4. **Investment policies.** Each company is required to register a statement of basic investment policy, which once stated may not be changed except with approval of stockholders.
5. **Management practices and procedures.** The act prohibits self-dealing, conflicts of interest, or breaches of trust; bars persons guilty of securities frauds from serving as officers or directors; requires that a majority of the board of directors be composed of persons not affiliated with investment bankers or with brokers; requires stockholders' approval of fundamental changes in the board of directors; calls for at least 40% of the directors to be persons who are not officers or investment advisers of the company; and requires that a majority of the directors of open-end companies be independent of the "sponsor" or sales distribution organization. Trafficking in management contracts and contracts to supervise the company's funds is prohibited. In addition, investment companies may not purchase over a nominal percentage of voting securities of other investment companies.

The act (Sec. 31) provides statutory authority for periodic inspection by the SEC of investment companies. These inspections indicated in some instances noncompliance with the act in such areas as the following:

1. Improper selling practices by salespeople who promoted the sale of mutual fund shares just prior to dividend dates without explaining that the amount of dividend to be paid was included in the purchase price of the shares on which a sales-load was paid and that receipt of the dividend would represent a return of capital on which the shareholder would be liable for income taxes
2. Deviations from fundamental policy without approval of stockholders
3. Improper composition of boards of directors because of the affiliations of directors
4. Acquisition of securities during an underwriting where an affiliated relationship existed between underwriter and company
5. Sale of securities to a company by an affiliated person acting as a principal
6. Failure to file an appropriate fidelity bond
7. Noncompliance with the requirements for the custody of the portfolio securities of a company under Section 17 of the act
8. Failure to obtain approval of stockholders or the board of directors for an investment advisory contract.

In addition to noncompliance with standards and regulations under the act, such inspections revealed instances where books and records were inadequate or lacking. Problems included failure to record the d te and time of requests for redemption, thus making it impossible to determine whether the investors received their correct net asset value; failure to maintain purchase and sales journals, and failure to maintain ledger accounts for broker-dealers used by the company for its portfolio security transactions; failure to keep proper vouchers for out-of-pocket expenses; and considerable delay in the transmission to the investment companies of funds received by dealers selling the mutual fund shares. Also found were instances where the custodian did not adhere to the terms of the custodianship agreement or the SEC's regulations on the safekeeping of portfolio securities of the company.

The vast growth of investment companies in the 1960s and the resulting changes created situations that were not anticipated in the original drafting of the Investment Company Act of 1940. As a result of the Securities and Exchange Commission's original proposals in 1967 plus subsequent modifications, the following recommendations were presented to the 91st Session of Congress:

1. Compensation received by investment advisers and other persons affiliated with investment companies should be "reasonable" and there should be opportunity for judicial enforcement of this standard.
2. Contracts that base any part of the adviser's fee on a specified percentage of the company's capital appreciation should be pro-hibited, but fees that increase and decrease proportionately on the basis of investment performance measured against an appropriate index of securities prices or other appropriate measure of performance would be permissible.

INVESTMENT COMPANY

3. The so-called front-end load on periodic payment plus certificate plans (i.e., certificates issued in connection with contractual plans for the accumulation of fund shares on an installment basis) should be abolished or restricted.
4. The National Association of Securities Dealers should be given authority to make rules to prevent excessive sales charges, subject to the Securities and Exchange Commission's oversight.
5. Exclusion from the act of those oil and gas funds that issue redeemable securities or sell their securities on the installment plan should be terminated; however, oil and gas funds in which investors make only a single payment and do not receive a redeemable security would still be excluded from the definition of an investment company.
6. The imposition of surrender charges should be abolished.

In late 1970, the 91st Congress passed the Mutual Fund Bill (P.L. 91-547), pursuant to which the NATIONAL ASSOCIATION OF SECURITIES DEALERS, INC.(NASD) submitted its proposed "full service" maximum sales load rule to the SEC. As proposed, the rule, which was designed to prevent excessive sales loads, taking into account all related circumstances, permitted mutual funds or single payment contractual plans to charge a maximum sales load of 8.5% (declining to 6.25% for larger purchases), but conditioned the right to charge the maximum on the fund's offering of dividend reinvestment at net asset value, rights of accumulation, and volume discounts, as defined in the rule. The rule was adopted by NASD's board of governors on January 28, 1975, and was subsequently approved by the NASD membership for SEC approval.

The section of the law that regulates contractual plans allows the sponsors of such plans to operate under two alternatives. The first alternative retains the 50% maximum first-year sales load and the 9% overall sales charge provisions previously in effect. If a periodic plan certificate is sold with such a load, the following refund provisions apply. The holder may surrender the certificate at any time within the first 18 months after issuance and receive the value of his account plus the excess of any sales load above 15% of his total payments. The registered investment company issuing the certificate, or any depositor of an underwriter for such company, must give written notice of these redemption rights. This notification must be made to each certificate holder who has missed three payments or more within 30 days following the expiration of 15 months after the issuance of the certificate. A second alternative allows not more than 20% of any one payment to be deducted for sales load, and provides that the entire deduction during the first four years may not exceed 64% of the total payments. Again, the total sales charge may not exceed 9% of the total investment over the life of the plan. Under this alternative a seller is entitled to deduct a 16% sales load each year for the four-year period or 20% in each of the first three years and 4% in the fourth year.

The law also gives a specific fiduciary duty to a fund's investment adviser, which would allow either the Securities and Exchange Commission or a shareholder to sue an investment adviser for a breach of fiduciary duty, particularly regarding compensation for his services.

In 1970, the Securities and Exchange Commission issued an official policy statement on the acquisition and holding of restricted securities by investment companies. These securities, sometimes referred to as "letter stock," are securities that are acquired in private placements or that for some other reason require registration under the Securities Act of 1933 before they may be resold to the public. The commission set a 10% limitation in terms of net assets on such restricted securities by open-end investment companies, so as to avoid possible liquidity problems.

Pros and cons of the load charge on open-end shares are as follows. The load is necessary to compensate the distributor for its sales promotion efforts, important for growth of the company, and the dealers selling to investors. The load is only on purchases by the investor, most companies making no or only a nominal charge on redemptions of shares. The following are the cons of the load charge. The load frequently may be more than the dividends plus appreciation, if any, of the first year of holding. There is no point in paying a load for open-end shares when just as reputable and suitable open-end companies charge no load, and when reputable and suitable closed-end company shares are available in the market either at asset values, or reasonable premiums, or even discounts below current asset values; closed-end companies do not redeem shares, but many have their shares listed on stock exchanges and traded actively in the over-the-counter market. That loads are profitable is indicated by the usually strong demand for shares of distributor organizations, some of which first made their shares publicly available in recent years.

Tax Status. Both open-end and closed-end investment companies may elect to qualify irrevocably as "regulated investment companies" for tax purposes under the Internal Revenue Code. Practically all have so elected because of the tremendous tax advantages obtained, i.e., in effect making them largely tax-free, thus reducing extra multiple taxation (taxation still is multiple—issuers of securities pay income taxes, and individual holders of investment company shares pay personal income taxes). To be eligible for the tax-regulated category, investment companies must be registered under the Investment Company Act of 1940; must qualify as to minimum diversification under the code (readily met by reason of the Investment Company Act's own requirements); and must distribute at least 90% of net investment income as taxable dividends (no requirement that capital gains be distributed). Such a regulated investment company pays federal income taxes solely on any part, up to 10%, of investment income retained, and on retained capital gains. Since 1956, moreover, the tax paid by the regulated investment company on retained capital gains is for the account of the shareholders, i.e., the individual shareholder reports and gets credit on his tax return for such tax paid by the investment company in his behalf, and writes up the cost of his investment company shares by the amount of the capital gains tax paid by the company. At the end of the year, each shareholder of an investment company receives therefrom a notification of the taxable basis for dividends received, ordinary dividend income, depletion dividends (return of capital), and dividends from capital gains, so that the shareholder may appropriately report such respective portions in his tax return. Capital gains tax paid on retained capital gains by the investment company is also reported to the shareholder.

Uses for Investment Company Shares. Individual investors find in investment company shares a medium for the practice of diversification for any amount invested. The diversification will be in accordance with the registered investing policy. Thus the individual can select that investing policy consistent with his own objectives. Classified as to investing policy, open-end companies include the common stock or equity companies, investing in diversified holdings of common stocks; the balanced funds, investing in bonds, preferred stocks, and common stocks in appropriate ratios of "defensive" and "aggressive" selections from such media; and the speciality funds, with portfolios specializing intensively in particular classes and qualities of securities, e.g., investing solely in high-grade bonds; medium-grade bonds; speculative bonds; high- and medium-grade preferred stocks; high-grade, medium-grade, and speculative common stocks; or stocks of companies in particular industries such as steel stocks, chemical stocks, etc., without diversification outside the industry selected.

Dual Funds, which first appeared in 1967, are closed-end companies with a specified duration (usually 15 years), which afford two types of leveraged shares: income shares, which contribute half the original capital but are entitled to all of the investment income, including a specified current minimum if earned dividend and dividend arrears if any, and capital shares, which also contribute half of the original capital but are entitled to all of the capital gains presumably accumulated when the fund is eventually liquidated, after allowing for original capital investment of the income shares and any of their dividend arrears. The capital shares therefore receive no dividends during the duration of the fund and depend upon the residual upon eventual liquidation for long-term capital gains.

Hedge funds (in fact, nonpublic limited partnerships, run by general partners) engage in both margin buying and short selling to realize capital gains. Swap funds, which first appeared in 1960, are exchange funds accorded tax-free status (Sec. 351 of the Internal Revenue Code) for the securities of participants originally accepted in setting up the fund, who thus postpone capital gains tax that would have to be paid if their holdings were first sold and the net proceeds used to participate in the fund. Such funds are "one-shot" formations, no continuous offering of shares being permitted pursuant to the code.

No-load funds are simply mutual funds that sell their shares to the public without the sales charge (load) above asset value. They can be readily identified in the list of quoted mutual fund shares by the fact that offered prices are exactly the same as bid prices (asset values).

Investment company shares are suitable for DOLLAR AVERAGING with automatic diversification provided by the portfolio of the company pursuant to its investing policy; for execution of FORMULA PLANS, defensive investment company shares being bought as well as aggressive investment company shares in the desired ratios and thereafter adjusted pursuant to the formula followed; for investment and in general for investors who do not have either the time or skill to select and administer their own direct selections.

BIBLIOGRAPHY

DONOGHUR's *Money Fund Report.*
WISENBERGER SERVICES, INC. *Investment Companies.* Annual.

INVESTMENT COMPANY ACT OF 1940 An act designed to control many abuses associated with investment companies and investment advisers. This complex act is described by the Commission of the Securities and Exchange Commission as follows:

> Under this act, the activities of companies engaged primarily in the business of investing, reinvesting, and trading in securities and whose own securities are offered and sold to and held by the investing public, are subject to certain statutory prohibitions and to Commission regulation in accordance with prescribed standards deemed necessary to protect the interests of investors and the public.

All companies whose business comes under this act must register with the SEC. Disclosure of the financial condition and investment policies of the company is required. This provision enables investors to have access to complete information concerning the activities of the investment companies. Such disclosures must be updated periodically.

Other major provisions of the act prohibit (1) anyone guilty of security frauds from being associated with investment companies, (2) transactions between the companies and their directors, officers, or affiliated companies without prior commission approval, and (3) pyramids of such companies and cross-ownership of their securities or the issuance of senior securities, except under certain conditions.

SEC supervision and regulation of the investment activities of the companies does not give assurance that securities offered by such companies will be good investments, except to provide that reports of company activities must be provided to stockholders at least semiannually. The registration statements and reports of regulated investment companies contain detailed financial statements and schedules which must be certified by independent public accountants. Accountants must conduct periodic unannounced examinations of the securities held by the companies and report the results to the SEC. Accountants are also required to certify not only the financial statements but also many of the items in the reports. This requirement provides "negative assurance" with respect to such items.

INVESTMENT EXPENDITURES At the macroeconomic level, investment expenditures include fixed business investment, residential construction, and changes in inventories. Fixed business investment (capital) represents the purchase of plant and equipment by firms and is roughly 70% to 75% of all investment expenditures. Fixed business investment is necessary in order for firms to replace old plant and equipment and then to expand the stock of capital.

Investment expenditures are an important category in the expenditure approach to the calculation of gross national product (GNP). See appended exhibit of the investment expenditures for the economy for selected years.

INVESTMENT COMPANY INSTITUTE Formerly the National Association of Investment Companies, the institute was founded in 1941. It represents its members—mutual funds, their managers, and their underwriters—and their shareholders in matters of legislation, regulation, taxation, public information and advertising, statistics, and economic and market research. The institute provides a clearinghouse to which interested persons and communications media may turn for information about the mutual fund industry in the United States, and serves as spokesman and factfinder in many areas affecting its members, their shareholders, and the investing public. The institute is located at 1725 K Street N.W., Washington, D.C. 20006.

Year	Gross Private Domestic Investment ($billions)
1950	$ 55.1
1960	78.2
1970	148.8
1980	437.0
1981	515.5
1982	447.3
1983	502.3
1984	664.8
1985	641.6
1986	671.0
1987	716.4

Source: Economic Report of the President, 1988.

INVESTMENT CREDIT Long-term CREDIT furnished to finance the purchase of durable goods, fixed assets, etc. A purchaser of corporation bonds or real estate mortgages is a lender of investment credit.

INVESTMENT INCOME INCOME derived from invested cap-ital as distinguished from income derived from services. In insurance company accounting, investment income is current income (interest, dividends, etc.) from securities held in portfolios, as contrasted with capital gains or losses derived from actual sale of securities, and book appreciation or depreciation on retained securities. Insurance companies generally keep their own dividends to stockholders within investment income alone, thus assuring stability of dividends to stockholders and the "ploughing back" of all other gains (underwriting, turnover of securities, and book appreciation) into surplus. This normally results in large ploughed back gains, with consequent compounding of growth in equity values over a period of years.

See INSURANCE COMPANY STATEMENTS.

INVESTMENT MARKET The channels or outlets for distributing bonds and other investments. The chief market for bonds exists among the following classes of purchasers: investing public (private investors); banks—commercial, savings, and trust companies; speculative public; insurance companies; business concerns; investment companies; trusts, estates, and trustees; eleemosynary institutions; foundations; labor unions, fraternal orders and clubs; endowments.

INVESTMENT MEDIA The various types of property in which capital may be invested rationally for gain, whether enhancement of principal, current return, or both, rather than just conservation of principal. Besides INVESTMENT in a going business, the most usual types of investment media available may be summarized as follows.

1. Savings accounts (in commercial banks, savings banks, credit unions, and savings and loan associations)
2. Time deposits and certificates of deposit
3. U.S. savings bonds and stamps
4. U.S. postal savings certificates
5. U.S. government bonds, Treasury notes, certificates of indebtedness, and bills
6. U.S. government-guaranteed obligations
7. U.S. government agency obligations
8. State, political, subdivision, and municipal obligations
9. Insurance—ordinary, limited payment, endowment, etc.
10. Annuities—life, terminable, perpetual
11. Notes, acceptances, and bills of exchange
12. Commodities
13. Precious metals, jewels
14. Objets d'art
15. Corporate bonds
16. Corporate stocks
17. Real estate bonds and mortgages—insured by the Federal Housing Administration, guaranteed by the Veterans Administration, or "conventional"—on urban property (commercial, industrial, and residential) and farm property
18. Chattel mortgages on various types of personal property

INVESTMENT METHODS AND STRATEGIES

19. Foreign bonds and stocks
20. Foreign exchange and gold
21. Real estate—urban property (commercial, industrial, and residential) and farm property.

In recent years, the precious metals and objets d'art including paintings, jewels, etc., have become more popular as "inflation hedges." As investments, however, they provide no current income; their value is subject to varying appraisal; their marketability is subject to negotiation and vulnerable to changes in industrial, personal, and governmental demand and tastes; and their proper storage usually involves carrying charges.

INVESTMENT METHODS AND STRATEGIES

Various theories have been advanced to determine the best method of selecting securities. The theories differ primarily in the distinction drawn between speculative and investment strategies. These theories can be concisely described in the following terms:

Theory	Strategy	Analysis
Technical selection	Speculative	Price and trading volume charts
Fundamental selection	Mixed	Valuation of future cash flows and cash assets
Efficient market selection	Investment	None—hold widely diversified portfolio with acceptable risk

Technical selection assumes that security prices usually move in identifiable patterns that can be determined through chart techniques to extrapolate trends. Fundamentalists rely heavily upon an analysis of discounted future cash flows to estimate the intrinsic worth of securities. Those who accept the efficient market theory hold that all important information associated with securities is already reflected in existing prices. Hence, analysis is not required.

A glossary of investment methods and strategies is shown here.

Glossary of Investment Methods and Strategies

Advance-decline Breadth of market. If advances consistently outnumber declines, the market is considered to be in a bullish phase. When declines are more numerous than advances, the market is considered to be in a bearish phase. When the Dow Jones averages advance and the advance/decline ratio either does not advance or levels off, the advance is probably false. If the advance/decline ratio is strong but the Dow levels off, the Dow should begin to rise.

Averaging up The technique of buying additional shares of a particular stock as the price of the stock rises to reduce the average cost of the stock.

Bear market A down market; a stock market after it has developed a downward trend. A bear market will usually not last as long as a bull market; it declines more rapidly than a bull market goes up. When the Dow Jones industrial average fails to penetrate the peak of the preceding intermediate advance, a bear market is signaled. A bear market is confirmed when the next intermediate dip penetrates the low point of the preceding decline. The bear market will con-tinue as long as these conditions exist. Chartists look for broad movement and increasing volume before they signal a primary trend. Can use effectively short selling, selling against the box, buying bonds, and options.

Blue chips The common stock of well-established, profitable, and large U.S.companies, such as IBM, GE, GM, and many others.

Bond Strategies include switching back and forth between stocks and bonds, depending upon market levels.

Breadth-momentum index A comparison of the amount of movement up or down of the advance-decline line with the movement of the New York Stock Exchange Index of stock prices. See advance-decline.

Breakouts Sharp and strong upward or downward stock price movements from a previously horizontal pattern. Breakouts signal a significant move in the price of the stock. False breakouts are common.

Bull market An up market; the market in an established upward movement. Bull markets typically last longer than do bear markets. Many signals are available to determine the end of a bull market, such as, low dividend yields on common stock and the floating of many new stock issues. When the Dow Jones industrial average fails to penetrate the low point of the preceding intermediate decline, a reversal of the bear (down) trend is possible. The bull market is confirmed when the next intermediate rise in the Dow penetrates the preceding peak. As long as these conditions keep recurring, the bull market continues.

Buy-and-hold The strategy of buying common stock and holding it for an indefinite period. Investor ignores market fluctuations. Can be justified for selling the security if there are major changes in the corporation or in the security.

Cash flow per share Net income plus expenses such as depreciation that do not involve actual cash outlays. Some analysts consider this ratio to be more significant than earnings per share; others maintain that it can be very misleading.

Cash position Some investors hold large amounts of cash or Treasury Bills during a bear market or during the last stages of a bull market, anticipating more favorable opportunities in the future. During periods of declining market prices, investors hold a cash cushion to invest at a later date. A fully invested position, usually less than 3% cash, is a bearish signal; a strong cash position, over 10%, is bullish. Companies having strong (weak) cash positions, can make (cannot make) substantial purchases and help the market rise.

Charts Graphic presentation of stock prices and volume of trading frequently used to forecast the market. Examples of charting include simple-line charts, trend-line charts, moving-average charts, point-and-figure charts, and many others. Used frequently in technical analysis. See entry on Charting.

Climax Sudden, sharp price trend changes on stock charts along with great increases in the volume of trading that signal immediate concern or opportunity.

Concept stocks Stocks to which a big idea can be associated, such as a scientific breakthrough, a new drug discovery, and a new merchandising approach. Sharp price fluctuations are often associated with concept stocks.

Confidence index Investor optimism and pessimism. A ratio of the yield on Barron's High-Grade Bond index to the yield on the Dow-Jones Composite Bond Average. Suggests the confidence of experienced investors in medium-grade corporate bonds relative to high-grade bonds. When lower-grade bond issues outperform high-grade bonds, the confidence index rises, which is an optimistic sign for stock prices. Investors are not worrying about safety and are willing to purchase a lower-quality bond. The converse is also true.

Consensus of indicators An averaging by various statistical methods of many stock market price indicators (for example, volume, short sales, free credit balance, advance-decline line at market tops and total short interest at market bottoms, and the odd-lot short sales ratio at market tops).

Constant-dollar plan A plan that keeps a fixed number of dollars in stock with a fluctuating amount in bonds or other defensive instruments. If stocks rise, some shares are sold and the extra money beyond the previously decided fixed amount is used to buy bonds. If stocks go down, bonds are sold and the money is used to buy shares to bring the dollars in the stocks up to the desired amount.

Constant-ratio formula A plan which keeps a fixed ratio of money in stock and bonds (for example, 50% in stocks and 50% in bonds). As the market fluctuates, stocks are sold and bonds bought, or vice versa, so as to keep the ratio constant. This plan is supposed to work well in a complete market cycle that includes some wide swings.

Contrary opinion Action that differs from what the general investing public does at a certain time. Its purpose is to outsmart the market. The underlying idea of this theory is that what a majority of investors know is not worth knowing.

Convertible bonds Convertibles may offer the stability of a bond in down markets and the capital gains opportunity of common stock in up markets. Provides some downside protection.

INVESTMENT METHODS AND STRATEGIES

Divergence analysis Analysis of the difference between the actions of sophisticated and unsophisticated investors (for example, short-sellers and specialists (sophisticated) versus odd-lot investors (unsophisticated)).

Diversification Holding more than one stock of a security to reduce overall risk, especially to spread risk among various counterbalancing industries and among different corporations within each industry. Diversification can presumably be attained for an individual investor by holding between five to fifteen different securities. Diversification can also be achieved through investing in mutual funds.

Dollar averaging Investing an equal amount of money at stated intervals (monthly, quarterly) in a particular security or group of securities. This practice should result in buying at low price levels to balance buying at higher prices. Dollar averaging is sometimes modified to allow increasing the amount of periodic investment when stock prices are low and decreasing the amount when stock prices are high.

Federal Reserve Board actions Noting actions taken by the Board of Governors of the Federal Reserve System that can influence business and the stock market (for example, discount (interest) rates, margin requirements, and member bank's reserves (money supply)) to serve as an indicator of stock market behavior.

Gold stock price Observe the prices of gold-mining companies stocks which tend to move in a direction opposite to that of the stock averages.

Government bonds Purchase government bonds on margin when a business recession is due because the government will undoubtedly adopt easy money policies that will result in a drop in interest rates and an increase in bond prices. Government securities are usually purchased for the safety factor.

Graham formula An investment timing plan that involves computing a normal or central value for earnings on the Dow-Jones Industrial Average and the yield on Moody's Corporate Aaa Bond Average. The formula involves a fundamental approach to investing.

Growth stocks Stocks of companies with earnings above the average at an annual rate are assumed. Growth stocks tend to become overvalued and to move in comparatively wide swings.

Hedging A sale or purchase of a contract for future delivery against a previous purchase or sale of an equal quantity of the same commodity or an equivalent quantity of another commodity that has a parallel price movement, and when it is expected that the transaction in the contract market will be cancelled by an offset transaction at the time the contemplated spot transaction is completed and before the futures contract matures; or, the practice of buying or selling futures to counterbalance an existing position in the trade market, thus avoiding the risk of unforseen major movements in price. Hedging may be accomplished in different ways in the stock market (for example, using options, to have a long position in stocks viewed favorably along with short positions in stocks viewed unfavorably; 50% long, 50% short; stable convertible bond and a common stock that fluctuates with the market in a bear market).

High-low index A measure of the difference between the number of stocks making new highs in price for the year and those making new lows. Considered a good indicator of bull market tops; provides early warning signal for the market in general.

Income stocks Stocks of companies that pay liberal and reliable dividends. However, the higher the yield, the higher the risk. Growth prospects should usually be considered.

Insider transactions The buying and selling activities of directors, officers, and large stockholders, reported monthly in the Official Summary of Security Transactions and Holding (the Insider's Report, compiled by the SEC). Insider transactions can provide clues to stock prices.

Institutional investing The investing activities of funds and other large investors of other people's money that dominate the stock market and sometimes provide clues concerning the volatility of stocks, diversification, risk, and other factors.

Investment advisory services Advice about stock and bond markets, typically made available in newsletter form (for example, *Value Line Investment Survey*).

Investment clubs Groups who agree to pool investment funds which meet regularly to determine jointly investment opportunities and decisions.

Leadership Stocks leading the advance or decline in a market. The quality of the stocks providing market leadership is important. Following a long advance, if low-priced stocks are attracting the most value, the investor understands that the public is heavily invested. This could indicate a top. If the volume leaders are the blue-chip stocks, the advance has further to go.

Leverage The advantage (or disadvantage) obtained by the use of borrowed money. In a rising market, the practice causes the asset value of the common stock to appreciate more rapidly percentage-wise than investing without the use of borrowed funds. Gains and losses are magnified through the use of leverage. Leverage in the stock market can be obtained through the use of margin, warrants, margined warrants, options, and convertibles.

Low-priced stocks Stocks selling below a relative low amount (for example, $10), which are frequently noted for price volatility. One theory suggests buying such stocks toward the bottom of a typical yearly price range and selling toward the top of the range. When a preponderance of low-priced stocks among the leaders exists, the market is nearing the end of a rally. The beginning of an upswing reflects an investor preference for quality stock; after they have been bid up in price, the investor turns to the lower-quality issues. If the Dow Jones industrial average is rising and the average price of the leaders is high, the bull market should continue.

Margin Credit A strategy that requires the investor to be willing to accept considerable losses. Margin requirements imposed by the SEC can also be used as an indicator of stock price movement.

Money supply The expansion or contraction of the money supply has a relationship to stock prices, interest rates, and other factors affecting the market. Monetary indicators include net free bank reserves, member banks' borrowings, Treasury bill rates, the federal funds rate, the discount rate, interest rates, and others.

Monthly investment plan An investment strategy that requires small investors to buy individual stocks in small dollar amounts on a periodic basis. Such plans are supposed to develop a habit of thrift in individuals.

Most active stocks Stocks showing the largest volume of trading during a certain period (for example, daily, weekly, annually) can provide clues to market trends. For example, an increasing number of negative price movements in lists of most active stocks is often a signal of a bear market.

Moving average An arithmetic mean that changes according to a specified period of time (for example, a three- or five-year moving average). Moving averages have been used to determine market trends and the rate of change of stock prices.

Municipal bonds Debt issues of cities, states, and other local governments. Interest income is usually free of federal income tax and some state and local taxes. Municipals usually provide safety and a reasonable after-tax yield comparison with taxable securities, especially for taxpayers in a higher tax bracket.

Mutual funds Companies that pool investment money from individuals and others that provide diversification and professional management.

New issues Common stock issues of companies that are going public and are selling stock to the public for the first time. The term is also applied to new issues of corporate or municipal bonds. Studies indicate that the odds against new common stock issues are unfavorable.

New York Stock Exchange seat prices The cost of membership on the exchange is considered by some investors to reflect optimistic or pessimistic expectations for the market in general.

Normal-value plans Formula investment plans which rely on determining a normal stock market level that should exist at a particular time. The formula typically relates a stock market average to fundamental values, such as earnings, dividends, or interest rates.

Odd-lot short sales Short sales in less than one hundred shares are sales by unsophisticated investors who are considered by some to be losers. A significant rise in the volume of odd-lot short selling is interpreted to mean that the stock market will improve, thus providing the odd-lot short seller a typical loss. The odd-lot short sales ratio is the ratio of odd-lot short sales to regular odd-lot sales.

Options activity ratio A speculative index based on the level of options activity compared with the volume of trading in the stock market.

Over-the-counter stocks Unlisted stocks that sometimes offer the possibility of finding young and relatively small corporations that show promise.

Price/earnings ratio A ratio of the market price of a stock to the stock's annual earnings per share. This ratio can indicate whether a particular stock is properly priced. A very high price/earnings ratio suggests high expectations for the future, which may be based merely on psychology. For some investors, the price/earnings ratio establishes a relationship between the intrinsic value, or justified price, of a stock and its current market price.

Intrinsic value = Earnings per share x P/E ratio

The P/E ratios are inversely related to interest rates because interest rates are directly related to rates of return.

Psychology The emotional and behavioral patterns of investors and speculators is a factor in determining stock prices and trends.

Scale trading An investment strategy involving buying a specified number of shares of a particular stock whenever the price of the stock moves downward by a certain amount (for example, a half point), and selling the same number of shares each time the price of the stock rises by a greater amount (for example, a full point).

Seasonal variations Stock prices fluctuate according to the hour, the day, the month, the season, the year, a series of years, and other periods. Experts often expect short-term price changes for stocks to be random movements. Cyclical movements involve longer times and reflect stock movements through periods of recession, depression, recovery, and inflation. Industries that tend to resist recession include health and food.

Selling strategy An investment plan established to suggest a point when a security should be sold. Many investors suggest that one should sell a stock if he or she would not want to buy more of the stock. Many share signals have been proposed (for example, a decline in the price-earnings ratio of a stock).

Short interest The number of shares that have been sold short of a particular stock or of the market as a whole. The short interest ratio is the ratio of total short interest on the New York Stock Exchange to daily average stock volume. A ratio of more than approximately 2.00 is considered bullish; a ratio of less than 2.00 is considered bearish. This ratio is commonly considered to be a contrary opinion indicator (short sellers are usually wrong). A falling short interest is considered to be bullish. The greater the number of shares sold short, the stronger the technical position. Speculators must back the securities they sold. A market with a large short position is in a strong position to rally rapidly if the market remains strong. Short sellers become anxious during a rally and cover their short positions.

Short selling A strategy that generally goes against the market. Short selling is generally considered to be speculative and risky. Folklore says that one should never stay short after the short interest becomes very large. Relatively active short selling by members of the New York Stock Exchange tends to reflect sophisticated selling and indicates a possible negative stock market.

Special situations Conditions that promise large capital gains with limited risk accompanied by an uncertain time factor. Special situations include mergers and reorganizations, large liquid assets, liquidations, stocks with high volatility, litigations, changes in law, management changes, technological innovations, marketing innovations, turnaround situations, and many more.

Speculation index A ratio of lower quality stocks to activity in higher-quality stocks. A high level of volume on the American Stock Exchange (considered speculative) compared with the volume on the New York Stock Exchange could indicate considerable speculative interest in the market.

Stock-Bond yield spread The difference between the average dividend yield on common stocks and the average yield from interest on high grade corporate bonds. A stock yield of 10% and a bond yield of 8% would be considered a negative spread and could indicate that stocks are overvalued.

Stop-loss orders An order left with a broker to sell a stock if it drops to a certain price in order to stop the loss.

Support and resistance levels A support level is a price level that a stock or the market has difficulty in breaking through on the downside; a resistance level is the same on the upside. Buying activity increases support levels; selling pressures increase resistance levels. Levels of support and resistance can indicate a major change in the market.

Tape trading Reading the stock market tape is a very short-term method of forecasting stock movements, often used by professional traders. Through a careful examination of the tape as transactions occur, the astute tape reader hopes to anticipate price changes and to take advantage of such changes when they occur.

Tax investing Investing strategy in which the tax consequences are the major considerations.

Trends Strategies based on the tendency of stock prices to follow established trends or directions (for example, bull or bear markets). Matters to consider are how steep is the trend, has the trend been tested, and similar questions.

Undervalued and overvalued securities Stocks or bonds that are priced below or above what is a reasonable or normal value as related to underlying net assets, earning power, or other securities may offer opportunities for profitable investment. Searching for undervalued securities is a form of bargain hunting.

Upside-downside volume A comparison of the trading volume of stocks with rising prices with those of stocks with falling prices can provide clues of the market direction.

Volume of trading The number of shares of stock traded during a particular period of time can provide a basis for trading or not trading. The volume of trading typically slows before the top of a bull market and before the bottom of a bear market.

Warrants Warrants giving the holder the right to buy a specified amount of a particular common stock at a certain price within a specified period of time can be attractive securities where leverage is a factor.

INVESTMENT RATING   See BOND RATINGS.

INVESTMENT RISKS   The basic risks in INVESTMENT are financial risk (risk of nonpayment by the obligor or issuer), also known as credit risk; interest rate risk (risk of open market price depreciation should interest rates rise, applicable to high-grade bonds and obligations), also known as money risk; and purchasing power risk (risk of decline in purchasing power of principal and income because of rise in the price level), also known as inflation risk. Investment ratings (quality ratings) reflect primarily financial risk.

Other risks include governmental and political risk; foreign exchange and expropriation risk; risk of institutional change (in social and economic system); risk of war and international tension.

INVESTMENT SECURITIES   Generally, all classes of bonds and stocks, regardless of quality. In the strict sense, however, INVESTMENT securities are those obligations and equities whose characteristics are distinctly or predominantly conservative.

General tests of investment securities are as follows.

1. Security of principal, which depends upon the character of the issuer, nature of the business, type of security, class of lien, nature of the collateral pledged, protective provisions in the mortgage or indenture, and provisions for recourse in the event of default.
2. Regularity of income, which depends upon the nature and stability of the business, and type of security.
3. Fairness of yield, a relative factor.
4. Efficiency and conservatism of management, an intangible factor of basic importance.
5. Marketability, which depends on such factors as legality for investment by fiduciaries, degree of seasoning, and maintenance of active listed or unlisted markets for the issue.
6. Investor convenience, including collateral value or

acceptability as security for loans, acceptability of denomination and maturity, registration privilege, place of payment of interest and principal, exemption from taxation, and interchangeability of denominations.
7. Financial factors of safety, depending basically upon equities, earning power, and position in capitalization.

INVESTMENT SECURITIES REGULATIONS
See COMPTROLLER'S REGULATION, NATIONAL BANK SECURITIES REGULATIONS.

INVESTMENT STOCKS
Stocks suitable for purchase because of their stability of earnings and income, and relative stability of market value. Even the high-grade common stocks, however, do not have as great stability of market value over a period of years as high-grade bonds (see FLUCTUATING PRINCIPLE). Nevertheless, for income and growth, even the most defensive INVESTMENT programs should include a selection of high-grade and good-grade common stocks for diversification.
See SPECULATION.

INVESTMENT TAX CREDIT
The Revenue Act of 1962 allowed companies to reduce their federal income taxes by an investment tax credit equal to a specific percentage of the cost of certain depreciable properties. A major purpose of this legislation was to encourage investments in productive facilities and to stimulate economic growth.

In accounting for the investment tax credit, the central issue is when the tax credit should affect income. Two acceptable methods are currently used to account for the tax credit. The flow-through method requires that the tax credit should reduce income taxes in the year the credit is taken for tax purposes. The cost reduction or deferral method requires that the credit should be allocated over the life of the asset and used to reduce income taxes over the life of the asset; the tax effect of the investment tax credit is postponed to future periods.

The Internal Revenue Code treats the credit as a direct reduction of taxes payable for the year in which the credit arises.

The 1986 tax revision eliminated the investment tax credit.

INVESTMENT TRUST
A term formerly applied indiscriminately to the INVESTMENT COMPANY, regardless of whether or not the form of organization was the technical business trust. Investment companies themselves years ago officially eliminated the term "investment trust" from their designation and literature, because of the negative connotation and implication of rigidity in the word "trust." Federal regulation (Investment Company Act of 1940) and state regulation ("blue sky" laws and regulations) have also eliminated the now obsolete term.

BIBLIOGRAPHY

AMERICAN INSTITUTE OF CERTIFIED PUBLIC ACCOUNTANTS. *Audits of Investment Companies*, 1985.
BROUIVER, K. *Mutual Funds: How to Invest with the Pros*, 1988.
DONOGHUR, W. E. *Donoghur's Mutual Funds Almanac*, 1988.
DORF, R. *The New Mutual Fund Investment Advisor*, 1988.

INVESTMENT VALUE
The intrinsic value of a security, as measured generally by the basic yardsticks of earnings, income, and asset value. Appraisal of investment values is one of the functions of INVESTMENT.

INVESTMENTS FOR SAVINGS BANKS
See SAVINGS BANK INVESTMENTS.

INVESTMENTS FOR TRUST FUNDS
See TRUST FUND INVESTMENTS.

INVESTOR
A person who buys securities for INVESTMENT as contrasted with the trader or speculator who is primarily interested in short-term turnover at a profit.
See SPECULATION.

INVISIBLE HAND
Adam Smith in *The Wealth of Nations* explained that individuals will act in a way that promotes their own self interest. But, by doing so, as if "led by an invisible hand to promote an end which was no part of his intention," he is also promoting the general welfare. Because of this, according to Smith, government interference in the economy is unnecessary. This belief underscored Smith's view of the virtues of free markets and free trade.

INVISIBLE IMPORTS
Such items in a country's international balance of payments as transportation charges, travel expenditures, payment of interest and dividends on investments, private remittances, and purchase of miscellaneous services, in and to foreign countries. By contrast, the visible imports are merchandise imports on current trade account.

For the U.S., in recent post-World War II years, private transportation items have usually been net credits by small margins, travel expenditures and private remittances abroad have been net debits by large margins, and private income from investments has yielded large net credits. Private long-term net capital investment, however, reflecting large-scale investment by U.S. firms abroad, has resulted in recent years in large debits, offset to some extent by net credits from buildup of foreign short-term balances in the U.S.

U.S. government accounts, reflecting military aid payments to allies, other grants and payments, and expenditures by U.S. military forces abroad, have resulted in large debits, both during World War II and in post-World War II years.
See INTERNATIONAL BALANCE OF PAYMENTS.

INVISIBLE SUPPLY
The amount of a commodity—grain, cotton, or other agricultural product—that is in the possession of farmers and so has not yet reached the primary markets.
See VISIBLE SUPPLY.

INVOICE
A sales slip; an itemized bill given by a seller to a purchaser of goods showing all the particulars of the sale, e.g., date, name of buyer and seller, salesperson's number, quantity and description of articles, unit prices, extensions, discounts (if any), total footing, etc. The invoice is in reality an original entry record, and since the billing system has come into general use, a duplicate of each invoice frequently is retained by the seller from which the monthly statement is prepared.

INVOLUNTARY BANKRUPTCY
See BANKRUPTCY.

IRISH DIVIDEND
A stock market expression humorously denoting an assessment upon stock. Instead of receiving a dividend, the stockholder is called upon to pay an assessment.

IRREDEEMABLE BONDS
Bonds with a fixed maturity but not subject to prior redemption; bonds that cannot be called for redemption by the issuer (payer or obligor) before maturity. They should not be confused with perpetual bonds or intermediate bonds.
See PERPETUAL BOND.

IRREDEEMABLE DEBENTURE
A perpetual type of debenture, called DEBENTURE STOCK, issued particularly by the British railroads, which had no fixed date of maturity or other provision for repayment of the principal, except in case of liquidation. Debenture stock of the British railroads was issued in both redeemable and irredeemable types, with interest rates ranging from 2.5% to 5%. The British government took over the British railroads in 1939 as a war measure at a fixed annual rental, and under the terms of the Transport Act of 1947, approved August 6, 1947, the British railroads were nationalized as of January 1, 1948. Security holders, including holders of irredeemable debenture stock, received 3% Guaranteed British Transport Stock, with maturities of 1978-1988 and 1968-1973.

IRREDEEMABLE PAPER MONEY
Money that a government has made legal tender in payment of debts but that is not redeemable in standard money, i.e., gold or silver, the metals commonly used as a basis for currency in all commercial countries.

Irredeemable paper money usually becomes the circulating money and tends to drive metallic money out of circulation or places it at a premium through the operation of GRESHAM'S LAW. It is usually subject to wide fluctuations in value and causes similar fluctuations, though in inverse ratio, in commodity prices. In the United States, paper and metallic money in circulation are irredeemable in gold; the country has been on an international gold bullion standard of the restricted type since the GOLD RESERVE ACT OF 1934.

IRREGULAR Indicates unevenness or variation in prices on a stock market, with some stocks advancing and others declining.

IRREGULARITIES Informalities or infirmities that make a negotiable instrument technically invalid. A small percentage of the checks and other items presented to a bank, especially through a clearinghouse, contain some formal irregularity. This necessitates their return to the presenting bank or firm for correction or reissue. Banks usually provide themselves with printed forms to be attached to such checks explaining the reason for their return.

The chief formal irregularities that require the return of checks are alteration, counter-signature missing, dated ahead, drawn against uncollected funds, duplicate paid, endorsement not exactly as drawn, endorsement illegible, endorsement incorrect, endorsement missing, filling (words and figures differ), guarantee of amount needed, guarantee of endorsement needed, insufficient funds, no account, no advice to pay, no instructions to pay, not due, not handled through exchange, original paid, past due, payment stopped, recalled, sent wrong, signature incorrect, signature missing, signature unknown, two signatures required, etc.

IRREVOCABLE CREDIT See LETTER OF CREDIT.

IRREVOCABLE LETTER OF CREDIT A letter of credit in which the specified payment is guaranteed by the bank if all terms and conditions are met by the drawee. A revocable letter of credit can be canceled or altered by the drawee (buyer) after it has been issued by the drawee's bank.

IRREVOCABLE STOCK POWER See STOCK POWER.

IRREVOCABLE TRUST See TRUST.

IRRIGATION BONDS Bonds issued to finance the construction of irrigation projects, both by public bodies and private corporations.

Many sections of the U.S., especially the far western states, must resort to artificial irrigation in order to carry on successful agriculture; such irrigation has opened up additional areas for cultivation. Among MUNICIPAL BONDS, many irrigation district bonds have been issued as an additional type of "district" financing. Irrigation district bonds underwent a baptism of fire during the 1932 depression—the depression's effects upon agriculture and abandonments of irrigated lands in the district by landowners hit by the depression affected tax collections for service on the irrigation district's bonds. Subsequent recovery in agricultural conditions has revived the investment standing of irrigation bonds as a group.

IRRIGATION DISTRICT BONDS IRRIGATION BONDS issued by an irrigation district as distinguished from Carey Act irrigation bonds or irrigation bonds issued by a private corporation. Irrigation district bonds belong to the quasi-municipal class.

ISSUE As a verb, to give out, emit, pass for delivery, or distribute. A government issues currency, bonds, etc.; a bank issues notes, cashier's checks, money orders, letters of credit, etc.; a corporation issues checks, notes, bonds, stocks, etc.

As a noun, in underwriting and investment finance, a new flotation of securities placed on the market for distribution to the investing public.

ISSUED CAPITAL STOCK That portion of the stock of a corporation that is outstanding in the hands of the stockholders, or repurchased and held by a corporation as TREASURY STOCK. It is not required that all of the authorized stock of a corporation be immediately issued. Issued CAPITAL STOCK is the difference between the authorized and unissued capital stock.

ISSUE OF MONEY See MINT, MONEY, REDEMPTION OF MONEY.

ISSUE PRICE The price at which a new flotation or issue of stock or bonds is offered to the public. This price is fixed by the last nondelaying amendment to the REGISTRATION STATEMENT filed on nonexempt issues under the Securities Act of 1933, and remains fixed during the offering period, assisted by price stabilization operations by the SYNDICATE manager for the UNDERWRITING group of investment banking houses handling the deal, subject to rules of the Securities and Exchange Commission.

The pricing of a new issue is one of the crucial factors in its success. Usually the price is determined by reference to the prevailing market prices at which comparable issues outstanding are selling; fixing it somewhat below such justified price will "sweeten" the offering and enhance its chances of success. The offering price is one of the material provisions of the purchase agreement (between the purchase group and the issuer), signed usually a few days before the expected effective date of the registration statement. Based thereon, the registration statement is amended the day before or on the morning of the effective date. The amendment specifies the proposed maximum aggregate offering price and offering price per unit. The price to the public, underwriting discounts and commissions, and proceeds to the registrant issuer, both per unit and total, are also required to be shown in tabular form on the first page of the prospectus, as to all securities registered that are to be offered for cash (estimated if necessary).

Pricing in COMPETITIVE BIDDING procedure is more complex, involving official invitations for bids on the part of the issuer; awarding of the successful bid; determination of the public offering price by the successful bidders; and filing of the post-effective amendment as to actual public offering price, underwriting discounts or commissions, etc. Under formal rule of the SEC, the registration statement for securities involving competitive bidding was only effective for the purpose of inviting competitive bids, and a further order of the SEC was necessary to make effective the amendment filing the public offering price and the underwriting terms. Now, pursuant to Rule 115 of the SEC, under specified conditions the post-effective amendment reflecting the results of the bidding becomes effective upon filing, without further order of the SEC.

See INVESTMENT BANKER.

ITEMS In banking practice, negotiable instruments payable upon presentation, including checks; money orders; and matured drafts, acceptances, and notes. The term is usually employed in combination with a qualifying word, e.g., cash items, collection items, clearinghouse items, city items, out-of-town items, etc.

ENCYCLOPEDIA OF BANKING AND FINANCE

J

JAPANESE FINANCIAL MARKETS The Japanese economy has been one of the most conspicuous success stories of the twentieth century, rising from the devastation of World War II to a position of world leadership. The financial sector was no exception. The world's ten largest commercial banks, as ranked by deposits, are all Japanese, and the Tokyo Stock Exchange is the world's largest in terms of capitalization.

Japan's financial markets have changed drastically in the past two decades and are continuing to change rapidly as Japan integrates more and more completely into world markets. Because Japanese financial institutions are distinctly different from their Western counterparts, this has resulted in some tension between the governments of Japan, Europe, and the United States.

The modern economic history of Japan begins in 1868 with the Meiji Restoration, when the Japanese launched a national effort to transform their feudal society into a Western-style industrial state. The core financial markets were formed in the decades following this start. Prior to World War II financial dealings were completely dominated by the zaibatsu: family-owned, bank-centered holding companies that could be described as the first multinational conglomerates. By the end of World War II, when they were forcibly broken up by the American Occupation, there were 83 zaibatsu with approximately 4500 subsidiary companies.

The second stage of Japan's industrialization began when the American Occupation left in 1952. Although American-style antitrust laws had formally outlawed the zaibatsu, similar entities, organized as loose, voluntary associations quickly formed. They were know as keiretsu. To facilitate the rebuilding of Japan's industrial capacity the Japanese financial system was closely regulated and tightly compartmentalized. Even after formal legal controls were relaxed, the Ministry of Finance and the Bank of Japan maintained control of interest rates and monetary aggregates by the use of "administrative guidance," a stronger, more comprehensive version of the "moral suasion" used by the U.S. Federal Reserve. Tight control continued until the 1980s when, as Japan became a major player in world financial markets, international pressure began to break down the Japanese regulations, a process that continues today.

The remainder of this article describes the major institutions and markets in the Japanese financial system.

Banks. Historically, Japan's banking structure since World War II has been rigidly segregated. National banks are distinct from local banks, commercial banks are distinct from investment banks, various credit banks operate in almost complete isolation from each other, and all are regulated by the Ministry of Finance and Bank of Japan to such a degree that 1986 saw Japan's first post-war bank failure (the policy had been to arrange a merger whenever failure became imminent). Many of Japan's largest banks are the prewar zaibatsu banks.

The details are as follows. Operating at the national level are the Bank of Japan, 13 city banks, 7 trust banks, and 3 long-term credit banks. The Bank of Japan is the central bank, and because of the regulatory climate in Japan even with today's new freedoms it is able to exercise much greater control than the U.S. Federal Reserve or any European central bank. The city banks are the country's major banks and have branches in all the large cities. Their customers are major corporations, both domestic and foreign, and the local banks forming the next lower tier in the banking system. All are among the largest 70 of the world's commercial banks. The Bank of Tokyo is unique in that it once had a monopoly in foreign exchange and foreign trade transactions, an area in which it continues to specialize.

The three long-term credit banks and seven trust banks are investment banks and are also national banks. By 1985 Japan had become the world's leading international banker, attaining that position by virtue of its huge trade and current account surpluses, high domestic savings rate, and low equity-to-asset ratio relative to foreign banks.

At the local level are 64 regional banks and 69 mutual savings and loans banks. These are located in the smaller cities and serve the local businesses and individuals. At one time restricted to domestic, local banking, they are now branching out. The largest regional bank, the Bank of Yokohama, is as large as the smallest city bank.

Also at the local level are 450 credit associations and 480 credit cooperatives that serve as specialized banks and have no real counterparts in the West. The Zenshinren Bank serves as a sort of central bank for the credit associations, as the Norinchukin Bank does for the agricultural and fishing cooperatives and the Shoko Chukin Bank does for the small business cooperatives. These large specialized banks are gradually converting to investment banks.

Prior to World War II only eight foreign banks had branches in Tokyo. Another eight, primarily Asian, were added between 1950 and 1968. The next decade added 34 more, but special regulations continued to prevent competition with domestic banks. By 1987 a total of 79 foreign banks were represented in Japan, and international pressure is expected to continue to break down the barriers to competition with domestic banks.

Finally, there is the Postal Savings System, which is in the process of converting to a bank. Since it is not in the banking system it is unregulated. It provides tax-free savings accounts of up to three million yen, paying a higher interest than equivalent time deposits in commercial banks. The accounts are not monitored and no identification is necessary to open an account so the deposit ceiling is easily bypassed by opening several accounts. Postal savings represented about $685 billion in deposits in 1985, and with over 19,000 outlets they will make a powerful bank.

Stock Market. Stock exchanges first opened in May 1878. Because pre-World War II finance was dominated by the zaibatsu, Japanese companies developed a tradition of working closely with banks and raising most of their capital indirectly, through bank loans, rather than directly, through equity and other capital markets. By the 1930s, most stock trading was done within zaibatsu companies; very few shares were offered publicly. In 1937 wartime controls were put in place and in 1945 trading was suspended.

When the stock market reopened in May 1949, there were nine exchanges, which decreased to the current eight in 1967 when the Kobe exchange merged into the Osake Exchange. The zaibatsu had been broken up and outlawed by the U.S.-imposed antitrust laws, so the stock markets became a more important source of capital, but not as important as in Western economics. In part this is because the Japanese used the stock market to reform their conglomerates, calling them keiretsu. Each company in the group purchased between $1/2$% and 3% of each other company and agreed not to sell these shares. This strategy circumvented the antitrust laws and made the keiretsu immune to investor takeovers, allowing them to pursue company interests ahead of shareholder interests.

Nonetheless, the stock markets grew in influence. In 1961 a less stringent second section of listings was added to the Tokyo, Osake, and Nagoya exchanges. A number of new protective regulations were added in the period from 1961 to 1965 during a broad-based decline in the market. In 1969, the first public offering of new stock was made by a Japanese corporation. In the 1970s the market grew steadily; in the 1980s it rocketed up, more than quadrupling in value between 1980 and 1987. The October 1987 stock market crash hit Japanese exchanges less severely than the rest of the world; the Tokyo Exchange is so far the only exchange to recover completely and climb above its precrash levels.

Today the Tokyo Exchange is the first and the Osaka the third largest stock market in the world. A total of 1,848 domestic companies are listed on Japanese exchanges, 1,075 on the Tokyo first section and 424 on the second section. The first foreign listing came in 1973. By 1986 there were 52. Foreign trading volume is quite low because of trading and ownership restrictions and because Japanese investors focus on untaxed capital gains rather than the taxed dividends that are the major component of the yield on foreign stocks.

A strong social tradition against litigation makes domestic takeover attempts unlikely, so a hostile takeover invariably means a foreign takeover. At present this is virtually impossible, especially among the keiretsu companies. The excitement at Japanese shareholder meetings takes the form of the sokaiya—a form of corporate blackmail involving payment for not attending shareholder meet-ings and publicly revealing scandalous information about the personal or company conduct of officers. The ploy's effectiveness relies on the Japanese aversion to public dissent and embarrassment.

Securities Firms. Securities firms in Japan serve as brokers, dealers, and underwriters for all of the financial markets. They can be grouped into three tiers: the Big Four, who are among the top six worldwide; ten significantly smaller, but still large, companies; and the remaining 230 firms.

The Big Four, Nomura, Daiwa, Nikko, and Yamaichi, are similar to zaibatsu, each having about a dozen subsidiary (high status) companies and up to 30 affiliated (low status) firms. All practice lifetime employment after a probationary period of several years. Instead of firing or demoting nonperformers, the Big Four firms generally transfer them to lesser status firm. Their foreign offices have expanded enormously in the 1980s, and all are now primary dealers in U.S. Treasury issues and underwriters in the Eurobond market.

Commissions are the primary source of income for Japanese securities firms, representing 75% to 85% of the revenue of smaller companies and 40% to 50% of the Big Four's revenue. Commissions are nonnegotiable, determined by the Tokyo Exchange with the approval of the ministry of finance. These firms would experience a sharp decline in revenue if forced to compete in a free market with foreign brokerage firms. Many smaller firms would go under. But Japanese markets are slowly opening to foreign firms. Banned from Tokyo Stock Exchange membership until 1982, foreign firms now have ten of the more than one hundred members.

Unique to the Japanese financial system are the three securities finance companies. Consolidated in 1956 from the nine companies originally created in 1950, they provide equity and bond financing to securities companies, serve as lenders of last resort, and provide a link between securities and money markets.

Bonds. For the first half of this century, Japanese corporate bonds were unsecured. As a result of the many bankruptcies during the Depression, in 1933 it was decided that all corporate bonds would be secured. In 1979 this requirement began to be relaxed, and in 1985 the first unsecured straight bond in half a century was issued.

The first government bonds were issued in 1965 after the stock market collapse and recession led to abandonment of the postwar balanced budget policy. Bond financing became a major policy tool after the 1975 recession. Public bond prices are not determined at auction, they are assigned, and although they are generally below the market rate, they have become more competitive since they became a major policy tool.

Like all other sectors of the financial system, the integration of Japan's bond market with the rest of the world led to a number of innovations. Convertible bonds and bonds with warrants attached were allowed in 1981 and have become increasingly popular. Samurai bonds and Shibosai bonds (privately placed) are yen-denominated foreign issues and first appeared in 1970. Shogun bonds are foreign currency denominated. The first Euroyen issue was in 1977, with domestic issuers not allowed until 1984. The Eurobond market, which is unregulated, is a major source of pressure for the deregulation of Japan's domestic markets. For example, sushi bonds, a foreign currency bond issued in the Euromarket, allows Japanese companies to expand foreign currency assets while avoiding the restrictions on owning foreign securities. Postwar bond futures began in 1985 as part of an effort to encourage trading in government bonds as the large 1975 issue came due.

Money Markets. There are four major components of Japan's domestic money market.

1. *Bill discount market:* corresponds roughly to the bankers acceptances market.
2. *Call money market:* corresponds roughly to the Federal funds market.
3. *Gensaki market:* bond repurchase agreements.
4. Negotiable certificates of deposit.

The bill discount and call money markets are restricted to financial institutions and the gensaki market prohibits individual participation.

The call money market was established in 1902 and originally included the bill discount market. In May 1971 the bill discount market split off, taking the longer maturity (two to four months) portion of the market.

The call money market presently handles maturities ranging from half a day to a month minus a day: a June 1972 ruling prohibits maturities from extending beyond the end of a month. Transactions involve an exchange of promissory notes through the intermediation of a Tanshi company (broker) and are generally in the one million to one hundred million yen range. Interest is paid at maturity.

In the bill discount market, original bills between a bank and a borrower are combined into accommodation bills between the bank and a Tanshi company. The accommodation bills are the ones actually traded, and they must have a definite commercial purpose; purely financial or speculative bills are not permitted. Bill discount maturities must include at least two month-ends and must be held at least one month plus one day prior to resale. The minimum transaction is ten million yen, most are well over one hundred million. Until 1978, the rate on all bills was set by Tanshi companies in consultation with the Bank of Japan; by late 1979, all rates were market determined. Interest on bills is deducted at purchase. An important feature of these bills is that, because they are not true banker's acceptances, greater bank-client confidentiality is possible.

The gensaki market started in 1949 but did not become a major force until the 1970s. In May 1979 it was opened to participation by nonresidents. Maturities are not longer than one year, with most under six months. All transactions go through securities companies. Only financial institutions and companies listed on the first section of the Tokyo Stock Exchange can participate. Trading is restricted to government, government-guaranteed, municipal, public corporation, bank debentures, and nonconvertible corporation bonds or debentures.

The CD market opened in May 1979. Its maturities are from three to six months, and the minimum denomination is five hundred million yen.

Bank of Japan. The most important distinction between Japan's central bank and the central banks of Europe and the U.S. is the use of open market operations. Because Japanese financial markets were so tightly regulated, interest rates and the money supply were set directly. Open market operations began in the bill discount market in 1972 and in the gensaki market in 1980, but it was not until 1986 that it became a policy tool comparable in importance to the status of open market operations in Western central banks.

BIBLIOGRAPHY

Directory: Affiliates and Officers of Japanese Firms in USA and Canada. Jetro, New York, NY. Latest edition.

JAWBONING One element of cost-push inflation is rising wages. Government efforts to informally urge unions and companies to restrain their wage increases in an effort to curb or prevent inflation is known as jawboning. There is no definitive evidence of the effectiveness of this policy tactic. It has in recent years been used politically, primarily by Democratic presidents.

JETTISON To throw overboard a ship's cargo in order to lighten the vessel when there is danger of sinking. An ocean carrier, as usually indicated by the ocean bill of lading, does not assume liability for jettison. This risk should therefore be covered in the MARINE INSURANCE certificate.

ENCYCLOPEDIA OF BANKING AND FINANCE

JOBBER See STOCK JOBBER.

JOB LOTS In commodity exchange trading, contracts for lesser units of trading than the regular contract unit. On the grain exchanges, 5,000 bushels is the regular or standard contract unit. Trading is also carried on in units of 1,000 bushels each—the job lots—except for oats for which the minimum job lot is 2,000 bushels. Trading in job lots is separate from trading in regular contracts and must be liquidated separately. Thus, five job lots cannot be applied to the liquidation of one round lot contract in grain, or vice versa. Commissions on job lot trades are proportionately higher than commissions on regular contracts.

See CHICAGO BOARD OF TRADE, COMMODITY EXCHANGES.

JOINT ACCOUNT This term has three meanings:

1. A joint business venture or temporary partnership.
2. A bank account owned jointly by two or more persons. In banking parlance, the term "joint accounts" refers indiscriminately to checking, savings, or thrift accounts opened in the names of two people, whether as tenants in common or as joint tenants. The deposit agreement as well as the designation of the account should be specific, however, as the legal incidents are different.

   In the case of tenants in common, there is no right of survivorship, so that in the event of death of one of the codepositors, there is no right in the survivor to the entire balance of the account. Instead, the survivor shares the account equally with the estate of the deceased. During the lifetime of the codepositors, deposits may be made by either party, but withdrawals are required to be jointly made.

   Joint tenant accounts entitle the survivor of the codepositors to the entire balance in the account upon the death of one of the codepositors by operation of the right of survivorship. During the lifetime of the codepositors, either party may deposit or withdraw freely. The New York Banking Law protects banks in this connection by providing that, prior to notification received by the bank in writing and signed by one of the joint tenants not to pay, payment and receipt or acquittance by a joint tenant entitled to withdraw under the terms of the deposit agreement shall constitute a valid and sufficient release and discharge to the bank. Banks also protect themselves on withdrawals upon death by requiring proof of death, tax waivers, or a surrogate's certificate in the case of withdrawal by estate of the deceased cotenant in common.

3. The simplified form of the SYNDICATE in security underwriting operations, combining both purchasing and selling operations by the members. The joint account involves two firms on a particular deal, whereas the syndicate involves three or more houses and usually many more, separately organized into purchase and selling groups. Even in the joint account, however, one of the houses is designated as manager of the account, to keep the records and confirm all sales. The joint account agreement, usually informal, specifies the interest of each house in the transaction, usually 50%, the details of the purchase from the issuing company; the offering price to the public; the concession to purchasing dealers; and the period of duration of the account. At the end of the period, the account is closed out and each firm is credited with its share in the net profits, after deduction of expenses. Any bonds remaining unsold are charged to each member of the joint account in proportion to its interest.

JOINT AND SEVERAL NOTE See JOINTLY AND SEVERALLY.

JOINT BONDS Bonds, whether of the mortgage, collateral trust, or debenture variety, that are the joint obligations of two or more issuing debtor organizations. The Great Northern-Northern Pacific joint collateral trust $6^{1}/_{2}$s (no longer outstanding) were an example of this class of bonds. This issue was secured by stock of the Chicago, Burlington & Quincy Railroad, owned jointly by the obligor railroads. In modern railroad finance, terminal bonds are secured by mortgage on the terminal and also by joint and several guarantee of principal and interest by the using railroads. For example, the Chicago Union Station first mortgage $4^{5}/_{8}$s, due in 1988, are secured by first mortgage on the Chicago Union State, and by joint and several guarantee of principal and interest by the Penn Central, the "Burlington" (Chicago, Burlington & Quincy R.R., now part of the Burlington Northern), and the Chicago, Milwaukee, St. Paul & Pacific railroads.

JOINT COMMISSION ON THE COINAGE Established by the Coinage Act of 1965 (79 Stat. 258; 31 U.S.C. 301), the Joint Commission on the Coinage reviewed such matters as the needs of the economy for coinage, the standards for the coinage, technological developments in metallurgy and coin-selector devices, the supply of silver, and other considerations relevant to the maintenance of an adequate and stable coinage system.

The Joint Commission on the Coinage ceased its existence on January 4, 1975, under the provisions of Section 14 of the Federal Advisory Committee Act of October 6, 1972 (88 Stat. 776). But the work of the annual ASSAY COMMISSION, to examine and test the weights and finenesses of coins manufactured by the mints, has continued.

See TRIAL OF THE PYX.

JOINT DEPOSITS See JOINT ACCOUNT, ALTERNATE DEPOSITS.

JOINT ECONOMIC COMMITTEE A permanent joint committee of the Congress established by the EMPLOYMENT ACT OF 1946 (60 Stat. 24; 15 U.S.C. 1023), its statutory functions being to study matters related to the economic report prepared by the COUNCIL OF ECONOMIC ADVISERS; coordinate legislative programs to promote economic stability and growth pursuant to the act; and serve as a source of data, recommendations, and guidance to other committees of Congress in connection with the recommendations and programs contained in the economic report.

In addition to a chairman from the membership of the Senate and a vice-chairman from the membership of the House of Representatives, membership of the committee consists of seven other members of the Senate and seven other members from the House. The committee from time to time subdivides into functional subcommittees to consider various specific subjects, and is serviced by a permanent staff.

Besides holding hearings on the economic report, the committee has published a long line of special studies on various economic subjects, drawing upon members of the faculties of various educational institutions as well as its staff for such investigations and studies. By joint resolution (S.J. Res. 55, P.L. 120, 81st Congress; Ch. 237, 1st Session), the committee is also authorized to issue monthly the publication "Economic Indicators," prepared for the committee by the Council of Economic Advisers.

JOINT ENDORSEMENT An endorsement made by two or more payees or endorsees. Where an instrument is made payable to the order of two or more persons: (1) if in the alternative, it is payable to any one of them and may be negotiated, discharged, or enforced by any of them who has (sic) possession of it; (2) if not in the alternative, it is payable to all of them and may be negotiated, discharged, or enforced only by all of them (Sec. 3-116, Uniform Commercial Code).

See ENDORSEMENT.

JOINTLY AND SEVERALLY When a note, mortgage, or bond is signed by several makers, who "jointly and severally promise to pay," each maker is individually liable for the full amount. This differs from the liability of each separate maker when the wording is "we jointly promise to pay." In such case the makers are liable as a whole and not individually.

JOINT MORTGAGE A MORTGAGE signed by two or more mortgagors, being the joint obligation of the signing parties.

JOINT NOTE A note that is signed by two or more makers, containing the unconditional promise: "We promise to pay," the words "JOINTLY AND SEVERALLY" being omitted.

In case a joint note is not met at maturity, in order to recover, the holder must sue all the makers jointly. A note of a partnership, e.g., Brown & Smith, is a joint note in the same manner as a note signed by two or more individuals.

JOINT OWNERSHIP OF PROPERTY Ownership of property, real or personal, in JOINT TENANCY. Advantages of such type of ownership are as follows.

JOINT PRODUCTS AND BYPRODUCTS

1. There is right of survivorship, so that if one joint tenant dies, the entire property belongs to the survivor. This legal incident is of such substantial importance that in the absence of express language creating a joint tenancy, statutes and the courts are disposed to treat the tenancy as a TENANCY IN COMMON, without right of survivorship. To create the joint tenancy, the express language—for example, "Harry A. Jones and Mary E. Jones, as joint tenants with right of survivorship and not as tenants in common"—is necessary. Use of the word "jointly" alone is not enough. Where the property is held in a valid joint tenancy, it will pass to the survivor upon death of the other joint tenant, without necessity of a will and without involving the laws of descent.
2. Joint tenancy eliminates the necessity of administration for real property not subject to estate and inheritance taxes. In the case of personal property, however, tax waivers or clearances are necessary, as statutes impose penalties upon transfer agents, depositories, etc., that permit transfers or withdrawals without such waivers or clearances.
3. Except in unusual circumstances, creditors may not reach the property in the survivor for the deceased joint tenant's debts.
4. A joint tenant cannot devise his interest, but alienation of his interest during his lifetime would destroy the joint tenancy and make it a tenancy in common.
5. Curtesy and dower to not attach.
6. A joint tenant cannot create an easement on land which is binding against himself and his joint tenant.

Taxwise, however, the joint tenancy is not as advantageous as the tenancy in common. A joint tenancy does not affect income taxes, as the income is divisible. Joint tenancy property is taxable in the estate of the joint tenant who furnished the consideration. Also, all of the property is subject to lien for federal taxes, including estate and gift taxes, on the decedent's estate, so that if the estate's assets are insufficient to cover taxes, the surviving tenant's property by survivorship, even though it did not become part of the estate, is subject to payment of the tax lien. A transfer from severable interests into joint tenancy constitutes a gift to the extent of the interest involved in the joint tenancy. A joint tenancy, however, can be converted into a tenancy in common without liability for gift tax if equivalent interests are involved.

A special kind of joint tenancy, the TENANCY BY THE ENTIRETY, is still recognized in some states, applying to real property only, created where conveyance of such property is made to a husband and wife without express words to the contrary. Tenancy by the entirety has right of survivorship, as in the case of the joint tenancy, but it differs from the latter in that the tenancy by the entirety cannot be terminated without the consent of both parties.

In husband and wife tenancies, the Commissioner of Internal Revenue has been strict in the application of the code, and required the husband's estate to pay estate tax on all the jointly held property unless the surviving spouse could show that part was the result of her contribution in property or earnings. For community property states, the federal estate tax law also required since 1942 that the taxable estate of the spouse who dies first shall include all community property except such part as was derived from the surviving spouse's separate property or earnings. Beginning with the Revenue Act of 1948, permitting for the first time the marital deduction of up to half the net estate for property left to the surviving spouse, the estate of the spouse first dying now has this very important means of reducing estate taxes, because of the graduation of rates, which is what the community property states had been doing in taxing the state of the first spouse to die for only half the community property.

JOINT PRODUCTS AND BYPRODUCTS

Costs of simultaneously producing or acquiring two or more products (joint products) that are produced or acquired together. Joint products resulting from the single-production process usually require further processing. Typically, none of the joint products has a relative value of such a size that it can be designated a major product.

To illustrate the allocation problem associated with joint products, assume that the joint cost of producing Product A and Product B in a common manufacturing process is $90,000 (the joint costs up to the split-off point). It is now necessary to determine the inventory value of Products A and B. The relative sales value method of allocating the $90,000 to Products A and B is widely used. Assume that the 20,000 units of Product A have a sales value of $100,000 and Product B a sales value of $200,000. The $90,000 would be allocated to Products A and B in the amounts of $30,000 (one-third) and $60,000 (two-thirds), respectively. This can be illustrated as follows:

Joint cost, $90,000 | Product A, $30,000
                    | Product B, $60,000

Split-off point

Joint costs are sometimes allocated on a physical measure basis. Under this method, total joint costs are allocated to the joint products on the basis of some unit of product output, such as units, pounds, tons, or square feet.

Byproducts are those products emerging at the split-off point that have minor sales value as compared with those of the major products. In many operations, byproducts are the same as scrap. Byproducts frequently are not allocated to any of the total joint costs incurred in the process. If additional costs are incurred after the split-off to process further the byproducts, these costs are usually assigned to the byproduct.

JOINT-STOCK BANKS

The incorporated commercial banks of England as distinguished from the Bank of England and the private banks, banking partnerships, foreign banks, etc. These banks are also known as "London clearing banks," being members of the London Bankers Clearing House. The "Radcliffe Report" describes features of these banks as follows.

Nearly all the domestic banking business of England and Wales is in the hands of these 11 banks. Of the 11, the Barclays, Lloyds, Midland, National Provincial, and Westminster are commonly known as the "Big Five" since their resources are six-sevenths of the total and they all have offices throughout the country. The District and Martins banks (together about 8% of the total) also have branches all over the country, although relatively few in the south. Williams Deacon's and Glyn, Mills are both owned by the Royal Bank of Scotland; the Glyn, Mills bank is confined to London, while Williams Deacon's is predominantly a Lancashire bank although with increasing representation elsewhere. Coutts is in London, and is owned by the National Provincial. The National Bank is predominantly an Irish bank, but has a number of branches in the London area and in other large industrial and commercial centers in England and Wales. The first seven and the last banks named are publicly owned, with many shareholders.

The primary business of these banks is the receipt, transfer, and encashment of deposits repayable on demand. Such deposits (credit balances on current account) total about 60% of all deposits, draw no interest, and may be transferred by check, banker's order, or credit clearing. In addition to these deposits on current account, the banks receive balances on deposit account, repayable at seven days' notice, amounting to about 40% of total deposits. Interest is paid on such time deposits by agreement of the banks, generally 2% under the Bank of England bank rate. Such deposits are not subject directly to check, but in practice banks seldom raise objections to occasional transfers from deposit account to current account to enable a check to be met, or to encashment of such time deposits on demand, subject to penalty of loss of interest. Although they have always had many small accounts, historically the great English banks have depended little on small savings accounts, and in recent times, the clearing banks as a matter of deliberate and concerted policy have stood aside while small savings have gone to the building societies, savings banks, and other specialized financial intermediaries.

JOINT-STOCK COMPANY

A form of business organization having characteristics of both the PARTNERSHIP and the CORPORATION, sometimes called a "partnership with transferable shares."

Advantages over the partnership are continuity of existence of the firm, unaffected by death or disability of owners or transfer of shares, and centralization of management in a board of directors and officers. Advantages over the corporation are freedom from the formal incorporation procedure, except for some states such as New York that require specified procedure; exemption from state corporation taxes except franchise taxes in some states (federally, the tax liability of the corporation attaches to joint-stock companies); the fact that in the absence of statutory provision for joint-stock companies, the "common law" joint-stock company is regarded as a partnership. Disadvantages compared with the corporation are lack of legal entity, so that taking and conveyance of real property unless specially authorized has to be done in the name of the president, directors, or trustees for the benefit of the company; inability to sue or be sued in its own name unless the right is specifically provided by statute; unlimited liability of individual stockholders for the obligations incurred by the joint-stock company, unless express limitation of liability is provided in each contract.

In New York, the General Associations Law, formerly known as the Joint-Stock Associations Law, governs the legal incidents of joint-stock associations, which are defined to include every unincorporated joint-stock association, company, or enterprise having written articles of association and capital stock divided into shares, but not to include a corporation or a business trust. The New York law requires every joint-stock association transacting business within New York State to file a certificate within 60 days after formation and annually thereafter. This certificate, filed with the secretary of State and with the clerk of the county of principal place of business, is to be signed and verified by the president and treasurer, and states the name and date of organization of the association, the number of its stockholders, the names and places of residence of the officers, and the principal place of business. Associations doing business in New York State are also required to file with the secretary of State a certificate designating the latter official as agent for service of process within the state.

Up to the time when general incorporation laws of the various states provided for "free" incorporation (incorporation by any group fulfilling the requirements), corporations could only be chartered by special act of the legislature. Motivation for formation of common law joint-stock companies in such circumstances might be the inability to obtain a corporate charter. The joint-stock company has a long history in England. Prior to the 1722 "Bubble Act," requiring chartering by act of Parliament for every joint-stock company, there were common law and chartered types. (The Bubble Act was repealed in 1825.) The modern English joint-stock company might be either the incorporated type with limited liability or the common law type with unlimited liability (most are the former type).

Because of taxation like the corporation and the benefits of limited liability of the corporation, joint-stock companies are not a common form of business organization in the U.S.

JOINT-STOCK LAND BANK BONDS All joint-stock land bank bonds have matured or been called for redemption, and all of the 88 chartered JOINT-STOCK LAND BANKS have been liquidated.

JOINT-STOCK LAND BANKS These agricultural credit institutions were privately organized and owned under the provisions of the FEDERAL FARM LOAN ACT of 1916, which also set up the FEDERAL LAND BANKS. The Emergency Farm Mortgage Act of 1933 provided that as of the date of enactment of the act (May 12, 1933), no joint-stock land bank should issue any tax-exempt bonds or make any farm loans except such as were necessary and incidental to the refinancing of existing loans or bond issues, or to the sale of any real estate then owned or thereafter acquired by the joint-stock land banks. This act in effect prohibited joint-stock land banks from acquiring new business and restricted them to orderly liquidation of existing assets. The FARM CREDIT ADMINISTRATION assumed supervision over remaining operation and liquidation of the joint-stock land banks, which have completed liquidation.

JOINT TENANCY A type of estate in real or personal property in which two or more persons, by virtue of grant or devise, never by laws of descent or operation of law, are associated in joint ownership. Joint tenancies have the four "unities" attaching, as follows.

1. **Title.** The joint tenancy arises by virtue of the same deed, conveyance, or will.
2. **Interest.** Each joint tenant must have the same interest and estate in the property.
3. **Time.** The estate of each joint tenant must arise at the same time.
4. **Possession.** Each joint tenant holds by the fractional interest specified and by the whole undivided possession.

In order to create a joint tenancy, the language of the grant or devise must be express and must clearly indicate that a joint tenancy is intended, as otherwise, statutes and courts generally rule that a tenancy in common is created. This disinclination to find joint tenancies by implication arises because of the important legal incident of survivorship. If one joint tenant should die, the estate passes to the survivors as joint tenants. The interest of the deceased joint tenant does not descend to his heirs, nor can he devise his interest. A joint tenant can mortgage or convey his interest during his lifetime, but if he does so, the joint tenancy is destroyed as to the interest mortgaged or conveyed. Partition will also dissolve the joint tenancy. Death of all the joint tenants but one will likewise terminate the joint tenancy.

See TENANCY IN COMMON, TENANCY BY THE ENTIRETY.

JOINT VENTURE The combination of two or more firms into a single activity. Generally, these relationships are short lived, formed for the production of a specific product. Also, the relationships are generally informal in nature, although they can be formal. When formal in nature, the new enterprise formed by the joint venture is called the child. While public statistics are not available, it has been estimated that the incidence of joint ventures has been increasing steadily during the 1980s. One reason for this trend is the necessity for firms to bring new products to market faster than in the past in an effort to meet foreign competition.

BIBLIOGRAPHY

HARRIGAN, K. R. *Strategies for Joint Ventures*, 1985).

JOURNAL In bookkeeping, a book of original entry; a record in which transactions are entered chronologically, i.e., in the order in which they occur, and from which they are posted to a ledger. Original entry records are also sometimes known as registers and blotters. Frequently, moreover, the original entry record is not made in a book but on various forms of posting media, e.g., deposit slip, debit and credit tickets.

The process of recording events and transactions in a journal is called journalizing. A journal is often referred to as a book of original entry because events and transactions are typically initially recorded therein using the double-entry system of accounting.

In addition to the general journal, special journals are often used to facilitate the recording of a large number of similar transactions. Typical special journals are described here:

Type of Special Journal	Nature of Transactions
Sales journal	Sales of merchandise on credit
Purchases journal	Purchases of merchandise on credit
Cash receipts journal	All receipts of cash from any source
Cash payments journal	All payments of cash for any purpose

The general journal would be used to record any event or transaction that could not be recorded in a special journal.

JUDGMENT A pecuniary award ordered by a court as the result of a lawsuit. A judgment constitutes a liability of the JUDGMENT DEBTOR and should accordingly appear upon his books. Likewise the award from the viewpoint of the judgment creditor is an asset, or contingent asset, since although awarded, it may be uncollectible.

JUDGMENT CREDITOR A creditor whose claim has been validated in a court of law and has been reduced to a judgment against the debtor.

JUDGMENT DEBT A debt that has been contested in a lawsuit and found to be due; a debt validated and against which an award has been made by a court.

JUDGMENT DEBTOR A debtor against whom a creditor has secured a judgment, which has been placed on record.
See JUDGMENT DEBT.

JUDGMENT NOTE An ordinary promissory note given by a debtor to a creditor to avoid legal action by the latter. It is an acknowledgment of a debt due the creditor and usually contains a power of attorney permitting the creditor to appear in court and confess judgment for the debtor.

JUDICIAL SYSTEM The rules of law that exist today have evolved over the centuries. The law is broadly viewed as a body of rules for human conduct, enforced by a governing power, as the means by which the control of society is attained. Much of the current law in the United States was transferred from England. Common law was and still is widely used as a basis of law.

A lawsuit or legal action between persons is called a civil action. Its purpose is to compensate for injury sustained through the violation of a person's legal right. A lawsuit or legal action brought against a wrongdoer by the state is called a criminal action. The objective of a criminal action is punishment to deter others from committing such acts, to reform the wrongdoer, or to protect society by segregating the wrongdoer from society.

The usual individual remedies available in a lawsuit are an action for money damages or an action by the owner of certain property to recover its possessions when it is wrongfully withheld.

There are two types of courts in the judicial system in the United States: trial courts and appellate courts. Trial courts determine the facts of a case; appellate courts are concerned primarily with questions of law. Before a court can hear a case, it must have jurisdiction over the type of case and the parties involved. Each state has its own court system. The federal government has its own court system consisting of trial courts and courts of appeal. Trial courts of unlimited jurisdiction are classified by function: criminal courts; estate courts (jurisdiction over estates of deceased persons and the guardians of minors); general civil courts.

A summons is used to obtain jurisdiction over a person. The person must be served with a summons. A trial court is usually referred to as a circuit court or superior court. Small claims courts are used to judicate small cases. The justice of the peace court is also a court of limited jurisdiction. The highest state court is usually referred to as the supreme court or court of appeals. Intermediate appellate courts are provided in some states.

In the federal court system, courts have jurisdiction involving parties with different citizenship (diversity jurisdiction) and those involving federal questions (federal question jurisdiction). Cases get to the U.S. Supreme Court when a party appeals to that court or petitions it to issue a writ of certiorari.

A typical civil trial involves various stages--pleading the case. Pleadings are the formal written statements which the parties file with the court alleging what each party believes to be the facts upon which he or she bases the claim or defense. The plaintiff files a complaint (a declaration), and the defendant files an answer (a plea). The defendant may file a counterclaim against the plaintiff or other motions, such as a motion for summary judgment. The second stage in a trial is the discovery state, using written interrogatories, oral depositions, and motions to produce, or for physical examination. A jury is impaneled in the actual trial, if a jury is used. A subsequent stage is for the parties to make an opening statement and present evidence. In the United States, a plaintiff has the burden of proof and must establish a prima facie case. Otherwise, the judge can direct that a verdict be entered against the plaintiff. After the presentation of evidence, the judge instructs the jury as to the law that applies in the case. The jury then hears the final argument by attorneys for each party to the case. The jury retires and considers the evidence and arguments and arrives at its verdict. The plaintiff must prove his or her case by a preponderance of the evidence. Either party may appeal the decision to an appellate court which can affirm, reverse, or remand the decision of the trial court.

The time for taking an appeal or otherwise correcting the action of a trial court varies from a few weeks to a few months. If the proper time has passed without a reversal or correction, a civil judgment is usually considered final as to the rights and liabilities involved in the dispute.

Arbitration is being more widely used as a substitute for taking a case to court. Mediators are often used to help settle disputes outside of the official judicial system.

JUMBO CDs Certificates of deposit in minimum denominations of $100,000.

JUMBO MORTGAGE A mortgage sold in the secondary market above $153,100. As of January 1, 1987, the secondary market for mortgages for Fannie Mae and Freddie Mac accepts only up to $153,100.

JUNIOR BONDS Bonds that are preceded by another issue or issues in their claim against the property pledged as security therefor. In the case of foreclosure they constitute a claim against the property pledged as security only after all prior claims have been satisfied. Junior bonds may be any kind of bonds except first mortgage bonds, e.g., second mortgage bonds, general mortgage bonds, debenture bonds. They are the opposite of SENIOR BONDS.

JUNIOR ISSUE JUNIOR BONDS; junior stock (usually refers to common stock as distinguished from preferred stock).

JUNIOR LIEN See JUNIOR BONDS, JUNIOR ISSUE, JUNIOR MORTGAGE, LIEN.

JUNIOR MORTGAGE A low-ranking MORTGAGE; a mortgage that is preceded by another or others in its claim against the mortgaged property, and that in case of foreclosure would not be satisfied until all prior mortgages had been satisfied. A junior mortgage constitutes a junior lien upon the mortgaged property and is any mortgage other than the first, e.g., second, third, general, etc.
See JUNIOR BONDS.

JUNIOR STOCK Stock of a corporation that usually does not have voting or full voting, liquidation, or dividend rights and is convertible in the future into the corporation's regular common stock if certain corporate performance objectives are achieved. Junior stock is usually not transferrable and has lower market value than regular corporate common stock because of restrictions and the uncertainty of conversion. Junior stock has been used in junior stock plans.

JUNK BONDS The term "junk bonds" was first used to denote outstanding bonds issued by firms suffering current financial troubles. Many of these firms (often referred to as "fallen angels") were financially strong when the bonds were originally issued but had encountered difficulties that made bond default a strong possibility.

As used today, junk bonds refer to all speculative-grade debt, regardless of the financial condition of the issuing firm. Speculative-grade bonds are those with ratings below BBB- (from Standard & Poor's) or Baa (from Moody's). In recent years, these ratings frequently have been assigned to bonds issued by new firms that do not have an established performance record. In the past, such new firms may have been denied access to the bond market because of their low ratings and been forced to rely solely on equity finance or bank borrowings. The junk bond market has given such firms a new financing alternative.

The investment banking firm of Drexel Burnham Lambert is generally credited with making junk bonds acceptable by creating an active secondary market in these securities. When interest in takeovers and leveraged buyouts increased dramatically in the early 1980s, the demands of both corporate raiders and management swelled the demand for debt capital. Drexel Burnham Lambert worked actively to persuade certain institutions (including some mutual funds) and others to invest in high-yield, low-rate debt securities (i.e., junk bonds). Drexel developed substantial expertise in putting together deals that proved attractive to both investors and issuers, and this success catapulted the firm to the top of the investment banking business.

In the late 1980s, many junk bonds had stopped paying interest or were associated with companies restructuring their debt. Many bond issuers were in bankruptcy proceedings. Additional companies were on investors "watch lists." Moody's Investors Service estimated that an average of 3.3% of junk-bond issuers defaulted each year between 1970 and 1988, compared to an annual default rate of 0.06% for issuers of investment-grade bonds.

Junk bond funds were faced with high liquidity risks, especially if a manager has to unload the high-yield bonds quickly. One major junk bond fund had to liquidate, resulting in a 20% or more loss to investors of their original investment. In 1989, there were more than 90 open-end junk funds with holdings of more than $34 billion in assets.

Moody estimates default rates for 3,000 corporate bond issuers over different time periods as follows:

Bond Rating	1-Yr	5-Yr	10-Yr	15-Yr
Triple A	0.00%	0.2%	0.8%	2.1%
Double A	.00	0.5	1.4	2.2
Single A	.01	0.5	1.4	2.7
Baa	.16	1.6	3.7	5.9
Ba	1.56	8.3	14.2	18.9
Single B	6.69	22.3	29.3	32.9

Source: Moody's Investors Service

JURISDICTION The power to hear and determine the subject matter in controversy between parties, or to adjudicate or exercise any judicial power over them.

JUSTICE, DEPARTMENT OF The Department of Justice was established by act of June 22, 1870, with the attorney general as its head. The attorney general, as head of the Department of Justice and chief law officer of the federal government, represents the United States in legal matters generally and gives advice and opinions to the president and to the heads of the executive departments of the government when so requested. The attorney general appears in person to represent the government in the U.S. Supreme Court in cases of exceptional gravity or importance. The department is organized into offices (legislative affairs, public affairs, professional responsibility, legal policy, legal counsel, justice programs), divisions (justice management, criminal division, antitrust, civil, civil rights, land and natural resources, tax, immigration and naturalization, drug enforcement), bureaus (investigations, prisons), and boards. The department plays key roles in protection against criminals and subversion, in ensuring healthy competition of business, in safeguarding the consumer, and in enforcing drug, immigration, and naturalization laws as well as in effective law enforcement, crime prevention, crime detection, and prosecution and rehabilitation of offenders.

Source: Department of Justice.

BIBLIOGRAPHY

MECHAM, M. "Justice Department Vows Stronger Antitrust Policy on Mergers." *Aviation Week and Space Technology*, March, 13, 1989.
"Regulators, Lawmakers Step Up Scrutiny of Lending Practices." *Savings Institutions*, March, 1989.

JUST-IN-TIME (JIT) An operating and management philosophy in which all resources, including materials, personnel, and facilities, are used as they are needed, or in a just-in-time manner. The objective of JIT is to assure the continuous flow of resources so that each part of the production process works as a unit—production throughput, not inventory buildup. In JIT, the emphasis is on time, not cost. It is assumed that if the processing time of a product is materially reduced, operating costs will also decline. For example, costs of raw materials, work-in-process, and finished goods inventories are costly to store, maintain, insure, move, account for and tie up working capital. In JIT, customers' orders trigger manufacturing operations.

Approximately 15% of U.S. manufacturing companies have adopted JIT in some manner. Management literature dealing with JIT suggests that using JIT generally allows a company to obtain the following advantages:

Maintain minimum inventory levels.
Establish pull-through production planning and scheduling.
Purchase materials as required in small lot sizes.
Perform simple and relatively inexpensive machine setups.
Develop a multiskilled labor force.
Create a flexible manufacturing system.
Maintain product quality.
Develop effective preventive maintenance.
Promote work improvement techniques.
Improve morale.
Reduce labor, material, and overhead costs.

JIT changes product costing practices, budgeting and planning approaches, capital budgeting methods, and internal reporting.

K

KANSAS CITY BOARD OF TRADE A marketplace in which buyers and sellers trade futures contracts on hard red winter wheat and the Value Line Index of nearly 1,700 stocks. Wheat options are also traded. The Value Line Index is similar in concept to the Dow Jones industrial average in that each indicates prices for a specific group of stocks. Stocks represented in the average range from small companies to large oil and manufacturing companies.

In 1856, a group of Kansas City merchants formed the KCBT—an organization similar to a chamber of commerce. In 1876 "grain call" trading was established, which marked the beginning of futures trading in Kansas City. The KCBT is a membership organization composed of individual firms and individual traders. To become a member, the exchange requires that certain financial and character requirements are met and that a KCBT membership be purchased or leased. Brokers also must be registered with the National Futures Association. Trading on the KCBT is done by open outcry. The Clearing Corporation is a clearing house for trading activities. It matches trades, ensuring that the buyers' and sellers' records agree.

The KCBT provides numerous support services for its members: a computer system that displays and transmits prices, electronic price quote machines on the trading floor, and a marketing department that promotes KCBT contracts. The board also has an audits and investigations department that ensures members follow KCBT regulations as well as trading rules set by the federal government.

KEOGH RETIREMENT PLAN A retirement plan for self-employed persons who own their own business (H.R. 10 plan; Code Sec. 1402(a)). To participate in the plan, a person must have earned income from the trade or business for which the plan was established to take a deduction for income tax purposes for a contribution to the plan. Self-employment income includes net income from a sole proprietorship or a partnership, income earned as an independent contractor, income from consulting fees, directors' fees, royalties from books, and others. An individual with earned income can shelter part of it in a Keogh plan, even if an employee. Deductible contributions may only be made subject to certain adjusted gross income limitations. Contributions can be made retroactively up to the due date of the return. Anyone may be the trustee of the plan, including an owner-employee. H.R. 10 plans must be established by year-end.

A Keogh plan can be classified either as a pension plan or profit-sharing plan. Pension plans are classified into plans where either the contribution is fixed (defined contribution plans) or the retirement benefit is fixed (defined benefit plans). Deductible contributions to defined contribution are the lesser of 25% of earned income (reduced by the amount of deductible contributions made on behalf of the self-employed person) or $30,000. Contributions to a defined benefit plan are determined actuarially. In some cases, these contributions can exceed the $30,000 ceiling imposed on defined contribution plans. The current maximum benefit that can be provided is the lessor of 100% of income or $94,023. The latter amount is adjusted annually by the IRS to reflect increases in the cost of living.

Deductible contributions to profit-sharing plans are limited to the lesser of 15% of earned income (reduced by the amount of the deductible contribution made on behalf of the self-employed person) or $30,000.

A 10% penalty tax is levied on distributions made before a participant reached age 59 1/2. A 15% excise tax is imposed on excess distributions. Also, a mandatory distribution must begin by April 1 of the year following the year in which the beneficiary reaches age 70 1/2, regardless of whether or not the person is actually retired. The death benefit exclusion provides that $5,000 is available to anyone, including the estate or beneficiary of an owner-employee.

Participants of any qualified plan, if the plan permits, can borrow up to the lesser of $50,000 or one-half of vested benefits. In any event, the first $10,000 of vested benefits can be borrowed. The loan must be repaid within five years, unless it relates to a principal residence.

Depository institutions compete successfully for the large volume of retirement deposits available under H. R. 10.

BIBLIOGRAPHY

All You Should Know About IRA, Keogh, and Other Retirement Plans. Prentice Hall, Inc., Englewood Cliffs, NJ, 1987.

HACK, S. *Retirement Planning for Professionals.* John Wiley and Sons, New York, NY. 1987.

RICHARDS, R. W. *Dow Jones-Irwin Dictionary of Financial Planning.* Dow Jones-Irwin, Inc., Homewood, IL, 1986.

TACCHINO, K. B. *Retirement Planning for a Business and Business Owner.* The American College, Bryn Mawr, PA, 1988.

VICKER, R. *The Dow Jones-Irwin Guide to Retirement Planning.* Dow Jones-Irwin, Inc., Homewood, IL, 1987.

KERN AMENDMENT One of the amendments (P.L. 1007, 70th Congress, March 2, 1929) of the Clayton Anti-Trust Act, providing additional exemptions from the prohibition of interlocking directorates by Section 8 of the latter act. Subsequently, the BANKING ACT OF 1935 (49 Stat. 717) completely revised Section 8 of the Clayton Act.

See INTERLOCKING DIRECTORS.

KERR-SMITH TOBACCO CONTROL ACT An act, originally passed June 28, 1934, and amended August 27, 1935, that provided for processing taxes in the tobacco industry to finance a quota system for growers, including penalty taxes on marketing in excess of individual quotas. After the Agricultural Adjustment Act of 1933 was held to be unconstitutional on January 6, 1936, particularly because of the processing taxes imposed, the Kerr-Smith Tobacco Act was repealed February 10, 1936, as were sister acts (BANKHEAD COTTON CONTROL ACT, Potato Control Act).

KEYNESIAN ECONOMICS The system of aggregative economic analysis, and theory of income-determination based thereon, associated with the name of John Maynard Keynes, the English economist (1883-1946), particularly set forth in his landmark work, *The General Theory of Employment, Interest, and Money* (1936). The Keynesian "tools" of economic analysis have become standard, but the Keynesian policies invoking a more positive role for government in economic activity are controversial.

Albert G. Hart concisely states the causal chain of the Keynesian theory of income-determination as follows: "National product and employment are determined, given a 'propensity to consume function,' by 'investment.' Investment is determined, given a 'marginal efficiency of capital function,' by the rate of interest. The rate of interest is determined, given a 'liquidity preference function,' by the stock of money; *or* the rate of interest may be set by a policy decision if the authorities are willing and able to endow the public with the stock of money it will elect to hold (under its liquidity preference function) at the rate set."

Economists who advocate an active use of stabilization policies are called Keynesians. Keynes argues that deficient aggregate demand in the private sector is the major cause of recessions. Therefore, the appropriate policy is an expansionary fiscal policy that will ensure full employment in the economy.

Keynesians believe that business cycles arise from the instability of private sector expenditures such as fixed business investments, residential housing, and consumer durables. This instability periodically results in recessions. The purpose of the federal government's stabilization policies, according to Keynesians, is to bring about a stable and sustainable rate of long-run economic growth. Keynesians point with pride to the fact that the United States has avoided a major recession since the Employment Act of 1964 was passed by Congress. The recessions of 1920-1921 and 1937-1938, and the Great Depression of 1929-1933 were more severe than any post-World War II recession.

Keynesians argue that large gaps between actual and potential real GNP require expansionary fiscal policies in order to increase the aggregate level of expenditures. The magnitude of crowding out in the credit market is believed to be small because of the availability of unemployed resources. Furthermore, an expansion of the money supply moderates the increase in the interest rate and lessens crowding out. If the magnitude of crowding out is small in comparison to the increase in deficit spending, the increase in aggregate demand will substantially increase real output. Thus, stabilization policies that include both demand and supply management policies are effective tools that should be employed by the government to improve economic conditions.

Other economists are skeptical about whether stabilization policies can close the gap between actual and potential real GNP because crowding out nullifies the increase in government spending. These economists do not believe in the active use of stabilization policies for three reasons. First, the size of the gap between actual and potential real GNP is difficult to estimate and is changing over the business cycle. Second, policy changes have a lagged effect on economic activity and may even move the economy in the wrong direction once its full impact (including all secondary effects) is realized. Third, economic instability historically has been associated more with an inappropriate use of stabilization policies than with the instability of private sector expenditures.

See CONSUMPTION FUNCTION, LIQUIDITY PREFERENCE, MARGINAL EFFICIENCY OF CAPITAL, MULTIPLIER.

BIBLIOGRAPHY

DILLARD, D. *The Economics of John Maynard Keynes.* 1948.
KEYNES, J. M. *The General Theory of Employment, Interest and Money,* 1936.
———. *Essays in Persuasion,* 1932.
———. *Laissez-faire and Communism,* 1926.
———. *A Treatise on Money,* 1930.
KLEIN, L. R. *The Keynesian Revolution.* 1947.
ROBINSON, J. *An Essay on Marxian Economics,* 1942.
SCHUMPETER, J. A. "John Maynard Keynes, 1883-1946." *The Economic Journal,* September, 1946.

KICKBACK LAW A 1986 federal law that provides severe penalties for accepting or giving kickbacks (41 U.S.C 51-58).

KILLING Among stock or produce exchange speculators, an unusually large and unexpected trading profit.

KINKED DEMAND CURVE It is common in economic analysis to illustrate a firm's or an industry's demand curve by a linear or curvilinear graph of price against quantity demanded. It is believed that such a depiction accurately represents the price-to-quantity tradeoff. However, in an oligopolistic industry, early theorists conceptualized the industry demand curve to be kinked. That is, competitors would be relatively unresponsive to price increases (from the prevailing price) and very responsive to price decreases. While this pedagogical tool still occupies a prominent position in most economics texts, game theory models of competition in oligopolistic industries are the more modern tool of analysis.

KITING CHECKS Making use of fictitious balances by drawing against uncollected funds. Depositors are not entitled to draw against uncollected funds, but banks are not always careful in guarding against payment of funds deposited but not collected. Where this is true, it is possible for two persons living in different localities, by exchanging checks with one another and depositing them with their respective banks, to have use of the funds until the day of collection, when funds may be deposited to make good the amount.

Kiting may also be practiced by a single individual having two bank accounts. By depositing a check drawn on Bank A to the credit of his account in Bank B and depositing a check drawn on Bank B to the credit of his account in Bank A, a person may draw against the fictitious balances thus credited, expecting to "cover" before the checks are presented.

In the long run, banks are able to detect individuals who make a practice of kiting. This practice injures the depositor's credit standing and may result in his losing his account.

KITING STOCKS Forcing stock prices to unwarranted high levels; inflating or ballooning the prices of stocks.

L

LABOR Services provided by workers of all types and skills. In manufacturing firms, labor can be divided into two broad categories; production workers and nonproduction workers. Production workers are directly involved in the physical process of making a product, such as laborers on an assembly line. Non-production workers include those individuals who are involved in some aspect of management, such as technical researchers, and those who provide services. But even within these broad headings, workers differ with respect to their skills, experience, age, sex, race, and so on. Although economists are aware of the heterogeneous nature of the labor force, it is convenient in economic analysis to group the services of all workers under a broad category called labor. Table 2 shows the U.S. labor force, employment, and unemployment data.

An individual can allocate his or her time in two ways: toward labor or toward leisure. Economist teach that this allocation is influenced by the prevailing wage rate. As wages rise, individuals allocate more time to labor and less time to leisure. This tradeoff has limits depending on each individual's relative taste for income versus leisure.

The working age population includes individuals who are in the labor force plus those individuals over the age of 16 who are either retired or are not seeking employment. The labor force participation rate is the proportion of the working-age population who is in the labor force. The labor force participation rate varies across different categories of workers, as shown in the table below. Two trends are clear: The participation rate of males has fallen steadily since 1950 and that of females has increased steadily. These data also suggest that women entering the labor force are primarily white.

Table 1/ Participation Rates (in percent)

Year	Economy	Males	Females	Whites	Blacks/Others
1950	57.9	86.4	33.9	–	–
1960	60.6	83.3	37.7	58.8	64.5
1970	61.0	79.7	43.3	60.2	61.8
1980	64.1	77.4	51.5	64.1	61.7
1985	65.1	76.3	54.5	65.0	63.3
1986	65.6	76.3	55.3	65.5	63.7
1987	65.9	76.2	56.6	65.8	64.3

Source: Economic Report of the President, 1988.

Separate labor markets exist for individuals with different skills and career objectives. Most individuals acquire a professional or technical background in order to compete in a select number of markets. Within these narrowly defined markets, the supply of labor is positively related to the wage rate. An increase or decrease in the wage rate increases or decreases the quantity of workers willing to offer their labor services to that market. The demand for labor is a derived demand. It is derived from the market demand for the firm's final product. A change in the demand for a firm's final product causes a corresponding change in the demand for inputs, including labor. Given this demand, quantity demanded is inversely related to the wage rate.

Labor productivity refers to the amount of output produced by a worker. Generally, it is measured as the ratio of total output per unit of labor, where the units of labor could be in terms of number of workers or number of man-hours. Estimates of output per worker are published in the *Economic Report of the President* and other sources.

The labor theory of value states that the value of a good or service is proportional to the amount of labor used to produce that good or service. Karl Marx espoused this view, but its origins can be traced to the English philosopher John Locke. Economists rely on markets to determine value. The labor theory has been discredited in capitalistic economies.

LABOR BANK A bank which has been organized, and whose stock is owned, by a labor union and its members. Except for the fact that they are operated under the auspices of labor unions primarily (although dealings are in no sense restricted to union members), labor banks differ in no essential respects from other banks. A pioneer of these banks was the Locomotive Brotherhood Bank of Cleveland, Ohio, which was opened in November, 1920. Of the total stock of this bank, 51% was owned by the brotherhood as an organization, the remainder of the stock being held by members of the brotherhood individually. Stockholders were to receive no more than 10% in dividends, and any surplus that accrued was to be distributed to depositors as an increased interest rate. But with the adversities of the banking crisis in the U.S. in 1931-1933, this experiment in cooperative banking came to an end.

Other examples were the Brotherhood of Locomotive Engineers' Cooperative Trust Company of New York City, which opened for business on December 29, 1923, organized under the banking laws of the State of New York, and the Brotherhood of Locomotive Engineers' Cooperative Trust Company of Philadelphia, organized in February, 1924, also a state-chartered institution. The brotherhood banks in New York and Philadelphia were equipped to do a trust business. All labor banks performed savings bank functions.

In May 1920, the Mount Vernon Savings Bank was organized in Washington, D.C. with capital of $160,000, as the pioneer labor bank. From then on the drive to open labor banks spread rapidly. Even in the depression year 1921, the American Federation of Labor unions entered the movement, and ten labor banks were established by the end of 1922. Four years later there were 36 such banks in existence, with aggregate resources of $126.5 million. Deposits had increased from $697,000 on June 30, 1920, to $109 million on June 30, 1926.

Beginning with 1926, terminations began to exceed initiations of labor banks, and a gradual decline became evident. By June 30, 1930, there were only 14 labor banks left. Only four labor banks have survived: the Amalgamated Trust & Savings Bank of Chicago, established in 1922; the Brotherhood State Bank of Kansas City, established in 1924; Broad National Bank of Newark, N.J., established in 1925 as the Union National Bank (name changed on July 15, 1961); and the Amalgamated Bank of New York, established in 1923.

In addition to chartering banks, labor unions make investments in bank stocks substantial enough to be reflected in representation of the labor union involved on the board of directors of the bank concerned. An example is the United Mine Workers of America and the National Bank of Washington, D.C.

Labor banks may be found in European and Latin American countries, as well as in Puerto Rico and Israel. The concept of the workers' bank appears to have special appeal in developing countries.

LABOR UNION An organization of workers from a similar occupation. A union represents its members' interests in such areas as contract negotiations with management. These contractual agree-

Table 2 / Labor Force, Employment, and Unemployment
(Thousands of persons; monthly data are seasonally adjusted. Exceptions noted.)

Category	1986	1987	1988	1988[R] Oct.	Nov.	Dec.	1989[R] Jan.	Feb.	Mar.	Apr.	May
Household Survey Data											
1. Noninstitutional population[1]	182,822	185,010	186,837	187,333	187,471	187,618	187,859	187,979	188,102	188,228	188,377
2. Labor force (including Armed Forces)[1]	120,078	122,122	123,893	124,310	124,737	124,779	125,643	125,383	125,469	125,863	125,806
3. Civilian labor force	117,834	119,865	121,669	122,091	122,510	122,563	123,428	123,181	123,264	123,659	123,610
Employment											
4. Nonagricultural industries[2]	106,434	109,232	111,800	112,335	112,709	112,816	113,411	113,630	113,930	114,009	114,102
5. Agriculture	3,163	3,208	3,169	3,238	3,238	3,193	3,300	3,223	3,206	3,104	3,112
Unemployment											
6. Number	8,237	7,425	6,701	6,518	6,563	6,554	6,716	6,328	6,128	6,546	6,395
7. Rate (percent of civilian labor force)	7.0	6.2	5.5	5.3	5.4	5.3	5.4	5.1	5.0	5.3	5.2
8. Not in labor force	62,744	62,888	62,944	63,023	62,734	62,839	62,216	62,596	62,633	62,365	62,571
Establishment Survey Data											
9. Nonagricultural payroll employment[3]	99,525	102,310	106,039	106,475	106,824	107,097	107,442	107,711	107,888	108,094	108,195
10. Manufacturing	18,965	19,065	19,536	19,505	19,557	19,589	19,648	19,648	19,680	19,669	19,651
11. Mining	777	721	733	717	712	711	711	711	714	720	719
12. Contract construction	4,816	4,998	5,294	5,162	5,191	5,213	5,267	5,270	5,252	5,275	5,261
13. Transportation and public utilities	5,255	5,385	5,584	5,596	5,616	5,634	5,654	5,667	5,666	5,682	5,694
14. Trade	23,683	24,381	25,362	25,315	25,386	25,453	25,553	25,631	25,685	25,698	25,717
15. Finance	6,283	6,549	6,679	6,710	6,726	6,744	6,746	6,763	6,774	6,781	6,788
16. Service	23,053	24,196	25,464	25,986	26,111	26,230	26,318	26,434	26,520	26,647	26,711
17. Government	16,693	17,015	17,387	17,484	17,525	17,523	17,545	17,587	17,597	17,622	17,654

[1] Persons 16 years of age and over. Monthly figures, which are based on sample data, relate to the calendar week that contains the 12th day; annual data are averages of monthly figures. By definition, seasonality does not exist in population figures. Based on data from *Employment and Earnings* (U.S. Department of Labor).
[2] Includes self-employed, unpaid family, and domestic service workers.
[3] Data include all full and part-time employees who worked during, or received pay for, the pay period that includes the 12th day of the month, and exclude proprietors, self-employed persons, domestic servants, unpaid family workers, and members of the Armed Forces. Data are adjusted to the March 1984 benchmark and only seasonally adjusted data are available at this time. Based on data from *Employment and Earnings* (U.S. Department of Labor).

ments include wage and fringe benefits, working conditions, job retraining, and length of the work week. In 1988, less than 17 % of the labor force belonged to a union, and this percentage is falling. Unionized workers are in mostly clerical, operative, or teaching-related professions.

Typically, union workers' contracts are multiyear agreements. Although employers may want to respond to market pressure by lowering wages, they often do not have the ability because of a prior contractual agreement with union members and other workers under contract.

The two appended tables show (1) U.S. membership in AFL-CIO affiliated unions, by selected union: 1975 to 1987 and (2) U.S. union membership, by state: 1975 to 1982.

LAFFER CURVE The diagram below illustrates a nonlinear relationship between tax rates and tax revenues for an economy. Such a relationship was popularized by Arthur Laffer and is commonly known as the Laffer curve.

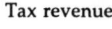

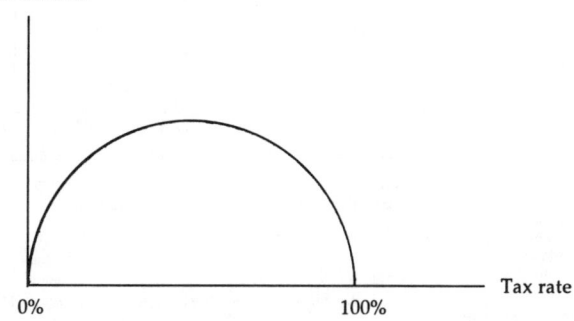

The Laffer curve shows that for either a zero tax rate or a 100 % tax rate (measured on the horizontal axis) no tax revenues (measured on the vertical axis) will be collected by the government. Tax revenues only will be positive at tax rates between 0% and 100% As illustrated, there is some tax rate at which tax revenues will be a maximum. The value of such a tax rate is not known for the U.S. economy.

LAGGING ECONOMIC INDICTORS Lagging ECONOMIC INDICATORS generally turn after the business cycle has turned. For example, the reciprocal of the average duration of unemployment will increase (decrease) after the business cycle indicates that the economy is growing (slowing). A lagging indicator, used with other indicators, is a useful measure for documenting a turning point in a business cycle.

LAISSEZ-FAIRE From laissez-nous faire; French for "allow us to do" or, idiomatically, "leave us alone." The term was supposedly used by the French businessman Legendre, in reply to a question by Louis XIV's finance minister Colbert as to how the state might aid business. In the eighteenth century it denoted a public policy of nonintervention and noninterference by government with business. In English economics, however, the term is particularly identified with the model of free enterprise with a minimum of governmental functions espoused by Adam Smith in his *Wealth of Nations* (1776).

In Smith's model, government is to perform those minimum functions which private enterprise could not or would not do because of the lack of capital or motivation of profits. The duties and functions of government are few:

1. National defense.
2. Domestic system of justice and police.
3. Maintenance of essential public works, such as harbors, canals, streets, highways, etc.
4. Contribution to support of schools and churches.

LAISSEZ-FAIRE

Table 1 / U.S. Membership in AFL-CIO Affiliated Unions, by Selected Union: 1975 to 1987
(In thousands. Figures represent the labor organizations as constituted in 1987 and reflect past merger activity. Membership figures based on average per capita paid membership to the AFL-CIO for the 2-year period ending in June of the year shown and reflect only actively-employed members.)

Labor organization	1975	1979	1985	1987
Total [1]	14,070	13,621	11,250	12,692
Automobile, Aerospace, and Agriculture (UAW)	X	X	974	998
Bakery, Confectionery, and Tobacco [2]	149	131	115	109
Boiler Makers, Iron Shipbuilders [2]	123	129	110	90
Bricklayers	143	106	95	84
Carpenters [2]	712	629	609	609
Clothing and Textile Workers (ACTWU) [2]	377	308	228	195
Communication Workers (CWA)	476	485	524	515
Electrical Workers (IBEW)	856	825	791	765
Electronic, Electrical and Technical [2]	255	243	198	185
Operating Engineers	300	313	330	330
Firefighters	123	150	142	142
Food and Commercial Workers (UFCW) [2]	1,150	1,123	989	1,000
Garment Workers (ILGWU)	363	314	210	173
Government, American Federation	255	236	199	157
Graphic Communications [2]	198	171	141	136
Hotel Employees and Restaurant Employees	421	373	327	293
Ironworkers	160	146	140	122
Laborers	475	475	383	371
Letter Carriers (NALC)	151	151	186	200
Machinists and Aerospace (IAM)	780	664	520	509
Musicians	215	206	67	60
Oil, Chemical, Atomic Workers (OCAW)	145	146	108	96
Painters	160	160	133	128
Paperworkers Int'l	275	262	232	221
Plumbing and Pipefitting	228	228	226	220
Postal Workers	249	245	232	230
Retail, Wholesale Department Store [2]	120	122	106	140
Rubber, Cork, Linoleum, Plastic	173	158	106	97
Service Employees (SEIU) [2]	490	537	688	762
State, County, Municipal (AFSCME)	647	889	997	1,032
Steelworkers	1,062	964	572	494
Teachers (AFT)	396	423	470	499
Transport Workers	95	85	85	85

X — Not applicable.
[1] Includes other AFL-CIO affiliated unions, not shown separately.
[2] Figures reflect mergers with one or more unions since 1975. For details see source.

Source: American Federation of Labor and Congress of Industrial Organizations, Washington, DC, *Report of the AFL-CIO Executive Council*, annual.

5. If absolutely necessary, levying of import duties for such essential functions as national defense.
6. Regulation of banking.
7. Enactment of usury laws.
8. Provision of free education for those unable to afford private education.
9. Fair and equitable regulation on behalf of labor.

Popularly, however, Smith is particularly identified with his view that if business is left free from governmental interference beyond the above minimal functions, it will although seeking private gain bring about general benefit; the businessperson or individual, acting in self-interest, serves the public interest:

Table 2 / U.S. Union Membership, by State: 1975 to 1982
(Data represent annual average, dues-paying full-time equivalent membership derived from financial records. Excludes unemployed members. In general, annual per capita revenues received by the parent organization were divided by the per capita rate to yield membership. For unions with multiple dues structures or other structures, other methods were used. A right-to-work State has laws which prohibit collective bargaining contracts from including clauses requiring union membership as a condition of employment.)

State	Total (1,000) 1975	1980	1982	Percent of employed [1] 1975	1980	1982
U.S. [2]	22,207	20,968	19,571	28.9	23.2	21.9
AL [3]	275	245	239	23.9	18.1	18.2
AK	67	56	59	41.2	33.1	30.4
AZ [3]	152	152	132	20.9	14.9	12.8
AR [3]	114	107	95	18.4	14.5	13.2
CA	2,694	2,693	2,495	34.5	27.3	25.4
CO	224	236	236	23.6	18.9	18.0
CT	338	267	269	27.7	18.7	18.9
DE	58	58	53	25.8	22.3	20.3
DC	191	216	199	33.0	35.1	33.4
FL [3]	427	348	359	15.6	9.7	9.6
GA [3]	249	282	279	14.4	13.1	12.7
HI	117	129	126	34.3	31.8	31.5
ID	52	56	50	19.4	17.1	16.1
IL	1,553	1,431	1,261	35.1	29.5	27.5
IN	610	627	505	31.6	29.5	25.1
IA [3]	232	238	211	23.4	21.4	20.5
KS [4]	128	121	110	16.0	12.8	12.0
KY	257	251	237	24.6	20.7	20.4
LA [5]	237	235	223	19.8	14.9	13.8
ME	74	87	76	20.7	20.7	18.5
MD	391	314	311	27.5	18.3	18.6
MA	565	515	517	24.3	19.4	19.7
MI	1,319	1,212	1,076	42.2	35.2	33.7
MN	426	431	419	29.0	24.3	24.5
MS [3]	84	78	74	12.6	9.5	9.3
MO	575	568	510	33.4	28.8	26.6
MT	76	70	59	31.8	25.0	21.7
NE [3]	107	104	98	19.3	16.6	16.3
NV [3]	99	103	90	37.4	25.8	22.1
NH	50	49	48	16.9	12.7	12.3
NJ	758	684	613	28.4	22.3	19.9
NM	62	59	61	17.0	12.6	12.8
NY	2,937	2,628	2,589	43.2	36.5	35.8
NC [3]	220	210	208	11.0	8.8	8.9
ND [3]	39	39	36	19.4	15.7	14.2
OH	1,449	1,312	1,132	36.1	30.0	27.4
OK	173	172	160	19.5	15.1	12.9
OR	282	289	264	33.9	27.6	27.5
PA	1,514	1,370	1,230	34.3	28.8	27.0
RI	90	76	76	26.3	19.1	19.4
SC [3]	66	73	68	6.8	6.2	5.8
SD [3]	28	25	24	13.3	10.7	10.3
TN [3]	324	305	292	21.7	17.5	17.3
TX [3]	705	755	782	16.0	12.9	12.5
UT [3]	99	99	94	22.4	18.0	16.8
VT	26	25	24	16.3	12.3	11.9
VA [3]	253	229	232	14.4	10.6	10.9
WA	540	543	517	44.7	33.8	32.9
WV	208	184	176	37.1	28.5	28.9
WI	527	492	457	31.5	25.4	24.5
WY [3]	33	37	34	22.6	17.5	15.6

[1] Nonagriculture employed.
[2] Includes Canal Zone, Guam, Puerto Rico, and Virgin Islands not shown separately.
[3] Right-to-work State.
[4] Right-to-work State for 1975 and 1980.
[5] Right-to-work State beginning 1980.

Source: Industrial Relations Data and Information Services, West Orange, NJ, *U.S. Union Sourcebook*.

"...he intends only his own gain, and he is in this, as in many other cases, led by an invisible hand to promote an end which was no part of his intention. Nor is it always the worse for the society that it was no part of it. By pursuing his own interest he frequently promotes that of the society more effectually than when he really intends to promote it. I have never known much good done by those who affected to trade for the public good. It is an affectation, indeed, not very common among merchants, and very few words need be employed in dissuading them from it"
(Wealth of Nations, Book 1, Ch. 2).

The essence of the Smithian model, therefore, is economic freedom:

"All systems either of preference or of restraint, therefore, being thus completely taken away, the obvious and simple system of natural liberty establishes itself of its own accord. Every man, as long as he does not violate the laws of justice, is left perfectly free to pursue his own interest his own way, and to bring both his industry and capital into competition with those of any other man, or order of men"
(Wealth of Nations, Book 4, Ch. 9).

But competition is essential to the working of the model:

"People of the same trade seldom meet together, even for merriment and diversion, but the conversation ends in a conspiracy against the public, or in some contrivance to raise prices. It is impossible indeed to prevent such meetings, by any law which either could be executed, or would be consistent with liberty and justice. But though the law cannot hinder people of the same trade from sometimes assembling together, it ought to do nothing to facilitate such assemblies, much less to render them necessary"
(Wealth of Nations, Book 1, Ch. 10).
See CAPITALISM.

LAMB An inexperienced speculator who plays the market, i.e., speculates blindly. Such a person is called a lamb because he follows the herd, buying or selling because others do so, and therefore is likely to be easy prey to losses. His transactions are not based on a knowledge of fundamental conditions or of intrinisic values, equities, or earning power, but on tips or hazy impressions. He trusts largely on chance, betting on the rise and fall of quotations. Whenever a lamb makes a profit, it is more accidental than otherwise. The Securities Act of 1933, the Securities and Exchange Act of 1934, the Commodity Exchange Act, and similar protective legislation aimed at fraud and manipulative practices cannot guarantee, of course, successful speculative operations or prudent investment by the lamb.

LAME DUCK A person who has become financially embarrassed, especially with reference to speculators.

LAND BANK COMMISSIONER The antecedent of this official was the farm loan commissioner member of the Federal Farm Loan Board, created to administer the Federal Farm Loan Act of July 17, 1916. Executive Order 6084 of March 27, 1933, transferred the functions of the board to the FARM CREDIT ADMINISTRATION (FCA), effective May 27, 1933. The order abolished the offices of appointed members of the board except the member designated as the farm loan commissioner, concurrently transferring all powers and functions of the board to the farm loan commissioner under the jurisdiction and control of the FCA. The title of farm loan commissioner was changed to land bank commissioner by the act of June 16, 1933, which gave the newly titled commissioner authority for extending land bank commissioner loans.

Authority to make land bank commissioner loans expired July 1, 1947, and the office was abolished by the act of August 6, 1953 (67 Stat. 393; 12 U.S.C. 636f).
See LAND BANK COMMISSIONER LOAN.

LAND BANK COMMISSIONER LOAN First see LAND BANK COMMISSIONER.

From May 13, 1933, to March 17, 1934, land bank commissioner loans to farmers were made from the $200 million fund which was made available to the land bank commissioner by Section 32 of the Emergency Farm Mortgage Act of 1933. Beginning March 17, 1934, the loans were made from the $2 billion bond authorization of the Federal Farm Mortgage Corporation, as provided in Section 9 of the Federal Farm Mortgage Corporation Act, of which $600 million could be used for this purpose.

Authority to make land bank commissioner loans expired July 1, 1947. From such date, activities of the Federal Farm Mortgage Corporation included orderly liquidation of outstanding land bank commissioner loans.

LAND BANKS In modern times particularly the FEDERAL LAND BANKS, which supply long-term farm mortgage credit through their Federal Land Bank associations.

In American colonial banking history, several experiments in so-called land banking were made. The earliest, established in 1681, was known as The Fund at Boston in New England. In 1714, a more elaborate land bank was established, known as A Projection for Erecting a Bank of Credit in Boston, New England, Founded on Land Security. Following these two projects were the New London Bank in 1732 and the Land Bank of 1740 (Massachusetts). Each of these banks was founded on the principle that land could be made the basis of credit and currency, being the ultimate security and redemption value therefor, and that paper currency could be collateraled by land as security without necessity for redemption in specie, which was scarce. For example, the currency issued by the Land Bank of 1740, secured by real estate, was redeemable in commodities. This land banking scheme was eventually liquidated after the English Parliament in 1741 amended the Bubble Act of 1720 to apply charters from Parliament.

LAND BONDS See FEDERAL FARM LOAN SYSTEM, JOINT-STOCK LAND BANK BONDS, MORTGAGE CERTIFICATE, MORTGAGE LOANS, REAL ESTATE BONDS.

LAND CONTRACT An installment land contract that allows the seller to hold onto his or her original below-market rate mortgage while "selling" the home on an installment basis. The installment payments are for a short term and may be for interest only. At the end of the contract, the unpaid balance, frequently the full purchase price, must be paid. The seller continues to hold title to the property until all payments are made. The buyer acquires no equity until the contract ends. If the borrower fails to make a payment on time, he or she could lose a major investment.

These loans are popular because they offer lower payments than market rate loans. Land contracts are also being used to avoid the DUE-ON-SALE clause (because the property will not be sold until the end of the contract).

LAND GRANT BOND A type of railroad bond secured by tracts of land granted to railroads by the federal government as well as by states and local governments. Federal land grants to railroads were discontinued after 1871, but states and local governments continued to give aid in land grants.

LAPPING An embezzlement scheme in which cash collections from customers are stolen. To avoid discovery, the embezzler corrects the customers' accounts within a few days by posting other cash receipts to the accounts from which the proceeds have been embezzled.
See FRAUD; KITING.

LAPSE In life insurance, the termination of an unmatured policy by reason of failure to pay the premium within the grace period, usually approximately one month after the due date of premium.

If the policy is for ordinary, straight, or permanent insurance coverage, it will have nonforfeiture values despite lapse. Nonforfeiture values include the following:

1. Cash surrender value, to which the holder of a lapsed policy is entitled. To avoid lapse, the policy may have provision for automatic premium loan, whereby the company upon specific arrangement will pay automatically any premium not paid by the insured when due, charging same against the cash surrender value until it is exhausted, at which time the policy would terminate, and have no further value.
2. Reduced paid-up life insurance, representing the application of the cash surrender value of a policy on which the insured can no longer pay the premiums to the amount of paid-up coverage

(requiring no further premium payments) it will buy at the age of the insured.
3. Extended-term insurance, representing the application of the cash surrender value of a policy on which the insured can no longer pay the premiums to the purchase of paid-up term insurance (not requiring further premium payments) for the period of time the cash surrender value will buy at the age of the insured.

Despite lapse, the policy may sometimes be reinstated upon payment of the overdue premiums and reexamination to determine whether the insured is still insurable.
See INSURANCE.

LA SALLE STREET The street in Chicago where most of the financial institutions are located; hence, by extension, a popular name for the Chicago financial district, as Wall Street is for New York, State Street is for Boston, and Lombard Street is for London.

LATIN MONETARY UNION   See LATIN UNION.

LATIN UNION A group formed in December, 1865—consisting of France, Belgium, Italy, and Switzerland—which adopted a common decimal coinage system based upon the French franc equivalent to $0.193 in United States money as the unit of value. Greece joined the union in 1868. These five nations agreed to accept without distinction, and to use as interchangeable, gold pieces not reduced in weight by natural abrasion more than 0.5%. Five-franc silver pieces conforming to certain conditions were also acceptable without distinction and were interchangeable. While the unit of value was the same in each country, it was known by different names; franc in France, Belgium, and Switzerland, lira in Italy, and drachma in Greece. Other countries which adopted the system without joining the union were Spain (peseta), Finland (finmark or markka), and Venezuela (bolivar).

In effect the union ceased to operate after the outbreak of World War I, and as early as 1921 its members signed a convention regulating the terms of its dissolution. But it was only in December, 1926, that Switzerland addressed a note to her partners informing them that she would consider the union terminated both in name and in fact on December 31, and, none of the partners having raised opposition, the union terminated on that date.

The original treaty of 1865 made uniform the content, weight, and form of the gold and silver currencies of the four countries signing it. Each was entitled to mint gold pieces of 100, 50, 10 and 5 francs and silver pieces of 5 francs without limit, and each undertook to accept these coins indiscriminately, so that the treaty sanctioned bimetallism. The depreciation of silver caused much difficulty almost from the outset of the union, however, and in 1879 the principle of bimetallism was partly abandoned. The countries agreed to stop the minting of silver coins, though the coins already existing continued to rank as legal currency with gold. This system, which has been called lame bimetallism, prevailed up to the outbreak of World War I.

The war witnessed the practical disappearance of all gold coins in the countries of the Latin Union, and even the silver ones vanished except in Switzerland. With the depreciation of the French, Italian Belgian, and Greek currencies after the war, Switzerland found silver pouring into its territory from all sides, the tendency accentuated by the fall in the price of silver. Switzerland had finally to prohibit the import of crowns emanating from the mints of the other partners to the union, but the crowns continud to come in secretly, and in 1920 all but Swiss crowns were declared illegal currency.

After the retirement of the forbidden crowns, for which a period of three months was allowed, Switzerland found itself possessed of 225 million francs in French, Italian, Belgian, and Greek silver pieces in addition to the silver already in the national bank. The countries concerned got together in 1921 and formed a convention for the solution of the problem, which involved the ultimate termination of the Latin Union. It was arranged with France that the 130 million French silver francs in the possession of Switzerland should be held until January 15, 1927, after which they would be returned in installments over a period of five years against 20 million francs gold plus the balance in Swiss francs, gold, or drafts on Switzerland. A similar arrangement was made with Italy and Belgium, except that Switzerland was given the right to melt down and transform into Swiss silver coins about half the Italian total of 65 million francs and three-fourths of the Belgian total of 29 million. As for the Greek silver pieces, the amount was so small that it was arranged that the whole should be transformed into Swiss coins.

LAW, JOHN   See MISSISSIPPI BUBBLE.

LAWFUL MONEY As defined by the attorney general of the United States, "every form of money which is endowed by law with legal tender quality." Since the AAA Farm Relief and Inflation Act of May 12, 1933, as amended by the Joint Resolution of Congress June 5, 1933, made legal tender all coins and currencies of the United States (including Federal Reserve notes, circulating Federal Reserve bank notes, and national bank notes), it follows that all forms of currency and coin are lawful money, as they are now endowed with legal tender quality.

Legal tender can also be defined as the kind of coin or money that the law compels a creditor to accept in payment of his or her debt, when tendered in the right amount. It is generally recognized that parties may contractually agree to payment in a form other than legal tender. For example, parties may stipulate that payment is to be in foreign coins, or currency, or through an exchange of goods or services, and such contracts are fully enforceable (60 Am. Jur.2d Payments P 25 (1972)).

Prior to 1982, the United States Code contained a provision stating that the "amount of account" of the United States shall be expressed in dollars, dimes, cents, and mills (31 U.S.C. P 371 (2976)). This section was amended and recodified as 31 U.S.C. P 5101 by Public Law 97-258 (1982), so that it no longer contains the expression "money of account," but simply provides:

United States money is expressed in dollars, dimes or tenths, cents or hundredths, and mills or thousandths. A dime is a tenth of a dollar, a cent is a hundredth of a dollar, and a mill is a thousandth of a dollar.

The omission of the phrase "money of account," as well as the historical background and meaning of that phrase, is discussed in the House report associated with the amendment, H.R. Rep. No. 97-651:

The word "money" is substituted for "money of account" to eliminate unnecessary words. As far as can be determined, the phrase "money of account" has not been interpreted by any court or government agency. The phrase was used by Alexander Hamilton in his "Report on the Establishment of the Mint" (1791). In that report, Hamilton posed six questions, including: "What ought to be the nature of the money unit of the United States?" Thereafter, Hamilton uses the phrase "money unit of the United States" and "money of account" interchangeably to denote the monetary system for keeping financial accounts. In short, the phrases simply indicate that financial accounts are to be based on a decimal money system:

...and it is certain that nothing can be more simple and convenient than the decimal subdivisions. There is every reason to expect that the method will speedily grow into general use, when it shall be seconded by corresponding coins. On this plan the unit in the money of account will continue to be, as established by that resolution (of August 8, 1786), a dollar, and its multiples, dimes, cents, and mills, or tenths, hundredths, and thousands.

Thus, the phrase "money of account" did not mean, by itself, that dollars or fractions of dollars must be equal to something having intrinsic or "substantive" value. This concept is supported by earlier writings of Thomas Jefferson in his "Notes on the Establishment of a Money Unit, and of a Coinage for the United States" (1784), and the 1782 Report to the President of the Continental Congress on the coinage of the United States by the Superintendent of Finances, Robert Morris, which was apparently prepared by the Assistant Superintendent, Governeur Morris.

The term lawful money, however, has also had a special connotation for bank legal reserve purposes. Vault cash eligible for legal reserve purposes of member banks prior to the 1917 amendment of the Federal Reserve Act was required to be gold or other lawful money (gold certificates, silver certificates, Treasury notes of 1890, United States notes, and silver coin). Other types of money could not serve as part of the vault cash for legal reserve at that time. The 1917 amendment of the Federal Reserve Act discontinued allowance for vault cash as part of legal reserves of member banks, and henceforth only balances in reserve accounts at the Federal Reserve banks could serve as such. Reserve accounts at the Federal Reserve banks may consist of any realized credits resulting from transactions in Federal Reserve credit, collections, currency, dealings with the Treasury, and gold transactions, etc. P.L. 86-114, July 28, 1959, again authorized the use of vault cash as part of member bank legal reserves; the Board of Governors of the Federal Reserve System, under such regulations as it may prescribe, may permit member banks to count all or part of their currency and coin as part of their legal reserves, there being no distinctions made as to types of currency and coin, either in the law or in regulation (Regulation D) of the board of governors.

Similarly, forms of currency still nominally stated to be redeemable in lawful money (United States notes, Federal Reserve notes, Federal Reserve bank notes, and national bank notes, the latter two being in process of retirement) may be redeemed in any other form of money, per the attorney general's opinion referred to above and the Joint Resolution of June 5, 1933.

Accounting information is expressed primarily in monetary terms. The monetary unit is the basic means of measuring assets, liabilities, and capital. It is the common denominator in business transactions. It is relevant, simple, universally available, useful, and understandable. Accountants have traditionally assumed that the dollar is the monetary unit of measuring in the United States. The stable unit concept offers an orderly basis for producing account balances and financial statements. The value of the monetary unit can change over time during periods of inflation or deflation. The stable monetary unit assumption is the accountant's basis for ignoring the effect of inflation and deflation and making no adjustments for the changing value of the dollar. FASB Statement No. 5 (1984) indicated that it expects the dollar unadjusted for inflation or deflation to continue to be used to measure items recognized in financial statements.

See LEGAL TENDER.

LAW OF DEMAND The quantity of a product consumers are willing to purchase. Economists maintain that there is a predictable negative relationship between price and quantity demanded, and they call this relationship the law of demand.

The law of demand states that the quantity of a product that individuals demand increases when the price of the product decreases, assuming all other factors that could influence purchasing decisions remain constant. Conversely, the law of demand predicts that the quantity demanded of a product decreases when the price increases, assuming all other factors that could influence purchasing decisions remain constant. The law of demand is graphically represented by a downward sloping relationship, a demand curve, between price and quantity demanded (as appended). This inverse relationship between price and quantity demanded can be derived mathematically and graphically from certain fundamental axioms in economics; however, there is also an intuitive explanation. At higher prices, less quantity is demanded because the sacrificed opportunities from having to pay the higher price are greater than they would be at lower prices. These sacrificed opportunities generally involve the ability to purchase a substitute product.

Typical Demand Curve

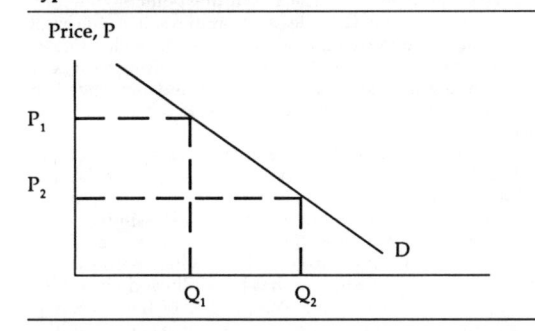

LAW OF DIMINISHING RETURNS The law of diminishing returns states that as increasing units of a variable factor (labor) are added to a fixed factor (capital), the output produced by the additional units of the variable factor will increase but eventually at a decreasing rate. Stated alternatively, when diminishing returns set in, output will begin to increase at a decreasing rate as more units of the variable factor are used. If diminishing returns were not a characteristic of production, then the world's supply of wheat (the output) could be grown in a flower pot (the fixed factor) by simply adding more and more seed (the variable factor).

In economics, the short run is defined as a period of time when at least one factor of production is fixed, generally capital. Labor, then, is the variable factor.

LAW OF SUPPLY There is no law of supply in economics. From the consumer side, there is the law of demand that leads to a graphical illustration of a downward sloping demand curve. However, the accompanying upward sloping supply curve comes from the theory of cost. From this theory, it follows that the marginal cost of production will increase (as a result of diminishing returns) and that firms make their short-run output decisions based on marginal cost. From this, it follows that supply curves are upward sloping.

LEAD FUTURES Futures trading on the COMMODITY EXCHANGE, INC. in lead was discontinued December 9, 1970, because of inactivity. For 1970, a total of only 35 contracts were traded, compared with 146 contracts in 1969.

LEADING INDICATORS A set of 12 ECONOMIC INDICATORS used to predict turns in the business cycle issued by the Bureau of Economic Analysis.

LEARNING CURVE A learning curve describes the relationship between direct labor hours per unit and cumulative units produced. When accumulated volume doubles, the labor hours per unit decrease by a constant percentage. An 80% learning curve indicates that when cumulative volume doubles, labor hours per unit are reduced by 20% to 80% of the previous level. As workers become familiar with a specific task, their productivity increases. This learning process is particularly noticeable in new products or processes. The learning curve was first used in World War II in the aircraft industry. The learning curve can be described algebraically as follows:

$$y(x) = ax - b$$

where $y(x)$ = direct labor hours required to produce x unit
 x = cumulative number of units produced
 a = number of hours required to produce first unit
 b = function the rate at which y(x) decreases as cumulative production increases.

Activities especially subject to learning curve analysis include:

1. Activities that have not been performed or not performed in their present operational form.
2. Activities being performed by new employees and others not familiar with the operations.
3. Activities that involve the use of a stated raw material for the first time or that involve a change in the way the material is used.
4. Production runs of short duration, especially if these runs are repeated.

To illustrate an application of the learning curve, assume that a ship builder estimates that it takes 4,000 labor hours to produce a yacht. The company expected to build eight yachts for various customers. The company estimates that its learning curve is 80% after the first yacht is built. The effect of the learning curve on labor hours is computed as follows:

Cumulative quantity	Cumulative Average hours per yacht	Cumulative hours
A	B	C
1	4,000	4,000
2	3,200 (4,000 x .80)	6,400
4	2,560 (3,200 x .80)	10,240
8	2,048 (2,560 x .80)	16,384

LEASE

Column A = Double the cumulative quantity.
Column B = Multiply the cumulative averages by the learning curve percentage.
Column C = Multiply the cumulative average by the cumulative quantity.

A learning curve chart is illustrated below.

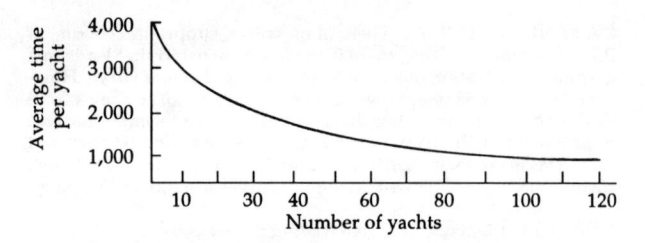

[Graph: Average time per yacht (y-axis: 1,000 to 4,000) vs Number of yachts (x-axis: 10 to 120), showing a decreasing curve]

A firm that accumulates experience the fastest can benefit competitively over a long-run period. A knowledge of how the experience curve operates can help companies develop strategies for new products and processes, pricing, expansion, and other plans.

LEASE A contract granting or letting the possession of lands, buildings, tenements, offices, machinery, or other chattels for a specified fixed or indeterminate period, for a stated consideration, usually a periodic payment known as rent or, in the case of land, ground rent. Since merely possession and use of the premises or property is conveyed by the landlord to the tenant in a lease, the property reverts to the landlord at the end of the term. Leases or assignments of leases whose terms run for more than one year from commencement of the terms must be in writing, under state versions of the statute of frauds, and subscribed by the parties charged or their agents, the latter authorized in writing. Leases that have no definite terms of duration create the tenancy at will, which may be terminated by either the lessor or the lessee at any time, in some states by giving reasonable notice of termination. The tenant under a lease (lessee) has a leasehold; the landlord (lessor), a reversion.

The lease is a flexible device for business use. Instead of tying up capital in acquisition of title to the real or personal property, the possession and use of the property may be had for the stated term in consideration of the rent or rental, which is a tax-deductible expense of doing business. The lease may also be resorted to as a combinational device. Various trunk-line railroads assembled various portions of their lines by means of long-term leases, for example, the Boston & Albany Railroad is leased to the New York Central Railroad for 99 years, to 1999. The lease also is the basis for the Philadelphia plan for railroad equipment trust financing, under which title to the railroad equipment is in the trustee, in trust for the beneficiaries (certificate-holding investors) and under which the railroad pays specified periodic rental payments to the trustee. Sale and lease-back arrangements are also a strategic use of the lease, whereby the owner and user of improved real property, for example, may sell the legal title to an investor, such as a life insurance company, and the life insurance company leases back the same property to the erstwhile owner, who now becomes a tenant for a long term of years. Motivations for the erstwhile owner include having the cash or other proceeds of the sale while continuing possession and use under fair rental, tax advantages of rental as compared with depreciation in ownership, and options to renew the lease for further long terms.

Lease classifications for financial accounting and reporting purposes can be summarized as to type and accounting method by lessee and lessor:

Type	Lessee	Lessor
Noncapitalized (no sale or purchase or sale of asset assumed)	Operating lease	Operating lease
Capitalized (sale and purchase of asset assumed)	Capital lease	Sales-type lease Direct-financing lease Leveraged lease

The lessee classifies a lease as a capital lease if it meets any one of the following criteria:

1. The lease transfers ownership of the property to the lessee by the end of the lease term.
2. The lease contains an option to purchase the leased property at a bargain price.
3. The lease term is equal to or greater than 75 percent of the estimated economic life of the leased property.
4. The present value of rental and other minimum lease payments equals or exceeds 90 percent of the fair value of the leased property less any investment tax credit retained by the lessor.

If none of these criteria is met, the lease is an operating lease.

For the lessor, a lease must meet one of the four criteria specified for the lessee and both of the following criteria:

1. Collectability of the minimum lease payments is reasonably predictable.
2. No important uncertainties surround the amount of nonreimbursable costs yet to be incurred by the lessor under the lease.

If these criteria are not met, the lease is an operating lease.

An operating lease merely requires the recognition of the rental agreement requiring periodic payments for the use of an asset during that period. Rent expense or rent income is recognized on the income statement of the lessee and lessor, respectively. No new assets or liabilities are recorded.

A capital lease is, in substance, the purchase of an asset and the incurrence of a liability. A capital lease transfers substantially all of the ownership privileges, including the benefits and risks of property ownership, and represents in economic substance but not in legal form a purchase or sale of an asset. Such leases should be accounted for by the lessee as the acquisition of an asset and the incurrence of a liability.

A leveraged lease is a three-party lease involving a lessee, a lessor, and a long-term creditor, usually a bank or other financial institution. The long-term creditor provides nonrecourse financing to the lessor. The financing provides the lessor with substantial leverage in the transaction. For example, a contractor might agree to build an office building and lease it to a company. To finance the construction of the building, a bank lends money to the contractor (lessor). The contractor uses a relatively small amount of his own funds. The lessor-owner's return on the investment comes from lease rentals, investment tax credit, and income tax benefit from depreciation on the total cost of the property and interest expense deductions on the debt, and other expenses. The lessor classifies the leveraged lease as a direct financing lease.

A sale-leaseback occurs when an owner sells property and then leases the same property back. The seller-lessee usually has a tax advantage in that the entire lease payment can be deducted, which can include interest and amortization of the cost of land and partially depreciated other real property. The sale-leaseback is often used when financing is a problem. From an accounting point of view, any profit or loss incurred by the seller-lessee from the sale of the asset under a capital lease is deferred and amortized over the lease term or the economic life of the asset. If the lease is an operating lease, any profit or loss on the sale should be deferred and amortized in proportion to the rental payments over the period the asset is used by the lessee.

The ECONOMIC RECOVERY ACT OF 1981 liberalized leasing rules, especially by providing for the ACCELERATED COST RECOVERY SYSTEM (ACRS) and the transferability of tax benefits.

Depository financial institutions offer commercial leasing services, either directly or through a subsidiary of the holding company. Leasing is considered an alternative to borrowing, permitting a 100% financing by the borrower, and has been allowed since 1963 under a ruling by the Office of the Comptroller of the Currency. Regulatory authorities have placed restrictions on leasing activities by financial institutions. The Federal Reserve sets a minimum on the amount of a lease; leases must be fully amortized requiring that the total proceeds from the lease are to be repaid with the prescribed terms of the lease.

Leasing can be a very profitable activity for depository institutions, often generating a 12% to 28% return. Leasing provides opportunities for creating a portfolio suited to its specific requirements such as payback periods and fixed or fluctuating rentals. Equipment leasing can be profitable and can also provide a method for attracting customers, obtaining a competitive edge, and improving the bank's public image.

LEASE-BACKED Securities in which leases on plant and equipment serve as collateral.

LEASEHOLD Generally speaking, leasehold bonds are not well regarded among real estate bonds because of the fixed duration of the term of the lease, unless supplemented by options to renew on the part of the lessee, and because of the vulnerability of the leasehold which is the security to default on the part of the lessee under the varied provisions of the lease. Leasehold bonds are in effect junior to rental payments under the lease.

A contractual arrangement between a lessor and a lessee that grants the lessee the right to use specific property, owned or controlled by the lessor, for a specific period of time in return for stipulated, periodic cash payments; also known as an estate for years. The payments are generally considered lease expense on the books of the lessee. In cases where the lease agreement transfers substantially all of the benefits and risks incident to ownership of the property so that the economic effect is similar to that of an installment purchase, the lease is capitalized and classified as a tangible rather than an intangible asset. Such a lease is referred to as a capital lease. Leasehold improvements made to the leased property typically revert to the lessor at the end of the life of the lease.

See REAL ESTATE BONDS.

LEASING The Comptroller of the Currency (Interpretive Ruling 7.3400) has ruled that a national bank may do the following:

1. Become the legal or beneficial owner and lessor of specific personal property or otherwise acquire such property at the request of the lessee who wishes to lease it from the bank.
2. Become the owner and lessor of personal property by purchasing the property from another lessor in connection with its purchase of the related lease.
3. Incur obligations incidental to its position as the legal or beneficial owner and lessor of the leased property, if the lease is a net full-payout lease representing a noncancelable obligation of the lessee, notwithstanding the possible early termination of that lease.

For the purpose of this ruling the following types of leases are defined:

1. A net lease is a lease under which the bank will not, directly or indirectly, provide or be obligated to provide for any of the following:
   a. The servicing, repair, or maintenance of the lease property during the lease term.
   b. The purchasing of parts and accessories for the lease property. However, improvements and additions to the leased property may be leased to the lessee upon its request in accordance with the full-payout requirements of this ruling.
   c. The loan of replacement or substitute property while the leased property is being serviced.
   d. The purchasing of insurance for the lessee, except where the lessee has failed in its contractual obligation to purchase or maintain the required insurance.
   e. The renewal of any license or registration for the property unless such action by the bank is clearly necessary to protect its interest as an owner or financier of the property.
2. A full-payout lease is one from which the lessor can reasonably expect to realize a return of its full investment in the leased property plus the estimated cost of financing the property over the term of the lease from the following sources:
   a. Rentals.
   b. Estimated tax benefits.
   c. The estimated residual value of the property at the expiration of the initial term of the lease.

The Comptroller's ruling goes on to provide that the estimate by the lessor of the total cost of financing the property over the term of the lease should reflect, among other factors, the term of the lease;
the modes of financing available to the lessor; the credit rating of the lessor and/or the lessee, if a factor in the financing; and prevailing rates in the money and capital markets.

Where the calculation of the cost of financing according to this formula is not reasonably determinable, a lease may be considered to have met the test for recovering the cost of financing if the bank's yield from the lease is equivalent to what the yield would be on a similar loan.

Any unguaranteed portion of the estimated residual value relied upon by the bank to yield a full return under this subsection shall not exceed 25% of the original cost of the property to the lessor. The amount of any estimated residual value guaranteed by a manufacturer, the lessee, or a third party which is not an affiliate (as defined for the purpose of 12 U.S.C. 371c) of the bank may exceed 25% of the original cost of the property where the bank has determined, and can provide full supporting documentation, that the guarantor has the resources to meet the guarantee. In all cases, both the estimated residual value of the property and that portion of the estimated residual value relied upon by the lessor to satisfy the requirements of a full-payout lease must be reasonable in light of the nature of the leased property and all relevant circumstances, so that realization of the lessor's full investment plus the cost of financing the property primarily depends on the creditworthiness of the lessee and any guarantor of the residual value, and not on the residual market value of the leased item. Full-payout calculations on leases of personal property to domestic governmental entities may be based on reasonably anticipated future transactions or renewals.

If, in good faith, a national bank believes that there has been an unanticipated change in conditions which threatens its financial position by significantly increasing its exposure to loss, the limitations above shall not prevent the bank from taking these actions:

1. As the owner and lessor under a net full-payout lease, taking reasonable and appropriate action to salvage or protect the value of the property or its interests arising under the lease.
2. As the assignee of a lessor's interest in a lease, becoming the owner and lessor of the leased property pursuant to its contractual right, or taking any reasonable and appropriate action to salvage or protect the value of the property or its interests arising under the lease.

The limitations do not prohibit a national bank from including any provisions in a lease, or from making any additional agreements, to protect its financial position or investment in the circumstances in paragraphs (1) and (2) immediately above.

The ruling provides that nothing in the section shall be construed to be in conflict with the duties, liabilities, and standards imposed by the Consumer Leasing Act of 1976 (15 U.S.C. 1667 et seq.).

Leases permissible under the Comptroller's ruling are subject to the limitations on obligations under 12 U.S.C. 84 (lending limits) and on extensions of credit under 12 U.S.C. 371c (loans to affiliates). The Comptroller reserves the right to determine that such leases are also subject to the limitations of any other law, regulation, or ruling which limits potential financial risks associated with other forms of bank financing.

This section shall not apply to any leases executed prior to June 12, 1979. With respect to the applicability of the immediately preceding provision, the Comptroller indicates that when making new extensions of credit, including leases, to a customer, national banks must consider all outstanding leases regardless of the date they were entered into. Any lease entered into in good faith prior to such date that does not satisfy the requirements of the ruling may be renewed without violation of this section only if there is a binding agreement in the expiring lease which requires the bank to renew it at the lessee's option and the bank cannot otherwise reasonably or properly avoid its commitment to do so, or the bank in good faith determines and demonstrates by full documentation that renewal of the lease is necessary to avoid significant financial loss and recover its total investment plus the cost of financing.

BIBLIOGRAPHY

CUDWORTH, E. F. *Equipment Leasing Partnerships*, 1989.
WINDERS, T. J., and WILLIAMS, W. *Profitable Equipment Leasing: A Practical Guide for Bankers*. Bank Administration Institute, Rolling Meadows, IL, 1987.

LEGACY A gift of money or other personal property made by the will of a TESTATOR. Legacies are of three kinds: specific, demonstrative, and general. A specific legacy is a gift of some specific article or particular part of the estate, which can be identified and distinguished from all others of the same nature, and is to be satisfied only by the delivery of such specific gift, e.g. a painting, ring, etc. A demonstrative legacy is a gift of a stated sum of money or of securities, payable out of a particular fund or security, e.g. a gift of $5,000 payable out of the proceeds of certain described bonds. It differs from a specific legacy because if the fund out of which the legacy is to be paid fails, recourse may be had to the general assets of the estate. A general legacy is a gift payable out of the general assets of the estate without reference to any particular fund or property. It does not call for the delivery of any particular piece of property. Money gifts are usually construed to be general legacies. That portion of the estate remaining after the specific, demonstrative, and general legacies have been paid is known as the residuary estate.

The recipient of a legacy is known as a legatee. A legacy may be void if the legatee dies before the testator, depending upon the wording of the will. In many cases the will leaves no doubt that the deceased legatee's gift is to pass on to the residuary.

Unless there is provision in the will to the contrary, if the assets of the estate are insufficient to pay all the debts, there must be an abatement of the legacies. The deficiency will fall first upon the residuary estate; when this is exhausted, the burden of the deficiency will rest pro rata on the general legacies. Specific legacies do not abate until the residuary estate and the amount equal to the sum of the general legacies has been exhausted. General legacies abate prior to demonstrative legacies, except when the fund out of which the demonstrative legacy is to be paid is insufficient, in which case the demonstrative legacy abates with the general legacies. However, in case the fund is sufficient for the payment of the demonstrative legacy, the latter abates with the specific legacies.

LEGAL BOND A bond that is legal for investment (1) by savings banks, (2) by insurance companies, (3) by trust funds, or (4) to secure government or other deposits. The term is relative, since bonds may be legal for one purpose but not for another—for investment by savings banks, but not for trust funds, or as collateral to secure state deposits, but not for federal government deposits. A bond, moreover, may be a legal investment for savings banks in one state but not in another.

See LEGALITY OF SECURITIES, SAVINGS BANK INVESTMENTS, TRUST FUND INVESTMENTS.

LEGAL HOLIDAY A day declared by law (statutes or proclamations) as being exempt from legal incidents, such as judicial proceedings, service of process, demand, payment, or protest of negotiable instruments, etc.; a public holiday.

Each state has jurisdiction as to the declaration of legal holidays to be observed within its borders. The President of the United States and Congress proclaim or legislate legal holidays for the District of Columbia and federal government offices throughout the country.

When a holiday happens to fall on a Sunday, it is usually observed the Monday following. The following legal holidays are observed by all the states: January 1 (New Year's Day); July 4 (Independence Day); Labor Day (first Monday in September); Thanksgiving Day (fourth Thursday in November); and December 25 (Christmas). Federal legal public holidays are as follows: New Year's Day; Washington's Birthday (now statutorily fixed as the third Monday in February); Memorial Day (Decoration Day, statutorily fixed as the last Monday in May); Independence Day; Labor Day; Columbus Day (now statutorily fixed as the second Monday in October); Veterans Day (now statutorily fixed as the fourth Monday in November); Thanksgiving Day; and Christmas Day.

See BANK HOLIDAYS.

LEGAL INVESTMENTS See LIFE INSURANCE COMPANY INVESTMENTS, SAVINGS BANK INVESTMENTS, TRUST FUND INVESTMENTS.

LEGALITY OF SECURITIES In civil issues, except U.S. government securities, legality depends upon the following conditions:

1. Authority for issue. State and municipal issues must be authorized by the Constitution or statutory law. Some issues require a legislative or popular vote.
2. Purpose of issue. Issues of public bodies must be for a public purpose.
3. Process of issue. State and municipal issues must be issued as the result of competitive bidding by interested investment banking groups. The bidding specifications may require a floor on price (e.g., not lower than par) and/or a maximum interest rate, the latter statutorily required. The invitations to bid must be sufficiently advertised.
4. Conformity to tax and debt restrictions. State and municipal issues must conform to any constitutional or statutory restrictions on the debt limit of the obligor (some financing may be outside of such debt limits). Tax limits may prevent the levying of all taxes necessary for the purpose of paying the principal and interest.

In corporate debt financing, various states require authority of the stockholders, given at special meetings of stockholders called for the purpose upon proper notice. Corporate debt may be issued for value only, and the statutes of a few states provide for limiting the amount of a corporation's indebtedness. Charter and bylaw provisions must be complied with, and existing mortgage indenture provisions must be checked for compliance with their protective provisions restricting creation of additional or prior indebtedness.

Railroad issues, with minor exceptions, must be approved by the Interstate Commerce Commission. Public utility issues of companies subject to jurisdiction of the Securities and Exchange Commission under the Public Utility Holding Company Act of 1935 must be approved by that agency. In addition, public utility issues must usually be approved by the public utility regulatory commission of the state in which the utility is located. Both the ICC and the SEC require competitive bidding for issues of railroads and utilities under their jurisdiction.

U.S. government, state, municipal, and railroad issues are exempt from the registration requirements of the Securities Act of 1933, but nonexempt new issues must conform with such requirements.

Legal Opinion. One of the risks that a bond buyer assumes concerns the legality or validity of the issue he contemplates purchasing. The legality of issuance is extremely important, because without it there may be no legal means by which investors' money may be recovered.

Municipal bonds: It is established and conventional procedure in competitive bidding for state and municipal issues to bid subject to a satisfactory or marketable legal opinion, i.e., one unqualifiedly citing the full legality of issuance by firms of attorneys specializing in municipal law who command the confidence of investors. A particular group of law firms in this field have come to be regarded as particularly well known and reliable. Thus their legal opinion as to legality and regularity of issuance of the securities is marketable.

Corporate securities: In the underwriting of corporate bonds, the legal phases of the issue are examined by the corporation's counsel or by outside attorneys. In addition, the originating investment banking firm's own counsel renders a final approving opinion, the fees thereof usually being borne by the issuer as one of the expense of the underwriting assumed. This final opinion is secured because the well-known law firm's opinion forms the basis for bank loans and trustee investments. Thus there is a distinction between the preliminary and final legal opinion, the latter being the acceptable basis for a bank loan when the corporate bonds are to be used as collateral for loans. Some well-known corporation law firms make a specialty of giving legal opinions upon bond issues. Thus the prospectus on the bond issue will often include the phrase, "We have the legal opinion of ———," or "Legality approved by ———." The legal opinion is related to the engineer's report, as both are necessary features in the successful marketing of bond issues. The first is a statement of legality of issuance, the second a statement of the technological condition of the corporation's property.

In competitive bidding for corporate securities, it has become customary for the issuer to appoint and defray the expense of independent counsel to represent the underwriters in the preparation of the documents necessary for the issue (registration statement, including the prospectus; indenture in the case of bond and debenture issues; any necessary amendment to the issuer corporation's charter, bidding form and specification; purchase agreement, etc.), in the furnishing of a legal opinion as to legality and regularity of issuance, and in the furnishing of any necessary legal advice and assistance to the investment banking group awarded the issue in the competitive bidding.

See LEGAL BOND.

LEGAL RATE OF INTEREST The maximum rate of interest which a lender may charge a borrower for the use of money, fixed by the laws of the various states. Interest charged in excess of the legal rate, called USURY, is penalized in varying degree by the laws of the various states.

The Truth-in-Lending Act (15 U.S.C. 1601), part of the Consumer Credit Protection Act, pertains primarily to the disclosure of credit costs. It is implemented by Regulation Z of the Federal Reserve Board. It does not regulate or limit the annual percentage rates for such consumer credit. Maximum interest rates on insured or guaranteed mortgage loans are specified by the FHA and the VA, which provide such insurance or guarantees. The 1979 Housing and Community Development Act Amendments exempted FHA loans from state usury ceilings.

Federal Override of State Usury Laws. Title V of the DEPOSITORY INSTITUTIONS DEREGULATION AND MONETARY CONTROL OF 1980 provided the following aspects of federal override of state usury laws.

Mortgage usury laws: The provision of a state constitution or law limiting the rate or amount of interest, discount points, finance charges, or other charges is preempted with respect to loans, mortgages, and credit sales or advances made after March 31, 1980, that are secured by a first lien on residential real property, by a first lien on stock in a residential cooperative housing corporation, or by a first lien on a residential manufactured home if the loan on the residential manufactured home is in compliance with consumer protection regulations of the FEDERAL HOME LOAN BANK BOARD. A state may take action reinstating usury limitations on mortgage loans if after April 1, 1980, and before April 1, 1983, it adopts a law or certifies that the voters of such state have voted in favor of any provision, constitutional or otherwise, that states explicitly and by its terms that such state does not want the federal usury override to apply to mortgage loans made in that state.

Business and agricultural loans: The referenced act also preempts state usury laws in the case of business or agricultural loans in the amount of $25,000 or more. A rate is established at not more than 5% in excess of the discount rate of the Federal Reserve banks including any surcharge thereon, in effect at the Federal Reserve bank in the Federal Reserve district where the person making the loan is located. This preemption would expire April 1, 1983, or at an earlier date if the state expressly reinstituted a state usury ceiling.

Other loans: In order to prevent discrimination against state-chartered institutions, state usury ceilings are preempted by the referenced act to permit insured state banks, branches of foreign banks, insured savings and loan associations, insured credit unions, and small business investment companies to charge interest on loans at a rate of 1% above the basic Federal Reserve discount rate. In addition, any state restrictions on the rate or amount of interest that may be paid on deposits or accounts at depository institutions were eliminated by the referenced act.

Penalties. Section 5198 of the Revised Statutes specifies the following as a penalty for usury by national banks:

1. The taking, receiving, reserving, or charging of a rate of interest greater than is allowed by Section 5197, when knowingly done, shall be deemed a forfeiture of the entire interest which the note, bill, or other evidence of debt carries with it, or which has been agreed to be paid thereon.
2. If the greater rate of interest has been paid, the person by whom it has been paid, or his legal representative, may recover back, in an action in the nature of an action of debt, twice the amount of the interest thus paid, from the national bank taking or receiving same, provided such action is commenced within two years from the date the usurious transaction occurred.

Such penalty (twice the interest) for usurious payment is relatively mild, as penalties range upwards to forfeiture of the principal, as well as a multiple of the interest, in some jurisdictions.

LEGAL RESERVES In deposit banking, the coverage by spec-ified types of assets (vault cash and balances at district Federal Reserve banks per the DEPOSITORY INSTITUTIONS DEREGULATION AND MONETARY CONTROL ACT OF 1980) of transaction account balances and nonpersonal time deposits averaged for defined time periods, expressed in percentages of the deposit bases (flat percentages or variable within range of specified minimum and maximum); legal reserve requirements. Legal reserves are required by statute and/or administrative regulation in American practice.

Although apparently liquidity reserves to cover deposit liabilities, actually such legal reserve requirements are conventionally fractional (less than 100%), so that true liquidity depends upon the marketability, shiftability, and self-liquidating nature of the earning assets over and above the legal reserves maintained. Actually, legal reserve requirements serve to limit the ability to expand earning assets because of the required setaside in uninvested funds. Moreover, SECONDARY RESERVES in banking practice serve operational liquidity needs.

To the extent their ratios are variable (set by the Federal Reserve board within statutory minimum and maximum), legal reserve requirements have become an instrument of MONETARY POLICY.

See BANK RESERVE, RESERVE.

LEGAL TENDER Money which by law may be tendered by a debtor to a creditor in payment of the debt, when tendered in the correct amount and at the proper time and place. The effect of the tender, if refused by the creditor, is to stop the running of interest of the debt, but not to extinguish the debt. Thereafter the debtor is to keep the tender available for payment.

All coins and currencies in the U.S. have been full legal tender since 1933. The last sentence of Paragraph (1) of Subsection (b) of Section 43 of the AAA Farm Relief and Inflation Act of May 12, 1933, which was part of the popularly known Thomas Amendment, read as follows: "Such notes [United States notes, or greenbacks, provided for] and all other coins and currencies heretofore or hereafter coined or issued by or under the authority of the United States shall be legal tender for all debts public and private."

This sentence was completely revised by Section 2 of the Joint Resolution of Congress of June 5, 1933, reading as follows: "All coins and currencies of the United States (including Federal Reserve notes and circulating notes of Federal Reserve banks and national banking associations) heretofore or hereafter coined or issued, shall be legal tender for all debts, public and private, public charges, taxes, duties, and dues, except that gold coins, when below the standard weight and limit of tolerance provided by law for the single piece, shall be legal tender only at valuation in proportion to their actual weight."

The act of Congress approved July 23, 1965 (P.L. 89-81), the Coinage Act of 1965, repealed the provisions of law formerly contained in Section 43(b)(1) of the act of May 12, 1933, as amended (31 U.S.C. 462) with respect to the legal tender status of coins and currencies of the United States, including Federal Reserve notes. But it added a new provision of law to the same effect, now found in 31 U.S.C. 392.

The Gold Reserve Act of 1934, enacted January 30, 1934, declared the coinage of gold at an end, and vested title to all of the monetary gold stock in the Treasury of the United States. All gold and gold coin were required to be turned in to the Treasury in accordance with this act. Hence no gold coin has been either coined or circulated domestically since the Executive Order of April 5, 1933, which required all persons to deliver gold in any form (bullion, coin, or certificates) to Federal Reserve banks and receive other lawful money therefor, and the Gold Reserve Act of 1934, which transferred such gold holdings of the Federal Reserve banks to the Treasury.

For historical purposes only, the appended table lists the varying degrees of legal tender power of various forms of United States money prior to the above legislation. Present legal tender power of all coins and currencies of the United States is not qualified as to limitations of amounts for any form of same. Thus even the lowly cent piece is legal tender in unlimited amount. Of course any debtor who goes out of his way to assemble the required amounts of minor coin and transport these for effective legal tender to a creditor on a large debt would incur the extra expense of such arrangements.

See GOLD REPEAL JOINT RESOLUTION, GOLD RESERVE ACT OF 1934, UNITED STATES MONEY.

LEGAL TENDER BONDS CURRENCY BONDS.

LEGAL TENDER NOTES See UNITED STATES NOTES.

LEGAL TENDERS See UNITED STATES NOTES

ENCYCLOPEDIA OF BANKING AND FINANCE

LEGATEE

Legal Tender Power (prior to 1933)

Kind of money	Legal tender qualities
Minor coin	Legal tender up to $0.25.
Subsidiary silver coin	For amounts not exceeding $10 in any one payment.
Standard silver dollars	Full legal tender except when otherwise stipulated in the contract.
Gold coin	Full legal tender.
United States notes	Legal tender except for duties on imports and interest on the public debt.
Gold certificates	Full legal tender.
Silver certificates	Not legal tender but receivable for all taxes, customs and public dues.
Treasury notes of 1890	Full legal tender except where otherwise expressly stipulated in the contract.
Federal Reserve notes	Not legal tender, but receivable for all taxes, customs and public dues.
Federal Reserve bank notes	Not legal tender, but receivable for all public dues except duties on imports. Could not be used by government to pay interest or to redeem currency.
National bank notes	Same as Federal Reserve bank notes.

Source: Office of Secretary of the Treasury, Coins and Currency of the United States.

LEGATEE   *See* LEGACY.

LENDING FLAT   *See* LENDING RATE.

LENDING RATE   This term is used in two connections:

1. The rate at which funds are loaned by lending institutions as distinguished from the rate of interest paid on time and savings deposits of banks. The lending rate is what the lending institution receives on its loans and thus is income (interest or discount), while the deposit interest rate is an item of cost of the funds.
2. The terms on which the lender of stock agrees to make the stock available to a borrower who has sold the stock short. When stock is sold for short account (*see* SHORT SALE), i.e., by a speculator who does not own it, such stock must be delivered to the buyer just as in the case of a long sale. In order to make such delivery, however, the short seller's broker must borrow the stock, either from a customer who owns it, from his own holdings, or from another broker or holder. The lender of the stock is willing to make the loan of the stock because in exchange therefor its current market value, in cash, is tendered, and thereafter daily "mark to the market" notices will keep the cash current with current market value of the loaned stock. The cash comes from the short seller's proceeds on his short sale initially. It is a way for the lender of stock to have the use of money for 100% of the market value of the stock, compared with the loan value (effective since January 3, 1974) of 50% of market value if he borrowed on it at a bank for the purpose of purchasing or carrying stocks on margin, or credit for loan value at the broker.

Stocks will lend flat, at a premium, and at a rate. Flat lending has prevailed in recent years, in which there is neither extra compensation (premium) above the market value of the stock paid to the lender, nor interest on the market value (at a rate) paid to the borrower. When stock loans at a premium, it is in demand for short-selling purposes. The premium is charged per day. On the other hand, when stocks lend "at a rate," money is very tight, as was the case in the late 1920's. The rate was usually figured somewhat below the prevailing call money rate.

See BORROWED STOCK, PRIME RATE.

LENDING STOCKS   *See* BORROWED STOCK, LENDING RATE, SHORT SALE.

LEND LEASE   The lend lease program was established March 11, 1941, pursuant to an act entitled "An Act to Promote the Defense of the United States," which authorized the President of the United States to aid allied nations by permitting any agency of the government to sell, transfer, exchange, lease, lend, etc., goods and supplies, both military and civilian, necessary for prosecution of the war. Departments and agencies which served as procurement agencies for the program were the War Department, Navy Department, Maritime Commission, Procurement Division of the Treasury Department, and the Department of Agriculture.

The program was carried on beyond the end of the war, and to July 31, 1946, An aggregate of $50,442 million was reported appropriated since inception of lend lease, including $2,017 million after V-J Day (September 2, 1945). The principal recipients of lend lease were the British Empire, with $31,267 million (compared with $6,320 million in reverse lend lease to the United States), and Russia, with $11,260 million (compared with $2 million in reverse lend lease). The total reverse lend lease to July 31, 1946, aggregated $7,387 million, consisting of credits for shipping, railroad transportation, and other services, foodstuffs, petroleum, and building of capital installations for the United States.

Lend lease was one of the principal capital items during the war in the INTERNATIONAL BALANCE OF PAYMENTS.

LESSEE   *See* LEASE.

LESSOR   *See* LEASE.

LETTER   A deposit slip accompanying a remittance (checks, matured drafts and notes, coupons, cash, etc.) for deposit forwarded by an out-of-town depositor by mail. Letters are of two sorts, cash and collection. Cash letters are those for which the depositor receives credit for the amount of the total footing upon receipt. This amount is subject to reduction for such amounts as may be subsequently unpaid when presented. Collection letters are those for which the depositor instructs the bank to postpone crediting his account until such items have been reported paid.

Cash letters can be distinguished from collection letters by the difference in their wording and by the fact that in the case of cash letters the list of items is footed, whereas in collection letters it is not. Cash letters are usually worded as follows: "We enclose for credit," or "We enclose for collection and credit." Collection letters are phrased, "We enclose for collection," "We enclose for collection and credit when paid," "Please report by number," "We enclose herewith for collection and credit items entered below. Please do not advise credit of items until actually paid." The majority of items forwarded for collection bear collection numbers by which they are always referred to when their payment is advised.

LETTER OF ADVICE   This term has two applications:

1. In banking practice, a letter of instructions written by one bank to a customer (bank, firm, or individual) concerning some transaction mutually affecting them, e.g., a letter requesting a correspondent bank to honor the checks of the former's customer, enclosing therein the customer's specimen signature, or a letter to a foreign correspondent notifying it that a bill, fully described, has been drawn against it.
2. A special class of remittance whereby funds deposited by a first party are transferred (credited) to a second party for the use of a third. To illustrate the situation out of which a letter of advice might arise, suppose A. B. Company, brokers in New York City, have a branch office in Boston which keeps an account with the Q Bank of Boston, the latter being a correspondent of the R Bank of New York. The A. B. Company, however, does not have an account with the R Bank of New York. The most rapid, convenient, and economical way for the A. B. Company of New York to remit funds to its branch office in Boston is to deposit in cash, or by certified check, with the R Bank in New York for amount it wishes to make available to its branch office in Boston.

Two copies of letters of advice are made. The first, entitled "Letter of Advice" is addressed to the Q Bank in Boston with which the A. B. Company, Boston Branch, has an account. This states, "We credit your account for $——— which has been received from A. B. Company, New York, for the use of A. B. Company, Boston Branch." The second copy is a receipt containing the same information as the original, and is delivered to the A. B. Company of New York, the remitter. The funds may be made available the same day by a telegraphic advice, the letter of advice being forwarded by mail as a confirmation.

LETTER OF ALLOTMENT See ALLOTMENT NOTICE.

LETTER OF CREDIT Instrument by which a bank substitutes its own credit for that of an individual, firm, or corporation, to the end that domestic and foreign trade may be more safely economically, and expeditiously conducted. In the case *American Steel Company v. Irving National Bank* (266 Fed. 41), the court defined a letter of credit as follows:

> "A letter requesting one person to make advances to a third person on the credit of the writer is a letter of credit. These letters are general or special. They are general if directed to the writer's correspondents generally. They are special if addressed to some particular person."

From a functional standpoint, banks recognize two classes of letters of credit—commercial and traveler's—and the above definition includes both classes. Since a TRAVELER'S LETTER OF CREDIT is treated under that subject, only additional definitions of commercial letters of credit are given below.

A commercial letter of credit has been defined as follows:

> "An instrument by which a banker, for account of a buyer, gives formal evidence to a seller of its willingness to permit him to draw on certain terms and stipulates in legal form that all such bills will be honored, is what has come to be known as a commercial letter of credit" (Board of Governors of the Federal Reserve System, *Federal Reserve Bulletin*).

Sample Letter of Credit
_____

Letter of Credit No. _____
$ _____   New York _____ 19 _____

To the A.B.C. Company,
   Paris, France

Please note that under instructions from our principals _____

we hereby open a revocable (irrevocable) credit in favor of _____

to the extent of $ _____   available in _____

draft(s) on _____
when accompanied by BILLS OF LADING for merchandise _____
INVOICE TO READ: _____

and (other documents, if any) _____

We hereby agree with bona fide holders that all drafts issued by virtue of this credit and in accordance with the above stipulated terms shall meet with due honor upon presentation at the office of this bank if drawn and negotiated before _____ 19 _____

It is a condition of the credit that all shipments made herewith must fully meet all requirements, present and future, of our government.

If the terms of the credit are unsatisfactory to you in any detail, please communicate with your customers and have amended instructions sent to us.

This credit will remain in force until _____

unless previously revoked.

When drawing drafts against this credit, or referring to it, please quote our number as above, and return this letter with the documents.

Terms of this credit shall be interpreted in accordance with the regulations shown on the reverse side. [Generally, these are general rules adopted by the Seventh Congress of the International Chamber of Commerce, entitled "Uniform Customs and Practice for Commercial Documentary Credits."]

Yours respectfully,
Manager Foreign Department,
_____ Bank.

The following is a somewhat more complete definition: an instrument drawn by a bank, known as the credit-issuing bank (and eventually the drawee bank), in behalf of one of its customers (or in behalf of a customer of one of its domestic correspondents), known as the principal (who guarantees payment to the credit-issuing bank), authorizing another bank at home or abroad, known as the credit-notifying or negotiating bank (and usually the payer bank), to make payments or accept drafts drawn by a fourth party, known as the beneficiary, when such beneficiary has complied with the stipulations contained in the letter.

Interpretive Ruling 7.7016 of the Comptroller of the Currency provides that a national bank may issue letters of credit permissible under the Uniform Commercial Code or the Uniform Customs and Practice for Documentary Credits to or on behalf of its customers. As a matter of sound banking practice, the Comptroller of the Currency in the referenced ruling further states that letters of credit should be issued in conformity with the following:

1. Each letter of credit should conspicuously state that it is a letter of credit or be conspicuously entitled as such.
2. The bank's undertaking should contain a specified expiration date or be for a definite term.
3. The bank's undertaking should be limited in amount.
4. The bank's obligation to pay should arise only upon the presentation of a draft or other documents as specified in the letter of credit, and the bank must not be called upon to determine questions of fact or law at issue between the account party and the beneficiary.
5. The bank's customer should have an unqualified obligation to reimburse the bank for payments made under the letter of credit.

A common form of commercial letter of credit is appended.

Analyzed into its component elements it will be seen that a commercial letter of credit consists of the following parts: (1) heading, (2) address to the beneficiary, (3) promise to honor drafts, (4) tenor of drafts, (5) amount, (6) description of required documents, (7) nature of shipment, (8) expiration date, (9) privilege of cancellation, and (10) supplementary details, such as issue date, number, disposition of letter, and interpretation.

Commercial letters of credit are classified as follows:

1. Direction of shipment.
   a. Export.
   b. Import.
   c. Domestic.
2. Security.
   a. Documentary.
   b. Clean.
3. Tenor of drafts drawn thereunder.
   a. Sight.
   b. Time.
4. Form of letter.
   a. Straight.
   b. Revolving.
5. Form of currency.
   a. Dollar.
   b. Sterling.
   c. Continental currency.
   d. Asiatic currency.
6. Privilege of cancellation.
   a. Irrevocable-confirmed.
   b. Irrevocable-unconfirmed.
   c. Revocable-Unconfirmed.
7. Payment of principal.
   a. Paid.
   b. Guaranteed.

None of the above classifications is mutually exclusive. A letter of credit may, for instance, arise out of an import transaction and be straight, documentary, 60 days' sight, guaranteed, revocable-unconfirmed, and payable in dollars.

An export letter of credit is one arranged to finance the export of merchandise, while an import letter of credit finances the import of merchandise.

A documentary letter of credit is supported by a bill of lading and relative papers, while a clean credit is not.

LETTER OF CREDIT

A sight letter of credit is one in which the draft drawn thereagainst is payable on presentation, while a time or acceptance credit is one in which the draft is payable only when the stipulated number of days after date of acceptance has elapsed.

A straight letter of credit is one issued to finance the shipment of specified merchandise and thereupon becomes void, while a revolving letter of credit automatically renews itself for the original stipulated amount each time a draft is drawn thereagainst and does not exhaust itself until the expiry date.

A dollar letter of credit is one in which the amount is specified in dollars and in which the draft drawn thereagainst must be drawn in dollars, while a sterling letter of credit is one in which the draft drawn thereagainst is in sterling currency.

A revocable letter of credit is one in which the credit-issuing bank reserves the right to rescind its obligation to honor drafts drawn by the beneficiary by the phrase "good till canceled" or other similar expression. An irrevocable letter of credit is one in which the credit-issuing bank waives the right to revoke the credit prior to the expiry date, unless the consent of the beneficiary is obtained. The irrevocable letter of credit may be strengthened by having the notifying bank in the exporter's country add its own unqualified assurance that the credit-issuing bank's obligation will be performed, and that if the latter refused to honor the draft drawn against the credit the notifying bank will pay or accept in any event. Such a letter of credit is known as irrevocable-confirmed. But if the notifying bank merely transmits the issuing bank's obligation to the beneficiary without confirming the latter's undertaking, thereby not making the issuing bank's commitment its own, then the letter of credit is called irrevocable-unconfirmed.

A paid letter of credit is one in which funds are deposited by the principal (buyer) with the credit-issuing bank at the time of issue, but this is of rare occurrence. A guaranteed letter of credit, which is the usual type, is one in which the principal guarantees payment of the amount of the draft to the credit-issuing bank at its maturity. See GUARANTY.

In issuing letters of credit a bank is not called upon to part with cash, unless it discounts its own acceptances drawn under the terms thereof. The liability created in the issue of letters of credit is not restricted, but the national banking laws and the Federal Reserve Act place definite limitations upon the amount which a member bank may accept under such credits. See ACCEPTANCE CREDIT.

Summary. From a review of decisions on commercial letters of credit the following principles may be deduced:

1. A letter of credit is not a negotiable instrument.
2. It does not create a trust fund in favor of the beneficiary.
3. An issuer of a letter of credit may not dishonor drafts presented by a negotiating bank under a clean irrevocable letter of credit if all the terms of the credit are fulfilled.
4. An issuer may dishonor bills drawn in violation of the conditions specified in a documentary letter of credit.
5. The negotiator is not liable for the genuineness of either goods or documents.
6. The issuer is responsible to the party requesting the credit for the observance of the conditions by the beneficiary.
7. The contract between the issuer and the beneficiary is entirely independent of the contract of sale between the buyer and seller, and the issuer cannot, because of the seller's breach of contract of sale, refuse to honor drafts which comply with the terms of the letter of credit.

Standby Letters of Credit. As defined in Interpretive Ruling 7.1160 of the Comptroller of the Currency, the term "standby letter of credit" does not include commercial letters of credit and similar instruments where the issuing bank expects the beneficiary to draw upon the issuer, which do not guarantee payment of a money obligation and which do not provide for payment in the event of default by the account party.

Accordingly, the referenced ruling defines a standby letter of credit as any letter of credit, or similar arrangement however named or described, which represents an obligation to the beneficiary on the part of the issuer: (1) to repay money borrowed by or advanced to or for the account of the account party, (2) to make payment on account of any indebtedness undertaken by the account party, or (3) to make payment on account of any default by the account party in the performance of an obligation.

A standby letter of credit is subject to the limitations of 12 U.S.C. 84 and must be combined with any other nonexcepted loans to the account party by the issuing bank for the purposes of applying the referenced Section 84. Where the standby letter of credit is subject to a nonrecourse participation agreement with another bank or banks, this provision shall apply to the issuer and each participant in the same manner as in the case of a participated loan.

Exceptions to the application of lending limits to standby letters of credit, as specified by the Interpretive Ruling 7.1160(c), are as follows:

1. Where prior to or at the time of issuance, the issuing bank is paid an amount equal to the bank's maximum liability under the standby letter of credit.
2. Where prior to or at the time of issuance, the issuing bank has set aside sufficient funds in a segregated deposit account, clearly earmarked for that purpose, to cover the bank's maximum liability under the standby letter of credit.
3. Where the Comptroller of the Currency has found that a particular standby letter of credit or class of standby letters of credit will not expose the issuer to the similar risk of loss as would a loan to the account party.

Standby letters of credit and ineligible acceptances, as defind in the Comptroller's Interpretive Ruling 7.1160, constitute extensions

Letters of Credit

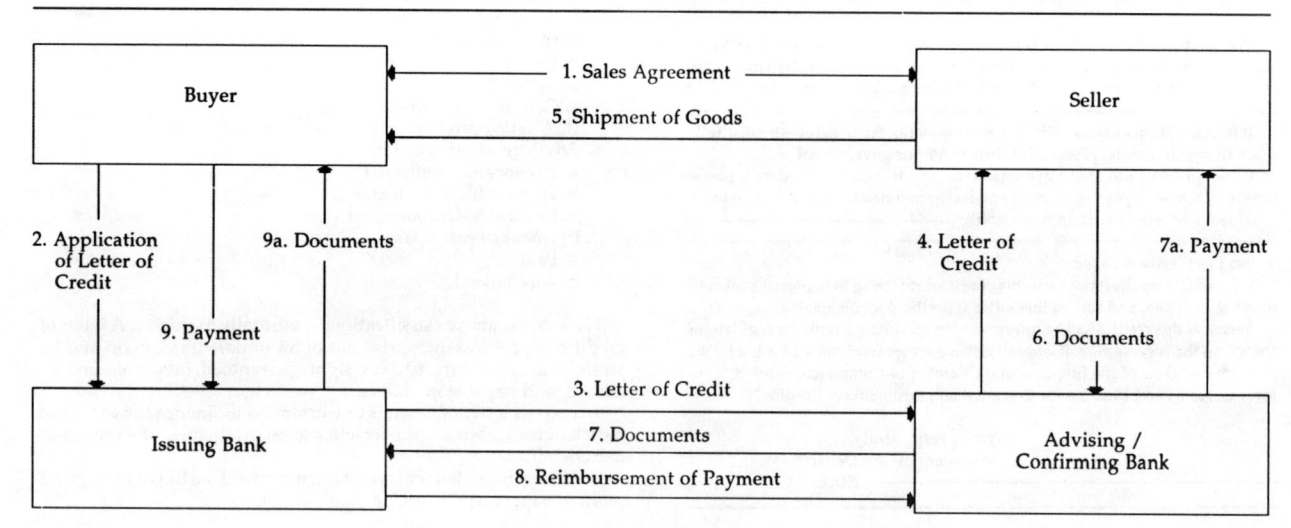

- Buyer ↔ Seller: 1. Sales Agreement; 5. Shipment of Goods
- Buyer → Issuing Bank: 2. Application of Letter of Credit
- Issuing Bank → Buyer: 9a. Documents; 9. Payment
- Issuing Bank → Advising/Confirming Bank: 3. Letter of Credit
- Advising/Confirming Bank → Issuing Bank: 7. Documents
- Issuing Bank → Advising/Confirming Bank: 8. Reimbursement of Payment
- Advising/Confirming Bank → Seller: 4. Letter of Credit; 7a. Payment
- Seller → Advising/Confirming Bank: 6. Documents

of credit within the meaning of 12. U.S.C. 371c (which refers to loans to affiliates) when they are issued on behalf of an affiliate.

The amount of outstanding standby letters of credit shall be stated in the bank's financial statement (12 CFR 11.7(c)(9)viii).

For legal aspects of letters of credit see Article 5, Uniform Commercial Code. The process for commercial and standby letters of credit is illustrated in the appended chart.

BIBLIOGRAPHY

"Catching Scams." *Global Trade*, March, 1989.
Powe, C. R. "E–470 Highway Moves Ahead with Foreign Letter of Credit," *ENR*, March 2, 1989.
Swieca, R. W. "Security Devices." *Business Credit*, November, 1988.

LETTER OF HYPOTHECATION See HYPOTHECATION CERTIFICATE.

LETTER OF IDENTIFICATION A letter given by the selling bank to a purchaser of a traveler's letter of credit, introducing him to the banks abroad which have agreed with the selling bank to honor all drafts drawn against the letter of credit.

See TRAVELER'S LETTER OF CREDIT.

LETTERS OF ADMINISTRATION An instrument in writing granted by a probate (or surrogate) court to a person appointed as administrator to settle the estate of a decedent who has left no will. These letters constitute the administrator's legal authority to act. In case the deceased person was a testator, but the person named in the will as executor is dead, incapable of acting, or declines to act, letters of administration with the will annexed are granted.

See ADMINISTRATOR.

LETTERS TESTAMENTARY An instrument in writing granted by a probate or surrogate court, or other official authority having jurisdiction over the probate of wills, empowering the executor named in a will to dispose of the estate in accordance with its terms. Letters testamentary make it known that the will in question has been properly proved and that the estate is in order to be settled.

See EXECUTOR, WILL.

LEVEE BONDS Bonds issued by a municipality or levee district, usually the latter, the proceeds of which are used for the purpose of constructing or maintaining levees for the reclamation or protection of land from submergence by water. Levee bonds belong to the general class of bonds known as reclamation issues, e.g., drainage bonds, reclamation bonds, irrigation bonds, etc. Wherever they are the direct obligation of a city or town, they rank in investment value with the other issues of such municipality. When issued by a levee district, their investment status is similar to that of any other type of district bond. The investor should investigate the wealth of the issuing jurisdiction, the necessity for the construction, the property values added, and the technological feasibility of the levee. As a class, levee bonds have proved fairly satisfactory and yield a high rate of return. Most of these bonds have been issued by levee districts in the South, particularly in the Mississippi Valley.

See MUNINCIPAL BONDS.

LEVERAGE The effect of trading on the equity, i.e., use of senior capital in capitalizations, in the form of borrowed funds, bonds, or preferred stock, ranking ahead of the junior equity, the common stock. In addition to such capitalization leverage, there is operating leverage, provided by relatively fixed operating expenses relative to expanding or contracting sales or revenues. There is also leverage provided by invested assets (for investment companies and insurance companies) and earnings assets or deposits (for banks), relative to stockholders' equity or book value.

In periods of rising earnings, leverage works very advantageously for the junior equity; but conversely, it works very adversely in periods of declining earnings. Thus, highly leveraged situations are quite speculative. Capitalization leverage, for example, works as follows:

1. Capitalization: $200 million 4% bonds, 100,000 shares of $5 preferred, and 10,000 shares of common stock.

2. With earnings available of $2 million, less bond interest of $800,000 and $500,000 preferred dividends, the common stock's equity in earnings is $700,000.
3. Should earnings increase 50%, the increase in common stock's earnings would be 143%, as follows:
With earnings available of $3 million, less bond interest of $800,000 and $500,000 preferred dividends, the common stock's equity in earnings is $1.7 million.
4. But should earnings decline 25%, the decline in common stock earnings would be 71%, as follows:
With earnings available of $1.5 million, less bond interest of $800,000 and $500,000 preferred dividends, the common stock's equity in earnings is $200,000.
5. Should earnings decline 35%, there would be no common stock earnings, as follows:
With earnings available of $1.3 million less bond interest of $800,000 and $500,000 preferred dividends, the common stock's earnings are zero.

Leverage is used to explain a firm's ability to use fixed-cost assets or funds to magnify the returns to its owners.

Leverage exists whenever a company has fixed costs. There are three types of leverage in financial management: operating, financial, and total leverage. Financial leverage is a financing technique that uses borrowed funds or preferred stock (items involving fixed financial costs) to improve the return on an equity investment. As long as a higher rate of return can be earned on assets than is paid for the capital used to acquire the assets, the rate of return to owners can be increased. This is referred to as positive financial leverage. Financial leverage is used in many business transactions, especially where real estate and financing by bonds or preferred stock instead of common stock are involved. Financial leverage is concerned with the relationship between the firm's earnings before interest and taxes (EBIT) and the earnings available to common stockholders or other owners. Financial leverage is often referred to as "trading on the equity." Operating leverage is based on the relationship between a firm's sales revenue and its earnings before interest and taxes. Operating leverage arises when an enterprise has a relatively large amount of fixed costs in its total costs. Total leverage reflects the impact of operating and financial leverage on the total risk of the firm (the degree of uncertainty associated with the firm's ability to cover its fixed-payment obligations).

Financial leverage arises as a result of fixed financial charges related to the presence of bonds or preferred stock. Such charges do not vary with the firm's earnings before interest and taxes. The effect of financial leverage is that an increase in the firm's earnings before interest and taxes results in a greater than proportional increase in the firm's earnings per share. A decrease in the firm's earnings before interest and taxes results in a more than proportional decrease in the firm's earnings per share. The degree of financial leverage (DFL) is measured by the following formula:

$$DFL = \frac{\text{Percentage change in earnings per share}}{\text{Percentage change in earnings before interest and taxes}}$$

The degree of financial leverage indicates how large a change in earnings per share will result from a given percentage change in earnings before interest and taxes. Whenever the degree of financial leverage is greater than one, financial leverage exists. The higher this quotient the larger the degree of financial leverage. Since debt financing incurs fixed interest charges, the ratio of debt to equity is considered a measure of financial leverage.

Operating leverage refers to the extent that fixed costs are utilized in the production process during an operating cycle. Operating leverage can also be used to measure the impact on earnings per share of having different levels of fixed to variable costs in manufacturing products. Earnings before interest and taxes are related to changes in the variable costs to fixed cost. As fixed oper-ating costs are added by the firm, the potential operating profits and losses are magnified, and are ultimately reflected in the variation in earnings per share of stock. The Degree of operating leverage (DOL) is computed as follows;

ENCYCLOPEDIA OF BANKING AND FINANCE

LEVERAGED BUYOUT

$$DOL = \frac{\text{Percentage change in earnings before interest and taxes}}{\text{Percentage change in sales}}$$

The degree of operating leverage indicates how large a change in operating profit will result from a given percentage change in sales. As long as the degree of operating leverage is greater than one, there is positive operating leverage.

The degree of total or combined leverage (DTL) is computed as follows:

$$DTL = \frac{\text{Percentage change in earnings per share}}{\text{Percentage change in sales}}$$

Whenever the percentage change in earnings per share resulting from a given percentage change in sales exceeds the percentage change in sales, total leverage is positive. The total or combined leverage for a company equals the product of the operating and financial leverages. Total leverage indicates a firm's ability to use both operating and financial fixed costs to magnify the effect of changes in sales on a firm's earnings per share. The appended exhibit illustrates the application of leverage to a firm's income statement. Observe that fixed expenses and interest expense remain unchanged. Note the section of the statement involved in the computation of operating, financial, and total leverage. Leverage arises from the fixed expenses and interest expenses that remain unchanged. Leverage analysis is an extension of break-even analysis and uses the same basic information: price, quantity, variable expenses, and fixed expenses.

BIBLIOGRAPHY

PETRUCELLO, R. M. "Investors Can Increase Leverage by Knowing How Lenders Think." *Real Estate Review*, Spring, 1988.

LEVERAGED BUYOUT A method of acquiring control of a corporation by borrowing against its assets, usually requiring a sale of assets to pay off the debt. The mechanism usually involves a raider seeking to expand his or her control or management buying out all public stockholders and taking the corporation private, using substantial amounts of borrowed capital by pledging as collateral the company to be acquired and its assets or additional financing from other investors. On a few occasions, employees have arranged to take control of a corporation in a leveraged buyout. Buyers typically contribute only a token amount of capital. Leverage buyouts are either cash flow-based or asset-based. Unsecured lenders carry much of the economic risk. Since 1982, the purchase price typically has included a premium over asset values.

The company's other stockholders are usually offered a premium for their equity to ensure the completion of the buyout. The buyer relies on the earnings and cash flows of the purchased company to retire the debt. Buyers also expect the company to grow and increase the value of their equity. Many buyers subsequently arrange for a public underwriting of the acquired company, a practice that often results in large profits to the management group at attractive capital gain rates.

Investment bankers, venture capital pools, insurance companies, pension funds, and other investors often become involved in company buyouts, either as lenders or investors, or both. It is estimated that such groups often contribute between 25% and 75% of the total equity. The capital structure of the firm often reflects a high debt/equity ratio. Insurance companies and pension funds sometimes provide mezzanine financing. Mezzanine financing protects senior creditors when mezzanine financiers accept either a subordinated debt position or preferred stock. Since 1984, high-yield, high-risk JUNK BONDS have been widely used as mezzanine financing.

Buyouts are especially attractive when the economy is growing and minimal inflation exists. Cost-cutting opportunities exist for the acquirer as well as opportunities to restructure the company and its products and product lines.

Lenders in buyouts should consider cash flows, aging of trade receivables, condition of inventories, appraised value versus book value of plant and equipment, short-term borrowing requirements, amount and terms of existing accounts payable and other debt, and operating income and expense levels. The quality of the company's earnings and assets and the realism of costs should be reviewed. Matters such as lease and labor contracts, relationship with suppliers, and management capabilities should be considered. Becoming a lender in a leveraged buyout has special risks and rewards which must be recognized.

Successful buyouts are often associated with noncyclical growth industries, but with many exceptions, with predictable cash flows. The acquired companies have large market share in a competitive industry. They are not often found in capital-intensive industries. The continuity of management is provided but is often temporary and selective.

Deal makers in buyouts identify the target company and often

Financial, Operating, and Total Leverage

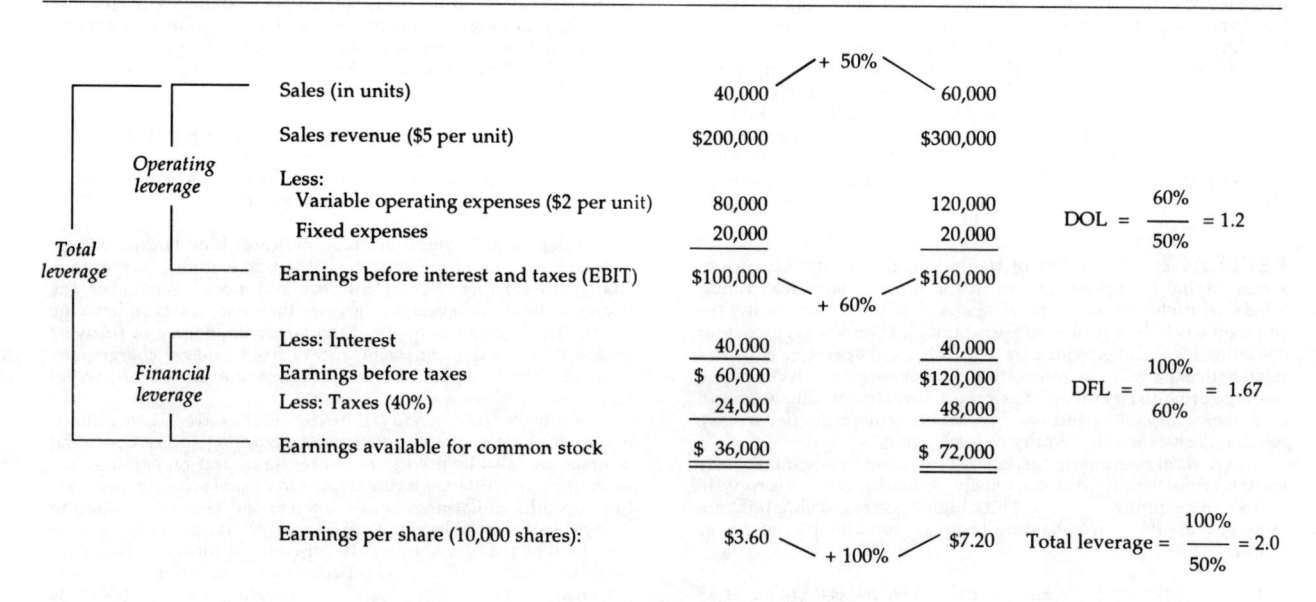

		40,000 → +50% → 60,000	
Sales (in units)		40,000 60,000	
Sales revenue ($5 per unit)		$200,000 $300,000	
Less: Variable operating expenses ($2 per unit)		80,000 120,000	
Fixed expenses		20,000 20,000	$DOL = \dfrac{60\%}{50\%} = 1.2$
Earnings before interest and taxes (EBIT)		$100,000 → +60% → $160,000	
Less: Interest		40,000 40,000	
Earnings before taxes		$60,000 $120,000	$DFL = \dfrac{100\%}{60\%} = 1.67$
Less: Taxes (40%)		24,000 48,000	
Earnings available for common stock		$36,000 $72,000	
Earnings per share (10,000 shares):		$3.60 → +100% → $7.20	Total leverage = $\dfrac{100\%}{50\%} = 2.0$

Operating leverage brackets: Sales through EBIT.
Financial leverage brackets: EBIT through Earnings available for common stock.
Total leverage brackets: entire statement.

structure the initial deal, arrange interim financing, and serve on boards of directors. Deal makers earn substantial fees for their services, often exceeding 15% of the equity.

BIBLIOGRAPHY

Leveraged Buyout: An Alternative to Plant Closings. The Conference Board, New York, NY, 1983.
BRANDT, S. J. "Avoiding the Legal Pitfalls of LBOs." *Bankers Magazine*, May-June, 1988.
Corporate Acquisitions, Mergers, and Divestitures. Prentice-Hall, Inc., Paramus, NJ. Looseleaf service.
Corporate Finance Sourcebook. Corporate Finance Sourcebook. New York, NY. Annual.
DIAMOND, S. C. *Leveraged Buyouts.* Dow Jones-Irwin, Inc., Homewood, IL, 1985.
Firstlist. First National Bank of Maryland, Baltimore, MD.
National Directory of the Leveraged Buyout Network. Leveraged Buyout Network, Arlington, TX. Annual.
SOLOMON, L. W. *Corporate Acquisitions, Mergers, and Divestitures.* Prentice Hall, Inc., Paramus, NJ. Looseleaf.
Who's Who of Corporate Acquisitions. The Hay Group, Philadelphia, PA. Annual.

LIABILITY Liabilities are probable future sacrifices of economic benefits arising from present obligations of a particular entity to transfer assets or provide services to other entities in the future as a result of past transactions or events. This definition makes a distinction between owners' equity and liabilities and emphasizes economic obligation rather than legal debt. Three essential characteristics of an accounting liability include the following:

1. A duty or obligation to pay exists.
2. The duty is virtually unavoidable by a particular entity.
3. The event obligating the enterprise has occurred.

Liabilities are usually classified as either current or noncurrent liabilities. Current liabilities are those obligations whose liquidation is reasonably expected to require the use of existing resources properly classified as current assets, or the creation of other current liabilities. This definition of current liabilities emphasizes a short-term creditors' claim to working capital rather than to the due date for classification purposes. Accounts payable, dividends payable, salaries payable, and taxes payable are examples of current liabilities. Liabilities that are not current are referred to as noncurrent or long-term liabilities. Bonds payable and mortgages payable are examples of long-term liabilities.

Contractual liabilities arise from events that are either expressly or implicitly contractual in nature. Some obligations are imposed on business enterprises by government or courts (such as taxes and fines), while others relate to nonreciprocal transfers from a business enterprise to owners or others (such as cash dividends and donations). A constructive liability is one that is implied from an arrangement, such as vacation pay and bonuses. Equitable obligations are neither contractual nor constructive obligations, but obligations arising from fairness, ethical and moral principles, or equity. An example of an ethical obligation is the responsibility of a monopoly supplier to deliver goods or services to dependent customers. Equitable liabilities are not currently recognized in financial statements. Contingent liabilities arise from an existing situation, or set of circumstances involving uncertainty as to possible gain or loss to an enterprise that will ultimately be resolved when one or more future events will occur or fail to occur. Only contingent losses are recognized. A contingent liability is accrued if (l) it is probable that a liability has occurred, or an asset has been impaired, and (2) it can be reliably measured. Examples of contingent liabilities include product warranties and pending litigation. Deferred liabilities are often found on financial statements. Deferred credits include (l) prepaid or unearned revenue involving a contractual obligation to provide a future good or service, such as for rent or interest received in advance, and (2) obligations arising from accounting principles which defer income recognition of the item, such as investment tax credits and deferred tax credits. The second type of deferred liabilities imposes no duty on the firm to transfer assets in the future. Such items arise from past transactions and are currently deferred from the income statement.

Liabilities may be classified in the following order of preference: (1) liabilities to preferred creditors, (2) liabilities to secured creditors, (3) liabilities to unsecured or general creditors, (4) contingent liabilities, and (5) liability (or accountability) to stockholders or other owners.

The chief liabilities of a bank are deposits, borrowings from the Federal Reserve bank or other banks, liabilities on account of letters of credit and acceptances, and capital accounts.

See CAPITAL LIABILITIES, CONTINGENT LIABILITIES, CURRENT LIABILITIES, FIXED LIABILITIES, NATIONAL BANK INDEBTEDNESS.

BIBLIOGRAPHY

GREENBAUM, S. I., and others. *Understanding Commercial Bank Contingent Liabilities*, 1986.
KIESO, D. E., and WEYGANDT, J. J. *Intermediate Accounting.* John Wiley and Sons, New York, NY, 1987.
NIKOLAI, L. A., and BAZLEY, J. D. *Intermediate Accounting.* PWK-Kent Publishing Co., Boston, MA, 1988.
WILLIAMS, J. R., and others. *Intermediate Accounting.* Harcourt Brace Jovanovich, San Diego, CA, 1989.

LIABILITY INSURANCE All the forms of property risks which are insurable; usually the insurance lines carried by casualty and surety companies, which include automobile liability, liability other than automobile, workers' compensation (employers' liability), fidelity, surety, glass, burglary and theft, boiler and machinery, automobile property damage, automobile collision, property damage and collision other than automobile, credit, etc.

See INSURANCE.

LIABILITY LEDGER A subsidiary ledger maintained in the loan and discount department of a bank in which the notes, acceptances, and bills of exchange discounted for and purchased from each borrower are recorded. Accounts are classified alphabetically, and from the record it is possible to ascertain, by reference to the balance column, the net liability of each borrower: (1) on his own paper, (2) on paper which he has endorsed for value, (3) on paper which he has made and which has been endorsed for value by others, and (4) on paper which he has endorsed as guarantor.

LIBEL In civil law, an untrue and malicious publication, expressed in printing, writing, or pictures, which tends to injure the reputation of a person, to hold him up to scorn or ridicule, or to injure him in his office, profession, or trade. The writing must involve a false accusation that is published and intended to injure a person's reputation or expose a person to public contempt or ridicule.

Recent libel cases have resulted in huge monetary awards. Proposals for changes in the libel law would eliminate most large libel damages; instead, plaintiffs would obtain a declaratory judgment or finding by the court concerning whether the statements of fact in dispute are true or not. The basic objective of libel law is to make libel victims whole. While some plaintiffs are motivated by the prospect of receiving money, others are more interested in repairing or protecting their reputation. Often a correction, retraction, or apology can resolve the problem, especially if it occurred before a suit was filed. Considerate treatment of the complainants is often recommended to reduce the impact of libel suits. Plaintiff lawyers often are retained on a contingency fee basis.

The avoidance of libel suits by banks expressing credit opinion unfavorable to a subject is highly important because the libel law places the burden on the defendant to prove absence of malice and plead the defenses. For this reason credit communications expressing opinions of financial responsibility should be given very carefully: (1) facts or knowledge, not mere belief, should be cited; (2) opinion or conclusions should be substantiated by facts and knowledge; (3) data should be furnished in generalized rather than specific form. In addition to giving credit information on a confidential basis, banks also use the disclaimer clause in credit information letters. An example is the following: "All statements on the part of the bank, or any of its officers, as to the responsibility or standing of any person, firm, or corporation, or as to the value of any securities, is a matter of opinion, given as such in answer to an inquiry, and solely as a matter of courtesy, for which no responsibility in any way is to attach to this bank or to any of its officers." Such a clause, however, does not protect the bank if in fact the statements were libelous. Generally, there are two defenses open to a defendant in a civil libel suit: that the publication is true, and that the circumstances surrounding the writing of the letter were such as to make it a conditionally privileged communication.

LIBERTARIANISM The school of thought advocating individual freedom as the cornerstone of the economic system. The belief is that individuals should be permitted to do as they like and that free markets will regulate such an economy. Associated with this laissez faire school of thought is Nobel Laureate Milton Friedman.

LIBERTY BONDS Bonds issued by the United States in 1917, 1918, and 1919, to finance our participation in World War I and to raise funds to lend to the Allied Powers. Four liberty bond issues and one victory loan issue were brought out between May 14, 1917, and April 21, 1919, the five issues (ten issues including the converted issues) aggregating approximately $21,478,357,000.

As of June 15, 1935, all the original issues of liberty bonds had been retired or converted into Treasury bonds or notes.

See UNITED STATES GOVERNMENT SECURITIES.

LIBOR LONDON INTERBANK OFFERED RATE.

LICENSE In real property law, permission to do acts upon the land of another which but for the permit granted would constitute a trespass. Licenses are personal to the licensee, are generally not assignable except by express agreement, and are generally revocable at will at any time, except for certain technical exceptions.

In securities regulation, state BLUE SKY LAWS of the preventive type require dealers and brokers seeking to offer securities in the state to obtain a license to do so from the securities commissioner or similar officer. In addition, licensed brokers and dealers are required to qualify the specific securities to be sold within the state.

In administrative law, licenses are permits granted by the sovereign or administrative bodies to which the sovereign power has been delegated in the exercise of the police power, to persons to carry on a profession, business, calling, or activity, or to engage in other relations vested with a public interest. Revenues from license fees constitute a particularly fruitful source of taxes in state tax systems.

LICENSING The grant of permission to do a specified activity, exercise a certain privilege, or carry on a particular business. To insure that certain business and professional practices maintain acceptable levels of services, states (and sometimes the federal government) require that licenses be obtained in order to operate. For example, medical doctors, dentists, and nurses must pass a state medical board examination before practicing. Lawyers and accountants must also pass a board examination. Real estate agents have to obtain a license before engaging in transactions. Restaurants must meet health standards in order to operate, and so on. From an economic perspective, licensing provides information to consumers as to which practitioners have met a preestablished minimum level of acceptance.

LIEN The right to hold any property given as a pledge or security until the debt which it secures is paid. To constitute a lien the debt must be enforceable in equity or law, e.g., a mortgage.

Liens are specific and general. A general lien comprises all the property belonging to the debtor. A specific lien comprises only the particular property subject to the lien, as specified in the instrument acknowledging the debt. A mechanic's lien is a specific lien, because it affects only the property upon which the laborer has expended material and labor.

A prior lien is not necessarily a first lien, it is simply one that takes precedence over others. A junior lien is not necessarily a second lien; it may be any lien other than the first.

LIENOR One who holds a lien.

LIFE ANNUITY See ANNUITY.

LIFE ESTATE A freehold estate created not by inheritance but by act of the parties, giving the life tenant the right to possession of the estate and to the income therefrom for the duration of his life or for the duration of the life or lives of another person or persons if so limited thereon.

Upon death of the life tenant or other person whose life determines the duration of the life estate, the property and income may, in accordance with the terms of the original grant, either revert to the grantor or his estate or become the possession of the REMAINDERMAN. Under modern statutes, not more than two successive life estates can be created where a remainder is limited thereon.

Life estates arising by operation of law are curtesy and dower.

See DESCENT, LAWS OF.

LIFE INSURANCE See INSURANCE.

LIFE INSURANCE COMPANY Life insurance companies are particularly vested with a high degree of public interest and concern because of their commitments with millions of policyholders to insure lives and provide investment for reserves. Accordingly, state laws throughout the United States regulate the investments of life insurance companies in varying degrees of strictness. Most life insurance companies, however, write business not only in the state of domicile but in other states as well. Thus the most stringent of these states will usually determine the level of quality of investments for the particular company, so as to qualify for licensing to do business even after adjustment for nonadmitted assets. Companies domiciled in the northeastern states account for the bulk of life insurance company assets, although numerically life insurance companies abound particulary in Texas and Louisiana.

The appended tables shows

Totals for region, division and state by policies, value, average per household and benefit payments.

The insurance law of New York, one of the representative northeastern states as to high level of insurance company regulation, regulates the investments of life insurance companies in three general respects: (1) most stringently, although governing a minor portion of funds, the minimum capital investment required for domiciled companies, (2) the deposit of securities of similar type for foreign companies admitted to do business within the state, and (3) for the bulk of funds, namely reserves plus any balance over minimum capital requirements and surplus, the generally applicable restrictions on investments, which on the whole are less stringent than for savings banks.

LIFE INSURANCE TRUST See INSURANCE TRUST.

LIFE INTEREST See LIFE ESTATE.

LIFE TENANT See LIFE ESTATE.

LIGHT COIN Coin reduced by natural abrasion below the standard weight fixed by law. Loss in weight of gold coins, if in excess of the limit of tolerance provided by law, reduces its legal tender value in proportion to such loss in weight.

Loss in weight of fractional silver, nickel, and copper coins does not affect their value as legal tender since these coins are worth less as metal than as coin

See LIGHT GOLD, TOKEN MONEY.

LIGHT GOLD Gold coins that are of reduced weight because of variation or percentage of error on the part of the mint or, more usually, abrasion resulting from circulation. For tolerance allowed the mint in fineness and gross weight, see TOLERANCE. The Revised Statutes, Section 3585, provided that any gold coin in the Treasury when reduced in weight by natural abrasion more than 0.5% below the standard weight prescribed by law should be recoined, and any gold coins reduced in weight by not more than 0.5% below the standard weight after a circulation of 20 years from date of coinage, and ratably for any period of less than 20 years, could be received at their nominal value by the Treasury.

The Joint Repeal Resolution of Congress of June 5, 1933, provided specifically that gold coins, when below the standard weight and limit of tolerance provided by law for the single piece, should be legal tender only at valuation in proportion to their actual weight.

However, under the Gold Reserve Act of January 30, 1934, no gold shall hereafter be coined, and no gold coin shall hereafter be paid out or delivered by the United States, except that coinage may continue to be executed by the mints of the United States for foreign countries. All gold coin of the United States, in accordance with the act, was withdrawn from circulation, to be formed together with all other gold owned by the United States into bars of such weights and degrees of fineness as the secretary of the Treasury may direct.

Table 1 / Life Insurance—Insurance in Force and Benefit Payments by State: 1986
(Applies to policyholders and payments in the U.S.)

Region, Division, and State	Policies (1,000)	Value (bil. dol.)	Average per household (dol.)	Benefit payments [1] (mil. dol.)
U.S.	394,883	7,452	82,800	71,432
Region:				
Northeast	83,229	1,686	89,800	19,665
Midwest	97,407	1,854	83,700	18,907
South	154,709	2,496	80,800	20,562
West	59,538	1.416	77,800	12,298
New England	20,893	443	92,500	4,567
Maine	1,935	31	68,800	291
New Hampshire	1,667	33	85,000	305
Vermont	852	15	73,600	169
Massachusetts	8,755	200	91,300	2,108
Rhode Island	1,823	31	85,300	304
Connecticut	5,861	133	111,700	1,390
Middle Atlantic	62,336	1,243	88,900	15,098
New York	27,958	590	87,800	7,498
New Jersey	12,042	286	102,000	3,365
Pennsylvania	22,336	367	82,500	4,235
East North Central	69,832	1,304	84,200	13,690
Ohio	18,451	334	82,900	3,483
Indiana	9,099	161	78,500	1,641
Illinois	19,907	388	90,800	4,160
Michigan	14,510	283	84,400	2,981
Wisconsin	7,865	138	77,100	1,425
West North Central	27,575	550	82,500	5,217
Minnesota	6,221	139	87,500	1,252
Iowa	4,578	86	80,200	998
Missouri	8,324	153	79,100	1,402
North Dakota	991	21	84,300	154
South Dakota	905	19	73,000	178
Nebraska	2,427	52	84,600	525
Kansas	4,129	80	84,700	708
South Atlantic	79,754	1,281	81,800	10,898
Delaware	1,313	26	109,000	238
Maryland	8,192	154	92,700	1,534
District of Columbia	2,053	46	185,600	337
Virginia	13,284	203	93,500	1,471
West Virginia	3,090	40	56,900	435
North Carolina	13,498	186	77,900	1,517
South Carolina	7,757	96	79,800	664
Georgia	12,646	208	92,200	1,427
Florida	17,921	322	67,300	3,275
East South Central	32,949	412	73,800	3,325
Kentucky	6,069	86	62,800	710
Tennessee	9,988	143	78,600	1,348
Alabama	12,704	123	83,200	849
Mississippi	4,188	60	65,600	418
West South Central	42,006	803	83,100	6,339
Arkansas	2,766	47	53,000	401
Louisiana	9,065	129	82,600	1,031
Oklahoma	4,445	87	96,700	916
Texas	25,730	540	90,500	3,991
Mountain	19,007	370	77,500	3,214
Montana	1,109	21	67,800	197
Idaho	1,308	23	65,000	215
Wyoming	630	13	74,900	125
Colorado	5,303	113	90,000	942
New Mexico	1,858	36	68,400	308
Arizona	5,057	94	75,400	865
Utah	2,437	45	87,600	364
Nevada	1,305	25	62,800	198
Pacific	40,531	1,046	77,900	9,084
Washington	5,025	125	71,100	1,135
Oregon	3,310	68	63,300	674
California	29,674	800	79,400	6,832
Alaska	656	15	84,800	123
Hawaii	1,866	38	112,000	320

1. Comprises death payments, matured endowments, disability and annuity payments, surrender values, and policy dividends.
Source: American Council of Life Insurance, Washington, DC, *Life Insurance Fact Book*, biennial.

LIMIT The definite price fixed by a customer in an order placed with a broker to buy or sell securities or commodities. A limit order is to be executed at the limit or better; e.g., a buy order for a round lot of X(U.S. Steel) at 70 shall be executed at a price of $70 per share or less; or a sell order of a round lot of J (Standard Oil of New Jersey) at 42 shall be executed at price of $42 per share or higher.
See ORDERS.

LIMITATIONS See ACCEPTANCE CREDIT, NATIONAL BANKING SYSTEM, STATUTE OF LIMITATIONS.

LIMITED COMPANY The term "Company," "Co.," "& Co.," or "& Company" in a firm title, without further wording indicating that the firm is corporate in nature, may indicate either a general or a limited partnership. In the latter form of business organization, which shall consist of one of more limited partners and one or more general partners, the limited partner(s) is not liable personally for firm debts, being limited in his liability to his investment in the firm.

The term "limited" in English terminology refers to the corporation whose stockholders, provided they hold fully paid and nonassessable shares, are not liable personally for firm debts. In American practice, the corporate form of organization is indicated by reference to "Corporation," "Corp.," "Incorporated," or "Inc." in the firm title.

Limited partnership associations are provided for statutorily in four states in the U.S. This type of organization is corporate in nature, with limited liability, division of ownership into shares of stock, and voting for a board of directors or managers. The shares may be transferred, but the transferee must be elected to membership by majority of the members and of the total shares of stock in order to be entitled to the voting privilege. A quirk of this form is that such transferee not elected to membership is entitled to the firm's purchase of his shares at fair value.

The business trust, also called the Massachusetts trust, may also enjoy limited liability for its beneficiaries (holders of transferable certificates of beneficial interest in the trust), but if such beneficiaries have the power of voting for the trustees, limited liability fails because of violation of the basic principle of the trust (power of beneficiaries to vote for or fail to reelect trustees implies control over legal title to the corpus [assets] and hence a merger of the legal and equitable interest), and so a mere partnership may be deemed to result, with personal liability for firm debts.
See CORPORATION, LIMITED LIABILITY.

LIMITED LEGAL TENDER See LEGAL TENDER, TOKEN MONEY, UNITED STATES MONEY.

LIMITED LIABILITY The liability of stockholders of the ordinary business corporation extends no further than to payment of the full par value of the issued and outstanding capital stock, such limited liability being one of the principal advantages of the corporate form of business organization. However, even for limited liability corporations, state statutes provide that every holder of shares of stock not fully paid shall be personally liable to the creditors of the corporation to an amount equal to the amount unpaid on the shares held by him for debts of the corporation contracted while such shares were held by the stockholder. Also, state statutes, e.g., New York's, provide that the stockholders of every stock corporation shall jointly and severally be liable personally for all debts due and owing to any of the corporation's laborers, servants, or employees other than contractors for services performed by them for such corporation under specified conditions.

National banks and state banks and trust companies once carried DOUBLE LIABILITY on their stock, stockholders being subject to assessment up to the par value of their shares in addition to losing their original investment. In accordance with the Banking Acts of 1933 and 1935, double liability for national bank stock has been ended, and most states have provided similar legislation for state banks and trust companies.
See LIMITED COMPANY.

LIMITED ORDER Limit order; a buy or sell order placed with a broker for execution at a specified price. Execution is to be effected at the limit or better.
See ORDER.

LIMIT OF TOLERANCE See LIGHT GOLD, TOLERANCE.

ENCYCLOPEDIA OF BANKING AND FINANCE

LIMPING STANDARD

Table 2 / Key Life Insurance Statistics

	1977	1986	1987	% Change 1986-85	% Change 1987-86
Life Insurance in Force in the United States (000,000 omitted)					
Ordinary	$1,289,321	$3,658,203	$4,139,071	12.7	13.1
Group	1,115,047	2,801,049	3,043,782	9.3	8.7
Industrial	39,045	27,168	26,668	− 3.8	− 1.8
Credit	139,402	233,859	242,977	8.3	3.9
Total	$2,582,815	$6,720,279	$7,452,498	11.0	10.9
Average Amounts of Life Insurance in Force in the United States					
Per Household	$ 34,800	$ 76,000	$ 82,800	9.0	8.9
Per Insured Household	$ 42,000	$ 93,800	$ 102,200	8.9	9.0
Life Insurance Purchases in the United States (000,000 omitted)					
Ordinary	$ 247,453	$ 933,592	$ 986,660	2.5	5.7
Group	115,839	374,741*	365,529	17.3	− 2.5
Industrial	6,504	418	324	− 42.1	− 22.5
Total	$ 369,796	$1,308,751*	$1,352,513	6.3	3.3
Benefit Payments in the United States (000,000 omitted)					
Payments to Beneficiaries	$ 10,196	$ 19,479	$ 20,530	6.9	5.4
Payments to Policyholders	10,999	26,169	26,586	− 3.2	1.6
Payments to Annuitants	5,267	22,657	24,316	6.6	7.3
Total	$ 26,462	$ 68,305	$ 71,432	2.7	4.6
Premium Receipts of U.S. Life Insurance Companies (000,000 omitted)					
Life Insurance	$ 33,765	$ 66,213	$ 76,737	10.1	15.9
Annuity Considerations	14,974	83,712	88,677	55.3	5.9
Health Insurance	23,580	44,153	47,549	5.5	7.7
Total	$ 72,319	$ 194,078	$ 212,963	24.5	9.7
Assets of U.S. Life Insurance Companies (000,000 omitted)					
Government Securities	$ 23,555	$ 144,616	$ 151,436	16.1	4.7
Corporate Bonds	137,889	341,967	405,674	15.2	18.6
Stocks	33,763	90,864	96,515	17.2	6.2
Mortgages	96,848	193,842	213,450	12.8	10.1
Real Estate	11,060	31,615	34,172	9.7	8.1
Policy Loans	27,556	54,055	53,626	− 0.6	− 0.8
Other Assets	21,051	80,592	89,586	12.0	11.2
Total	$ 351,722	$ 937,511	$1,044,459	13.5	11.4
Net Rate of Investment Income of U.S. Life Insurance Companies (Before Federal Income Taxes)					
Including Separate Accounts	6.89%	9.35%	9.09%	—	—
Excluding Separate Accounts	7.00%	9.64%	9.39%	—	—

* Includes Servicemen's Group Life Insurance of $51.0 billion and Federal Employees' Group Life Insurance of $10.8 billion.
Source: American Council of Life Insurance.

LIMPING STANDARD The monetary system of a country which, although the gold standard has been formally or informally adopted and the free coinage of silver has been suspended, nevertheless retains silver as a monetary medium with legal tender power. The limping standard in the U.S., from the effective date of the Bland-Allison Act on February 28, 1878, until repeal of the Sherman Silver Purchase Act in 1893, was in reality a survival of the era of BIMETALLISM, in which nominally both gold and silver were maintained as a joint standard at fixed mint ratios. The countries which constituted the LATIN UNION, once having had a bimetallic standard and still retaining silver coins in circulation, may also be said to have possessed a limping standard.

LINE *See* DEPOSIT LINE, LINE OF CREDIT.

LINE OF CREDIT The maximum amount which a person or concern is entitled to borrow from a bank at any given time, or normal limit of accommodation; also called the limit of credit, or credit line. It is the total credit force, or potential credit balance, at the disposal of a borrowing customer in return for which the customer is required to maintain proportional balances and prove to be an acceptable credit risk and an otherwise satisfactory account. The amount of a credit line is not definitely fixed, but varies from time to time according to the financial standing of the customer, as shown by submitted financial statements, the bank's loanable resources, and general money and trade conditions.

While a bank usually fixes a line of credit for its borrowing customers, it is usually reluctant to agree absolutely to provide for this amount because changing conditions, in the affairs of either the customer or the bank, may make it inadvisable, if not impossible, to grant the line agreed upon. In other words, while a bank is normally obligated to insure a line of credit agreed upon, it is not legally bound to do so. Any line of credit established is predicated upon the continuance of the same management and maintenance of a financial standing as good or better than that which was in existence at the time it was established.

Ordinarily a bank is able to provide its customers with as much credit as they are entitled to have in proportion to the value of their accounts and financial condition. For this reason, the well-established and conservatively conducted concern, having good banking connections, should never experience difficulty in obtaining all the credit it requires.

See CREDIT, CREDIT RISK, STATEMENT ANALYSIS, TWENTY PERCENT RULE.

Table 3 / Acquisitions of Investments
U.S. Life Insurance Companies (000,000 omitted)

Year	Government Securities	Corporate Securities Bonds	Stocks	Mortgages	Real Estate	Policy Loans	Total
1947	$ 1,941	$ 4,248	$ 307	$ 2,786	$ 219	$ 327	$ 9,597
1948	2,262	4,800	181	3,407	278	414	11,342
1949	1,065	3,674	251	3,440	264	478	9,182
1950	2,399	3,700	470	4,894	257	521	12,241
1951	7,691	4,379	278	5,134	273	535	18,290
1952	4,610	5,151	194	3,978	225	504	14,882
1953	3,939	4,631	233	4,345	205	579	13,932
1954	5,549	5,157	552	5,344	388	661	17,651
1955	6,176	4,687	382	6,614	371	669	18,909
1956	4,794	5,305	291	6,715	360	744	18,209
1957	3,933	6,044	294	5,230	458	916	16,775
1958	5,625	5,799	365	5,277	463	1,088	18,537
1959	5,613	6,318	514	5,975	446	1,156	20,022
1960	5,011	6,886	655	6,083	299	1,420	20,354
1961	6,478	9,113	918	6,785	429	1,427	25,150
1962	6,824	11,654	766	7,478	636	1,473	28,558
1963	6,018	14,200	788	9,172	485	1,504	32,167
1964	4,979	15,419	1,066	10,433	488	1,574	33,959
1965	4,273	20,128	1,463	11,137	448	1,702	39,451
1966	3,937	18,452	1,326	10,217	210	2,613	36,955
1967	3,949	25,930	2,065	8,470	668	2,365	43,447
1968	5,570	27,601	3,318	7,925	815	2,741	47,970

Year	Government Securities Long-Term	Total	Corporate Securities Bonds Long-Term	Total	Stocks	Mortgages	Real Estate	Policy Loans	Total
1969	$ 1,393	$ 4,655	$ 6,787	$ 31,883	$ 4,099	$ 7,531	$ 794	$ 4,118	$ 53,080
1970	796	4,612	6,808	41,405	4,086	7,181	859	4,149	62,292
1971	1,635	7,011	11,727	53,517	6,785	7,573	1,035	3,400	79,321
1972	1,604	8,989	14,257	68,240	8,468	8,696	976	3,252	98,621
1973	1,385	8,290	12,941	87,069	8,198	11,463	1,177	4,602	120,789
1974	1,456	7,609	11,266	86,656	4,932	11,339	1,294	5,332	117,0626
1975	3,695	13,644	16,567	96,534	5,955	9,595	2,115	4,600	132,443
1976	8,249	30,315	24,002	120,442	7,691	9,801	1,814	4,824	174,889
1977	7,498	34,908	30,183	147,114	7,588	14,176	2,059	5,115	210,960
1978	6,442	35,805	28,006	164,966	8,015	17,799	2,234	6,260	234,979
1979	6,866	41,566	23,170	186,195	10,374	20,689	2,793	8,739	270,356
1980	6,961	51,798	22,255	227,336	14,105	19,759	3,312	11,535	327,845
1981	10,620	72,879	22,966	312,707	19,498	13,478	4,467	12,641	435,670
1982	24,305	N.A.	32,939	N.A.	25,818	11,528	4,480	11,449	N.A.
1983	49,149	N.A.	50,766	N.A.	36,071	20,116	4,347	9,468	N.A.
1984	62,919	N.A.	68,709	N.A.	35,328	20,074	5,950	9,543	N.A.
1985	99,930	N.A.	98,344	N.A.	46,258	35,097	5,966	9,742	N.A.
1986	154,300	N.A.	137,456	N.A.	67,906	45,425	7,065	9,700	N.A.
1987	155,674		165,062	N.A.	74,452	44,223	7,068	10,181	N.A.

N.A. = Not available after 1981.
Source: American Council of Life Insurance.

LINE OF DEPOSIT *See* DEPOSIT LINE.

LINE OF STOCKS Commitments made on the long or short side of the market systematically bought or sold respectively on a scale.
See SCALING.

LIQUID ASSETS Among commercial and industrial concerns, CURRENT ASSETS; among banks, assets immediately available as cash, or quickly convertible into cash, e..g., call loans, amounts due from banks, exchanges for clearinghouse, loans eligible for rediscount, and securities enjoying a ready and reliable market. Liquid assets do not include time loans ineligible for rediscount, securities not enjoying a ready market, banking premises, etc.

The term liquid (or quick) assets also refers to current assets including cash, marketable securities, and receivables (excluding inventory and prepaid expenses). In computing the acid-test ratio to measure the liquidity of a firm, use the following ratio:

$$\text{Acid-test ratio} = \frac{\text{Liquid assets}}{\text{Current liabilities}}$$

LIQUIDATING MARKET A market in which selling in volume occurs, whether as the result of a concerted movement to reduce prices thought to be inflated or merely to take profits; as applied to stocks, the selling of long stock.
See BEAR MARKET, LIQUIDATION.

LIQUIDATING VALUE The net value realizable in liquidation of a business or particular asset. In security analysis, the term is most often associated with fire and casualty insurance stocks, to

Table 4 / Life Insurance Purchases in the United States
Exclusive of Revivals, Increases, Dividend Additions and Reinsurance Acquired

Year	Ordinary Policies (000 omitted)	Ordinary Amount (000,000 omitted)	Group Certificates (000 omitted)	Group Amount (000,000 omitted)	Industrial Policies (000 omitted)	Industrial Amount (000,000 omitted)	Total Number (000 omitted)	Total Amount (000,000 omitted)
1940	$ 3,855	$ 6,689	285	$ 691	14,017	$ 3,350	18,157	$ 10,730
1945	4,343	9,859	681	1,265	11,869	3,430	16,893	14,554
1950	5,279	17,326	2,631	6,068	14,924	5,402	22,834	28,796
1955	7,572	30,827	2,217	11,258*	14,356	6,342	24,145	48,427
1960	8,734	52,883	3,734	14,645	12,287	6,880	24,755	74,408
1965	9,937	83,485	7,007	51,385†	10,492	7,296	27,436	142,166†
1970	10,968	122,920	5,219	63,690†	7,582	6,612	23,769	193,122†
1975	12,549	188,003	8,146	95,190†	6,397	6,729	27,092	289,922†
1976	13,219	213,784	9,145	104,683	5,962	6,382	27,326	324,849
1977	13,679	247,453	9,599	115,839	5,859	6,504	28,137	369,796
1978	13,987	283,067	9,267	125,129	5,445	6,015	28,699	414,211
1979	14,259	329,570	9,245	157,906	4,457	5,335	28,961	492,812
1980	14,750	385,575	11,379	183,418	2,878	3,609	29,007	572,602
1981	15,838	481,895	11,923	346,702*†	1,791	2,419	29,552	831,114*†
1982	15,614	585,444	11,930	250,532	1,350	1,898	28,894	837,874
1983	17,737	753,444	13,450	271,690	834	1,388	32,021	1,026,441
1984	17,695	820,315	14,605	293,521	712	943	33,021	1,114,779
1985	17,104	910,944	16,243	319,503	533	722	33,880	1,231,169
1986	16,811	933,592	17,507	374,741*†	305	418	34,623	1,308,751*†
1987	16,225	986,660	16,698	365,529	230	324	33,153	1,352,513

Note: Figures from 1940-1973 exclude all credit life insuance. Beginning with 1974, data include long-term credit insurance (life insurance on loans of more than 10 years' duration).

* Includes Federal Employees' Group Life Insurance of $1.9 billion in 1955, $84.4 billion on 1981, and $10.8 billion in 1986.
† Includes Servicemen's Group Life Insurance of $27.8 billion in 1965, $17.1 billion in 1970, $1.7 billion in 1975, $45.6 billion in 1981, and $51.0 billion in 1986.

Sources: Life Insurance Marketing and Research Association and American Council of Life Insurance.

indicate stockholders' equity, however, rather than true estimated value in liquidation. It is generally computed by taking capital, surplus (at market values for security holdings), voluntary reserves, and the equity in unearned premiums reserve. For fire insurance stocks, such equity in unearned premiums is generally taken as a flat 40%, although the actual realizable equity generally is larger. For casualty insurance stocks, the equity in unearned premiums is usually figured closer, depending on average loss ratios for the particular lines of insurance outstanding. The liquidating value is generally expressed on a per share basis on the common capital stock.

See INSURANCE COMPANY STATEMENTS.

LIQUIDATION This term has three meanings:

1. Cash realization; the selling of holdings in stocks, bonds, or commodities, either to take profits or in anticipation of, or to prevent losses due to, lower prices. Liquidation may be forced or voluntary. Frequently liquidation is referred to as extending over a period of time. In this sense, liquidation forms that part of the BUSINESS CYCLE which is characterized chiefly by falling prices, business failures, and business inactivity.
2. The termination or winding up of a business by the conversion of its assets into cash and distribution of the proceeds, first to the creditors in their order of preference and the remainder, if any, to the owners in proportion to their holdings.
3. Liquidation is one relief procedure available to an insolvent debtor. Liquidation has as its basic purpose the realization of assets and the liquidation of liabilities rather than the continuation of the business as in a reorganization. Insolvency refers to the inability of a debtor to pay its obligations as they come due. Chapter 7, the Bankruptcy Reform Act of 1979, outlines the procedures for corporate liquidation. Chapter 7 is the basic liquidation procedure and is sometimes referred to as ordinary bankruptcy. Chapter 7 is available to most debtors other than a government unit, a bank, insurance company, or a railroad.

Liquidation can be started by a voluntary petition (debtor initiates the petition) or involuntary petition (creditors initiate the petition). In a liquidation, an interim trustee is appointed. Unsecured creditors have a right to elect a permanent trustee. In most cases, the interim trustee becomes the permanent trustee. The trustee liquidates the debtor's nonexempt property as soon as possible "with the best interests of parties in interest." The trustee proceeds to distribute the available proceeds to the debtor's creditors according to priorities assigned in Chapter 7. After the debtor's property has been converted into cash and a proper distribution has been made to creditors and others, the debtor receives a discharge. The court will grant the debtor a discharge unless certain conditions are present. Nonindividuals do not receive a discharge in a Chapter 7 case. Nonindividual debtors normally file a voluntary Chapter 7 petition to provide for an orderly liquidation of their assets and distribution of proceeds to their creditors.

See FORCED LIQUIDATION, LIABILITY.

LIQUIDATOR A person appointed by a court or designated by statute to wind up the affairs of a business. The state superintendent of insurance or cognate official is designated by statute to liquidate the affairs of insurance companies, title and mortgage companies, etc., placed in LIQUIDATION. Banking statutes designate receivers to wind up the affairs of closed banks. The Federal Deposit Insurance Corporation shall be appointed by the Comptroller of the Currency as receiver for closed insured national banks or insured District of Columbia banks. In addition, the corporation shall accept appointment as receiver for closed insured state banks if such appointment is tendered by the state banking authority and is authorized or permitted by state law.

LIQUIDITY The amount of time required to convert an asset into cash or pay a liability. For noncurrent assets, liquidity generally refers to marketability. Cash is a highly liquid asset. Accounts receivable and inventory are somewhat less liquid. Property, plant, and equipment would ordinarily be very nonliquid assets. Liquidity is important in evaluating the timing of cash inflows and outflows. The liquidity of an enterprise is a major indicator of its ability to meet its debts when they mature.

Liquidity ratios are often used to measure a firm's liquidity. These ratios typically relate to the enterprise's working capital—its current assets and current liabilities. Current assets include cash, short-term marketable securities, receivables, inventories, and prepaid items.

Current liabilities include such items as accounts payable, taxes, interest payable, and other such short-term payables. Major liquidity ratios include the current ratio and acid-test ratio computed as follows:

$$\text{Current ratio} = \frac{\text{Current assets}}{\text{Current liabilities}}$$

$$\text{Acid-test ratio} = \frac{\text{Quick assets}}{\text{Current liabilities}}$$

Quick assets include cash, short-term marketable securities, and accounts receivable. Inventories are excluded because there may be some delay in converting them into cash. Prepaid expenses are excluded because they cannot be converted into cash. The acid-test ratio is a more severe test of a company's short-term ability to pay its debts than is the current ratio.

BIBLIOGRAPHY

AMIHUD, Y., and MENDELSON, H. "Liquidity, Volatility, and Exchange Automation." *Journal of Accounting, Auditing and Finance*, Fall, 1988.
GLOSTEN, L. R. "Insider Trading, Liquidity, and the Role of the Monopolist Specialist." *Journal of Business*, April, 1989.
"Liquidity." *The Banker*, February, 1989.
WREN-LEWIS, S. "Supply, Liquidity and Credit: A New Version of the Institute's Domestic Econometric Macromodel [National Institute of Economic and Social Research; Britain]." *National Institute Economic Review*, November, 1988.

LIQUIDITY EFFECT Monetary policy has a direct effect on interest rates. When the money supply increases, for example, reserves in the banking system increase and lending thus increases. The market response to this increase in lending is for the interest rate to fall. This initial interest rate response to a monetary policy is called the liquidity effect.

LIQUIDITY PREFERENCE In Keynesian economics, the demand schedule for money, motivated by transactions motive (active circulation) and precautionary motive (reserves for future needs, risks, and uncertainty), both considered interest-inelastic, and speculative motive (shifts to and from liquidity vis à vis the markets), which is regarded as interest-elastic.

In its simplest formulation, the Keynesian concept of the rate of interest is the intersection of the curve representing supply of money (assumed interest-inelastic because fixed by the monetary authorities) and the curve of demand for money (liquidity preference).

Keynes developed the liquidity preference concept as another rebuttal of the classical theory that the rate of interest is determined by the intersection of the investment demand for funds and the supply of savings. He criticized the latter as indeterminate because the savings curve (supply of funds) will depend upon the level of real income, which is itself affected by the rate of interest through its effect upon investment.

The liquidity preference theory of interest rates was advanced by the British economist John Maynard Keynes in his classic work, *The General Theory of Employment, Interest, and Prices*, first published in 1936. To the transaction and precautionary motives for holding money, Keynes added a unique insight—the speculative demand for money. For simplification, Keynes looked at a case where the individual had only two means for storing wealth: either in money or in bonds. Keynes reasoned that in this case the individual would choose between storing wealth in bonds or in money balances based on some idea of the future direction of interest rates. If he thought interest rates were likely to fall, he would want to hold more of his wealth in bonds because when rates fall the value of bonds increases, so he would stand to make a capital gain from his investment in bonds. On the other hand, if the individual thought rates were likely to rise he would want to shift his wealth into money balances to avoid capital losses from investment in bonds.

Keynes advanced the idea that the interest rate and the consensus of individuals in the market about the future direction of rates were the principal determinants of the speculative demand for money. He explained that individuals usually have a conception of the normal rate of interest. If rates fall below this normal level, more and more individuals will begin to think that rates are likely to increase in the future. As a result, they will begin to shift more and more of their wealth portfolio out of bonds and into speculative money balances, increasing the speculative demand for money. Alternatively, when rates are above the normal level, more and more individuals will begin to bet that rates are going to fall, and they will shift wealth out of money balances and into bond investment, reducing the speculative demand for money. Keynes thus concluded that the speculative demand for money was negatively related to the rate of interest.

The total demand for money, arising from the demands of individuals for transaction, precautionary, and speculative money balances, was determined, Keynes argued, by the rate of interest and the level of income. Since money is valued in terms of what it can buy, the Keynesian theory of the demand for money is concerned with the demand for real as opposed to simply nominal money balances. The level of real money balances can be expressed as the level of nominal balances divided by some index of prices. Thus, according to the liquidity preference theory, a rise in the real stock of money will lower the rate of interest. Alternatively, a decline in the real stock of money will raise the rate of interest. An increase in the level of real income will raise the interest rate, other things being equal, and a decline in real income will lower it. The theory thus explains why interest rates tend to rise and fall over the business cycle as real income rises and falls.

Even Keynesians, however, concede that the Keynesian theory is also indeterminate, because the liquidity preference curve (demand for money) also will depend upon the level of real income. Thus the post-Keynesians have synthesized a combination of the loanable funds theory and the Keynesian concept to provide a determinate solution in theory. Demand factors (investment demand and shifts in savings relative to consumption), intersected by supply factors (liquidity preference and money supply), will provide a determinate theoretical explanation of how interest rates are determined.

BIBLIOGRAPHY

FERGUSON J. D., and HART, W. R. "Liquidity Preference or Loanable Funds: Interest Rate Determination in Market Disequilibrium." *Oxford Economic Papers*, March, 1980.
KALDOR, N., and TREVITHICK, J. "A Keynesian Perspective on Money." *Lloyd's Bank Review*, January, 1981.
LORIE, H.R. "Another Look at Liquidity Preference." *Quarterly Journal of Economics*, February, 1980.

LIST The total of securities traded on a stock exchange; LISTED SECURITIES.

LISTED SECURITIES Securities that have been approved and admitted or listed on a stock exchange. Each stock exchange has a listing policy and listing standards which must be complied with before a security is approved by it for trading. Such policy is voluntary; the Securities and Exchange Commission under the Securities Exchange Act of 1934 does not compel listing or impose uniformity of standards.

Such regulation, however, provides that a member of a national securities exchange or a broker or dealer may not effect any transaction in a security on an exchange unless the security is registered on that exchange under the Securities Exchange Act or is exempt from such registration. In general, the SEC points out, the act exempts from registration obligations issued or guaranteed by a state or the federal government or by certain subdivisions or agencies thereof, and authorizes the SEC to adopt rules of regulations exempting such other securities as the SEC may find necessary or appropriate to exempt in the public interest or for the protection of investors. Under this authority, the SEC exempted securities of certain banks, certain securities secured by property or leasehold interests, certain warrants, and on a temporary basis certain securities issued in substitution for or in addition to listed securities.

Section 12 of the Securities Exchange Act provides that an issuer may register a class of securities on an exchange by filing with the SEC and the exchange an application which discloses pertinent information concerning the issuer and its affairs, including information in regard to the issuer's business, capital structure, the terms of its securities, the persons who manage or control its affairs, the remuneration paid to its officers and directors, the allotment of options, bonuses and profit-sharing plans and financial statements certified by independent accountants. Section 13 in turn requires issuers having securities registered on an exchange to file periodic reports keeping current the information furnished in the application for registration. These periodic reports include annual reports, semiannual reports, and current reports. The latter are required to be filed for each month in which any of certain specified events have occurred, such as changes in control of the registrant, important acquisitions or dispositions of assets, the institution or termination of important legal proceedings, and important changes in the issuer's capital securities or in the amount thereof outstanding.

Development of the Listing Process. The SEC points out that the listing process has had a long evolution. As early as 1847, the New York Stock Exchange called for transfer books to be located in New York City. Its committee on stock list, created in 1869, promulgated rules protecting against forgery and overissuance of securities, and sought to obtain statements of conditions and lists of officers of issuers. The regular files of printed listing statements date from 1884. By 1900, the exchange had commenced to call upon applicants for agreements to public detailed statements and annual reports. The issuers' agreement with the exchange became more comprehensive over the years, providing for periodic earnings statements, independent auditing, prompt notification of issuer actions affecting their security holders, etc. With the advent of the SEC, the requirements of the listing agreements were supplemented by the requirements for registration along with listing.

The New York Stock Exchange provides the following historical account of development of its listing agreement. Since 1899, companies making applications for the listing of their securities have, as a regular part of the listing procedure, entered into a listing agreement with the exchange by which they commit themselves to a code of performance, after listing, in respect to the matters dealt with by the agreement. At the outset the items in the agreement were few in number and restricted in scope. Initially there were only three, two of which were concerned with mechanical necessities of the marketplace—the maintenance of transfer facilities and advance notice of record dates.

The third item represented the exchange's effort to satisfy, by a formal requirement, a public need which it had long recognized, but which its previous unsupported efforts had been unable to fill—the need of investors for regular financial reports by the companies whose securities they held. Supported by a rising popular demand for such information and the beginning of a show of interest by corporate management, the exchange sought, through the medium of the newly created listing agreement, to make the regular publication of annual financial statements a standard practice among listed companies. By contrast with the present situation, it is interesting to note that in 1866, the exchange, when requesting financial statements of a well-known railroad company of that day, was told by the company that it "made no reports and published no statements and had not done anything of the kind for the last five years."

From that beginning, as corporate policies and practices and those of the securities industry advanced and became more complex, and as the areas of warrantable public interest in corporate affairs broadened and became more clearly defined, the listing agreement advanced and expanded in scope as well as in number of requirements.

While that expansion, as measured from its beginning in 1899, has been considerable, it has also been gradual, in pace with the development of public policy in the fields of corporation finance, management, stockholder relations, and accounting. New requirements have been added only as the need for remedial measures became evident, or as they became useful in promotion of a trend toward improved practice among leading corporations. The exchange has been loath to adopt any new requirement affecting listed companies until that requirement has been proven to be not only sound in principle and an advancement of the public interest, but thoroughly workable as well.

One result of the evolutionary process by which the listing agreement has developed is that not all companies have an identical agreement with the exchange. The listing agreement as a whole is only renewed upon the occasion of an application for listing. The exact form of the agreement executed by any one company depends upon the form of agreement standard when it last made an application for listing any of its securities.

The exchange urges every listed company to be guided by the current standard form of agreement in the matters on which it bears, even though the specific agreement last executed by it may have been less comprehensive.

One of the most important and fundamental purposes and intents of the agreement, in combination with other procedures and policies of the exchange, is to assure that adequate and timely publicity is given to matters concerning listed companies of significance to the investing public. Reports made to the exchange pursuant to the listing agreement may be made available to the public and press by the exchange.

The principles underlying the agreement may also be useful as a guide to matters not specifically covered by it. In order to make it generally applicable and to hold the requirements within a reasonable number, it is restricted to matters of more or less common occurrence in the affairs of large, publicly owned companies. In all probability, there will arise from time to time unusual situations, not specifically covered by any paragraph of the agreement.

Objectives of the Listing Agreement. The listing agreement seeks to achieve the following objectives:

1. Timely disclosure, to the public and to the exchange, of information which may affect security values or influence investment decisions, and in which stockholders, the public, and the exchange have a warrantable interest.
2. Frequent, regular, and timely publication of financial reports prepared in accordance with accepted accounting practice and in adequate but not burdensome detail.
3. Provision of timely information to enable the exchange to perform efficiently and expeditiously its function of maintaining an orderly market for the company's securities, and to enable it to maintain its necessary records.
4. Preclusion of certain practices not generally considered sound.
5. Provision of opportunities for the exchange to make representations as to certain matters before they become accomplished facts.

In addition to the reports specifically provided for, the exchange urges that prompt release should be made whenever there are important developments which might affect security values or influence investment decisions of stockholders or the investing public. For example, the listing agreement requires immediate publicity in respect to dividend action or the omission of such action. On the other hand, discovery of oil, development of a new important product, or any one of a number of other possible developments are too numerous and varied for specific definition in the listing agreement. For its part, the exchange maintains a stock watching procedure to check on unusual market developments affecting listed securities. Where appropriate, listed companies may be consulted to ascertain if there are any unusual developments which should be made public.

Dual Listings and Unlisted Trading Privileges. The SEC provides the following account of development of unlisted trading on national securities exchanges.

The classical method by which stock exchanges evolved was for a group of local brokers to commence trading in any available securities. For more than half a century after the 1792 formative meeting under the "Buttonwood Tree," any security could be called up for trading on the New York Stock Exchange at the pleasure of any member. By 1856, vote of a majority of members present came to be required for the placing of a security on the list to be called, but upon the payment of a $0.25 fine any member could have any other security temporarily inserted (this was in the days before inauguration of the specialist system of trading, when stocks were traded upon call by an official of the exchange of the specific issue). Unlisted trading on the New York Stock Exchange was finally abolished in 1910, upon the recommendation of the New York Governor's Committee on Speculation in Securities and Commodities (the Hughes Committee) because most of the stocks in the unlisted department were in any event becoming listed.

The leading regional stock exchanges began trading in much the same way. For example, the rule on the Philadelphia Stock Exchange as late as 1876 was that "members may call up the various stocks of any chartered company, whether on the regular list or not." A resolution adopted by the Boston Stock Exchange in 1869 provided that "securities dealt in at the New York or Philadelphia Stock Exchanges may be called once, after the regular list, without charge..." The rule on the Philadelphia Stock Exchange by 1932 was that no securities could be admitted to unlisted trading which were not listed on the New York Stock Exchange, New York Curb Exchange (American Stock Exchange), Boston Stock Exchange, Pittsburgh Stock Exchange, or Chicago Stock Exchange.

The American Stock Exchange (known as the New York Curb Exchange until 1953) was the principal center of exchange trading on an unlisted basis. In 1931-1932, it had over 1,800 stock and 850 bond issues on its unlisted roster. As a result of the New York State Attorney General's examination of unlisted trading practices, the number was substantially reduced during 1933-1934 by removal of issues inactively traded on the exchange. The New York Produce Exchange provided facilitiies for security trading from 1928 to 1935, and had about 750 stock and 150 bond issues available for unlisted trading. The New York Real Estate Securities Exchange operated from 1929 to 1941, and had about 100 stock and 200 bond issues available for trading on an unlisted basis. A number of other exchanges on which unlisted trading occurred ceased to operate in the early days of the SEC. The net number of securities admitted to unlisted trading on the exchanges prior to 1934 is not available, but clearly ran into thousands.

The original bills for promulgation of the Securities Exchange Act of 1934 proposed abolition of unlisted trading on stock exchanges. The proposals were opposed by the American Stock Exchange and other smaller exchanges as compelling too sharp a transition. Accordingly, Congress directed the SEC to study the problem and submit its recommendations, which was done in a "Report on Trading in Unlisted Securities upon Exchanges," dated January 3, 1936. The recommendations were adopted, and the present Section 12(f) of the Securities Exchange Act of 1934 was enacted in May, 1936.

Under Section 12(f) of the act, the SEC may approve applications by national securities exchanges to admit securities to unlisted trading privileges without action on the part of the issuers, if it finds such admissions are necessary or appropriate in the public interest or for the protection of investors. Such admissions impose no duties on issuers beyond any they may already have under the act. Section 12(f) provides for three categories of unlisted trading privileges. Clause (1) provides for continuation of unlisted trading privileges existing on the exchanges prior to March 1, 1934. Clause (2) provides for granting by the SEC of applications by exchanges for unlisted trading privileges in securities listed on other exchanges. Clause (3) provides for granting by the SEC of applications for unlisted trading privileges conditioned, upon other things, upon the availability of information substantially equivalent to that required to be filed by listed issuers.

Included under Clause (1) of Section 12(f) are securities which had unlisted trading privileges on some exchanges prior to March 1, 1934. These fall into two groups: (a) those also listed and registered on some other exchange or exchanges, and (b) those admitted only to unlisted exchange trading. Issuers of securities in group (a) are subject to the statutory reporting requirements by reason of the listing and registration of their securities. Issuers of securities in group (b) may or may not be issuing public reports.

Dual listings and their share volume had become important to region stock exchanges (those outside of New York City) in the past, in some cases accounting for most of trading volume. Since July, 1964, the effective date of the 1964 amendments to Section 12(f), additional securities may be granted unlisted trading privileges on exchanges only if they are listed and registered on another exchange.

SEC Action on Withdrawals of Listings and Registration. Pursuant to Rule 12d2-1(b) under Section 12(d) of the Securities Exchange Act, applications may be made to the SEC by issuers to withdraw their securities, or by exchanges to strike any securities from listing and registration on exchanges. The SEC may not deny such applications if made in accordance with the appropriate exchange rules, but may impose such terms as it may deem necessary for the protection of investors. Also, Section 19(a)(4) of the act authorizes the SEC summarily to suspend trading in any registered security on a national securities exchange for a period not exceeding ten days if, in its opinion, such action is necessary or appropriate for the protection of investors and the public interest so requires.

Summary. Listing is no guarantee of the worth of a security, e.g., that it is of highest quality and will not fluctuate in value. It does not mean that such listed stocks will pay dividends, and be consistent earners. Nor does it even mean that such listed securites will be assured high market activity, although listing tends to promote marketability. The stock exchange concerned cannot assume responsibility for the business risk involved in operations of the companies whose securities are listed, or for fluctuations in market prices.

The advantages of listing, however, are important. The requirement of the publication of financial condition and operations provides publicity, enhancing knowledge by providing facts for informed judgment on security values. Listing prevents secret dividends, since due notice must be given of dividend payments, and assures advance notice on capital changes. The independent transfer agent and registrar requirement serves to prevent fraudulent issues and overissues. Listing tends to enhance marketability, and adds to acceptability as collateral because lenders accord importance to marketability in the event of default and necessity for disposal. Finally, the work of exchanges such as the New York Stock Exchange in prescribing accounting standards and notice of changes therein has elevated corporate practice and promoted the investor interest.

See AMERICAN STOCK EXCHANGE, NEW YORK STOCK EXCHANGE, STOCK EXCHANGES.

LISTING The admission of a security to full listing on a stock exchange, as compared with unlisted trading privileges allowed for non-fully listed securities by some stock exchanges.
See LISTED SECURITIES.

LITTLE BOARD *See* BOARD.

LIVESTOCK LOAN *See* CATTLE LOANS.

LIVING TRUST A form of TRUST by which the person who creates it (known as the trustor, donor, creator, or grantor) transfers title to certain property (securities, real estate, etc.) to a trustee with instructions to apply the income according to the terms of the trust agreement. The agreement may call for reinvestment of the income, or for a distribution of the income in whole or in part to designated beneficiaries and often to the trustor himself. The trustee renders a statement of account to the trustor at stated intervals.

This form of trust, also known as an inter vivos trust or as a voluntary trust, differs from the testamentary trust in that it becomes operative during the lifetime of the creator. It may be so drawn as to render unnecessary the making of a will, or in case only a part of the creator's property is placed in trust, his will need dispose only of the remainder. Special kinds of living trusts are retirement trusts, life insurance trusts, pension and profit-sharing trusts, etc.

Living trusts may be made revocable and subject to change, or irrevocable and not subject to change, even by the creator himself. If the trust is irrevocable, the property transferred becomes subject to the federal gift tax. If it is revocable and other incidents of ownership are retained by the settlor, the property will be subject to the federal estate tax at death of the settlor as part of his estate. These trusts make it possible for persons of means to retire from the active management of their businesses by being relieved of all details in connection with the administration of the affairs of their property. Thus the trustee becomes bound to maintain the property intact; to collect all rents, interest, dividends, and profits; and to remit the proceeds to the beneficiary, wherever he may reside.

The most usual sales arguments advanced in favor of the voluntary trust are the following:

1. It may save taxes. This is a highly technical and empirical subject, depending on the tax position, from the standpoint of gift taxes and estate and inheritance taxes, of the particular estate.
2. It gives the grantor an opportunity to see the trust in operation during his lifetime. This argument implies that if the voluntary trust proves satisfactory it can be left unchanged in details and allowed to operate similarly after the grantor's death, and if unsatisfactory it can presumably be changed or revoked. The best type of voluntary trust for older settlors is one irrevocable and nonamendable, to which this implication does not apply. The amendable type of trust could be changed, and the revocable type could be terminated and be succeeded by an altered trust during the grantor's lifetime; it is usually preferred for younger settlors during whose lives conditions might change.
3. The voluntary trust offers, through the ability of the corporate fiduciary as trustee, expert management of the investments.

The risks to which an estate is subject do not begin at the owner's death. The money which the owner has today, and of which he has settled the future disposition by will, may be gone before death of the testator and probate of the will. Assurance of provision for beneficiaries, without the danger that the loss of the settlor's fortune during his remaining lifetime would wipe out such provision, is provided effectively and surely by the living trust.

See INSURANCE TRUST.

LLOYD'S An association of English insurance underwriters, known as Underwriters of Lloyd's the oldest insurance organization in existence. Policies are not written as an organization by Lloyd's but rather by individual underwriters, supervised by the governing committee, although each policy bears the Lloyd's seal.

Starting in the seventeenth century as a small group of underwriters meeting in Edward Lloyd's coffee house, Lloyd's has become a powerful insurance association, the most famous in the world, whose members underwrite as individuals. Although the organization is particularly known for the underwriting of marine risks and such business as is incidental thereto, e.g., publication of Lloyd's Register, there is probably no class of calculable risk, however fantastic, which these underwriters will not insure. Besides underwriting risks, the organization has agents all over the world collecting information, aiding ships in distress, salvaging damaged goods, and adjusting insurance claims.

The underwriters at Lloyd's are actually the "names" (members of groups of the underwriters), who are monied individuals elected to membership upon sponsorship by the underwriting agents and interview by the committee of Lloyd's. The names are required to possess a minimum in unencumbered capital; they agree to unlimited personal liabilities for any underwriting losses allocated to each member of the group or syndicate and, on the other hand, participate in the final profits based on each individual's share of the risk. As of the end of 1989, there were approximately 32,000 investors represented in 360 more or less syndicates, of whom a significant number were located in other countries. Actual acceptance of the risks offered for underwriting by the Lloyd's brokers in the "room" is made by the underwriting agents representing their respective underwriting groups or syndicates. Eight large brokerage firms, all of which also own underwriting agencies, do about 60% of the premium income; the total number of brokerage firms is some 270. Financial statements are issued by Lloyd's every three years. Lloyd's prides itself on the financial strength of its underwriting groups.

For the protection of American underwriting liabilities, a trust fund aggregating as of December 31, 1981, over $3.5 billion, was originally established August 28, 1939, known as the Lloyd's American Trust Fund, with Citibank, N.A. of New York City as trustee. Premiums and claims arising out of policies of Lloyd's underwriters issued in the U.S. in dollars are paid into or out of such trust fund, which pursuant to the last revision of its provisions in October 1963, provides for neither variation, modification, nor declaration of closing date prior to December 31, 1987, except with the written consent of the American trustee. The fund cannot be revoked prior to December 31, 1987, and then only if Great Britain is not engaged in war with a European power.

The chairman of Lloyd's attributed Lloyd's high prestige to four reasons: (1) its policies are first-class security; (2) it has gained a reputation for prompt, just, and liberal settlement of all straightforward claims; (3) the market is readily adaptable to new risks and the changing needs and conditions of business; and (4) Lloyd's is the center of the finest shipping news service in the world, connected by tradition and by name with the great institution known as Lloyd's Register. Lloyd's Register has become the recognized information bureau for all world shipping. This register contains a list of the ships of all nations, giving their names and such descriptive details as length, breadth, depth, displacement, cargo space, horsepower, country of registry, etc.

Lloyd's has a representative or agent in every principal seaport of the world who forwards information continually in regard to vessel movements, disasters, and storms to London. These agents do not themselves underwrite insurance risks, but are representatives only of the Lloyd's organization, appointed to look after Lloyd's interests, collect information, assist in the adjusting or appraising of losses, etc.

As of the early 1990s, the 302 year-old exchange was experiencing difficult times brought on by competition, outmoded operating organizational structures and procedures, and unprecedented disasters, including the 1989 earthquake in California's Bay Area, the 1988 Piper Alpha oil-rig disaster in the North Sea, the 1988 Pan Am airline disaster over Lockerbie, Scotland, and Hurricane Hugo. As a result, Lloyd's is said to have lost more than 1,750 members in 1988 alone. Inadequate returns, 6.5% in 1986 and 2.1% in 1985, were a major factor in the exodus. Between 1981 and 1985, Lloyd reported claims of over 3.6 billion pounds and reserves against future losses of 1.35 billion pounds.

Competition intensified during the 1980s reducing already low profit margins. A major competitor is the Institute of London Underwriters, an association of more than 100 insurers, including Cigna Corp., Allianz Versicherungs AG of West Germany and Britain's Commercial Union Assurance PLC. Lloyd's difficulties have been compounded because its structure does not permit underwriters to deal directly with clients but through brokers, inhibiting quick responses to competitors. In addition, large oil, chemical, and airline companies are self-insuring many ventures which otherwise might have been insured through Lloyd's. Should the modernization procedures currently being considered by Lloyd's be successfully implemented, Lloyd's could regain its premier position as an insurer of catastrophic events.

Innovative underwriting, however, led to heavy losses in recent years for Lloyd's underwriting syndicates. Included in the losses on innovative risks were losses on coverage of computer leasing companies against cancellation of computer leases, coverage against cancellation of American participation in the Olympic Games in the U.S.S.R., insurance on arson-plagued tenements in the South Bronx, N.Y., ghetto; and coverage for a lost satellite launched by an American corporation. Moreover, on traditional Lloyd's shipping insurance, record maritime losses were incurred in 1979, including the collision and sinking of a loaded supertanker.

The South Bronx tenement losses on insurance, arranged by an authorized American agent of the underwriting syndicate at Lloyd's whose appointment evidently was not cleared at Lloyd's in accordance with internal procedure, led to the refusal of members of that underwriting syndicate to absorb the losses out of their personal resources in accordance with agreed unlimited personal liability. On the contrary, a suit by members of that syndicate was filed against the Lloyd's administration for alleged failure to follow internal controls and procedures for such an appointment.

BIBLIOGRAPHY

"Bad Luck Forces Updating at Lloyd's of London." *Business Week,* February 25, 1980.
BAILEY, E. "Lloyd's Has Second Thoughts: Restructuring Bill May Prove Overly Broad."*New York Times* June 20, 1981.
HINSEY, J. "The New Lloyd's Policy Form for Directors and Officers Liability Insurance—An Analysis." *Business Lawyer,* April 1978.
STUART, D. "Fisher Report on Self-Regulation at Lloyd's" *Best's Review,* August, 1980.
YOUNG, J. S. "New York's Insurance Industry: Perspective and Prospects." Federal Reserve Bank of New York. *Quarterly Review,* Spring, 1979.

LOAD This term has two meanings:

1. In connection with open-end investment company shares, the difference between the selling price of the shares and the net asset value of the underlying securities. No part of this charge goes to the INVESTMENT COMPANY itself. The distributor (sponsor) shares the load with the brokers who directly sell the shares to the investing public. It represents the cost of a number of factors, e.g., organizational and distribution costs including profit, advertising and promotion, and compensation to brokers as commission for sales. The load normally ranges from 6% to 9% over net asset value. A few investment companies sell directly to investors and charge no load. Either none or a nominal charge is made by open-end investment companies upon the redemption of shares.

2. In connection with electric utility operations, the peak or average use of the facilities of the company. An electric utility, for example, may have an available capacity of 1 million kW. The load placed upon the capacity will vary according to the time and volume use of electricity by the utility's customers. The maximum use at a given time is called the peak load. In the above case, if 600,000 kW is the peak usage, the load is 60% of capacity (peak load), as compared with lower average load over, for example, a 24-hour period. A utility must have capacity to supply the peak load requirements on both a diurnal and a seasonal basis with a reserve margin to spare. Thus the higher

the average consumption (load), the more optimum will be the absorption of fixed and constant costs necessitated by the investment in capacity.
See PUBLIC UTILITY INDUSTRY.

LOAD UP To purchase a security or commodity to the limit of one's financial capacity for speculative purposes. To be loaded up means to be "long" of an undesirable security or commodity which cannot be easily disposed of except at a loss.

LOAN A sum of money let out or rented by a lender to a borrower, to be repaid with or without interest. Long-term and intermediate-term loans covering a period of over one year may be formally evidenced by bonds, debentures, mortgages, deeds of trust, or certificates of indebtedness. Short-term bank loans are evidenced by notes, bills of exchange, acceptances, and loan and collateral contracts, and intermediate- or longer-term loans, by term loan agreements.

There are numerous possible classifications of bank loans, some of the most significant of which are as follows:

1. According to maturity.
    a. Demand loans, terminable at the option of either the lender or the borrower.
    b. Time loans which have a fixed or determinable maturity.
2. According to the character of the borrower.
    a. Commercial loans made to business concerns (producers, manufacturers, wholesalers, jobbers, and retailers) to supplement working capital for financing of current production and/or distribution. These loans are usually seasonal, being required only temporarily to finance the peak inventory requirements, and are usually paid after such peak is passed. Commercial loans are regarded as self-liquidating because they are repaid through the proceeds of sale of the goods financed. Such loans, therefore, are usually represented by current or quick assets of the borrower, such as receivable and inventories, which in the ordinary course of operations are converted into cash. Short-term commercial loans, usually ranging from 30 days to 6 months in maturity, but mostly preferred by commercial banks to be not over 90 days' maturity because of the requirement that they be eligible for rediscount at the Federal Reserve bank should the need arise, should, in traditional commercial banking theory, constitute the bulk of loans of a commercial bank. In recent decades commercial banks have developed substantial volume in term loans, representing advances for maximum maturities of 5 to 10 years, but amortized annually or more frequently, for such investment purposes as working capital, refunding, payment of debt, and capital assets, in competition with finance companies and life insurance companies active in term loans, as well as financing by corporations through investment bankers in the capital markets.
    b. Stock exchange or brokers' loans made to stock exchange brokers upon stock exchange collateral, amply secured pursuant to Regulation U of the Board of Governors of the Federal Reserve System where margin transactions are thus financed.
    c. Government security dealers' loans made upon the security of U.S. government securities to carry inventories and/or finance subscriptions to Treasury offerings.
    d. Other security loans, either purpose loans (made to individuals for the purchase or carrying of securities on margin), which are subject to Regulation U of the Board of Governors of the Federal Reserve System, or nonpurpose loans, which are made upon securities collateral to finance business purposes other than securities operations.
    e. Real estate mortgage loans secured by liens on improved real estate, including farm land and business or residential properties, either on real estate owned in fee simple by borrowers or, subject to rules and regulations of the Comptroller of the Currency, on leaseholds whose term extend at least 10 years beyond the maturity date of the loans.

    Formerly, under the National Bank Act, national banks were not allowed to make loans upon real estate. Lending upon real estate mortgage security was regarded as a function of saving banks since savings deposits are subject by provision in passbooks to 30 or 60 days' prior notice of withdrawal, and normally turnover and volatility of withdrawals should be much lower than for demand deposits. With inauguration of the Federal Reserve System, providing for sharply lower legal reserve requirements on time and savings deposits, the volume of time and savings deposits began to expand over time in national banks. Accordingly, Section 24 of the Federal Reserve Act has been amended some twelve times since 1916 to authorize real estate mortgage loans not to exceed (1) $66^2/3$% of the appraised value if such real estate is unimproved; (2) 75% of appraised value if such real estate is improved by offsite improvements such as streets, water, sewers, or other utilities; (3) 75% of appraised value if such real estate is in the process of being improved by a building or buildings to be constructed or in the process of construction; or (4) 90% of the appraised value if such real estate is improved by a building or buildings. If any such loan exceeds 75% of the appraised value of the real estate or if the real estate is improved with a one- to four-family dwelling, installment payments shall be required which are sufficient to amortize the entire principal of the loan within a period of not more than 30 years. The preceding specifications do not apply to guaranteed or insured mortgages. Mortgage loans may also be made upon forest tracts, not to exceed, when added to any outstanding prior mortgages, liens, and encumbrances, $66^2/3$% of the appraised fair market value of the growing timber, lands, and improvements. At the time a real estate loan is made, the aggregate outstanding real estate loans made or purchased may not exceed the unimpaired capital plus the unimpaired surplus of the bank, or 100% of the time and savings deposits of the bank, whichever is greater. Up to 10% of the total permissible amount of real estate loans need not comply with the individual loan restrictions of 12 U.S.C. 371.

    Construction loans to finance the construction of industrial or commercial buildings and having maturities of not over 60 months, where there is a valid and binding agreement entered into by a financially responsible lender to advance the full amount of the bank's loan upon completion of the buildings, and construction loans to finance the construction of residential or farm buildings and having maturities of not over 60 months shall not be considered according to the statute as loans secured by real estate, but "shall be classed as ordinary commercial loans whether or not secured by a mortgage or similar lien on the real estate upon which the building or buildings are being constructed." Such loans, however, are subject to a specific limitation under the statute of not over 100% in the aggregate of the national bank's unimpaired capital and surplus fund. By contrast, no national bank shall make forest tract loans in an aggregate sum in excess of 50% of its capital stock paid in and unimpaired plus 50% of its unimpaired surplus fund.

    But perhaps the most revealing vestige of bias against national bank lending on conventional real estate mortgage loans is the restriction of such loans, including forest tract loans, to not excess of the capital stock of the bank paid in and unimpaired plus its unimpaired surplus fund, or 100% of the amount of the bank's time and savings deposits, whichever is greater. Government insured or guaranteed mortgage loans are not subject to these limitations.
    f. Agricultural loans made to farmers for the purpose of financing the planting or harvesting of crops or the raising and marketing of livestock. Due to the longer time involved in these pursuits, these loans are of longer maturities than commercial credits. The Federal Reserve Act permits loans made upon agricultural paper, with maturity not exceeding 9 months (6 months before the Agricultural Credit Act of 1923 was passed) to be eligible for rediscount at the Federal Reserve banks. Subdivisions of agricultural loans include livestock loans and dairy cattle dealers' paper, as well as the specific types of commodities involved in the credits.
    g. Consumption loans. The loans referred to above are made for productive or investment purposes. When loans are made for the purpose of financing the purchase of goods for consumption, e.g., automobiles, household appliances,

LOANABLR FUNDS

Table 1 / Purchases and Sales of Mortgage Loans, by Lender: 1970 to 1987
(In billions of dollars. Covers all types of property.)

Lender	Purchases					Sales				
	1970	1980	1985	1986	1987	1970	1980	1985	1986	1987
Total	16.4	78.1	257.7	497.9	462.3	18.9	77.1	224.3	418.5	365.3
Savings associations[1]	3.7	13.2	65.0	71.3	64.6	1.0	16.1	103.2	164.6	123.6
Savings banks	1.8	1.2	2.9	3.4	3.5	.3	.8	6.0	13.0	12.9
Commercial banks	.8	4.9	12.0	42.8	58.2	2.0	8.4	19.2	40.1	52.6
Mortgage companies	.1	3.4	20.9	55.2	50.1	12.5	37.0	78.0	181.2	166.5
Federal credit agencies	5.7	16.3	33.0	39.5	25.2	2.6	10.5	8.0	15.9	7.2
Mortgage pools	2.7	29.4	114.3	260.4	230.6	.3	4.1	5.5	1.4	.3
Other	1.6	9.7	9.6	25.3	30.2	.3	.3	4.4	2.3	2.3

[1] Includes Federal savings banks insured by the Federal Savings and Loan Insurance Corporation.

Source: United States League of Savings Institutions, Washington, DC, *Savings Institutions Sourcebook,* annual. Data from U.S. Department of Housing and Urban Development.

furniture, etc., or of services, e.g., vacation trips, medical expenses, etc., such loans are not self-liquidating. In recent years, commercial banks have engaged in the fields of sales financing and personal, and consumers' loans in substantial volume, in competition with sales finance companies and personal loan companies.

h. Financial institutions loans made to the securities industry, finance companies, insurance companies, banks, and thrift institutions.

i. Government loans to governmental entities.

j. Industrial loans related to receivable-inventory financing, factoring, and leasing. These are often high-risk loans.

k. Export-import lending, which is often complex due to documentation requirements and trading practices.

3. According to security.

a. With collateral security, i.e., supported by valuable property which is transferable and may have a ready and reliable market, e.g., bonds, stocks, bills of lading, warehouse receipts, mortgages, real estate, etc.

b. With personal security, as evidenced by the endorsement or GUARANTY of a name or names other than the maker of the note. Such loans may be co-maker loans, two-name or three-name paper, etc.

c. Without either collateral or personal security. Contrary to popular impression, unsecured loans may actually involve less risk than those specifically secured. On the other hand, interbank loans, including advances from a district Federal Reserve bank to a member bank, are conventionally collateralized, although the business risk in the usual operational situation is minimal.

4. According to obligation or number of names responsible for payment.

a. One-name paper, for which only one party is responsible for payment.

b. Two-name paper, for which two names, either as joint makers or with one party as endorser, guarantor, or accommodation party, are responsible for payment. Trade and bankers acceptances are of necessity at least two-name paper, the acceptor becoming primarily liable and the drawer being secondarily liable (besides which there may be endorsers). For the reason that acceptances are at least two-name paper, they are generally preferred as investments, all things being equal, over single-name paper.

c. Three-name paper, etc., in which three or more names are responsible for payment. The party or parties are primarily liable, with any number of parties secondarily liable.

5. According to whether interest is paid at the time the loan is made or at maturity.

a. Loans on which interest is paid at maturity. Interest on demand loans usually is charged monthly, quarterly, or upon payment. Interest on time loans usually is chargd quarterly, semiannually, or at maturity.

b. Discounts on which the interest is deducted in advance at the time the loan is made, thus giving rise to unearned discount until earned by passage of time of the loan.

Table 2 / Commercial Bank Loans Outstanding in the US
(Billions, year-end)

	1978	1985	1986	1987
Loans outstanding	$ 782.6	$ 1,513.4	$ 1,667.3	$ 1,897.9
Total Assets	1,303.9	2,483.8	2,572.8	2,851.4
Loan / Asset Ratio	.60	.61	.65	.67

Loans may also be classified according to rate of interest, location of the borrower, business of the borrower, and whether eligible for rediscount with a Federal Reserve bank.

Exhibit Commercial loans outstanding in the United States, Total Assets, and Loan Ratio is appended. Also appended is a Table showing purchasing and sales of mortgage loans by lenders 1970-1987.

See AGRICULTURAL PAPER, AMORTIZATION LOANS, BILLS DISCOUNTED, CALL MONEY MARKET, CATTLE LOANS, COLLATERAL, COMMERCIAL PAPER, CREDIT, DISCOUNT, ELIGIBLE PAPER, FARM CREDITS ACT, FARM MORTGAGES, FEDERAL INTERMEDIATE CREDIT BANKS, LINE OF CREDIT, MORTGAGE LOANS, NATIONAL BANK LOANS, OPEN MARKET OPERATIONS, PERSONAL LOANS, SMALL LOAN BUSINESS, TERM LOANS.

LOANABLE FUNDS THEORY A supply and demand theory of the determination of nominal interest rates. Very simply, the nominal rate of interest is assumed to be determined by the demand and supply of loanable funds in the financial market.

The demand for loanable funds arises from the demands of individuals, businesses, and government. In each of these sectors of the economy, loanable funds are desired because the current spending plans of some individuals, businesses, and governments are greater than their current incomes. These deficit spenders need to borrow funds to bridge the gap between their spending plans and their current incomes.

The demand for loanable funds is assumed to be sensitive to the rate of interest that must be paid on borrowed money. The higher the rate of interest, the less they are likely to want to borrow. The demands are also affected by the level of income: the higher the income, the more likely individuals, businesses, and governments are likely to want to borrow.

The supply of loanable funds is influenced by the decisions of individual savers—persons, businesses, and governments. The separate decisions of these individual saving units regarding the amount they will save is a principal determinant of the supply of loanable funds in the market.

The decisions to supply loanable funds in the market (that is, to save and lend money) are influenced by the rate of interest and the levels of income. The higher the rate of interest, the more funds are likely to flow into the market as individuals, businesses, and governments curtail their spending plans to reap the rewards of higher interest rates.

Savings and thus the supply of loanable funds is sensitive also to the level of income. The higher the level of income the higher the level of savings and thus the supply of loanable funds.

The supply of loanable funds is also influenced by the amount of new money creation on the part of the banking system. The supply of new money is affected by the decisions of the central bank as well as the actions of individual commercial banks.

The supply and demand for loanable funds interact in the market to determine the nominal rate of interest. This interaction is illustrated in the appended exhibits: panels I and II. An increase in the propen-sity of individual economic units to save will shift the supply of loanable funds in panel I from S to S', resulting in a fall in the nominal rate of interest. Similarly, a rise in new money creation brought on by a change in Federal Reserve policy also will shift the supply schedule in panel I outward from S to S', lowering the nominal rate of interest at least in the short run.

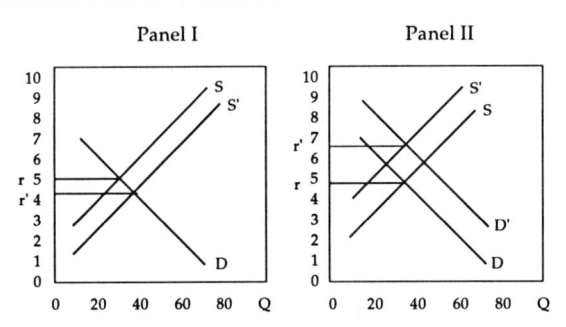

Panel I   Panel II

The effects of inflation on the supply and demand for loanable funds is illustrated in panel II of the appended exhibit. Inflation tends to increase the demands of borrowers as they try to spend to beat the next round of price increases. Accordingly, this effect is shown as a shift in the demand for funds from D to D'. Inflation also reduces the level of savings that flow into the financial system because individuals and businesses tend to invest their excess funds in real assets such as land, art, gold, and foreign currency. This effect is shown as a shift inward in the supply of loanable funds from S to S'. The net effect of the shifts in both demand and supply is to increase the nominal interest rate from r to r'.

The loanable fund theory provides a method to understand and assess the impact of certain specific changes in such variables as the level of savings, new money creation, and inflation on financial markets. As with any economic theory, it is highly abstract and in its simplest form does not allow properly for the interaction and feedback effects from the rest of the economy.

BIBLIOGRAPHY

Cooper, S. K., and Fraser, D. R. *The Financial Marketplace*, Chapter 6, 1986.

LOAN AND TRUST COMPANY   See TRUST COMPANY.

LOAN CAPITAL   That portion of the capital of a corporation furnished by long- and short-term creditors, e.g., bondholders, noteholders, banks, etc., evidenced by instruments having definite maturities, as distinguished from share capital which is contributed by the stockholders.

LOAN CERTIFICATES   See CLEARINGHOUSE LOAN CERTIFICATES.

LOAN CONTRACT   See GENERAL LOAN AND COLLATERAL AGREEMENT.

LOAN CROWD   Formerly, those brokers, members of a stock exchange, who desired either to borrow or to lend stocks and who usually met at a designated spot of the exchange.
See BORROWED STOCK, SHORT SALE.

LOAN DEPARTMENT   The department of a bank which, under the direction of the loan officers, executes the clerical details in connection with loan transactions. This involves the preparation of notes for signature, examination of collateral or guaranty contracts, and the proper keeping of the loan records. Loans usually are recorded on a card and in the loan register, loan ledger, maturity tickler, and rate sheet. The loan department is also charged with seeing that the collateral loans are adequately margined, that notes are presented for collection on the date of maturity, that collateral comparisons are made periodically, that interest statements are promptly forwarded, and that substitutions in collateral are made at the request of stock exchange borrowers.

BIBLIOGRAPHY

Bank Administration Institute. *Complete Guide to Loan Documentation*. Bank Administration Institute, Rolling Meadows, IL, 1986.
———. *A Practical Guide to the Law of Secured Lending*, 1986.
———. *Profitable Consumer Lending*, 1984.
Born, B. D. "How to Prepare a Loan Package." *National Public Accountant*, October, 1987.
Clarke, P. S. *The Complete Guide to Asset-Based Lending*. Bank Administration Institute, Rolling Meadows, IL, 1986.
———. *Complete Guide to Loan Documentation*. Bank Administration Institute, Rolling Meadows, IL, 1986.
———. *A Banker's Guide to Secured Lending and Documentation*, Bank Administration Institute, Rolling Meadows, IL, 1988.
———. *Asset-Based Lending*, 1985.
Glantz, M. "Maxims for Seasonal Lending." *Commercial Lending Review*, Spring 1988.
Groves, M. *Loan Review: A Guide*, 1987.
Holmes, E. M., and Shedd, P. J. *A Practical Guide to the Law of Secured Lending*, 1986.
Korsvik, W. J., and Meiburg, C. O. *The Loan Officer's Handbook*, 1986.
McCuistion, D. *The Prevention and Collection of Problem Loans*, 1988.

LOAN LEDGER   See LIABILITY LEDGER.

LOAN MARKET   See CALL MONEY MARKET, MONEY MARKET, REDISCOUNT RATE.

LOAN ORIGINATION   The evolving secondary market for loan servicing has helped to develop a new type of enterprise in the home finance industry in the late 1980s—companies that specialize in loan origination but do not service loans thereafter. Some traditional lenders have sold or closed their loan origination offices and retained their service function. The nonservicing loan originators are classified as:

1. Loan brokers—entities that transfer the right to fund and service loans for a fee.
2. Correspondents that originate, fund, and sell loans at a mark-up.

It is estimated that approximately one-third of the existing members of the Mortgage Bankers Association do not service loans.

Financial Accounting Standards Board Statement No. 91, "Accounting for Nonrefundable Fees and Costs Associated with Originating or Acquiring Loans and Initial Direct Costs of Leases," requires that most up-front commitment and origination fees be deferred by portfolio lenders and recognized as a yield adjustment over the life of the loan instead of being recognized in current income. Substantial amounts of direct and direct non-incremental costs must be expensed currently. For the mortgage banker, fee income and origination costs are recognized currently because the loans are sold quickly into the secondary mortgage market.

FASB Technical Bulletin No. 87-3 tightened accounting rules for determining the minimum loan servicing fee when calculating the gain or loss from selling a package of loans with servicing rights retained by the seller.

LOAN RATE   See CALL MONEY MARKET, MONEY MARKET, REDISCOUNT RATE.

LOAN REGISTER   A journal or register in which time loans are entered in the order in which they are granted. Since time loans usually are consecutively numbered, entries are in numerical as well as chronological order. This register is an original entry record and contains the complete details of the terms of each loan.
See BILLS DISCOUNTED REGISTER.

LOANING RATE   See LENDING RATE.

ENCYCLOPEDIA OF BANKING AND FINANCE

LOANS, PARTICIPATION IN See PARTICIPATION LOANS.

LOGARITHM A mathematical system of great usefulness in shortening long multiplication and division. A logarithm is defined as the exponent of the power necessary to raise a fixed number (the base) to produce a given number. Thus the logarithm of 100 is 2, because 10 raised to the second power (10^2) equals 100. Logarithms of numbers between 1 and 10 consist of decimals; of numbers between 10 and 100, the integer 1 and a decimal, of numbers between 100 and 1,000, the integer 2 and a decimal; etc. By recourse to a table of logarithms and formula, the most accurate BOND YIELD to maturity may be computed.

LOMBARD LOANS In England and certain European countries, loans secured by bonds and shares. The term derives its name from Lombard Street, the Wall Street of London, but is also used in other countries. Strictly speaking, the term usually refers to collateral loans made by the central bank to commercial banks. Lombard loans are similar to what are called collateral or "street" loans in the United States, except that Lombard loans are time loans while in the United States these loans are usually demand loans. Lombard loans are at somewhat higher interest rates than commercial loans and are limited in time duration by the policy of the central bank in regard to time duration of its discounts. The term is often used to designate collateral loans generally, without reference to its technical central reserve bank origin.
See BANK OF ENGLAND.

LOMBARD STREET An expression referring to financial London in the way Wall Street refers to financial New York. As described by one English writer, Lombard Street represents "the clearing banks of London, the discount houses, the bill brokers, and all the moneyed interests."

LONDON EQUIVALENT Under normal conditions, the price at which a security in London must be quoted to equal the New York price, being greater or less depending upon the rate of exchange, cost of shipment, loss of interest, etc. Thus ARBITRAGE in securities may be effected.

Free adjustment of London and New York security prices in the past had been impeded by transfer regulations and exchange restrictions. As of October 24, 1979, however, exchange control was abolished, except for controls on transactions with Southern Rhodesia, which exception was removed effective December 13, 1979. There are thus no exchange controls:

1. There is no prescription of currency requirements.
2. Payments for imports may be made freely.
3. Banks are allowed to engage in spot and forward exchange transactions in any currency, and they may deal among themselves and with residents and nonresidents in foreign notes and coin at market rates of exchange.
4. Payments for invisibles may be made freely.
5. Virtually all exports are free of export control, and there are no requirements affecting export proceeds.
6. Receipts in foreign currencies on account of invisibles may be retained or may be sold for sterling, and British and other banknotes may be brought into the United Kingdom freely.
7. There are no restrictions on capital transfers by residents of the United Kingdom into the beneficial ownership of residents of other countries.

LONDON EXCHANGE See STERLING EXCHANGE.

LONDON INTERBANK OFFERED RATE The rate at which banks in London place Eurocurrencies and/or Eurodollars with each other. Since the London Interbank Offered Rate (LIBOR) is a prime bankers' rate, it is often used in international banking as a basic rate, e.g., "LIBOR plus $1/8$ of 1%," in referring to an interest rate negotiated.

LONDON MONEY MARKET The London money market formerly had distinguishing institutional and operational characteristics which were summarized by the Division of International Finance of the Board of Governors of the Federal Reserve System as follows.

The Bank of England discounts directly only for London discount houses forming the London Discount Market Association who make a market for short-term government and commercial paper, and are financed by secured loans from the highly concentrated London clearing banks. If the clearing banks reduce their call loans to the discount houses, the latter in turn attempt to become liquid again by selling some of their holdings to nonbank money market institutions and, failing this, by resort to discounting at the BANK OF ENGLAND at a rate posted as the bank rate (subsequently termed the minimum lending rate).

As of August 20, 1981, however, a number of changes occurred structurally and operationally, including the following:

1. The minimum lending rate was abolished, and instead the Bank of England will seek to influence short-term interest rates in the London money market within a range not publicly disclosed by the purchase and sale of bills of exchange and government securities.
2. Acceptances of an enlarged list of banks became eligible for discount at the Bank of England.
3. The banks' reserve asset ratio was abolished, and the London clearing bank's maintenance at the Bank of England of deposits equal to 1.5% of specified liabilities was changed to a 0.5% cash ratio applicable to all banks. The Banking Act of 1979, effective October 1, 1979, had already decreed that no new deposit-taking institution to which the act would apply could legally be established without prior authorization from the Bank of England. These measures were intended to facilitate control by the Bank of England over monetary aggregates and money market operations.

The Bank of England can influence money market rates in a desired direction by open market operations or by refusing either to relieve shortages or to absorb surpluses of funds resulting from seasonal or cyclical developments. In a period of monetary restraint, the banks may thereby be unable to obtain added reserves to keep credit expansion going. In times when the bank wishes to encourage easier money market conditions, it may offer to purchase assets directly from the market at current rates. The Bank of England's transactions in the short-term securities market are carried out by its bill broker, one of the London discount houses. Longer-term securities (over five years) are handled by the bank's government broker, one of the large private brokers in the government bond market.

BIBLIOGRAPHY

BANK OF ENGLAND. *Annual Report.*
———. *Quarterly Bulletin.*
BARNETT, J. *Inside the [British] Treasury,* 1981.

LONDON RATES Rates of exchange for the different classes of sterling bills (cables; checks; 30-, 60-, and 90-day bills; etc.) as quoted in London.
See FOREIGN EXCHANGE, FOREIGN MONEYS.

LONDON STOCK EXCHANGE One of the most important of the European stock exchanges and one of the best-known security markets in the world. It was formally organized in July, 1773, as The Stock Exchange, after informal development from the time of the reign of William III, in the coffee houses in 'Change Alley, Jonathan's, and Garraway's; in the Royal Exchange; and in offices of the East India Company, Hudson's Bay Company, and New Jonathan's. The New Jonathan's building was subsequently outgrown, and a new building was opened in March, 1802, near the Bank of England. In 1853, the stock exchange building was rebuilt, and the membership enlarged to 2,000. Growth necessitated extension in 1881, when the building was enlarged to accommodate 1,500 more members. The reorganization plan of 1947, among other things, called for the rebuilding of the building and increasing facilities.

On February 9, 1970, the exchange moved from the old Throgmorton Street building that had housed the London Stock Exchange since 1853 to temporary quarters pending the completion in late 1972 of a new 26-story Stock Exchange Tower just west of the old Exchange Building. The expansion involved some $26.4 million in expenditure, including a new low building constructed on the site of the old exchange building and containing a trading floor of some 23,350 square feet, compared with 16,000 square feet in the temporary quarters and previous space of 15,000 square feet, reduced from the old quarters' full 23,550 square feet of trading floor when part of the old building was demolished in 1966.

The beginnings of automation also marked the shift to expanded quarters. On February 9, 1970, the exchange introduced its Market Price Display Service, a 22-channel closed circuit television system that transmits prices on some 700 stocks and company announcements to over 200 offices of brokers and banks. An intercommunication telephone system, linking all member firms, also was installed. Gone was the old system of waiters (pages) who, upon being telephoned by the brokerage office, would scurry to locate the broker's floor member, who in turn would dispatch a "blue button" (an apprentice wearing a blue badge) to a jobber to get the quotation desired.

Members of the exchange are of two classes, brokers and jobbers. The regulations provide that no member shall carry on business both as broker and as jobber; no partnerships between brokers and jobbers shall be created; and no member shall change his status from broker to jobber or vice versa without first giving a month's notice. No person is eligible for membership who is engaged as principal or employee in any other business, or whose wife is so engaged.

Brokers deal with the outside public, executing their clients' orders to buy and sell with the jobbers, who are analogous to dealers, making a market for securities for their own account, and unlike specialists on the New York Stock Exchange, not being bound to trade or to place public orders and interest first. The broker's compensation is the commission charged for executing the order, while the jobber's profit consists of the difference between his buying and selling prices. Jobbers are prohibited from dealing with the public.

Business on the exchange is divided into markets, each composed of a number of jobbers and brokers who specialize in securities of a certain broad class. Each market has its own separate position on the floor. A broker wishing to buy or sell securities goes to the place on the floor where the market is maintained. Many jobbers may compete in markets for particular stocks. There is no unit of trading as such, except customary market usage. On receiving an order from a client, the broker buys or sells from a jobber, as the case may be. Unless the client's LIMIT can be met, however, the order cannot be executed. If the order is executed, the broker forwards a contract note to the client in which the amount due and the settlement day are indicated.

A large number of issues are listed on the London Stock Exchange, reflecting the direct role that the exchange plays in the underwriting procedure and the absence of any separate curb or over-the-counter market. Sparse trading in options (puts and calls) also occurs. (In addition to the London Stock Exchange, there are a number of provincial stock exchanges, whereon securities are quoted that do not enjoy a London quotation.) Only a minor portion of the total list, however, will trade at any time. In corporate financing, except in cases where the security will be placed privately and held without dealings, obtaining a quotation on a stock exchange—preferably the London Stock Exchange because of its prestige—is an integral part of the financing procedure.

A stock exchange quotation for a company's securities may be obtained in connection with any of the following:

1. **Introduction.** This procedure does not involve new financing for a public company, but instead the qualification of the outstanding shares, pursuant to exchange regulations requiring publication of a statement setting forth full information about the company on the standard required for a prospectus in a public offering, where-upon the stock is authorized to be quoted on the exchange.
2. **Placing.** A company's brokers or issuing house will first place the issue with a relatively small number of clients, usually institutional investors, and then obtain a quotation therefor on the exchange, after which additional subscriptions are invited from a limited number of investors who are furnished printed particulars (also furnished to the exchange) but without the comprehensiveness of the full statement of an introduction.
3. **Public issue.** Pursuant to the Companies Act, a prospectus in full is required to be advertised and distributed in the form approved by the exchange, which will grant the quotation for such public issue. It is customary for the company's bankers to have a firm of brokers represent it before the council of the exchange and make the application, satisfying the council as to the marketing arrangements. While the stock exchange does not thereby incur any responsibility to the investor or anyone else for the documents, the fact that a stock exchange quotation is being obtained is regarded as a hallmark of respectability. Shares may not be issued at a price less than nominal (par) value (no par value stock is not authorized in England); hence the company has a vital interest in having a substantial premium over nominal value prevail in the quotation for the shares which serves as a basis for public sale.

The London Stock Exchange operates on a periodic instead of a daily settlement plan. There are two settlements per month, one near the middle and the other near the end of the month. All transactions within the period are to be settled at the next settlement day. There is some business done on a cash and immediate delivery basis, as on the New York Stock exchange. If a client does not wish to complete a purchase on the settlement day, his broker may arrange to carry payment over to the following settlement day. But for this service the client pays CONTANGO.

See SETTLEMENT DAYS.

LONG   When a buyer or holder of stocks or bonds, usually on margin, owns more than he has contracts to deliver; the opposite of short. When bulls have been buying in expectation of an advance in prices, they are long of the market or long of stock. Long stock is held by bulls in distinction to short stock needed by bears. Those who are long of stock constitute the long interest in the market.

See SHORT SALE.

LONG ACCOUNT   First read LONG. Long account or long interest, which may refer to one security or to the general market, is the aggregate of securities purchased or held, usually on margin, in expectation of a rise.

LONG BILL   A long-term bill; a bill of exchange drawn at 30 days' sight or more. Long bills are usually drawn from 60 to 90 days after sight, and in Far Eastern shipments from four to six months after sight.

See FOREIGN BILLS OF EXCHANGE.

LONG DATED BILL   *See* LONG BILL.

LONG INTEREST   LONG ACCOUNT. *See* LONG.

LONG MARKET   An OVERBOUGHT market.

LONG OF EXCHANGE   To hold more exchange on a given country than one has sold.

LONG ON THE MARKET   *See* LONG.

LONG PULL   The purchase or sale of a security with full expectation of holding it for a considerable period of time before a profit can be realized; a speculative commitment made with the realization that the position must be maintained for a relatively long period. A long pull is to be distinguished from commitments made for a turn. Speculators for the long pull naturally anticipate a larger profit on a single transaction than those who buy or sell for a turn.

LONG RATE   This term has two meanings:

1. In foreign exchange, the rate at which long bills, drawn at 30 days' sight or more and payable in another country, will be bought by the quoting bank or foreign exchange broker. Long rates are usually quoted for 30-, 60-, and 90-day bills, and are to be distinguished from the rate for cables, checks (demand drafts), and short bills. The long rate is determined as follows. The check rate is the basic rate. From this subtract interest at the discount rate abroad for the period of the tenor, and then add the necessary revenue stamps, correspondent's collection charge, etc. The result is subject to further slight modification under exceptionally heavy or slack demand for the particular class of bill.
2. In fire insurance, a rate made for a premium covering a policy to remain in force for more than one year. Thus a three-year policy is given a long rate which is twice the annual rate. The rate for a five-year policy is three times the annual rate.

LONG RUN In economics, activities are classified as long-run and short-run events. The distinction cannot be quantified into terms of calendar time. Rather, the short run is a time period in which at least one factor of production is fixed, usually capital. The long run is a time period where all factors of production are variable.

LONG SIDE *See* LONG, LONG ACCOUNT.

LONG STERLING Time bills of exchange drawn on London at 30 days' sight or more.
See LONG BILL.

LONG STOCK *See* LONG.

LORENZ CURVE A graphic device used by economists to illustrate the distribution of incomes (or similar data) for an economy, or the like. As seen from the appended figure, 60% of all U.S. families account for 40% of all earned income. If incomes were equally distributed, 40% of all families would account for 40% of earned income. The area between the 45-degree line and the Lorenz curve illustrates income inequality.

Lorenz Curve

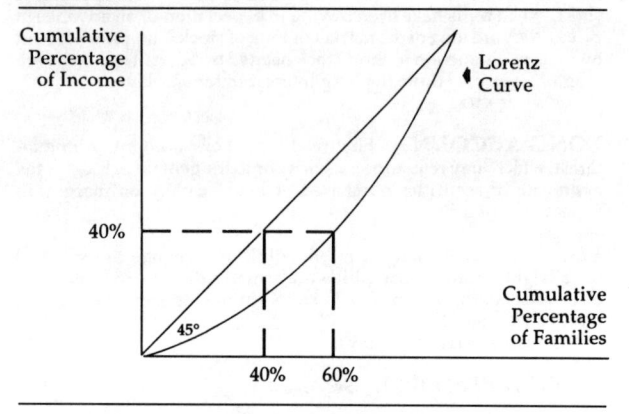

LORO ACCOUNTS In international banking, current accounts of banks with foreign banks of a foreign currency held on behalf of customers.
See FOREIGN EXCHANGE.

LOS ANGELES STOCK EXCHANGE This important regional national securities exchange consolidated with the San Francisco Stock Exchange in January, 1957, to form the present PACIFIC COAST EXCHANGE.

LOSSES Decreases in equity (net assets) from peripheral or incidental transactions of an entity and from other transactions and other events and circumstances affecting the entity during a period except those that result from expenses or distributions to owners. Losses can arise from such transactions and events as the sale of investments in marketable securities and from the disposition of used equipment. Losses can be classified as operating or nonoperating, depending on their relation to the enterprise's major ongoing or central operations.

The chief losses to which a bank is subject are due to bad loans and investments; forged, altered, or stop payment checks; counterfeit, defalcations or thefts by dishonest employees; and trading losses in foreign exchange or in securities. Some of these losses can be insured against.
See BAD DEBTS, CARE OF SECURITIES.

LOSS LEADER A marketing strategy in which a product is sold close to or below cost to induce customers to purchase other items with higher profit margins while in the store. Loss leaders have been used occasionally to market financial services but without marked success.

LOTTERY BOND A bond which may be called by lottery for redemption prior to maturity, for which the holder is paid, in addition to the principal and interest, a substantial varying cash bounty much larger than the ordinary small premium involved in a callable bond. In consideration of such lottery premiums, the lottery bonds may pay no current interest. Lottery bonds bear the usual identification numbers, and certain numbers are selected for repayment at the specified lottery premiums each year, thus introducing the gambling feature which makes them attractive to a certain class of investors. Advertisements of the sale of lottery bonds are prohibited from the United States mails and shipments are prohibited from interstate commerce. Lottery bonds, therefore, cannot be legally marketed in this country, but they have been a customary form of financing for the U.S.S.R. and its satellite nations in recent years, and have also been common among French and Belgium internal municipal issues.

LOTTERY TICKETS An act of Congress approved December 15, 1967 (P.L. 90-203) added Section 9A to the Federal Reserve Act, effective April 1, 1968, to prohibit state member banks from fostering or participating in gambling activities, and particularly the sale of lottery tickets inauguarated by various states.

A similar statute is 12 U.S.C. 25A, which reads in detail as follows:

(a) A National bank may not:
  (1) Deal in lottery tickets;
  (2) Deal in bets used as a means or substitute for participation in a lottery;
  (3) Announce, advertise, or publicize the existence of any lottery;
  (4) Announce, advertise, or publicize the existence or identity of any participant or winner, as such, in a lottery.
(b) A National bank may not permit:
  (1) The use of any part of any of its banking offices by any person for any purpose forbidden to the bank under subsection (a) of this section, or
  (2) Direct access by the public from any of its banking offices to any premises used by any person for any purpose forbidden to the bank under subsection (a) of this section.
(c) As used in this section:
  (1) The term "deal in" includes making, taking, buying, selling, redeeming, or collecting.
  (2) The term "lottery" includes any arrangement whereby three or more persons (the "participants") advance money or credit to another in exchange for the possibility or expectation that one or more but not all of the participants (the "winners") will receive by reason of their advances more than the amounts they have advanced, the identity of the winners being determined by any means which includes:
     (A) A random selection;
     (B) A game, race, or contest; or
     (C) Any record or tabulation of the result of one or more events in which any participant has no interest except for its bearing upon the possibility that he may become a winner.
  (3) The term "lottery ticket" includes any right, privilege, or possibility (and any ticket, receipt, record, or other evidence of any such right, privilege, or possibility) of becoming a winner in a lottery.
(d) Nothing contained in this section prohibits a National bank from accepting deposits of, cashing or otherwise handling checks or other negotiable instruments, or performing other lawful banking services for a State operating a lottery, or for an officer or employee of that State who is charged with the administration of the lottery.
(e) The Comptroller of the Currency shall issue such regulations as may be necessary to the strict enforcement of this section and the prevention of evasions thereof.

Penalty. The penalty for knowingly violating the above referenced statutes, as well as Section 20 of the Federal Deposit Insurance Act, shall be a fine of not more than $1,000 or imprisonment for not more than one year, or both.

LOUVRE ACCORD An international agreement arising out of a meeting of the finance ministers and central bank governors of six major industrial countries (Canada, France, the Federal Republic of Germany, Japan, the United Kingdom, and the United States) on

ENCYCLOPEDIA OF BANKING AND FINANCE

February 22, 1987, at the Palais du Louvre in Paris. The accord promised intensified efforts at economic policy coordination to promote more balanced economic growth and to reduce existing imbalances. In the communique (known as the Lourvre Accord), the parties to the agreement noted the progress that had been made in achieving sustainable, noninflationary expansion. They stated that "surplus countries committed themselves to following policies designed to strengthen domestic demand and to reducing external surpluses." Concurrently, "deficit countries committed themselves . . . to encourage steady, low-inflation growth while reducing their domestic imbalances and external deficits. The parties further agreed to cooperate "to foster stability of exchange rates around current levels."

LOWER OF COST OR MARKET An accounting procedure that provides the basis for reporting inventory and investments in the financial statements. Inventory and equity marketable securities are frequently valued in the financial statements at lower of cost or market. In applying the lower-of-cost-or-market method, the cost of the ending inventory or portfolio of marketable equity securities, is determined by an appropriate method, and is compared with market value at the end of the period. If market value is less than cost, an adjusting entry is made to record the loss and restate the inventory or securities. For inventory applications, market in "lower of cost or market" is interpreted as replacement cost with upper and lower limits that cannot be exceeded. For example, market or replacement cost should not exceed the net realizable value (i.e., estimated selling price in the ordinary course of business less reasonably predictable costs of completion and disposal); and market should not be less than net realizable value reduced by an allowance for an approximately normal profit margin.

When applied to marketable equity securities, the lower-of-cost-or-market method is applied separately to short-term and long-term portfolios of securities. Losses in market value related to the short-term portfolio are reported as part of income from continuing operations for the period. Losses in market value related to the long-term portfolio are reflected directly in the shareholders' equity section of the balance sheet in an owners' equity contra account. The lower-of-cost-or-market method is a conservative accounting method that avoids valueing inventory or marketable equity securities on the balance sheet at more than replacement cost. The method is somewhat inconsistent in that market decreases are recognized, while market increases are not recognized. However, most accountants prefer to reflect the loss in the utility of an asset in the period the impairment is first recognized and can be estimated while gains should be recognized only when realized.

LYONS Liquid yield option notes. *See* FINANCIAL INSTRUMENTS: RECENT INNOVATIONS.

M

M1 See MONEY SUPPLY.

M2 See MONEY SUPPLY.

M3 See MONEY SUPPLY.

MACMILLAN COMMITTEE The Committee on Finance and Industry, appointed by the British government on November 5, 1929, "to inquire into banking, and finance and credit, paying regard to the factors both internal and international which govern their operation, and to make recommendations calculated to enable these agencies to promote the development of trade and commerce and the employment of labor." It was composed of leading and distinguished experts in banking and finance and was headed by Lord MacMillan.

One of the findings of this committee, which submitted its report in midsummer, 1931, was that the gold reserve of the BANK OF ENGLAND should be not less than L150 million compared with gold reserves reported at the close of August, 1931, of some L134 million. On September 21, 1931, England went off gold when the Bank of England was relieved of the obligation to sell gold at fixed statutory price.

See GOLD STANDARD.

MACROECONOMICS That branch of ECONOMICS which deals with the economy as a whole, including such topics as national income determination, employment and unemployment, productivity, economic growth, government budgets and national debt, the level of prices, inflation, fiscal policy and monetary policy, international balance of payments and exchange rates, foreign trade and capital flows, and other aggregative data domestic and international. By contrast MICROECONOMICS primarily deals with the theory and facts of market structures and the operation of individual firms and industries that constitute the supply side, as well as the theory and behavior of consumers.

BIBLIOGRAPHY

BARRO, R. J. *Macroeconomics*. John Wiley and Sons, Inc., New York, NY. Latest edition.
DORNBUSCH, R., and FISCHER, S. *Macroeconomics*. McGraw-Hill Book Co. Latest edition.
GORDON R.J. *Macroeconomics*. Scott Foresman Co., Glenview, IL, 1987.
HALL, R. E., and TAYLOR, J. B. *Macroeconomics: Theory, Performance, and Policy*, 1985.
SARGENT, T. J. *Dynamic Macroeconomic Theory*, Harvard University Press, Cambridge, MA, 1987.

MAIL PAYMENT A means sometimes employed in remitting small sums of money abroad, differing in no essential respect from remitting by means of check. For example, if A in New York wished to remit $100 worth of francs to B in Paris, A would apply to his bank in New York to provide the payment to B in Paris, requesting the bank to charge his account for the amount and costs. The bank then would ascertain the current rate for francs and compute the number of francs that $100 would buy. To this would be added the cost of postage. In addition, because mail payment remittances are for small amounts, rates are somewhat higher than for checks; and when mail payments are made in dollars, a small commission is charged in addition to postage.

The issuing bank then writes to its Paris correspondent asking it to pay B in Paris the specified number of francs and to charge its account therefor. The Paris correspondent then makes payment by means of the most convenient method. (1) sending B a check drawn on itself, (2) sending actual currency by registered mail, or (3) requesting B to call personally for the funds.

MAIL TELLER The teller of a bank (sometimes known as the fourth teller) in charge of receiving, sorting, proving, and accounting for deposits which arrive by mail. Among larger city banks, deposits from individual customers and correspondent banks located out of town are as heavy in volume as deposits received over the receiving teller's window. A large clerical force is needed to attend to the detail necessary to dispose properly of these deposits, and it is the duty of the mail teller to supervise this work. A large part of this detail consists of sorting the checks according to the various collection agencies and proving the deposits with the deposit slips. Some will be collected through the local clearinghouse, others by messenger, others through the transit department, and the home debits will be charged to customers' accounts. Usually the mail teller also administers the work of sorting clearinghouse items among the various clearinghouse banks and has charge of the outgoing exchanges.

MAINTENANCE Costs or procedures that are incurred or undertaken to maintain tangible assets (buildings, equipment, systems, structures, and similar assets) in their operating conditions but do not increase the asset's economic benefits. In railroad accounting, maintenance of way and structures and maintenance of equipment, two expense items in railroad income accounts which are of more than passing interest to the investor in railroad securities because to an important extent their provision is controllable by railroad management.

The maintenance account in railroad retirement accounting determines the proportion of gross revenues provided for depreciation and repairs. Originally, in the system of accounts prescribed for railroads by the Interstate Commerce Commission in 1914, depreciation of fixed improvements was left to the discretion of railroad management. However, depreciation of equipment has been required since 1928, and effective January 1, 1943, the Interstate Commerce Commission has also required railroads to depreciate their fixed property (except for track accounts).

See RAILROAD EARNINGS.

MAJORITY STOCKHOLDERS The stockholders representing the controlling interest in a corporation. Ownership of over 50% of the stock is necessary for this purpose, but in large publicly owned corporations, effective control is usually achieved by minority holdings combining their votes with effective use of proxies from remaining scattered small holders.

In CUMULATIVE VOTING, MINORITY STOCKHOLDERS owning less than a majority of voting stock may be able to vote in at least one of the directors of the corporation.

See PROXY, MINORITY INTEREST.

MAKER The person (or persons) who executes a promissory note and thus is primarily liable on the instrument. The maker of a negotiable instrument by making it engage that he will pay it according to its tenor and admits the existence of the payee and his then capacity to endorse (Sec. 60, Uniform Negotiable Instruments Law). The maker of a check or draft is known as the DRAWER.

ENCYCLOPEDIA OF BANKING AND FINANCE

MAKING A BOOK When SPECIALISTS receive limit and stop orders, either with time limits or as open orders, such orders are entered in sequence in the book, a ring binder for each stock assigned to the specialist which limits the detail of the orders; price, number of shares (in number of round lots), name of the broker for whom entered, and type of order. The left-hand page of the ring binder is the buy side, listing the orders appropriately under the price groupings, which are graduated by eighths (e.g., for price 50, printed at the top of the page, space is provided under each one-eighth variation—and for the entering of the orders) with the lowest bids at the top of the page. The right-hand page is the sell side, similarly listing the orders, with the lowest offers at the top of the page and highest offers at the bottom of the page.

Orders at the market may also be handled by the specialist.

The book is the working tool of the specialist, its contents being confidential in view of the buying and selling data it contains. The book's entries measure the specialist's brokerage function; his dealings for own account, relative to the orders in the book, are restricted by rules.

MAKING A MARKET Standing ready to quote firm quotations (bid and asked) to buy and sell particular issues, particularly on the OVER-THE-COUNTER-MARKET. This usually involves maintaining a position (inventory) on the issue concerned.

In stock exchange practice, the floor members of commission brokers perform a brokerage function for their principals (the public customers for whom orders are executed on the floor). Under the specialist's bid or specialist's offer technique authorized in recent years for facilitating transactions in large blocks on the New York Stock Exchange and not as part of the regular auction market on the floor, the specialist is making a market in such blocks for his own account. Specialists and the floor members are also allowed to trade for their own accounts, subject to restrictions.

On the NEW YORK STOCK EXCHANGE, the registered competitive market makers (RCMM) is a member who has specific obligations to trade for his own or his firm's accounts—when called upon by an exchange official—by making a bid or offer that will narrow the existing quote spread or improve the depth of an existing quote. An RCMM may also be asked to assist a commission broker or a floor broker in executing a customer's otherwise unexecutable order.

In underwriting practice, when the syndicate manager engages in stabilization operations, subject to rules of the Securities and Exchange Commission, to prevent the open market price of the security from declining below the public offering price and thus ruining the public offering, he will engage in buying and selling and thus to this extent be involved in making a market. This trading account of the syndicate manager, lasting for the duration of the syndicate, will also absorb any offerings of the just publicly offered security which instead of staying placed with buyers are thrown back on the market during the offering period.

MAKING A PRICE When a seller quotes a price that he is willing to accept at the request of the buyer, or vice versa. This term is also used to refer to a practice on the LONDON STOCK EXCHANGE.

MAKING-UP PRICE The delivery price of a security. On the London Stock Exchange, it is the price at which a security is carried over from one settlement day to another.

MALTHUSIAN THEORY OF POPULATION The Reverend Thomas Malthus advocated in his *Essay on the Principle of Population* (1798) that unchecked population increases at a geometric rate and subsistence increases only at an arithmetic rate. Accordingly, population growth will eventually lead to starvation. Malthus underestimated humans' ability to innovate and to control their population growth.

MANAGED CURRENCY Essentially, any currency that in-volves application of central bank credit policy (MONETARY POLICY) and the latter-day concept of FISCAL POLICY. In the U.S. under the Employment Act of 1946 and the Full Employment and Balanced Growth Act of 1978 (also known as the Humphrey-Hawkins Act), these perhaps more conventional means are to be coordinated in the achievement of the goal of maximum employment, production, and stability of purchasing power consistent with growth.

In the more technical sense, however, managed currency schema particularly refer to more unconventional means of money management. In the 1930s, the term became associated particularly with currencies not anchored to gold (not on established gold par values or inconvertible) which were thus more susceptible to manipulation of their international exchange values and/or domestic purchasing powers. Managed currency practices thus included going off gold and the manipulation by exchange stabilization funds of the FOREIGN EXCHANGE values of currencies relative to the subject country's currency, with the aim of achieving either stabilized low levels or fluctuating levels relative to particular currencies, so as to stimulate exports artificially (at least temporarily, before other nations retaliated with similar measures and there ensued competitive exchange depreciation). Among nations, chronic debtors in their international balance-of-payments position, as well as inframarginal nations experiencing adverse trends in their gold flow and balance of payments and other nations resorting to defensive use of these devices, would resort to exchange depreciation, stabilization funds, trade restrictions, EXCHANGE RESTRICTIONS, inconvertibility, and other chimerical departures from the discipline of a metallic standard with established par values.

Floating Exchange Rates. When the Second Amendment to the Articles of Agreement of the International Monetary Fund became effective on April 1, 1978, all member countries were required to notify the fund of the exchange arrangements that they intended to apply thereafter. Many countries have accordingly revised their exchange rate systems in the new era internationally of abandonment of maintenance of the par value of a currency in terms of gold. (*See* FOREIGN MONEYS.)

Theoretical Systems. The problem of achieving stabilization of purchasing power of the money unit, while still remaining on the gold standard (even if variable), was the gist of Professor Irving Fisher's *Stabilizing the Dollar* (1920). Under this scheme, the currency would consist of certificates redeemable into gold, but the gold content of the certificate (e.g., the dollar) would be varied: (1) whenever the price level *fell*, the gold content of the dollar would be *raised* (therefore, on given gold stock resulting in *fewer* dollars as money supply); (2) whenever the price level *rose*, the gold content of the dollar should be *lowered* (thus increasing the money supply). To foil speculators, a 1% spread would be maintained between the buying and selling price of gold in terms of the dollar certificates redeemable in gold. The gold content would change 1% every two months for as long as the increase or decrease would be necessary to correct the fluctuation in the price level. This scheme ignored velocity as a factor in the money supply and presupposed domestic sensitivity to redemption values. Internationally, the changes in gold content would of course mean variation in par values and exchange rates (for example, a lowering of the gold content by thus cheapening the dollar might stimulate exports). Domestically, a lowering of the gold content by creating "free gold" would lead to additional issuance of certificates, expanding the currency supply, and thus (on principles of the quantity theory of MONEY) arrest a decline in prices. The scheme primitively ignored the fact that the bulk of the money supply is not currency but bank demand deposits.

Dr. Fisher's later idea, *100 Per Cent Money* (1935), therefore addressed itself to bank deposit currency. Ignoring control by variation in legal reserve requirements which are assumed fixed, this scheme proposed that all demand deposits be covered by 100% cash reserve. To obtain such complete cash reserves, banks would have to sell their earning assets to a monetary authority or pledge them to it on loans for the purpose. This would in effect transfer control over supply of demand deposits to the monetary authority, which could thereafter permit expansion in demand deposits by buying securities in the open market or contract the supply of demand deposits by selling securities in the open market, these operations supplying or reducing cash reserves in the banks. The justification for this scheme was eliminating the unstabilizing effects of bank credit expansion and contraction upon business activity and prices, and substituting stabilization through the monetary authority. The multiple expansion power of fractional reserve requirements (below 100%) would be eliminated by adoption of the 100% reserve; in the name of stability, the ability of the banking system to finance credit needs that were a multiple of dollars per dollar of cash reserves would be eliminated. The plan would also ignore time deposits, which would continue on the fractional reserve system; in fact, the plan stressed continuation of time deposits and the types of credit extended by time deposit institutions (which include commercial banks)—a loophole as far as the alleged objective of eliminating instability was concerned. By hindsight, this plan appears to have been an example of the extremes to which the search for stability could lead, for the basis of bank credit expansion (excess reserves) may be conventionally managed by variation in legal reserve requirements and open market operations without destroying the multiple expansion power of the banking system.

In his *Storage and Stability* (1937), Dr. Benjamin Graham proposed a commodity-reserve currency, the standard being a defined quantity of various commodities, rather than a monetary metal; e.g., a $100 unit might be defined in terms of specific quantities of wheat, corn, cotton, wool, rubber, coffee, tea, sugar, tobacco, petroleum, coal, wood pulp, pig iron, copper and tin, warehouse receipts for which would be bought and sold by the monetary authority for money, thus adjusting the money supply relative to prices for such basic commodities in the interest of stability of the price level. Instead of one monetary metal to worry about, there would be 15 commodities for the monetary authority to be concerned with, each with its own supply and demand characteristics and yield variations. This plan was expanded by Dr. Graham to an international basis in his *World Commodities and World Currency* (1944). In the 1930s, this plan appealed to those concerned with the farm problem as an additional means of price support for commodities for such monetary purposes.

BIBLIOGRAPHY

FISHER, I. *Stabilizing the Dollar*, 1920.
———. 100 Per Cent Money, 1935. Graham, B. *Storage and Stability*,1937.
———. *World Commodities and World Currency*, 1944.

MANAGEMENT The process by which human efforts are coordinated and combined with other resources to accomplish organizational goals and objectives. Management has been defined as "the art of getting things done through people" (Mary Parker Follett). Management requires an understanding of the economic principle of division of labor, which breaks tasks down into subtasks, and the coordination of effort, which reorganizes the subtasks into an efficient whole.

Managers perform five basic functions: planning, organizing, directing, leading, and controlling as noted in the appended exhibit.

Planning is the means of coordinating an idea into a reality—that is, determining the goals and objectives of the organization and the means of attaining them. Planning involves making decisions about a course of action and establishing priorities relating to the action.

Organizing and directing an enterprise requires that managers establish patterns of relationships (structures, hierarchies) among people and other resources that work to produce an output or accomplish a common goal or objective. Organizing and directing relate to the flow of work through the organization under guidance.

Leadership is required if organizational goals are to be achieved. Leadership influences persons to act for a common end or purpose. A skillful leader knows the personality, character, wants, behavior patterns, and organizational requirements of subordinates.

Controlling involves taking appropriate actions to ensure that organizational goals and objectives are planned and carried out, i.e., that the firm attains maximum effectiveness.

Management by objectives (MBO) is a relatively recent innovation in management that often improves performance and morale. MBO involves the joint establishment of objectives and performance review procedures in an effort to improve productivity. This principle is based on the theory that people find satisfaction in their work and accept responsibility for their performance. To be effective, MBO should have the approval and commitment of top management, provide for participation by subordinates in the setting of objectives, a degree of self-determination in implementing plans, and a periodic review of performance.

BIBLIOGRAPHY

ABBOUD, A. R. *Money in the Bank: How Safe Is It?*. Dow Jones Irwin, Inc., Homewood, IL, 1987.
ANSOFF, H. I., ed. *Strategic Management*. Halsted Press, New York, NY, 1979.
BANK ADMINISTRATION INSTITUTE. *Commercial Bank Management*, Bank Administration Institute, Rolling Meadows, IL, 1985.
———. *The Effective Bank Supervisor*, 1985.

The Management Process

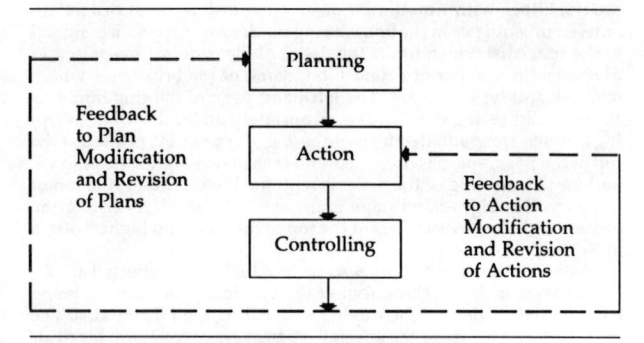

```
    ┌──────────► Planning ◄──┐
    │                ▼        │
Feedback          Action    Feedback
to Plan             ▼       to Action
Modification   Controlling  Modification
and Revision        │       and Revision
of Plans            │       of Actions
    └───────────────┘
```

———. *The Effective Branch Manager*, 1980.
———. *Job Descriptions for Financial Institutions: A Comprehensive Reference Guide*, 1987.
———. *Human Resources Management for Banks*, 1987.
———. *Personnel Policies: Guides for Bank Management*, 1980.
———. *The Product Management Handbook: A Practical Guide for Bank Product Managers*, 1983.
———. *Quality Management in Financial Services*,1985.
———. *Teller Management: Policies and Practices*, 1988.
———. *Effective Teller Management*, 1987.
———. *Modern Teller Training 3* (Video and workbook formats).
———. *A Banker's Guide to Interactive Terminals*, 1987.
BERRYMAN-FINK, CYNTHIA. *The Manager's Desk Reference*. AMACOM, New York, NY, 1989.
BITTEL, L. R., and RAMSEY, J. E., eds. *Handbook for Professional Manager*. McGraw-Hill Book Co., New York, NY, 1985.
Business Software Database. Information Sources, Inc., Berkeley, CA. Online data base.
California Management Review.
Decision Science.
JANNOTT, P. F. *Improving Bank Profits: How to Decrease Operating Expenses and Increase Income*. Bank Administration Institute, Rolling Meadows, IL, 1988.
JOHNSON, S., and BLANCHARD, K. *The One Minute Manger*. William Morrow and Co., Inc., New York, NY, 1982.
Journal of Management.
Journal of Operational Research.
Operations Research.
Organizational Behavior and Human Decision Processes.
Organizational Dynamics.
MCMANHON, R. J. *Bank Marketing Handbook*. Bankers Publishing Co., Boston, MA, 1986.
OLDHAM, F., JR., and SEGLIN, J. L. *Job Descriptions in Banking*, Bank Administration Institute, Rolling Meadows, IL, 1988.
Personnel.
Personnel Management.
Personnel Psychology.
RAU, E. S. "Managing Diversity: Banking's Next Strategic Challenge." *Bankers Magazine*, May-June, 1988.
REIDENBACH, R. E. and GRUBBS, M. R., *Developing New Banking Products: A Manager's Guide*. Prentice-Hall, Inc., Englewood Cliffs, NJ, 1986.
VOLK, R. T. "The Changing Role of the Branch Manager." *Bankers Magazine*," May-June, 1988.
WILLIAMSON, M. *Bank Record Retention Guidelines*. Bank Administration Institute, Rolling Meadows, IL, 1988.

MANAGEMENT ACCOUNTING A segment of accounting that deals specifically with how accounting data and other financial information can be used to manage businesses, governmental agencies, or not-for-profit entities. Management accounting focuses primarily on internal management needs. Its major function is to assure that an entity's resources are used efficiently and effectively. It provides financial information to help management make sound economic decisions. It maintains the accounting records, prepares financial statements, compiles analyses, interprets cost data, prepares special reports for planning and control decisions, and coordinates budgeting and reporting. The essence of management accounting is that it should provide the basis for a system of accountability.

Unlike financial accounting, management accounting is not directly affected by generally accepted accounting principles. The management system must ultimately motivate and assist managers in attaining their organizational objectives in a timely and efficient manner.

BIBLIOGRAPHY

COLE, L. *Management Accounting in Banks.* Bank Administration Institute, Rolling Meadows, IL, 1988.
HANSEN, D. R. *Management Accounting.* PWS-Kent Publishing Co., Boston, MA, 1990.

MANAGEMENT ADVISORY SERVICE Management advisory services, or simply advisory services, consist of advice and assistance on organization, personnel, planning, operations, controls, and other managerial and administrative concerns provided to clients by accountants, management consultants, and others. Such services provide advice and technical assistance to help clients improve their operations. When providing forecasting services, accountants must adhere to general professional standards such as competence, due care, planning and supervision, and sufficient relevant data. Technical standards are established for management advisory service engagements. For example, for an audit client a practitioner must not assume the role of management or any role that might impair objectivity. Responsibilities for management advisory services are now found primarily in AICPA Statements for Management Advisory Services (SSMAS), which became effective in 1982.

MANAGEMENT AND BUDGET, OFFICE OF By Executive Order 11541 of July 1, 1970, all functions transferred to the President of the United States by Part I of Reorganization Plan 2 of 1970 were delegated to the director of the Office of Management and Budget. Such functions are to be carried out by the director under the direction of the President. The office's functions include the following:

1. To aid the President to bring about more efficient and economical conduct of government service.
2. To assist in developing efficient coordinating mechanisms to implement government activities and to expand interagency cooperation.
3. To assist the President in the preparation of the U.S. Budget and the formulation of the fiscal program of the government.
4. To supervise and control the administration of the budget.
5. To conduct research and promote the development of improved plans of administrative management and to advise the executive departments and agencies of the government with respect to improving administrative organization and practice.
6. To assist the President by clearing and coordinating departmental advice on proposed legislation and by making recommendations as to presidential action on legislative enactments, in accordance with past practice.
7. To assist in the consideration and clearance—and, where necessary, in the preparation—of proposed executive orders and proclamations.
8. To plan and promote the improvement, development, and coordination of federal and other statistical services.
9. To plan and develop information systems to provide the President with program performance data.
10. To plan, conduct, and promote evaluation efforts to assist the President in the assessment of program objectives, performance, and efficiency.
11. To plan and develop programs to recruit, train, motivate, deploy, and evaluate career personnel.
12. To keep the President informed of the progress of activities by agencies of the government with respect to work proposed, work actually initiated, and work completed, together with the relative timing of work between the several agencies of the government, all to the end that the work programs of the several agencies of the executive branch of the federal government may be coordinated and that the moneys appropriated by the congress may be expended in the most economical manner with the least possible overlapping and duplication of effort.

Summary. The preceeding official listing of functions indicates the emphasis on managerial functions (in addition to the budgetary functions) of the new OMB many of which had already been functioning in the old Bureau of the Budget.

MANAGEMENT BY EXCEPTION A management control system that focuses on matters that require a manager's attention. Reports to managers frequently show whether actual results are in accordance with planned accomplishments, and whether the resources required to produce the planned accomplishments are actually in line with the plan. The reporting period must be short enough to allow managers to correct situations that are out of control.

MANAGEMENT BY OBJECTIVES (MBO) A management control system in which managers and workers jointly establish objectives over a specified time period and meet periodically to evaluate their progress in attaining the established goals. Most difficulties associated with MBO have arisen from too strict adherence to the original plan and a lack of flexibility in the system.

MANAGEMENT LETTER A written correspondence from the auditor to an official of the client containing suggestions and recommendations for improving procedures, operations, and controls relating to auditing, tax, and management services. The letter is usually addressed to the board of directors, its audit committee, the chief executive officer, or to a designated official.

MANAGEMENT REPRESENTATIONS Assertions or representations by management to its auditors associated with the following:

1. Existence or occurrence of assets or liabilities on a particular date or whether recorded transactions actually occurred within a period.
2. Completeness—whether accounts and transactions that should be in the financial statements are included therein.
3. Rights and obligations—whether assets are the rights of, and liabilities the obligations of, an entity on a particular date.
4. Valuation or allocation—whether assets, liabilities, revenue, and expense amounts in the financial statements are proper.
5. Presentation and disclosure—whether this is proper classification, description, and disclosure of financial statement items and categories.

The auditor must use professional judgment to determine how much to rely upon such representations when determining the nature, timing, and extent of audit procedures to be used.

MANAGEMENT THEORIES Cultural values and technological developments are primary elements of most management theories. Several major theories include:

1. Classical organization theory.
2. Scientific management.
3. Modern behavioral organization theory.
4. Information systems theory.
5. Quantitative management science.

Modern management theory includes elements of each of these theories and, in that sense, can be considered eclectic.

Classical organization theory focused attention on the functions or processes of management. Some principles of management frequently associated with the classical theory include authority, discipline, unity of command, chain of command, unit of direction, centralization, order, and equity.

Scientific management had its origins with Frederick W. Taylor who applied principles of engineering to designing financial incentive systems to motivate workers. Time and motion studies were outgrowths of Taylor's scientific management theory. Such studies contributed to improvements in the utilization of human and natural resources, primarily at the shop level.

Modern behavioral organization theory focuses on human behavior: individual, group, organizational, and environmental. With the oncoming of the computer age, management theory began to deal with management information systems as they impacted on management practice and thought. Organizations are conceptualized as a set of interrelated systems, each with its set of inputs, processing, and outputs. How systems operate and how systems interface with each other and the external environment are major interests of information systems theories.

Quantitative management science focuses on decision making and uses economic effectiveness criteria measured in terms of costs as a major objective. Mathematical models and computers provide powerful analytical tools and techniques which are widely used in quantitative management science's approach to management.

BIBLIOGRAPHY

BAKER, KENNETH R. and DEAN H. KROPP, *Management Science*. John Wiley & Sons, New York, 1985.

MANIFEST A formal schedule or statement of a cargo taken on board a ship, prepared by the manifest clerks under the direction of the ship's master. It is in reality a summary of all the bills of lading covering the ship's cargo and is at once an operating, clearance, entry, and accounting document. Its preparation is required and its form prescribed by the United States and by governments of the various foreign countries. A manifest is sworn to before the customs officials of the port of debarkation. One copy is forwarded to the customs officials at the port of entry, another to the ship owners, and a third retained as a part of the records of the ship.

MANIPULATION In the broadest sense, the artificial advancing and depressing of prices by those who have the ability to do so. The course of prices on an organized market could be artificially influenced in greater or lesser degree by numerous devices, including pools (inside and outside), rings, cliques, wash sales, matched orders, bucketing corners, and unlisting legitmate securities, as well as by disseminating tips, false reports, or "alleged information." Manipulative practices on national securities exchanges are prohibited by Sections 9 and 10 of the Securities Exchange Act of 1934, and such practices on commodity exchanges are prohibited by Sections 4b and 4c of the Commodity Exchange Act. In addition to being subject to such regulation by the Securities and Exchange Commission and the Commodity Futures Trading Commission, securities exchanges and commodity markets by rules of their own prohibit such practices and engage in self-policing. Despite such regulation and self-policing, the spreading of tips and rumors is quite impossible to prevent, so that the best protection against such still remains to inquire into the sources of information so as to distinguish between fact and rumor. The ultimate purpose of manipulation is to profit at the expense of the lambs (inexperienced speculators). Excessive or improvident speculation, whether based on unfounded rumor or on established facts, is not manipulation.

See BUCKET SHOP, CLIQUE, CORNER, MATCHED ORDERS, POOL, RING, TIP, WASH SALE.

MANUALS Periodic publications containing financial statistics and other descriptive information and used as reference sources by brokerage firms, financial institutions and investors. The term particularly refers to the services published by the leading publishers of factual and interpretive investment data—STANDARD & POOR'S CORPORATION (Standard & Poor's Corp., subsidiary of McGraw-Hill, Inc.) and Moody's (MOODY'S INVESTOR SERVICE, INC., subsidiary of Dun & Bradstreet, Inc.) A summary of these services follows.

Standard & Poor's. Publication services include *The Outlook* (weekly investment advisory service); *S&P Investment Advisory Survey* (weekly); *Stock Guide; Stock Summary; Bond Guide; Industry Surveys* (with complementing Statistical Section); *Corporation Records* (six volumes and Daily New Section), the basic reference for factual financial information on corporations); *Earnings Forecaster* (weekly new and revised earnings estimates on various companies); *Standard N.Y.S.E. Stock Reports; American Stock Exchange Stock Reports; Unlisted Stock Reports; Facts and Forecasts (daily); Bond Outlook; Municipal Bond Selector; Opportunities in Convertible Bonds; Convertible Bond Reports; Analysts Handbook; Transportation Service; Dividend Record; Status of Bonds; Called Bond Record; Registered Bond Interest Record; CUSIP Master Directory; Poor's Register of Corporations, Directors and Executives; Security Dealers Directly; Commercial Paper Reports Service; International Stock Report; Financial Green Book* (monthly summary of most recent financial results and market data on leading foreign and domestic stocks and bond issues); *Review of Securities Regulations; Trendline Publications* [daily basis] *Stock Charts; Current Market Perspectives;* and *OTC* [over-the-counter] *Chart Manual.* Computer-derived and automated services include ISL [Investment Securities Laboratory] Punched Cards; Corporate Pricing Service; ISL Price Tapes; Punched Card Dividend Service; Municipal Pricing and Leasing Services; Punched Card Registered Bond Interest Service; Punched Card Index Library; ISL Stock Price Books; and White's Tax Exempt Bond Market Ratings. An affilated company, Standard & Poor's Counseling Corp., provides individual and institutional clients with a continuing, personalized, and confidential investment service.

Moody's. Moody's bound volumes, supplemented by news supplements for ring binders, include *Municipals and Government, Public Utilities, Transportation, Industrial, Banks and Finance,* and *OTC* [over-the-counter] *Industrials.* Other factual services include *Moody's Dividend Record and Bond Record; Moody's Stock Guide; Moody's Bond Guide;* and *Moody's Handbook of Common Stocks.* Advisory and interpretive services include Stock Survey; Bond Survey; Moody's Advisory Reports; Moody's Personal Management Service; Moody's Supervisory Service for Banks and Trust Companies; and Moody's Estate and Trust Service.

Other. Among other financial publications in active use with brokerage firms, institutions, and investors are

Alfred M. Best Co.—*Best's Insurance Reports* [manuals] *on Life, Fire and Marine,* and *Casualty and Surety Companies; Best's Digest of Insurance Stocks.*
Bond Buyer—*Directory of Municipal Bond Dealers; Municipal Bond Sales Book.*
Commerce Clearing House, Inc.—Loose-leaf tax and business law reporting service.
Commodity Research Bureau, Inc.—*Commodity Yearbook.*
Dun & Bradstreet Publications Corp.—*Exporter's Encyclopedia.*
Fairchild Publications—*Fairchild's Financial Manuals; Industrial Textile Directory.*
Financial Information, Inc.—Daily Called Bond Service; Financial Daily Card Service, Financial Stock Guide.
Robert D. Fisher—Manuals on obsolete securities.
Fitch Investors Service, Inc.—Fitch Rating Register.
Monthly Stock Digest Service.
National Quotation Bureau—National Daily Quotation Service; National Quotation Bond Summary; National Stock Summary; National Municipal Bond Summary.
R. L. Polk & Co.—*Polk Bankers' Encyclopedia.*
Prentice-Hall, Inc.—Loose-leaf services on taxes and regulation.
Rand McNally & Co.—*Rand McNally Bankers' Directory.*
Research Institute of America, Inc.—Investors Service; *Tax Guide.*
The Spectator—*The Spectator Magazine; Insurance Yearbook.*
United Business Service—Weekly service on business and investing developments.
Value Line (Arnold Bernhard & Co., Inc.)—Value Line Investment Survey; Value Line Convertible Survey; Value Line OTC [over-the-counter] Special Situations Service.
Walker's Manuals—*Walker's Manual of Western Corporation and Securities; Vol. I, Financial; Vol. II, Industrial and General* (with manual supplements), *Walker's Weekly Newsletter.*

See BUSINESS FORECASTING SERVICES, FINANCIAL MAGAZINES, FINANCIAL NEWSPAPERS, MERCANTILE AGENCIES.

MAPS Market auction preferred stock. *See* FINANCIAL INSTRUMENTS: RECENT INNOVATIONS.

MARGIN Legally, a payment on account of a purchase, conferring ownership with its attendant risks and privileges upon the buyer, but subjecting him to a lien on the purchase to the extent that credit is advanced to finance the full purchase price secured by the purchase. Such margins are dollar margins; e.g., where a customer deposits in a brokerage account $1,000 on the purchase of 100 shares of a stock at $25 per share, his dollar margin is $10 per share or ten points. Equity margins—the type specified by the margin requirements regulation of the Board of Governors of the Federal Reserve System and by stock brokers in modern times—are measured not by the amount of cash deposited on the purchase but by the ratio between the customer's equity and the current market value of the purchased securities (on which the lending broker has a lien for the credit extended). Equity margins may be computed readily by the appended formula:

$$\frac{\text{Current market value of the security purchased} - \text{Debit balance}}{\text{Current market value of the collateral}} = \text{Equity margin}$$

Thus, if 100 shares of stock were bought at a total purchase cost (including commissions) of $50 per share on 50% margin, the current market value of the collateral (the stock bought is pledged for the margin credit) of $5,000, minus the debit balance (the amount owed by the buyer for the margin credit extended, which will be charged interest monthly) of $2,500, divided by the current market value of the shares ($5,000) indicates percentage margin of 50%. Should the market price decline to $40 per share, the percentage margin would be 37.5% (new current market value of $4,000, minus the debit balance of $2,500 [ignoring interest], divided by current market value of $4,000).

A further distinction as to margins is the difference between initial margins and maintenance margins. Margin requirements prescribed by the Federal Reserve Board of Governors are only initial margins (although the board has the power to prescribe maintenance margins); should the market price of stock bought on margin decline subsequent to purchase, the account would become restricted, but the board's regulations do not require the posting of additional equity by the purchaser to restore the percentage margin to the initial margin. However, Regulation T of the board of governors does not prevent a brokerage firm from imposing additional requirements, particularly maintenance requirements. Rule 431 of the New York Stock Exchange (NYSE) provides a maintenance margin rule that must be applied by a broker; and Section 220.7(e) of Regulation T provides that nothing in the regulation shall prevent brokerage firms from imposing maintenance requirements.

For the purpose of effecting new securities, transactions and commitments, the NYSE rule requires that margin shall be at least the greater of the amount specified in the regulations of the Board of Governors of the Federal Reserve System or by the above NYSE requirements, or such great amount as the exchange may from time to time require for specific securities, with a minimum equity in the account of at least $2,000 except that cash need not be deposited in excess of the cost of any security purchased. These minimum equity and purchase provisions shall not apply to "when distributed" securities in cash accounts and the exercise of rights to subscribe.

In addition to assigning a current loan value to margin stock generally, Regulations T and U of the board of governors permit special loan values for convertible bonds and stock acquired through the exercise of subscription rights.

Margin requirements of both the Board of Governors of the Federal Reserve System and the New York Stock exchange also apply to short sales. In figuring percentage margins on short sales the following formula may be used:

$$\frac{\text{Net proceeds of short sale} + \text{Initial Margin}}{\text{Current market value of stock}} - 1 = \text{Percentage margin}$$

Thus if 100 shares of a stock are sold short at $50 per share net (net proceeds after deduction of commissions, stock transfer tax, and SEC fee).

$$\frac{\$5,000 + \$2,500}{\$5,000} - 1 = 50\%$$

Subsequently, should the stock *rise* (unfavorable for the short seller) to $55 per share, the percentage margin would then be

$$\frac{\$5,000 + \$2,500}{\$5,500} - 1 = 36.4\%$$

BIBLIOGRAPHY

BOARD OF GOVERNORS OF THE FEDERAL RESERVE SYSTEM. *Annual Report.*
CURLEY, M. T. *Understanding and Using Margin*, 1989.

MARGIN ACCOUNT Customers buying stocks on MARGIN or engaging in short sales must have a general account (sometimes called a margin account), which also may be used for cash transactions. the strictly cash account permits only cash transactions.

In opening the general account, the customer signs the customer's agreement or margin agreement, which provides for the following standardized clauses:

1. *Hypothecation and rehypothecation clause:* "Any and all securities or commodities, or contracts relating thereto, nor or hereafter held or carried by you in any of my accounts (either individually or jointly with others), are to be held by you as security for the repayment of any liability to you in any of said accounts, with the right on your part to transfer moneys or securities from any one of my accounts to another when in your judgement such transfer may be necessary, and all such securities and commodities may, from time to time, and without notice, be pledged and repledged by you, either separately or in common with other securities or commodities, for any amount due upon my account(s), or for any greater amount, without retaining in your possession or control for delivery a like amount of similar securities or commodities."

    Hypothecation is the pledge of the securities to the broker as collateral for credit extended on margin purchases. Rehypothecation, in turn, is the use by the broker of the securities thus pledged to obtain security loans from banks. It is a rule of the New York Stock exchange that a member may not pledge a customer's securities for more than is "fair and reasonable in view of the indebtedness of the said customer to the said member firm or corporation." It will be noticed also that the above clause permits commingling of the customer's securities by the broker for the purpose of obtaining security loans from banks. Commingling consent must be expressly given by the customer.

2. "You shall have the right, whenever in your discretion you consider it necessary for your protection, or in the event that a petition in bankruptcy or for appointment of a receiver is filed by or against me or an attachment is levied against my account(s) with you (whether carried individually or jointly with others), to buy any or all securities and commodities which may be short in such demand for margin or additional margin, notice of sale or purchase, or other notice or advertisement, and any such sales or purchases may be made at your discretion on any exchange or other market where such business is then usually transacted, or at public auction or private sale; and in case of a sale at public auction or on an exchange, you may be the purchasers for your own account, it being understood that a prior demand, or call, or prior notice of the time and place of such sale or purchase shall not be considered herein provided, and it being further understood that I shall at all times be liable for the payment of any debit balance owing in any of my accounts with you upon demand, and that I shall be liable for any deficiency remaining in any such account(s) in the event of the liquidation thereof in whole or in part by you or by me."

    Although this language permits the broker to sell out a margin customer without notice and thus is a one-sided agreement (most customers do not bother to read the fine print of these provisions), in practice brokers do give notice on calls for more margin and notice of sale.

3. "The monthly debit balance in my account(s) shall be charged, in accordance with your usual custom, with interest at a rate which shall include the average rate paid by you on your general loans during the period covered by such balances respectively and any extra rates caused by market stringency, together with a charge to cover your credit service and facilities."

    In practice, interest on debit balances on small accounts of accounts with low activity tends to be somewhat higher than the current cost of credit to the broker, with the larger and more active accounts being given the benefit of variations in the cost of money to the broker. Interest compounds unless paid.

ENCYCLOPEDIA OF BANKING AND FINANCE

4. "All communications, whether by mail, telegraph, telephone, messenger, or otherwise, sent to me at my address as given to you from time to time shall constitute personal delivery to me." This provision covers the provision of law otherwise that call for margin and notice of sale must reach the attention of the customer.

See MARGIN BUYING.

MARGINAL ANALYSIS
Marginal analysis is the single most pervasive concept in economics. Decision making is described in terms of marginal benefits and marginal costs, that is the additional (marginal means additional) benefits associated with a decision and the additional costs associated with that same decision.

This marginal rule is applicable to a number of important economic questions. Marginal benefits and costs are considered when deciding how to allocate scarce resources (land, labor, air, water, etc.). Similarly, firms seeking to maximize profits do so by producing a level of output where marginal revenue equals the marginal cost of production. Also, decisions between alternative investments are made on the basis of the marginal return from each.

MARGINAL EFFICIENCY OF CAPITAL
That rate of discount which equates present value of net expected revenue from an investment of capital to its cost; a Keynesian concept. The concept plays a major role in the Keynesian theory of investment; the level of investment is determined by the marginal efficiency of capital relative to the rate of interest. If the marginal efficiency rate is higher than the rate of interest, investment will be stimulated; if not, investment will be discouraged. A fall in the rate of interest will stimulate investment, assuming the decline is below the given marginal efficiency rate. Marginal efficiency returns should then rise (based on higher anticipations of returns from investment), and such rise above a given prevailing rate of interest will stimulate investment.

The concept is based on the ordinary mathematical technique of computing present value of a given series of returns discounted at a specified discount rate. If an investment in equipment cost $4,450 and is expected to yield returns of $1,000 per year for five years, such returns,

$$\frac{\$1,000}{1+r}, \frac{\$1,000}{(1+r)^2}, \frac{\$1,000}{(1+r)^3}, \frac{\$1,000}{(1+r)^4}, \text{ and } \frac{\$1,000}{(1+r)^5}$$

will equate with the cost of $4,450 for the investment if the rate of discount (marginal efficiency of capital) is 4%. If the prevailing interest cost of money to finance such investment is actually below 4%, the investment will be stimulated; if it is above 4%, the investment will be discouraged.

In income-expenditure analysis, the marginal efficiency of capital is a prime factor in determining whether businesses are going to borrow and invest. The rate of interest is a passive factor because businesses do not borrow merely because the interest rate is low. A stable and material gap between the marginal efficiency of capital and the rate of return will result in an increase in the level of economic activity.

The marginal efficiency of capital is determined to some extent by the expectation of profits compared to the replacement cost of capital assets. The marginal efficiency of capital can ordinarily be improved by an increase in productivity, sales, or prices, or by a decrease in the costs of production. Generally, it is the relationship between the marginal efficiency of capital and the rate of interest that causes expansion, equilibrium, or contraction in the economy.

The term net expected revenue anticipations refers to net return over depreciation. Productivity theories of investment and their justification of interest date back at least to the work of the famous Austrian Bohm-Bawerk and the early work of Dr. Irving Fisher of Yale, but in the Keynesian schema the marginal efficiency of capital was adapted as one of the three major aspects of the Keynesian model, the other two being the liquidity preference concept of determination of interest rates and the consumption function.

See KEYNESIAN ECONOMICS.

MARGINAL PRODUCT
The additional output produced by an additional unit of input. For example, the marginal product of labor is the additional output produced by adding one additional unit of labor to the production process, holding capital fixed. The marginal product of capital is the additional output produced by adding one additional unit of capital—to the production process, holding labor fixed.

MARGINAL PRODUCTIVITY THEORY OF INCOME DISTRIBUTION
John Bates Clark (1847-1938) advocated in *The Distribution of Wealth* (1899) that factors of production should be paid according to their marginal product. Those factors contributing more to output should be rewarded accordingly. While this proposition is the basis for much of modern microeconomic theory, it is difficult to translate Clark's prescription into practice owing to the difficulty in measuring marginal products precisely.

MARGINAL PROPENSITY TO CONSUME OR SAVE
The portion of each additional dollar earned that consumers allocate to consumption as opposed to savings. Thus, the marginal propensity to consume (mpc) plus the marginal propensity to save (mps) sum to unity:

$$mpc + mps = 1.$$

In the U.S. economy, the mpc has historically been about .90. It has averaged slightly higher than .90 during the 1980s.

MARGINAL REVENUE
The additional revenue earned by a firm from selling one additional unit of its product. If a product can always be sold at the same price, then the additional revenue earned from selling one additional unit of the product equals the product's price. In general, however, a firm will have to lower its price to increase its quantity demanded (according to the law of demand); therefore, marginal revenue will decrease as additional units are sold. For a firm to maximize profit, economics teaches that the firm should produce to the point where marginal revenue equals marginal cost.

MARGINAL ROAD
A railroad whose earnings available for charges just about cover fixed charges, thus rendering it vulnerable to any decline in earning power. Bonds of marginal roads are in the speculative class and normally sell at large discounts.

See RAILROAD BONDS.

MARGIN BUYING
When the purchaser furnishes only a specified fraction of the total purchase price of the securities bought and the broker furnishes the balance, charging interest on that amount (the debit balance) until the customer either sells the stock or pays off the loan and thus takes up the stock. The broker in turn may obtain the funds for carrying margin accounts from banks by rehypothecating the securities bought on MARGIN by customers with the customer's permission, granted in advance in the customer's agreement for opening a MARGIN ACCOUNT.

With the passage of the SECURITIES EXCHANGE ACT OF 1934, on June 6, 1934, margin requirements on national securities exchanges became subject to regulation by the Board of Governors of the Federal Reserve System, Section 7 (a) of the act states the objective of such regulation:

"For the purpose of preventing the excessive use of credit for the purchase or carrying of securities, the Federal Reserve Board shall, prior to the effective date of this section and from time to time hereafter, prescribe rules and regulations with respect to the amount of credit that may be initially extended and subsequently maintained on any security (other than an exempted security) registered on a national securities exchange." The purpose is to prevent the excessive use of credit, not to influence the level or trend of stock prices. Also, the board is given power in the act to prescribe initial as well as maintenance margins; it has prescribed only initial margins from the beginning of such regulation.

Regulation T of the board of governors, pursuant to Sections 7 and 8(a) of the act, became effective October 1, 1934. It applies to extension and maintenance of credit by every member of a national securities exchange and to every broker and dealer who transacts a business in securities through the medium of any such member.

On May 1, 1936, Regulation U of the board of governors, pursuant to Section 7 of the Securities Exchange Act of 1934, became effective. It applies to loans by banks for the purpose of purchasing or carrying any stock registered on a national securities exchange.

Regulation G of the board of governors, "Collection of Noncash Items," was revoked effective September 1, 1967, when the board of governors concurrently revised its Regulation J, "Collection of Checks and Other Items by Federal Reserve Banks." A new regulation G was promulgated by the board of governors, effective March 11, 1968, applicable to credit by persons other than banks, brokers, or dealers for the purpose of purchasing or carrying registered equity securities.

Regulation X of the board of governors was adopted by the board in 1971 to carry out provisions of the Foreign Bank Secrecy Act of 1970. Regulation X implements Section 7(f) of the act and generally applies to borrowers obtaining credit from within the United States or borrowers obtaining credit from outside the United States who are (1) United States Persons, (2) foreign persons controlled by United States persons, or (3) foreign persons acting on behalf of or in conjunction with United States persons.

Special margin requirements for bonds convertible into stocks were also adopted by the board of governors effective March 11, 1968.

Effective July 8, 1969, Regulations T, U, and G were amended principally to implement the provisions of P.L. 90-437, adopted in 1968, which authorized the board of governors to expand the margin regulations to cover credit extended for the purchase of over-the-counter stocks having specified market activity characteristics and company size and stock distribution criteria, and bonds convertible into such stocks (the board of governors issues the limit of such specific over-the-counter stocks).

Regulations T, U, G, and X limit the amount of credit to purchase and carry margin stocks that may be extended on securities as collateral by prescribing a maximum loan value which is the specified percentage of the market value of the collateral at the time the credit is extended; thus margin requirements are the difference between the market value (100%) and the maximum loan value.

Brokers. Section 8 of the act makes it unlawful for any member of a national securities exchange, or any broker or dealer transacting business in securities through the medium of any such member, to borrow in the ordinary course of business on any security (other than an exempted security) registered on a national securities exchange except (1) from or through a member bank of the Federal Reserve System, (2) from any nonmember bank which shall have filed with the Board of Governors of the Federal Reserve System an agreement undertaking to comply with all provisions of the act, or (3) in accordance with any rules and regulations of the board of governors permitting loans between such members and such brokers or dealers.

Exempt securities (U.S. government securities, direct or guaranteed; state and municipal securities; etc.) are not subject to the margin requirements of Regulation T. Thus the much lower margins prescribed by the New York Stock Exchange would apply to its members as minimum margins on such exempt securities.

Banks. Since members of national securities exchanges and brokers or dealers doing business through them must borrow from member banks of the Federal Reserve System or nonmember banks which have agreed to abide by the act, the Board of Governors of the Federal Reserve System comprehensively controls stock market credit at the bank level by Regulation U, which reaches borrowing by brokers and direct borrowing by customers on purpose loans (loans to finance the purchasing or carrying of securities on margin).

Regulation U controls loans from banks by brokers both for the latter's own accounts and for the purpose of financing customers' margin accounts; loans to brokers for their own accounts are subject to the Regulation U margin requirement (set by the board of governors), but loans to brokers representing rehypothecation of customers' securities carried for the account of such customers are *not* subject to Regulation U margin requirement (set by the board of governors), instead being subject to the bank's own voluntary margin requirements (varying with the quality, mix, and market characteristics of the securities offered as collateral), which normally are less than the board's margin requirement.

Other bank loans on securities collateral exempt from the Regulation U requirement on margin include loans by banks to any bank, loans to dealers to aid in the distribution of securities to customers (not through an exchange), loans to brokers and dealers to meet emergencies, day loans, loans to finance arbitrage transactions of customers of the broker, or loans to odd-lot dealers

Nonpurpose loans, i.e., loans not for the purpose of purchasing or carrying securities on margin, are exempt from Regulation U margins, the bank's own voluntary margins applying, even if the securities are registered on a national securities exchange and non-exempt if used for purpose loans. Such loans are extended to firms and individuals for a variety of purposes. An administrative problem arises in connection with proper policing of such nonpurpose loans to ensure that this type of loan on securities does not develop into a loophole for circumvention of Regulation U.

Regulation U applies specifically to the making by banks of any loans secured directly or indirectly by any *stock* for the purpose of purchasing or carrying any stock registered on a national securities exchange. Thus, it does not apply if the purpose is to finance the purchase or carrying of any bonds registered on a national securities exchange, or any unlisted stocks or bonds. The bank's own voluntary margins would apply in such cases. For example, convertible bonds listed on a national securities exchange could be purchased by an individual and financed by a bank loan at the bank's own margin requirement, and Regulation U would not apply even if the convertible bonds were converted into a stock listed on a national securities exchange during the duration of the loan.

Other Lenders. Persons other than banks, brokers, or dealers who in the ordinary course of business extend or arrange to extend credit totaling $50,000 or more in any calendar quarter, or have outstanding at any time during the calendar quarter a total of $100,000 or more in such credit, secured directly or indirectly, in whole or in part, by collateral that includes any registered equity securities, are subject to the provisions of Regulation G, including registration with the Board of Governors of the Federal Reserve System through the district Federal Reserve bank. Among the provisions of the regulation is that Regulation G lenders obtain from the borrower a signed statement providing for, among other things, an indication of the purpose of any stock-secured loan, that they determine in good faith that the statement was correct, and that they sign it as so accepted. This requirement also applies to banks (Regulation U), but since loans by brokers or dealers generally are for the purpose of purchasing or carrying securities, no statement of purpose would ordinarily be required in connection with such loans.

Regulation X. Title III of the Foreign Bank Secrecy Act (P.L. 91-508) which was enacted October 26, 1970 to become effective November 1, 1971, made margin regulations of the Board of Governors of the Federal Reserve System for the first time directly applicable to U.S. borrowers and to foreign borrowers controlled by them or acting for them. In July 1971, the board of governors published for comment proposed amendments to its Regulation T, U, and G, to implement the new statute. The board of governors reports that the comments received prompted it instead to combine the changes in a new regulation, designated Regulation X.

The board of governors summarizes Regulation X as in essence providing that subject borrowers obtaining credit in the U.S. or abroad must comply with the margin regulation applicable to the lender, or if none applies, they must treat the borrowing as if it were subject to Regulation G, the margin regulation applicable to extensions of credit by persons other than banks, brokers, or dealers. Exemptions were provided for (1) individuals permanently resident abroad who obtain $5,000 or less in purpose credit (for the purpose of purchasing or carrying securities on margin) at any one time or in any one year, (2) foreign subsidiaries of U.S. corporations making markets in Eurobonds, and (3) extraordinary circumstances in which the board of governors may deem it justifiable to grant individual exemptions by order, if the obtaining of the credit is consonant with the purpose of the Foreign Bank Secrecy Act.

Leverage in Margin Buying. With high margin requirements, the leverage possible on margin trading is low. The purpose of buying on margin is to increase the possibility of gain with available cash. The advantage of buying on margin can be illustratd by the following example. Assume a speculator with cash of $10,000 wishes to purchase as much as possible of a certain stock selling at $100 per share. If he bought the stock for cash and delivery, he would be able to buy only 100 shares (ignoring commission costs). On a 10% margin, however, such as prevailed in the late 1920s, he would be able to buy 1,000 shares, the broker putting up $9,000 and the speculator $1,000 per 100 shares. In this way, the speculator could purchase ten times as much stock as he could by purchasing it outright. If the stock rises one point, a profit of $1,000 is made, whereas in an outright purchase the profit would be only $100. This advantage of leveraged possibility of gain, however, is offset by the disadvantage of equal possibility of loss, and therein lies the danger of low margins. If the stock declines one point, the speculator loses

$1,000. The broker will carry the stock provided there is adequate margin to protect the account; a broker will rarely carry a stock until the minimum maintenance (percentage) margin of the New York Stock Exchange is reached (25%), particularly in an active and rapidly declining market.

When a customer's percentage equity in a margin account falls below a level considered adequate by the broker, a MARGIN CALL is sent to the customer; if there is not a prompt response, the broker has the right to sell out the customer either wholly or partially, the latter in order to restore the account to a properly margined position. The customer under New York Stock Exchange rule may not be permitted by a member firm to make a practice of effecting transactions requiring initial or additional margin and then furnishing such margin by liquidation of the same securities or other securities. The required margin must be obtained as promptly as possible, but in any event before the end of the four full business days following the date of the transaction. Cash will of course cover the margin call; if securities are used, they must be listed securities with the necessary loan value; e.g. with 50% margins, the loan value is 50% of market value of such securities tendered in response to a margin call.

Restricted Accounts. An unrestricted account is one whose percentage equity is at least the prevailing board of governors' initial margin. A restricted account is one whose equity percentage has dropped below the board's initial margin; the board's regulation does not require that a margin call be sent to the customer to restore the margin to the initial margin level, but it does restrict the freedom of action of the customer with respect to such an account. Some of the restrictions are as follows.

The general rule is that no withdrawal of cash or registered or exempted securities will be permitted if the adjusted debit balance of the account would exceed the maximum loan value of the securities in the account after such withdrawal.

The following exceptions to the general rule are available only in the event no cash or securities need to be deposited in the account in connection with a transaction on a previous day, and none would need to be deposited thereafter in connection with any withdrawal of cash or securities on the current day:

1. Registered or exempted securities may be withdrawn upon the deposit in the account of cash (or registered or exempted securities counted at their maximum loan value) at least equal to the retention requirement (50% of current market value for registered securities other than exempted issues and maximum loan value for exempted securities) of the securities withdrawn.
2. Cash may be withdrawn upon the deposit in the account of registered or exempted securities having a maximum loan value at least equal to the amount of cash withdrawn.
3. Upon the sale (other than short sale) of registered or exempted securities in the account, there may be withdrawn in cash an amount equal to the difference between current market value of the securities sold and the retention requirement of those securities.

Substitutions in a restricted account, i. e., changes in holdings by purchases and sales on the same day, may be made provided the net result would not cause any change in the status of the account in regard to existing margin requirements.

Special subscription accounts, in connection with the exercise of stockholders' rights to subscribe to additional shares, call for satisfaction of initial and maintenance margin requirements and thereafter for four quarterly payments equal to 25% of the difference between initial equity in the account and initial margin percentage of market value of the stock at the time of the subscription.

Special miscellaneous accounts may be credited with the excess over margin requirements in a margin account occurring by reason of a rise in market value (which must be withdrawn on the same day it occurs) or dividends (which must be withdrawn in 35 days).

NYSE Margin Trading. The New York Stock Exchange (NYSE) points out that prior to July 8, 1969, brokers were permitted to extend regulated credit on stocks and convertible bonds listed or traded only on registered exchanges. Effective July 8, 1969, the Federal Reserve amended the regulations to permit brokers also to extend regulated credit on a selected list of stocks traded over the counter (OTC). OTC margin stocks are those determined by the Board of Governors of the Federal Reserve System to have characteristics similar to stock registered on national exchanges.

Margin customers whose equity is below the prevailing federal initial margin requirement are considered restricted. Retention requirements determine the amount of funds that restricted margin customers must apply to their debit balance following a sale of margined securities.

In addition to federal regulations of margin credit, the NYSE has certain credit requirements of its own. No person may open a margin account with a member firm without depositing a minimum account or its equivalent in securities. The exchange also sets requirements for the maintenance of margins, as distinguished from the initial margin requirements of the Federal Reserve Board. Generally speaking, a customer's equity may at no time be less than 25% of the market value of securities carried. (Member organizations frequently have house rules which are higher than 25%.) Should his equity fall below this level, the customer is required to put up more margin or the securities are sold by the broker. Also, the exchange may impose higher margin requirements in special circumstances on individual issues which show a combination of volume, price variation, and turnover of unusual dimensions.

These requirements are intended to discourage the use of credit for undue speculation in certain issues and to assist in maintaining fair and orderly markets. Also, customers whose accounts show a pattern of "day trading"—i.e., purchasing and selling the same listed issue on the same day—are required to have the appropriate margin in their accounts before transactions in securities subject to the special margin requirements can be effected. Generally, the NYSE has imposed special margin requirements infrequently since 1972. In 1980, one issue had a 100% requirement for a short period early in the year.

Commodity Margins. In speculative commodity futures trading, the situation is essentially different from that in securities because of the character of futures trading. All such trading is done on margin unless and until delivery of the cash commodity should occur. Original margins, usually averaging about 15% of the original purchase or sale, are required by futures commission houses, and additional margin is called for whenever price declines reduce the margin, usually to 75% of the original requirements. Should, in his judgment, the speculator accept delivery of the actual commodity, much more substantial margin is required. The commodity exchanges generally prescribe minimum margins, and futures commission houses are free to require higher margins than the minimum. In commodity exchange regulation, margins are not prescribed by the Commodity Futures Trading Commission, but regulation includes restriction on daily trading limits, as well as the maximum long or short positions that may be held by any speculative account at any time in any one commodity and the amount of speculative trading that may be done by any person on any one day. The segregation of funds belonging to customers, including margins deposited and profits on past transactions, is required on the books of futures commission houses.

Summary. Margin buying has been criticizd in the past, at times of severe declines in securities, as a factor exaggerating price movements and as a factor involving undue use of bank credit for such speculative purposes. Congress, instead of abolishing it and thus eliminating a type of activity making for broader markets, placed it under regulation (Securities Exchange Act of 1934) so that unduly low margins and excessive use of bank credit might be prevented.

MARGIN CALL   A notice sent by a broker to a customer, or by a bank to a borrowing banker, requiring additional security or a partial payment of a loan in order to offset or make good a loss in the value of the collateral due to a decline in the market price of securities pledged. The following is an example of a typical margin notice:

"As the present market value of the securities pledged to us as collateral against your indebtedness is not sufficient to give the customary margin, please send us at once additional satisfactory securities or cash to make good the margin, and oblige."

The additional margin should be forthcoming immediately. If not, the broker or the bank has the right, in accordance with the loan or margin agreement, to sell the securities pledged in order to satisfy the loan and any interest due, returning the remaining balance if any, or changing a deficiency to the borrower.

See MARGIN ACCOUNT.

MARGIN NOTICE MARGIN CALL.

MARGIN OF SAFETY The extent or degree by which the principal of a loan or issue of securities is protected by property equities and earning power. The first requisite of a sound investment is safety of principal, and the second is regularity (or prospect of maintenance) of the income. Strictly speaking, not even the best investment is absolutely safe either as to principal or as to income, and any sum invested must be regarded as carrying some risk. There is a wide range of risks in the multifarious investment media available, and the degree of safety—or, inversely, the degree of risk—is measured by the margin of safety, also sometimes called the factor of safety. Specifically, margin of safety refers to separate factors.

Excess Value. First, the phrase may apply to the excess value (in dollar amount or in percentage) of the specific lien security, specific pledge of assets or collateral, or general (but unpledged) assets supporting a loan or security issue. For example, in conservative mortgage finance the amount of the mortgage loan is rarely more than $66^2/_3\%$ of the appraised value of the mortgaged property. Thus a mortgage loan of $20,000 on a property appraised at $30,000 would have a margin of safety of $10,000 or 50%. The protection afforded this mortgage loan may also be viewed as the amount by which the value of the property could shrink and still leave a sum sufficient to pay off the mortgage. The degree of protection from this viewpoint, which might more logically be called the margin of risk, would also be $10,000, but $33^1/_3\%$ instead of 50%.

In the case of brokers' call loans on stock exchange collateral, banks require a specific pledge of stocks (or stocks and bonds mixed) which at market value equal from 120 to 130% of the amount of the loan. The 20 to 30% excess value of the collateral over the amount of the loan is called margin and must be continually kept good. If the loan is for $100,000 and the market value of the securities is $125,000, the margin of safety is $25,000, or 25%. The margin of risk, which is the amount by which the collateral security could decline in value and still leave a balance sufficient to pay off the loan, would be $25,000, but 20% instead of 25%.

The margin of safety for the principal of a mortgage bond issue is the excess of value of mortgaged property, or value of the remaining equity if subject to prior lien issues, over the par value of the amount outstanding. In practice, it is difficult, of course, to determine the market value of properties that are mortgaged for bond issues—especially railroad and public utility properties. However, engineering reports are of value in this connection, and in railroad mortgage bond issues there are certain well-established ratios of reasonable bonded indebtedness per mile of road. A bond issue may have excellent protection for the principal amount even though no lien or collateral security is offered. If the general unencumbered net assets of a company, conservatively valued, are twice the amount of debenture bonds outstanding and there are no prior bond issues, then the margin of safety for the principal of such a debt would be 100%.

The term "margin of safety" as a measure of the degree of protection afforded the principal sum invested in stocks seems never to have been used, since the value of stocks is usually thought to be dependent wholly on earnings available for such stocks. In theory, however, the principle could as well be extended to stocks as to bonds or any other form of debt. For example, if a corporation which has no funded debt, or debt other than current liabilities, has $250,000 in net tangible assets against $100,000 of preferred stock and $100,000 of common stock, the theoretical margin of safety for the paramount of preferred stock would be the excess of net tangible assets over the amount of preferred stock outstanding, e.g., $150,000, or 150%. Similarly, the margin of safety for the par amount of common stock outstanding would be the excess of the net tangible assets over the combined preferred and common stocks outstanding, e.g., $50,000, or 50%. If a corporation's books represent the true state of affairs, the margin of safety for the par amount of the common stock would be the amount of the total corporate surplus. If the common stock were purchased for 50% of par, the margin of safety in *equity* value would be $100 per share, or 200%.

The margin of safety, expressed either in dollars or as a percentage, shows how much sales can be reduced without sustaining losses.

Actual sales − Break-even sales = MS in dollars

$$\frac{\text{Excess of actual sales over break-even sales}}{\text{Actual sales}} = \text{MS as a percentage}$$

Excess of Earnings. Second and probably of considerably more importance, is the use of the term to denote the excess of earnings available for the payment of interest charges on a debt (whether short-term or long-term) and of earnings available for the payment of dividends over dividend requirements (or current dividend rates). In bond investments, much importance is attached to the margin of safety, particularly as determined over a period of years, as a key to investment values. The determination of the margin of safety (earnings available for a bond issue over interest requirements) is normally the chief factor used by various bond rating services in fixing bond ratings.

Wherever a corporation has only one bond issue, e.g., $1 million bearing 5%, and has had an income available for interest changes on this issue for the past five years of $150,000 a year, the average margin of safety is $100,000 a year, or 200%. In usual parlance, however, it is said to be earning its bond interest charges three times over. The earnings protection afforded by this corporation for its bond interest requirements, like the property protection afforded the principal amount of a debt as mentioned above, may be viewed as the extent by which the sum available for bond interest charges (usually called gross income or total income) could decline and still cover bond interest requirements. In this instance, the sum would be $100,000 annually, or $66^2/_3\%$. As stated previously, a more suitable designation for this percentage would be margin of risk.

It is customary in investment circles to regard the margin of safety for a corporation's fixed charges, or for its preferred dividend and common dividend requirements, as the number of times such charges or dividend requirements are earned. Thus, a corporation having annual fixed charges of $100,000 and earning $400,000 for such charges is said to earn its fixed charges four times over. The margin of safety—or better, margin of risk—would be better stated as 75%, i.e., the sum available for such charges could decline by as much as 75% and still leave enough to cover such charges. Likewise, such a corporation having earnings of $300,000 available for its preferred stock on which dividend requirements are $100,000 is said to be earning such requirements three times. The margin of risk would be computed on the amount by which the sum available for interest charges could decline and still pay all prior charges *plus* the preferred dividends, i.e., 50%. If the present common dividend is $100,000 annually (referring to the above example), the margin of safety (or margin of risk) would be computed on the amount by which the sum available for interest charges could decline and cover not only interest charges and the preferred dividend but the common dividend as well, i.e., 25%.

Wherever a corporation's earnings for interest charges are less than the interest charges, a minus margin of safety arises. For example, if earnings available for interest are $150,000 and interest charges are $200,000, 75% of the charges are being earned, making a margin of safety of minus $33^1/_3\%$, meaning that the sum available for interest charges must increase $33^1/_3\%$ in order to cover such charges.

See INVESTMENT SECURITIES.

MARGIN REQUIREMENTS *See* MARGIN BUYING.

MARINE INSURANCE Marine insurance policies specify the specific coverage and maximum liability to the insured (who may be the owner of the vessel or of the cargo) by the underwriter in consideration of payment of premiums for a specific voyage or other term and against specified risks, usually perils of the seas, fire, assailing thieves, criminal barratry of the master and mariners, and all other like perils and losses.

After the ocean bill of lading, the marine insurance certificate is the most important shipping document which accompanies a foreign bill of exchange, without which the shipper and the bank financing the shipment would take all the risks incident to marine transportation. Marine insurance is provided to cover the various marine hazards incident to overseas shipments, as protection to both the shipper and the bank that advances funds against the shipment.

While the law holds railroads (as common carriers and bailees) to strict responsibility in undertaking the transportation of goods and makes them liable for practically all losses and damage, e.g., theft breakage, fire, etc. (all except those caused by a public enemy or the so-called acts of God), the HARTER ACT has relieved ocean carriers of many specified marine risks. To provide for their liability to shippers, railroads insure themselves against all risks assumed as common carriers by the blanket insurance policies. Ocean carriers, being relieve of responsibility for cargoes, provide only for insurance to cover the vessel, passing on the burden of insuring the shipments constituting the cargo to the shippers.

Each ocean shipment should be covered against general marine risks and other risks to which it may be especially exposed, e.g., pilferage or breakage. The customary insurance policy covers only certain risks, and it is advisable that a proper understanding of the limitations and conditions of the insurance be reached between shipper and insurance agent in order to avoid future controversy. Insurance is usually obtained from the point of origin to the ultimate destination, and the insurance certificate is issued in the name of the shipper. An endorsement in blank is desirable, just as in the case of a bill of lading, when the documents are delivered to the accepting bank.

The amount of insurance should fully cover the cost of the goods. It is even advisable to insure for a greater amount that the invoice value, say 10%, to cover the shipper's profit and such transportation charges as are already incurred. It is important that the insurance policy cover all the important risks and, in time of war, war risk.

See AVERAGE.

MARK DOWN   In banking practice, the reappraisal of the value of securities pledged as collateral to stock exchange loans whenever there is a severe decline in the stock market. This procedure is necessary whenever securities decline, say on an average of four points or more, as a protection to the bank's loans and out of recognition of the principle that margin requirements must be kept continually good. The procedure requires examining the collateral cards of each stock exchange loan and changing the value of the securities to conform with the latest quotations. It is therefore a reinventorying of the collateral in acordance with the prevailing or most recent market quotations. When the change in the value of each security in the collateral to each loan has been noted, the total value of the securitues is then ascertained. Whenever the total value of the collateral computed under the reappraisal is insufficient to furnish the required margin, the loan is undermargined, and a margin notice is forwarded to the borrowing broker.

In management accounting, mark-down refers to a reduction in price below the original sale price, usually because of a decrease in the general level of prices, special sales, soiled and damaged goods, overstocking, and competition. Mark-down cancellations occur when the mark-downs are partially offset at a later date by increases in the prices of goods that had been marked down below the original sales price. Mark-down cancellations cannot exceed the original mark-down.

See MARGIN CALL.

MARKED CHECK   In some instances depositors have arranged with their banks that each check drawn by them shall bear a certain distinguishing mark known only to the depositor and the bank. The purpose of the marked check is to prevent forgery. The bank is bound not to pay checks for such depositors which do not bear the distinctive mark.

MARKET   In its broadest sense, any interaction of buying and selling interest for goods or services. Although a market is usually thought of as a locality, it is rather the buying and selling interest that establishes a market and thus the determination of quotations or prices of actual transactions in goods and services.

There are several classifications of markets. The chief classification is that based upon the kinds of media traded in, e.g., stock market, produce market, grain market, money market, cotton market, livestock market, real estate market, wood market, lumber market, foreign exchange market, etc. Markets may be formal and organized or informal and descentralized. When organized, they are usually called exchanges or boards, e.g., the NEW YORK STOCK EXCHANGE, CHICAGO BOARD OF TRADE, COMMODITY EXCHANGE, INC., Minneapolis Grain Exchange. The markets for unlisted securities, foreign exchange, real estate, etc., are decentralized. Organized markets are closed, while decentralized markets are open; i.e., trading in the former is limited to members of the exchange, while in the latter trading is open to any buyers and sellers.

Markets may be classified in accordance with the breadth of the demand for various products, e.g., world, national, and local markets. With the perfection of means of communication, many commodities now enjoy a world market, e.g., internationals among securities, sterling and dollar exchange, wheat, cotton, wood, etc. A national market is one in which the goods or services are traded in by buyers and sellers coming from any part of the country. A local market is one in which the goods or services are exchanged only within a restricted area.

Markets are primary and secondary. A primary market is one located in a center of consumption where large quantities are available for distribution and stored in warehouses, elevators, or railroad or shipping terminals. Chicago is thus a primary market for wheat and other grains. A secondary market is one near the points of production. It is the place where commodities are collected and not distributed. A market in a small prairie town, for example, would be a secondary market. As applied to securities, primary markets refers to the markets for new issues of securities publicly offered through investment bankers (the capital market), and secondary markets refers to the markets for already outstanding securities after such issues have been publicly floated. In U.S. security market practice, security exchanges and over-the-counter markets in already outstanding issues are thus secondary markets in this sense. Primary markets in securities may also refer to those maintained by the principal firms maintaining or making such markets, other firms, trading on such primary markets, are thus said to be secondary in over-the-counter practice.

Markets may also be said to be continuous or discontinuous, not because transactions occur every second, but because the facilities are available continuously or discontinuously for trading. A trading session of the New York Stock Exchange, for example, provides a continuous market for listed stocks and bonds. The market for unlisted stocks and bonds may be continuous. An AUCTION is a discontinuous market.

See AMERICAN STOCK EXCHANGE; CHICAGO MERCANTILE EXCHANGE; COFFEE, SUGAR & COCOA EXCHANGE, INC.; MARKETABILITY; MARKET PRICE; MARKET VALUE; NEW YORK COTTON EXCHANGE; OVER-THE-COUNTER-MARKET; REAL ESTATE BOARD OF NEW YORK, INC.; WINNIPEG COMMODITY EXCHANGE.

MARKETABILITY   The relative ease and promptness with which a security or commodity may be sold when desired, at a representative current price, without material concession in price merely because of the necessity of sale. Marketability connotes the existence of current buying interest as well as selling interest and is usually indicated by the volume of current transactions and the spread between the bid and asked price for a security—the closer the spread, the closer are the buying and selling interests to agreement on price resulting in actual transactions. To look at it from the standpoint of a dealer maintaining the MARKET, the closer his bid to current transactions and the smaller his mark-up as to asking prices, the larger the volume will be. By contrast, inactive securities that rarely trade or for which buyers have to be located or sales negotiated are characterized by large spreads between the bid and asked prices.

Whether marketability should be emphasized as a characteristic of a security to be purchased depends upon the likelihood of sale by the holder if the security is bought. Commercial banks investing for their secondary reserves must emphasize high marketability in such investments, for such securities may have to be sold to adjusting legal reserve position, to create excess reserves for loan demand, or to create excess reserves to meet deposit withdrawals. On the other hand, the investment portion of the securities portfolio need not stress so highly the factor of marketability, although such securities also should be marketable.

See COMPTROLLER'S REGULATION.

Mere LISTING on an established exchange does not guarantee marketability, as indicated by "Post 30" trading on the New York Stock Exchange for inactive issues; it is current buying and selling interest that creates marketability. Thus, some issues traded over-the-counter on active, firm markets maintained by dealers may have more marketability than some stocks listed on the New York Stock Exchange. Publicity given to prices and trading volume as well as to company developments of listed issues does tend to attract more attention to listed issues and to that extent encourage marketability; but some issues upon being listed lose activity because of loss of active sponsorship (advertising, preparation of analyses, recommendations, etc.) of over-the-counter firms previously dealing in them.

ENCYCLOPEDIA OF BANKING AND FINANCE

Loans on securities collateral should stress marketability as well as diversification of the securities offered as collateral, because of the possibility of necessity for sale in the event of default and in order to maintain an adequate market value for mix in collateral above the amount of the loan.

Commodities enjoy both spot (cash) markets and futures markets on the various commodity exchanges, both contract markets and other markets providing facilities for the meeting of buying and selling interests. Again, in the case of commodities the determinant of marketability is the degree of buying and selling interest resulting in transactions. Usually, exchange markets for commodities tend to be active because such exchanges attract (for hedging purposes) processors and manufacturers of the commodity concerned, as well as speculators.

Fixed assets, especially real estate, have low marketability, because negotiation is normally required in bringing buyers and sellers together and, in the case of specialized fixed assets, the range of the potential market (possible buyers or sellers) is usually limited.

MARKET AVERAGES One of the chief barometers upon which investors and speculators rely in making market commitments, for an indication of price trends as well as levels. Although the prices of securites fluctuate according to the particular demand and supply conditions affecting each, prices tend to rise and fall sympathetically, establish movements collectively which develop into upward, downward, or approximately horizontal trends when plotted on a chart. It is a function of market averages to measure such collective movements for representative samples of the market. An average, however, is just that, and fluctuations, movements, and trends of individual stocks, commodities, etc., in an average will vary from the average. Such variations from the average of individual items may in fact be emphasized in taking long or short positions.

Sympathetic price fluctuation, movements, and trends of individual securities or commodities are such a general phenomenon that Wall Street or LaSalle Street speaks of the entire market as being bearish or bullish or of prices being in general too high or too low, basing such characterizations by reference to averages which may be composed of a relatively small sampling of total items traded. This sympathy in price movements is but a corollary of the principle of interdependence of all prices, economic conditions or technical market influences tending to affecting particular securities or commodities also tending to affect others.

Current Averages. Among the principal averages compiled regularly and referred to generally are the following:

1. DOW JONES AVERAGES. Although based on relatively small samples of industrial, transportation, and public utility stocks, the Dow Jones stock, averages are still very conventionally referred to as indicators of general market levels and trends. The DOW THEORY continues to be based on the Dow Jones industrials and the transportation average (formerly on the DJ industrials and DJ railroad averages).
2. *Standard & Poor's averages.* These are constructed on the index method (1941-1943 = 10). The price of each stock multiplied by the company's outstanding shares of the common stock gives the current market value of the entire issue; total market values of all the stocks in each index are added together, and such composite current value is then expressed relative to the uniform 1941-1943 base market value. The basic indexes consist of 400 industrials, 20 transportation, 40 utilities, 40 financials, and 500 combined stocks. These are common stocks representing more than 90% of the market value of all common stocks listed on the New York Stock Exchange. They are computed at the opening, at each hour of the market day, and at the close, thus providing for the day the open, high, low, and close. Daily indexes (high, low, and close) are published in many newspapers and in Standard & Poor's own *Daily News Service, Facts & Forecasts, Outlook* (weekly), and the Statistical Section (available separately, bound in loose-leaf form and containing a comprehensive collection of business statistics).

In Addition to the daily indexes, Standard & Poor's publishes (as of Wednesday) closing prices each week, detailed group indexes (81 industrial groups and subgroups; 5 public utilities groups and subgroups; 4 transportation groups; and 11 financial groups, i.e., banks, insurance, finance companies, brokerage firms, real estate investment trusts, investment companies [both closed-end and bond funds], and savings and loan holding companies). Besides these groups and subgroups, additional weekly stock price indexes include 105 capital goods, 191 consumer goods, 25 high-grade common stocks, and 20 low-price common stocks. Also computed weekly are the yields and price-earnings ratios on each of the basic indexes, average price and yield on preferred stocks; yields on bonds (composite, industrials, and utilities) for each of the four highest quality ratings (AAA, AA, A, and BBB) as well as prices on the corporate AAA bonds; and yields and prices on government securities (long-term, intermediate, short-term) and on municipals.

3. *Moody's averages.* In Moody's stock averages, each stock is weighted by the number of its shares currently outstanding. In computation of the averages, adjustments are made for all stock splits and stock dividends, so that the series are comparable throughout the periods covered. These are price averages of 125 industrials, 20 rails, and 25 electric utilities. In addition, price averages are compiled for 9 New York City bank stocks and 9 insurance stocks, and various series of yield averages for preferred stocks; industrial preferred stocks, high-dividend series (high-grade, medium-grade, and speculative-grade); low-dividend series (high-grade and medium-grade industrials, and high-grade and medium-grade utilities). Moody's also prepares corporate bond yield averages by Moody's quality ratings (Aaa, Aa, A, and Baa) for average corporate as well as average for each of the quality ratings; average railroads, as well as average for Aa, A, and Baa quality ratings; average public utility, as well as average for each of the quality ratings; and average industrial, as well as average for each of the quality ratings. In addition, Moody's prepares yield averages for U.S. Treasury issues (91-day bills, 182-bills, 3- to 5-year issues, and long-term issues) daily, as well as 3-year, 5-year, and 10-year indexes.
4. *Value Line stock average.* The Value Line stock average of the 1700 stocks supervised by the Value Line Investment Survey is computed by expressing the daily closing price of each stock as a ratio of the preceding day's closing price, then averaging these ratios for all the stocks geometrically and relating the composite daily ratios to the base of June 30, 1961 = 100. This method gives equal weight to each stock without regard to corporate size, total shares outstanding, or investment stature; and the average, moreover, includes a comprehensive number of stocks.
5. *Barron's averages.* Besides publishing daily opening, hourly, and closing levels on the Dow Jones stock averages, Barron's publishes weekly the ten most active stocks (daily average closings, as well as ratio of ten most active stocks to total trading); hourly trading volume on New York Stock Exchange, hourly trading volume, separately, for the Dow Jones 30 industrials, 20 transportation, 15 utilities, and 65 combined stocks; Dow Jones weekly averages (first, high, low, and last), as well as cumulative-for-year first, high, low, and last; Dow Jones price-earnings ratios (industrials, transportation, and utilities) for current week, previous week, one year ago, and two years ago; Dow Jones weekly averages on bonds (first, high, low, and close) for 10 high-grade rails, 10 second-grade rails, 10 utilities, 10 industrials, and 40 combined bonds, as well as 10 rail income bonds; daily averages for these bond averages as well as U.S. government securities average; yield averages (weekly) on the Dow Jones averages of stocks and bonds, including municipal bond yield average; and spread between Barron's high-grade bond yield average and the Dow Jones industrials average yield, as well as ratio of Barron's high-grade bond yield average to the average yield on the Dow Jones 40 bonds (confidence index). Also Barron's publishes weekly the computed index and ratio of volume of 20 low-priced stocks to total volume of the Dow Jones industrials. The Barron's 50-stock average (weekly) is also regularly published, along with earnings and yield data thereon. Barron's group stock averages (simple arithmetical averages based on closing prices as of Thursday each week) are also published on 32 groups.

Institutionally Prepared Averages.

1. *New York Stock Exchange indexes.* The common stock price index is based on the total market value of NYSE common stocks, adjusted to eliminate the effects of capitalization changes, new listings, and delistings and based on the price of each stock

MARKET INFLUENCES

weighted by the number of shares listed. The aggregate market value is the sum of the individual market values and is expressed relative to the base period market value (December 31, 1965 = 50). In addition to the composite index, four subgroup indexes are computed (industrial, transportation, utility, and finance). All indexes are available on a day-to-day basis, along with the range each day. The daily composite index is available on a weekly basis from January 7, 1939, to May 28, 1964, and on a daily basis from that date to the present. The four subgroups are available from December 31, 1965. Currently 1520 stocks are in the indicator.

2. *American Stock Exchange indexes*. These indexes consist of three market indicators; the price level index, the breadth of market index, and the price earnings index. The price level index reflects the current price level of issues traded and changes in the price level over a period of time. It is calculated by adding the price changes from the previous close of each common stock and warrant and dividing the total by the number of common stocks and warrants. The net change is then added to or subtracted from the index level at the previous close. The index is available on a day-to-day basis. The breadth of market index is computed daily at the close of trading and shows the distribution of issues according to price changes. The price earnings index is computed monthly and relates the price of a stock to the latest available per share earnings of the company issuing that stock.

3. *NASDAQ indexes (National Association of Security Dealers Automated Quotations)*. The NASDAQ index was inaugurated May 17, 1971, as the over-the-counter market's first continuously available index (distributed at 5-minute intervals and constantly available through any of the electronic desk-top units that disseminate NASDAQ data). The newswire service receives a three-times-a-day dissemination, with the closing values available within minutes after the market closes at New York at 3:30 P.M. (Eastern time). The index is based on all the 3,500 domestic common stocks in the NASDAQ quotation system, reflecting the weighted effect of every change in the representative bid price of each security. The method of weighting utilizes the increment or decrement to the actual market value (shares times price) to move the index. At the same time, the index values are stabilized against the impact of any capitalization changes in securities in the base (new issues, splits, or deletion of issues). In addition to the composite index, separate indexes on six subgroups are also calculated, extracted from the full common stock base: industrials, banks, insurance, other finance, transportation, and utilities. Continuous posting of the net change from the previous day's close is provided with each index; and for all the indexes, the day's high and low is displayed with the index value at each five-minute point. Each index uses a base point of close of business as of February 5, 1971 = 100. Volume of trading in the NASDAQ issues is reported daily in the aggregate, as well as for the ten most actively traded issues.

Other Stock Averages. In addition to the above market averages, the NATIONAL QUOTATION BUREAU publishes a 35-stock industrial stock average of over-the-counter issues (using the constant divisor method, adjusted for splits and stock dividends) and a 15-stock insurance stock average (same method). The *New York Times* publishes daily price averages of its own (25 industrials, 25 rails, and 50 combined), as well as bond price averages (20 rails, 10 industrials, and 10 utilities, as well as combined).

Summary. Market technicians who emphasize price and volume data for individual stocks as well as averages in the development of their systems and theories for judging market trends and forcasting price movements make use of the above generally available averages as well as a variety of their own specialized averages. A stock average may be constructed as a simple average of prices of the stocks selected, on the index method, or on the weighted average (special weights, not automatic weighting by number of shares as for the index method) basis. A simple price average, such as the Dow Jones stock averages, faces the problem of eliminating distortions caused by split-ups and substantial stock dividends by using either the multiplier method (multiplying new stock by the multiple of the stock split or stock dividend) or the constant divisor method (used by Dow Jones; *see* DOW JONES AVERAGES). The index method automatically adjusts for such splits or stock dividends. The weighted average must adjust the special weights used on each stock affected by splits and stock dividends. All methods also face the common problem of the representativeness of the sample of stocks selected for the average; the larger the slice, the more representative the average will likely be but the more difficult the work of regular computation.

A bond average may be a simple average of prices or yield, or it may be an adjusted average of a specified number of issues (adjusted, e.g., to a uniform 4% rate and 20-year maturity). The reciprocal of a yield average of bonds—most often found in averages of high-grade bonds because of their fluctuation in sympathy with interest rates—is the composite market price for the average concerned. Thus yields on bonds may be plotted inversely on a chart so as to show the price trend.

MARKET INFLUENCES Almost everything that happens in business has a direct or indirect influence on the markets. Followers of the fundamental theory of security prices believe that market prices ultimately respond to the fundamental or real factors of economic developments for the economy as a whole, for industries, and for specific companies and specific securities. Commodity prices respond even more sensitively to such fundamentals as weather conditions, crop reports, and disposition of surpluses. Political developments may also be directly influencing.

In addition to fundamental factors, market influences include the technical factors pertinent to the market itself, such as size of short interest, profit-taking corrections of advances, particular volume and price behavior of specific stocks, reaction to news, breadth of the market generally and specifically for particular stocks, and market following for particular stocks which are of interest particularly to the traders seeking to profit from short-run trading swings. Fundamental and technical influences may frequently be linked in a cause-and-effect relationship—a special company development (merger, consolidation, split-up, stock dividend, new product, etc.) might lead to such a reduction of the floating supply of a stock that its market becomes thin and easily responsive in run-ups to bidding interest, or such a special development might lead overnight to a delayed or arranged opening, suspension of stop orders, etc.

It is the function of financial and economic news to supply the markets with the raw material of facts and developments upon which the markets may turn, after analysis and interpretation.

Much of this material is prepared for periodic release for publication, including such specific company developments as dividend actions, annual and interim reports, and comments by management at regular annual meetings. Other data become available intermittently, such as capitalization changes (announcement of split-ups, stock dividends, exchanges, etc.) and mergers or consolidations. Strikes, court decisions of particular economic portent, and monetary and fiscal developments are also in this category.

The appended tabulation provides a calendar of dates of publication for various types of economic and market data regularly issued.

CALENDAR OF NEWS RELEASES

Automobile Production
  Automobile Mfrs. Assoc.—Weekly, Mondays
  Automotive News—Weekly, Tuesdays
  Dow Jones & Co. (Wall St. Journal)—Weekly, Fridays, monthly estimates, on 2nd or 3rd day of following month
  Ward's Automotive Reports—Weekly, Saturdays
Automobile Sales (Regulations)
  Automotive News—Weekly, as State reports become available
  Dow Jones & Co.—In 10-day periods, with 1 week lag, monthly estimates, by end of first week of following month
  Ward's Automotive Reports—Weekly, Saturdays
Bank Clearings
  Dun & Bradstreet, Inc.—Weekly, Fridays
Bank Debits
  Board of Governors of Federal Reserve System—Monthly, about mid-month
Bank of England Return—Weekly, Fridays
Bank Statements, Federal Reserve System
  Board of Governors of Federal Reserve System:
  Factors Affecting Bank Reserves and Condition Statement of Federal Reserve Banks (H.4.1)—Weekly, Fridays

Condition Report of Large Commercial Banks in New York and Chicago (H.4.3)—Weekly, Fridays

Reserve Positions of Major Reserve City Banks (H.5)—Weekly, Fridays

Assets and Liabilities of All Commercial Banks in the U.S. (H.8)—Weekly, Thursdays

Condition Report of Large Commercial Banks and Domestic Subsidiaries (H.4.2)—Weekly, Thursdays

Deposits, Reserves and Borrowings of Member Banks (H.7)—Weekly, Thursdays

Aggregate Reserves and Member Bank Deposits (H.3)—Weekly, Wednesdays

Assets and Liabilities of All Member Banks by Districts (G.7.1)—Monthly, mid-month

Assets and Liabilities of All Commercial Banks, by Class of Ba (E.3.4)—Semi-annual, May and November

Brokers' Loans
Federal Reserve Reports on Banks (H.4.3, H.8, H.4.2, G.7.1, and E.3.4)—See above
Federal Reserve Report FR-240—Monthly, first week of month

Building Construction
F. W. Dodge (McGraw Hill) Construction Statistics (Indexes, Floor Area, Value)—Monthly, late month
Bureau of the Census (Commerce Dept.), Housing Starts and Building Permits; Value of New Construction Put in Place—Monthly
Advance Planning, Engineering News Record—Weekly, Fridays

Carloadings
Association of American Railroads—Weekly, Fridays

Chain Store Sales
Company Reports, Monthly Sales—1st and 2nd weeks of following month
New York Times Summary—About mid-month

Consumer Credit
and Consumer Instalment Credit at Commercial Banks (Federal Reserve Releases G.19 and G.18)—Monthly, first week
Finance Companies (Federal Reserve Release G.20)—Monthly, first week

Coal Production
Bituminous, National Coal Association—Weekly, Saturdays
Bituminous and Anthracite, Bureau of Mines—Weekly, Saturdays

Copper
Production, Deliveries, Stocks, U.S. and Outside U.S., Copper Institute— Monthly, about mid-month

Cotton
Volume of Trading, Open Interest, Commodity Exchange Authority—Daily, as of 2nd day preceding
Ginning Reports, Bureau of the Census (Commerce Dept.)—Monthly, August to December; also in January and March

Crop Reports
U.S. Dept. of Agriculture—Monthly, about first week of month

Electric Output
Edison Electric Institute—Weekly, Thursdays

Employment Statistics
Bureau of Labor Statistics, U.S. Dept. of Labor—Monthly, mid-month

Exports and Imports
U.S. Dept. of Commerce—Monthly, preliminary about mid-month; final figures about 25th of month

Failures—Business
Dun & Bradstreet—Weekly, Mondays; Monthly, latter part of 3rd week of month

Gas Sales
Manufactured and Natural Gas, American Gas Association—Monthly, near end of month

Grain Statistics
Grain Futures, Trading Volume and Open Interest, Commodity Exchange Authority—Daily, as of 2nd day preceding

Grain Purchases
by Commodity Credit Corp.—Weekly, Tuesdays
Visible Grain Supply, Chicago Board of Trade—Weekly, Tuesdays

Gross National Product
and Disposition of Personal Income, Bureau of Economic Analysis, Commerce Dept.—Preliminary quarterly, about 20th of month

Industrial Production Indexes
Federal Reserve (G.12.3)—Monthly, about mid-month

International Balance of Payments
Bureau of Economic Analysis, Commerce Dept.—Quarterly, about mid-month

Iron and Steel Production
American Iron & Steel Institute—Weekly, Tuesdays

Margin Account Debt
Equity Status, and Stock Market Credit, Federal Reserve—Federal Reserve Bulletin—Early in month
Stock Margin Accounts, Customers' Equity, Free Credit Balances, Stock Margin Debt, N.Y. Stock Exchange—Monthly, early month

Money and Money Rates
(Federal Reserve)
Money Stock Measures (H.6)—Weekly, Fridays
Selected Interest and Exchange Rates for Major Countries and the U.S. (H.13)—Weekly, Fridays
Weekly U.S. Government Security Yields and Prices (H.15)—Weekly, Mondays
Open Market Money Rates and Bond Prices (G.13)—Monthly, 1st week of month
U.S. Government Security Yields and Prices (G.14)—Monthly, 1st week of month

Paper Production
Newsprint, Production, Shipments and Stocks U.S. and Canada, Newsprint Service Bureau and Newsprint Assn. of Canada—Monthly, about 20th
U.S. Production, Shipments from Mills, Consumption by Publishers, American Newspaper Publishers Assn.—Monthly, about 20th
Paperboard Production, Orders, National Paperboard Assn.—Weekly, Wednesdays
Petroleum Production and Stocks
American Petroleum Institute—Weekly, Thursdays

Prices
Consumer Price Index, Bureau of Labor Statistics, U.S. Department of Labor—early in last week of month
Producer Price Index, Bureau of Labor Statistics, U.S. Department of Labor—about 18th of the month

Profits, Quarterly
Dow Jones & Co., Summary of Company Reports—As received (summary in 2nd month)
New York Times, Summary of Company Reports—As received

Railroad Earnings
Association of American Railroads, Estimates for Class 1 railroads—Early in following 2nd month
I.C.C. Report—About 2-month lag

Short Interest on N.Y. Stock Exchange—Monthly, about 20th of month

Statistical Indicators
Leading Indicators Index, U.S. Department of Commerce—About end of month

Supreme Court Decisions—Mondays, when Court is in session
See BUSINESS BAROMETERS.

MARKETING The activities that bring buyers and sellers together. Banks and other financial institutions are using mass media advertising as basic marketing tools. They also use direct mail and personal business solicitation techniques extensively. Marketing has truly come of age in the banking industry.

Marketing activities include communicating with customers and managing, distributing, and pricing products and services. The tasks of marketing are usually to create, develop, revitalize, or main-tain demand for a product or service. Strategic and tactical planning is required to produce a total marketing plan. Strategic planning is long term and performed by top-level executives. Tactical planning is short term and usually performed by middle-level marketing managers. Strategic planning involves defining the firms' mission, determining strengths and weaknesses, specifying objectives, product analysis, identifying alternatives, evaluating objectives, and making a decision. Tactical marketing forecasts industry and product demands, establishing tactical objectives, developing action programs, and implementing and monitoring the plan.

The principles and practices of marketing and distribution have been intensively analyzed and synthesized into an independent branch of study. Among the factors studied are physical distribution (including such factors as market methods employed in assembling, transporting, storage, sales, distribution, financing, risk taking, etc., as well as channels of distribution, the functions and methods of jobbers, types and methods of retailers, cooperative marketing, general problems confronting

MARKETING

manufacturers, and present-day merchandising methods) and "mental" distribution (including such factors as forces in marketing, analysis of a commodity, trademarks and brands, sales methods and sales management, advertising plans and media, advertising copy and display, together with the process involved in correlating all these factors in a complete marketing campaign). Besides inte-grated studies in such principles, a large volume of case material illustrative of principles in action has been accumulated and published.

As in the case of other areas of business and finance, marketing has been subjected in recent years to increasing quantitative analysis and technique, including model building, simulation, management games, and computer applications.

A glossary of basic marketing concepts is provided here; the list is not meant to be complete:

Advertising The presentation and promotion of ideas, goods, and services.

Bait-and-switch advertising Illegal practice of putting a product or service on sale with the intent of transferring the customer to a more expensive product.

Brand A name or symbol that identifies a good or service of a seller or group of sellers.

Channel of distribution Organized network that links producers of goods or services with users.

Cold canvassing Making calls on a potential aaccount without prior acquaintance or contact.

Competitive parity budgeting A form of budgeting in which a bank adjusts its advertising budget to be comparable to that of the leading bank in the industry.

Cooperative advertising A form of retail advertising in which the cost of advertising is shared by the retailer and the manufacturer on a percentage basis.

Culture A set of values or attitudes that shape human behavior.

Demographics Data associated with age, sex, income, nationality, race, or other factors that serve as the basis for analysis.

Derived demand Demand for a good or service that is dependent upon the demand for another product or service.

Elastic The sensitivity of a good, service, or market to change in price.

Endless-chain method A method of generating leads for customers that requires asking customers for the names of others who might become customers.

Experience curve A theory that holds that as a producer of goods or services increases the amount of the product, it experiences significant production cost decreases.

Frequency The average number of exposures to a specific advertisement received by prospects in a target market.

Inelastic A situation or product where a reduction in price results in a decrease in revenue.

Latent demand Demand that exists when there is a significant amount of unmet need.

Law of diminishing marginal utility A situation that occurs when additional purchases of a product or service result in decreasing incremental benefits.

Learning The process whereby behavior is established or modified.

Loss leader A product or service that is sold at or below cost to promote the sale of other products or services.

Marginal utility The change in total utility resulting from a one-unit change in the quantity of a product.

Mark-down A discount from the original selling price to stimulate sales and/or reduce inventories.

Market segmentation A technique for modifying or adjusting a firm's product or services to meet the needs of special market segments instead of the total market.

Marketing audit A review or examination of the total marketing operations of an entity.

Marketing concept A marketing philosophy that emphasizes identifying and matching customers' needs with a firm's products or services.

Marketing research The systematic accumulation, recording, analyzing, and interpreting of data about marketing issues, products, or services.

New-product committee A group of employees having different backgrounds organized to deal with evaluating and developing new products.

Objective-and-task method An advertising budgeting method that establishes the budget based on specific tasks to accomplish agreed-upon objectives.

Percentage-of-sales method An advertising budgeting method that establishes the budget based on a percentage of past or projected sales.

Point-of-purchase display A sales promotion technique used to direct attention at the point of purchase.

Positioning The structuring of a readily identifiable image for a product or service.

Price discrimination A difference in prices charged to different customers for the same product.

Price fixing An agreement between sellers on the price that will be charged for a product or service.

Pricing objective An entities pricing goals or targets.

Pricing strategies The overall goals to be attained through pricing.

Pricing policy See PRICING POLICY

Primary demand The overall demand for products or services.

Product Goods or services that are designed to produce consumer satisfaction.

Product life cycle The stages that a product or service passes through from the time it is introduced to the market to the time it is no longer available.

Product mix Products and services that an entity sells.

Psychological pricing Using psychological factors to determine prices.

Puffery Exaggerations used in selling.

Reference group A group that has influence on attitudes, behavior, or decisions.

Subculture A social group within an identifiable segment of a culture.

Target pricing Setting price at a level that will produce a certain share of a targeted market.

Trading area Geographic area from which customers are drawn.

Tying agreement A contractual agreement in which a seller agrees to sell or lease a product or service on the condition that the customer will also purchase other merchandise.

Unitary elasticity A situation that occurs when a change in price has no effect on total revenue.

See PRICING POLICY.

BIBLIOGRAPHY

BANK ADMINISTRATION INSTITUTE. *Effective Customer Service.* Bank Administration Institute, Rolling Meadows, IL, 1986.
———. *Telephone Techniques.*
———. *Bank Marketing Handbook,* 1986.
———. *Creating a Sales Culture in a Community Bank,* 1988.
———. *Effective Bank Product Management: How to be Profitable in a Competitive Environment,* 1988.
———. *Pricing Retail Deposit Products: A Case Study Approach,* 1986.
———. *The Product Management Handbook: A Practical Guide for Product Managers.*
———. *Products, Marketing & Technology* (Monthly).
———. *Sales Incentive Programs for Branch Personnel,* 1988.
———. *Selling Financial Services: A Handbook for Organizing a Bank Calling Program,* 1987.
———. *Small Business Banking: A Guide to Marketing and Profits,* 1987.
———. *A Personal Financial Planning Decision Guide,* 1985.
———. *Personal Financial Planning in Banks,* 1986.
———. *A Practical Guide to Market Research,* 1983.
CUNNINGHAM, W. H., and others. *Marketing: A Managerial Approach.* South-Western Publishing Co., Cincinnati, OH, 1987.
DONNELLY, J. H., JR., BERRY, L. L., and THOMPSON, T. W. *Marketing Financial Services.* Bank Administration Institute, Rolling Meadows, IL, 1985.
FURLONG, C. *Marketing Money: Excelling in Today's Financial Services,* 1989.
Journal of Advertising.
Journal of Advertising Research.
Journal of Marketing.
Journal of Marketing Research.
Marketing Research. U.S. Superintendent of Documents (Subject bibl., 125).
KERNS, S., *Marketing Financial Products & Services.* Probus Publishing Co., Inc., Chicago, IL, 1989.

McMahon, R. J. *Bank Marketing Planner: A Workbook for Preparing Your Bank's Annual Marketing Plan.* Bank Administration Institute, Rolling Meadows, IL, 1987.

Moeb, G. M., *Pricing Financial Services.* Dow Jones-Irwin, Inc., Homewood, IL, 1986.

Moran, J. L. *Marketing Strategies for Community Banks.* Bank Administration Institute, Rolling Meadows, IL, 1987.

Reidenbach, R. E., and Grubbs, M. R. *Developing New Banking Products: A Manager's Guide.* Prentice Hall, Inc., Englewood Cliffs, NJ, 1986

———. *Effective Bank Marketing: Issuers, Techniques and Applications,* 1987.

Ritter, D. *Cross-Selling Financial Services.* John Wiley and Sons, Inc., New York, NY, 1988.

Sinclair, A. C. "A Primer on Buying Commercial Loans." *Journal of Commercial Bank Lending,* July, 1988.

University Training Systems. *A Guide to Effective Custome Service.* Bank Administration Institute, Rolling Meadows, IL, 1986.

MARKET LEADERS Those stocks which act as bellwethers of their respective industry groups in market action. Examples of market leaders are General Motors, Ford, and Chrysler among the U.S. automobile manufacturers; General Electric among the electrical equipment companies; I.B.M. among the computer manufacturers and supplies; Eastman Kodak among the photography and film producers; Dupont among the chemical groups; American Telephone & Telegraph among the utilities; Exxon and Texaco among the oils, etc. This position of market leader reflects the position of the respective companies in their industry, as well as the popularity of the stocks with investors and with speculators who wish to buy or sell the market. The appended table shows U.S. Industrial Companies with largest sales in 1987.

MARKET LETTERS Practically every brokerage house issues a daily market letter, which it posts in its customers' room for the information of its clients and transmits by telegram to its branch offices. Such a letter is a short summary of the more prominent political, business, financial, and technical market factors bearing upon the immediate price trend. Advise is sometimes given as to commitments, recommendations for purchase and sale in certain groups, or specific securities being volunteered. Although some market letters have tended to deteriorate into meaningless technical jargon and pointless hedging and straddling, and although the popularity of market letter writers is ephemeral, such literature has achieved a definite place in the scheme of market influences.

In addition to the daily market letters described, many brokerage houses publish a more elaborate review every week or month. Such reviews contain a summary of business and financial conditions, analyses of particular stocks or bonds which the house favors, opinions of leading financial writers, statistical charts, and special features.

A summary of the leading financial and commodity markets appears in the newspapers of the larger cities as a regular department. Business reviews are published by all of the 12 Federal Reserve banks and by many of the metropolitan commercial banks.

MARKET LIQUIDITY RISK The possibility that a financial instrument cannot be sold quickly and at full market value.

MARKET MAKER A brokerage firm in the over-the-counter market that purchases and sells shares in one or more OTC stocks for its own account. The market maker acts as a principal on one side of a transaction.

MARKET OFF Denotes that the prices on a security or commodity have declined for the day.

MARKET ORDER An order given to a broker to be executed at the best price obtainable for the particular security or commodity immediately after its receipt. If no price is stated in an order, it is always understood to be "at the market."

See orders.

MARKET PRICE The price which is currently being realized for a particular security or commodity.

See market ratio, market value, mint price of gold.

U.S. Industrial Corporations with Largest Sales in 1987

Company (1986 rank)	Sales [1] (billions)	Income[1] (or loss) in (millions)
General Motors (1)	$101.7	$3,550
Exxon (2)	76.4	4,840
Ford Motor (3)	71.6	4,625
IBM (4)	65.2	5,258
Mobil (5)	51.2	1,258
General Electric (6)	39.5	2,915
Texaco (8)	34.3	(4,407)
AT&T (7)	33.5	2,044
Du Pont (9)	30.4	1,786
Chrysler (11)	26.2	1,289
Chevron (10)	26.0	1,007
Philip Morris (12)	22.2	1,842
Shell Oil (15)	20.8	1,230
Amoco (13)	20.1	1360
United Technologies (7)	17.1	591
Occidental Petroleum (19)	17.0	240
Procter & Gamble (18)	17.0	327
Atlantic Richfield (20)	16.2	1,224
RJR Nabisco (14)	15.8	1,209
Boeing (16)	15.3	480
Tenneco (21)	15.0	(218)
BP America (35)	14.6	564
USX (22)	13.8	219
Dow Chemical (27)	13.3	1,240
Eastman Kodak (26)	13.3	1,178
McDonnell Douglas (23)	13.1	313
Rockwell International (24)	12.1	635
Allied-Signal (25)	11.5	656
PepsiCo (34)	11.5	594
Lockheed (30)	11.3	421
Kraft (37)	11.0	489
Philips Petroleum (31)	10.7	35
Westinghouse Electric (28)	10.6	738
Xerox (32)	10.3	578
Goodyear Tire & Rubber (24)	10.1	770
Unisys (46)	9.7	578
Minnesota Mining & Manufacturing (39)	9.4	918
Digital Equipment (44)	9.3	1,137
General Dynamics (36)	9.3	437
Sara Lee (40)	9.1	267
Conagra (59)	9.0	148
Beatrice (*)	8.9 Est.	N.A.
Sun (35)	8.6	348
Georgia-Pacific (50)	8.6	458
ITT (41)	8.5	1,018
Unocal (45)	8.4	181
Anheuser-Busch (43)	8.2	614
Caterpillar (47)	8.1	350
Hewlett-Packard (51)	8.0	644
Johnson & Johnson (53)	8.0	833

*Not ranked in 1986.
N.A. = not available.
[1] Fiscal year.
Source: Fortune magazine.

MARKET RATE OF INTEREST The rate of interest charged by banks for the particular class of loans at issue, different rates being quoted for call loans, time loans (with mixed, industrial, and government bond collateral), commercial paper, bankers acceptances (eligible and ineligible), etc.

See bank discount, interest rate ceiling, money market, rediscount rate.

MARKET RATE STANDBY A formal commitment that provides the option to deliver loans at the current mortgage interest rate.

MARKET RATIO The ratio at which equal weights of gold and silver exchange in the market, as distinguished from their coinage or mint ratio; also known as the commercial ratio. Since the success of bimetallism depended upon the maintenance of equivalence between the market and mint ratios of gold and silver, the governments on a bimetallic standard would attempt to establish a mint ratio equal to the current market ratio. Experience showed, however, that the market ratio of gold and silver varied according to the demand and supply of these metals, which in a free bimetallic standard would be available without restriction in the markets. Thus, the defined mint ratio could never be sure of equating with the fluctuating market ratio. This was the situation that the United States encountered from the standard's establishment in the nation until the bimetallic standard was abandoned (defacto abandonment may be said to have begun with the "Crime of 73," the act of February 12, 1873, which failed to provide for coinage of the silver dollar). As the market ratio fluctuated relative to the fixed mint ratio, the overvalued metal at the mint—either gold or silver, depending on the particular time—would be presented to the mint, and the country was actually on either a current gold or a current silver standard.

MARKET SENTIMENT The prices of securities on a stock market are affected by many factors, commonly referred to as "sentiment," that exert considerable influence in the determination of prices. An unfavorable earnings report of a large corporation, for instance, tends to depress prices, even though the general outlook is favorable. A sudden reduction in the call money rate would sentimentally have a favorable influence on prices, even though the lower rate might later prove to be only temporary. Likewise, strength or weakness in the grain and cotton markets and in the foreign exchanges is likely to impart strength or weakness to the stock market, even though the connection between them is remote.

The term is also used to denote the general tone or feeling of operators toward the immediate future course of prices. Thus, market sentiment may be bullish (cheerful), bearish (gloomy), or mixed (divided) for the current day, immediate future, or "long pull."

See MARKET INFLUENCES.

MARKET SPOTS See SPOTTED.

MARKET STABILIZATION Although pegging, fixing, and stabilization of security prices are forms of manipulation generally prohibited by the SECURITIES AND EXCHANGE ACT OF 1934, Section 9a(6) of the act vests in the SECURITIES AND EXCHANGE COMMISSION (SEC) the discretionary power to allow such pegging, fixing, and stabilizing of the price of a security in accordance with such rules and regulations as the commission may prescribe as necessary or appropriate in the public interest or for the protection of investors. Situations where the public interest would be served by allowing such stabilization of price would arise, for example, in connection with a securities distribution or in connection with offering of subscription rights to subscribe to stock.

Following its statement of policy in 1940, rather than promulgate specific rules in connection with stabilizing practices, the SEC had depended upon informal interpretations, some of which were issued in the form of releases but most of which were individually rendered by letter or telephone in answer to specific requests. The Committee on Interstate and Foreign Commerce of the House recommended in a report, dated December 30, 1952, that the SEC "should earnestly and expeditiously grapple with the problem of stabilization with the view either of the early promulgation of rules publicly covering these operations, or of recommending to the Congress such changes in legislation as its experience and study show now to be desirable."

Accordingly, during the 1954 fiscal year, the SEC engaged in the formulation and release for public comment of rules relating to the stabilization of securities under the Securities Exchange Act. The proposed rules were circulated for public comment on May 18, 1954, and after hearings, the rules were promulgated as follows:

Rule X-10b-6, Prohibitions Against Trading by Persons Interested in a Distribution
Rule X-10B-7, Stabilizing to Facilitate a Distribution
Rule X-10b-8, Distribution Through Rights.

X-10b-6, although entitled negatively, actually defines the situations in which bidding for or purchasing securities for the purpose of the stabilization of the price of a distribution or public offering may be engaged in. X-10b-7 specifies the details of allowable stabilization of prices on one or more markets for a security, requires disclosure of such stabilization, and prescribes reports and notices thereof to the SEC. In general, the purpose of allowable stabilization is to prevent a decline in the price below the price fixed on the offering or distribution, not to raise it above the fixed price. In public offerings, the disclosure requirement is satisfied by complying with Rule 426 under the Securities Act of 1933, which requires in connection with stabilization that the prospectus set forth, either on the outside front cover page or on the inside front cover page, a statement in substantially the following form in capital letters, printed in boldface roman type at least as large as 10-point modern type and at least two points leaded:

IN CONJUNCTION WITH THIS OFFERING, THE UNDERWRITERS MAY OVER-ALLOT OR EFFECT TRANSACTIONS WHICH STABILIZE OR MAINTAIN THE MARKET PRICE OF [identification of each class of securities in which such transactions may be effected] AT A LEVEL ABOVE THAT WHICH MIGHT OTHERWISE PREVAIL IN THE OPEN MARKET. SUCH TRANSACTIONS MAY BE EFFECTED ON [identification of each exchange on which stabilizing transactions may be effected; if none, this sentence may be omitted]. SUCH STABILIZING, IF COMMENCED, MAY BE DISCONTINUED AT ANY TIME.

X10b-8 specifies the details of price stabilization allowed in connection with bids for and purchases of stock and/or rights involved in distributions through rights.

MARKET STRUCTURE The composition of firms in a market. There are four distinct market structures discussed in economics: perfect competition, monopolistic competition, oligopoly, and monopoly. With perfect competition, there are numerous sellers of a homogeneous product (oats); there are no barriers to entry. With monopolistic competition, there are many sellers of a differentiated product (breakfast cereal); there are some minor barriers to entry. With an oligopoly, there are a few sellers of a product that may be identical (steel) or differentiated (toothbrushes); there may be barriers to entry. And, with a monopoly, there is only one seller; entry barriers may be severe.

MARKET SWINGS See BUSINESS CYCLE, SPECULATIVE CYCLE, SWINGS.

MARKET VALUES EARNING RATIO In comparative value of common stocks, the ratio most often used in judging current market value, or fair current market value, is the multiple of market value relative to annual earnings (projected earnings for the coming year, as even the immediate past year's earnings are of merely historical interest). Although the ratio is most often expressed as the multiple, some analysts prefer the expression of the ratio in percentage (earnings divided by market value, as percentage), so that such earnings ratio may be more readily compared with the yields, which are expressed in percentage.

The market times earnings ratio or its alternative form, the earnings on market (percentage), represents the capitalization of earnings by market value.

There is some difference in usage among analysts who prefer the yield basis for comparison, as against the market times earnings or earnings on market. The basis for this preference is that the yield (annual dividend divided by market price) represents the money actually paid out to stockholders, relative to the market price. Although the yield basis of comparison may be made in its own right, particularly in judging comparative yields of income-type common stocks (those bought for stability of dividends), the earnings ratio should be primarily used in judging current market values because it reflects the full earning power of the firm. Just as in buying an interest in an unincorporated business, the investor in a corporation's common stock should note the capitalization of earning power which the current market price represents. Using earnings as a basis, moreover, indicates the extent of coverage of the current annual dividend and the plow-back of retained earnings. The latter should not be ignored in analysis, as they enlarge the earning base (net worth) and, even if the earnings rate (rate of return on net worth) remains constant, they will result in growth in total dollar earnings and thus in dollar dividends (even if the dividend payout ratio remains constant).

When common stocks on the average were expected to yield 6% and dividend payout ratio was expected to be on the order of 60% of earnings, the resultant earnings of 10% on the market (or market times earnings of ten times) led to the frequently found tabloidal yardstick that common stocks are cheap when they sell at ten times earnings. Actually, even at 10 times earnings a specific stock may or may not be cheap compared with others at the time, depending upon its outlook and standing in comparison with other stocks. The valuation of earnings by market varies over the cycle, investors being willing to pay more for earnings in prosperous stages of the cycle and less for earnings in times of recession or depression (if there are earning in an average, the deficit earnings stocks pull down aggregate earnings and make the overall market times earnings ratios misleadingly high). This is no phenomenon exclusive to security markets, as it is also found in other lines and in purchases of businesses. A normal or core market times earnings ratio is an empirical matter depending upon the specific period chosen, which should be at least inclusive of a full business cycle for representativeness, e.g., a moving ten-year average of the market times earnings ratio would normally be long enough in time to include full business cycles (inventory recessions and intermediate cycles). Overemphasis should be avoided, however, of such past earnings, as *future* earnings (certainly difficult to forecast, but after all, anticipations in futurity are the motivations for investment) are more relevant and should normally be available projected for the year ahead, at least, based on company budgeting

In years of prosperity, various GROWTH STOCKS have sold at market times earnings ratios far above the general average, reflecting premium prices because of their growth prospects for the future. Such growth stocks typically plow back a large percentage of current earnings, thus self-financing to some extent their financial requirements for growth. The problem in pricing such stocks is to avoid overpaying for future earnings allowing for growth, which boils down to the necessity for obtaining projections of future earnings that are as firm as possible. Obviously, mere extrapolations of past earnings growth rates are not reliable guides to future earnings growh of such stocks.

A further problem in usage of the market times earnings ratio in the comparison of common stocks is the variation among corporations in accounting policy and treatment of such items as inventory valuation, taxes, and depreciation (including accelerated depreciation and investment tax credits), and inclusion in operating statements of nonoperating items such as gains or losses of a capital nature. The analyst will adjust the reported earnings of corporations as much as possible for these factors, so as to arrive at as much comparability as possible. One technique in use in recent years to distort reported earnings by varying depreciation and tax accruals is adding back to reported net income the depreciation (a simplistic concept of cash earnings) and computing the market times earnings ratio thereon.

See INVESTMENT.

MARKET VALUE The current or prevailing price of a security or commodity as indicated by current market quotations, and therefore the price at which additional amounts presumably can be purchased or sold. At any given time, the market value of a given security is taken to be that indicated by the last sale; for inactive securities, where no current quotations are available, the latest bid price applies. In the case of unlisted securities, the market value may be determined by the last private sale or by competent appraisal. The market value constantly fluctuates in active issues and may change frequently during the course of a single day's trading.

MARKING DOWN RATES In banking practice, reducing the rate charged on outstanding call loans. It is usually the practice for brokers who have borrowed call money to ask the lending bank for a decrease in the rate when the renewal rate is reduced to a rate below that at which the loan previously stood. Most banks automatically mark down the rate on standing call loans when the renewal rate changes in favor of the borrower.

See CALL LOAN.

MARKING TIME Denotes that prices on a stock or commodity exchange are in a hesitating, stationary, unchanged, trendless condition preparatory to a move. Such a market exists when there is no change in fundamental conditions to warrant changes in price, and operators are waiting for events capable of either favorable or unfavorable interpretation, in the meantime preferring to proceed experimentally.

MARKING UP RATES Banks lending call money notify the borrowing brokers whenever the renewal rate on outstanding call loans is changed to a higher figure than that at which the loan was originally arranged or previously standing.

See CALL LOAN.

MARK SIGNATURE When a person is unable to write his own name, his signature to any legal instrument e.g., check, note, mortgage, passbook, etc., is affixed by means of an X or other distinguishing mark. The name of the signer is then written next to the mark by a witness in the following manner:

$$\text{John} \quad \overset{\text{his}}{\underset{\text{MARK}}{X}} \quad \text{Doe}$$

The witness signs his own name as witness.

Savings banks which serve communities where illiterates are numerous must provide for mark signatures or other means of identification. Usually the mark signature is supplemented by additional data which may be used as a basis for test questions for the purpose of future identification. Such data usually consist of age, date of birth, father's name, mother's name, occupation, color of eyes, color of hair, height, distinguishing marks, etc. When the passbook is presented for the purpose of withdrawing money, test questions are put to the customer based upon the data.

See FINGERPRINT IDENTIFICATION.

MARSHALING OF ASSETS Orderly disposal of assets between partnership creditors and partners' personal creditors in the termination of a partnership. Partnership creditors have first priority to partnership assets; any excess goes to personal creditors. Usually, personal creditors have first priority to personal assets; any excess goes to partnership creditors. However, the Bankruptcy Reform Act of 1979 revised this so that the trustee in bankruptcy of a partnership is entitled to share pro rata with unsecured creditors of a partnership.

Banks should request that the general partners of a partnership-borrower guarantee the debt so that the bank is not subject to a marshalling of assets doctrine by having to exhaust all efforts against the partnership, such as asset conversion or liquidation, before taking legal action against the partners.

MARTIN ACT The New York State blue sky law, constituting Article 23-A of the General Business Law, originally added by Chapter 649 of the laws of 1921.

The act has been expanded in recent years, both in statutory scope and in administration. Besides the original regulatory requirements for registration of broker-dealer and anti-fraud emphasis, Article 23-A now includes the New York State Intrastate Financing Act (effective November 1, 1968, imposing requirement for filing a prospectus on subject offerings), the New York Real Estate Syndication and Cooperative Law, the Investment Advisory Registration Act, and the New York Theatrical Financing Act. Administratively, the former Bureau of Securities in the attorney general's office (broker-dealer registrations, new requirement of fingerprinting fraud) and the former Condominium, Theatre and Syndication Financing Bureau (real estate securities offerings, theatrical financing, and New York intrastate financing) were combined early in 1971 into the Bureau of Securities and Public Financing.

The New York Intrastate Financing Act establishd for the first time the requirements for the filing of an offering prospectus making "full and fair disclosures of all material facts" for strictly intrastate offerings, exempting offerings subject to or specifically exempted from the federal securities laws, including private placements, but "while substantial Federal and Stock Exchange and NASD rules exist for protection of the public, which are often effective to a greater or lesser degree, State regulatory agencies provide an important role as partner in the protective process." According to the assistant attorney general of New York in charge of the Bureau, the main thrust is in areas inadequately covered or not covered by existing regulations but requiring immediate public protection, such as the franchise industry, real estate offerings not involving specific property, "hot issues" of allegedly fraudulent companies and promoters, shell corporations, and the like.

See BLUE SKY LAWS.

ENCYCLOPEDIA OF BANKING AND FINANCE

MARX, KARL Karl Marx (1818-1883), author of *Das Kapital*, may be the most influential social philosopher of the past century. The central theme in Marx's writings is that society can achieve its highest level through a communist system. Such a system, guided by social planning, would stress the equality of resources. This system, in theory, would be void of political hierarchial structures. No communist society today parallels Marx's vision.

MASSACHUSETTS TRUST Sometimes applied to the business trust, because of the fact that it was developed in Massachusetts as a form of business organization, quasi-corporate in character at a time when corporations were limited to Massachusetts in their powers to hold and deal in real estate and own controlling interests in Massachusetts public utility companies. Although these restrictions have since been removed, the business trust form still persists in a minority of instances as the form of business organization.

In organizational details the business trust is like a regular trust, being set up under a declaration of trust in which organizational details are provided and being limited as to maximum duration by the particular state's version of the RULE AGAINST PERPETUITIES. Legal title to the property of the business trust is vested in the trustees who issue transferable participation certificates to the beneficiaries (analogous to stockholders). In order to avoid unlimited liability for the debts of the trust, the declaration of trust must specify that no such unlimited liability will attach to the trustees. Also, where the beneficiaries are reserved the right to vote for trustees, court decisions have interpreted the arrangement to attach unlimited personal liability for debts of the trust to the beneficiaries, unless the trustees specify in all contracts that the beneficiaries will not be so liable, a cumbersome method of limitations of liability.

Since business trusts are subject to federal corporate income taxes and since their original purposes in Massachusetts are no longer applicable, they are generally considered a cumbersome variation of the standard form of business organization. State tax advantage in Massachusetts, however, still serves as a motivation.

MATCHED ORDERS A form of MANIPULATION by which an operator buys a particular stock from one broker and sells it through another, thus artifically giving the appearance of activity. The purpose of matched orders is to induce buying of the stock by the public as a result of the display of activity and change in price and to unload when the price has risen sufficiently to permit a satisfactory profit. The brokers receiving the orders to buy and sell usually have no knowledge of the purposes of the transaction and carry out their orders in good faith. This is an expensive method of manipulation and is likely to prove costly for the unsuccessful manipultor. Matched orders are prohibited by the Securities Exchange Act of 1934.

MATCHED SALE-PURCHASE AGREEMENTS
As defined by the Board of Governors of the Federal Reserve System, "When the Federal Reserve makes a matched sale-purchase agreement, it sells a security outright for immediate delivery to a dealer or foreign central bank, with an agreement to buy the security back on a specific date (usually within seven days) at the same price. Matched sale-purchase agreements are the reverse of repurchase agreements and allow the Federal Reserve to withdraw reserves on a temporary basis."

MATCHING PRINCIPLE An accounting principle that requires that revenues generated and expenses incurred in earning those revenues should be reported in the same income statement. In this way, sacrifices (expenses) are matched against benefits or accomplishments (revenues). Revenues are recognized according to the realization principle (when earned and when an exchange has taken place). Expenses are determined in accordance with the matching principle. General guidelines associated with applying the matching principle include the following:

1. **Associating cause and effect.** Expenses that cause or result in revenue and which can be directly associated therewith should be reported on the same income statement.
2. **Systematic and rational allocation.** If revenues and expenses cannot be related causually, the expenses should be allocated in a systematic and rational method (such as depreciation and amortization).
3. **Immediate recognition.** Otherwise, costs are charged to the current period as expenses (or losses) immediately because no future benefit is anticipated or no connection with revenue is apparent.

MATERIALITY The magnitude or significance of something that would be of interest to an informed investor or creditor in making evaluations and decisions. Materiality implies significance, substance, importance, and consequence. Although materiality is primarily quantitative in nature, it is not exclusively so. Magnitude alone, without considering the nature of the item and the circumstances surrounding the decision being made, generally is not a sufficient basis for making a materiality decision. An item is material for accounting purposes if the omission or misstatement of it, in light of surrounding circumstances, would change or influence the judgment of a reasonable person relying on the information.

Materiality judgments are concerned with levels or thresholds. Immaterial items that have little or no consequences to statement users can be handled as expediency, fairness, and professional judgment require. The Financial Accounting Board decided not to establish materiality rules in Statement of Financial Accounting Concepts No. 2, but rather left the decision on materiality up to the judgment of those who have all of the facts. The FASB stated that, "No general standards of materiality could be formulated to take into account all the considerations that enter into an experienced human judgment," and that when the board imposes materiality rules, it is "substituting generalized collective judgments for specific individual judgment, and there is no reason to believe that collective judgments are always superior." The FASB did qualify the above by stating that materiality rules may be written into some standards, which, in fact, has been done.

MATURITY The terminating or due date of a note, time draft, acceptance, bill of exchange, bond, etc; the date a time instrument of indebtedness becomes due and payable, e.g., a 60-day note become due and payable at the expiration of that period. A check or sight or demand instrument matures upon presentation for payment.

Time drafts or bills of exchange drawn 30 days after sight mature 30 days after acceptance, the maturity being fixed by computing the date 30 days thereafter. Time drafts should therefore be presented for acceptance as soon as possible whenever it is desirable to bring the maturity at the earliest possible date.

See DAYS OF GRACE.

As to maturity, bonds may be classified in four groups: (1) obligatory maturity without provision for PRIOR REDEMPTION, (2) obligatory maturity with prior redeemability with or without a premium, (3) indeterminate maturity, i.e., no definite maturity indicated but redeemable after a certain date at the option of the issuer, and (4) perpetual bonds issued without provision for optional or obligatory maturity, except in case of default in interest payments. Some common stocks of the classified type, such as Class A, and preferred stocks generally are issued subject to redemption, in whole or in part, and usually at a premium.

MATURITY DISTRIBUTION In high-grade bond holdings, the diversification of maturities as to short-term, intermediate-term, and long-term, aiming at a straddle on the problem of open market price depreciation versus normally higher yields on longer-term maturities. The market prices of high-grade bonds respond inversely to fluctuations in money rates and yields on high-grade paper and obligations, i.e., when interest rates, open market money rates, and yields on such obligations *rise*, their open market prices *decline* in order to afford higher yields, because the rate of interest payments that such bonds pay is fixed as of the time of their issuance.

Moreover, because normally long-term maturities yield more than short-term maturities, a given magnitude of change in money rates and yields will have more impact on long-term high-grade bonds, and hence on their open market prices, than on short-term maturities. The latter, therefore, are more stable in open market prices, normally, than long-term maturities; in addition, they can be more easily held to the final short-term maturity, allowing one to bypass the problem of open market price depreciation by preplanned holding to final maturity.

Thus long-term maturities normally yield more but are more vulnerable to open market depreciation, should money rates and yields on high-grade obligations rise in the intervening years before final maturity and should they have to be sold instead of held to final maturity. Of course, if long-term high-grade bonds can be held readily to final maturity, the problem of open market price depreciation in the intervening years will be bypassed, since there should be no question of payment in full of high-grade obligations at final maturity, and since institutional investors such as commercial banks (see COMPTROLLER'S REGULATION) and life insurance companies may carry such high-grade bonds at book values (less amortization of premium in cost if any), thus ignoring open market depreciation if any.

A completely short-term maturity concentration (e.g., maturities of under one year) will normally entail lower yields and hence lower income from investments, a particular problem when investments constitute the bulk of earning assets, but it provides highest protection against open market depreciation in the event of sale before maturity (so-called money risk or interest risk rate). On the other hand a completely long-term maturity concentration will provide higher yields and hence income from investments, but greatest exposure to risk of open market depreciation in the event of sale before final maturity. Spacing maturities in a diversified manner among shorts, intermediates, and longs, therefore, provides the following advantages: (1) overall yields on the portfolio are improved, (2) in the course of time, the maturity of the shorts periodically provides funds for reinvestment in longs at prevailing yields, (3) the portfolio will always have a layer of shorts as a secondary reserve which, in the event of required sale, will have least risk of open market depreciation.

Execution of a program of maturity distribution requires the availability of desired maturities in the market. Such diversification of maturities is available particularly in U.S. government securities.

MATURITY INDEX   See TICKLER.

MATURITY TICKLER
A record indicating the date upon which each loan, bill discounted, bond, investment, or other time instrument matures.

See TICKLER.

MAXIMAX CRITERION
Uncertainty is a situation in which the decision maker does not have information about the outcomes of his or her actions, and no estimates can be made about the probabilities associated with alternative outcomes. One criteria for guiding managers in such a situation is the maximax criterion. The rule is to select the alternative (such as an investment opportunity) that will yield the maximum possible outcomes under the best (maximum) of all possible situations. This is a criterion of optimism.

MAXIMIN CRITERION
Uncertainty is a situation in which the decision maker does not have information about the outcomes of his or her actions, and no estimates can be made about the probabilities associated with alternative outcomes. One criterion for guiding managers in such a situation is the maximin criterion. The rule is to select the alternative (such as an investment opportunity) that will yield the maximum possible outcomes under the worst (minimum) of all possible situations. This is a criterion of pessimism.

MCFADDEN ACT
A significant banking act passed in 1927 that permitted national banks to establish full-service branches within the cities in which they were located if state banks had similar authority. Following the passage of the McFadden Act, states began to increase restrictions on bank branching activities.

See PEPPER-MCFADDEN ACT.

MCCLEAN-PLATT ACT
An act passed September 17, 1919, under which national banks, without restriction to the amount of their capital and surplus, were permitted to subscribe in amounts not exceeding 5% of their capital and surplus to the stock of foreign banking corporations as a further means of providing for the capitalization of institutions engaged in financing foreign trade. This act was superseded by the EDGE ACT.

MEAN-VARIANCE EFFICIENCY
A model of the optimal selection of portfolios by investors. It is based on Harry Markowitz's idea that the only characteristics of a portfolio that an investor is interested in are its mean, or average, return and the variance of that return. The variance is interpreted as a measure of the portfolio's riskiness; the higher the variance the greater the risk.

The selection of a portfolio proceeds by the following steps:

1. Using the means, variances, and covariances of the individual assets calculate the means and variances of the possible portfolios.
2. Select a set of mean-variance efficient portfolios which have the properties that if some portfolio in the set has a higher mean it must also have a higher variance (otherwise delete the lower mean portfolio) and that no group of portfolios in the set can be combined into a new portfolio with a higher mean and an equal or lower variance than another member of the set (or, again, delete the lower mean portfolio).
3. From this efficient set select the portfolio that best corresponds to the individual's preference for risk versus return.

MEASUREMENT
The assignment of numbers to objects, events or situations in accord with some rule or guideline. The property of the objects, events, or situations that determines the assignment of numbers is called the measurable attribute (or magnitude). The number assigned is called its measure (the amount of its magnitude). The rule or guideline defines both the magnitude and the measure.

In accounting, assets and liabilities currently reported in financial statements are measured by different attributes, depending on the nature of the item and the relevance and reliability of the attribute measured. Five different attributes of assets and liabilities are used in present accounting practice:

1. The historical cost of an asset is the amount of cash or its equivalent paid to acquire it. Historical cost for a liability is the historical proceeds received when the liability is incurred.
2. Current cost of an asset is the amount of cash or other consideration that would be required today to obtain the same asset or its equivalent. For liabilities, current proceeds is the amount that would be received today if the same obligation were incurred.
3. Current exit value is the amount of cash or its equivalent that would be received currently if an asset were sold under conditions of orderly liquidation. For liabilities, current exit value is the amount of cash that would have to be paid currently to eliminate the liability.
4. Expected exit value is the nondiscounted cash flows associated with the expected sale or conversion of an asset at some future date. For liabilities, expected exit value is the amount of cash expected to be paid to settle the liability in the due course of business.
5. Present value of expected cash flows is the cash flows associated with the expected sale or conversion of an asset at some future date discounted at an appropriate rate of interest. For liabilities, the discounted amount of cash expected to be paid to settle the liability in the due course of business.

Historical cost (or historical exchange price) method underlies the conventional accounting system. Inventories, property, plant, and equipment are often recorded at historical or acquisition cost. Current cost is also used in measuring inventories. Current exit value is usually used for marketable equity securities. Expected exit value is often used for accounts receivable and accounts payable. Present value of expected cash flows is frequently used for long-term receivables and payables.

The monetary unit of measurement used in current practice is nominal units of money, unadjusted for changes in purchasing power of money over time.

MEASURE OF ECONOMIC WELFARE (MEW)
Although real gross national product (GNP) is a measure of the level of economic activity in our economy, it is not a measure of economic well-being. On the one hand, an increase in economic activity does not necessarily translate into an increase in our standard of living. Wars and disasters often stimulate economic activity because they generate an increase in government purchases in the case of a war and an increase in public and private spending in the case of a disaster. On the other hand, many positive contributions to economic welfare are not included in GNP estimates. The value of personal home repairs and household work is not included in the

national income accounts. The value of leisure time, which many view as contributing to well-being, is also not included in GNP.

Depreciation of business capital equipment is deducted from GNP to provide a measure of net national product (NNP). However, no other costs of production are subtracted, such as damage to the environment from production or depreciation of government-owned capital, highways, schools, or bridges.

An alternative measure to GNP was proposed nearly two decades ago by William Nordhaus and James Tobin. It is called measure of economic welfare (MEW). MEW includes the value of leisure time and work done outside of the marketplace and subtracts the cost of pollution and urban congestion, to note a few. Current estimate of MEW are larger than GNP, but MEW has been growing over time more slowly than GNP. MEW is not an official government index.

MEAT PACKING See PACKERS.

MECHANIC'S LIEN
A claim, created by statute law in most states, in favor of persons who have performed work or furnished materials in and for the erection or repair of a building. A mechanic's lien attaches to the land as well as to the building. It is a preferred claim and secures to the holder priority of payment, i.e., payment before that of other secured and general claims, except taxes.

MEDIUM OF EXCHANGE
In economic transactions money serves as a medium of exchange. Without money (a unit of account), all exchanges would take place through barter. With money, exchanges occur more efficiently.

The most important characteristic of any medium of exchange is that it is widely accepted. Gold, silver, and bank notes were, at one time, acceptable mediums of exchange. Confederate money also had its period of acceptance. Today, the U.S. currency is the accepted unit of account for exchanges in the United States.

BIBLIOGRAPHY

KING, R. G., and PLOSSER, C. I. "Money as the Mechanism of Exchange." *Journal of Monetary Economics*, January 1986.

MEETING
The types of corporate meetings may be illustrated by reference to business corporation law combined with provisions pertaining to business corporation in the general corporation law and stock corporation law. Provisions vary from state to state.

Directors' meetings are either regular meetings or special meetings, both of whch may be held at any place within or without the state unless otherwise provided by the certificate of incorporation or the BYLAWS. A majority of the entire board shall constitute a quorum, unless the certificate of incorporation requires a greater proportion or unless the certificate of incorporation or the bylaws specify less than a majority of the entire board but not less then one-third thereof. Unless the bylaws provide otherwise, regular meetings of the board may be held without notice if the time and place of such meetings are fixed by the bylaws or the board. Special meetings of the board, however, shall be held upon notice to the directors. But notice of meetings need not be given to any direcor who submits a signed waiver of notice (whether before or after the meeting) or who attends the meeting without protesting prior thereto or at its commencement the lack of notice.

Other provisions require written notice at least 10 days and not more than 50 days prior to a stockholder's meeting; the notice shall state who calls the meeting unless it is the annual meeting. Stockholders' meetings include the following types:

1. The annual meeting of stockholders for the purpose of electing directors. Section 602(b) requires that a meeting of shareholders shall be held annually for the election of directors and the transaction of other business on a date fixed by or under the bylaws.
2. Special meetings of stockholders. Such meetings may be called by the board of directors and by such person(s) as may be so authorized by the certificate of incorporation or the bylaws.
3. A special meeting of stockholders to oust holdover directors. If for a period of one month after the date fixed by or under the bylaws for the annual meeting of stockholders (or a period of 13 months after the formation of the corporation or the last annual meeting if no date has been so fixed) there is a failure to elect a sufficient number of directors to conduct the business of the corporation, the board of directors shall call a special meeting for the election of directors. But if the board does not call such special meeting within two weeks after the expiration of such period, or it is called but there is a failure to elect such directors for two months after the expiration of such period, holders of 10% of the shares entitled to vote for the election of directors may in writing demand the call of a special meeting for the election of directors, specifying the date and month (which shall not be less than two nor more than three months from the date of such call).

Upon receiving such written demand, the secretary of the corporation shall promptly give notice of such a meeting. If he fails to do so within five business days thereafter, any shareholder signing such demand may give such notice for the meeting, which shall be held at the place fixed in the bylaws or, if place is not so fixed, at the office of the corporation. For the purpose of electing directors but not for the transaction of any other business, a quorum at such a meeting shall be the shareholders attending in person or by PROXY entitled to vote in an election of directors, rather than the usual quorum of a majority of the shares entitled to vote.

In voting for directors, most states permit the certificate of incorporation of a business corporation to provide for CUMULATIVE VOTING. The certificate of incorporation or the bylaws are also permitted to provide for rotated (or staggered) directors by dividing the directors into two, three, or four classes, each to include not fewer than three directors.

MELON
In the stock market, a STOCK DIVIDEND or large extra cash dividend. When any extraordinary distribution of corporate profits is declared, the directors are said to have "cut a melon."

MELTDOWN
A term describing the precipitous drop in the stock average in October 1987. The term has a reference to the impact of the meltdown of an atomic reactor.

MEMBER BANK CALL REPORT
Statements of condition reported by member banks in response to calls from the Comptroller of the Currency, in the case of national banks, and from the Board of Governors of the Federal Reserve System, in the case of state member banks, are combined in the periodic *Member Bank Call Report*, a publication of the Board of Governors of the Federal Reserve System.

Calls by the Comptroller of the Currency and by the Board of Governors of the Federal Reserve System for statements of condition have been for identical dates since 1922. All member banks are required by law (Sec. 5211, Revised Statues, for national banks; Sec. 9 of the Federal Reserve Act) to be subject to not less than three calls a year, although customarily four calls per year have been issued. Each national bank in addition to submitting its official copy of its call statement to the Comptroller of the Currency, forwards a copy of the statement to its local federal Reserve bank. State member banks submit two copies of their call statements to their local Federal Reserve bank, one of which is forwarded to the board of governors. Tabulation of the national bank call figures is done by the Comptroller and of the state member banks figures by the board. The board of governors then combines its figures with those of the Comptroller of the Currency for publication in the *Member Bank Call Report*.

See CALL REPORT.

MEMBER BANKS
According to the Federal Reserve Act, "any National bank, State bank, or bank or trust company which has become a member of one of the Federal Reserve Banks." Since all national banks are required to join the FEDERAL RESERVE SYSTEM, they are, ipso facto, member banks.

The Federal Reserve defines a member bank as a "depository institution that is a member of the Federal Reserve. All national banks are required to be Federal Reserve System members, and state-chartered commercial banks and mutual savings banks may elect to become members. Member banks own stock in Federal Reserve Banks and elect some of the Federal Reserve Bank directors."

MERCANTILE AGENCIES
Companies engaged in the business of supplying credit information. Mercantile agencies are of

two classes, general and special. Of the general agencies, Dun & Bradstreet, Inc., is the oldest, best established, and most generally used. This company has been in existence for over 100 years (one of its antecedents having been the first general agency, established in New York City in 1841), and the entire country is served by its many branch offices. Its services are national in scope, the company is prepared to issue reports on practically any business house (producers, manufacturers, jobbers, wholesales, retailers, brokers, and traders) in the United States. Special agencies are those that limit their services to a single line or related lines of trade, and operate nationally or in a local field. Practically every trade association in the country has organized its own credit information exchange bureau. In addition, credit interchange bureaus, such as the National Association of Credit Management, exchange credit information among members, and the credit bureaus, such as those organized as the Associated Credit Bureaus of America, supply credit information and reports.

The general mercantile agencies furnish two kinds of reports, general and special. The general reports are contained in the reference or credit rating books, which are published quarterly. These books are leased (not sold) to the subscribers and contain many names—the *Dun & Bradstreet Reference Book* contains some 3 million names. Each name is given a capital and credit rating. The capital rating is based on the information contained in the financial statement that the agency endeavors to procure from each listed name every six months. The CREDIT RATING denotes the grade of credit to which the name is entitled in the opinion of the agency.

The special reports are usually limited to certain lines of business or to the more important names; the general agencies do not attempt to furnish such reports on all names. Special reports are obtained under contract, the price varying with the number requisitioned per year. The information furnished in special reports is of a general nature, but oftentimes quite extensive. As a rule these reports embody the following points: history, antecedents, and past record of the concern; present personnel; nature of the business; latest statement; total assets and liabilities from previous statements; location or properties; character and capacity of management; fire record; court record; general credit standing; opinion of the trade; and business outlook. From the standpoint of a bank undertaking a credit investigation, the special reports of the agencies are valuable in (1) furnishing the history of the concern, (2) furnishing leads which may be helpful in detecting other important information, and (3) corroborating information obtained from other sources.

Information obtained by the mercantile agencies is collected from various sources: (1) direct investigation of the name, (2) trade creditors and banking connections, (3) public records, and (4) insurance records. These agencies maintain a corps of reporters who call on trade, and written questionnaires and forwarded semi-annually to all business houses throughout the country to be answered and returned. Most businesspeople recognize the value of establishing and maintaining their credit position and consequently are willing to accede to the request of mercantile agencies for information. If this information cannot be secured directly, the facts are obtained from neighboring business houses or banks in their community.

Public records are also investigated. Usually the county clerk of each community is engaged to forward a report upon all items of interest to the central office of the agency. In large cities, agencies engage their own representatives to search these records. For instance, the records of the county recorder's office are searched for mortgages and other encumbrances, and various court records are searched for suits in civil or criminal cases, petitions and discharges in bankruptcy, and judgments and appeals.

The investigation of losses by fire, burglary, etc., constitutes an important part of the work of the general agencies. By special arrangements with the fire patrol of each city, local and national boards of fire underwriters, city and state fire marshals, and insurance companies, agencies are able to secure a vast amount of information concerning business insurance. Whenever a fire occurs, reports are made by the city fire patrol, local board of fire underwriters, etc., so that the agency can determine the amount of the loss, whether the business is insured, and the extent of the fire adjustment, in order to establish the net loss.

MERCANTILE EXCHANGE Some COMMODITY EXCHANGES offer interested dealers, processors, and speculators the facilities and advantages of futures trading in perishable commodities and thus are termed mercantile or produce markets, the specific commodities traded varying with each exchange.

Futures trading in perishable commodities was conducted in 1980 on the contract markets listed in the appended table, subject to regulation by the Commodity Futures Trading Commission.

In addition to the above markets, there are many regional spot markets throughout the country, for grain as well as other commodities.

MERCANTILE PAPER Notes, acceptances, and bills of exchange made or endorsed by concerns engaged in the jobbing, wholesaling, or retailing of commodities, as distinguished from obligations arising out of the production or manufacture of commodities. The short-term obligations of a wholesale grocery would be mercantile paper, whereas those of a farmer or steel manufacturer would not. Mercantile paper is a subclassification of COMMERCIAL PAPER.

Commodities Futures Trading

Market	Commodities
Chicago Mercantile Exchange	fresh eggs, potatoes, live hogs, pork bellies (frozen), live cattle, feeder cattle, broilers
Citrus Associates of the New York Cottom Exchange	orange juice (frozen concentrated)
New York Mercantile Exchange	imported lean beef, potatoes
Chicago Board of Trade	soybeans, soybean oil, soybean meal, iced broilers (besides grain)
MidAmerica Commodity Exchange	soybeans, live cattle, live hogs
Minneapolis Grain Exchange	sunflower seeds, wheat, oats
New York Coffee, Sugar & Cocoa Exchange	coffee ("C"), sugar (Nos. 11 and 12), cocoa
New York Cotton Exchange	cotton No. 2

MERCANTILISM Mercantilism, a term originally used by Adam Smith, refers to the theory that a country can grow stronger in world markets by exporting more goods than it imports. By so doing, this country is increasing its holding of gold. Smith explained the fallacy of this theory. True economic strength rests, he claimed, with the productive capabilities of a nation rather than with its monetary wealth.

MERCHANDISE TRADE ACCOUNT A trading country is both an importer and an exporter. A country may have either a trade surplus or a trade deficit, depending on the relative amounts of goods imported and exported. A trade surplus occurs when the value of exported goods is greater than the value of imported goods. A trade deficit occurs when the value of the imported goods exceeds the value of the exported goods. These calculations are based on estimates of the total payments for imports and the total receipts for exports. The estimates for all imported and exported goods are recorded in the merchandise trade account.

MERCHANT BANK Commercial and investment banks frequently found in European countries. Merchant banks frequently lend, borrow, underwrite, deal in securities, and provide other banking services. Certain aspects of merchant banking are prohibited for U.S. banks by the Glass-Steagall Act. However, U.S. banks are allowed to act as merchant banks in foreign countries with regulatory approval.

MERCHANTS' RULE A method for allowing interest credit on partial payments made on an installment basis. One variation of the merchants' rule requires that both debt and all partial payments are considered to earn interest up to the final date. The final amount due is their difference.

MERCHANDISE TURNOVER The rate at which the stock of merchandise of a concern is moved. It is also known as the momentum of sales or the sales-to-merchandise ratio. The merchandise turnover is properly determined by dividing the annual cost of goods sold by the average inventory, but in practice it is usually computed by dividing the annual net sales by the average inventory.

The merchandise turnover varies in different lines of business, each having a standard peculiar to itself. The merchandise turnover among wholesale groceries is naturally greater than in ship-building, jewelry, or the furniture business. It may be from seven to twelve in the former and two in the third and fourth. This ratio is an important barometer of the internal condition of a single business, and taken in the aggregate, it is a barometer of general business conditions. It is an indicator of overstocking or slow merchandising or of the rapid moving of goods, accordingly to whether the ratio is high or low. No greater amount of capital than necessary should be tied up in inventories; the faster goods can be turned, the greater the profit on the capital invested. Assuming the same margin of gross profit or markup, it is more profitable to move $50,000 of goods twenty times a year than $100,000 of goods ten times, because in the first instance the business can be carried on with half the capital of the second. Relatively high merchandise turnover indicates the capacity of the management to move its goods quickly and discloses a favorable condition.

In analysis of credit risks, wherever the merchandise turnover is high, insistence on a high current ratio is less important.

MERGER A combination of two or more corporations wherein the dominant unit absorbs the passive unit, the former continuing operations usually under the same name. By contrast, in a consolidation two units combine and are succeeded by a new corporation, usually with a new title.

State laws usually prescribe the conditions and procedures under which mergers of domestic corporations with other domestic corporations, or with "foreign" corporations (those chartered in other states), may be effected. Such statutory mergers have as a distinguishing characteristic that, under such special statutory procedure, the merger of one corporation with another will automatically terminate the corporate existence of the merged corporation upon issuance by the state of a final certificate of merger. Requirements for issuance of such a certificate usually are ratification by the stockholders' specified minimum consent (majority, two-thirds, three fourth, 80%—the prescribed ratios of consent of stockholders entitled to vote thereon vary among the states) at special meetings of stockholders called to act on the proposal of merger; filing of the article of merger with the state agency concerned (usually the office of the state's Secretary of State) together with franchise taxes and fees required; and compliance by such articles with all the provisions of the state law. State laws usually provide that stockholders dissenting from the merger may upon proper procedure be entitled to receive in cash the appraised (fair) value of their shares (right of appraisal).

Table 1 / Mergers and Acquisitions—Historical Summary: 1965 to 1987

Item	Unit	1965	1970	1980	1981	1982	1983	1984	1985	1986	1987
Mergers and acquisitions, net [1]	Number	2,125	5,152	1,889	2,395	2,346	2,533	2,543	3,001	3,336	2,032
Dollar value paid	Bil. dol.	NA	16.4	44.3	82.6	53.8	73.1	122.2	179.8	173.1	163.7
$100 million-plus deals	Number	NA	10	94	113	116	138	200	270	346	301
Method of payment:											
Cash	Percent	67	29	47	42	38	32	43	51	42	41
Stock	Percent	30	52	31	34	29	35	26	23	32	34
Combination	Percent	3	16	21	23	31	33	30	26	26	24
Debt	Percent	([2])	3	1	1	2	—	1	—	—	1
Divestitures	Number	191	1,401	666	830	875	932	900	1,218	1,259	807
Acquisitions of publicly traded sellers	Number	NA	NA	173	168	180	190	211	336	386	286
Acquisitions of privately held sellers	Number	NA	NA	988	1,330	1,222	1,316	1,351	1,358	1,598	855
Foreign sellers, total	Number	NA	NA	102	101	121	146	147	175	180	142
Foreign buyers, total	Number	NA	NA	187	234	154	125	151	197	264	220
Average P/E paid	Percent	19.4	23.1	15.2	15.6	13.9	16.7	17.2	18.0	22.2	23.3
Average premium paid over market	Percent	NA	33.4	49.9	48.0	47.4	37.7	37.9	37.1	38.2	38.3
Cancelled transactions	Number	NA	527	178	163	189	162	218	236	199	155

— Represents zero
NA - Not available.
[1] Represents announcement.
[2] A separate count for debt payments began in 1970.

Table 2 / Merger and Acquisition Transactions—Number and Value, by Industry: 1983 to 1987
(Represents transactions for which valuation data are publicly reported.)

Industry classification of seller	Number of mergers					Nominal value (mil. dol.)				
	1983	1984	1985	1986	1987	1983	1984	1985	1986	1987
Total	2,533	2,543	3,001	3,336	2,032	73,081	122,224	179,768	173,137	163,686
Oil and gas	111	102	86	58	30	12,076	42,982	23,160	3,247	15,442
Banking and finance	331	251	381	415	262	13,628	5,846	14,037	19,442	16,209
Insurance	67	66	67	94	38	2,966	3,006	2,694	5,413	2,484
Mining and minerals	18	12	16	14	8	2,946	347	356	148	676
Food processing	74	58	82	101	78	1,164	7,095	11,838	4,707	3,316
Conglomerate	13	18	14	20	6	2,745	6,983	16,302	15,307	6,839
Transportation	36	36	48	58	34	5,255	1,252	2,877	6,829	4,956
Broadcasting	60	83	93	123	64	3,747	1,918	15,013	8,107	8,729
Retail	90	130	136	147	150	1,489	6,673	10,030	13,683	17,039
Brokerage and investment firms	63	86	49	47	32	1,455	1,460	579	1,710	3,492
Other	1,670	1,701	2,029	2,259	1,330	25,609	44,662	82,882	94,544	84,504

Source: W. T. Grimm & Co., Chicago, IL, *Mergerstat Review*, 1987. (Copyright)

Table 3 / Largest Corporate Mergers or Acquisitions in U.S.
As of mid-1988

Company	Acquirer	Dollars	Year
Gulf Oil	Chevron	13.3 bln.	1984
Getty Oil	Texaco	10.1 bln.	1984
Conoco	DuPont	8.0 bln.	1981
Standard Oil	British Petroleum	7.9 bln.*	1987
Marathon Oil	U.S. Steel	6.5 bln.	1981
Beatrice	Kohlberg Kravis Roberts	6.2 bln.	1986
RCA	General Electric	6.2 bln.	1986
Superior Oil	Mobil Oil	5.7 bln.	1984
General Foods	Philip Morris	5.6 bln.	1985
Safeway Stores	Kohlberg Kravis Roberts	5.3 bln.	1986
Southern Pacific	Santa Fe Railroad	5.2 bln.	1983
Southland	J.T. Acquisition	5.1 bln.	1987
Hughes Aircraft	General Motors	5.0 bln.	1985
Nabisco	R.J. Reynolds	4.9 bln.	1985
Signal Cos.	Allied Corp.	4.9 bln.	1986
Sperry	Burroughs	4.8 bln.	1986
Connecticut General	INA	4.3 bln.	1981
Borg-Warner	AV Holdings	4.2 bln.	1987
Texasgulf	Elf Aouitane	4.2 bln.	1981
Cities Service	Occidental Petroleum	4.0 bln.	1982
Dome Petroleum	Amoco	3.8 bln.	1987
R.H. Macy	various investors	3.7 bln.	1986
American Hospital	Baxter Travenol	3.7 bln.	1986
Owens-Illinois	Kohlberg Kravis Roberts	3.6 bln.	1987
Belridge Oil	Shell Oil	3.6 bln.	1979
Allied Stores	Campeau	3.5 bln.	1986
Fort Howard Paper	FH Acquisition Corp.	3.5 bln.	(1)
ABC Broadcasting	Captial Cities Comm.	3.5 bln.	1985
Viacom	National Amusements	3.4 bln.	1987
Chesebrough-Ponds	Unilever N.V.	3.1 bln.	1987
MidCon	Occidental Petroleum	3.0 bln.	1986
Texas Oil and Gas	USX Corp.	3.0 bln.	1986
Carnation	Nestle	2.8 bln.	1984
Celanese	American Hoechst	2.7 bln.	1987
G.D. Searle	Monsanto	2.7 bln.	1985
Esmark	Beatrice Foods	2.7 bln.	1986
G.D. Searle	Monsanto	2.7 bln.	1985
Continental Group	Kiewit-Murdock	2.7 bln.	1984
St. Joe Minerals	Fluor	2.6 bln.	1981
Electronic Data Systems	General Motors	2.6 bln.	1984
Associated Dry Goods	May Dept. Stores	2.5 bln.	1986

*For the 45% of Standard Oil that British Petroleum did not already own.
(1) Still pending, Sept. 1988.
In 1987, there were 3,469 mergers and acquisitions completed or pending, a sharp drop from the 4,024 mergers of 1986. The value of the deals was $150 billion, compared with $190 billion in 1986.

Upon issuance of the certificate of merger from the state, the merger is effective, no conveyances, deeds, or other instruments of transfer of property between the corporations involved being necessary, with the continuing corporation being entitled to all the assets and rights of the combining corporations, but also being liable for all the undisturbed debts, claims, and other liabilities of the component corporations in the merger.

State laws pertaining to mergers of state-chartered banks and trust companies, insurance companies, and other financial institutions make special provision for the procedures and requirements involved in the banking and insurance laws governing such institutions. For a discussion of banking mergers, *see* BANK (CONSOLIDATION OF BANK, MERGER).

Motivations for mergers include additional capacity; expand market share (horizontal); diversification of products (conglomerate); backward (vertical) integration (manufacturers acquiring raw material supply companies); forward (vertical) integration (manufacturers acquiring sales outlets); additional capacity located in new markets; and a special kind of motive, acquisition of tax-loss corporations by profit-making companies in order to reduce tax liability, a type of merger now restricted by the tax laws (*see* REVENUE ACT).

Takeover activity in recent years has been stimulated by the inflation in costs of expansion by acquiring firms, as compared with market prices frequently prevailing below fair "real" values for takeover candidates, which situation makes it more economic to acquire such existing firms rather than expand and build extra capacity by the acquiring firms. Under SEC rules, any acquisition of voting stock of 5% or more must be reported. A frequently used tactic to enlarge holdings in the takeover candidates is the tender offer, also subject to SEC and state rules as to disclosure of principals involved and full details, which is aimed at stockholders of the targeted takeover firms. The acquiring firm offers to pay a premium over prevailing market price for a specified time period and maximum total of shares accepted at the tender offer's price.

It should be noted that use of the HOLDING COMPANY charter powers of an acquiring company eliminates the necessity for the stockholders' minimum ratio of approval of the proposed acquisition as well as the necessity for payment of the right of appraisal of fair value in cash to the dissenting stockholders of both the acquiring company and the acquired firm in the case of merger or consolidation. The holding company as the acquiring company simply buys enough of the voting securities of the acquired company in order to vote in a majority or all of the directors of the acquired company, thus gaining control of the acquired company, which instead of being disolved may be continued in existence as an affiliate or subsidiary of the acquiring company.

In 1985, the Supreme Court approved the concept of regional interstate banking arrangements. This ruling upheld Florida and Massachusetts laws that established the pattern for regions throughout the United States. Various states have joined to sanction interstate mergers and to remove certain barriers in New England, the Southeast, the Midwest, and the far West.

The Federal Deposit Insurance Corporation has arranged mergers or acquisitions of insolvent banks. The 1987 Regulators' Bill gave the FDIC authority to establish "bridge banks" to facilitate the disposition of large failing banks. The FDIC was given authority to establish an interim organization to stabilize the deteriorating condition of the insolvent bank and to obtain time to prepare an orderly merger or acquisition. The bridge bank concept raised considerable concern over government control and ownership of banks.

Whether or not specific mergers are violative of the ANTITRUST LAWS is a question of fact and law. Under the Clayton Act, the Federal Trade Commission has concurrent jurisdiction with the Department of Justice with regard to enforcement of prohibitions of monopolistic devices specified in the Clayton Act. The commission also has jurisdiction over "unfair methods of competition" (Sec. 5 of the Federal Trade Commission Act). The Department of Justice, however, has been particularly active in antitrust cases. Informally, the Department of Justice will advise beforehand as to whether or not a proposed merger of business corporations will be violative. If upon full disclosure the department does not find a proposed merger violative, it will not be stopped subsequently from bringing civil action against the executed merger, but the affirmative advisory will at least mean no criminal action against the parties involved in a merger.

In 1982 and again in 1984, the Department of Justice, at the urging of President Ronald Reagan, relaxed its antitrust criteria regarding mergers and business combinations. This policy intensified the trend of increased merger activity that began in the early 1970s. During the Reagan administration there have been more than 250,000 merger-related activities valued at over $2 trillion. Critics suggest that this rash of mergers will reduce domestic competition, but proponents point to the fact that there is little empirical evidence in support of that argument. There is some evidence that merger activity has slightly reduced private research and development (R&D) activity in the United States owing to the fact that post-merger firms extinguish the smaller firm's R&D program.

The appended tables compare the total number of mergers and aquisitions from 1965 to 1987 along with supporting details. The largest corporate mergers or acquisitions in the U.S. as of mid-1988 is also appended.

BIBLIOGRAPHY

ALBERTS, W. W. "Have Interstate Acquisitions Been Profitable." American Banker, September 18, 1986.
ARTHUR ANDERSEN & Co. *Buying and Selling Banks*. Arthur Andersen & Co., Chicago, IL, 1985.

AUSTIN, D. V. "The Herfindahl-Hirschman Index: Analyzing Its Effectiveness." *Issues in Banking Regulation,* Summer, 1988.

CATES, D. C. "Bank Analysis For a Takeover Era." *Magazine of Bank Administration,* December, 1988..

Directory of Financial Sources for Buyouts & Acquisitions. Venture Economics. Latest Edition

"Hostile Bank Takeovers."*Issues in Bank Regulation,* Winter, 1989.

KERWIN, J. S., and ROBINSON, R. A. "Chartering a Bank's Value: Number Analysis and Beyond." *ABA Banking Journal,* July, 1986.

McKinsey and Co. *Bankers' Merger and Acquisition Choices: Mapping a Course Through Consolidation,* 1985.

Mergers and Acquisitions.

PERRY, L. T. "Merging Successfully: Sending the 'Right' Signals." *Sloan Management Review,* Spring, 1986.

RIZZI, J. V. "Acquisition Analysis for Banks." *Bankers Magazine,* January-February, 1988.

ROSE, P. S. *Bank Mergers in a Deregulated Environment Scrutinizing the Promises, Avoiding the Pitfalls,* 1988.

———. "The Changing Bank Customer." *Canadian Banker,* 1987.

———. "The Impact of Mergers in Banking: Evidence from a Nationwide Sample of Federally Chartered Banks." *Journal of Economics and Business,* November, 1987.

SCRANTON, D. "Managing of Credit Risks in a Bank Merger." *Journal of Commercial Bank Lending,* January, 1986.

SULLIVAN, M. P. "Understanding of Cultures Is Critical in Managing Acquisitions." *American Banker,* November, 26, 1986.

WELKEN, D. L. "Thrift Competition: Does It Matter?" *Economic Review,* Jan./Feb., 1986.

MESSENGER A name given to certain employees of banks and brokerage houses. The chief function of bank messengers is to collect, by direct presentation, items (checks, notes, acceptances, etc.) not drawn on clearinghouse banks and not collectible through the clearinghouse. They also collect special items drawn on individuals, brokers, corporations, etc., such as arrival drafts and drafts with stocks and bonds attached. Collections made by messengers are frequently known as collections by hand. The larger banks maintain a large corps of messengers usually under the supervision of the city collection or note teller's department. They are given specific instructions, are not allowed to use their own discretion, may accept only cash or certified checks in payment of items, and must demand the return of all unpaid items.

Brokers' messengers are employed to effect the transfer and delivery of securities and are frequently entrusted with large amounts of valuable papers. Protection from possible loss by the dishonesty of messengers should be provided through fidelity and theft insurance. Increasing use of central securities depositories has reduced the necessity for such brokers' messengers, often called "runners."

METAL EXCHANGE See COMMODITY EXCHANGE, INC.

METALS See ALUMINUM, COPPER, GOLD BARS, GOLD PRODUCTION, SCRAP, SILVER, STEEL, STEEL ALLOYS, TIN, ZINC.

METHODS OF TRADING See TRADING METHODS.

METRIC SYSTEM A decimal system of weights and measures which originated in France. The basic unit of the system is the meter, which is approximately one ten-millionth of the distance on a meridian from the equator to the pole, or about 39.37 inches.

Proposed U.S. Conversion to Metric System. In accordance with the Metric Study Act of 1968, the Secretary of Commerce presented to the Congress on July 30, 1971, a report prepared by the department's National Bureau of Standards, "A Metric America—A Decision Whose Time Has Come," representing the results of three years of studies, surveys, and analyses by the bureau with the cooperation of many individuals and organized professional educational, business, labor, and consumer groups throughout the country. In endorsing the report's basic conclusion in favor of "going metric," the Secretary of Commerce recommended a coordinated, ten-year changeover to the metric system, done through a coordinated national program.

Measures of Length

Metric denomination and value		Equivalent in common use
myriameter	10,000 meters	6.2137 miles
kilometer	1,000 meters	0.62137 mi. (3280 ft. 10 in.)
kectometer	100 meters	328 feet, 1 inch
decameter	10 meters	393.7 inches
meter	1 meter	39.37 inches
decimeter	1/10 meter	3.937 inches
centimeter	1/100 meter	0.3937 inch
millimeter	1/1,000 meter	0.03937 inch

Measures of Capacity

Metric denomination and value			Equivalent in common use	
Name	Liters	Cubic measure	Dry measure	Liquid measure
kiloliter (stere)	1,000	1 cu. meter	1,308 cu. yds.	264.18 gals.
hectoliter	100	0.1 cu. meter	2,838 bu.	26.42 gals.
decaliter	10	10 cu. dm.	9.08 qts	2.64 gals.
liter	1	1 cu. dm.	0.908 qt.	1.0567 qts.
deciliter	1/10	0.1 cu. dm.	6.1025 cu. in.	0.845 gill
centiliter	1/100	10 cu. cm.	0.6102 cu. in.	0.338 fl. oz.
milliliter	1/1,000	1 cu. cm.	0.061 cu. in.	0.27 fl. dr.

Measures of Surface

Metric denomination and value		Equivalent in common use
hectare	10,000 sq. meters	2.471 acres
are	100 sq. meters	119.6 square yards
centare	1 sq. meter	1,550 square yards

Weights

Metric denomination and value			
Name	Grams	Water at maximum density	Equivalent in common use avoirdupois weight
millier (tonneau)	1,000,000	1 cu. meter	2,204.62 pounds
quintal	100,000	1 hectoliter	220.46 pounds
myriagram	10,000	1 decaliter	22.046 pounds
kilogram	1,000	1 liter	2.2046 pounds
hectogram	100	1 deciliter	3.527 ounces
decagram	10	10 cu. centimeters	0.3527 ounces
gram	1	1 cu. centimeter	15.432 grains
decigram	1/10	0.1 cu. centimeter	1.5432 grains
centigram	1/100	10 cu. millimeters	0.1543 grain
milligram	1/1,000	1 cu. millimeter	0.0154 grain

The secretary suggested that the Congress assign the responsibility for guiding the change, and anticipating the kinds of special problems described in the report, to a central coordinating body.

In releasing the report, the secretary stated that "for many years, this nation has been slowly 'going metric', and it would continue to do so regardless of national plans and policies. At the same time, the worldwide use of the metric system is increasing, and today ours is the only major nation which has not decided to take such a step. As the Report states, a metric America would seem to be desirable in terms of our stake in world trade, the development of international standards, relations with our neighbors and other countries, and national security."

With regard to the problem of conversion costs, the secretary recommended that "in order to encourage efficiency and minimize the overall costs to society, the general rule should be that any changeover costs shall 'lie where they fall'."

The appended tables list metric values and their common English system equivalents.

Congress legislated a voluntary metric conversion program, with a national board of 17 members to plan and coordinate the conversion, and the President signed the bill on December 23, 1975. On insistence of organized labor, and because of earlier opposition by small business based on the questions of subsidies to small business and assistance to workers to buy metric calibrated tools, Congress made it clear in the legislation that it did not call for compulsory conversion to the metric system to be a national goal.

The U.S. Metric Board, established by the above referenced legislation, the Metric Conversion Act of 1975, was terminated as such in September, 1983, in connection with the overall program of government deregulations of business by the Reagan administration, and what remains of it is an office in the Department of Commerce where it continues to have the objective of encouraging conversion to the metric system in the U.S.

But metrification by 1983 had already made progress in adoption in such lines as the automobile industry (General Motors, Ford); electronics industry (computers, communications equipment, etc.); chemical industry; sports equipment; cameras and film; wine, liquor, milk, and soft drink containers, and to some extent, at gasoline pump stations.

The American National Metric Council, an industry-sponsored group, points out that as of 1983 the only countries in the world that were either on the way to metrification or completely metrified were the U.S., Burma, and Brunei. The Council particularly stresses the importance of metrification in facilitating foreign trade and participation in sports abroad.

In many jurisdictions, however, measurements are required to be stated both metrically and conventionally on the container of comsumer goods. And the American National Metric Council concedes that conversion of such structure as football fields, baseball diamonds, and railroad trackage and other transportation signs and installations would not be feasible; nor would conversion of money or time.

The U.S. Metric Board pointed out that Congress first legalized the use of the metric system in the U.S. in 1866 and supplied each state with a set of standard metric weights and measures. In 1875, the U.S. was among 17 signatory nations to the Treaty of the Meter, which led to establishment of the metric system at the international system of measurement. The conventional or customary measurements—the foot, pound, etc.—actually has been defined in relation to the meter and kilogram since 1893 in the U.S.

BIBLIOGRAPHY

NATIONAL BUREAU OF STANDARDS, U.S. Department of Commerce. *What About Metric?*
———. *Some References on Metric Information. Charts on All You Need to Know About Metric and Metric Conversion Factors.*
U.S. METRIC BOARD. *U.S. Metric Board—An Introduction.*

METRIC TON A unit of weight used in European countries, particularly in measuring grains. A metric ton is equal to 2,204.62 avoirdupois pounds.

See METRIC SYSTEM.

MICROECONOMICS It is common practice to divide the study of economics into two parts, microeconomics and MACROECONOMICS. Microeconomics (micro meaning small) is the study of the allocation or exchange of scarce resources among market participants—consumers and producers (firms). Many argue that microeconomics is the foundation for macroeconomics because within microeconomic theory the fundamentals of exchange are developed.

MIDAMERICA COMMODITY EXCHANGE (MidAm) Founded in the 1860, the MidAm originally was incorporated as the Chicago Open Board of Trade. The exchange adopted its present name in 1972. In March 1986, the MidAm officially became affiliated with the Chicago Board of Trade. Under the agreement, all MidAm and full Chicago Board Options Exchange members have access to all MidAm contracts. All MidAm transacitons are cleared through the Board of Trade Clearing Corporation.

The MidAm offers a broad array of futures and options on futures geared specifically for the smaller hedger and speculator. The exchange's products are typically one-fifth to one-half as large as similar contracts at other exchanges. The contract listings include livestock, foreign currencies, grains, and metals.

MIDWEST STOCK EXCHANGE This stock exchange, second largest in trading volume among the regional national securities exchanges, dates from December 1, 1949, representing a merger of the Cleveland, Minneapolis-St Paul, and St. Louis STOCK EXCHANGES with the Chicago Stock Exchange. The Chicago Stock Exchange dated from March 21, 1882, when it was organized by a group of 131 Chicago businessmen.

In various aspects of its program of expansion and innovation, the Midwest Stock Exchange's trading floor has been rearranged and expanded, and a computerized system of order routing has been installed, under which a member firm is able to check the market on the Midwest Stock exchange (MSE) for possibly better executions of orders for duals (stocks traded on the Midwest Stock Exchange as well as fully listed on the New York Stock Exchange).

MILKING A process employed by the management of some companies of exploiting their business by squeezing the last cent of profit from operations, e.g., by failing to reserve a part of earnings for expansion and improvements, by not charging sufficient depreciation, by paying flagrantly over-liberal salaries, or by engaging in other improper, although perhaps legal, accounting methods. The term was also applied to the directors of public utility holding companies whose financial practices tended to enrich the stockholders at the expense of the operating companies and their public through malmanagement rather than mismanagement.

MILL A monetary unit of account of U.S. currency having a value of one-tenth of one cent. It is not coined, but is used in money calculations where precision in fractions of a cent is required.

MILLING The ridged or furrowed edge forming the circumference (rim) of coins. The nickel and bronze coins of the United States are not milled. The purpose of milling is to prevent the clippping or filing of the edges and the sale of such clippings by dishonest persons, by making the filing or mutilation so obvious that the coin could not be easily passed. Coins are designed to be thicketst at the edges in order to protect better the engraved figures on the obverse and reverse surfaces.

See ABRAISION, COINAGE.

MINIMUM EFFICIENT SCALE The output level that corresponds to a firm's ability to capture all economics of scale. Minimum efficient scale occurs where long-run average cost is a minimum. In other words, the firm, even through capital expansion, can not produce its product at a lower average cost. There are circumstances in which minimum efficient scale is so large that it is economically efficient for there to be only one producer of the product. If the industry were competitive, each firm would be producing at a higher average cost than under the monopoly situation. When such a situation exists, as in the case of the production and distribution of electricity, monopoly privilege is granted, but the company's price is regulated so that excessive profits are not earned. Such monopolies are called natural monopolies.

MINIMUM WAGE The concept of minimum wage was first developed by Pope Leo XIII in his 1891 letter to church bishops, *Rerum Novarum* (new matters). Therein, he argued that workers must earn a "living wage" sufficient for them to live a truly human

MINIMUM FREE BALANCE

life and to face their family responsibilities with dignity. However, it was not until the early 1900s that support for a minimum wage began to grow in the United States. Proponents believed that legislation was needed to protect industrial workers from exploitation and allow them to live at a reasonable standard. Opponents believed that wage rates should be market determined through the interaction of supply and demand.

A minimum wage is the least amount a worker can earn per hour, as set by law. The first minimum wage law (applicable only to women and children) was enacted in Massachusetts in 1912. Other states followed with similar legislation. However, in 1928 the Supreme Court ruled that the minimum wage in the District of Columbia was unconstitutional because it violated individual's freedom to contract. The first federal minimum wage law was enacted in 1931 as part of the Davis-Bacon Act. The act established that local labor market wages were to be the minimum wage paid to workers on federally financed construction projects. After several unsuccessful efforts to enact a general minimum wage law by the Roosevelt Administration, the Fair Labor Standards Act was passed in 1938, establishing a minimum wage of $0.25 per hour for both men and women. Since 1938, the minimum wage has increased, as shown in the data below.

Effective Date	Minimum Wage Per Hour
10/24/38	$0.25
10/24/39	0.30
10/24/45	0.40
1/25/50	0.75
3/1/56	1.00
9/3/61	1.15
9/3/63	1.25
2/1/67	1.40
2/1/68	1.60
5/1/74	2.00
1/1/75	2.10
1/1/76	2.30
1/1/78	2.65
1/1/79	2.90
1/1/80	3.10
1/1/87	3.35

Source: U.S. Department of Labor

In December 1989, enacted legislation raised the minimum wage as of April 1991 to $4.25 from the April 1990 $3.80. The increase was the first increase in the minimum wage in more than nine years. The minimum wage package also introduced a training wage differential for individuals entering the workforce who are under age 20—$3.35 an hour minimum April 1990 and $3.61 (85% of the minimum wage) in April 1991.

MINIMUM FREE BALANCE In checking or nonborrowing accounts, the AVERAGE BALANCE, also known as the compensating balance, maintained by a borrowing account. Cost accounting systems for checking accounts customarily allow an interest credit, based on the average rate of return earned on earning assets, on the minimum free balance in determining the service charge for activity of the account. Some banks offer checking services in a variety of forms featuring no requirement of minimum balances, operating instead on a flat charge per check or per account up to a maximum number of items handled.

See BANK COST ACCOUNTING, COMPENSATING BALANCES.

MINING SECURITIES The stock and bonds of coal, copper, silver, lead, zinc, and gold mining companies. In general, this class of securities is the most speculative of all, especially if the properties are undeveloped. In considering the purchase of mining securities, one should carefully distinguish between producing and undeveloped companies. A veteran analyst distinguished among producers that pay dividends, producers that do not pay dividends, corporations in the development stage which may or may not produce, and prospects consisting of leases or options upon property thought to contain mineral deposits.

In computing the worth of producing mining properties, the most important factors to consider are the extent of ore reserves, the cost of mining the given metal in comparison with its selling price, and the accounting policy with regard to DEPLETION.

Nowadays it is usually implied that mining technology has advanced to a point where ore reserves can be exactly estimated. This is far from the truth in the case of precious metals, where there is no way of accurately determining the length of a vein except by exploitation and exploration. In the case of coal and copper, however, more or less accurate estimates can be made.

There is a wide difference in the cost of production of a given mineral from mine to mine and, within a given mine, from ore to ore according to grade. Thus, within every producing district there will be relatively high-cost and low-cost producers.

When the raw material, coal or ore, has been entirely extracted from a mine in commercially practicable quantities, the property, including the machinery and equipment is almost worthless. It is specialized machinery, and the cost to move it would be nearly as much as it is worth. For this reason a mining company must provide, in addition to earnings, an amount sufficient to liquidate the original investment. In order to retire its capital investment, a mining company must formulate a policy of depletion which will permit periodically setting aside out of earnings a sum which, when the mineral assets have become exhausted, will equal the original investment. The perfection of the depletion policy depends upon the accuracy with which estimates of ore reserves are made and then revised as development and exploration proceed. Many mining companies do not make charges for depletion and therefore do not build up depletion reserves. When this is the case, dividends on stocks of such mining companies consist not only of a distribution from current earnings, but also of a return of investment.

Bonds are rare among mining companies as a class, but various well-established coal companies have issued them. Mining bonds should always be of the sinking fund variety, which provide for the periodic setting aside out of earnings sums with which to retire the bonds, particularly in proportion to extraction of the mineral asset if reserves are relatively low and the rate of production high.

MINNEAPOLIS GRAIN EXCHANGE A central marketplace for grain produced in Minnesota, North Dakota, South Dakota and eastern Montana. The exchange provides an auction site for the buyers and sellers of grain: farmers/producers, merchants, processors, shippers, country and terminal elevator operators, and brokers.

Prices on the exchange are negotiated between the buyer and the seller. The exchange records the price and other details of the transaction and provides a centralized meeting place for buyers and sellers. The trading room is the heart of the exchange. An average of one million bushels of grain are traded each day at the cash tables, including wheat, barley, oats, rye, sunflower seed, flax, corn, and soybeans, millet, milo, and rapeseed. When a sale is made at the cash tables, the grain is delivered to the buyer.

The futures market includes hard spring wheat, oats, and high-fructose corn syrup contracts that are traded in pits. Hand signals are often used to signify offers and bids. Trading is done by open outcry. A futures contract for wheat usually involves a round lot of 5,000 bushels, although a smaller job lot of 1,000 bushels is sometimes specified. The contract specifies a certain grade of grain to be delivered. Prices from the cash and futures markets are reported three times daily via phone at 9:45 A.M., 11:30 A.M., and 2:00 P.M.

The Minneapolis Grain Exchange has a membership of more than 400 individuals, representing about 140 firms. Membership is open to anyone 21 years old or older who has a reputation for fair and honest business dealings.

MINOR COINAGE PROFIT The SEIGNIORAGE profit which the Bureau of the Mint derives in coining MINOR COINS from the constituent metals. It is equal to the difference between the monetary value of the coins and the commercial value of the metals consumed in their coinage. Because all coins for domestic circulation produced in recent years have had cupronickel metallic content (copper and nickel), the MINT has reported total seigniorage.

During the fiscal year 1986, the Mint deposited $518.1 million in the general fund of the U.S. Treasury. Seigniorage on U.S. coins accounted for $392.4 million of the total. The 1986 total seigniorage compared with $515.9 million for 1985, $498.4 million for 1984, $477.5 million for 1983, $390.4 million for 1982, and $450.2 million for 1981. From January 1, 1935, through September 1986, the Mint-reported total seigniorage was $13,204.1 million.

MINOR COINS In the currency system of the U.S. the nickel (five-cent piece) and the cent (one-cent piece).

Composition of the nickel coin currently coined consists of a homogeneous alloy of 75% copper and 25% nickel, with a total standard weight of 77.16 grains, coined under the authorizing acts of May 16, 1866, and February 12, 1873. For a short period, from October 1, 1942, until expiration of the authority on Decembr 31, 1945, the silver nickel was coined under the authority of the act of March 27, 1942, as amended with the same total weight of 77.16 grains, but consisting of 56% copper, 35% silver, and 9% manganese.

Composition of the one-cent coin currently coined consists of 2.5% copper plated to a 97.5% zinc core, with a total weight of 38.58 grains. This (CPZ) cent was phased in with the bronze one-cent piece during 1982. From 1983 on, all one-cent coins were of the CPZ composition. Composition of the former bronze one-cent consisted of a homogeneous alloy of 95% copper and 25% nickel, with a total weight of 48 grains, which was authorized by the act of September 5, 1962, which amended Section 3515 of the revised statutes as amended (31 U.S.C. 317), calling formerly for composition of 95% copper and 5% tin and zinc, in such proportions as shall be determined by the director of the Mint. Under legislation enacted December 18, 1942 the use of tin in the alloy was discontinued, and the copper-zinc cent was coined by order of the secretary of the Treasury, dated December 16, 1943, from January, 1944, until expiration of the authority on December 31, 1946. After this emergency legislation expired, the use of tin in the alloy was resumed, as specified by law, but at the discretion of the director of the Mint it was resumed in infinitesimal quantities, approximately 0.1%. The 95% copper-5% zinc composition had proved entirely satisfactory as to the life, quality, and appearance of the coins produced. Also during the war year 1943, the zinc-steel cent was coined by orders of the secretary of the Treasury on December 23, 1942 and May 15, 1943.

The historical record of production of the minor coins by the U.S. Mint since 1793 is shown on the appended table.

Output of Minor Coins (billions of pieces)

	5-cent denomination	1-cent denomination
1793-1900	0.4	1.4
1901-1950	3.9	17.9
1951-1970	6.8	47.4
1971-1986	13.2	162.6

Source: U.S. Mint Annual Reports

MINORITIES The Community Reinvestment Act specified the need to support and encourage minority enterprises. The act requires that bank credit policies must be administered equitably within a community. Minority concerns also arise in the area of equal opportunity employment and affirmative action.

MINORITY BUSINESS DEVELOPMENT AGENCY

An agency of the federal government whose purpose is to develop and coordinate a national program for minority business enterprise. The agency was created to assist minority business in achieving effective and equitable participation in the American free enterprise system and in overcoming social and economic system disadvantages that have limited their participation in the past. MBDA provides national policies and leadership in forming and strengthening a partnership of business, industry, and government with the nation's minority businesses.

MBDA conducts most of its activities through its six regional offices (Atlanta, Chicago, Dallas, New York, San Francisco, Washington) and four district offices.

MINORITY INTEREST The interest of other shareholders in a subsidiary when a parent company owns less than 100% of the subsidiary; the noncontrolling interest in a subsidiary. Under proportional consolidation, the parent consolidates only its ownership in each of the subsidiary's finance statement items (such as 90% of cash, inventory, sales, and so on). Under full consolidation, the parent consolidates the entire amount of each of the subsidiary's individual assets, liability, and income statement accounts with those of the parent company. The additional amounts consolidated represent the minority interest. The minority interest in the subsidiary's net assets and net income are reported as separate items in the consolidated financial statements. The full consolidation method is commonly used in the preparation of consolidated financial statements.

In practice there is no complete uniformity in presenting the minority interest in consolidated financial statements. Most companies report the minority interest either as a part of the liability section or between the liability and stockholders' equity section of the balance sheet. A few companies classify the minority interest as a part of stockholders' equity.

MINORITY STOCKHOLDERS Those owning less than a majority controllng interest in the stock of a corporation. The majority of the stock of a corporatiopn may be held by another corporation (see HOLDING COMPANY) or by a few individuals who control its policy by using the voting power of the stock they own to elect a majority of the board of directors.

By means of CUMULATIVE VOTING, minority stockholders who hold at least the minimum number of voting shares necessary to elect one director may elect one or more directors and thereby have representation on the board, a situation not possible under ordinary (statutory) voting of one vote per share of voting stock.

MINT A place where metallic MONEY is manufactured or coined. The Bureau of the Mint, also known simply as the Mint, is one of the bureaus in the organization of the Treasury Department and is headed by the director of the Mint.

The principal mission of the United States Mint is to manufacture an adequate volume of coins for the nation to conduct its trade and commerce. The other major responsibilities of the Mint include the manufacture of medals of a national character; the manufacture and sale of annual proof and uncirculated sets; the manufacture and sale of numismatic items authorized by Congress and the president, normally for occasions of national prominence; the manufacture of gold and silver bullion coins; the production of coins for foreign governments when schedules permit; the custody, processing, and movement of bullion; the disbursing of gold and silver for authorized purposes; the distribution of domestic coins for general circulation through the facilities of the Federal Reserve banks and branches; the receipt and processing of uncurrent and mutilated coins; the compilation and publishing of world-wide coinage data; and other such functions as required by law and regulation.

The Mint distributes coins through the Federal Reserve Bank and branches. It also maintains physical custody of the Treasury's monetary stocks of gold and silver at Philadelphia, Denver, San Francisco Assay Office and San Francisco Old Mint, Fort Knox, Ky. (gold storage), and West Point, N.Y. (gold and silver storage). A mint museum is located at the San Francisco Old Mint.

The 90% silver coinage was phased out when the Coinage Act of 1965 eliminated all silver from the dime and quarter and reduced the silver content of the half dollar to 40%. The remaining silver content was removed from the silver half dollar in 1970. In 1978, Congress approved weight and size design changes in the standard silver dollar. In 1979, a smaller dollar coin bearing the image of Susan B. Anthony and the Apollo II moon landing were released to the public. In 1982, the copper-plated cent replaced the 95% copper cent. The government has produced numismatic coins to note the 250th anniversary of George Washington's birth, the 1984 Olympic games, and the 200th anniversary of the U.S. Constitution. Congress authorized the U.S. Mint to begin the production and sale of legal tender gold and silver bullion coins known as American eagle bullion coins. The gold coin has a face value of $50 (1 oz.), $25 ($^1/_2$ oz.), $10 ($^1/_4$ oz.), and $5 ($^1/_{10}$ oz.). The coins contain .9167 fine gold. The silver bullion coin has a face value of $1 and contains one troy ounce of .999 fine silver. For the 1986 fiscal year, the Philadelphia Mint produced 6,478.4 million coins; the Denver Mint produced 5,964.2 million coins; and the West Point Depository produced 150 million coins for general circulation.

MINT FINE BARS Bars of GOLD or SILVER of 0.995 fineness and upward.

Under orders of the secretary of the Treasury of December 28, 1933, and January 11 and 15, 1934, all gold coin domestically owned, with minor exceptions, was required to be delivered to the mints against payment in lawful money, and under the Gold Reserve Act of January 30, 1934, all gold coin was withdrawn from circulation and formed into bars. On January 31, 1934, a presidential proclamation reduced the gold content of the dollar from 23.22 fine grains to 13.71 fine grains, thus raising the monetary price for gold from $20.67 to $35 per ounce. Although gold continued to be nationalized, gold bars, regular issue or commercial sizes, could be purchased from the mint at $35 per ounce, plus 0.25% handling charge, under license for export in settlement of official international exchange transactions, pursuant to the Articles of Agreement of the International Monetary Fund (IMF) and under permit for use in industry and the arts. This system was continued despite the necessity for formation of the London gold pool late in 1960 following agreement of the New York Federal Reserve Bank and a group of European central banks (those of Belgium, West Germany, Italy, the Netherlands, Switzerland, United Kingdom, and France) to seek a stabilized London price for gold (by offering gold in the market when the market's price rose above the U.S. selling price plus cost of shipment of gold from New York to London, and by buying gold in the market when the price was at or below the U.S. selling price). However, the London gold pool scheme was abandoned in 1968, bringing into existence the two-tier gold market: (1) the official market among the central banks for the IMF member nations concerned, under which the U.S. continued to supply gold for official accounts at $35 per fine ounce plus the handling charge, and (2) the free market left to respond to supply and demand conditions (the supply of new gold production to come mainly from South Africa, with U.S. and Western European central banks first agreeing not to buy such newly mined output from South Africa, but subsequently [late 1969] being obliged to agree with South Africa to have it supply gold to the IMF at $35 per ounce in the event of payments deficits and/or a drop in the free market price for gold to $35 per ounce or less). Under these arrangements for strictly official buying and selling of gold among U.S. and Western European central banks, U.S. industry and the arts now had to obtain their gold (through U.S. licensed dealers, in turn deriving their supply from the free market in London) through free market channels.

On March 21, 1972, the Par Value Modification Act was signed, devaluing the U.S. dollar by approximately 7.89% (raising the official monetary price for gold from $35 to $38 per fine ounce). The Par Value Modification Act was amended on September 21, 1973, pursuant to which, effective October 18, 1973, the U.S. monetary price of gold per fine troy ounce was increased from $38 to $42.22, a further rise of 11.11%.

Silver, after having been nationalized by the presidential proclamation of August 9, 1934, pursuant to the Silver Purchase Act of 1934 requiring delivery of all silver in the continental U.S. to the mints, was denationalized on April 29, 1938, when the referenced presidential proclamation was revoked. Hence there has since been a domestic open market for silver bullion in the U.S. pegged at times by U.S. Treasury offerings of silver to the market at specified price. On November 10, 1970, the U.S. Treasury terminated its 1st program of offerings of silver to the market (mainly to industrial users), totaling between 300,000 ounces and 3.3 million ounces of silver per week. These offerings, through the General Services Administration, had been in effect since August 4, 1967. Its last auction of 1.5 million ounces, at about $1.84 per ounce, ended its supply of marketable silver.

Mint requirements for silver coinage purposes have been considerably relaxed, except for such special purposes as coinage of Eisenhower silver dollars; commemorative halves honoring George Washington's 250th birthday; silver dollars depicting the 1984 Olympics, the Statue of Liberty, the bicentennial of the Constitution; and 1 ounce American eagle bullion coins. The silver required for the latter two programs was obtained from the GSA silver stockpile.

Also, gold coins were issued at a premium in conjunction with the above programs, except the GW commemorative half dollar. All gold came from Treasury reserves, except that used for the American eagle bullion program, which came from newly mined domestic sources.

MINT MARK The unobtrusive mark on a coin which indicates the mint at which it was made.

MINT PAR OF BULLION See MINT PRICE OF GOLD.

MINT PAR OF EXCHANGE The ratio of one country's standard unit of money to that of another country on the same metallic basis; the bullion content of the monetary unit of one country expressed in terms of that of another. For any given nation, it is determined by dividing the weight of pure gold contained in its standard monetary unit into the weight of pure gold contained in the standard coin or monetary unit of another, the value of the alloy being disregarded. For instance, the established par of exchange of the pound sterling relative to the dollar became $2.40 upon the pound's 14.3% devaluation in November, 1967 (2.132810 grams of fine gold content of the pound sterling or 2.4 times the 0.888671 grams of fine gold for the dollar at that time). However, when the gold content of the U.S. dollar was reduced in 1972 to 0.820312 fine grams of gold, the new par of exchange of the pound sterling relative to the U.S. dollar became $2.60 (as of 1972, the pound sterling was floated, i.e., permitted to fluctuate in the foreign exchange market beyond the narrow 1% band below the par, preliminary to the establishment of a new par for the pound sterling). Article IV of the revised Articles of Agreement of the INTERNATIONAL MONETARY FUND (Second Amendment, which became effective on April 1, 1978) gave member countries substantial freedom in the selection of their exchange arrangements, including floating rates, but it established general obligations and specific undertakings that each member must meet in pursuit of its exchange policies. In addition to collaborating with the fund and other members to assure orderly exchange arrangements and to promote a stable system of exchange rates, each member is to endeavor to direct economic and financial policies toward fostering orderly underlying economic and financial conditions.

MINT PRICE OF GOLD The monetary equivalent of the statutorily defined weight of gold of standard fineness (0.900 fine) in the standard monetary unit.

Under the free gold coin standard that prevailed from 1900 (Gold Standard Act) to 1933—free in the sense that private parties could tender gold to the mint or offer it in the private market—the monetary unit of the U.S. (dollar) was statutorily defined to contain 25.8 grains of gold, 0.900 fine, or 23.22 grains of fine gold. Since 23.22 grains, therefore, of fine gold was equal to monetary value of $1.00, the mints or assay offices received and paid for pure gold at the rate of $20.67 per fine ounce. This was determined in the following manner: since there are 480 grains in one troy ounce, and 23.22 grains equaled money value of $1.00, it took $20.67 to buy a full fine ounce (480 grains), i.e., 480 divided by 23.22; $18.60 was paid per standard ounce (0.900 fine), this amount being exactly nine-tenths of $20.67. Slight coinage charges were made when gold offered was less fine than standard gold.

Statutory authority (Trading with the Enemy Act of October 6, 1917), confirmed and broadened by the Act of March 9, 1933 (Emergency Banking Act), provided the basis for a series of executive orders by the President in March (March 10, 1933) and April (April 5, 1933, and April 20, 1933), the effect of which was to take the United States temporarily off the gold standard. Title III of the Act of May 12, 1933 (Thomas Amendment) empowered the President to reduce the gold content of the dollar by as much as 50%. The Gold Reserve Act, January 30, 1934 (in addition to nationalizing gold, i.e., transferring title to all gold coin and bullion held by Federal Reserve banks to the United States and instituting a restricted gold bullion standard by terminating all further coinage of gold except for the account of foreign countries if any) narrowed the range of reduction of gold content to not more than 50% nor less than 40%; and the presidential proclamation of January 31, 1934, pursuant to the Gold Reserve Act, reduced the weight of the defined gold content in the dollar from 25.8 grains troy weight, 0.900 fine or 23.22 grains fine, to $15^{5}/_{12}$ grains, 0.900 fine or $13^{5}/_{7}$ grains fine (59.06% of the former fine gold content). Thus the new fine gold content was equivalent to a monetary value for gold of $35 per ounce.

Under the nationalized, restricted gold bullion standard that resulted, no domestic open market for gold bullion or coin existed, and all monetary gold imported into the U.S. or newly produced domestically had to be turned in to the mints for payment at the $35 per ounce monetary equivalent (less the handling charge of 0.25%). Conversely, gold was available for official international accounts (foreign governments, central banks, etc.) for monetary settlements at $35 per ounce plus the handling charge, under the International Monetary Fund's Articles of Agreement; and gold was available for industry and the arts, under license, at the same price. The latter availability for industry and the arts changed upon organization of the gold pool (an agreement among central banks of Western European nations and the U.S.) in 1960 and subsubsequent termination of

Relationship to Instruments of Credit Policy

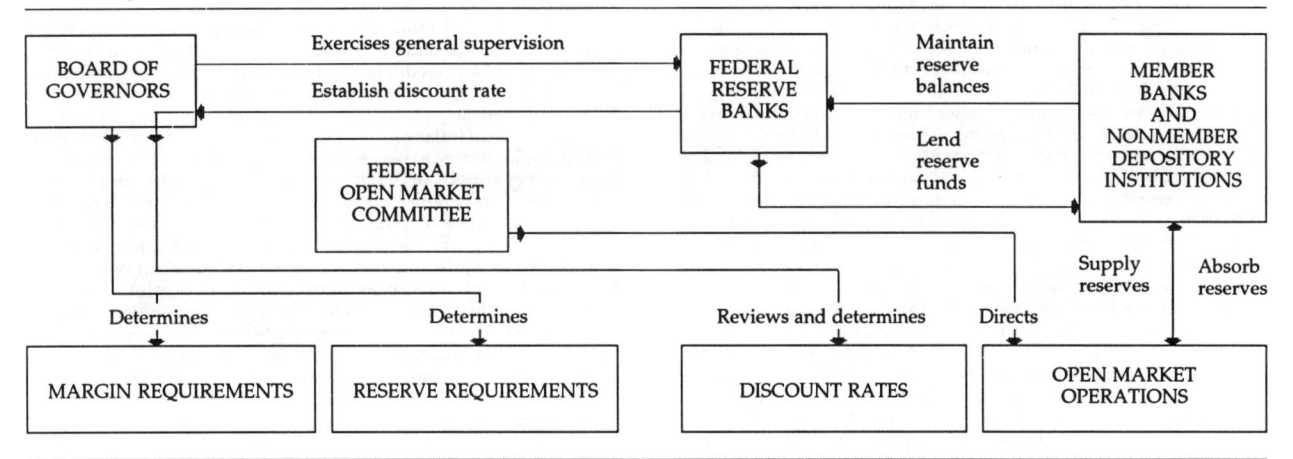

```
BOARD OF              Exercises general supervision        FEDERAL        Maintain          MEMBER
GOVERNORS   ─────────────────────────────────────────────> RESERVE  <──── reserve  ──────   BANKS
            ─────────── Establish discount rate ─────────> BANKS          balances          AND
                                                                                            NONMEMBER
                   FEDERAL                                          Lend                    DEPOSITORY
                   OPEN MARKET                                      reserve ──────────────> INSTITUTIONS
                   COMMITTEE                                        funds

                                                                                    Supply      Absorb
                                                                                    reserves    reserves
    Determines          Determines        Reviews and determines     Directs

   MARGIN              RESERVE                  DISCOUNT RATES              OPEN MARKET
   REQUIREMENTS        REQUIREMENTS                                         OPERATIONS
```

Source: Board of Governors, *The Federal Reserve System: Purposes and Functions.*

the gold pool in 1968; under the two-tier system of international gold transactions that resulted, which allowed both official central bank transactions and private gold transactions through licensed U.S. dealers, domestic U.S. gold for industry and the arts has to be obtained through the latter and the open gold market in London. The mint price of gold became $38 per ounce upon passage of the Par Value Modification Act on March 21, 1972 (internationally, upon notification to the IMF).

On August 15, 1971, the "gold window" (availability of gold of the U.S. to foreign nations and their official bodies at then official monetary price of gold of $35 per ounce) was closed, and has been kept closed since. The official monetary price of gold continues to be $42.22 per ounce in the U.S. but the U.S.'s official monetary gold remains completely nationalized; no use for coinage or paper money issuance; no redemption in any form of U.S. money into gold; and no availability of gold from the U.S.'s monetary stock to foreigners, whether governmental and official agencies or to private and banking channels.

See FOREIGN MONEYS, MINT PAR OF EXCHANGE.

MINT REMEDY   *See* REMEDY ALLOWANCE, TOLERANCE.

MINUTES   The proceedings of directors' and stockholders' meetings of a corporation, formally kept in permanent record in the MINUTES BOOK.

MINUTES BOOK   One of the CORPORATE RECORDS of a corporation, which include the stock certificate book, the stock transfer book, the stock ledger, and the minutes book. The minutes book records in formal permanent record all the actions and proceedings at meetings of directors and stockholders and thus is a vital corporate record. In a bank, the minutes book is usually kept by the cashier; in a business corporation, by the secretary.

See BYLAWS.

MISSISSIPPI BUBBLE   The final unfortunate outcome of a series of speculative financial ventures under the leadership of John Law, a Scottish financier and paper money advocate, with the aid of the French government. In May 1716, John Law obtained a franchise to organize in Paris France's first financial institution, known as the Banque Generale. This bank was empowered to issue notes (in reality paper currency) payable at sight in the weight and value of the money mentioned at the time of issue. In 1717, the notes were decreed as acceptable in payment of taxes, the immediate effects being to reduce interest rates and to cause the notes to command a premium. Having obtained the confidence of the regent, Law was granted control of Louisiana for purposes of trade and colonization.

Accordingly, in 1717, Law founded the Compagnie de la Louisiane et de l'Occident which later absorbed the Compagnie du Canada and companies with similar powers in East India, China, and Africa. The company was commonly known during its life as the Mississippi Company, but after its failure as the Mississippi Bubble. The early success of the scheme made it possible for the company to take control of the mint and the powers of "receivers-general," thus assuming vast importance in both home and colonial affairs. The Banque Generale was restyled Banque Royale in 1718, and in 1720 Law became comptroller-general of finance, the bank and company becoming one. After a great speculative craze, based on the overissue of paper money, the bank and its schemes collapsed in May, 1720, forcing Law to leave the country.

MIXED COLLATERAL   *See* COLLATERAL.

MIXING RATES   In multiple foreign exchange rate systems, the required application of various rates of exchange to specified categories of foreign trade items. For example, Brazil as of December 31, 1970, had five different buying rates: (1) rates on coffee exports calculated on the basis of the official market rate (listed in cruzeiro payment per bag) and the minimum registration price, (2) rates on exports of cocoa beans and paste based on the official market rate less 5% contribution quota, (3) rates on exports of cocoa derivatives based on the official market rate less 5% contribution quota, (4) rates on foreign bank notes and traveler's checks based on the manual market rate, and (5) rates on all other export proceeds and other receipts based on the official market rate. As of the same date, there were two selling rates: (1) on foreign bank notes and traveler's checks, the manual market rate, and (2) on imports, invisibles, and capital, the official market rate, except for a different effective rate on certain remittances of profits and dividends. In addition to such rate differentials, special regulations applicable to types of commodities and the foreign investment law constituted positive constraints.

See EXCHANGE RESTRICTIONS.

MMP   Money market preferred stock or dutch auction preferred stock. *See* FINANCIAL INSTRUMENTS: RECENT INNOVATIONS.

MOMENTUM OF SALES   *See* MERCHANDISE TURNOVER.

MONETARY COMMISSION   *See* NATIONAL MONETARY COMMISSION.

MONETARY POLICY   Broadly construed, any policy relating the supply or use of money in the economy. The coordinated adaptation of the credit control powers of the monetary authorities of a country exercised through the central bank upon the banking system, pursuant to a policy, e.g., of ease or restraint, relative to the economic situation. The usual objectives of such a policy would be to achieve stability in prices by countercyclical action upon the money supply, allowing over time for growth in the economy. Since the bulk of the effective money supply in modern credit systems is bank deposit currency created by expansion in bank loans and investments, monetary policy affects the money supply through effect upon available (excess) reserves of the banks, which are the basis for their expansion in loans and investments and hence in bank deposits. Monetary policy also affects the cost of bank credit by changes in the central bank's rates for rediscounts, loans, and advances to the banks, which would be reflected in turn in bank lending rates to customeers and open market money rates.

In the U.S., monetary policy is determined by the Board of Governors of the Federal Reserve System. Although the Federal Reserve Act contains no preamble or statement of monetary policy in general, the goals of economic stability consistent with growth and of maximum employment, production and purchasing power, as set forth in the EMPLOYMENT ACT OF 1946, are official goals of public policy for monetary policy and FISCAL POLICY, under the general directive in the Employment Act of 1946 to "coordinate and utilize all ... plans, functions, and resources" of government in achieving its goals. Moreover, the Full employment and Balanced Growth Act (HUMPHREY-HAWKINS ACT) approved October 27, 1978, provided that the Board of Governors of the Federal Reserve System shall transmit to the Congress, not later than February 20 and July 20 of each year, independent written reviews and analyses of recent developments affecting economic trends, the objectives and plans of the board of governors and the Federal Open Market Committee with respect to the ranges of growth of the monetary and credit aggregates for the calendar year, and the relation of such objectives and plans to short-term goals set forth in the most recent *Economic Report of the President* and to any short-term goals approved by the Congress. The July 20 report is also to include a statement of objectives and plans with respect to the ranges of growth of the monetary and credit aggregates for the next calendar year. The board of governors is to consult with the appropriate committees of the Congress, which will then submit their views and recommendations with respect to the board's intended policies. (The board of governors in its 1978 *Annual Report* commented that while nothing in the act requires the board to fulfill its plans for the monetary and credit aggregates set out in its reports if the board and the Federal Open Market Committee determine that the plans cannot or should not be achieved because of changing conditions, the act does require the board to explain any revision of that kind in subsequent consultations.)

The relationship of the Federal Reserve System's instruments to monetary policy is illustrated in the appended chart.

The coordination between monetary policy and fiscal policy, consistent with the independence of monetary policy as to its own responsibilities, was officially expressed in the accord of March 4, 1951, a joint statement by the Board of Governors of the Federal Reserve System and the Treasury to the effect that they had "reached full accord with respect to debt management and monetary policies to be pursued in furthering their common purpose to assure the successful financing of the government's requirements and, at the same time, to minimize monetization of the public debt."

With the outbreak of the Korean War in June, 1950, the debt-financing requirements of the government had increased and with them the importance from the Treasury's standpoint of a monetary policy which would assure low-interest cost of borrowing, stable money rates, an adequate supply of bank excess reserves to absorb a larger volume of government securities, and stable markets for government securities pegged at a fixed pattern of yields by the Federal Reserve, as had been done during World War II. On the other hand, monetary policy had to reckon with the danger of inflationary pressures being built up in the money supply through continuance of automatic liquidity for bank holdings of an expanded supply of government securities that were assured of the peg in prices. "Monetization of debt" is the expansion in bank deposits created by Treasury debt financing through commercial banks, a process which in turn could, if not restrained, be further parlayed into a multiple expansion of excess reserves brought into the banks by automatic liquidity for holdings of government securities.

The instruments of monetary policy are open market operations and variations in rates for rediscounts, loans, and advances in legal reserve requirements (*see* FEDERAL RESERVE SYSTEM). These have an impact upon both the availability and the cost of bank credit. They are aggregative (nonselective) in nature, the only selective credit control of the Board of Governors of the Federal Reserve System being their power, under the Securities Exchange Act of 1934, to vary by regulation the MARGIN requirements for the purchasing or carrying of securities on margin. In practice, obviously there are no precise formulas for monetary policy, its determination and execution being empirical by constant contact with business and credit conditions and "leaning against the wind" of the prevailing trends, as necessary.

The efficiency of monetary policy, through its effect upon the money supply, is best in the demand-pull type of inflation financed extensively by bank credit, i.e., and expanded money supply relative to the supply of goods and services, causing a rise in prices. The efficacy of monetary policy is challenged, however, in meeting the cost-push type of inflation, i.e., a rise in prices caused by the shifting forward of increases in costs even under short-term relative stability of the money supply. In the latter situation, the conventional instruments of monetary policy are said to be ineffective in reaching areas of such price inflation in the short run and may even be harmful to other business activity by raising the cost of credit, restricting its availability, and affecting investment. Implicit in such criticisms is the suggestion that direct price controls are the only solution for such cost-push type of inflation, a method of control used heretofore only in time of war and even then having problems of efficacy of its own. A little price control will not work, the free sectors attracting resources and activity from the controlled sectors; and comprehensive price controls, besides posing tremendous burdens of administration, are repugnant to a free enterprise system except in wartime.

A solution within the framework of conventional monetary policy would be to institute more selective credit controls. A wide variety of selective controls, for example, characterize the German banking system. West Germany's system of selective credit controls being the outstanding example of successful monetary policy in the post-World War II years in financing sustantially increased economic activity without serious price inflation. Selective credit controls, however, are not viewed with favor in the U.S., first because of the administrative burdens involved, and second, because our money markets are said to be highly developed enough to enable aggregative controls to work. But certainly West Germany's money markets are highly developed as well, and the administrative burdens are justified if the problem is serious enough to require effective action.

A New Approach to Monetary Policy. The Board of Governors of the Federal Reserve System on October 6, 1979, announced a series of complementary actions "that should assure better control over the expansion of money and bank credit, help curb speculative excesses in financial, foreign exchange, and commodity markets, and thereby serve to dampen inflationary forces."

The basic change in monetary policy was a change in the method used to conduct monetary policy to support the objective of containing growth in the monetary aggregates within the ranges adopted by the Federal Reserve. These ranges would be consistent with moderate growth over the months ahead. Basically, this action involves placing greater emphasis in day-to-day operations on the supply of bank reserves and less emphasis on confining short-term fluctuations in the federal funds rate. It was approved unanimously by the Federal Open Market Committee.

The Fed targets three principal measures of money for monetary control. M1 (formerly M1-B), which consists of currency in the hands of the public, demand deposits, and interest-bearing deposits against which checks can be written; M2, which includes assets in M1 plus all deposit liabilities of depository institutions (except large-denomination time deposits) as well as money market funds, overnight repurchase agreements issued by commercial banks, and certain overnight Eurodollars, and M3, which includes all of M2 plus large-denomination time deposits, term Eurodollars, and other repurchase agreements. In general, as Axilrod points out, the best definition of money is one that is both capable of reasonably accurate measurement and related in a highly predictable way to desirable performance of the economy. But "a number of money measures are currently in use precisely because it is not clear at this time which particular measure does consistently bear the most predictable relationship to economic objectives." An even broader measure of liquid assets, L, is also reported regularly by the Fed. Four quarterly growth rates of M2 and M3 are specified as targets semiannually by the Fed and reported to the Congress. Two- to four-month growth rates of M2 are also used as short-term targets.

Summary. Monetary policy may be clear in objectives, but necessarily has to be eclectic in operating guides and procedures.

See CREDIT CONTROL, MONEY SUPPLY.

BIBLIOGRAPHY

BOARD OF GOVERNORS OF THE FEDERAL RESERVE SYSTEM. *Monetary Policy Objectives for 1987*. Alan Greenspan testimony, February 21, 1988.

———. *1988 Monetary Policy Objectives, Summary.* Report to Congress pursuant to the Full Employment and Balanced Growth Act of 1978, February 23, 1988.
———. *Monetary Policy and Reserve Requirements.* Handbook.
BROCK, P. L. "Reserve Requirements and the Inflation Tax." *Journal of Money, Credit and Banking,* February, 1989.
CUTHBERTSON, K., and TAYLOR, M. P. "Monetary Anticipations and the Demand for Money in the United States." *Southern Economic Journal,* October, 1988.
FISHER, I. *The Purchasing Power of Money.* Augustus M. Kelley Publishers, New York, NY, 1911.
———. *A Program for Monetary Stability,* 1959.
GOODFRIEND, M., and KING, R. G. "Financial Deregulation, Monetary Policy, and Central Banking." *Economic Review,* May/June 1988.
GOODFRIEND, M. "Discount Window Borrowing, Monetary Policy, and the Post-October 1979 Federal Reserve Operating Procedure." *Journal of Monetary Economics,* September, 1985.
———. "Monetary Mystique: Secrecy and Central Banking." *Journal of Monetary Economics,* January, 1986.
———. Monetary Policy in Practice, Federal Reserve Bank of Richmond, 1987.
KEYNES, J. M. *The General Theory of Employment, Interest, and Money.* Harcourt Brace Jovanovich, San Diego, CA, 1936. *Keynes in the Modern World.* Proceedings of a conference held on the hundredth anniversary of Keynes's birth, 1983. Cambridge University Press.
KOHN, D. L. "Monetary Policy in an Era of Change." *Federal Reserve Bulletin,* February, 1989.
Monetary Policy and Reserve Requirements Handbook. Federal Reserve System. Monthly updates.
"Monetary Policy Report to the Congress. *Federal Reserve Bulletin,* March, 1989.
U.S. LIBRARY OF CONGRESS. Congressional Research Service. *Monetary Policy: After Volcher,* by G. Thomas Woodward,
———. *Monetary Policy: Basic Principles, Current Conditions, and Its Likely Course,* by G. Thomas Woodward, March 27, 1988.
———. *Targets for Monetary Policy,* by G. Thomas Woodward, March 23, 1988.
———. *The Federal Reserve Discount Rate: Its Significance In Monetary Policy,* by G. Thomas Woodward, Feb. 6, 1987.
WALLACE, N. "A Legal Restrictions Theory of the Demand for 'Money' and the Role of Monetary Policy." Federal Reserve Bank of Minneapolis *Quarterly Review,* 1983.

MONETARY STANDARDS The type of STANDARD MONEY (money of ultimate redemption) in a monetary system. The two basic types of monetary standards, therefore are commodity standards and flat standards.

Commodity Standards. The two commodities principally used as standard money in monetary history have been gold and silver.

1. Gold standards may be classified as follows:
   a. Gold coin standard.
   b. Gold bullion standard.
   c. Gold exchange standard.
2. Silver standards may be classified as follows:
   a. Silver coin standard.
   b. Silver bullion standard.
   c. Silver exchange standard.
3. Bimetallic standards—in which the STANDARD OF VALUE is defined as either of the two monetary metals, gold and silver, in specific quantity and fineness for each—may be similarly classifiable as to:
   a. Bimetallic coin standard.
   b. Bimetallic bullion standard.
   c. Bimetallic exchange standard.
4. Symmetallic standard (never tried)—in which the standard of value is defined as a specific *total* quantity of a fusion or combination of two (or more) monetary metals, in specified proportions—could be
   a. Symmetallic coin standard.
   b. Symmetallic bullion standard.
   c. Symmetallic exchange standard.
5. Compensated standard (never tried)—in which the quantity of the monetary metal in the standard unit would be changed to offset changes in the purchasing power—could not feasibly be a compensated coin standard, but it could be
   a. Compensated bullion standard.
   b. Compensated exchange standard.

Fiat Standards. Fiat standards define the standard unit as a unit of fiat money (irredeemable into any other kind of money); the paper, metal, or other constituent material of the currency is worth much less intrinsically than the monetary denomination specified. A fiat standard therefore specifies full legal tender for the standard fiat money. It is possible to have a fiat exchange standard in addition to the Fiat money standard as such.

Tabular Standard. The tabular standard (never tried) would involve adjustment of deferred payments in line with changes in prices, whatever the monetary standard might be. Thus it is not, properly speaking, a monetary standard as such.

Credit Money. Actually circulating media for the monetary standard might include various forms of credit money (or representative money), redeemable into the standard unit of the monetary standard.

See MONETARY UNIT.

MONETARISTS Monetarists argue that fiscal policies have little effect on real gross national product (GNP) because monetary growth is the most important factor determining economic activity. Furthermore, stabilization policies of any kind are not likely to be effective because policy makers have difficulty implementing the correct policies at the right time. The most notable advocate of monetarism is Nobel Laureate Milton Friedman.

The equation of exchange ($M \times V = P \times y = Y$) is central to the monetarist's analysis of economic activity. With the assumption that the velocity of money (V) is predictable and independent of the quantity of money (M) in the economy (this assumption is questionable, especially in the economic environment that has characterized the 1980s), the equation of exchange becomes the quantity theory of money. The quantity theory of money asserts that there is a causal relationship from changes in the money supply to changes in nominal GNP (Y) (equal to real GNP (y) times an average price level (P).

Monetarists also believe that stable fiscal and monetary policies will establish confidence in the economy and are conducive to long-run investment decisions. Their recommendation is to put the Federal Reserve Board on autopilot and to have the money supply increase at a predetermined and announced rate of growth.

MONETARY BASE The liabilities of the Federal Reserve System are its currency and the deposits of member banks. The total of these two liabilities is called the monetary base. Changes in the monetary base, through an open market operation, for example, are the first step toward changes in the money supply.

MONETARY STOCK The aggregate of all kinds of money issued by a government, including that held in the treasury, in the central banks and other banks of issue, and in circulation. The monetary stock of the United States consists of that held in U.S. Treasury and the mints, in the Federal Reserve banks, and in circulation (outside the Treasury and Federal Reserve banks).

The bulk of U.S. money in circulation is provided by FEDERAL RESERVE NOTES, which, as of March 31, 1987, accounted for over 92% of total currency and coin in circulation and were the only form of paper money being currently issued except for a continuing small amount of UNITED STATES NOTES.

All forms of paper money and coin in circulation, other than Federal Reserve notes (Federal Reserve Bank notes), national bank notes, GOLD CERTIFICATES (series issued prior to January 30, 1934), silver certificates, Treasury notes of 1890, United States notes, and coin (dollars and fractional coin) are Treasury liability currency.

The largest component of currency in circulation is the liability of the Federal Reserve. And in turn, the Federal Reserve notes compose the largest of the Federal Reserve's liabilities. As of December 31, 1986, $195,360 million in Federal Reserve notes were issued. The remaining $262,284 million liabilities largely consisted of deposits of private and government institutions.

The assets of the Federal Reserve at the same time were $266,030 million, most of which consisted of U.S. government securities totaling $211,316 million. Other Federal Reserve assets include a gold certificate account, special drawing rights certificates account, federal agency obligations, and foreign currency-denominated assets. Each of these accounted for less than 5% of total assets.

MONETARY TARGETS

In accordance with the Gold Reserve Act of January 30, 1934, title to all of the U.S. monetary gold stock, including some $3.5 billion held by the Federal Reserve banks, was vested in the Treasury of the United States. The gold certificates or credits therefor held by Federal Reserve banks and agents represented monetization of the payment (at the old rate for gold of $20.67 per ounce, compared with the $35 per ounce resulting January 31, 1934, when a presidential proclamation pursuant to the GOLD RESERVE ACT OF 1934 devalued the dollar) to the Federal Reserve banks by the Treasury when these institutions turned in their monetary gold. Only Federal Reserve banks and agents may hold such gold certificates, series of 1934, which do not appear in circulation. Their functions included (1) to serve as legal reserve requirement against Federal Reserve notes outstanding and total deposits of Federal Reserve banks (P.L. 89-3, March 3, 1965, eliminated such requirement against deposits, minimum of which was 25% at that time), and (2) to serve as gold cover (gold certificates collateral) against Federal Reserve notes outstanding (P.L. 90-269, March 18, 1968, eliminated such requirement, minimum of which prevailing at the time was 25%. Use for settlements for the Interdistrict Settlement Fund continued.

The Special Drawing Rights Act (P.L. 90-349, June 19, 1968), mainly authorizing U.S. participation in the special drawing rights arrangement established within the INTERNATIONAL MONETARY FUND, also authorized the secretary of the Treasury to sell to the Federal Reserve banks certificates against the special drawing rights of the U.S. and authorized the Federal Reserve banks to use such certificates for specified purposes.

MONETARY TARGETS Projections of monetary aggregate and credit growth that give some indication of monetary policy intentions of the Federal Reserve. Monetary targets (ranges) are announced in periodic reports by the Federal Reserve submitted to Congress as required by the Full Employment and Balanced Growth Act of 1978. The projections cover the annual periods from the fourth quarter of one year to the fourth quarter of the following year.

MONETARY UNION See LATIN UNION, SCANDINAVIAN UNION.

MONETARY UNIT The unit selected by a government to serve as the unit of account and which by law contains a prescribed weight (and fineness) of the metal selected to serve as the standard of value. The gold dollar, although no longer coined, is the monetary unit of the United States. Since the United States possesses a decimal coinage system, the dollar is a multiple of fractional coins and an aliquot part of coins of higher denomination. The weight of the standard unit was fixed at 23.22 grains of pure gold, or 25.8 grains of gold 0.900 fine, prior to the suspension of the gold standard on April 19, 1933. On January 31, 1934, presidential proclamation permanently fixed, pursuant to the Gold Reserve Act of 1934, the standard weight of the dollar at $15\,^{5}/_{21}$ grains, 0.900 fine, or 13.7137 grains pure gold, being 59.06% of the former gold content.

Pursuant to the Par Value Modification Act, signed March 21, 1972, the gold content of the U.S. dollar became 12.6588 grains fine a devaluation of approximately 7.69% compared with the former fine gold content. This action, internationally effective upon formal notification to the INTERNATIONAL MONETARY FUND, followed the floating of the U.S. dollar from its previous international par value as one of the measures in the administration's INCOMES POLICY on August 15, 1971.

The Par Value Modification Act was amended on September 21, 1973, pursuant to which, effective October 18, 1973, the U.S. monetary price of gold per fine troy ounce was increased from $38 to $42.22 (reduction in indicated gold content to 11.37 grains).

See GOLD COINS, MINT PRICE OF GOLD.

Although many countries have similarly retained gold as the standard of value, most of them have instituted a prohibition of gold coinage and internal circulation of gold coin similar to such prohibitions in the United States. For the various monetary units of other countries, see FOREIGN MONEYS.

See MONEY OF ACCOUNT, STANDARD MONEY, STANDARD OF VALUE.

MONEY A medium of exchange; an instrument, token, or commodity, whether metal or paper, by which payment is made for the transfer of values from one person to another. The essential characteristic of good money is that it is readily acceptable in payment for goods and services and in settlement of debts, without reference to the credit worthiness of its specific form or of the person tendering it in payment. Acceptability of specific forms of money in settlement of debts is imparted by the law's prescribing them to be LEGAL TENDER, i.e., money which by law a debtor is authorized to offer in payment of debt.

The role of government in the definition and maintenance of a high quality of money has been fundamental from ancient times. Aristotle (*Ethica Nichomachea*) was the precursor of modern theorists of money management by government in writing. "Money has become by convention 'money' [*nomisma*]—because it exists not by nature but by law [*nomos*] and it is in our power to change it and make it useless." The history of money from ancient times is replete with examples of governmental tinkering with money systems in accordance with this nominal theory of money. King Dionysius of Syracuse (432-367 a.c.) ordered in all drachmas, decreed each to be worth two, returned one new for evey two old, and used the profit to pay the public debt—as modern a devaluation as any present-day nominalist could conceive. The pathology of money is largely a history of nominalism in action. The ultimate in nominalism is FIAT MONEY, money decreed by government: (1) without any redemption into standard money, (2) without intrinsic value or having a declared monetary value far above any intrinsic value, and (3) having legal tender power as the exclusive or the preponderant basis of its value as money. Nominalism run wild leads to deterioration of money's acceptability as a medium of exchange and store of value until the money is rendered worthless, trade and exchange becomes impossible, and the wreckage wipes out or creates heavy losses for creditors, people on fixed money incomes, and all recipients of labor income.

The primary quality of good money that people and the economic system are entitled to, therefore, is stability of value. Stability of value connotes stability not only of the declared monetary value, but also of the purchasing power of money, i.e., its value in terms of goods and services. Modern monetary theory emphasizes that the meaningful function of money management by government is not monetary tinkering or exploitation, but furtherance of the neutrality of money in fulfilling its functions (1) as a measure of value, (2) as a medium of exchange, (3) as a standard of deferred payments, and (4) as a store of value. Implicit in an objective of the EMPLOYMENT ACT OF 1946 of maximum purchasing power is such management of the money supply relative to the level of prices.

By "money supply" is meant not only forms of money in circulation but also the bank deposit currency (demand deposits subject to check) that constitutes the principal means of payment in modern credit systems (although checks are basically credit instruments and not money) and the velocity (turnover) of both. The various forms of money used by the principal commercial nations of the world may be classified as follows:

1. PAPER MONEY
   a. Government notes or promises to pay.
      (1) Secured by gold reserve, full or partial (specie reserve).
      (2) Secured by government securities (collateral cover).
      (3) Unsecured (fiat money).
   b. Bank notes (usually exclusive with central banks as banks of issue).
      (1) Secured by gold reserves.
      (2) Secured by government securities.
      (3) Secured by commercial paper.
      (4) Secured by general assets.
      (5) Secured by any combination of the above.
2. Metallic money.
   a. Gold coin (prohibited or restricted in domestic circulation of most countries in recent years).
   b. Full legal tender silver coin.
   c. Subsidiary coins with full or limited legal tender.
   d. Minor coins, with full or limited legal tender.

Other qualities of good money conventionally include such factors as durability and malleability, which imply that metallic money is superior. Actually, because of its great advantage of portability, paper money has come to predominate in most currency systems of the world in denominations of the standard unit or higher, as it fully qualifies as to other conventional qualities—divisibility, homgeneity, and cognizability.

Gold constitutes the basic monetary metal for the currency and credit systems of the world, serving as reserve (invariably fractional) for currency and deposits. Over time, by resort to paper money and circulating coin in other metals (silver, copper, nickel, aluminum, etc.), great economy in the use of gold has been achieved, which has permitted great expansion in the money supply to meet the needs of exchange. A distinguishing feature of financially developed nations is the widespread use of checks, giro accounts, money orders, etc., as means of payment, which further economize on the use of basic metals for monetary purposes.

The appended table shows comparative totals of money in circulation for selected dates.

See COINAGE, CURRENCY, FOREIGN MONEYS, GOLD PRODUCTION, GOLD RESERVE, GOLD STANDARD, LATIN UNION, MINT, MONETARY STOCK, MONETARY UNIT, MONEY CIRCULATION, MONEY SUPPLY, QUANTITY THEORY OF MONEY, REDEMPTION OF MONEY, REPRESENTATIVE MONEY, SCANDINAVIAN UNION, TOKEN MONEY, UNITED STATES MONEY.

BIBLIOGRAPHY

FRIEDBERG, R. *Paper Money of the United States.* Coin and Currency Institute, Inc., Clifton, NJ.
Hard Money Digest.
Know Your Money. U.S. Secret Service. Annual.
KING, R. G., and PLOSSER, C. I. "Money as the Mechanism of Exchange." *Journal of Monetary Economics,* January, 1986.
KRAUSE, C. L., and LIMKE, R. F. *United States Paper Money.* Krause Publications, Inc., Iola, WI, 1986.
MEHRA, V. "Recent Financial Deregulation and the Interest Elasticity of M1 Demand." *Economic Review,* July/August 1986.

Table 1 / Comparative Totals of Money in Circulation—Selected Dates

Date	Amounts (in millions)	Per capita[1]
June 30, 1987	$ 215,128.6	$ 883.45
June 30, 1986	199,309.2	883.45
June 30, 1985	185,890.7	776.58
June 30, 1984	175,059.6	739.64
June 30, 1983	162,027.1	691.74
June 30, 1980	127,097.2	558.28
June 30, 1975	81,196.4	380.08
June 30, 1970	54,351.0	265.39
June 30, 1965	39,719.8	204.14
June 30, 1960	32,064.6	177.47
June 30, 1955	30,229.3	182.90
June 30, 1950	27,156.6	179.03
June 30, 1945	26,746.4	191.14
June 30, 1940	7,847.5	59.40
June 30, 1935	5,567.1	43.75
June 30, 1930	4,522.0	36.74
June 30, 1925	4,815.2	41.56
June 30, 1920	5,467.6	51.36
June 30, 1915	3,319.6	33.01
June 30, 1910	3,148.7	34.07

[1] Based on Bureau of the Census estimates of population.
The requirement for a gold reserve against U.S. notes was repealed by Public Law 90-269 approved Mar. 18, 1968. Silver certificates issued on and after July 1, 1929 became redeemable from the general fund on June 24, 1968. The amount of security after those dates has been reduced accordingly.

Millions Magazine.
Money.
Paper Money.
Treasury Bulletin. U. S. Department of the Treasury, Washington, DC. Quarterly.
World Currency Yearbook. Currency Analysis Inc., Brimingham, AL. Annual.

MONEY BROKER A person of firm that acts as intermediary between borrowers and lenders of money. With discontinuance of the money desk of the New York Stock Exchange at the end of World War II, the usefulness of such brokers increased. The market for federal funds, for example, is facilitated by the services of several firms (e.g., Garvin, Bantell & Co. in New York) and banks (e.g., Irving Trust Co. in New York). Regulations of the Board of Governors of the Federal Reserve System require that members of national securities exchanges borrow either from member banks of the Federal Reserve System or from nonmember banks who agree to submit to such regulation.

See MONEY MARKET.

MONEY CIRCULATION Currency (coin and paper money) in circulation, outstanding outside of the Treasury and Federal Reserve banks. Since most business in the United States (about 90%, judging from bank debits to checking accounts and estimated turnover of currency supply) is transacted by means of the bank check, money circulation is of secondary importance compared with demand deposits as part of the effective money supply. Indicating the turnover (velocity) of demand deposits (excluding interbank and U.S. government demand deposits), debits to such accounts reached a then record high of $206, 689.6 billion seasonally adjusted annual rate, or a turnover of 560.7 times the indicated total of 308.3 billion, seasonally adjusted, in demand deposits averaged for December 1986, including New York. Major New York City banks alone had a demand deposit turnover rate of 2251.6 times on the same basis, while other banks carried in the Federal Reserve's series on bank debits and deposit turnover had a demand deposits turnover rate of 340.0 times (all seasonally adjusted at annual rates). Such turnover rates afford an indication of the true effective supply of demand deposits, the primary form of transaction deposits. Turnover rates of demand deposits at New York City banks are much higher than those of other banks because of the concentration of financial transactions in New York City, involving both domestic and international funds. (For monthly data on bank debits and deposit turnover, see current issues of the *Federal Reserve Bulletin.*)

The bulk of money circulation in the U.S. consists of FEDERAL RESERVE NOTES. As of 1986, United States notes were the only other form of paper currency issued regularly, the only form of treasury liability currency in paper circulation, dollars and fractional coin are also treasury currency because the Treasury is responsible for their issuance or retirement.

Although of secondary importance compared with demand deposits (checking accountes) as a means of payment, paper currency and coin in money circulation have expanded in a steady uptrend which appears to indicate a permanently higher level of money circulation compared with pre-World War II years. Money circulation as of year-end 1986 was about 24 times larger than that of year-end 1940, and about 48 times larger than that of year-end 1929. On a per capita basis, money in circulation reached a record high of 855.0 as of March 31, 1987.

Among the reasons for this expansion are the much larger volume of employment and payrolls, expansion in retail trade and thus requirements for till money, elimination of interest on demand

Table 1 / U.S. Money in Circulation, by Denominations
Outside Treasury and Federal Reserve Banks (millions of dollars)

Fiscal Year	Total in circulation	Coin	$1	$2	$5	$10	$20	$50	$100	$500	$1,000	$5,000	$10,000
1950	27,741	1,554	1,113	64	2,049	5,998	8,529	2,422	5,043	368	588	4	12
1960	32,869	2,427	1,533	88	2,246	6,691	10,536	2,815	5,954	249	316	3	10
1970	57,093	6,281	2,310	136	3,161	9,170	18,581	4,896	12,084	215	252	3	4
1975	86,547	8,959	2,809	135	3,841	10,777	28,344	8,157	23,139	175	204	2	4
1980	137,244	12,419	3,499	677	4,635	11,924	40,739	13,731	49,264	163	189	2	3
1985	170,739	15,150	3,571	707	4,939	11,363	51,586	21,715	76,516	154	179	2	3

Source: U.S. Treasury Department, Financial Management Service

MONEYED CORPORATION

Table 2 / U.S. Money Circulation
(as of June 30 each year)

As of June 30:	Total (000,000 omitted)	Per capita
1800	$ 26,500	$ 4.99
1840	186,305	10.91
1850	278,762	11.98
1860	435,407	13.82
1865	1,083,541	30.35
1870	774,966	19.42
1875	833,789	18.50
1880	973,382	19.37
1885	1,292.569	22.81
1890	1,429,251	22.67
1895	1,801,968	23.02
1900	2,081,231	27.35
1905	2,623,340	31.30
1910	3,148,684	34.07
1914	3,459,434	34.90
1915	3,319,582	33.01
1916	3,649,258	35.79
1917	4,066,404	39.32
1918	4,481,697	42.87
1919	4,876,638	46.42
1920	5,467,589	51.36
1921	4,910,992	45.25
1922	4,463,172	40.55
1923	4,823,275	43.08
1924	4,849,307	42.50
1925	4,815,208	41.57
1926	4,885,266	41.61
1927	4,851,321	40.75
1928	4,796,626	39.81
1929	4,746,297	38.98
1930	4,521,988	36.74
1931	4,821,933	38.87
1932	5,695,171	45.62
1933	5,720,764	45.56
1934	5,373,470	42.52
1935	5,567,093	43.75
1936	6,241,200	48.74
1937	6,477,056	50.05
1938	6,460,891	49.77
1939	7,046,743	53.84
1940	7,847,501	59.46
1941	9,612,432	72.16
1942	12,382,866	91.95
1943	17,421,260	127.63
1944	22,504,342	162.98
1945	26,746,438	191.56
1946	28,244,997	200.34
1947	28,297,227	196.33
1948	27,902,859	190.31
1949	27,492,910	184.33
1950	27,156,290	179.03
1951	27,809,230	180.17
1952	29,025,925	184.90
1953	30,124,952	188.72
1954	29,921,949	184.23
1955	30,229,323	182.91
1956	30,715,189	182.64
1957	31,081,913	181.52
1958	31,171,739	179.08
1959	31,914,173	180.20
1960	32,064,619	177.61
1961	32,404,685	176.45
1962	33,679,527	180.98
1963	35,469,798	187.30
1964	37,733,694	196.41
1965	39,719,801	204.14
1966	42,554,022	216.10
1967	44,712,443	224.55
1968	47,640,463	236.82
1969	50,936,026	250.65

Table 2 / U.S. Money Circulation (continued)

As of June 30:	Total (000,000 omitted)	Per capita
1970	54,350,972	265.39
1971	58,393,190	282.08
1973	67,771	322.11
1974	73,833	348.44
1975	81,196	380.08
1976	88,878	413.17
1977	96,653	445.78
1978	106,288	486.42
1979	116,575	528.89
1980	127,097	570.51
1981	138,080	600.86
1982	148,170	638.51
1983	162,027	691.69
1984	175,060	739.85
1985	185,891	778.38

Note: In accordance with the Gold Reserve Act of 1934, $287 million in gold coin shown in Treasury records as outstanding was dropped from the statement of money in circulation (reflected in above 1934 figure).
Source: Secretary of the Treasury, Annual Reports; Statistical Abstract of the U.S.

deposits (Banking Act of 1933), increased service charges on checking accounts, and reduction in the number of banks in specific communities (although the number of banking offices in the aggregate has increased). Sales taxation and preference for cash payments instead of checks (it is speculated that the tax evasion motive and the underground economy may be importantly responsible) are the factors. Money in circulation by denominations on Table 1 is appended for selected years.

Total circulation reported outstanding (as of June 30 each year) and circulation per capita in the United States since 1800 have compared as listed on Table 2, appended.

MONEYED CORPORATION A corporation formed under or subject to the banking law or the insurance law. Stock corporations may be classified as moneyed corporations railroad corporations, transportation corporations, business corporations, and cooperative corporations.

MONEY MARKET In a broad sense, any demand for and supply of funds and credit; in the technical sense, the open market, as contrasted to personalized borrower-lender relationships for short-term funds and the capital market for longer-term funds (government and municipal bonds, and corporate bonds and stocks) provided by dealers and underwriters (both outstanding and new issues). The national money market in the U.S. is the New York money market.

Structurally, the New York money market has the following sectors:

Federal funds
Treasury bills
Bankers acceptance (bills)
Commercial paper
Certificates of deposit
Eurodollar certificates of deposit

At one time, when open market call and time loans to brokers could be arranged through the money desk of the New York Stock Exchange, such brokers' loans could also be classified as part of the money market. At the close of World War II, however, the money desk was discontinued, and such brokers' loans are now arranged directly between the banks and brokers concerned.

The primary dealers of U.S. government securities include the following banks and nonbanks (all of New York except where noted):

Banks
Bank of America NT & SA
Bankers Trust Co.
Chase Manhattan Government Securities Inc.
Chemical Bank

ENCYCLOPEDIA OF BANKING AND FINANCE

Citibank NA
Continental Illinois National Bank and Trust Co., Chicago
Crocker National Bank, San Francisco
First Interstate Bank of California, Los Angeles
First National Bank, Chicago
Harris Trust and Savings Bank, Chicago
Manufacturers Hanover Trust Co.
Morgan Guaranty Trust Co.
Security Pacific National Bank

Nonbanks
Bear, Stearns & Co.
Briggs, Schaedle & Co., Inc.
Carroll McEntee & McGinley Inc.
Daiwa Securities America
Dean Witter Reynbolds Inc.
Discount Corp of New York
Donaldson, Lufkins & Jenrette Securities Corp.
Drexel Burnham Lambert Government Securities Corp.
First Boston Corp.
Greenwich Capital Markets Inc., Greenwich, Conn.
Goldman, Sachs & Co.
E.F. Hutton & Co. Inc.
Kidder, Peabody & Co. Inc.
Kleinwort Benson Government Securities Inc.
Aubrey G. Lanston & Co. Inc.
Lehman Government Securities Inc.
Merrill Lynch Government Securities Inc.
Morgan Stanley & Co. Inc.
Nomura Securities International
Paine Webber Inc.
Wm. E. Pollock Government Securities Inc.
Prudential-Bache Securities Inc.
Refco Partners L.F.
Rothschild, Unterberg, Towbin Salomon Brothers Inc.
Smith Barney Government Securities Inc.
Thomson McKinnon Securities

Federal Funds. These are immediately available claims upon reserve accounts of member banks at the Federal Reserve Bank. Member banks resort to federal funds for the adjustment of reserve positions when needed for legal reserve purposes. Lending banks, in turn, earn some return on idle excess reserves at the Fed without tying up the funds on the loan for more than a day. For example, Bank A has excess reserves at the Fed; Bank B needs reserves for legal reserve requirements. Bank A will make the desired sum available to Bank B on the day needed by a simple and convenient exchange of checks: Bank A draws a check on its reserve account at the Federal Reserve Bank, payable to Bank B, and delivers it to Bank B in return for Bank B's cashier's check, payable to Bank A, for the same principal sum plus one day's interest at the current federal funds rate. Bank B will receive immediate credit to its reserve account for its Fed deposit of Bank A's check on the same day; Bank A will present Bank B's cashier's check at the clearinghoue and settlement will be made the following day. Net result: a loan of federal funds from Bank A to Bank B for one day at the prevailing rate for federal funds.

New York banks might borrow similarly from out-of-town banks or lend to out-of-town banks (usually correspondents). Bank C in New York City needs reserves; Bank D in New York State has excess reserves. Bank D telephones the New York Federal Reserve Bank (confirming by wire) to make available the desired amount to Bank C, which is done immediately. The following day, Bank C will repay the principal sum plus interest for one day at the prevailing rate for federal funds; this may be done by simple credit to Bank D's correspondent account with Bank C or by instructions to the Fed to charge Bank C's reserve account and credit Bank D's reserve account for the principal plus interest.

If the lending and borrowing banks are located in different Federal Reserve districts, the Federal reserve banks concerned will figure in the loan of federal funds. Bank X in New York, having excess reserves, upon request from Bank Y in Chicago or from a money broker on Y's behalf, will instruct the New York Federal Reserve Bank to transfer the desired sum by the Federal Reserve System's wire transfer system to the Chicago Federal Reserve Bank,

Table 1 / Money Market Interest Rates and Mortgage Rates: 1970 to 1987
(Percent per year. Annual averages of monthly data, except as indicated.)

Type	1975	1970	1978	1979	1980	1981	1982	1983	1984	1985	1986	1987
Federal funds, effective rate	5.82	7.18	7.93	11.19	13.36	16.38	12.26	9.09	10.23	8.10	6.80	6.66
Commercial paper, 3-month [1,2]	6.25	NA	7.94	10.97	12.66	15.33	11.89	8.88	10.10	7.95	6.49	6.81
Prime rate charged by banks	7.86	7.91	9.06	12.67	15.27	18.87	14.86	10.79	12.04	9.93	8.33	8.20
Eurodollar deposits, 3-month	7.03	8.52	8.78	11.96	14.00	16.79	13.12	9.57	10.75	8.27	6.70	7.07
Finance paper, 3-month [2,3]	6.15	7.18	7.80	10.47	11.49	14.08	11.23	8.70	9.73	7.77	6.38	6.54
Bankers acceptances, 90-day [2,4]	6.29	7.31	8.06	10.99	12.72	15.32	11.89	8.90	10.14	7.92	6.39	6.74
Large negotiable certificates of deposit, 3-month, secondary market	6.44	7.56	8.22	11.22	13.07	15.91	12.27	9.07	10.37	8.05	6.52	6.86
Federal Reserve discount rate [5]	6-$7^3/4$	$5^1/2$-6	6-$9^1/2$	$9^1/2$-12	10-13	12-14	$8^1/2$-12	$8^1/2$	8-9	$7^1/2$-8	$5^1/2$-$7^1/2$	$5^1/2$-6
U.S. Government securities: [6]												
3-month Treasury bill	5.78	6.39	7.19	10.07	11.43	14.03	10.61	8.61	9.52	7.48	5.98	5.77
6-month Treasury bill	6.09	6.51	7.58	10.06	11.37	13.80	11.07	8.73	9.76	7.65	6.03	6.03
1-year Treasury bill	6.28	6.48	7.74	9.75	10.89	13.14	11.07	8.80	9.92	7.81	6.08	6.32
Prime 1-year municipals [7]	3.91	4.35	4.15	5.34	6.25	7.92	7.88	5.29	6.05	5.12	4.33	4.44
Home mortgages (HUD series [8]):												
FHA insured, secondary market [9]	9.19	9.03	9.70	10.87	13.44	16.31	15.31	13.11	13.82	12.24	9.91	10.12
Conventional, new-home [10,11]	9.10	8.52	9.68	11.15	13.95	16.52	15.79	13.43	13.80	12.28	10.07	10.13
Conventional, existing-home [10]	9.14	8.56	9.70	11.16	13.95	16.55	15.82	13.45	13.81	12.29	10.09	10.14

NA - Not available.
[1] Based on daily offering rates of dealers.
[2] Yields are quoted on a bank-discount basis, rather than an investment yield basis (which would give a higher figure).
[3] Placed directly; averages of daily offering rates quoted by finance companies.
[4] Based on the most representative daily offering rates of dealers. Beginning Aug. 15, 1974, closing rates were used, and from Jan. 1, 1981, rates of top-rated banks only.
[5] Federal Reserve Bank of New York, low and high. The discount rates for 1980 and 1981 do not include the surcharge applied to frequent borrowings by large institutions. The surcharge reached 3 percent in 1980 and 4 percent in 1981. Surcharge was eliminated in Nov. 1981.
[6] Averages based on daily closing bid yields in secondary market, bank discount basis.
[7] Averages based on quotations for one day each month. *Source:* Salomon Brothers, Inc., New York, NY, *An Analytical Record of Yields and Yield Spreads.*
[8] HUD - Housing and Urban Development.
[9] Averages based on quotations for 1 day each month as compiled by FHA.
[10] Primary market.
[11] Average contract rates on new commitments.

Source: Except as noted, Board of Governors of the Federal Reserve System, *Federal Reserve Bulletin,* monthly, and *Annual Statistical Digest.*

for credit to Bank Y's reserve account. Bank Y will repay, the following day, the principal sum by reversing the wire transfer and the interest usually by check directly to Bank X or by credit to Bank X's correspondent account.

Money brokers, if they figure in federal funds deals, may charge no commission, in return for the expectation that the bank provided the service will continue to favor the broker with security orders (e.g., such brokers may be New York Stock exchange members, such as Garvin, Bantel & Co., which also deal in government securities), or may charge a fractional commission (annual rate of $1/16$th or $1/8$th of 1%). Banks acting as brokers in such federal funds deals do so without charge for correspondents. See MONEY BROKER.

Alternative methods of obtaining reserves might involve two or more days; federal funds, if available, provide the quickest and cheapest way for member banks to obtain reserves at the Fed.

The *rediscount rate* of the New York Federal Reserve Bank normally acts as the ceiling for the New York federal funds rate, for the alternatives of loans or advances at the bank would be cheaper if the federal funds rate went higher. Whenever money is easy, the federal funds rate will be well below the rediscount rate, reflecting an ample supply of excess reserves of member banks. Because of its sensitive reflection of member banks' money positions, the federal funds rate is regarded highly by the New York Federal Reserve Bank as an indicator of money market conditions, although its attention in latest years has primarily been on the monetary aggregates for purposes of MONETARY POLICY.

Repurchase agreements (sales by government securities dealers to member banks, with an agreement to buy back the securities one or more days later) and loans by out-of-town banks to government securities dealers are often settled in federal funds. The New York Federal Reserve Bank also utilizes such repurchase agreements to assist the money position of U.S. government securities dealers.

Treasury Bills. These shortest term of the U.S. government's obligations (*see* TREASURY BILLS, UNITED STATES GOVERENMENT SECURITIES) provide the heaviest volume of outstanding and trading activity of the money market. Open market operations of the FEDERAL RESERVE SYSTEM are normally conducted in Treasury bills. Commercial banks are their largest buyers and sellers, operating through government securities dealers to adjust their reserve positions or secondary reserves. Weekly new offerings are bid for competitively on Mondays, awards are made Tuesdays, and payment therefor is made on Thursdays, either in federal funds or in maturing bills. Major money market money flows, therefore, occur through the medium of Treasury bills.

Negotiable Time Certificates of Deposit. Beginning in 1961, the larger banks began to offer negotiable time certificates of deposit (CDs), a new money market instrument intended to attract and to keep corporate funds that otherwise would find investments in other money market instruments. Time CDs have short-term maturities, with yields which increase in proportion to the length of the maturities, and are issued in larger denominations of $0.5-$1.0 million minimum for the larger banks (no less than $100,000 for smaller banks).

Certificates of Deposit. First introduced to the domestic money market in 1961, negotiable certificates of deposit issued by U.S. banks domestically have become among the most important sources of funds of U.S. money market banks in recent years. The instrument specifies the amount of the deposit, the length of the maturity, the rate of interest (domestic certificate of deposit rates are quoted on an interest-bearing basis, rather than on a discount basis), and the terms of calculation of the interest (actual number of days to maturity, on a 360-day year basis, fixed or variable when paid, etc.). Rates are free to reflect prevailing levels of money rates on such certificates of deposit above $100,000, although the minimum denomination for market trading is actually $1,000,000. Since the offering bank can tailor the maturity and yield to compete successfully with Treasury bills of comparable maturity (for example, a return 25 basis points better than that on the bills), the offering bank can be successful in keeping the deposits of large corporate depositors that otherwise would leave to be invested in the bills; and by changing the classification of the deposits from demand to time, the bank can gain excess reserves because of the lower legal reserve requirements on time deposits compared to demand deposits.

Eurodollar Certificates of Deposit. These are dollar-denominated negotiable certificates of deposit issued by banks abroad, either by foreign branches of U.S. banks or by foreign banks, with the market centered in London. Also called Euro CDs, Eurodollar certificates of deposit were introduced to the market in London in 1966 by a U.S. bank and trading therein has grown substantially in recent years.

Bankers Acceptance. These are obligations of those banks which accept drafts drawn pursuant to commercial letters of credit (largely in foreign trade). Instead of holding them for investment until their final maturity and payment, their holders may sell them to bill dealers in the money market, who in turn sell them largely to other banks desiring such a high-grade short-term obligation for investment, especially foreign banks. Bill volume is secondary in size and activity to that in Treasury bills. See LETTER OF CREDIT.

Commercial Paper. These are short-term promissory notes (four-to six-month maturities as a rule) of nationally known and highly rated companies, placed through commercial paper dealers, who in turn sell the paper to commercial banks and other buyers. The largest finance companies place their own paper directly with investors in the New York money market without using dealers. Some major industrial conglomerates have also taken to direct placement of their commercial paper. The volume of commercial paper is larger than that of bankers acceptances, but both are by far secondary to volume and activity to Treasury bills.

Summary. The appended tables compare average annual rates for various sectors of the money market and annual money market instruments amounts outstanding for selected years.

BIBLIOGRAPHY

COOK, T. Q., and ROWE, T. D. *Instruments of the Money Market*. Federal Reserve Bank of Richmond, 1986.
DARST, D. M. *The Handbook of the Bond and Money Markets*. McGraw Hill Book Co., New York, NY, 1981.
DUFEY, G., and GIDDY, I. H.*The International Money Market*, Prentice Hall, Inc., Englewood Cliffs, NJ, 1978.
DUFFIELD, J. G., and SUMMERS. "Bankers' Acceptances." *Instruments of the Money Market*, 1981.
FEDERAL RESERVE BANK OF RICHMOND. *Instruments of the Money Market*.
STIGUM, M. *The Money Market*. Dow Jones-Irwin, Inc., Homewood, IL, 1983.
VAN HORNE, J. C. *Financial Market Rates and Flows*. Prentice Hall, Inc., Englewood Cliffs, NJ, 1984.

MONEY MARKET CERTIFICATE Certificates authorized for commercial banks and thrift institutions with minimum denominations originally at $10,000 and reduced to $2,500; interest rate based on the 26-week U.S. Treasury bill rate.

MONEY MARKET DEPOSIT ACCOUNT (MMDA)
A savings account authorized in 1982 under the Depository Institutions Deregulation Act (Garn-St. Germain Act). MMDAs are in effect a relatively high-yielding, liquid savings account with no interest rate ceiling. Rates are set by the bank. A seven-day hold is permitted on withdrawals; up to six preauthorized third-party withdrawals are permitted per month, of which three can be checks. Regulatory rules phased in minimum deposit requirements. The original minimum balance requirement of $2,500 was lowered to $1,000 on January 1, 1985, and eliminated in 1986.

MONEY MARKET FUNDS As defined by the Investment Company Institute, mutual funds whose primary objective is to make higher-interest securities available to the average investor

Table 2 / The Principal Money Market Instruments:
Amount Outstanding
($ billions)

Type of Instrument	1960	1970	1984	1985
Negotiable CDs (Large Denomination)	0	25	410	427
U.S. Treasury Bills	32	81	374	381
Commercial Paper	4	33	246	273
Bankers' Acceptances	2	7	75	68
Repurchase Agreements	0	3	118	141
Eurodollars	1	2	95	92
Federal Funds	1	20	70	84

who wants immediate income and high investment safety; also called liquid asset or cash funds. This is accomplished through the purchase of high-yield money market instruments such as U.S. government securities, bank certificates of deposit, bankers acceptances, and commercial paper.

Growth. In 1981, total assets of money market funds soared to some $182 billion, compared with $74 billion in 1980. According to the Investment Company Institute, money market funds in 1981 paid dividends to shareholders of $18 billion, "almost triple the amount they would have earned if the dollars had been held in 5 1/2 per cent savings accounts" (5 1/2 percent was the ceiling rate as of 1981 on passbook savings accounts of savings departments of commercial banks). The money market funds have been able to pay such superior returns because of their specialization in short-term money market investments, whose yields have risen in recent years in reflection of the antiinflation monetary policy adopted by the Board of Governors of the Federal Reserve System. With thrift institutions limited in the rates they may pay on passbook savings accounts as well as on time savings certificates of varying maturity to levels below those prevailing in the money market and afforded by money market funds, the drawing power of the money market funds off thrift funds has been a serious problem in recent years for thrift institutions. Disintermediation (outflow of thrift funds from the thrift institutions), compounded by the problem of operating losses incurred because of the higher interest cost of deposits and other expenses above current earnings from older portfolios of mortgages paying fixed rates below current rates paid on deposits, has been threatening net worths. (See SAVINGS AND LOAN ASSOCIATIONS, SAVINGS BANKS.)

Money market funds features include (1) opening of accounts with low initial amounts, e.g., $1,000 or $2,500, (2) free checkwriting for withdrawal of cash at any time without penalty, (3) dividends declared daily, compounded, or paid monthly, (4) same-day telephone withdrawals, (5) portfolio holdings that may be diversified in the various sectors of the money market or specialized in holdings of U.S. government securities alone, and (6) the advantages of scale provided by investing in the large wholesale amounts necessary in the money market (for example, $1,000,000 trading minimum in negotiable time certificates of deposit). Also the no-load feature and the low expenses are appealing.

Since the appeal of money market funds is their superior yield compared to the ceiling rates imposed on thrift institutions, the gradual elimination of such ceiling rates (see DEPOSITORY INSTITUTIONS DEREGULATION AND MONETARY CONTROL ACT OF 1980), as well as any appreciable declines in money market yields, might well dilute the appeal of money market funds to investors.

The appended table indicates the growth in recent years of money market funds.

Money Market Funds Yearly Data

End of year	Number of money market funds	Total assets (in millions)
1974	15	$ 1,715
1975	36	3,696
1976	48	3,686
1977	50	3,888
1978	61	10,858
1979	76	45,214
1980	138	74,447
1981	159	181,636

Source: Investment Company Institute.

Monetary Control. Money market fund shares are included by the Board of Governors of the Federal Reserve System in their M2 classification of the money supply for monetary control purposes (See MONEY SUPPLY) because of the checking privileges granted by money market funds to their holders.

Early in 1980, the Federal Reserve initiated a series of extraordinary actions to curb inflation, some of which were taken under authority of the Credit Control Act of 1969, which was invoked by the President for the first time. That act provides that "whenever the President determines that such action is necessary or appropriate for the purpose of preventing or controlling inflation generated by the extension of credit in an excessive volume, the President may authorize the Board [Board of Governors of the Federal Reserve System] to regulate and control any or all extensions of credit."

Among the severe restraints imposed on inflationary forces announced on March 14, 1980, was the imposition on money market funds of special deposits by the Federal Reserve equal to 15% of the net increases in their assets after March 14, 1980. Such a setaside in cold cash reduced the yields afforded by the money market funds subject to the action, but the mutual fund industry responded by organizing "clone" money market funds, new money market funds having the same features which continued to attract investors. However, both short- and long-term interest rates "dropped precipitously as money and credit demands fell off and signs of economic decline multiplied" (Fed's review) in reaction to the severe restraints imposed by the Fed. Accordingly, the Fed reduced its discount rate a full percentage point in May and again in June, announced a partial phaseout of the special credit restraint measures on May 22, and finally on July 2 announced plans to complete the phaseout, including lifting of the special deposits requirement imposed on money market funds.

With the entry into the financial services field in latest years of nonbanks, offering such services as cash management accounts with checking privileges, an open question as of 1982 continued to be whether legislation might in the future subject such nonbanks, including money market funds, to monetary regulation and control.

See INVESTMENT COMPANY.

BIBLIOGRAPHY

Donoghur's Money Fund Report. Periodic.
INSTITUTE FOR ECONOMETRIC RESEARCH. *Money Fund Safety Ratings.* Periodic.
INVESTMENT COMPANY INSTITUTE. *Fact Book.* Annual.
Weisenberger Investment Companies Service.

MONEY MULTIPLIER The factor by which a change in total reserves changes the M1 money supply. The money multiplier equals the reciprocal of the reserve requirement ratio ($1/rr$). Therefore, the change in demand deposits (ΔDD) resulting from a change in total reserves (ΔTR) from an open market operation will equal ($\Delta TR \times (1/rr)$):

$$\Delta DD = \Delta TR \times (1/rr)$$

where ($1/rr$) is the money multiplier. If the reserve requirement ratio is 10%, then the value of this money multiplier is ($1/.10$) = 10. Therefore, a $1 increase in total bank reserves will have a $10 impact on demand deposits.

MONEY OF ACCOUNT The kind of money in which the bookkeeping of a nation is carried on. In the United States, business houses keep accounts in dollars and cents; in England, in pounds, shillings, and pence; in France, in francs and centimes; etc.

Prior to 1982, the United States Code contained a provision stating that the "money of account" of the United States shall be expressed in dollars, dimes, cents, and mills. This section was amended by Public Law 97-258 (1982) so that the expression "money of account" is replaced by the term "money."

MONEY ORDERS A form of credit instrument calling for the payment of money to the named payee and providing a safe and convenient means for persons not having checking accounts to remit funds. There are three parties to a money order: the remitter (payer), the payee, and the drawee. Money orders have been issued by the Post Office Department; by American express Co., various other private organizations, and their franchised retail stores; and by some commercial and savings banks and savings and loan associations. In handling, an advantage of money orders as compared to checks is that presentation to their original place of purchase is not required for payment. A further advantage may be lower cost. The scale of fees for domestic postal money orders as of 1989 was as shown on the appended table.

ENCYCLOPEDIA OF BANKING AND FINANCE

MONEY POOL

1989 Postal Money Orders

Amount of money order	Amount of fee
$ 0.01 to $ 35	$ 0.75
Over $ 35	$ 1.00

MONEY POOL In past periods of financial stringency in the CALL MONEY MARKET, when bank lenders were generally calling in such loans, borrower brokers found themselves in a bind, with insufficient funds offered to take up the called loans. On various such occasions, a money pool was formed by a group of the larger banks as an emergency measure to relieve the stringency.

MONEY RATES In a broad sense, the levels of interest rates and yields on high-grade securities generally and the cost of credit to borrowers of various types. Customarily, however, the term is used in connection with open market rates in the New York money market, the money center of the nation.

The levels of money rates, like those of any other free market in a free enterprise economy, should be allowed to adjust themselves in accordance with supply and demand on a competitive basis. An aim of MONETARY POLICY, however, is to intervene in the money market and in the EXCESS RESERVES situation of banks, so as to influence both the cost and availability of bank credit in line with the desired objective of ease or restraint and the level of open market rates. The conventional instruments to effect monetary policy are open market operations and variation in rediscount rates and in legal reserve requirements.

High money rates undoubtedly reflect increased demand for credit relative to supply. The impact of monetary policy, however, should also be considered as a major determinant. When credit expansion progresses to the inflationary level, countercyclical monetary policy, by turning to the stage of restraint, will further tighten availability of bank credit and raise money rates, as the basic conditions necessary to arrest undue and inflationary credit expansion.

The open market rates most sensitive to supply and demand situation in money are the federal funds and Treasury bill rates. The REDISCOUNT RATE of Federal Reserve banks may act as a ceiling for the federal funds rate, if the member bank has not excessively turned to the discount window of the Fed. In turn the rediscount rate usually has been above the Treasury bill rates, although this is a generalization marked by numerous exceptions empirically, one reason for markup in rediscount rates would be to bring the latter into line with open market rates, particularly Treasury bill rates. One reason for keeping the rediscount rate above the Treasury bill yields would be to minimize any tendency to increased borrowings from Federal Reserve banks in order to invest in Treasury bills at the spread in net current yield. The same situation is true as to prime bankers acceptances, with 90-day maturities. Commercial paper rates, however, although for prime names, have longer maturities (usually four- to six-month paper), and these as well as banks' own prime lending rates to customers would therefore be above the rediscount rate.

See MONEY MARKET for tabular comparison of annual average rates on commercial paper, bankers acceptances, and new issues of Treasury bills.

MONEY RESERVE See BANK RESERVE, GOLD RESERVE, RESERVE.

MONEY RISK The risk of open market price depreciation in the price levels of high-grade obligations (and other types of high-grade fixed interest rate or dividend rate securities) should interest rates and yields generally rise and market prices of such securities have to adjust downward in order to afford the higher prevailing returns and yields; also known as interest rate risk.

See INVESTMENT, as well as the cross references under RISK.

MONEYS OF THE WORLD See FOREIGN MONEYS.

MONEY STOCK See MONETARY STOCK, MONEY CIRCULATION.

MONEY SUPPLY The Board of Governors of the Federal Reserve System targets three principal measures of money and the money supply for purposes of monetary control:

M1-A: Demand deposits of all commercial banks other than those due to domestic banks, the federal government, and foreign banks and official institutions, less cash items in the process of collection and Federal Reserve float; currency outside the Treasury, Federal Reserve banks, and the vaults of commercial banks; and traveler's checks of nonbank issuers.

M1-B: M1-A plus negotiable orders of withdrawal (NOW and automatic transfer services (ATS) accounts) at banks and thrift institutions, credit union share draft accounts, and demand deposits at mutual savings banks.

M2: M1-B plus savings and small-denomination time deposits at all depository institutions, overnight repurchase agreements at commercial banks, overnight Eurodollars held by U.S. residents other than banks at Caribbean branches of member banks, and money market fund shares.

M3: M2 plus large denomination time deposits at all depository institutions and term repurchase agreements (RPs) of commercial banks and savings and loan associations.

L: M3 plus other liquid assets such as term Eurodollars held by U.S. residents other than banks, bankers' acceptances, commercial paper, Treasury bills and other liquid Treasury securities, and U.S. savings bonds.

Nonfinancial debt is the sum of the following sectors' outstanding debt: U.S. government, state and local governments, nonfinancial domestic businesses, and households.

The "L" concept of the money stock is the broadest and comprehends liquid assets rather than components of the money stock customarily considered to be transactional in nature.

In its report submitted to Congress July 13, 1988, the Fed again did not set targets for M1 growth. This was a repeat of the practice it began in February 1987. For three years before that, M1 grew above the target range set by the Fed in previous reports. In July 1986, M1 was deemphasized. The continued abnormal behavior of velocity is somewhat responsible for the Fed not establishing any range for 1987 and 1988.

In February 1988 the target ranges for M2 was set at 4% to 8%. These were lower than the rate set for 1987 by 0.5 percentage point at the high end and 1.5 points at the low end. They were one percentage point lower at the low end of the range than the rates tentatively set for 1988 in July 1987. These targets remained the same in the objectives set out in July 1988.

The lack of M1 targets does not mean that the behavior of M1 will be ignored. Presumably, M2 and M3 have assumed greater roles in policy. Some attention may be paid to M1A, a measure of M1 similar to that which existed before financial deregulation led to the inclusion of a number of new types of accounts in the early 1980s.

The items included in the concept of the money supply are, in M1, varied in nature and in velocity (turnover in use as money in the transactions sense, or as a medium of exchange), and, in M2 and M3, varied in the degree to which they are readily substitutable for media of exchange.

Summary. Entirely aside from the crucial determination of what stance to adopt for MONETARY POLICY (tight or easy), determination of what to measure (and how to measure it) in the various components of money supply presents a continuing problem of definition and research for the Fed.

BIBLIOGRAPHY

DOTSEY, M. "Monetary Control Under Alternative Operating Procedures." *Journal of Money, Credit and Banking,* August, 1989.
FALK, B., and ORAZEM, P. F. "The Role of Systematic Fed Errors in Explaining the Money Supply Announcements Puzzle."
Journal of Money, Credit and Banking, August, 1989.
Revisions to Money Stock Data. Federal Reserve Bank, July, 1989.

MONEY TRANSFER The transmission of funds from one place to another by means of the public or private telegraph. The larger offices of the telegraph companies provide for the transfer of funds by wire to other important centers. The paying office requires the person presenting the telegram that requests payment to prove identification, unless identification is waived.

The money transfer business is dominated by Western Union, the pioneer of money transfers, located in Upper Saddle River, N.J. Western Union has over 130 years experience in providing this service and has over 13,000 agents. In 1988, American Express

MONEY TRANSFER

Money Stock, Liquid Assets, and Debt Measures
(Billions of dollars, averages of daily figures)

Item	1985 Dec.	1986 Dec.	1987 Dec.	1988 Dec.	1989 Feb.	1989 Mar.	1989 Apr.	1989 May
					Seasonally adjusted			
1 M1	620.5	725.9	752.3	790.3	787.4	786.3	783.2	773.4
2 M2	2,567.4	2,811.2	2,909.9	3,069.4	3,069.2	3,078.7	3,081.3	3,072.8
3 M3	3,201.7	3,494.9	3,677.6	3,913.0	3,927.7	3,949.5	3,957.6	3,954.3
4 L	3,830.6	4,137.1	4,340.2	4,673.5	4,689.7	4,723.0	4,739.2	NA
5 Debt	6,733.3	7,596.9	8,310.7	9,052.1	9,172.3	9,229.4	9,283.5	NA
M1 components								
6 Currency	167.8	180.5	196.4	211.8	214.3	215.6	215.9	216.4
7 Travelers checks	5.9	6.5	7.1	7.6	7.5	7.3	7.3	7.3
8 Demand deposits	267.3	303.2	288.3	288.6	284.8	284.3	281.5	278.2
9 Other checkable deposits	179.5	235.8	260.4	282.3	280.9	279.1	278.5	271.5
Nontransactions components								
10 In M2	1,946.9	2,085.3	2,157.7	2,279.2	2,281.8	2,292.4	2,298.1	2,299.4
11 In M3 only	634.3	683.7	767.6	843.6	858.5	870.8	876.4	881.5
Savings deposits								
12 Commercial Banks	125.0	155.8	178.5	192.5	190.3	188.6	185.6	182.5
13 Thrift institutions	176.6	215.2	237.8	238.8	234.3	232.2	227.3	222.4
Small-denomination time deposits								
14 Commercial Banks	383.3	364.6	385.3	443.1	461.0	472.0	485.6	497.2
15 Thrift institutions	499.2	489.3	528.8	582.2	587.4	589.0	597.6	608.9
Money market mutual funds								
16 General purpose and broker-dealer	176.5	208.0	221.1	239.4	247.2	256.0	260.2	259.9
17 Institution-only	64.5	84.4	89.6	87.6	89.6	87.6	87.7	91.6
Large-denomination time deposits								
18 Commercial Banks	285.1	288.8	325.4	364.9	378.2	385.5	392.6	395.7
19 Thrift institutions	151.5	150.1	162.0	172.9	173.4	173.4	175.2	176.3
Debt components								
20 Federal debt	1,585.3	1,805.8	1,957.5	2,114.0	2,140.4	2,162.6	2,171.8	NA
21 Nonfederal debt	5,147.9	5,791.1	6,353.1	6,938.1	7,032.0	7,066.7	7,111.7	NA
					Not seasonally adjusted			
22 M1	633.5	740.4	766.4	804.4	772.3	775.1	791.3	767.2
23 M2	2,576.2	2,821.1	2,918.7	3,077.1	3,056.7	3,072.1	3,092.9	3,063.3
24 M3	3,213.3	3,507.4	3,688.5	3,922.8	3,915.6	3,944.3	3,963.2	3,944.2
25 L	3,843.7	4,152.0	4,354.5	4,687.0	4,686.6	4,719.6	4,741.0	NA
26 Debt	6,723.5	7,581.¡1	8,292.8	9,037.5	9,136.4	9,190.2	9,246.3	NA
M1 components								
27 Currency	170.2	183.0	199.3	214.9	211.9	213.9	215.1	216.6
28 Travelers checks	5.5	6.0	6.5	6.9	7.1	7.0	7.0	7.1
29 Demand deposits	276.9	314.0	298.6	298.8	275.7	275.8	283.3	273.3
30 Other checkable deposits	180.9	237.4	262.0	283.7	277.6	278.3	286.0	270.2
Nontransactions components								
31 M2	1,942.7	2,080.7	2,152.3	2,272.8	2,284.4	2,297.0	2,301.5	2,296.1
32 M3 only	637.1	686.3	769.8	845.7	859.0	872.2	870.3	880.8
Money market deposit accounts								
33 Commercial Banks	332.8	379.6	358.8	352.5	342.5	340.1	336.3	327.1
34 Thrift institutions	180.7	192.9	167.5	150.3	142.9	140.2	135.0	129.9
Savings deposits								
35 Commercial Banks	123.7	154.2	176.6	190.3	188.2	187.8	186.2	183.7
36 Thrift institutions	174.8	212.7	234.8	235.6	230.5	230.7	227.9	223.8
Small-denomination time deposits								
37 Commercial Banks	384.0	365.3	386.1	444.1	462.8	473.0	483.6	493.5
38 Thrift institutions	499.9	489.8	529.1	582.4	591.6	592.0	598.5	605.8
Money market mutual funds								
39 General purpose and broker-dealer	176.5	208.0	221.1	239.4	247.2	256.0	260.2	259.9
40 Institution-only	64.5	84.4	89.6	87.6	89.6	87.6	87.7	91.6
Large-denomination time deposits								
41 Commercial Banks	285.4	289.1	325.8	365.6	378.1	387.0	390.5	394.4
42 Thrift institutions	151.8	150.7	163.0	174.0	174.3	173.2	173.7	175.2
Debt components								
43 Federal debt	1,583.7	1,803.9	1,955.6	2,111.8	2,133.6	2,149.0	2,155.1	NA
44 Nonfederal debt	5,139.8	5,777.2	6,337.2	6,925.7	7,002.8	7,041.2	7,091.3	NA

NA - Not available.

ENCYCLOPEDIA OF BANKING AND FINANCE

introduced a product similar to that offered by Western Union, called a MoneyGram. Citicorp offered Express Money in 1987 but withdrew from the market 14 months later. Start-up costs are very high, and a broad distribution network is needed. Fees vary based on the amount of money transferred. In 1989, Western Union charged $14 for each $100. American Express charged $11 for the same service.

Money transfers are also made by means of private telegraph lines controlled by the larger banks, including the Federal Reserve banks. Suppose, for instance, that Bank B of Joliet, Illinois, which normally maintains balances with Chicago Bank A and New York Bank C, wishes to place itself in immediate possession of New York funds, which have suddenly become exhausted. Supposing Banks A, B, and C are correspondents with reciprocal balances, Bank B may instruct Bank A to telegraph funds for its account with Bank C. Upon receipt of the instructions over the private wire, Bank C will credit the account of Bank B and charge the account of Bank A. At the same time Bank A will charge the account of Bank B. Thus a transfer of funds has occurred without actual currency shipments. Confirmatory advices will be sent by mail from Bank A to Bank C, and return advices from Bank C to Bank A and from Bank A to Bank B.

MONEY VALUE The value of an asset expressed in terms of the national currency, as contrasted with its barter value in terms of other goods and commodities. Money value is the standard expression of value for labor, services, wealth of all kinds, etc., in advanced commercial societies. Stated money values may be nominal or current, depending on whether they are arbitrarily fixed or reflect current realizable values.

MONOMETALLISM A system in which only gold or silver is made the basis of the standard money of a nation, other metals being used for subsidiary monetary purposes only. This means that the coins of only one metal are endowed with full legal tender qualities and are coined without limitation as to quantity. Leading commercial nations now have a monometallic gold system, also known as the SINGLE STANDARD and distinguished from BIMETALISM, but most countries are on a bullion standard and prohibit or restrict internal circulation of gold coin.

MONOPOLISTIC COMPETITION A market structure in which there are many sellers of a differentiated product (such as breakfast cereal) and only minor barriers to entry. Generally, competition in this type of industry is not in terms of price, as in a competitive market, but rather in terms of product attributes. Firms will advertise appealing characteristics of their produt in an effort to atract new customers.

MONOPOLY A market structure in which there is only one supplier of a product and significant barriers to entry. Having no competition from producers of identical or closely substitutable products, the monopolist will set a price to maximize profits. The price arrived at will be greater than the price that would prevail under perfect competition, and the corresponding output level will be less than what would prevail under perfect competition.

Monopoly is a theoretical construct used in economics to illustrate the opposite extreme to perfect competition, thereby demonstrating the economic efficiencies associated with competition. There are no pure monopolies in the United States, by law.

BIBLIOGRAPHY

WANG, L. F. S., and CONANT, J. L. "Corporate Tax Evasion and Output Decisions of the Uncertain Monopolist." *National Tax Journal*, December, 1989.
GLOSTEN, L. R. "Insider Trading, Liquidity, and the Role of the Monopolist Specialist." *Journal of Business*, April, 1989.
SAPPINGTON, D. E. M., "Regulating a Monopolist with Unknown Demand." *American Economic Review*, December, 1988.

MONOPSONY A market situation in which there is only one buyer of a product. One example of such a situation relates to mill towns wherein the mill is the dominant employer of labor. In such a situation, the monopsonist has significant control over the offer wage.

MONTHLY INVESTMENT PLAN A "pay-as-you-go" plan for the periodic investment in designated listed stocks by individual investors, inaugurated January 25, 1954 by the NEW YORK STOCK EXCHANGE for member firms; now no longer actively promoted. The plan was designed for small investors, calling for the investment, monthly or quarterly, of any amount from $40 to $999 in any one stock over any period from one to five years.

During 1970, participation in the Monthly Investment Plan (MIP) reached an all-time high. The MIP, sponsored by member organizations of the New York Stock exchange, was officially described by the NYSE as a method of acquainting the public with investing through the accumulation of small amounts of listed securities with small periodic payments. Full shares or fractional interest in a share was bought with each payment received. No credit was involved. Over 98% of the plans called for the automatic reinvestment of dividends.

The NYSE reported that a major element in the growth of the MIP could be attributed to the increase in employee stock purchase plans using the MIP procedure. This was an arrangement whereby companies permitted their employees to purchase stock through regular payroll deductions.

Special features of such plans were:

1. The company paid the commission on purchases made with funds deducted from employee paychecks.
2. Where possible, purchases were made in round lots and later prorated among the participants, thus stretching the buying power of the deduction for each employee.
3. Some companies also made a contribution—usually a percentage of the amount deducted from payroll—thereby increasing employee interest and participation in the plan at a relatively low cost to the company.

In the opinion of the New York Stock Exchange, the MIP opened a new era in the history of personal development, by offering individuals the opportunity to become owners, on a budgeted cash payment basis, of any of the stocks listed on the New York Stock Exchange. It was designed for "people who want the double advantage of regular thrift plus dividends and profit possibilities." The MIP, however, was not intended to be a substitute for such emergency financial reserves as a savings account or a life insurance policy.

Summary. In comparison with the MIP, mutual fund shares, another medium for investment by small investors, afford wider diversification automatically, each share representing an interest in the entire portfolio of the fund. Mutual fund shares are also cheaper for the small investor on full round turns (purchase and subsequent redemption) for periodic noncontractual cash accumulation. Their sales loads (premiums over asset value) are typically 6% to 9%, but there is no charge for odd lots and many funds do not change on redemption of shares (others have a nominal charge).

See INVESTMENT COMPANY.

MONTREAL CURB MARKET *See* MONTREAL EXCHANGE.

MONTREAL EXCHANGE Along with the TORONTO STOCK EXCHANGE and the Vancouver Stock Exchange, the latter especially active in low-priced mining issues, this exchange and its affiliated Canadian Stock Exchange (formerly known as the Montreal Curb Market) provide securities exchange facilities in Canada. The first exchange in Canada to receive its charter has as its main objective to provide an efficient market for the trading of listed securities and to facilitate public financing of companies. The Montreal Exchange is a nonprofit organization belonging to its members. The affairs of the exchange are supervised by its governing committee, consisting of 17 governors, including 11 member governors, 6 public governors and the president. The ME was the first exchange in Canada to make provisions for the appointment of public representatives to its governing body.

In 1863, a Board of Stock Brokers was formed in Montreal, consisting of 11 members who met daily. They made rules regarding membership, commissions, and listing fees for stocks. In 1874, the Board of Stock Brokers became the Montreal Stock Exchange, incorporated under that name with a charter from the government of the province of Quebec. In 1904, the exchange moved from St. Sacrament Street, where it had been operating since 1883, to St. Francois Xavier Street, in the heart of Montreal's financial district.

The Montreal Stock Exchange is now called the Montreal Exchange (ME) and is located in the Stock Exchange Tower on Square Victoria. Its name was changed in 1982 to reflect the growing prominence of financial instruments other than stocks on its trading floor. Early in 1926, the Montreal Curb Market was organized by members of the Montreal Stock Exchange with a view to providing organized trading facilities for unlisted securities which could not meet the listing requirements of the Montreal Stock Exchange. The name was changed from Montreal Curb Market to Canadian Stock Exchange on March 30, 1953.

During the 1970s, serious negotiations to merge the Montreal and Canadian stock exchanges were under way, and on January 1, 1974, the merger occurred. As of January 7, 1988, the ME had 76 full members, 5 individual members and 17 associate members. There are four distinct categories of associate membership. One provides direct electronic access to the ME floor. The other memberships provide access to each of the three ME divisions: the International Options Market, the Mercantile Division, and the International Division.

Broadly speaking, the main requisites for a corporation wishing to have its shares listed on the Montreal Stock Exchange have been a sound financial position, a distribution of the various securities of the applying corporation which would assure a public interest in the said securities, and competent management. By and large, the Canadian Stock Exchange, whose listing requirements were not as exacting, was a seasoning ground for securities prior to their graduating to listing on the Montreal Stock Exchange. The Canadian Stock Exchange was located in the Montreal Stock Exchange Building.

The ME is currently recognized as the fastest growing Canadian stock exchange. Its listing department watched over the listing of 6 new companies in 1982; during 1987, the same department had over 123 new entrants to its stock list. As of December 31, 1987, there were 738 companies listed with approximately 1,196 issues from across Canada and elsewhere. Many products are traded on the floor of the ME, such as equities, rights and warrants, options on stocks, bonds, Treasury bills, gold, platinum, the Canadian dollar and gold, and platinum and silver certificates. The Montreal Exchange has approximately 17% and 27% of the Canadian equity market and options market, respectively.

MOODY'S INVESTORS SERVICE One of the three statistical services, founed by John Moody in 1903. The business was incorporated in New Jersey on June 30, 1914. Late in 1961, the merger of Moody's with DUN & BRADSTREET INC. was announced. Moody's continued as a separate entity operating under its own management.

The company publishes the Moody's Manuals, consisting of the following volumes with semiweekly supplements:

Municipals and Governments
Banks and Finance
Industrials
OTC [over-the-counter] Industrials
Public Utilities
Transportation
International

In addition, the following services are published:

Stock Survey
Bond Survey
Dividend Record
Bond Record
Advisory Reports
Handbook of Widely Held Common Stocks

The company also provides several forms of investment services and does specialized research and economic and advisory work for banks, brokers, financial institutions, corporations, estates, pension funds, and individual investors.

Moody's originated investment ratings, familiarly known as Moody's Bond Ratings, which are widely used by bankers and investors and were formerly recognized in regulations of the Comptroller of the Currency and other bank supervisory agencies as one of the rating systems to be used as a guide in judging the quality of bonds eligible for purchase by banks.

See MANUALS.

MORAL RISK In loaning money, that part of the risk which depends upon the integrity or honestly of the borrower or prospective borrower. In one-name, straight, or uncollateraled loans, if not all loans, the moral risk is the most important of all the elements of the credit. The personal equation dominates all others, since without character and integrity no person can be trusted, irrespective of the ability and property he may possess. In judging the moral risk involved in the application for a loan one must investigate several elements, e.g., the reputation for honesty, sobriety, veracity, and standard of business ethics. Does the risk make a practive of welching on contracts when the market goes against him? Does he engage in unfair competition? Is he conservative in his commitments? Are his past performances and antecedent connections above reproach? What reputation does he have in the trade and among his banking connections?

See BUSINESS RISK, CREDIT, CREDIT RISK, PROPERTY RISK.

MORAL SUASION An informal process used by the Federal Reserve to attempt to advise major financial institutions of the Fed's position or proposed course of action without taking formal action. Moral suasion is an attempt on the part of the Federal Reserve to influence member banks. The Federal Reserve can control the money supply using three tools: open market operations, changes in reserve requirements, and changes in the discount rate. To reinforce the efficiency of changes in the discount rate, the Fed will often exert moral suasion (persuasion) on member banks. This is an informal, yet forceful, request to member banks to curb borrowing activity.

MORATORIUM An order by a government making it lawful to defer payment of all or certain kinds of debts for a certain period of time beyond the original maturity, issued in order to prevent general bankruptcy or a collapse of credit by legally protecting debtors against their creditors in times of public danger. Holdsworth defined a moratorium as "an official declaration or degree by the Government postponing all or certain types of maturing debts for a given period" (*Money and Banking*)

In later United States financial history, moratoria have been invoked in connection with banks and mortgage debts. Banking moratoria began on February 14, 1933, when Michigan ordered all banks in that state closed for eight days. Other states quickly invoked similar action, and the crisis culminated in the national bank holiday invoked by the President on March 6, 1933. The Emergency Banking Relief Act of March 9, 1933, authorized the Comptroller of the Currency to appoint conservators for any national bank when considered necessary in order to conserve its assets; provide for issuance of preferred stock by national banks and preferred stock and capital notes or debentures by state banks to the Reconstruction Finance Corporation to strengthen capital funds of banks; and authorized reorganization of national banks upon approval of the Comptroller and 75% of depositors or 66 2/3% of the stockholders or both. Sound banks were allowed to reopen promptly after termination of the holiday.

Moratoria in connection with mortgage debts were also invoked by states during the depth of the real estate depression to avoid wholesale foreclosures of mortgagors unable to meet principal installments and interest payments. Later these moratoria were continued on a modified basis and general recovery permitted full resumption of amortization and interest payments.

MORRIS, ROBERT, ASSOCIATES *See* ROBERT MORRIS ASSOCIATES.

MORRIS PLAN A pioneer system of personal loans which took its name from Arthur J. Morris, who founded the first Morris Plan bank (actually, a personal loan company making comaker loans to individuals) in 1910, the Fidelity Savings & Trust Company of Norfolk, Virginia.

Morris Plan loans were made on the modern monthly repayment basis for personal loans, with the first month's installments deducted from the face amount of the loan when made and the balance repayable monthly. Such an arrangement makes the effective rate of interest about twice the nominal rate, because the borrower has effective use of only half the loan proceeds over the year. Because of the then prevailing lack of banking law authorization for such loans and the usury law's limitation on interest rate, the plan evolved as a loan for the amount desired, nominally to purchase an investment

MORTGAGE

Schedule M Mortgage

Statutory Form M

This mortgage, made the _____ day of _____ nineteen hundred and ____, between _____ (insert residence), the mortgagor, and _____ (insert residence), the mortgagee.

Witnesset, that to secure the payment of an indebtedness in the sum of _____ dollars, lawful money of the United States, to be paid on the _____ day of _____ , nineteen hundred and _____ , with interest thereon to be computed from _____ at the rate of _____ per centum, per annum, and to be paid, according to a certain bond or obligation bearing even date herewith, the mortgagor herby mortgages to mortgagee _____ _____ (description).

And the mortgagor covenants with the mortgagee as follows:

1. That the mortgagor will pay the indebtedness as herinbefore provided.

2. That the mortgagor will keep the buildings on the premises insured against loss by fire for the benefit of the mortgagee; that he will assign, and deliver the policies to the mortgagee; and that he will reimburse the mortgagee for any premiums paid for insuring the buildings or in so assigning and delivering the policies.

3. That no building on the premises will be removed or demolished without the consent of the mortgagee.

4. That the whole of said principal sum and interest shall become due at the option of the mortgagee: after default in the payment of any installment of principal or of interest for
days; or after default in the payment of any tax, water rate or assessment for _____ days after notice and demand; or after default after notice and demand either in assigning and delivering the policies insuring the buildings against loss by fire or in reimbursing the mortgagee for premiums paid on such insurance, as hereinbefore provided; or after default upon request in furnishing a statement of the amount due on the mortgage and whether any offsets or defenses exist against the mortgage debt, as hereinafter provided.

5. That the holder of this mortgage, in any action to foreclose it, shall be entitled to the appointment of a receiver.

6. That the mortgagor will pay all taxes, assessments or water rates and in default thereof, the mortgagee may pay the same.

7. That the mortgagor within _____ days upon request in person or within _____ days upon request by mail will furnish a written statement duly acknowledged of the mount due on this mortgage and whether any offsets or defenses exist against the mortgage debt.

8. That notice and demand or request may be in writing and may be served in person or by mail.

9. That the mortgagor warrants the title to the premises.

In witness whereof this mortgage has been duly executed by the mortgagor.

In presence of: _____

---

certificate, to be paid for in monthly payments with the credit for the monthly payments going to the certificate account rather than the loan account. A variation would credit the monthly payments to a deposit account. In either case, the effective rate of interest, about twice the nominal rate, would not technically violate the usury law. Over the years, many states have amended their banking laws to authorize personal loans on such a basis, so that Morris Plan companies and industrial banks no longer need resort to the certificate device.

An additional feature of personal loans pioneered by the Morris Plan companies was insurance on the lives of borrowers through the Morris Plan Insurance Society. Borrowers could procure life insurance policies for the full amount of their loans, which in the event of death during the pendency of the loans would be applied to full repayment of the loans, with the remainder paid to the family or estate, thus relieving comaker and dependents from liability.

The Morris Plan Corporation of America, incorporated in Virginia in 1925 to assume the function of a holding company for the Morris Plan interests in banking, insurance, and other fields, changed its name to Financial General Corporation in 1956, and in turn adopted its present name (Financial General Bankshares, Inc.) in April, 1970.

Mortgage Debt (Flow of Funds Outstandings 1970-87)
(in Millions)

	Total	Home	Multi-family residential	Commercial	Farm
1970	470.4	294.4	60.1	85.6	30.3
71	519.0	320.9	70.1	95.9	32.2
72	590.9	360.3	82.8	112.7	3501
73	667.6	403.3	93.1	131.7	39.5
74	729.0	437.4	100.0	146.9	44.7
75	786.6	476.9	100.6	159.3	49.7
76	871.6	539.5	105.7	171.2	55.3
77	999.9	632.7	114.0	189.7	63.5
78	1151.1	742.8	124.9	211.8	71.6
79	1317.7	861.0	134.9	236.3	85.6
80	1448.8	955.2	142.3	255.5	95.8
81	1557.6	1032.1	142.1	277.5	105.8
82	1631.3	1074.7	145.8	300.8	110.0
83	1814.9	1191.4	189.9	351.0	112.6
84	2035.2	1320.5	184.8	418.4	111.6
85	2269.2	1469.6	213.5	480.4	105.7
86	2564.5	1667.4	246.3	554.0	96.8
87	2908.1	1888.2	273.7	656.2	90.0

Source: Federal Reserve Bulletin.

The company is now a registered bank holding company whose subsidiaries and affilates are engaged in banking, real estate management, and finance group activities.

MORTGAGE Mortgages in legal contemplation are of two types: (1) the common law mortgage, which conveys title to the land which is security for debt to the mortgagee, subject to the subsequent condition that upon payment of the debt with interest as convenanted, the conveyance shall be void, and (2) the legal lien mortgage, which merely entitles the mortgagee to a legal lien upon the land. The legal lien concept has been recognized by statutes of many states.

In form, the mortgage may in various jurisdictions be the deed of trust wherein the borrower (mortgagor) conveys to an intermediary trustee, in consideration of the indebtedness recited and trust created, in trust with power of sale, the described property, to secure to the lender (mortgagee) the repayment of the mortgage debt evidenced by the borrower's promissory note. The final holder of the note secured by the deed of trust, upon full payment, will direct the trustee to cancel the note and the deed of trust upon delivery of same to the trustee and to reconvey, without warranty, all the estate held by the trustee under the deed of trust to the person(s) legally entitled thereto.

The mortgagee, i.e., lender, should make certain that the title to mortgaged property is in the name of the mortgagor. A lawyer may be engaged to search the title, or else the services of a title insurance company may be secured. These companies make a business of searching titles and guaranteeing their validity. An abstract of the title is given by the lawyer of title insurance company to show the succession of ownership of the property and the encumbrances thereon, if any. Whenever a mortgage covers buildings or other property destructible by fire, the property should be adequately insured.

When the mortgage has been delivered to the mortgagee, it should be recorded in the office of the registrar of deeds at the county seat. This is necessary in order to circumvent the possibility of the same mortgagor giving a subsequent mortgage upon the property which may be recorded prior to the first.

Alternative Mortgage Instruments. The standard fixed payment mortgage (SFPM), or fully amortized level-payment fixed-term mortgage, including the longer-term fully amortized mortgage that became attractive to commercial banks as a result of the FHA-insured mortgage program that began in 1934, became prevalent in home mortgage lending by all types of mortgage lenders in the 1930s.

However, under conditions of widely fluctuating interest rates and inflation prevailing as of the late 1970s and early 1980s, the SFPM has come to be considered ill-suited for mortgage lenders. Accordingly, a number of alternative mortgage instruments (AMIs) have made their appearance. [The following discussion relies heavily

Table 2 / Mortgage Activity by Lender: 1970 to 1987
(In billions of dollars. Loans outstanding are as of end of year. Bank and savings and loan data include Puerto Rico.)

Item	1970	1975	1979	1980	1981	1982	1983	1984	1985	1986	1987
Savings and loan associations:											
Loans acquired [1,2]	22.0	58.3	104.6	81.7	58.5	67.2	148.9	194.2	210.6	289.6	275.0
Loans outstanding [3]	150.3	278.6	475.8	502.8	517.9	492.2	512.9	641.4	658.2	667.0	731.3
FHA-insured	10.2	16.5	13.0	12.8	12.0	12.1	12.8	12.3	11.1	8.8	5.0
VA-guaranteed	8.5	14.0	15.6	15.0	14.2	14.0	15.5	15.0	13.7	11.1	7.8
Conventional	131.7	248.0	447.2	475.0	491.7	466.1	484.6	614.1	633.4	647.1	718.6
Commercial banks: [4]											
Loans outstanding	73.3	136.2	243.8	262.3	282.7	299.0	328.0	374.8	425.3	497.9	582.5
Nonfarm residential	45.6	82.9	158.1	170.2	181.7	185.5	196.2	212.9	229.2	259.7	297.1
FHA-insured	7.9	6.3	4.8	4.4	4.5	4.6	5.6	5.8	5.7	7.0	8.8
VA-guaranteed	2.6	3.1	2.7	2.4	2.4	2.7	3.1	3.0	3.3	4.1	5.3
Conventional	35.1	73.5	150.6	163.3	174.7	178.2	187.5	204.1	220.2	248.6	283.0
Other nonfarm	23.3	46.9	77.1	83.5	92.7	105.1	122.4	151.3	164.8	225.4	270.9
Farm	4.4	6.4	8.6	8.5	8.3	8.4	9.3	10.5	11.4	12.8	14.5
Life insurance companies:											
Loans acquired [1]	6.6	8.8	19.6	18.3	13.0	10.0	18.8	19.2	31.7	40.6	39.5
Nonfarm	6.3	7.7	16.8	16.5	11.8	9.3	17.6	18.2	30.6	39.4	38.5
Farm	.3	1.1	2.8	1.8	1.2	.7	1.2	1.0	1.1	1.2	1.0
Loans outstanding	74.4	89.2	115.1	127.9	135.6	138.5	148.4	154.5	167.9	190.4	209.3
Nonfarm	68.7	82.4	103.0	115.0	122.5	125.7	135.7	142.1	156.1	179.4	199.4
FHA-insured	11.4	7.9	5.8	5.5	5.1	4.8	4.4	4.1	3.2	2.7	2.1
VA-guaranteed	5.4	3.9	3.0	2.8	2.6	2.5	2.3	2.0	1.5	1.2	1.0
Conventional	51.9	70.6	94.2	106.7	114.8	118.4	129.0	136.0	151.4	175.5	196.3
Farm	5.6	6.8	12.2	12.8	13.1	12.8	12.7	12.4		11.0	9.9

[1] Mortgage loans on all types of property acquired either by origination or purchase. Long-term loans only, excluding construction and land loans.
[2] Includes Guam.
[3] Includes shares pledged against mortgage loans, junior liens, and real estate sold on contract.
[4] Includes loans held by nondeposit trust companies; excludes holdings of trust departments of commercial banks.

Source: U.S. Dept. of Housing and Urban Development, *The Supply of Mortgage Credit, 1970-1979;* and monthly and quarterly press releases based on the Survey of Mortgage Lending Activity.

on an article by J. A. Mckenzie, a member of the Office of Policy and Economic Research of the Federal Home Loan Bank Board.]

1. *Adjustable rate mortgages (ARMs).* The interest rate on such mortgages is not fixed but will vary according to some interest rate index selected at the time the mortgage loan is made. If the index rises lenders are not required to raise the interest rate on the mortgage, but they are required to lower the interest rate if the index declines. Minimum and maximum size of the interest rate change may be subject to limitations. A change in the interest rate may result in a change in the monthly payment, the term of the loan, the outstanding balance of the loan, or some combination thereof. The interest rate might change every three or six months, but the payment changes every one, two, or three years, if an increase in the interest rate results in the monthly payment being insufficient to pay all the interest for the month, the unpaid interest will be added to the loan balance (negative amortization).

    Adjustable mortgages made by federal savings and loan associations are known as AMLs (adjustable mortgage loans); adjustable mortgages made by national banks are known as ARMs (adjustable rate mortgages); variable rate mortgages (VRMs) and renegotiable rate mortgages (RRMs) are specific types of adjustable mortgages.

2. *Graduated payment mortgages (GPMs).* Such a mortgage has a fixed interest rate, but the payments start out at a lower level than those of a fixed rate mortgage. The payments on a GPM increase at a specified rate during the earlier years of the loan; for example, on the most popular GPM plan, the payments increase by 7.5% each year for the first five years of the loan. Payments on a GPM ultimately rise to a level higher than on a comparable fixed-payment mortgage. Because the payments on a GPM start out at a low level, they may be insufficient to pay all the interest owed so that the portion of the monthly interest in excess of the monthly payment is added to the loan balance. Thus the outstanding balance on most GPMs actually increases for the first several years. (Such GPMs are especially suitable for newly married couples who anticipate that their income will rise in several years.)

3. *Pledged account mortgages (PAMs).* The pledge account mortgage is a special type of GPM. As noted, on most GPM plans the low initial payments are insufficient to pay all the interest owed. On a PAM, that portion of the interest due that is not covered by the monthly payment is deducted from a savings account pledged by the borrower.

4. *Graduated payment adjustable mortgage loans (GPAMLs).* This instrument combines the flexible-yield feature of a mortgage with an adjustable interest rate and the low-initial-payment feature of a mortgage with graduated payments. "The GPAML is a very complex instrument but may be thought of as a mortgage with two interest rates." The first is the debit rate, which is the rate at which the borrower is charged interest. The second is the payment rate, or the rate at which payments are computed. The common features of all GPAMLs are variable debit rates and an initial payment rate lower than the debit rate.

    All GPAML variations involve a deferral of some of the interest owed during the early years of the loan. This will result in some negative amortization, which can amount to a significant amount of negative amortization if the debit rate increases during the initial period of low payments. Some GPAML plans have payments rising by a set amount each year for the first several years; other plans fix the low payments for the first three or five years; the number of possible GPAML variations is limitless.

    The regulation under which federal savings and loan associations may write GPAMLs is extremely broad. This regulation encompasses the old GPM regulations because a GPM is simply a GPAML with a fixed interest rate. In addition, the GPAML will permit a wide variety of mortgage plans in which the borrower and lender agree to a certain pattern of payments. For example, the GPAML regulation will permit certain types of accelerated equity build-up mortgages, where the payment increases by a specified amount from a level that is sufficient to amortize the loan. On such a loan, the initial payment may be

Federal Regulations of ARM Lending by National Banks

Requirement to offer fixed-rate mortgage instrument to borrower	None
Limit to amount of ARMs that may be held	None
Indexes governing mortgage rate adjustments for the ARM mortgages	One of three national rate indexes: a long-term mortgage rate, a Treasury bill rate, or a three-year Treasury bond rate
Limit on frequency of rate adjustments	Not more often than every six months
Limit on size of total rate adjustment over life of mortgage	None
Allowable methods of adjustment to rate changes	Changes in monthly payment or rate of amortization
Limit on amount of negative amortization	Limits are set, and monthly payments must by adjusted peiodically to amortize fully the loan over the remaining term
Advance notice of rate adjustments	30 to 45 days prior to scheduled adjustments
Prepayment restrictions or charges	Prepayment without penalty permitted after notification of first scheduled rate adjustment
Disclosure requirements	Full disclosure of ARM characteristics no later than time of loan application.

based on a 30-year amortization schedule but the loan will be repaid in a much shorter period.

5. *Balloon mortgages.* A balloon mortgage is any mortgage that has not been fully paid off by the maturity of the loan. Balloon mortgages may be of two basic forms. The first is known as an interest-only balloon, where the payments have covered only the interest and no principal amortization. The interest-only balloon has a maturity of three or five years. The second type of balloon mortgage is known as a partially amortizing balloon, on which the monthly payments have been the same as on a long-term mortgage, but the loan becomes due before all the principal has been repaid. Partially amortizing balloon mortgages may have fixed or variable interest rates, and maturities as long as 15 years are not uncommon.

When a balloon mortgage matures, the mortgagor may still owe a substantial amount on the mortgage. If the borrower intends to sell the house before the loan matures, the proceeds may cover the amount still owed on the mortgage. On the other hand, if the borrower does not move or sell the house, the balloon mortgage is typically refinanced, but the original lender is under no obligation to refinance the loan, and if he does so, the borrower may again have to pay some or all of the costs associated with closing the loan at refinancing.

6. *Shared appreciation mortgages (SAMs).* A shared appreciation mortgage is a mortgage loan in which the borrower agrees to share the property's appreciation with the lender in return for an interest rate below that on a standard mortgage. SAMs have a contingent interest feature—a portion of the total interest due is contingent or dependent upon the appreciation of the property. At either the sale or transfer of the property or the refinancing or maturity of the loan, the borrower must pay the lender a share of the appreciation of the property securing the loan. Payments on an SAM are based on a long amortization schedule, but the loan may become due at the end of five or ten years.

The borrower and the lender jointly determine the size of the interest rate discount the term of the loan, and the share of the appreciation due the lender. Since the amount of appreciation is not known at the time of origination of the loan, the total interest due and the effective interest rate are also uncertain. Although SAMs have a relatively low initial payment, the mortgagor's mortgage payment can increase very significantly if the lender's share of the appreciation and remaining principal balance have to be refinanced at market rates.

7. *Price level adjusted mortgages (PLAMs).* The price level adjusted mortgage is different from all other mortgage types because the balance on a PLAM is indexed to account for actual inflation. Since the *balance* is indexed, the interest rate does not have to include an inflation premium. The interest rate on a PLAM is a real interest—an interest rate net of any inflation premium; real interest rates typically are in the range of 3%.

There are two potential problems with a PLAM. First, if the mortgagor's income does not grow at the same rate as inflation, the real payment burden can increase significantly during the term of the mortgage. Second, if the property value does not increase at the same rate as inflation, then situations could arise where the outstanding balance would exceed the value of the property. In such a case, the loan would not be fully secured, and some borrowers might default.

Both problems can be remedied by developing a modified premium PLAM, in which the contract rate explicity includes an inflation premium. For example, a modified PLAM could have an interest rate of 8%—3% real interest plus 5% inflation premium. Thus if the actual inflation rate turned out to be 9%, the balance on the modified PLAM would increase by only 4% at the end of the first year.

The tax angle, however, may make the PLAM unattractive for lenders: indexing of the loan balance represents income to the lender, who on an accrual basis would have to pay taxes at the balance indexed rises without actually receiving an immediate cash flow.

8. *Wraparound mortgages (WRAPs).* The wraparound mortgage is a technique whereby a homebuyer can assume a low-interest-rate mortgage from the seller. For example, if a buyer needs a $50,000 mortgage and the previous owner has an assumable mortgage with a relatively low interest rate and remaining balance of $30,000, the buyer might obtain a wraparound mortgage for $50,000. Payments to the wraparound lender must be sufficient to continue the payments on the assumed mortgage and to amortize the additional $20,000 loan. The advantage to the buyer is that the blended interest rate is lower than new mortgage rates, and the payments to the wraparound lender are lower than the payments would be on a new $50,000 at prevailing interest rates.

Standardized Mortgage Documents. In view of the variety of alternative mortgage instruments recently developed, the erstwhile drive to develop standardized mortgage documents will now have to contend with more nonstandardization than ever. The conventional programs begun in 1971 provided for the purchase of both single-family and multifamily conventional loans over the counter, as well as a forward commitment for multifamily loans. All loans purchased had to be on the Federal Home Loan Mortgage Corporation's approved mortgage documents. These documents, for each of the 50 states, were designed in conjunction with the Federal National Mortgage Association (FNMA) and with the active involvement of builders, consumer representatives, lenders, title companies, attorneys, and political leaders. The forms allowed the lender and the borrower to decide major loan terms, including such items as interest on escrow payments which the lender shall apply to pay taxes, assessments, insurance premiums, and ground rents; the amount of late charges; and prepayment penalty, such last being assessable only in the event of refinancing by the borrower, prepayment of the loan on sale of the home or for any other reason other than refinancing being allowable.

Consumers are advised to shop for home mortgage financing. Key factors to consider when evaluating financing sources are:

Affordability: total housing costs, including loan payments (now and in the future), maintenance, property taxes, and anticipated income changes.
The sales price minus the down payment, or amount to finance the length, or maturity of the loan.

How often the term may change.
How much the term may change.
The size of the monthly payments.
The interest rate or rates.
Whether the payments or rates may change.
How often and how much the payments or rates may change.
The index that rate, payment, or term changes are tied to.
The limits, if any, on negative amortization.
Whether there is an opportunity for refinancing the loan when it matures, if necessary.

The home buyer should not rule out the possibility of negotiating with the seller or lender for better terms. The homeowner should also consider hiring an attorney or a real estate broker to represent him or her. The borrower should be aware that creditors are required to give the borrower a statement of loan costs and terms before the agreement is signed. This information includes the annual percentage rate (APR), which measures total credit costs, including interest, points, and mortgage insurance.

Table 1 shows mortgage debt by categories: 1970-1987. Table 2 shows mortgage activity by lender: 1970-1987.

See CHATTEL MORTGAGE, FARM MORTGAGES, MORTGAGE BOND, MORTGAGE CERTIFICATE, MORTGAGE LOANS, PURCHASE MONEY MORTGAGE.

BIBLIOGRAPHY

ALLEN, P. "Count the Ways to Boost Mortgage Business." *Savings Institutions*, August, 1988.
BARRET, P. M. and MCKENZIE, J. A. *Alternative Mortgage Instruments*, 1984, Supplemented 1985, 1986, 1987. Warren Gorham and Lamont, Inc., New York, NY.
BIBLE, D. S. "An Empirical Study of Residential Mortgage Foreclosures With an Emphasis on Appraised and Assessed Values." *Real Estate Appraiser and Analyst*, Winter, 1988.
CARREL, H. L. "Under Reconstruction—Making Servicing Portfolios Pay." *Mortgage Banking*, November, 1988.
FABOZZI, F. J. *Handbook of Mortgage-Backed Securities*. Probus Publishing Co., Chicago, IL, 1988.
Financial Monthly Mortgage Handbook. Financial Publishing Co. Francis, T. "Software Focus: Mortgage Lending." *Magazine of Bank Administration*, January, 1989.
FRIEDMAN, R. "At Your Fingertips." *United States Banker*, January, 1989.
GELTNER, S., and HEWITT, J. R. "Mortgage Markets: Speaking the Local Language." *Mortgage Banking*, November, 1988.
KAPLAN, P. E. "Regulatory Facts of Life." *Mortgage Banking*, December, 1988.
KAPPELER, A. J. "Servicing: Do You Run a Quality Shop?" *Mortgage Banking*, November, 1988.
Mortgage Bankers Association. *The Mortgage Lender's Guide to REO*. Mortgage Bankers Assocation of America, Washington, DC, 1989.
NYSTROM, W. K. "Automated Mortgage Financing." *United States Banker*, February, 1989.
OXENHAM, L. *Modern Mortgage Banking*. Bank Administration Institute, Rolling Meadows, IL, 1988.
SCHNEIDER, H. "Building Business Ties With Realtors." *Mortgage Banking*, November, 1988.
SHERLOCK, P. M. "Strategic Planning at the Crossroad." *Mortgage Banking*, November, 1988.
THOMSETT, M. C. *Real Estate Dictionary*. McFarland & Co., Inc., Jefferson, NC.

MORTGAGE-BACKED SECURITIES Securities backed by mortgages usually issued by banks to large institutional investors and by the Government National Mortgage Association (GNMA or Ginnie Mae), Federal Home Loan Mortgage Corporation (FHLMC or Freddie Mac), and Federal National Mortgage Association (FNMA or Fannie Mae); collateralized mortgage obligations; pay-through bonds. The underlying collateral is a pool of mortgages. Investors receive payments from the interest and principal on the underlying mortgages.

MORTGAGE BANKER See MORTGAGE COMPANY.

BIBLIOGRAPHY

BUTLER, J. R., JR. "Working Out Workouts." *Mortgage Bankers*, August, 1988.

Mortgage Bankers.
MORTGAGE BANKERS ASSOCIATION OF AMERICA. *Mortgage Banking Terms*, Mortgage Bankers Association of America, Washington, DC, 1982.
———. *Mortgage Banking: Financial Statements and Operations Ratios*. Annual.
Mortgage Banking Magazine.
National Directory of Home Mortgage Lenders. SMR Research Corp., Budd Lake, NJ, 1989.

MORTGAGE BROKER An intermediary between the mortgage borrower and the lender. The mortgage broker does not make loans or provide significant servicing of loans.

MORTGAGE BOND A bond secured by a mortgage on property, whether real or personal or both. Mortgage or secured bonds are to be distinguished from debenture or unsecured bonds. In the United States mortgage bonds are more popular than debentures, whereas the reverse is the case in England.

See CONSOLIDATED MORTGAGE BONDS, FIRST MORTGAGE BONDS, GENERAL MORTGAGE BONDS, REFUNDING FIRST MORTGAGE BONDS, SECOND MORTGAGE BONDS.

BIBLIOGRAPHY

ANDREW, J. *Buying Municipal Bonds*, 1987.
CECALA, G. D. "Dealing in Mortgages." *The Banker*, January, 1989.
COONER, J. J. *Investing in Municipal Bonds*, 1987.
CORCORAN, P. J. "Commercial Mortgages: Measuring Risk and Return." *Journal of Portfolio Management*, Winter, 1989. *Credit and Capital Markets*. Bankers Trust Co., New York, NY. Annual.
FELDSTEIN, S. and FABOZZI J. *The Dow Jones-Irwin Guide to Municipal Bonds*, 1986.
FHA Monthly Report of Operations: Home Mortgage Programs. U.S. Department of Housing and Urban Development, Washington, DC.
FHA Monthly Report of Operations: Project Mortgage Insurance Programs. U.S. Department of Housing and Urban Development, Washington, DC.
Financial Monthly Mortgage Handbook. Financial Publishing Co., Boston, MA, 1985.
FREER, J. "Leveraging Home Loans." *United States Banker*, January, 1989.
HEWITT, J. R. "Custodians: Coming Into the Limelight." *Mortgage Banking*, January, 1989.
MBA National Delinquency Survey. Mortgage Bankers Association of America, Washington, DC. Quarterly.
Modern Real Estate and Mortgage Forms. Warren, Gorham and Lamont, Inc., Boston, MA. Looseleaf.
NATIONAL ASSOCIATION OF BANK LAWYERS. *Fundments of Municipal Bank Law*, 1988.
Relocation Report. Kinsale Corp., Stamford, CT. Biweekly.

MORTGAGE CERTIFICATE A former modified form of mortgage or real estate bond, also known as a mortgage participation certificate, no longer issued as the result of unfavorable operating and legal experiences with them during the 1929-1932 real estate depression. Many mortgage companies formerly issued mortgage certificates, and usually guaranteed the payment of both interest and principal, based upon and representing an interest in first mortgages which they owned. Such guarantees, however, proved worthless when invoked in volume, because the ratio of outstanding guarantees to capital funds was 20:1 and even as high as 40:1, and the companies went into reorganization or liquidation. There were several types of mortgage certificates. In some cases, certificates represented shares or participations in a specific bond and mortgage of large denomination held by the mortgage company and in which a precise description of the property securing the mortgage was recited. In other cases, the certificates were secured by a general pledge of mortgages equal in value to the certificates which were not specifically enumerated or described but deposited with a trustee. Mortgages so deposited were accompanied by: (1) a certificate of appraisal showing that the value of the property covered by the mortgage was at least twice the principal of said mortgage (to meet this requirement, actual practice tended to be over-liberal in appraisals), (2) a fire insurance policy fully protecting the holders of the certificates against loss in case of fire, and (3) a title insurance policy, guaranteeing the validity of the mortgage.

First mortgage certificates on property in New York State were formerly legal investments for trust bonds, but a 1936 amendment to the Decedent Estate Law and the Personal Property Law specifically declared the intention of prohibiting any future investments in parts of bonds and mortgages for trust funds.

MORTGAGE COLLATERAL TRUST BONDS
See COLLATERAL MORTGAGE BONDS.

MORTGAGE COMPANY
A company whose business consists of lending funds upon mortgage security and usually also transacting related activities such as title insurance, mortgage servicing, and investing operations including purchase and sale as middlemen of outstanding mortgages. Title and mortgage companies are subject in New York State to the Insurance Law, and hence are moneyed corporations. In New York, various mortgage companies engaged in the sale of guaranteed mortgages and mortgage certificates were placed in reorganization or liquidation following the breakdown caused by the 1929-1932 depression in real estate. The New York State Mortgage Commission was formed to take over some $800 million in mortgages securing mortgage certificates which had been sold by these companies with their guarantee.
See FARM MORTGAGE COMPANIES.

MORTGAGE CONSTANT
The amount of annual debt service (stated as a percent) required to pay interest at a stated rate and the entire principal over the amortization period. The mortgage constant is shown by the following formula:

Annual debt service = Loan amount x Mortgage constant

MORTGAGE DEBENTURE
MORTGAGE BONDS; a title used in countries where debenture is synonymous with bond.

MORTGAGEE
See MORTGAGE.

MORTGAGE GUARANTY INSURANCE COMPANY TAX AND LOSS BONDS
See TREASURY SECURITIES.

MORTGAGE IMPAIRMENT INSURANCE
An insurance policy that protects only the mortgage when a loss occurs and the mortgagor has not renewed his or her hazard insurance policy.

MORTGAGE INSURANCE
See FEDERAL HOUSING ADMINISTRATION.

MORTGAGE INVESTMENT COMPANY
A mortgage lending and investing institution similar to the MORTGAGE COMPANY, acting both for its own account and as middleman in the creation, purchase, or sale of mortgages on urban or farm property.
See FARM MORTGAGE COMPANIES.

MORTGAGE LOAN AND INVESTMENT COMPANY
A variant designation for MORTGAGE COMPANY and MORTGAGE INVESTMENT COMPANY.
See FARM MORTGAGE COMPANIES.

MORTGAGE LOANS
Loans made on real estate collateral, urban or rural, residential or business, in which a mortgage is given to secure payment of principal and interest.

Commercial Bank Mortgage Lending. Over a period of years, the trend of legislation and regulation has been to liberalize the comparatively stringent restrictions on real estate mortgage loans by national banks. As a series of regulatory changes permitted commercial banks (and also thrift institutions) to offer a variety of adjustable rate mortgages (ARMs), and the federal preemption of state mortgage rate ceilings removed that impediment to ARM expansion. In March, 1981, a new regulation was issued to govern conventional ARM lending by national banks (and shortly thereafter, revised regulations were approved for federally chartered S&Ls and federal mutual savings banks).

As summarized by the Fed, the major characteristics of the new federal regulations governing adjustable home mortgage lending by national banks are as shown in the appended table.

12 U.S.C. 371. This statute is the basic statutory authority for the real estate loans of national banks. Any national bank may make real estate loans secured by liens (the statute formerly read first liens) upon improved real estate, including improved farm land and improved business and residential properties. For loans to be real estate loans within the meaning of 12 U.S.C. 371, the real estate must be improved (i.e., substantial and permanent construction or development has contributed substantially to its value) and the real estate must be owned in fee simple (but the statute specifies also that under such rules and regulations as may be prescribed by the Comptroller of the Currency, the obligation may be secured by first lien on a leasehold under a lease which does not expire for at least ten years beyond the maturity date of the loan)

The interpretive ruling by the Comptroller of the Currency specifies that requirements for all real estate loans secured by leaseholds within the meaning of 12 U.S.C. 371 must comply with the following: (1) the leasehold must be on improved real estate, (2) the security must be a first lien on the leasehold, (3) the security instrument must be a mortgage, trust deed, or similar instrument, (4) the loan must mature at least ten years before the date on which the lease is due to expire (this requirement may be met by an option to renew for a period of ten years beyond the term of the mortgage), and (5) the loan must be amortized as are loans secured by first lien on real estate owned in fee simple.

Any national bank may purchase any obligation so secured in whole or in part and at any time or times prior to the maturity of such obligation.

Interpretive Ruling 7.2040 of the Comptroller of the Currency on first liens, dated December, 1979, provides among other things that a subordinate lien on real estate may be treated as a first lien within the meaning of 12 U.S.C. 371 if: (1) the bank has right to pay off the prior liens and become a first lien holder; and (2) the bank actually holds funds pledged by or on behalf of the borrower in an amount sufficient to pay off the prior liens, or the borrower is obligated for all funds advanced by the bank including any amount advanced to perfect or secure the bank's first lien position and the bank, at the inception of the loan, could fund the amount advanced to the borrower plus the amount outstanding on prior liens without violating any statute, regulation, or ruling.

Moreover, if a national bank holds a first and junior mortgage on real estate and there is no intervening lien, the combined mortgages will be regarded as merged into one first lien with the combined indebtedness being considered as a single loan with respect to application of the provisions of 12 U.S.C 371. But a lien which arises only upon the bank's election of its remedy under mortgage insurance or guaranty, applicable to the first lien, is not an intervening lien.

In general (Interpretive Ruling 7.2155 of the Comptroller of the Currency), the aggregate outstanding balance of real estate loans made or purchased may not exceed at the time of making a real estate loan the unimpaired capital plus the unimpaired surplus of the national bank or 100% of the time and savings deposits of the national bank, whichever is greater. But up to 10% of the total permissible amount of real estate loans need not comply with the individual loan restrictions of 12 U.S.C. 371.

The amount of any such loan hereafter made shall not exceed 50% of the appraised value of the real estate offered as security and no such loan shall be made for a longer term than five years, except that:

1. Any such loan may be made in an amount not to exceed 66 $^{2}/_{3}$% of the appraised value of the real estate offered as security and for a term not longer than ten years if the loan is secured by an amortized mortgage, deed of trust, or other such instrument under the terms of which the installment payments are sufficient to amortize 40% or more of the principal of the loan within a period of not more than ten years.
2. Any such loan may be made in an amount not to exceed 66 $^{2}/_{3}$% of the appraised value of the real estate offered as security and for a term not longer than 20 years if the loan is secured by an amortized mortgage, deed of trust, or other such instrument under the terms of which the installment payments are sufficient to amortize the entire principal of the loan within a period of not more than 20 years.
3. Any such loan may be made in an amount not to exceed 90% of the appraised value of the real estate offered as security and for a term not longer than 30 years if the loan is secured by an amortized mortgage, deed of trust, or other such instrument under the terms of which the installment payments are sufficient to amortize the entire principal of the loan within the period ending on the date of its maturity.

MORTGAGE LOANS

The foregoing limitations and restrictions shall not apply to:

1. Real estate loans which are insured under the provisions of Title II, Title VI, Title VIII, Section 8 of Title I, or Title IX of the National Housing Act. These are FHA-insured mortgages.
2. Real estate loans insured by the secretary of Agriculture pursuant to Title I of the Bankhead-Jones Farm Tenant Act, or the act entitled "An Act to promote conservation in the arid and semiarid areas of the United States by aiding in the development of facilities for water storage and utilization, and for other purposes," approved August 28, 1937, as amended.
3. Real estate loans which are fully guaranteed or insured by a state or by a state authority for the payment of the obligations of which the faith and credit of the state is pledged, if under the terms of the guaranty or insurance agreement the national bank will be assured of repayment in accordance with the terms of the loan.

Notwithstanding the foregoing limitations and restrictions, any national bank may make loans or purchase obligations for land development which are secured by mortgages insured under Title 10 of the National Housing Act or guaranteed under Title 4 of the Housing and Urban Development Act of 1968.

Other types of real estate loans that national banks may make are:

1. Real estate loans secured by first liens upon forest tracts which are "properly managed in all respects." Such loans shall be in the form of obligation(s) secured by mortgage, trust deed, or other such instrument. Any national bank may purchase any obligation so secured when the entire amount of such obligation is sold to the bank. Limitations on such loans are:
   a. The amount of any such loan shall not exceed 60% of the appraised fair market value of the growing timber, lands, and improvements thereon offered as security, and the loan shall be made upon such terms and conditions as to assure that at no time shall the loan balance exceed 60% of the original appraised total value of the property then remaining.
   b. No such loan shall be made for a longer term than 3 years except that any such loan may be made for a term not longer than 15 years if the loan is secured by an amortized mortgage, deed of trust, or other such instrument, under the terms of which the installment payments are sufficient to amortize the principal of the loan with a period of not more than 15 years and at a rate of at least $6^2/_3$% per annum.
   c. All such loans secured by first liens upon forest tracts shall be included in the permissible aggregate of all real estate loans prescribed (see below) in the statute, but no national bank shall make forest-tract loans in an aggregate sum in excess of 50% of its capital stock paid in and unimpaired plus 50% of its unimpaired surplus fund.
2. Loans made to finance the construction of industrial or commercial buildings and having maturities of not to exceed 60 months, where there is a valid and binding agreement entered into by a financially responsible lender to advance the full amount of the bank's loan upon completion of the buildings, and loans made to finance the construction of residential or farm buildings and having maturities of not to exceed 60 months. Such loans shall not be considered as loans secured by real estate within the meaning of the statute, but "shall be classed as ordinary commercial loans whether or not secured by a mortgage or similar lien on the real estate upon which the building or buildings are being constructed."

However, no national bank shall invest in or be liable on any such loans in an aggregate amount in excess of 100% of its actually paid-in and unimpaired capital, plus 100% of its unimpaired surplus fund.

Notes representing loans made under this section to finance the construction of residential or farm buildings and having maturities of not to exceed nine months shall be eligible for discount as commercial paper, within the terms of the second paragraph of Section 13 of the Federal Reserve Act, if accompanied by a valid and binding agreement, entered into by an individual, partnership, association, or corporation acceptable to the discounting bank, to advance the full amount of the loan upon the completion of the building.

Industrial loans are not subject to the restrictions or limitations imposed upon loans secured by real estate. (Such loans are those made to established industrial or commercial businesses which are made under the provisions of Secs. 102 or 102a of the Housing Act of 1948, as amended by the participation or purchase of the secretary of Housing and Urban Development, who was substituted for the Housing and Home Finance administrator by amendment contained in P.L. 90-19, May 25, 1967; former Sec. 13b of the Federal Reserve Act, authorizing loans and commitments for commercial and industrial purposes by Federal Reserve banks, was repealed by the Small Business Investment Act of 1958.)

Loans in which the Small Business Administration cooperates through agreements to participate on an immediate or deferred basis under the Small Business Act shall not be subject to the restrictions or limitations of this section imposed upon loans secured by real estate.

Home improvement loans which are made in substantial reliance upon the credit standing of the borrower, insurance, collateral, or combinations of these factors are not real estate loans (Par. 7.2000, Interpretive Rulings of the Comptroller of the Currency), and additional security in the form of junior mortgages, taken as a matter of prudent banking practice, need not meet the requirements of 12 U.S.C. 371. That statute specified that home improvement loans which are insured by the FHA (Sec. 203(k) or 220(h) of the National Housing Act) may be made without regarde to the first lien requirements of 12 U.S.C. 371.

Also, loans to manufacturing and industrial businesses where the national bank looks for repayment out of the operations of the borrower's business (relying primarily on the borrower's general credit standing and forecast of operations, with or without other security), but also wishes to take a mortgage on the borrower's real estate as a precaution against contingencies, shall not be considered as real estate loans within the meaning of this section, but shall be classed as ordinary commercial loans.

Quantitative Limitations on Real Estate Loans. No national bank shall make real estate loans (other than real estate loans upon forest tracts) in an aggregate sum in excess of the amount of the capital stock of such national bank paid in and unimpaired plus the amount of its unimpaired surplus fund, *or* in excess of 100% of the amount of its time and savings deposits. whichever is the greater.

But up to 10% of the total permissible amount of real estate loans need not comply with the individual loan restrictions of 12 U.S.C. 371.

Loans secured by mortgages insured under Section 203 of the National Housing Act (FHA-insured mortgages) shall not be taken into account in determining the amount of real estate loans which a national bank may make in relation to the capital and surplus or its time and savings deposits.

Also, any loan to veterans at least 20% of which is guaranteed by the Veterans Administration under 38. U.S.C., Chapter 37, may be made by any national bank without regard to limitations and restrictions of any other law relating to (1) ration of amount of loan to the value of the property, (2)maturity of the loan, (3) requirement for mortgage of other security, (4) dignity of the lien, or (5) percentage of assets which may be invested in real estate loans.

All real estate loans of national banks secured by first liens upon forest tracts shall be included in the permissible aggregate of all real estate loans, but no national bank shall make forest-tract loans in an aggregate sum in excess of 50% of its capital stock, paid in and unimpaired, plus 50% of its unimpaired surplus fund.

The term "conventional mortgage loans" refers to mortgage loans not insured by the Federal Housing Administration or guaranteed by the Veterans Administration.

Limitation of Interest on time and Savings Deposits. Since 70% of the volume of its time and savings deposits usually is the larger quantitative base for its aggregate of real estate loans of the conventional type, a national bank interested in real estate loan business might tend to attract such deposits by paying high interest rates thereon.

However, the rate of interest which a national bank may pay upon such time deposits or upon savings or other deposits shall not exceed the maximum rate authorized by law to be paid upon such deposits by state banks or trust companies organized under the laws of the state in which such national bank is located. Moreover, under Section 19 of the Federal Reserve Act, the Board of Governors of the Federal Reserve System is directed to limit by regulation the rate of interest which member banks may pay on time and savings deposits.

ENCYCLOPEDIA OF BANKING AND FINANCE

Mortgage Loan Practice. The papers incidental to a conventional mortgage loan are (1) a note or bond (as evidence of debt), (2) a mortgage duly executed (as security for the loan), (3) a certificate of appraisal (indicating the value of the mortgaged property and its excess of value over the loan), (4) an abstract of title, or a policy of title insurance, indicating that there are no prior liens against the property and, in the case of the policy of title insurance, guaranteeing the validity of the title, and (5) insurance papers (to protect the lender against loss in case of destruction of the mortgaged property by fire).

In applying for a conventional mortgage loan upon urban property, the applicant would be expected to supply the lending institution with such information as

1. The amount of money desired
2. The location of the property
3. The dimensions of the ground
4. The dimensions of the building
5. The building materials
6. The purposes for its use
7. The value of the ground
8. The value of the building
9. The annual rental
10. The amount of insurance.

The signature of the bondsman or mortgagor (borrower) is then attached to the application.

For reference to FHA-insured and VA-guaranteed loans see FEDERAL HOUSING ADMINISTRATION, GI LOANS.

The essentials of security in mortgage loans are (1) the extent of the margin of safety, i.e., the excess of the appraised value over the total liens on the property, (2) the possibility of depreciation in neighborhood values, (3) the earning power of the property in rentals and the amount of their excess over taxes, insurance, repairs, and all other charges, (4) the adaptability of buildings for other uses, (5) the location with reference to function.

See FARM MORTGAGES, LIFE INSURANCE COMPANY BENEFITS, NATIONAL BANKING SYSTEM, SAVINGS BANKS, TRUST FUNDS.

MORTGAGE PARTICIPATION CERTIFICATES

The FEDERAL HOME LOAN MORTGAGE CORPORATION (FHLMC), organized in 1970 as part of the Federal Home Loan Bank system to establish an active secondary market for mortgages, originated in 1975 its guaranteed mortgage certificates, structured like bonds, which provide undivided interests in conventional (neither FHA-insured nor VA-gurarantееd) residential mortgages underwritten and purchasecd by the FHLMC.

The FHLMC also issues participation certificates, structured like passthroughs, which also provide undivided interests in conventional residential mortgages held by it.

Each of these types of mortgage-backed securities is backed by pools of conventional mortgage loans. The FHLMC guarantees the punctual payment of interest at the rate specified by the certificate, as well as payment of principal. Final payment date on guaranteed mortgage certificates is nominally 30 years from date of issuance, but holders have the option of requiring the FHLMC to repurchase the certificate at par on dates specified, which may be 15, 20, or 25 years from date of issuance of the particular certificate. Final payment date on the participation certificates is also nominally 30 years from issuance date, but monthly repayments of principal and anticipated prepayments are assumed to provide average weighted maturity of approximately 12 years.

See MORTGAGE CERTIFICATE.

MORTGAGE SWAP AGREEMENT

An instrument designed to replicate an actual, on-balance-sheet investment in mortgage instruments (synthetic mortgage swap). Transactions associated with this instrument are supposed to provide an institution with the same cash flows, capital gains, and capital losses it would obtain had the institution actually purchased a share of a specified set of GNMA pools, placed them on the books, and funded them with short-term, LIBOR-based liabilities. To establish this synthetic mortgage investment, the mortgage swap establishes an agreement between the investment banking firm (the counterparty) and the institution that includes three primary components:

1. An interest rate swap with a declining notional principal such that the institution receives fixed payments from the counterparty in exchange for making floating payments. The decline of the notional principal is based upon the paydown experience of an actual set of underlying mortgage pools with a particular coupon and maturity range. This component replicates the interest inflows and outflows that would be associated with the actual, on-balance-sheet position.
2. A cash adjustment to the regular swap payments that accounts for the return of principal and subsequent reduction in the funding liabilities that would occur with the actual investment in mortgages as paydowns occur.
3. A forward commitment such that the institution agrees to purchase, or cash settle, mortgage securities, at the end of the mortgage swap's life from the counterparty. The purchase price is agreed upon at the beginning of the contract and is typically set near the current market price of the underlying mortgage pools.

If the institution chooses to take delivery of the mortgages, then this feature allows the institution to continue to hold its position in the mortgages after the contract expires. If the institution chooses to cash settle the commitment, the institution then has essentially captured the same capital gains or losses it would have had with holding and then selling the actual position.

The arrangement generally provides a favorable funding cost, pool diversification, and administrative efficiency. The mortgage swap, on a stand-alone basis, carries substantial interest rate risk. The mortgage swap is not primarily an interest rate risk hedging tool (versus the traditional interest rate swaps).

Source: Federal Home Loan Bank of Atlanta, Mortgage Product Spotlight, April 1989, Number 1.

MORTGAGOR   See MORTGAGE.

MOTIVATION

An internal pressure or drive that encourages, urges, or prompts a person or group to act or not act in a certain manner. Classical motivation theory maintains that humans maximize their own self-interest. This conceptualization is reflected in Adam Smith's economic philosophy expressed in *The Wealth of Nations*. Humans are motivated primarily by economic concerns. Economic incentives in the industrial setting are under the control of the organization; employees are to be controlled and motivated by the organization. As rational economic creatures, human must not allow their emotions and feelings to interfere with economic activities, including motivation.

Advances on the classical theory suggested that basic human needs were the source of motivations and these needs were structured in a hierarchy: physiological satisfaction; safety and security; social needs; self-esteem and the respect of others; and self-actualization. The unsatisfied needs motivate human behavior. Individuals satisfy their lower-level needs before proceeding to a higher level of need satisfaction that influences behavior. If a lower-level need is threatened, individuals will revert to that level.

Douglas McGregor developed the well-known theory of human behavior commonly referred to as Theory X and Theory Y. Individuals respond differently under the two theories of behavior. Theory X assumes a negative/passive approach to employees' motivation; Theory Y assumes a positive/active approach. Theory X focuses on external direction and control factors, and Theory Y focuses on integration and self-actualization as major behavior determinants. Theory X-type individuals dislike work, prefer directions, require control, and respond to threats; they are not ambitious, desire security above other needs, and are irresponsible. Theory Y-type people look for meaning in their work, possess initiative, are self-directing and problem-solving, and are committed to a job if it is satisfying; they are ambitious and seek responsibilities. According to many behaviorists, tasks could be structured to motivate, supervise, and direct people according to Theory X or Theory Y.

As might be expected, a Theory Z was proposed. William G. Ouchi undertook a study of the philosophy underlying Japanese business practice which concluded that Western businesses would probably be more successful, healthier, and happier workplaces if they adopted policies and practices found in Japanese industry. Qualities found desirable in Japanese organizations include lifetime employment, equality of worth, mutual respect, job flexibility, loyalty to the company, and nonspecialization.

MOTOR CARRIERS Growth of the motor carrier industry was marked in 1935 by passage of the Motor Carrier Act of August 9, 1935, which is Part II of the Interstate Commerce Act, placing interstate carriers under regulation of the INTERSTATE COMMERCE COMMISSION.

Enactment of the Motor Carrier Act on July 1, 1980 (49 U.S.C. 10101 note) marked a statutory change in the mandate of the Interstate Commerce Commission (ICC) toward less regulation of the motor carrier industry. Among the act's changes were (1) lessening of barriers to entry into the industry, (2) creation of the concept of a "zone of freedom" permitting the carriers to adjust their rates without prior approval of such rates as just and reasonable, and (3) the possible elimination of restricted routes. The act brings about increased competition among the different classification of motor carriers (common carriers, contract carriers, private carriers, and owner-operator carriers).

Common carriers offer their services to the general public for transportation of goods between designated points at published rates under the authority of a certificate of public convenience and necessity issued by the ICC. Certificates are restrictive as to territory, routes, services, and commodities to be carried.

Contract carriers offer service to a designated group of shippers under operating authority from the ICC which specifieds territory to be served and commodities carried. The Motor Carrier Act substantially liberalized the rules for contract carriage. Prior to the act, contract carriers were restricted to one type of carriage or geographical area and limited to a maximum of eight contracts; most of these restrictions have now been eliminated, making it possible for contract carriers to compete better for the increased tonnage handled by private and owner-operator carriers.

Private carriers—firms that operate their own trucks to transport their own freight—are not subject to ICC regulation if they qualify under the criteria for classification as such.

Owner-operator carriers are generally operator who (1) own or lease the trucks they drive, (2) do not possess ICC operating authority, and (3) provide intercity truckload service. Under proposals of the ICC as of 1980, private carriers would have the ability to trip lease equipment and drivers to common carriers as if they were owner-operators, which would further encourage competition and divert truckload revenues from the common carriers. Also, the ICC proposed to allow independent owner-operators to be leased by private carriers as well as by common carriers.

(Exempt carriers, another classification, are exempt from ICC regulations as to routes, areas, and rates, by reason of the nature of their tonnage—unprocessed agricultural products, livestock, newspapers, etc.)

Because of deregulation, the motor carrier industry has experienced increased competition among the different types of carriers. For about two years before passage of the Motor Carrier Act of 1980, the ICC had been taking steps leading to more competition in the industry, including assuming the power of approval for the tariffs established by regional rate bureaus of the industry for various classes of freight. Adding to the industry competition, as of March, 1981, the ICC under the authority of the Staggers Act of 1980 granted the railroads' piggyback service (*see* RAILROAD INDUSTRY) exemption from ICC authority and rate regulation, as to both prior and subsequent movement of such piggyback freight when hauled in railroad-owned motor vehicles.

Common and contract carriers are required to file with the ICC surety bonds, insurance policies, or other security to insure payment, within limits prescribed, of any judgement against such a carrier for personal injury or death or for damage or loss to property of others. The act also requires every motor carrier to file with the board of each state in which it operates the name of an agent upon whom process may be served, copies being required to be filed with the ICC.

The task of regulation of the motor carrier industry is complicated by two facts. First, unlike the railroads, which are virtually all common carriers, most carriers in the motor carrier industry are contract and private carriers. Second, the number of small motor carriers is large.

The Motor Carrier Act exempts from regulation other than safety regulation (1) motor vehicles operated by farmers in transporting their farm produce and supplies, (2) farm commodity carriers (motor vehicles exclusively transporting livestock, fish, or agricultural products), and (3) motor vehicles owned or controlled by agricultural cooperatives, among others.

BIBLIOGRAPHY

COMPTROLLER GENERAL OF THE U.S. *ICC Needs to Eliminate Improper Leasing Practices by Certified Motor Carriers* (Report to the chairman, Committee on the Judiciary, United States Senate), December 31, 1980.
INTERSTATE COMMERCE COMMISSION. *Annual Report.*
LIDDELL, F. W. *Financial Analysis of the Motor Carrier Industry*, Citibank, N.A., 1981.

MOVE An upward or downward course in the price of a particular stock or in the general market, brought about by the appearance of favorable or unfavorable conditions or by professional or public participation.

MOVEMENT *See* SWINGS.

MOVEMENT OF CROPS The principal grain crops are moved from the farms to the milling centers and eastern seaboard for export trade in the interval from August to October, the peak usually being reached in September. On account of the demand for money and credit required by the purchasers to pay the farmers at this period, large amounts of funds used to be transferred from the eastern banks to western banks. After settlement with the farmers had been made and the farmers in turn had paid their debts and made their autumn purchases, these funds gradually found their way back to the east as deposits in the larger banks of the money centers. The crop moving period was, for this reason, a period of money strain and was usually accompanied by temporarily higher money rates, especially affecting the New York call money market, the first to feel the influence of a money squeeze. It was significant that most of the business recessions or even full-fledged panics originated during the crop moving period on account of the intensity of the demand for funds at this time.

Because of the establishment of the Federal Reserve System and federal agencies for supplying agricultural credit (e.g., Federal Intermediate Credit banks and Banks for Cooperatives), and because of the ease with which banks can secure funds through the rediscount process from the Reserve banks, the crop moving period is now passed without the same fear of a money disturbance that formerly attended it.

See CROP REPORTS.

MULTIFAMILY PASS-THROUGHS Securities backed by multifamily mortgages where the principal and interest are passed through to the investor.

MULTILATERAL DEVELOPMENT BANKS International, multilateral financial institutions that provide financial and technical resources for social and economic development to less-developed nations. Resources of such institutions are derived primarily from direct contributions of industrialized or oil-exporting countries and from borrowing in the capital markets of the world. Multilateral development banks have been organized into the following categories:

1. Global—World Bank.
2. Regional—African, Asian, Inter-American Development Banks.
3. Specialized—Arab Bank for Economic Development in Africa, Arab Fund for Economic and Social Development, Caribbean Development Bank, Development Bank of the Great Lakes Countries, East African Development Bank, Inter-Asian Development Bank, Islamic Development Bank.

MULTINATIONAL CORPORATIONS Typically giant business corporations literally transnational in operations and allegedly international in policy and viewpoint, as compared with business corporations domestic to particular countries, which emphasize national policy and interests.

According to the U.S. Department of State, although certain aspects of multinational business corporation (MNC) behavior with respect to operations in the developing countries may be criticized the positive contributions of MNCs to the development of international trade and investment must be recognized. In contrast, some developing countries appear to assume the existence of an adversary relationship between MNCs and host countries, with the former's economic power pitted against the latter's allegedly weaker soverign power, and a number of developing countries maintain that the system needs to be changed to strengthen their bargaining power vis à vis MNC's and to increase their share of the benefits of international investment.

U.S. Policy. The U.S. Department of State reiterates that the United States has long held that a largely open international economic system without government intervention provides the most efficient allocation of resources. The fundamental U.S. policy on international investment, therefore, is conceived to be neither to promote nor to discourage inward or outward investment through government intervention: "we respect each country's right to determine the climate in which foreign investment takes place within its borders, although a liberal and stable investment climate clearly facilitates international flows of capital and technology."

Moreover, the U.S. Department of State, in its advisory on policy, indicates that the United States supports the development of principles of behavior for governments and MNCs. Such guidelines can affirm standards of good practice for both governments and enterprises, contribute to improved relations between them, and limit unilateral government intervention in investment. They can reduce conflicts between governments over investment issues, thereby strengthening the liberal climate for international direct investment. The United States can support, in the view of the Department of State, guidelines or codes relating to MNCs that are voluntary, that do not discriminate against MNCs in favor of purely national enterprises, that are balanced to include references to the responsibilities of governments as well as of MNCs, and that apply to all enterprises regardless of whether their ownership is private, government, or mixed.

International action. Many international organizations have MNC issues under review, but the most significant activities have taken place in the Organization for Economic Cooperation and Development (OECD), the United Nations, and the International Labor Organization (ILO).

The OECD has developed guidelines for MNCs as part of a broader understanding on investment issues. In June, 1976, the OECD ministers signed a Declaration on International Investment and Multinational Enterprises, which includes the following elements:

1. Reaffirmation by OECD members that a liberal international investment climate is in the countries' common interest.
2. Agreement that they should give equal treatment to foreign-controlled and national enterprises.
3. A decision to cooperate to avoid "beggar thy neighbor" actions pulling or pushing particular investments in or out of their jurisdictions.
4. Voluntary guidelines, defining standards for good business conduct which the ministers collectively recommended to MNCs operating in their territories; and
5. A consultative process under each of the above elements.

The OECD formally reviews the MNC guidelines and other portions of the elements for consideration of possible revisions. Thus its Committee on International Investment and Multinational enterprises, and the OECD Council of Ministers reviewed and reaffirmed the OECD's 1976 guidelines, in June of 1979.

The focus of the United Nations (UN) on MNCs is on its Commission on Transnational Corporations (TNCs) and the related Centre on TNCs. The United Nations Conference on Trade and Development (UNCTAD) on April 22, 1980, published its *Set of Multilaterally Agreed Equitable Principles and Rules for the Control of Restrictive Business Practices*, and UNCTAD's Commission on Transnational Corporations (TNCs) has, through its Intergovernmental Working Group on a Code of Conduct for Transnational Corporations, entered into a series of negotiating sessions to implement the proposed UN Code for Transnational Corporations. The position of the United States has been that the proposed Code does not state clearly that it is intended to be voluntary (as the OECD guidelines are); that important definitions are lacking and those that are shown are vague, and that there is no provision of nondiscriminatory application. The last point, in particular, involved the argument of representatives of socialist countries that state-owned or controlled enterprises not be exempt from application of the Code.

The ILO, like the OECD, is considered by the U.S. State Department to have made significant progress in providing for its "Tripartite Declaration of Principles" concerning multinational enterprises and social policy, which was completed in April, 1977, and approved by the Tripartite Advisory Committee the same month, followed by approval by the ILO's Governing Council in November, 1977. The Declaration strongly supports such principles as freedom of association and equality of treatment in employment, and also embodies a number of principles contained in the OECD guidelines. The U.S. subsequently became a member of the ILO, but even then indicated its support for the incorporation of the ILO's tripartite declaration in UN codes of conduct to cover employment and industrial relations.

Illicit Payments. The problem of illicit payments added to the controversy over the role of MNCs. In the United States, the Foreign Corrupt Practices Act of 1977 imposed a strict statutory prohibition on illicit payments in connection with international trade and investment. Following the initiative by the U.S., the UN's Economic and Social Council (ECOSOC) decided in August, 1976, to establish a group of experts to work on an international agreement to cover such payments, its Ad Hoc Intergovernmental Working Group on the Problem of Corrupt Practices.

The OECD's *Declaration* also included reference to bribery [or other improper benefit, direct or indirect, to any public servant or holder of public office" in connection with international trade or investment. And the International Chamber of Commerce (ICC), a private business organization, adopted on November 29, 1979, its "Extortion and Bribery in Business Transactions," providing for a voluntary set of "Rules of Conduct to Combat Extortion and Bribery."

Summary. Much of the steam has gone out of the debate concerning the role and practices of multinational corporations, because developing countries themselves (including the Newly Industrialized Countries—NICs) are establishing multinational organizations, e.g., the OPEC firms established in tax-haven countries, as well as such countries as Argentina, Brazil, Columbia, Hong Kong, India, Republic of Korea, Peru, the Philippines, Singapore, and Taiwan, for trading and investing abroad. Thus although multinationals of the private sector continue to be importantly substantial factors in the international trade and investment, their alleged threat to the sovereignty of host counties has yielded to positive restraints by host countries as well as their favoritism to domestic firms.

Since World War II, the size and sophistication of multinational business activity have increased substantially, and a new format for international business activity has developed. Firms now very often make direct investments in fully integrated operations abroad, rather than merely buying resources or selling manufactured products. Many companies have become worldwide entities operating in many different countries and controlling all phases of the production and distribution process—from extraction of raw materials, through manufacturing, to marketing and delivery to consumers throughout the world.

The evolution of the multinational corporation has greatly increased global economic and political interdependence. For the most part, multinational corporations are free to pursue profit opportunities and allocate resources across international boundaries. Thus, they may borrow in the capital markerts of one country to finance expansion in another, or transfer products and personnel from one overseas subsidiary to another.

In the chase for global profit opportunities, the actions of multinational corporations often come into conflict with the goals of the nation states in which they operate. Countries may want multinational corporations operating within their borders to produce more product domestically, to hire more local labor, and to export more. But such demands by host countries may conflict with global corporate profit strategies. When this happens, political tensions rise, and nation states may seek to impose certain controls on the operations of multinational corporations. Yet despite these inevitable stresses, multinational corporations have become an important force for global economic integration.

BIBLIOGRAPHY

Belkaoui, A. *International Accounting: Issues and Solutions*, 1985.
Borner, S. *Internationalization of Business*, 1986.
Buckley, P. S. *The Theory of the Multinational Enterprise*, 1987.
Edge, A. G. *The Multinational Management Game*, 1989
Graham, J. *International Business Negotiations*, 1988.

MULTIPLE CURRENCY BONDS Bonds the principal and/or interest of which may be payable in the currencies of specified nations other than the nation in which the bonds are issued. Issues denominated in multicurrency units are reported to have expanded substantially in international capital markets in recent years, permitting the investor, in principle, to select the currency in which repayment is to be made.

See FOREIGN DOLLAR BONDS, FOREIGN GOVERNMENT BONDS.

MULTIPLE DISCRIMINANT ANALYSIS (MDA)
A credit scoring system used to predict whether a borrower is creditworthy or not, based on such factors as time with present employer, income, bank accounts, time in present residence, and others. The system determines the statistical significance of each characteristic and how the characteristics can be combined to score borrowers. The multiple discriminant analysis technique has been subjected to some criticism and should be used with caution.

MULTIPLE LISTING AGREEMENT A real estate contractual arrangement in which the property owner signs a listing agreement with a particular broker who is also part of the multiple listing agreement, which provides that any broker who is a member of that agreement may show and sell the property. The commissions earned are divided among the brokers according to the multiple listing agreement. In an exclusive agency or exclusive listing, the property owner agrees that the property will not be listed with any other broker during the period of the agency.

MULTIPLIER In Keynesian economics, the factor k is the coefficient by which a given increment in autonomous spending or investment will increase income. In the Keynesian model, change in income (dY) is the sum of change in consumption (dC) plus the change in investment (dI), but Keynes postulated that C depends upon Y, so that the active determinant of dy is dI. As Y changes, C will change also in the same direction but by a smaller amount, the ratio dC/dY being the marginal propensity to consume, which is thus assumed to be greater than zero but less than 1. Upon an increment of 1 into the economy, Y increases by a factor times dI which is the reciprocal of the marginal propensity to save (1 minus the marginal propensity to consume).

Mathematically, this is derived as follows. Let dI equal dY minus dC (rearranging the definitional equation, dY equals dC plus dI). Dividing both sides by dY, we get

$$\frac{dI}{dY} = 1 - \frac{dC}{dY}$$

the reciprocal of which is

$$\frac{dY}{dI} = \frac{1}{1 - \frac{dC}{dY}}$$

Multiplying both sides by dI, we get:

$$dY = dI \; \frac{1}{1 - \frac{dC}{dY}}$$

or, in effect, dY is determined by dI times a factor, called k or the multiplier (the term for 1 divided by 1 minus the marginal propensity to consume), which is the reciprocal of the marginal propensity to save.

The larger the marginal propensity to consume, the larger will be the arithmetical value of the multiplier, and vice versa. Thus, if the marginal propensity to consume is $1/2$, the multiplier is 2; if $2/3$, 3; if $9/10$, 10; etc.

The basic principle involved, i.e., the relationship between increments in investment and increments in income, had been recognized in previous economic literature (e.g., Tugan-Baranowsky and Wicksell), but with the lead of R.F. Kahn ("The Relation of Home Investment to Unemployment," *Economic Journal*, June, 1931), Keynes is credited with precisely stating the relationship in mathematical terms and thus developing a new tool of economic analysis.

Although the mathematical setting for the multiplier gives it precision, it does not follow that the problems of economic analysis and forecasting are made any easier. The value of the multiplier may fluctuate over the consumption-expenditure time period, or leakages may occur, such as through the use of increments in income to pay off debts, to increase savings, etc; in the short run the relationship between consumption and income may not be normal. Keynes did not develop the additional tool of the accelerator, or the ratio between change in consumption and the derived change in investment induced thereby. The interaction between the multiplier and the accelerator will magnify the total change in income in a cyclical pattern.

See ACCELERATION PRINCIPLE.

MUNICIPAL BANKRUPTCY ACT The act of May 24, 1934 (P.L. 251, 73rd Congress) added a new Chapter IX (Secs. 78-80) to the National Bankruptcy Act Authorizing readjustments of the debts of municipalities and political subdivisions. This statute was declared unconstitutional in part on May 25, 1936, by the U.S. Supreme Court (*C. L. Ashton et al. v. Cameron County Water Improvement District No. 1*, 298 U.S. 513). Congress had already passed P.L 515 (74th Congress) on April 11, 1936, amending Section 80(a) and (d) of Chapter IX, pertaining to readjustments.

Accordingly, P.L. 302 (75th Congress) on August 16, 1937, then added new Sections 81-84 authorizing compositions of indebtedness of municipalities and political subdivisions on a temporary basis, to June 30, 1940. On March 4, 1940, P.L. 425 (76th Congress) amended Section 83(a) pertaining to compositions. P.L. 669 (76th Congress) on June 28, 1940, amended Sections 81, 83(b), 83(e), and 84, among other things extending to June 30, 1942, authorization for compositions. This deadline was further extended to June 30, 1946, by P.L. 622 (77th Congress, June 22, 1942). On July 1, 1946, P.L. 481 (79th Congress) placed Sections 81-83 of Chapter IX on a permanent basis, applicable to compositions for indebtedness of municipalities and political subdivisions of states, repealing the former time limitation.

The 1946 version of Chapter IX, however, was criticized on procedural grounds by the Commission on the Bankruptcy Laws of the United States in its 1973 *Report*; and on April 8, 1976, P.L. 94-260 created a new Chapter IX of the Bankruptcy Act to provide for improved and expeditious proceedings for municipal adjustment of debt. Further changes were enacted in the New Chapter 9 (not Chapter IX any longer) of the extensive revision of the bankruptcy laws contained in P.L. 95-598, November 6, 1978, which is brief in its new Chapter 9 and indeed includes by summary reference other sections of the new act as applicable to municipal proceedings:

1. A Chapter 9 case is now entirely within the jurisdiction of the bankruptcy court, instead of being exclusively within the jurisdiction of the U.S. district court, and instead of being termed the "petitioner," the municipal unit is referred to as the "debtor."
2. The former requirement in the petition as to preparation of a plan and its negotiation is no longer in effect, the active requirement being that the municipal unit cannot pay its debts as they mature and that the state law does not preclude proceeding under the new Chapter 9.
3. Section 362 of the act, providing in general for an automatic stay upon filing of the petition by debtors under the act as a whole, is specifically included as applicable to municipal proceedings (Sec. 901). This would serve to stay proceedings against the debtor commenced before filing of the petition; to stay the enforcement, collection, or assessment of any claims or liens similarly commenced; and to stay the setoff of any debt owing to the debtor that also arose before commencement of the case. This last situation would be of special interest to banks owning securities or other debt of the municipal unit but also holding deposits of the municipal unit. Section 922 of the act specifically provides that a petition filed under Chapter 9 operates as a stay, in addition to the stay provided by Section 362 of the act and applicable to all entities, of (1) the commencement or continuation, including the issuance or employment of process or of judicial, administrative, or other proceeding against an officer or inhabitant of the debtor that seeks to enfoce a claim against the debtor, and (2) the enforcement of a lien on or arising out of taxes or assessments owed to the debtor.

The debtor municipal unit shall file a list of creditors, and the plan's confirmation will occur if such plan has been accepted by creditors that hold at least two-thirds in amount and more than one-half in number of the allowed claims of the class of claims held by creditors—a general provision contained in Section 1126(c) of the act and made applicable to municipal proceedings by reference.

The court shall confirm a plan only if, among other things, the plan is "in the best interest of creditors and is feasible."

See BANKRUPTCY.

MUNICIPAL BONDS Bonds that are obligations of a county, city, town, village, tax district, or other civil division of a state, as distinguished from U.S. government bonds, state bonds, and bonds of business corporations. Municipal bonds constitute one of the basic types of civil (governmental) issues. The fundamental difference between municipal bonds and corporation bonds is that whereas the latter are paid out of earnings, municipal bonds of the general "full faith and credit" type are paid off through taxes levied on taxpayers in the jurisdiction.

Municipal obligations may be issued, pursuant to basic or special borrowing authority, for a variety of public purposes, including school houses and equipment; water works and mains; public buildings; street improvements; sewers; drainage; irrigation, and reclamation projects; parks and museums; bridges; fire equipment; public housing; public markets; etc.

The types of obligations classified from the standpoint of liability for payment, are:

1. Direct and general obligations, for which the full faith and credit of the issuing municipality are pledged. The principal source of revenues for municipalities is the property tax, but a variety of other taxes, including sales taxes, income taxes, unincorporated business taxes, personal property taxes, taxes on gross receipts of designated businesses, and license and other charges, as well as grants-in-aid from the federal government and tax-sharing distributions from the state, have increased their proportionate contribution to municipal revenues in recent decades.
2. Revenue bonds, which are payable from specified revenues only, usually from the property or facilty financed by the revenue bonds, and which do not pledge the full faith and credit of the municipality. Variations, however, may provide for general taxes to make up any deficiencies in revenue from the specified activity; such bonds would then classify as general obligations.
3. Special assessment bonds, which are payable from assessments upon property deriving benefits from the improvements financed by the bonds and do not bind the full faith and credit of the municipality.
4. Tax anticipation warrants or notes, which are issued in anticipation of the collection of taxes levied or assessed and are usually a first claim upon such tax receipts.

All municipal financing is of course obligational in nature, there being no such thing as stock offerings, even where the municipality is engaged in specific business-type activity, such as operating an electric or gas plant, a water system, a transit system, a liquor business, etc. Revenue bonds in recent years have been issued under the name of the special municipal authority created for specified activities, such as bridge and tunnel, airport, or highway operation. Also, municipal obligations are never secured by the pledge of specific assets, instead, the pledge is of general or specified revenues, which are dependent on varying yields therefrom.

The legality (or validity) of the issue is the first and fundamental consideration in judging the safety of municipal bonds. If the obligations are issued in full compliance with all applicable general or special authority therefor, they constitute valid obligations enforceable against the issuer. In bidding for municipal issues (competitive bidding is in virtually all instances required by law), it is customary for bidding syndicates to bid subject to a marketable legal opinion, i.e., an opinion as to the legality of the issue prepared by well-known law firms specializing in municipal law and readily acceptable by investors.

Since municipalities may be sued, bondholders may have effective recourse to the courts if the obligations are valid and binding on the issuer.

Other factors in analysis are:

1. Whether or not there are limits to the taxing power of the municipality, which would render the full faith and credit pledge in effect of a limited nature. Although most states impose tax limits upon municipalities and subdivisions, debt service may be excluded from such limits.
2. The good faith of the issuer (willingness to pay), as shown by its past record.
3. The ability to pay, measured by such tests as ratio of net debt to assessed value, ratio of annual debt service requirements to total annual revenues, net debt per capita, trend of debt, debt retirement, and the more general considerations of economic resources, trends and conditions in the jurisdiction, and ability of the financial administration. Financial data for municipalities, however, are not uniform, reflecting in turn varying practices as to assessment bases, tax limits, inclusion of overlapping debt, and accounting practices.

In an analysis of the financial statements of municipalities, the assessed value of taxable property, which is the basis for the most important source of revenues (the property taxes), is fundamental, as is the assessment basis used by the municipality in taxation. Assessment bases vary widely throughout the United States, so the mere figure for assessed valuation of property is not significant unless the asssessment basis is also given. Sinking funds should be deducted from gross debt to determine net debt. Using net debt as the basis, debt per capita and net debt percentage to assessed value of taxable property are two basic financial indicators of municipal credit. In comparisons of these ratios, municipalities should be classified in groups comparable as to population and total assessed valuation of property (adjusted for variation in assessment bases), as such ratios appearing high for small cities would not be considered high for larger cities. Comparisons of the prevalent tax rate with the legal limit (if any), as modified by exclusion of debt service from tax limits (if any), are also of interest, as well as the *trend* of general revenues and general expenditures and the volume of tax delinquencies. A high tax rate, with rising delinquencies and budget deficits, would indicate credit difficulties.

Municipal securities range widely in quality, from high grade through intermediate quality to low grade. High-grade municipal obligations, like other high-grade bonds, will fluctuate inversely with interest rates. The rate of interest they bear is importantly affected by exemption from federal income tax for all municipal obligations, a feature of particular value to high-income-bracket investors who therefore are willing to take a lower nominal rate of interest on municipal issues. The winning bid in competitive bidding for municipal issues is on a lowest cost of money basis (premium or discount on principal and interest cost for the maturity), which will vary with market conditions and level of interest rates and yields. Other factors influencing rates of interst and maturities are specific types (general obligations, revenue bonds, special assessment bonds, etc.); size, importance, and location of the issuing municipality; and the past record of the municipality and its present financial and credit trends. Maturities may be serials or single maturities with sinking funds. A sign of good financial management by municipalities would be the absence of the bunching of maturities at particular dates, as bunching may pose a financial problem of payment necessitating heavy refunding at such times.

A competitive bidding procedure by municipalities starts with publication of official notices of sale (really a set of specifications) inviting bids from interested bidding groups and usually published in local newspapers as well as the *Daily Bond Buyer*, a daily (with a weekly edition on Saturdays) which is widely subscribed to by firms, underwriters, and dealers specializing in municipal securities. Bids must be submitted on a specified date, at a specified location, sealed and accompanied by a good faith check from all bidders for 1% to 5% of the issue (losing bidders will be returned their checks). Bidders organize into bidding syndicates which, upon being awarded an issue, will in turn reoffer the bonds to investors, offering others a dealer's concession from offering price to help in the sale. Since municipal securities are exempt from registration of the Securities Act of 1933, there is no registration of the securities and no waiting period before a registration statement becomes effective. Neither is a prospectus necessary, but in practice an offering circular is prepared by the offering firms to facilitate sale by describing the issue and its features. (*Note:* all securities, exempt and nonexempt from the registration requirements of the Securities Act of 1933, are subject to the anti-fraud provisions of the act.)

The papers required of the issuing jurisdiction in authorizing a municipal bond issue are (1) a copy of the minutes in which the resolution authorizing the issue states the amount, maturities, purpose, date of issue, interest rate, location where payable, form of the bond, vote of officers (trustees) of the jurisdiction and the citation of law under which the bonds are issued; (2) a copy of the bond form; (3) an attorney's opinion as to the legality of the issue which states that the resolution has been examined, that the general code has been examined, and that in his opinion the bonds are (or are not) a binding obligation; (4) a transcript of the record of proceedings, which includes the title of the issue, the name of the jurisdiction, the names of its regularly constituted officers, the fiscal statistics of the jurisdiction (i.e., the population, debt, tax rate and application of taxes), the resolution to issue bonds, a legal notice of sale, proof of publications, a bond and financial statement, the minutes of the meeting accepting the successful bid, a treasurer's certificate that bonds have been paid for, a signature identification certificate containing signatures of officers who have signed the bonds, and satisfactory evidence that no litigation is threatened or pending against the jurisdiction affecting the validity of the bonds or the right of the officers to hold office.

The marketability of municipal securities varies widely from the inactive, relatively small, locally held issues to the highly marketable, large, well-distributed issues for which many municipal dealers will maintain close, active markets. Although increased interest by individual investors has developed in recent years, the market is still largely institutional in character, when blocks are put up for sale, negotiation may be required and dealers may be needed to locate buyers. Acceptability as collateral for bank loans varies with quality and marketability.

State Finances
Revenues, Expenditures, Debts, Taxes, and U.S. Aid (fiscal year 1986)

	Revenue (thousands)	Expenditures (thousands)	Debt (thousands)	Per cap. debt	Per cap. taxes	Per cap. U.S. aid
Alabama	$ 6,800,976	$ 6,347,706	$ 3,751,658	$ 926	$ 740	$ 434
Alaska	6,115,297	4,220,878	6,961,334	13,085	3,490	1,244
Arizona	6,037,995	5,074,152	1,482,590	449	975	357
Arkansas	3,622,940	3,355,403	1,086,677	458	770	474
California	63,987,002	57,370,220	20,122,437	745	1,144	419
Colorado	5,994,542	4,952,058	1,998,322	612	708	374
Connecticut	6,965,528	6,009,104	7,317,104	2,292	1,202	471
Delaware	1,774,650	1,415,325	2,634,531	4,162	1,343	495
Florida	15,950,334	13,759,262	5,679,591	486	780	278
Georgia	9,390,541	8,530,053	2,450,622	402	806	448
Hawaii	2,994,786	2,471,954	2,828,037	2,655	1,400	446
Idaho	1,743,619	1,516,579	658,164	657	743	434
Illinois	19,437,185	17,822,767	11,987,958	1,038	848	434
Indiana	8,485,339	7,548,547	2,180,275	396	810	363
Iowa	5,314,115	4,852,394	1,600,792	562	863	434
Kansas	3,947,736	3,521,814	352,393	143	777	359
Kentucky	6,779,264	5,950,666	4,109,579	1,103	863	479
Louisiana	8,359,377	8,217,991	10,478,904	2,329	807	463
Maine	2,388,932	2,156,438	1,558,447	1,330	940	573
Maryland	9,139,682	8,131,927	5,410,424	1,213	1,047	439
Massachusetts	13,121,432	12,449,251	11,843,997	2,030	1,314	528
Michigan	20,207,296	17,562,829	7,084,150	775	1,019	476
Minnesota	9,540,193	8,281,248	3,759,541	892	1,163	501
Mississippi	4,433,609	3,835,688	1,183,841	451	731	512
Missouri	7,490,675	6,476,921	3,750,916	741	712	391
Montana	1,753,593	1,642,736	1,240,239	1,518	755	723
Nebraska	2,334,278	2,205,044	1,309,164	819	700	413
Nevada	2,390,950	1,916,667	1,224,223	1,266	1,084	434
New Hampshire	1,547,740	1,348,160	2,383,510	2,321	472	394
New Jersey	17,557,784	16,043,098	16,899,079	2,216	1,096	440
New Mexico	3,925,064	3,300,139	2,137,298	1,445	989	479
New York	50,908,739	43,138,967	36,371,158	2,044	1,278	697
North Carolina	10,801,092	9,369,491	2,605,893	412	881	360
North Dakota	1,564,661	1,537,096	742,822	1,094	907	638
Ohio	23,020,914	19,010,295	8,858,693	824	843	443
Oklahoma	5,905,230	5,629,075	3,829,963	1,158	895	423
Oregon	5,524,208	4,925,280	7,141,919	2,643	715	497
Pennsylvania	22,120,293	19,278,331	7,801,623	656	898	481
Rhode Island	2,361,835	2,167,041	2,949,547	3,025	908	585
South Carolina	6,393,561	5,640,568	3,725,616	1,102	863	391
South Dakota	1,241,496	1,074,034	1,303,054	1,840	570	646
Tennessee	6,812,908	6,080,204	2,156,403	449	682	443
Texas	23,102,789	20,781,744	5,432,198	325	667	313
Utah	3,311,126	3,070,914	1,325,512	796	820	485
Vermont	1,184,865	1,094,716	984,145	1,819	923	617
Virginia	9,963,660	8,872,739	3,842,665	663	836	345
Washington	10,668,300	9,668,571	3,572,162	800	1,169	427
West Virginia	3,821,655	3,651,514	2,131,681	1,112	954	554
Wisconsin	10,885,758	9,124,918	4,659,656	974	1,148	483
Wyoming	2,003,511	1,632,973	825,059	1,627	1,569	929
United States	$ 481,279,035	$ 424,205,290	$ 247,715,163	$ 1,030	$ 948	$ 460

Source: Census Bureau, U.S. Commerce Dept.

MUNICIPAL DEBT

Municipal Bond Funds. The popularization of small investor interest in municipal bonds, however, has proceeded with the organization in recent years of municipal bond funds. At first the most common type was the unit investment trust, holding a fixed portfolio, with the indenture providing that the trust would terminate upon the maturity, redemption, sale, or other disposition of the last of the bonds held in the trust. More recent years have seen the growth of diversified open-end municipal bond investment companies qualifying to pay exempt-interest dividends as permitted by the Tax Reform Act of 1976.

BIBLIOGRAPHY

NATIONAL CITY MANAGEMENT ASSOCIATION. *Municipal Yearbook.*

MUNICIPAL DEBT Debt of state and local governmental units, apart from debt of the federal government. In addition to the federal government and the 50 states, there were over 81,500 local governmental units in the U.S., down from 102,341 such units in 1957, including 18,862 municipalities in 1977 and 17,215 municipalities in 1957.

The appended Table shows the debt of the states as of fiscal 1986 along with comparable data for revenue, expenditures and related per capita statistics.

A particular trend in state debt since the close of World War II has been the substantial rise in nonguaranteed debt (non-full faith and credit), reflecting the substantial expansion in authority, revenue bond financing and other types of non-full faith and credit borrowing. At the close of 1946, nonguaranteed state debt totaled 15.4% of aggregate state gross long-term debt. By 1956, such non-guaranteed debt totaled 50.9% of the aggregate; by 1979, 55.9%.

The debt of political subdivisions of states (counties, districts, municipalities, etc.) has run at a multiple of over two times the aggregate of debt of the states in recent years.

Cities in particular have felt the pressure of increased costs of and demand for services. Although in the aggregate expenditures have ben kept within revenues in recent years, debt has steadily risen.

The financial stringency caused by increased demands for services and facilities, on the one hand, and increased costs, on the other, at both state and local levels has led to a record volume of state and municipal financing in recent years and makes acutely felt any rise in interest rates increasing the cost of such heavier financing.

See MUNICIPALS.

MUNICIPAL OPTION PUT SECURITIES Bonds that can be sold back to the issuer at specific dates. The put option is sold separately from the bond.

MUNICIPALS The market designation for MUNICIPAL BONDS. The market for municipals is over the counter by many firms that specialize in this technical sector of the securities business.

Demand for state and municipal issues in recent years has come largely from the commercial banks, which are attracted to tax-exempts because of their comparatively high taxable equivalent yields, the rise in volume of interest-paying time and savings deposits, and the higher interest rates paid in recent years (subject to ceilings prescribed by the Board of Governors of the Federal Reserve System).

MUNICIPAL WARRANT As defined by the Board of Governors of the Federal Reserve System, warrants "shall be construed to mean bills, notes, revenue bonds, and warrants with a maturity from date of purchase of not exceeding six months, and the term municipality shall be construed to mean State, county, district, political subdivision, or municipality in the continental United States, including irrigation, drainage, and reclamation districts." Under Section 14 (b) of the Federal Reserve Act, any Federal Reserve bank can purchase warrants issued by a municipality in anticipation of the collection of taxes, or in anticipation of the receipt of assured revenues, provided they are general obligations of the entire municipality and other conditions.

A municipal warrant may originate as an order given by a municipal official acting under proper authority upon the treasurer of such municipality to pay a certain person, firm, or corporation a certain sum of money for goods or services advanced. When stamped as follows, "Presented but not paid on account of lack of funds. This warrant bears interest from this date until paid at the rate of percent," and signed by the treasurer, the order becomes a WARRANT. The details of the warrant are then entered, i.e., registered in the treasurer's records. A warrant may be payable to bearer or to order.

When a municipality having warrants outstanding accumulates funds available for their redemption, a call is inserted in a local newspaper announcing that warrants of designated numbers will be paid upon presentation, naming the date when interest will cease. A person who invests in warrants must provide for some method of automatic notification so that when a call is announced, prompt presentation may be made in order to avoid loss of interest.

See FEDERAL RESERVE BOARD REGULATIONS (REGULATION F).

MUNIMENT OF TITLE A muniment is a document by which rights are fortified or maintained. One of the legal characteristics of a BILL OF LADING is that, besides being a receipt for goods and a contract to ship, it is a muniment of title.

MUTILATED CURRENCY Coins that are cut, punched, trimmed, etc., and paper money that is torn or badly worn.

Paper money received by banks for deposit may be so mutilated and worn as to be unfit for circulation. It devolves upon the banks dealing with the public to redeem such money and to pay out, so far as possible, only clean crisp bills.

The Federal Reserve Bank of New York reports on the way responsibility for maintaining the physical quality of circulating U.S. paper currency is shared by the 12 Federal Reserve banks and the U.S. Treasury Department.

Each day, the millions of dollars of deposits made by depository institutions in Federal Reserve banks are scrutinized. Worn or mutilated notes are removed from circulation and destroyed. Since 1966, the Federal Reserve banks have been authorized by the secretary of the Treasury to destroy Federal Reserve notes, which now account for 99.5% of all paper currency in circulation. From the mid-1960s to early 1981, the Federal Reserve banks had found about $123 billion in folding money to be unfit for circulation and had had it canceled and cut. It was burned, shredded, or pulverized, depending upon the Federal Reserve bank's destruction method.

Currency destruction is rigidly controlled. At the new York Federal Reserve Bank, where more than $7 million in paper currency is destroyed daily, the procedure begins in the area where currency is sorted and counted. Workers who count currency as a fulltime job verify the deposits made by depository institutions, separate unfit notes by denomination, and place them into packages of 100. Counterfeit notes that are detected are forwarded to the Secret Service, a part of the U.S. Treasury.

Bundles of 1,000 notes of the same denomination are formed and about 300 bundles are sealed in a rolling trunk, to be moved to the bank's canceling and cutting area, a part of its Cash Department. There, bundles are again broken into packages which are fed into a canceling and cutting machine. The machine simultaneously punches four diamond-shaped holes into the notes and slices the packages in half lengthwise. The shapes and the number of cancelation holes vary at each Federal Reserve bank. A vacuum attachment collects the punched-out diamond-shaped particles into a large plastic bag.

Before destruction begins, a sample of the packages of lower halves is randomly selected for manual verification. When the examination is completed the batch of currency is deemed ready for destruction.

Upon arrival at the incinerator, the number of half-note bundles is once more verified against the number previously canceled and cut. The bundles are stacked on a rising conveyor platform which automatically feeds them into the furnace. The burning process takes about four hours for 2,200 bundles. The temperature inside the furnace reaches 1,800 degress Fahrenheit.

Currency destruction also involves maintenance and cleaning of the furnace and its environmental controls. Ashes are removed daily from the furnace room and sifted into barrels. Remaining bits of currency are extracted and burned with the next day's batch so that destruction can be complete.

The 12 Federal Reserve banks destroy all denominations of paper currency, except gold certificates issued prior to 1934 and old currency issues. Both of these categories of notes are destroyed in conjunction with the U.S. Treasury. After being canceled, the bottom halves, bearing the signature of the Treasurer of the U.S. and the secretary of the Treasury, are forwarded to Washington, D.C. The top halves are held at the Federal Reserve Bank until receipt of the

ENCYCLOPEDIA OF BANKING AND FINANCE

bottom halves is acknowledged by the Treasury. Then the top halves are burned with the day's unfit currency.

In recent years, the Federal Reserve Bank of New York has begun using high-speed equipment to electronically sort, count, and destroy unfit currency. High-speed machines can inspect up to 67,000 notes per hour, a 100% increase from the 30,000 notes per hour processed by medium-speed machines. Before destruction, the currency is moved to the high-speed area in the same way as to other counting rooms. There workers sort 1,000-note bundles into 100-note packages separated by instruction cards which are loaded into the machine. The cards instruct the machine to repackage the notes. Each note is electronically inspected to determine whether it is fit for return to public use. Notes deemed fit are restrapped into 100-note packages.

Notes unfit for circulation because of excessive soiling or mutilation are automatically sent to the machine's shredder and destroyed. High-speed machines destroy about $5 million or about one ton of currency daily. The shredder's blades cut unfit notes lengthwise into $1/16$-inch strips. the strips are sent by vacuum tube to a disposal area and compressed by machine into 400-pound bales. Currently, the bales are discarded. Some Federal Reserve banks, under U.S. Treasury rules, sell destroyed currency to businesses.

Redemption of Damaged Money. Paper that has been mutilated or partially destroyed may in some cases by redeemable at full face value. If clearly more than half of a note remains intact, it may be redeemed at its full face value by Federal reserve banks and their branches. If less than half of its original area still exists, it will not be redeemed unless the Treasurer of the U.S. is satisfied, on the basis of evidence submitted, that the remainder of the note was totally destroyed. (Until January 1, 1971, a mutilated note could be redeemed at full face value only if clearly more than three-fifths of its original area remained intact; portions clearly larger than two-fifths but less than three-fifths of the original were redeemable at half of their face value. Prior to 1889, mutilated paper money was sometimes redeemed at discounts of 10%, 20%, and so on, depending on the size of the fragments presented.) More seriously damaged currency must be sent to the Department of the Treasury for redemption.

Mutilated coins, may be redeemable, with their redemption value depending on their type, denomination, and the extent of the mutilation. Redemption of mutilated coins is handled by the Treasury Department's New York Assay Office. Coins that are merely bent or worn slick through natural wear are not considered mutilated and are exchangeable at full face value.

See LIGHT COIN, LIGHT GOLD, REDEMPTION OF MONEY.

MUTUAL ASSOCIATIONS Savings banks, savings and loan associations, insurance companies, and credit unions that are not organized as stock corporations but are owned by depositors, policyholders, or others. In 1986, there were 370 mutual savings banks, 3,078 savings and loan associations (down from 5,669 in 1970), and 16,910 credit unions. Savings and loan associations and credit unions are either state or federally chartered. Deposit insurance is available from state and federal insurance agencies for these institutions.

Mutual savings banks, savings and loans, and credit unions are permitted to sell federal mutual certificates that can assist these institutions in building their net worth and reserves. Such certificates are subordinated to savings accounts, savings certificates, and debt obligations of the associations. They are counted as part of the general reserve and net worth of the association. In 1982, the Federal Home Loan Bank Board lowered the target net worth/resources ratio from 4% to 3% to respond to the severe capital problems of these institutions. In 1986, the Federal Home Loan Bank Board increased the net worth/liability ratio to 6% to be gradually phased in.

Mutual federal credit unions have two targets of reserves to risk assets (total assets less cash), U.S. government securities, and loans free of credit risk. The targets are determined by age and size:

Mutual Funds—Summary: 1970 to 1987

Type of Fund	Unit	1970	1975	1980	1981	1982	1983	1984	1985	1986	1987
Number of funds, total	Number	361	426	564	665	857	1,026	1,246	1,531	1,843	2,324
Money market funds	Number	X	36	96	159	281	307	329	348	360	389
Equity funds	Number	294	286	267	286	320	374	466	574	700	847
Income and bonds funds	Number	67	104	149	154	169	201	240	323	409	566
Municipal bond funds	Number	X	X	42	46	50	78	114	174	247	368
Short-term municipal bond funds [1]	Number	X	X	10	20	37	66	97	112	127	154
Shareholder accounts, total	Millions	NA	9.9	12.1	17.5	21.4	24.6	28.2	35.0	46.1	54.7
Equity, bond, and income funds	Millions	NA	9.7	7.3	7.2	8.2	12.1	14.4	20.0	29.8	37.0
Money market funds and short-term municipal bond funds [1]	Millions	NA	.2	4.8	10.3	13.2	12.5	13.8	15.0	16.3	17.7
Assets, total	Bil. dol.	47.6	45.8	134.7	241.4	296.6	292.9	370.7	495.5	716.3	769.9
Money market funds	Bil. dol.	X	3.6	74.4	181.9	206.6	162.5	209.7	207.5	228.3	254.7
Equity funds	Bil. dol.	45.1	37.5	44.4	41.2	53.6	77.0	83.1	116.9	161.5	180.6
Income and bond funds	Bil. dol.	2.5	4.7	11.1	11.0	15.8	22.0	33.3	95.4	187.0	196.2
Municipal bond funds	Bil. dol.	X	X	2.9	3.1	7.4	14.6	20.8	39.4	75.7	77.0
Short-term municipal bond funds [1]	Bil. dol.	X	X	1.9	4.2	13.2	16.8	23.8	36.3	63.8	61.4
Sales, total	Bil. dol.	4.6	10.1	247.5	472.2	627.0	547.8	680.1	953.8	1,205.7	1,251.6
Money market funds	Bil. dol.	X	6.8	232.2	451.9	581.8	463.0	572.0	730.1	792.3	869.1
Equity funds	Bil. dol.	4.2	2.6	5.6	6.0	8.3	22.4	20.3	30.1	57.7	72.1
Income and bond funds	Bil. dol.	.4	.7	2.6	2.3	4.0	8.8	15.7	64.8	118.3	89.7
Municipal bond funds	Bil. dol.	X	X	1.8	1.5	3.5	9.1	9.8	19.4	39.9	28.9
Short-term municipal bond funds [1]	Bil. dol.	X	X	5.3	10.5	29.4	44.5	62.3	109.4	197.5	191.8
Redemptions, total	Bil. dol.	3.0	9.6	216.5	362.6	588.4	565.8	607.0	864.9	1,015.6	1,178.8
Money market funds	Bil. bol.	X	5.9	204.5	346.7	559.6	508.7	531.0	732.3	776.3	865.7
Equity funds	Bil. dol.	2.8	3.3	5.7	5.1	5.2	9.3	10.9	18.2	27.2	40.2
Income and bond funds	Bil. dol.	.2	.4	1.5	1.6	1.7	3.1	5.1	11.1	30.7	58.6
Municipal bond funds	Bil. dol.	X	X	1.0	.8	.7	2.3	4.1	4.3	9.1	17.4
Short-term municipal bond funds [1]	Bil. dol.	X	X	3.8	8.3	21.2	42.4	55.9	98.8	172.3	196.9

NA — Not available.
X — Not applicable.
[1] The average maturity of the portfolio is generally less than two years.

Source: Investment Company Institute, Washington, DC, *Mutual Fund Fact Book*, annual.

Less than four years old or below $500,000 assets: 10%
More than four years old or above $500,000 assets: 6%

MUTUAL CAPITAL CERTIFICATE
A long-term debt security issued by a federal mutual institution, subordinated to all other claims on assets; not covered by federal insurance of accounts; may be counted as net worth for regulatory purposes.

MUTUAL FUNDS
INVESTMENT COMPANIES that issue and sell redeemable securities that represent an undivided interest in the assets held by the fund. Mutual fund assets usually include stocks, bonds, government securities, and real estate. Primary advantages to investors are portfolio diversification and professional money management. Mutual funds are typically classified as income funds (money market: taxable or tax free; fixed income; income with growth), growth funds (international; metals; specialty; growth with income; growth; aggressive growth), or a combination of both income and growth.

The Securities Act of 1933 requires the fund's shares to be registered with the Securities and Exchange Commission prior to their sale. The Securities Exchange Act of 1934 regulates the purchase and sale of all types of securities, including mutual fund shares. The Investment Advisers Act of 1940 regulates certain activities of the investment advisers to mutual funds. The Investment Company Act of 1984 is a highly detailed regulatory statute applying to the fund itself. This act contains numerous provisions designed to prevent self-dealing and other conflicts of interest, provide for the safekeeping of fund assets, and prohibit the payment of excessive fees and charges by the fund and its shareholders.

Investment companies can be classified as management companies or unit investment trusts. Management companies actively manage a pool of assets for its shareholders. Management companies can be either open-end or closed-end. An open-end fund continuously offers new shares to investors and guarantees redemption at net asset value per share. A closed-end management company has a fixed number of shares outstanding and does not issue or redeem shares on demand. A unit investment trust issues redeemable securities that represent an undivided interest in a unit of the specified securities. The unit of assets is fixed at the beginning so that there is no management of the portfolio required. Investors usually retain their certificates to maturity. The appended table shows statistics for various types of funds.

The following terms are used frequently in mutual fund discussions:

Adviser The organization employed by a mutual fund to manage the fund's assets and offer advice on its investments.
Aggressive growth fund A fund that seeks to maximize capital appreciation by accepting larger than ordinary risks, such as investing borrowed money to provide leverage, short selling, hedging, and trading options and warrants.
Automatic reinvestment An option available to mutual fund shareholders to leave dividends and capital gain distributions in the fund to purchase additional shares.
Balanced fund A fund that generally has as objectives conserving the investors' initial principal, paying current income, and promoting long-term growth of both principal and income. Balanced funds have a portfolio mix of bonds, preferred stocks, and common stocks.
Bond fund A fund that invests in medium- to high-grade corporate bonds, convertible bonds, and preferred stock. The fund's objective is security of principal with as much income as possible.
Capital gains distributions Payments to mutual fund shareholders of gains realized on the sale of securities held by the fund.
Common stock fund A fund whose portfolio consists primarily of common stocks.
Corporate bond fund A fund that seeks a high level of income by purchasing bonds of corporations for the majority of the fund's portfolio.
Custodian The organization that holds in safekeeping the securities and other assets owned by a fund.
Distributions The payments to shareholders of a fund's interest dividends or capital gain income. Shareholders may take distributions in cash or in additional shares of the fund.
Diversification The procedure of spreading investments among many different securities to reduce risks.

Exchange privilege Enables a fund shareholders to transfer investments from one fund to another (usually within the same mutual fund family). A transaction charge is sometimes made.
Expense ratio The proportion that a mutual fund's annual expenses bear to the fund's average net assets for the year.
Flexible portfolio fund A fund that may be 100% invested in stocks or bonds or money market instruments, depending on market conditions.
GNMA or GINNIE MAE fund A fund that invests in mortgage securities backed by the Government National Mortgage Association.
Global bond fund A fund that invests in the debt securities of companies and countries worldwide.
Global equity fund A fund that invests in securities traded worldwide.
Growth and income fund A fund that seeks both capital growth and current income.
High-yield bond fund A fund that maintains at least two-thirds of its portfolios in lower-rated corporate bonds (Baa or lower by Moody's rating service and BBB or lower by Standard and Poor's rating service).
Income fund A fund whose primary objective is current income. Investments are often in bonds and dividend-paying stocks.
Index fund A fund with an investment objective to match the investment performance of a large group of publicly traded common stocks, such as the Standard & Poor's 500 Composite Stock Price Index.
International fund A fund that invests in equity securities of companies located outside the U.S. Two-thirds of their portfolios must be so invested at all times to be categorized here.
Investment objective The goal that the investor and the mutual fund seek.
Load The sales charges or commissions assessed by a mutual fund.
Management fee The amount paid by a mutual fund to the investment adviser for its services.
Market timing The shifting of assets into or out of a mutual fund to maximize investment returns based on anticipated market changes.
Money market fund A mutual fund that invests in short-term money market securities, such as bankers' acceptances, certificates of deposit, short-term government securities, and others.
Municipal bond fund A fund that invests in tax-exempt bonds issued by states, cities, and other local governments.
Net asset value per share The market worth of one share of a mutual fund. This figure is obtained by taking a fund's total assets, deducting liabilities, and dividing by the number of shares outstanding.
Net investment income Dividends and interest earned by a fund on securities minus the fund's expenses.
Prospectus The official booklet that describes a mutual fund and must be provided to investors. It includes information concerning the fund's investment objectives, policies, services, and fees.
Redemption price The amount per share (shown as the "bid" in newspaper tables) that mutual fund shareholders receive when they cash in shares. The value is the same as net asset value per share.
Reinvestment privilege An option available to mutual fund shareholders in which fund dividends and capital gains distributions are automatically turned back into the fund to purchase new shares and increase holdings.
Specialty fund A fund that specializes in securities of certain industries or regions.
Turnover ratio A ratio of a fund's annual purchase and sale activity of securities in its portfolio.

See INVESTMENT COMPANY.

BIBLIOGRAPHY

CLARK, D. M. "Community Banks Test the Waters of Mutual Funds." *ABA Banking Journal*, December, 1987
DORF, R. C. *The New Mutual Fund Investment Advisor*. Probus Publishing Co., Chicago, IL, 1986.
The Handbook for No-Load Fund Investors. McGraw-Hill Book Co., New York, NY, 1980-. Annual.
INVESTMENT COMPANY INSTITUTE. *An Investment Company Institute Publication*, 1989.
KAMPNER, R. I. "Banks Must Dispel Myths About Mutual Funds. "*Trusts and Estates*, December 1987.

Moody's Bank & Finance Manual, 1955-. Twice weekly.
Mutual Fund Fact Book. Investment Company Institute, New York, NY, 1966. Annual.
RUGG, D. D. *The Dow Jones-Irwin Guide to Mutual Funds*. Dow Jones-Irwin, Inc., Homewood, IL, 1986.
Wiesenberger Investment Companies Services. Warren Gorham and Lamont, Inc., New York, NY, 1941-. Annual.

MUTUAL HOUSING ASSOCIATIONS (MHSs)
Nonprofit organizations that are defined and supported by the community. Originating as a European concept, two main types have evolved in the United States since 1979. One type owns and serves one or more housing projects. MHAs of this type may be developers as well as owners of housing projects. Residents in these projects are charged an initial share fee that gives them rights to lifetime lease agreements as long as they live in the project. Because there is no resale of units, project-owning MHAs keep housing costs under control. They also provide management services and help teach shareholders how to govern their association and maintain their homes. The other type of MHA is purely a service organization, providing professional housing services to independent, limited-equity cooperative housing projects (co-ops) whose housing units are owned by the occupants. MHAs of this type sell management and resident training services and provide operational support to the co-ops at relatively low cost. They also can provide technical assistance to community organizations, developers, co-op projects, and government housing agencies."
Source: Federal Reserve Bank of Richmond.

MUTUAL MORTGAGE INSURANCE See NATIONAL HOUSING ACT.

MUTUAL SAVINGS BANK See SAVINGS BANKS.

MUTUAL SECURITY PROGRAM
Under the European Recovery Program (Marshall Plan) authorized by the Economic Cooperation Act of April 3, 1948 (Title I of the Foreign Assistance Act of 1948), the emphasis was on assistance by the U.S. in post-World War II economic recovery. On December 31, 1951, the Economic Cooperation Administration was terminated and replaced by the Mutual Security Agency, which continued to administer the European Recovery Program until formal termination on June 30, 1952.

With enactment of the Mutual security Act of October 10, 1951, a broader program of military, economic, and technical assistance was authorized for friendly countries "to strengthen the mutual security and individual and collective defenses of the free world [and] to develop their resources in the interests of their security and independence . . . " The Mutual Security Program combined all foreign aid programs under the centralized direction of the director for mutual security. The three principal components of the program were:

1. The Mutual defense Assistance Program (MDAP) administered by the Department of Defense.
2. The defense support and economic and technical assistance program, administered by the Mutual Security Agency, which replaced the Economic Cooperation Administration.
3. The Point 4 Program of technical aid to less developed countries (except in Southeast Asia, which area was administered by the Mutual Security Agency) administered by the Technical Cooperation Administration (TCA), Department of State.

In order to achieve more unified direction and integrated operation of the foreign assistance programs, as well as economy and greater efficiency, the organizational set-up within the executive branch to administer foreign aid was revised in 1953, although the three basic types of aid (military, economic, and technical aid) were continued. On June 1, 1953, an executive order of the President transferred responsibility for certain technical assistance programs formerly vested in the secretary of State to the jurisdiction of the director for mutual security. The director also assumed operating functions with respect to U.S. participation in international programs of technical assistance, relief and rehabilitation, and refugees. Effective August 1, 1953, foreign assistance and related economic operations were regrouped under a single agency, the Foreign Operations Administration (FOA). The office of the director for mutual security and the Mutual Security Agency were abolished and the functions transferred to the FOA.

Effective June 30, 1955, the FOA was abolished and its functions transferred to the Department of State and the Department of Defense; a semiautonomous organization in the Department of State, the INTERNATIONAL COOPERATION ADMINISTRATION, was established as successor to the FOA.

In turn, the International Cooperation Administration was abolished by the Foreign Assistance Act of 1961 (22 U.S.C. 2382), and its functions were redelegated to the AGENCY FOR INTERNATIONAL DEVELOPMENT (AID), An agency within the Department of State, AID was established by State Department Delegation of Authority 104 (November 3, 1961), pursuant to direction and authority contained in executive Order 10973 (November 3, 1961), which was in turn based on statutory authority to the President to exercise his functions under the Foreign Assistance Act of 1961.

The International Development Cooperation Agency. The INTERNATIONAL DEVELOPMENT COOPERATION AGENCY (IDCA) was established by Reorganizations Plan No. 2 of 1979 (44 FR 41165), effective October 1, 1979, to be a focal point within the U.S. government for economic matters affecting U.S. relations with developing countries. The director of the IDCA serves as the principal international development adviser to the President and to the secretary of State, subject to guidance from the secretary of State concerning the foreign policy of the United States.

The IDCA director has a wide range of authorities to assist in furtherance of the agency's mission, as follows:

1. The Agency for International Development (AID) is an organizational component of the IDCA, and its administrator reports to the IDCA director.
2. The Trade and Development Program (TDP) is also an organizational unit within the IDCA, and the TDP director reports to the IDCA director.
3. The Overseas Private Investment Corporation (OPIC) is a component of the IDCA, and the IDCA director serves as chairman of the board of directors of the corporation.

IDCA has lead budget and policy responsibility for U.S. participation in programs of the United Nations (UN) and of the Organization of American States (OAS) whose purposes are primarily developmental. These include the UN development Program (UNDP) and the UN Children's Fund (UNCEF), the World Food Program, and the OAS Technical Assistance Funds.

U.S. participation in the multilateral development banks (MDBs)—the World Bank Group and the regional development banks—is a shared responsibility of the director of IDCA and the secretary of the Treasury in the selection of the U.S. executive directors of the multilateral banks. The IDCA director advises the secretary and the U.S. representatives on development programs and policies and on each development project of the multilateral banks. Such advise is normally determinatitive, except in cases where the secretary of the Treasury finds that compelling financial or other nondevelopmental reasons (legislative requirements) require a different U.S. position. Differences between the director and the secretary may be submitted to the President for resolution.

The direction of the Food for Peace Program (P.L. 480) is a shared responsibility of the IDCA and the Department of Agriculture.

The IDCA also plays an important role in the implementation of the U.S. Economic Support Fund and a number of other development-related activities and programs.

The director of IDCA and senior agency staff chair and participate in a wide range of interagency committees. The director is a member of the National Advisory Committee on International and Monetary Affairs, the Trade Policy Committee, and the Advisory Committee on Agricultural Assistance. The director chairs the Development Coordination Committee, a broad interagency body that coordinates development and development-related policies and programs. As chair of this committee, the IDCA director annually prepares and submits to the Congress a report on development coordination. This report reviews the efforts undertaken to promote international economic development, and it discusses key issues facing policymakers in the development field.

IDCA has responsibility for policy instructions for a number of U.S. programs affecting developing countries. The IDCA director provides policy guidelines for the bilateral assistance programs to use in developing projects and programs. The director also works with other agencies in formulating the position the United States will take in international conferences or negotiations on many issues of concern to developing countries.

Budget Outlays for International Affairs. Budget outlays for International Affairs, Code 150, consist of the following largest categories: Code 151, Foreign Economic and Financial Assistance, and Code 152, International Security Assistance.

Summary. The Comptroller General of the U.S. in a report to the Congress on the subject notes that development of developing countries has become more complex with the shift to an emphasis upon multilateral aid, with the trend toward project assistance in the U.S. aid program, and with the growing importance of nonaid resource transfers. These and other changes had led to a dispersion of authority and responsibility for development activities.

Thus the creation of the IDCA in October, 1979, was considered to provide a new opportunity to improve development coordination.

N

NAKED OPTIONS In writing (offering) OPTIONS, writers of the call, put, or straddle type of options may write them "naked," without either owning or being short the underlying stock that is the subject of the option.

NAKED RESERVE Federal Reserve banks since 1968 have been free of any reserve requirements of their own against their Federal Reserve notes issued and their deposits. P.L. 90-269 (March 18, 1968) eliminated the provision of Section 16 of the Federal Reserve Act under which the Federal Reserve banks were required to maintain reserves in gold certificates (Series of 1934) of not less than 25% against Federal Reserve notes. Previously, P.L. 89-3 (March 3, 1965) had eliminated the requirement also formerly contained in Section 16 of the Federal Reserve Act for the maintenance of reserves in gold certificates (Series of 1934) of not less than 25% against Federal Reserve bank deposit liabilities. The preceding legal reserve ratios have been reduced from reserve in gold certificates, Series of 1934, equal to at least 40% of Federal Reserve notes issued, and reserve in gold certificates, series of 1934, or lawful money equal to at least 35% of deposits, by act of June 12,1945 (59 Stat. 237). Such reserves in gold certificates, Series of 1934, could also count as part of the "cover" (asset collateral) in gold certificates, Series of 1934, required to be posted with the Federal Reserve agent at each Federal Reserve bank as part of the 100% asset cover against Federal Reserve notes issued.

The "naked" or adjusted reserve of each Federal Reserve bank was a derived figure, calculated to indicate the true reserve position of each Federal Reserve bank. It was ascertained by adding to the bank's actual reserves the amount of its lendings (through rediscounts) to other Federal Reserve banks subtracting from them the amount of its own such borrowings. In this way the adjusted or naked reserve was correspondingly increased or decreased in absorbing the net effect of the changes in inter-Federal Reserve bank rediscounts. Under the Federal Reserve Act (Sec. 11b), the Board of Governors of the Federal Reserve System upon affirmative vote of at least five members may still require Federal Reserve banks to rediscount the discounted paper of other Federal Reserve banks at rates of discount to be fixed by the board of governors. Thus a Federal Reserve bank in a strong reserve position could be required to rediscount the paper of another Federal Reserve bank in a weak reserve position. The provisions used to be important because under Section 11c of the Federal Reserve Act (still in effect) the Board of Governors of the Federal Reserve System could suspend any reserve requirements specified in the act, but was to establish a graduated tax upon the amounts by which the reserve requirements fell below the minimum levels, which tax was to be paid by the Federal Reserve bank concerned. But even more important, the concerned Federal Reserve bank was to add the penalty tax to the rediscount rates of the bank, a rigid provision which could have been in conflict with the discount policy of the system. On March 3, 1933, the board of governors suspended reserve requirements of Federal Reserve banks for 30 days, and established the tax on the deficiency in reserves. By the end of March, 1933, however, the average daily RESERVE RATIO of the Federal Reserve banks had improved substantially, and thereafter rapid improvement occured.

NAME DAY See SETTLEMENT DAYS.

NARROW MARKET In the stock market, a market in which the volume of business is light, trading is inactive, and no sales are made at all in many issues. Because of the scarcity of, and spread between, bids and offers, relatively large changes in prices occur on a small volume of transactions.

Applied to a particular security, narrow market means that bids are infrequent and originate from but few sources. Thus, unlisted stocks of small companies not widely known, and even stocks listed on one of the large exchanges, may have a narrow market. For that reason they usually sell at lower prices than active stocks of equal earnings and property values. Active stocks command higher market quotations because they can be more readily disposed of without concessions in price.

NATIONAL ADVISORY COUNCIL ON THE INTERNATIONAL MONETARY AND FINANCIAL POLICIES Originally established as a statutory body (by the Bretton Wood Agreements Act of July 31, 1945), this council now operates under Executive Order 11269 of February 14, 1966, as amended by Executive Order 11334 of March 7, 1967, to coordinate the policies and operations of the representatives of the U.S. on the following institutions.

International Monetary Fund
International Bank for Reconstruction and Development
International Development Association
International Finance Corporation
Inter-American Development Bank
Asian Development Bank
Export-Import Bank of the United States
All other agencies of the U.S. government "to the extent that they make or participate in the making of foreign loans or engage in foreign financial exchange or monetary transactions."

The council also advises the secretary of the Treasury with regard to the performance by the secretary of his functions of instructing the U.S. representatives to the international financial organizations and giving the consent of the U.S. to certain actions of the international financial organizations.

NATIONAL AGRICULTURAL CREDIT CORPORATIONS Banking corporations authorized by the Agricultural Credits Act of March 4, 1923, intended to serve as privately capitalized corporations in the short-term livestock credit field, analogous to the joint-stock land banks in the farm mortgage field.

These corporations could be organized and controlled by private capital under the general supervision of the Comptroller of the Currency, with a minimum capital stock of $250,000. No national agricultural credit corporation could commence business until it had deposited with the district Federal Reserve banks U.S. government securities in an aggregate face amount of at least 25% of its paid-in capital stock. Any member bank of the Federal Reserve System could upon permission of the Comptroller of the Currency invest a limit of 10% of capital stock and surplus in the stock of one or more of these corporations. The corporations were empowered to make loans for agricultural purposes on chattels, livestock, growing crops, and personal credit up to a period of nine months, except that in the case of breeding stock and daily herds, the period could be extended to three years. Against the paper thus financed, debentures could be issued up to an amount prescribed by the Comptroller of the Currency. Also, such corporations could rediscount with the Federal Intermediate Credit banks. Section 14 (f) of the Federal Reserve Act was added by the Agricultural Credit Act of 1923 to provide,"whenever the Board of Governors of the Federal Reserve System shall declare that the public interest so requires," for open market purchase and sale of acceptances of such corporations.

"Very little use was made of the provision for establishing national agricultural credit corporations. Three were established, two for the purpose only of handling commodity loans for a temporary period, after which they liquidated voluntarily. The third was established in Oregon and proved fairly successful. However, it never issued debentures as had been planned in the Act but sold loans to its sponsor or discounted them with the Federal Intermediate Credit Bank of Spokane" (C.R. Arnold, FARMERS BUILD THEIR OWN PRODUCTIONS CREDIT SYSTEM, Farm Credit Administration, August, 1958). Section 77 of the Farm Credit Act of 1933 provided that after the date of enactment (June 16, 1933) no national agricultural credit corporation could be formed.

See FEDERAL INTERMEDIATE CREDIT BANKS, PRODUCTION CREDIT ASSOCIATION.

NATIONAL ASSOCIATION OF BANK WOMEN

A national organization founded in New York in 1921 as an association of women financial executives. By 1985, its membership had grown to more than 30,000 members. The goal of the NABW is to advance women's careers by providing them with management and educational programs. While originally focused solely on banking, its membership today covers all financial services industries.

NATIONAL ASSOCIATION OF CREDIT MANAGEMENT

A member-owned and -controlled organization of some 80 affiliated local association in the U.S., Europe; formerly known as the National Association of Credit Men. The National Association of Credit Management (NACM) was founded in 1896 to promote legislation for sound credit, protect business against fraudulent debtors, improve the interchange of credit information, develop better credit practices and methods, and establish a code of ethnics. Membership in an NACM-affiliated credit association includes membership in the national organization. Members of the NACM, who as of 1987 numbered about 41,000, are credit and financial executives, primarily representing manufacturers, wholesalers, financial institutions, and varied service organizations.

Credit interchange is one of the oldest NACM services to members. It is a nationwide system for assembling and distributing to participating member actual ledger experience of creditors. Today thousands of members participate in this activity through credit interchange bureaus operated by NACM-affiliated associations. Supplementing and extending the services of credit interchange are hundreds of special industry credit groups under the management of local affilatated associations. Other services include the collection service, operated locally with worldwide coverage provided; the adjustment service, in which NACM-approved bureaus engage in the rehabilitation or liquidation of distressed businesses, with greater return to creditors than from the average bankruptcy liquidation; and active legislative programs in behalf of members at both federal and state levels.

Educational services include the Graduate School of Credit and Financial Management, conducted for advanced credit and financial executives at Dartmouth, Baylor and Santa Clara, CA (course runs two weeks a year for three years), and the National Institute of Credit, which offers courses in cooperation with U.S. colleges and universities and also offers correspondence courses. NACM publications include the following:

1. *Business credit, formerly credit and financial management*, the only national publication covering the field of business credit and finance.
2. *Credit manual of commercial laws*, a comprehensive digest of laws affecting credit and finance, revised yearly since 1908.
3. *Digest of commercial laws of the world*, with seven volumes of concise summaries of commercial laws of 73 countries and two volumes covering patent and trademark laws and two volumes of state Violations of Commercial Law.
4. *Credit and collection letters*, a compilation of successful credit and collection letter.

In addition, a complete service in standard forms is available to members, including trade acceptances, credit applications, account review, and types of financial statements forms.

NATIONAL ASSOCIATION OF SECURITIES DEALERS, INC.

A countrywide membership association of securities brokers and dealers organized upon passage of the Maloney Act, an amendment to the Securities Exchange Act in June, 1938, and registered with the Securities and Exchange Comission for the purposes of the act. The following descriptive data are furnished by the association.

The National Association of Securities Dealers, Inc. is the out growth of the Code of Fair Competition for Investment Bankers, drawn up by representatives of the securities business under provisions of the National Industrial Recovery Act (NRA). When this legislation was declared unconstitutional by the Supreme Court of the United States in 1935, the securities industry undertook to preserve and make operative, on a voluntary basis, the provisions of the code looking toward perfection of a code of ethics and its enforcement. This was accomplished with the cooperation of the SECURITIES AND EXCHANGE COMMISSION, which for three years supported efforts of the business to obtain the necessary legislation giving the code idea legal substance.

In June, 1938, Congress adopted the legislation, popularly known as the "Maloney Act" after its sponsor, the late senator from Connecticut. The Maloney Act was introduced as an amendment (Sec. 15A) to the Securities Exchange Act. Specifically, it permits the organization of brokers and dealers into membership associations that register with the Securities and Exchange Commission for the purposes of the act. Upon passage of the Maloney Act, the National Association of Securities Dealers, Inc. was formed. It is the only association operating under the act.

The NASD regulates the entire OTC market by regulating its more than 6,700 member firms and their 460,000 professional employees at the end of 1988 under the oversight of the SECURITIES AND EXCHANGE COMMISSION. The NASD also owns and operates the NASDAQ System, the automated communications facility for the NASDAQ market. While it operates by statutory authority, the NASD is financed entirely by the securities industry and NASDAQ issuers.

The NASD is controlled by its 31-member Board of Governors, two thirds of whom are chosen from the securities industry and one-third of whom are selected from fields associated with the industry. Except for the president who is a member of the board, the governors serve without compensation. The NASD has many committees including arbitration, international institutional investors, investment companies (or mutual funds), municipal securities, options, qualifications, real estate, trading, and variable contracts.

The NASD fulfills its regulatory responsibilities through an integrated program that includes: (1) nationwide field inspections of member firms, (2) centralized, computerized surveillance of the trading of nearly 6,000 securities in the NASDAQ (NASD Automated Quotations) market, (3) enforcement of rules governing special product areas, such as municipal securities and government securities, (4) review of underwriting arrangements for the public distribution of securities, (5) qualifications testing of personnel, and (6) cooperative action with the exchanges, the states and the SECURITIES AND EXCHANGE COMMISSION. Firms for which the NASD is the examining authority are subject to at least one on-site inspection per year. Special examinations are conducted for cause, as information and circumstances warrant.

For inclusion in NASDAQ a company must have: SEC registration; total assets of at least $2 million; capital and surplus of at least $1 million; public float of 100,000 shares; 300 shareholders of record; and at least 2 market makers. If an operating company wishes to have its stock included in the NASDAQ National Market System, it must also have net income of $300,000 in the latest fiscal year or two of the last three years; a float of 350,000 shares; a minimum market value of float of $2 million; and a minimum bid of $3.

The appended table shows NASDAQ securities listed and volume of trading 1985 to 1987.

NATIONAL ASSOCIATION OF SECURITIES DEALERS AUTOMATED QUOTATIONS SYSTEM

A computerized communications facility for the NASDAQ market. The central computer complex for the NASDAQ system, located in Trumbull, Connecticut, utilizes a Sperry 1100/90 system and 16 Tandem TXP processors. Three regional concentrators connect 3,000 terminals, leased to securities firms and financial institutions, to the central processors over approximately 80,000 miles of leased telephone lines. Through this network and computer complex, the NASDAQ system processes over 1.7 million transactions each day,

NASDAQ— Securities Listed and Volume of Trading: 1975 to 1987

Item	Unit	1975	1979	1980	1981	1983	1984	1985	1986	1987
Companies listed	Number	2,467	2,643	2,894	3,353	3,901	4,097	4,416	4,417	4,706
Issues	Number	2,579	2,670	3,050	3,687	4,467	4,723	1,784	5,189	5,537
Shares traded	Million	1,390	3,541	6,692	7,823	15,909	15,159	20,699	28,737	37,890
Average daily volume	Million	5.5	14.4	26.5	30.9	62.8	59.9	82.1	113.6	149.8
Value of shares traded	Bil. dol.	21.2	44.3	68.7	71.1	188.3	153.5	233.5	3782	499.9

Source: National Association of Securities Dealers, Washington, DC, *Fact Book*, Annual.

with an average response time of two seconds. Central processor availability has been a consistent 99.9 percent or higher.

The NASDAQ ystem provides three basic services: the NASDAQ Quotation System, the Small Order Execution System, and the Trade Acceptance and Reconciliation Service.

NASDAQ Quotation System collects, validates, and distributes quotation information to subscribers. The system provides subscribers with quotation display through both its own terminals and the terminals of market data vendor organizations. Level 1 service is distributed through more than 180,000 terminals leased by subscribers from market data vendors, such as Quotron, Reuters, Telekurs, ADP/Bunker Ramo and others. This service distributes the best bid and asked prices in all securities to salespeople and dealers. The system also broadcasts last-sale price and volume information on the more than 3,000 issues of the NASDAQ National Market System to market data vendors. Level 2 service is provided through NASDAQ-owned terminals. On inquiry, this service supplies to both member and nonmember subscribers: a composite display with individual current quotes submitted by the market makers in each issue; the inside market quotation, which is the best bid and ask prices; and indexes, volume, and market summary information. Level 3 service allows registered, authorized market makers to maintain their quotations and report trades and daily volume to the system, in addition to receiving Level 2 information.

A Tandem-based system, the Small Order Execution System (SOES), enables orders in all securities to be executed automatically by computer, without the customary telephone call from one trader to another. The size limit for a single trade is 1,000 shares for the 3,000 NASDAQ National Market System issues and 500 shares for nearly 3,000 other NASDAQ issues.

Another Tandem-based system, Trade Acceptance and Reconciliation Services, helps the back offices of member firms resolve their uncompared and advisory OTC trades processed through participating clearing organizations.

NASDAQ is linked to London's International Stock Exchange, the first intercontinental market-to-market linkage.

NATIONAL BANK   A bank incorporated under a charter granted by the federal government upon the authority of the NATIONAL BANK ACT. Under a 1927 amendment of the act, national bank charters now have an indeterminate duration, as against a former duration fixed at 99 years and an earlier duration of 20 years.

See NATIONAL BANKING SYSTYEM.

NATIONAL BANK ACT   The act which created the NATIONAL BANKING SYSTEM, passed in February 25, 1863, and amended importantly in June 3, 1864. As amended many times since, the National Bank Act continues to serve as the basic banking law for national banks. Most of the U.S. Revised Statutes which contain the national banking laws are contained in Title 12 if the U.S. Code; the criminal provisions appear in Title 18 of the U.S. Code; and a scattering of other provisions appear in other titles of the U.S. Code.

One of the important original motivations for enactment of the National Bank Act was to provide for a uniform national bank note circulation. Neither the original act nor the subsequently amended act provided for prohibition of issuance of circulating noted by state banks. In February, 1865, however, the federal government imposed a tax of 10% on the issuance or payment of state bank notes, effective August 1, 1866, a tax which continues in the present-day Internal Revenue Code (Subchapter E, Secs. 4881-4886). The severity of this tax drove state bank notes out of existence, but the tax's constitutionality was upheld in VEAZIE BANK *v.* FENNO, 8 Wall. 533, 19 L. Ed. 482.

With enactment of the Federal Reserve Act, December 23, 1913, inaugurating the issuance of Federal Reserve notes, now the bulk of currency circulation, the importance of national bank notes declined, and since 1935 the latter have been in the process of retirement.

In organizational and operational aspects, however, the National Bank Act as amended continues to govern national banks. Reference should also be made to the FEDERAL RESERVE ACT and the FEDERAL DEPOSIT INSURANCE ACT for other provisions affecting national banks in their status as member banks of the Federal Reserve System and as insured banks.

NATIONAL BANK CALL   Four times each year each national bank must submit to the Comptroller of the Currency a report of the condition of the commercial department (since national bank charters are of the commercial type, the trust department, if any, is subject to separate examinations and reports). The Comptroller may also call for additional reports of condition from all national banks and special reports of condition from any national bank whenever he determines that such reports are necessary for the performance of his supervisory duties. Report of condition shall be submitted to the Comptroller on such dates and in such forms and shall contain sucn information as may be determined by the Comptroller. National banks are furnished with "report of condition" forms and instructions for their preparation, filing, and publication to the extent required by law.

When required by the Comptroller of the Currency, each national bank that has one or more affliates must submit with its report of condition a report of condition of each such affiliate. The Comptroller furnishes "affiliate report" forms and instructions for their preparations, filing, and publication to the extent required by law. However, reports of affiliates are no longer required unless specifically requested by the Comptroller (Comptroller of the Currency, Interpretive Rulings, Par. 7.7540)

Each national bank must also submit annually to the Comptroller of the Currency a report of its income and dividends for the 12-month period ending December 31. The Comptroller furnishes "report of income and dividends" forms and instructions for their preparations and filing.

Each national bank that exercises fiduciary powers must submit annually to the Comptroller of the Currency a report of the condition of its trust department. The Comptroller furnishes "Trust Department annual report" forms and instructions for their preparations and filing. If a national bank administers collective investment funds, it shall keep its fiduciary records seperate and distinct from other records of the bank. All fiduciary records shall be so kept and retained for such time as to enable the bank to furnish such information or reports with respect thereto as may required by the Comptroller of the Currency (Comptroller of the Currency, Regulation (12 CFR 9.8).

The Internation Operations Regulations (12 CFR 20) requires that a national bank notify the Comptroller of the Currency (1) upon application to the Board of Governors of the Federal Reserve System to establish the initial branch of a national bank in any foreign country; and 30 days prior to the establishment of any additional branches in a foreign country, dependency, or insular possession of the United States or foreign country; (2) upon application to the Board of Governors of the Federal Reserve System to directly or indirectly acquire a controlling interest in an EDGE ACT corporation, agreement corporation, or foreign bank; and (3) at least 30 days prior to the direct or indirect acquisition of less than a controlling interest in any Edge Act corporation, agreement

ENCYCLOPEDIA OF BANKING AND FINANCE

NATIONAL BANK CIRCULATION

corporation, or foreign bank, if the cost of such acquisiton exceeds $1 million.

The Comptroller of the Currency is the banking authority for each bank or trust company located and doing business in the District of Columbia that is not a national bank and that is not a member of the Federal Reserve System. Such institutions must maintain a reserve on the same basis and subject to the same conditions as prescribed for national banks located in the District of Columbia. Such reserve must be established and maintain with a national bank or a state member bank that is approved for such purposed by the Comptroller of the Currency. Each such District of Columbia bank or trust company must submit to the Comptroller each week a report of net deposits and reserves required. The depository national bank or state member bank must submit to the Comptroller each week a report of reserve held.

Call report dates. Since national banks must be insured by the FEDER DEPOSIT INSURANCE CORPORATION, the FDIC shall have access to reports of examininations by, and reports of conditons made to, the Comptroller of the Currency or any Federal Reserve bank, and to all revisions of reports of conditons made to either of them; and they shall promptly advise the FDIC of any revisions or changes in respect to deposit liabilities made or required to be made in any report of conditon. Four reports or condition annually shall be made by each insured state nonmember bank (except a district bank) to the FDIC, each insured national bank and each insured district bank to the Comptroller of the Currency, and each insured state member bank to the Federal Reserve bank of which it is a member, upon dates that shall be selected by the chairman of the board of directors of the FDIC, the Comptroller of the Currency, and the chairman of the Board of Governors of the Federal Reserve System, or a majority thereof.

The date selected shall be the same for all insured banks, except that when any said reporting date is a nonbusiness day for any bank, the preceding business day shall be its reporting date. Two dates shall be selected within the semiannual period of January to June, inclusive, and the reports for such dates shall be the basis for the certified statements to be filled with the FDIC in July pertaining to insured deposits; and two dates shall be selected within the semiannual period of July to December, inclusive , and the reports on such dates shall be the basis for the certified statements on insured deposits to be filed with the FDIC in January.

Verification of reports. Each report of condition shall contain a declaration, by the president, a vice-president, the cashier or the treasurer, or any other officer designated by the board of directors or trustees of the reporting bank to make such declaration, that the report is true and correct to the best of his or her knowledge and belief. The correctness of the report of condition shall be attested by the signatures of at least three of the directors or trustees, with the declaration that the report has been examined by them and to the best of their knowledge and belief is true and correct. At the time of making such reports of condition, each insured national, district, and state member bank shall furnish to the FDIC a copy thereof containing such signed declaration and attestations.

Publication of call reports. Each national bank call report shall be transmitted to the Comptroller of the Currency within ten days after the receipt of request thereof from him. The statement of resources and liabilities in the same form in which it is made to the Comptroller shall be published in a newspaper published in the place where such national bank is established, or if there is no newspaper in the place, then in the one published nearest thereto in the same county, at the expense of the national bank, and such proof of publication shall be furnished as may be required by the Comptroller. Any reports of affliates prescribed by the Comptroller shall be similarly published by the national bank under the same conditions as govern its own condition reports.

Penalty for failure to make reports. Every national bank that fails to make and transmit any report required under all of the covering statue (12 U.S.C. 161) shall be subject t a penalty of $100 for each day after the periods therein mentioned that it delays to make and transmit its report.

Uses of the call report. The statement of condition prescribed in the call report, sometimes called the "legal" statement of condition, is limited to the figures called for in the instructions for preparation, and as of the call date prescribes. Consolidated figures of the banks having important international operations would be more comprehensive (availiable in the voluntary published statements, as of conventional end-of-quarter-dates which may differ from the call dates). For banks owned by bank holding companies statements, the consolidated holding company statements, reflecting both banking and related operations, are most approriate for the bank stock investor since the public would have availiable for investment the senior holding company's securities. The senior holding company's annual and interim reports to stockholder are useful for their commentary on operations as well as figures thereon, in both the statement of conditons and the income statement.

See BANK STATEMENT, CALL REPORT.

NATIONAL BANK CIRCULATION   *See* NATION BANKNOTES.

NATIONAL BANK DEPOSITORY   *See* DEPOSITORY.

NATIONAL BANK EXAMINER   Under Section 5240, Revised Statutes (Sec. 21, Pars. 2-3, Federal Reserve Act), the Comptroller of the Currency, with the approval of the secretary of the Treasury, shall appoint examiners who shall examine every national bank twice in each calendar year, but the Comptroller, in the exercise of his decretion, may waive one such examination shall not be exercised more frequently than once during any two-year period.

The examiner making the examination of any national bank shall have power to make a thorough examination of all the affairs of the bank and in so doing shall have power to administer oaths and to examine any of the officers and agents of the bank under oath, making a full and detailed report of the conditions of the bank to the Comptroller of the Currency. It is further provided that in making the examination of any national bank, the examiners shall include such an examination of the affairs of all its affiliates other than member banks as shall be necessary to disclose fully the relations between such bank and such affiliates, and the effect of such relations upon the affairs of such bank.

In the event of the refusal to give any information required in the course of the examination of any such affilate, or in the event of the refusal to permit such examinations, the penalty is severe: all the rights, priviledges, and franchises of the bank shall be subject to forfeiture on accordance with Section 2, Federal Reserve Act, as amended (12 U.S.C. 501a).

Normally, reports of examination are kept confidential, but Section 5240, Revised Statues, give the Comptroller of the Currency the power to publish the report of his examination of any nation bank or affiliate which shall not within 120 days after notification of the recommendations or suggestions of the Comtroller, based on said examination, have complied with the same to his satisfaction. Ninety days's notice prior to such publicity shall be given to the bank or affliate.

Similarly, the examiner making the examination of any affiliate of a national bank shall have power to make thorough examination of all the affairs of the affiliate and in doing so shall have power to administer oaths and to examine any of the officers, directors, employees, and agents thereof under oath, making a report of his findings to the Comptroller of the Currency.

The expense of examinations of such affliliates may be assessed by the Comptroller if the Currency upon the affiliates examined in proportion to assets or resources held by the affiliates upon the dates of examination of the various affiliates. If any such affiliate shall refuse to pay such expenses or shall fail to do so within 60 days after the date of such assessment, then such expenses may be assessed against the affiliated national bank and, when so assessed, shall be paid by such national bank. However, if the affiliation is, with two or more national banks, such expenses may be assessed against and collected from any or all of such national banks, in such proportions as the Comptroller of the Currency may prescribe.

To carry out this heavy examining load, the Comptroller of the Currency has built up an organization of examiners, organized under 14 regional administrators of national banks. The examiners and assistant examiners making the examinations of nation banks and their affiliated, and the chief examiners, reviewing examiners, and other persons whose services may be required in connection with such examinations or the reports thereof, are employed by the Comptroller of the Currency with the approval of the secretary of the Treasury. The employment and compensation of examiners, chief examiners, reviewing examiners, assistant examiners, and other employees of the office of the Comptroller of the Currency whose compensation is and shall be paid from the assessments on banks or affliates shall be made without regard to the provisions of other

ENCYCLOPEDIA OF BANKING AND FINANCE

laws applicable to officers or employees of the United States. The funds derived from such assessments may be deposited by the Comptroller of the Currency in accordance with Section 5234, Revised Statutes (12 U.S.C. 192), and shall not be construed to be government funds or appropriated monies. The Comptroller of the Currency is authorized by Section 5240, Revised Statutes, and empowered to prescribe regulations governing the computation and assessment of the expenses of examinations and the collecting of such assessments from the banks and/or affiliated examined.

If any affiliate of a national bank shall refuse to permit the examiner to make an examination of the affiliate, or shall refuse to give any information required in the course of any such examination, the national bank with which it is affiliated shall be subject to a penalty of not more than $100 for each day that any such refusal shall continue. Such penalty may be assessed by the Comptroller of the Currency and collected in the same manner as expenses of examinations.

See BANK EXAMINATION, BANK EXAMINERS.

NATIONAL BANK INDEBTEDNESS No national bank, according to Section 5302 of the Revised Statutes (12 U.S.C. 82), as amended, shall at any time be indebted, or in any way be liable, to an amount exceeding the amount of its capital stock at such time actually paid in and remaining undimished by losses or otherwise plus 50% of the amount of its unimpaired surplus fund, except on account of the following types of liabilities:

1. Notes of circulation. (Liability for all national bank notes has been transferred to the Treasury, and national bank notes have been in process of retirement since 1935.)
2. Monies deposited with or collected by the national bank.
3. Bills of exchange or drafts drawn against money actually on deposit to the credit of the national bank for dividends and reserve profits.
4. Liabilities to the stockholders of the national bank, or due there to.
5. Liabilities incurred under the provisions of the Federal Reserve Act.
6. Liabilities incurred under the provisions of the Federal Deposit Insurance Act.
7. Liabilities created by the endorsement of accepted bills of exchange payable abroad actually owned by the endorsing bank and discounted at home and abroad.
8. Liabilities incurred under the provisions of Section 202 of Title II of the Federal Farm Loan Act, approved July 17, 1916, as amended by the Agricultural Credits Act of 1923.
9. Liabilities incurred on account loans made with the express approval of the Comptroller of the Currency under Paragraph (9) of Setion 5200 of the Revised Statues as amended (12 U.S.C. 84(9)).
10. Liabilities incurred under the provisions of Section 352a of Title 12 U.S.C. (this was Sec. 13b of the Federal Reserve Act, repealed effective August 21, 1959, by the Small Business Investment Act of August 21, 1958).
11. Liabilities incurred in connection with sales of mortgages, or participations therein, to the Federal National Motgage Association or the Federal Home Loan Mortgage Corporation.

The principal amount of capital debentures outstanding at any time, when added to all other outstanding indebtedness of the national bank, except those forms of indebtedness exempt from the provisions of 12 U.S.C. 82, shall not exceeed an amount equal to 100% of the bank's unimpaired paid-in capital stock plus 50% of the amount of its unimpaired surplus fund (Comptroller's Regulations, 12 CFR 14.5)

See NATIONAL BANK LOANS, NATIONAL BANK SECURITIES REGULATIONS.

NATIONAL BANKING ASSOCIATION Another name for national bank. This designation is employed throughout the Revised Statutes incorporating the National Bank Act, and codified in the U.S. Code.

NATIONAL BANKING SYSTEM A system of federally chartered, privately owned banks, established under the authority of the NATIONAL BANK ACT, originally motivated among other aims by the desire to provide for a uniform national currency (national bank notes) backed by U.S. government bonds. The plan for the system, outlined in 1861 by Salmon P. Chase, then secretary of the Treasury, became law February 25, 1863; was superseded by Act of June 3, 1863 (the National Currency Act); and was importantly amended and redesignated as the National Bank Act in 1874. There have been many amendments since, including amendments by the Federal Reserve Act and amendments thereto.

For details of requirements and/or authorized of issuance of national bank notes, see NATIONAL BANK NOTES. National banks no longer have any national banks notes outstanding for which they are liable, such liability having been transferred in 1935 to the U.S. Treasury as the U.S. bonds bearing the circulation priviledge were called and became unavailable, and national banks deposited lawful money with the Treasury to retire circulating notes still outstanding. The power to issue and circulate national banks notes still is found in the Revised Statutes which contain provisions of the National Bank Act (Par. 7, Sec. 5136 of the Revised Statutes: "to exercise by its board of directors or duly authorized officers and agents, subject to law, all such incidental power as shall be necessary to carry on the business of banking; . . . by obtaining, issuing, and circulating notes according to the provisions of this title."); and also still extant are the statutes providing the detail in connection with issuance and redemption of national bank notes (for a full list, see the appendix to NATIONAL BANKING LAWS AND RELATED STATUTES, Office of the Comptroller of the Currency, December 31, 1959).

Organization. No national bank may be organized with a capital of less than $100,000 except that national banks with a capital of not less than $50,000 may be organized in any place where the population does not exceed 6,000. No national bank may be organized in a city with population of over 50,000 with a capital of less than $200,000, except that in the outlying districts of such a city where the state laws permit the organization of state banks with a capital of $100,000 or less, national banks may, with the approval of the Comptroller of the Currency, have a capital of not less than $100,000. In addition, no national bank may commence business until it shall have paid-in surplus equal to 20% of it capital. The Comptroller may waive this requirement as to a state bank converting into a national bank, but each such state bank converting into a national bank shall, before the declaration of a dividend on its common stock, carry not less than 50% of its net profits of the preceding half year to its surplus fund until it shall have a surplus equal to 20% of its capital. Moreover, until the surplus fund of a national bank shall equal its common capital, no dividends shall be declared unless there has been carried to the surplus fund not less than one-tenth of the national bank's net profits of the preceding half year (in the case of quarterly or semiannual dividends), or not less than one tenth of the net profits of the preceding two consecutive half-year periods (in the case of annual dividends).

Parenthetically, it should be noted that the Comptroller of the Currency considers adequacy of capital funds for a proposed national bank relative to its particular planned scope of operations, volume of deposits, and competitive environment, so that the population-based figures in the statute are really minima. In line with this adequacy principle for beginning capital funds, the Comptroller in recent years has also favored an "adequate" paid-in sum for starting undivided profits.

All national banks are required to be members of the Federal Reserve bank of their district and to invest in the capital stock of such bank in the amount required by the Federal Reserve Act, which is 6% of the national bank's capital and surplus, of which 3% is actually called for payment. National banks are also required to be insured by the Federal Deposit Insurance Corporation.

National banks are charted and supervised by the Comptroller of the Currency. Application for a charter, which will be indeterminate in duration pursuant to the 1927 amendment, must be filed with the Comptroller of the Currency, and contain the following information: names and addresses of the prospective organizers (shareholders), at least five in number; number of shares subscribed by each; their residence, businesses, and financial strength (the latter at least twice their stock subscriptions); the proposed title for the bank, and its capital and surplus; the banking experience of the organizers, and data on the population of the community to be served, existing banking facilities, etc.; statement that no fees or commissions for securing subscriptions or selling stock are involved.

Through a national bank examiner in the region where the proposed bank is to be located, the Comptroller of the Currency conducts an investigation of the proposed bank, especially as to the character and experience of the organizers, existing banking facilities,

NATIONAL BANKING SYSTEM

and the reasonable prospects for success of the proposed bank. Upon approval, the office of the Comptroller forwards the necessary documents for execution, such as the articles of association, the organization certificate, standard bylaws, certificate of payment of capital stock and compliance with legal requirements or certificate of payment of capital stock installments, and oaths of directors. Authority to commence business is granted by the Comptroller's issuance of the certificate of authority to commence business, although affidavit of publication of charter (for 60 days) and notification of commencement of business are also required filings.

The following general powers are possessed by a national bank upon executing and filing the articles of association and the organization certificate, from date of execution of the organization certificate as a body corporate.

1. General corporate powers—adopting and using a corporate seal, having succession, making contracts, suing and being sued, electing or appointing directors, by it biard of directors appointing a president, vice-president, cashier, and other officers and prescribing bylaws, etc.
2. Discounting and negotiating promissory notes, drafts, bills, or exchange, and other evidences of debt.
3. Receiving deposits.
4. Buying and selling exchange, coin, and bullion.
5. Loaning money on personal security and other collateral security with specified limitations on the amount to a singe borrower.
6. Making real estate for own use or in order to avoid loss of defaulted loans.
7. Issuing circulating notes upon the deposit of government bonds having the circulation priviledge.
8. Holding real estate for own use or in order to avoid loss on defaulted loans.
9. Making acceptances covering domestic, export, and import transactions, or creation dollar exchange, subject to prescribed limitations, and issuing letters of credit.
10. Establishing and maintaining branch offices subject to limitations.
11. Carrying on a safe deposit business, directly or through subsidiaries, subject to limitations.
12. Purchasing investment securities for own account under limitations and restrictions prescribed by the Comptroller of the Currency.
13. Exercising trust powers upon special permit from the Board of Governors of the FEDERAL RESERVE SYSTEM, when not in contravention of state or local law.
14. Establishing branches in foreign countries, U.S. dependencies, or insular possessions if capital and surplus total $1 million or more, upon approval of the Board of Governors of the Federal Reserve System, and investing not over 10% of paid-in capital stock and surplus in the stock of one or more banks or in the U.S. or state corporations principally engaged in foreign banking or banking in a dependency or insular possession, provided such corporations abide by limitations and restrictions prescribed by the Board of Governors of the Federal Reserve System.
15. Acting as depositaries of public money, under such regulatons as may be prescribed by the secretary of the Treasury, and acting as financial agents of the U.S. government.
16. Acting as insurance agent and as broker or agent in making or procuring loans on real estate located within 100 miles of location, in places of less than 5,000 population.
17. Underwriting and dealing in U.S. government securities and general obligations of states, state subdivisions, and other specified government agencies.
18. Servicing mortgages sold out of own assets as agent for others.
19. Managing and selling real estate for others if the bank has authorized trust powers.
20. Providing travel services for customers, etc.

See FEDERAL RESERVE BOARD REGULATIONS (Regulation Y) for diversification in holdings of bank holding companies.

The above enumeration of diversified operational powers indicates that although national banks are primarily commercial banks, they may engage in activities providing a great variety of banking and related services, which for practical purposes may make them "department store" banks engaging in the three basic forms of banking: commercial, savings, and trust business. In turn, in most states, trust companies are permitted to engage in commercial banking, and state-chartered commercial banks in trust business. Through their personal LOAN departments, national banks may also engage in competition with the personal finance companies, and through their discounting of installment paper of dealers and buyers on the installment plan, in competition with savings banks and savings and loan associations. Through their mortgage loan departments, national banks engage in competition savings banks and savings and loan associations. Through their permissible underwriting activities and term loans, national banks may engage in competition with investment bankers, and in their permissible security trading activities, in competition with security dealers. Life insurance companies also are vied with for tetm loans, policy loans. and mortgage loans. These competitive activities indicate the development of competing types of financial institutions over the years, and the defensive or aggressive measures or national banks in meeting the changed and increasingly competitive market for credit of various types.

With the expanded organizational use of the HOLDING COMPANY by banking in recent years, additional diversifications of the "congeneric" type is possible in that such bank holding companies may acquire interests in nonbanking activities subject to certain restrictions and upon certain conditions.

CHANGES SINCE 1933. Since 1933 and 1935 many important changes affecting national banks have been made, either by direct amendment to the Revised Statutes or the Federal Reserve Act or in cognate banking laws. The following are among the most important of these revisions.

1. Member banks of the Federal Reserve System were prohibited from the payment of interest on demand deposits, effective June 16, 1933. The Board of Governors of the Federal Reserves System was also required to prescribe by regulation the maximum interest paid on time and savings deposits. (The DEPOSITORY INSTITUTIONS DEREGULATIONS COMMITTEE, established by Title II of the DEPOSITORY INSTITUTIONS DEREGUATION AND MONETARY CONTROL ACT OF 1980 was directed by the act to provide for the orderly phaseout and elimination of the limitations on interest and dividends on deposits, and to work toward providing all depositors with market rate of return on their savings with due regard for the safety and soundness of depository institutions.)
2. Stock of national banks, whether old or new stock, ceased on July 1, 1937, upon six months' published notice, to be subject to "double liability."
3. Commercial banking and the investment banking business were compulsorily separated through the prohibition beginning July 16, 1934, of the owning or controlling of "security affiliates" (companies engaged in the underwriting, distribution, and trading of securities generally) and the prohibition of underwriting activity bank itself except in prescribed governmental securities.
4. Member banks have been prohibited from acting as agent for the account of others in making loans to brokers or dealers. Loans to brokers or directly to others for the purpose of purchasing or carrying listed securities on margin are subject to margin regulations prescribed by the Board of Governors of the Federal Reserve System.
5. Member banks have been restricted in lending their funds to any executive officer. An executive officer must report to his board of directors concerning loans from banks.
6. In additons to quantitiave restrictions in the banking laws, member banks have been subjected to qualitative regulation of investment securities eligible for purchase for own account. Investment in affiliates is restricted, as well as loans thereto.
7. Bank holding companies have been brought under regulations, FIRST BY THE BANKING ACT OF 1933 and then in more extended form by the Bank Holding Company Act of 1956 as well as the Bank Holding Company Act Amendments of 1970. The change in the Bank Control Act (Title VI of the Financial Institutions Regulatory and Interest Rate Control Act of 1978) gave the federal banking agencies power to approve or disapprove proposed changes of control of banks and bank holding companies.
8. Branch banking powers have been generalized insofar as capital requirements are concerned (aggregate capital of every national bank and its branches shall at no time be less than the aggregate minimum capital required law for the established of

ENCYCLOPEDIA OF BANKING AND FINANCE

an equal number of national banks situated in the location of the bank and its branches), but to continue to be subject to state authorization for state banks, including the requirement generally that no national bank shall establish a branch outside the city of location inless it has the combined capital stock and surplus required by the state for state banks.

9. Nationwide deposit insurance was inaugurated on January 1, 1934, under a temporary plan providing for $2,500 deposit insurance (later raised to $5,000 per account), and then continue on August 31, 1935, under the permanent system providing $5,000 deposit insurance (raised to $10,000, September 21, 1950; to $15,000, October 16, 1966; to $20,000, December 23, 1969; to $40,000, November 27, 1974; and to $100,000, March 31, 1980).

10. The power to make loans was extended for various types of loans (e.g., 80% to 90% maximum ratio of appraised value, maximum term from 25 to 30 years on amortized first mortgage conventional real estate loans; maximum term from 36 to 60 months for commercial building construction loans; expansion in power to make loans or purchase obligation for land development [Urban Growth and New Community Development Act of 1970]; liberalization of restrictions with respect to loans on forest tracts; rise from 60% to 70% and to 100% on proportion of a national bank's time and savings deposits that may be invested in real estate loans.)

11. The number of directors of all member banks', including national banks, was prescribed to be not less than 5 nor more than 25. Every such director must own in his own right at least $1,000 par value of the bank's stock (unless the capital of the bank does not exceed $25,000, in shich case the requirement is at least $500).

12. Cumulative voting for directors of national banks, on a compulsory basis, was prescribed by the BANKING ACT OF 1933.

See BANKING ACT OF 1935, DEPOSITS, DOUBLE LIABILITY, NATIONAL BANK INDEBTEDNESS, NATIONAL BANK LOANS, NATIONAL BANK SECURITIES REGULATIONS, NATIONAL BANK TAXES.

NATIONAL BANK LOANS

Limitations imposed by Section 5200 of the Revised Statutes (12 U.S.C. 84) upon national banks restrict the amounts which a national bank may legally lend to any one borrower. On obligations generally (whether secured or unsecured), the limit is 10%. The term "obligations" embraces

1. The direct liability of maker or acceptor (including accommodation makers acceptors) of paper discounted with, or evidencing loans by, the bank.
2. The liability of the endorser, drawer, or guarantor who obtains a loan from or discounts paper with or sells paper under his guaranty to such national bank (but does not include accommodation endorsers).
3. In the case of obligations of copartnership or unincorporated association, the obligations of its several members.
4. In the case of obligations of a corporation, the obligations of all subsuduarues in which the corporation ownsa majority interest.

The Comptroller of the Currency has issued an outline if the exceptions to these limitations.

Exceptions to the General 10% Limitation on Bank Loans.

	Limits imposed by Sec. 5200 (i.e. maximum percentage of bank's unimpaired capital and surplus which may be loaned to any one borrower)
1. Drafts or bills of exchange drawn in good faith against actually existing values. (Exception 1 embraces only 2-name paper; it need not be secured.)	No limit
2. Commercial or business paper. (Exception 2 embraces only 2-name paper which must (1) be given by a purchaser to a seller in payment for a commodity; (2) bear the full recourse endorsement, of an actual owner; and (3) be negotiable.)	No limit
3. Obligations (including 1-name paper) secured by goods or commodities in process of shipment. The term "in process of shipment" is construed to mean in the hands of a carrier.	No limit
4. Obligations as endorser or guarantor of notes, other than commercial or business paper, taken under Exception 2, having maturity of not more than 6 months and owned by the party negotiating same.	15%, in addition to general 10% limit (25% total)
5. Bankers accptances of other banks of the kinds described in Sec. 13 of the Federal Reserve Act.	No limit
6. a. Notes or drafts secured by shipping documents, warehouse receipts, or other such documents (similar in nature to shipping documents and warehouse receipts—not including trust receipts) transferring or securing title covering readily marketable nonperishable staples which must be insured if it iscustomary to insure such commodities.	In addition to genera; limit of 10%, add 15% if security 115% 5% if security 120% 5% if security 125% 5% if security 130% 5% if security 135% 5% if security 140% (50% total)
b. Notes or drafts secured by shipping documents, warehouse receipts, or other such documents transferring or securing title covering refrigerated or frozen readily marketable stables if fully insured. Obligations arising from the same transaction or secured upon the identical staples for more than 10 months (6a); or for more than 6 months (6b), do not fall within the exception.	In addition to general limit of 10%, add 15% in security is 115% (25% total) (*Note:* The value of the security must be computed at "market value" and the required margin must be maintained at all times during the life of the loan.)
7. a. Noted and drafts secured by shipping documents or instrument transferring or securing title covering, or giving a lien on livestock.	15% in addition to general 10% limit (25% total)
b. Obligations arising out of the discount by cattle dealers of paper given in payment for dairy cattle, bearing full recourse endorsement, or uncon-ditonal guaranty of the seller, and secured by cattle sold.	15% in addition to general 10% limit (25% total)
8. Obligations secured by not less than a like amount of the following: a. Bonds or notes of the United States issued since April 24, 1917. b. Certificates of indebtedness of the United States. c. Treasury bills of the United States. d. Obligations fully guaranteed as to principa; and interset by the United States.	No limit, pursuant to regulation (12 CFR 6) of the Comptroller of the Currency, with approval of secretary of the Treasury (superseding, limits in the statute as provided for)

NATIONAL BANK NOTES

	Limits imposed by Sec. 5200 (i.e. maximum percentage of bank's unimpaired capital and surplus which may be loaned to any one borrower)
9. Loans to a national or state bank or to a representative in charge of the business thereof, when approved by the Comptroller of the Currency.	No limit
10. Obligations secured or covered by "unconditional" (as defined by the Comptroller) guaranties, commitments, or agreements to take over or to purchase for cash or its equivalent (within 60 days after demand) made by an Federal Reserve bank or the United States, including any department, bureau, commission, established, or corporation wholly owned directly by the United States.	No limit
11. Obligations of local public agency or public housing agency with a maturity of not more than 18 months of secured by agreement between obligor agency and the Housing and Home Finance Administraton or Public Housing Administration where the latter agrees to lend the agency prior to maturity and amount which will suffice to pay the principal and interest to maturity.	No limit
12. a. Obligations insured by the secretary of Agriculture under the Bank head-Jones Farm Tenant Act, or the Act of August 28, 1937, as amended, relating to the conservation of water resources. b. Amendment. The Consolidated Farmers Home Administration Act of 1961 superseded and repealed Titles I, II, and IV of the Bankhead-Jones Farm Tenant Act. Exception 12 should be contrued as also applying to obligations insured pursuant to provisions of the Consolidated Farmers Home Administration Act which amended or superseded provisions of the Bankhead-Jones Farm Tenamt Act.	15% in addition to general 10% limit (25% total)
13. Negotiable or nonnegotiable installment consumer paper with full recourse endorsment or unconditional guaranty of actual owner.	15% in addition to general 10% limit (25% total) (Note: If the bank's files or the knowledge of its officers of the financial condition of each maker is reasonably adequate, and an officer of the bank has certified that the responsibility of the maker has been evaluated and the bank is relying upon him for payment, then the limitation, shall apply solely to the maker.)

Section 23A of the Federal Reserve Act limits loans and credit to, repurchase agreements with, investments in and obligations of affiliates. The aggregate of all to one affiliate is limited to 10% of capital and surplus. The aggregate of all to all affiliates is limited to 20% of capital and surplus. (See Sec. 23A of Federal Reserve Act, Para. 2 and 3, for exceptions.) Loans secured by obligations of collateral credit of any kind must be in the form of stocks, bonds, debentures, or other such obligations having a market value of 20% more than advances; except if issued by state or political subdivision, value may be 10%. Section 24 states that loans to or secured by stock of corporation owning banking house, together with investment in and/or stock and obligations of corporation owning premises, together with amount of indebtedness incurred by such corporation which is affiliated with the bank, are limited to the amount of capital stock (unless the Comptroller of the Currency approves a greater amount).

Also, under Paragraph (m) of Section 11 of the Federal Reserve Act, the Board of Governors of the Federal Reserve System shall have power, upon the affirmative vote of not less than six of its members, to fix from time to time for each Federal Reserve district the percentage of individual bank capital and surplus which may be represented by loans secured by stock or bond collateral made by member banks within such district. But no such loan shall be made by any such bank to any person in an amount in excess of 10% of the unimpaired capital and surplus of such bank. Security loans secured by U.S. government bonds or notes issued since April 24, 1917, certificates of indebtedness of the United States, Treasury bills, or obligations fully guaranteed both as to principal and interest by the United States shall be exempt from this limitation, but state member banks shall be subject to the same limitations and conditions as are applicable in the case of national banks under Paragraph (8) of Section 5200 of the Revised Statutes.

Any percentage so fixed by the board of governors shall be subject to change from time to time upon ten days' notice. It shall be the duty of the Board of Governors of the Federal Reserve System to establish such percentages with a view to preventing the undue use of bank loans for the speculative carrying of securities. The statue empowers the board of governors to direct any member bank to refrain from further increase of its loans secured by stock or bond collateral for any period of up to one year under penalty of suspension of all rediscount privileges at Federal Reserve banks.

See LOAN.

BIBLIOGRAPHY

BOARD OF GOVERNORS OF THE FEDERAL RESERVE SYSTEM. *Federal Reserve Regulary Service.*
COMPTROLLER OF THE CURRENCY. *Comptroller's Manual for National Banks.*

NATIONAL BANK NOTES A uniform type of national currency issued by national banks under the authority of the NATIONAL BANK ACT, passed originally June 3, 1864, as the National currency Act and in 1874 designated as the National Bank Act.

Under the act, national banks were required, as a condition for charter, to transer and deliver to the Treasurer of the United States an amount, determined by their capitalization, of U.S. government interest-bearing registered bonds. Upon such transfer and delivery, the banks were entitled to receive from the Comptroller of the Currency circulating notes (in the form of demand promissory notes of the issuing bank) equal in amount to 90% of the current market value of the bonds deposited, but not exceeding 90% of their par value if bearing interest at a rate not less than 5%. Issues for each bank were limited to an amount equal to the paid-in capital of the bank, and the total for all banks was limited to $300 million. Circulation could be retired only through return of the notes to the Treasury, except in the case of liquidating banks, which after the lapse of one year could deposit lawful money to cover the retirement of outstanding notes and recover the bonds held by the Treasurer of the United States.

National bank notes were receivable at par in payment of taxes, excises, public lands, and all other dues to the United States, except duties on imports, and also for all salaries and other debts and demands owed by the United States to individuals, corporations, and associations within the United States, except interest on the public debt and the redemption of national currency (i.e., national bank notes). They were receivable by national banks for any debt or liability to such banks, and were required to be redeemed by the issuing bank, in lawful money, at the bank of issue and at designated agencies in enumerated redemption cities (after 1874, known as reserve cities), by the Act of June 20, 1874, national bank notes were made redeemable only at the bank of issue and the Treasury.

The office of the secretary of the Treasury (*Coins and Currency of the United States*) traces as follows the various and material amendments to the basic act, pertaining to national bank notes, beginning with the Act of March 3, 1865.

1. The aggregate amount of circulating notes of all banks, which was apportioned according to population and banking requirements by the Act of March 3, 1865, was increased from $300 million to $354 million by the Act of July 12, 1870, and finally by the Act of January 14, 1875, was freed from restrictions both as to total and as to apportionment.
2. By the Act of June 20, 1874, reserve requirements for notes were abolished, in favor of a 5% redemption fund deposited with the Treasurer of the United States. This fund was also counted as part of the required reserve against deposits, and notes were made redeemable only at the bank of issue and the Treasury.
3. Provision was made by the Act of June 20, 1874 (and by amendments approved July 12, 1882; July 14, 1890; and March 4, 1907) for the retirement of circulation of active banks upon the deposit of lawful money with the Treasurer of the United States.
4. The Act of July 14, 1890, provided for covering such deposits into the general fund of the Treasury as miscellaneous receipts.
5. By the Act of March 14, 1900, the tax on circulation secured by 2% bonds was fixed at 0.25% semiannually. Capital requirements for organization of national banks were lowered, and the amount of issuable circulation was increased from 90% of par to the full par value, but not exceeding the market value, of the bonds deposited.
6. The Act of May 30, 1908 (Aldrich-Vreeland Act) amended the National Bank Act by providing for the issuance, as an emergency currency, of additional circulation of national banks secured otherwise than by the deposit of United States bonds. Methods and conditions of issue were set forth on the act, and the additional circulation was authorized to be issued only at such times and under such conditions as in the judgment of the secretary of the Treasury warranted an increase in the national bank circulation. The Act of May 30, 1908, would have expired by limitation on June 30, 1914, but was amended and extended one year by the Federal Reserve Act of December 23, 1913. The act was further amended on August 4, 1914, and to meet an emergency then present, immediate steps were taken for the organization of all national banks into 45 national currency associations, through which additional circulation to a total amount of $381,592,145 was issued to national banks. The Aldrich-Vreeland Act expired by the revised limitation on June 30, 1915; prior to that date, deposits of lawful money had been made to cover the additional circulation issued, and the retirement of the notes proceeded in regular course. Meanwhile, the Federal Reserve banks had been organized, and Federal Reserve notes were available to meet the currency requirements of the country.

Circulation Privilege Bonds. Even before the enactment of the Federal Reserve Act, the Congress by various acts had taken occasion not to increase the amount of outstanding U.S. government bonds that might be used as security for the issuance of national bank notes. The Panama Canal loan bonds, issued in 1906-1908, carrying 2% interest, were the last bonds issued bearing the circulation privilege, except for temporary authorization provided by the Act of July 22, 1932, *infra*. The Act of June 25, 1910, which authorized the issue of postal savings bonds, provided that such bonds should not be receivable by the Treasurer of the United States as security for the issue of circulating notes by national banks. In each subsequent act authorizing bonds, similar provision was made.

The Federal Reserve Act, enacted December 23, 1913, provided that national banks thereafter organized should not be required to deposit United States bonds as a condition precedent to being authorized to commence business, although banks organized after that date might be banks of issue in accordance with previously existing law. The Federal Reserve Act further provided that after two years from its passage, and for 20 years thereafter, any member bank desiring to retire the whole or any part of its circulation might file with the Treasurer of the United States an application to sell for its account, at par and accrued interest, United States bonds securing the circulation to be retired. Provision was also made for the purchase by Federal Reserve banks of the bonds offered for sale by the national banks, the purchase money to be deposited in the Treasury for the redemption of the circulation to be retired. The Federal Reserve banks purchasing the bonds would thereby acquire bonds against which FEDERAL RESERVE BANK NOTES might be issued. They could, however, convert any 2% bonds against which no circulation was outstanding into securities not bearing the circulation privilege. At that time (December 31, 1913), the outstanding bonds available for deposit as security for the issuance of national bank notes were as follows.

2% consols of 1930	$646,250,150
2% Panama Canal loans of 1916-1936 and 1918-1938	84,631,980 63,945,460
3% loan of 1908-1918	118,489,900
4% loan of 1925	
	$913,317,490
Then held to secure circulation	$743,066,500

Under these provisions of the Federal Reserve Act, $56,256,500 of the 2% bonds were converted into securities not bearing the circulation privilege. The 3% bonds of 1908-1918 were paid at maturity August 1, 1918, and the 4% bonds of 1925 were called for redemption February 2, 1925. This left the 2% bonds, which were outstanding in the amount of $674,625.630, as the only bonds available as security for national bank notes. As an emergency measure, however, the Act of July 22, 1932, attached the circulation privilege with respect to national bank notes and Federal Reserve bank notes for a three-year period to all outstanding United States bonds bearing interest at a rate not exceeding 3.375%. The 2% consols of 1930 were called for redemption July 1, 1935. The 2% Panama Canal loan bonds of 1916-1936 and 1918-1938 were called for redemption August 1, 1935. The circulation privilege granted by the Act of July 22, 1932, expired July 22, 1935.

Thus, as the bonds that were deposited as collateral for national bank notes were called or otherwise became unavailable, national banks deposited lawful money to retire the circulation so secured, thereby ending their liability for national bank notes and transferring it to the United States (U.S. Treasury). As of the close of November, 1981, approximately $19 million in national bank notes was still in circulation (outside the Treasury and Federal Reserve banks), but when unfit for further circulation they are canceled and retired upon receipt at the Treasury, all of such still outstanding circulation being Treasury liability currency.

See MONETARY STOCK, UNITED STATES MONEY.

NATIONAL BANK REPORT *See* NATIONAL BANK CALL.

NATIONAL BANKRUPTCY ACT The power of Congress to legislate uniform laws on the subject of BANKRUPTCY throughout the United States is one of the powers expressly delegated to the federal government by the U.S. Constitution (Art. 1, Sec. 8).

Acting under this authority, several federal bankruptcy laws were passed prior to 1898, when the National Bankruptcy Act, basis of the present law, was enacted. This act in turn has been amended many times since, the most important amendments occurring since 1933, especially the fundamental amendments included in the Chandler Act effective September 22, 1938, and November 6, 1978. As now constituted (codified and enacted as Title 11 of the United States Code, entitled "Bankruptcy," per P.L. 95-598, 95th Congress), the act provides diversified relief for various types of debtors of the reorganization type (involving extension, composition, or reorganization), as well as the basic remedy of liquidation in bankruptcy.

Termed the Bankruptcy Reform Act of 1978, and effective October 1, 1979, the new bankruptcy act is a comprehensive revision of the federal bankruptcy court system, procedures, and law.

New United States bankruptcy courts are established, under the supervision of the director of the Administrative Office of the United States Courts, to which effective on April 1, 1984, cases, matters, and proceedings pending in the former Bankruptcy Act as of the end of

September 30, 1983, shall be transferred (cases commenced prior to October 1, 1979, continued under the appropriate provisions of the prior Bankruptcy Act).

Under the new Act, Chapter 7 pertains to liquidation, and Chapter 11, deals with reorganization. Involuntary petitions are applicable only to Chapter 7, providing for liquidation proceedings in which an interim trustee may be appointed by the court to operate the business, issue financing if necessary on an unsecured basis, and keep or change management as authorized by the court. he debtor would be required to post a bond as required by the court if it desired to resume operation of the business.

Chapter 11 of the new act, by contrast, provides for the debtor to remain in possession and operation of the firm (unless the court otherwise directs). Formerly, Chapter X provided for appointment of a trustee to work out the reorganization, whereas former Chapter XI continued the debtor in possession and operation. The new Chapter 11 combines the former Chapters X and XI, for reorganization relief, while continuing the debtor in possession, and is believed to expedite reorganization by making possible direct negotiation among the debtor, creditors, and stockholders. The new Chapter 11 applies to all types of business reorganizations, and authorizes the SECURITIES AND EXCHANGE COMMISSION to enter its appearance in any reorganization case and to raise or to present its views on any issue in a Chapter 11 case.

An important substantive feature of the new Chapter 11 proceedings for reorganization is that the "absolute priority rule" required in reorganization treatment under the former Chapter X, whereby senior creditors must be provided for in full before junior creditors and other claims may share, no longer is applicable. In its place, direct negotiation may result in junior claims and stockholders being able to share, where otherwise under the full priority rule they would be shut out. Such possibility of sharing, however, would depend upon the willingness of senior creditors to accept less than full priority treatment.

As experience with the new act and its provisions accumulates, there will no doubt be appropriate amendments in the future.

See INSOLVENCY, MUNICIPAL BANKRUPTCY ACT.

BIBLIOGRAPHY

See Bibliography under BANKRUPTCY.

NATIONAL BANK SECURITIES REGULATIONS

The business of dealing in securities and stock by national banks is limited by Paragraph 7, Section 5136 of the Revised Statutes as amended (12 U.S.C. 24) to purchasing and selling such securities and stock without recourse soley upon the order and for the account of customers, and in no case for its own account. The national bank shall not underwrite any issue of securities or stock, with the following exceptions.

1. The national bank may purchase for its own account investment securities under such limitations and restrictions as the Comptroller of the Currency may by regulation prescribe. (See COMPROLLER'S SECURITY for details of the regulations of the Comptroller of the Currency pertaining to investment securities of national banks.)
2. In general, subject to specified exceptions, the total amount of the investment securities of any one obligor or maker held by the national bank for its own account shall not exceed at any time 10% of its capital stock actually paid in and unimpaired and 10% of its unimpaired surplus fund. This limitation did not require any national bank to dispose of any securities lawfully held by it on the date of enactment of the Banking Act of 1935 (August 23, 1935).
3. National banks are governed in their security investments by Paragraph 7 of 12 U.S.C. 24 and by the Investment Securities Regulation of the Comptroller of the Currency (12 CFR 1). The referenced statute requires that for a security to qualify as an investment security it must be marketable and not predominantly speculative.
   a. "Type I security" means a security which a bank may deal in, underwrite, purchase, and sell for its own account without limitation other than the exercise of prudent banking judgement. These include obligations of the United States, general obligations of any state of the United States or any political subdivision thereof, and other obligations listed in Paragraph 7 of 12 U.S.C. 24, the latter as follows.
   (1) Obligations of the Washington Metropolitan Area Transit Authority which are guaranteed by the secretary of Transportation under Section 9 of the National Capital Transportation Act of 1969.
   (2) Obligations issued under authority of the Federal Farm Loan Act, as amended, of issued by the 13 Banks for Cooperatives or any of them.
   (3) Obligations of the Federal Home Loan banks.
   (4) Obligations which are insured by the secretary of Housing and Urban Development under Title XI of the National Housing Act, or obligations which are insured by the secretary of Housing and Urban Development pursuant to Section 1713 of this title (12 U.S.C.), if the debentures to be issued in payment of such insured obligations are guaranteed as to principal and interest by the United States.
   (5) Obligations, participations, or other instruments of or issued by the FEDERAL NATIONAL MORTGAGE ASSOCIATION or the GOVERNMENT NATIONAL MORTGAGE ASSOCIATION.
   (6) Mortgages, obligations, or other securities which are or ever have been sold by the FEDERAL HOME LOAN MORTGAGE ASSOCIATION pursuant to Section 1454 or Section 1455 of this title (12 U.S.C.).
   (7) Obligations of the Federal Financing Bank.
   (8) Obligations of the Environmental Financing Authority.
   (9) Obligations of other instruments or securities of the Student Loan Marketing Association.
   (10) Obligations of any local public agency (as defined in Sec. 1460(h) of Title 42 U.S.C.) as are secured by an agreement between the local public agency and the secretary of Housing and Urban Development in which the local public agency agrees to borrow from the secretary and the secretary agrees to lend to the local public agency monies in an aggregate amount which (together with any other monies irrevocably committed to the payment of interest or such obligations) will suffice to pay, when due, the interest on and all installments (including the final installment) of the principal of such obligations, which monies under the terms of said agreement are required to be used for such payments.
   (11) Such obligations of a public housing agency (as defined in the United States Housing Act of 1937, as amended) as are secured
      (a) By an agreement between the public housing agency and the secretary in which the public housing agency agrees to borrow from the secretary and the secretary agrees to lend to the public housing agency, prior to the maturity of such obligations, monies in an amount which (together with any other monies irrevocably committed to the payment of interest on such obligations) will suffice to pay the principal of such obligations with interest to maturity thereon, which monies under the terms of said agreement are required to be used for the purpose of paying the principal of and the interest on such obligations at their maturity.
      (b) By a pledge of annual contributions under an annual contributions contract between such public housing agency and the secretary if such contract shall contain the covenant by the secretary which is authorized by Section 1437d(g) of Title 42, and if the maximum sum and the maximum period specified in such contract pursuant to Section 1437d(g) of Title 42 shall not be less than the annual amount and the period of payment which are requisite to provide for the payment when due of all installments of principal and interest on such obligations.
      (c) By a combination of (a) and (b).
   b. "Type II security" means a security which a bank may deal in, underwrite, purchase, and sell for its own account, subject to a 10% limitation (10% of the bank's capital and surplus). These include the following:
   (1) Obligations of the International Bank for Reconstruction and Development, the Inter-American Development Bank, the Asian Development Bank, and the Tennessee Valley Authority.

NATIONAL BANK SECURITIES REGULATIONS

(2) Obligations issued by any state or political subdivision or any agency of a state or a political subdivision for housing, university, or dormitory purposes.

c. "Title III security" means a security which a bank may purchase and sell for its own account, subject to a 10% limitation of the bank's capital and surplus for each obligor, but which the bank may neither deal in nor underwrite.

d. Types II and III securities are subject to the following purchase standards.

(1) Evidence of the obligor's ability to perform, and of marketability. A bank may purchase a security of Type II or III for its own account when in its prudent banking judgment (which may be based in part upon estimates which it believes to be reliable), it determines that there is adequate evidence that the obligor will be able to perform all that it undertakes to perform in connection with the security, including all debt service requirements, and that the security is marketable, that is, that it may be sold with reasonable promptness at a price which corresponds reasonably to its fair value.

(2) Judgment based predominantly upon reliable estimates. The limitation is reduced to 5% of capital and surplus for all obligors in the aggregate where the purchase judgment is predicated on reliable estimates. The term "reliable estimates" refers to projections of income and debt service requirements or conditional ratings when factual credit information is not available and when the obligor does not have a record of performance. Securities purchased subject to such 5% limitation may, in fact, become eligible for the 10% limitation once a satisfactory financial record has been established.

(3) Securities ruled eligible by the Office of the Comptroller of the Currency. A bank may consider as a factor in reaching its prudent judgement with respect to a security a ruling published by the OCC on the eligibility of such security for purchase. Consideration must also be given, however, to the possibility that circumstances on which the ruling was based may have changed since the time of the ruling.

When a ruling published by the OCC provides that a security is eligible for purchase subject to a specified limitation, a bank may not at any time thereafter purchase such security if after such purchase the bank's holdings of such security would be in excess of the specification of limitation. Any bank may request the OCC to rule on the applicability of the investment Securities Regulation or Paragraph 7 of 12 U.S.C. 24 to any security which it holds, or desires to purchase for its own account as an investment security; or which it holds, or desires to deal in, underwrite, purchase, hold, or sell as a security of Type I or II.

e. The concept of capital and surplus is broadly defined as follows:

(1) Capital includes the preferred stock, if any, issued (authorized by Sec. 14.4 12 CFR 1).

(2) The definition of the term "unimpaired surplus fund" is applicable in determining the base by which a national bank's investment securities are limited (12 U.S.C. 24). Paragraph 7.1100(b) of the Comptroller's Interpretive Rulings. "Unimpaired surplus," defines the term as follows:

The term "unimpaired surplus fund"... shall consist of the amounts reportable in the following items as defined in the instructions for preparation of the report of condition form:

1. Fifty percent of the reserve for possible loan losses;
2. Subordinated notes and debentures;
3. Surplus;
4. Undivided profits; and
5. Reserve for contingencies and other capital reserves (excluding accrued dividends on preferred stock).

Paragraph 7.745 of the Comptroller's Interpretive Rulings specifically provides that the preceding concept of unimpaired surplus fund shall be applicable to the capital requirements by which a national bank's investment securities are limited.

The par value, not the book value or purchase price, of the security is the basis for computing the limitations. However, the limitations do not apply to securities acquired through debts previously contracted.

f. When a bank purchases an investment security that is convertible into stock or has stock purchase warrants attached, entries must be made by the bank at the time of the purchase to write down the cost of the security to an amount representing the investment value of the security, exclusive of the conversion feature or the attached stock purchase warrants. Purchase of securities convertible into stock at the option of the issuer is prohibited (12 CFR 1.10).

4. Except as provided or permitted by law, purchase by a national bank for its own account of any shares of stock of any corporation is not authorized.

Exceptions are summarized in the appended table.

History. Specific statutory authorization for the investment in bonds by National banks was first contained in the Act of February 25, 1927 (McFadden-Pepper Act); previously, Section 5136, Revised Statutes, had merely permitted the discount and negotiation of "promissory notes, drafts, bills of exchange, and other evidences of debt," the latter part of this provision being interpreted administratively by the Comptroller of the Currency to permit investment in bonds. The McFadden-Pepper Act specifically permitted national banks to invest in "bonds, notes, or debentures commonly known as investment securities, under such further definition of the term 'investment securities' as may by regulation be prescribed by the Comptroller of the Currency." The Comptroller's first ruling was that only marketable obligation may be purchased by banks; "under ordinary circumstances, the term 'marketable' means that the security in question has such a market as to render sales at intrinsic values readily possible."

Following enactment of the Banking Acts of 1933 and 1935, the Comptroller's Regulation of February 15, 1936, for the first time established qualitative as well as quantitative standards for bank investments; and as subsequently amended effective July 1, 1938, it made special provision for investment in bonds not enjoying a public market where an adequate sinking fund provided for at least 75% retirement of principal by maturity. The 1936 Comptroller's Regulation had for the first time referred (in a footnote) to the rating service: "The terms employed herein may be found in recognized rating manuals, and where there is doubt as to the eligibility of a security for purchase, such eligibility must be supported by not less than two rating manuals." (At that time, there were four rating services—Standard Statistics, Moody's, Poor's, and Fitch.) With regard to securities rated by any one of the then three rating services, the Comptroller of the Currency in enforcing the 1938 regulation and the Federal Deposit Insurance Corporation in examining banks agreed with respect to designation as to banking quality that (1) a security rated by only one service would be designated as of banking quality if rated within the first four grades by that service; (2) a security rated by only two services would be designated as of banking quality if rated within the first four grades by both services; and (3) a security rated by three services would be designated as of banking quality if rated within the first four grades by two of those services. The "purchase of investment securities in which the investment characteristics are distinctly or predominantly speculative, or the purchase of securities which are in default, either as to principal or interest" was prohibited.

On August 16, 1957, the investment securities regulation was revised by the Comptroller of the Currency, omitting reference to the rating manuals and specifying that "all investments securities shall be supported by adequate information in the files of the bank as their investment quality." Accordingly, Standard & Poor's, for example, analogously put it that "under present commercial bank regulations, bonds rated in the top four categories (AAA, AA, A, BBB or their equivalent) generally are regarded as eligible for bank investment." The September 12, 1963 revision of the regulation, termed by the then incumbent Comptroller as "the first major revision since 1934," restated and reinterpreted the broad authority of national banks to invest in investment securities, among other respects, in the following ways.

NATIONAL BANK SECURITIES REGULATIONS

Permitted Stock Holdings by National Banks

Type of Stock	Authorizing statute and limitation
Federal Reserve bank	12 U.S.C. 282—subscription *must* equal 6% of the bank's capital and surplus, 3% paid in (Regulation I, Federal Reserve Board; 12 CFR 209)
Safe deposit corporation	12 U.S.C. 24—15% of capital and surplus.
Corporation holding bank premises	12 U.S.C. 371(d)—100% of capital. Limitation includes total direct and indirect investment in bank premises in any form. Maximum limitation may be exceeded with permission of the Regional Administrator of National Banks (12 CFR 7.3100).
Small business investment company	15 U.S.C. 682(b)—5% of capital and surplus. After January 10, 1968, national banks are prohibited from acquiring shares of such a corporation if, upon making the acquisition, the aggregate amount of shares in small business investment companies then held by the bank would exceed 5% of its capital and surplus.
Banking service corporation	12 U.S.C. 1861 and 1862—10% of capital and surplus. Limitation includes direct and indirect investment in any form. Also, the corporation must be owned by two or more banks.
Foreign banking corporation	12 U.S.C. 601 and 618—10% of capital and surplus with the provision that capital and surplus must be $1 million or more.
Corporation authorized under Title IX of the Housing and Urban Development Act of 1968 (amendments not included)	12 U.S.C. 1718(f)—no limit.
Federal National Mortgage Association	12 U.S.C. 1718(f)—no limit.
Bank's own stock	12 U.S.C. 83—Shares of the bank's own stock may not be acquired or taken as security for loans, except as necessary to prevent loss from a debt previously contracted in good faith. Stock so acquired must be disposed of within 6 months of the date of acquisition.
Corporate stock acquired through debts previously contracted (DPC) transaction	Case law has established that stock of any corporation may be acquired to prevent loss from a debt previously contracted in good faith. However, if the stock is not disposed of within a reasonable time period, it loses its status as a DPC transaction and becomes a prohibited holding under 12 U.S.C. 24(7). The maximum time such stock can be retained generally is regarded to be 5 years. The maximum time limit for stock of affiliates acquired through a DPC transaction, and not held within the limitations of specific statutes, is 2 years.
Corporate stock acquired as a dividend from a small business investment company (SBIC)	12 CFR 7.7535—no limit. Stock of any corporation may be acquired and retained, if received as a dividend on SBIC stock.
Operating subsidiaries	12 CFR 7.10—no limit. Stock of any operating subsidiary corporation, the functions or activities of which are limited to those authorized to a national bank, may be acquired and held without limitation, provided that at least 80% of the voting stock of the subsidiary is owned by the bank. The establishment of an operating subsidiary requires the prior approval of the OCC (12 CFR 7.7376 and 7.7378 through 7.7380).
State housing corporation incorporated in the state in which the national bank is located	12 U.S.C. 24—5% of its capital stock, paid in and unimpaired, plus 5% of its unimpaired surplus fund when considered together with loans and commitments made to the corporation.
Agricultural credit corporation	12 U.S.C. 24—20% of capital and surplus unless the national bank owns over 80%. No limit if the national bank owns 80% or more.
Government National Mortgage Association	12 U.S.C. 24—no limit.
Student Loan Marketing Association	12 U.S.C. 24—no limit.
Minibank capital corporation	12 CFR 7.7480—2% of capital and surplus of the national bank. Aggregate investment in all such projects should not exceed 5% of the bank's capital and surplus.
Charitable foundations	12 CFR 7.7445—contribution in any one year not to exceed income tax deduction.
Bankers' banks	12 U.S.C. 24—10% of capital stock and paid-in and unimpaired surplus. Bankers' bank must be insured by the Federal Deposit Insurance Corporation, owned exclusively [a] by other banks, and engaged solely in providing banking services to other banks and their officers, directors, or employees. Ownership shall not result in any bank acquiring more than 5% of any class of voting securities of the bankers' bank.

Source: Comptroller of the Currency, *Handbook for National Bank Examiners*.
[a] Word "by" appears in the Comptroller's *Handbook for National Bank Examiners* (See 203.1, February 1982) and in the statute.

1. A bank might deal in, underwrite, purchase, and sell "public securities" (including obligations of the United States and general obligations of any state of the United States or of any political subdivision thereof) for its own account, subject only to the exercise of prudent banking judgment. In the case of underwriting or investment, such prudence was considered to require a consideration of the obligor's resources and obligations, as well as a determination that such resources were sufficient to provide for all required payments in connection with the obligation.
2. In purchasing an investment security, a bank was required to make certain determinations with respect to the obligor's ability to perform. These determinations could be based, in part, upon estimates. Ordinarily, a bank's holdings of the investment securities of any one obligor were limited to 10% of the bank's capital and surplus. However, when the bank's determinations were based predominately upon estimates, the bank's total holdings of all such obligors were limited to 5% of the bank's capital and surplus.

NATIONAL BANK TAXES National banks are deemed instrumentalities of the Federal government and hence, under the doctrine of *McCulloch* v. *Maryland* (4 Wheat. 316, 4 L. Ed. 579), decided in 1819 by the U.S. Supreme Court (option of Chief Justice Marshall), that the "power to tax involves the power to destroy," states may not tax national banks discriminatorily. The last paragraph of that opinion, however, indicated that such nondiscriminatory taxation would be valid. In Section 5219, Revised Statutes as amended (12 U.S.C. 548) permanently by P.L. 91-156 (December 24, 1969), Congress provided a new approach as follows.

For the purposes of any tax law enacted under authority of the United States or any State, a National bank shall be treated as a bank organized and existing under the laws of the State or other jurisdiction within which its principal office is located. [Effective January 1, 1972.]

Section 5219, Revised Statutes, had read as follows:

The legislature of each State may determine and direct, subject to the provisions of this section, the manner and place of taxing all the shares of National banks located within its limits. The several States may (1) tax said shares, or (2) include dividends derived therefrom in the taxable income of an owner or holder thereof, or (3) tax such National banks on their net income, or (4) according to or measured by their net income, provided the following conditions are complied with:

1.
   (a) The imposition by any State of any one of the above four forms of taxation shall be in lieu of the others, except as hereinafter provided in subdiv. (c) of this clause.
   (b) In the case of a tax on said shares the tax imposed shall not be at a greater rate than is assessed upon other moneyed capital in the hands of individual citizens of such State coming into competition with the business of National banks: Provided, That bonds, notes, or other evidence of indebtedness in the hands of individual citizens not employed or engaged in the banking business or investment business and representing merely personal investments not made in competition with such business, shall not be deemed moneyed capital within the meaning of this section.
   (c) In the case of a tax on or according to or measured by the net income of an association, the taxing State may, except in case of a tax on a net income, include the entire net income received from all sources, but the rate shall not be higher than the rate assessed upon other financial corporations nor higher than the highest of the rates assessed by the taxing State upon mercantile, manufacturing, and business corporations doing business within its limits; provided, however, that a State which imposes a tax on or according to or measured by the net income of, or a franchise or excise tax on, financial, mercantile, manufacturing, and business corporations organized under its own laws or laws of other States and also imposes a tax upon the income of individuals, may include in such individual; income dividends from national banks located within the State on condition that it also includes dividends from domestic corporations and may likewise include dividends from national banks located within the State on condition that it also includes dividends from foreign corporations, but at no higher rate than is imposed on dividends from such other corporations.
   (d) In case the dividends derived from the said shares are taxed, the tax shall not be at a greater rate than is assessed upon the net income from other moneyed capital.
2. The shares of any National bank owned by nonresidents of any State shall be taxed by the taxing district or by the State where the National bank is located and not elsewhere; and such National bank shall make return of such shares and pay the tax thereon as agent of such non-resident shareholders.
3. Nothing herein shall be construed to exempt the real property of national banks from taxation in any State or in any subdivision thereof, to the same extent, according to its value, as other real property is taxed.
4. The provisions of sec. 5219 of the Revised Statutes of the United States as heretofore in force shall not prevent the legalizing, ratifying, or confirming by the States of any tax heretofore paid, levied, or assessed upon the shares of National banks, or the collecting thereof, to the extent that such tax would be valid under such said section.

The same act of Congress approved December 24, 1969 (P.L. 91—156) that permanently amended Section 5219, Revised Statutes, as shown above, temporarily amended the latter by adding to the end thereof the following:

5.
   (a) In addition to the other methods of taxation authorized by the foregoing provisions of this section and subject to the limitations and restrictions specifically set forth in such provisions, a state or political subdivision thereof may impose any tax which is imposed generally on a nondiscriminatory basis throughout the jurisdiction of such state or political subdivision (other than a tax or intangible personal property) on a national bank having its principal office within such state in the same manner and to the same extent as such tax is imposed on a bank organized and existing under the laws of such state.
   (b) Except as otherwise herein provided, the legislature of each state may impose, and may authorize any political subdivision thereof to impose, the following taxes on a national bank not having its principal office located within the jurisdiction of such state, if such taxes are imposed generally throughout such jurisdiction on a nondiscriminatory basis:
      (1) Sales taxes and use taxes complementary thereto upon purchases, sales, and use within each jurisdiction.
      (2) Taxes on real property or on the occupancy of real property located within such jurisdiction.
      (3) Taxes (including documentary stamp taxes) on the execution, delivery, or reordation of documents within such jurisdiction.
      (4) Taxes on tangible personal property (not including cash or currency) located within such jurisdiction.
      (5) License, registration, transfer, excise, or other fees or taxes imposed on the ownership, use, or transfer of tangible personal property located within such jurisdiction.
   (c) No sales tax or use tax complementary thereto shall be imposed pursuant to this paragraph 5 upon purchases, sales, and use within the taxing jurisdiction of tangible personal property which is the subject matter of a written contract of purchase entered into by a National bank prior to September 1, 1969.
   (d) As used in this paragraph 5, the term 'State' means any of the several States of the United States, the District of Columbia, the Commonwealth of Puerto Rico, the Virgin Islands, and Guam.

The preceding temporary amendment of Section 5219, Revised Statutes, was specified to be effective from December 24, 1969 (date of enactment of the act) until the effective date of the permanent amendment thereto (January 1, 1972, was the original date specified).

By act approved December 22, 1971 (P.L. 92-213), Congress among other things extended from January 1, 1972, to January 1, 1973, the date upon which a national bank would, for the purposes of any state tax law, be treated as a bank organized under the law of the state within which its principal office is located. The same act directed the Board of Governors of the Federal Reserve System to make a study of the probable impact of the extension of the termination date of the above interim provisions on the revenues of state and local governments through intangible personal property taxes on national banks. The board of governors was to report the results of its study to the Congress not later than six months after the date of approval of this extension. This provision for study and report accorded with the view of the chairman of the board of governors that equal treatment of state and national banks in the home state was clearly called for, but that determination of whether changes should be made in other states should await further study.

The position of counsel for the office of the Comptroller of the Currency on the issue of intangible personal property taxes on national banks by states was as follows: "This office perceives no objection to adding these taxes to the list, with the exception of an intangible personal property tax. Intangible assets, such as loans and investment securities, constitute the great bulk of any financial institutions' assets and worth. Since the States are already permitted to levy a share tax, measured by the net worth of the bank's assets, it would constitute a form of double taxation to permit a direct tax on its intangible assets . . ."

The issue has since been settled, the Board of Governors of the Federal Reserve System having reported affirmatively to the Congress, and the old-numbered Section 5219 of the Revised Statutes (*supra*) now numbered 12 U.S.C. 548 with the exact language of the old-numbered statute, providing for nondiscriminatory state taxation of national banks in the home state.

Federal Taxation. For provisions of the federal tax laws regarding taxation of commercial banks, *see* TAXES. The Comptroller of the Currency has ruled (Interpretive Ruling 7.7505) that in order that a national bank may benefit from widely practiced and generally accepted accounting procedures available under the Internal Revenue Code to other taxpayers, the bank may use for income tax purposes the method(s) of depreciation currently set forth in the Internal Revenue Code as amended, and apply a generally accepted nonaccelerated method for financial accounting purposes with respect to certain newly acquired assets selected by the bank (fixed assets entitled to depreciation allowances). Once the dual depreciation treatment is applied to a given asset, it must be continued until the asset is fully depreciated. Upon adoption of the above practice, accounting recognition must be given to deferred income taxes applicable to the excess of depreciation allowed for income tax purposes over depreciation expense recorded for financial accounting purposes, if such taxes are material in amount.

NATIONAL BUDGET The Budget and Accounting Act of June 10, 1921 (42 Stat. 20; 31 U.S.C. 11-16) provided that the President of the United States shall transmit to Congress the proposed annual BUDGET of the United States, together with other budgetary information. The same act created the BUREAU OF THE BUDGET (BoB), now located organizationally in the Executive Office of the President pursuant to Reorganization Plan I of 1939; the BoB assists the President in the preparation of the budget and the formulation of the fiscal program of the federal government and supervises and controls the administration of the budget.

In preparing the budget, the Bureau of the Budget has authority "to assemble, correlate, revise, reduce, or increase the estimates of the several departments and establishments." Moreover, the director of the bureau issues and administers the instructions and regulations to guide the departments in making systematic reviews of their operations on a continuing basis (Title X of the Classification Act of 1949 and Executive Order 10072 of July 29, 1949). Section 3679 of the Revised Statutes as amended (31 U.S.C. 665) made agency systems of administrative control of funds subject to the director's approval, prescribed procedures by which the director apportions appropriations, and authorized the establishment of budgetary reserves.

In addition, the Budget and Accounting Procedures Act of 1950 (64 Stat. 834; 31 U.S.C. 18a, 18b) provided authority for the revision and simplification of budget and accounting procedures and made clear the bureau's responsibilities with regard to statistical information and the development of better organization, coordination, and management of the Executive branch. Thus additional functions of the bureau are managerial—to advise the executive departments and agencies of the federal government with respect to improved administrative organization and practice, to conduct research in the development of improved plans of administrative management, to aid the President to bring about more efficient and economical conduct of government service, and to plan and promote the improvement, development, and coordination of federal and other statistical services.

Reflecting the increasingly managerial functions of the BoB, the Office of Management and Budget was established in the Executive Office of the President, pursuant to Reorganization Plan 2 of 1970, effective July 1, 1970; and in turn, by Executive Order 11541 of July 1, 1970, all such functions transferred to the President of the United States by Part I of such Reorganization Plan 2 of 1970 were delegated to the director of the Office of Management and Budget, such functions to be carried out by the director under the direction of the President. The office's functions include the following:

1. To aid the President to bring about more efficient and economical conduct of government service.
2. To assist in developing efficient coordinating mechanisms to implement government activities and to expand interagency cooperation.
3. To assist the President in the preparation of the budget and the formulation of the fiscal program of the government.
4. To supervise and control the administration of the budget.
5. To conduct research and promote the development of improved plans of administrative management, and to advise the executive departments and agencies of the government with respect to improved administrative organization and practice.
6. To assist the President by clearing and coordinating departmental advise on proposed legislation and by making recommendations as to presidential action on legislative enactments, in accordance with past practice.
7. To assist in the consideration and clearance and, where necessary, in the preparation of proposed executive orders and proclamations.
8. To plan and promote the improvement, development, and coordination of federal and other statistical services.
9. To plan and develop information systems to provide the President with program performance data.
10. To plan, conduct, and promote evaluation efforts to assist the President in the assessment of program objectives, performance, and efficiency.
11. To plan and develop programs to recruit, train, motivate, deploy, and evaluate career personnel.
12. To keep the President informed of the progress of activities by agencies of the government with respect to work proposed, work actually initiated, and work completed, together with the relative timing of work between the several agencies of the government, all to the end that the work programs of the several agencies of the Executive branch of the government may be coordinated, and that the monies appropriated by the Congress may be expended in the most economical manner with the least possible (sic) overlapping and duplication of effort. (See reviews of management performance and program results by the General Accounting Office, which audits the receipt, expenditure, and application of public funds by the departments and agencies of the federal government; the primary purpose of these audits is to make for the Congress independent examinations of the way in which government agencies are discharging their financial responsibilities, including examining the efficiency of operations and program management, determining whether government programs are achieving the purposes intended by Congress and determining whether alternative approaches have been examined which might accomplish these objectives more effectively and more economically.)

Budgetary Reform. The planning-programming-budgeting system (PPBS), along the lines of the system in effect in the Department of Defense, was ordered instituted in all of the major civilian agencies of the federal government by the President (statement by the President to members of the Cabinet and heads of agencies, August 25, 1965).

Congress still acts on the budget in terms of "object categories" (e.g., for the Department of Defense budget, so much for military personnel, operation and maintenance, procurement, military construction, research and development, etc.), but also on the basis of programs (e.g., for the Department of Defense budget, so much for strategic forces, general-purpose forces, intelligence and communications, airlift and sealift, etc.).

The PPBS, therefore, presents the budget in terms of grouped programs in support of specific objectives, which in turn are designed to achieve general objectives of public policy. Each program consists of various program elements, the smallest units of planning and analysis, extending as far into the future as the nature of the program elements calls for and as is justified by necessity for full analysis. Benefit-cost analysis, whether analysis of quantified benefits discounted to present value whether analysis of quantified benefits discounted to present value of explicitly quantitative "cost effectiveness" analysis, can play its part in the evaluation of alternative program elements to be selected for the accomplishment of designated specific objectives. Changes in the programs may be made for any year, as program reviews and evaluation occur; flexibility may also be achieved by annual variation in emphasis on specific programs and program elements within the fiscal limits considered feasible.

The Unified Budget. The administrative budget, the type of budget presented prior to the 1969 fiscal year, covered receipts and expenditures of the federal funds (funds owned by the government) and excluded funds held in trust by the federal government. In the case of public enterprise funds, intragovernmental funds and reimbursements which by law are mingled with appropriations, the administrative budget offset receipts against expenditures; otherwise, it presented receipts and expenditures gross, except for refunds. While the administrative budget was not coextensive with either the finances requiring annual action or the expenditures subject to legislative and administrative control, it was usually the focus of attention as the principal financial plan for the government. Actually, it always included a number of appropriations and funds in which money became available each year without new action by the executive or legislative branches, the most import being interest on the public debt. Similarly, it excluded a few items on which annual action was required, but which were in the nature of trust funds.

Because of the above limitations of the administrative budget, the consolidated cash statement ("cash budget" for short) was calculated to reflect the transactions between the government and the public. It was "consolidated" in the sense that it included both federal funds and trust funds. It was "cash" also in the sense that its totals were basically on a checks-paid basis as distinguished from the checks-issued basis used in the administrative budget. As the trust funds, particularly those derived from taxes and social insurance payments, became of greater importance, the consolidated cash statement took on a greater significance in the presentation of federal finances and in analysis of the relationships between federal finances and the remainder of the economy. The consolidated cash statement followed the same rules as the administrative budget with respect to grossing and netting; most trust funds were reported gross, but a few, designated as trust revolving funds, were included on the basis of the net excess of expenditures over receipts. The consolidated cash statement also included among government-sponsored enterprises two privately owned groups of government agencies—the Federal Home Loan banks and the Federal Land banks—which at one time were of mixed ownership.

Also prior to the 1969 fiscal year, the budget document included a special analysis explaining the relationship between the federal sector of the national income accounts ("national income accounts budget") and the administrative budget and consolidated cash statement. The national income accounts budget is simply a presentation of the budget estimates in national income terms, indicating the relationship of the budget to the federal sector of the national income accounts. In accordance with the recommendations of the President's Commission on Budget Concepts, neither the administrative budget nor the consolidated cash statement has been utilized as a major measure of federal finances beginning with the 1969 fiscal year, but the special analysis containing the national income accounts budget has been continued.

Since the beginning of the 1969 fiscal year, the unified budget has been utilized to present the total financial plan for the government, along the lines recommended by the President's Commission on Budget Concepts in its report of October 10, 1967. The basic principles are that the unified budget encompasses all programs of the federal government and its agencies, with the outlay and deficits (of recent years) divided between the expenditure account and the loan account, and with proprietary receipts offset against outlays, regardless of the funding structure at any particular time. Payments between funds are eliminated from the totals, as is conventional in statements that consolidate data for a number of funds. The unified budget also includes a summary of congressional action on the budget (budget authority); summary of budget financing (borrowing from the public, or reduction in cash balances); total oustanding debt (gross, and amount held by the public); and, in memorandum form, the total of direct loans (in the Loan Account) and of guaranteed and insured loans outstanding.

The appended tabulation presents a comparative summary of the unified budget, with the above subdivisions, including the memorandum data.

The Commission on Budget Concepts considered it important that the "surplus" or "deficit" indicated by the budget should be calculated by comparison of expenditures other than loans with total budget receipts, for purposes of providing a measure of the economic impact of federal programs. Loans, like other government expenditures, result in acquisition of cash by recipients, and the borrowed funds will presumably be spent; however, the borrowers have assumed obligations for subsequent repayments, plus interest, which distinguish loan transactions from other expenditures in economic effects. Therefore, the separation of nonloan receipts and expenditures from loans and repayments thereof provides an expenditure account surplus or deficit as a fiscal policy yardstick (Report of President's Commission on Budget Concepts, pp.48-49).

Yet, as indicated by the appended comparative summary, the two calculations (expenditure netting and net lending) are combined for a "total budget" calculation of the budget surplus or deficit. Such combining of the two concepts makes the commission's budget surplus smaller or the commission's budget deficit greater than the expenditure account surplus or deficit, where the loan account shows the usual net lending.

The commission rejected the longstanding idea of a separate capital budget for the federal government, in the sense of separate outlays for capital goods, excluded from the total of budget expenditures in computing the budget surplus or deficit, and construction. Such outlays are left out of the current account. The commission argued that a number of foreign countries that previously used capital budgets have abandoned the practice, and that in other countries, where the "semblance" of a capital budget has been maintained, the division of transactions between those which go "above the line" in the regular budget and those which go "below the line" in the capital budget "has become so arbitrary as to make the result virtually meaningless." Moreover, the commission argued, use of a capital budget would seriously understate the current impact by the government upon the economic resources of the private sector, and thus likely lead to distortion in decisions as to allocation of resources, tending to promote the priority of expenditures for "brick and mortar" projects relative to other federal programs for which future benefits "could not be capitalized (including health, education, manpower training, and other investment in human resources)." Implicitly, this indicated a low opinion by the commission of the capitalization of future benefits from such programs under the planning-programming-budgeting system, *supra*. "Even if a capital budget were otherwise desirable, there would be a formidable array of difficult accounting problems and issues, such as the definition of assets (inclusion of military hardware, for example) and the measurement of depreciation on government property"—as if such accounting questions should be substantive blocks to the merits.

Much of the commission's position against a capital budget in conjunction with an operating budget appeared to rest on the possibility of unsound administration of such a budgetary system (e.g., "in any event, proponents of new spending programs would be tempted to stretch the capital budget rules on inclusion, so that the immediate impact of the program in increasing the current deficit, or reducing the current surplus, would be less, and the program itself therefore less visible"—pp. 33-34 of the commission's report). The merits of a capital budget-operating budget system are fundamentally that such a separation, on the contrary, would be likely to prevent bias against needed capital improvements and construction outlays, involving large outlays, because of their bulging of current expenditures, thus causing reduced surpluses or larger deficits on current basis. Current costs of such capital expenditures—debt service (interest and retirement of debt), depreciation, and operating costs—would be included in current expenditures from year to year, in conformity with the "matching principle" of matching flow of benefits from such capital improvements extending over a period of years of useful life with such current costs. Visibility of such capital

Summary Tables
Total Receipts and Outlays 1789-1992 (in millions of dollars)

Fiscal year	Receipts	Outlays	Surplus or deficit (-)
1789-1849	1,160	1,090	+70
1850-1900	14,462	15,453	-991
1901	588	525	+63
1902	562	485	+77
1903	562	517	+45
1904	541	584	-43
1905	544	567	-23
1906	595	570	+25
1907	666	579	+87
1908	602	659	-57
1909	604	694	-89
1910	676	694	-18
1911	702	691	+11
1912	693	690	+3
1913	714	715	.*
1914	725	726	.*
1915	683	746	-63
1916	761	713	+48
1917	1,101	1,954	-853
1918	3,645	12,677	-9,032
1919	5,130	18,493	-13,363
1920	6,649	6,358	+291
1921	5,571	5,062	+509
1922	4,026	3,289	+736
1923	3,853	3,140	+713
1924	3,871	2,908	+963
1925	3,641	2,924	+717
1926	6,795	2,930	+865
1927	4,013	2,857	+1,155
1928	3,900	2,961	+939
1929	3,862	3,127	+734
1930	4,058	3,320	+738
1931	3,116	3,577	462
1932	1,924	4,659	-2,735
1933	1,997	4,598	-2,602
1934	2,955	6,541	-3,586
1935	3,609	6,412	-2,903
1936	3,923	8,228	-4,304
1937	5,387	7,580	-2,193
1938	6,751	6,840	-89
1939	6,295	9,141	-2,846
1940	6,548	9,468	-2,920
1941	8,712	13,653	4,941
1942	14,634	35,137	-20,503
1943	24,001	78,555	-54,554
1944	43,747	91,304	-47,557
1945	45,159	92,712	-47,553
1946	39,296	55,232	-15,936
1947	38,514	34,496	+4,018
1948	41,560	29,764	+11,796
1949	39,415	38,835	+580
1950	39,443	42,562	-3,119
1951	51,616	45,514	+6,102
1952	66,167	67,686	-1,519
1953	69,608	76,101	-6,493
1954	69,701	70,855	-1,154
1955	65,451	68,444	-2,993
1956	74,587	70,640	+3,947
1957	79,990	76,578	+3,412
1958	79,636	82,405	-2,769
1959	79,249	92,098	-12,849
1960	92,492	92,191	+301
1961	94,388	97,723	-3,335
1962	99,676	106,821	-7,146
1963	106,560	111,316	-4,756
1964	112,613	118,528	-5,915
1965	116,917	118,228	-1,411
1966	130,935	134,532	-3,698
1967	148,822	157,464	-8,643
1968	152,973	178,134	-25,161
1969	186,992	183,640	+3,24
1970	192,807	195,649	-2,842
1971	187,139	210,172	-23,033
1972	207,309	230,681	-23,373
1973	230,799	245,707	-14,908
1974	263,224	269,359	-6,035
1975	279,090	332,332	-53,242
1976	298,060	371,779	-73,719
TQ	81,232	95,973	-14,741
1977	355,559	409,203	-53,644
1978	399,561	458,729	-59,168
1979	463,302	503,464	40,162
1980	517,112	590,920	-73,808
1981	599,272	678,209	-78,936
1982	617,766	745,706	-127,940
1983	600,562	808,327	-207,764
1984	666,457	851,781	-185,324
1985	734,057	946,316	-212,260
1986	769,091	989,815	-220,725
1987 est.	842,390	1,015,572	-173,182
1988 est.	916,571	1,024,328	-107,756
1989 est.	976,197	1,068,963	-92,766
1990 est	1,048,295	1,107,795	-59,501
1991 est.	1,123,155	1,144,445	-21,290
1992 est.	1,191,208	1,178,942	12,2672

* 500 thousand or less
Data for 1789-1939 are for the administrative budget; data for 1934 and all following years are for the unified budget.
Beginning in 1937, includes amounts for social security trust funds but are off-budget.

Source: Budget of the United States Government, Fiscal year 1988.

expenditures would be maintained by the separate capital budget, with supporting schedules of projects; by cost-benefit analysis under the planning-programming-budgeting system, which includes analysis of opportunity costs and impact upon allocation of resources; and by flow of funds analysis as to impact upon stabilization and other objectives of fiscal policy.

Full Employment Budget. This derived set of budgetary data is designed to indicated the amounts of expenditures and receipts that would occur under existing tax rates if the economy were operationg at some specified "full employment" level. The value of such data is that they provide an indication of the way in which receipts and expenditures would change as the economy moved from its existing position to one defined as "full employment." If this sort of analysis were combined with similar types of data for other sectors of the economy, information might be gleamed that would be useful in determining appropriate public policies to move toward full employment. A mechanistic adaptation of such data would be the view that if edpenditures were provided at such full-employment level, the multiplier effects would tend to create the revenues and other features of the very full employment figured.

Gramm-Rudman-Hollings Act. The act provided for automatic, across-the-board spending cuts if Congress failed to meet specified deficit targets. It also provided for deficit reductions without requiring Congress to record votes on individual programs that could have strong constituency support. The original act established deficit targets for each fiscal year beginning FY 86. The courts ruled this unconstitutional on the ground that the act vested executive power in a legislative branch officer (the comptroller general). In 1987, Congress enacted procedures designed to overcome the constitutional objections. The Balanced Budget and Emergency Deficit Control Reaffirmation Act liberalized the budget targets by extending the deficit reduction timetable. The revision restored the automatic procedure for sequestration by vesting the trigger with the director of the Office of Management and Budget. As amended, the act extended the process two years, calling for a balanced budget in FY 93. Corresponding changes in the deficit targets for each year were also provided. Sequestration occurs if the estimated deficit exceeds a $10 billion margin of error.

See NATIONAL DEBT, PUBLIC DEBT.

NATIONAL BUREAU OF STANDARDS Created in 1901 and organizationally within the Department of Commerce since 1903, the bureau has as its overall goal to strengthen and advance the nation's science and technology and facilitate their effective application for public benefit. To this end, the bureau conducts research and provides the following:

1. A basis for the nation's physical measurement system. A study prepared by the bureau ("A Metric America: A Decision Whose Time Has Come"), presented by the secretary of Commerce to

the Congress on July 29, 1971, recommended that the United States adopt the METRIC SYSTEM. The bureau's Institute for Basic Standards provides the central basis within the United States of a complete and consistent system of physical measurement, coordinates that system with the measurement systems of other nations, and furnishes essential services leading to accurate and uniform physical measurements throughout the nation's scientific community, industry, and commerce.
2. Scientific and technological services for industry and government. The bureau's Institute for Materials Research conducts materials research leading to improved methods of measurement standards and data on the properties well-characterized material needed by industry, commerce, educational institutions, and government; develops, produces, and distributes standard reference materials; relates the physical and chemical properties of materials to their behavior and their interaction with their environment; and provides advisory and research services to other government agencies.
3. A technical basis for equity in trade.
4. Technical services to promote public safety. The bureau's Institute for Applied Technology provides technical services to promote the use of available technology and to facilitate technological innovation in industry and government, cooperates with public and private organizations in the development of technological standards and test methodologies, and provides advisory and research services for federal, state, and local government agencies. The bureau's Center for Computer Sciences and Technology conducts research and provides technical service designed to aid government agencies in the selection, acquisition, and the effective use of automatic data processing equipment; and it also serves as the principal focus for the development of federal standards for automatic data processing equipment, techniques, and computer languages.

See COMMERCE, DEPARTMENT OF.

NATIONAL COMMISSION ON FRAUDULENT FINANCIAL REPORTING See TREADWAY COMMISSION.

NATIONAL CONSUMER COOPERATIVE BANK

A bank established by the National Consumer Cooperative Bank Act (12 U.S.C. 3001), approved August 20, 1978, to encourage the development of new and existing consumer and self-help cooperatives in the areas of health care, housing, consumer goods, and others.

The bank is governed by a 15-member board of director, appointed by the President with the advice and consent of the Senate: 8 members from among the heads of executive departments and agencies and the remaining 7 from among those members of the general public with experience in the cooperative field.

The bank operates as an independent, mixed-ownership financial institution that provides financial and technical assistance to eligible cooperatives. The bank assists in improving the quality and availability of goods and services to consumers, encourages ownership of its equity securities by cooperatives, and encourages broad-based ownership, control, and active participation by members in eligible cooperatives.

The bank provides loans to creditworthy cooperatives at a market interest rate. Cooperatives that cannot qualify for credit from the bank may be eligible to receive special financial and technical help from the bank's Office of Self-Help Development and Technical Assistance located at 2001 S. Street, N.W., Washington, D.C. 20009.

Conversion to Private Status. P.L. 97-35 provides for the orderly conversion, over time, of the bank to a private financial institution. The first step in this process was the conversion, on December 31, 1981, of class "A" notes owned by the United States. The capital of the bank consisted of this capital borrowed from the government as well as equity purchased by borrowers from the bank (class "B" stock) and by borrowers or organizations eligible to borrow (class "C" stock). The bank is authorized to raise capital through the sale of its bonds, debentures, notes, and other evidences of indebtedness. P.L. 95-351 provides that the United States is not responsible for any obligation of the bank.

P.L. 97-35, approved August 13, 1981, authorized the establishment of a nonprofit corporation (Sec. 501(c)(3) of the Internal Revenue Code of 1954) to assume the duties and responsibilities of the Self-Help Fund. This organization was created in 1982 to take over the duties of the Office of Self-Help Development and Technical Assistance, these duties consisiting of capital investment, advances and interest supplements to eligible cooperatives that do not qualify for loans from the national Consumer Cooperative Bank, technical assistance to cooperatives, research into matters relating to cooperatives, and investigations of new types of services that could be provided through cooperative not-for-profit organizations. The new nonprofit corporation will continue these activities without additional appropriated funds.

NATIONAL CREDIT UNION ADMINISTRATION

A federal administration responsible for chartering, insuring, supervising and examining federal credit unions, and for administering the National Credit Union Share Insurance Fund. The administration also manages the Central Liquidity Facility, a mixed-ownership government corporation whose purpose is to supply emergency loans to member credit unions.

A credit union is a financial cooperative that aids its members by encouraging thrift and by providing members with a source of credit for provident purposes at reasonable rates of interest. Federal credit unions serve occupational, associational, and residential groups. The idea of credit unions originated in Europe and was imported to North America in 1900. In 1908, the first legally chartered cooperative credit society was established in Manchester, New Hampshire, by a special act of the state's legislature. By 1933, enactment of state laws permitting formation of credit unions had been largely accomplished. In 1934, the Federal Credit Union Act was signed, giving additional impetus to the movement. This act provides for the chartering and supervision of federal credit unions and the insuring of member accounts of federal and state-chartered credit unions through the National Credit Union Share Insurance Fund.

The National Credit Union Administration (NCUA) was established by act of March 10, 1970 (84 Stat. 49; 12 U.S.C. 1752), and reorganized by act of November 20, 1978 (92 Stat. 3641; 12 U.S.C. 226), as an independent agency in the executive branch of the federal government. NCUA regulates and insures all federal credit unions and insures state-chartered credit unions that apply and qualify for share insurance. In size and amount of business transacted, federal credit unions have shown a steady growth. At year-end 1987 there were some 9,400 operating federal credit unions with 32 million members and more than $105 billion in assets. During 1987, federal credit unions paid more than $5.6 billion in dividends to their shareholder members. Loans outstanding were in excess of $64.1 billion.

The NCUA board grants federal charters to groups sharing a common bond of occupation, association, or groups within a well-defined neighborhood, community, or rural district.

The act of October 19, 1970 (84 Stat. 994; 12 U.S.C. 1781 et seq.), provides for a program of share insurance. The insurance is mandatory for federal credit unions and for state-chartered credit unions in 12 states (Alabama, Arkansas, Connecticut, Maine, Michigan, Minnesota, Mississippi, Nebraska, North Dakota, South Carolina, Vermont, and Wisconsin), while optional for other state-chartered credit unions that meet NCUA standards. Credit union members' accounts are insured up to $100,000. The National Credit Union Share Insurance Fund requires each insured credit union to place and maintain a 1% deposit of its insured savings with the insurance fund.

Members of credit unions exercise democratic control of the credit union by attending and participating in regular and special membership meetings, and by electing the board of directors. In encouraging members to save, a credit union may offer a variety of share accounts: regular shares, share drafts, share certificates, money markets, and retirement plan accounts. Other accounts include escrow, nonmember, and public unit accounts. Share accounts and share certificate accounts are the credit union's primary source of funds. Loans to members represent a federal credit union's major investment. The board of directors has the responsibility for setting written loan policies and is afforded considerable flexibility by Section 107(5) of the Federal Credit Union Act and Section 701.21 of the NCUA Rules and Regulations. A federal credit union may grant unsecured and secured loans. Unsecured loans are consumer-type loans. Comaker loans, share-secured loans, and automobile loans are common types of secured loans. Of significance are the following other kinds of secured loans: home equity loans, residential real estate loans, member business loans, line of credit and open-end loans, and guaranteed and insured loans.

NATIONAL CURRENCY

The National Credit Union Share Insurance Fund (NCUYSIF) was launched without the benefit of appropriated or taxpayer monies. The fund is managed under the direction of a three-person NCUA board and is audited annually by an independent accounting firm.

Congress created the Central Liquidity Facility (CLF) within NCUA to improve general financial stability by providing credit unions with a source of loans to meet their liquidity needs such as banks and savings and loan associations have available to them through the Federal Reserve System and Federal Home Loan banks. The CLF provides loans to meet unexpected share outflows, seasonal needs, and needs arising from emergencies such as strikes, plant closings, and local or national economic difficulties. A credit union may join the CLF directly as a regular member or through a corporate credit union that is an agent member of CLF. To become a regular member, a credit union must invest ¼ of 1% of its paid-in and unimpaired capital and surplus in the CLF. An additional ¼ of 1% is on call and must be kept in liquid form.

The Community Development Revolving Loan Program for Credit Unions (Part 705 of NCUA Rules and Regulations) enables both federal and state-chartered credit unions meeting certain qualifications to apply for and receive loans of up to $200,000 at a low fixed interest rate. Participating credit unions must serve a predominantly low-income member base and provide basic financial and related services to the members in the communities they serve. Loans from the fund must be matched, dollar for dollar, by increased shares in the credit union. All loans must be repaid in full within five years.

Other laws affecting federal credit unions include Truth in Lending Act, Regulation Z; Equal Credit Opportunity Act, Regulation B; Electronic Fund Transfer Act, Regulation E; Preservation of Consumers' Claims and Defense Rule (Federal Trade Commission rule); Fair Credit Reporting Act; Real Estate Settlement Procedures Act, Regulation X; Fair Debt Collection Practices Act; Home Mortgage Disclosure Act, Regulation C; Bank Bribery Amendments Act; Currency and Foreign Transaction Act; Right to Financial Privacy Act; Soldiers' and Sailors' Civil Relief Act; Fair Housing Act; Privacy Act; Government Securities Act of 1986; Federal Election Campaign Act; state laws dealing with abandoned property; Depository Institution Management Interlocks Act; Regulation G (loans secured by margin securities); and Expedited Funds Availability Act, Regulation CC.

A federally insured credit union may merge with one or more credit unions provided they comply with requirements set forth in Part 708 of NCUA Rules and Regulations and secure the prior approval of NCUA. A federal credit union may convert to a state-chartered credit union under the provisions of Section 125 of the Federal Credit Union Act. A state-chartered credit union may also convert to a federal credit union.

If a federal credit union liquidates, the liquidation is conducted in accordance with the requirements of Part 710 of NCUA Rules and Regulations. The board is to conduct the liquidation in such a manner that the interests of the members, the insurance fund, and the creditors of the credit union are safeguarded. If the credit union becomes insolvent during liquidation, the NCUA Board may either provide assistance of the Federal Credit Union Act and restore solvency or place the credit union into involuntary liquidation and pay out the members. The same alternatives apply when an operating credit union becomes insolvent. Involuntary liquidations are supervised by NCUA and the members' shares are paid directly from the National Credit Union Share Insurance Fund up to the $100,000 insurance limit. In 1988 there were 60 liquidations of federally insured credit unions of which 35 were recorded as involuntary liquidations and resulted in a $8 million loss to the NCUSIF. The remaining 25 were voluntary liquidations that were completed without loss to the fund. In 1988, 19 of the 35 involuntary liquidations evolved into purchase and assumption arrangements whereby the fund acquires segments of the failing credit union's assets and liabilities; the remaining are merged into an acquiring credit union.

The NCUSIF uses full accrual accounting under generally accepted accounting principles (GAAP). GAAP accounting for any insurance program requires adequate estimates, or balance sheet reserves, for known and anticipated losses. Deposit insurance accounting under GAAP requires two such estimates: one anticipates future cash outlays under guarantees issued when credit unions are merged with assistance or their assets are sold to third parties. The other reserve anticipates future losses from problem credit unions, i.e., those currently classified as "weak" or "unsatisfactory." The fund's adherence to GAAP is unique among the federal deposit insurers. Key statistics on federally insured corporate credit unions are appended.

Source: Federal Credit Union Administration.

NATIONAL CURRENCY NATIONAL BANK NOTES AND FEDERAL RESERVE BANK NOTES.

NATIONAL DEBT In its restricted sense, the aggregate of bonds, notes, certificates of indebtedness, bills, and other direct obligations of the United States government. For total internal debt of the United States, public and private, *see* INTERNAL DEBTS.

Total federal government debt is customarily reported gross, without deduction for holdings of U.S. government agencies and trust funds (special issues as well as public issues). Government guaranteed debt is reported separately. In addition to interest-bearing gross debt, the total includes matured debt on which interest has ceased, and debt bearing no interest (e.g., special notes of the United States issued to the International Monetary Fund, U.S. savings stamps). Technically, currency obligations of the U.S. Treasury, consisting of U.S. notes, national bank notes (in process of retirement), and certain other currency liabilites, are also non-interest-bearing debt. Government direct obligations are further divided into marketable public issues, nonmarketable public issues, and special issues to government trust funds and agencies.

In 1987 the national debt was $2,255.3 billion, of which about 80% was held by the public in the form of bonds. It is estimated that the national debt will rise to nearly $3,000 billion in 1990.

World War I gross debt reached an absolute peak on August 31, 1919, totaling $26,597 million and averaging an interest rate on interest-bearing debt of 4.196%. The gross debt in the subsequent post-World War I period reached the lowest point on December 31, 1930, totaling $16,026 million and averaging an interest rate of 3.75%.

World War II gross debt reached an absolute peak on February 28, 1946, totaling $277,912 million and averaging an interest rate of 1.972%. On a per capita basis, these fluctuations in gross debt have been as follows: August 31, 1919, $250.18; December 31, 1930, $129.66;

Key Statistics on Federally Insured Corporate Credit Unions
December 31 (Dollar amounts in millions)

	1984	1985	1986	1987[1]	1988[2]
Number	29	29	29	30	30
Assets	$4,046.1	$9,060.6	$12,182.1	$12,473.4	$13,554.2
Loans	465.7	459.8	621.0	1,302.8	1,068.4
Shares	5,273.6	8,024.2	10,851.0	10,699.4	11,808.7
Reserves	71.0	84.1	104.1	126.8	134.9
Undivided earnings[3]	31.2	38.4	45.3	56.2	63.3
Gross income	661.9	663.9	785.5	927.5	479.2
Operating expenses	17.6	21.2	25.4	29.5	16.0
Interest on borrowed money	37.4	45.5	47.9	75.7	55.1
Dividends and interest on deposits	584.9	575.9	685.9	790.6	393.1
Reserve transfers	12.0	10.5	17.2	17.5	8.3
Net income	10.0	11.4	9.0	14.7	6.8
SIGNIFICANT RATIOS					
Reserves to assets	1.2%	0.9%	0.9%	1.0%	1.0%
Reserves and undivid. earnings to assets	1.7	1.4	1.2	1.5	1.5
Reserves to loans	15.2	18.3	16.8	9.7	12.6
Loans to shares	8.8	5.7	5.7	12.2	9.0
Operating expenses to gross income	2.7	3.2	3.2	3.2	3.3
Salaries and benefits to gross income	1.1	1.1	1.2	1.3	1.4
Dividends to gross income	88.4	86.7	87.3	85.2	82.0
Yield on average assets[4]	11.0	8.7	7.4	7.3	7.4
Cost of funds to average assets[4]	10.4	8.1	6.9	6.8	6.9
Gross spread[4]	1.4	0.6	0.6	0.5	0.5
Net income divided by gross income	1.5	1.7	1.1	1.6	1.4
Yield on average loans[4]	12.0	7.8	7.1	7.5	9.1
Yield on average investments[4]	10.8	8.8	7.5	7.6	7.3

[1] Revised
[2] Data for June 30, 1988.
[3] 1988 figure includes net income of credit unions that did not close books as of June 30, 1988.
[4] Ratios for June 1988 annualized.

ENCYCLOPEDIA OF BANKING AND FINANCE

and February 28, 1946, $1979.61. As of September 30, 1981, total gross debt, at $997.855 million, equaled $4,301 per capita, both new highs.

In management of the national debt, the Treasury is guided by the following major objectives:

1. To secure funds as much as possible from "true savers," rather than from commercial banks, in order to reduce the inflationary potential of Treasury financing during a period of rising economic activity. The Treasury is referring in this connection to the "monetization of debt" (increase in deposits) that is generated by Treasury financing through commercial banks.
2. To secure the necessary funds at as reasonable cost to the taxpayer as possible, consistent with the primary goal of contributing to sound economic growth. The computed annual interest rate on the interest-bearing public debt stood at 11.486% as of September 30, 1981, compared to 9.032% the previous year and compared to a low of 1.929% for the 1944 fiscal year-end; 3.946% as of June 30, 1929; and 4.339% as of June 30, 1921.
3. To reduce the frequency of Treasury resource to the market and otherwise plan borrowing programs consistent with appropriate fiscal policy and monetary policy.

Table appended herewith shows the gross federal debt, as of each fiscal year from 1955 to recent years.
See NATIONAL DEBT, PUBLIC DEBT.

NATIONAL DEFENSE ADVISORY COMMISSION

The prototype of defense agencies created by the Roosevelt administration to coordinate and advise on defense mobilization. In creating the commission, officially entitled the Advisory Commission to the Council of National Defense, the President acted under statute of Congress enacted in 1916, which directed the appointment of a Council of National Defense to consist of the secretary of War, secretary of Navy, secretary of the Interior, secretary of Agriculture, secretary of Commerce, and secretary of Labor. In addition, the statute further directed the commission to nominate and the President to appoint an advisory Commission to consist of not more than seven members, each whom shall have a special knowledge of some industry, public utility, or the development of some natural resource, or be otherwise qualified in the opinion of the council.

The commission was appointed May 28, 1940, to coordinate and advise in the organization of the nation's resources of men and materials for defense purposes through the following divisions:

Industrial Materials Division: Edward R. Stettinius, former chairman of the U.S. Steel corporation, chief.
Production Division: William S. Knudsen, former president of the General Motors Corporation, chief.
Transportation Division: Ralph Budde, president of the Chicago, Burlington & Quincy, chief.

Table 1 / Federal Debt at the End of Year: 1955-1986

	In millions of dollars					As percentages of GNP				
	Gross Federal debt	Less: held by Federal Government accounts	Equals: held by the public	Held by the Federal Reserve System	Other	Gross Federal debt	Less: held by Federal Government accounts	Equals: held by the public	Held by the Federal Reserve System	Other
1955	274,366	47,751	226,616	23,607	203,009	71.0%	12.4%	58.6%	6.1%	52.5%
1956	272,763	50,537	222,226	23,758	198,468	65.2	12.1	53.2	5.7	47.5
1957	272,353	52,931	219,421	23,035	196,386	61.8	12.0	49.8	5.2	44.6
1958	279,693	53,329	226,363	25,438	200,925	62.1	11.8	50.3	5.7	44.6
1959	287,767	52,764	235,003	26,044	208,959	59.8	11.0	48.8	5.4	43.4
1960	290,862	53,686	237,177	26,523	210,654	57.4	10.6	46.8	5.2	41.6
1961	292,895	54,291	238,604	27,253	211,351	56.5	10.5	46.0	5.3	40.8
1962	303,291	54,918	248,373	29,663	218,710	54.4	9.8	44.5	5.3	39.2
1963	310,807	56,345	254,461	32,027	222,434	52.9	9.6	43.3	5.4	37.8
1964	316,763	59,210	257,553	34,794	222,759	50.3	9.4	40.9	5.5	35.4
1965	323,154	61,540	261,614	39,100	222,514	48.0	9.1	38.9	5.8	33.1
1966	329,474	64,784	264,690	42,169	222,521	44.6	8.8	35.8	5.7	30.1
1967	341,348	73,819	267,529	46,719	220,810	43.0	9.3	33.7	5.9	27.8
1968	369,769	79,140	290,629	52,230	238,399	43.5	9.3	34.2	6.1	28.1
1969	367,144	87,661	279,483	54,095	225,388	39.5	9.4	30.1	5.8	24.2
1970	382,603	97,723	284,880	57,714	227,166	38.6	9.9	28.8	5.8	22.9
1971	409,467	105,140	304,328	65,518	238,810	38.8	10.0	28.8	6.2	22.6
1972	437,329	113,559	323,770	71,426	252,344	37.9	9.8	28.1	6.2	21.9
1973	468,426	125,381	343,045	75,181	267,864	36.6	9.8	26.8	5.9	20.9
1974	486,247	140,194	346,053	80,648	265,405	34.3	9.9	24.4	5.7	18.7
1975	544,131	147,225	396,906	84,993	311,913	35.7	9.7	26.1	5.6	20.5
1976	631,866	151,566	480,300	94,714	385,586	37.2	8.9	28.3	5.6	22.7
TO	646,379	148,052	498,327	96,702	401,625	36.0	8.2	27.8	5.4	22.4
1977	709,138	157,295	551,843	105,004	446,839	36.7	8.1	28.5	5.4	23.1
1978	780,425	169,477	610,948	115,480	495,468	35.9	7.8	28.1	5.3	22.8
1979	833,751	189,162	644,589	115,594	528,995	34.1	7.7	26.3	4.7	21.6
1980	914,317	199,212	715,105	120,846	594,259	34.2	7.5	26.8	4.5	22.3
1981	1,003,941	209,507	794,434	124,466	669,968	33.6	7.0	26.6	4.2	22.4
1982	1,146,987	217,560	939,427	134,497	794,930	36.5	6.9	29.6	4.3	25.3
1983	1,381,886	240,114	1,141,771	155,527	986,244	41.6	7.2	34.4	4.7	29.7
1984	1,576,748	264,159	1,312,589	155,122	1,157,467	42.8	7.2	35.6	4.2	31.4
1985	1,827,470	317,612	1,509,587	169,806	1,340,051	46.4	8.1	38.3	4.3	34.0
1986	2,130,060	383,919	1,746,141	190,855	1,555,286	51.2	9.2	41.9	4.6	37.4

Source: Department of the Treasury

Labor Division: Sidney Hillman, president of the Amalgamated Clothing Workers Union, chief.

Agriculture Division: Chester Davis, member of the Board of Governors of the Federal Reserve System, chief.

Division of Price Stabilization: Leon Henderson, member of the Securities and Exchange Commission, chief.

Division of Consumer Protection: Harriet Elliott, Dean of Women, University of North Carolina, chief.

Defense Housing Coordinator: Charles F. Palmer, president of the National Association of Housing Officials, chief.

Bureau of Research and Statistics: Stacy May, of the Rockefeller Foundation, chief.

Division of State and Local Cooperation: Frank Bane, Executive Director of the Council of State Governments, chief.

Administrator of Export Control: Lt. Col. Russell L. Maxwell, chief (coordinating with the State Department).

Coordinator of Commercial and Cultural Relations Between the American Republics: Nelson Rockefeller.

The Office of the Coordinator of National Defense Purchases was created by Executive Order in June, 1940, to maintain close contact with defense procurement agencies and the commission.

The following year, 1941, the administration of national defense was reorganized and grouped under some 35 separate divisions, agencies, and offices, and the Council of National Defense became inoperative as its functions were absorbed by these new executive agencies.

See ASSIGNMENT OF CLAIMS ACT.

NATIONAL FARM LOAN ASSOCIATIONS
See FEDERAL LAND BANK ASSOCIATIONS.

NATIONAL HOUSING ACT
Approved June 27, 1934 (48 Stat. 1246; 12 U.S.C. 1702), the act orginally had the following main provisions:

1. Insurance against loss on property improvement loans. Lending institutions would be insured against loss up to 20% of all the loans made. The loans would be made without requirement of collateral, on more reasonable terms than had been previously available. The agency providing the insurance, established by the act, would be the FEDERAL HOUSING ADMINSTRATION (FHA). This "modernization credit plan," as it was then called, was intended as a pump-priming measure to operate for one and a half years.

2. Mutual mortgage insurance on homes and low-cost housing. This was considered the heart of the program and was intended to be permanent. FHA insurance was provided for mortgages made on terms including loan-value ratios up to 80%, maturities up to 20 years, and amortization by monthly payments. Only first mortgages would be insured. The insurable amount would be related to an adequate appraisal of the property but could not exceed $16,000. Interest could be not more than 5%, or up to 6%, if the market required, and the transaction had to be "economically sound." The borrower's regular mortgage payment would include a mortgage insurance premium which the lender would pay annually to the FHA. In time, the accumulation of premiums was intended to make the agency self-supporting and possibly provide dividends for mortgagors. Insurance claims would be paid in long-term interest-bearing debentures. Debentures issued in exchange for mortgages insured before July 1, 1957, were to be guaranteed by the United States (in 1938, the guarantee was made permanent). Mortgage insurance in amounts up to $10 million on low-cost rental housing built by limited-divident corporations was also provided.

3. National mortgage associations. The FHA was authorized to charter national mortgage associations with capital stock of at least $5 million. The associations would buy and sell FHA-insured mortgages to help make mortgage money available more consistently in all parts of the country and to reduce interest rates where rates were high.

4. Insurance of savings and loan accounts. The FEDERAL SAVINGS AND LOAN INSURANCE CORPORATION was established under the direction of the FEDERAL HOME LOAN BANK BOARD to insure the accounts of savings and loan associations.

The act has been amended since on numerous occasions, although the basic provisions of the act have never needed radical revision. Revisions have included the following.

In April, 1936, the modernization credit plan was extended to April 1, 1937. The liability for losses was reduced from the $200 million authorized in 1934 to $100 million, and the amount of insurance was reduced from 20% to 10% of all loans made. The authority to insure property improvement loans, except for disaster loans, expired in April, 1937, and was not renewed until February, 1938.

The Housing Authority Act of 1937 provided for combined federal and local subsidies to reduce rents for the low-income tenants, and for local government responsibility for development, ownership, and management as a matter of federal public housing policy.

The amendments to the act in 1938 were the first important changes in the original law. Title II was rewritten, and for the first time provided for more liberal terms on new low-cost, owner-occupied homes (90% mortgages with maturities of up to 25 years). The Treasury guarantee of FHA debentures was made permanent. Property improvement loan insurance authority was restored and has been continued in effect ever since by periodic extensions. Loans up to $2,500 (so-called Class 3 loans) to finance the construction of homes was authorized under Title I; Section 207 was revised to include housing built for profit. A separate Housing Insurance Fund was established for this section. Provision was made for setting up the Federal National Mortgage Association (FNMA) to buy and sell insured mortgages. FNMA was incorporated on February 10, 1938, and was then owned and operated by the Reconstruction Finance Corporation.

On June 3, 1939, two significant amendments were made to the Act.

1. An insurance premium of not more than 0.75% was provided for the first time on property improvement loans. The administrator fixed the charge at this rate, where it remained until 1954. Several reductions since have brought it down to 0.5%
2. A prevailing wage provision for multifamily housing under Section 207 was enacted.

In March, 1941, a new Title VI, Defense Housing Insurance (later renamed War Housing Insurance), was added to the act and soon became the dominant vehicle for FHA mortgage insurance. Requirement of "ecomomic soundness" was omitted. A special insurance fund was established to provide for losses.

On May 26, 1942, Section 608 was added t the Title VI of the act to stimulate the production of rental housing for war workers.

The Veterans' Emergency Housing Act of 1946 revised and extended FHA authority to insure mortgages under Title VI of the National Housing Act. "Necessary current cost" replaced "estimated replacement cost" as the basis for determining insurable mortgage amounts.

In 1946, because of the housing emergency, alternatives to minimum property requirements for multifamily housing were made acceptable if the project was structurally sound and well designed with continuing rental appeal. Elevator structures became acceptable for the first time. Amortization of Section 608 mortgages was reduced so as to lengthen the maturity by five years or longer. Working capital requirements were reduced. Forms were simplified and procedures streamlined to facilitate quick action on applications.

In 1947, Class 3 loans under Title I of the act, which had been discontinued during the war, were revived. Congress authorized FHA insurance of short-term loans to housing manufacturers, available in seven subsequent years.

The Housing Act of 1948 provided the following: (1) Section 611 was added to Title VI of the act to encourage application of cost-reduction techniques through large-scale modernized site construction of housing (this section became inactive in 1953); and (2) 95% mortgages and 30-year maturities were authorized for the first time under Section 203 on low-cost homes, and 90% morgages with 40-year maturities under Section 207 on low-cost and cooperative projects. Various other amendments to the act were made with the object of increasing the supply of housing for families of limited income. A new Title VII was added, providing for FHA insurance of yields on rental housing for families of moderate income where no mortgage financing was involved (but no insurance has ever been written under this title). FHA authority to issue commitments on new construction under Section 603 of Title VI expired finally on April 30, 1948.

On August 8, 1949, Title VIII was added to the act, authorizing the FHA to insure mortgages on rental housing for personnel of the Armed Services upon certification by the secretary of Defense. The Housing Act of 1949 authorized a public housing program and separate slum clearance program and under Title I, provided for an urban development program that later evolved into the "urban renewal" program. This act was the first housing act to specify the goal of "a decent home and suitable living environment for every American family."

The Housing Act of April 20, 1950, amended the act so as to encourage greater production of housing for middle-income families. It added a new Section 8, authorizing FHA insurance of mortgages on low-cost homes in outlying areas, and a new Section 213 for mortgage insurance on cooperative housing projects.

After FHA credit restrictions had been imposed July 19, 1950, because of the outbreak of the Korean War, on October 12, 1950, Regulation X of the Board of Governors of the Federal Reserve System became effective. FHA administrative rules for insured mortgages were amended to conform substantially with its provisions, which restricted loan-value and loan-cost ratios and restricted the maturities of loans above $2,500. FHA-insured property improvement loans of $2,500 or less were subject to the provisions of Regulation W of the board of governors affecting consumer credit.

The Defense Housing and community Facilities and Services Act of 1951 added a new Title IX to the act, providing for mortgage insurance on programmed housing in critical defense areas.

Credit controls were relaxed during 1952, and by April 21, 1953, all had been removed. FHA activity under the controlled materials plan was discontinued at the end of 1952.

The Housing Act of 1954 liberalized home financing terms with special provisions included for servicemen's homes. New FHA mortgage insurance programs in conjunction with urban renewal were authorized. Title VI was made inactive. The act also rechartered the FNMA and provided it with special assistance funds for the purchase of mortgages, modified urban renewal to permit production of lower-cost housing under Section 220 FHA mortgage insurance programs, and required that a local government develop a workable program for community improvement to be eligible for the public housing, urban renewal, and subsequent Section 221(d)(3) programs.

The Capehart Act in 1955 rewrote the military housing provisions of the act.

The Housing Act of 1956 made special provision for housing for the elderly.

During 1957 and 1958, minimum down payments for home mortgage transactions were reduced. FHA regulations were amended in 1957, to make it possible for the first time for mortgagees to sell securities to the public, backed by insured mortgages. A new certified agency program initiated in 1957 proved successful in extending FHA services to smaller localities and subsequently was made nationwide.

The Housing Act of 1959 for the first time utilized the BMIR (below market interest rate) technique of subsidizing housing, in that case Section 202 direct loans for rental projects for the elderly and handicapped. It departed from previous restriction in such programs to public sponsors and operators, to extend such programs to nonprofit sponsors in the private sector.

The Housing Act of 1961 marked the entry of the FHA into the subsidization of moderate-income housing with its addition of Section 221(d)(3) to the National Housing Act, authorizing the FHA to insure long-term BMIR loans for multifamily rental housing. The FNMA was the funding agency subsidizing the loans made by private lending institutions for the difference between the market rate and the average rate paid on outstanding federal debt, on projects restricted to limited-dividend, nonprofit, and cooperative associations. Because of the subsequent rise in interest rates paid on federal debt to about the 4% level in 1965, the Housing Act of 1965 pegged the BMIR level at no higher than 3%.

The Housing Act of 1965 also marked the new approach of direct rent subsidies; the FHA-admininstered rent supplement program, authorizing the FHA to make rental payments on behalf of qualified tenants of housing produced by limited-dividend, non-profit, or cooperative associations insured under the BMIR provisions of Section 221(d)(3), and, to lesser extent, other programs.

The Housing Act of 1968, amended and amplified by the Housing and Urban Development Acts of 1969 and 1970, on top of previous legislation, culminated in a variety of government programs and in the reaffirmation of housing goals. Section 1601 of the 1968 act specified the following goal: "The Congress finds that the supply of the Nation's housing is not increasing rapidly enough to meet the national housing goal, established in the Housing Act of 1949, of the 'realization as soon as feasible of the goal of a decent home and a suitable living environment for every American family.' The Congress reaffirms this national housing goal and determines that it can be substantially achieved within the next decade by the construction or rehabilitation of twenty-six million housing units, six million of these for low and moderate income families."

The following were among the specific programs of the 1968 act:

1. Section 235 provided for insurance of mortgages from private lenders to lower-income families at market rates of interest, with down payments as low as $200, applicable to new and substantially rehabilitated housing units, including one- or two-family homes, condominiums, and cooperative apartments, subject to maximum mortgage amounts; the FHA would make monthly payments on behalf of the homeowner to the mortgagee in the amount necessary to make up the difference between 20% of the family's monthly income and the required monthly payments under the mortgage for principal, interest, taxes, insurance, and mortgage insurance premium; payment limits would be the difference between the market interest rate and 1%.
2. Section 235(j) provided for assistance to lower-income families in acquiring standard existing or rehabilitated homes through purchase from nonprofit and public sponsors. The project mortgage, covering all of the dwelling units, was insured under Section 235(j)(1). During the period of rehabilitation, the nonprofit sponsor would pay interest on the advances made at the market rate, but after final approval by the Department of Housing and Urban Development, the lender would receive interest reduction payments which would bring the sponsor's interest rate down to 1%. Upon sale of individual units to qualified purchasers, the individual mortgage was insured under, and assistance payments were made on behalf of, the homeowner. Only nonprofit sponsors were eligible.
3. Section 236 provided for interest subsidies paid to the mortgage lender in order to reduce rents, and carrying charges for tenants in rental and cooperative units. Each tenant and cooperative owner would pay charges equivalent to 25% of monthly income; the interest subsidies could reduce payments on a project mortgage to the amount required for a mortgage bearing an interest rate of 1%. This Section 236 program modified the Section 221(d)(3) BMIR program and would probably replace it.

Among other provisions were Section 103(a), adding new Section 223(e) to the National Housing Act, which allowed the FHA to relax its standards for approving mortgage insurance on low- and moderate-income housing in older and declining urban areas; Section 102(a), adding Section 237 to the National Housing Act, which allowed the FHA to relax its credit standards for purchasers of low- and moderate-income housing; creation of the National Corporation for Housing Partnerships, designed as a federally chartered and privately funded corporation to organize a national housing partnership involving the participation of private investors in low- and moderate-income housing; various provisions pertaining to subsidizing low-rent public housing, to a new form of phased urban renewal (neighborhood development program) with increased grants for rehabilitation and redevelopment of blighted areas and projects in the selected Model Cities programs, and to leasing of land in urban renewal areas at written-down prices for housing assisted under the new low- and moderate-income housing programs; and specification that a majority of housing units in a subsidized project redeveloped for predominantly residential uses had to be for low- and moderate-income families, with at least 20% of such units allocated for low-income families or individuals.

In addition, the former Federal National Mortgage Association was split into two separate corporations: a new FEDERAL NATIONAL MORTGAGE ASSOCIATION (FNMA), a government-sponsored private corporation devoted entirely to providing liquidity and stability to the home mortgage market by the buying and selling of FHA-insured and VA-guaranteed mortgages, and the new GOVERNMENT

NATIONAL MORTGAGE ASSOCIATION (GNMA), which operates as a public agency, administering the special subsidy functions for federally assisted housing programs.

The GNMA covers the programs of the Department of Housing and Urban Development to assist in making mortgage credit available and to stabilize financing of selected types of mortgage loans. These activities include GNMA management and liquidating functions, the guarantee of mortgage-backed securities, and trustee functions in connection with participation certificates that are backed by loan obligations of various agencies.

1983 Assistance under Sections 235 and 236. For 1983, no new activity was planned under the Section 235 program, which provided home ownership subsidies for lower-income families. The Housing and Urban Development Act of 1968, as amended, authorized the Section 236 rental housing assistance program, which subsidized the monthly mortgage payment that an owner of a rental or cooperative project was required to make; this interest subsidy reduced rents for lower-income tenants.

"Troubled projects operating subsidies" provided payments to owners of eligible multifamily housing projects insured or formerly insured under the national Housing Act, as amended, under the Housing and Community Development Amendments of 1978. These subsidies were intended to prevent potential losses to the Federal Housing Administration Fund resulting from project insolvency and to preserve these projects as a viable source of housing for low- and moderate-income tenants. Funding was provided for essential repairs to correct deficiencies from deferred maintenance. No appropriation was requested for 1983; however, an estimated carry-over balance of $8 million, together with an estimated $24 million from the Rental Housing Assistance Fund, would be used to provide $32 million in financial assistance to approximately 98 projects.

For 1983, the budget proposed a major reform to the basic Section 8 program (housing assistance payments program, authorized by the Housing and Community Development Act of 1974, providing housing assistance payments to participating private owners and public housing agencies to provide housing for low-income families at rents they could afford), involving also the Section 202 elderly housing loan program of the Housing Act of 1959. All subsidies for new construction or substantial rehabilitation would be discontinued except for 10,000 units financed under the Section 202 loan program. All other activity in 1983 would be directed toward existing housing and would "make use of a revised, more cost-effective subsidy mechanism"—based on the concept of providing to eligible low-income households housing certificates which will permit them to find decent housing in the private market. While the subsidy would be based on the difference between an established rent payment standard for each market and a fixed percentage of family income, tenants would be given much greater freedom to determine how much of their income they actually would spend to obtain standard housing. In addition, program administration was expected to be much less complex under the housing certificate approach and the actual subsidy costs lower.

Summary. The FHA, formerly criticized as stimulating the exodus from the cities to the suburbs by facilitating the ownership of the one-family home, beginning in 1961 has been provided statutorily with a variety of subsidized programs to aid moderate- and low-income urban housing. The number and variety of public housing programs have also been expanded since the Housing Act of 1937. Regretably, the pressure to achieve results, combined with loose administration and controls, led to abuses and fraud in attracting private enterprise to programs in the early 1970s. With recognition of the "bankruptcy of subsidized housing" had emerged a new approach of giving needy families the means to find good housing for themselves, by subsidizing demand for housing by families, instead of designing programs to stimulate the supply side by subsidies.

NATIONAL INCOME

Net value of all goods and services produced, at "factor cost." National income is specifically derived as follows. Gross national product (market value of the output of final goods and services produced, before deduction of depreciation charges and other allowances for business and institutional consumption of durable capital goods) less depreciation and other allowances for consumption of capital equals net national product. Net national product less indirect business taxes, nontax liability, business transfer payments, current surplus of government enterprises minus subsidies, and "statistical discrepancy" equals national income.

In turn, national income minus undistributed corporate profits, corporate profits tax liability, corporate inventory valuation adjustment, contributions for social insurance, and excess of wage accruals over disbursements, plus net interest paid by government, government transfer payments, and business transfer payments, equals personal income.

Study and development of estimates of the national income were begun originally by the U.S. Department of Commerce in 1932, pursuant to 'Senate Resolution 220, 72nd Congress, which directed the secretary of Commerce to prepare a report including "estimates of the portions of the national income originating from agriculture, manufacturing, mining, transportation and other gainful industries and occupations, and estimates of the distribution of the national income in the form of wages, rents, royalties, dividends, profits, and other types of payments." The first report was issued in 1934 (Senate Document No. 124, 73d Congress), covering the years 1929-1932. The estimates have been compiled regularly in succeeding years.

Following pioneering work in concepts and methodology, as well as early estimates of national income by King, Kuznets, Martin, the National Bureau of Economic Research, and the National Industrial Conference Board, the Department of Commerce published its first estimates in 1935, covering the years 1929-1934. (The empirical development and use of the necessary data and the methodology followed in estimating the various income and product components are outlined in *National Income—1954 Edition*, U.S. Department of Commerce; data sources and procedures are discussed in Chapter 8 of *U.S. Income and Output*. 1958, U.S. Department of Commerce.) Beginning in 1951, the Department of Commerce has also published figures in "constant" dollars for gross national product and components (current dollar figures deflated by price deflator indexes). GNP data are published by the Department of Commerce quarterly, on a seasonally adjusted annual basis, in releases to the press and in its *Survey of Current Business*; the July issue of this publication in particular, and on occasion the August issue, contains comprehensive data on the national income and gross national product accounts, including any revisions of current and historical data called for, with explanation of the sources and nature of the revisions.

Gross national product is designed to be the most comprehensive measure of the output of the economy. It takes into account the value of all final products currently produced, including both capital goods and commodities available for current consumption, together with change in inventories of all types of goods. These goods and services are valued as nearly as possible at market prices, and no deduction from the total is made for the value of fixed capital used up in the process of production, i.e., depreciation and other capital consumption allowances. Only value added in successive stages of intermediate production is included, in order to avoid duplication. Also, the series is confined strictly to goods and services currently produced. It does not attempt to measure all transactions or changes in value. Hence, transfers of real estate, securities, and other existing assets are not taken into account. Likewise, capital gains and losses and gambling and other windfall profits are excluded, as well as payments such as unemployment compensation or pensions which are not related to current production. Because of its comprehensiveness, GNP is not as sensitive to cyclical influences as the most sensitive component, gross private domestic investment (new construction, including residential excluding farm, nonresidential excluding farm, public utilities, farm construction, petroleum and natural gas well drilling, and other private and new public construction; producers' durable equipment; and change in business and farm inventories). Other components of GNP are personal consumption expenditures, net exports of goods and services, and government (federal, state and local) purchases of goods and services.

National income is a summation of the amounts earned by labor, proprietors and landlords, corporation, and lenders (compensation of employees, proprietors' and rental income, corporate profits, and net interest) on account of current production, after allowance for depreciation and other capital consumption allowances. Like the GNP, national income also leaves out capital gains, including profits or losses arising from changes in inventory values due to price fluctuations. It also excludes indirect business taxes such as excises since they are not a reward to any of the factors of production, although they are included in market prices and hence in the GNP. The national income series, therefore, is more suitable than the GNP for studies of income distribution or for the analysis of long-range problems when weight should be given to the maintenance and replacement of fixed capital.

Personal income figures are especially useful for short-range economic analysis. They include only income actually received by persons (including nonprofit institutions and unincorporated enterprises as well as individuals) in cash or in kind. Thus, they exclude the retained earnings of corporations, which are not available for expenditure by persons. They include, on the other hand, Social Security benefits and other "transfer payments," which are not derived from factor payments in production but which are available for private expenditure. Personal income minus personal taxes and nontax liabilities is known as disposable personal income. The latter series is the basis for many studies of consumer expenditure and saving. Disposable personal income minus personal consumption expenditures equals personal saving.

As indicated in "The National Income and Product Accounts of the United States: An Introduction to the Revised Estimates for 1929-1980," in the December, 1980, issue of the *Survey of Current Business*, the Bureau of Economic Analysis (BEA) of the Department of Commerce completed a comprehensive revision of the national income and product accounts, the seventh of its kind. Such a revision, often called a benchmark revision, is the occasion for the incorporation of newly available and revised source data; the improvement of de4finitisons, classifications, and estimating procedures; the introduction of new series; and the redesign of tables to make them more convenient and informative. The appended tables, show national income by industry type or income fro selected years. The third Table shows Gross National Product, Net National Product, National Income, and Personal Income for selected years: 1960-19.

BIBLIOGRAPHY

EISNER, R. *The Total Incomes System of Accounts*, 1989.

Table 1 / Gross National Product, 1929–1981
(billions of dollars except as noted)

Year	Gross national product	Personal consumption expenditures	Gross private domestic investment	Net exports	Exports	Imports	Total	Total	National defense	Non-defense	State and local	Percent change from preceding period, gross national product*
1929	103.4	77.3	16.2	1.1	7.0	5.9	8.8	1.4	-	-	7.4	6.5
1933	55.8	45.8	1.4	.4	2.4	2.0	8.2	2.1	-	-	6.1	-4.2
1939	90.9	67.0	9.3	1.2	4.6	3.4	13.5	5.2	1.2	3.9	8.3	7.0
1940	100.0	71.0	13.1	1.8	5.4	3.6	14.2	6.1	2.2	3.9	8.1	10.0
1941	125.0	80.8	17.9	1.5	6.1	4.7	24.9	16.9	13.7	3.2	8.0	25.0
1942	158.5	88.6	9.9	.2	5.0	4.8	59.8	52.0	49.4	2.6	7.8	26.7
1943	192.1	99.4	5.8	-1.9	4.6	6.5	88.9	81.3	79.7	1.6	7.5	21.3
1944	210.6	108.2	7.2	-1.7	5.5	7.2	97.0	89.4	87.4	2.0	7.6	9.6
1945	212.4	119.5	10.6	-.5	7.4	7.9	82.8	74.6	73.5	1.1	8.2	.9
1946	209.8	143.8	30.7	7.8	15.1	7.3	27.5	17.6	14.8	2.8	9.9	-1.2
1947	233.1	161.7	34.0	11.9	20.2	8.3	25.5	12.7	9.0	3.7	12.8	11.1
1948	259.5	174.7	45.9	6.9	17.5	10.5	32.0	16.7	10.7	6.0	15.3	11.3
1949	258.3	178.1	35.3	6.5	16.3	9.8	38.4	20.4	13.2	7.2	18.0	-.5
1950	286.5	192.0	53.8	2.2	14.4	12.2	38.5	18.7	14.0	4.7	19.8	10.9
1951	330.8	207.1	59.2	4.4	19.7	15.3	60.1	38.3	33.5	4.8	21.8	15.5
1952	348.0	217.1	52.1	3.2	19.1	15.9	75.6	52.4	45.8	6.5	23.2	5.2
1953	366.8	229.7	53.3	1.3	18.0	16.7	82.5	57.5	48.6	8.9	25.0	5.4
1954	366.8	235.8	52.7	2.5	18.7	16.2	75.8	47.9	41.1	6.8	27.8	.0
1955	400.0	253.7	68.4	3.0	21.0	18.0	75.0	44.5	38.4	6.0	30.6	9.0
1956	421.7	266.0	71.0	5.3	25.0	19.8	79.4	45.9	40.2	5.7	33.5	5.4
1957	444.0	280.4	69.2	7.3	28.1	20.8	87.1	50.0	44.0	5.9	37.1	5.3
1958	449.7	289.5	61.9	3.3	25.2	21.0	95.0	53.9	45.6	8.3	41.1	1.3
1959	487.9	310.8	78.1	1.4	24.8	23.4	97.6	53.9	45.6	8.3	43.7	8.5
1960	506.5	324.9	75.9	5.5	28.9	23.4	100.3	53.7	44.5	9.3	46.5	3.8
1961	524.6	335.0	74.8	6.6	29.9	23.3	108.2	57.4	47.0	10.4	50.8	3.6
1962	565.0	355.2	85.4	6.4	31.8	25.4	118.0	63.7	51.1	12.7	54.3	7.7
1963	596.7	374.6	90.9	7.6	34.2	26.6	123.7	64.6	50.3	14.3	59.0	5.6
1964	637.7	400.5	97.4	10.1	38.8	28.8	129.8	65.2	49.0	16.2	64.6	6.9
1965	691.1	430.4	113.5	8.8	41.1	32.3	138.4	67.3	49.4	17.8	71.1	8.4
1966	756.0	465.1	125.7	6.5	44.6	38.1	158.7	78.8	60.3	18.5	79.8	9.4
1967	499.6	490.3	122.8	6.3	47.3	41.0	180.2	90.9	71.5	19.5	89.3	5.8
1968	873.4	536.9	133.3	4.3	52.4	48.1	199.0	98.0	76.9	21.2	101.0	9.2
1969	944.0	581.8	149.3	4.2	57.5	63.3	208.8	97.6	76.3	21.2	111.2	8.1
1970	992.7	621.7	144.2	6.7	65.5	69.0	220.1	95.7	73.6	22.2	124.4	8.2
1971	1,077.6	672.2	166.4	4.1	68.8	64.7	234.9	96.2	70.2	26.0	138.7	8.6
1972	1,185.9	737.1	195.0	.7	77.5	76.7	253.1	101.7	73.1	28.5	151.4	10.1
1973	1,326.4	812.0	229.8	14.2	109.6	95.4	270.4	102.0	72.8	29.1	168.5	11.8
1974	1,434.2	888.1	228.7	13.4	146.2	132.8	304.1	111.0	77.0	33.9	193.1	8.1
1975	1549.2	976.4	206.1	26.8	154.9	128.1	339.9	122.7	83.0	39.7	217.2	8.0
1976	1,718.0	1,084.3	257.9	13.8	170.9	157.1	362.1	129.2	88.0	43.2	232.9	10.9
1977	1,918.0	1,205.5	322.3	-4.2	193.3	187.5	394.5	143.9	93.3	50.6	250.6	11.6
1978	2,163.8	1,346.4	386.5	-1.1	219.1	220.3	432.1	154.8	100.2	53.3	278.3	-
1979	2,418.5	1,507.1	423.0	13.2	281.3	268.1	474.3	168.3	119.4	56.5	306.0	-
1980	2,633.1	1,667.1	402.3	25.2	339.2	314.0	538.3	197.1	131.4	65.8	341.2	-
1981	2,937.7	1,843.2	471.5	26.0	367.3	341.3	597.4	229.5	154.3	75.2	368.9	-

Source: Department of Commerce, Bureau of Economic Analysis.
*Changes are based on unrounded data and therefore may differ slightly from changes computed from data shown here.

Table 2 / National Income by Industry
(Billions of dollars)

	1960	1965	1970	1975	1980	1985	1987
National income without capital consumption adjustment	428.6	583.6	835.1	1,315.0	2,263.9	3,398.6	3,644.4
Domestic industries	425.1	577.8	827.8	1,297.4	2,216.3	3,363.3	3,614.9
Private industries	371.6	500.8	695.4	1,088.3	1,894.5	2,867.6	3,085.7
Agriculture, forestry, fisheries	17.8	21.0	25.9	46.5	61.4	81.5	88.2
Mining	5.6	6.1	8.4	21.2	43.8	30.4	31.0
Construction	22.5	32.3	47.4	69.9	126.6	185.1	196.7
Manufacturing	125.3	171.6	215.6	317.5	532.1	686.4	727.4
Durable goods	73.4	105.6	127.7	185.0	313.7	405.7	419.4
Nondurable goods	52.0	66.1	87.9	132.5	218.4	280.7	308.0
Transportation, public utilities	35.8	47.0	64.4	101.1	177.3	266.6	276.8
Transportation	18.5	23.7	31.5	48.0	85.8	112.8	120.7
Communication	8.2	11.5	17.6	26.8	48.1	73.6	76.3
Electric, gas, and sanitary services	9.1	11.7	15.2	26.2	43.4	80.2	79.9
Wholesale trade	25.0	32.5	47.5	83.0	143.3	203.4	213.6
Retail trade	41.3	55.1	79.9	123.1	189.4	298.8	316.2
Finance, insurance, and real estate	51.3	67.4	96.4	143.9	279.5	475.5	524.0
Services	46.9	67.9	109.8	182.1	341.0	639.8	711.6
Government, government enterprises	53.5	76.9	132.4	209.1	321.8	495.7	529.2
Rest of the world	3.5	5.8	7.3	17.5	47.6	34.9	29.5

Source: Bureau of Economic Analysis, U.S. Commerce Department.

Table 3 / National Income by Type of Income
(Billions of dollars)

	1960	1965	1970	1975	1980	1986	1987
National income	424.9	585.2	832.6	1,289.1	2,203.5	3,437.1	3,678.7
Compensation of employees	296.7	399.8	618.3	948.7	1,638.2	2,507.1	2,683.4
Wages and salaries	272.8	363.7	551.5	814.7	1,372.0	2,094.0	2,248.4
Government	49.2	69.9	117.1	176.1	260.1	393.7	420.1
Other	223.7	293.8	434.3	638.6	1,111.8	1,700.3	1,828.3
Supplements to wages, salary	23.8	36.1	66.8	134.0	266.3	413.1	435.0
Employer contrib. for social ins.	12.6	18.3	34.3	68.0	127.9	217.0	227.1
Other labor income	11.2	17.8	32.5	65.9	138.4	196.1	207.9
Proprietors' income	52.1	65.1	80.2	125.4	180.7	286.7	312.9
Farm	11.6	13.0	14.7	25.4	20.5	36.4	43.0
Nonfarm	40.5	52.1	65.4	100.0	160.1	250.3	270.0
Rental income of persons	15.3	18.1	18.2	13.5	6.6	12.4	18.4
Corp. prof., with inv. adjust	49.8	76.2	69.5	123.9	194.0	298.9	310.4
Corp. profits before tax	49.9	77.4	76.0	134.8	237.1	236.4	276.7
Corp. profits tax liability	22.7	30.9	34.4	50.9	84.8	106.6	133.8
Corp. profits after tax	27.2	46.5	41.7	83.9	152.3	129.8	142.9
Dividends	12.9	19.1	22.5	29.6	54.7	88.2	95.5
Undistributed profits	14.3	27.4	19.2	54.3	97.6	41.6	47.4
Inventory valuation adj.	-.2	-1.2	-6.6	-11.0	-43.1	8.3	-18.0
Net interest	11.3	20.9	41.2	83.8	200.9	331.9	353.6

Source: Bureau of Economic Analysis, U.S. Commerce Department.

PYATT, G. and ROUND, J. I. *Social Accounting Matrices*, 1985.
UNITED NATIONS. *Handbook of National Accounting*, 1986.

NATIONAL INDUSTRIAL CONFERENCE BOARD

A board founded in May, 1916, to provide a bureau of scientific research, a clearinghouse of information, a forum for discussion, and a means of cooperative action on matters vitally affecting the industrial development of the United States. The fundaments purpose of the conference board is to bring together the collective experience of those engaged in industry and the pertinent industrial facts secured by scientific inquiry and to translate knowledge and matured opinion into constructive action by the application of trained judgment.

The National Industrial Conference Board was organized with a directorate of executives in the principal branches of U.S. industry and with a trained staff of economists, statisticians, and engineers. Leading industrialists serve as officers and executive members of the board. The conference board is not a commercial organization. The major part of its income is derived from voluntary contributions of optional amounts from all classes of employers and others interested in the welfare of industry. Under the auspices of the board many reports, pamphlets, and books on business economics have been published.

NATIONAL INDUSTRIAL RECOVERY ACT

An act approved June 16, 1933, creating the National Recovery Administration (Blue Eagle Codes) and the Public Works Administration. Among other things the act:

1. Declared it to be the policy of Congress, in the then existing national emergency of widespread unemployment and disorganization of industry, to encourage national industrial recovery, to foster fair competition, and to provide for the construction of useful public works.
2. Covered all industries engaged in or affecting interstate or foreign commerce and provided for a comprehensive program of public works.

NATIONAL INDUSTRIAL RECOVERY ACT

Table 4 / Gross National Product, Net National Product, National Income, and Personal Income
(Billions of dollars)

	1960	1970	1975	1980	1986	1987
Gross national product	515.3	1,015.5	1,598.4	2,732.0	4,240.3	4,526.7
Less: Capital consumption allowances	46.4	88.8	161.8	303.8	455.9	480.0
Equals: Net national product	468.9	926.6	1,436.6	2,428.1	3,784.4	4,046.7
Less: Indirect business tax and nontax liability	45.3	94.0	140.0	213.3	348.4	366.3
Business transfer payments	2.0	4.1	7.4	12.1	25.1	28.1
Statistical discrepancy	-2.8	-1.1	2.5	4.9	-13.6	-8.1
Plus: Subsidies less current surplus of government enterprises	.4	2.9	2.4	5.7	12.6	18.3
Equals: National income	424.9	832.6	1,289.1	2,203.5	3,437.1	3,678.7
Less: Corporate profits with inventory valuation and capital consumption adjustment	49.5	74.7	117.6	177.2	298.9	310.4
Net interest	11.3	41.2	83.8	200.9	331.9	353.6
Contributions for social insurance	21.9	62.2	118.5	216.5	378.1	399.1
Wage accruals less disbursement	.0	.0	.1	.0	0	0
Plus: Government transfer payment to persons	27.5	81.8	185.7	312.6	496.0	520.6
Personal interest income	24.9	69.3	122.5	271.9	499.1	527.0
Personal dividend income	12.9	22.2	28.7	52.9	82.8	88.6
Business transfer payments	2.0	4.1	7.4	12.1	25.1	28.1
Equals: Personal income	409.4	831.8	1,313.4	2,258.5	3,531.1	3,780.3

Source: Bureau of Economic Analysis, U.S. Commerce Department.

3. Created the National Recovery Administration, the Industrial Recovery Board, the Federal Emergency Administration of Public Works and Board.
4. Relieved industries or integral units, during the emergtncy, from antitrust restrictions provided that they functioned under codes of fair competition, voluntary or imposed, agreements, or licenses.
5. Provided for the adoption of voluntary codes, subject to the President's approval, if the adopting body was of open, representative membership, if the code did not promote discrimination or monopolistic practices, and if labor was protected by rights to collective bargaining, prohibition of "yellow dog" contracts, and establishment of maximum hours, minimum rates of pay, and proper working conditions.
6. Provided that codes might be imposed by the President, upon his own initiative or complaint, after public hearing, to eliminate abuses inimical to the public.
7. Authorized employer-employee agreements on maximum hours, minimum rates of pay, and working conditions, standards so established to have the same effect as codes of fair competition.
8. To avoid administrative conflict with the Agricultural Adjustment Act, authorized the President to delegate to the secretary of Agriculture any of his powers and functions with respect to trades, industries, or subdivisions engaged in handling agricultural commodities.
9. Empowered the Federal Trade Commission, on the President's request, to conduct any necessary investigations.
10. Provided that violations of codes, agreements, or licenses should be deemed unfair competition to be restrained by United States district courts upon application of the attorney general or district attorneys.
11. Provided for petroleum control empowering the Interstate Commerce Commission upon the President's order to institute proceedings to control pipelines and fix rates, and that interstate transportation of petroleum drawn from storage in excess of amounts permitted by state law or regulations might be prohibited.
12. Stipulated that the Federal Emergency Administration for Public Works might function for two years, and authorized its administrator to prepare a program covering highways, water systems, conservation and development of natural resources, prevention of soil erosion, water power and electric transmission development, river and harbor improvements, flood control, low-cost housing and slum clearance, and, subject to suspension under treaty, naval and aircraft construction, army housing, motorization, and mechanization.
13. Terminated loans under the Emergency Act of 1932 and decreased the RFC's outstanding obligations $400 million.

14. Appropriated $3 billion; established a 2.5% sinking fund; allotted $400 million for state highways and $50 million for national-forest, Indian-reservation, and public-land roads; provided a $25 million revolving fund for subsistence homestead loans to facilitate population redistribution.
15. Provided for revenue from these sources: gasoline tax increase from $0.01 to $0.015; 5% excise tax on dividends paid to any one other than domestic corporations; $1 per $1,000 excise tax on corporation capital, domestic or foreign, employed in the United States; 5% excess-profits tax; all to terminate on President's proclamation at the close of the first fiscal year for which the budget is balanced or upon repeal of the Eighteenth Amendment, whichever should come earlier.

Act Invalidated. Section 3 of the act, the codes of fair competition section, was declared unconstitutional by a unanimous decision of the United States Supreme Court on May 27, 1935. The case involved in this decision was *A.L.A. Schechter Poultry Corp. et al v. U.S.* (295 U.S. 495). Highlights from the Supreme Court's decision in this case follow.

Extraordinary conditions may call for extraordinary remedies, but the argument necessarily stops short of an attempt to justify action which lies outside of the sphere of constitutional authority. Congress cannot delegate legislative power to the President to exercise an unfettered discretion to make whatever laws he thinks may be needed or advisable for the rehabilitation and expansion of trade or industry. (Delegation of legislative power by Congress to the President was the issue of this case; even Mr. Justice Cardozo, siding with the majority, wrote: "This is delegation running riot.")

In view of the nature of the few restrictions that are imposed, the discretion of the President in approving or prescribing codes, and thus enacting laws for the government of trade and industry throughout the country, is virtually unfettered.

If the commerce clause were construed to reach all enterprises and transactions that could be said to have an indirect effect upon interstate commerce, the federal authority would embrace practically all the activities of the people, and the authority of the state over its domestic concerns would exist only by sufferance of the federal government.

If the federal government may determine the wages and hours of employees in internal commerce of a state, it would seem that a similar control might be exerted over other elements of cost such as the number of employees, rents, advertising, methods of doing business, etc.

But the authority of the federal government may not be pushed to such an extreme as to destroy the distinction that the commerce clause itself establishes between commerce among the several states and the internal concerns of a state.

Without in any way disparaging this motive, it is enough to say that the recuperative efforts of the federal government must be made in a manner consistent with the authority granted by the Constitution.

NATIONAL LABOR RELATIONS ACT A 1935 act, also known as the Wagner Act. This legislation permitted the formation of labor unions that could represent workers in collective bargaining activities. One aspect of this act was the establishment of the National Labor Relations Board (NLRB) to oversee the establishment of unions and their activities.

NATIONAL METAL EXCHANGE Formerly the principal metal market of the United States, located in New York City. This exchange was merged with the COMMODITY EXCHANGE, INC. on July 5, 1933.

NATIONAL MONETARY COMMISSION The panic of 1907, perhaps the most serious monetary disturbance in the history of the United States, revealed the weakness of our banking monetary and credit system, and renewed interest in devising methods of reform. As a result of the panic and the revival of public interest in banking reform, on May 30, 1908, Congress passed the so-called Aldrich-Vreeland Law as a temporary relief measure until such time as new and thorough-going constructive banking legislation could be formulated. With this end in view, the act created the National Monetary Commission, the function of which was to make an examination of the monetary and banking systems of the leading commercial nations of the world and to submit a report. The sections creating the National Monetary Commission are as follows.

> Section 17: That a commission is hereby created, to be called the "National Monetary Commission," to be composed of nine members of the Senate, to be appointed by the presiding officer thereof, and nine members of the house of representatives, to be appointed by the speaker thereof; and any vacancy on the commission shall be filled in the same manner as the original appointment.
> Section 18: That it shall be the duty of this commission to inquire into and report to Congress, at the earliest date practicable, what changes are necessary or disirable in the monetary system of the United States, or in the laws relating to banking and currency, and for this purpose they are authorized to sit during the sessions or recess of Congress, at such times and places as they may deem desirable, to send for persons and papers to administer oaths, to summon and compel the attendance of witnesses and to employ a disbursing officer and such secretaries, experts, stenographers, messengers, and other assistants as shall be necessary to carry out the purposes for which said Commission was created. The Commission shall have power, through subcommittee or otherwise, to examine witnesses and to make such investigations or examinations in this or other countries, of the subjects committed to their charge, as they shall deem necessary.

After four years of investigation, which included a study of banking, credit, and currency systems at home and abroad, and with the cooperation of economists, bankers, and business leaders, the commission published its findings in 46 volumes, which are listed below. These volumes stimulated widespread interest and constitute one of the most informative, painstaking, scientific, and exhaustive research studies on banking, credit, and currency compiled on the U.S. banking system prior to institution of the Federal Reserve System.

Personnel. The membership of the National Monetary Commission was as follows:

Nelson W. Aldrich, Rhode Island, chairman
Edward B. Vreeland, New York, vice-chairman
Julius C. Burrows, Michigan
Eugene Hale, Maine
Philander C. Knox, Pennsylvania
Theodore E. Burton, Ohio
John W. Daniel, Virginia
Henry M. Teller, Colorado
Hernando D. Money, Mississippi
Joseph W. Bailey, Texas
Jesse Overstreet, Indiana
John W. Weeks, Massachusetts
Robert W. Bonygne, Colorado
Sylvester C. Smith, California
Lemuel P. Padgett, Tennessee
George F;. Burgess, Texas
Arsene P. Pujo, Louisiana
Arthur B. Shelton, secretary
A. Platt Andrew, special assistant to commission

In January, 1912, the commission reported in full to Congress and submitted a bill which later came to be known as the Aldrich Plan, after Senator Aldrich, the commission's chairman. Many of the best features of this plan were later embodied in the Federal Reserve Act, so that the recommendations with modifications of the monetary commission found tangible expression in the act which controls our banking, credit, and currency system today.

NATIONAL MORTGAGE ASSOCIATION Under Title III, entitled "National Mortgage Association," of the National Housing Act of 1934, authorization was provided for the organization of an association to purchase and sell first mortgages on real estate held under fee simple or under lease for not less than 99 years, and to borrow funds for the conduct of its business through the issuance of notes, bonds, or debentures in the open market. The FEDERAL NATIONAL MORTGAGE ASSOCIATION was organized pursuant to the provisions of Title III of the National Housing Act, as amended. In turn, pursuant to Section 808 of the Housing and Urban Development Act of 1968, the original Federal National Mortgage Association was split into the two present entities; the new Federal National Mortgage Association, a government-sponsored private corporation devoted entirely to providing liquidity and stability to the home mortgage market by its buying and selling operations in FHA-insured and VA-guaranteed mortgages, and the GOVERNMENT NATIONAL MORTGAGE ASSOCIATION (GNMA), which covers the programs of the Department of Housing and Urban Development to assist in making mortgage credit available and to stabilize financing of selected types of mortgage loans. GNMA activities include management and liquidating functions, the guarantee of mortgage-backed securities, and trustee activities in connection with participation certificates that are backed by loan obligations of various trustor agencies.

NATIONAL PRODUCTION AUTHORITY Organized in the Department of Commerce on September 11, 1950, by Executive Orders under the Defense Production Act of 1950. The National Production Authority (NPA) participated on behalf of the Department of Commerce in the mobilization program of the Korean War effort. Its two primary objectives were to represent the business point of view and provide business information on war-time industrial requirements and to develop administrative measures for industrial preparedness.

One specific function of the authority was to develop orders and regulations for control of materials in the civilian economy which were essential for defense requirements. The CONTROLLED MATERIALS PLAN, a full control system for the allotment of steel, copper, and aluminum, was replaced by the DEFENSE MATERIALS SYSTEM, a limited control system, on July 1, 1953. The authority also reviewed and made recommendations on applications for certificates of necessity permitting accelerated amortization under the Internal Revenue Act of 1950 on essential facilities, and reviewed applications for loans based on Title III of the Defense Production Act of 1950.

By order of the secretary of Commerce dated October 1, 1953, the NPA was abolished and its functions were merged into the Business and Defense Services Administration of the Department of Commerce.

NATIONAL QUOTATION BUREAU Established in 1913, to provide a daily quotation service on unlisted stocks and bonds for dealers and brokers, as well as a monthly summary service. The quotation service, published five days a week except stock exchange and legal holidays, is intended for houses of the better type that have a real interest in the OVER-THE-COUNTER MARKET. The service is for the exclusive use of subscribers in the offices to which the service is delivered. The bureau's standards and requirements confine the use of its service to listings that indicate a genuine interest in each security both as to quantity and price, although all wants and offerings listed are subject to previous sale or change of price. Thus upon consulting the service a subscriber refers to houses that are ready to trade on "inside" or wholesale markets for the stocks and bonds listed. The service is not intended for the public, but by facilitating the communication of buyers and sellers among trading dealers and brokers, it creates better markets in unlisted securities and thus benefits the public. As a requisite for listings in the service, a broker-dealer must have a minimm net worth of $50,000 if a corporation, and $10,000 if a partnership (revised early in 1962 from $25,000 for corporations and $5,000 for partnerships.

The service is nationwide, there being an eastern section, a western section, and coast sections. Messenger service is maintained at each of the bureau's offices in New York, Chicago, and San Francisco to collect listings from subscribers locally. Listings from subscribers located elsewhere are received by mail and by prepaid telegraph, telephone, or Bell System teletype. The monthly national corporation bond, stock, and municipal bond summaries are valuable reference sources for quotations on unlisted securities.

NATIONAL RAW SILK EXCHANGE
Merged with the COMMODITY EXCHANGE, INC. as of July 5, 1933.

NATIONAL SECURITIES CLEARING CORPORATION
The 1975 Amendments to the SECURITIES EXCHANGE ACT OF 1934 (Section 17A) established a system of regulation extending to all facets of the securities handling process, designed to promote prompt and accurate clearance and settlement of securities transactions. Clearing agencies were required to register with and report to the SECURITIES AND EXCHANGE COMMISSION, which would review the rules of such clearing agencies to determine whether they complied with the statute's objectives. The primary enforcement and inspection responsibilities over clearing agencies that are banks were assigned to whatever bank regulatory agency was appropriate. Rulemaking authority concerning the safeguarding of funds and securities by bank clearing agencies was to be shared by the SEC and the appropriate bank regulatory agency.

The 1975 Amendments allocated certain rule-making enforcement and other responsibilities between the SEC and bank regulatory agencies. This was accomplished by introducing a new term, "appropriate regulatory agency," whose definition delineated which agency would have authority over which persons or transactions. Other provisions sought to promote cooperation between and efficiency among the several regulatory agencies concerned with municipal securities dealers and the activities of transfer agents and clearing agencies.

Section 17A(e) of the 1975 Amendments also required the SEC to eliminate the physical movement of securities certificates during the settlement process. In addition, the SEC was directed, in Section 12(m), to study the practice of registering securities in "street name," i.e., in a name other than that of the beneficial owner, and to report to Congress its conclusions.

Approval of the NSCC as Clearing Agency. Among the organizations which filed application for registration as a clearing agency during the 1977 fiscal year was the National Securities Clearing Corporation. The NSCC was formed to combine the clearing operations conducted by three registered clearing agencies in New York:

1. The STOCK CLEARING CORPORATION, a subsidiary of the NEW YORK STOCK EXCHANGE;
2. The American Stock Exchange Clearing Corporation; and
3. The National Clearing Corporation, of the NATIONAL ASSOCIATION ASSOCIATION OF SECURITIES DEALERS, INC.

On January, 13, 1977, the SEC granted the NSCC's registration subject to specified conditions. This SEC order was confirmed by the U.S. Court of Appeals for the District of Columbia Circuit, which remanded the case back to the SEC for further consideration of matters of competitive bidding for the NSCC's facilities management contract and "geographic price mutualization" (GPM, the practice of charging all participants the same fee regardless of whether the participants deal with the clearing agency at its main facility or through a branch office). Pursuant to the remand, the SEC affirmed in substance both the NSCC's selection of the Securities Industry Automation Corporation (SIAC) as the facilities manager of its consolidated system and the NSCC's use of GPM, as of February 20, 1981.

The SEC viewed registration of the NSCC as a key step in achieving a national clearance and settlement system, to service the National Market System mandated by Congress in the 1975 Amendments to the Securities Acts.

"Street Name " Study. The 1975 Amendments to the Securities Acts required the SEC to examine the practice of recording the ownership of securities in other than the name of the beneficial owner (commonly referred to as "street" and "nominee" name registration) in order to determine whether the practice is consistent with the purposes of the Securities Exchange Act and whether issuer-shareholder communications could be improved while retaining the benefits of practice. In its final report, submitted in December, 1976, the SEC examined the benefits of the practice and concluded that the use of street and nominee name registration is essential to the establishment of a national system for the clearance and settlement of securities transactions and the facilitation of securities processing generally. The final report, however, at the same time recommended several steps to improve the performance of the system, including:

1. Requiring issuers to make more timely inquiries concerning the number of beneficial owners that broker-dealers represent;
2. Requiring broker-dealers to respond promptly to those inquiries;
3. Requiring issuers to supply requested proxy materials and annual reports in a timely manner; and
4. Requiring broker-dealers to forward those materials to their customers promptly.

The SEC adopted Securities Exchange Act Rule 14b-1 and amendments to Securities Exchange Act Rule 14a-3(d) to implement the recommendations.

The SEC's final report also examined the effects of the practice of street and nominee name registration of securities on the disclosure and dissemination of information regarding the beneficial owners of securities. It concluded that prevailing approaches to disclosure might not satisy fully the objective of making publicly available information identifying shareholders who potentially may influence corporate management or affect the market in an issuer's securities. Accordingly, the final report recommended legislation which would require those owners of more than 5% of an issuer's securities who are not covered by other ownership reporting requirements of the Securities Exchange Act to file with the SEC a short statement disclosing the person's identity; the number of shares; the nature of the interest; and the time and manner of acquisition. Such disclosure, among other things, was provided by legislation enacted December 20, 1977 (P.L. 95-213).

Securities Depositories. Development of the National Market System has also been facilitated by the expansion of interfaces among securities depositories. Thus in 1979 the SEC approved rule changes filed by The Depository Trust Company of New York and the Philadelphia Depository Trust Company establishing an interface between them which permits a participant in either depository to make book entry movements of securities either to its own account or to an account of another participant in the depository. This eliminates the need for the actual withdrawal and physical movement of securities in order to settle transactions among depository participants.

See DELIVERIES, GOOD DELIVERY, STOCK TRANSFERS.

NATIONAL SECURITIES EXCHANGES
See STOCK EXCHANGES.

NATIONAL SECURITY COUNCIL
Established by the National Security Act of 1947 (61 Stat. 496; 50 U.S.C. Sup. 402), as amended by the National Security Act Amendments of 1949, to advise the President regarding national security policies. The council is composed of the President, the Vice-President, the secretary of State, the secretary of Defense, the director of the Office of Civil and Defense Mobilization, and, as appointed by the President, by and with the advice and consent of the Senate, the secretaries and undersecretaries of other executive departments and of the military departments.

Under the direction of the council is the Central Intelligence Agency, Organizationally a part of the council are the NSC Planning Board and the Operations Coordinating Board. The NSC Planning Board consists of the special assistant to the President for National Security Affairs, as chairman and principal executive officer for the council, and other members of the assistant-secretary level appointed by the President on nomination of the departments or agencies participating in the council. The board's function is to formulate policy recommendations to be considered by the council. The Operations Coordinating Board is active in advising with the agencies concerned as to planning for the execution of policies adopted, in coordinating interdepartmental execution of policies and in initiating new proposals for action within national security policies. Members include the under secretary of State for Political Affairs, the deputy secretary of Defense, the director of Central Intelligence, the director of the U.S. Information Agency, the director of the International Cooperation Administration, one or more representatives designated by the President, and a representative of any other agency assigned responsibilities for implementation of national security policies dealt wih by the board.

Accordingly, the National Security Council is the highest echlon of staff agencies in the Executive Department concerned with matters involving national security.

NATIONAL SECURITY RESOURCES BOARD Functions of this agency in the Executive Office of the President were transferred in 1953 to the Office of Defense Mobilization by Reorganization Plan 3 of 1953, which abolished the board and its offices of chairman and vice-chairman.

Originally established by the National Security Act of 1947 as an independent agency, the National Security Resources Board was transferred to the executive Office of the President by Reorganization Plan 4 of 1949. Its membership consisted of a chairman and vice-chairman, appointed by the President from civilian life with the advice and consent of the Senate, and the secretaries of State, Treasury, Defense, Interior, Agriculture, Commerce, and Labor. Its function was to advise the President concerning the coordination of military, industrial, and civilian mobilization, including policies concerning industrial and civilian mobilization in order to assure most effective mobilization and maximum utilization of manpower in the event of war; programs for the effective use in time of war of natural and industrial resources for military and civilian needs, for the maintenance and stabilization of the civilian economy in time of war, and for the adjustment of the economy to war needs and conditions; and policies for establishment and conservation of adequate reserves of strategic and critical materials and for strategic relocation of industries, services, government, and economic activities essential to security.

See DEFENSE MOBILIZATION.

NATIONAL STOCK EXCHANGE Formerly this exchange had its own trading floor in the Mercantile Exchange building at 91 Hudson Street, in downtown New York City. Facilities included a relatively spacious trading floor with trading posts and the latest electronic communication and clearing systems with a widespread ticker (tape) system to carry the latest prices and quotations to interested brokerage offices throughout the country. A "specialist" system was provided to maintain steady and active markets in listed securities. As of 1971, there were ten stock specialists. The exchange had 209 individual members and 71 member firms; 49 of these were also members of the New York Stock exchange. A membership in the National Exchange was available for $500 to members of the new york mercantile exchange. The majority of its listings were over-the-counter securities.

The National Stock exchange discontinued operations on January 31, 1975, because of low trading volume.

NATIONAL WEALTH The "real" or tangible assets of a country, i.e., land, structures, equipment, inventories, etc. This concept excludes representative forms of wealth—stocks, bonds, negotiable instruments, etc.; intangible assets; and paper money.

Until publication of the estimates contained in the *Institutional Investor Study for the Securities and Exchange Commission*, the only comprehensive detailed estimates of U.S. national wealth and its components were those of Raymond W. Goldsmith (*National Wealth of the United States in the Postwar Period*, 1962), published by the National Bureau of Economic Research.

Goldsmith's study included a comparison of the structure of U.S. national wealth with that of other countries for which similar estimates were available; and its appendixes provided detailed statistics of the components of national wealth and their derivation.

The subsequent two volumes by Goldsmith and associates (*Studies in the National Balance Sheet of the United States*, 1963) presented further details on the structure and uses of the estimates. Volume 1 (by Raymond W. Goldsmith and Robert E. Lipsey) presented the main features of national and sectoral balance sheets in the post-World War II period, summarized some of the statistical problems involved in their construction, and showed how the balance sheet approach can be applied to specific problems—the influence of price changes on net worth and residential housing. Volume II presented the basic data on the balance sheets and fund flows (by Raymond W. Goldsmith, Robert E. Lipsey, and Morris Mendelson). Analysis using total flow of funds as an aggregative technique is now regularly provided by data published in the *Federal Reserve Bulletin;* the flows of funds associated with the gross national product through the four sectors of persons, business, international, and government are provided monthly in *Economic Indicators*, published by the Joint Economic Committee, and annually in the annual reports of the Council of Economic Advisers.

NATION'S ECONOMIC ACCOUNTS An ex-post reconciliation of national aggregate income and aggregate disposition of income in a given period (usually a year) by major economic sectors; a concept developed by the COUNCIL OF ECONOMIC ADVISERS. Originally termed "economic budget," the compilation has been continued in recent years in the annual reports of the Council of Economic Advisers under the heading "Group National Product: Receipts and Expenditures by Major Economic Groups," a presentation of the GNP accounts by sectors. The council explains this concept and its use as follows:

It is in the nature of the accounting concepts used that for the economy as a whole, total income received and total output (or expenditures) are always equal. The sum of the components of income, such as rents, wages, profits, and interest, must equal the value of the output of goods and services (the "triple identity"— spending equals income equals output). Thus, in the nation's economic accounts, receipts and expenditures add up to the same total, which is the gross national output or expenditure. It follows that if the receipts of any one sector of the economy exceed the expenditures of that sector, this will be balanced by an excess of expenditure over receipts in another sector. The accounts are like a snapshot taken for a given period, and the causal elements creating changes are revealed by a succession of such static pictures. Although income and expenditure for the economy as a whole are equal for any period, the expenditure of one period may differ from the income of the receding period. This results from the fact that collectively, all the economic units may wish to buy more than current output (spend more than current income), thereby stimulating increases in prices, production, or both, or they may be trying to reduce spending below the level of income and output, which tends to bring prices down, reduce production, and cause unintended inventory accumulation.

Only by rare coincidence will the aggregates of individual, business, and government decisions to spend or save match up so that the desire to save by some is exactly counterbalanced by plans to spend more than income by others. When this does happen, the economy remains stabilized at a given level of output and prices. When it does not happen, forces are set in motion that operate to change either the physical volume of activity, the price level, or both. It follows, concludes the council, that if there is to be steady expansion of the economy at stable prices, total spending in each succeeding period must rise somewhat above the income of the preceding period.

Flow of Funds Accounts. For comprehensiveness, the analytical matrix of flow of funds throughout sectors of the economy includes changes in financial assets and liabilities associated not only with current output but also with financial transactions. Originally developed by Morris A. Copeland (*A Study of Moneyflows in the United States*, National Bureau of Economic Research, 1952), the flow of funds concept has been adopted and revised by the Board of Governors of the Federal Reserve System (*Flow of Funds Accounts*, 1945-1968. 1970, provided definitions of terms and concepts).

See NATIONAL BUDGET, FOR REFERENCE TO THE NATIONAL INCOME ACCOUNTS BUDGET CONCEPT.

NATURAL GAS See GAS, for a review of both short-term and long-term concept.

NATURAL MONOPOLY Under certain circumstances it may be efficient for there to be only one supplier of a product. Such circumstances exist when the minimum efficient scale of production is very large. Because the technical nature of such a production process suggests that it is natural for the firm to be a sole supplier, the term natural monopoly is used.

In most local areas there is only one electric power company providing electricity to residential and commercial users. It is not cost efficient for there to be more than one because the minimum level of output needed to achieve economies of scale is so large. In the case of electric power, there is also a public service commission to regulate the price of the electricity.

NATURAL RESOURCES Resources that are exhausted as the physical units representing them are removed, processed, and sold. Natural resources include oil and gas reserves, timber, coal, sulphur, iron, copper, and silver ore. Natural resources are also considered long-term inventories acquired for resale or use in production over a period of years.

Natural resources are initially recorded in the accounts at their acquisition cost. The periodic allocation of the cost of a natural resource to the income statement is called depletion. Depletion reflects the physical exhaustion of a natural resource. Depreciation reflects the exhaustion of the service potential of a tangible fixed asset, such as property plant, and equipment.

The cost of a natural resource minus any residual value is systematically depleted as the natural resource is transformed into inventory. The depletion charge is usually computed by the unit-of-production method as follows:

Step 1 Compute the depletion charge per unit:

$$\frac{\text{Cost} - \text{Salvage value of the natural resource}}{\text{Estimated number of units in the natural resource}}$$

Step 2 Compute the depletion charge for the period:

Unit depletion charge x Number of units converted during the period

The Internal Revenue Code authorizes the use of percentage depletion for income tax purposes. According to the code, a percentage of gross income from the property is charged against operations when arriving at taxable income. Percentage depletion is a function of gross income rather than of production. Percentage depletion is allowable even after the cost of the asset has been fully recovered.

NEAR MONEY Highly liquid assets excluding currency, i.e., certain short-term Treasury securities and similar items. Most economist argue that other liquid assets, besides currency and demand deposits, such as time deposits, are part of the nation's overall money supply. These broader definitions of money are denoted as M_2 and M_3.

NEGATIVE AMORTIZATION A situation that arises when monthly payments on a loan are too low to cover the interest rate agreed upon in the mortgage contract. Instead of paying the full interest costs currently, the borrower pays them later—either in larger payments or in more payments. The borrower is paying interest on that interest. The lender postpones collection of the funds owed by increasing the size of the debt. In extreme cases, the borrower may lose the equity purchased with the down payment.

NEGATIVE ASSURANCE Legal and accounting expression meaning that "nothing came to our attention." Negative assurances are sometimes written by professionals to serve as a "comfort letter" to clients.

NEGATIVE GOODWILL Excess of net assets acquired over the cost of purchased subsidiary. This excess is allocated to reduce proportionately the value assigned to noncurrent assets (except long-term investments in marketable securities) to determine their fair values. Such a situation arises if a corporation acquires the shares of another corporation at a bargain purchase price, that is, at an amount that is less than the fair market value of the net assets of the acquired company.

NEGATIVE INCOME TAX A negative income tax is an alternative to our present welfare system. Under a negative income tax scheme, a family would receive a guaranteed income subsidy. As gross earnings of the family increase from $0, the negative income tax payments would decrease, but at a rate less than 100% Therefore, recipients have a financial incentive to earn additional income.

NEGLIGENCE A TORT related to behavior that results in injuries for which the perpetrator of the act may be held liable; intentional misconduct; inattention or carelessness. Typical negligence cases are associated with accidents and with medical and legal malpractice. Legal elements of negligence include:

1. Duty—the accused owed a duty of care to the plaintiff.
2. Breach of duty—the duty was breached.
3. Causation and injury—the defendant behaved in a negligent manner and caused the injury.

In evaluating the extent of negligence liability the courts consider various factors, including carelessness, causation, injury, foreseeability of injury, plaintiff's contributory misconduct, and burden of proof.

Negligence in product liability cases allows the ultimate purchaser to recover from the manufacturer in spite of the absence of privity. The plaintiff must prove that the manufacturer could foresee that a user could be injured as the result of negligence in the manufacture of the product and was negligent. The defendant's available defenses include contributory negligence and assumption of risk.

The Uniform Commercial Code provides that any person who by his or her negligence substantially contributes to a material alteration of a negotiable instrument or to the making of an unauthorized signature is precluded from asserting the alteration or lack of authority against a holder in due course or against a drawee or other payor who pays the instrument in good faith and in accordance with the reasonable commercial standards of the drawee's or payor's business.

The IRS definition of negligence has been expanded to include any failure to make a reasonable attempt to comply with the provisions of the code. The penalties also apply to careless, reckless, or intentional disregard of rules and regulations.

NEGOTIABLE DOCUMENTS All forms NEGOTIABLE INSTRUMENTS and other paper that is negotiable by mere delivery (e.g., bearer checks, drafts, or notes; bearer bonds or bond coupons) or by delivery and endorsement (e.g., order checks, drafts, or notes; order bills of lading). Technically, a negotiable instrument is one that calls for the payment of money. Since bills of lading and warehouse receipts call for delivery of merchandise they cannot be considered negotiable instruments in the technical sense, but still they may be negotiated if made order documents. The doctrine of "bona fide purchaser" in the case of securities is analogous to that of holder in due course in the case of negotiable instruments, in that when a purchaser for value, in good faith, and without notice of any adverse claim takes delivery of a security in bearer form or in registered form issued to him or endorsed to him in blank, he acquires the security free of any adverse claim in addition to acquiring the rights of a purchaser (Secs. 8-301(a) and 8-302, Uniform Commercial Code).

Negotiable documents is a term employed to designate all paper that may be negotiated, whether a negotiable instrument or not.

The principal negotiable instruments in the United States are checks, bills of exchange, promissory notes, and acceptances.

See NEGOTIABLE INSTRUMENTS LAW, NEGOTIABLE SECURITIES.

NEGOTIABLE INSTRUMENTS Written orders or promises to pay money that may be transferred from one person to another by delivery, or by endorsement and delivery, the full legal title thereby becoming vested in the transferee. The negotiation of such an instrument to a holder in due course gives such holder the same rights as held by the original payee (promisee), free from defenses (except real defenses) that might defeat them. Article 3 of the Uniform Commercial Code, entitled "Commercial Paper," is concerned with notes, drafts, checks, and certificates of deposit. Most such instruments are negotiable in form. Other types of negotiable property interests that are not commercial paper (e.g., stock and bond certificates, order or bearer bills of lading and warehouse receipts) are covered in other sections of the code, primarily Article 7.

ENCYCLOPEDIA OF BANKING AND FINANCE

NEGOTIABLE INSTRUMENTS

Laws relating to commercial paper developed among traders and merchants in Europe through customs and practices considered to be appropriate for the fair and efficient conduct of business. The body of common law provided a legal basis for the form and structure of commercial paper. At a later time, the rules of law relating to commercial paper were codified by legislation. The Uniform Negotiable Instruments Law was the first of the uniform business statutes drafted under the guidance of the Commissioners on Uniform State Laws. The Uniform Negotiable Instruments Law has been adopted by all the states and is the basic pattern for Article 3 of the Uniform Commercial Code.

A negotiable instrument is commercial paper (promissory notes, checks, drafts or bills of exchange, and certificates of deposit). A promissory note is an unconditional promise in writing made by one person to another, signed by the maker, engaging to pay on demand or at a fixed or determinable future time a sum certain in money to order or to bearer. A bill of exchange is an unconditional order in writing addressed by one person to another, signed by the person giving it, requiring the person to whom it is addressed to pay on demand or at a fixed or determinable future time, a sum certain in money to order or to bearer. A check is a bill of exchange drawn on a bank payable on demand. A certificate of deposit is an acknowledgment by a bank of a receipt of money with an engagement to repay it.

A negotiable instrument must meet the following four requirements:

1. It must be in writing and signed by the maker or drawee.
2. It must contain an unconditional promise or order to pay a certain sum in money and no other promise, order, obligation, or power except such as is authorized by Article 3 of the Uniform Commercial Code.
3. It must be payable on demand, or at a definite time.
4. It must be payable either to order or to bearer.

There is no express requirement concerning the materials with which or on which a negotiable instrument must be written. "Signed" includes any symbol executed or adopted by a party with present intention to authenticate a writing. A conditional promise or order (unnegotiable) is evident (1) if it states that it is subject to or governed by any other agreement or (2) if it states that it is to be paid only out of a particular fund or source (with some exceptions). For a sum to be certain, the amount must be capable of being calculated from data on the face of the note. To be payable in money requires that it be paid in the medium of exchange adopted by the government as its currency.

A promise is an undertaking to pay and must be more than an acknowledgment of an obligation. An order is a direction to pay and must be more than an authorization or request. Instruments payable on demand include those payable at sight or on presentation and those in which no time for payment is stated. Order paper is negotiated by the transferor's endorsing the paper and delivering it to the new holder. It is possible to negotiate bearer paper by delivery without an endorsement; however, a transferee will usually ask for an endorsement so as to obtain the advantage of the broader contract liability.

A holder in due course is one who has taken the instrument under the following conditions:

1. That it is complete and regular upon its face.
2. That the individual became the holder of it before it was overdue, and without notice that it was previously dishonored, if such was the fact.
3. That the holder took it in good faith and for value.
4. That at the time it was negotiated, the holder had no notice of an infirmity in the instrument or defect in the title of the person negotiating it.

It is generally held that a holder in due course holds the instrument free from any defect of title of prior parties, and free from defenses available to prior parties among themselves, and may enforce payment of the instrument for the full amount thereof against all parties liable thereon. The holder of a note is presumed to be the owner thereof, and may sue thereon in his or her own name.

Various forms of ENDORSEMENT include:

Special endorsement	Pay to the order of John Doe Signed: Bill Doe
Blank endorsement	Signed: Bill Doe
Restrictive endorsement	Pay to John Doe only Signed: Bill Doe
Qualified endorsement	Pay without recourse to order of John Doe Signed: Bill Doe
Conditional endorsement	On the election of the mayor in Greensboro, NC, Pay to the order of John Doe Signed: Bill Doe

An unqualified endorser, who receives consideration, warrants to the transferee and to any subsequent holder who receives the instrument in good faith:

1. That the endorser has good title to the instrument, or represents a person with title, and that the transfer is otherwise rightful.
2. That all signatures are genuine or authorized.
3. That the instrument has not been materially altered.
4. That no defense of any prior party is good against him or her.
5. That the endorser has no knowledge of any insolvency proceeding involving the payor.

A transferor without endorsement, who receives consideration, warrants to the transferee only who receives the instrument in good faith the same warranties.

Unless the instrument specifies otherwise, two or more persons (multiple signers) who sign as maker, acceptor, drawer, or endorser and as a part of the same transactions are jointly and severally liable. An accommodation party is one who signs the instrument in any capacity for the purpose of lending his or her name to another party to it. When the instrument has been taken for value before it is due, the accommodation party is liable in the capacity in which he or she has signed.

An unqualified endorser is released from liability on his endorser's promise if the holder failed to make due presentment to the payor or to give the endorser prompt notice of the payor's dishonor. The lability of a person on commercial paper may be discharged by (1) cancellation or renunciation and (2) discharge of secondary liability by changing primary contract.

An instrument is dishonored when a necessary or optional presentment is duly made and due acceptance or payment is refused or cannot be obtained within the prescribed time.

The Uniform Negotiable Instrument Act states that "where a signature is forged or made without authority of the person whose signature it purports to be, it is totally inoperative, and no right to retain the instrument, or to give a discharge, or to enforce payment thereof against any party thereto, give a discharge, or to enforce payment thereof against any party thereto, can be acquired through or under such signature, unless the party, against whom it is sought to enforce such right, is precluded from setting up the forgery or want of authority."

The act also states that "an instrument is not invalid for the reason only that it is antedated or past-dated, provided this is not done for an illegal or fraudulent purpose. The person to whom an instrument so dated is delivered, acquired title thereto as of the date of delivery."

The act states that "where a negotiable instrument is materially altered without the assent of all parties liable thereon, it is voided, except as against a party who has himself made, authorized or assented to the alteration and subsequent indorser. But when an instrument has been materially altered and is in the hands of a holder in due course, not a party to the alteration, he may enforce payment thereon according to its original tenor." However, any person who by his negligence substantially contributes to a material alteration of the instrument or to the making of an authorized signature is precluded from asserting the alteration or lack of authority against a holder in due course or against a drawee or other payor who pays the instrument in good faith and in accordance with the reasonable commercial standards of the drawee's or payor's business.

Banks have a debtor-creditor relationship with depositors. Even though a depositor has funds in the bank, a payee cannot force a drawee bank to make payments. The drawer could possibly have an action against a bank-drawee for wrongfully dishonoring a check. Generally, banks are not obligated to pay on a check presented more than six months after date but can pay in good faith and charge the customer's account. Banks are liable to a drawer for payment on bad checks unless the drawer was negligent. Drawer is required to promptly examine returned checks for irregularities or be held liable for bank's losses resulting from insufficient care and vigilance. A bank is considered to know the signature of endorsers and can collect from the party that cashed the check. Generally, oral stop payment orders are good for 14 days; written stop payment orders are good for six months and are renewable. A bank is entitled to a depositor's endorsement on deposited checks. If the endorsement is missing, the bank can supply it.

Contradictions sometimes appear in negotiable instruments. Generally the following rules apply: words control over figures; hand-written terms control over typewritten and printed terms; typewritten terms control over printed terms; an instrument stating "I promise to pay" and signed by two persons which results in joint liability for both parties.

See NEGOTIABLE INSTRUMENTS LAW, NEGOTIABLE SECURITIES.

BIBLIOGRAPHY

See any university business law textbook.

American Business Law Journal.
BROWN, G. W., and others. *Business Law with UCC Applications* 1989.
CLARK, L. S., and KINDER, P. D. *Law and Business,* 1987.
Journal of Business Law.
TILLMAN, G. B., and JOUNSON, K. W. "Lender Litigation: Variable Interest Rates and Negotiability." *American Business Law Journal,* Spring, 1989.

NEGOTIABLE INSTRUMENTS LAW The law relating to negotiable instruments, which has undergone two major codifications in an attempt to achieve greater uniformity among the various states. Beginning in 1897, the original Uniform Negotiable Instruments Law (UNIL), was legislated by all the various states, with variations and departures from the "uniform" model for specific states. The Uniform Commercial Code (UCC) constitutes a more comprehensive attempt to achieve greater uniformity in the fields of sales, commercial paper, bank deposits and collections, letters of credit, bulk transfers, warehouse receipts, bills of lading, other documents of title, investment securities, and secured transactions, including sales of accounts, chattel paper, and contract rights. The UCC, first offered to the states for adoption in 1952 and first enacted by Pennsylvania in 1953, had by 1971 been adopted by the District of Columbia, the Virgin Islands, and every state except Louisiana (which, however has adopted Articles 1, 3, 4, 5, and 7).

The term "commercial paper" of the UCC comprehends "negotiable instruments," the subject of the UNIL.

Prior to the codification and enactment of the UNIL, cases growing out of litigation concerning bills, notes, and checks, were governed by case law, the so-called law merchant—a body of rules, customs, and principles that had been practiced for centuries in England and recognized legally by the law courts beginning in the eighteenth century, particularly by the famous English jurist, Lord Mansfield, sitting on the Court of King's Bench. The case law, based on the law merchant and involving litigation in modern times as well, is still resorted to in those rare cases not covered "on all fours" or on moot points arising under the codes. The first statement of the principles of the law merchant was the British Bills of Exchange Act, enacted in 1882. The U.S. UNIL was to a larger extent influenced by the English law.

The UCC is composed of ten articles, as follows:

Article 1, General Provisions. Part 1, Short Title, Construction, Application and Subject Matter of the Act; Part 2, General Definitions and Principles of Interpretation.

Article 2, Sales. Part 1, Short Title, General Construction and Subject Matter; Part 2, Form, Formation, and Readjustment of Contract; Part 3, General Obligation and Construction of Contract; Part 4, Title, Creditors, and Good Faith Purchasers; Part 5, Performance; Part 6, Breach, Repudiation, and Excuse; Part 7, Remedies.

Article 3, Commercial Paper. (Reproduced below.)

Article 4, Bank Deposits and Collections. (Also reproduced below, in view of the provision that Article 3 is subject to the provisions of Article 4.)

Article 5, Letters of Credit.

Article 6, Bulk Transfers.

Article 7, Warehouse Receipts, Bills of Lading and Other Documents of Title. Part 1, General; Part 2, Warehouse Receipts: Special Provisions; Part 3, Bills of Lading: Special Provisions; Part 4, Warehouse Receipts and Bills of Lading: General Obligations; Part 5, Warehouse Receipts and Bills of Lading; Negotiation and Transfer; Part 6, Warehouse Receipts and Bills of Lading: Miscellaneous Provisions.

Article 8, Investment Securities. Part 1, Short Title and General Matters; Part 2, Issue—Issuer; Part 3, Purchase; Part 4, Registration.

Article 9, Secured Transactions: Sales of Accounts, Contract Right and Chattel Paper. (Also reproduced below, in views of the provision that Article 3 is subject to the provisions also of Article 9.)

Article 10, Effective Date and Repealer

Because of persisting although reduced variation in the specific provisions of enacted state versions of the UCC, reference should be made to the particular state law in each jurisdiction, along with the interpretive case law of the jurisdiction, which sometimes has construed particular statutory provisions with variation as compared with other jurisdictions.

Text of Articles 3, 4, and 9 of the UCC is appended herewith, for general information and as a basis for noting the variations or departures therefrom by the particular state's statutes.

Article 3
Commercial Paper

Part I
Short Title, Form and Interpretation

Section 3-101. *Short Title.*

This Article shall be known and may be cited as Uniform Commercial Code—Commercial Paper.

Section 3-102. *Definitions and Index of Definitions.*
(1) In this Article unless the context otherwise requires
  (a) "Issue" means the first delivery of an instrument to a holder or a remitter.
  (b) An "order" is a direction to pay and must be more than an authorization or request. It must identify the person to pay with reasonable certainty. It may be addressed to one or more such persons jointly or in the alternative but not in succession.
  (c) A "promise" is an undertaking to pay and must be more than an acknowledgment of an obligation.
  (d) "Secondary party" means a drawer or endorser.
  (e) "Instrument" means a negotiable instrument.
(2) Other definitions applying to this Article and the sections in which they appear are:
"Acceptance," Section 3-410.
"Accommodation party." Section 3-415.
"Alteration." Sections 3-407.
"Certificate of deposit." Section 3-104.
"Certification." Section 3-411.
"Check." Section 3-104.
"Definite time." Section 3-109.
"Dishonor." Section 3-507.
"Draft." Section 3-104.
"Holder in due course." Section 3-302.
"Negotiation." Section 3-202.
"Note." Section 3-104.
"Notice of dishonor." Section 3-508.
"On demand." Section 3-108.
"Presentment." Section 3-504.
"Protest." Section 3-509.
"Restrictive Indorsement." Section 3-205.
"Signature." Section 3-401.
(3) The following definitions in order Articles apply to this Article:
"Account." Section 4-104.
"Banking day." Section 4-104.
"Clearing house." Section 4-104.
"Collecting bank." Section 4-105.
"Customer." Section 4-104.

NEGOTIABLE INSTRUMENTS LAW

"Depositary bank." Section 4-105.
"Documentary draft." Section 4-104.
"Intermediary bank." Section 4-105.
"Item." Section 4-104.
"Midnight deadline." Section 4-104.
"Payor bank." Section 4-105.

(4) In addition Article I contains general definitions and principles of construction and interpretation applicable throughout this Article.

Section 3-103. *Limitations on Scope of Article.*
(1) This Article does not apply to money, documents of title, or investment securities.
(2) The provisions of this Article are subject to the provisions of the Article on Bank Deposits and Collections (Article 4) and Secured Transactions (Article 9).

Section 3-104. *Form of Negotiable Instruments; "Draft"; "Check"; "Certificate of Deposit"; "Note".*
(1) Any writing to be a negotiable instrument within this Article must:
 (a) be signed by the maker of drawer; and
 (b) contain an unconditional promise or order to pay a sum certain in money and no other promise, order, obligation or power given by the maker or drawer except as authorized by this Article; and
 (c) be payable on demand or at a definite time; and
 (d) be payable to order or to bearer.
(2) A writing which complies with the requirements of this section is:
 (a) a "draft" ("bill of exchange") if it is an order;
 (b) a "check" if it is a draft drawn on a bank and payble on demand;
 (c) a "certificate of deposit" if it is an acknowledgment by a bank of receipt of money with an engagement to repay it;
 (d) a "note" if it is a promise other than a certificate of deposit.
(3) As used in other Articles of this Act, and as the context may require, the terms "draft," "check," "certificate of deposit," and "note" may refer to instruments which are not negotiable within this Article as well as to instruments which are so negotiable.

Section 3-105. *When Promise or Order Unconditional.*
(1) A promise or order otherwise unconditional is not made conditional by the fact that it:
 (a) is subject to implied or constructive conditions; or
 (b) states its consideration, whether performed or promised, or the transaction which gave rise to the instrument, or that the promise or order is made or the instrument matures in accordance with or "as per" such transaction; or
 (c) refers to or states that it arises out of a separate agreement or refers to a separate agreement for rights as to prepayment or acceleration; or
 (d) states that it is drawn under a letter of credit; or
 (e) states that it is secured, whether by mortgage, reservation of title or otherwise; or
 (f) indicates a particular account to be debited or any other fund or source from which reimbursement is expected; or
 (g) is limited to payment out of a particular fund or the proceeds of a particular source, if the instrument is issued by a government or governmental agency or unit; or
 (h) is limited to payment out of the entire assets of a partnership, unincorporated association, trust or estate by or on behalf of which the instrument is issued.
(2) A promise or order is not unconditional if the instrument:
 (a) states that it is subject to or governed by any other agreement; or
 (b) states that it is to be paid only out of a particular fund or source except as provided in this section.

Section 3-106. *Sum Certain.*
(1) The sum payable is a sum certain even though it is to be paid:
 (a) with stated interest or by stated installments; or
 (b) with stated different rates of interest before and after default or a specified date; or
 (c) with a stated discount or addition if paid before or after the date fixed for payment; or
 (d) with exchange or less exchange, whether at a fixed rate or at the current rate; or
 (e) with costs of collection or an attorney's fee or both upon default.
(2) Nothing in this section shall validate any term which is otherwise illegal.

Section 3-107. *Money.*
(1) An instrument is payable in money if the medium of exchange in which it is payable is money at the time the instrument is made. An instrument payable in "currency" or "current funds" is payable in money.
(2) A promise or order to pay a sum stated in a foreign currency is for a sum certain in money and, unless a different medium of payment is specified in the instrument, may be satisfied by payment of that number of dollars which the stated foreign currency will purchase at the buying sight rate for that currency on the day on which the instrument is payable or, if payable on demand, on the day of demand. If such an instrument specifies a foreign currency as the medium of payment, the instrument is payable in that currency.

Section 3-108. *Payable on demand.*
Instruments payable on demand include those payable at sight or on presentation and those in which no time for payment is stated.

Section 3-109. *Definite time.*
(1) An instrument is payable at a definite time if by its terms it is payable:
 (a) on or before a stated date or at a fixed period after a stated date; or
 (b) at a fixed period after sight; or
 (c) at a definite time subject to any acceleration; or
 (d) at a definite time subject to extension at the option of the holder, or to extension to a further definite time at the option of the maker or acceptor or automatically upon or after a specified act or event.
(2) An instrument which by its terms is otherwise payable only upon an act or event uncertain as to time of occurrence is not payable at a definite time even though the act or event has occurred.

Section 3-110. *Payable to Order.*
(1) An instrument is payable to order when by its terms it is payable to the order or assigns of any person therein specified with reasonable certainty, or to him or his order, or when it is conspicuously designed on its face as "exchange" or the like and names a payee. It may be payable to the order of:
 (a) the maker or drawer; or
 (b) the drawer; or
 (c) a payee who is not maker, drawer or drawee; or
 (d) two or more payees together or in the alternative; or
 (e) an estate, trust or fund, in which case it is payable to the order of the representative of such estate, trust or fund or his successors; or
 (f) an office, or an officer by his title as such in which case it is payable to the principal, but the incumbent of the office or his successors may act as if he or they were the holder; or
 (g) a partnership or unincorporated association, in which case it is payable to the partnership or association and may be indorsed or transferred by any person thereto authorized.
(2) An instrument not payable to order is not made so payable by such words as "payable upon return of this instrument properly indorsed."
(3) An instrument made payable both to order and to bearer is payable to order unless the bearer words are handwritten or typewritten.

Section 3-111. *Payable to Bearer.*
An instrument is payable to bearer when by its terms it is payable to:
 (a) bearer or the order of bearer; or
 (b) a specified person or bearer; or
 (c) "cash" or the order of "cash," or any other indication which does not purport to designate a specific payee.

Section 3-112. *Terms and Omissions Not Affecting Negotiability.*

(1) The negotiability of an instrument is not affected by:
  (a) the omission of a statement or any consideration or of the place where the instrument is drawn or payable; or
  (b) a statement that collateral has been given to secure obligations either on the instrument or otherwise of an obligor on the instrument or that in case of default on those obligations the holder may realize on or dispose of the collateral; or
  (c) a promise or power to maintain or protect collateral or to give additional collateral; or
  (d) a term authorizing a confession of judgment on the instrument if it is not paid when due; or
  (e) a term purporting to waive the benefit of any law intended for the advantage or protection of any obligor; or
  (f) a term in a draft providing that the payee by indorsing or cashing it acknowledges full satisfaction of an obligation of the drawer; or
  (g) a statement in a draft drawn in a set of parts (Section 3-801) to the effect that the order is effective only if no other part has been honored.
(2) Nothing in this section shall validate any term which is otherwise illegal.

Section 3-113. *Seal.*
An instrument otherwise negotiable is within this Article even though it is under a seal.

Section 3-114. *Date, Antedating, Postdating.*
(1) The negotiability of an instrument is not affected by the fact that is is undated, antidated, or postdated.
(2) Where an instrument is antedated or postdated the time when it is payable is determined by the stated date if the instrument is payable on demand or at a fixed period after date.
(3) Where the instrument or any signature thereon is dated, the date is presumed to be correct.

Section 3-115. *Incomplete Instruments.*
(1) When a paper whose contents at the time of signing show that it is intended to become an instrument is signed while still incomplete in any necessary respect, it cannot be enforced until completed, but when it is completed in accordance with authority given it is effective as completed.
(2) If the completion is unauthorized, the rules as to material alteration apply (Section 3-407), even though the paper was not delivered by the maker or drawer; but the burden of establishing that any completion is unauthorized is on the party so asserting.

Section 3-116. *Instruments Payable to Two or More Persons.*
An instrument payable to the order of two or more persons
  (a) if in the alternative is payable to any one of them and may be negotiated, discharged or enforced by any of them who has possession of it;
  (b) if not in the alternative is payable to all of them and may be negotiated, discharged or enforced only by all of them.

Section 3-117. *Instruments Payable with Words of Description.*
An instrument made payable to a named person with the addition of words describing him
  (a) as agent or officer of a specified person is payable to his principal, but the agent or officer may act as if he were the holder;
  (b) as any other fiduciary for a specified person or purpose is payable to the payee and may be negotiated, discharged or enforced by him;
  (c) in any other manner is payable to the payee unconditionally and the additional words are without effect on subsequent parties.

Section 3-118; *Ambiguous Terms and Rules of Construction.*
The following rules apply to every instrument:
  (a) Where there is doubt whether the instrument is a draft or a note the holder may treat it as either. A draft drawn on the drawer is effective as a note.
  (b) Handwritten terms control typewritten and printed terms, and typewritten control printed.
  (c) Words control figures except that if the words are ambiguous, figures control.
  (d) Unless otherwise specified, a provision for interest means interest at the judgment rate at the place of payment from the date of the instrument, or if it is undated from the date of issue.
  (e) Unless the instrument otherwise specifies, two or more persons who sign as maker, acceptor or drawer or indorser and as a part of the same transaction are jointly and severally liable even though the instrument contains such words as "I promise to pay."
  (f) Unless otherwise specified, consent to extension authorizes a single extension for not longer than the original period. A consent to extension, expressed in the instrument, is binding on secondary parties and accommodation makers. A holder may not exercise his option to extend an instrument over the objection of a maker or acceptor or other party who in accordance with Section 3-604 tenders full payment when the instrument is due.

Section 3-119. *Other Writings Affecting Instrument.*
(1) As between the obligor and his immediate obligee or any transferee the terms of an instrument may be modified or affected by any other written agreement executed as part of the same transaction, except that a holder in due course is not affected by any limitation of his rights arising out of the separate written agreement if he had no notice of the limitation when he took the instrument.
(2) A separate agreement does not affect the negotiability of an instrument.

Section 3-120. *Instruments "Payable Through" Bank.*
An instrument which states that it is "payable through" a bank or the like designates that bank as a collecting bank to make presentment but does not of itself authorize the bank to pay the instrument.

Section 3-121. *Instruments Payable at Bank.*
Note: If this Act is introduced in the Congress of the United States, this section should be omitted. (States to select either alternative)
Alternative A—
A note or acceptance which states that it is payable at a bank is the equivalent of a draft drawn on the bank payable when it falls due out of any funds of the maker or acceptor in current aqccount or otherwise available for such payment.
Alternative B—
A note or acceptance which states that it is payable at a bank is not of itself an order or authorization to the bank to pay it.

Section 3-122. *Accrual of Cause of Action.*
(1) A cause of action against a maker or an acceptor accrues:
  (a) in the case of a time instrument on the day after maturity;
  (b) In the case of a demand instrument upon its date or, if no date is stated, on the date of issue.
(2) A cause of action against the obligor of a demand or time certificate of deposit accrues upon demand, but demand on a time certificate may not be made until on or after the date of maturity.
(3) A cause of action against a drawer of a draft or an indorser of any instrument accrues upon demand following dishonor of the instrument. Notice of dishonor is a demand.
(4) Unless an instrument provides otherwise, interest runs at the rate provided by law for a judgment:
  (a) in the case of a maker, acceptor or other primary obligor of a demand instrument from the date of demand;
  (b) in all other cases from the date of accrual of the cause of action.

Part 2
Transfer and Negotiation

Section 3-201. *Transfer: Right to Indorsement.*
(1) Transfer of an instrument vests in the transferee such right as the transferor has therein except that a transferee who has himself been a party to any fraud or illegality affecting the instrument or who as a prior holder had notice of a defense or claim against it cannot improve his position by taking from a later holder in due course.
(2) A transfer of a security interest in an instrument vests the

foregoing rights in the transferee to the extent of the interest transferred.
(3) Unless otherwise agreed, any transfer for value of an instrument not then payable to bearer gives the transferee the specifically enforceable right to have the unqualified indorsement of the transferor. Negotiation takes effect only when the indorsement is made and until that time there is no presumption that the transferee is the owner.

Section 3-202. *Negotiation.*
(1) Negotiation is the transfer of an instrument in such form that the transferee becomes a holder. If the instrument is payable to order, it is negotiated by delivery with any necessary indorsement; if payable to bearer, it is negotiated by delivery.
(2) An indorsement must be written by or on behalf of the holder and on the instrument or on a paper so firmly affixed thereto as to become a part thereof.
(3) An indorsement is effective for negotiation only when it conveys the entire instrument or any unpaid residue. If a purports to be of less, it operates only as a partial assignment.
(4) Words of assignment, condition, waiver, guaranty, limitation or disclaimer of liability and the like accompanying an indorsement do not affect its character as an indorsement.

Section 3-203. *Wrong or Misspelled Name.*
Where an instrument is made payable to a person under a misspelled name or one other than his own he may indorse in that name or his own or both; but signature in both names may be required by a person paying or giving value for the instrument.

Section 3-204. *Special Indorsement; Blank Indorsement.*
(1) A special indorsement specifies the person to whom or to whose order it makes the instrument payable. Any instrument specially indorsed becomes payable to the order of the special indorsee and may be further negotiated only by his indorsement.
(2) An indorsement in blank specifies no particular indorsee and may consist of a mere signature. An instrument payable to order and indorsed in blank becomes payable to bearer and may be negotiated by delivery alone until specially indorsed.
(3) The holder may convert a blank indorsement into a special indorsement by writing over the signature of the indorser in blank any conteract consistent with the character of the indorsement.

Section 3-205. *Restrictive Indorsements.*
An indorsement is restrictive which either:
(a) is conditional; or
(b) purports to prohibit further transfer of the instrument; or
(c) includes the words "for collection," "for deposit," "pay any bank," or like terms signifying a purpose of deposit or collection; or
(d) otherwise states that it is for the benefit or use of the indorser or of another person.

Section 3-206. *Effect of Restrictive Indorsement.*
(1) No restrictive indorsement prevents further transfer or negotiation of the instrument.
(2) Any intermediary bank, or a payor bank which is not the depositary bank, is neither given notice nor otherwise affected by a restrictive indorsement of any person except the bank's immediate transferor or the person presenting for payment.
(3) Except for an intermediary bank, any transferee under an indorsement which is conditional or includes the words "for collection," "for deposit," "pay any bank," or like terms (subparagraphs (a) and (c) of Section 3-205) must pay or apply any value given by him for or on the security of the instrument consistently with the indorsement, and to the extent that he does so he becomes a holder for value. In addition such transferee is a holder in due course if he otherwise complies with the requirements of Section 3-203 on what constitutes a holder in due course.
(4) The first taker under indorsement for the benefit of the indorser or another person (subparagraph (d) of Section 3-205) must pay or apply any value given by him for or on the security of the instrument consistently with the indorsement, and to the extent that he does so he becomes a holder for value. In addition

such taker is a holder in due course if he otherwise complies with the requirements of Section 3-203 on what constitutes a holder in due course. A later holder for value is neither given notice nor otherwise affected by such restrictive indorsement unless he has knowledge that a fiduciary or other person has negotiated the instrument in any transaction for his own benefit or otherwise in breach of duty (subsection (2) of Section 3-304).

Section 3-207. *Negotiaton Effective Although It May Be Rescinded.*
(1) Negotiation is effective to transfer the instrument although the negotiation is
(a) made by an infant, a corporation exceeding its powers, or any other person without capacity; or
(b) obtained by fraud, duress or mistake of any kind; or
(c) part of an illegal transaction; or
(d) made in breach of duty.
(2) Except as against a subsequent holder in due course such negotiation is in an appropriate case subject to recission, the declaration or a constructive trust or any other remedy permitted by law.

Section 3-208. *Reacquisition.*
Where an instrument is returned to or reacquired by a prior party he may cancel any indorsement which is not necessary to his title and reissue or further negotiate the instrument, but any intervening party is discharged as against the reacquiring party and subsequent holders not in due course and if his indorsement has been cancelled is discharged as against subsequent holders in due course as well.

Part 3
Rights of a Holder

Section 3-301. *Rights of a Holder.*
The holder of an instrument whether or not he is the owner may transfer or negotiate it and, except as otherwise provided in Section 3-603 on payment or satisfaction, discharge it or indorse payment in his own name.

Section 3-302. *Holder in Due Course.*
(1) A holder in due course is a holder who takes the instrument
(a) for value; and
(b) in good faith; and
(c) without notice that it is overdue or has been dishonored or of any defense against or claim to it on the part of any person.
(2) A payee may be a holder in due course.
(3) A holder does not become a holder in due course of an instrument:
(a) by purchase of it at judicial sale or by taking it under legal process; or
(b) by acquiring it in taking over an estate; or
(c) by purchasing it as part of a bulk transaction not in regular course of business of the transferor.
(4) A purchaser of a limited interest can be a holder in due course only to the extent of the interest purchased.

Section 3-303. *Taking for Value.*
A holder takes the instrument for value:
(a) to the extent that the agreed consideration has been performed or that he acquires a security interest in or a lien on the instrument otherwise than by legal process; or
(b) when he takes the instrument in payment of or as security for an antecedent claim against any person whether or not the claims is due; or
(c) when he gives a negotiable instrument for it or makes an irrevocable commitment to a third person.

Section 3-304. *Notice to Purchaser.*
(1) The purchaser has notice of a claim or defense if
(a) the instrument is so incomplete, bears such visible evidence of forgery or alteration, or is otherwise so irregular as to call into question its validity, terms or ownership or to create an ambiguity as to the party to pay; or
(b) the purchaser has notice that the obligation of any party is

voidable in whole or in part, or that all parties have been discharged.
(2) The purchaser has notice of a claim against the instrument when he has knowledge that a fiduciary has negotiated the instrument in payment of or as security for his own debt or in any transaction for his own benefit or otherwise in breach of duty.
(3) The purchaser has notice that an instrument is overdue if he has reason to know:
   (a) that any part of the principal amount is overdue or that there is an uncured default in payment of another instrument of the same series; or
   (b) that acceleration of the instrument has been made; or
   (c) that he is taking a demand instrument after demand has been made or more than a reasonable length of time after its issue. A reasonable time for a check drawn and payable within the states and territories of the United States and the District of Columbia is presumed to be thirty days.
(4) Knowledge of the following facts does not of itself give the purchaser notice of a defense or claim:
   (a) that the instrument is antedated or postdated;
   (b) that it was issued or negotiated in return for an executory promise or accompanied by a separate agreement, unless the purchaser has notice that a defense or claim has arisen from the terms thereof;
   (c) that any party has signed for accommodation;
   (d) that an incomplete instrument has been completed, unless the purchaser has notice of any improper completion;
   (e) that any person negotiating the instrument is or was a fiduciary;
   (f) that there has been default in payment of interest on the instrument or in payment of any other instrument, except one of the same series.
(5) The filing or recording of a document does not of itself constitute notice within the provisions of this Article to a person who would otherwise be a holder in due course.
(6) To be effective notice must be received at such time and in such manner as to give a reasonble opportunity to act on it.

Section 3-305. *Rights of a Holder in Due Course.*
To the extent that a holder is a holder in due course he takes the instrument free from:
(1) all claims to it on the part of any person; and
(2) all defenses of any party to the instrument with whom the holder has not dealt except:
   (a) infancy, to the extent that it is a defense to a simple contract; and
   (b) such other incapacity, or duress, or illegality of the transaction, as renders the obligation of the party a nullity; and
   (c) such misrepresentation as has induced the paty to sign the instrument with neither knowledge nor reasonable opportunity to obtain knowledge of its character or its essential terms; and
   (d) discharge in insolvency proceedings; and
   (e) any other discharge of which the holder has notice when he takes the instrument.

Section 3-306. *Rights of One Not Holder in Due Course.*
Unless he has the rights of a holder in due course, any person takes the instrument subject to:
   (a) all valid claims to it on the part of any person; and
   (b) all defenses of any party which would be available in an action on a simple contract; and
   (c) the defenses of want or failure of consideration, nonperformance of any condition precedent, non-delivery, or delivery for a special purpose (Section 3-408); and
   (d) the defense that he or a person through whom he holds the instrument acquired it by theft, or that payment or satisfaction to such holder would be inconsistent with the terms of a restrictive indorsement. The claim of any third person to the instrument is not otherwise available as a defense to any party liable thereon unless the third person himself defends the action for such party.

Section 3-307. *Burden of Establishing Signatures.* Defenses and Due Course.
(1) Unless specifically denied in the pleadings each signature on an instrument is admitted. When the effectiveness of a signature is put in issue:
   (a) the burden of establishing it is on the party claiming under the signature; but
   (b) the signature is presumed to be genuine or authorized except where the action is to enforce the obligation of a purported signer who has died or become incompetent before proof is required.
(2) When signatures are admitted or established, production of the instrument entitles a holder to recover on it unless the defendant establishes a defense.
(3) After it is shown that a defense exists a person claiming the rights of a holder in due course has the burden of establishing that he or some person under whom he claims is in all respects a holder in due course.

Part 4
Liability of Parties

Section 3-401. *Signature.*
(1) No person is liable on an instrument unless his signature appears thereon.
(2) A signature is made by use of any name, including any trade or assumed name, upon an instrument, or by any word or mark used in lieu of a written signature.

Section 3-402. *Signature in Ambiguous Capacity.*
Unless the instrument clearly indicates that a signature is made in some other capacity, it is an indorsement.

Section 3-403. *Signature by Authorized Representative.*
(1) A signature may be made by an agent or other representative, and his authority to make it may be established as in other cases of representation. No particular form of appointment is necessary to establish such authority.
(2) An authorized representative who signs his own name to an instrument:
   (a) is personally obligated if the instrument neither names the person represented nor shows that the representative signed in a representative capacity;
   (b) except as otherwise established between the immediate parties, is personally obligated if the instrument names the person represented but does not show that the representative signed in a representative capacity, or if the instrument does not name the person represented but does show that the representative signed in a representative capacity.
(3) Except as otherwise established, the name of an organization preceded or followed by the name and office of an authorized individual is a signature made in a representative capacity.

Section 3-404. *Unauthorized Signatures.*
(1) Any unauthorized signature is wholly inoperative as that of the person whose name is signed unless he ratifies it or is precluded from denying it; but it operates as the signature of the unauthorized signer in favor of any person who in good faith pays the instrument or takes it for value.
(2) Any unauthorized signature may be ratified for all purposes of this Article. Such ratification does not of itself affect any rights of the person ratifying against the actual signer.

Section 3-405. *Impostors; Signature in Name of Payee.*
(1) An indorsement by any person in the name of a named payee is effective if:
   (a) an impostor by use of the mails or otherwise has induced the maker or drawer to issue the instrument to him or his confederate in the name of the payee; or
   (b) a person signing as or on behalf of a maker or drawer intends the payee to have no interest in the instrument; or
   (c) an agent or employee of the maker or drawer has supplied him with the name of the payee intending the latter to have no such interest.
(2) Nothing in this section shall affect the criminal or civil liability of the person so indorsing.

Section 3-406. *Negligence Contributing to Alteration or Unauthorized Signature.*
Any person who by his negligence substantially contributes to a

NEGOTIABLE INSTRUMENTS LAW

material alteration of the instrument or to the making of an unauthorized signature is precluded from asserting the alteration or lack of authority against a holder in due course or against a drawee or other payor who pays the instrument in good faith and in accordance with the reasonable commercial standards of the drawee's or payor's business.

Section 3-407. *Alteration.*
(1) Any alteration of an instrument is material which changes the contract of any party thereto in any respect, including any such change in:
   (a) the number or relations of the parties; or
   (b) an incomplete instrument, by completing it otherwise than as authorized; or
   (c) the writing as signed, by adding to it or by removing any part of it.
(2) as against any person other than a subsequent holder in due course:
   (a) alteration by the holder which is both fraudulent and material discharges any party whose contract is thereby changed unless that party assents or is precluded from asserting the defense;
   (b) no other alteration discharges any party and the instrument may be enforced according to its original tenor, or as to incomplete instruments according to the authority given.
(3) A subsequent holder in due course may in all cases enforce the instrument according to its original tenor, and when an incomplete instrument has been completed, he may enforce it as completed.

Section 3-408. *Consideration.*
Want or failure of consideration is a defense as against any person not having the rights of a holder in due course (Section 3-305), except that no consideration is necessary for an instrument or obligation thereon given in payment of or as security for an antecedent obligation of any kind. Nothing in this section shall be taken to displace any statute outside this Act under which a promise is enforceable notwithstanding lack or failure of consideration. Partial failure of consideration is a defense pro tanto whether or not the failure is in an ascertained or liquidated amount.

Section 3-409. *Draft Not an Assignment.*
(1) A check or other draft does not of itself operate as an assignment of any funds in the hands of the drawer available for its payment, and the drawee is not liable on the instrument until he accepts it.
(2) Nothing in this section shall affect any liability in contract, tort or otherwise arising from any letter of credit or other obligation or representation which is not an acceptance.

Section 3-410. *Definition and Operation of Acceptance.*
(1) Acceptance is the drawee's signed engagement to honor the draft as presented. It must be written on the draft and may consist of his signature alone. It becomes operative when completed by delivery or notification.
(2) A draft may be accepted although it has not been signed by the drawer or is otherwise incomplete or is overdue or has been dishonored.
(3) Where the draft is payable at a fixed period after sight and the acceptor fails to date his acceptance, the holder may complete it by supplying a date in good faith.

Section 3-411. *Certification of a Check.*
(1) Certification of a check is acceptance. Where a holder procures certification the drawer and all prior indorsers are discharged.
(2) Unless otherwise agreed a bank has no obligation to certify a check.
(3) A bank may certify a check before returning it for lack of proper indorsement. it if does so, the drawer is discharged.

Section 3-412. *Acceptance Varying Draft.*
(1) Where the drawee's proffered acceptance in any manner varies the draft as presented, the holder may refuse the acceptance and treat the draft as dishonored in which case the drawee is entitled to have his acceptance cancelled.
(2) The terms of the draft are not varied by an acceptance to pay at any particular bank or place in the United States, unless the acceptance states that the draft is to be paid only at such bank or place.
(3) Where the holder assents to an acceptance varying the terms of the draft, each drawer and indorser who does not affirmatively assent is discharged.

Section 3-413. **Contract of Maker, Drawer and Acceptor.**
(1) The maker or acceptor engages that he will pay the instrument according to its tenor at the time of his engagement or as completed pursuant to Section 3-115 on incomplete instruments.
(2) The drawer engages that upon dishonor of the draft and any necessary notice of dishonor or protest he will pay the amount of the draft to the holder or to any indorser who takes it up. The drawer may disclaim this liability by drawing without recourse.
(3) By making, drawing or accepting the party admits as against all subsequent parties including the drawee the existence of the payee and his then capacity to indorse.

Section 3-414. **Contract of Indorser; Order of Liability.**
(1) Unless the indorsement otherwise specifies (as by such words as "without recourse") every indorser engages that upon dishonor and any necessary notice of dishonor and protest he will pay the instrument according to its tenor at the time of his indorsement to the holder or to any subsequent indorser who takes it up, even though the indorser who takes it up was not obligated to do so.
(2) Unless they otherwise agree, indorsers are liable to one another in the order in which they indorse, which is presumed to be the order in which their signatures appear on the instrument.

Section 3-415. **Contract of Accommodation Party.**
(1) An accommodation party is one who signs the instrument in any capacity for the purpose of lending his name to another party to it.
(2) When the instrument has been taken for value before it is due, the accommodation party is liable in the capacity in which he has signed even though the taker knows of the accommodation
(3) As against a holder in due course and without notice of the accommodation, oral proof of the accommodation is not admissible to give the accommodation party the benefit of discharges dependent on his character as such. In other cases the accommodation character may be shown by oral proof.
(4) An indorsement which shows that it is not in the chain of title is notice of its accommodation character.
(5) An accommodation party is not liable to the party accommodated, and if he pays the instrument has a right of recourse on the instrument against such party.

Section 3-416. **Contract of Guarantor.**
(1) "Payment guaranteed" or equivalent words added to a signature means that the signer engages that if the instrument is not paid when due he will pay it according to its tenor without resort by the holder to any other party.
(2) "Collection guaranteed" or equivalent words added to a signature mean that the signer engages that if the instrument is not paid when due he will pay it according to its tenor, but only after the holder has reduced his claim against the maker or acceptor to judgment and execution has been returned unsatisfied or after the maker or acceptor has become insolvent or it is otherwise apparent that it is useless to proceed against him.
(3) Words of guaranty which do not otherwise specify guarantee payment.
(4) No words of guaranty added to the signature of a sole maker or acceptor affect his liability on the instrument. Such words added to the signature of one of two or more makers or acceptors create a presumption that the signature is for the accommodation of the others.
(5) When words of guaranty are used, presentment, notice of dishonor and protest are not necessary to charge the user.
(6) Any guaranty written on the instrument is enforcible notwithstanding any statute of frauds.

Section 3-417. *Warranties on Presentment and Transfer.*
(1) Any person who obtains payment or acceptance and any prior

transferor warrants to a person who in good faith pays or accepts that:
(a) he has a good title to the instrument or is authorized to obtain payment or acceptance on behalf of one who has a good title; and
(b) he has no knowledge that the signature of the maker or drawer is unauthorized, except that this warranty is not given by a holder in due course acting in good faith:
  (i) to a maker with respect to the maker's own signature; or
  (ii) to a drawer with respect to the drawer's own signature, whether or not the drawer is also the drawee; or
  (iii) to an acceptor of a draft if the holder in due course took the draft after the acceptance or obtained the acceptance without knowledge that the drawer's signature was unauthorized; and
(c) the instrument has not been materially altered, except that this warranty is not given by a holder in due course acting in good faith
  (i) to the maker of a note; or
  (ii) to the drawer of a draft whether or not the drawer is also the drawee; or
  (iii) to the acceptor of a draft with respect to an alteration made prior to the acceptance if the holder in due course took the draft after the acceptance, even though the acceptance provided "payable as originally drawn" or equivalent terms; or
  (iv) to the acceptor of a draft with respect to an alteration made after the acceptance.

(2) Any person who transfers an instrument and receives consideration warrants to his transferee and, if the transfer is by indorsement, to any subsequent holder who takes the instrument in good faith that:
(a) he has a good title to the instrument or is authorized to obtain payment or acceptance on behalf of one who has a good title and the transfer is otherwise rightful; and
(b) all signatures are genuine or authorized; and
(c) the instrument has not been materially altered; and
(d) no defense of any party is good against him; and
(e) he has no knowledge of any insolvency proceeding instituted with respect to the maker or acceptor or the drawer of an unaccepted instrument.

(3) By transferring "without recourse" the transferor limits the obligation stated in subsection (2) (d) to a warranty that he has no knowledge of such a defense.

(4) A selling agent or broker who does not disclose the fact that he is acting only as such gives the warranties provided in this section, but if he makes such disclosure warrants only his good faith and authority.

Section 3-418. *Finality of Payment or Acceptance.*
Except for recovery of bank payments as provided in the Article on Bank Deposits and Collections (Article 4) and except for liability for breach of warranty on presentment under the preceding section, payment or acceptance of any instrument is final in favor of a holder in due course, or a person who has in good faith changed his position in reliance on the payment.

Section 3-419. *Conversion of Instrument; Innocent Representative.*
(1) An instrument is converted when:
(a) a drawee to whom it is delivered for acceptance refuses to return it on demand; or
(b) any person to whom it is delivered for payment refuses on demand either to pay or to return it; or
(c) it is paid on a forged indorsement.
(2) In an action against a drawee under subsection (1) the measure of the drawee's liability is the face amount of the instrument. In any other action under subsection (1) the measure of liability is presumed to be the face amount of the instrument.
(3) Subject to the provisions of this Act concerning restrictive indorsements a representative, including a depositary or collecting bank, who has in good faith and in accordance with the reasonable commercial standards applicable to the business of such representative dealt with an instrument or its proceeds on behalf of one who was not the true owner is not liable to conversion or otherwise to the true owner beyond the amount of any proceeds remaining in his hands.

(4) An intermediary bank or payor bank which is not a depositary bank is not liable to conversion solely by reason of the fact that proceeds of an item indorsed restrictively (Sections 3-205 and 3-206) are not paid or applied consistently with the restrictive indorsement of an indorser other than its immediate transferor.

Part 5
Presentment, Notice of Dishonor and Protest

Section 3-501. *When Presentment, Notice of Dishonor and Protest Necessary or Permissible.*
(1) Unless excused (Section 3-511) presentment is necessary to charge secondary parties as follows:
(a) presentment for acceptance is necessary to charge the drawer and indorsers of a draft where the draft so provides, or is payable elsewhere than at the residence or place of business of the drawee, or its date of payment depends upon such presentment. The holder may at his option present for acceptance any other draft payable at a stated date;
(b) presentment for payment is necessary to charge any indorser.
(c) In the case of any drawer, the acceptor of a draft payable at a bank or the maker of a note payable at a bank, presentment for payment is necessary, but failure to make presentment discharges such drawer, acceptor or maker only as stated in Section 3-502(1)(b).
(2) Unless excused (Section 3-511):
(a) notice of any dishonor is necessary to charge any indorser;
(b) in the case of any drawer, the acceptor of a draft payable at a bank or the maker of a note payable at a bank, notice of any dishonor is necessary, but failure to give such notice discharges such drawer, acceptor or maker only as stated in Section 3-502(1)(b).
(3) Unless excused (Section 3-511), protest of any dishonor is necessary to charge the drawer and indorsers of any draft which on its face appears to be drawn or payble outside of the states and territories of the United States and the District of Columbia. The holder may at his option make protest of any dishonor of any other instrument and in the case of a foreign draft may on insolvency of the acceptor before maturity make protest for better security.
(4) Notwithstanding any provision of this section, neither presentment nor notice of dishonor nor protest is necessary to charge an indorser who has indorsed an instrument after maturity.

Section 3-502. *Unexcused Delay: Discharge.*
(1) Where without excuse any necessary presentment or notice of dishonor is delayed beyond the time when it is due
(a) any indorser is discharged; and
(b) any drawer or the acceptor of a draft payable at a bank or the maker of a note payable at a bank who, because the drawee or payor bank becomes insolvent during the delay, is deprived of funds maintained with the drawer of payor bank to cover the instrument may discharge his liability by written assignment to the holder of his rights against the drawee or payor bank in respect of such funds, but such drawer, acceptor or maker is not otherwise discharged.
(2) Where without excuse a necessary protest is delayed beyond the time when it is due, any drawer or indorser is discharged.

Section 3-503. *Time of Presentment.*
(1) Unless a different time is expressed in the instrument, the time for any presentment is determined as follows:
(a) where an instrument is payable at or a fixed period after a stated date, any presentment for acceptance must be made on or before the date it is payable;
(b) where an instrument is payable after sight, it must either be presented for acceptance or negotiated within a reasonable time after date or issue whichever is later;
(c) where an instrument shows the date on which it is payable, presentment for payment is due on that date;
(d) where an instrument is accelerated, presentment for payment is due within a reasonable time after the acceleration;
(e) with respect to the liability of any secondary party presentment for acceptance or payment of any other instrument is due within a reasonable time after such party becomes liable thereon.
(2) A reasonable time for presentment is determined by the nature

of the instrument, any usage of banking or trade and the facts of the particular case. In the case of an uncertified check which is drawn and payable within the United States and which is not a draft drawn by a bank the following are presumed to be reasonable periods within which to present for payment or to initiate bank collection:
  (a) with respect to the liability of the drawer, thirty days after date or issue whichever is later; and
  (b) with respect to the liability of an indorser, seven days after his indorsement.
(3) Where any presentment is due on a day which is not a full business day for either the person making presentment or the party to pay or accept, presentment is due on the next following day which is a full business day for both parties.
(4) Presentment to be sufficient must be made at a reasonable hour, and if at a bank during its banking day.

Section 3-504. *How Presentment Made.*
(1) Presentment is a demand for acceptance or payment made upon the maker, acceptor, drawee or other payor by or on behalf of the holder.
(2) Presentment may be made:
  (a) by mail, in which event the time of presentment is determined by the time of receipt of the mail; or
  (b) through a clearing house; or
  (c) at the place of acceptance of payment specified in the instrument or if there be none at the place of business or residence of the party to accept or pay. if neither the party to accept or pay nor anyone authorized to act for him is present or accessible at such place, presentment is excused.
(3) It may be made:
  (a) to any one of two or more makers, acceptors, drawees or other payors; or
  (b) to any person who has authority to make or refuse the acceptance or payment.
(4) A draft accepted or a note made payable at a bank in the United States must be presented at such bank.
(5) In the cases described in Section 4-210 presentment may be made in the manner and with the result stated in that section.

Section 3-505. *Rights of Party to Whom Presentment Is Made.*
(1) The party to whom presentment is made may without dishonor require:
  (a) exhibition of the instrument; and
  (b) reasonable identification of the person making presentment and evidence of his authority to make it if made for another; and
  (c) that the instrument be produced for acceptance or payment at a place specified in it, or if there be none at any place reasonable in the circumstances; and
  (d) a signed receipt on the instrument for any partial or full payment and its surrender upon full payment.
(2) Failure to comply with any such requirement invalidates the presentment, but the person presenting has a reasonable time in which to comply and the time for acceptance or payment runs from the time of compliance.

Section 3-506. *Time Allowed for Acceptance or Payment.*
(1) Acceptance may be deferred without dishonor until the close of the next business day following presentment. The holder may also in a good faith effort to obtain acceptance and without either dishonor of the instrument or discharge of secondary parties allow postponement of acceptance for an additional business day.
(2) Except as a longer time is allowed in the case of documentary drafts drawn under a letter of credit, and unless an earlier time is agreed to by the party to pay, payment of an instrument may be deferred without dishonor pending reasonable examination to determine whether it is properly payable, but payment must be made in any event before the close of business on the day of presentment.

Section 3-507. *Dishonor; Holder's Right of Recourse; Term Allowing Re-Presentment.*
(1) An instrument is dishonored when
  (a) a necessary or optional presentment is duly made and due acceptance or payment is refused or cannot be obtained within the prescribed time or in case of bank collections the instrument is seasonably returned by the midnight deadline (Section 4-301); or
  (b) presentment is excused and the instrument is not duly accepted or paid.
(2) Subject to any necessary notice of dishonor and protest, the holder has upon dishonor an immediate right of recourse against the drawers and indorsers.
(3) Return of an instrument for lack of proper indorsement is not dishonor.
(4) A term in a draft or an indorsement thereof allowing a stated time for re-presentment in the event of any dishonor of the draft by nonacceptance if a time draft or by nonpayment if a sight draft gives the holder as against any secondary party bound by the term an option to waive the dishonor without affecting the liability of the secondary party, and he may present again up to the end of the stated time.

Section 3-508. *Notice of Dishonor.*
(1) Notice of dishonor may be given to any person who may be liable on the instrument by or on behalf of the holder or any party who has himself received notice, or any other party who can be compelled to pay the instrument. In addition an agent or bank in whose hands the instrument is dishonored may give notice to his principal or customer or to another agent or bank from which the instrument was received.
(2) Any necessary notice must be given by a bank before its midnight deadline and by any other person before midnight of the third business day after dishonor or receipt of notice of dishonor.
(3) Notice may be given in any reasonable manner. It may be oral or written and in any terms which identify the instrument and state that it has been dishonored. A misdescription which does not mislead the party notified does not vitiate the notife. Sending the instrument bearing a stamp, ticket or writing stating that acceptance or payment has been refused or sending a notice of debit with respect to the instrument is sufficient.
(4) Written notice is given when sent although it is not received.
(5) Notice to one partner is notice to each although the firm has been dissolved.
(6) When any party is in insolvency proceedings instituted after the issue of the instrument, notice may be given either to the party or to the representative of his estate.
(7) When any party is dead or incompetent, notice may be sent to his last known address or given to his personal representative.
(8) Notice operates for the benefit of all parties who have rights on the instrument against the party notified.

Section 3-509. *Protest; Noting for Protest.*
(1) A protest is a certificate of dishonor made under the hand and seal of a United States consul or vice consul or a notary public or other person authorized to certify dishonor by the law of the place where dishonor occurs. It may be made upon information satisfactory to such person.
(2) The protest must identify the instrument and certify either that due presentment has been made or the reason why it is excused and that the instrument has been dishonored by nonacceptance or nonpayment.
(3) The protest may also certify that notice of dishonor has been given to all parties or to specified parties.
(4) Subject to subsection (5) any necessary protest is due by the time that notice of dishonor is due.
(5) If, before protest is due, an instrument has beebn noted for protest by the officer to make protest, the protest may be made at any time thereafter as of the date of the noting.

Section 3-510. *Evidence of Dishonor and Notice of Dishonor.*
The following are admissible as evidence and create a presumption of dishonor and of any notice of dishonor therein shown;
  (a) a document regular in form as provided in the preceding section which purports to be a protest;
  (b) the purported stamp or writing of the drawee, payor bank or presenting bank on the instrument or accompanying it stating that acceptance or payment has been refused for reasons consistent with dishonor;
  (c) any book or record of the drawee, payor bank or any collecting bank kept in the usual course of business which

shows dishonor, even though there is no evidence of who made the entry.

Section 3-511. *Waived or Excused Presentment, Protest of Notice of Dishonor or Delay Therein.*
(1) Delay in presentment, protest or notice of dishonor is excused when the party is without notice that it is due or when the delay is caused by circumstances beyond his control and he exercises reasonable diligence after the cause of the delay ceases to operate.
(2) Presentment or notice or protest as the case may be is entirely excused when
   (a) the party to be charged has waived it expressly or by implication either before or after it is due; or
   (b) such party has himself dishonored the instrument or has countermanded payment or otherwise has no reason to expect or right to require that the instrument be accepted or paid; or
   (c) by reasonable diligence the presentment or protest cannot be made or the notice given.
(3) Presentment is also entirely excused when
   (a) the maker, acceptor or drawee or any instrument except a documentary draft is dead or in insolvency proceedings instituted after the issue of the instrument; or
   (b) acceptance or payment is refused but not for want of proper presentment.
(4) Where a draft has been dishonored by nonacceptance, a later presentment for payment and any notice of dishonor and protest for nonpayment are excused unless in the meantime the instrument has been accepted.
(5) A waiver of protest is also a waiver of presentment and of notice of dishonor even though protest is not required.
(6) Where a waiver of presentment or notice or protest is embodied in the instrument itself, it is binding upon all parties; but where it is written above the signature of an indorser it binds him only.

Part 6
Discharge

Section 3-601. *Discharge of Parties.*
(1) The extent of the discharge of any party from liability on an instrument is governed by the sections on
   (a) payment or satisfaction (Section 3-603); or
   (b) tender of payment (Section 3-604); or
   (c) cancellation or renunciation (Section 3-605); or
   (d) impairment or right of recourse or of collateral (Section 3-606); or
   (e) reacquisition of the instrument by a prior party (Section 3-208); or
   (f) fraudulent and material alteration (Section 3-407); or
   (g) certification of a check (Section 3-411); or
   (h) acceptance varying a draft (Section 3-412); or
   (i) unexcused delay in presentment or notice of dishonor or protest (Section 3-502).
(2) Any party is also discharged from his liability on an instrument to another party by any other act or agreement with such party which would discharge his simple contract for the payment of money.
(3) The liability of all parties is discharged when any party who has himself no right of action or recourse on the instrument
   (a) reacquires the instrument in his own right; or
   (b) is discharged under any provision of this Article, except as otherwise provided with respect to discharge for impairment of recourse or of collateral (Section 3-606).

Section 3-602. *Effect of Discharge Against Holder in Due Course.*
No discharge of any party provided by this Article is effective against a subsequent holder in due course unless he has notice thereof when he takes the instrument.

Section 3-603. *Payment or Satisfaction.*
(1) The liability of any party is discharged to the extent of his payment or satisfaction to the holder even though it is made with knowledge of a claim of another person to the instrument unless prior to such payment or satisfaction the person making the claim either supplies indemnity deemed adequate by the party seeking the discharge or enjoins payment or satisfaction by order of a court of competent jurisdiction in an action in which the adverse claimant and the holder are parties. This subsection does not, however, result in the discharge of the liability
   (a) of a party who in bad faith pays or satisfies a holder who acquired the instrument by theft or who (unless having the rights of a holder in due course) holds through one who so acquired it; or
   (b) of a party (other than an intermediary bank or a payor bank which is not a depositary bank) who pays or satisfies the holder of an instrument which has been restrictively endorsed in a manner not consistent with the terms of such restrictive endorsement.
(2) Payment or satisfaction may be made with the consent of the holder by any person including a stranger to the instrument. Surrender of the instrument to such a person gives him the rights of a transferee (Section 3-201).

Section 3-604. *Tender of Payment.*
(1) Any party making tender of full payment to a holder when or after it is due is discharged to the extent of all subsequent liability for interest, costs and attorney's fees.
(2) The holder's refusal of such tender wholly discharges any party who has a right of recourse against the party making the tender.
(3) Where the maker or acceptor of an instrument payable otherwise than on demand is able and ready to pay at every place of payment specified in the instrument when it is due, it is equivalent to tender.

Section 3-605. *Cancellation and Renunciation.*
(1) The holder of an instrument may even without consideration discharge any party
   (a) in any manner apparent on the face of the instrument or the endorsement, as by intentionally cancelling the instrument or the party's signature by destruction or mutilation, or by striking out the party's signature; or
   (b) by renouncing his rights by a writing signed and delivered or by surrender of the instrument to the party to be discharged.
(2) Neither cancellation nor renunciation without surrender of the instrument affects that title thereto.

Section 3-606. *Impairment of Recourse or of Collateral.*
(1) The holder discharges any party to the instrument to the extent that without such party's consent the holder
   (a) without express reservation of rights releases or agrees not to sue any person against whom the party has to the knowledge of the holder a right of recourse or agrees to suspend the right to enforce against such person the instrument or collateral or otherwise discharges such person, except that failure or delay in effecting any required presentment, protest or notice of dishonor with respect to any such person does not discharge any party as to whom presentment, protest or notice of dishonor is effective or unnecessary; or
   (b) unjustifiably impairs any collateral for the instrument given by or on behalf of the party or any person against whom he has a right of recourse.
(2) By express reservation of rights against a party with a right of recourse the holder preserves
   (a) all his rights against such party as of the time when the instrument was originally due; and
   (b) the right of the party to pay the instrument as of that time; and
   (c) all rights of such party to recourse against others.

Part 7
Advice of International Sight Draft

Section 3-701. *Letter of Advice of International Sight Draft.*
(1) A "letter of advice" is a drawer's communication to the drawee that a described draft has been drawn.
(2) Unless otherwise agreed, when a bank receives from another bank a letter of advice of an international sight draft, the drawee bank may immediately debit the drawer's account and

stop the running of interest pro tanto. Such a debit and any resulting credit to the account covering outstanding drafts leaves in the drawer full power to stop payment or otherwise dispose of the amount and creates no trust or interest in favor of the holder.

(3) Unless otherwise agreed and except where a draft is drawn under a credit issued by the drawee, the drawee of an international sight draft owes the drawer no duty to pay an unadvised draft but if it does so and the draft is genuine, may appropriately debit the drawer's account.

Part 8
Miscellaneous

Section 3-801. *Drafts in a Set.*
(1) Where a draft is drawn in a set of parts, each of which is numbered and expressed to be an order only if no other part has been honored, the whole of the parts constitutes one draft, but a taker of any part may become a holder in due course of the draft.
(2) Any person who negotiates, indorses or accepts a single part of a draft drawn in a set thereby becomes liable to any holder in due course of that part as if it were the whole set, but as between different holders in due course to whom different parts have been negotiated the holder whose title first accrues has all rights to the draft and its proceeds.
(3) As against the drawee the first presented part of a draft drawn in a set is the part entitled to payment, or if a time draft to acceptance and payment. Acceptance of any subsequently presented part renders the drawee liable thereon under subsection (2). With respect both to a holder and to the drawer payment of a subsequently presented part of a draft payable at sight has the same effect as payment of a check notwithstanding an effective stop order (Section 4-407).
(4) Except as otherwise provided in this section, where any part of a draft in a set is discharged by payment or otherwise the whole draft is discharged.

Section 3-802. *Effect of Instrument on Obligation for Which It Is Given.*
(1) Unless otherwise agreed, where an instrument is taken for an underlying obligation
  (a) the obligation is pro tanto discharged if a bank is drawer, maker or acceptor of the instrument and there is no recourse on the instrument against the underlying obligor; and
  (b) in any other case the obligation is suspended pro tanto until the instrument is due or if it is payable on demand until its presentment. If the instrument is dishonored, action may be maintained on either the instrument or the obligation; discharge of the underlying obligor on the instrument also discharges him on the obligation.
(2) The taking in good faith of a check which is not postdated does not of itself so extend the time on the original obligation as to discharge a surety.

Section 3-803. *Notice to Third Party.*
Where a defendant is sued for breach of an obligation for which a third person is answerable over under this Article, he may give the third person written notice of the litigation, and the person notified may then give similar notice to any other person who is answerable over to him under this Article. If the notice states that the person notified may come in and defend and that if the person notified does not do so he will in any action against him by the person giving the notice be bound by any determination of fact common to the two litigations, then unless after seasonable receipt of the notice the person notified does come in and defend he is so bound.

Section 3-804. *Lost, Destroyed or Stolen Instruments.*
The owner of an instrtument which is lost, whether by destruction, theft or otherwise, may maintain an action in his own name and recover from any party liable thereon upon due proof of his ownership, the facts which prevent his production of the instrument and its terms. The court may require security indemnifying the defendant against loss by reason of further claims on the instrument.

Section 3-805. *Instruments Not Payable to Order or to Bearer.*
This Article applies to any instrument whose terms do not preclude transfer and which is otherwise negotiable within this Article but which is not payable to order or to bearer, except that there can be no holder in due course of such an instrument.

Article 4
Bank Deposits and Collections

Part 7
General Provisions and Definitions

Section 4-101. *Short Title.*
This Article shall be known and may be cited as Uniform Commercial Code—Bank Deposits and Collections.

Section 4-102. *Applicability.*
(1) To the extent that items within this Article are also within the scope of Articles 3 and 8, they are subject to the provisions of those Articles. In the event of conflict the provisions of this Article govern those of Article 3, but the provisions of Article 8 govern those of this Article.
(2) The liability of a bank for action or non-action with respect to any item handled by it for purposes of presentment, payment or collection is governed by the law of the place where the bank is located. In the case of action or non-action by or at a branch or separate office of a bank, its liability is governed by the law of the place where the branch or separate office is located.

Section 4-103. *Variation by Agreement; Measure of Damages; Certain Action Constituting Ordinary Care.*
(1) The effect of the provisions of this Article may be varied by agreement except that no agreement can disclaim a bank's responsibility for its own lack of good faith or failure to exercise ordinary care or can limit the measure of damages for such lack or failure; but the parties may by agreement determine the standards by which such responsibility is to be measured if such standards are not manifestly unreasonable.
(2) Federal Reserve regulations and operating letters, clearing house rules and the like have the effect of agreements under subsection (1), whether or not specifically assented to by all parties interested in items handled.
(3) Action or non-action approved by this Article or pursuant to Federal Reserve regulations or operating letters constitutes the exercise of ordinary care and, in the absence of special instructions, action or non-action consistent with clearing house rules and the like or with a general banking usage not disapproved by this Article, prima facie constitutes the exercise of ordinary care.
(4) The specification or approval of certain procedures by this article does not constitute disapproval of other procedures which may be reasonable under the circumstances.
(5) The measure of damages for failure to exercise ordinary care in handling an item is the amount of the item reduced by an amount which could not have been realized by the use of ordinary care, and where there is bad faith it includes other damages, if any, suffered by the party as a proximate consequence.

Section 4-104. *Definitions and Index of Definitions.*
(1) In this Article unless the context otherwise requires
  (a) "Account" means any account with a bank and includes a checking, time, interest or savings account;
  (b) "Afternoon" means the period of a day between noon and midnight;
  (c) "Banking day" means that part of any day on which a bank is open to the public for carrying on substantially all of its banking functions;
  (d) "Clearing House" means any association of banks or other payors regularly clearing items;
  (e) "Customer" means any person having an account with a bank or for whom a bank has agreed to collect items and includes a bank carrying an account with another bank;
  (f) "Documentary draft" means any negotiable or non-negotiable draft with accompanying documents, securities or other papers to be delivered against honor of the draft;
  (g) "Item" means any instrument for the payment of money even though it is not negotiable but does not include money;
  (h) "Midnight deadline" with respect to a bank is midnight on its next banking day following the banking day on which it receives the relevant item or notice or from which the time

for taking action commences to run, whichever is later;
(i) "Properly payable" includes the availability of funds for payment at the time of decision to pay or dishonor;
(j) "Settle" means to pay in cash, by clearing house settlement, in a charge or credit or by remittance, or otherwise as instructed. A settlement may be either provisional or final;
(k) "Suspends payments" with respect to a bank means that it has been closed by order of the supervisory authorities, that a public officer has been appointed to take it over or that it ceases or refuses to make payments in the ordinary course of business.
(2) Other definitions applying to this Article and the sections in which they appear are
"Collecting bank." Section 4-105.
"Depositary bank." Section 4-105.
"Intermediary bank." Section 4-105.
"Payor bank." Section 4-105.
"Presenting bank." Section 4-105.
"Remitting bank." Section 4-105.
(3) The following definitions in other Articles apply to this Article:
"Acceptance." Section 3-410
"Certificate of deposit." Section 3-104.
"Certification." Section 3-411.
"Check." Section 3-104.
"Draft." Section 3-104.
"Holder in due course." Section 3-302.
"Notice of dishonor." Section 3-508.
"Presentment." Section 3-504.
"Protest." Section 3-509.
"Secondary party." Section 3-102.
(4) In addition Article I contains general definitions and principles of construction and interpretation applicable throughout this Article.

Section 4-105. *"Depositary Bank"; "Intermediary Bank"; "Collecting Bank"; "Payor Bank"; "Presenting Bank"; "Remitting Bank."*
In this Article unless the context otherwise requires:
(a) "Depositary bank" means the first bank to which an item is transferred for collection even though it is also the payor bank;
(b) "Payor bank" means a bank by which an item is payable as drawn or accepted;
(c) "Intermediary bank" means any bank to which an item is transferred in course of collection except the depositary or payor bank;
(d) "Collecting bank" means any bank handling the item for collection except the payor bank;
(e) "Presenting bank" means any bank presenting an item except a payor bank;
(f) "Remitting bank" means any payor or intermediary bank remitting for an item.

Section 4-106. *Separate Office of a Bank.*
A branch or separate office of a bank (maintaining its own deposit ledgers) is a separate bank for the purpose of computing the time within which and determining the place at or to which action may be taken or notices or orders shall be given under this Article and under Article 3.
Note: The words in preceding parentheses are optional.

Section 4-107. *Time of Receipt of Items.*
(1) For the purpose of allowing time to process items, prove balances and make the necessary entries on its books to determine its position for the day, a bank may fix an afternoon hour of two P.M. or later as a cut-off hour for the handling of money and items and the making of entries on its books.
(2) Any item or deposit of money received on any day after a cut-off hour so fixed or after the close of the banking day may be treated as being received at the opening of the next banking day.

Section 4-108. *Delays*
(1) Unless otherwise instructed, a collecting bank in a good faith effort to secure payment may, in the case of specific items and with or without the approval of any person involved, waive, modify or extend time limits imposed or permitted by this Act for a period not in excess of an additional banking day without discharge of secondary parties and without liability to its transferor or any prior party.
(2) Delay by a collecting bank or payor bank beyond time limits prescribed or permitted by this Act or by instructions is excused if caused by interruption of communication facilities, suspension of payments by another bank, war, emergency conditions or other circumstances beyond the control of the bank provided it exercises such diligence as the circumstances require.

Section 4-109. *Process of Posting.*
The "process of posting" means the usual procedure followed by a payor bank in determining to pay an item and in recording the payment including one or more of the following or other steps as determined by the bank:
(a) verification of any signature;
(b) ascertaining that sufficient funds are available;
(c) affixing a "paid" or other stamp;
(d) entering a charge or entry to a customer's account;
(e) correcting or reversing an entry or erroneous action with respect to the item.

Part 2
Collection of Items: Depositary and Collecting Banks

Section 4-201. *Presumption and Duration of Agency Status of Collecting Banks and Provisional Status of Credits: Applicability of Article; Item Indorsed "Pay Any Bank."*
(1) Unless a contrary intent clearly appears and prior to the time that a settlement given by a collecting bank for an item is or becomes final (subsection (3) of Section 4-211 and Section 4-212 and 4-213) the bank is an agent or sub-agent of the owner of the item and any settlement given for the item is provisional. This provision applies regardless of the form of endorsement or lack of endorsement and even though credit given for the item is subject to immediate withdrawal as of right or is in fact withdrawn; but the notice of ownership of an item by its owner and any rights of the owner to proceeds of the item are subject to rights of a collecting bank such as those resulting from outstanding advances on the item and valid rights of setoff. When an item is handled by banks for purposes of presentment, payment and collection, the relevant provisions of this Article apply even though action of parties clearly establishes that a particular bank has purchased the item and is the owner of it.
(2) After an item has been endorsed with the words "Pay any bank" or the like, only a bank may acquire the rights of a holder
(a) until the item has been returned to the customer initiating collection; or
(b) until the item has been specially endorsed by a bank to a person who is not a bank.

Section 4-202. *Responsibility for Collection; When Action Seasonable.*
(1) A collecting bank must use ordinary care in
(a) presenting an item or sending it for presentment; and
(b) sending notice of dishonor or non-payment or returning an item other than a documentary draft to the bank's transferor or directly to the depositary bank under subsection (2) of Section 4-212 (*see note to Section 4-212*) after learning that the item has not been paid or accepted, as the case may be; and
(c) settling for an item when the bank receives final settlement; and
(d) making or providing for any necessary protest; and
(e) notifying its transferor of any loss or delay in transit within a reasonable time after discovery thereof.
(2) A collecting bank taking proper action before its midnight deadline following receipt of an item, notice or payment acts seasonably; taking proper action within a reasonably longer time may be seasonable but the bank has the burden of so establishing.
(3) Subject to subsection (1) (a), a bank is not liable for the insolvency, neglect, misconduct, mistake, or default of another bank or person or for loss or destruction of an item in transit or in the possession of others.

Section 4-203. *Effect of Instructions.*
Subject to the provisions of Article 3 concerning conversion of instruments (Section 3-419) and the provisions of both Article 3 and

this Article concerning restrictive endorsements, only a collecting bank's transferor can give instructions which affect the bank or constitute notice to it and a collecting bank is not liable to prior parties for any action taken pursuant to such instructions or in accordance with any agreement with its transferor.

Section 4-204. *Methods of Sending and Presenting; Sending Direct to Payor Bank.*
(1) A collecting bank must send items by reasonably prompt method taking into consideration any relevant instructions, the nature of the item, the number of such items on hand, and the cost of collections involved and the method generally used by it or others to present such items.
(2) A collecting bank may send
   (a) any item direct to the payor bank;
   (b) any item to any non-bank payor if authorized by its transferor; and
   (c) any item other than documentary drafts to any non-bank payor, if authorized by Federal Reserve regulation or operating letter, clearing house rule or the like.
(3) Presentment may be made by a presenting bank at a place where the payor bank has requested that presentment be made.

Section 4-205. *Supplying Missing Endorsement; No Notice from Prior Endorsement.*
(1) A depositary bank which has taken an item for collection may supply any endorsement of the customer which is necessary to title unless the item contains the words "payee's endorsement required" or the like. In the absence of such a requirement a statement placed on the item by the depositary bank to the effect that the item was deposited by a customer or credited to his account is effective as the customer's endorsement.
(2) An intermediary bank, or payor bank which is not a depositary bank, is neither given notice nor otherwise affected by a restrictive endorsement of any person except the bank's immediate transferor.

Section 4-206. *Transfer Between Banks.*
Any agreed method which identifies the transferor bank is sufficient for the item's further transfer to another bank.

Section 4-207. *Warranties of Customer and Collecting Bank on Transfer or Presentment of Items; Time for Claims.*
(1) Each customer or collecting bank who obtains payment or acceptance of an item and each prior customer and collecting bank warrants to the payor bank or other payor who in good faith pays or accepts the item that
   (a) he has a good title to the item or is authorized to obtain payment or acceptance on behalf of one who has a good title; and
   (b) he has no knowledge that the signature of the maker or drawer is unauthorized, except that this warranty is not given by any customer or collecting bank that is a holder in due course and acts in good faith.
      (i) to a maker with respect to the maker's own signature; or
      (ii) to a drawer with respect to the drawer's own signature, whether or not the drawer is also the drawee; or
      (iii) to an acceptor of an item if the holder in due course took the item after the acceptance or obtained the acceptance without knowledge that the drawer's signature was unauthorized; and
   (c) the item has not been materially altered, except that this warranty is not given by any customer or collecting bank that is a holder in due course and acts in good faith
      (i) to the maker of a note; or
      (ii) to the drawer of a draft whether or not the drawer is also the drawee; or
      (iii) to the acceptor of an item with respect to an alteration made prior to the acceptance if the holder in due course took the item after the acceptance, even though the acceptance provided "payable as originally drawn" or equivalent terms; or
      (iv) to the acceptor of an item with respect to an alteration made after the acceptance.
(2) Each customer and collecting bank who transfers an item and receives a settlement or other consideration for it warrants to his transferee and to any subsequent collecting bank who takes the item in good faith that
   (a) he has a good title to the item or is authorized to obtain payment or acceptance on behalf of one who has a good title and the transfer is otherwise rightful; and
   (b) all signatures are genuine or authorized, and
   (c) the item has not been materially altered; and
   (d) no defense of any party is good against him; and
   (e) he has no knowledge of any insolvency proceeding instituted with respect to the maker or acceptor or the drawer of an unaccepted item.

In addition each customer and collecting bank so transferring an item and receiving a settlement or other consideration engages that upon dishonor and any necessary notice of dishonor and protest he will take up the item.
(3) The warranties and the engagement to honor set forth in the two preceding subsections arise notwithstanding the absence of endorsement or words of guaranty or warranty in the transfer or presentment and a collecting bank remains liable for their breach despite remittance to its transferor. Damages for breach of such warranties or engagement to honor shall not exceed the consideration received by the customer or collecting bank responsible plus finance charges and expenses related to the item, if any.
(4) Unless a claim for breach of warrant under this section is made within a reasonable time after the person claiming learns of the breach, the person liable is discharged to the extent of any loss caused by the delay in making claim.

Section 4-208. *Security Interest of Collecting Bank in Items, Accompanying Documents and Proceeds.*
(1) A bank has a security interest in an item and any accompanying documents or the proceeds of either
   (a) in case of an item deposited in an account, to the extent to which credit given for the item has been withdrawn or applied;
   (b) in case of an item for which it has given credit available for withdrawal as of right, to the extent of the credit given whether or not the credit is drawn upon and whether or not there is a right of charge-back; or
   (c) if it makes an advance on or against the item.
(2) When credit which has been given for several items received at one time or pursuant to a single agreement is withdrawn or applied in part, the security interest remains upon all the items, any accompanying documents or the proceeds of either. For the purpose of this section, credits first given are first withdrawn.
(3) Receipt by a collecting bank of a final settlement for an item is a realization on its security interest in the item, accompanying documents and proceeds. To the extent and so long as the bank does not receive final settlement for the item or give up possession of the item or accompanying documents for purposes other than collection, the security interest continues and is subject to the provisions of Article 9 except that
   (a) no security agreement is necessary to make the security interest enforceable (subsection (1)(b) of Section 9-203); and
   (b) no filing is required to perfect the security interest; and
   (c) the security interest has priority over conflicting perfected security interests in the item, accompanying documents or proceeds.

Section 4-209. *When Bank Gives Value for Purposes of Holder in Due Course.*
For purposes of determining its status as a holder in due course, the bank has given value to the extent that it has a security interest in an item provided that the bank otherwise complies with the requirements of Section 3-302 on what constitutes a holder in due course.

Section 4-210. *Presentment by Notice of Item Not Payable by, Through or at a Bank; Liability of Secondary Parties.*
(1) Unless otherwise instructed, a collecting bank may present an item not payable by, through or at a bank by sending to the party to accept or pay a written notice that the bank holds the item for acceptance or payment. The notice must be sent in time to be received on or before the day when presentment is due and the bank must meet any requirement of the party to accept or pay under Section 3-505 by the close of the bank's next banking day after it knows of the requirement.

(2) Where presentment is made by notice and neither honor nor request for compliance with a requirement under Section 3-505 is received by the close of business on the day after maturity or in the case of demand items by the close of business on the third banking day after notice was sent, the presenting bank may treat the item as dishonored and charge any secondary party by sending him notice of the facts.

Section 4-211. *Media of Remittance; Provisional and Final Settlement in Remittance Cases.*
(1) A collecting bank may take in settlement of an item
 (a) a check of the remitting bank or of another bank on any bank except the remitting bank; or
 (b) a cashier's check or similar primary obligation of a remitting bank which is a member of or clears through a member of the same clearing house or group as the collecting bank; or
 (c) appropriate authority to charge an account of the remitting bank or of another bank with the collecting bank; or
 (d) if the item is drawn upon or payable by a person other than a bank, a cashier's check, certified check or other bank check or obligation.
(2) If before its midnight deadline the collecting bank properly dishonors a remittance check or authorization to charge on itself or presents or forwards for collection a remittance instrument of or on another bank which is of a kind approved by subsection (1) or has not been authorized by it, the collecting bank is not liable to prior parties in the event of the dishonor of such check, instrument or authorization.
(3) A settlement for an item by means of a remittance instrument or authorization to charge is or becomes a final settlement as to both the person making and the person making and the person receiving the settlement
 (a) If the remittance instrument or authorization to charge is of a kind approved by subsection (1) or has not been authorized by the person receiving the settlement acts seasonably before its midnight deadline in presenting, forwarding for collection or paying the instrument or authorization is finally paid by the payor by which it is payable;
 (b) if the person receiving the settlement has authorized remittance by a non-bank check or obligation or by a cashier's check or similar primary obligation of or a check upon the payor or other remitting bank which is not of a kind approved by subsection (1) (b)—at the time of the receipt of such remittance check or obligation; or
 (c) if in a case not covered by subparagraphs (a) or (b) the person receiving the settlement fails to seasonable present, forward for collection, pay or return a remittance instrument or authorization to it to charge before its midnight deadline—at such midnight deadline.

Section 4-212. *Right of Charge-Back or Refund.*
(1) If a collecting bank has made provisional settlement with its customer for an item and itself fails by reason of dishonor, suspension of payments by a bank or otherwise to receive a settlement for the item which is or becomes final, the bank may revoke the settlement given by it, charge-back the amount of any credit given for the item to its customer's account or obtain refund from its customer whether or not it is able to return the items if by its midnight deadline or within a longer reasonable time after it learns the facts it returns the item or sends notification of the facts. These rights to revoke, charge-back and obtain refund terminate if and when a settlement for the item received by the bank is or becomes final (subsection (3) of Section 4-211 and subsections (2) and (3) of Section 4-213).
(2)(Within the time and manner prescribed by this section and Section 4-301, an intermediary or payor bank, as the case may be, may return an unpaid item directly to the depositary bank and obtain reimbursement. In such case, if the depositary bank has received provisional settlement for the item, it must reimburse the bank drawing the draft and any provisional credits for the item between banks shall become and remain final.)

Note: *Direct returns is recognized as an innovation that is not yet established bank practice, and therefore Paragraph 2 has been placed in parentheses. Some lawyers have doubts whether it should be included in legislation or left to development by agreement.*

(3) A depositary bank which is also the payor may charge-back the amount of an item to its customer's account or obtain refund in accordance with the section governing return of an item received by a payor bank for credit on its books (Section 4-301).
(4) The right to charge-back is not affects by
 (a) prior use of the credit given for the item; or
 (b) failure by any bank to exercise ordinary care with respect to the item, but any bank so failing remains liable.
(5) A failure to charge-back or claim refund does not affect other rights of the bank against the customer or any other party.
(6) If credit is given in dollars as the equivalent of the value of an item payable in a foreign currency, the dollar amount of any charge-back or refund shall be calculated on the basis of the buying sight rate for the foreign currency prevailing on the day when the person entitled to the charge-back or refund learns that it will not receive payment in ordinary course.

Section 4-213. *Final Payment of Item by Payor Bank; When Provisional Debits and Credits Become Final; When Certain Credits Become Available for Withdrawal.*
(1) An item is finally paid by payor bank when the bank has done any of the following, whichever happens first:
 (a) paid the item in cash; or
 (b) settled for the item without reserving a right to revoke the settlement and without having such right under statute, clearing house rule or agreement.
Upon a final payment under subparagraphs (b), (c) or (d) the payor bank shall be accountable for the amount of the item.
(2) If provisional settlement for an item between the presenting and payor banks is made through a clearing house or by debits and credits in an account between them, then to the extent that provisional debits or credits for the item are entered in accounts between the presenting and payor banks or between the presenting and successive prior collecting banks seritim, they become final upon final payment of the item by the payor bank.
(3) If a collecting bank receives a settlement for an item which is or becomes final (subsection (3) of Section 4-211, subsection (2) of Section 4-213) the bank is accountable to its customer for the amount of the item and any provisional credit given for the item in an account with its customer becomes final.
(4) Subject to any right of the bank to apply the credit to an obligation of the customer, credit given by a bank for an item in an account with its customer becomes available for withdrawal as of right
 (a) in any case where the bank has received a provisional settlement for the item—when such settlement becomes final and the bank has had a reasonable time to learn that the settlement is final;
 (b) in any case where the bank is both a depositary bank and a payor bank and the item is finally paid—at the opening of the bank's second banking day following receipt of the item.
(5) A deposit of money in a bank is final when made but, subject to any right of the bank to apply the deposit to an obligation of the customer, the deposit becomes available for withdrawal as of right at the opening of the bank's next banking day following receipt of the deposit.

Section 4-124. *Insolvency and Preference.*
(1) Any item in or coming into the possession of a payor or collecting bank which suspends payment and whic item is not finally paid shall be returned by the receiver, trustee or agent in charge of the closed bank to the presenting bank or the closed bank's customer.
(2) If a payor bank finally pays an item and suspends payments without making a settlement for the item with its customer or the presenting bank which settlement is or becomes final, the owner of the item has a preferred claim against the payor bank.
(3) If a payor bank gives or a collecting bank gives or receives a provisional settlement for an item and thereafter suspends payments, the suspension does not prevent or interfere with the settlement becoming final if such finality occurs automatically upon the lapse of certain time or the happening of certain events (subsection (3) of Section 4-211, subsections (1) (d), (2) and (3) of Section 4-213).
(4) If a collecting bank receives from subsequent parties settlement for an item which settlement is or becomes final and suspends

NEGOTIABLE INSTRUMENTS LAW

payments without making a settlement for the item has a preferred claim against such collecting bank.

Part 3
Collection of Items: Payor Banks

Section 4-301. *Deferred Posting, Recovery of Payment by Return of Items; Time of Dishonor.*
(1) Where an authorized settlement for a demand item (other than a documentary draft) received by a payor bank otherwise than for immediate payment over the counter has been made before midnight of the banking day of receipt, the payor bank may revoke the settlement and recover any payment if before it has made final payment (subsection (1) of Section 4-213 and before its midnight deadline it
   (a) returns the item; or
   (b) sends written notice of dishonor or nonpayment if the item is held for protest or is otherwise unavailable for return.
(2) If a demand item is received by a payor bank for credit on its books, it may return such item or send notice of dishonor and may revoke any credit given or recover the amount thereof withdrawn by its customer, if it acts within the time limit and in the manner specified in the preceding subsection.
(3) Unless previous notice of dishonor has been sent, and item is dishonored at the time when for purposes of dishonor it is returned or notice sent in accordance with this section.
(4) An item is returned:
   (a) as to an item received through a clearing house, when it is delivered to the presenting or last collecting bank or to the clearing house or is sent or delivered in accordance with its rules; or
   (b) in all other cases, when it is sent or delivered to the bank's customer or transferor or pursuant to his instructions.

Section 4-302. *Payor Bank's Responsibility for Late Return of Item.*
In the absence of a valid defense such as breach of a presentment warranty (subsection (1) of Section 4-207), settlement effected or the like, if an item is presented on and received by a payor bank the bank is accountable for the amount of
   (a) a demand item other than a documentary draft whether properly payable or not if the bank, in any case where it is not also the depositary bank, retains the item beyond midnight of the banking day of receipt without settling for it or, regardless of whether it is also the depositary bank, does not pay or return the item or send notice of dishonor until after its midnight deadline; or
   (b) any other properly payable item unless within the time allowed for acceptance or payment of that item the bank either accepts or pays the item or returns it and accompanying documents.

Section 4-303. *When Items Subject to Notice, Stop-Order, Legal Process or Setoff; Order in Which Items May Be Charged or Certified.*
(1) Any knowledge, notice or stop-order received by, legal process served upon or setoff exercised by a payor bank, whether or not effective under other rules of law to terminate, suspend or modify the bank's right or duty to pay an item or to charge its customer's account for the item, comes too late to so terminate, suspend or modify such right or duty if the knowledge, notice, stop-order or legal process is received or served and a reasonable time for the bank to act thereon expires or the setoff is exercised after the bank has done any of the following:
   (a) accepted or certified the item;
   (b) paid the item in cash;
   (c) settled for the item without reserving a right to revoke the settlement and without having such right under statute, clearing house rule or agreement;
   (d) completed the process of posting the item to the indicated account of the drawer, maker or other person to be charged therewith or otherwise has evidenced by examination of such indicated account and by action its decision to pay the item; or
   (e) become accountable for the amount of the item under subsection (1)(d) of Section 4-213 and Section 4-302 dealing with the payor bank's responsibility for late return of items.

(2) Subject to the provisions of subsection (1) items may be accepted, paid, certified or charged to the indicated account of its customer in any order convenient to the bank.

Part 4
Relationship Between Payor Bank and Its Customer

Section 4-401. *When Bank May Charge Customer's Account.*
(1) As against its customer, a bank may charge against his account any item which is otherwise properly payable from that account even though the charge creates an overdraft.
(2) A bank which in good faith makes payment to a holder may charge the indicated account of its customer according to
   (a) the original tenor of his altered item: or
   (b) the tenor of his completed item, even though the bank knows the item has been completed and unless the bank has notice that the completion was improper.

Section 4-402. *Bank's Liability to Customer for Wrongful Dishonor.*
A payor bank is liable to its customer for damages proximately caused by the wrongful dishonor of an item. When the dishonor occurs through mistake, liability is limited to actual damages proved. If so proximately caused and proved, damages may include damages for an arrest or prosecution of the customer or other consequential damages. Whether any consequential damages are proximately caused by the wrongful dishonor is a question of fact to be determined in each case.

Section 4-403. *Customer's Right to Stop Payment; Burden of Proof of Loss.*
(1) A customer may by order to his bank stop payment of any item payable for his account but the order must be received at such time and in such manner as to afford the bank a reasonable opportunity to act on it prior to any action by the bank with respect to the item described in Section 4-303.
(2) An oral order is binding upon the bank only for fourteen calendar days unless confirmed in writing within that period. A written order is effective for only six months unless renewed in writing.
(3) The burden of establishing the fact and amount of loss resulting from the payment of an item contrary to a binding stop payment order is on the customer.

Section 4-404. *Bank Not Obligated to Pay Check More Than Six Months Old.*
A bank is under no obligation to a customer having a checking account to pay a check, other than a certified check, which is presented more than six months after its date, but it may charge its customer's account for a payment made thereafter in good faith.

Section 4-405. *Death or Incompetence of Customer.*
(1) A payor or collecting bank's authority to accept, pay or collect an item or to account for proceeds of its collection if otherwise effective is not rendered ineffective by incompetence of a customer or either bank existing at the time the item is issued or its collection is undertaken if the bank does not know of an adjudication of incompetence. Neither death nor incompetence of a customer revokes such authority to accept, pay, collect or account until the bank knows of the fact of death or of an adjudication of incompetence and has reasonable opportunity to act on it.
(2) Even with knowledge a bank may for ten days after the date of death pay or certify checks drawn on or prior to that date unless ordered to stop payment by a person claiming an interest in the account.

Section 4-406. *Customer's Duty to Discover and Report Unauthorized Signature or Alteration.*
(1) When a bank sends to its customer a statement of account accompanied by items paid in good faith in support of the debit entries or holds the statement and items pursuant to a request or instructions of its customer or otherwise in a reasonable manner makes the statement and items available to the customer, the customer must exercise reasonable care and promptness to examine the statement and items to discover his

unauthorized signature or any alteration on an item and must notify the bank promptly after discovery thereof.
(2) If the bank establishes that the customer failed with respect to an item to comply with the duties imposed on the customer by subsection (1) the customer is precluded from asserting against the bank
   (a) his unauthorized signature or any alteration on the item if the bank also establishes that it suffered a loss by reason of such failure; and
   (b) an unauthorized signature or alteration by the same wrongdoer on any other item paid in good faith by the bank after the first item and statement was available to the customer for a reasonable period not exceeding fourteen calendar days and before the bank receives notification from the customer of any such unauthorized signature or alteration.
(3) The preclusion under subsection (2) does not apply if the customer establishes lack of ordinary care on the part of the bank in paying the item(s).
(4) Without regard to care of lack of care of either the customer or the bank, a customer who does not within one year from the time the statement and items are made available to the customer (subsection (1) discover and report his unauthorized signature or any alteration on the face or back of the item or does not within three years from that time discover and report any unauthorized endorsement is precluded from asserting against the bank such unauthorized signature or endorsement or such alteration.
(5) If under this section a payor bank has a valid defense against a claim of a customer upon or resulting from payment of an item and waives or fails upon request to assert the defense, the bank may not assert against any collecting bank or other prior party presenting or transferring the item a claim based upon the unauthorized signature or alteration giving rise to the customer's claim.

Section 4-407. *Payor Bank's Right to Subrogation on Improper Payment.*
If a payor bank has paid an item over the stop payment order of the drawer or maker or otherwise under circumstances giving a basis for objection by the drawer or maker, to prevent unjust enrichment and only to the extent necessary to prevent loss to the bank by reason of its payment of the item, the payor bank shall be subrogated to the rights
(a) of any holder in due course on the item against the drawer or maker; and
(b) of the payee or any other holder of the item against the drawer or maker either on the item or under the transaction out of which the item arose; and
(c) the drawer or maker against the payee or any other holder of the item with respect to the transaction out of which the item arose.

Part 5
Collection of Documentary Drafts

Section 4-501. *Handling of Documentary Draft; Duty to Send for Presentment and to Notify Customer of Dishonor.*
A bank which takes a documentary draft for collection must present or send the draft and accompanying documents for presentment and upon learning that the draft has not been paid or accepted in due course, must seasonably notify its customer of such fact even though it may have discounted or bought the draft or extended credit available for withdrawal as of right.

Section 4-502. *Presentment of "On Arrival" Drafts.*
When a draft or the relevant instructions require presentment "on arrival," "when goods arrive," or the like, the collecting bank need not present until in its judgment a reasonable time for arrival of the goods has expired. Refusal to pay or accept because the goods have not arrived is not dishonor; the bank must notify its transferor of such refusal but need not present the draft again until it is instructed to do so or learns of the arrival of the goods.

Section 4-503. *Responsibility of Presenting Bank for Documents and Goods; Report of Reasons for Dishonor; Referee in Case of Need.*
Unless otherwise instructed and except as provided in Article 5 a bank presenting a documentary draft

(a) must deliver the documents to the drawee on acceptance of the draft if it is payable more than three days after presentment; otherwise, only on payment; and
(b) upon dishonor, either in the case of presentment for acceptance or presentment for payment, may seek and follow instructions from any referee in case of need designated in the draft or, if the presenting bank does not choose to utilize his services, it must use diligence and good faith to ascertain the reason for dishonor, must notify its transferor of the dishonor and of the results of its effort to ascertain the reasons therefor and must request instructions.

But the presenting bank is under no obligation with respect to goods represented by the documents except to follow any reasonable instructions seasonably received; it has a right to reimbursement for any expense incurred in following instructions and to prepayment of or indemnity for such expenses.

Section 4-504. *Privilege of Presenting Bank to Deal with Goods: Security Interest for Expenses.*
(1) A presenting bank which, following the dishonor of a documentary draft, has seasonably requested instructions but does not receive them within a reasonable time may store, sell or otherwise deal with the goods in any reasonable manner.
(2) For its reasonable expenses incurred by action under subsection (1) the presenting bank has a lien upon the goods or their proceeds, which may be foreclosed in the same manner as an unpaid seller's lien.

Article 9
Secured Transactions; Sales of Accounts,
Contract Rights, and Chattel Paper

Part 1
Short Title, Applicability and Definitions

Section 9-101. *Short Title.*
This Article shall be known and may be cited as Uniform Commercial Code—Secured Transactions.

Section 9-102. *Policy and Scope of Article.*
(1) Except as otherwise provided in Section 9-103 on multiple state transactions and in Section 9-104 on excluded transactions, this Article applies so far as concerns any personal property and fixtures within the jurisdiction of this state
   (a) to any transaction (regardless of its form) which is intended to create a security interest in personal property or fixtures including goods, documents, instruments, general intangibles, chattel papers, accounts of contract rights; and also
   (b) to any sale of accounts, contract rights or chattel paper.
(2) This Article applies to security interests created by contract including pledge, assignment, chattel mortgage, chattel trust, trust deed, factor's lien, equipment trust, conditional sale, trust receipt, other lien or title retention contract and lease or consignment intended as security. This Article does not apply to statutory liens except as provided in Section 9-310.
(3) The application of this Article to a security interest in a secured obligation is not affected by the fact that the obligation is itself secured by a transaction or interest to which this Article does not apply.

Note: The adoption of this Article should be accompanied by the repeal of existing statutes dealing with conditional sales, trust receipts, factor's liens where the factor is given a non-possessory lien, chattel mortgages, crop mortgages, mortgages on railroad equipment, assignment of accounts and generally statutes regulating security interests in personal property.

Where the state has a retail installment selling act or small loan act, that legislation should be carefully examined to determine what changes in those acts are needed to conform them to this Article. This Article primarily sets out rules defining rights of a secured party against persons dealing with the debtor; it does not prescribe regulations and controls which may be necessary to curb abuses arising in the small loan business or in the financing of consumer purchases on credit. Accordingly, there is no intention to repeal existing regulatory acts in those fields. See Section 9-203(2) and the Note thereto.

Section 9-103. *Accounts, Contract Rights, General Intangibles and Equipment Relating to Another Jurisdiction; and Incoming Goods already Subject to a Security Interest.*
(1) If the office where the assignor of accounts or contract rights keeps his records concerning them is in this state, the validity and perfection of a security interest therein and the possibility and effect of proper filing is governed by this Article; otherwise by the law (including the conflict of laws rules) or the jurisdiction where such office is located.
(2) If the chief place of business of a debtor is in this state; this Article governs the validity and perfection of a security interest and the possibility and effect of proper filing with regard to general intangibles or with regard to goods of a type which are normally used in more than one jurisdiction (such as automotive equipment, rolling stock, airplanes, road building equipment, commercial harvesting equipment, construction machinery and the like) if such goods are classified as equipment or classified as inventory by reason of their being leased by the debtor to others. Otherwise, the law (including the conflict of laws rules) of the jurisdiction where such chief place of business is located shall govern. If the chief place of business is located in a jurisdiction which does not provide for perfection of the security interest by filing or recording in that jurisdiction, then the security interest may be perfected by filing in this state. (For the purpose of determining the validity and perfection of a security interest in an airplane, the chief place of business of a debtor who is a foreign air carrier under the Federal Aviation Act of 1958, as amended, is the designated office of the agent upon whom service of process may be made on behalf of the debtor.)
(3) If personal property other than that governed by subsections (1) and (2) is already subject to a security interest when it is brought into this state, the validity of the security interest in this state is to be determined by the law (including the conflict of laws rules) of the jurisdiction where the property was when the security interest attached. However, if the parties to the transaction understood at the time that the security interest attached that the property would be kept in this state and it was brought into this state within 30 days after the security interest attached for purposes other than transportation through this state, then the validity of the security interest in this state is to be determined by the law of this state. If the security interest was already perfected under the law of the jurisdiction where the property was when the security interest attached and before being brought into this state, the security interest continues perfected in this state for four months and also thereafter if within the four month period it is perfected in this state. The security interest may also be perfected in this state after the expiration of the four month period; in such case perfection dates from the time of perfection in this state. If the security interest was not perfected under the law of the jurisdiction where the property was when the security interest attached and before being brought into this state, it may be perfected in this state; in such case perfection dates from the time of perfection in this state.
(4) Notwithstanding subsections (2) and (3), if personal property is covered by a certificate of title issued under a statute of this state or any other jurisdiction which requires indication on a certificate of title of any security interest in the property as a condition of perfection, then the perfection is governed by the law of the jurisdiction which issued the certificate.
(5) Notwithstanding subsection (1) and Section 9-302, if the office where the assignor of accounts contract rights keeps his records concerning them is not located in a jurisdiction which is a part of the United States, its territories or possessions, and the accounts or contract rights are within the jurisdiction of this state or the transaction which creates the security interest otherwise bears an appropriate relation to this state, this Article governs the validity and perfection of the security interest and the security interest may only be perfected by notification to the account debtor.)

Note: The last sentence of subsection (2) and subsection (5) are in parentheses to indicate optional enactment. In states engaging in financing of airplanes of foreign carriers and of international open accounts receivable, (the) language in parentheses will be of value. In other states not engaging in financing of this type, (the) language in parentheses may not be considered necessary.

Section 9-104. *Transactions Excluded from Article.*
This Article does not apply
(a) to a security interest subject to any statute of the United States such as the Ship Mortgage Act, 1920, to the extent that such statute governs the rights of parties to and third parties affected by transactions in particular types of property; or
(b) to a landlord's lien; or
(c) to a lien given by statute or other rules of law for services or materials except as provided in Section 9-310 on priority of such liens; or
(d) to a transfer of a claim for wages, salary or other compensation of an employee; or
(e) an equipment trust covering railway rolling stock; or
(f) to a sale of accounts, contract rights or chattel paper as part of a sale of the business out of which they arose, or an assignment of accounts, contract rights or chattel paper which is for the purpose of collection only, or a transfer of a contract right to an assignee who is also to do the performance under the contract; or
(g) to a transfer of an interest or claim in or under any policy of insurance; or
(h) to a right represented by a judgment; or
(i) to any right of setoff; or
(j) except to the extent that provision is made for fixtures in Section 9-313, to the creation or transfer of an interest in or lien on real estate, including a lease or rents thereunder; or
(k) to a transfer in whole or in part of any of the following: any claim arising out of tort; any deposit, savings, passbook or like account maintained with a bank, savings and loan association, credit union or like organization.

Section 9-105. *Definitions and Index of Definitions.*
(1) In this Article unless the context otherwise requires:
(a) "Account debtor" means the person who is obligated on an account, chattel paper, contract right or general intangible;
(b) "Chattel paper" means a writing or writings which evidence both a monetary obligation and a security interest in or a lease of specific goods. When a transaction is evidenced both by such a security agreement or a lease and by an instrument or a series of instruments, the group of writings taken together constitutes chattel paper;
(c) "Collateral" means the property subject to a security interest, and includes accounts, contract rights and chattel paper which have been sold;
(d) "Debtor" means the person who owes payment or other performance of the obligation secured, whether or not he owns or has rights in the collateral, and includes the seller of accounts, contract rights or chattel paper. Where the debtor and the owner of the collateral are not the same person, the term "debtor" means the owner of the collateral in any provision of the Article dealing with the collateral, the obligor in any provision dealing with the obligation, and may include both where the context so requires;
(e) "Document" means document of title as defined in the general definitions of Article 1 (Section 1-201);
(f) "Goods" includes all things which are movable at the time the security interest attaches or which are fixtures (Section 9-313), but does not include money, documents, instruments, accounts, chattel paper, general intangibles, contract rights and other things in action. "Goods" also include the unborn young of animals and growing crops;
(g) "Instrument" means a negotiable instrument (defined in Section 3-104), or a security (defined in Section 8-102) or any other writing which evidences a right to the payment of money and is not itself a security agreement or lease and is of a type which is in ordinary course of business transferred by delivery with any necessary endorsement or assignment;
(h) "Security agreement" means an agreement which creates or provides for a security interest;
(i) "Secured party" means a lender, seller or other person in whose favor there is a security interest, including a person to whom accounts, contract rights or chattel paper have been sold. When the holders of obligations issued under an

indenture of trust, equipment trust agreement or the like are represented by a trustee or other person, the representative is the secured party.
(2) Other definitions applying to this Article and the sections in which they appear are
"Account." Section 9-106.
"Consumer goods." Section 9-109 (1).
"Contract right." Section 9-106.
"Equipment." Section 9-109(2).
"Farm products." Section 9-109(3).
"General intangibles." Section 9-106.
"Inventory." Section 9-109 (4).
"Lien creditor." Section 9-301 (3).
"Proceeds." Section 9-306 (1).
"Purchase money security interest." Section 9-107.
(3) The following definitions in other Articles apply to this Article:
"Check." Section 3-104.
"Contract for sale." Section 2-106.
"Holder in due course." Section 3-302.
"Note." Section 3-104.
"Sale." Section 2-106.
(4) In addition Article 1 contains general definitions and principles of construction and interpretation applicable throughout this Article.

Section 9-106. Definitions: *"Account"; "Contract Right"; "General Intangibles."*
"Account" means any right to payment for goods sold or leased or for services rendered which is not evidenced by an instrument or chattel paper. "Contract right" means any right to payment under a contract not yet earned by performance and not evidenced by an instrument or chattel paper. "General intangibles" means any personal property (including things in action) other than goods, accounts, contract rights, chattel paper, documents and instruments.

Section 9-107. Definitions: *"Purchase Money Security Interest."*
A security interest is a "purchase money security interest" to the extent that it is
(a) taken or retained by the seller of the collateral to secure all or part of its price; or
(b) taken by a person who by making advances or incurring an obligation gives value to enable the debtor to acquire rights in or the use of collateral if such value is in fact so used.

Section 9-108. *When After-Acquired Collateral Not Security for Antecedent Debt.*
Where a secured party makes an advance, incurs an obligation, releases a perfected security interest or otherwise gives new value which is to be secured in whole or in part by after-acquired property, his security interest in the after-acquired collateral shall be deemed to be taken for new value and not as security for an antecedent debt if the debtor acquires his rights in such collateral either in the ordinary course of his business or under a contract of purchase made pursuant to the security agreement within a reasonable time after new value is given.

Section 9-109. *Classification of Goods; "Consumer Goods"; "Equipment"; "Farm Products"; "Inventory."*
Goods are
(1) "consumer goods" if they are used or bought for use primarily for personal, family or household purposes;
(2) "equipment" if they are used or bought for use primarily in business (including farming or a profession) or by a debtor who is a non-profit organization or a governmental subdivision or agency, or if the goods are not included in the definitions of inventory, farm products or consumer goods;
(3) "farm products" if they are crops or livestock or supplies used or produced in farming operations or if they are products of crops or livestock in their unmanufactured states (such as ginned cotton, wool-clip, maple syrup, milk and eggs), and if they are in the possession of a debtor engaged in raising, fattening, grazing or other farming operations. If goods are farm products, they are neither equipment nor inventory;
(4) "inventory" if they are held by a person who holds them for sale or lease or to be furnished under contracts or service or if he has so furnished them, or if they are raw materials, work in process or materials used or consumed in a business. Inventory of a person is not to be classified as his equipment.

Section 9-110. *Sufficiency of Description.*
For the purposes of this Article any description of personal property or real estate is sufficient whether or not it is specific if it reasonably identifies what is described.

Section 9-111. *Applicability of Bulk Transfer Laws.*
The creation of a security interest is not a bulk transfer under Article 6 (see Section 6-103).

Section 9-112. *Where Collateral Is Not Owned by Debtor.*
Unless otherwise agreed, when a secured party knows that collateral is owned by a person who is not the debtor, the owner of the collateral is entitled to receive from the secured party any surplus under Section 9-502(2) or under Section 9-504(1), and is not liable for the debt or for any deficiency after resale, and he has the same right as the debtor
(a) to receive statements under Section 9-208;
(b) to receive notice of and to object to a secured party's proposal to retain the collateral in satisfaction of the indebtedness under Section 9-505;
(c) to redeem the collateral under Section 9-506;
(d) to obtain injunctive or other relief under Section 9-507(1); and
(e) to recover losses caused to him under Section 9-208(2).

Section 9-113. *Security Interests Arising Under Article on Sales.*
A security interest arising solely under the Article on Sales (Article 2) is subject to the provisions of this Article except that to the extent that and so long as the debtor does not have or does not lawfully obtain possession of the goods.
(a) no security agreement is necessary to make the security interest enforceable; and
(b) no filing is required to perfect the security interest; and
(c) the rights of the secured party on default by the debtor are governed by the Article on Sales (Article 2).

Part 2
Validity of Security Agreement and Rights of Parties Thereto

Section 9-201. *General Validity of Security Agreement.*
Except as otherwise provided by this Act a security agreement is effective according to its terms between the parties, against purchasers of the collateral and against creditors. Nothing in this Article validates any charge or practice illegal under any statute or regulation thereunder governing usury, small loans, retail installment sales or the like, or extends the application of any such statute or regulation to any transaction not otherwise subject thereto.

Section 9-202. *Title to Collateral Immaterial.*
Each provision of this Article with regard to rights, obligations and remedies applies whether title to collateral is in the secured party or in the debtor.

Section 9-203. *Enforceability of Security Interest: Proceeds, Formal Requisites.*
(1) Subject to the provisions of Section 4-208 on the security interest of a collecting bank and Section 9-113 on a security interest arising under the Article on Sales, a security interest is not enforceable against the debtor or third parties unless
(a) the collateral is in the possession of the secured party; or
(b) the debtor has signed a security agreement which contains a description of the collateral and in addition, when the security interest covers crops or oil, gas or minerals to be extracted or timber to be cut, a description of the land concerned. In describing collateral, the word "proceeds" is sufficient without further description to cover proceeds of any character.
(2) A transaction, although subject to this Article, is also subject to ....*, and in the case of conflict between the provisions of this Article and any such statute, the provisions of such statute control. Failure to comply with any applicable statute has only the effect which is specified thereon.

NEGOTIABLE INSTRUMENTS LAW

Note: At* in subsection (2) insert reference to any local statute regulating small loans, retail installment sales and the like. The foregoing subsection (2) is designed to make it clear that certain transactions, although subject to this Article, must also comply with other applicable legislation.

This Article is designed to regulate all the "security" aspects of transactions within its scope. There is, however, much regulatory legislation, particularly in the consumer field, which supplements this Article and should not be repealed by its enactment. Examples are small loan acts, retail installment selling acts and the like. Such acts may provide for licensing and rate regulation and may prescribe particular forms of contract. Such provisions should remain in force despite the enactment of this Article. On the other hand if a Retail Installment Selling Act contains provisions on filing, rights on default, etc., such provisions should be repealed as inconsistent with the Article.

Section 9-204. *When Security Interest Attaches; After-Acquired Property; Future Advances.*
(1) A security interest cannot attach until there is agreement (subsection (3) of Section 1-201) that it attach and value is given and the debtor has rights in the collateral. It attaches as soon as all of the events in the preceding sentence have taken place unless explicit agreement postpones the time of attaching.
(2) For the purposes of this section the debtor has no rights
   (a) in crops until they are planted or otherwise become growing crops, in the young of livestock until they are conceived;
   (b) in fish until caught, in oil, gas or minerals until they are extracted, in timber until it is cut;
   (c) in a contract right until the contract has been made;
   (d) in an account until it comes into existence.
(3) Except as provided in subsection (4) a security agreement may provide that collateral, whenever acquired, shall secure all obligations covered by the security agreement.
(4) No security interest attaches under an after-acquired property clause
   (a) to crops which become such more than one year after the security agreement is executed, except that a security interest in crops which is given in conjunction with a lease or a land purchase or improvement transaction evidenced by a contract, mortgage or deed of trust may if so agreed attach to crops to be grown on the land concerned during the period of such real estate transactions;
   (b) to consumer goods other than accessions (Section 9-314) when given as additional security unless the debtor acquires rights in them within ten days after the secured party gives value.
(5) Obligations covered by a security agreement may include future advances or other value whether or not the advances or value are given pursuant to commitment.

Section 9-205. *Use or Disposition of Collateral Without Accounting Permissible.*

A security interest is not invalid or fraudulent against creditors by reason of liberty in the debtor to use, commingle or dispose of all or part of the collateral (including returned or repossessed goods) or to collect or compromise accounts, contract rights or chattel paper, or to accept the return of goods or make repossessions, or to use, commingle or dispose of proceeds, or by reason of the failure of the secured party to require the debtor to account for proceeds or replace collateral. This section does not relax the requirements of possession where perfection of a security interest depends upon possession of the collateral by the secured party or by a bailee.

Section 9-206. *Agreement Not to Assert Defenses Against Assignee; Modification of Sales Warranties Where Security Agreement Exists.*
(1) Subject to any statute or decision which establishes a different rule for buyers or lessees of consumer goods, an agreement by a buyer or lessee that he will not assert against an assignee any claim or defense which he may have against the seller or lessor is enforceable by an assignee who takes his assignment for value, in good faith, and without notice of a claim or defense, except as to defenses of a type which may be asserted against a holder in due course of a negotiable instrument under the Article on Commercial paper (Article 3). A buyer who as part of one transaction signs both a negotiable instrument and a security agreement makes such an agreement.
(2) When a seller retains a purchase money security interest in goods, the Article on Sales (Article 2) governs the sale and any disclaimer, limitation or modification of the seller's warranties.

Section 9-207. *Rights and Duties When Collateral Is in Secured Party's Possession.*
(1) A secured party must use reasonable care in the custody and preservation of collateral in his possession. In the case of an instrument or chattel paper reasonable care includes taking necessary steps to preserve rights against prior parties unless otherwise agreed.
(2) Unless otherwise agreed, when collateral is in the secured party's possession.
   (a) reasonable expenses (including the cost of any insurance and payment of taxes or other charges) incurred in the custody, preservation, use or operation of the collateral are chargeable to the debtor and are secured by the collateral;
   (b) the risk of accidental loss or damage is on the debtor to the extent of any deficiency in any effective insurance coverage;
   (c) the secured party may hold as additional security any increase or profits (except money) received from the collateral, but money so received, unless remitted to the debtor, shall be applied in reduction of the secured obligation;
   (d) the secured party must keep the collateral identifiable but fungible collateral may be commingled;
   (e) the secured party may repledge the collateral upon terms which do not impair the debtor's right to redeem it.
(3) A secured party is liable for any loss caused by his failure to meet any obligation imposed by the preceding subsections but does not lose his security interest.
(4) A secured party may use or operate the collateral for the purpose of preserving the collateral or its value or pursuant to the order of a court of appropriate jurisdiction or, except in the case of consumer goods, in the manner and to the extent provided in the security agreement.

Section 9-208. *Request for Statement of Account or List of Collateral.*
(1) A debtor may sign a statement indicating what he believes to be the aggregate amount of unpaid indebtedness as of a specified date and may send it to the secured party with a request that the statement be approved or corrected and returned to the debtor. When the security agreement at any other record kept by the se-cured party identifies the collateral, a debtor may similarly re-quest the secured party to approve or correct a list of the collateral.
(2) The secured party must comply with such a request within two weeks after receipt by sending a written correction or approval. If the secured party claims a security interest in all of a particular type of collateral owned by the debtor, he may indicate that fact in his reply and need not approve or correct an itemized list of such collateral. If the secured party without reasonable excuse fails to comply, he is liable for any loss caused to the debtor thereby; and if the debtor has properly included in his request a good faith statement of the obligation or a list of the collateral or both, the secured party may claim a security interest only as shown in the statement against persons misled by his failure to comply. If he no longer has an interest in the obligation or collateral at the time the request is received, he must disclose the name and address of any successor in interest known to him and he is liable for any loss caused to the debtor as a result of failure to disclose. A successor in interest is not subject to this section until a request is received by him.
(3) A debtor is entitled to such a statement once every six months without charge. the secured party may require payment of a charge not exceeding $10 for each additional statement furnished.

*Part 3
Rights of Third Parties;
Perfected and Unperfected Security Interests;
Rule of Priority*

Section 9-301. *Persons Who Take Priority Over Unperfected Security Interests; "Lien Creditor."*

ENCYCLOPEDIA OF BANKING AND FINANCE

(1) Except as otherwise provided in subsection (2), an unperfected security interest is subordinate to the rights of
  (a) persons entitled to prior under Section 9-312;
  (b) a person who becomes a lien creditor without knowledge of the security interest and before it is perfected;
  (c) in the case of goods, instruments, documents and chattel paper, a person who is not a secured party and who is a transferee in bulk or other buyer not in ordinary course of business to the extent that he gives value and receives delivery of the collateral without knowledge of the security interest and before it is perfected;
  (d) in the case of accounts, contract rights and general intangibles, a person who is not a secured party and who is a transferee to the extent that he gives value without knowledge of the security interest and before it is perfected.
(2) If the secured party files with respect to a purchase money security interest before or within ten days after the collateral comes into possession of the debtor, he takes priority over the rights of a transferee in bulk or of a lien creditor which arise between the time the security interest attaches and the time of filing.
(3) A "lien creditor" means a creditor who has acquired a lien on the property involved by attachment, levy or the like and includes an assignee for benefit of creditors from the time of assignment, and a trustee in bankruptcy from the date of the filing of the petition or a receiver in equity from the time of appointment. Unless all the creditors represented had knowledge of the security interest, such a representative of creditors is a lien creditor without knowledge even though he personally has knowledge of the security interest.

Section 9-302. *When Filing Is Required to Perfect Security Interest; Security Interests to Which Filing Provisions of This Article Do Not Apply.*
(1) A financing statement must be filed to perfect all security interests except the following:
  (a) a security interest in collateral in possession of the secured party under Section 9-305;
  (b) a security interest temporarily perfected in instruments or documents without delivery under Section 9-304 or in proceeds for a ten-day period under Section 9-306;
  (c) a purchase money security interest in farm equipment having a purchase price not in excess of $2,500; but filing is required for a fixture under Section 9-313 or for a motor vehicle required to be licensed;
  (d) a purchase money security interest in consumer goods; but filing is required for a fixture under Section 9-313 or for a motor vehicle required to be licensed;
  (e) an assignment of accounts or contract rights which does not alone or in conjunction with other assignments to the same assignee transfer a significant part of the outstanding accounts or contract rights of the assignor;
  (f) A security interest of a collecting bank (Section 4-208) or arising under the Article on Sales (see Section 9-113) or covered in subsection (3) of this section.
(2) If a secured party assigns a perfected security interest, no filing under this Article is required in order to continue the perfected status of the security interest against creditors of and transferees from the original debtor.
(3) The filing provisions of the this Article do not apply to a security interest in property subject to a statute
  (a) of the United States which provides for a national registration or filing of all security interests in such property; or

Note: States to select either Alternative A or Alternative B.

Alternative A—
  (b) of this state which provides for central filing of, or which requires indication on a certificate of title of, such security interests in such property
Alternative B—
  (b) of this state which provides for central filing of security interests in such property, or in a motor vehicle which is not inventory held for sale for which a certificate of title is required under the statutes of this state if a notation of such a security interest can be indicated by a public official on a certificate or a duplicate thereof.

(4) A security interest in property covered by a statute described in subsection (3) can be perfected only by registration or filing under that statute or by indication of the security interest on a certificate of title or a duplicate thereof by a public official.

Section 9-303. *When Security Interest Is Perfected; Continuity of Perfection.*
(1) A security interest is perfected when it has attached and when all of the applicable steps required for perfection have been taken. Such steps are specified in Sections 9-302, 9-304, and 9-306. if such steps are taken before the security interest attaches, it is perfected at the time when it attaches.
(2) If a security interest is originally perfected in any way permitted under this Article and is subsequently perfected in some other way under this Article, without an intermediate period when it was unperfected, the security interest shall be deemed to be perfected continuously for the purposes of this Article.

Section 9-304. *Perfection of Security Interest in Instruments, Documents and Goods Covered by Documents; Perfection by Permissive Filing; Temprary Perfection Without Filing or Transfer of Possession.*
(1) A security interest in chattel paper or negotiable documents may be perfected by filing. A security interest in instruments (other than instruments which constitute part of chattel paper) can be perfected only by the secured party's taking possession, except as provided in subsections (4) and (5).
(2) During the period that goods are in the possession of the issuer of a negotiable document therefor, a security interest in the goods, is perfected by perfecting a security interest in the document, and any security interest in the goods otherwise perfected during such period is subject therein.
(3) A security interest in goods in the possession of a bailee other than one who has issued a negotiable document therefor is perfected by issuance of a document in the name of the secured party or by the bailee's receipt of notification of the secured party's interest or by filing as to the goods.
(4) A security interest in instruments or negotiable documents is perfected without filing or the taking of possession for a period 21 days from the time it attaches to the extent that it arises for new value given under a written security agreement.
(5) A security interest remains perfected for a period of 21 days without filing where a secured party having a perfected security interest in an instrument, a negotiable document or goods in possession of a bailee other than one who has issued a negotiable instrument therefor
  (a) makes available to the debtor the goods or documents representing the goods for the purpose of ultimate sale or exchange or for the purpose of loading, unloading, storing, shipping, transshipping, manufacturing, processing or otherwise dealing with them in a manner preliminary to their sale or exchange; or
  (b) delivers the instruments to the debtor for the purpose of ultimate sale or exchange or of presentation, collection, renewal or registration of transfer.
(6) After the 21 days period in subsections (4) and (5) perfection depends upon compliance with applicable provisions of this Article.

Section 9-305. *When Possession by Secured Party Perfects Security Interest Without Filing.*

A security interest in letters of credit and advices of credit (subsection (2)(a) of Section 5-116), goods, instruments, negotiable documents or chattel paper may be perfected by the secured party's taking possession of the collateral. If such collateral other than goods covered by a negotiable document is held by a bailee, the secured party is deemed to have possession from the time the bailee receives notification of the secured party's interest. A security interest is perfected by possession from the time possession is taken without relation back and continues only so long as possession is retained, unless otherwise specified in this Article. The security interest may be otherwise perfected as provided in the Article before or after the period of possession by the secured party.

Section 9-306. *"Proceeds"; Secured Party's Rights on Disposition of Collateral.*
(1) "Proceeds" includes whatever is received when collateral or

proceeds are sold, exchanged, collected or otherwise disposed of. The term also includes the account arising when the right to payment is earned under a contract right. Money, checks and the like are "cash proceeds." All other proceeds are "non-cash proceeds."

(2) Except where this Article otherwise provides, a security interest continues in collateral notwithstanding sale, exchange or other disposition thereof by the debtor unless his action was authorized by the secured party in the security agreement or otherwise, and also continues in any identifiable proceeds including collections received by the debtor.

(3) The security interest in proceeds is a continuously perfected security interest if the interest in the original collateral was perfected, but it ceases to be a perfected security interest and becomes unperfected ten days after receipt of the proceeds by the debtor unless
   (a) a filed financing statement covering the original collateral also covers proceeds; or
   (b) the security interest in the proceeds is perfected before the expiration of the ten day period.

(4) In the event of insolvency proceedings instituted by or against a debtor, a secured party with a perfected security interest in proceeds has a perfected security interest
   (a) in identifiable non-cash proceeds;
   (b) in identifiable cash proceeds in the form of money which is not commingled with other money or deposited in a bank account prior to the insolvency proceedings;
   (c) in identifiable cash proceeds in the form of checks and the like which are not deposited in a bank account prior to the insolvency proceedings; and
   (d) in all cash and bank accounts of the debtor, if other cash proceeds have been commingled or deposited in a bank account, but the perfected security interest under this paragraph (d) is
      (i) subject to any right of setoff; and
      (ii) limited to an amount not greater than the amount of any cash proceeds received by the debtor within ten days before the institution of the insolvency proceedings and commingled or deposited in a bank account prior to the insolvency proceedings less the amount of cash proceeds received by the debtor and paid over to the secured party during the ten day period.

(5) If a sale of goods results in an account or chattel paper which is transferred by the seller to a secured party, and if the goods are returned to or are repossessed by the seller or the secured party, the following rules determine priorities:
   (a) If the goods were collateral at the time of sale for an indebtedness of the seller which is still unpaid, the original security interest attaches again to the goods and continues as a perfected security interest if it was perfected at the time when the goods were sold. If the security interest was originally perfected by a filing which is still effective, nothing further is required to continue the perfected status; in any other case, the secured party must take possession of the returned or repossessed goods or must file.
   (b) An unpaid transferee of the chattel paper has a security interest in the goods against the transferor. Such security interest is prior to a security interest asserted under paragraph (a) to the extent that the transferee of the chattel paper was entitled to priority under Section 9-308.
   (c) An unpaid transferee of the account has a security interest in the goods against the transferor. Such security interest is subordinate to a security interest asserted under paragraph (a).
   (d) A security interest of an unpaid transferee asserted under paragraph (b) or (c) must be perfected for protection against creditors of the transferor and purchasers of the returned or repossessed goods.

Section 9-307. *Protection of Buyers of Goods.*

(1) A buyer in ordinary course of business (subsection (9) of Section 1-201) other than a person buying farm products from a person engaged in farming operations takes free of a security interest created by his seller even though the security interest is perfected and even though the buyer knows of its existence.

(2) In the case of consumer goods and in the case of farm equipment having an original purchase price not in excess of $2,500 (other than fixtures, see Section 9-313), a buyer takes free of a security interest even though perfected if he buys without knowledge of the security interest, for value and for his own personal, family or household purposes or his own farming operations, unless prior to the purchase the secured party has filed a financing statement covering such goods.

Section 9-308. *Purchase of Chattel Paper and Non-Negotiable Instruments.*

A purchaser of chattel paper or a non-negotiable instrument who gives new value and takes possession of it in the ordinary course of his business and without knowledge that the specific paper or instrument is subject to a security interest has priority over a security interest which is perfected under Section 9-304 (permissive filing and temporary perfection). A purchaser of chattel paper who gives new value and takes possession of it in the ordinary course of his business has priority over a security interest in chattel paper which is claimed merely as proceeds of inventory subject to a security interest (Section 9-306), even though he knows that the specific paper is subject to the security interest.

Section 9-309. *Protection of Purchasers of Instruments and Documents.*

Nothing in this Article limits the rights of a holder in due course of a negotiable instrument (Section 3-302) or a holder to whom a negotiable document of title has been duly negotiated (Section 7-501) or a bona fide purchaser of a security (Section 8-301) and such holders or purchasers take priority over an earlier security interest even though perfected. Filing under this Article does not constitute notice of the security interest to such holders or purchasers.

Section 9-310. *Priority of Certain Liens Arising by Operation of Law.*

When a person in the ordinary course of his business furnishes services or materials with respect to goods subject to a security interest, a lien upon goods in the possession of such person given by statute or rule of law for such materials or services takes priority over a perfected security interest unless the lien is statutory and the statute expressly provides otherwise.

Section 9-311. *Alienability of Debtor's Rights; Judicial Process.*

The debtor's rights in collateral may be voluntarily or involuntarily transferred (by way of sale, creation of a security interest, attachment, levy, garnishment or other judicial process) notwithstanding a provision to the security agreement prohibiting any transfer or making the transfer constitute a default.

Section 9-312. *Priorities Among Conflicting Security Interests in the Same Collateral.*

(1) The rules of priority stated in the following sections shall govern where applicable: Section 4-208 with respect to the security interest of collecting banks in items being collected, accompanying documents and proceeds; Section 9-301 on certain priorities; Section 9-304 on goods covered by documents; Section 9-306 on proceeds and repossessions; Section 9-307 on buyers of goods; Secion 9-308 on possessory against non-possessory interests in chattel paper or non-negotiable instruments; Section 9-309 on security interests in negotiable instruments, documents or securities; Section 9-310 on priorities between perfected security interests and liens by operation of law; Section 9-313 on security interests in fixtures as against interests in real estate; Section 9-314 on security interests in accessions as against interest in goods; Section 9-315 on conflicting security interests where goods lose their identity or become part of a product; and Section 9-316 on contractual subordination.

(2) A perfected security interest in crops for new value given to enable the debtor to produce the crops during the production season and given not more than three months before the crops become growing crops by planting or otherwise takes priority over an earlier perfected security interest to the extent that such earlier interest secures obligations due more than six months before the crops become growing crops by planting or otherwise, even though the person giving new value had knowledge of the earlier security interest.

(3) A purchase money security interest in inventory collateral has priority over a conflicting security interest in the same collateral if

(a) the purchase money security interest is perfected at the time the debtor receives possession of the collateral; and
(b) any secured party whose security interest is known to the holder of the purchase money security interest or who, prior to the date of the filing made by the holder of the purchase money security interest, had filed a financing statement covering the same items or type of inventory, has received notification of the purchase money security interest before the debtor receives possession of the collateral covered by the purchase money security interest; and
(c) such notification states that the person giving the notice has or expects to acquire a purchase money security interest in inventory of the debtor, describing such inventory by item or type.
(4) A purchase money security interest in collateral other than inventory has priority over a conflicting security interest in the same collateral if the purchase money security interest is perfected at the time the debtor receives possession of the collateral or within ten days thereafter.
(5) In all cases not governed by other rules stated in this section (including cases of purchase money security interests which do not qualify for the special priorities set forth in subsections (3) and (4) of this section), priority between conflicting security interests in the same collateral shall be determined as follows:
(a) in the order of filing if both are perfected by filing, regardless of which security interest attached first under Section 9-204(1) and whether it attached before or after filing;
(b) in the order of perfection unless both are perfected by filing, regardless of which security interest attached first under Section 9-204(1) and, in the case of a filed security interest, whether it attached before or after filing; and
(c) in the order of attachment under Section 9-204(1) so long as neither is perfected.
(6) For the purpose of the priority rules of the immediately preceding subsection, a continuously perfected security interest shall be treated at all times as if perfected by filing if it was originally so perfected and it shall be treated at all times as if perfected otherwise than by filing if it was originally perfected otherwise than by filing.

Section 9-313. *Priority of Security Interests in Fixtures.*
(1) The rules of this section do not apply to goods incorporated into a structure in the manner of lumber, bricks, tile, cement, glass, metal work and the like and no security interest in them exists under this Article unless the structure remains personal property under applicable law. The law of this state other than this Act determines whether and when other goods become fixtures. This Act does not prevent creation of an encumbrance upon fixtures or real estate pursuant to the law applicable to real estate.
(2) A security interest which attaches to goods before they become fixtures takes priority as to the goods over the claims of all persons who have an interest in the real estate except as stated in subsection (4).
(3) A security interest which attaches to goods after they become fixtures is valid against all persons subsequently acquiring interests in the real estate except as stated in subsection (4) but is invalid against any person with an interest in the real estate at the time the security interest attaches to the goods who has not in writing consented to the security interest or disclaimed an interest in the goods as fixtures.
(4) The security interests described in subsections (2) and (3) do not take priority over
(a) a subsequent purchaser for value of any interest in the real estate; or
(b) a creditor with a lien on the real estate subsequently obtained by judicial proceedings; or
(c) a creditor with a prior encumbrance of record on the real estate to the extent that he makes subsequent advances if the subsequent purchase is made, the lien by judicial proceedings is obtained, or the subsequent advance under the prior encumbrance is made or contracted for without knowledge of the security interest and before it is perfected. A purchaser of the real estate at a foreclosure sale other than an encumbrancer purchasing at his own foreclosure sale is a subsequent purchaser within this section.
(5) When under subsections (2) or (3) and (4) a secured party has priority over the claims of all persons who have interests in the real estate, he may, on default, subject to the provisions of Part 5, remove his collateral from the real estate; but he must reimburse any encumbrancer or owner of the real estate who is not the debtor and who has not otherwise agreed for the cost of repair of any physical injury, but for any diminution in value of the real estate caused by the absence of the goods removed or by any necessity for replacing them. A person entitled to reimbursement may refuse permission to remove until the secured party gives adequate security for the performance of this obligation.

Section 9-314. *Accessions.*
(1) A security interest in goods which attaches before they are installed in or affixed to other goods takes priority as to the goods installed or affixed (called in this section "accessions") over the claims of all persons to the whole except as stated in subsection (3) and subject to Section 9-315(1).
(2) A security interest which attaches to goods after they become part of a whole is valid against all persons subsequently acquiring interests in the whole except as stated in subsection (3) but is invalid against any person with an interest in the whole at the time the security interest attaches to the goods who has not in writing consented to the security interest or disclaimed an interest in the goods as part of the whole.
(3) The security interests described in subsections (1) and (2) do not take priority over
(a) a subsequent purchaser for value of any interest in the whole; or
(b) a creditor with a lien on the whole subsequently obtained by judicial proceedings; or
(c) a creditor with a prior perfected security interest in the whole to the extent that he makes subsequent advances if the subsequent purchase is made, the lien by judicial proceedings obtained or the subsequent advance under the prior perfected security interest is made or contracted for without knowledge of the security interest and before it is perfected. A purchaser of the whole at a foreclosure sale other than the holder of a perfected security interest purchasing at his own foreclosure sale is a subsequent purchaser within this section.
(4) When under subsections (1) or (2) and (3) a secured party has an interest in accessions which has priority over the claims of all persons who have interests in the whole, he may, on default, subject to the provisions of Part 5, remove his collateral from the whole; but he must reimburse any encumbrancer or owner of the whole who is not the debtor and who has not otherwise agreed for the cost of repair of any physical injury but not for any diminution in value of the whole caused by the absence of the goods removed or by any necessity for replacing them. A person entitled to reimbursement may refuse permission to remove until the secured party gives adequate security for the performance of this obligation.

Section 9-315. *Priority When Goods Are Commingled or Processed.*
(1) If a security interest in goods was perfected and subsequently the goods or a part thereof have become part of a product or mass, the security interest continues in the product or mass if
(a) the goods are so manufactured, processed, assembled or commingled that their identity is lost in the product or mass; or
(b) a financing statement covering the original goods also covers the product into which the goods have been manufactured, processed or assembled.
In a case to which paragraph (b) applies, no separate security interest in that part of the original goods which has been manufactured, processed or assembled into the product may be claimed under Section 9-314.
(2) When under subsection (1) more than one security interest attaches to the product or mass, they rank equally according to the ratio that the cost of the goods to which each interest originally attached bears to the cost of the total product or mass.

Section 9-316. *Priority Subject to Subordination.*
Nothing in this Article prevents subordination by agreement by any person entitled to priority.

Section 9-317. *Secured Party Not Obligated on Contract of Debtor.*
The mere existence of a security interest or authority given to the debtor to dispose of or use collateral does not impose contract or tort liability upon the secured party for the debtor's acts or omissions.

Section 9-318. *Defenses Against Assignee; Modification of Contract After Notification of Assignment; Term Prohibiting Assignment Ineffective; Identification and Proof of Assignment.*
(1) Unless an account debtor has made an enforceable agreement not to assert defenses or claims arising out of a sale as provided in Section 9-206 the rights of an assignee are subject to
   (a) all the terms of the contract between the account debtor and assignor and any defense or claim arising therefrom; and
   (b) any other defense or claim of the account debtor against the assignor which accrues before the account debtor receives notification of the assignment.
(2) So far as the right to payment under an assigned contract right has not already become an account, and notwithstanding notification of the assignment, any modification of or substitution for the contract made in good faith and in accordance with reasonable commercial standards is effective against an assignee unless the account debtor has otherwise agreed, but the assignee acquires corresponding rights under the modified or substituted contract. The assignment may provide that such modification or substitution is a breach by the assignor.
(3) The account debtor is authorized to pay the assignor until the account debtor receives notification that the account has been assigned and that payment is to be made to the assignee. A notification which does not reasonably identify the rights assigned is ineffective. If requested by the account debtor, the assignee must seasonably furnish reasonable proof that the assignment has been made and unless he does so the account debtor may pay the assignor.
(4) A term in any contract between an account debtor and an assignor which prohibits assignment of an account or contract right to which they are parties is ineffective.

Part 4
Filing

Section 9-401. *Place of Filing; Erroneous Filing; Removal of Collateral.*
First Alternative Subsection (1)
(1) The proper place to file in order to perfect a security interest is as follows:
   (a) when the collateral is goods which at the time the security interest attaches are or are to become fixtures, then in the office where a mortgage on the real estate concerned would be filed or recorded;
   (b) in all other cases, in the office of the (Secretary of State).
Second Alternative Subsection (1)
(1) The proper place to file in order to perfect a security interest is as follows:
   (a) when the collateral is equipment used in farming operations, or farm products, or accounts, contract rights or general intangibles arising from or relating to the sale of farm products by a farmer, or consumer goods, then in the office of the _____ in the county of the debtor's residence or if the debtor is not a resident of this state then in the office of the _____ in the county where the goods are kept, and in addition when the collateral is crops in the office of the in the county where the land on which the crops are growing or to be grown is located;
   (b) when the collateral is goods which at the time the security interest attaches are or are to become fixtures, then in the office where a mortgage on the real estate concerned would be filed or recorded;
   (c) in all other cases, in the office of the (Secretary of State) and in addition, if the debtor has a place of business in only one county of this state, also in the office of _____ of such county, or, if the debtor has no place of business in this state, but resides in the state, also in the office of _____ of the county in which he resides.

Note: One of the three alternatives should be selected as subsection (1).

(2) A filing which is made in good faith in an improper place or not in all of the places required by this section is nevertheless effective with regard to any collateral as to which the filing complied with the requirements of this Article and is also effective with regard to collateral covered by the financing statement against any person who has knowledge of the contents of such financing statement.
(3) A filing which is made in the proper place in this state continues effective even though the debtor's residence or place of business or the location of the collateral or its use, whichever controlled the original filing, is thereafter changed.
Alternative Subsection (3)
(3) A filing which is made in the proper county continues effective for four months after a change to another county of the debtor's residence or place of business or the location of the collateral, whichever controlled the original filing. It becomes ineffective thereafter unless a copy of the financing statement signed by the secured party is filed in the new county within said period. The security interest may also be perfected in the new county after the expiration of the four month period; in such case perfection dates from the time of perfection in the new county. A change in the use of the collateral does not impair the effectiveness of the original filing.)
(4) If collateral is brought into this state from another jurisdiction, the rules stated in Section 9-103 determine whether filing is necessary in this state.

Section 9-402. *Formal Requisites of Financing Statement; Amendments.*
(1) A financing statement is sufficient if it is signed by the debtor and the secured party, gives an address of the secured party from which information concerning the security interest may be obtained, gives a mailing address of the debtor and contains a statement indicating the types, or describing the items, of collateral. A financing statement may be filed before a security agreement is made or a security interest otherwise attaches. When the financing statement covers crops growing or to be grown or goods which are or are to become fixtures, the statement must also contain a description of the real estate concerned. A copy of the security agreement is sufficient as a financing statement if it contains the above information and is signed by both parties.
(2) A financing statement which otherwise complies with subsection (1) is sufficient although it is signed only by the secured party when it is filed to perfect a security interest in
   (a) collateral already subject to a security interest in another jurisdiction when it is brought into this state. Such a financing statement must state that the collateral was brought into this state under such circumstances;
   (b) proceeds under Section 9-306 if the security interest in the original collateral was perfected. Such a financing statement must describe the original collateral.
(3) A form substantially as follows is sufficient to comply with subsection (1):

Name of Debtor (or Assignor)
Address
Name of Secured Party (or Assignee)
Address
1. This financing statement covers the following types (or items) of property:
   (Describe)
2. (If collateral is crops) The above described crops are growing or are to be grown on:
   (Describe Real Estate)
3. (If collateral is goods which are or are to become fixtures) The above described goods are affixed or to be affixed to:
   (Describe Real Estate)
4. (If proceeds or products of collateral are claimed) Proceeds-Products of the collateral are also covered.
   Signature of Debtor (or Assignor)
   Signature of Second Party (or Assignee)

(4) The term "financing statement" as used in this Article means the original financing statement and any amendments but if any amendment adds collateral, it is effective as to the added collateral only from the filing date of the amendment.

(5) A financing statement substantially complying with the requirements of this section is effective even though it contains minor errors which are not seriously misleading.

Section 9-403. *What Constitutes Filing; Duration of Filing; Effect of Lapsed Filing; Duties of Filing Officer.*
(1) Presentation for filing of a financing statement and tender of the filing fee or acceptance of the statement by the filing officer constitutes filing under this Article.
(2) A filed financing statement which states a maturity date of the obligation secured of five years or less is effective until such maturity date and thereafter for a priod of 60 days. Any other filed financing statement is effective for a period of five years from the date of filing. The effectiveness of a filed financing statement lapses on the expiration of such 60 day period after a stated maturity date or on the expiration of such five year period, as the case may be, unless a continuation statement is filed prior to the lapse. Upon such lapse the security interest becomes unperfected. A filed financing statement which states that the obligation secured is payable on demand is effective for five years from the date of filing.
(3) A continuation statement may be filed by the secured party (i) within six months before and 60 days after a stated maturity date of five years or less, and (ii) otherwise within six months prior to the expiration of the five year period specified in subsection (2). Any such continuation statement must be signed by the secured party, identify the original statement by file number and state that the original statement is still effective. Upon timely filing of the continuation statement, the effectiveness of the original statement is continued for five years after the last date to which the filing was effective whereupon it lapses in the same manner as provided in subsection (2) unless another continuation statement is filed prior to such lapse. Succeeding continuation statements may be filed in the same manner to continue the effectiveness of the original statement. Unless a statute on disposition of public records provides otherwise, the filing officer may remove a lapsed statement from the files and destroy it.
(4) A filing officer shall mark each statement with a consecutive file number and with the date and hour of filing and shall hold the statement for public inspection. In addition the filing officer shall index the statements according to the name of the debtor and shall note in the index the file number and the address of the debtor given in the statement.
(5) The uniform fee for filing, indexing, and furnishing filing data for an original or a continuation statement shall be $..............

Section 9-404. *Termination Statement.*
(1) Whenever there is no outstanding secured obligation and no commitment to make advances, incur obligations or otherwise give value, the secured party must on written demand by the debtor send the debtor's statement that he no longer claims a security interest under the financing statement, which shall be identified by file number. A termination statement signed by a person other than the security party of record must include or be accompanied by the assignment or a statement by the secured party of record that he has assigned the security interest to the signer of the termination statement. The uniform fee for filing and indexing such an assignment or statement thereof shall be $.................... If the affected secured party fails to send such a termination statement within ten days after proper demand therefor, he shall be liable to the debtor for $100 and in addition for any loss caused to the debtor by such failure.
(2) On presentation to the filing officer of such a termination statement he must note it in the index. The filing officer shall remove from the files, mark "terminated" and send or deliver to the secured party the financing statement and any continuation statement, statement of assignment or statement of release pertaining thereto.
(3) The uniform fee for filing and indexing a termination statement including sending or delivering the financing statement shall be $.................

Section 9-405. *Assignment of Security Interest; Duties of Filing Officer; Fees.*
(1) A financing statement may disclose an assignment of a security interest in the collateral described in the statement by indication in the statement of the name and address of the assignee or by an assignment itself or a copy thereof on the face or back of the statement. Either the original secured party or the assignee may sign this statement as the secured party. On presentation to the filing officer of such a financing statement the filing officer shall mark the same as provided in Section 9-403(4). The uniform fee for filing, indexing and furnishing filing date for a financing statement so indicating an assignment shall be $...................
(2) A secured party may assign or record all or a part of his rights under a financing statement by the filing of a separate written statement of assignment signed by the secured party of record and setting forth the name of the secured party of record and the debtor, the file number and the date of filing of the financing statement and the name and address of the assignee and containing a description of the collateral assigned. A copy of the assignment is sufficient as a separate statement if it complies with the preceding sentence. On presentation to the filing officer of such a separate statement, the filing officer shall mark such separate statement with the date and hour of the filing. He shall note the assignment on the index of the financing statement. The uniform fee for filing, indexing and furnishing filing data about such a separate statement of assignment shall be $.....................
(3) After the disclosure or filing of an assignment under this section, the assignee is the secured party of record.

Section 9-406. *Release of Collateral; Duties of Filing Officer; Fees.*
A secured party of record may by his signed statement release all or a part of any collateral describd in a filed financing statement. The statement of release is sufficient if it contains a description of the collateral being released, the name and address of the debtor, the name and address of the secured party, and the file number of the financing statement. Upon presentation of such a statement to the filing officer, he shall mark the statement with the hour and date of filing and shall note the same upon the margin of the index of the filing of the financing statement. The uniform fee for filing and notice such a statement of release shall be $.............

Section 9-407. *Information from Filing Officer.*
(1) If the person filing any financing statement, termination statement, statement of assignment or statement of release furnishes the filing officer a copy thereof, the filing officer shall upon request note upon the copy the file number and date and hour of the filing of the original and deliver or send the copy to such person.
(2) Upon request of any person, the filing officer shall issue his certificate showing whether there is on file on the date and hour stated therein, any presently effective financing statement naming a particular debtor and any statement of assignment thereof and if there is, giving the date and hour of filing of each such statement and the names and addresses of each secured party therein. The uniform fee for such a certificate shall be $................... plus $................. for each financing statement and for each statement of assignment reported therein. Upon request the filing officer shall furnish a copy of any filed financing statement or statement of assignment for a uniform fee of $................. per page.

Note: *This new section is proposed as an optional provision to require filing officers to furnish certificates. Local law and practices should be consulted with regard to the advisability of adoption.*

Part 5
Default

Section 9-501. *Default; Procedure When Security Agreement Covers Both Real and Personal Property.*
(1) When a debtor is in default under a security agreement, a secured party has the rights and remedies provided in this Part and, except as limited by subsection (3), those provided in the security agreement. He may reduce his claim to judgment, foreclose or otherwise enforce the security interest by any available judicial procedure. If the collateral is documents, the secured party may proceed either as to the documents or as to the goods covered thereby. A secured party in possession has the rights, remedies and duties provided in Section 9-207. The

rights and remedies referred to in this subsection are cumulative.
(2) After default, the debtor has the rights and remedies provided in this Part, those provided in the security agreement and those provided in Section 9-207.
(3) To the extent that they give rights to the debtor and imposed duties on the secured party, the rules stated in the subsections referred to below may not be waived or varied except as provided with respect to compulsory disposition of collateral (subsection (1) of Section 9-505) and with respect to redemption of collateral (Section 9-506) but the parties may by agreement determine the standards by which the fulfillment of these rights and duties is to be measured if such standards are not manifestly unreasonable:
  (a) subsection (2) of Section 9-502 and subsection (2) of Section 9-504 insofar as they require accounting for surplus proceeds of collateral;
  (b) subsection (3) of Section 9-504 and subsection (1) of Section 9-505 which deal with disposition of collateral;
  (c) subsection (2) of Section 9-505 which deals with acceptance of collateral as discharge of obligation;
  (d) Section 9-506 which deals with redemption of collateral; and
  (e) subsection (1) of Section 9-507 which deals with the secured party's liability for failure to comply with this Part.
(4) If the security agreement covers both real and personal property, the secured party may proceed under this Part as to the personal property or he may proceed as to both the real and the personal property, in accordance with his rights and remedies in respect of the real property in which case the provisions of this part do not apply.
(5) When a secured party has reduced his claim to judgment, the lien of any levy which may be made upon his collateral by virtue of any execution based upon the judgment shall relate back to the date of perfection of the security interest in such collateral. A judicial sale, pursuant to such execution, is a foreclosure of the security interest by judicial procedure within the meaning of this section, and the secured party may purchase at the sale and thereafter hold the collateral free of any other requirements of this Article.

Section 9-502. *Collection Rights of Secured Party.*
(1) When so agreed and in any event on default, the secured party is entitled to notify an account debtor or the obligor on an instrument to make payment to him whether or not the assignor was theretofore making collections on the collateral, and also to take control of any proceeds to which he is entitled under Section 9-306.
(2) A secured party who by agreement is entitled to charge-back uncollected collateral or otherwise to full or limited recourse against the debtor and who undertakes to collect from the account debtors or obligors must proceed in a commercially reasonable manner and may deduct his reasonable expenses of realization from the collections. If the security agreement secures an indebtedness, the secured party must account to the debtor for any surplus, and unless otherwise agreed, the debtor is liable for any deficiency. But, if the underlying transaction was a sale of accounts, contract rights or chattel paper, the debtor is entitled to any surplus or is liable for any deficiency only if the security agreement so provides.

Section 9-503. *Secured Party's Right to Take Possession After Default.*
Unless otherwise agreed a secured party has on default the right to take possession of the collateral. In taking possession a secured party may proceed without judicial process if this can be done without breach of the peace or may proceed by action. If the security agreement so provides, the secured party may require the debtor to assemble the collateral and make it available to the secured party at a place to be designated by the secured party which is reasonably convenient to both parties. Without removal a secured party may render equipment unusable, and may dispose of collateral on the debtor's premises under Section 9-504.

Section 9-504. *Secured Party's Right to Dispose of Collateral After Default; Effect of Disposition.*
(1) A secured party after default may sell, lease or otherwise dispose of any or all of the collateral in its then condition or following any commercially reasonable preparations or processing. Any sale of goods is subject to the Article on Sales (Article 2). The proceeds of disposition shall be applied in the order following to
  (a) the reasonable expenses of retaking, holding, preparing for sale, selling and the like, and, to the extent provided for in the agreement and not prohibited by law, the reasonable attorneys' fees and legal expenses incurred by the secured party;
  (b) the satisfaction of indebtedness secured by the security interest under which the disposition is made;
  (c) the satisfaction of indebtedness secured by any subordinate security interest in the collateral if written notification of demand therefor is received before distribution of the proceeds is completed. If requested by the secured party, the holder of a subordinate security interest must seasonably furnish reasonable proof of his interest, and unless he does so the secured party need not comply with his demand.
(2) If the security interest secures an indebtedness, the secured party must account to the debtor for any surplus, and, unless otherwise agreed, the debtor is liable for any deficiency. But if the underlying transaction was a sale of accounts, contract rights or chattel paper, the debtor is entitled to any surplus or is liable for any deficiency only if the security agreement so provides.
(3) Disposition of the collateral may be by public or private proceedings and may be made by way of one or more contracts. Sale or other disposition may be as a unit or in parcels and at any time and place and on any terms, but every aspect of the disposition including the method, manner, time, place and terms must be commercially reasonable. Unless collateral is perishable or threatens to decline speedily in value or is of a type customarily sold on a recognized market, reasonable notification of the time and place of any public sale or reasonable notification of the time after which any private sale or other intended disposition is to be made shall be sent by the secured party to the debtor, and except in the case of consumer goods to any other person who has a security interest in the collateral and who has duly filed a financing statement indexed in the name of the debtor in this state or who is known by the secured party to have a security interest in the collateral. The secured party may buy at any public sale and if the collateral is of a type customarily sold in a recognized market or is of a type which is the subject of widely distributed standard price quotations, he may buy at private sale.
(4) When collateral is disposed of by a secured party after default, the disposition transfers to a purchaser for value all of the debtor's rights therein, discharges the security interest under which it is made and any security interest or lien subordinate thereto. The purchaser takes free of all such rights and interests even though the secured party fails to comply with the requirements of this Part or of any judicial proceedings
  (a) in the case of a public sale, if the purchaser has no knowledge of any defects in the sale and if he does not buy in collusion with the secured party, other bidders or the person conducting the sale; or
  (b) in any other case, if purchaser acts in good faith.
(5) A person who is liable to a secured party under a guaranty, indorsement, repurchase agreement or the like and who receives a transfer of collateral from the secured party or is subrogated to his rights has thereafter the rights and duties of the secured party. Such a transfer of collateral is not a sale or disposition of the collateral under this Article.

Section 9-505. *Compulsory Disposition of Collateral; Acceptance of the Collateral as Discharge of Obligation.*
(1) If the debtor has paid sixty per cent of the cash price in the case of a purchase money security interest in consumer goods or sixty per cent of the loan in the case of another security interest in consumer goods, and has not signed after default a statement renouncing or modifying his rights under this Part, a secured party who has taken possession of collateral must dispose of it under Section 9-504 and if he fails to do so within 90 days after he takes possession, the debtor at his option may recover in conversion or under Section 9-507(1) on secured party's liability.

(2) In any other case involving consumer goods or any other collateral a secured party in possession may, after default, propose to retain the collateral in satisfaction of the obligation. Written notice of such proposal shall be sent to the debtor and except in the case of consumer goods to any other secured party who has a security interest in the collateral and who has duly filed a financing statement indexed in the name of the debtor in this state or is known by the secured party in possession to have a security interest in it. If the debtor or other person entitled to receive notification objects in writing within 30 days from the receipt of the notification or if any other secured party objects in writing within 30 days after the secured party obtains possession, the secured party must dispose of the collateral under Section 9-504. In the absence of such written objection the secured party may retain the collateral in satisfaction of the debtor's obligation.

Section 9-506. *Debtor's Right to Redeem Collateral.*

At any time before the secured party has disposed of collateral or entered into a contract for its disposition under Section 9-504 or before the obligation has been discharged under Section 9-505(2) the debtor or any other secured party may unless otherwise agreed in writing after default redeem the collateral by tendering fulfillment of all obligations secured by the collateral as well as the expenses reasonably incurred by the secured party in retaking, holding and preparing the collateral for disposition, in arranging for the sale, and, to the extent provided in the agreement and not prohibited by law, his reasonable attorney's fees and legal expenses.

Section 9-507. *Secured Party's Liability for Failure to Comply with This Part.*
(1) If it is established that the secured party is not proceeding in accordance with the provisions of this Part, disposition may be ordered or restrained on appropriate terms and conditions. If the disposition has occurred, the debtor or any person entitled to notification or whose security interest has been made known to the secured party prior to the disposition has a right to recover from the secured party any loss caused by a failure to comply with the provisions of this Part. If the collateral is consumer goods, the debtor has a right to recover in any event an amount not less than the credit service charge plus ten per cent of the principal amount of the debt or the time price differential plus ten per cent of the cash price.
(2) The fact that a better price could have been obtained by a sale at a different time or in a different method from that selected by the secured party is not of itself sufficient to establish that the sale was not made in a commercially reasonable manner. If the secured party sells the collateral in the usual manner in any recognized market therefor or if he sells at the price current in such market at the time of his sale or if he has otherwise sold in conformity with reasonable commercial practices among dealers in the type of property sold, he has sold in a commercially reasonable manner. The principles stated in the two preceding sentences with respect to sales also apply as may be appropriate to other types of disposition. A disposition which has been approved in any judicial proceeding or by any bona fide creditors' committee or representative of creditors shall conclusively be deemed to be commercially reasonable, but this sentence does not indicate that any such approval must be obtained in any case nor does it indicate that any disposition not so approved is not commercially reasonable.

Summary. William A. Schnader, Esq., who first proposed the Uniform Commercial Code when he was president of the National Conference of Commissioners on Uniform State Laws in 1940, believed tht "if the state and other jurisdictions having the Code on their books fail to render their Codes uniform by the end of 1968, it may become necessary to have Congress enact the Code in order to have the commercial law of the United States uniform throughout the nation." Diversity, however, continues both in statutory variation and in case law of the various jurisdictions (see "The UCC and the Automatede Society," *Business Lawyer*, November, 1968; and with regard to negotiable instruments, the article therein by G. T. Dunne, "The Checkless Society and Articles 3 and 4").

NEGOTIABLE ORDER OF WITHDRAWAL (NOW)

An interest earning account on which checks may be drawn. Withdrawals from NOW accounts may be subject to a 14-day or more notice requirement, although it is rarely imposed. NOW accounts can be offered by commercial banks, mutual savings banks, and savings and loan associations and may be owned only by individuals and certain nonprofit organizations and governmental units. In effect, the NOW account is an interest-bearing checking account. The depositor is allowed to make third-party payments through the use of negotiable orders of withdrawal.

The NOW account was first offered by the Consumer Savings Bank of Worcester, Massachusetts, in June 1972. The spread of NOWs was originally confined to savings banks in Massachusetts and New Hampshire, but in 1980 they became available nationally.

NEGOTIABLE PAPER Those NEGOTIABLE INSTRUMENTS that evidence the borrowing of money on a short-term basis for commercial purposes, e.g., notes, trade and bankers acceptances, bills of exchange, etc.

NEGOTIABLE SECURITIES Coupon or bearer bonds (whether issued by a government, state, municipality, railroad, public utility, or industrial corporation), certificates of indebtedness, notes, warrants, coupons, and stock certificates that by their terms permit transfer of title by delivery or assignment.

See GOOD DELIVERY.

NEGOTIATE To transfer the title of a negotiable instrument from one person to another by endorsement and delivery, or by mere delivery, so that the transferee becomes the holder and is vested with all the rights of the holder in due course under specified conditions. Negotiation also implies a sale or passing of value. Therefore, in a collateral sense, since negotiating a note involves relinquishment of its title by the transferor, the term means to sell or discount, i.e., to borrow money.

NEGOTIATING PROCESS Negotiating is a basic form of decision making. Many different and conflicting theories of negotiating exist. Most theories contain one or more of the strategies of organizational influence identified by David Kipnis and Stuart M. Schmidt:

Strategy	Behavior
Reason	The use of facts and data to support the development of a logical argument. *Sample tactic:* "I explained the reasons for my request."
Coalition	The mobilization of other people in the organization. *Sample tactic:* "I obtained the support of co workers to back up my request."
Ingratiation	The use of impression management, flattery, and the creation of goodwill. *Sample tactic:* "I acted very humbly while making my request."
Bargaining	The use of negotiation through the exchange of benefits or favors. *Sample tactic:* "I offered an exchange (if you do this for me, I will do something for you)."
Assertiveness	The use of a direct and forceful approach. *Sample tactic:* "I demanded that he or she do what I requested."
Higher authority	Support of higher levels in the organization to back up requests. *Sample tactic:* "I obtained the informal support of higher-ups."
Sanctions	The use of organizationally derived rewards and punishments. *Sample tactic:* "I threatened to give him or her an unsatisfactory performance evaluation."

Success in negotiating involves many factors, including:

1. Negotiate strategically: focus on corporate goals and culture; external environment; ethical position.
2. Develop personal characteristics and skills: trust, coping, confrontation, assertiveness, stress-handling capacity,

leadership, interpersonal skills, exercise of power and authority, persuasive skills, logical reasoning, networking, and others.

Research into traits of successful negotiators suggest that the following traits are important:

1. The ability to plan and prepare for negotiations.
2. The ability to reason clearly under stressful conditions.
3. The ability to listen carefully and express oneself clearly and persuasively.
4. High self-esteem and personal integrity.
5. High level of aspiration and expectation, high level of negotiating skills, and high level of perceived power.

BIBLIOGRAPHY

BANK ADMINISTRATION INSTITUTE. *Winning Negotiation Strategies, for Bankers.* Bank Administration Institute, Rolling Meadows, IL, 1987.
BAZERMAN, M. H., and R. J. LEWICKI, *Negotiating in Organizations* (Sage Publications, Beverly Hills, Calif., 1983).
DAWSON, R. *You Can Get Anything You Want, But You Have to Do More Than Ask.* Simon & Schuster, Inc., New York, NY, 1987.
Inside Negotiations. Aries Productions. Monthly.
JANDT, F. E. *Win-Win Negotiating: Turning Conflict into Agreement.* John Wiley and Sons, Inc., New York, NY, 1988.
KUHN, R. L. *Dealmaker: All the Negotiating Skills & Secrets You Need.* John Wiley and Sons, Inc., New York, NY, 1988.
Negotiation Journal. Plenum Publishing Corp., New York. Quarterly.
STEERS, R. M., and L. W. PORTER, *Motivation and Work Behavior* (McGraw-Hill, New York, 1983).

NEGOTIATION   See NEGOTIABLE INSTRUMENTS, NEGOTIATE.

NET
The balance after all possible deductions, offsets, and allowances have been made from the gross amount, bringing it to its lowest terms, e.g., net weight, NET PRICE, net wealth, net assets, NET DEBT, and NET PROFITS.

NET ASSETS
Net assets of an enterprise are the excess of total assets over total liabilities as reported on the balance sheet. Net assets also equal owners' equity. Equity is defined as the residual interest in the assets of an entity that remains after deducting its liabilities. In a business enterprise, the equity is the ownership interest. The relationship between net assets and ownership interest can be illustrated as follows:

   Assets − Liabilities = Net assets
   Assets − Liabilities = Equity (or ownership interest)
   Therefore,
   Net assets = Equity (or ownership interest)

NET AVAILS
The proceeds of a discounted note: the sum of money given to the borrower in discounting a note, equivalent to the face of the note less the discount. It is also known as PROCEEDS.

NET BONDED DEBT
The aggregate of bonds issued, less those repurchased by the corporation and held in the treasury, or those retired and canceled, and less sinking fund assets, if any, set aside to redeem them.

NET CHANGE
The advance or decline of a security for a day or other period. The net change in stocks is released by stock exchanges to the daily newspapers for publication in the financial section, and is determined by taking the difference between the last sale for the current day and the last sale for the first preceding day on which such sale occurred. Normally, net change measures the difference between last sales of two consecutive days, but in the case of inactive stocks which rarely trade, the period covered by net change may vary widely.

NET DEBT
As applied to a corporation, the total fixed and current debt (liabilities), less sinking fund and cash or other assets specifically set aside for their payment. As applied to municipal or state finance, the term refers to the total funded and floating debt outstanding, less sinking fund accruals.

NET EARNINGS
In bank acclounting, both the Comptroller of the Currency (Securities Act Disclosure Rules, 12 CFR 11) and the Board of Governors of the Federal Reserve System (Regulation F) prescribe the same forms for financial statements for national banks and state member banks of the Federal Reserve System, respectively. The earnings reports called for are both annual and quarterly (the quarterly form providing also for cumulative fiscal year to date). The statement of income (annual) calls for the following main sections.

1. Operating income.
2. Operating expenses. Included in operating expenses is provision for loan losses, a departure compared to previous practice, as follows.
   a. Banks shall include a provision for potential losses in the current loan portfolio based on bank management's evaluation of the loan portfolio in light of all relevant factors.
   b. Banks shall furnish in a note to financial statements an explanation of the basis for determining the loan loss provision.
   c. Banks that do not provide for loan losses on a reserve basis shall include the amount of actual net chargeoffs (losses less recoveries) for the current year.

(*Note: The balance of the reserve for possible loan losses that is shown as a deduction in the statement of condition is only the valuation portion that has been established through charges against income. The reserve for possible loan losses allowable under Internal Revenue Service regulations is made up of three parts: valuation portion, contingency portion, and deferred tax portion. The balance in the valuation portion is increased by the amount of provision for possible loan losses charged to income in each period since December 31, 1968, and the amount of loan recoveries in each period since December 31, 1968, and reduced by the loan losses charged to the reserve for possible loan losses in each period since December 31, 1968. The resulting balance is the valuation portion of the reserve, which is required to be deducted from total loans in the statement of condition. Only the valuation portion of the reserve for loan losses is available for absorbing loan losses.*

The contingency portion represents the cumulative amount of transfers from undivided profits to the IRS reserve for bad debts. This amount, net of applicable income tax reduction benefit, is to be allocated to equity capital and shown in the statement of condition as "reserve for contingencies and other capital reserves."

The deferred tax portion represents the tax effect on the difference between the deduction for loan losses claimed for income tax purposes, pursuant to IRS rulings, and the "provision for possible loan losses" claimed for financialo reporting purposes. Such deferred tax portion is to be reported in "other liabilities" in the statement of condition.)

3. Income before income taxes and securities gains (losses). This is the net of the operating income and the operating expenses.
4. Applicable income taxes. These are the federal and state taxes applicable to the net (3). But they do not include taxes applicable to net security gains (or losses) and extraordinary items; such taxes (or tax reductions) are reported in items 6 and 8 below.
5. Income before securities gains (or losses). This is the difference between items 3 and 4.
6. Net security gains (or losses), less related tax effect of (amount to be specified).
7. Net income, the sum or difference of items 5 and 6. But if extraordinary items are reported (item 8), the caption to this item should read, "income before extraordinary items."
8. Extraordinary items, less related tax effect of (amount to be specified). These items are the material results of nonrecurring transactions that have occurred during the current reporting period. Only the results of major events outside of the ordinary operating activity of the bank are to be reported herein. Such events would include, but be limited to, material gain or loss from sale of bank premises, expropriation of properties, and major devaluation of foreign currency. Less than material results of nonrecurring transactions are to be included in other operating income (part of operating income) or other operating expenses (part of operating expenses) as appropriate. (*Note: Materiality can be importantly affected by items netted against*

particular extraordinary items, and is a concept in accounting generally allowing for managerial flexibility in reporting.)
9. Net income (sum of difference of items 7 and 8).
10. Earnings per common share. The per share amount of securities gains (losses) may be stated separately; if extraordinary items are reported, the per share amount of income before extraordinary items and the per share amount of the extraordinary items shall be stated separately. Such "earnings per common share" are the per share amounts applicable to the common stock of the bank, including common stock equivalent (for the accounting meaning of this technical concept, see "Accounting Principles Board Opinion No. 15, Earnings per Share"), and per share amounts on a fully diluted basis (again, this technical concept is found in "APB Opinion No. 15"). The basis of computation, including the number of shares used, shall be furnished in a note to the statement.

The quarterly report, in summarized form, contains the above breakout of main sections, with less subdivisions under each section than are called for in the annual report.

Basis is the registrant bank unconsolidated or, if the bank files on a consolidated basis (including its consolidated subsidiaries), the bank and its consolidated subsidiaries.

Summary. *See* BANK STATEMENT, for discussion of the changes in bank reporting of income reflecting the concepts generally used in accounting. Although the accountants won with their proposal to include normal provision for loan losses in operating expenses and to designate a specific net income figure, flexibility still exists in net concepts (income before securities gains or losses, net income, net income before extraordinary items), although the per share computation is subject to the accountants' concepts of "primary earnings per share, including common stock equivalents" and "fully diluted earnings per share" in general application to statements of industrial companies.

In the case of firms other than financial institutions, the terms "net earnings," "net profits," and "net income" are often used interchangeably to refer to the net remaining after all expenses and accruals, including income taxes, are deducted from the net sales or revenues. It has become conventional, however, to apply the terms "revenues" and "net income" in the case of public utility and railroad companies, and "sales" and "net income" in the case of other nonfinancial corporations. See *Accounting Terminology Bulletin No. 2*, American Institute of Certified Public Accountants.

NET INCOME According to *Accounting Terminology Bulletin No. 2*, American Institute of Certified Public Accountants, the excess of revenues or net sales over expenses. (When expenses exceed revenues or net sales, the result is net loss.) In the case of railroads and public utility corporations whose accounting is prescribed by the regulatory agencies concerned, net income refers the excess of operating revenues and other income over total operating expenses. In the case of railroads, income taxes are deducted from the net income before income taxes to compute the net income; but in the case of public utility corporations, income taxes are included in operating expenses as an allowable type of expense in determining the fair rate of return (net income) on the fair value of the assets devoted to providing the utility service.

NET INDEBTEDNESS *See* NET DEBT.

NET INTEREST MARGIN The spread between the average cost of funds and the average return on invested funds.

NET NATIONAL PRODUCT (NNP) In national income accounting, net national product (NNP) equals gross national product (GNP) less depreciation of the nation's capital stock. GNP is more easily measured and more frequently referred to in both economic analyses and in the popular press. However, many economists believe that NNP is a more accurate count of the output of the economy in a given year.

NET PRICE The price of a commodity or item of merchandise after deduction of all discounts, commissions, and allowances. In the buying and selling of securities, the commission for buying is added to the purchase price, and the commission for selling and the state and federal taxes are deducted from the sale proceeds.

NET PROFITS The excess of net sales and other income overall expenses, including income taxes, calculated on taxable net income. NET INCOME is now the preferred term in reference to such excess (*Accounting Terminology Bulletin No. 2*, American Institute of Certified Public Accountants). The term "profit" is to be used to refer to the gain on a given transaction, e. g., sale of an asset or other transaction.

NET REALIZABLE VALUE Settlement value; the nondiscounted amount of cash, or its equivalent, into which an asset is expected to be converted in due course of business less direct cost necessary to make that conversion.

NET SURPLUS Formerly used in corporation accounting to refer to the accumulated retained earnings, as well as to the capital surplus or paid-in surplus arising from such sources as subscription price paid in excess of par value or stated value of the shares, donations, and treasury stock transactions. Accountants now prefer the use of "retained earnings" ("free and unappropriated," after breakout of "retained earnings appropriated" for such purposes as plant expansion, equalization of dividends, working capital, contingencies, etc.).

In bank charts of accounts, the SURPLUS ACCOUNT may include paid-in elements (capital surplus) originally paid in as well as increases arising from transfers in round sums from the undivided profits account and/or reserves. In bank accounting the surplus account is always maintained at a fixed round sum, subject to change by action of the board of directors; in combination with capital stock accounts, it is often statutorily the basis for establishing limits on maximum loans to any one borrower, maximum holding in securities of any one obligor, subscription to Federal Reserve bank stock, maximum acceptance powers, etc. The undivided profits account (which might also include some paid-in original portion, from present practice of the Comptroller of the Currency, e.g., to prescribe an original "adequate" paid-in undivided profits sum when the national bank is organized, in addition to the adequate capital and surplus paid in) serves as the current retained earnings account, reflecting net additions or net deductions from net income or net losses from operations, after deduction of any cash dividends paid or declared and appropriations for reserves.

NETTING An account analysis methoc or procedure which allows a shortfall in one period to be netted with an excess in a subsequent period.

NET TRANSACTION ACCOUNTS Under Section 19 of the FEDERAL RESERVE ACT, as amended by the DEPOSITORY INSTITUTIONS DEREGULATION AND MONETARY CONTROL ACT OF 1980, the term "transaction account" has replaced the former term "demand deposit" for the purposes of computing net transaction accounts and reserve requirements. The term "transaction account" means a deposit or account on which the depositor or account holder is permitted to make withdrawals by negotiable or transferable instruments, payment orders of withdrawal, telephone transfers, or other similar items for the purpose of making payments or transfers to third persons. Transaction accounts include demand deposits, negotiable order of withdrawal accounts, savings deposits subject to automatic transfers, and share draft accounts.

In determination of the reserve requirement on such transaction accounts, the amount of cash items in process of collection and balances subject to immediate withdrawal due from other depository institutions located in the United States (including such amounts due from United States branches and agencies of foreign banks and Edge Act and agreement corporations) may be deducted from the amount of gross transaction accounts. Required reserves are computed on the basis of the daily average deposit balances during a seven-day period ending each Wednesday (the "computation period"). Reserves are held in the form of vault cash, a balance maintained directly with the district Federal Reserve bank, or a passthrough account, the last-named being considered a balance maintained with the Federal Reserve. For details, *see* RESERVE.

NET WORTH From an accounting standpoint, the excess of assets over liabilities; also known as proprietorship or capital. In the case of a corporation, it is represented by the capital stock, paid-in capital in excess of par or stated value (formerly called "surplus paid in"), and other free and clear equity reserve accounts, if any.

NET WORTH CERTIFICATE

Among partnerships, it is represented by the sum of the partners' capital accounts, and in the case of an individual, by the capital account.

From a legal standpoint, net worth represents the equity of the owners in the business, i.e., the net assets determined by subtracting all liabilities from the going value of the assets.

From the standpoint of the credit analyst engaged in judging credit risks, the net worh of a corporation is the sum of the capital stock, paid-in capital in excess of par or stated value, and equity reserves, less goodwill, patents, and other intangible assets, if any. Only actual tangible assets are included in the determination of net worth of a company applying for credit. It is a rule of thumb among bank credit analysis that unsecured loans should not exceed one-third of a company's net worth. Among security analysts, book value of a stock is also figured on a net tangible equity basis.

See INTANGIBLES

NET WORTH CERTIFICATE A special security issued by a depository institution with a net worth deficiency; it is then exchanged for a promissory note from the FDIC or FSLIC; the institution redeems its NWC when it returns to profitability and can make all required allocations to net worth.

NET WORTH METHOD An income tax method of estimating a taxpayer's income. The net worth method is sometimes used where the taxpayer has not maintained records or has falsified or destroyed records. The IRS reconstructs income by calculating the change in net worth during the period and adding estimated living expenses.

NET YIELD The part of the gross yield that remains after deducting all costs, such as servicing, and any reserves for losses.

NEW BUSINESS DEPARTMENT A department organized separately in the larger banks, corresponding to the sales promotion department among manufacturing and mercantile concerns. It is also known as the business extension or business development department, or the marketing research department, and may control or be associated with the advertising or PUBLICITY DEPARTMENT. This group of departments in banks represents a new role in modern banking and has arisen out of the increasing competition for new business and the campaign to educate the public to a great use of banking facilities. The chief objectives of the new business department are to secure more accounts, to maintain satisfactory relations with old accounts, and to build up small and dormant accounts. The primary objective of bank advertising is to increase the institution's deposits and therefore its available funds. There are three ways of accomplishing this purpose: by securing new depositors, by stimulating accounts already customers, and by encouraging customers of one department or service to become active customers of other departments and services.

The work of the department is usually put in the charge of a senior official, reflecting the new importance of business development as one of the most insistent problems of bank management. This work may be divided under three heads: correspondence, solicitation, and records. Correspondence is conducted with the list of prospects, compiled from customers and noncustomers; some of the larger banks maintain a fulltime staff of solicitors to find new sources of business.

The chief record of the department is usually the CENTRAL FILE. This file should contain a card for each customer and prospect, and show the principal items of information that maybe necessary to a continuous followup of the accounts. The file may be computerized, in which case the customer and/or prospect information is stored in a record on a computer storage device.

The department works in close cooperation with the credit department, the latter often furnishing leads and checking prospective accounts. Names of prospects are developed from the work of the new business representatives, applicants for particular kinds of services who might be interested in other services, applicants for information, officers, employees, reports of new incorporations, removal notices, news of business developments, etc.

NEW DEAL The self-adopted political description of the Franklin D. Roosevelt administration, beginning March 4, 1933. It represented a distinct break with the past, advocating a trend away from "rugged individualism" and industrial freedom toward social control of industry, banking, finance, transportation, agriculture, and markets. It did not advocate general public ownership of business, except in public utility projects such as the TVA, not alter the basis of private property, but imposed strict regulation and supervision of the major departments of economic life in and attempt to achieve a more equitable distribution of the national income through economic balance. In theory, the New Deal contemplated no abrogation of property or constitutional rights, and laws were enacted to legalize the changes in economic life brought about, the most important being the National Industrial Recovery Act, the Agricultural Adjustment Act, the Emergency Banking Relief Act, the Gold Reserve Act, and the Securities Act of 1933. The province of the government was held to be not to change the character of corporate or individual action, but to serve as umpire in the prominent areas of controversy.

The New Deal denied any affinity with fascism, communism, state socialism, or dictatorship under any banner. Both communism and state socialism imply government ownership of important instruments of production and a rejection of parliamentary processes. Fascism implies both a dictatorship with compulsions on industry and a limitation of the political and economic rights of individuals.

Various labels have been given to the New Deal, such as controlled capitalism, regulated capitalism, federal capitalism, disciplined democracy, cooperative state, balanced social state (Wallace), and economic constitutional order (Roosevelt). Among the aims attributed to the New Deal were substitution of a planned or managed economy for private, individualistic, laissez-faire enterprise; government intervention in business as umpire and planner; redistribution of wealth; use of managed currency and credit to provide a dollar with approximately the same purchsing and debt-paying power in one generation as in another; prevention of accumulation of great private fortunes; and provision against the hazards and insecurities of life by the Social Security system and unemployment insurance.

New Deal Legislation. The appended table shows the major pieces of legislation under the New Deal affecting agriculture, banking, finance, business, labor, securities, and securities markets. Invalidated and repealed acts are indicated by footnotes.

New Deal Legislation

Date approved	
1933	
March 3	Bankruptcy Act Amendment (individuals, railroads, and farmers)
March 9	Emergency Banking Relief Act
May 12	Agricultural Adjustment Act, carrying Thomas Inflation Amendment (Title III); also known as the AAA Farm Relief and Inflation Act [a]
May 12	Federal Emergency Relief Act
May 18	Tennessee Valley Authority Act [b]
May 27	Securities Act of 1933
June 5	Gold Repeal Joint Resolution [c]
June 10	Reconstruction Finance Corporation Amendments
June 12	Reciprocal Tariff Act
June 13	Home Owners' Refinancing Act of 1933
June 16	Banking Act of 1933
June 16	Farm Credit Act of 1933
June 16	National Industrial Recovery Act [d]
June 16	Emergency Railroad Transportation Act
1934	
Jan. 30	Gold Reserve Act of 1934 [c]
Jan. 31	Farm Mortgage Refinancing Act
Feb. 23	Crop Loan Act
April 7	Jones-Connally Farm Relief Act
April 21	Bankhead Cotton Control Act [e]
April 27	Home Owners Loan Act of 1934
May 9	Jones-Costigan Sugar Act
May 10	Revenue Act of 1934
May 24	Municipal Bankruptcy Act (supplementing National Bankruptcy Act) [f]
June 6	Securities Exchange Act of 1934

New Deal Legislation (continued)

Date approved

June 7	Corporate Bankruptcy Act (supplementing National Bankruptcy Act)
June 16	Bank Deposit Insurance Act
June 19	Communications Act of 1934
June 19	Silver Purchase Act of 1934
June 27	National Housing Act
June 28	Frazier-Lemke Bankruptcy Act

1935

Jan. 31	Reconstruction Finance Corporation Extension Act
Feb. 22	"Hot-Oil" Act [g]
April 8	Work Relief Act (Appropriation $4 billion)
April 27	Soil Erosian Act
May 15	Livestock Bankruptcy Act
May 28	Home Mortgage Relief Act
June 3	Farm Credit Act of 1935
June 14	Rail Extension Act (extending for one year the Emergency Railroad Transportation Act of 1933)
June 14	NRA Extension Act [d]
June 28	Deposit Insurance Extension Act
June 29	Farm Research Act
July 5	Wagner-Connery Labor Relations Act
Aug. 9	Motor Carrier Act of 1935
Aug. 14	Social Security Act
Aug. 23	Banking Act of 1935
Aug. 24	Act to Amend the Agricultural Adjustment Act (including the Potato Act of 1935) [a]
Aug. 26	Public Utility Holding Company Act of 1935
Aug. 27	Gold Clause Act [h]
Aug. 28	Frazier-Lemke Farm Mortgage Act (providing limited three-year moratorium) [h]
Aug. 29	Wagner-Crosser Rail Retirement Act [i]
Aug. 30	Guffey Coal Conservation Act [j]
Aug. 30	Revenue Act of 1935
Aug. 31	Tennesee Valley Amendment Act

1936

Jan. 27	Bonus Act
Feb. 10	Cotton-Tobacco-Potato Repeal Act
Feb. 29	Soil Conservation and Domestic Allotment Act
April 10	Commodity Credit Act
April 25	Tobacco State Compact Act
April 30	National Housing Act Amendment
May 20	Norris-Rayburn Rural Electrification Act
May 27	Unlisted Securities Trading Act
June 16	Commodity Exchange Act
June 20	Robinson-Patman Price Discrimination Act
June 23	The Revenue Act of 1936
June 30	Walsh-Healey Public Contracts Act

---

[a] Invalidated as to agricultural provisions, January 6, 1936, by 6-3 decision. Time required for adjudication, 29 days.
[b] Upheld as to certain provisions only, February 17, 1936, by 8-1 decision. Time required for adjudication, 59 days.
[c] Upheld, February 18, 1935, by 5-4 decision. Time required for adjudication, 41 days.
[d] Invalidated, May 27, 1935, by 9-0 decision. Time required for adjudication, 25 days.
[e] Repealed in conformity with invalidation of AAA on February 10, 1936.
[f] Invalidated, May 25, 1936, by 5-4 decision.
[g] Invalidated by 8-1 decision. Time required for adjudication, 28 days.
[h] Invalidated by 9-0 decision. Time required for adjudication, 29 days.
[i] Invalidated by 5-4 decision. Time required for adjudication, 54 days.
[j] Invalidated, May 18, 1936, by 6-3 decision. Time required for adjudication, 67 days.

New Deal Legislation (continued)

Date approved

1937

April 26	Bituminous Coal Act of 1937
Aug. 16	Bankruptcy Act Amendment (relating to municipal bankruptcy compositions)
Aug. 26	Revenue Act of 1937

1938

Feb. 16	Agricultural Adjustment Act of 1938
March 8	Commodity Credit Corporation Act
June 21	Natural Gas Act
June 22	Chandler Bankruptcy Act (amendment of the Bankruptcy Act)
June 23	Civil Aeronautics Act
June 25	Fair Labor Standards Act
June 25	Railroad Unemployment Insurance Act

1939

March 4	Act continuing functions of the Reconstruction Finance Corporation
March 4	Act continuing functions of the Commodity Credit Corporation and the Export-Import Bank
April 12	Public Salary Tax Act
June 3	National Housing Act Amendments
June 29	Revenue Act of 1939
June 29	Extension of Hot Oil Law
July 6	Extension of President's powers relative to the stabilization fund and dollar devaluation
July 28	Bankruptcy Act Amendment (for railroads in temporary financial difficulties)
July 30	Amendment of Liberty Loan Act (to permit issuance of long-term federal bonds beyond former $30 billion limit)
Aug. 3	Trust Indenture Act of 1939
Aug. 7	Amendments of Agricultural Adjustment Act
Aug. 10	Amendment of Social Security Act

1940

Jan. 1	Federal Power Act
June 25	Revenue Act of 1940
July 1	Bankruptcy Act Amendment
Aug. 22	Investment Company Act of 1940; Investment Advisers Act
Sept. 18	Transportation Act of 1940
Oct. 8	Excess Profits Tax Act of 1940 (Title VI of this act is the National Service Life Insurance Act of 1940)

1941

Feb. 19	Public Debt Act
March 7	Excess Profits Tax Amendments
March 11	Lend-Lease Act
Sept. 20	Revenue Act of 1941

1942

Jan. 30	Emergency Price Control Act
March 28	Public Debt Act of 1942
June 22	Bankruptcy Act Amendments
Oct. 21	Revenue Act of 1942

1943

April 11	Public Debt Act of 1943

1944

Feb. 25	Revenue Act of 1943 (became law Feb. 25, 1944, over President's veto)

NEW DEAL AGENCIES

New Deal Legislation (continued)

Date
approved

March 11	Farm Mortgage Relief Act
March 11	Bankruptcy Act Amendments
June 9	Public Debt Act of 1944
June 22	Servicemen's Readjustment Act of 1944
Oct. 3	Surplus Property Act

1945

April 3	Public Debt Act of 1945
July 31	Tax Adjustment Act of 1945
July 31	Export-Import Bank Act of 1945
July 31	Bretton Woods Agreement Act
Nov. 8	Revenue Act of 1945

BIBLIOGRAPHY

Babson, R. W. *The New Dilemma*, 1934.
Bingham, A. M., and Rodman, S. *Challenge to the New Deal*, 1934.
Claire, G. S. *Administocracy*, 1935.
The Economist (London). *The New Deal: An Analysis and Appraisal*, 1937.
Frambes, R. *Free Right to Contract and the New Deal*, 1934.
Frank, G. *America's Hour of Decision*, 1934.
Fruchs, M. I. *The New Bastille*, 1934.
Greenwood, E. *Spenders All*, 1935.
Hacker, L. M. *A Short History of the New Deal*, 1934.
Hubbard, J. B. *Current Economic Policies*, 1934.
Ickes, H. L. *The New Democracy*, 1934.
Lawrence, D. *Beyond the New Deal*, 1934.
Mills, O. L. *What of Tomorrow?* 1934.
Ogburn, W. F. *Social Change and the New Deal*, 1934.
Piquet, H. S. *Outline of the New Deal Legislation*, 1934.
Raushenbush, C. *Labor and the New Deal*, 1934.
Rice, S. *The New Deal*, 1934.
Robey, R. W. *Roosevelt Versus Recovery*, 1934.
Stolberg, B., and Vinton, W. J. *The Economic Consequences of the New Deal*, 1935.
Tayler, A. E. *The New Deal and Foreign Trade*, 1935.
Tugwell, R. G. *The Battle for Democracy*, 1934.
"Unofficial Observer," *The New Dealers*, 1934.
Wallace, H. A. *America Must Choose*, 1934.
"Unknown", *New Frontiers*, 1934.
Wallace, S. C. *The New Deal in Action*, 1934.
Warburg, J. P. *It's Up to Us*, 1934.
Williams, E. W. *Industrial Control for People*, 1934.
Woll, M. *Labor, Industry and the Government*, 1935.

NEW DEAL AGENCIES The appended table lists NEW DEAL agencies, popularly known as "alphabetical agencies," created during the Franklin D. Roosevelt administration.

New Deal Agencies

AAA	Agricultural Adjustment Administration
ACA	Advisory Committee on Allotments
ACAA	Agricultural Conservation and Adjustment Administration
ALB	Automobile Labor Board
AMA	Agricultural Marketing Administration
AOA	Administration of Operation Activities
ARA	Agricultural Research Administration
BAC	Business Advisory Council
BAE	Bureau of Agricultural Economics
BEW	Board of Economic Welfare
BFC	Banks for Cooperatives
BPA	Bonneville Power Administration
BWC	Board of War Communications
CAA	Civil Aeronautics Administration
CAB	Civil Aeronautics Board, Consumers Advisory Board
CAP	Civil Air Patrol
CCC	Civilian Conservation Corps, Commodity Credit Corporation
CCCR	Coordinator of Commercial and Cultural Relations
CEA	Commodity Exchange Administration
CES	Committee on Economic Security
CFB	Combined Food Board
CMB	Combined Munitions Board
COI	Coordinator of Information
CPA	Council of Personnel Administration
CPLO	Crop Production Loan Office
CPRB	Combined Production and Resources Board
CRMB	Combined Raw Materials Board
CSAB	Combined Shipping Adjustment Board
CSB	Central Statistical Board
CSC	Cotton Stabilization Corporation
CWA	Civil Works Administration
DAI	Division of Applications and Information of the Works Relief Administration
DCADA	District of Columbia Alley Dwelling Authority
DCB	Defense Communications Board
DGIAB	Durable Goods Industries Advisory Board
DHC	Defense Homes Corporation
DLB	Deposits Liquidation Board
DLC	Disaster Loan Corporation
DPC	Defense Plants Corporation
DSC	Defense Supplies Corporation
EC	Executive Council
ECFL	Emergency Crop and Feed Loans
ECNR	Executive Council for National Recovery
ECW	Emergency Conservation Works
EHC	Emergency Housing Corporation
EHFA	Electric Home and Farm Authority
EIB	Export-Import Bank
EPCA	Emergency Price Control Act
FAC	Federal Aviation Commission
FACA	Federal Alcohol Control Administration
FCA	Farm Credit Administration
FCC	Federal Communications Commission
FCIC	Federal Crop Insurance Corporation
FCT	Federal Coordinator of Transportation
FCU	Federal Credit Unions
FCUS	Federal Credit Union System
FDA	Food Distribution Administration
FDIC	Federal Deposit Insurance Corporation
FEA	Foreign Economic Administration
FEHC	Federal Emergency Housing Corporation
FEPC	Fair Employment Practices Committee
FERA	Federal Emergency Relief Administration
FESO	Federal Employment Stabilization Office
FFC	Foreign Funds Control
FFMC	Federal Farm Mortgage Corporation
FHA	Federal Housing Administration
FHLB	Federal Home Loan Banks
FHLBB	Federal Home Loan Bank Board
FICB	Federal Intermediate Credit Banks
FISC	Fur Industry Salvage Commission
FLA	Federal Loan Agency
FLB	Federal Land Banks
FMC	Federal Mortgage Corporation
FPC	Federal Power Commission
FPHA	Federal Public Housing Authority
FPI	Federal Prison Industries
FREB	Federal Real Estate Board
FSA	Farm Security Administration, Federal Security Agency
FSHC	Federal Subsistence Homesteads Corporation
FSCC	Federal Surplus Commodity Corporation
FSLA	Federal Savings and Loan Associations
FSLIC	Federal Savings and Loan Insurance Corporation
FSRC	Federal Surplus Relief Corporation
FTC	Federal Trade Commission
FTZB	Federal Trade Zones Board
FTSA	Special Adviser to the President on Foreign Trade
FWA	Federal Works Agency
GFA	Grain Futures Administration
GSC	Grain Stabilization Corporation
HIF	Housing Insurance Fund
HLB	Home Loan Bank, Home Loan Board
HOLC	Home Owners' Loan Corporation

IAB	Industrial Advisory Board
ICCP	Interdepartmental Committee on Commercial Policy
IEB	Industrial Emergency Board
JEB	Joint Economic Board
JSLB	Joint-Stock Land Banks
LAB	Labor Advisory Board
LBC	Land Bank Commissioner
MRC	Metals Reserve Company
NACA	National Advisory Committee for Aeronautics
NBAPC	National Business Advisory and Planning Council
NCB	National Compliance Board
NDAC	National Defense Advisory Commission
NDMB	National Defense Mediation Board
NEC	National Emergency Council
NHA	National Housing Agency
NIRA	National Industrial Recovery Act
NIRB	National Industrial Recovery Board
NLRB	National Labor Relations Board
NMB	National Mediation Board
NPB	National Planning Board
NPPC	National Power Policy Committee
NRA	National Recovery Administration
NRAB	National Railroad Adjustment Board
NRB	National Resources Board
NRC	National Resources Committee
NRRB	National Recovery Review Board
NRPB	National Resources Planning Board
NRS	National Re-employment Service
NSLRB	National Steel Labor Relations Board
NWLB	National War Labor Board
NYA	National Youth Administration
OADR	Office of Agricultural Defense Relations
OAPC	Office of Alien Property Custodian
OAWR	Office for Agricultural War Relations
OBCCC	Office of Bituminous Coal Consumers Council
OC	Office of Censorship
OCD	Office of Civilian Defense
OCIAA	Office of Coordinator of Inter-American Affairs
OCR	Office of Civilian Requirements
OCS	Office of Civilian Supply
ODB	Office of Dependency Benefits
ODHWS	Office of Defense and Health Welfare Services
ODT	Office Defense Transportation
OEM	Office of Emergency Management
OES	Office of Economic Stabilization
OFC	Office of Fishery Coordination
OFEC	Office of Foreign Economic Coordination
OFF	Office of Facts and Figures
OFRRO	Office of Foreign Relief and Rehabilitation Operations
OGR	Office of Government Reports
OLLA	Office of Lend-Lease Administration
OPA	Office of Price Administration
OPACS	Office of Price Adminstration and Civilian Supply
OPCW	Office of Petroleum Coordination for War
OPM	Office of Production Management
OSFCW	Office of Solid Fuels Coordinator for War
OSRD	Office of Scientific Research and Development
OSS	Office of Strategic Services
OWI	Office of War Information
OWM	Office of War Mobilization
PA	Petroleum Administration
PAB	Petroleum Administrative Board
PAW	Petroleum Administration for War
PBA	Public Buildings Administration
PCC	Production Credit Corporation
PCES	President's Committee on Economic Security
PIWC	Petroleum Industry War Council
PRA	Public Roads Administration
PRRA	Puerto Rico Reconstruction Administration
PWA	Public Works Administration
PWAP	Public Works Arts Projects
PWEHC	Public Works Emergency Housing Corporation
PWRCB	President's War Relief Control Board
RA	Resettlement Administration
RACC	Regional Agricultural Credit Corporations
REA	Rural Electrification Administration
RFC	Reconstruction Finance Corporation
RRA	Rural Resettlement Authority
RRC	Rubber Reserve Company
RRRB	Railroad Retirement Board
SA	Sugar Agency
SAB	Science Advisory Board
SAPFT	Special Adviser to President on Foreign Trade
SCS	Soil Conservation Service
SEC	Securities and Exchange Commission
SES	Soil Erosion Service
SHD	Subsistence Homesteads Division
SLIC	Savings and Loan Insurance Corporation
SLRB	Steel Labor Relations Board, State Labor Relations Board
SMA	Surplus Marketing Administration
SPAB	Supply Priorities and Allocations Board
SSB	Social Security Board
SSS	Selective Service System
SWPC	Smaller War Plants Corporation
TFI	Textile Foundation, Inc.
TVA	Tennessee Valley Authority
TVAC	Tennessee Valley Associated Cooperatives, Inc.
TWAB	Textile Work Assignment Boards
UNRRA	United Nations Relief and Rehabilitation Administration
USECC	U.S. Employees Compensation commission
USES	U.S. Employment Service
USHA	U.S. Housing Authority
USHC	U.S. Housing Corporation
USIS	U.S. Information Service
USMC	U.S. Maritime Commission
USTB	U.S. Travel Bureau
WAB	War Allotment Board
WDC	War Damage Corporation
WEPL	War Emergency Pipe Lines, Inc.
WFA	War Food Administration
WLB	War Labor Board
WMC	War Manpower Commission
WMI	War Materials, Inc.
WMPC	War Man Power Commission
WPA	Works Progress Administration
WPB	War Production board
WRA	War Relocation Authority, Work Relief Administration
WSA	War Shipping Administration
WSTIB	Woolen and Silk Textiles Industries Board
WWB	Writers War Board

NEW ORLEANS COTTON EXCHANGE The second largest cotton exchange in the United States, until it suspended trading on July 9, 1964. Incorporated January 17, 1871, not long after organization of the NEW YORK COTTON EXCHANGE in 1870. The New Orleans Cotton exchange operated under its charter of May 6, 1873, as amended.

The New Orleans Cotton Exchange subsequently moved to Chicago in 1983 as a result of an agreement with the MidAmerica Commodity Exchange and operates under the name of the Chicago Rice and Cotton Exchange. In 1986, the CRCE rough rice futures contract began trading on the Chicago Board of Trade trading floor. CRCE contracts are cleared through the Board of Trade Clearing Corporation.

NEW YORK BLUE SKY LAW The MARTIN ACT. See BLUE SKY LAWS.

NEW YORK CLEARING HOUSE ASSOCIATION See CLEARINGHOUSE.

NEW YORK COCOA EXCHANGE See COFFEE, SUGAR & COCOA EXCHANGE, INC.

NEW YORK COFFEE AND SUGAR EXCHANGE See COFFEE, SUGAR & COCOA EXCHANGE, INC.

NEW YORK COTTON EXCHANGE Organized as the New York Board of Cotton Brokers in 1868. In 1870 officers and a board of managers were elected on August 15, the constitution and bylaws were adopted on September 7, and the exchange was opened for business on September 10 at 142 Pearl Street, New York City. The exchange was incorporated by an act of the New York Legislature on April 8, 1871.

The exchange is now located in rented premises at 4 World Trade Center, New York City, where other commodity exchanges in New York City have concentrated their location.

The New York Cotton Exchange is the oldest cotton exchange in the world, and ranks domestically as the most important of the cotton futures and options markets, which formerly included the New Orleans Cotton Exchange and the Chicago Board of Trade. Abroad, the Liverpool Cotton Association, which resumed trading May 18, 1954, is the chief international market for U.S. and other cottons in Europe.

In the late 1960s and early 1970s the exchange innovated. In 1966 a citrus futures and options market was formed by the Citrus Associates of the New York Cotton Exchange. In 1970 a wool futures market was formed by the Wool Associates, and in 1971 a tomato futures market was formed by the Tomato Products Associates of the exchange. The latter two have since been discontinued.

All futures and options contracts traded on the New York Cotton Exchange (including the FINEX division) and on the Citrus Associates of the New York Cotton Exchange, Inc., include:

Futures and options	Futures
Cotton	European Currency Unit
Five-year U.S. Treasury note	Two-year U.S. Treasury note
U.S. Dollar Index	
Frozen concentrated orange juice	

Cotton. The mainstay of activity on the New York Cotton Exchange, the No. 2 cotton contract, trades in all months, with a contract size of 50,000 pounds net weight (approximately 100 bales with allowance of 1% more or less). Prices are quoted in cents and hundredths of a cent; minimum fluctuation is one one-hundredth of a cent, equivalent to $5 per contract. Daily limits on price movement are $0.02 above or below the settlement price of the previous market session.

Basis of the contract is strict low middling 1 $^1/_{16}$ inch U.S.-grown white cotton. Staples deliverable include 1 $^1/_{32}$ inch and longer; 1 $^1/_{32}$ inch cotton, which will be discounted 125% of the quoted difference between 1 $^1/_{32}$ inch and 1 $^1/_{16}$ inch cotton; 1 $^3/_{32}$ inch cotton, which will qualify for full premium; and 1 $^1/_8$ inch and longer cotton, which will be deliverable at the same premium as 1 $^3/_{32}$ inch cotton. Grades deliverable include low middling through good middling in white grades and middling light spot through good middling light spot in light spotted category. No spotted cotton is tenderable. Cotton must micronaire not less than 3.5 nor more than 4.9 to be tenderable. The average grade and staple premiums and discounts for tenderable qualities quoted for Greenville, South Carolina, Greenwood, Mississippi, Memphis, Tennessee, Dallas, Texas, and Phoenix, Arizona, will be used to determining settlement prices. Delivery points under the new contract are as follows: Galveston, Houston, New Orleans (freight bills acceptable on refund value to group B); and Greenville, South Carolina (freight bills not acceptable).

Trading in cotton futures has been active in recent years (See COMMODITIES, for commodity futures trading volume).

Citrus. The successful "F.C.O.J." contract (trading in frozen orange concentrate), conducted by the Citrus Association of the New York Cotton Exchange for deliveries in January, March, May, July, September, and November, calls for a contract unit of 15,000 pounds of range solids, 3% more or less. Frozen orange concentrate is quoted on a pound price, showing as "9515" for example, or $0.9515 per pound. Fluctuations are recorded in multiples of $0.0005 per pound, with a minimum $0.0005 fluctuation representing $7.50 on each contract of 15,000 pounds. Contract grade for delivery is U.S. Grade A with a Brix value of not less than 51°, a ratio of Brix value to acid of not less than 13 to 1 nor more than 19 to 1, and a minimum score of 94, with th factors of color and flavor each scoring 37 points or higher, and defects at 19 or better, provided that the frozen concentrated orange juice with a Brix value of more than 65° shall be calculated as having 7.135 pounds of solids per gallon delivered. Deliveries must be made in exchange-licensed warehouses in Florida. Daily limits on price movement are $0.05 ($750 per contract) above or below the settlement price of the previous market session, except when three or more contract months closed at the limit in the same direction for three successive business days, when the limit would be raised to $0.08 per pound above or below the settlement price of such month of the preceding session of the exchange. The limit would remain at $0.08 per pound until less than three contract months closed at the limit in the same direction; then on the next business day the limit would revert to the original level of $0.05 per pound. Minimum margins are set by the Citrus Associates of the New York Cotton Exchange.

Volume of trading in orange juice concentrate futures has been active and responsive to weather and temperature conditions.

Other contracts. Contract specifications for U.S. Dollar Index futures and options on U.S. Dollar Index futures include:

1. *Futures:* Contract size: $500 times the U.S. Dollar Index. Contract months: March, June, September, and December. Price quotation: Price is quoted as a percentage of the index value as of March 1973, calculated to two decimal places (for example, 101.57). Minimum price fluctuation: .01 of a U.S. Dollar Index point, which is equivalent to $5 per contract. Daily limit on price movements: none. Last day of trading: third Wednesday of the expiring contract month. Delivery: cash settlement, based on the settlement value of the U.S. Dollar Index at 10:00 A.M. on the last day of trading for an expiring contract.
2. *Options:* Contract size: one FINEX U.S. Dollar Index futures contract. Contract months: March, June, September, and December. Price quotation: Price is quoted in U.S. Dollar Index points and hundredths of a point. Strike prices: intervals of two U.S. dollar index trading points (200 ticks). Minimum price fluctuation: .01 of a U.S. Dollar Index futures point, which is equivalent to $5 per contract. Daily limit on price movement: none. Last day of trading: two Fridays before the third Wednesday of the expiring contract month. Exercise: until 5 P.M. on the last trading day.

The European currency Unit is a basket of ten currencies of the ten member states of the European Economic Community. The ECU contract offers an efficient and effective way to hedge and trade the ECU. Contract specifications include: Contract size: ECU 100,000. Contract months: March, June, September, and December. Price quotation: Price is quoted in U.S. cents and hundredths of a U.S. cent per ECU, with each cent representing $1,000 per futures contract. Minimum price fluctuation: .01 of a cent per ECU, which is equivalent to $10 per futures contract. Trading limits: none. Last day of trading: two business days prior to third Wednesday of expiring contract month. Settlement: physical delivery of ECU.

Contract specifications for five-year U.S. Treasury note futures include the following: Trading unit: U.S. Treasury notes with a face value at maturity of $100,000. Contract months: March, June, September, and December. Price quotation: points, 32nds, and $^1/_2$ of 1 $^1/_{32}$ of a point. For example, 88-025 equals 88 points and 2 $^1/_2$ thirty-seconds of a point. Minimum price fluctuation: one half of $^1/_{32}$ nd of a point, or $15.625 per contract. Daily limit on price movement: none. Last day of trading: 1:00 P.M. on the 98th last business day of the delivery month. Delivery: physical delivery of notes.

Contract specification on the two-year U.S. Treasury note futures contract, which began trading on February 22, 1989, include: Trading unit: face value at maturity of $200,000. Months: March, June, September, and December. Price quotation: Price is quoted as a percentage of par in minimum increments of $^1/_{32}$ of $^1/_{32}$ of a point, or $15.625 per contract. Daily limit on price movement: none. Last day of trading: 1:00 p.m. on the 8th last business day of the expiring contract month. Delivery: Federal Reserve book-entry system.

Source: New York Cotton Exchange.

NEW YORK CURB EXCHANGE See AMERICAN STOCK EXCHANGE.

NEW YORK DOLLARS Funds payable in New York, without deduction for interest or other charges, as distinguished from funds available at other points in the United States, or elsewhere, though payable in dollars. Banks in this country having accounts with correspondents abroad may issue letters of credit against which the holder may draw drafts against such correspondents. Instructions are usually given to such correspondents to provide for reimbursement upon cashing such drafts when presented, by a charge against the American bank's account, or else by drawing against the American bank in New York dollars.

NEW YORK EXCHANGE A check drawn upon a bank in New York. New York being the financial center, a check drawn upon New York should be acceptable in all places, but banks anywhere have an understandable disinclination to cash checks for strangers, requiring personal identification or preferably the endorsement of a depositor of the bank, as a protective measure against the risk of payment on bad checks or to the wrong payee.

The Federal Reserve System par collection system has placed most clearings and collections in the United States on a par basis, without deduction of exchange charges.

See FEDERAL RESERVE CHECK COLLECTION SYSTEM, PAR LIST.

NEW YORK FEDERAL RESERVE About one-fourth of all the earning assets of reporting member banks are within the New York Federal Reserve district. The New York Federal Reserve Bank reports also about one-fourth of the total resources of the 12 Federal Reserve banks. The New York Federal Reserve Bank was opened for business on November 16, 1914, with a staff consisting largely of workers lent to the new organization by neighbor New York City banks. The quarters occupied were in a small building at 62 Cedar Street. In the succeeding few weeks, the temporary employees were replaced by a permanent staff, which consisted on January 1, 1915, of 5 officers and 36 other employees.

In the early months of its existence, the principal activity of the bank consisted of taking into custody the reserve funds that all national banks were required by law to deposit as soon as the bank opened. During the first two years of the bank's existence, the earning assets were mainly in the form of open market purchases of acceptances and holdings of municipal warrants; there was no large demand from member banks for loans, and it was not until later that the subsidiary services, such as check and note collections and wire transfers, became major activities. The offices at 62 Cedar Street were unsatisfactory and provided no opportunity for expansion, so on May 1, 1916, the bank relocated on the first and fifth floors of the Equitable Building.

With the country's entrance into the war in April, 1917, the character of the work underwent a transformation. As new tasks were undertaken, it became necessary to increase rapidly the staff of the New York Federal Reserve Bank. By January 1, 1918, the employees numbered 845, a total nearly five times as large as that of one year before. The quarters on the first and fifth floors of the Equitable Building became inadequate. Additional space was secured in that building, and the entire building at 50 Wall;Street was also occupied. The capacity of the vault was so taken up with liberty bonds and other material requiring safe storage that it was necessary to use in addition, through the courtesy of the New York Clearing House, one of the vaults belonging to that organization.

The growth of the bank in 1917 and 1918 may in considerable measure be attributed to its use as an emergency institution, but there were developing at the same time other services of a more permanent nature, which engaged a constantly increasing proportion of the bank's staff. What may be called the ordinary services of the bank included collection of checks for member banks, collection of notes and drafts, telegraphic transfer of funds from one part of the country to another, settlement of current balances through the interdistrict settlement fund in Washington, payment of checks and warrants for the government, exchange of government bonds, payment of coupons upon government bonds, sale and redemption of U.S. certificates of indebtedness, custody and sale of securities for the U.S. Treasury and other government agencies and member banks, shipment of wrapped coin and currency, and maintenance of statistical and other services to aid member banks.

Throughout the period of most rapid growth, the housing of the bank's working force was a continual problem. This was solved in 1921 by construction of the bank's own $14 million building, located on the entire block bounded by Nassau, Liberty, Maiden Lane, and William Streets, in the New York financial district.

The Federal Reserve Bank of New York on January 1, 1917, was authorized to establish an agency with the Bank of England, and from that date it assumed a position of unofficial leadership in the FEDERAL RESERVE SYSTEM in international financial relations with European central banks and bankers, particularly under the governorship of Benjamin Strong. The Banking Act of 1933 specifically amended the Federal Reserve Act, however, to provide that the Board of Governors of the Federal Reserve System shall exercise special supervision over all relationships and transactions of any kind entered into by any Federal Reserve bank with any foreign bank or banker, or with any group of foreign banks or bankers. All such relationships and transactions shall be subject to such regulations, conditions, and limitations as the board may prescribe. In fact, no officer or other representative of any Federal Reserve bank shall conduct negotiations of any kind with the officers or representatives of any foreign bank or banker without first obtaining the permission of the board of governors. A full report of all conferences or negotiations, all understandings or agreements arrived at or transactions agreed upon, and all other material facts pertaining to such conferences or negotiations shall be filed with the board of governors in writing by a duly authorized officer of each Federal Reserve bank that shall have participated in such conferences or negotiations. These provisions, found in Section 14 (g) of the act, were aimed particularly at the Federal Reserve Bank of New York.

Under the governorship of Benjamin Strong, the New York Federal Reserve Bank led the way in development of open market operations as an instrument of credit control. Prior to the Banking Act of 1935, the 12 Federal Reserve banks had a good deal of independence to open market operations and could decide not to participate in open market operations upon 30 days notice. The Banking Act of 1935 established a new FEDERAL OPEN MARKET COMMITTEE, of which the board of governors assumed control, and provided that no Federal Reserve bank shall engage in or decline to engage in open market operations except in accordance with the directives of the committee.

Operations. The Federal Reserve Bank of New York serves the Second Federal Reserve District. Its territory includes New York State, the 12 northernmost counties in New Jersey, and Fairfield County, Connecticut. The New York Fed has a branch in Buffalo, New York, serving 14 western counties of the state. Additionally, there are five regional check processing centers within the district— one at the Buffalo branch; one each in Utica, New York, and Cranford, New Jersey; and two in Jericho, Long Island. Although it serves a geographically small area, the New York Fed is the largest Federal Reserve bank in terms of assets and volume of activity. Its location in the banking center of the world also makes it unique in other aspects.

At the direction of the Federal Open Market Committee (FOMC), the New York Fed conducts domestic open market operations on behalf of the entire Federal Reserve System. The FOMC, composed of all 7 of the board of governors and 5 of the 12 presidents of the district Federal Reserve banks, is the top policy-making unit of the Federal Reserve System. Open market operations—the buying and selling of U.S. government securities—provide the means through which the system conducts MONETARY POLICY, by influencing the cost and availability of credit. The president of the New York Fed is a permanent voting member of the FOMC and traditionally is selected its vice-chairman. The other 11 presidents of district Federal Reserve banks serve one-year rotating terms. Thus each year 4 of the other presidents serve as voting members of the FOMC. However, the nonvoting presidents attend the meetings and participate in the discussions. The first vice-president of the New York Fed is traditionally the only second-in-command who may substitute as a voting member of the committee in the absence of the New York Federal Reserve Bank president. When other voting presidents are unable to attend an FOMC meeting, an alternate reserve bank president votes. FOMC meetings are usually held about ten times a year in Washington, D.C.

All foreign exchange trading for the Federal Reserve System is done at the New York Fed, which buys and sells foreign currencies in the New York Foreign exchange market at the direction of the FOMC. Similarly, the foreign exchange desk operates in the foreign exchange market for the U.S. Treasury. Most foreign exchange transactions are aimed at stabilizing disorderly foreign exchange market conditions.

The New York Fed also stores "official" gold owned by about 80 foreign nations, central banks, and international organizations. The vault of the New York Fed, containing the largest known accumulation of gold in the world, rests on the bedrock of Manhattan, 80 feet below the street level. The vault as of November, 1980, held about $15 billion in gold bars, based on the official price of $42.22 per fine troy ounce, representing about a quarter of the known gold reserves of the world. Foreign official gold reserves have been held at the

New York Fed since 1924 for numerous reasons, including the stability of the U.S. political system, the concentration of international trade and finance in the New York money market, and the convenience of centralizing gold holdings in a place where international payments can be made quickly.

NEW YORK FUNDS See NEW YORK EXCHANGE.

NEW YORK FUTURES EXCHANGE
The COMMODITY FUTURES TRADING COMMISSION (CFTC) approved the New York Futures Exchange (NYFE) as a contract market in 1980 to trade futures contracts for certain foreign currencies and U.S. government instruments, and in 1981 to trade futures contracts in domestic bank certificates of deposit. Trading on the NYFE began August 7, 1980, when 3,581 futures contracts in U.S. Treasury 20-year bonds were traded. The NYFE was authorized to trade in futures in five foreign currencies—the British pound, the Canadian dollar, the Deutsche mark, the Japanese yen, and the Swiss franc—a field dominated by the Chicago Mercantile Exchange, through its International Monetary Market.

NYFE inaugurated trading in a new futures contract based on domestic bank certificates of deposit (CDs) on July 9, 1981.

The New York exchanges started late in their entry into the financial futures field (the AMERICAN STOCK EXCHANGE experimented with financial futures trading beginning in August, 1978, but after 24 months merged into the New York Futures Exchange; the COMMODITY EXCHANGE, INC. expanded its futures trading in 1979 to include Treasury bills and GNMA CDs, with further expansion into Treasury notes in 1980; and the NEW YORK MERCANTILE EXCHANGE discontinued its trading foreign currency futures {British pound, Canadian dollar, Deusche mark, Japanese yen, Belgian franc, and Swiss franc}, begun in 1978, in 1980) as compared with the pioneering Chicago exchanges which have established themselves in this growing financial futures field.

NEW YORK HIDE EXCHANGE
This exchange no longer exists as a separate entity. Its activities were merged with the COMMODITY EXCHANGE, INC. on July 5, 1933.

NEW YORK MERCANTILE EXCHANGE
Organized in 1872 to provide a national marketplace for trading in cash and futures contracts of various commodities. The exchange in recent years has become a diversified marketplace, where trading in futures ranges from agricultural commodities to precious metals to energy and crude oil options. The New York Mercantile Exchange (NYMEX), however, is still known for its active round white potato market, initiated in 1941 and popular with farmers, commercial interests, and others. In 1980 a new expanded contract was introduced with great success.

Round White Potato Futures Contract. During 1980, the NYMEX received approval from the COMMODITY FUTURES TRADING COMMISSION to open an expanded contract which included potatoes grown in the states of Maine, Connecticut, and New York. Previously, the NYMEX countract had been limited to Maine-grown potatoes. The inclusion of New York and Connecticut as deliverable sources enhanced the contract's usefulness by expanding the supply base and providing additional liquidity in the market. Trading in the revised contract opened on May 19, 1980, and open interest surpassed the 5,000 mark within one month. On December 31, 1980, open interest stood at 11,301 contracts. Annual trading volume in the round white potato futures contract totaled 393,759 contracts during 1980, an increase of 114% over 1979 volume. Price volatility accounted in part for this increase in volume, as a small fall crop nationwide created a "bull market"—for example, prices for the April, 1981, contract ranged from a low of $8.25 per hundred pounds on May 19, 1980, to a high of $17.75 recorded on January 16, 1981.

The round white potato futures contract unit is 50,000 pounds (1,000 fifty-pound bags). Minimum permitted delivery is 42,000 pounds (840 fifty-pound bags). Deliverable potatoes are round white varieties (except cobbler and warba types) grown in the states of Maine, New York, and Connecticut, and delivered in straight carloads or truckloads. Grade and size are U.S. No. 1, size A, 2-inch minimum, 4-inch maximum. Permitted substitutions (on the April and May contracts only) are U.S. commercial grade potatoes (same origin, varieties, and sizes as above) in straight carloads or trucks at a discount of 25% from the last settling price for the delivery month. The grade standards are U.S. Department of Agriculture standards for grades of potatoes in effect. Packaging is in 50-pound, properly enclosed new kraft or white paper bags, with ten extra empty bags required per shipment.

Price quotation basis is dollars and cents per 100 pounds, including freight costs to New York City. Minimum price fluctuation is $0.01 per 100 pounds; maximum daily price fluctuation is $0.50 per 100 pounds above or below the preceding day's settling price (maximum daily price fluctuation is subject to variable limits formula). Delivery months are February, March, April and November. Trading may also be conducted in other months as determined by the exchange's board of governors.

No. 2 Heating Oil Futures Contract. Since its introduction in November, 1978, the New York Mercantile Exchange's No. 2 heating oil futures contract has experienced substantial growth, becoming the dominant hedging vehicle in the heating oil industry and the most active commodity at the NYMEX. When first introduced, heating oil futures were received with curiosity and skepticism by investors and industry members alike, who believed that heating oil prices would only rise. However, such factors as weather, conservation, government policy, and world political events quickly disproved belief in the heating oil market's one-sided price movement. More than 3.1 million crude oil options were traded. The NYMEX heating oil market is now one of the most widely used price discovery and hedging mechanisms in the petroleum industry. The results of the NYMEX extensive market development efforts came to fruition in 1980: total trading volume for the year was 238,284 trades, and increase of 600% over 1979; open interest reached a record high of 13,519 contracts; and daily trading volume averaged more than 3,000 trades. In 1987, more than 3 million crude oil options were issued.

Amendments to the heating oil contract that were approved by the Commodity Futures Trading Commission (CFTC) during 1980 expanded the number of trading months available, making it possible to plan more than a year into the future. The success of the contract, which calls for New York Harbor delivery, prompted the NYMEX to apply to the CFTC for approval of a new contract specifying Gulf Coast delivery, which was expected to be approved and opened for trading. To accommodate this new Gulf Coast contract, reconfiguration of the trading floor was necessary.

In addition, two gasoline futures contracts, for leaded regular and unleaded, were pending CFTC approval. With the decontrol of petroleum prices by the government, the NYMEX indicates its aggressive pursuit of approval of these contracts and other energy-related futures contracts.

The No. 2 heating oil New York Harbor contract calls for 42,000 U.S. gallons as the contract unit (1,000 U.S. barrels). The delivery point is New York Harbor. Price quotation is in dollars and cents per gallon. Minimum price fluctuation is $0.0001 per gallon (equivalent to $4.20 per contract unit). Maximum daily price limit is $0.02, subject to expanded limit rules. Delivery months are all months.

The No. 2 heating oil Gulf Coast contract would have the same contract details and product specifications as the No. 2 heating oil New York Harbor contract, except that the delivery point would be the Gulf Coast area.

Platinum/Palladium Futures Contracts. Platinum trading was initiated at NYMEX in 1956 and has grown to become the exchange's dominant metals contract. Palladium trading, a more recently established market, began in 1968.

The platinum futures contract trading unit is 50 troy ounces, sheet or bar. Grade and quality specifications are minima of 99.5% pure platinum and 99.8% pure platinum and platinum metals (subject to pending request for revision of purity rules to minimum of 99.9% pure platinum). Delivery months are January, April, July, and October; trading may also be conducted in other months as determined by the exchange's board of governors. Price quotation basis is in U.S. dollars and cents per troy ounce, with minimum price fluctuation of $0.10 per ounce, and maximum daily price fluctuation of $20 per ounce above or below the preceding day's settling price (maximum daily price fluctuation may be increased subject to variable limits formula in the event settlement is subject to establishment at maximum daily fluctuation limit).

Contract unit on the palladium futures contract is 100 troy ounces. (Each contract unit must consist of no more than four pieces plate and/or ingot, with no individual piece weighing less than 10 ounces.) Grade and quality specifications call for a minimum specification of 99.8% pure palladium. Delivery months are March, June, September, and December, but trading may also be conducted in other months as determined by the exchange's board of governors. Price quotation basis is in U.S. dollars and cents per troy ounce. Minimum price fluctuation is $0.05 per ounce, with maximum daily price fluctuation $6 per ounce above or below the preceding day's settling price. (Maximum daily price fluctuation may be increased subject to variable limits formula in the event settlement is established at maximum daily fluctuation limit.)

Imported Lean Beef Futures Contract. Trading in the NYMEX imported lean beef futures contract was inaugurated on September 15, 1971. This innovative contract provides a hedging medium for importers, exporters, manufacturers, retailers, and commercial users of imported lean beef, all of whom are vulnerable to the volatile prices inherent in the meat industry.

Following the success of the heating oil contract, NYMEX expanded its offering of energy futures to the trading community. Contracts in leaded gasoline and crude oil were initiated in 1981 and 1985, respectively. In 1984, NYMEX introduced unleaded gasoline futures in response to the demands of a changing energy market. More than 2 million contracts for this product were traded in 1987, and more than 1.4 million were traded in the first half of 1988.

NYMEX crude oil futures became the most successful contract on the exchange within a year of its 1985 introduction. By 1987 trading volume grew almost 700%, and crude oil became the world's most actively traded physical commodity. By mid-1988, NYMEX crude oil was the world's third most actively traded futures contract, surpassed only by the Chicago Board of Trade's Treasury bond contract and the Chicago Mercantile Exchange's Eurodollar contract.

Crude oil options were added to the energy complex in November 1986. By 1987, they were the world's leading option on a physical commodity. In the first half of 1988, crude oil options trading was second only to Treasury bonds among options on futures contracts. Heating oil futures and propane futures began to trade in 1987. Natural gas futures began trading in 1989. The popularity of NYMEX is attributed largely to the recognition that energy futures protect oil market participants from price volatility.

NEW YORK PLAN *See* EQUIPMENT TRUST.

NEW YORK PRODUCE EXCHANGE *See* INTERNATIONAL COMMERCIAL EXCHANGE, INC.

NEW YORK REAL ESTATE BOARD REAL ESTATE BOARD OF NEW YORK, INC.

NEW YORK RUBBER EXCHANGE As a separate entity this exchange no longer exists. As of July 5, 1933, its activities were merged with the COMMODITY EXCHANGE, INC.

NEW YORK SAVINGS BANKS *See* INSTITUTIONAL INVESTORS MUTUAL FUND, INC.; INSTITUTIONAL SECURITIES CORPORATION; SAVINGS BANKS; TRUST COMPANY.

NEW YORK SOCIETY OF SECURITY ANALYSTS

A nonprofit membership corporation formed in 1937 to foster the interchange of information and opinion among analysts engaged in research in various branches of finance and economics, to improve analytical techniques, to establish and maintain a high standard of professional ethics, and to advance public understanding of the functions of financial analysts and the operation of the security and commodity markets.

Membership is divided, pursuant to amendments to the NYSSA constitution and bylaws late in 1980, into four classes of members: regular, retired (only the regular and retired regular members are eligible to hold office or become directors of the society), nonprimary (members who meet all the requirements of regular membership but have a primary membership in another constituent society of the Financial Analysts Federation, the national federation of security analysts' societies), associate (any person who was a "junior" member on December 22, 1980, subject to required application for regular membership within specified number of years), and affiliate (those who are not eligible for regular or associate membership but may be granted affiliate privileges by the discretion of the board of directors).

The New York Society of Security Analysts is headed by a 27-member board of directors, including the president, executive vice-president, two vice-presidents, a secretary, and a treasurer. It is the largest member society in the FINANCIAL ANALYSTS FEDERATION.

NEW YORK STATE INCOME TAX New York State's personal income tax, adopted in 1919 and first applicable to incomes for the year 1920, is New York State's largest single source of revenue.

NEW YORK STOCK EXCHANGE The major stock exchange in the world, where NYSE member brokers, acting for investors on six continents, trade millions of shares of the world's leading publicly owned corporations. Its functions are to maintain the most efficient marketplace in which anyone, anywhere, can quickly and conveniently buy and sell shares of the world's leading corporations. Approximately 1,600 corporations' shares are traded on the exchange. The aggregate market value is estimated to be nearly two trillion dollars—approximately half that of the U.S. gross national product. The NYSE had 600 member firms in 1988.

In May 1792, a group of 24 merchants and brokers met and agreed to give preference to one another in their dealings. Their written accord has come to be known as "The Buttonwood Agreement," after the tree under which much of their trading took place. Trading continued informally for several years in the street and in nearby coffeehouses where merchants gathered. Commercial activity sagged during the War of 1812, but by 1817 trading volume was sufficient to encourage brokers to create a formal organization. A constitution was adopted on March 8, 1817 which created the New York Stock and Exchange Board, the predecessor of the New York Stock Exchange. The brokers met in a "call" market. Twice a day, the president of the board read the list of securities while the members shouted bids and offers from the chairs assigned to them. This was the origin of the term "seat," which has signified a membership on the exchange. The marketplace moved into its first permanent home on Broad Street, just south of Wall Street, in 1865.

By 1876, continuous trading replaced the call market. Stocks were assigned to permanent locations at "trading posts" and brokers circulated about the floor to make their bids and offers. A "seat" became a term for membership.

The stock ticker, introduced in 1867, revolutionized market communications by making it possible to transmit market information nationwide. The installation of telephones in 1878 was another major innovation. In 1903 the marketplace moved to the corner of Broad and Wall Streets.

The stock market crash of 1929 focused critical attention on the securities industry. To supplement the exchange's own self-regulatory activities, Congress created the Securities and Exchange Commission in 1934 and inaugurated comprehensive federal regulation of the entire industry. After languishing during World War II, the market eventually recovered with the conversion to a peacetime economy.

In the Securities Acts Amendments of 1975, Congress called for expanding competition among the U.S. markets through technology aimed at creating a National Market System. This market system was implemented in subsequent years. Volume for a single day rose about 50 million shares on April 14, 1987, went over 100 million on August 18, 1982, soared over 200 million on August 2, 1984, and topped 300 million for the first time on January 23, 1987.

To be considered for listing on the NYSE, a company must meet or exceed specified levels of net earnings, assets, and trading volume, and its shares must be widely held by investors. The exchange also insists on evidence that trading interest in the company's shares is sufficient to warrant trading in the public auction market. A prospective listed company must also agree to meet the exchange's standards of disclosure, corporate governance, and shareholder participation. The major reason companies move to the NYSE after trading in other markets is to enhance their prestige and the marketability of their securities. Key factors in the decision to list include market liquidity, expanded trading activity, greater visibility, and a broader appeal to investors.

The NYSE surveillance team uses a variety of tools and techniques to carry out the exchange's self-regulatory obligations. One of the most important is the completely automated Stock Watch system that continuously monitors trading activity in all listed stocks. Stock Watch computers track NYSE trading activity in NYSE-listed stocks throughout each trading day. If trading in a stock falls outside predetermined price or volume guidelines, a computer printout alerts the exchange's market trading analysts. Data are analyzed to determine whether a violation may exist and an inquiry into the trading situation warranted.

ENCYCLOPEDIA OF BANKING AND FINANCE

NEW YORK STOCK EXCHANGE ABBREVIATIONS

Table 1 / Volume of Trading on New York Stock Exchange: 1970 to 1987
(Round lot: A unit of trading or a multiple thereof. On the NYSE the unit of trading is generally 100 shares in stocks. For some inactive stocks, the unit of trading is 10 shares. Odd lot: An amount of stock less than the established 100-share unit or 10-share unit of trading.)

Item	Unit	1970	1975	1979	1980	1981	1982	1983	1984	1985	1986	1987
Shares traded	Million	3,124	4,839	8,336	11,562	12,049	16,669	21,846	23,309	27,774	36,009	48,143
Round lots	Million	2,937	4,693	8,156	11,352	11,854	16,458	21,590	23,071	27,511	35,680	47,801
Average daily shares	Million	11.6	18.6	32.2	44.9	46.9	65.1	85.3	91.2	109.2	141.0	189.0
High day	Million	21.3	35.2	81.6	84.3	92.9	149.4	129.4	236.6	181.0	244.3	608.1
Low day	Million	6.7	8.7	18.3	16.1	23.9	36.8	53.0	46.4	62.1	48.9	86.7
By size:[1]												
At 100-900 shares	Percent	NA	42.1	27.5	24.7	21.1	16.2	14.6	11.3	10.6	10.8	13.6
At 1,000-4,900 shares	Percent	NA	31.4	33.7	32.2	31.0	28.5	26.7	25.1	24.1	25.7	21.1
At 5,000-9,900 shares	Percent	NA	8.7	11.4	11.4	12.1	12.8	12.7	13.8	13.8	13.9	14.1
At 10,000 or more shares[2]	Percent	NA	17.9	27.4	31.7	35.8	42.5	46.0	49.8	51.5	49.6	51.2
Odd lots	Million	186	146	180	209	196	211	256	238	263	329	342
Value of shares traded	Bil. dol.	102.5	131.7	244.5	382.4	396.1	495.1	775.3	773.4	980.8	1,388.8	1,888.7
Round lots	Bil. dol.	95.3	126.7	238.2	374.9	389.2	488.4	765.3	764.7	970.5	1,374.3	1,873.6
Odd lots	Bil dol.	7.2	5.0	6.3	7.5	6.9	6.7	10.1	8.7	10.3	14.5	15.1
Bond volume[3]	Mil. dol.	4,495	5,178	4,088	5,190	5,733	7,155	7,572	6,982	9,046	10,464	9,727
Daily average	Mil. dol.	17.7	20.5	16.2	20.5	22.7	28.3	29.9	27.6	35.9	41.4	38.4

NA — Not available.
[1] Share volume of reported trades by size (percent of total) on New York Stock Exchange.
[2] Includes bunched orders at the opening and re-opening of trading.
[3] Par value.

Source: New York Stock Exchange, Inc., *Fact Book*, annual.

Table 2 / Securities Listed on N.Y. Stock Exchange: 1970 to 1987
(As of December 31, except cash dividends are for calendar year.)

Item	Unit	1970	1975	1979	1980	1981	1982	1983	1984	1985	1986	1987
Bonds:												
Number of issuers	Number	843	1,066	1,043	1,045	1,049	1,031	1,034	1,024	1,010	951	885
Number of issues	Number	1,729	2,632	2,939	3,057	3,110	3,233	3,600	3,751	3,856	3,611	3,346
Face value	Bil. dol.	135	334	526	602	681	793	965	1,084	1,327	1,380	1,651
Market value	Bil. dol.	113	315	460	508	574	766	898	1,022	1,339	1,458	1,621
Average price	Percent	83.60	91.89	87.36	84.41	84.24	96.67	93.04	94.29	100.90	105.66	98.20
Stocks:												
Companies	Number	1,351	1,557	1,565	1,570	1,565	1,526	1,550	1,543	1,541	1,575	1,647
Number of issues	Number	1,840	2,111	2,192	2,228	2,220	2,225	2,307	2,319	2,298	2,257	2,244
Shares listed	Billion	16.1	22.5	30.0	33.7	38.3	39.5	45.1	49.1	52.4	59.6	72.0
Market value	Bil. dol.	636	685	961	1,243	1,144	1,305	1,584	1,586	1,950	2,199	2,216
Average price	Dollars	39.61	30.48	31.99	36.87	29.87	33.03	35.11	32.31	37.20	36.89	30.87
Cash dividends on common stock	Bil. dol.	19.8	26.9	46.9	53.1	60.6	62.2	67.1	68.2	74.2	76.2	84.4

Source: New York Stock Exchange, Inc., *Fact Book*, annual.

Bonds, options, and futures are also traded on the NYSE. The NYSE bond market is the world's largest. It offers investors a broad selection of some 4,000 bonds—with an aggregate par value of more than $300 billion—issued by the U.S. and foreign governments, U.S. and foreign corporations, and international banks.

In 1966, the exchange introduced the NYSE Common Stock Index—and four subindexes (industrial, transportation, utility, and finance)—to reflect the overall price changes of all common stocks listed on the exchange. If the index stands at 100.0 on a particular date, that means the average volume of all common shares listed on the NYSE on that date is twice as much as it was on the last business day of 1965. The exchange's stock index futures and options contracts are based on the NYSE Common Stock Index. Trading in standardized options contracts began in the early 1970s. The exchange also offers other options in addition to the Common Stock Index.

In 1992, the New York Stock Exchange will begin its third century as America's premier securities marketplace. Three appended tables present data showing (1) volume of trading on the New York Stock Exchange 1970-1987, (2) securities listed on the NYSE 1970 to 1987, and (3) data relating to prices and trading, customer financing, and margin requirements.

Source: New York Stock Exchange.

NEW YORK STOCK EXCHANGE ABBREVIATIONS

The abbreviations for stocks (stock symbols) assignd to stocks listed on the NYSE and used by the New York Stock exchange's systems of quotations and disseminations of reports of transactions.

How to Read the Consolidated Ticker Tape

1. 100-share-unit stock. Sales consisting of 100 shares of a stock in which the unit of trading is 100 shares will be printed with no quantity indicated. Thus a sale of 100 shares of XYZ Corp. at 39 1/2 will be printed XYZ39 1/2.
    a. Sales consisting of 200 or more shares of a stock in which the unit of trading is 100 shares is indicated by the number of units followed by the letter "s" on the lower line, and then the price. A sale of 200 shares at 39 1/2 will be printed XYZ2s39 1/2. 1,500 shares will print as 15s, 12,000 shares as 120s, etc.
    b. Sales of odd amounts of more than the trading unit will be printed as follows: XYZ125SHRS39 1/2.
2. The quantity of sales of stocks dealt in on a 10-share-unit basis will be designated by the letters •, on the lower line. A sale of 10 shares of the UWV Corp, at 23 1/2 will be printed 1•. 23 1/2, 200 shares as 20•. etc.

ENCYCLOPEDIA OF BANKING AND FINANCE

Table 3 / NYSE Trading Data and Margin Requirements

Indicator	1986	1987	1988	1988 Sept.	Oct.	Nov.	Dec.	1989 Jan.	Feb.	Mar.	Apr.	May
Prices and trading (averages of daily figures)												
Common stock prices												
1 New York Stock Exchange (Dec. 31, 1965 = 50)	136.00	161.70	149.91	151.47	156.36	152.67	155.35	160.40	165.08	169.73	169.38	175.55
2 Industrial	155.85	195.31	180.83	182.18	188.58	182.25	187.75	194.62	200.00	197.58	204.81	211.81
3 Transportation	119.87	140.39	134.01	136.27	141.83	137.51	144.06	153.09	162.66	153.85	164.32	169.05
4 Utility	71.36	74.29	72.22	71.83	74.19	79.28	74.81	75.87	77.84	87.16	79.69	84.21
5 Finance	147.19	146.48	127.41	133.15	136.09	130.05	128.83	132.26	137.19	146.14	143.26	146.82
6 Standard & Poor's Corporation (1941-43 = 10) [1]	236.34	286.83	NA	267.97	277.40	271.02R	281.28R	285.41R	294.01R	292.71R	302.25R	314.43
7 American Stock Exchange (Aug. 31, 1973 = 50) [2]	264.38	316.61	294.90	297.86	302.83	292.25	298.59	316.14	323.96	327.47	336.82	349.82
Volume of trading (thousands of shares)												
8 New York Stock Exchange	141,385	188,647	161,450	145,702	162,631	134,427	135,473	168,193	169,321	159,024	161,862	NA
9 American Stock Exchange	11,846	13,832	9,955	8,198	9,051	8,497	11,227	10,797	11,780	11,395	11,529	NA
Customer financing (end-of-period balances, in millions of dollars)												
10 Margin credit at broker-dealers [3]	36,840	31,990	32,740	32,770	33,410	33,640	32,740	32,530	31,480	32,130	32,610	33,140
Free credit balances at brokers [4]												
11 Margin-account [5]	4,880	4,750	5,660	4,725	5,065	4,920	5,660	5,790	5,605	5,345	5,450	5,250
12 Cash-account	19,000	15,640	16,595	14,175	14,880	15,185	16,595	15,705	16,195	16,045	16,125	15,965

Margin requirements (percent of market value and effective date) [6]

	Mar. 11, 1968	June 8, 1968	May 6, 1970	Dec. 6, 1971	Nov. 24, 1972	Jan. 3, 1974
13 Margin stocks	70	80	65	55	65	50
14 Convertible bonds	50	60	50	50	50	50
15 Short sales	70	80	65	55	65	50

[1] Effective July 1976, includes a new financial group, banks and insurance companies. With this change the index includes 400 industrial stocks (formerly 425), 20 transportation (formerly 15 rail), 40 public utility (formerly 60), and 40 financial.
[2] Beginning July 5, 1983, the American Stock Exchange rebased its index effectively cutting previous readings in half.
[3] Beginning July 1983, under the revised Regulation T, margin credit at broker-dealers includes credit extended against stocks, convertible bonds, stocks acquired through exercise of subscription rights, corporate bonds, and government securities. Separate reporting of data for margin stocks, convertible bonds, and subscription issues was discontinued in April 1984.
[4] Free credit balances are in accounts with no unfulfilled commitments to the brokers and are subject to withdrawal by customers on demand.
[5] New series beginning June 1984.
[6] These regulations, adopted by the board of governors pursuant to the Securities Exchange Act of 1934, limit the amount of credit to purchase and carry "margin securities" (as defined In the regulations) when such credit is collateralized by securities. Margin requirements on securities other than options are the difference between the market value (100 pecent) and the maximum loan value of collateral as prescribed by the board. Regulation T was adopted effective Oct. 15, 1934; Regulation U, effective May 1, 1936; Regulation G, effective Mar. 11, 1968; and Regulation X, effective Nov. 1, 1971.
On Jan. 1, 1977, the board of governors for the first time established in Regulation T the initial margin required for writing options on securities, setting it at 30% of the current market-value of the stock underlying the option. On Sept. 30, 1985, the board changed the required initial margin, allowing it to be the same as the option maintenance margin required by the appropriate exchange or self-regulatory organization; such maintenance margin rules must be approved by the Securities and Exchange Commission. Effective Jan. 31, 1986, the SEC approved new maintenance margin rules, permitting margins to be the price of the option plus 15% of the market value of the stock underlying the option.

Source: New York Stock Exchange, Inc., *Fact Book*, annual.

NEW YORK STOCK EXCHANGE, INC. See NEW YORK STOCK EXCHANGE SUBSIDIARIES.

NEW YORK STOCK EXCHANGE, SUBSIDIARIES

The consolidated financial statements of the New York Stock exchange, Inc. (the "Exchange") include the NEW YORK FUTURES EXCHANGE and all other wholly owned subsidiaries after elimination of significant intercompany transactions. Securities Industry Automation Corporation (SIAC), which is two-thirds owned by the exchange, is consolidated within the balance sheet, and its expenses applicable to the exchange and subsidiaries are included in the consolidated statement of net revenues and equity of members.

The exchange's investment in the DEPOSITORY TRUST COMPANY (DTC) and NATIONAL SECURITIES CLEARING CORPORATION (NSCC), which represent less than 50% ownership, are carried at cost since these companies are operated by separate management and have independent boards of directors.

Depository Trust Company. DTC is a central certificate depository. Under a shareholders' agreement, entitlement to own shares of DTC is redetermined each year, based on usage, with shares to be transferred as appropriate at the per share net worth determined as of December 31 of the preceding year.

National Securities Clearing Corporation. Effective January 1, 1977, the exchange merged the clearing operations of its wholly owned subsidiary, STOCK CLEARING CORPORATION, with similar operations of the American Stock Exchange Clearing Corporation and the National Clearing Corporation to form the NSCC. The exchange owns a one-third interest in NSCC, which operates the clearing systems for its participants.

Under the terms of the shareholders' agreement, NSCC was required to p[ay the exchange a fee for regulatory and other services based on its activity, up to a maximum of $15 million over the five-year period from 1977 through 1981.

Securities Industry Automation Corporation. SIAC is a two-

NEW YORK SUGAR EXCHANGE

thirds-owned consolidated subsidiary of the exchange. The remaining one-third is owned by the AMERICAN STOCK EXCHANGE, Inc. SIAC provides certain communications, clearing, and data processing operations and systems development functions to both exchanges and others. Under a service agreement, SIAC charges the users of its services their respective shares of its costs, representing primarily employee costs and payments for leased facilities and equipment.

See NEW YORK STOCK EXCHANGE.

NEW YORK SUGAR EXCHANGE *See*, COFFEE, SUGAR & COCOA EXCHANGE.

NEW YORK TIMES BUSINESS INDEX The *New York Times* weekly index of business activity is published every Sunday in the business and financial news section. It is a weighted composite of the most important and reliable trade indices for which weekly figures are promptly available. The index consists of five major components: freight carloadings, steel mill activity, electric power production, paperboard output, and lumber production. The index has an estimated "normal" because the base periods of its components vary. Seasonal adjustment is applied to all but steel, and long-term trend (the element of growth) is applied to steel and electric power. No series having a fluctuating price element is used; only those dealing with the actual physical volume of production are included. The statistics for each of the components appear on different days of the week and are combined in the Sunday index with an accompanying chart to give a broad, general picture.

This business index has been complied by the *New York Times* since January 5, 1929.

See BUSINESS BAROMETERS, INDEX NUMBERS.

NEXT OF KIN Those persons most closely related by blood; as construed by courts, relatives sharing in the estate according to the provision of the statutes of distribution. In New York State, all distinctions between persons who take as heirs at law or next of kin were abolished September 1, 1930, and the term "distributees" now covers both types of takers.

See HEIR.

NICKEL COIN The United States five-cent piece. it is classified as one of the MINOR COINS by the Treasury Department. Its composition is 75% copper (57.87 grains) and 25% nickel (19.29 grains), for a total weight of 77.16 grains. Under the Joint Resolution of Congress of June 5, 1933, all coins and currencies of the United States heretofore or hereafter coined or issued became legal tender for all public and private debts, public charges, taxes, duties, and dues. P.L. 89-81, approved July 23, 1965 (Coinage Act of 1965), repealed the legal tender provisions of 1933, but added a new provision of law to the same effect, codified in 31 U.S.C. 392.

NICKNAMES OF STOCKS Many of the leading stocks have nicknames by which they are popularly known on Wall Street. In many cases, nicknames have been derived from the ticker abbreviations for the stocks (*see* NEW YORK STOCK EXCHANGE ABBREVIATIONS). Examples among industrials are American Telephone & Telegraph, "Mama Bell"; Bethlehem Steel, "Bessie"; Coca Cola, "Knockout"; International Telephone & Telegraph, "Clara Bow"; and Kern County Land, "Casey."

NIGHT DEPOSITORY An after-hours depository or night drop. The following procedures are basic to sound night deposit operations:

1. The depositor should complete an application and signature card designed for this service. The card provides for signatures of the agents who will be permitted and authorized to pick up or open the bag for the customer.
2. The terms of the contract should be listed on the night depository envelopes. The envelopes are prenumbered for identification purposes and also include a space for the initials of the teller opening the envelope, the teller verifying the contents, and the date.
3. The bank's legal counsel should review the terms of the contract that exists between the bank and the customer.
4. The opening and recording of items deposited in the night depository should be under joint custody for the protection of the bank and its employees against possible customer claims.

NO ACCOUNT When a check is presented for collection through the clearinghouse for which the drawer as indicated has no account on the books of the drawee bank, the latter returns it to the presenting bank for credit, with the memorandum entitled "no account" attached.

See IRREGULARITIES.

NOBEL PRIZE WINNERS IN ECONOMICS Fourteen Americans have received the Nobel Prize in economics. They are:

Paul A. Samuelson	1970
Simon S. Kuznets	1971
Kenneth J. Arrow	1972
Wassily Leontief	1973
Milton Friedman	1976
Herbert A. Simon	1978
Theodore W. Schultz	1979
Lawrence R. Klein	1980
James Tobin	1981
George J. Stigler	1982
Gerard Debreu	1983
Franco Modigliani	1985
James M. Buchanan	1986
Robert M. Solow	1987

NO FUNDS When a check is presented for collection through the clearinghouse for which the drawer as indicated has no funds to the credit of his account with the drawee bank, the latter returns it to the presenting bank for credit, with the memorandum entitled "no funds" attached.

See IRREGULARITIES.

NOIL Short-fibered WOOL.

NOMINAL In economics, nominal value refers to monetary value. Nominal income refers to the actual monetary income earned. Nominal GNP refers to the monetary value of GNP in the year in question. A distinction is frequently made between nominal and real value. Real value is the nominal value adjusted for price change in order to permit a meaningful comparison of such terms over time.

NOMINAL ASSETS Assets of doubtful, indeterminable, or undetermined value, e.g., accounts and notes receivable, judgments, other claims, securities, obsolete items of machinery and equipment, etc. If carried on the books at all, these nominal assets should be carried at a nominal value, e.g., $1.

Sometimes the term is applied to the INTANGIBLES such as GOODWILL, patents, trademarks, etc. Where goodwill arises in connection with a corporate acquisition of another on a "purchase of assets" accounting basis, any goodwill arising thereby shall be capitalized and written off against the income account over a minimum of 40 years (2.5% per year). Such charge-off of amortized goodwill against current income is not tax deductible.

NOMINAL CAPITAL The capital of a corporation as determined by the par or stated value of its total outstanding shares as distinguished from the actual value of its net assets. The first is fixed by the certificate of incorporation; the second is indicated by the balance sheet reflecting current actual values of assets and fully listed liabilities.

The stated capital of a corporation may be reduced by amendment of the certificate of incorporation. Such reduction may also be achieved by a cancellation of shares. Directors may also act to reduce nominal capital by reducing PAR VALUE per share; but if the consideration received for no par value shares was fixed by shareholders, the directors may not reduce such stated capital unless the shareholders so authorize. The amount of such reduction, effected by cancellation without amendment of the certificate or by action of the directors, shall be disclosed to all shareholders in any event within six months of the date of such reduction.

Declaration and payment of dividends, to be legal and not impose criminal penalties upon the directors responsible, must be declared and paid not out of capital, but rather out of surplus only, so that remaining net assets of the corportion shall remain at least equal to the amount of its stated capital (the so-called trust fund doctrine, for minimum protection of creditors and other interested partiesx including stockholders). When any dividend is declared and paid from sources other than earned surplus ("retained earnings"), New York requires that it be accompanied by written notice stating its effect upon stated capital, capital surplus, and earned surplus (Sec. 510, BCL).

See NO PAR VALUE STOCK.

NOMINAL EXCHANGE

The rate of exchange based upon the nominal value of the MONETARY UNIT of the two trading countries, instead of the rate based upon the supply and demand of bills of exchange, i.e., market rate. While nominal exchange is synonymous with the MINT PAR OF EXCHANGE whenever the trading countries are on a gold basis—a free gold market being maintained between them— it differs whenever the standard unit between the two nations is a different metal (because of uneven market fluctuations), when the gold standard is suspended, or when gold is displaced by paper money.

See FOREIGN EXCHANGE.

NOMINAL PRICE

A price that is not a firm offer to buy or sell, but is quoted merely for information or to give an indication of what the firm price might be.

See NOMINAL QUOTATION.

NOMINAL PROFIT

An amount of profit that is neither excessive nor minimal but sufficient to induce a person or entity to remain in business.

NOMINAL QUOTATION

A price quotation which is not based upon an actual or firm bid or offering for a security, but is indicative of the possible price, based on last sale or firm quotation, obtainable through a "work-out" on a definite order or otherwise.

See BID AND ASKED QUOTATIONS.

NOMINAL RATE

See POSTED RATES.

NOMINAL VALUE

This term has two meanings:

1. Applied to securities, par or face value; market value existing in name only or so low as to be an arbitrary value.
2. Applied to coins, statutory or denomination value as distinguished from metal or bullion value.

NO MINIMUM BALANCE CHECKING ACCOUNTS

As the result of adoption by many banks of service charges and requirements for minimum free balances in checking accounts, the no minimum balance type of checking service, also known as pay-as-you-go checking services, has been developed in recent years to appeal to marginal bank prospects for checking service.

As the title indicates, a basic appeal of such plans is the absence of any requirement for a minimum balance in the account. Instead, there is a flat charge per check drawn and a small monthly charge (e.g., $0.25), and the depositor is merely required to have sufficient funds on deposit to cover checks issued.

See MINIMUM FREE BALANCE.

NONASSENTED SECURITIES

Securities, the owners of which have not consented to some proposed change in their status.

See ASSENTED SECURITIES.

NONASSESSABLE STOCK

Stock, the owners of which cannot be legally called upon for additional payments in case of insolvency or otherwise. Such limited liability is one of the basic advantages of the corporate form of business organization. Stocks are nonassessable if they are fully paid when issued. Stock not fully paid subjects the holder to personal liability to creditors of the corporation, in an amount equal to the amount unpaid on such stock, for debts of the corporation contracted while such stock was held by the holder. DOUBLE LIABILITY, or liability to assessment up to full par value of the stock in addition to loss of original investment, was formerly characteristic of bank stocks, but such double liability on bank stocks has been generally eliminated, following the lead of the Banking Act of 1935. Assessment liability to restore impairment of capital or to fully pay up capital stock continues for national bank stock under Section 5205 of the Revised Statutes (12 U.S.C. 55).

NONBANK BANKS

The Bank Holding Company Act (1956) defined banks as institutions that hold demand deposits and make business loans. Nonbank banks are banks that hold demand deposits or make business loans, but do not do both. Nonbank banks were established by some bank holding companies that wanted to operate banks in other states but were prohibited from doing so by regulatory actions. Bank holding companies discovered that they could circumvent the restrictions imposed by law if, when they bought a bank in another state, they simply sold off either its business loan portfolio or its demand deposit accounts. Doing so allowed interstate banking mergers to meet the approval of federal regulators.

The actions of federal regulators in approving the interstate mergers of nonbank banks were challenged in federal court. In 1986, the Supreme Court ruled the federal regulators could not legally halt the expansion of nonbank banks. In 1987, Congress passed the Competitive Equality Bank Act, which prohibited new nonbank banks and placed a temporary moratorium on the expansion of bank holding companies into the fields of insurance, real estate, and securities underwriting.

NONBROKERS' LOANS

The Weekly Consolidated Condition Report of Large Commercial Banks and Domestic Subsidiaries, issued by the Board of Governors of the Federal Reserve System (Release H.4.2,, issued for release on Fridays, and containing the figures as of Wednesdays, one week earlier), is given in full as follows so that the reporting context for loans "To others for purchasing and carrying securities (other than financial institutions and brokers and dealers)" (non brokers' loans) may be noted:

Federal funds sold (including securities purchased under agreement to resell)
    To commercial banks
    To nonbank brokers and dealers in securities
    To others
Other loans, gross
    Commercial and industrial
        Bankers acceptances and commercial paper
        All other
            U.S. addresses
            Non-U.S. addresses
    Real Estate
    To individuals for personal expenditures
    To financial institutions
        Commercial banks in the United States
        Banks in foreign countries
        Sales finance, personal finance companies, etc.
        Other financial institutions
    To nonbank brokers and dealers in securities
    To others for purchasing and carrying securities (other than financial institutions and brokers and dealers)
    To finance agricultural production
    All other
Less: Unearned income
        Loan loss reserve
Other loans, net
Lease financing receivables

Loans for the purpose of purchasing or carrying securities of the "other" classification indicate the volume of nonbrokers' SECURITY LOANS. It is generally assumed that individuals, partnerships, or corporations who borrow directly from their banks to finance security purchases tend to be more conservative, financially responsible, and experienced than the averge margin customer of brokers. Consequently, the trend in volume of such loans should reflect the market judgment and activities of the most astute and resourceful investors and speculators.

Loans by banks for the purpose of purchasing or carrying stocks registered on a national securities exchange are subject to regulation by Regulation U of the Board of Governors of the Federal Reserve System, the margin regulation twin to Regulation T applicable to brokers. In addition, Regulation G of the Board of Governors of the Federal Reserve System applies to lenders other than brokers, dealers, or banks. All of these regulations are issued pursuant to Section 7 of the Securities Exchange Act of 1934.

NONCALLABLE BONDS Bonds that by their terms cannot be retired before their obligatory maturity; bonds that have no provision for PRIOR REDEMPTION; bonds that have no optional maturity date.
See CALLABLE BONDS.

NONCLEARINGHOUSE STOCKS Stocks not designated by a stock exchange's clearing facilites for clearance through that institution because of their inactivity and the necessity for devoting capacity to the more active stocks.

The National Securities Clearing Corporation, one-third-owned subsidiary of the New York Stock Exchange, provides clearance and settlement facilities for all stocks listed on that exchange.
See NEW YORK STOCK EXCHANGE SUBSIDIARIES.

NONCONTINGENT PREFERENCE STOCK An English title for what corresponds to cumulative preferred stock in this country.

NONCUMULATIVE DIVIDENDS Dividends on noncumulative preferred stock. If dividends are not paid at the regular fixed dividend period because earnings are not sufficient, they are not in arrears and there is no obligation on the part of the corporation to pay them at any subsequent period before dividends are paid on the common stock. for example, if a corporation cannot pay the dividends upon its 7%, noncumulative preferred stock in 1981, the stockholders lose their right to claim these dividends forever, or if dividends are paid at 4%, the remainder is lost for all time. Such is the general rule among the states, except in the state of New Jersey (its so-called Cast Iron Pipe Doctrine, which holds that if there were annual net profits from which dividends on noncumulative preferred stock might have been paid, i.e., the preferred's dividends were earned, but were either wholly omitted or only partly paid, such noncumulative preferred stock would be entitled to such earned but unpaid dividends of past years). Noncumulative dividends, of course, are the reverse of CUMULATIVE DIVIDENDS.

Unless otherwise stated, all stock is noncumulative. If the stock of a corporation is all of one class, however, nothing is to be gained by inserting the word noncumulative, since dividends by their very nature are contingent upon earnings rather than fixed. Interest upon income bonds may be cumulative or noncumulative. As the result of reorganizations in recent years, particularly in the railroad industry, limited cumulative features have been attached to new preferred stocks or income bonds, e.g., cumulative up to a stated amount, say 15%, and noncumulative beyond that point.

NONEARNING ASSETS Assets under the control of a depository financial institution that do not produce any income. They are often the result of a default, foreclosure, or liquidation of loans or investments of customers. Nonearning assets also include cash held by a commercial bank in its vaults and as reserve deposits at a correspondent bank or at the Federal Reserve Bank. Checks in process of collection are also nonearning assets. Fixed assets are also classified as nonearning assets if they produce no income.

NONMEMBER BANKS Banks not members of the Federal Reserve System. The term is sometimes used to distinguish banks that are not members of a clearing house association.

NONMEMBER DEPOSITORY INSTITUTION A depository institution (commercial bank, mutual savings bank, savings and loan association, credit union, or U.S. agency or branch of a foreign bank) that is not a member of the Federal Reserve System. Nonmember depository institutions that offer transaction accounts or nonpersonal time deposits are subject to reserve requirements set by the Federal Reserve. Nonmember depository institutions have access to the Federal Reserve discount window and services on the same terms as member banks.

NONMONETARY EXCHANGE A reciprocal transfer between an enterprise and another entity in which the enterprise acquires nonmonetary assets by surrendering nonmonetary assets. Nonmonetary exchanges can also include services and liabilities. Monetary assets are fixed in terms of dollars and are usually contractual claims to a fixed amount of money. All other assets are nonmonetary. Nonmonetary assets include inventory, property, plant, and equipment. The cost of a nonmonetary asset acquired in a nonmonetary exchange is the fair value of the asset surrendered to obtain it, and a gain or loss should be recognized on the exchange. The gain or loss is computed by comparing the fair value of the asset surrendered to its book value. If a small amount of monetary consideration (referred to as boot) is given or received, the cost of the asset acquired can be computed as follows:

Cost = Fair value of asset surrendered + Boot given or − Boot received

When the nonmonetary exchange involves similar productive assets, the general rule stated above for recognizing gains and losses is modified. Similar productive assets are ones that are of the same general type, that perform the same function, or that are employed in the same line of business, such as a delivery truck for another delivery truck. When similar productive assets are exchanged, the exchange is not essentially the culmination of the earning process — the earnings expected from the original asset have not been completely realized but will be continued by the acquired asset. When similar productive assets are exchanged, the assets acquired are recorded at the book value of the asset surrendered, unless boot is involved in the exchange. The payor of the boot recognizes no gain on the exchange (losses are always recognized). The recipient of the boot recognizes gain on the exchange to the extent that the boot exceeds a proportionate share of the book value of the asset surrendered (losses are always recognized). Because boot has been received, the earning process is considered to have been completed to that extent and some gain can be recognized. When boot is received or paid, the book value of the similar productive asset acquired can be computed as follows:

Payor of boot:

Cost = Lower of book or fair value of asset surrendered − Boot paid

Recipient of the boot:

Lower of book or fair value of asset surrendered − Boot received + Gain recognized

NONNEGOTIABLE INSTRUMENTS In the hands of any holder other than a HOLDER IN DUE COURSE, a negotiable instrument is subject to all the defenses as if it were nonnegotiable. Title to nonnegotiable instruments, therefore, passes by assignment, the assignee "standing in the shoes" of the assignor as far as validity of title and rights are concerned. Any instrument that lacks any one of the requirements of negotiability, as specified in Section 3-104, Uniform Commercial Code, is nonnegotiable, and superior rights will not be vested in the transferee or assignee by operation of the doctrine of holder in due course. This does not mean that nonnegotiable instruments are any less valuable than NEGOTIABLE INSTRUMENTS, although for negotiation in the open market, negotiability is essential. Bills of lading, even though order bills in form, are not commercial paper under the Uniform Commercial Code because they are not instruments for the payment of money. Stock certificates, even though endorsed in blank and passing therefore by mere delivery, likewise are not negotiable instruments (commercial paper). However, bills of lading that specify that the goods are to be delivered to bearer or to the order of a named person are negotiable, and the rights of a holder of such a negotiable bill of lading are free from the claim that the former holder of the bill of lading was deprived of it by misrepresentation, fraud, accident, mistake, duress, undue influence, loss, theft, conversion, or that the goods had been surrendered by the carrier or had been stopped in transit (Sec. 7-502(2), Uniform Commercial Code). By contrast, a straight bill of lading, e.g., one that consigns the goods to a specified person, is nonnegotiable (Sec. 7-104(2), Uniform Commercial Code).

Similarly, in the case of stock certificates, a person acquiring the certificates in good faith and for value is free from specified defenses (Secs. 8-301, 8-311, and 8-315, Uniform Commercial Code).

On the other hand, checks, bills, notes, and bonds, even though instruments calling for the payment of a "sum certain in money," may be made nonnegotiable by failure to have the other requirements of negotiability.

ENCYCLOPEDIA OF BANKING AND FINANCE

NONNEGOTIABLE PAPER *See* NEGOTIABLE PAPER.

NONNOTIFICATION FINANCING Financing in which the lender does not notify the borrower's customers that accounts due from them are being used as collateral by the borrower as security for loans. The lender typically retains the right of notification to protect his or her rights.

NONPARTICIPATING PREFERRED STOCK
See PREFERRED STOCK.

NONPAYMENT *See* NOTORIAL PROTEST CERTIFICATE, PROTEST.

NONRESIDENT ALIEN An individual who is not a citizen or resident of the United States. Taxation depends on whether U.S. source income is effectively connected with the conduct of a U.S. trade or business.

NONSTOCK MONEYED CORPORATION Under New York statutes, a moneyed corporation is a corporation formed under or subject to the banking law or the insurance law. The term "nonstock corporation" includes every corporation other than a stock corporation or a public corporation. Thus, the term "nonstock moneyed corporation" refers to savings banks (no stock savings banks in New York), mutual charter savings and loan associations, mutualized insurance companies, credit unions, and other banking institutions organized without capital stock, being "owned" by the depositors or borrowers.

NONSUFFICIENT FUNDS (NSF) A term used to indicate that a depositor's balance is inadequate for the bank to pay a check drawn against the available balance.

NONTAXABLE SECURITIES *See* TAX-EXEMPT BONDS.

NONVALIDATING STAMP Banks that collect domestic drafts with bills of lading, warehouse receipts, or other documents attached usually place a nonvalidating stamp on the back of all accompanying drafts. The purpose of this practice is to protect the bank from being in any way responsible for the character of the goods designated in the bill of lading or other instrument accompanying the draft. The endorsement reads as follows:
"This bank hereby notifies all concerned that it makes no representation or guaranty, and assumes no responsibility as to the genuineness, regularity, or validity of bills of lading and/or other documents attached to this draft, nor as to the character, quantity, quality, or condition of merchandise mentioned in said bills of lading and/or other documents, nor as to any contract made by the endorser of this draft, or by consignor."

NONWAIVER A statement that failure to exercise a right under a contract is not be understood as a permanent relinquishment of the right.

NO PAR VALUE STOCK Stock that has no designated PAR VALUE. In 1912 New York State was the first state to authorize no par value stock, one of the motives being to prevent fraud in the sale of $100 par value stock under the misrepresentation to the uninformed that such par value meant actual asset or market value. Since then, all states have authorized no par value stock for business corporations. Banking corporations (banks, trust companies), other financial corporations (insurance companies, savings and loans, or building and loan associations), and holding companies issuing common stock for holding company purposes under the Public Utility Holding Company Act of 1935 (except with permission of the Securities and Exchange Commission) may not issue no par value stock.

No par value stock is entitled to status as "fully paid and nonassessble" when the full subscription price has been paid and credited to capital accounts. Certain states require a minimum capital to be subscribed and paid in, but the amount prescribed is low. New York has no such requirements. In no par value statutes, the amount over and above the stated value may be credited to paid-in surplus, and the board of directors is usually empowered by resolution to change the stated value per share. In a few states, dividends may be declared out of capital surplus created by reduction in stated value per share. An advantage of no par value stock is the flexibility of issuance at fair value from time to time without the rigidity of prescribed par value for entitlement to status as fully paid and nonassessable, as the nominal stated value may be readily changed by the directors. It should be noted, however, that the no par value device does not insulate directors against possible liability to creditors in the event the property or services that are the subject for stock issuance are grossly overvalued.

Until 1958, when the Federal stock transfer tax was changed, no par value stock was taxed the same as $100 par value stock, a factor that made more feasible the issuance of fractional par value stock (par value less than $100 per share). The federal stock transfer tax was eliminated effective December 31, 1965. A few states, e.g., New York, still tax no par value shares for incorporation taxes and annual franchise taxes ($0.05 per share), at a high rate compared with par value shares ($0.5% of the par value).

Under Section 501 of the New York Business Corporation Law, shares of stock of a business corporation may be all of one class or may be divided into two or more classes. Each class shall consist of either shares with par value or shares without par value. Shares without par value may be issued for such consideration as is fixed from time to time by the board of directors, unless the certificate of incorporation reserves to the shareholders the right to fix the consideration (Sec. 504 (d)). When the consideration for shares has been paid in full, the subscriber shall be entitled to all the rights and privileges of a holder of such shares and to a certificate representing his shares, and such shares shall be fully paid and nonassessable (Sec. 504(i)). Upon issuance by a corporation of shares without par value, the entire consideration received therefor shall constitute the stated capital, unless the board of directors within a period of sixty days after issuance allocates to surplus a portion, but not all, of the consideration received for such shares. But no such allocation shall be made of any portion of the consideration received for shares without par value that have a preference in the assets of the corporation upon involuntary liquidation, except all or part of the amount if any of such consideration in excess of such preference. Nor shall such allocation be made of any portion of the consideration for the issue of shares without par value that is fixed by shareholders pursuant to a right reserved in the certificate of incorporation, unless such allocation is authorized by vote of the shareholders (Sec. 506(b)).

The stated capital of a corporation, on the other hand, may be increased from time to time by resolution of the board of directors transferring all or part of the surplus of the corporation to stated capital. The board may direct that the amount so transferred shall be stated capital in respect of any designated class or series of shares (Sec. 506(c)).

Summary. From the above specification of statutory provisions, it is apparent that the use of no par value stock provides flexibility for the directors in determining by resolution the portion of consideration received for issuance of stock to be allocated to capital as such and to "surplus" ("capital surplus" or, pursuant to current approved terminology "contributed capital in excess of stated value, no par common stock" [or any other class of stock having no par value]). By contrast, a par value is established by the corporation's certificate of incorporation and normally can be changed only by amendment thereof. Most states require the entire amount received by a corporation from the sale of its no par value stock to be considered the minimum legal capital, and as such not available for dividend payments. On the other hand, a few states permit a business corporation issuing no par value stock to establish its minimum legal capital at the stated value, so that dividends could legally be declared from the consideration received in excess of the stated value per share.

No par value stock is not permitted for national banks and state-chartered institutions.

See WITHOUT PAR VALUE STOCK.

NO PROTEST It is customary banking practice to PROTEST all checks over $10 in amount when payment is refused unless instructions are given to the contrary. Most checks and some drafts and notes are accompanied by the instructions "no protest" when sent or deposited for collection; it is the usual practice to attach a "no protest" ticket to the item in order to indicate to the collecting bank or agent that it is not to be protested for nonpayment.

The reason for not protesting checks or other items of $10 or less is that the expenses of protesting are not warranted when the amount involved is so small. Messengers assigned to collecting items carrying no protest instructions should remove or erase them before presentation is made in order to circumvent the possibility of nonpayment. If the drawee is informed in advance of payment that an item drawn on him is not to be protested, he might take advantage of the knowledg, and for technical reasons refuse payment.

A protest of DISHONOR of a draft by nonacceptance or nonpayment, or of nonpayment of a promissory note, is not necessary unless the instrument appears on its face to be drawn or payable outside of the United States, its territories, and the District of Columbia. The holder, however, may protest the dishonor of any instrument, including domestic instruments, because according to the UNIFORM COMMERCIAL CODE, certain documents and records are admissible of dishonor and of any notice recited therein (the trier of the facts must accept such evidence in the absence of proof to the contrary [Sec. 3-510, UCC, and Sec. 1-201 (31), UCC]) Thus the certificate of protest has evidentiary value, placing the burden of going forward upon the defendant.

See NOTORIAL PROTEST CERTIFICATE.

NORMAL CROPS   See CROP REPORTS.

NORMAL DISTRIBUTION
A bell-shaped curve depicting a symmetric probability distribution of a continuous random variable. The distribution is defined by the mean and the standard deviation, such that approximately two-thirds of all observations fall within one standard deviation above and below the mean, and about 95 % will fall within two standard deviations above and below the mean.

The accompanying chart shows the normal distribution. Three shaded areas are indicated. The shaded area in the center of the curve is the portion that lies between the ordinate with a value of + 1 standard deviation (the square root of the arithemetic mean of the squared deviations of the individual items from the arithmetic mean) and the ordinate with a value of – 1 standard deviations on the X axis. The shaded area at the right of the curve is the portion that l above + 1.96σ standard deviations; the shaded area on the left is the portion that lies below – 1.96σ standard deviations.

Normal Distribution

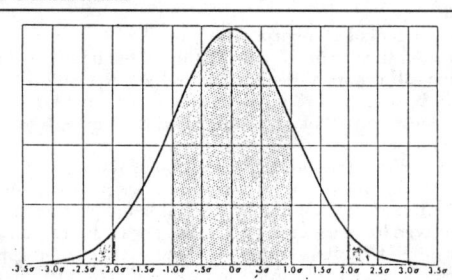

A table of the areas of the normal curve between maximum ordinate and ordinate at z = number of standard deviations away from the mean, (X – mean) / standard deviation), is also illustrated. The values in the table show the fraction of the area of the normal curve that lies between the maximum ordinate (Y) and the ordinate at various distances from the maximum ordinate. Reading down the table to z = 1.00, the fraction of the curve is .34. Since the normal curve is symetrical, slightly more that 68% of the area of the normal curve lies within the range of +1 or –1 standard deviations. This means that 68% of the individual values of a normal distribution fall within this range.

The percentage of items falling within any range expressed in standard deviation units can be computed in the same manner by doubling the fraction in the table. For example, 95% of the items in the normal distribution fall between + or 1.96 standard deviation; 99% fall within the range of + or – 2.576 standard deviation.

To illustrate the use of the normal curve, assume that an employee scores on an aptitude test are normally distributed about a mean = 60 with a standard deviation = 20. What proportion of the scores (a) exceed 85 and (b) fall below 50?

Case 1. From the areas of the normal curve table, where z = 1.25 (= 85 – 60) / 20), .39435 appears and represents the area of the normal curve between the maximum ordinate (50%) and the ordinate at z. The area above this ordinate represents the proportion of the scores that exceed 85, which is approximately 11% (50% – .39435).

Case 2. From the areas of the normal curve table, where z = –.50 (= 50–60), .19146 appears and represents the area of the normal curve between the maximum ordinate (50%) and the ordinate at z. The area below this ordinate represents the proportion of the scores that fall below 50, which is approximately 31% (+ .50 – .19146).

NORMAL GROWTH   See SECULAR TREND.

NORMATIVE ECONOMICS
The use of personal preferences and value judgments to argue for what ought to be. POSITIVE ECONOMICS or scientific economics is practiced when one predicts that if event A occurs, then event B will follow.

NOSTRO ACCOUNTS
A bank or other institution in this country having balances deposited with correspondent banks in foreign countries refers to such accounts as "nostro accounts," meaning "our accounts." Nostro accounts are kept in foreign currencies, i.e., the MONEY OF ACCOUNT of the country in which the funds are kept, with the equivalent dollar value noted in an adjacent column. The term is used among foreign exchange bookkeepers.

See VOSTRO ACCOUNTS.

NOTARIAL PROTEST CERTIFICATE
When a check, draft, or bill of exchange is dishonored, i.e. payment or acceptance is refused, the holder should have it protested before a notary public. The notary public presents it again to the drawee, and if payment is still refused a notarial protest certificate is prepared, together with a separate notice of protest to each of the endorsers. The notarial protest certificate is legal evidence of presentation and refusal to pay by the drawee or maker, and is a legal measure for the purpose of holding the endorsers liable on account of the item dishonored for payment by the maker. Such a certificate is legal evidence of presentation and refusal to pay; even in the case of an inland bill, for which protest is not required, it is preferable to procure a notarial certificate because of the prima facie evidentiary value such a certificate has in an action at law. The following is one form of a notarial protest certificate. (See NO PROTEST.)

Notarial Protest Certificate

UNITED STATES OF AMERICA
STATE OF NEW YORK   SS:
COUNTY OF NEW YORK

On the _____ day of _____ in the year _____ , at the request of the _____ Bank, of the City of New York, I the subscriber, a Notary Public of the State of New York, duly commissioned and sworn, did present the original (Check, Note, Draft, or Bill of Exchange) hereto annexed to (name of drawee or maker), in the City of New York, and demanded payment thereof, which was refused (reason for nonpayment).

Whereupon, I, the said Notary, at the request aforesaid, did Protest and by these presents do publicly and solemnly Protest, as well against the Drawers and Endorsers of said (Check, Note, Draft, or Bill of Exchange), as against all others whom it doth or may concern, for exchange, reexchange, and all costs, damages, and interest already occurred, and to be hereafter incurred for want of payment of said (Check, Note, Draft, or Bill of Exchange).

In testimony whereof, I have hereunto set my hand and affixed my seal at the City of New York, aforesaid.

                                        Notary Public
                                        for New York County
(Seal)

Endorsement on Notarial Protest Certificate

Please give notice of the within protest to all parties to the annexed _____ as soon as you receive this .

Notice to Each Party to the Item

                                               (Date)

Please take notice that a (check, draft, note, or bill of exchange) made by _____
for $ _____

Areas of the Normal Curve Between Maximum Ordinate and Ordinate at z

z or $\frac{X-\mu}{\sigma}$	.00	.01	.02	.03	.04	.05	.06	.07	.08	.09
0.0	.00000	.00399	.00798	.01197	.01595	.01994	.02392	.02790	.03188	.03586
0.1	.03983	.04380	.04776	.05172	.05567	.05962	.06356	.06749	.07142	.07535
0.2	.07926	.08317	.08706	.09095	.09483	.09871	.10257	.10642	.11026	.11409
0.3	.11791	.12172	.12552	.12930	.13307	.13683	.14058	.14431	.14803	.15173
0.4	.15542	.15910	.16276	.16640	.17003	.17364	.17724	.18082	.18439	.18793
0.5	.19146	.19497	.19847	.20194	.20540	.20884	.21226	.21566	.21904	.22210
0.6	.22575	.22907	.23237	.23565	.23891	.24215	.24537	.24857	.25175	.25490
0.7	.25804	.26115	.26424	.26730	.27035	.27337	.27637	.27935	.28230	.28524
0.8	.28814	.29103	.29389	.29673	.29955	.30234	.30511	.30785	.31057	.31327
0.9	.31594	.31859	.32121	.32381	.32639	.32894	.33147	.33398	.33646	.33891
1.0	.34134	.34375	.34614	.34850	.35083	.35314	.35543	.35769	.35993	.36214
1.1	.36433	.36650	.36864	.37076	.37286	.37493	.37698	.37900	.38100	.38298
1.2	.38493	.38686	.38877	.39065	.39251	.39435	.39617	.39796	.39973	.40147
1.3	.40320	.40490	.40658	.40824	.40988	.41149	.41309	.41466	.41621	.41774
1.4	.41924	.42073	.42220	.42364	.42507	.42647	.42786	.42922	.43056	.43189
1.5	.43319	.43448	.43574	.43699	.43822	.43943	.44062	.44179	.44295	.44408
1.6	.44520	.44630	.44738	.44845	.44950	.45053	.45154	.45254	.45352	.45449
1.7	.45543	.45637	.45728	.45818	.45907	.45994	.46080	.46164	.46246	.46327
1.8	.46407	.46485	.46562	.46638	.46712	.46784	.46856	.46926	.46995	.47062
1.9	.47128	.47193	.47257	.47320	.47381	.47441	.47500	.47558	.47615	.47670
2.0	.47725	.47778	.47831	.47882	.47932	.47982	.48030	.48077	.48124	.48169
2.1	.48214	.48257	.48300	.48341	.48382	.48422	.48461	.48500	.48537	.48574
2.2	.48610	.48645	.48679	.48713	.48745	.48778	.48809	.48840	.48870	.48899
2.3	.48928	.48956	.48983	.49010	.49036	.49601	.49086	.49111	.49134	.49158
2.4	.49180	.49202	.49224	.49245	.49266	.49286	.49305	.49324	.49313	.49361
2.5	.49379	.49396	.49413	.49430	.49446	.49461	.49477	.49492	.49506	.49520
2.6	.49534	.49547	.49560	.49573	.49585	.49598	.49609	.49621	.49632	.49643
2.7	.49653	.49664	.49674	.49683	.49693	.49702	.49711	.49720	.49728	.49736
2.8	.49744	.49752	.49760	.49767	.49774	.49781	.49788	.49795	.49801	.49807
2.9	.49813	.49819	.49825	.49831	.49386	.49841	.49846	.49851	.49856	.49861
3.0	.49865	.49869	.49874	.49878	.49882	.49886	.49889	.49893	.49897	.49900
3.1	.49903	.49906	.49910	.49913	.49916	.49918	.49921	.49921	.49926	.49929
3.2	.49931	.49934	.49936	.49938	.49940	.49942	.49944	.49916	.49948	.49950
3.3	.49952	.49953	.49955	.49957	.49958	.49960	.49961	.49962	.49964	.49965
3.4	.49966	.49968	.49969	.49970	.49971	.49972	.49973	.49974	.49975	.49976
3.5	.49977									
3.6	.49984									
3.7	.49989									
3.8	.49993									
3.9	.49995									
4.0	.49997									

dated _____
payable _____
(endorsed) _____
(made) by you is protested for nonpayment and that the holders look you for the payment thereof.

NOTARY PUBLIC A person commissioned by a state and authorized to administer oaths, to take acknowledgements and depositions, and to protest negotiable instruments for nonpayment or nonacceptance. The legal advantages of an instrument sworn to before a notary are admissibility into court as prima facie evidence of execution and admissibility as a court record.

A notary has authority to administer oaths in all matters connected with the exercise of his office; to take the acknowledgment or proof of instruments in writing relating to commerce or navigation, and to certify the same under his seal; to demand acceptance and payment of bills of exchange, promissory notes, and other commercial paper, and to protest them for nonacceptance or nonpayment.

NOTE A promise to pay as distinguished from an order to pay, such as a draft or check. Formally defined, a note is a written promise of the maker to pay a certain sum of money to the person named as payee, on demand or at a fixed or determinable future date. The Board of Governors of the Federal Reserve System has defined a promissory note as "an unconditional promise, in writing, signed by the maker, to pay, in the United States, at a fixed or determinable future time, a sum certain in dollars to order or to bearer."

Consideration is always deemed prima facie to exist in the case of NEGOTIABLE INSTRUMENTS, and lack of consideration between the original parties is not a defense against the HOLDERS IN DUE COURSE. Notes may be issued by individuals, partnerships, corporations, institutions, and governments. Federal Reserve notes and United States notes are monetary forms of promises to pay on demand without interest, and furnish a part of the circulating monetary medium. A note may be drawn without interest, but if it is drawn with interest with the rate omitted, the maximum legal rate of the state in which it is made is presumed.

One of the essential characteristics of notes is that they are ordinarily negotiable, i.e., superior rights may be vested in the holder in due course. Negotiation is achieved by delivery, i.e., handing it from one person to another, when the note is made payable "to bearer" or where the endorsement is "in blank," or by endorsement and delivery when it is made payable "to order." A note will be nonnegotiable if the words of negotiability, "bearer" or "order" are omitted from its face.

Notes should be presented for payment at the place named. If no place is indicated, presentment should be made at the maker's usual place of business or residence during business hours. The note should be presented on the due date in order to hold the endorsers (if any) liable; in case of refusal to pay, protest should be made. The liability of the maker is in no way voided by postponement of presentation beyond the due date, and the note may be protested for nonpayment even if past due. When a bill or note is lost, destroyed, or wrongly detained from the person entitled to hold it, protest may be made on a copy or on written particulars thereof, so that loss of a note will not affect the rights and liabilities of the parties.

Formerly three DAYS OF GRACE were allowed to persons obligated to pay notes, i.e., three days beyond the indicated maturity date. Under the NEGOTIABLE INSTRUMENTS LAW and Uniform Commercial Code, this practive was abolished so that an instrument matures on the date which it fixes.

Classified by methods of determining maturity, notes are of two forms: payable upon a specified date or payable a certain number of days after a fixed date. The first is known as a "fixed date" note and the second as a "days after date" note. The first reads: "On July 1, 1981, I promise to pay"; the second reads: "Sixty days after date, I promise to pay." In the second case, the note must be "timed" in order to determine the maturity date, and in this timing the exact number of days must be counted. For example, if a note is dated July 20 and runs for 60 days, it becomes due on September 18. If that date happens to be a Sunday or holiday, then the note is due on the next business day.

Banks frequently furnish customers blank forms for notes and usually insist upon their own forms to evidence loans extended to their borrowers. The following is a form of a promissory note without collateral where the payee is a bank.

A Promissory Note Without Collateral

New York, _____ 19 ___ $ _____ months (days) after date for value received I (we) promise to pay to the Bank on order, the sum of _____ Dollars, with interest at ___ per centum per annum.

It is further agreed that if the undersigned shall become insolvent or make a general assignment for the benefit of creditors, or file a voluntary petition in bankruptcy, or if a petition in bankruptcy shall be filed against the undersigned, or a receiver shall be appointed over the property or assets, or any thereof, of the undersigned, then this note and all other present or future demands of any and all kinds against the undersigned, whether created directly or acquired by assignment, whether absolute or contingent, shall for with be due.

Payable at the _____ Bank.
No. _____ Due _____

(Name of maker)

A collateral note ordinarily has the same form as the regular promissory note (above illustrated), together with the following or its equivalent.

A Promissory Note with Collateral

The undersigned has deposited with said bank as collateral security for the payment of this and any and every liability or liabilities of the undersigned to the said bank direct or contingent, due or to become due, or which may hereafter be contracted or existing, the following property:

(here the specific collateral is described)

together with all other securities in the possession of said bank belonging to the undersigned or in which the undersigned has an interest, hereby agreeing to deliver to said bank additional securities to its satisfaction, upon demand of said bank, also hereby giving to said bank a lien for the amount of all said liabilities of the under-signed to said bank upon all property and securities which now are or may hereafter be pledged as collateral with said bank by the undersigned, or in the possession of said bank in which the undersigned has an interest, and also upon any balance of the deposit account of the undersigned with said bank. On the nonperformance of this promise, or upon the nonpayment of any liabilities above mentioned, or upon the failure of the undersigned forthwith to furnish satisfactory additional securities on demand, at the option of said bank, this obligation shall become immediately due and payable, and then and in every such case, full power and authority are hereby given to said bank to sell, assign, and deliver the whole or said securities or any part thereof or any substitutes therefor or any additions thereto through any stock exchange, or broker or at private sale, without either advertisement or notice, the same being hereby expressly waived, or said bank itself may purchase the same or any part thereof free from any right of redemption on the part of the undersigned, which is hereby expressly waived and released. In case of sale for any cause, after deducting all costs and expenses of every kind, said bank may apply the residue of the proceeds of such sale, as it shall deem proper, toward the payment of any one or more or all of the liabilities of the undersigned to said bank, whether due or not due, returning the overplus, if any, to the undersigned, who agrees to be and remain liable to said bank for any and every deficiency after application as aforesaid, upon this and all other of said liabilities, the undersigned hereby authorizing the transfer or assignment of said securities and property to the purchaser thereof. And I hereby authorize any attorney-at-law to appear in any court of record in the United States, after the above obligation becomes due, and waive the issuing and service of process and confess a judgment against me in favor of the _____ Bank of _____ , or any holder of this note, for the amount then appearing due together with the costs of suit, and thereupon to release all errors and waive all right of appeal and stay of execution.

The term note also is sometimes applied to short-term bonds whether corporate or civil issues, especially if unsecured, e.g., United States Treasury notes.

See GENERAL LOAN AND COLLATERAL AGREEMENT, JOINTLY AND SEVERALLY JOINT NOTE, NATIONAL BANK NOTES.

NOTE BROKERS Dealers or COMMERCIAL PAPER houses whose business it is to act as middlemen between the issuers of commercial paper and banks, insurance companies, and private investors, who constitute the market on the demand side. Note brokerage firms are usually partnerships having ample capital resources, capital, and valuable bank connections to enable them to secure an adequate supply of funds to finance their transactions. Commercial paper borrowing is a means of temporarily raising funds for financing seasonal inventory requirements. Note brokers derive their profit by buying notes from the makers at one rate of discount and selling them at another, although some of the business may be done on the basis of a small commission that is charged the borrower.

The paper marketed by note brokers is varied in character and includes single-name paper, double-name trade paper, collateral notes, and trade and bank acceptances. Much of the paper dealt in by note brokers is single-name paper of well-known commercial houses.

A large portion of the paper is sold upon a ten days' option to give the proposed buyer an opportunity to investigate the standing of the maker. At the end of the option period it may be retained or returned. Note brokerage is a specialized machinery for facilitating commercial borrowing by prime credit risks in the open market.

NOTE LIABILITY The liability in connection with promissory notes outstanding will be reflected in financial statements as notes receivable or notes payable, as appropriate. Such items will be included among current assets (notes receivable) by business concerns that strive to "window dress" their financial statements as to working capital and current ratio (ratio of current assets to current liabilities). Unless such notes receivable arise out of normal credit terms in the sale of goods, however, they should be listed among noncurrent assets, even though nominally with maturity under 12 months. For example, a customer on credit sales might be slow in payment of the invoice on due date (e.g., "net 30," or 30 days from date of invoice), and in collection efforts his promissory note to pay in 30 or 60 days might be obtained. Such a note does not belong among current assets as it merely reflects in note form a slow accounts receivable. Notes representing loans to "insiders" of a firm also should not be included among current assets, but among the noncurrent assets; because these notes do not arise from normal operations and a collection is in the hands of the debtors themselves, who are in control of the firm, their liquidity is not unquestionable.

National banks formerly carried note liability for outstanding NATIONAL BANK NOTES, but such liability no longer is outstanding as national bank notes have been in process of retirement since 1935. Federal Reserve bank notes similarly have been in process of retirement, leaving only liability for FEDERAL RESERVE NOTES for Federal Reserve banks.

NOTES PAYABLE Aggregate of notes, acceptances, etc., held by others representing sums of money to be paid at a future time and constituting a liability of a business. From an accounting point of view, notes payable is the aggregate of notes contracted to be paid, also known as bills payable, and due to others.

NOTES RECEIVABLE A negotiable promissory note is an unconditional promise in writing made by one person to another engaging to pay on demand or at a fixed or determinable future time a sum of money to order or to bearer. Negotiability makes the instrument readily transferable and increases its usefulness because the seller can discount it or use it as collateral for a loan. The person promising to pay is the maker of the note; the person to be paid is the payee. Promissory notes may be either interest-bearing or non-interest-bearing.

If a note is not paid at maturity, it is said to have been dishonored. A payee of a note who sells it prior to maturity is discounting the note. The note can be discounted either "with recourse" or "without recourse." When a note is discounted "with recourse," the payee is contingently liable for the payment of the note if it is dishonored at maturity by the payee. To illustrate the discounting of a note receivable, assume that a $1,000, 90-day, 4 percent note dated September 3 is discounted at a bank on October 3 (60 days from maturity). The bank discount rate is 8%. The cash proceeds from the discounting is computed as follows:

1. Compute the maturity value of the note:

   $1,000 \times 0.04 \times 90/360$ = $10 interest plus $1,000 face

   value = $1,010

2. Calculate the discount charged by the note buyer on the maturity value of the note for the number of days from the date of discount to the date of maturity:

   $1,010 \times 0.08 \times 60/360$ = $13.47

3. Calculate the proceeds that the company receives from the discounted note:

   $1,010 - $13.47 = $996.53

If a "with recourse" discounted note is dishonored by the maker at maturity, the endorser is required to make good on the note, pay any interest due at maturity, and pay a protest (collection) fee.

NOTE TELLER Among small banks, an employee, sometimes also known as the third teller, who supervises the collection of notes and drafts at maturity and such demand items (checks and drafts) and special collection items as are not drawn on members of the clearinghouse association and must be collected by messenger.

Among larger banks, the note teller's department is usually a miscellaneous department of the bank, since it not only supervises the collection of nonclearinghouse checks but also disposes of miscellaneous types of transactions not important enough to be departmentalized.

NOTES TO FINANCIAL STATEMENTS Notes or footnotes to financial statements are procedures used to present additional information not included in the accounts on the financial statements. Generally accepted accounting principles consider notes to be an integral part of financial statements. Accounting principles require that certain information be disclosed in notes, such as narrative discussion, additional monetary disclosures, and supplementary schedules. One of the notes typically describes the major accounting policies used in preparing the financial statements (for example, inventory cost flow assumptions, depreciation method). The notes to financial statements are usually factual rather than interpretative.

NOTE TICKLER *See* TICKLER.

NOT-FOR-PROFIT ORGANIZATIONS Nonbusiness enterprise or organization is a term often used to refer to governmental units and to all other not-for-profit organizations. The major distinguishing characteristics of nonbusiness organizations, according to the Financial Accounting Standards Board, include:

1. Receipts of significant amounts of resources from providers who do not expect to receive either repayment or proportionate economic benefits.
2. Operating purposes that are other than to provide goods or services at a profit or profit equivalent.
3. Absence of defined ownership interests that can be sold, transferred, or redeemed, or that convey entitlement to a share of a residual distribution of resources in the event of liquidation of the organization.

Nonbusiness organizations include most human service organizations, churches, foundations, and private nonprofit hospitals and schools that receive a significant portion of their financial resources from sources other than the sale of goods and services. Nonprofit organizations can be distinguished by a difference in the source of the financial resources. One type includes organizations whose financial resources are obtained primarily from revenues from the sale of goods and services. Another type obtains a significant amount of its resources from sources other than from the sale of goods and services.

Generally accepted accounting principles (GAAP) applicable to most nonbusiness organizations are reflected in the AICPA's Statement of Position 78-10, "Accounting Principles and Reporting Practices for Certain Nonprofit Organizations." Refer to entry Generally Accepted Accounting Principles for guidance on GAAP for colleges and universities, hospitals, voluntary health and welfare organizations, and governments.

The objectives of financial reporting by nonbusiness organizations include the following as described by the Financial Accounting Standards Board in its Statement of Financial Accounting Concepts No. 4, "Objectives of Financial Reporting by Nonbusiness Organizations":

Financial reporting by nonbusiness organizations should provide information that is useful to present and potential resource providers and other users in making rational decisions about the allocation of resources to those organizations.

Financial reporting should provide information to help present and potential resource providers and other users in assessing the services that a nonbusiness organization provides and its ability to continue to provide those services.

Financial reporting should provide information that is useful to present and potential resource providers and other users in assessing how managers of a nonbusiness organization have discharged their stewardship responsibilities and about other aspects of their performance.

Financial reporting should provide information about the economic resources, obligations, and net resources of an organization, and the effects of transactions, events, and circumstances that change resources and interests in those resources.

Financial reporting should provide information about the performance of an organization during a period. Periodic measurement of the changes in the amount and nature of the net resources of a nonbusiness organization and information about the service efforts and accomplishments of an organization together represent the information most useful in assessing its performance.

Financial reporting should provide information about how an organization obtains and spends cash or other liquid resources, about its borrowing and repayment of borrowing, and about other factors that may affect an organization's liquidity.

Financial reporting should include explanations and interpretations to help users understand financial information provided.

The objectives in the statement apply to general purposes external financial reporting by nonbusiness organizations. The objectives are affected by the economic, legal, political, and social environment in which financial reporting takes place.

BIBLIOGRAPHY

FINANCIAL ACCOUNTING STANDARDS BOARD. *Statement of Financial Accounting Concepts No. 4*, "Objectives of Financial Reporting by Nonbusiness Organizations, 1980.
HOPKINS, B. R. *Law of Tax-Exempt Organizations.* John Wiley and Sons, Inc., New York, NY, 1983.
MCLAUGHLIN, C. P. *The Management of Nonprofit Organizations.* John Wiley and Sons, Inc., New York, NY, 1986.
Non-Profit Administrator's Master Guide. Master Guide Information Services, Salt Lake City, UT. Monthly.
PETERSON, J. C. *Voluntary Associations: Structure and Process*, Praeger Publishers, New York, NY, 1985.
WOLF, T. *Nonprofit Organizations: An Operating Manual.* Prentice Hall, Inc., Englewood Cliffs, NJ, 1984.

NOTICE OF INTENTION In the organization of a national bank, the first step is the informal application to organize sent to the Comptroller of the Currency, stating the title of the proposed national bank, the request to reserve such title until the formal application to organize is submitted, and the location and proposed capital of the proposed bank. If the proposed title is satisfactory, the Comptroller will normally reserve the title for 60 days and forward upon request the formal application for charter. Along with the intention to organize the national bank, the formal application states the following:

1. Title, location, capital, and surplus.
2. Whether it will succeed some existing bank.
3. Whether a banking house will be purchased or built.
4. Amount to be invested in banking house and fixtures or, if banking quarters are to be leased, amount of rental.
5. Certification that no fees or commissions are being paid for obtaining subscriptions or selling stock in the bank.
6. Signatures of at least five applicants who are prospective stockholders and preferably also officers or directors, together with their residences, businesses, financial strength in figures, amount of shares subscribed, and other banks with which the applicants have served as officers or directors.
7. Endorsement of the application by three prominent public officials of the place where the bank is to be located.

In most states, incorporators desiring to organize a state bank must sign a notice of intention to organize, setting forth their names, title of the proposed corporation, amount of its capital stock, and location. This notice is filed with the state banking department, and a copy must be published in a newspaper in the city of intended location for a certain period in advance of obtaining the charter. Other banks in the location must also be served with a copy of such intention. The foregoing is the practice in New York State.

NOTICE OF PROTEST *See* NOTARIAL PROTEST CERTIFICATE.

NOW ACCOUNTS SAVINGS ACCOUNTS from which payments can be made by draft. State-chartered mutual SAVINGS BANKS began offering NOW accounts in Massachusetts after a May, 1972, state court ruling authorized such deposits. NOWs were offered by state-chartered mutual savings banks in New Hampshire in September, 1972, with the approval of that state's bank commissioner. Beginning in January, 1974, Congress authorized all depository institutions in the two above-mentioned states to offer NOWs. Beginning in March 1976, Congress authorized NOW accounts at all depository institutions in Connecticut, Maine, Rhode Island, and Vermont. This authority was extended to New York State in November, 1978, and to New Jersey in December, 1979.

Finally, the DEPOSITORY INSTITUTIONS DEREGULATION AND MONETARY CONTROL ACT OF 1980 authorized all depository institutions that are federally insured to offer NOW accounts, beginning 12/31/80.

NOWs are negotiable drafts written on savings accounts at banks, mutual savings banks, and SAVINGS AND LOAN ASSOCIATIONS. Share drafts written on accounts at credit unions can be either negotiable or nonnegotiable. While in practice both NOWs and share drafts are honored as demand drafts, they are legally time drafts on which financial institutions have the right to delay payment for up to 30 days. NOWs offered by thrift institutions are "payable through" instruments, i.e., they are cleared through normal check-clearing channels and are paid by a commercial bank with which the issuing thrift maintains a correspondent banking relationship.

In connection with the authorization of NOW accounts to financial institutions in all parts of the nation beginning December 31, 1980, the staff of the Board of Governors of the Federal Reserve System made available NOW account eligibility restrictions as follows, per the law:

NOW accounts are available only to individuals and to qualifying organizations. Qualifying organizations must meet two separate tests of eligibility. First, they must be operated primarily for religious, philanthropic, charitable, educational, or other similar purposes. Second, they must not be operated for profit. This class of entities is almost identical to the class formerly eligible under Regulation Q to maintain a NOW account in New England, New York, and New Jersey only. Although Regulation Q does permit fraternal organizations to maintain NOW accounts, the statute omits such fraternal organizations from the list of eligible NOW depositors. In the judgment of the board of governors of the Federal Reserve System, since the statutory provisions were based on Regulation Q, it is believed that the omission of the term "fraternal" was unintentional and without significance, and that accordingly nonprofit organizations operating primarily for fraternal purposes, such as social and recreational clubs, will be regarded by the board as within the scope of the statute (Title III of the Depository Institutions Deregulation and Monetary Control Act of 1980) consistent with the intent of Congress as to the type of entities eligible to maintain NOW accounts. Governmental units, even though not operated for profit, generally do not qualify to hold NOW accounts since they are not organizations operated primarily for the qualifying purposes. However, independent governmental entities that are separately constituted, such as school districts, most state university systems, and local housing and redevelopment authorities, are eligible to hold NOW accounts since they are operated primarily for a qualifying purpose. In addition, funds held in a fiduciary capacity may be classifed as a NOW account so long as an individual (or individuals) or a qualifying organization has the entire beneficial interest in the funds. thus a profit-making organization could hold a NOW account as a trustee or other fiduciary for an entity that is qualified to hold a NOW account in its own capacity.

The Federal Reserve has advised member banks in states where NOW accounts were already available that the class of depositors eligible to hold NOW accounts under the act is virtually identical to the class of depositors eligible to hold savings deposits without limit (except for governmental units).

Maximum Interest Rate Payable. Effective December 31, 1980, the maximun interest rate payable on negotiable order of withdrawal accounts was 5.25%. This compared with 5% previously effective from January1, 1974, for federally insured commercial banks, savings and loan associations, cooperative banks, and mutual savings banks in Massachusetts and New Hampshire; from February 27, 1976, for similar institutions throughout New England; from November 10, 1978, in New York State; and from December 28, 1979, in New Jersey (authorization to issue NOW accounts was extended to similar institutions nationwide effective December 31, 1980).

Legal Reserve Requirements. NOW accounts are included in the M1 classification by the Board of Govenors of the Federal Reserve System, a classification that basically consists of currency in circulation, the public's demand deposits, the NOW accounts, traveler's checks of nonbank issuers, automatic transfer service accounts at banks and thrift institutions, and credit union share drafts. These balances, as basically transaction balances, are subject to legal reserve requirements on "net transaction accounts" (effective November 13, 1980, at 3% on such balances of net transaction accounts from $0 to $26 million, and at 12% on such balances of net transactions accounts over $26 million).

See FEDERAL RESERVE BOARD REGULATIONS (Regulation Q).

NUNCUPATIVE WILL An oral will; under the Model Execution of Wills Act, a nuncupative will is a will verbally declared within the hearing of atleast two disinterested witnesses. The various states, however, vary widely in provision for noncupative wills, with 5 states having no authority at all for such wills and 13 other states restricting nuncupative wills to soldiers and sailors.

O

OATS A cereal grass grown in cool, temperate climates. Like other food grains, including the most important (corn), most oats production remains on the farm for feed and seed. North central states are the principal producers, notably Iowa, Minnesota, Illinois, and Wisconsin. Russia is the largest producer of oats in the world followed by the U.S.

Futures contracts based on oats are traded on the Chicago Board of Trade, the MidAmerica Commodity Exchange, and the Winnipeg Commodity Exchange. The CBT contract is based on 5,000 bushels of oats delivered via warehouse receipt from warehouses in Chicago at par or at Minneapolis or St. Paul at a 7 1/2-cent discount. The trading months are July, September, December, March, and May. July is the first contract month of the new crop. The MCE contract is for 1,000 bushels and is identical to the CBT contract in other ways. The Winnipeg contract is based on the delivery of a 100-tonne broad lot, 20-tonne job lot of Canadian oats at Thunder Bay, Ontario. The contract is traded in Canadian dollars. Futures contracts on soybeans, wheat, and corn are used for speculation far more than oats futures contracts.

The U.S. Department of Agriculture provides much information on the production of grains in the United States. Of special interest are the USDA *Wheat Situation Report*, *Winter Wheat Seedling*, *Feed Situation Report*, *Feed Market News*, *Grain Market News*, *Stocks in All Positions*, *Export Sales Report*, and *Weekly Roundup of World Production*, and *Foreign Agriculture*. The CTB's annual report provides important information on the cash and futures grains markets.

OATS PIT *See* PIT.

OBJECTIVES OF FINANCIAL REPORTING FASB Concepts Statement No. 1, "Objectives of Financial Reporting by Business Enterprises", describes the broad purpose of financial reporting, including financial statements. The objectives in Statement No. 1 apply to general purpose external financial reporting and are directed toward the common interests of many users. The objectives arise primarily from the needs of external users who lack the authority to obtain the information they want and must rely on information management communicates to them. According to Statement No. 1, financial reporting should provide information that will help investors, creditors, and others to:

Make rational investment, credit, and other financial decisions.

Assess the amounts, timing, and uncertainty of prospective net cash inflows to the related enterprise. Their prospects for receiving cash from investments, from loans, or from participation in the enterprise might hinge on its cash flow prospects.

Evaluate the economic resources of an enterprise, the claims to those resources (obligations of the enterprise to transfer resources to other entities and owners' equity), and the effects of transactions, events, and circumstances that change resources and claims to those resources.

Concepts Statement No. 1 gives specific guidance about the kinds of information the financial reporting should provide:

Information about an enterprise's economic resources, obligations, and owners' equity.

Information about an enterprise's performance provided by measures of earnings and comprehensive income, with their components measured by accrual accounting. Information about how an enterprise obtains and spends cash, its borrowing and repayment practices, its capital (equity) transactions, including cash dividends and other distributions of enterprise resources to owners, and other factors that may affect liquidity or solvency.

Information about how management of an enterprise has discharged its stewardship responsibility to owners (stockholders) for the use of enterprise resources entrusted to it.

Statement No. 1 emphasizes that earnings information is the primary focus of financial reporting. According to this statement, earnings should be measured by accrual accounting. This requires that the financial effects of economic transactions, events, and circumstances be reported in the period when they occur instead of when cash is received or paid.

The statement indicates that management is responsible for the custody and use of the entity's resources and that financial reporting should provide information concerning that stewardship function. Reports should include quantitive information and management's explanations that would be helpful to external users.

BIBLIOGRAPHY

SFAC No. 1, *Objectives of Financial Reporting by Business Enterprises* (FASB, 1978).

OBJECTIVES OF FINANCIAL REPORTING BY NONBUSINESS ORGANIZATIONS The Financial Accounting Standards Board's Statement of Financial Accounting No. 4, "Objectives of Financial Reporting by Nonbusiness Organizations", establishes the following broad objectives of financial reporting by nonbusiness organizations:

1. Financial reporting by nonbusiness organizations should provide information that can help present and potential resource providers and other users decide how to allocate resources.
2. Financial reporting should provide information to help present and potential resource providers and other users to assess the services that a nonbusiness organization provides and its ability to continue those services.
3. Financial reporting should provide information that is useful to present and potential resource providers and other users in assessing how managers of a nonbusiness organization have discharged their stewardship responsibilities and about other aspects of their performance.
4. Financial reporting should provide information about the economic resources, obligations, and net resources of an organization, and the effects of transactions, events, and circumstances that change resources and interests in those resources.
5. Financial reporting should provide information about the performance of an organization during a period. Periodic measurement of the changes in the amount and nature of the net resources of a nonbusiness organization and information about the service efforts and accomplishments of an organization are most useful in assessing its performance.
6. Financial reporting should provide information about how an organization obtains and spends cash or other liquid resources,

about its borrowing and repayment of borrowing, and about other factors that may affect an organization's liquidity.

7. Financial reporting should include explanations and interpretations to help users understand financial information provided.

The objectives arise from the common interest of those who provide resources to nonbusiness organizations in the services they offer and their ability to continue those services. The objectives apply to general purpose external financial reporting.

BIBLIOGRAPHY

SFAC No. 4, *Objectives of Financial Reporting by Nonbusiness Organizations* (FASB, 1981).

OBJECTIVITY Verifiability or the ability to perform a function without bias. The measurement that results from an objective application of accounting principles and methods should be capable of duplication by another person. In auditing, objectivity refers to an auditor's ability to be impartial in the performance of an audit. Where there is considerable uncertainty in the measurement process, the most objective measurement method should usually be followed. For example, the cost of a building arrived at in an arm's-length transaction is usually more objective than a real estate appraiser's estimate of value.

OBLIGATION Generally, all classes of indebtedness, the fundamental idea being that the debtor is bound to pay and that the creditor has legal power to compel payment. Frequently, when one business is absorbed by another, the latter is said to assume the former's obligations. Bonds are frequently referred to in this country as obligations. In France, the term obligation is the equivalent of our bond.

The Revised Statutes of the United States define obligations to mean "all bonds, certificates of indebtedness, national bank currency, coupons, United States notes, Treasury notes, gold certificates, silver certificates, fractional notes, certificates of deposit, bills, checks or drafts for money, drawn by or upon authorized officers of the United States, stamps and other representatives of value, of whatever denomination, which have been or may be issued under any Act of Congress."

A direct obligation is an obligation of the original maker of a loan contract. For instance, a note is a direct obligation of the maker and an indirect obligation of the endorser.

A general obligation is one in which the creditor's relation to the debtor is that of a general creditor. In other words, a general obligation is an unsecured one, and subject to prior claims, e.g., preferential claims (wages, taxes, mechanics' liens) and secured claims (mortgages, mortgage bonds, and notes payable secured by a specific pledge of collateral). The term general obligation as applied to municipal bonds indicates those which bind the full faith and credit and are a lien upon the revenues of the entire issuing jurisdiction and not merely upon a part of the jurisdiction or a part of its revenues.

OBLIGATOR OBLIGOR.

OBLIGATORY MATURITY The absolute, final, or compulsory maturity of a note or bond, as distinguished from the optional maturity or prior redemption date. Bonds which by their terms may be retired at the option of the obligor before the obligatory maturity are known as callable, optional, or (less accurately) redeemable bonds.

OBLIGEE A creditor; one who can enforce payment of a debt, e.g., a note or bond holder.

OBLIGOR A debtor; a person, firm, or corporation that is bound to perform an obligation, such as payment of a note or bond. A corporation that has issued bonds is an obligor corporation. The United States government is obligor in the case of United States government bonds.

OBSOLETE SECURITIES Bonds that have matured and have been retired and canceled; stocks or bonds of corporations that are abandoned or defunct or that have temporarily suspended operations without actually dissolving.

BIBLIOGRAPHY

FISHER, ROBERT D. *Manual of Valuable and Worthless Securities:*
Vols. V and VI (1937 and 1938);
Vol. VII (1940), including the Robert D. Fisher Mining Manual, Vol. I (1940);
Vol. VIII (1941), including the Robert D. Fisher Mining Manual, Vol. II (1941);
Vol. IX (1942), including index;
Vol. X (1944-1945);
Vol. XI (1946), including index to Robert D. Fisher Mining Manual Vols. I and II and to Vol. X;
Vol. XII (1957).
———. *Manual of Valuable Securities*, 1943.
———. *Stock Detective*, 1958.
SCUDDER, MARVYN. *Manual of Extinct or Obsolete Companies:*
Vol. I (1926);
Vol. II (1928);
Vol. III (1930);
Vol. IV, index to Vols. I, II, and III.
SMYTHE, R. M. *Obsolete American Securities and Corporations*, 1904-1911, two vols.:
Valuable Extinct Securities (1929);
Valuable Extinct Securities Guide (1939)

OCEAN BILL OF LADING All ocean bills of lading issued must be subject to the Carriage of Goods by Sea Act of 1936, which enacted into law the Hague Convention Rules of 1921, and must so provide in a paramount clause.

See BILL OF LADING.

ODD LOT On stock exchanges, a smaller unit of trading than the standard unit of trading, known as a board or full or round lot, which on the New York Stock Exchange and other exchanges is 100 shares of stock for active stocks. Rule 55 of the New York Stock Exchange provides, however, that in the case of stocks so designated by the exchange, the unit of trading shall be a lesser number as may be determined by the exchange, and ten shares has been customary as the round lot for such less active stocks. The unit of trading in bonds is $1,000 original principal amount. Similarly, except as otherwise designated by the exchange, transactions in rights to subscribe are on the basis of one right accruing on each share of issued stock, and the unit of trading in rights is 100 rights. An odd lot, therefore, in 100-share round-lot stocks is any lot from 1 to 99 shares and in 10-share round-lot stocks is any lot from 1 to 9 shares.

On March 3, 1976, the NEW YORK STOCK EXCHANGE exercised its option to purchase the odd-lot processing system of the last remaining odd-lot dealer, Carlisle DeCoppet & Company, completing this $3.5 million purchase on May 24, 1976.

Previously, in December, 1975, the largest brokerage firm asked the Securities and Exchange Commission to allow the firm to begin to make its own market in odd lots, and this firm started to make its own markets in New York Stock Exchange-listed odd lots on January 2, 1976, away from the stock exchange floor. Another large member firm began making its own markets in odd lots of all New York Stock Exchange-listed stocks on August 16, 1976.

Accordingly, since that time there have been two channels for execution of orders in New York Stock Exchange odd lots: (1) the New York Stock Exchange system, now handled with the aid of electronics, through the specialists, and (2) the in-house markets of member firms that have chosen to make available odd lots in New York Stock Exchange-listed stocks.

The New York Stock Exchange's Odd-Lot System.

Order processing: Odd-lot order processing begins with the entry and validation of the orders. There are two methods for order entry. Most large member firms use computer systems and telecommunication networks to accept orders from their branch offices and direct them to the Securities Industry Automation Corporation (SIAC) common message switch (CMS). Other member firms utilize computer systems and/or networks supplied by private vendors for this same purpose. Firms sending their orders directly into CMS are called machine firms (MF) and account for over 75% of the order volume.

The second method of order entry is by means of the New York Stock Exchange Input Center, which is equipped and staffed by the exchange. Firms that use telephone or teletype to get their orders to their booths on the perimeter of the trading floor are called nonmachine firms (NMF). These firms then send their orders by the New York Stock Exchange pneumatic tubes to the New York Stock Exchange Input Center, where exchange operators enter these orders into the CMS. NMF order entry requires multiple steps and normally takes more time than the direct entry method of the machine firms.

The CMS validates all odd-lot orders for conformance to the exchange's standard order format. Any significant errors result in the order being returned to the member firm for correction and reentry. All properly edited orders are then sent to the odd-lot service computers for processing.

Order pricing: The odd-lot service computer system used for pricing orders is called APARS for automatic pricing and reporting system. APARS receives all orders from CMS and stores them in a pending execution file. APARS also receives New York Stock Exchange round-lot sales information from the exchange's market data system (MDS). APARS then matches the round-lot sales data to the file of pending orders to start the pricing process.

Market orders: Market orders are priced automatically using the next round-lot sale received by APARS after receipt of the order. Market orders to sell short are priced on the next sale that is higher than the price of the last different round-lot sale (*see* SHORT SALE). These sales are referred to as having a plus tick (a tick is the minimum price fluctuation of $0.125) or a zero plus tick.

Each odd-lot dealer can direct APARS to charge or not to charge a differential. Currently, until the system can accommodate other options, the differential, if any, is one-eighth of a point ($0.125) per share. Each dealer can elect to charge or not charge this differential on an individual stock basis. Additionally, each dealer has the option to charge or not charge the differential on market orders received before the exchange opening and an independent option for market orders received after the exchange opening. The exchange opening, for the purpose of the differential option, is currently set at 9:50 A.M. to allow each dealer to be fully advised of odd-lot shares to be priced on each stock's opening round-lot sale. This time can be adjusted to compensate for any emergency causing a delay in the official exchange opening.

Nonmarket orders: Limit and other orders, such as those that require a bid or offer execution, are considered nonmarket orders. Each dealer has the option of charging or not charging the oneeighth differential on these orders, regardless of the time of entry. These orders are filed by price in time sequence by stock. APARS maintains a record of the highest buy limit order price and the lowest sell limit order price awaiting execution. In maintaining this record, APARS takes into account whether or not a differential is to be charged. A pending buy limit order is filled on the next round-lot sale that is below the specified limit by the amount of the differential, if any, or by a greater amount. The differential, if any, is added to this price. A pending sell long limit order is filled on the next round-lot sale that is above the specified limit by the amount of the differential, if any, or by a greater amount. The differential, if any, is subtracted from this price. As with market orders, sell short limit orders can only be priced on a plus tick or zero plus tick transaction.

The price of the highest buy limit order and the price of the lowest sell limit order create what is known as the range of unexecuted limit orders. The computer monitors these prices to determine when limit order pricing is to be done. When a round-lot sale occurs at or below the low range (the price of the highest buy order) or at or above the up range (the price of the lowest sell order), the computer checks the file for orders to be executed. When this occurs, the range is broken and the computer must update its record to reflect the new highest buy or lowest sell price, to control its monitoring of future round-lot sales prices. The computer also checks the limit prices of all new orders and updates the range price if necessary; for example, if a new buy price is higher than the then current highest buy price, the new order price will become the new low range.

Stop orders are processed in a manner similar to that used for limit orders. Buy stop orders are filed with sell limits, and sell stop orders are filed with buy limits. Each stock's range of order prices controls both stop and limit orders. When a stop order is elected (that is, the stop price is met), it becomes a regular market order and is priced accordingly. When a stop limit order is elected, it is refiled and processed as a regular limit order.

Cancel orders: Odd-lot orders can be entered as day orders, that is, orders which expire if unfiled at the market close on the day of entry. They can also be entered as good-till-canceled (GTC) orders, in which case they are maintained as open orders indefinitely. Normally the open order file is purged once a year of all orders more than a year old, and the member firms are requested to reenter any such orders that they wish to retain in force.

From time to time, a customer will choose to cancel or change an order, either one entered that same day or one in the open order file from prior days. This can be done with a simple cancel order or with a cancel and replace order. These orders can be for any combination of market and limit orders, i.e., a market order replacing a market order, a limit replacing a limit, a market replacing a limit, or a limit replacing a market. In recent years, member firms were encouraged to enter two separate orders, one order to cancel and one to replace the previous order, particularly where a limit was being replaced by a market or vice versa. This procedure results in faster handling and more accurate executions. If the order to be canceled is on file and still unexecuted, the cancel will be applied and the new order will be filed to await execution. If no former order is found on a cancel and replace order, the new order will still be filed to await execution. The member firm will be informed that there was no order to cancel.

Execution reports: APARS creates a standard format execution report for each order as it is priced. Most orders are priced and reported automatically by the computer system. The pricing and reporting of any order that requires manual handling is initiated by keyboard entry via on-line computer terminals. Orders that are priced on the same day as entered require minimum data entry to supplement the computer's files. Entries for orders open from prior days require more extensive data entry. Regardless of how the report is initiated, automatically or by keyboard entry, all orders are priced and reported in the same manner. The execution reports are sent to CMS for distribution to the clearing firm designated on the order. CMS routes the reports to the machine firm's system via its own network for its own internal distribution. CMS sends nonmachine firm reports to printers on the trading floor, where they are distributed to the firms' floor booths.

Inventory management: APARS is designed to assist each dealer with the management of the inventory of shares required to service the odd-lot public. Executed customer buy orders reduce the inventory, while executed customer sell orders result in share accumulations. Many thousands of customer transactions are processed during each trading day, resulting in a turnover of several hundred thousand shares of stock daily. The APARS inventory control system is designed to minimize a dealer's market risk and to enable profitable operation. This is facilitated by advising each dealer, as quickly as possible, of odd-lot market order activity and large accumulations of shares in the limit open order file near the current market price.

Each dealer selects a value for total share accumulations for each stock on which he wants to be advised. Unless instructed otherwise, APARS will use the normal unit of trading, 100 shares or 10 shares. This value is called the inventory line. Each line is assigned a numerical code for simplicity of operation. Each code represents a long value and a short value.

Each dealer can change his line code selection at any time, to any code/value that is available in the system. For control purposes, such change requests must be made in writing, with a minimum of ten days' notice.

Limit alerts: Each odd-lot dealer is advised of large share accumulations in the file of open limit and stop orders near the current market. These advisory messages are called limit alert messages. Each morning the dealer is given a start-of-day limit alert informing him of all shares in the overnight file, i.e., the file after the prior day's close. This start-of-day message includes all shares for the full dollar closest to the down range, i.e., the highest buy orders and an additional dollar down, as well as all shares for the full dollar closest to the up range, i.e., the lowest sell orders and an additional dollar up.

During the day, additional limit alerts are sent to the dealer whenever the share accumulation of new limit or stop orders at or between the range of highest buy and lowest sell orders exceeds the line value. All limit alerts sent during the day replace all previous alerts sent during that day except the start-of-day alert. They include only shares of unexecuted orders as adjusted by cancels received that day. All during the day, alerts must be added to the start-of-day shares for complete up-to-the-minute totals of open orders.

The limit alert messages list the shares at the round-lot price which will execute the orders. APARS compensates for the dealer's option of whether or not a differential is charged, so that the alerts are consistent, regardless of differential.

In addition to these automatic limit alerts, additional alerts are available on request. For example, accumulations of prices not listed on the start-of-day alert can be requested before the opening or during the day if the market is moving away from the range that existed earlier in the day. A dealer can request a new alert for any dollar value in his stocks. Telephone facilities are provided at each post for contacting the odd-lot service clerks to request such an alert.

Position alarms: The computer maintains an approximate inventory position based on odd-lot activity. All market customer buy order shares are subtracted from and market customer sell long order shares are added to this position when they are received; limit order shares and market sell short order shares are added to or subtracted from the position (tallied) when they are executed. Each time the computer's position exceeds the line value for the stock as set by the dealer, a position alarm is generated. The alarm advises the dealer to plus or minus his inventory as a result of odd-lot trading activity. Each alarm also indicates the stock's line code, as well as the total number of round-lot units to plus or minus sent for the day, including the current alarm, i.e., six would indicate the total so far was plus 600 shares and three would indicate minus 300 shares. As soon as an alarm is sent, the computer considers it done, reduces its position to an odd-lot value, and starts to accumulate anew. This residual odd-lot position is also shown on the alarm.

Position alarms are suppressed until about 9:30 each morning, so that each dealer normally receives one major alarm for the round-lot share accumulation before the exchange opening. Since no trade has taken place, it can be assumed that these are net of dealers' starting odd-lot positions and unexecuted market orders received by this time (brought forward from the previous day). This reduces the number of alarms that would otherwise be sent from 8:30 to 9:30. All alarms are for the line value, but cannot be less than a round-lot unit of trading or a multiple thereof.

End of day processing: When the market closes each day, APARS performs various end-of-day procedures. All "on close" and "basis" orders are executed. All unexecuted day orders expire and are purged from the files. Where appropriate, certain buy limit and sell stop order prices are reduced to reflect dividends. Orders executed after the close and corrections processed after the close can result in inventory position changes that cannot be offset until the following day.

The odd-lot service then processes all executed orders as a prelude and introduction to the clearance system. All trades are doublechecked for valid information, cancellation of duplicates, and application of same-day change requests for the member firms. When this processing is completed, the trades are listed in complete detail for each specialist odd-lot dealer. They are also summarized for use in the dealers' profit and loss calculations.

In-House Odd-Lot System. The following briefly describes the in-house odd-lot system of the largest brokerage firm.

Customers with odd-lot orders have different choices. If the customer has an odd-lot market order, the firm's odd-lot program will afford an execution at the prevailing bid or offer without going to the exchange floor. Thus the customer has the opportunity to buy and sell odd lots to and from the firm at the currently reported bid and asked price prevailing when the order is entered rather than when it reaches the floor, giving the customer the advantage of a known fixed price at the time of entry of the order. Another advantage for the customer is the elimination of the one-eighth-point odd-lot differential on market orders.

On the other hand, if the customer prefers, the firm will execute his odd-lot order on the exchange floor; but, unless the order is entered on the opening of the market, a one-eighth-point differential will be added to or subtracted from the execution price. Price will be based upon the next sale except when such orders are entered on the opening of the market. Saving the one-eighth-point differential does not necessarily mean that the execution will be better. When the spread between bid and asked prices is greater than one-eighth point, the customer may be able to do better with a floor execution.

The firm's odd-lot program also offers in-house execution of odd-lot limit orders. In the case of orders with price limits, there would be no difference between the execution offered by the firm and that available on the floor of the exchange.

Odd-Lot Theory. The conventional belief historically that the "odd lotter is always wrong" in timing net purchases and sales at market tops and bottoms has not been supported by the facts. For example, research by Cleveland Trust Company's *Business Bulletin* (November, 1974) into the behavior of odd-lot volume from 1966 to 1974 established that in fact odd lotters' sales increased faster than purchases near market peaks, and their purchases increased faster than sales near market lows, as measured by the Dow Jones industrials average.

The completeness of stock exchange-reported odd-lot volume has been affected in recent years by in-house odd-lot transactions made available to customers by major member firms and by dividend reinvestment plans made available by leading corporations to their stockholders. In a representative example of the latter, all registered stockholders are eligible to participate in the company's dividend reinvestment and stock purchase plan. The plan permits the purchase of additional shares of the company's stock at a 5% discount from the market price through reinvestment of all or a portion of the dividends. Participants can also purchase additional shares, up to $25,000 worth annually, through a voluntary cash payment option. Shares purchased through this option are made at full market price. The company pays any brokerage commissions and bank fees related to both the reinvested dividends and voluntary cash purchases.

ODD-LOT DEALERS The highly specialized business of providing a market at all times for odd lots of stocks on the New York Stock Exchange, which originated as far back as 1871, became in January, 1970, centered in one firm, Carlisle DeCoppet & Co., as the result of the merger of Carlisle & Jacquelin with DeCoppet & Doremus.

In turn, on May 24, 1976, the New York Stock Exchange itself announced completion of the previously announced $3.5 million purchase of the computerized securities processing system of Carlisle DeCoppet & Co. and inauguration of its own ODD LOT system handled through specialists. On the AMERICAN STOCK EXCHANGE, its specialists have handled odd lots, there being no specialized odd-lot dealer system such as formerly prevailed on the New York Stock Exchange.

BIBLIOGRAPHY

SECURITIES INDUSTRY AUTOMATION CORPORATION. *NYSE Odd Lot Trading Specialist Guide.*

OFF A stock market expression indicating prices below preceding level. It also denotes "without," e.g., "dividend off" means "without dividend."

OFF-BALANCE SHEET FINANCING Borrowing in such a way that the obligation is not recorded on the borrower's financial statements (hence the term "off-balance-sheet" activities). Various techniques are available, including sales of receivables with recourse, product financing arrangements, leasing, and research and development arrangements. Financial accounting disclosure requirements have dealt with off-balance-sheet financing to some extent, which tends to promote an efficient market philosophy.

Regulators, security analysts, and the financial press have expressed special concerns about the rapid growth of off-balance-sheet activities in such contingent obligations as loan commitments, financial futures and options contracts, letters of credit, and foreign exchange contracts. These contingent obligations involve interest rate, credit, and/or liquidity risks. Such activities can increase a bank's overall risk because they offer more leverage than do a bank's lending and investment activities.

Off-balance-sheet financing offers a company the following advantages:

1. The company's debt/equity ratio improves for borrowing purposes, as does the market value of its stock.
2. Borrowing capacity is enhanced, especially if there are contractual limits or restrictions related to balance sheet items.
3. Borrowing costs are reduced from an improved balance sheet.
4. Management compensation plans are improved if they are related to ratios or earnings that are favorably affected by off-balance-sheet financing.
5. Risk sharing and tax management opportunities can be created through limited partnership arrangements and in-substance debt defeasance.
6. Loans are easier to arrange and at lower interest rates because of the improved debt structure on the balance sheet.

BIBLIOGRAPHY

Cooper, K. "Coming to Grips with Off-Balance-Sheet Risks." Federal Reserve Bank of Minneapolis, *Annual Report*, 1982.

OFF-BUDGET ACTIVITIES Not all activities are reported in the government's budget statements. Those that are not directly reported are referred to as off-budget activities. For example, student loans are not accounted for in the federal deficit figures, although many argue that they should be so noted.

OFFER This term has two meanings:
1. A bid; a price named at which one is willing to buy.
2. In stock exchange parlance, the price at which one is willing to sell. Thus: "The stock is offered at 35; the best bid is 30."

OFFERED DOWN Indicates that sellers are offering a security (or commodity) for sale at a price lower than that of the last transaction or latest quotation.

OFFERED FIRM Indicates that sellers are offering a security (or commodity) at a specified price, giving the prospective buyer a certain time for its acceptance. Thus, a bond may be offered firm at 95 and accrued interest for three days. Offered firm differs from offered subject to sale or offered subject to prior sale in that in the latter two cases the offer is good only if the securities are not previously sold to other buyers. A dealer who offers securities subject to prior sale is not liable if he refuses to sell to a party who bids for the offering after they have been sold elsewhere.

When one makes a bid at a definite price to hold good for a certain time, it is known as a firm bid.

OFFERING BOOK A book or list maintained by a dealer in bonds, stocks, commercial paper, etc., which contains a description of each security offered for sale, the price included.
See OFFERING SHEET.

OFFERINGS Bonds, stocks, notes, commercial paper, etc., of-fered for sale to customers.

OFFERING SHEET A list of commercial paper offered by a note broker. Large banks that offer participation loans to their bank customers also prepare offering sheets to show the names of loans in which they offer participations. In the investment business, an offering sheet differed from a bond circular in pre-SEC days in that the former contained a brief description of a number of issues, whereas the latter contained a more formal description of a single issue. The offering sheet usually closed with a statement such as the following: "We offer for subscription, subject to prior sale or allotment (such of these bonds as may not be taken up by others through the exercise of rights) when, as, and if issued and received by us, and subject to the approval of counsel." The offering sheet is still used today in the case of U.S. government, municipal, railroad, and other exempt securities (exempt from the Securities Act of 1933), but public offerings of nonexempt securities under the act must be accompanied by a prospectus.
See BOND CIRCULAR, SYNDICATE, UNDERWRITING.

OFFICE AUDIT An audit conducted by the Internal Revenue Service on the IRS premises. An office auditor conducts office audits, whereas opposed a Revenue Agent conducts field audits.

OFFICE PAPER Finance bills.
See FINANCE BILL.

OFFICERS Under various laws, the directors of a stock corporation may appoint or elect from their own number a president. The president of the corporation typically has the implied power and the apparent authority to perform any act on behalf of the corporation that can be ratified by the board of directors. Directors must designate the powers of the officers in the bylaws, but any such express limitations are of no avail as to outside parties relying on the apparent authority of the president, unless such outside parties have actual knowledge of such limitations.

The directors typically may appoint or elect one or more vice-presidents, a secretary, a treasurer, and other officers, agents, and employees as they may determine, or as may be provided in the bylaws of the corporation. Such officers need not be directors. As in the case of the president, these officers shall have such powers and perform such duties in the management of the property and affairs of the corporation, subject to the control of the directors, as may be prescribed by the directors in the bylaws. The directors may require any officer, agent, or employee to give security for the faithful performance of his duties and may remove him at their pleasure.
See BANK OFFICERS.

OFFICIAL CHECKS A broad classification including checks drawn by the bank against itself as well as checks that have been certified by the bank. Such checks represent the direct obligations of the bank and are included with other demand deposits in the report of condition. Official checks include cashier's checks, bank money orders, expense checks, dividend checks, certified checks, and personal money orders.

OFFICIAL LIST A short title for "The Stock Exchange Daily Official List," which is the London counterpart of the New York Stock Exchange list of security quotations. It is published twice daily, with a weekly edition which is a summary of the week's business.
See LONDON STOCK EXCHANGE.

OFFICIAL LISTING NOTICE A formal notice sent to a corporation that has applied to the committee on stock list or to a similar department of a stock exchange for permission to list its securities on the stock exchange, indicating that the application has been granted.
See LISTED SECURITIES.

OFFSHORE BANKING By popular usage, the establishment and operation of U.S. banks in such offshore "tax havens" as the Bahamas and the Cayman Islands.

Branches of member banks of the Federal Reserve System in the Bahamas and Cayman Islands as of year-end 1979 numbered 150, against 142 at year-end 1978, with reported total deposits of $63.9 billion as of year-end 1979, an increase of 33% compared to the $48.1 billion as of year-end 1978.

Amendment of Regulations D and Q by the Board of Governors of the Federal Reserve System, effective December 3, 1981, authorized the establishment in the U.S. of international banking facilities (IBFs) by U.S. depository institutions, Edge Act and agreement corporations, and branches and agencies of foreign banks located in the U.S. Under the rules adopted by the board of governors, an IBF may accept deposits from foreign residents (including banks) or from other IBFs. Such funds are exempt from the reserve requirements of Regulation D and from the interest rate limitations of Regulation Q. IBFs are permitted to offer to foreign nonbank residents large-denomination time deposits with a minimum maturity or required notice period prior to withdrawal of at least two business days. In addition, IBFs are permitted to offer overnight time deposits to foreign offices of U.S. depository institutions or foreign banks, to other IBFs, to foreign central banks, or to the institution establishing the IBF. Funds raised by an IBF can be used only to extend credit to foreign residents, to other IBFs, or to the institution establishing the IBF. Funds derived by an institution from its own IBF are subject to Eurocurrency reserve requirements.

The Board of Governors of the Federal Reserve System believed that the establishment of IBFs at U.S. banking offices would enhance the international competitive position of banking institutions located in the U.S. Parenthetically, establishment of the IBFs was considered to be a move to attract offshore banking business back to the U.S.
See INTERNATIONAL BANKING.

OFF THE BOARD Refers to transactions in unlisted securities in the OVER-THE-COUNTER MARKET.

The term also refers to special transactions in blocks of listed securities not executed on the floor of the NEW YORK STOCK EXCHANGE and not reported as part of the regular volume on the floor. Such procedures as exchange distributions, special offerings, secondary offerings, and specialists' bids and offers are part of the arrangements authorized by the New York Stock Exchange to facilitate transactions in blocks of listed securities. Block transactions in listed securities off the board also refer to the third market and fourth market.

ENCYCLOPEDIA OF BANKING AND FINANCE

OIL

OIL Petroleum; a natural resource. The Soviet Union and the United States are the largest producers of crude. The Organization of Petroleum Exporting Countries (OPEC) was formed in 1960 by Iran, Iraq, Kuwait, Saudi Arabia, and Venezuela. Qatar, Indonesia, Libya, Abu Dhabij Algeria, Nigeria, Ecuador, and Gabon later joined. These countries have organized loosely into six groups: the moderate Arabs, the radical Arabs, the Africans, the Asians, the Iranians, and the South Americans. Four major international oil companies (Chevron, Exxon, Mobil, and Texaco) are often referred to as the "Aramco partners." These companies initially owned Aramco, which produces most of Saudi Arabia's oil. Saudi took over Aramco ownership in 1980.

In the early 1970s, OPEC imposed an oil embargo that ended a relatively stable petroleum distribution system and prices. The Iranian crisis during 1978 and 1979 resulted in a further deterioration of the worldwide oil situation. During the early 1980s the crude production of most of the eastern oil-producing countries declined. Energy conservation methods reduced the demand for oil during these years, leading to an oversupply of the product and hence to price declines by the mid-1980s. By the late 1980s, OPEC's influence had been reduced to a great extent. OPEC had de facto abandoned fixed prices. Its official price in 1986 was $18 per barrel; the average price of the seven OPEC countries was around $15.

Crude oil is categorized in terms of sulfur content, density, and field of origin. The demand for oil comes almost exclusively from refineries. Long-term agreements and the spot market are frequently found in oil distribution. Swap transactions are common.

Futures contracts in petroleum and petroleum products began in 1978 when the New York Mercantile Exchange introduced heating oil No. 2 futures. Additional futures contracts are available for gasoline (leaded and unleaded), crude oil, propane (LPB) and gas oil. Futures are traded on the New York Mercantile Exchange, the New York Cotton Exchange, and the London International Petroleum Exchange. Units of trading are 1,000 barrels, except for gas oil which is 100 metric tons. Minimum price fluctuations are $0.01 per gallon, except for gas oil which is $0.25 per metric ton.

The appended table shows world produciton of crude oil, 1960-1987.

BIBLIOGRAPHY

AMERICAN PETROLEUM INSTITUTE. *Standard Definitions for Petroleum Statistics.*

PENWELL PUBLISHING COMPANY, *International Petroleum Encyclopedia.* Periodicals include: *Energy User News; Fuel Oil Week; National Petroleum News; Oil and Gas Journal; Oil Buyer's Guide; Oil Daily; The Petroleum Economist; The Petroleum Intelligence Weekly; Platt's Oilgram.*

U.S. DEPARTMENT OF ENERGY, *Crude Petroleum, Petroleum Products, and Natural Gas Liquids; Energy Data Report; Monthly Energy Review; Monthly Petroleum Statement; Petroleum Market Shares; Sales of LP Gases and Ethane; and Weekly Petroleum Status Report.*

OIL SECURITIES Stocks and bonds of oil-producing and -refining companies. The oil industry is becoming less speculative and is now one of the most strongly organized industry groups, dominated by relatively few powerful interests, both domestic and international. These companies are highly integrated and normally control all stages of the industry from prospecting and drilling wells to marketing gasoline. A completely integrated oil company combines at least four essential divisions: production (ownership of oil lands with proven production, oil wells, storage tanks, etc.), refining, transportation (pipelines, tank cars, tankers, etc.), and marketing (distribution stations, tank trailers, and in many cases retail gasoline stations). Domestic companies with large crude oil reserves are especially attractive for takeovers by major companies seeking buildup of such reserves.

In considering the purchase of oil securities, the investor should distinguish between three groups: (1) undeveloped properties consisting of leases and option lands, i.e., unproved territory, (2) properties that are producing but are not profitable, and (3) properties that are both producing and profitable.

World Production of Crude Oil [1], 1960-1987
(Millions of barrels per day)

Year	Total [2] OPEC	Canada	China	Mexico	United Kingdom	United States	U.S.S.R.	Other Non-OPEC	Total World
1960	8.70	0.52	0.10	0.27	([3])	7.04	2.91	20.96	1.42
1961	9.36	0.61	0.11	0.29	([3])	7.18	3.28	22.43	1.60
1962	10.51	0.67	0.12	0.31	([3])	7.33	3.67	24.32	1.71
1963	11.51	0.71	0.13	0.32	([3])	7.54	4.07	26.13	1.85
1964	12.98	0.75	0.18	0.32	([3])	7.61	4.60	28.36	1.92
1965	14.34	0.81	0.23	0.32	([3])	7.80	4.79	30.30	2.01
1966	15.77	0.88	0.29	0.33	([3])	8.30	5.23	32.93	2.13
1967	16.85	0.96	0.28	0.37	([3])	8.81	5.68	35.37	2.42
1968	18.79	1.19	0.30	0.39	([3])	9.10	6.08	38.64	2.79
1969	20.91	1.13	0.48	0.46	([3])	9.24	6.48	41.69	2.99
1970	23.41	1.26	0.60	0.49	([3])	9.64	6.97	45.29	2.92
1971	25.33	1.35	0.78	0.49	([3])	9.46	7.44	47.84	2.99
1972	27.09	1.53	0.90	0.51	([3])	9.44	7.88	50.26	2.91
1973	30.99	1.80	1.09	0.47	([3])	9.21	8.33	55.57	3.69
1974	30.73	1.68	1.32	0.57	([3])	8.77	8.86	55.77	3.84
1975	27.16	1.44	1.49	0.71	0.01	8.38	9.47	52.76	4.12
1976	30.74	1.30	1.67	0.83	0.25	8.13	9.99	57.19	4.30
1977	31.30	1.32	1.87	0.98	0.77	8.25	10.49	59.52	4.55
1978	29.81	1.31	2.08	1.21	1.08	8.71	10.95	59.87	4.72
1979	30.93	1.50	2.12	1.46	1.57	8.55	11.19	62.35	5.04
1980	26.89	1.44	2.11	1.94	1.62	8.60	11.46	59.23	5.17
1981	22.65	1.29	2.01	2.31	1.81	8.57	11.55	55.55	5.36
1982	18.87	1.27	2.05	2.75	2.07	8.65	11.62	52.90	5.64
1983	17.58	1.36	2.12	2.69	2.29	8.69	11.68	52.65	6.24
1984	17.48	1.44	2.30	2.78	2.48	8.88	11.58	53.83	6.90
1985	16.07	1.47	2.48	2.74	2.53	8.97	11.25	52.95	7.46
1986	18.51	1.47	2.61	2.43	2.55	8.68	11.62	55.74	7.88
1987 P	18.15	1.51	2.69	2.54	2.47	8.31	11.79	40.75	8.21

[1] Includes lease condensate, excludes natural gas plant liquids.
[2] Current membership of the Organization of the Petroleum Exporting Countries includes Algeria, Ecuador, Gabon, Indonesia, Iran, Iraq, Kuwait, Libya, Nigeria, Qatar, Saudi Arabia, United Arab Emirates, and Venezuela.
[3] United Kingdom available beginning 1975.
P — Preliminary.
Source: Energy Information Administration, *Annual Energy Review*, 1987.

Oil securities embody many of the same characteristics as MINING SECURITIES.

OKUN'S LAW An important statistical relationship in economics, called Okun's Law, exists between real output growth and the unemployment rate. Okun's Law states that a 3.5% to 4.0% growth rate in real output leaves the unemployment rate unchanged. In other words, the creation of new jobs when real growth is between 3.5% and 4.0% approximately equals the increase in the number of people entering the labor force. Unemployment rates will fall only when real output growth is above this range. Conversely, if real output growth is below this range, unemployment rates will begin to rise.

OLD LADY OF THREADNEEDLE STREET A nickname for the BANK OF ENGLAND, the main entrance of which is on Threadneedle Street, London.

OLD LINE RAILS The stocks of the well-known standard railroad corporations of the United States which have a reputation for good management, as shown by the high standard of maintenance of their properties, conservative financing, large earnings, and uninterrupted dividend record over a long period of years.

ON ACCOUNT A part payment on the purchase price is a payment on account.

ON A SCALE See AVERAGING, SCALING.

ONE-DAY CERTIFICATES The Federal Reserve is authorized by Section 14(b) of the Federal Reserve Act, as amended frequently at short intervals (e.g., latest series of amendments, by 89 Stat. 638, November 12, 1975; 91 Stat. 49, April 19, 1977; 91 Stat. 1131, October 12, 1977; 91 Stat. 1256, November 7, 1977; 93 Stat. 35, June 8, 1979; and 94 Stat. 140, March 31, 1980), to provide temporary financing, under special circumstances, directly to the U.S. Treasury. The aggregate amount of such obligations acquired directly from the United States which may be held by the 12 Federal Reserve banks under this provision shall not exceed $5 billion. Congress has kept this special authority on renewable two-year terms. Such precautions are motivated by the desirability of having the Treasury go to the open market for its borrowing, rather than resort directly to the Federal Reserve banks and thus bypass the market, lest monetization of the debt so easily accomplished through the central bank, as certain other nations have done, generate inflation in financing government deficits.

Under the legislation, the Treasury can borrow cash directly from the Federal Reserve only after the Board of Governors of the Federal Reserve System, by an affirmative vote of at least five members, has determined that "unusual and exigent circumstances" exist. In all other circumstances, Federal Reserve assistance is limited to lending securities to the Treasury from the System's portfolio; in turn, the Treasury would be expected to sell the securities in the open market to obtain cash, and must repurchase and return the securities within six months. Until June 1979, Treasury borrowings were accomplished through Federal Reserve purchases of interest-bearing "Special Certificates" issued by the Treasury.

In recent years the large balances maintained by the Treasury in the general fund and the system of weekly bill borrowing have largely eliminated the necessity for these special certificates. Another factor keeping the Treasury comfortably in cash resources in recent years of heavy issuance of government securities has been the book credit method of subscription to government securities by member banks, whereby the Treasury is credited deposits for the amount of the subscriptions. Whenever the Treasury has needed funds, therefore, it has given notice to the member banks to call upon these government deposits through the Federal Reserve banks.
See UNITED STATES GOVERNMENT SECURITIES.

ONE-DAY LOAN See DAY LOANS.

ONE-MAN COMPANY A corporation that is dominated by one person, either by ownership of the majority of the stock or by force of his personality and influence in the trade at large. Among credit people such a company is not considered as good a credit risk as one in which the control is more widely distributed, for the reason that the death of the one man in control may detract from the future of the concern by leaving it destitute of high-grade managerial ability.

ONE-NAME PAPER See SINGLE-NAME PAPER.

ON-LINE, REAL-TIME SYSTEM (OLRT) A system that provides immediate feedback of actual conditions, often used in control situations so that corrections can be made at the time the event itself is taking place. Processing time is instantaneous in an on-line system. OLRT systems require that related records and programs are on-line (disk files) and not in an off-line library. On-line refers to a terminal or input device in direct communication with the central processing unit. Real-time means that the data files are updated immediately after data input. The user receives the information in time to affect decisions.

OPEN See OPEN ACCOUNT, OPENING, OPEN MARKET OPERATIONS, OPEN MARKET RATES, OPEN MORTGAGE, ORDERS.

OPEN ACCOUNT When monthly or other periodic settlements arranged for purchases made and charged to the buyer's account are not evidenced by a note, the buyer is said to be buying on open account and the seller extending open credit. Whenever open accounts are established, there should be a definite promise of settlement, e.g., payment by the tenth of the succeeding month.

Open book accounts, known also as accounts receivable, are regarded as assets as good as notes or bills receivable, although the latter are prima facie evidence of debt and open accounts are not. The amount of credit extended on open account is usually limited, the maximum being known as the line of credit.
See ASSIGNED BOOK ACCOUNTS.

OPEN BOOK ACCOUNT See OPEN ACCOUNT.

OPEN CREDIT See CREDIT, OPEN ACCOUNT.

OPEN-END BONDS Mortgage bonds, usually those of a public utility company, in which the amount of bonds issuable under the mortgage is left indefinite or authorized in large aggregate, the mortgage permitting the subsequent issue of additional bonds in series within specified limits as to asset and/or earnings coverage of total fixed charges. Open-end bonds are more familiarly known as OPEN MORTGAGE bonds and are to be distinguished from closed mortgage bonds.
See BOND, CLOSED END MORTGAGE.

OPENING The hour at which trading begins on an organized exchange. The opening of the New York Stock Exchange is at 10 A.M.

OPENING PRICE The price at which the first sale for the day of any security is made. Opening prices are furnished by leading exchanges to the wire services for daily newspapers which publish stock quotations, together with the high, low, and close.

OPEN INTEREST In futures trading in grains, cotton, and other commodities, the quantity in bushels, bales, or other units of a given commodity involved in unclosed trading contracts entered into by speculators or others, either long or short, in futures. Open interest provides an indication of speculative interest. For example, if the total of long futures contracts of all options in wheat held by brokers for the account of all customers is 80 million bushels, that represents the open interest in that grain. Thus the open interest is the amount carried on open contracts, not yet closed out or terminated by sale or acceptance of delivery in the case of longs, or bought back in the case of shorts.

The COMMODITY FUTURES TRADING COMMISSION and commodity exchanges themselves may require reports on the volume of trading and open interest daily.

OPEN MARKET In OPEN MARKET OPERATIONS of the Federal Reserve System, the MARKET maintained by government securities dealers, through which firms the open market account of the system transacts operations. In Treasury borrowing operations, the open market is the money market in the case of short-term obligations, or the capital market in the case of long-term obligations.

In general, the term refers to a broad and freely competitive market, a market which is open to many buyers and sellers, and in which prices (whether commodities, securities, or money rates) are determined by such competition. Although organized markets, such as commodity exchanges and stock exchanges, restrict floor trading to members only, buyers and sellers among the public maintaining accounts with members may freely transact business on such markets through such accounts.

OPEN MARKET COMMITTEE *See* FEDERAL OPEN MARKET COMMITTEE.

BIBLIOGRAPHY

FEDERAL RESERVE BOARD OF GOVERNORS. *Annual reports.*
SARGENT, T. J., and SMITH, B. D. "Irrelevance of Open Market Operations in Some Economies with Government Currency Being Denominated in Rate of Return." *American Economic Review*, March, 1987.

OPEN MARKET OPERATIONS The New York Federal Reserve Bank is authorized to conduct transactions for the system open market account, pursuant to directives of the FEDERAL OPEN MARKET COMMITTEE, including the following: purchase and sale of government securities in the open market and exchange of such securities at maturity; purchase and sale of bankers acceptances in the open market for its own account; purchase of securities and acceptances under REPURCHASE AGREEMENTS; purchase and sale of foreign currencies in the form of cable transfers in the open market for the system open market account and maintenance of reciprocal currency arrangements with foreign banks (*see* SWAP NETWORK); direct purchase of government securities from the United States as may be necessary for the temporary accommodation of the Treasury Department as authorized (12 CFR 270.4(c) and (d)).

The purposes of open market operations may be summarized as follows: (1) to contract or expand the volume of excess reserves of member banks and thus affect the credit expansion power of member banks, (2) to influence the level of money rates through the quantitative effect upon bank excess reserves, (3) to provide orderly markets for government securities, (4) to influence the market for bills and commercial paper and levels of rediscounting and borrowing by member banks, and (5) to exercise effect upon foreign exchange markets and international capital movements through the effects upon money rates.

Although open market operations are considered to be the most flexible instrument of monetary policy at the initiative of the system, it is apparent that the most effective instrument from the standpoints of uniformity of effects as of effective dates upon member bank excess reserves and pervasiveness throughout the member banks is variation in legal reserve requirements. The latter, however, is considered more appropriate for the intermediate- and longer-term effectuation of policy.

BIBLIOGRAPHY

MEEKS, P. *Open Market Operations.* Federal Reserve Bank of New York, 1985.

OPEN MARKET RATES Money rates established for different classes of paper in the open market, or MONEY MARKET, as distinguished from the rates charged by banks to their own customers and from rates for advances and rediscounts established by Federal Reserve banks for member banks.

Open market rates are generally lower than the rates charged by banks to their own customers, including prime rates charged to most highly rated customers borrowing in large amounts. Thus one of the motivations for open market borrowing via commerical paper is the generally lower rates on such paper than on direct bank loans. Open market rates and yields on paper eligible for open market operations of the Federal Open Market Committee, such as Treasury bills and other short-term government securities and bankers acceptances, are also usually below the prime discount rates of Federal Reserve banks, although there is more correlation between Treasury bill rates and discount rates of the Fed. Thus Federal Reserve bank discount rates are usually under the market, as contrasted to the Bank of England's bank rate above the market.

See PRIME RATE.

OPEN MORTGAGE A mortgage that does not exclude the possibility of issuance of further debt thereunder, as distinguished from a CLOSED END MORTGAGE. In an open mortgage, there is no maximum amount of debt in bonds or notes authorized for issuance under its terms, although in practice protective or restrictive covenants actually limit the total amount of debt, including new debt, to prescribed minimal ratios in relation to assets and defined earnings coverages. A variation of the open mortgage is the limited open-end mortgage in which the total authorization, although fixed, is very high relative to actual financing needs, so that a large margin for additional financing is available, subject usually to protective covenants. Under the open or limited open-end mortgage, specific issues of bonds are issued in series from time to time.
See OPEN-END BONDS.

OPEN ORDER *See* ORDERS.

OPERATING ASSETS TURNOVER In financial statement analysis, one indicator of relative capital investment requirements of comparative firms and industries is the ratio of sales or revenues for a given year to the average total investment in tangible operating assets. The concept of tangible operating assets comprehends total assets involved in actual operations, excluding such nonoperating assets as investments in subsidiaries and excluding intangible assets such as goodwill. The ratio will indicate how much in sales or revenues is generated by operating assets in a given accounting year. Heavy-capital-using industries, such as the public utilities and railroads, have low turnovers of operating assets; by contrast, wholesale and retail trade firms have high turnovers of operating assets.
See STATEMENT ANALYSIS.

OPERATING COMPANY Any company that performs actual manufacturing or merchandising operations; one that conducts business operations as distinguished from a controlling or holding company, which does not itself operate but controls the policies of its subsidiary operating companies through stock ownership. Operating companies are underlying or subsidiary companies, the majority of the stock of which presumably is owned by a controlling company.

OPERATING CYCLE The time between the acquisition of inventory and the conversion of the inventory back into cash. The operating cycle of a business is also referred to as the cash cycle and the earnings cycle. For some industries such as a distillery, the operating cycle may extend 10 years or longer. For a grocer, the operating cycle would be measured in days. The normal operating cycle of a business is crucial to what determines whether assets and liabilities are current or noncurrent. For example, current assets include cash and other assets that are expected to be turned into cash, sold, or exchanged within the normal operating cycle of the enterprise or one year, whichever is longer. Current liabilities are liabilities that come due within the normal operating cycle or one year, whichever is longer. The normal operating cycle of a business is illustrated here:

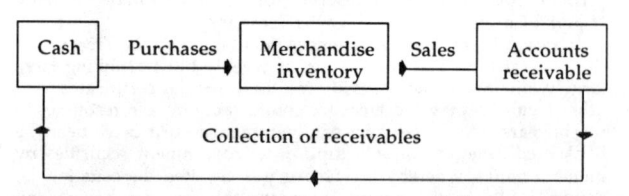

| Cash | Purchases | Merchandise inventory | Sales | Accounts receivable |

Collection of receivables

OPERATING EXPENSES The costs of conducting business exclusive of what are designated as fixed charges. In an industrial concern, operating expenses include manufacturing (factory) costs and selling and general administrative expenses, except taxes and interest on funded debt. In a merchandising concern, operating expenses are determined in the same way except that the cost of merchandise sold is substituted for manufacturing costs. In a railroad or public utility corporation, operating expenses consist of all expenses, except interest on bonds, rentals, and taxes. The Interstate Commerce Commission defines railroad operating expenses to consist of five groups of costs: (1) maintenance of way and structures, (2) maintenance of equipment, (3) conducting transportation, (4) traffic expenses, and (5) general expenses.

OPERATING RATIO The ratio of operating expenses to sales or revenues, which is a test of operating efficiency, measuring the total operating expenses per dollar of gross.

In manufacturing or trading concerns, the ratio of gross trading profit, after deduction of cost of goods sold from sales, indicates the extent of the mark-up or gross margin of profit. After selling and administrative expenses are deducted, the net operating profit in relation to sales indicates the overall operating ratio, including overhead.

In the case of railroads and public utilities, the operating ratio is the ratio of total operating expenses to gross revenues. The lower the ratio, the greater the ability to carry a larger burden of fixed charges and thus to incur additional debt.

OPERATORS Persons who speculate more or less actively in securities, either for their own accounts or as agents for principals. The term especially implies those who treat speculation professionally and whose dealings ordinarily have considerable influence upon price fluctuations. A synonymous term is TRADER, although traders characteristically seek to profit from secondary or intermediate price fluctuations, whereas operators take substantial long or short positions for cyclical as well as intermediate swings.

OPINION An AUDIT opinion expresses the auditor's conclusion concerning the financial statements. Audit opinions can be unqualified, qualified, adverse, or a disclaimer (the auditor cannot express an opinion). Reporting standards for auditing require that the auditor comment in a report on whether the financial statements are presented in accordance with generally accepted accounting principles, the accounting principles have been consistently applied from period to period, and that the disclosures in the financial statements are reasonably adequate.

If an unqualified opinion is not warranted, the audit may be required to modify the opinion. Such situations arise because the statements do not conform to generally accepted accounting principles, uncertainties exist concerning a contingency on the statements, limitations have been imposed on the scope of the auditor's examination, accounting principles have not been consistently applied, other auditors have performed a part of the examination, or the auditor wants to explain or emphasize a particular matter.

OPOSSMS Options to purchase or sell specified mortgage-backed securities.
See FINANCIAL INSTRUMENTS: RECENT INNOVATIONS.

OPPORTUNITY COST The cost of foregoing one thing—an investment, capital asset—to get an acceptable alternative. Opportunity costs are used primarily in decision making and not in product costing.
See OPPORTUNITY COST ANALYSIS.

OPPORTUNITY COST ANALYSIS The profit, or contribution, that is lost or foregone by using limited resources for a particular purpose. Opportunity costs arise from diverting an input factor from one use to another. Such costs do not require cash receipts or disbursements. Opportunity costs do not appear in the accounting records because they do not reflect a completed transaction.

Opportunity cost analysis is especially useful when evaluating alternatives. For example, there is an opportunity cost involved in using a machine to manufacture one product instead of another. To illustrate opportunity cost analysis, assume that a company can purchase some parts that it needs for production purposes for $10,000 from a supplier. It can make the parts for $8,000. However, if it makes the parts, it must use plant space that could be rented for $3,000. Opportunity cost analysis proceeds as follows:

	Make	Buy
Cost of obtaining parts	$ 8,000	$10,000
Opportunity cost: rental income lost	3,000	
Total	$11,000	$10,000

The company should purchase the parts from the outside supplier at a lower cost than it can make the parts when opportunity costs are considered.

OPTIMIZATION Economic decision making emphasizes the efficient allocation of resources to maximize or minimize an objective, such as maximizing profits or minimizing costs. The mathematical solution to such problems is optimization.

OPTIMUM SCALE OF OPERATION Scale or size of operation at which the lowest point on the average cost curve is attained.

OPTIONAL BONDS *See* CALLABLE BONDS.

OPTION DAY The day on which an option, e.g., a PUT (to sell) or a CALL (to buy), will expire unless exercised. If it is not profitable to exercise the option, the cost of the option may be considered a minor cost, in either the speculative sense or the protective sense (use of the put or call to protect an existing long or short position).

OPTION PERIOD The duration of an option as specified in the option contract, during which the person holding the option has the privilege of deciding whether or not he will exercise it, i.e., buy or sell, as the option might call for. The longer the duration, all things being equal, the more valuable the option. Under the Internal Revenue Code of 1954, "restricted stock options" may be exercised within ten years from the date of granting of the option.
See OPTIONS.

OPTIONS The privileges of buying and/or selling specified securities or commodities in specified amounts, at specified prices, and for a specified duration of time. Since consideration passes for such options, they are legally binding contracts for their duration. Most customary options are those to buy or sell securities, commodities, or real estate, but option contracts may be made for almost any good or service. Rights under options are sometimes sufficiently valuable to command substantial premiums.

Methods of trading on the New York Stock Exchange include seller's options calling for delivery times longer than the regular way basis of fourth full business day after date of transaction. On the stock exchanges, also, it is customary for the exchange's rules to specify that neither a member acting as specialist, nor a member organization in which such member is a participant, nor any other participant in such member firms shall directly or indirectly acquire or grant any option to buy or sell or to receive or deliver shares of the stock in which such member is a specialist. Such a rule is Rule 105 of the New York Stock Exchange. No member while on the floor shall initiate the purchase or sale on the exchange for his own account, or for any account in which he, his member firm, or any participant therein is directly or indirectly interested, of any stock in which he holds or has granted any put, call, straddle or option, or in which he has knowledge that his member organization or any participant therein holds or has granted any such options (Rule 96). Such rules reflect the concern that interests in options might lead to manipulation, as options were a favorite device of POOL operators.

Standardized Options Trading. Options are traded on 14 exchanges in the United States. Daily volume often exceeds a million contracts. Many options are also traded in the over-the-counter market.

These options give a holder the right to buy from the OPTIONS CLEARING CORPORATION, in the case of a call, or sell to the Options Clearing Corporation, in the case of a put, the number of shares (typically 100 shares) of the underlying security covered by the option at the stated exercise price by the proper filing of an exercise notice with the Options Clearing Corporation prior to the fixed expiration time of the option. The designation of a stock option includes the name of the underlying stock, the expiration month, the exercise price, and whether the option is a call or a put.

The settlement procedures of the Options Clearing Corporation are designed so that for every outstanding option there is a writer-and a clearing member who is or who represents the writer-of an option of the same series who has undertaken to perform the obligations of the clearing corporation in the event an exercise notice for the option is assigned to him. As a result, no matter how many options of a given series may be outstanding at any time, there will always be a group of writers of options of the same series who, in the aggregate, have undertaken to perform the clearing corporation's obligations with respect to such options.

Once an exercise notice for an option is assigned to a particular writer, that writer is contractually obligated to his broker to deliver the underlying security, in the case of a call, or to pay the aggregate exercise price, in the case of a put, in accordance with the terms of the option. This contractual obligation of the writer is secured by the securities or other margin which the writer is required to deposit with his broker with respect to the writing of all options.

The clearing member representing the writer is also contractually obligated, whether or not his customer performs, to perform the clearing corporation's obligations on an assigned option. Standing behind a clearing member's obligations are (1) the clearing member's net capital, (2) the clearing member's margin deposits with the clearing corporation, (3) the clearing corporation's lien on certain of the clearing member's assets, and (4) the clearing fund. The clearing fund is the minimum initial deposit of each clearing member, upon admission to membership, of $10,000 plus such additional amount as may be fixed by the clearing corporation, redetermined on a monthly basis pursuant to a formula prescribed in the rules of the clearing corporation. All clearing fund deposits must be made in cash or by the deposit of securities issued or guaranteed by the U.S. government and having a maturity of ten years or less.

Each clearing member is required, with respect to each stock option for which it represents the writer (such positions in options are referred to as short positions), either to deposit the underlying stock (in the case of a call) or U.S. Treasury bills in an amount at least equal to the exercise price (in the case of a put) or in the alternative to deposit and maintain specific margin with the clearing corporation amounting to 100% or such greater percentage as the clearing corporation prescribes (as of June 30, 1981, 130%) of the closing asked quotation for the option on the exchanges on the preceding business day.

Until June 1985 each class of options was assigned to one of three expiration month cycles: the January-April-July-October cycle, the February-May-August-November cycle, or the March-June-September-December cycle. Trading in options of a particular expiration month normally began approximately nine months earlier, so that at any given time there were generally three different expiration months open for trading, at 3-month intervals, in each class of options. For example, on the day following the expiration of January options, trading in options expiring in the following October would normally be opened (and trading in options expiring in April and July had been previously opened). From time to time exchanges changed the expiration month cycles to which particular classes of options were assigned.

In June 1985 CBOE piloted sequential expiration of stock options in 20 option classes. This pilot met the needs of market participants trading primarily in near-term series, while enhancing volume and liquidity in those classes. CBOE and other options exchanges expanded the sequential expiration pilot floorwide in August 1987.

The SEC, as of October 22, 1989, approved the options exchanges subsequently implemented the fixing of exercise prices at 5-point intervals for stocks trading at up to 100; and at 10-point intervals for stocks trading above 100. When trading is introduced in a new expiration month, an exchange ordinarily selects the two or three standard exercise prices surrounding the current market price of the underlying stock. For example, if the underlying stocks trades at 37 during the period when exercise prices are being selected for a new expiration month, two new series of options would ordinarily be introduced with exercise prices at 35 and 40.

However, as of April 1985, CBOE offered 2 1/2 point strike price intervals for options on stocks trading below $25, to enhance depth and liquidity in lower-priced options by giving investors more near-the-money strikes for hedging purposes.

In May 1987 CBOE applied to the SEC for approval of long-term two-year options in SPX (The Standard and Poor's 500 index option) with strike price intervals of 25-points, compared with SPX's current (as of August 1987) 5-point strike prices. Long-term options were designed to protect institutional portfolios from long-term market moves.

The appended table shows the volume of various options traded on the exchanges and in the over-the-counter market.

Uses of Options. Options may be purchased or sold through securities brokers, many of whom are members of one or more of the exchanges. The price (premium) of an option, which is paid by the purchaser and is received by the writer (seller) of the option, is determined in the exchange's auction market. Both purchasers and writers pay the transaction costs, which may include commissions charged or incurred in connection with the options transactions and may be significant. Once an option has been issued by the clearing corporation, the contractual ties between the holder and the writer of the option are severed. Instead, the holder of an option looks to the clearing corporation and not to any particular writer for performance in the event of exercise. Since each time an option is issued to a holder there is a writer of an option of the same series contractually obligated to the clearing corporation (through a clearing member), the aggregate obligations of the clearing corporation to holders of options are backed up by the aggregate obligations that writers owe to the clearing corporation. Upon exercise of an option, the clearing corporation assigns an exercise notice to a clearing member's account with the clearing corporation selected at random from among all clearing member accounts reflecting the writing of options of the same series as the exercised option.

The Option Clearing Corporation's prospectus lists the following possible uses for exchange-traded options.

1. Using calls for leverage potential. Because the premium of a call is considerably less than the cost of the underlying security covered by the call, a given amount of funds may purchase calls covering a much larger quantity of such security than could be purchased directly. By so leveraging his funds, the purchaser of calls has the opportunity to benefit from any significant increase in the price of the security to a greater extent than had he purchased the security outright. However, if the call is not sold while it has remaining value and if the security does not appreciate during the life of the call, the call purchaser may lose his entire investment in the call; whereas had he purchased the security directly, he might have had no loss or only a paper loss. Moreover, if the underlying stock pays dividends, they would have been received by the investor as a stockholder, but not as the holder of calls. In addition, except where the time value of the remaining life of a call may be realized in the secondary market afforded by the exchange-trading of the options, for a call purchase to be profitable the market price of the underlying security must exceed the exercise price by more than the premium and transaction costs paid in connection with the purchase of the call *and* its sale or exercise.

Volume of Exchange—Traded Options
(Thousands)

	Call contracts	Put contracts
CBOE (Includes all CBOE options contracts)		
1976	21,501	—
1977	23,583	1,257 *
1978	30,743	3,979
1979	29,918	5,250
1980	42,941	9,954
1981	40,799	16,783
1982	50,214	25,507
1983	57,858	24,610
1984	78,933	44,341
1985	100,156	48,733
1986	114,788	65,570
NYSE		
1985	126 *	37 *
1986	952 *	99 *

	Total options volume
NASDAQ	
1985	107
1986 (January through July)	46

* Equities only
Sources: Securities and Exchange Commission and The Chicago Board Options Exchange.

2. Using calls as an alternative to investing in the underlying stock. This use of calls assumes that an investor who anticipates a rise in the price of the underlying stock, but does not think it prudent to subject himself to the risk of a severe price decline by buying the underlying stock outright, will invest the entire difference between the cost of the call and the cost of the underlying stock in a relatively risk-free manner (such as a savings account or Treasury bills), the income from which helps to offset the cost of the call. To the extent this is not done, the call investment becomes more of a leverage device, *supra*. Moreover, a call investor does not have the choice of waiting out an unexpected downturn in the security price beyond the expiration date of the call. In addition, the very security that might be considered more conservative from a direct purchase standpoint could be more risky as a call investment, because its high stability may also mean that its price is less likely to rise significantly during the relatively short duration of a call.
3. Hedging a short position against a price increase. A call gives the holder the right to acquire the underlying security at a fixed price, so that an investor intending to sell a security short in anticipation of a decline in the price of the security may buy calls to hedge against a rise instead in the price of the security. If the security's price remains the same for the life of the call, the investor will have lost the amount of the call's premium and transaction costs. If it declines, any profit made in the short-selling transaction will be reduced by the amount of the premium and transaction costs. However, should the price of the security rise, the short seller may be protected against a substantial loss he would otherwise have had to incur if he had to cover his short position at the increased market price. Such hedged short selling, although less risky than unhedged short selling, is considered suitable only for sophisticated investors.
4. Fixing the price of a future security purchase. If an investor anticipates the purchase of a security at some time in the future, such as when funds become available, and considers the present price of the security to be attractive, he may fix that price (plus the premium and transaction costs) as the purchase price of the security by buying a call that does not expire until after the time the purchase is anticipated. At that time, he can merely exercise the call to acquire the security (unless the market price of the security has declined below the exercise price, in which event the security can be bought in the open market and the call allowed to lapse without exercise).

The following are possible uses for put options.

1. Buying puts in anticipation of a price decline in the underlying security. This use contemplates the purchase of puts by an investor who does not own the underlying security. The put buyer, like the short seller, seeks to benefit from a decline in the market price of the underlying security. Unlike the short seller, the put buyer does not become subject to margin and margin calls, nor to the theoretically unlimited risk of the short seller should the price of the underlying security rise instead of declining. On the other hand, if the put is not sold when it has remaining value and if the market price of the underlying security remains equal to or greater than the exercise price during the life of the put, the put buyer will lose his entire investment in the put option. Moreover, unless the put may be sold in a closing sale transaction, in order for the purchase of a put to be profitable the market price of the underlying security must decline sufficiently below the exercise price to cover the premium and transaction costs. As the put buyer acquires puts covering a greater number of shares than he might have sold short directly, he is in a more highly leveraged position and is subject to the increased risks of that position. Accordingly, the use of puts for leverage is extremely risky and is considered unsuitable for investors who do not have the financial capability to withstand large losses.
2. Buying puts to hedge a long position in the underlying security against a price decline. Puts may be purchased to protect the profits in an existing long position in an underlying security, or to protect a newly acquired position in an underlying security against a substantial decline in its market value. In either case, the protection is provided only during the life of the put, when the holder of the put is able to sell the underlying security at the put exercise price regardless of any decline in the market price of the underlying security. An investor using puts in this manner will have reduced any profit he might otherwise have realized in his long security position by the premium paid for the put and transaction costs.

Writing options. The writer of a call assumes an obligation to deliver the underlying security covered by the call against payment of the aggregate exercise price upon the assignment to him of an exercise notice by the Options Clearing Corporation. This obligation continues until the writer closes out his position in the option; but once a writer has been assigned an exercise notice in respect of the option, he will thereafter be unable to effect a closing purchase transaction in that option and will be required to delivery the underlying security.

A principal reason for writing calls on a securities portfolio is to attempt to realize, through the receipt of premium income, a greater return than would be earned on the securities alone. The covered call writer (who owns the underlying security) has in return for the premium given up the opportunity for profit from a price increase in the underlying security above the exercise price so long as his writer obligation continues, but has retained the risk of loss should the price of the security decline. The call writer may be required to sell his securities at the exercise price at any time upon being assigned an exercise notice, and in such circumstances the net proceeds that he realizes from the sale of his securities at the exercise price may be substantially below the prevailing market price.

Where the writer of a call owns neither the underlying security nor some other security (such as a warrant or option or convertible security for the underlying security) to acquire the underlying security, his naked option position is extremely risky and he may incur larger losses. Such an uncovered call writer generally hopes to realize income from the writing transaction, but without the necessity of commiting capital to the purchase of the underlying security. However, he is required to maintain margin with his broker, and as distinguished from the covered call writer, he stands to incur an out-of-pocket loss if the price of the underlying security increases above the exercise price; the extent to which the current market value of the underlying security exceeds the aggregate exercise price (which theoretically can be without limit), reduced by the premium but increased by transaction costs, represents the uncovered call writer's loss. Because of the potentially large (theoretically unlimited) losses which may be incurred, such transactions in uncovered calls are considered suitable only for sophisticated investors having the financial capacity to sustain such losses, including liquid assets available to meet margin calls and to cover by purchasing the underlying security, unless they are engaged in arbitrage or hedge transactions.

Like the writer of a call, a put writer hopes to realize premium income. If the put writer does not have a short position in the underlying security or a long position in another put covering the same underlying securities (that expires no sooner than the put written and that has an exercise price not less than the exercise price of the put written), the put writer must either maintain margin with his broker on account of writing the put or else deposit with his broker or an approved bank or other depository an amount equal to the aggregate exercise price. The risk position of a put writer who does not hold either a short position in the underlying security or another put of the same class is similar to that of a covered call writer who owns the underlying securities: the put writer stands to incur a loss if and to the extent that the price of the underlying security falls below the exercise price, reduced by the premium received for writing the option but increased by the transaction costs. If the put writer deposits an amount equal to the aggregate exercise price of the put with an approved bank or other depository in lieu of maintaining margin on his position and if the deposited funds are invested for the writer's account (or if the writer independently invests an amount equal to the aggregate exercise price), the put writer will receive the income earned on that investment in addition to premium income.

Puts may also be written by investors as a means of acquiring the underlying security at a net cost which is less than the current market price. If the put is exercised, the put writer's cost of acquiring the underlying security will be the exercise price less the premium. If the put is not exercised, the put writer will not have acquired the underlying security, but will nonetheless have earned the premium for writing the put.

If an investor writes a put covering an underlying security that he has sold short, the investor still hopes to realize premium income in the writing transaction, but his risk position is different from that of the put writer without such a short position. In the former case, the investor may still incur a loss in his put writing transaction if the price of the underlying security falls below the exercise price, but this loss may be offset by a profit realized in the related short security position. The put writer who is also a short seller of the underlying security bears the risk of his short security position. Thus if the price of the underlying security should increase instead of decline, such an investor stands to incur a loss in covering his short security position, offset to the extent of the premium received in the put writing transaction. Potential losses which may be incurred in short selling transactions are limited only by the extent of the increase in the price of the security sold short. Accordingly, writing puts against short positions in the underlying security is risky, and is considered suitable only for sophisticated investors who have the means to meet margin calls and to sustain large losses.

A put writer may liquidate his position prior to the assignment of an exercise notice by purchasing a put of the same series as the put previously written. To the extent that the cost of such a liquidating purchase plus transaction costs exceeds the premium initially received, the put writer will have incurred a loss in the put transaction.

Spread positions. A spread position is one in which an investor is the holder of one or more options of a given class and concurrently maintains a position as a writer of one or more options of different series within that same class, e.g., a spread position in which the investor is the holder of an XYZ April 35 call and the writer of an XYZ January 35 call. Spread positions may involve holding an option with a different expiration date from that of the option written, as in the preceding example, or holding and writing options with different exercise prices but with the same expiration date, or holding and writing options in which both the expiration date and the exercise price differ.

Spread positions may be undertaken to fulfill a variety of investing strategies, and they are among the most complicated of all option transactions. No investor should establish spread positions unless he thoroughly understands the mechanics and risks involved and is financially able to bear the risks. In addition to the same risks that are involved in the purchase and writing of options, spreads are subject to certain special risks, including difficulty of execution, the risk of exercises, and the increased risk arising from closing out one side of the spread transaction. An investor who writes a spread side is subject to being assigned at any time prior to the option's expiration an exercise notice to purchase or deliver the underlying security, so that he will no longer be in a spread position and instead will be subject to the risks of the other side of the original spread.

Straddles. A straddle is an equivalent number of puts and calls covering the same underlying security and having the same exercise price and expiration date. An investor may buy a straddle or may write a straddle. As with spreads, straddle orders are more difficult to execute than orders for puts or calls alone, because they require the execution of orders covering different options at or about the same time. An investor who buys a straddle generally anticipates relatively large price fluctuations in the underlying security, but is unsure as to the direction in which the price may move. Because the purchase of a straddle represents the purchase of two options, the premium for a straddle is greater than that for a put or a call alone. This means that the price of the underlying security must rise or fall enough to permit the investor to recover the premium paid for the straddle plus transaction costs before a profit may be realized.

An investor who writes a straddle generally wishes to earn more premium income than he would earn from writing a put or a call alone. It should be noted that if the price of the underlying security both rises and falls during the life of straddle, both the put and the call could be exercised, thus resulting in heavy losses. These risks may be somewhat moderated if the investor buys the underlying security at the same time that he writes a straddle covering that security, which serves to cover his obligation as a writer of the call component of the straddle. As in the case of other options transactions, writers of straddles are subject to the applicable margin requirements.

The intrinsic value of an option reflects the amount by which a option is in the money (the amount of the intrinsic value). At a time when the current market price of ABC stock is $56 a share, an ABC $50 call would have intrinsic value of $6 a share. If the price of the stock drops below $50, the call has no intrinsic value. Time value refers to whatever value the option has in addition to its intrinsic value. For example, when the market price of the ABC stock is $50 a share, an ABC $50 call may command a premium of $4 a share. The $4 is time value and reflects the expectation that, prior to expiration, the price of ABC stock will increase by an amount that would enable an investor to sell or exercise the option at a profit. An option may have both intrinsic value and time value, i.e., its premium may exceed its intrinsic value. For example, with the market price of the ABC stock at $55, an ABC $50 call may command a premium of $6 a share—an intrinsic value of $5 a share and a time value of $1 a share.

Incentive Compensation Stock Options. In the field of corporation finance, options granted to members of management have become an increasingly widespread type of incentive compensation in recent years.

The incentive stock option (ISO) authorized by the 1981 Tax Act provides within its limits more attractive tax treatment for the recipient, similar to that which applied to the formerly authorized qualified stock option. The recipient does not pay tax when he exercises the option, the tax being deferred until the stock is sold, which must be not earlier than one year after the date of exercise and two years after the date of granting the option. At such time of sale, the difference between the exercise price and the sale price is taxable not at ordinary income tax rates, as in the case of nonqualified options whether or not the stock was sold, but at capital gains rates. But the issuing corporation cannot take the difference between the exercise price and the sale price as a tax deductible form of compensation, as in the case of nonqualified options. Moreover, the corporation is limited in ISOs to a maximum dollar amount of stock per recipient executive in a calendar year (although if the corporation does not grant an option in a given year, it may carry forward half of the unused amount for three years).

In the case of STOCK APPRECIATION RIGHTS (SARs), the recipient is paid the difference between the exercise price and the market price. But there is an accounting disadvantage to the corporation in that the increase in value of the outstanding stock appreciation rights must be charged to current earnings of the corporation, which could prove to be an appreciable depressant to the corporation's earnings.

In investment banking, the investment banker underwriting new issues, particularly speculative issues of relatively new and untried firms, might specify, in addition to the usual underwriting spread (the difference between public offering price and net proceeds to the issuing corporation), additional underwriters' compensation in the form of options on additional stock at low prices as compared with the public offering price on current issue. Thus if the new issue is successful and the public offering price is maintained or commands a premium, the underwriters are in position to exercise such options profitably within the option period. The same principle would apply in the case of stock purchase warrants issued to the underwriters in such situations.

Summary. In addition to the market risks inherent in options transactions, there are special risks relating to the systems and procedures of the exchanges and the clearing corporation. Because of the technicalities of the options and option combinations, as well as rules of the exchanges concerned and of the Options Clearing Corporation, and the necessity for keeping closely posted on market behavior of the underlying stock and appurtenant positions of the investor in options, investors should become thoroughly familiar with the contents of the prospectus and the procedures of the Options Clearing Corporation. Success in option operations also requires a close relationship between the investor and his account executive and knowledge by the latter of the investor's goals and objectives.

BIBLIOGRAPHY

Major brokerage firms have numerous publications explaining options and options trading.

OPTIONS CLEARING CORPORATION A Delaware corporation whose stock is equally owned by the Chicago Board Options Exchange, the American Stock Exchange, the Philadelphia Stock Exchange, and the Pacific Stock Exchange. It is registered as a clearing agency under the Securities Exchange Act, and it and its clearing members are subject to the Exchange Act and the regulatory jurisdiction of the Securities and Exchange Commission.

See OPTIONS.

ORDER INSTRUMENTS *See* PAY TO ORDER.

ORDERS This term has two meanings:

1. Written instructions to pay money, such as checks, drafts, bills of exchange, money orders, etc.
2. Instructions to buy or sell securities (or commodities) to a broker.

In securities market practice, orders of various types have conventionally come to be associated with certain implied characteristics and treatment. The following summary illustrates the various types of orders for round lots in stock exchange practice:

1. Basic instructions in order.
    a. Buy order-margin account or cash account.
    b. Sell order-sell short (margin required) or sell long. The SHORT SALE is to be executed under specific rules and procedures.
2. Size of order.
    a. Round lot.
    b. ODD LOT.
3. Price instructions.
    a. Market order-to be executed as promptly as possible, at the best possible prevailing price, by the broker in competition with other brokers on the floor for executions.
    b. Limit order-to be executed at the price limit or better (if buy order: at no more than the limit price, lower if possible; if sell order: at not less than the limit price, higher if possible).
4. Special orders.
    a. Stop order. Stop orders, whether to buy or to sell, specify a price. When the market for the stock touches that price, the stop order is elected, and it immediately thereafter is to be treated as a market order, i.e., to be executed as promptly as possible, at best possible price. The stop order, therefore, differs from the limit order in that the price specified is not determining of price limit; in a stop order, the price specified is the point for treatment as a market order. Thus, stop orders are in effect deferred market orders. In times of unusual market activity in specific stocks, to prevent aggravation of volatile market action, stock exchange rules reserve the right of the stock exchange administration to suspend stop orders in such stocks. In a declining market, for example, elected stop orders would act like land mines, exploding into market orders to sell as the market declined, and snowballing the market decline.
        (1) To buy. Placed at specified price *above* the market; for example, a short seller having sold short at 60 would place a stop order to buy (cover) at 61 or 62, so that in case the stock goes up instead of down, the stop order will stop loss.
        (2) To sell. Placed at specified price *below* the market; for example, a person long of stock at 60 places a stop order to sell at 59 or 58. In case the stock goes down instead of up, the stop order will stop loss.
    b. Stop and limit order-a combination of both the stop order, becoming elected when the price specified is touched by the market, and the limit order, thereafter to be treated as a limit order with regard to price (to be executed at limit or better). For example, a person has just bought 100 shares of U.S. Steel at 90. He places an order: "Sell 100 shares U.S. Steel at 87 stop, limit 86." Should the market drop to 87, the order is elected for action, but to be executed at not less than 86, higher if possible. Like the straight limit orders, stop and limit orders because of their price limitation may cause the customer to miss the market in the event of a pronounced uptrend or downtrend, as the case may be.
        (1) To buy, price specified *above* current market.
        (2) To sell, price specified *below* current market.
    c. Other types of orders.
        (1) Discretionary order, completely discretionary (name of stock, number of shares, buy or sell, price, timing) or partially so (discretion as to price and timing in the broker). Completely discretionary orders are not forbidden under New York Stock Exchange rule, but they must be initialed by a general partner of the member firm as of date of entry. Partially discretionary orders are not subject to this rule. Most brokers discourage such orders because of the extra responsibility involved.
        (2) Cancel orders.
            (a) Straight cancel, simply canceling an existing order.
            (b) Cancel former order (CFO order), canceling previous order, but replacing it with details in current order.
            (c) Immediate or cancel order (fill or kill order) to be executed immediately or else canceled. This type of order might be used to test the market in a stock.
5. Time specification.
    a. Day order, good only until the close of the trading session on the day of entry. All orders, unless time is otherwise specified, are day orders. All market orders are day orders automatically; limit orders, however, may specify a longer time limit.
    b. Other time orders, e.g., week order (GTW order) or month order (GTM order), good this week or good this month.
    c. Open orders (GTC orders), good 'til canceled. Under New York Stock Exchange rules, GTC orders must be reconfirmed by customers at least every six months (last trading day of April and October). Open buy orders are marked down by the dividend on ex-dividend dates.

In volume, market orders and day orders constitute the bulk of orders handled.

ORDINARY RECEIPTS In accounting, SALES or revenues from normal operations, excluding nonoperating income, whether of a recurring or nonrecurring nature.
See REVENUE.

ORDINARY SHARES The English equivalent of U.S. common stock. In England, ordinary shares are often divided into two classes, preferred shares and deferred shares.

ORGANIZATIONAL BEHAVIOR Planning, control, budgeting, and pricing activities of management are influenced by and have influence on the behavior of people who work in the organization. Major areas in organizational behavior include:

1. *Organizational theory and decision making:* This area deals with such matters as organizational structure (centralized/decentralized; functions of organizations; line and staff structures).
2. *Motivation and perception:* Human needs, levels of needs, and relationships.
3. *Communications:* Formal and informal communication structures and networks.
4. *Behavioral science:* Behavioral impacts of management and managerial activities.
5. *Ethical issues:* Competence, independence, integrity, and fairness (equity).

Behavior in organizations is conditioned by many factors including organizational structure, management styles, control systems, and others.

BIBLIOGRAPHY

DRESSLER, GARY, *Organization Theory* (Prentice-Hall, Englewood Cliffs, N.J., 1986).
STEERS, RICHARD M., *Introduction to Organizational Behavior* (Scott, Foresman, 1984).

ORGANIZATION CERTIFICATE One of the documents executed and filed in the organization of a bank. The execution of this instrument is one of the steps requisite to the organization of a national bank.

An applicant cannot conduct banking business until final approval (a charter) is received. If preliminary approval is granted, certain procedural actions must be taken by the applicant before a charter can be granted. These actions include establishing the bank as a body corporate, with directors, articles of association, and bylaws. Appropriate forms and instructions will be furnished with a preliminary approval letter. The bank does not become a body corporate until the organization certificate and articles of association have been accepted for filing by the regional administrator.

Organization certificate forms (CC 7020-20) for national banks are furnished by each regional office and by the Bank Organization and Structure Division, Office of the Comptroller of the Currency, Washington, D.C. They must state the name of the proposed bank, its location, capital, number of shares, and the name, address, financial worth of, and number of shares to be held by each stockholder. The organization certificate must be executed in duplicate before a notary; one copy is forwarded to the regional administrator, the other retained by the bank. It must be signed and acknowledged by the same persons who sign the ARTICLES OF ASSOCIATION. When all the necessary papers have been filed and the subscription to Federal Reserve bank stock has been paid (3% payment of the subscription of 6% of capital and surplus), a certificate of authority to commence business (to be published for specified 60-day period) will be issued to the bank by the Comptroller of the Currency.

ORGANIZATION COSTS Costs related to getting an enterprise started. Organization costs are incurred during the formation of the enterprise and prior to income-producing operations. Expenditures usually classified as organization costs include such items as promoters', attorneys', and accountants' fees, underwriters' commissions, securities registration and listing fees, printing costs, etc. Such costs are ordinarily capitalized as an intangible asset or deferred charge and amortized (written off) over a period of time not to exceed 40 years. Expenditures relating to the organization of the enterprise are assumed to benefit the future and are considered assets in that without them the company could not have been started. In practice, some accountants treat organization costs as a reduction of contributed capital. This treatment is justified on the grounds that organization charges reflect a reduction of the receipts associated with the financing of the corporation.

ORGANIZATION FOR ECONOMIC COOPERATION AND DEVELOPMENT Succeeding the ORGANIZATION FOR EUROPEAN ECONOMIC COOPERATION (OEEC), this new organization came into being September 1, 1961, upon ratification of its convention, signed in Paris on December 15, 1960. OECD is headquartered in Paris. As of 1981 membership included all 18 European countries that participated in the OEEC (Austria, Belgium, Denmark, France, Federal Republic of Germany, Greece, Iceland, Ireland, Italy, Luxembourg, the Netherlands, Norway, Portugal, Spain, Sweden, Switzerland, Turkey, and the United Kingdom), Canada, the United States, Australia, Finland, Japan, and New Zealand, with Yugoslavia as an associate member. The organization is patterned after that of the OEEC, with the council of ministers being the chief governing body, whose decisions on matters referred to it must be unanimous. Organization for Economic Cooperation and Development (OECD) committees include Economic Policy Committee, Economic and Development Review Committee, Trade Committee, and Payments Committee (the EUROPEAN MONETARY AGREEMENT was continued under the OECD, for certain of the OECD countries, without the membership of Canada and the U.S.). These functional committees are concerned with their specialized areas among the objectives of the OECD, which are chiefly

1. To help member countries to achieve the highest sustainable rate of economic growth and of employment, to increase living standards, and at the same time to maintain financial stability;
2. To contribute to sound economic expansion, in member countries as well as in nonmember countries in the process of economic development;
3. To contribute to the expansion of world trade on a multilateral, nondiscriminatory basis, in accordance with existing international obligations.

Operating objectives include the extension and strengthening of the OEEC's practice of consultation on economic policies of member countries, with special attention to the harmonizing of national policies in their international effects. The new OECD took over and maintains the OEEC's codes of current invisible transactions and of capital movements, and it was contemplated that member obligations under these codes would be extended to transactions with all members of the INTERNATIONAL MONETARY FUND. When the OECD came into existence, the OEEC's code of trade liberalization was expiring.

Special emphasis of the OECD is on growth and development. Thus, it took over and continues the Development Assistance Group, formed by the OEEC in 1960 as the Development Assistance Committee, which is concerned with the formulation of policy on aid to the less developed countries.

ORGANIZATION FOR EUROPEAN ECONOMIC COOPERATION This organization has been replaced by the ORGANIZATION FOR ECONOMIC COOPERATION AND DEVELOPMENT (OECD). The following is included for historical interest.

This permanent form of group organization of the European countries receiving U.S. foreign aid had its genesis in the Committee of European Economic Cooperation, formed at a conference of the 16 recipient nations on July 12, 1947. The committee surveyed the needs of the respective countries and presented its report on requirements under the European Recovery Program (Marshall Plan).

The organization was formally organized under a special charter signed in Paris on April 16, 1948, the structure including (1) a council, composed of all members (18 European countries including West Germany) and headed by a chairman and two vice-chairmen, (2) an Executive Committee consisting of 7 members designated annually by the council; and (3) a secretary general, assisted by a first and second deputy secretary general, all three appointed by the council.

The Organization for European Economic Cooperation (OEEC) is credited with having been at the center of the movement toward European economic cooperation and having played a vital role in Western European economic recovery. It was a force, with its trade liberalization code, in reducing trade restrictions among its members. Its members established the European Payments Union (EPU) in 1950 as a clearing and credit mechanism for transactions among its members; upon establishment of currency convertibility for nonresidents by most of the member nations, the EPU was succeeded by the European Monetary Agreement (1958), providing for the European Fund (to make short-term credit available to member countries on an ad hoc basis in order to assist in temporary balance of payments difficulties) and the Multilateral System for Settlements, a means whereby participating members have the alternative of settling their claims and debts with one another either through market channels at any time or through the system at the end of each month. It continued to work in a variety of fields of common economic interest to members, including formulation and implementation of stabilization programs (e.g., for Turkey and Spain, the latter having become on July 20, 1959, the eighteenth member of the OEEC). A natural result of the OEEC's work has been establishment of the European Economic Community (Common Market) in 1957. The OEEC's EPA (European Production Agency) was created in 1953 as the operational agency of the OEEC, originally aimed at fostering increased European productivity in industry and agriculture, but later emphasizing sponsorship of cooperative research projects and providing various kinds of assistance to its less developed members.

ORGANIZATION OF A BANK See BANK ORGANIZATION.

ORGANIZATION OF ARAB PETROLEUM EXPORTING COUNTRIES The origins of the Organization of Arab Petroleum Exporting Countries (OAPEC) before its formal organization in Beirut in January, 1968, may be said to have been the meeting of oil and finance ministers of Arab countries in Baghdad in August, 1967, including producers and nonproducers of oil. The objectives were primarily political-to pressure pro-Israel countries by use of the oil weapon. Since the ORGANIZATION OF PETROLEUM EXPORTING COUNTRIES (OPEC) was already in existence, the charter of the OAPEC provided that determinations by the OPEC would also apply to OAPEC member countries. Also antedating the OAPEC, the Arab League (League of Arab States) was formed in March, 1945, in Cairo and served as a mediating and coordinating group among its members, besides coordinating military, diplomatic, and economic efforts against Israel. When Egypt signed a peace treaty with Israel, the league expelled Egypt and moved its headquarters to Tunis.

ORGANIZATION OF PETROLEUM EXPORTING COUNTRIES (OPEC) The formation of the Organization of Petroleum Exporting Countries (OPEC) in Baghdad on November 14, 1960, was precipitated by the decision of one of the giant Seven Sisters (Exxon, Texaco, Socal, Gulf, Mobil, British Petroleum, and

Shell) to cut its posted price per barrel for Arabian OIL by 7.5%, thus causing a loss of about $30 million in revenues or 10% for Saudi Arabia alone; and by the urging of Dr. Juan Perez Alfonzo, the Venezuelan oil minister, that the oil countries unite in control of supply, based on his observation of the success of the Texas Railroad Commission in administering its system of control of supply and allocation of "allowables."

At the beginning, the modest price objective was to restore the stable pre-1960 posted prices of the oil companies for output; and the organization did not achieve mandatory allocations of supply among its member nations, although agreement on price and supply objectives subsequently was sought at meetings of the OPEC (headquarters in Vienna). But the OPEC turned effectively aggressive even before the 1973-1974 embargo of shipments to the United States, Holland, and Denmark, by threatening to cut off shipments in 1967 and by entering into an effective agreement on higher prices. Following the Yom Kippur war, the ORGANIZATION OF ARAB PETROLEUM EXPORTING COUNTRIES (OAPEC) met in Kuwait on October 16, 1974, at which time the OPEC members asserted and took over from the oil companies the right to set posted prices and agreed on reducing production, demonstrating the ability to control prices as well as output along cartel lines.

The cumulative current account surplus for the years 1974-1981 of such OPEC members as Kuwait, Libya, Oman, Saudi Arabia, and the United Arab Emirates totaled some $350 billion, compared with the cumulative account surplus for the same period of $38 billion for other OPEC members (Algeria, Ecuador, Gabon, Indonesia, Iran, Iraq, Nigeria, and Venezuela). The pull of such surpluses upon oil-importing countries wreaked havoc upon their balances of payments, offset to an imperfect extent by the investments abroad of OPEC surpluses in short-term and long-term investments and bank deposits in such havens as the money and capital markets in the U.S. and U.K. and in turn the recycling of such funds by those centers to needy non-oil-producing countries. Besides reductions in flows of OPEC surpluses for investment in the international money and capital markets, the smaller OPEC surpluses may lead to switching from long-term to short-term holdings by the OPEC countries for easier repatriation in case of need. It is estimated that 75% of OPEC funds have flowed into U.S. dollars.

In the early 1980s, the price of crude oil in the United States peaked at nearly $36 per barrel. Recessions and curtailed world demand for oil have caused the price of crude oil to fall and the stability of OPEC to wain. In 1989, OPEC was not a significant factor in the world oil markets.

BIBLIOGRAPHY

ORGANIZATION OF PETROLEUM EXPORTING COUNTRIES. *Annual Review and Record.*

ORGANIZING FUNCTION Organizing is a major function of management. The primary purpose of organization is to provide for the efficient and effective accomplishment of the goals and objectives of the enterprise. The goals and objectives that are developed through the planning process serve as the basis of the organizing function.

Organizing an organization requires that managers establish patterns of relationships (structures, hierarchies) among people and other resources that work to produce an output or accomplish a common objective. Organizing is related to how work flows through the organization under guidance. It involves assigning responsibilities through the division of labor and the coordination of the parts into a cohesive whole. The coordination of effort requires the development of effective communications throughout the enterprise. Finally, organization requires the establishment of an authority structure that defines decision-making powers.

Organization theory has identified certain principles that can be used effectively in designing an organization structure:

1. *Specialization:* The tasks assigned to individuals should be limited.
2. *Objectivity:* Activities and functions that are directed towards achieving an enterprise's goals and objectives are to be provided.
3. *Specification:* Authority and responsibilities should be clearly communicated, preferably in writing.
4. *Authority and responsibility:* Authority given should be commensurate (equal) to responsibilities assigned.
5. *Unity of command:* Subordinates should have only one superior. Exceptions must be appropriately justified.

The organizational chart can also be designed to show line and staff relationships. Line positions involve persons who are directly associated with operations and who are directly responsible for creating and distributing the goods or services of the organization. Line authority is reflected by the typical chain of command that begins with the board of directors and extends down through various levels in the enterprise. Production and sales departments are examples of line activities. Staff refers to persons or groups in an enterprise whose major function is to provide advice and service to the line positions. Personnel and internal auditing departments are staff activities. An organizational chart for a firm with both line and staff positions is appended. Observe that authority flows from top to bottom. No individual is subject to more than one person with respect to one task. These command relationships reduce or prevent confusion, inefficiencies, and frustration.

Line and Staff Relationships

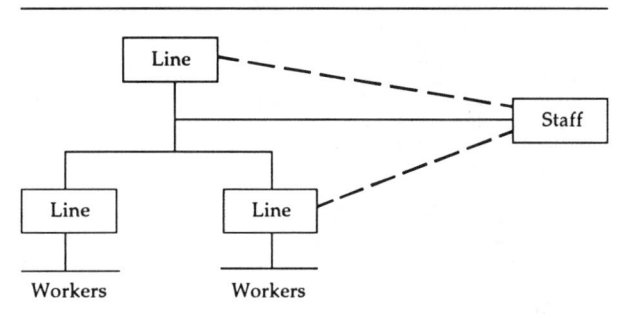

ORIGINAL BILL Foreign checks and bills of exchange are issued in duplicate and designated either as original and duplicate or as first and second of exchange.
See FIRST OF EXCHANGE.

ORIGINATOR An investment banking house that originates or promotes a new issue of stock or bonds. An originator is not necessarily an UNDERWRITER.

OTHER COMPREHENSIVE METHODS OF ACCOUNTING Financial statements prepared in accordance with comprehensive bases of accounting (OCBOA) other than generally accepted accounting principles (GAAP). Four criteria exist for financial statements prepared according to OCBOA:

1. A basis of accounting that the reporting entity uses to comply with the requirements of financial reporting provisions of a government regulatory agency to whose jurisdiction the entity is subject. Examples are a basis of accounting used by railroad companies reporting to the Interstate Commerce Commission and insurance companies reporting to a state insurance company.
2. A basis of accounting that the reporting entity uses or expects to use to file its income tax return for the period covered by the financial statements.
3. The cash receipts and disbursements basis of accounting and modifications of the cash basis having substantial support, such as recording depreciation on fixed assets or accruing income taxes.
4. A definite set of criteria having substantial support that is applied to all material items appearing in financial statements, such as the price level basis of accounting.

Accountants generally apply certain guidelines when determining the appropriate basis of accounting where GAAP are not required:

1. Does the additional cost of preparing GAAP exceed the benefits?
2. Do financial statements prepared under OCBVOA differ substantially from those prepared according to GAAP?

Cash basis and tax basis statements do not report financial position

OUT OF LINE

and results of operations in accordance with GAAP. It is recommended that they not be referred to as "balance sheet" or "income statement" without some modifications. Titles such as "statement of assets and liabilities on a cash basis," "statement of cash revenues received and expenses paid," and "balance sheet— modified cash basis" are often used.

BIBLIOGRAPHY

AMERICAN INSTITUTE OF CPAs, *Audit and Accounting Manual (AICPA)*.

OUT OF LINE Used by speculators and investors to refer to particular securities, the prices of which are thought to be either above or below that warranted by the general level or average. For example, two stocks may bear the same dividend rate, have the same asset value and the same present and future earning power, and still command widely divergent prices or yields on the market. One may be said to be out of line with the other or with the general level of securities of like nature.

OUT-OF-TOWN CHECKS A check drawn on a bank located in another place is an out-of-town item to the bank receiving it for credit to the account of the depositor. Out-of-town checks are collected through the FEDERAL RESERVE CHECK COLLECTION SYSTEM or through correspondent banks with whom arrangements have been made to act as collecting agents therefor.
See TRANSIT DEPARTMENT.

OUT-OF-TOWN CLEARINGS See FEDERAL RESERVE CHECK COLLECTION SYSTEM, FEDERAL RESERVE INTERDISTRICT COLLECTION SYSTEM, TRANSIT DEPARTMENT.

OUT-OF-TOWN COLLECTIONS See COLLECTION ITEMS.

OUTSIDE BROKER One not belonging to the principal stock exchange in a particular location. Thus, in New York City an outside broker is one not a member of the New York Stock Exchange.

OUTSIDE MARKET A securities market other than the New York Stock Exchange. Originally, it referred specifically to the Curb (the New York Curb Market, now known as the American Stock Exchange).

OUTSIDERS The general public; the nonprofessional speculating element; speculators who are not in possession of the financial statements and other information regarding the corporations in the securities of which they deal in advance of their publication, i.e., in advance of their being made available to the public. The outsiders also usually know nothing about the market's TECHNICAL POSITION. An outsider trades on the basis of external facts, FUNDAMENTAL CONDITIONS, etc., rather than advance or inside information.
See INSIDER.

OUTSIDE SECURITIES Securities not listed or quoted on the principal exchange in the location, i.e., traded on an outside market. Thus, in New York City securities not traded on the New York Stock Exchange are outside securities.

OUTSTANDING BONDS The aggregate of bonds (or stocks in the case of outstanding stocks) that have actually been issued and sold, as distinguished from the amount authorized. The maximum amount of stock which a corporation is authorized to issue is determined by the certificate of incorporation. Under New York statutes, stock corporations have the power to borrow money and contract debts when necessary for the transaction of business, but consent of at least two-thirds of the stockholders is required for the execution of any mortgage, except purchase money mortgages, to secure such debt.
See AUTHORIZED BONDS, AUTHORIZED CAPITAL STOCK.

OVERALL BASIS In investment analysis, the extent or degree of coverage of all fixed charges by earnings available for such charges. The importance of the term may be illustrated with the case of a company having three bond issues, each having a lien rank ahead of the other, in accordance with the following example.

Income available for bond interest		$600,000
Charges, first lien bonds	$150,000	
Charges, second lien bonds	150,000	
Charges, third lien bonds	100,000	400,000
Balance available for surplus		$200,000

On an overall basis, this company covered its total charges 1.5 times ($600,000 divided by $400,000). Such a comparison is less favorable than might be stated for each of the bond issues considered separately. Thus, charges on the first lien bonds were earned 4 times ($600,000 divided by $150,000); charges on the second lien bonds after requirements on first lien bonds were earned 3 times ($450,000 divided by $150,000); charges on third lien bonds were also earned 3 times after requirements on first and second lien bonds combined, thus giving the superficial appearance of being as well covered as the second lien bonds. However, if income available for bond interest should shrink by $150,000 to $450,000, the overall coverage would be 1.13 times, and charges on the third lien bonds would be earned only by 1.5 times, after allowing for requirements on first and second lien bonds, instead of 3 times as before. In other words, a shrinkage of only 25% in income available for bond interest would reduce the safety margin for the third lien bond by one-half. Instead of the single issue method of computation, the overall or cumulative method would therefore count as requirements for each issue not only that issue's requirements, but also any preceding requirements. Thus, the times earned ratios for each issue would be as follows:

Income available for bond interest	$600,000	$450,000
Times earned:		
First lien bonds	4.00	3.00
Second lien bonds	2.00	1.50
Third lien bonds	1.50	1.13

OVERBOUGHT The condition of a market when speculative buying has been heavy in spite of advancing prices, leaving it in a weak technical position, susceptible to declining prices through profit-taking and probable renewed short selling because of the latent desire of speculators (the long interest) to take their profits and the probable temporary elimination of the short interest.

OVERCAPITALIZATION A condition that exists in a corporation when the value of its net assets is less than the par value of its shares. If shares were fully paid for when issued and property values subsequently kept intact, overcapitalization would not occur. It has been held among courts that capital stock should not exceed the market value of a corporation's net assets, but among financiers and accountants this principle is not regarded as altogether sound or practicable. From the point of view of the latter, overcapitalization does not exist until and unless the capital stock outstanding is so great that the corporation is unable to earn a reasonable and ordinary return upon it. In other words, the test of proper capitalization is not asset value, but the earning power of the assets.

Overcapitalization in the case of a railroad or other public utility is likely to result in a receivership and reorganization by which a scaling down of securities bearing a fixed rate of interest must be effected.
See WATERED STOCK.

OVERCERTIFICATION The practice of certifying a check by a bank for an amount greater than the balance credited to the account of the drawer. In effect, overcertification is tantamount to a temporary loan, since any check so certified by a bank shall be a good and valid obligation against the bank. Section 5208 of the Revised Statutes (12 U.S.C. 501) provides that it shall be unlawful for any officer, director, agent, or employee of any Federal Reserve bank or of any member bank to certify any check drawn upon such bank unless the person, firm, or corporation drawing the check has on deposit with such bank an amount of money not less than the amount specified in such check.

The penalties are severe. Such act of overcertification by any officer, director, agent, or employee of any Federal Reserve bank or of any member bank shall, at the discretion of the Board of Governors of the Federal Reserve System, (1) subject such Federal Reserve bank to the penalties of Section 11(h) of the Federal Reserve Act (suspension or liquidation or reorganization of the bank), (2) subject such member bank, if a national bank, to the liabilities and proceedings by the Comptroller of the Currency provided in Section 5234 of the Revised Statutes (12 U.S.C. 192), which provides for appointment of a receiver for the bank by the Comptroller, and (3) subject such member bank, if a member bank other than a national bank, to the penalties imposed by Section 9 of the Federal Reserve Act (forfeiture of membership in the Federal Reserve System upon hearing by the board of governors).

Moreover, whoever, being an officer, director, agent, or employee of any Federal Reserve bank or member bank of the Federal Reserve System, certifies a check before the amount thereof has been regularly deposited in the bank by the drawer thereof, or resorts to any device, or receives any fictitious obligation, directly or collaterally, in order to evade any of the provisions of law relating to certification of checks, shall be fined not more than $5,000 or imprisoned for not more than five years, or both (18 U.S.C. 1004).

See CERTIFIED CHECK, DAY LOANS.

OVERCHECK   To overdraw one's account.
See OVERDRAFTS.

OVERCOMMITMENT   Making contracts involving financial responsibility in excess of the amount of one's capital or credit—for example, buying securities on a thin margin; similar to OVEREXTENSION.

OVERDRAFTS   An account appearing upon the general ledger and financial statement of a bank to indicate the aggregate amount by which depositors have overdrawn their accounts. From a bookkeeping standpoint, the overdraft occurs when a depositor overchecks, i.e., when not only has the credit balance been exhausted, but a debit balance has been created in the account.

Overdrafts are thus equivalent to unsecured loans, which occur through the oversight of a customer or through delay in deposit remittances. Since overdrafts appear as an asset to offset the amount by which depositors' accounts are increased, they obviously increase gross deposits.

There is no statutory reference to overdrafts in the national banking laws. Administratively, the Comptroller of the Currency does not consider overdrafts to be illegal, but considers involuntary overdrafts to be irregular and an improper practice criticizable by examiners. Voluntary overdrafts, whereby banks agree with customers to honor any overdrafts on their accounts for a fee and treat the deficits as unsecured advances, are, however, considered by the Comptroller of the Currency to be a legal means of extending credit, although significantly sizable overdrafts will be reviewed for credit quality and adherence to statutory lending limits in the same manner as other loans (Interpretive Ruling 7.1161). Despite the best efforts to police depositors' accounts, involuntary overdrafts will occasionally occur, but as a criticizable practice they should be held to the unavoidable minimum.

In banking practice, when overdrafts are detected by ledger clerks, such checks are reported to the bank officer concerned for a decision as to whether or not to honor such checks. Frequently, as a matter of courtesy and service, the depositor concerned is notified and given the opportunity to make good the deficit immediately, thus obviating the necessity for returning the check on account of not sufficient funds or no funds and perhaps having it protested. In such cases, the check is held awaiting the action of the depositor, who is sent a notice as follows:

"Your account appears to be overdrawn $_____ . This notice is sent in the regular course of business in order that the matter may receive your prompt attention in case the overdraft has been caused by a delayed deposit or remittance."

In the case of popular no-minimum-balance checking accounts, however, the heavy volume of such checks handled and the extra burden of providing such overdrawn notices may make it impracticable to provide such notices; consequently, the overdrawn checks will be returned marked "NSF" (not sufficient funds). To penalize overdrawing and to cover extra costs of handling, banks may make an extra charge of, say, $5 per such debit notice to the no-minimum-balance checking account.

OVERDRAW   To draw a check that more than exhausts one's credit balance at a bank, thereby creating a debit balance.
See OVERDRAFTS.

OVERDUE BILLS   Bills (or notes in the case of overdue notes) that have not been paid at maturity. When an endorsed note is not paid at maturity, it should, unless it contains a waiver of protest, be protested in order to hold the endorsers liable. Bills or notes not paid at maturity are transferred from the time loans or bills discounted accounts, which should contain only unmatured items, to an account entitled "bills discounted overdue." For the disposition of bills long overdue, see BAD DEBTS.

OVEREXPANSION   Roughly equivalent to INFLATION; the construction of plant facilities and production of goods in excess of reasonable near-term production requirements and sales probabilities. Such a condition is characterized by overaccumulation of inventories, tying up working capital and freezing any bank loans used to finance inventory expansion. Thus overexpansion in business generally has the effect of placing commercial loans of banks in an overextended position.
See BUSINESS CYCLE.

OVEREXTENDED ACCOUNTS   From a broker's standpoint, accounts that are undermargined; from a banker's standpoint, loans that the borrower cannot pay at maturity, thereby requiring renewal.

OVEREXTENSION   From the point of view of a lender, credit is overextended when a line out of proportion to the risk's capital rating, moral responsibility, and business ability is granted. From the point of view of a trader, overextension is a condition of having purchased securities or commodities in excess of an amount justified by his capital and borrowing power; in the case of declining prices, such overextension is apt to lead to losses through an inability to furnish proper margin or otherwise through pressure by creditors. From the standpoint of business, the term refers to expansion of facilities and equipment beyond the immediate or prospective needs of the concern.

OVERISSUE   An issue of stock or bonds by a corporation in excess of the amount authorized. The purpose of a STOCK REGISTRAR is to prevent an overissue.
See AUTHORIZED BONDS, AUTHORIZED CAPITAL STOCK.

OVERLYING MORTGAGE   A mortgage before which one or more other mortgages have prior claim upon the company's property. An overlying mortgage is, therefore, not a first mortgage, and overlying bonds are junior lien bonds. Overlying mortgage is a synonym of JUNIOR MORTGAGE and an antonym of UNDERLYING MORTGAGE.

OVERNIGHT LOAN   In the New York MONEY MARKET a special category of very short-term credit accommodation for dealers in securities, primarily government securities dealers and those dealing in over-the-counter securities. The overnight loan provides credit for such dealers by which to pay off any day loans, the latter incurred in order to pay for securities against delivery or to obtain release from pledge of securities in order to deliver. Overnight loans, like day loans, are evidenced by specific notes for specific amounts; but they are fully secured by securities placed in possession of the bank lender, whereas day loans are secured by lien on securities in the process of being received or delivered. Also, overnight loans are subject to maximum loan values and varying interest rates like other security loans, whereas day loans' rate is fixed and day loans are not subject to margin requirements.

OVERPLUS   Practically equivalent to surplus, or a balance over all expenses.

OVERS AND SHORTS   In banking practice, an account in which items that are either over (credits) or short (debits), producing a state of unbalance, are kept in suspense until they can be located and adjusted. The amount of overs and shorts, if any, is entered in daily department proofs and later consolidated by the general bookkeeping or auditing department. This department, by having access to the details of all the transactions of the bank, is in a position to locate differences and adjust them.

ENCYCLOPEDIA OF BANKING AND FINANCE

OVERSEAS PRIVATE INVESTMENT CORPORATION (OPIC)

A federal agency for encouraging mutually beneficial American business investment in the world's developing nations. OPIC began operations in 1971. The agency encourages investment projects that will help the social and economic development of over 100 developing countries. At the same time, OPIC also helps the U.S. balance of payments through the profits returned to the United States, as well as the U.S. jobs and exports created. OPIC helps U.S. investors find investment opportunities, insurance to protect their investments and loans, and guarantees to help finance their projects.

OPIC is governed by a 15-member board of directors—8 appointed from the private sector and 7 from the federal government.

By reducing or eliminating certain perceived political risks for investors and providing financing and assistance not otherwise available, OPIC helps to reduce the unusual risks and problems that can make investment opportunities in the developing area less attractive than in advanced countries. At the same time, it reduces the need for government-to-government lending programs by involving the U.S. private sector in generating capital and strengthening private sector economies in developing countries.

OPIC insures U.S. investors against the political risks of expropriation, inconvertibility of local currency holdings, and damage from war, revolution, insurrection, or civil strife. It also offers a special insurance policy to U.S. contractors and exporters against arbitrary drawings of letters of credit posted as bid, performance, or advance payment guaranties. Other special programs are offered for minerals exploration, oil and gas exploration, and development and leasing operations.

OPIC offers U.S. lenders protection against both commercial and political risks by guaranteeing payment of principal and interest on loans up to $50 million made to eligible private enterprises.

Its direct investment fund loans, offered to small- and medium-sized businesses, generally cover terms of from 7 to 12 years, and usually range from $100,000 to $4 million with varying interest rates, depending on assessment of the risks of the project financed.

OPIC is self-sustaining and has received no public funds beyond its original startup appropriations, which have been returned to the U.S. Treasury.

Financial highlights for 1988 include the following:

Insurance:	
Total insurance in force (in millions)	$8,407
Investment guaranties (in millions):	
Commitments: 1	732.8
Outstanding	367.1
Direct investment (in millions)	
Commitments	77.7
Investment loans outstanding	47.4

OVERSOLD The condition of a market when selling, especially short selling, has been in heavy volume at declining prices, placing the market in a technical position to rally through the latent urgency of covering by the short interest.

OVERSPECULATION A condition existing when the aggregate of trading in securities or commodities on any exchange is in excess of that needed to furnish a ready market and to keep prices in harmony with actual values.

OVERSTAYED Describes a trader who, having a paper profit (an unrealized profit), waits for a larger profit and then, because of a sudden decline in prices, finds that the profit is reduced or canceled or even converted into a loss. He is said to have overstayed his market.

OVERSUBSCRIPTION When the aggregate of subscriptions contracting to buy an issue of securities offered to the public exceeds the amount of the issue. In such cases, subscriptions over $1,000 in bonds or, say, ten shares of stock are usually reduced pro rata by the syndicate manager in order to equalize the subscriptions and the amount of the issue, and the larger subscriptions are frequently cut down by a greater percentage than the smaller.

OVER-THE-COUNTER MARKET The largest of all securities markets because of the large quantities of debt securities traded in it. U.S. government securities (which alone make up the biggest of all sectoral markets), issues of states, contries and municipalities and most corporate bonds are traded over the counter, by dealers making markets in such securities. The total value of debt instruments traded in this fashion in a year in the U.S. alone has been estimated at $90-$100 trillion, with U.S. government securities the overwhelming part of the total.

Dealers in this market are subject to monitoring and on-site inspection and examination by the National Association of Securities Dealers, Inc. The NASD is the self-regulatory organization for the over-the-counter market, operating under the oversight of the Securities and Exchange Commission. Congress, by the Securities Acts Amendments of 1975, assigned the NASD the responsibility for examining dealers in municipal securities for their compliance with federal securities laws and the rules of the Municipal Securities Rulemaking Board. In 1986, Congress passed the Government Securities Act, which gave the NASD the further responsibility of monitoring, inspecting and examining firms dealing in government securities.

Many corporate bonds are listed for trading on the New York Exchange. However, it is generally understood that the exchange trading volume in such bonds is a minuscule percentage of that done by over-the-counter bond dealers.

Equity issues listed on stock exchanges are traded over-the-counter in the so-called third market. Wile exchange member firms are forbidden by exchange rules from trading listed stocks off the floors of the exchanges, firms not belonging to the exchanges are under no such prohibition. A number of non-exchange member firms specialize in off-board block transactions.

There are also an estimated 11,000 other equity securities traded over-the-counter, issues that generally are too small to qualify for inclusion in the computerized NASDAQ market or for listing on an exchange. These issues continue to be traded with the aid of the "pink sheets," daily bulletins that indicate which firms make markets in these stocks but seldom quote bid and asked prices. The aggregate share and dollar volume in these securities is very small, compared to the NASDAQ.

The SEC has recently become concerned about the regulation of this non-NASDAQ market, and has asked the NASD to become more active in it. Accordingly, the NASD is requesting dealers in non-NASDAQ securities to report their trading activity to the NASD by electronic means. This permits the market surveillance department of the NASD to capture non-NASDAQ trade data and to analyze them for possible instances of wrongdoing. The NASD has also built an electronic bulletin board display service, which makes the non-NASDAQ trade data available to registered dealers. This provides the dealers and their customers with better information on the non-NASDAQ markert, and introduces into it some of the orderliness that the NASD's automated NASDAQ system provides to the NASDAQ market.

BIBLIOGRAPHY

COLLINS, J. O. *The Individual Investor's Guide to OTC Stocks*, 1989.
Moody's Handbook of O-T-C Stocks. Quarterly.
Moody's OTC Industrial Manual. Annual, with weekly supplements.
Moody's OTC Unlisted Manual. Annual, with supplements.
NASD Manual. Commerce Clearing House, Chicago, IL. Looseleaf.
National Association of Securities Dealers Manual. Commerce Clearing House, Chicago, IL. Annual.
OTC Chart Manual. Standard and Poor's Corp., New York, NY. Bimonthly.
OTC Penny Stock Digest. C. S. Metos, Publisher. Annual.
Over-the-Counter Securities Handbook. Review Publishing Co. Annual.

OVERTRADING Trading in securities or commodities on too small a margin, i.e., buying an amount out of proportion to a given capital. To hold securities on too small a margin is as risky as buying unsound securities.

OVERTURN TURNOVER.
See MERCHANDISE TURNOVER.

OWNERSHIP CERTIFICATES The Internal Revenue Code calls for a variety of information returns to be filed with the commissioner of internal revenue so as to permit checking of the tax returns of the recipients of various types of income. Ownership certificates are information returns prepared on payment of corporate bond interest payments. When the interest coupons are presented for payment, the ownership certificate is to be executed by the payee. Form 1000 is used where the payee is a citizen, resident alien, resident fiduciary, resident partnership, or nonresident partnership all of whose members are citizens or residents, and where the bond concerned was issued before January 1, 1934, and has a tax-free covenant. Form 1001 is used where the payee is a nonresident alien, nonresident partnership (consisting wholly or partly of nonresident aliens), or nonresident foreign corporation, and where the bond concerned was issued by any U.S. domestic corporation, resident foreign corporation, or nonresident foreign corporation with a fiscal agent in the U.S.

In the case of registered bonds, ownership certificates are to be executed upon payment of interest, as in the case of coupon bonds. If such ownership certificates are not furnished by the registered owner of the registered bonds, the withholding agent must prepare them (a withholding agent is any person required to withhold a tax, as in the case of tax-free covenant bond interest payments and payments to nonresident payees).

No ownership certificates are required where the issuer was an individual or partnership or a state, state agency, or state subdivision. Ownership certificates likewise are not required where the owner of the obligation is a domestic corporation, resident foreign corporation, or foreign government.

Information returns as to ownership are also prepared in the case of dividends received on stock by a record owner where the stockcertificate has not yet been transferred to the new owner but, through dividend due-bill, the record owner as seller has delivered to the buyer a due-bill check for such dividend (the stock having been bought dividend on). Otherwise, the record owner, through filing by the paying corporation of Form 1099-DIV, will be charged for tax purposes with having received the dividend. Form 1087-DIV is executed by the record owner to show the actual owner and payee.

P

PACIFIC STOCK EXCHANGE A consolidation of the San Francisco Stock Exchange, which was founded in 1882, and the Los Angeles Stock Exchange, which was founded in 1899. The unification of these two exchanges, bringing together the west's two principal security markets, was effected in January, 1957, after years of planning and study. Each former exchange is now a division of the Pacific Stock Exchange. Each division has its own executive officers and staff, while management is vested in a board of governors of eight, four from each division, under a chairmanship that alternates annually between Los Angeles and San Francisco.

Purpose. The unification of the Los Angeles and San Francisco stock exchanges was instigated and accomplished better to serve industry and public investors in the growing and dynamic west. It has created an active and broader marketplace, providing many advantages for investors, corporations, security dealers, banks, and financial institutions. Stock issues of corporations on the Pacific Stock Exchange benefit greatly by an extended and more fluid trading market now available as the result of the consolidation.

Both trading floors operate as one. Orders to buy or sell receive instantaneous execution on both floors even though they are 400 miles apart. Modern high-speed communication makes this possible. A unique direct voice communications system connects both trading floors, enabling floor members to execute orders as if they were in the same room. This special telephone circuit joining both floors has no duplicate outside the Civil Aeronautics Authority (transferred to the Federal Aviation Agency in 1958). Through it a seller on one trading floor can find a buyer on the other in seconds. For example, a member on the Los Angeles floor receives an order to sell 300 shares of XYZ stock at 15. He relays it to the Los Angeles specialist in XYZ. The Los Angeles specialist looks at his book and sees he can take 200 shares at that price. For the other 100 shares, he lifts a specialist handset telephone from its cradle and presses the talk button that puts him instantly through to the San Francisco floor. He utters the words "XYZ," and his voice emerges from the 15 small loudspeakers on the posts of as many specialists in San Francisco. The San Francisco specialist in XYZ picks up his handset and hears the Los Angeles specialist say, "There are 300 shares of XYZ at 15. I'll take 200. How about you?" The San Francisco specialist looks at his book and says, "I'll take the other 100." Elapsed time would be only about 10 seconds.

The intermarket trading system (ITS), by providing other markets with the ability to view the PSE's quotes and send orders to its specialists, has provided a more equal opportunity for exchanges such as the PSE to compete for equity order flow. This has stimulated active interest in new floor brokerage and specialist operations in both the Los Angeles and San Francisco floors, where additional specialist posts have been established in recent years.

In particular, the PSE has led the industry in the development of automated order processing, offering the first communication and execution system of its kind over a decade ago. This service was continually improved and expanded to keep pace with the changing requirements of its participants. With recent developments in the national marketplace, the needs of the retail brokerage firm became even more demanding, requiring both fast and efficient handling of a customer's order and nationwide execution capabilities. The PSE met these requirements in December, 1979, inaugurating its Scorex system, an update of the industry's first automated securities communication, order routing, and execution system. An exclusive development of the PSE, Scorex combines the best features of the modern national market and automated order processing with the proven benefits of auction market trading.

See STOCK EXCHANGES.

BIBLIOGRAPHY

PACIFIC COAST STOCK EXCHANGE, INC. *Annual Report.*
SECURITIES AND EXCHANGE COMMISSION. *Annual Report; Monthly Statistical Review.*

PACKERS The Packers and Stockyards Administration was established on October 1, 1981, in accordance with Memorandum No. 1000-1 of the secretary of Agriculture, issued pursuant to the Reorganization Plan No. 2 of 1953 (7 U.S.C. 2201). Packers and stockyards activities were formerly performed by the Agricultural Marketing Service.

The official goal of this program is to assure fair play in the marketing of livestock, meat, and poultry. Its principal purpose is to maintain effective competition for livestock, meat, and poultry marketing to assure that farmers and ranchers receive the true market value for their livestock and poultry. Consumers and members of the livestock, poultry, and meat industries are also protected against unfair business practices in the marketing of meat and poultry, and from restrictions on competition which would unduly increase meat and poultry prices.

The Packers and Stockyards Act of 1921 as amended (7 U.S.C. 181 et seq.) was intended to assure fair competition and fair trade practices in the marketing of livestock, meat, and poultry, as well as meat and poultry products. The act set forth rules for fair business practices and free, open, and competitive markets. Its objectives are the following: (1) to assure that farmers and ranchers obtain fair market value for their livestock and poultry, (2) to protect consumers against unfair business practices in marketing of meats and poultry, and (3) to protect members of the livestock, poultry, and meat industries against unfair practices of competitors. The P&SA administers the act by regulations.

PACKING LIST A list accompanying a shipment of goods, indicating the number of packages and their contents but omitting prices.
See CERTIFICATE OF INSPECTION.

PAID CHECKS CANCELED CHECKS.

PAID CREDIT A short title for paid letter of credit. A commercial LETTER OF CREDIT is paid in advance only in rare instances, but a TRAVELER'S LETTER OF CREDIT is usually paid for when issued.

PAID-UP CAPITAL That part of the subscribed capital stock which has been issued and paid for, the remainder being subject to CALL and representing uncalled capital. Federal Reserve bank stock, for example, must be subscribed for by member banks in amounts equal to 6% of the combined capital and surplus of the subscribing bank, but up to the present time only 50% of the amount subscribed has been called.

PAID-UP SHARES FULLY PAID STOCK.

PANIC A sudden, excited, unreasoning collapse of confidence in the ability of banks and creditors generally to meet their obligations. In the financial history of the United States, it has been primarily a financial rather than a business phenomenon, and has been immediately traceable to a collapse in the credit structure, usually precipitated by the failure of a conspicuous bank or business house, or a succession of failures without previous warning. This operated as a signal that all banks might not be solvent, and runs on banks and demand for cash payments developed like wildfire. Hence banks were the storm centers of panics.

Fundamentally, a panic has been a reaction against stringent cre-dit conditions, rising security and commodity prices, and difficult collections, finally culminating in a buyers strike. It has been anticipated by feverish industrial production; rising price, wage, and interest levels; expanding bank loans and falling reserves; extreme prosperity; overexpansion of plant facilities; and overextension of credit.

During panics businesspeople strove to protect their cash position and to maintain financial solvency. There usually have been plenty of goods and collateral but a shortage of currency, so creditors pressed their debtors for cash payments. But collections were achieved only with great difficulty. For this reason, securities and commodities were thrown on the market for what they would bring in order to raise cash. Panics have usually been of short duration, and have been followed by a period of liquidation and industrial depression. A panic should be distinguished from CRISIS, DEPRESSION, and LIQUIDATION.

Provision for ELASTIC CURRENCY in the Federal Reserve Act appears to have solved the shortage of currency problem. Through the rediscount process and advances on government securities and other assets, additional currency can be created with discounted notes as security. As long as the requirements as to deposits and Federal Reserve note liabilities of the Federal Reserve banks themselves are met, additional Federal Reserve currency and reserves can be injected into the member banks. The most critical banking panic of the United States began with declaration of the initial state moratorium by Michigan in February, 1933, and culminated in the banking holiday declared for the entire nation in March, 1933. Panics of varying intensities occurred in 1907, 1903, 1900, 1893, 1873, 1857, 1846, 1837, and 1825.

See BUSINESS CYCLE.

BIBLIOGRAPHY

MIRON, J. A. "Financial Panics, the Seasonality of the Nominal Interest Rate, and the Founding of the Fed." *American Economic Review*, 1986.
SPRAGUE, O. M. W. *History of Crises Under the National Banking System*. Natonal Monetary Commission. Augustus M. Kelley, Pubs., New York, NY. 1910.

PAPER All short-term evidences of debt not under seal, i.e., negotiable instruments used in borrowing short-term funds, especially funds for commercial purposes. The following classes of paper are frequently referred to: AGRICULTURAL PAPER, BUSINESS PAPER, COMMERCIAL PAPER, COMMODITY PAPER, CORPORATION PAPER, MERCANTILE PAPER, and TRADE PAPER.

PAPER BASIS When a country does not employ or no longer employs a metallic basis for its currency system, and commodity prices and foreign exchange rates are based upon (usually) depreciated PAPER MONEY.

PAPER MONEY Paper instruments, e.g., Federal Reserve notes, silver certificates, U.S. notes, Treasury notes of 1890, Federal Reserve bank notes, and national bank notes (now in process of retirement), which serve as substitutes for metallic money and form the principal part of the circulation media. For the principles underlying paper money, see MONEY.

The advantages of paper money over metallic money are as follows: (1) greater portability, i.e., convenience in handling; (2) saving of loss from abrasion; (3) economy of time in counting and weighing (gold coin, now withdrawn from circulation, formerly had to be weighed to determine the extent of abrasion); (4) greater security in case of loss or theft; (5) saving of interest for the amount by which the value of paper money exceeds that of the metallic money kept in reserve for its redemption; (6) greater cleanliness since paper money can be frequently reissued.

For a description of different kinds of United States paper money, and legal tender and redemption qualities thereof, see MONETARY STOCK and UNITED STATES MONEY.

BIBLIOGRAPHY

Know your Money. U.S. Secret Service.
FRIEDBERG, R. *Paper Money of the United States: A Complete Illustrated Guide with Valuations*. Coin and Currency Institute, Inc., Clifton, NJ, 1986.
KRAUSE, C. L., and LIMKE, R. F. *United States Paper Money*. Krause Publications, Incv., Iola, WI, 1986.
Paper Money. Paper Money Collectors., Florissant, MO. Bimonthly.
Treasury Bulletin. U.S. Department of the Treasury.
United States Currency. Board of Governors of the Federal Reserve System.
World Currency Yearbook. Currency Analysis, Inc., Birmingham, AL. Annual.

PAPER MONEY INFLATION The issue of paper money in quantities in excess of the value of the metallic or documentary (government bonds, commercial paper, etc.) reserve behind it. Wherever it is impossible for a government to redeem its paper currency in standard money on demand, monetary INFLATION exists.

PAPER PROFITS Unrealized profits; profits not yet taken; profits existing because of a rise in the market price of a security or commodity over its purchase price, or a decline in the market price below the selling price, if sold short. For instance, if 100 shares of United States Steel have been bought at 80 and the price is currently quoted at 85, a paper profit of 5 points, or $500, has arisen. But the profit does not become certain until the stock has actually been sold and converted into cash.

PAR In the original sense, state of equality, or 100%, without premium or discount. PAR VALUE may refer to the face or nominal value of a share of stock, the value imprinted or engraved on a bond or stock certificate, or the principal amount at which a bond will be redeemed at maturity.

See FOREIGN EXCHANGE, MINT PAR OF EXCHANGE.

PARADOX OF THRIFT More savings may not always be good for the economy. This is a paradox because economics teaches that more savings leads to more investment, which in turn leads to economic growth. However, if everyone increased savings, consumption activity would decrease and national income would fall. As income falls, investment will also fall, and this is not good for the economy.

PAR CLEARANCES Clearinghouse checks, i.e., those passing through a local clearinghouse association, are collected at par, no charge being made to the payee or endorser by the collecting bank which receives the check for deposit, or to the drawer by the bank on which it is drawn.

The term usually refers, however, to out-of-town collections. The FEDERAL RESERVE CHECK COLLECTION SYSTEM provides for compulsory collection of out-of-town checks among its members and clearing members at par. (The Federal Reserve reported that as of December 31, 1980, there were no nonpar banking offices.) This means that the system provides that all checks be accepted and remitted for by the drawee bank at par. It does not mean that a bank accepting an out-of-town check for deposit and credit may not make a charge. Such a charge, however, is not a collection or exchange charge—it is an interest or discount charge. If a bank accepts for deposit and credit a check drawn on a bank located at a point five days away, the charge which the collecting bank makes is for the loss of interest incurred while the check is in the process of collection. The depositor is not entitled to draw against uncollected funds. In the case of savings deposits or time deposits (demand deposits as of 1982 were still not permitted to draw interest), interest may be credited from the date of deposit. The charge made by the collecting bank is exactly parallel to the charge made for discounting a note due in five days.

See FEDERAL RESERVE INTERDISTRICT COLLECTION SYSTEM, INTERDISTRICT SETTLEMENT ACCOUNT.

PAR COLLECTION OF CHECKS See CLEARINGHOUSE EXCHANGE RATES, FEDERAL RESERVE CHECK COLLECTION SYSTEM, FEDERAL

RESERVE INTERDISTRICT COLLECTION SYSTEM, INTERDISTRICT SETTLEMENT ACCOUNT, PAR CLEARANCES.

PARENT COMPANY A business corporation owning full or majority interest in other corporations called subsidiaries. Ownership of stock in other business corporations is not an inherent power of a business corporation, and must be authorized in the state's corporation laws and in turn included specifically in the corporation's certificate of incorporation. All but some nine states now permit business corporations to hold stock of other business corporations, led originally by New Jersey in 1888. Parent companies may operate exclusively as holders of stock in other corporations, in which case they are pure holding companies; or they may engage in operations of their own besides holding stock in other corporations, in which case they are holding-operating or mixed holding companies, or simply parent companies. The extent of the holding need not be a majority interest for actual control, as a concentrated minority block of voting stock may achieve working control if other holdings of the same stock are dispersed. Thus the Public Utility Holding Company Act of 1935 (Sec. 2(7)) defines a holding company, for the purposes of that act, as "any company which directly or indirectly owns, controls, or holds with power to vote, 10% or more of the outstanding voting securities of a public-utility company or of a company which is a holding company... and ... any persons which the (Securities and Exchange Commission) determines, after notice and opportunity for hearing, directly or indirectly to exercise (either alone or pursuant to an arrangement or understanding with one or more persons) such a controlling influence over the management and policies of any public utility or holding company as to make it necessary or appropriate in the public interest or for the protection of investors or consumers that such person be subject to the obligations, duties, and liabilities imposed in this title upon holding companies."

Most leading U.S. corporations are of the holding-operating type, such as American Telephone & Telegraph, DuPont, and General Motors. Despite the expenses of maintaining separate corporate organizations, including extra taxation (regular corporation income tax upon 15% of the dividends received from subsidiaries), parent companies are motivated to operate separately incorporated subsidiaries rather than direct divisions of the parent company because of the following advantages: (1) domestic status for a subsidiary incorporated under the laws of a particular state; (2) decentralization along with accountability of the separately incorporated division; (3) adaptability to the varying corporation laws of different states; (4) preservation of goodwill value of the subsidiary corporation's name; (5) insulation (limited liability of the parent company) against liabilities of separately incorporated subsidiaries; (6) relative ease of disposal of separately incorporated subsidiaries; (7) flexibility in financing for separately incorporated subsidiaries; etc.

The income of a parent company is derived from dividends, interest, royalties, rents, etc., from its subsidiaries and, where it is also an operating company, its own net profits from operations.

Equity Method of Accounting. The Accounting Principles Board of the American Institute of Certified Public Accountants, as of March, 1971, issued its "APB Opinion No. 18, The Equity Method of Accounting for Investments in Common Stock." The board reaffirmed its conclusion that investments in common stock of unconsolidated domestic subsidiaries should be accounted for by the equity method in consolidated financial statements. It extended this conclusion to investments in common stock of all unconsolidated subsidiaries, foreign as well as domestic, in consolidated financial statements. Under the equity method, the investing parent company records the investment in the stock of the investee at cost, and adjusts the carrying amount of the investment to recognize the investing parent's share of the earnings or losses of the investee after date of acquisition. The amount of the adjustment is included in the determination of net income by the investing parent. The APB, however, caveats that the equity method is not a valid substitute for consolidation and should not be used to justify exclusion of a subsidiary when consolidation is otherwise appropriate.

See HOLDING COMPANY, OPERATING COMPANY.

BIBLIOGRAPHY

COMMERCE CLEARING HOUSE. *APB Accounting Principles.* Latest edition.

PARETO'S LAW Vilfredo Pareto in his *Manual of Political Economy* (1906) defined a Pareto optimum exchange as one in which at least one party in the exchange is better off and no one is worse off. This concept of optimality is used in economics to evaluate and compare various income redistribution and resource reallocation schemes.

PARIS BOURSE The Paris Stock Exchange, the full title of which is The Company of the Paris Bank, Exchange, Trade and Finance Brokers (Compagnie des Agents de Change de Paris). Although the Paris Bourse is one of the oldest in the world, dating from official recognition by Louis XV in 1724, it is predated by bourses at Lyon and Toulouse and by the oldest of all stock exchanges, the Bruges Bourse, dating from the thirteenth century. The modern Bourse may be said to date from 1801, and its present building, the Palais de la Bourse, was built in 1808.

The Paris Bourse actually consists of three major markets:

1. The parquet, or formal market, which trades in the more seasoned issues and is composed of a restricted number of licensed brokers. These brokers assemble within an enclosure called the corbeille on the floor for their outcry of bids and offers. There are no specialists.
2. The coulisse, corresponding to a curb market.
3. The hors-cote, or unlisted market.

In September, 1944, the Bourse recommenced business after having been freed from German control during World War II.

Purchases of shares may be made on a cash basis (comptant) or on a future basis usually on margin (marche à terme). The margin requirement was reduced by the government early in 1960 from 80% to 70%. In marche à terme buying, the buyer may specify a prime (e.g., 5 to 10 points per share) to cover himself in case the stock bought for future delivery has declined by the liquidation (settlement) date, usually the twenty-first of the month. If so, the buyer may be relieved from his futures contract to take delivery of the stock by paying the seller the prime. The buyer must notify the seller of his election either to take delivery or to pay the prime on the day before the liquidation, called the réponse des primes. Settlement, in turn, may be made either by taking delivery or by arranging a report (carryover of the futures contract to the next settlement date). As of early 1960, marche à terme trading constituted about half of trading volume. Reflecting economic recovery in France and revival of investor interest, trading activity in recent years has been substantial, accompanied by rising prices stimulated also by inflation hedging.

PARITY In ARBITRAGE, equivalence; derived from par, meaning the equivalent price for a certain security or currency relative to another security or currency, or relative to another market for the security of currency, after adjustments for exchange rates, loss of interest, and other factors.

See FOREIGN EXCHANGE, LONDON EQUIVALENT.

The parity concept has played a basic part in U.S. agricultural policy since the 1930s, when the price support program was provided. The Department of Agriculture reviews its historical development as follows.

Parity prices for farm products were first defined by the AGRICULTURAL ADJUSTMENT ACT OF 1933. Agricultural leaders recognized that high or low prices for farm products are not in themselves of primary significance—of far greater significance is what farm products will buy in terms of food, clothing, feed, machinery, fertilizer, and other things that farmers need for living and for production. Giving this idea legislative definition, the Agricultural Adjustment Act of 1933 declared it to be the policy of Congress to "reestablish prices to farmers at a level that will give agricultural commodities a purchasing power with respect to articles that farmers buy, equivalent to the purchasing power of agricultural commodities in the base period." Parity prices came to be the most commonly used parity standard. They were the prices that would give a unit of a farm commodity the same purchasing power, or exchange value in terms of goods and services bought by farmers, as farm commodities had in a selected base period (1910-1914), during which these price relationships were considered to have been reasonably well balanced. In short, parity prices were a yardstick for measuring how close prices received by farmers were to the prices Congress defined as a fair goal or objective.

The parity price formula did not measure cost of production, standard of living, or income parity. It was not a comprehensive measure of the economic well-being of farmers. It was based on price relationships which are only one component of cost of production and income. Inasmuch as the old formula basis of comparison specified by laws was 1910-1914, the ratio-to-parity comparisons did not take into account the many technological developments that have occurred over the last several decades, affecting the efficiency of input utilization in the production of many crops and livestock products.

Parity income has sometimes been held to be the goal of the agricultural industry, and definitions of it were incorporated in agricultural legislation, for example in the Agricultural Act of 1948. As defined therein, "\"parity' as applied to income, shall be that gross income from agriculture which will provide the farm operator and his family with a standard of living equivalent to those afforded persons dependent upon other gainful occupation. "Parity' as applied to income from any agricultural commodity for any year, shall be that gross income which bears the same relationship to parity income from agriculture for such year as the average gross income from such commodity for the preceding ten calendar years." However, parity income has never been used in the operation or administration of any agricultural program.

Old Parity Price Formula. The parity price formula in use before January 1, 1950, was often referred to as the old formula. The old formula was designed to arrive at prices for individual agricultural commodities which would have the same purchasing power in terms of prices paid by farmers as they had in some base period. The base period provided by the original act of 1933 was August, 1909, to July, 1914, for all commodities except tobacco. The base period for tobacco was August, 1919, to July, 1929. Parity prices were calculated by multiplying the average price received for a commodity during the base period by the appropriate index of prices paid by farmers.

Steps in calculating parity prices during the 17-year period prior to January 1, 1950, were as follows:

1. A base price was determined. For most commodities for which satisfactory monthly price data were available, this was done by averaging the prices received by farmers for the 60 months August, 1909-July, 1914. The average price of cotton was $0.124 a pound; corn, $0.642 a bushel; and wheat, $0.884 a bushel. Base prices for potatoes, tobacco, and several fruits and vegetables were averages of the season average prices for the marketing periods that fell within the period August, 1919-July, 1929, or within the 60 months August, 1934-July, 1939, or August, 1936-July, 1941.
2. An index of prices paid, including interest and taxes, was calculated using prices for about 80 items used in family living and about 90 items used in farm production. These included items in the following groups of commodities: clothing, household supplies, food, furniture and furnishings, building materials, automobiles, trucks and tractors, feed, farm machinery, fertilizer, equipment and supplies (including gas, oil, and tires), and seed. The estimated quantity of each commodity bought by farmers was used to combine these prices into an index. Allowances for farm real estate taxes and interest payable on mortgages secured by farm real estate were also included. This procedure gave the overall index of prices paid, interest, and taxes, which was published each month. After January, 1950, this index was identified and published as the unrevised index, to distinguish it from the PARITY INDEX, which covers more commodities and includes wage rates as well as interest and taxes, and which is used under the parity formula prescribed in the Agricultural Acts of 1948 and 1949. In January, 1965, the last commodity went over to the new formula, so the old index was discontinued.
3. The base price was multiplied by the index of prices paid, interest, and taxes (or by the index of prices paid if the base period was other than August, 1909-July, 1914).

New Formula. Experience with the old parity formula indicated that the 1910-1914 base period was so remote that changes in the relationship among prices of agricultural commodities, such as those resulting from new technology in production and marketing or from changes in consumption habits of the population, were not reflected in the parity prices. In creating its modernized or new formula, Congress sought to maintain the overall 1910-1914 balance between prices received and prices paid by farmers, but at the same time to have the parity prices reflect the current relationship among prices of individual farm commodities.

Modernized parity became effective January 1, 1950, following enactment of the Agricultural Acts of 1948 and 1949. These acts, as well as the Act of July 17, 1952, the Agricultural Act of 1954, and the Agricultural Act of 1956, amended Section 301(a) of the Agricultural Adjustment Act of 1938, pertaining to the calculation of parity prices, to read as follows.

(1) (A) The Parity Price for any agricultural commodity, as of any date, shall be determined by multiplying the Adjusted Base Price of such commodity as of such date, by the Parity Index as of such date.

(B) The Adjusted Base Period Price of any agricultural commodity, as of any date, shall be (i) the average of the prices received by farmers for such commodity at such times as the Secretary of Agriculture may select during each year of the 10-year period ending on the 31st of December last before such date, or during each marketing season beginning in such period if the Secretary determines use of a calendar year basis to be impracticable, divided by (ii) the ratio of the general level of prices received by farmers for agricultural commodities during such period to the general level of prices received by farmers for agricultural commodities during the period January, 1910, to December, 1914, inclusive.

(The period used for computing the adjusted base period price was moved forward a year at a time in order to keep the relationship between commodities more nearly in alignment with current conditions and in order to make it possible to calculate parity prices for new commodities which became increasingly important after the pre- and post-World War I base periods prescribed by early legislation.)

Briefly, the chief differences between the new and the old formulas were as follows:

1. The adjusted base-period price under the new formula took into consideration price relationships among commodities in the most recent 10-year period, whereas the old formula retained the relationship that existed in the original base period.
2. The 10-year average in item 1 above was adjusted to a 1910-1914 level, using the average of the index of prices received for all commodities for the same 10 years.
3. An allowance for wage rates paid farm labor was included in the parity index.

The change from the old formula to the new formula for computing parity prices would have involved a sharp drop in parity prices for basic commodities. In order to graduate the changeover, transitional parity prices were also provided by the 1948 act, limiting the drop from old to new parity to steps of not more than 5% of the old parity per year, but providing that beginning January 1, 1950, modernized parity prices should govern. The 1949 act suspended the effective date of modernized parity by providing that the parity price for any basic agricultural commodity—corn, cotton, wheat, peanuts, rice, and tobacco—as of any date during the period January 1, 1950, through December 31, 1953, should not be less than its old parity (the old formula meant higher parity prices for wheat, corn, cotton, and peanuts, but the new formula resulted in higher prices for rice and tobacco). The Act of July 17, 1952, extended for two additional years (through December 31, 1955) the requirement that the effective parity price for the six basic commodities be the higher of parity prices computed under both the old and new parity formulas. The Agricultural Act of 1954 did not extend this suspension of changeover to new parity, and so the transitional parity formula went into effect January 1, 1956, with respect to the basic commodities. The Agricultural Act of 1956, however, froze transitional parity for corn, peanuts, and wheat during 1957. Transitional parity provisions again became effective for the basics on January 1, 1958. The last commodity went over to the new parity in January, 1965, and after that time no transitional parities were calculated; adjusted base period prices were recalculated in January of each year.

The actual method of computation under the new formula was as follows:

1. The average of prices received by farmers for individual commodities for the 10 preceding years was calculated (e.g., for 1969, the period was 1959-1968). An allowance for unredeemed

loans and for other supplemental payments resulting from price support operations was included for those commodities for which applicable.
2. This 10-year average was divided by the average of the index of prices received by farmers for the same preceding calendar years, adjusted to include an allowance for unredeemed loans and other supplemental price support operations, to give an adjusted base price.
3. Parity prices were computed by multiplying the adjusted base prices by the current parity index (with 1910-1914 = 100).

The level of support directed or authorized by price support legislation was almost always expressed in terms of a percentage, or within some percentage range, of the parity price for the commodity at the beginning of its marketing year. Later, when the required statistics became available and the formula could actually be computed, the level of support could be re-expressed in terms of dollars and cents.

New Target Price Concept. New with the Agriculture and Consumer Protection Act of 1973 is the concept of guaranteed, or target, prices and deficiency payments for wheat, feed grains, and upland cotton. Deficiency payments are not made as long as the average market price received by farmers during the first five months of the marketing year (or in the case of cotton, during the calendar year in which the crop is planted) remains above the target level. It is only when the average market price drops below target levels that a farmer's cash price is supplemented; and then it is only supplemented on allotment production on the amount that average price exceeds the larger of the loan rate or the five-month national average price, weighted by the historical quantity of production sold in each month. This arrangement provides a farmer with a guaranteed return on the portion of the crop produced on his allotment, freeing him to concentrate on all-out production without fear that a market decline will drop prevailing prices below the level of profitability.

Escalator provision: An escalator provision was included in the Agriculture and Consumer Protection Act of 1973 that could raise target prices. Under this escalator provision, the target prices increase if the cost of production goes up more than overall farm productivity. The formula is as follows: cost of production increase is measured by the Department of Agriculture's cost of production index, adjusted by the productivity change as measured by the national average yield for the preceding three years compared with the yield of the three years previous to the preceding year. For example, for the 1976 crop, the 1973-1975 average yield was compared with the 1972-1974 average yield. This assures that if the national average costs of production rise faster than the national average crop productivity, the target prices will reflect such a change.

Disaster payments. Also new under the Agriculture and Consumer Protection Act of 1973 is the provision under which a producer may be considered for payment at a special rate when prevented by natural disaster from planting any portion of his wheat or feed grain allotment to wheat, feed grains, or other nonconserving crops, or when a natural disaster causes total actual production to be less than two-thirds of normal production on allotment acres. Other nonconserving crops may be substituted for wheat and feed grains in evaluating this two-thirds provision. The disaster deficiency payments are included to help free the farmer to work toward all-out production without the worry of excessive risk.

1988 Crop Target Prices and Loan Rates

	Target price	Regular loan rate	Acreage[a] reduction	Paid Land[b] diversion
Per bushel:				
Wheat	$4.23	$2.21	27.5%	NA
Corn	2.93	1.77	20.0%	10%
Grain Sorghum	2.78	1.68	20.0%	10%
Barley	2.51	1.44	20.0%	10%
Oats	1.55	.90	5.0%	NA
Per pound:				
Upland cotton	0.759	0.518	12.5%	NA

Source: USDA
[a] To be eligible for program benefits, including CCC loans and target price coverage, producers are required to participate in acreage reduction and diversion programs.
[b] Optional

Set-aside. The Agriculture and Consumer Protection Act of 1973 also provided authority for the secretary of Agriculture to specify set-aside when the secretary considers land retirement to be a necessity. If a set-aside is in effect, producers must set aside and devote to approved conservation uses an acreage of cropland equal to the specified percentage of their allotments in order to be eligible for loans, purchases, or payments. Cost-sharing for the control of erosion, insects, weeds, and rodents, or for the establishment of wildlife food plots or habitat, is authorized on set-aside. The secretary may provide for additional voluntary set-aside at fair and reasonable rates if it is needed to help balance crop production. The secretary also has the discretionary authority to impose or suspend the conserving base requirement.

Later Legislation. The target price concept has been continued since the Agriculture and Consumer Protection Act of 1973, which was amended by the Food and Agriculture Act of 1977, which in turn was amended by the Emergency Agricultural Act of 1978, the Agricultural Adjustment Act of 1980, and the Agriculture and Food Act of 1981.

Loan Program. While the loan program does not guarantee the participating farmer a profit, it does offer definite safeguards and advantages if his commodity is eligible for loan. The loan program gives farmers an opportunity to obtain cash and hold their crops for later sale. In practice, if the producer cannot profitably pay off his loan and sell the commodity, the loan may be satisfied in full by letting the COMMODITY CREDIT CORPORATION take over the commodity, without recourse. The loan program tends to even out marketings. In order to meet operating costs, farmers would otherwise be inclined to market their crops at harvest time. This sometimes makes for market gluts, undue burdening of the transportation system, and lower prices. Price swings and transportation bottlenecks are minimized to a great extent by spreading commodity marketing over the season. The loan program gives producers a chance to exercise greater independence in their marketing operations and to benefit from price increases that often come later in the season after harvest.

For many commodities, Congress has established a specific parity level at which—or a range within which—rates are to be set for loans, purchases, and payments. The parity price for an agricultural commodity is the dollars and cents price, determined by formula, that will give such commodity the same buying or purchasing power, in terms of goods and service bought by farmers and certain costs of their farming operations, that such commodity had in the 1910=1914 base period, with an adjustment based on the commodity's most recent 10-year average farm price, divided by the ratio of the general level of prices for all farm commodities during such 10-year period to the general level of prices received for all commodities during the 1910-1914 base period. The parity price of a commodity is therefore a general or overall standard.

Summary. During the 1980s the target price concept, was in effect the following commodities: wheat, corn, upland cotton, and rice. Minimum loan and purchase levels are established for wheat, feed grains, upland cotton, and rice. Deficiency payments for each of the four commodities are required when the target price for the commodity exceeds the national average market price or the loan rate, whichever is higher. The target prices for grain sorghum and oats—and, if designated by the secretary of Agriculture, for barley—are established at a level which is "fair and reasonable" in relation to the target prices established for corn.

PARITY INDEX Under Title III, Subtitle A, Section 301(a) of the Agricultural Adjustment Act of 1938, as amended by the Agricultural Acts of 1948 and 1949, "the ratio of (i) the general level of prices for articles and services that farmers buy, wages paid to hired farm labor, interest on farm indebtedness secured by farm real estate, and taxes on farm real estate, for the calendar month ending last before such date, to (ii) the general level of such prices, wages, rates, and taxes during the period January 1910 to December 1914, inclusive." The concept of parity index has been replaced by that of target price.

Uses. The parity index was prescribed for use in the computation of parity prices by Section 301 of the Agricultural Adjustment Act of 1938 as amended. Parity prices were computed by multiplying the adjusted base prices (*see* PARITY) by the current parity index (with 1910-1914 = 100). Decisions as to the level at which prices would be supported, pursuant to prevailing provisions of law, and the dates on which price support activity would be started or terminated were dependent in part on parity prices as determined by such computations using the parity index.

Indexes of Prices Received and Prices Paid by Farmers
(1977 + 100)

Year	Prices received by farmers (all farm products)	Prices paid by farmers (all commodities, services, interest, taxes, and wage rates)
1946	52	30
1947	60	35
1948	63	38
1949	55	36
1950	56	37
1951	66	41
1952	63	42
1953	56	40
1954	54	40
1955	51	40
1956	50	40
1957	51	42
1958	55	43
1959	53	43
1960	52	44
1961	53	44
1962	53	45
1963	53	45
1964	52	45
1965	54	47
1966	58	49
1967	55	49
1968	56	51
1969	59	53
1970	60	55
1971	62	58
1972	69	62
1973	98	71
1974	105	81
1975	101	89
1976	102	95
1977	100	100
1978	115	108
1979	132	123
1980	134	138
1981	138	150
1982	133	159
1983	135	161
1984	142	165
1985	128	163
1986	123	159
(Prelim. 1987)	127	162

Source: U.S. Department of Agriculture, 1988

Coverage. The Department of Agriculture points out that the coverage of prices paid series did not include all of the major areas of expenditures of farm families. Each such area was represented by a sample of items, since the proliferation of items offered in the modern markets for purchase defied complete coverage. The areas covered by the prices paid series were divided into two main groups, those bought for family living and those bought for production purposes. In the former group were food, clothing, household furnishings, household operation, autos and auto supplies, and building materials bought for farm home construction and repair. In the production group were feed, feeder livestock, motor supplies, motor vehicles, farm machinery, building materials for service buildings, fencing materials, fertilizer, farm supplies, and seed. Among the areas of farm family expenditure not included in the data collection program (because of lack of resources) were prices of medical, dental, and hosptial services; a variety of personal and financial services; and an increasing number of services performed on a custom or fee basis for farm operations.

Computation. Summarization procedures included listing and editing data reports and computing straight averages and weighted averages where valid weights were available. Such weights were usually confined to production items, since weights for items used in family living were not available for geographic units smaller than states. The various indications of data were then used by state statisticians in making recommended state average prices. Upon being received in Washington, the data were transcribed to a national summary for each commodity. After adoption of state estimates for each commodity by the Crop Reporting Board, regional and U.S. averages were computed. Weighting of state data to compute regional and U.S. average prices was on the basis of current use, if available, or on the basis of average purchases per farm as determined by special surveys of farm expenditures and numbers of farms. The national averages were used in the computation of the various subgroup and group indexes of prices paid needed in the computation of the parity index.

The appended table compares the index of prices received with the index of prices paid by farmers. (The prices paid index was frequently referred to as the parity index. The parity ratio was computed by dividing the index of prices received by the parity index and multiplying the result by 100.) The relationship between the two indexes, although they are no longer presented on their original base of 1910-1914 = 100, is relevant in indicating the ratio between what farmers receive and what farmers pay, updated to the 1977 base. It will be noted that in 1986 and 1987 the ratio of prices received divided by prices paid dipped to 77 and 78, respectively, constituting one often-cited indication of farm difficulties.

BIBLIOGRAPHY

U.S. DEPARTMENT OF AGRICULTURE. *Agricultural Prices.*

PARITY PRICE Price per bushel (or pound or bale) that would be necessary for a bushel today to buy the same quantity of goods (from a standard list) that a bushel would have bought in the 1910-14 base period at the prices then prevailing. Generally, it would be the price per bushel of wheat that farmers would need today to purchase a suit of clothes with the same number of bushels that it took in 1910-14.

PARITY RATIO A measure of the relative purchasing power of farm products; the ratio between the index of prices received by farmers for all farm products and the index of prices paid by farmers for commodities and services used in farm production and family living. The parity rate measures price relationships (prices received and prices paid). It does not measure farm income (units of production per acre and per animal have increased, and fewer farmers share total farm income). It does not measure the farmers' total purchasing power, because individual farms are larger, and total farm production is higher. It does not measure farmers' welfare to reflect off-farm income, government payments, farmers' assets, and other factors.

PARKING SECURITIES An illegal means used in corporate takeovers whereby the party attempting to acquire a corporation arranges for arbitragers to hold large blocks of stock that can be acquired quickly. The raider hopes to gain an effective hold on a corporation before acquiring the 5% ownership that triggers public disclosure of stock purchases. This procedure sometimes involves illegal INSIDER TRADING activity.

Stock parking has also been used to create illegitimate tax losses through prearranged securities transactions. In such transactions, one party sells securities at a loss and then repurchases them by prior agreement at the same or slightly higher prices. In 1989, the government successfully brought a major case involving stock parking in a racketeering trial of securities firm officials. The case involved acts of conspiracy; racketeering; and securities, wire and mail fraud.

PAR LIST The banks throughout the United States which accept and remit to presenting banks at out-of-town points for checks drawn upon themselves at par. Member banks of the Federal Reserve System are automatically placed on the par list. Other banks that are willing to accept and remit for checks drawn upon themselves at par may be placed upon the par list and are known as clearing members. As of December 31, 1980, there were no nonpar banking offices, according to the Federal Reserve. Clearing member banks are entitled to collect out-of-town checks through the FEDERAL RESERVE CHECK COLLECTION SYSTEM, a service which was formerly free of charge but is now subject to specified charges pursuant to the DEPOSITORY INSTITUTIONS DEREGULATION AND MONETARY CONTROL ACT OF 1980.

PAR OF EXCHANGE *See* MINT PAR OF EXCHANGE.

PAR POINTS Locations (cities and towns) which, with relation to a given central location, were considered to be within the par area of collections. No charge was made to a depositor who deposited for credit items drawn on banks located at par points. For any given location, the local clearinghouse association usually determined which points were par points by designating the area within a certain radius as the par area, and the area beyond this boundary as the nonpar area. In this way, bank members of the clearinghouse were governed by the same procedure, and standardized minimum exchange rates were fixed for all nonpar points.

The DEPOSITORY INSTITUTIONS DEREGULATION AND MONETARY CONTROL ACT OF 1980 gave all depository institutions access to the Federal Reserve System's check collection services. The Board of Governors of the Federal Reserve System therefore on August 12, 1981, approved an amendment to Regulation J that expanded the definitions of "bank" and "sender" to include those nonmember institutions (see FEDERAL RESERVE BOARD REGULATIONS).

Regulation J's statutory provisions provide that every Federal Reserve bank shall receive on deposit at par from depository institutions or from Federal Reserve banks checks and other items, including negotiable orders of withdrawal (NOWs) and share drafts and drafts drawn upon any of its depositors, and, when remitted by a Federal Reserve bank, checks and other items, including negotiable orders of withdrawal (NOWs) and share drafts and drafts drawn by any depositor in any other Federal Reserve bank or depository institution upon funds to the credit of said depositor in said Reserve bank or depository institution.

Moreover, "nothing herein contained" (in the statute, 12 U.S.C. 360) shall be construed as prohibiting a depository institution from charging its actual expense incurred in collecting and remitting funds or for exchange sold to its patrons. The Board of Governors of the Federal Reserve System shall, by rule, fix the charges to be collected by the member banks from patrons whose checks are cleared through the Federal Reserve bank, and the charge which may be imposed for the service of clearing or collection rendered by the Federal Reserve bank.

See FEDERAL RESERVE CHECK COLLECTION SYSTEM.

PARTIAL PAYMENT When a check is accepted that specifies that it is in full settlement of a claim, its acceptance will operate as a discharge of the claim in full, and the ordinary rule will not apply that a dispute exists as to the amount due and that independent consideration exists to support the accord and satisfaction. (See Section 3-408, Uniform Commercial Code.) Of course, payment by check is conditional and is defeated as between the parties by dishonor of the check on due presentment (Sec. 2-511(3), Uniform Commercial Code), unless it is expressly accepted as absolute payment.

PARTIAL PAYMENT PLAN Investment and odd-lot dealers formerly permitted small investors to buy bonds and the more conservative classes of stocks by means of partial payments. Such sales plans are now no longer operative because of the applicability of margin requirements under the SECURITIES EXCHANGE ACT OF 1934. The down payments, or initial deposits, were usually the same as margins required in margin buying. Monthly payments were then required until the full purchase price was paid. Interest was charged for the amount of the unpaid balance. Some dealers permitted as little as one share to be bought under this plan, with an initial deposit as low as $10.

The owner of a partial payment account could sell the securities in order to realize a profit which had accrued on his securities, even though the balance had not yet been paid. For this reason, the partial payment plan was closely akin to margin buying. In case of a sudden decline in the price of securities held, the broker was entitled to demand additional payments, although not yet due.

The MONTHLY INVESTMENT PLAN of the New York Stock Exchange was *not* a partial payment plan. It was a "pay as you go" method of purchasing designated securities.

PARTICIPANT A party—bank, investment house, etc.—which is invited to take and accepts membership in a distributing syndicate organized for the purpose of selling an issue of securities, or to which is given a share or partial interest in a loan granted by another bank.

See PARTICIPATION, PARTICIPATION LOAN.

PARTICIPATING BOND A bond, also known as a dividend or profit-sharing bond, which, in addition to bearing a minimum fixed rate of interest, is entitled to share in additional payments from profits of the issuing corporation. Participating bonds differ from INCOME BONDS in that while the minimum interest rate is fixed in the former and is an enforceable obligation, the maximum rate is only nominal in the latter and is subject to nonpayment, partial payment, or full payment only if earned. The additional participation by participating bonds above the minimum fixed rate may be limited by a certain maximum rate or else the participating bonds may share in the earnings ratably with, and as fully as, the equity securities (preferred or common stock).

Participating bonds are not common. Like CONVERTIBLE BONDS, they are securities which attempt to combine the creditor status of bonds with the ownership appeal and right to net profit of the equity. They are sometimes secured, oftentimes being collateral trust bonds, but most often are unsecured debentures "sweetened up" with such participating features.

PARTICIPATING PREFERRED STOCK See PREFERRED STOCK.

PARTICIPATION The portion or share of securities that is allotted to each member of a distributing syndicate, known as a participant, by the syndicate managers when an issue of securities is floated by a SYNDICATE. The amount of participation allotted to each member depends upon the size of the bank (in the case of government and municipal securities, which banks are still allowed to underwrite) or investment banking firm or securities dealer, the size of the territory served, the ability of the member to dispose of previous allotments, etc.

The interest of each member of a JOINT ACCOUNT is also known as a participation.

A participation agreement spells out the warranties and responsibilities of the lead lender and includes terms as the percentage of the loan to be taken by the participant(s), the dollar limit, if any, of the participant's share of the loan, the frequency of notification of the account's status, the rate of interest, a termination clause, and the frequency of settlement between the lead bank and the participant. The lead bank provides the participant bank with credit information and history of the borrower and with copies of all documents pertaining to the loan.

If the loan participation is legally classified as securities, four securities laws can affect the participation:

1. Registration provisions of the Securities Act of 1933.
2. Antifraud provisions of the Securities Exchange Act of 1934.
3. Broker-dealer registration requirements of the 1934 act.
4. Glass-Steagall Act.

Historically, participations have played a significant role in banking. They are desirable financing opportunities for both borrowers and lenders, especially for large or complex loans.

PARTICIPATION CERTIFICATE See PARTICIPATION LOANS.

PARTICIPATION LOANS Loans made by one bank in which another bank is given a part interest. This is a common practice among many of the large banks in the money centers, which maintain accounts with interior banks, by which the latter are given an investment outlet for their available funds in time and demand loans. This method of investing available funds of bank correspondents is a convenient one for the interior banks, since the loans can be made and terminated at their option and without inconvenience. Small correspondent banks use this method of investing temporarily idle funds as a substitute for commercial paper. The correspondent bank usually allows the bank in which the deposits are kept to select the names of the paper in which the participation is granted.

Care must be taken not to permit a participation loan which exceeds the participant's legal maximum loan to one borrower. Participation certificates, containing the details of the transaction, are issued to the participant as evidence of the participation loans.

The following is a typical form of participation certificate.

ENCYCLOPEDIA OF BANKING AND FINANCE

Sample Certificate of Participation

$ _____   No. _____

CERTIFICATE OF PARTICIPATION
issued by
Blank National Bank of New York

has allotted to _____ Bank
in participation of _____
in a note for $ _____
made by _____
dated _____
with interest at _____ % per annum.

PARTICULAR AVERAGE In marine insurance, insurance with particular AVERAGE, without limitation of percentage, covers any partial loss resulting from marine perils.

PARTIES The parties to a check are the drawer, payee, drawee, and endorsers; to a draft or bill of exchange, the DRAWER, DRAWEE (called acceptor after he accepts it), payee (often the same party as the drawer), and endorsers; to a note, the MAKER, PAYEE, and endorsers.

PARTNER'S CAPITAL The amount of money contributed by the partners of a firm for investment in the partnership business. This term is also sometimes applied to the capital contributed by the stockholders of a corporation, presumably represented by the aggregate amount of preferred and common stock outstanding, as distinguished from the amount of capital represented by bonds and other forms of fixed indebtedness. Stocks are sometimes referred to as share capital, while bonds, notes, mortgages, debentures, equipment trust certificates, etc., are called loan capital.

PARTNERSHIP A general partnership is a form of business organization in which two or more persons (no limit as to the number) are associated as coowners for the purposes of business or professional activities for private pecuniary gain. Each general partner is a general agent for the others and may bind the partnership for acts within the scope of the partnership's business. It is a contractual relationship needing no written partnership agreement to arise. It is preferable, however, to prepare written articles of copartnership, especially in order to define the duties of each partner and respective authorities which will be binding as among the partners and to specify the agreed sharing of profits and losses which otherwise in the absence of specification will be implied to be equal.

As distinguished from the corporation, the general partnership requires no formal legal proceedings in the form of charter or franchise from the state, although legal incidents of the general partnership have been enacted by all states except Georgia and Louisiana by their versions of the Uniform Partnership Law, declaratory of common law principles which will otherwise prevail in other jurisdictions which have not enacted statutes. Moreover, the general partnership has no separate legal existence apart from the partners, and so is not taxed as a firm for income tax purposes as is the corporation. Because of such lack of legal entity, however, the general partnership is subject to unlimited personal liability by the general partners for any of the partnership debts, each general partner being jointly and severally liable for the firm debts. In recovering from personal assets of the partners, however, firm creditors are subject to the rule of marshaling of assets, pursuant to which personal creditors have first claim upon personal assets in the event of conflict as to priorities. In turn, personal creditors are subject to the firm creditors' first claim upon firm assets. In addition, because of the lack of legal entity for the general partnership as a firm, the firm's existence is very fragile, being subject to *dissolution* (not necessarily *liquidation* in each case) by reason of the death, withdrawal, bankruptcy, or legal disability of any of the general partners. Usually such lack of permanence of duration of the firm is a disadvantage insofar as long-term firm financing is concerned. This factor, as well as the divisibility of ownership into conveniently sized units (shares) enjoying limited liability and transferring readily without legal difficulty, makes the corporation the feasible form of business organization where substantial external financing is required for a firm.

Unlike the general partnership, the limited partnership is purely statutory and will arise by implication and without written articles of copartnership. A limited partnership is formed by express written agreement, pursuant to statute of the home state, between one or more general partners and one or more limited partners. The limited liability feature applies only to the limited partners, provided they are merely investors in the firm and actually do not have a voice in the management. The general partners in the limited partnership are subject to all the legal incidents of general partnership law. Most states have enacted their versions of the Uniform Limited Partnership Act. A limited partnership, like the corporation and unlike the general partnership, has no freedom of movement and will be simply a general partnership in any jurisdiction other than the home state of creation. State procedural requirements for the creation of the limited partnership, including the filing of a certificate or articles of partnership and publication thereof, are not onerous. Specific compliance, however, is necessary in order to achieve limited liability for the limited partners. Moreover, the limited partners' claims as to withdrawal of capital investment, sharing in profits, or withdrawal of loans to the firm must not impair the ability of the firm to provide for firm creditors. As investor-partners, however, limited partners enhance the financial resources of a partnership, the usual motivation for such form of organization. The disadvantage of impermanence of the firm because of the dissolution incidents of the general partnership will also apply to the limited partnership insofar as the general partners are concerned. As far as the limited partners are concerned, their withdrawal pursuant to agreement or transfer of their interest will not work a dissolution of the firm. A limited partner may legally demand a dissolution, however, if after notice and without injury to the claims of creditors, the return of his investment is not forthcoming.

Other forms of partnership are the following:

1. The joint venture modified as to (a) limitation of existence for a single undertaking or specified period, and (b) centralized authority in the manager.
2. The mining partnership modified as to (a) coownership only as to profits, tenancy in common of the individuals as to the mine; (b) possibility of issuance of stock for transferable ownership interests in the mine; (c) no general agency authority in each of the partners to bind the partnership within the scope of the business, a manager usually having limited authority for necessary labor, supplies, etc.; and (d) personal liability of partners for firm debts incurred while they were owners or until notice of retirement is given to creditors.
3. The limited partnership association modified as to (a) formal organizational procedure, akin to that of the corporation, including organization tax; (b) legal entity for the firm so that limited liability applies; (c) division of the capital into shares of stock; (d) election by the shareholders of a board of managers or directors akin to that of the corporation; (e) transferability of stock subject to the requirement that new shareholders must be accepted by a majority of the existing stockholders in order to vote. Should the new shareholder be denied election, he may, pursuant to law, demand the purchase of his shares by the association, either by negotiations or pursuant to appraisal by court-appointed appraiser. This requirement for cash might prove embarrassing to the liquidity of the firm. Like the limited partnership and corporation, the limited partnership association is a creature of statute of the home state and will not have freedom of movement as such into other states. Only four states provide for this variation of the partnership, with their own variations of the form in each case.

Partnerships are treated as separate accounting entities from the partners. A partner's capital interest in a partnership is a claim against the net assets of the partnership as reflected in the partner's capital account. A partner's interest in profit and loss determines how the partner's capital interest changes as a result of subsequent operations.

Advantages associated with the partnership form of business organization include the ease of formation and dissolution, its ability to pool capital and personal talents and skills, its nontaxable status for income tax purposes, and the relative freedom and flexibility partners enjoy in business matters. Disadvantages of partnerships include their limited life, the ability of a partner to commit the partnership in contractual matters, the unlimited personal liability of partners, and the difficulties of raising large sums of capital and of transferring ownership interests as contrasted with the corporate form of business organization.

A person may become a partner in an existing partnership by purchasing an interest from one or more of the existing partners and by investing cash or noncash assets in the partnership. A person can be admitted to a partnership only with the consent of all continuing partners in the new partnership enterprise.

The tax bases for assets contributed by the partners to the partnership are the same tax bases that applied to the individual partner making the contribution. The tax basis of a partner's interest in capital of a partnership is the sum of the tax bases of the assets contributed by the partner, increased by the personal liabilities of other partners which the partner assumes, and decreased by the partner's personal liabilities assumed by other partners. The sum of the tax bases of the partnership assets equals the sum of the tax bases of the partners' separate interests in capital.

Summary. Numerically, business firm population in the United States is about 80% simple proprietorships, with 10% partnerships and 10% corporations. Corporations account for the bulk of business assets, sales, and employment in the aggregate. This reflects their advantages for assembling large aggregations of capital. The partnership form is required in some states for firms involved with professional responsibility of a personal nature to clients. Law and accounting firms are often formed as partnerships.

BIBLIOGRAPHY

"Capital Account Safe Harbors Explained." *Journal of Taxation*, October, 1988.
Corporation-Partnership-Fiduciary Filled-in Tax Return Forms. COMMERCE CLEARING HOUSE, INC., Chicago, IL. Annual.
Federal Income Tax Specimen Returns: Corporation, Partnership and Fiduciary. PRENTICE HALL, INC., Englewood Cliffs, NJ. Annual.
How to Save Time and Taxes Preparing the Federal Partnership Return. MATTHEW BENDER & CO., INC., New York, NY. Looseleaf.
Partnership Taxation. SHEPARD'S/McGRAW-HILL BOOK CO., Colorado Springs, CO. Looseleaf.
"Protecting Yourself Against Your Partners. *Canadian Business*, November, 1988.
SCHLOSSBERG, R L., and PRUSIECKI, J. F. "How Partnerships Can Reduce Taxes in LBO Acquisitions." *Mergers and Acquisitions*, November/December, 1988.
THOMAS, S. G. "Why Partnerships Break Up." *Inc.*, November, 1988.
WYLIE, P., and GROTHE, M. "Breaking Up Is Hard to Do." *Executive Female*, November/December, 1988.

PAR VALUE Face value or nominal value.

Bonds. The PAR or face value of a bond is the principal amount (DENOMINATION) at which the obligor (issuing corporation) contracts to redeem the bond at maturity. It is also the basis upon which the cash interest rate on the bond is computed. Although bonds are usually originally issued at an interest rate sufficiently attractive to assure their sale approximately at par or at slight discount, they will subsequently fluctuate in accordance with the trend of money rates and yields (if high-grade) and general business conditions (if second-grade or speculative) and earnings available for charges of the issuer. Whether a bond commands an open market premium or discount, the closer it approaches maturity, the closer the market value should approximate the par value, unless there is serious question about the ability to repay or refund by the issuer. At the date of maturity, it should be worth precisely par, since that is its redemption value. In the United States, business corporation bonds are usually issued in denominations of $1,000, although $500 and $100 denominations are not infrequent. Higher denominations such as $5,000 and $10,000 occur in relatively fewer instances, designed for institutional investors.

Stocks. The par or face value of shares of stock is not uniform, although $100 was formerly the most common par value. Shares may be given any specified par value, e.g., $50, $25, $10, and even smaller or odder denominations especially as the result of split-ups. In speculative enterprises, such as in the oil and mining industries, the par value of shares is usually small, and in turn the number of shares on a given dollar amount of capital is large. This is done in order to attract a wider market than would be possible if shares were of higher par value and hence there were fewer shares on a given dollar amount of capital, resulting in higher per-share figures for earnings, asset value, dividend (if any), and market price. In many states, shares may be issued without par value, in which cases the shares are assigned a stated or declared value for purposes of the capital stock account. In relatively rarer cases, par value of business corporations may be a multiple of $100, e.g., $500, $1,000, etc.; this may be done by privately owned or closely held corporations to restrict the number of holders. The significance of par value is that it must be fully paid (in the case of business corporations, issuable for cash, property, or services) in order that the stock may attain nonassessable status (limited liability). In the case of no par value shares, the subscription price must similarly be fully paid, even though the stated or declared value may be a fraction of the subscription price. But the subscription price on subsequent issues may be varied flexibly in line with market conditions as compared with the rigid par value requirement in the case of par value shares.

The treasury stock device in connection with the promotion of new speculative enterprises has been rendered obsolete by no par value shares and by fractional par values (something less than $100). That device would call for issuance of stock to the promoter for his services (subject to a test of reasonableness of the value thereof) at full par value. Next, the promoter would then donate back to the corporation a portion of his holdings, allowing the corporation thereafter to sell the treasury stock thus donated at any price to investors in the speculative venture, such resold treasury stock being entitled to fully paid and nonassessable status (having been originally issued at full par value). Thus the new corporation would be able to raise cash needed for the venture.

See WITHOUT PAR VALUE STOCK.

PASS A DIVIDEND When a board of directors omits to declare a regular or expected dividend, it is said to pass a dividend.

PASSBOOK A bank book; a book in which deposits, or deposits and withdrawals, are recorded. Passbooks are provided for both commercial and savings accounts. In commercial checking accounts the passbook is merely a memorandum of deposits. It is neither a book of original entry nor a statement of account. The DEPOSIT SLIP is the original entry and the important record from a legal point of view. Unlike the savings bank passbook, the nonsavings account passbook is not a contract. Entries should not be considered as absolute receipts admissible as court records, but rather as acknowledgments of receipts of deposits corresponding in amount to the footing of the accompanying deposit slips. It is not necessary to present a passbook when making deposits in a commercial checking account. It is only necessary to fill out a deposit slip, a duplicate being rendered if desired. The acceptance of a deposit for absolute receipt and credit, except for cash, is usually conditional upon the collection and payment of such deposit. Deposits of checks, in other words, are subject to final payment and therefore to cancellation of credit for such portions as may be returned unpaid.

In order that commercial depositors may understand the purpose of a passbook and the conditions under which deposits are accepted, a notation such as the following should be imprinted on the flyleaf.

> This passbook is issued for the convenience of customers and is intended for a record of deposits only. It is not a book of original entry, nor a statement of account. Statements of account will be rendered monthly.
>
> All items, other than money, are subject to cancellation of credit if not paid on presentation. It must be understood that the liability of the bank is limited to the observance of due diligence in selecting its immediate correspondents for the presentation and collection of items in this city and elsewhere and that the endorsement "Pay to any bank or banker," or its equivalent, shall not exceed such liability, and this bank will not be responsible for loss of any kind due to the acts of negligence of such correspondents in the selection of subagents for presentation and collection, etc., or for loss in or through the mails, or for any failure to present, demand, or collect on any Saturday or holiday.

The status of a savings account passbook is legally very different from that issued for a checking account. In savings bank practice, it is used as a voucher or receipt, both for money deposited and for money withdrawn. It must be presented whenever a deposit or withdrawal is made, and periodically for the credit of interest accumulated on the balance. It is also the evidence of the contract existing between the bank and the depositor. Whenever withdrawals are made, the depositor is identified by some means other than through the possession of the passbook. In case he is not personally known to the teller, his signature is compared with that on record. Test questions may also be asked. Among illiterates, many SAVINGS BANKS use the fingerprint method of identification.

A savings bank passbook is not negotiable, but may be assigned for the purpose of obtaining a loan, except where a bank prohibits assignments in its bylaws.

Lost Passbook. The loss of a passbook for a commercial account is of no serious consequence since the passbook is only a memorandum of deposits; it cannot be used by another person for making withdrawals.

Among savings banks, however, the passbook is an important instrument, being at once a contract and the only means by which the depositor makes both deposits and withdrawals.

Most New York City savings banks, merely require that upon identification, with proof of loss satisfactory to the bank, payments may be made, upon proper receipts therefor, of balances due on such accounts in accordance with the books of the bank, and such accounts closed. The officials of the bank may require that such loss be advertised in a newspaper circulating in New York City and may further require that 30 days shall elapse thereafter before such payments be made.

See FINGERPRINT IDENTIFICATION.

PASS-THROUGH CERTIFICATE A mortgage-backed security that gives an owner an undivided interest in the underlying asset pool (the mortgage) and an income stream linked directly to the return (the mortgage payments) on that pool. Typically, pass-through certificates are issued or guaranteed by a special payment vehicle that is a separate corporation or trust to which the mortgage originator transfers the pooled assets.

PASS-THROUGH SECURITY A security representing an interest in an underlying pool of mortgages. Payments received on the underlying pool are passed through to the security investor.

PAST-DUE BILLS See OVERDUE BILLS.

PATENT An exclusive right given to an individual or firm to use a particular process or to make or sell a specific product for a predetermined period of time—17 years in the United States. During that period of time, the patent holder has a monopoly over the patented product or process because the patent gives the inventor the right to prevent others from using his or her patented process or making or selling his or her patented product. The Patent and Trademark Office celebrated the issuance of the one millionth patent produced under its computerized printing process in FY 1987.

The rationale behind the patent system is based on the belief that innovations benefit society. Therefore, some incentive should be provided to individuals and firms for incurring the risks associated with innovative activity. This rationale is well founded. Innovations often lead to technological improvements, which, in turn, can increase the well-being of society through the development of new or improved products, and through changes in production processes that lower costs or increase efficiency. There is, however, a risk associated with innovative activity because many ideas may never develop into a commercial process or product. Furthermore, new products and processes can easily be stolen before the inventor receives enough final benefits to cover all of the related costs. A patent protects the innovator or innovating firm from some degree of these pressures and thereby encourages the search for new knowledge. The patent system also provides incentives to invest in research and development, to commercialize new technology, and to make public inventions that would otherwise go unnoticed.

New and useful production processes and products are patentable, but the discovery of basic knowledge is not. The variety of things patentable ranges from a new chemical compound used in producing a drug to a new circuit configuration for high-speed computers, to a new design for a child's toy. The initial cost to obtain a patent may be only a few hundred dollars; however, the cost to firms to retain legal counsel to enforce their patents can run into hundreds of thousands of dollars a year.

The patent system in the United States is administered by the Patent and Trademark Office (PTO) and was established by Congress under Article 1, Section 8 of the U.S. Constitution "... to promote the progress of ... the useful arts ...." PTO examines applications for three kinds of patents: design patents (issued for 14 years), plant patents, and utility patents (issued for 17 years), including reissue patents. Reexamination of patents still in force began July 1, 1981. Under legislation effective May 8, 1985, PTO began issuing statutory invention registrations, which have the defensive but not the enforceable attributes of a patent. PTO also processes international applications for patents under the provisions of the Patent Cooperation Treaty, including, as of July 1, 1986, the examination provisions of Chapter II of the treaty. Patents may be reviewed and searched in the PTO and in more than 60 public libraries around the country.

The appended table shows patents granted, by industry, from 1970 to 1987.

BIBLIOGRAPHY

AGRES, T. "Archaic Patent File System Strangles." *Research & Development*, January, 1989.
Intellectual Property Law Review. Clark Boardman Co., New York, NY. Annual.
Patent Law Fundamentals. Clark Boardman Co., New York, NY. Looseleaf.
Patents. MATTHEW BENDER & CO., INC., New York, NY. Looseleaf.
Patents and Trademarks. U.S. Superintendent of Documents, Washington, DC. (Subject bibl. 21).
ROSENBERT, P. D. *Patent Law Fundamentals.* Clark Boardman Co., New York, NY. Looseleaf.

PATENT AND TRADEMARK OFFICE A federal office that examines applications for three kinds of patents: design patents (issued for 14 years), plant patents, and utility patents (issued for 17 years), including reissue patents. The office issues statutory invention registrations, which have the defensive but not the enforceable attributes of a patent. About 77,000 patents were issued for fiscal year 1986 that provide inventors with exclusive rights to the results of their creative efforts. Patents may be reviewed and searched in the office and in more than 60 public libraries around the country. The patent system is intended to promote incentives to invent, to invest in research and development, to commercialize new technology, and to make public inventions that would otherwise go unnoticed.

A trademark includes any distinctive word, name, symbol, device, or any combination thereof adopted and used by a manufacturer or merchant to identify goods or services and distinguish them from those manufactured or sold by others. Trademarks, registered for 20 years with renewal rights, are examined by the office for compliance with various statutory requirements to prevent unfair competition and consumer deception. More than 55,000 trademarks were registered for 1986.

The appended table shows patents and trademarks issued from 1961 to 1987.

PAWN A pledge for the payment of a debt. In this country the term applies to the pledge of personal belongings—jewelry, furniture, clothing, musical instruments, etc.—for a loan from a pawnbroker who is licensed and permitted to exact extra-legal rates of interest. A pawnbroker requires the actual deposit of the articles pledged for the loan he provides and is permitted to sell or otherwise dispose of articles pledged in case the loan is not paid at a specified maturity. In England, the term applies to the deposit of collateral as security for a bank loan, as distinguished from hypothecation in which the property itself is not deposited as security but merely the evidence thereof, such as a mortgage, bill of lading, etc.

PAWNBROKER See PAWN.

PAYABLE-THROUGH CHECK A check payable by one bank but "payable through" another. On May 27, 1988, the Federal Reserve Board issued Regulation CC: Availability of Funds and Collection of Checks to Implement the Expedited Funds Availability Act of 1987. As initially issued, Regulation CC required a check payable by one bank but "payable through" another, and sent to the "payable-through" bank for payment or collection, to be local or nonlocal—for the purpose of funds-availability schedules—depending on the location of the "payable-through" bank. As a

Patents, by Industry: 1970 to 1987
(Includes all patents for inventions granted to residents of the United States, its territories, and foreign citizens. Number of patents by industry may not add to total since a patent may be recorded in more than one industry category.)

SIC[1] code	Industry	1970	1975	1980	1985	1986	1987
X	Total	64,429	70,002	61,819	71,661	70,860	82,952
X	Durable goods:						
32	Stone, clay, glass, and concrete products	2,118	2,335	2,106	2,382	2,300	2,553
33, 3462-3	Primary metals	793	1,032	764	783	822	794
34	Fabricated metal products[2]	7,646	8,870	7,429	8,295	8,328	9,748
35	Machinery, except electrical	18,349	20,365	17,056	20,185	19,568	21,907
36, 3825	Electrical and electronic equipment, and supplies	14,333	13,103	11,612	15,295	15,341	19,995
37, 348	Transportation and other public utilities	4,100	5,210	4,047	4,966	4,924	6,047
38	Professional and scientific instruments[3]	8,085	8,930	8,477	10,139	10,567	12,536
X	Nondurable goods:						
20	Food and kindred products	508	705	515	576	462	500
22	Textile mill products	717	715	636	800	780	821
28	Chemicals and allied products	9,616	12,909	10,746	11,300	10,123	11,273
13, 29	Petroleum, oil and gas extraction	859	810	783	1,018	849	954
30	Rubber and miscellaneous plastics products	4,728	5,711	4,909	5,897	5,591	6,232
	All other SIC[1] groups	6,260	7,216	6,319	6,684	7,180	8,131

X — Not applicable.
[1] Standard Industrial Classification.
[2] Excludes SIC groups 3462, 3463, 348.
[3] Excludes SIC group 3825.

Source: U.S. Patent and Trademark Office, *Patenting Trends in the United States, State Country Report, 1963-1987*.

Patents and Trademarks: 1961 to 1987
(In thousands. Calendar year data. Covers patents issued to citizens of the United States and residents of foreign countries.)

Item	1961-1970	1971-1980	1980	1981	1982	1983	1984	1985	1986	1987
Patent applications filed	967.8	1,091.5	113.0	114.5	118.4	112.4	120.6	127.1	133.0	139.8
Inventions	912.3	1,019.4	104.3	106.4	109.6	103.7	111.3	117.0	122.4	127.9
Designs	51.6	65.8	7.8	7.4	8.2	8.1	8.7	9.6	9.9	11.2
Botanical plants	1.2	1.7	.2	.2	.2	.3	.3	.2	.3	.4
Reissues	2.7	4.6	.6	.5	.4	.3	.3	.3	.3	.4
Patents issued	618.3	731.0	66.2	71.0	63.3	62.0	72.7	77.2	76.9	89.4
Inventions	585.1	687.8	61.8	65.8	57.9	56.9	67.2	71.7	70.9	83.0
Individuals	143.3	152.0	13.3	14.1	11.9	10.5	12.3	12.9	13.3	15.3
Corporations: U.S.	343.1	343.3	29.4	29.5	25.8	25.7	30.1	31.3	29.6	33.8
Foreign[1]	83.8	176.4	18.2	21.0	19.2	19.6	23.6	26.4	27.0	32.9
U.S. Govenment	14.9	16.1	1.0	1.1	1.0	1.0	1.2	1.1	1.0	1.0
Designs	30.2	38.1	3.9	4.7	4.9	4.6	4.9	5.1	5.5	6.0
Botanical plants	1.0	1.6	.1	.2	.2	.2	.2	.2	.2	.2
Reissues	2.1	3.4	.3	.4	.3	.4	.3	.3	.3	.2
Published applications[2]	.6	1.3	Z	.1	Z	Z	Z	Z	.2	.2
Foreign country residents[3]	124.3	237.3	24.7	26.5	24.0	25.4	30.5	33.9	34.9	41.7
Certificates of trademarks issued	235.1	309.0	24.7	48.6	48.4	46.8	54.0	71.7	51.8	51.4
Trademarks	196.1	250.6	18.9	42.7	42.4	40.5	48.6	65.8	46.7	47.3
Trademark renewals	39.0	58.4	5.9	5.9	6.0	6.2	5.4	5.9	5.1	4.1

Z — Less than 50.
[1] Includes patents to foreign governments.
[2] Abstracts of technical disclosure of patent published at request of applicant or owner. The practice called "Defensive Publications" began Nov. 1968 and ended July 1986. The current practice, called "Statutory Invention Registrations," began May 1985.
[3] Includes patent inventions and patents for designs, botanical plants, and reissues. Beginning 1986, also includes published applications.

Source: U.S. Patent and Trademark Office. Fiscal-year figures are published in the *Commissioner of Patents and Trademarks Annual Report*.

result of a lawsuit by credit unions, the Federal Reserve Board adopted a final rule amending the definition of paying bank to include the bank through which a check is payable and to which it is sent for payment or collection, if the check is not payable by a bank.

The final rule requires any bank that issues payable-through checks to have the checks conspicuously labeled with the name, location, and the first four digits of the routing number of the bank on which it is written. The checks would also have to bear the name and location of the payable-through bank and the legend "payable through." This procedure would make these items more readily identifiable. The first four digits of the nine-digit routing number and the location of the bank where the check is payable must be in the same check-processing region. This rule will become effective February 1, 1991.

A bank that issues payable-through checks that do not meet these requirements will bear the risk of any loss suffered by a depository bank that would not have occurred if the check had complied with the rule. The bank will be liable to the extent that the return from the nonlocal payable-through bank took longer than would have been required if the check had been returned expeditiously.

PAYABLE THROUGH THE CLEARINGHOUSE

Some checks are stamped with "Payable through the Clearinghouse," "Through the Clearinghouse," or a similar expression. Such checks cannot be presented at the drawee bank and cashed, but must be deposited for credit and in turn collected through the clearinghouse. During the panic of 1907 checks stamped in this way aided the banks in increasing the supply of money, since clearinghouse balances were settled not by actual cash, but with clearinghouse loan certificates. These certificates passed as money between members only.

PAYABLES

In accounting, a catchall reference to the combined aggregate of notes and accounts payable.

See ACCOUNTS PAYABLE, NOTES PAYABLE.

PAYABLE WITH EXCHANGE See WITH EXCHANGE.

PAY DAY

Account or SETTLEMENT DAY; the last day of the fortnightly settlement on the London Stock Exchange.

PAYEE

The party (person, firm, or corporation) in whose favor a check, note, draft, or money order is made payable. In the case of a note, the payee is the party to whom the promise to pay is made. The payee may be the maker, drawer, drawee, or any third party. Where the instrument is payable to order, the payee must be named or otherwise indicated with reasonable certainty.

See NEGOTIABLE INSTRUMENTS LAW (Sections 3-1110, 3-116, 3-117, and 3-203, Uniform Commercial Code).

PAYER

The party (person, firm, or corporation) upon whom payment devolves, as in the case of a check, draft, note, or bond. In the case of a check, the payer is the drawer; in the case of a draft, the drawer (acceptor after he accepts it); in the case of a note, the maker; and in the case of a bond, the obligor (issuer). Makers of promissory notes and acceptors of drafts are primarily liable parties and their liability is unconditional.

See NEGOTIABLE INSTRUMENTS LAW (Sections 3-413, 8-201, 8-202, and 3-511, Uniform Commercial Code).

PAYING BANK

The bank upon which a check is drawn and which pays a check, acceptance, or sight draft to a collecting bank or holder; drawee bank.

Article 4, Bank Deposits and Collections, of the Uniform Commercial Code adopts many of the provisions of the American Bankers Association's Bank Collection Code, which had been enacted in some 18 states.

PAYING TELLER

The first teller; the most important teller of a bank.

Although the paying teller is usually associated with the paying of cash against checks presented for payment and the custodianship of that part of the bank's money stock necessary for counter use, his functions are considerably more comprehensive.

The following outline shows the functions of the paying teller in detail:

1. Paying out money (cashing checks, bank drafts, and matured coupons, etc.) upon identification.
2. Custodianship of money.
   a. Receiving.
      (1) Shipments inward from correspondent or other banks.
      (2) Shipments from other banking departments, e.g., receiving teller, collection department, etc.
      (3) Shipments from original government sources:
         (a) Federal Reserve bank of district.
         (b) United States Treasury.
         (c) United States Assay Office.
   b. Counting, examining, strapping, and storing money.
   c. Redeeming worn and mutilated money at original sources.
   d. Detecting counterfeits and raised bills.
   e. Maintaining adequate supply of various kinds and denominations of money.
3. Shipping money to correspondent and other banks.
4. Certifying checks.
5. Settling clearinghouse balances.
6. Making disbursement for petty expenses.
7. Disbursing payroll cash.
8. Depositing excess cash with Federal Reserve bank or other depository or depositories.
9. Verifying signatures of principals of accounts.
10. Verifying stop-payments.
11. Proving daily work.

Often the work of counting and inspecting money and of certifying checks is so heavy that separate sections are created, but always under the supervision of the paying teller.

See CERTIFICATION DEPARTMENT.

PAYMENT CAPS

Terms of certain loans that place an upper limit on the amount of periodic payments. If the interest rate on an adjustable-rate loan increases and the loan has a payment cap, the monthly payments can rise to the limit set by the cap. They may increase by less than changes in the index would require.

PAYMENT FOR HONOR

The payment of a check or bill of exchange after it has been protested for nonpayment by an outside party for the purpose of saving the honor of any person liable thereon. Such payment for honor should be attested by a notarial act of honor. The payer for honor is entitled to receive the bill and the notarial protest certificate upon which the notarial act of honor is appended.

See NEGOTIABLE INSTRUMENTS LAW (Section 3-603, Uniform Commercial Code).

PAYMENTS MECHANISM

In a comprehensive sense, payments in coin and currency would be included in a country's payments system, in addition to transfers of funds effected by check, draft, or similar paper instrument. But in view of the ELECTRONIC FUND TRANSFER ACT (Title IX of the Consumer Credit Protection Act as amended (15 U.S.C. 1601 et seq.) and Regulation E of the FEDERAL RESERVE BOARD REGULATIONS, the board of governors has issued official staff commentary as follows. (Parenthetical references pertain to Regulation E.)

1. Payments in currency are not electronic fund transfers because they do not debit or credit a customer's account (Sec. 205.2 (g)).
2. Check truncation systems are not covered because the fund transfer by means of the truncation is initiated by check, draft, or similar paper instrument (Sec. 205.2(g)).
3. A transfer initiated by a draft drawn against the consumer's account is not an electronic fund transfer. But transfers via the AUTOMATED CLEARINGHOUSE are subject to the regulation (Sec. 205.2(g)).
4. Deposits of currency and checks at an automated teller machine (ATM) are electronic fund transfers for purposes of Regulation E if there is a special agreement between the financial institution and the consumer for the provision of EFT services to or from the particular account to which the deposit is made (Sec. 205.2(g); Sec. 205.9 (b)(1)(iv), footnote 4a).
5. If an employer or other payor delivers a composite check made payable to a financial institution for crediting to consumers' accounts at the institution on which the payee information is contained on magnetic tape, such transfers are not electronic fund transfers (Sec. 205.2(g)).
6. On the other hand, if a company obtains authorization from consumers to debit their accounts and the financial institution debits the customers' accounts in accordance with billing information contained on magnetic tape provided by the payee and sends the payee a composite check, such transfers are electronic fund transfers (Sec. 205.2(g)).
7. Transfers under the U.S. Treasury's direct-deposit program, whereby Social Security benefits are sent via the ACH to the consumer's financial institutions and institutions receive fund transfers through a correspondent bank which sends a computer printout listing the payee and payment amounts, together with a composite check payable to the financial institution, are electronic fund transfers (Sec. 205.2(g)).

Thus the particular mode of effecting payments and the payments mechanism selected determine whether or not the transfers are subject to the Electronic Fund Transfer Act and Regulation E, which establish and carry out the basic rights, liabilities, and responsibilities of consumers who use electronic money transfer services and of financial institutions that offer these services. The board of governors points to the intent of the act primarily to protect individual consumers engaged in electronic transfers, and emphasizes the corresponding care that should be exercised by financial institutions in order to avoid the liabilities under the act and regulation that otherwise might develop.

BIBLIOGRAPHY

BOARD OF GOVERNORS OF THE FEDERAL RESERVE SYSTEM. *Federal Reserve Regulatory Sevice.*

PAYMENT STOPPED *See* STOP PAYMENT.

PAYMENT TABLES   Financial tables that show monthly payments (principal and interest) for loans that fully pay off the debt over the loan term for various annual interest rates and amounts financed.

PAYROLL TAXES   The Federal Social Security Act provides a variety of programs for qualified individuals and families, including a federal old-age and survivors' benefits program with medical care for the aged and a joint federal-state UNEMPLOYMENT insurance program. Benefits are based upon the average earnings of the worker during the period of employment in covered industries. Funds to support these programs come from payroll taxes imposed under the Federal Insurance Contribution Act (FICA) and the Federal Unemployment Tax Act (FUTA).

Social Security taxes are imposed on both employer, employees, and the self-employed. The employer deducts the tax from the employee's gross pay and remits it to the government along with the employer's share. Both parties are taxed at the same rate based on the employee's gross pay up to an annual maximum limit.

Employers are also subject to the Federal Unemployment Tax Act, which supports a system of unemployment insurance. This tax is levied by the federal government in cooperation with state governments. A rate is applied against income earned by covered employees up to a specified amount. The employer is allowed a credit against the federal tax for unemployment taxes paid to the state. In some states, employers with favorable employment records are entitled to a reduction in taxes.

Employers are required to withhold from employees' pay an amount estimated for federal income taxes. Employers remit the withholdings to the federal government. The amount withheld depends primarily upon the employee's earnings and the number of exemptions the employee is entitled to claim. Many states have income taxes and withholding procedures similar to those used by the federal government.

PAY TO BEARER   A negotiable instrument, (e.g., check, draft, note) made payable to bearer, cash, or currency is payable to bearer, and title may be negotiated by mere delivery without endorsement. Instruments that are payable to bearer, known as BEARER instruments, include all forms of money; checks, drafts, and notes made payable to bearer; coupon or bearer bonds; and coupons detached from bonds.

See NEGOTIABLE INSTRUMENTS LAW(Section 3-111, Uniform Commercial Code).

PAY TO ORDER   A negotiable instrument that is made payable to order can be negotiated only by endorsement and delivery. A check written "Pay to the order of John Doe" or "Pay to John Doe or order" is an order instrument, and must be endorsed by John Doe before it may be negotiated to another person by delivery thereto.

See NEGOTIABLE INSTRUMENTS LAW (Section 3-110, Uniform Commercial Code).

PEER REVIEW   The American Institute of Certified Public Accountants established a voluntary organization, the Division of CPA Firms (consisting of firms having an SEC practice), in 1977 to maintain and improve the quality of the accounting and auditing services performed by member firms. A peer review of a member firm, conducted by other CPAs under the auspices of the AICPA, provides considerable assurance that the firm has an appropriate quality control system for its accounting and auditing practice and that it is complying with that system. Firms are expected to undergo a peer review every three years. A major purpose of peer reviews is to recognize the public's interest in reliable financial statements. The Private Companies Practice Section of the AICPA (consisting primarily of smaller CPA firms) also has established a peer review process that is similar to that required by the Division of CPA Firms.

Peer reviewers are required to evaluate a firm's quality control system against standards and comprehensive guidelines established by the AICPA. They also test a representative sample of a firm's accounting and auditing engagements for compliance with professional standards. Reviewers are expected to determine whether a firm's policies and procedures are adequate to meet quality control standards. The reviewers issue a written report on their peer review. If the report indicates the need for corrective action, the firm is expected to indicate in writing what it will do to correct the problem. In serious cases of inadequacy, a firm may be required to undertake additional education, agree to a revisit, or submit to another peer review within a short time. Most CPA firms receive unqualified opinions.

The AICPA has identified nine basic elements of quality control for a CPA firm: independence, assignment of personnel, consultation, supervision, hiring, continuing professional education, advancement, client acceptance and continuance, and inspection. Additional criteria required include assignment of responsibilities to personnel to provide for effective implementation, effective communication of the policies and procedures throughout the firm, and monitoring the system so that it is effective.

PEGGED PRICE   The price of a security or commodity is pegged when it is not permitted by those in control to advance above or decline below a certain fixed point. The market as a whole is pegged when prices remain stationary without moving perceptibly in one direction or the other.

Pegging, fixing, or stabilizing prices of securities on national securities exchanges is unlawful under Section 9 of the Securities Exchange Act of 1934 if in contravention of such rules and regulations as the Securities and Exchange Commission may prescribe as necessary or appropriate in the public interest or for the protection of inventors. By Rule 10b-7, the SEC permits stabilizing to facilitate a distribution or offering of a security, subject to restriction and reports on stabilizing activities (Rule 17a-2).

Under the Commodity Exchange Act (Sec. 5d), a commodity exchange may be designated by the secretary of Agriculture as a contract market when the rules of the exchange among other things provide for the prevention of manipulation of prices and the cornering of any commodity by any dealer or operator upon such exchange. Such exchange rules restrict the daily price fluctuation to some maximum range (daily trading limits), relative to the previous day's settlement or closing price. In some instances, trades shall not be made in any one day at an advance of more than the daily trading limit above the lowest previous price on that day, or at any decline of more than the daily trading limit below the highest previous price on that day. The objective of such daily trading price limits is to prevent unusual conditions of optimism or pessimism from booming or demoralizing prices. In addition, as a means of preventing large-scale operations by market "plungers," the Commodity Exchange Act's amendments of 1936 authorize the Commodity Exchange Commission to fix limits on the amount of any person's speculative trading and open contracts.

PENCE   The plural of PENNY.
See ENGLISH MONEY TABLE.

PENNY   In the new English coinage system, effective February 15, 1971, the penny is a plain-edge, bronze coin having a diameter of 2.0320 centimeters and weight of 3.5640 grams. The equivalent value, in terms of the old coinage system, is 2.4 pence.

The name is also given to the one-cent piece in the U.S.
See ENGLISH MONEY TABLE, MINOR COINS.

PENNY STOCKS   Loosely applies to low-priced equity issues, usually thinly traded and high risk issues. At one time it did refer to stocks under one dollar a share, but given that a dollar today is worth less than a third of a 1967 dollar, stocks priced under five dollars a share are generally called penny stocks. Many of the issues do not trade on a formal exchange but trade in the OVER-THE-COUNTER MARKET. Some of the more established issues are monitored on the

NATIONAL ASSOCIATION OF SECURITIES DEALERS AUTOMATED QUOTATION systems (NASDAQ).

Low-priced stocks that do not trade on a formal exchange usually do not see a lot of movement on a day-to-day basis. This inactivity can be deceptive. All stocks trade with a bid and ask price or spread. This spread is usually a much larger share of what the investor pays as compared with higher-priced issues. A very low-priced stock may have to appreciate 50% or more before an investor can realize a gain on a penny stock investment.

Low-priced stocks have seen periods of popularity from time to time. Usually they are associated with young start-up companies. One of the first periods of penny stock popularity was in the late 1800s, when mining operations in Colorado sought capital. It was found that selling many shares of a stock at a low price was more attractive than a few shares or even parts of a share of higher-priced stocks. Colorado to this day appears to have the most favorable laws for these stocks, so many investment firms specializing in penny stocks have their headquarters in that state.

During the favorable business climate of the 1960s many noted companies such as International Business Machines and Xerox went public as penny stocks. In retrospect, many who did not buy these stocks when they had the opportunity regret their decision. But a resurgence in penny stocks to finance oil concerns in the early 1980s, and the subsequent collapse of the bulk of these issues, shows that this area of the market deserves some caution.

In 1989, the Securities and Exchange Commission adopted regulations to hopefully eliminate fraudulent penny stock operations by making it impossible to close sales of such stock over the phone. When selling low-priced stocks that are not listed on an exchange or on the NASDAQ system, brokers must obtain a written sales agreement from the buyer who is not a regular customer. Brokers must also get information about a buyer's investment experience and financial condition. The regulation is aimed at eliminating boiler-room operations that often use high-pressure telephone sales pitches to sell stocks which often are worthless or become worthless soon after the sale. Only stocks selling for less than $5 a share and issued by companies with less than $2 million net tangible assets come under the regulation.

BIBLIOGRAPHY

OTC Penny Stock Digest. Chis S. Metos, Publisher. Annual.
Penny Stock News. Penny Stock News, Inc. Semimonthly.
Penny Stock Preview. Idea Publishing Corp. Monthly.

PENSION An arrangement whereby an employer agrees to provide benefits to retired employees, usually in the form of an allowance, annuity, or subsidy. A pension plan may be either contributory or noncontributory. In a contributory plan, both employer and employee contribute to the fund from which benefits are to be paid. In a noncontributory plan, only the employer makes contributions to the fund.

A single-employer plan is a pension plan established unilaterally by an employer. Multiemployer plans are sometimes established within an industry.

The funding aspect of pension plans are important. Funding means to pay to a funding agency. It also refers to assets accumulated by a funding agency to provide retirement benefits when they come due. Pension costs that have been paid over to a funding agency are said to have been funded. A funding agency is an organization or individual, such as an insurance company or a trustee, who accumulates assets for the payments of benefits under the plan and who administers the program. Terminal funding occurs when the benefits payable to a retired employee are funded in full at the time the employee retires; there is no funding for active employees. Pay-as-you-go funding does not provide any prior funding for retirement benefits but provides resources for the pensions as they come due after retirement.

In an insured pension plan, annuities are purchased for employees under individual or group annuity contracts between an employer and an insurance company. The insurance company guarantees the payment of benefits. Noninsured plans are generally funded by a trust agreement between an employer and a trust company.

When pension benefits are no longer contingent on an employee's continued employment, the employee's benefits under the plan are said to be vested. When benefits vest, an employee's pension rights cannot be reduced or taken away.

A defined benefit plan is a plan that states the benefits to be received by employees after retirement or the method of determining such benefits. A defined contribution plan is one in which the employer's contribution is based on a specified formula. Future benefits are limited to those that the plan can provide. A defined contribution plan specifies the amount of the periodic contributions to be paid by the plan's sponsor (and not the benefits to be received by a participant). Benefits are usually based on the amount credited to an individual's account.

BIBLIOGRAPHY

All Your Should Know About IRA, Keogh, and Other Retirement Plans. J. K. Lasser Tax Institute Staff. Prentice Hall, Inc., Englewood Cliffs, NJ, 1987.
BULOW, J. "The Effect of Inflation on the Private Pension System." *Inflation: Causes and Effects,* 1982.
———. "What Are Corporate Pension Liabilities?" *Quarterly Journal of Economics,* August, 1982.
CONGRESSIONAL BUDGET OFFICE. "Tax Policy for Pensions and Other Retirement Savings." *Government Printing Office,* Washington, DC, 1987.
DAVIS, E. P. "Financial Market Activity of Life Insurance Companies and Pension Funds." Bank for International Settlements, 1987.
Employee Benefit Plan Review, C. D. Spencer and Associates, Inc., Chicago, IL. Monthly.
ERISA: The Law and the Code. Bureau of National Affairs, Inc., Washington, DC. Annual.
EZRA, D. D., and AMBACHTSHEEJR, K. P. "Pension Funds: Rich or Poor?" *Financial Analysts Journal,* March/April, 1985.
FELDSTEIN, M., and RANDALL MORCK. "Pension Funds and the Value of Equities." *Financial Analysts Journal,* September/October, 1983.
FINANCIAL ACCOUNTING STANDARDS BOARD. *Statement of Financial Accounting Standards No. 87: Employers' Accounting for Pensions.* Norwalk, CN, 1985.
Guidebook to Pension Planning. Commerce Clearing House, Inc., Chicago, IL. Annual.
IPPOLITO, R. *Pensions, Economics and Public Policy.* Dow Jones-Irwin, Inc., Homewood, IL, 1986.
———. "The Economic Burden of Corporate Pension Liabilities." *Financial Analysts Journal,* January/February, 1986.
———. "The Labor Contract and True Economic Pension Liabilities." *American Economic Review,* December, 1985.
IRA Compliance Manual: Individual Retirement Arrangements, Keogh Plans, Simplified Employee Pensions. Prentice Hall, Inc., Paramus, NJ. Looseleaf.
Journal of Pension Planning and Compliance.
Know Your Pension Plan. U.S. Department of Labor, Washington, DC.
LANGETIEG, T. C., and OTHERS. "Measuring the Effective Duration of Pension Liabilities." *Solomon Brothers,* New York, NY, November, 1986.
LEIBOWITZ, M. "Liability Returns: A New Perspective on Asset Allocation." *Solomon Brothers,* May, 1986.
MALLEY, S. L., and JAYSON, S. "Why Do Financial Executives Manage Pension Funds the Way They Do?" *Financial Analysts Journal,* November/December, 1986.
MCGILL, D. *Fundamentals of Private Pensions.* Richard D. Irwin, Inc., Homewood, IL, 1984.
MUNNELL, A. *The Economics of Private Pensions.* Brookings Institute, Washington, DC, 1982.
Pension and Employee Benefits: Code-ERISA-Regulations. Commerce Clearing House, Inc., Chicago, IL. Annual.
Pension Benefit Guaranty Corporation. *Promises at Risk: SEPPAA Premium Study Report.* Pension Benefit Guaranty Corporation, Washington, DC, 1987.
Pension Reform Handbook. Prentice Hall, Inc., Paramus, NJ. Annual.
Pension Regulations Manual Service. Warren, Gorham and Lamont, Inc., Boston, MA. Two volumes, plus monthly bulletins.
Pensions and Investments Age. Crain Communications, Inc., Chicago, IL. Biweekly.
Pension World. Communciation Channels, Atlanta, GA. Monthly.
Qualified Retirement Plans. West Publishing Co., St. Paul, MN. Periodic Supplementation.
U.S. GENERAL ACCOUNTING OFFICE. "Benefit Levels of Nonfederal Retirement Programs." Government Printing Office, Washington, DC, 1985.

WARSHAWSKY, M. J. *The Funding of Private Pension Plans.* Staff Study. Board of Governors of the Federal Reserve System, Washington, DC, 1987.

WYATT CO. *The Tax Reform Act of 1986: Analysis of Employee Benefits and Compensation Provisions,* 1986.

PENSION BENEFIT GUARANTY CORPORATION (PBGC)

A federal government agency established to administer two mandatory insurance programs covering most private defined benefit pension plans. Under its single-employer program, the PBGC pays guaranteed pension benefits to participants in terminated single-employer plans, and under its multiemployer program, the PBGC provides financial assistance to multiemployer plans so that they can provide guaranteed benefits. The PBGC was established by Title IV of the Employee Retirement Income Security Act of 1974, 29 U.S.C. S 1301 *et seq.* (ERISA). ERISA has been amended on several occasions, most recently by the Pension Protection Act of 1987.

The PBGC is a self-financing, wholly owned United States Government corporation subject to the provisions of the Government Corporation Control Act, 31 U.S.C. S 9101 *et seq.* (1982). It is governed by a board of directors consisting of the secretaries of labor, commerce, and the Treasury. The secretary of labor is chairman of the board. In addition, a seven-member advisory committee, composed of two representatives of employee organizations, two representatives of employers, and three representatives of the general public, advises the PBGC. All members are appointed by the president.

Coverage. Title IV of ERISA provides for coverage of most tax-qualified private defined benefit pension plans. These are pension plans that provide a benefit, the amount of which can be determined from a formula in the plan—for example, one based on factors such as age, years of service, average or highest salary. The PBGC administers two benefit insurance programs: one for single-employer pension plans and one for multiemployer pension plans. More than 39 million workers participate in more than 112,000 covered plans.

At the close of the fiscal year 1987, the single-employer program had accumulated assets of $2.2 billion and liabilities of $3.7 billion. The multiemployer program had accumulated assets of $113.6 million and liabilities of $45.2 million.

Single-employer insurance program. Under Title IV of ERISA, the PBGC guarantees payment of basic pension benefits any time a covered single-employer plan terminates without sufficient assets to pay those benefits. Amendments to Title IV in 1986 and 1987 restrict voluntary plan terminations to those situations in which either the plan has sufficient assets and can provide all "benefit liabilities", *i.e.*, all liabilities under the plan (a "standard" termination), or the employer sponsoring the plan can satisfy certain specified tests of financial distress (a "distress termination").

Termination notice requirements: The plan administrator is required to notify each affected party at least 60 days prior to the proposed termination date for a standard or distress termination. (The PBGC is an affected party for this purpose for distress terminations only.) In a standard termination, the plan administrator must notify each participant of his or hers benefit amount and of the information used to determine that amount, e.g. age, salary, and length of service. A standard or distress termination notice, whichever applies, must be submitted to the PBGC as soon as practicable after the 60-day advance notice to affected parties is given. All plan terminations require the plan administrator to submit to the PBGC actuarial information certified by an enrolled actuary.

Standard termination: Only a plan that has sufficient assets to fund all benefit liabilities may terminate in a standard termination. The plan administrator closes out the plan in the private sector by purchasing irrevocable commitments from an insurer or otherwise fully satisfying all benefit liabilities.

Distress termination: The circumstances under which an underfunded pension plan may be terminated by a plan administrator were limited by amendments to ERISA made in 1986 and 1987. The contributing sponsor and all members of its controlled group must meet one of four distress tests, although the PBGC may institute involuntary termination proceedings under other circumstances. The distress tests enumerated by ERISA are: (1) liquidation in bankruptcy or insolvency proceedings; (2) reorganization in bankruptcy or insolvency proceedings (the bankruptcy court must find that the controlled group will be unable to pay all its debts pursuant to a plan of reorganization and continue in business outside the reorganization unless the pension plan is terminated); (3) determination by PBGC that termination of the pension plan is required to enable the controlled group to pay debts while staying in business; (4) determination by PBGC that termination of the pension plan is necessary to avoid unreasonably burdensome pension costs caused by a declining work force. Distress terminations and most terminations instituted by the PBGC result in joint and several liability for the contributing sponsor and all members of the contributing sponsor's controlled group. (See Liability Under Section 4062 of ERISA below). In addition, the PBGC as trustee of the plan collects contributions owed to the plan.

PBGC-initiated termination: THE PBGC also may institute termination proceedings when certain events specified in ERISA indicate that such action may be necessary.

Guarantees: ERISA limits the total monthly benefit that the PBGC may guarantee for one individual to $1,909.09 per month for plans terminating during 1988 and requires that the PBGC guarantee recent benefit increases only on a phased-in basis. Under the 1987 amendments to ERISA, the PBGC also pays a portion of plan benefits above the guaranteed amount, based on the percentage of its recovery of termination liability.

Multiemployer insurance program. Under Title IV of ERISA, the PBGC, prior to 1980, guaranteed basic benefits for multiemployer plans in a fashion similar to that for single-employer plans. However, the payment of guaranteed benefits was at the PBGC's discretion under the provisions of the law that remained in force until August 1, 1980. The Multiemployer Pension Plan Amendments Acts of 1980 (MPPAA), 94 Stat. 1208; 29 U.S.C. 1381-1461 (1982), revised the law applicable to multiemployer pension plans by changing the insurable event from plan termination to plan insolvency. In accordance with this act, the PBGC provides financial assistance to plans that are unable to pay basic benefits. The plans are obligated to repay such assistance. MPPAA also makes an employer withdrawing from a plan liable to the plan for a portion of the unfunded vested benefits.

Guaranteed benefits under a multiemployer plan differ from guaranteed benefits under a single-employer plan. Under a multiemployer plan, the guaranteed benefit is limited to 100% of the first $5 of the employees' accrual rate plus a fraction (either 65% or 75%) of the lesser of $15 or the accrual rate, if any, in excess of $5, times years of credited service. Financially troubled multiemployer plans are allowed to reduce their benefits and insolvent plans are required to reduce certain benefits, but not below guaranteed levels.

Premiums. All covered defined benefit pension plans are required to pay prescribed premium rates to the PBGC. The annual premium per plan participant for multiemployer pension plans was $2.20 though September 24, 1988 and increases to $2.60 for plan years starting on or after September 25, 1989. As of January 1, 1988 the basic premium for single-employer plans was $16 per participant per year for all plans and an additional amount for underfunded plans of $6 per $1,000 of underfunding up to a maximum of $50 per participant.

GAO Audit. The Government Corporation Control Act 31 U.S.C. S9101 *et seq.* (1982)—requires the General Accounting Office (GAO) to audit the financial statements of the PBGC at least once every three years. The GAO's audit for fiscal 1980 was the second since the PBGC's inception in September 1974. The first reported audit was issued on May 3, 1979, and resulted in a disclaimer of opinion. The disclaimer was based on (1) material accounting and estimating problems (primarily in estimating the liability for the present value of guaranteed future benefits), (2) internal control problems, and (3) other factors beyond the corporation's control. The GAO did not assert that the liabilities reported for the present value of guaranteed future benefits were incorrect, but rather that the available data upon which they were based were inadequate to provide a reliable estimate. The GAO has noted significant improvements since then.

Budgetary status of the PBGC. PBGC programs are required by ERISA to be self-financing. PBGC's operations are financed through the premiums collected from ongoing covered plans, investment income, assets acquired from terminated plans, and the collection of employer liability payments due under ERISA as amended. In addition, the PBGC may borrow up to $100 million from the Treasury to finance its operations, but no debt was outstanding in connection with this borrowing authority as of September 30, 1987. The fiscal 1987 annual report indicated that no use of this borrowing authority was contemplated. ERISA provided under Title IV that the U.S.

government is not liable for any obligation or liability incurred by the PBGC.

ERISA originally provided that the receipts and disbursements of the PBGC should not be included in the totals of the budget of the United States government. However, the Multiemployer Pension Plan Amendments Act provided that for the fiscal years beginning after September 30, 1980, PBGC's receipts and disbursements should be included in the totals of the budget of the United States government.

Liability to the PBGC. Under Section 4062 of ERISA, a contributing sponsor's controlled group incur joint and several liabilities to the PBGC whenever a single-employer plan is terminated in a distress termination or is involuntarily terminated by the PBGC. The amount of this liability is the difference between the value of the plan's assets and the value of the plan's liabilities. The liability to the PBGC is measured as of the date of termination of the plan and accrues interest from that date. If after demand by the PBGC, any liable party fails to pay this debt, the PBGC has a lien to the extent that the amount of the liability does not exceed 30% of the collective net worth of the contributing sponsor and all of the members of its controlled group.

Financial statements. For its financial statements, the PBGC compiles an inventory of all terminated pension plans that have been or are expected to be trusteed. Such total increased from 1,128 in fiscal year 1984 to 1,201 in 1985, 1,355 in 1986, and 1,415 in 1987. The PBGC's total reserve liabilities for guaranteed benefits for terminated plans and net claims for pending terminations were carried at $3,666,650,000 as of September 30, 1987, compared with $5,540,610,000 as of September 30, 1986. As of September 30, 1987, the deficiency in assets in the PBGC's balance sheet was $1,480,141,000 (the assets included $48,474,000 in assets of terminated plans not in trusteeship and $362,344,000 in amounts due for employer contributions and employer liability) compared with $3,781,640,000 as of September 30, 1986 (including $45,988,000 in assets in terminated plans not in trusteeship and $266,617,000 in amounts due for employer contributions and employer liability). A significant portion of the reserve for guaranteed benefits is based upon estimated data, since a final actuarial determination has not yet been made by the PBGC. However, the valuations for assets of terminated plans not in trusteeship and the amounts due for employer liability, as well as other receivables are also reflective of estimates.

The fiscal 1987 statements representing assets and liabilities of the 1,415 plans with known termination dates prior to October 1, 1987, that the PBGC had trusteed or expected to trustee included 1,405 single-employer plans and 10 multiemployer plans. The single-employer and multiemployer funds are separate entities, and gains from one cannot be used to offset losses from the other fund.

Background and general summary. In the 1960s, public awareness about the integrity of pension plans was heightened by news of abuses by pension plan administrators. Few plans actually failed, but complaints about restrictive age and service requirements, mismanagement of funds, and termination of coverage for employees who were close to retirement were frequent.

The closing of the Studebaker plant in South Bend, Indiana, in 1964, which inflicted heavy pension losses on workers, led to congressional hearings. Subsequent hearings on related pension concerns preceded the passage of the EMPLOYEE RETIREMENT INCOME SECURITY ACT (ERISA) on Labor Day 1974. Although this law does not require that an employer have a pension plan, it does provide partial protection to the participants in plans by setting standards for participation, vesting, funding, and fiduciary responsibility.

Statistical highlights of the PBGC for 1988 are appended. The PBGC summarized its activities for FY 1988 as follows: The PBGC protects some 31 million American worker and retirees in about $105,000 single-employer pension plans and another 8.3 million participants in some 2,300 multiemployer pension plans; the PBGC is trustee for 1,476 total plans; plan terminations in 1988 were nearly 11,000; landmark pension reforms brought stability to the single-employer program's financial condition. The multiemployer program, already solvent, continued to improve and revenues again exceeded expenses; with a new variable-rate premium in effect part of the year, the PBGC's premium revenues increased by nearly 70%, reaching a total of $481.7 million; the PBGC paid $324.7 million in benefits to almost 113,000 participants and is obligated to pay another 104,000 people when they become eligible for benefit payments in the future. Three LTV plans in litigation have about 61,000 additional retirees receiving

Single-Employer and Multiemployer Programs Combined
(Dollars in millions)

At Fiscal Yearend	FY 1987	FY 1988
Assets	$2,276.9	$2,551.7
Liabilities	$3,757.1	$4,002.9
Accumulated Deficit	$(1,480.1)	$(1,451.3)
Accumulated Number of Plans (trusteed, pending trusteeship, and pending termination)	1,415	1,476
Total Number of Participants Owed Guaranteed Benefits*	217,000	217,000
Number of Participants Being Paid*	112,500	112,800

For the Fiscal Year	FY 1987	FY 1988
Premium Income	$284.4	$481.7
Investment and Other Income	$264.7	$11.7
Results of Operations (loss)	$2301.5	$28.9
Benefits Paid	$303.6	$324.7
Number of Plans Trusteed	60	104

*Population size remained stable primarily because certain large plans pending termination in FY 1987 did not terminate.
Source: Pension Benefit Guaranty Corp.

approximately $332.3 million in benefits annually and about 30,000 other participants.

In general, ERISA has worked well to ensure that the pension promises made to millions of American workers and their families are kept by American employers. That success, however, had been threatened by inadequate funding standards and termination rules that encouraged employers to terminate plans and unload unfunded pension liabilities on PBGC. The 1987 legislation reduced the opportunities for employers to jeopardize benefit promises through systematic underfunding of liabilities.

BIBLIOGRAPHY

COMPTROLLER GENERAL. "Disclaimer of Opinion on the Financial Statements of the Pension Benefit Guaranty Corporation for the Fiscal Year Ended September 30, 1980." *Report to the Congress of the United States*, June 23, 1982.
COMPTROLLER GENERAL. "Review of the Pension Benefit Guaranty Corporation's Progress Towards Improving Accounting and Internal Control Weaknesses." *Report to the Congress of the United States*, November 22, 1983.
PENSION BENEFIT GUARANTY CORPORATION. *Annual Report and Financial Statements* for the Fiscal Years Ended September 30, 1986 and 1987.

PEPPER-MCFADDEN ACT The most important revision of the national bank laws since the passage of the Federal Reserve Act of 1913, but related to national banks rather than to Federal Reserve Banks. The Pepper-McFadden Act, also widely known as the McFadden Act, passed on February 25, 1927, which was also the month and day of enactment of the original NATIONAL BANK ACT OF 1863.

The most drastic modification provided by this act was the removal of some of the handicaps under which national banks had been competing with state commercial banks by permitting branch banking to national banks in states where the laws granted such powers to state institutions. Because of the greater liberality of most of the state laws in the matter of branch banking, there had been a strong tendency since World War I for national banks to convert to state charters. At the time of the passage of this act, the position of the national banks was weaker than that of the state commercial banks, their number being less than half that of the state commercial banks, and their total resources, deposits, and capital, and surplus also being less than that of state banks and trust companies combined. The tendency toward abandonment of national bank charters in favor of state charters threatened to weaken the Federal Reserve System, since only national banks were made compulsory members. In a report, the Comptroller of the Currency said: "Each time a national bank abandons its charter the Federal government loses an instrumentality through which it maintains a direct control over banking policy and banking operations. Each withdrawal constitutes the loss of a unit in the basic membership of the Federal Reserve System."

In equalizing the powers of national banks and state commercial banks in the matter of branch banking, the act was not aiming to encourage branch banking in the broadest sense, e.g., as practiced in Canada and most European countries, but rather to limit branch banking to the degree enjoyed by state banks, which in no case permits banking by a state institution outside the state of incorporation. While the law placed national banks on the same legal basis as state banks, it went no further and perhaps did not go far enough. In no case could a national bank operate branches outside of the city in which it was located, even though as in California, state banks were permitted to operate branches (with certain limitations) anywhere in the state. It was definitely prescribed that state institutions that operated branches outside of the city in which the main office was located had to relinquish such branches or stay out of the Federal Reserve System.

Among the other provisions of the McFadden Act were the following:

1. It permitted national banks, with approval of the Comptroller of the Currency and by vote of two-thirds of stockholders, to increase capital stock by a stock dividend, provided the remaining surplus was equal to at least 20% of the increased capital stock.
2. It granted national banks the right to deal directly in investment securities. Prior to the act, national banks had no power to join underwriting syndicates or deal in investment securities except as purchasers for own account.
3. It permitted national banks to have par values of less than $100 per share.
4. It liberalized capital requirements to the extent that a national bank, notwithstanding the requirement of $200,000 minimum capital in cities of over 50,000, could be organized, subject to the approval of the Comptroller, with capital of less than $100,000 in outlying districts of such cities where the state laws permitted the organization of state banks with capital of $100,000 or less.
5. It permitted a national bank to make five-year first mortgage loans (whole loans, fractional interests not being considered real estate loans for the purposes of this provision) on 50% of value of improved real estate, including improved farm land located within its Federal Reserve district or within a 100-mile radius from the head office, irrespective of district lines. Such real estate loans could aggregate 25% of capital and 25% of surplus, or 50% of savings deposits, at the bank's election.

PER CAPITA CIRCULATION See MONEY CIRCULATION.

PER CAPITA DEBT See NATIONAL DEBT.

PER CAPITA INCOME See NATIONAL INCOME.

PER CAPITA WEALTH See NATIONAL WEALTH.

PERCENTAGES Interest rates, dividend rates, and statistical comparisons are expressed by means of percentages, indicating hundredths. Thus, 6% interest on $100 for a year is $6.00. A 6% dividend on a share of stock of $100 par value is $6.00; $50 par value, $3.00; $25 par value, $1.50. A 6% interest rate on a $1,000 bond means interest of $60 annually; on a $500 bond, $30; and on a $100 bond, $6.

PERFECT COMPETITION The process through which firms adjust to changes in the activities of other firms. The adjective "perfect" refers to a theoretical ideal degree of rivalry among firms. This theoretical case is studied in economics in order to establish a benchmark against which the competitive behavior of firms in the real world can be compared.

The assumptions that underlie the perfect competition case are: a large number of homogeneous firms, each producing a homogeneous product in the industry and each having only a small portion of total industry output, free entry and exit from the industry, and perfect information on the part of consumers. One important result from the perfect competition case is that in equilibrium all firms will earn zero economic profit.

PERFORMANCE INDICATORS Critical factors that contribute to the attainment of goals and objectives, especially profitability. In banking, the key performance indicators include the following:

Achievement of objectives
Budget to actual performance
Staff efficiency and effectiveness
Compliance
Margins
Return on investment
Return on equity
Adequacy of staffing levels
Expense levels
Loan quality
Interest sensitivity and gaps
Asset/liability relationships
Liquidity
Solvency
Backlogs and errors
Expectations attained
Accuracy, timeliness, and focus reporting
Earnings and earnings quality
Earnings per share
Cash flows
Loan ratings and policy compliance
Profitability
Yields
Revenues
Cost of funds
Response time
Marketing effectiveness
Market share

Key indicators can be developed to provide relevant information to different levels of management and on different products. Key indicators offer an early warning system; a procedure to monitor risks; and a way to gain knowledge of operations, improve communications, and utilize resources more effectively. Indicators should be measurable, timely, relevant, and reliable.

PERFORMANCE RATIOS Financial ratios that are used to measure the performance of an entity, division, department, or personnel. Performance ratios can provide insights into a bank's profitability, return on investment, capital adequacy, and liquidity. Standard performance ratios for banks include the following:

1. Profitability
    As a percentage of average total assets:
        Net interest revenue
        Noninterest income
        Noninterest expense
        Pretax income before securities gains or losses
    Return on investment
    Return on assets
    Return on earning assets
    Noninterest income to noninterest expense
    Noninterest income to operating income
    Service charges to deposits
    Credit quality
    As a percentage of total loans
        Net loan charge-offs
        Loan loss reserves
    Nonperforming assets as a percentage of total assets
2. Capital adequacy
    Primary capital as a percentage of total assets
    Equity capital as a percentage of total assets
    Total capital as a percentage of total assets
3. Productivity
    Average total assets per employee
    Net operating income per employee
    Operating earnings per employee
    Personnel expense per employee
    Personnel expense as a percentage of average total assets
    Deposits per employee
    Overhead as a percentage of operating income
    Efficiency ratio

4. Liquidity
   Loans as a percentage of earning assets
   Net purchased liabilities as a percentage of total assets
   CDs to deposits

Specific areas of performance that typically deserve oversight in banking include: (1) spreads and margins associated with interest yields, (2) leverage, (3) asset allocation, (4) asset quality, (5) earnings quality, and (6) overhead cost control. These areas are essential to developing satisfactory rates of return on assets, equity, and growth of capital.

Polk's *World Bank Directory* and Rand McNally's *International Bank Directory* are sources of commercial banking performance statistics. The Sheshunoff data are a widely used source of financial performance data for commercial banks. Decision Research Sciences, Inc., publishes detailed statistics for commercial banks, savings and loan associations, mutual savings banks, and credit unions. The Federal Reserve System, the Federal Home Loan Bank Board, the National Credit Union Administration, the Office of the Comptroller of the Currency, the Treasury Department, and many state regulatory authorities publish banking statistics that are useful for comparative purposes.

BIBLIOGRAPHY

Cole, L.P. *Managaement Accounting in Banks*, BAI, 1986.

PERIOD OF DISTRIBUTION   In SYNDICATE operations, the duration of the offering period during which the security is publicy offered through the members of the selling group. The term most often refers to that period near the top of short-, intermediate-, and long-term speculative cycles when the better informed and usually shrewder speculators take their profits and sell.
   See DISTRIBUTION, PERIOD OF.

PERLS   Principal exchange-rate-linked securities.
   See FINANCIAL INSTRUMENTS: RECENT INNOVATIONS

PERMANENT ASSETS   Fixed or capital assets.
   See FIXED ASSETS.

PERMANENT CERTIFICATE   See DEFINITIVE BOND.

PERMANENT INVESTMENTS   Real estate, mortgages, stocks, bonds, etc., purchased by investors with the intention of holding them indefinitely (in the case of bonds, until maturity) for the purpose of deriving an income therefrom and without the intention of trading therein. Bonds held by insurance companies or savings banks are generally regarded as permanent investments, whereas bonds held by an investment house in current position are trading assets.

PERPETUAL ANNUITY   See ANNUITY.

PERPETUAL BOND   A bond that has no prescribed maturity date; a bond with a very long maturity date, which therefore for practical purposes might well be considered a perpetual obligation. Perpetual bonds, in effect, are a contradiction in terms, since by definition a bond is a promise to pay both principal and interest on specified future dates. They are also known as INDETERMINATE BONDS and sometimes, but not properly, as IRREDEEMABLE BONDS.

British Consols, specifically 2.5% Consolidated Stock of 1921 or thereafter, nominally have no maturity date but are redeemable at any time at par on such notice and in such amounts as Parliament may determine. In the U.S., perpetual bonds have not been popular with issuers. For examples,
   See ANNUITY BONDS.

PER PRO   See PER PROCURATION.

PER PROCURATION   A signature given by an agent who has limited authority to sign for, or on behalf of, his principal. The authority may be given orally, by power of attorney, or by other written evidence. Banks and trust companies frequently empower certain clerks to sign in this manner, especially where official signatures are required in volume, as in stock registrar and transfer activity.

A signature by procuration operates as a notice that the agent's authority to sign is limited and that the principal is liable only if the agent acts within the actual limit of his authority. For this reason, persons accepting per pro signatures should ascertain the extent of the agent's authority in order to assure against the possibility of the agent's exceeding such authority. The recipient of per pro signatures is entitled to a statement of authority for such signatures. A per pro signature may read either:

   The Blank Bank
   Per Pro John Doe

or:

   Per Pro Blank Bank
   John Doe

The term is abbreviated Per Proc. or Per Pro. or P.P.
   See NEGOTIABLE INSTRUMENTS LAW (Sec. 3-403, Uniform Commercial Code).

PERSONAL CHECK   A check drawn by an individual as distinguished from one drawn by a partnership, corporation, or bank.

PERSONAL CREDIT   Credit given to an individual, or to which an individual is entitled, as distinguished from that given to a firm for business purposes. At first, the personal loan departments of commercial banks comprehended loans for such personal purposes as payment of medical and dental fees, tuition, etc. But subsequent expansion of the permissible purposes to include the financing of installment purchases of various kinds has led to change in classification of such credit to CONSUMER CREDIT.

PERSONAL ESTATE   See PERSONAL PROPERTY.

PERSONAL FINANCE   Coincident with the large expansion in CONSUMER CREDIT in recent years, the subject of personal finance has assumed specialized importance. An increasing number of works are devoting detailed attention to this subject, including such matters as management and control of personal spending through the use of personal budgets and accounts; proper allocation of living expenses; how to plan for medical expenses, taxes, insurance premiums, and debt payments; how to manage income and to plan for estate growth and retirement; most feasible procedures in financing a home, investing in securities, selecting amounts and types of insurance, buying on the installment plan, and meeting financial emergencies; how to buy or borrow wisely; how to provide for children's expenses, education, and insurance, etc.

The personal finance companies, also known as consumer credit companies or small loan companies, have been in the enlightened forefront of this trend toward increased literature on management of personal finances, particularly in advice against overborrowing and improper management of personal finances which might result in inability of their borrowers to meet debts as they mature.

The record volume of consumer installment credit has stimulated debate as to its economic role as a stimulant or depressant. On the positive side, consumer credit makes possible a higher standard of living by making available an increased range of higher-priced consumer durables, such as automobiles, television sets, household appliances, air conditioning and heating units, household furniture, etc., that otherwise might not be bought on a strictly cash basis. On the negative side, it is alleged that the increase in consumer fixed charges on debt, either short- or intermediate-term (installment or noninstallment arrangements) or long-term (such as amortization of mortgages and insurance premiums), reduces personal savings, thins reserves, and might in the event of a decline in personal income result in a more than proportionate decline in consumption spending.

PERSONAL FINANCIAL PLANNING   The evaluation of a person's current financial position and financial goals leading to a presentation of a plan to achieve those goals. A typical financial plan includes the following:

1. A balance sheet analysis.
2. Cash flow projection.
3. Long-term accumulation plans for retirement, education, etc.
4. Statement of individual's goals.
5. Insurance analysis.

PERSONAL FINANCIAL STATEMENTS

6. Estate and tax planning.
7. Projection of income taxes.
8. Overview of weaknesses and strengths in the individual's financial outlook.
9. Recommendations for implementing the plan.

When determining an investment strategy prior to retirement, one should:

1. Analyze one's ability to tolerate different types of risk.
2. Determine the retirement time horizon.
3. Establish personal investment objectives such as growth, income, or stability.
4. Obtain a thorough knowledge of investment options.
5. Formulate an individual investment strategy and begin the selection process.
6. Consider seeking investment counseling.

Financial planners charge clients in one of three ways: a fee-only basis, a fee-and-commission basis, or a commission basis.

Two professional organizations currently accredit planners after they have completed certain educational and professional requirements: The College for Financial Planning confers the Certified Financial Planner (CFP) designation, and the American College confers the Chartered Financial Consultant (ChFC) designation. Two major professional organizations are associated with financial planning: the International Association for Financial Planning and the Institute of Certified Financial Planners.

Research done by Bank Administration Institute suggests that if personal financial planning is done on a stand-alone basis, profitability is difficult to achieve. Profitability usually accompanies revenue generated from the sale of other products used to implement the financial plan's recommendations and from relationship building and cross-selling.

BIBLIOGRAPHY

ARTHUR D. LITTLE, INC. *A Personal Financial Planning Decision Guide.* Bank Administration Institute, Rolling Meadows, IL, 1985.

BLUMBERT, D. A. *Personal Financial Planning in Banks.* Bank Administration Institute, Rolling Meadows, IL, 1986.

———. *Tactical Investing: Strategies for Getting the Most Out of Your Money,* 1985.

DOMINI, A. L., and others. *The Challenges of Wealth: Mastering the Personal and Financial Conflicts.* Dow Jones-Irwin, Inc., Homewood, IL, 1988.

ELSKEN, B., and CRAMER, K. "Just Living Together." *Money,* January, 1989.

Family Law Handbook. Bureau of National Affairs, Inc., Washington, DC, 1985.

Family Tax Planning. Matthew Bender & Co., Inc., New York, NY. Two volumes.

FERGUSON, S., and NAIRNE, M. E. "Diversify, Diversify." *CA Magazine,* November, 1988.

HALLMAN, G. V., and ROSENBLOOM, J. S. *Personal Financial Planning,* 1987.

JONES, H. S. *Planning Your Financial Futures: Personal Financial Planning That Helps You.* John Wiley and Sons, Inc., New York, NY, 1988.

KESS, S., and WESTLIN. *Commerce Clearing House Estate Planning Guide Including Financial Planning.* Commerce Clearing House, Chicago, IL, 1983.

LEIMBERG, S., and OTHERS. *Tools and Techniques of Financial Planning.* National Underwriter, Cincinnati, OH, 1986.

PETTERLE, E. A., and KAHN, R. C. *Legacy of Love: How to Make Life Easier for the Ones You Leave Behind—A Practical Workbook and Planning Tool.* Shelter Pubns., Bolinas, CA, 1986.

PERSONAL FINANCIAL STATEMENTS The reporting entity of personal financial statements is either an individual, a husband and wife, or a group of related individuals. Personal financial statements should provide adequate disclosure of information relating to the financial affairs of an individual reporting entity.

For each reporting entity, a statement of financial position (or balance sheet) is now required to present estimated current values of assets and liabilities, a provision for estimated taxes, and net worth. A provision should also be made for estimated income taxes on the differences between the estimated current values of assets, the

Personal Financial Statements

John and Mary Doe
Statement of Financial Condition
December 31, 1990 and 1991

Assets	1991	1990
Cash	$ 5,000	$ 3,000
Investments		
Marketable securities (Note 1)	20,000	17,000
Clix, Inc., a closely held corporation	100,000	80,000
Residence	200,000	120,000
Personal effects	30,000	25,000
Total assets	$355,000	$245,000

Liabilities and Net Worth		
Credit cards	$ 1,500	$ 1,000
Income taxes—current year balance	5,500	4,000
Demand note payable to bank, 16%	10,000	–
Mortgage payable, 10% (Note 2)	100,000	110,000
Total	117,000	115,000
Estimated income taxes on the differences between the estimated current values of assets, the current amounts of liabilities and their tax bases (Note 3)	10,000	5,000
Net worth	228,000	125,000
Total liabilities and net worth	$355,000	$245,000

estimated current amount of liabilities, and their respective tax bases. Comparative statements for one or more periods should be presented. A statement of changes in net worth is optional. Such a statement would disclose the major sources of increases and decreases in net worth. Increases in personal net worth arise from income, increases in estimated current value of assets, decreases in estimated current amount of liabilities, and decreases in the provision for estimated income taxes. Decreases in personal net worth arise from expenses, decreases in estimated current value of assets, increases in estimated current amount of liabilities, and increases in the provision for income taxes.

Personal financial statements should be presented on an accrual rather than a cash basis. A classified balance sheet is not used. Assets and liabilities are presented in the order of their liquidity and maturity, respectively. A business interest that constitutes a large part of an individual's total assets should be shown separate from other assets. Such an interest would be presented as a net amount and not as a pro rata allocation of the business's assets and liabilities. An illustration of a personal financial statement is appended.

BIBLIOGRAPHY

AMERICAN INSTITUTE OF CERTIFIED PUBLIC ACCOUNTANTS, *AICPA Auditing and Accounting Manual,* 1982.

BAILARD, THOMAS E., et al., *Personal Money Management,* Science Research Associates, Inc., Chicago, 1986.

PERSONAL HOLDING COMPANY The Revenue Act of 1934 for the first time defined personal holding companies and imposed special surtax rates on their undistributed profits as a means of taxing this device which had been developed by moneyed individuals in high tax brackets to reduce their tax liability. Such an individual, with tax bracket higher than corporate rates, would transfer income-producing investments to a closely held personal holding company, which would pay the regular corporate rates on taxable income and plow back (accumulate) the undistributed earnings. After a number of years the individual could liquidate the personal holding company and be taxed merely at the capital gains rates. If he died, the heirs could liquidate the personal holding company and the accumulated earnings would have avoided the individual income tax.

A personal holding company is a closely held corporation (1) that is owned by 5 or fewer shareholders who own more than 50% of the corporations' outstanding stock at any time during the last half of its taxable year and (2) whose PHC income equals at least 60% of the corporation's adjusted gross income for the tax year. The personal holding company tax is equal to 28% of the undistributed personal holding company income. The purpose of the tax is to prevent closely held companies from converting an operating company into a nonoperating company.

PERSONAL INCOME   *See* INCOME TAXES, NATIONAL INCOME.

PERSONAL LOAN BROKER   A type of licensed lender under the New York State banking law. Any personal loan company or personal loan broker duly authorized to do business in 1932, when the article was revised by the New York State version of the Small Loan Act, was deemed by virtue of such "grandfather" clause to have a license to continue business under the revised article, which requires licensing for such personal loan lenders or brokers in the small loan field.

See SMALL LOAN BUSINESS.

PERSONAL LOAN COMPANY   Small loan companies; specialists in personal loans, i.e., cash loans directly to individual borrowers for such personal purposes as to refinance the payment of bills; to pay medical bills, taxes, insurance premiums, etc.; and to provide cash for transactions which will permit cost savings.

The field is closely regulated. Consumer finance companies, the broadest classification of companies in the field, are subject to statutes in each of the 50 states, the District of Columbia, and Puerto Rico. Most of the installment loans of consumer finance companies are made under the various state versions of the Uniform Small Loan Law, or the Model Consumer Finance Act, prepared and offered to the states by the Russell Sage Foundation and the National Consumer Finance Association, respectively. In addition, consumer finance companies operating thereunder are subject to additional state laws governing sales financing and revolving credit, insurance premium financing, home repair financing, second mortgages on homes, and maximum interest (usury) laws. The Uniform Consumer Credit Code codifies all the various laws pertaining to consumer credit. In addition, consumer finance companies in general are subject to the Federal Consumer Credit Protection Act. Features of regulation include the following, in addition to regulatory requirements of full disclosure of charges and annual percentage rate thereof; proper receipting, record keeping, and reports; and truthful advertising.

1. *Loan limits.* Small loan statutes specifying maximum loan limits among the states had been revised to such maxima in individual states as $25,000, $35,000, $45,000, $55,000, and higher.
2. *Rates.* Under the original draft of the Uniform Small Loan Law, rates on "small loans" were limited to maximum of 3.5% per month, and various states in recent years still specify 36% per year on the first dollar bracket of graduated loan rates, as the maximum, the incremental rate decreasing in subsequent dollar brackets of total loan. However, increasingly in recent years, state small loan laws have been revised to permit any agreed rate (either on any amount, or any agreed rate over specified maximum incremental amount). The original Russell Sage Foundation hoped by its Uniform Small Loan Law specifying maximum rates and amounts on small loans, above general level of interest rates, to attract reputable lenders to the field and drive out the small loan sharks, but the latter persist where borrowers have ceased to qualify for credit by the reputable lenders.
3. *Duration.* Average length of outstanding loans has become longer in recent years within the limits usually specified in state small loan laws. In practice, duration is influenced by purposes of the loan and trend of interest rates.

Operations. Personal loan companies may be classified as chains (multiple-office companies operating in many cities and/or states) and independents (the smaller companies operating one or a few offices in a single city). Because borrowers are mostly wage earners in the lower income brackets, the chains select locations such as industrial centers and larger cities that will generate sufficient volume and will not operate in any jurisdictions that do not authorize sufficiently high loan limits and rates necessary for profitable operation.

Personal loan companies' receivables are mostly unsecured. Prime consideration is the ability of the borrower to repay the loan out of monthly income. Because of the frequent emergency nature of loan applications, emphasis is on speedy streamlined application procedures and prompt availability of loans. Applications are checked as to information by calls to employers, credit bureaus, etc., or by field investigators who combine collection work with their investigative duties. Because collection costs and loss of interest and principal collections constitute a substantial part of costs, emphasis is on keeping loans current, which may be achieved for slow loans by refinancing. Small loan laws permit interest to be collected on total unpaid balances, including delinquent payments. Fluctuation of total volume tends to be countercyclical. Volume tends to increase in times of general economic recession, which adds to the risks involved.

Because of the greater uniformity of operations imposed by regulation, the personal loan companies are susceptible of uniform statistical analysis. Among the more important calculations used in analysis are the following:

1. *Total debt to net worth.* Personal loan companies derive their funds by equity investment, bank credit, and financing in the capital markets. A normal debt-to-net worth ratio is 2:1 or 2½:1, which is modest leverage.
2. *Cash to current debt.* This ratio indicates the cash position carried, which is fairly high in order to accommodate loan demand and to maintain cash balances under outstanding bank lines of credit.
3. *Delinquency analysis.* Because of the usual refinancing of loans in difficulty, delinquencies are best analyzed on the basis of most recent payments on outstanding loans: (1) 90-day accounts (no collections received for 90 days or more); (2) 60- to 89-day accounts (no collections received for 60 to 89 days); and (3) interest-only accounts (only interest and charges, no payments on principal, received in last 60 days).
4. *Collection factor.* Rate of collections (collection factor) is the averge total of cash principal collections to average monthly outstanding receivables.
5. *Liquidating period.* This concept determines the theoretical liquidating period necessary to liquidate debt from receivable collections. Net debt is computed by deducting cash from total unsubordinated debt. Rate of collections (collection factor) then is applied to current volume of receivables outstanding to determine the number of months of collections necessary, as well as total amount of receivables necessary, to liquidate the net debt. Any excess of receivables thus arrived at is considered collateral margin.
6. *Analysis of volume.* Receivables are analyzed as to new or former customers, and as to additional loans to present borrowers, with and without additional loan advanced. A renewal loan with additional amount advanced is considered a better account than one without additional advance, indicating the company considered the risk justified the additional sum. The volume of renewals is normally substantial, accounting for 70% to 75% of annual volume.
7. *Reserve for losses to outstanding receivables.* This ratio of loss reserve is judged as to adequacy on the basis of quality of the receivables, actual losses and recoveries, and current economic conditions.
8. *Net losses to receivables.* The net of chargeoffs, after deducting recoveries, is expressed as a percentage of average outstanding receivables.
9. *Net profit to net worth.* Net profit to average net worth indicates the overall profitability of operations.

During the 1980s, the consumer contributed significantly to the continued expansion of the economy. This in turn contributed to the profitability of personal loan and finance companies. Debt as a percentage of disposable income has been as high as 19% excluding home equity loans, an historical high. More consumers are in the 25- to 54-year-old bracket, which is considered the peak consumer borrowing period. It is expected that the growth rate of the "baby boomers" will slow to less than 1% annually through the 1990s. The appended table offers a broad picture of consumer and mortgage debt compared to disposal income, 1979 to 1988.

Personal loan companies as licensed lenders in the personal loan field are socially desirable, responsible lenders in this marginal

PERSONAL LOANS

credit field, supplying a necessary form of credit that otherwise would go by default largely to loan sharks extorting exorbitant charges from necessitous borrowers. Like other forms of CONSUMER CREDIT, personal loans have expanded in volume to record totals in recent years, attracting increased competition to personal loan companies from commercial banks and other financial institutions.
See PERSONAL LOANS.

BIBLIOGRAPHY

HAYES, D. A. "Retail Banking in an Interest-Sensitive World." *Bankers Magazine*, July-August, 1980.
NATIONAL CONSUMER FINANCE ASSOCIATION. *Finance Facts Yearbook.*
SHANAHAN, R. B. "The Organization and Operation of a Consumer Loan Department." In BAUGHN, W. H., and WALKER, C. E., eds., *The Bankers' Handbook*, rev. ed., 1978.
SMITH, C. W., JR. "On the Theory of Financial Contracting: The Personal Loan Market." *Journal of Monetary Economics*, July, 1980.
Steinberg, E. I. "Consumer Credit, 1960-1980." *Survey of Current Business*, February, 1981.

PERSONAL LOANS As defined by the Board of Governors of the Federal Reserve System for its consumer credit statistical series, all installment loans not covered by automobile paper, other consumer goods paper (credit extended for the purpose of purchasing automobiles and other consumer goods and secured by the items purchased), and repair and modernization loans (FHA-insured and noninsured loans made to finance maintenance and improvement of owner-occupied dwelling units). Such personal loans are made to individuals for consumer purposes, mostly for consolidation of consumer debts; payment of medical, educational, or travel expenses; and payment of personal taxes or insurance premiums. Some personal loans are used for the purchase of consumer goods, but they are not included under automobile paper or other consumer goods paper unless they are secured by the goods purchased.

Although personal loans are the specialized field of the consumer finance companies (which, however, so overlap into other operations that they are grouped with sales finance and other finance companies as finance companies), the field is an important one also for commercial banks. Commercial banks participate indirectly, through loans to consumer finance companies. In addition, the commercial banks account for a large proportion of total personal loan volume.

The earliest personal loan departments of commercial banks date from about 1923. In 1928, the National City Bank of New York (now First National City Bank) inaugurated its personal loan department, followed in 1929 by the Bank of America of California, leading to greater participation by other commercial banks in subsequent years in this field of retailing of bank credit. The year 1934 is considered a turning point marking major interest by commercial banks in consumer installment loan departments. In order to do this type of business, commercial banks needed enabling amendments to banking laws in the particular home states of operation, authorizing the higher effective rates necessary for personal loans.

A series of valuable operating manuals for the guidance of commercial banks in the field of personal loans and other forms of installment credit have been published by the Committee on Consumer Credit of the American Bankers Association. Its *Bank Manual on Installment Loans* in particular covers the credit requirements and operating procedures for commercial banks interested in this field.
See CONSUMER CREDIT, PERSONAL LOAN COMPANY.

PERSONAL PROPERTY All tangible and intangible movable goods or possessions, e.g., money, securities, accounts receivable, merchandise, furniture, livestock, harvested crops, etc. Legally, all property can be divided into two classes; personal property (personalty) and REAL PROPERTY (realty).

Personal property is bequeathed, the beneficiary being known as the legatee; whereas real property is devised, the beneficiary being known as the devisee.
See CHATTEL.

PERSONAL SECURITY There are two general classes of security, personal and COLLATERAL. When a loan is made upon personal security, the note which evidences the debt is signed not only by the maker, but also by another financially responsible person acting as endorser, surety, or guarantor. There is no implication that personal security is based upon the moral risk alone. The financial worth and capacity of the guarantor are also taken into consideration. In personal security, however, there is no specific pledge of collateral.
See GUARANTY.

PERSONAL SERVICE CORPORATION A corporation having as its principal activity the performance of personal services that are substantially performed by employee-owners (a tax concept). Employee-owners are employees who own, on any day of the tax year, more than 10% of the personal service corporation's stock.

PERSONAL TRUST See LIVING TRUST, TRUST.

PERSONALTY See PERSONAL PROPERTY.

PERSONNEL DEPARTMENT A department organized among the larger banks to coordinate the problems arising in securing and training an adequate supply of clerical workers. The scope of the department may be indicated by the following outline of activities:

1. Engaging new employees, receiving applications and interviewing candidates for employment, eliminating undesirable material, and keeping all applicable records including:
   a. Application form.
   b. References form.

Consumer and Mortgage Debt Comparisons Related to Disposable Income *
(In millions of dollars)

As of Dec. 31	Disposable income (Bil. $)	Automotive	Mobile homes	Revolving	All other **	Total	% of disposable income	Home mortgage debt	% of disposable income	Total consumer installment & mortgage debt	% of disposable income
1988	3,471.8	289,823	25,552	185,755	165,061	666,191	19.2	2,017,041	58.1	2,683,232	77.3
1987	3,209.7	267,180	25,957	159,307	160,578	613,021	19.1	1,925,197	60.0	2,538,218	79.1
1986	3,019.6	246,109	26,883	136,381	162,460	571,833	18.9	1,698,524	56.2	2,270,357	75.2
1985	2,838.7	209,636	26,834	122,013	159,272	517,754	18.2	1,488,099	52.4	2,005,763	70.7
1984	2,668.6	173,704	25,795	100,212	142,827	442,538	16.6	1,318,545	49.4	1,761,083	66.0
1983	2,428.1	143,799	23,704	78,667	121,698	367,869	15.2	1,189,811	49.0	1,557,680	64.2
1982	2,261.4	124,218	22,833	66,243	110,242	323,536	14.3	1,074,670	47.5	1,398,206	61.8
1981	2,127.6	118,956	20,302	60,838	110,586	310,682	14.6	1,065,294	50.1	1,375,976	64.7
1980	1,917.9	111,936	18,621	54,894	112,115	297,566	15.5	986,979	51.5	1,284,545	67.0
1979	1,729.3	112,475	18,207	53,357	112,444	296,483	17.1	878,938	50.8	1,175,421	68.0

* All data have been revised.
** Includes personal loans and other consumer goods paper.

Source: Federal Reserve Board and Department of Commerce.

c. Correspondence relating to employment.
d. Fidelity insurance applications.
2. Transferring employees.
3. Answering inquiries concerning former employees.
4. Training employees—general and banking education.
5. Attending to discharges of employees.
6. Making salary adjustments.
7. Preparing personal history cards, showing:
   a. Name and address.
   b. Marital condition.
   c. Age.
   d. Telephone number.
   e. Antecedent educational history.
   f. Antecedent work history.
   g. Date of entry.
   h. Initial salary.
   i. Department originally assigned to.
   j. Occupation in that department.
   k. Records of department transfers.
   l. Records of salary revisions with dates.
   m. Record of resignation or discharge with dates and reason.
8. Rating employees in degree of efficiency.
9. Preparing turnover and other statistics regarding the working force.
10. Making job analysis.
11. Promoting healthful employer-employee relations.
12. Conducting the house organ.

PET BANKS This term has two meanings:

1. In American banking history, the state-chartered banks designated as Treasury depositaries by the Jackson administration, beginning in 1833, after Jackson's veto in 1832 of a bill rechartering the second Bank of the United States. After the Panic of 1837 caused wholesale suspensions by such banks, the Independent Treasury System of sub-treasuries was enacted by the Van Buren administration in 1840. It was repealed in 1841 by the Harrison administration, but reenacted in August, 1846. The system endured until 1920, when the Sub-Treasury Act was repealed; the functions of the sub-treasuries transferred in 1921 to the Federal Reserve banks as fiscal agents of the federal government.
2. In modern times, the central depositaries designated by large business firms to receive remittances by customers, addressed to such banks at specified post office lock box numbers. Such a bank collects such mail, lists the remittances received, deposits the checks received, and accounts over to the firm concerned for the total receipts, with resultant expedited handling and convenience. A variation on such a depositary system is for such banks to report regularly to a designated money center bank, which will consolidate such reports and present a consolidated cash position to the firm's treasurer each business day, in addition to serving as the focal point for centralized management of the deposits thus accumulated.

PETRODOLLARS Term applied to Eurodollar deposits held by petroleum-exporting countries or their citizens. Petrodollars are distinguishable from other Eurodollars only by the identity of their owners.

PETROLEUM See OIL.

PETTY CASH FUND A fund from which is disbursed cash in payment of petty expenses, e.g., telegrams, postage, carfare, taxi fare, small supplies, etc. Vouchers are kept for each disbursement, and periodically petty expenses are analyzed and charged to various expense accounts. In the meantime they are held as a part of petty cash.

PHILADELPHIA-BALTIMORE-WASHINGTON STOCK EXCHANGE See PHILADELPHIA STOCK EXCHANGE.

PHILADELPHIA PLAN See EQUIPMENT TRUST.

PHILADELPHIA STOCK EXCHANGE America's oldest securities marketplace, tracing its official organization back to 1790, when the Philadelphia Board of Brokers was organized. In 1981, trading and clearing facilities of the Philadelphia Stock Exchange (PHLX) were centralized in the PHLX's new building, and the branch office and clearing facilities formerly in Baltimore (as a result of the merger of the Baltimore Stock Exchange in 1919) and in Washington, D.C. (as a result of the merger of the Washington Stock Exchange in 1953) were closed. The Pittsburgh Stock Exchange, which had been operating together with the PHLX in previous years, was also merged by the PHLX at close of 1969.

The first regional stock exchange to trade stock options (1975), the PHLX was reported to be doing 50% of its business in calls and puts.

Operations. Trading on the PHLX is linked electronically with that of other markets by the intermarket trading system (ITS). The PHLX's own expanded PACE system provides customer orders with executions based on immediate price comparisons available from other market centers, "offering the best executions quicker than any other automated system." Both of these systems indicate the commitment of the PHLX to the development of the National Market System mandated by Congress in the 1975 amendments to the Securities Acts and pushed by the Securities and Exchange Commission.

Changes and improvements have placed the PHLX's STOCK CLEARING CORPORATION of Philadelphia (SCCP) in closer automated contact with other organizations in the national clearance and settlement system. As the PHLX was the first regional exchange to participate in the ITS, SCCP helped to forge the first ITS clearing arrangement and played an important role in implementing further improvements. The PHLX also completed the funding arrangements which permitted the SCCP to develop a trust company for the purpose of operating PHILADEP, the clearing corporation's depository. This subsidiary provides simplified lower-cost settlement and custody services for members choosing to settle their trades in the depository, whether they be Philadelphia trades or trades originating in other marketplaces and settled in Philadelphia.

See STOCK EXCHANGES.

BIBLIOGRAPHY

DIAMOND, D. "New Steps at an Innovative Exchange." *New York Times*, June 6, 1982.
PHILADELPHIA STOCK EXCHANGE, INC. *Annual Report*.
SECURITIES AND EXCHANGE COMMISSION. *Monthly Statistical Review*.

PHILIPPINE GOVERNMENT DEPOSITARIES Since the independent Republic of the Philippines was proclaimed July 4, 1946, the designation of fiscal agents or depositaries in the continental United States by the Philippine government no longer is subject to its former insular status. Under Section 15 of the Federal Reserve Act, deposit of public funds of the Philippine Islands was prohibited in any bank not a member of the Federal Reserve System.

PHILLIPS CURVE In macroeconomic theory, the graph depicting the concept of a trade-off between reduction in the unemployment rate and rise in the inflation rate (i.e., reduction in the rate of unemployment through fiscal-monetary policies is at the expense of rise in the inflation rate).

As developed by the research of A. W. Phillips for the United Kingdom in the years 1862-1957, the Phillips curve, plotted with the vertical scale measuring the rate of inflation and the horizontal scale measuring the rate of unemployment, had a continuously rising curvature traced from the highest rate of employment upward past the "full employment" rate (unemployment rate of approximately 4%) to higher levels of the inflation rate. This conflicted with the conventional macroeconomic theory that inflation would not occur while the economy had idle resources and labor, and that if the "full employment" rate of economic activity were reached, excess demand would merely result in inflation.

Conversely, the Phillips curve implied that fiscal-monetary measures to reduce the rate of inflation would be at the expense of rise in the rate of unemployment.

Research in the U.S. has led to varying conclusions as to the actual shape and position of the Phillips curve, and to an emphasis on the importance of improving productivity and quality of the labor force, instead of merely applying expansionary fiscal-monetary policies.

BIBLIOGRAPHY

GORDON, R. J. "Hystersis in History: Is There Even a Phillips Curve?" *American Economic Review*, May 1989.

FISCHER, S., and SUMMERS, L. H. "Should Government Learn to Live with Inflation? *American Economic Review*, May, 1989.

PHYSIOCRATS The first formal school of economists. The intellectual leader of this group was Francois Quesnay. Writings of the group were published in France beginning in the late 1750s. The hallmark of the physiocrat contribution was the formulation of a theoretical model or framework from which solutions could be derived. Fundamental to their theoretical circular flow of economic activity was the agricultural sector, as would logically be expected given the economic environment of their day.

BIBLIOGRAPHY

EKELUND, R. B., and R. F. HEBERT. *A History of Economic Theory and Method*, McGraw Hill, New York, 1989.

PIK Pay-in-kind preferred stock.
See FINANCIAL INSTRUMENTS: RECENT INNOVATIONS.

PIG IRON Defined by the American Iron and Steel Institute, a metallic product, the result of blast furnace or electric smelting of iron ores, which is used as part or all of the initial metallic charge in STEEL making, puddling, and producing molten metal for foundry use. Thus it is a basic product in the iron and steel industry.

PINCH A sudden advance in prices. An advance in money rates would be called a money pinch or SQUEEZE. If security prices suddenly advance when there is a large short interest in the market, the shorts are said to be pinched.

PINK SHEETS A term that refers to approximately 11,000 thinly traded over-the-counter stocks that are not on NASDAQ, the National Association of Securities Dealers Automated Quotations system. The pink sheets are published daily by the National Quotation Bureau of Jersey City, N.J., a unit of Commerce Clearing House Inc., Riverwood, Ill. The quotation data are printed on thin, pink sheets of paper. Pink sheet issues are usually considered highly speculative.
In 1990, the OTC Bulletin Board was developed by the National Association of Securities Dealers and approved by the SEC. This electronic system was designed to facilitate trading and surveillance of pink sheet stocks. It was also expected that this computerized market would improve the visibility of smaller stocks and make them less susceptible to fraud.

PIT The active center of trading activity on the floor of a commodity exchange. On the CHICAGO BOARD OF TRADE, for example, there are seven pits located on the trading floor, one each for wheat, corn, oats, soybeans, rye, soybean oil and meal, and lard. These are the points at which traders transact their business. Structurally a pit consists of a series of concentric steps arranged in the configuration of an octagon, leading up from the outside and down to the center. This arrangement permits traders to communicate with one another in the minimum of space. The term "pit" is synonymous with market, except that only one commodity is dealt in at a single pit. A pit in a commodity exchange is similar to a POST on a stock exchange.
Trading in the pits is carried on by open outcry of every offer to sell and every bid to buy the futures contract traded, supplemented by a code of hand signals. Fingers of the signal hand held up vertically show the number of round lots; palm turned outward from the person indicates offer to sell, palm turned inward to the person indicates bid to buy; fingers held horizontally in various positions indicate fractions of a cent bid or offered, the full cents price being kept posted on blackboards on the walls of the trading floor. Traders buying and selling job lots (1,000 bushels as compared with 5,000-bushel round lots) are grouped in one area of the grain pits.

PITTMAN ACT An act passed April 23, 1918, designed to aid in the stabilization of the currencies of China and India, where a shortage of silver increased the world price of this commodity to high levels. The act provided for the release of approximately 208 million standard silver dollars held in the Treasury as collateral for silver certificates. The silver-purchasing provisions of this act (effective June 1, 1920) provided for the replacement of this silver, and the United States mint was required to purchase the entire domestic silver output at a price of $1 an ounce until the entire amount should be replaced. Purchases under the Pittman Act ceased about July, 1923. U.S. silver producers benefited under the terms of this act, since the mint paid $1 an ounce against an average world market price during 1921 of $0.63 and during 1922 of $0.67.

PLAIN BONDS Debentures; unsecured bonds; certificates of debt.
Designation of title for such bonds usually is given a more appealing title than just "plain bonds," although one railroad, the Boston & Maine, did actually so entitle one of its issues outstanding years ago.
See DEBENTURE BONDS.

PLANNING A major function of management. Planning is a process that establishes goals and objectives and develops a decision model for selecting the means of attaining those goals and objectives.
The strategic planning model consists of four components:

1. Basic research and analysis of internal and external environments and identification of macro-and micro-level trends.
2. Identification and analysis of alternative goals and objectives.
3. Statement of goals and objectives.
4. Development of policy alternatives and resource utilization.

Planning requires that an organization make choices regarding:

1. Its goals and objectives (what the organization wants to do and why).
2. The means of attaining these ends (when, where, and how to do them).

Following is a hierarchy of planning showing types of planning, levels, and scope:

Type	Level	Scope
Goals and objectives of the organization	Top management	Broad, companywide and long-term
Policies, departmental	Middle management	Narrow, variable terms, tactical, flexible
Procedures and methods	Line and supervisory	Narrow, variable terms, detailed

BIBLIOGRAPHY

ALTMAN, E. "Managing the Commercial Lending Process." In *Handbook for Banking Strategy*, 1985.
ASPINWALL, R. C. and EIXENBEIS, R. A. *Handbook for Banking Strategy*. John Wiley and Sons, Inc., New York, NY, 1985.
BANK ADMINISTRATION INSTITUTE. *The Wall Street Journal on Management: The Best of the Manager's Journal*. Bank Administration Institute, Rolling Meadows, IL, 1985.
———. *Banker's Handbook for Strategic Planning*, 1985.
BELOW, P. J., and OTHERS. *Executive Guide to Strategic Planning*. Jossey-Bass, Inc., San Francisco, CA, 1987.
BURTON, E. J., and MCBRIDE, W. *Business Plan Manual*. John Wiley and Sons, Inc., New York, NY, 1988.
Business Strategies Bulletin. Commerce Clearing House, Inc., Chicago, IL. Monthly.
CLARKE, P., and PAQUETTE, L. "Financial Management with Lotus 1-2-3." Accountancy, December, 1988.
COWEN, S. S., and MIDDAUGH, J. K. "Designing an Effective Financial Planning and Control System." *Long Range Planning*, December 1988.
FALLON, WILLIAM K., ed., *AMA Management Handbook*. AMACOM, New York, 1983.
GARDNER, J. R./, and OTHERS, EDITORS. *Handbook of Strategic Planning*. John Wiley and Sons, Inc., New York, NY, 1986.
Journal of Business Strategy. Long Range Planning. Pergamon Press, Inc., Elmsford, NY. Bimonthly.
Looking Ahead and Projection Highlights. National Planning Association, Washington, DC. Monthly.

"The New Gospel of Financial Planning." *Money*, March, 1989.

Planning. American Planning Association, Chicago, IL. Monthly.

PARSON, M.J., *Back to Basics Planning*. Facts on File Publications, New York, 1985.

Planning Review.

Planning Under Uncertainty: Multiple Scenarios and Contingency Planning. The Conference Board, Inc., New York, NY. Conference Board Report No. 741.

"Reassessing Your Financial Plans." *Management Accounting*, November, 1988.

REINHARTH, L., H. SHAPIRO, E. KALLMAN, *Planning: Strategic, Administrative, Operational*. Van Nostrand Reinhold, Florence, Kentucky, 1980.

SAPP, R. W., and SMITH, R. W. *Strategic Management for Bankers*. The Planning Forum, Oxford, OH, 1984.

WOELFEL, C. J., and MECIMORE, C. D. *The Operating Executive's Guide to Profit Planning Tools and Techniques*. Probus Publishing Co., Chicago, IL, 1986.

PLANT A manufacturing establishment; production unit; works; factory; mill; the buildings, machinery, appliances, tools, implements, and equipment used in production; the fixed investment used to carry on a business.

PLANT ASSETS The fixed assets of a business, except land, permanently employed for production. They include buildings, machinery, tools, instruments, implements, equipment, and appliances, against which a reserve for depreciation and obsolescence should be provided.

PLANT VISIT A factory inspection or industrial survey undertaken as a regular part of an investigation by an investment banker (who frequently retains an industrial engineer to inspect the physical equipment) to determine the efficiency of production, the relation between costs and market prices, the probable future developments of the territory served, and the need for and probable return on the new capital which he has been asked to provide by underwriting an issue of securities.

A plant visit is not usually undertaken when a commercial loan is sought, but is sometimes employed where conditions are without precedent, or where there is doubt whether the credit should be granted. When desirable, such an investigation in commercial banking practice need not be technical, since it is the financial condition rather than the plant condition that determines the safety of a short-term loan. It is only insofar as the plant condition may affect the financial condition that the plant visit may be particularly important. In the majority of cases, where it seems advisable at all, it can be undertaken by an experienced credit man or loan officer. The principal points to be considered are location, transportation facilities, plant layout, modernness of equipment, efficiency of workers, and cost accounting methods.

PLEDGE When COLLATERAL, e.g., stocks, bonds, etc., is delivered to a bank as security for a loan, the delivery constitutes a pledge for the payment of a debt. A pledge implies a relinquishment of the property by the borrower and the transfer of its custody to the lender. The property pledged must be in negotiable form in order to permit the lending bank to assign it in case of the failure of the borrower to redeem his note.

See HYPOTHECATION, PAWN.

PLEDGED ACCOUNT BUY-DOWN MORTGAGE WITH AN ADJUSTABLE RATE. *See* BUY-DOWN.

PLEDGEE The party to whom a PLEDGE is made, i.e., to whom securities or other assignable property are pledged as security for payment of a loan.

PLEDGOR One who pledges or hypothecates securities or other property as security for the payment of a loan.

See PLEDGE.

PLUM Extraordinary company profits distributed in the form of an extra cash or stock dividend; a MELON.

PLUNGE Reckless speculation on a large scale.

PLUNGER One who takes enormous risks in the expectation of correspondingly large gains.

POINT The unit of price in which fluctuations in quotations and gains and losses are expressed in stocks, bonds, and commodities. On security markets, a point is $1 per share, but the smallest unit of price fluctuation, except for rights and very low-priced stocks, is one-eighth of a point ($0.125 per share for stocks and $1.25 for bonds, except U.S. government bonds which are traded in minimum price fluctuations of one-thirty-second of a point or $0.3125). In connection with obligations quoted on a yield basis, basis points refer to the yield; e.g., a 2% coupon bond with a current yield of 2.5% is said to be yielding 50 basis points higher than the coupon rate.

On commodity exchanges, the minimum fluctuation's equivalent on the contract will depend upon the definition of the contract's size. Thus in grains, the minimum fluctuation of $0.00125 per bushel (wheat, rye, corn, oats, and barley) is equivalent to $6.25 per contract because the round lot is 5,000 bushels; the minimum fluctuation in cotton futures of $0.0001 is equivalent to $5.00 per round lot of 100 bales or 50,000 pounds, etc.

POINT IV PROGRAM The fourth of four points of foreign policy proposed by President Truman in his inaugural address on January 20, 1949. It has been a technical cooperation program, which has been administered by the foreign aid agency under its various organizational changes since original statutory authority for the program (Title III of Chapter II of the Mutual Security Act).

In the 1970 fiscal year, emphasis was shifted to technical assistance activities, particularly new and innovative techniques to overcome bottlenecks to development. Grants began to be used in developing countries for the following purposes: (1) to provide the advisers, teachers, training, and equipment required for the improvement of educational, administrative, technical, and professional skills; (2) to assist in the control and eradication of major diseases and other menaces to health; (3) to establish and improve institutions which further economic and social development programs and projects; (4) to assist family planning programs; and (5) to finance research and development of U.S. universities and other institutions concerned with problems of economic development.

Technical assistance, energy, research, and related development problems are one of the classifications of programs provided by the AGENCY FOR INTERNATIONAL DEVELOPMENT (AID), a component organization of the INTERNATIONAL DEVELOPMENT COOPERATION AGENCY (IDCA). The director of the IDCA serves as the principal international development adviser for the President and the secretary of State, subject to guidance concerning the foreign policy of the United States from the secretary of State.

See MUTUAL SECURITY PROGRAM.

POINT-OF-SALE TERMINALS On-line electronic terminals located in retail establishments that allow for transfer of funds between accounts, authorizations for credit, verification of checks, and provision of related services at the time of purchases. They allow customers of participating financial institutions to effect transactions through the use of machine-readable debit cards containing a magnetic stripe indicating the customer's account number, bank number, and types of accounts. When the PIN (personal identification number) is inserted, the bank's computer, with which the POS terminal is connected, will provide such banking services as deposits, withdrawals, funds transfer, loan and bill payments, and overdrafts, including shift of funds for payment to the store.

POS terminals depend upon the volume of customers and transactions at the retail establishments selected for installation, which therefore ideally should be active retail centers in shopping centers drawing customers in large numbers from the surrounding geographic area.

Large retail establishments, such as supermarkets, might instead provide space for automatic teller machines (ATMs), or for customers provide check-cashing service or a range of other financial services such as sale of mutual fund shares and insurance (e.g., the Kroger Co. financial center located in its supermarkets).

See ELECTRONIC FUND TRANSFER ACT.

POLICY A written contract between the insurer and the person insured.

The policy specifies in detail the terms and conditions under which the parties are bound, the property covered, and the risks insured against in consideration of payment of the premiums. Basic provisions of insurance policies within each major class of insurance—life, fire, and casualty—are subject to state regulation and standardization in the industry, but new forms of coverage developed over the years and variables in terms allow for sales appeal and competition among companies.

See INSURANCE.

POOL This term has two meanings:

1. A combination of persons—brokers, professional traders, or other interests—who organized for the purpose of exploiting a certain stock or stocks. A pool was a joint venture or temporary association of speculators. A definite prearranged agreement specified such details as (1) the designation of a manager with full power to act for the members of the agreement; (2) the specific stock and maximum shares or dollar amount of position either long or short at any time, with purchases and sales to be made at such times and in such amounts as the discretion of the manager would call for; (3) the specified interest of each member who deposited at least initial margin as a condition for becoming a member; and (4) the specified duration of the account, usually subject to extension for further specified period at the manager's discretion. While the pool agreement was in force, its members agreed not to trade individually in the security being exploited.

In order to be successful, the pool had to have astute management, capital, and knowledge of technical market conditions. Pools were by no means always successful. It soon became apparent when a pool was operating, so it was not impossible for observing outsiders to take advantage of its operations, which if carried too far would result in defeat of the pool's objectives and result in loss for its members. The terms clique, syndicate, and ring were sometimes used with much the same significance as pool. Different speculative pools were given special names in accordance with the type of agreement entered into among its members—e.g., inside pools, blind pools, bobcat pools, etc. Pools were either bull pools (for the rise) or bear pools (for the decline) or both. The operational stages of a bull pool were as follows: (1) period of accumulation, when the pool's interest was in keeping prices stable so the block of accumulation could be assembled with least disturbance to the market price and the floating supply could be cleaned up; (2) markup, when the pool generated unusual trading activity and price run-up in the stock, thus attracting an outside following for it, further spiraling the price in view of the thin floating supply (the pool manager might have to feed the market stock at this stage to prevent too rapid a run-up prematurely, or be prepared to absorb offerings as the price rose to prevent a swamping of the rise); (3) stage of distribution, either at the end of the rise, if the market was broad enough in outside buying interest, or on a scale from the stock's top, as outsiders bought on a mild decline in expectation of the stock's recovery to its high.

To accomplish its purposes, the pool capitalized on company developments, such as higher earnings, dividends, merger or consolidation, etc., and the dissemination of tips, rumors, etc. It resorted to all available technical means of manipulation, including matched orders, wash sales, jiggles, and collusion with company insiders and specialists in the stocks concerned. The trading pool accumulated its position in the open market; the option pool operated on low-priced options from the company itself or large holders which assured it of a supply of stock at low prices. According to the report of the Senate Banking Committee (*Stock Exchange Practices*, Senate Report No. 1455, 73d Congress, 2d Session), one of the most successful pools was that in Sinclair Consolidated Oil stock in 1929, which realized a $12.6 million profit. The famous radio (RCA) pool of 1929 made a profit of $4.9 million. The same report distinguished between good and bad pools as follows:

> The testimony before the sub-committee again and again demonstrated that the activity fomented by a pool creates a false and deceptive appearance of genuine demand for the security on the part of the purchasing public and attracts persons relying upon this misleading appearance to make purchases which relieve the pool of its holdings in the end.

Attempts have been made to differentiate between "beneficient" pools and "nefarious" pools. Pools operated for the purpose of stabilizing the market prices during periods of secondary distribution or while liquidating blocks of stock held by estates or creditors have been placed in the category of "beneficient" pools, whereas pools operated merely for the purpose of raising the price of securities so that the participants might unload their holdings at increased prices have been characterized as "nefarious" pools.

From the viewpoint of the purchaser outside of the pool circle, there is no substantial or ethical difference in these two types of pool. Although the purposes may by different, the means employed are identical.

In all cases, fictitious activity is intentionally created and the purchaser is deceived by an appearance of genuine demand for the security. Motive furnishes no justification for the employment of manipulative devices.

Accordingly, the Securities Exchange Act of 1934 prohibited pool operations under penalties (Sec. 9). Moreover, Rule 105 of the New York Stock Exchange provides that neither a member acting as a specialist, nor a member firm in which such member is a participant, or any other participant in such member firm shall be directly or indirectly interested in a pool dealing or trading in the stock in which such a member is a specialist; nor shall any such member, member firm, or participant therein directly or indirectly acquire or grant any option to buy or sell or to receive or deliver shares of the stock in which such member is a specialist. Similar rules are provided by other exchanges. Pursuant to discretionary power under the Securities Exchange Act, however, the Securities and Exchange Commission by regulation (Rule 10b-7) permits, under restrictions and safeguards, stabilizing to facilitate a distribution. Such permissible manipulation by a distribution syndicate is a recognition of a beneficent pool-type activity.

2. More or less formal groupings of competing firms for the purpose of control of prices, patents, markets, output, income, etc. Such pools are violative of the antitrust laws because their motivation is to eliminate or lessen competition or to effect monopoly. It should be noted, however, that a patent pool per se is not a violation of the antitrust laws, if in fact not motivated by such violation but to effect patent cooperation, avoid litigation, etc. (e.g., *Standard Oil Co. (Indiana)* v. *U.S.*, 283 U.S. 163 (1931)).

In railroad regulation, pooling of traffic or revenues of competing carriers was prohibited by the original Interstate Commerce Act of 1887. But the Transportation Act of 1920 provided that pooling agreements deemed by the Interstate Commerce Commission to be in the public interest, not unduly restricting competition, would be permissible. The Reed-Bulwinkle Act of 1948 provided that agreements among railroads as to rates, fares, classifications, divisions, allowances, or charges would be exempt from the antitrust laws if approved by the Interstate Commerce Commission as in the public interest.

POOLING OF INTERESTS Accounting for a business combination can be accomplished by two methods: pooling of interests method and purchase method. APB Opinion No. 16 established 12 conditions that must be met before the pooling-of-interests method can be used to account for a business combination.

The concept behind the pooling-of-interests method is that the holders of the common stock in the combining companies continue as holders of the common stock in the combined company. The business combination is accounted for by adding together the book value of the assets and equities of the combined enterprises. The combining corporation records the assets and liabilities received from the combined companies at book values recorded on the books of the combined companies. The equity of the acquired company is combined with the equity of the acquiring company. The allocation of the acquired company's equity among common stock, other contributed capital, and retained earnings may have to be restructured as a result of the differences in the par value of the stock issued and the par value of the stock acquired. The pooling-of-interests method can be contrasted with the purchase method of accounting for a business combination.

BIBLIOGRAPHY

Accounting Research Bulletin No. 48, Business Combinations. AICPA, Committee on Accounting Procedure, 1958.

POPULATION The Bureau of the Census is the major source of population statistics in the United States. The bureau conducts a decennial census of population, a monthly population survey, a program of population estimates and projections, and other periodic surveys relating to population characteristics.

The U.S. Constitution provides for a census of the population every ten years to establish a basis for apportionment of members of the House of Representatives among the states. The first census was taken in 1790. In 1902, the Bureau of the Census was established as a permanent federal agency and was assigned the responsibility of enumerating the population and for compiling statistics on other matters.

The census is a complete count. An attempt is made to account for every person, for each person's residence, and for other characteristics (sex, age, family relationships, and others). Since the 1940 census, additional data have been obtained from representative samples of the population. In the 1980 census, two sampling rates were used. For most of the county, one in every six households (about 17%) received the long form or sample questionnaire; areas estimated to have fewer than 2,500 inhabitants, every other household (50%) received the sample questionnaire. Census workers in 1990 are expected to count about 250 million people and 106 million households, relying heavily on automation and computers. Approximately 400,000 temporary census takers were employed between summer 1989 and summer 1990.

Table 1 appended shows the U.S. population by official census from 1900 to 1988. Table 2 shows U.S. population centers from 1790 to 1980. Table 3 shows resident population by sex, race, residence, and median age, from 1790 to 1987. Figure 1 shows state population, percent change, 1980 to 1987.

The estimated population of the United States according to the Bureau of the Census on January 1, 1988, was 244.6 million, representing an 8% increase over the 1980 census count of 226.5 million. Of the 38 metropolitan areas of a million or more, Dallas-Forth Worth's 25% increase since the 1980 census was exceeded only by the 26% increase in the Phoenix area. It is estimated that approximately 78% percent of the U.S. population live in metropolitan areas. Before 1980 to 1987, the South and West accounted for 15 million of the nation's 17 million population increases, or 90% of the growth.

The nation's population center continues to move south and west in Missouri since the 1980 census, to about ten miles northwest of Potosi in west-central Washington County as of 1985. The center is generally considered to be where the country would balance perfectly if it were a flat surface and every person on it had equal weight.

During the 1980-87 period, the country's Hispanic population increased 30% to 18.8 million, increasing more than four times faster than the U.S. total. The Census Bureau estimates that Hispanics present 8% share of the population may increase to 19% by 2080.

It is estimated that more than 37 million Americans have a disability and that 13.5 million cannot perform basic physical activities.

Elementary and high school enrollments were significantly lower in 1986 than in 1980. The college level was higher. The farm population continued to fall, decreasing by 7% to 5.3 million from 1984 to 1985. Approximately one of every 45 (2.2%) people live on farms.

The nation's median age in 1987 was 32.1 years versus 30.0 years in 1980. The baby boom apparently was becoming middle aged. There were approximately 89.5 million households in the United States in 1987. This represented a 1.2 million average annual increase since 1980.

Household income averaged $22,650 in 1985, an increase over the previous year of 0.9% after adjustment for inflation.

The Bureau of the Census provides the medium projection of the world's population for the year 2000 to be approximately 6,350 million, representing a 55% increase over the 1975 estimate and a 150% increase since 1950. Some recent projections indicate a possible stabilization of total world population at about 10 billion late in the next century; the estimate could be affected by delays in attaining lowered fertility levels. Population expansion in many less-developed countries has substantially offset development efforts as well as foreign aid. Food production has not kept pace with population growth in many parts of the world. Pressure of population growth upon food supply could revive the somewhat discredited Malthusian specters of famine, pestilence, and disease, as well as social and political unrest.

Table 1 / Population: 1900 to 1988.
(In thousands, except percent. Estimates as of July 1. Prior to 1940, excludes Alaska and Hawaii. Total population includes Armed Forces abroad; civilian population excludes Armed Forces.

Year	Resident population	Year	Total Population	Percent change	Resident population	Civilian population	Year	Total Population	Percent change	Resident population	Civilian population
1900	76,094	1950	152,271	1.7	151,868	150,790	1970	205,052	1.2	203,984	201,895
1905	83,822	1951	154,878	1.7	153,982	151,599	1971	207,661	1.3	206,827	204,866
1910	92,407	1952	157,553	1.7	156,393	153,892	1972	209,896	1.1	209,284	207,511
1915	100,546	1953	160,184	1.7	158,956	156,595	1973	211,909	1.0	211,357	209,600
1920	106,461	1954	163,026	1.8	161,884	159,695	1974	213,854	.9	213,342	211,636
1925	115,829	1955	165,931	1.8	165,069	162,967	1975	215,973	1.0	215,465	213,788
1930	123,077	1956	168,903	1.8	168,088	166,055	1976	218,035	1.0	217,563	215,894
1935	127,250	1957	171,984	1.8	171,187	169,110	1977	220,239	1.0	219,760	218,106
1940	132,457	1958	174,882	1.7	174,149	172,226	1978	222,585	1.1	222,095	220,467
1941	133,669	1959	177,830	1.7	177,135	175,277	1979	225,055	1.1	224,567	222,969
1942	134,617	1960	180,671	1.6	179,979	178,140	1980	227,757	1.2	227,255	225,651
1943	135,107	1961	183,691	1.7	182,992	181,143	1981	230,138	1.0	229,637	227,989
1944	133,915	1962	186,538	1.5	185,771	183,677	1982	232,520	1.0	231,996	230,327
1945	133,434	1963	189,242	1.4	188,483	186,493	1983	234,799	1.0	234,284	232,589
1946	140,686	1964	191,889	1.4	191,141	189,141	1984	237,001	1.0	236,477	234,762
1947	144,083	1965	194,303	1.3	193,526	191,605	1985	239,279	1.0	238,736	237,031
1948	146,730	1966	196,560	1.2	195,576	193,420	1986	241,613	1.0	241,096	239,374
1949	149,304	1967	198,712	1.1	197,457	195,264	1987	243,915	1.0	243,400	241,661
		1968	200,706	1.0	199,399	197,113	1988	246,113	1.0	245,602	243,910
		1969	202,677	1.0	201,385	199,145					

Source: U.S. Bureau of the Census, *Current Population Reports*, series P-25, Nos. 802, 1023, and 1029.

POPULATION

Table 2 / U.S. Center of Population, 1790-1980

Center of Population is that point which may be considered as center of population gravity of the U.S. or that point upon which the U.S. would balance if it were a rigid plane without weight and the population distributed thereon with each individual being assumed to have equal weight and to exert an influence on a central point proportional to his distance from that point.

Year	N. Latitude °	′	″	W. Longitude °	′	″	Approximate location
1790	39	16	30	76	11	12	23 miles east of Baltimore, MD.
1800	39	16	6	76	56	30	18 miles west of Baltimore, MD.
1810	39	11	30	77	37	12	40 miles northwest by west of Washington, D.C. (in VA.)
1820	39	5	42	78	33	0	16 miles east of Moorefield, W. VA. [1]
1830	38	57	54	79	16	54	19 miles west-southwest of Moorefield, W. VA. [1]
1840	39	2	0	80	18	0	16 miles south of Clarksburg, W. VA. [1]
1850	38	59	0	81	19	0	23 miles southeast of Parkersburg, W. VA. [1]
1860	39	0	24	82	48	48	20 miles south by east of Chillicothe, OH.
1870	39	12	0	83	35	42	48 miles east by north of Cincinnati, OH.
1880	39	4	8	84	39	40	8 miles west by south of Cincinnati, OH. (in KY.)
1890	39	11	56	85	32	53	20 miles east of Columbus, IN.
1900	39	9	36	85	48	54	6 miles southeast of Columbus, IN.
1910	39	10	12	86	32	20	In the city of Bloomington, IN.
1920	39	10	21	86	43	15	8 miles south-southeast of Spencer, Owen County, IN.
1930	39	3	45	87	8	6	3 miles northeast of Linton, Greene County, IN.
1940	38	56	54	87	22	35	2 miles southeast by east of Carlisle, Sullivan County, IN.
1950 (Incl. Alaska & Hawaii)	38	48	15	88	22	8	3 miles northeast of Louisville, Clay County, IL.
1960	38	35	58	89	12	35	6 1/2 miles northwest of Centralia, IL.
1970	38	27	47	89	42	22	5 miles east southeast of Mascoutah, St. Clair County, IL.
1980	38	8	13	90	34	26	1/4 mile west of DeSoto, MO.

[1] West Virginia was set off from Virginia Dec. 31, 1862, and admitted as a state June 20, 1863.

Source: U.S. Bureau of the Census.

Table 3 / Resident Population by Sex, Race, Residence, and Median Age: 1790 to 1987
(Thousands, except as indicated)

Date	Sex Male	Female	Race White	Black Number	Black Percent	Other	Residence Urban	Rural	Median age (years) All races	White	Black
Conterminous U.S. [1]											
1790 (Aug. 2)	NA	NA	3,172	757	19.3	NA	202	3,728	NA	NA	NA
1810 (Aug. 6)	NA	NA	5,862	1,378	19.0	NA	525	6,714	NA	16.0	NA
1820 (Aug. 7)	4,897	4,742	7,867	1,772	18.4	NA	693	8,945	16.7	16.5	17.2
1840 (June 1)	8,689	8,381	14,196	2,874	16.8	NA	1,845	15,224	17.8	17.9	17.3
1860 (June 1)	16,085	15,358	26,923	4,442	14.1	79	6,217	25,227	19.4	19.7	17.7
1870 (June 1)	19,494	19,065	33,589	4,880	12.7	89	9,902	28,656	20.2	20.4	18.5
1880 (June 1)	25,519	24,637	43,403	6,581	13.1	172	14,130	36,026	20.9	21.4	18.0
1890 (June 1)	32,237	30,711	55,101	7,489	11.9	358	22,106	40,841	22.0	22.5	17.8
1900 (June 1)	38,816	37,178	66,809	8,834	11.6	351	30,160	45,835	22.9	23.4	19.4
1920 (Jan. 1)	53,900	51,810	94,821	10,463	9.9	427	54,158	51,553	25.3	25.6	22.3
1930 (Apr. 1)	62,137	60,638	110,287	11,891	9.7	597	68,955	53,820	26.4	26.9	23.5
1940 (Apr. 1)	66,062	65,608	118,215	12,866	9.8	589	74,424	57,246	29.0	29.5	25.3
United States											
1950 (Apr. 1)	75,187	76,139	135,150	15,045	9.9	1,131	96,847	54,479	30.2	30.7	26.2
1960 (Apr. 1)	88,331	90,992	158,832	18,872	10.5	1,620	125,269	54,054	29.5	30.3	23.5
1970 (Apr. 1) [2]	98,926	104,309	178,098	22,581	11.1	2,557	149,325	53,887	28.0	28.9	22.4
1980 (Apr. 1) [3]	110,053	116,493	194,713	26,683	11.8	5,150	167,051	59,495	30.0	30.9	24.9
1985 (July 1, est)	116,160	122,576	202,769	28,870	12.1	7,097	NA	NA	31.5	32.4	26.6
1967 (July 1, est)	118,531	124,869	205,820	29,736	12.2	7,844	NA	NA	32.1	33.0	27.2

NA — Not available.
[1] Excludes Alaska and Hawaii.
[2] The revised 1970 resident population count is 203,302,031, which incorporates changes due to errors found after tabulations were completed. The race and sex data shown here reflect the official 1970 census count while the residence data come from the tabulated count.
[3] The race data shown for April 1, 1980 have been modified.

Source: U.S. Bureau of the Census.

ENCYCLOPEDIA OF BANKING AND FINANCE

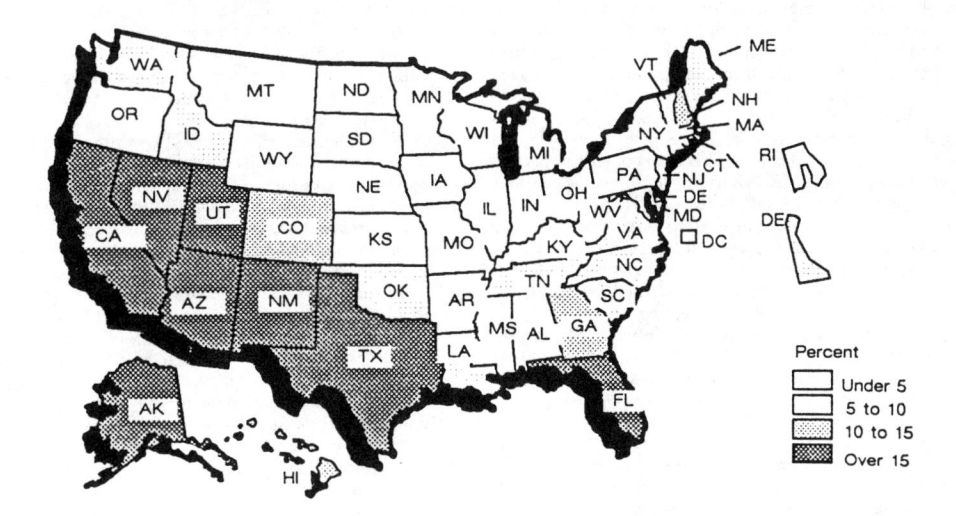

Figure 1 / State population—Percent Change: 1980-1987

Percent
- Under 5
- 5 to 10
- 10 to 15
- Over 15

Source: Chart prepared by U.S. Bureau of the Census.

BIBLIOGRAPHY

Bureau of the Census Catalog. U.S. Bureau of the Census. Annual.
Census. U.S. Government Printing Office.
County Business Patterns. Bureau of the Census. Annual.
Current Population Reports. Bureau of the Census.
Historical Statistics of the United States, Colonial Times to 1970: A Statistical Abstract Supplement. Bureau of the Census. Two volumes.
"1992 Metro Market Projections." *Sales Marketing and Management,* November 7, 1988.
Population and Development Review. Quarterly.
Population Bulletin. Bimonthly.
Population Index. Quarterly.
"Population Growth of Large Metropolitan Areas. *Statistical Bulletin.* Metropolitan Life Insurance Co., April/June, 1989.
RAYMONDO, J. C. "How To Choose a Projection Technique." *American Demographic,* February, 1989.
RICHE, M. F. "California Here It Comes." *American Demographics,* March, 1989.
Ross, J. A. *International Encyclopedia of Population.* Macmillan Publishing Co., New York, NY, 1982.
"Tomorrow's Fastest-Growing Markets: Population Growth Rates, 1987-92." *Sales Marketing and Management,* November 7, 1988.
"Tomorrow's Negate-Growth Markets: Rates of Decline, 1987-92." *Sales Marketing and Management,* November 7, 1988.
"2010 [Census Bureau Projections]." *American Demographics,* February, 1988.

PORPHYRY Any compound rock or ore; in finance, a copper mine containing reserves of ore of comparatively low grade. By extension the term is used to refer to a copper company or group of copper companies which extract copper from low-grade copper ores, as distinguished from the companies engaged in developing mines containing native copper or ore with a high copper content. The porphyry copper companies are also known as the high-cost producers, because the cost of developing low-grade ores is greater than that of developing high-grade ores.

PORTFOLIO Holdings of loans and securities. A Federal Reserve bank is said to have added to its portfolio of bill holdings, or a bank to have liquidated its portfolio of government securities. The portfolio of an investment company, likewise, is its total list of security holdings.

PORTFOLIO INSURANCE A form of hedging that uses STOCK INDEX FUTURES contracts and index options to limit the downside risk of holding a diversified portfolio of common stocks. PI programs are offered by major banks, brokerage firms, insurance companies, and other financial institutions. They have attracted many large institutional holders of common stocks like pension funds and mutual funds.

When the stock market declines, holders of common stocks traditionally begin to move some portion of their assets out of stocks and into cash to protect themselves against further declines in the market. PI programs attempt to hedge against the possibility of a market decline by selling stock index futures contracts or stock index options (buying stock index put options). The more the market falls, the more futures and options contracts are sold by PI programs. If the market continues to fall, the rise in the value of the portfolio's futures and options positions cushions the decline in the value of the portfolio's common stocks. PI managers believe that such HEDGING programs using futures and options involve lower transaction costs and provide greater liquidity than the traditional method of actually selling stocks and buying Treasury bills.

Portfolio insurance differs from true insurance in that it does not guarantee protection in the event of a market downturn. In the market crash of October 19, 1987, many PI programs had to be shut down because trading in financial futures and options was suspended. As a result, many portfolio managers were surprised to find that their PI programs provided little or no protection. Many PI programs were discontinued after the crash because the increased market volatility raised the cost of PI programs to unacceptable levels by increasing the implicit cost of futures and options premiums. PI programs also have been blamed for exacerbating the market's turmoil during and following the 1987 crash.

POSITION This term has two meanings:

1. A reference to the month in which one's futures contracts mature, i.e., delivery becomes due. In all of the future markets, e.g., grain, cotton, sugar, coffee, etc., contracts for delivery at some future date, designated by months, are bought and sold. For example, a contract which matures next December is known as a December position. The Commodity Exchange Authority of the U.S. Department of Agriculture reports daily the volume of trading and open interest in commodity futures trading upon regulated commodity exchanges.
2. The current trading inventory of securities of security dealers.

ENCYCLOPEDIA OF BANKING AND FINANCE

POSITION SHEET An accounting summary designed to show the commitments of a bank or foreign exchange house in foreign currencies. A position sheet is usually prepared daily to show exactly the bank's position with regard to its foreign balances, and the total amount for which it is committed both on spot and future contracts. In reality, it is a summary of the foreign exchange ledgers and shows whether the bank is long or short of each foreign currency. If a bank is long in its sterling position, the aggregate of its sterling accounts, with correspondents abroad, will show a net credit balance on the latter's books. A bank is short of sterling when the opposite condition prevails, i.e., when the aggregate of sterling accounts with correspondents abroad shows a net debit balance on the latter's books. Thus a bank is short of sterling when it has not only exhausted available sterling balances against which it can sell sterling drafts but overdrawn such accounts, leaving a net debit balance which must be made good. To even up accounts, it will be necessary for the bank to cover—that is, to purchase sterling.

In determination of the position for each day, future contracts are considered as well as spot. The position sheet shows the average cost and current market rate of all commitments, and approximately shows the bank's daily profit or loss in each foreign currency.

POSITIVE ECONOMICS Objective inquiry in economics is called scientific or positive economics. Positive economics is practiced when one predicts that if event A occurs, then event B will follow. This prediction is based on the objective evaluation of facts; that is, that event B is the logical result after event A. The distinguishing characteristic of positive economics is that the predictions are testable if given sufficient information. Thus, positive economics may be either true or false.

POST A point or position on the floor of a stock exchange at which certain stocks are bought and sold. Specific stocks are assigned to specific posts for the purpose of centralizing trading; thus Post 2 on the New York Stock Exchange is where the floor member of a commission house will go on the floor to execute orders on "X" (U.S. Steel common). The New York Stock Exchange has assigned its list to 18 active posts and 1 additional post, Post 30, for 10-share-unit stocks and inactive stocks.

Actually, the posts on the New York Stock Exchange since 1928 have not been posts in structure and appearance, being instead U-shaped structures some 8 feet high and 100 square feet in area, inside and outside of which are stationed the employees assigned to the post; specialists, odd-lot brokers, and varying "crowds" (commission brokers, floor traders, floor brokers) engaging in transactions.

Corresponding to the posts on the floor of stock exchanges are the pits on commodity exchanges, or rings in which trading in commodities is transacted.

POSTAL SAVINGS SYSTEM An act of Congress dated March 28, 1966 (80 Stat. 92; 39 U.S.C. 5225-5229) provided for the closing of the postal savings system. At a time when national banks had not yet been authorized to accept savings deposits, the postal savings system, originally established in 1911 under the Postal Savings Act of June 25, 1910 (36 Stat. 814; 39 U.S.C. 751, 753), provided for a nationwide system of savings offices in post offices which provided savings facilities for communities without them.

The funds on hand in the postal savings system as of July 1, 1967, representing deposits remaining unclaimed as of that date, were transferred to the U.S. Treasury in a trust fund account. The official record of the account will be retained at the post office where it was opened, and the department will continue to assist holders to process their claims.

POST-DATED CHECK A CHECK that is dated ahead, i.e., bears a date that has not yet arrived. A bank has no authority to pay a post-dated check. It may pay checks only when dated as of the day of presentation or a date prior thereto. A check is a draft drawn on a bank and payable on demand. When the check is post-dated, i.e., given a date later than the date when execution and delivery occur, the post-dating changes the check from a demand instrument to a time instrument, and the check is not payable until that specified date.

POSTED RATES There is no centralized single place for the open Monday market in New York City; instead, prevailing rates are established by checking the banks, brokers, and dealers in various types of funds constituting the MONEY MARKET. Until about 1946, the money desk on the floor of the New York Stock Exchange received listings of credit needs and offerings by banks which the desk clerk could use to place borrowing brokers and lending banks in communication for the arrangement of call loans. Since that time, however, call loans have been customer loans, arranged between individual broker customers and specific banks, with a continuance of activity by money brokers.

Nevertheless, a centralized command post for learning prevailing money rates is the New York Federal Reserve Bank, which is constantly in touch with the market in connection with its constant check of money market conditions. In addition, the various leading money market banks post each morning at about 11 A.M. their dealer loan rates on loans to government securities dealers secured by government securities, both on renewals and new loans. Thus, "$3^1/_4$–$3^1/_4$" or "$33^1/_4$ across" indicates for the bank thus quoting that renewal loans (first quotation) and new loans (second quotation) will both be made at $3^1/_4$%; "3–$3^1/_4$" indicates renewals at 3% and new loans at $3^1/_4$%; or "$3^1/_4$–0" indicates renewals at $3^1/_4$%, no new loans available. Similarly, a check of quotation of banks, dealers, and brokers in such segments of the money market as federal funds, bankers acceptances, and commercial paper will establish prevailing rates for such funds.

In the foreign exchange market, posted rates are quoted daily by banks and dealers in foreign exchange, indicating the quotations at which specific currencies are offered for sale. Posted rates usually govern small transactions, differing from actual rates determined directly between banks or dealers and large buyers by negotiation, which will fluctuate in accordance with transactions and will not necessarily correspond with the posted rates. As with other quotations, when actual rates are quoted, they are intended for immediate action, and they will not hold firm for any time unless specifically stated.

POSTIL In bookkeeping, an explanatory marginal note written against an item in a journal or ledger. The Boston ledger provides postil spaces.

POTATOES Futures trading in potatoes is conducted on the NEW YORK MERCANTILE EXCHANGE and the CHICAGO MERCANTILE EXCHANGE, both of which are contract markets designated by the secretary of Agriculture and are regulated by the Commodity Exchange Authority. Of these two futures markets, the more active market for potato futures is that on the New York Mercantile Exchange.

A contract unit on the New York Mercantile Exchange (NYMEX) for the round white potato futures contract is 50,000 pounds (1,000 fifty-pound bags), the minimum permitted delivery being 42,000 pounds (840 fifty-pound bags). Deliverable potatoes are the round white varieties (except cobbler and warba types) grown in the states of Maine, New York, and Connecticut, and delivered in straight carloads or truckloads. The year 1980 was eventful for the NYMEX round white potato futures contract. During the year, the exchange received approval from the COMMODITY FUTURES TRADING COMMISSION to open an expanded contract for potatoes, which includes potatoes grown in the above-mentioned states. Previously the NYMEX contract had been limited to Maine-grown potatoes only.

Grade and size are U.S. No. 1, Size A, 2-inch minimum, 4-inch maximum. Permitted substitutions on the standard contract (April and May contracts only) are U.S. commercial grade potatoes (same origin, varieties, and sizes as above) in straight carloads or trucks at a discount of 25% from the last settling price for the delivery month. The grade standards are U.S. Department of Agriculture standards for grades of potatoes in effect.

The price quotation basis is in dollars and cents per 100 pounds including freight costs to New York City. Minimum price fluctuation is $0.01 per 100 pounds (no limit on last trading day). Maximum daily price fluctuation is $0.50 per 100 pounds above or below the preceding day's settling price (maximum daily price fluctuation is subject to variable limits formula). Delivery months are February, March, April, and November. Trading may also be conducted in other months as determined by the exchange's board of governors.

In delivery procedure, the seller has a choice of transportation: properly enclosed insulated trucks or refrigerator rail cars on track. The buyer may choose to take delivery at the point of origin without a final inspection or in New York City with grade guaranteed. In New York City, the truck delivery location is New York Fruit Auction Corporation, Hunts Point Food Center, Hunts Point, Bronx,

ENCYCLOPEDIA OF BANKING AND FINANCE

N.Y. 10474, and the rail delivery location is Harlem River Yards, Bronx, N.Y. Transfer of ownership to the buyer is upon completion of good delivery at New York City or the point of origin. Freight charges with rail delivery are paid by the buyer from the point of origin to the destination if different from the Harlem River Yards, Bronx, N.Y.; but the seller will provide allowance to the buyer of the freight rate from the point of origin to the Harlem River Yards, Bronx, N.Y. Freight charges with truck delivery are prepaid by the seller to the final inspection point; when the buyer takes delivery at the point of origin, there is an allowance by the seller to the buyer, as established and published by the exchange, for trucking charges from the point of origin to New York City.

Price Support Status. Potatoes have not been price-supported since the beginning of 1951. The Agricultural Act of 1949 made support mandatory for Irish potatoes, but the Act of March 31, 1950, provided that potato prices could not be supported unless marketing quotas were in effect. Since no legislative authority was enacted for the imposition of marketing quotas on potatoes, the 1950 act had the effect of prohibiting price support for potatoes. The Agricultural Act of 1954 removed potatoes from the category of designated nonbasic commodities and also repealed the section of the Act of March 31, 1950, which prohibited price support on Irish potatoes unless marketing quotas were in effect. The Commodity Credit Corporation reported a total loss of $178.1 million was incurred in price support previously provided for Irish potatoes, the heaviest loss experienced on any supported commodity. The commodity is difficult to support successfully because of perishability, difficulties in storage for support purposes, and sharp fluctuations in supply despite acreage reduction. These factors have made potatoes one of the most erratic and speculative farm crops.

POUND This term has two meanings:

1. A unit of weight equal to the following equivalents: 16 ounces, 7,000 grains, 454 grams, 0.454 kilogram, and 14.58 troy ounces.
2. POUND STERLING.

POUND STERLING The standard monetary unit of the British Commonwealth and a number of other countries (*see* FOREIGN MONEY). Generally known as the pound sterling or simply sterling (to distinguish it from the unit of weight), the English pound as of November 18, 1967, was given a reduced gold content of 2.13281 grams of gold and thus a new par value relative to the U.S. dollar of $2.40 at the INTERNATIONAL MONETARY FUND. The former par value was $2.80 (2.48828 grams of gold). Under the new par, a troy ounce of gold was the equivalent of 14.5833 pounds sterling. A U.S. dollar at the new par was the equivalent of 0.416667 of a pound sterling (or, conversely, the par value of the pound sterling was $2.40).

From June 23, 1972, however, the U.K. foreign exchange authorities did not maintain the exchange rate of the pound sterling within announced margins. Therefore all transactions in the official exchange market, except those in currencies maintaining a fixed relationship with the pound sterling, took place at a fluctuating exchange rate. Thus the U.K. was already floating the exchange rate of the pound sterling when most other major industrial countries began turning to floating rates in 1973. (The new Article IV of the Articles of Agreement of the International Monetary Fund became effective in 1977.) On March 13, 1979, the EUROPEAN MONETARY SYSTEM (EMS) was formally implemented. Although the U.K. is a member of the EMS, it does not participate in the common margins arrangement with respect to exchange rates among members of the EMS.

Sterling has been the domestic currency of England since the eleventh century. Since the early part of the nineteenth century, a basic international currency, the sterling bill on London, has been an international means of financing world trade. The pound sterling is also known as the sovereign. It derives its name from the fact that it originally represented a pound of silver.

Under the new decimal money system of the United Kingdom, effective February 15, 1971, the pound sterling domestically is equivalent to 100 new pence.

See ENGLISH MONEY TABLE.

POVERTY LEVEL A government-defined level of income to meet the minimal food, housing, clothing, medical, and transportation needs of individuals and families. In 1986, the poverty level for a family of four was $10,700. With inflation, the poverty level increases over time.

The percent of individuals below the poverty level has varied over time. In 1970, 12.6% of all individuals were below the poverty level. This percentage was 11.1 in 1973, but rose to 13.0% in 1980. In 1986, 13.6% of all individuals were below the poverty level.

POWER OF ATTORNEY A document witnessed or acknowledged, authorizing the person named therein to act in place of the signing party. A power of attorney may be general or special. In the latter, the authority of the agent is limited and is valid only for acts defined therein. In financial transactions, a power of attorney is usually special or limited, and is frequently used in the transfer of stock certificates and proxies for voting. It must set forth the powers conferred upon the agent. The common form of assignment and power of attorney approved by the committee on stock list of the New York Stock Exchange for the purpose of transferring stock, appearing on the reverse side of most certificates, is as follows.

Sample Power of Attorney

For value received _____
I (We) _____ hereby sell, assign and transfer unto _____
_____ shares of the capital stock represented by the within certificate and do hereby irrevocably constitute and appoint attorney to transfer the said stock on the books of the within named company with full power of substitution in the premises.
Dated _____
In the presence of _____

See PROXY.

POWER OF SUBSTITUTION A form that is stamped or written on the reverse side of a stock certificate when an attorney who has been named for the purpose of transferring the stock is exercising the privilege of appointing a substitute, according to the terms of the POWER OF ATTORNEY.

In such cases, the following form is signed by the attorney appointed in the assignment. The substitute is named in the body of the power of substitution.

Sample Power of Substitution

I (We) hereby irrevocably constitute and appoint _____
my (our) substitute to transfer the within named stock under the foregoing Power of Attorney, with like power of substitution.
Dated _____
In the presence of _____

See STOCK TRANSFERS.

PREAUTHORIZED DEBITS Arrangements that provide for preauthorized deductions from a customer's account and deposits into a company's account for mortgage, insurance, or utility payments.

PRECISION AND RELIABILITY Precision is the measure of the accuracy of an estimate—the closeness of the estimate to the true population value. The indicated reliability level, R, is the probability of achieving that degree of accuracy. When evaluating means, the precision interval is the range surrounding the sample mean, which has an R percent probability of including the true population mean.

PREEMPTIVE RIGHT Stockholders' privilege to subscribe to new issues of voting stock, usually the common stock or securities convertible into voting stock, before such offerings are made to nonstockholders. A preemptive RIGHT is often referred to as a privileged subscription right. The preemptive right has been eroded in recent years.

PREFERENCE BONDS Usually railroad income or adjustment bonds, especially when issued in series as first, second, and third, or Series A, Series B, Series C, etc. Interest on preference bonds is paid on each series in the order of preference. Thus interest may be earned and declared on Series A and B, but not on Series C.

See INCOME BONDS.

PREFERENCE INCOME BONDS PREFERENCE BONDS.

PREFERENCE STOCK The English equivalent for preferred stock. The term is also used in America in preferred stock nomenclature to designate different classes of PREFERRED STOCK, such as PRIOR PREFERENCE STOCK.

PREFERRED CREDITOR One who has preferred claims that legally take precedence over those of other creditors. For instance, in the dissolution of an insolvent company, the claims of laborers for wages, the claims of the government for taxes, and mechanics' liens take precedence over all others, whether secured or unsecured.

See LIABILITY.

PREFERRED DIVIDENDS See PREFERRED STOCK.

PREFERRED STOCK Stock that has a claim upon the earnings (and sometimes upon the assets and control) of a corporation prior to the common or other class of stock. Preferred stock represents an equity in the corporation which ranks after all bonds and floating debt, but ahead of common stock. Dividends must be paid upon the preferred stock before any distribution may be made to the common stockholders. Sometimes preferred stock is issued in series, e.g., Preferred A, Preferred B, etc.; Class A, Class B, etc.; or First Preferred Stock, Second Preferred Stock, etc. In such cases, dividends must be paid on the first series before a distribution can be made on the second, and on the second before on the third.

Dividends on preferred stock may be cumulative or noncumulative. A cumulative dividend is one that carries over from year to year and accumulates if it is not paid in one year, i.e., profits are not sufficient to pay the dividend at the full rate in any given year, then it is said to be in arrears and so long as it is unpaid constitutes a claim on earnings prior to dividends on the common stock. Common stockholders, therefore, are not entitled to receive dividends so long as dividends upon cumulative preferred stock remain in arrears. Noncumulative dividends are a prior claim in any given year, but if profits are insufficient to pay the dividend in full, there is no obligation on the part of the corporation to make up the deficiency in any subsequent year prior to paying dividends on the common stock. In other words, the dividends not paid in any given year are lost to the stockholders forever. The courts have held that dividends upon preferred stock are cumulative unless otherwise stated.

Dividends upon preferred stock may be at a fixed rate or on an "if earned" basis. Dividends on the latter basis are payable if declared by directors. This feature is related to the cumulative or noncumulative provisions; if earned, the dividend may or may not accumulate according to whether or not the dividend is cumulative.

Preferred stock may also be preferred as to assets and as to control. But in no case are preferences more than those specifically set forth. When stock is preferred as to assets, the full preference value must be paid in case of dissolution or insolvency before any payment (liquidating dividend) is made to the common shareholders. Prior claims as to voting sometimes rest with the preferred stock, but usually this class of stock has no voting power, the theory being that the common stockholders, bearing the greater part of the risk, should have the control. In other cases of less frequent occurrence, preferred and common stockholders rank equally in voting power.

Preferred stocks have been referred to as hybrid securities, affording the disadvantages of fixed return and lack of voting power of bonds while at the same time affording none of the legal rights and recourse upon default that bonds provide because of their status as equities. However, as senior equities, preferred stocks have their appeal for income purposes. Their range of yields varies with quality and stability of earnings of the issuer. Many high-grade preferred stocks fluctuate, like high-grade bonds, in accordance with the trend of money rates. Normally high-grade preferred stocks afford somewhat better returns than those available on high-grade bonds.

The attractiveness of preferred stocks may be increased by additional provisions designed to provide further features for the investor who purchases this class of securities. Some of these measures to secure further protection are the following: (1) preference as to assets; (2) cumulative dividends; (3) limited issue; (4) provision for partial or total redemption of the issue at some subsequent date by means of a sinking fund and usually at a premium; (5) provision requiring that net current assets shall at all times equal or exceed the amount outstanding; (6) provision requiring that net surplus be kept at a certain percentage of capital; (7) provision for automatically placing control in the hands of preferred stockholders in case of failure to pay dividends, etc.

Innovations in preferred stock in recent years have included floating-dividend-rate preferred stock and term preferred stock subject to mandatory sinking fund. The latter requires that to the extent that the company does not satisfy its mandatory sinking fund obligation in any year, such obligation must be satisfied in the succeeding year or years. If the company is in arrears in the redemption of the preferred stock pursuant to the mandatory sinking fund requirement, the company shall not purchase, otherwise acquire for value, or pay dividends on common stock. For balance sheet purposes, pursuant to SEC requirement, such term preferred stock (so called because operation of the sinking fund would eventually retire all of the preferred stock by a given future year) is listed separately and prior to other preferred stocks of the company not having such sinking fund feature.

Participating preferred stock carries the right to earn dividends in excess of the specified dividend rate in an amount, under simple participation, equal to the rate paid upon the common stock. Under this arrangement, the preferred stockholders share in extreme prosperity along with the common stockholders without relinquishing any of their rights of priority, and in no case can common stockholders receive dividends at a higher rate than the preferred stockholders.

Convertible preferred stock gives the owner the option of converting his preferred shares into common shares at a stated rate of exchange. In case of appreciation of the market value of the common shares, the convertible preferred would reflect the rise in market value, and a profit would be made by converting. Thus participating preferred and convertible preferred stock have additional speculative attractions.

Preferred stocks create a special type of ownership with less risk than common stock, but with definite limitations of control and income.

See CAPITAL STOCK, STOCK CERTIFICATE.

PREMISES This term has two meanings:

1. Within a legal document, such as a deed, conveyance, or mortgage, the term used to refer to the subject matter.
2. BANKING HOUSE.

PREMIUM This term has four meanings:

1. The percentage of price which a security commands over its face value.
   A share of stock of $100 par value selling at 110 is at a premium of 10%, or $10 a share. The amount of the premium is based upon par value. If the stock has a par value of $50 and it sells for $60, it is at a 20% or $10, premium. Premium is the opposite of DISCOUNT. For the mathematics and accounting involved in writing off the premiums on bonds, see AMORTIZATION.
2. AGIO. Gold or silver coin is at a premium when it is necessary to pay more than statutory face value for it in paper money of the same denomination.
3. The annual (or less frequent) sum paid by an insured party upon an insurance policy.
4. The price paid on an option contract or other privilege.

See PRIVILEGES.

PREMIUM BONDS Bonds that are retired at their maturity (or at an optional prior date) at an amount above their par value customarily much larger than the ordinary premium involved in interim call of ordinary bonds, which are retirable at maturity at face amount of principal without premium. The size of the premium in premium bonds gives them a lottery appeal. Such bonds are not permitted in this country, but are frequent in Europe.

Bonds bought or quoted at a premium are sometimes (but in a loose sense) called premium bonds.

See LOTTERY BONDS.

PREPAID EXPENSE A good or service purchased by a company for use in its operations but not fully consumed by the end of the accounting period. At the end of the accounting period these items that have been used up in the process of generating revenue must be matched as expenses against the current revenues; the

ENCYCLOPEDIA OF BANKING AND FINANCE

unused cost remains an asset on the balance sheet. Examples of prepaid expenses include office supplies, prepaid insurance, and prepaid rent.

Prepaid expenses can also be conceptualized as expenses of a future period that have been paid in advance. Prepaid expenses are classified as current assets even though they will never be converted into cash as the typical current assets would be. Current asset classification for prepaid expenses is justified on the basis that if the expenditure for the item had not occurred, cash would have to be expended in the future.

PRESENTATION PRESENTMENT.

PRESENTATION DRAFT Demand DRAFT.

PRESENTMENT
The exhibiting of a matured note, acceptance, or bill of exchange to the maker, acceptor, or drawee for payment is known as a presentment for payment. When a draft or bill of exchange is handed to the drawee for acceptance, it is known as a presentment for acceptance. Notes and bills of exchange should be presented on the due date in order legally to hold the endorsers. A notarial protest certificate is legal evidence of formal presentment and refusal to pay or accept.

See NEGOTIABLE INSTRUMENTS LAW (Section 3-501 through Section 3-511, inclusive, Uniform Commercial Code, "Presentment, Notice of Dishonor, and Protest").

PRESENT STANDARD OF WEIGHT AND FINENESS
Some bonds and other longtime contracts still outstanding and calling for the payment of money specify that the amount due shall be paid in gold coin of the United States according to the present standard of weight and fineness. The purpose of this specification was to avoid future litigation in case any question arose as to the kind of money in which the debt was payable, or in case of a change in the coinage laws to avoid payment in a depreciated currency.

The Joint Resolution of Congress of June 5, 1933, declared that "every provision contained in or made with respect to any obligation which purports to give the obligee a right to require payment in gold or a particular kind of coin or currency, or in an amount in money of the United States measured thereby, is declared to be against public policy; and no such provision shall be contained in or made with respect to any obligation hereafter incurred. Every obligation, heretofore or hereafter incurred, whether or not any such provision is contained therein or made with respect thereto, shall be discharged upon payment, dollar for dollar, in any coin or currency which at the time of payment is legal tender for public and private debts."

An act of Congress approved October 28, 1977 (P.L. 95-147) repealed the Joint Resolution to Assure Uniform Value to the Coins and Currencies of the United States, approved June 5, 1933 (31 U.S.C. 822a(a)). The intended effect of repeal was to permit inclusion of gold and multicurrency clauses in private contracts.

PRESENT VALUE
The net amount of discounted expected cash flows relating to an asset or liability. Stated another way, present value is the principal that must be invested at time period zero to produce the known future value. The process of converting the future value to the present value is referred to as discounting. Present value problems can assume this form: If $1,688.96 is to be received four years in the future, what is its present value if the discount rate is 14%? The present value in this illustration can be computed by using the following formula:

$$pv = f \frac{1}{(1+i)^n}$$

where pv = present value of any given future amount due in the future

f = a future amount
i = interest rate
n = number of periods.

The present value of $1,688.96 received at the end of four years discounted at 14% is $1,000 calculated as follows:

$$pv = (\$1,688.96) \frac{1}{(1+.14)^4} = \$1,000.$$

The present value of an annuity is the amount that must be invested now and, if left to earn compound interest, will provide for the receipt or payment of a series of equal rents at regular intervals. Over a period of time, the present value balance increases periodically for interest and decreases periodically for each rent paid or received.

Tables are available that make present value computations relatively easy.

BIBLIOGRAPHY

WOELFEL, CHARLES J. *Financial Managers Desktop Reference to Money, Time, Interest and Yield.* Probus, Chicago, 1986.
WOOLRIDGE, J., and SHUEY, K. "Floating Rate Preferred Stock An Innovation in Bank Capital." *The Bankers Magazine*, May/June, 1983.

PRICE
The VALUE of anything exposed for sale expressed in money terms; exchange value in money terms; amount of money necessary to purchase goods and services; money asked by a seller to relinquish title to goods or services. Actual price is sale price. Asked price is the price placed upon goods by a seller (i.e., offering price). Bid price is that which a buyer is willing to pay. Blanket price is that named for an entire lot of miscellaneous goods. Cash price is the amount of money that must be paid at the time goods are sold or delivered. Close prices indicate that bid and offering prices vary but fractionally. Closing prices refer to the last price for the day on the exchange or organized market. Cost-plus price is the price determined by adding a stipulated fixed profit or percentage profit to the actual cost, as in the case of government manufacturing contracts. Current price is that which prevails at the present. Fair price is one that takes into consideration all factors of value, giving the seller a normal profit without injustice to the buyer. Firm price is a price OFFERED FIRM. List price is one published in a price catalogue or schedule from which discounts at varying rates may be offered. Market price is that currently prevailing in the market. Net price is that after deducting discounts and allowances. Nominal price is an approximation to the market price or a bookkeeping price. Offered price is that which a seller is willing to take. Opening price is the price of the first sale on the market. Quoted price is that named by a seller for communication with possible buyers. Selling price is that at which sales actually occur. Settling price is the same as MAKING-UP PRICE. Unit price is the pro rata price of a single unit in a lot. Upset price, a term used at auction or foreclosure sales, is the lowest price that will be accepted.

See EXHAUST PRICE, ISSUE PRICE, MINT PRICE OF GOLD, PRICES.

PRICE CEILING
A shortage will arise in a market when a price is set below the equilibrium price. A price set below equilibrium is called a price ceiling, which means that the price cannot increase above that level.

In 1973 and 1974, due to the OPEC oil embargo, the government set a price ceiling on gasoline. This ceiling was below the equilibrium price that would have prevailed in an open market. As a result, a shortage of gasoline at the artificially low price resulted. In response, long lines for gasoline appeared, and states, in response, initiated gasoline rationing schemes. Similarly, a shortage of low-cost apartment housing exists in many urban areas because of rent control programs. Under rent control, the rental price is set below the market equilibrium price, thereby creating an excess demand.

PRICE ELASTICITY OF DEMAND
A measure of responsiveness in the quantity demanded of a good or service to a change in the price of that good or service. It is calculated as the percentage change in quantity demanded divided by the corresponding percentage change in price.

Demand is said to be elastic if the elasticity of demand is greater, in absolute value, than -1.0. For example, if the price elasticity of demand for a product were -2, then a 1% increase (decrease) in that product's price would lead to a 2% decrease (increase) in the quantity demanded of that product, everything else remaining the same. If the price elasticity of demand is less, in absolute value, than -1 (such as -0.8), then demand is said to be inelastic.

PRICE FLOOR A minimum price set by the government. A price artificially set above the equilibrium price is referred to as a price support or price floor. When such artificially high prices are imposed, a surplus results.

Agricultural prices have been supported above equilibrium since the federal government intervened in 1930 to stabilize farmers' incomes. The minimum wage is also an example of a price support. In both cases, a surplus results. Excess agricultural products are produced and the quantity of workers willing to work at the minimum wage is greater than the quantity supplied.

PRICE INDEX A comparison of the prices of goods and services in the current year to those in a base year. In economics, a number of price indexes are used, such as the consumer price index, GNP deflator, producer price index, and wholesale price index.

PRICE INDEX NUMBERS *See* INDEX NUMBERS.

PRICE LEADERSHIP In an oligopoly there is an interdependence among producers. One type of behavior that results from this interdependence is price leadership. Price leadership connotes a behavior where the dominant (leader) firm increases price as a signal for the other firms to follow. Such action, by itself, is not illegal; however, if it arises from collusion it is as illegal as price fixing.

PRICE MOVEMENTS *See* BUSINESS CYCLE, FLUCTUATING PRINCIPLE, INDEX NUMBERS, SPECULATIVE CYCLE, SWINGS.

PRICE RIGIDITY Some economists argue that prices are inherently rigid under an oligopoly because if any one firm raises its price, no other firm would follow and hence the initial firm's revenues would fall. If any one firm lowered its price, all firms would follow, thereby eliminating the anticipated revenue increase. Owing to this type of interdependence among oligopolistic firms, prices are inherently rigid. There is little empirical support for this theoretical notion, frequently call the kinked demand curve of oligopoly.

PRICES The universal expression of the exchange value of goods and services; the most important determinants of production and consumption in a competitive system. Upon the given selling prices in relation to costs of production depends the supply of output for future sale, and upon the given market prices in relation to incomes depends the effectiveness of demand and consumption. Freely flexible prices are essential for a competitive system, if they are to fulfill their function as efficient regulators and allocators of production and consumption, responding to real supply and demand factors. All things being equal, high prices would attract new firms, increase investment, expand supply, and reestablish a new level of equilibrium relative to effective demand. Low prices, conversely, would divert resources to other more profitable uses, but in turn, as supply in those sectors would become low relative to demand, low prices would be similarly self-corrective. In such a model of flexible prices and mobile resources, therefore, the objective market is the determinant of income, consumption, investment, and level of utilization of resources. Needless to say, fluctuation instead of stability is of the essence in such a system, and the role of government is conceived to be the enforcement of free competition and a minimum of interference with the price system.

Such a rigorous model, however, in practice has been modified by private and governmental vested interests and value judgments, which interfere with the free working of the price system. Pure competition supposes undifferentiated products besides freedom of entry of firms and absence of price control by firms. Perfect competition supposes perfect knowledge and mobility of resources into alternative uses. Even in an industry characterized by freedom of entry, product differentiation in such respects as physical, locational, service, and advertising factors inevitably exists to afford the firms concerned degrees of monopolistic control over prices, so that competition is no longer pure. The complexity of markets, the lack of perfect knowledge by consumers, and the power of advertising impair the rationality of consumer choices (consumer sovereignty). Thus competition is in the more customary situation neither pure nor perfect, and instead monopolistic competition (Chamberlin's concept) is the more prevalent type of market. The firm in monopolistic competition can raise its price above the purely competitive price, maximizing its profits at a point of less than purely competitive output. The same is true in situations of oligopoly (few sellers) and monopoly (one seller). Such social cost, in the form of higher prices and less than maximum output, and existence of imperfect rather than perfect competition are argued to call for more positive governmental intervention, for maximum social advantage: (1) for more rational allocation of resources (directed growth); (2) for greater stability (to control inflation and mitigate the business cycle); and (3) for regulation of monopoly and monopolistic pricing practices (intervention into the pricing process).

The contra view is that private rigidities in the economic system are not solved by the substitution therefor of governmental rigidities; that the sapience of governmental economic administration is vastly overrated, particularly because of political considerations; and that the role of government should continue to be as noninterventionist as possible in maintaining a maximum competitive environment for business, particularly where pricing is involved. An intermediate viewpoint is the more pragmatic approach of tolerating monopolistic elements if the end results are abundance of output, technological progress, and reasonable prices and quality (workable competition).

Thus, vis à vis the goals of the Employment Act of 1946, of economic growth, high employment, and stable prices, the behavior of prices, pricing policies, and price control have been the subject of increased study and controversy in recent years, particularly as to the role that government should play. A particular issue is administered prices (Gardner C. Means's term for prices fixed or controlled by sellers or buyers). The alleged prevalence of administered prices in the economy is said to create rigidity instead of flexibility in prices, resulting in costs of lower output, diversion of purchasing power, and creation of creeping inflation of the cost-push type which is more difficult to control than demand-pull type of inflation by conventional fiscal and monetary measures, so that selective direct price and cost controls are advocated for effective control. There is considerable disagreement, however, with both the diagnosis and the prognosis.

See BID PRICE, BIDS AND OFFERS, EXHAUST PRICE, INDEX NUMBERS, MARKET AVERAGES, QUOTATIONS, PRICE.

PRICE SUPPORT Agriculture in the U.S. since 1933 has been the beneficiary of a diversified number of programs of assistance, classified in a 1960 study by the Joint Economic Committee as follows: (1) stabilization of farm prices and income; (2) conservation of resources; (3) credit and related programs for electrification, telephone facilities, farm purchase, maintenance, operation, and housing; (4) research, education, marketing, and regulatory; (5) school lunch and donations; (6) Farm Credit Administration; (7) wartime consumer subsidies on agricultural commodities; and (8) wartime, defense, special, and other needs. Of these, the first category includes the commodity price support program, which puts a floor under prices of specified agricultural commodities, and the parity payment programs, which are intended to bring the prices of specified agricultural commodities nearer or up to their parity level, with controversial results in actual practice.

An official review of price-support and related legislation through the years is provided by the Agricultural Stabilization and Conservation Service of the U.S. Department of Agriculture as follows. Price-support operations have been carried out by the COMMODITY CREDIT CORPORATION since 1933. Throughout this period, supports have been directed or authorized by specific legislation highlighted hereafter.

The Early Program (1933-1937). The principal legislative tool for stabilizing agricultural prices and income during the 1933-1937 period was the AGRICULTURAL ADJUSTMENT ACT of 1933. This act provided for production controls, implemented by payments from funds acquired by processing taxes, on certain commodities. Acreage control programs were in effect for cotton, corn, peanuts, rice, sugar, tobacco, and wheat. Rental and benefit payments were made to producers of these commodities in an effort to reduce acreage and production.

However, it became apparent in the fall of 1933 that the strengthening of farm income through production controls would be a slow process. Thus, the Commodity Credit Corporation (CCC) was created under the President's emergency powers and the first price-support loans, similar to those made today, were extended on corn and cotton. Only these two of the major commodities were supported during the 1933-1937 period. Support was accomplished through nonrecourse loans. Price support, not mandatory at the time, was carried out under authority granted to the CCC by its

Delaware charter. Per-bushel support prices for corn during the five-year period were from $0.45 to $0.55. Per-pound supports for cotton during the period were from $0.09 to $0.12.

The Supreme Court in January, 1936, declared unconstitutional the production control features of the Agricultural Adjustment Act of 1933 and also voided processing taxes. Later the Soil Conservation and Domestic Allotment Act of 1936 became law. This legislation provided for soil-conserving and soil-building payments to cooperating farmers. Soil-building payments were made for soil-building practices, and soil-conserving payments were made for shifting acreage from soil-depleting to soil-conserving crops. Although this legislation made for better land use, it provided inadequate authority for the price and income stabilization operations deemed necessary by farm leaders.

Large crops of wheat and cotton in 1937, accentuating the twin problems of surplus and low prices, led to passage of the Agricultural Adjustment Act of 1938, the first legislation that made price support mandatory for certain commodities (corn, cotton, and wheat).

The Prewar Years (1938-1940). The Agricultural Adjustment Act of 1938, which is still in effect in amended form, provided for the following: (1) mandatory price-support loans on certain basic commodities so that the commodities could be stored in time of plenty and returned to the market when supplies became scarce—the "ever-normal granary" idea, and (2) marketing quotas on certain basic commodities, keyed to acreage allotments, which were intended to keep supplies in line with market demand.

The Agricultural Adjustment Act of 1938, as originally enacted, made supports mandatory at 52% to 75% of parity for corn, wheat, and cotton.

The Agricultural Adjustment Act of 1938 authorized the CCC to make loans on agricultural commodities including dairy products. The CCC had authority under its charter to support virtually any agricultural commodity. Permissive commodities supported during the 1938-1940 period included butter, dates, figs, hops, turpentine, rosin, pecans, prunes, raisins, barley, rye, grain sorghums, wool, winter cover crop seeds, mohair, and peanuts and tobacco for which, at that time, supports were not mandatory.

There were no specific limits on supports for permissive commodities other than the overall objectives of the act, but the mandatory commodities could not be supported at levels above 75% of parity.

The War Years (1941-1948). An April 3, 1941, amendment to the Agricultural Adjustment Act of 1938 made supports on peanuts mandatory at 50% to 75% of parity.

The Act of May 26, 1941, directed the CCC to make loans to cooperators (producers who did not exceed their farm acreage allotments) on the 1941 crops of rice, tobacco, cotton, corn, and wheat at 85% of parity. The act was amended December 26, 1941, to add peanuts to the list of commodities to be supported at the 85% level, and to extend applicability of the act to the 1942-1946 crops.

Section 8(a) of the Stabilization Act of 1942 directed the CCC to make loans to cooperators at 90% of parity upon any crop of cotton, corn, wheat, rice, tobacco, and peanuts (the basic agricultural commodities) harvested after December 31, 1941, and before two years after the end of hostilities. This period ended with the 1948 crops of these commodities.

The Act of June 30, 1944, increased the rate of support on cotton harvested after December 31, 1943, to 92.5% of parity. The Act of October 3, 1944, increased the rate still further to 95% of parity with respect to crops of cotton harvested after December 31, 1943, and planted prior to January 1, 1945.

The Act of July 28, 1945, required that the support rate on fire-cured tobacco be 75% of the rate for burley tobacco, and that the rate for dark air-cured and Virginia sun-cured tobacco be 66<2/3>% of the burley rate. This was modified in 1957.

Section 4 of the Act of July 1, 1941, the so-called Steagall Amendment, required support at not less than 85% of parity or comparable price for those nonbasic commodities for which the secretary of Agriculture or the War Food Administrator requested an expansion of production for war purposes and made public announcement to that effect. By the Act of October 2, 1942, the minimum rate of support was increased to 90% of parity and support at that rate was required to be continued for two years after the end of the war— December 31, 1948.

The Steagall commodities were the following: hogs, eggs, chickens (with certain exceptions), turkeys, milk, butterfat, dry peas of certain varieties, dry edible beans of certain varieties, soybeans for oil, peanuts for oil, flaxseed for oil, American-Egyptian cotton, potatoes, and sweet potatoes.

Among the 140 or so other commodities supported during the war years were the following: wool, turpentine, rosin, American hemp, sugar beets, sugarcane, blackeye peas and beans, certain fruits for processing, certain vegetables for processing, barley, grain sorghums, rye, Sea Island cotton, certain vegetable seeds, winter cover crop seeds, and hay and pasture seeds.

The Act of August 5, 1947, required support of wool prices until December 31, 1948, at the 1946 support level.

Postwar Years (1949-1950).

Agricultural Act of 1948: The Agricultural Act of 1948 made price support on 1949 crops of the basic commodities mandatory at 90% of parity.

For Steagall commodities, support on 1949 production of hogs, chickens, eggs, and milk and its products was fixed at 90% of parity through December 31, 1949.

Support on 1949 production of dry beans, dry peas, turkeys, soybeans, flaxseed, peanuts, American-Egyptian cotton, and sweet potatoes was set through December 31, 1949, at not less than 60% of parity or comparable price nor higher than the level at which the commodity was supported in 1948.

Support on potatoes harvested on or before December 31, 1948, and marketed through December 31, 1949, was maintained at 90% of parity. Support on potatoes harvested after December 31, 1948, and marketed through December 31, 1949, was set at not less than 60% of the parity price nor more than the 1948 support level.

Support was made mandatory on wool marketed through June 30, 1950, at the 1946 level of $0.423 per pound for shorn wool, grease basic.

Supports were authorized on other commodities through December 31, 1949, if funds were available, at levels in a fair relationship with the basics, "Steagalls," and wool.

The act provided that beginning January 1, 1950, parity prices for individual crops be computed so as to take into consideration, in addition to the 1910-1914 base period, average prices for the previous ten years. The act also provided for transitional parity^that is, limiting the drop from the old to the new parity to steps of not more than 5% of old parity per year.

Agricultural Act of 1949: Support for 1950-crop basics was made mandatory at not more than 90% of parity nor less than certain minimums based on the supply percentage at the beginning of the marketing year. However, the act provided that if marketing quotas were in effect for tobacco, the level of support for tobacco should be 90% of parity. The act also assured mandatory 90% supports for the 1950 crops of the other basics (and 80% for the 1951 crops) if producers had not disapproved quotas on any crop for which marketing quotas or acreage allotments were in effect.

Support was made mandatory on wool, including mohair, at the 60%-90% of parity level, but it was provided that the level should be established so as to encourage an annual production of 360 million pounds of shorn wool. This latter provision made support for shorn wool mandatory at 90% of parity.

Support was made mandatory for tung nuts, honey, and Irish potatoes at the 60%-90% of parity range.

Support was also made mandatory on milk, butterfat, and the products of milk and butterfat at the 75%-90% of parity range; for other nonbasic commodities, support was made permissive at not to exceed 90% of parity.

The act provided that the parity price for any basic agricultural commodity—corn, cotton, wheat, peanuts, rice, and tobacco^as of any date during the period January 1, 1950-December 31, 1953, should not be less than its parity price as computed by the old parity formula. The old formula meant higher parity prices for wheat, corn, cotton, and peanuts, whereas the new formula resulted in higher prices for rice and tobacco.

Korean War Period (1951-1954). Although the Agricultural Act of 1949 provided flexible supports on most basic commodities within the 80%-90% of parity range for the 1951 crops with a lower minimum for subsequent crops, flexible provisions did not become operative for some time. South Korea was invaded by North Korea in June, 1950, and the Department of Agriculture, as part of the United Nations defense effort, maintained supports on all 1951-crop basics at the 90% level so as to stimulate production.

Section 106(a) of the Act of June 30, 1932, provided for price support at 90% of parity on the basic commodities under any program announced while Title IV of the Defense Production Act

PRICE SUPPORT

(authorizing price controls) was in effect. Title IV expired as of April 30, 1953.

Flexible provisions were postponed still further by the Act of July 17, 1952, which amended the Agricultural Act of 1949 to provide for 90% of parity price support for the 1953 and 1954 crops of any basic commodity with respect to which producers did not disapprove marketing quotas. The act also made supports mandatory on extra long staple cotton for the first time.

Support continued to be mandatory under the Agricultural Act of 1949 as follows: wool and mohair, 60% to 90% of parity, although the provision with respect to encouraging an annual production of 360 million pounds of shorn wool assured wool support at 90% of parity; tung nuts and honey, 60% to 90% of parity; and milk and butterfat, 75% to 90% of parity.

The Act of March 31, 1950, prohibited price support on potatoes of the 1951 and subsequent crops unless marketing quotas were in effect. Inasmuch as there was no legislation authorizing quotas for potatoes, mandatory support for potatoes was, in effect, brought to an end with marketing of the 1950 crop.

Support was permissive on other nonbasic commodities at any level not to exceed 90% of parity.

The Act of July 17, 1952, extended for two additional years (through December 31, 1955) the requirement that the effective parity price for the six basic commodities should be the higher of parity prices computed under both the old and new parity formulas.

Post-Korea (1955 to date).

Agricultural Act of 1954: For basic commodities, the Agricultural Act of 1954 provided for flexible price support on 1955 basic crops (other than tobacco) at 82.5% to 90% of parity. Since no limitation was imposed with respect to 1956 and later crops of these commodities, the flexible provisions of the 1949 act became effective beginning with the 1956 crop at the 75% to 90% range.

The act also provided for set-asides of 400 million to 500 million bushels of wheat and 3 million to 4 million bales of cotton, the set-asides to be excluded in the computation of price-support levels, but to be included in the computation of acreage allotments and marketing quotas.

The act provided for price support on 1955 and subsequent crop extra long staple cotton at the minimum level of support determined in accordance with the table of supply percentages (75% to 90% of parity). Subsequent legislation required the 1957 crop to be supported at the same level as the 1956 crop and the 1958 and subsequent crops to be supported at not in excess of the 1956 level but not less than 60% of parity.

Support continued to be mandatory on tung nuts and honey at 60% to 90% of parity and on milk and butterfat at 75% to 90% of parity.

The 1954 act removed Irish potatoes from the list of designated nonbasic agricultural commodities, thereby moving Irish potatoes to the category of "other nonbasic agricultural commodities."

The National Wool Act of 1954 (Title VII of the Agricultural Act of 1954) provided for a new price support program on wool and mohair, effective April 1, 1955. Wool was to be supported at the level determined necessary to encourage an annual domestic production of 300 million pounds, but not to exceed 110% of parity, and mohair was to be supported at a related level. Payments were authorized as a means of price support.

Support on other commodities continued to be permissive, at any level between zero and 90% of parity.

Agricultural Act of 1956: The Soil Bank Act, which was enacted as a title of the Agricultural Act of 1956, authorized a program of annual acreage diversion for wheat, corn, rice, cotton, peanuts, and several types of tobacco (acreage reserve program). It also provided for long-term land retirement (conservation reserve program). The acreage reserve program terminated in 1958, but land could be placed under 10-year conservation reserve contracts through 1960.

The 1956 act required corn producers to comply with farm base acreages and to divert certain acreage to receive price support at the full rate. Price support was made mandatory on grain sorghums, barley, rye, and oats on the 1956 crop at 76% of parity and, if price support was made available in the commercial corn-producing area to producers not complying with acreage limitations, on the 1957 crop at not less than 70% of parity.

The 1956 act provided that whenever the price of either cottonseed or soybeans is supported, the price of the other shall be supported at such level as will cause them to compete on equal terms on the market.

December 31, 1955, marked the expiration of the special requirement that the effective parity price for the six basic commodities be the higher of the parity prices computed under the old and new parity formulas; thus the transitional parity mechanism went into effect January 1, 1956, with respect to basics. The Agricultural Act of 1956, however, froze transitional parity for basics during 1957. This affected corn, peanuts, and wheat, for which transitional parity was higher. By January, 1960, all the basics had effected the transition, and for their 1960 crops all were under the new parity formula.

Agricultural Act of 1958: For basic commodities, the Agricultural Act of 1958 provided for a referendum of corn producers to determine if they favored continuing with their current price support program, which made support available within a 75% to 90% of parity range for those producers who complied with their acreage allotments, or shifting to a new program which discontinued acreage allotments and made support available to all producers at 90% of the average price received by producers during the three preceding calendar years, but in no event at less than 65% of parity. In the referendum held November 25, 1958, a majority of the growers voting favored the latter program, and it became effective with the 1959 crop.

Under other provisions of the act, producers of upland cotton were given a choice of supports for their 1959 and 1960 crops based on two different acreage allotments. Under choice A, a producer who complied with his regular acreage allotment was assured support on his 1959 crop at not less than 80% of parity and on his 1960 crop at not less than 75% of parity. Under choice B, a producer who complied with an allotment which might be as much as 40% larger than his regular allotment, at the discretion of the secretary of Agriculture, was assured support for either or both of these two years at a level 15% of parity below the level of support established for producers electing choice A. For subsequent years, a return to a single no-choice program was specified, with the range of support set at 70% to 90% of parity for 1961, and at 65% to 90% of parity for subsequent years. Beginning with the 1961 crop, the exact level of support was not required to be based upon the supply percentage, and the support price was based on the average quality of the crop.

For rice, beginning with the 1959 crop, the minimum level of support was not based on the supply percentage. For the 1961 crop, the support price range was from 70% to 90% of parity, and for the 1962 and subsequent crops, the range of price support was from 65% to 90% of parity.

In line with the 1956 act, the Agricultural Act of 1958 took oats, barley, rye, and grain sorghums out of the permissive price-support category and in effect made them designated nonbasics by requiring that, beginning with the 1959 crop, price support should be made available for each of these crops at such level of its parity price as the secretary of Agriculture determined to be fair and reasonable in relation to the level of support made available for corn. Since support for corn was and still is mandatory, this had the effect of making support mandatory also for these other feed grains.

Act of February 20, 1960: This act provided for price support on the 1960 crop of tobacco at the same level as on the 1959 crop, and on the 1961 and each subsequent crop at a level determined by adjusting the support level for the 1959 crop by the ratio of prices paid by farmers in the preceding three calendar years to the prices paid in the calendar year 1959.

Act of March 22, 1961: This legislation provided for an acreage diversion program for corn and grain sorghums under which payments could be made to producers who diverted acreage to conserving uses. Payments in kind from CCC stocks were authorized as a method of paying participants. The level of price support for the 1961 crop of corn was to be not less than 65% of parity. Since a higher level of support was authorized for the 1961 crop of corn than the level of support for the 1959 and 1960 crops, and since the requirement that the support for oats, rye, barley, and grain sorghums be fair and reasonable in relation to corn support was not changed, the act also indirectly authorized a higher level of support for oats, rye, barley, and grain sorghums. Price support for corn and grain sorghums was limited to the normal production of the 1961 acreage of these commodities based on the 1959-1960 average per-acre yield. This legislation was the forerunner of the feed grain programs which were to be in effect throughout the 1960s.

The Agricultural Act of 1961: Approved August 8, 1961, the act continued the 1961 feed grain provisions basically unchanged for 1962 crops except for the addition of barley as a diverted acre crop. The act continued the level of support for 1962-crop wheat within the

75% to 90% of parity range, but tightened eligibility requirements for price support. It extended acreage diversion provisions to wheat and provided for a 10% reduction in the 55-million-acre minimum national wheat allotment. It limited support to producers in the commercial wheat-producing area who participated in the special 1962 wheat program authorized by this act.

Food and Agriculture Act of 1962: This act (P.L. 87-703, approved September 27, 1962) provided for 1963 wheat and feed grain programs and for programs for 1964 and future crops of these commodities. Provisions for crops after 1963 never became fully effective.

For 1963 wheat, the legislation authorized an emergency wheat program including voluntary diversion of wheat acreage. Participants who diverted wheat acreage were eligible for support at an average of $2 per bushel. This was made up of a loan of $1.82 per bushel and an $0.18-per-bushel price-support payment. Since the program was authorized after many farmers had begun fall plantings, producers who harvested within acreage allotments but did not divert acreage were eligible for loans only.

For 1963-crop feed grains, the legislation continued the price-support eligibility provisions for acreage diversion of corn, grain sorghums, and barley, and continued the corn support at not less than 65% of parity. It also provided for part of the price support in the form of payments in kind from CCC's stocks. This was set at $0.18 per bushel for corn and comparable amounts for barley and grain sorghums.

For 1964 and subsequent crops of wheat, the act provided for a marketing certificate program with price support between 65% and 90% of parity on wheat used for food in the United States, and on a share of the exports to be determined by the secretary of Agriculture. Remaining wheat was to be supported at a level related to its feed value and the world wheat price. This program was dependent upon marketing quotas being in effect. However, more than one-third of the producers in a 1963 referendum did not approve marketing quotas. A feature of this legislation eliminated the minimum 55-million-acre national allotment and authorized the secretary to estimate a year's requirements for wheat and set an acreage allotment to meet those requirements.

For 1964 and subsequent crops of corn, the act provided for price support at such level—from 50% to 90% of parity—as the secretary determined would not result in increasing the CCC's stocks of corn.

This legislation also authorized the substitution of feed grains for wheat acreage, and wheat for feed grain acreage, during any year in which an acreage diversion program is in effect for feed grains, with price support to be from 65% to 90% of parity for any crop of corn for which an acreage diversion program is in effect.

Feed Grain Act of 1963: The Feed Grain Act of 1963 (P.L. 88-26) approved May 20, 1963, authorized a voluntary feed grain program for the 1964 and 1965 crops similar in principle to that in effect for 1963.

Agricultural Act of 1964: The Agricultural Act of 1964 (P.L. 88-297) approved April 11, 1964, authorized a two-year program for the 1964 and 1965 crops of cotton and wheat.

For upland cotton, a support price of $0.30 per pound for middling one-inch cotton was provided for the 1964 crop. Under the 1958 act, the support price for the 1965 crop was to be at a level within 65% to 90% of parity. In addition, the 1964 act provided for a price-support payment on 1964 and 1965 crop cotton at not more than 15% of the basic level of support for those producers planting within their domestic allotments. Domestic allotment was that portion of the national allotment needed to produce the cotton for domestic consumption. Payments in kind (cotton equalization payments) were authorized to persons other than producers in amounts which would make upland cotton produced in the U.S. available for domestic use at a price not in excess of the price of exportable cotton.

For wheat, the legislation authorized a two-year voluntary wheat certificate and acreage diversion program. Marketing quotas were suspended. It provided for price support for wheat accompanied by domestic certificates at between 65% and 90% of parity, and for wheat unaccompanied by certificates at a level not in excess of 90% of parity, as the secretary of Agriculture determined appropriate taking into account competitive world prices, the feed value of wheat, and the level of support for feed grains. Price support was also provided for wheat accompanied by export certificates.

Act of April 16, 1965: This act provided for acreage-poundage farm marketing quotas on tobacco. When such quotas are in effect, price support is to be available on not to exceed 110% (120% for burley) of the quota for the farm. Acreage-poundage quotas have been in effect only for flue-cured tobacco.

Food and Agriculture Act of 1965: Approved November 3, 1965, this act provided four-year commodity programs (1966-1969 crops) for feed grains, wheat, and upland cotton. It continued the payment method for wool. It authorized a Class I milk base plan for the 75 federal milk marketing orders, and a long-term diversion of cropland under a cropland adjustment program. The act was extended for one year, through December 1970, by P.L. 90-559, approved October 11, 1968.

Basically, the Food and Agriculture Act of 1965 continued the feed grain diversion and payment programs and the wheat diversion and certificate program with modifications. It also extended the payment and diversion program to cotton. It provided for market support of cotton, feed grains, and wheat prices through price support loans and payments (certificates, in the case of wheat).

P.L. 90-475: Approved August 11, 1968, this legislation provided for lower price-support loans for extra long staple cotton, supplemented by price-support payments.

Agricultural Act of 1970: This act, approved November 30, 1970, and applicable through 1973, initiated a cropland set-aside approach for participating producers in the wheat, feed grains, and cotton programs for the 1971-1973 crop years and established the payment limitation a person could receive annually under the program.

Agriculture and Consumer Protection Act of 1973: This act, which amended the Agricultural Act of 1970, initiated established or target prices for wheat, feed grains, and upland cotton, with payments to eligible producers based on allotted acres to be made under specific conditions. No payment would be made as long as the average market price received by producers during the first five months of the marketing year—or, in the case of upland cotton, during the calendar year in which the crop was planted^remained at or above target level. If the average market price for the stated period dropped below the target level, a payment on the allotment (for cotton, the acreage planted within the allotment) would be made to eligible producers equal to the difference between the target price and the higher of the loan level or the average market price. The target prices for 1974 and 1975 were set in the act ($0.38 per pound for upland cotton, $2.05 per bushel for wheat, and $1.38 per bushel for corn), with reasonable rates to be set for grain sorghum (and barley, if designated) in relation to the rate for corn.

Target prices for the 1976 and 1977 crop years would be set by taking an established price for each year, and increasing or decreasing it to reflect changes in prices paid by producers and productivity. The former is shown by an index of production costs (production items, interest, taxes, and farm wage rates) published by the Department of Agriculture, and the latter is measured by comparing the most recent national three-year average for each crop with the three-year average ending with the preceding year.

The act also authorized disaster payments (plantings affected by drought, flood, or other natural disaster or condition beyond control), calling for payment for the portion affected at the larger of the regular calculated rate or one-third of the target price. Moreover, if because of the same circumstances, the total quantity of the commodity or authorized substitute crop harvested were substantially less than the expected production, the payment rate for the deficiency in production below 100% would be the larger of the regular calculated rate or one-third of the target price. (Expected production is the farm payment yield multiplied by the farm acreage allotment for the grains and the farm base acreage allotment for cotton.) Provision was also made to establish a disaster reserve of inventories not to exceed 75 million bushels of wheat, feed grains, and soybeans to alleviate distress caused by a natural disaster.

Food and Agriculture Act of 1977: The 1977 act amended the Agriculture and Consumer Protection Act of 1973, as amended, and prior legislation. It substituted a national program acreage (NPA) determined by the secretary of Agriculture for the acreage allotment system for wheat and feed grains. The NPA represents the estimated acreage needed to meet domestic and export needs (less imports) plus any desired adjustment in stocks. The target prices concept was continued.

The 1977 act was amended by the Emergency Agricultural Act of 1978, the Agricultural Adjustment Act of 1980, and the Agricultural Act of 1980 to cover the 1978-1981 wheat and feed grain crop years. In the case of upland cotton, the 1977 act prescribed a complicated method of determining the loan rate. The loan level for strict low

PRICE SUPPORT LEVEL

No. 1123. Price Support Operations—Selected Commodities: 1983 to 1987

Crop and year	Support of target price [1] (dol. per bu.)	National average loan rate (dol. per bu.)	Quantity under support [2] Amount (mil. bu.)	Percent of production
Corn: [3]				
1983	2.86	2.65	162	4
1984	3.03	2.55	1,097	14
1985	3.03	2.55	3,168	36
1986	3.03	1.92 [4]	4,888	59
1987	3.03	1.82	4,200 [5]	59
Soybeans: [3]				
1983	X	5.02	101	6
1984	X	5.02	278	15
1985	X	5.02	518	25
1986	X	4.77 [4]	327	17
1987	X	4.77	276 [5]	14
Wheat: [6]				
1983	4.30	3.65	635	26
1984	4.38	3.30	284	11
1985	4.38	3.30	843	35
1986	4.38	2.40 [4]	515	25
1987	4.38	2.28	475 [5]	23
Cotton: [7]	Cents per lb.		1,000 bales [8]	
1983	76.0	55.0	1,744	22
1984	81.0	55.0	2,957	23
1985	81.0	57.3	7,291	54
1986	81.0	55.0 [4]	6,170	63
1987	79.4	52.3	5,350 [5]	38
Sorghum: [3]	Dol. per cwt.		Mil. cwt.	
1983	4.86	4.50	8	3
1984	5.14	4.32	36	7
1985	5.14	4.32	201	32
1986	5.14	3.25 [4]	222	42
1987	5.14	3.11	210 [5]	51
Rice: [7]	Dol. per cwt.		Mil. cwt.	
1983	11.40	8.14	40	40
1984	11.90	8.00	58	42
1985	11.90	8.00	75	56
1986	11.90	7.20 [4]	132	99
1987	11.66	6.84	126 [5]	99

X — Not applicable.
[1] Guaranteed on normal production from participating farms.
[2] Represents loans made, purchases, and purchase agreements entered into.
[3] For years beginning September 1
[4] 1986 annual loan rates were reduced 4.3 percent for budget purposes (e.g. corn became $1.84 per bu.).
[5] Preliminary.
[6] For years beginning June 1.
[7] For years beginning August 1.
[8] Bales of 480 lb. net weight.
Source: U.S. Dept. of Agriculture, Agricultural Stabilization and Conservation Service. Data published in *Agricultural Statistics*, annual.

middling $1^1/_{16}$-inch upland cotton, micronaire 3.5 through 4.9, at average U.S. location would be the smaller of the following prices:

1. 85% of the average price (weighted by market and month) of such quality of cotton as quoted in the designated U.S. spot markets during three years of the five-year period ending July 31 in the year in which the loan level is announced, excluding the year in which the average price was the lowest in such period, or:
2. 90% of the average price, for the 15-week period beginning July 1 of the year in which the loan is announced, of the five lowest-priced growths quoted for strict middling $1^1/_{16}$-inch cotton, c.i.f. Northern Europe, this amount to be adjusted downward by the average difference, during the period April 15 through October 15 of the year in which the loan is announced, between such average Northern Europe price quotation and the spot market quotations for strict low middling $1^1/_{16}$-inch cotton, micronaire 3.5 through 4.9. If the Northern Europe calculation is less than the spot market calculation, the loan level may be increased up to the spot market calculation. In no event, however, can the loan level be less than $0.48 per pound.

The upshot of this complicated formula was a 1981 loan rate of $0.5246 per pound, compared with a 1981 target price of $0.7087 per pound for upland cotton.

The Federal Crop Insurance Act of 1980 extended the disaster payment program through the 1981 crop year. Producers on farms who elected to obtain federally subsidized crop insurance would waive disaster payments on the crop.

Agriculture and Food Act of 1981: This act amended the Food and Agriculture Act of 1977 as amended and prior legislation. The act provided the statutory basis for an acreage reduction program to be in effect for the 1982 wheat crop. Participating farmers were required to reduce their acreage of wheat planted for harvest by at least 15% from an established wheat base. Only farmers who took part would be eligible for target price protection and regular price support or farmer-owned reserve loans.

Summary. A basic dilemma of U.S. price support programs is that while such programs have been intended to reduce supply and have induced a decline in farm population over time, record yields and other agricultural efficiencies have been stimulated, and the remaining farm population has record productivity.

See PARITY, PARITY INDEX.

BIBLIOGRAPHY

BOEHM, W. T. "Agricultural Policy: Some Hard Choices Ahead." *Southern Journal of Agricultural Economics*, July, 1981.

BOGGESS, W. G., and HEADY, E. O. "A Sector Analysis of Alternative Income Support and Soil Conservation Policies." *American Journal of Agricultural Economics*, November, 1981.

EVANS, S. "Acreage Response to the Target Price and Set-Aside Provisions of the Food and Agriculture Act of 1977." *Agricultural Economics Research*, October, 1980.

GARDNER, B. L. *The Governance of Agriculture*, 1981.

HALCROW, H. G. *Economics of Agriculture*, 1980.

HAZELL, P. B. R., and POMAREDA, C. "Evaluating Price Stabilization Schemes with Mathematical Programming." *American Journal of Agricultural Economics*, August, 1981.

JOHNSON, D. G., ed. *Food and Agricultural Policy for the 1980s*, 1981.

KITE, R. C., and ROOP, J. M. "Changing Agricultural Prices and Their Impact on Food Prices Under Inflation." *American Journal of Agricultural Economics*, December, 1981.

MORSUCH, B. J., WEAVER, R. D., and HELMBERGER, P. G. "Wheat Acreage Supply Response Under Changing Farm Programs." *American Journal of Agricultural Economics*, February, 1980.

PENN, J. B. "Commodity Programs and Inflation." *American Journal of Agricultural Economics*, December, 1979.

ROY, E. P., CORTY, F. L., and SULLIVAN, G. D. *Economics: Applications to Agriculture and Agribusiness*, 3rd ed., 1981.

PRICE SUPPORT LEVEL The price for a unit of a farm commodity (bushel, pound) that the government will support through price support loans or payments. Price support levels are determined by law and are set by the Secretary of Agriculture.

PRICE THEORY Microeconomic theory. The theory of prices studies the flow of goods and services from business firms to households, the compositon of such flows and the determination of the prices of goods and services in the flow. Price theory also studies the flow of services of economic resources (land, labor, and capital) from resource owners to business firms and how the prices of these resources are determined. One component of price theory would state: If the price of a commodity rises, then the quantity demanded of the commodity declines (demand theory). In a free enterprise economic system, problems of price and scarcity are solved by the price mechanism.

See THEORY, VALUE.

PRICING POLICY Pricing is a profit-planning situation in which management evaluates the profit consequences of various pricing policies before reaching a decision. Pricing policy refers to the principles and practices that determine pricing decisions. Theory and practice vary widely where pricing policies are determined, even within the same industry. Practices range from rule-of-thumb judgments to conventional practices, to the application of microeconomic principles.

Administered Pricing. Administered pricing is a pricing policy in which a seller can exert an influence on the price charged for a product or service because of the absence of competition. Large and powerful producers are occasionally in a position to adopt administered pricing.

Conversion Cost Pricing. Conversion costs include direct labor and factory overhead costs. Costs of materials used in the product are not considered. Conversion costing is occasionally used when a customer provides the material. Conversion cost pricing requires that factory capacity is limited in terms of labor and overhead cost constraints. Companies direct their efforts to products or services requiring less labor and overhead (scarce resources) because more units can be produced and sold. For example, assume the following information:

	Product X	Product Y
Direct material	$10	$10
Conversion costs:		
Direct labor	5	1
Factory overhead	9	4
Total production cost	$24	$15

If the firm desires a 10% markup on conversion cost, the sales price for each product is:

	Product X	Product Y
Full cost	$24.00	$15.00
Markup on conversion cost:		
10% x $14	1.40	
10% x $5		.50
Sales price	$25.40	$15.50

More units of product Y can be produced because product Y requires less conversion cost. Each product produces the same profit per unit of scarce resource.

Cost-Plus Pricing. Cost-plus pricing requires a firm to add a predetermined, markup to an established or known average cost. The size of the markup depends upon what the firm calculates it can obtain. This form of pricing usually establishes a target rate of return on its investment and uses this rate to establish prices. Cost-plus pricing generally does not take into consideration the elasticity of demand or the relationship of marginal cost to marginal revenue. As a result, the price established may not be the most profitable price attainable. Costs should be used in pricing primarily to forecast the impact on profits of alternative pricing policies. Cost usually refers to full costs. Cost-plus pricing is in essence a backward cost pricing method. A desired percentage for profit is added to the full cost of the product or service to establish the price. Highway construction, defense, and housing contracts frequently use cost-plus pricing methods. Cost-plus pricing usually involves the difficult task of allocating fixed costs that cannot be traced directly to a project.

A problem with full-cost pricing occurs when two or more products or projects are produced or worked on. How should common costs be allocated to the products or projects and how large should the markup be? In spite of these and other problems, full-cost pricing is widely used because the economic model of pricing is difficult to apply. Managers consider full-cost pricing to be safe, and intuitively managers believe that in the long run all costs, fixed and variable, must be recovered if the firm is to survive. However, full-cost pricing cannot guarantee any of these assumptions.

Differential Cost Pricing. A differential cost is the increase in total costs resulting from the production of additional unit(s). A desired markup based as a percentage of differential cost is added to full cost. Differential cost pricing focuses on the contribution to fixed costs and profit that an additional order will produce.

Direct Cost Pricing. Direct costs include the direct cost of material and labor along with variable factory overhead costs. When direct cost pricing is used, selling prices are set at a percentage above these direct costs incurred in manufacturing or producing the good or service. Direct cost pricing is valid if the cost characteristics of a company's product lines are similar. If the indirect costs that should be allocated to each product line are not essentially the same percentage of direct costs, and if the assets employed by product lines are not similar, direct cost pricing can produce inequities in the pricing process. This method does not base pricing on indirect costs, which are often arbitrarily allocated to products.

Discounts. A discount is a reduction of a stated price. Major types of discounts include quantity, trade, cash, and seasonal discounts. Other discounts are based on geographical factors (zonal pricing based on delivery distance); delivery methods (discounts for customer collection); trade-in allowances on old equipment. Discount can be based on physical volume or dollar sales, a percentage discount or a cash difference from a list price, a flat sum rebate, or a net price. Discounts can also be published, discretionary, negotiated, or a combination thereof. Major types of discounts and the reasons for using them are outlined here:

Type	Method	Objective
Quantity discount	1. Single order: based on volume purchased at one time.	Relates to individual customer. Encourages large orders. Passes on cost savings and economies in large orders.
	2. Cumulative: based on volume purchased over a fixed period of time.	Discourages small orders. Encourages repeat orders.
Trade discount	Percentage discount from a specific list price that supposedly represents distributors' expenses and profits. Trade discounts may be expressed as a flat rate or combined with a quantity discount.	Assists in controlling final selling price. Discriminating between different distributors (retailers, wholesalers). Eliminates need to change catalogues, since discounts can be changed, not list prices.
Cash discount	Deductions offered by seller if payment is within a specified time period.	Encourages early payment of account, reducing credit and collection risks.
Seasonal	Different prices depending on the season, day of week, where demand has a cyclical pattern and supply is fixed.	Encourages spreading of demand, avoidance of peak loading, and increasing demand during low periods (hotels, cinemas, and electricity).

PRICING POLICY

Economic Theory of Pricing. In a free enterprise system, supply and demand determine prices. Demand is a schedule of the total quantities that purchasers will buy at different prices at a given time. A demand curve shows the number of units of a good or service that consumers will buy at a given time and at various prices. The typical demand curve moves downward to the right, indicating that more will be sold at lower prices. An increase in demand means that a greater quantity will be purchased at each price. A decrease in demand means that a smaller quantity will be bought at each price.

The market supply of a good consists of the total quantity of the good that sellers are ready to sell at different prices at a given time. A supply curve is a line indicating the number of units of a good or service that will be offered for sale at different prices. The supply curve rises from left to right because as the price continues to rise the intersection of lines drawn from prices and quantities climbs higher and higher to the right. An increase in supply means that a larger amount will be offered; a decrease in supply means that a smaller amount will be offered at the same price.

Under perfect competition, the price of a good is determined by the intersection of the market demand curve and the market supply curve for the product. This is referred to as the equilibrium price.

In a monopoly, the firm has one distinctly downward sloping demand curve. By varying its output, the monopolist can affect the price for its product. To maximize profits, the monopolist increases output as long as marginal revenue from the increased output exceeds the marginal cost of such output. This point on a graph is at the intersection of the marginal revenue and the marginal cost curves. This point determines both output and price at the average revenue curve. Profit is the difference between average cost per unit and average revenue per unit. The monopolist has an influence over price because of his ability to control the quantity of goods or services produced.

Under monopolistic competition, a firm is able to differentiate its product from similar products. The producer has a downward-sloping demand curve (average revenue curve) which indicates that as prices decline, demand increases. In the short run, firms operating under conditions of monopolistic competition have an equilibrium position similar to the monopolistic firm, i.e., at the point where marginal cost equal marginal revenue from below and where price is equal to or larger than average variable cost. The firm makes an economic profit but not as large a profit as a firm would make under monopolistic conditions. Firms operating under conditions of monopolistic competition usually have excess capacity because they are not operating at a level of output where average cost is lowest. In the long run, new firms enter the market because of the presence of economic profit. Firms do not operate at the optimum of their cost curves and so have not attained their greatest efficiency.

Under oligopolistic market conditions, firms in the arrangement are interdependent and recognize this fact. Any action taken by one member will usually result in a reaction by the other firms, which are rivals. If the firms agree to maximize the join profits of all the firms in the market, each firm may maximize its own profits. However, a firm may attempt to pursue policies designed to maximize its individual profits, ignoring the reaction of its rivals. The behavior of the rivals will determine the success or failure of this effort. There are no standard models to illustrate oligopolies.

"Fair" Pricing. "Fair" pricing is an ethical concept of pricing goods and services. Under fair pricing, an organization prices its goods and services at a price that allows the full recovery of all costs plus an equitable profit. Costs incurred for factors of production (land, labor, and capital) are supposed to be in amounts that provide for a fair standard of living for the parties involved. The concept of fair pricing is difficult to apply because what is fair or equitable is difficult to define.

Peak Load Pricing. Utilities must have the capital equipment to meet the peak load demand for their product, such as electricity. If peak load occurs only once a day and demand is lower throughout the rest of the time period (a day, usually), then a sufficient amount of capital equipment is in place but not used on a regular basis. Economists have long recommended peak load pricing as one way to even demand through a day. Under such a pricing scheme, those using the product during the peak hours would pay a higher price that those using the product during off-peak hours. In the case of residential electricity, demand increases between the hours of 5:00 P.M. and 9:00 P.M. due to the heavier demand for hot water, dish washers, and clothes dryers. A peak load pricing scheme would provide a financial incentive to individuals to use these during off-peak hours thereby reducing the level of peak demand. Some electrical utilities are now using time-of-day pricing on a limited basis.

Penetration Pricing. Companies have occasionally used penetration pricing to gain entrance into a market. In penetration pricing, the company introduces a product at a low price and then hopefully moves up to a higher price. Penetration pricing is sometimes used when the competition dictates a price ceiling. Where a high volume of sales is required to make a product profitable, penetration pricing with its low prices might produce the necessary volume.

Proximate Value Pricing. (copyrighted) Proximate Value Pricing maintains that products or services should be priced and promoted according to their value from a customer's viewpoint, and not on a cost basis or on what the traffic will allow. According to this concept, there are four elements of value pricing: product utility to satisfy customer needs, customer alternatives, customer perception of the ability of the product to satisfy a need, and buyer capacity to pay for the product.

Return on Assets. Some firms establish a price for their product or service based on a desired rate of return on assets employed in the company. The desired markup on cost can be determined according to the following formula and illustration; the company desires a 10% return on $60,000,000 assets employed in the business and annual costs total $45,000,000:

$$\text{Percent markup} = \frac{\text{Assets employed}}{\text{Total annual costs}} \times \begin{array}{c}\text{Desired rate of}\\ \text{return on}\\ \text{cost capital employed}\end{array}$$

$$\text{Percent markup on cost} = \frac{\$60,000,000}{\$45,000,000} \times 10\%$$

Percent markup = 13.3%

The sales volume would then be computed using this formula:

$$\text{Sales volume} = \text{Total annual costs} + (\text{Total annual costs} \times \text{Percentage markup on cost})$$

Sales volume = $45,000,000 + ($45,000,000 x 13.3 percent)

Sales volume = $50,985,000 (rounded to $51,000,000)

If one million units are expected to be sold, the sales price should be $51.00 ($51,000,000/1,000,000 units).

Skim-Off-the-Top Pricing. A company with a unique product or service may be able to take advantage of this situation until the market demand declines or competitors enter the field. Pricing under such conditions is referred to as skim-off-the-top pricing, or price skimming. As long as the company maintained an exclusive market for this product, it could charge a higher than normal price for the product in the early marketing stages. Generally, a higher price will produce a larger dollar volume of sales initially than would a low initial price.

Standard Costs. Standard costs are costs that could be attained with efficient production methods at a normal capacity. In standard cost systems, a standard cost for material, labor, and factory overhead is developed. When a standard costs pricing policy is adopted, the company adds a desired markup to standard costs to establish a price.

Stay-Out, Floor, and Going-Rate Pricing. Stay-out pricing refers to low initial pricing, which is directed at discouraging potential competitors from entering the market. When stay-out pricing is used, profit margins are low and competitors may find it difficult to compete under such circumstances.

Floor pricing involves lowering prices to meet competitors' prices. A floor-pricing policy frequently results in little or no profit but is justified on the basis that such pricing is required for the firm to keep its product(s) in the market.

Many firms simply adopt a manufacturer's or wholesaler's suggested retail price as a convenience or because contracts require it.

Going-rate pricing requires a seller to base his prices on prices established by competitors in his market.

Transfer Pricing. Divisions of an enterprise frequently buy and sell to one another. A price must be established for these transfers. This price is referred to as the transfer price. Various alternatives to establishing a transfer price include the following:

1. The transfer price should be set equal to the manufacturing cost of the selling division.
2. The transfer price should be the amount for which the selling division could sell the product to an outside firm.
3. The transfer price should be the amount for which the buying division could purchase the product from an outside firm.
4. The transfer price should be a negotiated amount agreed upon by the buying and selling divisions.
5. The transfer price should be the costs incurred to the point of transfer plus the opportunity costs for the firm as a whole. The opportunity cost would be the next best alternative for the firm. For example, if the selling division was operating at less than full capacity, the opportunity cost would be zero. If the selling division was operating at full capacity, the opportunity cost would be the lost contribution margin (selling price minus variable costs) resulting from forgoing outside sales to sell to the buying division.

The choice of method depends upon a number of factors, such as the autonomy allowed to divisions, the degree of market competition, the extent to which the goals of the division are expected to correspond to the goals of the firm, short-run supply and demand relationships, and how divisions are evaluated by the firm.

Variable Cost Pricing. Variable cost pricing requires that a firm identify its variable and fixed costs. When this distinction can be made, a company's contribution margin (sales minus variable costs) can be computed. The effect on contribution margins of different prices can be related to fixed costs. Assume that a company produces two products and the variable cost of material, labor, and factory overhead for product X is $20 and for product Y is $30. If a 25% markup on variable cost is used, the sales price is:

	Product X	*Product Y*
Full cost (assumed)	$50	$40
Markup on variable cost:		
10% x $20	2	
10% x $30		3
Sales price	$52	$43

A major advantage of variable cost pricing is that the difficult problem of allocating indirect, fixed costs can be avoided. Variable pricing is often useful in pricing a special order at a special price, in a dumping situation, or in a distress case. In difficult times, a company may need to make some revenue above variable cost as an alternative to no revenue. Special-order pricing may involve discriminatory prices that may have to be justified in order not to violate the Robinson-Patman Act.

Bank Pricing. In general terms, banks use the standard pricing formula for pricing their products and services:

Profit = Volume x (Unit price − Unit cost)

The objective is to increase profits by increasing volume of services sold or by increasing the margin of profit or by a combination of both increasing volume and profit margins. This pricing represent a form of bottom-line pricing.

Banks must not ignore the role of demand and supply in the market mechanism and pricing decisions. The price elasticity or inelasticity of demand of products or services must also be considered, including cross-elasticity and income elasticity of demand. Price elasticity of demand is influenced by the nature of the product, the price in relation to total expenditures, its durability, the availability of substitutes, and the number of uses. The degree of competition, monopoly, monopolistic competition, and oligopoly existing within the market structure can also influence pricing policies and practices, as can other economic considerations.

Developing a pricing strategy for loan and deposit products is a complex process for most financial institutions. Typically, the objectives affecting deposit generation activities fall into one of five categories: market penetration, market skimming, early cash recovery, rate of return, or product line promotion. In planning to meet one or a combination of these objectives, financial institutions have pursued four types of strategies in pricing retail deposit products: regulator-set pricing, follow-the-competition pricing, cost-oriented pricing, and value/demand-oriented pricing. (Jeffrey L. Seglin, *Bank Administration Manual*, BAI).

Pricing policy for banks and other financial institutions has been regulated by government agencies and legislation. Regulation Q authorized the Federal Reserve to set levels and types of interest rates that could be paid on specific deposit accounts. This regulation established artificial ceilings on interest that did not represent the open market value of money. The truth in lending regulation, Regulation Z, required specific disclosures on consumer credit. This regulation was directed at unfair practices in the financial industry. The cost incurred in complying with this regulation increased the price of credit to consumers. Regulations G, M, T, U, and X placed restrictions on the financing of securities transactions, especially as they related to the purchase or carrying of securities and borrowings associated with such transactions. These regulations affected the pricing policies of financial institutions. The 50 states have also imposed regulations governing financial services, which directly or indirectly affect pricing, especially those that imposed interest rate caps for borrowing and USURY laws.

The Depository Institutions Deregulation Act of 1980 provided for the gradual deregulation of banking and the phaseout of the interest rate restrictions of Regulation Q. Section 202.(a) of the Depository Institutions Deregulation and Monetary Control Act of 1980 noted that the Congress finds that:

1. Limitations on the interest rates which are payable on deposits and accounts discourage persons from saving money, create inequities for depositors, impede the ability of depository institutions to compete for funds, and have not achieved their purpose of providing an even flow of funds for home mortgage lending.
2. All depositors, and particularly those with modest savings, are entitled to receive a market rate of return on their savings as soon as it is economically feasible for depository institutions to pay such a rate.
3. It is the purpose of this title to provide for the orderly phaseout and the ultimate elimination of the limitations on the maximum rates of interest and dividends that may be paid on deposits and accounts by depository institutions by extending the authority to impose such limitations for six years, subject to specific standards designed to ensure a phaseout of such limitations to market rates of interest.

The Garn-St. Germain Depository Institutions Act of 1982 clarified the Depository Institutions Deregulation and Monetary Control Act in a variety of ways as they affected pricing services. Thrifts were allowed to offer a commercial demand deposit account tied to a loan relationship. The lending powers of thrifts were extended to commercial lending. The act provided for the creation of a money market deposit account that allowed a market rate of interest to be paid on deposits of $2,500 or more with a phaseout of this minimum over the next three and a half years. The legal limits on lending for national banks were increased from 10% of capital and surplus to 15%. The effect of this legislation was to allow prices to become competitive by reducing or eliminating the pricing constraints placed on financial institutions.

See COMPETITION, MONOPOLY.

BIBLIOGRAPHY

BJORK, W. E. "Spread-Pricing for Financial Institutions." *The Magazine of Bank Administration*, March 1986, pp. 72-78.

COLLETTI, D. "Pricing Retail Deposit Products." *The Magazine of Bank Administration*, August 1986, pp. 22-26.

GIARDINI, V. *Internal Transfer Pricing of Bank Funds*, Rolling Meadows, IL.: Bank Administration Institute, 1983.

MOEBS, G. M. *Pricing Financial Services*, Dow Jones Irwin, Homewood, IL, 1986.

PRIMARY DEPOSITS

Prime Rate (1965-1987)

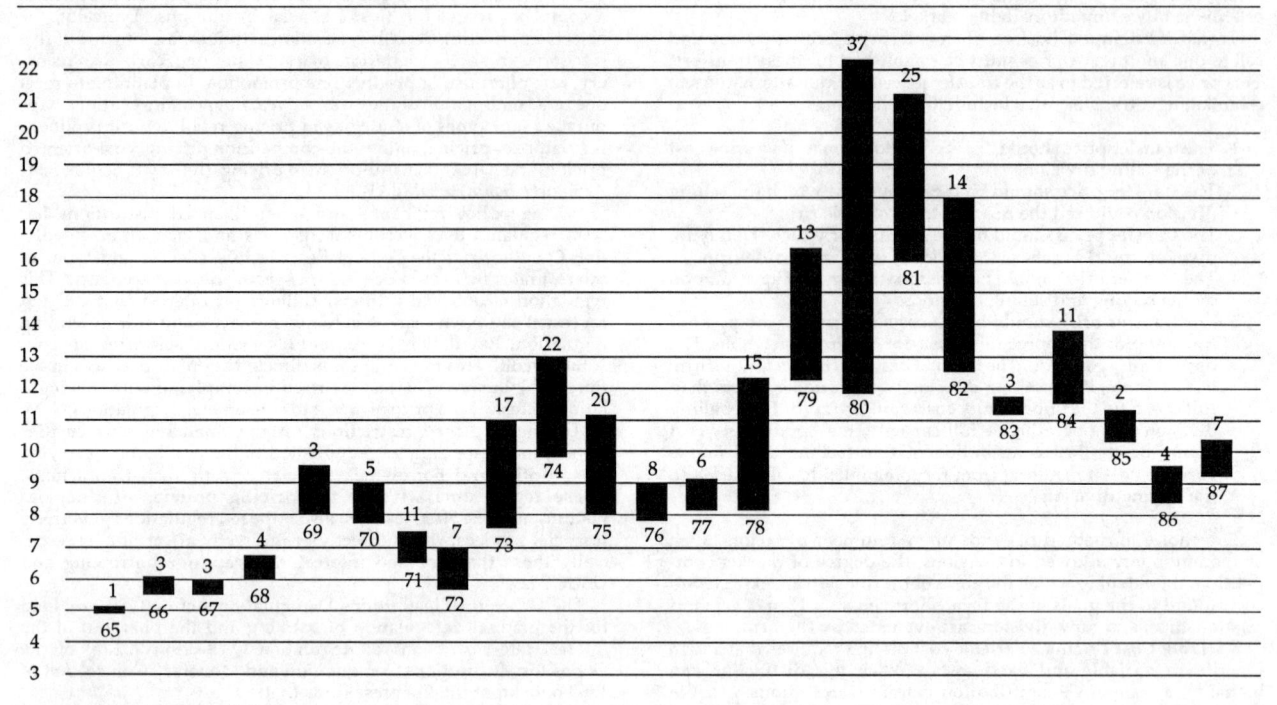

Source: National Bank of Detroit
Note: Reflects the yearly range and number of times prime rate changed during the course of each year at NBD.

PRIMARY DEPOSITS Deposits which arise from actual lodgment in a bank of cash or its equivalent, as distinguished from derivative deposits which are deposit credits created by granting loans and crediting the borrowers' accounts for the proceeds.

PRIMARY LIABILITY A direct liability as distinguished from a contingent one.
See LIABILITY.

PRIMARY MARKET See MARKET.

PRIMARY POINTS The large cities where grain is received from the country districts and stored in elevators and warehouses, to be distributed to the various consuming centers as needed. The chief primary points are Chicago, Minneapolis, Duluth, Kansas City, St. Louis, Detroit, Toledo, and Buffalo.

PRIMARY RECEIPTS Total daily receipts of grain at the PRIMARY POINTS.

PRIME In reference to an investment (bond, acceptance, commercial paper), first-class, high-grade, gilt-edge, conservative, etc.

PRIME RATE The interest rate most closely approximating the riskless or pure rate for money, i.e., most devoid of financial risk (highest-quality credit with least or negligible premium for credit risk).

Among security yields, the yields on U.S. government securities are conventionally considered to be the most closely approximating riskless rates. Thus, the differential between yields on AAA corporate bonds and on U.S. government obligations of comparable maturities would measure approximately the added premium for risk. Federal Reserve bank rediscount rates on eligible commercial paper and on advances to member banks secured by U.S. government securities are the Federal Reserve bank's prime rates.

In commercial bank loans, the prime rate is the interest rate charged for the very best credits of short-term maturity. Determination of the prime lending rate is a function of a bank's lending policy, which is in turn influenced by the prevailing monetary policy, inflation, the general level of money rates, the availability of excess reserves, and general business conditions. Variation in the prime rate charged by banks (the series reported regularly in the *Federal Reserve Bulletin*) has been since 1965 as indicated in the appended chart.

Rates on business loans of banks reflect, in addition to the factors enumerated above, the size of the loan (all things being equal, the larger the loan, the lower the rate); maturities of loans (short-term, long-term, and revolving credits); and geographical variation (rates in the money centers tend to be lowest). The prime rate on commercial bank loans is a guideline, not a firm indication of rates actually charged on bank commercial loans; borrowers may be charged points above prime or even rates shaving (below) the prime, depending upon details of the loans and the bank's credit policy.
See MONEY MARKET, MONEY RATES.

PRINCIPAL This term has two applications:

1. The face amount or par value of a note or other evidence of debt; that is, the amount exclusive of interest or premium which the holder is entitled to receive at maturity. It is also the sum on which interest is computed.
2. The amount of money employed for profit or interest-bearing purposes; the amount invested for the purpose of yielding an income under the name of interest, as distinguished from such income.

PRINCIPLE OF SUBSIDIARITY A social and political principle that implies that each higher unit in the economy of body politic exists to give assistance to or to benefit lesser units.

PRIORITIES The claims of creditors against a business, estate, or landed property have certain priorities or preferences. For the priority of claims against insolvent businesses, see LIABILITY. For the preferences accorded preferred stockholders, see PREFERRED STOCK. In the case of an estate, every executor or administrator shall pay, out

ENCYCLOPEDIA OF BANKING AND FINANCE

of the first monies received, the reasonable funeral expenses of the decedent, which expenses shall be preferred to all debts and claims. Payment of legal and proper expenses of administration and the statutorily prescribed commissions of the executor or administrator is also authorized. Debts of the decedent shall also be paid before distributions to the distributees, debts ranking in the following prescribed priorities:

1. Debts entitled to a preference under the laws of the United States and State of New York;
2. Taxes assessed on property of the deceased prior to his death;
3. Judgments docketed and decrees entered against the deceased according to the priority thereof; and
4. All recognizances, bonds, sealed instruments, notes, bills and unliquidated demands and accounts.

PRIOR LIEN *See* LIEN.

PRIOR LIEN BONDS Bonds secured by a mortgage taking precedence over another or other mortgages against the company's property. These bonds are not necessarily, as the title might imply, first mortgage bonds. The title generally occurs only among railroad issues. It is necessary to investigate the terms of the mortgage in order to determine the exact nature of the security.
See LIEN.

PRIOR-PERIOD ADJUSTMENTS A few profit and loss items are reported as prior-period adjustments on financial statements and require a restatement of retained earnings. These items are the corrections of errors of a prior period and adjustments that result from the realization of income tax benefits of preacquisition operating loss carryforwards of purchased subsidiaries.

Material errors in the financial statements of one accounting period that are discovered in a subsequent period usually involve an asset or liability and a revenue or expense of a prior year. In the year of the correction, the asset or liability account balance should be corrected and the related revenue or expense should be made directly to the retained earnings account and should not affect the income statement for the current year. For example, assume that the Blue Company discovered that it failed to record $100,000 of depreciation expense for 1990 and discovered the error in 1991. This error overstated 1990 income before income taxes by a similar amount. Assume that after considering the income tax effect of this error, the error resulted in a net overstatement of income in 1990 of $85,000. The January 1, 1991, retained earnings balance of the Blue Company is assumed to be $500,000. The correction would be disclosed on the December 31, 1991, statement of retained earnings as a prior period adjustment as shown here:

Retained earnings, as previously reported January 1, 1991	$500,000
Less: Correction of overstatement in 1990 net income due to depreciation understatement (net of $15,000 income taxes)	85,000
Adjusted retained earnings, January 1, 1991	$415,000

If comparative financial statements are presented, the prior-year statements should be restated to show the effect on net income, retained earnings, and asset or liability balances for all periods reported.

PRIOR PREFERENCE STOCK A rarely used title indicating that two or more classes of preferred stock have been issued, but the stock so named is entitled to dividends in full before the second or third class receives anything. It is more usual, when preferred stock is issued in series, to designate it as first, second, and third preferred stock, or as series or class A, B, C, etc.

PRIOR PREFERRED STOCK First preferred stock.
See PRIOR PREFERENCE STOCK.

PRIOR REDEMPTION The act of calling redeemable or optional bonds for redemption at a date prior to the obligatory maturity. Unless provision is made in the terms of an issue, bonds are not subject to prior redemption.

PRIOR SALE *See* OFFERED FIRM.

PRIVATE BANKING Banking conducted as a partnership or individual proprietorship, as distinguished from incorporated banking. Private banking is the oldest form of banking. The private banking houses of Europe for centuries have played an important role in European finance, and in the United States various private banking houses occupy positions of comparable influence and prestige.

Until passage of the BANKING ACT OF 1933, Congress had not referred in federal statutes to private bankers, and their supervision and regulation were left to the states. In some states, such as New York, regulation of private banks is now comparable in detail to that of incorporated banks, but in other states, regulation has been liberal. In still others, the banking business is denied to unincorporated banks.

Congress in Section 21 of the Banking Act of 1933 provided that after the expiration of one year after the date of enactment of the act, which was June 16, 1933, it shall be unlawful for any person, firm, corporation, association, business trust, or other similar organization engaged in the business of issuing, underwriting, selling, or distributing, at wholesale or retail, or through syndicate participation, stocks, bonds, debentures, notes, or other securities, to engage at the same time to any extent whatever in the business of receiving deposits subject to check or to repayment upon presentation of a passbook, certificate of deposit, or other evidence of debt, or upon request of the depositor. This general prohibition does not prohibit national banks or state banks or trust companies (whether or not members of the Federal Reserve System) or other financial institutions or private bankers from dealing in, underwriting, purchasing, and selling investment securities to the extent permitted to national banks under Section 5136 of the revised statutes (that statute, found in 12 U.S.C. 24, permits national banks to purchase for own account investment securities under limitations and restrictions prescribed by the Comptroller of the Currency; but otherwise limits dealings in securities to the purchase and sale without recourse, solely upon the order and for the account of customers and in no case for own account, and limits the underwriting of securities to U.S. government securities, general obligations of states and municipalities, and securities of specified federal agencies). This general prohibition does not affect such right as any banking institution may otherwise possess to sell, without recourse or agreement to repurchase, obligations evidencing loans on real estate.

Section 21 of the Banking Act of 1933 further provided that it shall be unlawful for any person, firm, corporation, association, business trust, or other similar organization to engage, to any extent whatever with others than his or its officers, agents, or employees, in the business of receiving deposits subject to check or to repayment upon presentation of a passbook, certificate of deposit, or other evidence of debt, or upon request of the depositor, unless such person, firm, corporation, association, business trust, or other similar organization

1. Shall be incorporated under and authorized to engage in such business by the laws of the United States or any state, territory, or district, or
2. Shall be permitted by any state, territory, or district to engage in such business and shall be subjected by the law of such state, territory, or district to examination and regulation, or
3. Shall submit to periodic examination by the banking authority of the state, territory, or district where such business is carried on and shall make and publish periodic reports of its condition, exhibiting in detail its resources and liabilities, such examination and reports to be made and published at the same times and in the same manner and under the same conditions as required by the law of such state, territory, or district in the case of incorporated banking institutions engaged in such business in the same locality (as amended by the Banking Act of 1935).

Prior to passage of the Banking Act of 1933, most private banking houses combined the business of receiving deposits subject to check and doing a foreign exchange, acceptance, loan, and discount business with the purchase, sale, and distribution of securities through underwriting and participation in underwriting groups. Thus, Section 21 of the act required such private banking houses to make an election between their commercial banking and deposit business and their securities business. The private banking house of J. P.

Morgan & Co., for example, elected to stay in the banking business, and incorporated as a state institution entitled J. P. Morgan & Co., Inc. (subsequently merged with the Guaranty Trust Company to form the present Morgan Guaranty Trust Company). The securities business of the firm was divorced and independently organized as the investment banking firm of Morgan Stanley & Co.

Congress also provided in the amended Section 8 of the Clayton Act, pertaining to interlocking directorates, that no private bankers shall be at the same time directors, officers, or employees of any other bank, banking association, savings bank, or trust company organized under the National Bank Act or organized under the laws of any state or of the District of Columbia, or any branch thereof, except that the Board of Governors of the Federal Reserve System may by regulation permit such service as directors, officers, or employees of not more than one other such institution or branch thereof.

Prior to 1933, besides the major private banking houses doing an international business (what the French call "hautes banques"), such as J. P. Morgan & Co., Kuhn, Loeb & Co., Dillon, Read & Co., etc., and the mainly domestic investment banking firms, there was a third classification of private bankers engaging in banking business chiefly in foreign-born neighborhoods of large cities. The tightening of state regulation of private bankers particularly reached this previously loosely regulated group.

BIBLIOGRAPHY

"Are Private Banking Operations Successful?" *Journal of Commercial Bank Lending*, April, 1989.
LAURIE, S. "Are You Being Served?" *The Banker*, April, 1989.

PRIVATE WIRE Banks, investment houses, and members of stock and commodity exchanges frequently lease telephone or telegraph wires for their own use exclusively, or jointly with other parties, for the purpose of keeping in immediate and convenient contact with their branches or correspondents located in other places, or with certain other houses in the larger centers.

PRIVATE WIRE HOUSES Members of the New York Stock Exchange, American Stock Exchange, Chicago Board of Trade, etc., which maintain private wire connections with their branch offices or correspondents located in other cities and towns throughout the country, and thus do a large volume of commission business in the execution of orders on the various markets. Because of the costly overhead involved in maintaining such systems of private wires, and the necessity for large volume to cover expenses, the number and scope of facilities of the large wire houses have been affected by years of low trading volume, and their number has often declined through mergers.

PRIVILEGE BROKER A put and CALL broker and dealer, dealing in PRIVILEGES, e.g., puts, calls, spreads, and straddles.

PRIVILEGED BONDS CONVERTIBLE BONDS and bonds with warrants attached.
See STOCK PURCHASE WARRANT.

PRIVILEGED COMMUNICATION *See* LIBEL.

PRIVILEGE OF REGISTRATION Coupon bonds sometimes give the holder the option to have them registered, either as to principal and interest or as to principal only.
See REGISTERED BOND.

PRIVILEGES Specific financial contracts made with the view of permitting one of the parties to exercise some right, option, or privilege, such as to purchase securities or commodities, for a limited time, a price being paid for such privilege. Specific forms of privileges are the option, PUT, CALL, SPREAD, STRADDLE.
See OPTIONS.

PRIVITY The contractual relationship between the parties to a contract.

PROBABILITY The likelihood of the occurrence of any particular form of an event. For example, if a coin is tossed into the air, one of two events will occur—heads or tails. This probability can be expressed as

$$p = 1/2$$

and the possibility of a tail turning up as:

$$q = 1 - p = 1/2$$

Problems in which the probability of occurrence of an event remains constant or can be assumed to do so can be solved by using the binomial theorem.

When $p = 1/2$, the binomial distribution is symmetrical. As n (number of combinations) increases, the binomial distribution approaches the symmetrical curve known as the normal distribution. The binomial formula can be written as:

$$(a + b)^2 = a^2 + 2ab + b^2$$

Probability analysis can be used in analyzing many financial and other business problems and opportunities, including capital budgeting, return on investment, pricing, risk in an investment, and break-even analysis.
See NORMAL DISTRIBUTION.

PROBATE The formal establishment and proof of execution of a document as the last will and testament of the deceased. In its broader legal meaning, probate refers to all matters over which probate courts, variously designated among the states as probate court, surrogate's court, orphans' court, etc., have jurisdiction. Probate proceedings are initiated by the filing of petition for probate of the will by specified interested persons. After a will has been admitted to probate by decree of the probate judge or surrogate, any person entitled to LETTERS TESTAMENTARY thereunder who is competent by law to serve and who appears and qualifies will be issued such authority to act under the will.

PROCEEDS This term has three applications:

1. The sum that a borrower receives from a bank when a note is discounted. The proceeds are equal to the face amount of a note less the DISCOUNT, and are sometimes known as the net avails.
2. The sum realized from the sale of any property, whether securities, commodities, land, etc., after deduction of the expenses of sale.
3. The sum collected upon a check after deduction of exchange or collection charges.

PRODUCE EXCHANGES Spot markets in produce (perishable provisions such as butter, eggs, vegetables, fish, poultry, etc.) are maintained in most consumption centers of population. In the larger cities, such produce markets are supplemented by public markets operated by the municipality.

Such markets are part of the agricultural marketing system through middlemen. Because the perishability and quality variation of produce magnify the problem of fair marketing for the producer, federal legislation in this area is designed to eliminate fraud and sharp practices. The Produce Agency Act of 1927 applies to the handling and disposition of products received in interstate commerce for sale on consignment by any persons receiving fruit, vegetables, dairy products, poultry, or other perishable products. It punishes as a misdemeanor such practices as fraudulent accounting, false or misleading statements with intent to defraud, and the dumping of produce without good cause.

The more comprehensive Perishable Agricultural Commodities Act of 1930 requires the licensing of all persons doing business as commission merchants, dealers, or brokers handling fresh or frozen fruits or vegetables in interstate or foreign commerce. The act prohibits such unfair practices as failure to deliver or rejection of goods without reasonable cause; false and misleading statements; incorrect accounting on consignments; failure to pay promptly for commodities purchased or received on consignment; misrepresentation of goods, quality, condition, or state or country of origin; and alteration of federal inspection certificates. Licensees are required to keep adequate accounts and records for two years, to facilitate investigation of complaints which may be filed with the Department of Agriculture. In addition to formal proceedings (culminating in suspension of license for failure to pay a determined reparation award) and disciplinary proceedings, as authorized in the act, the Department of Agriculture has instituted informal arbitration of bona fide disputes for quick and inexpensive settlements, upon written consent to such arbitration by all the parties concerned.

To provide an opportunity for individuals and firms holding positions in particular types of produce to hedge against price changes, futures contract trading is available on two commodity exchanges designated as contract markets by the secretary of Agriculture. The CHICAGO MERCANTILE EXCHANGE and the NEW YORK MERCANTILE EXCHANGE provide futures trading in butter, eggs, and potatoes. The function of such commodity futures markets is more valuable than trading volume alone would indicate, for example, in butter, in which futures trading volume is relatively modest. Most creameries sell butter directly to customers under sales agreements providing for specified premiums over the price quotation on the Chicago or New York Mercantile Exchange, so that these exchanges facilitate the distribution of the bulk of butter sold directly without going through these exchanges.

Outlets for producers of produce commodities include sale directly to consumers, through local middlemen, to processors and manufacturers, and to terminal (central) markets. The trend is toward more decentralization of the marketing of produce, bypassing the central markets, as particularly exemplified by the more direct and local buying by the large chain stores and supermarkets.

BIBLIOGRAPHY

U.S. DEPARTMENT OF AGRICULTURE, *Marketing* (Yearbook of Agriculture)

PRODUCER PRICE INDEX (PPI) An index that measures the average price change in producer (nonfinal) goods. In calculating this index, the U.S. Department of Labor, Bureau of Labor Statistics, uses nearly 3,000 producer products ranging from feeds to fibers to fuels. The PPI varies from year to year in a manner similar to the consumer price index (CPI). Listed below are the annual rates of change in the PPI and the CPI from 1980 through 1987.

	Annual Percentage Change	
Year	PPI	CPI
1980	11.8	12.4
1981	7.1	8.9
1982	3.7	3.9
1983	0.6	3.8
1984	1.7	4.0
1985	1.8	3.8
1986	2.3	1.1
1987	2.2	4.4

Source: *Economic Report of the President*, 1988.

PRODUCT DIFFERENTIATION Consumers choose between homogeneous products strictly on the basis of their price. Producers often differentiate their products in order to provide a second dimension through which consumers may make purchasing decisions. The strategy in differentiating one's product is to separate consumer choice from the product's price. This gives the producer the ability to raise price without loosing many customers, and thus increase revenues. Breakfast cereals, underwear, and shampoos are a few products marketed on the basis of differential characteristics.

PRODUCT FINANCING ARRANGEMENTS Transactions in which a company sells a portion of its inventory to another entity with the intent to reacquire that inventory in the future. Such arrangements generally allow one party to finance the product and still retain control over its ultimate disposition. For example, Company A sells (i.e., transfers or parks) inventory to Company B and agrees to repurchase the inventory at a specified price and time. Company B uses the inventory as collateral for a bank loan. The proceeds of the bank loan are used by Company B to pay Company A for the inventory. At a later date, Company A repurchases the inventory from Company B plus related holding costs incurred by Company B; Company B uses these proceeds to repay the bank loan. A chart illustrating a product financing arrangement is appended.

For accounting purposes, Company A is financing its inventory even though legal title has passed to Company B. Company B might be interested in such an arrangement because it may want to work out a similar arrangement with Company A in the future or for other business reasons. Since the economic substance of the transaction did not involve a sale, the inventory transferee to Company B is included in Company A's inventory. The proceeds from the sale are recognized by Company A as a liability and not as revenue. This treatment requires Company A to report the product and liability (a financing arrangement) on its balance sheet.

PRODUCTION The creation or addition of utility. Utility is the ability of a good or service to satisfy want. The four basic types of utility are: form (usefulness increases by changing its form or shape); place (more utility in one location than in another); time (more utility at one time than at another); and possession (occurs when a good or service is transferred from one person to another). The relationship between factor of production (land, labor, capital, and entrepreneurship) inputs and product output is referred to as the production function of the firm.

PRODUCTION AND MARKETING ADMINISTRATION Under the reorganization of the Department of Agriculture announced by the secretary of Agriculture in November, 1953, the former Production and Marketing Administration's functions were distributed to (1) the former Commodity Stabilization Service (name changed to Agricultural Stabilization and Conservation Service by the secretary's Memorandum 1458 of June 14, 1961, effective June 5, 1961), and (2) the former Agricultural Marketing Service (name changed to Consumer and Marketing Service by the secretary's Memorandum 1567, Supplement 1, of February 8, 1965).

See AGRICULTURE, DEPARTMENT OF.

PRODUCTION CREDIT ASSOCIATIONS Local cooperative organizations of farmers and stockmen, originally chartered by the FARM CREDIT ADMINISTRATION under the provisions of the Farm Credit Act of 1933. In addition to their operations in discounting agricultural and livestock paper for various types of financing institutions, the FEDERAL INTERMEDIATE CREDIT BANKS (FICB) supervise and assist the production credit associations in making credit available to farmers and stockmen. The FICB presently operate under the authorities contained in Title II of the Farm Credit Act of 1971, P.L. 92-181, as amended.

Of the total Federal Intermediate banks' loans and discounts outstanding, the bulk are for the production credit associations (PCAs), which own all of the banks' outstanding Class B stock. The associations acquired the Class B stock through required purchases and by receiving patronage refunds paid in the form of such stock.

Product Financing Arrangement

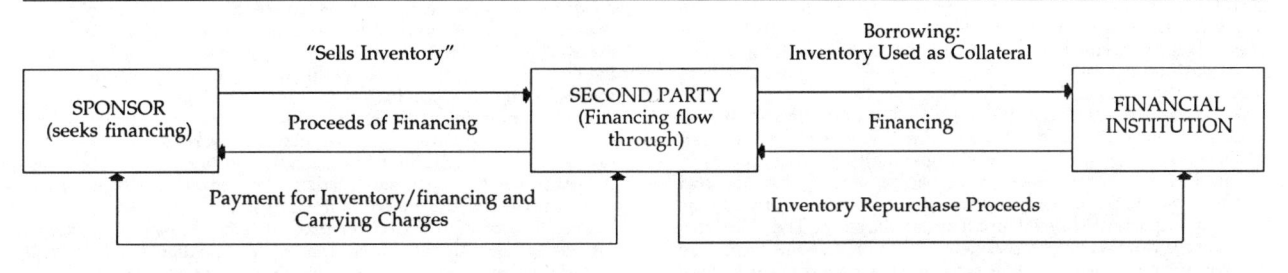

The banks do not make loans directly to farmers. They function as banks of discount, and supervise and assist the PCAs in their furnishing of credit to farmers. Interest rates charged by the banks to the PCAs and other financing institutions depend to a large extent upon the rates the banks have to pay for their debentures issued in the open market. Total net earnings or savings of the banks, after paying all operating expenses and after building and maintaining required legal reserves, are returned to the PCAs and other financing institutions using the banks as patronage refunds. This refunding of savings by the banks to the PCAs reduces the farmer-members' cost of borrowing.

In all farm credit districts, the PCAs have adopted mutual loss sharing plans, participating loan plans, or both. These agreements, which have been in existence for several years, have the effect of putting the net worth of the PCAs more directly behind the net worth of the Federal Intermediate Credit banks and their outstanding debentures.

Lending Procedure. Farmers borrow short- and intermediate-term agricultural credit through their PCAs. PCAs lend money for almost every farm, farm home, and farm family expense. A farmer may obtain money to buy seed, feed, fertilizer, or livestock. Through his PCA, a farmer may finance a new truck, tractor, or other farm machinery. He may borrow to repair farm buildings or to modernize his farm home. He may even finance a college education for his children. PCA loans of up to 7 years may be made to bona fide farmers or ranchers, persons engaged in performing on-the-farm services to farmers, and rural residents. Loans to commercial fishermen may be extended up to 15 years. PCAs also may participate in loans with other PCAs or with commercial banks.

Farmers become members of the PCA nearest their farms when they get their first loan. A farmer does this by buying Class B (voting) stock equal to 5% of his loan. This is usually just added to the amount of the loan so that he does not have to provide cash to purchase the stock. If he borrows more funds as his operations grow, he buys enough additional stock to make his total investment equal to 5% of his loans. Members frequently buy larger amounts of stock to help their associations take care of farmers' growing credit needs.

When members repay their loans, they usually keep their Class B stock and use it again when they need another loan. If a member does not borrow for two years, his stock is converted to Class A (nonvoting) stock. By holding their stock as an investment, members help to strengthen the financial structure of the association. The conversion to nonvoting stock keeps the control in the hands of farmers who are actually using the association. Farmers run their associations through boards of directors democratically elected from among the member-borrowers. Every active member of the PCA has one vote, regardless of the size of his loan or the amount of stock he owns in the PCA. Each member of the board of directors of the PCA is a farmer who lives in the area and is a member of the PCA. He knows what it takes to farm successfully in that particular locality. The board sets overall policies for the PCA as provided for in its bylaws and hires a manager to conduct its day-to-day business affairs. He may carry the title of secretary-treasurer, manager, or president, and may have several people on his staff, depending on the size of the PCA, its volume of business, and the number of members it serves. Many large PCAs have branch offices for added convenience to their members. As of the 1982 fiscal year, there were 423 PCAs throughout the country serving farmers on a fulltime basis.

The board of directors must also see that the PCA is operated in an efficient manner, and in accordance with its policies and the laws which govern PCAs. In addition to setting policies, hiring the manager, and being responsible for the operation of the PCA, the board may also appoint various committees. Most important of these is the loan committee, which usually consists of the manager and two directors. The function of the loan committee is to review loan applications. Because members of the committee are themselves farmers elected to the board by their fellow members, they are in a good position to render fair and knowledgeable judgments in conducting this basic part of the PCA's business.

The farmer is not charged interest on any part of his PCA loan until the money is made available to him. When he repays any part of the loan, no further interest is charged on the portion repaid.

The Federal Intermediate Credit banks, the suppliers of loan funds to the PCAs, return their earnings in the form of stock to the PCAs in proportion to the interest they pay the banks. The FICBs also allocate their net worth reserves to the PCAs on the same basis. The PCA, in turn, returns its earnings to farmer-members in the form of dividends on their stock and in patronage refunds in proportion to the interest they have paid during the year.

Summary. Production credit associations are local credit cooperatives, designed to be retail outlets for the intermediate-term lending of funds made available at wholesale from the Federal Intermediate Credit banks. At the time of formation of the PCAs in 1933, other (private) intermediate-term farm credit institutions, such as livestock loan companies, agricultural credit corporations, and commercial banks, were alleged to be unable fully to meet farmers' credit needs of this type. In the intermediate credit system, however, Federal Intermediate Credit banks purchase and discount notes of farmer-borrowers of national or state banks, trust companies, agricultural credit corporations, and livestock loan companies, besides those of production credit associations.

See FARM CREDIT ACTS.

PRODUCTION CREDIT CORPORATIONS Originally established under the Farm Credit Act of 1933, the 12 production credit corporations, one in each of the farm credit districts, supervised the operations of the PRODUCTION CREDIT ASSOCIATIONS. They also assisted in the organization of these associations and provided their initial capital, the production credit corporations themselves being entirely owned by the federal government. Pursuant to the Farm Credit Act of 1956, each production credit corporation was merged into the Federal Intermediate Credit Bank in each district as of January 1, 1957.

Restructuring. The Agricultural Act of 1987 mandated a restructuring of the Farm Credit System. The Federal Land bank and the Federal Intermediate Credit bank in each Farm Credit district were required to merge. The resulting Farm Credit Bank will be a federally chartered instrumentality of the United States with corporate powers similar to those formerly held by the FLB and the FICB.

Within six months of the mergers of the FLBs and FICBs, the board of directors of each FEDERAL LAND BANK ASSOCIATION and PRODUCTION CREDIT ASSOCIATION that share substantially the same geographic territory must submit a plan to their stockholders for merging the two associations. The plan must first be approved by the district Farm Credit bank and the Farm Credit Administration. If the plan is approved and adopted by the stockholders, the resulting association will be a direct lender and obtain its loan funds from the Farm Credit Bank in the same manner as PCAs now obtain loan funds from the FICBs. The boards of directors of associations, whether merged or not, will be elected from among their stockholders, except that at least one member will be elected by the other directors and shall not be a director, officer, employee, or stockholder of any system institution.

See FEDERAL INTERMEDIATE CREDIT BANKS.

PRODUCTION FUNCTION A production is a relationship between inputs and output. If output is denoted as Q and inputs are denoted as K (for capital) and L (for labor), then

$$Q = f(K,L)$$

denotes that there is a systematic relationship between these inputs and output. In economics this function is often quantified mathematically. There are many theoretical functions studies in economics. The most frequently studied is the Cobb-Douglas production function.

PRODUCTION INDEX The total index of industrial production, prepared monthly by the Board of Governors of the Federal Reserve System and published in the monthly *Federal Reserve Bulletin*, is "probably the most widely used as a coinciding measure of conditions." It is designed to measure changes in the physical volume or quantity of output of manufacturing and mining establishments and electric and gas utilities. The gross product originating in the industries covered by the index contributes about 30% of total gross national product.

The 235 monthly series are grouped into two separate classifications. Each of the 235 series is assigned to a market grouping as well as to an industry grouping. For example, the auto production series is a component of consumer goods in the market classification and of transportation equipment in the industry classification.

The classification based on type of end-use has as its major categories consumer goods, equipment, intermediate products, and materials. The consumer goods grouping, which accounted for 28%

of the total index in the 1967 period, is further subdivided into automotive products, home goods (including appliances, furniture, television sets, etc.), clothing, and consumer staples. The equipment series, which accounted for 20% of the total in 1967, is further divided between business equipment and defense and space equipment. Intermediate products, which accounted for 13% of the total, represent construction and business supplies that leave the industrial sector at this point.

The materials component consists of three major categories: durable goods materials, nondurable goods materials, and energy materials. Durable goods materials, which accounted for 20% of the total index in 1967, include materials or components used primarily in the manufacture of finished durable goods. They range from metal mining and logging materials to semiconductors and original equipment auto tires. Nondurable materials, which were 10% of the total in 1967, include containers, textile materials, chemical materials, paper materials, and other nondurable materials. Energy materials consist of primary and converted fuel materials.

Industry Groupings. The classification by producing industry is based on the 1967 edition of the Standard Industrial Classification (SIC) and has as its principal categories durable manufactures, nondurable manufactures, mining, and utilities. Durable manufactures include 11 of the SIC major groups^primary metals; fabricated metals; electrical machinery; nonelectrical machinery; transportation equipment; instruments; ordnance; stone, clay, and glass; lumber; furniture; and miscellaneous manufactures. That category also includes measures of the manufacturing activities for the Department of Defense. In the 1967 base period, these durable manufactures accounted for 52% of the weight of the total index.

Nondurable manufactures include 10 of the SIC major groups—food and beverages; tobacco; textiles; apparel; paper; chemicals, which includes representation of the manufacturing establishments owned by the Department of Energy; printing and publishing; petroleum; rubber and plastics; and leather. During the 1967 base period, it accounted for 36% of the total index. Mining activities, which accounted for 6% of the index in this same period, include coal and metal mining, oil and gas extraction, and production of stone and earth materials. Utility output of electricity and gas includes both private- and government-owned establishments, and accounted for 6% of the total index in the 1967 base period.

The monthly series are adjusted periodically to more comprehensive annual levels based in large part on Bureau of the Census comprehensive censuses of manufactures and annual surveys of manufactures. Extensive use is made of the most recent benchmark indexes, which are based on shipments for about 10,000 individual products covered in the 1963 and 1967 censuses of manufactures. The data, adjusted for inventory change, were converted to constant dollars using price relatives. The major sources of the price relatives were the producer price indexes from the Bureau of Labor Statistics and unit values from the Bureau of the Census.

Adjustment for seasonal variation is made to all individual series. In addition, the seasonal factors for the basic aggregate series in both the market and industry groupings are subject to continuous review and editing. To diminish the effect on the seasonal factors of the sharp recession in 1974 and recovery in 1975, data for those years were excluded from the calculation of seasonal factors for most series.

Revisions in the Index. Since it was first published in 1927, the index has undergone several major revisions. A major revision was completed in 1959, with revised indexes and new groupings carried back to January, 1947. The principal changes were the following:

1. Adjustment of individual monthly series to levels shown by the census of manufactures and other data.
2. Broadening of coverage to include electric and gas utility output, and introduction of new component series in a number of manufacturing and mining industries.
3. Introduction of new market groupings.
4. Adoption of the 1957 Standard Industrial Classification.

The next major revision was introduced in early 1972. Several major statistical changes were made at that time, including the following:

1. Adjustment to census benchmark levels through 1963 and to annual indexes based on the *Annual Survey of Manufactures* (ASM) through 1968.

2. Introduction of kilowatt hour data adjusted for output per kilowatt hour to replace many but not all hours worked series.
3. Major market groupings extended back through World War II.
4. Introduction of alternative (supplementary) value of product dollar weights for the product portion of the market groupings.
5. Introduction of initial base-weight years that were then linked to provide 1967 = 100 indexes.
6. Adoption of the 1967 Standard Industrial Classification.

In 1976, the index was further revised as follows:

1. To reflect 1963 to 1967 benchmark indexes and the ASM through 1973.
2. To increase the number of basic series from 227 to 235 by the addition of 26 new series and the deletion of 18 former series.
3. To allow for changes in market groupings to improve the representation of automotive products and energy materials.
4. To shift the value of product weights to 1972 dollars.

Uses. The Federal Reserve index of industrial production is used with related data on employment, inventories, trade, prices, and other economic variables in analyzing short- and long-run developments in the economy. The component indexes are used to determine the areas in which important changes accounted for the observed changes in the total index. They may also be used in analysis related to individual industries—for example, studies of a company's output and sales figures in relation to the output movements of the industry.

The *1980 Supplement to Economic Indicators* points out that the scope of the index is limited to manufacturing, mining, and electric and gas utilities. It should not be used as a measure of total production because agriculture, construction activity, transportation, trade, and various other sectors are not included. But it should be noted that changes in the output of manufactures, minerals, and utilities are especially significant because they account for much of the cyclical variation in total economic activity.

The appended table compares the yearly levels of the industrial production index since 1929.

See BUSINESS BAROMETERS, INDEX NUMBERS.

PRODUCTIVITY AND PRODUCTIVITY GROWTH

Productivity is the relationship between the quantity of inputs (land, labor, tractors, feed) employed and the quantity of outputs produced. An increase in productivity means that more outputs can be produced from the same inputs or that the same outputs are produced with fewer inputs. Single-factor and multifactor indexes are frequently used to measure productivity. Single-factor measures examine the output per unit of one input at the same time other inputs may be changing. Multifactor productivity indexes consider all productive resources as a whole, netting out the effects of substitution among inputs. Crop yield per acre, output per work hour, and livestock production per breeding animal are all single-factor productivity indicators. The total farm output per unit of input index is a multifactor measure.

Productivity and productivity growth are vital to the economic well-being of a nation because they enhance standards of living and the quality of life. Productivity growth improves production efficiency, which in turn enhances the competitive, financial, and military position of a nation within the international community. It increases income, which potentially can be reallocated toward improving conditions of social concern such as environmental pollution or poverty and thereby enhancing quality of life. Productivity advances ameliorate inflationary pressures and thus helps establish economic stability. Productivity growth also stimulates market competition within an economy and among economies, thus improving resource allocation in general.

One phenomenon responsible for productivity growth is technological progress. Technological change brings about production efficiencies, which in turn lead to productivity growth.

There is no single, generally accepted way to measure productivity or productivity growth at either the aggregate level or the level of one particular firm (or organization within the firm). The more common measures begin with a conceptual representation of an input-to-output transformation process usually referred to as a production function.

PRODUCT LIFE CYCLE

Industrial Production Indexes (1967 = 100)

Year	Total	Total	Durable	Nondurable	Mining	Utilities
1967 proportion	100.0	87.95	51.98	35.97	6.36	5.69
1929	21.6	22.8	22.5	23.2	43.1	7.4
1930	18.0	18.7	16.7	21.1	37.4	7.6
1931	14.9	15.3	11.5	19.9	32.1	7.3
1932	11.7	11.8	7.0	17.5	26.8	6.8
1933	13.7	14.0	9.1	19.9	30.6	6.7
1934	15.0	15.3	11.1	20.4	32.0	7.1
1935	17.3	18.0	14.2	22.7	34.8	7.7
1936	20.4	21.5	18.4	25.2	10.0	8.7
1937	22.3	23.4	20.8	26.7	45.1	9.6
1938	17.6	18.0	13.3	23.7	39.0	9.7
1939	21.7	21.5	17.7	26.1	42.1	10.7
1940	25.0	25.4	13.5	27.5	46.8	11.8
1941	31.6	32.4	31.4	33.3	49.7	13.3
1942	36.3	37.8	39.9	34.6	51.3	14.9
1943	44.0	47.0	54.2	37.1	52.5	16.5
1944	47.4	50.9	59.9	38.6	56.2	17.5
1945	40.7	42.6	45.2	38.5	55.1	17.8
1946	35.0	35.3	31.6	39.7	54.2	18.6
1947	39.4	39.4	37.7	41.3	61.3	20.1
1948	41.1	40.9	39.3	42.7	64.4	22.4
1949	38.8	38.7	35.7	42.0	57.1	23.9
1950	44.9	45.0	43.5	46.7	63.8	27.2
1951	48.7	48.6	48.9	48.3	70.0	31.0
1952	50.6	50.6	51.9	49.2	69.4	33.7
1953	54.8	55.2	58.7	51.2	71.2	36.5
1954	51.9	51.5	51.8	51.6	69.9	39.3
1955	58.5	58.2	59.2	57.2	77.9	43.9
1956	61.1	60.5	61.1	60.1	82.0	48.2
1957	61.9	61.2	61.6	61.1	82.1	51.5
1958	57.9	57.0	53.9	61.6	75.6	53.9
1959	64.8	64.2	61.9	67.7	78.7	59.3
1960	66.2	65.4	62.9	69.3	80.3	63.4
1961	66.7	65.6	61.8	71.5	80.8	67.0
1962	72.2	71.5	68.6	75.8	83.1	72.0
1963	76.5	75.8	73.1	80.0	86.4	77.0
1964	81.7	81.0	78.3	85.2	89.9	83.6
1965	89.8	89.7	89.0	90.9	93.2	88.7
1966	97.8	97.9	98.9	96.7	98.2	95.5
1967	100.0	100.0	100.0	100.0	100.0	100.0
1968	106.3	106.4	106.5	106.2	104.2	108.4
1969	111.1	111.0	110.6	111.5	108.3	117.3
1970	107.8	106.4	102.3	112.3	112.2	124.5
1971	109.6	108.2	102.4	116.6	109.8	130.5
1972	119.7	118.9	113.7	126.5	113.1	139.4
1973	129.8	129.8	127.1	133.8	114.7	145.4
1974	129.3	129.4	125.7	134.6	115.3	143.7
1975	117.8	116.3	109.3	126.4	112.8	146.0
1976	130.5	130.3	122.3	141.8	114.2	151.7
1977	138.2	138.4	130.0	150.5	118.2	156.5
1978	146.1	146.8	139.7	156.9	124.0	161.4
1979	162.2	153.2	146.3	163.3	125.3	166.1
1980	147.0	146.7	136.7	161.2	132.7	168.3
1981	151.0	150.4	140.5	164.8	142.2	169.1

Source: Board of Governors of the Federal Reserve System.

BIBLIOGRAPHY

Bureau of Labor Statistics. U.S. Department of Labor.
Executive Productivity. Executive Productivity, Boca Raton, Fl. Monthly.
GOLDBERG, J. A. *Manager's Guide to Productivity Improvement.* Praeger Publishers, New York, NY, 1985.
How to Boost Company Productivity and Profits. Dartnell Corp., Chicago, IL. Looseleaf.
Index of Output Per Man-Hour, Selected Industries. U.S. Bureau of Labor Statistics.
LINK, ALBERT N., *Technological Change and Productivity Growth.* Harwood Academic Publishers, London, 1987.
National Productivity Review. Quarterly.
Productivity. Productivity, Inc., Stamford, CO. Monthly.
Productivity and the Economy: A Chartbook. Bureau of Labor Statistics.
SCHERMERHORN, J. *Management for Productivity.* John Wiley and Sons, Inc., New York, NY, 1985.
SCICTUELLA, J. "Using Employee Participation to Enhance Productivity." *The Bankers Magazine,* November/December, 1988.
STILLER, B. "Are Banks Overdosing On Technology Buying?" *Bankers Monthly,* December, 1988.

PRODUCT LIFE CYCLE Over time, the sales of a new product will first increase as the product gains market acceptance, and then decrease as competing products are introduced. All products go through such cyclical sales patterns. In the figure below, the four phases of a somewhat typical product life cycle are shown along with the pattern of sales that characterizes each stage. During the maturity stage, competitors are in their growth stage.

Product Life Cycle

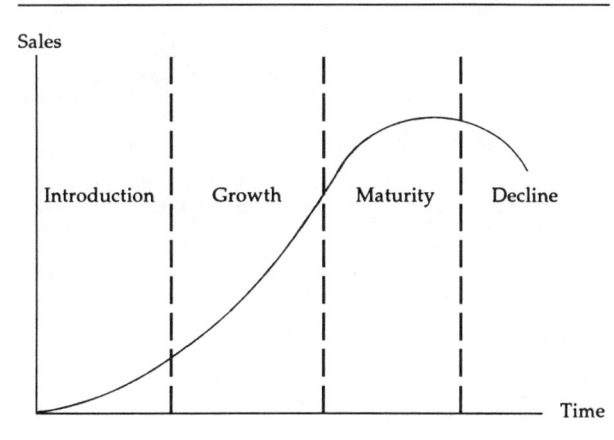

```
Sales
  |                                              
  |         |         |          |
  |         |         |          |
  |  Intro- |  Growth |  Maturity | Decline
  |  duction|         |          |
  |         |         |          |
  |_____|_____|_____|_____ Time
```

PROFESSION An association of individuals engaged in a vocation or occupation that generally is expected to meet the following criteria:

1. It renders essential service to society.
2. It depends upon a body of specialized knowledge acquired through formal education.
3. It has developed a language of its own.
4. It has requirements for admission that are regulated by law.
5. Its members are governed by ethical principles that emphasize the virtues of honesty, probity, and devotion to the welfare of those served.
6. It has procedures for disciplining those whose conduct violates ethical standards.

Typical professions include medicine, law, accounting, education, the ministry, and nursing. Many would also include banking.

The accounting profession is typically subdivided into public accountants, who function as independent experts and perform services for clients and internal accountants, who work for a particular entity. The profession can be further subdivided as follows:

Public Accountant	Internal Accounting
External auditor	Financial or general accountant
Management consultant	Cost accountant
Tax specialist	Internal auditor
	Tax accountant
	Systems analyst

A certified public accountant (CPA) is an accountant who has fulfilled certain requirements established by a state law for the practice of public accounting and becomes licensed to practice public accounting in that state. To become a CPA, an accountant must pass a comprehensive examination in accounting theory, practice, auditing, and law. In addition to the CPA examination, other professional examinations have been developed to test the competency level of practitioners. These include the Certificate in Management Accounting (CMA) and the Certified Internal Auditor (CIA).

BIBLIOGRAPHY

CAREY, JOHN L., *Getting Acquainted with Accounting*. Houghton Mifflin, Boston, 1973.

PREVITS, GARY JOHN, *The Scope of CPA Services*. John Wiley & Sons, N.Y., 1985.

PROFESSIONAL An operator who habitually makes a business of speculating in the stock market, commodity markets, or both. Speculators are divided into two classes, the professionals and the public. Professionals are traders who engage in speculation as a vocation; the public are amateur traders who enter the market as an avocation, either occasionally or continuously.

The stock market is said to have a professional appearance when the public is out of it or when participation by the public is small, and prices consequently are controlled by the professionals.

See OPERATORS.

PROFIT This term has three meanings:

1. In economics, the concept of reward of the entrepreneur for risk taking and management.
2. In business operations, the gain from manufacturing, merchandising, and selling operations after all expenses are met. Since profit normally is added to net worth, it may be measured by the increase in net worth over that of the previous accounting period. The amount of a concern's profits thus may be determined not only through the profit and loss statement, but also by a comparison of the earned surplus or net worth in balance sheets, which, however, is the residue of profits after dividends and any other appropriations and does not reveal details of sources of income and expenses, such as are found in the profit and loss statement.
3. In speculative transactions, the excess of the net selling price over the cost (including all charges) of the security or commodity traded in.

Profit is a motivating factor behind many managerial activities. Much has been written about the role (as opposed to the method of calculation) of profit. Profit plays three important roles in a capitalistic society. Profit is the financial reward for taking risk; profit is the financial reward for having monopoly power; and profit is the financial reward for having efficient management. The promise of profit provides a strong incentive to owners and managers to act efficiently. Therefore, it is common in economic theory to hypothesize that the guiding criterion by which to evaluate the actions of firms is profit maximization.

See NET PROFITS.

PROFIT AND LOSS In bookkeeping, the temporary or summary account through which all expenses and profits are cleared in order to determine the net profit or loss for the accounting period. Expenses and losses are entered on the debit side, and sales or other income items on the credit side. In banking practice, the balance of this account is carried to undivided profits. P. & L. is the abbreviation for profit and loss.

PROFIT PLANNING Planning and control are the two key ingredients involved in profit making. PLANNING is a process that (1) establishes goals and objectives, and (2) develops a decision model for selecting the means of attaining those goals and objectives. One of the major decision models used for implementing the planning process is budgeting. Three types of planning are basic to goal realization: strategic planning (a business plan), short-run planning (forecasting and budgeting), and project and situation planning.

Control is primarily the act of (1) determining that actions undertaken are in accordance with plans, and (2) using feedback to assure that goals and objectives are being attained. Control provides information concerning how well a job is being done, how effectively goals and objectives are being achieved, and how efficiently resources are being used. Controlling involves five distinct steps:

1. Establish standards to use for evaluating performance.
2. Obtain feedback information on performance.
3. Determine whether any modifying action is required under the circumstances.
4. Determine what action, if any, is required.
5. Take the necessary action to modify the situation.

Controls are usually developed around responsibility centers within the enterprise, such as cost centers, profit centers, or investment centers. Managers generally need score-card information (How well or poorly are we doing?), attention-directing information, and problem-solving information.

PROFIT SHARING BONDS *See* PARTICIPATING BONDS.

PROFIT TAKING The selling of securities or commodities when the price has advanced over that of the purchase price in order to convert paper profits into cash, i.e., to realize a profit on a speculative transaction through selling at a higher price. In a case of short selling, profit taking consists in buying (covering) when the current price has fallen below the original selling price.

PRO FORMA A statement or presentation that reports a statement or presentation that would have been shown if a different accounting principle or method had been in effect in an earlier period. For example, for certain accounting changes in the current year that affect a previous year(s), such as a change from straight-line depreciation to an accelerated depreciation method, income before extraordinary items and net income must be computed on a pro forma (as if or for the sake of form) basis for all periods presented as if the newly adopted principle had been applied during all periods affected.

PROGRAM TRADING Arbitrage between the market for stock index futures and the stock market itself. Arbitrage traders attempt to profit by buying in one market and selling in another. Program traders try to buy a stock index futures contract, such as the S&P 500 stock index, when it is cheap relative to the prices of the underlying stocks, and sell it when it is high. If the price of the futures contract becomes overvalued, program traders sell the futures and buy the stocks.

Using computers, program traders constantly track prices on the futures market and prices on the stock exchange. The computers also keep abreast of interest and dividend rates. Then if prices in the futures market get substantially out of line with what traders think they should be based on mathematical equations, the computers issue buy or sell orders. Computer information is vital to quickly identify buying and selling opportunities in the market.

By selling futures and buying the stocks at the same time, program traders create a fully hedged position. They also capture a spread, since the futures usually sell at a premium over the value of the stock (because the interest rate is usually higher than the dividend rate). When the futures contract expires, the spread goes to zero because the value of the expiring contract must equal the price of the stocks. The traders then "unwind" the programs—selling the stocks and letting the futures expire. When this occurs, they pocket the risk-free profits from the original spread, sometimes far beyond what is available on Treasury bills. In 1985, the spreads were so large that program traders could earn annualized returns that were 400 to 600 basis points above the prevailing three-month Treasury bill rate. Since that time, because more and more firms have set up program trading operations, the returns from program trading are reported to have declined.

At the end of every quarter, program traders must unwind their positions because the index futures and options expire. The last hour of trading on the stock exchange during the last day of each quarter has come to be known as the "triple witching hour," the hour at which futures, options, and index options contracts all expire at the same time. Some of these days have been marked by extreme volatility in the market, as program traders have dumped large volumes of stock on the market. This has led to concerns in some quarters as to how this volatility should be managed.

In 1989, many major players in program trading withdrew from all forms of program trading and criticized rival brokerage firms about their role in this controversial trading strategy. This computer-aided strategy for buying and selling baskets of stocks and offsetting amounts of stock-index futures has been criticized for disrupting the market and adversely affecting its integrity. Some maintain that brokerage firms compete with their customers when they employ this technique.

PROGRESSIVE TAX A tax that takes a larger percentage from higher income individuals than from lower income individuals. The federal individual income tax system is a progressive tax reflecting the ability-to-pay principle of taxation.

PROGRESSIVE DISCOUNT RATES Federal Reserve banks were permitted under the Phelan Bill, which amended Section 14(d) of the Federal Reserve Act and became law April 13, 1920, to increase the rediscount rates of those member banks whose rediscounts exceeded a specified base to which the normal rate applied. The purpose of the progressive discount rate plan was to discourage further borrowing and rediscounting at times when the volume of credit outstanding was dangerously high and when prices reached excessive levels. In the latter months of 1920, effective use was made of progressive rates in two Federal Reserve districts. The plan was put forward because the general raising of the normal REDISCOUNT RATE throughout the United States did not sufficiently restrict rediscounting operations, and as an alternative to the plan of refusing to accept certain classes of paper for rediscount regardless of the discount rate.

Section 14 (d) of the Federal Reserve Act was further revised by the Act of March 4, 1923, and the Banking Act of 1935 (August 23, 1935), so that today the section merely provides generally that every Federal Reserve bank shall have power to establish from time to time, subject to review and determination of the Board of Governors of the Federal Reserve System, rates of discount to be charged for each class of paper, which shall be fixed with a view of accommodating commerce and business.

PROMISOR One who promises to do or to forbear to do an act.

A promisor is legally responsible for fulfilling a promise made in contemplation of legal relations, provided it has been made for legally sufficient consideration and its fulfillment is not contrary to law. The maker of a note or the acceptor of a bill is a promisor, and his liability as a primary party is absolute.

PROMISSORY NOTE As defined by the Negotiable Instruments Law, an unconditional promise in writing made by one person to another, signed by the maker, engaging to pay on demand or at a fixed or determinable future time a sum certain in money, to order or to bearer.

The promissory note and the bill of exchange (draft and check) are the instruments encompassed by the Negotiable Instruments Law. Under the Uniform Commercial Code, by contrast, the broad term "commercial paper" encompasses drafts, checks, certificates of deposit, and notes.

PROMOTER A person who brings together a newly conceived business enterprise and financiers; that is, one who secures the necessary capital from financial interests, bankers, underwriters, private investors, etc., to inaugurate a new business. The promoter is a kind of middleman who discovers business opportunities and sells them to capitalists.

The function of a promoter of a new enterprise is to conceive or discover the proposition, assemble the factors, test its technical and legal feasibility, procure options upon property, patents, etc., issue the informal prospectus (not the prospectus required under the Securities Act of 1933), aid in the flotation of securities, and launch the enterprise. The promoter is in reality an entrepreneur pro tem.

Under Regulation C of the Securities and Exchange Commission, which governs every registration of securities under the Securities Act of 1933, the term "promoter" is defined to include the following:

1. Any person who, acting alone or in conjunction with one or more other persons, directly or indirectly takes initiative in founding and organizing the business or enterprise of an issuer.
2. Any person who, in connection with the founding and organizing of the business or enterprise of an issuer, directly or indirectly receives in consideration of services or property, or both services and property, 10% or more of any class of securities of the issuer or 10% or more of the proceeds from the sale of any class of securities. However, a person who receives such securities or proceeds either solely as underwriting commissions or solely in consideration of property shall not be deemed a promoter within the meaning of this definition if such person does not otherwise take part in founding and organizing the enterprise.

Since compensation of the promoter is an integral part of the registration statement, it is subject to the review of the Securities and Exchange Commission. Compensation of promoters and their activities are also subject to the blue sky laws of the various states.

There are both occasional and professional promoters. Occasional promoters may be bankers, lawyers, engineers, or business executives who, because of their business contacts and knowledge of the technical, legal, and financial phases of business, are in a position to discover propositions the exploitation of which appears to promise large returns. The professional promoter is regarded with more or less suspicion, due to the fact that in the nature of things he may optimistically attempt promotions which lack feasibility.

The promoter performs an incalculable service for society by setting into motion ideas by which the wealth of the nation is enhanced.

PROMOTERS' STOCK A special form of stock peculiar to England, sometimes also known as DEFERRED STOCK or FOUNDERS' SHARES. Such stock is issued with limited and deferred privileges as payment for the services of the promoters who have been instrumental in organizing a corporation.

In the U.S., compensation of the PROMOTER or promoters has usually been in the common stock, the extent of the compensation being dependent on the importance of the promoter's services and his bargaining power. Speculative enterprises, involving much promotion, usually provide high compensation for the promoter.

PROMOTION *See* PROMOTER.

PROPENSITY As conceived by Maynard Keynes, the propensities were the propensity to consume, the propensity to hoard (for liquidity), and the propensity to save. The propensity to consume was defined as the functional relationship between a given level of income and consumption spending out of that income. The basis for such a functional relationship was the finding that ordinarily the most important determinant of consumption spending of individuals is their level of income. In Keynes's view, changes in consumption follow changes in income ordinarily in fairly stable fashion in the same direction but by a smaller amount. From this premise, he evolved the concept that the marginal propensity to consume would ordinarily be less than "unity" (less than one), and thus the MULTIPLIER could be worked out mathematically.

The propensity to hoard was called by Keynes the liquidity function, or LIQUIDITY PREFERENCE. In Keynes's model a functional relationship between the given stock of money and the demand for liquidity (liquidity preference) determines the rate of interest.

The propensity to save, or disposition to refrain from consumption at given levels of income, was found by Keynes to be a function of income and not of the rate of interest, the latter factor being assigned minor importance as a stimulant or deterrent to saving.

In post-Keynesian terminology, F. W. Paish also introduced the concept of the marginal propensity to import, indicative of the tendency for a country to import more as its income rises, so that, paradoxically, the country's international merchandise trade balance might turn unfavorable (excess of imports over exports) as it becomes more prosperous.

BIBLIOGRAPHY

BELL, D., and KRISTOL, I., eds. *The Crisis in Economic Theory*, 1981.
LAWSON, T. "Keynesian Model Building and the Rational Expectations Critique." *Cambridge Journal of Economics*, December, 1981.
MARTY, A. L. "The Aggregate Supply Function Once Again (A Study of Keynes' Theory of Effective Demand)." *Economic Inquiry*, April, 1981.
REDHEAD, K. J. "On Keynesian Economics and the Economics of Keynes: A Suggested Interpretation." *Bulletin of Economic Research*, May, 1981.

PROPERTY As defined by the courts, the right to possession, enjoyment, and disposition of all things subject to ownership. Popularly, however, the term property is generally applied to the things themselves which are the subject of ownership.

Property is broadly classified as REAL PROPERTY and PERSONAL PROPERTY. Real property consists of land, all things growing therein or appurtenant thereto, and all rights or interests issuing out of or concerning the land. Personal property, by exclusion, is everything else that is not real property, and is defined by New York statute (Sec. 39, General Construction Law) as chattels, money, things in action, and all written instruments themselves, as distinguished from the rights or interests to which they relate by which any right, interest, lien, or encumbrance in, to, or upon property, or any debt or financial obligation, is created, acknowledged, evidenced, transferred, discharged, or defeated, wholly or in part.

In older property systems, real property constituted the major basis of wealth. In modern times, however, as the result of the development of the corporation as the principal form of business organization and diffusion of corporate ownership through widespread distribution of equities and stocks, personal property has become the more important type of property.

Eight states have community property systems. The rest are classified as common law jurisdictions. The major differences between the two systems center around property rights possessed by married persons. In a common law system, each spouse owns whatever he or she earns. In a community property system, one-half of the earnings of each spouse is considered owned by the other spouse.

PROPERTY LAW Property is either real property, personal property, or a fixture. Real property (realty) includes land and anything permanently attached the land. A building and the land on which it stands are real property. Personal property (personalty) includes all property not classified as real property or a fixture. A fixture is an item that was formerly personal property but which is affixed to real property and is considered a part of the real property.

Interest in property includes present interests (1) fee simple absolute: includes most ownership rights; may be transferred while living, without will, or by will; may be subject to mortgages, state laws, etc.; (2) fee simple defeasible: the estate reverts to a grantor upon the occurrence of a stated event.

A transfer of the legal title to real estate is done by a written instrument referred to as a deed. Deeds include warranty deeds, bargain and sale deeds, and quit-claim deeds. A warranty deed contains unconditional promises by the grantor that the grantor has title and right to convey it and that the property is free from encumbrances except as disclosed in the deed. The deed ensures quiet enjoyment (grantor nor third party with rightful claim will disturb grantee's possession), further assurance (grantor will procure documents to perfect title), and general warranty (grantor will defend title against claims of others). Bargain and sale deeds generally promise only that grantor has done nothing to impair title to the property (has not created any encumbrances) and does not warrant against prior impairments. Quit-claim deeds convey only what interest in property the grantor has. The grantor makes no warranty of title.

Recording a deed gives constructive notice to others of the grantee's ownership and serves to protect the grantee (new owner) against subsequent purchasers. A deed is valid between immediate parties without recording.

Title insurance is used to insure that title is good and covers the warranties made by the seller. Without title insurance, a purchaser's recourse is against the grantor. Standard title insurance policies generally insure against all defects of record and defects grantee may be aware of, excluding defects disclosed by survey and physical inspection of the premises. The title insurance company is liable for damages or expenses if there is a title defect or encumbrance that is insured against. Title insurance does not pass to subsequent purchasers of the property.

A lien is a claim held by one person against the property or property interest of another. Important liens against real estate include mortgage liens, judgment liens, and mechanics' liens. Mechanics' liens are claims arising from labor or material that has improved or added to the value of property. Architects, builders, subcontractors, and material suppliers usually have a right to obtain mechanics' liens.

A mortgage is a nonpossessory lien on real property to secure the performance of an obligation (usually a debt). A mortgage is an interest in real property and must be in writing. Debtor usually retains title. Debt is usually evidenced by a promissory note included in the mortgage agreement. Purchase-money mortgages are created when a seller takes a mortgage from the buyer at the time of a sale or a lender furnishes the money with which property is purchased. Mortgages are usually recorded; recording gives the same benefits as recording a deed.

When mortgaged property is sold, the buyer may assume the mortgage (the buyer becomes personally liable). The seller remains liable unless released by the mortgage holder by a novation. A novation occurs when a purchaser assumes a mortgage and the mortgagee (lender) releases the seller in writing from the mortgage. When a buyer takes "subject to" a mortgage, the buyer accepts no liability for the mortgage and the seller is primarily liable. Buyer may pay the mortgage and the mortgage holder must accept.

Mortgage holders can foreclose on the property even in the hands of the buyer.

The mortgagor (owner) retains possession and the right to use the property and may transfer the property subject to the mortgage. The mortgagor (creditor) has a lien on the property and can assign the mortgage to third parties or foreclose on the land to satisfy the debt upon default. Property properly recorded is subject to the mortgage. Foreclosure requires judicial action that directs a foreclosure sale. Court will sometimes refuse to confirm a sale if the price is so low as to be clearly unfair. The mortgagor can usually redeem the property by paying interest, debt, and related expenses. This right exists until the foreclosure sale. After the foreclosure sale, the debtor may redeem the property by paying off the loan within a statutory period. If a mortgagee forecloses and sells the property, the mortgagee must return any excess proceeds from the sale to the mortgagor. If the proceeds are insufficient to pay the obligation, the mortgagor remains indebted to the mortgagee for the deficiency.

A lease establishes a relationship between a lessor (landlord) and a lessee (tenant) resulting from contracting for possession of property for some period of time in exchange for consideration. The property reverts to the landlord at the termination of the lease. A lease is both a contract and a conveyance. Leases for more than one year must be in writing under the statute of frauds.

The tenant under the lease has a leasehold; the landlord (lessor), a reversion. A leasehold may be period to period or for a definite period of time (a lease for years). A period-to-period lease is for a fixed and determinable period of time, such as a month or year. Notice of termination must usually be given in the same amount of time as rent or tenancy period. Leases for a definite period are for a fixed amount of time and end automatically at the date of termination. Holdovers by a tenant after a definite period of time with express or implied approval of the landlord create a period-to-period lease.

Lessor promises tenant right to possession, quiet enjoyment, and fitness for use. Lessee may assign or sublease unless lease provides otherwise. Where a sublease is involved, the lessee (sublessor) remains liable on the lease. Lessor cannot take action against sublessee for rent. The lessee has the duty to pay rent at the end of the term or period of tenancy unless otherwise agreed upon. The lessee generally has the obligation to make ordinary repairs to the property, but structural repairs are the responsibility of the lessor. If a tenant wrongfully retains possession after the termination of the lease, the lessor can evict the lessee, treat as a holdover tenant, or the tenancy becomes one of period-to-period imposing upon the lessee a liability for rent under the same conditions as in the expired lease.

Leases can be terminated by an expiration of the lease, proper notice in a tenancy from period-to-period, surrender by lessee and acceptance by lessor, death of lessee (except for a period of years), and eviction.

PROPERTY, PLANT, AND EQUIPMENT Long-lived (fixed), tangible (possessing physical substance) assets that are owned by business enterprises for use in operations and are not held for investment or for resale. Property refers to a resource such as land and can include building sites, parking areas, roads, etc. Plant refers to buildings, including structures, facilities, and attached appurtenances (e.g., lighting systems, air-conditioning or heating systems, docks). Equipment includes such items as office and delivery equipment, machines, furniture, fixtures, and motor vehicles.

Property, plant, and equipment are usually presented in financial statements at historical (or acquisition) cost, adjusted for accumulated depreciation. Acquisition cost is the cash or cash equivalent required to acquire the asset, including expenditures required to put the asset into proper condition and location for use. Depreciation is a process that allocates the cost of a tangible long-lived asset, less salvage value, over its useful life in a systematic and rational manner. Except for land, other items included in property, plant, and equipment are subject to depreciation. Property, plant, and equipment are usually classified on the balance sheet after current assets and investments.

PROPERTY TAXES Governmental authorities such as counties, cities, and school districts levy taxes on real and personal property. Assessed values of property are used as the basis for setting a tax rate sufficient to raise tax revenue that will meet budget requirements. Tax rates usually are determined by using a formula similar to the following:

$$\text{Tax rate} = \frac{\text{Revenue required}}{\text{Assessed property valuation}}$$

Tax rates are usually expressed as a certain number of dollars per $100 of assessed valuation.

Accountants use various methods for accruing real and personal property taxes. The preferable method is monthly accrual using the fiscal period of the taxing jurisdiction. Property taxes are usually recognized as expenses except where capitalized (as assets) while property is being developed or prepared for use.

BIBLIOGRAPHY

DEBOER, I., and CONRAD, J. "Do High Interest Rates Encourage Property Tax Delinquency? *National Tax Journal*, December, 1988.
LADD, H. F., and BRADBURY, K. L. "City Taxes and Property Tax Bases." *National Tax Journal*, December, 1988.
POND, J. D. "Challenging Your Property Tax Assessment." *Management Accounting*, May, 1989.
VANCE, M. *Assessment for Taxation*. Vance Bibliographies, Monticello, IL, 1986.
———. *The Property Tax*, 1986.
———. *Real Property Valuation*, 1986.

PROPERTY RISK That risk involved in lending money which varies according to, and therefore is determined by, the value of the net assets or net worth of the borrower. For a loan to be well protected, the borrower should possess unpledged net tangible assets which if converted into cash would be sufficient to cover the amount of the loan, whether secured or unsecured. In the case of bills discounted, bank or trade acceptances, or unsecured commercial paper where no collateral security is offered, there is always the presumption that the borrower has current assets which, if converted into cash, would be more than sufficient to liquidate the loan. The property risk can be determined by an examination of the borrower's statement. The lending bank should always determine whether the prospective borrower had already borrowed from other lending institutions and in what amount.

The property risk is distinguished from the MORAL RISK and the BUSINESS RISK. Together they constitute the classical threefold divisions of a credit risk. Property risk is usually regarded as less important than the moral or business risk.

See CREDIT, CREDIT RISK.

PROPORTIONAL TAX A tax that takes the same percentage of income from each individual. Advocates of a flat federal income tax system are proponents of proportionalism.

PROPRIETARY COMPANY A controlling company, or PARENT COMPANY. A proprietary company is usually not an operating company.

PROPRIETORSHIP A firm owned by one individual called a proprietor. In this type of organization the owner makes all of the business decisions and earns all of the profits. Legally, the owner is responsible for all of the firm's debts and liabilities. As one might expect, individual proprietorships are generally small and operate with only a few employees. In comparison with other forms of firm ownership — partnerships and corporations — proprietorships are the largest in terms of numbers, but they have grown in number at the slowest rate (about 2% per year).

PRORATION Restriction of output of crude OIL through allocation of production, imposed on either a voluntary or a compulsory basis, for the purpose of conservation and maintaining orderly markets for crude oil.

Proration is imposed by the states in varying degrees of strictness, ranging from the compulsory proration imposed by Texas through its Railroad Commission (the State Public Service Commission) to the largely voluntary proration imposed by the Oil Conservation Committee of California. On the other hand, no proration at all is imposed by Illinois, one of the important producing states. The Interstate Oil Compact among the states is given recognition by Congress, which under the Connally Hot Oil Act prohibits the interstate shipment of oil produced in excess of that established as allowable by state proration laws. The basis for establishing the allowables under state proration laws is the monthly estimate of demand for crude oil prepared by the Bureau of Mines in the U.S. Department of the Interior.

PROSPECT This term has two meanings:

1. A possible customer; a person, firm, or corporation whose business is desired and solicited, but with whom no business relations have been established.
2. In extractive industries, a new development such as a mine or a newly drilled well.

PROSPECTUS In September 1980, the SEC established the first of a series of revisions intended to improve disclosure and bring about the integration of the disclosure systems under the 1933 and 1934 acts. Final rules were announced relating to (1) amendments to the annual report, Form 10-K, and related forms, rules, regulations, and guides; (2) amendments to Regulations S-X, which proposed to eliminate the differences between the requirements of generally accepted accounting principles and Regulation S-X; and (3) uniform financial statement instructions for forms and reports required under the federal securities laws. These changes make it easier to incorporate a number of items required in the Form 10-K by reference to the annual report. The ultimate goal of the SEC is to find a way to differentiate between user constituencies, to improve financial reporting in general, and reduce the costs of compliance.

The new procedures allow for an abbreviated format for registering securities issued in business combinations that do not significantly affect the issuer. Abbreviation is accomplished and duplication is avoided by having the issuer provide its annual report to security holders. The prospectus contains only information about the particular transaction and about the company being acquired.

A document that describes a new security issue. The prospectus is in the form of a circular, letter, notice, or advertisement that offers a security for sale and is filed with the SECURITIES AND EXCHANGE COMMISSION as part of the registration statement. The securities acts of 1933-1934 were intended to provide the investing public with full and fair disclosure of information necessary to evaluate the merits of security offerings. The acts requires that a registration statement be filed with the SEC. To give the investing public information included in the registration statements, a prospectus is to be provided potential investors before or at the time of the sale or delivery of the securities.

The significance of the requirement of the prospectus under the Securities Act of 1933 is that it is the direct means whereby the full disclosure of material facts concerning a publicly offered security may be communicated to investors. The prospectus is an integral part of the REGISTRATION STATEMENT, which is on public record and available to all in all its detailed entirety. But it is the prospectus which is required to reach the investor and which will execute the objective of the act.

It has been argued that in practice the average lay investor has neither the time nor the background to analyze and comprehend the prospectuses sent him, and that therefore the requirement is a waste of effort and money. The objective of the act, however, is satisfied if the investor is supplied the facts; if the investor ignores them or, lacking personal knowledge and capacity, fails to have them interpreted for him by qualified analysts, that is the investor's personal risk of lack of diligence. Certainly, as compared with the bulky, technically worded prospectuses that first appeared following the passage of the act, the modern prospectus has become more summarized and readable for the lay investor. The Securities and Exchange Commission requires that "all information required to be included in a prospectus shall be clearly understandable without the necessity of referring to the particular form or to the General Rules and Regulations. Except as to financial statements and information required in tabular form, the information set forth in a prospectus may be expressed in condensed or summarized form. Financial statements included in a prospectus are to be set forth in comparative form if practicable, and shall include the notes thereto and the accountants' certificate." No matter how condensed, however, the prospectus is an objective statement of material facts without puffing or slanting, not sales literature. Interpretation and value judgments are for the investor to make.

Related to the problem of content of the prospectus has been the problem of its use for dissemination of information prior to the effective date of the registration statement. Prior to amendment of the Securities Act of 1933 by P.L. 577 (68 Stat. 683), approved August 10, 1954, and effective October 10, 1954, the act prohibited the offering of a security for sale as well as the actual consummation of a sale prior to the effective date. The SEC took the view that it has always been a basic purpose of the act that information concerning securities to be offered to the public should be given widespread distribution during the waiting period (minimum of twenty days) between the date of filing and the effective date of the registration statement. Nevertheless, sellers of securities considered it a difficult distinction that it was lawful and desirable to disseminate information during the waiting period but illegal to offer to sell or to solicit offers to buy. The amended act now permits written offers during the waiting period by means of a prospectus (standard "red herring" prospectus, or preliminary summary prospectus) which meets the requirements of the SEC's rules. The act, however, continues to make actual sales, contracts of sale, and contracts to sell unlawful before the registration statement becomes effective. Delivery of the final (statutory) prospectus is still required, no later than at the time of delivery of the security after sale (Sec. 5(b)(2) of the act), whether the preliminary prospectus ("red herring") or the summary prospectus is used, so that they represent extra expense for the issuer.

The "red herring" prospectus is a standard prospectus, except for the omission of information with respect to the offering price, underwriting discounts or commissions, discounts or commissions to dealers, amount of proceeds, conversion rates, call prices, or other matters dependent upon the offering price. The outside front cover must carry, in red ink, the caption "Preliminary Prospectus," the date of its issuance, and the following statement printed in type as large as at of the body of the prospectus:

A registration statement relating to these securities has been filed with the Securities and Exchange Commission, but has not yet become effective. Information contained herein is subject to completion or amendment. These securities may not be sold nor may offers to buy be accepted prior to the time the registration statement becomes effective. This prospectus shall not constitute an offer to sell or the solicitation of an offer to buy nor shall there be any sale of these securities in any State in which such offer, solicitation or sale would be unlawful prior to registration or qualification under the securities laws of any such State.

The summary prospectus, an even more summarized version of the standard prospectus, is now permitted (Rule 434a) under specified conditions (reports or minimum size and earning power of registrants). This "tabloid" prospectus may be used prior to the effective date of the registration statement, in which event it must carry the "red herring" statement (see above) as a "Preliminary Summary Prospectus," or on and after the effective date. Either type must set forth at its beginning or end a conspicuously printed statement that COPIES OF A MORE COMPLETE PROSPECTUS MAY BE OBTAINED FROM (INSERT NAME OR NAMES). "All information included in a summary prospectus... may be expressed in such condensed or summarized form as may be appropriate in the light of the circumstances under which the prospectus is to be used. The information need not follow the numerical sequence of the items used for registration and no information, other than the capitalization table and the summary of earnings, need be given in tabular form" (Rule 434a). Abbreviated as this prospectus may be, and twice removed from the complete exposition of the registration statement, it is still a vast improvement over the one-page models of brevity which characterized offering circulars in pre-Securities Act times.

Other release of information by issuers whose securities are in registration has been the basis for the issuance of guidelines by the Securities and Exchange Commission (Securities Act of 1933, Release No. 5180, August 16, 1971). The SEC emphasizes that there is no basis in the securities acts or in any policy of the commission which would justify the practice of nondisclosure of factual information by a publicly held company on the grounds that it has securities in registration under the Securities Act of 1933. However, neither a company in registration nor its representatives should instigate publicity for the purpose of facilitating the sale of securities in a proposed offering; and any publication of information by a company in registration other than by means of a statutorily authorized prospectus should be limited to factual information and should not include such things as predictions, projections, forecasts, or opinions with respect to value.

Emphasizing the objective role of the Securities and Exchange Commission, every prospectus must set forth on the outside front cover page the following statement in boldface capital letters: THESE SECURITIES HAVE NOT BEEN APPROVED OR DISAPPROVED BY THE SECURITIES AND EXCHANGE COMMISSION NOR HAS THE COMMISSION PASSED UPON THE ACCURACY OR ADEQUACY OF THIS PROSPECTUS. ANY REPRESENTATION TO THE CONTRARY IS A CRIMINAL OFFENSE.

If the registrant or any underwriter knows or has reasonable grounds to believe that there is an intention to overallot or that the price of any security may be stabilized (pursuant to SEC rules) to facilitate the offering of the registered securities, the following statement must appear in the prospectus, either on the outside front cover page or on the inside front cover page, substantially in the following form: IN CONNECTION WITH THIS OFFERING, THE UNDERWRITERS MAY OVERALLOT OR EFFECT TRANSACTIONS WHICH STABILIZE OR MAINTAIN THE MARKET PRICE OF (identifying each class of securities in which such transactions may be effected) AT A LEVEL ABOVE THAT WHICH MIGHT OTHERWISE PREVAIL IN THE OPEN MARKET. SUCH TRANSACTIONS MAY BE EFFECTED (identifying each exchange on which stabilizing transactions may be effected). SUCH STABILIZING, IF COMMENCED, MAY BE DISCONTINUED AT ANY TIME. Such stabilizing of the price of a security in order to facilitate an offering is expressly permitted (Rule 10b-7, under the Securities Exchange Act of 1934), subject to enumerated constraints and to reporting requirements (Rule 17a-2).

Another problem related to the prospectus is its use after effective date of registration. The act requires sellers of securities to deliver prospectuses to purchasers in the initial distribution of a security, regardless of how long the distribution might take. Prior to its amendment by P.L. 577, *supra*, the act also required the delivery of the prospectus by securities dealers in trading transactions for one year after the commencement of an offering, even though the initial distribution of the security had been long since completed. The amendment reduced the one-year period to 40 days after the effective date or after commencement of the public offering, whichever was later. However, if the issuer has not made a previous offering under an effective registration statement under the act, the aforementioned 40-day period is extended to 90 days. A dealer still disposing of an unsold allotment or otherwise still participating in an initial distribution must continue to deliver the prospectus as long as he is still thus engaged. Investment companies which continuously offer their securities (the open-end or mutual funds) must under the amended act use prospectuses in all transactions, so long as securities of the same class are currently being offered or sold by the issuer or by or through an underwriter.

To keep the content of prospectuses up to date, before amendment the act required that prospectuses which are used more than 13 months after the effective date of a registration statement should contain information as of a date within one year of such use. As amended, the act provides that where a prospectus is used more than 9 months after the effective date, the information contained therein shall be as of a date within 16 months of such use.

The act (Sec. 3(b)) authorizes the Securities and Exchange Commission to exempt, by its rules and regulations and subject to such terms and conditions as it may prescribe, any class of securities from regular registration under the act if it finds that the enforcement of such requirement with respect to such securities is not necessary in the public interest and for the protection of investors, by reason of the small amount involved or the limited character of the public offering.

Rule 242. On January 17, 1980, the SEC adopted Rule 242, pursuant to Section 3(b) of the Securities Act of 1933. This rule provides an exemption from the registration provisions, and hence from the requirement of the prospectus, for sales by domestic small corporate issuers of securities up to $2 million in any 6-month period to an unlimited number of accredited investors, as defined in the rule, and to 35 nonaccredited persons. The rule itself does not require the issuer to furnish an offering circular to investors if only accredited persons are involved in such a Rule 242 offering, based upon the presumption that these types of investors "are able to fend for themselves." If, however, a Rule 242 offering involves one or more nonaccredited persons, the issuer must furnish all purchasers, including both accredited and nonaccredited persons, the same kind of information as that specified in Registration Form S-18 to the extent it is material, except for certain financial information.

Form S-18 is the simplified registration form for small businesses, calling for substantially less narrative and financial disclosure than Form S-1, which is the form such issuers would otherwise use for registration of their securities. In a further effort to reduce the registration burden on small issuers, the SEC designed the Form S-18 to contain all the disclosure requirements within the confines of the form itself so that the preparer need not seek out any cross references to other rules and forms. Form S-18 is available to certain domestic and Canadian corporate issuers for the registration of up to $5 million of their securities to be sold for cash.

BIBLIOGRAPHY

ELTON, E. J., and others. "New Public Offerings, Information, and Investor Rationality: The Case of Public Offered Commodity Funds." *Journal of Business*, January, 1989.
SECURITIES AND EXCHANGE COMMISSION. *Annual Report*.

PROSPERITY   That phase of the trade cycle characterized by business activity, as shown by the volume of trade and bank clearings, rising prices, large profits, low percentage of business failures, high wages, liberal buying, etc. This phase of the business cycle usually follows the period of recuperation, which in turn follows a depression. The close of a period of prosperity is likely to be characterized by inflated bank credit and currency, low bank reserves, high money rates, high commodity prices and wages, and speculative activity and profiteering, until finally a crisis arises, which is a reaction against the period of high prices and marks the end of prosperity.

See BUSINESS CYCLE.

PROTECTIONISM   Governmental or political pressure, policy, and/or regulation intended to improve the position of a domestic producer relative to a foreign producer (as opposed to free trade policies). Typical policies include increasing the home market price of the foreign product, decreasing the cost of domestic producers, or restricting the access of foreign producers to the home market. Arguments for restricting trade include national defense, income redistribution favoring some disadvantaged group, optimum tariff argument related to the exercise of economic power, job protection, protection of infant industries, spillover effects to other industries, support of a strategic trade policy, reciprocity and the "level playing field," and the balance of trade policies. Major protectionist devices include tariffs, quotas, regulatory barriers, subsidies, and exchange controls.

TARIFFS are taxes imposed on goods entering a country from abroad. U.S. tariff rates peaked in the twentieth century following the Smoot-Hawley Tariff of 1930. QUOTAS limit the number of products importers can sell in the home market over specific periods. Orderly marketing agreements or voluntary export restraints have been employed in recent years. The U.S.-Japan automobile agreement in the 1980s is one such example. Regulatory barriers are often found in the tariff code. Product standards are a form of regulatory barriers. Subsidies are sometimes associated with an industry or with export activities of an industry. The U.S. shipbuilding industry has received subsidies that include credit programs, special tax incentives, and direct subsidy payments. Exchange controls restrict access to the foreign money required to buy foreign goods. The central bank can be used to hold down the exchange rate by buying foreign exchange with domestic currency.

Haufbauer, Berliner, and Elliott (1986) examined the cost of protectionism in the United States in 31 cases in which trade volume exceeded $100 million and the United States imposed protectionist trade restrictions. Their figures indicate that annual consumer losses exceeded $100 million in all but six of the cases. The largest losses, $27 billion per year, came from protecting the textile and apparel industries. There were also large consumer losses associated with protection in carbon steel ($6.8 billion), automobiles ($0.8 billion) and dairy products ($5.5 billion). Domestic producers were the primary beneficiaries of protectionist policies although foreign producers also realized large gains. Total losses to consumers is enormous. A study (1982) by the Organization for Economic Cooperation and Development analyzed the costs and benefits of protectionist policies in manufacturing in OECD countries. The study indicates that costs generated far exceeded benefits obtained.

BIBLIOGRAPHY

Hufbauer, Gary Clyde, Diane T. Berliner, and Kimberly Ann Elliott. *Trade Protection in the United States: 31 Case Studies.* Institute for International Economics, 1986.
Hickok, Susan. "The Consumer Cost of U.S. Trade Restraints," Federal Reserve Bank of New York, *Quarterly Review.* Summer 1985, pp. 1-12.
Krugman, Paul R. *Strategic Trade Policy and the New International Economics*, MIT Press, 1986.
Organization for Economic Co-Operation and Development (OECD). *Costs and Benefits of Protection.* (1985).
World Bank. *World Development Report*, 1987, Oxford University Press, 1987.

PROTECTIVE DEVICES Being depositories for large amounts of cash and other valuables which are negotiable by delivery, banks are subject to attacks by hold-up men, burglars, and safe-blowers. Defensive measures have kept pace with offensive tactics. Among the banks in larger cities, the employment of special guards in uniform is an almost universal practice. Their purpose is preventative as well as furnishing a means of apprehending hold-up men in case an assault is attempted. The daring of hold-up men is in direct proportion to chances of success, and hold-ups are not likely where the promise of success is slight.

Modern banks are equipped with various kinds of protective equipment. Safes and vaults are now made with armor plate consisting of an alloy steel that is as nearly burglar-proof as possible. Other means of protecting a bank, and especially its cash, are the following:

1. Electric signal systems communicating with a local burglar alarm company, prepared upon alarm to dispatch detectives in case of trouble. For night protection this system involves a periodic turning in of signals from electric signal boxes located in various parts of the bank building.
2. Emergency alarms with buttons placed at the fingertips of tellers to call special guards located at other stations in the bank.
3. Bulletproof armored glass in front of the teller's cage to protect the paying teller and the cash in his cage.
4. Automatic door-closing devices operating from the paying teller's cage to close all means of escape to hold-up men who may attempt an assault.
5. A time lock and a burglar alarm signal on the door of the vault or safe.

For the protection of checks against alterations and forgeries, see CHECK PROTECTING DEVICES.

See FINGERPRINT IDENTIFICATION, FEDERAL RESERVE BOARD REGULATIONS (Regulation P), VAULT.

PROTECT PROFITS STOPS Stop orders placed with a broker by a client to protect profits on a security once they have accumulated. Stop orders are generally regarded as stop loss orders, and in a sense they are since they are placed at a point below the current market and if executed give a realized amount something less than the maximum that might have been attained. Many stop orders are placed, however, to ensure the realization of a part of the paper profit that has accumulated. In this sense, such a stop order is for the purpose of protecting profits rather than preventing increased losses.

See STOP LOSS ORDER.

PROTEST The written certification by a notary public that a negotiable instrument has been presented for acceptance or payment and has been dishonored (nonaccepted or payment refused). Protest normally is executed under the hand and seal of a notary public, but it may also be made by a respectable citizen in the presence of two or more credible witnesses. Foreign bills of exchange (drawn in one state and payable in another) must be protested, as failure to do so will discharge the endorsers and the drawer. Inland bills of exchange (drawn and payable in the same state) need not be protested, as oral or any kind of notice will be sufficient to bind the endorsers and drawer. Because of the evidentiary value of the notarial protest certificate as prima facie evidence of presentment, dishonor, and notice which shifts the burden of proof upon being produced, it is desirable to have the instrument protested even if it is an inland bill or if the foreign bill does not show on its face that it is foreign. For the necessary elements of protest, see NOTARIAL PROTEST CERTIFICATE.

See NEGOTIABLE INSTRUMENTS LAW (Section 3-501, Uniform Commercial Code).

PROTEST FEES Fees paid to the notary public before whom PROTEST of a negotiable instrument is made, and any other incidental charges in connection with protest. Protest fees are ordinarily paid by the holder of the instrument at the protest. Where such protest is necessary in order to fix the liability of the parties, as in the case of a foreign bill of exchange, protest fees may be recovered by the holder from the drawer, the acceptor, or the last endorser, as they are in the nature of special damages or expenses arising out of the dishonor. Where protest is not necessary in order to charge the parties, as in the case of inland bills of exchange, there is a conflict of authority among the courts as to whether the drawer would be chargeable with protest fees.

PROTEST FOR NONACCEPTANCE Protest of a time foreign (out of state) bill of exchange for refusal of the drawee to accept. When a foreign bill appearing on its face to be such is dishonored by nonacceptance, it must be duly protested for nonacceptance. If it is not so protested, the drawer or any endorsers are discharged. (See NEGOTIABLE INSTRUMENTS LAW (Sec. 3-502, Uniform Commercial Code).) Protest of a domestic time bill of exchange for nonacceptance is not required, but is desirable because of the evidentiary value of the notarial certificate.

See NOTARIAL PROTEST CERTIFICATE.

PROTEST FOR NONPAYMENT See PROTEST.

PROTEST WAIVED When there are no endorsements on a negotiable instrument or when the endorser writes "protest waived," or words of similar import, above his signature as an endorser on the instrument, protest is not necessary to hold the endorser liable. When the waiver is embodied in the instrument itself, it is binding on all parties. According to Section 13 of the Federal Reserve Act, when notes are rediscounted for a member bank, they must be endorsed by such bank, and such endorsement shall be deemed a "waiver of demand, notice and protest."

See NEGOTIABLE INSTRUMENTS LAW (Section 3-511, Uniform Commercial Code).

PROXY Authority given in writing, legally witnessed, by which a stockholder confers upon other person(s) the power to vote the voting stock owned by him at a specified meeting of stockholders or adjournment thereof. In most large corporations, many of the stockholders find it impossible, even if interested, to attend stockholders' meetings in person. Since shares of voting stock carry the right to vote as one of the rights of ownership, the right may be conferred upon someone else by statutory authority of the state corporation laws. In common law, however, the stockholder cannot vote by proxy; a vestige of this tradition persists in modern times in the practices of special kinds of corporations such as religious corporations. State business corporation laws usually impose a limitation on the valid duration of a proxy. For example, Delaware provides that a proxy not specifying a longer duration will expire three years from its date; New York provides for expiration in eleven months unless the proxy specifies a longer definite duration. The proxy is a revocable power of attorney; it may be superseded by a later dated proxy or by appearance of the stockholder in person to vote at the specified meeting.

In modern corporate practice, a proxy committee nominated by the board of directors is elected by stockholders at the annual meeting. The proxy committee's members are the individuals whose names will appear on the "management" proxies sent to stockholders and who will vote for the "management" slate of directors at the meeting. Thus a high enough proxy vote will assure election of the management's nominees as directors. In the case of large corporations, with the majority of stock held by thousands of small holders, this proxy system is conducive to continuation of control by existing management and its nominees. If the management merits such perpetuation, the best interests of the corporation are served. If not, the proxy system affords a position of entrenchment for incumbents, which is difficult to overcome.

SEC Proxy Rules and Information Rules. Regulation 14A of the Securities and Exchange Commission under the Securities Exchange Act of 1934, implementing Section 14(a) of that act, governs the manner in which proxies or other authorizations may be solicited from the holders of securities registered under Section 12 of that act, whether for the election of directors, approval of other corporate action, or some other purpose. This regulation also applies to security holders of registered public utility holding companies (Public Utility Holding Company Act of 1935) and their subsidiaries and registered investment companies (Investment Company Act of 1940).

As summarized by the SEC, the regulation requires that in any solicitation, whether by the management or by minority groups, disclosure must be made of all material facts concerning the matters on which such holders are asked to vote, and they must be afforded an opportunity to vote "yes" or "no" on each matter. The regulation also provides, among other things, that where the management is soliciting proxies, any security holder desiring to communicate with other security holders "for a proper purpose" may require the management to furnish him with a list of all security holders or to mail his communication to security holders for him (such holder to defray the reasonable expenses thereof to be incurred by the issuer). A security holder may also require the management to include in its proxy material any appropriate proposal which he wants to submit to a vote of security holders. But he is subject to certain limitations: (1) submission of such proposal at least 60 days prior to the first date on which the management proxy material is released to security holders, and (2) statement by the security holder of the proposal in not more than 100 words, if the management opposes the proposal. Further, if the proposal as submitted is not a proper subject for action by security holders under the laws of the issuer's domicile or if it "clearly appears that the proposal is submitted by the security holder primarily for the purpose of enforcing a personal claim or redressing a personal grievance against the issuer or its management" or "primarily for the purpose of promoting general economic, political, racial, religious, social, or similar cause," the management is not required to include the proposal.

Any security holder or group of security holders may at any time make an independent proxy solicitation upon compliance with the proxy rules, whether or not the management is making a solicitation. Additional detailed provisions of the regulation apply where a contest for control of the management of an issuer or representation on the board of directors is involved.

Among the circumstances under which the management may omit a proposal and any statement in support thereof from its proxy statement and form of proxy is the repetitive situation. Where substantially the same proposal has previously been submitted to security holders in the management's proxy statement and form of proxy relating to any annual or special meeting of security holders held within the preceding five calendar years, it may be omitted from the management's proxy material relating to any meeting of security holders held within the three calendar years after the latest such previous submission, in the following situations:

1. If the proposal was submitted at only one meeting during such preceding period, and it received less than 3% of the total number of votes cast in regard thereto; or
2. If the proposal was submitted at only two meetings during such preceding period, and it received at the time of its second submission less than 6% of the total number of votes cast in regard thereto; or
3. If the proposal was submitted at three or more meetings during such preceding period, and it received at the time of its latest submission less than 10% of the total number of votes cast in regard thereto.

Similarly subject to omission would be a proposal merely consisting of a recommendation or request that the management take action with respect to matters relating to the conduct of the ordinary business operations of the issuer.

Copies of proposed proxy material must be filed with the Securities and Exchange Commission in preliminary form prior to the date of the proposed solicitation. Where preliminary material fails to meet the prescribed disclosure standards, the management or other group responsible for its preparation is notified informally and given an opportunity to correct the deficiencies in the preparation of the definitive proxy material to be furnished to security holders.

Under Section 14(c) of the Securities Exchange Act of 1934, issuers of securities registered under Section 12 must, in accordance with rules and regulations prescribed by the commission, transmit information comparable to proxy material to security holders from whom proxies are not solicited with respect to a stockholders' meeting. Regulation 14C of the commission implements this provision by setting forth the requirements for information statements.

Special provision (Rule 14a-11) is made for solicitations of proxies and submissions of material in election contests (otherwise known as proxy battles). Such solicitors of proxies are required to file with the SEC (Schedule 14B) information as to identity and background, interests in securities of the issuer and details of acquisition, and information on arrangements or understandings with respect to future employment or transactions with the issuer. Three copies of any soliciting material shall be filed in advance with the SEC, which thus may apply fair disclosure standards without becoming involved in censorship.

Amendments to Proxy Regulation. The SEC on December 6, 1978, approved various amendments to Regulation 14A and to Schedule 14A which call for more detail to be furnished to stockholders concerning such additional details of corporate governance as structure, composition, and functioning of issuers' board of directors; resignation of directors; and the terms of settlement of any proxy contests. Specific parts of Regulation 14A were amended as follows.

In Item 6(b), new information as to composition of the board of directors calls for a brief description, in tabular form, "to the extent possible," of any of "certain significant economic and personal relationships which exist between a director and an issuer." Examples include the following:

1. Whether the nominee or director has had a principal occupation or employment with any of the issuer's parent companies, subsidiaries, or affiliates during the last five years.
2. Information as to "any blood, marriage, or adoption relationships (except relationships more remote than first cousins)" of a nominee or director to a person holding office as an executive officer of the issuer's parent companies, subsidiaries, or affiliates.
3. Details of the "economic relationships" with the issuer by a nominee or director who is or has been within the last two fiscal years an officer, director, employee, or owner of an interest in excess of 1% of the equity of an entity which as customer or supplier of the issuer has had or will have business transactions of specified size with the issuer.
4. Information as to whether "the nominee or director is a member or employee of or is associated with a law firm which the issuer has retained in the last two full fiscal years or proposes to retain in the current fiscal year."
5. Information as to the nominee or director being a director, partner, officer, or employee of any investment banking firm which has performed services for the issuer other than as a participating underwriter in a syndicate in the last two full fiscal years or which the issuer proposes to have perform services in the current year.
6. Information as to whether the nominee or director is a "control person of the issuer" (other than solely as a director of the issuer).
7. Any other relationships between the nominee or director and the issuer or its management substantially similar in nature and scope to the preceding.

In addition, Item 6(d) of Regulation 14A now calls for information as to "whether or not the issuer has a standing audit, nominating and compensation committee of the board of directors, or committees performing similar functions." As to the nominating committee, the issuer is asked to indicate "whether that committee will consider nominees recommended by shareholders," and if so, to indicate the procedures to be followed by shareholders in submitting such recommendations. Item 6(e) requires information as to "the total number of meetings of the board of directors (including regularly scheduled and special meetings) held during the last full fiscal year" and identification of any "incumbent director who during the last full fiscal year attended fewer than 75 percent of the aggregate of (1) the total number of meetings of the board of directors (held during the period for which he has been a director) and (2) the total number of meetings held by all committees of the board on which he served (during the period that he served)."

Item 6(f), moreover, states that if a director has resigned or declined to stand for reelection since the date of the last annual meeting because of a disagreement as to the issuer's "operations, policies, or practices, and if the director has furnished the issuer with a letter describing such disagreement and requesting that the matter be disclosed, the issuer shall state the date of resignation or declination to stand for reelection and summarize the director's description of the disagreement."

If the issuer intends to include in the proxy solicitation statement a statment in opposition to a resolution proposed by a shareholder, a copy of this statement must be sent to such shareholder not later than ten days before the issuer's proxy materials are filed with the SEC. The regulation also requires that settlements of election contests be specified as to terms. Item 8 of Schedule 14A calls for the proxy statements issued after September 30, 1978, to contain such details on services provided by the issuer's independent accountant as the following:

1. The services provided in the last fiscal year.
2. The percentage relationship of the aggregate fees for all nonaudit services paid to the accountant to the audit fees.
3. Whether the issuer's board of directors or its audit or comparable committee approved each such service.
4. Circumstances and details of any services provided by the accountant "that were furnished at rates or terms that were not customary."
5. Any existing direct or indirect understanding or agreement placing a limit on current or future years' audit fees, "including fee arrangements that provide fixed limits on fees that are not subject to reconsideration if unexpected issues involving accounting or auditing are encountered."

Shareholder Proposals. Typical of stockholder proposals submitted to a vote of security holders are resolutions relating to amendments to charters or bylaws to provide for cumulative voting for the election of directors; limitations on the granting of stock options and their exercise by key employees and management groups; the sending of post-meeting report to all stockholders; changing the place of the annual meeting of stockholders; and the approval by stockholders of management's selection of independent auditors.

Policy Toward Proxy Contests. The ultimate form of protest against inefficient management is the sale of holdings by the individual or institutional holder. *Pension Funds and Economic Freedom*, by Robert Tilove, published by the Fund for the Republic, reports that institutional holders "vote their proxies persistently on the management side of the proposals submitted to stockholders," including the "independent proposals" directed "innocuously" toward the above objectives. Motivations are various, but it would seem important for such investing institutions as investment companies to keep their informal pipelines of contacts with corporate managements intact by staying friendly with managements, even when investing policy might call for recurrent shifts in holdings. Such contacts are invaluable for keeping posted on corporate developments and trends, and are vital for diligent administration of holdings. Where more serious situations develop, such as proxy battles between opposing managerial factions, ad hoc consideration of the relative merits of the rivals would lead to more variation in attitude of institutional investors and investing institutions.

Voting by proxies by members of national securities exchanges is subject to rules of the exchanges, requiring the member firms to give proxy for stock registered in the name of the firm at the direction of the beneficial owner.

See NEW YORK STOCK EXCHANGE (Rules 450-460).

BIBLIOGRAPHY

ACEITUNO, T. A. "1988 Proxy Season Established New Force in Corporate America." *Pension World*, April, 1989.
SECURITIES AND EXCHANGE COMMISSION. *Annual Report*.

PRUDENT MAN RULE A legal concept of prudence. For example, a prudent man will not invest in speculative securities, will diversify to spread risks and avoid a catastrophic loss, and will remain relatively liquid so that distributions and payments can be made. The prudent man rule has special applications to situations involving estates and trusts.

PUBLIC ACCOUNTANT A professional accountant or auditor whose services are available for the auditing of books, installation of accounting systems, and preparation of financial statements, tax returns, valuations, etc. If the public accountant passes an examination provided by the state, he is given a certificate and is entitled to call himself a CERTIFIED PUBLIC ACCOUNTANT.
See AUDITOR.

PUBLIC ADMINISTRATOR A public official who is appointed to administer the estates of intestate persons whose heirs cannot be immediately determined or located or who is appointed in lieu of a private administrator.
See ADMINISTRATOR.

PUBLIC CREDIT The credit enjoyed by a national government, state, county, municipality, etc. The same principles govern public credit as govern commercial, agricultural, banking, and other forms of credit. Thus, a government, state, or municipality may have a good or bad credit standing, depending upon its reputation and ability to pay its obligations.

PUBLIC DEBT A debt associated with the NATIONAL DEBT because of official reference to the federal government's debt as the "public debt of the United States." Although the term is thus in practice restricted in meaning to the federal debt, in the nontechnical sense it is applicable to all public debt incurred by sovereign jurisdictions—the federal government, the states and political subdivisions thereof, and municipalities.

See INTERNAL DEBTS, NATIONAL BUDGET.

The federal government debt consists of the direct and guaranteed obligations issued by the U.S. government and its instrumentalities. Treasury obligations are issued pursuant to authority of the second Liberty Bond Act, approved September 24, 1917, as amended. Section 21 (31 U.S.C. 757b) as amended imposes a debt limit on the face amount of obligations issued under the act and obligations guaranteed as to principal and interest by the United States. The appended table shows the public debt and interest paid of the federal government: 1940-1987.

The variety of issues as to types and maturities indicates the tailoring by the Treasury of offerings so as to reach a maximum market. In both new money and refunding operations in debt management, the Treasury is guided by major objectives as follows: first, to secure the funds as much as possible from true savers rather than from commercial banks, in order to reduce the inflationary potential of Treasury financing during a period of rising economic activity; second, to secure the necessary funds at as reasonable cost as possible, consistent with the primary goal of contributing to sound economic growth; third, to reduce the frequency of its operations and otherwise plan its borrowing programs so as to interfere as little as possible with Federal Reserve conduct of monetary policy.

For further data on types of U.S. government issues and financing, *see* UNITED STATES GOVERNMENT SECURITIES, TREASURY SECURITIES.

PUBLIC DEPOSITS Deposits in banks by the federal government, states, political subdivisions, and municipalities.

Under Section 10 of the Act of June 11, 1942 (12 U.S.C. 265), all insured banks designated for the purpose of the secretary of the Treasury may be depositaries of public monies of the United States.

Beginning in March, 1951, special depositories of public monies designated under the provisions of Treasury Circular No. 92 were permitted to accept for deposit in their Treasury tax and loan accounts, funds representing checks of $10,000 or more received by collectors of Internal Revenue on account of income taxes, excess profits taxes, and interest or penalties, including deficiencies and payments of estimated taxes. These checks drawn on a bank could be carried by the bank as such Treasury deposits after the checks had been deposited by tax collectors for the Treasury's account in the Federal Reserve banks. The credits arising in Treasury tax and loan accounts from these tax payments were designated "x" balances, and would be drawn on first before calls were made on other credits in tax and loan accounts. As a result, there would be no immediate impact on bank reserves resulting from the heavy payment of taxes, since the commercial banks involved would simply transfer funds from the taxpayers' accounts to Treasury deposits and the Treasury would draw on these funds over a period of time.

Under authority of P.L. 95-147, the Treasury implemented a program on November 2, 1978, to invest a portion of its operating

No. 496. Public Debt and Interest Paid of the Federal Government: 1940 to 1987

(Total *public debt* is restricted to borrowing by the Treasury and the value of savings bonds at current redemption value. Minus sign (−) indicates decrease.)

Year	Public debt Total[1] (bil. dol.)	Average annual percent change[2]	Per capita[3] (dol.)	Interest paid Total (bil. dol.)	Percent of Federal outlays[4]
1940	43.0	8.4	325	1.0	10.5
1945	258.7	43.0	1,849	3.8	4.1
1950	256.1	−.1	1,688	5.7	13.4
1955	272.8	1.3	1,651	6.4	9.4
1960	284.1	.9	1,572	9.2	10.0
1965	313.8	2.0	1,613	11.3	9.6
1970	370.1	3.3	1,814	19.3	9.9
1971	397.3	7.4	1,921	21.0	10.0
1972	426.4	7.3	2,037	21.8	9.4
1973	457.3	7.2	2,164	24.2	9.8
1974	474.2	3.7	2,223	29.3	10.9
1975	533.2	12.4	2,475	32.7	9.8
1976	620.4	16.4	2,852	37.1	10.0
1977	698.8	10.1	3,170	41.9	10.2
1978	771.5	10.4	3,463	48.7	10.6
1979	826.5	7.1	3,669	59.8	11.9
1980	907.7	9.8	3,985	74.9	12.7
1981	997.9	9.9	4,338	95.6	14.1
1982	1,142.0	14.4	4,913	117.4	15.7
1983	1,377.2	20.6	5,870	128.8	15.9
1984	1,572.3	14.2	6,640	153.8	18.1
1985	1,823.1	16.0	7,616	178.9	18.9
1986	2,125.3	16.6	8,793	187.1	18.9
1987	2,350.3	10.6	9,630	195.4	19.5

[1] Adjusted to exclude nonmarketable issues to the International Monetary Fund and other international institutions for 1950, 1955, 1960, 1965, and 1970-1974.
[2] From preceding year shown; for 1940, change from 1935.
[3] 1940-1976, based on estimated July 1 population; thereafter, based on October 1 resident population; prior to 1960, excludes Alaska and Hawaii.
[4] Calculated on total expenditures not reduced by interfund transactions representing interest and certain other payments to Treasury through 1950. Beginning 1955, total budget outlays.

Source: U.S. Dept. of the Treasury, *Statistical Appendix to the Annual Report of the Secretary of the Treasury on the State of the Finances* through fiscal 1980; thereafter, *Monthly Statement of the Public Debt of the United States*, and *Final Monthly Treasury Statement of Receipts and Outlays of the U.S. Government.*

cash in obligations of depositaries maintaining tax and loan accounts. Under the Treasury's tax and loan investment program, depositary financial institutions select the manner in which they will participate in the program. Depositaries that wish to retain funds deposited in their tax and loan accounts in interest-bearing obligations participate under the note option; depositaries that wish to remit the funds to the Treasury's account at district Federal Reserve banks participate under the remittance option.

Deposits to tax and loan accounts occur in the normal course of business under a uniform procedure applicable to all financial institutions whereby customers of financial institutions deposit with them tax payments and funds for the purchase of government securities. In most cases the transaction involves merely the transfer of funds from a customer's account to the tax and loan account in the same financial institution. On occasions, to the extent authorized by the Treasury, financial institutions are permitted to deposit in these accounts proceeds from subscriptions to public debt securities entered for their own account as well as for the accounts of their customers.

The tax and loan system permits the Treasury to collect funds through financial institutions and to leave the funds in note option depositaries and in the financial communities in which they arise until such time as the Treasury needs the funds for its operations. In this way, the Treasury is able to neutralize the effect of its fluctuation operations on note option financial institution reserves and the economy.

Funds of states, political subdivisions, and municipalities similarly require pledged collateral and legal reserves, but as demand deposits would not receive any interest. Such public monies have unique characteristics as far as withdrawal and inflow are concerned, as compared with commercial and individual deposits. Whether such deposits should be solicited, therefore, is to be determined in the light of their behavior and the feasible earning assets for such funds.

See GOVERNMENT DEPOSITARY, GOVERNMENT DEPOSITS.

BIBLIOGRAPHY

SECRETARY OF THE TREASURY. *Annual Report.*
U.S. DEPARTMENT OF THE TREASURY. *Treasury Bulletin* (monthly).

PUBLIC DEBT, BUREAU OF A bureau of the federal government that supports the management of the public debt, prepares Treasury Department curculars offering public debt securities, directs the handling of subscriptions and making of allotments, formulates instructions and regulations pertaining to security issues, and conducts or directs transactions in outstanding securities. The bureau performs the final audit of retired securities and interest coupons; maintains accounting control over public debt receipts and expenditures, securities, and interest costs; keeps individual accounts of owners of book-entry and registered securities and authorizes the payment of principal and interest; and adjudicates claims on account of lost, stolen, destroyed, or mutilated securities.

PUBLIC FINANCE In its ministerial concept, public finance is concerned with the revenues (taxation), expenditures, and debt management of government. In its broader concept, public finance is concerned with all activities of government creating economic benefits or costs, a concept that encompasses not only the field of finance and economics, but also the other social sciences. In any system of public finance, there is inherent an underlying FISCAL POLICY, which may range from the relatively ministerial policy of the cameralists of the seventeenth and eighteenth centuries (the "fathers of public finance"), primarily concerned with the raising of revenues and efficient administration of the public finances, to the modern fiscal policies concerned with normative criteria (ability to pay, equality of sacrifice, minimum total sacrifice, etc.) and the adaptation of public finance to macroeconomic planning in such areas as countercyclical measures, economic growth, and stability.

The subject has been very extensively covered by its international literature. The following is a selection from recent U.S. publications.

BIBLIOGRAPHY

"GAO Reports Urge Restructuring [IRS, bank regulation and federal financial management]." *Journal of Accountancy*, February, 1989.
LEWIS, C. W. "Ethics and the Public Finance Function." *Government Finance Review*, October, 1988.
WOLF, F. D. "The Growing Need For Reform of Federal Financial Management." *CPA Journal*, December, 1988.

PUBLIC HOUSING ADMINISTRATION Functions, powers, and duties of this former constituent agency of the Housing and Home Finance Agency were transferred to the Department of Housing and Urban Development by an act approved September 9, 1965 (79 Stat. 667; 5 U.S.C. 624 note).

See HOUSING AND URBAN DEVELOPMENT, DEPARTMENT OF.

PUBLICITY DEPARTMENT A department, also termed public relations or advertising department, organized among the larger banks usually under the supervision of a vice-president and under direct charge of a manager. The chief function of this department is to assist in selling the bank's services and to create new business by attracting prospects and stimulating the interest of existing customers. In many instances the activities of such a department are grouped together with those of the NEW BUSINESS DEPARTMENT.

Bank advertising and publicity may be general or direct. General publicity is that which makes an indirect appeal, usually through the medium of newspaper and magazine advertising. The material most frequently used for this purpose is the statement of condition of the bank. Direct publicity consists of advertising materials, circulars, pamphlets, etc., distributed to a mailing list of selected prospects or present customers. This material may call attention to a new service, e.g., a consumer credit or checking account service; it may be informative, calling attention of prospects to some service of the bank; or it may be entirely general in character for the purpose of keeping the bank's name and services before the bank's public.

The nature of the materials used depends largely upon the type of institution and its new business policy. Some of the larger commercial banks distribute among their customers and prospects a monthly analysis of business and financial conditions. Flyers (conveniently sized circulars) on specific services are often used by commercial banks "retailing" services to the public. The same type of material is often used by mutual savings banks in advertising their popular services and savings bank life insurance. Trust department literature, on the other hand, is likely to be more formally informative, since the average person is likely to know little about trust services.

Other possibilities for publicity are conventional recourse to established advertising media, as well as the preparation of releases to the press on activities of the bank, promotions, addresses of officers, etc. Advertising campaigns usually involve the retaining of an advertising agency.

BIBLIOGRAPHY

AMERICAN BANKERS ASSOCIATION. *Effective Public Relations and Communications: A Handbook for Banks*, 1982.
BERNAYS, E. L. "Restoring Public Confidence in Our Banks." *Bankers Magazine*, September-October, 1980.
FELDMAN, S. "The Sad State of Bank PR." *Bankers Magazine*, January-February, 1980.
PLUMMER, F. A. "Bank Investor Relations—A New World." In BAUGHN, W. H., and WALKER, C. E., eds., *The Bankers' Handbook*, rev. ed., 1978.

PUBLIC LOAN Obligations issued by a sovereign, whether a federal government, state, province, political subdivision thereof, or a municipality, for public purposes and for the public welfare. Public loans are either temporary or short term, to meet temporary deficits or unanticipated deficiencies in revenues, or long term or permanent, to finance the cost of permanent public improvements or supplement current revenues by capitalizing future taxes in the present. Public credit is reflected in the terms of public loans and ordinarily commands better terms than private credit, so the riskless cost of money is most closely indicated by the short-term or long-term cost of public loans.

PUBLIC PARTICIPATION Public participation in the securities markets is usually directly indicated by the volume of buying and selling in ODD LOT transactions.

PUBLIC REGULATION In politics, economics, and business, the intervention of public authority, i.e., the federal or state government, in business affairs. Public regulation is considered the mean between the evils of monopoly or of unrestrained competition on the one hand and public ownership or even some form of socialism on the other. The purpose of regulation is to secure the benefits of private initiative and ownership and at the same time prevent the abuses of monopoly power and evils of severe competition.

Public regulation was first applied to the public service industries, the railroads and public utilities. Competition in these industries is wasteful because of the necessity of duplicating extensive and expensive productive and distributive facilities, so public grants of monopolistic position in these fields have come to be accepted as a fundamental necessity. To prevent the abuse of such monopolistic power, particularly with reference to reasonableness of charges and adequacy of service, regulation of industries in the public service category has become thoroughly institutionalized. Grounded on common law regulation of common callings, public regulation has been extended by statute over rates and service of firms covered by the public utility concept, or businesses "affected with a public interest" in the narrow legal sense. The landmark case of *Munn* v. *Illinois* (94 U.S. 113) in 1877 upheld state imposition of maximum rates and licensing and bonding requirement upon grain elevators on common law principles. This led to extension of the principle to railroads, water companies, grist mills, stockyards, and companies in the gas, telephone, and electric industries. It was further extended to the regulation by a state of fire insurance rates (*German Alliance Insurance Co.* v. *Kansas*, 233 U.S. 389, 1914). But when Kansas in 1920 enacted a statute requiring compulsory arbitration of disputes concerning wages and work conditions of all firms manufacturing, preparing, or transporting food, clothing, and fuel, as businesses "affected with a public interest," the U.S. Supreme Court unanimously rejected the further extension of the public utility concept (*Wolff Packing Co.* v. *Kansas*, 262 U.S. 522).

Further extension of public regulation, however, is considered possible on legal grounds of a different concept. In 1894, in *Brass* v. *North Dakota* (153 U.S. 391), the U.S. Supreme Court found constitutional state imposition of maximum rates for storage of grain on the ground that the Court would not be justified in imputing the wisdom or expediency of the state legislature in passing such a law. And in the landmark case of *Nebbia* v. *New York* (291 U.S. 538, 1934), the Supreme Court upheld state fixing of minimum wholesale and retail prices of milk through a Milk Control Board, by a five-to-four decision, even though the dairy business is not a public utility, considering it a proper subject of regulation through the state "police power" (to safeguard health). The crucial reasoning of the majority opinion read as follows: "If the law-making body within its sphere of government concludes that the conditions or practices in an industry make unrestricted competition an inadequate safeguard of the consumer's interests, produce waste harmful to the public, threaten ultimately to cut off the supply of a commodity needed for the public, or portend the destruction of the industry itself, appropriate statutes passed in an honest effort to correct the threatened consequences may not be set aside because the regulation adopted fixes prices reasonably deemed by the legislature to be fair to those engaged in the industry and to the consuming public."

Public regulation may possibly be further extended on the basis of another concept, as yet undeveloped. Constitutional limitations have been held to apply to a private concern if it is performing a public function (such as operating a company town, *Marsh* v. *Alabama*, 326 U.S. 501, 1946). Thus, A. A. Berle, Jr. asks: "Today, one wonders whether a corporation having attained power to control the life of an individual may not have moved into the category of "conducting a public function' by that very fact." And on the common law doctrine of illegal concerted refusals to deal with anyone, he raises the question of whether a single firm's refusal to deal with an individual constitutes boycotting. Moreover, "concentration of power in corporate hands is being accompanied by a rudimentary and growing system of *ad hoc* economic planning, increasingly translating itself into explicit law, in which the government stands ready both to enforce the plan and, if need be, to give financial or other assistance to make it feasible."

The web of public regulation of business has been growing over time. Besides state regulation, the principal federal laws under which the regulation of industry was enforced prior to the New Deal are the following:

1. Interstate Commerce Act of 1887 with its amendments,
2. Sherman Anti-Trust Act of 1890,
3. Panama Canal Act of 1913,
4. Clayton Act of 1914 with amendments,
5. Federal Trade Commission Act of 1914,
6. Webb-Pomerene Act of 1918,
7. Transportation Act of 1920,
8. Federal Water Power Act of 1920,
9. Packers and Stockyards Act of 1921, and
10. Grain Futures Act of 1922.

Public regulation was greatly extended under the NEW DEAL administration beginning March 4, 1933, affecting agriculture, banking, public utilities, radio and television, airlines, motor carriers, exchanges, securities business, and industry (especially labor, wages and hours, price discrimination, and fair trade laws). The Reagan administration, by contrast, espoused furtherance of the start toward deregulation begun in preceding administrations, with M. L. Weidenbaum, a leading proponent of deemphasis on regulation, named chairman of the COUNCIL OF ECONOMIC ADVISERS.

BIBLIOGRAPHY

Aranson, P. H., and Ordershook, P. C. "Regulation, Redistribution and Public Choice." *Public Choice*, 1981, 37 (1).
Fraser, D. A., and Byrom, F. L. *Failing Industries: The Role of Government*, 1980.
Fromm, G., ed. *Studies in Public Regulation*, 1981.
Gatti, J. F., ed. *The Limits of Government Regulation*, 1981.
Haveman, R. H., and Christiansen, G. B. "Environmental Regulations and Productivity Growth." *Natural Resources Journal*, July, 1981.
Kelman, S. "Regulation and Paternalism." *Public Policy*, Spring, 1981.
Kemp, K. "Symbolic and Strict Regulation in the American States." *Social Science Quarterly*, September, 1981.
Lave, L. B. *The Strategy of Social Regulation: Decision Frameworks for Policy*, 1981.
Lee, L. W. "A Theory of Just Regulation." *American Economic Review*, December, 1980.
Peskin, H. M., Portney, P. R., and Kneese, A. V. "Regulation and the Economy: Concluding Thoughts." *Natural Resources Journal*, July, 1981.
Peterson, H. C. *Business and Government*, 1981.
Poole, R. W., Jr., ed. *Instead of Regulation: Alternatives to Federal Regulatory Agencies*, 1982.
Portney, P. R. "The Macroeconomic Impacts of Federal Environmental Regulation." *Natural Resources Journal*, July, 1981.
Reynolds, L. "Foundations of an Institutional Theory of Regulation." *Journal of Economic Issues*, September, 1981.
Schwert, G. W. "Using Financial Data to Measure Effects of Regulation." *Journal of Law and Economics*, April, 1981.
Sherman, R. "Pricing Inefficiencies Under Profit Regulation." *Southern Economic Journal*, October, 1981.
Voytko, J. M. "The Business-Government Problem." *Journal of Policy Analysis and Management*, Fall, 1981.
Weidenbaum, M. L. *Business, Government and the Public*, 2nd ed., 1981.

PUBLIC SERVICE COMMISSION State administrative agencies for regulating and supervising public utility corporations. All states and the District of Columbia have such agencies (although in some states they are not called public service commissions), but the comprehensiveness of jurisdiction of the agencies varies among the states as to classes of public utilities regulated. The purpose of these agencies is to harmonize the public interest, insofar as consumers are concerned, with the interests of the companies and their investors. The degree of regulation similarly varies. Such regulation finds tangible expression in control of entry of firms through franchises and certificates of convenience and necessity, extensions and abandonments of service, adequacy and standards of service, rates, capital issues, and accounting regulations.

See PUBLIC UTILITY INDUSTRY.

PUBLIC TRUSTEE A government bureau or office exercising trust powers. A public trustee office by which the functions of executor, administrator, and trustee are exercised was created by statute in New Zealand. A public trustee law became operative in England and Wales on January 1, 1908. Under its provisions, trust functions are undertaken by an office established by the government. In the case of such a sovereign trustee, a beneficiary has no legal power to enforce the trust without its consent, on the legal principle that a sovereign cannot be sued except with its consent. In the United States, there is no comparable office of public trustee in the federal government or the states, but any public jurisdiction (the federal government, the states, political subdivisions, and municipalities) has the perfect power to act as trustee, and instances are numerous where property has been conveyed in trust to a state or municipality for a stated public use.

See TRUST.

PUBLIC UTILITY See PUBLIC UTILITY INDUSTRY.

BIBLIOGRAPHY

Chambliss, L. "Utilities." *Financial World*, December 27, 1988.
Cudahy, R. D. "Return on Investment and Fairness in Regulation." *Public Utilities Fortnightly*, February 2, 1989.
Moody's Public Utility Manual. Moody's Investors Service, Inc., New York, NY. Annual.
Pfeffer, J. L. "Sharing Increased Value in Utility Acquisitions, Mergers, and Restructurings." *Public Utilities Fortnightly*, December 8, 1988.
Public Utilities Fortnightly. Public Utilities Reports, Inc., Arlington, VA. Biweekly.
Smartt, L. E. "An Accounting Survey Profiles an Industry." *Public Utilities Fortnightly*. January 5, 1989.
Updegrave, W. L. "Total Return: the Two-Lane Approach to Wide Profits." *Money*, December, 1988.

PUBLIC UTILITY BONDS Bonds that are obligations of a PUBLIC UTILITY CORPORATION engaged in furnishing such utility services as electric light and power, gas, water, telephone, and transportation (traction), as distinguished from railroad and industrial bonds. Because of the heavy investment in fixed assets required in these industries and thus availability of such assets as collateral for bonded debt, it is customary for most utility companies to finance by means of mortgage bonds. In the electric industry, where continuing financial requirements are necessary as companies keep capacity ahead of growing service demand, the typical mortgage bond issues are part of a single large open-end mortgage indenture, with various issues from time to time in series. Such open-end indentures contain protective provisions to prevent dilution of asset and earnings coverages on existing bonds as additional series are issued. Among such protective provisions are the following: (1) limitation of additional bonds to a ratio, usually 60% to 75%, of net new property added; (2) requirement that total fixed charges on existing and additional bonds be earned by a specified minimum, such as two times. In lieu of a conventional sinking fund, an improvement fund might be specified at the rate analogous to that of a sinking fund (say, 1% per year on amount of bonds outstanding), to be paid in cash (for application to purchase or redemption of bonds), or in bonds, or by certifying net additions to property at 60% or 75% thereof. Also, to assure provision for maintenance at minimum of, say, 15% of gross revenues, the indenture might contain a provision requiring the cash deposit of any deficiency in such minimum maintenance any year. The conventional call provision is found in utility mortgage bonds, providing for redemption on usually 30 days' notice on any interest date, at either flat or scaled premiums over par. The conversion feature is rarer in utility mortgage bonds, but is found particularly in telephone company debentures as a form of deferred equity financing.

As a group, utility companies resort to bonded debt in higher ratio than do railroad and industrial companies. On the average, electric utilities finance about 50% of their capital structures in bonds, with another 10% in preferred stock and 40% in common equity. Natural gas companies may go even higher in ratio of bonds. Safety of such recourse to leverage is assured by the relative essentiality and stability of earnings, which should cover fixed charges even in years of recession in earnings by comfortable margins of safety. Such leverage magnifies the rate of return permitted by public utility regulation on the property devoted to the service, reflecting cost of capital of approximately 15% in recent years of inflation. For example, a 15% rate of return on $100 million of assets financed 50% by 10% bonded debt, 15% by 12% preferred stock, and the balance in common equity would cover interest charges by three times and overall interest charges plus preferred dividends (income taxes are permitted to be included in operating expenses) by 2.21 times, and show a rate of return on the common equity alone of 23.43%.

In addition to analysis of a financial nature such as balance sheet and income account analysis, analysis of utility bonds is also concerned with such fundamental factors as the franchise (ideally, it should be an exclusive, "indeterminate" as to duration, and with flexibility of rates authorized based on cost of service), the territory served (ideally, a growth area in population and economic development), competitive position, and the reasonableness of regulation. In the area of earnings, factors conducive to high quality ratings for utility bonds include a high proportion of residential sales, as compared with more cyclical industrial and commercial sales; high average consumption, so as to absorb optimally the fixed costs of capacity necessary to cover peak loads with margins to spare; and high margins of safety for fixed charges, even at worst of earnings over the cycle.

PUBLIC UTILITY COMMISSION PUBLIC SERVICE COMMISSION.

PUBLIC UTILITY CORPORATION A corporation that supplies services "affected with a public interest," i.e., indispensable to the consuming public. Railroads, traction lines, electric light and power, gas, telephone and telegraph, bus and ferry lines, and water companies are public utility or public service corporations, usually operating under grants of FRANCHISE and/or certificates of convenience and necessity from public authority which grant them complete or varying degrees of monopoly in providing the service in specified territories. Although in legal principle railroads are fundamentally of the same general classification as regulated public service corporations, in classifications of the securities of these companies, railroads are placed in a separate category.

Public utility corporations operate under regulation based on statutes and common law principles which require these corporations to (1) serve all who apply for services without discrimination, (2) charge reasonable rates, (3) charge nondiscriminatory rates (this does not mean the same rates for all users and all volume of use, as differential rates may be justified on reasonable classification), and (4) provide adequate service. Railroads and public utilities operating interstate are subject to federal regulation (Interstate Commerce Commission for railroads, Federal Power Commission for operating utility companies, and Securities and Exchange Commission for utility holding companies and their subsidiaries). In addition, railroads and utilities operating intrastate are subject to the regulation of state agencies (Public Service Commission or the equivalent) in the states in which operations are conducted.

Usually public utility corporations are unique in having a public monopoly of operation in their field and in the territory of operation, granted by the state or municipality in the form of a certificate of convenience and necessity and franchise. Such authorizing documents limit free entry into the field by other firms and serve as the quid pro quo basis for imposition of regulation.

PUBLIC UTILITY HOLDING COMPANY ACT OF 1935

An act providing for the control and regulation of public utility holding companies and "for other purposes," approved August 26, 1935 (49 Stat. 803; 15 U.S.C. 79-79z-6). Title I of the act was the Public Utility Holding Company Act of 1935; Title II was the Federal Power Act.

Title I provided for federal control of public utility holding companies through the Securities and Exchange Commission. It applied to gas and electric holding companies, defined as any company owning, holding, or controlling 10% or more of the voting stock of a utility operating company or of any other holding company so doing; or such companies which, while not owning such proportion, nevertheless were found by the commission to exercise such control as to subject them to regulation in the public interest. Such companies were required to register with the SEC, filing detailed data on organization, intercorporate relationships, contracts, control, finances, etc. If they did not register, they could not engage in interstate commerce or use the mails.

The act required the SEC, as soon as practicable after January 1, 1938, to require physical integration of properties and simplification of financial structure. Integration involves the limitation of operations to a single integrated public utility system and such other businesses as are reasonably incidental or economically necessary or appropriate to the operations of such an integrated public utility system. The commission was statutorily directed to permit a registered holding company to continue to control one or more additional integrated public utility systems if, after notice and opportunity for hearing, it found that the following criteria were met: (1) each of such additional systems could not be operated as an independent system without the loss of substantial economies which could be secured by the retention of control by such holding company; (2) all of such additional systems were located in one state or in adjoining states, or in a contiguous foreign country; and (3) the continued combination of such systems under the holding company's control was not so large (considering "the state of the art and the area or region affected") as to impair the advantages of localized management, efficient operation, or the effectiveness of regulation. Moreover, the commission could permit as reasonably incidental, or economically necessary or appropriate to the operations of one or more integrated utility systems, the retention of an interest in any other business (other than a utility company) which the commission found necessary or appropriate in the public interest or for the protection of investors or consumers, and not detrimental to the proper functioning of such system.

In administering this part of the statute, the SEC administratively ruled that gas and electric businesses could not be integrated in a single system unless substantial economies resulted from such combination. The SEC also ruled on a basic one-area location of the principal system, with an additional system if permitted; on limited size if inconsistent with efficient operation and localized management; and on divestment of most other businesses. As a result, reorganization plans approved by the SEC entailed drastic changes and divestments in the composition of many systems in compliance with the physical integration requirement.

For simplification of financial structure, the statute directed the SEC to take such steps, after notice and hearing, as necessary to ensure that the corporate structure or continued existence of any company in the holding company system does not unduly or unnecessarily complicate the structure, or unfairly or inequitably distribute voting power among security holders—including, if necessary, the elimination of holding companies. The SEC, in correcting pyramiding of holding companies, simplified the use of holding companies to no more than two vertical tiers of holding companies in addition to the operating companies. Overcapitalization and write-ups of asset values were corrected in approved simplification plans. Such simplification of holding company structures involved drastic overhaul of many systems, eliminating holding companies beyond "the second degree."

On a permanent basis, the act also gave the SEC regulatory powers over the financial operation of registered holding companies and their subsidiaries, including regulation of securities issuance and capital structure, acquisitions and dispositions of holdings and other intercompany transactions, service contracts, and accounting. The "dust had long since settled" with regard to major work by the SEC in connection with the Public Utility Holding Company Act.

Title II of the act gave the Federal Power Commission regulatory power over rates of federal licensees or electric companies engaged in interstate distribution at wholesale or transmission. Rates must be just and reasonable, and be filed with the commission. Approval of the commission is necessary for issuance of securities, which issuance must be for "lawful object" and "reasonably necessary and appropriate." Regulation also extends to mergers and combinations, connections, and accounting. The act specifically directs the FPC to cooperate with state commissions to assist in state regulation of public utilities. Since this encompassed public utility type of regulation and did not involve integration or simplification, this portion of the act was readily adjusted to by the companies concerned, as compared with the drastic Title I.

Summary. The Public Utility Holding Company Act of 1935 provides for the physical integration and corporate simplification of holding company systems of public utilities. According to the Securities and Exchange Commission, integration standards restrict a holding company's operations to an "integrated utility system." Such a system is defined as one: capable of economical operation as a single coordinated system; confined to a single area or region in one or more states; and not so large that it negates the advantages of localized management, efficient operations, and effective regulation. To be authorized by the SEC, the acquisition of securities and utility assets by holding companies and their subsidiaries must meet the following standards: the acquisition must not tend toward interlocking relations or concentrating control detrimental to investors or the public interest; any consideration paid for the acquisition must not be unreasonable; the acquisition must not complicate the capital structure of the holding company system or have a detrimental effect on system functions; and the acquisition must tend toward economical, efficient development of an integrated public utility system. The SECURITIES AND EXCHANGE COMMISSION regulates public holding companies under this act.

Proposed security issues by any holding company must be analyzed by the staff and approved by the commission. Other phases of the act provide for regulation of dividend payments; intercompany loans; solicitation of proxies, consents, and other authorizations; and insider trading. Upstream loans from subsidiaries to their parents and upstream or cross-stream loans from public utility companies to any holding company in the same holding company system require commission approval.

See PUBLIC UTILITY INDUSTRY.

PUBLIC UTILITY INDUSTRY

The principal characteristic that differentiates a public utility from other industrial and commercial firms is that a public utility operates as a monopoly within

PUBLIC UTILITY INDUSTRY

its service area. This privilege is usually granted because of the large amount of capital investment required to provide a desired service. The public utility industry is highly regulated by federal and state authorities to assure a reasonable amount of fair dealings between the utility and the public it serves. The following federal agencies are charged with regulating the public utility industry:

Federal Energy Regulatory Commission (FERC)—electricity, gas, and oil. Prior to 1977, the regulatory agency was the Federal Power Commission. The FERC is an independent agency in the Department of Energy.
Atomic Energy Commission (AEC)—nuclear fuel.
Federal Communications Commission (FCC—telephone.
Securities and Exchange Commission (SEC)—public utility holding companies and all utilities with public ownership.

States have established public service commissions to regulate the intrastate activities of a utility. Generally, regulatory bodies have the authority to (1) designate operating areas, (2) fix rates for services, (3) establish accounting policies and a uniform chart of accounts, (4) make accounting policy rulings, (5) process complaints by customers, and (6) prescribe operating methods. The National Association of Regulatory Utility Commissioners (NARUC) makes recommendations for regulatory activities.

The rate-making process establishes a series of rate schedules that the utility may charge classes of customers: industrial, commercial, and residential. Subcategories are usually established within each class on the basis of quantity, time of service, or frequency of service. Rates are normally designed to be sufficient for the utility to recover its costs of operations, provide for replacements and improvements in equipment and facilities, pay for its cost of borrowed capital, and return a fair profit to its investors.

The largest segment of the public utility industry is the electric light and power companies. Since the early years of the century, electric output has approximately doubled every decade. By 1980 the industry had grown to a generating capacity of over 600,000 megawatts; it has been estimated that capacity will exceed 800,000 megawatts before the year 2000.

The earliest use of electricity was for illumination, but so successful have the electric companies been in developing other uses for power, including appliances, air conditioning, and commercial and industrial uses, that nighttime loads are now lower than daytime loads and summer loads of various utilities are now seasonally the highest.

The first electric company to use incandescent lamps was the Edison Electric Illuminating Company of New York, incorporated in 1880 and commercially operated for the first time in 1882 with a power load of about 10 kw, serving 85 customers. This company was the forerunner of the present massive electric industry. Necessarily involved in the initial development was not only Edison's invention of the incandescent bulb but also a complete system of generating equipment, distribution lines, meters, and other essential equipment. Over the course of the next two generations electricity almost entirely supplanted gas for both interior and outdoor lighting purposes. Gas, after a period of readjustment, emerged as a valuable fuel for domestic cooking and heating and, either straight or as mixed natural gas, for industrial use (*see* GAS).

The early financial history of the first Edison companies throughout the country was typically the same, with the original capital provided by local citizens through subscription to common stock. The growth of the business was so rapid that additional financing, a continuing financial problem of the industry to this day, soon became necessary. The original capitalization of the New York company of $1 million had to be increased in five years by 150%, bringing the total to $2.5 million in 1887, which had to be doubled in 1890.

The next major phase of development of the industry was toward the consolidation of small companies into larger operating companies. In August, 1892, for example, the Brush Electric Light Company and the Thomson Houston Electric Light & Power Company of Buffalo were consolidated to form the Buffalo General Electric Company, serving the entire city of Buffalo. In 1907, the Chicago Edison Company and the Commonwealth Electric Company were consolidated to form the Commonwealth Edison Company. In New York, on May 1, 1901, the original Edison Electric Illuminating Company was consolidated with the New York Gas & Electric Light, Heat & Power Company to form the New York Edison Company, in turn a predecessor of the present Consolidated Edison Company.

During the latter part of the 1920s, the holding company was particularly used as the acquisitive device for assembling interests in utility and nonutility operating companies, resulting in a number of large heterogeneous systems often scattered geographically throughout the country. The depression of the early 1930s revealed the structural weaknesses of such systems, overcapitalized, overusing the holding company with excessive leverage, and conducive to abuse of operating companies by holding companies under the pressure of high fixed charges and depression in earnings. Following passage of the PUBLIC UTILITY HOLDING COMPANY ACT OF 1935, compulsory integration of physical properties and simplification of holding company structures involved a drastic reorganization of the industry under surveillance of the Securities and Exchange Commission. From June 15, 1938, to June 30, 1959, a total of 2,064 holding and operating-holding companies were either released from regulatory jurisdiction under the act or ceased to exist as separate corporate entities, in compliance with reorganizations either approved by or initiated by the SEC on notice and hearings. Drastic as this readjustment was, it unquestionably strengthened the industry for the growth which subsequently was resumed.

The Regulatory Climate. A review by the Comptroller General of the U.S. (*Electric Power: Contemporary Issues and the Federal Role in Oversight and Regulation*) has pithily contrasted the change in the long-term trend of the electric power industry that occurred in the 1960s and 1970s.

From its inception and into the 1960s, the industry grew steadily to meet broadening markets and increasing uses for electricity. Electricity growth, to a large extent, corresponded to the nation's economic growth. With few exceptions, the demand for electrical power increased every year and doubled about every 10 years. The construction of fewer but larger generating units resulted in highly centralized power systems, reduced the unit costs of power production, and led to lower electric rates for consumers. Throughout most of its development, the industry was characterized by steady growth in sales and power production, dependable cost estimates and schedules for construction of power plants, plentiful fuel supplies, and limited public concern for the environmental or social impacts of new facilities.

Regulatory actions, relating to the propriety of power rates, environmental impacts, and other factors, played a modest role in the growth of the industry. For many years productivity growth more than offset expansion costs, and the industry's ability to offer increasingly better service, coupled with stable or lower rates, minimized confrontations with regulators and consumers. The regulatory process faced by electric utilities was a relatively simple one, and the outcomes of rate proceedings and reviews of major expansion plans were largely predictable. Controversies over electric power plans and policies were rare.

Unfortunately for utilities and consumers alike, these conditions have changed greatly. In the late 1960s and throughout the 1970s, a series of changes shattered the stability of utility operations. Changing public interests and public reaction to power interruptions focused national attention on the electric power industry. Service reliability became a public issue, as did the environmental costs of generating and transmitting power.

The 1973 oil embargo and subsequent price increases, combined with rapidly escalating construction costs, elongated construction schedules, and the increased public concern about the impacts of large power plants abruptly changed the industry's historical patterns. Retail power rates doubled between 1973 and 1979. Higher consumer prices, economic downturns, and the emergence of a national conservation ethic slowed growth in electricity demand. Domestic power sales have increased about 3% a year since 1973, compared with an 8% a year increase from 1950 to 1970. Unanticipated reductions in demand growth left some utilities with excess generating capacity and others facing hostile reviews of their construction plans. Some utilities face similar problems in the 1980s, when more large new power plants are scheduled to come on line.

The 1970s were also characterized by very significant changes in the regulatory climate. State and federal officials became much more active in asserting the public interest in the management of power resources. It was no longer self-evident that new power plants should be built to meet utilities' forecasts of future demand growth. Regulatory officials in some cases have begun scrutinizing utility forecasts and requiring new generating plants to be economically justified, environmentally and socially acceptable, and capable of reducing the nation's dependence on imported fuels.

ENCYCLOPEDIA OF BANKING AND FINANCE

Concerns about the viability of nuclear energy as a safe and economical source of electricity had been growing for a decade. But the March, 1979, accident at the Three Mile Island nuclear plant in Pennsylvania increased the public's awareness of the potential risks of nuclear power. The response of capital markets and new regulatory requirements reflecting these concerns will intensify cost pressures and could lead to even longer lead-times for nuclear power plants.

Because of these and other recent developments, the utility industry has been abruptly moved from a position of generally amicable public relations to one in which many utility officials perceive skeptical public attitudes as a major problem to be overcome.

Capital Requirements. The electric power industry is the nation's most capital-intensive industry. Capital requirements are likely to increase in the future because construction cost escalations are resulting in substantially higher prices for new facilities.nuclear capacity would appear to be overprojected.

See TELEPHONE SECURITIES, WATER COMPANY BONDS.

PUBLIC UTILITY STOCKS Preferred and common stocks of public utility companies in the electric light and power, natural gas, manufactured gas, water, telephone, telegraph, and traction industries. Seasoned operating-company equities of well-established companies in these fields, with the exception of most traction company equities, were traditionally held in high regard as defensive investments, for relative stability and assurance of dividends. In addition, many public utility common stocks in recent years had scored substantial capital gains, reflecting wider market realization of the substantial growth factor in utility equities. With the worsening of inflation, however, resulting in higher interest costs of financing and in higher fuel costs, together with lags in rate increases as relief from shrinkage in rates of return and higher construction costs, public utility equities incurred a decline in regard as investments which only lately, with the ebbing in the rate of inflation and lower interest rates generally, has begun to return to former levels. Although railroads are also public service corporations by definition, railroad equities have been generally held in lower regard as investments, being instead more appreciated as trading media when properly timed, in view of their much higher susceptibility to the business cycle.

Merits of public utility stocks may be summarized generally as follows: (1) the protected nature of operation conferred by franchises and certificates for specified territories served; (2) essential nature of the services rendered; (3) state and federal regulation which, in the interests of both the consumers and the investors, regulates rates, rates of return, capitalizations and security issues, financial practices, and accounting systems; (4) expansion and growth through economic development of territories served, increase in population, extensions of markets and uses for service, and rise in average load factor. Although the rate levels permitted by public regulation generally authorize modest rates of return on the rate base of assets devoted to service, public regulation permits, as safe in the circumstances, a relatively high degree of resort to leverage in capital structures by recourse to debt securities (as well as preferred stocks as far as common equities are concerned). Such leverage magnifies the basically modest rates of return allowed on asset bases into attractive earnings rates on common equities alone, with substantial coverage of fixed charges and preferred dividends, and also magnifies the rates of increase in common stock earnings as overall earnings rise. Moreover, public utility equities are steady dividend payers.

As the result of the break-up of holding-company systems required in compliance with the Public Utility Act of 1935, an increased number of operating-company equities became available to the public for the first time. Divestment plans often called for the listing of the operating-company equities distributed, and as a result the number of utility equities listed on the exchanges has increased, with resultant wider variety of choice to investors in utility equities.

See PUBLIC UTILITY BONDS, PUBLIC UTILITY INDUSTRY.

PUBLIC WAREHOUSE See WAREHOUSE COMPANY.

PUBLIC WORKS ADMINISTRATION Originally created by the National Industrial Recovery Act, passed June 16, 1933, as the Federal Emergency Administration of Public Works, and later reorganized as the Public Works Administration (PWA). Under the government reorganization plan of 1939, the Public Works Administration was transferred to the FEDERAL WORKS AGENCY. Essentially a pump-priming agency to stimulate national recovery, the PWA was subsequently placed in liquidation and was reported wholly liquidated.

PUMP PRIMING Under the NEW DEAL, federal government expenditures designed to stimulate general business recovery by injecting government spending into the money stream. Pump-priming expenditures were provided for federal public works, allocations to state and local governments for public works projects, subsidies and grants to farmers in consideration of reduction of production, unemployment relief, etc.

For the fiscal years 1933-1941, federal expenditures for the agricultural aid program and unemployment relief as shown in the appended table.

Federal Pump-Priming Expenditures, 1933-1941
(in millions)

Fiscal year	Agricultural adjustment program	Unemployment relief
1933	–	$ 345
1934	$ 289	1,846
1935	712	2,351
1936	533	2,309
1937	527	2,432
1938	362	1,914
1939	787	2,595
1940	1,002	1,919
1941	877	1,694
Totals	$5,089	$17,405

Source: Board of Governors of the Federal Reserve System.

PURCHASE ACCOUNTING Purchase accounting is an accounting method that is used under certain circumstances in accounting for a business combination, such as a merger, consolidation, or stock acquisition. Accounting for a business combination by the purchase method follows principles normally applicable under the historical-cost method for acquisitions of assets and issuances of stock. The cost to the purchasing entity of acquiring another company in a business combination treated as a purchase is the amount of cash disbursed or the fair value of other assets distributed or securities issued. The cost of the assets recorded on the acquired company's books is not recorded by the acquiring company as the cost of the purchased assets, as would be the case when the pooling-of-interests method is used. Because the assets acquired are recorded at their fair market value, any excess of cost over these fair values of total identifiable net assets is assigned to intangibles, such as goodwill. Goodwill is amortized over a period not to exceed 40 years. The purchase method of accounting must be used for a business combination unless all conditions prescribed for a pooling of interests are met.

In purchase accounting, postacquisition earnings of the acquired entity are combined with the surviving entity's earnings. Restatement of the financial statements of prior years is not required.

PURCHASE MONEY BONDS Bonds secured by PURCHASE MONEY MORTGAGE, a type of mortgage so called because it is executed as part of the consideration and in part payment for property acquired. The proceeds of issue of purchase money bonds are used to purchase the property by which they are secured. This type of issue is usually resorted to whenever there are outstanding mortgage bonds with "after acquired" clauses therein, under which any property subsequently acquired would come under the lien. By issuing purchase money bonds, the issuers avoid the operations of the after acquired clause of existing mortgage bonds.

PURCHASE MONEY MORTGAGE A MORTGAGE given by the purchaser to the seller at the time of conveyance of land to the purchaser, designed to secure the unpaid balance of the purchase price. The New York Civil Practice Act (Sec. 514) provides that where real property is sold and conveyed and at the same time a mortgage thereupon is given by the purchaser to secure the payment of the whole or a part of the purchase money, the lien of the mortgage upon that real property is superior to the lien of a previous judgment wholly or partly for a sum of money or directing the payment of a sum of money against the purchaser. Independent of statute, however, New York case law holds that a purchase money mortgage executed and recorded at the same time as another mortgage given in the same transaction has priority over such other mortgage.

PURCHASED PAPER Commercial paper that has been purchased outright, as distinguished from paper that has been discounted. The Federal Reserve Act defines it as "paper bought through brokers or others with whom the purchasing bank has no direct business relations."

PURCHASING POWER Ability to buy, as determined by income in relation to the price level. The purchasing power of a fixed income, for example, varies inversely with the general price level. That is, a rising price level diminishes the purchasing power of a fixed income, whereas a falling price level increases it. An index of purchasing power can be computed by reversing an index of commodity prices. In fact, the Bureau of Labor Statistics computes an index of purchasing power which is a reciprocal of this organization's commodity price index. A COST OF LIVING INDEX is, in effect, a purchasing power index if considered reciprocally.

PURCHASING POWER RISK Among INVESTMENT RISKS, the risk of decline in purchasing power of principal and income from an investment because of rise in the price level; also known as inflation risk.

Although the consumer price index (*see* COST OF LIVING INDEX) is not really an index of living costs and thus reciprocally of the purchasing power of money, it is often so used in the absence of any more comprehensive index.

Any fixed-return security (debt securities, preferred stocks, or even common stocks whose dividends remain unchanged over the years of rise in the price level) would be vulnerable to purchasing power risk. The hedges against purchasing power risk, therefore, are common stocks that rise in market price and increase dividends at least in step with the rise in the price level—a problem of selectivity in investing.

See INFLATION, INVESTMENT.

PUSH-DOWN ACCOUNTING In a purchase business combination, push down accounting requires the revaluation of the assets and/or liabilities of the acquired company on its books based on the price paid for some or all of its shares by the acquiring company. Push-down accounting has no impact on the presentation of consolidated financial statements or on the separate financial statements of the parent (investor) company. The SEC has maintained that where ownership of 100% of the entity has changed hands, the new cost basis to the acquiror should be reflected in the financial statements of the acquired entity. The accounting profession has not reached a consensus on this matter.

PUT A contract that entitles the holder thereof, at his option, to sell to the maker (in the New York Put and Call Market, through the endorser, a member firm of the New York Stock Exchange) at any time within the life of the contract a specified number of shares of a specific stock, at the price fixed in the contract.

A put is the opposite of a CALL. A STRADDLE is both a put and a call on the same stock, written at the same price and at the same time and identical as to the number of shares and life of the contract. A SPREAD is both a put and a call on the same stock and identical as to the expiration of the contract; like a straddle, the spread is really two separate options and either or both may be exercised during the life of the contracts. Contract price for both options of the straddle is usually the current market price of the stock, whereas the put and call sides of the spread are priced at points away from the market (e.g., relative to a current market price of 50, the put price might be 47 and the call price 53).

These options are dealt in by put and call dealers, who in New York have organized the Put and Call Brokers and Dealers Association, Inc. Puts and calls sold by members of this association carry a guarantee by a member firm of the New York Stock Exchange that the contract will be fulfilled, and such endorsement adds to the strength of the contract. Members of the New York Stock Exchange are not permitted to deal in options or privileges on the floor of the exchange.

The protective function of puts and calls is perhaps the most important advantage of use of such privileges. The holder of stock who buys a put or the short seller who buys a call is hedged for the duration of the option. Thus, the owner of stock when he purchases a put knows that if the market price of the stock on which he is long moves downward, he can, during the life of his put, sell stock at the price specified in his put contract by exercising the put contract on or before the time by expiration. But puts or calls need not necessarily be purchased at the time a stock is bought or sold. Individuals who have a substantial profit on their purchases or short sales as the result of subsequent market action may protect such profits by a put or a call.

See OPTIONS.

PUT OF MORE *See* CALL OF MORE, PUT.

PUTS AND CALLS *See* OPTIONS.

PYRAMIDING This term has at least four meanings.

1. In stock market transactions, the practice of borrowing against unrealized paper profits to make additional purchases; a series of buying or selling operations during an upward or downward trend in the stock market, working on margin with the profits made in the transaction. The objective is to make additional profits without investing one's own resources to obtain leverage.
2. In finance, the practice of creating a speculative capital structure by means of a series of holding companies or other strategies, whereby a relatively small amount of voting stock in the parent company controls a large corporate system or assets.
3. In real estate transactions, the practice of financing 100% or more of the value of the property.
4. A fraudulent scheme involving the use of a small amount of one's own resources to acquire a relatively large amount of resources from others without an economic foundation to the transaction(s).

PYROTECHNICS In speculative circles, the rapid moving of the price of a stock up or down over a wide range as a result of manipulation. The expression "gyrations" is sometimes used to indicate the same phenomenon.

PYX *See* TRIAL OF THE PYX.

Q

QUALIFICATIONS FOR DIRECTORS *See* DIRECTORS.

QUALIFIED ACCEPTANCE *See* ACCEPTANCE.

QUALIFIED ENDORSEMENT *See* ENDORSEMENT.

QUALIFIED OPINION In the auditing of a firm's accounts by an independent accountant, a report or opinion stating specific exceptions made by the accountant as the result of his audit.

A qualified opinion is issued when the financial statements present the firm's financial position, results of operations, and cash flows in conformity with GAAP except for the matter associated with the qualification (reservation). Qualified opinions are issued generally when (1) a scope limitation exists, (2) a departure from generally accepted accounting principles exists, and (3) other auditors are involved and their work cannot be relied upon.

When the auditors' reservations are more serious, a disclaimer of opinion or an adverse opinion may be issued. The adverse opinion states that the financial statements do not present fairly the financial position of the company, the results of its operations, and the cash flows in conformity with generally accepted accounting principles. A disclaimer of opinion is issued when the auditors cannot give an opinion because of scope limitations, the existence of significant uncertainty because the auditor is not independent with respect to the entity being audited, or for some other reason.

See UNQUALIFIED OPINION.

QUALITATIVE CHARACTERISTICS OF ACCOUNTING INFORMATION Qualities or ingredients of accounting information that make it useful. The FASB's Statement of Financial Accounting Concepts No. 2, "Qualitative Characteristics of Accounting Information," discusses the qualitative characteristics that make accounting information useful. Key terms are defined below. The appended diagram outlines what is referred to as a hierarchy of accounting information qualities.

Definitions:
Qualitative Characteristics of Accounting Information

Bias Bias in measurement is the tendency of a measure to fall more often on one side than the other of what it represents instead of being equally likely to fall on either side. Bias in accounting measures means a tendency to be consistently too high or too low.
Comparability The quality of information that enables users to identify similarities in and differences between two sets of economic phenomena.
Completeness The inclusion in reported information of everything material that is necessary for faithful representation of the relevant phenomena.
Conservatism A prudent reaction to uncertainty to try to insure that uncertainty and risks inherent in business situations are adequately considered.
Consistency Conformity from period to period with unchanging policies and procedures.
Feedback Value The quality of information that enables users to confirm or correct prior expectations.
Materiality The magnitude of an omission or misstatement of accounting information that, in the light of surrounding circumstances, makes it probable that the judgment of a reasonable person relying on the information would have been changed or influenced by the omission or misstatement.
Neutrality Absence in reported information of bias intended to attain a predetermined result or to induce a particular mode of behavior.
Predictive Value The quality of information that helps users to increase the likelihood of correctly forecasting the outcome of past or present events.
Relevance The capacity of information to make a difference in a decision by helping users to form predictions about the outcomes of past, present, and future events or to confirm or correct prior expectations.
Reliability The quality of information that assures that information is reasonably free from error and bias and faithfully represents what it purports to represent.
Representational Faithfulness Correspondence or agreement between a measure or description and the phenomenon that it purports to represent (sometimes called validity).
Timeliness Having information available to a decision maker before it loses its capacity to influence decisions.
Understandability The quality of information that enables users to perceive its significance.
Verifiability The ability through consensus among measures to ensure that information represents what it purports to represent or that the chosen method of measurement has been used without error or bias.

Source: FASB, Accounting Standards: Statement of Financial Accounting Concepts 1-6. McGraw-Hill Book Company, New York, N.Y., 1986.

The hierarchical arrangement is used to show certain relationships among the qualities. The hierarchy shows that information useful for decision making is the most important. The primary qualities are that accounting information shall be relevant and reliable. If either of these two qualities is missing, the information cannot be useful. To be relevant, information must be timely, and it must have predictive value or feedback value or both. To be reliable, information must have representational faithfulness and it must be verifiable and neutral. Comparability, including consistency, is a secondary quality that interacts with relevance and reliability and contributes to the overall usefulness of information. Two constraints are shown on the chart: Benefits must exceed costs and materiality. To be useful and worth providing, the benefits of information should exceed its cost. All of the qualities described are subject to a materiality threshold. Materiality refers to whether the magnitude of an omission or misstatement of accounting information would influence the judgment of a reasonable person relying on the information.

Information provided by financial reporting should be understandable to those who have a reasonable understanding of business and economic activities and are willing to study the information with reasonable diligence.

The hierarchy of qualitative characteristics does not rank the characteristics. If information is to be useful, all characteristics are required to a minimum degree. At times various qualities may conflict in particular circumstances, in which event trade-offs are often necessary or appropriate. For example, the most relevant information may be difficult to understand, or information that is easy to understand may not be very relevant.

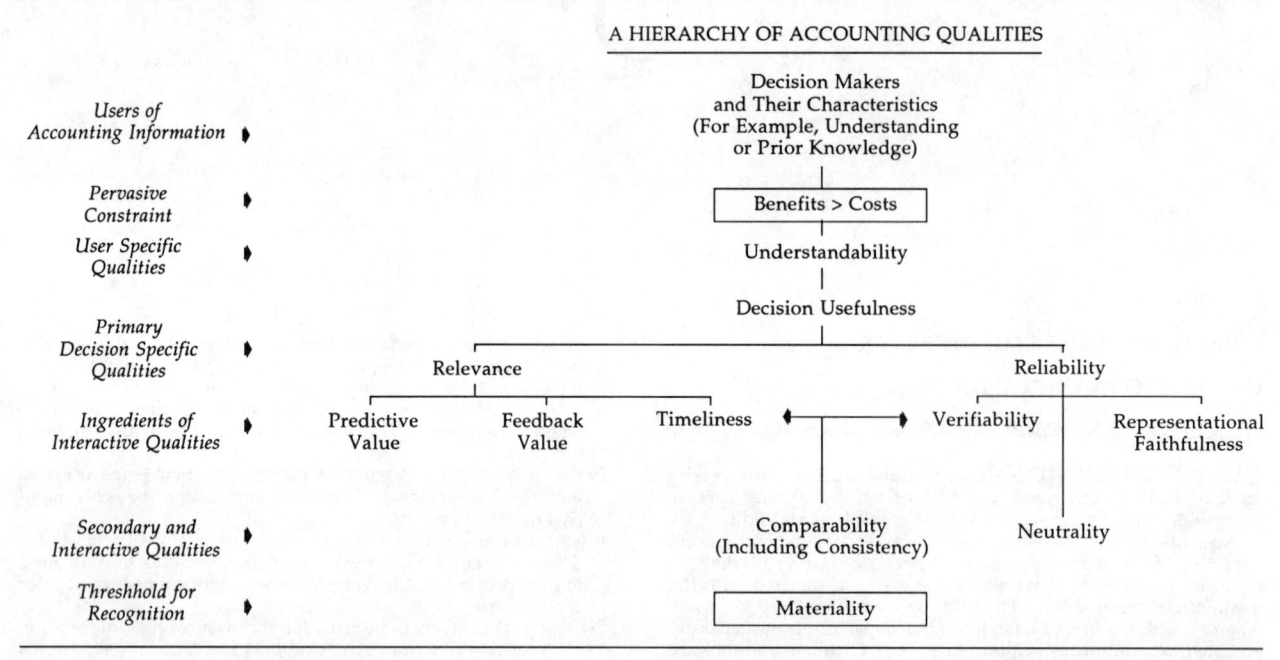

Qualitative Characteristics of Accounting Information

A HIERARCHY OF ACCOUNTING QUALITIES

- **Users of Accounting Information** → Decision Makers and Their Characteristics (For Example, Understanding or Prior Knowledge)
- **Pervasive Constraint** → Benefits > Costs
- **User Specific Qualities** → Understandability
- Decision Usefulness
- **Primary Decision Specific Qualities** → Relevance | Reliability
- **Ingredients of Interactive Qualities** → Predictive Value, Feedback Value, Timeliness | Verifiability, Representational Faithfulness
- **Secondary and Interactive Qualities** → Comparability (Including Consistency), Neutrality
- **Threshhold for Recognition** → Materiality

Source: Statement of Financial Accounting Concepts No. 2, "Qualitative Characteristics of Accounting Information" (Stamford, FASB, May 1980). Copyright by Financial Accounting Standards Board, High Ridge Park, Stamford, Connecticut 06950, U.S.A. Reprinted with permission.

BIBLIOGRAPHY

SFAC No. 2, Qualitative Characteristics of Accounting Information (FASB, 1981).

QUALITY CIRCLES Small groups of workers who meet periodically to consider work-related problems and opportunities, including quality of work, quantity of work, costs, evaluations, and other matters. The major improvements in production and quality of Japanese industry have been attributed, in part, to quality circles (QCs).

Quality circles are claimed to have certain advantages as a management technique:

1. They satisfy needs of employees to participate in planning and improving their work.
2. They provide challenges and growth opportunities for the employees.
3. They are positive motivators for the workforce.

When implementing quality circles as an organizing arrangement, management should:

1. Prepare the organizational environment before introducing the procedure.
2. Have a long-term commitment to the project.
3. Make its support and involvement visible and consistent.
4. Clearly establish the authority and responsibilities of the QCs.
5. Thoroughly train participants in the process and techniques associated with QCs.
6. Give serious consideration to recommendations coming from QCs.

BIBLIOGRAPHY

INGLE, SUD, *Quality Circles Master Guide*. Prentice-Hall, Englewood Cliffs, N.J., 1982.

QUALITY CONTROL Quality is considered one of the components of efficiency, the others being speed, resource utilization, service, and changeability. Quality control refers to adherence to standards or requirements for goods and services produced or received. Quality control provides a degree of assurance to product/service performance. Total quality performance has been defined by A.V. Feigenbaum as "an effective system for integrating the quality development, quality maintenance and quality improvement efforts of the various groups in an organization so as to enable production and service at the most economical level which allow for full customer satisfaction." Inspection and observation are the major activities by which qualitative or quantitative quality controls are monitored. Quality control has its costs:

1. *Cost of conformance:* Costs associated with preventing defects (product design review, vendor approval, process controls, inspection, testing, etc.).
2. *Cost of nonconformance:* Costs associated with product/service defects or failure (rework or redesign, returns and allowances, product liability, etc.).

Quality can be improved if management includes quality in both its short-and long-range planning activities and commits to a policy of quality control. Quality control is essentially management's responsibility. Personnel motivation can be a strong and effective factor in developing product and service quality. Zero-defect programs in production processes can be an effective quality control technique if top management is committed and involved.

BIBLIOGRAPHY

BESTERFIELD, D. H. *Quality Control: A Practical Approach.* Prentice-Hall, Inc., Englewood Cliffs, NJ, 1986.
BUTLER, L. R., and DYNAN, F. J. "Putting Service Quality Into Practice: A Case Study." *Journal of Retail Banking*, Winter, 1988.
COLLETTI, D. L. "Retail Banking Success: A Question of Quality." *Magazine of Bank Administration*, April, 1987.
"Do It Right, Not Over Again." *ABA Banking Journal*, February, 1989.
GOODMAN, J. A., and others. "Converting a Desire for Quality Service into Action with Measurable Impact." *Journal of Retail Banking*, Winter, 1988.
JACKSON, D. M. "Service Quality Improves with Branch Automation," *Magazine of Bank Administration*, March, 1988.
Journal of Quality Technology. Quarterly.

Quality. Monthly.
Quality Control: Meeting the New Competition. American Management Association, New York, NY. Looseleaf.
Quality Progress. Monthly.
RADDON, G. H. "Quality Service—A Low-Cost Profit Strategy." *Bank Marketing*, September, 1987.
SINHA, M. N., and WILLBORN, W. W., *Management of Quality Assurance*, John Wiley and Sons, Inc., New York, NY, 1985.
WADSWORTH, H. M., and others. *Modern Methods for Quality Control and Improvement.* John Wiley and Sons, Inc., New York, NY, 1986.
WAGNER, G. M. "Take An Active Role in the Quality Crusade." *Bank Marketing*, August, 1987.

QUANTITATIVE METHODS Because of the complexity of management, managers have turned to quantitative techniques and models as tools for solving many problems. Such methods are frequently referred to as OPERATIONS RESEARCH (OR).

A rational approach to quantitative decision making involves establishing a well-defined objective, selecting a mathematical or logical model, and arranging an optimization process. Quantitative methods include simulation models and models that establish equations that can be solved mathematically.

Linear programming. Linear programming is a powerful mathematical procedure designed to assist in planning. Most linear programming problems call for the maximization or minimization of some economic objective such as net income, net loss, or costs. These problems often involve the determination of the optimum scheduling routine, product mix, production routing, or transportation route. In such problems, constraints usually exist on available alternatives—for example, constraints on available resources, machine time, manpower, or facilities.

Queuing model. Queuing theory, or waiting-line theory, is concerned primarily with processes that have random arrival intervals and random servicing of customers. Operating, marketing, and production managers have opportunities to apply this analytical tool. Queuing theory involves minimizing overall costs; that is, the waiting costs imposed on customers or businesses and the cost of providing extra service facilities and/or personnel. Examples of waiting-line applications include:

Repair personnel servicing machines.
Parking for trucks and cars.
Docks for transportation.
Clerks for spare-parts counter.
Windows for merchandise returns.
Clerks at check-out counters.

Many waiting-line problems can be solved by managerial intuition or past experience. However, there are many situations too complex for these procedures. Many models are available for dealing with waiting-line problems. One is the single channel exponential service time model. This model uses the following symbols:

A = mean arrival rate
S = mean service rate

A bank has one teller. Persons arrive at an average rate of four per hour. Service time averages twelve per hour (five minutes per customer). The following equations have been developed by management scientists for this model; solutions to the problem are provided:

1. System utilization = Probability that the servers are busy = A/S

$$\frac{4}{12} = 33.4\% \text{ busy}$$

2. Average number in the system = Number of units in the queue plus number being served = A/(S - A)

$$\frac{4}{(12-4)} = .5 \text{ average number in line}$$

3. Average number waiting for service to begin = Number of units in the queue = A squared/S(S - A)

$$\frac{4 \text{ squared}}{12(12-4)} = \frac{16}{96} = \frac{1}{6} \text{ person}$$

4. Average time spent waiting in the system = Queue time plus plus service time = 1/S - A

$$\frac{1}{(12-4)} = \frac{1}{8} \text{ of an hour}$$

5. Average time spent waiting before service begins = Time in que = A/S(S - A)

$$\frac{4}{12(12-4)} = \frac{4}{96} \text{ of an hour}$$

6. Percent of idle time = 1 - A/S

$$1 - 33.4\% = 66.7\% \text{ idle time}$$

QUANTITY THEORY OF MONEY The theory that prices (and therefore the value of money) vary, other things being equal, with the quantity of money in circulation. In its simplest form, the quantity equation, the theory is an old one, found, for example, in the writings of Bodin, Hume, Locke, and Montesquieu. Expressed mathematically, the purely quantitative approach would read as follows:

$$P = \frac{M}{T}$$

in which P is the general price level, M is the quantity of money, and T is the total volume of transactions. P varies directly with M; thus, assuming T remains constant, variations in M have corresponding variations in P. P varies inversely with T; thus, assuming M remains constant, an expansion in T will lower P and vice versa.

In the U.S., the quantity theory was reexamined and statistically investigated by E. W. Kemmerer, Sr. and Irving Fisher, the latter particularly in his *The Purchasing Power of Money* (rev. ed. 1926). In the original edition of this work in 1911, Dr. Fisher developed the cash transactions or transactions-velocity version of the equation, which retained the fundamental theory of causal effect between the factors. The cash transactions version would read as follows:

$$P = \frac{MV + M^1V^1}{T}$$

in which the new factors are V, velocity or turnover of the basic money supply (coin and paper currency); M^1, bank deposit money (demand deposits subject to checking); and V^1, velocity or turnover of M^1. P is passive, determined by interaction of the other variables. T (assuming full employment) can be regarded as fairly constant over the short run, although in the long run economic development (expansion in volume of transactions) would produce a net expansion in transactions. Velocities (V and V^1) could also be regarded as normally stable, being reflective of the payment habits of the population and firms. M^1, in Fisher's view, normally maintains a constant proportion to M. Therefore, the active factor causing changes in P is M, since it causes proportional changes in M^1 and both together directly affect P, the other factors being normally constant. Modern economists disagree with Fisher's analysis of the behavioral characteristics of the above variables, including the alleged passivity of P.

In England, such economists as Marshall, Pigou, and Robertson (the Cambridge school) developed the cash balances version of the quantity theory. Instead of using velocity, this version keeps the stock or volume magnitudes, modifying the concept to equate M with the total price volume of trade (PT) by adjusting PT to the extent of fraction (k) to show the portion of total spending represented by cash balances on hand. The cash balances approach would read as follows:

$$M = PT \times k$$

QUARANTINE

n which k may be assumed to be constant, since it reflects cash holding habits of the population and firms; T also may be assumed to be constant in the short run (assuming full employment, as Fisher does), so that an increase in spending of the floating supply of M (assuming no increase in total M in the economy) will cause a rise in P, given a constant T.

Another version of the quantity theory is that developed by J. W. Angell (*The Behavior of Money*, 1936) which relates the ratio of national income (the product of average price of total goods produced times their physical volume) to the stock of money to establish the income velocity of money.

As definitional equations, the quantity theory's versions would arouse no challenges; it is when the equations are used as the framework for pinpointing causative variables, however, leading to recommendations as to policy actions, that criticism is aroused. In back of the cost-push explanation for price inflation of recent years in the U.S., for example, as opposed to the demand-pull explanation, is the concept that P is not passive as Fisher supposed.

See INFLATION.

QUARANTINE This term has two meanings:

1. In navigation law, the period of time during which a vessel is detained in the harbor or treatment station before passengers or crew may go ashore, while segregation and treatment for infectious disease proceeds; also, the regulation relating to this period of time. Every ship clearing a foreign port for a port in the United States is required under U.S. navigation laws to obtain from the consular officer of the United States thereat a bill or certificate of health for the vessel, covering its cargo, crew, and passengers.
2. In real estate law, the common law right of a widow to continue living in her deceased husband's residence for a period of forty days following his death.

QUARTER This term has three meanings:

1. The U.S. quarter dollar, or $0.25 piece. Pursuant to the Coinage Act of 1965 (P.L. 89-81, July 23, 1965), silver has been completely eliminated from the coin. The two outer layers are composed of a cupronickel alloy of 75% copper and 25% nickel, metallurgically bonded to a center core or inner layer of pure copper. The obverse and reverse sides are white in appearance, and the copper core gives the coin a copper-colored edge. The clad quarter weighs 5.67 grams, compared with 6.25 grams for the former silver (90% silver, 10% copper) quarter.

   The referenced Coinage Act of 1965 repealed Section 43(b)(1) of the act of May 12, 1933, as amended (31 U.S.C. 462), with respect to the full legal tender status of all coins and currencies of the United States, including Federal Reserve notes, and added a new law to the same effect codified in 31 U.S.C. 392.
   See TOKEN MONEY.
2. A unit of measure used in English markets, chiefly in connection with grains. A quarter is eight bushels.
3. A short expression for quarter-year, or three months, often used in connection with interim financial statements and dividend payments on a quarterly basis.

QUARTER DAYS The days marking the beginning of each quarter of the calendar year—January 1, April 1, July 1, and October 1. Quarter days are the most usual dividend and interest payment dates. In law, quarter days are those days on which rent, debt installments, etc., payable quarteryearly are by law or custom payable.

Most bond interest is paid semiannually, on January 1 and July 1. However, February 1, May 1, August 1, and November 1 quarterly payment dates for stocks have increased in popularity with corporations and dividend disbursing agents as a means of spreading the load.

See QUARTERLY DISBURSEMENTS.

QUARTER EAGLE A formerly coined U.S. gold coin with a denomination of $2.50, one-fourth of the full denomination of the eagle ($10).

The Gold Reserve Act of 1934 (January 30, 1934) provided that all the monetary gold of the United States thereafter would be in bullion form and all gold coinage would be ended, pursuant to nationalization of gold originally provided for by an executive order of April 5, 1933 (requiring all persons to deliver monetary gold in any form to Federal Reserve banks for other lawful money). The Gold Reserve Act of 1934 required the Federal Reserve banks to transfer all gold coin and bullion to the U.S. Treasury.

See GOLD COINS.

QUARTERLY DISBURSEMENTS Dividends on stocks usually are paid quarterly. The most popular quarterly dates are the calendar quarter days, January 1, April 1, July 1, and October 1, or "JAJO," the first letters of the quarter-months involved. The next most popular quarterly dates are February 1, May 1, August 1, and November 1, or "FMAN."

Although bond interest is sometimes paid quarterly, it is usually paid semiannually, on January 1 and July 1. Income bond interest is customarily paid annually, usually on April 1 or May 1, if earned and declared by directors out of earnings for the preceding calendar year. Bonds that carry a mixed rate—the interest rate being partly in fixed interest and partly in contingent interest dependent upon earnings and declaration by directors—usually provide for regular semiannual payment of the fixed portion of the rate and for annual payment of the contingent portion, usually on April 1 or May 1, out of earnings for the preceding calendar year.

Corporations that do their own paying of interest and dividends on bonds and stocks or appoint fiscal agents to distribute interest and dividends are torn between the desire to place their securities on an investment basis by affording investors periodic disbursements during the year and the cost-minded objective of keeping down the cost of such disbursements by having fewer disbursement dates. A basic advantage of investing in INVESTMENT COMPANY shares is the function of investment companies in collecting interest and dividends paid by corporations on varying disbursement dates and in turn paying out their own dividends to shareholders based on dividend and interest income on uniform dates, usually quarterly or semiannually.

In former years, when money rates were sensitive to changes in EXCESS RESERVES of banks, the volume of interest and dividend disbursements (particularly on the heaviest dates of January 1 and July 1), like the volume of income tax payments on income tax dates, used to affect money rates temporarily because of the money pinch caused until the payments flowed back to the banks.

QUASIMUNICIPAL BONDS *See* SEMIMUNICIPAL BONDS.

QUASI-REORGANIZATION When a corporation encounters financial difficulties, it may attempt to reorganize its capital structure through formal court proceedings. To avoid the problems and expense of court proceedings, a procedure called quasi-reorganization can be undertaken that will accomplish basically the same objective. The purpose of a quasi-reorganization is to absorb a deficit (debit balance in the retained earnings account) and give the enterprise a fresh start. In a quasi-reorganization, a deficit is eliminated against contributed capital. If legal capital is being reduced, state approval is normally required; otherwise, only stockholders' approval is required. Once the deficit is eliminated, the corporation can proceed as though it had been legally reorganized. If the corporation operates profitably after the quasi-reorganization, dividends can be declared which would not have been possible in most states if the deficit had not been eliminated.

Subsequent to the quasi-reorganization, the new retained earnings account shown in the balance sheet must be dated to show it runs from the effective date of the readjustment. This dating should be disclosed in the statements as long as it has special significance, usually until after a post-reorganization earnings pattern has been established. A balance sheet disclosure in the stockholders' equity section could be as follows:

Retained earnings accumulated since October 31, 1992, at which time a $500,000 deficit was eliminated as a result of a quasi-reorganization	$80,000

QUICK ASSETS All those assets that in the ordinary course of business will be converted into cash, or that in case of an emergency can be quickly realized upon without appreciable sacrifice (thus constituting a comprehensive concept of liquidity). In the practice of financial STATEMENT ANALYSIS, the quick asset ratio is the ratio of cash and receivables only to total current liabilities (ACID TEST ratio). Includible also would be any marketable securities which a firm might have of the secondary reserve type. This latter concept emphasizes liquidity in the operating sense, as opposed to the liquidating sense. Inventory would be excluded.

See CURRENT ASSETS.

QUINTAL A metric measure of weight, consisting of 100 kilograms and equivalent to 220.46 pounds.

See METRIC SYSTEM.

QUIT-CLAIM DEED A type of DEED in which the grantor releases to the grantee any and all title or interest which the grantor has in the described property, but which contains no warranty or covenants of title.

QUORUM The Comptroller of the Currency requires that the bylaws of all national banks be in conformity with their own articles of association and the National Bank Act. The definition of what constitutes a quorum for the board of directors must be stated in the bylaws. The specimen bylaws which are furnished by the Comptroller of the Currency on request provide that a majority of DIRECTORS is required to constitute a quorum and that no business can be transacted without a quorum. It is accordingly the custom among all banks to provide that a majority of the board of directors be present in order to constitute a quorum for the transaction of business.

QUOTA This term has three meanings:

1. In immigration restrictions, the allowable immigration annually for specified nationalities under the Immigration Act of 1924 (*see* POPULATION).
2. In operations of the INTERNATIONAL MONETARY FUND, the membership subscriptions of fund members into the fund. The Interim Committee considering the seventh general review of the quotas of members reported its view as of October 25, 1978 that there was a need for an increase in total quotas if the expected need for conditional liquidity over the next five years was to be met, and that such an increase would strengthen the available sources of balance-of-payments financing by enhancing the ability of the fund to provide such financing without heavy recourse to borrowing and by furthering the process of international adjustment.
3. In connection with restrictive practices in international trade, quantitative import controls and restrictions. Quotas are imposed by the federal government to protect domestic producers in selected industries from foreign competition by limiting the supply of certain imported products. There are benefits and costs from the use of quotas as a protectionist device. Economic gains to the producers and employees in the protected industries are often substantial, as measured by increased profitability. Industries wanting to limit foreign competition can exert a great deal of political pressure by lobbying for quotas. Consumers, however, bear the cost of this action because prices for the protected products are higher than they would be if there were freer trade, and the range of product choices to consumers is generally smaller.

See GENERAL AGREEMENT ON TARIFFS AND TRADE.

QUOTATIONS Prices at which securities, commodities, and other property for which there is a large and ready market are being currently quoted, i.e., being bid or offered. A full quotation will express what will be paid (bid) and the offered price (asked). The normal order for quotations is the bid first, the asked price next. Quotations may be nominal (an approximation of the current bidding and selling prices, aided by such indications as last recorded transaction, current inquiries, and prevailing market trends), in which case the quoter does not stand ready to buy or sell at the nominal prices, or firm, in which case the quoter stands ready to transact business at the quoted prices. In the latter case, the size either way—bid or asked—will usually be given. Activity will be indicated by the amount of the spread between bid and asked; in essence this represents how close buyers and sellers are as to price, so that actual transactions occur in volume. Firm quotations may be left with the inquirer for a reasonable period of time, but usually only on a subject basis—subject to prior sale or prior purchase, as the case may be, by the quoter. Dealers checking one another's quotations will create uniformity in the market, as differences will be quickly detected and appropriate transactions effected to close the gaps.

Market Data System. The New York Stock Exchange's Market Data System (MDS), operated by the Securities Industry Automation Corporation (SIAC), went into full operation in 1966. The MDS computer began operating the ticker system in June, 1966, from optical-scanning card readers at posts on the trading floor. All posts were phased into the system by the close of 1966. As each post was converted from manual to direct computer input, a post printer and automatic call-out of all transactions at the post also went into operation. The system provides instantaneous collection of transaction and quotation data, linking the trading floor with display devices at member firms' offices throughout the U.S. and abroad. A new Market Data Control Division was formed within the Ticker and Quotation Department to oversee the various functions of the Market Data System.

In turn, quotations may be obtained at a member firm's office by means of an electronic interrogation device which has instant access to a computer center that receives current market information (bid and asked and sales data) from the Market Data System.

NASDAQ. In 1966, the Board of Governors of the National Association of Securities Dealers, Inc. (NASD) appointed a special Automation Committee to investigate the feasibility of automated quotations in the over-the-counter market. During the 1968 fiscal year, an independent management consulting firm, under the direction of the Automation Committee, conducted a study of the economic feasibility of such a system. The findings of the consultant and detailed specifications concerning a proposed NASD automated quotations system known as NASDAQ (National Association of Securities Dealers Automated Quotations) were submitted to several private firms. Following consideration of proposals received from these firms, the Automation Committee selected the firm which in its opinion could best supply and operate the physical equipment for the system under the direction and supervision of the NASD. The NASDAQ system became operational in February, 1971, and in February, 1976, NASDAQ, Inc., a wholly owned subsidiary of the NASD, purchased the assets of the NASDAQ system from its builder and operator, the Bunker Ramo Corporation.

NASDAQ involves the use of electronic data processing equipment in combination with communications facilities in a three-level system designed to meet the quotations needs of professional traders in the over-the-counter markets. Level I provides a current representative interdealer bid and asked price for any security registered in the system for the information of registered representatives and customers of retail firms. Level II is designed for use by firm trading departments and supplies upon request a list of market makers, together with their respective current bid and asked prices for each security registered in the system. Level III is also for use by trading departments, but differs from Level II chiefly in providing input facilities allowing authorized market makers to enter, change, or update bid and asked prices.

NASDAQ enables the NASD to provide newspapers with up-to-date bid and asked prices, thereby providing a more reliable indication of current markets. Another feature of the NASDAQ System is the publication of over-the-counter stock indices. These indices, together with volume figures and other statistical information gleaned from NASDAQ, provide an overview of trends and operations of the over-the-counter market heretofore not available.

The NASD supplies to newspapers bids and offers quoted by over-the-counter dealers to each other as of approximately 4:00 P.M. (Eastern time); such quotations do not include retail markup, markdown, or commission, and do not represent transactions. The over-the-counter weekly list, consisting of a group of unlisted securities less widely held than those on the daily over-the-counter list, is quoted on a similar basis.

Stock tables published in the newspapers list the open, high, low, and close, as well as change for the day and reported volume, on actual transactions for stocks traded on the principal exchanges. High and low range and information on dividends paid are also provided. Closing bid and asked prices of stocks not traded during the day are published by newspapers providing comprehensive coverage. The Associated Press, which supplies stock tables to newspapers throughout the United States and in foreign countries, provides automated transmission of stock tables. Some newspapers

QUOTATION TICKER

carry such stock tables of actual transactions on leading exchanges for the more widely held stocks only, rather than complete tables.

The *Bank and Quotation Record,* published by the *Commercial and Financial Chronicle,* provides a reference source for data on transaction prices as well as quotations for listed and unlisted issues. The *National Stock Summary* provides recapitulation of bids and offers by dealers in over-the-counter securities.

QUOTATION TICKER   *First see* TICKER.

The tickers of the NEW YORK STOCK EXCHANGE (NYSE) and AMERICAN STOCK EXCHANGE normally carry prices of actual transactions. Half an hour after the opening, however, if space and activity permit, quotations may appear on the tape, showing the bid and asked prices after an actual transaction is recorded and a change in quotation occurs. Thus:

1/X 31.B.30 3/4... 31 1/4

would indicate a transaction of a round lot (100 shares) of U.S. Steel common at 31, followed by a new quotation of 30 3/4 bid, offered at 31 1/4.

After the close of trading, the ticker will run quotations, including the basis prices set by the ODD-LOT DEALERS.

Under normal trading conditions, the New York Stock Exchange's 900-character-per-minute stock ticker reports NYSE transactions on the tape within seconds after they are entered into the Market Data System, operated by the Securities Industry Automation Corporation (SIAC), a joint subsidiary of the New York and American stock exchanges. Trading in exchange-listed issues in other markets is also entered into the system and transmitted to tickers, cathode-ray-tube units, and moving bulletin boards across the country.

See TAPE.

ENCYCLOPEDIA OF BANKING AND FINANCE

R

RACKETEER INFLUENCED AND CORRUPT ORGANIZATIONS ACT (RICO) Federal legislation providing for harsh penalties, including seizure of assets and profits earned through illicit activities, originally intended as tool for fighting organized crime but later used for other purposes, including white-collar crimes such as futures trading fraud and insider trading. In mid 1989, traders on the Chicago futures markets were charged under RICO with defrauding customers—mail fraud and wire fraud and crimes in the trading pits. Tactics used to get around the exchanges' open outcry trading procedures included:

1. *Prearranged trading:* Trading when two or more traders buy and sell futures among themselves without offering the orders in the pits.
2. *Front-running:* Brokers trade ahead of large customer orders they are expected to execute, thereby profiting from the market effect of the orders.
3. *Bucketing:* A method for skimming customers' profits.

RICO has been criticized as being improperly or unfairly employed in certain cases. Government attorneys have frequently obtained temporary restraining orders (TRO) upon the filing of RICO indictment to preserve all forfeitable assets of the defendant until the trial is completed and judgment entered. Some attorneys have objected to this on the grounds that such action prior to conviction violates basic constitutional rights, including seizure of property without due process. In addition, TROs have sometimes had harsh impacts on third parties who have done business with defendants. In 1989, the criminal division of the Department of Justice imposed restrictions on the use of TROs in RICO prosecutions. The restrictions require that the prosecution show that other remedies cannot preserve the assets for forfeiture in the event of a conviction. The prosecution must also state the anticipated impact that forfeiture and the TRO might have on noninvolved third parties. The forfeiture must be proportionate to the defendant's asserted crime. Further, the government must state that it will not seek to disrupt the legitimate business activities of the defendant or to take from third parties assets legally transferred to them.

RAID The free selling of stocks by professional operators who take advantage of a situation—a temporarily overbought market, unfavorable news, or knowledge that the market is honeycombed with stop orders not far below current quotations—to depress prices in order to be able to cover at a profit. The term is usually used in connection with the term "bear." Market reviewers sometimes report: "The bears raided the market."

RAILROAD BONDS Bonds of railroad corporations may be classified as follows:

1. *As to class of lien:*
   a. First mortgage.
   b. Second mortgage.
   c. General mortgage.
   d. Debenture.
   e. Adjustment.
   f. Income.
2. *As to security:*
   a. Mortgage issues.
   b. Equipment trust issues.
   c. Collateral trust issues.
   d. Debentures (unsecured).
3. *As to purpose:*
   a. Divisional bonds.
   b. Extension bonds.
   c. Equipment bonds.
   d. Terminal bonds.
   e. Consolidated mortgage bonds.
   f. Refunding bonds.

"Underlying" (senior) bonds of long-established railroad corporations are among the most seasoned of corporation bonds, since they have been on the market longer than many other issues and the value of the underlying properties and earning power of the various issues are matters of historical record and tested by time. As a class, therefore, the higher-grade railroad bonds customarily enjoyed in the past a higher investment regard than public utility or industrial bonds. This regard was shaken during the 1929-1932 depression, when the large number of railroads which went into receivership and the decline in margins of safety in earnings coverage of charges, even for higher-grade issues, led to a decline in investment regard for railroad bonds. In recent years, regard for railroad credit has been restored to appropriate levels for the highest-grade liens. Since the railroads have not been dynamically in the market for new bond money, the supply of high-grade railroad liens is relatively low and closely held by institutional investors.

See ADJUSTMENT BONDS, COLLATERAL TRUST BONDS, CONSOLIDATED MORTGAGE BONDS, DEBENTURE BONDS, DIVISIONAL BOND, EQUIPMENT TRUST, EXTENSION BOND, FIRST MORTGAGE BONDS, GENERAL MORTGAGE BONDS, INCOME BOND, REFUNDING BONDS, SECOND MORTGAGE BONDS, TERMINAL BONDS.

RAILROAD CONTINGENT FUND *See* CONTINGENT FUND, RECAPTURE CLAUSE.

RAILROAD EARNINGS Railroad earnings in general are characterized by both negative and positive aspects. On the one hand, it is pointed out that revenue ton-mileage gains have lagged behind gains in the Federal Reserve Board's production index's manufacturing component, as well as gross national product; that the decline in average ton-mile revenue after 1958 has coincided with decline in the Interstate Commerce Commission's index of carload freight rates; that rise in labor costs has largely offset productivity gains; and that operating margins have shrunk.

On the other hand, it is argued that there has been substantial improvement in cost control with the use of advanced techniques including data processing equipment; that the quality of many types of traffic has improved in the sense of reduced cyclical fluctuation; and that operating leverage and capital structure leverage should magnify upturns in profit margins as revenues improve. Moreover, it is pointed out that lifting the load of unprofitable passenger operations off the railroads should help earnings, as should merger savings, diesel power savings, and gains from diversified holdings of railroads and/or their holding company parents.

BIBLIOGRAPHY

ASSOCIATION OF AMERICAN RAILROADS. *Analysis of Class I Railroads.* Annual.
———. *Economic ABZs of the Railroad Industry.*

RAILROAD EQUIPMENT BONDS See EQUIPMENT TRUST.

RAILROAD INDUSTRY One of the oldest basic industries in the United States, the railroad industry has undergone the full cycle of promotion and development, growth, and maturity since the first railroad in the United States, the Baltimore & Ohio, was opened in 1829.

Until 1850, the railroads were in a trial period of promotion and experimentation; the canals were dominant in inland transportation until about the 1870s. In 1850, however, the railroads began to expand aggressively, aided by land grants from the federal government and the states and subsidies of various types from states and localities. In 1869, the first transcontinental line was completed; in the decade beginning in 1880, total mileage was more than doubled; and in 1887, the federal government stepped in for the first time with regulation through the Interstate Commerce Act, supplementing regulation by the states. The development period may be said to have culminated by 1890, when total mileage owned reached a total of 163,597 miles, with 1,013 steam railroads operating and $8 billion investment in road and equipment.

In the period 1890-1920, the railroad industry may be said to have reached the zenith in growth. During this period, the number of steam railroads reached a high of 1,564 (1907), and mileage owned reached a high of 254,251 miles (1916). Investment in road and equipment jumped from $8 billion in 1890 to $19.8 billion in 1920, and mileage owned, from 163,597 miles to 252,845 miles. Total operating revenues increased from $1,052 million in 1890 to $6,310 million in 1920. In the latter year the Transportation Act of 1920 was enacted, marking the fullest stage of federal regulation.

In 1920, however, a period of maturity set in which witnessed declines in the number of railroads, mileage, and gross revenues. In the two decades from 1920 to 1940, the number of railroads was reduced from 1,085 to 574; mileage owned, from 252,845 miles to 233,670 miles; and gross revenues, from $6,310 million to $4,355 million, a low point in gross revenues of $3,138 million being set in 1933. In the period 1930-1939, a total of 110 railroads with total mileage of 80,957 miles, or about one-third of all owned mileage, went into receivership or trusteeship. Rate of return upon net property investment declined from 5.35% in 1926 to 1.61% in 1938. During this period, many factors combined to make the railroads a sick industry—the loss of passenger business and short haul traffic to the automobile and truck, competition from the airlines, pipelines, and water carriers, inadequate rates, and the adverse effect of leverage in railroad capitalizations and operations during the decline in gross revenues—and the "transportation problem" became a chronic subject of study.

Fortunately for the railroad industry, the railroads remained under private operation during World War II, and with competing forms of transportation curtailed by war conditions, a resurgence of railroad prosperity enabled the railroads to regain their best financial and operating position since that enjoyed before the federal government took over their operation in World War I. The railroads took advantage of their refound prosperity by reducing debt and fixed charges, increasing maintenance and capital outlays, strengthening working capital, and emerging from receivership or reorganization with scaled down capitalizations and charges. Thus, from 1940 to 1947, funded debt was reduced from $10.6 billion to $8.5 billion; fixed charges, from $619 million to $435 million; capital expenditures increased from $429 million to $865 million; maintenance outlays rose from $497 million for roadway and structures and $819 million for equipment to $1.2 billion for roadway and structures and $1.6 billion for equipment; and net working capital, despite the large capital expenditures and retirement of debt, increased from $536.5 million at the close of 1940 to $1.6 billion at the close of 1947.

In the post-World War II years, substantial rate relief and a more sympathetic attitude on the part of the Interstate Commerce Commission toward earnings problems were of material assistance to the railroads in seeking to retain their margins in the face of fluctuation in volume and inflationary rise in costs. Beginning in 1951, under stimulation of the Korean War defense effort, operating revenues passed the $10 billion mark for the first time, averaging $10.2 billion for the years 1951-1955 and dipping below the $10 billion level only in the recession year 1954 ($9.4 billion). Passenger revenues responded to Korean War stimulation with rises to $900 million and $906 million in 1951 and 1952, compared with $813 million in 1950; but by 1953 they had started a decline which is still continuing. By contrast, freight revenues reached their Korean peak of $8,950 million in 1953, compared with $8,788 million in 1952, $8,634 million in 1951, $7,817 million in 1950, and $7,048 million in 1949. They did this on revenue ton-mileage of 605.8 billion in 1953, against 614.8 billion in 1952 and 646.6 billion in 1951, thanks to higher freight rates. After setbacks to $7.79 billion in freight revenues and to 549 billion in revenue ton-miles for 1954, freight revenues rose to $8,538 million in 1955 and peak of $8,951 million in 1956, on revenue ton-mileage of 623.6 billion in 1955 and 647.1 billion in 1956.

The year 1955 proved to be the best post-World War II year for profitability: (1) although 5.2% less than in 1953, the 1955 operating revenues showed an appreciable 7.8% gain over those for 1954; (2) with operating expenses holding at a level only 3.5% above those for 1954, a well-leveraged 29.1% increase occurred in net railway operating income; (3) at $1,128 million, net railway operating income topped the previous post-World War II record of $1,109 million (1953); (4) net income rose to $925 million, an all-time high; and (5) rate of return (profit) on investment reached 4.22%, close to the best post-World War II level of 4.31% (1948).

In the period 1955-1970, revenue ton-miles rose a total of 22.3%; average revenue per ton-mile rose from $0.01370 to $0.01432 in 1970, the highest level since the 1957, 1958, and 1959 levels of $0.01445, $0.01463, and $0.01445, respectively; and operating revenues rose to a new all-time high of $11,983 million, compared with $10,106 million in 1955.

With such a strong showing in revenues and volume, the railroads should have been able to bring down a reasonable proportion of the revenue gains, with even no more than a fair experience with costs. Instead, the horrendous rise in costs wiped out all of the revenue gains: (1) operating ratio (operating expenses to total revenues) rose from 75.7% to 81.2%; (2) transportation expenses (which include wages of conductors, engineers, trainmen, yardmen, and station employees; fuel and supplies; and other expenses involved in the handling of traffic) rose to new highs in 1970, totaling 40.8% of revenues compared with 37.3% in 1955 and alone eating up by their rise 60% of the rise in revenues between the two years; (3) rise in maintenance expenses ate up another 35% of the rise in revenues; (4) total expenses (including general, miscellaneous), and the preceding categories) rose $2,083 million, compared with the total rise in revenues of $1,877 million, totally wiping out the gain in revenues and then some; (5) payroll taxes more than doubled, rising $292 million; (6) equipment and joint facility rents (net expenses) tripled to $776 million, versus $252 million in 1955; and (7) interest charges rose about 70%, from $311 million to $522 million. As a result, net income (ordinary income, before extraordinary and prior period charges and credits) plummeted from $927 million in 1955 to less than $127 million in 1970, and thus the indicated net profit margin (as percentage of revenues) dropped from 9.2% in 1955 to 1.1% in 1970.

Moreover, the rate of return (net railway operating income) on net investment (investment in transportation property, net of depreciation and amortization) came down from 4.22% in 1955 to 1.47% in 1970, its lowest since the depression year of 1932.

Industry's Status and Outlook. Characterizing railroading as a "sick industry, finding it more and more difficult to meet the public's needs," ASTRO (America's Sound Transportation Review Organization, created by the board of directors of the Association of American Railroads in September 1969) in its 1970 prospectus on the industry summarized the situation as follows:

1. Railroads must regain financial strength if they are to remain in private enterprise.
2. Railroad earnings are falling at a serious rate.
3. Low earnings prevent an adequate return on the fixed investment in railroads.
4. Even appropriating earnings from nontransportation sources, railroad income continues to decline.
5. Because of marginal earnings, capital improvement programs are falling further behind.
6. The decline in earnings has continued.
7. Published figures may even understate the railroads' capital shortage.
8. Poor results, year in and year out, have nationwide consequences beyond the localized effects of difficulties of particular carriers or certain regions.

The Interstate Commerce Commission, in its 1969 *Annual Report*, agreed with the unfavorable appraisal of the outlook for the railroads: "Given competitive pressure, continued inflation, and unsatisfactory rates of return, the general financial condition of railroads may be expected to remain poor, capital expenditures to remain minimal, and reduction in employment extended."

Yet the volume outlook called for more railroad freight service in the future. In the 20 years ended with 1969, intercity ton-miles increased by 107% and railroad ton-miles by 46%; and in the 8 years ended with 1969, the increases were 4.8% per annum in intercity ton-miles and 4% in railroad ton-mileage. Assuming a growth rate of 3.5% per annum through 1980, and assuming the railroads' share of total intercity ton-mileage remained at 41%, total intercity ton-mileage would have been 2,774 billion in 1980, compared with 1,900 billion in 1969; and the railroads' intercity ton-mileage would have been 1,140 billion in 1980, compared with 780 billion in 1969. For the railroads, that would have been 46% greater volume by 1980. Actually, the railroads' share of total intercity freight ton-mileage declined in 1980 to 37%, but that was still a rise compared to 35.7% for 1979, and total freight ton-mileage of the railroads did achieve a 19.5% rise compared to 1969.

Moreover, because of freight rate increases since 1969, the volume achieved in 1980 meant total freight revenues of $26.3 billion, compared with $10.3 billion in 1969, an increase of over 2.5 times in freight revenues.

The appended table shows major operating and financial statistics for Class 1 railroads 1987-1989.

It should be noted, however, that such growth has been distributed differentially among the different districts and railroads servicing them. Moreover, over time railroads have become proportionally heavier movers of bulk industrial materials and products, and thus their revenues are more vulnerable to the effects of economic fluctuations.

Conrail. The Consolidated Rail Corporation (Conrail), created by the Regional Rail Reorganization Act of 1973 (45 U.S.C. 701) as a for-profit corporation, began operations on April 1, 1976, when it assumed major portions of six bankrupt railroads: Penn Central, Central of New Jersey, Lehigh Valley, Lehigh and Hudson River, Erie-Lackawanna, and Reading. Conrail thus took over a 17,000 route-mile (34,000 track-mile) system that served 16 northeastern and midwestern states, the District of Columbia, and two Canadian provinces.

Conrail was created under a reorganization plan prepared by the United States Railway Association (USRA). The reorganization plan projected that Conrail would incur losses through 1978 but would begin earning a profit in 1979. The reorganization plan also anticipated that Conrail would need financial help to cover operating losses in its early years and to support a massive capital rehabilitation and improvements program. Accordingly, Congress provided $3.3 billion in federal funds for Conrail until the company could generate enough from its own operations to become self-sufficient. However, through December 31, 1980, Conrail piled up net losses from operations of $1.3 billion.

The Northeast Rail Service Act, signed August 31, 1981, called for the federal government to sell Conrail by June, 1983, if it had achieved profitability and was thus saleable, or else liquidate it. The secretary of Transportation was directed in the referenced act to retain an investment banker as soon as practicable. Conrail's operations improved steadily in 1981.

Conrail recorded its first annual profit in 1981, a $39 million net income based on generally accepted accounting principles. The company pointed out that this profit was achieved despite an 8% decline in total carloadings in 1981 compared to 1980, when Conrail incurred a loss of $244 million. In addition to recurring operations, Conrail's 1981 financial results reflected the effects of provisions for losses on disposition of assets, sales of tax benefits, and other unusual transactions.

During the 1980s and 1990s, the rail industry improved its profitability, efficiency, and financial statements. In 1970 the year of the Penn Central bankruptcy, the industry had a return on investment of 1.7% and experienced a net working capital deficit of an estimated $60 million. Long-term debt approximated 65% of equity. Subsequently, deregulation provided by the Railroad Revitalization and Regulatory Act of 1976 and the Staggers Act of 1980 along with infusions of federal funds have rescued the industry. In 1987, Class I railroads had an ROI of 5.1% and positive working capital in excess of $700 million. Revenue adequacy has not yet been attained, but progress has been evidenced. The industry has had difficulty in earning a return on investment equal to the cost of capital (11.6% in 1987). Featherbedding remains a difficult problem for the industry as do numerous work rules that promote inefficiencies and inflate costs. To reduce costs, the industry has focused on modern technology, improved efficiency, and consolidation to reduce employment and increase productivity.

Passenger Deficits. The Rail Passenger Service Act of 1970 provided that operation of intercity passenger trains on railroads electing to participate was to be handled under contract for the newly formed National Railroad Passenger Corporation. Trains not included in its "Amtrak" network (formerly called "Railpax") could be discontinued. The plan was expected to reduce, and perhaps eventually to eliminate, the deficits attributable to intercity railroad passenger service.

That deficit in passenger service totaled $470 million for 1970, compared with $464 million in 1969, having run in the range of $394 million (1962) to $724 million (1957) since the beginning of the 1950s. The deficit related solely to passenger service (reflecting directly assigned expenses) was $250 million for 1970, up successively from $225 million in 1969, $198 million in 1968, $138 million in 1967, $31 million in 1966, $44 million in 1965, $18 million in 1964, and $9 million in 1963. These directly charged passenger service costs included passenger service expenses, taxes, and rents. In addition, under the formula and accounting prescribed by the Interstate Commerce Commission, common expenses were apportioned statistically to the freight services and to the passenger services.

The National Railroad Passenger Corporation (Amtrak) was created "when it appeared that rail passenger service could no longer be supported by private railroad companies" (report by the Comptroller General of the U.S.). Specifically, the Rail Passenger Service Act of 1970 as amended (84 Stat. 1327; 45 U.S.C. 541) created the National Railroad Passenger Corporation as a for-profit corporation "to provide a balanced transportation system by improving and developing intercity rail passenger service."

The federal government had given Amtrak billions for its capital acquisition and improvement programs. This has been necessary because Amtrak has not become the for-profit corporation that was planned in 1970, when initial funding for it came from the government and from private railroads giving up passenger service. Federal financing authorized for Amtrak in 1971 amounted to $40 million for operating expenses and $100 million in loan guarantees for capital acquisitions. The railroads had a choice of taking either common stock or a tax writeoff for their payments. Four railroads (the Burlington Northern, Grand Trunk Western, Milwaukee Railroad, and Trustees of the Penn Central) elected to take common stock that had a total par value of $94 million. Since 1971, a "unique" relationship has evolved between Amtrak and the federal government. While Amtrak has remained a private corporation, like a public entity it supplies a service to the public and is significantly controlled and financed by the federal government. Such control includes controlling the board of directors' selection and makeup, providing for accountability requirements related to Amtrak's status as a mixed-ownership corporation (such as annual audits by the General Accounting Office), and determining route structures.

Table 1 / Rail Forecast—Class I Railroads

Item	R1987	P1988	E1989
Operating revenues (bil. $)	$26.5	$28.0	$27.9
Yr.-to-yr. change	+1.5%	+5.7%	–0.4%
Operating profits (bil. $)	$2.75	$3.10	$3.63
Yr.-to-yr. change	+109.6%	+12.7%	+17.1%
Operating ratio	89.6%	88.9%	87.0%
Ton miles (in billions)	948.0	1001.0	995.0
Yr.-to-yr. change)	+9.3%	+5.6%	–0.6%
Revenues per ton-mile (Yr.-to-yr. change)	–6.8%	–0.4%	+0.4%
Return on Net Invst	5.2%	5.7%	6.5%
Change in industrial output	+3.8%	+5.7%	+2.7%

E-Estimated.
R-Revised.
Note: Operating profits in 1987 penalized by $607 million of special charges. Profits in 1988 reduced by $733 million by charges.
Source: Standard & Poor's Corp.

RAILROAD LEGISLATION

Table 2 / Amtrak Passengers, Passenger Miles, Daily Train Miles Revenues, Costs, Deficit and Ratios—Fiscal Years: 1976-1986

Category	1976	1977	1978	1979	1980	1981	1982	1983	1984	1985	1986	%Change 1985-86	%Change 1976-86
Passenger (millions)	16.9	19.2	18.9	21.4	21.2	20.2	19.0	19.0	19.9	20.8	20.3	−2.3	20.1
Passenger Miles (billions)	3.8	4.3	4.0	4.9	4.6	4.8	4.2	4.2	4.6	4.8	5.0	4.2	31.6
Daily Train Miles	85.7	86.7	86.4	86.5	81.1	84.1	78.5	79.8	79.4	82.2	79.2	−3.6	−7.6
Operating Revenue	277.8	311.2	313.0	381.3	436.8	612.2	630.7	664.4	758.8	825.8	861.4	4.3	210.1
Corporate Costs	56.4	56.8	60.2	45.3	50.5	84.1	145.2	120.0	36.9	34.0	33.4	−1.8	−40.8
Operating Costs	665.8	784.2	830.1	952.8	1,102.8	1,2525.5	1,280.6	1,349.4	1,485.2	1,566.1	1,530.2	−2.3	129.8
Total Costs	715.5	842.4	890.3	988.1	1,153.3	1,336.6	1,425.8	1,469.4	1,522.1	1,600.1	1,563.6	−2.3	118.5
Deficit[1]	437.9	531.2	577.3	616.8	716.5	724.4	795.1	804.9	763.3	774.3	702.0	−9.3	60.4
Revenue/Costs Ratio[2]	0.405	0.386	0.365	0.415	0.431	0.421	0.5	0.54	0.56	0.58	0.6	6.9	53.1

[1] Deficit before federal operating payments, but after state subsidies.
[2] Interest and depreciation removed from Total Costs before calculating the ratio.

Amtrak's basic route system was designated by the Secretary of Transportation in 1971. Additions to the route structure were authorized by Congress, designated experimental by the Secretary of Transportation, and later officially made by Amtrak's board of directors upon request from state, regional, or local agencies under funding arrangements set by the Rail Passenger Service Act.

The appended table shows basic statistics related to Amtrak.

Mergers. In the Transportation Act of 1920, the Interstate Commerce Commission was directed to draft plans for consolidating the nation's railroads into a limited number of systems, and the ICC proposed to create 21 independent rail networks. This plan, however, never became effective, and although other major merger plans were developed later, the Emergency Railroad Transportation Act of 1933 halted all of them. The Transportation Act of 1940 relieved the ICC of its original statutory directive to draft national merger plans, and returned to the railroads the initiative for developing merger proposals. The Association of American Railroads "scorecard" of railroad mergers indicates that the modern railroad merger movement began in January, 1955, with a petition (subsequently granted) to merge the Louisville & Nashville and the Nashville, Chattanooga & St. Louis. Many mergers have occurred in recent years.

Under a policy announced in September, 1980, the Interstate Commerce Commission indicated that it would favor mergers which improved railroad efficiency and reduced excess capacity. The Chessie System merger with the Seaboard Industries, for example, was managerially expected to result in annual savings of over $60 million after three years. On the other hand, the ICC indicated that it would disapprove mergers if the combined carrier did not provide "adequate service to shippers on reasonable demand," or if transportation alternatives available to shippers would be substantially reduced and the benefits from the mergers were achievable in "less competitive" ways.

When major mergers occur or are proposed, rival railroad systems assess their impact upon their own competitive position, and thus further mergers may be stimulated defensively if not aggressively in reaction to the impact.

Railroad Holding Companies. Under the pressure of poor railroad operating results, a number of leading railroad managements have organized holding companies to control the railroad as a subsidiary and in addition to acquire subsidiaries operating in nonrailroad fields, congeneric or conglomerate, including real estate, mining, oil exploration, gas, coal, chemicals, consumer goods, foundry works, even a life insurance company, in the hope of diversifying into profitable lines, boosting consolidated profits, and even showing dynamic growth. In the process, such holdings in companies at least as to nonrail activities were free from direct regulation by the Interstate Commerce Commission (although stimulated by the Penn Central failure, railroad holding company legislation was proposed).

For investors in holding company equities, the problem of analysis of present position and outlook is complicated by the nonrailroad holdings, frequently of a widely diversified nature, in addition to the railroad. Moreover, complete analysis would call for nonconsolidated statements of each of the major holdings, liquidity, and intra-holding company shifts of funds.

Summary. With the advent of the railroad conglomerate-type holding company, a new era has emerged in railroad equities, complicating the problems of regulation and analysis and holding forth the possibility of either restoring interest in the field as a growth area or compounding earnings and financial difficulties through poor choices for diversification into nonrail lines. It should be noted that for years various railroads had directly owned important subsidiaries in such related lines as land holdings, timber, mining, oil and gas, and real estate, and that "other income" (other than from railroad operations) had been important sources of support for net incomes.

BIBLIOGRAPHY

Annual Report of Interstate Commerce Commission. Interstate Commerce Commission. Annual.
Cars of Revenue Freight Loaded. Association of American Railroads, Washington, DC. Weekly.
INTERSTATE COMMERCE COMMISSION. *Annual Report.*
Jane's World Railways. Jane's Publishing Co., New York, NY. Annual.
Official Railway Guide. North American Freight Service Edition. National Railway Publication, Co., New York, NY. Bimonthly.
Official Railway Guide. North American Travel Edition. National Railway Publication Co., New York, NY. Monthly.
Rail Rates and Routing. G. R. Leonard and Co., New york, NY. Frequent revision.
Railway Age. Railroad Research Information Service Bulletin. U.S. Department of Commerce.
Railway Age Review and Outlook Issue. Simmons-Boardman Publishing Corp., New York, NY. Annual.
Railway Directory and Year Book. Business Press International, Ltd., Sutton, Endland. Annual.
Transport Statistics in the United States. U.S. Interstate Commerce Commission.
Thomas Cook International Timetable. Forsyth Travel Library. Shawnee Mission, KS. Monthly.
Trains: The Magazine of Railroading. Kalmbach Publishing Co. Milwaukee, WI. Monthly.
U.S. DEPARTMENT OF TRANSPORTATION, FEDERAL RAILROAD ADMINISTRATION. *Railroad Freight Traffic Flows,* 1990.
Yearbook of Railroad Facts. Association of American Railroads, Washington, DC.

RAILROAD LEGISLATION Beginning in the last quarter of the nineteenth century when transportation by railroad was essentially monopolistic, the history of railroads in the United States was largely a conflict between the railroads on the one hand, restive under restraints of increasing regulation, and the states and federal government on the other, imposing requirements as to fair and reasonable rates, restraints on discriminatory practices, and service and safety requirements. At the federal level, regulation reached its most comprehensive stage with enactment of the Transportation Act of 1920, which imposed the "fair rate of return on fair value" principle and otherwise comprehensively regulated the railroads. As the railroad industry has matured and has encountered problems of inadequate rates, competition from favorably entrenched modes of transportation, and high costs, the punitive philosophy of regulation has given way to regulation emphasizing equalized competitive conditions, adequate rates, and awareness of railroads' cost problems.

Staggers Rail Act of 1980. The (Harley O.) Staggers Rail Act of 1980 (P.L. 96-448, October 14, 1980) was termed by various parties at interest as follows: (1) the Maine Central *Messenger:* "A complex and comprehensive bill which is probably the most important railroad legislation to be considered by Congress in many decades" (the article went on to say that the Staggers Rail Act of 1980 is not by any means total rail deregulation, but "it is a significant restructuring of the railroad regulatory process"); (2) the Association of American Railroads: "The new law, while short of wholesale deregulation, nevertheless substantially eases the regulatory burden on the railroad industry, providing significant changes in rules governing ratemaking, car control and other areas of railroading"; and (3) the Interstate Commerce Commission: "An important step forward giving railroads the pricing freedom necessary to earn adequate revenues and in expanding competition in the transportation industry."

Summary. Appended herewith is a historical chart showing the evolution of forms of railroad practices to prevent unrestrained competition, forms of control, and the specific federal railroad legislation pertaining thereto since 1830. For bankruptcy legislation pertaining to railroads, *see* BANKRUPTCY, NATIONAL BANKRUPTCY ACT.

RAILROAD STATISTICS Principal sources of statistics on U.S. railroads are the Interstate Commerce Commission and the Association of American Railroads.

The Interstate Commerce Commission publishes annual reports, Carrier Financial and Statistical Reports, Decisions, Orders, Reports, and traffic statistics.

The Association of American Railroads publishes the following:

Analysis of Class I Railroads.
Annual Report.
Economic ABZs of the Railroad Industry.
Operating and Traffic Statistics (annual).
Property Investment and Condensed Income Account (annual).
Rail News Update (every two weeks).
Revenues, Expenses and Income (quarterly).
Statistics of Class I Railroads (annual).
Trends (releases on carloadings, piggyback volume, freight equipment, etc.).
Yearbook of Railroad Facts.

The *Analysis of Class I Railroads* is a comprehensive intraindustry profile presenting over 600 selected financial and operating statistics for each Class I railroad, as well as consolidations by district and for the United States as a whole.

The report provides extensive data within the following subjects:

1. Physical characteristics.
2. Operations-freight service (utilization, traffic characteristics, and commodity data), passenger service.
3. Employment.
4. Fuel.
5. New worth and investment base.
6. Revenues, expenses, and income.

Evolution of Railroad Legislation and Control

Period	Device used by roads to secure cooperation and prevent unrestrained competition among railroads	Forms of control	Federal railroad legislation
1830-1850		Unrestrained competition.	
1850-1860	Agreements to maintain rates		
1860-1870	Pooling—traffic	Control by state legislation.	
1870-1897	Pooling—money	Judicial control (state and federal).	
1887-1898	Joint traffic associations	Commission with advisory powers (no power to fix rates).	Interstate Commerce Act (1887); Sherman Anti-Trust Law (1890).
1898-1904	Stock control—formation of securities companies.	Vesting in Interstate Commerce Commission (in 1906) of power to fix maximum rates (subject to test of reasonableness in courts).	Hepburn Act (1906); Northern Securities Co. dissolved (193 U.S. 197, 1904).
1904-1918	Long- and short-haul clause (type of rate discrimination). Railroad ownership or control of Panama Canal water competing carriers. Interlocking directorates.	Strengthening of Interstate Commerce Commission's power over long- and short-haul practice; banning of railroad control of competing water carriers.	Mann-Elkins Act (1910); Panama Canal Act (1912); Clayton Act (1914).
1918-1920	Governmental operation; regional cooperation.	Governmental administration (complete powers).	Federal Control Act (1918).
1920	Permissive consolidations pursuant to ICC regional plans; pooling and interlocking directors subject to ICC approval.	Vesting in Interstate Commerce Commission of full plenary control; maximum, minimum, and precise rate fixing; security issues; accounting; fair return (recapture clause).	Transportation Act (1920).
1933-1936	Repeal of recapture clause; new rate-making rule of lowest cost consistent with adequate and efficient service; motor regulation.	Establishment of Federal Coordinator of Transportation for special studies and recommendations (expired 1936).	Emergency Transportation Act (1933); Motor Carrier Act (1935).
1940	Equalized competition among competing modes of transportation through fair and impartial regulation.	Repeal of requirement that consolidations follow ICC plans; water carrier regulation; widened aid from R.F.C.	Transportation Act of 1940.
1948	Agreements relating to fares, classifications, divisions, allowances or charges exempt from antitrust laws.	Requirement of ICC approval.	Reed-Bulwinkle Act (1948).

ENCYCLOPEDIA OF BANKING AND FINANCE

RAILROAD STOCKS

7. Replacement of plant and equipment: locomotives, freight cars, ties, rails, and gross capital expenditures.

The *Economic ABZs of the Railroad Industry* presents more than 120 tables describing contemporary railroad economics within the following subjects:

1. Industry consist.
2. Capital investment.
3. Cost of operations.
4. Demand and traffic.
5. Energy.
6. Financial performance.
7. Rates.
8. Resource availability and utilization.
9. Profiles.

Each table has a "fighting title"—in essence, a conclusion about some aspect of railroad economics. Thus a mere reading of the table of contents provides the reader with basic economic tenets about the railroad industry. Additional tables will be added from time to time.

Although the ABZs will be updated annually and available in May of each year, the complete report, offering time series data and indices, will be published every five years beginning in 1980. In each intermittent year, a supplemental document providing raw data of the previous year will be offered.

The statistical services (*see* MANUALS) also provide factual and interpretive services on railroads and their securities; specifically, Moody's *Railroads* (annual manual) and semiweekly news supplements and Standard & Poor's Railroad Securities Service (interpretive and advisory) and Corporation Records (factual).

RAILROAD STOCKS Equities of railroads, both preferred and common stocks. GUARANTEED STOCKS of railroads are a separate classification.

Because of the earnings leverage provided by funded debt and other fixed charges in railroad capitalizations and by the high proportion of relatively fixed expenses in operations, railroad equities are ordinarily subject to wide variation in earnings. Consequently, relatively few railroad equities have achieved long-term investment status. With the advent in recent years of railroad holding companies, owning control of the railroad concerned as well as investing in other diversified interests, a new complicating factor has entered into consideration of railroad equities, i.e., the extent to which the nonrail interests of the holding company add to or detract from the basic railroad equity appeal.

BIBLIOGRAPHY

ASSOCIATION OF AMERICAN RAILROADS. *Analysis of Class I Railroads.* Annual.
———. *Economic ABZs of the Railroad Industry.*

RAILROAD TRANSPORTATION (EMERGENCY) ACT OF 1933 An act, approved June 16, 1933, which, among other things:

1. Established a system of railroad control headed by a federal coordinator of transportation to work in cooperation with the roads and with labor to effect economies, but not at the expense of wage earners.
2. Provided that appeals from the decisions of this coordinator, appointed by the President with Senate consent, might be

Evolution of Railroad Legislation and Control (continued)

Period	Device used by roads to secure cooperation and prevent unrestrained competition among railroads	Forms of control	Federal railroad legislation
1958	Specially expedited ICC action on intrastate rates discriminating against interstate commerce. Specified authority of ICC to discontinue or change operation of unprofitable trains in interstate and intrastate service. New rule of rate-making for ICC (giving more competitive weight to rates.) Government-guaranteed loans to railroads. Restriction of commodities exemption of Motor Carrier Act.	Additional or changed powers of ICC.	Transportation Act of 1958
1967	Creation of the U.S. Department of Transportation.	Transfer of jurisdiction over carrier safety practices previously vested in ICC.	Department of Transportation Act, effective April 1, 1967
1970	Revitalization of the rail passenger service.	Creation of National Railroad Passenger Corp. (Amtrak); assignment of responsibility for standards of adequate service by railroads operating intercity passenger trains to ICC.	Rail Passenger Service Act of 1970
1973	Creation of Consolidated Rail Corp. (Conrail).	Establishment of government-directed and -funded plan to reorganize bankrupt railroads in northeast quarter of U.S.	Regional Rail Reoprganization Act of 1973,
1976	Reduction in degree of regulation by ICC; increase in flexibility given railroad management to raise and lower freight rates; expending of ICC action.	Significant changes in way ICC regulates rail transportation; provisions of $6.5 billion in grants, loans, and loan guarantees for Conrail, passenger services, and needs of other qualifying railroads.	Railroad Revitalization Act, Regulatory Reform Act of 1976, or 4R.
1980	Substancial loosening of economic regulation governing railroads.	Granting to railroads of pricing freedom necessary to earn adequate revenues in face of expanding competition.	Staggers Rail Act of 1980

ENCYCLOPEDIA OF BANKING AND FINANCE

taken to the Interstate Commerce Commission, his orders, unless revoked by the commission, to have the force and effect of orders of the commission.
3. Authorized the creation of three coordinating committees to operate with the coordinator, one each for the eastern, southern, and western groups of roads, each committee containing seven members, five representing the major roads, one representing steam roads with operating revenues under $1,000,000 in 1932, and another representing electrical systems, not connected with steam railways. The act provided that the railroads were to be assessed $1.50 a mile to cover the expenses of this set-up.
4. Required the coordinator and the committees to encourage, promote, and require action by the carriers to avoid waste and preventable expense; to promote financial reorganization of the carriers, with due regard to legal rights; to reduce fixed charges to the extent required by public interest and improve carrier credit; and also to provide for the immediate study of other means of improving conditions surrounding transportation in all its forms.
5. Set aside the antitrust laws whenever necessary to carry out the coordinator's orders.

RAILS In stock market parlance, railroad stocks as a class, as distinguished from the "industrials," meaning industrial stocks.
See RAILROAD STOCKS.

RAISED BILLS Paper money the denominations of which have been fraudulently raised. Raised bills are much more frequent and persistent in their recurrence than counterfeits. There are two methods of raising the denominations on paper money. One is to cut off the figures on the corners of a large-denomination bill and paste them over the figures on the corners of a smaller-denomination bill. Another method is to bleach out by acid the figures on small denominations and skillfully insert higher ones with waterproof ink. Raised bills are much more readily detected than counterfeits. With knowledge of the engraved portraits that the genuine bills carry, it is a simple matter to distinguish a raised bill. Paying tellers, receiving tellers, money clerks and other employees handling money should acquaint themselves with the portraits appearing on each denomination of various kinds of paper money. (For instance, the $1 silver certificate and United States note carry the portrait of Washington; the $5 Federal Reserve note carries the portrait of Lincoln; etc.) These are given in a chart under DENOMINATIONAL PORTRAITS.

RAISED CHECK A check on which the amount has been fraudulently increased.
See ALTERATION, CHECK, CHECK PROTECTING DEVICES.

RALLY In stock market parlance, a rise in prices following a sudden decline.

RANDOM WALK Many economists and financial analysts contend that the price fluctuations of stocks are random, meaning that their movements from one time period to the next are unpredictable. The term used to describe this fact is random walk, meaning that the path of stock prices is random. The random walk model is a model of the behavior of market prices of common stock over time. The model states that next period's price is equal to this period's price plus (or minus) some unknown, unpredictable change. The idea, first presented in 1900 by Louis Bachelier in his doctoral dissertation, was revived briefly in 1934 by Holbrook Working and finally resurfaced in the works of many researchers in the late 1950s. The random walk model is closely related to the EFFICIENT MARKET HYPOTHESIS. All forms of the efficient markets hypothesis imply that prices follow a random walk. However, prices following a random walk imply only the "weak form" of efficient markets.

RAPID PAYOFF MORTGAGE See GROWING EQUITY MORTGAGE.

RATE See BANK RATE, FOREIGN EXCHANGE, MONEY MARKET, RATE OF EXCHANGE, REDISCOUNT RATE.

RATE BASE In public utility regulation, the valuation placed upon property in use for the purpose of authorizing an overall fair return on such property investment, in recent years usually 5.5% to 6%, in the absence of franchise restrictions. Despite state provision for administrative agencies (see PUBLIC SERVICE COMMISSION) to regulate both the fair value of the rate base and the fair return thereon, the courts from an early period have been involved in cases litigating the reasonableness of rate bases and rates of return.

For many years, under the rule of Smyth v. Ames (169 U.S. 466, 1898), the courts emphasized the formula or basis for determination of fair value of the rate base, its general rule being so general that all relevant methods of valuation, probable earning capacity, and required operating expenses had to be considered in valuation cases, lest the determination run afoul of the challenge of "due process." Since the decisions did not show consistency in favoring any particular method of valuation and the "rule of Smyth v. Ames" was considered legally and economically unsound, in addition to being impracticable, the U.S. Supreme Court finally abandoned the rule in the 1944 case of Federal Power Commission v. Hope Natural Gas Co., 320 U.S. 591. In the latter case, considered to stand for the newer doctrine of "end result" or total effect of a rate order, the majority opinion held: "Under the statutory standard of 'just and reasonable', it is the result reached not the method employed which is controlling. It is not theory but the impact of the rate order which counts. If the total effect of the rate order cannot be said to be unjust and unreasonable, judicial inquiry under the Act is at an end. The fact that the method employed to reach that result may contain infirmities is not then important."
See PUBLIC UTILITY INDUSTRY, VALUATION.

RATE CAP A limit on the amount the interest rate may change that limits the borrower's risk in an adjustable-rate loan.

RATE OF EXCHANGE The market or commercial price at which a foreign currency is quoted; the price of the money of one country quoted; the price of the money of one country quoted in the money of another. "The rate of exchange is that rate expressed in terms of local currency which bills of exchange drawn on foreign currency payable at a foreign point, command" (L. H. Langston).
See FOREIGN EXCHANGE.

RATE OF INTEREST See INTEREST, MONEY MARKET.

RATE OF RETURN ON SECURITIES The rate of return on a security is a major factor associated with evaluating and selecting an investment. All security-pricing models involve computing the present values of future cash flows the security is expected to pay. For common stocks, cash flows represent periodic cash dividends. For bonds, cash flows represent periodic coupon payments plus the face value of the bond at maturity.

Various methods are available for computing the rate of return on a security. The single-period rate of return is one such measure. This rate is the percentage price appreciation plus the percentage cash return (current yield on a bond; dividend yield on a stock) during a given period. The rate is typically expressed as an annualized value. The single-period rate of return can be computed using the following equation:

$$\text{Single-period return} = \text{Percentage price appreciation} + \text{Percentage cash return}$$

$$R_t = \frac{P_t - P_t - 1}{P_t - 1} + \frac{C_t}{P_t - 1}$$

where

R_t = Return during the period ending at date t
P_t = Security price at date t
P_t-1 = Security price at date t
C_t = Cash flow received at date t

The equation can also be used to measure future expected single-period returns. The symbol "E" is used to mean expected return, price, etc. The following data can be used to illustrate the computation of the actual rate of return on a stock and the expected rate of return on the stock:

ENCYCLOPEDIA OF BANKING AND FINANCE

RATING

Data	Description	Stock
P_0	Last year's closing price	$20.00
C_1	This year's cash flow	$ 1.00 dividend
P_1	Today's closing price	$18.00
$E(C_2)$	Next year's expected cash flow	$ 1.00 dividend
$E(P_2)$	Next year's expected closing price	$22.00

Last year's actual rate of return on the stock:

$$R_1 \text{ on stock} = \frac{\$18-20}{\$20} + \frac{\$1}{\$20} = -5.00\%$$

Expected returns for the coming year would be:

$$E(R_2) \text{ on stock} = \frac{\$22 - \$18}{\$18} + \frac{\$1}{\$18} = +27.8\%$$

BIBLIOGRAPHY

BERNSTEIN, LEOPOLD A., *Financial Statement Analysis,* Irwin, Homewood, IL., 1983.
COLEMAN, ALMAND, et al., *Financial Accounting and Statement Analysis: A Manager's Guide,* Robert F. Dame, Richmond, VA., 1982.

RATING Grade; classification. A credit rating is a letter or number used by a mercantile or other agency in reports and credit rating books to denote the ability and disposition of various businesses (individual proprietorship, partnership, or corporation) to meet their financial obligations.

Ratings are used as a guide to the investment quality of bonds and stocks, based on security of principal and interest (or dividends), earning power, mortgage position, market history, and marketability.

See BOND RATINGS, CAPITAL RATING, CREDIT, CREDIT RATING, GRADING.

RATIO An expression of a mathematical relationship between one quantity and another. The ratio of 400 to 200 is 2:1 or 2. If a ratio is to have any utility, the elements that constitute the ratio must express a meaningful relationship. For example, there is a relationship between accounts receivable and sales, between net income and total assets, and between current assets and current liabilities. Ratio analysis can disclose relationships that reveal conditions and trends that often cannot be noted by inspection of the individual components of the ratio.

Ratios are generally not significant of themselves but assume significance when they are compared with previous ratios of the same firm, ratios of other enterprises in the same industry, and ratios of the industry within which the company operates.

It is helpful to organize ratios in terms of areas to be analyzed and interpreted. At least three major areas can be identified:

1. Short-term liquidity.
2. Capital structure (and long-term solvency).
3. Earnings and profitability.

Short-term liquidity refers to the ability of a firm to meet its current obligations as they mature. The relationship of current assets to current liabilities is an important indicator of the degree to which a firm is liquid. Working capital and the components of working capital also provide measures of the liquidity of a firm.

The capital structure of an enterprise consists of debt and equity funds. The sources and composition of the two types of capital determine to a considerable extent the financial stability and long-term solvency of the firm. A company's capitalization usually depends on the industry, the financial position of the company, and the philosophy of management. Long-term debt and preferred stock can add "leverage" to a company's capital structure. Capital structure ratios provide information on the debt capacity of the company and its level of financial risk. Financing decisions frequently involve determining the type of arrangements to be used and the amount of indebtedness to be incurred.

Operating and profitability performance ratios reflect the results

R. N. Services Company
Balance Sheet
December 31, 19X1 and 19X0

	19X1	19X0
Assets		
Current assets:		
Cash	$ 50,000	$ 35,000
Marketable securities	100,000	65,000
Accounts receivable	200,000	250,000
Inventories	80,000	60,000
Total current assets	430,000	400,000
Property, plant, and equipment	1,000,000	800,000
Less accumulated depreciation	(600,000)	(500,000)
	400,000	300,000
Goodwill	100,000	125,000
Total assets	$1,330,000	$825,000
Liabilities and Shareholders' Equity		
Current liabilities:		
Accounts payable	$ 100,000	$100,000
Notes payable	15,000	15,000
Income taxes payable	100,000	85,000
Total current liabilities	215,000	200,000
Long-term debt:		
Bonds and notes payable	500,000	350,000
Total liabilities	715,000	550,000
Shareholders' equity:		
Common stock, 10,000 shares outstanding	250,000	200,000
Contributed capital in excess of par	100,000	100,000
Retained earnings	265,000	25,000
Total equity	615,000	325,000
Total liabilities and shareholders' equity	$1,330,000	$825,000

R. N. Services Company
Income Statement
For the years ended December 31, 19X1 and 19X0

	19X1	19X0
Net sales	$625,000	$225,000
Costs and expenses:		
Cost of goods sold	100,000	70,000
Selling and administrative expense	150,000	100,000
Interest expense	50,000	30,000
Total costs and expenses	300,000	200,000
Income before income taxes	325,000	25,000
Income taxes	75,000	5,000
Net income	250,000	20,000
Retained earnings at end of period	25,000	5,000
Dividends	10,000	0
Retained earnings at end of period	$265,000	$ 25,000

Additional information:
Market price per share of common stock, $75.
Average daily purchases of inventory, $50,000.

Source: Charles J. Woelfel, *Corporate Finance and Accounting,* Probus Co., Chicago, IL, 1987. The following ratios are derived from these financial statements.

Table 1 / Financial Statement Ratios

Ratio	Formula	Solution to case	Interpretation
Liquidity ratios			
a. Current (or working capital) ratio	$\dfrac{\text{Current assets}}{\text{Current liabilities}}$	$\dfrac{\$430,000}{\$215,000} = 2$	Short-term debt-paying ability (i.e., dollar amount of current assets from which to obtain funds necessary to liquidate each dollar of current liabilities).
b. Acid-test (or quick) ratio	$\dfrac{\text{Quick assets, i.e., cash marketable securities, receivables}}{\text{Current liabilties}}$	$\dfrac{\$350,000}{\$215,000} = 1.6$	A more severe test of the short-term debt-paying ability than the current ratio since it excludes inventory (which awaits sale) and prepaid expenses.
c. Cash ratio	$\dfrac{\text{Cash}}{\text{Current liabilities}}$	$\dfrac{\$50,000}{\$215,000} = .23$	The severest test of short-term debt-paying ability.
Measures of the movement or turnover of current assets and liabilities			
a. Receivables turnover	$\dfrac{\text{Sales (net)}}{\text{Average receivables (net)}}$	$\dfrac{\$625,000}{\$225,000} = 2.7$	The efficiency in colleting receivables and in managing credit.
b. Age of receivables	$\dfrac{365}{\text{Receivables turnover}}$	$\dfrac{365}{2.7} = 135$	The number of days it takes on the average to collect accounts receivable; the extent of control over credit and collection.
c. Inventory turnover	$\dfrac{\text{Cost of goods sold}}{\text{Average inventory}}$	$\dfrac{\$100,000}{\$70,000} = 1.4$	Marketability of inventory, efficiency in the management of inventory, and the reasonableness of the quantity of inventory on hand.
d. Days in inventory	$\dfrac{365}{\text{Inventory turnover}}$	$\dfrac{365}{1.4} = 261$	The average number of days required to use or sell inventory (e.g., the average period that an item is held in inventory). For a manufacturing company, the number of days should correspond closely with production time.
e. Working capital turnover	$\dfrac{\text{Net sales}}{\text{Average working capital}}$	$\dfrac{\$625,000}{\$207,500} = 3$	The extent to which a company is using working capital to generate sales.
f. Number of days' purchases in ending accounts payable	$\dfrac{\text{Accounts payable}}{\text{Average daily purchases}}$	$\dfrac{\$100,000}{\$50,000} = 2$	The extent to which the company is paying its bills promptly.
Solvency ratios			
1. Measures of capital structure:			
a. Owners' equity to total assets	$\dfrac{\text{Total owners' equity}}{\text{Total assets (net)}}$	$\dfrac{\$615,000}{\$1,330,000} = .46$	Proportion of firm's assets provided by owner.
b. Owners' equity to total liabilities	$\dfrac{\text{Total owners' equity}}{\text{Total liabilities}}$	$\dfrac{\$615,000}{\$715,000} = .86$	Relative claims of owners and creditors to rest of firm.
c. Fixed assets to total equity	$\dfrac{\text{Total owners' equity}}{\text{Fixed assets (net)}}$	$\dfrac{\$615,000}{\$400,000} = 1.53$	Relationship of owners' investment to the company investment in fixed assets (i.e., the higher the ratio, the less owners' capital is available for working capital).
d. Book value per share of common stock	$\dfrac{\text{Common stock equity}}{\text{Number of common shares outstanding}}$	$\dfrac{\$615,000}{10,000} = \$61.50$	Net assets reported on financial statement per share of common stock.
2. Measures of debt structure (debt management):			
a. Total liabilities to total assets	$\dfrac{\text{Total liabilities}}{\text{Total assets (net)}}$	$\dfrac{\$715,000}{\$1,330,000} = .53$	Protection available to creditors and the extent to which the company is trading on equity.
b. Total liabilities to owners' equity	$\dfrac{\text{Total liabilities}}{\text{Owners' equity}}$	$\dfrac{\$715,000}{\$615,000} = 1.2$	Relationship between total debt and equity financing. "What is owed to what is owned."
Profitability (earnings) ratios			
1. Net income to sales	$\dfrac{\text{Net income}}{\text{Net sales}}$	$\dfrac{\$250,000}{\$625,000} = .4$	Profit margin per dollar of sales.
2. Operating ratio	$\dfrac{\text{Cost of goods sold + operating expenses}}{\text{Net sales}}$	$\dfrac{\$100,000 + \$150,000}{\$625,000} = .4$	Profit margin per dollar of sales.

Table 1 / Financial Statement Ratios (continued)

Ratio	Formula	Solution to case	Interpretation
3. Sales to total assets (or asset turnover)	$\dfrac{\text{Net sales}}{\text{Average total assets}}$	$\dfrac{\$625,000}{\$1,077,000} = .57$	Productivity of all assets in generating sales.
4. Earnings per share of common stock	$\dfrac{\text{Net income—preferred dividend requirements}}{\text{Average number of common stock}}$	$\dfrac{\$250,000}{10,000} = \$25$	Return on common shareholders' investment per share of
5. Price/earnings ratio	$\dfrac{\text{Market price per share of common stock}}{\text{Net income per share of common stock}}$	$\dfrac{\$75}{\$25} = \$3$	Price paid for stock per dollar of earnings (i.e., the price of earnings). Newspaper include this information in daily stock tables.
6. Dividends yield	$\dfrac{\text{Annual cash dividends per share of common stock}}{\text{Market price per share of common stock}}$	$\dfrac{\$1}{\$75} = .013$	Cash yield or return on common stock.
7. Return on investment (or return on assets)	$\dfrac{\text{Net income}}{\text{Average total assets}}$	$\dfrac{\$250,000}{\$1,077,000} = .23$	Return on investment in total assets. Sometimes net operating income is used as the numerator while intangibles and investments are excluded from the denominator.
8. Return on common stockholders' equity	$\dfrac{\text{Net income}}{\text{Average common stockholders' equity}}$	$\dfrac{\$250,000}{\$470,000} = .53$	Return on the investment by common stockholders.
9. Payout ratio	$\dfrac{\text{Cash dividends}}{\text{Net income}}$	$\dfrac{\$10,000}{\$250,000} = .04$	The extent to which a company distributes current earnings to stockholders in the form of dividends i.e., the "generosity" of the Board of Directors.
10. Cash flow from operations per share of common stock	$\dfrac{\text{Net income adjusted for noncash items}}{\text{Average number of shares of common stock outstanding}}$	$\dfrac{\$395,000}{10,000} = \$39.50$	The amount of cash generated from operations for each share of stock.

of the profit-seeking activities of an enterprise. Many of the data required for evaluating performance are obtained directly from the income statement that summarizes the results of operations. However, performance should be related to the assets that produce the earnings and how outsiders (for example, the stock market) perceive the performance and earnings of the enterprise. Measures of operating performance usually provide answers to the following questions: How much profit does the company make on each dollar of investment? How much profit does the company make on each dollar of sales? The profitability of investment usually relates to the following:

1. Return on total assets (total investment).
2. Return on invested capital (debt and equity).
3. Return on owners' investment (shareholders' equity).

The profitability of sales focuses on specific contributions of purchasing, production, administration and overall profitability as reflected in gross profit margin, operating profit margin, and net profit margin.

Several important profitability ratios are referred to as market value ratios. Most of these ratios relate to the valuation of stock and are of considerable importance to financial analysts and stockholders.

These ratios include earnings per share, dividends per share, yield on common stock, dividend payout, and book value per share of common stock. Major financial ratios are illustrated in appended table. Data for the problem illustrated are also provided in accompanying financial statements.

The purpose of FINANCIAL STATEMENT ANALYSIS is to examine past and current financial data so that a bank's performance and financial position can be evaluated and future risks and potentials estimated. Financial statement analysis can yield valuable information about trends and relationships, the quality of the bank's assets and earnings, and the strengths and weaknesses of its financial position. Typical financial ratios related to banks are appended.

Failed banks typically have indicated higher loan-to-asset ratios, lower capital-to-assets ratios, lower efficiency, and lower profitability in years preceding their failure than have successful banks.

Federal and state regulatory agencies publish statistical data related to banks. Private sources such as Sheshunoff & Co., Bacon Whipple & Co., American Bankers Association, and others publish voluminous statistical data related to banking in the United States.

A table of selected indicators associated with FDIC-insured commercial banks for selected years 1984-1989 is appended.

See CREDIT BAROMETRICS, CURRENT RATIO, FEDERAL RESERVE STATEMENT, RESERVE RATIO.

BIBLIOGRAPHY

HAWKINS, DAVID F. *Corporate Financial Reporting and Analysis*, Irwin, 1986.
HERRICK, *Bank Analyst's Handbook*, John Wiley & Sons.
MCGLADREY & PULLEN, *Banking Industry Manual*, 1987.
ERNST & WHINNEY, *Profitability Measurement for Financial Institutions: A Management Information Approach*, Bank Administration Institute, 1987.
GARCIA, F.L. *How to Analyze a Bank Statement*, Bankers Publishing Company, 1985.
KOLTVEIT, JAMES M. *Accounting for Banks*, Matthew Bender, 1988.
WOELFEL, CHARLES J. *Financial Statement Analysis*, Probus Publishing Co., 1988.

RATIO ANALYSIS In STATEMENT ANALYSIS, the technique of reducing aggregate data into meaningful ratios, for further specialized study and analysis thereof.

The study of ratios as a technique of analysis dates from the work of Alexander Wall and Robert Morris Associates, a national association of bank credit analysts, the former's pioneer article in 1912 illustrating the use of ratios in analysis being one of the earliest on this subject. Among the formal works of Mr. Wall are *Ratio Analysis of Financial Statements* (1928) and *Basic Financial Statement Analysis* (1942).

RATIO ANALYSIS

Financial Statement Ratios for Banks

Area measured	Ratio	Formula	Description
Liquidity	Liquid Assets to Borrowings	$\dfrac{\text{LIQA}}{\text{BORR}}$	Liquid Assets (Due from Banks plus Federal Funds Sold plus Trading Securities plus Securities with less than 1 year to maturity) divided by Federal Funds purchased plus Other Borrowings.
	Liquid Assets to Borrowings & Large CDs	$\dfrac{\text{LIQA}}{\text{BORR} + \text{CD}}$	Liquid Assets (see preceding description) divided by Federal Funds Purchased plus Other Borrowings plus Large Denomination CDs with less than 1 year maturity.
	Loans to Deposits	$\dfrac{\text{TLOANS}}{\text{TDEP}}$	Total Loans divided by Total Deposits. Measures amount of deposits committed to loans by the bank.
Risk	Earnings Volatility	$\dfrac{\text{SD}}{\text{Mean}}$	Standard Deviation of annual year-to-year earnings growth divided by the Mean of the year-to-year earnings growth (5 years if available). Measures earning volatility.
	Rate Sensitivity Mismatch	$\dfrac{\text{VRA-VRL}}{\text{TA}}$	Variable Rate Assets minus Variable Rate Liabilities divided by Total Average Assets.
	Loss Coverage Ratio	$\dfrac{\text{NI} + \text{TAX} + \text{LP}}{\text{NCO}}$	Net Income plus Taxes plus Loss Provision divided by Net Charge-offs.
	Loan Loss Reserve to Loans	$\dfrac{\text{LLR}}{\text{TLOAN}}$	Loan Loss Reserve divided by Total Average Loans. Measures loan quality.
	Equity to Assets or Capital Ratio	$\dfrac{\text{EQ}}{\text{TA}}$	Total Shareholders' Equity divided by Total Assets.
	Equity + LLR to Loans	$\dfrac{\text{EQ} + \text{LLR}}{\text{TLOANS}}$	Total Shareholders' Equity plus Loan Loss Reserve to Total Loans.
	Capital to Risk Assets	$\dfrac{\text{EQ} + \text{DBT} + \text{LLR}}{\text{TA-CASH-LIQA}}$	Total Shareholders' Equity plus Long-Term Subordinated Debt plus Loan Loss Reserve divided by Total Assets less Cash and Liquid Assets.
	Net Charge-Offs to Loans	$\dfrac{\text{NCO}}{\text{TLOANS}}$	Net Charge-offs to Total Average Loans. Measures loan quality.
Growth	Earnings Per Share	$\dfrac{\text{CYE/S}}{\text{PYE/S}} - 1$	Current Year Earnings Per Share divided by Prior Year Earnings Per Share minus 1.
	Dividends Per Share	$\dfrac{\text{CYD/S}}{\text{PYE/S}} - 1$	Current Year Dividends Per Share divided by Prior Year Dividends Per Share minus 1.
	Total Assets	$\dfrac{\text{CYTA}}{\text{PYTA}} - 1$	Current Year Total Average Assets divided by Prior Year Total Average Assets minus 1.
	Total Loans	$\dfrac{\text{CYTL}}{\text{PYTL}} - 1$	Current Year Total Loans divided by Prior Year Total Loans minus 1.
	Total DDA & Savings	$\dfrac{\text{CYDDA} + \text{S}}{\text{PYDDA} + \text{S}} - 1$	Current Year Total DDA & Savings divided by Prior Year Total DDA & Savings minus 1.
	Total Deposits	$\dfrac{\text{CYTD}}{\text{PYTD}} - 1$	Current Year Total Deposits divided by Prior Year Total Deposits minus 1.
	Equity	$\dfrac{\text{CYEQ}}{\text{PYEG}} - 1$	Current Year Total Shareholder Equity divided by Prior Year Total Shareholder Equity minus 1.
	Growth in assets	$\dfrac{\text{Current year's assets}}{\text{Previous year's assets}} - 1$	
	Growth in loans	$\dfrac{\text{Current year's loans}}{\text{Previous year's loans}} - 1$	
	Growth in deposits	$\dfrac{\text{Current year's deposits}}{\text{Previous year's deposits}} - 1$	
	Growth in income	$\dfrac{\text{Current year's income}}{\text{Previous year's income}} - 1$	
	Growth in equity	$\dfrac{\text{Current year's equity}}{\text{Previous year's equity}} - 1$	
	Growth in dividends	$\dfrac{\text{Current year's dividends}}{\text{Previous year's dividends}} - 1$	
	Dividend payout ratio	$\dfrac{\text{Current year's dividend}}{\text{Net income}}$	

RATIO ANALYSIS

Financial Statement Ratios for Banks (continued)

Area measured	Ratio	Formula	Description
Profitability	Return on Assets (ROA)	$\dfrac{NOI}{TA}$	Net Operating Income (after tax) divided by Total Average Assets.
	Net Interest Margin	$\dfrac{NII}{TA}$	Net Interest Income divided by Total Average Assets. Measures ability of management to generate net income.
	Other Income Contribution	$\dfrac{TOI}{TA}$	Total Other Income divided by Total Average Assets.
	Loss Provision	$\dfrac{LP}{TA}$	Provision for Loan Loss divided by Total Average Assets.
	Shareholder Return	$\dfrac{DIV. + APPREC.}{BEG.\ MV}$	Cash Dividends per share plus share price appreciation (Ending share price minus Beginning share price) divided by Beginning Market Value (i.e., share price).
	Return on Equity (ROE)	$\dfrac{NOI}{EQ}$	Net Operating Income (after tax) divided by Average Shareholder's Equity.
	Dividend Payout	$\dfrac{DIV}{NI}$	Cash Dividends declared divided by Net Income.
	Security Gains & Losses	$\dfrac{SG/L}{TA}$	Security Gains and Losses (net of Taxes) divided by Total Average Assets.
	Yield on Average Earning Assets	$\dfrac{\text{Interest Income}}{\text{Average Earning Assets}}$	Earning assets include balances of loans, securities, and other interest-bearing assets. Measures the yield on earning assets.
	Rate Paid on Funds	$\dfrac{\text{Interest Expense}}{\text{Average Interest-bearing Liabilities}}$	Measures the cost of funds employed by the bank.
	Net Interest Margin	$\dfrac{\text{Interest Income - Interest Expense}}{\text{Average Earning Assets}}$	Measures the spread and relationship of interest-bearing assets to interest-bearing liabilities.
Capital Structure			
	Capital Ratio	$\dfrac{\text{Shareholders' Equity}}{\text{Total Assets}}$	Relationship of stockholders' equity to total assets. Measures the adequacy of capital.
	Capital to Debt	$\dfrac{\text{Shareholders' Equity}}{\text{Total Liabilities}}$	Relationship of stockholders' equity to total debt.

Table 2 / Selected Indicators, FDIC-Insured Commercial Banks

	1989*	1988*	1988	1987	1986	1985	1984
Return on assets	0.94%	0.66%	0.83%	.010%	0.63%	0.70%	0.64%
Return on equity	14.70	10.92	13.43	1.54	9.99	11.15	10.48
Equity capital to assets	6.41	6.07	6.28	6.02	6.19	6.19	6.14
Primary capital ratio	7.99	7.83	7.85	7.76	7.55	7.42	7.20
Nonperforming assets to assets	2.22	2.48	2.14	2.46	1.95	1.46	1.60
Net charge-offs to loans	0.72	0.88	0.99	0.93	0.99	0.84	0.75
Asset growth rate	4.41	4.04	4.36	2.03	7.71	8.86	7.11
Net operating income growth	63.72	1.54	2018.29	-85.27	-20.65	6.30	3.40
Percentage of unprofitable banks	8.78	13.08	14.24	18.62	20.65	17.10	14.05
Number of problem banks	1,289	1,491	1,394	1,559	1,457	1,098	800
Number of failed/assisted banks	64	54	221	201	144	118	78

* Through March 31; ratios annualized where appropriate

Source: FDIC

ENCYCLOPEDIA OF BANKING AND FINANCE

Since 1932 the mercantile credit agency Dun & Bradstreet, Inc. has published annual studies of the "14 Important Ratios" for specific lines of activity grouped under manufacturing, wholesaling, and retailing categories. The specific number of firms is indicated for each line of activity covered, and the upper quartile, median, and lower quartile of the particular ratio shown.

The "14 Important Ratios" regularly published by Dun & Bradstreet, Inc. are as follows:

1. Current Assets to Current Debt.
2. Net Profits on Net Sales.
3. Net Profits on Tangible Net Worth.
4. Net Profits on Net Working Capital.
5. Net Sales to Tangible Net Worth.
6. Net Sales to Net Working Capital.
7. Collection Period.
8. Net Sales to Inventory.
9. Fixed Assets to Tangible Net Worth.
10. Current Debt to Tangible Net Worth.
11. Total Debt to Tangible Net Worth.
12. Inventory to Net Working Capital.
13. Current Debt to Inventory.
14. Funded Debt to Net Working Capital.

The significant ratios vary with the line of business and with the meaningful relationships of balance sheet and operating data peculiar to it. Thus, in addition to the above mercantile and industrial ratios, other technical ratios would be found in railroad, public utility, bank, insurance, and mining ratio analysis.

BIBLIOGRAPHY

Bank Administration Institute and Robert Morris Associates. *Customer Profitability Analysis: A Tool for Improving Bank Profits.* Bank Administration Institute, Rolling Meadows, IL, 1985.
———. "Bank Analysis for a Takeover Era." *Magazine of Bank Administration,* December, 1988.
Cates, D. "Bank Analysis: Why Measures of Performance Don't Work." *Bank Accounting and Finance,* Fall, 1987.
Dun & Bradstreet Credit Services. *Industry Norms and Key Business Ratios, 1982/83.* Annual.
Compustat. Standard and Poor's, Englewood, CO. Online data base.
Disclosure Database. Disclosure, Inc., Bethesda, MD. Online data base.
Federal Deposit Insurance Corp. *Bank Operating Statistics.* Annual.
Federal Trade Commission and U.S. Securities and Exchange Commission. *Quarterly Financial Report for Manufacturing, Mining, and Trade Corporations.*
Mortgage Bankers Association of America. *Mortgage Banking: Financial Statements and Operating Ratios.*
NAARS. American Institute of Certified Public Accountants, New York, NY. Online data base.
Robert Morris Associates. *Annual Statement Studies, 1923.* Annual.
Sources for U.S. Financial and Operating Ratios. Banker Library Mini-List Number Five, Publications Office, Harvard Business School, Boston, MA. Annual.
Troy, L. *Almanac of Business and Industrial Financial Ratios.* Prentice Hall, Inc., Englewood Cliffs, NJ, 197-. Annual.

RATION BANKING The Ration Banking Program, as announced in the *Federal Reserve Bulletin* for August, 1947, was terminated effective July 1, 1947. The Ration Banking Plan, as described in the *Federal Reserve Bulletin* for February, 1943, was developed by the Office of Price Administration with the cooperation of federal and state bank supervisory authorities, the American Bankers Association, and representative bankers. After having been tested in 33 banking offices in the Albany-Troy-Schenectady area of New York, the plan was placed in operation on a nationwide basis in January, 1943. Under ration banking, ration stamps, coupons, certificates, tokens, and other ration evidences taken in by storekeepers, wholesalers, and other sellers of rationed commodities in the course of business from their customers were deposited with the participating banks to the credit of the ration accounts of the depositors. Ration bank accounts were handled in much the same manner as regular bank accounts except that they were kept in units of measure instead of units of value. The ration depositor drew ration checks on his ration account in favor of his supplier of goods. The general public did not participate in ration banking. In addition to thousands of commercial banks which participated in the Ration Banking Program, the Federal Reserve banks and their 24 branches participated by effecting the clearance of ration checks.

Although now terminated, the Ration Banking Program is noteworthy as evidence of the broadened business policies of commercial banks in recent years.

See NEW BUSINESS DEPARTMENT.

RATIO OF CURRENT ASSETS TO CURRENT LIABILITIES CURRENT RATIO.

RATIO OF CURRENT ASSETS TO TOTAL LIABILITIES One of the tests applied to a financial statement by bank credit analysts in the appraisal of a credit risk. The purpose of this test is to determine the immediate position of the prospective borrower in case of forced liquidation. Fixed assets cannot be converted into cash in a short time; consequently, if the current assets are more than sufficient to liquidate the entire liabilities, the position is regarded as sound. A 2 to 1 ratio would be highly satisfactory. Wherever bonds mature within a short time and no sinking fund or other assets exist with which to redeem the issue, a 1 to 1 ratio between current assets and total liabilities is obviously insufficient, unless it is intended to refund the bonds. Where there are no fixed liabilities, this ratio will be identical with the CURRENT RATIO.

See STATEMENT ANALYSIS.

RATIO OF DEBT TO NET WORTH One of the tests applied to a financial statement by bank credit analysts in the appraisal of a credit risk. The purpose of this test is to determine the proportion of the capital used in the business which has been furnished by the owners as compared with that furnished by creditors, i.e., the relation between "share capital" and "loan capital." Each type of business must set its own standard; this ratio should be studied from year to year in order to determine what ratio is normal to a particular business. The idea of normality can also be gained by comparison with conditions among other concerns in the same line of business. If the proportion of total debt to net worth is too high, overtrading on the equity may expose solvency to danger, because earnings upon borrowed capital may not be sufficient to pay the cost of carrying it.

Generally speaking, total debt should not exceed net worth. A business that has a low ratio of debt to net worth is in a better credit situation than one that has a high ratio. From a comparative standpoint, if the tendency from year to year is toward increasing net worth rather than increasing total debt, the condition may be regarded as favorable; contrariwise, as unfavorable.

See STATEMENT ANALYSIS.

RATIO OF FIXED ASSETS TO NET WORTH One of the tests applied to a financial statement by bank credit analysts in the appraisal of a credit risk. The purpose of this test is to determine whether the investment in fixed assets has been furnished by the owners of the business. Properly the owners should furnish all the capital required for plant and in addition a considerable portion of the working capital, since it gives them greater power to expand their business and draw upon the credit of banks.

Generally speaking, the lower the ratio of fixed assets to net worth, the better the condition disclosed.

See STATEMENT ANALYSIS.

RATIO OF MERCHANDISE TO RECEIVABLES One of the tests applied to a financial statement by bank credit analysts in the appraisal of a credit risk. This ratio is determined by dividing the value of merchandise by the sum of the accounts and notes receivable. Usually these items constitute the greater part of the current assets, but they are quite dissimilar in nature. Receivables represent claims against others, while merchandise represents possession of physical goods. The value of the former depends upon the credit standing of the names to which goods have been sold and therefore does not represent certain value, since experience shows that losses are bound to occur in converting receivables into cash. Merchandise, however, represents value in hand, since it may be sold for cash as well as for credit. On the other hand, profits have been anticipated in receivables, whereas merchandise is still carried at cost or market (whichever is lower). While it cannot be absolutely stated that receivables represent a better asset than merchandise, under normal conditions where credits are cautiously extended and

RATIO OF MERCHANDISE TO SALES

where the merchandise is specialized in character and subject to wide market fluctuations, they are ordinarily regarded as superior.

The purpose of this ratio is to determine the relative balance between receivables and merchandise particularly with reference to (1) whether the business is overbuying or overproducing, and (2) whether the accounts are fully collectible. If receivables increase relatively faster than merchandise, laxity in collection methods or a too liberal policy may be indicated, but if merchandise increases relatively faster than receivables, then overbuying or overproducing may be indicated. Generally speaking, a swing toward receivables accompanied by a rising current ratio is a favorable indication.
See STATEMENT ANALYSIS.

RATIO OF MERCHANDISE TO SALES MERCHANDISE TURNOVER.

RATIO OF NET PROFITS TO NET WORTH One of the tests applied to a financial statement by bank credit analysts in the appraisal of a credit risk. The purpose of this test is to determine the capacity of the business to make sustained profits over a period of time. The rate of profits for a single year is not necessarily significant. The period of review should include both prosperous and depressed times. In application of this test, note should be taken of the following points: (1) whether the rate of net profits is normal for the type of business in question; (2) to what extent profits are due to a rise in inventory values; and (3) whether the trend of the ratio is upward, downward, or stationary.
See STATEMENT ANALYSIS.

RATIO OF PLANT TO NET WORTH RATIO OF FIXED ASSETS TO NET WORTH.

RATIO OF RESERVES TO LIABILITIES See RESERVE RATIO.

RATIO OF SALES TO RECEIVABLES ACCOUNTS RECEIVABLE TURNOVER.

REACTION A decline in the volume of business transacted in the country, i.e., a period of depression; a reversal of the price trend which up to the time of the reaction has been upward. A temporary reaction in prices in an advancing market is sometimes said to be normal and healthy.
See BUSINESS CYCLE.

READILY MARKETABLE STAPLES As defined by the Board of Governors of the Federal Reserve System in Regulation C, "an article of commerce, agriculture, or industry of such use as to make it the subject of constant dealings in ready markets with such frequent quotations of price as to make (a) the price easily and definitely ascertainable, and (b) the staple itself easy to realize upon by sale at any time."

According to rulings of the Board of Governors of the Federal Reserve System, while nonperishable commodities are not expressly restricted as eligible staples, banks, as a matter of prudence, should not consider as eligible any staple which is in its nature so perishable as not to be reasonably sure of maintaining its value as security, at least for the life of the draft which is drawn against it.
See ELIGIBLE PAPER, REDISCOUNT.

READJUSTMENT This term has two meanings:

1. A proceeding similar to a reorganization, except that it is done voluntarily by the security holders under company jurisdiction without resort to the courts, rather than being under court jurisdiction under a receiver of trustee. The Mahaffie Act of 1948 permits railroads, under Interstate Commerce Commission supervision, to effect readjustment plans upon consent of 75% of each class of security affected, without the necessity of invoking Bankruptcy Act reorganization procedure.
See RECAPITALIZATION.
2. That phase of a business cycle following a crisis, or panic and emergency liquidation, in which the normal equilibrium between demand and supply is in the process of being restored. It is characterized by a curtailment of production in most lines but in varying degrees, lower production costs achieved through increased efficiency in labor and management, lower prices, smaller profits, greater thrift exercised by the consuming public, etc. The readjustment period precedes the period of recuperation which leads finally to prosperity. The period of readjustment immediately follows the period of industrial or business depression.
See BUSINESS CYCLE.

REAL ESTATE Real property, including the land, structures, and other improvements that are permanently attached.

The nonlegal term for real property, comprising land, buildings, and appurtenances thereto. Mortgage companies, real estate brokers, agents, and operators generally classify land as rural, farm, or urban (city) property, the last term also including suburban property. City real estate is further classified as "essential" or "nonessential." Residences and business property (stores, offices, and factory sites) are essential; theatres, museums, club houses, churches, and other buildings of like specialized character, as well as outlying vacant land, are nonessential. General-purpose and special-purpose classifications are perhaps more indicative of what is basically meant by the terms "essential" and "nonessential," as the latter terms are not intended to be disparaging of the uses involved.

Residential property is subdivided into single- and multiple-family dwellings (apartments or tenement houses). Business property is subdivided into retail, wholesale, factory, and office building. Among business properties, buildings occupied by retail stores are usually considered to offer the better class of security.

A short glossary of terms associated with real estate, exclusive of terms described elsewhere in this encyclopedia, is provided here:

Acceleration clause A condition in a loan contract or mortgage note that allows the lender to demand immediate repayment of the balance if the contract is breached.
Adaptive reuse The process of recycling older structures into different use.
Adverse possession A way of obtaining title to property occupying it under a claim of ownership for a period of years as specified by state law.
Agent A person who represents another (the principal) in dealing with third parties. A real estate broker is the agent of the individual who retains the broker to purchase, sell, lease or otherwise represent him or her in a real estate transaction.
Agreement of sale A contract that identifies the property, purchase price, and other terms of a sale.
Alienability The right to convey rights to real property.
Allodial system A system of individual land ownership in fee simple.
Amortization The process of retiring debt or recovering a capital investment through systematic repayments of principal.
Anchor tenant A major unit in a shopping center assumed to generate the most customer traffic, e.g., a supermarket or drugstore.
Appraisal An estimate or opinion of value of property by an expert as of a specific date, supported by the presentation and analysis of pertinent data. An appraisal is usually made by the cost approach (cost to reproduce the property), the market approach (comparison with similar properties), or the income approach (capitalization of actual or projected income data).
Assessed value The value of property determined by a taxing authority for purposes of assessing property taxes; assessed value usually has a fixed relationship to market value established by the taxing authority.
Assumption of mortgage The assumption by a second purchaser of the responsibility for repaying existing indebtedness secured by property, which ordinarily relieves the first purchaser of the original obligation.
At-risk A tax concept that limits a taxpayer's loss deductions to the amount of his or her capital investment.
Axial theory A real estate theory that urban areas grow by developing outward around major transportation arteries from the central business district.

Balloon mortgage A mortgage loan that requires periodic payments but which leaves the loan less than fully amortized at maturity, requiring a final large payment referred to as the "balloon."
Bid rent curve A graphic description that maps site rent per square foot to distance from a central business district.
Blanket mortgage A mortgage that covers more than one property.
Breakeven ratio A measure of the relationship of debt service and operating expenses to gross income; the occupancy level to make neither a profit nor a loss.

ENCYCLOPEDIA OF BANKING AND FINANCE

REAL ESTATE

Broker A person who acts as the agent in buying, selling, leasing, or managing property for a commission.
Brokerage license The privilege or right conferred by a state to conduct a business of a real estate broker. The candidate for the license must usually pass a written examination and meet other requirements.
Builder's method A method of estimating reproduction cost by totaling direct labor and materials costs and indirect costs to estimate the cost to reproduce a new structure or improvement.
Building code State or local ordinance that regulates minimum building and construction standards to protect the general health, safety, and welfare.

Capital improvement An expenditure that will extend or improve the life of a capital structure.
Capitalization The mathematical procedures of discounting net operating income by an appropriate rate to estimate the value of something.
Capitalization rate The rate of return used to value a given cash flow or income stream.
Carrying costs Cash outlays to continue maintaining an investment, such as interest.
Cash flow Revenue remaining after all cash expenses are paid; noncash charges such as depreciation are not included in the computations.
Certificate of occupancy A certificate issued by a zoning board or building commission to indicate that a structure complies with the building code and be legally occupied.
Collateral An asset, such as real estate or securities, which a borrower pledges as security. A mortgage typically gives a creditor the right to seize the collateral after nonperformance of the debtor.
Color of title A title that appears to be correct but actually has a defect.
Commercial real estate Improved property held for the production of income.
Commitment A promise to make an investment or loan at some time in the future if certain specified conditions are met. A "take-out" commitment is provided by the anticipated long-term lender. A "gap" commitment is an anticipated short-term loan to provide part of the final "take-out" that the long-term lender will not advance until certain conditions are met. The amount above the basic loan is the "gap." "Standby" commitments occur when a lender and borrower use to reassure a short-term construction lender that the construction lender will be repaid if, after completion of a building, the borrower cannot find adequate long-term financing.
Comparable properties Other properties that can be used to compare a property to make a judgement about market value.
Comparative unit method A method used to estimate reproduction or replacement cost by using actual costs of similar property and dividing it by the footage therein to yield a unit cost per footage.
Complementary land use Relationship between property sites that support one another.
Concentric circle theory A theory that describes urban growth in circles around a central business district.
Condominium A form of fee ownership of whole units or separate portions of multiunit buildings that enables the formal filing, recording and financing of a divided interest in real property, such as apartments, offices, and professional buildings.
Conformity A concept that property attains its maximum value when it conforms to neighborhoods, land use, and architectural integrity.
Constant The agreed-upon periodic payments required to pay the face interest rate, with any residual amount used to amortize the loan.
Construction loan A loan used for the construction of property, usually from six months to two years. A construction loan is usually disbursed in increments (draws or draw-downs), as the construction proceeds; a construction loan is usually repaid through the proceeds of a permanent loan.
Construction loan draw One of a series of payments made by a lender under a construction loan.
Contract rent The agreed-upon rent.
Conversion A change or modification in the use of property.
Cooperative A form of property ownership whereby a structure is owned by a corporation whose stockholders are entitled to lease a specific unit in the building. The property is owned by a corporation or trust with individual owners holding stock in the corporation or an interest in the trust.
Coownership An ownership interest in property by more than one person.
Counteroffer Under the law of contract, an alternative offer by an offeree to the offeror.

Dead land Land that because of its location is incapable of being developed.
Dealer One who buys and sells property as a part of normal business operations.
Debenture An obligation in the form of a bond secured only by the general credit of the issuing entity.
Debt coverage ratio The ratio between net operating income and the debt service on a loan. It is interpreted to mean that the higher the ratio, the lower the risk to the lender.
Deed A written instrument that conveys title to real property.
Deed of conveyance A deed given by a trustee to a beneficiary at the termination of the trust relationship under a trust deed.
Deed of trust A written, three-party (borrower, lender, trustee) instrument used to provide security for a debt, instead of a mortgage.
Default To fail to complete a contractual obligation.
Defeasible fee A fee simple interest in land that can be terminated on the happening of a specific event.
Deficiency judgment A judgment against the mortgagor when the amount obtained at a foreclosure sale is less than the amount due on the mortgage or deed of trust.
Density The number of persons or improved space within a specified unit of land.
Discount center A shopping center characterized by a major anchor tenant and surrounded by complementary shops, grocery stores, and other merchants.
Discounted present value The value of property computed by discounting expected future cash flows over a period of time.
Discount rate An interest rate used to convert a future stream of payments or cash into a single present value.
Draw A request from a borrower to obtain partial payment from a lender as related to a loan commitment.

Easement An interest in land that gives the holder a right of way to use the land for a specific purpose.
Easement appurtenant An easement that passes with the land on its conveyance to a subsequent owner.
Enjoyment The right of a fee simple interest to be free from interference from prior owners.
Equalization The process of adjusting property assessments or valuations in a taxing district to achieve a uniform proportion between assessed values and actual cash values to assure property owners are taxed at an equal rate.
Equity The interest of an owner or shareholder in property or a company. Equity refers to (1) the difference between the current market value of a property and the liens or mortgages that encumber it, or (2) the cash that makes up the difference between the mortgage and the construction or sale price.
Equity kicker A loan guarantee that the lender will receive a percentage of property appreciation over a specified period of time and/or a percentage of income from the property.
Equity participation The right of an investor to participate to a specified extent in the increased value of a property, project, or income from the property or project.
Escalation clause An arrangement in a lease that allows the landlord to pass through increases in certain expenses to tenants, such as taxes and operating expenses.
Escheat The reversion of property to the state when a person dies intestate without known heirs.
Escrow An agreement providing that the lender is to collect and hold property taxes and insurance due on mortgage property until due.
Estate at sufferance The rights of a tenant after a lease expires and the tenant remains without permission from the landlord.
Estate at will The right of a tenant that automatically renews for a period specified in the original lease, until terminated by owner or tenant.
Estate from period to period A leasehold interest that terminates after a fixed period of time.
Exclusive agency An agreement giving a real estate broker an exclusive agency right to sell or lease the property of the owner. The

ENCYCLOPEDIA OF BANKING AND FINANCE

REAL ESTATE

owner can nevertheless sell or lease directly without being liable for a commission. In an exclusive right of sale, the owner would be liable for a commission if he or she sells or leases the property.

Exculpatory clause A clause in a contract that relieves one party of liability for injuries or damages to another.

Face value The value or amount that is shown on the face of an instrument such as a bond, note, or stock.

Feasibility study Research into the financial, economic, and other factors that provide information concerning the use of property and expected returns from the project.

Fee or fee simple Title to a property that is absolute, good, and marketable, without condition.

Fee simple absolute Absolute ownership subject to the limitations of police power, eminent domain, escheat, or private restrictions of record.

Fee simple determinable A fee simple that ends on the happening of a stated condition.

Festival A shopping mall without an anchor tenant characterized by a festive atmosphere which gives a social or tourist orientation.

FHA Federal Housing Administration.

FHLBB Federal Home Loan Bank Board.

FHLBS Federal Home Loan Bank System.

FHLMC Federal Home Loan Mortgage Corporation (Freddie Mac).

Fiduciary A relationship of trust between a person charged with a duty to act on behalf of another and a person to whom such duty is owed, e.g., guardians, trustees, executors, and directors.

First mortgage A mortgage which has a prior claim over all other liens against real estate. In many jurisdictions, real estate taxes, mechanics liens, court costs, and certain other involuntary liens can take priority over a first mortgage lien.

Floating rate A variable interest rate charged for the use of borrowed money. The rate is usually a specified percentage above a fluctuating base rate, usually the prime rate of a major commercial bank or the rate associated with a government debt instrument.

FNMA Federal National Mortgage Association (Fannie Mae).

Foreclosure The legal process that forces a sale of mortgaged property to provide funds to pay off a loan upon the default by a mortgagor. Upon foreclosure, the debt may not be fully discharged. In such a situation, a "deficiency judgment" may be obtained which places the creditor in a position similar to that of any other creditor.

Foreclosure by action and sale A foreclosure requiring the lender to take court action before selling property held as collateral for a loan.

Foreclosure by power of sale A foreclosure stemming from a deed of trust in which the trustee can dispose of the property without court action.

FSLIC Federal Savings and Loan Insurance Corporation.

Gap financing Financing provided by a second lender to a borrower when the financing provided by the first lender was insufficient.

General warranty deed A deed stating that the grantor is liable for title defects that were created during his or her ownership and all previous owners.

Good title Unencumbered title to property that provides a marketable title.

Highest and best use The use of property that at a given time provides the greatest net return.

Hypermarkets A shopping mall format designed to allow shoppers to get all of their shopping done in one trip through the checkout line.

HUD Department of Housing and Urban Development.

Infrastructure Roads, highways, water and sewer system, fire and police protection, parks and recreation, schools, and similar services and facilities provided by the federal or state governments or a municipality.

Industrial park A large area of improved land used for industrial and manufacturing purposes wherein individual sites are purchased or leased by users.

Intermediate-term loan A loan for a term of three to ten years that usually is not completely amortized at maturity, often used by developers.

Interim loan A loan that is to be repaid from the proceeds of another loan. The loan is usually not self-liquidating.

Junior mortgage loan A mortgage loan in which the lien and the right of repayment is subordinate to another mortgage loan(s).

Leap-frogging Land development that skips to outlying areas for purpose of development.

Lease A contract that gives the lessor the right of possession for a period in return for rents by lessee.

Leasehold estate A tenant's interest in property resulting from a lease.

Leasehold improvements The cost of improvements to property leased for a period of years, usually paid for by the tenant. The improvements typically become the property of the lessor/owner on the expiration of the lease.

Leverage The use of borrowed funds in financing property or a project with the expectation of obtaining a profit above the cost of borrowing.

Lien The right to hold property as security until a debt that is secured by the lien is paid.

Life estate An interest in property that provides control and use of the property during the holder's life.

Life tenant One who has an estate for life in real property.

Limited partnership A partnership that limits limited partner(s) (usually investors) to the amount of their investment. In a limited partnership, at least one partner is a general partner who has unlimited liability for the obligations of the partnership.

Line of credit An agreement between a bank and a borrower under which the bank agrees to provide unsecured credit to the borrower upon specified terms and conditions.

Listing agreement A contract between a seller and a real estate broker.

Listing broker The broker who has a contractual arrangement with the seller to sell or lease the property.

Littoral rights Shoreline rights of owners whose land abuts lakes, rivers, or oceans that allows use of the water without restriction.

Loan run-off The rate at which an existing mortgage portfolio will reduce to zero if no new loans are added to the portfolio.

Location A major factor affecting the value of property.

Manufacturers' outlet center A shopping format designed to be a destination or attraction composed of direct manufacturer's outlet stores, and restaurants, having off-price retailers.

Map A plat. A survey of a tract of land prepared by a survey or showing boundaries of parcels, roads, highways, and other units.

Market study Research that analyzes the general demand for property or product.

Market value The probable price that property would bring if available for sale in the open market in a knowledgeable, arm's length transaction.

Mechanic's lien A claim that attaches to property to protect the rights of one who performs labor or provides material in connection with construction activities.

Metes and bounds survey A survey describing land by identifying boundaries through terminal points and degrees of latitude and longitude.

Moratorium A period of time in which payments of debts or other performance of a legal obligation is temporarily suspended.

Mortgage An instrument used to make real estate security for a debt. In some states, a mortgage is an actual conveyance of the property to the creditor until the mortgage is satisfied. A note secured by the mortgage typically reflects the arrangement. Mortgages assume many forms: first, junior, short-term, long-term, wraparound, construction, development, and others.

Mortgage banker A nondepository lender that originates real estate loans and then sells them (packages) to institutional lenders and other investors. Mortgage bankers frequently service these mortgages.

Mortgage broker An entity who arranges financing with a permanent lender for a borrower for a fee.

Mortgage constant The total annual payments of principal and interest (annual debt service) on a mortgage with a level-payment amortization schedule, expressed as a percentage of the initial principal amount of the loan.

Mortgage insurance Insurance that provides protection for a mortgage lender in the event of default by a borrower.

Multiple listing service A selling technique used by brokers whereby a listing with any one broker automatically becomes available to all brokers participating in the service. When a sales results, the commission is divided between the brokers.

Neighborhood A section of a city or town that has common features distinguishing it from adjacent areas.
Neighborhood centers Strip centers or small shopping centers.
Nuisance The use or condition of property that unreasonably interferes with the rights of others.

Offer A promise to perform in return for a promise to act.
Open-end mortgage A mortgage that allows the lender to make additional advances in the future.
Open listing Offering property for sale or lease through a broker in which the broker has no exclusive agency or right of sale.
Option The right given by the owner to another to acquire or lease property at a specific price within a period of time. If the option is not exercised, the consideration is forfeited.
Origination The process by which a loan is created, including the finding of the opportunity, analysis and structuring of the financing, and the review and acceptance procedures by which the commitment is ultimately issued.
Origination fee A fee charged by a lender at the beginning of a loan to cover administrative costs.

Package mortgage A mortgage loan that packages what would normally be two separate loans, such as a construction loan and a permanent loan.
Participation mortgage A single mortgage loan made by more than one lender.
Passivity A condition of not actively managing an investment or property.
Points A point is one percent of the loan, usually charged by the lender at the beginning of a loan to increase the effective yield. A point is an additional compensation to the lender and cost to the borrower.
Power center A shopping format designed to have no major anchor store but five or more nationally known stores that have the ability to draw customers alone but that have even greater pull when combined in one location.
Prepayment clause A provision in a loan agreement allowing the borrower to repay the loan before maturity.
Prepayment penalty A fee charged a borrower for the right to pay off a loan before it is due.
Prime lending rate The rate at which commercial banks will lend money to their most creditworthy customers. The rate is used as a base for most loans to financial intermediaries and other borrowers.
Principal The buyer or seller in a real estate or investment transaction; the sum of money loaned.
Prior lien A lien ranking ahead of another lien(s).
Progression The concept that inferior property's value is enhanced as a result of being associated with superior properties.
Proration A division of taxes, interest, insurance, and similar charges so that the seller and buyer each pay the portion representing the period of his or her ownership.
Purchase money mortgage A mortgage that is taken by a seller from a buyer in place of purchase money. The seller finances the loan in whole or in part.

Quit-claim deed A deed in which the grantor makes no warranties to the grantee.

Real estate investment trust (REIT) A trust established for the benefit of a group of investors which is managed by a trustee(s) who hold title to the assets for the trust and control its acquisitions and investments, at least 75% of which are real estate holdings. No federal income tax is paid by the trust if certain conditions are met.
Redlining A specific geographic area identified for the purpose of making loans or lending terms that are different from the norm; often represents a discriminatory lending practice.
Replacement cost The cost of creating a building or improvement having similar utility on the basis of current costs and usage.
Reproduction cost new The cost of creating a building or improvement which exactly replaces an existing structure on the basis of current prices and uses.
Restrictive covenant A limiting clause in a deed that regulates the use of property.
Return on equity A ratio which consists of net income for the period divided by equity usually expressed as a percentage.

Riparian rights Rights of an owner abutting water to access and use of the water within limits.

Sale-leaseback A form of real estate transaction in which the investor buys property from and simultaneously leases it back to the seller. The previous owner or developer "cashes out" of an existing property while retaining control.
Sealed bid A sales technique where all prospective buyers submit offers in a sealed envelope. The property goes to the highest bidder.
Second mortgage A junior mortgage.
Senior mortgage A mortgage that has first priority.
Self-liquidating loan A loan that will be repaid at maturity as a result of amortization payments.
Short-term mortgage A real estate loan for a term of three years or less.
Sinking fund An arrangement under which a portion of a bond or preferred stock issue is retired periodically. Assets are typically set aside to provide for the payments.
Site analysis A study of the physical, economic, and legal characteristics of a site.
Special interest centers Highly specialized shopping centers which target specific limited niches, e.g., automotive centers and ethnic centers.
Specialty centers Shopping centers that have no anchor tenant and consist of regular-price specialty retailers, usually upscale.
Special warranty deed A deed in which the grantor is liable only if the problem arose through the actions of the grantor or during his or her ownership.
Stand-alone destination A store that has the capacity to draw customers by itself from great distances. The store usually sells only private-label products.
Standby fee A fee charged to induce the lender to remain willing to lend on preestablished terms for a specified period at the borrower's option.
Sunbelt Areas located in the south and southwestern part of the United States.
Syndicate A group of investors who unite to transact business for a limited period and usually for a single purpose. A syndicate is a form of a short-term partnership.
Subordinated debt Junior debt subordinated to secured and unsecured senior debt.

Takeout commitment A permanent loan commitment associated with a project to be constructed.
Tax shelter An investment that provides relief from income taxes or an opportunity to claim deductions from taxable income. Tax shelters are currently scrutinized by the Internal Revenue Service.
Time sharing The division of ownership or use of a resort unit or apartment on the basis of time periods.
Title Evidence of ownership of property related to indicate the right to possess, use, and dispose of property.
Title closing The actual transfer of title to property.
Title company A company that examines titles to property to determine its validity and any limitations on the title. The title company insures the validity of the title to the owner or lender.
Title examiner A person or firm trained in examining public land record to determine if the present owner has good title.
Title insurance Insurance provided by a title company to insure the validity of title to property.
Topography The contours of the surface of a site.

Upzoning Upgrading the classification of property.

VA Veterans Administration.
Variance A difference allowed from a standard or code.

Warehouse clubs Retailers that have membership fees or other restrictions and offer a no-frills, low-price alternative to traditional retail outlets.
Wraparound A form of secondary financing in which the amount of the second loan equals the balance of the first loan plus the amount of the new financing.

Yield In real estate transactions, yield refers to the effective annual amount of income that is being accrued on an investment expressed as a percentage of its value.

Zoning An ordinance that is used by local governments to assess land uses and to regulate lot size and height of building and other restrictions on land use.
See REAL PROPERTY.

BIBLIOGRAPHY

ALLAWAY, W. J., et al. MODERN REAL ESTATE PRACTICE. Real Estate Education Co., Chicago, IL, 1988.
Analyzing Real Estate Opportunities: Market and Feasibility studies. Prentice Hall, Inc., Englewood Cliffs, NJ, 1987.
ESTE, J. *Handbook of Loan Payment Tables, 1976.*
GLOVER, T. "Investors Expect Real Benefits." *Accountancy,* October, 1987.
GROSS, J. S. *Illustrated Encyclopedic Dictionary of Real Estate.* Prentice Hall, Inc., Englewood Cliffs, NJ, 1987.
JOHNSON, L. M. *The Individual Investor's Guide to Real Estate Investing.* International Publishing Corp, Chicago, IL, 1989.
KASSTER, L. R. "The Due Diligence Obligations of Institutions that Sell Real Estate Securities." *Real Estate Review,* Winter, 1988.
Journal of Property Management. Institute of Real Estate Management, Chicago, IL. Bimonthly.
Journal of Real Estate Taxation. Warren, Gorham and Lamont, Inc., Boston, MA. Quarterly.
MADEN, C., AND BORTZ, J. *The Dow Jones-Irwin Guide to Real Estate Investing.* Dow Jones-Irwin, Inc., Homewood, IL, 1983.
National Real Estate Investor. Communication Channels, Inc., Atlanta, GA. Monthly.
The Real Estate Appraiser and Analyst.
Real Estate Issues.
Real Estate Law Journal.
Real Estate Review.
Real Estate Today.
Realty and Building.
SEDLIN, M. *The Real Estate Handbook.* Dow Jones-Irwin, Inc., Homewood, IL, 1989.
SIROTA, D. *Essentials of Real Estate Investment.* Real Estate Education Co., Chicago, IL, 1988.
STANGER, R. A. *Evaluating Real Estate Partnership Investments,* 1987.
THORNDIKE, D. *Thorndike Encyclopedia of Banking & Financial Tables.* Warren Gorham and Lamont, Inc., New York, NY, 1987.
VENTOLO, W. L., and others. *Mastering Real Estate Mathematics.* Real Estate Education, Co., Chicago, IL, 1984.
WOFFORD, L. E. *Real Estate.* John Wiley and Sons, Inc., New York, NY, 1986.
WURTZEBACH, C. H., and MILES, M. E. *Modern Real Estate.* John Wiley and Sons, New York, NY, 1987.

REAL ESTATE BONDS Bonds secured by mortgages or trust conveyances of real estate. In the investment sense, real estate bonds are a series of bonds issued in convenient denominations with a mortgage on real estate as security. Usually such bonds were issued by a mortgage or investment company, which, in addition to furnishing mortgage security, guaranteed bonds by endorsement. Mortgage certificates are a variant of real estate obligations.

The investment quality of real estate bonds depends upon (1) the productivity of the mortgaged real estate; (2) the ratio of bonds issued to the conservative value of the mortgaged property; (3) whether the real estate is adequately insured; (4) provision for amortization of the loan by the mortgagor; and (5) the financial standing of the issuing company. Where real estate bonds are lawfully issued and in conformity with conservative principles of mortgage finance, they are comparable in safety with mortgage loans, but the 1929-1932 depression exposed weaknesses in many real estate bonds traceable chiefly to nonobservance of conservative financing practices during the boom of the late 1920s.

See MORTGAGE BOND, MORTGAGE CERTIFICATE, MORTGAGE LOANS.

REAL ESTATE INVESTMENT TRUSTS The modern real estate investment trust (REIT) has been called by the Securities and Exchange Commission a "result of the Federal tax laws."

Sections 856-858 of the Internal Revenue Code of 1954 established a new form of REIT entity to serve as a tax-free conduit for income distributed to shareholders. Sections 856-858 of the Code as amended and the regulations thereunder define what constitutes the REIT, provide how it and its beneficiaries will be taxed, and prescribe the types of investments in which the REIT may engage.

Under provisions of the Real Estate Investment Trust Act, REITs are exempt from corporate taxes on net income distributed to their shareholders if the trust complies with provisions of the trust law and regulations adopted by the Internal Revenue Service. To be considered a real estate investment trust for purposes of the federal income tax laws, the REIT must elect to be so treated and must meet strict requirements, including the following:

1. 90% or more of earnings must be distributed to shareholders.
2. At the end of each fiscal quarter of its taxable year, at least 75% of the value of the total assets of the trust must consist of real estate assets (including interests on loans secured by mortgages on real property and shares in other realty trusts), cash, cash items, and government securities.
3. Beneficial ownership of the trust must be held by 100 or more trust shareholders during at least 335 days of a taxable year of 12 months. More than 50% of the outstanding shares may not be owned, directly, indirectly, or constructively, by or for five or fewer individuals, at any time during the last half of the taxable year.
4. The trust may not hold real property primarily for sale in the ordinary course of business.
5. At least 75% of the gross income of the trust must be derived from rents, mortgage interest, and gains from the sale of real estate.
6. An additional 15% of the gross income of the trust must be derived from the same sources or from dividends or lawful interest or gains from the sale or other disposition of stock or securities, or any combination of the foregoing.
7. Not more than 25% of the value of a trust's total assets may be represented by securities.
8. Gross income from sales or other disposition of stock or securities held for less than six months and of real property held for less than four years must be less than 30% of gross income.

These features are in general similar in nature to those applicable to the open-end investment companies ("mutual funds") and enable the smaller investor to share in a portfolio professionally managed, especially at a time of real estate prosperity. But structurally REITs are more akin to the closed-end investment companies, since they do not stand ready to redeem shareholders' shares at prevailing asset value and since they are permitted to finance in debt securities as well as equity. Such capital structure leverage resulted in accelerated declines in asset values and income when the boom in real estate ended in the late 1960s and the early 1970s, causing financial difficulties for many REITs and banks that had loans outstanding to such REITs. Those REITs which have survived are in position to participate in turnarounds in real estate values and earning power.

REAL ESTATE LOANS See MORTGAGE LOANS.

REAL ESTATE MORTGAGE See MORTGAGE, MORTGAGE BOND, MORTGAGE LOANS.

REAL ESTATE MORTGAGE INVESTMENT CONDUIT The 1986 Tax Reform Act authorizes the creation of a new tax structure for issuers of mortgage-backed securities called the real estate mortgage investment conduit (REMIC). Through its REMIC provisions, the 1986 tax law allows issuers of mortgage-backed securities to choose the REMIC tax vehicle through which to transfer payments by mortgagors to investors. The principal effect of the REMIC structure is to reduce the importance of federal tax considerations in designing mortgage security transactions.

Under the REMIC structure, claims to a pool of mortgages or mortgage-backed securities can be sold to investors. The dominant form of investor interest in a REMIC is a regular interest. Regular interests can be issued in varying classes. For example, interests may be divided into maturity classes so that the earliest mortgages to repay can be assigned to the fast-pay regular interests, while the last mortgages to pay can be assigned to the slow-pay regular interests, just like a collateralized mortgage obligation (CMO). Regular interests can also be issued with differing priorities in the event of defaults by mortgagors. In theory, the REMIC structure allows the cash flows from a pool of mortgages to be rearranged into an almost infinite series of different types of regular interests.

The other kind of investor interest in a REMIC is a residual interest. There can be only one class of investors who own residual interests, and all of the residual interests must be undivided pro rata interests. Residual interests consist of rights to payments that are contingent on a certain speed of mortgage repayments or the rights to earnings on reserve funds that are not needed to pay the amounts guaranteed to holders of regular interests.

REMICs are tax-free entities. All of the taxable income that accrues to a REMIC is passed through to the holders of residual interests, after deduction for the amount of REMIC income allocated to the holders of regular interests.

For foreign investors, REMIC investments are exempt from the 30% U.S. withholding tax. For thrift institutions and real estate investment trusts, REMIC investments are considered the same as real estate loans, as long as the underlying collateral qualifies as such.

REAL ESTATE SETTLEMENT PROCEDURES ACT
An act that requires disclosure of information about the services and costs involved at "settlement," when real property is transferred from seller to buyer.

REAL ESTATE TRANSACTIONS
Real estate sales are divided into two broad accounting categories: retail land sales and other real estate sales. Retail land sales involve sales of real estate on a volume basis with relatively small down payments. The seller usually develops the land by subdividing the property, selling the lots, and making improvements such as paving and landscaping. Revenue is recognized on retail land sales when the following conditions are met: the refund period has expired, the cumulative payments equal or exceed 10% of the sales price, the receivables are collectible and are not subordinate to new loans on the property, and the seller either is not obligated to make improvements on the lots sold or has made progress on improvements promised. Depending upon the circumstances, revenue is recognized under one of the following methods: full accrual method, deposit method, installment method, or percentage of completion method.

Other real estate sales include any real estate except retail land sales. A sale should be recorded upon the closing of a transaction involving a transfer of the usual risks and rewards of ownership for a consideration. Profit recognition should be deferred until specific criteria have been met, including the adequacy of the purchaser's down payment, the purchaser's continuing commitment to the investment, and the seller's continuing commitment for performance. If these criteria are not met, then one of the following methods should be used depending upon the circumstances: deposit method, installment method, or cost recovery method.

BIBLIOGRAPHY

SFAS No. 66, *Accounting for Sale of Real Estate* (FASB, 1982).

REALIZATION
The process of converting noncash resources and rights into money. This term is used in accounting and financial reporting to refer to sales of assets for cash or claims to cash. The terms "realized" and "unrealized" identify revenues or gains or losses on assets sold and unsold, respectively. Accrual accounting recognizes revenue as being realized when it is earned.

Revenue is generally considered as being earned when the earning process is completed and an exchange has taken place, as when a manufacturer makes and then sells a product. Revenue is realized when the sale takes place (not when the product is manufactured) because the earning process is substantially completed and an exchange took place. Revenue from sales of products is often recognized at the date of sale, usually interpreted to mean the date of delivery to customers. Revenue from services rendered is recognized when services have been performed and are billable. Revenue from permitting others to use enterprise resources, such as interest, rent, and royalties, is recognized as time passes or as the resources are used.

Modification of the revenue realization principle described above include the following:

1. Revenue recognized during production. In long-term construction contracts, contractors can recognize revenue during the construction period using the percentage-of-completion method. This method can be used when the contract price is definite, when a reasonable estimate can be made of progress towards the completion of the project, and the costs incurred or to be incurred are known or can be estimated.
2. Revenue recognized at the completion of production. Revenue is sometimes recognized when production is completed. Precious minerals and some agricultural commodities trade in markets that have a readily determinable and realizable market price. Revenue could be recognized for such product when production is completed and before a sale occurs.
3. Revenue recognized when cash is collected. When considerable uncertainty exists concerning the collectability of an account, revenue can be recognized as cash is received after the sale. The installment sales method or the cost recovery method would be appropriate for recognizing revenue under these circumstances.

BIBLIOGRAPHY

SFAC No. 5, *Recognition and Measurement in Financial Statements* (FASB, 1984).

REALIZATION VALUE
The price at which an asset is actually sold, as distinguished from its book, cost, or inventory value; the prices realized through liquidation.

REAL MONEY
Roughly, metallic money; money made of a commodity (in the leading commercial nations, one of the precious metals having value otherwise than in its money function); money manufactured from a metal having known and recognized commodity (commercial) value, e.g., gold, silver, nickel, copper. Such money is not necessarily standard money, although gold is a standard with most nations. Real money is to be distinguished from paper money, which is representative money (e.g., Federal Reserve notes or silver certificates), or credit or fiduciary money with or without a specific pledge of assets as security. Real money is also to be distinguished from such money equivalents as checks, drafts, promissory notes, and money orders.

REAL PROPERTY
In law, land, that which is erected upon or growing upon or affixed to land, and rights issuing out of land.
See PERSONAL PROPERTY, REAL ESTATE.

REAL RATE
Nominal rate adjusted to remove the effect of a changing price level, i.e., a rate measured in dollars of constant purchasing power.

REAL STOCK
"Long" stock; stock held and deliverable by outright or margin owners, as distinguished from stock that has been sold short.

REALTY
See REAL ESTATE, REAL PROPERTY.

REAL VALUE
The value of money stock, the GNP, an interest rate, or any other economic quantity adjusted for changes in the price level. The term "real" is used to suggest that the value reflects the actual purchasing power in terms of goods and services. Some examples of real value are:

Real GNP The nominal GNP divided by the GNP deflator (the price index).
Real consumption Nominal consumption divided by the consumer price index (CPI).
Real inventories Inventories divided by an appropriate price index, possibly the producer price index.
Real interest rate The nominal interest rate minus the inflation rate. In most cases, the correct inflation rate will be the percentage change in the CPI.

REBATE
In banking practice, a deduction, drawback or allowance extended if a borrower, for example, pays interest in advance on a six months' note and then, by consent of the lender, pays off the debt one month before maturity. Wherever a note is liquidated before maturity with the lender's consent, the borrower is entitled to receive back interest. This is called a rebate of interest.

Rebates on freight rates were prohibited by the original Interstate Commerce Act of 1887.
See INTERSTATE COMMERCE ACT.

REBATED ACCEPTANCE ANTICIPATED ACCEPTANCE.

RECAPITALIZATION Any voluntary changes in respect to the capitalization of a business corporation, effected by the corporation by consent of the holders of the respective types of securities without resort to the jurisdiction of the courts, as in judicial REORGANIZATION.

As an example of a state law, the New York Business Corporation Law was amended in 1962 and 1963 to facilitate amendments and changes to the business corporation's certificate of incorporation from time to time. Following are among the possible amendments and changes relating to capitalization: to increase or decrease the aggregate number of shares, or shares of any class or series, with or without par value, which the corporation shall have authority to issue; to eliminate from authorized shares any class of shares, or any shares of any class, whether issued or unissued; to increase the par value of any authorized shares of any class with par value, whether issued or unissued; to reduce the par value of any authorized shares of any class with par value, whether issued or unissued; to change any authorized shares, with or without par value, whether issued or unissued, into a different number of shares of the same class or into the same or a different number of shares of any one or more classes or any series thereof, either with or without par value; to fix, change, or abolish the designation of any authorized class or any series thereof or any of the relative rights, preferences, and limitations of any shares of any authorized class or any series thereof, whether issued or unissued, including any provisions in respect of any undeclared dividends, whether or not cumulative or accrued, or the redemption of any shares, or any preemptive right to acquire shares or any securities; as to the shares of any preferred class, then or theretofore authorized, which may be issued in series, to grant authority to the board of directors or to change or revoke authority of the board to establish and designate series and to fix the number of shares and the relative rights, preferences, and limitation as between series (Sec. 801).

Moreover, the corporation may reduce its stated capital by amendment of its certificate of incorporation (Sec. 801) which reduces the par value of any issued shares with par value; changes issued shares so as to bring about a reduction of stated capital, and eliminates from authorized shares shares that have been issued and reacquired by the corporation (TREASURY STOCK).

Amendments of the certificate of incorporation may be authorized by vote of the holders of a majority of all outstanding shares entitled to vote thereon at a meeting of shareholders (Sec. 803). No amendment or change, however, shall affect the existing rights of persons other than shareholders (Sec. 806(5)). If class voting applies, the affirmative vote of a majority of each class or series is also required (Secs. 803 and 804), when such amendments or changes of the class or series would exclude or limit their right to vote on any matter; reduce par value; change any authorized shares into a different number of shares of the same class, or into the same or a different number of shares of any one or more classes or any series thereof; or change the relative rights, preferences, and limitations of any shares of any authorized class or series thereof.

A holder of any adversely affected shares who does not vote for or consent in writing to the actions enumerated below shall (by complying with the statutory procedure, Sec. 623, to enforce shareholder's right to receive payment for shares) have the right to dissent and to receive payment for such shares if the amendment alters or abolishes any preferential right of any outstanding shares having preferences; creates, alters, or abolishes any provision or right in respect of the redemption of any outstanding shares; alters or abolishes any PREEMPTIVE RIGHT of such holder; or excludes or limits the right of such holder to vote on any matter (Sec. 806(6)).

Any holder intending to enforce such right of appraisal shall file with the corporation, either before the authorizing shareholders' meeting or before the vote thereat, written objection to the action indicating intent to demand payment for his shares if the action is taken. The corporation then sends written notice of the authorization to such objecting stockholders by registered mail. Within 20 days of such notice, the dissenting shareholder shall make written demand upon the corporation for payment of the fair value of his shares, and within a month shall submit his stock certificates to the corporation or its transfer agent for marking thereon that they are dissenting shares and return to the shareholder; because upon filing of the notice of dissent, the shareholder ceases to have any of the rights of shareholders except the right to be paid the fair value of his shares under the right of appraisal statute (Sec. 623).

Right of appraisal for dissenting shareholders also applies to dissent from merger of subsidiary corporation (Sec. 905) and merger or consolidation of domestic and foreign corporations (Sec. 907).

RECAPTURE CLAUSE Part of Section 15a of the Interstate Commerce Act, as amended in Section 422 of the Transportation Act of 1920, repealed retroactively by the Emergency Railroad Transportation Act of 1933. The recapture clause, in effect from 1920 to 1933, provided that if any carrier received for any year a net railway operating income in excess of 6% of the value of its railway property, it was to pay over one-half of such excess to the commission for the purpose of establishing and maintaining a general railway contingent fund. The other half of the excess was to be placed in a reserve fund. The carriers that earned in excess of 6% on property value might draw upon this reserve fund to the extent that their net railway operating income for any year was less than a sum equal to 6% of the value of their property devoted to the service of transportation. When this fund equaled 5% of the value of the railway property, such excess railway operating income as was payable to the carrier might be used for any lawful purpose, including extra dividends.

This clause was sustained in a decision rendered in December, 1923, by the United States Supreme Court in an appeal taken by the Dayton-Goose Creek Railway Company (in which 19 other large railroads joined) from the decision of the United States District Court for the Eastern District of Texas.

Repeal of the recapture clause was provided for in the Emergency Transportation Act of 1933, which stated:

"All moneys which were recoverable by and payable up to the Interstate Commerce Commission, under paragraph (6) of Section 15A of the Interstate Commerce Act, as in force prior to the enactment of this act, shall cease to be so recoverable and payable; and all proceedings pending for the recovery of any such moneys shall be terminated.

"The general railroad contingent fund established under such section shall be liquidated and the Secretary of the Treasury shall distribute the moneys in such fund among the carriers which have made payments under such section, so that each such carrier shall receive an amount bearing the same ratio to the total amount in such fund that the total of amounts paid under such section by such carrier bears to the total of amounts paid under such section by all carriers; except that if the total amount in such fund exceeds the total of amounts paid under such section by all carriers such excess shall be distributed among such carriers upon the basis of the average rate of earnings (as determined by the Secretary of the Treasury) on the investment of the moneys in such fund and differences in dates of payments by such carriers."

The amount that had been paid into the railroad contingent fund during the approximately 13 years of effectiveness of the recapture clause was about $10 million.

See RAILROAD TRANSPORTATION (EMERGENCY) ACT OF 1933, TRANSPORTATION ACT OF 1920.

RECEDE To incur a setback in commodity and security prices; to experience a decline or shrinkage in values. When business activity is said to recede, a mild intermediate recession is indicated rather than a major cyclical downswing.

See BUSINESS CYCLE.

RECEIPT An evidence of payment; a written acknowledgment given by one who receives money or other property to one who pays money or delivers property. The use of formal receipts has been practically abandoned in modern business. It is more customary for creditors to render statements of account to debtors periodically, and if payment is made in cash, the statement is stamped "Paid." Payments are usually made by check, however, and since the check must be endorsed by the payee (creditor), it constitutes satisfactory evidence of payment after it has been returned to the drawer by his bank. Many concerns print upon their statements a notice to the following effect: "No receipt necessary. Your canceled check is your voucher." An ordinary receipt acknowledging payment of a debt is not a promise to pay money and thus is not negotiable under the Negotiable Instruments Law. On the other hand, nonnegotiable instruments made to order, such as an order bill of lading or a warehouse receipt, can be assigned by endorsement.

See CANCELED CHECKS, TEMPORARY RECEIPTS, TRUST RECEIPT, WAREHOUSE RECEIPT.

RECEIVABLES A claim against others for the future receipt of money, goods, or services. Receivables include accounts receivable (sometimes called trade receivables), installment sales receivable, notes receivable, receivables from officers or employees, claims against insurance companies for damages to property, and many other claims.

Accounts receivable arise from the sale of goods or services on account. A major problem associated with accounts receivable is determining what recognition should be given to the possibility that the amount owed may not be collected. The allowance method and the direct write-off method are employed to deal with uncollectible accounts. Under the allowance method, an estimate of uncollectible accounts is made at the end of each accounting period and reported in the income statement as an expense. On the balance sheet, estimated uncollectible receivables are deducted from the gross amount of accounts receivable. This deduction serves as a contra asset or valuation account. The estimated amount of uncollectible accounts is determined as a percentage of credit sales for the period, a percentage of the ending accounts receivable, or by aging the accounts receivable. The allowance method is used when there is high probability that some receivables will not be collected and when the seller can estimate the dollar amount considered to be uncollectible. When the direct write-off method is used, the account is written off and an expense is recognized in the income statement when a customer actually defaults on payment. The write-off method cannot be used when uncollectible amounts are significant and can be estimated.

RECEIVER A person appointed by an equity court to take custody of the property of a debtor and to preserve the business for the benefit of creditors under supervision of the court. In nonstatutory equity receiverships, the receiver's duties and powers are defined by the order of the court appointing the receiver, but where statutes apply, the receiver's duties and powers are governed by the statutes under the supervision of the court. The federal statute is the NATIONAL BANKRUPTCY ACT as amended. Where federal statutes do not apply, state bankruptcy statutes if any will govern; should there be no applicable state statutes, equity receivership under principles of equity jurisprudence will be applied by a court of equity. Equity receiverships, however, with the objective of continuing the business of a debtor in reorganized condition, are now relatively obsolete in view of the comprehensive remedies available in the amended federal statute, which provides not only for liquidation but also for reorganization and whose great advantage is the binding of dissenters to a plan of reorganization if the minimum consent is obtained, instead of payment of dissenters' claims in cash as is necessary in equity receivership.

Duties of the receiver are custodial in nature. The active duty of working out a plan of reorganization, if feasible, or recommending liquidation of a debtor after study of the facts and circumstances is charged to the trustee in bankruptcy under the National Bankruptcy Act. In equity receiverships, the work of bringing in a plan of reorganization was in practice in the hands of a reorganization committee drawn from the protective committees formed for each class of securities or creditors affected.

See RECEIVERSHIP, REORGANIZATION.

RECEIVER'S CERTIFICATES Obligations issued by a RECEIVER with the approval of the court having jurisdiction, to provide working capital for an insolvent concern, the affairs of which are in the custody of the receiver. Issuing receiver's certificates is the most convenient means by which additional capital can be secured to revive a business, since business failures are often caused by a lack of adequate capital.

In order to ensure a ready market for receiver's certificates, the court usually permits them to take precedence over first mortgage bonds, or other debt of the debtor, especially in the case of a railroad, or other public utility corporation, where public necessity demands its continuance as a going concern. They are usually short-term obligations and are ordinarily unsecured.

Because of the conditions under which they are issued and practical certainty that both principal and interest will be paid, receiver's certificates are entitled to an investment rating at least equal to that of the first mortgage bonds of the debtor in receivership. Receiver's certificates are not preferred claims, such as taxes and wages.

RECEIVERSHIP The legal status of a debtor placed in either equity or statutory proceedings as an insolvent. Equity receiverships refer to nonstatutory proceedings, governed by principles of equity jurisprudence, resorted to for continuance on a reorganized basis of the business of a debtor firm in the absence of statutes providing for such judicial reorganization; statutory receiverships are governed by the details of the applicable statutes. The National Bankruptcy Act, as amended in 1933 and subsequent years to provide for reorganization procedures, made obsolete recourse to equity receiverships. Under the continued bankruptcy provisions of the act, providing for the remedy of liquidation of the debtor, the court may appoint a receiver in bankruptcy, whose duties are to take charge of the property and conduct the business until such time as the trustee in bankruptcy is elected or appointed or the petition is dismissed. Under the reorganization provisions, the trustee in reorganizations under the National Bankruptcy Act not only has the duties of custody of the business and operation thereof of the receiver in equity receiverships, but also has positive duties pertaining to study of the debtor's circumstances and preparation and filing of plan of reorganization, if feasible.

In receiverships, the debtor is placed in the jurisdiction of the court, and the management loses control. The court initially appoints the receiver, whose duties are prescribed in the court order appointing him, and usually include, in addition to the basic duty of taking custody of and preserving the property of the debtor, the operation and administration of the business, including the borrowing of money, with court approval, for current purposes through issuance of RECEIVER'S CERTIFICATES.

Bank receiverships are statutory in nature. Under the Federal Deposit Insurance Act, the FEDERAL DEPOSIT INSURANCE CORPORATION shall be appointed by the Comptroller of the Currency as receiver for any closed national bank or District of Columbia bank, closed either by its board of directors or by the Comptroller of the Currency on account of inability to meet the demands of its depositors. It shall be the duty of the corporation as such receiver to realize upon the assets of the closed bank, having due regard to the condition of credit in the locality; to enforce the individual liability of directors thereof; and to wind up the affairs of such closed bank in conformity with the provisions of law relating to the liquidation of national banks except as modified by provisions of the Federal Deposit Insurance Act (other laws relating to receiverships of national banks include Secs. 5205, 5220, and 5234 of the Revised Statutes and Sec. 31 of the Banking Act of 1933). The corporation shall retain for its own account such portion of the amounts realized upon such liquidation as it shall be entitled to receive on account of its subrogation to the claims of depositors paid off their deposit insurance of up to $100,000 per account, and shall pay to depositors and other creditors the net amounts available for distribution to them on remaining claims. With respect to such closed bank, the corporation as receiver shall have all rights, powers, and privileges possessed by or granted by law to a receiver of an insolvent national bank.

Similarly, whenever any insured state bank (except a District of Columbia bank) shall have been closed by action of its board of directors or by the authority having supervision of such bank, on account of inability to meet the demands of depositors, the Federal Deposit Insurance Corporation shall accept appointment as receiver therefor, if such appointment is tendered by the authority having supervision of such bank and is authorized or permitted by state law. With respect to any such insured state bank, the corporation as receiver shall possess all the rights, powers, and privileges granted by state law to a receiver of a state bank.

RECEIVING TELLER The teller, sometimes known as the second teller, whose function it is to receive deposits of cash items from customers over the window. His duties are exactly opposite of those of the paying teller, but the two tellers jointly handle the inflow and outflow of the bank's cash. In a commercial bank, the deposits over the receiving teller's window consist of cash (metallic and paper money), checks, drafts, and matured coupons, checks being in the great majority. The receiving teller receives only those deposits that are the equivalent of cash and for which the depositor receives credit at the time of deposit before collection is actually effected. Checks may not be drawn on uncollected balances, and interest on out-of-town checks is deferred until collection is made. All items, except cash, are subject to cancellation of credit in case they are returned unpaid.

The receiving teller's responsibilities are second in importance only to those of the PAYING TELLER. In receiving deposits he is required to observe the following points:

1. Compare the title of the account on the passbook with that on the deposit slip for agreement. This is important since depositors may have several special accounts, e.g., payroll account, dividend account, interest coupon account, named officer as treasurer account, sinking fund account, etc.
2. See that the deposit slip is correctly dated. It is an original entry record and as such is admissible into court as evidence. If it is found to be incorrect, the receiving teller should correct it.
3. After separating the cash from the checks, count the cash first. Should the cash be in excess of the amount listed on the deposit slip, it is advisable to notify the depositor personally or over the telephone. The depositor's instructions may be to increase the deposit by the difference, or to return the amount of the difference. If the cash is short, the amount of the deposit is reduced accordingly. In this case the depositor should be required to submit a corrected deposit slip.
After the cash is counted, the amount is entered on the cash sheet, the cash amount on the deposit slip checked to indicate that it is correct, and the entry recorded. While the cash is being counted, it should be examined for counterfeits and raised bills.
4. Prove the checks with their listing on the deposit slip, or with the adding machine list accompanying it. While theoretically the receiving teller should examine the endorsement of all the checks deposited, it is usually only practical for him to examine the endorsement on the last check in a bundle. Whenever checks in large volume are deposited, they are not examined in detail at the time of receipt, because of the time such examination would consume. Entry is made in the passbook to correspond with the deposit slip and is subject to revision, if later found to be incorrect. The work of detailed examination of a check is left to the receiving teller's clerks, or to an hour in the day when the receiving teller is not busy at the window. In practice, it is only possible for the receiving teller to verify the actual cash with each deposit, the checks being examined and proved, in case of volume, by means of the BLOCK SYSTEM.

RECESSION A downturn in economic activity. The economy naturally undergoes business cycles, comprising recessions and growth periods. The most severe recession in this century in the United States occurred between 1929 and 1933 and is known as the Great Depression. The most recent recession was during 1981 and 1982. Since then, the economy has been growing at a slow but steady pace.

RECIPROCAL TARIFF ACT The original "Reciprocal Tariff Act" (Trade Agreements Act of June 12, 1934, 19 U.S.C. 1351-1354) contained a three-year delegation of power to the President to raise or lower tariffs by 50% within the "frame of reference" of then existing rates. The authority has been extended by Congress from time to time. The latest extension, in 1958, was for four years, the longest extension of any of the reciprocal tariff acts, making possible longer-term trade agreements with other countries, considered particularly necessary in connection with negotiations with the countries in the European Common Market (see EUROPEAN ECONOMIC COMMUNITY).

The 1958 extension provided for a reduction in tariff rates to the lowest rate obtainable by any one of three alternative methods: (1) reducing the July 1, 1958, rate by not more than 20%; (2) reducing the July 1, 1958, rate by not more than two percentage points; and (3) reducing an existing rate to not less than 50% ad valorem. Tariff reductions could not be made in more than four stages, nor could separate stages be less than a year apart; the last stage could not be later than three years after the first stage. The act authorized the President to raise duties as much as 50% over the rates that existed on July 1, 1934; previously, the applicable date had been January 1, 1945, and since the 1934 rates on many items were substantially higher than the 1945 rates, this change in the base date increased the extent to which duties on such items could be raised. Another amendment provided by the extension act was that, if the President should reject a Tariff Commission recommendation to raise tariffs under the "escape clause," Congress could override the President by a two-thirds majority of each house. The extension act also provided authority in "escape clause" cases to impose a duty as high as 50% ad valorem on items formerly duty-free.

The program of reciprocal (bilateral) tariff reductions begun in 1934, under the sponsorship of Secretary of State Cordell Hull, had resulted by July 19, 1952, in bilateral trade agreements with some 46 countries, many of which have been superseded by the overriding multilateral modifications of tariffs among member nations of the GENERAL AGREEMENT ON TARIFFS AND TRADE.

See TARIFF, for discussion of the bilateral and multilateral programs of tariff reductions of the U.S.

RECOGNITION The process of formally including an item into the financial statements of an entity such as an asset, liability, revenue, or expense. Items are recognized in the statements in both words and numbers. An item and information about the item must meet four fundamental recognition criteria to be recognized, subject to a cost_benefit constraint and a materiality threshold:

1. *Definition:* The item must meet the definition of an element of financial statements.
2. *Measurability:* It has a relevant attribute measurable with sufficient reliability.
3. *Relevance:* The information about it is capable of making a difference in users' decisions.
4. *Reliability:* The information is representationally faithful, verifiable, and neutral.

The amount of revenue recognized in the financial statements is measured by different attributes (for example, historical cost, current cost, current market value, net realizable value, and present value of future cash flows).

Revenues and gains are generally not recognized as components of earnings until realized or realizable and earned. The basic rule is that revenue is recognized when the earning process is completed and an exchange has taken place. This is usually at the point of sale or when a service has been performed. Certain departures form this principle are allowed.

BIBLIOGRAPHY

SFAC No. 5, Recognition and Measurement in Financial Statements (FASB, 1984).

RECOINAGE The melting and manufacturing into new coins of abraded, mutilated, and short weight coins. This expense is borne by the government mint.
See LIGHT COIN, LIGHT GOLD.

RECONCILEMENT OF ACCOUNTS The verification by a bank of its accounts with depositors. Periodic reconcilement of accounts is one of the important tests of clerical efficiency and accuracy in handling bank accounting transactions. The approved and most convenient means of reconciling accounts is to attach a reconcilement blank as a stub or separate form to each statement of account as rendered. These are usually forwarded to customers periodically (monthly), or when they call in person. The reconcilement blank requests the customer to report the correctness of the statement immediately and to note any errors. When the reconcilement blank is returned signed, a mutual verification of accounts has been established. If errors are reported, the bank can proceed to trace and investigate them and adjust any differences.

A typical form of reconcilement blank is appended.

RECONSTRUCTION This term has two meanings:

1. READJUSTMENT; that phase of the business cycle in which business is attempting to restore the normal equilibrium between supply and demand.
2. The English equivalent of the U.S. term REORGANIZATION.

RECONSTRUCTION FINANCE CORPORATION Under P.L. 163 (R.F.C. Liquidation Act) of July 30, 1953, the lending authorization of the Reconstruction Finance Corporation (RFC) was terminated effective September 28, 1953. Its lending activities under

Reconcilement Blank

Please Return Promptly

_____ , 19 _____

TO THE _____ BANK.

Your accounts rendered to the close of business _____
_____ showing balance
$___ due _____ agree with
our books, with the exceptions noted below.

Yours truly,

_____
(Authorized Signature)

Please use signature of officer or principal as now authorized to us.

---

the Federal Civil Defense Act of 1950 and the Defense Production Act of 1950 were transferred to the Treasury as of that date. The same law provided for establishment of the SMALL BUSINESS ADMINISTRATION to continue the small loans program.

The RFC formally went out of existence June 30, 1954, in accordance with the liquidation act. Certain loans, securities, and other assets were transferred to the Federal National Mortgage Association, the Small Business Administration, and the Export-Import Bank, and the Treasury assumed responsibility for completing liquidation of other activities.

In its heyday, the RFC was the leading federal domestic financing and credit agency, at first providing aid on an emergency basis "to stop deflation in agriculture and industry and thus to increase employment by the restoration of men to their normal jobs" and subsequently developing into a financer of domestic recovery and later of war projects during World War II. As originally created by the Reconstruction Finance Corporation Act, approved January 22, 1932, the corporation was limited in capital to $500 million, but this was later expanded by amendments and other laws adding to the powers and scope of the corporation. In the year 1933-1934, the financial strength of the corporation was increased and the scope of its lending activities was broadened. Loans were made to banks, railroads, insurance companies, agricultural credit institutions and mortgage banks, industries, and public works. Large amounts were also granted to states for work and direct relief without necessity of repayment. In 1948, after a World War II period as financier for defense projects, the corporation had its charter extended for six more years, but lending power was reduced from $2 billion to $1.5 billion, the corporation retaining the authority to buy insurance company preferred stock and to maintain a secondary mortgage market. In particular, the RFC continued to be a source of loans for small business until replaced by the Small Business Administration in 1953.

RECOURSE A legal term indicating that the purchaser of a financial asset from an original creditor has a claim on the original creditor in case the debtor defaults. A contract with recourse can assume many forms: an explicit guarantee that credit losses will be reimbursed or the assets replaced by assets of similar quality; an agreement to repurchase assets before maturity; indemnification by a third-party guarantor for any losses that occur.

The term is frequently found in the law of negotiable instruments, wherein the endorsement "without recourse" is recognized as a qualified endorsement. The endorser "without recourse" nevertheless makes the warranties specified in Section 3-417, Uniform Commercial Code.

See ENDORSEMENT.

RECOVERY This term has three meanings:

1. Whenever a bank collects a note, or a part payment thereon, that has been previously written off as a loss and charged to reserves or undivided profits. Since the amount of such a recovered note has already been charged off, it is allowable to credit reserves or undivided profits account for the amount recovered.

2. As used in financial reviews, an advance in prices following a previous decline.
3. In a broad commercial sense, roughly equivalent to business revival or recuperation. It indicates a period of business betterment following a period of liquidation and depression.

See BUSINESS CYCLE.

REDEEMABLE Both bonds and preferred stock are sometimes issued with the redeemable feature—that is, optional retirement before the obligatory maturity.

See CALLABLE BONDS, PREFERRED STOCK.

REDEEMABLE BONDS *See* CALLABLE BONDS.

REDEMPTION The act of redeeming a debt; payment of a debt; retirement of an issue of bonds or notes; the cancellation of a debt, whether on a date prior to maturity or upon the date of obligatory maturity.

The redemption feature on bonds, debentures, or preferred stock is often referred to as the call feature.

See CALL, CALLABLE BONDS.

REDEMPTION AGENT Any agent designated to perform the function of redeeming debts, debt securities, or currency.

In the Washington, D.C., area, the Treasurer of the United States issues and redeems government bonds and other securities, a function which in other parts of the country is performed by Federal Reserve banks and their branches.

Current forms of U.S. paper money (Federal Reserve notes and United States notes) have not been redeemable into the monetary metal, gold, since 1933 and 1934 (*see* UNITED STATES MONEY). Nor are the 5% redemption funds formerly statutorily required to be maintained with the Treasurer of the United States for national bank notes and Federal Reserve Bank notes (in process of retirement since 1935 and 1945) any longer required. Redemption privilege of silver certificates into standard silver dollars expired June 24, 1968. The 5% redemption fund in gold certificates, formerly required to be maintained with the Treasurer of the United States against Federal Reserve notes, no longer is required. The Office of the Treasurer continues to handle claims for partially destroyed paper currency; replacement of paper currency that has become worn out is handled by Federal Reserve banks by verification and destruction. Unfit currency delivered to the Treasury in the Washington, D.C., area is verified and destroyed by the Treasurer of the U.S.

REDEMPTION BONDS Practically the same as REFUNDING BONDS. To be precise, the term redemption bonds should be reserved for issues supplanting those called for redemption, whereas the term refunding bonds should be reserved for those supplanting maturing issues. Redemption bonds are not to be confused with redeemable, i.e., optional, bonds.

REDEMPTION CHECK A special form of check issued by banks belonging to a clearinghouse association in payment of items that have passed through the clearinghouse but that are not acceptable by the drawee bank because of technical irregularities or invalidities, and therefore are returned. Redemption checks are payable only to members of the clearinghouse association, are not negotiable, and are payable only through such clearinghouse association.

REDEMPTION FUND P.L. 90-269, March 18, 1968, eliminated the provision of Section 16 of the Federal Reserve Act under which the Federal Reserve banks were required to maintain reserves in gold certificates (Series 1934) of not less than 25% against Federal Reserve notes, and with this the requirement for a redemption fund with the Treasurer of the United States of 5% (minimum) less the amount of gold certificates (Series 1934) held by the Federal Reserve agent at each Federal Reserve bank as collateral against Federal Reserve notes issued. Such deposit of gold certificates was counted and included as part of the gold certificates reserve formerly required to be maintained against Federal Reserve notes outstanding.

The idea of a redemption fund against Federal Reserve notes was in the original Federal Reserve Act, and had as its basic antecedent the requirement of a 5% redemption fund required to be maintained against national bank notes, with the Treasurer of the United States, by national banks pursuant to the National Bank Act. The redemption fund against Federal Reserve notes eliminated by P.L. 90-269 was combined with the gold certificate fund of the Federal Reserve System.

Federal Reserve bank notes and national bank notes, which are in the process of retirement, were also required to maintain similar redemption funds. Balances have been on deposit with the Treasury since March, 1935, for retirement of all outstanding Federal Reserve bank notes and since August, 1935, for retirement of all outstanding national bank notes.

See FEDERAL RESERVE BANK NOTES, FEDERAL RESERVE NOTES, FIVE PERCENT REDEMPTION FUND, NATIONAL BANK NOTES.

The Gold Standard Act of 1900 provided for the redemption in gold coin of United States notes or "legal tenders" when presented to the Treasury. In order to secure prompt and certain redemption of these notes, the secretary of the Treasury was required to set apart in the Treasury a reserve fund of $150 million in gold coin and bullion, which could be used for this purpose alone. If, on account of redemption of these notes, the fund fell below $100 million, the secretary of the Treasury was authorized to restore the fund to the original amount by issuing United States bonds therefor. In accordance with the Gold Reserve Act of 1934, no currency of the U.S. is now redeemable in gold, and since March, 1968, the reserve of $156 million against United States notes (and Treasury notes of 1890 through June 30, 1961) no longer is set aside against Treasury gold stock.

See also UNITED STATES NOTES.

REDEMPTION NOTICE   See SINKING FUND REDEMPTION NOTICE.

REDEMPTION OF MONEY   In accordance with Section 6 of the Gold Reserve Act of 1934, no currency of the United States would be redeemed in gold, except to the extent permitted in regulations which may be issued by the secretary of the Treasury with the approval of the President. This general prohibition is also subject to the proviso that gold certificates owned by the Federal Reserve banks shall be redeemed at such times and in such amounts as in the judgment of the secretary of the Treasury are necessary to maintain an equal purchasing power of every kind of currency in the United States, an action which it has not found since to be necessary.

P.L. 95-147, enacted October 28, 1977, among other things repealed the "Joint Resolution to Assure Uniform Value to the Coins and Currencies of the United States," approved June 5, 1933 (31 U.S.C. 463), the intended effect of such repeal being to permit the inclusion of gold and multicurrency clauses in private contracts. But through 1982, no action had ever been taken under the Gold Reserve Act of 1934 to restore gold redemption of U.S. money, and talk of "restoration of the gold standard" as a possibility indicated no gold redemption of money, but rather prescription of gold reserve as a "golden brake" on Federal Reserve credit expansion.

Under authorization of the Act of May 29, 1920, which discontinued the functions of assistant treasurers and subtreasuries, the secretary of the Treasury transferred to the Federal Reserve banks and branches the functions performed by the former assistant treasurers of the United States in connection with the issue, exchange, and replacement of United States paper currency and coin and the receipt for redemption of national bank notes and Federal Reserve bank notes. Except for the duties in this respect performed by the Treasurer of the United States as may be indicated from time to time by the secretary of the Treasury, distribution of available supplies of United States paper currency and coin, exchanges and replacements thereof, and payments on account of redemption of currency and coin were, so far as practicable, transferred to the Federal Reserve banks and branches. Federal Reserve banks and branches were instructed by the Treasury to make an equitable and impartial distribution of available supplies of United States paper currency and coin in all cases, and applications therefor thereafter were to be made to the Federal Reserve bank or branch located in the same district with the applicant.

See MONETARY STOCK, MONEY CIRCULATION, UNITED STATES MONEY.

REDISCOUNT   The discounting for a second time of commercial paper (notes, acceptances, and bills of exchange), by one bank for another or by a Federal Reserve bank for a member bank; also such rediscounted paper itself. Since the FEDERAL RESERVE SYSTEM has been in operation, the term has applied almost solely to the discounting of paper by a Federal Reserve bank for a member bank. In substance, however, any note is rediscounted whenever an endorser negotiates it.

The term "discount rate" has come to be applied to rates generally for loans and advances by the district Federal Reserve banks to member banks (and to depository institutions in general, under the DEPOSITORY INSTITUTIONS DEREGULATION AND MONETARY CONTROL ACT OF 1980). Reserve banks may lend to depository institutions either through advances secured by acceptable collateral or through the discount of certain types of paper. But credit extended by the Federal Reserve generally takes the form of an advance.

Even before the Federal Reserve System, rediscounting was a common practice among banks. Banks that had exhausted their loanable resources or lacked sufficient reserve resorted to this practice as an expedient to obtain additional reserves. Consequently, it was often regarded as evidence of weakness on the part of the borrowing bank. There should be, however, no stigma attached to rediscounting under the Federal Reserve Act, as the rediscount process is one of the normal operating procedures contemplated by the act.

The authority for extensions of credit by Federal Reserve banks is found in Sections 10(a), 10(b), 13, 13a, and 19 of the Federal Reserve Act and Section 7(b) of the International Banking Act of 1978 relating to extensions of credit by Federal Reserve banks to depository institutions and others.

Regulation A of the Board of Governors of the Federal Reserve System establishes the rules under which Federal Reserve banks may extend credit to depository institutions and others. Extending credit to depository institutions, as indicated by the Board of Governors of the Federal Reserve System in its Federal Reserve Regulatory Service, is a principal function of Federal Reserve banks. While OPEN MARKET OPERATIONS are the primary means of affecting the overall supply of reserves, the lending function of the Federal Reserve banks is an effective method of supplying reserves to meet the particular credit needs of individual depository institutions.

The lending functions of the Federal Reserve System, states the board of governors, are conducted with due regard to the basic objectives of MONETARY POLICY and the maintenance of a sound and orderly financial system. These basic objectives are promoted by influencing the overall volume and cost of credit through actions that affect the volume and cost of reserves to depository institutions. Borrowing by individual depository institutions, at a rate of interest that is adjusted from time to time in accordance with prevailing economic and money market conditions, has a direct impact on the reserve positions of the borrowing institutions and thus on their ability to meet the credit needs of their customers. However, concludes the board of governors, the effects of such borrowing do not remain localized but have an important bearing on overall monetary and credit conditions.

Availability and terms are described by the Board of Governors of the Federal Reserve System as follows (Sec. 201.3 of Regulation A):

1. **Short-term adjustment credit.**   Federal Reserve credit is available on a short-term basis to a depository institution under such rules as may be prescribed to assist the institution, to the extent appropriate, in meeting temporary requirements for funds, or to cushion more persistent outflows of funds pending an orderly adjustment of the institution's assets and liabilities. Such credit generally is available only after reasonable alternative sources of funds, including credit from special industry lenders, such as Federal Home Loan banks, the National Credit Union Administration's Central Liquidity Facility, and corporate central credit unions, have been fully used. Under certain circumstances, a surcharge may be imposed above the basic rate of interest normally charged by Federal Reserve banks.
2. **Extended credit.**
    a. *Seasonal credit.* Federal Reserve credit is available for periods longer than those permitted under adjustment credit to assist smaller depository institutions in meeting regular needs for funds arising from a combination of expected patterns of movement in their deposits and loans. Seasonal credit is available only if similar assistance is not available from other special industry lenders. Seasonal credit will ordinarily be limited to the amount by which the depository institution's seasonal needs exceed certain percentages, established by the board of governors, of the institution's average total deposits in the preceding calendar year. Such credit will be available if the Federal Reserve bank is satisfied that the institution's qualifying need for funds is seasonal

and will persist for at least four weeks. Need for credit at depository institutions will also be given consideration when institutions are experiencing unusual seasonal demands for credit in a period of liquidity strain. To the extent practicable, a depository institution should arrange in advance for seasonal credit for the full period during which such credit is expected to be required. Under certain circumstances, a surcharge may be imposed above the basic rate of interest normally charged by Federal Reserve banks.

b. *Other extended credit.* Federal Reserve credit is available to depository institutions under extended credit arrangements where similar assistance is not reasonably available from other sources, including special industry lenders. Such credit may be provided where there are exceptional circumstances or practices involving only a particular depository institution. Exceptional circumstances would include situations where an individual depository institution is experiencing financial strains arising from particular circumstances or practices affecting that institution—including sustained deposit drains, impaired access to money market funds, or sudden deterioration in loan repayment performance. Extended credit may also be provided to accommodate the needs of depository institutions, including those with long-term asset portfolios, that may be experiencing difficulties adjusting to changing money market conditions over a longer period, particularly at times of deposit disintermediation. A special rate or rates above the basic discount rate established by the Federal Reserve banks, subject to review and determination by the board of governors, may be applied to other extended credit.

c. *Emergency credit for others.* In unusual and exigent circumstances, a Federal Reserve bank may, after consultation with the board of governors, advance credit to individuals, partnerships, and corporations that are not depository institutions if, in the judgment of the Federal Reserve bank, credit is not available from other sources and failure to obtain such credit would adversely affect the economy. The rate applicable to such credit will be above the highest rate for advances in effect for depository institutions. Where the collateral used to secure such credit consists of assets other than obligations of, or fully guaranteed as to principal and interest by, the United States or an agency thereof, an affirmative vote of five or more members of the board of governors is required before credit may be extended.

A Federal Reserve bank may discount for any Federal Intermediate Credit bank (1) agricultural paper, or (2) notes payable to and bearing the endorsement of the Federal Intermediate Credit bank that cover loans or advances made under Subsections (a) and (b) of Section 2.3 of the Farm Credit Act of 1971 (12 U.S.C. 2074) and that are secured by paper eligible for discount by Federal Reserve banks. Any paper so discounted shall have a period remaining to maturity at the time of discount of not more than nine months.

Practice. The statutory and regulatory framework, the New York Federal Reserve Bank indicates (*Fedpoints 18*), generally provides rather broad latitude to the Federal Reserve banks for the exercise of judgment and discretion in the operation of the discount window. Thus, the window can be equitably administered in a manner responsive to the needs of individual institutions and the local and regional conditions affecting those institutions. In fulfilling this broad administrative responsibility, Federal Reserve banks consider, among other things, an institution's size, access to the money markets and other sources of funds, the special circumstances facing the institution, and the geographic and economic environment in which the institution is operating.

The general practice at the New York Federal Reserve Bank has been to limit maturities on adjustment credit advances to not more than two weeks for smaller banks, to the end of the weekly reserve period for larger banks, and to overnight for the largest banks. Discount window loans may generally be renewed beyond their initial maturity if institutions need the additional time to make adjustments in their assets and liabilities.

Extended credit at the New York Federal Reserve Bank is provided through three programs designed to assist depository institutions in meeting longer-term needs for funds:

1. One program provides seasonal credit, for periods up to six months, to smaller depository institutions which generally lack continuous access to market funds (*Fedpoints 16*).
2. A second program assists institutions that experience special difficulties arising from exceptional circumstances or practices involving only that institution. Assistance in these cases is provided only when funds are not available from other sources.
3. In situations where more general liquidity strains affect a broad range of institutions—such as thrift institutions that emphasize longer-term mortgage assets—credit may be provided to address the problems of the institutions being affected by the general situation.

Discount Rates. Each discount rate is required by law to be set by the board of directors of each district Federal Reserve bank every 14 days, subject to "review and determination" by the Board of Governors of the Federal Reserve System. The board of governors does not initiate discount rate changes, but acts on recommendations of the boards of directors of district Federal Reserve banks. The board of governors has three options when it receives a recommendation: the governors may approve the rate, disapprove the rate, or make no decision. In either of the last two circumstances, the directors of the district Federal Reserve bank may continue to recommend a rate change. In addition, the board of governors may act on one petition or may wait until it has requests from several Federal Reserve banks before acting. The board of governors also may act on any day to approve a rate.

Starting in September, 1980, the four types of credit enumerated above became available to eligible depository institutions—short-term adjustment credit and three types of extended credit. (These classifications of the New York Federal Reserve Bank differ in format from those specified in Regulation A.)

Previously, there were five types of credit available: short-term adjustment; seasonal; emergency; special for individuals, partnerships, and corporations; and special for foreign central banks, foreign governments, and monetary authorities.

Interest on the four types of credit available since September, 1980, is scaled as follows. On adjustment credit, the rate is generally the basic rate plus any surcharge which might be applied depending upon the length and frequency of the borrowing. On seasonal credit, the rate is also the basic rate, plus any surcharge. On other extended credit, the rate may be more than the basic rate, depending on policy considerations and money market conditions. On emergency credit, the rate must be in excess of the highest discount rate in effect for depository institutions.

As part of the March, 1980, Credit Restraint Program, the Federal Reserve instituted a surcharge on borrowings by large commercial banks, to discourage frequent use of the discount window and speed bank adjustments in response to restraint on bank reserves. The surcharge of three percentage points was applied in April, 1980, to banks with deposits of $500 million or more which borrowed in two consecutive weeks, or in more than four weeks in a calendar quarter. In May, 1980, this surcharge was eliminated, although the authority to impose surcharges remained in effect.

Uniformity of discount rates was generally maintained from the founding of the Federal Reserve System in 1914 to the mid-1920s. Variations developed in subsequent years, reflecting regional credit conditions. Discount rate uniformity returned to the system in recent times in the recognition that the discount rate reflected national credit policy rather than regional credit conditions.

Historically, the basic discount rate generally has been changed infrequently over the course of a year. In only six years through 1980 has the rate changed five times or more at the New York Federal Reserve Bank: in 1921, 1930, and 1958, five times each; in 1971, six times; and in 1973, 1978, and 1980, seven times each.

Selected Federal Reserve Board discount rates for the period 1976 to 1988 are appended.

Summary. Federal Reserve regulations emphasize that borrowing at the discount window of Federal Reserve banks is a "privilege, not a right," and that such borrowings are not to be considered a source of capital. As an instrument of monetary policy, the discount rate's changes have "announcement effects," and "can on occasion be interpreted as a signal of a change in Monetary Policy." But borrowing at the discount window is at the initiative of the depository institutions, as a source of more reserves, whereas open market operations are at the initiative of the Federal Open Market Committee as an instrument of monetary policy which in addition to having

Federal Reserve Board Discount Rate

Effective Date		Rate
1976:	Jan. 19	5 1/2
	Nov. 22	5 1/4
1977:	Aug. 31	5 3/4
	Oct. 26	6
1978:	Jan. 9	6 1/2
	May 11	7
	July 3	7 1/4
	Aug. 21	7 3/4
	Sept. 22	8
	Oct. 16	8 1/2
	Nov. 1	9 1/2
1979:	July 20	10
	Aug. 17	10 1/2
	Sept. 19	11
	Oct. 8	12
1980:	Feb. 15	13
	May 30	12
	June 13	11
	July 28	10
	Sept. 26	11
	Nov. 17	12
	Dec. 13	13
1981:	May 5	14
	Nov. 2	13
	Dec. 4	12
1982:	July 20	11 1/2
	Aug. 2	11
	Aug. 16	10 1/2
	Aug. 27	10
	Oct. 12	9 1/2
	Nov. 22	9
	Dec. 15	8 1/2
1984:	April 9	9
	Nov. 21	8 1/2
	Dec. 24	8
1985:	May 20	7 1/2
1986:	March 7	7
	April 21	6 1/2
	July 11	6
	Aug. 21	5 1/2
1987:	Sept. 4	6
1988:	Aug. 9	6 1/2
In effect	Sept. 1, 1988	6 1/2

Source: Federal Reserve Board of Governors.

primarily quantitative effects upon depository institutions' reserves also thereby has effects on rates. Critics of the discount rate, therefore, as an instrument of monetary policy believe that the discount rate and discount window availability represent "leakages" in effectiveness of monetary policy.

BIBLIOGRAPHY

BAKER, H. K., and MEYER, J. M. "Impact of Discount Rate Changes on Treasury Bills." *Journal of Economics and Business,* Fall, 1980.

BOARD OF GOVERNORS OF THE FEDERAL RESERVE SYSTEM. *Federal Reserve Regulatory Service.*

———. *Reappraisal of the Federal Reserve Discount Mechanism,* Vols. 1 and 2, 1971; Vol. 3, 1972.

BOLTZ, P., and O'BRIEN, J. "Tying the Discount Rate to Market Rates of Interest." *Federal Reserve Staff Study,* May, 1980.

BROWN, K. H. "Effect of Changes in the Discount Rate on the Foreign Exchange Value of the Dollar, 1973 to 1978." *Quarterly Journal of Economics,* August, 1981.

FEDERAL RESERVE BANK OF NEW YORK. "Discount Rates." *Fedpoints 30,* March, 1981.

GILBERT, R. A. "Access to the Discount Window for All Commercial Banks: Is It Important for Monetary Policy?" Federal Reserve Bank of St. Louis *Review,* February, 1980.

GRAHAM, S. L. "Is the Fed's Seasonal Borrowing Privilege Justified?" Federal Reserve Bank of Minneapolis *Quarterly Review,* Fall, 1979.

KEIR, P. "Impact of Discount Policy Procedures on the Effectiveness of Reserve Targeting." *New Monetary Control Procedures,* Federal Reserve Staff Study, Vol. 1, January, 1981.

REDISCOUNT RATE The rate of discount charged by Federal Reserve banks for rediscounting commercial, industrial, or agricultural ELIGIBLE PAPER or other paper. Under Section 14 (d) of the Federal Reserve Act, every Federal Reserve bank has the power to establish from time to time, subject to review and determination of the Board of Governors of the FEDERAL RESERVE SYSTEM, rates of discount to be charged by the Federal Reserve bank for each class of paper, which shall be fixed with a view of accommodating commerce and business. Each Federal Reserve bank shall establish such rates every 14 days, or oftener if deemed necessary by the board of governors. Rediscounting of such eligible paper, the original basis, has given way over the years to lending on a variety of collateral.

Whenever member banks have low volume of excess reserves or are "in at the Fed" for additional reserves to cover legal reserve requirements, reflecting tightness in reserve position as the result of credit expansion, or policy, the REDISCOUNT rate assumes increased importance as a regulator of the cost of Federal Reserve credit to the member banks. Raising the rediscount rate, making it more costly for member banks to obtain Federal Reserve credit, may or may not act as a deterrent to member bank credit expansion, depending on the level of returns from loans and investments available to the banks and alternatives available in the money market for adjusting reserve positions. Usually, rediscount rate changes follow changes in money market rates rather than precede them (especially changes in Treasury bills and other prime short-term paper, rediscount rates normally keeping somewhat ahead of these rates); and these prime open market rates are normally sensitive to changes in bank excess reserves, in turn a function of bank credit expansion and/or Federal Reserve policy. Thus for most effective credit control, a combination of negative open market operations (net selling of government securities on balance by the system open market account) and rise in rediscount rate would act both quantitatively upon bank reserves and ratewise upon the cost of Federal Reserve credit to the banks desiring or needing additional reserves not otherwise feasibly obtainable. In this connection, it should be remembered that recourse to Federal Reserve credit by rediscounting or advances is a privilege rather than an absolute right, being subject to Federal Reserve bank policing of any chronic or undue use thereof by specific member banks, especially since rediscount rates are normally below rates charged by banks to their customers, even their "prime" lending rates. Also, most banks are normally reluctant to borrow from the "Fed," and to this extent, recourse to Federal Reserve credit would be credit of "last resort," after other available alternatives prove to be either unavailable or higher ratewise. In particular, the "federal funds" market (lending rate for excess reserves at Federal Reserve banks by member banks having such available funds) is most sensitive of all the rates to tightness or ease in bank reserve positions.

On the other hand, when bank reserves are ample, changes in the rediscount rate, other than for indication of Federal Reserve policy and their "psychological" effect, have no direct impact on the member banks because they do not require substantial Federal Reserve credit at such times. Thus, in 1953, the discount rate was raised from 1.75% at year-end 1952 to 2%, but with member banks' excess reserves rising from a net deficiency of $570 million at the close of 1952 to an excess of $763 million at the close of 1953, member banks' total discounts and advances dropped from $105.5 billion in 1952 to $93.4 billion in 1953, totaling $28 million at the close of 1953 against $156 million at the close of 1952. And of course under conditions comparable to the glut in reserves in 1940, when excess reserves totaled $6.6 billion at year-end, the rediscount rate would be of merely academic interest to the member banks.

As an instrument of monetary policy, the rediscount rate (or, as it is more customarily referred to, the discount rate) was overshadowed during World War II and the post-World War II years prior to 1951 of "easy money" by the increased importance of open market operations and by the "peg" on government securities at a fixed pattern of yields, which assured member banks of "automatic liquidity" or their government securities at the Fed. A basic point at issue between the Board of Governors of the Federal Reserve System and the Treasury, culminating in their agreement or accord of March, 1951, was not the rate level, but the level of bank reserves. As the result of that accord, the independence of the Federal Reserve as to monetary policy and restrictive open market operations brought about an increase in rediscounts and advances during 1952, and thus restoration of the importance of the rediscount rate.

As a monetary tool, variation in the discount rate has an impact on money market rates and yields beyond the immediate effect on the cost of reserve bank credit to depository institutions and a "psychological" effect on cost of financing expectations because of the indication given of monetary policy. Monetary policy actions affecting the supply of bank excess reserves (open market operations and, less frequently, variation in legal reserve requirements) also have an impact on money rates, and usually discount rate variations are made in conjunction with such open market operations' effect on volume of commercial bank excess reserves, as a supplementary type of actions.

See Bibliography under REDISCOUNT.

REDLINING The practice of refusing to grant loans in certain neighborhoods regardless of the quality of the structure or the ability of the borrower to repay. To discourage this practice, the Home Mortgage Disclosure Act (1985) compels lenders to publicly disclose the areas in which they have made loans. The act is governed by the Federal Reserve System's Regulation C, and is administered by the regulatory agency for the particular lending institution. In 1977, Congress passed the Community Reinvestment Act to encourage institutions to make mortgage loans in low-income areas. Each depository institution must define the community it serves and develop a Community Reinvestment Act statement, outlining its lending policies in the community. A notice of this statement must be posted in its lobby, and it must be made available to interested persons. The institution must maintain a file of public comments on its lending policies, and it must review its Community Reinvestment Act statement annually.

REDRAFT A bill of exchange drawn by a holder of a dishonored bill upon either the drawer or an endorser, for the amount of the original bill plus the protest fees; also known as a "cross bill." Where foreign exchange is involved, the redraft or cross bill also includes the amount of "re-exchange" measured by the rate of exchange where the drawer or endorser is located.

See BILL OF EXCHANGE.

REFINED SUGAR See SUGAR.

REFLATION The employment of the monetary powers of the government to stop deflation and to induce the opposite course, i.e., INFLATION, in sufficient measure to counteract the preceding deflation. The term was apparently coined in the years 1932-1933. Reflation implies monetary and/or credit manipulation to restore prices to a preconceived "desirable" level, and not excessive inflation which would ruin the value of money. Reflation advocates are those who favor a MANAGED CURRENCY.

REFUND ANTICIPATION LOAN A loan contract between the taxpayer and a financial institution with the preparer acting as broker. The income tax refund is collateral for the loan and is used to repay the loan through direct deposit. IRS is not a party to the loan contract. The financial institution and the return preparer may share in a fee for this service as long as the amount is not based on a percentage of the refund and is the same for all loans.

REFUNDING The process of refinancing a debt that cannot conveniently be paid when due; more especially, selling a new issue of bonds from the proceeds of which a maturing issue will be retired. Railroads and other public utility corporations secure a large part of their capital by means of bond issues that are never intended to be permanently retired. Instead, capital is permanently secured by the refunding process, which is legitimate finance where property values are kept intact. For accounting purposes, the issuing of the new bonds and the cancellation of the old issue are considered two separate transactions. Retiring the old bonds results in a realized gain or loss equal to the difference between the carrying amount of the bonds and the price paid to retire the bonds. The gain or loss is recognized in the accounting period when the bonds are retired and is not deferred to be amortized in future periods.

See REFUNDING BONDS.

REFUNDING BONDS Bonds issued for the purpose of providing funds to retire bonds previously issued, either to effect a reduction in interest rate (such refunding interest savings being important in a period of low money rates) or to replace bonds about to mature. Strictly speaking, refunding bonds should not be authorized to exceed the amount of the original issue (except when mortgages are consolidated) and should be for the same purpose. Frequently, however, new issues entirely unrelated to the issues being retired have the effect of refunding as well as bringing in additional working capital. To make clear the purpose of a refunding issue, it is advisable to clarify the title by adding a word descriptive of such purpose—refunding water bonds or refunding first mortgage bonds.

In the case of civil refunding bonds, i.e., bonds of states, counties, and other political subdivisions, arbitrary statutory limits are placed on their terms in some states. In fact, some states and their political subdivisions are altogether prohibited from issuing refunding bonds. In no case should civil refunding bonds be allowed when the asset purchased by the proceeds is not permanent. Thus, refunding bonds are justifiable and permissible to replace bonds issued to acquire parks, playgrounds, or land for streets but not to replace bonds issued for school buildings, fire stations and apparatus, local relief purposes, etc.

Because of the historically very high interest rates at which new issues of bonds have been floated in recent years such as the 1970s, 1980, and 1981, various issues carry in their indentures a limitation on the refunding of such issues (which otherwise might readily occur on long-term issues should interest rates subsequently recede to lower levels). An example is the issue of Series TT 9% bonds, due 2001, by Pacific Gas & Electric, issued in 1969; the earliest refunding call price was specified as 109.23, in 1974 (thus assuring five years of enjoyment of the 9% interest rate for investors, free from risk of refunding).

REFUNDING FIRST MORTGAGE BONDS A refunding bond (usually issued by a railroad or public utility corporation) that is secured by a first mortgage and has, therefore, the same security as the issue whose place it takes. Refunding first mortgage bonds are not to be confused with FIRST REFUNDING MORTGAGE BONDS.

REFUNDING RECEIVER'S CERTIFICATES Receiver's certificates issued to provide funds to pay off maturing RECEIVER'S CERTIFICATES.

REGIONAL AGRICULTURAL CREDIT CORPORATION Pursuant to the Emergency Relief and Construction Act of 1932, the RECONSTRUCTION FINANCE CORPORATION established 12 regional Agricultural Credit Corporations, one in each of the 12 farm credit districts, to provide short-term agricultural credit. The FARM CREDIT ADMINISTRATION took over their supervision in 1933, and in 1934, with establishment of the Production Credit Corporation and associations, the 12 district regional Agricultural Credit Corporations were merged into the single Regional Agricultural Credit Corporation of Washington, D.C., which engaged in intermittent lending activity of an emergency and wartime nature. In 1949, the Regional Agricultural Credit Corporation of Washington, D.C., was terminated, and its remaining assets and records were transferred through the secretary of Agriculture to the FARMERS HOME ADMINISTRATION.

REGIONAL BANK Each of the 12 Federal Reserve banks is known as a regional bank, or regional reserve bank, because each serves a single, clearly defined Federal Reserve district. Before the passage of the Federal Reserve Act, two plans were proposed. One recommended the establishment of one central reserve bank (the Aldrich Plan) such as exists in England and France. The other provided for "regional banks, each to be operated by a different board of directors and owned by member banks within its district." The latter was adopted in order to prevent concentration of control in the east. Although each regional bank is a separate institution and serves a given territory, cooperation of the 12 regional banks is secured through control by the Board of Governors of the Federal Reserve System, which was increased by the Banking Acts of 1933 and 1935. For instance, this body has power to require one Federal Reserve bank to rediscount the discounted paper of another. Thus, the regional banks combine the features of centralization and decentralization.

See FEDERAL RESERVE SYSTEM.

REGIONAL CHECK PROCESSING CENTERS

Regional check processing centers are operated by Federal Reserve banks to expedite check collection. These centers clear checks and sort them according to the depository institution upon which the checks are drawn. This complements regional clearing arrangements established by depository institutions in the same locality to exchange checks and settle net balances.

In 1971, the Board of Governors of the Federal Reserve System recommended establishing RCPCs to help improve the nation's payments mechanism. The following year, the first center, the Baltimore-Washington RCPC of the Federal Reserve Bank of Richmond, became fully operational after a one-year pilot test.

RCPCs serve depository institutions within areas not necessarily confined to a Federal Reserve district or state lines. Since the function of the centers is to accelerate nationwide check collection, RCPC boundaries are determined by check flows. For example, Fairfield County, Connecticut, is part of the New York Reserve district. However, many checks deposited in Fairfield County institutions are drawn on banks in the Boston Reserve district. Thus, Fairfield County is served by the Boston Fed's Southwestern New England RCPC in Windsor Locks, Connecticut. RCPCs routinely receive checks drawn on participating institutions from four sources: other participating member banks, other RCPCs, Federal Reserve banks and their branches, and "direct sending" member banks. A direct sending member bank is one authorized by its Reserve bank to send checks drawn on banks in other Reserve districts directly to the appropriate Reserve bank, branch, or RCPC. The direct sending bank gets credit for those checks in its reserve account at its own Reserve bank.

As a result of the INTERNATIONAL BANKING ACT OF 1978 and the DEPOSITORY INSTITUTIONS DEREGULATION AND MONETARY CONTROL ACT OF 1980, all depository institutions in the U.S., except for certain agencies, have been granted limited deposit access to local facilities. Depository institutions include member and nonmember commercial banks, savings banks, savings and loan associations, and credit unions.

Prior to these two acts, RCPCs also accepted checks deposited by the local participating banks that were not members of the Federal Reserve, providing the checks were drawn on other banks in the same RCPC area.

The primary objective of RCPCs is to collect checks overnight. To accomplish this, RCPCs sort, clear, and deliver checks rapidly by eliminating various handling stages. Personal and corporate checks constitute the bulk of items deposited at RCPCs. These checks are generally delivered to the RCPC by private carriers hired by the participating banks. Other cash items deposited at RCPCs include checks drawn on the Treasury, postal money orders, and redeemed food coupons, items deposited by the participating depository institutions. However, RCPCs do not handle cash or securities.

Finally, in addition to providing speedy clearance, the processing of checks at an RCPC results in quicker identification of fraudulent and other invalid items.

As a result of the Monetary Control Act, Federal Reserve banks are authorized to charge institutions, at explicit prices, for central bank services, including check-related operations.

See AUTOMATED CLEARINGHOUSE, CLEARING HOUSE INTERBANK PAYMENTS SYSTEM, CLEARINGHOUSE, FEDERAL RESERVE BOARD REGULATIONS (Regulation J).

REGISTER CHECK SERVICE

A copyrighted checking service offered to banks as more profitable, simpler to operate, and more popular with customers than money orders or other forms of streamlined popularized checking services. The service features a small flat fee, usually $0.10, for each Register Check, which the customer obtains at the bank and fills out. The Register Check is then presented to the Register Check window, where a teller completes it, hands it back to the customer, and notes it on a credit slip which is kept on file until the check is presented for payment. A minimum of bookkeeping through the credit slips and Register Check account is involved.

See BANK MONEY ORDER, NO MINIMUM BALANCE CHECKING ACCOUNT.

REGISTERABLE AS TO PRINCIPAL ONLY

When the principal and not the coupons of a bond may be registered in the name of the owner, the bond is said to be "registerable as to principal only."

See REGISTERED BOND, REGISTERED COUPON BOND.

REGISTERABLE BOND See REGISTERED BOND.

REGISTERED BOND

Classified as to form, bonds may be registered or coupon bonds. Registered bonds may be subdivided into those which are "registered both as to principal and interest" and those which are "registered as to principal only."

The name of the owner of a registered bond is written on its face, and it cannot be negotiated except by endorsement and transfer on the books of the issuing organization. In other words, registered bonds are transferred in the same manner as stock certificates. The bonds contain a form of assignment and transfer on the reverse side. Registration is a privilege offered optionally in the sale of certain issues of coupon bonds to appeal to those investors who may wish to avail themselves of the opportunity to protect the equitable owner, in case of theft.

The registration of bonds necessarily entails the maintenance of complete records by the issuing organization. Usually, therefore, a bank or trust company is appointed to act as registrar. The registrar maintains the necessary records, which show the owner's name and address, when sales occur, and the name of the transferor and transferee. In this way, the ownership of each bond can be traced.

When bonds are registered as to principal only, coupons are attached, but such coupons are negotiable by delivery just like those detached from coupon bonds. The principal, however, can only be negotiated by endorsement and transfer of title to the buyer on the book of the registrar. These are known as registered coupon bonds.

When bonds are registered both as to principal and interest, no coupons are attached. Checks for the interest are remitted to the registered holder at each coupon date and a check for the principal at maturity.

The market price of registered bonds is usually somewhat less than that of coupon bonds of the same issue because of the inconvenience incident to transfer.

REGISTERED COUPON BOND

A coupon bond that is registered as to principal only. Coupons attached to such bonds are negotiable by delivery and are payable to bearer, just like those attached to coupon bonds.

REGISTERED REPRESENTATIVES

Account executives; customers' brokers; formerly, customers' men. These are personnel in brokerage offices who have contact with and service the public and who are analogous to salespeople in investment houses. Registered representatives handle customers' orders, inquiries, and other contacts. The New York Stock Exchange requires these personnel to register by filing a detailed personal history and to complete successfully courses and examinations in the procedure and practice of the exchange. Revocation of registration occurs upon any finding of failure to observe ethical standards and to adhere to principles of just and equitable trade. Registered representatives may solicit margin transactions by calling personally upon a customer at his home, provided the customer has previously given express permission in writing and provided also that the customer's home is not situated more than a reasonable distance from the brokerage office. Under no circumstances may a registered representative guarantee a customer against loss in his account. Another rule of the New York Stock Exchange forbids payment of commissions to registered representatives based directly upon volume of business, as this would technically constitute splitting of commissions, which is forbidden. In paying its registered representatives an annual salary rather than commissions based on volume of business, a brokerage house, it is believed, avoids setting up the temptation for these personnel to stimulate unwarranted activity in accounts.

REGISTERED SECURITIES EXCHANGE

Beginning with the effective date of application, October 1, 1934, it has been unlawful to transact business on any securities exchange not registered with or exempted from registration by the Securities and Exchange Commission. See Section 6 of the Securities Exchange Act of 1934. For a list of registered exchanges, see STOCK EXCHANGES.

REGISTERED STOCK

Stock that cannot be transferred without placing of the signature of the owner upon the books of the issuing corporation and delivery of the certificate. The owner of the certificate may, however, appoint an attorney to act in his stead.

All stock in U.S. corporations is "registered," since the name of the stockholder is recorded on the stock transfer books and dividends are mailed to stockholders of record. In England, "coupon" stock is more commonly found, the stock certificates having coupons that are detachable for collection of dividends declared. Imperial Oil of Canada stock is issued in both coupon and registered form. In England, INSCRIBED STOCK is also commonly found.

REGISTRAR A corporate agent appointed to perform the function of authenticating issues of stocks and bonds, and thus to prevent overissue of spurious bonds or stocks.

See STOCK REGISTRAR.

REGISTRATION OF MORTGAGES Under Section 235 (g) of the Banking Law of New York State, every mortgage and assignment of a mortgage taken or held by a savings bank shall immediately be recorded or registered in the office of the proper recording officer of the county in which the real property described in the mortgage is located. The objectives of the Recording Act are to preserve the evidence of real estate conveyances and to afford protection to purchasers in good faith and without notice from these claiming title to land. A recorded mortgage has priority over a mortgage subsequently recorded. The New York Recording Act requires that the mortgagee be a "purchaser" in good faith and for a valuable consideration. Thus, a recorded mortgage given to secure an antecedent debt (past consideration) has been held to be not paramount to a prior unrecorded mortgage, because past consideration is not held to be a "valuable consideration" under the Recording Act.

See TORRENS SYSTEM OF LAND TITLE REGISTRATION.

REGISTRATION OF STOCK See STOCK REGISTRAR.

REGISTRATION PRIVILEGE See REGISTERED BOND.

REGISTRATION STATEMENT Under Section 5 (a) of the SECURITIES ACT OF 1933, unless a registration statement is in effect as to a nonexempt security, it shall be unlawful for any person, directly or indirectly, to make use of any means or instruments of transportation or communication in interstate commerce or of the mails to sell such security through the use or medium of any prospectus or otherwise; or to carry or cause to be carried through the mails or in interstate commerce, by any means or instruments of transportation, any such security for the purpose of sale or for delivery after sale.

Sections 6, 7, and 8 of the act further relate to the registration statement. Section 6 prescribes the filing of the registration statement in triplicate, at least one copy of which shall be signed by each issuer and its principal officers and majority of the board of directors. Section 7 prescribes that the information specified in Schedule A outlined in the act shall be contained and required in the registration statement, subject to any further requirements prescribed by regulations of the Securities and Exchange Commission. Section 8 prescribes that normally the effective date of a registration statement shall be the twentieth day after the filing thereof. (Actually, because of workload, the effective date has averaged longer.)

Section 11 of the act then prescribes the civil liabilities arising on account of any false registration statement. In case any part of the registration statement, when such part becomes effective, contains an untrue statement of a material fact or omits to state a material fact required to be stated therein or necessary to make the statements therein not misleading, any person acquiring such security (unless it is proved that at the time of such acquisition he knew of such untruth or omission) may, either at law or in equity, in any court of competent jurisdiction, sue every person who signed the registration statement; every person who was a director of or partner in the issuer at time of filing; every person who with his consent is named in the registration statement as being or about to become a director or partner; every accountant, engineer, or appraiser, or any person whose profession gives authority to a statement made by him who has with his consent been named as having prepared or certified any part of the registration statement; and every underwriter.

An integral part of the registration statement is the PROSPECTUS which contains the same statements made in the registration statement but need not include detailed documents required for the registration statement.

Dissemination of Information. "In registration" refers to the entire process of registration, at least from the time an issuer reaches an understanding with the broker-dealer which is to act as managing underwriter in a public offering of a nonexempt security, prior to the filing of a registration statement, and the period during which dealers must deliver a prospectus containing the information specified by Section 10 of the act, including among other data the issuer's financial condition, business, property, management, and specified information about the offering including the manner of the offering and the intended use of the proceeds received. The registration and prospectus requirements reflect the basic purpose of the Securities Act of 1933, to require dissemination of adequate and accurate information concerning issuers and their securities in connection with the offer or sale of securities to the public, without fraud.

A basic question for issuers, therefore, was the information that may be released while securities are in registration. Securities Act of 1933 Release No. 5180 of the SECURITIES AND EXCHANGE COMMISSION clarified the question by stating that while issuers and their representatives should not initiate publicity when in registration, they should nevertheless respond to "legitimate" inquiries for *factual* (italics ours) information about the company's financial condition and operations. But care should be exercised, stated the commission, so that predictions, projections, forecasts, estimates, and opinions concerning value are not given with respect to such things as sales and earnings and value of the issuer's securities. The Securities and Exchange Commission stated that as a matter of policy it encourages the flow of factual information to shareholders and the investing public, and issuers in this regard should:

1. Continue to advertise products and services.
2. Continue to send out customary quarterly, annual, and other periodic reports to stockholders.
3. Continue to publish proxy statements and send out dividend notices.
4. Continue to make announcements to the press with respect to factual business and financial developments; i.e., receipt of a contract, the settlement of a strike, the opening of a plant, or similar events of interest to the community in which the business operates.
5. Answer unsolicited telephone inquiries from stockholders, financial analysts, the press, and others concerning factual information.
6. Observe an "open door" policy in responding to unsolicited inquiries concerning factual matters from securities analysts, financial analysts, security holders, and participants in the communications field who have a legitimate interest in the corporation's affairs.
7. Continue to hold stockholder meetings as scheduled and to answer shareholders' inquiries at stockholder meetings relating to factual matters.

On the other hand, in order to curtail problems in this area, issuers should avoid:

1. Issuing forecasts, projections, or predictions relating but not limited to revenues, income, or earnings per share.
2. Publishing opinions concerning values.

The SEC concluded that the determination of whether an item of information or publicity could be deemed to constitute an offer (a step in the selling effort) in violation of Section 5 must be made by the issuer in the light of all the facts and circumstances surrounding each case.

"Red Herring" Prospectus. Consistent with the preceding principles, the SEC authorized the use, for dissemination of information subject to completion or amendment on a public offering without solicitation of orders, of the preliminary prospectus, or "red herring" prospectus. Such prospectus takes its popular name from the requirement by the SEC that its nature be shown in red ink on the front cover, as follows, vertically along the left margin:

A Registration Statement relating to these securities has been filed with the Securities and Exchange Commission but has not yet become effective. Information contained herein is subject to completion or amendment. These securities may not be sold nor may offers to buy be accepted prior to the time the Registration Statement becomes effective. This prospectus shall not constitute an offer to sell or the solicitation of an offer to buy nor shall there be any sale of these securities in any state in which such offer, solicitation or sale would be unlawful prior to registration or qualification under the securities laws of any such state.

Revisions of Registration Statement Forms. Since the publication of the *Report of the Advisory Committee on Corporate Disclosure to the Securities and Exchange Commission* in 1977, the SEC has implemented as rapidly as possible the commission's recommendation to integrate the disclosure systems under the Securities Act as well as the Securities Exchange Act and to avoid "duplicative, unnecessary, or impractical reporting requirements." The implementation began with the promulgation of Regulation S-K as the source of uniform disclosure items and has included the revision of Securities Act registration statements' forms to reflect the revised S-K data appropriately called for.

New Registration Form. A new form adopted in 1980 provided an abbreviated format for registering securities issued in business combinations that do not significantly affect the issuer. Abbreviation is accomplished and duplication is avoided by the delivery of multiple documents, and information about the issuer is provided by delivering its annual report to security holders. The prospectus (Securities Act registration statement) contains only information about the particular transaction and about the company being acquired.

Small Business Form S-18. The SEC's Office of Small Business Policy monitors the content and quality of disclosure in smaller offerings, pursuant to both Regulation A and Form S-18, which is the simplified registration procedure for small businesses. Form S-18 calls for substantially less narrative and financial disclosure than does Form S-1, which is the form such issuers would otherwise use for registration of their securities. Form S-18 is available to certain domestic and Canadian corporate issuers for the registration of up to $5 million of their securities to be sold for cash. In order to facilitate processing for the issuer, the form may be filed with the regional offices of the SEC as well as in Washington, D.C.

Rule 242. Also in connection with small business, the SEC on January 17, 1980, adopted Rule 242, pursuant to Section 3(b) of the Securities Act. This rule provides an exemption from the registration provisions of the Securities Act for sales by domestic corporate issuers of up to $2 million in securities in any six-month period to an unlimited number of "accredited investors," as defined in the rule, and to 35 nonaccredited persons. The rule itself does not require the issuer to furnish an offering circular to investors if only "accredited persons" are involved in a Rule 242 offering, based upon the presumption that these types of investors are "able to fend for themselves." If, however, a Rule 242 offering involves one or more nonaccredited persons, the issuer must furnish all purchasers, including both accredited and nonaccredited persons, the same kind of information as that specified in Form S-18 to the extent material, except certain financial information.

Summary. The SEC's Division of Corporation Finance in the 1980 fiscal year experienced its first major reorganization in 20 years, restructuring its disclosure operations section so as to concentrate review responsibilities for reporting companies engaged in the same industries in one of the five major operating sections. In connection with this reorganization and the program of integrating disclosure requirements for both the Securities Act and Securities Exchange Act, the SEC's Division of Corporation Finance has been moving toward a system of selective review. The developing system seeks to concentrate review resources on areas of greatest priority, while eliminating the review of other documents except on an audit or sample basis. Thus continues the marasmus of the registration procedures of the SEC.

BIBLIOGRAPHY

SECURITIES AND EXCHANGE COMMISSION. "Release on Revaluation of *Guides for the Preparation and Filing of Registration Statements and Reports Under the Securities Act of 1933 and the Securities Exchange Act of 1934*," Securities Act Release No. 6163, December 5, 1979.

REGRESSION AND CORRELATION ANALYSIS

Regression analysis is a statistical procedure for estimating mathematically the average relationship between a dependent variable and an independent variable or variables. Simple regression involves one independent variable; multiple regression involves two or more variables. Correlation analysis provides a description of the strength of such relationships.

Regression analysis is widely used to forecast sales by product lines and to forecast income and other financial data. Data required varies, but several years' of monthly or quarterly history can serve as the basis for establishing meaningful relationships. Mathematically, it is necessary to have two more observations than there are independent variables. Regression analysis is usually very effective in short- and intermediate-term analysis. It is considered very good for identifying the turning point in financial relationships.

Regression analysis describes or estimates the value of one variable (the dependent variable on the basis of one or more other variables (the independent or explanatory). If a sales manager desires to predict auto sales for the next year (the dependent variable) on the basis of disposable income, regression analysis can be used to attempt to predict or estimate the value of the dependent variable (car sales).

Simple linear regression is defined by the following formula:

$$y = a + bx$$

where

y = dependent variable
x = independent variable
a = a constant or y intercept of regression line constant that represents the value of y when b is zero
b = slope of the regression line (the amount of change in y when x changes)

The method of least squares attempts to find a line of best fit for the graph of a regression equation. The method of least squares fits a regression line between the observation points such that the sum of the squared vertical differences between the regression line and the individual observations is minimized.

To illustrate the computation of the regression line, assume the following data of sales and salespersons' salaries:

Salaries (in hundreds of dollars)		Sales (in thousands)		
x	y	xy	x^2	y^2
$11	14	154	121	196
17	18	306	289	324

Data for 10 additional observations omitted

Total $174 $225 $3,414 $2,792 $4,359

The regression line, $y = a + bx$, is determined by the following two normal equations for a regression line:

$$Sy = na + b(Sx)$$

$$Sxy = a(Sx) + b(Sx2)$$

where

n = number of observations (12 in this case)
x = salaries (a measure of volume)
y = sales
S = sum of

Solving the equations gives the following results:

a = 10.5836
b = 0.5632

The regression line is:

$y = \$10.5836 + \$0.5632(x)$

If salaries are $10, sales projections would be $16.2156:

$y = \$10.5836 + \$0.5632(10)$
$y = \$16.2156$

An advantage of the least squares regression analysis is that a correlation analysis can be performed to quantitatively measure how well the regression line fits the data points. A variety of statistics can be used to describe the accuracy and reliability of the regression results, especially the correlation coefficient (r) and the coefficient of determination (r^2).

The correlation coefficient (r) is computed to measure the association between two variables; in this case, salaries and sales. Correlation analysis is the relationship between variables. If the variables move with each other, they have a direct relationship (positive correlation) as in graph I that follows. If the variables move in opposite directions, they have an inverse relationship (negative correlation). If there is little or no relationship, the data appear widely scattered and unrelated.

The degree and direction of correlation is measured from –1 to 1. The sign indicates either the relation is inverse or direct. The coefficient of correlation is measured by

$$\frac{\text{Amount of variation explained}}{\text{Total variation}}$$

When all the observations in a scatter diagram are in a straight line, all of the variations would be explained and the coefficient of correlation would be 1 or –1. If there is no correlation, the coefficient of correlation is 0. (See appended illustration.)

Regression and Correlation Analysis

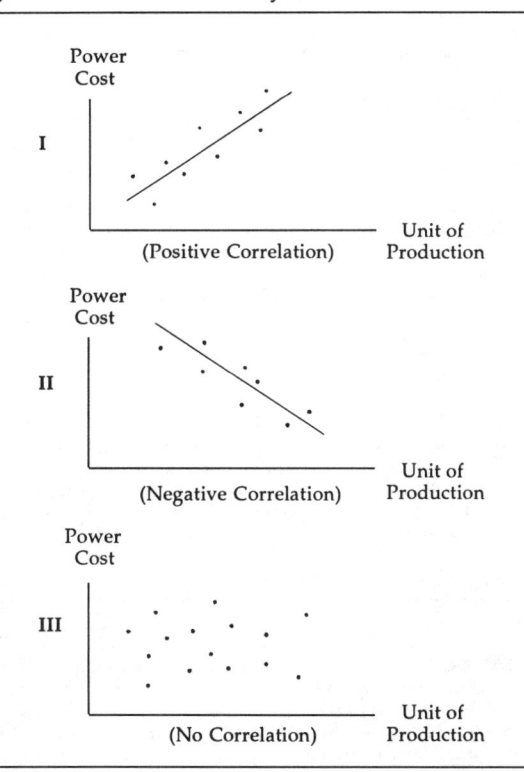

I — (Positive Correlation), Power Cost vs Unit of Production

II — (Negative Correlation), Power Cost vs Unit of Production

III — (No Correlation), Power Cost vs Unit of Production

A test of significance for a value of correlation requires the calculation of the probability that such a value of correlation would occur in random sampling from a universe in which there was no correlation.

The coefficient of determination represents the proportion of the total variation in y that is explained by the regression equation. Its value ranges between 0 and 1. For example, where sales is a function of salespersons' salaries with $r^2 = 0.61$, 61% of the total variation in sales is explained by the regression equation (or the change in salaries) and 39% is explained by some other factor (such as price, income). This somewhat low coefficient of determination suggests that salepersons' salaries is not a very good way to estimate sales.

Nearly every statistical software package has a routine for estimating a regression line.

REGRESSIVE TAX   A tax that takes a smaller percentage from higher-income individuals than from lower-income individuals. Overall, Social Security is a regressive tax because there is a maximum income limit beyond which no taxes are paid. Therefore, very wealthy individuals pay a lower percentage of their total income to Social Security than do lower-income individuals.

REGULAR DIVIDEND   A dividend established on a periodic basis of so much annually, payable semiannually, quarterly, or monthly, as the case may be. Seasoned and well-established companies place their stocks on a regular dividend basis in order to enhance the investment appeal of their securities by affording stockholders steady income. The regular dividend should be established at a point well within average earning power, so that it need not be often changed should earning power fluctuate and may be supplemented by extra dividends or special dividends as earnings warrant. On the other hand, companies whose earnings are subject to wide fluctuation prefer not to establish a regular dividend basis, as it would be liable to frequent changes, and instead pay periodic dividends as earnings, working capital needs, and the earnings outlook warrant, retaining the freedom to change the amount as necessary. Nevertheless, in a long period of good business, such companies may pay a consistent amount regularly, thus giving rise to an "indicated" annual rate which has empirical regularity.

REGULAR LOT   The standard unit of trade on a stock or commodity exchange; the full or BOARD LOT.

REGULAR WAY   The customary method of trading on the securities markets.
   See TRADING METHODS.

REGULATION   See PUBLIC REGULATION.

REGULATIONS OF BOARD OF GOVERNORS OF FEDERAL RESERVE SYSTEM   See FEDERAL RESERVE BOARD REGULATIONS.

REHYPOTHECATE   To repledge; to pledge collateral a second time. Whenever a bank, broker, or other lender advances funds against collateral (in the form of stocks, bonds, or notes) and uses the collateral so pledged to secure in turn a loan from another lender, the process is called rehypothecation. The most typical example of rehypothecation is that which occurs when stock exchange brokers repledge collateral held as security against balances due on margin accounts with a bank as security for a loan. Member banks sometimes pledge securities held against customers' loans as collateral for loans from a Federal Reserve bank. Rehypothecation is legally permissible if the customer's consent thereto is obtained in writing. Loan agreements usually provide for such power on the part of the pledgee (lender).
   See HYPOTHECATION, PLEDGE.

REICHSBANK   The central bank of Germany and the dominant financial institution in the country, operating both as a bankers' bank and banker for the public through its large system of countrywide branches until operations ceased following the defeat of Germany in World War II.
   See BANK OF GERMANY.

REIMBURSEMENT DRAFT   A draft remitted by a foreign bank in payment of items (bills of exchange, checks, postal orders, etc.) forwarded to it for collection. For example, suppose bank A in New York sends a draft for one thousand pounds to bank B in London for collection, with instructions to remit the proceeds by draft. Bank B, upon collecting the funds, will forward a draft to bank A drawn upon a domestic bank, perhaps bank A itself, for one thousand pounds less collection charges.

REINVESTMENT   Buying additional securities with the interest and dividends on present holdings, or new securities with the proceeds of sale or funds realized upon maturity of old ones. The term usually refers to the investment of the principal of bonds that have matured, or interest derived therefrom. Since the heaviest bond and interest coupon maturities fall on January 1 and July 1, a large demand for reinvestment of capital normally occurs on these dates.

RELATED PARTY TRANSACTIONS For accounting purposes, related parties may be any of the following: affiliates; principal owners and close kin; management and close kin; parent companies and subsidiaries; equity method investors and investees; trusts for the benefit of employees, such as pension or profit-sharing trusts managed by or under the trusteeship of management; or any other party that can significantly influence the management or operating policies of the reporting enterprise, to the extent that it may be prevented from operating in its own best interest. Such other parties could include an officer or director of a corporation, a stockholder, and a partner or joint venturer in a partnership or venture. An affiliate is a party that controls, is controlled by, or is under common control with another enterprise, directly or indirectly. Principal owners are owners of more than 10% of an enterprise's voting interest. Management includes persons who have policy-making and decision-making authority within an enterprise and who are responsible for attaining an enterprise's objectives. Next of kin refers to immediate family members whom a principal owner or a member of management might control or influence or by whom they might be controlled or influenced because of the family relationship.

In related party transactions, one party is in a position to control a transaction or the effect of a transaction on another party. In such situations, a conflict of interest or transactions with insiders may occur. Examples of related party transactions that commonly occur in the normal course of business include the following: sales; purchases; transfers of realty and personal property; services received or furnished; use of property and equipment; borrowings and lendings; guarantees. Transactions between related parties cannot be presumed to be arm's-length transactions.

Financial statements must include disclosures of material, related party transactions, except compensation arrangements, expense allowances, and other similar items in the normal course of business. Disclosure must include the nature of the relationship, a description of transaction(s), dollar amount of transactions, and amounts due to and from related parties. An auditor's responsibility in related party transactions is to make reasonable inquiry to determine that all material relationships are identified and disclosed and that such transactions do not violate fiduciary relationships.

RELEASE In general, the relinquishment or discharge of any right, claim, or privilege, either expressly, impliedly, or by operation of law. A mortgage may be discharged by satisfaction, by payment, by tender of payment (which extinguishes the lien and stops the running of interest, although it does not satisfy the mortgage debt), by merger of the mortgage interest and the legal title to the mortgaged land in one person at the same time, by extinguishment where the owner of the land acquires the mortgage, and by lapse of time. A release or satisfaction of a mortgage is a statutory instrument in New York and is a conveyance within the meaning of the Recording Act.

REMAINDERMAN The person who receives the remainder of an estate after the termination of a prior interest set up in the estate by the terms of the creation thereof by the testator or settlor. The remainderman may come into possession of the estate upon the death of the life tenant, or at the end of a certain period designated in a trust. It is the duty of a trustee to harmonize the interests of both the life tenant and the remainderman and to preserve the remainder of the estate for the remainderman.
See TRUST.

REMAINING MORTGAGE BALANCE TABLE
A table that enables a person to compute the remaining mortgage balance at a given time. A portion of the table appears as follows:

Remaining balance at 15.50% interest amortized monthly

	Original term in years			
Age of loan	10	15	20	25
1	95.46	98.17	99.20	99.64
5	68.35	87.22	94.41	97.48

The unpaid balance on a $100,000, 20-year mortgage at 15.5% interest amortized monthly interest after five years is computed as follows:

$100,000 × 94.41 = $94,410 unpaid balance

REMARGINING Placing additional margin against a loan collateraled by securities that have declined in value. In stock exchange loans, the amount of the margin must be kept constantly good. Most brokers advise margin customers to keep a comfortable credit balance, in order to avoid the risk of the account's being placed in the restricted category under Regulation T in the event of a sudden market decline. If there is a decline in the market, the borrower is required to furnish additional securities or to pay a part of the loan.
See MARGIN.

REMEDIAL LOANS See SMALL LOAN BUSINESS.

REMEDY ALLOWANCE A technical term used by the British mint to indicate the permitted variation of actual weight and fineness of coins from the exact weight and fineness defined by the Coinage Act. The remedy for fineness is two parts in one thousand for gold coins and four parts in one thousand for silver coins. The remedy allowed in weight per English sovereign is 0.20 of a grain.

In the United States the legal variation allowed in coinage is known as the "Remedy of the Mint."
See TOLERANCE.

REMITTANCE This term has two applications:

1. Any form of payment in cash or its equivalent, in satisfaction of a debt, which is forwarded from one point to another.
2. In banking practice, the forwarding for credit of deposits (checks, cash, money orders, matured coupons, etc.) by customers through the mails; more properly, a check from a bank in payment of the proceeds of checks previously sent to it for collection.

REMITTANCE ACCOUNT Among transit and collection departments, a collecting agent or correspondent with whom arrangements have been made to remit by check the proceeds from checks previously sent to it for collection. Such collection agents are to be distinguished from those with whom arrangements have been made to offset items sent for collection by charges to their accounts on the books of the forwarding bank.

REMITTANCE LETTER See RETURN REMITTANCE.

REMONETIZATION The endowment of a metal with the power to act as a monetary standard, i.e., permitting its coinage without limit as to quantity and giving the coin manufactured from it full legal tender powers, after such coin has once been deprived of this power by reason of being degraded to the rank of token money.
See DEMONETIZATION.

RENEGOTIATED-RATE LOANS Loans whose interest rates or repayment terms have been revised as a result of credit deterioration.

RENEWAL When a bank extends a loan by permitting a borrower to substitute a new note for a maturing note, the new note is called a renewal and in the legal sense constitutes a novation if the old note is surrendered. The renewal of a loan should always entail the cancellation of the maturing note and the making of a new one, and bookkeeping records should show such cancellation and renewal. In many classes of loans, renewals are regularly expected. Real estate mortgage loans, both on farm and urban property, and livestock loans are usually subject to renewal. The buyer of commercial paper sold in the open market by note brokers is under no obligation to renew.
See FROZEN CREDITS.

RENEWAL BONDS Bonds issued to extend a maturing issue; another title for what are virtually extended bonds and are practically equivalent to refunding bonds.
See EXTENDED BOND, REFUNDING BONDS.

RENEWAL RATE In the New York money market, the renewal rate on time loans to brokers by banks is the current rate for renewals of the notes with specific maturity dates which govern collateral loans. Demand or "call" loans are governed by a general

agreement under which continuing loans and repayments may be made or terminated on short notice by either party ("calls" have been rare in recent years), with interest computed daily at current rate.
See MONEY MARKET.

RENTES This term has two applications:

1. The annual interest payable upon the bonded debt of the governments of France and other European countries.
2. By extension of the above meaning, the government bonds themselves—for example, French rentes.

A novel feature of French government bond issues is the "gold hedge" provision. On June 17, 1958, the government floated a 54-year 3.5% issue, amortizable in annual drawings (but no accelerated amortization prior to 1970). Amortization was linked to the price of the 20-franc gold coin (the "napoleon") on the Paris market. The sum repaid when the bonds fall due would be equal to the nominal value of the bonds plus a percentage; this percentage, to be determined before May 31 each year, would be equal to the percentage by which the average price of the napoleon during the 100 market days preceding May 15 exceeds the market price of the napoleon in mid-June, 1958 (F 3,600). If the price during such a period is equal to or below such base market price, the bonds would be redeemed at par. In May, 1952, a similar 60-year 3.5% loan was issued, with its amortization also linked to the price of the napoleon. Both issues are exempt from all taxes.

REORGANIZATION The judicial financial readjustment of a corporation under procedures prescribed by federal or state statutes, as compared with voluntary READJUSTMENT. The NATIONAL BANKRUPTCY ACT as revised, codified as Title 11, U.S.C., provides for reorganization procedures under court supervision, including Subchapter IV of Chapter 11 for railroads and Subchapter II of Chapter 11 for other corporations. These statutory reorganization procedures, as revised and codified by the Federal Bankruptcy Reform Act of 1978, effective October 1, 1979, were enacted to meet the shortcomings of equity receiverships for reorganization, particularly the necessity for paying off in full the claims of dissenting security holders. Under the statutory reorganization procedures, the required ratio of consents upon acceptance (two-thirds in amount and more than one-half in number of allowed claims) and confirmation of the reorganization plan by the court binds the dissenting minorities.

The principal causes leading to the necessity for reorganization among corporations are (1) overcapitalization (especially errors in capitalization which involve excessive fixed charges), and (2) errors in scale of operation and excessive fixed costs. Among railroads, the chief causes of reorganization have been overcapitalization through issuance of excessive volume of obligations and prolonged business depression which causes the leverage of fixed charges in capitalization and fixed costs in operations to operate adversely on net operating income. The special causes necessitating railroad reorganization are (1) the accumulation of large or pressing floating debt, (2) large fixed charges on funded debt, and (3) low working capital and/or unexpectedly low earnings. No class of business organizations has resorted to reorganization more consistently than railroads over time. Approximately one-third of total railroad mileage went into receivership or trusteeship during the period 1930-1939. As the result of some quite drastic reorganizations since, however, resort to reorganization may not be as characteristic of railroads in the future (see RAILROAD INDUSTRY).

The most usual specific objects to be accomplished in a reorganization are (1) to raise additional capital, (2) to reduce fixed charges, (3) to pay off floating debt, (4) to eliminate unprofitable departments of the operations, (5) to scale down the capital issues or substitute contingent obligations for fixed ones, and (6) to convert previously excessive proportion of obligational securities in the capitalization into equity securities, preferred stock, or common stock. In order to prepare for future operation on a reorganized basis, it might also be necessary to raise additional funds, both current and of a capital nature, the latter for example to modernize facilities. Unless the court orders otherwise, the trustee may operate the business during the reorganization period, but the debtor may continue in possession subject to court limitations or conditions and may file a plan.

The chief rules to be observed in a reorganization plan are as follows. (1) The maximum charges under the reorganization should be covered by a reasonable margin by the worst of the anticipated earnings on a reorganized basis. (2) Instead of the former "absolute priority rule," the holder of claim or interest of each class should receive or retain under the plan not less than amount the debtor would receive if the business were liquidated under Chapter 7 (which provides for liquidation rather than reorganization). The aggregate capitalization should be determined realistically by "capitalizing" at a suitable rate the average earnings reasonably projected for the reorganized business.

Reorganization under Chapter 11 of the Bankruptcy Reform Act of 1978 contemplates the continuation of the business enterprise and its eventual rehabilitation, rather than Chapter 7 bankruptcy, which has for its purpose the orderly liquidation and distribution of the estate to creditors according to their rank. Chapter 11 is available primarily for businesses, although individuals are eligible. Filing a petition under Chapter 11 effectively stays the debtor's creditors. A Chapter 11 process involves the following procedures:

1. Proceedings are initiated either voluntarily by the debtor or involuntarily by (a) at least three creditors with claims of at least $5,000 (where more than 12 creditors exist) or (b) fewer than three creditors with $5,000 or more in claims where fewer than 12 creditors exist;
2. The court may appoint a trustee who has custody of the property; a creditors' committee consisting of the largest creditors is established.
3. A plan of reorganization is proposed; a debtor in possession has exclusive right to file a plan during the first 120 days after the date of the order for relief. If a trustee has been appointed or if the debtor's plan has not met the 120-day deadline, other parties may file a plan. Whoever proposes the plan must come forward with a disclosure statement that provides specific information about the debtor, its history and prospects, and details about the plan.
4. The court may approve or disapprove this informational document.
5. The plan and disclosure statement are submitted to those whose claims and interest are impaired by the plan.
6. Finally, if the plan has been accepted by every class of impaired creditors and equity security holders, the court confirms the plan if specified minimum criteria are satisfied, i.e., if it is in best interests of creditors and is feasible. Confirmation of the reorganization plan discharges a nonbusiness debtor from most or all of its debts.

See BANKRUPTCY.

BIBLIOGRAPHY

FRANK, J. R., AND TOROWS, W. N. "An Empirical Investigation of U.S. Firms in Reorganization." *Journal of Finance*, July, 1989.
SECURITIES AND EXCHANGE COMMISSION. "Corporate Reorganizations." *Annual Report*.
GINSBERG, ROBERT E., *Bankruptcy* (Prentice-Hall, Englewood Cliffs, N.J., 1985).

REORGANIZATION BONDS Bonds issued in connection with a reorganization, usually issued in exchange for bonds authorized and outstanding under the old capitalization, and customarily in railroad reorganizations issued in "packages" of so much per new bonds, plus stock or cash, in exchange for the old securities. The title ADJUSTMENT BONDS indicates that such bonds are issued in connection with reorganization, but many new income bonds issued in reorganizations of recent years do not carry the term "adjustment" as part of their title.

REORGANIZATION COMMITTEE Under equity receivership practice, the investors in the debtor's securities, acting through their REORGANIZATION committees, developed and presented a reorganization plan for approval of the court. Under the Reorganization Chapter of the Bankruptcy Act of 1978 (Chapter 11), creditors' and equity security holders' committees continue to be provided for, as in the former versions of the NATIONAL BANKRUPTCY ACT.

Chapter 11 (Sec. 1102) of the Bankruptcy Act of 1978 provides as follows:

1. As soon as practicable after the order for relief has been granted, the court shall appoint a committee of creditors

holding unsecured claims. The committee of creditors holding unsecured claims shall ordinarily consist of the persons willing to serve who hold the seven largest claims against the debtor of the kinds represented on such committee, or of the members of a committee organized by creditors before the order for relief was granted, if such committee was fairly chosen and is representative of the different kinds of claims to be represented.
2. On request of a party in interest, the court may order the appointment of additional committees of creditors or of equity security holders if necessary to assure adequate representation of creditors or of equity security holders. The court also shall appoint any such committee.
3. A committee of equity security holders appointed as above shall ordinarily consist of the persons willing to serve who hold the seven largest amounts of equity securities of the debtor of the kinds represented on such committee.
4. On request of a party in interest and after notice and a hearing, the court may change the membership or the size of a committee appointed to represent unsecured claims or additional committees of creditors or of equity security holders, if the membership of such committee is not representative of the different kinds of claims or interests to be represented.

At a scheduled meeting of a committee appointed in accordance with the preceding provisions, at which a majority of the members of such committee are present, the committee, with the court's approval, may select and authorize the employment of one or more attorneys, accountants, or other agents to represent or perform services for such committee.

A committee appointed in accordance with the preceding provisions may:

1. Consult with the trustee or debtor in possession concerning the administration of the case.
2. Investigate the acts, conduct, assets, liabilities, and financial condition of the debtor, the operation of the debtor's business and the desirability of the continuance of such business, and any other matter relevant to the case or to the formulation of a plan.
3. Participate in the formulation of a plan, advise those represented by such committee of such committee's recommendations as to any plan formulated, and collect and file with the court acceptances of a plan.
4. Request the appointment of a trustee or examiner under Chapter 11, if a trustee or examiner, as the case may be, has not previously been appointed under Chapter 11 in the case; and perform such other services as are in the interest of those represented.

As soon as practicable after the appointment of a committee, the trustee shall meet with committee to transact such business as may be necessary and proper.
See BANKRUPTCY.

REPARATIONS The amount of damages assessed at the Treaty of Versailles in 1919 by the victorious Allies against Germany and other defeated nations of the world war.
See WAR DEBTS.

BIBLIOGRAPHY

WHEELER-BENNETT, J. W. *The Wreck of Reparations*, 1933.

REPLEDGE To rehypothecate; to pledge collateral a second time. When a lender who holds collateral as security for a loan becomes a borrower and deposits the same collateral with the consent of his borrower as security for his own loan, the collateral is repledged. A bank or broker might deposit securities pledged as collateral against customers' loans with another institution as collateral for a loan.
See REHYPOTHECATE.

REPRESENTATIVE MONEY Paper money issued against, and secured by, monetary metal deposited in a national treasury or other public depository in amounts sufficient to redeem such money in full. Thus, silver certificates were examples of representative money, since they were payable on demand and sufficient silver was deposited to redeem them in full. Federal Reserve notes, the principal form of paper money outstanding in the United States, although fully secured by gold certificates, special drawing rights, government securities, and eligible paper collateral and payable in lawful money, are not representative money because they are not supported by a 100% metallic reserve.
See MONEY, UNITED STATES MONEY.

REPUDIATION Wilful refusal to pay a debt; the dishonor or rejection of an obligation or contract, as distinguished from an unavoidable failure or DEFAULT. Repudiation may be complete or partial. The term is usually applied to the refusal of a government or civil subdivision thereof to pay a bonded obligation. Whenever a sovereign power, e.g., a national government or state, repudiates its debts, the citizens who have bought its bonds have no recourse, since an individual has no power to sue a sovereign power without its consent. A municipality, however, may be sued.

Although a national government may repudiate its obligations, very few instances of such repudiation are on record. The United States has never repudiated any of its bonds. Several of the states and certain counties have been guilty of repudiation, illegality of the issue being the chief excuse. According to Lawrence Chamberlain, there were two periods of repudiation in the United States. The first, from 1837 to 1844, was due to the depressed conditions which followed the panic of 1837; and the second, from 1870 to 1884, is characterized as a "period of bad faith." In the depression of the early 1930s, it is estimated that some 3,000 local governmental units and districts defaulted.

REPURCHASE AGREEMENTS Two simultaneous transactions in which a holder of securities sells securities to an investor with an agreement to repurchase them at a fixed price on a fixed date. A reverse repo is the same transaction from the perspective of the lender. The security buyer in effect lends the seller money for the period of the agreement, and the terms of the agreement are structured to compensate the buyer for this. Dealers use repurchase agreements (repos) to finance their positions. In effect, a repo is a short-term, collateralized loan from an investor to a dealer. The Federal Reserve uses repos to supply reserves to the banking system and reverse repos to drain its reserves.

Repurchase agreements can be done on an overnight basis, for a fixed term, or on the basis of a continuing contract. Fixed-term repos are usually made for less than 30 days. When executed under a continuing contract, repo contracts usually contain a clause to adjust the interest rate on a day-to-day basis. Interest rates on overnight repurchase agreements usually are lower than the federal funds rate by as much as 25 basis points. The additional security provided by the loan collateral employed with repos lessens their risk relative to federal funds. Repos are usually negotiated in large dollar amounts.

The use of repos became common after World War II among a few government security dealers and large money center banks. Since the 1960s, the volume of transactions and the number of participants have grown substantially. In 1985, the annual average volume of transactions outstanding on the books of major government security dealers amounted to $320 billion. Repos have proved to be very popular cash management vehicles for individuals, firms, and governments with unpredictable cash flows. Repos have been associated in recent years with widely publicized scandals involving the failure of government security dealers. A publication of the Federal Reserve Bank of Atlanta concluded that losses to investors can be avoided if investors (1) operate under the terms of a clearly specified and executed master repurchase agreement, (2) properly assess counterparties including their corporate structure and capital strength, (3) use appropriate procedures for obtaining control of securities, and (4) evaluate securities appropriately and monitor them regularly, making margin calls when necessary.

Repurchase agreements have two major applications.

1. Bonds are sometimes sold by one bank or investment house to another with the privilege of repurchase. This transaction is tantamount to securing a loan equal to 100% of the collateral offered. For instance, should an investment house desire to borrow funds with bonds as collateral, it may, instead of applying for a loan, arrange to temporarily sell them to a bank with an agreement to repurchase them at the same price at some specified future date—when the need for the funds has passed. When such an agreement is concluded, the bank pur-

chases the bonds outright at a flat price, or a flat price plus accrued interest, with an agreement to sell them back to the borrowing institution at the same price plus interest at a stipulated rate upon the expiration of a certain period. The price agreed upon for purchase and resale is usually at or a few points below the prevailing market price.

Regulations of the Comptroller of the Currency authorize member banks to enter into repurchase or resale agreements only when the member bank concerned has the sole right or option under the agreement.

Appended is a typical form of bond repurchase agreement.

General Bond Repurchase Agreement

AGREEMENT MADE THIS DAY OF _____ , 19 _____
Between
_____ Bank
and
_____

WHEREAS, in consideration of the agreement to purchase hereinafter expressed, _____ Bank has this day agreed to purchase from _____
at a price of _____ flat.
The _____ Bank hereby agrees to resell said lot of bonds to the _____ on or before 60 days from the purchase date at the same price _____ flat, plus interest on the purchase price at the rate of _____
_____ percent per annum, and the said
_____ hereby agrees to repurchase said lot of bonds from the _____ Bank on or before 60 days from the selling date, at the said price _____ flat, plus interest on the sale price at the rate of _____
percent per annum.

THE _____ BANK
By _____
Cashier

2. Member banks may borrow from a Federal Reserve bank through the instrumentality of a repurchase agreement, which, to all intents and purposes, is a collateral advance. Eligible collateral is of four classes: Treasury bonds, certificates of indebtedness, bankers' acceptances, and eligible commercial paper.

The form of repurchase agreement used by Federal Reserve banks is appended.

Federal Reserve Repurchase Agreement

New York, _____ , 19 _____
TO FEDERAL RESERVE BANK, _____
NEW YORK, N.Y. _____

The _____ Bank hereby offers for rediscount for _____ days from date the bills and/or notes which are listed on this application and agrees on _____ , 19, _____ to pay you the face value of the same which are thereupon to be released to us. If such payment is not made on said date, you are hereby authorized to charge to our account the face value of said bills and/or notes and to hold them for collection for our account, subject to our order.

_____ Bank
Cashier

See RETAIL REPURCHASE AGREEMENTS.

RESCHEDULING DEBT
An arrangement in which the maturity of a loan is lengthened to improve the chances of a borrower making loan payments.

RESEARCH AND DEVELOPMENT COSTS
Costs related to developing or modifying products, processes, services, or techniques. Research is a planned search or critical investigation aimed at discovery of new knowledge; development refers to bringing research findings into a plan or design for further action. Development includes the conceptual formulation, design, and testing of product alternatives, construction of prototypes, and operation of pilot plants. It does not include routine or periodic alterations to existing products, production lines, manufacturing processes, and other ongoing operations.

All research and development (R&D) costs should be charged to expense when incurred. This implies that the future expected value of research and development cost does not merit recognition as an asset because of the risks, uncertainties, and estimates involved.

The cost of materials, equipment, and facilities that are acquired or constructed for research and development activities and that have alternative future uses should be capitalized when acquired or constructed. However, when such equipment and facilities are used, the depreciation of such items and the materials consumed should be included as research and development costs. The following activities are generally considered research and development costs:

1. Laboratory research aimed at discovery of new knowledge.
2. Searching for applications of new research findings or other knowledge.
3. Testing to search for or evaluate product or process alternatives.
4. Modification of the formulation or design of a product or process.

BIBLIOGRAPHY

LINK, ALBERT N., *Research and Development Activity in U.S. Manufacturing* (Praeger, New York, 1981).
R&D Partnerships: Structuring the Transactions; A How-to-Guide for Lawyers, Accountants and Tax Shelter Professions. Clark Boardman Co. Annual.
Research and Development.
Research Technology Management.
SFAS No. 2, ACCOUNTING FOR RESEARCH AND DEVELOPMENT COSTS (FASB, 1974).

RESERVATION
Before passage of the Securities Act of 1933, in printing descriptive circulars it was customary for the issuing investment house or syndicate to append a statement purportedly precluding any liability which might accrue because of misstatements or inaccuracies which might be contained. Following are typical examples of such reservations:

"The information contained in this circular is not guaranteed, but is believed to be correct."

"The statements and figures presented herein are not guaranteed, but are taken from sources which we believe to be accurate."

"All information given herein is from official sources or from sources which we regard as reliable, but in no event are the statements herein contained to be regarded as representations of the undersigned."

"The statements contained herein are based upon information which we consider entirely trustworthy. While we do not guarantee the information, we believe it to be correct."

Although the legal efficacy of such "disclaimer" clauses is subject to actual litigation and the facts of each case, such hedge clauses have continued to be generally used. In view of the principle of disclosure of interest of the Securities Act of 1933, it is now customary to add an indication of the interest that the firm issuing such descriptive circulars has in the security described. An example of the modern hedge clause follows:

"The data contained herein have been obtained from reports of the company to its stockholders and from various statistical services and other sources which we believe reliable, but without further verification or investigation by us. This information is not intended to and should not be relied upon as comprising a complete report or analysis. Neither the facts herein presented nor the opinions herein expressed constitute representations by us. We deal, as principals or agents, in the security described herein."

RESERVE This term has four applications.

Accounting. In accounting, a reserve, as distinguished from RESERVE FUND, is an account appearing among stockholder equity to indicate a reservation of retained earnings. Usually a reserve account is specifically named to indicate its purpose, but it represents neither cash nor other assets in any earmarked form. It is merely a part of the proprietorship (net worth) of the business.

In recent years, as the result of dissatisfaction with the term "reserve," the Committee on Accounting Terminology of the American Institute of Accountants recommends that the term "reserve" be applied only to accounts that are allocations of retained income and that accounts which provide for asset deductions (valuation accounts) be referred to as "allowances," e.g., allowance for bad debts, allowance for depreciation, allowance for depletion, etc. Accruals should be properly identified as such, e.g., accrued taxes, accrued interest payable, etc., rather than referred to as "reserves."

An accounting reserve is used only to describe an appropriation of retained earnings. Only the board of directors can appropriate retained earnings. The major purpose of appropriating retained earnings is to provide more information to the users of the financial statements. Reasons for appropriating retained earnings include contractual agreements requiring such appropriations (for example, a bond indenture may place a limitation on dividends), state law (for example, required by some states when treasury stock is acquired that could impair the capital of the company), and voluntary actions by the board to retain assets in the business for future use. The creation of a reserve is the result of an accounting entry and does not set aside cash or any other asset of the company.

When the reserve is no longer needed, the appropriation can be returned to retained earnings. The return of the appropriation to retained earnings increases unappropriated retained earnings without affecting the assets or current position of the company.

If an enterprise desired to set aside cash or other assets to provide for contingencies or other purposes, it could do so by establishing a fund (not a reserve). This action would represent a transaction that has economic significance.

Life Insurance. In life insurance, the policy reserves are the accumulating fund from such portions of premiums as are not currently used to pay mortality claims and expenses and are instead compounded to the credit of outstanding policies for future years. In fire and marine and casualty insurance, unearned premiums, representing the premiums paid in advance but not yet earned, are required by law to be set up in the unearned premiums reserves.

Banking. In banking, the term has several applications, each having a technical meaning quite different from those of accounting and insurance.

Primary reserves: "Primary reserves" refers to the assets in the form of cash maintained in a bank's own vault or claims on cash on deposit with compulsory or optional depositories. When compulsory pursuant to banking laws, such cash primary reserves are referred to as "legal reserve requirements." In the United States, the amount of reserve requirement against demand and time deposits, the method of its computation, the place of deposit thereof, and composition (for Federal Reserve banks) are prescribed by banking law.

The origin of legal reserve requirements in the United States is generally credited to the 1842 banking law of Louisiana, which included the requirement of a specie reserve of one-third of all obligations to the public (at that time, deposits and bank notes), a provision emulated in varying degree by many other states prior to the Civil War. The principle of legal minimum reserves against deposits became firmly entrenched when the National Bank Act of 1863 included such provision.

The purpose of legal reserve requirements originally was apparently to maintain the ability of the banks to pay their liabilities in cash. Actually, however, since these requirements are fractional (below 100%) and are not freely available inasmuch as required against outstanding deposit liabilities, this liquidity motivation in modern times is considered to be of minor importance. Instead, the primary function of legal reserve requirements is to serve as a "brake" on expansion in loans and investments of the banks and thus in their deposits. Since such expansion in effect "uses up" excess reserves (i.e., primary reserves in excess of the legal minimum required against existing deposits), the ability of the banking system as a whole to expand loans and investments (and thereby deposits) is measured by the reciprocal of the average legal reserve requirement. Thus, with an average legal reserve requirement of approximately 12% (on transaction accounts), the banking system may optimally expand its loans and investments by $8\,^1/_3$ times per dollar of excess reserves. The individual bank in the system, however, has no such multiple expansion power, for in addition to suffering the "cost" in excess reserves in the form of additional legal reserve requirements against increased deposits created by credit expansion, it invariably will lose some derivative or created deposits to other banks in the system as such deposits are checked out by the recipients. How much such "withdrawals" cost in excess reserves will be for the individual bank is an empirical matter, depending on such factors as compensating balance requirement, if any, by the bank; the extensiveness of operations of the bank, which may result in a return flow of a portion of the check-outs back to the same bank because recipients of the check-outs also happen to be depositors in the same bank; and the area of spending of the check-outs (in the same community or in other areas). If there is no compensating balance requirement by the bank and there is no return flow whatsoever of check-outs, it is obvious that an individual bank will be able to expand only on a 1:1 basis if the derivative deposits are checked out in full.

Revision of legal reserve requirements: The DEPOSITORY INSTITUTIONS DEREGULATION AND MONETARY CONTROL ACT OF 1980 (Title I of P.L. 96-221; 94 Stat. 132), enacted on June 4, 1980, imposes legal reserve requirements on depository institutions that maintain transaction accounts or nonpersonal time deposits. Such reserve requirements are variable within a given statutory range and hence are a means by which the Board of Governors of the Federal Reserve System may conduct monetary policy. On August 15, 1980, the board of governors adopted a revised Regulation D of the FEDERAL RESERVE BOARD REGULATIONS to implement the provisions of the act.

The term "depository institutions" encompasses any federally insured commercial or savings bank, or any commercial or savings bank that is eligible to become insured by the FEDERAL DEPOSIT INSURANCE CORPORATION; any mutual or stock savings bank; any savings and loan association that is a member of the FEDERAL HOME LOAN BANK SYSTEM and that is insured by, or eligible to apply for insurance with, the FEDERAL SAVINGS AND LOAN INSURANCE CORPORATION; and any credit union that is insured by, or eligible to apply for insurance with, the NATIONAL CREDIT UNION Administration Board. In addition, Regulation D applies to United States branches and agencies of foreign banks with total worldwide consolidated bank assets in excess of $1 billion, and to Edge Act and agreement corporations.

Reserve requirements are computed on the basis of an institution's average daily net deposit balances during the seven-day period beginning each Thursday (the "computation period"). Required reserve balances must be maintained at a Federal Reserve bank during the seven-day period (the "maintenance period") beginning on the second Thursday following the end of the computation period. When the amount of the required reserve balance is determined, the average daily United States currency and coin held during the computation period is deducted from the institution's reserve requirements.

Effective February 2, 1984, Paragraphs (c) and (d) of Section 204.3 of Regulation D were amended to modify the manner in which depository institutions maintain required reserves. The changes adopted by the Board of Governors of the Federal Reserve System introduce contemporaneous reserve requirements on transaction accounts for medium-size and larger depository institutions, instead of the "lagged" system in effect since 1968. The board of governors, like monetary analysts, believes that shortening the lag between the computation and maintenance of required reserves on transaction accounts will enhance the conduct of monetary policy by strengthening the linkage between the supply of reserves and the money supply.

The term "transaction account" includes demand deposits; negotiable order of withdrawal (NOW) accounts; savings accounts subject to automatic transfers; share draft accounts; accounts that permit payments to third parties through the use of a check, draft, negotiable instrument, debit card, or other similar items; accounts under the terms of which a depositor is *permitted* (italics by the board of governors in their *Federal Reserve Regulatory Service*) to make more than three preauthorized or telephone transfers per month; and accounts that permit a depositor to make payments to third parties through automated teller machines (ATMs) or remote service units.

The appended table shows the reserve requirements in effect as of December 1988, accompanied by explanatory footnote disclosures of significant concepts.

Table 1 / Reserve Requirements of Depository Institutions [1]
(Percent of deposits)

Type of deposit, and deposit interval [2]	Depository institution requirements after implementation of the Monetary Control Act	
	Percent of deposits	Effective date
Net transaction accounts [3,4]		
$0 million-$41.5 million	3	12/20/88
More than $41.5 million	12	12/20/88
Nonpersonal time deposits [5]		
By original maturity		
Less than 1 1/2 years	3	10/6/83
1 1/2 years or more	0	10/6/83
Eurocurrency liabilities		
All types	3	11/13/80

[1] Reserve requirements in effect on Dec. 31, 1988. Required reserves must be held in the form of deposits with Federal Reserve Banks or vault cash. Nonmembers may maintain reserve balances with a Federal Reserve Bank indirectly on a pass-through basis with certain approved institutions. For previous reserve requirements, see earlier editions of the *Annual Report* and of the *Federal Reserve Bulletin*. Under provisions of the Monetary Control Act, depository institutions include commercial banks, mutual savings banks, savings and loan associations, credit unions, agencies, and branches of foreign banks, and Edge corporations.

[2] The Garn-St Germain Depository Institutions Act of 1982 (Public Law 97-320) requires that $2 million of reservable liabilities (transaction accounts, nonpersonal time deposits, and Eurocurrency liabilities) of each depository institution be subject to a zero percent reserve requirement. The Board is to adjust the amount of reservable liabilities subject to this zero percent reserve requirement each year for the succeeding calendar year by 80 percent of the percentage increase in the total reservable liabilities of all depository institutions, measured on an annual basis as of June 30. No corresponding adjustment is to be made in the event of a decrease. On Dec. 20, 1988, the exemption was raised from $3.2 million to $3.4 million. In determining the reserve requirements of depository institutions, the exemption shall apply in the following order: (1) net NOW accounts (NOW accounts less allowable deductions); (2) net other transaction accounts; and (3) nonpersonal time deposits or Eurocurrency liabilities starting with those with the highest reserve ratio. With respect to NOW accounts and other transaction accounts, the exemption applies only to such accounts that would be subject to a 3 percent reserve requirement.

[3] Transaction accounts include all deposits on which the account holder is permitted to make withdrawals by negotiable or transferable instruments, payment orders of withdrawal, and telephone and preauthorized transfers in excess of three per month for the purpose of making payments to third persons or others. However, MMDAs and similar accounts subject to the rules that permit no more than six preauthorized, automatic, or other transfers per month, of which no more than three can be checks, are not transaction accounts (such accounts are savings deposits subject to time deposit reserve requirements.)

[4] The Monetary Control Act of 1980 requires that the amount of transaction accounts against which the 3 percent reserve requirement applies be modified annually by 80 percent of the percentage increase in transaction accounts held by all depository institutions, determined as of June 30 each year. Effective Dec. 20, 1988 for institutions reporting quarterly and Dec. 27, 1988 for institutions reporting weekly, the amount was increased from $40.5 million to $41.5 million.

[5] In general, nonpersonal time deposits are time deposits, including savings deposits that are not transaction accounts and in which a beneficial interest is held by a depositor that is not a natural person. Also included are certain transferable time deposits held by natural persons and certain obligations issued to depository institution offices located outside the United States. For details, see section 204.2 of Regulation D.

Source: Federal Reserve Board of Governors.

Moreover, if at least five members of the Board of Governors of the Federal Reserve System find that "extraordinary circumstances" require such action, the board of governors, after consultation with the Congress, may impose a reserve requirement at any ratio on any liability of depository institutions for periods of 180 days.

Legal reserves on transaction accounts are to be uniformly applied to all depository institutions, but those on nonpersonal time deposits may vary according to maturity. No legal reserve requirements are specified by the Monetary Control Act of 1980 against personal time deposits including savings accounts.

Regulation D of the Board of Governors of the Federal Reserve System treats certain types of accounts as personal time deposits even though they are held by the depository institution as trustee. Individual retirement account (IRA) and Keogh plan time deposits fall into this category, as do escrow accounts of natural persons. In addition, any nontransferable time deposit held in the name of a trustee or other fiduciary, whether a natural person or not, will be regarded as a personal time deposit if the entire beneficial interest is held by natural persons.

The board of governors also has determined that the term "time deposit" will also include, regardless of maturity, a promissory note, an acknowledgment of advance, or a similar obligation that is issued to any non-U.S. office (i.e., located outside the United States) of another depository institution or another foreign bank, or to institutions whose time deposits are exempt from interest rate limitations under Regulation Q.

Promissory notes (commercial paper), ineligible acceptances ("finance bills"), due bills, acknowledgments of advance, repurchase agreements against assets other than obligations of or fully guaranteed by the United States government, and funds supplied from nondepository affiliates are regarded as deposits. Generally, such obligations with original maturities of less than 14 days will be regarded as demand deposits and will be subject to the reserve requirement on transaction accounts. Those with maturities of 14 days or more will be regarded as nonpersonal time deposits, if transferable or held by a depositor other than a natural person.

Subordinated capital debt of member banks, however, is not regarded as a deposit subject to reserve requirements or interest rate limitations as long as certain conditions, including a minimum maturity of seven years or more, are met. Subordinated capital debt of thrift institutions is treated similarly.

An institution is required to maintain reserves against obligations issued by a nondepository affiliate if the proceeds of such obligations are channeled to the institution. An obligation issued by an affiliate of a depository institution will not be regarded as a deposit of the affiliated depository institution if the obligation has a maturity of four years or more or if the obligation would not have been a deposit had it been issued directly by the affiliated depository institution.

A due bill will not be treated as a reservable deposit if it is collateralized with a similar security within three days of issuance. A security is "similar" if it is of the same type and if its maturity is comparable to that of the obligation purchased by the customer. A due bill that remains uncollateralized after three business days is a deposit from that time forward.

Regulation D of the Board of Governors of the Federal Reserve System identifies as reservable net borrowings from related foreign offices, loans to United States residents made by overseas offices of depository institutions located in the United States, sales of assets by depository institutions in the United States to their overseas offices, and proceeds of sales to foreign branches of all assets. The legal reserve ratio established November 13, 1980, on Eurocurrency transactions is 3%.

The reserves of a depository institution may be held in the form of vault cash or a balance maintained at a Federal Reserve bank, either directly or indirectly on a passthrough basis. A depository institution that is a member of the Federal Reserve System must hold its required reserve balances directly with its Federal Reserve bank. A nonmember depository institution may either hold its required reserve balances directly with its Federal Reserve bank or pass its required reserve balances to the Federal Reserve bank through a correspondent. Such a correspondent may be a depository institution that holds a required reserve balance directly with the Federal Reserve, a Federal Home Loan bank, or the National Credit Union Administration Central Liquidity Facility.

The board of governors has the authority to specify the portion of vault cash that a depository institution may use to meet its reserve requirements. Regulation D permits a depository institution (since the initial reserve requirements were established under the Monetary Control Act of 1980 as of November 13, 1980) to use all of its vault cash as eligible reserve assets. Vault cash consists of United States currency and coin and does not include securities or earning assets of any type.

In an effort to reduce the reporting and reserve management burdens of very small depository institutions and to reduce the processing burden of the reserve banks, the Federal Reserve was requiring depository institutions with total deposits of less than $5 million to report their deposits for a seven-day computation period only once each calendar quarter, and to maintain reserves over the following three-month period based on such deposit reports.

The Federal Reserve Board extended through the end of 1982 the deferral of deposit reporting and reserve requirements for

RESERVE

Table 2 / Aggregate Reserves of Depository Institutions and Monetary Base
(Billions of dollars, averages of daily figures)

Item	1985 Dec.	1986 Dec.	1987 Dec.	1988 Dec.	1988 Oct.	1988 Nov.	1988 Dec.	1989 Jan.	1989 Feb.	1989 Mar.	1989 Apr.	1989 May
Adjusted for Changes in Reserve Requirements [2]					*Seasonally adjusted*							
1. Total reserves [3]	48.49	58.14	58.69	60.71	60.86	60.85	60.71	60.37	60.26	59.85	59.46	58.74
2. Nonborrowed reserves	47.17	57.31	57.92	58.99	58.56	57.99	58.99	58.71	58.77	58.04	57.17	57.02
3. Nonborrowed reserves plus extended credit [4]	47.67	57.62	58.40	60.23	60.34	60.31	60.23	59.75	59.82	59.38	58.88	58.22
4. Required reserves	47.44	56.77	57.66	59.67	59.80	59.73	59.67	59.23	59.11	58.90	58.69	57.71
5. Monetary base [5]	219.51	241.45	257.99	275.50	273.66	274.38	275.50	276.78	277.55	278.61	278.67	278.33
					Not seasonally adjusted							
6. Total reserves [3]	49.59	59.46	60.06	62.21	60.37	60.96	62.21	62.07	59.37	58.94	60.01	57.72
7. Nonborrowed reserves	48.27	58.64	59.28	60.50	58.07	58.10	60.50	60.40	57.88	57.13	57.72	56.00
8. Nonborrowed reserves plus extended credit [4]	48.77	58.94	59.76	61.74	59.85	60.42	61.74	61.45	58.93	58.46	59.43	57.20
9. Required reserves	48.53	58.09	59.03	61.17	59.31	59.84	61.17	60.92	58.22	57.98	59.23	56.69
10. Monetary base [5]	222.73	245.25	262.08	279.71	272.29	275.32	279.71	277.92	274.36	275.62	278.11	277.49
Not Adjusted for Changes in Reserve Requirements [6]												
11. Total reserves [3]	48.14	59.56	62.12	63.74	61.92	62.41	63.74	63.47	60.69	60.21	61.29	58.91
12. Nonborrowed reserves	46.82	58.73	61.35	62.02	59.62	59.55	62.02	61.81	59.21	58.40	59.00	57.19
13. Nonborrowed reserves plus extended credit [4]	47.32	59.04	61.83	63.27	61.40	61.87	63.27	62.85	60.26	59.73	60.71	58.39
14. Required reserves	47.08	58.19	61.09	62.70	60.85	61.29	62.70	62.32	59.54	59.25	60.51	57.88
15. Monetary base [5]	223.53	247.71	266.16	283.18	275.78	278.65	283.18	281.31	277.66	278.94	281.52	280.54

[1] Latest monthly and biweekly figures are available from the Board's H.3 (502) statistical release. Historical data and estimates of the impact on required reserves of changes in reserve requirements are available from the Monetary and Reserves Projections Section. Division of Monetary Affairs. Board of Governors of the Federal Reserve System, Washington, D.C. 20551.
[2] Figures incorporate adjustments for discontinuities associated with the implementation of the Monetary Control Act and other regulatory changes to reserve requirements. To adjust for discontinuities due to changes in reserve requirements on reservable nondeposit liabilities, the sum of such required reserves is subtracted from the actual series. Similarly, in adjusting for discontinuities in the monetary base, required clearing balances and adjustments to compensate for float also are subtracted from the actual series.
[3] Total reserves not adjusted for discontinuities consist of reserve balances with Federal Reserve Banks, which exclude required clearing balances and adjustments to compensate for float, plus vault cash held during the lagged computation period by institutions having required reserve balances at Federal Reserve Banks plus the amount of vault cash equal to required reserves during the maintenance period at institutions having no required reserve balances.
[4] Extended credit consists of borrowing at the discount window under the terms and conditions established for the extended credit program to help depository institutions deal with sustained liquidity pressures. Because there is not the same need to repay such borrowing promptly as there is with traditional short-term adjustment credit, the money market impact of extended credit is similar to that of nonborrowed reserves.
[5] The monetary base not adjusted for discontinuities consists of total reserves plus required clearing balances and adjustments to compensate for float at Federal Reserve Banks and the currency component of the money stock plus, for institutions not having required reserve balances, the excess of current vault cash over the amount applied to satisfy current reserve requirements. Currency and vault cash figures are measured over the weekly computation period ending Monday.
The seasonally adjusted monetary base consists of seasonally adjusted total reserves, which include excess reserves on a not seasonally adjusted basis, plus the seasonally adjusted currency component of the money stock and the remaining items seasonally adjusted as a whole.
[6] Reflects actual reserve requirements, including those on nondeposit liabilities, with no adjustments to eliminate the effects of discontinuities associated with implementation of the Monetary Control Act or other regulatory changes to reserve requirements.

Source: Federal Reserve Board of Governors.

nonmember depository institutions that had less than $2 million in total deposits as of December 31, 1979. The board acted to avoid burdening very small nonmember banks and thrift institutions with reporting and reserve maintenance requirements, in view of legislation pending as of May, 1982, that would give small depository institutions a permanent exemption.

State requirements: States have varying requirements with respect to legal reserves. A majority of the states distinguish between demand and time deposits and provide for a higher requirement on the former classification. The great majority also provide the option to the bank of keeping legal reserves against demand and time deposits with either depository banks or vault cash. Legal reserve requirements against demand deposits vary between 7% and 30% (the latter in a single instance), with a strong leaning toward 15%. Requirements against time deposits vary between 0% and 10%, with most requiring 5%. Variable legal reserve requirements against demand and time deposits within a statutory range of variation are found in 23 states and the District of Columbia. Geographic differentiation in legal reserve requirements is found in a decided minority of the states.

"Competition" in the level of legal reserve requirements between federal and state requirements might or might not be a factor influencing nonmembership of state-chartered banks in the Federal Reserve System, depending upon the materiality of the differential if any.

Other types of banking reserves: "Secondary reserves" are earning assets of unimpeachable quality and highest marketability, usually of short-term maturity, such as short-term government securities, bankers' acceptances, commercial paper, call loans, etc. Treasury bills are particularly used by banks for secondary reserve purposes. "Excess reserves" in banking are total assets eligible to satisfy legal reserves in excess of the legal reserve requirements.

Having the power to set reserve requirements gives the Federal Reserve an important tool that can be used to affect the money supply and the profitability of financial institutions. If it raises reserve requirements, the Fed reduces the amount of deposits that financial institutions can maintain, resulting in a decline in the supply of money. In addition, since reserve balances earn no interest, raising the level of required reserves lowers the profitability of depository institutions. Alternatively, a reduction in reserve requirements leads to an expansion of the money supply and an increase in the profitability of banking institutions.

Changing reserve requirements is such a powerful policy instrument and the effects of such changes are so profound that the Fed employs this instrument only very seldom. Instead, it normally uses its open-market operations to pursue its monetary objectives. The reserve requirement tool is brought into use only in real financial crises.

Some economists have suggested that reserve requirements be abolished altogether because of their deleterious effects on bank profitability. Others, like Milton Friedman, have argued for 100% reserve requirements, asserting that such requirements would give the Fed better control over the money supply. Both of these proposals are extreme and adoption of either appears remote.

International Monetary Usage. In international monetary terminology, the term "reserves" refers to the country's gold stock, including exchange stabilization fund, special drawing rights, holdings of foreign currencies, and reserve position available at the INTERNATIONAL MONETARY FUND.

The appended table shows aggregate reserves of depository institutions and monetary base, 1985 to 1989.

See BANK RESERVE, GOLD RESERVE, NAKED RESERVE, RESERVE RATIO.

BIBLIOGRAPHY

FEDERAL RESERVE BOARD OF GOVERNORS. *Annual reports.*
———. *Monetary Policy and Reserve Requirements.* Handbook.
———. *Federal Reserve Regulation Service.*
Federal Reserve Bulletin.

RESERVE AGENT Historically, another term for reserve depository (not to be confused with FEDERAL RESERVE AGENT). A state bank or trust company designated by a State Banking Department or a national bank located in a central reserve city or reserve city, which, with the approval of the Comptroller of the Currency, could act as a reserve depository for a portion of the legal reserve requirements of banks.

Prior to the establishment of the Federal Reserve System, national banks located in reserve cities were permitted to keep one-half of their legal reserve with reserve agent banks located in central reserve cities, and national banks located in other cities were permitted to keep three-fifths of their legal reserve with reserve agents located in either central reserve cities or reserve cities.

With the advent of the Federal Reserve System, the district Federal Reserve banks became the depositories for the legal reserve requirements of the member banks in their respective districts, with the amounts of the legal reserve requirements varying according to the location of the member banks in CENTRAL RESERVE CITIES, RESERVE CITIES, or other cities (so-called COUNTRY BANKS) within the Federal Reserve district.

Legal Reserve Depositories for Nonmember Institutions. Under the DEPOSITORY INSTITUTIONS DEREGULATION AND MONETARY CONTROL ACT OF 1980, Regulation D of the Board of Governors of the Federal Reserve System specifies that a nonmember of the Federal Reserve System required to maintain reserve balances ("respondent") may select only one institution to pass through ("passthrough rules") its required reserves. Eligible institutions through which a respondent's required reserve balances may be passed through ("correspondents") are Federal Home Loan banks, National Credit Union Administration Central Liquidity Facility, and depository institutions that maintain required reserve balances directly at a Federal Reserve bank office.

In addition, the Board of Governors of the Federal Reserve System reserves the right to permit other institutions, on a case-by-case basis, to serve as passthrough correspondents.

The correspondent chosen must subsequently pass through the required reserve balances of its respondents directly to the appropriate Federal Reserve bank office and be responsible for reserve account maintenance.

U.S. branches and agencies of foreign banks and Edge Act and agreement corporations may act as passthrough correspondents for any nonmember institution required to maintain reserves, or pass through their own required reserve balances through correspondents.

See RESERVE, RESERVE DEPOSITORY.

RESERVE BANK According to the Federal Reserve Act, a FEDERAL RESERVE BANK. Prior to creation of the FEDERAL RESERVE SYSTEM, national banks located in central reserve and reserve cities were called reserve banks.

RESERVE BANK OF INDIA The central bank of India, not to be confused with the STATE BANK OF INDIA. Established in 1935, the Reserve Bank of India has the mission "to regulate the issue of bank-notes and the keeping of reserves with a view to securing monetary stability. . . and generally to operate the currency and credit system of the country to its advantage." By statute, it is provided that the Reserve Bank of India will always hold a minimum of 55% of stock of the State Bank of India, which succeeded the Imperial Bank of India and is the institution designated to establish nationwide banking facilities by acquisition of other banking companies, especially state-associated banks, and extensive branch banking, particularly in rural and semirural areas.

RESERVE CITIES The Federal Reserve Act (Sec. 19) conferred upon the Board of Governors of the Federal Reserve System the power to classify or reclassify reserve and central reserve cities, or to terminate their designation as such, for the purpose of legal reserve requirements. In view of the amendment of Section 19 by P.L. 86-114 (July 28, 1959), changing the statutory range of variation in legal reserves and particularly providing for termination of the classification CENTRAL RESERVE CITIES on July 28, 1962, the board of governors as of February 10, 1960, suspended until further notice its triennial review of classification of central reserve and reserve cities.

At the time of the triennial designation of reserve cities effective March 1, 1957, five cities (Pueblo, Colorado; Kansas City, Kansas; Topeka, Kansas; Wichita, Kansas; and Toledo, Ohio) that did not fall within the standards of classification as reserve cities under the board's Rule for Classification of Reserve Cities were nevertheless continued as reserve cities at the request of member banks in those cities, as permitted by the rule in such circumstances.

Under the 1947 Rule, as then in effect, member banks in those cities were entitled to assume that they would have an opportunity to reconsider the situation at the time of the triennial review in 1960. In view of the board's suspension of triennial reviews and the seeming inequitableness of indefinitely continuing to classify cities as reserve cities against the wishes of member banks in those cities, the board's rule was amended to provide in such circumstances for termination of reserve city designation.

Such requests for termination were subsequently received and approved by the board of governors for termination of the reserve city designations of Kansas City, Kansas; Topeka, Kansas; and Wichita, Kansas.

Giving effect to elimination of the preceding cities as reserve cities, classification as of early 1960 was as follows:

1. Reserve cities are the city of Washington, D.C., and every city except New York and Chicago in which there is located a Federal Reserve bank or branch of a Federal Reserve bank. These cities are as follows:

Atlanta	Memphis
Baltimore	Minneapolis
Birmingham	Nashville
Boston	New Orleans
Buffalo	Oklahoma City
Charlotte	Omaha
Cincinnati	Philadelphia
Cleveland	Pittsburgh
Dallas	Portland
Denver	Richmond
Detroit	St. Louis
El Paso	Salt Lake City
Helena	San Antonio
Houston	San Francisco
Jacksonville	Seattle
Kansas City	
Little Rock	
Los Angeles	
Louisville	

2. Additional cities designated by the board of governors as reserve cities were as follows:

RESERVE DEPOSITORY

Columbus, Ohio
Des Moines, Iowa
Fort Worth, Texas
Indianapolis, Indiana
Miami, Florida
Milwaukee, Wisconsin
National City (National Stock Yards), Illinois
Pueblo, Colorado
St. Paul, Minnesota
Toledo, Ohio
Tulsa, Oklahoma

See RESERVE.

RESERVE DEPOSITORY A bank designated and authorized to act as depository for a portion of the legal reserves against deposits which other banks are required by law to maintain.

Every member bank of the Federal Reserve System is required to establish and maintain reserve balances against demand and time deposits as required by the Federal Reserve Act, partly in vault and partly with the Federal Reserve bank of its district.

Legal reserves against deposits of state banks are required by state laws to be kept in part on hand and in part with designated reserve depositories. The New York State Banking Law defines "reserve depository" as a banking corporation designated by the Superintendent of Banks as a depository for reserves on deposits. Section 106 of the Banking Law specifically provides that no bank or trust company shall deposit any of its funds with any other banking corporation or private banker unless such corporation or banker has been designated as a depository for the funds of the bank or trust company by a vote of the majority of the directors of the bank or trust company, exclusive of any director who is an officer, director, trustee, or partner of the depository designated. In any case where a banking corporation or private banker is so designated, a bank or trust company shall not deposit therewith an amount in excess of 25% of the capital stock, surplus fund, and undivided profits of such bank or trust company unless such other banking corporation or private banker is located within the State of New York and has been approved by the superintendent as a depository for the purpose of this section, in which case the amount so deposited may equal, but shall not exceed, 100% of the capital stock, surplus fund, and undivided profits of such bank or trust company. These restrictions do not apply to deposits that any New York State bank or trust company shall maintain with a Federal Reserve bank.

See RESERVE.

RESERVE FUND An asset in the form of cash, securities, or other specific assets which has been set aside for some particular purpose and has no accounting relation per se to the liability account "reserve." This accounting term is sometimes incorrectly used as synonymous with the accounting term RESERVE.

Some accountants establish the asset "reserve fund" for a particular purpose and at the same time earmark surplus by creating a "reserve" for the same purpose. Once the reserve fund has been applied to the purpose intended, however, the reserve on the liability side for the same purpose serves no useful function and should be closed out to general reserves or surplus.

In England, the term is equivalent to the U.S. term earned surplus. This account is created by retaining portions of the earnings in the business, instead of disbursing them as dividends.

RESERVE RATIO A short term for the full title "Federal Reserve Ratio of Reserves to Deposit and Federal Reserve Note Liabilities." This ratio appeared weekly in the published statement of each Federal Reserve bank and of the 12 Federal Reserve banks combined. The ratio was years ago regarded as an important barometer of credit conditions and money supply, but the Board of Governors of the Federal Reserve System pointed out that in general Federal Reserve credit policy was determined on the basis of the broad needs of the credit and business situation and not on the basis of variations in the reserve ratio. The varying conditions in the different Federal Reserve districts were shown by variations in the ratio of the individual Federal Reserve banks, while the consolidated ratio for all Federal Reserve banks showed the condition for the entire system.

The reserve ratio was the ratio of total reserves to deposits and Federal Reserve note liabilities combined. The Act of June 12, 1945 (59 Stat. 237) reduced the statutory reserve requirements of the Federal Reserve banks from 40% to 25% in gold certificates against deposits, and from 35% in gold certificates or lawful money to 25% in gold certificates against FEDERAL RESERVE NOTES in actual circulation. Subsequently, P.L. 89-3 (March 3, 1965) eliminated the requirement for the maintenance of reserves in gold certificates of not less than 25% against Federal Reserve bank deposit liabilities. Then P.L. 90-269 (March 18, 1968) eliminated the "gold cover" against Federal Reserve notes, i.e., maintenance by Federal Reserve banks of reserves in gold certificates of not less than 25% against Federal Reserve notes which could also be counted as part of the collateral behind such notes. Consequently, in analysis of Federal Reserve figures the reserve ratio is no longer statutorily relevant; nevertheless, it would be of interest to continue its calculation for comparative purposes.

Computation of Reserve Ratio. The table appended herewith compares the reserve ratio of the 12 Federal Reserve banks at the close of December each year since 1914 (such end-of-year date tends to see about the lowest ratios of the year because of the seasonal expansion at such a time of year in Federal Reserve notes circulation).

It is apparent that complete elimination of the reserve requirements was called for by the steady erosion in the reserve ratio since 1964. What would have happened, had the 25% reserve ratio requirement been continued in effect, was spelled out in the Federal Reserve Act as follows:

1. Under Section 11, Paragraph 4, of the Federal Reserve Act, the Board of Governors of the Federal Reserve System is authorized to suspend for a period not exceeding 30 days any reserve requirements specified in the act, and from time to time to renew such suspension for periods not exceeding 15 days. But such action would have been a short-time measure and would have proven embarrassing by its required repetition.

12 Federal Reserve Bank's Ratio of Gold, Gold Certificates, and Special Drawing Rights to Deposits and Federal Reserve Note Liabilities Combined

End of Year	Percent	End of Year	Percent
1948	100.3	1914	48.9
1949	94.1	1915	54.7
1950	81.4	1916	49.4
1951	59.1	1917	46.4
1952	48.0	1918	46.2
1953	39.6	1919	44.5
1954	43.3	1920	45.1
1955	70.2	1921	44.4
1956	72.5	1922	44.6
1957	75.3	1923	46.3
1958	73.0	1924	42.1
1959	69.0	1925	39.9
1960	71.4	1926	37.4
1961	66.4	1927	34.8
1962	63.3	1928	31.8
1963	69.6	1929	29.7
1964	73.7	1930	27.5
1965	66.5	1931	23.3
1966	62.9	1932	20.7
1967	63.8	1933	17.6
1968	70.8	1934	14.5
1969	77.6	1935	13.8
1970	80.1	1936	14.1
1971	79.9	1937	12.1
1972	83.7	1938	12.1
1973	86.7	1939	12.3
1974	90.8	1940	11.7
1975	90.8	1941	10.7
1976	76.3	1942	10.4
1977	62.6	1943	10.1
1978	49.0	1944	9.2
1979	41.7	1945	8.7
1980	43.5	1946	8.8
1981	48.3	1947	8.9

Source: Board of Governors of Federal Reserve System, *Banking and Monetary Statistics; Federal Resrve Bulletin.*

2. The same section and paragraph, however, as amended in 1945, required that if the reserve held against Federal Reserve notes should fall below 25%, the Board of Governors of the Federal Reserve System should establish a graduated tax of not more than 1% per annum upon such deficiency until the reserves fell to 20% per annum; and when the reserve should fall below 20%, tax at the rate increasingly of not less than 1.5% per annum upon each 2.5% or fraction thereof that such reserve should fall below 20% per annum. The tax would be paid by the Federal Reserve bank, but the Reserve bank should add an amount equal to said tax to the rates of interest and discount fixed by the Board of Governors of the Federal Reserve System. Thus, such deficiency would have acted upon the discount rate in an automatic fashion, regardless of the merits of such rise in the discount rate from a monetary policy standpoint.

Thus the issue would have been posed: automatic rules or discretionary management. The Congress by its successive lowering of the reserve ratio never allowed this "golden brake" to operate.

It might be noted that all of the U.S. gold stock has been "monetized" by the U.S. Treasury and is reflected in full in gold certificate holdings of the 12 Federal Reserve banks, which are included in the calculations. But the U.S. gold stock is carried at its statutory price of $42.22 per troy ounce, far below prevailing market prices for gold.
See GOLD RESERVE.
See FEDERAL RESERVE SYSTEM.

RESERVE REQUIREMENTS See RESERVE.

RESIDUARY DEVISEE A person to whom real property of an estate is devised in the residuary clause of a will after the specific devisees have received their shares. Real property is devised; personal property is bequeathed.
See DEVISE.

RESIDUARY LEGATEE A person named in the residuary clause of a will who shares in the distribution of the personal property of the testator, after the estate debts and expenses have been paid and the specific, demonstrative, and general legacies have been distributed.
See LEGACY.

RESISTANCE POINT The price level at which a stock in a declining market tends to stop, i.e., "resist" further selling, or a stock in an advancing market refuses to rise. Speculators who operate on the basis of charts take the former situation to mean that those familiar with the stock (insiders) regard the stock as intrinsically cheap at that price and are willing to support the market at that level by taking all that is offered. In the latter case, it is reasoned that the price "resists" further gains because those most familiar with the conditions behind the stock believe that the price is higher than is warranted by underlying conditions. It is by studying these "resistance points" in the market for individual stocks that some operators and chartists obtain their "signals" for market operations.

RESOLUTION TRUST CORPORATION A federal agency established by Congress to oversee the disposal of the assets of failed S&Ls in the wake of the thrift crisis of the 1980s. The Resolution Trust Corp. was created in August 1989 to clean up the leftovers of the thrift crisis of the 1980s resulting from mismanagement, miscalculation, greed, theft, deregulation, and adverse economic conditions. It has become the largest financial institution in the world.

The RTC was given a portfolio of $104 billion assets from the 262 failing S&Ls that federal regulators had seized since February 1989. The corporation was expected to close hundreds of additional S&Ls and eventually accumulate assets of over $400 billion. The RTC would attempt to sell to banks or other investors the healthy portions of savings institutions taken over, such as portfolios of home loans. Undesirable real estate and problem business ventures would be disposed of as the opportunity arose. Approximately $150 billion of assets were estimated to be in this category, including shopping centers, churches, and miscellaneous other assets. This made the RTC the largest real estate owner and manager in history. Money received from the sale of assets would help the government recoup part of the cost of funds expended on supporting the federal deposit insurance program that guaranteed deposits up to $100,000 relating to failing thrifts.

The legislation establishing the RTC listed six economically distressed states where the RTC could not sell property for less than 95% of market value: Arkansas, Colorado, Louisiana, New Mexico, Oklahoma, and Texas. This provision was to avoid depressing the real estate market in these states and giving away assets at unrealistic prices.

President Bush named an oversight board consisting of Treasury Secretary Nicholas F. Brady, Federal Reserve Board Chairman Alan Greenspan, Secretary of Housing and Urban Development Jack Kemp, and two private citizens. Day-to-day operations of the agency are directed by L. William Seidman, chairman of the Federal Deposit Insurance Corporation. The FDIC supplies the personnel for the RTC. Additional employees are recruited from subcontractors as property managers, disposal experts, sales agents, auctioneers, and others.

The agency was required to prepare and publish an inventory of its properties by January 1990. The RTC was expected to first attempt to sell seized S&Ls to healthy thrifts and banks that would be interested in expanding their branches and deposits. Where available real estate and investments were of questionable or junk value, the RTC would attempt to dispose of such items before attempting to sell an S&L.

The RTC was assigned the mission of disposing of the properties assigned to it by December 31, 1996, the date it is scheduled to complete its mission. This schedule seemed also impossible to meet.

RESPONDENTIA An instrument by which the master of a ship pledges its cargo as security for money borrowed in order that necessary repairs may be made at a foreign port.
See BOTTOMRY BOND.

RESPONSIBILITY ACCOUNTING Responsibility accounting focuses on the collection of data to place responsibility for cost incurrence on managers to achieve cost control. The emphasis is on people who incurred the costs. Responsibility accounting is also referred to as profit-centered accounting and performance reporting.

Responsibility accounting is based on these assumptions:

1. All spending can be controlled.
2. Responsibility for spending must be assigned and assigned fairly.

Assigning responsibility in an organization requires that authority to act be clearly assigned. When responsibilities are assigned, commensurate authority to carry out those responsibilities also must be assigned. These relationships are usually presented in the organizational chart and the chart of accounts. The organizational chart should reflect a plan of organization that provides an appropriate segregation of functional responsibilities. Accounting reports should be prepared to summarize the performance of each responsibility center. Such reports should include only those items over which the center has control.

Responsibility accounting requires that costs be collected by responsibility centers so that individuals assigned responsibilities can receive appropriate performance reports. Management practice has accepted four major types of responsibility centers:

1. Expense (or cost center: an organizational unit that is held accountable for the incurring of expense).
2. Revenue center: an organizational unit that is held accountable only for revenue.
3. Profit center: an organizational unit that is held accountable for revenue and expense.
4. Investment center: an organizational unit whose management is held accountable for attaining a satisfactory rate of return on capital.

BIBLIOGRAPHY

MILLER, E. L., *Responsibility Accounting and Performance Evaluations* (Van Nostrand Reinhold, Florence, KY., 1982).

REST A title given to the surplus account that appears in the published statement of the Bank of England. Elsewhere in English

Responsibility Accounting Reports

RESPONSIBLE COMPANY
Assembly Shop A
Foreman Report
March 31, 19X1

Expense	Budget This Mo.	Budget Year to Date	Actual This Mo.	Actual Year to Date	Variances Favorable/(Unfavorable) This Mo.	Variances Favorable/(Unfavorable) Year to Date
Direct material	$ 15,000	$ 45,000	$ 16,000	$ 50,000	$ (1,000)	$ (5,000)
Direct labor	30,000	90,000	25,000	80,000	5,000	10,000
Supplies	5,000	10,000	5,500	12,000	(500)	(2,000)
Other	100,000	250,000	90,000	295,000	10,000	(45,000)
	$150,000	$395,000	$136,500	$437,000	$13,500	$(42,000)

RESPONSIBLE COMPANY
Plant Superintendent: Plant 1
Plant Expense Report
March 31, 19X1

Expense	Budget This Mo.	Budget Year to Date	Actual This Mo.	Actual Year to Date	Variances Favorable/(Unfavorable) This Mo.	Variances Favorable/(Unfavorable) Year to Date
Assembly Shop A	$150,000	$ 395,000	$136,500	$ 437,000	$13,500	$(42,000)
Assembly Shop B						
Assembly Shop C			(Details omitted)			
Assembly Shop D						
Superintendent's office						
	$500,000	$1,300,000	$490,000	$1,280,000	$10,000	$ 20,000

RESPONSIBLE COMPANY
Vice-President Manufacturing
Expense Report
March 31, 19X1

Expense	Budget This Mo.	Budget Year to Date	Actual This Mo.	Actual Year to Date	Variances Favorable/(Unfavorable) This Mo.	Variances Favorable/(Unfavorable) Year to Date
Plant No. 1	$ 500,000	$1,300,000	$ 490,000	$1,280,000	$ 10,000	$ 20,000
Plant No. 2						
Plant No. 3			(Details omitted)			
Vice-President's office						
	$3,000,000	$9,300,000	$3,100,000	$9,500,000	$(100,000)	$(200,000)

RESPONSIBLE COMPANY
President
Expense Report
March 31, 19X1

Department	Budget This Mo.	Budget Year to Date	Actual This Mo.	Actual Year to Date	Variances Favorable/(Unfavorable) This Mo.	Variances Favorable/(Unfavorable) Year to Date
Manufacturing	$3,000,000	$ 9,300,000	$3,100,000	$ 9,500,000	$(100,000)	$(200,000)
Purchasing						
Sales						
Treasurer			(Details omitted)			
Controller						
President's office						
	$9,000,000	$27,700,000	$9,500,000	$28,300,000	$(500,000)	$(600,000)

bank accounting, this account is entitled "reserve fund" and corresponds to the combined surplus and undivided profits accounts in U.S. bank accounting practice.

RESTRICTIVE ENDORSEMENT Any endorsement that results in the endorsee becoming an agent or trustee for the endorser. An example is "Pay A for collection." Such an endorsement prohibits the further negotiation of the negotiable instrument.

RESULTING TRUST In the law of trusts, a TRUST that will be held to arise as a matter of law as the result of the acts of the parties, regardless of any actual intent by them to create an express trust. For example, a resulting trust will be held to arise where one party transfers property under such facts and circumstances that the inference arises that such conveyor does not intend that the transferee and holder of the legal title thereto shall enjoy the beneficial interest therein. Resulting trusts are to be distinguished from constructive trusts; in the latter, a trust "implied in law" will be held to arise where a court of equity, in order to prevent injustice, will charge the holder of the legal title with a duty to convey it to another person.

See TRUST COMPANY.

RESUMPTION OF SPECIE PAYMENTS See SPECIE PAYMENT.

RETAIL REPURCHASE AGREEMENTS The "sale" by a financial institution to a customer of an interest in U.S. government or federal agency securities, in a denomination of less than $100,000, with an agreement by the institution to "repurchase" the interest at a date not more than 89 days in the future, with interest. The development of this new form of bank "liability management" is of regulatory interest to banks as well as the "thrift" institutions (savings and loan associations and mutual savings banks especially, as institutions particularly affected by DISINTERMEDIATION in recent years).

During 1981, the Securities and Corporate Practices Division of the Office of the Comptroller of the Currency, in conjunction with the Chief National Bank Examiner's Office, developed guidelines for national banks using retail repurchase agreements (repos). These guidelines, which were contained in OCC Banking Circular No. 157, addressed a number of banking and securities law issues and supervisory concerns raised by retail repo programs. The division also provided assistance to the staff of the SECURITIES AND EXCHANGE COMMISSION in connection with an SEC release regarding the status of retail repo programs under the statutes administered by the SEC.

If banks and thrift institutions follow the guidelines issued by the regulatory agencies as to " in particular, each United States security should be specifically matched as security for a particular group of Repurchase Agreements" (Home Loan Bank Board Guideline, supra), investors in retail repos will be perfected in their security interest.

See REPURCHASE AGREEMENTS.

RETAIL SALES Retail sales *trend* is noted for evidence of consumer sentiment and consumer buying. Consumer *expectations* (consumer buying intentions) are the subject of regularly published surveys of such intentions conducted by the Bureau of the Census, based on methodology developed by the Bureau of the Census and National Bureau of Economic Research and available quarterly in "Consumer Buying Intentions" (Series P-65 in Current Population Reports of the Bureau of the Census). The Board of Governors of the Federal Reserve System also publishes regularly in the *Federal Reserve Bulletin* an index of total retail sales (1967 = 100), based on Census Bureau figures. See appended table for retail sales 1955-1987. The data indicate a dynamic growth trend, reflecting growth in physical volume as well as the effects of price inflation.

RETAINED EARNINGS Earnings of a corporation that have not been distributed in the form of dividends. The major factors that affect retained earnings include:

1. Net income or loss, including income (loss) from continuing operations, discontinued operations, extraordinary gains or losses, and the cumulative effects of changes in accounting principles.
2. Dividends (cash, property, script, stock, liquidating).
3. Prior period adjustments, primarily the correction of errors of prior periods.
4. Appropriations of retained earnings (legal, contractual, and discretionary).

A deficit is a negative retained earnings balance. A deficit is usually the result of accumulated prior net losses or dividends in excess of earnings.

RETIREMENT The paying off of an obligation at maturity or prior thereto. The term is practically synonymous with redemption and may be used in connection with bonds, notes, acceptances, or paper money (promises to pay) issued by the government or by Federal Reserve or national banks. When bonds are subject to redemption, optional retirement is provided (see CALLABLE BONDS). When paper money is retired, it is withdrawn from circulation and canceled.

RETREAT A stock market expression used by financial writers to indicate a general decline in security values.

RETURN This term has two usages:

1. The current return or YIELD on bond or stock as found by dividing the price into the annual dividend or interest payment.
2. An exhibit of banking statistics, such as a combined statement of assets and liabilities of a clearinghouse association.

In England, a bank statement of condition or balance sheet is called a bank return—for example, return of the Bank of England.

See BANK OF ENGLAND RETURN.

Kind of business	1986	1987
Retail trade, total	$1,437,497	$1,510,579
Durable goods, total	538,618	559,105
Automotive dealers	320,338	326,850
Motor vehicle, other miscellaneous automotive dealers	294,445	299,838
Auto and home supply stores	25,891	27,012
Furniture, home furnishings, equipment stores	80,374	84,148
Furniture, home furnishings stores	41,947	44,210
Household appliance, radio, and TV stores	33,290	34,462
Building materials, hardware, garden supply, and mobile home dealers	75,874	78,005
Building materials and supply stores	66,402	71,983
Hardware stores	12,335	14,095
Nondurable goods stores, total	898,879	951,474
Apparel and accessory stores	74,765	79,069
Men's, boys clothing, furnishings	8,980	9,049
Women's clothing, specialty stores, furriers	29,663	31,171
Shoe stores	13,433	14,586
Food stores	301,762	314,287
Grocery stores	284,126	296,105
General merchandise group stores	165,074	175,885
Department stores	137,316	146,520
Variety stores	8,276	8,438
Eating and drinking places	135,308	147,645
Restaurants, lunchrooms, cafe	73,483	80,990
Drinking places	11,665	12,512
Gasoline service stations	97,277	103,154
Drug stores	51,631	56,000
Liquor stores	19,635	19,506

Total retail stores sales (*millions of dollars*)—(1955) 183,851; (1958) 200,353; (1959) 215,413; (1960) 201,529; (1961) 218,992; (1962) 235,563; (1963) 246,666; (1964) 261,870; (1965) 284,128; (1966) 303,956; (1967) 292,956; (1968) 324,358; (1969) 346,717; (1970) 368,403; (1971) 406,234; (1972) 449,069; (1973) 509,538; (1974) 540,988; (1975) 588,146; (1976) 657,375; (1977) 725,212; (1978) 806,773; (1979) 899,116; (1980) 959,561; (1981) 1,041,327; (1982) 1,072,100; (1983) 1,174,298; (1984) 1,289,373; (1985) 1,379,626.

Source: Bureau of the Census, U.S. Department of Commerce.

RETURNED ITEMS Checks, or other demand or matured items, returned by a drawee bank to the presenting bank because of certain technical IRREGULARITIES or invalidities which might involve the drawee bank in a loss if the items were accepted. They are returned so that the presenting bank may correct the defect or take such other action as may be necessary.

RETURN ON INVESTMENT (ROI) A comprehensive measure of financial performance. The basic formula for computing return on investment involves the following:

$$\text{ROI} = \text{Capital turnover} \times \text{Margin as a percentage of sales}$$

$$= \frac{\text{Sales}}{\text{Capital employed}} \times \frac{\text{Net income}}{\text{Sales}}$$

The relationship of ROI to balance sheet and income statement items is shown in the appended exhibit. Note that ROI is computed in this exhibit as follows:

$$\text{ROI} = \text{Turnover} \times \text{Earning Ratio}$$

where

$$\text{Turnover} = \frac{\text{Sales}}{\text{Capital employed}}$$

$$\text{Earning ratio (or margin)} = \frac{\text{Net income}}{\text{Sales}}$$

Capital turnover is the ratio of sales to capital employed in generating the sales. Capital turnover is a measure of the use of assets in relation to sales. Generally, the larger the volume of sales that management can generate on a given investment in assets, the more efficient are its operations. Margin is the ratio of net income to sales.

Capital employed can be interpreted to mean total assets, total assets less current liabilities (that is, working capital plus noncurrent assets), or stockholders' equity. When management performance is being evaluated, either the first or second concept of capital employed should be used because management should be held responsible for assets available to them. When stockholders' equity is used as the measure of capital employed, the analysis stresses the long-range ability of the firm to make use of the investments of its owners.

The ROI formula takes into account all of the items that go into the balance sheet and income statement and so represents a comprehensive overview of performance. The appended exhibit shows a structural outline of the relationships that make up ROI.

The following various actions can be taken to improve ROI:

1. Increase total sales by increasing volume, sales price, or some combination thereof, while maintaining or improving the margin on sales.
2. Decrease expenses, thereby increasing net income.
3. Reduce the amount of capital employed (for example, reduce the inventory level, improve collection of accounts receivable) without decreasing sales.

Advantages claimed for ROI analysis include the following:

1. Focuses management's attention upon earning the best return on total assets.
2. Serves as a measure of management's efficiency and effectiveness.
3. Integrates financial planning, budgeting, sales objectives, cost control, and profit-making activities.
4. Provides a basis for comparing companies.
5. Provides a motivational basis for management.
6. Identifies weaknesses in the utilization of assets.

BIBLIOGRAPHY

WOELFEL, C. J., and MECIMORE, C., *The Operating Executive's Handbook of Profit Planning Tools and Techniques* (Probus, Chicago, IL, 1986).

RETURN REMITTANCE A check forwarded by a bank acting as collection agent or correspondent, in payment of the proceeds of check previously forwarded by, and collected for, an out-of-town bank with whom arrangements for collection have been established. The letter accompanying the return remittance lists the collected checks and is known as a remittance letter.

See REMITTANCE ACCOUNT.

REVENUE For accounting purposes, actual or expected cash inflows (or the equivalent) that have occurred or will eventually occur as a result of the enterprise's ongoing major or central operations during the period. Gains are not revenue. Gains are increases in equity (net assets) from peripheral or incidental transactions of an entity and from all other transactions and other events and circumstances affecting the entity during a period except those that result from revenues or investments by owners.

Accounting revenue arises primarily from one or more of the following activities:

1. Selling products.
2. Rendering services.
3. Permitting others to use the entity's assets (leasing, renting, lending).
4. Disposing of assets other than products.

Return on Investment (ROI) Relationships

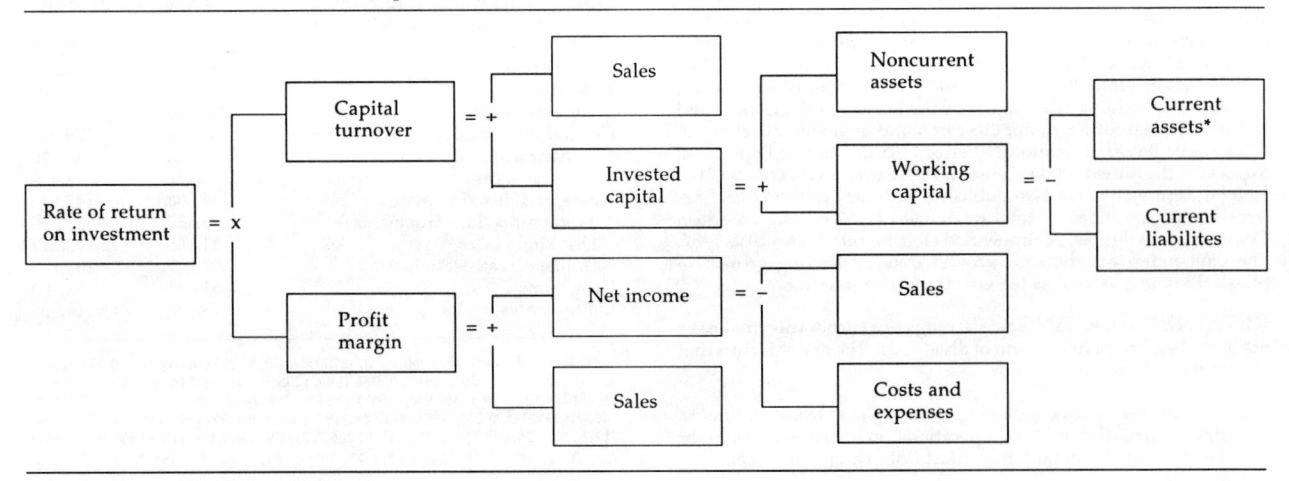

Rate of return on investment = Capital turnover × Profit margin

Capital turnover = Sales ÷ Invested capital

Profit margin = Net income ÷ Sales

Invested capital = Noncurrent assets + Working capital

Net income = Sales − Costs and expenses

Working capital = Current assets* − Current liabilities

* Includes cash, accounts receivable, and inventory

Revenues are generally realized when the earning process is complete or virtually complete, and an exchange has taken place. The earning process consists of all those activities that produce revenue, including purchasing, producing, selling, delivering, administering, and others.

RECOGNITION is the process of formally recording an item in the financial statements of an entity. Revenue is usually recognized at the time a product has been sold or when services have been rendered. Revenue is sometimes recognized before the point of sale. For example, the percentage-of-completion method is sometimes used to recognize revenue from long-term construction contracts based on the progress of the construction.

Some long-term service contracts recognize revenue on the basis of proportional performance. Revenue is sometimes recognized after the point of sale where there is great uncertainty about the collectability of the receivable involved in a sale. Under such circumstances, revenue can be recognized on the installment method or cost recovery method when cash is collected. Under the installment method, a proportion of gross profit on the sale is recognized with each cash collection. Under the cost recovery method, gross profit is not recorded until the full cost of the item sold is recovered.

Revenue from service transactions should be recognized on the basis of the seller's performance of the transaction. Service industries include engineering, legal services, management consulting, medical, mortgage banking, accounting, architecture, and many others. Performance is the execution of a defined act (or acts) that occurs with the passage of time. Four different methods of accounting for revenues on service transactions have been proposed: specific performance method (at the time the act takes place), completed performance method, proportional performance method (in proportion to the performance of each act when more than one act is required), and the collection method (when a significant degree of uncertainty surrounding the collectability of service revenue exists).

Funds raised by a government for public purposes and consisting of taxes, including direct taxes and excises, licenses, fees, special assessments, fines, etc. are considered governmental revenue; income from publicly owned and operated projects or services; and miscellaneous receipts, such as proceeds of sale of publicly owned properties, interest on government funds, etc. Revenues are further classified as to INTERNAL REVENUE and customs duties or other foreign-derived revenues.

Proceeds from loans or borrowing are not classified as revenue, as although they add to current receipts, they also give rise to concurrent borrowing liabilities.

BIBLIOGRAPHY

SFAC No. 3, *Elements of Financial Statements of Business Enterprises* (FASB, 1981).
SFAC No. 5, *Recognition and Measurement in Financial Statements of Business Enterprises* (FASB, 1984).

REVENUE ACT Any fiscal legislation concerned with the raising of public revenues and containing tax provisions. The Internal Revenue Code of 1939 brought together all current revenue acts and other laws pertaining to internal revenue, codifying them in an orderly manner. The Internal Revenue Code of 1954 went further, overhauling the tax laws, changing the arrangement and content of provisions of the 1939 code, and containing new substantive provisions. Between the enactment of the 1939 code and that of the 1954 code, there were at least 21 revenue acts or other laws passed pertaining to federal internal revenues, and since enactment of the 1954 code, additional legislation has been enacted from time to time, amending specific provisions of the code. The 1954 code, however, still stands as a basic collection of features, since further developed, pertaining to internal revenue which deserve historical review. Its principal structural changes were summed up by the U.S. Treasury as follows:

1. *Depreciation.* Computation of depreciation was permitted under the declining balance method at twice the straight-line rate. The Treasury characterized this as conforming more closely to "true" depreciation, since about two-thirds of the depreciable cost under this method is written off during the first half of the asset's life, as compared with only one-half under the straight-line formula. The sum-of-the-digits method was also authorized (actually, for accelerated depreciation, the decreasing charges variant of the sum-of-the-digits method), which in some respects is more liberal than the 200% declining balance method. Any other consistent method was also allowed, as long as it would not produce larger deductions than those allowable under the 200% declining balance method during the first two-thirds of the useful life of the asset.

(The 200% declining balance method and sum-of-the-digits method of computing depreciation, by bunching most of the depreciation in the earlier years of useful life of the asset, such as plant, machinery, and other equipment, might appeal more to firms than the straight-line method (1) to save taxes in those years if rates are high; (2) to increase retained cash earnings, since depreciation is a noncash expense; and (3) to stimulate more frequent replacement of assets and increased investment in capital goods, since there is nothing to prevent a firm, having already taken most of the depreciation under the accelerated methods, from trading in machinery and equipment for new models, especially if the latter incorporate major improvements in technology, without waiting for expiration of the full estimated useful life of the original asset.)

2. *Double taxation of dividends.* Under the code, each stockholder was permitted to exclude from his gross income up to $50 of dividends and was allowed a credit against tax equal to 4% of the dividends in excess of the exclusion. The amount of the credit was limited to 2% of the stockholder's total taxable income in 1954, and to 4% in later years.

(This was merely token relief from "double taxation" of stockholders, i.e., the corporations in whose stock they invest pay income taxes on all net income, and then the stockholders individually have to pay taxes on dividends received from the corporations. Investment companies [see INVESTMENT COMPANY] have achieved tax-freedom under specified conditions.)

3. *Research and experimental expenditures.* The new code gave all taxpayers the option to deduct such expenses currently or to "capitalize" them and write them off over a period of not less than five years.

4. *Carryback of operating losses.* The period for the carryback of losses was extended from one to two years, thus providing, in combination with the five-year carryforward, a total span of eight years for absorbing losses.

5. *Tax on unreasonable accumulation of surplus.* Instead of requiring a showing of an immediate and specific need for retained earnings, the 1954 code required the taxpayer to show only that the retained earnings were necessary to meet "reasonably anticipated" business requirements. An accumulation of $60,000 could be made without threat of penalty (a concession to "small business"); and the tax, when imposed, was applied only to the portion of the retained earnings found to be unreasonable.

6. *"Preferred stock bail-outs."* The code taxed as ordinary income the proceeds of the sale or redemption of preferred stock acquired through distributions by a corporation to common stockholders as nontaxable stock dividends in preferred stock and later redeemed.

7. *Net operating loss carryovers.* As a means of reducing the trafficking in "tax-loss corporations," the code eliminated the carryover when more than 50% of the stock of the loss corporation was purchased by new owners within a two-year period and the loss corporation thereafter did not continue in the same business.

8. *"Collapsible" corporations and partnerships.* The code tightened the provisions applicable to such corporations, formed and liquidated for the purpose of converting ordinary income tax liability into capital gains tax and imposed restrictions on collapsible partnerships.

Tax Reform Act of 1969. The Tax Reform Act of 1969 (December 30, 1969) was termed "one of the most sweeping and complex since the adoption of the income tax in 1913." The sweeping coverage of the act is indicated by the following summary of some of the topics covered:

1. *Rate reductions for individuals.* The act provided for overall rate reductions for individuals, primarily those in the lower tax brackets, involving an estimated $1.4 billion in 1970 and rising to $9.1 billion for 1974. Techniques for such reductions included increasing the personal exemption and credit for dependents (raising the per person allowance from $600 to $625 in 1970,

$650 in 1971, $700 in 1972, and $750 in 1973 and thereafter) and raising the standard deduction from 10% ($1,000 maximum) to 13% ($1,500 maximum) in 1971, 14% ($2,000 maximum) in 1972, and 15% ($2,000 maximum) in 1973 and subsequent years.

2. *Low-income allowance.* The administration in April, 1969, recommended a low-income allowance designed to relieve persons and families with incomes below the "poverty level" (as defined by the Department of Health, Education and Welfare) from any tax liability. As enacted, the low-income allowance replaced the minimum standard deduction of $300 plus $100 per dependent. The allowance, set for 1970 at $1,100, was phased out completely for a family of four as its income rose to $4,500, and for 1970 was automatically taken into consideration in the tax tables for taxpayers. For 1971 the allowance was $1,050, phased out more gradually, and for subsequent years was $1,000.

3. *Single persons.* One of the "horizontal inequities" in the federal income tax had been the disproportionately high tax burden on single persons in relation to that of married persons who enjoy the benefits of income splitting. The act provided a new schedule of rates for single persons which limited the tax thereon to not over 120% of the tax on joint returns with same taxable incomes.

4. *Earned income rate limitation.* The administration strongly supported the concept of a maximum tax rate on earned income, so as to provide a strong incentive to the earning of income by personal services, both by employees and by self-employed persons, and, by contrast, to minimize resort to the devices for conversion of ordinary income into capital gains and for deferment of income in order to avoid the burden of very high bracket rates. The marginal top rate on earned income (wages, salaries, professional income, and up to 30% of profits from trade or business) was made 60% for 1971 and 50% for subsequent years.

5. *Minimum tax on tax preference income.* On the other hand, the act provided for a new concept, the minimum tax (10%) on "tax preference income." Previous tax code imposed no limit on the amount of economic income that an individual could exclude from taxes through preferential treatment provided in various provisions of the code. These preferences were intended to be incentives to investment, but they contained no adequate limits on their use. Thus, in recent years many high-bracket individual taxpayers had used these preferences alone or in combination so as to pay little or no taxes. The new minimum tax of 10% on tax preference income was computed on the net tax preference income after deduction from such income of the regular federal income tax and $30,000 (or, in the case of married persons filing separate returns, $15,000 on each). Among the tax preference income types were included (1) half of net long-term capital gains (excess over net short-term capital losses) for individuals; (2) 37.5% of such net long-term capital gains for corporations; (3) the excess of percentage depletion over cost depletion; (4) the excess of accelerated depreciation or rapid amortization over straight-line depreciation on real property, or personal property subject to net leasing, or pollution control facilities, or railroad rolling stock, or rehabilitation expenditures; (5) the excess of interest on debt, incurred by individuals to purchase or carry investment assets, over net investment income reported in ordinary income; (6) in the case of financial institutions, bad debts deducted in excess of the actual average past loss experience; and (7) in the case of stock options, the difference between the option price and the fair market value of the stock at the time the option is exercised by the holder.

6. *Income averaging.* The act substantially liberalized the income averaging provisions, so that averaging would be available whenever income exceeded by $3,000 120% (formerly 133 $1/3$%) of the base period (average of four preceding years). Those resorting to income averaging, however, would not be entitled to the new earned income rate limitation, or the alternative capital gains rate.

7. *Charitable contributions.* The act provided for an increase generally in the limitation on the charitable contributions deduction from 30% to 50% of adjusted gross income, for gifts to churches, educational institutions, and publicly supported charities, as recommended by the administration. But for specified cases, the formerly allowed unlimited charitable deductions were discontinued for the years subsequent to 1974. And in order to limit some of the present tax advantages of gifts of appreciated property in particular cases, the act provided that in specified situations charitable contributions of appreciated property had to include any capital gains over purchase price or other basis, in gross income; in such situations taking capital gains into account, half of the long-term capital gains involved would not be included in deductions.

8. *Alternative capital gains tax for individuals.* For individuals, the alternative capital gains tax included in its computation the 25% ceiling rate on the first $50,000 of net long-term capital gains. On net long-term capital gains of over $50,000, the effect of the computation was to tax the first $50,000 of net long-term capital gains at 25% and the balance of the gains at higher rates (for higher tax brackets, rates on capital gains over $50,000 rose to 29.5% for 1970, 32.5% for 1971, and 35% for 1972 and later years). Prior to January 1, 1970, both short-term and long-term capital *losses* were considered at 100% in arriving at the limited capital loss allowance; but beginning January 1, 1970, only 50% of net long-term capital loss could be used (e.g., $2,000 of net long-term capital losses would be needed to result in a $1,000 deduction), the maximum allowable capital loss deduction being $1,000.

9. *Farm losses.* The administration's studies had demonstrated that large farm losses generally represented capital expenditures which had been deducted under the liberal cash method of accounting. The cash method of accounting had been allowed to farmers primarily to help small farmers, but taxpayers with large farm losses generally turned out to be wealthy investors obtaining a "tax shelter." Accordingly, the act required taxpayers having a farm loss of over $25,000 for a year and adjusted gross income from nonfarm sources of $50,000 and over to maintain an "excess deductions account" (EDA) for farm losses of over $25,000. On any subsequent sale of the farm property, any gain—to the extent it would otherwise be taxed as a long-term capital gain—would be treated as ordinary income to the extent of the net balance in the EDA (net after deduction of any net ordinary farm income in any years from the accumulated farm losses).

10. Among other provisions affecting individuals were provisions liberalizing types of expenses allowable as deduction for employee moving expenses, although the distance test for such deduction was lengthened from 20 to 50 miles, and disallowing deductibility of losses in a business not operated for a profit ("hobby losses").

Besides various of the preceding provisions applicable, the act contained the following provisions affecting business:

1. *Repeal of the 7% investment tax credit.* The act provided for repeal of the 7% investment tax credit effective as of April 18, 1969 (with transitional provisions similar to those employed when the credit was suspended in 1966). (The investment tax credit has since bounced back into the revenue acts in modified forms.)

2. *Liberalized amortization.* On the other hand, amortization provisions were extended as follows: (1) amortization of water or air pollution control facilities over 60 months, if installed before January, 1975, to plants in operation December 31, 1968, and pertaining to proportion of cost for first 15 years of normal useful life; (2) amortization option extended to railroads for rolling stock over a 5-year period, as well as for gradings and tunnel borings over a 50-year basis, all subject to specified limitations; and (3) amortization option, instead of depreciation, over five years for safety equipment in coal mines.

3. *Restricted real estate depreciation.* The administration then felt that there was unduly heavy reliance on tax incentives as a means of achieving national housing goals, and the act's restrictions reflected this policy. Accelerated depreciation methods (double declining balance and sum-of-the-years'-digits) were eliminated for new commercial, industrial, and other nonresidential buildings; such accelerated depreciation methods, however, were still allowed for new rental housing. Accelerated depreciation for other new real estate was restricted to the 150% declining balance method, and old buildings could be depreciated only on the straight-line basis, except for provision for the 125% declining balance method in the case of used residential real estate with over 20 years' useful life. Still, capital expenditures to rehabilitate low-cost rental housing,

made through 1974, could be amortized over a five-year period. Moreover, the act amended the recapture provisions of the code to deny long-term capital gains treatment on the sale of real estate to the extent of all depreciation claimed in excess of straight-line, except for residential housing, on which the amount subject to recapture is marked down by one percentage point per month after one hundred full months of holding the property; and also except for specified federally assisted projects and other limited-return publicly assisted housing, on which the prior more favorable recapture provisions were continued.

4. *Tax-free corporate dividends.* Under prior provisions, a cash dividend was a distribution out of earnings and profits, so that a dividend exceeding the earnings and profits was treated as a return of capital (i.e., tax-free, although serving to mark down cost basis). In the view of the administration, through the use of accelerated depreciation, many companies, especially in the utility and real estate fields, were able to distribute "substantial" amounts to shareholders without current tax to the shareholders. Accordingly, the act provided that for tax years beginning after June 30, 1972, companies were required to compute earnings and profits by using only the straight-line method of depreciation for the purpose of determining such taxability.

5. *Allowances on natural resources.* The act reduced the percentage-depletion rates from 27.5% to 22% (of gross income) for gas and oil wells, with the limitation remaining that depletion allowance should not be over 50% of net income, and made reductions in depletion allowances (generally by one percentage point) for other minerals. The administration did not recommend the reductions but did not oppose them. On the other hand, the act extended the depletion allowance to any minerals (except salt and water) extracted from any perennial saline lake in the U.S. However, deductions for mining exploration expenditures made after 1969 would be subject to recapture upon the mine's reaching the production stage, and the act treated mineral production payments as loan transactions or sale of property subject to mortgage, thus putting an end to previous tax benefits of such "carved out" production payments.

6. *Restricted depreciation for regulated utilities.* Regulated public utility companies, explained the Treasury Department, generally account for depreciation on a straight-line basis for rate-making purposes. Where accelerated depreciation is taken for tax purposes, therefore, the actual federal tax paid is lower than the tax liability that would result from straight-line depreciation taken for rate-making purposes. Some regulatory commissions permit their regulated utilities to "normalize" their tax for rate-making purposes, i.e., they treat as a cost the tax that would have been imposed if straight-line depreciation had been used and treat the difference between this amount and the actual tax as a reserve for future taxes. Other regulatory commissions require their regulated companies to include in current costs of operations only the actual tax paid, with the result that the tax reduction due to accelerated depreciation is "flowed through" to the customers as a reduction in rates, thus further reducing profits and income tax revenues. At the time of introduction of the 1969 tax act bill, many regulatory commissions were switching from normalization to flow-through, and others were even imputing the use of accelerated depreciation where the utility in fact was using straight-line depreciation for tax purposes. This trend would have forced utilities to switch to accelerated depreciation for tax purposes, and the "flow-through" would have had a double effect in reducing tax revenues, in the Treasury's view, since it would have resulted in a reduction in utility gross revenues as well.

Thus the Treasury supported the act's prohibition on extension of "flow-through," i.e., utility companies (electric, telephone, gas pipeline, steam transporters, "Comsat," water supply companies) were limited for tax purposes to straight-line depreciation unless the regulatory commission concerned permitted the company to use accelerated depreciation and normalize its tax reduction resulting therefrom.

7. *Taxability of stock dividends.* Distribution of common stock dividends on common stock does not normally represent a taxable event to the shareholder, since the shareholder simply receives additional shares to represent the same unchanged equity interest in the corporation. The previous code provision did provide for taxing distributions of stock dividends where the shareholder had an election to receive either cash or stock, but the Treasury felt a general provision was necessary to tax all stock dividends which changed the proportionate interest of the shareholder in the corporation where such change was related to a cash dividend or other outstanding shares, especially in view of the development in recent years of many new sophisticated types of stock which avoided the impact of the general rule, bearing such features as increasing and decreasing conversion ratios. Accordingly, the act made clear that an increase in a shareholder's interest in a corporation, when related to a taxable dividend paid to other shareholders, was to be taxed, and provided more detail on applicable situations, with transitional provisions.

8. *Corporate securities issued in mergers.* The Treasury sought to curb tax benefits obtained by conglomerates and other acquisition-minded corporations by the substitution of deductible interest for nondeductible dividends on securities issued, e.g., convertible debentures or other debt instruments having equity characteristics, used to effect a merger or acquisition. The act provided that deductibility of interest would be denied where the debt securities are subordinated to a "significant segment" of the other creditors; the debt securities are convertible into common stock, or were issued with warrants to purchase common stock; the corporation's debt-equity ratio is over 2:1; or the corporation giving effect to the acquisition would fail on a *pro forma* basis to earn its annual interest expenses by at least three times. The denial of the interest deductibility would be terminated after the corporation met the debt-equity criterion and showed the referenced earnings coverage for at least three consecutive years. The Internal Revenue Service was given authority by the act to issue regulations "providing tests for distinguishing generally whether bonds or debentures are in fact debt or equity."

(This introduction of administrative interpretation of equity elements in debt securities, to determine eligibility for tax deductibility of the interest charges involved, presumes that such use of debt securites of the "hybrid" type (with conversion feature, warrants, or subordination) can be indulged in freely, whereas in fact the market disciplines overuse of debt securities in capital structures, and Accounting Principles Board Opinion No. 15, "Earnings per Share," calls for the adjustment of earnings per share on the common stock to "primary" and "fully diluted" bases, giving effect to "common stock equivalents" in the debt structure and other *pro forma* exercise of equity features in debt securities. Actually, a 2:1 ratio in debt-to-equity proportions would be considered high, higher than is conventionally tolerated by the market for even stable-earning, well-established utilities.)

9. *Multiple corporations.* Also adopted, in modified form, by the act was the administration's recommendation to limit to a controlled group of corporations (as enacted, for a six-year transition period) the entitlement to multiple surtax exemptions and other tax benefits for small business.

10. *Financial corporations.* As compared with previous code entitlement to an absolute reserve of 2.4% of outstanding uninsured loans in computing allowance for bad debts, commercial banks under the act were subjected to a maximum of 1.2% of eligible loans for the first six years, followed by 0.6% in the next six years and then actual loss experience. Net operating losses of commercial banks could be carried back for ten years. Realized gains on sale of bonds by commercial banks would be treated as ordinary income, rather than capital gains, similar to realized bond losses; gains on bonds held July 11, 1969, continuing to have entitlement to capital gains treatment if realized within 13 years. *See* BAD DEBTS, with its discussion of bad debt reserves of banks.

Mutual savings banks and savings and loan associations were subjected to the same treatment of realized bond gains and losses as prescribed for commercial banks. These savings institutions were no longer entitled to special deduction for bad debts based on 3% of increases in real estate loans, and their alternative deduction of 60% of taxable income was reduced over a ten-year period to 30% of taxable income; in the alternative, these institutions could opt to use the formula allowed commercial banks.

11. *Minimum corporate tax.* Like individuals, corporations were subjected to a 10% minimum tax on "preference income" in

REVENUE BONDS

excess of $30,000 plus regular federal income tax, on most items considered preference income for individuals.

Tax Reduction Act of 1975. Act of Congress approved March 29, 1975 (P.L. 94-12), provided a $22.8 billion tax cut by amending the Internal Revenue Code of 1954 to, among other things:

1. Provide a 10% rebate of 1974 taxes up to a maximum of $200.
2. Temporarily (for 1975) increase the low-income allowance, increase the percentage standard deduction to 16% of adjusted gross income up to a maximum of $2,600, provide a $30 tax credit for each $750 personal exemption, and provide a 10% earned income credit for certain low-income taxpayers.
3. Provide an increase in the income limitation for the deduction of child care expenses from $18,000 to $35,000.
4. Authorize a tax credit of 5% of the purchase price of a new principal residence, up to $2,000.
5. Extend the time in which a taxpayer must purchase a new principal residence in order to defer recognition of gain on the sale of a former residence from the prevailing 1 year to 18 months, and, if the taxpayer constructs a home, from the prevailing 18 months to 2 years.
6. Provide a $50 one-time payment to U.S. residents who receive a Social Security, supplementary security income, or railroad retirement benefit for the month of March, 1975.
7. Authorize an increase in the investment tax credit (increase from 4 to 10% for utilities, and from 7 to 10% for all other businesses, on equipment acquired after January 21, 1975, and placed in service before January 1, 1977).
8. Provide an increase in the corporate surtax exemption from $25,000 to $50,000, with a corresponding reduction of the tax rate on the first $25,000 of corporate income from 22 to 20%.

Revenue Adjustment Act of 1975. Act approved December 23, 1975 (P.L. 94-164), continued the 1975 tax cut reductions, at an $8.4 billion level, through June 30, 1976, by among other things:

1. Providing 6 months of tax cuts for individuals, sufficient to allow prevailing withholding rates to remain unchanged.
2. Incorporating a statement of principle that, subject to economic conditions or unforeseen circumstances, any additional tax cuts-beyond June 30, 1976-would be accompanied by dollar-for-dollar reductions in federal spending.
3. Increasing the minimum and maximum standard deductions for individuals for 6 months.
4. Increasing the tax credit for individuals to the larger of $35 per capita or 2% of the first $9,000 of taxable income.
5. Increasing the low-income allowance.
6. Extending for 6 months the temporary increase in the corporate surtax exemption (to $50,000) and temporary decrease (to 20%) in the tax rate on the first $25,000 of corporate profits.

Tax Revision. By P.L. 94-331, approved June 30, 1976, Congress extended the tax cuts, provided by the Tax Reduction Act of 1975, for two months, until September 1, 1976.

However, Act of Congress approved October 4, 1976 (P.L. 94-455), extensively revised the nation's tax laws. Among other things, the new law:

1. Imposed new restrictions on investments in tax shelters.
2. Made major revisions in federal estate and gift taxation.
3. Continued personal and corporate tax cuts passed in 1975.
4. Increased the minimum tax.
5. Made numerous changes in the taxation of foreign income.
6. Imposed new safeguards in the administration of federal tax laws.
7. Denied certain tax benefits to persons who paid bribes to foreign officials and participated in international boycotts.

Tax Reduction and Simplification Act. Act of Congress approved May 23, 1977 (P.L. 95-30), among other things:

1. Provided a standard deduction of $2,200 on single-income tax returns and $3,200 on returns filed jointly.
2. Authorized a "new jobs" tax credit for employers of up to $100,000 each, equal to 50% of the first $4,200 of wages paid to each additional employee hired in 1977 and 1978 over the average number of workers on the payroll in 1976 after adjustment to allow for 2% annual growth (with the amount of an employer's deduction for wages to be reduced by the amount of such credit).
3. Extended for an additional year, through 1978, the tax credit of $35 per individual (or 2% of the first $9,000 of taxable income) and the low-income credit for families earning less than $8,000.
4. Restored through December 31, 1976, the sick pay exclusion eliminated by the Tax Reform Act of 1976.
5. Waived penalties and interest incurred with respect to the 1976 tax year by individuals and corporations as a result of changes made by the 1976 act.
6. Authorized $435 million additional funding for federal work incentive (WIN) programs for fiscal years 1978 and 1979 and an additional $2.25 billion for countercyclical revenue sharing with states and localities.

Revenue Act of 1978. P.L. 95-600, approved November 6, 1978, did the following:

1. Liberalized personal income tax provisions, largely by lowering the schedule of tax rates. It replaced the general tax credit, which was due to expire at the end of 1978, with an increase in the personal exemption from $750 to $1,000.
2. Provided for a five-step schedule for corporate tax rates with a maximum tax rate of 46% and made the investment tax credit of 10% permanent.
3. Expanded the earned income tax credit for the working poor and reduced the effective rate on individual capital gains, the latter reducing revenues by nearly $2 billion in 1979, according to official estimates.
4. Stated the intention of the tax-writing committees of the Congress to report legislation providing "significant tax reductions for individuals when certain goals for Federal expenditures are met and when justified in the light of prevailing and expected economic conditions over the next 4 years."

Reagan Administration's Tax Acts. The Reagan administration has had major tax laws enacted since the Administration took office in January 1981:

1. ECONOMIC RECOVERY TAX ACT OF 1981. The administration considered this act to be an integral part of the administration's economic recovery program, providing incentives for work, saving, and investment by reducing tax receipts by $82.6 billion in 1983, $130.3 billion in 1984; $158.2 billion in 1985, and $202.3 billion in 1986. The major provisions of this act included an across-the-board reduction in individual income tax rates and other reductions in individual income taxes; beginning in 1985, annual inflation-related adjustment of the zero bracket amount, the personal exemption, and individual income tax brackets; and on increase in accelerated cost recovery of capital expenditures.
2. TAX EQUITY AND FISCAL RESPONSIBILITY ACT OF 1982. In the administration's judgment, this act improved the fairness of the tax system while preserving the incentives for work, saving, and investment enacted in 1981. This act *increased* receipts primarily by eliminating the unintended benefits and obsolete incentives, increasing taxpayer compliance, and improving collection techniques. The provisions of this act were expected by the administration to increase receipts by $17.3 billion in 1983, $38.3 billion in 1984, $42.2 billion in 1985, and $52.1 billion in 1986.

After ERTA in 1981 and TEFRA in 1982, the next major tax legislation was the Deficit Reduction Act (DRA) of 1984. In 1986, Congress passed the Tax Reform Act, which made substantial changes in the tax law. This massive overhaul of the 1954 Internal Revenue Code resulted in changing the title of the Code to the Internal Revenue Code of 1986.

The appended table shows Internal Revenue Gross Collections by Source, 1970-1986.

See APPROPRIATION, ESTATE TAXES, EXCISES, GIFT TAX, INCOME TAXES, INTERNAL REVENUE.

REVENUE BONDS Bonds issued by municipalities with principal and interest payable from revenues or income from

Internal Revenue Gross Collections, by Source: 1970 to 1986
(For fiscal year ending in year shown.)

Source of Revenue	Collections (bil. dol.)				Percent of total			
	1970	1980	1985	1986	1970	1980	1985	1986
All taxes	195.8	519.4	742.9	782.3	100.0	100.0	100.0	100.0
Individual income taxes	103.7	287.5	396.7	416.6	53.0	54.9	53.4	53.2
Withheld by employers	77.4	223.8	299.0	314.4	39.5	43.1	40.2	40.1
Employment taxes [1]	37.4	128.3	225.2	244.4	19.1	24.7	30.2	31.2
Old age and disability insurance	35.7	122.5	215.6	234.9	18.2	23.6	29.0	30.0
Unemployment insurance	.8	3.3	5.7	5.7	.4	.6	.8	.7
Corporation income taxes	35.0	72.4	77.4	80.4	17.9	13.9	10.4	10.2
Estate and gift taxes	3.7	6.5	6.6	7.2	1.9	1.3	.9	.9
Excise taxes	15.9	24.6	37.0	33.7	8.1	4.7	5.0	4.3
Alcohol	4.7	5.7	5.4	5.6	2.4	1.1	.7	.7
Tobacco	2.1	2.4	4.5	4.6	1.1	.5	.6	.5
Manufacturers	6.7	6.5	10.0	9.9	3.4	1.3	1.3	1.3
Windfall profits tax	NA	3.1	5.1	8.9	NA	.6	.7	1.1
Other	2.4	6.9	12.0	4.7	1.2	1.3	1.6	.6

NA – Not applicable.
[1] Includes railroad retirement, not shown separately.

Source: U.S. Internal Revenue Service, *Annual Report of the Commissioner and Chief Counsel of the Internal Revenue Service.*

municipally owned or state-owned plants, toll roads or bridges, or public works, such as water works, electric light and power plant, port authority, railroad, etc. Thus, revenue bonds are secured by the property and income of a city-owned or state-owned enterprise. The full faith and credit of the state or municipality, however, are not pledged behind revenue bonds, so such issues are classified as "limited liability" debt of the issuing governmental unit. Particularly in the case of municipalities, since World War II an increasing proportion of financing has been in the form of revenue bonds, given mounting outstanding debt pressing against debt limits, surging needs involving capital facilities to be financed by debt, and receptivity of the municipal market for bonds of the revenue type well secured by their earnings.

In some instances, revenue bonds are secondarily backed by the full faith and credit of the issuing governmental unit, which makes such issues "double barreled" in this respect and raises a close question as to whether or not such hybrid issues are really general obligation bonds.

Commercial banks, pursuant to the Banking Act of 1933, are allowed to underwrite, and to invest in without usual limitations, only general obligation state and municipal issues.

Revenue bonds are to be distinguished from industrial aid bonds, issued by various municipalities under statutory authority of the states concerned and involving the leasing of plant facilities to a specific business corporation; such bonds depend for their soundness upon the ability of the business corporation concerned to continue in business and to pay the specified lease rentals which furnish the income to service such bonds.

See MUNICIPAL BONDS.

REVENUE EXPENDITURES See CAPITAL AND REVENUE EXPENDITURES.

REVENUE SHARING The federal government shares revenues with states in the form of unrestricted grants. In 1985-86, state and local total revenues were $641,407,000, of which $113,099,000 came from the federal government.

REVERSE MORTGAGE A mortgage where the lender pays the homeowner (borrower) monthly payments, establishes a line of credit that the homeowner can draw on when desired, or provides for monthly payments to the homeowner and a line of credit; borrowings secured by home real estate. Reverse mortgages are designed to assist people, especially senior citizens, who have little ready cash but have built up equity in their homes. Reverse mortgages allow a lender to pay the homeowner monthly payments. Then, at some point agreed upon in advance, usually when the homeowner dies, the home is sold and the lender is repaid. An annuitized reverse mortgage in one in which a lender (a bank or heir) provides the owner a life annuity and takes over the home upon the owner's death. The owner retains a lien on the property to assure that the payments will be made.

In the late 1980s, the federal government established a demonstration program for reverse mortgages limited to 2,500 loans. For a test, HUD selected one lender in each state by lottery. Each lender would be allowed to offer 50 reverse mortgages. The test would run through 1991.

The government's reverse mortgage program is operated by the Federal Housing Administration. It provides government-backed insurance to local, private, and public lenders making reverse mortgages to senior borrowers in their areas. The FHA will insure loans that assume any of three basic payment formats, plus some additional features: tenure loans in which a homeowner is guaranteed to receive monthly checks of an agreed-upon amount for as long as he or she occupies the house as a principal residence; term loans with a definite repayment date; line-of-credit loans that allow borrowers to withdraw money in amounts and frequencies of their own choosing, up to a maximum. The FHA program allows lump-sum drawdowns on any of the plans. FHA insures fixed-rate and adjustable-rate reverse mortgages. The program also allows homeowners and lenders to work out a lower rate on the loan in exchange for the lender receiving a percentage of future appreciation of the property (equity sharing).

Maximum payments on FHA reverse mortgages are related to borrower's age, the interest rate, the form the loan takes, and the property value up to a maximum claim amount. According to an FHA schedule, a 75-year-old widow with a $100,000 debt-free house would qualify for a $812-a-month maximum payment on a five-year fixed-term reverse mortgage at a 10% rate, with no appreciation sharing. A ten-year loan would provide monthly payments of up to $510. If the loan was a tenure loan (guaranteed payments for an indefinite period), the maximum monthly payment would be $357.

Eligibility for the FHA program is limited to homeowners 62 and older. If the borrowers are married, the younger spouse must be at least 62. Homes must be relatively debt free. Property eligible under the program include single-family houses, town houses and condominiums. Cooperatives are not included.

The lender must provide access to counseling on reverse mortgages to assure that the borrower is aware of alternatives and consequences.

BIBLIOGRAPHY

"New FHA Program: Pilot Promises Elderly Money From Home." *ABA Banking Journal*, December, 1988.
SCHELMAN, L. "Reverse Mortgage." *United States Banker*, January, 1989.
TOPOLNICKI, D. M. "Reverse Mortgages: An Idea Whose Time Is Finally Coming." *Money*, March, 1989.

REVERSE SWAP One form of activity in the secondary swap market. A reverse swap offsets the interest rate or currency exposure on an existing swap. Reverse swaps can be written with the original counterparty or with a new counterparty. In either case, they are typically executed to realize capital gains.

REVERSING ENTRIES After the accounting records have been adjusted and closed at the end of the accounting period, reversing entries can be made on the first day of the new period to turn around (or reverse) certain adjusting entries. This accounting procedure often simplifies the recording of certain transactions in the new period. For example, assume that the following adjusting entry was made to record accrued salaries:

| December 31 | Salaries expense (debit) | 5,000 |
| | Salaries payable (credit) | 5,000 |

The reversing entry on January 1 of the new year is as follows:

| January 1 | Salaries payable (debit) | 5,000 |
| | Salaries expense (credit) | 5,000 |

REVIEW To perform inquiry and analysis that provide the accountant with a reasonable basis for expressing limited assurance that the statements need no material modifications in order to conform with generally accepted accounting principles or, if applicable, with another comprehensive basis of accounting. The objective of a review is to provide the accountant with a basis for expressing limited assurance that there are no material modifications that should be made to the financial statements.

REVOCABLE CREDIT A LETTER OF CREDIT that the issuing bank can cancel without consulting the beneficiary.

REVOLVING ASSETS CURRENT ASSETS.

REVOLVING CHECK CREDIT An innovation in personal loan credit introduced by a Boston bank in 1955 and adopted by a number of additional banks beginning in 1958.

A typical plan's procedure was summarized by the Philadelphia Federal Reserve Bank as follows:

1. The customer fills out an application stating the amount he can afford to repay each month.
2. If the bank approves, this figure is multiplied by a fixed number of months-from 12 to 24, depending on the bank's policy-to determine the maximum amount he may borrow. Thus if it is decided that repayments of $50 a month can be handled and the bank's plan is for 20 months, the limit of the line of credit is $1,000.
3. The customer then receives a supply of checks which he may use just like any personal check. When one of these checks is written and is presented to the bank for payment, it is charged to the revolving credit account and becomes a loan to the customer.
4. Monthly repayments begin once a debt is incurred. They are usually in the predetermined size regardless of the amount borrowed, although a few plans provide for payments as a fraction of the outstanding balance.
5. The customer may continue to write checks until he reaches his maximum line. Once repayments bring his debt below the limit, he may start borrowing all over again.
6. There is no charge while the account is not in use. When the customer borrows, he must pay interest on the amount of the credit outstanding (generally, advances prior to April 1, 1981, were subject to interest rates on the order of 1% or 1.5% per month, but as of 1982 they were on the order of 1.65% per month, or 19.8% annual percentage rate). With the advent in 1969 of Regulation Z of the FEDERAL RESERVE BOARD REGULATIONS, as amended since, checking accounts with such overdraft lines of credit are subject to the requirements of full disclosure to borrowers as consumer credit extended or offered to a consumer primarily for personal, family, or household purposes, including the expression of defined finance charges on an annual percentage rate basis. Variations in the extension of such check credit include the "checking plus" type of account, which involves authorization to the customer to draw checks in excess of the balance in the checking account up to a prearranged maximum amount, and the "ready credit" type of account, whereby the customer upon approval of his application is given a special book of checks to be used in drawing on the agreed line of credit. In the case of revolving plans, the credit is restored, up to the specified ceiling, as payments are made. Although this idea is compared to the practice by European banks of honoring overdrafts on depositors' accounts, actually it is a deferred line of personal or consumer credit-to be drawn on by check when actually needed, with the revolving feature keeping the line of credit on a continuing basis. The latter feature eliminates the expense of periodic renewals of conventional personal loans. Banks that are aggressive in "retail" or consumer credit should find this innovation to be stimulative of additional volume, as it is another form of "easy credit" so popular with consumers in recent years (see CREDIT CARDS). The Philadelphia Federal Reserve Bank reports the note of caution that the initial credit investigation should be thorough, and that there should be a periodic review of each account, in view of the possibility of deterioration in creditworthiness of the borrower over the term of the credit. Check credit as of 1982 had been adopted by numerous banks, especially those with large number of branches doing consumer banking, after many such banks had taken a ""wait and see" attitude to profit from the experience of the pioneers and early adopters of this innovation.

REVOLVING CREDIT A commitment by a bank to lend to a customer under predefined terms; open-end credit. The commitments generally contain covenants allowing the bank to refuse to lend if there has been a material adverse change in the borrower's financial condition.
See LETTER OF CREDIT.

RICH MAN'S PANIC Any period in which there is a sudden and violent decline in security prices caused by the outpouring of new isues that have not been fully digested, rather than fundamental economic causes; a name given particularly to the panic of 1903. The panic of 1903 was one of "undigested securities," in which security prices dropped precipitously because of the conversion into cash of large holdings by wealthy and influential investors and speculators. Such a panic does not create widespread financial disarrangement, nor does it mark the beginning of a period of serious depression-it concentrates itself on the stock and bond markets. It therefore primarily affects "rich men" rather than the public at large.

RICO RACKETEER INFLUENCED AND CORRUPT ORGANIZATIONS ACT.

RIGGING THE MARKET The manipulation of security prices by professional operators to their advantage. Manipulative practices on stock and commodity exchanges are prohibited by the SECURITIES EXCHANGE ACT OF 1934 and the COMMODITY EXCHANGE ACT. The term is used more frequently on European exchanges than in this country. There it refers to the practice of creating a false show of activity and strength by artificially forcing prices upward with the intention of inducing the public to buy. If the manipulatory tactics are successful, securities are unloaded on the public at prices higher than those at which they were accumulated.

RIGHT The "preemptive right" of the stockholders of the voting stock of a corporation, i.e., the right to subscribe for the same proportionate interest as that now held, in additional voting stock. This right is recognized in the common law and in the corporation laws of various states. Its purpose is to afford the present stockholders equal opportunity to subscribe to the additional stock and thus to maintain the same proportionate interest. Otherwise, the additional voting stock might be issued solely to a specified group or person, and thus dilute the interest in voting power and in equity of the excluded stockholders.

To illustrate, a small corporation might have 1,000 shares of common stock, the sole issue with voting power, and have a common stock equity of $100,000, or $100 per share. Stockholder A might own 52%, or 520 shares, and thus have a 52% interest in the equity. Assuming an additional 1,000 shares are issued at $100 per share to stockholders other than A, A's interest in the doubled common stock and in the equity would be reduced to 26%, converting his previous majority holding to a minority holding. The preemptive right therefore entitles A to subscribe to 52% of the additional 1,000 shares, so that he can still maintain a 52% interest (owning 1,040 shares of the new 2,000-share common capitalization).

In practice, the dilution in the above example of exclusion of A would be worse than depicted, because it has become conventional to price the additional stock at an attractive price, usually measured by subscription price below the market value, as an incentive for stockholders issued rights to subscribe and exercise same. Thus, assuming $100 per share also happens to be the market value in the above example, the new stock might be priced at $80 per share, or $20 below the market value. This premium of market price over subscription price gives the rights a definite value; with the old stock carrying the rights to subscribe selling at $100 per share, the rights would be worth $10 apiece. This is calculated on the basis of the following convenient formula:

$$\frac{\text{market price of old stock ("rights on")} - \text{subscription price}}{1 + \text{number of rights required for one new share}}$$

or, numerically computed,

$$\frac{100 - 80}{1 + 1}$$

or $10 value per right, to the stockholder receiving same. The factor of 1 used in the denominator is an adjustment factor to allow for the fact that the market price of the old stock ("rights on") includes the value of the one right that each old share is entitled to.

Arithmetically, another way of arriving at the same result would be as follows. To become entitled to the one right necessary for one new share, the holder has to have one old share, worth $100; exercising the one right received, at $80, would result in the holder's owning two shares costing a total of $180, or $90 per share. The difference between the current market value of $100 and such average cost of $90 is the value of the one right, $10.

The issuance of rights to subscribe to additional stock involves formal action by the board of directors of a corporation, including if necessary the amendment of the certificate of incorporation, and formal resolution by the board of directors prescribing (1) the date as of which the stockholders of record will be forwarded the rights (record date); (2) the issuance date for the rights; (3) the expiration date of the subscription privilege, which usually is short term, say 30 to 60 days; and (4) the subscription price. Since the additional stock thus offered to stockholders is a public offering, the company has to file a registration statement or notification with the Securities and Exchange Commission, pursuant to the Securities Act of 1933, if required under this act and regulations of the SEC to do so.

Only stockholders of record receive the rights on the issuance date. Therefore, on the first "ex-rights" (without rights) date for the old stock, buyers thereof will find the price adjusted downward by the value of the rights; in the above example, if $100 is still the market price, the "ex-rights" price of the old stock will be $90, since buyers of the old stock now will receive no rights. The formula for compuntation of the value of the rights on the first ex-rights date and thereafter is as follows:

$$\frac{\text{market price of old stock ("ex-rights")} - \text{subscription price}}{1 + \text{number of rights required for one share}}$$

or, numerically computed,

$$\frac{90 - 80}{1}$$

or $10 value per right. Arithmetically, the buyer wishing to obtain stock via the subscription method would now have to buy one right costing $10 and pay the subscription price of $80; thus total price for the old stock (ex-rights) would be $90. The price for the old stock (ex-rights) and the value of the rights would have to be in approximate equivalence (allowing for commission costs, etc.), as otherwise arbitrage would close the gap. For example, if the old stock ex-rights should be available (bid) at $95 and the rights cost $10, an arbitrageur would concurrently buy one right and sell the old stock, using the stock obtained by subscription (costing a total of $90) to deliver against the stock sold at $95 and thus clearing the difference as gross profit. Such selling of the old stock and buying of the rights would depress the price of the former and raise that of the latter until an equivalence was restored.

Rights are assignable; if the holder upon their receipt does not wish to exercise the rights, he may sell and transfer the rights to another. Stock exchanges often list rights that may issue out of shares listed thereon. Failing to exercise rights results in a shirinkage of proportionate interest in the corporation of the stockholder; a stockhohould never let the rights expire without either their exercise or their sale.

From the standpoint of the corporation, authorization and issuance of rights is a form of "internal" raising of additional funds (from existing stockholders). As a device for additional financing, subscription rights offered at discounts from prevailing market (subscription price under the market), in order to create value for the rights and serve as an incentive for their exercise, unquestionably are usually costlier than open market financing (sale of the additional stock to the public through investment bankers) at current market price, less the usual underwriting "spread" or commissions. Thus in the above example, the 20% discount in subscription price, or $20,000, is a high cost for financing, and usually a corporation could achieve a much better realization through investment bankers on a public offering. For example, sale of the new stock in the open market by public offering, at a market price of $100, less 5% to 10% underwriting spread and other offering costs, would generate $100,000 proceeds to the company with less cost in terms of both money and number of shares. Accordingly, costly form of raising new money. And since a subscription rights a very costly form of raising new money. And since a subscription rights offering is fraught with risk, a "standby" underwriting agreement may have to be resorted to anyway to assure the corporation of success.

The risks are that despite the high discount price placed on the new stock, relative to the current market value for the old stock, the market price for the old stock might decline below the subscription price during the duration of the rights offering period (30 to 60 days, say). This would ruin the offering, since stockholders would see no point in paying $80 subscription price for new stock when the old stock was available at $70. And, if the stock offered has to be registered with the SEC, there will be another 20 days at least (normal waiting period), before the registration statement becomes effective. Thus a standby agreement by underwriters, usually at a flat fee on all shares plus the normal underwriting spread on any shares taken up by the underwriters upon nonsubscription by stockholders, has to be arranged if the corporation desires assurance of obtaining the full gross proceeds counted on, either from subscribing stockholders or from the standby investment bankers. For, even in the rights offering considered successful, there are always some stockholders who do not wish to subscribe because they already have too much stock, because they do not have the funds, etc.

Accordingly, to allow flexibility in the preemptive rights provision, some state laws now do not require compulsory offering to stockholders of additional shares have voting power, or senior securities (bonds, debentures, preferred stock) convertibile into the voting stock, by making it possible for the certificate of incorporation to limit or to deny the preemptive right of stockholders. A feasible provision in the certificate of incorporation is to allow the directors discretion as the subscription offerings to stockholders or open market offerings. Such limitations or denials of the preemptive right on a compulsory basis are usually justifies on the grounds that it is primarily concerned with maintenance of voting power, and that the average stockholder of the modern large, publicly financed corporation has little interest in voting power.

In any event, even at common law, the following situations are held to be not subject to the rule of preemptive right: (1) sale of original subscription stock, when the corporation is being formed; and (2) issuance of stock for property, or in settlement of claims of debts. No preemptive rights are held to attach to treasury stock. Frequently, in order to facilitate sale of stock under employees' stock purchase programs or other issues of additional stock, the stockholders might be asked to waive their preemtive rights thereto, where the preemptive right is compulsory.

Preemptive Rights on National Bank Stock. The Comptroller of the Currency in his Interpretive Ruling 7.6050 requires that the articles of association of a national bank, by affirmative vote of the holders of two-thirds of the bank's outstanding voting shares, must provide for or specifically negate the vesting of preemptive rights in the shareholders

RING This term has two meanings:

1. In security manipulation before passage of the securities exhange act of 1934, a clique or informal pool composed of individuals who had a community of interests and cooperated in order to achieve a certain end, such as to raise or lower the price of a certain security. Unlike a pool, a ring involved no written contract delegating management to one member and binding the individual members to share profits or losses. The members were free to manage their own commitments as they chose.
2. On commodity exchanges, the structure on the trading floor aroung which brokers and traders gather to trade in futures. On the grain exchanges, it is called the PIT.

RISK The probability that the actual return on an investment will differ from its expected return. For example, a Treasury bill is considered by many investors to have practically no risk. This cannot be said of a 30-year bond of any major corporation in the United States. Risk is the major constraint on investments; return on investment is the major opportunity or benefit. Other constraints on investments include taxes and the cost of investing. Large potential risks are associated with large potential returns. Small potential risks are associated with small potential returns. Investors are typically risk averse. They will not assume risk for its own sake, nor will they incur a given level of risk without being reasonably compensated for doing so. Investors have various risk-return tradeoffs that are reflected in their investing activities.

Risks associated with investing are identified as interest rate risk, market risk, inflation risk, business risk, financial risk, and liquidity risk. Interest rate risk results from changes in the level of interest rates. Security prices move inversely to interest rates. Interest rate risks are associated primarily with bonds, but they can also affect stocks. Market risk refers to the variability in returns resulting from fluctuations in the market. All investments in securities are subject to market risk. Inflation risk refers to a loss in purchasing power due to the changes in the general purchasing power of the dollar. Inflation risk is directly related to interest rate risk. Interest rates tend to rise as inflation increases; lenders demand premiums to compensate them for loss in purchasing power. Business risk refers to the risk of investing in a particular business or industry. Financial risk refers to the risk related to the use of debt financing by companies. Companies that use debt rather than equity to finance their assets typically assume a larger financial risk than those that do not. Financial risk and leverage are closely linked. Liquidity risk is the risk associated with securities that cannot be purchased or sold quickly and without major price concessions. The more uncertainty there is concerning the liquidity of an investment the larger the liquidity risk.

Additional risks include governmental and political risk, foreign exchange and expropriation risk, risk of war, and default risk (risk that a borrower will be unable to make interest or principal payments on debt). Credit rating services can be useful in identifying various types of risks.

Another important risk to consider is purchasing power risk, also known as inflation risk. It reflects the impact of inflation on an investment, i.e., the likelihood of decreased purchasing power. The eroding effect of inflation on investments or savings can be illustrated as follows where a firm has $20,000 annual income:

Year	Value with 4% inflation	Value with 5% inflation	Value with 6% inflation
1	$19,231	$19,048	$18,868
3	17,780	17,277	16,792
5	16,439	15,671	14,945
10	13,511	12,278	11,168
20	9,128	7,538	6,236

In brokerage usage, speculation often refers to the purchase of a security for short-term gain. Investing usually refers to the acquisition of a security for a relatively long period of time. Investors and speculators often have different risk tolerances, but both groups evaluate technical market data (prices, price trends, volume) and fundamental data (dividends, earnings, asset values).

An investor's risk tolerance is usually based on emotional temperament and attitude toward fluctuations in the value of one's investments. A person's current financial status and prior investment experiences will determine one's risk tolerance.

See BUSINESSMAN'S RISK, BUSINESS RISK, CREDIT RISK, DISTRIBUTION OF RISK, DIVERSIFICATION, GAMBLE, INSURANCE, INVESTMENT RISKS, MORAL RISK, PROPERTY RISK, SETTLEMENT RISK, TRANSFER RISK, SPECULATION.

BIBLIOGRAPHY

BANK ADMINISTRATION INSTITUTE. *Risk & Other Four-Letter Words*. Bank Administration Institute, Rolling Meadows, IL, 1986.
BHALA, R. *Risk-Based Capital Adequacy Rules*. Bank Administration Institute, Rolling Meadows, IL, 1989.
MUELLER, P. H. *Perspective on Credit Risk*,
OBERHOFER, G. D. *Rate Risk Management*. Probus Publishing Co., Chicago, IL, 1988.
THORNHILL, W. T. *Effective Risk Management*. Bank Administration Institute, Rolling Meadows, IL, 1989.

RISK ASSET RATIO In recent years, the Comptroller of the Currency has evolved the concept of "capital funds cushion" for banks. Cross assets (reserves for bad debts and valuation reserves not deducted), exclusive of cash or its equivalent, U.S. government obligations, and loans or portions of loans guaranteed or insured by federal government agencies, are the "risk" assets, i.e., loans, municpal and corporate bonds, and other assets. Against these risk assets, the capital funds (capital, surplus and undivided profits) and reserves are compared, the arrive at the risk asset ratio—for example, risk assets 5.80 times capital funds and reserves. Any bank with a risk asset ratio of over 6 times would be criticizable as to low strength of capital funds cushion and urged to obtain additional proprietorship funds through subscription to new stock.

Like all ratios, the risk asset ratio if used arbitrarily, without consideration of actual quality of the so-called risk assets, would fail to allow for qualitative differences among banks criticized on the ground of too high a risk asset ratio. Nevertheless, as a general standard for judging the sufficiency of capital cushion of banks, the risk asset ratio is of course superior to the old rule of deposits no more than 10 times capital funds. The latter rule was obviously oblivious to the composition of the assets constituting the investment of the available funds (capital funds and deposits), including the "nonrisk" assets within the Comptroller's exemption above. As a result of expansion in deposits, many banks have gone considerably over the 10:1 deposits to capital funds level, but the unfavorable connotations of such high deposits to capital funds ratios have been neutralized by high concentrations in "nonrisk" assets, especially U.S. government obligations.

RISK PREMIUM The additional required rate of return due to extra risk incurred by an investor.

ROBERT MORRIS ASSOCIATES A national association of bank loan and credit officers founded in 1914 and organized primarily to conduct research in bank credit. Membership is limited to national and state commercial banks, savings banks, trust companies, Federal Reserve banks, and private banks or bankers engaged in a general banking business, discount or acceptance houses, commercial paper dealers, and U.S. agencies of foreign banks doing a discount or deposit business in the United States. The publication of this organization is the *Bulletin of the Robert Morris Associates* (monthly). The corporation is chartered by the Commonwealth of Pennsylvania.

RMA has more than 3,000 commercial banks and thrift institutions, representing almost 14,500 commercial loan and credit officers and related personnel in all 50 states. RMA was named after the American patriot who signed the Declaration of Independence and who was largely responsible for financing the Revolutionary War. Morris was also instrumental in helping establish the U.S. banking system. The association's original purpose was to facilitate the flow and interchange of credit information. The purpose today has been expanded to include working continuously to improve the principles and practices of commercial lending, loan administration, and asset management in commercial banks. RMA provides commercial bankers with programs, products, and services required to increase their proficiency in lending, credit, and related areas.

ROBINSON-PATMAN ACT In an effort to strengthen the Sherman Act, the Clayton Act and the Federal Trade Commission Act were passed in 1914. Section 2 of the Clayton Act forbade price discrimination among purchasers of commodities where the effect of such discrimination was to lessen competition. That section was amended in 1936 with the passage of the Robinson-Patman Act. Robinson-Patman broadened the illegality of price discrimination to include not only impingements on competition, but also any injuries to other competitors.

ROLLOVER A process whereby a new offering is subscribed for inmaturing obligations, a term used particulary in connection with the financing of UNITED STATES GOVERNMENT SECURITIES in recent years. Holders of the maturing obligations are afforded the privilege of subscribing to the new issue by turning in holdings of the maturing obligations in payment. Thus, the maturity "rolls over" and the operation is similiar to a refunding.

ROLLOVER MORTGAGE A variation of the adjustable-rate mortgage that fixes the interest rate for a period of time—three to five years, for example—with the understanding that the interest rate will then be renegotiated. Loans with periodically renegotiated rates are called rollover mortgages.

ROOM TRADER A stock exchange member who does not maintain a commission house for the execution of customers' orders, but who trades solely for his own account; a floor trader; a FLOOR TRADER. A room trader is usually a professional speculator who takes out an exchange membership in order to save the expense of paying commissions on his voluminous transactions and to have the priviledge of trading on the floor of the exchange board room where he can take advantage of price fluctuations as they occur.

ROTATION One of the characteristics of a bull. Not all stocks rise simultaneously or uniformly in an advance. The movement starts in groups previously deflated and working into a favorable industrial position. As these groups tire of rising they rest, and the advance is communicated to others. Then, as other groups improve their earnings posittion, they, in turn, participate. In a broad bull market there may be several distinct periods of rise in a group of stocks, or in individual stocks.

ROUND LOT The regular unit of trading in a stock exchange transation, which for most stocks is 100 shares and for bonds is $1,000. Ten shares is the unit of trading for less active or high-priced stocks on the New York Stock Exchange, designed as ten-share-unit stocks. An amount less than the unit of trading is an ODD LOT.

ROUND TRANSACTION A completed trading transaction, i.e., the sale of a security or commodity previously purchased, or a purchase to cover a previous short sale.

ROUND TURN ROUND TRANSACTION.

ROUTE ITEMS Nonc300learinghouse checks and other items that are collected by a messenger. Banks in the larger cities map out certain routes or areas which are assigned to individual messengers. Each messenger collects the items drawn on banks or individuals located within the boundaries of his route, whence the origin of the term.

ROYAL EXCHANGE A building in London where foreign exchange is widely dealt in and where Lloyd's underwriters are located. It is not to be confused with the London Stock Exchange.

ROYALTY A payment made to an inventor or to an author by a manufacturer or publishers, respectively, in return for the exclusive right to manufacture or publisher, respectively, in return for the exclusive right to manufacture and sell the inventor's or author's product. The royalty is usually based on a certain percentage of the sales, or a specified return on each sale, of the patented article, copyrighted book, etc. The term also applies to a return on a concession, or to payments due to an owner or landlord by a operting company for minerals or ores taken from mines or quarries located on his property.

Oil royalty interests have been defined by the Securities and Exchange Commission in its Regulations B and B-T, conferring exemption under certain conditions to offerings of less than $100,000, as follows:

Landowners' royalty interests means fractional undivided interests in the royalty reserved by a landowner or fee owner upon the creation of an oil or gas lease.

Overriding royalty interests means fractional undivided interests or rights of participation in the oil or gas, or in the proceeds from the sale of the oil or gas, produced from a specified tract, which are limited in duration to the terms of an existing lease and which are not subject to any portion of the expense of development, operation, or maintenance.

Working interests means fractional undivided interests or rights of participation in the oil or gas, or in the proceeds from the sale of oil or gas, produced from a specified tract, which are limited in duration to the terms of an existing lease and which are subject to any portion of the expense of development, operation, or maintenance.

Oil or gas payments means fractional undivided interests or rights of participation in the oil or gas, or in the proceeds from the sale of oil or gas, produced from a specified tract, which are limited to a maximum amount fixed in barrels of oil, cubic feet of gas, or dollars.

RUBBER One of the essential raw materials of the world, the value of which is greatly enhanced by manufacture into a great variety of finished articles, consumer as well as industrial. Natural rubber is an international commodity, being produced and exported principally by Indonesia and Malaya and consumed chiefly by the U.S., the United Kingdom, Japan, West Germany, and France. The synthetic rubber industry, stimulated under wartime conditions because of the cutoff of natural rubber supplies, reached new high levels of production and consumption in the post-World War II period.

Despite expansion in world demand, natural rubber production in the past periodically outran concumption, in consequence of which producing interests from time to time sought restrictive agreements to bring production more in line with demand. Following earlier attempts to control production which proved unsuccessful, the so-called Stevenson plan for limiting production and exports was adopted on November 1, 1922, without the cooperation of Dutch interests, and continued in force until 1928. Although the plan was successful at first and resulted in a sharp rise in the price of natural rubber up to 1925 (when a maximum price of $1.21 a pound was recorded), it later failed, in large measure because production in the unrestricted areas was stimulated by such high prices and in minor measure because of increased use of reclaimed rubber in consuming countries.

Besides the market in London (London Commodity Exchange), natural rubber also has a spot market in New York.

The contract unit of rubber futures is 15 tons. Minimum fluctuations are expressed in terms of pounds: 0.001/ton resulting in a profit or loss per contract of 5.00 pounds/ton. The daily price limit is in pounds: 0.03. Contract months are January, March, April, June, July, September, October, and December.

BIBLIOGRAPHY

Grilli, E. R. "Natural Rubber: A Better Future?" *Finance and Development*, June, 1981.
"Rubber in Decline." *Financial Times*, (London), July 2, 1982.
U. S. Department of Commerce, Bureau of Industrial Economics. *1982 U. S. Industrial Outlook for 200 Industries with Projections for 1986*, January, 1982.

RULE AGAINST PERPETUITIES The rule against undue suspension of alienation of property, founded upon reasons of publich policy; rule against remoteness of vesting; a common law rule that makes void any estate or interest in property so limited that it will not take effect or vest within a period measured by a life or lives in being at the time of the creation of the estate plus 21 years and the period of gestation. The rule or modifications thereof has been made statutory in about 14 states and the District of Columbia.

In New York State, the Real Property Law provides that successive estates for life cannot be limited, except to persons in being at the creation thereof; where a remainder is limited on more than two successive estates for life, all the life estates subsequent to those of the two persons first entitled thereto become void, and on the death of the two persons, the remainder takes effect in the same manner as if no other life estates had been created.

See TRUST.

RULE OF 69 A rule stating that an amount of money invested at i percent per period will double in $69/i + 0.35$ periods. For example, at 10% per period, a sum will double in $69/10 + 0.35 - 7.25$ periods.

RULE OF 72 The computation of the time it takes for money at interest to double. It is computed as (72/interest rate). For example, principal invested at 6% will double in approximately 12 years ($^{72}/_6$).

RULE OF 78 A procedure followed by some finance companies for allocating interest on loans among the months of a year using the sum-of-the-months'-digits basis when equal monthly payments from the borrower are to be received. For example, the sum of digits from 1 through 12 is 78. Therefore, $^{12}/_{78}$ of the year's earnings are allocated for the first month of the contract, $^{11}/_{78}$ to the second month, etc.

RULE OF 115 (TRIPLING) To determine how long it takes $1 to triple ($3) at different rates of return, divide the rate of return into 115. For example, at 10% per annum, an investment will triple in 11.5 years ($^{115}/_{10}$).

RUNNER A bank's or broker's MESSENGER.

RUN ON A BANK A concerted movement of depositors to withdraw deposits from a bank, out of fear of its inslovency, especially in times of panic or money or credit disturbance. Since a bank's customary cash reserve is a small percentage of its deposits, a wholesale run might easily cause the bank to suspend cash payments, even though its assets were entirely sufficient to pay off all liabilities. If a bank is in a position to liquidate its quick assets and pay deposits promptly, confidence may be restored and the run stopped. Runs on banks were common during the panics of 1837, 1957, 1873, 1893, 1900, and 1907. The most serious runs on banks occurred during the years 1932-1933, finally culminating in state banking "holidays" and eventually the nationwide bank suspension declared by the President. One of the primary purposes of the Federal Deposit Insurance System is to maintain the confidence of depositors in banks, the lack of which was chiefly responsible for bank runs in the past.

RURAL CREDITS See AGRICULTURAL CREDIT, FARM MORTGAGES, FEDERAL FARM LOAN SYSTEM.

RURAL CREDITS ACT See AGRICULTURAL CREDITS ACT, FARM CREDIT ADMINISTRATION, FEDERAL FARM LOAN ACT, FEDERAL INTERMEDIATE CREDIT BANKS.

RURAL DEVELOPMENT INSURANCE FUND A fund established on October 1, 1972, pursuant to Section 116 of the Rural Development Act of 1972 (P.L. 92-419, approved August 30, 1972) to make community facility and business and industrial loans and loan guarantees to both profit and nonprofit organizations. The Rural Communication Development Fund, an account under the Rural Development Insurance Fund, was established pursuant to Secretary's Memorandum No. 1988 approved May 22, 1979. This memorandum transferred certain financing authorities under the Consolidated Farm and Rural Development Act (7 U.S.C. 1921 et seq.) from the FARMERS HOME ADMINISTRATION to the RURAL ELECTRIFICATION ADMINISTRATION for the purpose of financing and administering community antenna television services or facilities in rural areas. The fund is used to make or guarantee loans for community antenna television services or facilities.

RURAL ELECTRIFICATION ADMINISTRATION An agency created to finance electric and telephone facilities in rural areas of the United States and its territories. About 1,000 rural electric and 900 rural telephone utility systems in 47 states have received loans from the Rural Electrification Administration (REA).

The REA does not own or operate rural electric or telephone facilities. Its functions are to provide, throught self-liquidating loans and technical assistance, adequate and dependable electric and telephone service to rural people under rates and conditions that permit full and productive use of these utility services.

The agency was established originaly on May 11, 1935, by Executive Order No. 7037 as an emergency relief program. Statutory authority was provided by the Rural Electrification Act of 1936 (7 U.S.C. 901-950(b)). The act established REA as a lending agency with responsibility for developing a program for rural electrification. An October 28, 1949, amendment to the Rural Electrification Act authorized the REA to make loans to improve and extend telephone service to rural areas. On May 11, 1973, authority to guarantee loans made by non-REA lenders was authorized by an amendment to the act. The REA administrator is appointed by the President, subject to Senate confirmation. Both the Rural Electrification Administration and the RURAL TELEPHONE BANK organizationally are under the under-secretary of Agriculture for Small Community and Rural Development.

REA Loans. REA loans are made from the Rural Electrification and Telephone Revolving Fund in the U.S. Treasury. These funds are generally loaned at a rate equal to the average market yield on outstanding marketable obligations of the United States with a comparable maturity. The fund is replenished through collections on outstanding and future REA loans, through borrowings from the secretary of the Treasury, and through sales of beneficial ownership interests in borrowers' notes held in trust by REA.

REA Loan Guarantees. The REA also guarantees loans to facilitate the obtaining of financing for large-scale electric and telephone facilities from non-REA sources. Gurantees are considered if such loans could have been made by the REA under the act, and may be made concurrently with an REA loan. Guaranteed loans may be obtained from any legally organized lending agency qualified to make, hold, and servie the loan. All policies and procedures of the REA are applicable to a guaranteed loan. In 1974, the REA entered into an agreement with the Federal Financing Bank (FFB) whereby the FFB agreed to purchase obligations guaranteed by the REA administrator. The REA acts as the agent for the FFB, and all the borrowers' dealings are with the REA. (The FFB is an arm of the Treasury Building in Washington, D.C.)

Supplemental Financing. Borrowers meeting specified criteria are required to obtain part of their financing from non-REA sources. The National Rural Utilities Cooperative Finance Corporation, BANKS FOR COOPERATIVES, and other financial institutions provide a substantial portion of the borrowers' capital needs.

Electric Program. In the field of rural electricfication, the REA is empowered by Congress through the Rural Electrification Act of 1936, as amended, to make loans to qualified borrowers, with preference to nonprofit and cooperative associations and to public bodies. The loans finance the construction and operation of generating plants and transmission and distribution lines to provide initial and continued adequate electric service to persons in rural areas.

Highlights of REA Loan Programs*

Electric (since 1935)

All loans	$51.1	billion
REA direct loans	$20.3	billion
Loan guarantees	$30.8	billion
Consumers	13	million
Miles of line	2.2	million
Generating capacity	31	million kilowatts

Telephone (since 1949)

All loans	$ 8.4	billion
REA direct loans	$ 5.4	billion
RTB loans	$ 2.4	billion
Loan guarantees	$ .7	billion
Subscribers	5.6	million
Miles of line	962	thousand

* as of June 30, 1988
Source: Rural Electrification Agency.

Telephone Program. In authorizing the telephone loan program in 1949, Congress directed that it be conducted to "assure the availability of adequate telephone service to the widest practicable number of rural users of such service." About two-thirds of the telephone systems financed by the REA are commercial companies, and about one-third are subscriber-owned cooperatives.

Highlights of REA Loan Programs as of November 1988 is appended.

RURAL TELEPHONE BANK An agency of the United States, established in 1971. Bank loans are made, in preference to rural electrification administration (REA) loans, to telephone systems able to meet its requirements. The bank's management is vested in a governor (the REA administrator) and a board of directors, including six who are elected by the bank's stockholders. Bank loans are made for the sam purposes as loans made by the REA, but bear interest at a rate consistent with the bank's cost of money. In addition, loans may be made to purchase stock in the bank required as a condition of obtaining a loan. The bank uses the facilities and services of the REA and other Department of Agriculture agencies.

RYE The leading rye-producing state is South Dakota, where one-fourth of the U.S. crop is grown. North Dakota and Nebraska combined raise another third of the U.S. rye crop. Russia, Poland, East Germany, and West Germany are the world's largest producers.

After reaching a high of 49.2 million bushels during the 1971 "rye glut," rye production in recent years has ranged between 14.9 million bushels and 24.1 million bushels, making it one of the lesser agricultural crops. Rye has not been included in the feed grain program for target price level and disaster provision protection.

Support, however, is available to growers through nonrecourse loans and purchases from county Agricultural Stabilization and Conservation Service offices. Loans mature on demand, but no later than the last day of the ninth calendar month following the month the loan is made. Loan rates are established for all counties. These are adjusted subject to quality determinations and location differentials for individual producers.

Rye is the only cereal grass other than wheat that is used to make bread. Rye is used in the United States and Canada for human and animal food, industrial applications, and seed.

Rye futures are traded on the Winnipeg Commodity Exchange for delivery during October, December, March, May, and July. The contract size is 100-tonne broad lot, 20-tonne job lot for delivery in Thunder Bay, Ontario. The standard weight of rye for futures delivery is 56 pounds.

S

SAFE DEPOSIT COMPANY A financial warehouse. A company organized to provide facilities for the systematic safekeeping of securities, contracts, wills, insurance policies, jewelry, plate, and other valuable documents and property, either as a separate institution or in connection with a bank or trust company. The safe deposit facilities are usually in the basement of a fireproof building. Extensive vaults must be maintained, safe against fire, water, burglary, and mob violence. The vault itself is usually constructed of armor steel, heavily encased in brick or concrete with double doors, which are equipped with a time lock and special emergency alarm apparatus. The combination locks on the outer and inner doors are usually subject to joint control; access requires at least two persons. The larger companies place special watchmen on duty day and night to furnish additional protection. Inside the vault are separate steel compartments of various sizes to be rented to customers, each with a separate door and lock.

Safe deposit boxes vary in capacity and shape, from a small drawer to a moderate-sized safe, the rental charge being in proportion to space occupied. Access can be gained only by the renter in person or by a duly authorized attorney ("deputy"). Each box is unlocked only through joint control. No renter can enter the vault without being accompanied by the vault attendant, who has a master key to each compartment drawer. The compartment must be unlocked by the vault attendant before it can be unlocked by the renter. Within the locked compartment drawer is a separate box, usually of steel, with a lock of its own. This box can be withdrawn by the renter. Often private rooms are furnished so the owners may clip the coupons, examine valuables, and otherwise administer their affairs in privacy. A strict guard is kept at all times.

The relationship between a safe deposit company and a box renter is that of bailor and bailee. The safe deposit company is responsible for the safety of the renter's possessions. The renter is bound to pay his rent and to submit to the regulations necessary for the safety of his own property and for that of his fellow renters. Upon the death of the renter, the agreement between the safe deposit company and the renter usually provides that the register of wills or other similar public officer, or his authorized representative, may, at the discretion of the safe deposit company and when accompanied by an officer of the company and by one or more other persons having an interest in a search of the box, be permitted to open the safe to look for and remove a will or to list the property of the renter therein. Otherwise, the box may be opened only by the legal representative of the estate of the deceased, on a certificate of the surrogate or probate court of the jurisdiction assuring the safe deposit company of the legal right of such representative to the control of the property of the deceased.

The records of a safe deposit company, while comparatively simple, must provide means of certain identification. Records must be kept containing signatures, addresses, rental terms (contracts), and such information as number of box, number of key, and the renter's appointment of deputies. A visitor's register shows the time of arrival and departure of each renter who visits a box. In New York State, for example, the forms of records are prescribed by the superintendent of banks and all safe deposit companies are subject to regulation by the state banking department.

Safe deposit companies are state-chartered. In carrying on the safe deposit business, a national bank shall not invest in the capital stock of a corporation organized under the law of any state to conduct a safe deposit business in an amount in excess of 15% of capital and surplus. But the general limitation (Sec. 23A, Federal Reserve Act) on member bank loans to affiliates (not over 10% of capital and surplus to any one affiliate, and not over 20% of capital and surplus to all affiliates) specifically does not apply to any affiliate "engaged solely in conducting a safe deposit business." While there is no specific provision in the National Bank Act or Federal Reserve Act empowering national banks to maintain safe deposit boxes, the Comptroller of the Currency ruled that directors of a national bank may, at their discretion, invest a moderate sum in the construction of safe deposit vaults for the use of customers. National banks have the specific power to hold securities in custody for customers.

See NATIONAL BANK LOANS, NATIONAL BANK SECURITIES REGULATIONS.

History of Safe Deposit Function. The safekeeping function is perhaps the oldest form of banking, out of which evolved lending and investing operations involving monies on general deposit. The modern safe deposit box, however, was a comparatively late development in U.S. banking. The novel feature of a safe deposit box is that it gives each individual renter independent control of his private box and its contents without giving knowledge of the value or nature of the contents to others. This feature required the ingenious invention of the safe deposit lock with its two keys, the guard key held by the vault custodian and the renter's private access key fitting his own safe deposit box and giving him or his deputy exclusive control of the box. As a result of this invention, safe deposit companies, or vault systems of banks, developed.

The first safe deposit vault in the world was organized and opened for business in New York City by Francis H. Jenks in June, 1865, with the establishment of the Safe Deposit Company of New York. The second safe deposit vault was opened in Philadelphia on November 26, 1866, by the Fidelity Trust Company (now Fidelity Bank). The third vault was opened in Boston on January 1, 1868, under the name of Union Safe Deposit Vaults. The business developed rapidly after 1890, and in recent years has been promoted by commercial as well as savings banks as one of the diversified services for the public in "retail" banking. Safe deposit associations or sections of banking associations are found in many states.

Tax Visitation. In various jurisdictions, the overriding taxation power of the state has led safe deposit companies to include a specific clause in contracts with box renters giving the safe deposit company discretion, upon the death of the renter, to allow authorized representatives of the taxing authority to open the safe deposit box to look for and remove a will or to list the property of the renter therein, when accompanied by an officer of the safe deposit company and by one or more other persons having an interest in such search or list.

See CUSTODIANSHIPS.

SAFETY-FUND BANKS In 1829, New York State adopted the safety-fund system for the insurance of bank deposits and note issues. The plan provided for the annual payment by each bank of 0.5% of its capital into a fund held in trust by the state comptroller. In practice, the fund was used to redeem the notes rather than the deposits of failed banks, since the fund was insufficient to pay both. The safety-fund banks were granted special charters; since a new constitution passed in 1846 prohibited special charter banks, the system was abandoned with the expiration of the safety-fund bank charters. This system was the forerunner of required reserves against deposits, which started with the National Bank Act, and of the later tendency toward compulsory GUARANTY OF BANK DEPOSITS by state legislation.

SAFETY OF PRINCIPAL The prime essential of a good INVESTMENT.

SAG A tendency to slight price declines on the stock and commodity exchanges. Price declines in a sagging market are less severe than price declines in a weak market.

SAKELLERIDES A type of Egyptian COTTON.

SALE-LEASEBACK An arrangement whereby an owner sells property and then immediately leases it back from the buyer. The lessee often enters into such a lease to get working capital and certain tax advantages. The lessor usually enters into such an arrangement because it is profitable.

From an accounting viewpoint, the sale and the leaseback are considered as a single transaction involving a secured loan. When certain conditions are met, any profit from the sale is deferred and amortized in proportion to the amortization of the leased asset, if a capital lease is involved, or in proportion to rental payments over the time the asset is used if an operating lease is involved.

SALES The gross charges to customers for the goods and services provided during the accounting period. Net sales are gross sales less any sales returns or allowances available to customers and sales discounts taken by credit customers.

Sales are major business transactions involving the delivery of goods, merchandise, services, properties, and rights in exchange for cash or money equivalents, such as accounts and notes receivable. Most sales represent the normal, ongoing transactions of the enterprise. Other sales may be incidental, unusual in nature, and infrequent in occurrence. For accounting purposes including recording and reporting, sales are usually classified as regular sales, sales from discontinued operations, and extraordinary sales on the income statement. Sales can also be classified according to the outline appended.

The total reported as "sales" should include only receipts from regular operations of the firm; receipts from nonoperating sources should be shown separately in the profit and loss statement's "other income" section. Also, only goods and services actually sold to customers should be included as sales; transfers of goods to warehouses or branches of the firm and shipments on consignment, whether to agents or customers, are not sales. Goods on consignment are unsold inventory until a transfer of title to customers occurs.

Net sales is a key figure in analysis of the profit and loss statement for profitableness of operations and in study of trends of both the firm and the industry. Ratios such as the OPERATING RATIO and more detailed expense ratios, net profit margin, AVERAGE COLLECTION PERIOD, and TURNOVER ratios depend on the net sales figure.

In railroad and public utility accounting, "operating revenues" is the term analogous to sales.

See REVENUE.

SALES FINANCE COMPANIES Finance companies that primarily engage in the discounting of installment receivables of dealers and retailers, and thus engage in "indirect" financing of consumers buying automobiles and other consumer goods on time.

In addition to the companies affiliated with leading automobile manufacturers and specializing in the discounting of automobile dealers' installment receivables, other leading sales finance companies have widely diversified operations. For example, one of the largest companies furnishes the following outline of the diversified operations of its subsidiaries.

Its finance companies are involved in the following:

1. *Wholesale financing* of current wholesale purchases by distributors and dealers from manufacturers, especially of automobiles, refrigerators, radios, television sets, heating equipment, time and labor-saving machinery, and other labor-saving equipment usually sold on the installment plan while still carried in stock.

2. *Installment financing* of the retail sale of similar products sold on the installment plan by manufacturers, distributors, and dealers.

3. *Commercial financing* of current open accounts receivable (discounting) of manufacturers, wholesalers, mills, and converters, on the "nonnotification" plan (not giving notice to customers of the assignment of the invoices), on three bases as to assumption of liability by the finance company: entirely without recourse as to credit losses on approved accounts, with limited liability on credit losses, or with full guarantee by the sellers. Firms selling (discounting) their receivables to the finance company continue to pass on their credits and make collections directly from their customers; they receive 80% to 95% cash upon delivery of shipping evidence, the balance when collected. Advances are also made on inventories, fixed assets, other security, and open credit.

4. *Factoring* (the purchase of current open accounts receivable from mills, manufacturers, converters, and wholesalers and the assumption of all credit risk thereon). Firms can "factor" their entire annual sales volume. The factor passes on credits, purchases the approved accounts receivable, makes all collections directly from the customers ("notification" basis), and assumes all credit losses on approved accounts. Advances are also made by the factor on inventories, fixed assets, other security, and open credit.

5. *Direct loans* made through subsidiary industrial banks or personal loan companies to individual owners of automobiles, secured by liens thereon, and usually with insurance against fire, theft, collision, and accidental physical damage. Some of these subsidiaries also make loans with liens upon other articles usually sold on the installment plan, as well as unsecured "character" and "co-maker" loans.

Classification of Sales

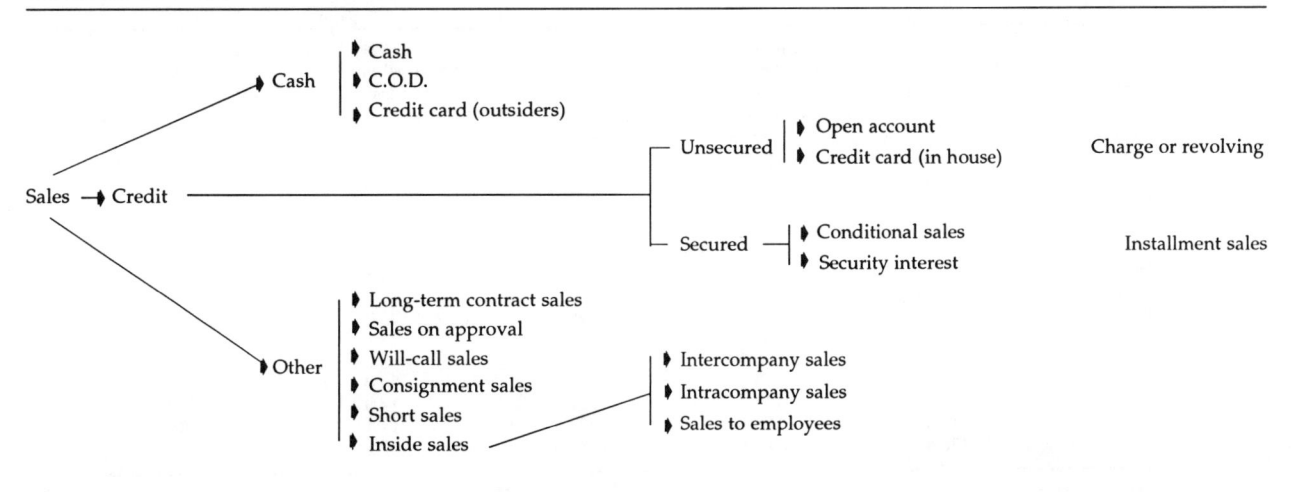

```
Sales ─┬─ Cash ─┬─ Cash
       │        ├─ C.O.D.
       │        └─ Credit card (outsiders)
       │
       ├─ Credit ─┬─ Unsecured ─┬─ Open account          ─── Charge or revolving
       │          │             └─ Credit card (in house)
       │          │
       │          └─ Secured ─┬─ Conditional sales       ─── Installment sales
       │                      └─ Security interest
       │
       └─ Other ─┬─ Long-term contract sales
                 ├─ Sales on approval
                 ├─ Will-call sales
                 ├─ Consignment sales
                 ├─ Short sales
                 └─ Inside sales ─┬─ Intercompany sales
                                  ├─ Intracompany sales
                                  └─ Sales to employees
```

ENCYCLOPEDIA OF BANKING AND FINANCE

Its insurance companies are involved in the following:

1. *Credit insurance* for manufacturers, wholesalers, mills, and converters against excessive losses on their accounts receivable. Such firms pass on their own credits, carry and collect their receivables, and are reimbursed by the credit insurance company for losses in excess of an agreed-upon percentage of annual sales. The credit insurance company also guarantees payment of accounts by individual customers and maintains collection service for its clients.
2. *Health insurance* (individual or group health and accident insurance, including hospitalization and surgical benefits).
3. *Automobile insurance* on new and used automobiles and trucks against loss by fire, theft, collision, and accidental physical damage. The fire insurance company subsidiary usually confines its insurance to articles sold on the installment plan and financed by the finance companies.

This giant sales finance company also has subsidiaries in widely different manufacturing fields; it has gone beyond the role of financier in the process of diversifying.

Sales finance companies were pioneers in meeting the credit needs of the automobile dealers and are credited with a major role in the mass distribution of automobiles facilitated by installment terms made available to buyers. Since the middle 1930s especially, commercial banks have entered this field in substantial aggregate volume and provide the principal competition to the sales finance companies.

In the last half of the 1970s, finance companies increased their share of the total automobile installment paper market to 19% or $9.7 billion. This was approximately one third of the commercial bank share of 55% or $28.6 billion. At the end of March, 1987, the market share was 38% or $93.0 billion.

Finance companies have generally ranked second behind commercial banks with regard to consumer installment credit. By March 1987, the total was $579.5 billion. Commercial banks had a 45% share with $262.3 billion. Finance companies had a 23% share with $136.1 billion.

In financing their portfolios of discounted paper, the sales finance companies offer their own short-term paper, including direct offerings (placed directly with investors by the companies) in the commercial paper market.

See CONSUMER CREDIT, FACTOR, MONEY MARKET, PERSONAL FINANCE.

SALES WITH RIGHT OF RETURN Sales contracts often permit the buyer to return merchandise for a full refund or allow for an adjustment to be made to the amount owed. Such contracts are common in such industries as publishing, records and tapes, and sporting goods.

Where a right to return exists, revenue is not recognized from the sale until all of the following criteria are met:

1. The sales price is fixed or determinable at the date of sale.
2. The buyer has paid or will pay the seller, and the obligation is not contingent upon resale of the product.
3. The buyer's obligation to the seller would not be changed by theft or damage to the merchandise.
4. The buyer has an economic substance apart from the seller.
5. The seller does not have sufficient obligations for future performance to directly bring about the resale of the product by the buyer.
6. The amount of future returns can reasonably be estimated.

BIBLIOGRAPHY

SFAS No. 48, *Revenue Recognition When Right of Return Exists* (FASB, 1981).

S&P BASKET A stock "basket" product referred to as an exchange stock portfolio, which allows investors to buy and sell all the stocks in the Standard & Poor's 500 stock index in $5 million blocks with a single execution. The basket concept allows large investors to buy and sell a broad slice of the market instead of single stocks or stock index futures.

SAN FRANCISCO STOCK EXCHANGE *See* PACIFIC COAST STOCK EXCHANGE.

SATISFICING The process of allocating one's personal resources — time, talent, energy, etc. — to maximize one's own well-being. Academic researchers suggest that managers "satisfice" owners by performing at a minimum acceptable level and then, once this level is reached, pursuing activities to maximize their own well-being. For example, a manager may maximize short-term profits in order to have a list of completed accomplishments. With such a list, a manager may be able to obtain another job at a higher salary. However, the original employer bears the cost of this short-run behavior because it is in the company's best interest to maximize long-run profits.

SATURATION The point at which the offerings of new securities are greater than the demand, without substantial concessions in price. This term is used among investment bankers to indicate that new investment securities have for the time being absorbed the available supply of capital awaiting investment. Investment bankers and syndicate managers detect the saturation point whenever attractive offerings cannot be sold within the syndicate period. Thus, when securities become a drug on the market, the saturation point is reached.

The term may also be used for commodities.

SAVINGS In microeconomics, consumers are assumed to do two things with their disposable (after tax) income — consume and

Domestic Finance Companies Year-End Data
(billions)

Year	Accounts receivable, gross			Less reserves for unearned income and losses	Accounts receivable, net
	Consumer	Business	Total		
1972	$31.9	$27.4	$59.3	$7.4	$51.9
1973	35.4	32.3	67.7	8.4	59.3
1974	36.1	37.2	73.3	9.0	64.2
1975	36.0	39.3	75.3	10.5	72.9
1976	38.6	44.7	83.4	12.7	86.5
1977	44.0	55.2	99.2	12.7	86.5
1978	52.6	63.3	116.0	15.6	100.4
1979	65.7	70.3	136.0	20.0	116.0
1980	73.6	72.3	145.9	23.3	122.6
1981	85.5	81.0	166.5	28.9	138.1
1982	75.3	100.4	194.3	33.2	161.1
1983	83.3	113.4	217.3	34.0	183.2
1984	89.9	137.8	251.1	38.0	213.5
1985	113.4	158.3	300.6	44.1	256.5
1986	136.5	174.8	345.0	37.2	297.8

Source: *Federal Reserve Bulletin.*

save. Savings represent a source of loanable funds for financial organizations such as banks. Thus, increased savings should have a dampening impact on interest rates and spur investment activity.

Personal savings have been falling in recent years. Savings were $136.9 billion in 1980, $164.1 billion in 1984, and $120.2 billion in 1987.

SAVINGS ACCOUNTS According to the regulations of the Board of Governors of the Federal Reserve System, "those accounts of the bank in respect to which, by its printed regulations, accepted by the depositor at the time the account is opened-(a) the pass book, certificate, or other similar form of receipt must be presented to the bank whenever a deposit or withdrawal is made, and (b) the depositor may at any time be required by the bank to give notice of an intended withdrawal not less than 30 days before a withdrawal is made."

National banks, state banks, and trust companies are permitted to receive time DEPOSITS and to pay interest thereon. In such institutions, there is no requirement that such time deposits be segregated from demand deposits and invested in earning assets in a special manner. As to savings deposits as such (passbook savings accounts) in commercial banks, such deposits are time deposits for legal RESERVE purposes because of the customary provision for prior notice of withdrawal in the bylaws governing such savings accounts (as a matter of practice, as in the case of mutual savings banks and SAVINGS AND LOAN ASSOCIATIONS, commercial banks waive such notice). The newly developed "savings certificates of deposit" are also treated as time deposits for legal reserve purposes if the remaining maturity is 30 days or more. Technically, such savings certificates are really time deposits and are not passbook savings. This distinction is reflected in the lower legal reserve requirement prescribed by the Board of Governors of the Federal Reserve System against "savings deposits" as such versus such requirement against "time deposits," and in the differentials in ceiling interest rates that may be paid on "savings" compared to those permitted on other time deposits (including savings certificates), the latter varying according to length of maturity.

In the opinion of counsel for the Board of Governors of the Federal Reserve System, the banking laws of the states, not being controlling as to instrumentalities of the U.S. government, may not prohibit national banks from advertising and soliciting savings accounts and employing the term "savings" when so doing. Moreover, the savings (time) deposits of national banks cannot be invested in the same manner as deposits of (mutual) savings banks pursuant to state statutes and regulation, but only as prescribed by the Revised Statutes and the Federal Reserve Act. In a "legal list" state like New York State, therefore, savings deposits of national banks are not restricted to investments on such legal list or the other restricted types of earning assets prescribed by the state's banking laws and regulations of the banking board and superintendent of banks for the state's mutual savings banks.

No national bank shall make loans permitted on real estate security (of the conventional type, versus the FHA-insured, VA-guaranteed, or other government-insured mortgage loans) in excess of the amount of its capital stock paid in and unimpaired plus its unimpaired surplus fund or in excess of 100% of the amount of its time and *savings* deposits, whichever is greater. Any such national bank may continue to receive time and savings deposits and to pay interest on same, but the rate of interest that such national bank may pay upon such time deposits or upon savings or other deposits shall not exceed the maximum rates authorized by law to be paid upon such deposits by state banks or trust companies organized under the laws of the state in which such national bank is located (12 U.S.C. 371).

SAVINGS AND LOAN ADVISORY COUNCIL An independent, statutory advisory body that consults with the Federal Home Loan Bank Board in its administration of the Federal Home Loan Bank System, the Federal Savings and Loan Insurance Corporation, and the Federal Savings and Loan System. The council meets three or more times yearly. It makes recommendations on matters within the jurisdiction of the bank board. The council consists of 24 members—one elected from each Federal Home Loan Bank district and 12 appointed by the Federal Home Loan Bank Board annually. The elected members are usually chosen from the ranks of active savings and loan managers.

SAVINGS AND LOAN ASSOCIATIONS Savings and home financing institutions, mostly mutual organizations having no capital stock; also known as savings associations, building and loan associations, building associations or building societies, cooperative banks, and homestead associations. The earliest savings and loan association in the U.S. was the Oxford Provident Building Association of Philadelphia, organized in 1831, modeled after the English building society. The original 40 members agreed to save a specified amount each week and pool such funds for home loans to members. The limited funds generated by such a closed system led most associations by 1850 to invite savings accounts from the public generally and thus become public savings institutions. By 1890, associations were to be found in every state and territory of the U.S.

Though originally voluntary unincorporated associations, by the close of the century many associations had incorporated under the general corporation laws or had chartered under special state provisions where required. In recent years, some 16 states permitted the approximately 700 associations concerned to issue "guarantee" stock, which is permanent capital stock, transferable but not withdrawable, and which must be maintained in specified minima relative to total assets or savings carried. Prior to the 1930s, such stock companies used to "guarantee" interest on savings deposits, but this is no longer done. Most of the some 4,613 savings and loan associations today are of the mutual (nonstock) type. Stock associations are controlled by their stockholders. In federal associations, which are largely nonstock but may also include federal stock-chartered associations per 1980 Federal Home Loan Bank Board (FHLBB) regulation, and usually among state mutuals, voting power per mutual-type charter is one vote per person for borrower-members and one vote per $100 or fraction of savings accounts for savings members, with a maximum voting power of no more than 50 votes for any member. Voting is for directors of the association and on specified corporate actions, as in business corporation practice; proxy voting, including having the savings member sign a proxy when opening the account, is permitted and widely practiced. Proxies are revocable, but to prevent an incumbent management from freezing out an "opposing" member, federally chartered associations may not discriminatorily close or redeem any share account, per FHLBB ruling. Normally, however, there is no activity of this nature. In practice, most savings members have little or no interest in voting, and some probably do not even read the agreement opening an account which contains the proxy or realize they have voting power, in the belief that they are depositors, as in commercial or savings bank practice. The savings and loan association accounts in the mutual-type associations, however, by law are not deposits but shareholder accounts; the income paid on savings accounts is not interest but dividends. The point may be considered academic if the shareholder accounts are insured up to the $100,000 per account by the FEDERAL SAVINGS AND LOAN INSURANCE CORPORATION (FSLIC).

Types of Charters. Beginning in 1933, when the HOME OWNERS' LOAN ACT was passed, federal charters (then solely of the nonstock type) were available, thus creating a "dual" federal-state system in this field, as in the case of commercial banking. The federal chartering authority is the HLBB, pursuant to Section 5 of the Home Owners' Loan Act of 1933 (48 Stat. 132) as amended, which exercises supervision and provides analogous central banking facilities for members. Federal charters may be obtained new or by way of conversion from state charters. Federally chartered associations must belong to the Federal Savings and Loan Insurance Corporation; state-chartered institutions may become members. In many states, membership in both of these federal institutions is a prerequisite for a state charter. As of December 31, 1980, there were 1,985 federally chartered savings and loan associations, with combined assets of $348.5 billion, and 2,628 state-chartered savings and loan associations, with total assets of $281.4 billion, all of the 4,613 federally and state-chartered associations being found in all 50 states, the District of Columbia, Guam, and Puerto Rico. In chartering an association, the Home Loan Bank Board, in accordance with the tests provided in Section 5(e) of the act, considers all available information, particularly as to the character and responsibility of the applicants, the need for such an institution in the community to be served, the prospects for its usefulness and success, and whether it could be established without undue injury to properly conducted existing local thrift and home-financing institutions. Before applications are approved, the applicants and any parties protesting are granted an opportunity to present information at a public hearing. In considering applications for conversion to federal charter by an uninsured state-chartered

SAVINGS AND LOAN ASSOCIATIONS

institution, the board applies the same eligibility standards as if such an association were seeking insurance of accounts under state charter.

The board also considers applications for branch offices by federal associations on the basis of the same tests used for new federal charters. Approvals are granted only when there is satisfactory evidence that there is a need for the proposed branch in the community and that it can be operated successfully and without undue injury to existing local thrift and home-financing institutions. It is the practice of the board to provide for a public hearing before granting approval for the establishment of any new branches, at which hearing protests may be presented in person or in writing. Decisions of the board are based on the hearing record and such other information as is available to the board. Because of competition and expansion, the board's attitude toward branches, as well as new charters for federal associations, has been of increasing interest to state supervisors of associations, who as interested parties send representatives to such hearings. As of December 31, 1980, the total of 4,613 savings and loan associations operated a total of 16,757 branches, raising the total number of offices to 21,370 as of that date. In the decade 1971-1980, the number of branches more than tripled, from 4,961 at year-end 1971 to 16,757 at year-end 1980.

Types of Accounts. Until the mid-1960s, the passbook account was the major savings instrument issued by the savings and loan associations. Any amount could be added to or withdrawn from a passbook account at any time. This account flexibility meant that associations were in the difficult position of "borrowing short" (savings withdrawals on demand) and "lending long" (earning assets being chiefly 20- to 30-year mortgage loans). The U.S. League of Savings Associations gave the following explanation.

In 1966, Congress enacted legislation giving the Federal Home Loan Bank Board explicit power to set the maximum rate that may be paid on different types of savings accounts. Until that time, association rates had been unregulated, although commercial bank rates had been controlled since 1933. The new law and regulations had the effect of preventing rate wars that could have put some associations into an unsound financial position. Unfortunately, the regulations also raised the specter of DISINTERMEDIATION-people withdrawing their funds from financial intermediaries, including the savings and loan associations, to make direct market investments (such as money market funds, money market instruments, and general securities) whenever general interest rates, and therefore yields, rose above savings account ceilings.

To help stem such periodic outflows, the FHLBB authorized a variety of certificate accounts, on which the associations could pay a higher rate for a specified minimum amount of funds that remained on deposit for a specified term.

At first, the rate ceilings for associations were set at 0.5% higher than for banks. This was intended to reflect the historical fact that an association typically paid savers more than a bank did. The rate differential also helped to assure a steady supply of funds for housing. That is, it let savings and loan associations compete effectively for savings dollars, since banks were able to offer the consumer a broader range of financial services.

In mid-1973, the differential was reduced to 0.25%, partly as a result of the gradual regulatory implementation of significant new asset and liability powers that had been granted to associations by the 1968 Housing Act. At the same time, all ceilings and most other restrictions were removed from deposits of $100,000 or more ("jumbo" CDs). (In the DEPOSITORY INSTITUTIONS DEREGULATION AND MONETARY CONTROL ACT OF 1980, Congress extended rate ceiling authority and the 0.25% differential for six years, in combination with the plan to phase out rate controls entirely over that period.)

The authority to issue longer-term savings certificates helped to stabilize the associations' deposit base. By the end of 1973, association savers for the first time held more than half of their funds in certificate accounts.

However, as inflation intensified throughout the 1970s, it became increasingly difficult for savings associations and other institutions to attract and hold the savings of the nation's households, despite the growing popularity of certificates. The increased volatility of savings flows into and out of associations contributed much to the boom-or-bust nature of the housing industry.

In May, 1978, the federal regulators took a new approach in response to market pressures that once more were slowing savings gains. They authorized the six-month money market certificate, a short-term savings instrument requiring a mininum deposit of $10,000. The money market certificate (MMC) is a fixed-rate certificate, but the maximum allowable rate on new certificates is subject to change each week, the ceiling being based on the average yield on six-month Treasury bills in the most recent weekly auction.

The new MMC proved to be far more popular than had been anticipated. Beginning with the first offerings in mid-1978, savers quickly moved funds into MMCs, and the account structure of associations began a rapid change. By year-end 1980, more than one-third of all savings dollars were in these short-term, rate-sensitive money market certificates.

Small savers-those with less than the $10,000 MMC minimum to invest-began calling for a market-rate certificate within their reach. Accordingly, a four-year version was authorized beginning July 1, 1979, but it did not prove to be successful. On January 1, 1980, it was replaced by a similar instrument with a 30-month maturity, which attracted nearly $50 billion in its first year.

Associations continue to offer a variety of other accounts, although each represents a small percentage of total savings.

The 90-day notice account has no minimum balance or term and no restrictions on the frequency or size of additions, but the saver must give 90 days' notice of withdrawal in order to earn 0.5% more than the passbook rate.

INDIVIDUAL RETIREMENT ACCOUNTS (IRAs) and KEOGH RETIREMENT PLANS are in effect trust accounts that provide retirement pension funds for people who are not covered by an employer-sponsored plan. Savers place a portion of their annual income in one of these accounts until the savers reach at least 59 1/2 years of age. The dollars deposited are excluded from taxable income for federal income tax purposes, and tax on the interest earned is deferred until withdrawals are begun, presumably when the saver has retired and therefore is in a lower tax bracket. (The "new" IRA became available January 1, 1982, enabling savers to save on 1982 taxes while saving money for the future. Every working person could put up to $2,000 a year into an IRA, and could shelter another $250 if the spouse was not employed. Even if a working person already participated in a company-sponsored plan, he could open up his own individual IRA account. Generally, withdrawals were required to begin between the ages of 59 1/2 and 70 1/2 to avoid tax penalties.)

NOW ACCOUNTS (negotiable order of withdrawal) allow checklike drafts to be drawn against the funds on deposit in the account, the funds earning interest in the meantime. These interest-bearing checking accounts were authorized nationwide December 31, 1980.

Eurodollar certificates allow associations to attract overseas dollars whenever domestic interest rates are higher than those in the international markets. Although the possibilities of attracting such funds are considered intriguing, the importance of such Eurodollar certificates as of 1981 had been negligible.

By the end of 1980, more than half of all savings held by savings and loan associations were in rate-sensitive deposits-MMCs, 30-month and 4-year market rate certificates, and jumbo CDs. Furthermore, well over half of the deposits held by associations at year-end 1980 had short terms (MMCs and many jumbo CDs) or no term (passbooks). These funds tended to be volatile, being more susceptible to withdrawals than long-term certificate funds.

The net impact of these changes in account structure of savings and loan associations has been a substantial increase in the cost of funds to savings and loan associations and a severe squeeze on earnings in 1979, 1980, and 1981, as short-term interest rose to record highs and continued to prevail not much below such levels.

New Powers. In addition to new home lending empowerments, federal associations now have increased authority to engage in correspondent activities, to offer consumer leasing services, to act as depositary and fiscal agents, to issue credit cards, to engage in financial options market trading, and, through increased authority, to invest in service corporations (see Depository Institutions Deregulation and Monetary Control Act of 1980, below). Federal associations are now in a position to diversify further in meeting the competition of nondepository institutions in providing financial services (e.g., the Federal Home Loan Bank Board gave approval to limited brokerage investment advisory services by federal savings and loan associations through subsidiaries of service corporations of the associations).

Moreover, in connection with the expanded power to provide commercial loans, a federally chartered west coast association announced plans in February, 1983, to form a nationwide alliance of savings and loan associations to pool their lending abilities in syndicating large corporate loans, in addition to providing capital for real estate development, commercial lines of credit, equipment leasing, insurance and escrow functions, and other aspects of property management.

Two landmark acts have comprehensively broadened the operating powers of savings and loan associations and fundamentally changed their ability to compete for the future in providing diversified financial services.

Garn-St. Germain Depository Institutions Act of 1982: In the opinion of the chairman of the Federal Home Loan Bank Board, the GARN-ST. GERMAIN DEPOSITORY INSTITUTIONS ACT OF 1982 "will allow the flexibility for (savings and loan) associations to choose how to structure themselves and what risks they would like to bear" in providing not only their traditional specialty of housing finance, but also their diversified financial services.

The act broadened the operating powers of savings and loan associations in seven areas.

1. Individual and corporate demand deposits authority. "Federals" (federally chartered institutions) may accept individual and corporate demand deposits.
2. Overdrafts. Overdraft loans may be issued with respect to any transaction account of a federal association, including the new individual and corporate demand accounts as well as NOW (negotiable order of withdrawal) accounts.
3. Commercial investment authority, including the following.
   a. Commercial loans. Federal savings and loan associations can invest 5% of their assets in commercial loans upon enactment of the act (which was October 15, 1982), and up to 10% after January 1, 1984. Federally chartered savings banks are initially authorized by the act to invest up to 7.5% of their assets in such loans.
   b. Commercial real estate loans. Up to 40% of assets may consist of loans secured by liens on nonresidential real estate. The liens do not have to be first liens.
   c. Inventory, floor planning, and consumer loans. Such loans may amount to 30% of assets.
   d. Equipment leasing. Up to 10% of assets may be invested in vehicles, mobile homes, machinery, equipment, furniture, and other tangible personal property for lease or sale.
4. Governmental securities. Up to 100% of assets may be invested in obligations of state and local governments. Except for investments in general obligation securities, however, investments in obligations of any one issuer are limited to 10% of the association's total capital and surplus.
5. Education loans. The act expands the scope of then current 5% of assets education loans authority to include any loan for educational purposes.
6. Time deposits in savings and loan associations. The act allows associations to invest in one another's time and savings deposits.
7. New money market account. The act amends the Depository Institutions Deregulation Act of 1980 to specifically mandate that the DEPOSITORY INSTITUTIONS DEREGULATION COMMITTEE authorize the new money market deposit account, not later than 60 days after date of enactment of the act, to be directly "equivalent to and competitive with Money Market Mutual Funds registered with the Securities and Exchange Commission under the Investment Company Act of 1940" (the committee authorized the new money market deposit account for depository institutions effective December 14, 1982). It also authorized "Super-NOW" accounts January 5, 1983.

Depository Institutions Deregulation and Monetary Control Act of 1980: The second landmark act "significantly [impacting] S & Ls" (*see* Marcis and Riordan in bibliography), the DEPOSITORY INSTITUTIONS DEREGULATION AND MONETARY CONTROL ACT OF 1980 (DIDMCA), included the following new powers for savings and loan associations.

1. Authorization to issue NOW (negotiable order of withdrawal) accounts nationwide by January 1, 1981.
2. Authorization for federal savings and loan associations to engage in trust fiduciary business and credit card activities.
3. Authorization to invest up to an aggregate limit of 20% of assets in consumer loans, commercial paper, corporate debt securities, and bankers acceptances.
4. New real estate lending authority. Federal S&Ls are permitted to make second mortgage loans and residential mortgage loans without any geographic restriction, and to invest in home mortgage loans of up to 90% of the appraised value of property which includes a building. (The mortgage may be 65% of the appraised value of an unimproved lot and 75% of the appraised value of an improved lot without a building.)
5. Permanent federal override of state usury ceilings for mortgages, and a 3-year preemption for business and agriculture loans over $25,000.
6. Increased investment authority in service corporation activities. The percentage of assets that an association can invest in the activities of a service corporation was increased from 1% to 3%. Any increase above 1% must be equally divided between community investment or community development activities and the regular business of the service corporation.
7. Federal associations are permitted to issue mutual capital certificates and provide that such certificates pay dividends rather than interest so that the certificates can be considered equity. In addition, the mutual capital certificates would be eligible for inclusion in insurance reserves. Mutual capital certificates are considered to hold the potential for providing mutual institutions with much-needed capital in the 1980s in order to continue growth without having to convert to the stock form of charter.
8. Phasing out of Regulation Q interest rate ceilings on deposits, regarded as perhaps the most controversial feature of the DIDMCA in that thrift institutions have traditionally regarded deposit interest rate controls and the "interest rate differential" of thrift institutions (in permitted rates higher than those permitted to commercial banks) as important to the viability of their operations.

Regulation Q would be phased out over a period of six years according to the act. The Deregulation Committee, consisting of representatives of each of the federal regulatory agencies and the Treasury Department, had the authority to raise or not to raise deposit rate ceilings on passbook accounts in accordance with the following targets established in the act.

1. During the first 18 months following passage of the act (on March 31, 1980), the target is a 25-basis-point increase in the rate on passbook accounts.
2. During the next 18 months, the target is a 50-basis-point increase.
3. During years four through six, the target is also 50 basis points each year. At the end of the sixth year, all rate control authority will cease and interest rates paid on deposits will be determined by the market.

The DIDMCA for the first time imposed "legal reserve requirements" against deposits of all depository institutions, besides member banks of the Federal Reserve System, in the form of nonearning deposits at a district Federal Reserve bank and cash on hand at the institution. After implementation of the act, nonmember institutions could maintain reserves on a "passthrough" basis with specified approved institutions. The required level of reserves is based on the total of transaction accounts (NOW, checking, and other third-party payment accounts) and nonpersonal time deposits (i.e., those not of natural persons)-12% on transaction balances over $25 million (adjustable according to annual increase percentage), 3% on transaction accounts below $25 million, and 3% on nonpersonal time deposits of original maturity of less than four years.

Although the act thus places nonbank institutions under the jurisdiction of the Federal Reserve for such legal reserve requirement purposes, and all depository institutions have access to the Federal Reserve "discount window" for loans, the respective regulatory agency of the nonbank depository institution continues to have regulatory jurisdiction over matters other than legal reserve requirements; the Fed's policy expects that each category of nonbank institution would first resort to its regulatory agency's channels for loans before turning to the Fed's discount window for funds. In the case of savings and loan associations, advances (loans) from the Federal Home Loan banks are the major type of borrowed funds, although some associations borrow directly in the nation's financial markets.

Specifics of Federal Home Loan Bank Board (FHLBB) regulation over associations include the following.

ENCYCLOPEDIA OF BANKING AND FINANCE

SAVINGS AND LOAN ASSOCIATIONS

1. Liquidity requirements. Mandated liquidity ratios are computed against withdrawable savings deposits and borrowings repayable on demand or in one year or less. Qualifying investments for regulatory liquidity, subject to specific maturity limits, include cash, demand deposits, U.S. government and federal agency securities, commercial bank time deposits, bankers acceptances, and state and municipal securities. The same types of investments, with shorter maturities, are eligible for the short-term liquidity requirement. The FHLBB is empowered by law to vary the overall liquidity ratio between 4% and 10%.
2. Liability reserves and net worth requirements, set by the FHLBB for all associations insured by the Federal Savings and Loan Insurance Corporation (FSLIC). Subordinated debt securities and mutual capital certificates (for a mutual association) may also be included as part of net worth, as may permanent stock (for a stock institution). The FHLBB has the power to vary the net worth requirement between 3% and 6%.

Types of Loans. Savings and loan associations offer a broad range of mortgage options for home-financing needs. Mortgages may be conventional (i.e., not insured or guaranteed by the FHA or VA) or may be made under a variety of government-sponsored programs. Private mortgage insurance also may be used on conventional loans to reduce risk.

Although most associations continued to offer the traditional fixed-rate, fixed-term mortgage loan, many also were moving into the area of alternative mortgage instruments, including graduated payment, reverse annuity, variable rate, and adjustable mortgage loans. A common feature of these newer types of loans is the provision for periodic interest rate adjustments.

Besides mortgage loans, almost all associations make a variety of consumer loans. The bulk of these loans were traditionally closely related to housing, such as mobile home and home improvement loans. Pursuant to 1980 legislation, associations are now allowed to finance other common consumer needs, such as automobile and credit card purchases.

Although mortgages generally are written with maturities of 25 or more years, loan portfolios turn over at a comparatively steady rate and provide a stream of loanable funds that, unlike volatile savings flows in recent years of high interest and returns in competing alternatives for savings, are predictable and constant for associations. These funds come into associations as scheduled payments on amortized principal, prepayments, loan payoffs because of the sale of the mortgaged properties, and proceeds from secondary mortgage market sales from the existing portfolio.

Secondary Mortgage Market. The secondary mortgage market is the aggregate buying, selling, and trading of existing mortgage loans and mortgage securities. Investors may buy whole loans, participations (ownership shares in a group of loans), or a variety of mortgage-backed securities.

Mortgage holders may set up pools by packaging FHA, VA, or conventional mortgages and issuing securities that represent shares in the package. The creator of the pool continues to make collections of payments from the borrowers. Payments to the investors may be passed on monthly as received, payments may be made monthly whether or not received, or interest may be paid semiannually and principal at designated intervals. Also, the securities may be guaranteed by the GOVERNMENT NATIONAL MORTGAGE ASSOCIATION (GNMA) or partially insured by a private mortgage insurance company.

Lenders that wish to free funds from their existing portfolios sell loans, participations, or securities. In times of high interest rates, sellers generally prefer to issue securities. This permits them to use old, low-rate loans to raise new funds without having to sell them at a discount.

Federal agency lenders operate primarily in the secondary market; they generally are net purchasers. In the private sector, mortgage companies dominate the selling side, while associations normally are the largest buyers of loans. In a typical year, associations' purchases account for 10% to 15% of their total loan acquisitions. In more recent years, associations have also become more interested in originating mortgage loans for subsequent sale to investors, such as pension funds and insurance companies.

Mergers. In recent years, associations experienced a steep decline in net income as a result of the interaction of high and volatile interest rates with their savings deposit and mortgage portfolio structure. When interest rates move higher, market-rate savings accounts offered by the associations attract a larger volume of funds compared to passbook savings. The cost of savings to the association rises, and the higher rates in alternative offerings must be paid or savings will flow to other institutions and other types of investments (disintermediation). At the same time, the interest rates on Federal Home Loan bank advances and other borrowed money also rise. Most of the association's mortgage portfolio, on the other hand, is still tied up in long-term, fixed-rate mortgages carrying low rates of years ago. High interest rates slow portfolio turnover further, as people defer home construction and purchases until rates decline, and as those who do buy homes in such a period often want to assume the existing lower-rate mortgage on the property. The rate of return on the portfolio therefore increases only slowly under such conditions.

The number of association mergers increased in the 1980s. The merger of a problem association into one that is financially and managerially strong is the rescue technique most frequently used for insured associations by the Federal Savings and Loan Insurance Corporation (FSLIC); such mergers can occur interstate across the country. In protecting the funds of savers, the FSLIC has a wide choice of remedies when a member institution's financial position becomes uncertain. It can make loans, grant contributions, purchase assets, or use any combination of these. These actions help put the member institution back on a firm footing or allow time for a merger or orderly liquidation to be arranged. Regulatory changes by the FHLBB liberalized rules and limits whereby FSLIC members could plan and consummate mergers.

Income Taxes. Associations were first made subject to federal corporate income tax in 1951. In general, they are taxed like other corporations, the major difference being that associations may use a special formula to make tax-free additions to reserves of otherwise taxable income. Like other corporations, associations are subject to a minimum tax on preference items of income, including accelerated depreciation on real property, capital gains, and any additions to loss reserves that exceed actual bad debt experience.

In order to claim special tax status as a "domestic building and loan association," an institution must pass three tests: a supervisory test, which requires that the institution be supervised by a state or federal agency; a business operations test, which requires that at least 75% of the deposits of an association be held by the general public and that at least 75% of gross income be derived primarily from mortgage loans; and an assets test, which requires that 60% of an association's assets be held in cash, residential mortgages, and certain other specified investments.

Summary. Because of lowered earnings in recent years of higher interest and other costs, associations have not been in a good position to move aggressively into the new areas and powers authorized by new legislation and regulations.

As the U.S. League of Savings Associations points out, whether the institution wants to establish a consumer lending operation, set up a trust services department, begin issuing credit cards, or move into some other newly authorized area, initial costs can be significant, and it can be some time before the operation begins to return a profit. Thus in the operating climate of 1980, many associations simply have been unable to bear the additional costs of entering these new and potentially profitable areas.

Moreover, in addition to increased competition for savings funds from traditional competitors (commercial banks, mutual savings banks, and credit unions), savings and loan associations face new competition, as do their traditional competitors, from the emerging "near banks" offering cash management accounts, personal lines of credit, free checking privileges, credit/debit cards, passthrough investments, money market funds and other mutual fund shares, broker participations, and other specialized financial services.

Thrift crisis. The thrift industry in the United States has been in turmoil since the 1970s, when interest rates were deregulated on deposits, but not on assets. Rising inflation pushed deposit rates above the yields on fixed-rate mortgages held by thrifts, resulting in major losses in the thrift industry. To remain competitive with similar rapidly expanding financial institutions, thrifts adjusted deposit rates more quickly than the rates charged for loans and other services.

The Garn-St. Germain Depository Institutions Act of 1982 attempted to place thrifts back in competition with other financial institutions by increasing the scope of their lending activities. The FEDERAL HOME LOAN BANK BOARD and the Federal Savings and Loans Insurance Corporation (FSLIC) were given some capability for dealing with thrifts in serious financial difficulty. They authorized an emergency program to assist institutions that had strained finances but relatively sound operations.

Rapid increases in oil and gas prices boosted the economies of the oil-and gas-producing states, which exerted pressure on the economy to keep pace with this expanded economic growth. Ill-advised lending practices and speculation by many institutions, especially ones in Texas, became rampant. The regulatory system was not prepared for this development at the state or federal level. The federal examination staff, centralized in Washington, was not equipped to cope with the problem. In mid-1985, the Federal Home Loan Bank Board decided to move the examination and supervision function out of Washington to the 12 district banks and to remove it from salary and hiring limitations.

During 1987, thrifts continued to attempt to meet their primary function of helping Americans build and purchase their own homes. They originated two-fifths of the home mortgages written, in the amount of $254 billion. Home mortgage holdings grew 10.5% in 1987. Prior to the crash, the sum of withdrawals outpaced deposits at thrifts on net by an average of $1.5 billion per month. A very low savings rate and households putting a larger portion of savings directly into market instruments or paying off existing debts contributed to this decline.

After the market collapse on October 19, 1987, depositors made large deposits in savings accounts; new deposits averaged $4.5 billion a month from October through April, due mainly to the high risks perceived in equity investments versus the protection offered by federally insured thrift institutions. The seven-month trend was reversed in May.

Thrifts began to be classified into two distinct segments: institutions that were solvent and generally well managed made up 90% of the industry; the remaining 10% were insolvent. The 10% experienced massive losses that resulted in the failure of many thrifts and attempts to rescue others by regulatory authorities and ultimately Congress and the American taxpayer. The insolvent thrifts lost $10.2 billion in 1987, while the industry had a net loss of $7.8 billion, compared with 1986 earnings of $131 million.

The institutions that produced these losses were concentrated in the energy and farm states, principally in the Dallas and Topeka districts of the FHLBS. The Dallas district accounted for more than 60% of 1987 losses. A major downturn in oil and gas production precipitated by a softening in the world price of crude oil caused a severe economic reversal in the "oil patch" areas. Economic distress in the farming sector was a contributing factor, as was the contraction in office building and multifamily residential construction nationally.

The resultant stress in the affected regions raised the cost of funds, fueled by insolvent institutions competing for a finite number of dollars under unfavorable conditions. The average cost of funds in the Dallas district in the fourth quarter of 1987 exceeded the national average by 47 basis points, and in the first quarter of 1988 it declined to 44 basis points over the national average.

The Federal Home Loan Bank Board developed and implemented a "Southwest Plan," which represented a strategy for consolidating ailing thrifts with healthy ones, in order to reduce costs and restore vitality to the industry without sacrificing service to the consumer.

The passing of the Competitive Equality Banking Act of 1987 brought about the $10.825 billion recapitalization of the FSLIC insurance fund. Shortly after enactment, the bank board put into place the regulations and resolutions required to implement its provisions. The board chartered the Financing Corporation (FICO) to manage the debt issue, authorizing it to issue up to $3.75 billion in any one year. FICO's organization consisted of a three-member directorate appointed by the bank board. The members included two Federal Home Loan Bank presidents and the director of the Office of Finance of the Federal Home Loan Bank System. FICO has made public and private sales of the 30-year maturity bonds, with yields varying in 1987-1988 from 9.42% to 10.73%. Total debt outstanding on June 30, 1988, was $2.9 billion. Bank trust departments, pension and retirement funds, mutual funds, insurance companies, and foreign investors made up 75% of the buyers. FICO bonds are noncallable instruments whose principal is guaranteed through the purchase of zero-coupon bonds financed by investments in FICO stock by the 12 Federal Home Loan banks. The bonds are held in a segregated account in the Federal Reserve Bank of New York City. Interest will be repaid from assessments on the federally insured thrift industry. The Federal Reserve Board's discount window accepts the bonds for open market operations and also as collateral. In 1988, Standard & Poor's had qualified FICO's debt securities as eligible investments for AAA rated financing.

Examinations of savings and loan institutions are under the supervision of the Federal Home Loan banks. If these periodic examinations reveals a problem, the district bank appoints a supervisory agent to monitor the institution without involving FSLIC. If an unassisted acquisition is deemed impossible, the agent may require that the institution be transferred into FSLIC, where an effort is made to resolve the problems. FSLIC hoped to resolve all of its cases by merger or acquisition because this method is usually the most economical solution for FSLIC on a case-by-case basis compared with liquidation or insured account payout. During 1987, FSLIC resolved 48 troubled thrifts at an estimated cost of $4.5 billion. Thirty-one were resolved by assisted sales to other financial institutions and corporate and private investors.

In 1987, 17 cases were resolved by insurance action. This involves transferring the insured deposits and branch offices of the closed thrift to another FSLIC-insured institution, without disrupting service to the insured depositors. Acquiring institutions paid FSLIC premiums totaling $24 million to take over the insured accounts.

The FSLIC is empowered to place an institution in its Management Consignment Program (MCP). MCP is an early intervention process for a thrift whose assets are being dissipated. It is an interim solution for a thrift that has been declared insolvent by the bank board. MCP thrifts are rechartered and new management is put in place, temporarily, to operate the institution on a day-to-day basis. The new institution assumes all assets, liabilities and deposits of its predecessor. As of 1987, 80 associations had been placed in the program since its inception in April 1985.

Since 1981, the tax laws have contained a number of provisions designed to help FSLIC fulfill its statutory mandate of protecting the safety and soundness of insured institutions.

The bank board's Office of Enforcement coordinates formal administrative enforcement activities throughout the bank system when violations of law or unsafe practices are found. These actions are halted before they do major harm, so losses to the institutions or FSLIC are reduced. Enforcement may prosecute matters by administrative or civil litigation, but it usually resolves them by obtaining enforcement orders or consent agreements. In 1987, the office obtained 25 cease and desist orders. Enforcement has been actively involved in making criminal referrals. In 1987 the Justice Department established a criminal prosecution task force of 50 lawyers, investigators, and accountants to assist with prosecutions. In the beginning, the task force concentrated its efforts in Texas because of the many thrift problems there.

The thrift industry deteriorated even further in 1988 and 1989. It was losing an estimated $20 million a day during the latter months of this period. The government became more deeply involved in attempting to rescue the thrifts. Insolvent thrifts placed under FDIC control (zombie thrifts) were permitted to offer extremely high rates to depositors. Insolvent thrifts felt that they had nothing to lose by paying high rates for deposits that could be used to make potentially high-return but very risky investments, such as JUNK BONDS. Throughout the thrift crisis, charges were made that the bank board was improperly influenced by the thrift industry and its lobbyists. The Justice Department brought several criminal cases against thrift personnel and officers during these years.

Thrift bailout. On August 10, 1989, President Bush signed legislation providing for a historic savings and loan bailout—the Financial Institutions Reform, Recovery and Enforcement Act of 1989. This legislation came two years after the August 10, 1987, bailout of the S&L insurance fund, which had been depleted while attempting to rescue ailing thrifts. The legislation provided funding for the bailout, imposed stricter financial standards on S&Ls activities, and brought about the most extensive overall changes of the regulatory bureaucracy in 50 years. The burden of the 1989 bailout falls on the taxpayers. The legislation calls for the government to borrow $50 billion over the 26-month period following enactment of the legislation, $20 billion before the 1989 fiscal year ended on September 30, and $30 billion in 1990 and 1991. An additional $15 billion in short-term debt to be issued before September 30, 1989, is to be refinanced as part of the Treasury's regularly scheduled borrowing program.

Funds were infused into the S&L system to replace high-rate certificates of deposits—the "Texas premium"—offered by ailing S&Ls. The objective was to cover the operating losses at 262 of the most seriously troubled institutions then under government control

SAVINGS AND LOAN ASSOCIATIONS

until the government could permanently rescue them and to improve the capital ratios of thrifts. Some of these institutions had been rate leaders, offering high interest rates to attract deposits they could not otherwise have obtained because of their weak financial condition. It was anticipated that this would take pressure off other institutions to offer high rates just to remain competitive. The 1989 legislation requires thrifts to have tangible capital (the excess of real assets over liabilities), or equity, of 1.5% of assets and core capital of 3% (a capital to asset ratio). Core capital includes goodwill acquired through takeover or merger with other institutions. By January 1995, 3% must be in tangible assets. This means that thrifts will have to attract more than $20 billion in new capital before 1995. They will have to keep almost 70% of their assets in mortgage-related investments, whereas they previously had almost unrestricted investment capabilities.

Professionals estimate that regulators will spend at least $166 billion to close or sell hundreds of insolvent savings institutions over the following decade. The result will be a dismantling of the $1.4 trillion thrift industry by arranging the removal of about 750 thrifts from the field. Commercial banks will be free to acquire healthy thrifts, and healthy thrifts can choose to convert themselves into banks. Experts in the field estimate that between 1,000 and 2,000 thrifts will fail or sell out; industry assets will shrink by more than $250 billion. The act provided for the creation of a bond-issuing agency—Resolution Financing Corporation—and a Resolution Trust Corporation to take over certain thrifts.

The restructuring of the thrift industry is expected to have many ripple effects. Depositors and mortgage borrowers will find it more difficult to locate bargains made available by ailing thrifts striving to survive. Commercial banks and money market funds will get most of the savings flowing out of the thrift industry. Cost of funds is expected to decline. Shareholders of healthy thrifts can expect to receive premiums for their shares from thrift acquires. Premiums paid by banks into the federal deposit-insurance fund will almost double, to $1.50 for every $1,000 of deposits; thrift premiums will rise to $2.30 in 1990 and could possibly reach $3.25. The lucrative tax breaks made available in 1988 to investors in restructured thrifts are no longer available.

It is estimated that commercial banks pay 8 to 20 cents for each dollar of deposits when they acquire bank branches, which is considered expensive. Healthy thrift stocks were considered cheap in 1989, frequently 50% or more below the price/earnings multiple of bank stocks. This would enable banks to acquire S&Ls for the equivalent of 4.5 cents per dollar of deposit. This arithmetic has made S&Ls attractive to commercial banks. Source: Federal Home Loan Bank Board.

The appended table shows the top 20 U.S. thrifts, ranked by size of deposits.

See FEDERAL HOME LOAN BANK SYSTEM.

BIBLIOGRAPHY

"America's Thrift Crisis: From Drama to Farce." *Economists*, January 21, 1989.
Audits of Savings and Loan Associations. American Institute of Certified Public Accountants, New York, NY.
BALDWIN, W. "The Money Has Already Been Borrowed." *Forbes*, February 20, 1989.
BARTH, J. R., and BRADLEY, M. G. "The Ailing S&Ls: Causes and Cures." *Challenge*, March/April, 1989.
"Capital Outlook." *United States Banker.* January, 1989.
COLLINS, S. H. "No Wonderful Life for Savings & Loans." *Journal of Accountancy*, December, 1988.
CROCKETT, J. H. "The Good Bank/Bad Bank Restructuring of Financial Institutions." *The Bankers Magazine*, November/December, 1988.
DICKERSON, C. S. *Commercial Lending by Thrift Institutions.* Robert Morris Associates, Philadelphia, PA, 1987.
EDGERTON, J. "You Owe Us $100 Billion." *Money*, March, 1989.
Fact Book of Savings Institutions. National Council of Savings Institutions, Washington, DC, 1988.
FEDERAL HOME LOAN BANK BOARD. *Annual Report.*
———. *All Operting Savings and Loan Associations: Selected Balance Sheet Data and Flow of Savings and Mortgage Lending Activities.* Monthly.
MOODY'S RATING OF THRIFTS. *United States Banker*, January, 1989.
Savings Institutions.
National Savings and Loan League Journal. Monthly.
Savings and Loan Source Book. United States League of Savings Associations, Chicago, IL. Annual.
Savings Institutions. United States League of Savings Institutions, Chicago, IL. Monthly.
Sourcebook: Savings Institutions. United State League of Savings Institutions, Chicago, IL. Latest edition.
The U.S. Savings Institutions Directory. Rand McNally. Skokie, IL, 1989.
"Who Is To Blame for the S&L Crisis?" *Fortune*, March 13, 1989.
YANG, C., and ZIGAS, D. "Only the Strong Will Survive the Thrift Rescue." *Business Week*, May, 1989.

Top 20 Thrift Institutions, Ranked by Size of Deposits—December 31, 1987

Rank	Savings & Loan Association	Location	Assets ($000) 12/31/87	12/31/86
1	American Savings & Loan Assn.	Stockton, CA	33,843,873	33,933,294
2	Home Savings of America FA	Irwindale, CA	30,533,471	27,789,661
3	Great Western Bank, FSB	Beverly Hills, CA	28,526,110	27,405,368
4	California Federal Savings & Loan Assn.	Los Angeles, CA	23,219,400	20,540,400
5	Glendale Federal Savings & Loan Assn.	Glendale, CA	23,206,137	17,451,589
6	Meritor Savings Bank	Philadelphia, PA	19,016,456	18,447,272
7	First Nationwide Bank FSB	San Francisco, CA	17,177,903	15,044,316
8	Great American First Savings Bank	San Diego, CA	15,242,243	13,064,815
9	Goldome FSB	Buffalo, NY	15,153,370	14,669,199
10	Home Federal Savings & Loan Assn. of San Diego	San Diego, CA	14,109,123	12,074,620
11	CrossLand Savings FSB	Brooklyn, NY	13,774,567	10,095,697
12	Gibraltar Savings	Beverly Hills, CA	13,480,564	11,406,157
13	World Savings FS&LA	Oakland, CA	12,837,910	12,439,262
14	Coast Savings & Loan Assn.	Los Angeles, CA	11,951,980	9,725,362
15	First Federal of Michigan	Detroit, MI	11,882,593	11,271,916
16	Columbia Savings & Loan Assn.	Beverly Hills, CA	11,227,256	10,222,652
17	Dime Savings Bank of New York	Garden City, NY	10,944,187	8,366,595
18	Imperial Savings Assn.	San Diego, CA	10,869,882	8,911,820
19	Empire of America, FSB	Buffalo, NY	10,855,983	6,301,574
20	City Federal Savings Bank	Bedminster, NJ	10,810,794	10,728,053

Source: The American Banker.

SAVINGS AND LOAN BANK OF NEW YORK

Originally created by the New York State Legislature in 1914, this institution began operations in January, 1915, as the Land Bank of the State of New York. The legislature changed its title to the Savings and Loan Bank of the State of New York in 1932, converting it into a central bank owned by the SAVINGS AND LOAN ASSOCIATIONS of the state of New York and servicing them with short- and long-term funds, as well as accepting their deposits. In its last years, it also operated a data processing facility at Fishkill, New York, which has been closed after having been leased to I.B.M. The institution was placed in voluntary liquidation in 1968. Creditors and depositors were reported paid off.

Chapter 322, New York State Laws of 1970, authorized savings and loan associations in New York State to invest in a trust company or other New York corporation whose stock is owned exclusively by at least 20 New York State-chartered savings and loan associations or federal savings and loan associations located in New York State.

SAVINGS AND LOAN HOLDING COMPANIES

The Savings and Loan Holding Company Amendments of 1967, signed February 14, 1968, provided for comprehensive regulation of holding companies in the industry. These institutions were required to register with the Federal Savings and Loan Insurance Corporation, to file periodic reports on their financial condition, and to submit to regular examinations by the FSLIC. The 1968 legislation was a set of amendments to Section 408 of the National Housing Act, previously known as the Spence Act. The stated purpose of the Spence Act was to promote and preserve local management of SAVINGS AND LOAN ASSOCIATIONS by protecting them against encroachment by holding companies. But in its original form, "it was only effective to a limited extent." Although the Spence Act put some restraints on acquisitions by holding companies, the Federal Home Loan Bank Board had found significant abuses in areas not dealt with by that act. For example, it did not give the board access to books and records of holding companies and their affiliates. By this omission, the board was denied knowledge of transactions between subsidiary associations and their holding company affiliates, even where such transactions were prohibited by the act. The new legislation strengthened the board's ability to cope with holding company practices. As amended, Section 408 of the National Housing Act now provides the FSLIC, acting through the board, with the necessary regulatory and supervisory powers.

A holding company or its subsidiaries that are not savings and loan associations cannot engage in activities on behalf of its savings and loan subsidiaries that would evade any law or regulation applicable to such subsidiaries; nor can a holding company that controls more than one association engage in certain activities unrelated to the savings and loan industry. (The divestment deadline was extended to February 14, 1973.)

The act prohibits certain transactions between the subsidiary-insured associations and their holding company affiliates. It also authorizes the board to pass on other affiliated transactions. It requires prior written approval by the board for any acquisition by a holding company of an additional insured institution, whether by purchase of stock or assets or by merger. Prior written approval by the board also is necessary before any company that is not a savings and loan holding company can acquire one or more insured associations. The act authorizes the board to control the incurrence of debt by a holding company, other than a "diversified savings and loan holding company," in excess of 15% of its consolidated net worth.

Under the law, a "diversified savings and loan holding company" is one in which that segment of its business embracing savings and loan and related activities represents less than 50% of its consolidated net worth and 50% of its consolidated net earnings. Such a company is exempt from the debt control provisions of the law.

To avoid an immediate violation of the prohibition against interlocking management, Section 584.9(b) of the regulations provided in effect a moratorium until May 15, 1968. Thereafter continuation of an interlock required board approval. The board established the principle that such management interlocks could be approved only when they were instituted at the behest of the board. In the latter part of 1969, the board transferred the responsibility for processing all applications filed by holding company-controlled associations from the Washington office to the supervisory agent at the district Federal Home Loan bank where the applicant is located. A further move toward decentralization was made when the board delegated authority to the director and the deputy director, Office of Examinations and Supervision, to pass on debt applications involving amounts of not more than $500,000. These officers may also pass on applications for deregistration. Supervisory agents were authorized to grant extensions of time for filing registration statements and periodic reports.

Financial Institutions Regulatory and Interest Rate Control Act of 1978 (P.L. 95-630, November 10, 1978). The FINANCIAL INSTITUTIONS REGULATORY AND INTEREST RATE CONTROL ACT OF 1978 was notable for the improved enforcement powers provided for the Federal Home Loan Bank Board in those parts of the act affecting the FHLBB or the institutions under its jurisdiction.

Title I, increased supervisory authority: The FHLBB can now obtain cease-and-desist orders against individual directors, officers, employees, agents, and other persons participating in the affairs of an insured institution. Such orders can also be issued against service corporations of mutuals as well as savings and loan holding companies and their uninsured affiliates. Previously, cease-and-desist action was possible only against insured institutions.

The FHLBB under Title I can now require a savings and loan holding company to terminate activities, ownership, or control of any noninsured subsidiary, if such activities, ownership, or control constitute a serious risk to the financial safety, soundness, or stability of an insured subsidiary and are inconsistent with either the sound operation of an insured institution or the purposes of Section 408 of the NATIONAL HOUSING ACT (governing savings and loan holding companies) or the Financial Institutions Supervisory Act. In addition, the existing authority to suspend and to remove individual officers and directors was expanded to enable the FHLBB to proceed against such persons.

Included in Title I was provision for greatly improving the ability of the Federal Savings and Loan Insurance Corporation (FSLIC) to deal with institutions in financial difficulty by authorizing the FSLIC to purchase assets, assume liabilities, and make loans or guarantees in order to facilitate the merger of an insured institution in danger of default or sale of its assets (with assumption of liabilities). In addition, the prior requirement that contributions or guarantees must not be in excess of the amount reasonably necessary to save the expense of liquidating the institution was modified to provide for an exception in cases where the FSLIC determined that the continued operation of the institution was essential to provide adequate savings or home-financing services to its community.

Title II, interlocking directorates: Under Title II, restrictions were placed on management official interlocks between depository institutions or depository holding companies and other depository institutions or depository holding companies not affiliated therewith.

1. Geographic restriction. A management official of a depository institution or a depository holding company may not serve as a management official of any other depository institution or depository holding company not affiliated therewith, except for depository institutions having assets less than $20 million, if an office of one of the institutions or any depository institution that is an affiliate of such institutions is located within the same SMSA (standard metropolitan statistical area) as an office of the other institution or any depository institution that is an affiliate of such other institution, or within the same city, town, or village as an office of the other institution or any depository institution that is an affiliate of such other institution, or within any city, town, or village contiguous or adjacent thereto.

2. Size restriction. Management officials of depository institutions or depository holding companies (or affiliates) having assets greater than $1 billion are prohibited from serving as management officials of any other nonaffiliated depository institution or depository holding company (or affiliate) having total assets greater than $500 million.

3. Exceptions to interlock prohibitions. The geographic and size prohibitions do not apply to an institution in liquidation or in the hands of a receiver or conservator, an Edge Act corporation, a credit union being served by a management official of another credit union, a depository institution or depository holding company that does not do any business in the U.S. except as an incident to activities outside the U.S., a state-chartered savings and loan guaranty corporation, or a Federal Home Loan bank or any other organization specifically organized to serve depository institutions. Furthermore, the FHLBB may prescribe regulations to permit otherwise prohibited service.

SAVINGS AND LOAN INSURANCE CORPORATION
See FEDERAL SAVINGS AND LOAN INSURANCE CORPORATION.

SAVINGS BANK INVESTMENTS
Savings banks are restricted by state laws in the investment of their assets to prescribed types of securities and other investments, largely fixed income producing and of conservative quality. The chief reason for such supervision is to prevent speculation with savings deposits and to enforce conservatism, and thus to make savings banks as sound as possible. Regulating states may be "legal list" states (those publishing specific list of securities eligible for savings bank investment) or "non-legal list" states (those prescribing the standards by statute but not specifying the securities). Even in states that publish a legal list of securities, however, the selection of particular securities from the legal list is still a function and responsibility of savings bank management.

First mortgage loans are legal investments for savings banks in all states, as well as investment in government, state, and municipal bonds. High-grade railroad bond and equipment trust obligations and public utility (electric, gas, telephone) obligations are generally eligible. Bank stocks with specified investment characteristics are permitted investments in New England states, but stocks in general have only in recent years been authorized under qualitative and quantitative limitations. Loans secured by mortgages and securities themselves eligible for investment are generally legal, as are bankers' acceptances, bills of exchange, and loans secured by passbook. Direct investment in real estate is not permitted except for real estate acquired as a place of business for the bank and its branches.

SAVINGS BANKS
Banking institutions organized especially to encourage thrift among persons of modest means by paying interest-dividends on savings deposited therein. Originally, savings banks were regarded as semiphilanthropic institutions that provided facilities for collecting the savings of the poor and investing such savings in high-grade investments, to the end that income therefrom might provide periodic interest-dividends to depositors. Although modern mutual savings banks continue to be classified as nonprofit institutions, they are no longer regarded as semiphilanthropic institutions for the poor. Nevertheless, one feature of savings banks has remained dominant, i.e., the public promotion of thrift and strict supervision of the investment of deposits as a means of protecting a class of depositor that can least afford to lose such personal lifetime and precautionary savings, but that is least capable of making a wise selection of a bank.

The concept of a savings bank is said to have originated with Daniel DeFoe, the English author, who in 1697 suggested the organization of "Friendly Societies for Provident Habits in General." The first Friendly Society, however, was not organized until 1765, and development was slow. The name "savings bank" was not applied until 1810, when the Rev. Henry Duncan of Ruthwell Village, Dumfrieshire, Scotland, established a small bank for his parishioners, which received about $750 in deposits the first year.

Following are among the earliest savings institutions in the United States. The Philadelphia Savings Fund Society, sponsored by wealthy businessman and philanthropist Condy Raquet, began operations in December, 1816, although it was not chartered until 1819. The Provident Institution of Savings in the Town of Boston, chartered in mid-December, 1816, began operations in February, 1817. The Savings Bank of Baltimore and the Salem Savings Bank (Massachusetts) were founded in 1818. The Bank for Savings in the City of New York, Society for Savings of Hartford (Connecticut), Savings Bank of Newport (Rhode Island), and Providence (Rhode Island) Institution for Savings were started in 1819; and the Institution for Savings in Newburyport and Vicinity (Massachusetts) and Albany Savings Bank (New York) began operations in 1820. The third largest savings bank in the country, the Bowery Savings Bank of New York City, with total deposits at mid-year 1981 of $4,867 million, dates from 1834. The period of greatest expansion in savings bank chartering occurred in the two decades from 1850 to 1870, particularly in the post-Civil War period and in the eastern states. Most "mutual" savings banks are to be found in ten states in the northeast. With the rise of savings and loan associations and the acceptance of savings deposits by commercial banks, including national banks following the enactment of the National Bank Act, the spread of the mutual type of savings bank to other parts of the country slowed. By 1900, there were 492 mutual savings banks, with total deposits of some $2 billion.

The mutual-type charter is distinctive in being nonstock, although corporate in nature, and in providing for self-perpetuating trustees, the depositors having no voting power (under the federal [mutual] savings bank charter [see below], depositor voting of the trustees must be adopted six years after conversion). The nonstock feature means that depositors as general creditors are the residual interest and share proportionately in the earnings, after expenses and allocations to reserves and surplus (sometimes called "guaranty fund") by the trustees. Deposits in savings banks, whether mutual or stock type, are liabilities, and depositors are creditors. In any liquidation, it is a moot question whether the present depositors are entitled to a pro rata distribution of all the reserves and surplus built up from the past retention of earnings from all depositors, both present depositors and former depositors. The nonstock feature has also entitled mutual savings banks to a tax classification as nonprofit institutions, and thus to special tax treatment; but unlike depositors in other cooperative financial institutions, depositors have no voting power. The management of a mutual savings bank is headed by its board of trustees or managers; "by State legislation and long precedent, they are committed in practice to the theory that they will be better run if their trustees are chosen by the existing board from the best talent available among the successful and experienced business men and citizens of the community" (*American Banker*). This traditional practice probably is grounded in the origin of mutual savings banks as thrift institutions for the poor and wage-earners, a class of depositors not expected to be knowledgeable enough for intelligent voting, and on the high degree of fiduciary and public responsibility chargeable to trustees. Nevertheless, in some states, the trustees are elected by a larger group of "corporators"; the state banking official might demur to the nominee's background in a board's designation of a new trustee (as in the case of alleged nepotism in a large New York City institution), and many trustees are not banking experts and thus are actually dependent upon the expertise of the officers the trustees appoint. The responsibilities of trustees under representative state laws include the following.

1. Observance of the trustee's oath, which in one state must be reaffirmed each year. Similar to the oath of national bank directors, the trustee's oath affirms that the trustee will diligently and honestly administer the affairs of the bank. Some states prohibit service as a trustee to any individual who has ever been involved in recourse to any insolvency law-an unfair restriction since the determining factor should be the character and ethics of the individual concerned.
2. Fiduciary responsibility to depositors for performance of duties with care and diligence. If loss or damage to depositors occurs because of lack of proper care and diligence, the trustees may be held personally liable.
3. Active participation in management, including examining the bank; overseeing bank mortgage loans and investments by service on trustee committees; declaring dividends consistent with earnings and with statutes; and determining general policies for the officers to execute as to operations, investments, etc.
4. Absence of conflicts of interest. In nearly all states a trustee may not obtain loans from his own bank or have any interest in profits of the bank, including any salary for service as trustee or, in some states, fees for attendance at meetings, etc. Trustees serving, however, are entitled to compensation for their services as officers and for their services for the bank as attorney, but no commissions or fees are permitted for obtaining any loans or investments from the bank.

Any trustee (or officer) of a savings bank is subject to removal from office, on notice and hearing, for violations of law, for continuation of unsafe or unsound practices, or for actions contrary to the best interests of the bank.

In lieu of capital stock, the original incorporators of a mutual savings bank contribute to an original fund, which thereafter is repayable gradually from earnings. Thus although nominally "nonprofit" in purpose, savings bank organization actually depends upon the likelihood of successful operation. State laws varyingly prescribe the minimum "guaranty fund" (surplus) that must be maintained. In general, a surplus of 10% to 15% is considered adequate relative to deposits.

Regulation of Loans and Investments. Another distinctive feature of the mutual savings bank is the detailed nature of regulation of operations. For an example of such regulation of investments, that of New York State, *see* SAVINGS BANK INVESTMENTS. Stock savings banks are not regulated as intensively as the mutual type as to investments by the states chartering them, but some of these states impose detailed regulation comparable to that in the "mutual" states.

Impact of the DIDMCA of 1980. The Depository Institutions Deregulation and Monetary Control Act of 1980, signed into law by the President on March 31, 1980, included the following provisions relevant to savings banks.

Phaseout of Regulation Q and the "differential": Federal deposit interest rate control was extended for six years, to March 31, 1986. Authority to establish rates during the phaseout period was transferred to the DEPOSITORY INSTITUTIONS DEREGULATION COMMITTEE (DIDC), which was directed "to provide for the orderly phase-out and the ultimate elimination" of interest rate controls "as rapidly as economic conditions warrant" and with "due regard for the safety and soundness of depository institutions."

During the phaseout period, the committee was authorized to increase the ceilings on existing categories of accounts, to create new categories of accounts not subject to limitations, or to remove ceilings entirely. However, the committee could not increase ceilings above market rates. Targets were established to increase passbook and similar savings account rates by at least 0.25% in the first 18 months and by 0.5% by the end of each of the third through sixth years. These rate increases were not mandatory, the National Association of Mutual Savings Banks (NAMSB) pointed out; rather, the committee has leeway to adjust ceilings higher or lower than the established targets, and during the six-year period, the 0.25% thrift institution differential must be maintained on all categories of accounts in existence as of December 19, 1975.

During 1980, the NAMSB criticized various DIDC actions, suggested a need for new legislation to assure the rate differential (between thrift institutions and commercial banks on payment of interest on deposits), and supported an amendment to a 1980 housing bill that would have added the secretary of Housing and Urban Development to the deregulation committee.

Mandatory reserve requirements: Mandatory reserve requirements were imposed by the DIDMCA upon all financial institutions offering transaction accounts (defined as demand deposits, NOW accounts, automatic transfers, telephone bill paying plans, or similar third-party payment orders). Reserves of 3% were set on the first $25 million in transaction account balances, with reserves on balances over $25 million to range from 8% to 14%, the initial rate set at 12%. In addition, nonpersonal time deposits were subject to 3% reserves initially, with the Federal Reserve permitted to vary this requirement from 0% to 9%. The act also authorized the imposition of supplemental, interest-bearing reserves of up to 4% on transaction accounts, if monetary policy necessitated such action.

The NAMSB's position on the issue of mandatory reserve requirements imposed on all financial institutions had been that a persuasive case had not been made for the need to extend reserve requirements to transaction balances held by thrift institutions. The NAMSB pointed out that savings banks are strongly influenced by Federal Reserve policies through the impact of OPEN MARKET OPERATIONS on interest rate levels, and through changes in Regulation Q ceilings. There was great concern that extending the reserve-setting authority of the Federal Reserve to nonmembers could establish a precedent, so that at some future time reserve requirements might be applied not only to transaction accounts of thrift institutions, but to their regular savings and time deposits as well.

Corporate powers for federal savings banks: The DIDMCA authorized corporate banking powers for federal mutual savings banks, but not for federal SAVINGS AND LOAN ASSOCIATIONS (that expansion of powers for federal savings and loan associations was later provided by the GARN-ST. GERMAIN DEPOSITORY INSTITUTIONS ACT OF 1982). Federal savings banks were permitted under the act to make commercial, corporate, and business loans up to 5% of assets, provided such loans were made within the state or within 75 miles of the bank's headquarters. Federal savings banks could also "accept demand deposits in connection with a commercial, corporate, or business loan relationship." These powers (and others listed below) were granted in addition to those which already existed under state law; the latter would therefore be "grandfathered" in connection with a conversion of charter from state charter to federal savings bank charter.

Federal mutual savings banks and federal savings and loan associations were authorized by the act to invest to an aggregate of 20% of their assets in secured and unsecured consumer loans, commercial paper, and corporate debt securities. They were also granted other new powers in the areas of issuance of credit cards, liberalized real estate lending, trust operations, and issuance of mutual capital certificates (form of debt financing).

Federal charter authority has been provided by Title XII of the FINANCIAL INSTITUTIONS REGULATORY AND INTEREST RATE CONTROL ACT OF 1978 (FIRIRCA), which gave savings banks the option to convert to federal savings banks in the 17 states in which they operate. Such institutions will be supervised by the FEDERAL HOME LOAN BANK BOARD (FHLBB) and insured by the FEDERAL SAVINGS AND LOAN INSURANCE CORPORATION. The federal charter title does not authorize the de novo chartering of savings banks in any state; thus, only institutions that previously existed as state-chartered savings banks may convert to federal mutual savings banks.

Subject to approval by the Federal Home Loan Bank Board, a savings bank that converts to federal charter is permitted to do the following.

1. Continue all of the activities it was engaged in as of December 31, 1977.
2. Retain or make all types of investments held at year-end 1977, except that its equity, corporate bond, and consumer loan investments cannot exceed the average ratio of such investments to total assets for the five years immediately preceding the application to convert.
3. Establish branch offices and other facilities as prescribed by state law, except that the state's numerical limitations on branching do not apply, and the savings bank is permitted to branch within its own standard metropolitan statistical area (SMSA), within its county, or within 35 miles of its home office regardless of state law-but not across state lines.

If, at the time of conversion, the FHLBB determines that antidiscrimination laws and regulations covering the extension of home mortgage credit, or any requirements implementing the Consumer Credit Protection Act, are more stringent than the comparable federal provisions, the state law will govern the federal savings bank.

Title XII of the FIRIRCA also stipulated that a federal mutual savings bank may not subsequently convert from the mutual to the stock form of ownership.

The NAMSB hailed passage of the FIRIRCA as for the first time providing savings banks with access to the benefits of the dual banking system, "a privilege which has long been available to all of the nation's other depository institutions."

On September 11, 1980, the application of the Newport Savings Bank in Newport, New Hampshire, to convert from a state to a federal charter was approved by the Federal Home Loan Bank Board. It was the nation's first savings bank to receive federal charter approval under the FIRIRCA of 1978, which authorized a system of federal chartering for mutual savings banks. (The Newport Savings Bank changed its name upon conversion to Newport Savings Bank fsb, and subsequently to Lake Sunapee Savings Bank fsb.) As of May, 1981, federal charter conversions had also been completed by the Anchor Savings Bank fsb, New York City, and Citizens Savings Bank fsb, Ithaca, New York; several other applications were pending.

For other provisions, *see* DEPOSITORY INSTITUTIONS DEREGULATION AND MONETARY CONTROL ACT OF 1980.

Disintermediation Problems: For the first time during the postWorld War II period, the savings bank industry reported negative bottom-line earnings in 1980. The 1980 loss was equivalent to $205 million, or 0.12% of total assets, compared with net income of $741 million, or 0.46% of total assets, in 1979. Increases in deposit interest expenses outpaced gains in gross operating income by a substantial margin, with interest paid to depositors rising a record $2 billion in 1980, the effective interest rate paid on savings bank deposits in 1980 being 7.85%, 105 basis points higher than in 1979. The substantial rise in interest paid on deposits in 1980 resulted from the variety of deposit arrangements paying more than the permitted ceiling passbook rate, offered by savings banks in an attempt to staunch the heavy outflow of deposits to higher-yielding money market funds and other alternatives available for depositors. These deposit arrangements included sharply increased rates paid on 6-month money market certificates of deposits by the savings banks, accelerated shifts within the savings banks from fixed-rate to market-linked accounts, higher rollover expenses on maturing money market certificates throughout much of the year, considerable growth in $2\frac{1}{2}$-year market-linked certificates of deposit, and ceiling rate increases on both 6-month and 30-month certificates of deposit.

By 1981, the equity accounts of some savings banks were so weakened by continued operating losses that emergency mergers, involving even giant institutions, began to appear. Early in 1981, a study by the Federal Reserve focused on the general issue of affiliation between commercial banks and thrift institutions. The NAMSB continued to oppose any action by the Federal Reserve Board to permit bank holding companies to acquire thrift institutions. A bill passed by the U.S. Senate in September, 1980, supported by the NAMSB, would have imposed an indefinite moratorium on the acquisition of thrift institutions by commercial banks *except in cases where a takeover was deemed necessary to prevent an insolvency* (italics ours). The position of the NAMSB is that Congress, rather than the regulatory agencies, should decide the issue in a manner that will ensure the "continued integrity of the thrift industry as the major competitors of commercial banks."

Impact of Garn-St. Germain Depository Institutions Act of 1982. This legislation has finally provided the authority for the effective federal assistance program for thrift institutions, particularly savings banks, which the thrift institutions had been urging.

Title I of the act, entitled Deposit Insurance Flexibility, enhanced the ability of the FEDERAL DEPOSIT INSURANCE CORPORATION (FDIC) and the Federal Savings and Loan Insurance Corporation (FSLIC) to aid institutions in need of assistance by expanding the forms of financial assistance that could be provided by these agencies, by broadening the circumstances under which such assistance could be granted, and by providing specific procedures for the agencies to follow to facilitate the acquisition or merger of failed or failing institutions. Broadened conservatorship powers with respect to certain of the insuring agencies were granted.

Title II of the act, entitled Net Worth Certificates, provided authorization for an income capital assistance program designed to assist insured institutions having a net worth equal to or less than 3% of assets. In order to qualify for such assistance, institutions must have a net worth equal to or greater than 0.5% of their assets after issuance of such net worth certificates (capital notes), which may be counted as part of the surplus of the institutions. If the surplus falls to between 2% and 3% of assets, the institution is eligible for capital infusion equal to 50% of its net operating loss for the two previous quarters; and if surplus falls to between 1% and 2% of assets, the capital infusion could be equal to 60%, rising to 70% of the net operating loss for the two previous quarters if the surplus falls between 0.5% and 1%. Assistance under Title I of the act does not preclude assistance under Title II. But should surplus fall below 0.5% of total assets, the institution is not eligible for Title II capital infusion.

The FDIC reported in January, 1983, that it had provided some $175 million in assistance to 15 savings banks, most of them in the New York City area, still faced with continuing operating losses as the result of the higher interest cost of deposits necessary to stem the drain of disintermediation, especially in competition with money market funds, compared to still low earnings rates on portfolios of mortgage loans made years ago at then prevailing low interest rates.

The Garn-St. Germain Depository Institutions Act also mandated the authorization by the DEPOSITORY INSTITUTIONS DEREGULATION COMMITTEE (DIDC) of the money market deposit account (authorized December 14, 1982) to depository institutions. The DIDC further authorized the new "Super-NOW" accounts as of January 5, 1983. Both of these accounts, in conjunction with trend toward lower rates in the money markets, have eased the competitive problem in attracting and keeping deposit funds at lower rates, thus making it possible to add to earning assets, including new mortgages at a favorable interest rate spread over cost of deposits, and to improve operating income.

See SAVINGS BANK INVESTMENTS.
See also SAVINGS AND LOAN ASSOCIATIONS.

BIBLIOGRAPHY

FEDERAL DEPOSIT INSURANCE CORPORATION. *Annual Report.*
FEDERAL SAVINGS INSURANCE FUND. *Annual Report.*
National Fact Book. National Council of Savings Institutions. Washington, DC. Annual.
Savings Bank Journal.
Taxation of Financial Institutions. Matthew Bender & Co., Inc., New York, NY. Looseleaf.

SAVINGS BONDS   *See* UNITED STATES SAVINGS BONDS.

SAVINGS DEPOSITS   *See* SAVINGS ACCOUNTS, SAVINGS AND LOAN ASSOCIATIONS, SAVINGS BANKS.

SAY'S LAW   Supply creates its own demand. A "law" named after economist Jean Baptiste Say (1767-1832).

SCALE BUYING   *See* BUYING ON A SCALE.

SCALING   A method of trading in securities or commodities in which orders to buy are placed at regular intervals downward from the prevailing market price and orders to sell are placed at regular intervals upward from the prevailing market price.
See BUYING ON A SCALE.

SCALPER   A speculator who sells at every opportunity to make a fractional, one-point, or two-point profit.
See SCALPING.

SCALPING   The realization of a fractional, one-point, or two-point trading profit, especially when turns are made in quick succession; taking advantage of any small gain.

SCANDINAVIAN UNION   A monetary union formed by Norway, Sweden, and Denmark in 1873, in which the single gold standard and the same monetary unit were adopted-the krone. In 1905, Norway dissolved its political union with Sweden and elected its own king.
See LATIN UNION.

SCARCITY   The limited availability and quantity of resources in relation to the unlimited needs and wants of human beings. Scarcity is a condition that faces every society.

SCHEDULE SHOWING WHEN PROCEEDS OF ITEMS WILL BECOME AVAILABLE   In connection with the FEDERAL RESERVE CHECK COLLECTION SYSTEM, each district Federal Reserve bank publishes operating circulars for the guidance of member banks and others concerned who send checks to the Fed or are presented checks for payment. Such circulars are issued pursuant to Regulation J of the Board of Governors of the Federal Reserve System, Collection of Checks and Other Items and Wire Transfers of Funds.

Regulation J of the Board of Governors of the Federal Reserve System, as amended effective August 12, 1981, governs the collection of checks and other cash items and the collection of noncash items by the Federal Reserve banks. Subpart A of the regulation covers the sending of items to the Federal Reserve banks, the warranties of the banks, and the remittance and payment for the items. Subpart B of the regulation defines the rights and responsibilities of member banks using the Federal Reserve Communications System for "wire transfer of funds"; this subpart does not govern other electronic payments, such as point-of-sale transactions and payments processed through automated clearinghouses (ACHs).

The check collection cycle begins with the deposit of a check at a depository institution. If the check is drawn on that institution, the collection is completed internally. If the check is drawn on another depository institution, other steps are required before funds can be transferred from the depository institution upon which the check is drawn.

1. Checks may be sent by the depository institution receiving them as deposits directly to the depository institution on which they are drawn. In such cases, the two institutions settle directly with each other.
2. Alternatively, checks may be sent to correspondent banks that provide clearing and collection services.
3. Checks also may be cleared through a clearing association of which both depository institutions are members.

Checks that are not handled through any of the preceding arrangements are likely to be processed through the Federal Reserve's check collection system.

The depositing depository institution will receive credit from the receiving Federal Reserve bank according to the Federal Reserve bank's published Deferred Availability Schedule, with the time ranging from the same day the checks are received to a maximum of two business days later. On the day such credit is due, the depositing institution's reserve account balance at the Federal Reserve bank is increased, and on the day payment is made, the paying institution's reserve balance is reduced.

Assuming the collection process goes smoothly, the day the credit is available for use by depositing institutions will correspond to the day payment is received. However, for a variety of reasons, the Federal Reserve bank may be prevented from obtaining payment from the depository institution on which the checks are drawn on the same day that credit automatically is given. Checks received in poor condition must be processed at Federal Reserve offices on semiautomatic equipment, slowing the collection process. Or delays may occur due to unexpected volume or equipment malfunctions. Another factor may be transportation delays that arise from bad weather, strikes, or mechanical breakdowns. In certain circumstances, some depository institutions and the Federal Reserve bank may be open, while other depository institutions in the same district are closed.

When checks in the process of collection do not reach their destination as scheduled, credit is given to the depositing institution's reserve account balance at the Federal Reserve bank anyway. At that moment, FLOAT is created. Federal Reserve float thus created affects the monetary aggregates, since it creates reserves in the banking system. Therefore, depending upon monetary objectives, OPEN MARKET OPERATIONS of the Federal Reserve System may have to be used to offset movements in float.

See AUTOMATED CLEARINGHOUSE.

SCHOOL BONDS   A subclassification of municipal bonds issued for the purpose of raising funds for the construction and equipment of public schools.

See MUNICIPAL BONDS.

SCHOOL DISTRICT BONDS   Bonds issued by a school district (organizational unit organized to manage and control the schools of a certain section and having taxing power) for the purpose of building public schools. The school district is the typical unit of school finance in the U.S., and there are some 70,000 such districts. Many states, however, use the township or county as the financial and administrative organization for schools. School district bonds are payable from taxes on all property encompassed by the district, as general lien obligations of the communities included.

See MUNICIPAL BONDS.

SCHOOL SAVINGS BANKS   Savings systems adopted by many public schools for the purpose of inculcating habits of thrift among schoolchildren. In the U.S., the pioneers in adapting the idea from European practice were S. T. Merillo of Beloit Savings Bank, Wisconsin in 1882 and J. H. Thiry, a Long Island City (N.Y.) school commissioner, in 1883. By receiving authority from the local board of education and enlisting the cooperation of the teaching staff, savings banks throughout the U.S. have organized many school savings departments, or junior departments.

Different plans have been used for collecting and administering school savings. In some cases, the money is collected periodically by the teachers and turned over to the principal, who places it in the savings bank in the name of each depositor. Special passbooks and other special forms are provided for this purpose. Another method is to issue and sell stamps that are pasted in a book as evidence of deposits. In other cases, the pupils make their deposits over the window. The American Bankers Association (Savings and Mortgage Division) actively promotes the participation by banks in school savings banking and in the sale of U.S. savings bonds and stamps in schools, and has devised inexpensive savings systems for use by banks.

See SAVINGS BANKS.

SCHUMPETERIAN HYPOTHESIS   The hypothesis that firms with greater market power will be more innovative than those with less because the former can appropriate the benefits of innovation to a greater degree. Joseph Schumpeter, the foremost economics writer in the—German Historical School of the early to mid-1900s, described innovation by means of a production function. The production function, he wrote, describes the way the quantity of product varies with the quantity of inputs. If the form of the production function is varied, rather than the quantity of inputs, there has been an innovation.

S CORPORATION   A small business corporation that meets various requirements and has validly elected not to be taxed at the corporate level. Small businesses are those that meet the 35-shareholder limitation, certain types of shareholder restrictions, and the one class of stock restriction. For an S corporation, items of income or loss are passed through to shareholders in a manner similar to the way partnerships pass through of such items to partners.

SCRAP   Steel scrap is waste, dismantled, and salvaged iron and steel products. Scrap is a basic raw material, since open hearth and electric furnaces utilize scrap in conjunction with pig iron in mixtures for making steel. Some furnaces use close to 100% scrap. The use of scrap effects a conservation of domestic iron ore resources; since scrap is the metallic equivalent of pig iron, every ton of scrap consumed saves two tons of ore (average grade of domestic iron ore is about 50%). The domestic scrap supply also relieves dependence upon foreign iron ore (in recent years U.S. companies have developed substantial iron ore sources in Canada and Venezuela); such dependence leaves the U.S. vulnerable to the cutting of long transportation lines of supply in the event of war. Thus, a strong domestic scrap industry is considered essential for national defense purposes.

The previously chaotic domestic scrap industry was organized in a businesslike manner by the Institute of Scrap Iron & Steel in 1928. "Revert scrap," also called "home scrap," is the result of the manufacture of steel and steel products by the mills themselves. Industrial scrap is scrap recovered from finished products, such as automobiles, farm equipment, ships, etc. The scrap industry collects and processes scrap into different grades for the requirements of customers; there are approximately 75 different grades or sizes into which unprepared scrap may be segregated and processed, necessitating a substantial investment by scrap processors in processing and handling equipment.

As may be expected, steel scrap prices are highly sensitive to fluctuation in the operating rates and the inventory position of the steel industry. A continuing problem is the technological improvement in steelmaking, which reduces requirements for scrap. The industry, however, "has little doubt but that scrap will continue to be used in large tonnages by the steel and foundry industries over the years."

See STEEL.

SCRIP   A temporary certificate issued for exchange at a later date for money, a permanent certificate, or whatever the scrip entitles the holder to receive. The term is frequently used to refer to fractional shares of stock issued during a reorganization or stock conversion, or to represent dividends not paid in cash but deferred to a later definite or uncertain date. Scrip certificates representing fractional shares may be combined and exchanged for whole shares. In still another and probably the original sense, this term is less frequently used to denote paper currency of fractional denominations, known as shinplasters, current during the Civil War.

Finally, the term has been used synonymously (but incorrectly) with emergency currency, such as CLEARINGHOUSE LOAN CERTIFICATES.

SCRIP CERTIFICATE   A fractional share of stock. Dividends are not paid on SCRIP.

SCRIP DIVIDEND   A type of dividend payable in short-term promissory paper, called SCRIP, in order to conserve cash at the particular dividend period. Scrip dividends are relatively rare, as most corporations prefer to defer or omit dividends entirely if the cash position does not justify payment, or to declare dividends in stock.

See STOCK DIVIDEND.

SEALED BID   See AWARD.

SEASONAL VARIATION   The more or less regular swings of almost any series of economic data attributable to the influence of the changing seasons. For example, bank debits in December are normally larger than in other months of the year; egg prices in January are almost without exception higher than in May; railroad carloadings reach their annual peaks in the fall. As generally applied, the term is a misnomer, a more appropriate designation being "monthly variation" or "quarterly variation," depending on the frequency of the data. Quarterly data, seasonally adjusted, is converted to an annual rate in the case of such magnitudes as gross national product and its components.

The reference "adjusted for seasonal variation" (or "adjusted for normal seasonal variation") means that in the data so described allowance has been made for the usual or average month-to-month or quarter-to-quarter change, and the resulting figures are free from the normal seasonal influence. In statistical practice, an index of seasonal variation is usually computed for each series of data. The simple average method takes into account the percentage that each of the 12 months is of the average for the year. To adjust a series for seasonal variation, one merely divides successive unadjusted monthly data by the corresponding index of seasonal variation. There are many methods of computing indexes of seasonal variation for use in adjusting historical data, one of the best known being the "link-relative method" developed by Warren M. Persons. As in the case of adjusting for SECULAR TREND, the purpose is to reveal cyclical movement in business data. Techniques for compiling the strictly seasonal adjustment index seek to exclude cyclical influences as much as possible so as to isolate the cyclical factors in the data.

BIBLIOGRAPHY

CHANG, E. C., and PINEGAR, J. M. "Seasonal Fluctuations in Industrial Production and Stock Market Seasonal." *Journal of Financial Quantitative Analysis*, March, 1989.
GARDNER, E. S., JR., and MCKENZIE, E. "Seasonal Exponential Smoothing With Damped Trends." *Management Science*, March, 1989.
SASTRI, T. "Multipass Seasonal Adjustment Filter." *Management Science*, January, 1989.

SEASONED SECURITIES Securities of recognized merit and of long standing, issued by corporations engaged in the production of basic staples, whose officers are skilled in operating and financial management, whose properties and net assets leave a safe equity for securities, and whose earnings have been sufficiently stable to ensure interest payments and dividend disbursements over a long period of time. The chief significance of this term is to indicate that such securities are subject to a smaller price fluctuation range than other securities and are consequently more satisfactory for investment and collateral purposes.

SEAT A membership on a stock exchange. No actual seats are now provided for member brokers; the term is a carryover from the days when each broker was assigned a seat in the board room of a stock exchange. The cost of seats varies with the demand and supply and the activity of the market.
See NEW YORK STOCK EXCHANGE.

SECONDARY DISTRIBUTION A special block procedure used for effecting executions of extremely large blocks of securities, outside of and without upsetting the regular market of the stock on the floor of the securities exchange. In a secondary distribution, the member firm usually acts as a dealer, combining with other members and nonmembers to effect the sale of the BLOCK, usually after trading hours and usually at a fixed price less a concession to the dealers participating. The securities exchanges generally require members to obtain the approval of the exchange before organizing a secondary distribution. On the New York Stock Exchange, Rule 393 specifies the filing of an application for approval; the factors bearing on approval or disapproval, including whether or not the regular floor market for the stock can absorb the block within a reasonable time and at a reasonable price and whether or not the other block procedures (special offering or exchange distribution) are more feasible; announcement by the exchange on the ticker tape of the terms and conditions of the distribution; minimum discounts to dealers and to members of the selling group, which may be headed by a syndicate manager; and reporting requirements (daily and at the termination of the distribution summarizing all transactions and listing all participants in the group).

Both in number and volume, secondary distributions have been by far the most active of the SPECIAL BLOCK PROCEDURES in recent years.

SECONDARY LIABILITY Contingent or indirect liability. Unqualified endorsers of negotiable instruments (on blank and special endorsements) have conditional liability, i.e., upon presentment to and dishonor by the primary party and notice thereof, they are obligated to pay the instrument (Sec. 66, Uniform Negotiable Instruments Law).
See CONTINGENT LIABILITIES.

SECONDARY MARKET An organized market for trading existing assets. It can involve physical facilities, such as organized exchanges, or a network of electronically linked trading rooms located throughout the world. These facilities provide liquidity to the secondary market.

SECONDARY RESERVES Those earning assets of a bank, other than the "investment" type, that are intended to supplement (in invested form) the primary reserves (cash and claims to cash) by providing standby liquidity for deposit withdrawals or availability for expansion in loans. Secondary reserves represent the excess primary reserves generated by deposit increases and/or decline in loans, put into highest-grade, short-term, and highly marketable items that normally can be converted into cash quickly, in substantial amounts, and with minimized risk of loss when the funds are once again needed for deposit withdrawals and loan expansion. Seasonal and random fluctuations in deposits and loans are the types of fluctuation customarily adjusted to with the technique of secondary reserves. Provision for cyclical and secular fluctuation is rarer in practice.

Open market items such as call loans, short-term government securities, short-term highest-grade municipals, bankers acceptances, and prime commercial paper are considered suitable for secondary reserve purposes. In practice, however, Treasury bills and other short-term government securities are particularly used by banks for secondary reserves because of their ready markets for substantial blocks and their variety of specific maturities. For example, if Treasury bills are appropriately selected to mature when the funds will be needed, the run-off of maturities will provide the funds, instead of the turnover in the market.

The overall liquidity capability of a bank includes the realizability, by sale or borrowing, on all available assets. Ordinarily, however, banks rely on secondary reserves for normal operating liquidity requirements, keeping investment items intact for earnings purposes. In addition to the conventional availability of the DISCOUNT WINDOW for eligible paper in the "note pouch" and advances on government securities collateral from Federal Reserve banks, the availability of Federal Reserve credit to member banks in times of emergency was increased by Sections 10(a) and 10(b) of the Federal Reserve Act authorizing Federal Reserve banks to make advances to any member bank "secured to the satisfaction of such Federal Reserve Bank" and to groups of five or more member banks on acceptable assets (both sections were added by the Act of February 27, 1932, in the worst depression year). The adjustment of legal reserve position may be accomplished by secondary reserve items, particularly Treasury bills, and recourse to federal funds if necessary.

One authority recommends that banks also provide secondary reserve liquidity for the full maximum legal reserve requirements (difference between prevailing legal reserve requirement and the statutorily authorized maximum) because of the frequency of legal reserve changes in recent years by the Board of Governors of the Federal Reserve System. This recommendation is unquestionably conservative, but if generally followed would mean the banking system would be, in effect, operating at maximum legal reserve requirements, whether or not the board currently prescribed them, and would render minimal the impact of legal reserve changes. Banks would find such a practice costly in impact upon earnings, and instead they operate at current legal reserve requirements (naturally wanting them low and stable), adjusting earning assets in the event of changes in such requirements.

SECOND BANK OF THE UNITED STATES See BANK OF THE UNITED STATES.

SECOND-CLASS PAPER Notes, trade acceptances, and bills of exchange that are obligations of names not as well known as those classified as first class and thus are not entitled to the highest credit rating. The term is not derogatory and does not imply that the risk in purchasing this paper is unduly high, but only that the standing of the maker is somewhat inferior to that of the maker of paper classified as first class. Paper may also fall into a third or lower class.

SECOND LIBERTY LOAN ACT One of the World War I financing acts, approved September 24, 1917. Section 8 of the Second Liberty Loan Act grants authority to the secretary of the Treasury to make deposits of proceeds arising from the sale of government securities and arising from the payment of income and excess profits taxes, in government depositories and "war-loan accounts" in such incorporated banks and trust companies as he may designate. Section 19 of the Federal Reserve Act specifically contravenes the further provision of Section 8, the First Liberty Bond Act (approved April 24, 1917), and the Third Liberty Loan Act (approved April 4, 1918) that no reserves are required against such government deposits in requiring legal reserves to be maintained by banks against such government deposits, which also require a specific pledge of security.

See GOVERNMENT DEPOSITARY, GOVERNMENT DEPOSITS, PUBLIC DEPOSITS.

Section 21 of the Second Liberty Bond Act, as amended many times since, is also the authority for the statutory limitation on the PUBLIC DEBT of the federal government. The present interest rate ceiling of 4.25% on U.S. government bonds dates from the Third Liberty Loan Act (April, 1918) and the Fourth Liberty Loan Act (July, 1918).

However, in recent years the Treasury has been specifically authorized by legislation to issue maximum amounts of bonds exempt from any interest rate limitation. In 1971 it received authorization to issue up to $10 billion in such bonds; as of 1982, as the result of successive further authorizations, it was authorized to issue up to $70 billion in such bonds. See UNITED STATES BONDS.

SECOND MORTGAGE A mortgage placed upon real property that is already encumbered with a first mortgage. An owner of a piece of real estate appraised at $50,000, who has borrowed $25,000 by placing a first mortgage on it, may wish to borrow an additional $5,000 by giving a second mortgage as security, making the total indebtedness equal to $30,000. In case of failure to pay either the principal or the interest, the holder of either the first or the second mortgage is entitled to foreclose his mortgage in order to satisfy his claim. In case of foreclosure by the first mortgage holder and sale of the property, the holder of the second mortgage is not entitled to receive anything until the first mortgage holder has been paid in full. Since the protection offered to a second mortgage holder is less than that for a first mortgage holder, lending on a second mortgage is attended with greater risk than lending on a first mortgage. The degree of risk on a second mortgage depends on the margin between the appraised value and the total claims against the property. To compensate for the greater risk in second mortgage loans, a higher interest rate is charged.

National banks may make first mortgage loans (12 U.S.C. 371(a)(1)), and, as specified in the Interpretive Rulings (7.2040(2)) of the Comptroller of the Currency, a subordinate lien on real estate may be treated as a "first lien" within the meaning of 12 U.S.C. 371 if:

1. The bank has the right to pay off the prior liens and become a first lien holder; and
2. The bank actually holds funds pledged by or on behalf of the borrower in an amount sufficient to pay off the prior liens; or the borrower is obligated for all funds advanced by the bank, including any amount advanced to perfect or secure the bank's first lien position, and the bank, at the inception of the loan, can fund the amount advanced to the borrower plus the amount outstanding on prior liens without violating 12 U.S.C. 84, 12 U.S.C. 371, 12 U.S.C. 371c, or any other statute, regulation, or ruling.

State banks and trust companies in some states are permitted to make second mortgage loans, but with certain restrictions. In most states savings banks are prohibited from making second mortgage loans.

See MORTGAGE, MORTGAGE LOANS, SECOND MORTGAGE BONDS.

BIBLIOGRAPHY

CECALA, G. D. "Dealing in Mortgages." *United States Banker*, January, 1989.
FRIEDMAN, R. "At Your Fingertips." *United States Banker*, January, 1989.
SICHELMAN, L. "Misplaced Benefits." *United States Banker*, March, 1989.

SECOND MORTGAGE BONDS Bonds secured by a mortgage upon property that is already encumbered with an issue of first mortgage bonds. Second mortgage bonds occur most frequently among railroad issues, and constitute a second lien upon the property specified in the mortgage and the earnings of the company. Consolidated mortgage bonds, general mortgage bonds, first and consolidated mortgage bonds, first and refunding mortgage bonds, etc., are usually bonds in which a part of the security consists of a second mortgage.

See SECOND MORTGAGE.

SECOND OF EXCHANGE See FIRST OF EXCHANGE.

SECOND PREFERRED STOCK See PREFERRED STOCK.

SECOND TELLER See RECEIVING TELLER.

SECULAR TREND Long-term or normal trend. The concept of a normal value for any series of statistical data at a given time, or projected or extrapolated into the future, is useful primarily as base or reference point in judging the effects of economic factors other than the growth factor. The phrase "corrected for secular trend," frequently encountered in connection with business statistics, means that the data presented have been adjusted to allow for computed long-term growth or secular trend. The secular trend in itself is an indicator of "normals" at any given points in the progression of the data, which will indicate how much above or below such normals the current data are; thus the raw data are frequently shown in conjunction with the secular trend line derived from the data. The secular trend is thus a statistically derived concept, depending on the representativeness of the total period covered. It may be fitted visually into a chart of the raw data, or it may be computed exactly by such methods as the least squares method, the moving average method, or the semiaverage method.

SECURED BILLS Documentary bills of exchange; bills of exchange that are accompanied by a bill of lading giving title to the merchandise specified therein. The term is also applied to notes, acceptances, or bills of exchange that are secured by bonds, stocks, warehouse receipts, short-term paper, or other securities.

SECURED CREDITOR A creditor who holds some form of collateral or legal right to claim certain assets of the person, firm, or corporation to which a loan or advance has been made, or to whom goods have been sold. Thus, a mortgagee, mortgage bond holder, or bank that lends against any kind of collateral at least equal in value to the face of the loan is a secured creditor.

A general depositor in a bank is an unsecured creditor, except in the case of the government or a civil division thereof (state, county, city), which requires a depository collateral for such deposits.

See LIABILITY.

SECURITIES That class of investments represented by engraved, printed, or written documents evidencing ownership or creditorship in a corporation or other forms of business organization, or a creditorship relation to public bodies. The term therefore includes bonds, stocks, mortgages, notes, coupons, scrip, warrants, rights, options, etc., of every kind.

As defined by the Securities Act of 1933, the term "security" means any note, stock, treasury stock, bond, debenture, evidence of indebtedness, certificate of interest or participation in any profit-sharing agreements, collateral-trust certificate, reorganization certificate or subscription, transferable share, investment contract, voting-trust certificate, certificate of interest in property, tangible or intangible, or, in general, any instrument commonly known as a security, or any certificate of interest or participation in, temporary or interim certificate for, receipt for, or warrant or right to subscribe to or purchase, any of the foregoing.

The term is semantic, since "securities" are all insecurities in varying degrees and respects.

The appended tables show securities prices 1970 to 1987 and sales of stocks and options on registered exchanges: 1970 to 1987.

See INVESTMENT.

SECURITIES ACT OF 1933

Table 1 / Security Prices: 1970 to 1987
(Annual averages of monthly figures, except as noted.)

Class or item	1970	1975	1980	1981	1982	1983	1984	1985	1986	1987
Bond prices (dollars per $100 bond):										
Standard & Poor's: Municipal [1,2]	72.3	68.9	57.4	43.2	41.8	51.4	48.0	53.0	65.1	62.7
Dow Jones and Co., Inc.: [3]										
Yearly high	69.7	69.7	76.6	65.8	71.5	77.8	72.9	83.7	93.7	95.5
Yearly low	64.4	66.2	61.0	55.0	55.7	69.4	64.8	72.3	83.7	81.3
Stock prices:										
Standard & Poor's common index										
(500 stocks) (1941-43 = 10) [4]	83.2	86.2	118.7	128.0	119.7	160.4	160.5	186.8	236.3	268.8
Industrial	91.3	96.6	134.5	144.2	133.6	180.5	181.3	207.8	262.2	330.5
N.Y. Stock Exchange common stock index (Dec. 31, 1965 = 50):										
Composite	45.7	45.7	68.1	74.0	68.9	92.6	92.5	108.1	136.0	161.7
Yearly high [5]	52.4	51.2	81.0	79.1	82.4	99.6	98.1	121.9	145.8	188.0
Yearly low [5]	37.7	37.1	55.3	65.0	58.8	79.8	85.1	94.6	117.8	125.9
Industrial	48.0	50.5	78.6	85.4	78.2	107.5	108.0	123.8	155.9	195.3
Transportation	32.1	31.1	60.5	72.6	60.4	89.4	85.6	104.1	119.9	140.4
Utility	37.2	31.5	37.3	38.9	39.8	47.0	46.4	56.8	71.4	74.3
Finance	54.6	47.1	64.3	73.5	72.0	95.3	89.3	114.2	147.2	146.5
American Stock Exchange Market Value Index (Aug. 31,1973 = 50)	48.3	41.6	150.6	171.8	141.3	216.5	208.0	229.1	264.4	316.4
NASDAQ OTC composite [6]	NA	77.6	202.3	195.9	232.4	278.6	247.4	324.9	348.8	402.9
Industrial	NA	81.0	261.4	229.3	273.6	323.7	260.7	330.2	349.3	422.9
Insurance	NA	80.9	166.8	194.3	226.4	257.6	283.1	382.1	404.1	425.5
Banks	NA	72.4	118.4	143.1	156.4	203.8	229.8	349.4	412.5	465.1
Dow Jones and Co., Inc., total										
(65 stocks) [1,7]	243.9	247.3	328.2	364.6	345.4	472.2	463.1	541.6	702.5	849.5
Industrial (30 stocks)	753.2	802.8	891.4	932.9	884.4	1,190.3	1,178.5	1,328.2	1,792.8	2,276.0
Transportation (20 stocks)	152.4	163.4	307.2	398.6	359.8	544.6	513.8	645.1	785.4	929.2
Public utility (15 stocks)	108.8	79.8	110.4	108.6	112.0	130.0	131.8	157.6	195.2	201.7
Wilshire 5000 equity index [8]										
(Dec. 31, 1980 = 1404.596)	830.3 [9]	763.8	1,220.7	1,343.7	1,233.7	1,691.5	1,644.6	1,923.6	2,418.8	2,843.7
Standard & Poor's:										
Dividend-price ratio (percent)	3.83	4.31	5.26	5.20	5.81	4.40	4.64	4.25	3.48	3.06
Earnings-price ratio (percent)	6.45	9.14	12.66	11.87	11.60	8.02	10.02	8.12	6.09	5.48

NA — Not available.
[1] Source: U.S. Bureau of Economic Analysis.
[2] Derived from average yields on basis of assumed 4 percent, 20-year bond; Wednesday closing prices.
[3] Source: Dow Jones and Co., Inc., New York, NY. Effective 30, 1976, the Dow Jones averages of 20 income railroad bonds were discontinued. With the dropping of the rail averages, which had been part of the Dow-Jones 40-bond average, the 40-bond average became a 20-bond average consisting of 10 utility bonds and 10 industrial bonds.
[4] Effective July 1976, the index includes 400 industrial stocks (formerly 425), 20 transportation (formerly 15 rail), 40 public utility (formerly 60), and 40 financial stocks, not previously covered.
[5] Source: New York Stock Exchange, Inc., New York, NY, *Fact Book*, annual.
[6] Source: National Association of Securities Dealers, Washington, DC, *Fact Book*, annual, OTC = over-the-counter.
[7] Based on stocks listed on the New York Stock Exchange.
[8] Represents return on the market value of all common equity securities for which daily pricing is available. For 1970-1975, annual average of end of month figures; thereafter, annual average of daily figures. Source: Wilshire Associates, Santa Monica, CA, releases.
[9] Represents Dec. 31, 1970.

Source: Except as noted, Board of Governors of the Federal Reserve System, *Federal Reserve Bulletin*, monthly.

BIBLIOGRAPHY

AMIHUD, Y., and MENDELSON, H. "Liquidity, Volatility, and Exchange Automation." *Journal of Accounting, Auditing, and Finance*, Fall, 1988.

"Assault On Insider Trading." *Mergers and Acquisitions*, January/February, 1989.

BANK ADMINISTRATION INSTITUTE. *Securities Activities: An Overview for Bankers*. Bank Administration Institute, Rolling Meadows, IL, 1988.

CHAMBLISS, L. "Bounty Hunters' Special." *Financial World*, November 19, 1988.

DEAN WITTER REYNOLDS, INC. *Understanding the Securities Markets*, 1987

"Kaufman: The World Needs a Good Cop, or a Good Panic." *Euromoney*, November, 1988.

MAHONEY, J. J., and THEIS, J. A., "Beyond the Rules—SEC Staff Administrative Positions on Financial Statement Requirements For Business Acquisitions." *CPA Journal*, October, 1988.

O'BRIEN, E. I. "Synchronize Financial Markets." *Futures*, October, 1988.

SMITH, A. "Global Security Processing: Global Headaches?" *ABA Banking Journal*, March, 1989.

SECURITIES ACT OF 1933 An act (48 Stat. 74; 15 U.S.C. 77a et seq.), approved May 26, 1933, and subsequently amended, representing the federal "Truth in Securities" Act. The act did not and has not supplanted the state BLUE SKY LAWS now found in all of the continental states except Nevada, the first of which was enacted in 1911. The two basic principles of the Securities Act of 1933 are full disclosure of material facts and antifraud. The principal features of the act are as follows.

1. **Registration requirement.** Securities offered for public sale in interstate commerce or through the mails, whether by the issuing company or by any person in a "control relationship" to the issuer, must first be registered under the act, by the filing of a registration statement with the SECURITIES AND EXCHANGE COMMISSION (SEC). Exemptions from the registration requirement include federal government, state, and municipal securities; bank stocks; negotiable instruments arising out of current transactions; any securities of nonprofit institutions (religious, educational, charitable, etc.), savings and loan associations, farmer cooperatives, or common carrier railroads; receiver or trustee certificates; insurance or endowment policies; and purely intrastate offerings. In 1978, the SEC amended its Regulation A,

Sales of Stocks and Options on Registered Exchanges: 1970 to 1987
(Excludes over-the-counter.)

EXCHANGE	Unit	1970	1975	1980	1981	1982	1983	1984	1985	1986	1987
Market value of all sales, all exchanges [1,2]	Bil. dol	136	173	522	532	657	1,023	1,004	1,260	1,868	2,492
New York	Bil. dol	108	143	398	416	515	816	815	1,024	1,453	1,987
American	Bil. dol	15	6	47	40	34	48	32	38	63	102
Midwest	Bil. dol	5	7	21	25	35	60	62	79	102	122
Chicago	Bil. dol	–	6	28	22	32	39	35	38	56	124
Pacific	Bil. dol	5	5	13	13	21	31	31	40	55	71
Philadelphia	Bil. dol	3	3	11	11	14	20	19	23	35	48
STOCKS [3]											
Shares sold, all exchanges [2]	Million	4,539	6,226	15,488	15,910	22,414	30,146	30,456	37,046	48,338	63,771
New York	Million	3,213	5,056	12,390	12,843	18,211	24,253	25,150	30,222	39,258	53,038
American	Million	879	541	1,659	1,472	1,550	2,209	1,584	2,115	2,999	3,496
Midwest	Million	149	252	598	735	1,144	1,662	1,843	2,274	2,784	3,329
Pacific	Million	165	199	435	457	810	1,070	1,006	1,352	1,750	2,034
Market value, all exchange [2]	Bil. dol	131	157	476	491	603	957	951	1,200	1,705	2,284
New York	Bil. dol	103	134	398	416	514	815	814	1,023	1,450	1,983
American	Bil. dol	14	6	35	26	20	31	21	26	43	53
Midwest	Bil. dol	5	7	21	25	35	60	62	79	102	122
Pacific	Bil. dol	5	5	11	11	18	27	28	37	51	57
OPTIONS [4]											
Contracts traded, all exchanges [2]	Million	(NA)	18	97	109	137	149	197	233	289	305
Chicago	Million	(NA)	14	5	58	76	82	123	149	180	182
American	Million	(NA)	4	29	35	39	39	40	49	65	71
Market value of contracts traded, all exchanges [2]	Bil. dol	(NA)	6.4	45.9	41.7	53.7	64.2	53.0	59.1	87.9	118.9
Chicago	Bil. dol	(NA)	6.3	27.9	22.4	32.3	39.4	34.9	38.4	55.9	76.9
American	Bil. dol	(NA)	(NA)	12.5	13.8	14.3	15.8	10.5	11.6	19.0	25.7
Options exercised:											
Number of contracts	Million	(NA)	.3	4.9	7.4	9.2	13.6	11.9	10.5	14.5	17.0
Value	Bil. dol	(NA)	1.3	20.4	34.6	37.1	65.1	55.6	49.5	72.8	85.9

– Represents zero. NA = Not available. [1] Includes market value of rights and warrants and, through 1975, bond sales. Excludes the value of options exercised.
[2] Includes other registered exchanges, not shown separately. [3] Includes voting trust certificates, American Depository Receipts, and certificate of deposit for stocks.
[4] Includes non-equity options as of October 1982.
Source: U.S. Securities and Exchange Commission, *SEC Monthly Statistical Review*.

providing instead for an increase from $500,000 to $1.5 million in the exemption from regular registration requirements and eligibility thereof under Regulation A registration and offering and an increase from $50,000 to $100,000 in the minimum for such offerings not requiring any offering circular under Rule 257 of Regulation A. As of early 1982, the SEC staff was reported working on the possibility of a single uniform exemption applicable to all kinds of offerings of less than $5 million under both federal and state securities laws, which would "result in substantial savings of time and money in the multi-State offering of securities."

Registration statements must contain financial and other information that will permit an informed analysis of the securities and an appraisal of their value by investors to whom they are offered for sale. To that end, a PROSPECTUS containing pertinent facts set forth in the registration statement must be delivered to purchasers of the securities and to persons receiving written offers through the mails or interstate commerce. Upon filing of the registration statement and prior to its "effective date," the securities may be offered for sale, but written offers may be made only in accordance with rules of the SEC, and unless and until the registration statement becomes effective, the securities may not legally be sold or contracts entered into for their sale.

Registration statements filed are examined by the SEC Division of Corporation Finance. The registration statement may be refused or suspended (after notice and hearing) if it is found to contain material misstatements or omissions of fact, thus barring the sale of the securities until the registration statement is appropriately amended.

Registration of securities does not ensure investors against loss in their purchase, but merely serves to inform investors of the essential facts upon which the securities may be realistically evaluated. Also, registration is not to be taken as approval of the merits of the securities by the SEC or a finding by the SEC as to the accuracy of the facts disclosed, and it is unlawful to so represent in the offer and sale of the securities. If, however, the disclosures in the registration statement and prospectus are materially defective, the persons responsible for filing false information with the SEC subject themselves to the risk of fine, imprisonment, or both, and the issuing company, its responsible directors and other officials, and the underwriters may be liable in damages to purchasers of the registered securities.

2. **Antifraud provisions.** The Securities Act of 1933 also contains prohibitions against false representations and other fraudulent activities in connection with the sale of securities in interstate commerce and through the mails. These antifraud provisions apply to all securities thus sold, even though the securities may be exemptions or exceptions from the registration requirement.

SECURITIES AND EXCHANGE COMMISSION

A federal agency created by the SECURITIES EXCHANGE ACT OF 1934 and organized on July 2, 1934, to carry out the provisions of that act and to take over from the Federal Trade Commission the administration of the SECURITIES ACT OF 1933. In addition to these acts, the Securities and Exchange Commission (SEC) has responsibilities under the Public Utility Holding Company Act of 1935, the Trust Indenture Act of 1939, the Investment Company Act of 1940, and the Investment Advisers Act of 1940. The commission also advises U.S. district courts in connection with reorganization plans of debtor corporations

The Organization of the SEC

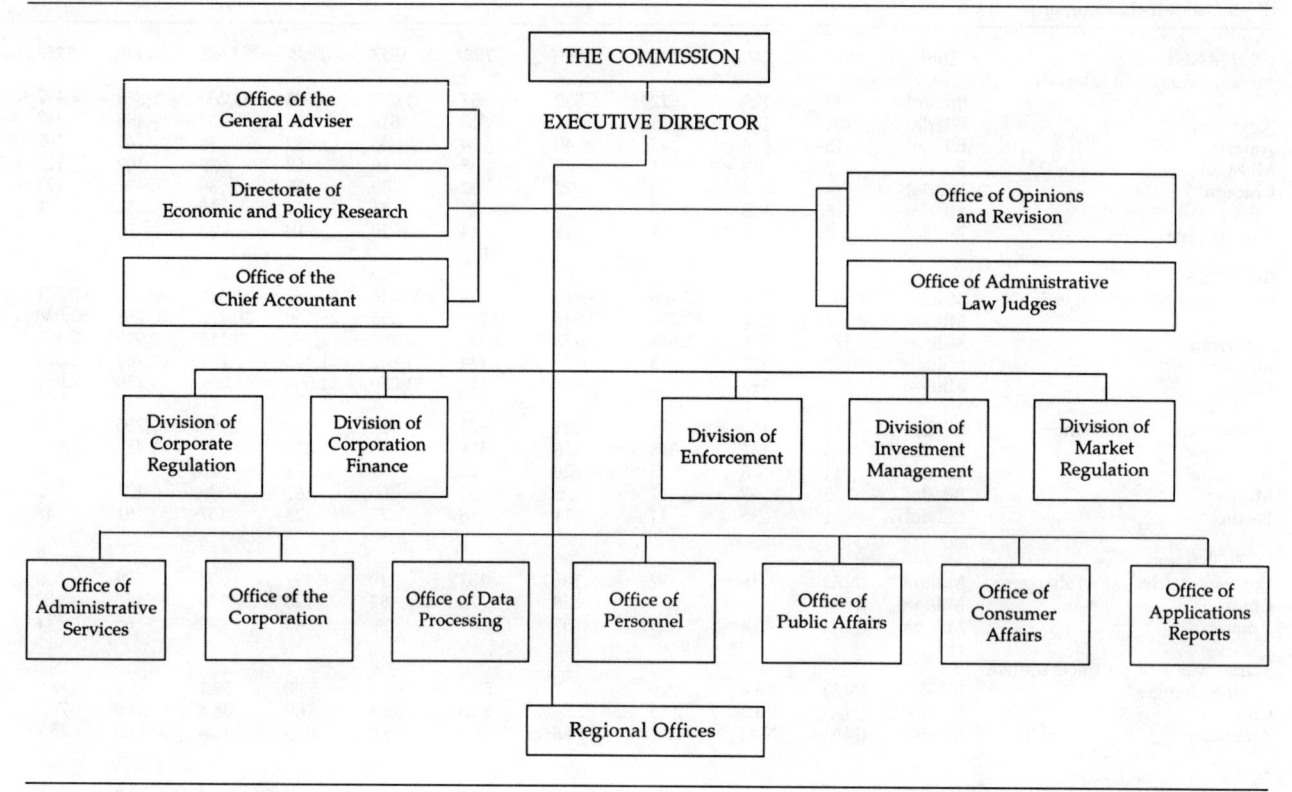

```
                                    THE COMMISSION
        Office of the                      |
        General Adviser  ───────── EXECUTIVE DIRECTOR

        Directorate of                                        Office of Opinions
    Economic and Policy Research  ──────────────────────────  and Revision

        Office of the                                         Office of Administrative
        Chief Accountant                                      Law Judges

    Division of      Division of      Division of    Division of       Division of
    Corporate        Corporation      Enforcement    Investment        Market
    Regulation       Finance                         Management        Regulation

  Office of      Office of the   Office of Data   Office of    Office of       Office of      Office of
  Administrative Corporation     Processing       Personnel    Public Affairs  Consumer       Applications
  Services                                                                     Affairs        Reports

                                    Regional Offices
```

Source: The Federal Reserve System

filed under the National Bankruptcy Act, exempts from registration securities of the International Bank for Reconstruction and Development (Sec. 15 of the Bretton Woods Agreements Act of 1945), and certifies for tax exemption the status of investment companies furnishing capital to development corporations (Sec. 851(e), Internal Revenue Code of 1954).

The SEC has three major responsibilities: ensuring the provision of full and fair disclosure of all material facts concerning securities offered for public investment, initiating litigation for fraud cases when detected, and providing for the registration of securities offered for public investment.

The commission's functions are quasi-judicial in nature, appeals from its decisions being taken to U.S. courts of appeals. Its membership consists of five commissioners, not more than three of whom may be members of the same political party, appointed by the President (with the advice and consent of the Senate) for five-year terms, rotated. The chairman is designated by the President (Sec. 3, Reorganization Plan 10 of 1950).

An organizational chart of the SEC is appended.

A period of crisis developed among securities firms in 1967-1969, caused chiefly by "fails" to deliver, and the SECURITIES INVESTOR PROTECTION CORPORATION was established in December, 1970, to protect investors against losses in the event of failure of brokerage firms.

Development of National Market System. The 1975 Securities Acts Amendments directed the SEC to facilitate the establishment of a national market system for securities as well as a nationwide system for the clearance and settlement of securities transactions. The SEC has since continued its efforts toward the development of such a system, and as of early 1982 had ordered an electronic link between seven stock exchanges and the over-the-counter market, initially involving 30 stocks. The commission had achieved implementation toward a national market system by the introduction of a consolidated tape for reporting securities transactions and a composite quotation system.

The 1975 amendments (Sec. 17A) also established a system of regulation extending to all facets of the securities handling process, designed to promote prompt and accurate clearance and settlement of securities transactions. Clearing agencies must be registered with and report to the SEC, which will review the rules of such clearing agencies to determine whether they comply with the statute's objectives. The primary enforcement and inspection responsibilities over clearing agencies that are banks are assigned by the amendments to whichever bank regulatory agency is the appropriate regulatory agency. Rule-making authority concerning the safeguarding of funds and securities by bank clearing agencies is shared by the commission and the appropriate bank regulatory agency.

The Securities Exchange Act was further amended by the 1975 amendments to require transfer agents other than banks to register with the SEC. Bank transfer agents must register with the appropriate bank regulatory agency. The SEC is granted broad rule-making power over all aspects of a transfer agent's activities. Nevertheless, as with clearing agencies, where a transfer agent is a bank, inspection and enforcement responsibilities are vested in the appropriate bank regulatory agency, and rule-making authority concerning the safeguarding of funds and securities by bank transfer agents is shared by the SEC and the appropriate bank regulatory agency.

Section 17A(e) of the 1975 amendments also required the SEC to eliminate the physical movement of securities certificates during the settlement process. In addition, the commission was directed in Section 12(m) to study the practice of registering securities in "street name," i.e., in a name other than that of the beneficial owner, and to report to Congress its conclusions.

Municipal Securities. The new Section 15B of the 1975 amendments initiated a comprehensive pattern for the registration and regulation of brokers, dealers, and banks that buy, sell, or effect transactions in municipal securities as part of their regular business in other than a fiduciary capacity. Issuers of municipal securities continue to be exempt from the registration provisions of the federal securities acts.

A municipal securities rule-making board was created to prescribe rules regulating the activities of brokers, dealers, and municipal securities dealers relating to transactions in municipal securities. The SEC is required to take affirmative action on rules proposed by the board and is authorized to abrogate, add to, or delete from any board rule. The SEC may directly regulate fraudulent, manipulative, and deceptive acts and practices, pursuant to Sections 10(b) and 15(c) of the Exchange Act.

However, the board does not have any power to conduct inspections or to enforce its rules. Instead, the act assigns these responsibilities to the NATIONAL ASSOCIATION OF SECURITIES DEALERS, INC. (NASD) for securities firms that are members of the NASD (Secs. 15A(b)(7) and 15B(c)(7)). Similarly, such responsibilities are assigned to the bank regulatory agencies for municipal securities dealers that are banks (Secs. 15B(c)(5) and 17(b)).

Accountants. Public accountants deal primarily with the corporate finance division and with the office of the chief accountant. The corporate finance division has primary responsibility to assure that the financial information given to the public in securities offerings is complete and not misleading. The chief accountant is the principal adviser to the commission on matters relating to accounting and auditing. Regulation S-X (form and content of financial statements), the accounting series releases (ASRs), and a recently initiated series of financial reporting releases (FRRs) are the major documents that prescribe the form, content, and methods used in reporting to the SEC. Although the SEC has developed its own rules and procedures, it has generally allowed the private sector to formulate generally accepted accounting principles.

Bank accounting and financial reporting. The Securities Act of 1933 generally requires that securities offered for public sale be registered with the commission. The Securities Exchange Act of 1934 requires publicly held companies to comply with the commission's regulations regarding the appropriate disclosure of financial information in the following areas: registration of classes of securities, periodic reports, proxy solicitations and information statements, and tender offer documents. Commission authority in the above areas covers holding companies that own banks and savings and loan associations. Securities issued directly by depository institutions are generally exempt from the Securities Act registration requirements. Currently approximately 1,000 banks and approximately 70 savings and loan holding companies file Exchange Act reports with the commission. Approximately 400 banks file their Exchange Act reports with the three bank regulators, which are responsible for reviewing such reports. Section 12(i) requires each bank regulator to issue regulations "substantially similar" to those issued by the commission under certain provisions of the Exchange Act. Generally, the commission specifies the accounting principles and other requirements that must be followed in preparing the Exchange Act disclosure documents of publicly held, federally insured banks. The bank regulators require all depositories to follow GENERALLY ACCEPTED ACCOUNTING PRACTICES for the majority of transactions. Commission Regulation S-X provides that financial statements filed with the commission will be presumed misleading unless prepared in accordance with GAAP. Audited financial statements prepared in accordance with GAAP are the basis of financial disclosures to investors under the commission's disclosure system. Bank regulators do not require that all bank financial statements be audited by independent public accountants. The Federal Reserve Board requires that financial statements of bank holding companies be so audited where consolidated assets equal or exceed $150 million.

The commission has authority under the federal securities laws to investigate and take enforcement action with respect to securities law violations, including securities fraud committed by a bank, bank holding company, or associated persons. The commission has addressed violations of the federal securities laws in a variety of ways: injunctions; administrative proceedings to require compliance with the reporting provisions of the act; disciplinary proceedings against professionals, including accountants and auditors; and limitations on a professional's ability to practice before the commission. Since 1981, the commission has brought more than 15 enforcement and disciplinary actions relating to banking institutions for: improper loan loss reserves, the making of false and misleading statements concerning financial condition and the results of operations, overstatement of net income and net loans outstanding, fraud, and various types of reporting and filing violations.

In order to provide full disclosure to investors through its filings, the commission has adopted disclosure standards for bank holding companies to supplement disclosure required by GAAP, including the following:

1. Article 9 of Regulation S-X prescribes the form and content of financial statements for bank holding companies in commission filings. Article 9 also requires general disclosures concerning foreign activities.
2. Industry Guide 3 requires disclosure of distributions of assets, liabilities, and equity; information concerning the investment portfolio; types of loans, including domestic loan concentration (by industry) and foreign loan concentration; interest rate sensitivity; risk elements; and loan loss experience.
3. Staff Accounting Bulletins 49 and 49A call for disclosures by bank holding companies about loans to foreign countries that are experiencing liquidity problems. They also provide guidance concerning additional disclosures concerning the restructuring of existing debt in foreign countries, fundings of additional borrowings, and related matters.
4. Staff Accounting Bulletin 50 reports staff's view on financial statement and Industry Guide disclosure requirements in filings involving the formation of one-bank holding companies.
5. Staff Accounting Bulletin 56 reports staff's views concerning disclosures about allocated transfer risk reserves mandated by the bank regulators for purposes of the supervisory and regulatory functions of those agencies.

Commission Regulations S-X and the commission's financial reporting releases set forth the accounting principles that must be employed in preparing financial statements for inclusion in these commission filings. Staff accounting bulletins provide additional guidance.

Corporate reorganization. Chapter 11 of the Bankruptcy Code authorizes the SEC to appear in any reorganization case and to present its views on any issue. Chapter 11 applies to all types of business reorganizations. The commission generally limits its participation to proceedings involving significant public investor interest—protecting public investors holding the debtor's securities and participating in legal and policy issues of concern to public investors. It may comment on the adequacy of reorganization plan disclosure statements and participate where there is a commission law enforcement interest. Reorganization plans often involve publicly held debtors issuing new securities that may be exempt from registration under Section 5 of the Securities Act of 1933. Source: Securities and Exchange Commission.

See NEW YORK STOCK EXCHANGE.

BIBLIOGRAPHY

Accountants SEC Practice Manual. Commerce Clearing House Inc. A monthly reference service.
Federal Securities Law Reporter Commerce Clearing House Inc.
SEC Compliance, Prentice-Hall, Inc. A reference service.
Securities Regulations Prentice-Hall, Inc. A monthly reference service.
SKOUSEN, K. F. *An Introduction to the SEC,* 1987.
SEC Publications:
Annual Reports
News Digest
SEC Docket
The Work of the Securities and Exchange Commission
Statistical Bulletin

SECURITIES COMPANY HOLDING COMPANY; a company organized to hold the shares of its subsidiary companies. The term sometimes is applied to an investment house or company that deals in securities at retail. Among banks, prior to the Banking Act of 1933, the security affiliate engaged in underwriting and dealing in securities without restriction. The Banking Act of 1933 required the "divorcement" of such security affiliates one year after passage of the act on June 16, 1933.

SECURITIES EXCHANGE ACT OF 1934 An act (48 Stat. 881; 15 U.S.C. 78a to 78jj) approved June 6, 1934, as amended, that seeks to outlaw misrepresentation, manipulation, and other abusive practices in securities markets and to establish and maintain "just and equitable principles of trade which would be conducive to open, fair and orderly markets." The act marked the first time that the securities markets were brought under uniform regulation; in addition, it contains provisions affecting corporate practices.

1. Registration of listed securities. The act extends the disclosure principle by requiring every company that has securities listed on an exchange to register with the SECURITIES AND EXCHANGE COMMISSION (SEC) and to file annual and other periodic reports disclosing financial and other data for the information of the investing public. In practice, once a listing application for securities to be newly listed has been approved by the exchange concerned, the exchange forwards a certificate of such approval to the SEC. Registration with the SEC normally becomes effective 30 days after the SEC receives the exchange's certification, on which effective date trading may begin in the security on the exchange.

   Similar registration and annual and other reports must also be filed, pursuant to the Securities Act Amendments of 1964, by companies whose equity securities are traded over-the-counter, if such a company has $1 million in assets and 500 or more, but less than 750, shareholders. Proxy solicitation, "insider trading" provisions, and the registration requirement referred to, which theretofore were applicable principally to securities traded on exchanges, were also made applicable to such over-the-counter securities. In addition, P.L. 90-437 (July 29, 1968) extends margin requirements to specified securities traded over-the-counter, to be similarly set by regulation of the Board of Governors of the Federal Reserve System.

2. "Insider" trading in listed securities. The act requires that "insiders" (officers, directors, and 10% owners) regularly report their holdings of and transactions in all equity securities of the particular issuer with whom they are associated to the SEC and the exchange concerned. Also, in order to curb the misuse of "inside" information by such persons, insiders are made liable by the act to account to their companies for their profits on any purchase and sale, or sale and purchase, that occurs *within* a six-month period.

3. Proxy solicitation. Management officials of listed companies must disclose in their solicitation of proxies basic financial and other information reflecting the company's financial condition and the results of its operation. The commission has promulgated, pursuant to the act, a set of "proxy rules" that require disclosure of the basic facts pertinent to the subject matter of the meeting and vote. In addition, the form of proxy must give the stockholder freedom of action to vote for or against different proposals, and may not bind him to vote on an "all-or-none" basis. The proxy rules also entitle independent or minority stockholders to include, in management solicitations, any proper proposals that they wish to have put to a vote of the stockholders. The rules facilitate the independent solicitation of proxies by minority stockholders, including the solicitation of proxies for the election of their own nominees to the board of directors.

4. Registration of stock exchanges and broker-dealers. The act provides for the registration with the SEC of stock exchanges and of brokers and dealers in the over-the-counter markets. A prerequisite to stock exchange registration is a requirement that its rules shall proscribe practices by members that may not be just and equitable, and that the exchange must be empowered to suspend, expel, or otherwise discipline members for violations of such rules. The SEC has a residual power to see that the exchange's rules are modified or supplemented to accomplish these objectives. Basically, it is a system of self-regulation by the exchanges themselves, with the SEC in an overseer role.

   The Maloney Act, a 1938 amendment to the Securities Exchange Act, provided for the organization of associations of over-the-counter dealers to self-regulate their membership. One such association, the NATIONAL ASSOCIATION OF SECURITIES DEALERS, INC. (NASD), has been organized. It has adopted and enforces a code of fair practice governing the conduct of its members and their dealings with investors. Such brokers and dealers must register with the NASD before they may engage in the securities business in interstate commerce. At the end of December, 1981, 3,265 brokers and dealers were registered with the NASD. The SEC may deny or revoke the registration of a broker-dealer in cases of fraud in securities transactions or other misconduct in the securities business, when the commission, after notice and hearing, finds such denial or revocation in the public interest. The SEC may also, on similar grounds, suspend or expel a member from membership in the NASD or in a stock exchange.

5. Policing of trading practices. Under the act, the SEC maintains surveillance of securities trading practices on both the exchanges and the over-the-counter markets. Its rules prescribe, among other things, the limitations upon short selling and the maintenance at all times of a minimum capital position relative to liabilities by brokers and dealers. The latter rule is designed to minimize the possibility of firm insolvency, which would endanger customers' free credit balances and securities held in custody. Broker-dealer inspections are made to assure compliance.

6. The act provides the statutory authority for the prescription by the Board of Governors of the Federal Reserve System of margin requirements regulating the amount of credit that brokers and banks may extend on the purchase of listed securities. The SEC has the duty of enforcing compliance by brokers and dealers in securities with the Fed's regulations.

7. Enforcement. The act authorizes the SEC to take testimony under oath and to subpoena books and records for the purpose of developing the facts with respect to possible violations, and to obtain federal court orders of injunction against continuance of acts and practices violative of the act or SEC rules. The act also provides for criminal prosecutions for willfull violations through the Department of Justice.

1975 Amendments. The Securities Acts Amendments of 1975 (P.L. 94-29), enacted June 4, 1975, significantly revised and expanded the Securities Exchange Act of 1934. Among other things, the Securities and Exchange Commission was directed to facilitate the establishment of a national market system for securities and a nationwide system for the clearance and settlement of securities transactions, clarify and strengthen the commission's oversight role with respect to self-regulatory organizations, and provide for broad regulation of brokers, dealers, and banks trading in municipal securities. The 1975 amendments further contained the prohibition of imposition of any schedule or fixing of rates of commissions, allowances, discounts, or other fees (even before enactment of the amendments, the SEC had adopted Rule 19b-3, providing for the elimination of fixed commission rates as of May 1, 1975).

Integrated Disclosure System. During the 1980 fiscal year and continuing into the 1981 fiscal year, the prime focus of the SEC in the area of disclosure policy was on the integration of the full disclosure system administered by the SEC. The program had several major objectives: integration of disclosures required by the SECURITIES ACT OF 1933 and the SECURITIES EXCHANGE ACT OF 1934; narrowing of the differences between information supplied by registrants to the commission in formal filings and information supplied to various segments of the public through informal means; improvement of disclosure requirements through revision of obsolete rules and standardizing of requirements; and refocusing of the staff review process. The SEC pointed out that the 1933 act established a system of transaction-oriented disclosures, with the focus on particular offerings of securities, while the 1934 act established a system of continuous disclosure, with the focus on public companies and their ongoing reporting obligations to the commission and to their shareholders. These two systems developed and operated independently over more than 40 years, resulting in an unnecessary degree of duplication in the disclosure documents produced.

SECURITIES INVESTOR PROTECTION CORPORATION

A corporation federally chartered following passage by the Congress of the Securities Investor Protection Act of 1970, in December, 1970. Patterned after the FEDERAL DEPOSIT INSURANCE CORPORATION, which insures bank deposits, the Securities Investor Protection Corporation (SIPC) is designed to protect investors against losses in the event a brokerage firm is forced to liquidate. An amendment to the act enacted October 10, 1980, raised the limits of protection to $500,000 for customer cash claims and no more than $100,000 of which may be a claim for cash as opposed to securities. The act mandates the protection of cash balances in a customer's securities account, provided the cash was deposited for the purchase of securities. The intent of the customer, therefore, must be determined. The payment of interest would be one relevant factor in determining such intent. Accounts in which cash is deposited solely to earn interest and not for the purpose of purchasing securities would not, therefore, be protected by the SIPC.

No limit, however, applies on the return of securities registered or in the process of being registered to customers of a firm that has failed. Nor is there a limit on the distribution, pro rata to customers, of remaining cash and securities of customers held by the firm.

The money required to protect customers beyond that which is available from the property in the possession of a failed broker-dealer is advanced by the SIPC from a fund maintained for that purpose. Sources for the SIPC fund are assessments collected from SIPC members and interest on investments in U.S. government securities. If the need arises, the SECURITIES AND EXCHANGE COMMISSION (SEC) has the authority to lend the SIPC up to $1 billion, which the SEC in turn would borrow from the U.S. Treasury.

From 1971 through 1977, the statute required the SIPC to assess members 0.5% of their gross revenues from the securities business to build up the SIPC fund. The fund achieved the statutory minimum level of $150 million in 1977, and assessments were reduced during the first half of 1978 and eliminated during the second half of 1978. Beginning in 1979, each member's annual assessment became $25. The SIPC fund aggregated $380 million in cash and U.S. government securities on December 31, 1987. The highest amount advanced for customer protection in a single year up to that date was $35 million (1973). Net SIPC advances for customer protection totaled $63 million since SIPC's inception in 1981. Net SIPC advances for customer protection totaled $218 million since 1970; by contrast, the fund earned interest of $249 million during the same period.

Under the law, all registered broker-dealers and members of national securities exchanges must be members of the SIPC unless exempt under the act. Exempt are broker-dealers who deal exclusively in the distribution of shares of registered open-end investment companies or unit investment trusts, in the sale of variable annuities and of insurance, or in the business of rendering investment advisory services to one or more registered investment companies or insurance company separate accounts. Persons whose principal business, in the determination of the SIPC, taking into account business of affiliated entities, is conducted outside the United States and its territories and possessions are also exempt.

The self-regulatory organizations—the exchanges and the National Association of Securities Dealers, Inc. (NASD)—and the SEC report to the SIPC concerning member broker-dealers who are in or are approaching financial difficulty. If SIPC determines that the customers of a member require the protection afforded by the act, the SIPC initiates steps to commence a customer protection proceeding. This requires that the SIPC apply to a federal district court for the appointment of a trustee to carry out the liquidation, although under certain circumstances the SIPC may pay customer claims directly. Stronger brokerage firms have been able to withstand the vicissitudes of the market because of refinements in the self-regulatory organizations, modernization of member operations, higher minimum capital requirements, and more stringent requirements for entry into the securities business. Nevertheless, as the result of the collapse of the boom in speculative low-priced new issues, the number of securities firm failures was reported to be increasing in early 1982. Although these failures were of relatively small firms, advances from the SIPC's fund to liquidation trustees reportedly had caused a decline in the fund from $215.7 million at mid-year 1981 to some $160 million as of March, 1982.

As a result, the SIPC obtained SEC approval in February 1982, to assess each member 0.25% of its gross revenues from securities operations, which could mean a substantial increase from the low $25 per year rate prevailing in recent years. Assessments at that level commenced in May 1983, and continued until April 1986, when assessments were set at $100 per annum for each SIPC member. On April 1, 1986, SIPC also entered into an agreement with a consortium of banks for a confirmed line of credit in the amount of $500 million. That agreement runs until March 31, 1989.

Organization. A board of seven directors determines policies of the SIPC and governs operations. Five directors are appointed by the President of the United States, subject to Senate approval. Three of the five directors represent the securities industry, and two are from the general public. One director is appointed by the secretary of the Treasury and one by the Federal Reserve Board from among the officers and employees of those organizations. The chairman, who is the SIPC's chief executive officer, and the vice-chairman are designated by the President from the public directors.

The headquarters of the SIPC is in Suite 800, 805 Fifteenth Street, N.W., Washington, D.C. 20005, where copies of their copyrighted brochure, "How SIPC Protects You," may be obtained.

Pre-SIPC Situation. Prior to the SIPC assumption of responsibility for the protection of its members' securities customers, more than 160 NEW YORK STOCK EXCHANGE member firms—and an undisclosed but presumably larger number of non-NYSE brokerage firms—went out of business. Most of the NYSE firms either merged with or were acquired by other NYSE firms, often through arrangements facilitated or initiated by the exchange itself. Some 80 firms dissolved, retired from the securities business, or self-liquidated, without "undue public concern or inconvenience to customers." In most of the remaining situations, mergers or acquisitions were also arranged "without serious inconvenience to customers." Public attention, however, did focus on the affairs of 17 particular firms that got into difficulties.

The principal instrument of the exchange's voluntary financial assistance to the customers of member firms in liquidation had been the special trust fund, originally established by the exchange in 1964. The special trust fund reached an initial goal of $10 million, supplemented by $15 million in standby credit, in 1965. The fund was augmented by an exchange contribution of $5 million at the end of 1969, at which time the standby credit was reduced to $10 million. In June, 1970, the program was expanded to $55 million to permit assistance to firms that had recently been placed in liquidation by the exchange.

When Congress passed the Securities Investor Protection Act at the end of December, 1970, the New York Stock Exchange announced the termination of its voluntary customer assistance program and planned the phasing out of the special trust fund. The exchange, however, would fulfill its prior commitments with respect to firms already in its customer assistance program at that time.

SECURITIES LEDGER A ledger in which transactions in bonds or other securities are recorded. Accounts are classified alphabetically, according to the name of the security. The information that a typical securities ledger contains is shown by the headings of the columns in the form below.

DR	CR
Date of purchase	Date of sale
Descriptive details	Descriptive details
Pare value	Par value
Unit purchasing price	Proceeds of sale
Commission	Commission
Total cost	Interest accrued
Accrued interest paid	General ledger account cr.
Balance	Interest credited
(a) Par	Profit or loss
(b) Money	Disposition
Trading value	Remarks
Book value	
Remarks	

SECURITIES MARKETS Security transactions take place in either the primary market or the secondary market. In the primary market, the purchaser gives the original issuer of the security cash in exchange for the security. In a primary market, the original security issuer receives cash; the public now holds a security that did not previously exist. Weekly T-bill offerings by the U.S. Treasury and municipal bond sales by a city occur in the primary market. Following the primary offering of a security, the security is said to trade in the secondary markets between members of the public. The NEW YORK STOCK EXCHANGE, the AMERICAN STOCK EXCHANGE, and the OVER-THE-COUNTER market are considered secondary markets.

Investment bankers specialize in the creation and placement of securities in the primary market. These organizations provide advice, underwriting, and distribution services to their clients. The advice provided by investment bankers usually relates to the type of security offering (debt or equity), the timing of the offering, the legal characteristics of the issue, and the price at which the security can be sold.

Underwriting refers to the investment bankers' practice of absorbing the price risks the issuer is unwilling to accept. Underwriting takes various forms:

1. *Firm commitment:* The underwriter commits to purchase the full amount of the issue from the seller at an agreed-upon price.

The banker then reoffers the security to the public. The underwriter's spread represents compensation to the underwriter. The investment banker frequently forms a purchase group consisting of other investment bankers who participate in the purchase of the securities. The lead underwriter is primarily responsible for negotiating the agreement with the issuer and maintaining the records.

2. *Standby agreement:* The underwriter agrees to help sell the new issue for a given period of time. After this period passes (often 30 days), the underwriter is required to purchase any unsold securities at a predetermined price. Standby agreements are frequently used in stock sales that utilize a rights offering.
3. *Best-effort basis:* The banker acts as a broker and returns unsold securities to the issuer. The banker assumes no risk for unsold securities. Best-effort underwriting is often used when the issuer is confident that the issue can be sold or when the issuer is relatively small and unestablished.

Securities are distributed by various methods. Some issuers market their issues directly to the public (for example, the U.S. government). Common stock offerings using rights can often be marketed directly by the issuer. Syndicates consisting of investment bankers are often formed to assist in the distribution of securities. Members of the purchase syndicate frequently develop a selling group that actively distributes the securities to their clients. The selling group usually consists of members of the purchase group and various retail brokerage houses. A selling group agreement establishes the term of the agreement; the division of the underwriter spread among the manager, the purchase group, and the selling group; and the accounting procedures. The agreement requires that no member will sell beneath the offering price. During the early days of the offering to the public, the managing underwriter may stabilize the market by purchasing the security at a fixed price—a form of legal price manipulation.

Private placements refer to the distribution of securities to fewer than 25 private buyers. Private placements do not require registration with the SEC. Bond issues are frequently distributed through private placements.

The established stock exchanges and the over-the-counter market represent the secondary markets. On the New York Stock Exchange, members are classified as:

1. *Commission brokers:* partners in a brokerage firm who execute orders for their clients on the floor of the exchange.
2. *Floor brokers:* commission brokers who handle overflow transactions with the commission brokers.
3. *Floor traders:* members who buy and sell solely for their own account.
4. *Specialists:* members who are assigned a number of stocks in which they act as brokers by maintaining a limit book and as dealers by selling and buying shares in which they specialize. Specialists provide a continuous and liquid market in securities.

Stock and bond transactions that are not handled on one of the organized exchanges are traded in the over-the-counter (OTC) market. This market is not centrally located but consists of a network of brokers and dealers who communicate by telephone or computer terminals. Mutual fund shares, many bank and finance stock, most corporate bonds, and U.S. government and municipal obligations are traded in the OTC market.

A third market in securities refers to OTC transactions in a security that is also traded on an organized exchange. Institutional investors often trade large blocks of stock in this market. Negotiated fees are typical in this market.

A fourth market in securities refers to transactions that occur directly between a buyer and a seller of a large block of securities. In the fourth market, brokers and dealers are eliminated. A wire network provides current information subscribers are willing to buy or sell at specified prices.

Securities commissions have been negotiated rates since May 1, 1975. However, brokerage firms establish firmwide rates for various types of transactions and classes of customers. Discount brokerage firms offer low commissions but provide little, if any, investment counseling and advice.

Flow charts of a trade execution and of the clearing process are appended.

Trade Execution

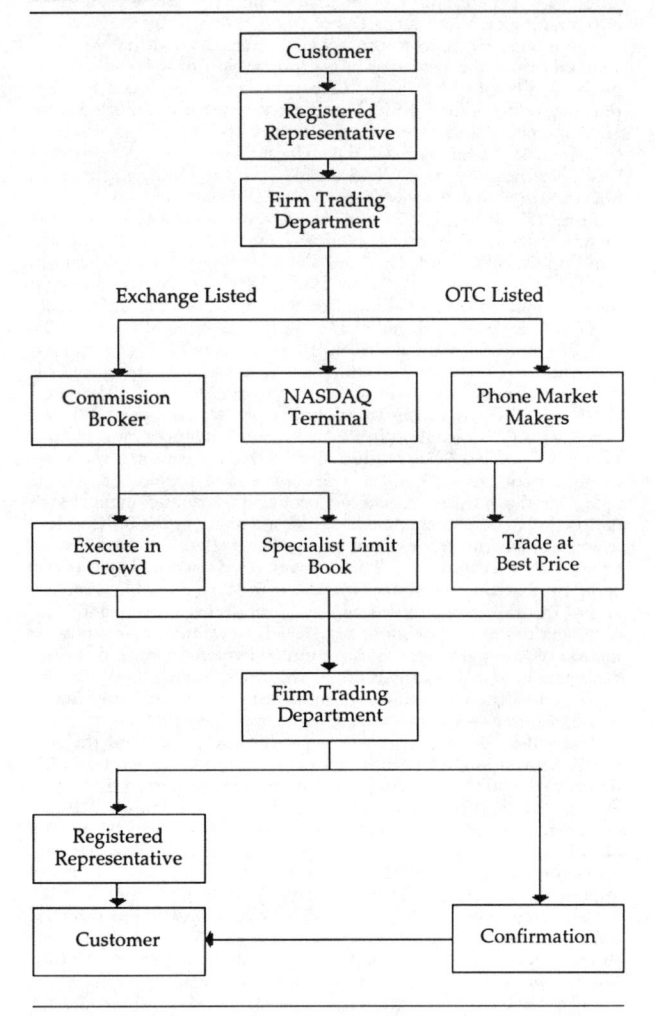

Customer → Registered Representative → Firm Trading Department

Exchange Listed:
- Commission Broker → Execute in Crowd
- NASDAQ Terminal → Specialist Limit Book

OTC Listed:
- Phone Market Makers → Trade at Best Price

→ Firm Trading Department → Registered Representative → Customer ← Confirmation

Source: Robert C. Radcliffe, *Investment: Concept, Analysis, and Strategy,* Scott, Foresman and Company, Glenview, IL., 1982.

SECURITIES REGULATIONS See COMPTROLLER'S REGULATION, INVESTMENT SECURITIES, LIFE INSURANCE COMPANY INVESTMENTS, SAVINGS BANK INVESTMENTS, TRUST FUND INVESTMENTS.

SECURITIZATION The pooling and repackaging of similar loans into marketable securities that can be sold to investors. Many types of loans are currently being securitized: residential mortgage loans, automobile, and other commercial loans. Securitization is distinguished from whole loans and loan participations.

Securitization provides a process for improving the liquidity of assets and capital-to-asset ratios while increasing earnings. Fees obtained through securitization increase a bank's earnings. Savings in regulatory costs and in economies of scale are also possible. Securitization can enable banks to reduce credit risks associated with variable-rate loans.

Securitization can result in the deterioration of bank assets because investors require high-quality loans. The purchaser must usually depend on the originator or some other party for servicing, which can be a disadvantage.

BIBLIOGRAPHY

MORRIS, D. *Selling and Securitizing Commercial Bank Assets,* 1988.
PAVEL, C. "Securitization." *Economic Review,* 1986.
ROSENTHAL, J., and OCAMPO, J. *Securitization of Credit,* 1988.

Clearing Process

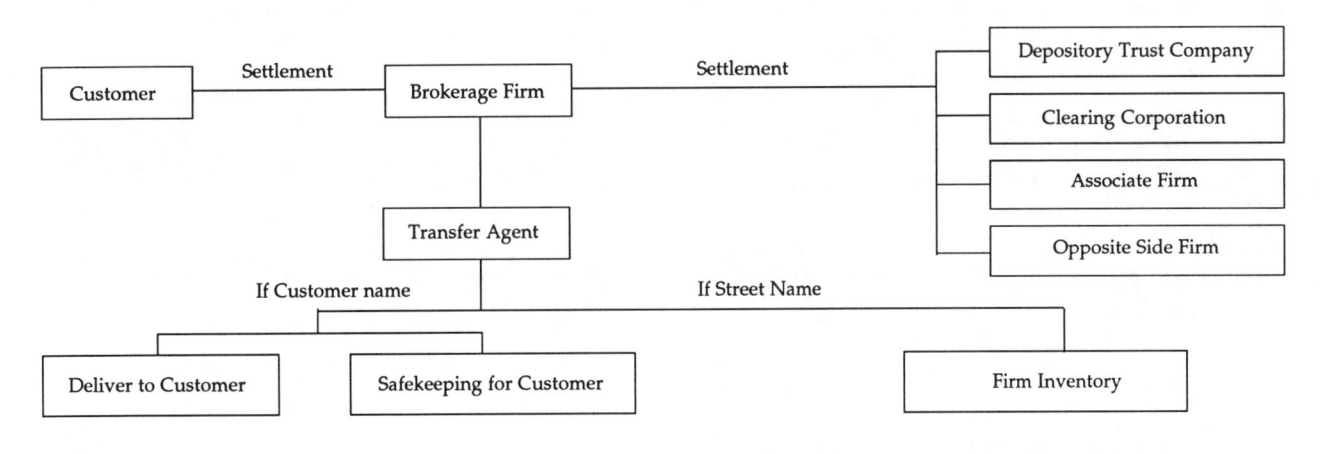

```
Customer --Settlement-- Brokerage Firm --Settlement-- Depository Trust Company
                                                       Clearing Corporation
                                                       Associate Firm
                                                       Opposite Side Firm
              Transfer Agent
     If Customer name              If Street Name
Deliver to Customer | Safekeeping for Customer        Firm Inventory
```

Source: Robert C. Radcliffe, *Investment: Concept, Analysis, and Strategy*, Scott, Foresman and Company, Glenview, IL., 1982.

SECURITY A pledge of property or of good faith for the payment of a debt.

There are two classes of security: collateral or property security and personal security. Collateral security is any property, negotiable interest, or documentary evidence of a claim against, or ownership in property, conveying title to the holder as a pledge for the repayment of money lent, or as guarantee for the performance of a contract.

Personal security is the GUARANTY of the payment of money by one person for another person whose credit standing is not sufficient to justify the credit on his single name. In personal security, there is no pledge of property, but simply the signature (endorsement, guaranty, or SURETY) of some person having financial responsibility. Personal security, therefore, is only valuable where the person's moral standing is high.

Banking laws permit banks to make loans without security within generally applicable restrictions, and the basic LINE OF CREDIT calls for unsecured loans where the credit risk so justifies. Where the credit risk is high, a protective device is the pledge of specific collateral; it does not eliminate the credit risk, but it provides the additional recourse to the pledged property and the status of secured creditorship in the event of default. Unsecured loans are justified on the basis of high credit ratings indicated by reliable financial statements. In countries where business renders financial statements unreliable, the secured loan is typical.

The wide diversification of secured bank lending in recent years is indicated by the types of specific collateral or property security for bank loans, including bonds, stocks, notes, trade acceptances, bank acceptances, bills of lading, warehouse receipts, certificates of deposit, mortgages on real estate, chattel mortgages, assigned book accounts (accounts receivable), assigned syndicate agreements, trust receipts, assignable insurance policies having cash surrender values, savings passbooks, etc.

See HYPOTHECATION, REHYPOTHECATE.

BIBLIOGRAPHY

BANK ADMINISTRATION INSTITUTE. *1988 I.D. Checking Guide.* Bank Administration Institute, Rolling Meadows, IL, 1988.

SECURITY AFFILIATES The affiliate securities companies of commercial banks that prior to the Banking Act of 1933 engaged in a general securities business, including underwriting and purchasing and selling of securities, both as dealers and brokers.

The forerunner of the security affiliates was the First Security Co., organized by the First National Bank of the City of New York in 1908, when it was found that nothing in the national banking laws prohibited the formation and operation of such affiliates. The greatest popularity of security affiliates developed in the 1920s, when leading banks organized such companies in order to participate in the then highly profitable securities business. The depositors of the bank were generally utilized as a primary line of customers by the security affiliate.

With collapse of the security markets following 1929, many of the security affiliates became a drain on their parent banks; in some cases, such as was the case of the BANK OF UNITED STATES (New York), which closed its doors in December, 1930, the drain proved fatal. Accordingly, the Banking Act of 1933, passed June 16, 1933, required that within one year after passage of the act, security affiliates should be divorced from banks. It had been the general practice to have each share of bank stock carry with it a proportionate interest in the security affiliate by trusteeing the security affiliate's stock for the benefit of the bank stockholders.

SECURITY ANALYSIS The dissection of all pertinent data of individual companies—nature of the business, position in the industry, quality, demand for and diversity of products, capability of management, financial condition, capital structure, record of past earnings in relation to sales and investment, current and prospective earnings, relative stability of sales, earnings and payments, book as well as "hidden" asset values, yields, price-earnings relationships, and developments within the company and industry. The objectives of security analysis are a determination of the grade of the specific security and the determination of valuation therefor (current comparative valuation and "normal" value judgment).

See INVESTMENT, SPECULATION.

BIBLIOGRAPHY

PESSIN, A. H. *Fundamentals of the Securities Industry.* New York Institute of Finance, New York, NY, 1985.

SECURITY LOANS Loans secured by the pledge of securities collateral. Loans by banks on securities for the purpose of purchasing or carrying listed stocks on margin are subject to Regulation U of the Board of Governors of the Federal Reserve System, requiring the same initial margin requirements as for loans to brokers to finance such customers under Regulation T of the board and as for credit extended by lenders other than banks, brokers, or dealers under Regulation G of the board. The margin requirement has fluctuated over the years from a low of 25% in 1934 to 100% (no margin), in accordance with the board's view as to proper margin in the light of the overall credit position. By curbing the leverage provided by margin buying, margin regulation tends to be a stabilizing influence on the market; conversely, a reduction in margin requirements adds to such leveraged buying power. Because of relatively high margin requirements in recent years, security loans have not been the problem they were in the late 1920s, when brokers' loans by banks reached record totals, with banks attracted by high rates and allowed to act for "others" in placing such loans.

An additional direct power to curb the volume of security loans is vested in the Board of Governors of the Federal Reserve System by

Section 11(m) of the Federal Reserve Act, which provides that upon the affirmative vote of not less than six of its members, the board of governors shall have power to fix from time to time the percentage of individual bank capital and surplus that may be represented by loans secured by stock or bond collateral made by a member bank within each Federal Reserve district. No such loan shall be made by any such bank to any person in an amount in excess of 10% of the unimpaired capital and surplus of the bank.

See BROKERS' LOAN.

SEGMENT PERFORMANCE
A part of an entity whose activities represent a major line of business or class of customer. A segment is a part of an enterprise that sells primarily to outsiders for a profit. Examples of a segment of a business include a subsidiary, a division, a department, a product, a market, or other separations where the activities, assets, liabilities, and operating income can be distinguished for operational and reporting purposes.

Information about segments of a business, especially for diversified companies, is useful to investors of large, complex, heterogenous, publicly traded enterprises in evaluating risks, earnings, growth cycles, profit characteristics, capital requirements, and return on investments that can differ among segments of a business. The need for segment information is the result of many environmental factors including the growth of conglomerates, acquisitions, diversifications, and foreign activities of enterprises.

A reportable segment is determined by the following procedures:

1. Identifying the enterprise's products and services.
2. Grouping the products and services into industry segments.
3. Selecting the significant industry segments by applying various tests established for this purpose.

Segment information that must be disclosed in financial statements includes an enterprise's operations in different industries, foreign operations and export sales, and major customers. Detailed information must be disclosed relating to revenues, segment's operating profit or loss, and identifiable assets. Segment information is primarily a disaggregation of the entity's basic financial statements.

BIBLIOGRAPHY

SFAS No. 14, *Financial Reporting for Segments of a Business Enterprise* (FASB, 1976).

SEIGNIORAGE
Technically, the charge made by a government for minting standard bullion; by extension, the profit made by the government in issuing currency (the difference between the bullion or metal price and the denominational value of the currency). Such profit has been accounted for in the U.S. Treasury's statements as a miscellaneous receipt. The term originated in the Middle Ages, when the sovereigns or kings (seigneurs) made such a charge for minting coin.

Seigniorage on Coin and Silver Bullion

Fiscal year	Total
Jan. 1, 1935–June 30, 1965 cumulative	$ 2,525,927,763.84
1968	383,141,339.00 [1]
1970	274,217,884.01
1972	580,586,683.00
1974	320,706,638.49
1975	660,898,070.69
1980	662,814,791.48
1982	390,407,804.91
1983	477,479,387.58
1984	498,371,724.09
1985	515,906,969.31
1986	392,445,674.57
1987	458,070,694.43
Cumulative, Jan. 1, 1935–Sept. 30, 1987	$13,256,964,791.12

[1] Revised to include seigniorage on clad coins.

The appended table shows the seigniorage on coin and silver bullion for selected years.

Seigniorage should be distinguished from brassage, which involved a charge covering costs of minting, without a profit.

See COINAGE, MINT.

SELF-CHECK A check deposited for credit or presented for payment at the bank on which it is drawn, i.e., a home debit. When deposited for credit, a self-check involves a credit to the last endorser's account and a debit to the drawer's account. Obviously, a self-check does not pass through the clearinghouse.

SELF-LIQUIDATING LOAN A short-term commercial loan, so called because it is automatically discharged through the proceeds of the sale of the merchandise that it finances.

See ELIGIBLE PAPER.

SELF-REGULATORY ORGANIZATIONS Non-government organizations that have statutory responsibility to regulate their own members, such as the NEW YORK STOCK EXCHANGE, the AMERICAN STOCK EXCHANGE, and the NATIONAL ASSOCIATION OF SECURITIES DEALERS (NASD).

SELLER TAKEBACK A mortgage provided by the seller. This mortgage is frequently a second trust and is combined with an assumed mortgage. The second mortgage provides financing in addition to the first assumed mortgage, using the same property as collateral. In the event of default, the second mortgage is satisfied after the first. Seller takebacks frequently require payments for interest only, with the principal due at maturity.

SELLER'S OPTION See TRADING METHODS.

SELLING AGAINST THE BOX Selling stocks owned without relinquishing ownership of the certificate deposited in a safe deposit box. That is, an owner of stocks may sell stock that he owns without delivering the certificates to the broker. Thus, he is technically "short" in his brokerage account, though in reality he is not short. Such a sale offers a method of protecting assets in a declining market. After sales have been consummated, the stocks may be repurchased, presumably at a profit, and the original position is maintained. If the price rises, the owner may deliver his stocks from his strong box. Another advantage of selling against the box is that the source of the liquidation is not disclosed, since the original owner's name appears on the transfer books.

SELLING CLIMAX The end of a wave of heavy short selling necessitating liquidation of impaired margin accounts. Such a situation tends to build up a climax, i.e., a quick termination of the sharp selling movement, as a result of which the market is placed in a position to respond to an automatic rally. A selling climax terminates a period of heavy selling with rapid price declines. A market may decline slowly over a period of time as a result of important liquidation, however, without developing a selling climax.

SELLING FLAT See FLAT.

SELLING ON A SCALE See BUYING ON A SCALE, SCALING.

SELLING ON A BALANCE See BUYING ON BALANCE.

SELLING ORDER See ORDERS.

SELLING OUT The exercise of the legal right accorded a broker to close out an account of a customer, or of a bank to close out a broker's loan, for failure to furnish additional margin when demanded. An account or loan is sold out in a declining market in order to protect the lender from the loss that might accrue due to the decline in the value of the collateral below the face value of the loan. Loans are usually sold out at or near the EXHAUST PRICE. However, most brokers advise customers to maintain more than adequate credit balances and usually notify customers informally of the necessity for increasing credit balances lest the account become a restricted account under Regulation T.

See MARGIN BUYING.

SELLING SHORT See SHORT SALE.

SELLING STOP ORDER See STOP LOSS ORDER.

SEMIANNUAL INTEREST Interest that is payable twice a year. The interest upon the majority of bonds and mortgages is payable semiannually. The heaviest interest dates are January 1 and July 1. Interest dates occur most frequently on the first and fifteenth of the month.

See QUARTERLY DISBURSEMENTS.

SEMIMUNICIPAL BONDS Bonds that are not necessarily the obligation of all the taxpayers of the issuing municipality, but that are obligations of such taxpayers as secure the benefit of the improvements constructed from the proceeds of those bonds; thus, district drainage, irrigation, or reclamation bonds, levee district bonds, and sometimes street-paving bonds belong to this class. In purchasing municipal bonds, investors should inquire whether they are obligations of all or only a part of the taxpayers of the issuing civil division. Semimunicipal bonds are not entitled to as high a rating as MUNICIPAL BONDS.

SENIOR BONDS Bonds that have a claim upon the assets and earnings of a corporation prior to other bonds. For example, first mortgage bonds are senior to second mortgage bonds, and all mortgage bonds are senior to the debentures of the same corporation. The term senior is used as an antonym of junior and indicates, in a general way, that the securities have first claim upon assets and earnings.

When a corporation is capitalized by means of stocks or bonds, the bonds are the senior obligations; when a corporation is capitalized without bonds, the preferred stock is referred to as the senior issue and the common stock as the junior issue.

SENIOR ISSUE See SENIOR BONDS.

SENIOR LIEN See LIEN.

SERIAL BONDS Bonds having multiple maturities instead of a single maturity for payment of principal. An issue of bonds may mature in its entirety on a single maturity date, or in installments. Serial bonds are retired by the latter method, a certain portion specified in the indenture maturing at regular intervals. For example, a $1 million issue of bonds dated July 1, 1970, may mature in serials, the first $100,000 on July 1, 1971, and subsequent $100,000 installments every year thereafter (ten serials of $100,000 each).

Serial bonds are issued when there is no intention of refunding; their purpose is similar to that of sinking fund bonds, i.e., regular provision for retirement of the debt. The entire issue of serial bonds may carry the same interest rate, or it may carry differing interest rates for differing maturities. In turn, the yields of the various serials may differ because of sale at varying prices, depending upon the term. The advantage of serial bonds from the standpoint of the issuer is therefore flexibility in pricing portions of the total issue, so as to reflect varying capital market conditions for short-, intermediate-, and long-term maturities, and to maximize sale to include investors interested solely in particular maturities. Thus the shorter maturities might command better market prices than the longer maturities, resulting in better overall markets than a single long-term maturity with a sinking fund feature. In contrast to the sinking fund method of providing regular retirement, serial bonds shorten the average term of the total borrowing and eliminate the necessity for sinking fund arrangements. Serial bonds are especially used in EQUIPMENT TRUST financing and in state and municipal issues.

See MUNICIPALS.

SERVICE CORPORATION A subsidiary of a bank or thrift institution that provides services, excluding the deposit function, for the entity that owns the service corporation or customers. Services provided are described as "nonbanking" for banks and as "real estate activities" for savings and loan service entities.

SERVICE SALES TRANSACTION A transaction between a seller and a buyer in which, for a mutually agreed price, the seller performs, agrees to perform, or agrees to maintain readiness to perform an act or acts, including permitting others to use enterprise resources that do not alone produce a tangible commodity or product as the principal intended result (FASB). Following are examples of types of business that offer services:

Advertising agencies.
Computer service organizations.
Employment agencies.
Entertainment.
Engineering firms.
Retirement homes.
Accounting firms.
Architecture firms.
Law firms.
Travel agencies.

Revenue from service transactions is recognized on the basis of the seller's performance. Performance is the execution of a defined act or acts with the passage of time. Four methods of recognizing revenue are:

1. Specific performance method.
2. Completed performance method.
3. Proportional performance method.
4. Collection method.

When performance of services consists of the execution of a single act, revenue should be recognized when that action takes place—the specific performance method. For example, when dental service consists solely of the extraction of a tooth, revenue would be recognized when the tooth is pulled. When services are performed in more than a single act and the final act is so significant in relation to the service transaction taken as a whole that performance cannot be considered to have taken place until the execution of that act, revenue should be recognized only on the completion of the final act—the completed performance method. For example, a moving company would recognize revenue when the household furniture was transported to its destination. When performance consists of the execution of more than one act, revenue should be recognized based on the measurement of the sales value of each act—the proportional performance method. For example, recognition of revenue by an accounting firm for stages of work performed in auditing assignments, tax preparations, and related tasks would be on the proportional performance method. If a significant uncertainty exists with regard to the realization of service revenue, revenue should be recognized when cash is collected.

SERVICING The collection of mortgage payments, securing of escrow funds, payment of property taxes and insurance from the escrowed funds, monitoring delinquencies, and accounting for and remitting principal and interest payments to the investor.

SET OF BILLS See FIRST OF EXCHANGE.

SET OF EXCHANGE See BILLS IN A SET, FIRST OF EXCHANGE.

SETTLED PRODUCTION The steady or even rate of flow of an oil well, indicative of large reserve supplies.

SETTLEMENT This term has three applications.

1. In general, the striking of a balance between two or more parties having mutual dealings with one another and the payment of the debit balance by the debtor (debtors) to the creditor (creditors).
2. The striking of balances among members of a CLEARINGHOUSE association.
3. The process by which purchases and sales of securities among brokers are determined and the balances paid off at the stock exchange clearinghouse; the process by which interbroker, nonclearinghouse securities transactions or produce exchange transactions are paid off.

See SETTLEMENT DAYS, TRADING METHODS.

SETTLEMENT CLERK In banking practice, the name given to the clerk who receives packages of checks delivered from each presenting bank and determines the total amount of checks so presented at the CLEARINGHOUSE each day. The settlement clerk is the representative of the bank at the clearinghouse and reports to the clearinghouse manager the total of checks presented by and against the bank, leading to the determination of the debit or credit balance.

ENCYCLOPEDIA OF BANKING AND FINANCE

SETTLEMENT DAYS On the London Stock Exchange, settlements of security transactions are regularly made twice a month, once about the middle of the month and once at the end of the month. Transactions "for cash" are settled by immediate payment, regardless of the regular settlement day.

Each settlement requires three days: the first is known as contango day (also continuation, carrying over, or making-up day), the second is name or ticket day, and the third is pay day, i.e., settlement day proper. All transactions, except for cash, occurring between settlement days must be paid for and delivered in accordance with the brokers' contracts at the next settlement period.

The advantage of periodic settlements, as compared with the daily settlements made in America, is the saving of time to brokers in making deliveries and payments.

SETTLEMENT RISK The possibility that operational difficulties will interrupt delivery of funds even where the counterparty is able to perform.
See RISK.

SETTLOR A trustor, donor, or creator; one who creates a voluntary TRUST—i.e., one who "settles" an income, or other benefit, on a beneficiary.
See LIVING TRUST.

SEWER BONDS Municipal or semimunicipal bonds, the proceeds of which are used in the construction of sewers.
See MUNICIPAL BONDS.

SHADE A slight concession in prices.

SHAKING OUT The process of elimination of speculators with thin margins or inadequate capital from the market, caused by a decline in securities or commodities which stimulates short selling and touches off STOP LOSS ORDERS on the way down, thus further adding to the supply. At the conclusion of a "shake-out," stocks are said to pass into stronger hands capable of maintaining positions. In view of the relatively high margin requirements of recent years, "shoestring" margin buying, such as occurred in the late 1920s, has been absent as a market factor.
See MARGIN BUYING.

SHALE See OIL.

SHARE In England and Canada, the equivalent for the U.S. term stock, the term stock being reserved to denote government bonds. In the United States this term is synonymous with stock, or share of stock, but is much less commonly used.

SHARE CAPITAL The part of the capital of a corporation that is represented by outstanding shares of stock as distinguished from "loan capital," which is represented by bonds and floating debt.

SHARED APPRECIATION MORTGAGE Shared equity; a MORTGAGE in which the borrower agrees to share with the lender a sizable percent (often 30% to 50%) of the appreciation in the property's value when the borrower sells or transfers the property, or after a specified number of years. Such mortgages often have relatively low interest rates.

SHAREHOLDER See STOCKHOLDER.

SHAREHOLDERS' EQUITY The excess of assets over liabilities (or net assets) of a corporation. This represents the book value of claims of the owners to a share in the entity's assets after debts have been settled. The claims of certain classes of owners may have priority over others, especially where both common and preferred stock are outstanding. The preferred stock would usually have a higher priority but limited rights to share in the net assets and earnings of the corporation. Common stockholders would have a residual interest in the assets and earnings.

Shareholders' equity is increased when shares are issued by the corporation and by additional equity capital arising from earnings. It is decreased by dividends, reacquisition of stock, or losses from operations. Other transactions can also change shareholders' equity.

In banking, five possible types of equity are included in shareholders' equity: preferred stock, common stock, surplus, undivided profits, and equity reserves. The preferred stock account reports the par value of preferred stock outstanding. The common stock account reports the total par or stated value of the bank's outstanding common shares. The surplus account is the difference between the total value received and the common stock's par value when it was issued. The surplus account is also increased by transfers from the undivided profits account. The undivided profits account is increased by net income and reduced by cash or stock dividends and capital transfers. Equity reserves include contingency reserves, such as reserves for security losses and the contingency portion of provision for possible loan losses. The book value of a bank's common stock is the summation of the common stock, surplus, undivided profits, and equity reserve accounts.

SHARE LOAN A passbook loan. A loan secured by savings account of a S&L member. Also commonly called a savings account loan, dividend-day loan, or dividend-anticipation loan.

SHARE-TENANT A farmer who owns no land but who produces crops on a share basis, i.e., for a percentage of the crop, on another's land. The share-tenant thus exchanges his labor for a share (frequently one-half to two-thirds) of the product raised on the landowner's land.

The Bankhead-Jones Farm Tenant Act approved July 22, 1937, as amended (7 U.S.C. 1000-1029), authorizes operating loans and direct and insured farm ownership loans. Loans are available from the FARMERS HOME ADMINISTRATION to tenant farmers, laborers, and sharecroppers, repayable over periods of up to 40 years.

SHARES WITHOUT PAR VALUE See WITHOUT PAR VALUE STOCK.

SHEARED See FLEECE.

SHELF REGISTRATION Under Rule 415 of the SECURITIES AND EXCHANGE COMMISSION (SEC), adopted by the SEC on February 24, 1982, for a nine-month trial period, widely traded leading corporations may file a single S-3 "shelf registration" statement form with the SEC under the SECURITIES ACT OF 1933 to cover the total of new bond and/or stock financing for the next two years, without the necessity of filing new registration statements and distributing new prospectuses, thus expediting the public offering without the customary "waiting period." The shelf registration and prospectus, however, are subject to posteffective amendments to reflect any facts or events that individually or in the aggregate represent a fundamental change in the information previously set forth, although incorporation by reference is permitted for periodic reports filed under the Securities and Exchange Act (annual and interim reports, etc.) in lieu of posteffective amendments. Also, posteffective amendments to the filed registration statement are required to include any information with respect to the plan of distribution, "including (but not limited to) any addition or deletion of a managing underwriter, other than as a co-manager"; this presumably will afford financing corporations greater flexibility in the choice of underwriters, whether on a negotiated or a competitive bidding basis, or even in the choice of private placements versus public offerings, lump sum versus periodic smaller offerings, etc.
See INVESTMENT BANKER.

BIBLIOGRAPHY

FOSTER, F. D. "Syndicate Size, Spreads, and Market Power During the Introduction of Shelf Registration." *Journal of Finance*, March, 1989.
KADAPPAKKAM, P. R., and KON, S. J. "The Value of Shelf Registration for New Debt Issuers." *Journal of Business*, April, 1989.

SHELTERING TRUST A TRUST created to provide an income for the support of a spouse, or the support and education of children, and at the same time to "shelter" them from the dangers of their own inexperience, the cupidity of security salesmen, and the errors of incompetent advisers; also known as a spendthrift trust.
See LIVING TRUST.

SHERMAN ANTITRUST ACT   One of the fundamental ANTITRUST LAWS, the pioneer federal statute in this field (passed July 2, 1890), and a cornerstone in the legal expression of public policy against restraint of trade and monopoly or attempts to monopolize. The Sherman Antitrust Act is a general statute without definitions, leaving to the courts the task of interpretation and application, and of wide scope. For example, "*every* contract, combination in the form of trust or otherwise, or conspiracy in restraint of trade or commerce among the several States, or with foreign nations" was made illegal (Sec. 1), and "*every* person who shall monopolize or attempt to monopolize or combine or conspire with any other person or persons to monopolize any part of the trade or commerce among the several States, or with foreign nations, shall be deemed guilty of a misdemeanor" (Sec. 2). But in the process of judicial interpretation and application of common law principles, *not* every restraint has been found violative, only *unreasonable* restraints of trade ("rule of reason" *obiter dicta* of *Standard Oil Co.* v. *U.S.*, 221 U.S. 1; and *U.S.* v. *American Tobacco Co.*, 221 U.S. 106, both in 1911), particularly if combined with intent to monopolize and abuse of such power. This "rule of reason," however, has not been applied to cases of express or implied conspiracies to fix prices, and the modern trend in interpretation of size and market power is toward finding them per se violative. (*See U.S.* v. *Aluminum Co. of America*, 148 F.2d 416 (1945) and *U.S.* v. *American Tobacco Co.*, 328 U.S. 781 (1946).)

The Clayton Act and the Federal Trade Commission Act, both passed in 1914 and amended since, supplement the Sherman Act by amplifying detail in the fields of antitrust and unfair competitive practices.

SHERMAN NOTES   *See* TREASURY NOTES OF 1890.

SHERMAN SILVER-PURCHASE ACT   An act passed July 14, 1890, as a substitute for the Bland-Allison Act repealed on the same day. This act directed the secretary of the Treasury to purchase monthly 4.5 million ounces of fine silver at the market price, payment to be made in Treasury notes. These notes were legal tender and made redeemable in gold or silver coin by the secretary of the Treasury at the discretion of the holder. On account of the piling up of overvalued silver dollars in the Treasury as a result of the Bland-Allison Act and the Sherman Silver-Purchase Act, a decline in the gold reserve through gold exports at this time, and the fact that banks called for redemption of the Treasury notes in gold, a strain was put upon public confidence as to the ability of the government to meet its paper currency in gold. Combining with these circumstances was a panic in the London silver market in 1893 which brought the market ratio between silver and gold to about 31 to 1, compared with a mint ratio of 15.988 to 1. At market prices the silver dollar was then worth about $0.50 in gold. With continual demands being made upon the Treasury for redemption of Treasury notes of 1890 and greenbacks in gold, it became evident that the continued purchase of silver, leading to an increased circulation of overvalued silver dollars, would soon seriously embarrass the Treasury Department. Accordingly, Congress repealed the purchasing clause of this act on November 1, 1893.

SHIFTING LOANS   The process of seeking other lending banks for ACCOMMODATION when banks call upon broker-borrowers to pay up their loans.
See CALL MONEY MARKET.

SHILLING   A former silver English coin, popularly known as a "bob," equal to one-twentieth of a pound or 12 pence. The shilling was eliminated in the conversion of the English coinage system to the decimal system on February 15, 1971; the coin of equivalent value in the new coinage system is the five-pence coin (cupronickel).
See ENGLISH MONEY TABLE.

SHINPLASTERS   A popular name given to fractional paper currency issued during the Civil War and to similar currency issued after the War of 1812 because of a shortage of metallic money.

SHIPPER'S LOAD AND COUNT   A clause sometimes used in a BILL OF LADING for the purpose of limiting the carrier's liability.

SHIPPING DOCUMENTS   The papers that may accompany a domestic or foreign bill of exchange. A bill of exchange supported by shipping papers is known as a documentary bill. In domestic transactions, the minimum shipping documents consist of the bill of lading and seller's invoice. In foreign bills of exchange, the minimum documents consist of the ocean bill of lading, marine insurance certificate, and seller's invoice.

Other documents that may accompany a foreign bill of exchange, depending upon the agreement between buyer and seller, the laws of the nations concerned, etc., are as follows.

Consular invoice
Certificate of analysis
Certificate of inspection and weight
Certificate of origin
Warehouse receipt
Dock receipt
War risk insurance certificate

SHOESTRING MARGIN   A thin, inadequate margin. Speculators with small, precarious margins are said to be "trading on a shoestring."

SHOGUNS   U.S. dollar bonds issued in Japan.

SHORT   *See* SHORT SALE.

SHORT ACCOUNT   The aggregate of securities that have been sold short, i.e., for the account of short sellers. The size of the short account is considered by financial reviewers as bearing upon the technical position of the market.

For tabulation of the aggregate short account, *see* SHORT SALE.

SHORT BILLS   Bills of exchange drawn by banks or commercial interests, but usually documentary and payable from 1 to 30 days after presentation, as distinguished from long bills, which are payable 90 or more days after sight. Some authors give 60 days as the dividing line between long and short bills.
See FOREIGN BILLS OF EXCHANGE.

SHORT COVERING   The purchase of stock (or commodities) by a short seller to close or complete a transaction. Since every SHORT SALE involves borrowing, a purchase must be made in order to fulfill the contract and permit the return of the borrowed stock (or commodity contract).

SHORT INTEREST   The aggregate of securities (or commodities) that have been sold short and not yet "covered"; practically the same as SHORT ACCOUNT.

For tabulation of short interest in recent years, *see* SHORT SALE.

SHORT OF THE MARKET   One is said to be short of the market when one has sold securities (or commodities) short and has not yet covered.
See SHORT SALE.

SHORT RATE   In connection with fire insurance premiums, a rate based on a period of less than one year which is more than proportional to the yearly rate.
See INSURANCE.

SHORT RUN   In economics, a period of time during which a firm is unable to vary all of its inputs. Generally, labor is variable but capital is not.

SHORTS   Speculators who have sold short.
See SHORT SALE.

SHORT SALE   As defined by the Securities and Exchange Commission (Rule 3b-3, General Rules and Regulations under the Securities Exchange Act of 1934), any sale of a security that the seller does not own or any sale that is consummated by the delivery of a security borrowed by or for the account of the seller. Types of short sales encompassed by this definition include the following.

1. The speculative and hedging types of short sales, in which the short seller does not own the particular stock sold short and must arrange either directly or through his broker to borrow it in order to make delivery on the sale. Unlike the speculative

ENCYCLOPEDIA OF BANKING AND FINANCE

short seller, who does not own any stock, the hedging short seller is "long" of certain stocks but, expecting a market decline, sells other stocks short and subsequently "covers" them at a profit which offsets the losses on his original holdings.

2. Short sales "against the box," in which the short seller owns the particular stock sold short but borrows other shares of the same stock to make delivery, later "covering" by either utilizing his own stock or buying shares in the open market. Such short sales against the box may be made for a variety of reasons: to carry over profits into the next tax period, to hedge, or to bypass current unavailability of shares for regular delivery on a long sale.

Tax carryover: As of December of a tax year A may have a paper profit on a stock previously bought at a lower price but not wish to include such realized gain in taxable income of the current tax year. He may therefore sell the stock short in December and "cover" in January by delivering his long stock, thus shifting the realized gain to the following tax year.

Hedge: B owns a block of a given stock. Anticipating a market decline, he sells that stock short, borrowing other shares of the same stock for the delivery on the sale. Subsequently, if the stock actually declines, he covers at a profit, which will offset the loss on his "long" stock. If the stock rises instead, his "long" profit offsets his loss on the short sale.

Delivery difficulty: C wants to sell a given stock, but the shares are not immediately available for regular delivery (he is having difficulty getting them out of a safe deposit box, the shares are located elsewhere, etc.). Therefore, he may sell the stock short, borrowing other shares of the same stock for the regular delivery; later, when the original stock becomes available, he utilizes it for delivery when he "covers" on the short sale.

3. Arbitrage short sales, which occur when securities are concurrently bought and sold in the same or different markets—a "technical" type of short sale.

Mechanics of Short Sales. In stock exchange practice, in order to sell short customers must have the general account, with the accompanying customers agreement. Because short sales require margin, stock must be borrowed by the broker to make delivery, and there are special restrictions on executions of orders to sell short. Every "sell" order itself must be marked "long" or "short" (SEC Rule 10a-1 (b)).

The price restriction rule (SEC Rule 10a-1 (a)) reads as follows:

"No person shall, for his own account or for the account of any other person, effect on a national securities exchange a short sale of any security (1) below the price at which the last sale thereof, regular way, was effected on such exchange, or (2) at such price unless such price is above the next preceding different price at which a sale of such security, regular way, was effected on such exchange. In determining the price at which a short sale may be effected after a security goes ex-dividend, ex-rights, or ex-any other distribution, all sale prices prior to the 'ex' date may be reduced by the value of such distribution."

The price restriction rule means that the market order to sell short may be executed at a price representing a "plus tick" or "zero plus tick" (a "tick" is the minimum multiple of price fluctuation in a stock, normally $1/8$ of a point).

Plus tick: Successive transactions in the stock at the trading floor post are 20, 19, and 19 $1/8$. The short sale order may *not* be executed at 19, because that price represents a decline of at least $1/8$ as compared with the immediately preceding transaction at 20. The short sale *may* be executed at 19 $1/8$, because that price represents a rise of minimum $1/8$ price fluctuation as compared with the immediately preceding transaction at 19.

Zero plus tick: Successive transactions in the stock at the trading floor post are 20, 19, 19 $1/8$, and 19 $1/8$. The short sale order *may* be executed at the time of the second 19 $1/8$ transaction, at 19 $1/8$, because that price, although "zero" in fluctuation as compared with the immediately preceding transaction, is up the $1/8$ minimum as compared with the next preceding *different* price of 19.

The short sale order, however, may not be executed at a "minus tick" or "zero minus tick."

Minus tick: Successive transactions in the stock at the trading floor post are 20, 20 $1/8$, and 20. The short sale order may not be effected at the last price of 20, because that price represents a minus tick as compared with the immediately preceding transaction.

Zero minus tick: Successive transactions in the stock at the trading floor post are 20, 20 $1/8$, 20, and 20. The short sale order may not be effected at the last price of 20, because although "zero" in fluctuation as compared with the immediately preceding transaction, that price is minus the $1/8$ minimum as compared with the next preceding *different* price of 20 $1/8$.

It is of course possible under the rule to sell short at a price at least $1/8$ above the latest transaction price, even when it is a "minus tick" or "zero minus tick" price; but whether the execution will be possible depends upon such bid appearing. To facilitate executions, each trading post on the floor has dials for each stock traded, indicating the last sale price and whether it is a plus or minus fluctuation.

The SEC rule exempts the following from the above pricing restriction:

1. Any sale by any person, for an account in which he has an interest, if such person owns the security sold and intends to deliver such security as soon as is possible without undue inconvenience or expense
2. Any "long" sale
3. Any sale of an odd lot
4. Any sale by an odd-lot dealer to offset odd-lot orders of customers
5. Any sale by an odd-lot dealer to liquidate a long position that is less than a round lot, provided such sale does not change the position of such odd-lot dealer by more than the unit of trading
6. Any sale in connection with arbitrage transactions between different markets
7. Any sale in connection with arbitrage transactions between different securities.

Margin Requirements: Short sellers are subject to margin requirements-not only those of the Board of Governors of the Federal Reserve System (Regulation T) but also, on the "Big Board," those of the New York Stock Exchange (NYSE) itself.

The Fed's margin requirement is an initial margin, determined at the time the short sale is made, and is computed subsequent to the day of sale on the basis of the closing sale price of the stock on the previous trading day. The Fed has been prescribing the same margin requirements on short sales as on margin buying (50% effective since January 3, 1974).

The NYSE margin requirement is both an initial minimum and a minimum maintenance margin. NYSE Rule 431 prescribes a minimum equity of $2,000 in an account for a short sale to be possible. Rule 431 also prescribes the following maintenance margins on short sales.

1. $2.50 per share or 100% of the market value, in cash, whichever amount is greater, of each stock short in the account selling at less than $5 per share; plus
2. $5 per share or 30% of the market value, in cash, whichever amount is greater, of each stock short in the account selling at $5 per share or above; plus
3. 5% of the principal amount or 30% of the market value, in cash, whichever amount is greater, of each bond short in the account.

Thus, for stocks selling at less than $5, a 100% margin is required; for stocks selling at $5 or over, the minimum is $5; and for a stock selling at $16 $3/4$ or over, the 30% alternative becomes advantageous.

A formula for figuring margins on short sales as is follows:

$$\frac{\text{Net proceeds of sale} + \text{Initial margin}}{\text{Market value}} - 1.00$$

Thus a sale of 100 shares X at *net* proceeds of $80 per share (after deducting brokerage commission, New York state stock transfer taxes, and the SEC fee) requires margin of $5,600 as follows (assume a current market price of 80):

$$\text{Margin} = \frac{8000 + 4000}{8000} = 1.50 - 1.00 = 50\%$$

If the stock thereafter rises to 90 and the short seller has not yet covered, the new margin in the account would be

$$\text{Margin} = \frac{8000 + 4000}{9000} = 1.33 - 1.00 = 33.33\%$$

If, on the other hand, the stock thereafter declines to 70 and the short seller has not yet covered, the new margin in the account would be

$$\text{Margin} = \frac{8000 + 4000}{7000} = 171.43 - 1.00 = 71.43\%$$

Short Sale Procedure. Once the order to sell short has been executed, the stock sold must be delivered "regular way" to the buyer on the fourth full business day after the date of the transaction. Since the speculative short seller does not have the stock to deliver, he must arrange for his broker to borrow the stock in order to make delivery.

One of the clauses in the standard customers agreement in the general account reads: "I hereby authorize you to lend either to yourselves or to others any securities held for me on margin." Thus the short seller's broker, by virtue of such agreements with his other customers, may have the stock available for delivery. More usually, the broker will borrow the stock from other brokers by contact between the respective "cashiers" of the firms involved. Firms lend stock because there is a concurrent posting in cash of the full market value of the stock lent. Where stocks lend "flat," use of such cash is interest-free; where stocks lend "at a rate," the lender of the stock pays interest on the cash quid pro quo for the stock lent. If stocks lend "at a premium," the borrower of the stock pays a daily fee and in addition posts the cash market value of the stock borrowed; premiums pursuant to Rule 157 of the NYSE must be quoted on a basis of specified dollars per hundred shares. Both "rate" and "premium" lending have been obsolete in recent years.

The net cash proceeds of the short sale, therefore, are not immediately available to the short seller, as they are used to post the cash for the stock borrowed. If the stock moves upward in price, the broker lending the stock will serve a "mark to market" notice upon the borrowing broker, requiring the posting of more cash, so as to keep the stock loan secured at all times by approximately 100% in cash at current market value. If the stock moves downward in price, the broker borrowing the stock serves a mark to market notice upon the lending broker calling for the return of the excess cash. The loan of the stock may be canceled on four business days' notice by either party (Rule 160 of the NYSE).

When the short seller finally covers (buys the stock originally sold short), the stock received on such covering will be tendered to the broker who lent the stock, causing the return of the cash quid pro quo, which in turn will serve to pay for the covering transaction. The net difference between the original transaction proceeds and the cost of the cover will be the net profit or loss on the short sale (short sellers have no debit balance on which to pay interest, as margin buyers do), which will be either a short-term or a long-term gain for tax purposes, depending on the six months' demarcation.

Pros and Cons on Short Selling. Short selling has been one of the most controversial market practices from early times. It is a sophisticated technique used particularly by "professionals," and in the days before the Securities Exchange Act of 1934, banning all forms of manipulation, short selling was often accompanied by "bear raids," which used varied devices to crack confidence in the stock sold short, such as dissemination of false rumors, tips, and information on the stock. Short selling was utilized by famous stock market operators such as Gould, Fisk, Vanderbilt, and Drew; it was the last-named who supposedly coined the doggerel, "He who sells what isn't his'n, must buy it back or go to prison." It is estimated that about three-fourths of all the short sales in modern times have been made by members of the exchange, half of which in turn were made by specialists in conducting normal operations in their assigned stocks. In 1830, a law was passed prohibiting short sales, but this law was repealed in 1858. Short selling, moreover, has been upheld in the courts, and the stock exchange has based its stand on the legality of short selling on several decisions. In *Bibb* v. *Allen* (149 U.S. 481), the U.S. Supreme Court said: "It is held settled that contracts for the future delivery of merchandise or perishable property are not void whether such property is in existence in the hands of the seller or to be subsequently acquired." In *Hurd* v. *Taylor* (181 N.Y. 231), the New York Court of Appeals said: "The purchase of stocks through a broker, though the party ordering such purchase does not intend to hold the stocks as an investment, but expects the broker to carry them for him, with the design on the part of the purchaser to sell the stocks when their market value has enhanced, is, however speculative, entirely legal. Equally so is a 'short' sale where the seller has not the stock he assumes to sell, but borrows it and expects to replace it when the market value has declined." In the case of *Irwin* v. *Williar* (110 U.S. 499), the U.S. Supreme Court said in part: "A person may make a contract for the sale of personal property which the vendor does not own or possess, but expects to obtain by purchase or otherwise, which is binding if an actual transfer of property is contemplated." The rules of the New York Stock Exchange upholding short selling were sustained by the N.Y. Supreme Court in the case of *Cohen* v. *Budd* (52 Misc. 217), which held that "stock exchanges have the power to enact such rules for the government of their affairs as are necessary to carry out their purpose when not contrary to the law of the land."

The pros for short selling may be summarized as follows.

1. It is analogous to commercial practice, such as a farmer selling his crop before harvesting, the manufacturer selling his output for months in advance, the subscriber paying in advance for a magazine subscription, etc.
2. It restrains high prices because short sales are stimulated by unduly high prices.
3. It provides a price "cushion" for the market because the short seller eventually covers.
4. It stabilizes prices by depressing unduly high prices and supporting prices justifying covering.
5. It counteracts the inflationary effect of margin buying.
6. It enhances market continuity by increasing the number of sellers and buyers.

The following are contra arguments against short selling.

1. It is not analogous to commercial practices because the latter are simply convenient ways of selling goods or services always in ownership or control of the seller.
2. Short selling actually increases in volume and impact when prices turn downward, and does little to restrain unduly high prices.
3. The price cushion provided by covering is at lower prices, after the price decline has been effected and when other bidding interest has been thinned by the decline.
4. It is deflationary, which may be just as bad as the inflationary effect of margin buying.
5. It may reduce market continuity by its "bearish" effect on sentiment.

In the writer's view, short selling is sustainable, free from "bear raiding" and under present restrictions as to price executions to prevent accelerative effect, as the free expression of price opinion in open competitive markets. The margin buyer, a "bull" on prices, is entitled to such price opinion; so is the short seller, a "bear" on prices. The market can only benefit from such full expression of price opinion; if the short seller is wrong and prices are justifiedly entitled to higher levels, prices will go up regardless of short selling. It must be remembered that theoretically there is no limit to the loss that a short seller may incur if the stock sold short keeps on rising and he keeps posting mark to market notices and at least the minimal margins required. If the short seller is right and prices are deflated to lower levels, the "bulls" prima facie could not justify the higher prices. The full interplay of price opinion, without manipulation, will make for sounder markets.

The Securities Exchange Act of 1934 did not abolish short selling in stock markets. Instead (Sec. 10), it left the issue up to the Securities and Exchange Commission, for prescription of rules and regulations. Section 16(c), however, forbids short selling by directors, officers, and owners of 10% or more of the stock of a corporation registered on a national securities exchange. The first rules of the SEC, promulgated in February, 1938, provided that no short sale could be executed at or below the price of the last sale; all had to be executed at least a "tick" above last sale. This severely reduced short selling, which revived subsequently when the present execution rules (see above) were promulgated in March, 1939.

Short Selling in the Unified Market. On March 6, 1974, the SEC proposed amendments to Securities Exchange Act (Rules 3b-3, 10a-1, and 10a-2) in order to establish uniform short sale rules, which

SHORT SIDE

were considered to be a necessary element of the consolidated reporting system. After "analyzing the comments received on the proposed amendments and concluding that no serious objections had been raised, the Commission announced their adoption to be effective October 4, 1974 [the October Amendments]." But in a letter to the commission, dated October 11, 1974, the New York Stock Exchange asserted that the October Amendments would create insurmountable technical, operational, and regulatory problems. Accordingly, in view of the problems noted by the NYSE, the commission temporarily suspended the effectiveness of the October Amendments to Rules 10a-1 and 10a-2.

The effect of that suspension was to leave the regulation of short sales on exchange markets as it had existed before adoption of the October Amendments, while the SEC continued to study the most efficient, effective, and fair manner to achieve uniform short-sales regulation in a central market system.

On March 5, 1975, the commission published for comment additional proposed amendments to Rule 10a-1 (the "March Proposals"). The commission noted that many persons believed that short selling should not be regulated at all, except to the extent it is used as a manipulative device. In the SEC's view, however, consideration of such arguments had been hampered by a lack of current statistical studies of the pattern of short selling in today's markets, particularly on regional securities exchanges and in the "third market." "In any event," the SEC concluded, "it would be premature to consider elimination of Short Sales regulation altogether or for any class of short sellers, before additional progress was made toward the establishment of a central market system." However, the commission specifically encouraged comments on the feasibility and probable effects of exempting from regulation short sales by persons other than brokers and dealers, or of eliminating the short-sale regulation entirely.

Network A of the Consolidated Market System commenced operation on June 16, 1975. In order to ensure comparable short-sale regulation of all transactions in reported securities in all markets reporting transactions to that system, the commission announced on June 12, 1975, the adoption of amendments to Rules 10a-1 and 10a-2 (effective June 16, 1975) which were material in all respects to the "March Proposals."

Paragraph (a) of Rule 10a-1 would not apply to short sales of any reported security until last sale information on that security was made available to vendors of market information on a real-time basis. When such information became available on a real-time basis, Paragraph (a) of Rule 10a-1 would govern short sales in all markets (including transactions effected on national securities exchanges and in the over-the-counter market). Additionally, national securities exchanges would have an option either to adopt their own short sale rules, subject to the commission's power under Section 19 of the SECURITIES EXCHANGE ACT OF 1934, or to be governed by Paragraph (b) of Rule 10a-1, the traditional form of the rule, which applies only to short sales effected on national securities exchanges.

Statistics on Short Interest. On May 25, 1931, the New York Stock Exchange began publishing the size of the outstanding short interest. Weekly figures showing the number of shares in the total short interest were released by the NYSE, compiled from information secured from its members, once each week from May 25, 1931, until September 21, 1931, when daily reports were required. Starting September 19, 1932, daily reports were discontinued and weekly reports resumed. As of June 5, 1933, weekly reports were discontinued, and thereafter monthly reports were required, starting June 30, 1933.

SHORT SIDE   SHORT ACCOUNT; those who have sold short and whose interest it is to work for a decline in prices.

SHORT STOCK   Stock that has been sold short.
See SHORT SALE.

SHORT-TERM NOTES   Notes with maturities of under one year. Such maturities are particularly characteristic of seasonal borrowing, including paper "eligible" for rediscount by Federal Reserve banks. Section 13 of the Federal Reserve Act specifies maximum maturities of 90 days, exclusive of grace, on paper drawn or issued for industrial or commercial purposes; Section 13a of the act specifies maximum maturities, at the time of discount and exclusive of days of grace, of 9 months for paper issued or drawn for agricultural purposes or based upon livestock.
See ELIGIBLE PAPER.

SICK MARKET   The stock market following a period of speculative activity in which prices have fallen and traders become discouraged. A condition of uncertainty and hesitancy prevails, and traders are casting about for news susceptible to favorable or unfavorable interpretation so that commitments may be made accordingly.

SIDELINES   A trader in securities or commodities is said to be on the "sidelines" when he is temporarily out of the market, having closed out his long or short position. Institutional investors or investing institutions that have the problem of continuous investment resort to shifts to liquidity (cash and government securities) when called for by market trends.
See INVESTMENT, SPECULATION.

SIGHT BILL OF EXCHANGE   A BILL OF EXCHANGE payable on presentation to the drawee.

SIGHT BILLS   Bills payable on presentation; demand bills and presentation bills.
See BILL OF EXCHANGE.

SIGHT CREDIT   A short title for "sight letter of credit"; a LETTER OF CREDIT that specifies the drawing of sight drafts thereunder.

SIGHT DRAFT   A DRAFT payable upon presentation.

SIGHTING A BILL   Presenting a bill payable at sight or so many days after sight for payment or acceptance to the drawee in order to bring it under his sight. A sight bill should be presented as soon after receipt as possible.

SIGHT RATE   The rate of exchange applicable to a demand draft or check; CHECK RATE.

SIGNATURE CARD   See SIGNATURE DEPARTMENT, SIGNATURES.

SIGNATURE DEPARTMENT   A separate department among larger banks, the function of which is to verify SIGNATURES on all home-debit checks before they are charged to the depositors' (drawers') accounts. Since a bank is responsible for paying checks signed by a forged or unauthorized name, the verification of the genuineness of signatures is important. The verification of signatures depends upon the keeping of an up-to-date signature card file containing all signatures with which the bank comes in contact and the employment of clerks who can memorize the signatures of the customers in order to discriminate between a genuine signature and a fictitious, forged, or otherwise unauthorized one, without constant comparison with the signature card.

When an account is opened, the signatures of principals of each account are secured on a signature card for future use. Some banks procure specimen signatures on three different cards to be used in the paying teller's and new business departments and at the check desk. Other banks make photographic copies of signature cards, thus obviating the necessity of requesting customers to sign more than one.

In partnership accounts, the signatures of all partners are required. In corporation accounts, the signature of each official authorized to sign, either as full authority, for countersignature, or PER PROCURATION, is obtained. The signatory power of each official is also indicated. Thus a bank official may be authorized to certify a check but not to sign a cashier's check. For authentication of the signatures of officials, a copy of the resolution of the board of directors empowering such officials to sign is also procured. Changes in authority to sign must be followed up and signature cards revised accordingly. The signature clerk must see not only that the person's signature is genuine but also, in case of an official signing for a corporation, that he has power to sign and that the power to sign is still in force.

Banks usually place the following additional information on the signature cards: occupation or business, address, date of opening the account, person making introduction.

SIGNATURES   A bank is required to know the signatures of all its customers, and is responsible if it pays a check on which the drawer's signature has been forged. For this reason it is essential that the signature upon each check be verified before it is paid and

ENCYCLOPEDIA OF BANKING AND FINANCE

charged to the customer's account. The method of verification is explained under SIGNATURE DEPARTMENT.

When checks are presented to the paying teller, the signature of which he does not recognize (as in the case of a new account), he must consult the signature file, which should be readily accessible. If the drawer's signature differs from the usual one so as to raise the question of genuineness, it is referred to an officer. In England, when the signature differs and it is difficult to communicate with the depositor, it is a customary practice to return the check with the explanation "signature differs."

Signatures may be representative of different types of accounts:

1. Individual.
2. Joint—where two or more persons have a joint interest in the account.
3. Copartnership—where two or more persons can sign checks binding a firm.
4. Corporation—where certain officials are authorized to sign by a resolution of the board of directors, which the bank should have on file.
5. Power of attorney—where an agent may be appointed to sign for another person. In this case a copy of the power of attorney, setting forth the agent's authority, should be on file.
6. Agent, manager, treasurer, special, etc. A person or corporation may have several special accounts for various purposes. The person authorized to sign checks for withdrawals from such an account does not need to reveal the principal.
7. Administrator, executor, trustee, sinking fund agent, etc. When a person is signing in a fiduciary capacity, proper authorization to act in such capacity must be on file.

SIGN IN BLANK In a nontechnical sense, the ENDORSEMENT of a negotiable instrument. Because such endorsement makes the instrument a bearer instrument, negotiation of the instrument may be effected by mere delivery, so that the warranties specified in Section 65, Uniform Negotiable Instruments Law, extend in favor of no holder other than the immediate transferee.

SIGNING BY MARK See MARK SIGNATURE.

SILVER One of the precious metals and also a highly versatile metal for industrial uses, particularly photography, electrical and electronic applications, sterling ware, brazing alloys, and electroplated ware—all these uses taking more silver annually than jewelry (which in latest years has accounted for a minor part of total silver consumption). Consumption of silver for coinage purposes has declined in recent decades, as many countries (including the U.S.) have converted to nonsilver coins in their coinage systems. Consumption of silver for the arts and industry has continued to run ahead of new silver output in recent years.

With excess of demand over new output characteristic, it would be supposed that silver prices should rise substantially. Actually, however, higher prices tend to dishoard existing supplies (other than new production) of silver, which results in estimated world supplies (excluding Communist-dominated areas) being a factor of constraint on higher market prices. In 1979, however, extraordinary market speculation in silver caused New York prices to rise from $5.40 an ounce in January to $28 an ounce late in December, 1979, and to $50.35 an ounce in the third week of January, 1980, only to end at below $11 an ounce in March, 1980.

The U.S. Treasury played an important role in supporting silver market prices in former years, but on November 10, 1970, with completion of its auction sales through the General Services Administration (GSA), begun on August 4, 1967, the Treasury ceased to supply silver (mainly to industrial users), and the silver market became wholly free from Treasury influence (the former "floor" for the market provided by offerings from the Treasury at $1.293 also ended in 1967). The Treasury therefore has been left with its stockpile at the GSA of 139.5 million ounces, in addition to any silver accumulated per authority in Section 104 of the Coinage Act of 1965. Section 104 reads that "the Secretary (of the Treasury) shall purchase at price of $1.25 per fine troy ounce any silver mined after the date of enactment of this Act (the Coinage Act of 1965, enacted July 23, 1965) from natural deposits in the United States or any place subject to the jurisdiction thereof and tendered to a United States mint or assay office within one year after the month in which the ore from which it is derived was mined." As of 1981, no action had been forthcoming

Table 1 / Silver

Year	Production[a] World	U.S.	U.S. consumption[a] Industry	Coinage	Average N.Y. price per fine ounce
1971	294.7	41.6	129.1	2.5	$ 1.546
1972	301.5	37.2	151.1	2.3	1.685
1973	307.9	37.8	195.9	0.9	2.558
1974	292.2	33.8	177.0	1.0	4.708
1975	303.0	34.9	157.7	2.7	4.419
1976	316.3	34.3	170.6	1.3	4.353
1977	340.2	38.2	153.6	0.1	4.623
1978	344.7	39.4	160.2	0.2	5.401
1979	344.5	38.1	157.3	0.1	11.094
1980	339.8	32.2	124.8	0.1	20.632 [b]

Source: U.S. Bureau of Mines, U.S. Dept. of Commerce
[a] In millions of fine ounces.
[b] Range of prices for 1980 was $48,000 high, $10,800 low

on the disposal of the 139.5 million ounces of silver in the strategic stockpile.

U.S. Legislation. The modern history of silver in the U.S. dates from 1933. Title III of the Act of May 12, 1933, delegated power to the President to alter the weight of the silver dollar and provide for unlimited coinage of silver and gold at fixed mint ratio (bimetallism), and authorized the President to accept up to 200 million ounces of silver at not over $0.50 an ounce in payment of foreign debts owed to the U.S., and to issue silver certificates against this silver. This legislation provided the authority for the President, beginning December 21, 1933, and continuing until passage of the Act of July 6, 1939, to direct the mints, by a series of proclamations, to accept all newly mined domestic silver tendered to them for coinage into silver dollars. The first proclamation provided that 50% seigniorage would be deducted, and in view of the statutory coinage value of silver of $1.29+ per fine ounce, this meant a net price of $0.6464+ per fine ounce. Subsequent proclamations provided for seigniorage deductions of 40% to 50%, or a range in net prices from $0.6464+ to $0.7757+ per fine ounce.

The Act of June 19, 1934, the Silver Purchase Act, authorized and directed the secretary of the Treasury to purchase silver with the objective of reaching and maintaining 25% of the monetary value of total monetary stocks of the U.S. in silver. Silver certificates were required to be issued up to at least the cost value, and might be issued up to the full monetary value ($1.29+ per fine ounce) of silver so purchased. The secretary of the Treasury was given authority to coin standard silver dollars for the redemption of all silver certificates. Foreign silver and domestic silver could be purchased under this act at a price not to exceed its monetary value ($1.29+ per fine ounce), except that the price paid for silver situated in the continental U.S. on May 1, 1934, could not exceed $0.50 per fine ounce.

The Act of July 6, 1939, directed the mints to receive for coinage into standard silver dollars any newly mined domestic silver mined subsequent to July 1, 1939, deducting 45% seigniorage (thus a net price of $0.7111+ per fine ounce).

The Act of July 31, 1946, which amended the Act of July 6, 1939, provided for the acquisition of domestic silver mined after July 1, 1946, tendered to any U.S. mint within one year after the ore from which it was derived was mined, at 30% seigniorage charge, or a net price for such newly mined domestic silver of $0.905+ per fine ounce. The bimetallism power of the President conferred by Title III of the Act of May 12, 1933, expired June 30, 1943. After the Gold Reserve Act of 1934 had amended the Act of May 12, 1933, to provide a two-year life for the authority from January 30, 1934, plus a one-year extension by proclamation, subsequent amendment had extended the duration of the power to June 30, 1943.

Also, the Silver Purchase Act of June 19, 1934, authorized the President to require delivery of all silver in the U.S. to the mints and to pay for it a fair market price (nationalization of silver). Nationalization was subsequently effected and later rescinded. On June 28, 1934, the Treasury prescribed licenses for the export of silver; and on August 9, 1934, presidential proclamation and executive order ordered all silver in the continental U.S. to be delivered to the mints, silver so delivered to be paid for in any currency at $0.5001 per fine ounce (not conflicting with the price then prevailing for *newly mined* domestic silver of $0.645 per fine ounce). Silver so delivered was to be coined or held as bullion for later coinage. Denationalization

SILVER

occurred on April 29, 1938, when presidential proclamation revoked the presidential proclamation of August 9, 1934, except as it applied to newly mined domestic silver, and when the Treasury order of June 28, 1934, and the Silver Regulations of August 17, 1934, were rescinded so as to remove restrictions on the free import and export of silver.

The Act of July 12, 1943 (Green Act), authorized the President, through the secretary of the Treasury and upon recommendation of the chairman of the War Production Board, to sell or lease domestically any silver held or owned by the U.S., provided that at all times the Treasury maintained the ownership and possession of control within the U.S. of an amount of silver of a monetary value equal to the face amount of all outstanding silver certificates. The price for such silver was to be not less than $0.7111 per fine ounce. This World War II authority expired on December 31, 1945. During World War II, the Treasury lent 900 million ounces to industry as a substitute for copper, shipped 410.8 million ounces under "lend lease" arrangements, and sold 150 million ounces. Thus by the end of World War II, the Treasury's stock of silver had declined from 2.5 billion ounces prewar to 950 million ounces.

The Act of July 31, 1946, authorized the Treasury to sell silver at not over $1.29+ per fine ounce and to buy silver at not less than $0.905 per fine ounce. On the day this act became law, the secretary of the Treasury announced that sales would be made at price of $0.91 per fine ounce. Beginning in 1961, however, the silver market lost its previous stabilization created by the coordination of the Mexican and U.S. governments. On November 28, 1961, the Treasury suspended sales of silver to the domestic industry. On June 4, 1963, P.L. 88-36 repealed pertinent portions of the Silver Purchase Act of 1934, the Act of July 6, 1939, and the Act of July 31, 1946; provided for maintenance of enough silver on hand at the Treasury to cover redemption in full of outstanding silver certificates for silver dollars; repealed the tax on transfers of silver bullion; and provided for issuance of $1 and $2 denominations for Federal Reserve notes. The silver market boiled up to a high of $1.293 per ounce, the effective price indicated by Treasury action of redemption of silver certificates, as compared with lows of $1.21 in 1963, $1.01 in 1962, and the stabilized price of $0.91375 in 1960 and 1961. The $1.293 per ounce price, first reached on September 9, 1963, in connection with large-scale redemption of silver certificates, "pegged" the market at that level for the years thereafter until 1967, when Treasury stabilization at that price ceased at midyear and the market rose to a high of $2.17 an ounce.

P.L. 89-81, July 23, 1965, the Coinage Act of 1965, confirmed the plans of the Treasury to convert the coinage system to reduced silver half-dollars and nonsilver quarters and dimes; to invoke in the meantime a ban on the exporting, melting, etc., of any U.S. coins if needed (for their silver content); and to hold the open market price at $1.293 per ounce as long as Treasury silver stocks' availability permitted. An open leakage, however, in such supplies was created by the large-scale redemption of silver certificates and the coinage demands. Thus, after the "horse had been stolen," the Treasury locked the barn, by gaining authorization (P.L. 90-29, 1967) to suspend the redemption of silver certificates one year later (June 24, 1968) and by following the recommendations of the new Joint Commission on the Coinage (established by the Coinage Act of 1965) on May 18, 1967, to issue regulations banning the exporting, melting, etc., of U.S. coins and to limit future sales of silver to domestic industrial users. Only two months later, on July 14, 1967, following a stampede to redeem silver certificates, the Treasury announced the complete suspension of Treasury sales of silver at $1.29 an ounce and the limitation of future sales to weekly auctions through the GSA at prevailing market prices. Market prices rose in 1967 to a high of $2.17 an ounce, followed by a 1968 peak of $2.565 per ounce. It was a period of speculation in silver, which hindsight shows might have been more controlled by both the Joint Commission on the Coinage and the Treasury. An example of the Joint Commission's inconsistent action was the recommendation in December, 1968, that legislation be enacted permanently banning private melting of U.S. coins and then on May 12, 1969, the opposite recommendation that the Treasury repeal its regulations prohibiting such melting. It should be pointed out, however, that the chairman of the Joint Commission on the Coinage is the secretary of the Treasury.

On November 10, 1970, Treasury sales of silver at going prices through the GSA ended. P.L. 91-607, Title II, December 31, 1970, provided for issuance of nonsilver dollars and half-dollars having the same composition as the cupronickel quarters and dimes previously authorized by the Coinage Act of 1965. The silver market was now completely free of any Treasury operations, except for any changes in the stockpile and any possible future offerings from U.S. mint holdings (some 39 million ounces as of 1980).

Repercussions of 1980 Silver Price Gyrations. The COMMODITY EXCHANGE, INC. (COMEX) reported that the reduced level of trading in silver in 1980 reflected a series of "extraordinary events" which commenced in the market during the fall of 1979. At that time, the COMEX board of governors was alerted to an apparent concentration of large silver market positions under the control of a limited number of traders. This serious situation in the COMEX silver market required the constant attention of the COMEX board of governors and the COMEX staff over a period of seven months.

In discharging its self-regulatory responsibilities, the COMEX board took a series of actions during the period from September, 1979, to March, 1980, designed to ensure the orderly liquidation of silver futures. These actions included raising margins on silver contracts to reflect increased volatility in silver prices; expanding daily trading limits; creating a Special Silver Committee, composed of disinterested board members, to investigate and monitor silver market positions; imposing speculative position limits; and temporarily restricting trading to liquidation only.

The Chicago Board of Trade, in connection with its trading in silver futures, imposed only a limited ban on new positions (February and March) and a 600-contract limit on individuals' holdings. The chairman of the COMMODITY FUTURES TRADING COMMISSION (CFTC) was reported to have raised the question of whether position limits in delivery months might be useful in preventing speculative excesses, although they would inhibit substantial volume.

P.L. 96-276, approved June 17, 1980, among other things provided that the Commodity Futures Trading Commission should establish a joint working group with the Board of Governors of the Federal Reserve System, the Department of the Treasury, and the SECURITIES AND EXCHANGE COMMISSION to analyze the events in the silver cash and futures markets from September, 1979, through March, 1980. The group was to report its findings to the appropriate committees of the Congress, together with recommendations for legislative changes that could prevent similar events in any futures market. A detailed study was submitted by the Commodity Futures Trading Commission on the events in the silver market in 1979 and 1980. The Federal Reserve Board's chairman also presented statements on the financial aspects of the silver situation; on May 1, 1980, he appeared before the Subcommittee on Agricultural Research and General Legislation of the Senate Committee on Agriculture, Nutrition, and Forestry, and on May 21, 1980, he appeared before the Subcommittee on Conservation and Credit of the Committee on Agriculture of the House of Representatives. In addition, the president of the Federal Reserve Bank of Minneapolis appeared on October 1, 1981, before the referenced House subcommittee to comment on the study by the CFTC; the Federal Reserve had previously submitted an "Interim Report on Financial Aspects of the Silver Market Situation in Early 1980."

Specific aspects of a financial nature included the following.

1. Bank credit to the Hunt interests, the major speculators for the rise in silver, is estimated to have peaked at about $1 billion, most of which apparently was used by the Hunts to meet margin calls as the price of silver dropped. From January until late March, 1980, the Federal Reserve, in view of the prevalent policy of "special" credit restraint by banks, would have had a special interest in such huge bank financing of a single speculative group, but "had no direct knowledge of the size of the Hunt positions or of the fact that they were financing margin calls by borrowings of any kind."

2. Subsequently, a $1.1 billion credit line was granted to the Placid Oil Company (owned by Hunt family trusts but not by the Hunt brothers themselves) by a syndicate of eleven domestic and two foreign banks. The Federal Reserve emphasizes that no official of the Federal Reserve initiated or participated in the negotiations, but that the Federal Reserve did have an interest in the outcome of the negotiations, which culminated in a restructuring of existing debt, secured in part or wholly by silver, into credit secured by the resources and earnings of the Placid Oil Company and supported by the collateralized guarantee of the Hunt brothers. The Fed's primary concern was that the terms and conditions of the loan agreement be consistent with the special voluntary credit restraint program then in effect; and that the proceeds of the loan not be used directly or

indirectly to support any renewed speculative activity by the Hunts, but instead that the silver be liquidated in an orderly manner. In the light of these stipulations and arrangements, including periodic reports about the credit from the lead banks to bank examination personnel, the Federal Reserve "interposed no objections to the loan." The Fed has subsequently expressed satisfaction that the broad purposes and protections that formed the basis for the Fed's interposing no objections are being observed, although "from time to time, the Federal Reserve has reminded the banks of the importance we give to these protections."

The magnitude of the silver crisis was indicated by Chairman Volcker's comment that "as the market values [of silver] collapsed, some of those institutions [which had funded the speculative positions with substantial amounts of credit], and certain market intermediaries (which had wittingly or not committed an excessive amount of their own capital) were placed in jeopardy, and their failure could in turn have triggered financial losses for others and severe financial disturbances."

Markets for Silver. Futures trading in silver is provided by the COMMODITY EXCHANGE, INC. in New York City (resumed in 1963) in 10,000-ounce contracts; by the CHICAGO BOARD OF TRADE (began 1969) in 5,000-ounce contracts and 1,000-ounce contracts; and by the MidAmerica Commodity Exchange in 1,000-ounce contracts. The WINNIPEG COMMODITY EXCHANGE began trading in 200-ounce silver futures in 1981. The London Metals Exchange trades in 10,000-troy-ounce silver futures.

The appended table provides basic statistics relating to silver.

See MARKET RATIO, MONETARY STOCK, SILVER CERTIFICATES, SILVER COINAGE, SILVER DOLLAR, UNITED STATES MONEY.

BIBLIOGRAPHY

"All that Glitters." *Futures*, September 1989.
COMMODITY EXCHANGE, INC. *Annual Report*.

SILVER BULLION SILVER ingots, usually cast for commercial purposes in bars assaying not less than 0.999 fineness, but with variation in weights from the basic weights of 1,000 or 1,100 troy ounces.

The U.S. Treasury completed its weekly auctions of silver, mainly to industrial users, which it had inaugurated August 4, 1967, on November 10, 1970. Sources of supply, therefore, are the commercial refiners (e.g., Handy & Harman) and imports from the London spot market for silver. In addition, futures trading is conducted in silver in the U.S. principally on the New York COMMODITY EXCHANGE, INC. and the CHICAGO BOARD OF TRADE.

Under P.L. 91-607, December 31, 1970, the nonsilver U.S. dollar and nonsilver half-dollar coins were authorized for general circulation, similar in composition to the completely nonsilver quarters and dimes authorized under the Coinage Act of 1965. Effective January 1, 1971, the former 40% (reduced) silver half-dollar, authorized by the Coinage Act of 1965, was discontinued. Therefore, on the part of the Bureau of the Mint in the U.S., monetary demand for silver bullion for regular issues of domestic coinage has ceased.

SILVER CERTIFICATES Formerly issued regularly in denominations of $1 (the "workhorse of circulation"), $2, $5, $10, $20, $50, $100, $500, and $1,000, engraved with green backs and stamped on their obverse side with a blue seal, silver certificates were first issued in 1878, following passage of the BLAND-ALLISON ACT.

On their face, silver certificates indicated that they were redeemable to the bearer on demand for $1 in silver. P.L. 90-29, effective June 24, 1967, provided that after one year therefrom (June 24, 1968), silver certificates would no longer be thus redeemable in silver.

With authorization and issuance of the new $1 denomination (and also $2 denomination), Federal Reserve notes, as authorized by P.L. 88-36, June 4, 1963, became the basic form of paper currency issued for circulation, aside from the minor amount of UNITED STATES NOTES still issued and chargeable to Treasury currency (liability of the U.S. Treasury).

See UNITED STATES MONEY.

SILVER COINAGE When the Coinage Act of 1965 (P.L. 89-81, July 23, 1965) was passed, SILVER coinage in the U.S. was actually confined to the subsidiary silver coins (HALF-DOLLAR, QUARTER, and DIME), since the standard SILVER DOLLAR had not been actually coined since 1935. Under the Act of April 2, 1792, establishing the first monetary system of the U.S., both gold and silver were standard monetary metals and were entitled to free coinage at the U.S. Mint. The bimetallic standard was in fact terminated by the Act of February 12, 1873 (the CRIME OF '73), which failed to provide for continued coinage of the standard silver dollar. Subsequent legislation, however (BLAND-ALLISON ACT, 1878; SHERMAN SILVER-PURCHASE ACT, 1890), authorized silver purchase programs and the issuance of silver

Table 2 / Silver—Summary: 1970 to 1987

Item	Unit	1970	1980	1981	1982	1983	1984	1985	1986	1987, prel.
Silver										
Ore produced [1,4]	1,000 sh. ton	934	2,936	5,579	6,636	8,658	9,392	5,347	6,425	8,000
Production, U.S.	1,000 fine oz.	45,006	32,329	40,683	40,248	43,431	44,592	39,433	34,220	37,280
Value	Mil. dol.	80	667	428	320	497	363	242	187	261
World production	1,000 fine oz.	300,991	342,804	361,617	371,159	387,711	413,930	422,093	415,625	429,081
Industrial consumption										
U.S., net [5]	1,000 fine oz.	128,404	124,694	116,670	118,840	116,464	114,841	118,555	118,940	115,271
Imports [2]	Mil. dol.	104	1,606	1,028	927	2,124	963	952	798	588
Canada	Mil. dol.	64	660	375	303	420	301	288	261	141
Mexico	Mil. dol.	9	282	228	205	340	336	251	257	200
Peru	Mil. dol.	19	354	273	143	269	197	76	57	40
Exports	Mil. dol.	49	1,910	332	209	377	206	161	143	180
Price per fine oz. [3,5]	Dollars	1.77	20.63	10.52	7.95	11.44	8.14	6.14	5.47	7.01
Production: [4]										
Idaho	Mil. fine oz.	19.1	13.7	16.5	14.8	17.7	18.9	18.8	11.2	—
Arizona	Mil. fine oz.	7.3	6.3	8.1	6.3	4.5	4.2	4.9	4.2	3.4
Utah	Mil. fine oz.	6.0	2.2	2.9	4.3	4.6	D	D	D	—
Colorado	Mil. fine oz.	2.9	3.0	3.0	1.9	2.1	2.2	0.5	0.6	—

— Represents zero.
D — Withheld to avoid disclosure.
Z — Less than $500,000.
[1] Gold and silver are also produced from base-metal ores and placers.
[2] 1970, general imports, thereafter, imports for consumption.
[3] Selling price.
[4] Includes gold-silver ore through 1986, silver ore only in 1987.
[5] Excludes coinage.

Source: U.S. Bureau of Mines, *Minerals Yearbook*.

SILVER DOLLAR

dollars and/or silver certificates, although it did not restore unequivocably the former BIMETALLISM. Subsidiary silver coinage was continued throughout, along with the standard silver dollar as a supplementary, not coequal, monetary unit, pursuant to the GOLD STANDARD ACT OF 1900, which unequivocably established the GOLD STANDARD in the U.S. until its suspension and subsequent modified reestablishment on January 30, 1934, by the GOLD RESERVE ACT OF 1934.

Silver was nationalized in the U.S. (August 9, 1934, by presidential proclamation and executive order), but subsequently denationalized (April 29, 1938, by presidential proclamation revoking the 1934 presidential proclamation except for authorized government purchase of newly mined domestic silver).

The Coinage Act of 1965 converted the former subsidiary silver coinage to 40% (reduced) silver half-dollars and nonsilver quarters and dimes. The Coinage Act of 1965, in turn, was amended by Title II of P.L. 91-607, December 31, 1970, to provide for the coinage of completely silverless dollar coins and fractional (formerly called subsidiary silver) coins, as follows.

Sec. 101. (a) The Secretary {of the Treasury} may mint and issue coins of the denominations set forth in subsec. (c) in such quantities as he determines to be necessary to meet national needs

(b) Any coin minted under authority of subsec. (a) shall be a clad coin. The cladding shall be an alloy of 75 per centum copper and 25 per centum nickel, and shall weigh not less than 30 per centum of the weight of the whole coin. The core shall be copper.

(c) (1) The dollar shall be 1.500 inches in diameter and weigh 22.68 grams.
(2) The half dollar shall be 1.205 inches in diameter and weigh 11.34 grams.
(3) The quarter dollar shall be 0.955 inches in diameter and weigh 5.67 grams.
(4) The dime shall be 0.705 inches in diameter and weigh 2.268 grams.

On May 12, 1969, the Treasury immediately adopted the recommendation of the JOINT COMMISSION ON THE COINAGE (established by the Coinage Act of 1965) and revoked the prohibition on melting down silver coins, which previously subjected violators to criminal penalties.

SILVER DOLLAR This coin dated from the first U.S. coinage act, the Act of April 2, 1792, and continued to have a weight of 412.50 grains of standard SILVER (0.9 fine) until its final demise and replacement by the cupronickel dollar coin, as authorized by Title II of P.L. 91-607, December 31, 1970 (actually, the standard silver dollar had not been coined since 1935). The history of the silver dollar was marked by a temporary lack of authorization (Act of February 12, 1873, the "Crime of '73"), but its coinage was subsequently resumed under the silver purchase programs provided by the BLAND-ALLISON ACT, 1878, and the SHERMAN SILVER-PURCHASE ACT, 1890 (the latter authorized the issuance of TREASURY NOTES OF 1890, without restoring the silver dollar to coequal bimetallic monetary status). Under the GOLD STANDARD ACT OF 1900, the secretary of the Treasury was directed to keep other forms of circulation (including the silver dollar) at "parity" with the gold dollar specifically enacted as the standard monetary unit of ultimate redemption.

The silver dollar was the heaviest of the coins, and silver dollars were therefore popularly referred to as "cartwheels." Except in silver-producing states such as Idaho, Utah, Montana, Arizona, and Nevada, silver dollars were not found extensively in circulation, SILVER CERTIFICATES instead being used in other states as a more convenient form of silver circulation.

The statutory coinage value for silver dollars was $1.2929+ per ounce, 0.9 fine, or $1.1636+ per ounce of standard silver. Thus coinage of silver dollars in former years, or issuance of silver certificates also formerly authorized, created a SEIGNIORAGE profit for the Treasury, and the bullion value of the silver dollar at any given time could be determined by dividing the average market quotation by the statutory price for silver ($1.2929+ per troy ounce).

See MONETARY STOCK, UNITED STATES MONEY.

SILVER PURCHASE ACT OF 1934 An act, approved June 19, 1934, which, among other things:

1. Declared it to be the policy of the United States that the proportion of silver to gold in the monetary stocks of the United States should be increased, with the ultimate objective of having and maintaining one-fourth of the monetary value of such stocks in silver.
2. Authorized and directed the secretary of the Treasury, whenever the proportion of silver in the stocks of gold and silver of the United States is less than one-fourth of the monetary value of such stocks, to purchase silver, at home or abroad, for present or future delivery, at such rates and times and upon such terms as deemed reasonable and most advantageous to the United States; but provided that no purchase of silver should be made at a price in excess of its monetary value, and that no purchase of silver situated in the United States on May 1, 1934, should be made at a price in excess of $0.50 a fine ounce.
3. Authorized the secretary of the Treasury, with approval of the President, to sell any silver acquired under the terms of the act, at such rates and times and upon such conditions as deemed reasonable and advantageous, whenever the market price of silver exceeds its monetary value or the monetary value of the stocks of silver is greater than 25% of the monetary value of the stocks of gold and silver.
4. Authorized and directed the secretary of the Treasury to issue and place "in actual circulation" silver certificates in such denominations as he might prescribe.
5. Provided that the Treasury should maintain as security for all silver certificates heretofore and hereafter issued, and at the time outstanding, an amount of silver bullion and standard silver dollars equal to the face value of the silver certificates.
6. Stipulated that all silver certificates should be legal tender for all debts, public and private, public charges, taxes, duties and dues, and should be redeemable on demand at the Treasury in standard silver dollars.
7. Vested in the secretary of the Treasury, with approval of the President, the power to investigate, regulate, and prohibit, by license or otherwise, the acquisition, importation, exportation, or transportation of silver "and of contracts and other arrangements made with respect thereto," and to require reports as to the facts involved, whenever necessary to effectuate the policy of the law—violations to be punishable by a maximum fine of $10,000, not over ten years imprisonment, or both.
8. Authorized the President, by executive order, to require the delivery to the mints of "any or all" silver by whomever owned or possessed, this silver to be coined into silver dollars or otherwise added to the monetary stocks as the President may determine; and provided that there should be returned therefor in standard silver dollars, or any other coin or currency of the United States, the monetary value of the silver so delivered less deductions for seigniorage, brassage, coinage, or other mint charges.
9. Provided that silver withheld in violation of this provision be forfeited to the government and, in addition, persons failing to comply with the provision be subject to a penalty equal to twice the monetary value of the silver withheld.
10. Amended the stamp-tax provisions of existing law to provide a transfer tax on silver bullion equal to 50% of the difference between the price for which any interest in silver is to be transferred and the cost of the bullion, plus allowed expenses.

SILVER STANDARD COUNTRIES See SILVER.

SIMPLE ARBITRATION OF EXCHANGE See ARBITRATION OF EXCHANGE.

SIMPLE INTEREST Interest on the principal (funds originally received or paid). The number of time periods passed or the amount of interest paid or accrued do not affect the computation of simple interest. Simple interest is computed as follows:

$$Interest = Principal \times Time$$

where time is a year, a fraction of a year, or a multiple of years.

In interest terminology, percent means per centum, i.e., per hundred. Therefore, 8% equals $8 per $100, which can be expressed in two ways:

as a ratio: $8\%/100 = .08$
as a rate: Ratio x 100

$$.08 \times 100 = 8\%$$

SINGLE-NAME PAPER Notes that are the obligations of one party only, i.e., the maker; also known as straight paper.

Single-name paper "represents loans to an individual, firm, or corporation on their own note of hand without any other responsibility than that of the general credit of the maker. Although two or more names may appear on a note either as makers or endorsers, it is still single-name paper if the names represent identical interests. Sometimes the members of a firm will endorse their firm notes personally, but unless they are possessed of considerable outside means entirely apart from their business, such endorsements merely strengthen the moral risk and the instrument is still single-name paper. Again, a firm may have a subsidiary organization trading under a separate name, but with identical interests, so that although both names appear on the note—one as maker and the other as endorser—the obligation is still essentially single-name paper. Failure to guard against this contingency has caused many bank losses, since a single failure may affect several allied companies" (O. H. Wolfe, *Practical Banking*).

A large proportion of the COMMERCIAL PAPER sold through the medium of note brokers is single-name paper.

SINGLE OPTION A put or a CALL.

SINGLE STANDARD A monetary system in which one metal, e.g., gold or silver, is made the basis of the STANDARD MONEY and coins manufactured from all other metals are subsidiary.

See GOLD STANDARD, STANDARD OF VALUE.

SINKING FUND A fund created by setting aside out of earnings at stated intervals monies sufficient to provide for the payment of all, or part, of a long-term debt, such as an issue of bonds, or of a senior stock, such as preferred stock. The creation of a sinking fund is a method of amortization or extinguishment of a debt not yet matured, and is as binding on the debtor organization (obligor) as any other provision of the contract.

A sinking fund is usually placed in the hands of a sinking fund trustee named under the terms of a mortgage deed. It may be invested in three ways: deposited in a bank to bear interest, invested in bonds of other organizations, and invested in bonds of the issuing organization. Since there is the opportunity for mismanagement of sinking fund investments, it is usually considered safer to apply sinking fund payments to the purchase of the company's own bonds being amortized, thus extinguishing the very debt for which the sinking fund was created.

There are three ways in which a sinking fund may be invested in a company's own bonds: purchasing and keeping alive parts of other issues, purchasing and keeping alive parts of the issue being amortized, and purchasing and canceling parts of the issue being amortized. The latter method is usually considered the best since it not only decreases fixed charges, but increases the equity of the owners and strengthens the security of the bondholders. It also prevents mismanagement of the sinking fund and tends to stabilize the price by making a market for the bonds.

The purchase of the bonds being amortized may be accomplished by open market transactions, or else the mortgage deed may provide for the purchase on certain interest dates of a certain number of bonds to be called by lot, usually at a premium. In the latter case, notice is given by the sinking fund agent that in accordance with the provisions of the mortgage and deed of trust it has designated by lot, for redemption on a certain date out of monies paid to the trustee by the issuing company, a certain sum of money for the redemption of bonds bearing the numbers stated in the notice.

"Mandatory" Sinking Fund on Preferred Stock. Preferred stock with a "mandatory" sinking fund of a specific dollar amount per year for retirement of the preferred stock at a specific sinking fund price(s) has led to the new classification of "term" preferred stock. Since the sinking fund provision will retire all of the preferred stock in a given number of future years, such preferred stock has been loosely referred to as having a future "maturity" and as being in the nature of "debt," to be included on the balance sheet as part of the long-term debt of the company.

Preferred stock, with or without a mandatory sinking fund, is stock, and preferred stock holders are *not* creditors as they would be in the case of debt. Moreover, examination of the provisions for a mandatory sinking fund indicates that default in providing the "mandatory" sinking fund does not create an act of default for failure to pay money owed, as in the case of debt. In case of failure to provide the mandatory sinking fund as agreed by the company in the preferred stock's provisions, typical provisions for such mandatory sinking fund preferred stock call for a penalty, for prohibition of the use of cash for common stock dividends, and for the repurchase by the company of its stock—serious consequences of course for the common stock holders, but not an act of default on debt, as in the case of a defaulted sinking fund called for in covenants of bonds and/or debentures.

The SECURITIES AND EXCHANGE COMMISSION (SEC) in its accounting release on the subject did not concur in including mandatory sinking fund preferred stock in the long-term debt of a company; but the SEC did provide for the listing of such preferred stock ahead of other preferred stock without such provision, in the preferred stock component of shareholders' equity.

SINKING FUND ASSETS An account that represents cash or securities in which the SINKING FUND is invested. From an accounting and credit standpoint, these assets should be considered as applicable to the reduction of the relative liabilities.

SINKING FUND BONDS Bonds issued under a SINKING FUND agreement, which requires the debtor organization (obligor) to periodically set aside out of earnings a sum which, with interest, will be sufficient to redeem the issue in whole or part at maturity. The purpose of sinking fund bonds is to give assurance to investors that systematic provision is to be made for the repayment of the loan, and sinking fund payments become obligatory as part of the contract. Sinking fund payments are usually made to a trust company or sinking fund trustee and are just as binding on the issuer as interest payments, e.g., failure to make sinking fund payments entitles the bondholders to the same legal rights as default in payment of interest.

Sinking fund bonds occur among both civil and corporate issues, but are more common among the latter. Sinking fund bonds are essential for the protection of the investor in the case of extractive industries, such as coal mining, oil, and the like, since the assets of those industries are of a wasting character. Among railroad and public utility corporations where the fixed assets must be kept intact in order that operations may continue, sinking funds are nevertheless quite common.

Among civil issues, the serial method of debt repayment has tended to replace the sinking fund method in recent years.

SINKING FUND REDEMPTION NOTICE A notice, published in accordance with the requirements of the bond indenture notifying holders of bonds that are callable for redemption before maturity, that certain bonds have been drawn by lot for current sinking fund redemption on a specified date and should be presented for payment, as interest will cease after the redemption date.

One of the continuing functions of custodianship and administration of securities is to be aware of and act promptly on such sinking fund notices, so as to minimize the loss of investment income from the called principal. Individual sinking fund notices are mailed to holders of registered bonds, but coupon (bearer) holders can only be reached through sinking fund advertisements published in the financial press, such as the appended example. One of the services of the statistical services is the collection and dissemination of financial notices of this type.

See SINKING FUND BONDS.

SIXPENCE On February 15, 1971, the United Kingdom replaced its traditional coinage system with its new decimal currency. The old sixpence (cupronickel, milled edge, weighing 43.636 grains) was eliminated (although it was retained for a transitional period); the new coins are the halfpenny, penny, two-pence, five-pence, ten-pence, and fifty-pence coins.

See ENGLISH MONEY TABLE.

SIX PERCENT 60-DAY RULE A method that simplifies interest computation in certain situations. Based on this rule, interest can be calculated by simply dividing the principal by 100. For example, the interest cost on a 60-day loan of $1,000 at 6% simple interest would be:

$$\$1,000/100 = \$10$$

The six percent 60-day rule can also be used to compute interest with other values for interest rate and number of days. For example, the interest cost of a two-year loan of $1,000 at 9% simple interest would be: Interest on $1,000 for 60 days at 6% (move decimal two places to left)

	$10
Multiply by the number of 60-day intervals in 2 years	x12
Interest on $1,000 for 2 years at 6%	$120
Interest = 9% = $^3/_2$ of 6%	x $^3/_2$
Interest on $1,000 for 2 years at 9%	$180

SIXTEEN TO ONE The popular title of the issue raised in the campaign of 1896 between Bryan and McKinley, having reference to the coinage ratio between silver and gold. Bryan advocated the reestablishment of BIMETALLISM on this basis. The coinage ratio of 16 to 1 between silver and gold was established by act of Congress in 1837, although the exact ratio was 15.988 plus.
See FREE COINAGE.

SKYROCKETING The rapid rise of a stock, or of the entire market, over a wide range in a short time. Such a rise is brought about by speculative enthusiasm generated by particularly favorable news.

SLAUGHTER The sale of securities at prices far lower than intrinsic values warrant.

SLIPPING A declining tendency of stock market prices.

SLOW ASSETS Fixed, permanent, or capital assets.
See FIXED ASSETS.

SLOW LOANS A classification in the examination of a bank's loans; doubtful loans. Reserves or outright chargeoff should be provided for such loans.
See EXAMINATION PROCEDURE.

SLUGGISH Denotes a state of inactivity in a market, i.e., a small number of transactions and slight price changes.

SLUMP This term has two applications.

1. The continued decline in prices in a market, especially when due to unfavorable trade reports.
2. A falling off in the volume of business in a trade or industry, or throughout the entire business structure.

SMALL BUSINESS ADMINISTRATION Created by the Small Business Act of 1953 (67 Stat. 232). The Small Business Administration (SBA) derives its present existence and authority from the Small Business Act (72 Stat. 384; 15 U.S.C. 631 et seq.), as amended, and from the following legislation: Small Business Investment Act of 1958 (72 Stat. 698; 15 U.S.C. 661), as amended; Section 213(a) of the War Claims Act of 1948, as amended (76 Stat. 1111; 50 U.S.C. App. 20171); Title IV of the Economic Opportunity Act of 1964 (78 Stat. 526, as amended; 42 U.S.C. 2901 et seq.); and Disaster Relief Act of 1970 (84 Stat. 1744; 42 U.S.C. 4401 et seq.). Also, the secretary of the Department of Housing and Urban Development, by authority in Section 312(f) of the Housing Act of 1964 (78 Stat. 791; 42 U.S.C. 1452), has delegated to the SBA certain responsibilities and functions under the loan program for rehabilitation of nonresidential property; and the secretary of Commerce has delegated to the SBA certain responsibilities and functions under Section 202 of the Public Works and Economic Development Act of 1965 (79 Stat. 556; 42 U.S.C. 3142).

The fundamental purposes of the Small Business Administration are to aid, counsel, assist, and protect the interests of small businesses; ensure that small business concerns receive a fair portion of government purchases, contracts, and subcontracts, as well as of the sales of government property; make loans to small business concerns, state and local development companies, and the victims of floods or other catastrophes, or of certain types of economic injury; and license, regulate, and make loans to small business investment companies.

The functions and activities of the SBA are officially described as follows.

1. **Financial assistance.** The Small Business Administration guarantees loans to small businesses that are unable to obtain private financing. Such loans must be of such value or so secured as reasonably to assure repayment. No loan may be made unless the financial assistance is not otherwise available on reasonable terms. Under the guaranty plan, the SBA agrees to purchase the guaranteed portion of the loan only upon default. In addition to providing financial assistance to the general small business community, the SBA gives particular emphasis to the following groups: businesses owned by socially and economically disadvantaged individuals; businesses that employ or are owned by handicapped individuals; small energy-oriented firms seeking to finance plant facilities and the acquisition of supplies and equipment necessary for specific energy measures; state and local development companies for plant construction, conversion, or expansion, including the acquisition of land; and small business concerns owned by low-income individuals or located in urban or rural areas with high proportions of unemployed or low-income individuals.
2. **Investment company assistance.** A primary function of small business investment companies (SBICs) is to provide a source of needed equity capital or long-term loans to new or expanding small businesses. The Small Business Investment Act, as amended, authorizes the SBA to purchase or to guarantee the timely payment of all principal and interest, as scheduled, on debentures issued by such companies. In addition, the SBA is authorized to purchase preferred securities (shares of non-voting stock or other securities having similar characteristics) from small business investment companies operating under authority of Section 30(d), which specifies that the investment policy of such companies will be to make investments solely in small concerns owned and operated by disadvantaged persons.
3. **Disaster loan fund.** This fund finances disaster loans made pursuant to Section 7(b) of the Small Business Act, as amended. Under this program, physical disaster loans are made at favorable terms to property owners for rehabilitation of property damaged by natural disasters such as floods, hurricanes, tornados, earthquakes, etc. For the 1983 fiscal year, approvals were estimated at $440 million.

    Appropriations for financing are authorized as capital to the extent required to carry out the authorized functions. However, a capital appropriation for this fund was not requested for 1983. Instead, the agency would initiate an "intensive" debt collection program resulting in an additional $65 million in loan repayments, over and above the normal amortization, for 1982 and 1983 fiscal years.
4. **Lease guarantees revolving fund.** The lease guarantees program was designed to provide prime space for those small business firms that could not compete with prospective tenants with AAA ratings. This program had been incurring excessive losses and had not been an important form of assistance to small businesses. As a result, the program for the 1983 fiscal year is limited to paying claims resulting from defaulted leases approved in prior years.
5. **Surety bond guarantees revolving fund.** P.L. 93-386, the Small Business Amendment Act of 1974, established this fund to finance the surety bond guarantees program. The SBA will guarantee a portion of the losses sustained by a surety company as a result of the issuance of a bid, payment, and/or performance bond to a small business concern.
6. **Pollution control equipment contract guarantee revolving fund.** P.L. 94-305, approved June 4, 1976, established this fund to alleviate the adverse impact of pollution regulations on small businesses. The SBA may, whenever it determines that small business concerns are at an operational or financial disadvantage with respect to the planning, design, or installation of pollution control facilities or the financing thereof, guarantee the payment of rentals or other amounts due under qualified contracts.

7. **Other SBA assistance to small business.** The programs under procurement assistance are aimed at assuring that small business receives a fair share of government procurements. In addition, the SBA maintains a Procurement Automated Source System, which is used by federal agencies and prime contractors to identify small businesses for contract opportunities. Through the Small Business Institute and Small Business Development Center programs, along with counseling services, training programs, and publications, small business owners and/or managers are assisted in their goal of improving the management and efficiency of their businesses.

The minority small business and capital ownership development activities provide assistance to minority small business firms—primarily in the area of federal procurement—and evaluate overall agency performance in promoting minority business development. The business development program assists in the establishment or expansion of firms that are owned by minority or other disadvantaged business persons and that have the potential to develop into viable competitive businesses in a reasonable period of time. In addition, Sections 7(j) (1) through (10) of the Small Business Act, as amended, provide authority to contract for professional management training and support to assist the socially and economically disadvantaged entrepreneur.

The international trade program is designed to promote and expand small business participation in exporting by directing small businesses to knowledgeable private sector resources and by encouraging nongovernment groups to provide necessary assistance to small exporters.

The SBA serves as the government's principal advocate of small business. The advocacy program also has the responsibility for the government's program to advance women's business enterprise.

Summary. As successor to the Reconstruction Finance Corporation's small business loans program, the SBA has expanded credits and functions over the years as Congress has grafted on additional authorizations. The SBA operates in marginal and subsidy areas of credits, and the loss ratios referred to above, particularly on direct credits, are not within tolerable levels for private credit institutions under normal economic conditions. It should be remembered, however, that SBA credits are extended on a noncompetitive basis, i.e., to firms unable to obtain loans from established credit channels, but the SBA will and prefers to participate with private lending institutions, such participations being up to as much as 90% of the loan, or to guarantee payment of loans made by private lending institutions up to the same percentage, providing for amortization over maturity (maximum, 10 years) and thus affording longer average use of the funds for the borrowing firms as compared with short-term credits.

See TERM LOANS.

SMALL LOAN BUSINESS

Licensed lending under the various state versions of the Uniform Small Loan Law, prescribing maximum loan amounts and an interest rate that may be charged per month on unpaid balances.

See CONSUMER CREDIT, PERSONAL FINANCE.

SMALL SAVER CERTIFICATE

A form of time deposit offered by commercial banks and thrift institutions. The maturity of the certificates is 18 to 30 months. Interest rates are related to the average yield of U.S. Treasury securities with comparable remaining maturity.

SMASH

An abrupt and violent decline in prices of securities or commodities, creating a condition bordering on panic; a stronger expression than BREAK.

SMITH, ADAM

A major economist who argued for economic freedom in the form of *laissez faire* that implied that nations could progress by the accumulation of wealth. Adam Smith is considered to be the founder of political economy. In his classic *The Wealth of Nations* (1776), Smith gave impetus to the development of a theoretical structure of the capitalist economic system by concluding that the private ownership and use of capital would lead, by an invisible hand, to the common good. Smith is attributed with erecting a system referred to as "classical economics." David Ricardo, Thomas Malthus, and John Stuart Mills are considered major proponents of classical economics.

Smith's central doctrine of *laissez faire, laissez passes* maintains that an economy functions best when it is free of governmental influence because each person seeks his or her own self-interest in the betterment of the entire economy.

Smith's discussion of the advantages of the division of labor as an economic force was emphatic: "The greatest improvement in the productive powers of labour, and the greater part of the skill, dexterity, and judgment with which it is anywhere directed, or applied, seem to have been the effects of the division of labor." Smith developed the "price system" of value economics, which dominated the development of the science of economics. The determinants of profit were explained by Smith as follows: "The increase of stock, which raises wages, tends to lower profit. When the stocks of many rich merchants are turned into the same trade, their mutual competition naturally tends to lower its profit . . ." According to Smith, economic activity consists in the pursuit of material wealth. Smith generally abstracted economic life from other human activities and motives.

Smith's critics maintain that he was a materialist and an individualist. His absolutism would displease the relativists and would lead to a narrow model. However, many important economic ideas can be traced directly to the *The Wealth of Nations*.

See PRICE THEORY, THEORY, VALUE.

SMITHSONIAN AGREEMENT

A last-ditch attempt to continue the fixed par value system (with permitted "ceiling" above and permitted "floor" below the declared par values) for currencies of the member nations of the INTERNATIONAL MONETARY FUND. The effort eventually was abandoned when the Second Amendment to the Articles of Agreement of the IMF was declared effective, leading to the era of "floating exchange rates."

On December 17 and 18, 1971, the ministers and central bank governors of the "Group of Ten" (leading industrial countries, members of the International Monetary Fund: Belgium, Canada, France, West Germany, Italy, Japan, the Netherlands, Sweden, the United Kingdom, and the United States) met at the Smithsonian Institution in Washington, D.C., and reached agreement on the realignment of the currencies of their countries.

The need for the Smithsonian Agreement arose from fears that continuation of the situation that developed following the closing of the "gold window" by the United States on August 15, 1971, and imposition by it of a 15% import surcharge, a period in which exchange rates "floated" without guidelines for their regulation or for reconciliation of conflicting national objectives and in which restrictive practices in international trade and finance increased, would "breed hesitation in private and public planning, procurement, and investment," with serious international deflationary consequences.

The agreement provided for a realignment of exchange rate relationships among major currencies as the first essential. In addition to the exchange rate changes, other important aspects of the agreement included an undertaking among the participants to consider long-term reform or improvement of the international monetary system, a provision for temporary wider margins of official exchange rate fluctuations, and agreement by the United States on an immediate removal of its import surcharge.

On December 18, 1971, the executive directors of the IMF adopted a decision providing for a "temporary regime" of wider margins of exchange rate fluctuations relative to central rates or par values. Under the IMF's "Central Rates and Wider Margins: A Temporary Regime," exchange rates in transactions involving a member's currency could move within a margin of 2.25% on either side of the parity rates. The maximum margin of 4.50% between the "floor" and the "ceiling" rates relative to the par values or central rates was designed to enable members to observe the purposes of the IMF to the maximum extent possible "during the temporary period preceding the resumption of effective par values with appropriate margins in accordance with the [IMF's] Articles."

Although formal action establishing a new par value for the U.S. dollar, based on an official price of $38 an ounce for gold, was not completed until May 8, 1972, the U.S. committed itself in the Smithsonian Agreement to provide for congressional approval of a 7.89% devaluation of the dollar in terms of gold (official price increase).

In April-May, 1972, agreement was reached by members of the European Economic Community (EEC) to limit fluctuations of their currencies in relation to each other to 2.25%, thus reducing by half

SOCIAL ACCOUNTING

the maximum range that would be associated with maintenance by the countries concerned with margins of plus or minus 2.25% in relation to the U.S. dollar. This agreement, accompanied by special arrangements for intra-EEC settlements of balances resulting from official interventions into the foreign exchange markets, was an important step (familiarly called the "snake," from the graph pattern of rate fluctuations of the currencies concerned relative to each other) toward implementation of the plan for monetary union of the EEC countries (See EUROPEAN MONETARY MYSTEM).

On June 23, 1972, because of heavy outflows of short-term capital which led to a large and accelerating decline in net U.K. reserves, the United Kingdom decided to allow the pound sterling to "float" in the foreign exchange markets, unfettered by the agreed Smithsonian Agreement limit of fluctuation. In response to that action on sterling, 15 member countries, whose trading and financial ties with the United Kingdom were close and whose currencies were pegged to the pound sterling, decided to maintain that peg, thus allowing their currencies to "float" with sterling.

In the two-year period following the August, 1971, decision by the U.S. to suspend convertibility of the U.S. dollar into gold, "the foreign exchange markets experienced the most severe and sustained series of crises since the end of World War II, according to the IMF." On April 1, 1978, the Second Amendment to the Articles of Agreement of the IMF, providing for the present system of broader international currency arrangements, became effective.

SOCIAL ACCOUNTING A subset of accounting that helps a business determine whether the operating goals and programs of the enterprise are beneficial to society. Social accounting reports on the social benefits and costs of doing business. Some financial statements include grants to hospitals, the arts, minority groups, urban development, educational institutions, and charitable foundations as a form of social accounting.

SOCIAL CREDIT A term used by a school of "New Economics" in offering a program in solution of the economic paradox of "penury amidst plenty." The plan would disturb the existing institutions of private capitalism, i.e., private property and individual initiative, only to a minimum extent. Its proponents, led by Major C. H. Douglas, a British engineer who has written extensively on the subject, claim that under a modern production system, goods of every description can be turned out with a continuously decreasing amount of human energy and labor. The technological genius of every country is working toward the replacement of labor by machines, and mercantile institutions are endeavoring to put the world out of work—thus creating a miscalled unemployment problem. To a considerable degree, this is blamed on banking and credit systems, the following situations being the roots of the difficulty.

1. Wages and dividends will not purchase total production–this difficulty is cumulative.
2. The only sources of buying power likely to make up this difference are loans and export credits.
3. All industrial nations are competing for export credits–making for fierce competition and sometimes war.
4. The main distribution of purchasing power is through wages and salaries to individuals. At the same time, the preponderating factor in production is improving processes and utilizing solar energy (such as coal, oil, steam, etc.).
5. This latter tends to displace wage payments and, in consequence, affects distribution of products to individuals. At the same time, the credit factor must increase in importance and dominates production.
6. Said production is, therefore, of a character calling for control of credit, and is capital production.
7. Therefore, the fundamental derivation of credit is from a community of individuals, and since individuals are ceasing in part to benefit by the use thereof, it is breaking down.

To remedy the faulty system of distribution of purchasing power, the proponents of the social credit doctrine propose the following.

1. The establishment of a "national credit account," which is in the nature of a vast revolving fund.
2. "National dividends," to be paid periodically to all adult inhabitants of this country from the national credit account. There may be some exceptions of too prosperous individuals, but nearly every adult person is to receive, quarterly or half-yearly in cash or in credit at some bank, his dividend in money provided by the national government from this proposed fund.
3. "The national discount" and the "just price." The national discount is to be determined by analyses and syntheses made by statisticians of the national government. These studies will pertain to actual "consumption" by the nation as a whole during a stated period—three months or six months—and to estimated "production" of goods and services nationally during the same period. From the ratio of the grand totals of such consumption and production statistics, the national discount is to be determined. The President, or other designated authority, shall promulgate an edict declaring the percentage of discount for the next quarter or half-year—25% perhaps, or 35%, or more, or less, or nothing, or less than nothing (an assessment instead of a discount). This discount is to apply throughout the nation on all retail purchases during the period in question. Retailers are to allow to all purchasers the declared discount from regular selling prices, such discount being in the nature of a subsidy or gift to every purchaser. This discount will establish "the just price." The necessity for such a just price is based upon much involved reasoning, calculation, and illustration by the proponents of social credit.
4. Rigorous control of credit. Issuance and recall of bank loans are to be removed from the banks by another presidential edict. These powers are to be bestowed upon a national council or board. This body shall be made analogous to the Supreme Court and shall determine the "going rates" for loans, the rates for national dividends, etc. The present banks are to continue operations, if they desire to do so, but shall not make loans in excess of their capital and surplus. They may not build up vast "bank-deposit accounts," which the social credit doctrine designates as "money," based upon loans to customers.

SOCIAL INSURANCE State-controlled insurance against the risks and hazards of a complex civilization, including, in its more comprehensive aspects, coverage for individual unemployment, sickness, industrial accident, permanent invalidity, old age, maternity, and widowhood. In many European countries, social insurance is regarded as a normal function of the government, but the development of social insurance has been slow and experimental. Some social insurance schemes are voluntary and contributory (on the part of the insured) in whole or part; others are compulsory. The trend in recent years is toward compulsion.

In 1889, Germany launched the first comprehensive social insurance program for any important country. Great Britain, in 1909, made its beginnings in this field, which have culminated in the Beveridge "cradle to the grave" concept. In the United States, the trend toward the various forms of social insurance has been rapid since 1911, when workers' compensation acts first appeared.

Social insurance may be noncontributory, in which case the state bears the whole of the cost, or it may be contributory, in which case the employer, the employed person, or both pay into a fund. The state may or may not add a subsidy to the accumulated contributory fund out of public money raised by taxation. Plans may be compulsory or voluntary, either as a whole or in part. Whether the plan is compulsory or voluntary, the state exercises supervision and may contribute subsidies. In most plans of social insurance, there is an income and property limit. Only those persons whose resources are within the limit are eligible, and certain benefits—for instance, pensions—may be graded inversely to those resources.

Social insurance falls into four broad categories: accident, including workers' compensation; sickness, including maternity; old age, including invalidity or physical incapacity to earn a living; and unemployment.

See SOCIAL SECURITY, UNEMPLOYMENT INSURANCE.

SOCIALISM According to Norman Thomas, successor to Eugene Debs as the "No. 1" American Socialist, "In its broadest sense, Socialism (evolutionary Socialism) is the doctrine that land, natural resources, and the principal means of production and distribution should be socially owned and democratically managed so that production should be for public use rather than private profit..."

Morris Hillquit, another American Socialist, stated in *Socialism*: "The Socialist programme advocates a reorganization of the existing industrial system on the basis of collective or national ownership of

ENCYCLOPEDIA OF BANKING AND FINANCE

the social tools. It demands that the control of the machinery of wealth creation be taken from the individual capitalist and placed in the hands of the nation, to be organized and operated for the benefit of the whole people."

The idea of Socialism, therefore, is the belief in the gradual evolutionary attainment of the socialist society; Socialism's advocacy of democracy, therefore, is not inconsistent with its tenets, and in fact such Socialists often refer to themselves as "social democrats." The goal of complete nationalization is also often modified by Socialists to partial nationalization of the "basic" industries, or a "mixed economy." Indeed, in recent years, the goal of even partial nationalization has been abandoned in the program of some Socialists, such as those of West Germany; in England, the previously nationalized iron and steel and truck transportation industries have been restored to private ownership (true, by the Conservative Party upon return to power, but that in itself indicated the shift of public support from the Laborite nationalization program).

In France, the election of a Socialist president for a seven-year term on May 10, 1981, led to an extensive program in just one year of nationalization of private banks and industrial sectors (electronics, chemicals, steel, and the arms industry, with possible further extension into the computer, pharmaceutical, and telephone industries), based on the rationale that "nationalization will provide us with the tools for the next century... If this is not done, far from being brought under national control, these companies will rapidly come under international control... nationalization is a weapon to protect France's production apparatus." Moreover, the official workweek was reduced from 40 to 39 hours, with a further reduction to 35 hours planned for 1985; paid holidays were increased by a fifth week for workers; the retirement age was reduced to 60; provision was made for labor representation on the companies' boards; etc.

In the eyes of militant Communists, who pursuant to Karl Marx (see COMMUNISM) advocate attainment of the Communist society by violent means, Socialists are hated "revisionists"of the basic Marxian doctrine, called "Scientific Socialism" by Marx to distinguish it from the ideas of "Utopian Socialism" prevalent at the time Marx wrote. The U.S.S.R. represents the nearest approach to an embodiment of Marxian Socialism, but it has never approached the Marxian ideal of the "classless society" of pure Communism; instead it has evolved institutionally as a dictatorship of the Communist Party.

BIBLIOGRAPHY

BAILEY, R. "The World Turns." *Forbes*, May 15, 1989.
HENDERSON, D. R. "Why Socialism Isn't Dead." *Fortune*, May 8, 1989.

SOCIAL SECURITY The Social Security programs under the Social Security Act, first enacted in 1935, have been broadened by amendments and new legislation many times since, from the original provision for old age retirement to benefits for dependents and survivors (added in 1939), provision for disability (1956), and health benefits (1966). Medicare, a broad program of health insurance for individuals 65 or older, was added in 1965. Catastrophic insurance for the elderly was proposed in 1989. Along the way, employments covered were expanded, minimum retirement ages were lowered, benefit levels were raised, the tax rates were increased, and the maximum taxable base was raised appreciably.

But Old Age Survivors and Disability Insurance (OASDI) programs became only a part of total federal cash benefit programs: income replacement programs, such as Social Security and unemployment insurance, relate benefits to wage histories; income support programs, such as public assistance, base payments on need; and income compensation programs, such as disability compensation for veterans, base benefits on some other measure of impairment to earning capacity. Moreover, programs providing for assistance in kind include health care programs (Medicare and Medicaid); food and nutrition programs, such as the food stamp program; and housing programs (public housing and rent supplements).

As a result, total income security outlays (Social Security, unemployment insurance, and all others) became the largest and one of the most steadily growing functions in the federal budget. Unemployment compensation outlays, which vary with the unemployment rate, have fluctuated widely both in absolute amounts and as a percentage of the GNP.

Increases in the cost of income security programs come largely from automatic cost-of-living adjustments and from growth in the number of beneficiaries. Most of the benefits are paid under entitlement standards established in law. However, the administration proposed and the Congress enacted some entitlement qualifications and made a number of other legislative changes in income security programs through the Omnibus Budget Reconciliation Act of 1981 (P.L. 97-35). These changes included the following.

1. Elimination of "inappropriate" Social Security payments to adult students, nondependent survivors, and disabled workers receiving more in public disability payments than they earned before their disability.
2. Concentration of extended unemployment benefits to workers in states experiencing high levels of unemployment.
3. Reforms in Aid to Families with Dependent Children (AFDC) to eliminate families with "substantial income" from the rolls, to create new work opportunities for those recipients who should be self-supporting, to correct inequities that failed to focus assistance on those in greatest need, and to streamline administration.
4. Provision for automatic increases in federal employee retirement programs once per year rather than twice per year.

Under the administration's federalism initiative, responsibility for AFDC and the food stamp program would be assumed by the state governments in exchange for the federal government's assuming the responsibility for the Medicaid program. This proposed exchange would begin in 1984. In addition, the responsibility for the low-income home energy assistance program would be assumed by the states.

In 1990, FICA contribution and benefit wage base rose $2,400 to $50,400. The effect on payroll and self-employed taxes is shown here:

	1990	1989
FICA tax wage base	$50,400	$48,000
Employee tax rate	7.65%	7.51%
Maximum employee tax	$3,856	$3,605
Self-employed tax rate*	15.30%	13.02%
Maximum self-employed tax	$7,711	$6,250

*The law provided a 2% tax credit in 1989. For 1990, self-employed individuals have the option to deduct a portion of their Social Security taxes for income tax or self-employment tax purposes.

Based on increases in the consumer price index, Social Security beneficiaries will receive a 4.7% cost-of-living adjustment increase in 1990.

The maximum monthly federal SSI payments in 1988 for an individual with no other countable income, living in his/her own household, was $354 ($532 for a couple).

Employers remit amounts withheld from employee wages for Social Security and income taxes to the Internal Revenue Service; employer Social Security taxes are also payable at the same time. Self-employed persons who have net earnings of $400 or more in a year must report and pay Social Security taxes along with their regular income tax forms. Social security taxes are transferred to the Social Security Trust Fund: Federal Old-Age and Survivors Insurance Trust Fund, the Federal Disability Insurance Trust Fund, and the Federal Hospital Insurance Trust Fund. Such taxes are used only to pay benefits, the cost of rehabilitation services, and administrative expenses. Money available after such distributions and not required for such purposes is by law invested in obligations of the federal government. Such investments pay interest and must be repaid when the obligations are redeemed or mature. Sources of funds and expenditures of the trust funds, 1970-1987, are shown in the appended table.

Economic Impact. Proponents of a liberalized scale of benefit payments of various types see an orderly evolution from the contributory principle to the social adequacy principle in financing income security programs. The logical end-result of the latter principle would be a provision from general taxes for minimum income for all. (This idea had already made its appearance as of 1972, in the form of the Family Assistance Program (FAP), under which it was proposed to replace the federal-state program of aid to families with dependent children (AFDC) with a new federal income maintenance program for *all* poor families with children, thereby aiding the *working* poor for the first time.) As transfer payments aiding such

SOCIAL SECURITY

Table 1 / Social Security Trust Funds
Old-Age and Survivors Insurance Trust Fund, 1940-87
(In millions)

	Receipts			Expenditures				
Calendar year	Net contrib. inc., reimbursements from gen'l rev.	Net interest received	Total	Cash benefit payments, rehabilitation services	Transfers to railroad retirement acct.	Administrative expenses	Total	Total assets at end of year
1940	$ 325	$ 43	$ 368	$ 35	—	$ 26	$ 62	$ 2,031
1950	2,667	257	2,928	961	—	61	1,022	13,721
1960	10,866	516	11,382	10,677	$ 318	203	11,198	20,324
1970	30,256	1,515	32,220	28,798	579	471	29,848	32,454
1980	103,456	1,845	105,841	105,083	1,442	1,154	107,678	22,823
1981	122,627	2,060	125,361	123,803	1,585	1,307	129,695	21,490
1982	123,673	845	125,198	138,806	1,793	1,519	142,119	22,088
1983	138,337	6,706	159,584	149,221	2,251	1,528	152,999	19,628
1984	164,122	2,266	169,328	157,841	2,404	1,638	161,883	27,117
1985	176,958	1,871	184,239	167,248	2,310	1,592	171,150	35,842
1986	190,741	3,069	197,393	176,813	2,585	1,601	181,000	39,081
1987	202,735	4,690	210,736	183,587	2,557	1,524	187,668	62,149

Disability Insurance Trust Fund, 1960-87

1960	$ 1,010	$ 53	$ 1,063	$ 568	$ -5	$ 36	$ 600	$ 2,289
1970	4,481	277	4,774	3,085	10	164	3,259	5,614
1980	13,255	485	13,871	15,515	-12	368	15,872	3,629
1981	16,738	172	17,078	17,192	29	436	17,658	3,049
1982	21,995	546	22,715	17,376	26	590	17,992	2,691
1983	17,991	1,569	20,682	17,524	28	625	18,177	5,195
1984	15,945	1,174	17,309	17,898	22	626	18,546	3,959
1985	17,191	870	19,301	18,827	43	608	19,478	6,321
1986	18,399	803	19,439	19,853	68	600	20,522	7,780
1987	19,691	648	20,303	20,519	57	849	21,425	6,658

Hospital Insurance Trust Fund, 1970-87
(In millions)

		Income						Disbursements			Trust Fund	
Fiscal year [1]	Payroll taxes	Transfers from railroad retirement account	Reimbursement for uninsured persons	Premiums from voluntary enrollees	Payments for military wage credits	Interest on investments and other income [2]	Total income	Benefits payments [3]	Administrative expense [4]	Total disbursements	Net increase fund	Fund at end of year
1970	$ 4,785	$ 16	617	—	$ 11	$ 137	$ 5,614	$ 4,804	$149	$ 4,953	$ 661	$ 2,677
1975	11,291	132	481	6	48	609	12,568	10,353	259	10,612	1,956	9,870
1980	23,244	244	697	17	141	1,072	25,415	23,790	497	24,288	1,127	14,490
1981	30,425	276	659	21	141	1,341	32,863	28,907	353	29,260	3,603	18,093
1982	34,390	351	808	25	207	1,829	37,611	34,343	521	34,864	2,747	20,840
1983	36,387	358	878	26	3,663 [5]	2,629	43,940	38,102	522	38,624	-7,121	13,719
1984	41,364	351	752	35	250	2,812	45,563	41,476	633	42,108	3,455	17,174
1985	46,490	371	766	38	86	3,182	50,933	47,841	813	48,654	4,103	21,277
1986	53,020	364	566	40	-714	3,167	56,442	49,018	667	49,685	17,370	38,648
1987	57,820	368	447	40	94	3,982	62,751	49,967	836	50,803	11,949	50,956

Note: Totals do not necessarily equal the sum of rounded components.
[1] For 1967 through 1976, fiscal years cover the interval from July 1 through June 30; fiscal years 1977-84 cover the interval from October 1 through September 30.
[2] Other income includes recoveries of amounts reimbursed from the trust fund which are not obligations of the trust fund and other miscellaneous income.
[3] Includes costs of Peer Review Organizations (beginning with the implementation of the Prospective Payment System on October 1, 1983).
[4] Includes costs of experiments and demonstration projects.
[5] Includes the lump sum general revenue transfer of -$805 million as provided for by Section 151 of P.L. 98-21.
Source: U.S. Social Security Administration

lower income groups, federal income security payments have a leveling impact upon income distribution.

Moreover, shifting by employers of their rising share of contributions could have an appreciable impact on employment and wages. And with the population growth rate in the U.S. decreasing (advocates consider zero-growth a welcome development from the standpoint of population control), the percentage of the aged (persons over 65) will rise, so that a decreased (working) proportion of the population will be supporting an increased (retired) proportion of the population. At higher tax rates and tax bases, the young workers of today cannot expect to have the value of their expected future retirement payments (for remainder of retirement years expected) equal the cost of contributions plus interest during their working years.

On the other hand, it is argued that provision for income maintenance programs out of general taxes, on a "pay-as-you-go" basis, would be desirable, instead of the current financing plan of accumulating an excess of receipts over current disbursements, the trust funds, which are invested in special U.S. Treasury obligations and the proceeds of which are spent currently by the Treasury—thus

Table / Social Security Trust Fund
Supplementary Medical Insurance Trust Fund, 1970-1987
(In millions)

	Income				Disbursements			
Fiscal year [1]	Premium from participants	Income Government contributions [2]	Interest and other income [3]	Total income	Benefit payments	Administrative expenses	Total disbursements	Balance in fund at end of year [4]
1970	$ 936	$ 928	$ 12	$ 1,876	$ 1,979	$ 217	$ 2,196	$ 57
1975	1,887	2,330	105	4,322	3,765	405	4,170	1,424
1976	1,951	2,939	104	4,994	4,672	528	5,200	1,219
1977	2,193	5,053	137	7,383	5,867	475	6,342	2,279
1978	2,431	6,386	228	9,045	6,852	504	7,356	3,968
1979	2,635	6,841	363	9,839	8,259	555	8,814	4,994
1980	2,928	6,932	415	10,275	10,144	593	10,737	4,532
1981	3,320	8,747	372	12,439	12,345	883	13,228	3,743
1982	3,831	13,323	473	17,627	14,806	754	15,560	5,810
1983	4,227	14,238	682	19,147	17,487	824	18,311	6,646
1984	4,907	16,811	807	22,525	19,473	899	20,372	8,799
1985	5,524	17,898	1,155	24,577	21,808	922	22,730	10,646
1986	5,699	18,076	1,228	25,004	25,169	1,049	26,217	9,432
1987	6,480	20,299	1,018	27,797	29,937	900	30,837	6,392

[1] For 1967 through 1976, fiscal years cover the interval from July 1 through June 30; fiscal year 1977-86 cover the interval from October 1 through September 30.
[2] The payments shown as being from the general fund of the Treasury include certain interest-adjustment items.
[3] Other income includes recoveries of amounts reimbursed from the trust fund which are not obligations of the trust fund and other miscellaneous income.
[4] The financial status of the program depends on both the total net assets and the liabilities of the program.
[5] Administrative expenses shown include those paid in fiscal years 1966 and 1967.

Source: U.S. Social Security Administration.

involving double taxation in providing for interest on such obligations (and eventually repayment of principal).

Also, the current principle of benefit payments for OASDI, the "retirement test," has evoked increasing criticism: retired workers under age 70 lose benefits in a ratio of $1 for every $2 earned above $6,000. By contrast, any other type of income exceeding the level does not invoke a similarpenalty. Such penalty provision is criticized on at least two counts: the $6,000 level is hardly adequate for living expenses; and the needy are least likely to have investment income and other types of income to supplement the low Social Security level, whereas the well-to-do have such nonemployment types of income, not subjected to any such penalty. However, instead of completely eliminating the employment earnings penalty, changes merely raised the permitted penalty-free level of employment earnings.

Moreover, the Social Security tax rates, being flat rates on the specified tax base, are criticized as regressive in imposing the largest proportionate burden on the lower income brackets. The higher the flat Social Security tax rates become, the greater the regressivity in impact will become. Thus proponents of providing for Social Security benefits out of general taxation argue that such a change would mean a less regressive impact, since federal tax revenues are largely derived from income taxation where "progressive" (graduated upwards) tax rates prevail.

BIBLIOGRAPHY

Aaron, H. J., and Burtless, G. "Fiscal Policy and the Dynamic Inconsistencies of Social Security Forecasts." *American Economic Review*, May, 1989.
Annual Statistical Supplement, 1989. Social Security Bulletin.
"Another Catastrophe [retirement payments]." *Fortune*, November 6, 1989.
Kotlikoff, L. S. "On the Contribution of Economics to the Evaluation and Formation of Social Insurance Policy." *American Economic Review*, May, 1989.
National Underwriter, *Social Security Manual*. 30th Edition. National Underwriter, Cincinnati, OH, 1989.
———. *All About Medicare*, 3rd Edition, 1989.
Social Security Bulletin.
Social Security Handbook. U.S. Department of Health, Education, and Welfare.
Social Security Programs Throughout the World. U.S. Department of Health, Education, and Welfare.

SOFT Applied to a stock, or to the entire stock market, when prices have a declining tendency.

SOFT LANDING A movement in the economy from a period of relative prosperity toward recession reflected by slower economic growth, declining inflation and interest rates, but no recession. A soft landing has the benefits of avoiding both a recession and a surge in inflation. However, a soft landing can inflict considerable suffering by swelling the unemployment rolls while reducing profits and the average family income.

The Federal Reserve, through its monetary policy, is primarily involved in the softlanding process. In 1989, when the U.S. economy was headed towards a soft landing, Chairman Greenspan testified before Congress that the Fed's focus had shifted from fighting inflation to avoiding a recession.

SOFT MONEY Paper money as distinguished from metallic or hard money.

SOFT SPOT Any single stock that stands out prominently in the day's quotations because of its weakness, when the rest of the list maintains its strength.

SOIL BANK The Soil Bank Act, Title I of the Agricultural Act of 1956, was initiated in 1956 to reduce production, to promote conservation, and to protect farm income by payments to "cooperators" for withholding cropland from production and diverting acreage to other uses. The Soil Bank had two parts: (1) the acreage reserve, an annual agreement program to reduce production of the basic crops immediately by dropping acreages below established allotments; and (2) the conservation reserve, a long-term three-, five- or ten-year contractual program to take general cropland out of production and put it to conservation uses.

The following summary is from the Agricultural Stabilization and Conservation Service, U.S. Department of Agriculture.

A total of $750 million was set in the act for any one year's operation of the acreage reserve program (ARP), with specific annual fund ceilings imposed for the designated allotment crops in surplus. The acreage reserve program was operative in 1956, 1957, and 1958, and then was discontinued. The conservation reserve program (CRP), with the long-term contracts entered into through 1960, had a limitation of $450 million each calendar year.

The conservation reserve program, authorized in 1956 under the Soil Bank Act, provided for contracts with participating farmers for up to ten years to take cropland out of production and to establish and maintain protective vegetative cover or other needed conservation practices, such as tree planting, water impoundments, and wildlife conservation. The program was offered during the period from 1956 through 1960. Mandatory extensions of some contracts were required because tree seedlings initially were unavailable for planting on all diverted acres. acres. Only a few contracts remained in effect under this program, and they expired not later than December 31, 1972. The Soil Bank Act was repealed by Section 601 of the Food and Agriculture Act of 1965 (P.L. 89-321). However, conservation reserve contracts entered into through 1960 were to remain in effect until they expired.

SOIL EROSION AND DOMESTIC ALLOTMENT ACT
See AGRICULTURAL ADJUSTMENT ACT.

SOLA
A foreign check or bill of exchange consisting of one document as distinguished from a check or bill drawn in a set, i.e., in duplicate or triplicate. Foreign checks and bills of exchange are normally issued in duplicate and transmitted separately. A sola check or bill is not of usual occurrence. Such a check or bill would be phrased, "Pay this sola bill of exchange to the order of," or the word "sole" would be printed in large type across the face. The term is used synonymously with sola bill, sole, sole of exchange, and solus.
See FIRST OF EXCHANGE.

SOLVENCY AND INSOLVENCY
In a popular sense, solvency means that a business is able to pay its debts as they come due. Insolvency means that the business is unable to do so. In Section 101 of the Bankruptcy Reform Act of 1978, insolvency means a financial condition such that the sum of the entity's debts is greater than all of the entity's property at fair valuation. According to this definition, a corporation could be solvent even though it may be temporarily unable to pay currently maturing debts because of the insufficiency of liquid assets.

Liquidity refers to the ability of a firm to meet its short-term obligations as they come due. Solvency and insolvency usually relate to long-term conditions.

A number of remedies are available to a firm that is in serious financial difficulty, ranging from voluntary agreements with creditors to involuntary arrangements. The courts may also become involved in the process. Nonjudicial and judicial remedies include the following:

Control	Nonjudicial	Judicial
Control by debtor	Extension of maturity date Composition agreement	Reorganization (debtor in possession)
Control by others	Creditor committee Voluntary assignment	Reorganization (trustee) Liquidation

Composition agreements are arrangements in which creditors accept a certain percentage of their separate claims in full settlement of those claims. Debtor and creditors may enter into a contractual agreement by which control of the debtor's business is given over to a committee formed by the creditors. In a voluntary assignment, a debtor executes a voluntary assignment of property to a trust for the benefit of the creditors. REORGANIZATIONS and LIQUIDATIONS are judicial methods for dealing with financially distressed companies. Under a Chapter 11 reorganization, the objective is the continuation of the business. In a liquidation, the objective is the liquidation of the business, the realization of assets, and the settlement of liabilities to the extent possible, and the discharge of unsettled liabilities.

In liquidations, a statement of affairs is usually prepared when a bankruptcy petition is filed. The statement of affairs outlines the legal status of the various creditors and the realizable value of the assets. A statement of realization and liquidation provides information to the court, debtors, and creditors concerning the progress being made in the liquidation of the business.

BIBLIOGRAPHY

MATZ, L. *Bank Soundness: A Banker's Guide to Controlling Asset Quality.* Bank Administration Institute, Rolling Meadows, IL, 1989.

———. *Bank Solvency: A Banker's Guide to Practical Liquidity Management.* Bank Administration Institute, Rolling Meadows, IL, 1986.

SOURCES OF FINANCIAL INFORMATION
The nonprofessional investor can find many sources of basic financial information in major newspapers, journals, and periodicals. Most brokerage houses also distribute market letters and recommendations to customers.

I. The financial press
   A. Newspapers (current business topics and market price data)
      1) *Wall Street Journal* (daily)
      2) *The New York Times* (daily)
      3) *Commercial and Financial Chronicle* (weekly)
      4) *Barron's* (weekly)
      5) *M/G Financial Weekly* (weekly)
      6) *Wall Street Transcript* (twice weekly)
   B. Journals and periodicals (general investment topics)
      1) *Business Week* (weekly)
      2) *Financial World* (biweekly)
      3) *Forbes* (biweekly)
      4) *Finance* (monthly)
      5) *Financial Executive* (monthly)
      6) *Fortune* (biweekly)
      7) *Institutional Investor* (monthly)
      8) *Financial Analysts Journal* (bimonthly)
      9) *OTC Review* (monthly)
II. Industry and company data (historical and statistical)
   A. *Statistical Abstract of the U.S.*
   B. *Business Statistics*
   C. *Standard & Poor's Statistical Basebook*
   D. *Predicasts*
   E. *U.S. Industrial Outlook*
   F. *American Statistics Index*
   G. U.S. government publications
III. Industry data (general information)
   A. Dun & Bradstreet key business ratios
   B. Robert Morris Associates annual studies
   C. Value Line Investment Survey
   D. Moody's manuals
IV. Company data (general)
   A. Corporate reports
   B. Security prospectus
   C. SEC reports (8 K, 9 K, and 10 K)
   D. Standard & Poors:
      1) *Corporate record*
      2) *Analysts handbook*
      3) *Stock reports*
      4) *Stock guide*
   E. Moody's manuals
   F. Value Line Investment Service
V. Money Market and Bonds
   A. *Money Manager* (weekly)
   B. *Weekly Bond Buyer* (weekly)
   C. *Bankers Trust Credit and Capital Markets*
   D. *Moody's Bond Survey* (weekly)
   E. *Value Line Options and Convertibles*
   F. *Moody's Bond Record*
   G. *Moody's Municipal and Government Manual*
   H. *Standard & Poor's Bond Guide*
   I. *Standard & Poor's Convertible Bond Report*
VI. Miscellaneous Investment Advisors
   A. *Value Line Options and Convertibles*
   B. *Vickers Guide to Investment Company Portfolios*
   C. *Weisenberger Investment Companies* (annual)
   D. *Investment Dealers Digest Mutual Fund Directory* (semiannual)
   E. *Mutual Fund Fact Book* (Investment Company Institute)
   F. *Commodity Yearbook*
   G. *Guide to World Community Markets*

SOVEREIGN
This term has two meanings:

1. In law, the supreme authority of government. In the U.S., there are 51 sovereigns—the federal government, with authority

derived from the U.S. Constitution and the people, and the 50 states. A sovereign may not be sued without its consent.

2. In the currency system of England, a gold coin with the value of one pound, no longer in circulation.

See ENGLISH MONEY TABLE, FOREIGN MONEYS.

SPACED MATURITIES A technique of adjustment to interest rate risk (the risk of market price depreciation in the event interest rates and yields should rise) in investment in high-grade bonds. A given rise in yields has least impact on the shortest-term maturities, but short-term maturities normally yield less than long-term maturities, which are hit most by the given rise in yields. Therefore, in order to obtain "livable yields" and yet maintain a degree of protection against open market depreciation, investors "space" holdings in short-, intermediate-, and long-term maturities as a diversification.

See MATURITY DISTRIBUTION.

SPECIAL AGENT *See* AGENT.

SPECIAL ASSESSMENT BONDS Bonds issued by municipalities for obtaining funds to finance improvements the benefits of which are purely local in character, such as parks, drainage ditches, sewers, sidewalks, etc. While these bonds are obligations of a municipality or district, the principal and interest are payable by levying a special tax upon the property benefited, and not on the municipality as a whole; thus, bonds issued for the construction of a drainage sewer may be repaid by levying taxes on the property benefited by such drainage. Usually the locality benefited organizes itself into a district which exists solely for the purpose of financing the proposed improvement and which alone bears the cost. As investments, special assessment bonds lie midway between municipal bonds and promises to pay by private obligors.

See SEMIMUNICIPAL BONDS.

SPECIAL BLOCK PROCEDURES The NEW YORK STOCK EXCHANGE provides special procedures for the handling of large blocks of stock, outside the regular market for the stock concerned on the floor, in order to attract such large orders from financial institutions, large estates, corporations, and other investors for executions within a reasonable time and at a reasonable price.

A member firm must obtain the exchange's approval for the use of any of these seven special block procedures, which are officially described briefly as follows.

1. **The specialist block purchase/specialist block sale.** The broker may negotiate a direct purchase or sale of stock for a customer, outside the regular auction market, with the NYSE specialist in that stock.
2. **The exchange distribution/exchange acquisition.** The broker may accumulate the necessary orders, and then fill the original block by "crossing" the orders on the floor in the auction market between the current bid and ask quotations.
3. **Special offering/special bid.** When the size of the block order or current market conditions make it necessary to enlist the marketing services of the entire "exchange community," the broker may announce the offering price or the bid price over the ticker, open to all members and their customers. The transactions are made on the exchange floor, but not as part of the auction market.
4. **Secondary distribution.** This method is used for extremely large sell orders. The member organization usually acts as a dealer, combining with other members and nonmembers to effect the sale of the block, usually after trading hours and usually at a fixed price. NYSE members account for approximately 75% of the shares sold in this manner.

Of the above special block procedures, the special bid, the exchange acquisition, and the specialist block sale were inaugurated on October 22, 1956, as the reverse of the other previously adopted methods for the sale of large blocks. As compensation for the additional services required of the broker, special commissions are paid by the customer who originates the large block order. The "other side" generally pays no commissions.

SPECIAL DEPOSITS *See* DEPOSITS.

SPECIAL DRAWING RIGHTS Because of the "limited possibilities for gold and the dollar to provide additional international monetary reserves" and the "unalterable opposition" of the U.S. to a rise in the price of gold as a solution for the problem, the 1967 annual meeting of the INTERNATIONAL MONETARY FUND (IMF) at Rio de Janeiro, Brazil, unanimously endorsed the outline plan for creation of a supplemental reserve asset, backed by the full faith and credit of participating nations, that would be universally accepted as a supplement to gold and dollars and could be issued in quantities sufficient to ensure adequate growth of total monetary reserves. Studies had started in 1964, and the establishment of special drawing rights (SDRs) resulted from these studies and from negotiations subsequently involving the IMF and the "Group of Ten" (the countries that had joined in the General Arrangements to Borrow supplement to the IMF's resources, i.e., Belgium, Canada, France, Germany, Italy, Japan, the Netherlands, Sweden, the United Kingdom, and the U.S.). The amendment to the Articles of Agreement of the IMF creating the special drawing rights became effective on July 29, 1969, upon ratification by the required 67 member countries having 80% of the voting power of the IMF.

SDRs are created by the IMF in appropriate total amounts and are allocated among the member countries in proportion to their fund quotas, thus increasing the reserves of member nations. The appropriate total amount of SDRs initially created for the dates January 1, 1970, January 1, 1971, and January 1, 1972, was $9.5 billion. The initial allocation of SDRs, aggregating approximately 3.4 billion units, equivalent to $3.4 billion at the U.S. dollar's parity, was made on January 1, 1970. The allocation of SDR 4.053 billion made as of January 1, 1981, was the final allocation in the third basic period, which ended December 31, 1981, and brought the total of SDRs to SDR 21.433 billion.

The SDR, which is the unit of account for fund transactions, is finding increasing acceptance as a unit of account (or as the basis for a unit of account) for private contracts and international treaties, as well as for use by other international and regional organizations. The reduction in the number of currencies in the SDR "valuation basket" from 16 to 5 on January 1, 1981, has further enhanced the usefulness of the SDR as a unit of account and has given fresh impetus, according to the IMF, to the issue of private financial obligations denominated in SDRs.

In addition to its role as a unit of account, the SDR also functions as a currency peg. When a member of the IMF pegs its currency to the SDR, the value of its currency is fixed in terms of the SDR and then is set in terms of other currencies by reference to the SDR value of the other currencies as calculated and published by the IMF. As of September 30, 1987, 9 members of the IMF were pegging their currencies to the SDR.

The Council of Economic Advisers (U.S.) summarized the action as permitting "an adequate but not excessive growth of official reserves." SDRs may be used when a participant has a need to use reserves. When a participant wishes to use SDRs to acquire desired currency for international payments, the IMF may designate the participant that has to receive them and to provide the user with a currency that must be a "currency convertible in fact" (defined in the amendment to the Articles of Agreement of the fund as a currency having interconvertibility at appropriate rates of exchange for balances arising in connection with the use of SDRs, and which in addition is convertible in the sense of being the currency of a participant that freely buys and sells gold (Art. IV, Sec. 4(b) of the Articles) or that has accepted the obligations to establish a par value (Art. VIII, Secs. 2, 3, and 4 of the Articles), as well as any other currency for which suitable arrangements exist for conversion, at rates of exchange prescribed by the fund, into any of the currencies in the group that are interconvertible).

Participants designated are those that have strong balances of payments and reserve positions, or that must acquire SDRs to meet obligations or for other reasons under the IMF's Articles of Agreement. A participant is obligated to accept SDRs on the fund's designation up to the point at which the participant's holdings are three times its allocation. SDRs may also be transferred between participants without fund designation or without need if the fund so decides in transactions for specified purposes. SDRs can be transferred to the IMF's general account in payment of charges or in repayment of a member's drawings.

Summary. Creation of SDRs, although it "will give nations more time to redress their balance-of-payments disequilibria in an orderly fashion," does not correct the imbalances, as correction depends upon adoption of appropriate domestic policies, adoption of appropriate selective measures, and adjustment in exchange rates.

SPECIAL ENDORSEMENT An unqualified ENDORSEMENT of a negotiable instrument, whereby the endorser makes all the warranties specified in Section 3-417, Uniform Commercial Code.

A special endorsement specifies the person to whom or to whose order it makes the instrument payable. Any instrument specially endorsed becomes payable to the order of the special endorsee and may be further negotiated only by his endorsement. The holder may convert a BLANK ENDORSEMENT into a special endorsement by writing over the signature of the endorser in blank any contract consistent with the character of the endorsement (Sec. 3-204, Uniform Commercial Code). An example of a special endorsement is "Pay to A. B. See. (Signed) John Doe." (It is not required that an endorsement read "to the order of," although the same is required on the face of the instrument.)

SPECIALISTS In the actual transaction of business, stock exchanges may be of two types: (1) the "call" type, in which an official of the exchange calls out the roster of listed stocks, and as each stock is "called," trading is transacted by the members present; or (2) the "specialist" type, in which members of the exchange are assigned the responsibility of maintaining markets in specified stocks at the trading "posts" to which the stocks are assigned upon being listed.

Under rules of the New York Stock Exchange, four classes of specialists are provided for: regular specialists, relief specialists, associate specialists, and temporary specialists. No member is allowed to act in the first three capacities unless he is registered with the exchange, and a floor official must authorize a temporary specialist to act as such. Relief specialists take over the "book" of the regular specialist in the latter's absence. Associate specialists assist the regular specialist in handling the book, but do not solicit orders or assist in the maintenance or stabilization of the market by purchases or sales for their own account; the handling of the book or the making of any bid or offer may be done by an associate specialist only if either the regular specialist or a relief specialist is present. Temporary specialists are appointed by a floor official in the event of an emergency or when the volume of business necessitates such help.

The regular specialist makes application to the exchange and receives formal approval. For approval, he must show that he can meet the capital requirements prescribed by the exchange. Minimum capital requirements for specialists have been increased sharply. In general, the exchange requires that each specialist unit be able to assume a position of 5,000 shares of each 100-share-unit common stock in which the unit is registered, compared to a required position of 1,200 shares in 1965. Moreover, the specialist unit should be able to assume a position of 1,000 shares in each convertible preferred stock. In addition, the net liquid asset requirement for each specialist unit is set at $500,000, or 25% of the value of the total position requirements, whichever is greater. (Many specialists employ a great deal more capital in servicing the stocks that they handle.) Some specialists use only their own funds, while others augment their capital with financing arrangements with other exchange member organizations or banks.

Each specialist has two functions. First, he executes limit orders (see ORDERS) that other members of the exchange may leave with him. These orders are booked with the specialist when the current market price is away from the prices of the orders, e.g., when a commission broker receives a limit order to buy at 55 a stock selling at 60. By executing these orders on behalf of other exchange members when the market price reaches the price stated on these orders, the specialist makes it possible for these members to transact other business elsewhere on the exchange floor. In handling these orders, the specialist acts as a broker or agent and receives a portion of the commission received by the commission broker (no added commission is charged to the public).

The specialist's second and more complex role is that of dealer or principal for his own account. As a dealer, the specialist is expected, insofar as reasonably practical, to maintain continuously fair and orderly markets in the stocks assigned to him. When there is temporary disparity, for example, between supply and demand, he usually is expected to buy or sell for his own account in order to narrow price changes between transactions and to give depth to the market. By doing this, the specialist keeps price continuity more orderly than it would be otherwise, and thereby contributes to the liquidity of the market. He thus makes it possible for investors' orders to be executed at better prices when temporary disparity exists.

The exchange gives this specific example of action by a specialist for his own account. A stock has just sold at 55; the highest price anyone is willing to pay is 54 $1/4$ (the best bid), and the lowest price at which anyone is willing to sell now is 55 $1/4$ (the best offer). The specialist, acting as dealer for his own account, may now decide to bid 54 $3/4$ for 100 shares, thus making the new quotation 54 $3/4$ bid, 55 $1/4$ asked, which thus narrows the spread between the bid and asked price to $1/2$ point. Now if a prospective seller wishes to sell 100 shares at the price of the best bid, "the specialist will purchase his stock at 54 $3/4$, and by doing this, the specialist not only provides the seller with a better price, but also maintains better price continuity, since the variation from the last sale is only one-fourth of a point" (whether such an original spread represented a disparity would be a question of fact).

On the other hand, the specialist may sell stock for his own account in order to maintain the market. A stock has just sold at 62 $1/4$; the best bid is 62, and the best offer is 63. The specialist may offer 500 shares at 62 $1/2$ for his own account, changing the quotation to 62 bid, 62 $1/2$ asked. Now if a prospective buyer wishes to buy 100 shares at the price of the best bid, the specialist will sell his stock at 62 $1/2$, thus making the stock available at a price one-half point cheaper. Thus better price continuity and depth of the market have been maintained.

In his efforts to maintain an orderly market, a specialist may sometimes make both the best bid and the best offer in a stock for his own account. When the specialist does not have sufficient stock in his inventory, he may sell "short" to maintain a market. In doing this, he must observe all the rules and regulations governing a SHORT SALE. But the specialist is not expected to prevent a stock from declining or to keep it from going up. He is expected to try to keep rises and declines fair and orderly, insofar as is practicable under the circumstances. "Obviously," points out the exchange, "a single specific formula cannot be applied to markets in individual stocks to determine whether they are fair and orderly. What is considered fair and orderly in one stock may be regarded as completely inadequate in another. It depends on such things as market conditions, price level of the stock, normal volume of transactions, number of outstanding shares, and how widely the stock is distributed."

The Specialist's "Book." The specialist enters limit orders in his book under each price category in the sequence in which they are received. For each order he shows the number of shares and from whom received. He represents these orders in the market, frequently competing against other members who are representing customers. As he is successful in executing the orders in his book, he sends reports to the members for whom he has acted according to the sequence of listing under each price category. When he makes a transaction for another broker, or when an order is canceled, he crosses it out in his book.

The specialist is prohibited by rule from buying for his own account at a given price while he holds an order to buy at that price for someone else. Also, the specialist must not buy stock at any price for his own account while holding an order to buy that stock "at the market" (the best available price). The same is true with respect to a specialist selling for his own account while holding a sell order for someone else. The specialist cannot compete at the same price, for his own account, with orders he holds as a broker's broker.

Arranging the Opening. Another crucial situation in which the specialist plays a key role is the opening for a stock assigned to him. The New York Stock Exchange portrays the specialist in such a situation as follows.

Most of the orders received by brokers on the floor before the opening of the market are left with the specialist. Using these orders and also dealing for his own account in varying degrees, the specialist arranges the opening price in each stock, usually near the previous close. In arranging the opening, the specialist must consider general market conditions and the market conditions in the particular stock.

Surveillance and Performance. The New York Stock Exchange's system for checking on the specialist and his performance includes the requirement that specialists submit to the exchange, about eight times a year, details of their dealings for unannounced one-week periods selected at random by the exchange. These figures and studies of price continuity, spreads in quotations, and depth are examined by the exchange to determine the specialist's effectiveness in maintaining fair and orderly markets.

In addition, the exchange maintains an on-line price surveillance program based on trading data obtained from the exchange's computers, which run the stock ticker. This program monitors all trades reported on the ticker throughout the market session. When the price movement of a stock exceeds preset standards, the computer prints the symbol, time, and price of the transaction on a teletypewriter machine in the exchange's surveillance section. The surveillance section retrieves from the computer's memory bank the chronological sequence of sales, which is then examined. If there is no apparent cause for the fluctuation, the surveillance section alerts a trading floor official in the area where the stock is traded. The official will then speak to the specialist to determine if a problem exists.

See the *1971 Annual Report* of the New York Stock Exchange, Inc., p. 20, for reference to the adoption of criteria for measuring the performance of specialists; this new approach to specialist surveillance was "intended to lead to further improvements in the continuity, spread, and depth provided by the specialist system."

The exchange publishes three aggregative measures of overall specialists' performance: "participation rate," determined by dividing specialists' purchases and sales for their own account by all reported purchases and sales; "stabilization rate," purchases at prices below or sales at prices above the last different price; and "price continuity"

Regulation. The mixture of broker-dealer functions in the specialist's operations posed a problem of regulation for the early Securities and Exchange Commission (SEC). The SEC's conclusions and recommendations in its 1936 *Report on the Feasibility and Advisability of the Complete Segregation of the Functions of Dealer and Broker* led to additional rules and procedures; and in 1963, the SEC's *Special Study of the Securities Markets* took another long look at the role of the specialist and found there was a need not for any broad and drastic change in the system, but for a number of improvements in specialists' practices and regulatory concepts and methods. Rule 11B(1) of the SEC's regulations, adopted not long thereafter, still specifies the guidelines for specialists in trading for their own account to maintain orderly markets for the stocks assigned to them.

The 1972 *Staff Study of the Regulation of Specialists on the New York and American Stock Exchanges,* by the Senate Securities Subcommittee of the Committee on Banking, Housing and Urban Affairs, criticized the SEC for allegedly insufficient inspections of specialists' operations (last major inspection of NYSE specialists occurred in 1970) and the NYSE for alleged footdragging in providing automated data that would provide readier access to activity in particular stocks by specialists, as well as alleged resistance to tighter regulation of specialists.

The specialist earns a floor brokerage commission by acting as an agent in executing the orders left with him by other members. The amount that a specialist derives from commissions is influenced to a great extent by the particular stocks in which he specializes. Stocks in which there is usually an active public interest are known as "bread and butter" stocks, and in these stocks the specialist acts principally as an agent, for which he receives commissions. Stocks in which there is less interest and in which the specialist's participation for his own account is a constant requisite are known as "dealer" stocks. The specialist, in risking his funds, also hopes to realize a profit on the transactions that he makes for his own account, which depends on his judgment and astuteness as well as general market conditions. Failure, however, to perform his dealer function properly could result in the loss of his registration.

The specialist also performs a key function by helping to execute large orders, on which the specialist may be able to assist the commission broker by taking or supplying part or all of the stock as dealer at a mutually agreeable price within the market, by locating willing buyers and sellers by drawing on his knowledge of the market, and by handling market or limited price orders given to him by a commission broker who is executing, on a piecemeal basis, a large order requiring time to fill. For those occasions in which recourse to the regular "auction" market may not be feasible, the NYSE has developed special methods for handling large blocks, including the specialist block purchase or sale.

Summary. The Martin Report (William McChesney Martin's *Report with Recommendations to the Board of Governors of the New York Stock Exchange,* August, 1971) stated that "a better system of maintaining a continuous and responsible market [than the specialist system] has not been suggested." The report, however, urged an increase in the resources of specialists and the development of methods to encourage and enable specialists to improve the performance of their functions in instances where securities are offered in unusually large volume.

SPECIAL REPORTS Auditors frequently are engaged to report on matters that are not financial statements prepared in conformity with generally accepted accounting principles. The American Institute of Certified Public Accountants has grouped special reports into four categories which require specific reporting procedures (SAS 14, "Special Reports"):

1. Reports on financial statements prepared in accordance with a comprehensive basis of accounting other than GAAP (including income tax basis, cash basis, price-level-adjusted basis, and prescribed regulatory basis).
2. Reports on specified elements, accounts, or items of a financial statement (royalties, profit participation, or a provision for income taxes).
3. Reports on compliance with aspects of a contractual agreement related to audited financial statements.
4. Reports on information presented in prescribed forms or schedules that require a prescribed form of auditor's report.

SPECIAL SITUATION In the stock market, a security having a unique speculative interest; a security in which some development, peculiar to itself, promises profit regardless of the general market trend. Such situations arise in connection with reorganization, recapitalization, clearance of dividend arrears, special distributions, merger or consolidation developments, etc.

The term is also sometimes applied to secondarily important issues from a speculative standpoint that become particularly attractive for trading purposes.

See SPECULATION.

SPECIE Metallic money—gold or silver coin—as distinguished from paper money and credit instruments (checks, notes, and the like). The term is also sometimes applied to gold and silver bullion. Since January 31, 1934, gold coin is no longer coined or in circulation in the United States. Pursuant to P.L. 91-607, December 31, 1970, nonsilver dollars and half-dollars are now minted for general circulation; coinage of the former 40% silver half-dollar (pursuant to the Coinage Act of 1965) was discontinued effective January 1, 1971. The Coinage Act of 1965 also brought about desilverization of the quarter and dime. All coins of the U.S. currently minted, therefore, are composed of the baser metals (cupronickel).

SPECIE PAYMENT Payment in coin and sometimes in bullion, as distinguished from payment in paper money, which may be convertible or inconvertible, i.e., not redeemable in coin. Practically all of the banks in the United States suspended specie payments on their notes during the panics of 1814, 1837, and 1857. The greenbacks issued by the United States government during the Civil War failed to specify a method or time of redemption. Since they were not supported by an adequate metallic reserve and were merely government promises to pay, they greatly depreciated in value. The Specie Resumption Act of 1875, however, provided that the secretary of the Treasury should, "on and after January 1, 1879, redeem in gold coin the United States legal tender notes outstanding, on their presentation for redemption at the office of the Assistant Treasurer of the United States in the City of New York, in sums of not less than $50." Even before this date and ever since, UNITED STATES NOTES (greenbacks) have been maintained on a parity with gold. The Thomas Amendment to the AAA Farm Relief and Inflation Act (May 12, 1933) and the Gold Repeal Joint Resolution of June 5, 1933, made United States notes full legal tender for all purposes. P.L. 89-81, July 23, 1965 (Coinage Act of 1965), repealed these legal tender provisions, but added a new provision of law to the same effect in 31 U.S.C. 392.

SPECIE POINT *See* GOLD POINTS.

SPECIE RESUMPTION ACT *See* SPECIE PAYMENT.

SPECIFIC LEGACY *See* LEGACY.

SPECIFICATIONS In foreign exchange, the terms applicable to bills of exchange drawn under letters of credit; in invitations for competitive bidding, the terms and conditions governing bids

SPECULATION

and with which bidders must comply. Letters of credit specify in minute detail the terms that must be followed in drawing drafts thereunder, e.g., amount, nature of shipment, terms of drafts, expiration date, currency, documents to accompany drafts, etc.

SPECULATION In its broadest sense, risk taking, i.e., taking investing risks with the anticipation of profit, but incurring the chances of loss. The rationality of speculation depends on how accurately the elements entering into the situation can be isolated and evaluated, and how future developments based upon such calculations can be forecast. Speculation is a necessary, inseparable, integral, noninsurable, and inescapable element in business and ownership of property, i.e., all business by its inherent nature is a continuous speculation, and property is liable to degrees of risk and uncertainty as to value and income. Speculation that is inherent in business is known as primary speculation, since it cannot be avoided completely. When speculation is incidental to the main business undertaken, e.g., stock market operations, it is called secondary or incidental speculation.

From a broad economic standpoint, speculation is a necessary function because venture capital, or assumption of risk inherent in riskier opportunities, is necessary for economic growth and development and financing of innovation and change. As compensation for the assumption of risk, the returns on speculation should include, in addition to the basic or "pure" (riskless) payment for use of capital, an added premium for the assumption of risk. When speculative risks are borne by the speculator, who is in a position to calculate the uncertain elements within reasonable limits of error and who can protect himself against disastrous losses by proper application of the principles of successful speculation (techniques of trading, hedging, options, stop loss orders, etc.), security and commodity markets develop added marketability; the shifting of the risk to speculators from manufacturers, processors, etc., unable to tolerate a high degree of risk enables the latter to carry on operations with minimized risk on inventories.

Normally, the type of gain most attractive to speculators is capital gain, i.e., the profit on turnover, rather than interest and dividend income, since turnover profits on holdings held for more than six months are taxable as "long-term capital gains" at a net effective rate of only 25%.

Gambling. Because of losses arising in speculative commitments, especially by the inexperienced who engage in secondary speculation without proper application of the principles of speculation, speculation is sometimes confused with gambling. However, gambling is based on pure chance without the shifting or assumption of business risk from the businessperson or investor primarily intent on investment. Gambling involves an unnecessary, artificially created, avoidable, or "synthetic" risk, such as wagering money on some future, fortuitous event, without any necessary relation to business operations or the acquisition and disposal of property.

Speculation differs from gambling in that speculation implies taking existing business risks that are subject to analysis, interpretation, and measurement, and thus become amenable to scientific forecast. Necessary speculation is a productive economic function, since it must be borne by businesspersons and investors in overcoming the uncertainties of the future, especially with reference to financial risk and price changes. Gambling serves no productive economic function of shifting risk from businesspersons and investors to speculators, although gambling by the professional and sophisticated may be based on careful calculation of odds, racing performance records of horses and dogs, etc. Even "blind" or uninformed speculation is not quite gambling, since it does involve a shifting of the risk from the businessperson or investor to such a speculator.

Investment. Speculation and INVESTMENT are also often confused. The line of demarcation between the two terms is difficult to draw because they are customarily used in a loose rather than a technical sense.

In brokerage circles, it is commonly assumed that purchasing a security with the intention of holding it permanently is investment, whereas purchasing a security with the intention of selling it as soon as a favorable opportunity presents itself is speculation. It is also generally supposed that a commitment purchased with the primary intention of deriving dividend and interest income therefrom is an investment; whereas a commitment based on anticipations of capital gain is a speculation. These are loose, popular interpretations of the terms and are not technically accurate.

Technically, the distinction between investment and speculation rests on the degree of safety of the capital sum committed (relative degree of risk). An investment is a commitment for any length of period of holding, whether for investment income or capital gain anticipations, in which the degree of risk is low; a speculation is a commitment in which the degree of risk is high. Thus the further popular impression that margin buying is pure speculation ignores the real significance of the difference between investment and speculation. Margin buying arrangements are merely a leveraged form of buying, and thus are procedural, not substantively related to the risks of the commitment involved. High-grade securities may be bought on margin. Similarly, the fact that margin buying is motivated primarily by capital gain anticipations is not conclusive that it is speculation. Maximization of gain, whether investment income or capital gain, should motivate the investor just as much as the speculator. The same test of degree of risk logically should apply to short selling; it may be difficult to accept the idea that a short sale is an investment because most thinking is conditioned to the idea that capital gain operations are per se speculation. But a short sale may be a high- or low-risk operation, depending on the forces determining the degree of risk; the short seller risks his money just as much as the long buyer.

Because both investment and speculation should be motivated by maximization of gain, whether investment income or capital gain, both investors and speculators should consider both "technical" market data (prices, price trends, volume, etc.) and "fundamental" data (earnings, dividends, asset values, money rates, company developments, etc.) for informed investing and speculating, so as to determine the degree of risk involved in commitments that affect both types of return. Doctrinaire market "technicians" who advocate completely ignoring the fundamental factor and instead recommend completely relying on technical market data as a basis for operations do not consider all relevant factors, since fundamental data are part of the forces bearing on commitments.

See BUSINESS BAROMETERS, BUSINESS CYCLE, BUSINESS FORECASTING SERVICES, FLUCTUATING PRINCIPLE, FUNDAMENTAL CONDITIONS, GAMBLE, INDUSTRIAL STOCKS, INVESTMENT, MARKET AVERAGES, MARKET SENTIMENT, PUBLIC UTILITY STOCKS, RAILROAD STOCKS, SECURITY ANALYSIS, SPECULATIVE CYCLE, WALL STREET.

SPECULATIVE CYCLE A period of rising security prices followed by a period of falling prices; a wavelike pattern in which security prices pass through a peak and valley, i.e., a successive major upward and downward swing. A speculative cycle is popularly described as possessing three stages. After a "bear market" has reached bottom, there is a period of accumulation, during which prices of stocks move forward very gradually. This is the first stage. The second stage is when the leading barometers indicate a return to normal conditions, ultimately leading to prosperity. This is called the period of advance, and is characterized by active bidding-up of security prices. The third and last stage is that of distribution. During this stage, business is at boom proportions, but credit becomes tight and interest rates rise. Insiders, experienced speculators, and investing institutions sell their stocks while prosperity is still prevailing and prices are still high, in anticipation of the "turn."

Stock movements may be classified as primary or cyclical—the major trend movements comprehending a complete cycle; secondary—the intermediate swings within the primary trend (reactions in a bull market and rallies in a bear market); and daily fluctuations. The primary movements have their source in economic fundamentals, the secondary movements are chiefly "technical," and the daily fluctuations are considered moot. "Technical analysis" of stock market trends is concerned with primary and intermediate trends.

See BUSINESS CYCLE, BUSINESS FORECASTING SERVICES, SWINGS.

SPECULATIVE INVESTMENTS Securities that are not entitled to an investment rating because of unstable characteristics, either as to earning power, equity position, or outlook. In an upswing of the speculative cycle, however, speculative securities command major attention and interest for traders interested in short-term price appreciation, as at such times speculative developments are favorable for such securities.

See SPECULATION.

SPECULATOR A person who engages in the practice of risktaking; one who hazards his money, effort, and time in the taking of risks of SPECULATION, for the purpose of gain. The speculator often attempts to make a gain on short-term price changes, as opposed to the investor, who normally has a longer time orientation.

SPIN-OFF A distribution of subsidiary stock to the shareholders of the parent corporation, giving them control of the subsidiary, without having to surrender any shares. The distribution is similar to an ordinary dividend distribution. For the distribution not to be taxable to the shareholders, the distributing corporation must distribute at least 80% of the outstanding stock of the controlled corporation.
See SPLIT-OFF, SPLIT-UP.

SPINs Standard & Poor's indexed notes.
See FINANCIAL INSTRUMENTS: RECENT INNOVATIONS.

SPLIT The execution of an order in two or more parts at different prices. For example, an order to sell 2,000 shares might be executed on two different days in lots of 1,000 shares at different prices, because of inability to find a market at suitable prices on one day.
See SPLIT-UP.

SPLIT-OFF A form of corporate separation in which a parent corporation distributes to its shareholders stock in a corporation that it controls, similar to a SPIN-OFF, except that the shareholders surrender a part of their stock in the parent corporation for the stock in the controlled corporation. No tax is recognized by the shareholders from the exchange of their shares.

SPLIT OPENING A rather wide difference in the price of a stock occurring immediately at the opening. This sometimes happens when important news concerning a stock is released overnight. For example, U.S. Steel might have an excited opening, and sales at different parts of the trading post might occur simultaneously at different prices, say 83 to 84. If 5,000 shares were sold at the opening gong at from 83 to 84, the ticker would report 50X 83-84. An odd lot order would be based on the average price, say 83 5/8.

SPLIT ORDER See SPLIT.

SPLIT PROOF SYSTEM BLOCK SYSTEM.

SPLIT-UP Increasing the number of shares of a corporation by some ratio or multiple; dividing each existing share of a corporation into a number of new shares of reduced par or stated value. For example, a corporation with 100,000 shares of common capital stock of $100 par value each might split its stock into 400,000 shares of $25 par value each. This would be a four-to-one split-up. Or, if the stock was no par value, the stated value per share of the new shares would be reduced on the books to 25% of the former figure. A stock split-up, like a nontaxable stock dividend, does not imply any actual distribution to stockholders. It is essentially a bookkeeping transaction, and the stockholders' equity in the assets and earnings of the corporation remain as before. The additional shares received in a stock split-up are in no event to be considered as income.

The chief purpose of a stock split-up is to reduce the market value of a stock to make possible a wider ownership. A stock selling at $200 per share finds a more limited market than one selling at $50 a share. The directors of a corporation are justified in ordering a stock split-up to achieve a broader distribution of shares and greater stability in quotations, since a split-up usually brings these corollary advantages. The importance of a stock split-up is usually overemphasized by speculators, although frequently it is true that the total market value of the shares is greater after the split-up than before the split-up. Normally, the dividend after a split-up is maintained in proportion to the split-up.

A stock split-up differs in a number of respects from a STOCK DIVIDEND. As heretofore explained, a stock split-up is an actual division of each existing share into a number of parts, each of which is thereafter considered to be a full share. Such a division involves an actual reduction of the par value or stated value of the stock. From an accounting standpoint, a stock split-up affects the capital account only. On the other hand, a stock dividend involves a capitalization of earned surplus and a maintenance of the old par or stated value.

Thus, if a company has 100,000 shares of $100 par stock and declares a two-for-one split-up, the capital account thereafter would show 200,000 shares of $50 par stock. But if a 100% stock dividend is declared instead, the 200,000 shares would remain at $100 par each, and it would be necessary to transfer $10 million, or $100 for each of the new 100,000 shares, from the surplus to the capital account.

If, however, this surplus of $10 million also existed in the case of the split-up, the position of the investor, as regards earnings and asset value per share, would be the same in both cases, since his new stock would reflect the earning power and asset value of the surplus, whether or not the latter was capitalized. Thus, the difference between a split-up and a stock dividend, from this standpoint, is largely a matter of accounting. In the case of a stock dividend, the old dividend rate is usually maintained, whereas in a split-up, the dividend rate is usually reduced in proportion.
See SPIN-OFF, SPLIT-OFF.

SPONSOR The banking house (the company's banker, the original underwriters, etc.) that has an interest in the price at which a particular issue sells. Speculators speak of a stock as having good or bad sponsorship in accordance with its market behavior.

Few listed stocks are so friendless as to be without a godfather. Virtually every important issue is sponsored by a group (investment banking house, investment group, brokers, or dealers) interested in the stock. Sponsorship varies in financial power, but is designed to protect the stock against neglect or inactivity in order to maintain a price in consonance with its warranted value. The sponsors are in close touch with the company's progress and normally are assisted in their efforts by cooperation of the issuer in policies and publicity.

Active sponsorship thus gives rise to support points on declines and resistance points on advances. The sponsors have in mind a minimum price at which their stock should sell under a given set of market conditions and are prepared to purchase at such a price should it drop thereto. The support points are usually provisional, since market conditions may become unfavorable, and it is a fundamental rule of finance not to peg a price, regardless of the resources of the supporters, when conditions become adverse. Should large quantities of the stock come on the market, the original support level is dropped to a lower point, and under circumstances of serious financial stress, as in a major decline, support may be entirely abandoned.

SPOT An adjective used in connection with foreign exchange and commodities, e.g., grains, cotton, sugar, coffee, etc., indicating trading for immediate, as distinguished from future, delivery. In grain trading, the spot price is called the cash price. Most commodity exchanges maintain spot markets in addition to FUTURES trading.

SPOT CASH Immediate cash available or given for a purchase involving immediate delivery.

SPOT PRICE Cash price; a price quoted for commodities, including foreign exchange, that are ready for immediate delivery for cash, as distinguished from the price quoted for futures, i.e., commodities for future delivery.

SPOT SALE A sale in which cash is paid for immediate delivery, as distinguished from a future sale.

SPOTTED Describes stock market prices when a few securities advance or decline, while the majority remain stationary. The securities that are conspicuous for resisting the trend, or that show a counter movement, are called market spots.
See HARD SPOT, SOFT SPOT.

SPOTTY See SPOTTED.

SPREAD This term has five meanings.

1. The difference between the bid and asked prices of a security. This difference may be "narrow" or "wide," depending upon the supply and demand of the particular issue and the activity of its market.
   See QUOTATIONS.
2. The difference between the public offering price fixed for a new issue and the net proceeds to the issuer, constituting the underwriters' compensation and any expenses of issuance borne by agreement of the issuer. The UNDERWRITING spread is compensation for underwriting risks assumed in the "firm" and "standby" types of underwriting, and is compensation for

ENCYCLOPEDIA OF BANKING AND FINANCE

preparation of the issue for market and for distributional expenses and services.
See SYNDICATE.
3. A combination of a PUT and a CALL by which the purchaser has the privilege of "putting" at one price, or "calling" at another price, the specified security within the contract period. A STRADDLE is similar to a spread except that the put and call prices are the same.
4. In commodity FUTURES trading, the difference between two delivery months, whether in the same market or in different markets.
5. In ARBITRAGE operations in foreign exchange, the difference in rates between two markets, which difference is larger than normal.
See ACK SPREAD.

SPREADING Using the difference between two prices to gain an advantage. The term "spread" has various applications: (1) differences between bid and offer prices on a commodity or financial instrument, (2) differences between yields or prices of two cash instruments, (3) difference between the two prices of futures contracts, (4) the profit margin of a dealer in a transaction, (5) the difference between a bid and an asked price of securities. As applied to grain, arbitraging in an attempt to secure a profit by a closing of the spread, or price difference, existing (1) between the future deliveries of the same grain (or other commodity), as, for example, October and May wheat; (2) between the same grain in different markets, as, for example, wheat in Winnipeg and Chicago; and (3) between two grains, e.g., corn and wheat, in the same market. Spreading may also be defined as consisting of the purchase of a futures contract for a certain amount of a particular cereal in a certain position and the simultaneous sale of an identical amount of that or some other cereal in the same or another position.

The relation between nearby and deferred futures within the same market is a most important one and attracts many spreaders who do not care to risk the hazards of intermarket commitments. Broadly speaking, the existence of liberal stocks of grain in terminal markets, particularly when the grades are applicable to delivery on futures contracts, results in carrying charges—a premium for deferred months over nearby.

In the case of position spreading, a certain grain future is bought in one market and sold in another. For example, May wheat is bought in Winnipeg and sold in Chicago simultaneously and in equal amounts. The purpose of this operation is to realize a profit, and the impelling motive is the belief that wheat is relatively cheaper in Winnipeg and dearer in Chicago than it should be, because of conditions that the spreader believes are temporary.

In addition to the spreads mentioned above, there is more or less constant spreading going on among Minneapolis, Kansas City, Duluth, and Chicago all the time. Minneapolis represents a spring wheat market and naturally reflects the supply-and-demand situation in spring wheat territory. Should there be an acute shortage in the spring wheat crop, it is logical to expect that Minneapolis futures will command a premium over Chicago futures.

The functions of the spreader and the economic reasons for his existence are apparent in that his operations serve the purpose of eliminating, or at least modifying, the tendency toward runaway movements of any particular positions, out of line with commercial surroundings. Spreading prevents the development of uncommercial situations, eliminates criticisms of manipulation, and makes it possible to carry on merchandising operations smoothly and economically.

SPURT A sudden and appreciable advance in stock or commodity market prices achieved by a series of fractional movements rather than by jumps of a point or more.

SQUEEZE The condition when short sellers are forced to cover their contracts at a loss because they fear that rising prices will mount higher.

A money squeeze refers to a temporary shortage in the supply of loanable funds accompanied by difficulty in borrowing and the marking-up of interest rates.

STABILIZATION POLICY The goal of stabilization policy is to moderate the business cycle, which means that the economy should operate as close to full employment as possible. Stabilization can be accomplished by increasing either aggregate demand—a demand management policy—or aggregate supply—a supply management policy.

STABILIZED DOLLAR A theoretical dollar having constant purchasing power, so named by Professor Irving Fisher of Yale University in his book entitled *Stabilizing the Dollar*. The theory behind the stabilized or compensated dollar is to convert the present gold standard into a true commodity standard, i.e., to standardize the dollar as a unit of purchasing power. Instead of a gold dollar having a constant weight and varying purchasing power, there would be a gold dollar of constant purchasing power and varying weight.

The proposed method by which this plan would become effective would be to increase the weight of the gold dollar to compensate for its depreciation in purchasing power. The degree of change in purchasing power would be ascertained by a reference to carefully prepared INDEX NUMBERS. Under this plan, gold coins would be relegated to the status of token coins that would entitle the holder to a varying quantity of gold bullion. Appraisals of changes in the value of money would be made quarterly or annually by reference to index numbers.

The chief criticisms directed against the stabilized dollar plan are that the increase in gold is only one of the causes of higher prices; that the plan would destroy the function of price since price fluctuations are guides to production and consumption; that it would not prevent sharp fluctuations from week to week, which are more dangerous than a general trend upward or downward, since in the latter the general scale is maintained; and that administration would be difficult.
See MONEY.

BIBLIOGRAPHY

FISHER, I., and COHRSSEN, H. R. L. *Stabilized Money*, 1934.
OWEN, R. L. *Stabilized Dollars*, 1936.
FINANCIAL ACCOUNTING STANDARDS BOARD. *Standard No. 33. Financial Reporting and Changing Prices*, 1979. Amended and partially superseded.
———. *Standard No. 82. Financial Reporting and Changing Prices: Elimination of Certain Disclosures*, 1984.

STAGFLATION A combination term, derived from the prevalence of STAGNATION (slow or no economic growth in "real" [inflation-adjusted] economic growth) accompanied by INFLATION (rising prices).

The COUNCIL OF ECONOMIC ADVISERS in its 1982 *Report* states that while the period from 1959 to 1973 witnessed average annual growth rates in real gross national product (GNP) of 4%, the rate from 1973 to 1979 was only 2.8%. "The irony of the 1970s was that the attempt to trade inflation for employment resulted in more inflation and rising unemployment. This period was characterized by relatively high unemployment rates and high rates of inflation, a phenomenon often called 'stagflation'." Government fiscal policy and monetary policy appeared to be unable to reduce inflation without, sooner or later, increasing inflation. This led many to argue that a permanent reduction in the rate of inflation brings about a permanent rise in the unemployment rate, the famous tradeoff implied by the "Phillips Curve" (developed by the English economist A. W. Phillips, based on his study of English unemployment and rate of change in wage rates in the United Kingdom for the years 1862-1957). The tradeoff would be the acceptance of some acceptable rate of inflation in consideration of lower unemployment.

But the Council of Economic Advisers (1982 *Report*) shows that there is no reason to expect a systematic association between the average unemployment rate and the average rate of price-level change, and that none is found in the data (in the U.S.) when one considers periods of several years or longer. "The failure of previous policymakers to accept this conclusion is one of the principal reasons we have had a decade of stagflation," according to the council.

STAGNATION The condition on a stock exchange, or in general business, when volume is low and trading inactive.

In the late 1930s, the "stagnation thesis" in economics, propounded by Prof. A. H. Hansen, pointed to various factors reducing private investment over the long term: the increase in saving as income expanded; the decline in rate of population growth; the absence of new, heavy, capital-using industries, such as the railroads or electric light and power industries; and the passing of the "frontier." Since private investment therefore would fall short of the level of investment necessary for maintaining full employment, the thesis held that government investment had to supply the secular deficiency. The stagnation thesis has been refuted by subsequent developments: consumption spending has been stimulated by rising standards of living and the expansion of consumer credit; population growth has accelerated; substantial private and public research and development have created increased investment requirements in such fields as atomic energy, automation, electronics, and a host of "growth industries"; and although the physical frontier disappeared in the last century, there are many "technological frontiers."

STAGs   Sterling transferable accruing government securities.
See FINANCIAL INSTRUMENTS: RECENT INNOVATIONS.

STALE CHECK   Under Section 4-404, Uniform Commercial Code, a bank is under no obligation to a customer having a checking account to pay a CHECK, other than a certified check, that is presented more than six months after its date. However, although the bank is not required to do so, "it may charge its customer's account for a payment made thereafter in good faith" (Sec. 4-404, UCC).

A check must be presented for payment within a reasonable time after its date of issuance. The UCC (Sec. 3-503(2)) provides that a "reasonable time" for presentment is determined by the nature of the instrument, any usage of banking or trade, and the facts of the particular case; the UCC then sets up two presumptions as to "reasonable time" in the case of uncertified checks drawn and payable within the U.S.: as to the drawer, 30 days after date of the check or date of issuance (whichever later); as to the endorser, 7 days after his endorsement.

STAMP TAX   Federal stamp taxes are levied on a variety of transactions, including those involving stock and bond issue and transfer, deeds (real estate conveyances), playing cards, foreign insurance policies, and silver bullion.
See STOCK TRANSFER TAX.

STAMPED SECURITY   A bond or stock that has been stamped at some time subsequent to the original issuing date to show some change in its status—a new condition to which it is subject or a privilege to which it is entitled. It implies an addendum to the original agreement for the purpose of reinforcing the security or otherwise. An EXTENDED BOND is very often stamped.

Sometimes the term is used to apply to securities that are subject to a stamp tax and on which such tax has been paid.

STANDARD   A criterion or norm; a level of excellence or attainment considered a goal or measure of adequacy. Standards provide several important economic functions:

1. *Information:* verified data, terminology, test and measurement methods for evaluating and quantifying product attributes.
2. *Compatibility:* properties that a product should have in order to be compatible with a complementary product or with other components within a system.
3. *Variety reduction:* limitations on the range or number of allowable levels of product characteristics, such as physical dimensions.
4. *Quality:* specification of an acceptable level of product performance along one or more dimensions including reliability, durability, efficiency, safety and environmental impact.

Accounting literature has described a standard cost as a yardstick; a benchmark; an index of waste or potential savings; a gauge. In this sense, a standard is an established measurement that serves as a reference in computing deviations from a norm. Generally, a standard cost is a cost that should be attained under an assumed set of conditions. The assumed set of conditions may reflect an ideal standard, a past performance standard, or an attainable good performance standard.

STANDARD & POOR'S CORPORATION   The largest "statistical service" organization in the U.S. in the securities field, representing a merger of the Standard Statistics Company and Poor's Publishing Company and, in 1960, the acquisition of some of the services of the Fitch Publishing Company. The many services provided are summarized in MANUALS.

STANDARD BULLION   Gold or silver bullion having precisely the same composition as gold or silver coins, i.e., bullion ready for COINAGE without refining. Standard bullion consists of 900 parts of pure gold or silver and 100 parts of copper alloy, i.e., gold or silver nine-tenths fine. The U.S. mints manufactured gold issue bars in 400-troy-ounce sizes, and silver issue bars in 1,000-troy-ounce sizes. (Gold and silver commercial bars are issued in miscellaneous sizes.) The seven active member countries of the Gold Pool have neither sold gold in private gold markets nor bought gold in the same since their agreement of March 17, 1968.
See MINT.

STANDARD INDUSTRIAL CLASSIFICATION (SIC)
Industry groupings established by the Bureau of the Census within the Department of Commerce for classifying production activity. The SIC is the statistical classification standard supporting all establishment-based federal economic statistics classified by industry. The classification extends to all fields of economic activities and defines industries according to the composition and structure of the economy. It is revised periodically.

The SIC facilitates the collection, tabulation, presentation, and analysis of data relating to establishments. It also promotes uniformity and comparability in the presentation of statistical data collected by various agencies of the United States government, state agencies, trade associations, and private research organizations.

Two-Digit SIC Industries within Manufacturing Sector

20: Food and kindred products
21: Tobacco manufactures
22: Textile mill products
23: Apparel and other textile products
24: Lumber and wood products
25: Furniture and fixtures
26: Paper and allied products
27: Printing and publishing
28: Chemicals and allied products
29: Petroleum and coal products
30: Rubber and misc. plastic products
31: Leather and leather products
32: Stone, clay, and glass products
33: Primary metal industries
34: Fabricated metal industries
35: Machinery, except electrical
36: Electric and electronic equipment
37: Transportation and related products
38: Instruments and related products
39: Miscellaneous manufacturing

Source: Department of Commerce.

An establishment is defined as "an economic unit, generally at a single physical location, where business is conducted or where services or industrial operations are performed." The SIC covers the following fields of economic activity: agriculture, forestry, fishing, hunting, and trapping; mining; construction; manufacturing; transportation, communications, electric, gas, and sanitary services; wholesale trade; retail trade; finance, insurance, and real estate; personal, business, professional, repair, recreation, and other services; and public administration. For example, within the manufacturing sector there are 20 major industrial groups, each coded by a two-digit classification number ranging from 20 through 39. These industry groups are referred as two-digit SIC groups. These industries are listed in the appended table. Within each two-digit SIC category there are a series of three-digit SIC industries corresponding to more finely defined product categories. For example, SIC 371 is motor vehicles and equipment within SIC 37. SIC categories go to the seven-digit level. SIC 3711321 is fire department vehicles.

Division H, finance, insurance, and real estate, includes banking and banking-related activities:

STANDARD MONEY

Major Group 60 Depository institutions

This group includes institutions that are engaged in deposit banking or closely related functions, including fiduciary activities:

601 CENTRAL RESERVE DEPOSITORY INSTITUTIONS
    6011 Federal Reserve banks
    6019 Central reserve depository institutions, not elsewhere classified

602 COMMERCIAL BANKS
    6021 Commercial banks and trust companies (accepting deposits) chartered under the National Bank Act. Trust companies engaged in fiduciary business, but not regularly engaged in deposit banking, are classified in Industry 6091.
    6022 State commercial banks
    6029 Commercial banks, not elsewhere classified

603 SAVINGS INSTITUTIONS
    6035 Savings institutions, federally chartered
    6036 Savings institutions, not federally chartered

606 CREDIT UNIONS
    6061 Credit unions, federally chartered
    6062 Credit unions, not federally chartered

608 FOREIGN BANKING AND BRANCHES AND AGENCIES OF FOREIGN BANKS
    6081 Branches and agencies of foreign banks
    6082 Foreign trade and international banking institutions

609 FUNCTIONS RELATED TO DEPOSITORY BANKING
    6091 Nondeposit trust facilities
    6099 Functions related to depository banking, not else where classified
        Automated clearing house
        Check cashing agencies
        Clearing house associations: bank or check
        Deposit brokers
        Electronic funds transfer networks
        Escrow institutions other than real estate
        Fiduciary agencies other than real estate or trust
        Foreign currency exchanges
        Money order issuance
        Regional clearing house associations
        Representative offices of foreign banks, excluding agents and branches
        Safe deposit companies
        Tax certificate sale and redemption agencies
        Traveler's check issuance

Major Group 61 Nondepository credit institutions
Major Group 62 Security and commodity brokers, dealers, exchanges, and services
Major Group 63 Insurance carriers
Major Group 64 Insurance agents, brokers, and service
Major Group 64 Real estate

Major Group 67 Holding and other investment offices

611 FEDERAL AND FEDERALLY SPONSORED CREDIT AGENCIES
    6111 Federal and federally-sponsored credit agencies
        Banks for cooperatives
        Commodity Credit Corporation
        Export-Import Bank
        Farmers Home Administration
        Federal Home Loan Mortgage Corporation
        Federal Intermediate Credit Bank
        Federal Land banks
        Federal National Mortgage Association
        Government National Mortgage Association
        National Consumer Cooperative Bank
        Rural Electrification Administration
        Student Loan Marketing Association
        Synthetic Fuels Corporation

614 PERSONAL CREDIT INSTITUTIONS
    6141 Personal credit institutions
        Automobile loans
        Consumer finance companies
        Financing of automobiles, furniture, appliances, personal airplanes, etc.
        Industrial loan "banks," not engaged in deposit banking
        Industrial loan companies, not engaged in deposit banking
        Installment sales finance, other than banks
        Loan companies, small, licensed
        Loan societies, remedial
        Morris plans not engaged in deposit banking
        Mutual benefit associations
        Personal finance companies, small loan, licensed

615 BUSINESS CREDIT INSTITUTIONS
    6153 Short-term business credit institutions, except agricultural
        Business credit institutions, short-term
        Credit card service, collection by central agency
        Direct working capital financing
        Factors of commercial paper
        Financing of dealers by motor vehicle manufacturers' organizations
        Installment notes, buying of
        Installment paper dealer
        Mercantile financing
        Purchasers of accounts receivable and commercial paper
        Trust deeds, purchase and sale of
        Working capital financing
    6159 Miscellaneous business credit institutions
        Agricultural loan companies
        Automobile finance leasing
        Credit institutions, agricultural
        Farm mortgage companies
        Financing leasing of equipment and vehicles
        General and industrial loan institutions
        Intermediate investment "banks"
        Investment companies, small business
        Livestock loan companies
        Loan institutions, general and industrial
        Machinery and equipment finance leasing
        Pri-mutuel totalizator equipment finance leasing and financing
        Production credit association, agricultural
        Truck finance leasing

616 MORTGAGE BANKERS AND BROKERS
    6162 Mortgage bankers and loan correspondents
        Bond and mortgage companies
        Loan correspondents
        Mortgage bankers
        Mortgage brokers, using own money
        Mortgage companies, urban
    6163 Loan brokers
        Agents, farm or business loan
        Brokers, farm or business loan
        Loan agents
        Loan brokers
        Mortgage brokers arranging for loans but using money of others

BIBLIOGRAPHY

OFFICE OF MANAGEMENT AND BUDGET, *The Standard Industrial Classification of Industries*, 1987.

STANDARD MONEY The money selected by a government to serve as the basis of its currency system. Standard money has three fundamental characteristics: it is freely coined by the government mint for private citizens without limitation as to quantity; it has full and unqualified legal tender value in payment of all debts; and it has full bullion value, i.e., the metal or bullion value is identical with the coin value (except in countries that charge seigniorage).

Gold is the standard money of the leading commercial nations, although silver is still used by China, India, and a few other countries.

Under BIMETALLISM, the coins manufactured from two metals, usually gold and silver, circulate concurrently as standard money. Bimetallism has been abandoned by all the countries that have tried the experiment.

See GOLD STANDARD, MONETARY UNIT, STANDARD OF VALUE.

STANDARD OF VALUE One of the basic functions of money; a common denominator or yardstick for determining valuation of another commodity or service that may be commanded in exchange. In the absence of a money system of valuation, every two commodities, etc., would have a unique ratio of exchange (price), and there would be no uniform pricing system because no commodity would be serving as *the* standard of value. This disadvantage of barter and the necessity for a double coincidence of demand are obviated by declaring (by monetary statute) a standard unit of value, with its multiples and fractions of denominations, to serve as money, i.e., an exchange medium of general acceptability.

In the U.S., the dollar is the standard unit of value, declared by monetary statute which also defines the type of monetary standard. Since the GOLD RESERVE ACT OF 1934, the U.S. has been on a restricted gold bullion standard (monetary gold is completely nationalized domestically and there is no domestic redemption into gold, but internationally the dollar is on a restricted bullion basis).

See GOLD STANDARD, MONETARY UNIT, STANDARD MONEY, STORE OF VALUE.

STANDARD OF WEIGHT AND FINENESS See PRESENT STANDARD OF WEIGHT AND FINENESS.

STANDARD STOCKS Tested or seasoned stocks; stocks of well-known companies having large assets, demonstrated earning power, a long dividend record, and a skillful and conservative management; stocks whose values, though influenced by current earnings, are relatively stable, being subject to only moderate fluctuations.

STANDARDS YEARBOOK See NATIONAL BUREAU OF STANDARDS.

STANDBY LETTER OF CREDIT A contractual arrangement guaranteeing financial or economic performance involving three parties—the "issuer" (bank), the "account party" (the bank customer), and the "beneficiary." The bank guarantees that the account party will perform on a contract between the account party and the beneficiary. The effect is to substitute the bank's liability for the account party's liability. The account party compensates the bank for the risk. The standby letter of credit contract typically includes provisions that allow the bank to (1) require the account party to deposit funds to cover anticipated payments the bank must make under the arrangement, (2) debit the account party's account to cover disbursements, (3) require collateral during the term of the arrangement, and (4) book any unreimbursed balance as a loan at interest and on terms set by the bank.

Standby letters of credit have played a significant role in bank failures. The Penn Square National bank in 1982 was such a case. Standby letters can increase bank risk materially. Outstanding standby letters grew from $80.8 billion in June 1982 to $153.2 billion in June 1985—a 90% increase. Most of the growth occurred at the 25 largest banks, which recorded more than a $40 billion increase in outstanding standby letters during the same period, according to an article in *Economic Review*.

The traditional commercial letter of credit is typically used to finance the shipment and storage of goods. Currently the standby letter of credit is being used for many additional purposes. The current standby letter is payable upon presentation of evidence of default or nonperformance by the account party. Such letters typically expire without being used. It is estimated that approximately one half of banks' standby letters back debt obligations.

Surety and insurance companies as well as other specialized providers offer guarantees as credit risk coverage (repayment of principal and interest). The expansion of direct financing markets has contributed to this growth. Inflation and deflation, resulting in volatility in asset prices and returns on investment, have also contributed to the expansion of such entities into this market. Banks that provide standby letters of credit to customers typically have lending and deposit relationships with these customers, thus giving them an advantage over the nonbank providers. In the late 1980s, fees ranged from 25 to 50 basis points on the outstanding amount; fees on longer-term and lower-quality credits ranged from 125 to 150 basic points or more, depending on the risk. Banks should consider portfolio diversification as a method for managing the credit risk involved in standby letters of credit and place limitations on the growth of standby letters.

BIBLIOGRAPHY

BENNETT, BARBARA. "Off Balance sheet Risk in Banking: The Case of Standby Letters of Credit", *Economic Review*, Winter 1986, Federal Reserve Bank of San Francisco.

STANDSTILL CREDITS Short-term bank credits tied up in German paper under the "Standstill Agreements" effected by Germany with banking creditors in the United States, England, and other countries following the collapse of German credit beginning in 1930. These foreign banking investors had been attracted to the German short-term paper by the relatively high interest rates. Under the Standstill Agreements, principal payments and lowered interest rates were provided for, but despite such collections over extended periods, most U.S. banks found such German credits an additional source of chargeoffs.

STARS Short-term auction rate cumulative preferred stock.
See FINANCIAL INSTRUMENTS: RECENT INNOVATIONS.

STATE BANK A bank organized under a charter granted by one of the states, as distinguished from trust companies and savings banks, which, although similarly organized under state laws, are authorized as a primarily different type or specialized business; and as distinguished from national banks, which are organized under charters issued by the Comptroller of the Currency. State banks, like national banks, are organized primarily to conduct a general banking business, and together these institutions constitute the class of banks generally known as commercial banks. Many institutions operating under trust charters, however, have diversified business to include commercial banking and thus have come to be included under the commercial category. In turn, many commercial banks have diversified operations to include trust and savings functions.

State banking laws in the older states antedated the National Bank Act, enacted originally in 1863, and thus served as the model in various respects for the act. In turn, the National Bank Act influenced state banking legislation subsequently, both in new states and in amendments of the laws of the older states. The "dual" banking system has competed to a certain extent, in organizational and operating respects, with the state requirements.

When state banks voluntarily join the Federal Reserve System, they must submit, however, to the same limitations and conditions with respect to the purchase, sale, underwriting, and holding of investment securities and stock as are applicable to national banks; and although a state bank upon becoming a member of the Federal Reserve System retains its full charter and statutory rights as a state bank or trust company, no Federal Reserve bank is permitted to discount for any state bank or trust company paper of any one borrower who is liable for borrowed money in an amount greater than that permitted for a national bank.

A condition of membership in the Federal Reserve System, to which national banks must belong, is the acceptance of checks drawn upon them at par. State banks, if not members of the Federal Reserve System, are not required to accept checks at par.

STATE BANK EXAMINERS See BANK EXAMINERS.

STATE BANKING DEPARTMENT The department in each state charged with the execution of the laws relating to the various types of banking institutions located in and chartered by the state. (The actual title of the department varies in some states.) In most states, including New York, the chief officer of this department, usually appointed by the governor, is called the superintendent of banks. In other states he is known by various titles, e.g., "commissioner of banking" (Massachusetts), "auditor" (Illinois), "commissioner of banking and insurance" (New Jersey).

The superintendent or head of the banking department is under

STATE BANK OF INDIA

bond and is authorized to appoint such deputies, examiners, and clerks as may be necessary to carry out the duties imposed upon him. The principal duties of the department are to examine all banks chartered by the state as often as required by law (usually twice a year), to pass upon applications for charters from petitioning organizers, and to terminate, liquidate, and distribute the assets of any bank that may become bankrupt, as prescribed by law. The expenses of the department are usually defrayed by assessments upon the banking institutions examined.

STATE BANK OF INDIA   The bank that succeeded the IMPERIAL BANK OF INDIA. It is not to be confused with the central bank of India—the Reserve Bank of India.

STATE BONDS   A subclassification of civil bonds; bonds that are the obligations of a state, as distinguished from bonds of the federal government. Types of state obligations as to liability are general obligations which are serviced from the general funds of the state, there being no specific pledge of any particular revenues; general obligations which however are payable primarily from specifically pledged particular revenues; and "revenue" type of obligations which are payable only out of specified revenues and are not general obligations, e.g., highway bonds.

Like the federal government, a state, being a sovereign power, cannot be sued without its consent. A state could repudiate its debts, therefore, and an investor would have no legal remedy to enforce payment against the will of the state. In the nineteenth century, various states repudiated their bonds; to this day, for example, an organization of English investors still makes a periodic request for payment on repudiated obligations of certain southern states. Certain states became marginal in finances in the 1929-1932 depression; for example, in 1932, the state of Arkansas was obliged to default on obligations which in subsequent years were lengthened in maturities and on which service was resumed on the extended basis. In modern times, the investment ratings of state obligations generally have improved, reflecting strengthened finances, but variation in quality ratings is still found, reflecting the marginal position of a few states and the particular position of specific issues such as the "revenue" type of obligations.

Several means have been adopted by a number of the states to strengthen their credit and develop a better market for their issues. One means is to place a provision in the obligations that provides consent to suit in case of default. Wherever the state constitution provides this sanction, the "strength of claim" factor in quality ratings is enhanced.

Another means of strengthening credit is to add a provision in obligations to levy certain taxes for the payment of principal and interest, backed in addition by the "full faith and credit" of the state. Since this is a contract and the federal constitution prohibits a state from impairing the obligation of contracts, such a provision is enforceable, thus adding to the "strength of claim."

State finances, however, generally depend heavily upon excise taxes of various kinds—gasoline, motor vehicle, beverage, sales, franchise, tobacco, etc.—as well as license fees and income taxes, and most states rely little on real estate taxes. By contrast, property taxes are the cornerstone of municipal finances. The revenue of most states, therefore, is highly sensitive to the business cycle.

State obligations are exempt from federal income taxes and are generally also exempt from income taxes of the state of issue, but they are not exempt from federal or state estate and inheritance taxes and may be subject to income and other taxes in other states.

STATE COMPTROLLER   A state officer whose responsibility it is to supervise and control the state's fiscal operations. In connection with the banking system, it is usually the state comptroller's function to approve the bond of the superintendent of banks and to designate depositaries for trust funds and moneys paid into court.

STATE, U.S. DEPARTMENT OF   The senior executive department of the U.S. government, established by act of July 27, 1789 (1 Stat. 28) under the name Department of Foreign Affairs and renamed Department of State by act of September 15, 1789 (1 Stat. 68). The secretary of state is the principal official of the department and performs duties enjoined or entrusted to him by the president.

The Department of State advises the president in the formulation and execution of foreign policy. As chief executive, the president has overall responsibility for the foreign policy of the United States. The department's primary objective in the conduct of foreign relations is to promote the long-range security and well-being of the United States. The department determines and analyzes the facts relating to American overseas interests, makes recommendations on policy and future action, and takes the necessary steps to carry out established policy. In so doing, the department engages in continuous consultation with the American public, the Congress, other U.S. departments and agencies, and foreign governments; negotiates treaties and agreements with foreign nations; speaks for the United States in the United Nations and in more than 50 major international organizations in which the United States participates; and represents the United States at more than 800 international conferences annually.

STATED VALUE   In the case of NO PAR VALUE STOCK, the value assigned by resolution of the board of directors of a corporation to each share of the authorized and outstanding stock for capital account purposes. Some states, e.g., Delaware, permit directors in the case of no par value stock to allocate a part of the paid-in capital, received upon subscription to shares, as surplus by assigning a lower value than the subscription price per share as the stated value. In order for no par value stock to be "nonassessable," subscribing purchasers must pay not less than the subscription price and not less than the stated value, in which event the stock becomes fully paid and entitled to limited liability status as far as personal liability of holders is concerned. Another expression for stated value is "declared value."

See WITHOUT PAR VALUE STOCK.

STATEMENT   This term has two applications:

1. A statement of condition, or BALANCE SHEET.
   See BANK STATEMENT.
2. STATEMENT OF ACCOUNT.

STATEMENT ANALYSIS   That part of the process of measuring a credit risk that is determinable through an analytical study of balance sheets and, in particular, comparative balance sheets taken over a period of years. In modern scientific credit granting, a prospective commercial borrower is required to submit financial statements in order that the business and property risks may be measured, to determine whether the property values therein indicated and the profits that such property yield form an adequate basis for securing the proposed loan.

When statements are received by a bank, they are first placed in analysis form on "statement comparison sheets." By comparing one period with another, one can establish the rate of growth or retrogression and changes in separate assets, liabilities, and equities. Actual conclusions are arrived at after a thorough study of the separate items on the statement and a scrutiny of the various balance sheet tests, e.g., current ratio, ratio of current assets to total liabilities, merchandise turnover, account turnover, etc.

See ACCOUNTS RECEIVABLE TURNOVER, CURRENT RATIO, FINANCIAL STATEMENT ANALYSIS, MERCHANDISE TURNOVER RATIOS, RATIO OF CURRENT ASSETS TO TOTAL LIABILITIES, RATIO OF DEBT TO NET WORTH, RATIO OF FIXED ASSETS TO NET WORTH, RATIO OF MERCHANDISE TO RECEIVABLES, RATIO OF NET PROFITS TO NET WORTH.

STATEMENT DEPARTMENT   The department of a bank or other financial institution that has charge of the preparation and forwarding of customers' statements of account. In modern banking, statements of account are rendered either by balancing passbooks or by the statement system, with the latter system nowadays practically universal. Statements are duplicates of the ledger accounts, except that all entries are shown in detail.

In many banks, statements are prepared on billing machines (combination typewriters and adding machines), which are provided with counters or registers that automatically record and print additions and subtractions with resulting balances. The debits are posted to the statements in complete detail, each separate check drawn by the depositor and each charge ticket or other posting medium being listed thereon. Likewise, each credit, whether posted from a deposit slip, letter, credit ticket, or other posting medium, is listed.

The statement department may be considered a part of the individual bookkeeping department. Whenever separate clerks operate the ledgers and statements, it is necessary that they verify their work frequently, and always before statements are forwarded to customers.

See STATEMENT OF ACCOUNT, VOUCHER DEPARTMENT.

STATEMENT OF ACCOUNT A continuous, daily posted record, showing in detail all debits and credits and balance as of the close of the period, usually one month. The statement of account is rendered by a commercial bank, broker, or other business to its customers. These accounts give dates and descriptions and permit the customer to verify the bank's record with his own. If differences occur, they can then be investigated when the customer reports back through the reconcilement blank usually enclosed with the statement.

See RECONCILEMENT OF ACCOUNTS.

STATEMENT OF CASH FLOWS A major financial statement that summarizes the effects of cash on the operating, investing, and financing activities of a company for a period. Cash includes not only cash, but also cash equivalents, such as short-term highly liquid investments. The statement classifies cash receipts and cash payments according to the company's major activities: operating, investing, and financing:

1. Operating activities include all transactions and events that are not investing and financing activities. Such activities include delivering or producing goods for sale and providing services. Such transactions and events enter into the determination of net income.
2. Investing activities include lending and collecting on loans and acquiring and selling investments and productive long-term assets.
3. Financing activities include cash flows relating to liabilities and owners' equity.

Information in a statement of cash flows can help investors, creditors, and others to evaluate the following: the entity's ability to generate future cash flows and to predict the amounts, timing, and uncertainty of future cash flows; the entity's ability to pay dividends and meet obligations; the reasons for the difference between net income and net cash flows from operating activities; the reliability of income numbers; the cash and noncash investing and financing transactions during a period (why assets and liabilities increased or decreased during the period).

The Financial Accounting Standards Board outlined the importance of the statement of cash flows on funds flows, liquidity, and financial flexibility:

Funds Flows. Information about past cash flows or other funds flows may help users of financial statements improve their understanding of the activities of an enterprise, understanding the effects on funds flows of income-generating activities, and evaluate the investing and financing activities of an enterprise. In those and other ways the information may be used as a basis for making assessments of future cash flows associated with operating, investing, and financing activities.

Liquidity. Liquidity is an indication of the "nearness to cash" of the assets and liabilities of an enterprise. Nearness to cash can be regarded as the time that must elapse before assets and liabilities result in cash receipts and payments through normal operations. Information about liquidity may help to identify the relationship between income-generating activities and the related receipts and payments of cash. It also may help to identify the pay-back period on investments in operating assets. A short pay-back period may indicate a high level of financial flexibility.

Financial Flexibility. Financial flexibility is the capacity to adapt to favorable and unfavorable changes in operating conditions. For example, financial flexibility may enable an enterprise to undertake a new investment or to introduce a new product line. Equity investors may be particularly interested in this aspect of financial flexibility. When change has an adverse effect, financial flexibility may be critical to the survival of an enterprise. Declining funds flows from operations and reduced liquidity may signal an impending cash flow problem. The solvency of an enterprise may depend on its financial flexibility. Sources of financial flexibility include the ability to generate additional cash flows by financing, by liquidating assets, and by modifying operations. Information about past funds flows and the liquidity of assets and liabilities may be useful in assessing financial flexibility.

Following is a sample of the direct method of preparing a statement of cash flows:

ABC Company
Statement of Cash Flows
For the year ended December 31, 19XX

Cash flows from operating activities:	
Cash received from customers	$ 76,000
Cash disbursed for operating activities	21,000
Cash provided by operating activities	55,000
Cash flows from investing activities:	
Purchase for plant assets	(8,000)
Proceeds from sale of land	2,000
Cash used by investing activities	(6,000)
Cash flows from financing activities:	
Proceeds of bond issuance	8,000
Payment to retire bonds	(5,500)
Proceeds from issuing capital stock	1,000
Dividends paid	(1,500)
Cash provided by financing activities	1,000
Net increase in cash	$50,000

Useful ratios using data from the statement of cash flows and income, and from the balance sheet can be constructed:

1. Quality of earnings (to support current level of operations and to generate future earnings)
   a) Net income to cash provided by operating income:
   Net income/Cash provided by operating activities
   b) Reinvestment activities:

   Capital investments/Depreciation + Proceeds from sale of assets

   c) Cash flow for adequacy:

   Cash provided by operating activities/Cash investments + Inventory additions + dividends + Debt uses

2. Financial management (reliance on outside financing for growth)
   d) Cash provided by sources
      (a) Cash provided by operating activities/Total sources of cash
      (b) Cash provided by investing activities/Total sources of cash
      (c) Cash provided from financing activities/Total sources of cash
   e) Productivity ratio:

   Cash from operating activities/Capital investments

   f) Cash flow per share of outstanding common stock:

   Net increase in cash/Number of common shares outstanding

3. Mandatory cash flows (primarily interest and repayment of principal)
   a) Long-term debt payment ratio:

   Cash applied to long-term debt/Funds supplied by long-term debt

   b) Total fund sources required for long-term debt:

   Cash applied to long-term debt/Total cash sources

4. Discretionary cash flows (e.g., for dividends, to acquire other companies, to invest in short-term securities)
   a) Discretionary cash uses/Total sources of cash
   b) Individual discretionary use (e.g., dividends)/Total discretionary uses
   c) Dividend payout of cash from operating activities/Cash from operating activities

In a statement of cash flows, cash includes not only currency on hand, but also demand deposits with banks and other financial institutions, and cash equivalents. Cash equivalents are short-term highly liquid investments that are (1) readily convertible to known amounts of cash, and (2) so near their maturity that they present insignificant risk of changes in value because of changes in interest rates. Generally, only investments with original maturities of three months or less to the entity holding the investment qualify as cash equivalents.

In 1989, the Financial Accounting Standards Board issued Statement 104, "Statement of Cash Flows—Net Reporting of Certain Cash Receipts and Cash Payments and Classification of Cash Flows from Hedging Transactions," that amends FASB Statement No. 95. The amendment affects bank reporting. Bankers requested the reconsideration of how certain gross data required under Statement 95 were to be reported by banks. Bankers maintained that certain gross data required under Statement No. 95 were of little value and were difficult and costly to accumulate.

The board concluded that for banks, savings institutions, and credit unions, the cost of providing information about certain gross cash receipts and payments generally exceed the benefit to users of their statements of cash flows. Banks, savings instsitutions, and credit unions are not required to report gross amounts of cash receipts and cash payments for (a) deposits placed with other financial institutions and withdrawals of deposits, (b) time deposits accepted and repayment of deposits, and (c) loans made to customers and principal collections of loans. When those enterprises constitute part of a consolidated enterprise, net amounts of cash receipts and cash payments for deposit or lending activities of those enterprises shall be reported separate from gross amounts of cash receipts and cash payments for other investing and financing activities of the consolidated enterprise.

BIBLIOGRAPHY

Stewart, J. E., and others. "Implementing the New Statement of Cash Flows for Banks." *Bank Accounting and Finance*, Spring, 1988.
Financial Accounting Standards Board. *Standard No. 95. Statement of Cash Flows*, 1987.
FASB *Statement of Financial Accounting Standards No. 95*, "Statement of Cash Flows," 1987.
FASB *Discussion Memorandum*, Reporting Funds Flow, Liquidity, and Financial Flexibility," 1980.

STATEMENT OF CONDITION

A daily record taken from the general ledger representing a trial balance or summary of accounts in the general ledger. This report is especially useful to bank executives in evaluating daily trends in the bank's financial position and operating relationships. The report is also useful in controlling reserve requirements. Periodically, banks are required to provide a formal statement of condition to authorized state or federal banking officials. Condensed statements are often made available in the bank lobby and are published in local and other newspapers.

STATEMENT OF FINANCIAL POSITION

A balance sheet; a report that shows the financial position of an enterprise at a particular moment of time, including the firm's economic resources (assets), economic obligations (liabilities), and the residual claims of owners (owners' equity). Assets are usually shown in the order of their liquidity (nearness to cash) and liabilities in the order of their maturity date.

The balance sheet provides information about the nature and amounts of investments in an enterprise's resources, obligations to enterprise's creditors, and the owners' equity in net enterprise resources. This information provides investors, creditors, and others with a basis for computing rates of return, evaluating the capital structure of the enterprise, and assessing the liquidity and financial flexibility of the enterprise. Limitations of the balance sheet are (1) it does not reflect current values, (2) judgments must be used in allocating costs, and (3) it omits many items that are of financial value and interest to the business but which cannot be recorded objectively.

The balance sheet is usually presented in one of the following formats:

1. Account form: Assets = Liabilities + Owners' Equity
2. Report form: Assets − Liabilities = Owners' Equity

The balance sheet discloses major classes and amounts of an entity's assets as well as major classes and amounts of its financing structure, including liabilities and equity. Major classifications used in a classified statement of financial position include:

1. Assets
   a) Current assets (cash, marketable securities, accounts receivable, inventory, prepaid expenses)
   b) Investments
   c) Property, plant, and equipment
   d) Intangible assets (patents, copyrights, goodwill)
   e) Deferred charges or other assets
2. Liabilities
   a) Current liabilities (accounts payable, notes payable, wages payable, accrued liabilities, unearned revenue)
   b) Long-term liabilities
3. Owners' equity
   a) Capital stock
   b) Paid-in capital in excess of par or stated value
   c) Retained earnings

Working capital is the excess of current assets over current liabilities and can be computed from data shown on the balance sheet. This significant figure is useful in determining the ability of the firm to finance current operations and to meet obligations as they mature. The relationship between current assets and current liabilities is referred to as the current ratio and is a measure of the liquidity of the enterprise.

Balance sheets are usually presented in comparative form. Comparative statements include the current year's statement and statements of one or more of preceding accounting periods. Comparative statements are useful in evaluating and analyzing trends.

Assets and liabilities reported on the balance sheet are measured by different attributes such as historical cost, current (replacement) cost, current market value, net realizable value, and present value of future cash flows, depending upon the nature of the item and the relevance and reliability of the attribute measured. Historical cost is the exchange price of the asset when it was acquired. Current cost is the amount of cash or its equivalent required to obtain the same asset at the balance sheet date. Current market value or exit value is the amount of cash that may be obtained at the balance sheet date from selling the asset in an orderly liquidation. Net realizable value is the amount of cash that can be obtained as a result of a future sale of an asset. Present value is the expected exit value discounted to the balance sheet date.

BIBLIOGRAPHY

SFAC No. 3, *Elements of Financial Statements of Business Enterprises*, (FASB 1981).
SFAC No. 5, *Recognition and Measurement in Financial Statements of Business Enterprises*, (FASB,1984).

STATEMENTS OF FINANCIAL ACCOUNTING CONCEPTS

A series of publications in the Financial Accounting Standards Board's conceptual framework for financial accounting and reporting. The statements set forth objectives and fundamentals that serve as the basis for developing financial accounting and reporting standards. The objectives are intended to identify the goals and purposes of financial reporting. The fundamentals are also intended to describe the underlying concepts of financial accounting that guide the selection of transactions, events, and circumstances to be accounted for, their recognition and measurement, and the means of summarizing and communicating them to interested parties. Taken as a whole, the conceptual framework is a coherent system of interrelated objectives and fundamentals that is expected by the FASB to lead to consistent standards and that prescribes the nature, function, and limits of financial accounting and reporting. Statements of financial accounting concepts do not establish standards prescribing accounting procedures or disclosure practices for particular items or events. Such standards are issued by the board as statements of financial accounting standards.

BIBLIOGRAPHY

FINANCIAL ACCOUNTING STANDARDS BOARD, *Accounting Standards: Conceptual Framework of Accounting Concepts 1-5* (FASB, 1985).

STATEMENTS OF FINANCIAL ACCOUNTING STANDARDS
Official pronouncements of the FINANCIAL ACCOUNTING STANDARDS BOARD considered to be generally accepted accounting principles that are binding in accounting practice. The FASB employs due process procedures in the preparation and review of proposed standards before issuing them.

Rule 203 of the rules of conduct of the AICPA Code of Professional Ethics covers statements of financial accounting standards:

> A member shall not express an opinion that financial statements are presented in conformity with generally accepted accounting principles if such statements contain any departure from an accounting principle promulgated by the body designated by Council... to establish such principles which has a material effect on the statements taken as a whole, unless the member can demonstrate that due to unusual circumstances the financial statements would otherwise have been misleading. In such cases, his report must describe the departure, the approximate effects thereof, if practicable, and the reasons why compliance with the principle would result in a misleading statement.

See ACCOUNTING PRINCIPLES, GENERALLY ACCEPTED ACCOUNTING PRINCIPLES.

BIBLIOGRAPHY

FINANCIAL ACCOUNTING STANDARDS BOARD, *Accounting Standards: Original Pronouncements* (McGraw-Hill, N.Y., most recent edition).

STATEMENT OF RETAINED EARNINGS
A financial statement that reconciles the beginning and ending balances in the retained earnings account. This statement can be presented as a separate statement or in a combined statement of income and retained earnings. Generally accepted accounting principles require that a retained earnings statement be present whenever comparative balance sheets and an income statement are presented. A retained earnings statement reporting a prior-period adjustment would appear as follows:

Beginning retained earnings	$100,000
Deduct: Adjustment for failure to record depreciation a prior year	10,000
Adjusted beginning retained earnings	90,000
Add: Net income for the period	110,000
Deduct: Dividends	20,000
Retained earnings at end of year	$ 90,000

STATE STREET
The street in Boston where most of the financial institutions are located; by extension, financial Boston.

STATISTICAL ANALYSIS
Business managers often employ statistical techniques to deal with decisions they are called upon to make or problems they must solve. Several of these basic statistical techniques will be discussed in this entry.

Arithmetic mean. The arithmetic mean is a measure of the central tendency of a distribution. The arithmetic mean (X) of a series of values of a variable is the sum of the values of the data divided by the number of values:

$$X = \frac{S(x)}{N}$$

where
X = arithmetic mean
S = sum of the value of the data
x = the value of an individual variable
N = the number of the values of the variable x

For example, the weekly sales of five employees are as follows:

Smith	$50,000
Jones	50,000
Red	60,000
Blue	40,000
White	300,000
Total	$500,000

The arithmetic average is $100,000, computed as follows:

$$X = \frac{\$500,000}{5} = \$100,000$$

The value of the arithmetic mean is based on all the observations and is influenced by all the values of the variable. This can give extreme values too much significance. The arithmetic mean can be manipulated algebraically.

Geometric mean. The geometric mean of a series of values is the nth root of the product of the values. The geometric mean is the average to use when rates of change or ratios are being averaged, assuming it is intended to give equal weight to equal rates of change.

Median. The median is the value of the middle item in an array arranged in order of magnitude. In the illustration of weekly sales of five employees, the median is $60,000 (Red's sales). The median is affected by the position of each item in the series; the value of each item is not a factor.

Mode. The value of the variable that occurs most frequently is called the mode. In the illustration of weekly sales of five employees, the mode is $50,000 (Smith and Jones).

Moving average. The moving average of a time series is the arithmetic or weighted average of a number of consecutive points of the series, where the number of data points is chosen to eliminate seasonal effects or irregularities. The marketing manager has compiled data for sales from Janaury through May, which reflect seasonal influences. To predict sales, the manager decides to use a three-month moving average to eliminate the impact of seasonal factors. (A minimum of two years' data should be used if seasonal influences are present.)

	Sales	3-month total	3-month average
January	50,000		
February	60,000	150,000	50,000
March	40,000	120,000	40,000
April	20,000	100,000	33,334
May	40,000		

The moving average is also useful for controlling inventory for low-volume items.

Standard deviation. The standard deviation is used to interpret the variability of a data set. It is a measure of the dispersion (scatter) of the data. About 68% of all values will fall within one standard deviation to either side of the mean; about 95% of all values will fall within two standard deviations to either side of the mean; and 99.73% of all values will fall within three standard deviations to either side of the mean.

Standard error of the mean. The standard error of the mean computes the standard deviation of the distribution of sample means. The "error" refers to sampling error.

Weighted arithmetic mean. A weighted mean is used when the observations have varying degrees of importance or frequency. For example, an employee scores 90% on a six-month evaluation and 80% on an annual evaluation. The manager assigns a weight of 5 and 20 to the evaluations, respectively. The weighted average evaluation would be computed as follows:

Grade	Weight		
	x	w	xw
Six-month evaluation	90	5	450
Final evaluation	80	20	1600
Total		25	2050

The weighted mean (X) is computed as follows:

$$X = \frac{S(xw)}{N} = \frac{2050}{25} = 82$$

See REGRESSION AND CORRELATION ANALYSIS, STATISTICS GLOSSARY.

STATISTICAL DEPARTMENT

In a bank, the ANALYSIS DEPARTMENT; in an investment or brokerage house, the ANALYTICAL DEPARTMENT.

STATISTICS GLOSSARY

Statistical techniques are frequently used in finance, management, and related disciplines. This glossary provides brief definitions of major statistical concepts. Some terms are defined more fully elsewhere in this book.

Analysis of variance A method for testing hypotheses about the means of two or more populations.

Area under the normal curve The proportion of the total frequencies of the normal distribution that falls between two points on the X axis.

Bernoulli trial A replication of an experiment in which one of two mutually exclusive and exhaustive outcomes must occur.

Bias One gives more weight to the facts that support his/her opinion than to conflicting data.

Binomial distribution Discrete probability mass function involving independent, repeated, Bernoulli trials.

Binomial theorem An algebraic method for raising a binomial to any power, invented by Sir Isaac Newton. For example, $(a + b)^2 = a^2 + 2ab + b^2$.

Central limit theorem Regardless of the parent population distribution, as n gets larger, the distribution of the mean will become more and more like a normal distribution.

Chi-square distribution A test used to determine the goodness of fit between a single sample and a theoretical population or to determine whether two attributes are dependent or independent (a test of independence) system.

Classification A process of separating a mass of individual facts or figures into groups on the basis of some similarity. For example, sales can be classified in terms of territory, salesmen, country, etc.

Cluster sampling Selecting randomly from groups, or clusters, having a similar characteristic.

Coefficient of determination Explained amounts of variation in y relative to the total to be explained.

Coefficient of variation A method of comparing amounts of different sizes by reducing them to a comparable percentage basis, e.g., each standard deviation is expressed as a percentage of the mean of the data from which system was computed.

Continuous variables Quantities that can take on any value within a given range.

Control limits Upper and lower bounds set on the key measures of a production process.

Convenience sampling Values taken according to what is convenient (nonprobabilistic sampling).

Correlation The relationship between two or more sets of variables. The more closely two (or more) series are related, the higher the degree of correlation. Nonlinear correlation is a method of measuring correlation when the relationship between two variables is described by a nonlinear regression line. Multiple regression analysis is a method of simultaneously considering the relationship between all variables when two or more independent variables are used in making estimates of the dependent variable. Partial correlation analysis is a method of measuring the net correlation or partial correlation between one independent variable and the dependent variable, eliminating the relationship with the other independent variables in the study.

Correlation coefficient A measure of the population linear association between x and y.

Cyclical variation Pattern repeated over periods of varying lengths, usually longer than a year.

Degree of freedom Number of values in a sample that are "free" to vary when calculating a sample statistic.

Descriptive statistics Methods of arranging, summarizing and conveying the basic characteristics of a set of numbers.

Discrete variables Quantities that occur only at certain values.

Econometrics Methods of statistical analysis of economic models.

Elasticity The percentage change in y for a 1% change in x.

Event A subset of the outcomes of an experiment.

Gauss-Markov theorem Theorem developed by K.F. Gauss and A.A. Markov which states that the least-squares estimators of the intercept and the slope in the population regression line are the best linear unbiased estimators.

Geometric mean The nth root of the product of a series of values. The geometric mean is the average to use when rates of change or ratios are being averaged, and it is intended to give equal weight to equal rates of change.

Irregular variation Unpredictable or random fluctuation.

Index number A ratio of two numbers expressed as a percentage.

$$\text{Index number} = 100 \times \frac{\text{Value in period } i}{\text{Value in base period}}$$

Judgment sampling Primary consideration is the judgment of the person in charge; nonprobabilistic sampling.

Kurtosis A measure of the shape of a distribution, indicating its degree of flatness or peakedness.

Laspeyres price index A price index constructed by weighing each price by the quantity consumed in the base year.

Measurement
  Nominal: categorize data by names only.
  Ordinal: scale has the property of order.
  Interval: scale has order plus a constant interval.
  Ratio: scale has order, a constant interval, m plus a unique zero-point that makes the ratio statements meaningful.

Median The middle value in a set of values.

Mode The value that occurs most frequently.

Moving averages A series of averages in which each average is the mean value over a fixed interval of time centered at the midpoint of each interval.

Normal distribution A symmetrical, bell-shaped continuous probability density function characterized by its two parameters, the mean and the variance.

Null hypothesis A statement that is set up to be tested. If the observed facts are inconsistent with this statement, it is considered discredited; otherwise it is tentatively accepted.

Paasche price index A price index constructed by weighing each price by the quantity consumed in year i.

Parameters Numerical characteristics of a population, e.g., its mean, median, a proportion, standard deviation, etc. The value of such a measure computed from a sample is called a statistic.

Percentiles Those values that separate a data set into 100 equal parts.

Population Relevant values in a particular context.

Probability The likelihood of the occurrence of any particular form of an event; a number greater than or equal to 0 and less than or equal to 1 that indicates how likely an event is to occur. If a coin is tossed, one of two events will occur—heads or tails. The probability of a head turning up is: $p = 1/2 = 50\%$

Probability density function A rule describing the height of $f(x)$ for a continuous random variable x.

Quantitative data Facts capable of being expressed numerically.

Quartile The point that has one-fourth of the frequencies smaller and three-fourths larger is the first quartile. The third quartile has one-fourth of the frequencies larger and three-fourths smaller. The second quartile is the medium.

Quota sampling A specified number of values collected (non-probabilistic sampling).

Range The absolute value of the difference between the smallest and the largest amounts.

Rank correlation A method used to analyze a relationship using ranks rather than actual observations.

Sample A subset of a population; a selected portion of the aggregate.

Sampling error The difference between a sample estimate and the

actual value of the population parameter that occurs because a sample is only a part of a population. Nonsampling errors are avoidable.
Seasonal variation Regular, periodic fluctuations repeated over a period of one year.
Secular trend A long-term, steady change that is inherent or structural in its nature. Growth and deterioration are examples of secular trends.
Sequential sampling Sample items not taken simultaneously, but sequentially.
Simple random sampling Every item and every group of items has the same probability of being in the sample.
Skewed distribution Any distribution that is not symmetric.
Standard deviation A measure of dispersion based on the deviation of all the values of the variable from a measure of typical size.
Standard error of the estimate Standard deviation of sample points about the sample regression line.
Statistical inference Making generalizations, predictions, or conclusions about a population based on a sample assumed to have been drawn from that population.
Statistical methods Methods of organizing, summarizing, and analyzing individual facts.
Straight line A straight line is represented by the equation $y = a + bx$. The value of a is the y intercept, or the value of the y variable when $x = 0$. The b value represents the amount that the trend changes for a change of one in the value of x, the slope of the trend line. The x variable represents time and the y variable is the series being classified on the basis of time. Any change in the time unit (x variable) gives the same change in the y value, resulting in a straight line when plotted on an arithmetic chart.
Sum of squares A sum of squared deviations about a mean.
Symmetric distribution A distribution with the same shape on both sides of the median.
Systematic sampling Selection of every kth item, starting from a random point.
t distribution A test of the significance of the sampling error.
Time series Periodic observations of a variable that is a function of time.
Trend Long-term movement in a time series.
Two-tail test A test used to determine whether a sample mean is different from the universe mean. A one-tailed test is used to determine whether a sample mean is larger than the universe, or whether a sample mean is smaller than the universe mean. That is, variation in only one direction is tested.
Type I error Rejecting a hypothesis that is true.
Type II error Accepting an hypothesis that is false.
Utility function A description of the relationship between various dollar amounts and the index used to measure the value to the decision maker.
Variance of x The expectation of the squared deviations of a random variable about its mean.
Weighted arithmetic mean A method of increasing the influence of a particular item on the average by including this item more than once in the total.

See REGRESSION AND CORRELATION ANALYSIS, STATISTICAL ANALYSIS.

BIBLIOGRAPHY

Statistical Publications. U.S. Superintendent of Documents (Subject bibl. 273).

STATISTICAL SERVICES *See* BOND RATINGS; BUSINESS FORECASTING SERVICES; FITCH INVESTORS SERVICE, INC.; MANUALS; MERCANTILE AGENCIES; MOODY'S INVESTORS SERVICE; STANDARD & POOR'S CORPORATION.

STATISTICS Quantitative (numerical) data. Statistical techniques are used in a variety of physical and social sciences as a means of collecting, assembling, analyzing, and presenting numerical data in meaningful visual and analytical forms. Particularly, in the field of business, there has been a proliferation of data in modern times, both governmental and public and both aggregative for the economy as a whole and microeconomic for specific industries and firms. As a result, the principles of statistics and statistical techniques have been increasingly applied to business data, so that they might serve informational, forecasting, and managerial functions.

See STATISTICAL ANALYSIS, STATISTICAL GLOSSARY.

BIBLIOGRAPHY

BERENSON, M. L., et al. *Applied Statistics,* 1988.
JOHNSON, R. R. *Elementary Statistics,* 1988.
VAN MATRE, J., and BILBREATH, G. H. *Statistics for Business and Economics,* 1987.

STATUTE OF FRAUDS Statute requiring that certain contracts must be in writing and signed by the party to be charged. A written contract is evidence that parties to the contract have voluntarily entered into an agreement that has certain and definite provisions. The statute of frauds can be used as a defense in breach of contract lawsuits in that noncompliance with the statute of frauds makes a contract unenforceable. The original statute of frauds was enacted in 1677 in England.

Generally, an agreement to sell land or any interest in land must be in writing. Such agreements include easements, leases longer than one year, mortgages, and contracts to sell real estate. An agreement that cannot be performed within one year from the making of the agreement usually falls within the statute of frauds. Any contract for the completion of a task that can conceivably be completed in one year may be oral. An agreement to answer for the debt or default of another (a contract of guaranty) must be in writing and signed. The statute also covers an agreement made upon consideration of marriage, an agreement by an executor or administrator to answer for debt of a decedent out of assets of the executor, agreement for sale of tangible and intangible goods above a specified amount provided by law, agreements creating in a creditor a nonpossessory security interest in goods, and agreements for sale of securities of any amount.

STATUTE OF LIMITATIONS The time period within which an action may be brought or during which the right must be enforced. Once the period has expired, the cause of action or right is barred from legal remedy. In all jurisdictions, as an incident of the right to sue on a cause of action, there is specified usually a statute of limitations on the action, either substantively (as an integral part of the cause of action itself) or adjectively (procedurally).

The statutes of limitations vary among the states of the United States, as well as among the types of actions. Statutes begin to run from the time the cause of an action accrues—a breach of contract. The running of a statute can be stopped by disability of the plaintiff to sue (e.g., insanity or legal disability) or as a result of the defendant's absence from the jurisdiction. In many states, the time limit is within six years from the date of breach. The time limit for bringing a suit for fraud does not begin to run until the fraud has been discovered or when the crime is committed. Murder is typically not covered by the statute.

For tax purposes, the major applications of the statute of limitation relates to the three-year period in which a tax deficiency may be assessed and the three-year period in which a taxpayer may claim a refund (subject to modifications and extensions).

The following table summarizes the statutes of limitations among the various states on promissory notes, open accounts, and ordinary contracts. Reference, however, should be made to the specific statutes for details pertinent to the particular cause of action.

STEADY In the stock market, denotes that prices generally, or for a certain group of stocks, are firm and show little fluctuation.

STEAGALL COMMODITIES In price support operations under the PARITY program for agricultural commodities, those commodities added by the Steagall Act to the program: hogs, eggs, chickens (certain exceptions), milk, butterfat, flaxseed, soybeans and peanuts for oil, potatoes and cured sweet potatoes, American-Egyptian cotton, turkeys, dry peas, and edible beans of specified varieties. The six basic commodities for price support under the parity program are cotton, wheat, corn, tobacco, rice, and peanuts (used as nuts).

See BASIC COMMODITIES, PARITY INDEX.

STEAMER DATE Formerly used among foreign exchange dealers to denote the time of departure of the next steamship carrying mail to the foreign port in question. The steamer date was important in calculating the probable time required for transmitting a foreign check, bill of exchange, or letter of credit to a given point abroad. Market bills (large bankers bills dealt in between banks)

STEEL

Statutes of Limitations Chart

State	Promissory notes, years	Open accounts, years	Ordinary contracts, years
Alabama	6	3	6 [a]
Alaska	6	6	6 [a]
Arizona	6 [a]	3	3 oral, 6 written [b]
Arkansas	5	3	3 oral, 6 written [a]
California	4 [c]	4	2 oral, 4 written [a]
Colorado	6	6	6 [a,d]
Connecticut	6	6	3 oral, 5 written [a]
Delaware	6	3	4 oral, 6 written [a]
District of Columbia	3	3	6 [a]
Florida	5	3	3 oral, 5 written [a]
Georgia	6	4	4 oral, 6 written [a]
Hawaii	6	6	6 [a]
Idaho	5	4	4 oral, 5 written
Illinois	10	5	5 oral, 10 written [a]
Indiana	10	6	6 oral, 20 written [a,e]
Iowa	10	5	5 oral, 10 written [a]
Kansas	3	3	3 oral, 5 written [a]
Kentucky	15 [f]	5 [g]	5 oral, 15 written [a]
Louisiana	5	3	10
Maine	6 [h]	6	6 [a]
Maryland	3	3	3 [a]
Massachusetts	6 [i]	6	6 [a]
Michigan	6	6	6 [a]
Minnesota	6	6	6 [a]
Mississippi	6	3	3 oral, 6 written [a]
Missouri	10	5	10 [a]
Montana	8	5	5 oral, 8 written [a]
Nebraska	5	4	4 oral, 5 written [a]
Nevada	6	4	4 oral, 6 written [a]
New Hampshire	6	6	6 [a]
New Jersey	6	6	6 [a]
New Mexico	6	4	4 oral, 6 written [a]
New York	6	6	6 [a]
North Carolina	3	32	3 [a]
North Dakota	6	6	6 [a,d]
Ohio	15	6	6 oral, 15 written [a]
Oklahoma	5	3	3 oral, 5 written [j]
Oregon	6	6	6 [a]
Pennsylvania	6	6	6 [a]
Rhode Island	6	6	6 [a]
South Carolina	6	6	6 [a]
South Dakota	6	6	6 [a]
Tennessee	6	6	6 [a]
Texas	4	2	2 oral, 4 written [a]
Utah	6	4	4 oral, 6 written [a]
Vermont	6 [k]	6	6 [a]
Virginia	5	3	3 oral, 5 written [a]
Washington	6	3	3 oral, 6 written [a]
West Virginia	10	5	5 oral, 10 written [a]
Wisconsin	6	6	6 [a]
Wyoming	10	8	8 oral, 10 written [a]

[a] Section 2-725, Uniform Commercial Code, provides 4-year statute of limitations as to sales contracts.
[b] 4 tears on instruments executed outside the state.
[c] On corporation notes.
[d] On contracts affecting real property, 10 years.
[e] On contracts to convey land, 15 years; on contracts for the payment of money, 10 tears.
[f] 5 tears if note is "placed on the footing of a bill of exchange."
[g] On merchant's account 5 years from January 1 next succeeeding the dates of delivery of the articles charged in the account.
[h] 20 years, if attested to by witnesses.
[i] 20 years, if attested to by witness and action brought by original payee or executor or administrator.
[j] 5-year statute of limitations as to sales contracts.
[k] 14 years if note is attested to by witnesses.

were usually payable to the seller on the steamer date. With the speed of communications and transportation achieved in recent decades, "spot" transactions in FOREIGN EXCHANGE in recent times include transactions that in times of slower communication and transportation were accorded the "time rate," for foreign exchange.

STEEL The most important of commercial metals and one of the most important basic industries of the U.S. and other leading industrial nations. To development of the "heavy" steel industry may be credited the expansion in capital goods and manufacturing capacity, the growth of cities, and the development of the railroads, which characterized the country's economic expansion following the turn of the century. Later, with development of the automobile, household appliance, and container industries, "light" steels, such as sheet and strip, assumed importance. In recent years, with the development of product applications and markets for alloy steels, the "age of alloy steels" has been developing.

The American Iron and Steel Institute provided the following data on the steel industry in 1988. During the 1980s, the steel industry was among the top ten largest industries in the United States, in aggregate value of shipments. In tonnage, steel accounts for more than 90% of all metals consumed in the United States. The steel industry in the United States comprises about 300 companies, of which 80 produce raw steel. Steel plants are located in 39 states and about 300 communities throughout the nation. The average number of hourly workers employed in steel production and shipment (exclusive of salaried employees) was 109,800 in 1987, down from 150,900 in 1985. The historic high was reached in 1953, when an average of 544,300 hourly paid workers were employed. The total employment cost per hour worked by an hourly employee during 1985 was $22.81. A record high of $26.29 was attained in November 1982. The employment cost averaged $23.05 in 1987. The steel industry paid $5.9 billion in wages and salaries in 1986, compared with $6.9 billion in 1985. Steel sector profits in 1981 had been $1.7 billion on sales of $43.1 billion. In 1985, losses totaled $1.8 billion on sales of $28.3 billion, and in 1986, an aggregate net loss of $4.2 billion on sales of $24.9 billion.

Raw steel production capability in 1977 was at a high of 160 million net tons. Closing of mills and production facilities since then brought the figure down to 127.9 million tons in 1986 and approximately 111.0 million tons in 1987. Capacity utilization was close to 90% in early 1981; In early 1987, the rate was approximately 71%.

In the recent 20 years, the use of basic oxygen furnaces has risen sharply, representing 59.5% in 1986. Production by open hearth furnaces has declined sharply, while production by the newer electric furnace process rose sharply.

Steel imports totaled 17.1 million tons in 1983 compared with 5.2 million tons in 1987. Since 1982, the developing countries, as a group, have moved ahead of Japan and the European Economic Community to become the leading sources of steel imports. Total demand in the United States has held steady at about 100 million tons a year through the 1980s. There has been essentially no shift away from steel, only a shift from domestic to imported steel. Imports filled more than 35% in 1984, 1985, and 1986.

It is estimated the capital investment was half of what should have been spent to keep the industry even by replacing work-out facilities. Capital expenditures continue to be larger than cash flow generated by steel operations. The amounts spent continue to be far below what the industry should spend to meet its modernization goals.

The 1984 United States program of voluntary restraint agreements under which the U.S. is supposed to induce foreign countries to hold down their shipments of steel to a total of about 20% of the U.S. market did not approach the reduction goals. The program was designed to give the steel industry a five-year breathing space. The program was only modestly successful. It is estimated in 1989 that excess steelmaking capacity in the world is about 200 million tons, roughly one-fifth of the world total and equal to the capacity of the entire Western hemisphere. The American steel industry has asked for enforcement of import-restraint agreements and petitioned the government to penalize imports of steel which are priced with the benefit of subsidies, or dumping, or both. The government has provided a modest sum appropriated for the Keyworth Program proposed by the president's science adviser, which is intended to leapfrog steelmaking technologies at government laboratories.

Recent Trends. The steel industry in the U.S. has had its share of

Crude Steel Production and Consumption: 1975 to 1985
[Production data cover both ingots and steel for castings and exclude wrought (puddled) iron. Consumption data represent apparent consumption (i.e. production plus imports minus exports) and do not take into account changes in stocks.]

Country	Production (mil. metric tons) 1975	1980	1984	1985	Consumption Total (mil. metric tons) 1975	1980	1984	1985	Per capita (kilograms) 1975	1980	1984	1985
World	642.5	699.4	677.1	679.5	NA	NA	NA	NA	NA	NA	NA	NA
United States	105.8[1]	101.5[1]	83.9[1]	80.1[1]	116.8	115.6	113.3	107.3	541	508	479	448
Argentina	2.0	2.6	2.5	2.8	4.2	3.4	2.7	NA	163	120	88	NA
Australia	7.9[2]	7.9[2]	4.6[2]	6.3[2]	6.3	6.1	5.7	5.8	453	414	369	366
Austria	4.1	4.6	4.9	4.7	2.2	2.7	1.9	1.8	284	358	257	235
Bangladesh	.1	.1	.1	.1	.2	.4	.4	.5	2	4	4	5
Belgium	11.6	12.3	11.4	10.8	3.2[3]	3.2[3]	3.6[3]	2.8[3]	314[3]	313[3]	354[3]	275[3]
Brazil	7.8	10.2	10.8	9.1	11.1	14.2	9.3	NA	106	117	70	NA
Bulgaria	2.3	2.6	2.9	2.9	2.2	2.8	2.9	3.0	252	315	323	336
Canada	13.0	15.9	14.7	13.5	13.2	12.9	13.2	11.9	581	538	525	471
China: Mainland	23.9	37.1	43.5	46.8	29.1	43.3	57.9	66.6	31	44	55	63
Czechoslovakia	14.3	15.2	14.8	15.0	10.8	11.2	10.8	11.0	731	729	700	709
East Germany	6.5	7.3	7.6	7.9	9.5	9.8	8.9	9.5	566	583	536	574
France	21.5	23.2	19.0	19.1	19.3	20.0	15.2	14.2	365	372	276	258
Greece	1.0[4]	1.1[4]	.8	1.0	1.3	2.0	1.5	1.6	143	206	149	164
India	7.9	9.4	10.3	11.1	8.4	11.5	NA	NA	14	17	NA	NA
Indonesia	.1	.4	1.0	1.4	1.4	2.3	2.5	2.3	11	16	16	14
Italy	21.8	26.5	24.1	23.9	17.8	26.1	20.9	20.7	321	463	367	362
Japan	102.3	111.4	105.6	105.3	64.7	73.4	68.5	66.7	580	629	571	553
Mexico	5.2	7.0	7.3	7.2	6.1	10.6	8.6	8.3	102	152	113	105
Netherlands	4.8	5.0	3.5	3.4	4.5	4.6	4.3	4.4	332	328	295	305
Nigeria	NA	Z	.2	.3	1.4	2.0	.6	.9	21	24	7	9
North Korea	2.9[4]	5.2[4]	6.5	6.5	2.9	5.9	6.3	8.4	186	326	319	413
Pakistan	NA	NA	NA	NA	.5	.6	.7	.7	8	8	7	7
Philippines	NA	NA	NA	NA	1.0	1.2	.6	.5	24	25	12	9
Poland	14.6	18.6	15.2	15.4	17.8	19.3	15.3	15.2	524	542	416	409
Romania	9.5	13.2	14.4	13.8	9.8	12.1	11.5	10.9	463	545	509	480
South Africa	6.6	9.1	7.8	8.6	7.5[5]	6.6[5]	5.4[5]	NA	259[5]	232[5]	172[5]	NA
South Korea	2.0	5.8	5.1	4.9	1.8	4.9	8.1	NA	52	128	198	NA
Soviet Union	141.3	147.9	154.2	154.7	141.0	NA	NA	NA	554	NA	NA	NA
Spain	11.1	12.6	13.4	14.7	10.9	8.9	6.5	9.9	306	238	170	257
Sweden	5.6	4.2	4.7	4.9	6.3	4.1	3.7	3.2	773	498	441	384
Turkey	1.5	1.7	2.8	3.1	2.7	3.4	5.1	NA	68	77	105	NA
United Kingdom	20.1	11.3	15.1	15.7	21.0	13.8	14.4	14.4	376	246	255	254
Venezuela	.9	1.8	2.8	3.1	2.3	3.0	3.0	3.2	185	199	177	186
Vietnam	NA	NA	NA	NA	.2	.2	.1	.1	4	4	2	1
West Germany	40.4	43.8	39.4	39.2	30.3	33.8	29.9	29.3	489	549	489	481
Yugoslavia	2.9	2.3	2.0	2.1	5.3	5.7	5.0	5.1	248	255	217	221

NA — Not available.
Z — Less than 50,000 metric tons.
[1] Excludes steel for castings made in foundries operated by companies not producing ingots.
[2] Year ending June 30.
[3] Luxembourg included with Belgium.
[4] Data from U.S. Bureau of Mines.
[5] Including Botswana, Lesotho, Namibia, and Swaziland.
Source: Statistical Office of the United Nations, New York, NY, *Statistical Yearbook*. (Copyright.)

severe structural and operating problems during the 1970s and the 1980s, yet optimistic projections for the decade of the 1980s were not lacking.

The Barometer of Trade. In business circles, the conditions in the iron and steel industries—the great basic industries—are regarded as indicative of the conditions that other industries are likely to experience and therefore reflective of general business conditions. "As steel goes, so goes the country" has been a truism accepted as axiomatic among bankers, businesspersons, and analysts. Given the growth in size and diversity of industry considered as a totality in the last two decades, the steel industry is probably not entitled to the barometric value it once had.

The appended table shows crude steel production and consumption 1975 to 1985.

See BUSINESS BAROMETERS, SCRAP.

STEEL ALLOYS Substances, mostly other metals, used in combination with iron to produce the desired type of finished STEEL. The older types of alloys were carbon and manganese; among the newer alloys are nickel, tungsten, vanadium, cobalt, chromium, molybdenum, aluminum, columbium, tantalum, and zirconium. Steel alloys are selected to serve specific purposes, as, for example, to attain increased strength, hardness, and resistance to fatigue, shock, abrasion, heat, rust, corrosion, and stain.

Steel itself is an alloy, being produced from iron and proportions of carbon and manganese. Alloy steel production has become increasingly important; relative to total output of steel ingots and castings, alloy steel output for 1981 rose to 1 ton for every 5.2 tons of steel ingots and castings, compared with 1 ton for every 9.3 tons of steel ingots and castings in 1970. Although "low" alloy steels have been made in the past in open hearths, the modern "high" alloy steels, requiring close control over composition, are made in electric furnaces, which now produce over one-third of total alloy steel production. Alloy steels are regarded as possessing great possibilities for expansion in demand and production that have opened up a new "alloy steel age."

STEPPED TAX-EXEMPT APPRECIATION ON INCOME REALIZATION SECURITIES Zero-coupon bonds for an initial period, after which they are converted to interest-bearing securities.

STERLING A common term for British money of any denomination, whether gold, silver, or bank notes. The British refer to their money as "pounds," "sterling," or "pounds sterling." By extension, this term has assumed a metaphorical meaning indicative of purity or high quality, e.g., "sterling silver," "sterling character," and the like.

See POUND, POUND STERLING.

STERLING AREA According to the INTERNATIONAL MONETARY FUND(IMF), as of June 30, 1981, the only currency whose exchange rate was maintained against the pound sterling was the dalasi (of The Gambia). The IMF further reported that whether or not the pound sterling's exchange rate is rising or falling, the intervention by the United Kingdom's foreign exchange authorities "is limited to small-scale smoothing operations to moderate excessive fluctuations and preserve orderly markets." Exchange controls have been abolished. Banks are allowed to engage in spot and forward exchange transactions in any currency, and they may deal among themselves and with residents and nonresidents in foreign notes and coin at free market rates of exchange. Payments for "invisibles" may be made freely; sterling banknotes may be dispatched to nonresidents against payment in sterling or in any foreign currency. For any type of travel, U.K. residents can obtain on demand from banks and travel agents such foreign exchange as they may require without limitation. Travelers may take out any amount in sterling or foreign currency notes; receipts in foreign currencies on account of invisibles may be retained or may be sold for sterling. There are no restrictions on capital transfers by residents of the U.K. into the beneficial ownership of residents of other countries, and all proceeds from the realization, redemption, or maturity of sterling capital assets (including direct investments) are remittable at the market rate of exchange.

Investments, whether direct or portfolio, may be freely made in the U.K. by nonresidents or abroad by residents. However, cases involving the takeover of existing U.K. companies that by their size or nature constitute a "vital part" of British industry may be subject to consideration under the provisions of the Fair Trading Act of 1973. The government also has powers under the Industry Act of 1975 to prevent or undo undesirable foreign takeovers of important manufacturing undertakings, "but these powers have never been used." There are no restrictions on transactions in sterling or foreign currency securities, which may be exported or imported without formality. Banks may freely accept foreign currency deposits and employ them in their foreign currency business or convert them to sterling (but following the abolition of exchange control, the Bank of England asked the banks to maintain control of their foreign currency exposure, and a more formal system of monitoring banks' open positions against agreed limits was introduced in 1981).

Payments for imports may be made freely; with specified exceptions, most imports are admitted without restriction under an open general import license. Virtually all exports are free of export control, and there are no requirements affecting export proceeds.

Formerly, with exchange control, restrictions on transactions between residents of the U.K. and residents of the "scheduled territories" were not imposed, so that exchange control applied mainly to transactions with residents of countries outside the scheduled territories. Considered and treated as scheduled territories, however, were countries in the "overseas sterling area" (OSA), and currencies of the following OSA countries were pegged to sterling as of 1974: Bangladesh, Barbados, The Gambia, Guyana, India, Ireland, Mauritius, Sierra Leone, Sri Lanka, and Trinidad and Tobago.

STERLING BILLS Bills of exchange payable in British currency, i.e., pounds sterling.

STERLING BONDS Bonds, the principal and interest of which are payable in British currency, i.e., pounds sterling.

STERLING CREDITS Letters of credit, the specifications for which call for drawing bills of exchange payable in pounds sterling.

STERLING EXCHANGE Exchange, i.e., checks and bills, drawn against bank balances on points in Great Britain. Since London is the banking center of Britain and the principal banks maintain head offices there, sterling exchange almost invariably affects balances in London banks. Sterling exchange is therefore practically synonymous with London exchange.

STIFFENED In the stock market, denotes that prices have hardened, i.e., slightly advanced.

STOCK This term has three meanings.

1. In the United States, CAPITAL STOCK; SHARE.
   See ASSENTED SECURITIES, AUTHORIZED CAPITAL STOCK, COMMON STOCK, FULLY PAID STOCK, GUARANTEED STOCKS, INDUSTRIAL STOCKS, INSCRIBED STOCK, MINING SECURITIES, NONASSESSABLE STOCK, PREFERRED STOCK, PUBLIC UTILITY STOCKS, RAILROAD STOCKS, TREASURY STOCK, WATERED STOCK.
2. In Great Britain, debenture bonds, whether issued by a corporation (company) or the government or a civil division thereof. For instance, government and municipal loans are referred to as government or corporation (meaning municipal in England) stock. Company stock is held and transferred in any multiples of one pound and sometimes less, while shares are for fixed denominations.
3. In business usage, goods, merchandise, or finished product; thus, stock of goods.
   See MERCHANDISE TURNOVER.

STOCK ALLOTMENT WARRANT See SUBSCRIPTION WARRANT.

STOCK APPRECIATION RIGHTS A form of incentive compensation for a firm's officers and/or employees, issuable as a part of stock options, which entitles the recipient to receive the appreciation in the market value of the optioned stock between the optioned stock's price as of issuance of the option and the stock's price as of date of exercise. Such appreciation in value may be received wholly in CASH from the issuing corporation, or partly in cash and partly in stock. The cash feature is particularly advantageous for the recipient, inasmuch as he does not have to raise the cash for exercise of the option for the stock; and while the cash received is subject to withholding income tax, there are not any transaction costs associated with the sale of the stock if the recipient chooses to sell the stock to realize the cash proceeds.

On the other hand, from the standpoint of the issuing corporation, stock appreciation rights payable in cash require that the appreciation in value be charged to earnings, which can be an appreciable depressant on reported earnings (APB Opinion No. 25, "Accounting for Stock Issued to Employees").

BIBLIOGRAPHY

"SARs—Type Rights Taxable When Convertible to Cash." *Journal of Taxation*, November, 1988.
WOOD, R. W. "How to Help a Client Choose a Stock or Stock-Related Compensation Plan." *Practical Accountant*, December, 1988.

STOCK ASSESSMENT See ASSESSMENT.

STOCK BILLS Bills of exchange drawn against and accompanied by stocks or investment securities that are deliverable upon payment of such bills. Shipping securities "draft attached" is a customary method of delivery to out-of-town points, in transactions between dealers in securities.

STOCK BROKER See BROKER.

STOCK CERTIFICATE A receipt or certificate of ownership signifying that the person whose name is written thereon is the owner of a certain portion of the capital stock of the designated corporation. The stock certificate is "representative" of the intangible personal property right involved—the stockholder's ownership in the corporation. The extent of ownership is indicated by the ratio of the number of shares held to the total number of shares outstanding; thus, if one owns ten shares in a corporation having an outstanding capital stock of $1 million ($100 par value), one owns 0.001 of the undivided assets. Stock certificates are printed, lithographed, or engraved forms. To guard against fraudulent and forged securities, the principal stock exchanges of the world require securities dealt thereon to be engraved. With this precaution, it is possible for a stock exchange to be sure of the physical genuineness of its securities.

Stock certificates may be divided into two types: simple certificates, which contain a plain statement of ownership, and certificates, which contain a digest of the terms governing the stock. The following are the essentials of a stock certificate.

1. Number of certificate.
2. Number of shares owned.
3. Par value (or without par).
4. Name of issuing corporation.
5. State of incorporation.
6. Total authorized capital stock.
7. Whether common or preferred.
8. Body.
    a. Simple certificate.
        (1) To whom issued (name of stockholder).
        (2) Number of shares issued to the owner.
        (3) How transferable.
    b. Agreement.
        (1) To whom issued (name of stockholder).
        (2) Number of shares owned.
        (3) Whether fully paid and unassessable.
        (4) Voting power.
        (5) If preferred, whether cumulative or noncumulative.
        (6) If preferred, what dividend rate.
        (7) How transferable.
        (8) Disposition of assets in event of dissolution.
9. Signatures of two officers.
10. Corporate seal.
11. Registrar.
12. Transfer agent.
13. On reverse side, blank form of assignment.

See CAPITAL STOCK, COMMON STOCK, PREFERRED STOCK, STOCKHOLDER.

STOCK CLEARING CORPORATION Effective January 1, 1977, the NEW YORK STOCK EXCHANGE merged the clearing operations of its wholly owned subsidiary, Stock Clearing Corporation (SCC), with similar operations of the American Stock Exchange Clearing Corporation and the National Clearing Corporation (NCC), and a new clearing entity, the National Securities Clearing Corporation (NSCC), was formed to operate the clearing systems.

See NEW YORK STOCK EXCHANGE SUBSIDIARIES.

STOCK COMPENSATION PLANS Most corporate compensation packages are either cash or stock. Bonuses are currently a function of both individual performance and corporate profits. Typical bonuses are a fixed percentage of corporate profit or of profits in excess of a specified return on stockholders' equity. Stock awards are assumed to create a positive relationship between the interests of top management and the shareholders. Disadvantages of stock awards include the possibility that top management will focus on short-term profits and/or an improper pattern of risk behavior.

Compensation plans for executives have been classified into three major categories:

1. *Market performance plans* include compensation plans in which the value received by the employee depends solely on the market price, or movements in the market price, of the employer's stock. In the traditional plan, the employee receives the right to purchase a specified number of a company's shares at a specified price over a specified period. In stock appreciation rights (SARs) plans, an employee is entitled to either cash or corporate stock in an amount equal to the excess of the market value of the company's stock over a predetermined price for a stated number of shares.
2. *Enterprise performance plans* are plans in which the value ultimately received by the employee depends solely on company performance. In performance unit plans, the employee is awarded performance units, each unit having a specified dollar value based upon specified performance goals during the performance period (typically three to five years). Such plans are cash plans. Book value plans are similar to performance unit plans only they are related to changes in the book value of a company. Phantom stock plans are awards in units of number of shares of stock. After qualifying for the receipt of the vested units, the executive receives in cash the number of units multiplied by the current market price of the stock.
3. *Combination market—enterprise performance plans* include those in which the value received by the employee depends on both company performance and the market price of the company's stock. These plans are similar to enterprise performance plans except that the award is in stock instead of cash. Junior stock plans and stock options with performance requirements fall under this category.

Various option pricing models have been proposed for management consideration. The minimum value option pricing method is expressed in a mathematical formula. The equation states that the value of a stock option cannot be negative and must be at least equal to the difference between the market value of the underlying stock and the present value (assuming a risk-free discount rate) of the sum of the exercise price and expected dividends during the exercise period. The minimum value of the stock option increases with:

An increase in the market value of the underlying stock.
A decrease in the exercise price.
A decrease in dividends paid by the company.
An increase in the exercise period.
An increase in the risk-free rate of return.

The Black-Scholes option pricing model is more complex but similar to the minimum value option. The Black-Scholes option pricing model takes into consideration probability estimates relating to the future variation of the market price of the underlying stock. According to this model, the riskier the stock, the more valuable the option.

Formula-based plans reduce some of the uncertainty and ambiguity about how performance will be evaluated. However, mechanistic formulas can lead to dysfunctional behavior. As a general rule, a company's incentive program should control for:

1. Increases or decreases in profits caused by accounting conventions instead of operating performance.
2. Increases in profits caused by the failure to adjust for price level changes.
3. Increases in profits resulting from concentrating on short-term rather than long-term performance measures.
4. Actions that maximize divisional performance measures versus overall corporate welfare.

STOCK DIVIDEND A DIVIDEND paid to stockholders in shares of stock of the issuing corporation. Such shares are issued to stockholders of record out of the unissued stock of the corporation, or, if all the stock has been issued, the charter is amended so as to authorize additional capital stock. For example, suppose a company with a single class of capital stock of $1 million issued and outstanding ($2 million authorized) and a surplus (accumulated out of earnings) of $500,000 finds that its earnings have averaged 12% on the outstanding stock for a period of ten years and that current dividends at 6% can in all probability be maintained on an additional issue of $200,000. In such a situation, a stock dividend of 20% may be declared without violating the rules of conservative corporation finance. If a 20% stock dividend is declared, the disbursement will entitle each present stockholder to receive one additional share for every five shares held. A stock dividend involves no payment of cash, but it is frequently advantageous because the psychology of the market is such that the market value of six shares after the stock dividend has been declared will probably be greater than that of five shares previous to the dividend announcement. More persons are able to buy a greater number of shares by reason of the lower price. Furthermore, while the stock dividend involves no cash, it confers upon the stockholders the right to increased dividends, provided the same rate is maintained. From an accounting standpoint, the stock dividend in the above example merely involves a transfer of $200,000 from the surplus account to the capital stock account. The net worth of the corporation is in no way changed, and in this sense a stock dividend is in reality no dividend at all, since the stockholder's equity in the assets of the corporation is no greater than before. There is only a presumption that the stockholder will receive increased dividends.

The new shares issued upon the disbursement of a stock dividend are fully paid, since they are charged against accumulated undivided profits previously earned and are retained by reinvestment in the business. Declaration of a stock dividend by the directors is popularly referred to as "cutting a melon."

In the past, a few corporations have issued small periodic stock dividends (sometimes as frequently as quarterly) in lieu of, or supplementary to, regular cash dividends. This practice has been defended on the ground that the cash was needed for reinvestment in the business. Otherwise, stockholders might be misled as to the true value of such dividends.

From a tax standpoint, whether or not a stock dividend is taxable depends on two factors.

1. If the stockholders' interest in the corporation after receipt of the dividend is different in kind or nature, the dividend is taxable.
2. If there is merely a reshuffling of evidence of ownership, without any actual severance of income available to the stockholders or change in prior ownership, there is no income, and hence the stock dividend is nontaxable.

Accordingly, split-ups and stock dividends in the same class of stock held by the stockholder result in the stockholder's owning the same proportionate interest in the company's assets as before the distribution, and hence are nontaxable. But a distribution that changes the proportionate interest, such as a dividend in common stock issued to holders of preferred stock, is taxable. Taxable also are dividends in stocks owned in other corporations, since these are obviously dividends paid in property owned by the corporation.

Accounting Procedure. The Committee on Accounting Procedure of the American Institute of Certified Public Accountants (*Accounting Research and Terminology Bulletin*, Final Edition, 1961) recommended that the "fair value," instead of merely the par value or stated value, of the stock issued in a stock dividend be transferred from retained earnings ("earned surplus") to the capital stock account in effecting the stock dividend; and that where the purpose of a stock dividend is to reduce the market price per share and the total of the stock dividend is more than 25% of the shares outstanding, the dividend should be properly termed "a split-up effected in the form of a dividend" although it may be effected on the books by transfer from retained earnings to capital stock at the par or stated value, not "fair value." This, it is submitted, is "confusion worse compounded."

Of course both a SPLIT-UP and a stock dividend, when effected, will result in an increase in the number of shares, so that the unit market price of the stock will be reduced. The two types of actions, however, are completely different in impact on the capital stock and surplus accounts. For example, in a 100% stock dividend, for each $100 par share of the present 100,000 shares outstanding, stockholders of record will receive another share. The number of shares doubles, so that with par value remaining the same, capital stock amount rises from $10 million to $20 million; the difference is transferred from retained earnings. By contrast, in a "2 for 1" split-up, stockholders receive two shares of $50 par value for each share of $100 par held. The number of shares doubles, but the dollar amount of the capital stock remains the same ($10 million); the surplus accounts remain unaffected. To call a stock dividend of 100% (in excess of 25%) a split-up is to confuse the basic difference in nature of the two types of actions.

STOCK EXCHANGE ABBREVIATIONS See NEW YORK STOCK EXCHANGE ABBREVIATIONS.

STOCK EXCHANGE BANKS Banks and trust companies in the Wall Street district that habitually lend a part of their credit resources to brokers, syndicates, and investment houses, for financing security transactions, investment purchases, and margin trading. The term "brokers' bank" is particularly applied to those institutions that tend to specialize in such accounts, such as the Continental Bank & Trust Company of New York, which did so for many years up to 1929.

STOCK EXCHANGE BROKER See BROKER.

STOCK EXCHANGE COLLATERAL See COLLATERAL.

STOCK EXCHANGE HOLIDAYS See BANK HOLIDAYS.

STOCK EXCHANGE LOANS Loans made to brokers, syndicates, and investment houses with securities traded on the New York Stock Exchange as collateral.
See BROKERS' LOAN, CALL LOAN, CALL MONEY MARKET.

STOCK EXCHANGE SEAT See NEW YORK STOCK EXCHANGE.

STOCK EXCHANGES Organized markets for the purpose of centralized trading in securities. Exchanges may be incorporated, or voluntary associations of members; in the U.S., the stock exchanges are voluntary associations. Details of organization include a constitution, bylaws, and rules and regulations governing the members and their trading in issues "listed," i.e., admitted by the exchange to be traded in by members pursuant to the listing policy of the exchange. Exchanges themselves do not trade in the listed securities; they merely provide the facilities for trading. Organizationally, income of the exchange is derived from membership dues (initiation fees and annual dues), listing fees (initial and annual), and charges for particular services, such as wires and tickers. The income is used to defray the expenses of organization, principally salaries and wages for fulltime personnel engaged in supervisory or operating duties. Required investment includes that needed for the real estate and the plant and equipment necessary to provide the facilities for members; other assets include the investment of surpluses in earning assets (government and other securities), which provide investment income and a cushion to absorb capital expenditures and any operating deficits pending adjustment in fees.

Stock exchanges are institutionally justified by their function of facilitating marketability in their listed securities by providing the trading facilities and publicity to volume and prices and by requiring the corporations whose shares are listed to observe standards of accounting and reporting, thus enhancing public confidence in the exchange and its listed securities. Mere listing on an exchange does not guarantee high marketability, which is a function of buying and selling interest, but the latter is facilitated by exchange functions. In U.S. practice, stock exchanges are strictly markets of a "secondary" nature, i.e., for securities already issued and outstanding and admitted through the listing process to trading. Exchanges are not involved directly, therefore, in the process of capital formation or in the flotation of new securities or additional issues of existing securities; but indirectly they facilitate financing by the timing and pricing guidance to new issues provided by their markets. To the extent that such markets result in better prices, fairly determined, financing is facilitated and added value is imparted by listing. Ready, continuous markets are naturally preferred by lenders on loans secured by securities, and thus listed securities having such high marketability command greater availability of credit and added collateral value.

Regulation. Prior to 1934, U.S. stock exchanges were not directly regulated by public authority; there was no federal regulation, and the states where stock exchanges were located had blue sky laws but no direct regulation of exchanges. Thus, the stock exchanges were left to their own sense of public responsibility in policing their stock list and trading practices.

The SECURITIES EXCHANGE ACT OF 1934 for the first time brought stock exchanges under public (federal) regulation. It did so by making it unlawful for any broker, dealer, or exchange, directly or indirectly, to make use of the mails or any means or instrumentality of interstate commerce for the purpose of using any facility of an exchange within or subject to the jurisdiction of the United States to effect any transaction in a security, or to report any such transaction, unless such exchange was registered as a national securities exchange with the SECURITIES AND EXCHANGE COMMISSION (SEC) or was exempted from such registration upon application by the exchange because, in the opinion of the commission, by reason of the limited volume of transactions effected on such exchange, it was not practicable and not necessary or appropriate in the public interest or for the protection of investors to require such registration.

Registration involved the filing of a registration statement in the form prescribed by the commission, containing the following agreements, information, and documents.

1. Agreement to comply and to enforce, so far as is within the powers of compliance by the exchange's members, with the provisions of the act and its amendments, and rules and regulations thereunder.

ENCYCLOPEDIA OF BANKING AND FINANCE

Stock Exchanges
N.Y. Stock Exchange Transactions

Year	Yearly volumes Stock shares	Bonds par values
1900	138,981,000	$ 579,293,000
1905	260,569,000	1,026,254,000
1910	163,705,000	634,863,000
1915	172,497,000	961,700,000
1920	227,636,000	3,868,422,000
1925	459,717,623	3,427,042,210
1929	1,124,800,410	2,996,398,000
1930	810,632,546	2,720,301,800
1935	381,635,752	3,339,458,000
1940	207,599,749	1,669,438,000
1950	524,799,621	1,112,425,170
1960	766,693,818	1,346,419,750
1970	2,937,359,448	4,494,864,600
1975	4,693,427,000	5,178,300,000
1980	11,352,294,000	5,190,304,000
1981	11,853,740,659	5,733,071,000
1982	16,458,036,768	7,155,443,000
1983	21,589,576,997	7,572,315,000
1984	23,071,031,447	6,982,291,000
1985	27,510,706,353	9,046,453,000
1986	35,680,016,341	10,475,399,000
1987	47,801,314,120	9,726,244,500

American Stock Exchange Transactions

Year	Yearly volume Stock shares	Bonds [1] princ. amts.
1929	476,140,375	$513,551,000
1930	222,270,065	863,541,000
1940	42,928,337	303,902,000
1945	143,309,392	167,333,000
1950	107,792,340	47,549,000
1960	286,039,982	32,670,000
1970	843,116,260	641,270,000
1980	1,626,072,625	355,723,000
1981	1,343,400,220	301,226,000
1982	1,485,831,536	325,240,000
1983	2,081,270,000	395,190,000
1984	1,545,010,000	371,990,000
1985	2,100,860,000	645,182,000
1986	2,978,540,000	810,264,000
1987	3,505,950,000	686,922,000

[1] Corporate

Source: N.Y. Stock Exchange and American Stock Exchange.

2. Data as to organization, rules of procedure, membership, and such other information as may be prescribed by the commission.
3. Copies of its constitution, articles of incorporation with all amendments, and existing bylaws and rules of the exchange.
4. Agreement to furnish to the commission copies of all amendments to the rules of the exchange "forthwith upon their adoption."

No registration shall be granted or remain in force unless the rules of the exchange include provision for the expulsion, suspension, or disciplining of a member for conduct or proceeding inconsistent with the just and equitable principles of trade and declare that the willful violation of any provisions of the act or regulations thereunder shall be considered conduct or proceeding inconsistent with just and equitable principles of trade.

Basically, the technique of regulation is to oversee self-regulation by the exchanges, operating under their own constitutions, bylaws, and rules considered adequate from a coverage and disciplinary standpoint. The act outlaws misrepresentation, manipulation, and other abusive practices in securities markets so as to promote open, fair, and orderly markets. Every corporation that has securities listed on an exchange must register with the SEC and file annual and other periodic reports disclosing financial and other data needed by the investing public in evaluating the securities—an extension of the "full disclosure" principle also effected by the Securities Act of 1933 for public offerings whether or not listed on an exchange. The act also directed the Board of Governors of the Federal Reserve System to prescribe margin requirements "for the purpose of preventing the excessive use of credit for the purchase or carrying of securities" and specified that short sales be subject to rules and regulations of the SEC, in addition to prohibiting short sales by corporate "insiders" of stock of their corporation, rendering proxy solicitation subject to rules of the SEC, requiring reports on holdings of corporate "insiders," and making recoverable to corporations short-term profits made by insiders in the corporation's stock.

Registered Exchanges. A total of 11 stock exchanges are registered under the Securities Exchange Act as national securities exchanges, as follows.

American Stock Exchange
Boston Stock Exchange
Chicago Board of Options
Chicago Board of Trade
Cincinnati Stock Exchange
Intermountain Stock Exchange
Midwest Stock Exchange
New York Stock Exchange
Pacific Stock Exchange
Philadelphia Stock Exchange
Spokane Stock Exchange

The appended table shows stock and bond volume on the N.Y. Stock Exchange and the American Stock Exchange for the years 1900-1987 amd 1929-1987, respectively.

The regional exchanges, through aggressive solicitation of listings, liberal membership rules, and lower commission charges on "duals," pose a continuing problem to the New York exchanges for maintenance of their predominant position in listings and volume.

Foreign Exchanges. The leading stock exchanges in Canada include the Toronto Stock Exchange, the Montreal Stock Exchange, and the Vancouver Stock Exchange. European stock exchanges have a long history and are to be found in principal cities of Europe.

See BOURSE, LONDON STOCK EXCHANGE, PARIS BOURSE.

National Market System. The Securities Acts Amendments of 1975 mandated the development of a National Securities Market by the Securities and Exchange Commission, which as of May 17, 1982, as a first step ordered the electronic linkage for 30 stocks of the New York Stock Exchange's trading system, which links seven of the stock exchanges, and the NATIONAL ASSOCIATION OF SECURITIES DEALERS AUTOMATIC QUOTATION SYSTEM, which links market makers in the over-the-counter (unlisted) markets. Such linkage, in the SEC's view, would stimulate competition between SPECIALISTS on the stock exchanges and over-the-counter market makers.

In the view of the New York Stock Exchange, its specialist system can hold its own in such competition, but the NYSE cautions that there should be a rule (not provided as yet by the SEC) to prevent internalization (i.e., firms matching buy and sell orders in-house rather than exposing them to the linkage competition).

STOCKHOLDER The legal owner of one or more shares of STOCK in a corporation. By law, the owner of a stock certificate is the person whose name appears on its face and to whom the stock is registered in the books of the company, although the certificate may have been assigned in blank and sold to another person who has not yet transferred the stock into his name and in whom the equitable title is vested.

The ownership of stock entitles the stockholder to four rights: proportionate ownership in the undivided assets of the corporation (*see* STOCK CERTIFICATE); the right to dividends when earned and declared by the board of directors; the right to proportionate control through voting power (unless specifically disallowed by the articles of incorporation or bylaws) and to receive notice of elections and

STOCKHOLDERS MEETING

meetings where voting power may be exercised; and the right to subscribe to additional stock before offerings are made to the general public (preemptive right), unless such preemptive right is specifically negated by the articles of incorporation or does not apply in specified instances, such as stock issued to effect a merger, consolidation, or reorganization or to satisfy conversion or option rights outstanding.

See PREFERRED STOCK, STOCKHOLDERS OF RECORD.

BIBLIOGRAPHY

Barron's National Business and Financial Weekly.
COULSON, D. R. *Profiting from Stock Market Inefficiencies.* Probus Publishing Co., Chicago, IL, 1987.
FEINBERG, P. "The Unlocking of Corporate America." *Pension World*, February, 1989.
Financial Planning: the Magazine for Financial Service Professionals. Financial Services Information Co., Atlanta, GA. Monthly.
Forbes.
HEERWAGEN, P. D. *Investing for Total Return.* Probus Publishing Co., Chicago, IL, 1988.
HIRT, G., and others. *Investor's Desktop Portfolio Planner.* Probus Publishing Co., Chicago, IL, 1988.
Institutional Investor. Institutional Investor, Inc., New York, NY. Monthly.
KNOWLTON, C. "Ready For Your Annual Meeting." *Fortune*, April 24, 1989.
LODERER C., and ZIMMERMANN, H. "Stock Offerings in a Different Institutional Setting: The Swiss Case, 1973-1983." *Journal of Banking and Finance*, September, 1988.
MEYER, W. "Showdown in Delaware: the Battle to Shape Takeover Law." *Institutional Investor*, February, 1989.
Technical Analysis of Stocks and Commodities: the Trader's Magazine. Technical Analysis, Inc., Seattle, WA. Monthly.
Wall Street Journal.

STOCKHOLDERS' MEETING There are various kinds of stockholders' meetings of business corporations: annual, special, extraordinary, etc. Thus, under the New York Business Corporation Law, stockholders' meetings include:

1. Annual meeting for the election of directors and the transaction of such other business as may come before the meeting on a date fixed by or under the bylaws (Sec. 602(b), N.Y. Business Corporation Law).
2. Special meeting called by the board of directors for election of directors. If for one month after the date fixed by or under the bylaws for the annual meeting of shareholders or, if no date has been fixed, for 13 months after formation of the corporation or the last annual meeting, there is a failure to elect a sufficient number of directors to conduct the business of the corporation, the board of directors shall call a special meeting for the election of directors (Sec. 603(a), N.Y. Business Corporation Law).
3. Special meeting called by the stockholders for election of directors. If the preceding special meeting is not called by the board of directors within two weeks after the expiration of the specified period of time, or if it is so called but there is a failure to elect such directors for a period of two months after the expiration of such period, holders of 10% of the shares entitled to vote in an election of directors may in writing demand the call of a special meeting for the election of directors. Such written demand shall specify the date and month for such special meeting for the election of directors, which shall be not less than two nor more than three months from the date of such call. The secretary of the corporation upon receiving the written demand shall promptly give notice of such meeting; if he fails to do so within five business days thereafter, any shareholder signing such demand may give such notice of meeting to be held at the place fixed in the bylaws therefor or, if a place is not so fixed, at the office of the corporation. At any such special meeting on demand of shareholders, the shareholders attending in person or by proxy and entitled to vote at an election of directors shall constitute a quorum for the purpose of electing the directors—but not for the transaction of any other business (Secs. 603(a) and (b), N.Y. Business Corporation Law).
4. Special meeting of stockholders (two-thirds approval of the holders of all outstanding shares entitled to vote thereon is required) to vote on sale, lease, exchange, or other disposition of assets (Sec. 909(a) (3), N.Y. Business Corporation Law).
5. Special meeting of stockholders (two-thirds approval of all outstanding shares entitled to vote thereon is required) to authorize a plan for merger or consolidation (Sec. 903(a)(1)(2) and (b), N.Y. Business Corporation Law).
6. Special meeting of stockholders (two-thirds approval of the holders of all outstanding shares entitled to vote thereon is required) to authorize voluntary, nonjudicial dissolution, unless the certificate of incorporation provides that any shareholder or holders of a specified number or proportion of shares may require the dissolution of the corporation at will or upon the occurrence of a specified event (Secs. 1001 and 1002, N.Y. Business Corporation Law).
7. Special meeting of stockholders to petition for judicial dissolution (by holders of 10% of all outstanding shares entitled to vote thereon, or a lesser proportion if authorized in the certificate of incorporation, who call for the meeting; but a majority of all outstanding shares entitled to vote thereon, or a greater proportion if specified in the certificate of incorporation, shall adopt such a resolution calling for petition to court for judicial dissolution [Sec. 1103, N.Y. Business Corporation Law]) on the grounds that the assets are not sufficient to discharge its liabilities, or that a dissolution is deemed to be beneficial to the shareholders.
8. Special meeting of stockholders to petition to court for judicial dissolution, in case of deadlock among directors or shareholders (Sec. 1104, N.Y. General Business Corporation Law). One or more of the following grounds shall be the basis for such a petition: that directors are so divided respecting the management of the corporation's affairs that the votes required for action by the board cannot be obtained; that the shareholders are so divided that the votes required for the election of directors cannot be obtained; that there is internal dissension and two or more factions of shareholders are so divided that dissolution would be beneficial to the shareholders.
9. Special meeting of stockholders to petition to court for judicial dissolution by resolution of the board of directors, if a majority of the board finds assets insufficient to cover liabilities or that a dissolution will be beneficial to shareholders (Sec. 1102, N.Y. Business Corporation Law).

At the regular annual meetings, annual financial reports of the corporation are customarily presented to stockholders, and questions on operations and finances of the corporation are answered by the management.

The president of the corporation or chairman of the board of directors usually presides as chairman of the meeting; although the stockholders present have the right to elect such chairman of the meeting, they usually elect such a senior officer or director.

STOCKHOLDERS OF RECORD The legal stockholders; stockholders whose names are registered in the stock registry and recorded in the stock ledger of a corporation. A STOCK CERTIFICATE may be assigned in blank and held by another person, lost, or stolen, but the privileges and rights to dividends, etc., still belong to the stockholder of record.

See BOOKS CLOSE.

STOCK INDEX FUTURES TRADING The latest innovation in FUTUREStrading as of 1982—organized futures contract trading based on prices of the selected stock index levels, together with the usual features of commodity futures trading including contract unit, minimum price change, daily price change limit (if any), specified delivery months, minimum customer margins, speculative limits (if any), and maturing contract trading termination and settlement.

With approval of the COMMODITY FUTURES TRADING COMMISSION, the following exchanges began trading in 1982 in stock index futures, based on the indicated selected stock indexes.

Unlike commodity futures, stock index futures call for no delivery of warehouse receipts for the commodity at maturing contract trading termination. Nor do stock index futures call for delivery of securities at final settlement. Basis for settlement is cash, representing the "marking to market" of remaining contracts based on the

Exchange	Stock index
Kansas City Board of Trade	Value Line Composite Index
Chicago Mercantile Exchange	Standard and Poor's Composite 500-Stock Index
New York Futures Exchange	New York Stock Exchange Composite Stock Exchange
Chicago Board of Trade	Major Market Index

level of the selected stock index at the close of trading on the last trading day of the expiring contract month.

Investors, underwriters, and market makers carrying current securities with "long" positions could hedge by the sale of a forward maturity of a stock index future. Such parties having "short" positions could hedge by the purchase of a forward maturity of a stock index future, as could writers of "naked" OPTIONS or buyers of put options.

See HEDGING.

STOCK JOBBER LONDON STOCK EXCHANGE members are of two classes: brokers and jobbers. Each class performs a distinct function, and by the rules of the exchange one is prohibited from performing the role of the other. A broker deals with the public, executing buying and selling orders. A jobber acts as an intermediary between brokers having securities to sell and those having securities to buy. The broker receives a commission from his customer, but the jobber's compensation consists of the difference between his buying and selling price.

STOCK MARKET See AMERICAN STOCK EXCHANGE, LONDON STOCK EXCHANGE, NEW YORK STOCK EXCHANGE, PARIS BOURSE, STOCK EXCHANGES.

BIBLIOGRAPHY

American Stock Exchange Weekly Bulletin. American Stock Exchange, New York, NY.
BASKIN, J. B. "The Development of Corporate Financial Markets in Britain and the United States, 1600-1914." *Business History Review,* Summer, 1988.
BURTON, M. *Random Walk Down Wall Street.* W. W. Norton and Co., Inc., New York, NY, 1985.
Block, F. E. *Security Analysis.* McGraw-Hill Book Co., New York, NY, 1987.
CHEN, NAI-FU, and others. "Economic Forces and the Stock Market." *Journal of Business,* July, 1986.
COMISKEY, E., MULFORD, C., and TURNER, D. "Bank Accounting and Reporting Practices for Interest Rate Swaps." *Bank Accounting and Finance,* Winter 1987-88.
COULSON, D. R. *Profiting from Stock Market Inefficiencies,* 1987.
Daily Stock Price Record. Standard and Poor's Corp., New york, NY. Quarterly.
DAVIS, C. D., and others. *Stock Market Volatility.* Board of Governors of the Federal Reserve System, August, 1987.
Dow-Jones Investor's Handbook. Dow Jones-Irwin, Inc., Homewood, IL. Annual.
Dow Theory Forecasts. Dow Theory Forecasts, Inc., Hammond, IN. Weekly.
Encyclopedia of Stock Market Techniques. Investors Intelligence, Inc., New Rochelle, NY. Looseleaf.
ERDMAN, P. *Paul Erdman's Money Book: An Investor's Guide to Economics and Finance,* 1984.
Financial World.
Forbes.
HUANG, R. D., and JO, H. "Tests of Market Models: Heteroskedasticity or Misspecification?" *Journal of Banking and Finance,* September, 1988.
LORIE, J. H., and others. *The Stock Market: Theories and Evidence.* Dow Jones-Irwin, Inc., Homewood, IL, 1985.
HENDERSON, S., and PRICE J. *Currency and Interest Rate Swaps.* Butterworth Legal Pubs., Stoneham, MA, 1984.
Moody's Handbook of Common Stock. Moody's Investors Service, New York, NY. Quarterly.
National Monthly Stock Summary. National Quotation Bureau, New York, NY. Monthly.

Assignment Form

For value received _____ hereby sell, assign and transfer unto _____
_____ ( ) Shares of the _____
Capital Stock of the _____
standing in _____ name on the books
of said _____
represented by Certificate No. _____
herewith and do hereby irrevocably constitute and appoint
_____ attorney to transfer the said stock on the books of the within named Company with full Power of _____ Substitution in the premises.

Date _____   _____

New York Stock Exchange Fact Book. New York Stock Exchange, New York, NY. Annual.
New York Stock Exchange Statistical Highlights. New York Stock Exchange, New York, NY. Monthly.
PTS F and S Index. Predicasts, Inc., Cleveland, OH. Online data base.
SHAPIRO, M. D. "The Stabilization of the U.S. Economy: Evidence from the Stock Market." *American Economic Review,* December, 1988.
SMITH, A.Y "Global Security Processing: Global Headaches?" *ABA Banking Journal,* March, 1989.
Standard and Pool's Daily Corporation News. Standard and Poor's, New York, NY. Online data base.
Standard and Poor's Stock Reports. Standard and Poor's Corp., New York, NY. Looseleaf.
Stock Market Values and Yields. Prentice Hall, Inc., Paramus, NJ. Annual.
Stock Trader's Almanac. The Hirsch Organization, Inc., Old Tappan, NJ. Annual.
UPDEGRAVE, W. L. "Seven Signals That Help You Answer the Toughest Question of All: When to Sell." *Money,* February, 1989.
WEINSTEIN, M. "Stock Debate: Go Global or Stick with U.S. Shares?" *Futures,* February, 1989.
ZBESKO, J. "Determinants of Performance in the Bull Market." *Journal of Portfolio Management,* Winter, 1988.

STOCK OPTIONS The right to purchase shares of common stock in accordance with an agreement, upon payment of a specified amount. Stock option plans are compensation schemes under which executives are granted options to purchase common stock over an extended option period at a stated price. Nonstatutory stock options are not approved by the IRS Code and do not give special tax advantages to employees. Companies sometimes grant stock appreciation rights (SAR) that allow the employee to receive cash, stock, or a combination of cash and stock based on the difference between a specified amount per share of the stock and the quoted market price per share at some future date.

In compensatory stock option plans, the excess of the market price of the stock over the exercise price is considered the compensatory portion of the plan. This amount is computed on the date that the number of shares an individual employee is entitled to receive and the option or purchase price of the shares is known. This date is referred to as the measurement date. Compensation expense is recorded as the services giving rise to the stock option are rendered.

Where stock appreciation rights are concerned, total compensation expense to be allocated is estimated by the excess of the market value over the designated price. This amount is allocated to expense over the service period.

STOCK POWER An instrument that effects the sale, assignment, and transfer of stock to a designated person and appoints a designated person attorney to transfer the stock on the books of the corporation. Stock certificates usually contain a stock power in blank on their reverse side. The following form is the assignment, separate from the certificate, that is approved by the New York Stock Exchange.

See GOOD DELIVERY.

STOCK PRICE AVERAGES Arithmetic or weighted averages, or INDEX NUMBERS, of selected groups of stocks, designed to afford a single-figure indication of market levels and trends that may be easily charted or cited. The smaller the list of stocks used in the average or index number, the less representative of the market as a whole it is liable to be, because of the constantly shifting leadership of the market. Thus, an average based on a group of high-quality, seasoned industrials is liable at stages of major speculative interest in medium- and lower-grade issues to fail to reflect advances in the latter groups. Accordingly, the larger the number of issues constituting the average, the more diversified representation it is likely to have, and therefore the more likely it is to be reflective of the broad market trend.

Stock price indexes or averages are prepared by a number of financial news publishers and statistical organizations. Among the daily averages currently published are the following.

1. DOW JONES AVERAGES.
2. Standard & Poor's indexes (1941-1943 = 10) for 400 industrials, 20 transportation, 40 utilities, 40 financial, and combined 500 stocks. The 500-stock index is used for the stock index futures of the CHICAGO MERCANTILE EXCHANGE.
3. NEW YORK STOCK EXCHANGE indexes. The (composite) common stock price index is based on the total market value of New York Stock Exchange common stocks, adjusted to eliminate the effects of capitalization changes, new listings, and delistings. The index is based on the price of each stock, weighted by the number of shares listed. The aggregate market (the sum of the individual market values) is expressed relative to the base period aggregate market value (December 31, 1965 = 50). In addition to the composite index, the exchange prepares and publishes the four subgroup indexes: industrials, transportation, utilities, and finance. All indexes are available on a daily basis, with high, low, and last. The basic composite index is available on a weekly basis from January 7, 1939, to May 28, 1964, and daily from that date to the present. The four subgroups are available on a daily basis from December 31, 1965. The NYSE composite index is used by the NEW YORK FUTURES EXCHANGE for its stock index futures.
4. Value Line index. Computed every three minutes by the investment advisory firm of Arnold Bernhard & Co., Inc., the Value Line index is a geometric composite price average of some 1,700 actively traded stocks, indexed to 1961 = 100. Unlike the Standard & Poor's indexes and New York Stock Exchange indexes, the Value Line index is based on a true price average, not weighted by the number of outstanding shares of each issuer. The Value Line composite index is used by the Kansas City Board of Trade for its stock index futures.

See MARKET AVERAGES.

STOCK PURCHASE WARRANT
An "equity privilege" sometimes attached to bonds, debentures, or preferred stocks, but more often separately issued, that entitles the holder to the right to purchase the specified number of shares per warrant of the common stock of the corporation within the exercise period, which may be a limited term (usually long-term, or even perpetual). Such warrants state on their face the terms under which the right to buy the stock may be exercised.

Warrants have become especially popular with traders interested in fast-moving trading media because prevailing market prices for the warrants may be much lower than prevailing market prices for the common stock itself, so that it takes less money to carry a given position in number of warrants, and because the warrants may have higher price appreciation "leverage" than the common stock itself.

To illustrate the preceding point, assume that a given issue of warrants entitles the holder to purchase two shares of common stock for each warrant at $10 per share, and that the common stock itself is selling at $12 per share. The theoretical value of one warrant would be:

Common stock's market price	–	Warrant's exercise price	x	No. of shares per warrant	=	Theoretical value per warrant
12		10		2		4

Now, if the common stock's market price should go up 50% (from 12 to 18), the theoretical value per warrant would rise 300% (from 4 to 16), as follows, or 6.0 times faster.

Common stock's market price	–	Warrant's exercise price	x	No. of shares per warrant	=	Theoretical value per warrant
12		10		2		4

In practice, when the appreciation leverage ratio between the warrants and the common stocks is very high, as in the second situation above, the warrants may command a premium over their basic theoretical value per warrant, which may become smaller or disappear as the warrants-common stock appreciation leverage ratio becomes very low. Thus, if the common stock should reach 50, a further rise of 50% (to 75) would mean merely a 62.5% rise in the theoretical value of the warrants, based on an implied rise (from 80 to 130), or a ratio down to 1.25 times between appreciation percentages of the warrants and the common stock.

From a financing standpoint, warrants at issuance are usually priced at a premium exercise price over the prevailing market price of the common stock, which would seemingly indicate a negative theoretical value; yet the warrants may be salable, depending upon the duration of the privilege to subscribe (the longer the term, all things being equal, the higher the price investors may pay) and upon the outlook for appreciation in the common stock over the term of the warrants. Warrants may be issued separately, as a separate form of financing; they may be attached to bonds, debentures, or preferred stock as a "sweetener"; or they may be issued in a "package" of a given unit of such senior securities plus a given number of warrants, at a given offering price for the package, the warrants in such case being physically separate from the senior security. Unlike the conversion privilege, warrants when exercised serve as a source of proceeds to the issuer company, while leaving the senior security still outstanding and providing its leverage; and like the conversion privilege, warrants as "sweeteners" of senior securities may result in lower interest rates and dividend rate costs on bonds, debentures, or preferred stock. SUBORDINATED DEBENTURES, instead of having a conversion privilege, may have warrants attached or issued physically separately in conjunction therewith, both to achieve a lower interest rate than might otherwise be required and to offset the negative connotation of the subordination feature.

Warrants serve a definite and useful purpose in corporation finance under certain circumstances. In theory, the use of warrants generally implies a willingness on the part of the stockholders of a business to share future increases in profits, if any, with those who furnish additional capital in the form of senior securities in return for a willingness on the part of the latter to accept a lower rate of fixed income than would otherwise be necessary.

The use of warrants is particularly well adapted to situations in which the company is unwilling or unable to pay the rate of interest or dividends that would be necessary on ordinary issues of bonds or preferred stocks, and to untried or unseasoned ventures, the senior securities of which investors are loath to buy unless some speculative privilege attached thereto offers a profit possibility in the event of successful operations.

From the standpoint of the common stockholders as owners of the business, the granting of such warrants to others may be fully justified by the necessity or desirability of raising additional capital on a favorable immediate basis.

See RIGHT, SUBSCRIPTION WARRANT.

STOCK QUOTATIONS
See QUOTATIONS, QUOTATION TICKER.

BIBLIOGRAPHY

PORT, O. "Turning Your Desktop Into a Person Big Board." *Business Week*, March 27, 1989.
Wall Street Journal.

STOCK RATINGS
The convenient expression, by letter grade, of the quality of preferred and common stocks, similar to BOND RATINGS but determined differently—not to be confused with the current market recommendation ("buy," "sell," or "hold").

The Standard & Poor's Corporation's common stock ratings include the following:

A+	Highest
A	High
A-	Above Average
B+	Average
B	Below Average
B-	Low
C	Lowest

Standard & Poor's point of departure is a scoring system based upon earnings and dividend records. The first step is to examine the earnings record of the past eight years. In measurement of earnings stability, a basic score is given for each year in which net per share equals or exceeds that of the preceding year. For any year in which earnings declined, the score is reduced by the percentage of that decline. The average of these eight annual scores, weighted for frequency of earnings declines, becomes Standard & Poor's first "basic earnings index."

This earnings stability index is then multiplied by a growth index, based on the square root of the percentage by which earnings increased between the base year period and the most recent three years. To prevent growth in extreme cases from dominating the rating, the growth factor is topped at 150%.

Scoring for dividend stability and growth is similar, with the principal exception being that a longer period is used and results are weighted for recency. A further weighting is applied for frequency of dividend reductions, because an erratic dividend policy is a matter affecting investment standing. The result is multiplied by a growth factor similar to that for earnings.

When this is completed, the two factors—earnings and dividends—are combined into a single numerical ranking. All the common stocks so graded are then grouped into seven classes. To these, Standard & Poor's has assigned the above-referenced letter grades.

These mathematically determined results are modified in some instances by special considerations. Nonrecurring costs, windfall profits, etc., must sometimes be allowed for. There are certain other exceptions. In the oil industry, for example, so-called cash flow is used rather than final net profit "in order to avoid the distortions that might be caused by differences in accounting practices."

Also, since earnings and dividends of regulated public utilities characteristically are more stable than those of most nonregulated industries, numerous other factors must be considered. Among these are capital structure, amount of depreciation reserves, condition of properties, growth potentialities for individual service areas, the regulatory environment, and the rate of return.

These scorings are not to be confused with bond quality ratings, which are arrived at by a necessarily altogether different approach. Additionally, they must not be used as a substitute for market recommendations; the price of a high-graded stock may at times be so high as to justify its sale, while a low-score stock may be attractively priced for purchase. Rankings based on earnings and dividend record are no substitute for analysis. Nor are they quality ratings in the complete sense of the term. They cannot take into account potential effects of management changes, internal company policies not yet fully reflected in the earnings and dividend record, public relations standing, recent competitive shifts, and a host of other factors that may be relevant to investment status.

An asterisk (*) preceding the ranking denotes a railroad guaranteed stock quality rating based on Standard & Poor's bond rating scale. N.R. (no ranking) may be indicated because of insufficient data, nonrecurring factors, or some other reason.

Quality ratings on preferred stocks are expressed by Standard & Poor's by symbols like those used in bond ratings. They are independent of the bond ratings, however, in the sense that they are not necessarily graduated downward from the ranking accorded the issuing company's debt. They represent a considered judgment of the relative security of dividends and of the prospective yield stability of the stock. The ratings are as follows:

AAA	Prime
AA	High Grade
A	Sound
BBB	Medium Grade
BB	Lower Grade
B	Speculative
C	Submarginal

Summary. Stock ratings are highly convenient tabloidal indications of quality based upon financial risk factors (earnings and dividends), but as Standard & Poor's cautions, they are no substitute for analysis by the individual or institutional investor. The "prudent man" rule as to investing diligence calls for independent analysis and justification data for an investing choice, not merely reliance upon a rating.

See INVESTMENT.

STOCK REGISTRAR A trust company, bank, or individual, authorized to act in a fiduciary capacity, which has been appointed by a corporation to certify that the number of its shares issued does not exceed the authorized amount and to check the work of the transfer agent. The rules of the New York Stock Exchange require that corporations whose stocks are listed thereon maintain separate registrars and transfer agents. The relation between a corporation and its registrar is fixed by contract. In the absence of any law fixing liability, this contract defines the liabilities of the registrar.

In the case of formation of a new corporation or issuance of additional stock, the work of the registrar is to compare the number of shares represented by the certificates with the number authorized and, if there are no irregularities, to register the certificates in its own records and sign its name to each stock certificate. In the case of outstanding shares, it is the registrar's duty to make certain that each new certificate issued by the transfer agent (which may be the corporation itself) is accompanied by a genuine certificate representing the same number of shares to be canceled. In other words, the registrar must see that there is a cancellation for each issuance, placing a "canceled" stamp on old certificates and validating new certificates by means of its signature.

STOCK RIGHTS The privilege attached to a share of common stock to purchase a specified number of shares of common stock or a fractional share. Stock rights indicate the price at which stock can be acquired (the exercise price), the number of shares that may be acquired for each right, and the expiration date. When a corporation issues stock rights to shareholders without compensation, one right is issued for each share. The number of rights required to purchase an additional share depends upon the agreement. Between the date on which the issuance of rights is announced and the date the rights are issued, the stock to which the rights relate is purchased and sold in the market rights on, which means that the value of the stock and the rights are united. After the rights are issued, the rights are traded separately from the stock and the stock is traded ex-rights.

Stock warrants (or stock purchase warrants) are securities that give to the holder the ability to buy a specified number of shares of stock at a stated price for a specified period of time. Stock warrants do not pay current income. Warrants are often used to sell bonds or stock to make the securities more attractive when they are being issued. Warrants are purchased from the issuing firm or in the marketplace for cash. Stock rights are usually issued free to current stockholders who are entitled to purchase additional shares from a pending new issue of a stock in proportion to their present holdings (a preemptive right).

STOCK SPLIT A distribution of company's own capital stock to existing stockholders with the purpose of reducing the market price of the stock, which would hopefully increase the demand for the shares. To accomplish the stock split, the par or stated value of the stock is adjusted. For example, a $10 par value stock that is split two for one will have a $5 par value after the split. Assume the following information about a stockholders' equity section of a corporate balance sheet. The stock is split 2:1.

	Before stock split	After stock split
Common stock, $10 par, 10,000 shares issued	$100,000	
Common stock, $5 par, 20,000 shares issued		$100,000
Additional paid-in capital	10,000	10,000
Retained earnings	90,000	90,000
Total	$200,000	$200,000

Note that after the stock split, the components of stockholders' equity are the same as before the split. Only the par value of the shares and the number of shares outstanding have changed.

A reverse stock split is a stock split in which the number of shares outstanding is decreased.

STOCK SUBSCRIPTIONS A contract to purchase corporate stock on an installment basis. The contract provides that the subscriber (investor) will purchase a certain number of shares at an agreed-upon price, with payment spread over a specified time period. A down payment is often required. Provisions for dealing with defaults are also provided. The shares are usually not issued until the subscriber has made complete payment of the subscription price. Most subscriptions are collected in full. If default occurs, the contract may provide for the return to the subscriber of the entire amount paid in; the amount paid in, less any costs incurred by the corporation to reissue the stock; a lesser number of shares based upon the payments received; the forfeiture of the amounts paid in.

The subscriptions receivable are listed as a contra-stockholders' equity account in financial statements (and not as an asset) because collection is uncertain—the SEC position. Other accountants would classify the subscriptions receivable as an asset. The common stock subscribed account is listed in the contributed capital section of stockholders' equity to indicate that the corporation has contracted to issue additional stock.

STOCK SYMBOLS *See* NEW YORK STOCK EXCHANGE ABBREVIATIONS.

STOCK TRANSFER AGENT *See* STOCK TRANSFERS.

STOCK TRANSFER JOURNAL A book in which transfers of stock of a corporation are authorized and recorded. It is practically a duplicate of the assignment appearing on the reverse of the stock certificate.

STOCK TRANSFERS Stock certificates are representative personal property, and one of the fundamental rights of stockholders is to pass their ownership from one person to another by assignment. In case of sale, however, the purchaser is not the stockholder of record on the stock book of the corporation until a transfer has been effected thereon. Until such transfer to the name of the new owner, the corporation is legally entitled to continue to treat the stockholder of record as the owner of the stock for all corporate purposes, such as forwarding thereto notices of meetings, proxies, dividends, rights, etc. Transfer involves the cancellation of the old certificate and the issuance of a new one or ones pursuant to the transfer instructions. It is the duty of the transfer agent, whether an officer or clerk of the corporation itself or an outside individual, bank, or trust company, to see that the act of transfer is properly executed.

When shares of stock are sold, it is necessary for the seller to present a GOOD DELIVERY to the buyer on the settlement day ("regular way" terms call for delivery on the fourth business day after the date of the transaction, in practice on the New York Stock Exchange and other security markets). For good delivery, the stock certificate shall be accompanied by a proper assignment, executed on the certificate itself or on a separate paper (Rule 195, N.Y. Stock Exchange). A separate assignment shall contain provision for the irrevocable appointment of an attorney, with power of substitution and a full description of the security, in the form approved by the New York Stock Exchange.

See POWER OF ATTORNEY.

The "attorney" specified in the power of attorney is the party who actually performs the act of transfer on the books of the corporation, as agent for the endorser. If a broker's name is inserted in an assignment as attorney, a power of substitution shall be executed in blank by such attorney (Rule 196) for good delivery. The name of the person in the stock transfer office who actually performs the transfer will be filled in as the attorney in the completed transfer. Because of the extra formality involved, the attorney is not usually named and the space therefor is left blank.

The signature to an assignment or power of substitution shall be technically correct, i.e., it shall correspond with the name as written upon the face of the certificate in every particular, without alteration, enlargement, or any change whatever, except that in the case of a firm the following may be written either way (Rule 198): "and" or "&," "Company" or "Co."

The signature to an assignment of a certificate not in the name of a member or member firm, except registered U.S. government securities, shall be guaranteed by a member or member firm, or by a commercial bank or trust company organized under federal or state laws and having its principal office in the vicinity of the exchange (Rule 209). In view of this required guarantee, the signature of a witness in the assignment is in practice considered superfluous. The date, however, is a material requirement to be filled in.

A certificate issued in the names of two or more individuals or firms shall be a delivery only if signed by all the registered owners, including joint accounts and tenancies in common. Stock in the name of a corporation shall be a delivery only if the statement "proper papers for transfer filed by assignor" is placed on the assignment and signed by the transfer agent, indicative of proper authority by the authorized agents of the corporation. Authorization is also required for fiduciaries.

It is no longer required that marital status of women (unmarried, married, or widow) be indicated on the face of a certificate. Endorsement by such registered married women is sufficient for good delivery, except where state law still restricts the power of married women to transfer without endorsement of consent of their husbands (Texas, Arizona, and New Mexico).

The listing agreement of the New York Stock Exchange requires maintenance by the corporation of a transfer agent (the company itself or a bank or trust company) in the financial district of New York, as well as an independent registrar in the financial district.

Governing the incidents of stock transfer is the state's version, in its adoption of the UNIFORM COMMERCIAL CODE, of Article 8 of the code, entitled "Investment Securities." A "security" is an instrument that is issued in bearer or registered form. If the security is in bearer form (running to bearer according to its terms and not by reason of any endorsement), voluntary transfer of possession shall be effective upon such delivery. If the security is in registered form (it specifies a person entitled to the security or its rights, its transfer may be registered upon books maintained for that purpose by or on behalf of the issuer, or it so states), delivery is effective upon endorsement to the transferee or in blank plus actual delivery. A "bona fide purchaser" is a purchaser for value in good faith and without notice of any adverse claim who takes delivery of a security in bearer form or of a security in registered form issued to him or endorsed in blank. A bona fide purchaser, in addition to acquiring the rights of a purchaser, also acquires the security free of any adverse claim to the extent of the interest purchased. But lack of genuineness of a security is a complete defense even against a purchaser for value and without notice. However, the true owner cannot assert the defense of unauthorized endorsement against a purchaser for value and without notice of adverse claims who has in good faith received a new, reissued, or reregistered security on registration of transfer. Nor may the following defenses prevail against an innocent purchaser for value: that his transferor did not own the stock, that the transferor had no authority to deliver the certificate, that the transfer was made in violation of restriction of transfer not specified on the certificate of stock itself, or that the certificate was obtained by fraud, duress, mistake, or without consideration.

The code also prescribes the procedure in the case of lost, destroyed, or stolen securities. When a security has been lost, apparently destroyed, or wrongfully taken and the owner fails to notify the issuer of that fact within a reasonable time after he has notice of it and the issuer registers a transfer of the security before receiving such a notification, the owner is precluded from asserting against the issuer any claim for registering the transfer under the code or any claim to a new security. But when the owner of a security claims that the security has been lost, destroyed, or wrongfully taken, the issuer must issue a new security in place of the original security if:

1. The owner requests a new security before the issuer has notice that the original security has been acquired by a bona fide purchaser.
2. The owner files with the issuer a sufficient indemnity bond.
3. The owner satisfies any other reasonable requirements imposed by the issuer.

If after the issuance of the new security, a bona fide purchaser of the original security presents it for registration of transfer, the issuer must register the transfer unless registration would result in overissue, in which event the issuer may be compelled by the person entitled to the issue to purchase and deliver such a security against surrender of the security if any held; or if the security is not available for purchase, the person entitled to issue may recover from the issuer the price he or the last purchaser for value paid for it, with interest from the date of his demand. In addition to any rights on the indemnity bond, the issuer may recover the new security from the person to whom it was originally issued or any person taking under him except a bona fide purchaser.

Endorsement of a STOCK CERTIFICATE in full (with the name of the transferee) may be completed by filling in the name of the transferee. Frequently, an old certificate may be reissued in separate names with a specified number of shares for each as desired. Proper stock transfer tax stamps must accompany the certificate, both for good delivery and for valid transfer on the books of the corporation. Certificates in street name are those registered in the name of a broker or brokerage firm, which upon assignment in blank constitute good delivery and also may be readily hypothecated for broker borrowing.

See ASSIGNMENT IN BLANK, STOCK REGISTRAR.

STOCK TRANSFER TAX The federal tax on stock transfers was terminated in 1965.

New York Stock Transfer Tax. New York State levied and collected a stock transfer tax which was turned over entirely to New York City from 1965 until 1975, when the proceeds were turned over to the New York State Municipal Assistance Corporation. Tax liability was incurred upon the sale of stock. As part of New York City's austerity budget for fiscal 1976, a "temporary" 25% surcharge was added to existing rates, at first for one year, effective July, 1975. This meant that for stocks selling above $20 per share, the rate increased from $0.05 per share to $0.0625 per share (individual sellers not residing or working in New York State paid half the rate), with corresponding 25% increases for the lower price ranges.

On August 2, 1978, a phaseout of the stock transfer tax was started with the elimination of the 25% surcharge which had been imposed each year since 1975. Through an annual reduction in the nonrebatable portion of tax (October 1, 1979, 1980, and 1981), the tax impact was completely eliminated as of October 1, 1981.

For the record, the original scale of the stock transfer tax rates, effective prior to July, 1975, was as follows:

Price range of stock	Effective tax per share prior to July, 1975
$0-4.99	$0.0125
5-9.99	$0.025
10-19.99	$0.0375
20+	$0.05

Bond Transfer Tax. Effective August, 1975, a transfer tax on bonds was levied for the first time in New York State. The revenue from the tax—$6.9 million by the end of 1975—was far below original expectations. This, together with the fact that the tax was providing an incentive for dealer firms to move to New Jersey where no bond tax existed, led to a repeal of the bond tax effective March 2, 1976. The tax had been $0.25 per $1,000 on corporate bonds, collected from both the buyer and the seller.

SEC Fee. The SECURITIES AND EXCHANGE COMMISSION charged a fee or fraction thereof of the money involved in transactions on any registered exchange.

STOCK TRUST CERTIFICATE A certificate, also known as trust certificate, issued in exchange for the stock of competing corporations entering the TRUST form of combination and deposited with trustees, who in exchange therefor issue trust certificates pursuant to the deposit agreement and who direct the affairs of the corporations included in the "trust" by reason of their voting power. By the time of passage in 1890 of the Sherman Act, the technical trust form of combination had given way to the HOLDING COMPANY.

STOCK TURNOVER See MERCHANDISE TURNOVER.

STOCK WATERING See WATERED STOCK.

STOP LOSS ORDER An order given to a broker by a customer, usually in order to protect a profit created by an advance or to limit a loss in case of a sudden decline. In the case of a short seller, a stop loss order is employed to protect profits created by a decline or to limit losses created by an advance. The following illustration indicates the use of a stop loss order by a speculator who has purchased stock in anticipation of a rise.

Suppose United States Steel is purchased at 85. While the speculator anticipates that the market will rise, he does not wish to take a large loss should his judgment prove wrong. He may therefore enter a stop loss order to sell at 80. This would not be touched in case of a small dip in prices, but if the market developed a declining tendency, the stock might drop to a point where the order would go into effect. The broker is not bound to sell the stock at the exact stop loss order price. There may be other orders to sell the stock at 80 ahead of any given order, or there may be no bids at that price, so the stock must be offered down until a purchaser is obtained. This means that, in reality, a stop loss order when touched off ("elected") becomes a market order and is executed at the best price obtainable at the time the market reaches the vicinity of 80.

The market is sometimes honeycombed with stop loss orders; in the event of a steady decline, stop loss orders will be touched off, thereby adding to the supply of stock on the downside.

STOP ORDER See STOP LOSS ORDER.

STOP ORDERS ON PASSBOOKS When a savings bank passbook is lost, a stop order should be issued by the depositor upon his bank. The stop order consists of a written notice addressed to the bank, stating that passbook No. belonging to has been lost, and includes a request to stop payment, signed by the depositor. The savings bank will then attach a slip to the depositor's ledger card with the words "Do not pay." This will serve to remind the teller to allow no withdrawals, should the passbook be fraudulently presented.

STOP PAYMENT A depositor has the legal right to stop payment on checks that he has previously drawn. An oral stop payment request is generally good for 14 days, and a written stop payment request is generally good for 6 months (the oral stop order may be binding on the bank only if confirmed in writing within that period, and the written order may be renewed in writing) (Sec. 4-403(2), Uniform Commercial Code). In order to make a bank liable, a written stop order must be presented in writing and reach the bank on which the stopped CHECK is drawn before the check is presented. A telegraphic request to stop payment is legally enforceable. Banks usually endeavor to stop payment on oral or telephonic instructions, but are not always able to do so. A satisfactory form of stop payment order is as follows.

Stop Payment Order

Date _____

Kindly stop payment upon a check drawn by _____
_____ to _____
(us or me) _____ (name of payee) _____
dated
The number of the check is _____

Very truly yours,

_____
(name of drawer)

The stop payment order gives four facts—the number, date, amount, and payee of the check. Paying tellers and check-desk clerks usually keep a list of the stop payment orders continually before them. This list is arranged in alphabetical order, according to the names of the drawers who have issued stop payment orders. The paying teller should keep in mind all stop payment orders, and in cases of doubt, the list should be scrutinized before a check is cashed.

Foreign banks issue checks in original and duplicate, or first and second of exchange. Duplicates are not paid until it is determined by inspecting the statement of account or canceled checks that the original has not been paid. At the time a duplicate check is paid, a stop payment order is automatically placed against the original. Since possible previous payment of the original is always verified when a duplicate is presented for payment, it is not necessary to place a stop against a duplicate at the time the original is paid. On the other hand, when the original is presented, provided there is no stop

STOPPED STOCK

payment against it, it is paid without verifying the payment of the duplicate through the statement or voucher records.

Acknowledgments of a stop payment order should be made by a form letter to read as shown.

Acknowledgment of Stop Payment

We are in receipt of your letter of _____ requesting us to stop payment of your draft No. _____ dated _____ , for $ _____ , to the order of _____ , and the matter will have our careful attention. The draft does not appear to have been paid since date of issue.

Acknowledgments are also made of cancellations of stop payment orders. This typical form letter reads as shown.

Acknowledgment of Cancellation

We are in receipt of your letter of the _____ , and in accordance with your instructions we have removed the stop payment order which we had placed against your draft No. _____ , dated _____ , in favor of _____ for $. _____ ,

Stop payment sheets should be duplicated for use at the check desk so that checks coming in through the clearinghouse upon which stop payment orders have been placed may be stopped and returned to the presenting bank.

The principal reasons for stopping payment are to cancel purchase orders, to prevent cashing of a lost check by a dishonest person who may have come into illegal possession of the check, and to prevent the payment of an original check when the duplicate has already been paid.

STOPPED STOCK A sale effected pursuant to an agreement entered into on the floor of an exchange, whereby one member, usually the specialist in such stock, guarantees to purchase or sell to another member a stated amount of the stock, either at the price of the next sale or at a specified price when the stock sells at such price. An agreement by a member to "stop" securities at a specified price constitutes a guarantee of the purchase or sale by him of the securities at that price or its equivalent. Members and member firms should report to their customers that securities have been "stopped" with another member only if the "stop" is unconditional and the other member has definitely agreed thereto.

Orders to buy and sell each individual stock are normally paired off or stopped in equal amounts at the opening of the exchange. Any excess orders to buy or to sell are executed, thereby establishing the price of the stopped stock. Stopped stock may be printed on the ticker if no other shares are offered or bid at that price.

A stop order (see STOP LOSS ORDER) to buy becomes a market order when a transaction in the security occurs at or above the stop price. A stop order to sell becomes a market order when a transaction in the security occurs at or below the stop price.

STOP TRANSFER ORDER When a stock certificate has been lost or stolen, the owner has the right to issue a stop transfer order to the transfer agent so as to prevent transfer in the name of a wrongful party. Transfer may also be stopped by a court order.

Before accepting stock certificates for transfer, transfer agents must ascertain whether stop orders have been issued against the stock certificates. It is customary to defer issuance of new certificates in place of lost or stolen certificates for one year after notice is iven, and then to issue the new certificates only upon the filing of a bond of indemnity, usually for a sum equal to double the value of the stock involved.

STORE OF VALUE A function of money. Because money has value and is accepted as a medium of exchange this year, next year, and for years into the future, it is one form in which wealth can be maintained. Thus, money serves as a store of value. It represents present and future purchasing power for those who hold it.

STRADDLE A combination of a put and a call, which grants to the holder the right to require the maker, within a specified time, to purchase and/or sell a specified security at a stipulated price. The price stipulated in a straddle is almost invariably the market price prevailing at the time the straddle is executed.

See SPREAD.

STRADDLE THE MARKET To be short of one or more stocks and long of another or others. Straddling the market is a form of hedging or insurance for protecting commitments in stocks when the future course of prices is uncertain. If one is short of one stock and long on another, should the next general movement of prices be down, the sum lost through the decline in value of long stocks ideally will be approximately offset by a profit in short stocks.

STRAIGHT PAPER Generally, all classes of unsecured notes, acceptances, and bills of exchange. A straight loan is one without collateral security.

See SINGLE-NAME PAPER.

STRAP An OPTION position consisting of the purchase of more calls than puts although all have the same exercise price and exercise date. While the trade expects an increase in price volatility, there is also an expectation that the price of the underlying instrument is more likely to rise than to fall.

STRAPS Stated-rate auction rate cumulative preferred stock.
See FINANCIAL INSTRUMENTS: RECENT INNOVATIONS.

STREET A popular name for the New York financial district.
See WALL STREET.

STREET BROKER A broker not belonging to any stock exchange who buys and sells unlisted securities for his clients. Such brokers also act as dealers for their own account in buying or selling unlisted securities. Member firms also often maintain unlisted trading departments. Since a market for inactive, unlisted securities is often difficult to locate, a street broker is useful to banks, investment houses, security dealers, and other brokers, as well as individual investors and traders. Street brokers' commissions and markups are self-regulated through the NATIONAL ASSOCIATION OF SECURITIES DEALERS, INC. (NASD). One of the NASD Rules of Fair Practice provides: "...if a member buys for his own account from his customer, or sells for his own account to his customer, he shall buy or sell at a price which is fair, taking into consideration all relevant circumstances, including market conditions with respect to such security at the time of the transaction, the expense involved, and the fact that he is entitled to a profit; and if he acts as agent for his customer ... he shall not charge his customer more than a fair commission or service charge ... "

See OVER-THE-COUNTER MARKET.

STREET CERTIFICATE A stock exchange broker's name for stock certificates that have been transferred in blank and on that account are negotiable by delivery without further endorsement or transfer upon the books of the company. A street certificate must be endorsed in blank by the registered owner, and the signature must be guaranteed by a member firm. The street certificate then may be bought, sold, and transferred any number of times without being transferred on the books of the company. Street certificates are the customary form of stock certificates serving as collateral to margin accounts. These certificates are adequate for trading on margin, but when the stock is purchased outright or taken up by a margin purchaser, the street certificate must be taken to the company's transfer office and a new certificate issued in the name of the purchaser. Should the new certificate, after being registered in the name of the owner on the books of the company, be sold, endorsed in blank by its registered owner, and properly guaranteed, it would again become a street certificate.

STREET IMPROVEMENT BONDS A subclassification of municipal or special assessment bonds issued for the purpose of paving or repairing streets. Usually these bonds are special assessment bonds, i.e., the obligation of the taxpayers whose property is benefited, and not of the entire municipality.

See EMIMUNICIPAL BONDS, SPECIAL ASSESSMENT BONDS.

STREET LOAN CALL LOAN.

ENCYCLOPEDIA OF BANKING AND FINANCE

STREET NAME A term used to refer to securities held in the name of brokers, or their nominees, instead of in the customer's name.

STREET RAILWAY BONDS A class of PUBLIC UTILITY BONDS, usually secured by street railway property. Street railways are natural monopolies and share with other public utilities the characteristic that as monopolies affected with a public interest, their rates are generally regulated. There are two methods by which the rates charged by street railways are limited: The rates may be specified and the rate regulating powers vested in the municipality by the franchise contract, or rates may be regulated by a public service commission. From the investor's point of view, the latter is more satisfactory. The modern tendency of public service commissions is to adjust the street railway fares to permit a fair return on the capital invested in the property; the recent attitude of public service commissions has been one of protecting the interests of the investor through the allowance of fare increases.

Generally speaking, street railway bonds are a good investment in cases where they are secured by property whose replacement value does not exceed the bond issue and where rate regulation is left to the public service commission. In recent years street railways have encountered competition from municipally owned or licensed bus lines, but have themselves converted to an increasing extent to motor buses or trolley buses, thus increasing the efficiency of operation and service.

STRIKE PRICE An OPTION's exercise price.

STRIPS Separate trading of registered interest and principal of securities. The U.S. Treasury's acronym for zero-coupon instruments derived from selected long-term notes and bonds. At a bondholder's request, the Federal Reserve, as the Treasury's fiscal agent, will separate a designated security into its individual coupon components and the corpus or principal payment. Each coupon calls for payment of a certain dollar amount on a specific date, while the body of the security calls for repayment of the principal amount at maturity. The pieces may be traded separately at a discount from face value and must be maintained on the Treasury's book-entry system. The value of zero coupons at any given moment is determined by the market.

According to the Federal Reserve Bank of New York, the Treasury's STRIPS program had several objectives, including an attempt to reduce the cost of financing the public debt by facilitating competitive private market initiatives. Zeros also broadened the appeal of U.S. government securities. The book-entry or computer record-only feature of STRIPS provides an efficient means of transferring ownership, thus enhancing the trading of zero-coupon instruments. The first Treasury securities made eligible for STRIPS were issued in mid-February 1985.

Zeros have become popular for investments on which taxes can be deferred, such as pension plans. They can also be tailored to meet a wide range of portfolio objectives because of their known cash value at specific future dates. For example, a 20-year bond with a face value of $20,000 and a 10% interest rate, could be stripped into 41 negotiable zero-coupon instruments. The main body, or principal, and each of the 40 semiannual interest coupons become one zero-coupon instrument. The body would be worth the $20,000 face value upon maturity. The other zeros created from the semiannual interest coupons would each be worth $2,000 (one-half the annual interest of $2,000) on the specified payment date. Each of the 41 zero-coupon instruments could be traded until its due date.

When physical securities in engraved certificate form are stripped, the investor may receive one or more actual coupons or that part of the security specifying payment of the principal. Since January 1, 1983, the U.S. Treasury has not issued new bearer notes or bonds, which are securities with coupons attached.

In August 1982, one major bond dealer began marketing receipts that evidenced ownership of Treasury zeros held by a custodian. The first of these receipt products were named Treasury Investment Growth Receipts, or TIGRs. Other firms entered the market with similar products, given names such as Certificates of Accrual on Treasury Securities, or CATS, Treasury receipts (TRs), and Lehman Investment Opportunity Notes (LIONS).

The STRIPS program provides that only depository institutions with book-entry accounts at Federal Reserve banks may request securities be stripped. The U.S. Treasury does not sell stripped securities. The market decides when and how much of an eligible Treasury security is separated and marketed. Eligible securities may be stripped at any time.

STRUCTURAL UNEMPLOYMENT Individuals who have involuntarily left a job as a result of a decrease in the long-term demand for products in that particular industry. New skills or additional education may be necessary for these individuals to find new employment. Because of structural unemployment, it is unreasonable to expect the economy ever to reach a zero rate of unemployment.

STRINGENCY A period in which credit is tight and borrowers are experiencing difficulty in procuring funds. During a stringency, money rates, especially in the call loan market, are high, and banks and business houses exercise caution and discretion in granting credit. If the stringency is severe, credit can be obtained only by the highest class risks who can furnish the most conservative collateral. A money stringency is one of the characteristics of a period of expansion, inflation, and speculation, reaching its highest expression at a time of crisis or panic, when it becomes the chief characteristic of such a crisis. Before the Federal Reserve System, which introduced elastic currency and perfected elastic bank credit, a money stringency was occasion for considerable alarm, usually precipitating a break in the security markets.

STRONG A market or a single security or commodity is said to be strong when there is a price advance.

STUB In general, a counterfoil or part of a bound set of printed, blank forms, e.g., checks, stock certificates, receipts, and the like, which may be detached from the main portion by tearing at the perforation. The stub is a memorandum containing essentially the same information as the main form, and is retained as a part of the permanent records of a business.

For check stubs, *see* CHECKBOOK.

STUDENT LOAN MARKETING ASSOCIATION A private corporation created by the Education Amendments of 1972 (amendments to the Higher Education Act of 1965) to expand funds available for student loans by providing liquidity to banks, educational institutions, and other lenders engaged in the guaranteed loan program.

The federal government, however, through the President of the United States, designates one-third of the 21 directors of the Student Loan Marketing Association (popularly known as Sallie Mae) and its chairman. Sallie Mae is also required to submit annual reports of operations and activities to the President and to the Congress, to submit to examination of its books by independent certified public accountants, and to submit report of such audit to the secretary of the Treasury.

As of 1982, Sallie Mae was offering three programs under its guaranteed student loan program: a loan purchase program; a warehousing advance program; and commitment programs, for lenders in this now-deemphasized program of student aid. A program of loan consolidation, purchase of loans made under the auxiliary loan program, and a program of loan participations or pooled interests in loans were among the other functions designed to provide liquidity for banks, thrift institutions, and educational institutions that engaged in the guaranteed student loan program. Sallie Mae also engaged in the health education assistance program for students. Loans originated under both the guaranteed student loan program and the health education assistance loan program were either directly insured by the U.S. government or reinsured by the U.S. government if guaranteed by state or nonprofit private agencies.

Sale of debt securities is the principal means of financing the requirements of Sallie Mae, mainly through the FEDERAL FINANCING BANK, which on March 9, 1981, agreed to lend Sallie Mae up to $5.0 billion, chiefly in the form of 15-year variable-rate notes, all of which had been borrowed and were outstanding as of January 9, 1982. The variable interest rate was 0.125% above the 91-day Treasury bill rate. Beginning in May, 1981, Sallie Mae also began to finance its secondary market operations in part through the issuance of nonguaranteed discount notes, which were unsecured and had maturities no longer than one year. In addition, in 1982 Sallie Mae began offering on a public basis nonguaranteed floating-rate notes with maturities of three years or over, the rate varying according to the bond yield equivalent of the 91-day Treasury bill rate; and from time to time it offers to the public intermediate- and long-term fixed-rate securities. The secretary of the Treasury is authorized at his discretion to purchase Sallie Mae's obligations to a maximum of $1.0 billion, in addition to any guaranteed obligations which may be outstanding to the FFB. To date, however, no borrowings had been made under this authorization.

The Sallie Mae's obligations issued are exempt from state, municipal, or local taxation, similar to U.S. government obligations.

The *Treasury Bulletin* reported that as of September 30, 1982, the Student Loan Insurance Fund had total assets of $1,717.9 million, compared to total liabilities of $2,095.2 million. Among the assets was $1,525.4 million in total loans receivable, against which was allocated a total allowance of doubtful collectibility of $1,030.4 million.

SUBJECT BID   A bid for a security, usually in connection with inactive stocks in over-the-counter markets or smaller stock exchanges, that is tentative or temporary rather than firm. The occasion for a subject bid arises when trading has been infrequent and a wide spread presumably exists between any actual bid and actual offer. One who places a subject bid is, in effect, endeavoring to locate a corresponding offer, but does not obligate himself to buy except on further negotiation or confirmation. Thus, a subject bid is not a dependable bid that can be used as a certain basis for a trade. It is a trial or locating bid, subject to confirmation, change, prior purchase, or possible cancellation.

SUBJECT OFFER   A tentative offer to sell an inactive stock, made in an effort to locate a bid. It is not necessarily a firm, final, or actual offer. For a fuller explanation, *see* SUBJECT BID.

SUBJECT TO CALL   *See* CALLABLE BONDS.

SUBJECT TO CHECK   Payable on demand. The term is used in conjunction with that type of bank account or deposit in which the depositor retains the right to withdraw funds immediately and without notice to the bank, by means of check. All commercial checking accounts are subject to check, and most of the deposits of a commercial bank are DEMAND DEPOSITS, i.e., subject to check.

SUBORDINATED DEBENTURES   A type of DEBENTURE in which the provision for "subordination agreement" in its indenture renders the claim of such subordinated debentures, in the event of liquidation, dissolution, bankruptcy, or reorganization, junior to present or future debt, defined as senior thereto. Such defined senior debt typically includes funds borrowed from banks, insurance companies, and other financial institutions, as well as all other forms of notes or other debentures not expressly subordinated. This results in the subordinated debentures, instead of sharing ratably with other unsecured claims of general status, becoming part of the equity base as far as such defined debt, made expressly senior, is concerned. Thus, it becomes easier to obtain bank and other loans entitled to such seniority because of the subordination agreement. Subordinated debentures have been particularly utilized by finance companies as a financing medium in recent years.

SUBROGATION   The substitution of another person in the place of the creditor. The person so substituted succeeds to all the rights of the original creditor, all debts owing to the creditor becoming payable to the substituted person. A subrogated note is one in which the person to whom it is payable has substituted another person as successor to his rights therein.

Under federal deposit insurance, the FEDERAL DEPOSIT INSURANCE CORPORATION, in the case of a closed national bank or District of Columbia bank, shall upon the payment to the depositor of his insured deposit be subrogated to all rights of the depositor against the closed bank to the extent of such payment. In the case of any other closed insured bank, the corporation shall not make any payment to any depositor until the right to be subrogated to the rights of such depositors on the same basis shall have been recognized, either by express provision of state law, by allowance of claims, by assignment of claims, or by any other effective method. Such subrogation shall include the right on the part of the corporation to receive the same dividends from the proceeds of the assets of the closed bank and recoveries as would have been payable to the depositor on a claim for the insured deposit, such depositor retaining his claim for any uninsured portion of his deposit.

SUBSCRIBER   One who subscribes for a certain number of shares of stock, or a certain amount (par value) of bonds, either by entering his name on a subscription list (blank) or by making some other agreement to purchase.

SUBSCRIPTION   An offer to purchase stocks or bonds, given to a corporation, or its authorized trustee or representative, by a subscriber. A subscription is merely an offer to purchase and can be revoked by the subscriber until accepted. In the case of subscription before incorporation, acceptance is made when the corporation comes into existence and makes an act of acceptance by a duly authorized officer, express or implied. In the case of subscription after incorporation, acceptance is simple, as the corporation is already in existence and merely accepts, thus giving rise to contract.

In order to have the status of a continuing offer, a subscription before incorporation must contain an agreement to form the corporation and to take a specified number of shares therein, as a mere agreement to subscribe to shares of stock in a corporation to be formed in the future is just an agreement to agree, there being no corporation in existence.

An acceptance of a subscription is subject to allotment. This provision protects the corporation against suit in case of oversubscription, which necessitates a pro rata reduction of subscriptions for amounts in excess of a certain minimum.

SUBSCRIPTION WARRANT   An instrument entitling the stockholders of record to "rights," or subscription privileges; a certificate issued by a corporation specifying the amount of stock and the terms and conditions under which each stockholder is entitled to subscribe to new shares that the corporation is about to issue. Subscription warrants are legal evidence of the ownership of subscription rights and are assignable.

See RIGHT.

SUBSIDIARY COINAGE   Coins manufactured from metals other than the standard metal. In the U.S., all fractional coin is now both nongold (the international monetary metal of the U.S., but completely nationalized domestically, with no gold coinage or gold circulation of any kind) and nonsilver. (This includes new issues of completely nonsilver dollars and half-dollars for general circulation, both similar in composition to the cupronickel quarters and dimes, the former pursuant to Title II of P.L. 91-607, December 31, 1970, and the latter pursuant to the Coinage Act of 1965.) MINOR COINS (nickels and cents) and SUBSIDIARY SILVER COINS (half-dollars, quarters, and dimes) are terms no longer used in reference to coins of denominations less than the standard unit of the dollar, in view of their now homogeneous cupronickel composition. Instead, the term fractional coin is used in such reference.

See FRACTIONAL CURRENCY, UNITED STATES MONEY.

SUBSIDIARY COMPANY   A corporation controlled by another corporation through partial or complete stock ownership of the voting class of security, interlocking directorate, lease, or community of interest. Many major corporations in the U.S. are of either the "pure" (exclusive) holding company type or the "mixed" holding company type, owning control of a number of subsidiaries, which may be in turn intermediate holding companies and/or operating companies. Carrying such interests in separately incorporated and controlled companies has the advantages of decentralizing management in separate boards of directors and officers, accountable to the parent company on a profit and loss basis autonomously; preserving goodwill values of the local name of subsidiaries and local management; bypassing any undue taxation of "foreign" corporations (those domestic to other states) by carrying local properties in subsidiaries domestic to the state of location; and separating particular activities or holdings in specified subsidiary corporations, thereby limiting liability and providing flexibility in the event of sale, dissolution, reorganization, or bankruptcy, with a minimum of disturbance organizationally to other holdings. Where the holdings of the parent corporation are "conglomerate" in nature (nonrelated and noncomplementary operations), the device of a separately incorporated subsidiary for each activity enhances specialization of its management, along with responsibility and accountability. Subsidiary corporations also make possible vertical, horizontal, and "circular" combinations with flexibility.

On the other hand, there are extra expenses and costs in maintaining multiple subsidiary corporations. Holding companies owning at least 80% of the stock of a subsidiary may file a consolidated tax return, at a cost of 2% additional tax imposed for the privilege. In a consolidated return, profits of profitable subsidiaries may be offset wholly or partly by losses of the unprofitable units. If separate returns are made, the parent corporation must pay the 15% tax on intercorporate dividends received from subsidiaries.

See HOLDING COMPANY.

SUBSIDIARY SILVER COINS The fractional silver coins formerly issued—the half-dollar, quarter, and dime. These contained only 385.8 grains troy, 0.9 fine (347.22 grains of pure silver) to the silver dollar, while the silver dollar itself contained 412.5 grains, 0.9 fine (371.25 grains pure silver).

Subsidiary silver coins are no longer issued by the U.S. Mint; the Coinage Act of 1965 provided for the issuance of 40% silver-clad half-dollars and completely nonsilver (cupronickel) quarters and dimes, and P.L. 91-607, December 31, 1970, authorized the issuance of nonsilver dollars and half-dollars for general circulation (cupronickel), the new issuance of the 40% silver half-dollar being discontinued effective January 1, 1971.

All fractional coinage is full legal tender. P.L. 89-81, July 23, 1965, known as the Coinage Act of 1965, repealed the original lender tender provisions contained in Section 43(b) (1) of the Act of May 12, 1933, as amended (31 U.S.C. 462), but added a new provision of law to the same effect codified in 31 U.S.C. 392.

SUBSIDY Governmental financial assistance given to designated public enterprises operating under private management—railroads, motor carriers, airlines, steamship operators and builders, agricultural activities, etc.—in order to encourage such industries, which otherwise might go undeveloped or remain inadequately developed.

Subsidies may be direct or indirect, may include grants for operations as well as construction subsidies, and may be "in kind" as well as financial in nature.

Subsidies in the broadest sense include tax expenditures and the federal credit budget.

SUBSTITUTION EFFECT One important theoretical premise upon which the law of demand is based. For two products, A and B, which are substitutes, as the price of product A falls (with the price of product B unchanged), the quantity demanded for product A will increase in part because individuals substitute out of the relatively higher-priced product B into the now relatively lower-priced product A.

SUBSTITUTIONS IN COLLATERAL The relinquishment of certain collateral pledged to secure a loan, and the deposit of other collateral of equivalent value in its stead. Substitutions are an essential part of the machinery of handling brokers' loans. They are also necessary whenever short-term paper is pledged as collateral against long-term notes, in rediscounted notes securing FEDERAL RESERVE NOTES and in the collateral supporting COLLATERAL TRUST BONDS.

Call loans and brokers' time loans are always secured by stock exchange collateral, i.e., stocks and bonds that are constantly being traded in. A broker obtains a loan from a bank by pledging this collateral, which has been purchased for the accounts of customers operating on margin. While these securities are owned by the brokers' customers, they are held by the brokers as security against the debit balances that they advance. Suppose a broker's customer orders the sale of some of the stock that the broker has rehypothecated with a bank. In order to make delivery, the broker must obtain physical possession of these shares previously pledged to secure his bank loan. It is therefore necessary to procure them at the bank where they are deposited as collateral. In the meantime, however, the broker has purchased stock for other accounts, and these he can offer in exchange for the stocks that have been sold but are deposited at the bank. Accordingly, a messenger is sent to the broker's bank with the securities to be substituted and with a request phrased as follows.

Substitution forms are signed by a member of the brokerage house who is authorized to sign, or by an authorized attorney.

Substitution Request

_____, 19 _____

Please deliver the following securities from our loan number, _____ dated _____.

We hand you in exchange _____

(Signature)

Substitution clerks who examine collateral substituted for collateral to be released should observe the following points: that the signature on the substitution request is authorized and genuine; that the character of the substituted collateral is acceptable, i.e., approximately equivalent to the character of the collateral being released; that the new collateral is negotiable; and that the market value of the substituted collateral is approximately equal to the value of the collateral to be released.

Since rediscounted commercial paper of not more than three months' duration (nine months for agricultural paper) may form a portion of the collateral supporting Federal Reserve notes, it would be necessary that the pledged stream of maturing notes be released from the custody of the Federal Reserve agent at each Federal Reserve bank (who has charge of this collateral and whose duty it is to supervise substitutions) and that the newly rediscounted paper be substituted.

Substitution of collateral in real estate mortgage bonds or in collateral trust bonds is permissible only on previously agreed upon terms specified in the indenture, and customarily responsibility for seeing that the character and value of the new collateral is as good as that of the released collateral is chargeable under the indenture to the trustee.

SUBTREASURY One of the branch offices of the United States Treasury performing government fiscal operations of the same character as those of the United States Treasury, and under the supervision of assistant treasurers. By an act of Congress dated May 29, 1920, the operation of the subtreasuries as a part of the fiscal system was required to terminate on June 30, 1921. Subtreasuries were located in New York City, Baltimore, Boston, Chicago, Cincinnati, New Orleans, Philadelphia, St. Louis, and San Francisco. By the act above referred to, these nine subtreasuries were closed and their functions taken over by the various Federal Reserve banks, which carry on the fiscal operations in the same manner as previously.

See TREASURY DEPARTMENT.

SUCCESSFUL-EFFORT ACCOUNTING An accounting method used in oil and gas operations that capitalizes such costs as exploration, drilling, and lease rentals associated with establishing the location of a natural resource only when the effort results in the discovery of a natural resource. Costs associated with unsuccessful wells are expensed. The full-cost method capitalizes the costs associated with all the wells, both successful and unsuccessful. Both methods of accounting for the cost of oil and gas properties are considered generally acceptable accounting methods and satisfy the needs of users of the financial statements.

Large companies generally use successful-effort accounting, while smaller companies often use the full-cost method in order to reduce current expenses and increase income. Neither method reflects the economic substance of oil and gas exploration in that they do not include the current value of the oil and gas reserves in the statements.

BIBLIOGRAPHY

AICPA, *Accounting and Reporting Practices in the Oil and Gas Industry* (AICPA).
TOUCHE ROSS & Co., *Oil & Gas Accounting: What Producers Must Know* (Touche Ross & Co., 1980).

SUGAR Sucrose, produced from both sugarcane and sugar beets.

Major sugar exporters include Cuba, Brazil, Australia, the Philippines, and France. Major importers include the United States, Japan,

Russia, and England. Major producers of sugar include Russia, France, Mexico, West Germany, Poland, and the United States.

The major use of sugar is the direct sale of the refined product in wholesale and retail outlets.

Sugar is included in the U.S. price support programs along with other grains. World sugar prices tend to be volatile, with long periods of surplus followed by shorter periods of shortages and price increases.

The New York COFFEE, SUGAR & COCOA EXCHANGE, INC. offers two sugar contracts for trading. The sugar no. 11 (world) contract is the more actively traded. This contract calls for delivery of cane sugar in bulk f.o.b. stowed from any of 27 foreign countries of origin as well as the United States. The sugar no. 12 (domestic) contract, which trades less actively than the no. 11 contract, calls for delivery of cane sugar in bulk, c.i.f. duty paid at named Atlantic and Gulf ports.

The sugar futures markets have been used primarily by sugar cane producers, industrial users, refiners, and sugar dealers. However, both the no. 11 and no. 12 contracts could be used for hedging purposes by persons involved in the production and processing of sugar beets. In addition, according to the exchange, the manufacturers and users of corn sweetener products could find sugar futures at times to be a viable hedge against their price risks.

SUGAR EXCHANGE See COFFEE, SUGAR & COCOA EXCHANGE, INC.

SUPERDOT An electronic order routing system by which member firms transmit market and limit orders in NYSE-listed securities directly to the specialist post where the securities are traded or to the member firm's booth. In 1988, 183 member firms participated as SuperDOT subscribers.

SUPERFUND ENVIRONMENTAL TAX A tax enacted to assist in paying for certain governmental actions in environmental matters. The tax is imposed at a 0.12% rate times the amount by which modified alternative minimum taxable income for the tax year exceeds $2,000,000. Modified alternative minimum taxable income equals alternative minimum taxable income excluding (1) any alternative net operating loss deduction (NOL) claimed or (2) any deduction claimed for the superfund environmental tax.

SUPERINTENDENT OF BANKS See STATE BANKING DEPARTMENT.

SUPER NOW ACCOUNT An account authorized for depository institutions starting January 1983 that is a combination of a NOW account (negotiable order of withdrawal) and a money market deposit account (MMDA). The super now account must have a minimum initial and average balance of at least $2,500; no interest rate ceiling exists except that no more than 5.25% must be paid when the average balance falls below $2,5000; a seven-day notice of withdrawal may be required but is rarely applied. Unlimited deposit and withdrawal transactions are allowed only to depositors eligible for NOW accounts, excluding for-profit businesses.

SUPERREGIONAL BANK A very large non-money center bank that owns banks in more than one state.

SUPPLY CURVE A graphic devise to illustrate that price and quantity supplies are positively related. The higher price is needed to provide the financial incentive for producers to make more of their product available, assuming all else remains constant. In the short run, a firm's supply curve is its marginal cost curve.

SUPPLY MANAGEMENT POLICIES Supply management policies focus on enhancing economic growth by creating new employment opportunities and improving resource efficiency. Economic decisions to allocate resources to the production process are influenced by changes in taxes and by regulatory policies. Therefore, supply management policies take two forms: a reduction of marginal tax rates aimed at increasing the amount of capital and labor in the production process and a reduction of government regulatory policies that affect the marginal cost of production.

SUPPLY-SIDE ECONOMICS The school of economics that developed in the U.S. in the late 1970s and early 1980s, emphasizing supply instead of demand in economic analysis, and particularly the disincentive effects of high taxes upon productivity, investment, and growth. Reduction in marginal tax rates, it was argued, would lead to higher after-tax marginal incomes (thus reducing the "wedge" or difference between before-tax and after-tax incomes), which would therefore lead to higher growth and employment and larger rather than smaller tax revenues.

This approach is not new in economic theory, having its roots in *Say's Law* of Markets (that supply creates its own demand) in Jean Baptiste Say's *Treatise on Political Economy*, 1803, and in David Ricardo's *Principles of Political Economy and Taxation*, 1817.

Publicity-wise, however, popular interest in supply-side economics appears to have been stimulated by Dr. Arthur Laffer's "Laffer Curve" and by the apparent adoption by the Reagan administration of the economic program developed by the supply-siders. The "Laffer Curve" is non-data-based and simply depicts on a diagram (vertical scale, tax revenue; horizontal scale, tax rate from 0 to 100%) a perfectly concave curve rising from 0 at the origin to a peak and then declining back to 0 at 100% tax rate. The area within the curve is divided into two hypothetical areas, "normal" and "prohibitive," by a vertical line, which on the horizontal scale would represent the "optimum" rate of tax. Any tax rates below the optimum would increase tax revenues on a declining marginal increase on the upward portion of the curve; but beyond the point indicated by the vertical line of demarcation, any further increases in tax rates would decrease tax revenues marginally until the last marginal increase in tax rates to 100% would yield no marginal increase in revenue.

Besides tax reduction, the supply-siders' economic program included reduced government and government spending, deemphasis on fiscal and monetary attempted targets and more emphasis on the free market, deregulation instead of increased regulation, and monetary objective restraints, even to the extent of restoring the discipline of a gold standard.

See FISCAL POLICY, MONETARY POLICY.

BIBLIOGRAPHY

BARTLETT, B. *Reaganomics*, 1981.
LAFFER, A. B. "Supply-Side Economics." *Financial Analysts Journal*, September-October, 1981.
KERAN, M. W. "The Supply-Side Miracle." *Journal of Portfolio Management*, Summer, 1989.

SUPPORT The active sponsorship of a single security, or a group of securities, by a syndicate, dealer group, individual speculators, or other special interests, to prevent further decline. Support usually is furnished to give a security, or the entire market, an appearance of strength for the purpose of arresting a downward movement and inspiring confidence, rather than with the intention of making immediate profits. Active support, however, in the face of declining market trend is rare, as best results for the stock supported are possible when general market conditions are not adverse.

SUPPORTING ORDERS Buying orders lodged with brokers for the purpose of furnishing SUPPORT.

SURETY This term has two applications.

1. A guarantor; a person or company that agrees to answer for the debt or performance of another in case of default.
2. Suretyship; a guaranty or security protecting a person against loss in case of default in the payment of a debt, or in the performance of a contract; an instrument or undertaking, ordinarily called a surety bond, given as evidence of the guaranty by which the surety becomes bound as the principal or original debtor is bound.

See SURETY COMPANY.

SURETY BOND See SURETY COMPANY.

SURETY COMPANY A company that guarantees the acts of others, i.e., acts as surety for a valuable consideration. One of the principal types of guarantees undertaken by a surety company is the insurance of the faithful conduct of employees handling money or valuable papers, guaranteeing any losses that may result from dishonesty. This is known as fidelity insurance. A surety company undertaking this class of risk keeps in touch with the history of employees and refuses to insure those who have police records. By attempting to secure conviction of defaulters and refusing to renew a surety bond when the insured has been guilty of misconduct, these companies tend to reduce dishonesty, defalcation, and embezzlement.

Originally surety contracts or guarantees were personal, i.e., one person guaranteed the faithful performance of another. Such personal suretyships were frequently abused and rarely compensated. About 1876, the idea of corporate suretyship was put into operation in this country, and a company undertook to assume, for a premium, all the responsibilities of acting as surety. In 1881, when Elihu Root, then counsel of the American Surety Company, presented to the New York Legislature the application of the company to do business, there were very few laws governing the methods by which a corporation might issue surety bonds and undertakings.

A corporate surety bond is a three-party instrument, involving the principal, the obligee or assured, and the surety. The principal is the individual, firm, or corporation on whose behalf the surety is issued. The obligee or assured is the individual, firm, or corporation in whose favor the suretyship is issued. The surety is the company issuing the guaranty.

The laws of today require a great many different bonds covering every phase of human relationship, from licensing a peddler to guaranteeing the honesty and faithful performance of duties of public officials, guardians, trustees, and executors; the fidelity of employees; and the performance of contracts.

By rigidly adhering to its underwriting standards created by years of experience and by only issuing suretyship for responsible applicants, the surety company is acting as a safeguard for all citizens and taxpayers. Under varying conditions and in the different states and municipalities, it has been possible for surety companies to build up a broad experience, which has been of inestimable assistance to legislatures in safeguarding funds.

SURPLUS The proportion of profits of a business for the current accounting period in excess of all costs, expenses, interest charges, and dividend payments, i.e., the amount available for carrying forward into the next accounting period (net profit); or the accumulated or undivided profits of past periods left invested in the business, i.e., the earned surplus. The first application, however, is not strict accounting terminology. The term "surplus" should not be used synonymously with net profits, but rather should designate undivided profits of a corporation—profits that have not been distributed in dividends to stockholders. The surplus, which in some cases exceeds capital stock, should be added to the latter, together with any unallocated equity reserves, in order to determine net worth.

The American Institute of Certified Public Accountants, in its *Accounting Terminology Bulletin No. 1*, has recommended that the term "surplus" be discontinued in balance sheet presentation, whether "capital surplus," "paid-in surplus," or "earned surplus." Among the terms that may appear in balance sheets, in lieu of the preceding terms, are the following more descriptive terms.

For "paid-in surplus": "contribution in excess of par or stated value," "paid-in capital in excess of par or stated value," or "additional paid-in capital." If the surplus arises from appraisal of fixed assets: "excess of appraised value of fixed assets over cost," "unrealized appreciation of fixed assets," "appraisal capital." If the surplus arises from donations: "capital arising from donation of shares of capital stock," "donated capital," "capital contributed by donation of (specified type of asset)."

For "earned surplus": "retained earnings," "earnings reinvested in the business," "accumulated retained earnings," etc. The proliferation of terms created in the effort to get away from the possible misinterpretation of the term "surplus" as in excess may be more descriptive, but standardization has been sacrificed.

In banking, surplus refers to a portion of stockholders' equity representing the effect of selling stock at a premium above its par value and by transfers from the undivided profits account.

In economics, surplus refers to a situation in which, at a given price, quantity supplied is greater than quantity demanded. To alleviate a surplus, price must fall.

See CAPITAL AND SURPLUS.

SURPLUS RESERVE The amount of a bank's RESERVE (held in a Federal Reserve bank if a member bank, or in its own vault or legal depositaries if a nonmember bank) in excess of the legal reserve requirement; more commonly known as EXCESS RESERVES. The term also applies to the surplus reserves of all the banks in a given clearinghouse association.

In accounting, the term is applied to that type of equity reserve that represents an earmarked portion of surplus and is not definitely allocated for any purpose. In accordance with the modern trend in accounting terminology, the term "surplus reserve" has been replaced by "appropriations of retained earnings," although the term "reserve" continues in use, e.g., "reserve for contingencies," "reserve for plant expansion," "reserve for expansion," "reserve for equalization of dividends," etc.

See RESERVE.

SURRENDER VALUE In connection with insurance policies, the cash sum that the insurance company agrees to pay the holder who exercises the option of surrender. The surrender value increases in proportion to the number of premiums paid and the growth of the policy reserve. The loan and surrender value of a policy are usually coincident.

SURROGATE COURT The name given in some states to the court, usually of county jurisdiction, having jurisdiction over probate of wills, administration of intestacies, supervision over executors and administrators, guardianships, etc. It is known in other states as PROBATE court, or orphan's court.

SUSHIS Eurobonds issued by Japanese entities that do not count against limits on holdings of foreign securities.

SUSPENSION This term has three meanings:

1. The termination of a business due to insolvency or bankruptcy.
2. The temporary closing of a bank that, though in a solvent condition, desires to liquidate a part of its assets in order to be in shape to meet the demands of its creditors.

See FAILURES.

3. Prohibiting members of a stock exchange from exercising their rights as members for a stated period for violating certain rules of the exchange. On the New York Stock Exchange, members may be suspended (as distinguished from expelled) not only for specific violations of rules, but also for certain acts not expressly defined. The rules of the New York Stock Exchange provide for suspension in the following cases: "conduct or proceeding inconsistent with just and equitable principles of trade," where failure "has been caused by recklessness or unbusinesslike dealings," and whenever a member has been "adjudged guilty of any act which may be determined by said [Board of Governors] to be detrimental to the interest or welfare of the exchange."

See NEW YORK STOCK EXCHANGE.

SUSPENSION OF GOLD PAYMENTS *See* GOLD REPEAL JOINT RESOLUTION, GOLD RESERVE ACT OF 1934, GOLD STANDARD.

SUSPENSION OF SPECIE PAYMENTS *See* SPECIE PAYMENT.

SWAP A financial transaction in which two counterparties agree to exchange streams of payments over time according to a predetermined rule. A swap is normally used to transform the market exposure associated with a loan or bond borrowing from one interest rate base (fixed term or floating rate) or currency of denomination to another. Central banks use swap arrangements as reciprocal short-term credit agreements to obtain foreign exchange for intervention in the foreign exchange market. The central bank obtains domestic currency in exchange for forcing currency.

In bond swapping, the switch is from one fixed-income security to another fixed-income security having the same or different coupon, maturity, quality rating, yield level, and other features. Investors usually swap bonds to gain increased current income or yield to maturity (yield-pickup swap); to obtain better price performance should there be a movement in interest rates (rate anticipation swap); to purchase or sell a security at a historically attractive yield relative to other similar issues (substitution swap); to purchase or sell a security at a historically attractive yield compared to other groups or types (sector swap); or to attain other investment objectives—tax minimization, portfolio diversification, portfolio concentration.

SWAP NETWORK

BIBLIOGRAPHY

ANDREWS, E. L. "Insurance for Rising Interest Rates." *Venture*, December, 1988.
BEIDLEMAN, C. *Financial Swaps*. Dow Jones-Irwin, Inc., Homewood, IL, 1985.
BICKSLER, J., and CHEN, A. "An Economic Analysis of Interest Rate Swaps." *The Journal of Finance*, July, 1986.
COOPER, R. "Still Plenty of Room to Grow." *Euromoney*, October, 1988.
SMITH, C. W., and others. "The Market for Interest Rate Swaps." *Financial Management*, Winter, 1988.

SWAP NETWORK A series of short-term, reciprocal credit lines in foreign currency operations. The swap network enables the Federal Reserve to exchange (swap) dollars for the currencies of 14 foreign nations through their central banks, up to previously agreed upon amounts. The BANK FOR INTERNATIONAL SETTLEMENTS (BIS) is also part of the swap network for the specified currencies it holds.

Any participant can initiate a swap drawing. Transactions are conducted through the Federal Reserve Bank of New York, which acts for the Federal Reserve System and the United States Treasury in foreign currency operations. As in domestic money market operations, the New York Fed acts under authorization and a directive from the Federal Open Market Committee (FOMC). It also consults closely with the U.S. Treasury on all operations.

The first swap line of $50 million was established with the Bank of France in March, 1962. Similar agreements with other central banks followed in 1962 and 1963. The last lines were established in 1967; however, most credit lines have been increased since then. The agreements establishing swap lines are limited to one year, but can be renewed annually, by mutual consent, for additional one-year periods.

Funds drawn under swap agreements are created by central banks. The Federal Reserve, for example, creates dollars through authority granted by Congress. Any undesired bank reserve creation can be offset by domestic open market operations. Other foreign central banks have similar power to create national currency. The BIS, however, acquires its swap funds either through borrowings from participants or through foreign exchange market operations.

Use of swap facilities was heavy through the early 1970s, as foreign central banks often drew on the lines to obtain dollars needed to finance foreign exchange market intervention. The Federal Reserve obtains foreign currencies either for foreign exchange market intervention or to purchase dollars that central banks would otherwise have converted into gold or other U.S. reserve assets. Throughout periods of heavy borrowing, swap drawings reduced the need for central banks to rely on gold and other reserve assets to settle their accounts.

Federal Reserve use of the swap network was suspended temporarily on August 15, 1971, when the U.S. "closed the gold window" by ending dollar-gold convertibility. The Federal Reserve resumed swap drawings for market intervention purposes in August, 1972. With the move to floating exchange rates by the major countries in 1973, the Federal Reserve and other central banks have subsequently made use of swap lines on numerous occasions to finance exchange market intervention. The objective of these interventions has been to counter disorderly trading conditions.

In keeping abreast of market developments, the New York Fed maintains close communications with other central banks in the network, on a daily basis in some instances. A drawing will usually be initiated by telephone, followed by an exchange of cables specifying terms and conditions. A swap is in the form of a foreign exchange contract—the sale of dollars by the Federal Reserve for the currency of the foreign central banks, with the simultaneous agreement to reverse the transaction three months later. The appropriate accounting entries are made by the New York Fed and the foreign central bank involved.

SWEATING A method of obtaining gold or silver dust from coins by rubbing them together in a box or bag.

SWEEP ACCOUNT A service provided by a depository financial institution to invest on an overnight basis all, or a portion, of a customer's idle balances.

SWEETENING A LOAN A Wall Street expression meaning to place additional securities on deposit to margin a loan after security values have declined, in order to keep the margin intact or to strengthen the margn.
See MARGIN CALL.

SWINDLING The selling of doubtful or worthless securities through misrepresentation. Swindling may be accomplished through advertisements that offer securities of high yield or promise exorbitant profits, or through circulars distributed gratis that are written deceptively and with an ulterior purpose, rather than to give bona fide disinterested analyses.

Another form of swindling consists of switching low-grade securities of doubtful or no value for high-grade securities of unquestionable merit.
See BLUE SKY LAWS, BUNCO, FALSE STATEMENT ACTS.

SWINGS The periodic movements upward and downward in business activity, commodity prices, security prices, or money rates. Proponents of the DOW THEORY classify price movements in stock prices as primary or major trend, indicating the basic direction of the market (primary "bull" or "bear" market); secondary movements or reactions, which are intermediate interruptions (declines or rallies) to the primary trend and which figure in its forecasting and determination; and daily movements (the "ripples"), which individually are disregarded by the theory but are accumulated and charted to delineate the intermediate swings.
See SPECULATIVE CYCLE.

Basic movements in economic activity in alternating periods of prosperity and depression, formerly referred to as "business cycles," have been further refined by analysis into three distinct types: the "Kitchin" short waves (named after Joseph Kitchin), particularly identified with inventory fluctuations; the "Juglar" nine- to ten-year waves (named after Clement Juglar); and the "Kondratieff" long waves (named after N. D. Kondratieff).
See BUSINESS CYCLE, BUSINESS FORECASTING SERVICES.

SWITCHING This term has two meanings.

1. When a speculator in grain, cotton, or sugar futures transfers his contract to mature in some future month.
2. The process of transferring one's interest to another security, i.e., liquidating one's holdings in one security for the purpose of placing proceeds in another security because the prospects appear to be more attractive, to increase one's income, or to strengthen one's position.

SYMBOLS *See* NEW YORK STOCK EXCHANGE ABBREVIATIONS.

SYMMETALLISM BIMETALLISM suffered from an inherent defect—the cheaper marketwise of the two defined monetary metals would be presented at the mint for coinage at the statutorily fixed mint ratio so that, in actuality, circulation would tend to be monometallic rather than bimetallic.

Symmetallism proposed to obviate this defect by requiring the presentation at the mint of *all* the required monetary metals (two or more) in the statutorily specified proportions, for coinage and bullion. Such coinage and bullion thus would be neither gold nor silver, for example, but an amalgam of both—a hybrid system. Symmetallism would suffer from the basic difficulties of determining the "par" of exchange relative to monometallic as well as bimetallic systems and combatting natural reluctance to present the metal undervalued at the mint. The U.S. tried the bimetallic system in its monetary history, but never resorted to symmetallism.
See MONOMETALLISM.

SYNDICATE In general, any joint venture; a temporary association of parties for the financing and execution of some specific business project. The UNDERWRITING syndicate is a group of investment banking houses, or broker-dealer firms, that organize to underwrite an issue from a corporation or governmentally, as distinguished from a single underwriter. The public offering and sale of relatively small aggregate issues might be accomplished by a single investment banking firm, the "originator"; but when the size of the issue is large, involving substantial risk and tie-up of the single originating firm's available capital and credit and requiring more selling power than the single firm can provide, the originating firm invites other investment banking firms to join it in functional syndicates. Following are the types of syndicate agreements.

1. Purchase agreement, the contract between the issuer and the purchase group of firms, a material provision of which is the agreement by the issuer to sell to each of the members of the purchase group and the agreement by the latter to buy their specified proportions of the total underwriting.
2. Purchase group agreement (agreement among the underwriters), which not only repeats the participation liability of each member firm found in the purchase agreement but also authorizes the syndicate manager, acting for the purchase group, to place the "give-up" portion through selected other firms in the selling group at a concession and to institutional investors directly at the public offering price.
3. Selling group agreement ("offering to selected dealers") between the syndicate manager, acting for the purchase group, and the invited dealers, mobilized thereby for greater distributive power for expeditious sale of the entire issue. Members of the purchase group, to the extent of their "take-down," also distribute at retail to such extent.

Purchase Agreement. The passage of the Securities Act of 1933, with its registration procedure for public offerings and a waiting period until the effective date for public sale of 20 days or more, introduced a greater degree of risk in underwritings of the firm commitment type (including the standby type). Thus, the purchase agreement now conventionally includes a "market out" or escape clause. This provides that the purchase contract may be terminated by the representative firm (originator acting on behalf of itself and other purchase group members aggregating 50% or more participation): "(a) if, prior to the time the post-effective amendment [to the registration statement] shall become effective, the market value of securities in general, or political, economic or financial conditions shall have so materially changed as in the judgment of the representative to render it inadvisable to proceed with such public offering; or (b) if, prior to the closing date [settlement with issuer for agreed proceeds of sale], the company shall have sustained a material and substantial loss by fire, flood, accident or other calamity which in the judgment of the representative shall render it inadvisable to proceed with the delivery of the securities, whether or not such loss shall have been insured." Although this might seem to impair the binding nature of liability, in practice it is rarely invoked even when market conditions become unstable, because of the natural desire of the purchase group to have a satisfied issuer client. The purchase agreement is also contingent upon the registration statement's reaching the effective date so that the securities may validly be publicly sold.

Purchase Group Agreement. This is the joint venture proper of the underwriting firms involved, covering such points as the liability of each participant ("several" liability conventionally in use limits liability of each participant to its agreed share of the total issue) and the appointment of the syndicate manager (usually from the originating firm) and granting of authority and discretion thereto in management of the syndicate on such matters as amount of give-up, formation of selling group and concession thereto from public offering price, necessary stabilization operations, termination or extension of the offering date, details of payment and delivery, manager's fee, and legal clauses such as indemnification, representations, and warranties.

Selling Group Agreement. A huge public offering might involve a relatively few members of the purchase group and hundreds of members of the selling group located throughout the country and abroad. The syndicate manager, pursuant to the purchase group agreement, selects the selling group members and their allocations, at the dealers' concession specified. Since no public offering of the issue may be made before the effective date, the selling group agreement and the final prospectus are sent to the dealers on the effective date, for acceptance of the allocation, which is subject to prior sale. It is often provided that the concession to the dealer will be withheld, or the shares returned to the dealer, with respect to any shares that the manager has had to purchase in stabilization operations (they may be traced to the dealer who was supposed to have sold them effectively). It is also conventionally provided that the selling group dealer in turn may make a specified "reallowance" (portion of his own concession) to other dealers not members of the selling group.

The total underwriting spread (difference between public offering price and net price to the issuer) will be distributed three ways: the management fee to the syndicate manager, the underwriting share (purchase group), and the selling commissions (selling group's concession). Expenses of the offering, some of which the issuer may specifically agree to bear in the purchase agreement, are deducted before making the division.

Competitive Bidding Practice. The above procedure refers to conventional underwriting by private negotiation. Competitive bidding, which is required for public utility issues under the Public Utility Act of 1935 (pursuant to rule of the Securities and Exchange Commission) and for railroad securities (pursuant to rule of the Interstate Commerce Commission), necessarily affects the procedure for syndicates. The process begins with the issuer's "statement of terms and conditions" and invitation for bids. (Some firms begin even sooner—as soon as the prospective financing is "firm" enough—so as to form strong syndicates.) The major firm forming the syndicate invites other firms to become members and confirm; a "major" participation would be one equal in size to that of the manager and of any other member, minor participations ranging downward therefrom. Before the effective date, the issuer stages "briefings" for the interested groups and supplies documentary and descriptive data. Each group in turn has meetings among its member firms, who a few days before submission of the bid execute and sign the agreement among such prospective purchasers, specifying participation (which may be increased by 10% without special agreement, usually, to allow for "dropouts"), appointment of the manager and determination of his fee, sharing of expenses whether or not the bid wins, the authorization of stabilization operations by the manager if the bid is successful, etc. The final meeting of the bidding group is usually held on the very morning of the day specified by the issuer for submission of bids, so that the bid may reflect the latest market conditions. Submission of the bid makes possible determination by the manager of the selling concession to dealers and the public offering price. Subject to the terms and specifications of the issuer, the winning bid is determined, usually on a "lowest cost of money" basis to the issuer. The successful group's manager then swings into action for distribution through the selling group and directly to institutions, and bidding group firms are allocated their "take-downs." The first act by the manager is to sign the purchase contract with the issuer, on behalf of the winning group, provisions of which were previously furnished to prospective bidders by the issuer for information.

Impact of "Shelf Registration." Rule 415 of the SECURITIES AND EXCHANGE COMMISSION under the Securities Act of 1933, adopted for a nine-month trial period on February 24, 1982, called for a corporate issuer to file a single S-3 registration to cover the total amount of securities it will put "on the shelf" for issuance in the next two years. Since the traditional underwriting firm that has handled the corporation's offerings on a negotiated basis in the past is not specified, it is expected that despite the traditional ties, fiercer competition for the business from other underwriting firms may develop and/or the corporation may more readily change its traditional underwriter ("originating" underwriter).

Banks as Underwriters. Pursuant to the BANKING ACT OF 1933, banks may underwrite only U.S. government securities and other "Federal area" securities, as well as general obligation state and municipal securities. In recent times the U.S. Treasury has offered Treasury bills on a competitive bidding basis, and other marketable securities on an auction basis. State and municipal securities are issued on a competitive bidding basis, a traditional requirement of state and municipal laws. Therefore, money center banks active in municipals form syndicates for bidding on such new issues, or become members of the same. Banks in recent years also have urged modification of the Glass-Steagall Act to permit their underwriting of revenue municipals, a move opposed by nonbank underwriters in this field.

See INVESTMENT BANKER.

BIBLIOGRAPHY

FOSTER, F. D. "Syndicate Size, Spreads, and Market Power During the Introduction of Shelf Registration." *Journal of Finance*, March, 1989.

SYNDICATED LOANS Loans participated in by multiple banks and other institutions where the overall credit involved exceeds an individual lender's legal lending or other limits. One bank in the syndicate usually acts as agent for the other institutions.

T

T-ACCOUNT A ledger summary of the assets and liabilities of any business, bank or other institution or individual. Assets are listed on the left side of the T, and liabilities are listed on the right. For the T-account to be in balance, total assets must equal total liabilities. An entry on the left side of the T is referred to as a debit; an entry on the right side is a credit. The dollar difference between the total debits and the total credits is called the account balance. The rules for recording increases and decreases in accounts are summarized as follows:

Debit an account to record:
1. Increase in an asset.
2. Decrease in a liability.
3. Decrease in equity.
4. Decrease in revenue.
5. Increase in expense.

Credit an account to record:
1. Decrease in an asset.
2. Increase in a liability.
3. Increase in equity.
4. Increase in revenue.
5. Decrease in expense.

TAFT-HARTLEY ACT The Labor-Management Relations Act of 1947, which amended the Wagner-Connery Act of 1935. With the passage of the Taft-Hartly Act in 1947, certain unfair labor practices by labor unions were forbidden: The scope of closed shops (a shop hiring only union workers) is limited; states have the right to adopt right-to-work laws; the government is empowered to obtain an injunction preventing any work stoppage for 80 days when a strike threatens the nation's health and welfare; unions cannot use union funds in connection with national elections; officers of unions must take an oath that they are not members of the Communist Party before the union can be certified (amended by the Landrum-Griffin Act); unions must file financial reports with the U.S. Department of Labor along with a membership list.

TAKE A FLIER See FLIER.

TAKE AND PAY CONTRACT An agreement in which one party guarantees to purchase an agreed-upon amount of a product, provided it is delivered.

TAKE OR PAY CONTRACT A contract in which a purchaser agrees with a seller to pay specified minimum payments even if delivery of the products or services is not taken. These contracts are often related to project financing arrangements.

TAKEOUT LOANS In construction loans by national banks, loans having maturities of not to exceed 60 months made to finance the construction of industrial or commercial buildings, the permanent financing covered by a valid and binding agreement entered into by a financially responsible lender to advance the full amount of the bank's loans upon completion of the buildings (12 U.S.C. 371, third paragraph).

A national bank may make a combined construction and permanent loan secured by residential, farm, industrial, or commercial property for a period of up to 30 years and 60 months. Section 371 does not require that the interim and the permanent financing be made separately (Par. 7.2405, Interpretive Rulings of the Comptroller of the Currency).

TAKEOVER The acquisition of one business enterprise by a person, a group, or another business. This is done by buying the assets of the business and/or enough equity issues with voting power to control the management of the firm. A friendly takeover occurs when the management of the companies involved negotiate cooperatively to merge their enterprises. A hostile or unfriendly takeover often begins with a tender offer for the shares of a target firm by another corporation alien to the management of the target firm. In a hostile takeover, the objective is to acquire sufficient shares to control votes and seize management authority from the target firm. In a proxy battle, groups of shareholders compete with management for changes in corporate policy by forming voting blocs.

Takeovers often begin with the acquisition of shares by the acquiring firm. If more than 5% of the outstanding shares of the target firm are acquired, the buyer must file Form 13D with the SEC, which has the effect of revealing the acquirer's intent. The acquiring firm may instead issue a tender offer for a controlling interest. Form 14D must be filed, giving the offer price and other details relating to the tender.

In hostile takeovers, management may attempt to defend itself by urging shareholders to reject the offer, seek a higher bid or bidder, or accept the candidate firm's own counteroffer. Management may borrow money to make a self-tender or make an exchange of shares for debt. In some cases, management has bought the shares acquired by the acquiring firm, often at a premium in return for an agreement to stop the takeover attempt. Such efforts are commonly called "greenmail." Special terms associated with takeover include:

Crown jewels A target company's most valuable assets, which could be sold to make it less attractive to a raider or to raise cash after a debt-structured raid.

Friendly takeover A situation in which the management of the target company recommends to its stockholders that the tender offer be accepted. In a friendly takeover, the acquiring company usually purchases a small amount of the target company's shares in the open market until a significant percentage (such as 10% or 15%) is acquired. The acquirer makes an offer to management to obtain the remaining shares, or a major portion thereof, to company shareholders. Management may respond favorably, after which the acquiror makes a tender offer to the shareholders. If the management of the company recommends to its stockholders that the tender offer be rejected, the tender offer would represent a hostile tender offer.

Golden parachute A strategy whereby the top management of the target company is to receive large rewards if the managers' positions are terminated as a result of a hostile takeover.

Greenmail A situation involving the sale of shares acquired by the hostile acquiror back to the company, often resulting at a handsome profit to the acquiror.

Hostile tender offer A situation in which the management of the target company recommends to its stockholders that the tender offer be rejected.

Leveraged buyouts A takeover in which the acquiror arranges the transaction so that a significant amount of debt and a relatively small amount of equity capital are used to accomplish the buyout. In leveraged buyouts, assets acquired in the buyout are usually pledged as collateral for funds borrowed to purchase the target company.

Pac-man A strategy in which the target company attempts to acquire the hostile takeoverer to foil the attempt.

Parking An illegal devise used in some takeovers whereby the person attempting the takeover arranges to have arbitragers hold large blocks of stock that could be purchased in a hurry. By this technique, the raider could gain an effective hold on a corporation before personally acquiring that 5% ownership that triggers public disclosure of stock acquisitions.

Poison pill A takeover defense in which the target company issues very large amounts of convertible preferred stock that can dilute the percentage of common stock to be acquired by the hostile acquiror. A comopany might also dispose of attractive assets to make the tarket company less attractive as a takeover prospect.

Scorched earth policy A situation whereby the target company liquidates a significant portion of its assets to make the company undesirable to a suitor.

Shark repellent Sections in a corporation's bylaws that are designed to discourage unfriendly takeovers. Such tactics include requiring a high percentage of the shareholders to approve a takeover.

Target company A company that is being considered for a takeover by another company. The book value of the target company is frequently significantly below the current market value of the target company's stock.

Tender offer A formal offer to purchase a specified amount of stock at a set price.

Tin parachute Generous severance benefits for ordinary employees, used as a poison pill.

White knight A strategy of finding another company friendly to the target company to acquire it before it can be acquired by the hostile aggressor.

TALE Contracts involving the payment of metallic money might call for payment by tale, meaning by count, as distinguished from by weight. If payment were made in gold coin, for instance, the total sum by tale would disregard abrasion, whereas the sum by weight would denote actual value. A given sum computed by tale would give a smaller value than if computed by weight.

P.L. 95-147, October 28, 1977, among other provisions repealed the "Joint Resolution to Assure Uniform Value to the Coins and Currencies of the United States," approved June 5, 1933 (31 U.S.C. 463). The intended effect of such repeal was to permit the inclusion of gold and multicurrency clauses in private contracts.

TALON In general, the portion of a bond that remains after all coupons have been removed. Depending upon the nature of the bond, the talon may have value.

In England, France, and Germany, the last portion of a bond, certificate, or rente remaining after the coupons have been detached, sometimes taking the form of a special coupon. When the talon is presented to the proper office of the government, the holder is entitled to receive a new certificate or rente with its full quota of coupons for the next period. French RENTES are usually issued with coupons attached for five-to ten-year periods.

TANGIBLE ASSETS Physical or material assets, e.g., real estate, buildings, machinery, inventories, and cash, as distinguished from intangible assets, e.g., goodwill, patents, trademarks, and the like.

On a balance sheet, property, plant, and equipment are the terms used to classify tangible noncurrent assets that are used in the normal operations of a business. Included in this category are assets that are held for use and not for investment, have an expected life of more than one year (a bundle of future services), and are tangible in nature (having physical substance). The major types of assets included in property, plant, and equipment are land, buildings, equipment, machinery, furniture and fixtures, leasehold improvements, and certain natural resources.

TANKER LOANS In the various specialized fields of INTERNATIONAL BANKING, one of the more volatile types of credits has been credits to private owners and operators of oil tankers in the world tanker market, extended principally by European and Far Eastern banks but also by a few of the major U.S. banks active directly or indirectly in international banking.

After the boom in tanker construction and chartering which occurred in the 1960s, overcapacity developed after the 1967 Arab-Israeli War, and prevailing charter rates weakened to below operating costs and payments on loans. Under the circumstances, reports of financial difficulties of two tanker groups raised concern regarding the shipping portfolio of U.S. banks.

Reportedly included among bank criteria in granting tanker loans are the following: (1) emphasis on cash flows discounted to present value on negotiated long-term charters and leases, typically to major oil companies and having final maturities beyond the maturities of loans, (2) preference for borrowers having other diversified sources of liquidity besides the tanker operations, especially in the case of tanker owners reluctant to accept modest rates on long-term charters and instead holding out for bulges in spot tanker rates, and (3) on vessel loans, loan-to-cost ratios normally at 50%, but adjustable between precommitment and closing dates to allow for changes in feasibility.

TAPE A narrow ribbon of paper used in quotation tickers on which prices transmitted by telegraph from market headquarters are printed by an electrically operated instrument.
See QUOTATION TICKER, TICKER.

TAPE ABBREVIATIONS See NEW YORK STOCK EXCHANGE ABBREVIATIONS, TICKER ABBREVIATIONS.

TAPE PRICES Prices as indicated on the ticker tape. These are printed on the tape in ticker abbreviations, or ticker symbols.
See QUOTATION TICKER, TICKER.

TARE Unproductive weight; weight of the container, package, crate, or vehicle in which goods are loaded for shipment or carriage, as distinguished from the gross weight and net weight. Thus, if a barrel of oil weighs 400 lbs., the barrel 40 lbs., and the oil 360 lbs., 400 lbs. represents the gross weight, 360 lbs. the net weight, and 40 lbs. the tare.

TARGET COMPANY A company selected as an attractive candidate for an ACQUISITION, MERGER, or CONSOLIDATION.
See TAKEOVER.

TARGETED MARKET A market segment selected as desirable for promotion purposes, such as the upscale market. Targeting is a common MARKETING practice in banking. Markets are targeted that best accommodate a bank's strengths, capacity to serve, and ability to compete. Targeting should be attempted only after researching a market and establishing a current data base.

TARGET EXAMINATION A mini-or selective examination. Targets Examinations were developed in the 1980s by the California Banking Department. CAMEL 1 and 2 rated banks were targeted to receive minimum on-site supervision by state banking regulators. The regulators accumulated sufficient data periodically to justify this practice. Procedures were developed to return to on-site examinations if conditions warranted.

TARIFF This term has three meanings:

1. In general, a schedule of charges for services or merchandise. This general use of the term, however, is tending to disappear in favor of specific references.
2. A schedule of freight or passenger tariff rates. Railroads and other transportation agencies post schedules of rates or charges for carrying various classes of merchandise or passengers, pursuant to statutory requirements of publicity. In order to ascertain the charge for carrying freight from one point to another, it is necessary to determine first the classification and then ascertain the tariff on goods within that classification.
3. The statutes under which duties on imports are imposed. Under the U.S. Constitution, no tax may be levied on exports (Art. I, Sec. 9, Par. 5), but Congress has the power to "lay and collect taxes, duties, imposts and excises." The states may not "without the consent of Congress" lay any imposts or duties on imports or exports, per Article I, Section 10, Paragraph 2 of the U.S. Constitution. The federal government has imposed duties on imports under various tariff acts since 1789. The purpose of a tariff may be to raise revenues, and until 1900, about half of the expenses of the federal government were defrayed from collection of customs duties. Other reasons may be for the protection of domestic industry to enable it to compete with imports which have to pay the protective duties upon entry or for regulatory purposes.

TARIFF

A Brief Outline of U.S. Tariff History to 1960.

Tariff Act of 1789—the first tariff act of the United States, passed on the recommendation of Alexander Hamilton, the first secretary of the Treasury, with mildly protective duties of 5% on most imports.

Tariff Act of 1816—duty on cotton and woolen goods established at 25% for three years, after which it became 20%.

Tariff Act of 1824—duty on cotton and woolen goods established at 33 1/3 %; duties increased on iron, wool, hemp, and bagging.

Tariff Act of 1828—duty increased on pig iron, bar iron, hemp, wool, and flax.

Tariff Act of 1832—woolens subjected to a simple *ad valorem* duty of 50%.

Tariff Act of 1833—so-called compromise tariff; duties generally reduced, with principle of gradual decreases until "a general level of 20% should be reached."

Tariff Act of 1842—a protective tariff, with higher rates.

Tariff Act of 1846—known as the Walker Tariff; rates reduced.

Tariff Act of 1857—duties decreased.

Tariff Act of 1861 (March 2)—known as the Morrill Tariff; duties increased on wool and iron.

Tariff Act of 1863 (March 3)—certain duties increased.

Tariff Act of 1864 (June 30)—certain duties increased.

Tariff Act of 1870 (July 14)—certain duties reduced.

Tariff Act of 1872 (May 1)—average duties decreased about 10%; tea and coffee put on free list.

Tariff Act of 1875 (March 3)—reductions repealed.

Tariff Act of 1883 (March 3)—duty on combing wool reduced; taxes on matches, bank checks, and savings bank deposits abolished.

Tariff Act of 1890 (Oct. 1)—known as the McKinley Tariff; rates generally raised; sugar put on free list.

Tariff Act of 1894 (Aug. 28)—known as the Wilson Tariff; rates lowered.

Tariff Act of 1897 (July 24)—known as the Dingley Tariff; rates generally raised, in some cases to extreme levels; sugar duty made specific.

Tariff Act of 1909—known as the Payne-Aldrich Tariff; rates slightly lowered; contained 121 pages and mentioned 3,500 articles, 360 duty-free.

Tariff Act of 1913—known as the Underwood Tariff; rates lowered.

Tariff Act of 1922—known as the Fordney-McCumber Tariff; rates increased.

Tariff Act of 1930—known as the Hawley-Smoot Tariff; rates increased to the most protective levels in U.S. history.

Reciprocal Tariff Act (June 12, 1934)^ushered in the reciprocal trade agreements program, particularly sponsored by Secretary of State Cordell Hull; extended by Congress on eleven separate occasions, usually for three-year periods, sometimes for one, two, or (1958) four years.

Escape clause: The 1955 extension of the Reciprocal Tariff Act of 1934 strengthened the escape clause (reservation in trade agreements of the right to revise any tariff that threatens to cause or is causing serious injury to a domestic competitive industry). This reservation, under the Trade Agreements Extension Act of 1951, as amended since, provides for investigations by the International Trade Commission and reports to the President as to actions which should be taken under the escape clause of trade agreements.

By executive order in 1947, the President had required that all new trade agreements contain the escape clause. Provisions substantially in accord with this executive order were included in the escape clause of the General Agreement on Tariffs and Trade.

Peril point: The peril point provision, originally enacted in the 1948 extension of the 1934 act, repealed in 1949, but restored in the 1951 extension, provided that the U.S. International Trade Commission shall survey all commodities on which the President proposes to negotiate agreements and shall specify rates of duty below which, in the commission's judgment, tariffs cannot be lowered without injury to U.S. industry or business. The President could reduce the tariffs below these points, but if he did so, he would be required to send an official communication to the Congress explaining the reasons for such action.

Trade Expansion Act of 1962. Signed by the President on October 11, 1962, the Trade Expansion Act of 1962 was characterized by the Joint Economic Committee as the most important development in U.S. tariff legislation since the Trade Agreements Act of 1934. The major features of the act provided new authority to reduce tariffs and new programs of adjustment assistance to firms and workers. The new presidential authority for tariff reduction included (1) general authority to decrease by 50% any rate of duty existing on July 1, 1962, and to modify other types of import restrictions; (2) special authority to negotiate with the European Economic Community (EEC) for reductions of up to 100% in duties on goods for which the EEC and the United States together furnished more than 80% of the free world's exports and agricultural goods, if the President determined such reduction would help to maintain or expand U.S. exports; (3) special authority to reduce by more than 50% or to eliminate duties on tropical agriculture or forestry products not produced in significant quantities in the United States, provided that the EEC would make a comparable nondiscriminatory commitment; and (4) special authority to reduce or to eliminate duties of less than 5% *ad valorem*. To administer tariff negotiations authorized by the act, provision was made for the appointment of a special representative for trade negotiations. The act also provided for the establishment of a cabinet-level interagency trade committee to advise and assist the President in carrying out the mandate of the act.

The Trade Expansion Act of 1962 also provided two types of adjustment assistance if increased imports arising primarily from tariff concessions granted under the act or any prior act were causing serious injury to an industry. One provided for the traditional authority of adjustment of tariffs or imposition of quotas; the other provided for direct assistance to firms and workers in injured industries. Upon proper certification and for a limited time period, technical, financial, and tax assistance to firms thus injured would be provided, and trade readjustment allowances of up to 52 weeks could be given to affected workers. In addition, similar assistance was provided to firms and workers injured as a result of imports without a finding of injury to the industry. In addition to the above provisions, the act contained a number of other important features: requirements for public notification and for public hearings when articles are being considered for trade concessions; reservation of certain articles from negotiations, notably those on which an escape clause action was in effect; provisions for withdrawing trade agreement concessions in the event of unreasonable import restrictions being imposed by foreign countries; and requirements for carrying out the negotiated tariff reduction in stages.

Trade Act of 1974 (P.L. 93-618). On January 3, 1975, the President signed the Trade Act of 1974 into law. This act had been pending before the Congress for nearly two years before final passage on December 20, 1974. It was the first major trade legislation since the Trade Expansion Act of 1962 and substantially revised basic U.S. trade law. As summarized by the U.S. Department of State, the Trade Act in many respects established a new framework for the formulation and implementation of U.S. trade policy.

Negotiating authorities: These authorities would exist for five years, with staging of duty reductions over ten years at a rate not to exceed 3% annually if the total reduction is 20% *ad valorem* or less, or at a rate not to exceed reductions per annum of one-tenth of the total reduction if the total reduction is more than 20%.

Tariff rates above 5% *ad valorem* may be reduced 60%; tariffs of 5% *ad valorem* or below may be eliminated.

Increases in tariffs may be used primarily to harmonize duty rate levels with those of other countries; they may be negotiated up to the greater of 50% above 1934 rates or 20% *ad valorem* above existing rates.

Agreements on reduction, elimination, or harmonization of nontariff barriers (NTBs) may be implemented under a fast-track procedure for affirmative congressional approval. No amendments to an implementing bill are allowed, and there are provisions for: (1) discharge of a committee from consideration of an implementing bill, (2) limitation on motions which can be made in connection with consideration of such bill, and (3) time limits on debate.

The main objectives of tariff negotiations are to obtain more open and equitable market access and to eliminate, reduce, or harmonize devices which distort trade or commerce. Other principal objectives are to

1. Obtain to the maximum extent feasible opportunities for appropriate manufacturing product sectors and the agricultural sector equivalent to those offered by the United States to similar products of foreign countries;
2. Enter into bilateral trade agreements if the President deter-

mines that such agreements will be more effective than multilateral ones in promoting U.S. economic growth and employment;
3. Conclude trade agreements which benefit both developing countries and the United States;
4. Obtain satisfactory international rules with respect to domestic safeguards (i.e., temporary adjustment to import competition); and
5. Negotiate supply access agreements.

Input into the negotiating process was provided for as follows:

Congressional participation was provided by appointment of five members each from the House Ways and Means and Senate Finance Committees as advisers to the U.S. trade negotiating delegation and by provision for consultations prior to the presentations of NTB agreements for congressional approval.

A network of public and private sector advisory committees operates throughout the prenegotiation and negotiation periods. The administration must report on its disposition of such advice, and the committees are to submit reports to Congress appraising trade agreements.

Prenegotiation procedures are required prior to the extension of any offers for basic tariff agreements and in connection with renegotiation and compensation agreements. The same procedures are required prior to the extension of generalized preferences to any article. Examples of these procedures are public listing of all articles being considered for duty reductions, International Trade Commission (ITC) and executive branch advice, and public hearings.

Other authorities: Other provisions of the Trade Act of 1974 established the following.

The President is to raise temporarily U.S. trade barriers (up to 15% *ad valorem* duty surcharge or quotas limiting imports at current levels) when large and serious balance-of-payments deficits or other fundamental international payments problems require such special important measures, but he may refrain from proclaiming any restrictions if the national economic interest requires. The President is also authorized to lower existing trade barriers (with duty reductions limited to 5% *ad valorem*) during periods of large and persistent balance-of-payments surpluses. If the President determines the imposition of restrictions for balance-of-payments purposes will be contrary to the national interest, he need not raise barriers but must consult with Congress. The time limit on actions under these authorities is 150 days, extendable by Congress.

Whenever import relief action has been taken, the President may reduce duties by not more than 30% in order to pay the compensation owed U.S. trading partners as a result of the import action. In determining whether to grant compensation, the President is to consider whether a country has violated trade agreements benefiting the United States and, if so, whether such country has compensated the United States—or the United States has taken offsetting action—for such violation.

In order to authorize minor housekeeping adjustments necessary after a major round of trade negotiations, the President is granted, for two years beyond the basic five-year negotiating authority, authority to reduce in each year by no more than 20% (and subject to the overall limitations of the tariff reduction authority) duties on no more than 2% of total U.S. imports for such year.

Authority to renegotiate duties is granted for two years beyond the five-year period of the basic negotiating authorities in the act, but is limited to unused residual negotiating authority and to no more than 2% of total U.S. imports in any one year.

All trade agreements under the act are to be subject to termination and withdrawal by the United States. Upon termination of or withdrawal from an agreement, the President may impose or raise duties to a rate not higher than 50% above the statutory rate or 20% *ad valorem* above the multilateral trade negotiating rate.

The act establishes a general rule that concessions should be extended on a nondiscriminatory basis. However, the President is required to determine at the conclusion of the multilateral negotiations whether any major industrialized country fails to make concessions in such negotiations affording competitive opportunities to U.S. producers substantially equivalent to those competitive opportunities afforded to producers of such country by U.S. concessions in such negotiations. If the President determines that any major industrialized country has failed to make such concessions, he is to recommend to the Congress legislation necessary to correct the balance of concessions.

Duties on articles subject to national security or import relief measures may not be reduced under the negotiating authorities of the act, nor may any barriers imposed for import relief or national security purposes be reduced. Further, other import barriers may not be reduced if their reduction would undermine the national security or import relief measures. Articles subject to national security or import relief measures also are ineligible for generalized preferences.

The President was directed, as soon as practicable, to enter into agreements which have the effect of amending GENERAL AGREEMENT ON TARIFFS AND TRADE (GATT) articles in order to achieve a fairer and more equitable trading system. Twelve specific objectives (including access to supplies, revision of the international safeguard mechanism, agreement on the use of subsidies, etc.) were enumerated. Because of the practical difficulties in amending GATT, the President was further directed to enter into agreements complementary to the GATT with interested countries in order to achieve reform of the international trading system. If the implementation of any such agreements would change federal law and such agreements are not implemented pursuant to a prior delegation of authority, they must be submitted to the Congress for approval. In order best to assure a final vote on their merits, such agreements may be submitted under the same expedited procedures as those provided for nontariff-barrier agreements under Section 102.

U.S. International Trade Commission: The name of the Tariff Commission was changed to the UNITED STATES INTERNATIONAL TRADE COMMISSION (USITC). The major structural changes in the operation of the commission were as follows: (1) terms of the commissioners are extended to nine years, (2) chairmanship and vice-chairmanship are to rotate among the members, and (3) the commission is to be independent of the executive branch for budget purposes.

Import relief: Temporary relief for domestic industry from import competition was made more accessible. Under prior law, the eligibility criteria for such relief often proved too strict. The Trade Act of 1974 modified previous law by eliminating the requirement of a causal link between increased imports and trade agreement concessions and requiring that increased imports be a "substantial" cause of serious injury or threat thereof, rather than the "major" cause, as was required in the past. Under previous law, "major" was defined as a cause greater than all other causes; under the Trade Act of 1974, "substantial" was defined as an important cause that is not less than any other cause.

Provision was also made in the Trade Act of 1974 for a finding of injury to a domestic industry located in a major geographical area if the following conditions are met: (1) production in the geographic area constitutes a major portion of production of the national industry, (2) the producers in the geographic area serve primarily the markets of such area, and (3) imports are concentrated in such geographic area.

Largely because import relief could be given under the Trade Act of 1974 on the basis of injury to industry in a geographic area, import relief could be imposed on either a selective or nondiscriminatory basis. In cases where a finding of injury to an industry in a geographic area resulted in the imposition of import relief, it would likely be preferable to impose barriers only against imports from the country or countries causing the injury.

Upon an affirmative determination of finding of injury by the ITC, the President must impose or increase quotas or negotiate an orderly marketing agreement (or take any combination of the above actions), unless he determines that the imposition of any such relief would be contrary to the U.S. economic interest. If the President either takes no action or takes action which differs from that recommended by the ITC, the Congress may, by concurrent resolution passed by majority vote of both houses, substitute the relief recommended by the ITC for that imposed by the President.

The Trade Act of 1974 for the first time introduced the possibility of an ITC finding that adjustment assistance offers a viable alternative to import relief for the adversely affected industry. Where the ITC finds that adjustment assistance "can effectively remedy the injury to an industry," the ITC may recommend the provision of such assistance.

Import relief would be temporary in nature. It may be granted for a five-year period, with one extension for three years if necessary, but is, to the extent feasible, to be phased down after the first three years.

TARIFF

Adjustment assistance: Adjustment assistance was made available to the following groups:

1. *Workers.* The Trade Act of 1974 would make adjustment assistance for workers displaced by increased imports more effective and more accessible than under previous law. Access criteria were significantly liberalized and benefits were increased. Benefits may now be provided equal to 70% of each worker's average weekly earnings prior to the time of unemployment, subject to a ceiling of 100% of the national average weekly wage in manufacturing, for a period of 52 weeks generally, and in the case of older workers and workers in training for a period of up to 78 weeks. Special provisions for job search, training, and relocation were also included.
2. *Firms.* As with worker adjustment assistance, adjustment assistance for firms under the Trade Act of 1974 would be more effective and more readily available. The secretary of Commerce was authorized to guarantee loans (up to $3 million per firm), to make direct loans (up to $1 million per firm), and to provide technical assistance.
3. *Communities.* For the first time, the Trade Act of 1974 introduced a concept of trade adjustment assistance to communities adversely affected by imports. The community adjustment assistance provisions were directed to attract new investment to trade-impacted areas. During the first year $100 million was authorized for loans and direct grants to firms locating in the adversely affected community; up to $1 billion in outstanding loans could be guaranteed at any one time.

Relief from unfair trade practices: The Trade Act of 1974 gave considerably more flexibility to the President in fashioning responses to unjustifiable or unreasonable foreign trade practices and tightened provisions of existing U.S. laws against foreign dumping, export subsidization, and unfair practices in connection with imports.

The President was authorized to withdraw trade agreement concessions or to impose duties or other import restrictions in response to unjustifiable or unreasonable foreign trade practices which adversely affect U.S. commerce. He may retaliate on either a nondiscriminatory or a selective basis, provided that, if the President retaliates on a nondiscriminatory basis, Congress may, by concurrent resolution, limit the effect of any retaliation to the offending country.

The antidumping laws were tightened. Time limits were imposed (an initial determination must be made within six months, or nine months for complicated cases, after publication of an antidumping proceeding, and a final determination must be made three months thereafter), and certain other procedural and technical changes were made. The Trade Act of 1974 provided U.S. manufacturers, producers, or wholesalers an automatic right to appear at antidumping hearings, and provided for judicial review of negative Treasury findings.

In addition, a new concept was introduced to the antidumping law. Provision was made for antidumping determination against MULTINATIONAL CORPORATIONS which operate in several foreign countries if they support low-priced exports to the United States through high-priced sales by other subsidiaries located in other foreign countries.

Time limits for countervailing duty determinations (six months for preliminary determinations, one year for a final determination) and express provision for judicial review of countervailing duty determinations were added to existing law. Furthermore, the Trade Act of 1974 also extended application of the countervailing duty law to duty-free imports, provided a finding of injury is made by the ITC. A finding of injury in connection with the imposition of countervailing duties on duty-free imports was necessary in order to make this new feature of the law compatible with U.S. international obligations (i.e., the GATT).

In order to encourage successful negotiation of nontariff barrier agreements, the secretary of the Treasury was authorized to suspend the application of countervailing duties during the four-year period ending January 3, 1979, providing he made determinations that:

1. Adequate steps have been taken to reduce substantially or eliminate the adverse effect of the bounty or grant on domestic producers;
2. There is a reasonable prospect that trade agreements on nontariff barriers will be entered into under Section 102 of the act; and
3. The imposition of countervailing duties would be likely to jeopardize seriously the satisfactory completion of such negotiations.

Section 337 of the Tariff Act of 1930 (providing for the exclusion of articles the import of which involve unfair trade practices, i.e., U.S. patent infringement) was substantially modified to authorize final determinations by the USITC, subject to an override by the President for policy reasons, within 60 days. Under previous law the Tariff Commission advised the President as to violations of Section 337, and upon receiving such advice, the President determined whether to exclude any article from entry.

The USITC: (1) must make its determination within one year (18 months in complicated cases), (2) must consult with appropriate government agencies, (3) may issue cease-and-desist orders as alternatives to exclusions, and (4) may prescribe a reasonable bond under which articles subject to exclusion orders may enter.

In connection with Section 337 cases, the USITC is to consider all legal and equitable defenses.

Nondiscriminatory tariff treatment of imports from state trading countries: The extension of nondiscriminatory (most-favored-nation or MFN) tariff treatment to U.S. imports from non-market economy countries not formerly receiving such treatment was authorized by the Trade Act of 1974, but only if the President finds that such countries are not denying their citizens freedom of emigration. The extension of U.S. government-financed credits and investment guarantees to such countries, either directly or indirectly, was also contingent upon such a finding by the President. This requirement concerning freedom of emigration could be waived for an initial period of 18 months and extended for a one-year period thereafter, if the President determined that such a waiver would promote freedom of emigration and received assurances that the emigration practices of the country concerned would lead substantially to freedom of emigration.

Extension of the waiver must initially be approved by the Congress by affirmative action (although if Congress does not act within a specified period, the waiver will continue in effect unless disapproved) and thereafter is subject to a one-house congressional veto. Further, the President is authorized to withhold MFN treatment and U.S. credits from countries not now receiving MFN treatment if he determines such countries are not cooperating in accounting for U.S. personnel missing in Southeast Asia.

Extension of nondiscriminatory treatment must be made pursuant to bilateral commercial agreements which must be approved by both houses of Congress. The act specifies certain provisions (safeguard procedures, national security reservations, provisions for the protection of patents, trademarks, copyrights, etc.) which are to be included in such agreements with non-market economy countries not presently receiving most-favored-nation treatment.

Relief from market disruption caused by imports from Communist countries is provided for if a "market disruption" test, which is easier to meet than the standard for triggering customary escape clause actions, is met. If the President determines that there is reason to believe that market disruption exists and that emergency action is needed, he may extend immediate relief pending ITC investigation of and findings on market disruption.

Any bilateral agreement under Title IV of the act with Czechoslovakia must include renegotiation of the settlement for payment by Czechoslovakia of amounts owed U.S. citizens and nationals.

An East-West Trade Board was established to monitor East-West trade. The board is to report periodically to Congress.

Generalized tariff preferences: Title V of the Trade Act of 1974 authorized the President to extend preferential duty-free treatment to a broad range of manufactured products and selected other products imported directly from beneficiary developing countries for a period of up to ten years (with provision for a report to and review by the Congress after five years). These preferences are designed to promote the economic development of developing countries through expanded trade opportunities and to improve U.S. economic relationships with them.

Before extending preferences the President must seek the advice of the USITC and interested executive agencies with respect to articles proposed for duty-free preferential treatment. In the process of formulating such advice, primarily focused on the effect of preferential duty reductions on domestic producers and consumers, both the USITC and the executive branch will hold public hearings.

TARIFF

The following requirements for the system of generalized preferences were prescribed by the Congress.

In addition to a list of developed countries which may not be granted preferences, preferences are not to be granted to:

1. Communist countries unless the products of such countries are receiving nondiscriminatory tariff treatment from the United States, such country is a contracting party to the GATT and a member of the INTERNATIONAL MONETARY FUND, and such country is not "dominated or controlled by international communism";
2. Members of the ORGANIZATION OF PETROLEUM EXPORTING COUNTRIES (OPEC) or other countries party to any other arrangement if such countries participate in any action pursuant to such arrangement the effect of which is to withhold supplies of vital commodities from international trade or to raise the price of such commodities to an unreasonable level and thereby cause serious disruption of the world economy (unless such countries are party to an agreement to which the United States is also a party which assures the United States fair and equitable access to supplies at reasonable prices);
3. Countries which grant reverse preferences to other developed countries, which have or are likely to have significant adverse effect on U.S. commerce, unless the preferences or their significant adverse effects were to be eliminated by January 1, 1976;
4. Countries which have nationalized property of U.S. citizens or businesses without making prompt, adequate, and effective compensation or which have not submitted the dispute to arbitration or otherwise taken steps to discharge their obligations under international law;
5. Countries which do not take adequate steps to prevent narcotic drugs and other controlled substances produced in, processed in, or transported from their borders from entering the United States unlawfully; and
6. Countries which do not act in good faith in recognizing or enforcing arbitral awards in favor of U.S. citizens or businesses.

The President may waive, for any country, the exclusions based on nationalizations, drug traffic, and arbitral awards for reasons of U.S. national economic interest.

The President may not designate the following as eligible articles for purposes of preferences:

1. Textile and apparel articles which are subject to textile agreements;
2. Watches;
3. Import-sensitive electronic articles;
4. Import-sensitive steel articles;
5. Specified categories of footwear articles;
6. Import-sensitive glass products; and
7. Any other article which the President determines to be import-sensitive in the context of generalized preferences.

To receive preferential treatment, an eligible article must be imported directly from the beneficiary developing country, and the local content in the developing country must be at least 35% in the case of an individual beneficiary country or 50% in a case where two or more members of an association of countries treated as one country for purposes of generalized preferences contribute to the value of an article.

Competitive need ceilings are designed to reserve the preferential benefits for developing country industries which have a need for such advantages and to provide a basis for withdrawing the preferences in cases where industries are demonstrably competitive. Whenever the President determines that imports of an individual article from any one beneficiary country (or association of countries treated as one country) exceed one or both ceilings, then the preference on that article will be withdrawn from that country in the subsequent year. These ceilings are as follows:

1. $25 million per country (with this amount to vary in subsequent years in proportion to changes in the gross national product (GNP) of the U.S. compared with the base year 1974) and/or
2. 50% of total U.S. imports of the article (provided that the 50% ceiling does not apply to articles for which no like or directly competitive article is produced in the United States).

General provisions. In addition to technical housekeeping provisions contained in Title VI of the Trade Act of 1974 (i.e., repeal of earlier laws), there are provisions for:

1. Annual reports by the President to the Congress on measures which countries are taking to prevent the entry of illegal drugs into the United States;
2. Exoneration from liability which might arise as a result of participating in the voluntary restraint agreement negotiated in connection with steel exports to the United States;
3. The gathering and reporting of certain statistical data on imports and exports;
4. An increase in the value of duty-free gifts which may be sent from certain insular possessions;
5. An extension by three years of the period for reviewing protests against the U.S. import surcharge of August 17, 1971;
6. Authorization of negotiation for a free trade area between the United States and Canada; and
7. Limitation on the loans, guarantees, or insurance which any U.S. government agency (except the COMMODITY CREDIT CORPORATION) may approve in connection with exports to the Soviet Union to an aggregate amount of $300 million. This amount, however, may be exceeded with congressional approval.

On October, 9, 1984, Congress cleared an omnibus trade bill (HR 3398—PL 98-573) that included more than 100 different measures, mostly requests for import relief for particular products. The bill was signed by President Reagan on October 30. The most controversial provisions of the bill included authority for the administration to begin free-trade talks with Israel, preferred treatment of exports for developing nations, and import relief for the steel and wine industries. Major impetus for the bill was a record-setting U.S. trade deficit of $70 billion in 1983. Many legislators maintained that unfair trade practices of other nations contributed to the significant increase in imports and to the trade deficit. The bill gave the Commerce Department the ability to act against foreign trade practices associated with export subsidies and unfair trade practices, including "downstream dumping" (a practice of adding subsidized components made in one country to exports assembled in another country). The political argument made in Congress was the necessity of providing a "level playing field" for United States companies.

In 1987, House and Senate were unable to agree upon a trade bill in spite of a record $166.3 billion merchandise trade deficit in 1986 and worse prospects for 1987. Congress was also caught up in efforts to deal with deficit reduction issues compounded by the October 19 stock market crash.

On January 1, 1989, the U.S.-Canada Free Trade Agreement became effective, after being approved by the U.S. Congress and the Canadian Parliament. Negotiated by the two countries in 1987, the agreement was designed specifically to phase out tariffs between the United States and Canada over a ten-year period. At the time, Canadian duties on U.S. products averaged 9% of the value of the products; U.S. tariffs on Canadian imports averaged 4%. The agreement also terminated certain restrictions on investments and services. The pact guaranteed U.S. access to Canadian oil, gas, and uranium. The agreement did not deal with government subsidies or intellectual property. However, disputes over subsidies and nontariff barriers were made subject to binding decisions by newly established U.S.-Canadian panels. The two countries retained their own antidumping and countervailing duty laws. The U.S.-Canada Free-Trade Agreement was the second U.S. bilateral freetrade agreement. The first such agreement was with Israel, approved in 1985.

In 1987, Congress passed a controversial textile quota bill (HR 1154), which was vetoed by the president on September 28. The House sustained the veto. The bill established permanent global quotas for imports of textiles, apparel, and shoes. President Reagan had previously vetoed a textile quota bill that imposed country-by-country quotas on textiles, which infuriated the textile industry.

Also in 1988, a massive omnibus trade bill was approved by Congress and signed by the president. The bill dealt with unfair foreign trade practices, tariffs, quotas, antisubsidy provisions, and relief for certain industries damaged by imports. Trade became a factor in U.S. policy making, reducing the impact of foreign policy and defense considerations. The bill provided for presidential authority to negotiate multilateral nontariff agreements. The bill also authorized the president to arrange multilateral tariff

ENCYCLOPEDIA OF BANKING AND FINANCE

TARIFF

agreements and, within defined limits, to change U.S. duties. Tariff reductions exceeding 50% and negotiated tariff increases required approval by Congress. The act transferred from the president to the U.S. trade representative the authority to determine whether a foreign practice harming U.S. trade was unfair and required investigation. The act gave the trade representative the authority to determine what action could be taken against an unfair foreign trade practice and to implement such action, subject to presidential discretion. Mandatory retaliation against violations of trade agreements or unjustifiable foreign trade practices was required. Retaliation would ordinarily include tariff restrictions.

Multilateral Program. Following World War II, an era of international multilateral cooperation was initiated. The charter of the International Trade Organization (ITO), completed in Havana in March, 1948, would have pledged the ratifying signatories, including the U.S., to principles of tariff reduction and elimination of other international trade barriers, administered by a permanent administrative body, the ITO. The ITO charter, however, was not ratified by the U.S. Senate, so the General Agreement on Tariffs and Trade, originally a temporary device pending ratification of the ITO charter, became a de facto substitute for the ITO charter as a working basis for international multilateral agreements on tariff reductions and barrier eliminations. As a result of the U.S. signature of the GATT as an executive agreement and participation therein, many of the reciprocal trade agreements concluded by the United States on a bilateral basis have become inoperative, because the United States and the country concerned as members of the GATT have entered into superseding GATT concessions.

Multilateral Tariff Reductions. Commencing with its first negotiating conference (Geneva, October 30, 1947, effective January 1, 1948), the General Agreement on Tariffs and Trade (GATT) has been the multilateral basis for tariff reductions; negotiating conferences followed in 1949 (Annecy, France), 1951 (Torquay, England), 1956 (Geneva), and 1960-1961 (Geneva). With enactment in the United States of its Trade Expansion Act of 1962, which authorized U.S. negotiators to enter into multilateral negotiations (originally intended by the administration to be across-the-board but changed in practice to item basis), came the Kennedy Round of negotiations, beginning in 1964 and not concluded until June, 1967.

The average *ad valorem* equivalent of collected duties declined from 47% in 1934 to 28% in 1945 and 12% in 1955. Of this indicated total decline of 35% in duty rates, the U.S. International Trade

Value of U.S. Exports, Imports, and Merchandise Balance
(Millions of dollars)

	Principal Census trade totals					Other Census totals		
Year	U.S. exports and re-exports, excluding military grant-aid	U.S. general imports f.a.s. transaction values [1]	U.S. merchandise balance f.a.s. [1]	U.S. general imports c.i.f.	U.S. balance exports f.a.s. imports c.i.f.	Military grant-aid shipments	Exports of domestic merchandise	Re-exports
1950	9,997	8,954	1,043	—	—	282	10,146	133
1955	14,298	11,566	2,732	—	—	1,256	15,426	128
1960	19,659	15,073	4,586	—	—	949	20,408	201
1965	26,742	21,520	5,222	—	—	779	27,178	343
1970	42,681	40,356	2,325	42,833	-152	565	42,612	634
1975	107,652	98,503	9,149	105,935	1,716	461	106,622	1,490
1980	220,626	244,871	-24,245	256,984	-36,358	156	216,668	4,115
1984	217,865	325,726 [2]	-107,861	341,177	-123,312	23	212,057	5,831
1985	213,133	345,276 [2]	-132,143	361,626	-148,493	13	206,925	6,221
1986	217,292	369,961 [2]	-152,669	387,082	-169,790	12	206,376	10,928
1987	252,853 [3]	405,901 [2]	-153,035	424,082	-171,223	13	243,859	9,007

Note: Export values include both commercially-financed shipments and shipments under government-financed programs such as AID and PL-480.

[1] Prior to 1974, imports are customs values, i.e. generally at prices in principal foreign markets.
[2] In 1981 import value changes back to customs value.
[3] Includes undocumented exports to Canada.

U.S. Foreign Trade, by Economic Classes
(Millions of dollars)

Economic class	1965	1970	1975	1980	1985	1986	1987
Exports, total	29,128	45,114	106,622	216,672	206,925	206,376	241,399 [2]
Excluding military grant-aid	—	—	106,161	216,515	206,912	206,364	228,280
Crude foods	2,587	2,748	11,804	9,695	7,938	9,120	10,197
Manufactured foods	1,590	1,921	4,221	13,197	9,947	9,303	10,312
Crude materials	2,887	4,492	10,883	18,776	13,319	10,729	11,973
Agricultural	1,942	2,524	5,747	—	—	—	—
Semimanufactures	4,114	6,866	12,815	37,312	38,006	36,335	41,594
Finished manufactures	16,008	26,563	66,379	126,518	137,717	140,889	167,323
Excluding military grant-aid	—	—	65,918	126,362	137,704	140,877	167,310
Imports, total [1]	22,293	40,748	99,305	245,262	345,276	369,961	405,901
Crude foods	2,008	2,579	3,642	7,737	9,351	11,125	10,123
Manufactured foods	1,877	3,519	5,953	10,385	12,562	13,058	14,225
Crude materials	3,709	4,126	23,570	76,380	44,404	41,395	38,645
Agricultural	864	797	1,280	2,336	2,593	2,601	2,870
Semimanufactures	4,964	7,263	17,326	34,072	44,043	41,395	44,820
Finished manufactures	8,871	22,464	46,411	112,620	234,914	268,096	298,088

[1] Customs values are shown for imports.
[2] Total exports includes undocumented exports to Canada.

Source: Office of Trade and Investment Analysis, U.S. Dept. of Commerce.

Commission has estimated that half (17.5%) could be attributed to tariff cuts under the trade agreements program. Reductions in U.S. tariffs under the Kennedy Round lowered the average tariff level of the United States to 7.8% by 1973.

The Tokyo Round of multilateral trade negotiations, the seventh since World War II, has been the most comprehensive and far-reaching since establishment of the GATT in 1947. Trade negotiators representing the major trading nations of the world, accounting for more than 90% of world trade, on April 12, 1979, agreed upon the "final substantive results." For the first time, agreements were reached which deal with a broad range of so-called nontariff obstacles to trade, such as national government policies and such practices as export subsidies, government purchasing requirements, import quotas and licensing procedures, product standard-setting, and customs valuation methods. These governmental interventions in the international commercial marketplace, whether or not designed for trade advantage, had displaced tariffs as the major distortion. Further, agreements were negotiated governing international trade in civil aircraft, steel, beef, and dairy products, and modernizing GATT rules with respect to antidumping, dispute settlement, and the rights and obligations of developing countries.

U.S. trade policy. As specified in the *Economic Report of the President* (January, 1979), the aims of U.S. trade policy are to enable the United States and other economies to benefit from the most efficient allocation of worldwide resources and to channel U.S. resources into sectors of comparative advantage. During 1978, the major activities of U.S. policy makers in this area involved the multilateral trade negotiations (MTN) in Geneva, the determination of domestic trade policy, and the development of the President's national export policy.

The trade package of the MTN (GATT) negotiations included codes on subsidies, government procurement, standards, customs valuation, and licensing. It also included a package of tariff cuts by the United States, with reciprocal cuts from trading partners of the United States. The U.S. cuts were projected to average about 30%. In addition, negotiators agreed to remove several particularly burdensome industrial and agricultural nontariff barriers. The trade package provided measures to improve the GATT framework for dealing with agricultural trade issues, trade with developing countries, balance of payments measures, export restrictions, and the general management of trade disputes.

With its national export policy, the Carter administration committed itself to a stronger emphasis on foreign markets for foreign goods by the following major policy provisions:

1. An increase in the size and flexibility of the EXPORT-IMPORT BANK activities;
2. A commitment from the SMALL BUSINESS ADMINISTRATION to channel up to $100 million of its loan guarantees to small export businesses;
3. An earmarking of $20 million of the budgets of the Department of Commerce and the Department of State to assist small- and medium-sized businesses in their marketing efforts abroad;
4. An increase in the level of short-term agricultural export credits by almost $1 billion; and
5. A decision to ask the Justice Department to clarify ambiguities about the enforcement of the Foreign Corrupt Practices Act and the international application of the ANTITRUST LAWS.

Summary. The appended two charts, prepared by the U.S. Department of Commerce, trace the trend since 1950 in total volume of U.S. and world trade exports and imports and U.S. foreign trade by economic classes.

Besides the above referrals to specific terms, *see also* BALANCE OF TRADE, FOREIGN TRADE, INTERNATIONAL BALANCE OF PAYMENTS, INVISIBLE IMPORTS, RECIPROCAL TARIFF ACT.

BIBLIOGRAPHY

American Import/Export Bulletin. North American Publishing Co. Monthly.
GATT Activities. Annual.
International Customs Journal. U.S. Bureau of Customers.
Custom Bulletin. Weekly.
Economic Report of the President (annual).
GENERAL AGREEMENT ON TARIFFS AND TRADE (GATT), *Annual Report.*

———. *Custom Regulation's of the United States.* U.S. International Trade Commission Publishers, *Tariff Schedules of the United States Annotated* [a classified list of import commodities, giving rates of duty for each].
———. *The Tariff Schedules of the United States Converted into the Format of the Brussels Tariff Nomenclature.*

TARIFF ACT OF 1930 Approved June 17, 1930; also known as the Smoot-Hawley Tariff. The rates of this tariff increased as a whole over those of the Fordney-McCumber Tariff Act of 1922, which was considered a highly protective tariff. Unlike preceding tariffs, however, it contained a provision for flexibility or changes in rates if approved by the President. The act empowered the Tariff Commission (now known as the United States International Trade Commission) to recommend increases or decreases to the President, which would become effective if signed, provided no increase exceeded 50%. Investigations into the costs of production of any domestic article for the purpose of making such suggestions could be made by the commission: first, upon the request of the President; second, upon resolution of either or both houses of Congress; third, upon its own motion; or fourth, upon application of any interested party if, in the judgment of the commission, there was sufficient reason.

The Smoot-Hawley Tariff was amended on June 12, 1934, by the Trade Agreements Act of 1934, delegating power to the President to raise or lower existing duties by as much as 50%. Under this legislation, the era of high protective tariff policy was replaced by the reciprocal trade agreements program, and a large number of such agreements were signed with such unilateral action, including most favored nation treaties which assured each of the signing nations of preferential treatment.

See TARIFF.

TARIFF COMMISSION Originally created by an act of Congress approved September 8, 1916 (39 Stat. 795), as the U.S. Tariff Commission. By the Trade Act of 1974 (P.L. 93-618, January 3, 1975), the name was changed to UNITED STATES INTERNATIONAL TRADE COMMISSION, and major structural changes were made in the operation of the commission.

TAX ABATEMENT A decrease of a tax improperly imposed.

TAX AND LOAN ACCOUNTS The operating cash of the U.S. Treasury is maintained in the Treasury's accounts with the Federal Reserve banks and branches and in tax and loan accounts in approved depositaries. As the balances in the accounts at the Federal Reserve banks become depleted, they are restored by calling in (withdrawing) funds from the thousands of financial institutions throughout the country authorized to maintain tax and loan accounts.

Under authority of P.L. 95-147, the U.S. Treasury implemented a program on November 2, 1978, to invest a portion of its operating cash in obligations of depositaries maintaining tax and loan accounts. Under the Treasury tax and loan investment program, depositary financial institutions select the manner in which they will participate in the program. Depositaries that wish to retain funds deposited in their tax and loan accounts in interest-bearing obligations participate under the note option; depositaries that wish to remit the funds to the Treasury's account at Federal Reserve banks participate under the remittance option.

Deposits to tax and loan accounts occur in the normal course of business under a uniform procedure applicable to all financial institutions, whereby customers of financial institutions deposit with them tax payments and funds for the purchase of government securities. In most cases the transaction involves merely the transfer of funds from a customer's account to the tax and loan account in the same financial institution. On occasions, to the extent authorized by the Treasury, financial institutions are permitted to deposit in these accounts proceeds from subscriptions to public debt securities entered for their own account and for the account of their customers.

The tax and loan account system permits the U.S. Treasury to collect funds through financial institutions and to leave the funds in note option depositaries and in the financial communities in which they arise until such time as the Treasury needs the funds for its operations. In this way, the Treasury is able to neutralize the effect of its fluctuation in operations on note option financial institutions' reserves and the economy.

BIBLIOGRAPHY

U.S. Treasury Department, Office of the Secretary. *Treasury Bulletin* (monthly).

TAX ANTICIPATION OBLIGATIONS
Obligations issued by a governmental unit in order to provide funds for current expenditures until taxes or other revenues due can be collected.

Tax anticipation obligations as such are issuable by states and municipalities to tide revenues over slack levels in anticipation of tax receipts in the short run; thus these obligations are short-term borrowing, often termed tax-relief or tax-arrearage obligations. They are not to be confused with REVENUE BONDS.

U.S. Treasury Tax Anticipation Bills (TABs). Beginning in 1951, the U.S. Treasury began to issue TREASURY BILLS of the type termed tax anticipation bills (popularly called TABs) as a means of offsetting seasonal dips in tax receipts. Issued through competitive bidding for actual issues ranging in maturities from 23 to 273 days, the TABs matured about one week after due dates for taxes but could be tendered at full par to pay income taxes on tax-payment dates. Thus they provided corporations with a convenient form of investment of funds for eventual payment of income taxes. Commercial banks serving as U.S. government depositories were usually given the option of paying for the TABs by the book-credit method (by crediting the U.S. government tax and loan deposit account on their books). The U.S. Treasury terminated the issuance of TABs in 1975 and has since issued cash management bills which replaced TABs as well as bill strips in U.S. Treasury short-term financing.

TAX AVOIDANCE
Tax avoidance includes legal efforts by a taxpayer to arrange his/her tax-related transactions and affairs so as to reduce one's tax liabilities. Judge Learned Hand in S.R. Newman declared:

> "Over and over again courts have said that there is nothing sinister in so arranging one's affairs as to keep taxes as low as possible. Everybody does so, rich or poor; and all do right, for nobody owes any public duty to pay more than the law demands: taxes are enforced extractions, not voluntary contributions. To demand more in the name of morals is mere cant."

The courts accept a corporation as being distinct from its shareholders. However, if it appears that a sham transaction occurs, the courts can rule that tax avoidance has taken place. For example, if there is no principal purpose for a tax-free acquisition, the courts can disallow deductions, credits or other allowances resulting therefrom. If there is a "principal purpose" other than stock avoidance, the taxpayer can have other purposes, such as tax savings.

TAX BASE
The value of the asset or object upon which the tax is levied.

TAX COMPLIANCE
The completion of a tax return accurately and on a timely basis. Tax planning is ordinarily required to assure tax compliance.

TAX COURT
The United States tax court is a legislative court under Article I, Section 8, Clause 9 of the Constitution. Its function is to review deficiencies assessed by the commissioner for income, estate, or gift taxes. Currently, the tax court consists of 19 judges. The chief judge is elected biennially from among the 19 judges of the court. The tax court tries and adjudicates controversies involving the existence of deficiencies or overpayments in income, estate, and gift taxes in cases where deficiencies have been determined by the commissioner of Internal Revenue. It also hears cases commenced by transferrees and fiduciaries who have been issued notices of liability by the commissioner.

The tax court has jurisdiction to redetermine excise taxes and penalties imposed on private foundations. Similar jurisdiction over excise taxes has been conferred with regard to public charities, qualified pension plans, real estate investment trusts, and the windfall profit tax on domestic crude oil. Simplified procedures may be utilized for the trials of small tax cases, provided that in a case conducted under these procedures the decision of the court would be final. The jurisdictional maximum for such cases is $10,000 for any disputed year. The tax court has jurisdiction to render declaratory judgments relating to the qualification of retirement plans, including pension, profit-sharing, stock bonus, annuity, and bond purchase plans; the tax-exempt status of charitable organizations, qualified charitable donees, private foundations, or private operating foundations; and the status of interest on certain government obligations.

All decisions other than small tax cases are subject to review by the United States courts of appeals and thereafter by the Supreme Court upon the granting of a writ of certiorari.

The office of the court and all of its judges are located in Washington, D.C., with the exception of a field office located in Los Angeles. The court conducts trial sessions at various locations within the United States as reasonably convenient to taxpayers as practicable. Each trial session is conducted by a single judge or a special trial judge.

In addition to the tax court, there are two additional courts of original jurisdiction or trial courts in which tax cases can be brought: the U.S. district court and the U.S. claims court. The taxpayer can select only one of the three courts to hear the case. If the taxpayer or government disagrees with the decision by the trial court, it has the right to appeal to either the U.S. court of appeals or the U.S. circuit court of appeals, whichever is appropriate in the particular case. Appeal can then be made to the Supreme Court, but such appeals are rarely granted. The following outline demonstrates the trial and appeal procedure for taxpayers and the government.

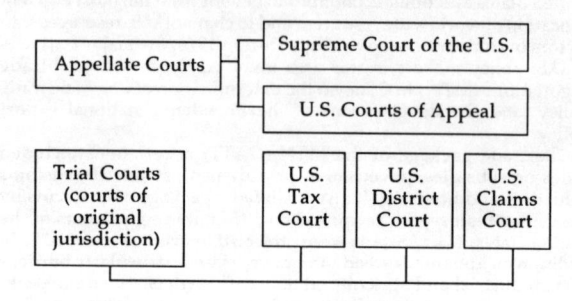

```
Appellate Courts ──┬── Supreme Court of the U.S.
                   └── U.S. Courts of Appeal

Trial Courts ──┬── U.S. Tax Court
(courts of     ├── U.S. District Court
original       └── U.S. Claims Court
jurisdiction)
```

TAX-BASED INCOMES POLICY
As an alternative to wage and price controls, tax-based incomes policy (TIP) was termed "an idea that deserves serious consideration" (1978 Joint Economic Committee *Report*) in controlling inflation. See WAGE AND PRICE GUIDEPOSTS.

The idea is not really new, since both Henry C. Wallich, a member of the Board of Governors of the Federal Reserve System, and Sidney Weintraub, of the University of Pennsylvania faculty, advocated a tax-based incomes policy in 1971. Governor Wallich repeated his personal advocacy of such a policy in an appearance before the Joint Economic Committee on February 8, 1978.

Both Wallich and Weintraub advocated the penalty approach to enforcement of their TIP version. The thousand or so largest companies would be required by enabling legislation to limit total wage and benefits increases to recent long-term productivity rate, plus one-half of the prevailing inflation rate. Firms subject to TIP would be penalized for violation of the guideline by a 5% corporate income tax surcharge. Since, according to Gov. Wallich, research indicates that prices are basically determined by wages and other compensation of labor which all told account for 75% of the gross national product, such an approach would be effective in reaching the basic cause of inflation, even though nonwage factors such as demand pressures and nonwage costs may play a role in price movements.

Professor Weintraub estimated that such a TIP approach imposed on the 2,000 largest firms would involve about 85% of the output in the private sector and about 25% of the wages and other labor income of the total economy. In addition, if government sectors were also included, the total labor income affected would come to about 35%. Since "these are the economy's pacesetters ... everybody else would soon fall into line," in Weintraub's extrapolation.

Okun Version of TIP. Arthur Okun, a former chairman of the Council of Economic Advisers and now with the Brookings Institution, advocated, instead of the penalty approach, a TIP rewarding firms and workers complying with the guideline on wages: (1) firms would receive a tax credit equal to 25% of the wage increase granted to workers complying with the guideline, and (2) in turn, the workers holding wage increases in line with the guideline would receive a tax credit equal to 1.5% of their wages up to $20,000.

Summary. Neither Wallich nor Weintraub reckoned with a principal cause of inflation in recent years, i.e., federal budget deficits and monetization of the debt. At the least, their penalty version would be politically unacceptable because of opposition from both business and labor. Okun's version, which similarly centers on wage push as the principal cause of inflation, would involve high costs for the Treasury in tax reductions which themselves would probably fuel further inflation.

TAX DODGE An illegal attempt to avoid taxes.

TAX EQUITY AND FISCAL RESPONSIBILITY ACT OF 1982 P.L. 97-248, signed by the President on September 3, 1982, providing for revenue increases of $17.9 billion in fiscal 1983, $37.6 billion in fiscal 1984, and $42.7 billion in fiscal 1985, for a total of $98.2 billion in increased revenues for the three fiscal years. The Tax Equity and Fiscal Responsibility Act of 1982 (TEFRA) was enacted approximately one year after the ECONOMIC RECOVERY TAX ACT OF 1981 (ERTA), which provided for revenue reductions of $93.4 billion in fiscal 1983, $149.6 billion in fiscal 1984, and $182.2 billion in fiscal 1985.

The Reagan administration maintained that TEFRA complied with the revenue-raising requirements of the first budget resolution, endorsed by the President and passed by the Congress in June, 1982, which called for the Congress to reduce budget deficits by $378 billion over the following three fiscal years ($280 billion in reductions of expenditures and $98 billion in revenue increases).

The administration further maintained that the supply-side (*see* SUPPLY-SIDE ECONOMICS) incentives provided for in the Economic Recovery Tax Act of 1981 were not affected by the TEFRA, which did not change (1) the third year of the tax cut provided for in ERTA (i.e., the 10% rate reduction on July 1, 1983); (2) the indexing of tax rates, after the full 25% rate reductions take effect; and (3) "most" of the accelerated cost recovery provisions for business contained in ERTA.

Moreover, it was estimated that one-third of the $98.2 billion increase in revenues—$31 billion—provided by TEFRA would not be from new taxes but from stepped up compliance provisions designed to collect taxes, and that more than three-fourths of the increased revenues to be derived through TEFRA would be derived from combined compliance provisions and the closing of tax loopholes.

Among the principal provisions of TEFRA, conference report of House and Senate conferees, are the following.

Compliance provisions are intended to reduce the "tax gap" from noncompliance, and the collection provisions are intended to improve and facilitate the collection of taxes already owed. These include increases in penalties for noncompliance, improvement and expansion in information reporting to the IRS, changes in interest computation rules, and revisions to pension withholding provisions. Rules are provided for access to tax information and for its use in nontax criminal investigations and prosecutions. Collection of corporate estimated income taxes is accelerated by changes which include increasing payments from 80% to 90% of the actual tax due.

Withholding at a flat rate of 10% is required on payments of interest and dividends after December 31, 1982, with special rules provided to minimize the financial and administrative burdens on financial institutions adjusting to the system. Interest payments of $150 or less are exempt. Low-income individuals whose tax liability for the prior year was less than $600 ($1,000 on a joint return) are exempt, as are individuals age 65 or over with tax liabilities under $1,500 ($2,500 for a married couple filing jointly). This exempts those over 65 with taxable incomes in 1984 of less than $14,450 ($24,214 on a joint return).

Existing alternative minimum tax is strengthened by shifting to the tax base all items currently subject to the add-on minimum tax and adding several new items to existing preferences.

Pension tax benefits for high-income individuals are limited by reduction in the maximum annual addition to a defined contribution plan from $45,475 to $30,000 and reduction in the maximum annual benefit under a defined benefit plan from $136,425 to $90,000. Where a combination of plans is provided, the maximum benefits allowable are reduced from 140% to 125%, applicable to dollar limits. Cost-of-living adjustments are suspended for 1984 and 1985. Loans that exceed the lesser of $50,000 or half the present value of the employees' nonforfeitable accrued benefit under retirement plans, but not less than $10,000, are deemed to be taxable distributions.

Deductions for casualty and theft losses are allowed only as to the excess over 10% of the adjusted gross income for the year (exclusion of $100 per loss is retained). Medical expense deductions are now subject to a floor of 5% instead of 3%, and the $150 deduction for health insurance is deleted (health insurance cost is to be treated as medical expenses).

Rules are provided for amortization for original issue discount bonds, and the unwarranted tax advantage for coupon stripping is eliminated (Keogh and individual retirement account holders are not affected, since they pay no current taxes).

The act repeals the more rapid recovery rates scheduled to take effect in 1985 and 1986 under the accelerated cost recovery system (ACRS).

The safe harbor leasing provisions contained in ERTA are repealed, effective after December 31, 1983. The rules are modified substantially to impose limits on the amount of property that may be leased and the amount of benefit from depreciation and investment tax credits available to lessors.

New rules generally require a 15% cutback in the availability to corporations of certain items of tax preference.

The rules now generally call for reduction in the basis of assets involved in the investment tax credit by 50% of the amount of the credit.

TEFRA requires corporations to capitalize and amortize over ten years interest and real property taxes attributable to the construction period of nonresidential real estate.

The telephone excise tax is increased to 3% for the calendar years 1983 through 1985, after which the tax is terminated.

The cigarette excise tax is doubled from $0.08 to $0.16 per pack for cigarettes removed from bonded premises after December 31, 1982, and before October 1, 1985.

The 5% tax on domestic air passenger tickets is raised to 8%. Tax rates on gasoline and fuels used in noncommercial aviation, air freight weighbills, and aircraft equipment are raised. The increases on tickets and fuels apply to purchases after August 31, 1982, to be extended to December 31, 1987, when they will be terminated.

The Federal Unemployment Tax Act (FUTA) wage base is increased to $7,000 effective January 1, 1983, and the tax rate is increased to 3.5%. Effective January 1, 1985, the tax rate is increased to 6.2%, which, in view of increased offset credit of 5.4%, means the effective federal tax rate is increased from 0.7% to 0.8%.

Tax incentives for corporate mergers and acquisitions are reduced.

Net extraction losses in foreign oil and gas operations in one country may offset net extraction income from such operations in other countries in the computation of oil and gas extraction taxes.

TEFRA requires the registration of most bonds.

Any payments to foreign officials or agents of a foreign government may be deducted as business expenses if such payments are not prohibited by the Foreign Corrupt Practices Act.

TAXES Compulsory payments imposed by a sovereign for public purposes.

Taxes may be classified as:

1. Direct taxes, those imposed upon the individual directly, such as a poll tax or a per capita tax. Under the U.S. Constitution, direct taxes shall be apportioned among the several states.
2. Indirect taxes, those imposed upon a privilege or right which a person exercises, such as the right to transmit or right to receive estate property (estate and inheritance taxes) or the right to make gifts of property (gift taxes). The U.S. Constitution also provides that duties, imposts, and excises imposed by the federal government shall be uniform throughout the country.

Taxes are levied on the basis of two broad principles: the benefit principle and the ability-to-pay principle. The benefit principle of taxation suggests that those consumers who directly receive the benefits from public goods and services should themselves finance these expenditures. User taxes, for example gasoline taxes earmarked to finance highway construction and repair, are levied according to the benefit principle. This principle underlies the rationale for every citizen being taxed to pay for public goods, such as national defense.

The ability-to-pay principle of taxation is based on the equity concept that those who earn more can afford to pay more taxes. This principle underlies the U.S. individual income tax program. The more income a person earns, the larger the percentage of that income that is taxed.

Taxes may also be classified as: (1) regressive (those graduated so as to impose highest rates on lowest incomes or property values), (2) proportional (those imposing the same proportional rates on all incomes or property values, whether large or small), and (3) progressive (those graduated so as to impose highest rates on highest incomes or property values). In the United States, progressive income taxation, based on the ability to pay, is the prevailing type in both federal and state taxation.

Business excise (licenses, gasoline taxes) and income taxes are the most important types of state taxes, followed by property taxes and inheritance taxes. Property taxes are the major source of local (municipal) taxes, but excises (sales taxes) are being increasingly resorted to as a source of municipal revenues.

See ESTATE TAXES, EXCESS PROFITS TAX, EXCISES, GIFT TAX, INCOME TAXES, INHERITANCE LAWS, INTERNAL REVENUE, NATIONAL BANK TAXES, REVENUE ACT, STOCK TRANSFER TAX, TARIFF, TAX-EXEMPT BONDS, TAX-FREE COVENANT, TAXES ON INVESTMENTS.

BIBLIOGRAPHY

All States Tax Handbook. Prentice Hall, Inc. Annual.
BERNSTEIN, P. W., ed. *The Arthur Young Tax Guide*, 1985-. Annual.
Federal Tax Coordinator. Research Institute of America, 1970-.
Federal Taxes. Prentice-Hall Information Services, Englewood Cliffs, NJ. Weekly.
Federal Tax Handbook. Prentice-Hall Information Services, Englewood Cliffs, NJ, 1947. Annual.
Government Quarterly Report: Quarterly Summary of State and Local Tax Revenue. Bureau of the Census. Quarterly.
Guidebook to Taxes. Commerce Clearing House, Inc., Chicago, IL. Annual.
INTERNAL REVENUE SERVICE. *Your Federal Income Tax*, 1943-. Annual.
———. *Individual Income Tax Returns.* Annual.
———. *Tax Information Publications.* Annual.
———. *Statistics of Income, Corporation Income Tax Returns*, 1916-. Annual.
———. *Statistics of Income Bulletin.* Quarterly.
———. *Statistics of Income, Source Book, Partnership Returns.*
J. K. Lasser's *Your Income Tax.* Simon and Schuster, New York, NY, 1937-. Annual.
Journal of Taxation. Master Federal Tax Manual. Research Institute of America, 1975-. Annual.
MILLER, R. B. *Tax Haven Investing: A Guide to Offshore Banking and Investment Opportunities.* Probus Publishing Co., Chicago, IL, 1988.
National Tax Journal.
State Tax Handbook. Commerce Clearing House, Inc., Chicago, IL. Annual.
Taxes.
Taxes and Taxation. U.S. Superintendent of Documents (Subject bibl. 195).
STANDARD & POOR'S. *Tax Reporter*, 1913-. Standard & Poor's, New York, NY. Weekly.
WESTIN, R. A. *A Lexicon of Tax Terminology*, 1984.
U.S. GENERAL ACCOUNTING OFFICE. *A Glossary of Terms Used in the Federal Budget and Related Accounting, Economic, and Tax Terms*, 1981.
U.S. Master Tax Guide. Commerce Clearing House, Chicago, IL, 1943-. Annual.
Selected tax software available 1990:
A-plus Tax 1040. Arthur Andersen & Co.
Digitax 1040. Digtax Inc.
GoSystem 1040. CLR/Fast-Tax.
Lacerte 1040. Lacerte Software Corp.
Master Tax. CPAid, Inc.
Software 1040. Prentice Hall, Inc.
Tax Machine. Accountants Microsystems.
Tax Partner 1040. Best Programs.
Tax Relief Plus. Micro Vision Software.
1040 Solution. 1040 Solutions, Inc.
1040 Tax Prep Program. Pencil Pushers.
TurboTax Pro Series 1040. Chipsoft, Inc.

TAX EQUIVALENT YIELD The federal income tax exempts municipal bonds from federal tax. For the bondholder who pays a federal income tax, a tax exempt bond has a taxable equivalent yield that exceeds the interest stated on the bond. Tables are available that provide this yield. Generally, the following formula provides the tax equivalent yield:

$$\text{Tax equivalent yield} = \frac{\text{Stated tax-free yield on bond}}{1 - \text{Marginal tax rate}}$$

A 9% tax-free bond for a taxpayer in the 28% marginal tax bracket would have a 12.5% tax equivalent yield.

$$\text{Tax equivalent yield} = \frac{.09}{1 - .28}$$

$$= 12.5\%$$

Taxpayers in a high tax bracket would obtain a substantial advantage in yield return on tax-exempt securities.

TAXES ON INVESTMENTS With the increased importance of securities as a form of taxable property and with increased rates of taxation, taxes on investments have become a major factor in the selection and turnover of securities, especially for investors who are subject to the higher tax brackets. Variables in the legitimate reduction of TAXES by investors include location of the taxpayer, location of his investments, and type of investments held.

Taxes on investments in the United States include federal income taxes, state income taxes, federal estate and gift taxes, state estate taxes, property taxes, and security transfer taxes. Income taxes are imposed upon the return from investments in interest and dividends, as well as upon capital gains or losses from sale. Estate, gift, and property taxes are imposed upon principal valuation of the securities. Transfer taxes are excises imposed at specified rates.

Some of the factors which investors may consider in legitimately reducing the load of taxation are as follows:

1. Strategic use of the capital gains and losses provisions. By control over the holding period and timely realization of capital gains or losses, it may be possible for investors to reduce their income taxes.
2. Resort to tax-exempt securities. This generally is feasible for the wealthier investors in high tax brackets and for institutional investors.
3. Location of securities in states having preferential taxation. This particularly applies in the case of creation of trusts and in estate taxation.

Investment income is defined as the taxpayer's gross income from interest, dividends, royalties, net short-term or long-term capital gains attributable to the disposition of investment property, and the ordinary income from recapture of depreciation or intangible drilling costs (under specified provisions of the code), to the extent the income is not derived from a trade or business. Investment expenses are all those deductions allowed as trade or business expenses (under a special provision of the code) real and personal property taxes, bad debt deductions provided in a special provision of the code, depreciation deductions, depletion, expenses incurred in connection with the production of investment income, and certain other expenses allowed under the code. Net investment income is the excess of the taxpayer's current investment income over investment expenses.

See TAX-EXEMPT BONDS.

TAXES ON STOCK TRANSFERS *See* STOCK TRANSFER TAX.

TAX EVASION Illegal activities that are designed to reduce the tax liability. To be guilty of evading taxes, the individual must already have a tax liability.
See TAS AVOIDANCE.

TAX-EXEMPT BONDS As the result of passage of an act of Congress on March 1, 1941, the exemption from federal income taxes of U.S. government securities was terminated, except for issues still outstanding after that date termed partially tax-exempt (exempt from all taxation except estate or inheritance or gift taxes imposed by federal or state authority, surtaxes on income, and excess profits or war-profits taxes, if any). U.S. government securities therefore are taxable (subject to federal income tax, as well as capital gains, estate, inheritance, gift, and excise taxes, whether federal or state, but exempt from income or property taxes as to principal or interest by any state, by any of the possessions of the U.S., or by any local taxing authority). Taxable U.S. government securities include all Treasury bills, certificates of indebtedness, notes and bonds, depositary bonds, U.S. savings bonds issued on or after March 1, 1941, Federal Housing Administration debentures issued on contracts dated on or after March 1, 1941, Governmental National Mortgage Association (GNMA) obligations, and instruments of Federal Land banks, Federal Intermediate Credit banks, Banks for Cooperatives, Federal Home Loan banks, and the Federal National Mortgage Corporation (FNMA), although exemption from state and local income or property taxes does not extend to GNMA and FNMA obligations issued since August 2, 1954. It should be noted, however, that certain issues of U.S. government bonds, if held by an individual at his death, may be tendered and reckoned at full par in payment of federal estate taxes on his estate (see FLOWER BONDS). It should also be noted that public housing agency (local authorities) and urban renewal program agencies' (local public agencies) project notes are exempt from federal income tax (and in nearly all cases, interest is also tax-exempt in states of issuance), as well as being backed by the full faith and credit of the United States.

The largest field of tax-exempt obligations, therefore, is now in state and municipal issues, which are exempt from federal income taxes as well as taxes by the home state or political subdivision thereof. Even in this field, however, tax exemption is a relative term, as such issues are subject to federal estate and gift taxes, as well as income, inheritance, and property taxes of states other than the home states. Moreover, federal capital gains taxes do apply.

See MUNICIPAL BONDS, UNITED STATES GOVERNMENT SECURITIES.

TAXFLATION   The hybrid term coined to refer to the impact of both higher INCOME TAXES and INFLATION.

As money incomes of households and business inflate, so do personal and corporate income tax payments as taxable incomes rise to the upper tax brackets. But the lower after-tax incomes then are hit also by lowered purchasing power because of continued inflation. The net result is lowered effective demand, causing slowdown in output and rise in unemployment.

Indexing of Tax Rates as the Solution. The *Economic Recovery Tax Act* of 1981 (ERTA), in addition to providing for increments of reductions in individual tax rates by 5% October 1, 1981, followed by a 10% reduction July 1, 1982, and a second 10% reduction July 1, 1983, provides that beginning in 1985, the tax brackets, zero bracket amount, and personal exemptions was adjusted to reflect annual changes in the consumer price index (see COST OF LIVING INDEX). Such indexing was applicable to the tax years beginning after December 31, 1984.

Evaluation. A concurrent rise in unemployment and in the rate of inflation has confounded both Keynesian economics and proponents of the PHILLIPS CURVE, the latter standing for the proposition that empirically there is a tradeoff between change in prices and unemployment rates—the cost of expansionary fiscal and monetary policies which increase aggregate demand and reduce unemployment is inflation. One explanation advanced for this concurrence of the rise in unemployment *and* inflation, as evidenced by the 1973-1975 experience, is that higher unemployment was *caused* by the sharp inflation, and that as money incomes inflated rapidly, the built-in automatic stabilizer effect of progressive (graduated upwards) tax rates meant a higher tax bite on money incomes accompanied by lower purchasing power caused by the inflation, thus reducing effective demand and leading to lower output (in real or uninflated terms) and higher unemployment. This is consistent with the problem defined by the Tax Equalization Act.

Whether indexation—either of salaries and wages or of taxes—is the appropriate solution, however, is a matter of opinion. Contrary opinion points out that no general indexing of inflation can protect real income efficiently and that in fact indexation may aggravate and build in inflation. Moreover, it is pointed out that taking out the bite of progressively higher tax rates on inflated incomes would destroy the automatic stabilizer characteristic of the progressive income tax structure, which deliberately aims to restrain inflation by lowering after-tax incomes and thus decreasing the ability to pay inflated prices. Proponents of the Tax Equalization Act argue that the inflation penalty inherent in the income tax structure is one of the basic causes of inflation, because income recipients realize that increases in income must be *in excess* of the cost-of-living increases simply to maintain the actual value of take-home income.

See AUTOMATIC STABILIZERS.

TAX-FREE BONDS   TAX-EXEMPT BONDS.

TAX-FREE COVENANT   The federal income tax law of 1913 contained a provision which required the normal tax on bonds which were subject to tax to be withheld at the source and also required that ownership certificates accompany all coupons detached from corporation bonds at the time of their presentation. This proved an annoyance to investors and hurt the sale of corporation bonds. Accordingly, issuers of corporate obligations floated their bonds with "tax-free covenants," whereby the obligor (issuer) agreed to pay any income tax which the law required the corporation to withhold from the interest paid to the bond owners.

The Revenue Act of 1918, however, raised the normal income tax rate above 2% and discontinued collection of the tax from the obligors, instituting instead the present practice of collection of the tax from the bondholders. Nevertheless, the new tax law made provision for withholding or payment of income tax of 2%, the former income tax rate, so that a holder of tax-free covenant bonds, under which the obligor usually assumed a tax of 2%, was relieved from income tax to this extent.

With passage of the Revenue Act of 1934, the requirement that the obligor withhold federal income tax up to 2% on tax-free covenant bonds was restricted to bonds issued on or before January 1, 1934. Whether or not bonds issued on and after January 1, 1934, carry the tax-free covenant, the obligor is now not required to withhold federal income tax in any amount, so that holders are required to pay the full federal income tax on such bonds.

Fundamentally, the purpose of the tax-free covenant was to shift the burden of the tax to the obligor, and at the time it was introduced, the assumption of tax, usually "up to 2%," no doubt was an inducement to investors in view of the low income tax rates then prevailing. In subsequent years, however, with the steady rise in income tax rates, the advantage to the bondholder of such 2% tax-free covenants became of minor significance.

TAX HAVEN   A country or municipality that provides low tax rates and other tax provisions that serve as incentives for individuals or other tax entities to accumualte capital or income therein to reduce, eliminate, or conceal such items that otherwise would be taxed in the home country.

TAX INCIDENCE   The point at which the burden of a tax ultimately rests. For example, the incidence of a tax on liquor is the consumer. Taxes on a retail store's activities can be passed forward to the buyer of the store's product, thereby shifting the incidence of the tax away from the store owner to the purchaser. Alternatively, the retailer could shift the incidence of the tax to his or her workers by lowering their salaries. If the retailer pays the tax from earned income, then the incidence of the tax is the retailer, where it was originally intended.

TAX LOOPHOLE   An unjustified discrimination or exemption from tax.

TAX-MANAGED MUTUAL FUNDS   A type of open-end INVESTMENT COMPANY that invests in corporate equities, not in tax-exempt securities.

Tax-managed mutual funds as a matter of deliberate policy pay out no dividends to their stockholders, retaining all net investment income and capital gains to add to asset value. As a result, such mutual funds do not qualify for the tax exemption available to regulated investment companies which, under the Internal Revenue Code, must pay to their stockholders at least 90% of their net investment income (any capital gains also distributed to their stockholders would be tax-exempt to regulated investment companies). Nevertheless, tax-managed mutual funds do have their income tax liability limited to their income tax rate times 15% of the dollar amount received in dividends (85% of such income from investments being excluded from the tax base, as in the case of other corporations receiving intercorporate dividends from corporations invested in). The remaining 15% of dividend income subject to taxes

TAX MULTIPLIER

is reducible further by deductibility of operating expenses of the funds, and further minimization of income taxes may result from offsetting devices by the management of the funds such as writing covered options on stocks owned.

From the standpoint of investors in the stock of tax-managed mutual funds, the basic appeal of such investment is the growth of asset value, which ideally will result in long-term capital gains taxable at a maximum of 20% (50% normal tax rate times the 40% of capital gains subject to tax, the other 60% of such gains being excluded) when realized, instead of the higher normal income tax rate applicable to dividend income when dividends are distributed from investment income. Of course capital appreciation is of the essence for success in such investment.

TAX MULTIPLIER A change in taxes will often have a multiplied impact on the economy. The tax multiplier quantifies what the impact will be. The tax multiplier equals the negative of the ratio of the marginal propensity to consume to the marginal propensity to save: -mpc/mps. If the mpc is .80 and the mps is .20 (mpc + mps = 1, always), then the value of the tax multiplier is -4.0. Therefore, a $1 increase in taxes will decrease national income by $4, or multiples thereof.

TAXPAYER IDENTIFICATION NUMBER (TIN)
A taxpayer's identification number represented by a nine-digit number with no alphabetic characters. A TIN is usually an individual's Social Security number or an employee identification number. The Interest and Dividend Tax Compliance Act of 1983 established information reporting requirements by banks and other institutions. All payors of interest and dividends are required to provide the Internal Revenue Service with substantial information on payments made to account holders. Institutions are required to show due diligence in obtaining a taxpayer's identification number or face a penalty of $50 for each Form 1099 that is filed with a missing or incorrect TIN. Aggregate penalties have totaled in the millions for certain payor institutions. The Internal Revenue Service has released a series of regulations describing how the rules are to be met.

BIBLIOGRAPHY

PRICE WATERHOUSE. *A Guide to TIN Compliance.* Bankers Publishing Co. Rolling Meadows, IL, 1988.

TAX RATES In 1988, a two-bracket system (15% and 28%) was implemented for individuals:

Married filing jointly, or surviving spouse	
0 to $29,750	15%
Over $29,750	28%
Single	
0 – $17,850	15%
Over $17,850	28%
Married filing separately	
0 – $14,875	15%
Over $14,875	28%
Head of Household	
0 – $23,900	15%
Over $23,900	28%

The Tax Reform Act of 1986 provided for an inflation adjustment to the tax brackets for tax years beginning after 1988 (for taxable income amounts at which the 28% rate starts). For tax years beginning in 1988, individuals having taxable income exceeding specified limits will be subject to an additional tax of 5% of taxable income. Upper-income married taxpayers filing jointly lose the benefit of the 15% tax rate. A 5% net adjustment to their taxable income will begin at $71,900. Heads of households' taxable income of between $61,650 and $123,790 will be subject to the five percent adjustment, as will single individuals' taxable income between $43,150 and $89,560. The rate adjustment for married taxpayers filing separately will apply when their taxable income is between $39,500 and $113,300. In 1989, corporate tax rates were as follows:

Taxable income	Rates
$1 – $50,000	15%
50,001 – 75,000	25
75,001 – 100,000	34
100,001 – 335,000	39
Over $335,000	34

Income tax rates for estates and trusts for taxable years beginning in 1987 were as follows:

If taxable income is:	The tax is:
Not over $500	11% of taxable income
Over $500 but not over $4,700	$55, plus 15% of the excess over $500
Over $4,700 but not over $7,550	$685, plus 28% of the excess over $4,700
Over $7,550 but not over $15,150	$1,483, plus 35% of the excess over $7,550
Over $15,150	$4,143, plus 38% of the excess over $15,150

For taxable years beginning in 1988:	
Not over $5,000	15% of taxable income
Over $5,000	$750, plus 28% of the excess over $5,000

TAX REFORM ACT OF 1986 President Reagan's 1986 budget called for a tax system that would be "simpler, more neutral, and more conducive to economic growth." The broad objectives of the Tax Reform Act of 1986 were fairness, revenue neutrality, long-term economic growth, and simplicity. Congress attempted to deal with broad public policy implications of the entire tax law instead of treating specific issues such as recessions, deficits, energy shortages, and others. The tax law had a major impact on how individuals and businesses save, invest, earn, and spend. Legislative discussions involved the modified flat tax, which would have far fewer tax brackets than the existing system. Many tax deductions would be eliminated, thereby increasing the individual's gross income; then the tax rates could be lowered. As it turned out, the scope of the changes was so comprehensive that the tax code was renamed the Internal Revenue Code of 1986.

The Tax Reform Act of 1986 repealed the investment credit the three-year rule for tax-free recovery of contributions to employee-annuities, for annuities starting after July 1, 1986; and the $1,000-a-year life insurance exclusion of interest received by a surviving spouse on installment proceeds of life insurance for amounts received for death occurring after October 22, 1986. Provisions repealed effective for 1987 and later years include: income averaging, dividend exclusion, 60% deduction for capital gains, deduction for estate and local sales taxes, deduction for qualified adoption expenses, deduction for a married couple when both work, credit for political contributions, and extra exemptions for age and blindness. These repealed provisions are replaced by the additional standard deduction.

Major provisions affecting individuals include:

1. No 60% deduction for long-term capital gains. After 1987, no distinction between short-term capital gains or losses. Capital gains will be taxed at ordinary rates. For 1988, the maximum rate on capital gains is 33 percent.
2. $3,000 of capital losses may offset ordinary income dollar for dollar.
3. Passive activity losses must offset passive activity income and are severely limited.
4. Income averaging completely eliminated after 1986.
5. Unemployment benefits totally includible in gross income.
6. Moving expenses become an itemized deduction.
7. Earned income credit increased to a maximum of $8900.
8. Medical expenses floor increased from 5% to 7.5%.
9. Consumer interest expenses phased out between 1987 and 1991.

ENCYCLOPEDIA OF BANKING AND FINANCE

10. Miscellaneous itemized deduction subject to a 2% adjusted gross income floor.
11. Business meals and entertainment expenses are only 90% deductible.
12. Tighter rules adopted on retirement plans.
13. Individual retirement accounts available for taxpayers with adjusted gross income under $25,000 ($40,000 for joint returns) and for taxpayers not covered by an employer pension plan. Deductions for IRAs totally phased out above $35,000 ($50,000 for joint returns).
14. Maximum contributions for tax-sheltered annuities curtailed.
15. Retirees lose favorable ten-year forward averaging for retirement plan distributions.

Major provisions related to corporations include:

1. Capital gains are no longer subject to preferential alternative tax rate. All corporate capital gains taxed at regular corporate tax rate, which can be as high as 34%.
2. No net operating loss carryforward.
3. Generally gains and losses from corporate liquidations will be recognized upon corporate liquidation distributions and sales with a complete liquidation.
4. The corporate deduction for dividends received is reduced from 85% to 80%.
5. The alternative minimum tax rate increased from 15% to 20%. The corporate exemption increased from $10,000 to $40,000 but phased out over $150,000.

Major provisions affecting business transactions:

1. Recovery periods and rates of recovery and the depreciation methods modified. Most business assets can use the 200% declining balance method.
2. The research tax credit extended for three years but reduced from 25% to 20%.
3. Industrial development bonds can no longer be used to finance convention, sports, trade show, parking, or pollution control facilities.
4. The reserve for bad debts method is generally no longer available.

TAX RELIEF BONDS See TAX ANTICIPATION obligations.

TAX SHELTER An investment at risk to acquire something of value, with the expectation that it will produce income and reduce or defer taxes and that its ultimate disposition will result in the realization of gain. Tax-sheltered investments are often public offerings that have been registered with the Securities and Exchange Commission for interstate sale or with a state agency. Private offerings are not registered. Most tax shelters are structured as limited partnerships in which the investors are the limited partners. Subchapter S corporations are also used to structure a tax shelter. The tax losses generated by most tax-sheltered investments are attributable to deductions for depreciation and interest on borrowed funds that provide leverage for the investment. Investment tax credits and rehabilitation credits frequently add to the attractiveness of tax shelters.

Tax shelters have frequently been abused. An abusive tax shelter is a transaction without any economic purpose other than the generation of tax benefits. Such shelters frequently overstate the valuation of assets. The Internal Revenue Service disapproves of abusive tax shelters.

BIBLIOGRAPHY

ARTHUR ANDERSEN & Co., *Tax Shelters—The Basics.* Arthur Andersen & Co., 1982.
J. K. Lasser's Guide to Tax-Deferred Investments. Simon & Schuster, Inc., New York, NY, 1987.
MILLER, R. B., *Tax Haven Investing: A Guide to Offshore Banking and Invetment Opportunities.* Probus Publishing Co., Chicago, IL, 1988.
MORTIMER, M., and NAMORATO, C. *Third Annual Tax Shelter Controversies: The IRS, Justice and SEC.* Harcourt Brace Jovanovich, San Diego, CA, 1987.
STEINER, B. R., and KENNEDY, D. W. *Perfectly Legal*, 1985.

TAX SHIELD A device for protecting income from taxation, such as depreciation; the tax saved because of the tax deductibility of an expenditure.

TAX TREATIES The United States has treaty agreements with many foreign countries dealing with tax and other matters. Where conflict arises, the provisions contained in a treaty override the rules contained in the Internal Revenue Code. The tax treaties are used to reduce or eliminate the burden of double taxation or to establish cooperation between the taxing authorities of the two nations.

T-BILLS See TREASURY BILL FUTURES, TREASURY BILLS.

TECHNICAL ANALYSIS In analysis of stock prices, the system and analytical approach of reliance exclusively upon price and volume data, whether in graphic form or otherwise, for deriving trends and formations (typical chart patterns) that will lead to conclusions as to present market position and possible future market action for the market as a whole (as measured by general stock averages), for stock groups, and for individual stocks.

Proponents of this approach to market analysis argue that market data are the most definitive and relevant because they will reflect what the marketplace's judgment of fundamentals (earnings, dividends, balance sheet data, income account data, management, etc.) is, and because they include in addition a very important factor which the fundamentals cannot include, i.e., the psychology of buyers and sellers prevailing in the market. Prices are determined by supply and demand and move in persisting trends the continuance or reversal of which can be detected and extrapolated by technical analysis.

As an indicator of primary trend, the DOW THEORY is a technical approach. Technical indicators include advance-decline indexes, odd-lot theory, the confidence index, moving average indexes, relative strength indexes, short interest and customers' credit balances data. Charting methods include line charting, bar charting, and point-and-figure charting, each type of charting yielding trend patterns in prices accompanied by volume fluctuation during the trends. Chart formations, each with their general characteristics and significance, include fans, triangles, head and shoulders formations (straight up and inverted), wedges, flags, rectangles, pennants, saucers, saucepans, bowls, "M and W" formations, gaps, islands, etc. Particular to the point-and-figure system is the fulcrum (compound fulcrum, inverse fulcrum). In all systems, the establishment by the data of trendlines and channels makes it possible to draw conclusions as to breakouts therefrom on the upside or downside and to estimate target projections for prices and levels of averages. Support and resistance points are also spotted on the basis of analysis of chart patterns.

Fundamentalist View. Although the extreme fundamentalist might regard technical analysis as an over-elaborate attempt to systematize the effects and not the underlying causes of rational stock market movements, the prudent analyst will check not only the fundamental position of a stock, a stock group, or the market (measured by general market averages), but also the technical position of same, because the latter approach unquestionably has followers who have their own impact upon market movements. Through checking of the stock charts and technical position, it may also be possible to detect an unusual rise in volume, accompanied by buoyant price movements, in stocks before fundamentalist data become generally available to explain the higher activity and prices. Moreover, because good information seldom is very fresh by the time it filters down to the general public, charts will show how much of a rise, accompanied by higher volume, has already occurred by the time the "good" information becomes available to the public, by which time such information will have already been acted upon by those institutions and individuals who received the information early.

Random Walk View. Random walk theory challenges the basic assumption of technical analysis of predictability of prices based on existing historical market data including patterns of price and volume fluctuation. Instead, random walk theory postulates that price changes are random because any nonrandom fluctuations in prices are quickly seized upon by knowledgeable market participants and thus eliminated as prices are restored to equilibrium reflecting intrinsic values justified by the relevant knowledge. This is the famous EFFICIENT MARKET HYPOTHESIS: (1) that market participants (at least sufficient numbers of them) are rational and have full access to all available relevant information, (2) that prices quickly reflect such relevant information, and (3) that therefore prevailing prices will promptly reflect intrinsic values as the result of such informed buying and selling. Consequently, all predictable price changes are already discounted, and so any price changes that occur will be random and follow a random walk.

Summary. Although the random walk theory has strong academic support, technical analysis refuses to die and continues to have its loyal adherents.

See BUSINESS BAROMETERS, CHARTIST, MARKET INFLUENCES, SPECULATION.

BIBLIOGRAPHY

ARNOTT, R. D., and FABOZZI, F. J. *Asset Allocation: A Handbook of Portfolio Policies, Strategies & Tactics*, 1988.

ENG, W. F. *Technical Analysis of Stocks, Options & Futures*, Probus Publishing Co., Chicgo, IL, 1988.

MEYERS, T. A. *The Technical Analysis Course: A Winning Program for Stock and Futures Traders and Investors*, 1989.

PISTOLESE, C. *Using Technical Analysis*, 1989.

SUTTON, D. P., and BENEDETTO, M. W. *Initial Public Offerings: A Strategic Planner for Raising Equity Capital.* Probus Publishing Co., Chicago, IL, 1988.

WEISS RESEARCH. *Timing the Market: How to Profit in Bull and Bear Markets with Technical Analysis.* Probus Publishing Co., Chicago, IL, 1986.

TECHNICAL CORRECTION ACT OF 1982
A tax law that made changes in major tax provisions including the accelerated cost recovery system, the investment credit, job credits, the credit for research costs, the incentive stock options, and the WINDFALL PROFIT TAX ACT.

TECHNICAL MARKET DATA
Market data in various relationships have been utilized in a variety of ways in a search for technical market indicators of high correlation and reliability. (By contrast, the random walk hypothesis holds that fluctuation in stock prices approximates a random walk so that past data provide no guide to future fluctuation and trend.) Among the data used are the following:

1. Volume-price relationships. The theory is that the behavior of the volume of trading relative to price changes indicates supply-demand conditions and hence provides a clue as to future trend.
2. Breadth of market. An increase in the total number of issues traded, in a rising market, is considered a favorable indicator for further advance, and vice versa.
3. Cumulative net advances or declines, charted as a continuous curve.
   These are generally considered to be a good indicator of short-term trend.
4. Net new highs and new lows, charted as a continuous curve. New highs less new lows, on a cumulative basis, indicate the ability of the market to break out into higher levels or, on the other hand, to resist sinking to lower levels.
5. Short interest (short sales still outstanding as of mid-month, reported monthly). The ratio of the short interest to average trading volume for the period will provide an indication of potential buying support (short sellers who would cover their outstanding short sales by buying and thus completing the transactions).
   Reported data on the short interest only cover issues reported by the New York Stock Exchange and do not include short interest on the regional exchanges or by third market (over-the-counter) firms trading in NYSE-listed issues; moreover, the reported data do not reflect growing use of the PUT option in hedging positions. As a result, it is anticipated that the usefulness of the reported data on NYSE short interest as technical market data may well be diminished as development of the unified national securities market proceeds.
6. Ratio of low-priced stocks' market average to high-priced stocks' market average, the former indicating speculative interest and the latter investment interest. In the early stages of a bull market, the ratio is low (initial market interest is attracted to the higher-quality issues), but the ratio rises past unity in the later stages of a bull market, as speculative issues outperform the higher-grade issues.
7. Corporate insiders (officers, directors, and owners of more than 10% of a company's stock) buying or selling.

Odd-Lot Data. The reliability of data on odd-lot volume on the New York Stock Exchange as a technical market indicator also has been affected by the emergence of important odd-lot volume in other markets, such as the COMEX System on the Pacific Stock Exchange and the PACE System on the Philadelphia Stock Exchange. Moreover, as West and Murphy of the New York Stock Exchange point out, the public's shift in the NYSE's odd-lot volume to constant sale balances in recent years can be attributed to factors other than investors' negative view on the market, such as the substantial increase in splits, stock dividends, mergers, dividend reinvestment plans, and employee participation plans, which have resulted in large additions to odd-lot holdings of investors without being reflected in odd-lot purchases in the market. Minimum commissions on transactions, even with discount brokers, also make odd-lot transactions regressively expensive for the public. Odd-lot short sales by the public (NYSE members rarely sell short in odd-lots) are the particular basis for the persisting generalization that "the public is always wrong" (empirical study of past data indicates that when the ratio of odd-lot short sales to NYSE odd-lot volume has risen, the market in the subsequent month has turned upward).

See TECHNICAL ANALYSIS.

TECHNICAL POSITION
Among stock speculators, the situation, circumstances, set of conditions, influences, or forces operating within the market itself, as distinguished from purely external or extrinsic factors, which favor a price movement upward or downward. From the standpoint of the bulls, the technical position is said to be good when the forces or influences in the market are favorable to an advance in prices and bad when favorable to a decline. It is well known in speculative circles that successful speculation depends upon a knowledge of the technical position of the market, as well as the outside influences or FUNDAMENTAL CONDITIONS, e.g., political events, trade reports, earnings statements, money rates, and general business conditions. Following are the chief elements affecting the technical position:

1. Whether the market is overbought or oversold,
2. The extent of the short interest,
3. Whether stocks are widely distributed or centered in the hands of a few,
4. The extent of public participation,
5. Activity,
6. The attitude of big operators,
7. The quantity of stop loss orders present above or below the current level of quotations,
8. The sensitiveness of speculators to bad news,
9. The extent to which the market has advanced or declined without reaction or rally,
10. The extent to which pyramiding is evident, and
11. Whether margins are thin or heavy.

Short-swing operators take advantage of their knowledge of the technical position and place their orders accordingly.

See TECHNICAL ANALYSIS.

TECHNOCRACY
Rule by technologists; a derived term. Representing a body of thought, technocracy was an interpretation of technology—an attempt to re-create a system or social mechanism based on a scientific use of technological forces. It claimed that the social problem of production and distribution on the North American continent is a technological one and hence would discard all orthodox or traditional approaches (i.e., political and economic) to the management of society and substitute a system in which the productive capacity of the physical equipment of the continent would be utilized at a full balanced load. Thus, technocracy was nonpolitical, nondemocratic, and nonphilosophical, contending that the complex modern industrial-economic-social-political problems cannot be solved by political and legalistic minds.

Technocracy had its inception in an organization known as the Technical Alliance of North America, which began functioning in 1919 in New York City. This group included Thorstein Veblen, Bassett Jones, Richard Tolman, Frederick L. Ackerman, Stuart Chase, and Howard Scott, who acted as chief engineer of the Technical Alliance.

The primary aim of this group was to ascertain the possibility of applying the achievements of science to social and industrial affairs. With this in mind, the alliance proceeded to make a survey of the energy and natural resources of the North American continent (all that territory included between the Panama Canal and the North Pole), studying the industrial evolution that had taken place therein. This survey showed graphically the operating characteristics of the present industrial system with its alleged waste and leakage and worked out a tentative design and a complete coordinated system of production and distribution. The chief objective was to provide a better standard of living for the people living in North America with the least possible waste of nonrenewable resources.

The chief conclusions of technocracy were (1) that there exists on the North American continent a potential condition of plenty such as is to be found nowhere else in the world: marvelous natural resources, an abundance of raw materials, huge productive machinery adequate for turning out vast quantities of goods, and a body of trained technicians and skilled workers—the finest in the world—capable of operating this productive machinery in the most efficient manner, (2) that the price system can no longer function adequately as a method of production and distribution of goods, (3) that the invention of power machinery has made it possible to produce goods in abundance with a relatively small amount of human labor, and (4) that as machines displace men, however, purchasing power is destroyed, for people cannot buy goods if they cannot work for wages and salaries.

With the advent of the Roosevelt administration and its New Deal in 1933, active interest in technocracy waned.

BIBLIOGRAPHY

ADAMSON, M., and MOORE, R. I. *Technocracy: Some Questions Answered*, 1934.
ARKWRIGHT, F. *The ABC of Technocracy*, 1933.
RAYMOND, A. *What Is Technocracy?* 1933.
SCOTT, H. *Introduction to Technocracy*, 1933.
WALSH, R. J. *An Introduction to Technocracy*, 1933.

TECHNOLOGICAL CHANGE Technology changing over time. The term technology has been used in a variety of ways. In a narrow sense, technology refers to specific physical tools, but in a broader sense it describes whole social processes.

One useful approach to this definitional issue is to conceptualize technology as the physical representation of knowledge. Any useful technological device is, in part, proof of the knowledge-based or informational assumptions leading to its creation. This informational view of technology implies that technology per se is an output from a consciously undertaken process. Such an idea highlights the role of research in the generation of technologies. Thus, technologies can be distinguished, although imperfectly, by the amount of embedded information.

Banks have become intensively involved in the technological revolution. Computers allow easy and inexpensive gathering, storing, analyzing, and retrieving of customer data and other banking-related information. The automated teller machine (ATM) has been widely used since the early 1980s. Bank transactions are currently made by electronic impulse away from the banks' physical location. Automatic clearing houses, direct payroll crediting, direct bill payment, use of debit cards, and point of sale (POS) terminals have become commonplace in banking. Competition and cost controls have contributed greatly to the significant advances in technological adaptation.

TECHNOLOGICAL UNEMPLOYMENT A term coined to refer to individuals displaced by technology. For example, automating an aspect of an assembly line production process will replace labor with machines. Individuals loosing their jobs because of this are said to be technologically unemployed.

TEFRA TAX EQUITY AND FISCAL RESPONSIBILITY ACT OF 1982.

TELEPHONE INDUSTRY Practically all telephone service in the United States is provided by privately owned companies that typically possess a monopoly within their service areas. As a result, state and federal regulations are a significant factor in the industry, especially with regard to pricing of telephone services. This practice is assumed to result in providing the greatest number of customers with the best service at the lowest price. It also is supposed to encourage capital formation by providing a reasonable return to investors. The Federal Communications Commission (FCC) has oversight and responsibility for enforcing the Communications Act of 1934. State public utility or public service commissions are responsible for local service franchises and activities.

Local telephone service is provided primarily by regional holding companies and independents. In January 1984, AT&T divested its 22 Bell operating companies in the form of seven regional holding companies (RHC) as a result of a 1982 consent degree that settled an antitrust suit filed by the Department of Justice: AMERITECH, BELL ATLANTIC, BELLSOUTH, NYNEX, PACIFIC TELESIS, SOUTHWESTERN BELL, AND U.S. WEST. Approximately 1,400 independents also provide service as regulated monopolies within specified territories. The RHCs are considered to be among the most financially sound corporations in the U.S. Investors view them as "cash cows."

AT&T is the major provider of long-distance telephone service. Other major providers include MCI Communications and US Sprint.

Cellular telephones represent a major innovation in the telephone industry. Cellular telephone service is named for small regions or cells into which a service area is divided. Each cell has a low-power transmitter/receiver referred to as a base station. A cell typically has a service radius of from two to ten miles. Each base station is connected to a mobile telephone switching office by means of telephone lines or microwave technology. A central switching point coordinates the calls for the service area.

BIBLIOGRAPHY

SIMON, S. A. *Divesture: The First Year*, 1985.
Telephone, Telegraph, and Television. U.S. Government Printing Office (Subject bibliography 199).

TELEPHONE SECURITIES Securities (bonds, debentures, preferred stock, and common stock) of companies in the telephone industry, the largest of the public communications industries, which include the telephone industry, the wire-telegraph industry (land lines and ocean cable), and the radio-telegraphic industry.

The telephone industry ranks as the second largest public service industry in the U.S., after the electric light and power industry. Over 1,500 other telephone companies, known as independents, served about half of the geographic area of the United States, mainly rural and suburban areas and small towns. Five holding companies accounted for about three-fourths of the independents' share of the market.

While accounting largely for total communications services, telephone service is just one of the types of telecommunications services provided by the industry, which has been engaged in a variety of research, development, and technological changes. Data transmission, for example, has been one of the fastest growing areas of the business. Other areas include transmission of radio and television programs; electronic switching systems (ESS), which provide faster call processing, increased reliability, and reduced maintenance costs; wave guide facilities, which offer greater capacity for transmission of all kinds of communications; laser beams, which can provide lightwave transmission of many messages through thin transparent glass fibers; data under voice (DUV), which makes possible transmission of data over microwave frequencies at the lower end of the band; traffic service position systems (TSPS), which permit person-to-person dealings; and commercial picturephone meeting service—a two-way voice and video service connecting picturephone service centers.

The debt ratio is of interest from a financing standpoint, because while a higher proportion of debt financing would lower the overall composite cost of capital (because interest on debt securities is tax-deductible, whereas dividends on preferred or common stock do not have such tax treatment to the company), excessive use of debt leverage might cause quality ratings on the debt securities to be lowered and financing costs to rise, inasmuch as the telephone industry, historically, has had more cyclical variability in revenues and operating revenues than the electric light and power industry, for instance. It should be noted, also, that because of heavy investment in facilities, fixed costs are relatively high, thus imparting high operating leverage as well.

Communications Satellites. The Communications Satellite Corporation (Comsat) was formed in 1963, pursuant to the 1962 Communications Satellite Act. Communications carriers owned 37% of Comsat's outstanding shares (29% owned by American Telephone & Telegraph), with the public owning 63%. Directors of Comsat include four elected by the carriers (three by AT&T), three appointed by the President of the United States, and eight elected by the general public.

TELEREGISTER
An electrically manipulated board for posting stock quotations as they are made, controlled from a central office. The boards, which may be installed in the board rooms of brokers' offices, were rented, as a service, from the Western Union Telegraph Company.

TELEX
In the expanding field of communications, Telex and TWX (the trademark of the Western Union Telegraph Company) utilize similar technologies for teletypewriter communications which provide both the sender and the receiver with written copies of messages.

For either type of system, to communicate with similarly equipped points throughout the United States, the user obtains a line from the Western Union Telegraph Company and a terminal consisting of a telephone dial for communication and a keyboard for the messages, which are printed out at the terminals at both the sending and receiving ends.

International telex messages may be sent by placing a call by WATS line (Wide Area Telecommunications Service) or direct distance dialing through the nearest international telex switch reached domestically by Western Union, Telex, or TWX. Competition has resulted in reduced rates. Some heavy users of international service, including banks, have achieved savings by using their own facilities instead to reach the international carriers.

TELLER
A bank employee who in one capacity or another transacts business with customers over the window. The paying and receiving tellers are the most familiar examples. Large banks also have the mail teller, NOTE TELLER, COLLECTION TELLER, COUPON TELLER, etc.

See PAYING TELLER, RECEIVING TELLER.

BIBLIOGRAPHY

BANK ADMINISTRATION INSTITUTE. *Effective Teller Management.* Bank Administration Institute, Rolling Meadows, IL, 1987.
———. *Modern Teller Training 3* (Video and workbook formats).
———. *Teller Management Policies and Practices*, 1988.

TEMPORARY BONDS
Bonds issued as temporary certificates for permanent or definitive bonds and which differ from temporary receipts in that they contain the same complete recitals that appear on the permanent forms and are not merely acknowledgments of payment and promises of delivery. The term also denotes bonds or certificates issued for temporary financing purposes; thus, receivers' certificates are temporary bonds.

TEMPORARY CERTIFICATES
See TEMPORARY BONDS.

TEMPORARY RECEIPTS
Corporations floating a new bond, note, or stock issue frequently desire to obtain possession of the new funds as soon as possible and before permanent, engraved certificates can be prepared for delivery. To provide for this contingency, temporary printed or lithographed receipts are issued to purchasers upon payment. These receipts are acknowledgments of payment and promises to deliver permanent or definitive bonds (or stock). They are held by the purchasers until the issuing corporation announces that definitive forms are ready for substitution upon surrender of the temporary receipts.

TENANCY
An interest in land based on relationships. A TENANCY IN COMMON is a form of coownership in which each tenant (owner) holds an undivided interest in property. The ownership interest of a tenant in common does not terminate upon the owner's prior death.

A joint tenancy provides for the undivided ownership of property by two or more persons with the right of survivorship. Right of survivorship gives the surviving owner full ownership of the property.

A TENANCY BY THE ENTIRETY is essentially a joint tenancy between husband and wife. As in a joint tenancy, upon the death of one tenant by entireties the entire title automatically and immediately vests in the survivor.

TENANCY BY THE ENTIRETY
In law, the particular type of tenancy created in real estate granted or devised to husband and wife, where no express words indicate the creation of a different estate. Each has the right to an undivided half in the real estate subject to the tenancy, and in the event of death of either, the right of survivorship enables the survivor to take the whole. During life, neither husband nor wife may convey his or her interest so as to cut off the right of survivorship. The interest of either party may be mortgaged, but in the event of foreclosure, the purchaser at foreclosure sale merely becomes a tenant in common with the other party, subject to the latter's right of survivorship.

Tenants by the entirety may terminate the tenancy by a joint deed of both husband and wife conveying the real estate. The tenancy may also be terminated by an absolute divorce, upon which the parties merely become tenants in common. A voluntary partition between the husband and wife may also terminate the tenancy by the entirety.

See JOINT TENANCY, TENANCY IN COMMON.

TENANCY IN COMMON
In law, the type of tenancy or estate created when real or personal property is granted, devised, or bequeathed to two or more persons, in the absence of express words creating a JOINT TENANCY. If the persons are husband and wife and the property is real estate, a TENANCY BY THE ENTIRETY will automatically arise, unless there are express words creating a joint tenancy or tenancy in common.

A tenant in common holds and may convey, mortgage, devise, or bequeath his undivided interest in the property, real or personal. There is no right of survivorship, as in the case of joint tenancy or tenancy by the entirety, so that death of a tenant in common does not vest his interest in the surviving tenants. In the event of conveyance, the purchaser (at the foreclosure of the mortgage), devisee or legatee, or distributee (in the case of intestacy) becomes a tenant in common with the other original tenants in common. The most customary method of termination of tenancy in common is by partition, either voluntary or by action to compel partition. Also, conveyance by tenants in common of their interests to a single tenant in common will terminate the tenancy in common by merger. A tenant in common is liable to other cotenants for waste and cannot purchase an outstanding claim to the exclusion of his cotenants or create an easement binding the real property against himself or his cotenants. Classified according to the number and relationship of owners, estates are in severalty, in joint tenancy, in tenancy in common, and in tenancy by the entirety.

TENANT
Generally, a person who is entitled to a terminable interest in the possession, enjoyment, or occupation of an estate, such as for life, for years, from year to year, at will, or by sufferance.

In the landlord-tenant relationship, the tenant is one who, not being the owner, occupies real property under consent of the owner and in subordination to the owner's title, but is entitled to exclusive possession, use, and enjoyment, usually in consideration of payment of rent as specified in the LEASE.

TENDER
This term has three meanings:

1. Bid. See BID PRICE
2. See LEGAL TENDER.
3. In law, the act of offering unconditionally to a claimant or creditor, in satisfaction of the claim, the sum of money or property considered to be due and owing.

TENDER OFFER
In takeovers of control of target companies by acquisitive companies, the invitation to stockholders of the target company to tender their shares for a specified price per share, usually at a premium over prevailing market prices as an incentive, subject to a maximum number of total shares to be accepted on the tenders and subject to a given time period for the tenders.

The tender offer thus aims to acquire sufficient shares in the target company to assure effective control despite opposition from management of the target company and usually is resorted to after friendly overtures to management of the target company have been unsuccessful. Under Sections 13(d) and (e) and 14(d), (e), and (f) of the Securities Exchange Act of 1934, enacted in 1968 and amended in 1970, the acquiring firm must give the management of the target firm and the Securities and Exchange Commission thirty days' notice of intention to effect the acquisition, and when purchases of stock are made through tender offers or by open market purchases, the beneficial owner of the stock must be disclosed as well as the name of the party providing the funds for the acquisition. The SEC's implementation of the statute provides for filing of Schedule 13D reports by persons or groups who have made acquisitions resulting in their ownership of more than 5% of a class of securities, as well as those making tender offers which if successful would result in more than 5% ownership. Schedule 14D reports are filed on solicitations or recommendations in a tender offer other than by the maker of the offer.

On the other hand, Rule 14d-2 under the Securities Exchange Act exempts from the requirement of Schedule 14D reports those communications from an issuer to its security holders which do no more than identify the tender offer, state that management is studying the proposal, and request that security holders defer making a decision on the tender offer until they receive management's recommendation, which must be made no later than ten days before expiration of the tender offer, unless the SEC authorizes a shorter period.

In addition, more than 30 states have antitakeover laws which may delay tender offers and thus afford the target company's management time in which to set up effective defenses against the takeover or seek more acceptable alternative offers for control.

See MERGER.

10-K The annual report filed by reporting companies with the SEC within 90 days after the close of the fiscal year that provides information disclosures of material facts concerning the company. Preparing the 10-K typically requires the cooperation of the firm's officers, attorneys, and auditors. Form 10-K contains the following items:

1. General instructions.
2. Cover page.
3. Disclosures relating to a company's business, properties, legal proceedings, and security ownership of certain beneficial owners and managements (Part I).
4. Information contained in the annual report to shareholders, including market price data, selected financial data, three years of audited financial statements, and management's discussion and analysis of the company's financial condition and results of operations (Part II).
5. Proxy disclosure information relating to directors and executive officers, and management's remuneration (Part III).
6. Financial statements not required in the annual report to shareholders and additional financial schedules and exhibits (Part IV).
7. Signatures.
8. Supplemental information.

1099 The income tax form used to report the payment of interest, dividends, and other fees to individuals.
See TAXPAYER IDENTIFICATION NUMBER.

TENNESSEE VALUE AUTHORITY The largest federal power agency, originally created by the Tennessee Valley Authority Act of May 18, 1933 (48 Stat. 58; 16 U.S.C. 831—831dd), to take over the Muscle Shoals Dam (Wilson Dam) and execute the provisions of the act with respect to flood control, development of water power, and reforestation, as well as the development of new types of fertilizers for use in agricultural programs. Executive Order 6161 of June 8, 1933, which implemented Sections 22 and 23 of the act, authorized the corporation to conduct investigations into additional legislation which might be enacted to aid further the proper conservation, development, and use of the resources of the region.

Organization. All functions of the Tennessee Valley Authority (TVA) are vested in its three-member board of directors, appointed by the President of the United States with the consent of the Senate. The board reports directly to the President. The general manager is the TVA's principal administrative officer and reports to the board of directors.

A system of dams built by TVA on the Tennessee River and its larger tributaries provides flood regulation on the Tennessee and contributes to regulation of the lower Ohio and Mississippi rivers. The dams harness the power of the rivers to produce electricity. They also provide other benefits, including a major asset for outdoor recreation.

TVA is a wholesale power supplier for many local municipal and cooperative electric systems serving customers in parts of seven states. At Muscle Shoals, Alabama, TVA operates a national laboratory for development of new and improved fertilizers and processes. Research results are made available to industry. In western parts of Kentucky and Tennessee, TVA operates Land Between The Lakes—a demonstration project in outdoor recreation, environmental education, and natural resource management.

Nonpower Activities. In addition to its power program, the TVA engages in regional development programs, including water resources and general resources development, as well as environmental research and development; a fertilizer and munitions development program; and general service activities such as topographic mapping, bridge maintenance, fallout shelter maintenance, and reimbursable services furnished at the request of other agencies.

Summary. The TVA was one of the most controversial of the New Deal projects, particularly because of its alleged role in providing a yardstick of power rates to retail consumers when its rates were obviously not comparable with private power rates principally because of nonpayment of federal taxes. In recent years, its expansion into the largest of the federal government's direct operations of a business-type activity has given concern to those who believe such projects should be deemphasized. The 1959 law limiting the TVA to its existing area is expressive of this philosophy; but like any major power project, TVA in supplying its customers has the obligation to keep its capacity ahead of peak demand loads, and with consumption (especially by defense customers) increasing, its expansion has been unavoidable on a sound business basis.

See PUBLIC UTILITY INDUSTRY.

BIBLIOGRAPHY

COMPTROLLER GENERAL OF THE U.S. "Electric Energy Options Hold Great Promise for the Tennessee Valley Authority." Report to the Congress, November 29, 1978.
TENNESSEE VALLEY AUTHORITY. *Annual Report.*

TENNESSEE VALLEY AUTHORITY ACT An act, approved May 18, 1933, which, among other things:

1. Created the Tennessee Valley Authority (TVA) to maintain and operate properties owned by the United States near Muscle Shoals, Alabama, in the interests of national defense and agricultural and industrial development of the Tennessee Valley and to improve navigation in the Tennessee River and control the flood waters of the Mississippi and Tennessee Rivers;
2. Authorized the TVA to acquire real estate and build dams, powerhouses, reservoirs, transmission lines, and power projects; unite power installations into one or more transmission line systems; contract with commercial producers for fertilizers; manufacture experimental fertilizers; make and sell explosives to the government at cost; produce, sell, and distribute power; lease nitrate plant No. 2 for the private manufacture of fertilizer; sell $50 million worth of 3.5% 50-year bonds to finance improvements; and, with presidential approval, complete dam No. 2 and the steam plant at the No. 2 nitrate plant at Muscle Shoals; and
3. Ordered the construction of the Cove Creek Dam across the Clinch River in Tennessee, with a power transmission line from Muscle Shoals.

TENOR In negotiable instruments, the length of time specified in a note (or draft for payment) between date of issuance (or date of acceptance of a time draft) and maturity date; USANCE.
See TERM.

TEN PERCENT RULE This term has two meanings:

1. *See* TWENTY PERCENT RULE.
2. The provision in the national bank laws that prohibits a national bank from lending, except under certain conditions, more than 10% of its capital and surplus to one person, firm, or corporation.

See NATIONAL BANK LOANS.

TEN-POINT MARGIN Initial margin, i.e., a partial payment, equal to $10 or ten points *per share* for each share purchased. Thus, $1,000 as margin on the purchase of 100 shares was a ten-point margin, whether the purchase price per share was $25 or $90. Another term for point margins was dollar margins. Instead of point margins, equity margins were prescribed by the New York Stock Exchange in 1933, when it voluntarily established the first uniform margin requirements. When the Board of Governors of the Federal Reserve System, pursuant to the Securities Exchange Act of 1934, established the first federally prescribed initial margin requirements in 1934, it too adopted the equity type, which are based on the relationship between the customer's equity in a margin account and the market value of the collateral (stocks purchased on margin).

Point margins therefore have not been used in modern times. Before inauguration of its rule on equity margins in 1933, the New York Stock Exchange by general rule simply provided that margins be "adequate," and left it to the discretion of the member firms to require specific margins, which varied with the quality, volatility, and price level of the stocks bought on margin. When used, point margins also varied with these factors.

See MARGIN BUYING.

TERM The period or duration of a contract, estate, note, acceptance, time draft, bill of exchange, or bond.

See MATURITY.

TERM BONDS Bonds of the same issue maturing on the same date. Serial BONDS have more than one maturity date.

TERM FEDERAL FUNDS FEDERAL FUNDS (reserve balances of institutions at district Federal Reserve banks) "sold" (lent) for periods of time longer than the customary overnight usage.

In recent years, the Federal Reserve Bank of New York reports, banks have borrowed immediately available federal funds for periods longer than a single day as a source of short-term funds in liability management of the bank's money position. According to the Fed, this form of borrowing of federal funds was developed by agencies of Canadian banks located in the United States. Term federal funds normally run for 30, 60, or 90 days' duration and may constitute a more advantageous alternative in liability management of a bank than certificates of deposit. CDs involve legal reserve requirements as well as deposit insurance, whereas term federal funds are classified as borrowings without such requirements and therefore may provide lower net cost to the borrowing (buying) bank even if the borrowing rate is fractionally higher. The term federal funds market has developed in recent years to the point where suppliers (lenders) include, besides Canadian agencies and other foreign banks, savings and loan associations (through their Federal Home Loan Bank System, which itself is a source of such funds to the market) and corporations (indirectly through offshore Eurodollar deposits, which in turn are lent by the receiving bank as term federal funds).

TERMINABLE ANNUITY See ANNUITY.

TERMINABLE BONDS Bonds that have a fixed compulsory maturity, as distinguished from indeterminate or perpetual bonds.

See INDETERMINATE BONDS, PERPETUAL BOND.

TERMINAL BONDS Bonds that are obligations of a terminal company, which in turn may be owned by, or the property of which may be leased to, one railroad or a number of railroads jointly, usually the latter. Proper terminal facilities are of the utmost importance to railroads, and upon these facilities depend the volume, dispatch, and cost with which traffic is handled. Terminal costs are usually large and many railroads cooperate in the use of terminal facilities, as evidenced by the frequency of union stations and joint freight terminals. The formation of a terminal company, the property of which (yards, buildings, tracks, etc.) can be mortgaged to secure additional capital, accounts for the origin of this class of bonds.

The revenue accruing to a terminal company is derived from charges to the railroad companies using the facilities, apportioned on the basis of traffic.

Terminal bonds are frequently guaranteed by the railroads sharing the company's facilities. When terminal bonds are secured by valuable property located at important railroad centers or shipping points, with earnings in excess of interest charges, or are guaranteed by railroads of high credit standing, they constitute a high-grade investment.

TERM LOANS Intermediate credit of a capital nature extended by commercial banks and the larger life insurance companies and finance companies to firms unable or unwilling to run the risks of capital market underwriting for new capital for such purposes as an increase in working capital or the purchase of equipment or other fixed assets. Commercial banks in particular began to extend such loans in the 1930s as an adjustment to changed credit conditions in which the demand for traditional short-term commercial loans has declined.

Term loans are characterized by regular periodic amortization of a fixed principal amount, occasionally followed by a large balloon final maturity, usually in the last year. Interest rates are graduated according to the serial maturities and on the average for the full term compare with capital market flotations of similar maturity. In addition to periodic amortization, the term loan agreement usually contains a number of protective provisions, such as maintenance of a minimum working capital or current ratio; restrictions on dividends from earnings realized subsequent to the loan and if the minimum working capital requirements are satisfied; restrictions on further borrowing, short-term or long-term; restrictions on pledging or mortgaging of assets or assumption of contingent liabilities; provisions for continuity of management; submission of budgets and financial statements, audited and unaudited; in the event of acts of default, acceleration of all remaining maturities; etc.

Since term loans are an investment banking type of credit, they are usually suitable only for the larger commercial banks with diversified loans and are confined to a suitable proportion of the volume of loans. Two developments have led to a larger volume of term loans by the more aggressive commercial banks^the change in emphasis in examination procedure to the importance of ultimate payment rather than the speed of payment and the change in the Federal Reserve Act (Sec. 10B) permitting Federal Reserve banks to made advances on satisfactory collateral of member banks if such need arises.

TERMS OF SALE This term has two meanings:

1. The price basis asked for something offered for sale.
2. The conditions other than price under which goods are sold and usually the conditions under which payment is to be made, particularly time of payment at the price named and discounts offered for payment before the stipulated date of payment. Wholesale trade and many retail accounts are arranged on a credit basis, with payment expected on certain dates after sale. Wherever goods are sold on credit, there is a definite understanding as to the time of payment. This statement of understanding is familiarly known as terms of sale or, since it refers to the time that the credit is allowed, terms of credit.

In retail trade, terms may be net without discount. That is, no discount is allowed from the price quoted at the time of the sale, but open charge accounts and billing at the end of the month may be afforded the better customers, e.g., in groceries and meats. In wholesale trade, however, groceries are generally sold to hotels, restaurants, etc., on terms of 1% discount if paid in 10 days, or 30 days for payment if no discount is taken. Terms of sale in the wholesale lumber trade are quoted 2% 10 days, net 30 days, meaning that the buyer has the option of paying the full amount of the bill in 30 days or of paying cash less 2% in 10 days. The latter is a cash discount transaction.

Examples of terms of sale in mercantile practice include the following:

1. *Prepayment terms:* C.B.O. (cash before order); C.W.O. (cash with order); C.O.D. (cash on delivery); sight draft, B/L (bill of lading) attached. Cash terms really involve credit, since the buyer customarily has a reasonable time in which to inspect the goods delivered and decide whether or not to accept delivery, with payment usually called for in ten days' time from invoice date.
2. *Individual order terms:* These vary as to credit period, depending upon a number of factors, including trade practice,

characteristics of demand, and characteristics of supply. They will also vary as to discount and discount period, if any, depending on the relative position of the seller and the buyer and economic conditions, as well as trade practice. Thus, "$^2/_{10}$, $^n/_{30}$" means 2% cash discount if invoice is paid within 10 days of invoice date, credit period 30 days. The cost of forgoing the cash discount on this basis, extrapolated to an annual basis, could be computed as follows: the buying firm would have the use of funds for 20 days if it did not pay on the final day of the discount period, so that on a $100 invoice, it would have the use of $98 for the 20 days; therefore, the implicit annual interest cost would be

$$\frac{2}{98} \times \frac{365}{20} = 37.2\%$$

Similar computation may be made where the terms vary, e.g., $^2/_{10}$, $^n/_{60}$ 14.9% annual rate; $^3/_{30}$, $^n/_{60}$ 37.3%; etc.

3. *Lumped-order terms:* When buyers buy frequently, all deliveries may be lumped by the seller and billed as of one date, with discount and credit periods beginning with this billing date, e.g., $^8/_{10}$ E.O.M., meaning (if all deliveries for the month of May, for example, are involved) billing as of the end of May, with payment on due date of June 10 entitled to 8% discount off invoice total, thus making the discount and credit periods identical; $^8/_{10}$ M.O.M., meaning billing as of the middle of May, payment due on May 25, when 8% cash discount would be allowed; and $^2/_{10}$ prox. net 30, meaning discount date of June 10, following shipments in May, and due date on June 30.
4. Extra dating would be exemplified by "$^2/_{10}$, 60 ex."; season dating would be exemplified by "$^{net}/_{60}$, 60 ex." or by citing regular terms on invoice dated ahead of the normal shipment date.

The terms of sale are influenced by the rate of turnover in the trade as well as by the system of marketing. Where the turnover is rapid, as in the case of meats and groceries, the terms of sale are short—in dry goods they are longer and in furniture still longer.
See AUCTION.

BIBLIOGRAPHY

DUN & BRADSTREET, INC. *Terms of Sale.*

TERRITORIAL BONDS Bonds issued by Hawaii, the Philippines, and Puerto Rico while these issuers still had territorial status.
See INSULAR BONDS.

TESTAMENT Now largely supplanted by the term WILL.

TESTAMENTARY TRUST A TRUST created by a will. For an example, *see* WILL (will of Robert W. de Forest).

TESTATOR One who makes a WILL.

TESTATRIX A woman who makes a will; feminine form of TESTATOR.

TEST NUMBER A code number or word prefixed or appended to cable transfers by banks and foreign exchange dealers in order to ensure the authenticity of the message. This test number usually changes with each message, and since the formula for computing or decoding a test number is kept under lock and key and subject only to official supervision, it authenticates a message just as an officer's signature validates a bank draft. An example of a typical test word formula is "Add together the day of the month upon which the message is sent, the number corresponding to the day of the week (accompanying table), the month (same table), and the numbers for the amount in thousands, hundreds, and units (same table). Then add your private number, which is _____."

As a further safeguard, the private number is usually fixed after the formula has been made, or it may be cabled separately. Although the above-mentioned formula numbers are permanent or are changed at infrequent intervals, the test number usually varies with each cable. It is more difficult to solve a test number without the formula than to forge a signature (O. H. Wolfe, *Practical Banking*).

TEST WORD *See* TEST NUMBER.

TEXAS PREMIUM A premium paid for deposits in financially weak Texas S&Ls during the later 1980s, when the thrift industry was in serious financial difficulty. Many of the ailing thrifts were in Texas and the Southwest during this period.
See THRIFT INDUSTRY CRISIS.

TEXTILES A production and marketing industry in which fiber is made into fabric products for sale to consumers or industrial users. The industry is concentrated in the Carolinas and Georgia. It is labor-intensive, and it depends on consumer spending for clothing and home furnishings. The cyclical nature of the industry is reflected in sharp earnings declines in 1974, 1980, 1982, and 1985. It is noted for its productive efficiency in recent years.

It is estimated that one out of every ten manufacturing jobs in the U.S. is in textile and apparel production. Total employment was approximately 1.8 million at year-end 1987. This represents a 22% decrease from 2.3 million in 1974.

The Department of Commerce estimated that textile company earnings in 1988 dropped 18.8% to $1.5 billion. Before 1989, apparel demand played a major role in textile shipments and order rates, which were volatile and unpredictable. By 1989, imports continued to slow while exports rose. Investors consider the outlook for the industry to be generally favorable.

The early and middle 1980s were hard on textiles due to a recessionary economy and stiff competition from low-cost imports. These problems resulted in a major restructuring of the industry, including restructuring, reductions in employment, and increased capital expenditures to modernize plants and technology. Involved in the consolidation of the industry were West Point-Pepperell, which acquired Cluett, Peabody & Company; Springs Industries, which merged with M. Lowenstein; Cannon Mills, which was acquired by David Murdock and sold to Fieldcrest Mills to establish a new company, Fieldcrest Cannon; and Wickes Companies, which acquired Collins & Aikman. Cone Mills, Burlington Industries (a $2.5 billion transaction), and Dan River went private. J.P. Stevens disposed of its finished fabric business and acquired Burlington's towel and sheet operations. By 1989, Fieldcrest Cannon, Springs Industries, and West Point-Pepperell were the only three remaining major, publicly traded textile companies. The trend was for textile companies to become market leaders in core businesses.

BIBLIOGRAPHY

American Fabrics and Fashion.
American Textiles.
GRAYSON, M., ed. *Encyclopedia of Textiles, Fibers and Non Woven Frabics.* John Wiley and Sons, Inc., New York, NY, 1984.
Textile Horizons.
Textile World.

THEORY A hypothesis that has been successfully tested by its ability to predict accurately and to explain; a systematic statement of principles that serve as a foundation and explanation for underlying phenomena. Theory is usually the product of deductive or inductive approaches. The deductive approach involves reasoning from the general to the particular; the inductive approach involves reasoning from the particular to the general. The objective of economic and accounting theory is to establish a framework or reference point to guide and evaluate economic and accounting reasoning and practice.
See PRICE THEORY.

THIN MARGIN A small margin; a shoestring margin; a margin that gives the owner only a small equity in his purchase; a narrow or insufficient margin that leaves the speculator's account in an exposed and precarious condition in case of a declining market. Brokers customarily do not carry stocks on margin for customers unless there is ample margin and will not continue carrying the stocks until the margin is exhausted.
See MARGIN BUYING.

THIRD MARKET The dealer market in large blocks that developed off the board in listed stocks, as the result of the growing institutionalization of the security markets. The third market, however, a dealer market, has been adversely affected by development of the fourth market, providing for direct electronic communication among institutions buying and selling large blocks.

See NEW YORK STOCK EXCHANGE.

THIRD MORTGAGE A MORTGAGE placed upon property already encumbered with a first and SECOND MORTGAGE. For instance, a piece of real estate appraised at $50,000 may be encumbered with a first mortgage of $20,000 and a second mortgage of $10,000. If the owner wishes to raise an additional $5,000 by using the property as security, a third mortgage will be created, making total mortgage indebtedness $35,000. In case of foreclosure, a third mortgage would not be paid until both the first and second mortgages had been fully satisfied.

In practice, third mortgages are rare, since it is difficult to find a lender on this class of security, although where the sum of the first and second mortgages constitutes a debt of less than one-half of the appraised value of the property, there is nothing intrinsically unsound in lending a small amount on a third mortgage. To avoid the stigma of borrowing on a third mortgage, the property owner in the above example would likely, if he desired to raise additional money, pay off the first and second mortgage loans and issue a single first mortgage for $35,000.

THIRD MORTGAGE BONDS Bonds secured by a mortgage upon property already encumbered with an issue of first and second mortgage bonds. Such bonds represent a third lien upon the assets and earnings of the issuing corporation. Third mortgage bonds are rare, but among certain railroads' general or consolidated mortgage issues, part of the property falling under such general or consolidated mortgages is often already encumbered with a first and second mortgage.

See THIRD MORTGAGE.

THIRD OF EXCHANGE See FIRST OF EXCHANGE.

THIRD TELLER MAIL TELLER.

THOMAS AMENDMENT The popular name for Title III of the AAA Farm Relief and Inflation Act, approved May 12, 1933. It was the first major legislation on gold and silver and was the antecedent of the Joint Resolution of June 5, 1933, the GOLD RESERVE ACT OF 1934, and the SILVER PURCHASE ACT OF 1934.

For a summary of the major provisions of the Thomas amendment, see SILVER (U.S. Legislation).

THREADNEEDLE STREET The street in London on which several banking institutions, including the BANK OF ENGLAND, are located; by extension, one of the popular names for the London banking district. LOMBARD STREET is another street in London around which financial activities are centered and is a more popular designation for the financial district than Threadneedle Street. The usage corresponds to our use of Wall Street as a popular designation for financial New York.

THREE CS OF CREDIT Character, capacity, and capital, which bankers traditionally use to analyze credit. Conditions (of the general economy, a specific industry, the firm, the firm's products or services), and collateral are sometimes added to make it five Cs of credit.

THREE-NAME PAPER Notes, bills of exchange, bank and trade acceptances—usually some form of commercial paper—with three signatures (either as makers or endorsers) responsible for payment and representing separate interests, e.g., a note signed by two makers and having one endorsement, or an acceptance with the name of the drawer, acceptor, and one endorser.

See SINGLE-NAME PAPER.

THRIFT DEPARTMENT A savings department operating in connection with state banks and trust companies in those states, e.g., New York, where the banking laws prohibit the use of the term "savings" when advertising or soliciting such accounts. State banks and trust companies, as well as national banks, may accept time deposits, and since savings deposits are a type of time deposits, there is nothing to prevent these banks from soliciting time deposit accounts if the use of the term "savings" is avoided. The purpose of this law, where enacted, is to restrict the use of the term "savings" to savings banks exclusively. To comply with the law, therefore, banks solicit accounts for this department under the name of thrift accounts, special interest accounts, compound interest accounts, or time deposit accounts.

See SAVINGS ACCOUNTS.

THRIFT INDUSTRY Savings banks and savings and loan associations whose primary function is obtaining retail deposits to invest in residential mortgage loans and real estate development activities. Savings and loans are usually insured by FSLIC. Savings banks are insured by the FDIC. In 1989, there were 2,949 S&Ls and 397 savings banks in the U.S. Thrifts hold approximately 50% of outstanding residential mortgage debt.

Most thrifts are relatively small and operate in a local lending area. In 1989, eight of the ten largest thrifts were located in California. Statistics indicate that approximately 12% of the nation's insured thrift have assets of less than $25 million; 66% have between $25 million and $250 million of assets; 1% have assets over $5 billion. Thrift can be classified as wholesale and retail focused.

Thrifts are highly regulated by state and federal authorities. The primary federal agency responsible for overseeing the savings and loan industry is the Federal Home Loan Bank Board which serves as regulator, central banker, and deposit insurance fund administrator. The FHLB system consists of 12 district banks that serve as lenders for member thrift. District banks are authorized to extend short- or medium-term credit. The district banks obtain their funds from issuing consolidated debt obligations with government agency backing. Member thrifts are required to own stock in their regional FHLB bank. They must maintain an average daily balance of liquid assets equal to at least 5% of net withdrawable accounts plus short-term borrowings each month. The FSLIC charges premiums for deposit insurance equal to 20.88 basis points (0.00208%) of outstanding deposits. FSLIC can assume management control of member institutions that do not comply with capital standards (the Management Consignment Program) or closure.

Thrifts are sensitive to interest rate changes. Profits vary inversely with interest rates because thrift liabilities are usually short term, while assets (mortgages) are long term. When interest rates rise, deposit costs tend to increase faster than mortgage yields, narrowing spreads. The converse reaction to interest rate changes is also typical. A table outlining mortgage lending and savings activities for all S&LS from 1978 to 1987 is appended.

The thrift industry underwent a major financial crisis during the 1980s. This is discussed at length under the entry SAVINGS AND LOAN ASSOCIATIONS.

THRIFT INSTITUTIONS ADVISORY COUNCIL
A council established following the passage of the Monetary Control Act of 1980 to provide information and views on the special needs and problems of thrifts. This group comprises representatives of saving banks, savings and loan associations, and credit unions.

Mortgage Lending and Savings Activity—All S & Ls
(In millions of dollars)

Year	Total savings	Net savings inflow *	Mortgage loans acquired	Mortgages outstanding
1987	1,142,446	49,934	372,927	822,289
1986	1,092,512	53,007	382,217	774,023
1985	1,039,505	52,099	288,710	760,296
1984	987,406	127,059	270,316	702,568
1983	860,347	137,190	216,650	618,655
1982	723,157	42,986	92,458	571,100
1981	680,171	15,034	80,303	612,867
1980	665,137	49,127	108,101	594,779
1979	616,010	42,356	141,939	566,170
1978	573,654	52,837	154,360	520,126

* All data revised.
Source: U.S. League of Savings Institutions.

THRIFT SOCIETY An association of employees in a business institution formed for the purpose of promoting habits of thrift among them by receiving their savings and investing them more profitably than would be possible in a savings bank. Frequently the company supervises the investment of the thrift fund and guarantees payment of the principal and interest at a certain rate.

TICKER The popular name given to the high-speed printing telegraph which carries reports of transactions on the floor of an exchange into the offices of subscribers. In the latter offices, the ticker tape may be projected, for reader viewing at large, by means of the TRANS-LUX, a movie-type projector; or the prices of transactions on specific stocks, as received over the wire, may be automatically posted electrically by means of the Teleregister electric stock boards. Or, in the most primitive method, the information on the tape printed by the ticker may be posted with chalk on blackboards by board boys. To facilitate such reporting of transactions on the ticker, stocks and bonds are assigned ticker symbols, i.e., TICKER ABBREVIATIONS of their titles.

Consolidated Tape. Under the consolidated tape plan, ticker systems of the New York Stock Exchange (NYSE) and American Stock Exchange on June 16, 1975, became Network A and Network B, respectively. Network A reports transactions that take place on the New York Stock Exchange or any of the participating regional stock exchanges and other markets in New York Stock Exchange-listed securities. Each transaction is identified according to its originating market. Similarly, transactions in American Stock Exchange-listed securities and certain other securities listed on regional stock exchanges are reported and identified on Network B.

Beginning on August 1, 1978, stock brokers and their customers could obtain through the consolidated quote system bid and asked price quotations, with size, from all market centers where listed stocks are traded.

On April 17, 1978, the Intermarket Trading System (ITS) began pilot operations. ITS consists of a central computer facility, a network of interconnected terminals that link each of the six participating market centers, and quotation displays on each participating trading floor. Through ITS, any broker or market maker can interact with counterparts in other markets whenever a better execution opportunity is available for the customer. Information on stock quotations in ITS stocks is electronically transmitted to each market center. The display on the NYSE shows the New York market and the best market (bid and asked) away from New York.

In December, 1966, the exchange completed installation of optical card readers on the trading floor, one at each trading post and one for floor supervisory personnel. With this step, reporting of transactions on the New York Stock Exchange became fully automated. Trading reports previously transmitted from the floor by pneumatic tubes or voice are sped to the computer system via direct electronic signals. This new automated system cuts from minutes to a split-second the interval between a trade's being reported and its appearance on the ticker tape. The card reader optically scans the details of a transaction marked on a special IBM card by a reporter at the trading post, and simultaneously transmits this information electronically—stock symbol, number of shares, and price—to the computer center, which in turn automatically transmits it to the thousands of exchange stock tickers and display devices.

Ticker services, therefore, are part of the total flow of information which is being subjected to electronic modernization on the New York Stock Exchange.

Dow Jones Ticker. In addition to the stock and bond tickers or commodity tickers, another important ticker service is that of the Dow Jones Company, the Dow Jones News Ticker, which constantly operates before, during, and after the trading session on the New York Stock Exchange, publishing news and quotations affecting the market as such news matter becomes available.

See QUOTATION TICKER, TICKER ABBREVIATIONS.

TICKER ABBREVIATIONS New York Stock Exchange ticker abbreviations may be explained as follows.

One price following the abbreviation of a stock signifies a sale of 100 shares. Thus, NP 20 means the sale of 100 shares of Northern Pacific at 20.

When more than 100 shares are sold, the number of shares sold precedes the price. Thus, NP 2.20 $^1/_2$ means the sale of 200 shares of Northern Pacific at 20 $^1/_2$. NP 3.20 $^3/_4$, $^1/_4$, $^1/_2$ means the sale of 300 shares of Northern Pacific at 20 $^3/_4$, followed by the sale of 100 shares at 20 $^1/_4$ and another 100 shares at 20 $^1/_2$.

An offer alone without a bid is preceded by an 0. Thus, NP 0.19 means an offer of 19 for Northern Pacific.

A bid alone without an offer is followed by a B. Thus NP 19 $^1/_2$ B means a bid of 19 $^1/_2$ for Northern Pacific.

When a sale is not reported in its right place, the price is preceded by the abbreviation SLD. Thus, NP.SLD. 20 $^1/_2$ means that a sale of Northern Pacific has not been reported in the right place.

When an error has been made by a reporter or in printing, the last letter or figure is repeated several times, indicating that the quotation is to be eliminated. Thus, NP 20 $^1/_2$ $^1/_2$ $^1/_2$ $^1/_2$ means that a sale of Northern Pacific is to be disregarded.

TICKET DAY *See* SETTLEMENT DAYS.

TICKLER A maturity index; a book in which the maturity dates of notes, discounts, acceptances, bonds, and sometimes dividends, interest payments, and the like are journalized to serve as a reminder to the bank or brokerage house that these instruments will need attention at some future date.

The most important tickler in a bank is that showing the maturity of notes and acceptances. It is essential that a note be presented on the maturity date in order to hold the endorser liable. The note maturity tickler, therefore, is indispensable in the management of a bank, whether large or small, in order to guarantee presentation of notes at maturity and thereby protect the bank from possible losses through the release of endorsers, should presentation be neglected.

The purpose of a note maturity tickler is to record all notes in such a way as to indicate the dates on which they mature. This is accomplished by journalizing (recording chronologically) notes by maturity dates at the time they are discounted or purchased. Consecutive pages in the tickler are devoted to consecutive maturity dates. By reference to the tickler, consecutive pages of which are headed with consecutive dates, it is possible to tell at a glance what notes are maturing on any given date and the amount of the total maturities for any given day.

Maturity ticklers are also maintained to indicate compulsory and optional maturity dates of bonds which a bank holds as its own investments.

TIER ONE CAPITAL Core capital or basic equity that serve as a buffer against losses; equity capital and disclosed reserves. Tier One capital is considered the sum of equity capital and disclosed reserves, as adjusted. Tier One capital is one element of risk-based capital. The adjustments involve goodwill and cumulative perpetual preferred stock. Goodwill must be deducted from the sum of equity capital and disclosed reserves (with some exceptions). Bank holding companies may include cumulative perpetual preferred stock in Tier One.

Equity capital includes common stock and noncumulative perpetual preferred stock. For bank holding companies, equity capital also includes cumulative preferred stock. Common stock includes paid-in capital at par value, or stated capital if no par stock is issued. Common stock must be issued and fully paid up. Noncumulative perpetual preferred stock has distinct features: Holders have a preference to dividend distributions or liquidation distributions ahead of common stockholders. Such stock is perpetual in the sense that it has no maturity date and cannot be redeemed at the option of the holder. Noncumulative refers to the fact that unpaid dividends do not accrue to the stockholder. The Federal Reserve warns against "overreliance" on preferred stock.

Disclosed reserves are included in Tier One. These are reserves "created or increased by appropriations of retained earnings or other surplus" according to the Basle Agreement. They also include minority interests in the equity of subsidiaries not wholly owned. Goodwill booked after March 12, 1988 (all goodwill after December 31, 1992 regardless of when recorded) is deducted as an adjustment.

See TIER TWO CAPITAL.

BIBLIOGRAPHY

BHALA, R. *Risk-Based Capital: A Guide to the New Risk-Based Capital Adequacy Rules*, 1989.

TIER TWO CAPITAL Undisclosed reserves, revaluation reserves, general provisions and general loan loss reserves, hybrid debt-equity instruments, and subordinated term debt available to absorb losses. Undisclosed reserves are accumulated after-tax retained profits that are not formally disclosed in the balance sheet. Revaluation reserves are reserve accounts on the balance sheet that are increased whenever an asset is revalued to reflect market value. Hybrid instruments are part equity and part debt, e.g., convertible debt. Subordinated debt is instruments with a maturity over five years that are subordinated to other debt or to limited life preferred stock. Investments in certain unconsolidated subsidiaries are deducted when computing Tier Two capital (if the subsidiary is engaged in banking and financial activities and the parent company has a direct or indirect ownership interest of 50% or more in the subsidiary).

See TIER ONE CAPITAL.

BIBLIOGRAPHY

BHALA, R. *Risk-Based Capital: A Guide to the New Risk-Based Capital Adequacy Rules*, 1989.

TIGHT MONEY The condition when credit is difficult to obtain, even though high-grade collateral is offered and high interest rates prevail.
See STRINGENCY.

TIGRs Treasury investment growth certificates.
See FINANCIAL INSTRUMENTS: RECENT INNOVATIONS.

TILL MONEY Money for use at the counter, as distinguished from that kept as reserve in the vault or deposited with other banks. The PAYING TELLER is usually exclusive custodian of the till money necessary for current over-the-window use.

TIMBER BONDS Bonds issued to finance logging and lumber-making operations and secured by timber lands. These bonds were formerly popular in the lumber industry as a means of raising needed capital, particularly after the turn of the century, when Chicago was the principal market for these issues and there were a number of independents operating in the Middle Western timber areas. Leading lumber companies publicly owned at present include the Georgia-Pacific Corporation and the Weyerhaeuser Timber Company. The center of the lumber industry has shifted to the Northwest.

TIME BILLS See BILL OF EXCHANGE, DRAFT, FOREIGN BILLS OF EXCHANGE.

TIME CERTIFICATE OF DEPOSIT As defined by Regulation D of the Board of Governors of the Federal Reserve System, a deposit evidenced by a negotiable or nonnegotiable instrument which provides on its face that the amount of such deposit is payable to bearer or to any specified person or to his order (1) on a certain date, specified in the instrument, not less than 30 days after the date of the deposit; or (2) at the expiration of a certain specified time not less than 30 days after the date of the instrument; or (3) upon notice in writing which is actually required to be given not less than 30 days before the date of repayment; and (4) in all cases, only upon presentation and surrender of the instrument. A deposit with respect to which the bank merely reserves the right to require notice of not less than 30 days before any withdrawal is made is not a time certificate of deposit within the meaning of the above definition.

Appended is a simplified form of a negotiable time certificate of deposit.
See CERTIFICATE OF DEPOSIT, TIME DEPOSITS.

TIME DEPOSITS Defined by Regulation D of the Board of Governors of the Federal Reserve System for the purposes of computation of legal reserve requirements of member banks as including (1) time certificates of deposit, (2) time deposits, open account, and (3) savings deposits.

1. Time certificates of deposit are DEPOSITS evidenced by a negotiable or nonnegotiable instrument which provides on its face that the amount of such deposit is payable to bearer or to any specified person or to his order (1) on a certain date, specified in the instrument, not less than 30 days after the date of the deposit; or (2) at the expiration of a certain specified time not less than 30 days after the date of the instrument; or (3) upon notice in writing which is actually required to be given not less than 30 days before the date of repayment; and (4) in all cases only upon presentation and surrender of the instrument.

2. Time deposits, open account, are deposits other than time certificates of deposit or savings deposits, with respect to which there is in force a written contract with the depositor that neither the whole nor any part of such deposit may be withdrawn, by check or otherwise, prior to the date of maturity, which shall be not less than 30 days after the date of deposit, or prior to the expiration of the period of notice which must be given by the depositor in writing not less than 30 days in advance of withdrawal.

3. Savings deposits are deposits evidenced by a passbook, consisting of funds deposited to the credit of one or more individuals, or of a corporation, association, or other organization operated primarily for religious, philanthropic, charitable, educational, fraternal, etc., purposes and not operated for profit, or in which the entire beneficial interest is held by one or more individuals or by such an organization, and in respect to which deposit (1) the depositor is required, or may at any time be required, by the bank to give notice in writing of an intended withdrawal not less than 30 days before such withdrawal is made, and (2) withdrawals are permitted in only two ways, either (a) upon presentation of the passbook, through payment to the person presenting the passbook, or (b) without presentation of the passbook, through payment to the depositor himself but not to any other person whether or not acting for the depositor. Every withdrawal made upon presentation of a passbook shall be entered in the passbook at the time of the withdrawal, and every other withdrawal shall be entered therein as soon as practicable after it is made.

Regulations of the Board of Governors of the Federal Reserve System require member banks to disclose the rules regarding withdrawal of time deposits before maturity in all advertising of interest paid on such deposits. Clear, conspicuous, and accurate notice must be given of the fact that federal law and regulations prohibit the withdrawal of time deposits in their various forms before maturity unless the required penalty is applied to the funds permitted to be withdrawn. A member bank may refuse to permit any premature withdrawal, but such a policy should be disclosed.

The practical importance of PERSONAL time deposits for depository institutions is that they are free entirely from reserve requirements, whereas net transaction accounts as defined are subject to reserve requirements (see RESERVE). Moreover, depository institutions may pay interest on time deposits, subject to rate ceilings which eventually (under the DEPOSITORY INSTITUTIONS DEREGULATION AND MONETARY CONTROL ACT OF 1980) will be phased out so that competitive market rates may be paid (see DEPOSIT INTEREST RATES, DEPOSITORY INSTITUTIONS DEREGULATION COMMITTEE) and DISINTERMEDIATION reduced or eliminated.

Trend. Since the close of World War II, and particularly since the mid-1950s, the ratio of total time deposits to total deposits has risen sharply, e.g., from 20% at year-end 1945 and 26% in 1956 to 74% as of June 30, 1982, for all commercial banks. Development and offering by commercial banks of such innovations as savings certificates (technically, time deposits paying interest rates quite competitive with those of savings institutions and certainly more competitive than the below-the-market interest rate ceiling on savings deposits as such at commercial banks) and time certificates of deposit, offered to business firms at better rates of return for comparable maturities than U.S. Treasury bills, for example, have induced business firms to keep funds on deposit at commercial banks. In the process, previous demand deposits of such business firms changed in classification from demand to time deposits, thus lowering appreciably the legal reserve required and helping to pay the higher interest cost of deposits resulting by releasing previously required reserves for investment in earning assets.

In the course of this basic shift in composition of deposits, commercial banks have also increased their holdings of tax-exempts (state and municipal securities, exempt from federal income tax as to interest income), which had risen from 3% of total loans and investments at year-end 1945 to 8% at year-end 1956 and relative to holdings of securities alone 43% of total securities held and 12% of combined loans and investments, as of June 30, 1982.

The fixing of interest rate ceilings on savings and time deposits has been a very sensitive matter for savings institutions (mutual savings banks, savings and loan associations, credit unions, investment companies of the income investment policy type, etc.), because higher yields available in the money market either directly or through money market funds have caused disintermediation (shift of funds from the savings intermediary institutions). But commercial banks as well have experienced an outflow of funds to the money markets as money market yields and yields on money market funds in particular have soared in recent years and attracted savings funds.

TIME DRAFT   *See* DRAFT.

TIME GROUP   Among collection and transit clerks, a group into which out-of-town checks are assembled to be forwarded for collection through the FEDERAL RESERVE CHECK COLLECTION SYSTEM. The proceeds of out-of-town checks became available as reserve to the sending bank in a certain number of days indicated by the Federal Reserve SCHEDULE SHOWING WHEN PROCEEDS OF ITEMS WILL BECOME AVAILABLE. This schedule divides out-of-town checks into a certain number of time groups, each Federal Reserve bank making its own schedule. For the New York Federal Reserve Bank, three time groups known as immediate credit points, one-day points, and two-day points are shown in the schedule.

See TRANSIT DEPARTMENT.

TIME LOAN   A loan that becomes payable on a future specified date and that is not terminable at the option of either borrower or lender before that time. In practice, a bank will usually accept payment of a time loan before compulsory maturity with a pro rata abatement of interest or discount.

See LOAN.

TIME LOCK   A mechanical contrivance for preventing the opening of the door of a vault, even though the combination is worked, before the hour set for opening by adjustment of the attached clock.

TIME MONEY   Money loaned for a definite period and payable on a specified future date, as distinguished from call or demand money.

See MONEY RATES.

TIME PAPER   All forms of notes, acceptances, bills, and drafts maturing on a specified future date, as contrasted with paper payable on demand.

See LOAN.

TIME-SHARING   A procedure whereby several people use computing systems or services on the same hardware. Time-sharing also refers to a form of property ownership for a stated period of time, along with other owners, often used in resort property promotions.

TIME TO RUN   The number of days elapsing between the date of discount and the maturity of a note. When a note evidencing a time loan is presented to a bank for discount, it must be timed in order to ascertain the precise maturity date and the amount of the discount. A 90-day note (its term is 90 days) dated April 1 may be presented for discount on April 15. In calculating the time to run, one must make an exact count of the number of days; e.g., in the above illustration the time to run is 75 days (discount is computed for 75 days) and the maturity date falls on June 29 (not June 30). If the maturity date should fall on a Sunday or a holiday, the note becomes payable, in most states, on the following business day. Accordingly another day may be added in computing the discount. In some states, notes falling due on Sunday are collectible on the Saturday preceding. Reference must be made to the laws governing the collection of notes in the various states, including the Uniform Commercial Code as adapted by the particular state.

TIME UTILITY   The usefulness that a commodity or service has at a point in time.

TIME VALUE   The imputed monetary value of an OPTION reflecting the possibility that the price of the underlying instrument will move so that the option will become more valuable. The total value of an option, or its price, consists of its intrinsic value and its time value.

TIME VALUE OF MONEY   The concept that a future sum of money is of less value than the same dollar amount today, because money today will increase to a larger sum through investments and interest. It is estimated that if the Indians who sold Manhattan Island to Peter Minuit in 1626 for $24 had invested that principal at 8% interest compounded annually, the principal would have grown to over $18 trillion in the early 1980s. This would probably be sufficient to buy back all of the property on the island today.   Another illustration: $1,000 invested annually in an IRA at 9.65% compounded annually would grow to $56,306.62 at the end of 20 years.

BIBLIOGRAPHY

FABOZZI, F. J. *Fixed Income Mathematics.* Probus Publishing Co., Inc., Chicago, IL, 1988.
WOELFEL, C. J. *The Desktop Guide to Money, Time, Interest & Yields.* Probus Publishing Co., Chicago, IL, 1987.

TIN   An international metal, with the principal sources of supply (such as Malaya, Bolivia, Indonesia, the Congo, Thailand, and Nigeria) distant from the major importing countries (United States and Europe). Tin has been subject since 1956 to international controls imposed by the International Tin Council. The council was set up under the first International Tin Agreement, drafted in 1953 and finally approved by the necessary producing and importing countries in the free world (exclusive of the United States) in 1956. By the setting of export quotas for the six major producers relative to demand from the importing nations, the council seeks a balancing of supply and demand and thus prevention of the wide gyrations in tin prices.

The Fourth International Tin Agreement was negotiated at the United Nations Tin Conference held in Geneva April 13-May 15, 1970. Meeting under the auspices of the UN Conference on Trade and Development (UNCTAD), the conference was attended by 38 countries producing and consuming tin. The United States is not a member of the Tin Council, but attended the conference in view of its standing as the world's largest tin-consuming nation. Objectives of the new agreement, which was designed to succeed the previous five-year agreement that was due to expire on June 30, 1971, remained basically unchanged. They included maintaining a balance between world production and consumption of tin, preventing excessive fluctuations in the market price, and increasing export earnings of the producer countries.

Finance and Development of the International Monetary Fund points out that in the Fifth International Tin Agreement (ITA), which became effective in July, 1976, greater emphasis was placed on buffer stock operations than on export controls. The maximum level of stocks that could be accumulated was considerably enlarged. First, the target set for members' contributions in the form of cash or metal was raised from 20,000 to 40,000 metric tons, equivalent to approximately 18% of world production. Second, it was established that in case of need, the International Tin Council could borrow additional resources from commercial banks by using its tin stocks as collateral.

However, since the Fifth International Tin Agreement came into effect, the problem has been a shortage of tin on the market, and the buffer stock has not been able to defend the ceiling price. In fact, tin prices throughout 1979 and into 1980 soared to new high levels of well over $8 a pound. The ITA has had little success in moderating the price increases, partly (as pointed out by the U.S. Treasury

Department) because its buffer stocks have been too small and partly because of variable production and export taxes in producing countries which have discouraged investment and production. Paradoxically, however, this was not be welcomed by Bolivia, a high-cost producer as compared with Southeast Asia, which uses the open-pit mining of tin, for Bolivian governmental and private mines have been operating unprofitably despite the substantial rise in tin prices.

The Sixth International Tin Agreement, valid for five years, was agreed upon on June 23, 1982, by representatives of four major tin producing nations—Indonesia, Malaysia, Thailand, and Australia—and 16 consuming nations (excluding the United States, which did not take part in the accord), meeting in Geneva to negotiate an accord to replace the Fifth Agreement, which expired on June 30, 1982.

Like its predecessors, the agreement was designed to prevent excessive fluctuations in the price of tin and to ensure long-term equilibrium between supply and demand through the use of a buffer stock facility, floor and ceiling prices, and export controls. The buffer stock facility, which would buy and sell tin on the world markets to keep prices within predetermined ranges, would consist of a maximum of 39,000 metric tons, with members financing 19,000 metric tons and the rest financed through loans.

Prices of tin on the London Metal Exchange rose $0.213 a pound to $5.08 in response to the announcement of the new tin agreement, but with world surplus of tin at some 45,000 metric tons at that time, price weakness prevailed so that the International Tin Council in April, 1982, ordered producing nations to hold back 10% of their potential export tonnage in the second quarter of 1982, and indications by the Council's president pointed to further export controls.

Signatories to the new agreement, which entered into force July 1, 1982, were eight fewer nations, but the producers joining the agreement—Indonesia, Malaysia, Thailand, and Australia—account for some 79% of world output, and the 16 consuming nations represent just less than 50% of world usage.

Malaysia, Thailand, and Indonesia concurrently announced that they had formed a separate producers' association which they disclaimed had intention to undermine the Tin Council or act as a cartel. Besides formation of such a tin producers association of the tin-producing nations of Southeast Asia, the Malaysian government also led in creation of a joint marketing agency to bypass the London Metal Exchange.

U.S. Policy. Except for minor domestic production, the U.S. imports virtually all primary tin, and is naturally interested in reasonably low tin prices. The General Services Administration's (GSA) stockpile holdings of tin.

Trading. The international center of trading in tin is the London Metal Exchange. A spot market for tin exists in New York.

TIN   *See* TAXPAYER IDENTIFICATION NUMBER.

TIP   An unsupported statement or advice given a person concerning the movement of a particular security, in supposed confidence and secrecy, but without revelation of the source of information or facts to demonstrate its logic. Tips are given by legitimate bankers, brokers, and insiders who have a knowledge of facts upon which to base their judgment but may not be in a position to disclose these facts. Such tips are honest. Tips are also given by unscrupulous brokers, professional tipsters, and charlatans with the intention to misrepresent and deceive. Most tips are based upon guesswork, rumor, or pure fabrication. No tip should be acted upon without investigation, or at least without knowledge of the reputation of the informant. Tips are one of the manipulative or deceptive devices prohibited by Section 9 of the Securities Exchange Act of 1934.
  See COPPER A TIP.

TIPSTER   One who gives advice to buy or sell a certain security without furnishing information and reasons; especially the professional charlatan who usually specializes in questionable or highly speculative securities. Such advice is usually offered with an ulterior motive and should not be acted upon. Tipsters of the professional type are banned by Section 9 of the Securities Exchange Act of 1934 and through the registration provisions of the Investment Advisers Act of 1940. The states also proceed against professional tipsters under local blue sky laws.
  See TIP.

TITLE   The evidence of a person's right to or ownership in a piece of property. In the case of real estate, the documentary evidence of ownership is the TITLE DEED.
  See ABSTRACT OF TITLE, TITLE INSURANCE.

TITLE COMPANY   *See* TITLE INSURANCE COMPANY.

TITLE DEED   The documentary evidence of a person's ownership of a pieceof land. Such a deed specifies in whom the legal estate is vested and the history of the ownership and transfers from one person to another from the original grant to the present owner. Title to land may be acquired in one of five ways: purchase, inheritance, devise, gift, or foreclosure of a mortgage.
  See ABSTRACT OF TITLE, TITLE INSURANCE.

TITLE GUARANTY   *See* TITLE INSURANCE.

TITLE INSURANCE   A contract by which the insurer, usually a title insurance company, for a valuable consideration agrees to indemnify the insured for a specific amount against any loss which may arise through the appearance of defects of title to real estate wherein the latter has an interest as purchaser, mortgagee, or otherwise. Such a contract is recognized as a true indemnity for loss actually sustained by reason of the defects or encumbrances against which the insurer covenants to indemnify. Title insurance involves a careful examination of the evidences of title by the insurer, who employs or is himself a skilled conveyancer.
  See TITLE INSURANCE COMPANY.

BIBLIOGRAPHY

Clearing Land Titles. West Publishing Co., St. Paul, MN.
Title Insurance & Real Estate Securities Terminology. Real Estate Publishing Co.
Title News.

TITLE INSURANCE COMPANY   A company, usually operated in conjunction with a mortgage company, which examines titles to real estate, determines their status at law, and insures their validity to interested persons, whether owners, purchasers, or lenders, whether or not the insuring company makes a loan on such property. A purchaser of or lender on (mortgagee) real estate is entitled to an abstract of title, and the seller or borrower must be able to transfer a clear title to the purchaser or mortgagee. Ordinarily, abstracts of title are prepared and the title is verified by a lawyer who only states an opinion and neither guarantees the validity of the title nor defends any claim that may be set up against it. A title insurance company, however, the personnel of which being composed in large part of lawyers, agrees to indemnify the owner of a title against any loss which may be sustained through the subsequent development of a defect. A title insurance policy is the evidence of the title insurance. Its cost depends upon the value of the property and the degree of risk involved, as shown by the condition of the title.

TO ARRIVE GRAIN   Grain to be shipped (not to arrive) from 3 to 90 days after purchase according to contract, as distinguished from cash grain and grain for future delivery.

TO BEARER   *See* PAY TO BEARER.

TOBACCO   Long ranked in agricultural history as a basic cash crop, tobacco is still a mainstay of the economies of such states as North Carolina, Kentucky, South Carolina, Tennessee, Virginia, and Georgia and is a major recipient of price support and related program assistance. Over one-third of the total crop is exported, and the United States is also a substantial importer of particular kinds of tobacco, making tobacco one of the major commodities in U.S. foreign trade. Government price support is mandatory for the kinds of tobacco produced under marketing quotas.

Consumption Trends. Although domestic consumption of cigarettes, which account for the bulk of tobacco consumption, has been affected by antismoking publicity in recent years, relative gains have been scored by the low-tar and -nicotine filter types which have been heavily promoted in the permitted advertising by tobacco companies. Exports, by contrast, have risen to new high levels, with leading markets being the European community and Japan.

BIBLIOGRAPHY

———. "Outlook for Tobacco." National Agricultural Outlook Conference (annual).

TOKEN COINS *See* TOKEN MONEY.

TOKEN MONEY As a result of the Coinage Act of 1965 (*see* UNITED STATES MONEY) and subsequent coinage decisions, all coins being issued in the United States are token coins, i.e., they do not have the intrinsic value called for by their nominal value. The characteristics of token money, in general, may be summarized as follows:

1. **Issued typically in small denominations.** Token money is primarily a means of making change.
2. **Made of metal other than the standard monetary metal.** Token coins are made of nickel and copper, rather than of gold or of silver, silver being the supplementary monetary metal formerly utilized in the United States for issuance of standard silver dollars (371.25 grains, troy weight, of pure silver) and subsidiary silver coins (345.6 grains, troy weight, of pure silver for two halves, four quarters, or ten dimes.)
3. **Short in weight.** Token coins do not have the intrinsic value called for by their nominal value. They are worth more as coins signifying purchasing power than as metal or bullion. The purpose of this provision is to prevent token coins from being melted, hoarded, or exported, thus insuring their permanence in circulation.
4. **Coined on government account only.** It is evident that if coins are issued at a nominal value, which is about the cost of the metal contained in them, the issuer—the government—makes a profit or seigniorage. This profit inures to the benefit of the government and not to a private person.
5. **Limited in amount coined.** Token coins are minted to the amount which experience shows is necessary for the purposes of trade. The purpose of this restriction is to keep token coins from falling below par.

The act of Congress approved July 23, 1965 (P.L. 89-81), known as the Coinage Act of 1965, repealed the provisions of the law formerly contained in Section 43(b)(1) of the Act of May 12, 1933, as amended (31 U.S.C. 462), providing for full unlimited legal tender of all coins and currencies of the United States, including Federal Reserve notes, but added a new provision of law to the same effect codified in 31 U.S.C. 392.

TOLERANCE Allowance made for the deviation of gold or silver coins from the specifications as to weight and fineness prescribed by statute. Tolerance is of two kinds: (1) for variation, or percentage of error, allowed to the Mint, also known as remedy or remedy of the Mint; (2) for abrasion, or reduction in weight through circulation, allowed without impairing full legal tender value. The tolerance allowed the Mint was for error in fineness and error in gross weight. The tolerance for error in fineness was 1/1000, i.e., a coin could be 0.901 or 0.899 fine and still be legal. The General Instructions and Regulations of the United States Mint, however, stated that no bullion should be coined that varied beyond the limits of 0.8997 and 0.9003. For silver dollars, the tolerance was one and one-half grains.

Under Section 5 of the Gold Reserve Act of 1934, no gold shall hereafter be coined, and all gold coin was withdrawn from circulation.

For the tolerance allowed for abrasion through circulation, *see* LIGHT COIN, LIGHT GOLD.

TOMBSTONE An advertisement used by underwriting syndicates that outlines a public sale of securities.

TON-MILE The unit of railway freight service and of costs and revenue, represented by the carriage of one ton of freight one mile. Annual freight revenues divided by ton-miles results in the average revenue per ton mile, a basic indicator of profitableness of railroad operation.

See RAILROAD EARNINGS.

TO ORDER *See* PAY TO ORDER.

TOP The conclusion of a period of rising prices on a stock or commodity market, i.e., when the highest prices for the upward movement have been attained. It is usually the point or plateau at which general optimism, as demonstrated by public participation in the market, is shown and professional operators distribute, i.e., unload their holdings. The top of a market is reached in a period of great prosperity, but before the turning point in stock or commodity prices.

See BUSINESS CYCLE.

TOPHEAVY Describes the condition of a single security or the market when prices have reached a level too high to be warranted by conditions and therefore may be expected to react; the condition of a market when prices have advanced rapidly and a decline is in prospect.

TOP PRICE The highest price quoted for a stock or commodity or the highest average price for the market as a whole for a single day's trading, for a movement, or for an entire speculative cycle.

TORONTO STOCK EXCHANGE Founded in 1852, the Toronto Stock Exchange has been the most important securities market in Canada since its merger in 1934 with the old Standard Stock and Mining Exchange (also located in Toronto). The Standard Stock and Mining Exchange was established in the latter part of the nineteenth century and had grown to be the world's largest purely mining stock exchange. The growth and importance of the Toronto Stock Exchange were officially recognized in 1878, when a special act of Parliament was invoked granting to the exchange "the right of constitution of a body politic and corporate." In 1887, a permanent place of business was obtained. As the largest Canadian securities exchange, the Toronto Stock Exchange fulfills a major function in the maintenance of a listed market for Canadian securities, thus aiding in this respect in Canadian financing. In recent years, the trading list in industrials has substantially expanded, while the exchange continues to be an active market for mining stocks; oil and gas issues are also traded actively.

TORRENS SYSTEM OF LAND TITLE REGISTRATION A system under which an owner of land may apply for a certificate of title to be issued by the registrar of the county, named after Sir Robert Torrens, who, as land commissioner and registrar general, established the system in Australia in 1858. The certificate is similar to a ledger page as commonly used in bookkeeping accounts. The original certificate constitutes one page in the title book in the registrar's office, upon which all the facts with regard to the title of the particular piece of ground affected are entered, i.e., description of the property, name of the owner in fee, and the mortgages and other liens or encumbrances standing against it. A duplicate of this certificate or ledger page is given to the owner as his evidence of title.

The certificate of title gives to the owner a declaration or statement of his title which is indefeasible and incontestable. In order to ascertain the condition of a title, it is necessary only to scrutinize this ledger page certificate; whatever may be noted there may be finally and absolutely accepted as the condition of the title. No mortgage, judgment, lien, dower claim, ancient right of heirs, or any other claim can be set up or claimed unless it is noted upon this certificate. By its policy of title insurance, a title company simply promises to defend a person's title in case of a lawsuit. The Torrens system, however, is calculated to prevent lawsuits, i.e., the law provides that no claim can be set up against the title or enforced in a court unless the claim is stated upon the certificate. This is accomplished by the fact that the first certificate issued is founded upon a final judgment of the court and backing every certificate is the sovereignty of the state declaring the title to be absolutely indefeasible and incontestable. After the first registration, no searching is required and the title cannot be questioned.

The chief defect of the present system is that no purchaser of real estate can be certain of his title until he has employed an attorney to examine the title from the current date back to the original grant. This examination is expensive and must be repeated with each sale, because no prospective purchaser will be content to buy without being assured of the title.

The success of the plan in Australia caused it to spread rapidly to various English colonies. England adopted such a law in 1862, and in 1897 it was made compulsory in London. In 1865, the system was established in Ireland. In Canada it is today practically universal.

In the United States registration laws have been established in 19 states as follows: California, 1897 (amended 1914); Colorado, 1903; Georgia, 1917; Illinois, 1897; Massachusetts, 1898; Minnesota, 1901; Mississippi, 1914; Nebraska, 1915; North Carolina, 1913; North Dakota, 1917; New York, 1908; Ohio, 1896 (constitution amended 1912); Oregon, 1901; South Carolina, 1916; South Dakota, 1917; Tennessee, 1917; Utah, 1917; Virginia, 1916; Washington, 1907. The system was adopted by the United States government for the Philippine Islands in 1902 and for Hawaii in 1903.

The certificate system of land registration has not met with success in every state. The Massachusetts law is one of the most successful and has served as a model for that of the Philippine Islands, Hawaii, New York, Minnesota, and a few other states.

TORTS AND CRIMES Violations of a standard of behavior established by society. A tort can be defined as a violation of an individual, noncontractual right, for which the law provides a remedy. Torts are usually classified as intentional and nonintentional, and then subdivided according to the general nature of the plaintiff's injury:

I. Intentional misconduct
   A. Physical violence or action
      1. To the plaintiff or property
         a. Directly (battery, conversion, trespass false imprisonment)
         b. Indirectly (mental or emotional violence; i.e., threat to commit a battery plus attempt to carry out the threat)
      2. Plaintiff sustains no physical or property injury
   B. Offensive or disturbing words
      1. Injury to reputation (slander, or oral defamation; libel, or written defamation)
      2. Public disclosure of plaintiff's private information (invasion of privacy)
      3. Defendant's words cause mental or emotional problems that then cause physical injury (insults, humiliations, faked claims, offensive language)
II. Unintentional (negligent) misconduct
   A. Personal injury or property damage caused by defendant's acts coming in physical contact with plaintiff or his/her property (negligent misconduct)
   B. Defendant disturbs plaintiff mentally or emotionally so as to cause him/her to suffer physical injury

Crimes are usually classified as felonies or misdemeanors. Felonies are the more serious crimes, usually resulting in a sentence to the penitentiary or heavy fine. Misdemeanors are lesser crimes, usually resulting in shorter sentences or smaller fines. To be charged with a felony, a person must be indicted by a grand jury. To arrest a person for committing a crime, an arrest warrant must be obtained. To search a person's house, a search warrant must first be obtained from the judicial branch of government. To be convicted of a crime, one must be proven guilty beyond a reasonable doubt. For a misdemeanor, one is usually charged by a document prepared by the district or state's attorney know as an "information." The document sets forth information similar to an indictment without requiring action by the grand jury.

Business crimes include antitrust crimes (e.g., restraint of trade or to price fixing), mail fraud, embezzlement (breach of trust leading to a victim being deprived of his/her property), larceny (similar to embezzlement but lacking the special confidential relationship between criminal and victim), and forgery (false writing or alteration of a written document with an intent to defraud).

TOTAL COST The sum of total variable cost and total fixed cost. In any time period, total cost represents the expenditures of an organization. Subtracting total cost from total revenue leaves profit.

TOTTEN TRUST An inter vivos trust created when a bank depositor deposits funds in an account as trustee for a designated beneficiary. Technically, the TRUST thus created is a revocable trust, but on death of the depositor, an absolute trust is deemed to arise by presumption as to the account and its remaining balance.

TRACTION SECURITIES Stocks and bonds of electric railway companies, whether surface, elevated, subway, or interurban railways, as distinguished from the securities of railroad companies.
See STREET RAILWAY BONDS.

TRADE ACCEPTANCE A bill of exchange drawn by the seller (drawer) on the purchaser of goods sold and accepted by such purchaser (drawee); as defined by the Board of Governors of the Federal Reserve System, "a bill of exchange drawn to order, having a definite maturity and payable in dollars in the United States, the obligation to pay which has been accepted by an acknowledgment, written or stamped, and signed across the face of the instrument by the company, firm, corporation, or person upon whom it is drawn; such agreement to be to the effect that the acceptor will pay at maturity, according to its tenor, such draft or bill without qualifying conditions."

In order to be eligible for a rediscount, a trade acceptance "must bear on its face or be accompanied by evidence in form satisfactory to the Federal Reserve Bank that it was drawn by the seller of the goods on the purchaser of such goods. Such evidence may consist of a certificate on or accompanying the acceptance, to the following effect: THE OBLIGATION OF THE ACCEPTOR OF THIS BILL ARISES OUT OF THE PURCHASE OF GOODS FROM THE DRAWER. Such certificate may be accepted by the Federal Reserve Bank as sufficient evidence; provided, however, that the Federal Reserve Bank, in its discretion, may inquire into the exact nature of the transaction underlying the acceptance."

Although use of the trade acceptance has been widespread in Europe for many years, its use has only partially supplanted the use of the check in this country. One of the aims of the Federal Reserve Act was to encourage the use of the acceptance in the United States. The purpose of the American Acceptance Council was to maintain an intensive campaign to foster the trade acceptance in U.S. business. The movement was also approved by the National Association of Credit Management, which stated, "Trade acceptances present conveniences and economies which should appeal to the encouragement and support of commercial credit grantors. The trade acceptance system would eliminate certain serious evils which have developed with the increase of commercial credits on an open account system, and of which unearned discounts, the abuse of sales terms, and the assignment of accounts receivable are the more prominent."

The procedure in trade acceptance practice is as follows. The seller of merchandise upon making shipment forwards with the shipping documents an acceptance form (in reality a time draft). This form is often sent in duplicate to enable the buyer to retain a copy for his files. If the goods are subject to cash discount, the buyer may avail himself of this opportunity by remitting immediately; otherwise the buyer is expected to sign the acceptance form by writing his name across the face of the instrument, indicating the date, and designating the bank where it is payable. In the great majority of cases, an acceptance is payable at the drawee's (acceptor's) bank. It may be made payable at any bank or trust company in the United States. It is then returned to the drawer (seller).

The Uniform Commercial Code (1962 official text), as presented to the states for their adoption, provided in Alternative A of Section 3-121 that a note or acceptance which states that it is payable at a bank is the equivalent of a draft drawn on the bank payable when it falls due out of any funds of the maker or acceptor in current account or otherwise available for such payment. If the particular state has adopted this alternative provision, when a trade acceptance is made payable at the acceptor's bank, it may be presented for payment and collected through banking channels in the same manner as a check. On the other hand, Alternative B of Section 3-121 does not so provide.

But there are many other advantages accruing to both buyers and sellers in the use of the trade acceptance. The advantages to the seller are as follows:

1. It completes the transaction by joining the evidence of the debt and means of payment with the shipment or invoice.
2. It compels definite payment at maturity. The seller has the buyer's negotiable promise that at a specified time and place the buyer will pay for the goods purchased from the seller.
3. It makes definite calculations possible, since sellers know in advance at what times their sales will become available as cash.
4. It prevents tying up capital in open book accounts.

5. It provides additional credit facilities. Trade acceptances can be discounted at 100% of their face value, while accounts receivable cannot be discounted even under the most favorable conditions for more than 95%. Furthermore, there is no limit to the amount of acceptance paper which a bank may take from one customer, since the 10% limitation (applying to national banks and to state banks in many states) does not apply.
6. It reduces collection expenses and petty annoyances.
7. It avoids making the seller perform banking functions.
8. It tends to prevent the cancellation of orders and the return of goods.
9. It increases the liquidity of the seller's assets.
10. It permits a lower discount rate. Trade acceptances command a preferential rate of interest, since they afford double security to the lending bank. Recognition of the superior security in the trade acceptance is demonstrated by the fact that the Federal Reserve rate of rediscount for this class of paper is usually the prime rate.
11. It promotes economy through the lower rate of discount and through the reduction of the cost of extending credit, losses on bad accounts, etc.

Many of the advantages to the seller also accrue to the buyer. In addition, the acceptance benefits the buyer in the following ways:

1. It strengthens his credit. In giving a trade acceptance, the buyer proves his good faith by binding himself to pay an honest debt in full when it becomes due. He assumes no obligation until after the seller has surrendered title to the merchandise. In other words, it brings the transaction out into the open and places the buyer on a merit basis.
2. It tends to develop careful buying. The purchaser will not overbuy when he realizes that the debt must be met at a definite maturity.
3. It reduces expenses of handling open accounts.
4. Acceptance buyers are preferred by sellers.

The use of the trade acceptance also benefits the banker in the following ways:

1. It tends to better the character of the bank's assets, since trade acceptances are two-name paper and are readily rediscountable.
2. It promotes a keener sense of responsibility in business.
3. It increases the amount of discounting business to be done.
4. It increases the amount that can be loaned to one borrower.
5. It makes possible a fuller utilization of commercial credit.
6. It prevents the secret assignment of open book accounts.

A trade acceptance must always represent a completed merchandise transaction and cannot be used as a means to enforce payment of debts past due or as an evidence of a loan, i.e., it is to be based solely in connection with a current merchandise transaction. Federal Reserve banks may rediscount trade acceptances or purchase them in the open market, provided they conform to the eligibility requirements. The Board of Governors of the Federal Reserve System has provided by regulation, "The Federal Reserve Bank shall take such steps as it deems necessary to satisfy itself as to the eligibility of the ... trade acceptance offered for rediscount and may require a recent financial statement of one or more parties to the instrument. The trade acceptance should be drawn so as to evidence the character of the underlying transaction, but if it is not so drawn, evidence of eligibility may consist of a stamp or certificate affixed by the acceptor or drawer in a form certificate to the Federal Reserve Bank."

Despite united efforts to promote the use of the trade acceptance, it has not caught on as a popular business practice, except perhaps as a means of making liquid accounts inclined to be slow on collections.

See ACCEPTANCE, BANK ACCEPTANCE.

TRADE ASSOCIATION An association of the units in a single line of business for mutual aid and protection of common interests. Practically all types of business in the United States are represented in trade associations, many of which meet annually in convention to discuss trade practices, establish rules of conduct, and organize other methods of cooperation.

Trade associations are not new in the United States or in other countries. In this country, organizations of competitors in given industries or branches of industries, encompassing a wide variety of trade interests, may be traced well back into the nineteenth century. In their present form, U.S. trade associations are generally recognized to have had their beginnings in the period of the Civil War, although several associations trace their establishment to earlier dates. Many associations had their inception during the period of increasing business activity marking the recovery from the panic of 1873.

Four major types of trade association activities of the past have been declared illegal by the courts. Broadly speaking, these four types of activities relate to unification in selling, exclusion from the market, curtailment of production, and price fixing.

Under the NATIONAL INDUSTRIAL RECOVERY ACT, the powers, purposes, and activities of trade associations were broadened. That act authorized the National Recovery Administration to employ existing trade or industrial associations or to establish new agencies if necessary to compel reforms in industry with respect to employment, hours of labor, wages, control of production, and prevention of unfair methods of competition. To achieve these ends, the act provided five principal methods: (1) voluntary trade association codes, (2) voluntary agreements within an industry, (3) codes limited to the subjects of hours of labor, wages, and conditions of employment, (4) compulsory codes imposed by the administration, and (5) a system of licensing in extreme cases where uncorrected abuses were shown to exist. Of these, the voluntary trade association codes were the most important. After the National Industrial Recovery Act was declared unconstitutional and the industry codes were abandoned, the stimulation of trade associational activities within permissible areas continued.

Among the many trade associations in the United States are the following:

Aerospace Industries Association of America
Air Transport Association of America
Aluminum Association
Aluminum Recycling Association
American Bankers Association
American Bureau of Metal Statistics
American Council of Life Insurance
American Farm Bureau Federation
American Forest Institute
American Frozen Food Institute
American Gas Association
American Insurance Association
American Iron & Steel Institute
American Leather Chemists Association
American Meat Institute
American Paper Institute
American Petroleum Institute
American Society of Association Executives
American Trucking Associations, Inc.
Architectural Aluminum Manufacturers Association
Asphalt Institute, The
Association of American Railroads
Automobile Manufacturers Association
Automotive Service Industry Association
Barley & Malt Institute
Bituminous Coal Research, Inc.
Chlorine Institute
Cooperative League of the U.S.A.
Copper Development Association
Eastern Railroad Association
Edison Electric Institute
Farm & Industrial Equipment Institute
Farmstead Equipment Association
Food Marketing Institute
Gas Appliance Manufacturers Association
Glass Container Manufacturers Institute, Inc.
Independent Petroleum Association of America
International Apple Institute
International Fabricare Institute
Machinery & Allied Products Institute
Manufacturing Chemists' Association
Millers' National Federation
National Aeronautic Association of the U.S.A.
National Association of Bedding Manufacturers
National Association of Business Men, Inc.

TRADE BALANCE

National Association of Electric Companies
National Association of Food & Dairy Equipment Manufacturers
National Association of Furniture Manufacturers
National Association of Home Builders of the U.S.
National Association of Life Underwriters
National Association of Manufacturers
National Association of Motor Bus Owners
National Association of Mutual Savings Banks
National Association of Recycling Industries
National Association of Retail Druggists
National Association of Retail Grocers of the U.S.
National Association of Wheat Growers
National Association of Wholesaler-Distributors
National Automobile Dealers Association
National Canners Association
National Coal Association
National Cotton Ginners Association
National Council of Farmer Cooperatives
National Electrical Manufacturers Association
National Forest Products Association
National Foundation for Consumer Credit
National Home Furnishings Association
National Independent Meat Packers Association
National Industrial Sand Association
National Lime Association
National LP-Gas Association
National Machine Tool Builders' Association
National Paint & Coatings Association
National Paper Box Association
National Petroleum Council
National Petroleum Refiners Association
National Restaurant Association
National Retail Hardware Association
National Retail Merchants Association
National Soft Drink Association
Northern Textile Association
Portland Cement Association
Potash Institute
Rayon Yarn Producers Group
Rubber Manufacturers Association
Securities Industry Association
Silk and Rayon Printers and Dyers Association of America
Southern Forest Products Association
Tanners Council of America
Thread Institute
Tile Manufacturers' Association, Inc.
Tire & Rim Association
Tobacco Merchants Association of the U.S.
Transportation Association of America
U.S. Beet Sugar Association
U.S. Brewers Association
U.S. Cane Sugar Refiners Association
U.S. League of Savings Associations
Western Wood Products Association
Wine Institute

Trade associations related to banking and financial services include, but are not limited to, the following:

American Bankers Association
American Society of Bank Directors
Association of Bank Holding Companies
Association of Reserve City Bankers
Bank Administration Institute
Bank Marketing Association
Conference of State Bank Supervisors
Bank PAC
Consumer Bankers Association
Credit Union National Association
Electronic Funds Transfer Association
Independent Bankers Association of America
Mortgage Bankers Association of America
National Association for Bank Cost and Management Accounting
National Association of Bank Women
National Association of Credit Union Supervisors
National Bankers Association
National Council of Savings Institutions
Robert Morris Associates
Securities Industry Association
U.S. League of Savings Institutions
Western Independent Bankers

TRADE BALANCE See BALANCE OF TRADE.

TRADE BAROMETERS See BUSINESS BAROMETERS.

TRADE CREDITOR A person, firm, or corporation to which a business is indebted for purchases on open account or as evidenced by its notes payable.

TRADE CYCLE BUSINESS CYCLE.

TRADE DEFICIT/TRADE SURPLUS A trading country is both an importer and an exporter. A country may have either a trade surplus or a trade deficit depending on the relative amounts of goods exported and imported. A trade deficit occurs when the value of imported goods exceeds the value of exported goods. A surplus occurs when the value of imported goods is less than the value of exports. The U.S. economy enjoyed a trade balance in the early part of the 1980s, but but the trade deficit has grown since that time.

TRADE DISCOUNT A deduction from the published list price allowed to the trade, as distinguished from cash discount. The purpose of trade discount is to permit manufacturers and merchants dealing in commodities with frequent and wide price fluctuations to adjust the fixed price as published to current market quotations; thus, trade discounts offered depend upon current market conditions.
See CASH DISCOUNT.

TRADE DOLLAR The trade dollar of 420 grains troy was authorized by theAct of February 12, 1873. It was intended for circulation in Oriental countries as a substitute for the Mexican dollar, which it slightly exceeded in weight, but by the terms of the authorizing act it was made legal tender in the United States in sums not exceeding $5. The following history is from the Treasury Department *Bulletin*.

This legal-tender quality was withdrawn by the joint resolution approved July 22, 1876, and the coinage was limited to such amount as the secretary of the Treasury should consider sufficient to meet the export demand. The Act of February 19, 1887, provided for the retirement of trade dollars and their recoinage into standard silver dollars or subsidiary silver. For six months after the passage of the act, they could be exchanged at the Treasury or any subtreasury, dollar for dollar, for standard silver dollars or subsidiary coin.

The total number of trade dollars coined was 36 million. The number redeemed under the Act of 1887 was 7.7 million, and from the bullion resulting from the melting of these dollars $2.7 million were coined in subsidiary silver and $5.1 million into standard silver dollars. Following expiration of the period of redemption, trade dollars were purchased as bullion when presented at the mints.

TRADE EXPANSION ACT OF 1982 Federal legislation empowering the president to negotiate certain tariff reductions, such as to the European Common Market, or to grant them on the basis of reciprocal trade agreements. The act also provides for the granting of technical and financial assistance to employers adversely affected by foreign competition.

TRADEMARK As defined by an act of Congress, "any word, name, symbol or device, or any combination thereof, adopted and used by a manufacturer or merchant to identify his goods and distinguish them from those manufactured or sold by others." Rights in trademarks (U.S. government agencies have adopted the term "trademark" as a single word, compounded from the former "trade mark") are acquired by use, which must continue if those rights are to be preserved. In order to be eligible for registration, a mark must be in use in commerce which may be lawfully regulated by Congress.

Trademarks are registered on the principal register and the supplemental register of the U.S. Patent and Trademark Office. "Coined, arbitrary, fanciful or suggestive marks, usually called technical marks, if otherwise qualified," may be registered on the principal register. A trademark that is merely descriptive of goods or their regional origin, or is primarily a surname, is placed on the supplemental register.

The Trademark Act of 1946 provides that "for the purposes of registration on the Supplemental Register, a mark may consist of any trademark, symbol, label package, configuration of goods, name, word, slogan, phrase, surname, geographical name, numeral, or device, or any combination of any of the foregoing, but such mark must be capable of distinguishing the applicant's goods or services."

A trademark cannot be registered if it comprises immoral, deceptive, or scandalous matter, or matter that may disparage or falsely suggest a connection with persons living or dead, institutions, beliefs, or national symbols. It cannot use the flag or coat of arms or other insignia of the United States, any state, municipality, or foreign nation. It cannot use a portrait, signature, or name of a living individual without his consent or those of a deceased President of the United States without consent of his widow.

An application for registration must be filed in the name of the owner of the mark, who may submit his case or be represented by an attorney at law or other person authorized to practice in trademark matters. A complete application comprises a written application, a drawing of the mark, five specimens or facsimiles, and the filing fee.

The Patent and Trademark Office publishes a pamphlet, "General Information Concerning Trademarks," which describes the way applications and drawings are to be prepared and gives sample forms for application. The Patent and Trademark Office, upon request, will supply forms for the registration of a trademark in the name of an individual, a firm, or a corporation. If facilities permit, the office will make drawings from the applicant's direction and at his expense. If the application is allowed, the trademark will be published in the *Trademark Official Gazette* so that anyone who considers that he will be damaged by the new mark may file his opposition within 30 days.

The Trademark Act of 1946 also provided for the registration of service marks, certification marks, and collective marks. A service mark is a title, symbol, or name used in sale or advertising of services to identify them. A certification mark is used by others than the owner to certify origin or quality, such as work by a union. A collective mark is used by members of a cooperative, an association, or other group and indicates membership in a union or other organization. A digest of registered trademarks may be inspected at the Patent and Trademark Office.

A trademark is registered for 20 years and may be renewed for periods of 20 years if still in use in commerce regulated by Congress, or if nonuse is due to special circumstances which excuse nonuse and is not due to any intention to abandon the mark.

The pamphlet "General Information Concerning Trademarks," is a general guide. The "Trademark Rules of Practice of the Patent Office with Forms and Statutes" is also published. The *Trademark Official Gazette*, issued weekly, contains information concerning trademarks published for opposition, registered, and renewed. The office also maintains a roster of agents and attorneys qualified to practice before the Patent and Trademark Office.

TRADE PAPER Notes or trade acceptances given rather than money in exchange for merchandise; BUSINESS PAPER.

TRADER A person who engages in speculation, buying and selling securities or commodities for price appreciation; a person who executes orders of others on the floor of an exchange or who, among dealers in unlisted securities, maintains a position or inventory in assigned stocks and engages in buying and selling operations in such stocks.

TRADE READJUSTMENT *See* BUSINESS CYCLE, READJUSTMENT.

TRADE REFERENCE The name of a business house (usually a creditor, but sometimes a debtor) given by another business house to a bank, business house, or mercantile agency in order that its credit reputation may be investigated. No organizations are in a better position to know the character, ability, and general standing of a given enterprise than its creditors. When a business house desires to open credit relations with another, it is customary for the latter to request names of references for investigative purposes pending the allowance or rejection of the application.

TRADE REPRESENTATIVE, OFFICE OF UNITED STATES A federal office of the Special Representative for Trade Negotiations created by Congress in the Trade Expansion Act of 1962. This act authorized the special trade representative to negotiate all trade agreements on behalf of the United States and to administer the trade agreements program under the Tariff Act of 1930 and the Trade Expansion Act of 1962. Congress established the office as a cabinet-level agency within the executive office of the president. In 1980, the office was renamed the Office of the United States Trade Representative.

The United States trade representative has three major responsibilities: he/she is the president's chief adviser on international trade policy; he/she has primary responsibility with the U.S. government for developing international trade policy and for coordinating its implementation; he/she is the nation's chief negotiator for international trade agreements.

TRADERS' MARKET In unlisted securities trading, the inside market, or that market with the closest spreads between bid and asked prices, maintained for trading between firms and not for the public. Traders' markets are published daily in the National Quotation Bureau's sheets (*see* NATIONAL QUOTATION BUREAU). Quotations released through regional offices of the NATIONAL ASSOCIATION OF SECURITIES DEALERS, INC. to the press reflect approximate quotations for the public. Necessarily, spreads in quotations for the public must allow for the expense of maintaining facilities for the public. Traders' markets may be likened to wholesale prices, while public quotations are retail prices.

TRADING ACCOUNT SECURITIES Securities acquired with the intention of selling them within a short period of time, as opposed to investment account securities. The Glass-Steagall Act restricts banks' securities trading but does not prohibit trading. Banks can underwrite debt obligations of the United States and general obligations of states or political subdivisions. They can also purchase securities for the customer accounts and for the bank's own account. A bank's trading activities and trading department are normally kept separate from its other investment activities and departments. Banks generate income from trading activities by commissions on transactions and by profits on transactions in trading securities. The Federal Deposit Insurance Corporation has concluded that certain transactions should be included in the trading account and not the investment account: when-issued securities trading, pair-offs, gains trading, corporate settlement on U.S. government and federal agency securities purchases, and short sales. The FDIC maintains that purchases of stripped mortgage-backed securities, residuals, and zero-coupon bonds may be unsuitable for the investment portfolio.

TRADING ASSETS Accounts receivables, inventory, and similar assets used in the noral operations of a business for trading or exchange purposes.

TRADING CORPORATION That type of management investment organization which seeks to secure profits from short-term trading swings and makes frequent shifts in positions.

See INVESTMENT COMPANY.

TRADING MARKET A narrow, dull, inactive market in which prices cover the same ground over and over; a market in which public participation is negligible, transactions being largely confined to those of professional traders, and therefore sometimes called a professional market. A trading market is a preparatory, hesitating condition preceding an impending movement upward or downward. In a trading market the range of stocks is kept within a few points, and the trading area is a small range between the limits of which the movement of prices is confined.

A trading market is a period of vacillation occurring at the conclusion of a decisive upward or downward swing. Preparatory to the next swing, prices vibrate within a narrow range, the amplitude of fluctuations demarking the limits of the trading area. It is a time of suspended judgment—a speculative question mark—and may be conceived of as a prolongation of a pause to permit digestion of the preceding move, while speculators wait for additional facts to provide an impetus for a fresh start in one direction or the other.

Referring solely to the movements of the averages, a trading area on a high plateau in a bull market almost invariably is an interlude in what later proves to be a resumption of the rise, or else the energy required to hold prices within the area would not have been expended. The technical rule is that the line of least resistance is

TRADING METHODS

motion, and stocks having risen to a temporary apex would be more apt to round off and with little hesitation start downward. Similarly, a trading area at the bottom of a sharp decline is a breathing space to take account of fundamentals. If the decline has gone too far, recovery, if there is to be one, will lose no time in asserting itself. Consequently, a trading area following a declining movement is usually the precursor of a resumption of the fall. Technically, then, a trading area is a compromise, since the rule of motion is violated.

What applies to the averages in regard to trading areas is not applicable to individual stocks. Frequently, what appears to be a trading area at the bottom of a decline in an individual stock is a zone of accumulation, with the next important movement upward. Similarly, the semblance of a trading area in an individual stock on a high plateau frequently turns out to be a level of distribution, with the next move downward.

A trading area offers one type of market situation in which the trader may have his decision made for him with a minimum of risk. Since a trading area is an interruption of the trend, the market will show, by its own action, what the direction will be when the trading market has terminated. Just as soon as the averages break out of their trading range in one direction or the other, the action can be followed almost blindly. Almost invariably, it is a signal for a continuation of that directional change.

See TECHNICAL ANALYSIS.

TRADING METHODS The bases for payment and delivery for transactions in stocks on the New York Stock Exchange are three: (1) cash (for delivery on the same day), (2) regular way (for delivery on the fifth full business day following the day of the transaction), and (3) seller's option, wherein the seller may deliver from six days to not more than sixty days from the day of the transaction, at his option, giving notice to the buyer one business day in advance.

The pertinent rules from the New York Stock Exchange *Directory and Guide* are as follows.

Bonds, Rights, and 100-Share-Unit Stocks—Rule 64. Bids and offers in securities admitted to dealings on an issued basis shall be made only as follows, and may be made simultaneously as essentially different propositions, but when made without stated conditions shall be considered to be "regular way": (1) "cash," i.e., for delivery on the day of the contract, (2) "regular way," i.e., for delivery on the fifth business day following the day of the contract, (3) "seller's option," i.e., for delivery within the time specified in the option, which time shall be not less than six business days nor more than sixty days following the day of the contract, except that the exchange may provide otherwise in specific issues of stocks or classes of stocks and except that on the second, third, fourth, and fifth business days preceding the final day for subscription, bids and offers in rights to subscribe shall be made only "next day," i.e., for delivery on the next business day following the day of the contract, and on the day preceding the final day for subscription shall be made only for cash.

Cash delivery must be specified in an order. It would be resorted to whenever there is need for maximum speed in the sale of a stock, such as for tax purposes, or to obtain stock quickly, such as for voting purposes. The seller's option basis is a deferred delivery; pursuant to Rule 137, written contracts (in forms approved by the exchange) must be exchanged between the parties not later than the second business day following the transaction.

Less than 100-Share-Unit Stocks—Rule 65. Stocks having a unit of trading of less than 100 shares, not assigned by the exchange for dealings by the use of cabinets as provided in Rule 85 (a procedure, off the floor, for trading in inactive stocks), shall be dealt in as provided in Rule 64 (above). Anything contained in the rules to the contrary notwithstanding, the following rule shall apply to deliveries of less than 100-share-unit stocks dealt in pursuant to this rule:

Unless the exchange directs otherwise, an odd lot of stock sold by an odd-lot dealer for his own account shall be delivered on the fourteenth day following the day of the contract, and may be delivered on any business day prior thereto, except that delivery shall not be made before the fifth business day following the day of the transaction, unless otherwise agreed.

U.S. Government Securities—Rule 66. Bids and offers in securities of the United States government admitted to dealings on an "issued" basis shall be made only as follows, and may be made simultaneously as essentially different propositions, but when made without stated conditions shall be considered to be "regular way": (1) "cash," i.e., for delivery on the day of the contract, (2) "regular way," i.e., for delivery on the business day following the day of the contract, (3) "seller's option," i.e., for delivery within the time specified in the option, which time shall be not less than two business days nor more than sixty days following the day of the contract, except that the exchange may provide otherwise in such securities.

Because regular way delivery is one day on U.S. government securities, the seller's option therefore runs from *two* days to not more than sixty days.

Repeal of Former Rules. When Rule 64 was amended on February 9, 1968, so as to pertain to bonds and rights, as well as 100-share-unit stocks, former Rule 67 (pertaining to convertible bonds), Rule 68 (pertaining to other bonds), and Rule 69 (pertaining to fourth day or delayed delivery and to disagreement) were repealed.

See DELIVERIES, EX- DIVIDEND, GOOD DELIVERY, STOCK CLEARING CORPORATION.

TRADING ON THE EQUITY The practice of using borrowed money at fixed interest rates or issuing preferred stock with constant dividend rates with the expectation of obtaining a higher rate of return on the money used than the interest or preferred dividends paid; LEVERAGE. Just as a company's gain can be magnified when trading on the equity, so can its losses.

TRADING SESSIONS ON STOCK EXCHANGE
See HAMMOND'S TIME, NEW YORK STOCK EXCHANGE.

TRADING UNIT The unit of trading on the New York Stock Exchange is 100 shares for active stocks, 10 shares for inactive stocks. Units of less than 100 shares for active stocks and less than 10 shares for inactive stocks are odd lots.

See ODD LOT.

TRADING VALUE Among traders or speculators, the price at which a purchase, whether a bond, stock, real estate, or commodity, must be sold in order for the owner to get out even; in the language of speculation, the price at which a purchase stands the owner, e.g., if a stock has been purchased at 90, it must be sold at that price if the owner is to avoid taking a loss. The trading value at the time of actual purchase is equal to the cost, market and book values.

Where trading operations are constantly engaged in, a record of trading values is extremely important, because these values are the indicators of the profitableness of individual transactions. To illustrate the use of trading value, suppose ten bonds having a par value of $1,000 each are bought for $9,000. The trading value is 90 (100 equals par); that is, ten bonds would have to be sold at 90 in order to avoid a loss. If, however, five of these bonds are sold for $5,000, the trading value for the remaining five is 80 because they may be sold at that price without this particular block of bonds being closed out at a loss. Bond and stock traders apply the profit made in one group of securities to losses made in others to determine net results and for tax purposes.

TRANSACTION ACCOUNT As defined by the Board of Governors of the Federal Reserve System, "a checking account or similar account from which tranfers can be made to third parties". Demand deposit accounts, negotiable order of withdrawal (NOW) accounts, automatic transfer service (ATS) accounts, and credit union share draft accounts are examples of transaciton accounts at banks and other depository institutions.

TRANSFER AGENT   See STOCK TRANSFERS.

TRANSFER BOOK The stock transfer ledger in which changes of ownership in stock are recorded, i.e., the transferor is debited and the transferee is credited. Under Section 624 of the New York Business Corporation Law, every stock corporation must maintain a stock book containing the names, alphabetically arranged, of all persons who are stockholders of the corporation, their places of residence, the number of shares held, the time when they became owners thereof, and the amount paid thereon.

See CORPORATE RECORDS.

TRANSFER IN BLANK The transfer or assignment of a stock certificate to another person by the person whose name is registered on its face through delivery to the person who has bought it, without inscription of the name of the person to whom it has been sold on the back of the certificate where the form of assignment is printed. When a stock certificate has been transferred in blank, it can pass by purchase from one owner to another any number of times, and while the holder is the legal owner, on the books of the corporation the stock is still in the name of the person who originally transferred it in blank. He would therefore get any dividends that might be declared and paid by the corporation and would be entitled to vote and receive any other rights, but in practice these dividends and rights would be conveyed to the current owner by way of a DUE BILL or other claim. Stock that has been transferred in blank usually represents FLOATING SUPPLY OF SECURITIES, and such certificates are known as street certificates.

See STREET CERTIFICATE, STOCK TRANSFERS.

TRANSFER ITEM An item that cannot be fully processed through a teller's cage. Such items are given to another teller with a transfer ticket.

TRANSFER OFFICE The office of the stock transfer agent designated by a corporation to handle transfers of its stock, or, where no agent is designated, the office of the corporation itself which handles the work. Listing requirements of the NEW YORK STOCK EXCHANGE require a corporation to maintain a stock transfer office and a stock registrar in the City of New York.

TRANSFER OF MORTGAGE Either the mortgagor (borrower) or the mortgagee (lender) may assign his interest in a MORTGAGE.

In the assignment of a bond and mortgage, the bond is the obligation to pay the debt for which the mortgage is security. An assignment of the bond alone has been held by New York courts to carry with it the mortgage security, but the assignment of the mortgage alone without the bond does not effect transfer of title to the mortgage.

The New York Real Property Law (Sec. 258, Schedule O) contains a short form of assignment of a bond and mortgage (Statutory Form I, Without Covenant), as appended.

Short Form of Mortgage Assignment

Know that , _____ assignor, in consideration of _____ dollars, paid by _____ assignee, hereby assigns unto the assignee, a certain mortgage made by _____ , given to secure payment of the sum of _____ dollars and interest, dated the _____ day of _____ ,recorded on the _____ day of _____ , in the office of the _____ _____ of the county of _____ in liber _____ of mortgages, at page _____ covering premises _____ , together with the bond or obligation described in said mortgage, and the moneys due and to grow due thereon with the interest.

To have and to hold the same unto the assignee, and to the successors, legal representatives and assigns of the assignee forever.

In witness whereof, the assignor has hereunto set his hand and seal this _____ day of _____ , nineteen hundred and _____ .

In presence of: _____

The New York courts, however, have held that the bond and mortgage are assignable by delivery without a writing or the payment of consideration by the assignee.

The grantee may be held as to any equities existing at the time of the assignment between the mortgagor and mortgagee, as the bond and mortgage are nonnegotiable instruments. The grantee may also be held as to any equities by third parties existing at the time of assignment against the assignor.

When land which is mortgaged is conveyed, the grantee may take the property *subject* to the mortgage, and thus be free from liability on the bond for any deficiency arising upon foreclosure, such liability remaining in the original mortgagor, or may take the property *assuming* the mortgage, whereby the grantee undertakes the personal liability to pay the mortgage debt and thus can be held on any deficiency. Assumption of the mortgage by the grantee is part of the consideration involved in the transaction.

See MORTGAGE LOANS.

TRANSFER OF STOCK *See* STOCK TRANSFERS.

TRANSFER PAYMENTS An amount of money that an individual receives from the federal government as a grant. This money is literally transferred from the government to individuals.

TRANSFER PRICING Divisions of an enterprise frequently buy and sell to one another. A price must be established for these transfers. This price is referred to as the transfer price. Various alternatives to establishing a transfer price include the following:

1. The transfer price should be set equal to the manufacturing cost of the selling division.
2. The transfer price should be the amount the selling division could sell the product to an outside firm.
3. The transfer price should be the amount the buying division could purchase the product from an outside firm.
4. The transfer price should be a negotiated amount agreed upon by the buying and selling divisions.
5. The transfer price should be the costs incurred to the point of transfer plus the opportunity costs for the firm as a whole. The opportunity cost would be the next best alternative for the firm. For example, if the selling division was operating at less than full capacity, the opportunity cost would be zero. If the selling division was operating at full capacity, the opportunity cost would be the lost contribution margin (selling price minus variable costs) resulting from foregoing outside sales to sell to the buying division.

The choice of method depends upon a number of factors, such as the autonomy allowed to divisions, the degree of market competition, the extent to which the goals of the division are expected to correspond to the goals of the firm, short-run supply and demand relationships, and how divisions are evaluated by the firm.

TRANSFER RISK A risk that arises when borrowers incur debts denominated (to be settled) in the currencies of other countries; a component of country risk. Government policies or economic conditions in a borrower's country sometimes prevent the borrower from obtaining the foreign currencies required to service its debts. In such cases, the position of the lender is weakened.

TRANSIT CLERK A bank clerk who has charge of the collection of out-of-town CASH ITEMS.

See COLLECTION CLERK.

TRANSIT DEPARTMENT The department of a bank that collects checks and other items drawn on out-of-town banks. The principal media of collection are through the FEDERAL RESERVE CHECK COLLECTION SYSTEM and through other banks acting as collecting agents.

TRANSIT FANFOLD MACHINE A special type of adding-typewriter used in the preparation of transit letters.

See TRANSIT LETTER.

TRANSIT ITEM *See* OUT-OF-TOWN CHECKS.

TRANSIT LETTER A letter or deposit slip addressed to a Federal Reserve bank or other bank acting as collecting agent, containing a list of the enclosed out-of-town checks to be collected for, the proceeds to be remitted to the sending bank. A transit letter describes each listed check with the following details: (1) transit number of the drawee (paying) bank (if the transit number is not used, the name and location of the bank are written out), (2) name or transit number of the sending (owning) bank, (3) amount, and (4) any special instructions, e.g., no protest, wire nonpayment, deliver documents upon payment only, etc.

TRANSIT NUMBER *See* NUMERICAL TRANSIT SYSTEM.

TRANSLATION The conversion of the assets, liabilities, and operating items of a foreign branch or subsidiary from stated amounts of foreign currency into U.S. dollars. When the account balances of a parent company and its foreign subsidiary or branch are stated in different currencies, it is necessary to translate the financial data of the subsidiary into terms of the currency of the parent to apply the equity method of accounting and prepare consolidated financial statements. The objectives of translation are to:

1. Provide information that is generally compatible with the expected economic effects of a rate change on an enterprise's cash flows and equity.
2. Reflect in consolidated financial statements the financial results and relationships of the individual consolidated entities as measured in their functional currencies in conformity with U.S. generally accepted accounting principles.

When translating the trial balance of a foreign entity and rates of exchange have changed, the translated dollar trial balance will not balance. This difference is accumulated in an account called the cumulative translation adjustment. This is the amount necessary to make the translated debits and credits in U.S. dollars balance. The amount can be either a debit or a credit and is reported as a separate component of stockholders' equity (and not in the income statement). Because assets and liabilities are translated at the current rate and equity accounts (except for retained earnings) at the date of the transaction (historical rate), an imbalance occurs. A change in the exchange rate between the U.S. dollar and a foreign currency results in a change in the U.S. dollar equivalent of the net investment in the foreign entity. If the foreign currency strengthens against the dollar, the U.S. dollar equivalent is enhanced. The translation adjustment reflects the unrealized economic effect of exchange rate changes on the net investment in the foreign entity. It has no effect on the net cash flows generated by the foreign entity.

TRANS-LUX Movie projector equipment used principally for market quotations by stock and grain exchanges and brokerage firms; sometimes called the movie ticker. The equipment is designed so that projections are made from behind the screens. The screen is a translucent or daylight type which permits exceptional clarity of visibility with a minimum of distortion in full daylight or artificial light. The paper tape of the usual Western Union stock ticker or a special cellophane tape with quotations printed on by the TICKER is mechanically drawn past the lens and magnified and projected across a screen, from left to right, at a moderate rate of speed. The equipment is also used for projecting news articles from the broad tape ticker service of newspapers and reporting agencies, such s the Dow-Jones Ticker Service. Other adaptations of special types are used for home movies, educational, advertising, and motion picture theatre purposes.

TRANSPORTATION For bibliography, see under RAILROAD INDUSTRY.

TRANSPORTATION, DEPARTMENT OF As had been proposed for some time, Congress finally passed the Department of Transportation Act on October 15, 1966 (80 Stat. 931), establishing the Department of Transportation for the "purpose of developing national transportation policies and programs conducive to the provision of fast, safe, efficient, and convenient transportation at the lowest cost consistent therewith." The act, however, left the INTERSTATE COMMERCE COMMISSION (railroads, motor carriers, bus lines, freight forwarders, water carriers, and transportation brokers), the Maritime Administration (aid to the U.S. merchant marine), and the Civil Aeronautics Board (civil aviation, within the United States and between the United States and foreign countries) as independent agencies, regulatory in nature.

The Department of Transportation (DOT), therefore, as of 1979 included the following components.

Federal Aviation Administration. Formerly the Federal Aviation Agency, the FAA became a part of the Department of Transportation in 1967 as a result of the Department of Transportation Act, supra. The FAA is charged with regulating air commerce to foster aviation safety, promoting civil aviation and a national system of airports, achieving efficient use of navigable airspace, and developing and operating a common system of air traffic control and air navigation for both civilian and military aircraft.

Federal Highway Administration. The FHWA became a component of the Department of Transportation pursuant to the Department of Transportation Act, supra. Its mission encompasses highway transportation in its broadest scope, carrying out the highway transportation programs of the department, and coordinating highways with other modes of transportation to achieve the most effective balance of transportation systems and facilities under federal transportation policies as contemplated by the act. Among its specific functions and activities is administration of the federal-aid highway program of financial assistance to the states for highway construction. This program provides for construction of the 42,500-mile national system of interstate and defense highways, financed on a 90% federal-10% state basis, and the improvement of 872,000 miles of other federal-aid primary and secondary roads and their extensions, with financing on a 50%-50% basis.

Urban Mass Transportation Administration (UMTA). Linked with the Federal Highway Administration (FHWA) in jointly issued regulations (23 CFR 450 and 49 CFR 613, September, 1975), the UMTA antedates both the FHWA and the DOT itself, having been created under authority of the Urban Mass Transportation Act of 1964, as amended (49 U.S.C. 1601 et seq.). The UMTA was brought into the DOT fold by Section 3 of the President's Reorganization Plan No. 2, effective July 1, 1968.

The specific missions of the UMTA are to assist in the development of improved mass transportation facilities, equipment, techniques, and methods; to encourage the planning and establishment of areawide urban mass transportation systems; and to provide assistance to state and local governments in financing such systems.

By contrast, the FHWA is concerned with the total operation and environment of the highway systems, with particular emphasis on improvement of highway-oriented aspects of highway safety. It does seek to coordinate highways with other modes of transportation to achieve the most effective balance of transportation systems and facilities under cohesive federal transportation policies as contemplated by the Department of Transportation Act.

But both federal highway and urban mass transit legislation require urban areas to establish a transportation planning process calling for the development of a single transportation plan for highways and transit that includes consideration of actions integrating automobiles, public transit, taxis, pedestrians, and bicycles. The regulations also made UMTA and FHWA urban transportation planning requirements consistent.

The General Accounting Office (GAO) reports that Congress, through its appropriations to the Department of Transportation's FWHA and UMTA, has provided funds to urban areas for such purposes as bus and railcar purchases, transit operating assistance, and major highway construction. Urban mass transit operating assistance was first authorized in 1974, and the Surface Transportation Assistance Act of 1978 authorized more than $1.5 billion per year for this program for the fiscal years 1979-1982.

The GAO reports that although urban areas have increased their emphasis on short-range planning, the joint regulations of the UMTA and FHWA have not had much of an impact on the planning process and the types of transportation projects being implemented because FHWA and UMTA are not administering the regulations jointly; metropolitan planning organizations are not able to coordinate the urban transportation planning process, integrating highways and public transit into a single transportation system through the cooperation of state and local groups and agencies; and various funding and legal provisions discourage the implementation of transportation systems management projects.

Federal Railroad Administration (FRA). Purposes of the FRA include the consolidation of government support of rail transportation activities, provision of a unified and unifying national rail transportation policy, administration and enforcement of rail safety laws and regulations, administration of financial assistance programs for certain railroads, the conducting of research and development in support of improved intercity ground transportation and the future requirements for rail transportation, provision for revitalization of Northeast corridor rail passenger service, and operation of the Alaska Railroad. The FRA was created by the Department of Transportation Act of 1966 (80 Stat. 932).

The secretary of Transportation serves as one of the directors of the United States Railway Association, established by the Regional Reorganization Act of 1973 (45 U.S.C. 701), approved January 2, 1974, to develop a system plan designed to provide adequate and efficient rail service in the midwest and northeast regions of the United States through restructuring of bankrupt railroads in those areas. The system plan provided for the creation of the Consolidated Rail Corporation (Conrail), for which the United States Railway

Association provides funds for working capital and rehabilitation by purchasing securities of Conrail.

The secretary of Transportation also serves as one of the directors of the National Railroad Passenger Corporation (Amtrak), created by the Rail Passenger Service Act of 1970 (45 U.S.C. 541), as amended, as a for-profit corporation to provide a balanced transportation system by improving and developing intercity rail passenger service.

See RAILROAD INDUSTRY.

National Highway Traffic Safety Administration. Established by the Highway Safety Act of 1970 (84 Stat. 1739), the administration carries out programs relating to the safety performance of motor vehicles and related equipment, motor vehicle drivers, and pedestrians under the National Traffic and Motor Vehicle Safety Act of 1966 (80 Stat. 731), as amended. In addition, under authority of the Motor Vehicle Information and Cost Saving Act (86 Stat. 947), as amended, the administration carries out programs and studies aimed at reducing economic losses in motor vehicle crashes and repairs through diagnostic inspection projects; administering the federal odometer law and a uniform national maximum speed limit; and promulgating average fuel economy standards for passenger and nonpassenger motor vehicles. Under authority of the Clean Air Amendments of 1970 (84 Stat. 1700), the administration also certifies as to the consistency of Environmental Protection Agency state grants with any highway safety program developed pursuant to Section 402 of Title 23 of the U.S. Code.

National Transportation Safety Board (NTSB). Previously an organizational part of the Department of Transportation, the NTSB was established as an independent agency of the federal government on April 1, 1975, by the Independent Safety Board Act of 1974 (49 U.S.C. 1901). The mission of the NTSB is to promote transportation safety by conducting independent investigations of accidents and other safety problems and by formulating safety improvement recommendations.

Saint Lawrence Seaway Development Corporation. Established by act of Congress approved May 13, 1954 (33 U.S.C. 981), as amended, the corporation was transferred to the Department of Transportation by the Department of Transportation Act. The corporation is now one of the operating administrations of the DOT and is self-sustaining, being financed from revenues received from tolls charged for the use of its facilities. The corporation, a wholly government-owned enterprise, is responsible for the development, operation, and maintenance of that part of the seaway between Montreal and Lake Erie within the territorial limits of the United States. It charges tolls in accordance with established rates for users of the seaway which it negotiates with the St. Lawrence Seaway Authority of Canada. The corporation coordinates its activities with its Canadian counterpart, particularly with respect to overall operations, traffic control, safety, season extension, and related programs designed to fully develop the "fourth seacoast."

United States Coast Guard. Established in 1915 by an act of January 28, 1915 (14 U.S.C. 1), it succeeded its predecessor, "The Revenue Marine," established in 1790 as a federal maritime law enforcement agency. It became a component of the DOT on April 1, 1967, pursuant to the Department of Transportation Act. The Coast Guard is a branch of the Armed Forces of the United States at all times and is a service within the DOT, except when operating as part of the U.S. Navy in time of war or when the President directs.

TRANSPORTATION ACT OF 1920 The RAILROAD LEGISLATION which marked the beginning of modern regulatory policies toward the railroad industry in its period of maturity. This act recognized for the first time the necessity for placing the railroad industry on a stable basis by affording adequate rates which would enable railroads to earn a fair return upon railway property. The act also permitted railroads to enter into pooling agreements and combinations, subject to approval of the Interstate Commerce Commission. It broadened the powers of the commission to include supervision over security issues, new construction, abandonments, etc., and set up new procedure for handling labor disputes. In connection with allowing fair rates of return, the act set up the provisions for recapture of earnings in excess of fair rate of return (the RECAPTURE CLAUSE), since repealed.

See INTERSTATE COMMERCE ACT, VALUATION ACT OF 1913.

TRANSPORTATION (EMERGENCY) ACT OF 1933
See RAILROAD TRANSPORTATION (EMERGENCY) ACT OF 1933.

TRANSPORTATION RATIO In railroad finance, the ratio of a railroad company's transportation expenses to total (gross) operating revenues, expressed as a percentage. Transportation expenses are those incurred in the conduct of train operations, chiefly the cost of fuel and the wages of train and station personnel. The transportation ratio is the best rough guide of a railroad's operating efficiency. The normal transportation ratio (on the average) is about 35%.

See RAILROAD EARNINGS.

TRAVELERS' CHECKS International checks; more technically, a modified form of a traveler's letter of credit, not drawn on any specified bank or banks, but payable at practically all banks throughout the world and guaranteed by some well-known institution. They furnish a convenient and safe currency for travelers and may be purchased at all principal banks for cash at a customary cost of 1% of face value. They are listed in convenient denominations, in U.S. dollars ($10, $20, $50, $100, and $500), but are also available in specified denominations in foreign currencies, such as Canadian dollars, French francs, German marks, Japanese yen, pounds sterling, and Swiss francs. The signature of the payee (usually also the buyer) is written on the face of the check at the time of purchase. Space is reserved for the beneficiary's countersignature in the presence of the person agreeing to cash the check, for purposes of identification. The signature written in the presence of the paying bank or other institution must correspond with the signature written at the time of the purchase, agreement of the two signatures usually being regarded as sufficient identification for the payment of the money. For this reason, a travelers' check should never be countersigned by the payee except in the presence of the person who agrees to accept it. These checks are almost universally acceptable abroad, and the principal hotels, railroads, airlines, steamship lines, and merchants accept them as freely as cash.

Where stability of exchange rates permits, travelers' checks issued in dollars may be issued payable at fixed rates of exchange. Whenever money (whether cash, personal checks, bank drafts, or travelers' checks) is converted from one currency to another, a foreign exchange transaction is involved, and, as in any business transaction, there is a cost for this service which is included in the rate of exchange received. Each of the following involves a currency exchange: (1) the purchase of any foreign currency travelers' checks with the currency of the home country, (2) the cashing of travelers' checks in any country other than the country in whose currency the checks are issued, and (3) the conversion of unused foreign currency travelers' checks back into the currency of the home country. In some countries, there are also government or banking association-imposed taxes or handling charges applied to the cashing of travelers' checks and other financial instruments.

Travelers' checks are also used domestically. They are usually acceptable as currency, i.e., without being first cashed, by railroads, airlines, hotels, gas stations, and principal merchants. Thus, they are equivalent to insured money.

Travelers' checks are both safe and convenient; if they are lost or stolen, no loss is likely to be incurred because of the fact that no person other than the payee can cash them, since the countersignature must be written in the presence of the person agreeing to accept them. In case of loss, however, owners of travelers' checks are reimbursed, provided the second signature has not been affixed. Unused travelers' checks are redeemable by the issuer. When presented for redemption they must be countersigned exactly as when cashed at any other place.

Banks sometimes issue guaranteed travelers' checks, in which case the payee does not pay for them at the time of issue but permits the bank to charge his account after they have returned from abroad and are presented to the payee's bank for collection.

TRAVELER'S LETTER OF CREDIT A letter issued by a domestic bank introducing the bearer to its correspondents in a foreign country and instructing such correspondents to honor drafts, up to a specified limit, drawn by the bearer, usually in the currency of that country. Traveler's letters of credit are issued for the convenience of foreign travelers and answer the same purpose as travelers' checks.

Traveler's letters of credit are of two types, circular and specially advised. A circular letter of credit, the more common of the two, enables the borrower to negotiate drafts at any one of a number of foreign correspondents which will pay against drafts so drawn to the borrower, thus enabling the borrower to obtain funds wherever he may be traveling. Appended is a form of circular letter of credit.

Circular Letter of Credit

No. ———

For $ ———
issued by
BLANK BANK
New York, ————— , 19 ——

Messrs. the Banks and Bankers
(mentioned on the accompanying list of correspondents).

Gentlemen:
We beg to introduce to you and to recommend to your courtesies ———————————— to whom kindly furnish funds in sums as desired up to an aggregate amount of ———————————— dollars against demand drafts on Blank Bank, New York City.

We engage that such drafts will meet with due honor at this bank if negotiated not later than ————————— , 19, ————— and marked "drawn under Blank Bank's Letter of Credit No. ——————— " upon the condition that the amount of each draft negotiated by you shall have been inscribed on the second page of this letter, the draft signed in your presence, and the signature carefully compared by you with holder's signature appearing on the inside of the cover of the accompanying list of correspondents duly certified to by this bank.

Kindly purchase drafts at the best rate at which you buy demand drafts on New York, deducting all your charges, if any, and please see to it that the present letter be canceled and attached together with the list of correspondents to the draft which exhausts the credit.

A specially advised letter of credit is designed for the benefit of a person who expects to remain in one city in which the bearer is entitled to draw drafts only against a single designated foreign correspondent.

Traveler's letters of credit are usually paid for in advance, and any unused portions may be redeemed at the expiration of the credit. A commission is charged at the time of issue. Sometimes traveler's letters of credit are issued without payment by the bearer in advance; instead, arrangements are made with the issuing bank to charge the bearer's account when drafts negotiated by the bearer with foreign correspondents are presented to the bank issuing the credit.

Letters of credit may be issued in dollars or a foreign currency, according to the wishes of the buyer. If they are issued in dollars, drafts drawn are converted into foreign currency by the paying bank at the current rate of exchange.

The purchaser of a circular letter of credit is entitled to the following papers from the issuing bank: (1) the letter of credit itself, (2) a booklet containing a complete list of correspondents which will pay against the letter of credit, (3) a travelers' telegraphic code by which the holder may communicate in code with the issuing bank or its affiliations concerning its credit or otherwise, and (4) a book of identification containing a specimen signature of the bearer which, in effect, is a letter to correspondent and other banks mentioned in the booklet (see sample appended).

Sample Letter of Identification

Dear Sir:
We beg to introduce to you the bearer of our traveler's circular letter of credit No. ————————— , a specimen of whose signature will be found below.

—————————————

Letters of credit are issued for a specified amount indicated on the face and are subject to a certain expiration date, after which checks drawn under the letter of credit will not be honored for payment by foreign correspondents.

When the beneficiary of a letter of credit wishes to procure funds, he presents the letter of credit to a correspondent and draws a draft for the amount desired, being careful to reserve the affixing of his signature until it can be made in the presence of the paying officer. The signature on the draft must correspond with the signature of the beneficiary as it appears in the letter of identification. This agreement of signatures completes the process of identification and certifies to the foreign bank paying the draft that the bearer of the letter of credit is entitled to the funds. On the second page of the letter of credit, payments are endorsed by each correspondent bank which honors the bearer's draft. The endorsement shows the date of payment, the name of the paying bank, and the amount written in figures and words. The bank that pays the last amount due takes up the letter of credit and forwards it to the issuing bank along wit the draft which it has paid.

TREADWAY COMMISSION   The National Commission on Fraudulent Financial Reporting. The commission, named after its chairperson, former SEC Commissioner James C. Treadway, was organized in 1985 to develop recommendations for fraudulent financial reporting. Its major recommendations include:

1. All public companies should establish audit committees consisting of independent directors.
2. The independent auditor's responsibility for the detection of fraudulent financial reporting should be increased, especially for the detection of errors and irregularities.
3. Auditors should use analytical procedures in all audit engagements to detect fraudulent financial reporting.
4. The auditor's report should clarify the role and responsibilities of the independent auditor and describe the extent to which the auditor has reviewed and evaluated the internal control structure.
5. Membership of the AICPA's Auditing Standards Board should include a larger representation of nonaccountants.

See AUDIT, ETHICS.

TREASURE TROVE   Coin, plate, or bullion found hidden in the earth, buildings, or other places, the owner of which is unknown. Where statutes so provide, title to treasure trove passes to the state; otherwise, the finder is entitled to treasure trove against all including the owner of the realty or soil where found, except against the true owner.

TREASURER   The accountant responsible for the monetary functions of granting credit, collecting and depositing money, disbursing money, and obtaining credit.

TREASURER OF THE UNITED STATES   See TREASURY DEPARTMENT.

TREASURY, SECRETARY OF THE   One of the cabinet officers, corresponding to what in other countries would be the Minister of Finance. The secretary of the Treasury has general supervision, management, and control of the TREASURY DEPARTMENT and the bureaus under that department, including the Bureau of the Mint; the Bureau of Alcohol, Tobacco, and Firearms; the Bureau of Government Financial Operations; the Federal Law Enforcement Training Center; the Bureau of Engraving and Printing; the Bureau of Public Debt; the Internal Revenue Service; the Office of the Comptroller of the Currency; and the U.S. Secret Service. The secretary is statutorily charged with the preparation of plans for the improvement and management of the public revenue and support of the public credit; the prescription of forms for keeping and rendering all public accounts and the making of returns; the issuance of all warrants for moneys to be paid from the Treasury pursuant to legal appropriations; the submittal of an annual report to the Congress upon the condition of finances, and publication the first of each month of the last preceding weekly statement of the Treasury; and in general, the performance of "all such services relative to the finances as he shall be directed to perform."

Besides his managerial and administrative duties, the secretary of the Treasury is in a position to recommend and influence fiscal policies. The analysis staffs of the Treasury Department coordinate the analytical activities in the Treasury Department relating to taxation, financing, and debt management, and the preparation of economic and statistical materials for the use of Treasury officials in the formulation of tax and debt policies. Among the important posts in which the secretary of the Treasury also serves are chairman, National Advisory Council on International Monetary and Financial Problems; U.S. governor of the International Monetary Fund, the International Bank for Reconstruction and Development, and the

Inter-American Development Bank; and member of the Council on Foreign Economic Policy. Decisions of the Treasury on terms and timing of new government debt financing importantly affect the money market and capital markets. Since the "accord" of March, 1951, monetary policy (determined and administered by the Board of Governors of the Federal Reserve System) has been free of complete subordination to fiscal requirements, but continues to be cooperative with FISCAL POLICY consistent with autonomy for objectives of monetary policy.

TREASURY BILL FUTURES The International Monetary Market (IMM) of the CHICAGO MERCANTILE EXCHANGE on January 6, 1976, began trading in futures contracts for 90-day U.S. Treasury bills.

The COMMODITY EXCHANGE, INC. of New York City inaugurated its financial futures market on October 2, 1979, for 90-day Treasury bills. The CHICAGO BOARD OF TRADE (CBT) also has a futures contract in 90-day U.S. Treasury bills.

The basic contract calls for $1 million in 90-day U.S. Treasury bills, the trading months being March, June, September, and December. Prices are quoted not in terms of the annualized yields on a 360-day basis, as in the government securities market, but in terms of what the IMM calls a price index (100.00 minus the yield), so as to express quotations in terms of price. Trading in contracts ends in the third week of the delivery month, on the second business day (normally Wednesdays) after the weekly auction of 90-day bills, followed by settlement of outstanding futures contracts on Thursdays, which also happens to be the day for settlement on the latest auctioned bills, so that new 90-day bills are thus available for delivery if desired. (As in the case of commodity futures, hedgers normally are interested in turning over the futures contracts, rather than taking delivery.)

Minimum price fluctuation for any one day, compared to the previous day's settling price, is 50 points, or $1,250. The settling price is the average of the prices at which the first and last trades occurred during the last minute of trading. However, expanded trading limits for daily price changes are permitted in the following circumstances: (1) when a contract closes at the normal daily trading limit *in the same direction* on two successive days, on the third day the daily price limit on *all* contract months rises to 150% of the normal trading limit, and (2) if on such third day any contract closes at the initially expanded daily price limit and in the same direction as the preceding daily price limit, the expanded daily price limit rises to 200% of the normal daily price limit, and remains at same for as long as any contract month continues to close at such additional expanded daily price limit.

The minimum margin specified by the IMM, as last reported, is $1,000 per contract, which initial margin is adjusted daily as price fluctuations occur. The IMM itself oversees margin requirements, which may be more than the minimum margin per contract if required by the particular brokerage firm through which transactions are effected. Commissions charged, which are roundturn commissions, vary among the brokerage firms selected for the execution of orders, as negotiated commissions prevail.

Uses for T-Bill Futures. The IMM points out that any institution that has a significant portion of its assets and/or liabilities committed to interest rate-sensitive vehicles can use a futures market to hedge this exposure. In addition to considering the proportion of rate-sensitive exposure, financial managers should also consider the impact of interest income or expense on their organizations' earnings. Potential hedgers in interest rate futures include banks, corporations, nonbank financial institutions, government securities dealers, trust departments, mutual funds, pension funds, real estate investment trusts, and finance companies.

The IMM cites several advantages for banks of hedging in T-bill futures. With a long hedge (buying futures) a bank can protect the government securities trading area against falling interest rates on future purchases, and a bank's trust department can hedge the return on the rollover of its short-term money market instruments.

With a short hedge (selling futures) a bank can hedge the cost of future certificate of deposit purchases, Eurodollar borrowings, repos (repurchase agreements), and federal funds.

The appended table shows a hypothetical example cited by the IMM to show how a money manager could use the T-bill futures market to establish the yield he will receive when he reinvests or rolls over his portfolio. The same technique could be used to establish in advance a rate on a money market instrument to be purchased at a future time by the money manager.

Example of Use of T-Bills Futures

Cash market		Futures market	
September 15:			
Bought $5 million in T-bills at 9%		Bought 5 Dec. contracts at 9% (IMM index: 91.00	
Cost	$4,886,250	Value	$4,887,500
December 10:			
Rolled over $5 million in T-bills at 7%		Sold (offset) 5 Dec. contracts at 7% (IMM index: 93.00)	
Cost	$4,911,528	Value	$4,912,500
Loss	$ 25,278	Profit	$ 25,000

Note: Commission and security deposit are not included in the example. The trader should consult his broker for this information.

It should be noted that high correlation (extent to which yields or price fluctuations of one money market instrument are matched by those of another) are essential for good hedges (perfect correlation would be relatively difficult to achieve). Knowledge and up-to-date correlation of the rate behavior and rate outlook for the money market media involved are necessary.

Borrowers in the money markets could also use interest rate futures to protect against increases in short-term rates with a short or sell hedge. The short hedge in futures markets is used to offset increased borrowing costs. The financial manager sells an interest-rate contract now for future delivery. If rates rise between the contract sale date and its delivery date, the value of the futures contract will drop, and the hedger can make a gain by buying back, for a lower price, the contract he sold previously at a higher price. With the gain from his futures contract, the borrower is able to offset the increase in his borrowing costs.

Bank Utilization of Futures Contracts. The Board of Governors of the Federal Reserve System, the Comptroller of the Currency, and the Federal Deposit Insurance Corporation have issued guidelines concerning such matters as accounting, internal bank control, monitoring credit risk, meeting disclosure requirements, and the role of the bank's board of directors; these guidelines cover all contracts entered into or renewed on or after January 1, 1980. National banks must ask for and receive approval from the Comptroller of the Currency to trade in the T-bill (and/or Government National Mortgage Association (GNMA)) futures contracts. The number of banks that have received such permission has increased substantially, led by the larger banks which have the experienced personnel and the large-scale commitments to justify operations in the futures markets, both for their own account and for correspondent banks.

TREASURY BILLS Treasury bills (T-bills) are debt obligations of the U.S. Government that mature in one year or less. The U.S. Treasury regularly sells bills with maturities of three months (13 weeks), six months (26 weeks), and one year (52 weeks). All bills are sold at discount so that the return to the investor is the difference between the purchase price of the bill and its face or par value.

The volume of bills outstanding has grown substantially in recent years because of the large federal budget deficits. T-bills are the most popular money market instrument.

Treasury bills are held by a wide variety of investors, including individuals, businesses, commercial banks, money market mutual funds, the Federal Reserve System, and foreigners. The popularity of T-bills stems from their unique characteristics. First, T-bills are considered to be essentially free from default risk. Second, they are highly liquid because there is a very large and efficient secondary market that enables investors to convert bills easily to cash. Third, the income earned on T-bills is exempt from state and local income taxes. And finally, bills are sold in minimum denominations as small as $10,000 and in multiples of $5,000, making them appropriate for the needs of both large and small investors.

The U.S. government first offered T-bills for sale in 1929. At present, the Treasury conducts public auctions of three- and six-month bills every week and one-year bills every month. Occasionally, the Treasury also sells cash management bills with maturities that have ranged from 3 to 168 days. These special issues are designed to bridge low points in the Treasury's cash inflows.

In order to reduce the cost of issue of the large volume of bills that the Treasury sells, T-bills are only issued in book-entry form. Purchasers do not receive actual physical certificates. Ownership is recorded in a book-entry account established at the Treasury, and investors receive only a receipt as evidence of purchase. The book-entry system for Treasury securities is a tiered custodial system whereby the ownership of T-bills is represented by entries on the books of a series of custodians. This system extends from the Treasury itself through the Federal Reserve banks and depository institutions to the ultimate owner.

The weekly auctions of three- and six-month bills are held each Monday. The amount of bills that the Treasury intends to sell at each weekly auction is announced on Tuesday. Bids must be presented at the Federal Reserve banks or their branches by 1:00 P.M. New York time of the day of the auction. Payment and delivery of bills is on Thursday following the Monday auction.

Potential investors may enter bids in two categories: competitive and noncompetitive. Under a competitive bid, the bidders state the amount of bills they are willing to purchase and the price they are willing to pay. Competitive bids are usually made only by large investors. Smaller investors may enter noncompetitive bids. Noncompetitive bidders state the quantity of bills they are willing to buy and agree to pay a price equal to the weighted average price of bills sold to investors in the competitive bid category. Noncompetitive bids are limited to a maximum of $1 million of each new offering.

The Treasury fills all noncompetitive bids first. In recent years, the volume of noncompetitive bids has averaged between 10% and 25% of the issues sold. The remainder of the issue after the noncompetitive bids have been filled is allocated to competitive bidders according to the price of their bid, from the top bidder down.

Investors wishing to buy bills other than at regular auction and those wishing to sell bills prior to maturity may do so easily in the secondary market. The secondary market in Treasury bills is the largest and most efficient of any money market instrument. One measure of its efficiency is the narrow spread between the bid and ask prices on bills. This spread is normally only between two and four basis points, that is only $200 to $400 per $1 million traded.

The secondary market in bills is maintained principally by a group of security dealers known as primary dealers. In 1986, there were 37 primary dealers, of which 14 were commercial banks. In addition, there is a large and growing number of secondary dealers.

Trading in bills takes place "over the counter," rather than on a formal exchange. Dealers are in almost constant contact over the telephone. Primary dealers are in contact also with the Federal Reserve, and the Fed conducts its open market operations in government securities only through primary dealers.

T-bills have lower rates than other money market instruments such as certificates of deposit (CDs) and commercial paper because investments in T-bills generally are considered to be free from default risk. The spread between the T-bill rate and that on other instruments is not constant but varies over time and with economic conditions. Over the past several decades, the spread between the CD rate and that on T-bills has ranged from a high of more than 200 basis points to less than 30. Commonly, the spread tends to widen in bad economic time as investors tend to seek the security of default-free T-bills and to narrow in good times as the market becomes less concerned about default risk.

Statutory authority for Treasury bills is found in 31 U.S.C. 3104, 3121. Governing regulations include the following: Department Circular No. 300, as revised (31 CFR, Part 306); Department Circulars, Public Debt Series Nos. 26-76 (31 CFR, Part 350) and 27-76 (31 CFR, Part 349); and Department Circular, Public Debt Series No. 2-86 (31 CFR, Part 357) for bills issued in Treasury Direct. For additional information, consult the Office of Financing, Bureau of the Public Debt.

BIBLIOGRAPHY

Cook, T. Q. and Rowe, T. D., eds. "Treasury Bills," *Instruments of the Money Market*, 1986.

TREASURY BONDS Treasury bonds come in $1,000, $5,000, $10,000, $100,000, and $1,000,000 denominations. The $500 denomination was eliminated on Treasury bonds issued since mid-1971. Treasury bonds are subject to federal taxes (income, capital gains, estate, and gift taxes), as are Treasury bills and notes, but exempt as to both principal and interest from all taxes of any state, interest rate varies from issue, maturity varies, but in practical bonds are issued for terms of more than 10 years. U.S. possessions, or local taxing authorities, except estate or inheritance taxes. Flower bonds are no longer being issued.

Treasury bonds are in book-entry form. Bonds issued before September 29, 1982, are in coupon, registered, and book-entry forms. Bonds issued from September 29, 1982, to August 14, 1986, are in registered and book-entry forms. STRIPS are in book-entry form.

Under the authorizing statute, a limitation is placed on the amount of bonds exceeding $4\,^{1}/_{4}\%$ per annum that may be outstanding and held by the public at any one time. By definition, this excludes bonds held by the Federal Reserve System Open Market Committee and by federal government accounts.

When so provided in the offering circulars, bonds may be called for redemption prior to maturity on 4 months' notice.

Statutory authority for Treasury bonds is 31 U.S.C. 3102, 3121. Governing regulations are found in Department Circular No. 300, as revised (31 CFR, Part 306), Department Circulars, Public Debt Series No. 2-86 (31 CFR, Part 357), for bonds issued in Treasury Direct, subject to provisions of the individual offering circular for each issue. Additional information is available from the Office of Financing, Bureau of the Public Debt.

In 1982, several major securities firms began to place with the investing public issues of receipts representing claims on principal of selected long-term Treasury bonds, sold at discounts from par, and, at discounts, receipts representing claims on the interest such bonds will pay over their remaining maturity, but neither the receipts on principal nor the receipts as to interest will make any payments prior to the call or eventual maturity. Actually, the underlying Treasury bonds is custodianed with a trust company, and both types of receipts are issued against such bonds. Thus, such Treasury bonds are not stripped of their interest coupons for sale of the bond certificates and interest coupons separately, which might create confusion in the market for the intact Treasury bonds with interest coupons attached. But such zero coupon Treasury bond receipts are highly suitable for Keogh and individual retirement account (IRA) investment, for they lock in the prevailing yields at discount prices to maturity without tax liability for imputed current accretion of the discounts as current income.

See UNITED STATES GOVERNMENT SECURITIES, ZERO-COUPON BONDS.

TREASURY CERTIFICATES *See* CERTIFICATE OF INDEBTEDNESS, UNITED STATES GOVERNMENT SECURITIES.

TREASURY DEPARTMENT Established by act of Congress approved September 2, 1789 (1 Stat. 65; 31 U.S.C. 1001). It performs three basic types of functions:

1. As a major policy adviser to the President, the secretary has primary responsibility for formulating and recommending domestic and international financial policy, formulating and recommending tax policy, participating in the formulation of broad fiscal policies that have general significance for the economy, and managing the public debt.
2. As Financial agent for the U.S. government, the department performs a variety of fiscal service operations, including accounting for public moneys, issuing and processing government checks, issuing and promoting the sale of savings bonds and other securities, collecting tax revenues and customs duties, supervising the national banks, and manufacturing coins, currency, and postage stamps.
3. As a department charged with major law enforcement responsibility, the Treasury guards the President and Vice-President and their families, and candidates for those offices, and detects and arrests counterfeiters, smugglers, bootleggers, and forgers of government checks or securities.

In addition to overseeing the above activities, the secretary of the Treasury serves in many positions as chief financial officer of the U.S. government, including serving as U.S. governor of the International Monetary Fund, the International Bank for Reconstruction and Development, the Inter-American Development Bank, the Asian Development Bank, and the African Development Fund. He also serves on numerous committees and advisory groups covering a wide variety of activities including the management of federal trust funds, such as the Old Age and Survivors Insurance Trust Fund.

In particular, the undersecretary for monetary affairs has responsibilities in international affairs through an assistant secretary who has jurisdiction over deputy assistant secretaries in the following fields: trade and investment policy, commodities and natural resources, international monetary affairs, developing nations, Saudi Arabian affairs, and the international monetary group. Through a fiscal assistant secretary, the undersecretary for monetary affairs also oversees the Bureau of Government Financial Operations and the Bureau of the Public Debt.

Responsible to the deputy secretary of the Treasury also are (1) the assistant secretary for domestic finance, having jurisdiction over deputy assistant secretaries for capital markets policy, debt management, and state and local finance and over the Office of Revenue Sharing; (2) the assistant secretary for economic policy, having jurisdiction over domestic economic analysis through a deputy assistant secretary, over the Office of Financial Analysis, and over international economic analysis through a deputy assistant secretary; and (3) the assistant secretary for tax policy, having jurisdiction over tax legislation and tax policy economics through respective deputy assistant secretaries, over the Office of Tax Analysis, over the Office of Tax Legislative Counsel, over the Office of International Tax Counsel, and over the Office of Industrial Economics.

An undersecretary of the Treasury includes in his jurisdiction the Treasurer of the United States, the U.S. Savings Bond Division, the Bureau of the Mint, and the Bureau of Engraving and Printing.

The Comptroller of the Currency, chartering and examining authority for national banks, is organizationally under the deputy secretary of the Treasury. So is the commissioner of the Internal Revenue Service. Included in the jurisdiction of the assistant secretary for enforcement and operations is the Bureau of Alcohol, Tobacco and Firearms, the U.S. Customs Service, the U.S. Secret Service, and the Office of Foreign Assets Control.

Reports. The secretary of the Treasury is required by law to submit an annual report to the Congress on the condition of the nation's finances. Other reports regularly published are Daily Treasury Statement (Cash and Debt Operations of the United States Treasury), Monthly Statement of the Public Debt of the United States, Monthly Treasury Statement of Receipts and Outlays of the U.S. Government, and Monthly Statement of United States Currency and Coin. The comprehensive monthly *Treasury Bulletin*, also regularly issued by the Office of the Secretary, contains data on federal fiscal operations; federal obligations; account of the U.S. Treasury; monetary statistics; federal debt; public debt operations; United States savings bonds; United States savings notes; the ownership of federal securities; the Treasury survey of ownership; the Treasury survey of commercial bank ownership; market quotations on Treasury securities; average yields of long-term bonds; international financial statistics; capital movements; foreign currency positions; and financial operations of government agencies and funds.

The appended tables show the consolidated financial statements of the United States government: Consolidated Statement of Financial Position as of September 30, 1988 and 1987; Consolidated Statement of Operations for the Years Ended September 30, 1988 and 1987; Consolidated Statement of Cash Flow for the Years Ended September 30, 1988 and 1987.

TREASURY DIRECT Investors in Treasury notes, bonds, and bills receive a statement of account, instead of engraved certificates, as evidence of their holdings in government securities. The securities are maintained in book-entry accounts on the records of the U.S. Treasury Department. Such securities are said to be held in Treasury Direct. This procedure is supposed to make investing in new issues of marketable Treasury securities easier, safer, and more convenient.

TREASURY NOTES Interest-bearing company obligations of the U.S. government with intermediate maturities of not less than one year or more than ten years (the latter was changed in 1976—prior maximum maturities were seven years).

Treasury notes are issued in minimum denomination of $5,000 if maturity is less than four years, and $1,000 if maturity is four years or more. Definitive securities were also issued in denominations of

Consolidated Financial Statements
United States Government Consolidated Statement of Financial Position as of September 30, 1988 and 1987 ($ billions)

	1988	1987
Assets		
Cash	44.4	36.4
Other monetary assets	133.4	150.4
Accounts receivable, net of allowances	70.6	67.6
Advances and prepayments	16.9	7.0
Inventories, net	212.5	182.1
Investments, at face value	2.6	3.3
Loans receivable, net of allowances	179.8	194.8
Property, plant, and equipment, net of accumulated depreciation	437.1	453.9
Other assets	87.1	70.1
Total assets	1,184.4	1,165.6
Liabilities		
Accounts payable	100.9	94.9
Interest payable	34.6	31.9
Accrued payroll and benefits	11.9	11.5
Unearned revenue	22.1	7.9
Debt issued under borrowing authority	2,047.8	1,906.3
Pensions and actuarial liabilities	1,257.0	1,265.0
Other liabilities	162.7	137.5
Total liabilities	3,637.0	3,455.0
Accumulated position	- 2,452.6	- 2,289.4

The accompanying notes are an integral part of this statement.

Source: U.S. Department of Treasury.

$10,000, $100,000, and $1,000,000. Interest rates vary from issue to issue.

Notes are now in book-entry form. Notes issued before January 1, 1983, are in coupon, registered, and book-entry forms. Notes issued from January 1, 1983, to August 14, 1986, are in registered and book-entry forms. STRIPS are in book-entry form.

On February 15, 1985, the Department of the Treasury initiated STRIPS (Separate Trading of Registered Interest and Principal of Securities) for notes authorized therefor by the terms of their issue. This program, which grew out of large demand for "stripped" Treasury securities, provides a more efficient treading method for the zero-coupon market and thus lowers the cost of financing the public debt. STRIPS enables depositary financial institutions that maintain book-entry securities accounts at Federal Reserve banks to request that eligible securities accounts be separated into their component parts (principal and interest). In general, Treasury plans

TREASURY NOTES

Consolidated Financial Statements
United States Government Consolidated Statement of Financial Position as of September 30, 1988 and 1987 ($ billions)

	1988	1987
Revenues		
Levied under the Government's sovereign power		
Individual income taxes	473.7	392.6
Corporate income taxes	109.7	83.9
Social insurance taxes and contributions	337.1	303.3
Excise taxes	35.3	32.5
Estate and gift taxes	7.8	7.5
Customs duties	17.9	15.0
Miscellaneous	17.5	18.0
	999.0	852.8
Earned through Government business-type operations		
Sale of goods and services	82.2	52.3
Interest	11.9	13.3
Other	36.9	51.6
Total revenues	1,130.0	970.0
Expenses by agency		
Legislative branch	1.6	1.9
Judicial branch	1.4	1.2
Executive branch		
Office of the President	21.8	24.2
Departments		
Agriculture	68.7	68.0
Commerce	2.3	2.5
Defense	322.8	262.1
Education	18.8	12.9
Energy	16.9	14.5
Health and Human Services	374.4	357.5
Housing and Urban Development	23.7	20.2
Interior	5.7	5.7
Justice	4.3	4.8
Labor	27.1	24.9
State	3.6	3.1
Transportation	26.8	9.8
Treasury	13.7	3.3
Interest on the public debt	168.9	166.2
Independent agencies	174.5	151.5
Total expenses	1,277.0	1,134.3
Excess of expenses over revenues	- 147.0	- 164.3

The accompanying notes are an integral part of this statement.

Consolidated Financial Statements
United States Government Consolidated Statement of Financial Position as of September 30, 1988 and 1987 ($ billions)

	1988	1987
Uses of funds		
Excess of expenses over revenues	147.0	164.3
Less charges not requiring cash in current period:		
Depreciation	44.5	45.8
Pension and payroll benefits	7.8	5.8
Interest	6.5	5.9
Bad debts	17.8	17.5
Cash used in operations	70.4	89.3
Purchase of property and equipment (net of sales of $12.2 in 1988 and $5.3 in 1987)	59.8	165.1
Increase in inventories	30.4	—
Increase in miscellaneous assets	26.9	—
Total uses of funds	187.5	254.4
Sources of funds		
Borrowing from the public	141.5	157.2
Decrease in receivables	12.0	38.9
Decrease in inventories	—	3.2
Decrease in investments	.7	.6
Decrease in miscellaneous assets	—	52.4
Increase in liabilities	40.5	2.3
Total sources of funds	194.7	254.6
Net increase in cash and monetary assets	7.2	.2
Change in valuation of gold at market value	- 16.2	—
Cash and monetary assets at beginning of year	186.8	186.6
Cash and monetary assets at end of year	177.8	186.8

The accompanying notes are an integral part of this statement.

to make the STRIPS program available for new securities with ten or more years of original maturity. Other securities with this feature are noted in the *Monthly Statement of the Public Debt*. On May 1, 1987, the Treasury began the reconstitution of securities within the STRIPS program. Reconstitution is the reassembly of a STRIPS book-entry security into a fully constituted book-entry security after it has been previously separated into its principal and interest components.

Statutory authority for Treasury Notes is found in 31 U.S.C. 3102, 3121. Governing regulations are found in Department Circular No. 300, as revised (31 CFR, Part 306), Department Circulars, Public Debt Series No. 2-86 (31 CFR, Pat 357), for notes issued in Treasury Direct, subject to provisions of the individual offering circular for each issue.

Under the Treasury's program of regular issuance of its basic types of debt issues (bills, notes, and bonds), the usual rotation has called for two-year notes to be auctioned about one week before the end of every month; four-year notes, about the last month of every quarter; and five-year notes, about the middle of the second month of each quarter. Three-year notes occasionally have been used in refunding packages about the middle of a quarter and seven-year and ten-year notes offered as options in quarterly refundings, dated midmonth. In advance of such quarterly refundings, the Treasury has adopted the practice of indicating its cash needs for the quarter and the types of financing being considered, a practice which permits orderly market adjustment and investment planning. They are subject, to full federal taxation (income, capital gains, estate, and gift taxes).

The TAX EQUITY AND FISCAL RESPONSIBILITY ACT OF 1982 requires Treasury notes issued after December 31, 1982, to be in registered or BOOK ENTRY form.

During World War II, the Treasury did not resort to note financing importantly, relying largely on bills and certificates of indebtedness. Beginning in 1949, the Treasury resumed important issuance of notes, particularly as a means of lengthening maturity of the public

Consolidated Financial Statements
United States Government Consolidated Statement of Financial
Position as of September 30, 1988 and 1987 ($ billions)

	1988			1987		
	Actual	Budget [1]	Budget [2]	Actual	Budget [3]	Budget [4]
Budget receipts						
Individual income taxes	401.2	393.4	405.2	392.6	364.0	392.8
Corporation income taxes	94.2	105.6	93.4	83.9	104.8	89.6
Social insurance taxes and contributions	334.3	331.5	335.0	303.3	301.5	301.9
Excise taxes	35.5	35.3	34.7	32.5	32.6	31.9
Estate and gift taxes	7.6	7.6	7.6	7.5	6.0	8.1
Customs duties	16.2	16.4	17.1	15.0	14.4	14.8
Miscellaneous receipts	20.0	19.4	20.4	19.3	19.1	19.4
Total budget receipts	909.0	909.2	913.4	854.1	842.4	858.5
Budget outlays						
Legislative branch	1.9	1.9	1.9	1.8	2.1	2.1
Judicial branch	1.3	1.4	1.4	1.2	1.2	1.2
Executive Office of the President	.1	.1	.1	.1	.1	.1
Funds appropriated to the President	7.3	5.2	9.4	10.4	11.8	12.2
Departments						
Agriculture	44.0	50.7	46.9	49.6	55.1	53.3
Commerce	2.3	2.5	2.5	2.2	2.4	2.5
Defense	304.0	299.6	299.6	294.6	295.1	295.0
Education	18.2	18.8	19.0	16.8	16.8	17.5
Energy	11.2	10.5	10.9	10.7	10.6	10.5
Health and Human Services	373.2	375.1	374.6	351.3	348.2	350.9
Housing and Urban Development	19.0	18.6	19.5	15.5	14.6	15.6
Interior	5.2	5.4	5.4	5.1	5.2	5.4
Justice	5.4	5.2	5.2	4.3	4.8	4.6
Labor	21.9	22.0	22.0	23.5	24.5	24.0
State	3.4	3.3	3.3	2.8	3.3	3.0
Transportation	26.4	26.3	26.1	25.4	26.2	26.8
Treasury	202.5	198.9	202.3	180.3	180.2	182.9
Independent agencies	95.3	88.1	94.4	80.7	85.2	82.5
Undistributed offsetting receipts	-78.5	-77.7	-78.7	-72.4	-71.8	-73.2
Total budget outlays	1,064.1	1,055.9	1,065.8	1,003.9	1,015.6	1,016.9
Total budget deficit	-155.1	-146.7	-152.4	-149.8	-173.2	-158.4

[1] FY 1989 Budget of the U.S. Government, released by the Office of Management and Budget on Feb. 18, 1988.
[2] Midsession review of the FY 1989 Budget, released by the Office of Management and Budget on July 28, 1988.
[3] FY 1988 Budget of the U.S. Government, released by the Office of Management and Budget on Jan. 5, 1987.
[4] Midsession review of the FY 1988 Budget, released by the Office of Management and Budget on Aug. 17, 1987.

debt into the intermediate range, and meeting demand from commercial banks and other institutional investors for spacing of maturities beyond the short-term range.

See UNITED STATES GOVERNMENT SECURITIES.

TREASURY NOTES: FOREIGN-TARGETED In October 1984, the Department of the Treasury began offering foreign-targeted securities. These are Treasury notes that are sold only to foreign institutions or to foreign branches of United States financial institutions, who certify that, as of the date of issuance, the notes are not being acquired for, or for offer to resell to, a Untied States person. However, the securities may be sold to or acquired by U.S. persons following a period of 45 days after the day the securities are auctioned. Foreign-targeted notes may be exchanged for companion domestic securities 45 days after the auction. Interest on these notes is paid annually. The interest rate varies from issue to issue, and is established in the auction of the companion domestic issue.

The notes are in book-entry form. They are also available in registered form 45 days after auction.

Foreign-targeted Treasury notes have a minimum denomination of $5,000 if maturity is less than four years, and $1,000 if maturity is four years or more. Definitive securities are also available in denominations of $10,000, $100,000, and $1,000,000.

Statutory authority for these notes is 31 U.S.C 3103, 3121. Governing regulations are found in Department Circular No. 300, as revised (31 CFR, Pat 306), subject to provisions of the individual offering circular for each issue. Additional information can be obtained from the Office of Financing, Bureau of the Public Debt.

TREASURY NOTES OF 1890 Notes authorized by the Act of July 14, 1890, commonly called the Sherman Silver Purchase Act. The secretary of the Treasury was directed to purchase each month 4,500,000 ounces of fine silver at the market price and to pay for the same with Treasury notes redeemable on demand in coin. It was provided in the act that when the notes should be redeemed or received for dues they might be reissued, but that no greater or less amount of such notes should be "outstanding at any time than the cost of the silver bullion and the standard silver dollars coined therefrom, then held in the Treasury, purchased by such notes."

The authority for the purchase of silver bullion under this act was repealed by the Act of November 1, 1893, up to which date the government had purchased 168.7 million fine ounces, at a cost of $155.9 million, for which Treasury notes were issued. Compounding the problem of shrinkage in the nation's gold caused by fears of currency inflation from issuance of such silver-backed Treasury notes of 1890, President Cleveland shortly after becoming President announced that Treasury notes of 1890 would be redeemed in gold, presumably to allay such fears but instead aggravating the run on the nation's gold. To replenish the nation's gold, the President resorted to the controversial purchase of gold coin from a syndicate of U.S. and foreign bankers, paid for by long-term government bonds at premium interest rates. With the success of the Republican Party in the presidential election of 1896, on a platform favoring the gold standard, domestic and international runs on the U.S. Treasury's gold supply abated, aided and abetted by inflows of gold from Europe as the result of higher prices and quantities for U.S. farm exports. The Gold Standard Act of 1900 definitely adopted the gold standard, by declaring the gold dollar to be the monetary standard of the nation, establishing a $150 million reserve in the Treasury for the redemption of paper money, and providing that all forms of money issued or coined be kept at a parity with gold. Treasury notes redeemed in standard silver dollars were canceled and retired in accordance with the requirements of the Act of 1890.

Sections 5 and 8 of the Act of March 14, 1900, also provided for the cancellation and retirement of Treasury notes to an amount equal to the coinage of standard silver dollars and subsidiary silver from the bullion purchased with such notes. By 1915, all but $2.25 million had been retired. Since these notes were retired as fast as received by the Treasury Department and supplanted by silver certificates supported by silver coin previously purchased with the Treasury notes, for all practical purposes, they ceased to be an active form of currency. In October, 1922, circulation statements began carrying the amount of Treasury notes of 1890 at about $1 million; in recent years, the amount has been "less than $500,000," apparently an irreducible amount traceable to export, loss, or other causes.

Before the Thomas Amendment of May 12, 1933, which made all forms of currency legal tender, and the joint resolution of Congress of June 5, 1933, these notes were legal tender for all debts, public and private, except where otherwise expressly stipulated in the contract.

See MONETARY STOCK; TREASURY, SECRETARY OF THE.

TREASURY SECURITIES Interest-bearing and non-interest-bearing obligations of the U.S. government issued by the Treasury as a means of borrowing money to meet government expenditures not covered by tax revenues and for other purposes.

Marketable Treasury securities fall into four categories (see separate entries for each of the following): TREASURY BILLS, TREASURY NOTES, TREASURY BONDS, AND FOREIGN-TARGETED TREASURY NOTES. Marketable Treasury obligations are currently issued in book-entry form; the purchaser receives a statement rather than an engraved certificate.

Nonmarketable issues include the following:
A. Offered to the general public (see separate entry under UNITED STATES SAVINGS BONDS):
  1. U.S. savings bonds, Series EE and HH
  2. U.S. savings bonds, Series E and H
  3. U.S. savings notes (withdrawn from sale)
  4. Foreign-targeted Treasury notes
B. Offered to specific investors:
  1. **State and local government series.** Form includes certificates of indebtedness, notes, and bonds in book-entry form. Denominations are $1,000 minimum; larger amounts in $100 multiples. Maturities are up to one year for certificates; one to ten years for notes; more than ten years for bonds. Interest rate varies, depending upon prevailing Treasury rates and the rate paid by state or local governments on their own financing, the proceeds of which are invested in these securities. Interest is accrued and added to principal daily. These bonds are offered to state and local governments as a medium for investing proceeds of their own financing in compliance with the arbitrage provisions of the Internal Revenue Service regulations. These securities may be redeemed prior to maturity on 15 days' notice, anytime after 25 days from issuance in the case of certificates and one year from issuance in the case of notes and bonds. An appropriate interest rate adjustment and penalty may be assessed in cases of redemptions prior to maturity.
  2. **Demand depositary securities.** These securities are certificates of indebtedness in book-entry form issued in denominations of $1,000 minimum and any increment above that amount. Interest rate varies, based on an adjustment of the federal funds rate. Interest is accrued and added to principal daily. The Tax Reform act of 1986 imposed arbitrage rebate requirements on issuers of tax-exempt bonds and directed the Treasury to offer a money market-type investment vehicle. The security is treated as a tax-exempt bond under the Internal Revenue Code and therefore enables entities to invest proceeds of tax-exempt bonds in an obligation that avoids the earning of rebatable arbitrage. Maturity is one day. Securities are automatically rolled over each day unless redemption is requested. One day's notice of redemption is required.
  3. **Depositary bonds.** Bonds in book-entry form, denominations of $1,000, maturity of 12 years from issue, and interest rate of 2%. These bonds are offered to depositaries and financial agents designated under the provisions of Title 12, U.S., for use as collateral to secure deposits of government moneys. These bonds may be redeemed prior to maturity on 30 days' notice by either party.
  4. **Rural Electric Authority bonds.** These securities are in the form of certificates of indebtedness and bonds in book-entry form with maturities of 12 years on bonds and 1 year on certificates. Interest rates are 2% on bonds and 5% on certificates. They are issued in denominations of $1,000. These securities are offered to electric and telephone cooperatives as an investment medium for unexpended loan proceeds from the Rural Electrification Authority or Rural Telephone Bank (in the case of certificates). The REA does not permit the draw-down of a loan until the monies are needed. R.E.A. series bonds are redeemable prior to maturity on not less than 30 days' nor more than 60 days' notice. Certificates are redeemable prior to maturity on one week's notice after one month from the issue date. REA approval is reburied for an investment in bonds, and they may be redeemed at the option of the United States or the owner.
  5. **Government account series.** These securities are in the form of bills, certificates, notes, and bonds in book-entry form. Denominations are in multiples of $1,000. Interest and maturity date varies. Interest rate depends on prevailing Treasury rates. Certain trust fund statutes require the secretary of the Treasury, as trustee, to invest the moneys held by the funds and authorize the issuance to the funds of nonmarketable "special" securities, not offered to the public. The following trust funds may obtain, under the terms of their authorizing statutes, special issuances of securities under Title 31 U.S.C.: Civil Service Retirement Fund; Social Security Trust Funds; Federal Deposit Insurance Corporation; Federal Savings and Loan Insurance Corporation; Railroad Retirement Funds; and Unemployment Trust Fund.
  6. **Foreign series—government.** These securities assume the form of bills, certificates of indebtedness, notes, and bonds in book-entry form. Maturities and interest rates vary from issue to issue. Treasury securities in the form of foreign currency series were first issued in 1961. These securities have been used to deal with some aspects of dollar accumulations by foreign financial authorities and to facilitate U.S. foreign exchange operations. Treasury securities in the form of foreign series issuances to foreign governments or foreign central banks have been issued since 1962. Special operations, primarily involving the Export-Import Bank's loans to foreign countries for military material purchases in the United States, gave rise to these securities. Short-term foreign currency-denominated issuances (bills and certificates) are usually redeemable at any time, in whole or in part, on two days' notice. Notes and bonds, as well as all dollar-denominated issuances, are redeemable prior to maturity, in whole or in part, as per agreement, which may call for notice as short as two days. Dollar-connected issuances, in certain cases, have penalty provisions connected with premature redemptions.
  7. **U.S. retirement plan bonds (withdrawn from sale).** The Self-Employed Individuals Tax Retirement Act provided a mechanism whereby self-employed individuals could establish pension plans for themselves and their employees to obtain tax-sheltered benefits similar to those available to participants in employer pension plans. U.S. retirement plan bonds were authorized as one alternative mode of investment under the terms of the act. These bonds were first issued January 1, 1983. Rates were increased to maintain parity with savings bonds. The securities were registered in names of natural persons in single ownership or beneficiary form and were nontransferable. The offering of these bonds was terminated as of April 30, 1982, based on the secretary's decision that the low volume of sales and the

existence of adequate other forms of Keogh investment did not warrant continuation of the offering.

8. **U.S. individual retirement bonds (withdrawn from sale).** The Employees Retirement Income Security Act of 1974 provided a mechanism whereby individuals not covered under any other pension plan could invest for retirement purposes in an IRA form of savings arrangement and obtain tax benefits similar to those of participants in other pension plans. U.S. individual retirement bonds were authorized to provide on alternative mode of IRA investment under the terms of the act. The offerings of these bonds were terminated as of April 30, 1982, based on the Secretary's decision that the low volume of sales and the existence of adequate other forms of IRA investment did not warrant continuation of the offering.

Non-interest-bearing debt includes Guaranty Insurance Company tax and loss bonds and certain matured and other debt:

a) **Mortgage Guaranty Issuance Company tax and loss bonds.** These are nonmarketable bonds with ten years maturity from date of issue registered in exact amount paid by purchaser and nontransferable. The bonds have been issued since March 18, 1968, and are offered for sale only to companies organized and engaged in the business of writing mortgage guaranty insurance within the United States. The securities are not subject to call for redemption by the secretary of the Treasury prior to maturity, but may be redeemed in whole or in part at the owner's option at any time after three months from issue date.

b) **Matured and other debt.** Matured and other debt may be classified as follows: (1) Matured securities described above that are still outstanding, (2) certain obsolete forms of currency (e.g., silver certificates, U.S. notes, fractional currency, etc.) that comprise outstanding debt but are not subject to the debt limitation, (3) outstanding matured securities that were not issued under Chapter 31 of Title 31, United States Code, and, therefore, are not subject to the debt limitation (e.g., postal savings bonds, first liberty bonds, Treasury savings certificates, thrift and Treasury savings stamps, and other old debt), (4) Federal Financing bank bills which, by the terms of their authorizing statute, are not subject to the debt limitation, and (5) various matured Chapter 31, Title 31, United States Code issuances that are still outstanding and subject to the debt limitation, but are not issued any longer (e.g., liberty bonds other than first liberty bonds, Victory notes, adjusted service bonds, Armed Forces leave bonds, Treasury bonds—Investment series excess profits tax refund bonds, and U.S. savings stamps).

Chapter 31, Section 3101, of Title 31, United States Code, as amended, provides a limitation on the amount of public debt the United States can have outstanding at any given time. The following items enter into the computation of the public debt that is subject to that statutory limit:

1. The total amount of outstanding public debt securities issued under Chapter 31 of Title 31, United States Code. These issuances are described in detail above.
2. Certain federal agency obligations that are guaranteed as to principal and interest by the United States by the statute authorizing their issuance. Currently, the only outstanding, nonmmatured securities of this type are certain Federal Housing Administration debentures. There are also negligible outstanding amounts of matured guaranteed issuances of the Federal Farm Mortgage Corporation and the Home Owners' Loan Corporation.
3. Certain participation certificates issued by the Federal National Mortgage Association and the Export-Import Bank.

For additional information consult the Office of Financing, Bureau of the Public Debt.
See PUBLIC DEBT, UNITED STATES GOVERNMENT SECURITIES.

BIBLIOGRAPHY

FABOZZI, F. J. *Handbook of Treasury Securities.* Probus Publishing Co., Chicago, IL, 1987.
Handbook of Securities of the United States Government and Federal Agencies. First Bost Corporation, latest edition.
The U.S. Government Securities Market. Harris Trust & Savings Bank. Latest edition.
STIGUM, MARCIA. *The Money Market.* Latest edition.

TREASURY STATEMENT In February, 1954, the Treasury's reporting of receipts and disbursements of the federal government was changed so as to convert the "Daily Statement of the U.S. Treasury" from a statement of classified receipts and disbursements into a statement of cash deposits and withdrawals affecting the general account of the Treasurer of the United States, together with closing cash balances for the day in the account of the Treasurer of the United States. Thus, the daily statement presented the government's cash condition. In addition, it reported a summary of Treasury assets and liabilities.

The revised "Daily Statement of the United States Treasury" went into effect July, 1974. It reflects current-day activity based on telephone and wire reports from the Federal Reserve System and internal Treasury sources. The statement has become fully functional, providing more timely and detailed information. It provides data as follows:

Table I: Operating Cash Balance (Combined Closing Balances in Federal Reserve Account, and in Tax and Loan Note Accounts).
Table II: Deposits and Withdrawals of Operating Cash, in detail.
Table III-A: Public Debt Transactions (Issues and Redemptions).
Table III-B: Adjustment of Public Debt Transactions to Cash Basis.
Table III-C: Debt Subject to (Statutory) Limit.
Table IV: Federal Tax Deposit System Activities.
Table V: Tax and Loan Note Accounts by Depository Category.
Table VI: Memorandum Information, Income Tax Refunds Issued.

A revised monthly budgetary statement, the "Monthly Statement of Receipts and Outlays of the U.S. Government," was concurrently established as the key statement with which all other government reports relating to receipts and expenditures shall be consistent (including the *Budget of the U.S. Government*, the *Combined Statement of Receipts, Expenditures and Balances of the U.S. Government*, the *Annual Report on the State of the Finances*, the monthly *Treasury Bulletin*, and other reports of government agencies showing cash receipts and disbursements prepared for use of the government and the public).

BIBLIOGRAPHY

U.S. TREASURY DEPARTMENT. Office of the Secretary. *Annual Report on the State of the Finances.* Annual.
———. *Treasury Bulletin.*

TREASURY STOCK A corporation's own capital stock that has been fully paid for by stockholders, legally issued, reacquired by the corporation, and held by the corporation for future reissuance. The reacquisition of the shares reduces shareholders' equity. Treasury stock is not an asset because the corporation cannot own itself. Neither can a corporation recognize a gain or a loss when reacquiring or reissuing its own stock. Treasury stock is treated as a reduction of stockholders' equity. Treasury stock does not possess voting rights or the preemptive right, nor does it share in dividend distributions or in assets at liquidation.

Treasury stock does not give the corporation the right to vote, to exercise preemptive rights as a stockholder, to receive dividends, or to receive assets upon corporate liquidation.

Corporations purchase their outstanding stock for a variety of reasons:

1. To meet employee stock compensation contracts or merger needs.
2. To increase earnings per share by reducing the shares outstanding.

3. To abort a takeover attempt or to reduce the number of stockholders
4. To make a market in the stock.
5. To facilitate a leveraged buyout.

Treasury stock is not an asset. When shares are acquired and held for reissue, the effect is a reduction in capital and is so reported in the financial statements as a deduction from stockholders' equity or as a deduction from issued shares of the same class. In rare instances, Treasury stock has been reported as an asset, especially if the shares have been reacquired to meet employee compensation contracts. Treasury stock is essentially unissued capital stock. It can be reported in the stockholders' equity section of the balance sheet as contra to shareholders' equity as follows:

Contributed capital:

Common stock	XXX
Additional paid-in capital	XXX
Total contributed capital	XXX
Retained earnings	XXX
Less: Treasury stock (10,000 shares at cost)	(15,000)
Total stockholders' equity	$XXXXXX

TREASURY TAX AND SAVINGS NOTES

Series A and B of Treasury tax and savings notes were first offered in 1941 to serve as media for the payment of taxes and were of interest to large taxpayers for investment of tax reserves pending payment of taxes. Beginning in 1942, only Series C notes were issued, which were three-year, noncallable, nontransferable notes, issued at par. The last issue outstanding matured April 15, 1956. The Treasury discontinued sales of Series C notes in October, 1953.

See UNITED STATES GOVERNMENT SECURITIES.

TREND

The direction that the economy or market is taking over an extended period of time. The secular trend of a time series is probably best represented graphically by a straight line or a smooth curve, since growth or decay typically proceeds gradually without abrupt changes in direction. A straight line on an arithmetic chart indicates that the amount of change was the same each year or period. A statistical measure of secular trend provides useful information about the change in the statistical series. It indicates how the series has grown in the past and can be used to forecast future changes. The trendline can also be used to adjust a series to take out the effect of the long-term trend to isolate nontrend fluctuations, such as the business cycle.

TRIAL OF THE PYX

An annual ceremony required by the British coinage laws for the purpose of testing the weight and fineness of gold and silver coins to see that the coinage laws are being complied with. The pyx is a box in which specimen coins made at the mint are preserved. The test is conducted by a jury consisting of the Goldsmiths' Company, summoned by the lord chancellor. When coinage was done by contract, the trial, held at irregular intervals, had some importance, since the contractors were not entitled to full payment until after such trial. Since coinage has been conducted by the government mint, the trial of the pyx is largely a perfunctory ceremony. Also, in modern times, the trend has been to increase circulation of paper currency and withdraw coinage, particularly gold coins.

In the United States, this term by analogy would refer to the annual trial of the coins by the annual ASSAY COMMISSION, a test of the fineness and weight of coins manufactured at each new minting to determine whether or not the variation is in excess of the limits of error permitted by the law.

See REMEDY ALLOWANCE, TOLERANCE.

TRIAL BALANCE

A list of ledger accounts and amounts. A trial balance provides evidence of the equality of total debits and credits in the ledger. The equality of debits and credits on a trial balance does not prove that the correct accounts were debited and credited. Trial balances can be taken at various times during the accounting cycle and therefore provide unadjusted, adjusted, and postclosing trial balances. A condensed trial balance would appear as follows:

	Debits	Credits
Assets	XXX	
Liabilities		XXX
Owners' equity		XXX
Revenues		XXX
Expenses	XXX	
Total	XXX	XXX

Note that assets and expense accounts usually have debit balances; revenue, liability, and owners' equity accounts usually have credit balances. This is a result of the basic rules for double-entry accounting.

TRIPLE WITCHING HOUR

At the end of every quarter, program traders must unwind their positions because the index futures and options expire. The last hour of trading on the stock exchange during the last day of each quarter has come to be known as the "triple witching hour," the hour at which futures, options, and index option contracts all expire. Some of these days have been marked by extreme volatility in the market, as program traders have dumped large volumes of stock on the market. This raised concerns in some quarters as to how this volatility should be managed.

TROUBLED DEBT RESTRUCTURING

A debt restructuring in which the creditor, because of the debtor's financial difficulties, grants a concession to the debtor at a point earlier than the scheduled maturity date. The two principal types of debt restructuring include a transfer of assets or equity interest from a debtor to a creditor in full settlement of a debt and a modification of terms. Modification of terms include such arrangements as interest rate reductions or maturity date extensions. Debtors experience gains and creditors recognize losses on troubled debt restructurings.

The accounting procedures for troubled debt restructurings can be summarized as follows for the debtor and creditor as shown in the appended table on the following page.

BIBLIOGRAPHY

FINANCIAL ACCOUNTING STANDARDS BOARD. *Statement of Financial Accounting Standards No. 15*, "Accounting by Debtors and Creditors for Troubled Debt Restructuring," 1977.

TRIANGULAR EXCHANGE

See ARBITRAGE.

TROY WEIGHT

A system of weights, used by the Mint, jewelers, and apothecaries. The apothecaries' table of weights is as follows:

20 grains = 1 scruple
3 scruples = 1 dram
8 drams = 1 ounce
12 ounces = 1 pound.

The Mint and jewelers' table of weights is as follows:

24 grains = 1 pennyweight
20 pennyweights = 1 ounce
12 ounces = 1 pound.

The grain is the same weight in both tables, there being 5,760 grains to the troy pound.

TRUNCATION

A system under which only a monthly statement is sent to the bank depositor who drew the checks by the bank on which the checks were drawn, without the canceled checks.

When the bank depositor draws the checks and sends them to the recipients for various types of payments, the first banks to receive the checks will be those banks with which the recipients of the checks make their deposits. Truncation would involve such first receiving

Troubled Debt Restructuring

Form of restructure	Accounting for debtor and creditor
Settlement of debt:	
Transfer of assets.	Debtor recognizes gain; creditor recognizes loss on restructure. Debtor recognizes gain or loss on asset transfer.
Granting an equity interest.	Debtor recognizes gain; creditor recognizes loss on restructure.
Modified terms; debt continues:	
Carrying amount of debt is less than total future cash.	No gain or loss is recognized on restructure; however, a new effective interest rate must be computed.
Carrying amount of debt is greater than total future cash.	Gain or loss is recognized on restructure; debt reduced to the amount of future cash flows. No interest expense or income is recognized in subsequent periods when only principal is repaid over the remaining life of the loan.

banks *not* sending the checks deposited on to the banks on which the checks are drawn for presentation via clearing and collection. Instead, the first receiving banks, it is proposed, would *keep* the checks deposited (drawn on the payor banks) and merely send payment instructions to the payor banks by electronic communication.

Consequently, the banks on which the checks are drawn would not receive any canceled checks to send to the depositor along with the monthly statement. A monthly statement would be sent out, but it would be a computerized statement of deposits and withdrawals in the bank depositor's account, including the debits represented by the payor bank's remittances to the first receiving bank (pursuant to the latter's instructions as to payment) for the checks deposited by check recipients with first receiving banks.

BIBLIOGRAPHY

BOARD OF GOVERNORS OF THE FEDERAL RESERVE SYSTEM. *Fee Schedule for Commercial Check Services*, Federal Reserve Regulatory Service, Volume III.

TRUST This term has two meanings:

1. A popular name for a business combination controlling a large number of plants or stores; a combination of business enterprises for the purpose of eliminating competition and securing greater economies of production and distribution. Technically, a trust obtains control of an industry by combining the leading companies therein through the medium of a trust agreement whereby all of the stock of member companies is centralized in a board of trustees and stockholders receive in exchange trustee certificates, evidencing a proportionate interest. The board of trustees chooses the directors of the member companies, can remove them at will, determines the allocation of earnings and dividends, and can order member companies to become inactive so as to centralize operations in a few members and thus lessen the supply of output for the industry at pegged prices. See SHERMAN ANTITRUST ACT.
2. As defined by Bogert, "a fuduciary relationship in which one person is the holder of the legal title to property, subject to an equitable obligation to keep or use the property for the benefit of another"; as defined by Blackstone, "an estate devised or granted in confidence that the devisee or grantee shall convey it, or dispose of the profits, at the will of or for the benefit of another; an estate held for the use of another."

From early times trusts have had for their purpose the preservation of property in order that favored individuals or institutions might benefit as recipients of the income from the principal of the trusts or come into the possession of the principal itself. In the establishment of a trust, there are customarily three principal parties involved: (1) the trustor, or party creating the trust, who is also known as the settlor, grantor, or donor, (2) the beneficiary, or one for whose benefit the fund is established, and (3) the trustee, who is charged with the management and preservation of the property which constitutes the trust estate.

The administration of trusts usually proceeds without any involvement of the courts. Trust administration involves primarily the prudent management of funds to provide continuing benefits to an income beneficiary and then to a remainderman. Estate administration is primarily a liquidating process.

Classified by origin, trusts may be created by a declaration or DEED OF TRUST or by WILL. The former, popularly known as living trusts, personal trusts, or voluntary trusts, may take effect immediately upon the execution of the instrument. Unless the trustor expressly reserves the right to modify or revoke, such a trust becomes irrevocable even by the trustor himself, except that in most jurisdictions a trust whose objects have been accomplished or a passive trust may be revoked with the consent of all parties beneficially interested. A LIVING TRUST may be created for the benefit of the trustor himself or for other persons, and the trustor may make himself a sole trustee or a trustee jointly with others for the benefit of a third party. The terms of a testamentary trust, i.e., one created by will, cannot be altered after the death of the testator.

Various circumstances have operated to increase public interest in trusts and in the creation of trust estates. Ambitious persons desire to create a competence for themselves in old age and to insure the education and support of their children during the period of their infancy. But if property is left in the children's own hands, there is always the possibility of its being dissipated. On the other hand, if it is given outright to relatives, the property may be squandered or the beneficiary may be the victim of unscrupulous persons or well-intentioned but inexperienced advisers. Consequently, trusts have been placed in the hands of trusted, experienced, and conscientious persons or corporations (banks and trust companies) that will administer the property and its income in accordance with the desire of the testator or trustor, as expressed in the will or deed of trust.

Among the various types of trusts in terms of provisions affecting distribution to the beneficiaries are the following: (1) trusts in which the income is to be periodically paid over to the trustor himself, or to the wife, child, parent, or friend of the trustor, or to a charitable or other institution, (2) trusts in which the income is to be accumulated for a minor until he or she arrives at the age of majority, (3) trusts in which the principal is to be paid over to one beneficiary at a certain age (the remainderman), the income in the meanwhile being paid to another or the same beneficiary (the life-tenant), and (4) trusts in which the principal is to be paid to the beneficiary upon marriage as a marriage settlement.

Because of the nature and responsibility of the relationship brought into existence by the establishment of a trust, the law has surrounded the administration of trust funds with numerous safeguards for the protection of all concerned. Among these safeguards are the following: (1) the trustee must keep accurate accounts of the funds held, invested, and distributed, and trust funds must be kept entirely segregated from individual or corporate assets, (2) the trustee must comply with the wishes of the trustor in carrying out the terms of the trust, (3) the trustee is not permitted to take advantage of his position to profit at the disadvantage of the beneficiaries, and (4) unless the character of the investments has been prescribed by the trustor, the trustee is bound to confine himself to the class of investments permitted by the law of the state as being legal for trust funds.

Although the law places safeguards around trust funds, it has also prevented the locking up of such funds beyond a reasonable length of time. To circumvent this tendency, which arises from the natural desire to retain in the family the property which it has acquired, two rules have been written into the trust laws of most states, e.g., New York. One of these is the RULE AGAINST PERPETUITIES, which makes a gift void if the vesting of title is postponed beyond two lives in being and the minority of a third life. The other law is that no funds may be placed in trust for the accumulation of income except during the period of legal infancy of one or more minor beneficiaries then in being. The objects of this law are to avoid concentration of wealth in one family and to insure the reentry of the trust funds into the normal channels of business.

The compensation of the trustee is usually agreed upon between the trustor and trustee; if not, the fee is determined by statutory provisions or court direction.

Elements associated with the creation of a trust include the following:

1. Trustor must have legal capacity.
2. Trustor must intend to create a trust.
3. The trust must have a trustee.
4. The beneficiary of the trust must be identifiable at the time the trust is created.
5. Trust property must exist at the time the trust is created.

There are a variety of trusts, some of which are noted here:

1. Inter vivos trust created by trustor while living.
2. Testamentary trust created by a will.
3. Charitable trust, which has as its object some recognized social benefit.
4. Clifford trust, in which the creator retains rights to possession of trust property after a stated period of time or upon the occurrence of a stated event.
5. Spendthrift trust, designed to protect a beneficiary from creditors or from his or her squandering the assets of the trust.
6. Implied trust, which is presumed by the court to exist or is imposed by a court.
7. Active trust, wherein the trustee has some specific duties to perform. Passive trusts do not impose specific duties on the trustee; the trustee merely holds the legal title of the trust property until ownership passes.
8. Totten trust relates to a bank savings account that depositor opens as "John Doe in trust for Bill Doe."
9. Discretionary trust, in which the trustee pays the beneficiary only as much as the trustee determines to be appropriate.
10. Support trust, in which the trustee pays the beneficiary only as much as is required to educate and support the beneficiary.

See TRUST COMPANY, TRUST FUND INVESTMENTS. For bibliography, see under TRUST COMPANY.

TRUST COMPANY As defined by the New York banking law, a "corporation organized for the purpose of taking, accepting and executing such trusts as may be lawfully committed to it, acting as trustee in the cases prescribed by law, receiving deposits of money and other personal property, and issuing its obligation therefor, and lending money on real and personal securities."

"Technically speaking, a trust company is a corporation organized for the purpose of accepting and executing trusts, acting as trustee under wills, bond issues, registrar of bonds and stocks, executor or administrator of estates, etc., although by law and practice trust companies may do a general banking business, but do not issue currency" (W. H. Kniffin, *The Practical Work of a Bank*).

In speaking of the diversity of trust companies' functions, Clay Herrick (*Trust Companies*) writes that the term "is applied to corporations whose functions vary greatly. Some are simply banks of deposit and discount; many are savings banks; some are safe-deposit companies; some are title-insurance or fidelity insurance companies; some serve chiefly as fiscal agents for corporations, and as registrars, transfer agents, intermediaries in reorganizations, promoters, etc.; some devote themselves to the care of estates and to services as executors, administrators, guardians, trustees, etc. Most companies combine two or more of these classes of functions, while a few undertake nearly all of them. In early years the life insurance and trust businesses were intimately associated."

Originally, trust companies were created to act as incorporated trustees. In acting in various trust capacities, administration of estates, custodianship of funds, trusteeship under mortgage indentures, etc., they naturally came into possession of large sums of money and securities, and accordingly it became necessary to extend their functions beyond those of a merely fiduciary character. Insofar as cash was handled, banking operations became necessary, and the handling of securities made necessary the development of investment and safe deposit departments. For these reasons, a modern trust company's operations are not much different from those of a large bank. Recent legislation has tended to eliminate the difference between trust companies and banks, and in most states trust companies are now permitted by law to perform all the functions of a bank in addition to trust functions.

The trust functions of a trust company are divided into two broad classes, individual trusts and corporate trusts. Individual trusts act in the following capacities: executor, administrator, trustee, guardian, conservator, custodian, committee in lunacy, etc. Corporate trusts act in the following capacities: fiscal agent (e.g., paying agent for interest coupons and dividends); registrar of stock; transfer agent; trustee under a deed of trust; depositary for protective committees, reorganization committees, etc.; escrow agent; etc.

Individual trusts might be established for the following situations listed below:

1. For individuals with lack of business experience.
2. For individuals in poor health.
3. For absentee property owners.
4. For the aged.
5. For persons traveling in foreign countries.

In such cases the trust company will take complete charge of the entire property and assets of the individual, collecting any income such as from interest, coupons, dividends, annuities, pensions, notes, accounts, bonds, mortgages, and land contracts. In case of real property, it keeps up repairs, taxes, and insurance and reinvests income and principal.

Corporate trusts provide any of the following functions:

1. Trustee under a mortgage securing an issue of bonds.
   a. Act as agent and representative for bondholders.
   b. Act as agent and representative for bondholders in case of acts of default or foreclosure.
   c. Serve as custodian and manager of sinking fund.
2. Fiscal or financial agent of municipal or private corporations.
   a. Pay bonds, coupons, and interest.
   b. Attend to publication and amending of notices.
   c. Act as agent for syndicate, managing voting trusts, etc., issuing and collecting calls for installment payments and computing and distributing to proper parties the amounts of participation in profits or proceeds.
   d. Serve as depository of cash and securities for underwriting syndicates, etc.
   e. Receive subscriptions to stocks and bonds and handle the same when issued.
3. Transfer agent and registrar. (Knowledge of laws and great care and accuracy are essential for a transfer agent; prevention of overissue is the function of the registrar, which must be a different organization from the issuer of bonds.)
4. Depositary for protective committees and reorganization committees.
5. Escrow agent.

Trust companies carry on and work in departments, the most common being banking, trust, and safe deposit. Larger trust companies are veritable financial department stores and may have in addition the following departments: bond and investment department, mortgage department, transfer (or registration) department, real estate department, organization department, title insurance department, and women's department.

Much of the business of a trust company can be divided into kinds of trustee work on this basis:

1. Business as trustee or agent for individuals under private agreement.
2. Probate business.
3. Real estate business.
4. Investment business.
5. Insolvency business.
6. Business as trustee or agent for corporations.
7. Business as transfer agent and registrar for corporations.
8. Corporate reorganization and financing.
9. Title insurance.
10. Safe deposit business.
11. Savings and banking business.
12. Miscellaneous business.

Trust companies lay claim to the following advantages over an individual trustee:

1. **Perpetual existence.** The trust company is permanent, while the individual trustee may resign, die, or become incapacitated.
2. **Superior responsibility.** The trust company is required to keep its trust funds separate from its banking assets. The trust department is subject to examination by the state banking department; in case of trust institution failure, trust funds are held intact for the beneficiaries and cannot be levied upon by the company's general creditors. In many states, moreover, a trust company must make a deposit of securities with the state banking department as a guarntee of faithful discharge of its duties.
3. **Permanent location.** The trust company has an established place of doing business; it does not move away and is accessible every business day.
4. **Superior facilities.** A trust company can employ experts on investments, and by maintaining a highly specialized accounting system and safe deposit and banking departments, it can furnish better facilities.
5. **Greater economy.** A trust company is not required to give bond, which is a saving to the estate. The presumption is that since a trust company is an authority on investments, better protection against unnecessary losses and a more certain income can be secured in the investment of trust funds. By making a specialty of the business, the trust company can better protect the interests of the estate.

BIBLIOGRAPHY

COMPTROLLER OF THE CURRENCY. *Comptroller's Manual for National Banks*, Part 9, Fiduciary Powers of National Banks and Collective Invetment Funds.
Trusts and Estates.

TRUST COMPANY STOCKS See BANK SECURITIES.

TRUST DEED See DEED OF TRUST.

TRUST DEPARTMENT The department of a national or state bank that engages in trust work.

National banks desiring to exercise fiduciary powers shall file an application with the Comptroller of the Currency pursuant to 12 CFR 4.7b. "Fiduciary powers" means the powers to act in any fiduciary capacity authorized by the Act of September 28, 1962, 12 U.S.C. 92a. Under that act, authorization for national banks to exercise fiduciary powers was transferred from the Board of Governors of the Federal Reserve System to the Comptroller of the Currency.

In the case of state-chartered banks becoming members of the Federal Reserve System, such banks shall retain their full charter and statutory rights as state banks or trust companies and may continue to exercise all corporate powers granted to them by the state in which they were chartered. Examinations of state member banks are a condition of membership of such banks in the Federal Reserve System, but directors of the district Federal Reserve bank may approve the examinations made by the state authorities and accept same in lieu of examinations made by Federal Reserve examiners.

In most states, state banks are permitted to organize trust departments. In all cases, a trust department of a bank must keep its trust records and assets segregated from its banking records and assets.

The bookkeeping must be regarded as distinct. If trust funds are deposited in the banking department, they must be secured by a deposit of U.S. bonds or other approved securities. Securities and assets belonging to each separate trust must, moreover, be kept separate from one another. Trust employees are required to furnish bond for the faithful performance of their duties.
See TRUST COMPANY.

BIBLIOGRAPHY

"The Small Guys." *United States Banker*, February, 1989.
TOBIN, M. "Shakeout in Trust." *United States Banker*, February, 1989.
"Trust Products: Consider the Risks." *Magazine of Bank Administration*, January, 1989.
WHITNEY, V. P. *Trust Department Administration and Operations.* Two looseleaf volumes. Periodic supplementation.

TRUST DEPOSITS DEPOSITS that are made by one person as trustee for another person. Such deposits are made under trustee account agreements executed in advance and are subject to the terms and conditions of such agreements. Despite the usual provisions in such agreements for acquittance and discharge of the bank for withdrawals by the trustee where a trustee has both a personal account and a trustee account in the same bank, the bank might become subject to constructive notice and duty of inquiry in cases of loss to beneficiaries through steady and large withdrawals from the trustee account to the personal account.

TRUSTEE A person or corporation to whom a trust is committed. Federal and state laws permit a trust company or trust department of a bank to accept and execute any trust which is lawful for an individual. Generally, any qualified person capable of taking legal title may become a trustee.
See TRUST.

TRUSTEE SHARES Certificates of beneficial interest in an investment company of the fixed trust type, representing an interest in the securities held under the trust. If there are no bonds or debentures and only one class of stock is issued against the securities held in the investment company, a single trustee share represents that proportion of the undivided equity in the total amount of securities in the trust as one trustee share bears to the total proportion of the undivided equity in the total amount of number issued.
See INVESTMENT COMPANY.

TRUST ESTATE An estate the equitable title to which belongs to one person, but the legal title, possession, and management of which are entrusted to another person or corporation as trustee. The income of such estate belongs to the equitable owner, i.e., the beneficiary, or CESTUI QUE TRUST.
See TRUST.

TRUST FUND INVESTMENTS The duty of a trustee with respect to authorized investments is determined by the instructions of the settlor (creator of the trust) in the trust instrument: (1) the instructions may specify the classes or types of investments in which the trustee shall invest; (2) retention and/or continued investment in the types of investments made by the settlor and conveyed in trust may be directed; or (3) the trustee may be given partial or complete discretion to invest. In discharging his responsibility, the trustee is required to follow the directions of the settlor with due prudence and skill. Courts may intervene to authorize trustees to take different action if following the settlor's instructions might work to the disadvantage of the beneficiaries. The courts hold trustees to a strict construction of the settlor's directions which deviate from usual trustee investments.

Where there are no settlor's instructions or court directions otherwise, the state statutes may govern, depending on whether they are mandatory or permissive. Where the trustee chooses to follow permissive statutes, he must still show exercise of reasonable care and skill. The trustee may choose to invest outside the statutes, but if so, he must likewise show care and skill. Besides trustees under formal trust instruments, such fiduciaries as executors, administrators, and other persons or institutions holding trust funds for investment are subject to the statutes and court decisions. Even if income payments to the beneficiaries are involved in a trust, the primary responsibility of the trustee is conservation of principal.

TRUST FUNDS

The two basic regulatory approaches to investing by fiduciaries are the statutory approach, prescribing limitations on such investing to specified classes of investments by general or detailed statute, and the prudent man rule (*Harvard College* v. *Amory*, 9 Pick. (Mass.) 446, 1831), authorized as such in the statute or the settled doctrine of cases and authorizing in general terms investment in such securities "as would be acquired by prudent men of discretion and intelligence in such matters who are seeking a reasonable income and the preservation of their capital."

The pressure for performance and the erosion in purchasing power of fixed incomes caused by inflation have contributed to the trend toward allowing equities, with the constraint of the prudent man rule, as legal investments for trust funds not bound by specific directions or constraints. But such investments in equities inevitably involve more instability in income and in value of principal, an important aspect of trustee's responsibilities in view of the traditional judicial emphasis upon conservation of principal. "Nothing succeeds like success," so successful investment programs of trustees involving equities will not be the subject of complaints from income beneficiaries and principal remaindermen. But such equity investment programs involve greater risks, so complaints and demands for surcharges for alleged nonexercise of prudence and diligence might occur.

See TRUST, TRUST COMPANY.

BIBLIOGRAPHY

AMERICAN BANKERS ASSOCIATION. *The Trust Business*, 1982.
COMPTROLLER OF THE CURRENCY. *Fiduciary Powers of National Banks and Collective Trust Funds*, 12 CFR 9.
WHITNEY, V. P. *Trust Department Administration and Operations*, 1981.

TRUST FUNDS Funds that have been placed in the possession of an individual or corporate trustee in accordance with a trust agreement, trust deed, or will or, in the absence of specific instructions, according to the law of the state. Investment of trust funds is usually restricted to securities approved by the states.

See TRUST, TRUST FUND INVESTMENTS.

TRUST INDENTURE ACT An act originally approved August 3, 1939, effective on February 3, 1940, and amended since (15 U.S.C. 77aaa et seq., 1970), requiring that bonds, debentures, notes, and similar debt securities offered for public sale, except specifically exempted issues, be issued under an indenture that meets the requirements of the act and has been duly qualified by the Securities and Exchange Commission (SEC).

The SEC points out that the provisions of the Trust Indenture Act are closely integrated with the requirements of the Securities Act of 1933. Registration pursuant to the Securities Act of 1933 of securities to be issued under a trust indenture subject to the Trust Indenture Act is not permitted to become effective unless the indenture conforms to the requirements of the Securities Act, designed to safeguard the rights and interests of the purchasers. Moreover, specified information about the trustee and the indenture must be included in the registration statement for the public offering.

The Trust Indenture Act of 1939 was passed after studies by the SEC had revealed the frequency with which trust indentures failed to provide minimum protections for security holders and absolved "so-called trustees" from minimum obligations in the discharge of the trusts. The act requires, among other things, that the indenture trustee be a corporation with a minimum combined capital and surplus and be free of conflicting interests which might interfe e with the faithful exercise of its duties on behalf of the purchasers of the securities, and it imposes high standards of conduct and responsibility on the trustee.

However, one source of possible conflict of interest which the act does not prohibit outright is the situation where a bank acts as an indenture trustee for an issuer which is a borrower from the commercial department of the same bank. For a comprehensive study of the problem of possible conflicts of interest in connection with a bank's serving as indenture trustee as well as being a lender to the same corporation in its commercial banking department, see Leo Herzel and Dale E. Colling, "The Chinese Wall and Conflict of Interest in Banks," *The Business Lawyer*, November, 1978.

TRUST OFFICER The manager of a trust department in a bank or trust company; the official in charge of the trust business. He is empowered to sign instruments, including checks, and to commit the institution, but only in connection with the trust business.

TRUSTOR The settlor; the person who creates a TRUST.

TRUST RECEIPT A contract or trust agreement between a bank and its debtor-borrower which is temporarily substituted for other collateral securing an advance. The object of the trust receipt is twofold: to evidence the delivery of certain property to the debtor-borrower by the lending bank and to obtain acknowledgement of the legal title to such property in the lending bank.

The trust receipt may be used in the following types of credit transactions: (1) in substitution of collateral, e.g., securities, notes and acceptances, receivables, or merchandise, on which the bank had made advances, (2) in exchange for documents representing title to goods in storage or transit, e.g., warehouse receipts, bills of lading (ocean or rail), or cotton tickets, and (3) in exchange for documents covering import shipments, whether the merchandise is to be sold, warehoused, processed, or manufactured.

The trust receipt is used principally in connection with import transactions in which the importer's bank holds the bill of lading and draft drawn against the shipment. The importer needs the bill of lading in order to obtain possession of the merchandise at the steamship terminal, but if the bill of lading is released by the bank, the latter surrenders its security for the advance. The terms of credit have probably been arranged, however, so that the draft will not be due until after the importer has had an opportunity to liquidate the merchandise. The purpose of the trust receipt is to bridge the gap between the release of the bill of lading by the bank and the maturity of the draft, at the same time placing the legal title of the goods (until such time as the draft is paid) in the name of the lending bank.

The legal status of the trust receipt has been variously adjudicated. It has been variously held to be a conditional sale, a chattel mortgage, and a secret lien. Courts have generally upheld the trust receipt except where banks have endeavored to press their claims against third parties. In order to maintain rights against these parties it is necessary for banks to record the trust receipt in all states except where the instrument is regarded as a chattel mortgage.

Trust receipts are not viewed as good collateral, and it is the disposition of banks not to take trust receipts from their customers unless their credit standing is sufficiently meritorious as to warrant an unsecured advance of like amount. Trust receipts are not considered as collateral by the Board of Governors of the Federal Reserve System unless the goods covered therein are earmarked and can be identified at all times or are to be replaced by warehouse receipts, or unless an actual sale of the goods has been completed (in which case the receipt becomes collateral only for a reasonable time).

A typical form of trust receipt is appended.

Sample Trust Receipt

To the ——————————— Bank: ———————
We acknowledge the receipt from you of the following merchandise, your property, specified in the bill of lading per ——————————— , dated ——————— , which bill of lading has been delivered by you to us without waiver of your ownership of the goods therein described. Said goods are marked and numbered as follows: (Here follows a description of the merchandise.)

It is understood that said goods are consigned to us by you for sale on your account, and in consideration thereof, we hereby agree to hold said goods in trust for you, and as your property, with liberty to sell same for your account, or to manufacture and remanufacture the same without cost or expense to you. We further agree to keep said goods and the manufactured product and also the proceeds thereof, whether in the form of money or bills receivable or account, separate and capable of identification as your property, and in case of sale to deliver, as soon as received, the full net proceeds thereof direct to you to apply against ———————————

on our account under the terms of letter of credit No. ——————
issued for our account, and for the payment of any other indebtedness of ours to you, whether due or to become due.

You may at any time cancel this trust and take possession of said goods or of the proceeds of such as may then have been sold, wherever the said goods or proceeds may then be found, and in the event of any suspension, insolvency, or bankruptcy on our part, or of the nonfulfillment of any obligation made or assumed by us under said credit, or under any other credit issued by you on our account, or of the nonpayment of any indebtedness on our part to you, all obligations, acceptances, indebtedness, and liabilities, whether due or to become due, shall thereupon at your option mature and be due and payable. We further agree to keep said property insured against fire, payable in case of loss to you, without cost or charge to you, hereby waiving any lien which we might otherwise have on said property for insurance duties or charges paid by us. Any insurance money received for any loss shall be subject to the trust herein contained in the same manner as the goods themselves.

Importer.

TRUTH IN LENDING SIMPLIFICATION AND REFORM ACT TITLE VI OF THE DEPOSITORY INSTITUTIONS DEREGULATION AND MONETARY CONTROL ACT OF 1980.

Following the passage of this act, the Federal Reserve Board issued its simplified version of Regulation Z with model forms and clauses on March 18, 1981. According to a summary in the *Bank Administration Manual*, this act provided:

1. That if the creditor requires a deposit as a condition of the transaction, the consumer must be informed that the annual percentage rate does not reflect the effect of the required deposit; however, the required deposit does not need to be included in the annual percentage rate calculation.
2. A *de minimis* finance charge tolerance of $5 for amounts of $1,000 or less and $10 for amounts of more than $1,000.
3. That if creditors make early disclosures, they will be required to redisclose before consummation only if the actual annual percentage rate varies by more than one-eighth of one percent from that previously disclosed in a regular transaction, or more than one-fourth of one percent in an irregular transaction.
4. That if a transaction involves a variable-rate feature, that fact must be disclosed and the creditor must design and provide a hypothetical example demonstrating the changes that would result from the variable-rate feature.
5. That only state law provisions that contradict federal requirements would be preempted. Since that time, the Truth in Lending Act has been amended through various acts, including the Cash Discount Act of 1981, International Banking Facility DepositInsurance Act of 1981, and the Higher Education Act of 1981.

The act has been amended through various acts: Cash Discount Act of 1981, the International Banking Facility Deposit Insurance Act of 1981, and the Higher Education Act of 1981. Regulation Z of the Federal Reserve covers the basic requirements of the act.

BIBLIOGRAPHY

CHAMNESS, ROBERT P. *Truth in Lending/Regulation Z: A Complete Reference for Bankers*. Cumulative Supplement No. 1 Rolling Meadows, IL.; Bank Administration Institute, 1982.

TURN A completed speculative transaction involving a purchase and sale.
See ROUND TRANSACTION.

TURN IN THE MARKET A change in or reversal of the price tendency; the beginning of a major swing upward after prices have declined or remained on a low plateau over a long period, or the beginning of a major swing downward after prices have risen or remained on a high plateau over a long period.

TURNOVER Loosely, the amount or rapidity of sales, as compared with another factor. Properly, however, the term should not be confined to sales turnover of merchandise and may be used to indicate the number of times and rapidity with which invested capital, total assets, or accounts are turned over or moved in a given period. It is therefore a ratio determined by dividing the amount of annual sales by the average invested capital, merchandise, or receivables, etc. For example, if the annual sales are $5,000,000 and the invested capital $4,000,000, the capital turnover is 1.25 times.
See ACCOUNTS RECEIVABLE TURNOVER, CREDIT BAROMETRICS, MERCHANDISE TURNOVER.

TURN THE CORNER In business forecasting and securities literature, to reverse the trend of affairs. An individual company, a group of securities, or business in general may turn upward after a prolonged period of depression or downward after a period of prosperity.

TWENTY PERCENT RULE The practice of some banks of requiring that borrowing customers maintain average deposit balances equal to about 20% of such borrowings. Although the practice of requiring a certain proportion between balances and borrowings is common among banks, the proportion is not uniformly 20%, but ranges from 10 to 25%. The greatest force of the application of this rule is felt in New York City. The chief reasons for requiring a 20% or other proportion of balances to borrowings are as follows:

1. Borrowers should maintain cash working balances sufficient to insure a safe liquid position, thereby protecting both the borrower and lending bank.
2. The right to credit must be earned, and since a bank could not lend freely unless certain proportions were kept on deposit, it prefers to select as borrowers customers who earn the right to a credit force by keeping adequate balances.
3. Commercial banks morally, though not legally, become bound to insure the borrowing customers' credit line, provided no change in financial status occurs, and the insistence on keeping balances in proportion to loans may be regarded as a premium to insure a credit force equal to the line granted.
4. Bank operating costs are considerably increased as the result of the exercise of the loan and credit functions, and this increased cost is passed on to borrowing customers.

TWO-CENT PIECE In the United States, coinage of the two-cent piece was discontinued in 1864.
See BRONZE COINS.

TWO-DOLLAR BROKER A floor broker on the NEW YORK STOCK EXCHANGE who executes orders for other exchange members and member firms. The term is derived from the former charge of $2 for purchasing or selling 100 shares of stock. Although the charge of the two-dollar broker is now higher, the term has remained as a designation of this type of floor member.

Two-dollar brokers, also known as independent brokers, are to be distinguished from registered traders, New York Stock Exchange members who trade for their own accounts, subject to rules of the Securities and Exchange Commission and the New York Stock Exchange which limit their activities. In May, 1978, the New York Stock Exchange created a new category of floor members^registered competitive market makers—who pass an examination prescribed by the exchange to serve as such and who have specific obligations set by the exchange to trade for their own and their firm's accounts on request of an exchange official by making a bid or offer that will reduce the existing quote spread (between the bid and asked prices) or improve the depth of an existing quote.

TWO-NAME PAPER Notes, bills of exchange, and trade and bankers acceptances with two signatures, each representing separate interests responsible for payment. Trade and bankers acceptances are automatically at least two-name paper, since both the drawer and the acceptor are liable to the discounting bank. Two-name paper is also known as double-name paper.
See SINGLE-NAME PAPER.

TWO-TIER GOLD SYSTEM On March 17, 1968, the governors of the central banks of the United States and six European countries (members of the GOLD POOL, see below) agreed in Washington, D.C., on the establishment of a two-tier price system for gold. Under the arrangement, official transactions among these countries would take place at the official gold price, which was then $35 an ounce; and the countries agreed to neither sell gold on the international gold market (e.g., London) nor buy more than a little gold from private sellers. Thus, until the two-tier gold system was terminated on November 10, 1973, there were two price systems for gold: (1) the official $35 per ounce price; and (2) the private international market prices for gold, principally in the most active international gold market in London.

Establishment of the Gold Pool. By 1947, the London private gold market, licensed by the Bank of England and with permitted transactions at premiums of not over 1% above the $35 an ounce official gold price, had become of sufficient concern to the INTERNATIONAL MONETARY FUND (IMF) that it called upon its members to prohibit private market transactions in gold at premiums because "such transactions tend to undermine exchange stability and to impair monetary reserves." Accordingly, the United Kingdom withdrew permission for free market gold dealings in London, as did a number of other countries.

However, with the French government obtaining IMF permission to establish a domestic gold market in Paris, and with South Africa (ranking with the U.S.S.R. as one of the two largest gold producers) arranging for sale in February, 1949, of 100,000 ounces of gold at a premium price of $38.20 an ounce "for manufacturing or artistic" purposes, pressure built up for restoration of the London gold market, particularly since South African and Russian supplies to the market exceeded the then nonmonetary demand (speculative demand as yet had not developed) and London prices had receded to $35 an ounce and below.

Accordingly, the London market was reopened in 1954, with the United States concurring, despite a warning by the Federal Reserve Bank of New York that such resumption of free market dealings might result in larger volume and premiums over $35 an ounce in the future which would invite profitable arbitrage (European central banks buying U.S. gold at $35 an ounce, the U.S. gold window being open, and turning it over at the market's premium, all in the interests of stabilizing the market, of course, back to or closer to the $35 level).

The Gold Pool, or "central bank gold syndicate," was nevertheless formed in 1961, consisting of the central banks of eight nations^Belgium, France, Italy, Switzerland, the Netherlands, West Germany, United Kingdom, and the United States. Each central bank other than that of the United States contributed a given rate to the pool, with the United States matching their total combined contribution. The Bank of England acted as agent for the pool in sales in the market, replenishing its supply by new purchases from the U.S. Treasury at the official U.S. price of $35 an ounce.

Thus the U.S. monetary gold supply became subject not only to central bank demand for gold reserves, but also to private demand, including the speculative demand for gold that built up as continuing balance-of-payments deficits of the United States threatened the foreign exchange and IMF position of the U.S. dollar as a key currency. From a total of $23 billion at the end of 1951 (64% of total official gold reserves), the U.S. total gold reserve had declined to a 12-year low of $10.547 billion by May 30, 1968. In the five months preceding March, 1968, about $3 billion in gold was supplied by the Gold Pool to the market, principally gold from the United States.

End of the Gold Pool and the Two-Tier Gold System. The Gold Pool was terminated with initiation of the Two-Tier Gold System on March 17, 1968. In addition, the foundation was laid for subsequent establishment of the SPECIAL DRAWING RIGHTS (SDRs), or paper gold, which would eventually replace gold as the means of effecting international settlements and replace the U.S. dollar in its role of key currency.

On August 15, 1971, the United States closed the gold window, thus ending the *raison d'etre* for continuation of the Gold Pool and the two-tier gold system. The end of the latter formally came at a meeting in Berne, Switzerland, of the central bank representatives on November 10, 1973. After the two devaluations of the U.S. dollar (8.57% on December 18, 1971, and 10% on February 12, 1973) and implementation of the Second Amendment to the IMF's Articles of Agreement on April 1, 1978, the United States in the new era of floating exchange rates with IMF surveillance achieved its foreign exchange objectives by swap arrangements, among other techniques.

See GOLD CONSUMPTION, GOLD MOVEMENTS, GOLD PRODUCTION, GOLD RESERVE, SWAP NETWORK.

TYPE-RATIO ANALYSIS *See* CREDIT BAROMETRICS.

U

ULTIMATE BENEFICIARY In a TRUST, the beneficiary who receives the final distribution of principal and who therefore is the principal beneficiary or REMAINDERMAN, as compared with the income beneficiary or intermediate beneficiary.

ULTRA VIRES Literally, beyond the powers. In CORPORATION law, since a corporation may act only within its charter powers (express, implied, and incidental) and statutory powers, any *ultra vires* acts of the corporation at common law are deemed to be null and void, and unenforceable.

The modern view, however, is reflected statutorily in most states in abolition of the defense of *ultra vires* in actions for breach of contract by or against a corporation. Nevertheless, if the contract is wholly executory on both sides, most courts still allow *ultra vires* as a defense. It follows that a corporation that has received the benefits of full performance may not itself plead *ultra vires* as a defense if sued itself for nonperformance. And if, by contrast, it is the corporation that has fully performed but the defendant party has not, the defense of *ultra vires* is unavailing.

Section 7 of the Model Business Corporation Law provides stockholders of corporations engaging in *ultra vires* acts with injunctive relief against the corporation and with representative suit against officers and directors. Moreover, in a *quo warranto* proceeding, the state attorney general of the home state of incorporation of the corporation engaging in *ultra vires* acts may enjoin the corporation from such further acts, or dissolve the corporation.

UNAMORTIZED DISCOUNT AND PREMIUM That portion of the original bond discount or premium or the excess of the face value of securities over the amount paid that has not been written off against or to earnings by the amortization process.

UNASSENTED SECURITIES Stocks or bonds, the status, i.e., the rights in or conditions, of which a corporation desires to change, but the owners have not agreed.

Under Chapter 11 of the National Bankruptcy Act, which provides for corporate reorganizations, written acceptances of creditors holding two-thirds in amount and over half in number of allowed claims are required before the reorganization plan may be confirmed. Should the court thereafter confirm the reorganization plan, it will be binding on the nonassenting creditors and stockholders.

Voluntary changes in capitalization, however, are subject under corporation laws to the right of appraisal by nonassenting stockholders. For example, under the New York Business Corporation Law (Sec. 806(b)(6)), a holder of any adversely affected shares who does not vote for or consent in writing to the taking of such actions as those listed below shall (subject to and by complying with the procedure to enforce shareholder's right to receive payment for shares, Sec. 623 of New York Business Corporation Law) have the right to dissent and to receive the appraised value for such shares, if the action taken in the certificate of amendment does any of the following: alters or abolishes any preferential right of any outstanding shares having preferences; creates, alters, or abolishes any provision or right in respect to the redemption of any outstanding shares; alters or abolishes any PREEMPTIVE RIGHT of such holder to acquire shares or other securities; or excludes or limits the right of such holder to vote on any matter, except as such right may be limited by the voting rights given to new shares then being authorized of any existing or new class.

See READJUSTMENT, REORGANIZATION.

UNCALLED CAPITAL The balance of subscription liability on capital stock of a corporation, subject to payment therefor pursuant to calls specified in the subscription contract. Subscribing stockholders are liable to the corporation for their uncalled subscription liability and, in the event of failure of the corporation, to the creditors' representative. *See* FULLY PAID STOCK for discussion of issuance of certificates for partly paid stock.

On the corporate books, a subscriptions ledger is used for the posting of entries from the supporting subscriptions journal, recording the collection of subscriptions upon the issuance of calls by the board of directors. In the general ledger, the subscriptions receivable account is debited for the amount of subscriptions received, and credited for the amount of payments by subscribing stockholders; any net debit balance is a current asset. In accounting for the capital stock, the total authorized amount is accounted for by the amount issued and outstanding, plus the subscribed but not yet issued stock (as indicated by the contra subscriptions receivable account).

UNCERTAINTY A situation in which a decision maker does not have information about the outcomes of an action. Unlike with risk, with uncertainty no estimates can be made about the probabilities associated with alternative outcomes. Decision making is guided by the consistent use of selected criteria, such as the MAXIMIN and MAXIMAX CRITERIA.

UNCLAIMED BALANCES Bank balances that have remained dormant without deposits or withdrawals over a long period of time; inactive or dormant accounts.

There is no specific provision in the National Bank Act or the Federal Reserve Act that governs disposition of unclaimed deposits of a national bank. Insured deposits, however, must be claimed as required by the Federal Deposit Insurance Act. If after the Federal Deposit Insurance Corporation shall have given at least three months' notice to the depositor by mailing notice to his last known address appearing on the books of the closed bank, any depositor in the closed bank fails to claim the insured deposit from the corporation within 18 months after appointment of receiver or fails within such period to claim or arrange to continue his deposit if it has been transferred to a new bank or to another insured bank, all rights of the depositor with respect to the insured deposit and against the new bank or other insured bank with respect to the transferred deposit shall be barred; all rights of the depositor against the closed bank and its shareholders, or the receivership estate to which the FDIC may have become subrogated, shall thereupon revert to the depositor. The amount of any transferred deposits not claimed within such 18 months' period shall be refunded to the FDIC.

If a national bank voluntarily dissolves, unclaimed deposits are transferred to the custody of the Comptroller of the Currency. When insured national banks or insured District of Columbia banks are closed for inability to meet demands of depositors, the Federal Deposit Insurance Corporation shall be appointed receiver, and one of its duties shall be to wind up the affairs of such closed banks in conformity with the provisions of law relating to liquidation of closed national banks, as modified by the Federal Deposit Insurance Act. One of these provisions is that all moneys received by the receiver are paid into the Treasury of the United States, and dividends to depositors are drawn on the balance in the Treasury to the credit of the insolvent bank. Any amounts unclaimed, therefore, remain in the Treasury.

Insofar as national banks are concerned, state laws pertaining to

ENCYCLOPEDIA OF BANKING AND FINANCE

unclaimed deposits ("escheat laws") which require no proof that dormant accounts have in fact been abandoned, or which burden performance of a national bank's functions such as compliance with the ratable distributions requirement of R.S. 5236, have been held invalid by federal courts, including the U.S. Supreme Court, in various cases. Otherwise, however, such state laws have been held to be constitutional and applicable to national banks located within the state.

Various states have enacted abandoned property laws, declaring defined types of funds unclaimed after specified periods of years to be abandoned and requiring the turning over of such funds to the state. Such laws require the filing of an annual report with the designated state official, specifying the details of the abandoned property as of the specified preceding date, and the publication of a public notice listing the names and last known addresses of persons entitled to such property.

UNCLAIMED DEPOSITS   See UNCLAIMED BALANCES.

UNCOLLECTED ITEMS   An account that appears among the assets in the weekly statement of the Federal Reserve System, representing the amount of items in the process of collection but not yet collected for member banks. It is ordinarily only partially offset by the account entitled DEFERRED AVAILABILITY ITEMS, thus giving rise to FLOAT.

UNCONFIRMED CREDIT   See LETTER OF CREDIT.

UNCOVERED PAPER MONEY   Irredeemable paper MONEY; paper money not supported or only partially supported by a specie reserve.
   See FIAT MONEY.

UNDERGROUND ECONOMY   The shadow, hidden, subterranean, irregular economy where goods and services—some legal, some illegal—are produced but not reported.

The underground economy hinders effective governmental policy making because it impacts on tax rates, tax programs, and budget deficits.

BIBLIOGRAPHY

BENNETT, J., and DILORENZO, T. *The Underground Government; The Off-Budget Public Sector*, 1983.

UNDERLYING BONDS   Prior lien bonds; senior bonds; bonds secured by a mortgage lying closer to the ground than other issues secured by junior liens on the same property; bonds secured by a first mortgage, or at least by a mortgage having priority over other mortgages on the same property. The term is an antonym of overlying or junior bonds.
   See UNDERLYING MORTGAGE.

UNDERLYING LIEN   A lien, i.e., a right to retain property given as security until the claim against it has been paid (e.g., a mortgage), that underlies or is prior to others. A first mortgage is an underlying lien, but a second mortgage is also an underlying lien when there is a third. Any lien is an underlying lien except the last. The use of this term presumes that overlying or junior liens exist.

UNDERLYING MORTGAGE   A mortgage constituting a prior lien over other mortgages on the same property. Although usually understood to be a first mortgage, an underlying mortgage is any mortgage that takes precedence over another mortgage on the same property; thus, a first mortgage is an underlying mortgage when there are two; first and second mortgages are underlying mortgages when there are three; first, second, and third mortgages are underlying mortgages when there are four; etc.

UNDERLYING SYNDICATE   See SYNDICATE.

UNDER THE RULE   Whenever a member of the New York Stock Exchange becomes insolvent or is unable to make good deliveries, his outstanding contracts are settled "under the rule." Actually, there are two sets of rules involved—those pertaining to insolvency and those involving failure to fulfill contracts. When an announcement is made of the suspension of a member or member firm pursuant to the provisions of Article XIII of the New York Stock Exchange Constitution, members or member firms having exchange contracts with the suspended member or firm for the purchase, sale, or loan of securities shall without unnecessary delay proceed to close such contracts on the exchange or in the best available market, pursuant to the bylaws or rules of the Stock Clearing Corporation which are applicable and provide the method of closing.

A contract in securities admitted to dealings on the exchange that has not been fulfilled according to the terms thereof may be officially closed by an officer or employee of the exchange authorized by the exchange to close such contracts. The order to close such contract shall be delivered to the exchange, and the member or member firm giving such order shall also deliver notice of intention to make such closing at the office of the member or member firm in default.

Delays in deliveries occurring through no fault of the contracting firm expose it to buy-ins, but before the drastic action of a buy-in is resorted to, the courtesy among cashiers of Wall Street is to give the defaulting firm a period of grace in which to make the delivery.
   See GOOD DELIVERY.

UNDERTONE   The fundamental underlying tendency of market prices, neglecting hour to hour fluctuations. The undertone of a day's market may be weak, steady, or strong.

UNDERWRITER   This term has two meanings:

1. An insurer; a person or company that undertakes any kind of INSURANCE contract for a compensation.
2. A person or company that underwrites an issue of securities.

As defined by the Securities Act of 1933, in Section 2 (11), the term underwriter means "any person who has purchased from an issuer with a view to, or sells for an issuer in connection with, the distribution of any security, or participates or has a direct or indirect participation in any such undertaking, or participates or has a participation in the direct or indirect underwriting of any such undertaking; but such term shall not include a person whose interest is limited to a commission from an underwriter or dealer not in excess of the usual and customary distributors' or sellers' commission."
   See SYNDICATE, UNDERWRITING.

UNDERWRITING   The act or process by an underwriting syndicate of guaranteeing the sale of an issue of securities by purchasing it at a stated price from the issuing corporation or governmentality. It devolves upon the underwriters constituting the purchase group to dispose of the securities to the investing public at a price sufficiently attractive to ensure their sale and yet yield the underwriters a profit.

Back when larger underwriting spreads were customary, and before passage of the Securities Act of 1933, which imposed civil liability upon underwriters, it was the practice to organize a second purchase group, larger than the original purchase group and usually composed of large distributing houses with large placement power among institutional investors. From the standpoint of the original purchase group, this second intermediate group between the original purchase group and the selling group, usually called the "banking group," assured the spreading of the risk and also additional aid in carrying any unsold bonds or other security involved in the underwriting. Since passage of the act, however, this intermediate group has practically disappeared, discouraged also by the narrower spreads available for allocation among the original purchase group members and any additional banking group members.

In addition to the straight underwriting of a public offering, involving a firm commitment, there is the standby type of underwriting, wherein the purchase group makes a firm commitment to take any balance of bonds or shares unsubscribed in a company offering of subscription rights to stockholders. There is also the "best efforts" type of underwriting, wherein the underwriters make no firm commitment but merely engage to use their best efforts to sell as much of the offering as possible.
   See INVESTMENT BANKER, SYNDICATE.

UNDESIGNATED CITIES   Cities not designated as reserve cities by the Board of Governors of the Federal Reserve System. P.L. 86-114, approved July 18, 1959, provided for the termination of the classification of "central reserve cities" for legal RESERVE purposes. This was effected by the board of governors, pursuant to the statute's authorization, beginning July 28, 1962. Member banks in undesignated cities are referred to as country banks, although the implication thereof that such banks are all located in rural areas of course is not accurate.

Amendments to Regulation D, Reserves of Member Banks, include the factors taken into account by the board of governors in considering requests from member banks located in reserve cities to carry lower reserves than other member banks in the same city, based on the character of the bank's business, including but not limited to the rate of activity of its demand deposits.

UNDIGESTED SECURITIES Securities issued in excess of the capacity of the investment market to fully absorb them; securities not owned outright by ultimate investors but held by syndicates, individual speculators, and bankers with the intention of disposing of them when a favorable market opportunity presents itself. Sometimes securities purchased by an underwriting syndicate cannot for one reason or another be entirely sold to the investment public. Such part as remains unsold in the hands of the syndicate members is said to be undigested. The severe decline of security prices in 1903 is sometimes referred to as the panic of undigested securities.

UNDIVIDED PROFITS The name of an account to which current net earnings or profits are credited; unappropriated profits. This title most frequently occurs in bank accounting and corresponds to what is usually known among manufacturing and mercantile corporations as retained earnings. It represents profits not distributed in dividends.

Banking institutions maintain two accounts-undivided profits and SURPLUS. Current net earnings are credited to the former account, which consists of undistributed earnings available for dividends and the amount retained to build up total equity; the latter account is a round sum account, which may be increased as the undivided profits account grows over time, by round sum transfers from the undivided profits account. Under the latest bank chart of accounts evolved by the banking agencies for bank statements, reserves, whether for contingencies or losses, are not shown with capital, surplus, and undivided profits; instead, reserve for possible losses in toto is netted out on the assets side of the statement of condition from the gross total of loans.

See BANK STATEMENT, CAPITAL AND SURPLUS.

UNEARNED INCREMENT Enhancement in the value of property arising from the growth of population and not from improvements effected therein by the owner. Such unearned or natural increases in value, however, are reflected promptly in increased assessments and taxes upon the property. Capital gains upon the sale or other disposition of the property are also taxed. In the event of population shifts, unearned decrements in the value of property are just as likely to occur.

The single tax, as advocated by Henry George in his *Progress and Poverty*, would be levied upon the rental value of the land alone, as distinct from the rental value of the improvements made thereon.

UNEARNED INTEREST AND DISCOUNT The title of a deferred income account set up to reflect interest or DISCOUNT paid in advance but not yet earned. In accounting terminology, this account is a liability or real account that, when the interest or discount is fully earned, becomes a nominal account and is closed out to the profit and loss account. If unearned interest and discount were not set up, true earnings would be overstated for a particular period. Proper accounting on the accrual basis therefore calls for accrual of interest and discount as earned.

Under the latest bank chart of accounts and instructions for their preparation and reporting evolved by the banking agencies for bank statements, the total of unearned interest and discount is deducted from the gross total of loans.

See BANK STATEMENT.

UNEMPLOYMENT Individuals are classified as employed, unemployed, or not in the labor force according to a monthly survey of 50,000 households by the U.S. Bureau of Labor Statistics. People are defined as employed if they are working full time or part time, or are absent from work because of vacation, strikes, or personal reasons. Individuals who would like to work but who are not actively looking for work are not counted as unemployed and are not in the labor force. Attention is usually given to the proportion of the labor force that is unemployed, the unemployment rate, rather than the portion that is employed because many government policies are developed with the intention of reducing unemployment. The aggregate unemployment rate for all individuals is listed below for selected years.

Year	Unemployment Rate
1970	4.8%
1975	8.3
1980	7.0
1985	7.1
1986	6.9
1987	6.1

Source: Economic Report of the President, 1988.

BIBLIOGRAPHY

Area Trends in Employment and Unemployment. U.S. Employment and Training Administration. Monthly.
BLS Labor Force. Bureau of Labor Statistics, Washington, DC. Online data base.
DWORACZEK, M. *Unemployment Insurance Benefits: A Bibliography.* Vance biographies, Monticello, IL.
How the Government Measures Unemployment. U.S. Bureau of Labor Statistics. Report number 505.
Labor Statistics (LABSTAT). U.S. Bureau of Labor Statistics. Online data base.
PEARSON, R. W. *Helping the Unemployed Professional.* John Wiley and Sons, Inc., New York, NY, 1988.

UNEMPLOYMENT INSURANCE The federal-state unemployment insurance system, initiated in the Social Security Act of 1935, offers the first economic line of defense against the ripple effects of unemployment. By cash payments made directly to laid-off workers, it ensures that at least a significant proportion of the necessities of life, most notably food, shelter and clothing, can be met on a week-to-week basis while a search for work takes place.

In the U.S., before passage of the SOCIAL SECURITY Act, Wisconsin was the only state that had adopted unemployment insurance. As a result of passage of the Social Security Act (Title III, which defines the conditions under which a state may receive federal grants for the administration of its unemployment insurance law), each state (as well as the District of Columbia and Puerto Rico) has its own unemployment insurance law and operates its own program.

In the FY 1987, $16.09 billion in unemployment compensation and related benefits was paid to 8.5 million unemployed workers, in the following programs:

Program	Amount	Beneficiaries
Regular unemployment compensation (UI); includes $.08 billion in extended benefits.	$15.05 billion	7.5 million
Unemployment compensation for federal employees (UCFE).	0.18 billion	0.1 million
Unemployment compensation for ex-service members (UCX).	0.13 billion	0.1 million
TOTAL	$15.36 billion	7.7 million

The administrative costs of the states, paid by federal grants, aggregated $1.6 billion. At the federal level, administration is conducted by the Unemployment Insurance Service of the Employment and Training Administration, Department of Labor, which in FY 1985 had 136 employees in the national office and 80 in regional offices.

UNEMPLOYMENT INSURANCE

During the fiscal year ending in September 1987, there were 97.9 million workers covered by the federal-state system. Some 5.3 million employers paid $19.1 billion in state unemployment compensation taxes.

As initiated in 1935 in the Social Security Act, the unemployment compensation system is a unique federal-state mechanism grounded upon federal law but executed in its relationship to the employer and the unemployed worker through state law and by state employees.

Conceptually, unemployment compensation is designed to provide benefits to most workers out of work due to no fault of their own for periods between jobs. Except in a few states where there are small employee payments, the system is financed by a payroll tax on employers. Originally, most states paid benefits for a maximum duration of 13 to 16 weeks; most states now pay a maximum of 26 weeks, and a few extend duration somewhat farther.

In periods of high unemployment in individual states, benefits are payable for up to 13 additional weeks, up to a maximum of 39 weeks. These extended benefits are funded on a shared basis: 50% from state funds and 50% from federal sources.

From time to time, in periods of national recession, when all states are impacted by high and sustained unemployment, federally funded programs of supplemental benefits have been adopted. There were two such programs during the 1970s and another, Federal Supplemental Compensation (FSC) program, was effective, from September 1982 until March 1985. This program provided for additional periods of benefit eligibility for individuals who had exhausted all regular state benefits, and, where applicable, extended benefits.

The Basic System. The unemployment insurance system in this country is the product of federal and state legislation. About 97% of wage and salary workers are now covered by the federal-state system, originally established by the Social Security Act. The federal taxing provisions are in the Federal Unemployment Tax Act, Chapter 23 of the Internal Revenue Code (FUTA). Railroad workers are covered by a separate federal program. Veterans with recent service in the Armed Forces and civilian federal employees are covered by a federal program, Chapter 85, Title 5, United States Code, with the states paying benefits as agents of the federal government.

The federal provisions in the Social Security Act and the Federal Unemployment Tax Act establish the framework of the system. If a state law meets minimum federal requirements, (1) employers receive a 5.4% credit against the 6.2% federal payroll tax, and (2) the state is entitled to federal grants to cover all the necessary costs of administering the program

Financing the Program. Under the provisions of the Internal Revenue Code, a tax is levied on covered employers at a current rate of 6.2% on wages up to $7,000 a year paid to an employee. The 6.2% federal tax will drop to 6.0% at the end of calendar year 1990. The law, however, provides a credit against federal tax liability of 5.4% to employers who pay state taxes under an approved state unemployment compensation program. This credit is allowed regardless of the amount of the tax paid to the state by the employer. Because all of the states now have approved unemployment compensation laws, the standard federal tax in every state is 0.8%. This federal tax is used to pay all of the administrative costs, both state and federal, associated with the unemployment compensation programs, to provide 50% of the benefits paid under the Federal-State Extended Unemployment Compensation Act of 1970, to pay the cost of benefits under the Emergency Unemployment Compensation Act of 1974 (from January 1975 through March 1977) and to maintain a loan fund from which an individual state may borrow (Title XII of the Social Security Act) whenever it lacks funds to pay the unemployment compensation benefits due for any month.

State Taxes: All states levy taxes on employers within the state. Four states (Alabama, Alaska, New Jersey, and Pennsylvania) also collect contributions from employees. These taxes are deposited by the state to its account in the unemployment trust fund in the federal Treasury, and withdrawn as needed to pay benefits. As of September 30, 1987, the total trust fund reserve of the 50 states that had positive balances was $22.9 billion; one state was supplementing its state unemployment compensation tax collections with loans from the federal account in order to meet benefit payments. At the end of FY 1987, five states had outstanding loans in a total amount of $2.9 billion.

Federal Requirements for Experience Rating: The federal law initially allowed employers additional credit for a lowered rate of contribution if the rates were based on not less than three years of "experience with respect to unemployment risk." In 1954, the three-year requirement was relaxed and states were permitted to assign a reduced rate, based on their "experience," to new and newly covered employers who had at least one year of experience immediately preceding the computation date. Since 1970, states may also grant reduced rates (but not less than 1%) for newly covered employers.

State Requirements for Experience Rating: All states, except Puerto Rico, provide for a system of experience rating by which employers' contribution rates are varied from the standard rate on the basis of their experience with the amount of unemployment encountered by their employees. In most states, three years of experience with unemployment means more than three years of coverage and contribution experience.

Liable Employers: Employers are subject to the federal unemployment tax if, during the current or preceding calendar year, they employed one or more individuals in each of at least 20 calendar weeks or if they paid wages of $1,500 or more during any calendar quarter of either such year. Variations on these requirements relate to employers in agriculture and domestic service: (a) in agriculture, employers are covered who have at least ten or more workers in a calendar year or a cash payroll of at least $20,000 in a calendar year; (b) in domestic service, employers are covered who have a cash payroll of at least $1,000 in any calendar quarter.

Taxable wages are defined as all remuneration from employment in cash or in kind with certain exceptions. The exceptions include earnings in excess of $7,000 in a year, payments related to retirement, disability, hospital insurance, or similar fringe benefits.

Taxable Wage Base: Thirty-six states have adopted a higher tax base than the $7,000 now provided in the Federal Unemployment Tax Act. Alaska's wage base is the highest at $21,100. In all states an employer pays a tax on wages paid to each worker within a calendar year up to the amount specified in state law. Most states also provide an automatic adjustment of the wage base if the federal law is amended to apply to a higher wage base than specified under state law.

Coverage. The Federal Unemployment Tax Act applies to employers who employ one or more employees in covered employment in at least 20 weeks in the current or preceding calendar year or who pay wages of $1,500 or more during any calendar quarter of the current or preceding calendar year. Also included are large employers of agricultural labor and some employment in domestic service. State legislatures tend to cover employers or employment subject to the federal tax because, while there is no compulsion to do so, failure to do so is of no advantage to the state and a disadvantage to the employers involved. While states generally cover all employment that is subject to the Federal tax, they also may cover some employment that is exempt from the tax, such as smaller employers of agricultural labor and domestic service.

Although the extent of state coverage is greatly influenced by the federal statute, each state is, with a single exception, free to determine the employers who are liable for contributions and the workers who accrue rights under the laws. The exception is the federal requirement that states provide coverage for employees of nonprofit organizations and employees of state and local governments, even though such employment is exempt from FUTA. Since January 1, 1978, the federal law has required that state unemployment insurance laws must provide coverage for virtually all employees of state and local governments and all but very small nonprofit employers.

Benefit Rights. There are no federal standards for benefits, qualifying requirements, benefit amounts, or duration of regular benefits. Hence, there is no common pattern of benefit provisions comparable to that in coverage and financing. The states have developed diverse and complex formulas for determining workers' benefit rights.

Under all state unemployment insurance laws, a worker's benefit rights depend on his or her experience in covered employment in a past period of time, called the base period. The period during which the weekly rate and the duration of benefits determined for a given worker apply is called his or her benefit year.

Source: U.S. Department of Labor.

Summary. In aggregative economics, unemployment insurance payments are considered to be an "automatic stabilizer." They increase, reflecting rise in initial claims, during recessions; but they decrease, reflecting rise in employment, during economic upturns. Controversial issues with respect thereto include whether benefits should be paid to strikers and whether there should be more equality of average weekly benefits among the state plans.

BIBLIOGRAPHY

Benefit Series Service, Unemployment Insurance. Employment and Training Administration, Washington, DC. Quarterly.
DWORACZEK, M. *Unemployment Insurance Benefits: A Bibliography,* Vance Bibliographies, Monticello, IL, 1987.
Unemployment Insurance Claims. U.S. Department of Labor. Monthly.
Unemployment Insurance Reports. Commerce Clearing House Inc. Chicago, IL. Weekly.
Unemployment Insurance Statistics. U.S. Department of Labor. Monthly.

UNENCUMBERED Free from all claims and debts. Real estate is unencumbered when there are no mortgages or other liens, e.g., taxes, against it.

UNEVEN Describes the stock market when prices fluctuate rapidly and over a wide range.

UNFUNDED DEBT Floating debt; short-term debt; indebtedness not represented by funded (long-term) debt.

UNIFIED BONDS See UNIFYING MORTGAGE BONDS.

UNIFORM BANK CALL REPORT A report required by regulatory authorities of national banks, state banks that are members of the Federal Reserve System, and insured state nonmember banks. These reports are typically reports of condition and income. They must be submitted on the report forms provided by the regulatory agencies for each report date.

UNIFORM BANK PERFORMANCE REPORT A report developed by the Federal Financial Institutions Examination Council that is used as an analytical tool for bank supervisory, examination, and management purposes. According to the council, the performance report:

... shows, in a convenient format, the impact of management decisions and economic conditions on a bank's performance and balance sheet composition. The performance and composition data contained in the report may be used as an aid in making decisions concerning the adequacy of earnings, liquidity, capital, asset and liability management, and growth management. Bankers and examiners alike may use the report to further their understanding of the bank's financial condition and through such understanding become more effective in the performance of their duties.

A performance report is produced for each commercial bank that is supervised by the Board of Governors of the Federal Reserve System, Federal Deposit Insurance Corporation, or the Office of the Comptroller of the Currency. Data are presented on the reports as ratios, percentages, and dollar amounts along with average data for the bank's peer group and percentile rankings for most ratios.

UNIFORM BILLS OF LADING ACT See BILL OF LADING.

UNIFORM COMMERCIAL CODE The Uniform Commercial Code (UCC), a project of the National Conference of Commissioners on Uniform State Laws and of the American Law Institute, is a comprehensive codification and modernization of commercial law (excluding law dealing with real property), which was offered to the various states with the objective of achieving greater uniformity in commercial laws. The UCC has been enacted, albeit without uniformity, in 49 states (exception: Louisiana), the District of Columbia, and the Virgin Islands. Such lack of substantial uniformity has led to proposals that there be federal enactment of the code (see below).

The scope of this work may be judged from its repealer article, Article 10, which provides upon its enactment by the particular state for repeal of the following specific acts:

Uniform Negotiable Instruments Act
Uniform Warehouse Receipts Act
Uniform Sales Act
Uniform Bills of Lading Act
Uniform Stock Transfer Act
Uniform Conditional Sales Act
Uniform Trust Receipts Act

Also to be repealed upon the code's enactment would be any laws regulating the following items:

Bank collections
Bulk sales
Chattel mortgages
Conditional sales
Factor's lien acts
Farm storage of grain and similar acts
Assignment of accounts receivable

Development of the Code. Initial impetus for promulgation of the Uniform Commercial Code began in 1940, and the work began in 1945. In 1952, a draft of the code was adopted by the National Conference of Commissioners on Uniform State Laws and the American Law Institute, and approved by the House of Delegates of the American Bar Association. Pennsylvania was the first state to enact the code, on April 6, 1953, effective July 1, 1954. After the Law Revision Commission of New York State had submitted a report on the code in 1956, the editorial board of the code prepared a new draft which was approved by the institute and the conference in mid-1957, reacting not only to the New York State report but also to suggestions from other jurisdictions and bodies. Massachusetts enacted substantially the 1957 draft in 1957, effective October 1, 1958, and there followed 47 other enactments, all by 1966. New York itself enacted the code in 1962, effective September 27, 1964.

Outline of Contents. In addition to Article 10, the effective date and repealer article, the code consists of the following articles:

Article 1. General provisions—intended to be applicable throughout the code.

Article 2. Sales—completely supersedes the Uniform Sales Act and adds much new matter.

Article 3. Commercial paper—replaces the Uniform Negotiable Instruments Law.

Article 4. Bank deposits and collections—contains many of the points in the Bank Collection Code prepared by the American Bankers Association and adopted by various states.

Article 5. Letters of credit—new matter containing basic rules applicable to this specialized field of commercial law.

Article 6. Bulk transfers—represents a model bulk transfers law.

Article 7. Warehouse receipts, bills of lading, and other documents of title—replaces the Uniform Warehouse Receipts Act, the Uniform Bills of Lading Act, and the portions of the Uniform Sales Act pertaining to documents of title.

Article 8. Investment securities—replaces in its entirety the Uniform Stock Transfer Act; also pertains to bearer and registered bonds and additional types of investment paper not previously covered in uniform laws.

Article 9. Secured transactions; sales of accounts, contract rights and chattel paper—replaces the Uniform Trust Receipts Act, the Uniform Conditional Sales Act, and Uniform Chattel Mortgage Act, as well as variety of acts dealing with assignment of accounts receivable, factor's liens, etc. Considered by proponents to be a great step forward in commercial law.

Recent Developments. The following are among the developments in business practice which as of 1981 were leading to proposals for amending the Uniform Commercial Code.

1. Amendment of Articles 3 and 4 of the Uniform Commercial Code to cover more satisfactorily recent developments in payments systems, including electronic funds transfers. In November, 1978, Congress enacted the Electronic Fund Transfer Act (Title IX of the Consumer Credit Protection Act as amended, 15 U.S.C. 1601 et seq.) and the Board of Governors of the Federal Reserve System issued its Regulation E, Electronic Fund Transfers (as amended to January 15, 1981), which provides *inter alia* that state laws that are inconsistent with the act and Regulation E shall be preempted, but then only to the extent of the inconsistency (a state law would not be inconsistent with the act and the regulation if it is more protective of a consumer).

2. Amendment of the code to cover specifically the leasing of

personal property, in view of the substantial growth in such types of transactions in recent years.
3. Revisions of Article 9 of the code (as of January 1, 1980, some 30 states, including New York and Massachusetts, had adopted the revisions, work on which originally started in November, 1968, by the review committee appointed by the Permanent Editorial Board), calling for refiling of financing statement in the event of changes in name of debtor of his transfer of the collateral, in order to constitute a perfected filing.

A problem for proponents of the code continues to be the lack of desired substantial (if not absolute) uniformity among the enacting states, considered necessary in this field in view of the large volume of interstate business transactions. These variations exist not only in departures from the basic Uniform Commercial Code, but also in failure among many states to enact proposed amendments to the code promulgated by the Permanent Editorial Board for the Uniform Commercial Code.

Proposed solution to lack of uniformity in applicability to interstate transactions is enactment by the Congress of a federal code, which it is argued would also lead to conformity therewith by the variant states for intrastate transactions.

See NEGOTIABLE INSTRUMENTS LAW.

BIBLIOGRAPHY

AMERICAN LAW INSTITUTE-AMERICAN BAR ASSOCIATION. *Resource Materials: Banking and Commercial Lending Law*, 2 vols., 1981.
BUSINESS LAWYER. *Uniform Commercial Code Annual Survey.*

UNIFORM CONSUMER CREDIT CODE Consumer credit law developed by the Commissioners on Uniform State Laws in 1968. The code has been adopted by almost a quarter of the states and covers many of the areas found in the Federal Consumer Protection Act. The code deals with truth in lending; establishes rate ceilings; treats referral sales and door-to-door sales, fine-print clauses, creditor's remedies, deficiency judgments, garnishments, and others. It also covers credit transactions involving most types of real-estate sales and goods and services by persons who regularly engage in credit selling.

UNIFORM GIFT TO MINORS ACT An act that provides a method of transferring property to minors. A custodian manages the property on behalf of the minor; the custodianship ends when the minor attains majority.

UNIFORM LIMITED PARTNERSHIP ACT An act regulating limited partnership acts initially written in 1916 and amended in 1976. Forty-six states have adopted the 1916 version. Only two states have adopted the 1976 version. A limited partnership is a partnership formed by two or more persons having as members one or more general partners and one or more limited partners. The limited partners shall not be bound by the obligations of the partnership.

UNIFORM NEGOTIABLE INSTRUMENTS LAW See UNIFORM COMMERCIAL CODE, NEGOTIABLE INSTRUMENTS LAW.

UNIFORM PARTNERSHIP ACT Legislation adopted by most of the states governing the formation, operation, and dissolution of partnerships in the United States. According to this act, a partnership is "an association of two or more persons to carry on as co-owners a business for profit."

The act contains provisions generally applicable to the formation, operation, and dissolution of partnerships in the United States. The Uniform Partnership Act has 45 sections that are separated into the following seven parts: preliminary provisions, nature of partnership, relations of partners to persons dealing with partnership, property rights of a partner, dissolution and winding up, miscellaneous provisions.

UNIFORM WAREHOUSE RECEIPTS ACT See WAREHOUSE RECEIPTS ACT.

UNIFYING MORTGAGE BONDS Bonds issued (usually by railroad companies) for the purpose of combining several issues of bonds into one issue supported by a single blanket mortgage. The purpose of such an issue is to simplify a company's finances. When unifying mortgage bonds are issued, the amount authorized is usually sufficiently large to provide for future expenditures for some time to come. This title is practically synonymous with GENERAL MORTGAGE BONDS and CONSOLIDATED MORTGAGE BONDS.

UNISSUED STOCK Stock that has been authorized to the corporation by its certificate of incorporation or certificate of capital changes but is as yet unissued. Although unissued stock is not an asset or a liability, it should be shown on the balance sheet, with indication of which portion if any is reserved for options, warrants, or conversion privileges. Unissued stock not earmarked for such purposes is available to directors for issuance for corporate purposes.

In the case of national banks, regulation of the Comptroller of the Currency (Sec. 14.2 of 12 CFR) provides that with the approval of the Comptroller and by a two-thirds vote of the bank's stock, the bank may increase its common stock in the category of authorized but unissued stock.

The approval of the Comptroller of the Currency of such an increase shall not be required where the resulting amount of common stock in the category of authorized but unissued stock will satisfy either of the following criteria.

1. Where the resulting total amount of authorized but unissued stock will be free of preemptive rights (see PREEMPTIVE RIGHT) of shareholders, and will not exceed 25% of the currently issued and outstanding stock. The 25% limitation may be calculated without regard to authorized but unissued stock that is specifically designated as being reserved for issuance in connection with employee stock option plans, employee stock purchase plans, employee bonus plans, or other similar programs, provided that such plans have been approved by the Comptroller of the Currency. Such 25% limitation also may be calculated without regard to authorized but unissued stock that is specifically designated as shares held for the purpose of satisfying the requirements of convertible capital notes or convertible preferred stock, subject to the Comptroller's approval of such convertible issues.
2. Where the resulting total amount of authorized but unissued stock, exclusive of that amount specifically reserved for issuance in connection with employee compensation programs and for satisfying requirements of the convertible securities of the bank as referred to in the preceding paragraph, will be subject to preemptive rights of shareholders and will not exceed 50% of the currently issued and outstanding stock.

Authorized but unissued stock may also be issued under 12 CFR 14.2 from time to time as stock dividends (see STOCK DIVIDEND) or for such other purposes and considerations as may be approved by the board of directors of the national bank and by the Comptroller of the Currency. Any request for approval of the Comptroller for such issuance should be in writing and submitted to the appropriate regional administrator of national banks.

Authorized but unissued stock may also be issued from time to time to employees of the national bank pursuant to a stock option or stock purchase plan adopted in accordance with 12 CFR 13 (employee stock option and stock purchase plans of national banks), or in exchange for convertible preferred stock or convertible capital notes or debentures in accordance with the terms and provisions of such securities.

A certified copy of every amendment to the Articles of Association of the national bank adopted by the shareholders in connection with any of the above shall be filed pursuant to 12 U.S.C. 21a (Amendment to Articles of Association), the original certificate to be forwarded to the Comptroller of the Currency at the Washington, D.C., office and a copy sent to the appropriate regional administrator of national banks.

See AUTHORIZED CAPITAL STOCK, BANK STATEMENT, CAPITAL STOCK, ISSUED CAPITAL STOCK, TREASURY STOCK.

UNIT BANK A bank that has no branches and operates independently out of one building in a state having unit banking law.

UNITED NATIONS An international organization that was established in accordance with the charter of the United Nations drafted by governments represented at the Conference on

International Organization meeting at San Francisco. The charter was signed on June 26, 1945, and came into force on October 24, 1945, when the required number of ratifications and accessions had been made by the signatories. In 1989, the United Nations consisted of 159 mem-ber states, of which 51 are founding members.

The purposes of the United Nations set out in the charter are: to maintain international peace and security; to develop friendly relations among nations; to achieve international cooperation in solving international problems of an economic, social, cultural, or humanitarian character and in promoting respect for human rights; and to be a center for harmonizing the actions of nations in the attainment of these common ends.

The principal organs of the United Nations are:

1. *General Assembly:* All states that are members of the United Nations are members of the General Assembly. Its functions are to consider and discuss any matter within the scope of the charter and to make recommendations to the members of the United Nations and other organs. It approves the budget of the organization, the expenses of which are borne by the members as apportioned by the General Assembly.
2. *Security Council:* The Security Council consists of 15 members, of which five—the People's Republic of China, France, the Union of Soviet Socialist Republics, the United Kingdom, and the United States—are permanent members and are elected each year. The ten nonpermanent members are elected for two-year terms by the General Assembly. The council acts on behalf of the members of the United Nations in maintenance of international peace and security.
3. *Economic and Social Council:* This organ is responsible, under the General Assembly, for the economic and social programs of the United Nations.
4. *Trusteeship Council:* This council considers reports from the member administering the Trust Territory, examines petitions from inhabitants of the Trust Territory, and provides for periodic inspection visits in the Trust Territory.
5. *International Court of Justice:* The court is the principal judicial organ of the United Nations. It has its seat at The Hague, the Netherlands. All members of the United Nations are ipso factor parties to the statute of the court. The jurisdiction of the court comprises all cases that the parties refer to it and all matters specifically provided for in the charter of the United Nations or in treaties and conventions in force. The court consists of 15 judges. They are elected for nine-year terms by the General Assembly and the Security Council, voting independently; they may be reelected.
6. *Secretariat:* The Secretariat consists of a secretary-general and staff. The secretary-general is appointed by the General Assembly on the recommendation of the Security Council. The secretary-general is the chief administrative officer of the United Nations. He/she may bring to the attention of the Security Council any matter that threatens the maintenance of international peace and security.

BIBLIOGRAPHY

Annual Review of United Nation Affairs. Oceana Publishing, Inc. Dobbs Ferry, NY. Annual.
UNITED NATIONS PUBLICATIONS, New York, NY:
  Basic Facts about the United Nations.
  Current Bibliographical Information.
  Demographic Yearbook.
  Everyone's United Nations.
  Industrial Statistics Yearbook.
  International Trade Statistics Yearbook.
  National Accounts Statistics.
  Your United Nations.
  UN Chronicle.
  United Nations Publications in Print; Check List: English.
    Annual Catalog.
  World Statistics in Brief.
United Nations Chronicle.

UNITED STATES BONDS Long-term, marketable types of direct obligations in the U.S. government's debt structure, which may be issued with any maturity but in practice are issued with maturities of over ten years, in view of the extension of maximum maturities of notes to ten years by legislation enacted in March, 1976.

Advance Refunding Technique. Refundings well in advance of maturities of issues were first utilized in the 1960 fiscal year as a preferable method of lengthening the debt, with minimum changes in ownership and minimum adverse effects on markets and the economy as compared with alternative methods. Under tax legislation enacted in September, 1959, the secretary of the Treasury may designate an advance refunding as a nontaxable exchange, involving no immediate taxation on exchanges of an existing issue par for par with a new issue. The Treasury classifies advance refundings as "senior" advance refundings, to shift 5- and 12-year maturities into longer terms, and "junior" advance refundings, to shift 1- and 5-year maturities into intermediate maturities.

See UNITED STATES GOVERNMENT SECURITIES.

Financing. All things being equal, it would of course be desirable to shift the bulk of maturities on the federal debt to longer-term maturities at relatively low interest rates and, in order to minimize the monetization of the debt through financing sale to commercial banks, to sell the bulk of issues to noncommercial bank investors including individuals. In meeting total financing needs, however, the Treasury as a practical matter has to "tailor" offerings so as to reach a maximum of its market with the least economic disturbance, bearing in mind the level of interest rates and the competition of its long-term needs with private long-term investment needs in such areas as home mortgage financing and corporate financing of capital expenditures. Thus, a variety of maturities, interest rates, and types of securities have been developed, along with bonds, to reach the maximum market, institutional as well as individual.

UNITED STATES DEPOSITARIES Federal Reserve banks and branch-es and some 15,500 authorized commercial financial institutions that provide the various departments and agencies of the U.S. government with banking and financial services. The Financial Management Service in the Treasury Department administers matters relating to the designation of government depositaries and the deposit of government funds with them. Depositaries may receive deposits directly from corporate taxpayers, directly from government agencies, or through the Treasury's lockbox network. Payments to the government are also made through the banking system by electronic fund transfers (EFT). With the exception of time deposits, government funds usually remain on deposit with commercial depositaries no longer than 24 hours before they must be remitted to a Federal Reserve bank for credit to Treasury's account.

The operating cash of the Treasury is held in Treasury accounts with Federal Reserve banks and branches and in tax and loan accounts of thousands of commercial banks, savings and loans, and credit unions throughout the country. Approximately 15,500 commercial financial institutions maintain Treasury tax and loan (TT&L) accounts. Each year, approximately 65% of the government's gross budget receipts is collected through the TT&L system.

The TT&L system functions as follows: As certain classes of taxes are deposited by business firms at local financial institutions, the funds are transferred on each institution's books from the taxpayer's account to the Treasury's tax and loan account. The depositary at the same time forwards "advices of credit" to its local Federal Reserve bank, which updates the depositary's account on its books and provides Treasury aggregate data for cash management purposes. Treasury directs the Federal Reserve banks to draw down the tax and loan balances as funds are needed to cover government disbursements.

Under authority granted by Public Law 95-147, implemented in 1978, Tax and Loan Depositaries voluntarily participate in the tax and loan account system under one of two options: the remittance option or the note option. Under the remittance option, the commercial financial institution accepts tax deposits and is allowed one business day to remit the funds to the Treasury's account at a Federal Reserve bank. Under the note option, the commercial financial institution accepts the tax deposits and retains the funds in its Treasury tax and loan note account until they are withdrawn by the Treasury. (Funds in the note accounts are interest-bearing at 25 basis points below the Fed funds rate.) All withdrawals are effected by an immediate charge to each depositary's reserve account or the reserve account of a member correspondent. (There is also a procedure for moving funds out of Treasury's accounts at the Fed to note option depositaries that have agreed to participate. That process is called a "direct investment," and it, too, is effected through the reserve

ENCYCLOPEDIA OF BANKING AND FINANCE

account structure.) Annual interest revenue from the program is in excess of $1 billion.

The TT&L system facilitates monetary policy and provides an efficient collection mechanism. It promotes smooth functioning of the economy by reducing the impact of government financial operations on the distribution and level of bank reserves and on the money market. The peaks and valleys in the timing of money flows between the public and the government can cause sharp changes in bank reserves, along with undesirable fluctuations in money market interest rates and the availability of loanable funds in the banking system. Treasury tax and loan accounts prevent these drastic swings. The Treasury draws down or builds up the tax and loan balances with depositaries so as to match the flow of collections with the flow of payments in Treasury's account at the Fed.

The regulations governing depositaries and financial agents of the government are in Title 31 of the Code of Federal Regulations (31 CFR) at Part 202. The regulations governing depositaries for federal taxes and tax and loan depositaries are found at 31 CFR Parts 214 and 203 respectively. Included in the regulations are the requirements for collateral to secure government funds in excess of insurance coverage.

BIBLIOGRAPHY

U.S.TREASURY DEPARTMENT. *Annual Report of the Secretary of the Treasury on the State of the Finances.*
———. *Treasury Bulletin* (monthly).

UNITED STATES GOVERNMENT SECURITIES

Securities that are obligations of the United States government and represent a debt that legally constituted federal authorities promise to pay on stated maturity dates. An act of Congress, September 2, 1789 (1 Stat. 65; 5 U.S.C. 241), established the Department of the Treasury and charged the secretary of the Treasury with the preparation of plans for the improvement and management of the revenue and the support of the public credit. As of March 17, 1971, P.L. 92-5 amended the Second Liberty Bond Act (31 U.S.C. 757b) to provide that the face amount of obligations issued under authority of that act, and the face amount of obligations guaranteed as to principal and interest by the United States, shall not exceed in the aggregate $400 billion outstanding at any one time, the so-called permanent debt ceiling. The Act of June 30, 1967 (P.L. 90-39) provided that the face amount of beneficial interests and participation certificates issued under Section 302(c) of the Federal National Mortgage Charter Act (12 U.S.C. 1717c) during the fiscal year 1968 and outstanding at any time shall be added to the amount otherwise taken into account in determining whether the requirements of the above provisions are met. House of Representatives Joint Resolution 520, June 23, 1982, provided for an increase in the debt limit to $1,290.2 billion ($890.2 billion temporary ceiling, to September 30, 1983, in addition to the permanent limit of $400 billion). The Senate finally approved House Resolution 520 on September 23, 1982. In view of the likelihood of continued high budget deficits, further increases in the temporary debt limit appear to be probable.

The Public Debt Act of 1942 delegated to the secretary of the Treasury complete discretion in the sale of marketable securities as to issuance on a competitive or other basis, on an interest-bearing or discount basis, on a combination basis, or at such price or prices as the secretary of the Treasury may prescribe.

Types of Issues.

Treasury bills: TREASURY BILLS are issued at a discount, and no interest as such is paid thereon. Therefore the investor obtains his return from the difference between purchase price and sale price or maturity face value, which shall be considered ordinary income or loss, not capital gain or loss, as provided in the Internal Revenue Code.

Three-month and six-month Treasury bills are normally auctioned weekly on Mondays, with payment due the following Thursday, through the district Federal Reserve banks as fiscal agents for the Treasury. Fifty-two-week bills are auctioned every four weeks, usually on Wednesdays. Special bills maturing shortly after tax dates may be offered a few times a year. Cash management or federal funds bills due usually within a few days are also auctioned occasionally, to tide over the Treasury during periods of shortfalls in the early part of some months, sold only in large blocks to market participants who submit minimum tenders of $10 million.

Tenders for Treasury bills are invited under competitive and noncompetitive bidding. Competitive tenders must be expressed on a price basis of 100, e.g., 99.334. Noncompetitive tenders, usually up to $500,000, without stated price are accepted in full at the average price of the accepted competitive bids. Bills are issued in book-entry form only, in a variety of denominations, increasing in multiples of $5,000 from a $10,000 minimum order, and may be exchanged for lower denominations only.

Certificates of indebtedness: The CERTIFICATE OF INDEBTEDNESS, a type of short-term issue with a maturity of one year, is no longer issued by the Treasury, having been displaced by Treasury bills.

Treasury notes: TREASURY NOTES have maturities of not less than one year nor more than ten years, and thus are in the "intermediate" maturities classification. The Treasury has issued two-year notes, four-year notes, and five-year notes on a regular basis; has issued three-year notes less frequently; and customarily has included offerings of notes in quarterly refunding operations, including seven-year and ten-year notes. Notes may be offered to the public for cash subscription, in exchange for outstanding or maturing issues, or for submission of bids (in terms of yield usually) by auction. Treasury notes pay interest, and are available in denominations ranging from $1,000 (except on notes with maturities of less than four years) to as much as $1 million, $100 million, and $500 million. As of June 30, 1982, there were 95 separate note issues outstanding, making the note issue the type of issue most often used in Treasury financing practice in recent years.

Bonds: See UNITED STATES BONDS.

Investment series B bonds of 1975-1980: These were nonmarketable 2.75% bonds, originally issued on April 1, 1951, on a par for par basis for marketable 2 1/2 s of June and December, 1967-1972, and additionally issued on April 30, 1952. These bonds were nontransferable, nonmarketable, and nonredeemable by the holder, but could be exchanged at the owner's option for 1.50% five-year marketable Treasury notes which were last issued dated October 1, 1979; bore interest from issuance date semiannually on April 1 and October 1; and, with their maturity only five years from issuance date, were down to only $21 million outstanding when the last of the series B bonds matured on April 1, 1980.

Miscellaneous issues: The most important types of nonmarketable issues are government account series, issued by the Treasury directly to government agencies, trust funds, and accounts; UNITED STATES SAVINGS BONDS; state and local government series, issued to state and local governments for reinvestment of proceeds of advance refundings of their tax-exempt debt, subject to Internal Revenue Service regulation of the practice; and foreign series and foreign currency series, the first denominated in dollars and the second in the currency of the country making the purchase, issuable in bills, certificates of indebtedness, notes, or bonds, to foreign governments and official institutions of foreign countries.

Position of Government Securities. Federal government securities represent the highest form of credit in the U.S. investment markets, since the obligations represent the full faith and credit of the U.S. government on direct and fully guaranteed issues. Thus in investment practice, the yields on U.S. government securities of varying maturities are the point of departure as "riskless" prime-quality returns for money, from the standpoint of financial risk (ability and willingness to pay). As the topmost sovereignty in the political system of the U.S., the federal government has powers which may be invoked to honor its public debt obligations: (1) the only national taxing power in the political system, in effect making the national wealth and national income a basis for revenues from which to meet obligations; and (2) the power to "coin money and regulate the value thereof," exclusively a federal power but not considered in conservative finance as an active support factor. A sound banking system, with coordination of fiscal policy with monetary policy, constitutes sounder assurance of ability of the Treasury to pay and refund obligations than the second factor, in view of the credit-creating power of the commercial banking system and the normally large volume of government securities taken by banks.

Besides the above factors of ability to pay, the willingness-to-pay record of the U.S. government has been exemplary in governmental finance, from the very beginning of the nation when Congress, at the instance of Alexander Hamilton, funded the federal debt of the Revolutionary War and postwar period.

Moreover, the large volume, well-distributed holdings, and active markets maintained by government securities dealers make government securities ideal for liquidity purposes of institutions as well as individuals. Marketable types provide "secondary reserves" for institutional investors and investing institutions. Savings bonds, although not marketable, are insulated from market fluctuation for individual holders, who may redeem them at specified redemption values.

Major Classifications of U.S. Government Securities.

1. *Marketable or nonmarketable.* Marketable issues include bills, certificates of indebtedness, notes, and bonds. Nonmarketable issues include savings bonds, depositary bonds, investment series bonds, special issues, and foreign series and foreign currency series.
2. *Fixed rate or discount obligations.* The only marketable discount type issues are Treasury bills, although the Treasury has full discretion to issue obligations on an interest-bearing or discount basis.
3. *Direct or guaranteed obligations.* The remaining unmatured guaranteed debt of U.S. government agencies as of February 28, 1979, consisted of $19.8 million of D.C. Armory Board and $586 million of Federal Housing Administration debentures (optionally issuable). The highest levels ever of guaranteed debt were $6,316.1 million outstanding on November 30, 1941 (pre-Pearl Harbor), and $5,497.6 million on June 30, 1940 (preceding defense program).
4. *Callable or noncallable prior to maturity.* For flexibility in debt management, the Treasury has issued some of its marketable bonds with optional call dates, so that it can redeem these bonds at par prior to final maturity on any semiannual interest date on notice (usually about four months). The first call date is the first date indicated in the bond's description; e.g., the 4s of February 15, 1988-1993, originally issued January 17, 1963, become callable on notice on February 15, 1988, and on any subsequent interest payment date, final maturity being February 15, 1993. As of June 30, 1982, 23 of the 47 bond issues outstanding were callable (deferred call) before final maturity. Since 1952, the Treasury has called outstanding bonds only if the refunding could result in interest saving compared with interest rate on the outstanding issues.

Agency Issues. Unguaranteed federal agency debt which is not direct debt of the U.S. government but involves "government sponsorship," has increased appreciably in recent years, reflecting increased open market financing by the agencies concerned. The clause "although the Government assumes no liability, direct or indirect, for them, the (obligations) are secured obligations of banks operating under Federal charter with governmental supervision" pertains to obligations issued in the capital markets by such federally sponsored corporations as Banks for Cooperatives, Federal Intermediate Credit banks, and Federal Land banks, and likewise, with respect to the joint and several obligations of the Federal Home Loan banks. The Federal National Mortgage Association (FNMA), constituted as a government-sponsored private corporation by the Housing and Urban Development Act of 1968, has a mixture of obligations. Its "mortgage-backed bonds" (Sec. 304(d) of the Charter Act) are general obligations of FNMA and are issued pursuant to the terms of the FNMA Mortgage Trust; timely payment of principal and interest due on such obligations is guaranteed by the General National Mortgage Association pursuant to Section 306(g) of the Charter Act, which provides that "the full faith and credit of the United States is pledged to the payment of all amounts which may be required to be paid under any guaranty (by GNMA) under this subsection." On the other hand, the FNMA capital debentures and convertible debentures were issued under Section 304(e) of the Charter Act, which provides for issuance of subordinated debentures which may be convertible into common stock. These are not guaranteed by the United States and do not constitute a debt or obligation of the United States or of any agency or instrumentality thereof other than the FNMA.

Under the Participation Sales Act of 1966, federal agencies (Small Business Administration, Department of Housing and Urban Development (including the FNMA), the Veterans Administration, the Export-Import Bank, the Farmers Home Administration (only for land acquisition loans, as well as for rural housing and crop production), and the Office of Education (only for loans for the construction of school facilities)) could pool agency assets (e.g., mortgages or loans) and, through the FNMA (later succeeded by the GNMA in this function) as trustee, sell participation certificates affording investors beneficial interest in the trusteed pool of agency assets. Originally, such participation certificates were not subject to the statutory public debt limit of the U.S. (Second Liberty Bond Act, 31 U.S.C. 757b); but the Act of June 30, 1967 (P.L. 90-39) provided that the face amount of beneficial interests and participations issued under Section 302(c) of the FNMA Charter Act (12 U.S.C. 1717(c)) during the fiscal year 1968 and outstanding at any time shall be added to the debt subject to the statutory public debt limit referred to.

Various of the federal agency issues referred to above have appeal to institutional investors because of their high marketability and yields 25 to 50 basis points higher than those of direct obligations with comparable maturities.

Growth in the public debt (federal as well as state and local) is indicated in PUBLIC DEBT; in the absolute as well as in percentage, growth in state and local debt has exceeded that of the federal debt on net basis (outstanding, held by the public), despite the "spinning off" of federally sponsored agencies in which there is no longer any federal proprietary interest (beginning in 1947, Federal Land banks; 1951, Federal Home Loan banks; 1968, Federal National Mortgage Association, Federal Intermediate Credit banks, and Banks for Cooperatives).

Tax Status of Government Securities.

Bills: Any income derived from Treasury bills, whether interest or gain from their sale or other disposition, does not have any exemption as such, and loss from the sale or other disposition of any such bills does not have any special treatment as such under the Internal Revenue Code. The bills are subject to estate, inheritance, gift, or other excise taxes, whether federal or state, but are exempt from all taxation now or hereafter imposed on the principal or interest thereof by any state, or any of the possessions of the United States, or any local taxing authority. For purposes of taxation, the amount of discount at which the bills are originally sold by the United States is to be considered as interest.

Certificates of indebtedness, notes, and bonds: Income derived from these securities is subject to all taxes now or hereafter imposed under the Internal Revenue Code. The securities are subject to estate, inheritance, gift, or other excise taxes, whether federal or state, but are exempt from all taxation now or hereafter imposed on the principal or interest thereof by any state, or any of the possessions of the United States, or any local taxing authority.

For savings bonds only, for the purposes of taxation, any increment in value represented by the difference between the price paid and the redemption value received (whether at or before maturity) shall be considered as interest.

Special issues, being investments of various government funds and payable only for the account of such funds, have no present tax liability.

Pursuant to a ruling by the Treasury, October 31, 1957, the exchange of 2.75% investment series B bonds, due 1975-1980, into five-year 1.50% notes creates no gain or loss for federal income tax purposes. The notes taken in exchange take the cost basis of the bonds exchanged for computation of gain or loss upon subsequent sale or other disposition of the notes. The entire period of continuous holding-of the bonds and later the notes-is considered for purposes of determining whether the capital gain or loss is long-term or short-term.

Market System for Government Securities. Marketable U.S. government and federal agency securities are virtually all traded in the OVER-THE-COUNTER MARKET, although government bonds are listed on the New York Stock Exchange, and trading in odd lots of government securities was recently instituted on the American Stock Exchange. Primary markets are maintained by bank dealers and nonbank dealers who in turn are serviced by government bond brokers who do not make markets and instead provide information on quotations and broker trades among dealers. In its OPEN MARKET OPERATIONS, the trading desk of the New York Federal Reserve Bank does business with only "recognized" or primary dealers.

The trading system for government securities has various unique features. Issues other than Treasury bills are normally quoted in bid and asked prices expressed in percentages (with minimum fluctuation of thirty-seconds) per $100 of face, e.g., "99.31" or "99-31" means $99 $^{31}/_{32}$, or $99.9687 per $100 of face value (on interest-paying issues, actual price paid will include in addition any accrued interest on the issue since its last payment date). The difference between the bid price and the asked price, both of which are net without commission in dealer markets, is called the spread, and is customarily very narrow on the more active issues so that the volume of the transaction involved is the dominant factor (e.g., on bills and other short-term issues, spread of $^1/_{32}$ to $^4/_{32}$ of a point [$312.50 to $1,250 per million]). Quotations may also be found expressed in sixty-fourths, e.g., "100.16+" means $100\,^{33}/_{64}$.

Treasury bills are quoted at net prices expressed on a discount rate percentage from full par, on a 360-day basis. Thus on bills with a maturity of six months or less, the annualized yield on a discount basis may be calculated on an "equivalent bond yield" basis (365 days). For example, Treasury bills with maturity of October 4, 1979, quoted on a 9.01% asked price basis for delivery on August 3, 1979, would have an annualized bond equivalent yield of 9.28%.

$$y = \frac{365 \times d}{360 - (d + t)} = \frac{365 \times 0.0901}{360 - (0.0901 \times 62)} = 9.28\%$$

where

y = annualized bond equivalent yield;
d = discount rate expressed as asked price (0.0901);
t = number of days of remaining maturity (62).

For Treasury bills with over six months' maturity, a more complex formula used by the Treasury and Federal Reserve results in a lower annualized bond equivalent yield because bonds (and other interest-paying issues) pay semiannual interest, whereas Treasury bills do not.

Regular way delivery on government securities is the next full business day following the day of the transaction; in addition, it is possible to arrange cash transactions (payment and delivery on the same day as the transaction) or delayed delivery, which will involve the accrual of interest to the deferred delivery date. In the case of odd-lot transactions, the normal delivery basis is five full business days following the day of the transaction.

Payment on deliveries of government securities is in federal funds, i.e., funds at the Federal Reserve bank. Since 1976, the U.S. Treasury has developed the book-entry system of effecting deliveries on government securities, whereby member banks of the Federal Reserve System keep the government securities at the Federal Reserve bank in accounts with computerized record keeping. Thus government securities dealers must clear through member banks who, by wire to the Fed, effect the necessary transfers of the securities kept there under the book-entry system to other member banks acting on behalf of their government securities dealers, against transfers of the funds in payment. Dealer banks would be so engaged for their own account.

Electronic Quotations. In recent years, the increasingly widespread use of electronic quotation systems has virtually revolutionized the quotation and trading procedures in the government securities market. Electronic quotation systems are classified as billboard and execution systems. The billboard system calls for identified contributor dealers to list their subject quotations on issues on video screens for the information of subscribers or recipients who, in turn, must contact the contributing dealer directly, usually by telephone, in order to effect transactions. The execution system also displays bid and asked firm quotations on the video screens, but the contributors who furnish the quotations are not identified. Thus in order to effect transactions, an interested participant who wishes to have actual transactions to buy or sell must contact the sponsor of the video screen, who will buy from or sell to the interested participant and simultaneously sell to or buy from the undisclosed contributing dealer who furnished the quotations.

Electronic quotation systems already have resulted in rapid, cheap, and widespread dissemination of bid and asked quotations on government securities. (Such systems also have been extended to other money market quotations and foreign exchange rates.) Since they provide firm bids and offerings to all participants simultaneously and thus continuous opportunities for actual trading, electronic execution systems are considered to have transformed dealer trading into a virtual auction process.

Summary. U.S. government securities fill a vital role in the investment and credit structure, providing liquid earning assets for institutions and individuals and serving as earning assets and media for collateral cover of the Federal Reserve notes, the largest form of paper currency in the money supply. Although no conservative viewpoint would desire overexpansion of the government debt, it would be difficult for the financial system to adjust to a substantial retirement reducing the supply and varieties of government securities available.

See NATIONAL BUDGET, PUBLIC DEBT, TREASURY BILL FUTURES, TREASURY SECURITIES, TREASURY TAX AND SAVINGS NOTES.

BIBLIOGRAPHY

BOARD OF GOVERNORS OF THE FEDERAL RESERVE SYSTEM. *Annual Report.*
——. *Federal Reserve Bulletin.*

UNITED STATES GOVERNMENT SECURITIES CROWD In bond trading on the New York Stock Exchange, the section of the ACTIVE CROWD that handles trading in marketable U.S. government securities. Because of the largely institutional character of the market for U.S. government securities, most trading volume in government securities is transacted off the board, usually in large blocks at low net spreads, by dealers in government securities, including trading departments of banks. Bids and offers in government securities are in minimum variations of one thirty-second of 1%.

UNITED STATES INDIVIDUAL RETIREMENT BONDS *See* TREASURY CERTIFICATES.

UNITED STATES INTERNATIONAL TRADE COMMISSION The U.S. Tariff Commission, originally created by act of Congress on September 8, 1916, had its name changed to United States International Trade Commission (USITC) by Section 171 of the Trade Act of 1974 (19 U.S.C. 2231). The commission's present powers and duties are provided for largely by the Tariff Act of 1930, the Antidumping Act of 1921, the Agricultural Adjustment Act, the Trade Expansion Act of 1962, the Trade Act of 1974, and, most recently, the Trade Agreements Act of 1979 (P.L. 96-39), a "most momentous and comprehensive act."

The Trade Agreements Act of 1979 (Sec. 2) implemented the results of the Tokyo Round of Multilateral Trade Negotiations (MTN) for the United States by approving the trade agreements submitted to the Congress on June 19, 1979, and the statement of administrative action to implement such agreements.

The following review of provisions of the Trade Agreements Act of 1979 details the procedures and duties involving the USITC.

Title I; Countervailing and Antidumping Duties.

Countervailing duties: Subtitle A of Title VII of the Tariff Act of 1930, as added by Section 101 of the referenced 1979 act, applies a new countervailing duty law to imports from countries that assumed the obligations (or substantially equivalent obligations) of the MTN agreement relating to subsidies and countervailing measures. Imports from seven developing countries could come under the new law under agreements in force on the day the referenced 1979 act was submitted as a bill to Congress, June 19, 1979. The existing countervailing duty law applies to all other imports.

Under the law, countervailing duties are imposed when the administering authority (reassigned to the INTERNATIONAL TRADE ADMINISTRATION and formerly mostly in the Treasury Department) determines that a country or person is providing a subsidy with respect to a class or kind of merchandise imported into the United States, and the USITC determines that the establishment of an industry is materially retarded or that an industry in the United States is materially injured or threatened with material injury by reason of imports of that merchandise. Material injury in the countervailing duty and antidumping statutes is defined to be harm that is not inconsequential, immaterial, or unimportant.

Countervailing duty investigations can be self-initiated by the administering authority or initiated by petition. Within 20 days after a petition is filed, the administering authority must determine whether the petition alleges the elements necessary for relief (material injury to a domestic industry by reason of subsidized imports) and includes information reasonably available to the petitioner supporting the allegations. If the determination is affirmative, an investigation to determine whether subsidization exists begins. If the determination is negative, the proceedings end.

Within 45 days after a petition is filed or an investigation is self-initiated, the USITC must determine whether there is reasonable indication that injury to a domestic industry by reason of subsidized imports exists. If the determination is negative, the proceedings end.

Within 85 days after a petition is filed or an investigation is self-initiated, the authority makes a preliminary determination, based on the best information available at the time, whether there is a reasonable basis to believe or suspect that a subsidy exists. In extraordinarily complicated cases, this determination is made within 150 days.

If the preliminary determination is positive, the administering authority requires bonds or cash deposits to be imposed on allegedly subsidized imports in an amount equal to the estimated net subsidy, and continues its investigation. The USITC initiates an investigation to determine whether injury exists. If the authority's preliminary determination is negative, the administering authority continues its investigation.

Within 75 days after its preliminary determination, the administering authority makes a final determination whether a subsidy exists. If the determination is negative, the proceedings end.

Within 120 days after the administering authority makes an affirmative preliminary determination, the USITC makes a final determination whether a domestic industry is being materially injured by reason of subsidized imports. In a case where the administering agency makes a preliminary determination that a subsidy does not exist, the USITC's final determination on material injury must be made within 75 days after the administering authority's affirmative final determination on subsidy.

If the final determination of the USITC is affirmative, a countervailing duty order requiring imposition of countervailing duties must be issued within 7 days of the USITC's determination.

An investigation can be suspended, prior to a final determination by the administering authority on the issue of subsidization, if (1) the government of the subsidizing country, or exporters accounting for substantially all of the imports of the merchandise under investigation, agree to eliminate the subsidy, to offset completely the net subsidy, or to cease exports of the merchandise to the United States within 6 months after suspension of the investigation; or (2) if extraordinary circumstances are present and the government or exporters described above agree to take action that will completely eliminate the injurious effect of the imports of the merchandise under investigation.

The USITC, upon petition, may review an agreement to completely eliminate the injurious effect to determine if that result is accomplished. If the USITC determines that the injurious effect is not eliminated, then the investigation must be completed.

If the administering authority determines that an agreement which resulted in suspension of an investigation is being violated, then the investigation is resumed. Unliquidated imports of the merchandise covered by the agreement are liable for retroactive countervailing duties if the goods entered on or before the later of 90 days before the date of the affirmative preliminary determination (which is issued on the day the investigation is suspended) or the date of the violation.

The deposit of estimated countervailing duties on imports that entered on or after the date a countervailing duty order is published is required at the same time the deposit of estimated normal duties is required, that is, within 30 days after release of the goods from customs custody. Final settlement of accounts with customs on imports subject to countervailing duties is required within 12 months after the end of an exporter's or manufacturer's fiscal year within which the imports were entered, or withdrawn from warehouse for consumption.

Countervailing duties are imposed retroactively from the date of a final finding of injury or threat of injury that, but for suspension of liquidation, would have been injury, to the date on which liquidation of entries of imports subject to investigation was suspended, usually the date of the preliminary determination. In "critical circumstances," countervailing duties are imposed retroactively from the date of a final finding of injury to the date 90 days before the date on which liquidation was suspended. Critical circumstances exist when the USITC determines there was injury which would be difficult to repair, caused by what the administering authority determined to be massive imports over a relatively short period benefiting from export subsidies.

Antidumping duties: Subtitle B of Title VII of the Tariff Act of 1930, as added by the referenced Trade Agreements Act of 1979, repealed the Antidumping Act of 1921 and replaced it with a comprehensive statute built upon the 1921 act and consistent with the MTN antidumping code. Under the new law, antidumping duties are imposed when the administering authority determines that a class or kind of merchandise is being or is likely to be sold in the United States at less than fair value and the USITC determines that the establishment of an industry is materially retarded or that an industry in the United States is materially injured or threatened with material injury by reason of imports of that merchandise.

Antidumping investigations can be self-initiated by the administering authority or initiated by petition. Within 20 days after a petition is filed, the administering authority determines whether the petition alleges the elements necessary for relief (material injury to a domestic industry by reason of dumped imports) and includes information reasonably available to the petitioner supporting the allegation. If the determination is affirmative, the authority initiates an investigation to determine whether dumping exists. If the determination is negative, the proceedings end.

Within 45 days after a petition is filed or an investigation is self-initiated, the USITC determines whether there is a reasonable indication that injury to a domestic industry by reason of dumped imports exists. If the determination is negative, the proceedings end.

Within 160 days after a petition is filed or an investigation is self-initiated, the authority makes a preliminary determination, based on the best information available at the time, whether there is a reasonable basis to believe or suspect that dumping exists. In extraordinarily complicated cases, this determination is made within 210 days.

If the preliminary determination is positive, the administering authority requires bond or cash deposits to be posted on allegedly dumped imports in an amount equal to the estimated margin of dumping, and continues its investigation. The USITC initiates an investigation to determine whether injury exists. If the authority's preliminary determination is negative, the administering authority continues its investigation.

Within 75 days (or 135 days upon request of exporters or petitioners) after its preliminary determination, the administering authority makes a final determination whether dumping exists. If the determination is negative, the proceedings end.

Within 120 days after the administering authority makes an affirmative preliminary determination, the USITC makes a final determination whether a domestic industry is being materially injured by reason of dumped imports. In a case where the administering authority makes a preliminary determination that dumping does not exist, the USITC final determination on material injury must be made within 75 days after the administering authority's final affirmative determination on dumping. If the final determination of the USITC is affirmative, an antidumping duty order requiring imposition of antidumping duties is issued within 7 days of the USITC determination.

An investigation can be suspended prior to a final determination by the administering authority on the issue of dumping if exporters accounting for substantially all of the imports of the merchandise under investigation agree to eliminate the dumping or to cease exports of the merchandise to the United States within 6 months after suspension of the investigation, or if extraordinary circumstances are present and the exporters referred to above agree to revise prices so as to completely eliminate the injurious effect of the imports of the merchandise under investigation.

The USITC, upon petition, may review an agreement to completely eliminate the injurious effect to determine if that result is accomplished. If the USITC determines that the injurious effect is not eliminated, then the investigation must be completed.

If the administering authority determines that an agreement that resulted in a suspension of an investigation is being violated, then the investigation is resumed and unliquidated imports of the merchandise covered by the agreement are liable for retroactive antidumping duties if entered on or after the later of 90 days before the date of the affirmative preliminary determination or the date of the violation.

Deposit of estimated antidumping duties on imports entered on or after the date of an antidumping duty order is required at the same time deposit of estimated normal duties is required, that is, within 30 days after release of the goods from customs custody. Final settlement of accounts with customs on imports subject to antidumping duties is required for most entries within 12 months after the end of an exporter's or manufacturer's fiscal year within which the imports were entered, or withdrawn from warehouse for consumption.

Antidumping duties can be imposed retroactively from the date of a final finding of injury or threat of injury that, but for suspension of liquidation, would have been injury to the date on which liquidation of entries of imports subject to investigation was suspended, usually the date of the preliminary determination. In "critical circumstances," antidumping duties can be imposed retroactively from the date of a final finding of injury to the date 90 days before the date on which liquidation was suspended. Critical circumstances exist when the authority determines that there is a history of dumping in the United States or elsewhere of the class or kind of merchandise under investigation or the importer of the merchandise knew or should have known that dumping was occurring, and that there have been massive imports of the merchandise in a relatively short period, and the USITC determines that the material injury is by reason of the massive imports to an extent that, in order to prevent such material injury from recurring, it is necessary to retroactively impose an antidumping duty.

Review of determinations: At least once during each 12-month period beginning on the anniversary of the date of publication of a countervailing duty or antidumping duty order, or a notice of the suspension of an investigation, the administering authority must review and determine the amount of any net subsidy, review and determine the account of any antidumping duty, and review the current status of and compliance with any agreement by reason of which an investigation was suspended.

In both antidumping and countervailing duty cases, whenever the administering authority or the USITC receives information concerning, or a request for the review of, an agreement that has resulted in suspension of an investigation, or a final determination that shows changed circumstances sufficient to warrant a review of the suspension or determination, it must conduct such a review. Absent good cause shown, such reviews will not be made before 24 months have elapsed since the notice of the determination or suspension was made.

All review, whether by petition or self-initiated, must include a hearing. Following review, the administering authority can revoke, in whole or in part, a countervailing or antidumping duty order or terminate the suspension of an investigation.

Definitions; special rules: The following are some key definitions applicable to antidumping or countervailing duty cases, or both.

The injury criteria in the countervailing duty and antidumping statutes are material injury to, threat of material injury to, or material retardation of the establishment of a domestic industry. "Material injury" is defined as harm that is not inconsequential, immaterial, or unimportant.

In determining whether injury exists, the USITC considers the volume of, and relative or absolute increases in the volume of, subsidized or dumped imports and their effect on the undercutting, suppressing, or depressing of prices, as well as the consequent impact of dumped or subsidized imports on domestic producers.

With respect to impact, the USITC evaluates all relevant factors including actual and potential decline in output, sales, market share, profits, productivity, return on investment, or utilization of capacity; factors affecting domestic prices; and actual and potential negative effects on cash flow, inventories, employment, wages, growth, and ability to raise capital or investment.

With regard to the volume, effect on prices, and impact of dumped imports, no one or several of the factors listed necessarily gives decisive guidance.

For purposes of determination of material injury in antidumping and countervailing duty cases, the term "industry" includes domestic producers as a whole of a product like the imported articles under investigation, or those domestic producers whose collective output constitutes a major proportion of total domestic production. Producers related to exporters or importers of the dumped product, or who import it, may be excluded. An injury finding may be based on effects in a geographical market under the following circumstances: first, producers in a market sell all or almost all their production there; second, demand in the market is not to any substantial degree supplied by producers located elsewhere; third, imports are concentrated in the market; and fourth, producers of all, or almost all, of the product in the market are injured.

"Like product" is defined as a product that is like, or in the absence of like, most similar in characteristics and uses to the imported article.

For purposes of the new countervailing duty law, the term "subsidy" means the same as "bounty or grant" under existing law, and includes, but is not limited to, the following:

1. The export subsidies listed in annex A to the agreement relating to subsidies and countervailing measures
2. The domestic subsidies set forth below when provided or mandated by governmental action to a specific enterprise, industry, or group of enterprises or industries, whether publicly or privately owned, and whether paid or bestowed directly or indirectly on the manufacture, production, or export of any class or kind of merchandise
3. The provision of capital, loans, or loan guarantees on terms inconsistent with commercial considerations
4. The provision of goods or services at preferential rates
5. The grant of funds or forgiveness of debt to cover operating losses sustained by a specific industry
6. The assumption of any costs or expenses of manufacture, production, or distribution.

The amount of a countervailing duty is equal to the net subsidy received by the producer, manufacturer, or exporter of the merchandise. The net subsidy received is computed by subtracting from the gross subsidy the following:

1. Application fees, deposits, and similar payments paid in order to qualify for, or receive, the benefit of the subsidy
2. The loss in the value of a subsidy resulting from its deferred receipt, if such deferral is mandated by government order
3. Export taxes, duties, or other charges levied on the export of the merchandise to the United States specifically intended to offset the subsidy received.

Hearings: The administering authority and the USITC are required to hold hearings during a countervailing duty or antidumping duty investigation. The hearings are not subject to the Administration Procedures Act (5 U.S.C. 554-557 and 702); however, a hearing record is required.

Verification of information: Verification of all information relied on by the administering authority in connection with a final determination in a countervailing or antidumping duty investigation is required. If information submitted cannot be verified, then decisions must be made on the basis of the best information available, which may include the information in the petition.

Access to information: The administering authority and the USITC must keep parties to antidumping and countervailing duty investigations informed of the progress of the investigation. A record must be maintained by the agencies of ex parte meetings held during the course of an investigation between interested parties, or other persons providing factual information, and the person in the respective agency charged with making the determination in the investigation, or any person charged with making a final recommendation to that person in the investigation.

Information properly designated as confidential is maintained in confidence during an investigation, except that the administering authority and the USITC may disclose confidential information received in a proceeding if it is disclosed in a form so that the information cannot be associated with, or otherwise be used to identify, the operation of a particular person. Certain confidential information submitted to the administering authority or the USITC may also be disclosed under an administrative protective order or pursuant to a court order.

Transitional rules for countervailing duty orders: With respect to countervailing duty orders in effect on the effective date of the new law, involving countries signing the subsidies agreement and under which countervailing duties have been waived under Section 303(d) of the Tariff Act of 1930, the USITC must determine whether material injury exists within 180 days after being notified by the administering authority of such a case. The waiver in that case continues until the determination by the USITC. If that determination is negative, the proceeding terminates. If it is affirmative, countervailing duties are imposed.

Title II; Customs Valuation.

Methods of valuation: The Trade Agreements Act of 1979 revises Section 402 of the Tariff Act of 1930, which specifies the methods for determining the value of an import for purposes of applying ad valorem duties to make it consistent with the customs valuation agreement negotiated in the multilateral trade negotiations (MTN). It also repeals the final list and American selling price methods of customs valuation.

The amended version of Section 402 now contains five methods—one primary method and four secondary methods—for determining customs value. The five methods are arranged in a hierarchical fashion, with an order of priority governing the application of each method.

The primary method of valuation under the new Section 402 is the transaction value of the imported merchandise; that is, the price actually paid or payable for the merchandise when sold for exportation to the United States with specified adjustments. The price actually paid is increased by the amounts attributable to various factors, including "assists," royalties, and license fees the buyer is required to pay as a condition of the sale of the merchandise to him and the proceeds of a subsequent resale, disposal, or use of the imported merchandise accruing to the seller, if these amounts are not otherwise included in the price actually paid or payable. Assists are defined as items or services supplied directly or indirectly by the buyer of the imported merchandise free of charge or at reduced cost for use in connection with the production or the sale for export to the United States of the imported merchandise.

Transaction value can be used in related-party transactions in appropriate cases. Two alternative tests are provided for determining whether the transaction value could be used in a related-party transaction. If an examination of the circumstances of sale of the merchandise indicates that the relationship did not influence the price, then the transaction value can be accepted. The second test compares the transaction value with a set of test values to see if the transaction value closely approximates one of the test values.

If the primary valuation method, i.e., the transaction value of the merchandise being appraised, cannot be accepted by the Customs Service, then the first alternative is the previously accepted and adjusted transaction value of identical merchandise sold for export to the United States and exported at or about the same time as the goods being valued. The second alternative is the previously accepted and adjusted transaction value of similar merchandise sold for export to the United States and exported at or about the same time as the goods being valued.

If the three previously mentioned value standards cannot be accepted, the customs value is determined on the basis of deductive value or computed value, in that order, unless the importer chooses to reverse the order of application of the two standards. The deductive value of imported goods is determined by subtracting from their resale price in the United States specific elements of value that have been added to the goods—that is, customs duties, selling expenses, etc.—to arrive at a value comparable to the transaction value.

The computed value of imported merchandise is the sum of the following:

1. The cost or value of the materials, fabrication, and other processing employed in the production of the imported merchandise
2. An amount for profit and general expenses equal to that usually reflected in sales of merchandise of the same class or kind as the imported merchandise that are made by producers in the country of exportation for export to the United States
3. Any assist, if not included in 1 or 2 above
4. The packing costs.

The final method of appraisement, to be used only when a value cannot be accepted under any of the previous valuation methods, is based on a value that is derived from one of the previous methods, with reasonable adjustments to the extent necessary to arrive at a value.

Presidential report: Section 203 of the Trade Agreements Act of 1979 directs the President to submit a report to Congress as soon as practicable after the close of the two-year period beginning on the date on which the amendments made by Title II of the act take effect, containing an evaluation of the operation of the customs valuation agreement, both domestically and internationally.

Final list and American selling price rate conversions: The U.S. valuation system was composed of two separate customs valuation laws, Sections 402 and 402a of the Tariff Act of 1930. The standards in Section 402a were the valuation standards established in the original Tariff Act of 1930. The Customs Simplification Act of 1956 added a new Section 402 to the Tariff Act of 1930 containing additional standards. The original standards were used to appraise only those articles for which dutiable value during the fiscal year 1954 would have been 5% less under the Section 402 standards added in 1956 than under Section 402a standards. These articles were determined by the secretary of the Treasury and were listed in regulations. They were known as the "final list" articles.

The American selling price (ASP) method of customs valuation existed under both Sections 402a and 402, and was virtually identical under both sections. The value of the import was based on the selling price of a U.S. manufactured article that was like or similar to the imported article. ASP was used only if required specifically by law. It was required to be used to value benzenoid chemicals, certain plastic- or rubber-soled footwear, canned clams, and certain gloves.

Sections 222 and 223 of the Trade Agreements Act of 1979 convert the rate of duty applicable to each article in the tariff schedules of the United States that was on the final list or valued on an ASP basis to a rate providing duty receipts equal to those received under the final list or ASP. ASP and final list are required.

Title III; Government Procurement. Title III of the Trade Agreements Act of 1979 implements the agreement on government procurement. The President is permitted to waive certain "buy American" restrictions in U.S. law or practice that discriminate against particular products of designated countries. Designated countries are countries that are parties to the agreement or that provide reciprocal procurement benefits to the United States. The President is permitted to prohibit federal government procurement of products from nondesignated countries. Furthermore, the President is permitted to withdraw or to limit waivers granted and, after consultation with the Congress and private sector, to grant new waivers.

The waiver authority enables the President to waive those portions of U.S. law, most notably the Buy American Act (41 U.S.C. 10a et seq.), that discriminate against purchases of foreign goods by federal government agencies. A waiver can apply only to goods that are the products of designated countries. Least developed (poorest) countries can be designated without condition. All other countries are required to provide reciprocal benefits for the United States in their government procurement, and major industrial countries are required to become parties to the agreement in order to be designated.

The annex to the agreement indicates those U.S. agencies whose procurement can be subject to waiver of discrimination against foreign goods. Procurement by those agencies accounted for about 15% of federal government procurement. Contracts of under $190,000 are excepted from the agreement and from the President's waiver authority.

The President is required to bar federal procurement of products subject to a waiver from any country that is not "designated." However, the President can delay this bar with respect to countries (other than major industrial countries) for up to two years; agency heads can waive the bar on a case-by-case basis; and procurement can continue with a country that is a party to a reciprocal procurement agreement with the Department of Defense.

The President is permitted to reduce or expand the coverage of waivers. However, an expansion of the coverage of a waiver to additional government procurement by an agency not listed in annex I of the agreement on the date of enactment of the referenced Trade Agreements Act of 1979 requires prior consultations with the Congress and the private sector.

Title III imposes substantial monitoring and reporting requirements with respect to both United States and foreign government procurement practices, and encourages negotiations to expand the agreement to cover more foreign government procurement.

Title IV; Technical Barriers to Trade (Standards). Title IV of the Trade Agreements Act of 1979 provides the statutory framework for United States' implementation of its obligations under the agreement to technical barriers to trade. Many of the practices covered by the agreement, such as notification of proposed standards-related activities and the provision of an opportunity for public comment, were already widely followed in the United States. However, certain of the agreement's provisions, while they are not a departure from U.S. practice, require implementation through legislation.

Obligations of the United States: The legislation does not prohibit standards-related activities that do not create unnecessary obstacles to the international trade of the United States. No standards-related activity is deemed to constitute an unnecessary obstacle to the international trade of the United States if the demonstrable purpose of the standards-related activity is to achieve a legitimate domestic objective, including, but not limited to, the protection of health or safety, essential security, environmental or consumer interests, and if such activity does not operate to exclude imported products that fully meet the objectives of such activity. United States' implementation of the agreement does not weaken the right of federal agencies, state agencies, or private persons to engage in standards-related activities that are deemed appropriate and necessary for reasons that are established in U.S. law.

Functions of federal agencies: The legislation attempts to avoid the establishment of new government offices by specifying, wherever possible, the use of existing offices and procedures. Current operations of the Departments of Commerce and Agriculture are used to implement aspects of the agreement within their expertise. The Office of the Special Representative for Trade Negotiations (STR) is given increased responsibilities for coordinating the standards-related activities of federal agencies which affect international trade. STR, U.S. embassies, and, where appropriate, the Departments of Commerce and Agriculture also monitor foreign implementation of the agreement. Finally, STR and the Departments of Commerce and Agriculture are responsible for coordinating federal government encouragement of state agencies and private persons to observe practices consistent with the obligations in the agreement.

Federal agencies are permitted to provide technical standards assistance to interested parties. Agencies are required to solicit technical and policy advice from the private sector advisory committees established under Section 135 of the Trade Act of 1974.

Administrative and judicial proceedings regarding standards-related activities Section 421 of the Trade Agreements Act of 1979 provides that, except as otherwise provided in Title IV of the act, the provisions of the subtitle will not create any right of action under the laws of the United States with respect to allegations that any standards-related activity engaged in within the United States violates the obligations of this country under the agreement. The STR is responsible for processing representations alleging U.S. violations of the agreement and participating, as necessary, in the settlement of disputes between the United States and other parties to the agreement.

Only parties or countries providing similar rights and privileges to U.S. interests can make representations to the STR alleging violations of U.S. obligations under the agreement. Federal agency proceedings on allegations against standards-related activities covered by the agreement are permitted only if the STR makes a finding of reciprocity or finds that the agreement dispute-settlement procedures are inadequate.

Definitions and miscellaneous provisions: Definitions of such key terms as "international standards organizations" and "standards" are contained in Title IV. Miscellaneous provisions specify persons or intra-agency activities not subject to the subtitle, a provisional effective date for Title IV of January 1, 1980, and the required future evaluation of the operation of the agreement by the STR.

Title V; Implementation of Certain Tariff Negotiations. Title V of the Trade Agreements Act of 1979 provides for the implementation of certain tariff concessions negotiated in the MTN agreement. Many of the tariff changes implemented under this title involve reductions or increases in rates of duty that exceed the limitations on the President's authority to proclaim a reduction or increase in a rate of duty under Sections 101 and 109 of the Trade Act of 1974. In other cases, changes in non-MTN duties or in headnotes, nomenclature, and classification affecting non-MTN duties are made. Non-MTN duties can only be changed by statute.

Title VI; Civil Aircraft Agreement. Title VI of the Trade Agreements Act of 1979 implements tariff changes required under the agreement on trade in civil aircraft. The President is permitted to eliminate duties on articles covered by the agreement—for example, airplanes and parts certified for use in civil aircraft. The 50% duty on repairs on U.S. civil aircraft performed in foreign countries is also eliminated.

Title VII; Certain Agricultural Measures. Title VII implements concessions to foreign countries under bilateral agreements relating to cheese, chocolate crumb (a mixture of chocolate and milk solids), and meat. The title increases the amount of cheese imports permitted under U.S. quotas; establishes procedures, in lieu of the countervailing duty law, to prevent subsidized cheese imports under quota from undercutting domestic cheese prices; increases the existing U.S. quotas on chocolate crumb; and establishes a 1.2 billion pound floor on meat import quotas under the meat import law.

Cheese: Section 701 of the Trade Agreements Act of 1979 permits the President to proclaim import quotas, at an annual level of up to 111,000 metric tons, on certain cheeses under the authority of Section 22 of the Agricultural Adjustment Act, without following the procedures of Section 22. The cheese import quotas can be increased above 111,000 metric tons only in accordance with the provisions and procedures of Section 22, except that the President cannot take emergency action under Section 22, that is, without a prior investigation and report by the USITC, unless the secretary of Agriculture finds that "extraordinary circumstances" exist.

About 85% of cheeses currently imported are subject to quotas. Certain specialty cheeses and soft-ripened cheeses (Brie, Camembert, and so on) are not under quota, but imports of other cheeses are limited, regardless of their price. Previous quotas did not limit imports of several types of cheese, if they were priced above $1.23 per pound. The new quota of 111,000 metric tons permits importation of about 15,000 more metric tons of cheese than was imported in 1978.

Section 702 provides for imposition of additional import fees or quotas on cheese subject to quotas to the extent necessary to prevent imports from undercutting, through use of subsidies, the wholesale price of comparable domestic cheeses. Action against price undercutting is required within a maximum of 68 days after a complaint.

Chocolate crumb: Section 703 of the Trade Agreements Act of 1979 provides for an increase of about 4.4 million pounds over the previous 21.68 million-pound quota on chocolate crumb. This accommodates quotas allotments to Australia (2,000 metric tons) and New Zealand (2 kilograms) negotiated in the MTN. This nominal allocation to New Zealand permits that country to export to the United States the amount of quota unused by other countries having significant quota allocations.

Meat: Section 704 of the Trade Agreements Act of 1979 amends the meat import law to provide that no quota may be imposed under that law at a level less than 1.2 billion pounds. This implements MTN commitments to Australia and New Zealand. Under previous law, which set import quotas at a level in direct proportion to domestic production, domestic production would have had to decline below 1978 levels before a quota below 1.2 billion pounds could have been established.

As a result of an agreement with Canada, the meat import law is also amended to make certain high-quality, portion-controlled cuts of beef subject to the restrictions under the law. The total amount of meat imports permitted under the meat import law were not increased thereby.

Title VIII; Treatment of Distilled Spirits.

Tax treatment: Title VIII repeals the wine-gallon method for determining the $10.50 per gallon tax on distilled spirits. As a result, both domestic and imported distilled spirits are now taxed uniformly under the proof-gallon method, which is based upon alcohol content. Title VIII also provides a half-month extension in the time period for payment of excise taxes on domestically bottled distilled spirits, to be phased in over a three-year period.

It also establishes the all-in-bond system for controlling the production of distilled spirits and collecting the excise taxes. This simplifies the tax collection process and reduces the number of government employees required to collect liquor excise taxes, as well as reduces ancillary capital investment by domestic producers necessary to comply with the current administrative system.

Tariff treatment: Title VIII repeals the wine-gallon method of duty assessment and makes imported distilled spirits dutiable on the basis of proof-gallon, that is, actual alcoholic content. Tariff rates on distilled spirits are converted to rates that yield the same revenues as were provided by the wine-gallon method of duty assessment and taxation. For example, the rate of duty on bottled whiskey was formerly $0.51 per wine-gallon; this rose to $2.30 per proof-gallon. Of the increase, about $1.70 reflects conversion to the proof-gallon method of taxation and about $0.08 reflects the conversion to the proof-gallon method of duty assessment.

The new tariff rates apply to products of countries that fail to provide to the United States reciprocal benefits for the wine-gallon repeal. For those countries affording reciprocal MTN benefits, the President is permitted to reduce the new duty on a proof-gallon basis to the rate formerly prevailing on a wine-gallon basis, that is, the rate on bottled whiskey can drop from $2.30 to $0.51 per proof-gallon. Until January 3, 1980, under Section 101 of the Trade Act of 1974, the President was also permitted to reduce the wine-gallon rate by up to an additional 60%, that is, from $0.51 to $0.202 cents per proof-gallon.

The President is permitted to raise the duty back to the full measure of protection, that is, $2.30 per proof-gallon on bottled whiskey, if a beneficiary country does not implement concessions granted to the United States. Furthermore, the President is required to withdraw, suspend, or modify equivalent concessions (but not necessarily the wine-gallon concession) if a foreign country fails to implement concessions benefiting U.S. export interests in distilled spirits.

Title IX; Enforcement of U.S. Rights. Title IX of the Trade

Agreements Act of 1979 revises Section 301 of the Trade Act of 1974 to permit enforcement of U.S. rights under the MTN agreements and to provide a procedure for private parties to request government action to remedy foreign violations of the agreements.

Section 301 of the Trade Act of 1974 permitted private parties to complain of foreign violations of international trade rules. It permitted the President to impose import restrictions as retaliatory action, if necessary, to enforce U.S. rights against "unjustifiable" or "unreasonable" foreign trade practices that burdened, restricted, or discriminated against U.S. commerce.

Title IX imposes time limits on investigations and recommendations by the Special Representative for Trade Negotiations and on presidential action under Section 301. The revision of Section 301 continues the ability of the United States to take "all appropriate and feasible action" within the President's power to obtain the elimination of any acts, policies, or practices that are unjustifiable, unreasonable, or discriminatory and that burden or restrict U.S. commerce. This mandate covers those actions that may not be specifically covered by international trade agreements or the GATT but that, in fact, burden or restrict U.S. commerce.

Title X; Judicial Review. Title X of the Trade Agreements Act of 1979 revises current law to provide increased opportunities for appeal of certain interlocutory and all final rulings by the administering authority or the USITC in antidumping and in countervailing duty cases. Title X also expands opportunities for judicial review of determinations by the Customs Service of the appraised value, classification, or rate of duty of imported goods. Furthermore, Title X provides for judicial review of Customs Service decisions regarding the certification of the "country of origin" of products covered by the Government Procurement Code.

Title X amends the Tariff Act of 1930 by adding a new Section 516A, which provides the specific judicial review procedures for countervailing duty and antidumping proceedings. The existing Section 516 is amended to delete those provisions dealing with antidumping and countervailing duty determinations, and thus include solely procedures for a domestic interested party's contest of appraised value, classification, or the rate of duty of imported merchandise.

Section 516A establishes the standards of review for those countervailing duty and antidumping duty determinations that are appealable. In general, the standard for interlocutory determinations is whether they are arbitrary, capricious, an abuse of discretion, or otherwise not in accordance with law. The standard for other determinations is whether they are not supported by substantial evidence on the record or are otherwise not in accordance with law. The act permits the Customs Court to enjoin, during the period of judicial review, liquidation or some or all entries of merchandise covered by a determination of the administering authority or the USITC during a countervailing or antidumping investigation.

The record before the court, unless otherwise stipulated by all interested parties participating, consists of all information presented to, or obtained by, the administering authority or the USITC during the course of a countervailing or antidumping proceeding and all government memorandums pertaining to the case on which the authority relied in making determinations. The record also includes a copy of the determinations sought to be reviewed, all transcripts or records of conferences or hearings, and all notices published in the *Federal Register*.

Title XI; Miscellaneous Provisions. Extension of nontariff barrier negotiating authority (Sec. 1101): The President's authority under Section 102 of the Trade Act of 1974 to enter into trade agreements to eliminate nontariff barriers and other distortions to trade adversely affecting U.S. commerce is extended until January 3, 1988. Any agreement becomes effective only after congressional consultation and enactment of an implementing bill under the legislative procedures in the Trade Act of 1974.

Auctioning of import licenses (Sec. 1102): The President is permitted to auction licenses used to administer quantitative restrictions under the following laws:

1. Sections 125, 203, 301, and 406 of the Trade Act of 1974
2. Trading with the Enemy Act
3. Section 204 of the Agricultural Act of 1956 (except relating to meat or meat products)
4. The International Emergency Economic Powers Act
5. The headnotes of the U.S. tariff schedules, except for restrictions imposed under Section 22 of the Agricultural Adjustment Act of 1933
6. Any legislation implementing an international agreement, including commodity agreements (except agreements relating to cheese or dairy products).

The auction authority applies only to quantitative restrictions imposed or modified after the date of enactment.

Private advisory committees (Sec. 1103): Private advisory committees established under Section 135 of the Trade Act of 1974 are continued for the following purposes: first, advising on trade negotiations and ensuring effective implementation of the MTN codes; second, evaluating and refining those codes; third, managing problems in key trading sectors; and fourth, advising on overall trade policy objectives and priorities. The mandate of advisory committees is broadened to include support of implementation of trade agreements and other trade policy activities. The President is given discretion to establish advisory committees on an appropriate basis when trade policy activities of the U.S. government warrant them, including committees on services.

The Trade Agreements Act of 1979 repeals the requirement that existing advisory committees write summary reports of trade agreements entered into under the Trade Act of 1974 after January 3, 1980. The act continues exemptions of the advisory committees from provisions of the Federal Advisory Committee Act and, in addition, exempts agriculture committees from the requirements of Title XVIII of the Food and Agriculture Act of 1977.

Study of possible agreements with North American countries (Sec. 1104): A study by the executive branch of the desirability of entering into trade agreements to promote the mutual economic growth of the United States, Canada, Mexico, and other appropriate countries in the northern portion of the Western Hemisphere was required. The study was to examine the agricultural, energy, and other sectors, and was to be submitted to the Committee on Ways and Means of the House of Representatives and the Committee on Finance of the Senate within two years after enactment of the act.

Section 337 of the Tariff Act of 1930 (Sec. 1105): A civil penalty is provided for a violation of a cease-and-desist order issued by the USITC under Section 337 of the Tariff Act of 1930. Section 337 permits the USITC to issue a cease-and-desist order with respect to unfair trade practices in the importation of a product. The penalty is a maximum of the higher of either $10,000 or the market value of the goods in question for each day in which an importation or sale of goods occurs in violation of the order. The penalty is recovered in a civil action brought by the USITC.

Section 337 is further amended to make clear that the statute does not cover actions within the purview of the countervailing duty law or the antidumping law. The USITC can suspend that part of an investigation under Section 337 which relates to such actions.

Reporting statistics on a cost-insurance-freight (CIF) basis (Sec. 1108): Import and balance-of-trade statistics are to be reported on a CIF basis. Also required is publication of all tariff rates that would be in effect if customs valuation were on a CIF rather than current basis.

Reorganizing and restructuring of international trade functions of the U.S. government (Sec. 1109): The President was required to submit proposed legislation restructuring the foreign trade policy-making and regulatory functions of the federal government by July 10, 1979. In order to ensure that the 96th Congress took final action on a comprehensive reorganization of trade functions as soon as possible, the appropriate committee of each house of Congress was to give the legislation proposed by the President immediate consideration and was to make its best effort to take final action on a bill to reorganize and restructure the international trade functions of the government by November 10, 1979.

Study of export trade policy (Sec. 1110): On or before July 15, 1980, the President was to submit to the Congress a study of the factors bearing on the competitive posture of U.S. producers in world markets and the policies and programs required to strengthen the relative competitive position of the United States in world markets. This study was also to include recommendations on the promotion of U.S. exports generally, and exports by small business particularly, and on the disincentives to exports created by the programs and activities of regulatory agencies.

Generalized system of preferences (Sec. 1111): The generalized system of preferences (GSP) under Title V of the Trade Act of 1974 is modified as follows.

The President is permitted to continue GSP treatment for eligible articles, and to designate new eligible articles, from beneficiary developing countries that exceed the competitive need limitation—that is, no more than 50% of total annual U.S. imports of an article eligible for GSP may come from one country, if total imports of the article are less than $1 million (adjusted annually to reflect changes in the GNP).

The customs union rule that permits such entities to be considered a single country, for GSP, is changed (1) to permit associations of countries contributing to comprehensive regional economic integration among their members to be designated as a single beneficiary developing country; (2) to permit application of the competitive need ceilings on GSP treatment (total annual imports of an eligible article from any one country may not exceed about $37 million, or 50% of total U.S. imports of the article) for a specific article from an association of countries described above to the individual member countries of such an association, rather than to the association as a whole; and (3) to reduce the minimum value-added requirement for GSP articles from such an association from 50% to 35%, the requirement applicable to individual countries.

The exclusion of ORGANIZATION OF PETROLEUM EXPORTING COUNTRIES (OPEC) member countries from GSP is modified to allow extension of GSP treatment to eligible articles from OPEC countries otherwise qualifying as beneficiary developing countries if they conclude bilateral product-specific trade agreements with the United States in the MTN and continue to supply petroleum to the United States.

Concession-related revenue losses to U.S. possessions (Sec. 1112): If a concession is granted in the MTN with respect to a product upon which are levied excise taxes that produced in 1978 a major share (10% or greater) of the revenues for the government of a U.S. possession, then the secretary of Commerce, with respect to fiscal year 1980 and the next four fiscal years, must determine within three months after the close of the fiscal year whether the concession contributed importantly to a loss of such revenues to the possession in the fiscal year concerned as a result of displaced sales of the product. In making this determination, the secretary must examine the extent to which any other factors were contributing to a loss of such revenues.

If the secretary determines a reduction in revenue exists, then the President can add to the budget amounts to be appropriated to the possessions concerned to offset in whole or in part the excise tax losses.

Summary. As indicated by the preceding explanation of the Trade Agreements Act of 1979, adapted from Senator Russell B. Long's presentation to the Senate (*Congressional Record*, July 23, 1979), the act approves the trade agreements submitted to the Congress on June 19, 1979, and specifies the proposed administrative actions to implement the agreements, which were reached at the Tokyo Round of Multilateral Trade Negotiations, insofar as they concern nontariff barriers to trade (the first significant revisions of international rules concerning nontariff barriers to trade since the adoption in 1947 of the General Agreement on Tariffs and Trade (GATT)]. In addition, the Tokyo Round agreements included significant reductions in tariffs, the U.S. reductions averaging about 30%; those of Japan, 22%; and those of the EUROPEAN ECONOMIC COMMUNITY, 27%.

The role of the International Trade Commission continues to be that of a fact-finding agency, having broad powers to study and to investigate all factors relating to U.S. foreign trade; its effect on domestic production, employment, and consumption; the competitiveness of U.S. products; and foreign and domestic customs laws. The commission may act on its own initiative or at the request of the President, other government agencies, the Senate Finance Committee, or the House Ways and Means Committee. The commission is composed of six commissioners, who are appointed by the President with the advice and consent of the Senate for a term of nine years, unless appointed to fill an unexpired term, and are not eligible for reappointment. The chairman and vice-chairman are designated by the President for two-year terms. Succeeding chairmen may not be of the same political party, nor may more than three commissioners be members of the same political party. The commission publishes results of investigations concerning various commodities and subjects, and also publishes a series of reports on chemicals. Other publications include *Summaries of Trade and Tariff Information*; an *Annual Report* to the Congress on the operation of the Trade Agreements Program; and an *Annual Report* to the Congress on commission activities.

See COMMERCE, DEPARTMENT OF; RECIPROCAL TARIFF ACT.

BIBLIOGRAPHY

ALLEN, M. "The Multilateral Trade Negotiations—A Background Note." *Finance and Development*, September, 1979.
BALASSA, B. "The Tokyo Round and the Developing Countries." *Journal of World Trade Law*, March-April, 1980.
BECSKY, G. "Duality of the U.S. Trade Policy." *Acta Oeconomica*, nos. 1-2, 1979.
DICKEY, W. L. "The Pricing of Imports into the United States." *Journal of World Trade Law*, May-June, 1979.
FIELEKE, N. S. "Trade Between the United States and Japan: Some Key Issues." *New England Economic Review*, November-December, 1979.
HOUCK, J. P. "Agricultural Trade: Protectionism, Policy, and the Tokyo-Geneva Negotiating Round." *American Journal of Agricultural Economics*, December, 1979.
MIDDLETON, R. W. "The GATT Standards Code." *Journal of World Trade Law*, May-June, 1980.
OLECHOWSKI, A., and SAMPSON, G. "Current Trade Restrictions in the EEC, the United States, and Japan." *Journal of World Trade Law*, May-June, 1980.
ROTIVAL, A. "GATT Promoted Programmes of Exports." *Management Training Review*, nos. 1-2, 1978.
SAMPSON, G. P. "Contemporary Protectionism and Exports of Developing Countries." *World Development*, February, 1980.
VAN BAEL, I. "Ten Years of EEC Anti-Dumping Enforcement." *Journal of World Trade Law*, September-October, 1979.

UNITED STATES MONEY

Coinage System. The COINAGE system of the U.S. underwent substantial changes when P.L. 89-81, July 23, 1965 (known as the Coinage Act of 1965), fundamentally changed the metallic content of the three denominations of subsidiary coins (the half-dollar, the quarter, and the dime).

The half-dollar clad coin, first produced December 30, 1965, by the Denver Mint as authorized by the act and bearing the date 1965, has an overall silver content of 40% (0.400 fineness) and is faced with an alloy of 80% silver and 20% coppper, metallurgically bonded to a center core containing approximately 21% silver and 79% copper. The gross weight of the clad half-dollar is 11.5 grams, of which 4.6 grams is silver. By contrast, the former 0.900 fineness silver half-dollar weighed 12.5 grams, of which 11.25 grams were silver.

Silver was completely eliminated from the quarter and the dime. The two outer layers of these denominations are composed of a cupronickel alloy of 75% copper and 25% nickel, metallurgically bonded to a center core or inner layer of pure copper. The obverse and reverse sides are white in appearance, and the copper core gives the coins a distinctive copper-colored edge. The clad quarter weighs 5.67 grams, compared with 6.25 grams for the 0.900 fine silver quarter. The clad dime weighs 2.268 grams, compared with 2.5 grams for the former 0.900 fine silver dime.

Three denominations of coins were left unchanged: the bronze one-cent piece, the cupronickel five-cent piece, and the standard SILVER DOLLAR of 0.900 fineness. Although the act stipulated that no silver dollars were to be manufactured during the five-year period dating from enactment of the act, and the Treasury indicated no plans for such coinage (last previous coinage of the standard silver dollar occurred back in 1935), the act created the JOINT COMMISSION ON THE COINAGE and left the future of the standard silver dollar subject to its recommendations.

The Joint Commission on the Coinage at its May 12, 1969, meeting recommended, among other things, that the Treasury Department request legislation authorizing the minting of a nonsilver dollar coin besides a nonsilver half-dollar. Specific legislation that eventuated was Title II of P.L. 91-607, December 31, 1970, which provided, among other things, for the minting of 150 million Eisenhower memorial dollars, containing 40% silver, to be distributed only in proof and uncirculated condition on a subscription basis, not for general circulation; the authorization of nonsilver dollar and half-dollar coins for general circulation, similar in composition to the clad quarters and clad dimes, the former 40% silver half-dollar being discontinued effective January 1, 1971; and the authorization through the General Services Administration for the auction of about 3 million 0.900 fineness silver dollars still held by the Treasury, completed on November 10, 1970.

Pursuant to the recommendation of the Joint Commission on the Coinage, the Treasury revoked the ban on melting down or exporting silver coins of the former content fineness, in view of their no longer being minted; such ban had been authorized the Treasury by Section 5 of the Coinage Act of 1965.

Anthony Dollar. P.L. 95-447, dated October 10, 1978, authorized the issuance of the new Susan B. Anthony dollar coin. It further provided that the minting of the Eisenhower circulating dollar coin be discontinued as of December 31, 1978. Pursuant to amendment by the referenced act of the Coinage Act of 1965, the new Anthony dollar is 1.043 inches in diameter and weighs 8.1 grams, compared to a diameter of 1.205 inches and a weight of 22.68 grams for the Eisenhower dollar coin. As a result, the cost of production of the Anthony dollar is $0.03 each, compared with $0.08 each for the Eisenhower dollar.

For the government, the promotional advantage cited for the Anthony dollar, as a substitute for the $1 denomination paper dollar, was that the $1 bill costs nearly $0.02 to produce but lasts only 18 months in circulation, frequently in bad shape, whereas the Anthony coin costs $0.03 to produce but lasts 15 years or more in good condition. The advantages for the financial community of substitution of the Anthony dollar for the $1 bill include elimination of the need to remove worn and torn bills from circulation, reduction in mistakes resulting from new $1 bills received being stuck together or being of mixed denominations, reduction in teller verification time, reduction of the possibility of counterfeiting, speeding up of teller transaction time and reduction in customer waiting time, and elimination of jamming of currency counting machines.

For the retail community, the advantages cited for the new Anthony dollar coin include saving of time and reduction in errors at cash registers, ease of withdrawal from and entry into cash drawers (bills by contrast are secured under a spring retainer in the cash register and must be straightened), saving in time and reduction in errors in either manual or automatic counting and handling operations (bills often stick together and cannot be distinguished by size), and ease and speed in separation by size (bills must be individually separated by denomination and placed face up in one direction, etc.).

Finally, the advantages cited for the consumer for the new Anthony dollar coin are that it is easy to carry with other coins and so eliminates fumbling in both sections of wallet or purse and allows higher bills to remain secure; it is easy to find in a pocket or change purse since it is sized between the quarter and half-dollar and weighs one-third as much as four quarters; it is easy for children to use; and it is easy to hear when dropped.

The new Anthony dollar coins were minted in Philadelphia, Denver, and San Francisco and distributed by the Federal Reserve banks. These regional mints began production in December, 1978, in order to accumulate an inventory of 500 million coins prior to their release to local banks in July, 1979, and production after such release was originally planned at the rate of 80 million per month.

The initial reception, however, of the new Anthony dollar coin as of late 1979, beyond high interest in the initial distribution, proved to be disappointing in terms of the stated goal of displacing the $1 denomination paper dollar, and the Treasury planned a greater promotion campaign. The Susan B. Anthony Dollar Coin Act of 1978 (P.L. 95-447) was the result of a comprehensive review of the coinage system of the U.S. conducted during the Ford administration by Research Triangle Institute.

Paper Money System. The PAPER MONEY system of the U.S. also has undergone fundamental changes in recent years. SILVER CERTIFICATES, originally dating from 1878 and issued in denominations of $1, $5, and $10 by the Treasurer of the United States against standard silver dollars, silver, or silver bullion held in the Treasury, where they could be redeemed upon demand in standard silver dollars, have not been issued since October, 1964.

P.L. 90-29, June 24, 1967, provided that by June 24, 1968, silver certificates would no longer be redeemable for silver. Pursuant to the authority vested in the secretary of the Treasury by P.L. 88-36 (June 4, 1963), silver certificates could be exchanged on demand at the U.S. Assay Offices in New York and San Francisco for silver bullion of equivalent value computed at the monetary value of silver of $1.2929 per fine troy ounce (pursuant to Act of August 27, 1935 [31 U.S.C. 773a]. Silver certificates could continue to be exchanged at the U.S. Treasury for coins and currency other than silver dollars, but that was meaningless contrasted with the expectations for market profits as silver rose in market prices). The Treasury also continued to accept, under the procedure established July 22, 1963 (28 F.R. 7530), requests for silver bullion in fine silver bars of approximately 1,000 ounces accompanied by tenders of funds other than silver certificates. Under this procedure, a person desiring silver bullion in this form could request the Federal Reserve Bank of New York or the Federal Reserve Bank of San Francisco to acquire silver certificates for his account in an equivalent amount and, upon completion of acquisition of the required amount of silver certificates, to accept them for the account of the Assay Office for exchange for silver bullion. Toward the end of the June 24, 1968, deadline for redemption of silver certificates, the Treasury began redeeming in silver of less than commercial fineness.

FEDERAL RESERVE NOTES were authorized in denominations as low as $2 and $1 by P.L. 88-36 (June 4, 1963). The new $1 denomination Federal Reserve note has successfully become the new workhorse of paper money circulation, displacing the $1 denomination silver certificate which formerly performed this function.

The new $2 denomination Federal Reserve note, however, has failed to catch on as a replacement for the $1 denomination bill. The $2 bill was introduced in November, 1975, when 525 million such bills were purchased by the Federal Reserve, which paid a cost of $15 per 1,000, or a total cost of $7,875,000, entirely aside from costs to the Treasury for designing the bill, preparing the die, and producing the bill. The Treasury projected annual savings of $10 million when and if the $2 bill importantly displaced the $1 bill, a savings projection based on cutting in half its production run on $1 bills. Only 225 million of the new $2 bills were put into public use, and the balance of 300 million $2 bills remained in Federal Reserve storage-seemingly permanent storage, because their destruction would be expected to make collectors' items of the $2 bills in circulation.

Before issuance of the new $2 denomination Federal Reserve note, the last printing of the $2 bill was the 1963-1963A series in May, 1965, of UNITED STATES NOTES, a vestige of Civil War currency issuance.

Paper MONEY forms no longer being issued include the following.

1. GOLD CERTIFICATES, issued prior to January 30, 1934. Holdings of the public were ordered turned in to Federal Reserve banks in 1933, and in turn turned in to the Treasury by Federal Reserve banks in January, 1934, in connection with the nationalization of gold in any monetary form. As of December, 1978, there were still $3 million (approximately) in circulation, the same amount (apparently irreducible) reported outstanding at the end of each year since 1974.
2. FEDERAL RESERVE BANK NOTES, all authority for issuance of which ended with the Act of June 12, 1945 (although no interest-bearing government securities carrying the circulation privilege have been outstanding since August 1, 1935). Still, some $48 million were reported outstanding at the close of December, 1978.
3. NATIONAL BANK NOTES, in the process of retirement since July 22, 1935, when the Act of July 22, 1932, temporarily attaching the circulation privilege to all outstanding U.S. government bonds bearing interest rates not over 3.375 expired, and no subsequent government bonds with the circulation privilege were issued. At the close of December 1978, there were still some $20 million of national bank notes in circulation, the same amount reported since 1969.
4. SILVER CERTIFICATES, not issued since October, 1964, and whose bearer redemption into silver was terminated June 24, 1968. At the close of December, 1978, there were still some $207 million in circulation.
5. TREASURY NOTES OF 1890, which, by the Act of March 14, 1900, were directed to be canceled and retired whenever received in the Treasury, in an amount equal to the coinage of standard silver dollars from the bullion purchased under the Act of July 14, 1890 (Sherman Silver Purchase Act). Less than $500,000 of such Treasury notes of 1890 have been in circulation in recent times.

Present United States Money System. The appended table shows the amounts of the various kinds of coin and paper money outstanding and in circulation.

Gold coin (double eagle [$20], eagle [$10], half eagle [$5], and quarter eagle [$2.50]), which up to the spring of 1933 was a part of the circulating money supply of the U.S., was called in and its holding made illegal on March 10, 1933, and the remaining amount that was

UNITED STATES NOTES

U.S. Currency and Coin Outstanding and in Circulation

Amounts Outstanding and in Circulation March 31, 1989

	Total currency and coin	Currency				Coin		
		Total	Federal Reserve notes	U.S. notes	Currency no longer issued	Total	Dollars	Fractional coin
Amounts outstanding	$287,267,007,128	$268,821,364,230	$268,231,138,325	$322,539,016	$267,686,889	$18,445,642,898	$2,024,703,898	$16,420,939,000
Less amounts held by:								
The Treasury	480,939,606	36,696,688	4,706,923	31,772,639	217,126	444,242,918	332,592,110	111,650,808
The Federal Reserve banks	43,856,442,669	43,373,823,940	43,373,790,541	213	33,186	482,618,729	110,262,359	372,356,370
Amounts in circulation	$242,929,624,853	$225,410,843,602	$224,852,640,861	$290,766,164	$267,436,577	$17,518,781,251	$1,581,849,429	$15,936,931,822

Source: Financial Management Service.

nominally outstanding but rendered no longer legal for circulation was deducted from the data on the money supply of the U.S. on January 31, 1934. Gold certificates issued prior to 1934 similarly were ordered turned in and became illegal for circulation. Gold certificates (Series of 1934) and gold certificate fund-Federal Reserve System are issued only to Federal Reserve banks against credits thereat established for the Treasurer of the United States.

United States notes, a vestigial part of Civil War financing originally called "greenbacks," are still required by the Act of May 31, 1878, to be reissued (denominations of $2 and $5).

Restoration of Gold Clauses in Contracts. Act of Congress approved October 28, 1977 (P.L. 95-147) among other things repealed the "Joint Resolution to Assure Uniform Value to the Coins and Currencies of the United States," approved June 5, 1933 (31 U.S.C. 463). The intended effect of this repealer is to permit the inclusion of gold and multicurrency clauses in private contracts. The referenced joint resolution had provided that "... every provision contained in or made with respect to any obligation which purports to give the obligee a right to require payment in gold or a particular kind of coin or currency, or in an amount in money of the United States measured thereby, is declared to be against public policy; and no such provision shall be contained in or made with respect to any obligation hereafter incurred. Every obligation, heretofore or hereafter incurred, whether or not any such provision is contained therein or made with respect thereto, shall be discharged upon payment, dollar for dollar, in any coin or currency which at the time of payment is legal tender for public and private debts. Any such provision contained in any law authorizing obligations to be issued by or under authority of the United States is hereby repealed, but the repeal of any such provision shall not invalidate any other provision or authority contained in such law."

Legal Tender. P.L. 89-81, the Coinage Act of July 23, 1965, provided for the restatement of legal tender in terms substantially identical to those of the provision of the Act of May 12, 1933, as amended by the Joint Resolution of June 5, 1933, in effect up to the date of enactment of the Coinage Act of 1965. "All coins and currencies of the United States (including Federal Reserve Notes and circulating notes of Federal Reserve Banks and national banking associations), regardless of when coined or issued, shall be legal tender for all debts, public and private, public charges, taxes, duties, and dues."

Monetary Standard. The Gold Reserve Act of 1934 (January 30, 1934) nationalized gold, provided that monetary gold of the U.S. shall be held in bullion form, and further provided that no currency of the U.S. (including circulating notes of Federal Reserve banks and national banks) should thereafter be redeemable in gold except to the extent permitted by regulations of the secretary of the Treasury with the President's approval. Domestically, therefore, the U.S. monetary standard has been an inconvertible paper standard, which permits no gold money in any form (bullion, coin, or gold certificates) and no conversion into gold of any other forms of monies. Internationally, as a result of membership since 1947 in the International Monetary Fund (IMF) international monetary system of fixed par values for currencies, based on respective gold contents with the U.S. dollar as the key currency and international gold convertibility for "official accounts" (governments and their official institutions), the U.S. has been on an international gold exchange standard. (On April 3, 1972, legislation authorizing the first devaluation of the U.S. dollar since Presidential Proclamation of January 31, 1934, devalued by 40.94%, thus raising the monetary gold price from $20.67 to $35 per ounce; this devaluation by approximately 8%, which was effected on May 8, 1972, raised the statutory price of monetary gold from $35 to $38 per ounce.) Further devaluation of the U.S. dollar by about 10% was effected October 18, 1973, thus raising the monetary gold price to $42.22 per ounce.

Summary. Giving effect to changes in recent years, the United States money system has the following characteristics.

1. All forms of current coinage are token coins—i.e., their intrinsic value does not match their denominational value. (If it did, the coinage would be fullbodied or "commodity" money.) Monetary gold is nationalized.
2. The old 0.900 standard silver dollars have premium value over denominational value if open market silver prices prevail above $1.29+ per ounce. The old 0.900 subsidiary silver coins have premium value over denominational value if open market silver prices prevail above $1.38 ounce. The old 40% silver clad half-dollar coins have premium value over denominational value if open market silver prices prevail above $3.38 per ounce. (As of mid-year 1979, silver spot prices at New York were up to over $8.70 an ounce.)
3. All forms of paper money currently issued (Federal Reserve notes and United States notes) are irredeemable paper money insofar as the standard metal, gold, is concerned. Silver certificates still outstanding are irredeemable insofar as their former redemption privilege into silver is concerned.
4. All forms of lawful money, however, are full legal tender.

See also FIAT MONEY, GOLD COINS, IRREDEEMABLE PAPER MONEY, MINOR COINS, MINT, MINT PRICE OF GOLD, MONETARY STOCK, QUANTITY THEORY OF MONEY, SUBSIDIARY SILVER COINS.

UNITED STATES NOTES Circulating notes created by several acts passed during the Civil War; also known as legal tender notes, "legal tenders," and "GREENBACKS," (because they were the first bills to be engraved with green backs). They were issued in denominations of $1, $2, $5, $10, $20, $50, $100, $500, $1,000 and $10,000, but mostly in small denominations of $2 and $5. On August 10, 1966, the Treasury Department announced that the $2 denomination would no longer be printed, and the last $5 denomination United States notes were checked out of the vault of the Treasurer of the United States on April 1, 1969. As required by the Act of May 31, 1878, the amount of United States notes outstanding is maintained at $322,539,016, of which $313,201,378 are in circulation and $9,337,633 are held by the Treasury.

The Act of February 25, 1862, authorized the issue of $150 million,

$50 million of which was in lieu of an equal amount of demand notes and could be issued only as the demand notes were canceled. A second issue of $150 million was authorized by the Act of July 11, 1862, $50 million of which however was to be a temporary issue for the redemption of a debt known as the Temporary Loan. A third issue of $150 million was authorized by the Joint Resolution of January 17, 1863, and the Act of March 3, 1863. The total amount authorized was $450 million, and the highest amount outstanding at any time was $449,338,902, as of January 30, 1864.

The reduction of $400 million from the original permanent issue to the amount at present still outstanding, $346,681,016, was brought about as follows.

1. Act of April 12, 1866, provided that United States notes might be retired to the extent of $10 million during the ensuing six months, and that thereafter they might be retired at the rate of not more than $4 million per month. This authority remained in force until suspended by the Act of February 4, 1868. The authorized amount of reduction during this period was about $70 million, but the actual reduction was only about $44 million.
2. No further change was made in the volume of United States notes outstanding until after the Panic of 1873 when, in response to popular demand, the government reissued $26 million of the canceled notes, bringing the amount outstanding to $382 million, where it remained until the Act of January 14, 1875, which provided for a reduction to $300 million.
3. Act of May 31, 1878, again stopped the process of reduction by requiring the notes to be reissued when redeemed or received in the Treasury on any account.

During the period of suspension of specie payments, January 3, 1862-January 1, 1879, no provision was made for redemption of United States notes in coin. The Credit-Strengthening Act of March 18, 1869, declared it to be the policy of the United States to provide for the redemption of United States notes in coin, and the Resumption Act of January 14, 1875, directed the secretary of the Treasury to prepare and provide for such redemption in coin on and after January 1, 1879. For this purpose, it authorized the use of surplus revenues and the sale of bonds authorized by the Refunding Act of July 14, 1870. Pursuant to this authority, $95.5 million of 4.5% and 4% bonds were sold, and the proceeds ($96 million in gold) were placed in the Treasury as a fund for such redemption; in time, this fund became known as the "gold reserve."

The steps by which such reserve came to total its eventual amount of $156,039,430.93 were as follows.

1. The Bank Act of July 12, 1882, provided for the suspension of issuance of gold certificates whenever the amount of gold coin and gold bullion in the Treasury reserved for the redemption of United States notes fell below $100 million.
2. The Act of March 14, 1900, making further provision for the redemption of United States notes (and Treasury notes of 1890), required the secretary of the Treasury to set up a reserve fund of $150 million in gold for the redemption of such notes, and prescribed the means for maintenance of such reserve fund.
3. The Aldrich-Vreeland Act of May 30, 1908, directed that taxes received on national bank circulation secured otherwise than by United States bonds (i.e., issuable as temporary emergency currency) should be credited to the reserve fund held for the redemption of United States notes.
4. The Federal Reserve Act of December 23, 1913, authorized application, at the discretion of the secretary of the Treasury, to such gold reserve fund of the net earnings derived by the United States from the Federal Reserve banks. The Act of March 4, 1923, made similar provision with respect to the net earnings derived by the United States from Federal Intermediate Credit banks. Through these means, $6,039,430.93 in gold was added to such gold reserve fund, making the aggregate of the fund $156,039,430.93.

However, Section 8 of the Act of Congress approved March 18, 1968 (P.L. 90-269) amended Section 6 of the Gold Reserve Act of 1934 (31 U.S.C. 408a) by striking out the provision for maintenance of such gold reserves by the Treasurer of the United States against United States notes and Treasury notes of 1890 (the latter had not thus been reserved since June 30, 1961).

Since the Gold Reserve Act of January 30, 1934, and Presidential Proclamation thereunder January 31, 1934, no currency may be redeemed in gold except as permitted by regulation issued by the secretary of the Treasury with approval of the President. Thus United States notes have been irredeemable in respect to the monetary metal, gold, since March, 1933, and then enactment of the permanent statute, the Gold Reserve Act of 1934, although the latter continued to specify the maintenance of gold reserve for United States notes and Treasury notes of 1890 until P.L. 90-269 (March 18, 1968), *supra*.

Title III of the Act of May 12, 1933, authorized the President, under certain circumstances, to direct the secretary of the Treasury to cause to be issued additional greenbacks in an aggregate amount not exceeding $3 billion. This authority was never exercised by the President, and was terminated by the Act of June 12, 1945.

By their various original authorizing acts, United States notes were declared to be "lawful money and a legal tender" for all debts, public and private, except duties on imports and interest on the public debt. The Act of June 17, 1930, authorized the acceptance of United States notes in payment of customs dues. The Act of May 12, 1933, as amended by the Joint Resolution of June 5, 1933, which declared all coins and currencies of the United States legal tender for all debts, public and private, public charges, taxes, duties and dues, removed all limitations on the legal tender quality of United States notes. P.L. 89-81, July 23, 1965 (Coinage Act of 1965) restated legal tender in substantially identical terms with the provision of the Act of May 12, 1933, as amended by the Joint Resolution of June 5, 1933.

BIBLIOGRAPHY

Barrett, D. C. *The Greenbacks and Resumption of Specie Payments*, 1862-1879, 1931.
Mitchell, W. C. *A History of the Greenbacks*, 1903.
U.S. Treasury Department. *Facts About United States Money*.

UNITED STATES POSTAL SAVINGS BANKS
See postal savings system.

UNITED STATES POSTAL SERVICE
The Postal Reorganization Act of 1970 (P.L. 91-375) converted the Post Office Department into the U.S. Postal Service, an independent establishment within the Executive Branch. The Postal Service commenced operations July 1, 1971, and was charged with providing patrons with reliable mail service at reasonable rates and fees.

The U.S. Postal Service is governed by an 11-member Board of Governors, including nine governors appointed by the President; a Postmaster General who is selected by the governors; and a Deputy Postmaster General who is selected by the governors and the Postmaster General.

Decisions on changes in domestic rates of postage and fees for postal services are recommended to the governors of the Postal Service by the independent Postal Rate Commission after hearing on the record under the Administrative Procedures Act. The Commission also recommends decisions on changes in the domestic mail classification schedule to the governors. Decisions of the governors on rates of postage, fees for postal services, and mail classification are final, subject to judicial review. Programs include all postal activities providing window services, processing, delivery, and transportation of mail; research and development; administration of postal field activities; and associated expenses of providing facilities and financing.

Financing. The activities of the U.S. Postal Service are financed from the following sources: (1) mail and services revenue; (2) reimbursements from federal and non-federal sources; (3) proceeds from borrowing; (4) interest from U.S. securities and other investments; and (5) appropriations by the Congress. All receipts and deposits are made to the Postal Service Fund and are available without fiscal year limitation for payment of all expenses incurred, retirement of obligations, investment in capital assets, and investment in obligations and securities.

Since 1973, transactions of the Postal Service Fund and the assets and liabilities of the U.S. Postal Service no longer appear within the totals of the U.S. budget.

Section 2005 of the Postal Reorganization Act authorizes borrowing authority of $10 billion with a yearly limitation of $2 billion, of which not more than $500 million may be used to cover operating expenses.

The Postal Service may require the secretary of the Treasury to purchase its obligations so long as the secretary's holdings from such required purchases do not exceed $2 billion at any one time. Obligations of the Postal Service may be fully guaranteed as to timely payment of principal and interest by the U.S. government if the Postal Service so requests and the secretary of the Treasury determines that the guaranty is in the public interest.

Bond Financing. Under Trust Indenture for a bond offering back on February 1, 1972, the Postal Service must (1) reserve an amount available under the $2 billion mandatory purchase authority at least equal to the aggregate principal amount of bonds outstanding under the Trust Indenture (currently $250 million), and (2) exercise such authority to the extent necessary to meet principal, premium if any, and interest payments on such obligations.

Postal Service bonds are not guaranteed by the U.S. government, but they are lawful investments and may be accepted as security for all fiduciary, trust, and public funds under the control and authority of the U.S. government. The bonds are also eligible as security for 90-day advances to depository institutions by the Federal Reserve System, and as collateral for treasury tax and loan accounts. United States Postal Service bonds are exempt from all state and local taxes except estate, inheritance, and gift taxes.

BIBLIOGRAPHY

EXECUTIVE OFFICE OF THE PRESIDENT, OFFICE OF MANAGEMENT AND BUDGET. *Budget of the United States of America*, Fiscal Year 1983.

UNITED STATES RETIREMENT PLAN BONDS
See TREASURY SERCURITIES.

UNITED STATES RULE
A rule stating that interest is computed on the unpaid balance of a debt. The payment is first applied to interest. The excess payment reduces the balance of the debt.

UNITED STATES SAVINGS BONDS
The United States government issues a variety of nonmarketable savings bonds issues.

Series EE Bonds: Nonmarketable issue.

Interest Rate: Series EE bonds issued on and after November 1, 1986, and held five years, will receive interest at 85% of the average return during that time on marketable Treasury securities with five years remaining to their maturity, or 6%, whichever is higher. Interest will be compounded semiannually. Thereafter, the variable rate will be determined in the same manner for the period from issue date to the end of each additional six-month period, until the bond's 12-year maturity. If cashed before being held five years, EE bonds earn 4.27% after one year, rising each six months to the minimum guaranteed five-year yield of 6%.

Series EE bonds bearing issue date (1) prior to November 1, 1982, if held until the first semiannual interest accrual date occurring on or after November 1, 1987, or (2) between November 1, 1982, and October 31, 1986, if held five years from the issue month, will receive a market-based return if it is higher than the guaranteed return of 7.5%. Established rates on outstanding bonds are guaranteed to the end of the original maturity period.

Series HH bonds issued on or after November 1, 1986, will pay interest semiannually by direct deposit/electronic funds transfer (DD/EFT) or Treasury check at a rate of 6% per annum. Older HH bonds will continue to receive their guaranteed interest rates to the end of their original maturity periods.

Maturity: 12 years for Series EE bonds with issue dates on and after November 1, 1986; 10 years for Series EE bonds with issue dates from November 1, 1982, through October 31, 1986; 8 years for Series EE bonds with issue dates from May 1, 1981, through October 31, 1982; 9 years for Series EE bonds with issue dates from November 1, 1980, through April 30, 1981; 11 years for Series EE bonds with issue dates from January 1, 1980, through October 31, 1980; 10 years for all Series HH bonds. No provision has been made to extend the bonds beyond their original maturities.

Denominations: Series EE: $50, $75, $100, $200, $500, $1,000, $5,000, and $10,000; Series HH: $500, $1,000, $5,000, and $10,000.

History and Purpose: Series EE and HH savings bonds were originally offered on January 1, 1980; the fixed interest rate was improved effective November 1, 1980 and again on May 1, 1981. On November 1, 1982, interest rates became market-based (with the initial guaranteed minimum set at 7 1/2%) to provide bondholders with an equitable return on their savings. On November 1, 1986, the guaranteed minimum rate, which kicks in if the market-based rate is lower, was reduced to 6% to reflect the decline in market interest rates. They are designed to replace the Series E and H bonds, the sale of which has been discontinued. Many of the characteristics of the Series E and H bonds are retained; however, there are some significant differences between Series EE and E bonds, e.g., the higher discount rate (50% vs. 25%), the higher minimum denomination ($50 vs. $25), the longer term to maturity (12 years vs. 5 years), and a longer minimum holding period (6 months instead of 2).

Other Distinctive Features:

1. Series EE are accrual bonds offered on a discount basis at 50% of face amount. Interest is paid at redemption as part of the current redemption value.
2. Series HH are current income bonds issued at par in exchange for eligible Series E bonds, Series EE bonds, and/or savings notes with level interest payments at semiannual intervals. Series HH bonds may also be obtained by reinvestment of matured Series H bonds.
3. Series EE bonds are payable at any time after six months from issue. They may be redeemed by some 45,000 qualified paying agents, the Federal Reserve banks and branches, and the Bureau of the Public Debt.
4. Series HH bonds are payable at any time after seven months from issue. They may be redeemed by the Federal Reserve banks and branches and the Bureau of the Public Debt.
5. Series EE interest is reportable for federal income tax purposes for the year in which the bonds are redeemed, mature, or are otherwise disposed of, whichever is earliest. Alternatively, the bond owner may elect to report interest each year as it accrues; however, such election must apply to all of the owner's accrual-type securities and cannot be changed without Internal Revenue Service approval. Series HH interest is taxable for the year in which it is received.
6. Series EE bonds, along with Series E bonds and savings notes, may be exchanged for Series HH bonds with continued deferral of taxation on the portion of accrued Series EE interest included in the purchase price of the Series HH bonds.

Series E and H Bonds (withdrawn from sale)

Statutory Authority: 31 U.S.C. 3105

Governing Regulations: Department Circular No. 530, as revised (31 CFR, Part 315), subject to the provisions of the offering circulars: D. C. No. 653 (31 CFR, Part 316) for Series E bonds and D. C. No. 905 (31 CFR, Part 332) for Series H bonds.

Interest Rate: Series E and H bonds were issued at varying rates of interest, from 2.9% to 6.5%, and have received the benefit of subsequent rate increases. Series E bonds held until their first semiannual interest accrual dates occurring on or after November 1, 1987, will receive the market-based rate or the applicable minimum guaranteed return. (Series E bonds issued before November 1947, which will mature prior to satisfying the five-year holding requirement, and are not eligible for the market-based rate.) Established rates on outstanding bonds are guaranteed to the end of the original or current extended maturity period. When bonds enter the next ten-year extension on or after November 1, 1986, the guaranteed minimum rate will be 6% per annum, compounded semiannually unless such yield is changed prior to the beginning of a future extended maturity period. Series H bonds will continue to receive their guaranteed interest rates to the end of the original, or current extended maturity period on or after November 1, 1986, will earn 6% per annum. Series E bonds issued after January 1951, and held until their first interest accrual dates in 1991, will receive a .5% bonus compounded semiannually, retroactive to the first interest accrual date in 1980.

Maturity: Series E bonds have had varying original maturity periods depending on their issue date, ranging from ten years for the oldest bonds to five years for the last ones issued. Series E bonds issued from May 1941 to November 1965 have been granted three ten-year extended maturity periods. Those issued thereafter have been granted two ten-year extended maturity periods.

Form: Registered and nontransferable.

Denominations: Series E - $10, $25, $50, $75, $100, $200, $500, $1,000, $10,000, and $100,000. (Note: eligibility to purchase the $10 and $100,000 Series E bonds was limited.) Series H - $500, $1,000, $5,000, and $10,000.

History and Purpose: Savings bonds were originally issued in 1935 to provide a secure and attractive instrument for small investors and an additional source of funds for the Treasury. Series E bonds were first issued in May 1941. They played a major role in financing World War II and continued as a stable method of debt financing. Series H bonds were first offered on June 1, 1952, as a companion series for investors who preferred to receive current income. Series E bonds were withdrawn from sale as of June 30, 1980, and Series H bonds as of December 31, 1979. They were replaced by Series EE and HH, respectively.

Other Distinctive Features:

1. Series E are accrual bonds that were issued at 75% of face amount. Interest is paid at redemption as part of the current redemption value.
2. Series H are current income bonds, issued at par; interest is paid semiannually by direct deposit/electronic funds transfer (DD/EFT) or by Treasury check.
3. All Series E and H bonds are payable upon presentation. Series E bonds may be redeemed by some 45,000 qualified paying agents, the Federal Reserve banks and branches, and the Bureau of the Public Debt. Series H bonds may be redeemed only by the Federal Reserve banks and branches and the Bureau of the Public Debt.
4. Series E interest is reportable for federal income tax purposes for the year in which the Series E bonds are redeemed, reach final maturity, or are otherwise disposed of, whichever is earliest; as with Series EE interest, the bond owner may elect to report Series E interest as it accrues. Series H interest is taxable for the year in which it is received.
5. Eligible Series E bonds, along with Series EE bonds and/or savings notes, may be exchanged for Series HH bonds with continued deferral of taxation on accumulated accrued interest included in the purchase price of HH bonds. Matured Series E bonds may continue to be exchanged for a period of one year from the date of final maturity; thereafter they are not eligible for exchange.

Savings Notes (withdrawn from sale)

Statutory Authority: 31 U.S.C. 3103, 3121

Governing Regulations: Department Circular No. 530, as revised (31 CFR, Part 315), subject to the provisions of the offering circular: Department Circular, Public Debt Series No. 3-67, as amended (31 CFR, Part 342).

Interest Rate: Savings notes held five years from their first interest accrual dates occurring on or after November 1, 1982, will earn the market-based rate applicable to Series E and EE bonds during the holding period or the guaranteed minimum, whichever is higher; notes redeemed during the holding period will earn the guaranteed return. The original interest rates were 4.74% per annum compounded semiannually for notes issued prior to June 1, 1968, and 5% for notes issued thereafter. Subsequent rate increases for Series E bonds were also applied to savings notes. Savings notes held until their first interest accrual dates in 1991 will earn a .5% bonus, compounded semiannually, retroactive to their first interest accrual dates in 1980.

Maturity: Original term was 4 1/2 years; two 10-year optional extension periods were granted. All notes are now in the second extended maturity period.

Form: Registered and nontransferable.

Denominations: $25, $75, $100.

History and Purpose: Purchase of savings notes could be made only in tandem with Series E bonds. The notes were withdrawn from sale as of June 30, 1970.

Other Distinctive Features:

1. The notes were issued on a discount basis of 81% of the face amount. Interest is paid at redemption as part of the current redemption value.
2. Savings notes are payable upon presentation. They may be redeemed by some 45,000 qualified paying agents, the Federal Reserve banks and branches, and the Bureau of the Public Debt.
3. Savings note interest is reportable for federal income tax purposes for the year in which the note is redeemed, matures, or is otherwise disposed of, whichever is earliest. Alternatively, the note owner may elect to report interest each year as it accrues; however, such election must apply to all of the owner's accrual-

type securities and cannot be changed without Internal Revenue Service approval.
4. Savings notes and Series E/EE savings bonds may be exchanged for Series HH bonds with continued deferral of taxation on the portion of accrued note interest included in the purchase price of the Series HH bonds.

Determination of the Market-Based Variable Investment Yield for Series E and EE Savings Bonds and Savings Notes. A new market-based interest rate formula has been in effect for savings bonds since November 1, 1982. To qualify for the market-based rate, bonds must be held for five years after the institution of the market-based return plan for bonds. Therefore, in order to receive the market-based rate, all Series E bonds and savings notes issued on or after November 1, 1987, must be held until their first interest accrual dates occurring on or after November 1, 1987, in order to qualify for the same market-based rate. New bonds held less than five years will continue to earn interest on a fixed, graduated scale. Bonds purchased November 1, 1986, and after have a guaranteed minimum rate of 6% if held five years or more. The market-based variable investment yield will be used to determine the redemption value of a bond, unless its applicable minimum investment yield produces a higher value.

Each market day, the Treasury records the yield on outstanding marketable Treasury securities with remaining terms to maturity of approximately five years, from closing bid yield quotations in the market for Treasury securities. The monthly average of these daily yields is calculated and rounded to two decimal places. For each six-month period beginning with May 1 or November 1, the monthly averages will be averaged and rounded to two decimal places. When ten consecutive six-month periods are recorded (the first such period will be May 1, 1982, through April 30, 1987), the average for the ten periods will be calculated and rounded to two decimal places. The market-based variable investment yield will be determined by taking 85% of this ten-period average and rounding it to the nearest 1/4 of 1%. For each additional half-yearly retention of the bond, computation of the market-based variable investment yield will include the next successive six-month market yield average.

Monthly averages of the market yield on outstanding Treasury securities with a remaining term to maturity of approximately five years are published in the quarterly *Treasury Bulletin* and by the Board of Governors of the Federal Reserve System. They may be found in the board's statistical releases G.13 and H.15, and in Table 1.35 of the monthly *Federal Reserve Bulletin*. For example, for the six months ended October 31, 1982, the averages were as follows:

1982	
May	13.75%
June	14.43
July	14.07
August	13.00
September	12.25
October	10.80
Six-Month Average	13.05%
85% of Six-Month Average	11.09%

The market-based rates announced by Treasury for each six-month period beginning November 1, 1982, through April 30, 1987, are:

1. 11.09% November 1, 1982 — April 30, 1983
2. 8.64%   May 1, 1983 — October 31, 1983
3. 9.38%   November 1, 1983 — April 30, 1984
4. 9.95%   May 1, 1984 — October 31, 1984
5. 10.94% November 1, 1984 — April 30, 1985
6. 9.49%   May 1, 1985 — October 31, 1985
7. 8.36%   November 1, 1985 — April 30, 1986
8. 7.02%   May 1, 1986 — October 31, 1986
9. 6.06%   November 1, 1986 — April 30, 1987
10. 5.84% May 1, 1987 — October 31, 1987

Tax Status. Interest on series EE and HH saving bonds is not subject to state or local income taxes. Both series EE and series HH bonds are subject to other taxes, such as estate, inheritance, and gift taxes—whether federal or state—but they are exempt from all other taxation imposed on principal or interest by any state, U.S. possession, or local taxing authority.

Summary. Historically, the Treasury has promoted the sale of United States savings bonds as a means of increasing such noninflationary increments of debt and lengthening maturities. However, the Treasury has had to downplay the attractiveness of savings bonds to avoid disintermediation (flight of savings from savings institutions). An egregious example of such Treasury-induced disintermediation, although it involved a marketable issue, was the famous " Magic 5s" (four-year, ten-month notes of October 15, 1959) which, because of their high coupon rate relative to rates paid by savings institutions at that time, attracted many individual investors.

Further information concerning U.S. savings bonds can be obtained from the Office of Financing, Bureau of the Public Debt. The Department of the Treasury Circulars, Public Debt Series, also provide additional information.

BIBLIOGRAPHY

For full details about series EE and series HH bonds, *see:* Department of the Treasury Circulars, Public Debt Series.
These are available from Federal Reserve banks and branches.

UNITED STATES TREASURER See TREASURY DEPARTMENT.

UNIT OF ACCOUNT Money provides a uniform way to measure the value of goods and services, so it is a unit of account. In the United States, all goods and services are priced by a single monetary unit, the dollar. In every economy, prices are specified in a monetary unit of account called money.

UNIT OF VALUE MONETARY UNIT.
See MONEY OF ACCOUNT, STANDARD OF VALUE.

UNIVERSAL COMMERCIAL CODE (U.C.C.) The Universal Commercial Code was drafted for the purpose of standardizing numerous state laws that affected commerce. The U.C.C. included various topics, including contracts for the sale of goods, negotiable instruments (commercial paper), secured transactions, and bulk sales. Various states have adopted all or part of the U.C.C. Article 4, bank deposits and collections, deals with many areas where the code has a significant impact on banks and banking.

UNIVERSAL NUMERICAL SYSTEM See NUMERICAL TRANSIT SYSTEM.

UNLAWFUL LOANS Loans made by banks in violation of the banking laws. Unlawful loans may be divided into four classes: those in excess of the maximum allowed to one borrower (*see* NATIONAL BANK LOANS); loans in excess of the legal rate of interest (*see* LEGAL RATE OF INTEREST, USURY); loans to certain persons such as bank officers, directors, and employees, which are criticizable among national banks and usually among state banks unless approved by a majority of the board of directors; and loans for certain purposes, e.g., a national bank may not loan upon real estate with a second mortgage as security.

UNLIMITED MORTGAGE An open end mortgage; a mortgage that is not limited to a certain amount, but nevertheless may be restricted by the bankers who are to sell the bonds secured thereby. The restrictions relate to earnings, purpose for which money is to be spent, probable earning power of the improvements, cost of improvements, etc. The limited open end mortgage, which occurs in public utility mortgages in particular, has the advantage of relieving the company of the trouble and expense of preparing frequent new mortgages as additional funds are needed to meet expansion. The limited open end mortgage also simplifies the financial plan of the company because all of its financing may be accomplished by issuing series of bonds under a single mortgage rather than by bringing out several issues under different mortgages.

See OPEN MORTGAGE.

UNLISTED SECURITIES Securities not admitted to registration, listing, or trading on organized securities exchanges, but traded in the OVER-THE-COUNTER MARKET. Trading in such securities is conducted by brokers and dealers for their customers and for their own account with other brokers, dealers, and customers wherever a market can be found, various firms "making markets" in particular issues. Over-the-counter firms make a specialty of dealing in unlisted securities, and many exchange members maintain unlisted securities departments.

The volume of transactions in unlisted securities, reported daily since late 1971 by the NASDAQ (NATIONAL ASSOCIATION OF SECURITIES DEALERS AUTOMATED QUOTATIONS SYSTEM), includes only transactions effected by NASDAQ market-making firms, but may include some duplication where such market-making firms trade with one another. Early in 1971, the system began supplying quotations fed into its computers on some 2,500 unlisted stocks, and it was planned to expand to some 20,000 unlisted issues eventually. The "pink sheets" (daily listing of bid and asked entries on specific stocks by subscribing dealers) continue to be published for the use of dealers (the inner, or wholesale market quotations) by the NATIONAL QUOTATION BUREAU on some 40,000 issues. NASDAQ supplies the newspapers with volume, bid and asked, and net daily change on the ten most active unlisted issues, as well as volume, bid change, and quotations on the full over-the-counter list. Such quotations do not include retail markup, markdown, or commissions.

Issues traded over-the-counter include U.S. government securities; issues of states, subdivisions of states, and municipalities; the bulk of corporate bonds (industrial, public utility, and railroad); all railroad equipment trust certificates; railroad leased line and guaranteed stocks; most bank and insurance stocks; most foreign securities, including Canadian issues; and some of the closed end investment company issues (open end investment company issues [mutual funds] are "tap" issues available from the companies concerned, through brokers in the case of "load" funds, but are quoted in the over-the-counter sections of the newspapers).

Act of Congress approved July 29, 1968 (P.L. 90-437) amended the Securities Exchange Act of 1934 to authorize the Board of Governors of the Federal Reserve System to extend the coverage of margin requirements to credit that banks and other lenders may extend for the purpose of purchasing and carrying securities traded over the counter (as distinguished from those traded on the national securities exchanges), and to permit brokers and dealers to extend credit on such securities, subject to margin requirements. The board of governors published its first list of over-the-counter margin stocks on July 8, 1969, and has revised it since from time to time.

See MARGIN BUYING; NATIONAL ASSOCIATION OF SECURITIES DEALERS, INC.

UNLISTED TRADING PRIVILEGES A security admitted to trading on a securities exchange upon the request of a member, as distinguished from the issuer, is said to be "admitted to unlisted trading privileges." Such privileges may be granted by an exchange, under the Securities Exchange Act of 1934, only with permission of the SECURITIES AND EXCHANGE COMMISSION (SEC). This reflects the public interest in having securities ostensibly listed on a securities exchange subject to control of the issuer by the exchange through the listing agreement.

Admissions to unlisted trading privileges are governed by Section 12(f) of the Securities Exchange Act and regulations of the Securities and Exchange Commission. The 1975 amendments (Act of June 4, 1975, P.L. 94-29) broadened that provision to include securities not listed on any other exchanges, but other changes, reflecting concern that such unlisted trading might affect development of a national market system, provided that such applications may not be granted if the effect would be to restrict competition. In its reports, the SEC refers to issues admitted to unlisted trading privileges under clauses 1, 2 and 3 of Section 12(f) of the Act.

"Clause 1" issues are issues admitted to unlisted trading privileges on an exchange prior to March 1, 1934. These are reported in two categories: those listed and registered on a securities exchange other than that where they are admitted to unlisted trading (duals), and those not listed and not registered on any exchange. The latter type were recruited from the over-the-counter markets, upon application of members to the exchange, and are the type particularly implied by the term "unlisted trading privileges of the grandfather clause type."

"Clause 2" issues are issues admitted to unlisted trading privileges pursuant to grants of applications by stock exchanges beginning in April, 1937. These grants of applications are based upon an existing listing and registration on some other stock exchange (duals).

"Clause 3" issues are those admitted to unlisted trading pursuant to grants of applications from stock exchanges conditioned upon the availability of information with respect to the stocks, which is substantially equivalent to that filed in the case of listed issues.

SEC sanction of the trading in duals on regional exchanges decentralizes trading to other exchanges on the strength of full listing on the home exchange; such a policy, of course, has not been favored by the New York Stock Exchange. The SEC, however, has been tougher in administering the true unlisted trading issues (grandfather issues under Clause 1, and Clause 3), and over time the importance of these has declined, particularly on the American Stock Exchange, an active center for such issues prior to 1934.

UNLOAD To sell securities or commodities to avoid a loss due to a falling market or any expected unfavorable development; "to get out from under" before prices collapse. In the absence of regulation, the "insiders," i.e., directors and officers of a corporation, might unload their holding of the securities of their corporation upon the market in anticipation of poor earnings or threatened insolvency. The expression is usually applied to transactions on a large scale.

Section 16 of the Securities Exchange Act and corresponding provisions in the Public Utility Holding Company Act of 1935 and the Investment Company Act of 1940 are designed to provide other stockholders and investors generally with information on insider securities transactions and holdings, and to prevent insiders from profiting from short-term trading in a company's securities through unfair use of confidential information.

UNQUALIFIED OPINION An auditor's opinion stating that the financial statements are presented fairly in conformity with GENERALLY ACCEPTED ACCOUNTING PRINCIPLES applied on a consistent basis and include all necessary disclosures. The opinion is interpreted to mean that the statements fairly present the financial position, results of operations, and cash flows. Otherwise the auditors must give a qualified opinion, an adverse opinion, or disclaim an opinion. A qualified opinion expresses certain reservations in the report related to the scope of the audit and/or the financial statements. If the reservations are more serious, the auditor can issue a disclaimer or an adverse opinion. In an adverse opinion, the auditor states that the financial statements do not present fairly the financial position of the company, the results of its operations, or its cash flows. In a disclaimer the auditor cannot give an opinion because of scope limitations or some other reason.

Following is an unqualified opinion.

To the Stockholders of ABC Company:

We have audited the accompanying balance sheet of ABC Company as of December 31, 1991, and the related statements of income, retained earnings, and cash flows for the year then ended. These financial statements are the responsibility of ABC Company's management. Our responsibility is to express an opinion on these financial statements based on our audit.

We have conducted our audit in accordance with generally accepted auditing standards. These standards require that we plan and perform the audit to obtain reasonable assurance about whether the financial statements are free of material misstatement. An audit includes examining, on a test basis, evidence supporting the amounts and disclosures in the financial statements. An audit also includes assessing the accounting principles used and significant estimates made by management, as well as evaluating the overall financial statement presentation. We believe that our audit provides a reasonable basis for our opinion.

In our opinion, the financial statements referred to above present fairly, in all material respects, the financial position of ABC Company as of December 31, 1991, and the results of its operations and its cash flows for the year then ended in conformity with generally accepted accounting principles.

Signed

New York, New York
February 25, 1992

See also QUALIFIED OPINION.

UNREGISTERED EXCHANGE A stock exchange that is exempted from registration with the Securities and Exchange Commission, under Section 5 of the SECURITIES AND EXCHANGE ACT OF 1934, upon application of the exchange, because, in the opinion of the commission, by reason of the limited volume of transactions effected on such exchange, it is not practicable and not necessary or appropriate in the public interest or for the protection of investors to require such registration.

See STOCK EXCHANGES.

UNSECURED CREDITOR A general creditor; a person or company that has no security or other legal claim upon specific property to satisfy a debt. An unsecured creditor shares in the distribution of the assets of a bankrupt equally with all other unsecured claims after preferred and secured claims have been met.

See LIABILITY.

UNSTEADY Describes the stock market when prices fluctuate widely, but close without showing a definite tendency.

UNVALUED SHARES *See* NO PAR VALUE STOCK, WITHOUT PAR VALUE STOCK.

URANIUM Uranium oxide (U_3O_8) concentrate, the basic raw material ("yellow cake") milled from uranium ore for processing into the nuclear rods used in nuclear power plants, is of particular importance to the PUBLIC UTILITY INDUSTRY.

BIBLIOGRAPHY

BUREAU OF MINES. Department of Energy.
Electrical World (bimonthly).

URBAN MORTGAGE DEBT Mortgage debt on non-farm property, including homes, apartment houses, office buildings, hotels, etc. Low-interest rates, availability of mortgage money from mortgage lending institutions, and appropriate economic conditions in the 1950s and 1960s led to substantial growth in mortgage lending on 1- to 4-family houses, which continued in the 1970s until higher interest, tighter availability of mortgage funds, and economic recession materially affected the volume of housing and mortgage activity in the late 1970s and early 1980s.

See FEDERAL HOME LOAN SYSTEM, SAVINGS AND LOAN ASSOCIATIONS, SAVINGS BANKS.

USANCE The nonstatutory period of time fixed by mercantile usage or custom for the payment of a bill of exchange drawn in one country and payable in another.

See FOREIGN BILLS OF EXCHANGE.

USURY From the Latin, "usura," meaning enjoyment, interest, i.e., money paid for the use of money. Although the term originally meant interest, in modern times it has come to mean excessive interest, particularly interest in excess of the maximum rate fixed by law.

In the United States, maximum legal interest rates are prescribed by the various state laws, which also prescribe the maximum contract rates. Every state in the United States has by statute fixed the legal or conventional rate of interest, which in former years was typically 6%, but which in recent years because of a general rise in interest rates has led to a number of higher legal rates. Most states also prescribe on contract rates of interest. In addition to these general usury laws, specific statutes provide special limitations for particular types of lenders; e.g., small loan laws of the various states prescribe the maximum rate that may be charged by licensed small loan lenders on remaining unpaid balances.

Penalties for violations of the usury laws vary in the different states.

See LEGAL RATE OF INTEREST.

The National Banking Act does not affirmatively prescribe federal legal rates of interest. Instead, national banks may charge maxima as follows: (1) rate allowed by the state, territory, or district wherein the national bank is located or 1% above the Federal Reserve bank discount rate on 90-day commercial paper, whichever is greater; (2) where a different rate is specified for banks organized under state laws, such special rate; (3) where no rate is prescribed, 7% or 1% in excess of the Federal Reserve bank discount rate on 90-day commercial paper, whichever is greater. Such interest may be taken in advance. The purchase, discount, or sale of bona fide bills of exchange, payable at a place other than place of such purchase, discount, or sale, at not more than the current rate of exchange for sight drafts in addition to the interest, shall not be considered as taking or receiving a greater rate of interest (Sec. 5197, Revised Statutes; 12 U.S.C. 85).

The penalty for violation, when knowingly done, shall be a forfeiture of the entire interest specified in the evidence of debt, or agreed to be paid thereon. In case the violative rate of interest has already been paid, the person paying it, or his legal representative, may recover twice the amount of the interest thus paid, provided the action is commenced within two years from the time the usurious transaction occurred (Sec. 5198, Revised Statutes; 12 U.S.C. 86).

See SMALL LOAN BUSINESS.

Impact of Usury Ceiling Rates on Mortgages. Because the rise in market interest rates close to or up to the fixed usury ceiling rates in recent years was causing relative declines in building and residential mortgage lending, various states have established, by amendments to usury laws, the floating type of usury rate ceiling. Floating ceilings are intended to avoid the impact of fixed ceilings while still providing protective limits. These floating usury ceilings are tied to various market interest rates, the most common being yields on long-term U.S. government bonds and the Federal Reserve discount rate. For a survey of specific state usury ceilings, see Federal Reserve Bank of St. Louis *Review*. April, 1979.

Federal Preemption of State Usury Ceilings. The DEPOSITORY INSTITUTIONS DEREGULATION AND MONETARY CONTROL ACT OF 1980 preempted state usury ceilings on certain residential mortgage loans for a broad spectrum of lenders. It also temporarily preempted limits on business and agricultural loans of $25,000 or more, authorizing lenders to charge a rate up to 5% above the Federal Reserve discount rate. The act also granted to other financial institutions the authority, previously limited to national banks, to set rates for all types of loans up to one percentage point above the discount rate. Institutions can benefit from this provision only when the indexed rate exceeds the state limit that would otherwise apply.

BIBLIOGRAPHY

LANGHOLM, O. *The Aristoelian Analysis of Usury*, 1985.
MARK, J. *An Analysis of Usury*, 1980.

UTILITIES, ELECTRIC An industry that provides electric and nuclear power. Electric utilities are natural monopolies subject to state and federal regulation, including rates, adequacy of service, issuance of securities, accounting systems used, and allowable rate of return on investment. Most utilities operate on an intrastate basis. The Federal Energy Regulatory Commission, formerly the Federal Power Commission, exercises some federal controls.

Investors have looked to utilities for yield and dividend growth. In recent years, emphasis has been placed on appreciation and a firm's capacity margin of power. In the late 1980s, electric sales remained strong due primarily to the growth in the industrial sector of the economy, additional commercial construction, and an increase in residential customers. Oil supplies were relatively stable and available. The decline in interest rates and reduced construction activities were reflected in reduced capital costs. Cash flows were typically strong. Dividend growth was limited by earnings potential.

Rate regulation reflects a U.S. Supreme Court decision of 1944 in *Federal Power Commission* v. *Hope Natural Gas*. The court ruled that there is no one method for determining "just and reasonable rates." The court stated that the final result of rate making determines fairness and reasonableness. In its ruling, the court established basic criteria for fair return on an invested rate base: The return to the equity owner should be commensurate with returns on investments in other enterprises with comparable risks; the return should be sufficient to ensure confidence in the financial integrity of the enterprise so that it can maintain its credit and attract capital. Utilities are not guaranteed a certain return on earnings.

UTILITY The ability of a good or service to satisfy a want; usefulness. Four major types of utility include: form, place, time, and possession. Form utility is associated with improving or increasing the usefulness of a commodity by modifying its form or shape. The yearly updating of automobile models represents adding form utility to the product. Place utility adds usefulness by moving a product to a more desirable location. Time utility is the result of having a commodity or service available at one time rather than another. Possession utility occurs when the ownership of a good or service is transferred from one person to another.

V

VALEURS The French equivalent for the term securities in the United States. In France, stocks are called *actions*, and bonds are called *obligations*. Obligations may also be known as *fonds d'état* (government funds, i.e., bonds), *fonds garantis* (i.e., guaranteed bonds), and *emprunts* (borrowings).

VALIDATION Proof or confirmation to ascertain whether an item, procedure, or transaction conforms to policy or legal requirements.

VALORIZATION The process of attempting to establish a higher market price for a commodity by governmental interference than would be obtained by free and open competition. The arbitrary market value is established in several ways, e.g., governmental maintenance of a purchasing fund, governmental loans to producers to enable them to hold their products awaiting a favorable market opportunity, etc. The government of Brazil in the past has attempted to valorize coffee, which had declined to a price far below its normal cost of production.

VALUATION Appraisal or act of appraisement; appraised value of specified assets. Methods of valuation may be on the following bases: original cost, less depreciation (accounting method); cost of reproduction; cost of replacement (replacing existing plant by new plant giving effect to latest technology); or annual appraisal, either by physical inventory or by application of price indexes. Variations of the original cost method include first original cost (cost of assets when first applied to service); prudent investment cost; and investment cost (actual cost to existing company).

In valuation work, the two variables are the specific assets to be included (tangible and intangible) and the valuation method (basis) to be used.

The valuation of property of the regulated industries (railroads and public utilities) has been a point of contention ever since the courts first entertained appeals to review the determinations of valuation of properties for rate-making and other purposes by administrative agencies of the federal government and the states. For years the landmark case that the U.S. Supreme Court followed in valuation cases was *Smyth* v. *Ames*, 169 U.S. 466 (1898), which laid down the rule that all elements should be considered in the determination of "fair value." In 1944, in the case of *Federal Power Commission* v. *Hope Natural Gas Co.* (320 U.S. 591), the Supreme Court abandoned emphasis on the fair value rule and instituted the doctrine of "end result" of the rate order, i.e., whether the total effect of a rate order resulted in just and reasonable earnings, regardless of the formula or method of valuation used. *See* FAIR RETURN.

The banking industry frequently uses the following measures of valuation:

1. Demand deposits and time deposits/Average assets to monitor the composition of its funding base.
2. Primary capital/Average assets to measure risk as perceived by bank regulators.
3. Net interest margin/Average assets to reflect the return available from risk acceptance.
4. Noninterest expense/Average assets to measure operational efficiency.
5. Price/earning to measure stock performance in relation to earnings.

For bases of valuation of bank investments, *see* COMPTROLLER'S REGULATION, NATIONAL BANK SECURITIES REGULATIONS.

BIBLIOGRAPHY

Appraisal Digest. Quarterly.
Appraisal Journal. Quarterly.
The Dictionary of Real Estate Appraisal. American Institute of Real Estate Appraisers, Chicago, IL, 1984.
Property Tax Journal. Quarterly.
VENTOLO, W., and WILLIAMS, M. *Fundamentals of Real Estate Appraisal*. Real Estate Education Co., Chicago, IL, 1987.

VALUATION ACCOUNT A contra account; an account that is related to and offsets, in whole or in part, one or more other accounts. A contra account can be deducted from the asset to which it is related to determine a carrying or book value.

VALUATION ACT OF 1913 An amendment of the INTERSTATE COMMERCE ACT of 1887, passed March 1, 1913, and amended February 28, 1920, which provided for the valuation of all railroad properties in the United States. Section 19-a of the Interstate Commerce Act, it was known as the Physical Valuation of Property Act. The rate-making section of the TRANSPORTATION ACT OF 1920 provided that as soon as the valuation of a railroad had been determined under Section 19-a of the Interestate Commerce Act, that valuation should be used in revising the tentative value of each rate territory for rate-making purposes.

The original purpose of the Valuation Act, which was sponsored by Senator Robert M. LaFollette, was to ascertain the physical valuation of the railroads in the belief that actual values were far exceeded by capital issues, i.e., the railroad capitalizations were excessive in terms of real value behind them. By June 30, 1934, practically all of the work of valuing the railroads had been completed by the Bureau of Valuation of the Interstate Commerce Commission. These valuations of individual railroad properties were as of various dates from 1914 on, and were not brought down to date. It was the consensus of opinion, however, that allowing for present values, railroad valuations were considerably above the par value of securities outstanding.

The Valuation Act did not specify the use of any particular basis of valuation, and generally stated that the Interstate Commerce Commission "shall investigate, ascertain, and report the value of all the property owned and used by every common carrier subject to the provisions of the Act. To enable the Commission to make such investigation and report, it is authorized to employ such experts and other assistants as may be necessary. . . . The Commission shall make an inventory which shall list the property of every common carrier subject to the provisions of the Act in detail, and show the value thereof as hereinafter provided, and shall classify the physical property, as nearly as practicable, in conformity with the classification of expenditures for road and equipment, as prescribed by the Interstate Commerce Commission. In such investigation said Commission shall ascertain and report in detail as to each piece of property owned or used by said common carrier for its purposes as a common carrier, the original cost to date, the cost of reproduction new, the cost of reproduction less depreciation, and an analysis of the methods by which these several costs are obtained, and the reason for their differences, if any. The Commission shall in like manner ascertain and report separately other values, and elements of value, if any, of the property of such common carrier, and an analysis of the methods employed, and of the reasons for any differences between any such value, and each of the foregoing cost values."

Valuation data in practice proved unsatisfactory as a basis both for the now-repealed "recapture clause" of the Transportation Act of 1920 and for rate-making. Accordingly, the Emergency Railroad Transportation Act of 1933 provided for a new rule of rate-making, under which the Interstate Commerce Commission is required to give due consideration to the effect of rates on the movement of traffic, to the need in the public interest of adequate and efficient railroad transportation service at the lowest cost consistent with the furnishing of such service, and to the need for revenues sufficient to enable carriers under honest, economical, and efficient management to provide such service.

See RAILROAD INDUSTRY, RAILROAD LEGISLATION.

VALUE Dictionary definitions of value include: fair price; a proper equivalent in money, commodities, etc. for something sold or exchanged; the worth of a thing in money or goods at a certain time; market price; estimated or appraised worth or price; purchasing power; that quality of a thing according to which it is thought of as being more or less desirable, useful, estimable, important, etc.; worth; the quantity or amount for which a symbol stands (mathematics).

In philosophy, value has various meanings, including the standards or principles of worth (what makes something have value) and the worthy things themselves (the valuables). A theory of value would be a set of guidelines for the analysis of the meaning and basis of value judgments.

In finance, one refers to the present value of money or an annuity and the future value of money or an annuity. These concepts reflect the TIME VALUE OF MONEY.

John Marshall (1842-1924), the founder of the neoclassical school of economics in England, defined value as "the worth of a commodity in exchange for other commodities." For the economist, the concept of value is connected with that of WEALTH. Adam Smith wrote: "The word *value* has two different meanings, and sometimes expresses the utility of some particular object and sometimes the power of purchasing other goods which the possession of that object conveys." The exchange value is the value of one thing in terms of another at any place and time, i.e., the amount of that second which can be obtained there and then in exchange for the first. The term is relative and expresses a relationship between two things at a particular place and time. Value of things are often expressed in prices. Utility of a thing is often considered a major determinant of value. Economists refer to the value of a marginal product of a factor of production. For example, a firm will employ a factor of production (land, labor, capital) only as long as it adds more to the total revenue than it adds to the total cost. If factor X is the only variable factor for the firm, the value of the extra output generated by the additional unit of factor X hired is equal to the extra output of the additional unit of factor A employed multiplied by the price at which the output is sold.

Socialists under the influence of Marx have maintained that the cost of labor is the measure of value. This is often referred to as the labor theory of value.

The term *value* is used in accounting accompanied by an adjective signifying many different ideas: book value, par value, no-par value, stated value, appraisal value, fair market value, disposal value, salvage value, scrap value, exit value, entry value, discovery value, replacement value, maturity value, carrying value, and others.

See ASSESSED VALUATION, INTRINSIC VALUE, INVENTORY VALUE, INVESTMENT VALUE, TRADING VALUE.

VALUE-ADDED STATEMENT Value added refers to a portion of the selling price of a commodity or service attributable to a specific stage of production. A value-added statement is used by many British companies to report on the wealth creation process. Value added represents the income of shareholders, suppliers of debt capital, employees, and governments. Value added can also be conceptualized as sales revenue minus the cost of materials and services which were brought in from outside suppliers. The value-added statement can be presented in the following format:

Sources

Sales		$500,000
Less: Brought-in materials, services	$100,000	
Depreciation	50,000	150,000
Total value added		$350,000
Applied as follows:		
To wages	200,000	
To interest (banks and other lenders)	25,000	
To taxes	75,000	
To dividends	30,000	
To retained earnings	20,000	
Total value added		$350,000

VALUE-ADDED TAX A value-added tax (VAT) is a tax levied on value added at each stage of production rather than only on the final selling price. VATs are common in Europe. The advantage of a VAT is that it is difficult for any producer to evade the tax, but a disadvantage is that final consumers are unaware of the total VAT at the time of purchase because little value is added by the retailer. Increased attention has been shown to the possibility of enacting a federal value-added tax, in view of its prevalence in European Common Market countries and the expectation that its revenue yield could result in lowering federal income tax rates as well as Social Security (FICA) taxes (the latter expectation based on the assumption that Social Security System revenues could be drawn from general revenues of the Treasury).

The value-added principle is used in gross national product accounting, to avoid double counting. Basically the value-added tax is a sales tax of the multiple-stage type, but instead of being levied on each turnover as the product progresses in stages from the raw material form to purchase by the consumer of the finished product, it is imposed on the increments of value added at each stage (gross receipts minus the cost of intermediate goods and services). The following simplified example illustrates the principle.

Stage of production	Total receipts	3% tax	Value added	3% tax
Raw wool	$ 50	$ 1.50	$40	$1.50
Processing of the wool	75	2.25	25	0.75
Manufacture of the woolens	95	2.85	20	0.60
Manufacture of apparel	130	3.90	35	1.05
Retail of apparel	180	5.40	50	1.50
Total tax		$15.90		$5.40

Alternatively, the value-added tax might be imposed at the last or consumption stage, so that the tax base would be total receipts minus cost of intermediate goods and services; it has been advocated that capital expenditures be subtracted also, so that the base would include consumer goods value only. In this form, the value-added tax would be a general retail sales tax on consumer goods only, with capital goods exempted because of their importance for economic growth and productivity.

The value-added tax would avoid the avalanche or parlayed accumulative effect of a tax on each turnover, and the idea that its high revenue yield might permit reduction of the income tax and Social Security tax load has appeal. However, it would still be a federal sales tax, and would be subject to criticism as regressive in impact upon the differing incomes of consumers unless reduced in regressivity by exemptions on necessities and/or a graduated rate structure.

BIBLIOGRAPHY

AGUIRRE, C. A., and SHOME, P. "The Mexican Value-Added Tax: Methodology For Calculating the Base." *National Tax Journal*, December, 1988.

DENCHER, S. "Annual Accounting: A New Way To Pay VAT." *Accountancy*, October, 1988.
HAFER, R. W., and TREBING, M. E. "The Value-Added Tax—A Review of the Issues." Federal Reserve Bank of St. Louis *Review*, January, 1980.
HERGERT, M., and MORRIS, D. "Accounting Data for Value Chain Analysis." *Strategic Management Journal*, March/April, 1989.
"LOOK BEFORE YOU LEAP INTO A VAT." *Nation's Business*, April, 1989.
"Shipwrecking 1992." *Economist*, September 17, 1988.
TURE, N. B. *Value-Added Tax: Facts and Fancies*, 1979.
YEH, C. "The Incidence of the Value-Added Tax in a Neoclassical Growth Model." *Public Finance*, 34,2, 1979.

VALUE DATE The date upon which the proceeds of a check or other instrument deposited for credit become available for withdrawal, i.e., have a value. The term is used particularly in foreign exchange bookkeeping to indicate the date upon which the proceeds of a draft become available for the use of a customer or correspondent, or upon which a remittance becomes available in the account of the purchaser abroad.

VALUE LINE INVESTMENT SURVEY MODEL
A statistical model of capital asset prices. The model is sometimes used for detecting under- or overvalued securities.

VARIABLE ANNUITY According to the American Council of Life Insurance (successor to the American Life Insurance Association), a type of annuity in which all or part of the basis may be common stock investments or a cost-of-living index; a variable life income contract. Part or all of the funds normally placed in common stocks or other investments are maintained in a separate investment account. Considerably more investment latitude is permitted with funds in separate accounts than with life insurance investments generally. With one type of variable annuity, income payments are fixed and guaranteed once they begin, although the initial size depends upon the value of the fund. With another type, the income payments vary with the current value of the investments on which the annuity is based. Many plans provide for a combination of fixed or variable incomes under one contract.

Variable annuities are purchased by premiums payable either in one lump sum or in periodic payments. Like conventional annuities, they provide income starting either immediately or at specified future time, payable annually, semiannually, quarterly, or monthly. Variations offered include an equivalent single life annuity, life annuity with guaranteed period, joint and survivorship annuity, etc. Types of variable annuities classified as to sources of demand include individual variable annuities; group variable annuities (employer-employee welfare and pension plans); variable annuities pursuant to HR 10 (Keogh Act), which permits the self-employed special tax treatment for pension or profit-sharing plans for themselves and their employees; Keogh Act variable annuities for associations (e.g., doctors, lawyers, accountants, etc.), franchise groups, and groups employed by eleemosynary institutions (religious, charitable, or educational).

Regulation. As late as 1961, only three states provided for both laws and regulations on variable annuities. By 1963, however, thirty-four states had some law, regulation, or procedure authorizing the sale of variable annuities, and by 1970 all but one state provided for the authorization of the sale of variable annuities and the creation of separate accounts in connection with their administration and operation.

The Internal Revenue Code specifies the tax treatment for pension and profit-sharing plans that qualify, and the Internal Revenue Service administers these tax aspects. As securities, variable annuities are subject to the federal securities acts (Securities Act of 1933; Securities Exchange Act of 1934, governing selling organizations as broker-dealers; and the Investment Company Act of 1940, since the separate accounts set up in connection with variable annuities have been ruled to be investment companies). Accordingly, the Securities and Exchange Commission has administrative jurisdiction under these acts. In addition, as securities, variable annuities in various states are subject to regulation (issuance and sale) under the state blue sky laws.

A new equity product, VARIABLE LIFE INSURANCE, had its beginnings in the United States in 1969.

Summary. Conventional annuities, since they depend for performance upon fixed-dollar investments, are vulnerable over time to the erosion of purchasing power caused by inflation in living costs. On the other hand, variable annuities, invested in appropriate equities, should provide the hedge against inflation desired in the long run, but are subject to greater fluctuation in market values. The balanced approach (combined investment of equal amounts in fixed-dollar annuities and variable annuities) attempts to combine the strengths of each type in a diversified holding.
See INSURANCE.

BIBLIOGRAPHY

AMERICAN COUNCIL OF LIFE INSURANCE. *Life Insurance Fact Book* (annual).
TEACHERS INSURANCE AND ANNUITY ASSOCIATION OF AMERICA. *Annual Report*.

VARIABLE COST Although some factors of production remain fixed in the short run, other inputs vary with the level of production. Variable cost is associated with these factors. Total variable cost (TVC) is the TOTAL COST associated with the variable factors of production. TVC increases with output. Average variable cost (AVC) is total cost per unit of output and it equals TVC divided by output. AVC is U-shaped: first AVC decreases and then increases. The economic reason for this shape comes from the LAW OF DIMINISHING RETURNS.

VARIABLE LIFE INSURANCE As defined by the American Council of Life Insurance, LIFE INSURANCE under which the benefit relates to the value of assets behind the contract at the time the benefit is paid. Under variable life insurance policies that have been proposed in the United States, the amount of death benefit payable would fluctuate but would never be less than the initial death benefit payable under the policy.

Variable life insurance policies do not have guaranteed cash values, as such values necessarily fluctuate with the values of holdings in the separate account for such policies, reflecting the investment policy pursued.
See VARIABLE ANNUITY.

BIBLIOGRAPHY

AMERICAN COUNCIL OF LIFE INSURANCE. *Life Insurance Fact Book*. Annual.

VARIABLE RATE MORTGAGES As of May 30, 1979, the FEDERAL HOME LOAN BANK BOARD voted to permit, on a nationwide basis, all federally chartered SAVINGS AND LOAN ASSOCIATIONS to originate, purchase, and participate in variable rate mortgages (VRMs), effective July 1, 1979. In December, 1978, the Federal Home Loan Bank Board had generally approved the VRM, but because of a competitive situation, had limited its authorization to federally chartered savings and loan associations in the state of California, effective in February, 1979.

In the VRM, interest rates may be changed only once a year, with a maximum increase of 0.5% yearly and 2.5% over the life of the MORTGAGE. Interest rate decreases, on the other hand, are limited to 0.5%, with no maximum total decrease over the life of the mortgage.

To assure full disclosure for an informed choice by the borrower, the VRM regulations require that the borrower receive materials describing the type of instruments offered and setting forth the following.

1. A side-by-side comparison of differing terms.
2. Payment schedules, including the "worst case" schedule and total payment difference for VRMs.
3. Information regarding the cost-of-funds index used as guideline for possible variation in the interest rate (see below).
4. A description of the borrower's options in the event of an increase in interest rate.
5. A statement that borrowers may elect a standard mortgage instrument.
6. Information regarding personnel at the district Federal Home Loan bank whom borrowers may contact with questions about the disclosures.

Interest rates on VRMs are tied to the index "Average Cost of Funds to Federal Savings and Loan Insurance Corporation-Insured Savings and Loan Associations, by Bank District," which is published in the monthly *Federal Home Loan Bank Board Journal*. The index, computed semiannually by the Federal Home Loan Bank Board, is based on interest and dividends paid on savings, Federal Home Loan bank advances, and other borrowed money during the period, as a percentage of average savings and borrowings. (Averages are based on 7 month-end figures for half years and 13 month-end figures for years. Half-year data are annualized by doubling.)

Summary. In addition to the VRM, there are two other alternatives to the standard fixed-payment mortgage (SFPM): the GRADUATED PAYMENT MORTGAGE (GPM) and the reverse annuity mortgage (RAM). Proponents of the VRM believe that variable rate mortgages should allow more stable mortgage flows, greater stability in housing markets, and higher returns on their deposits for savers of member savings and loan associations.

On the other hand, recognizing that lenders need flexibility on their assets side to balance variability in their liabilities, the president of the Federal National Mortgage Association (FNMA) has called attention to the following: there is no consensus as yet on the indexing mechanism that will deal equitably with the needs of home buyers, lenders, and long-term investors; there is still considerable concern that VRMs, like the current and proposed new GPMs, will in effect weave inflation further into the economy; and the advent of the new AIMs has renewed proposals for revamping or removing deposit interest ceilings imposed by Regulation Q, and increases in interest rates on deposits would inevitably result in higher interest rates on mortgages.

Attitudes of lenders and borrowers toward VRMs realistically may be expected to be influenced by the prevailing levels and trend of interest rates. When interest rates are rising, lenders will be likely to be interested in offering VRMs, but borrowers may not be receptive to them. When interest rates reach their peaks, lenders are likely to prefer to offer the conventional fixed interest rate mortgage, whereas borrowers may be much more likely to prefer the VRMs.

BIBLIOGRAPHY

FEDERAL HOME LOAN BANK BOARD. *Annual Report.*

VARIANCE In law, an active disagreement between two parts of a legal proceeding which should agree, as between a statement and the evidence offered in support of the evidence. In statistics, the variance is the average of the squared deviations (the square of the standard deviation), which is useful in statistical analysis, especially when a measure of dispersion is required.

In accounting, variance is the difference between actual and standard or between budgeted and actual expenditures or expenses. Variance analysis is based on the concept of management by exception. A variance system provides management with information only when conditions, performance, or activity varies from what they should be. Variance systems are designed and used primarily for control and evaluation purposes. An effective variance system would focus on matters which require management's attention. Variance analysis is also widely used to evaluate performance.

Variance systems typically require:

1. Accurate performance standards or benchmarks.
2. Variables that are subject to control.
3. Accurate measurement procedures for inputs and outputs.
4. Responsibilities assignable, preferably through responsibility centers.

Actual cost can differ from standard or budgeted cost because (1) the actual price or rate differs from the standard or budgeted and (2) actual usage or efficiency differs from the standard or budgeted. A price or rate variance indicates that more or less was paid for the cost factor than the standard or budgeted required. A usage or efficiency variance indicates that more or less of the cost factor was used than was anticipated by the standard or budgeted.

VAULT A secure space for the protection and storage of valuable property. Among banks three types of vaults are used—money vaults, record vaults, and storage vaults. Record and storage vaults are for the protection of current and old records, etc., and are safe against fire and water. Money vaults are designed to be safe against fire, water, burglary, and violence.

Money vaults vary greatly in size and construction; those of safe deposit companies often occupy an entire basement or ground floor. Many ingenious devices have been invented to secure protection against burglars, and among the larger banks a large number of these devices are in use. The larger vaults are equipped with two-foot-thick armor plate steel walls and three-foot-thick steel doors. Since most burglars gain access to a vault through the door by boring or drilling the combination, it is necessary to give the door added protection. Such added protection may consist of an electric signal alarm system communicating with the local burglar alarm company and setting off an alarm bell in the bank; a time lock; or an electric current running through the door. In some banks, a network of wires is run through the vault wall so that the slightest puncture will produce a contact that will notify the local burglar alarm company and set off an alarm in the bank. The time lock does not open the door automatically, but prevents it from being opened before a prearranged hour. The electric current grips any person tampering with the combination or bolts of the door. The vault wall itself is often embedded in a concrete case. If burglars do gain access to the interior of the vault, steam-jets may be arranged so as to fill the place with live steam in a few moments.

The interior of a vault is usually divided with many combination locks which, like the outside combination, are subject to joint control. The combinations to these locks are known by separate officers having custodianship over certain portions of the bank's assets; thus, one compartment may contain the bank's money reserve, another United States bonds, another other securities, another securities pledged as collateral, another securities for which the bank is custodian, another trust department assets, etc.

See SAFE DEPOSIT COMPANY.

VAULT CASH In early December, 1959, the Board of Governors of the Federal Reserve System modified its RESERVE requirement regulation, Regulation D, to permit member banks to count their vault cash in excess of specified percentages of their deposits as part of their required reserves. The action was taken under the authority of legislation enacted by the Congress in July, 1959 (P.L. 86-114, July 28, 1959), which authorized the board of governors to permit member banks to treat vault cash as reserves.

The modification by the board of governors of its Regulation D was designed in part to remedy inequities that had arisen because many banks, particularly smaller country banks, had found it necessary to hold relatively larger amounts of vault cash than other banks did for operating purposes.

VELOCITY Concepts of velocity, or rate of turnover for given time periods, include the following.

1. Transactions velocity, or rate of total money spending to money balances. In practice, since no records are kept on rates of spending of coin and currency, the data used for money balances are bank demand deposits of individuals, partnerships, corporations, states, and political subdivisions and bank savings deposits, excluding negotiable order of withdrawal (NOW) accounts and special club accounts such as Christmas and vacation club accounts. The data used for measuring turnover are debits to such demand deposits and savings deposits of accounts of "business" (corporations and other profit-seeking organizations, excluding commercial banks but including savings and loan associations, mutual savings banks, credit unions, the Export-Import Bank, and federally sponsored lending agencies) and others. The turnover ratio, or velocity, is computed as the ratio of debits to deposits. (See current issues of the *Federal Reserve Bulletin* for the statistical series "Bank Debits and Deposit Turnover.")
2. Income velocity, or ratio of gross national product to money supply. Since gross national product is the estimate of all final goods and services at market value produced in the economy in a given time period, it excludes transactions not involving current output of goods and services and does not therefore measure total spending. (See *Historical Chart Book* of the Board of Governors of the Federal Reserve System, issued annually.)

Both concepts of velocity have their merits as measures of the effects of the effective money supply upon business and credit conditions, after allowing for rates of turnover.

VELVET An easily made profit; bonus; net profit clear of expenses; a profit made on a speculative transaction.

VENDEE One to whom something is sold.

VENDOR One who sells, or who has sold, something.

VENTURE CAPITAL Capital to provide funds for start-up situations ("seed capital") and for existing high-risk small businesses suffering from capital deficiencies but having high profit potential as emerging growth companies, especially in the various fields of high technology.

In the private sector, sources of venture capital include wealthy individuals, either individually or organized into groups or funds by financial firms and investment bankers, and venture capital subsidiaries organized by such firms and bankers.

In the public sector, the subject of venture capital has been popular with Congress because of its identification with small business and because of low levels of innovation and productivity in the economy in recent years. The latest examples of legislation on the subject, H.R. 4326 (Small Business Innovation Act) and S. 881, were reconciled as amended and passed by both houses, the Senate concurring finally in the House-passed version of S. 881, the Small Business Innovation Development Act of 1982. The act provides that each federal agency that has an extramural budget for research or research and development (R&D) in excess of $100 million for fiscal year 1982, or any fiscal year thereafter, shall expend not less than 0.2% of its extramural budget in fiscal year 1983 or in such subsequent fiscal year as the agency has such budget, not less than 0.6% of such budget in the second fiscal year thereafter, not less than 1% of such budget in the third fiscal year thereafter, and not less than 1.25% of such budget in all subsequent fiscal years with small business concerns specifically in connection with small business innovation research programs which meet the requirements of the act and regulations thereunder.

In addition to the preceding requirements, each federal agency that has a budget for research or research and development in excess of $20 million for any fiscal year beginning with fiscal year 1983 or subsequent fiscal year shall establish research goals specifically for funding agreements for research or research and development to small business concerns, no such goal to be less than the percentage of the funding agreements thus reached with small business in the immediately preceding fiscal year.

Each federal agency required to have a small business innovation research (SBIR) program or to establish goals therefor shall report annually to the SMALL BUSINESS ADMINISTRATION the number of awards pursuant to grants, contracts, or cooperative agreements over $10,000 in amount and the dollar value of all such awards, and shall compare such SBIR awards in number and amount with awards to concerns other than small businesses.

The director of the Office of Science and Technology Policy, in consultation with the Federal Coordinating Council for Science, Engineering, and Research, shall, in addition to consulting as directed with the Small Business Administration, report not less than annually to the committees on small business of the Senate and the House of Representatives on all phases of the implementation and operation of SBIR programs within agencies required to establish an SBIR program, together with recommendations.

In addition, the Comptroller General of the U.S. shall, not more than five years after date of enactment of the act, transmit a report to the Senate and House on the implementation and nature of research conducted under the act, including the judgments of the heads of departments and agencies as to the effect of the act on research programs.

Background. In the course of consideration of the act, data furnished by members of Congress on the floor indicated that the set-aside programs of the act were necessary "because small businesses have suffered discrimination in the past by Government agencies in the awards of R&D contracts, and the political clout and connections of large corporations has resulted in a disproportionate share of Federal R&D moneys being funneled to them, while small businesses find themselves shut out unfairly."

Summary. It is hoped that such governmental provision of funds for small business ventures will not preclude the private sector from providing both "seed capital" and additional funds to finance operations out of the development stage. The field is fraught with high risk for private sector investors, but the rewards when realized can be very substantial, especially in high technology start-ups.

BIBLIOGRAPHY

BARTLETT, J. W. Venture Capital: *Law, Business Strategies, Investment Planning.* John Wiley and Sons, Inc., New York, 1988.
Business Capital Sources. International Wealth Success, Inc., New York, NY. Monthly.
Corporate Finance Sourcebook. Corporate Finance Sourcebook, New York, NY. Annual
Entrepreneur Magazine. Entrepreneur Group, Irvine, CA. Monthly.
Firstlist. First National Bank of Maryland. Quarterly.
Handbook of Business Finance and Capital Sources. American Management Association, 1985.
Inc.; The Magazine for Growing Companies. Inc. Publishers, Boston, MA. Monthly.
LINDSEY, J. *The Entrepreneur's Guide to Capital,* 1989.
PRATT, S., and MORRIS, J. K., eds. *Pratt's Guide to Venture Capital Sources.* Annual.
SUTTON, D. P., and BENEDETTO, M. W. *Initial Public Offering: A Strategic Planner for Raising Equity Capital,* 1988.
Venture.
Venture Capital.
Venture Capital Journal.

VERTICAL BULL CALL SPREAD and VERTICAL BEAR PUT SPREAD Limited risk/limited gain options strategies involving the purchase of a call (put) at one exercise price and sale of a call (put) at a higher (lower) strike price.

VERTICAL COMBINATION A business combination between companies in the same line of business but on different levels of operations. For example, a vertical combination would result if a furniture manufacturing company, a furniture wholesaler, and a furniture retailer were to combine.

VERTICAL INTEGRATION A firm is vertically integrated if it has some controls over inputs into its production process and/or some control over markets to which its product is sold. A firm is said to be backward integrated if it owns, for example, a plant that produced an input used in making its final product. A firm is said to be forward integrated if it controls, say, the distribution of its product to final consumers. Vertical relationships can be achieved through outright purchases or through vertical mergers.

VESTED INTEREST An immediate, fixed interest in real or personal property; the right of possession and enjoyment may be postponed until some future date or until the happening of some event.

VETERANS ADMINISTRATION (VA) An independent agency under the president that operates diverse programs to benefit veterans and members of their families. Benefits for war veterans have been provided by governments since ancient times. The U.S. benefit system traces its roots to 1636, when the Pilgrims of Plymouth Colony were at war with the Pequot Indians. The Pilgrims passed a law which provided that "if any man shalbee sent forth as a soldier and shall return maimed, he shalbee maintained competently by the collonie during his life." The Continental Congress in 1776 encouraged enlistments during the Revolutionary War by providing pensions for soldiers who were disabled. In 1865, Abraham Lincoln called upon Congress and the American people "to care for him who shall have borne the battle and for his widow, and his orphan." This phrase has become the motto of the VA.

The 1987 veteran population was nearly 28 million. War veterans living at this time accounted for 57% of all Americans who ever served in war during the country's two-century history.

Currently veterans benefits include: compensation payments for disabilities or death related to military service; pensions; education and rehabilitation; home loan guaranty; burial; and a medical care program incorporating nursing homes, clinics, and medical centers.

Credit assistance is provided so the housing credit needs of eligible veterans and active duty service personnel may be satisfied by private capital on more liberal terms than generally available to nonveterans. Assistance is provided chiefly through substituting the government's guaranty on loans made by private lenders in lieu of the down payments, shorter terms, and other requirements generally required in conventional home mortgage transactions. A system of direct financial grants is available to help certain

VETERANS ADMINISTRATION (VA)

permanently disabled veterans acquire specially adapted housing.

The major lending activities include appraising properties to establish their values; supervising the construction of new residential properties; passing on the ability of a veteran to repay a loan and the credit risk; servicing and liquidating defaulted loans; and disposing of real estate acquired as the consequence of defaulted loans. There are also substantial operations involved in managing and realizing loan assets. A counseling service is conducted to aid potential minority homebuyers both in obtaining housing credit and in discharging their obligations as homeowners and mortgagors.

Housing assistance. The VA's loan guaranty program provides housing credit assistance whereby mortgage credit needs of veterans and service personnel may be satisfied by private capital on more liberal terms than is generally available to nonveterans, without the assumption of undue risks by the federal government. Assistance is primarily through substituting the government's guaranty on loans in lieu of the substantial down payments, relatively short terms, and other investment safeguards applicable to conventional mortgage transactions.

Loans may be used to purchase a home; to purchase a residential unit in certain condominium projects; to build a home; to repair, alter or improve a home; to refinance an existing home; to improve a home by installing solar heating or other energy conservation measures; to buy a manufactured home, with or without a lot; or to buy a lot for a manufactured home the veteran already owns.

Over 481,000 veterans were assisted in home ownership during FY 1987. Approximately 40% of the total were guaranteed loans for refinancing purposes, primarily for the purpose of reducing monthly mortgage payments by refinancing original VA loans at a lower rate. A table comparing VA housing assistance for 1987 and 1988 is appended.

Housing Assistance: Comparative Highlights

Item	FY 1988	FY 1987	Percent Change
Number of loans guaranteed			
Home	232,638	474,391	-51.0
Manufactured home	2,071	5,100	-59.4
Average loan amount			
Home	$74,168	$73,322[1]	+1.2
Manufactured home	$23,207	$22,850	+1.6
Maximum interest rate[2]			
Home	11.0%	10.5%	—
Manufactured home	13.5%	13.0%	—
Minimum interest rate[2]			
Home	9.5%	8.5%	—
Manufactured home	12.0%	11.0%	—
GI home loans outstanding[3]	4,025,856	4,115,803	-2.2
GI home loans in default[3]	139,400	144,912	-3.8
As a percent of loans outstanding	3.46	3.52	-1.7
Substitutions of entitlement	1,798	1,556	+15.6
Properties on hand[3]	21,161	22,633	-6.5

[1] Data revised from FY 1987 Annual Report. *Source:* Veterans Administration.
[2] During year.
[3] End of year.

VA loans offer important advantages over most conventional loans: no down payments unless required by the lender; a comparatively favorable interest rate; limitations on closing costs; an assumable mortgage; long amortization terms; right to prepay without penalty in certain cases; inspection at various stages of the construction process; forbearance extended to worthy VA homeowners experiencing temporary financial difficulty.

To get a VA loan, a person must:

1. Be an eligible veteran who has available home loan entitlement.
2. Use the loan for an eligible purpose.
3. Occupy or intend to occupy the property as his or her home within a reasonable period of time after closing the loan.
4. Have enough income to meet the new mortgage payments on the loan, cover the costs of owning a home, take care of other obligations and expenses, and still have income left over for family support.
5. Have a good credit record.

VA-guaranteed loans are made by private lenders such as banks, savings and loan associations, or mortgage companies. If the loan is approved, the VA guarantees the loan when it is closed. The guaranty protects the lender against loss if the owner or a later owner fails to repay the loan. The VA will guarantee 60% of the loan amount up to a maximum of either $27,500 or the amount of entitlement a veteran has available. A veteran can borrow up to the reasonable value of the property as determined by VA or the purchase price, whichever is less.

A veteran is eligible for VA financing if he or she served within any of the following categories: wartime service; peacetime service; service after September 7, 1980 (enlisted) or October 16, 1981 (officer); and other types of service. Wartime service includes World War II, Korean conflict, or Vietnam era. The person must have served at least 90 days on active duty and been discharged or released under other than dishonorable conditions. A service-connected disability may extend these limitations. Peacetime service includes service between July 26, 1947 to June 26, 1950; February 1, 1955 to August 4, 1964, or May 8, 1975 to September 7, 1980 (enlisted) or to October 16, 1981 (officer). Service must have been at least 181 days of continuous active duty and been discharged or related under conditions other than dishonorable. If a person served less than 181 days, eligibility may be available if the discharge was because of a service-connected disability. Service after September 7, 1980 (enlisted) or October 16, 1981 (officer) provides eligibility if the person was separated from service which began after these dates and the individual completed 24 months of continuous active duty or the full period (181 days) for which he or she were called or ordered to active duty, and been discharged or released under conditions other than dishonorable; or completed at least 181 days of active duty with a hardship discharge, a discharge for the convenience of the government, or been determined to have compensable service-connected disability; or been discharged for a service-connected disability. Other types of service include certain U.S. citizens who served in the armed forces of a government allied with the United States in World War II; unmarried surviving spouses of the eligible persons who died as a result of the service or service-connected injuries; the spouse of any member of the Armed Forces serving on active duty who is listed as missing in action, or is a prisoner of war and has been so listed for a total of more than 90 days; and individuals with service as members in certain other organizations, services, programs, and schools may be eligible.

Ineligible service includes World War I service; active duty for training in the Reserves; or active duty for training in the National Guard (unless activated under the authority of title 10, U.S. Code).

VA-guaranteed financing is available to buy a home; to buy a townhouse or condominium unit in a project that has been approved by the VA; to build a home; to repair, alter, or improve a home; to simultaneously purchase and improve a home; to improve a home through installment of a solar heating and/or cooling system or other weatherization improvements; to refinance an existing home loan; to refinance an existing VA loan to reduce the interest rate; to buy a manufactured home and/or lot; to buy and improve a lot on which to place a manufactured home that the veteran already owns and occupies; and to refinance a manufactured home loan to acquire a lot.

The maximum VA home loan term is 30 years and 32 days. However, the term may never be for more than the remaining economic life of the property as determined by appraisal. The VA will guarantee loans to purchase homes made with the following repayment plans: traditional fixed-payment mortgage; graduated payment mortgage; buydowns (the builder of a new home or seller of an existing home may buy down the veteran's mortgage payments by making a large lump-sum payment up front at closing that will be used to supplement the monthly payments for a certain period, usually three to five years); and equity mortgage. The maximum interest rate on VA loans varies based on changes in the mortgage market. No commission or brokerage fees may be charged for obtaining a VA loan. However, the borrower may pay reasonable closing costs to the lender in connection with a VA-guaranteed loan. The closing costs generally include VA appraisal, credit report, survey, title evidence, recording fees, a 1% loan origination fee, and a VA funding fee. The closing costs and origination charge may not be included in the loan, except in VA refinancing loans. Generally, veterans are not allowed to pay discounts or points in connection with VA financing. Lenders may require discount points when they consider the maximum VA interest rate to be too low. The VA has no direct control over the charging of discounts.

As summarized by the Veterans Administration (VA), veterans' financial benefits include the following.

The VA is authorized to guarantee home loans made to eligible veterans by private lenders. Such loans may be for the purpose of purchasing a conventionally constructed home or mobile home (with or without a lot), refinancing an existing home mortgage, purchasing a condominium unit, or buying a farm home. Loans may also be guaranteed for home improvement purposes, including the installation of a solar heating and/or cooling system or other weatherization improvements.

Eligibility requirements vary based on the period of service. World War II, Korean conflict, and Vietnam war veterans must have 90 days of active duty (unless discharged earlier for service-connected disability) and a discharge or separation under other than dishonorable conditions. Post-World War II, post-Korean conflict, and post-Vietnam war veterans must have 181 days of active duty (unless discharged earlier for service-connected disability) and a discharge or separation under other than dishonorable conditions. Service personnel who have served at least 181 continuous days in active duty status, although not discharged, are eligible while their service continues without a break. Unmarried surviving spouses of veterans, including service personnel, who served between September 16, 1940, and 1981 and who died as a result of service-connected disabilities are eligible for home loan benefits. Spouses of service personnel on active duty who are officially listed as missing in action or prisoners of war and have been in such status for more than 90 days are also eligible for home loan benefits. Spouses of such prisoners of war or missing-in-action personnel are, however, limited to one loan. Loan guarantee benefits are available to all eligible veterans and service personnel until used. Certain U.S. citizens who served in the armed forces of a U.S. ally are also eligible.

The VA may guarantee the lender against loss for up to 60% of the loan amount or $27,500, whichever is less, on all types of home loans, except for mobile home loans for which the maximum guaranty is 50% of the loan amount or $20,000, whichever is less. There are no established loan maximums. However, no loan may exceed the property's value as established by the VA.

The VA makes no charge for guaranteeing a loan. No commission or brokerage fees may be charged to a veteran for securing a loan. However, the lender may charge reasonable closing costs, usually paid by a borrower; such closing costs generally include the VA appraisal, credit report, survey, title evidence, and recording fees. The lender, as provided in schedules issued by the VA, may also make a reasonable flat charge to cover all other loan origination costs. The closing costs and origination charge may not be included in the loan.

In addition to being declared eligible for a loan based on the veteran's period of service, the applicant must qualify by meeting the requirements of the governing law in respect to income and credit. The governing law requires that the applicant's income have a proper relation to the terms of repayment of the loan and other expenses. This means that the veteran's income must be sufficient to meet the anticipated mortgage payments on the loan, take care of other obligations and expenses, and leave an adequate amount to support the veteran and dependents. The applicant must also be a satisfactory credit risk.

Terms of VA home loans may extend to 30 years and 32 days under the law. They may be partially or fully paid at any time without penalty; part payments may not be less than one monthly installment or $100, whichever is less. The maximum interest rate at the time of origination of the loan may vary from time to time as announced by the VA, based on changes in the mortgage market (similar to the practice of the Federal Housing Administration on FHA-insured loans). Variation in market mortgage rates above such maxima, as has been the case in recent years of high interest rates generally, has been a factor causing low activity by mortgage lenders in FHA-insured and VA-guaranteed mortgages.

BIBLIOGRAPHY

Annual Report of the Administration of Veterans Affair. Veterans Administration, Washington, DC. Annual.
American Legion Magazine.
Federal Benefits for Veterans and Dependents. Veterans Administration, Washington, DC. Annual.
Once a Veteran: Benefits, Rights, Obligations. Veterans Administration, Washington, DC.
The Retired Officer.
VFW Magazine.

VISE An official endorsement on a passport or other document as an approval or attestation of its validity; certification that a document has been examined by the proper authorities and found to be correct and regular in all respects. The term "visa" is used by the U.S. State Department.

VISIBLE SUPPLY Stocks of goods subject to statistical measurement.

Visible supply is used particularly to denote the stocks of grain in public and private terminal elevators, at all terminal markets, and in transit, as distinguished from the amount held on the farms. It is also used to indicate the stocks of other commodities on hand at the principal sources of production, e.g., copper stocks at refineries; raw sugar supplies held by importers and refineries; hides held by packers, tanners, and importers; etc.

VISITORIAL POWERS Under the Federal Reserve Act (Sec. 21), no bank shall be subject to any visitorial powers other than such as are authorized by law or vested in courts of justice, or such as shall be or shall have been exercised or directed by Congress, by either the House of Representatives or the Senate, or by any committee of Congress or of either house duly authorized.

Member banks of the Federal Reserve System are subject to examination at least twice each year, or more often if it is considered necessary, by examiners appointed by the Comptroller of the Currency with the approval of the secretary of the Treasury. The Board of Governors of the Federal Reserve System, however, may authorize acceptance of examination by the state authorities in the case of state member banks, and may at any time direct the holding of a special examination of state member banks. In addition to the examinations made and conducted by the Comptroller of the Currency, every Federal Reserve bank may, with the approval of the Federal Reserve agent or the board of governors, provide for special examination of member banks within its district. At least once a year, the Federal Reserve banks themselves are subject to examination ordered by the board of governors. Upon joint application of ten member banks, the board of governors shall also order a special examination and report of the condition of any Federal Reserve bank.

State corporation laws usually specify details of judicial supervision of a corporation and of the officers and members thereof. In New York State, this is found in Article 6 of the General Corporation Law, Section 62, which states that such specification of judicial supervision shall not impair any vistorial power over a corporation vested in a corporate body or public officer.

See BANK EXAMINATION.

VITAL STATISTICS *See* POPULATION.

V-LOAN A loan guaranteed through Federal Reserve banks under Regulation V of the Board of Governors of the Federal Reserve System, pursuant to the Defense Production Act of 1950; also known as defense production loans.

Under the Defense Production Act of 1950, the following are authorized to guarantee loans for defense production that are made by commercial banks and other private financing institutions: the Departments of the Army, Navy, and Air Force; the Defense Logistics Agency of the Department of Defense; the Departments of Commerce, Interior, Agriculture, and Energy; the General Services Administration; the National Aeronautics and Space Administration; and the Nuclear Regulatory Commission. The Federal Reserve banks act as fiscal agents of the guaranteeing agencies under the board's Regulation V.

The maximum rate of interest that a financing institution may charge for a V-loan is the rate that the institution currently charges its most creditworthy business customers for loans of comparable maturity (unless the governmental guarantor decides that a particular loan bearing a higher rate of interest is necessary for national defense purposes).

See FEDERAL RESERVE BOARD REGULATIONS (Regulation V).

VOLATILE MARKET A market that is subject to wide price fluctuations. Volatility is often attributed to a lack of liquidity.

VOLATILITY The price variability of an instrument underlying an option contract, defined as the standard deviation in the logarithm of the price of the underlying instrument expressed at an annual rate. Expected volatility is a variable used in pricing options.

VOLUNTARY ASSOCIATION A rare form of business organization similar to that of a TRUST in the popular sense. In Massachusetts, voluntary associations exist in which the management of the business is given over to a number of trustees by a deed of trust from the stockholders. The stockholders receive transferable certificates which represent their interest in the association.

See MASSACHUSETTS TRUST.

VOLUNTARY BANKRUPTCY See BANKRUPTCY.

VOLUNTARY CREDIT RESTRAINT PROGRAM A program sponsored by the Federal Reserve System under the Defense Production Act of 1950, to help assure adequate financing for defense and defense-related activities and to curtail credit for nonessential and deferable purposes.

For about 14 months ending in May, 1952, private financial organizations cooperated in the voluntary credit restraint program. The board of governors pointed out that during this period, the program supplemented other measures of the board to limit credit and monetary expansion.

In April, 1952, at the request of the President, the financial actions of state and local governments were removed from the restrictions of the program. On May 12, 1952, operations under the program were discontinued, and the voluntary credit restraint organization was placed on a standby basis. On June 30, 1952, authority for the program was terminated by amendments to the Defense Production Act.

Early in 1965, the VOLUNTARY FOREIGN CREDIT RESTRAINT PROGRAM was inaugurated as part of a broad series of measures designed to effect improvement in the U.S. INTERNATIONAL BALANCE OF PAYMENTS position.

VOLUNTARY FOREIGN CREDIT RESTRAINT PROGRAM Established in early 1965 as part of a government wide effort to strengthen the U.S. INTERNATIONAL BALANCE OF PAYMENTS. According to Governor Andrew F. Brimmer of the Board of Governors of the Federal Reserve System, the Voluntary Foreign Credit Restraint Program (VFCR) was essentially a request that U.S. financial institutions restrain their capital outflow by limiting loans to foreigners and the acquisition of investments abroad.

The central feature of the program was a set of guidelines issued to U.S. banks and nonbank financial institutions by the Board of Governors of the Federal Reserve System. At the beginning of 1968, the board of governors received, by Executive Order 11387 dated January 1, 1968, authority to impose mandatory regulations relating to the foreign transactions of banks and other financial institutions. However, in view of the degree of cooperation financial institutions had exhibited since the program was instituted, the board of governors elected to continue it as voluntary in nature. The same executive order made mandatory the program administered by the Department of Commerce for nonfinancial corporations. On March 1, 1968, because of a difficult financial situation that developed for Canada early in the year, all transactions with that country were exempted from restriction under the U.S. balance-of-payments programs.

The program was one of the three sets of restraints on U.S. capital outflow-the voluntary foreign credit restraint program, applicable to U.S. banks and nonbank financial institutions, administered by the Board of Governors of the Federal Reserve System; the foreign direct investment program, regulating funds supplied by U.S. corporations to their overseas affiliates, administered by the Department of Commerce; and the INTEREST EQUALIZATION TAX, applicable to purchases by Americans of foreign stock, bonds, and other equity and debt securities.

Under the VFCR program, each bank and each nonbank financial institution was asked to keep its loans to foreigners and its other investments abroad within specified limits. Each institution, in making loans and investments under these ceilings, was to give priority to credits that financed U.S. exports and that met the financing needs of developing countries.

In addition to observing the overall ceilings, the institutions were asked to observe additional restraints on capital outflows to the developed countries of continental Western Europe, and lesser restraints on capital outflows to developing countries.

On January 29, 1974, the Board of Governors of the Federal Reserve System announced the termination of its VFCR guidelines. The VFCR was ended in conjunction with actions taken by the Treasury Department to reduce the interest-equalization tax to zero, and by the Department of Commerce to terminate its foreign direct investment restrictions.

VOLUNTARY TRUST See LIVING TRUST.

VOSTRO ACCOUNTS In foreign exchange bookkeeping, the accounts of foreign banks or other foreign correspondents having dollar balances on deposit with a domestic bank or other institution. The term literally means "your accounts" and is the antonym of NOSTRO ACCOUNTS.

VOTING POWER The ultimate power in a corporation is the voting power exercised by stockholders.

Stockholders vote by shares of stock held, except in the case of CUMULATIVE VOTING, as authorized by the certificate of incorporation, or other certificate filed pursuant to law, for elections of directors. In cumulative voting, each stockholder is entitled to as many votes as shall equal the number of votes that except for such cumulative voting provisions he would be entitled to cast for the election of directors with respect to his shares of stock multiplied by the number of directors to be elected. The stockholder may cast all such cumulative votes for a single director or may distribute them among the number of directors to be voted on, as he may see fit.

There are various ways of depriving the stockholder of voting power. For example,

1. By the stockholder's use of the PROXY.
2. By creation of the VOTING TRUST. A stockholder, by agreement in writing, may transfer his stock to a voting trustee or trustees for the purpose of conferring the right to vote thereon for a period not exceeding ten years upon the terms and conditions stated in the agreement.
3. By reclassifying a class of stock, so as to deprive the entire class of stock of voting power. The certificate of incorporation or other certificate filed pursuant to law may provide, either absolutely or conditionally, that the holders of any designated class or classes of stock shall not be entitled to vote, or it may otherwise limit or define the respective power of voting of the several classes of stock. However, in any proposal for classifying or reclassifying any already authorized or outstanding shares so as to deprive a class of stock of voting power, the holders of all shares of any class or classes that will be adversely affected by such action shall be entitled to vote, regardless of any provision to the contrary in the certificate of incorporation, other certificate of incorporation, or other certificate filed pursuant to law.

VOTING TRUST A trust created when the stockholders of a single corporation deposit their stock in the custody of designated trustees, called voting trustees, who issue stock trust certificates or voting trust certificates in exchange. The stockholders retain all rights in their stock except voting power, which is delegated to the trustees under the terms and during the life of the voting trust agreement. Voting trusts are usually created in reorganizations when it is desirable to concentrate the control in the hands of capable persons in order to tide the corporation over the difficult period. Otherwise, the purpose is to secure continuity in policies, management, and operation, e.g., a voting trust is often provided for in the case of companies closely owned so as to assure stability of management.

Under the New York Business Corporation Law (Sec. 621), a voting trust agreement is limited to ten years. Other states have enacted laws imposing similar limitations. Trust companies are often appointed by voting trustees to act as custodians of stock certificates, to issue and transfer voting trust certificates in exchange, and to disburse dividends received upon the stock to the proper owners.

VOTING TRUST CERTIFICATE A certificate issued by voting trustees to a stockholder as a negotiable receipt for stock certificates deposited with such trustees.

See VOTING TRUST.

VOTING TRUSTEES See VOTING TRUST.

VOUCHER A receipt; a receipted bill or statement; any paper evidencing a money expenditure or payment of a debt. Canceled checks are often called vouchers because they offer proof of payment. Originally, a voucher meant a person or paper that afforded proof or bore witness concerning some matter under examination.

VOUCHER CHECK A special form of check combining the features of a formal receipt and a check. On a voucher check, space is reserved in the left-hand margin, or on the reverse side, to indicate the goods, services, or debt owing, i.e., statement of account or invoice, for which the check is in payment. A variant form of the voucher check is a double-sized check folded in the middle, one sheet operating as a check and the other as a voucher.

The advantage of a voucher check is that each bill is identified with its payment, and when the check is returned from the bank endorsed by the payee (creditor), it constitutes unquestionable evidence of payment. The voucher check is in general use among large corporations where the voucher system is in operation. In personal checking transactions, an ordinary canceled check serves the purpose of a receipt just as well as a voucher check.

VOUCHER DEPARTMENT The department of a bank that cancels, verifies, files, stores, and forwards canceled checks or vouchers to the depositors who drew them, after they have been posted to the debit of depositors' accounts on the ledgers and statements. Checks are canceled as of the date they are paid and posted to the drawer's account. Cancellation is effected by means of a perforating machine which cuts the following words into the check: "Paid (date) Blank Bank." The canceled checks are then sorted by customers' accounts and filed until the statements are prepared. They are arranged in the order of payment, which is the same as the order in which they appear on the statement. When the statement is ready, the bank verifies the canceled checks by "checking" them against the entries. Individual customers' canceled checks are usually combined with the statement, placed in an envelope, and retained at the bookkeeper's window until called for by the customer. Canceled checks are sent to out-of-town customers by registered mail or express.

VOUCHER SYSTEM An accounting system developed to control cash payments and promote efficiency by eliminating the special purchases journal and the accounts payable subsidiary ledger. It accounts for all payments except those from the petty cash fund.

In a voucher system, each cash disbursement must be authorized by a voucher. A voucher is a serially numbered document that includes all pertinent information about the requested disbursement. The voucher must be signed by one to approve cash disbursements. Supporting documents for the expenditure, such as purchase invoices, freight bills, or receiving documents, must be attached to the voucher. After the voucher is authorized, it is filed in an unpaid voucher file which replaces the accounts payable subsidiary ledger. A voucher register and a check register are two journals used in the voucher system. A voucher register is a special journal used to record all liabilities approved for payment by voucher. A check register is used to record cash disbursements.

In a voucher system, individuals who are authorized to approve vouchers do not prepare or sign checks or have access to the voucher and cash registers. The individual who signs checks is allowed to do so only when a voucher for the payment has been authorized.

W

WAGE AND PRICE GUIDEPOSTS Originally presented in the January 1962 *Report of the Council of Economic Advisers* in the Kennedy administration as a voluntary system of wage and price controls in order to avoid inflation, the wage and price guideposts were aggregative in nature, rather than specific for particular types of labor and industries. They consisted of the following general guides.

The general guide for noninflationary wage behavior was that the rate of increase in wage rates (including fringe benefits) in each industry be equal to the trend-rate of overall productivity increase. General acceptance of this guide would maintain stability of labor cost per unit of output for the economy as a whole—although it was conceded that it would not for individual industries.

The general guide for noninflationary price behavior called for price reductions if the industry's rate of productivity increases exceeded the overall rate, for this would mean declining unit labor costs. On the other hand, it called for an appropriate increase in prices if the opposite relationship prevailed. But it called for stable prices if the two rates of productivity increase were equal.

These guideposts were advanced as general guides. To reconcile them with objectives of equity and efficiency, specific modifications concededly had to be made to adapt them in the circumstances of particular industries. If all of these modifications were made, each in the specific circumstances to which it applied, they would be consistent with stability of the general price level. It was urged that public judgments about the effects on the price level of particular wage or price decisions should take into account the modifications as well as the general guides.

The most important modifications were as follows.

1. Wage rate increases would exceed the general guide rate in an industry that would otherwise be unable to attract sufficient labor; or in which wage rates were exceptionally low compared with the range of wages earned elsewhere by similar labor, because the bargaining position of workers was weak in particular local labor markets.
2. Wage rate increases would fall short of the general guide rate in an industry that could not provide jobs for its entire labor force even in times of generally full employment; or in which wage rates were exceptionally high compared with the range of wages earned elsewhere by similar labor, because the bargaining position of workers had been especially strong.
3. Prices would rise more rapidly, or fall more slowly, than indicated by the general guide rate in an industry in which the level of profits was insufficient to attract the capital required to finance a needed expansion in capacity; or in which costs other than labor costs had risen.
4. Prices would rise more slowly, or fall more rapidly, than indicated by the general guide in an industry in which the relation of productive capacity to full employment demand showed the desirability of an outflow of capital from the industry; or in which costs other than labor costs had fallen; or in which excessive market power had resulted in rates of profit substantially higher than those earned elsewhere on investments of comparable risk.

Evaluation. Such wage and price controls were voluntary and essentially aggregative in nature, with necessary exceptions for special circumstances, and it was not the intention to freeze the respective shares of labor and nonlabor in total industrial income. As a result, they soon broke down under the pressure of specific exceptions to the general guideposts. By contrast, World War II and Korean War controls were mandatory with specific applicabilities, but even with their mandatory nature under wartime pressures, problems of compliance and effectiveness existed. The most extraordinary example of wage and price controls, the first attempted in the U.S. under peacetime conditions, was imposed by the Nixon administration, beginning with the freeze in August 1971. For review and discussion of those controls, see INCOMES POLICY.

BIBLIOGRAPHY

COUNCIL OF ECONOMIC ADVISERS. *Annual Reports* for 1962, 1963, and 1964.

WAGE-PRICE SPIRAL A form of cost-push inflation.

WAIVER Voluntary renunciation or relinquishment of a legal right.
See PROTEST WAIVED, WAIVER OF DEMAND, WAIVER OF NOTICE.

WAIVER OF DEMAND Unless excused, presentment is necessary to charge secondarily liable parties (for acceptance, as called for by a draft, or if the draft is payable at a place other than the residence or place of business of the drawee, or if date of payment depends upon presentment; or for payment, to charge any endorser); see NEGOTIABLE INSTRUMENTS LAW (Sec. 3-501, Uniform Commercial Code). Although such parties secondarily liable are entitled to receive notice of dishonor and refusal to pay, it is a right which they may waive (Sec. 3-511, Uniform Commercial Code).
See PROTEST WAIVED.

WAIVER OF NOTICE This term has two meanings:

1. See PROTEST WAIVED.
2. Corporation meetings under state statutes are of two basic types. Directors' meetings are the regular meetings and special meetings of the board of directors. Under state statutes, the bylaws may provide for a quorum for directors' meetings to be not less than a specified minimum, such as one-third of the board, and fix the dates of regular meetings of the directors. If the dates for regular meetings appear in the bylaws, the directors are not entitled to any additional notice. For special directors' meetings, notice is required, but such notice may be waived. Stockholders' meetings are the annual meetings, special meetings, meetings to oust holdover directors, and extraordinary meetings (those held by application to a court of equity, where there is difficulty in getting the required ratio of consent because of stockholder apathy in sending in proxies or attending in person, etc.). Notice is required for all these types of meetings, but may be waived in writing.
See MEETING.

WAIVER OF PROTEST See PROTEST WAIVED.

WALL STREET The financial district of New York and, by extension, the financial interests of the United States. The Wall Street district, or financial district, located in the area south of Chambers Street in New York City, includes not only the New York Stock Exchange, the American Stock Exchange, and the offices of their

ENCYCLOPEDIA OF BANKING AND FINANCE

member firms as well as over-the-counter firms, investment bankers, commercial paper and discount houses, and government and municipal securities dealers, but also the banks and trust companies, the Federal Reserve bank, the New York Clearing House, many of the general offices of the industrial, railroad, public utility, and insurance companies maintained in that area, a large number of the import, export, and steamship companies, the New York Chamber of Commerce, Customs House, and the New York mercantile, commodity, cotton, coffee, sugar, and cocoa exchanges.

Since finance is the key to the economic structure, any objective appraisal of the role of Wall Street must include among its conclusions the facts that it is a mechanism for the flow of capital from individual and institutional sources to public and private users of funds which is essential for economic development, and that it provides marketability for the large volume and varieties of paper and securities originating in the financial system.

BIBLIOGRAPHY

ALISON, E. W. *Raiders of Wall Sttreet*, 1986.
AULETTA, K. *Greed and Glory on Wall Street: The Fall of the House of Leheman*, 1986.
CARRENGTON, T. *The Year They Sold Wall Street*, 1987.
EICKSON, G. *Wall Street's Guide*, 1985.
HAYES, S. *Wall Street and Regulation*, 1987.
SHARP, R. M. *The Lore and Legends of Wall Street*, 1989.

WARD A minor child whose person and/or property is under the control of a GUARDIAN.

WAR DEBTS Credits extended by the United States to allied nations for the purpose of prosecuting war efforts.

World War I. The U.S. State Department reports that the original indebtedness to the United States from World War I totaled $12.4 billion, with outstanding debt and interest as of April, 1979, exceeding $28 billion. These debts present special problems. Most debtor governments have never denied the legality of the debts but maintain that payment depends on their receipt of World War I reparations from Germany. The 1953 London agreement on German external debts, which was ratified by the U.S. Senate and has the status of a treaty, deferred resolution of government claims against Germany arising from the war "until a final general settlement of this matter." Although the United States has never recognized the legal connection between World War I obligations owed to this country and reparation claims on Germany, there is therefore the referenced linkage in reality.

Although the United States never received reparations from Germany, it nevertheless financed German borrowing under the Dawes and Young plans. During the period 1924-1930, it is estimated that the net foreign debt of Germany was increased by 18 billion Rm. to 25 billion Rm., and that about 55% of the long-term debt and 37% of the short-term debt of Germany were financed in the United States. During the period 1924-1931, under the Dawes and Young plans, German payments to the United States on her debt aggregated 449 million Rm. Financing by the United States of German debt aided Germany in meeting reparations payments to the other allies, who in turn were aided by such payments at least indirectly in meeting war debt payments to the United States.

This circuitous flow of funds broke down in 1930 and 1931, and in June, 1931, the Hoover administration declared a moratorium of one year on war debt payments to the United States. The Lausanne Conference in June and July, 1932, eliminated an estimated 90% of Germany's reparations liability and substituted therefor the plan calling for delivery by Germany to the Bank for International Settlements of an issue of 3 billion Rm. in 5% bonds (approximately $715 billion), to be held by the bank three years and then publicly offered. Not long afterward, debtors of the United States began to default on war debt payments on the grounds of hardship, and in June, 1934, Germany proclaimed a transfer moratorium and suspended cash payments on foreign debts.

On April 13, 1934, the Johnson War Debt Default Act was approved, prohibiting financial transactions with any foreign government in default in the payment of its war debts. On March 10, 1941, the Lend-Lease Act was approved, and war debts for the prosecution of World War II were financed in large part under this act in subsequent years.

Overall Current Situation. The U.S. State Department reported in April, 1979, that as of September 30, 1978, debts owed to the United States, excluding those arising from World War I, totaled $45.7 billion. This reflected debts from many different types of transactions, such as the following:

1. War material delivered to U.S. allies during World War II.
2. The reconstruction effort in post-World War II Europe.
3. Provision of surplus foodstuffs to developing countries.
4. Loans to assist the developing countries.
5. EXPORT-IMPORT BANK loans to aid U.S. exports.

About 54% of the debt was owed by the non-oil exporting developing countries; 25% by western industrial countries (including Greece and Turkey); 9% by Israel; 7% by members of the Organization of Petroleum Exporting Countries (OPEC); and about 5% by the U.S.S.R. (Russia) and Eastern Europe. Six countries accounted for $18.4 billion, or over 40% of the total debt: Israel, $4.2 billion; India, $3.5 billion; the United Kingdom, $3.2 billion; Pakistan, $2.6 billion; Korea, $2.5 billion; and Brazil, $2.4 billion. Seven other countries—Indonesia, Turkey, Egypt, the U.S.S.R., Taiwan, Spain, and Chile—each owed the U.S. over $1 billion.

As of September 30, 1978, the 13 OPEC members owed the U.S. government $3.3 billion in long-term debt. Indonesia owed almost 60%; with a per capita income of $415 (1981), it was still receiving concessional assistance. The principal and interest payments on debts owed by OPEC countries were current, except for $37 million owed by Iran. That Iranian arrearage of 1945 and 1948 involving two surplus property agreements signed in those years (and since 1975, made subject by Iran to payment settling a claim it had against the U.S. for damage to Iranian railways by Allied forces during World War II) was relatively small compared to the claims against Iran by both the U.S. and U.S. nationals, which, however, became subject to review by the Iranian-U.S. Claims Tribunal, and as of 1982 were still in process of review, and negotiation, on the hostages episode and related events.

The U.S.S.R.'s long-term indebtedness totaled $1.1 billion in principal: $443 million was for Export-Import Bank loans to encourage U.S. export sales, and the remainder was owed under terms of the 1972 U.S.-U.S.S.R. LEND LEASE agreement. In accordance with that agreement, the Soviets made three unconditional payments totaling $48 million. Payments on the remaining lend-lease obligations of $674 million were conditioned on the granting by the U.S. of most-favored-nation treatment to Soviet exports as provided in the 1972 U.S.-U.S.S.R. Trade Agreement, which had not gone into effect as of 1982.

The U.S. State Department advises that U.S. lending agencies are careful to protect the U.S. right to repayment, and that most debts are paid on time. Collections, including interest, on long-term credits extended since 1940 exceeded $50 billion as of April, 1979, and in the fiscal year 1978, dollar repayments totaled roughly $4 billion. In contrast, principal and interest payments due and unpaid after 90 days or more totaled $612 million as of September 30, 1978. The State Department advises that most of these delinquencies stemmed from unique circumstances that impeded the ability of the U.S. to collect. For example, about one-third of current arrearages related to Korean conflict logistical support claims, whose validity had not been clearly established. Another one-third related to debt owed by China, Cuba, Cambodia, and Vietnam. Remaining delinquencies were distributed among many countries and related to a variety of lending and credit programs administered by U.S. agencies. According to the State Department, in most situations the delinquencies reflected technical factors rather than conscious decisions by foreign governments to avoid repayment.

Legislation authorizing government lending programs includes authority for debt renegotiation, "because unusual circumstances may require the modification of loan terms."

"We believe," advises the State Department, "that exceptional situations requiring debt reorganization to insure repayment should be addressed efficiently and equitably in a multilateral framework," as such a framework is essential so that all creditor countries should share the burden of any adjustments. "Equally important," according to the State Department, "debt renegotiation should be conditioned on debtor country willingness to undertake a comprehensive economic program to strengthen its balance-of-payments situation."

Since 1956, there have been about 40 multilateral negotiations involving 12 debtor countries, and the U.S. has participated in most

WAR DEBT DEFAULT ACT

of the agreements. Although many countries recently had faced considerable economic difficulty, the incidence of multilateral debt renegotiation had remained small. The April, 1979, advisory from the State Department indicated that in the last three years, five multilateral agreements had been concluded, with the U.S. participating in those for Zaire, Turkey, and Peru.

Summary. It will be noted that both economic and military assistance totals are reported by the U.S. Department of State in the above total foreign indebtedness to the U.S. government, excluding that arising from World War I. Such combining of economic and military assistance reflects the close association of the two types of assistance, during both World War II and the cold war since.

See AGENCY FOR INTERNATIONAL DEVELOPMENT, MUTUAL SECURITY PROGRAM, WAR DEBTS DEFAULT ACT.

BIBLIOGRAPHY

CLAYTON, JAMES L., ed. *The Economic Impact of the Cold War*, 1970.
MOULTON, H. G., and PASVOLSKY, L. *War Debts and National Prosperity*, 1933.
SIMONDS, F. H. *The ABC of War Debts*, 1933.
U.S. DEPARTMENT OF STATE. "Foreign Indebtedness to the U.S. Government." *Gist*, April, 1979.
WEIDENBAUM, MURRAY C. *The Economics of Peacetime Defense*, 1974.

WAR DEBTS DEFAULT ACT An act, approved April 13, 1934, sponsored by Senator Johnson of California, which had as its main object the prohibition of financial transactions with any foreign government in default in the payment of its obligations, or any part thereof, to the government of the United States. It also imposed a fine of not more than $10,000 and/or imprisonment for not more than five years for violation of this act.

Extensions of military and civilian aid during World War II for the purpose of prosecuting the war were administered under LEND LEASE, authorized by the Lend-Lease Act approved March 10, 1941.

WAR PAPER WAR LOAN.

WAREHOUSE ACT See WAREHOUSE RECEIPTS ACT.

WAREHOUSE CERTIFICATE WAREHOUSE RECEIPT.

WAREHOUSE COMPANY A company engaged in the business of storing goods and merchandise for hire. Such a company has a bailee's lien on property stored for the amount of the charges, and an insurable interest in such property to the extent of charges and any advances that may have been made thereon.

The term "public warehouse" applies to all storage buildings whose facilities are open to the public, as compared with the private warehouses of individual manufacturers and retailers used only for the products of the owner.

A distinct feature of the modern warehousing companies is the diversification of their service. In addition to furnishing storage space, many of the larger companies provide steamship piers, loft buildings for manufacture, cold storage plants, railroad connections with the trunk lines, and truck distributing services, all of these facilities operating as a closely coordinated unit. Thus there are several sources of revenue from a single customer. A manufacturer hiring storage space is likely to store his excess stock in nearby warehouses of the company. Similarly, it is likely that he will use the company's piers for his foreign trade and the company's trucks and railroad connecting facilities for his inland distribution. While the warehouse company profits from this diversification of services, the customer himself also benefits from the economy and convenience of storage and distribution facilities concentrated at a single point and under a single direction.

Field warehousing organizations in recent times have also developed field warehousing services, including the segregation, storage inspection, and protection of pledged goods stored on the premises of a borrower rather than in public warehouse space, thus facilitating loans by banks on field warehouse receipts. For banks, the advantages of such field warehouse receipt loans include the following: (1) open lines may be converted to secured loans; (2) the safety of loans is increased; and (3) new loan business secured by such warehouse receipts issued by bonded and licensed warehousing companies may be created. Included in the service provided by one warehouse company, operating nationally and offering field warehousing facilities, is an IBM commodity collateral report for loan officers, which materially reduces the cost of servicing commodity loans and keeps loan officers up to date on inventory values.

Future of Warehousing. In the future, experts see a greater reliance on computerized, automated warehousing and distribution inventory management, with today's fragmented trucking and warehousing company giving way to a more complex firm offering a full range of logistical services, transportation options, warehousing, package filling, final assembly services, order processing, and inventory control. In such an environment, the full-service public warehouses, located just about everywhere and linked through their national association, would enjoy certain advantages over own-company facilities in fixed locations: maximum flexibility in designated location and transportation costs and payment only for actually used space and labor.

BIBLIOGRAPHY

ADAMS, A. B. "Security Agreements Under the Uniform Commercial Code." *Journal of Commercial Bank Lending*, September, 1968.
DANIELS, F. C., LEGG, S. C., and YUILLE, E. C. "Accounts Receivable and Related Inventory Financing." *Journal of Commercial Bank Lending*, July, 1970.
FREDMAN, A. J., and TONIETTI, M. E. "Inventory Financing." *Credit and Financial Management*, March, 1976.
LOTT, K. L., and MYERS, R. G. "Secured Lending." In BAUGHN, W. H., and WALKER, C. E., eds., *The Bankers' Handbook*, rev. ed., 1978.
MOSKAL, B. S. "No Buck Rogers in Corporate Logistics," in "Future Focus." *Industry Week*, February 20, 1978.
SAYER, S. F. "Many Faces of Collateral." *Credit and Financial Management*, February, 1970.

WAREHOUSE LOAN A loan made against warehouse receipts, i.e., against the evidence of goods stored in a warehouse.
See WAREHOUSE RECEIPT.

WAREHOUSEMAN See WAREHOUSE COMPANY, WAREHOUSE RECEIPT.

WAREHOUSE RECEIPT The Uniform Warehouse Receipts Act, the Uniform Bills of Lading Act, and provisions of the Uniform Sales Act pertaining to negotiation of documents of title were consolidated and revised under Article 7, Warehouse Receipts, Bills of Lading, and Other Documents of Title, of the Uniform Commercial Code. The code codified substantially all of the provisions of these acts except for their criminal provisions.

A warehouse receipt is a receipt for goods stored in a warehouse. It represents an undertaking in which the warehouseman or warehouse company acknowledges receipt and agrees to be responsible for the safe custody and redelivery of the therein described goods upon surrender of the receipt properly endorsed and payment of the charges. For the owner or holder to whom the goods are deliverable, it also constitutes a document of title.

Warehouse receipts are issued in negotiable and nonnegotiable form, but usually the former so that they may serve as collateral for bank loans. Since they do not call for payment in money, they cannot technically be called NEGOTIABLE INSTRUMENTS. A nonnegotiable receipt states that the goods will be delivered to the depositor or to some other person designated on its face. A negotiable receipt states that the goods will be delivered to the bearer or to the order of some person named therein. Negotiable receipts are printed on a yellow form and nonnegotiable receipts on a white form.

Under the Uniform Commercial Code, a warehouse receipt may be issued by any warehouseman. It need not be in any particular form, but must contain the following essential terms: (1) location of the warehouse where the goods are stored; (2) date of issuance of the receipt; (3) consecutive number of the receipt; (4) statement as to whether the goods received will be delivered to the bearer, to a specified person, or to a specified person or his order; (5) rate of storage and handling charges, except that where goods are stored under a field warehousing arrangement, a statement of that fact is sufficient on a nonnegotiable receipt; (6) a description of the goods or of the packages containing them; (7) the signature of the warehouseman, which may be made by his authorized agent; (8) the fact of ownership if the receipt is issued for goods of which the warehouseman is owner, either solely or jointly or in common with others; and (9) a statement of the amount of advances made and of liabilities incurred for which the warehouseman claims a lien or security interest.

Warehouse receipts offer an important basis of commercial credit, and are frequently employed by importers, manufacturers, and merchants as collateral for bank loans. They are regarded as good collateral provided the merchandise stored is not subject to rapid physical deterioration or to excessive market depreciation. In case of deterioration or decline in value, the warehouseman is compelled to notify the depositor of the merchandise and the bank which has made advances against the receipt. Since the warehouseman is not responsible in case of loss or damage by fire, the receipt should be accompanied by a fire insurance certificate if offered as bank collateral.

See WAREHOUSE RECEIPTS ACT.

WAREHOUSE RECEIPTS ACT Prior to 1916, warehouse and elevator companies were under the regulation of the separate states. In New York State, the Uniform Warehouse Receipts Act was first enacted in 1907, and in 1909 was amended and incorporated into the General Business Law as Article IX (Secs. 90-143, inclusive). The Uniform Warehouse Receipts Act has been adopted by 46 states.

Federally, at the instigation of the Department of Agriculture, Congress passed the Federal Warehouse Receipts Act on August 11, 1916. The purpose of this act was twofold: (1) to standardize the type of warehouses storing agricultural products acceptable as collateral for bank loans, and (2) to standardize warehouse receipts in order to furnish more satisfactory evidence of storage and to provide more complete records. Under the federal act as since amended, warehouses are licensed and brought under the inspection service of the Department of Agriculture. Periodic reports are required of all warehousemen so that their financial condition, and the physical condition of their properties, may be known at all times.

The Uniform Commercial Code (Sec. 7) has codified substantially all of the provisions of the Uniform Warehouse Receipts Act (*see* WAREHOUSE RECEIPT).

The warehouse company must comply with the laws of the state in which it is located, including licensing laws. In establishing a field warehouse, the warehouseman must take the necessary steps to assure an effective bailment which will provide continuous, exclusive, and "notorious" possession of the goods. This requires leasing of a portion of the depositor's premises for the purposes of the field warehouse, to which none but the authorized representatives of the field warehousing company have accesss. It had been permissible for the field warehouseman to hire one of the employees of the depositor to act as the field warehouseman's representative, but this practice has not been permitted in administration of the Federal Warehouse Act.

BIBLIOGRAPHY

See bibliography under WAREHOUSE COMPANY.

WAR FINANCE CORPORATION A corporation created by the Act of April 5, 1918, for the purpose of aiding financing of essential war industries and the marketing of their products. The corporation during the years 1918-1923 provided financing for exports and agricultural intermediate credit. It may be regarded as an antecedent of the RECONSTRUCTION FINANCE CORPORATION, created by act of Congress on January 22, 1932.

WAR LOAN An organized finance drive by the government during and for the purpose of financing a war.

During World War II, the United States organized seven war loans and a victory loan, as follows:

1. **First war loan.** Offered November 30, 1942, consisting of $2,831 million in Treasury 2.5% bonds, due 1963-1968; $3,062 million in Treasury 1.75% bonds, due June 15, 1948; and $3,800 million in Treasury 0.875% certificates of indebtedness.
2. **Second war loan.** Offered March 12, 1943, consisting of $3,762 million in Treasury 2.5% bonds, due 1964-1969; $4,939 million in Treasury 2% bonds, due 1950-1952; and $5,251 million in Treasury 0.875% certificates.
3. **Third war loan.** Offered August 16, 1943, consisting of $3,779 million in Treasury 2.5% bonds, due 1964-1969; $5,257 million in Treasury 2% bonds, due 1951-1953; and $4,122 million in Treasury 0.875% certificates.
4. **Fourth war loan.** Offered November 22, 1943, consisting of $2,212 million in Treasury 2.5% bonds, due 1965-1970; $3,728 million in Treasury 2.25% bonds, due 1956-1959; and $5,048 million in Treasury 0.875% certificates.
5. **Fifth war loan.** Offered April 14, 1944, consisting of $2,909 million in Treasury 2.5% bonds, due 1965-1970; $5,825 million in Treasury 2% bonds, due 1952-1954; $1,948 million in Treasury 1.25% notes; and $4,770 million in Treasury 0.875% certificates.
6. **Sixth war loan.** Offered October 23, 1944, consisting of $3,448 million in Treasury 2.5% bonds, due 1966-1971; $7,922 million in Treasury 2% bonds, due 1952-1954; $1,550 million in Treasury 1.25% notes; and $4,395 million in Treasury 0.875% certificates.
7. **Seventh war loan.** Offered April 11, 1945, consisting of $7,967 million in Treasury 2.5% bonds, due 1967-1972; $5,284 million in Treasury 2.25% bonds, due 1959-1962; $2,635 million in Treasury 1.5% bonds, due December 15, 1950; and $4,799 million in Treasury 0.875% certificates.
8. **Victory loan.** Offered September 12, 1945, consisting of $11,689 in Treasury 2.5% bonds, due 1967-1972; $3,470 million in Treasury 2.25% bonds, due 1959-1962; and $3,768 million in Treasury 0.875% certificates.

In addition to these offerings of marketable securities, the Treasury organized large financing drives for the placement of UNITED STATES SAVINGS BONDS, first issued in 1935 and emphasized during the war loan drives for purchases by individuals either directly or through payroll savings plans.

See UNITED STATES GOVERNMENT SECURITIES.

WAR PAPER WAR LOAN.

WARRANT Tradeable instrument conferring on the holder the right to purchase from, or sell to, the warrant issuer a fixed-income security or equity stock under specified conditions for some period of time. Warrants have been used as a short-term obligation of a municipality or other political subdivision, constituting a part of its floating debt or as a revenue obligation issued in anticipation of tax collections. Recently, the most common warrants have been sold in conjunction with Euro-bond offerings and enable the holder to obtain a security identical to the original issue.

Federal Reserve banks are permitted to invest in such warrants as are defined by the Federal Reserve Act thus: "with a maturity from date of purchase of not exceeding six months, issued in anticipation of the collection of taxes or in anticipation of the receipt of assured revenues by any state, county, district, political subdivision, or municipality in the continental United States, including irrigation, drainage, and reclamation districts, such purchase to be made in accordance with rules and regulations prescribed by the Board of Governors of the Federal Reserve System." Regulation F of the board of governors regulates the purchase of such warrants.

See DIVIDEND WARRANT, INTEREST WARRANT, MUNICIPAL WARRANT, STOCK PURCHASE WARRANT.

BIBLIOGRAPHY

MESLER, D. *Warrants: Analysis and Investment Strategy.* Probus Publishing Co., Chicago, IL, 1986.

WARRANT ATTACHED *See* STOCK PURCHASE WARRANT.

WARRANTY A guarantee or promise by the seller relating to some aspect of the sale, such as the quality, quantity, or title of the goods. Warranties are either express (made part of the contract by seller's oral, written, or printed words) or implied (made part of the contract by operation of law without any action by the parties).

Express warranties can be an affirmation of fact or promise, description, sample, or model. "Puffing" and opinions are not warranties. An express warranty can be excluded or disclaimed by words or conduct if consistent with a written contract. Express warranties relating to the quality of goods can be made by promise or by description. Implied warranties include warranties of merchantability and fitness for a particular purpose. Such warranties are implied by law. A fitness-for-particular-purpose warranty can only be excluded or disclaimed in writing. A seller's title warranty relates to the assumption that the seller owns the goods and the goods are not subject to any security interests or liens held by other persons. A warranty of title can be excluded or modified only by specific language. A seller's infringement warranty is an implied warranty and affirms that the goods will not be subject to a patent or trademark infringement suit by a third party. A buyer's infringement warranty affirms that if the buyer supplies the specifications, the buyer warrants that the seller will not be subject to a patent or trademark infringement suit by a third party due to the seller's manufacturing.

The Magnuson-Moss Warranty Federal Trade Commission Improvement Act was passed in 1975 and applies to consumer goods sold to consumers. The act requires specified disclosures in any written warranty given for consumer goods that cost more than $15. The act does not require that a written warranty be issued, and it provides remedies for consumers who have been harmed.

Warranties for services result only if there is a sale of goods involved. There are no sales warranties for contracts involving services.

WARRANTY DEED   See DEED.

WASH SALE
A simultaneous transaction and a countervailing transaction that have the effect of eliminating the impact of the transactions. In tax law, a wash sale refers to the sale of a security when substantially identical stock is bought within 30 days before or after the sale. No deduction for losses is allowed on the sale of the stock or securities if, within a period beginning 30 days before the date of the sale and ending 30 days after the date of sale, substantially identical stock or securities are acquired. Stocks are substantially the same if their earning power, interest rate, value of assets, preferences, and other features are identical or nearly identical. The disallowed lost is added to the basis of the acquired stock.

In options trading, an illegal process in which simultaneous purchases and sales are made in the same commodity futures contract, on the same exchange, in the same month. No actual position is taken although the appearance indicates otherwise.

WASTING ASSETS
Exhausting assets; assets such as minerals, oil and gas, timber, and other natural resource deposits which are reduced as they are worked, or depleted. The Internal Revenue Code governs the allowance of annual deductions against income, thus enabling the recovery of the cost or other basis of the asset plus subsequent capital additions, as reasonable allowance for depletion and for depreciation of improvements.

The percentage depletion rates allowed in the code vary according to the type of natural resource involved, except timber. Depletion deduction is the specified allowable percentage of the gross income from the property, but may not exceed 50% of the taxable income from the property, computed without allowance for the depletion.

To compute percentage depletion, a percentage specified in the code is applied to the gross income from the property. Following are examples of 1989 depletion rates:

Natural resource	Percentage rate
Gravel, sand, and other items	5%
Shale and clay used for sewer pipes; or brick and clay, shale, and slate used for lightweight aggregates	7.5%
Asbestos, coal, sodium, chloride, and others	10%
Gold, silver, oil shale, copper, and iron ore from U.S. deposits	15%
Sulfur, uranium, and a series of minerals from U.S. deposits	22%
Metals, other than those subject to 22% or 15% rate	14%

As depletion reserves are thus accumulated, dividends therefrom may be paid; such dividends are not taxable, being a return of capital and thus to be deducted from cost of the stock held to determine new adjusted cost basis.

See DEPLETION.

WATER BONDS
A subclassification of municipal bonds, the purpose of which is to furnish the municipality with a supply of water. These bonds are of the highest-grade investments, since not only are they issued for an essential purpose, but in many cases the water plant of a municipality earns the interest on the water bonds, thereby making it unnecessary for the city to provide such interest out of taxes.

WATER COMPANY BONDS
The water supply industry is one of the oldest among public utilities, but because of increasing public ownership of water supply systems, there are only a relatively few privately owned water supply companies. These private companies in turn have a comparatively small aggregate of bonded debt outstanding, primarily because of the largely local nature of operations and the absence of extraterritorial connections and expansion as in the case of electric power and natural gas companies.

Water company bonds are characterized by limited floating supply caused both by the relatively small amounts outstanding and by the holding of such bonds by institutional investors for investment, particularly the life insurance companies. Although varying in quality, water company bonds deserve a generally favorable investment regard because of the investment characteristics of the industry itself. These include the following characteristics:

1. Essential nature of the service provided;
2. Stability of revenues, there being little industrial load in sales to industrial users, and sales being largely residential;
3. Assurance of growth arising from growth in population of the territory served;
4. Low operating ratio of expenses to revenues, despite a tendency in recent years toward higher costs;
5. Reduction in fixed charges in former years of low money rates by refunding into lower coupon bonds (although the ratio of plant and property, and therefore funded debt, to gross revenues is comparatively high, necessitated by the requirement of large capital investment for the business);
6. Relative freedom from pressure for rate reductions or burdensome state regulation;
7. Satisfactory franchises.

See PUBLIC UTILITY INDUSTRY.

WATERED CAPITAL   See WATERED STOCK.

WATERED STOCK
Stock the par value of which is in excess of the value of the net tangible assets which it represents. Watered stock is created in several ways: (1) by issuing stock for money or other property worth less than its par value; (2) by giving stock away to the promoters or organizers for their services, or to stockholders as a bonus; (3) by an impairment of assets through an operating deficit, and (4) by issuing stock against a fictitious or intangible asset.

The amount of watered stock in a corporation may be determined by the excess of the par value of its stock over its tangible assets. Inasmuch as the assets must be at least equivalent to the stock, the "water" is hidden under the name of some fictitious or intangible assets, e.g., goodwill, patents, trademarks, and the like, or an overvaluation of the tangible assets.

Many companies that were originally organized with watered stock have since squeezed the water out by retaining some of the earnings and reinvesting them in the business. In the cases of some enterprises which have been extraordinarily profitable, i.e., earning a large percent of return upon the capital invested, stock may have been watered for the purpose of concealing large profits. This may have been accomplished by increasing stock against some intangible asset, usually patents or goodwill. In such a case, although the stock is watered, the company cannot be said to be overcapitalized, since OVERCAPITALIZATION presupposes that the corporation cannot earn even a moderate return upon the capital outstanding.

WATER POWER ACT
The Federal Water Power Act of June 10, 1920 (16 U.S.C. 791-823) provided for the licensing by the Federal Power Commission of hydroelectric projects on U.S. government lands or on navigable waters of the U.S. It was amended in 1921 (41 Stat. 1353) to exclude water power projects in national parks or national monuments. By Title II of the Public Utility Act of 1935 (16 U.S.C. 791a-825r), the original Federal Water Power Act with certain amendments was made Part I of the Federal Power Act, and Parts II and III were added, vesting the commission with jurisdiction over the transmission and sale at wholesale of electric energy in interstate commerce and public utility companies engaged therein.

WATER POWER COMPANY BONDS Bonds of hydroelectric power companies, being a subclassification of public utility bonds. Large initial investment is required for the building of hydroelectric power plants and standby steam plants for use in periods of low water flow. When the hydroelectric plants are in operation, operating earnings are relatively high as compared with those from operation of steam generating plants, because of the basic advantage in elimination of fuel costs. When rainfall and water flow are low, however, and companies must resort to operation of the steam plants, the operating ratio of such a water power company rises and operating earnings are lowered. This fluctuating nature of earnings of a water power company results in variable margins of earnings over fixed charges of water power company bonds.

See PUBLIC UTILITY BONDS, PUBLIC UTILITY INDUSTRY.

WAYS AND MEANS COMMITTEE The U.S. House of Representative's Committee on Ways and Means drafts tax legislation, oversees customs, reciprocal trade agreements, bonded debt of the United States, deposits of public money, tax-exempt foundations and charitable trusts, the Social Security system, public assistance, and unemployment programs. Subcommittees include the following: trade, oversight, select revenue measures, health, Social Security, and human resources.

WEAK Denotes stock or commodity prices having a declining tendency. A weak security, commodity, or market is one in which prices are lower than for the previous day or in trend over a period of time.

WEALTH Things of value owned; the sum total of current economic goods. Some economists measure wealth by totaling the assets of the individuals and firms of the economy. Others would add to this total the property and assets of the government. Others would include resources not extracted or still in their original state. To include stocks, bonds, and mortgages in the total of wealth would be to count these intangible assets twice. Wealth is a stock concept; it is the total value of economic goods at any point in time. On the other hand, income is a flow concept; it is the total value of goods and services produced over a period of time, usually a year.

According to *Forbes* magazine, in 1989 six of the ten richest individuals in the world were Japanese. The United States led the world in the total number of billionaires with 55. Yoshiaki Tsusumi, the head of Japan's Seibu Railway Group, was at the top of the list of private billionaires, with a personal net worth of at least $15 billion, a decrease from $18.9 billion in the previous year because of the dollar's rise against other major currencies. Japan had 41 members on the list. The highest ranking American on the list was Sam Walton, founder of Wal-Mart Stores. It was estimated that he was worth approximately $8.7 billion, up from $6.5 billion.

The concept of NATIONAL WEALTH is essentially different from that of private wealth. National wealth is the aggregate of the wealth of individuals plus social wealth, i.e., the property of the federal government and its political subdivisions which include federal, state, and city public works, buildings, parks, museums, and the like. In computation of national wealth, care is taken to avoid double counting. For example, a railroad property is wealth, but it is represented also by stocks and bonds owned by individuals, which they in turn consider as part of their wealth; both the value of the railroad property and the value of its stocks and bonds must not be included in an estimate of national wealth.

WEALTH TRANSFER TAXES Estate and gift taxes that transfer the tax on the dispositions of property that occur as a result of the transferor's death or on lifetime transfers.

WEBB-POMERENE ACT An act passed on April 10, 1918, also known as the Export Trade Act or Webb Act. This act exempted from the prohibitions imposed by the Sherman Anti-Trust Act and the Clayton Act on monopolies and combinations in restraint of trade such export trade associations as might be formed by exporters for purposes of foreign trade, wherein they came into competition with foreign cartels and monopolies operating free from any restrictions upon quotas, prices, and selling policies.

Section 4 of the act, however, specifically provided that such export trade associations would not be exempt from the prohibition imposed by the Federal Trade Commission Act (approved September 26, 1914) against unfair methods of competition used against competing American exporters, even though such unfair methods were used outside the territorial jurisdiction of the United States. The FEDERAL TRADE COMMISSION was vested with the powers of supervision over such foreign trade associations, including registration, filing of reports, and power to make findings and recommendations to the Attorney General of the United States where it finds upon investigation that any acts of foreign trade associations are in restraint of trade within the United States or in restraint of the export trade of any domestic competitors of such foreign trade associations.

WELCHER One who fails to live up to an agreement which, though not enforceable at law, is a moral obligation, e.g., one who refuses to accept or deliver an order of goods, or cancels an order when the market goes against him.

WHEAT The U.S. wheat sector faced excess supplies in the 1980s and slow growth in exports. However, production remained large. Yields rose and wheat could be grown at low cost both in the Great Plains and Southeast, where it is double-cropped with soybeans. None of the many farm policies used in previous years have prevented periodic wheat surpluses or reduced them without great expense. Issues for farm legislation include the level and flexibility of income and price supports, ways of increasing exports, and the purposes and size of wheat reserves.

Wheat is the third leading field crop produced in the United States in terms of value of production. Only corn and soybeans are more important. There are five major classes of wheat grown in the United States: hard red winter, soft red winter, hard red spring, white, and durum. These classes are grown in distinct regions, have different end uses, and are marketed separately. The U.S. exports all five classes of wheat. The most important bread wheat is exported principally to the USSR, Brazil, China, and Japan. China is the largest customer for soft red winter wheat used for cakes, pastries, and crackers. White wheat is imported mostly by Asian countries, where it is used for noodle products. The largest importers of durum are Tunisia and Algeria.

Wheat has two distinct growing seasons. Winter wheat, sown in the fall, normally accounts for 70% to 80% of total production. Spring-sown wheat accounts for the remainder.

The increase in wheat production through the mid-1970s came mostly from larger yields per acre. In recent years, the growth in wheat production has come from significant gains in both area and yield. Factors affecting yield include weather, management practices, variety, total acreage level, and regional distribution of acreage.

Domestic uses of wheat include food, feed, seed, and industrial uses. Over time, consumer preferences have changed. The demand for wheat for food uses is relatively unaffected by changes in wheat prices and economic conditions.

Argentina is the main competitor for hard winter wheat. The Canadians sell mostly hard spring wheat, while the European community sells soft wheat. Australia exports white wheat. Over the past two decades, the United States, Canada, and Australia have supplied about three-fourths of world wheat exports.

The major objective of international commodity agreements is to stabilize world prices by getting importing and exporting countries to agree to trade within a mutually determined price band. The most successful international wheat agreement lasted from 1962 to 1967 when the United States and Canada began to export burdensome stocks.

Federal wheat policies trace back to World War I, when the U.S. government imposed export quotas and fixed wheat prices to prevent runaway inflation. During the 1920s, overproduction brought calls to raise wheat farm income through a two-price system. Bills were introduced in Congress to boost domestic wheat prices to "parity," a relationship between costs and prices that was defined to exist from 1910 to 1914. A federal farm program designed to stabilize prices and control surpluses was implemented by the Agricultural Marketing Act of 1929. A federally funded corporation was set up to make loans to marketing cooperatives that would purchase surplus wheat from farmers.

The Agricultural Adjustment Act of 1933 was enacted to raise farm incomes and control production. Producers were assigned an allotment based on an average of past acreage. They were given the opportunity to reduce area by a certain percentage of this allotment base and in return receive a cash payment on their domestic allotment, that part of their allotment that would be used for domestic food. Together with the Dust Bowl, the programs turned wheat surplus into scarcity by 1936. In January 1936, the Supreme Court ruled against processing taxes that had been imposed to finance production controls. The Agricultural Adjustment Act of 1938 introduced features contained in more recent legislation: nonrecourse loans, storage payments, parity payments, allotments, marketing quotas, export subsidies, and conservation incentives. Loan rates were to be set between 52% and 75% of parity. To receive parity payments, farmers had to abide by acreage allotments. If supplies exceeded 135% of total use, compulsory marketing quotas were to be announced, and if approved by two-thirds of the farmers, put into effect. If a marketing quota was in effect, all producers were required to comply with the announced program provisions. The first mandatory quotas were approved for the 1941 crop.

The Agricultural Acts of 1948 and 1949 revised the parity formula to reflect the relative levels of demand. The 1949 legislation pegged support rates at 90% of parity for 1950. The soil bank was established by the Agricultural Act of 1956 to withdraw farmland from production as a measure to help reduce the growing surpluses. Wheat surpluses built to immense levels by the early 1960. A voluntary paid diversion was implemented in 1962 and 1963.

During the mid-1970s, wheat generally enjoyed strong exports, and prices aided the move toward more market-oriented farm programs. The 1973 act made significant revisions in income programs and initiated the disaster payments programs. Set-aside programs in 1978 and 1979 reduced wheat acreage to some extent and raised prices. The act continued the wheat target price/deficiency payment program, farmer-owned reserve program, and set-aside program authority.

The impact of the 1980s programs was mixed. Deficiency, diversion, and in-kind payments did support income but added to high government costs. In recent years, direct payments made under the wheat program have been a significant portion of growers' income.

See CHICAGO BOARD OF TRADE, COMMODITY EXCHANGES, CROP REPORTS, FUTURES, HEDGING, INTERNATIONAL GRAINS ARRANGEMENT, PRICE SUPPORT.

BIBLIOGRAPHY

CHICAGO BOARD OF TRADE. *Chicago Board of Trade Statistical Annual.*

WHEAT PIT See PIT.

WHEN, AS, AND IF ISSUED See WHEN ISSUED.

WHEN ISSUED The method of trading in listed or unlisted securities whose issue has not been finally approved, or for which certificates or forms have not been issued or are not ready for delivery, and therefore in which execution of contracts is contingent upon such issue. Bids and offers in securities admitted to dealings on the New York Stock Exchange on a when issued or when distributed basis shall be made only on that basis, for delivery when issued or when distributed as determined by the exchange. However, written contracts in forms approved by the exchange must be exchanged not later than the business day following the transaction, and signatures to such contracts shall be affixed by a partner of the contracting firm.

Rule X-12D3 of the Securities and Exchange Commission, issued under the Securities Exchange Act of 1934, defines the requirements under which unissued warrants and unissued securities other than warrants may be registered for when issued trading on a national securities exchange. The requirement of the Securities Act of 1933 that a registration statement be in effect, if required, is incorporated in this regulation. Formal and official announcement by the issuer of plan or reorganization, exchange, subscription rights, etc., is also a requirement for registration for when issued trading on a national securities exchange. Included among types of when issued trading are exchanges or distributions resulting from the breakup of public utility holding companies under Section 11 of the Public Utility Act of 1935, securities issued under reorganizations pursuant to Chapter X of the National Bankruptcy Act, and railroad securities issued pursuant to Chapter VIII of the Bankruptcy Act (the former Sec. 77).

WHIPSAWED Denotes the suffering of a double loss as the result of buying at the top of a movement and then, when prices have reached the bottom, not only selling long stocks but also selling short stocks, which, because of a subsequent upward turn in the market, are covered at a loss. As stated by one writer, being whipsawed consists of "buying in the hope of a rise, but selling instead on a fall, then selling more, expecting a further fall, but being compelled to buy because the market goes up instead of down," i.e., "getting caught, coming and going."

WHITE ELEPHANT Any property that cannot be operated at a profit because the cost of operation would exceed the gross revenue; any business into which considerable capital has been invested that, because of changes in fashion or popular taste, obsolescence, or some other reason, cannot be profitably operated and could be sold only at a terrific loss, e.g., a large hotel located at a once fashionable summer resort no longer popular. The term is derived from the concept of the white elephant eating more than its services are worth.

WHOLESALE BANKING A banking function providing bank services, loan security, and loans to large corporate customers or nonprofit institutions. Managing wholesale banking involves human resource management, market management, and product management. Banks typically organize their wholesale banking function on the basis of geographic location, industry groupings, sales, asset size of the customer, or product line. Human resource management refers to such activities as recruiting, training, information and measurement systems, compensation, retention, and career path development. Market management involves techniques and procedures associated with market dynamics and relationships. Product management deals with developing, maintaining, and enhancing products offered by the bank.

BIBLIOGRAPHY

The Future of Wholesale Banking. BOSTON CONSULTING GROUP, Boston, MA, 1986.

WIDE OPENING The condition when opening prices for the same stock in an active market are wide apart.

WIDE PRICES The condition when bid and asked prices are not fractionally or at least normally close. Ordinarily the bid and asked prices for an active security are from one-eighth to three-fourths of a point apart; when they are several points apart, e.g., bid 10, asked 13 $^1/_2$, they are said to be wide.

WIDOW'S EXEMPTION For the benefit of a widow of a deceased debtor, a continuance of the immunity or privilege allowed by law to a debtor during his lifetime to hold a certain amount of property free from levy or seizure in payment of his debts. Legally, a widow's exemption is a continuation for the benefit of the wife of a deceased debtor of the immunity, privilege, and freedom from any charge or burden allowed by law to a debtor during his lifetime to hold property up to a certain amount, or certain classes of property free from all liability to levy and sale, on execution, attachment, or other legal process issued for the satisfaction of a money judgment.

WILD CAT BANKS Banks organized under the laws of the various states in the chaotic, uncontrolled, and unsound banking period between the years 1811 and 1863. These banks were permitted to issue bank notes against personal notes or bonds and mortgages of resident land owners, and in many cases were organized solely for the purpose of issuing paper money rather than carrying on a deposit and loan business. In Michigan, many of these institutions were said to be located "in the depths of forests where there were few human habitations, but plenty of wild cats." They were purposely made inaccessible to prevent redemption of their practically worthless notes. Bank failures were numerous, and since the security behind these notes was inadequate and illiquid, holders suffered large losses. There were approximately 1,600 different kinds of bank notes in circulation when the 10% federal tax, in 1866, put an end to the note issues of state banks.

WILD CAT COMPANY An unsound or highly speculative business venture in which the chance of success is slight; particularly a company organized to develop oil wells on leased lands before it is known positively that oil exists.

WILD CAT CURRENCY Notes issued by the WILD CAT BANKS before the period of sound banking in the United States; any depreciated or worthless money.

ENCYCLOPEDIA OF BANKING AND FINANCE

WILD CAT SECURITIES Highly speculative, fraudulent, or worthless securities; securities of companies organized to exploit an unsound, fanciful, or hazardous venture, but upon which the promoters promise large profits; securities of companies that represent nothing but "capitalized hopes."

See WILD CAT COMPANY.

WILL A formal written testament or final disposition of property to take effect after death, made by a person of sound and disposing mind, known as a testator. All persons are competent to make a will except idiots, infants, and persons of unsound mind. In some states, testaments of personal property may be made at an earlier age than wills of real property, but most states today make no distinction between wills and testaments as to the age at which each can be made.

Generally, laws of most states require that a will be in writing (although various states allow nuncupative or oral wills under specified conditions), signed by the testator or by some person in his presence and by his direction, and attested by witnesses, who must subscribe their names thereto in the presence of the testator. Most states require two witnesses, except a few which require three. Three witnesses are desirable even where only two are required.

Although the form or wording of a will is immaterial as long as its intent is clear, and only the subscription by the testator and signatures of the witnesses are absolute requisites, it is advisable to obtain competent legal advice when drawing and executing a will. Many things may render a will invalid, such as failure to sign it in the proper place or an insufficient number of witnesses. Erasures, interlineations, or other changes made at a later date than the will itself may not be valid. Unclear language or contradictory provisions may also defeat the testator's intent, particularly in the intricacies of specific legacies, demonstrative legacies, general legacies, and the residuary clause. Codicils may be written to supplement the matter contained in the will, but the same formalities must be observed. The laws governing the execution of wills differ in various states. It is unsafe for a layman to draw a will without consulting a lawyer. Even in cases where the property is small or where the disposition thereof appears not to be a complicated matter, competent legal counsel is essential both to avoid possible litigation (expense of which might be charged to the estate) and to ensure that the precise intentions of the testator are carried out.

In addition to allowing nuncupative or oral wills, most states allow holographic wills, those written entirely in the handwriting of the testator. In New York State, nuncupative wills are permitted only in the case of soldiers on active military duty, sailors at sea, and merchant seamen on the high seas, and must be made in the hearing of two persons and proved by at least two witnesses. New York allows a holographic will when written entirely in the handwriting of the testator even though the same be unattested.

There are a number of advantages to making a will over leaving an intestate estate:

1. The testator (one who makes a will) can designate to whom and in what proportions the property shall be left. He can designate relatives, friends, employees, or charitable institutions as legatees-more to some and less to others. In New York, neither spouse may devise or bequeath more than one-half of the net estate to a charity or for a charitable purpose where a husband, wife, child, descendant, or parent survives. Without a will, the property will be distributed according to the laws of descent in the state in which the testator was a resident. These laws operate rigidly. In New York, where dower and curtesy were abolished August 31, 1930, a personal right of election was given to a surviving spouse to take the same share as in intestacy despite a will made by the deceased spouse.
2. The testator can name his own executor and stipulate that he not be required to give bond. Otherwise, the court will appoint an administrator. An administrator is required to give bond and the premium will be charged to the estate. The heirs will be involved in the intricacies of court procedure, and their inheritance may become the prey of inexperienced or unscrupulous persons. Thus, with a will, the property is likely to be more economically and expeditiously distributed.
3. The testator can set up a testamentary trust. In this way, all or a part of the property may be conserved, with the income distributed to the persons designated in accordance with their needs and the principal distributed at some future date. Without a will, the principal of the estate is divided by law, and every beneficiary, if or when of age, comes into absolute control of his or her estate without regard to personal ability to take care of it. Only by a will can a life income be provided.
4. Real estate can be sold more readily. A testator can empower the executor to sell his real estate. Without a will, in some states the property can be sold only if all the heirs agree, or by means of a lengthy and expensive suit in partition. In New York, the administrator of a decedent dying after August 31, 1930, may sell, mortgage, or lease real property under the same conditions as for executors, requiring petition, hearings, and order by the surrogate.

See CODICIL; DESCENT, LAWS OF; EXECUTOR; LIVING TRUST; TRUST.

For illustrative purposes, the carefully drawn wills of two wealthy men, George F. Baker and Robert W. de Forest, both of which contain supplementary codicils, are reproduced herewith.

Will of George F. Baker

I, GEORGE F. BAKER, of the City of New York, do hereby make, publish and declare this my last will and testament:

ARTICLE FIRST—Section 1. I give and bequest unto my daughter, Evelyn B. St. George, the sum of $5,000,000.

Section 2. I give and bequeath unto my daughter, Florence B. Loew, the sum of $5,000,000.

Section 3. The above legacies to my daughters are in addition to provisions which I have made in my lifetime for them and their children.

ARTICLE SECOND—I give and bequeath unto my son, George F. Baker, Junior, and unto my daughter, Evelyn B. St. George, and unto my daughter, Florence B. Lowe, respectively, such of the furniture, furnishings, pictures, carpets, rugs, silverware, china, glass and other chattels usually contained in the dwelling house upon my country place in Tuxedo, New York, as my said son, George F. Baker, Junior, shall by a writing signed by him and filed with my executor, within six months after my death, determine to be desired by him or his sisters respectively.

ARTICLE THIRD—I give, devise and bequeath unto my granddaughter, Florence J. Loew, and her heirs forever, my country place at Tuxedo, New York, together with all buildings and improvements thereon and all appurtenances and all the furniture, both useful and ornamental, pictures, bric-a-brac, farming and garden tools and equipment, horses, wagons, automobiles, harness and articles of stable and garage equipment, and other chattels which at the time of my death shall be in or upon my said country place or ordinarily used in connection therewith, excepting only such of the articles above enumerated as are in and by the last preceding article of this will otherwise disposed of.

ARTICLE FOURTH—I give and bequeath the following legacies:

(a) To the New York Public Library, Astor, Lenox and Tilden Foundations, a corporation, the sum of $250,000.

(b) To the New York Exchange for Women's Work, a corporation, the sum of $25,000.

(c) To the Tuxedo Memorial Hospital, a corporation, the sum of $25,000.

In the event that I shall hereafter in my lifetime make any gift or gifts to any of the institutions or corporations to which I have bequeathed legacies in and by this fourth article of my will, such gift or gifts to any such institution or corporation shall be deemed to be in payment of, or on account of, the legacy so bequeathed to it in and by this article, and such gift or gifts shall operate to the extent thereof as in ademption or satisfaction of any such legacy.

If, in any case, I have committed myself during my lifetime to make certain gifts to one or more of such institutions or corporations, it is my will that the legacy herein given to any such institution or corporation shall be taken in full satisfaction and discharge of all such commitments.

ARTICLE FIFTH—In memory of my father, George E. Baker, and my mother, Eveline S. Baker, I give and bequeath unto the Protestant Episcopal Cathedral Foundation of the District of Columbia, the sum of $250,000. It is my wish that this legacy shall be devoted to the erection of an addition to the Washington Cathedral which will serve as a memorial to my father and mother.

WILL

ARTICLE SIXTH—I give and bequeath unto Frank Rysavy the sum of $25,000.

ARTICLE SEVENTH—In recognition of faithful service, I give and bequeath the following legacies:
(a) To Helen E. Reddy the sum of $10,000.
(b) To Claire Chaplin the sum of $10,000.
(c) To Michael Birish the sum of $15,000, but if he shall die before me leaving a widow me surviving, such widow shall take the legacy her husband would have taken had he survived me.
(d) To Mary Monahan the sum of $5,000.
(e) To William Ellings and his wife jointly the sum of $10,000, but if either of them shall die before me the survivor shall take the whole of this legacy.
(f) To Adla Backman the sum of $6,000.
(g) To Louise Holdtman the sum of $4,000.
(h) To Cecilia Fitzgerald the sum of $1,000.
(i) To Sophie McEnnis the sum of $2,000.
(j) To Catherine McDonnell the sum of $3,000.
(k) To Frank Healy the sum of $2,000.
(l) To John Rivoire the sum of $2,500.

ARTICLE EIGHTH—All the rest, residue and remainder of my property and estate, real and personal, of whatsoever nature and wheresoever situated and whether acquired before or after the execution of this will, I give, devise and bequeath unto my son, George F. Baker, Jr., and his heirs forever.

ARTICLE NINTH—I direct that all transfer, legacy, or inheritance taxes, or estate duties, or other taxes in the general nature thereof, which may become payable by reason of my death, shall be paid out of the capital of my residuary estate.

ARTICLE TENTH—I hereby appoint my said son, George F. Baker, Jr., to be the executor of this my will. I authorize my said executor in his discretion to sell and convey at public or private sale, for cash or upon credit, or partly for cash and partly upon credit, and upon such terms and conditions as he shall deem proper, any property, real or personal, belonging to my estate and not hereby specifically devised or bequeathed, and to borrow any moneys for any purposes which he may deem necessary or convenient in the administration of my estate and to secure such loans by the pledge or hypothecation of any securities belonging to my estate and no person making any such loan or loans to my executor shall be bound to inquire into the expediency or propriety thereof or to see to the application of the proceeds thereof, and the judgment of my executor as to the necessity or propriety of any such loan shall be final and conclusive upon all persons interested in my estate.

In the event that my said son shall die, or fail to qualify or resign as executor of this my will, I hereby appoint The First National Bank of the City of New York to be the executor thereof, with all the same powers, discretionary or otherwise, as are herein conferred upon my said son as executor.

I direct that no bond or other security shall ever be required of any executor hereby appointed by reason of non-residence in any jurisdiction in which this will may be proved, or for any other cause whatsoever.

LAST—I revoke all former wills by me at any time made.

In witness whereof I have hereunto set my hand and seal this 21st day of May in the year 1930.

GEORGE F. BAKER.

Signed, sealed, published and declared by George F. Baker, the testator above named, as and for his last will and testament, in our presence, and we, at his request, in his presence and in the presence of each other, have hereunto subscribed our names as witnesses this 21st day of May, 1930.

LEWIS CASS LEDYARD, 27 East Seventy-second Street, New York City.

JACKSON E. REYNOLDS, 33 Beekman Place, New York City.

SAMUEL A. WELLDON, 28 East Thirty-sixth Street, New York City.

The Codicil

I, GEORGE F. BAKER, of the City of New York, having heretofore and on the 21st day of May, in the year 1930, duly made, published and declared my last will and testament bearing date that day, do now make, publish and declare this codicil thereto:

FIRST—Whereas and by sub-division (k) of the seventh article of my said will I gave and bequeathed to Frank Healy the sum of $2,000, and whereas since the making of my said will the said Frank Healy has left my service; now I do hereby wholly revoke the said legacy to him given in said sub-division (k) of the seventh article of my said will.

LASTLY—Except as modified by this codicil, I do hereby in all things ratify, confirm and republish my said last will and testament.

In witness whereof I have hereunto set my hand and seal this 14th day of April, in the year 1931.

GEORGE F. BAKER.

Signed, sealed, published and declared by George F. Baker, the testator above named, as and for a codicil to his last will and testament, in our presence, and we, at his request, in his presence and in the presence of each other, have hereunto subscribed our names as witnesses on the day and year last above written.

LEWIS CASS LEDYARD, 27 East Seventy-second St., New York City.

JACKSON E. REYNOLDS, 33 Beekman Place, New York City.

WALTER S. GIFFORD, 111 East Seventieth Street, New York City.

Will of Robert W. de Forest

I deem it inappropriate in a will, which only concerns the disposition of property and is necessarily made public, to give any expression of my beliefs or affections. These are inherently private. I therefore confine the provisions of my will to its legal purposes.

FIRST. I give to The Metropolitan Museum of Art and to The Charity Organization Society of the City of New York, that is to each, the sum of fifty thousand dollars ($50,000). In so far as I may have given ten thousand ($10,000) at any one time subsequent to the date of this will to either of these institutions, such gifts shall be deemed advancements on account of the above legacies.

SECOND. I give to my children surviving me the sum of five thousand dollars ($5,000) for each of my grandchildren me surviving, making a total sum of five thousand dollars multiplied by the number of my grandchildren so surviving. I rely on my children to apply this gift so that each of my grandchildren shall remember me, but this reliance shall not affect the absolute quality of my gift to my children.

THIRD. If my wife survive me, I give:—
(1) to each of my children me surviving the sum of two hundred and fifty thousand dollars ($250,000).

To whatever extent I may have given to any of my children since January 1, 1923, the sum of not less than twenty thousand dollars ($20,000), either in money or in securities of that market value, such gift shall be an advancement on account of the legacy given to such child.

I devise to my son Johnston, as part of his legacy above mentioned, any or all of the real estate owned by me in Suffolk and Nassau counties, Long Island, at the time of my death, other than Wawapek Farm as hereinafter described, provided he elect within six months after probate of my will to take the same, or any part thereof designated by him, at the assessed valuations thereof as the same appear on the tax bills last paid before my death. He has been associated with me in the purchase of this property, he has been interested in its use and development, and I wish to give him this opportunity if he cares to avail of it.

(2) I give to my wife, Emily Johnston de Forest, all my personal effects other than money or securities.

ENCYCLOPEDIA OF BANKING AND FINANCE

I also give to her the sum of two hundred and fifty thousand dollars ($250,000).

There are friends whom I wish to remember. There are those who have been in my employ for many years whom I also wish to remember. There are public purposes to which I have given in my lifetime to which I may wish to give more. I expect to indicate to my wife in some form my desires in these and possible other particulars, and I rely on her to carry out any expressed intentions of mine, but this gift to her is not qualified in any respect by this reliance upon her, and is absolute.

(3) All the rest, residue and remainder of my estate, real and personal, wheresoever and whatsoever, I give to my executors named in my will, in trust, to hold the same and any reinvestments thereof during the life of my said wife, to apply the income thereof during the life of my said wife to her use semiannually, or oftener if practicable, and upon her death to divide the same equally among her and my children then surviving and the lawful issue of any children who have died before her, such issue to take its parent's share. Except, however, that as respect any part of my estate given to any grandchild who may not be of lawful age, it shall be held in trust for such grandchild as provided by (a) of the Fourth Article of my will.

FOURTH. If my wife die before me I give:

1. To my children me surviving all my personal effects other than money and securities (except those hereinafter specifically bequeathed), to be divided equally between them.
2. All the rest, residue and remainder of my estate, real and personal, wheresoever and whatsoever (except that hereinafter specifically given otherwise), I give, in equal shares, to my children me surviving, and the issue of any who may have predeceased me, such issue to take their parents' share and to divide it equally between them.
    (a) Except that as respects any part of my said gift given to any grandchild who may not be of a lawful age, part of my said gift to any grandchild who may not be of lawful age I direct that it be held in trust for such grandchild until he or she attains lawful age; that so much of the income thereof as may in the opinion of my executors and trustees be necessary for the education and maintenance of such grandchild be applied for it semiannually, or oftener if practicable, and that when such grandchild attains majority the principal thereof be paid over to it. Should any grandchild die before attaining majority such principal shall be paid over in equal parts to its brothers or sisters, as the case may be, or if there be no brothers and sisters, then to my next of kin in the proportions provided by law; and
    (b) Except also that I give to my eldest son me surviving any country-place known as Wawapek Farm, at Cold Spring Harbor, Long Island, intending by this description to include all the land owned by me within the election district of Cold Spring Harbor, together with all the furniture, equipment and other personal property there situated at the time of my death, and used or intended to be used in connection therewith, it being my expectation and desire that such son will maintain this family country home, with which all my children have many associations in common, so far as practicable as a permanent family home, in which my other children can share so far as my said eldest son deems expedient, but the expression of this expectation and desire is not intended to limit in any sense the absolute quality of this gift, or to impose any moral obligation on my said son; and
    (c) Except also that I devise to my son, Johnston, as part of his share in my estate, any or all of the real estate owned by me in Suffolk and Nassau counties, Long Island, at the time of my death, other than Wawapek Farm as above described, provided he elect within six months after probate of my will to take the same, or any part thereof to be designated by him, at the assessed valuation thereof as the same appear on the tax bills last paid before my death. He has been associated with me in the purchase of this property, he has been interested in its use and development, and I wish to give him this opportunity if he cares to avail of it.
    (d) As I have said in that part of my will which will be effective if my wife survives me, I wish to remember some friends, some who have been in my employment and possibly some public purposes in which I am interested, and I expect to indicate in some form my desires in these and possibly other particulars. I rely on my children to carry out any of my expressed intentions, but my gift to my children is not qualified in any respect by this reliance upon them and is absolute.

FIFTH. I appoint my wife, Emily J. de Forest, my brother, Henry L. de Forest, and my two sons, Johnston and Henry W. de Forest, executrix and executors of and trustees under this my will.

I authorize and empower my said executors and trustees to compromise and settle any claims against my estate in their discretion; to sell, convey and transfer any real or personal property of which I may die possessed, or to which I may die entitled, at such time and in such manner, and upon such terms, as in their discretion shall seem most advantageous to my estate; to hold as part of the trust funds to be held by them under this will any property or securities of which I die possessed; to reinvest, in their discretion, the proceeds of any property held in trust by them as part of said trust funds and sold by them, in any other property or securities selected by them for this purpose, and to execute and deliver any instruments of conveyance and transfer, and do all other acts, and take all other proceedings in relation to such sale, conveyance, transfer and reinvestment, as may, in their judgment, be requisite and proper.

I further authorize and empower my said executors and trustees to lease any real estate of which I may die possessed, or in which any of my estate given in trust may be invested pursuant to the powers of this will, for terms not exceeding twenty-one years, with renewals, and with such covenants for improvements as they may deem expedient, and also to improve any such real estate out of the proceeds of my personal estate.

I further authorize and empower my said executors and trustees to value, for the purpose of constituting the said trust funds, and also for the purpose of division, any of the property of which I may die possessed, their valuations to be final and conclusive, and to distribute any property to such trust funds, and to all persons entitled to share in my estate at such valuations, with like effect in all respects as if it were sold at such valuations and the proceeds thereof distributed in money.

I further authorize and empower such of my executors and trustees as may qualify, to appoint, under their hand and seal, with the consent of the beneficiary of any trust, if of age and without such consent if the beneficiary be not of age, a successor trustee or trustees in the place of any who may not qualify, or who, having qualified, may die or resign, or otherwise be incapacitated from performing the duties of trustee. This power to be exercised by successor trustees with like effect as if they had been originally appointed.

I direct that my executors and trustees, and my successors so appointed, be not required to give bonds.

LASTLY. I revoke all other wills and codicils to wills, by me at any time heretofore made.

IN WITNESS WHEREOF, I, ROBERT W. DE FOREST, have hereunto set my hand and seal at New York City this 5th day of February, in the year one thousand nine hundred and twenty-six.

ROBERT W. DE FOREST

Signed, Sealed, Published and Declared by ROBERT W. DE FOREST, the Testator, as and for his Last Will and Testament, in the sight and presence of us, who in his and each other's sight and presence, and at his request, have hereunto subscribed our names as witness thereto, this 5th day of February, A.D., 1926.

ROBERT D. ELDER, Short Hills, N.J.

WILLIAM McBRIEN, 10419-116th St., Richmond Hill, N.Y.

OLIVE M. CLEARWATER, 36 Raymond Ave., Rutherford, N.J.

A CODICIL to the Will of ROBERT W. de FOREST dated February 5, 1926.

FIRST. By the third article of my will, effective if my wife survive me, and by clause (3) of said article, I give a life estate in the rest, residue and remainder of my estate to my wife and provide that

WILL

upon her death this property is to be divided equally among her and my children then surviving, and the lawful issue of any children who have died before her, such issue to take its parent's share. I except from my property so to be divided equally among her and my children upon her death, my country place known as Wawapek Farm, at Cold Spring Harbor, Long Island, intending by this description to include all the land owned by me within the election district of Cold Spring Harbor, together with all the furniture, equipment and other personal property there situated at the time of her death, and used or intended to be used in connection therewith, and I give and devise the same to my eldest son then surviving. It is only all the rest, residue and remainder of my property with the above exception which is to be divided equally among my children then surviving and the lawful issue of any children who may have died before her, such issue to take its parent's share.

SECOND. I give the following legacies:

(1) To the American Federation of Arts the sum of ten thousand dollars ($10,000).

(2) To my wife my share of the Jekyl Island Club and the Jekyl Island Annex Association, together with all my property on Jekyl Island, real and personal. Also eighteen shares of the stock of the Adirondack Mountain Reserve and all my rights as lessee or otherwise in the camp and camp sites on the easterly side of the Upper Ausable Lake appurtenant to such stock.

(3) To my son, Henry L. de Forest, nine shares of the said stock and the camp site appurtenant thereto known as the Trumbull Camp.

(4) To my son, Johnston de Forest, my share in the Cascapedia Club, and all my fishing equipment.

(5) To my faithful and trusted secretary, William McBrien, the sum of thirty thousand dollars ($30,000).

(6) To Elizabeth E. Castello, an annuity of six thousand dollars ($6,000) a year, payable quarterly from the date of my death. This may be paid out of the income from securities to be set aside by my executors for this purpose, or by the purchase of an annuity for her in the Metropolitan Life Insurance Company, or any other company preferred by her.

(7) I revoke the appointment of my brother, Henry W. de Forest, as one of my executors and trustees under the fifth clause of my will. I do not wish to impose on him this burden, and I know that my wife and my two sons can always count on his advice and aid without having this burden upon him in addition to the many others he is carrying.

LASTLY. I revoke all other wills and codicils to wills by me at any time heretofore made, except my will dated February 5, 1926, and this codicil thereto.

IN WITNESS WHEREOF I have hereunto set my hand and seal this 16th day of July, 1928.

ROBERT W. DE FOREST

Signed, Sealed, Published and Declared by the Testator above named and for a Codicil to his Will dated February 5, 1926, in our presence, who at his request and in his and each other's presence have signed as witnesses thereto, this 16th day of July, 1928.

ROBERT THORNE, 863 Park Avenue, New York.

MARY MITCHISON, 44 Butler Place, Brooklyn, New York.

A second CODICIL to the Will of ROBERT W. DE FOREST.

This will is dated February 5, 1926, and the first codicil is dated July 16, 1928.

I give to my executors, in trust, the sum of fifty thousand dollars ($50,000), to apply the same, principal and interest and any accumulations of interest, to the maintenance and improvement of the Adirondack Mountain Reserve, of which I am now president. My purpose is to preserve the forests, lakes and mountains of the Upper Ausable Valley in their wild and natural condition, under the policy set forth in the present by-laws of the reserve or as these by-laws may be hereafter amended.

To effectuate this purpose I give my said trustees absolute power and discretion in the application of this gift. I do not wish it used for current expenses. I expect these will be met by our members, but I wish to safeguard the reserve against unusual outlay.

If in the opinion of my trustees my purposes cannot be wisely accomplished by this gift, I authorize them to terminate the trust as to any amount then in their hands, either in whole or in part, and distribute the same as part of my residuary estate.

Should any trustee die or become incapacitated, the surviving trustees or trustee may appoint, under hand and seal, a successor, who shall be vested with the same powers as if originally appointed by me.

This trust shall continue, unless sooner terminated, during the lives of my two sons.

My trustees are authorized to use my gift in any way which will, in their opinion, best accomplish my purpose. I suggest that my gift be constituted by fifty thousand dollars of certificates of the Provident Loan Society of New York, of that par value, if at the time of my death I own that amount.

IN WITNESS WHEREOF, I, ROBERT W. DE FOREST, have hereunto set my hand and seal at New York City, New York, this 9th day of October, in the year one thousand nine hundred and twenty-eight.

ROBERT W. DE FOREST.

Signed, Sealed, Published and Declared by ROBERT W. DE FOREST, the Testator, as and for a Second Codicil to his Last Will and Testament dated February 5, 1926, in the sight and presence of us, who in his and each other's sight and presence, and at his request, have hereunto subscribed our names as witnesses thereto, this 9th day of October, A.D., 1928.

ROBERT THORNE, 863 Park Avenue, New York.

MARY MITCHISON, 44 Butler Place, Brooklyn, New York.

A Third CODICIL to the WILL of ROBERT W. DE FOREST dated February 5, 1926 and to the two codicils thereto dated respectively July 16 and October 9, 1928.

FIRST. I give the following legacies:

(1) To the Metropolitan Museum of Art, one hundred thousand dollars ($100,000), in lieu of the fifty thousand dollars ($50,000) given to that institution by my will. It is my wish that this be held as a principal sum the income of which shall be applied every year to provide free concerts in the Museum. But the expression of this wish shall create no legal obligation.

(2) To the Charity Organization Society of the City of New York, the sum of one hundred thousand dollars ($100,000), in lieu of the fifty thousand dollars ($50,000) given to that Society by my will. The fifty thousand dollars I have recently given to the said Society shall be deemed an advancement on account of this legacy of one hundred thousand dollars.

(3) In so far as I may hereafter give to either of the said institutions at any one time twenty-five thousand dollars ($25,000) or more, such gifts shall be deemed advancements on account of these legacies.

(4) To Elizabeth E. Castello, twenty thousand dollars ($20,000), in addition to the annuity given by the codicil to my will dated July 16, 1928.

(5) To Helen Moore, ten thousand dollars ($10,000).

(6) To Mrs. Henry Parkman, twenty thousand dollars ($20,000).

(7) To Margaret N. Hogan, if she shall be in my employ at the time of my death, five thousand dollars ($5,000).

(8) To William McBrien, twenty thousand dollars ($20,000), in addition to the thirty thousand dollars given to him by the codicil to my will dated July 16, 1928.

SECOND. I direct that all estate or inheritance taxes upon the legacies given by this codicil, and my will, and any codicil thereto shall be paid out of my residuary estate, so that my legatees may receive the net amount of their legacies.

THIRD. Any legacies may be paid by my securities, at valuations fixed by my executors, not below market values.

LASTLY. I revoke all other wills and codicils to wills by me at any time made except my will dated February 5, 1926, and the two codicils thereto above mentioned, all of which I confirm.

IN WITNESS WHEREOF I have hereunto set my hand and seal this 26th day of July, 1929.

ROBERT W. DE FOREST

Signed, Sealed, Published and Declared by the testator above named as and for a Codicil to his Will dated February 5, 1926, in our presence, who at his request and in his and each other's presence have signed as witnesses thereto, this 26th day of July, 1929.

ERNEST C. MANSFIELD, 330 West 85th Street, New York City.

MRS. ELIZABETH GILWAY, 7 Washington Square, New York City.

I, ROBERT W. DE FOREST, residing at 7 Washington Square, New York City, New York, do hereby make, publish and declare the following as and for a fourth CODICIL to my Last Will and Testament dated February 5, 1926, and the three codicils thereto dated respectively July 16, 1928, October 9, 1928, and July 26, 1929.

FIRST. By the third article of my will, effective if my wife survives me, I give my residuary estate in trust to my executors, to hold and apply the income thereof to my wife and upon her death to divide it equally between her and my children her surviving.

I wish to except from this equal division my country place, known as "Wawapek Farm," at Cold Spring Harbor, Long Island, as described by section (b) of the fourth article of my will, and to give this property as so described to my eldest child her surviving. This as distinguished from dividing it. And I hereby modify my will in this particular.

SECOND. In addition to the powers given my executors by my said last will and testament and the said codicils thereto, and for the purpose of paying any debts of my estate, any taxes thereon or on the transfer thereof and any expenses of administering my estate, I hereby authorize and empower my said executors to borrow such sums of money as they may deem necessary and to pledge or mortgage as collateral security for the repayment thereof any property, real or personal, of which I may die seized or possessed.

THIRD. I increase to the sum of one hundred thousand dollars ($100,000), instead of fifty thousand dollars, the legacy given to my executors by the second codicil to my will for the maintenance and improvement of the Adirondack Mountain Reserve, with like effect in all respects as if I had named the sum of one hundred thousand dollars in that codicil.

FOURTH. I increase the annuity of six thousand dollars ($6,000), given by the Codicil to my will dated July 16, 1928 to Elizabeth E. Castello, to the amount of ten thousand dollars ($10,000), and like effect in all respects as if I had named said sum ten thousand dollars instead of six thousand dollars in that codicil.

FIFTH. I revoke any codicil to my will heretofore executed except those above named, and confirm my said will and the said three codicils thereto.

IN WITNESS WHEREOF, I have hereunto set my hand and seal this 22d day of May, 1930.

ROBERT W. DE FOREST.

Signed, Sealed, Published and Declared by Robert W. de Forest, the testator, as and for a Fourth Codicil to his Last Will and Testament dated February 5, 1926, in the sight and presence of us, who in his and each other's sight and presence and at his request, have hereunto subscribed our names as witnesses thereto this 22d day of May, 1930.

MARGARET N. HOGAN, 115 Henry Street, Brooklyn, N.Y.

MRS. ELIZABETH GILWAY, 7 Washington Square, New York City.

I, ROBERT W. DE FOREST, residing at 7 Washington Square, New York City, New York, do hereby make, publish and declare the following as and for a Fifth CODICIL to my Last Will and Testament dated February 5, 1926, and the four codicils thereto dated respectively July 16, 1928, October 9, 1928, July 26, 1929, and May, 1930.

I give the following legacies:

(1) To Elizabeth E. Castello thirty thousand dollars ($30,000) in addition to the annuity given by the codicil to my will dated July 16, 1928, making my gift to her in all fifty thousand dollars.

(2) To Margaret N. Hogan, if she be in my employ at the time of my death, five thousand dollars ($5,000) in addition to the five thousand dollars given to her by the third codicil to my will, making my gift to her in all ten thousand dollars.

(3) I revoke any codicils to my will heretofore executed except those named, and confirm my said will and the said four codicils thereto.

In witness whereof, I have hereunto set my hand and seal this 3rd day of November, 1930.

ROBERT W. DE FOREST.

Signed, sealed, published and declared by Robert W. de Forest, the testator, as and for a Fifth Codicil to his Last Will and Testament, dated February 5, 1926, in the sight and presence of us, who in his and each other's sight and presence and at his request, have hereunto subscribed our names as witnesses thereto this 3rd day of November, 1930.

WILLIAM MCBRIEN, 10419-116th Street, Richmond Hill, New York.

ELIZABETH GALLAGHER, 7 Washington Square, New York City.
See ESTATE TAXES.

BIBLIOGRAPHY

AMERICAN LAW INSTITUTE-AMERICAN BAR ASSOCIATION. *Resource Materials: Estate Planning in Depth.*
COMMERCE CLEARING HOUSE. *Estate Planning Guide.*
Drafting Wills and Trust Agreements: A Systems Approach. WARREN, GORHAM AND LAMONT, INC., Boston, MA. Looseleaf.
Estate Planning: Wills, Estates and Trusts. PRENTICE HALL, INC. Englewood Cliffs, NJ. Looseleaf.
INSTITUTE FOR BUSINESS PLANNING, INC. *Complete Book of Wills and Trusts.*
Murphy's Will Clauses: Annotations and Forms with Tax Effects. MATTHEW BENDER & CO., INC., New York, NY. Looseleaf.
NEW YORK STATE BAR ASSOCIATION. *Basic Will Drafting for Small Estates.*
———. *Estate Planning and Will Drafting for Estates Up to $500,000.*
PRACTICING LAW INSTITUTE. *Advanced Will Drafting.*
———. *Practical Will Drafting.*
PRENTICE-HALL, INC. *Complete Guide to Estate Accounting and Taxes.*
STOCKER, J. E. STOCKER ON DRAWING WILLS. Practicing Law Institute, New York, NY, 1987.
Wills-Estate Planning Forms. PRENTICE HALL, INC., Englewood Cliffs, NJ. Looseleaf.

WINDFALL PROFIT TAX A tax imposed on crude oil production. The tax is a temporary excise or severance tax on production, imposed at the wellhead as each barrel of oil is removed from the ground and sold. The tax is imposed on the holder of the economic interest in the oil, referred to as the producer. Primary collection responsibility is placed on the first purchaser of the crude oil.

WINDING UP LIQUIDATION; terminating a business by a voluntary dissolution or BANKRUPTCY, selling the assets, paying the debts, and distributing the balance, if any, to the owners. In modern bankruptcy statutes, the old theory of liquidation for the benefit of creditors has been replaced by the modern concepts of reorganizations and arrangements for the relief of debtors.

WINDOW DRESSING The practice of certain companies of temporarily arranging their affairs in order to make a more favorable showing on the date of their published financial statements than actual conditions warrant. In application to financial institutions, the term refers to temporarily increasing liquidity just prior to a statement date by calling loans or selling securities, in order to make it appear through the published statement that the reported liquidity is habitually carried.

See BANK STATEMENT, CALL REPORT.

WINNIPEG COMMODITY EXCHANGE

WINNIPEG COMMODITY EXCHANGE Originally established in 1887 as the Winnipeg Grain & Produce Exchange, this leading Canadian commodity market was incorporated in 1891. Following the opening of a grain futures market and a clearinghouse in 1901, the exchange was reorganized in 1908 as a voluntary, nonincorporated association under the name Winnipeg Grain Exchange, and continued development as a major market. The name was subsequently changed to the present title.

The appended table shows the futures trading in selected commodities on the Winnipeg Commodity Exchange as of 1981.

Futures Trading on the Winnipeg Commodity Exchange

Commodity	Trading Months	Contract size
Barley	May, July, Oct., Dec.	100 metric tons
Flaxseed	May, July, Oct, Nov., Dec.	100 metric tons
Gold, centum	Feb., May, Aug., Nov.	100 oz.
Gold, standard	Jan., Apr., July, Oct.	400 oz.
Oats	May, July, Oct., Dec.	100 metric tons
Rapeseed	Jan., Mar., June, Sept., Nov.	100 metric tons
(Vancouver)		
Rye	May, July, Oct., Nov., Dec.	100 metric tons
Wheat	May, July, Oct., Dec.	100 metric tons

Since Winnipeg is in the same time zone as Chicago, trading on the CHICAGO BOARD OF TRADE is concurrent with trading on the Winnipeg Commodity Exchange.

WIPED OUT Denotes the loss by a speculator of money put up as margin, occasioned by a drop in the value of the securities purchased and their consequent sale by the broker to protect his loan (customer's debit balance), or by extension, the total loss of one's wealth.

WIRE FATE ITEM A check, draft, or note sent for collection from an out-of-town depositor or bank correspondent with instructions to report by wire whether or not the item was collected, i.e., paid when presented.

WIRE HOUSE A large brokerage firm which operates nationally and internationally, with many branch offices which do a large commission business (execution of orders for the public), and thus maintains a large communications network, including a leased private wire system.
See BROKER, BROKERAGE OFFICE ORGANIZATION, NEW YORK STOCK EXCHANGE.

WITHDRAWAL Checking account deposits (individual, partnership, and corporation accounts) as demand deposits are subject to withdrawal by the depositor at any time, without notice, by check or in cash. Negotiable order of withdrawal (NOW) accounts serve transactional purposes without the requirement of prior notice of withdrawal, as do arrangements for automatic transfers from savings balances.

Passbook savings are subject to prior notice of withdrawal of 30 to 60 days, although such notice is customarily not invoked, so that in practice such savings are actually accorded demand availability.

TIME DEPOSITS, however, whether single-maturity or multiple-maturity, may be withdrawn only at specified maturities, since keeping the funds on deposit for the agreed maturity is consideration for the interest rates paid, which normally are higher the longer the agreed maturity. Premature withdrawals are subject to penalties, customarily loss of the premium interest rate as well as loss of three months' interest, per regulation of the banking agencies.

New Withdrawal Penalty. A new early withdrawal penalty in all deposit categories for new certificates issued or renewed after July 1, 1979, was announced by the banking agencies (Federal Reserve Board, Federal Deposit Insurance Corporation, and Federal Home Loan Bank Board). If deposits mature in more than one year, the minimum penalty will be six months' loss of interest. If the deposit matures in one year or less, the minimum penalty will be three months' loss of interest. The previous penalty of a loss of three months' interest and payment of interest on the funds withdrawn at only the passbook rate would continue to apply to all time deposits issued before July 1, 1979.

See CHECKING ACCOUNTS, DEMAND DEPOSITS, SAVINGS ACCOUNTS.

In COLLATERAL loan practice, the collateral loan agreement usually permits the substitution of collateral for items currently pledged, which may then be withdrawn, with the consent of the lender.
See SUBSTITUTIONS IN COLLATERAL.

WITH EXCHANGE When the words "with exchange" or "payable with exchange" are written on a draft or check, exchange charges or collection costs, in addition to the face of the instrument, are payable by the drawee or payer, respectively.

WITH INTEREST Accrued interest added. With interest bonds are bonds that carry a fixed interest rate and currently are paying their interest trade "and interest," i.e., the buyer, in addition to paying the market price, also pays the interest accrued since the last interest payment date of the bonds.
See ACCRUED INTEREST, FLAT.

WITHOUT PAR VALUE STOCK Stock that has no designated par value, commonly referred to as NO PAR VALUE STOCK.

WITHOUT RECOURSE This term has three meanings:

1. In the law of negotiable instruments, an ENDORSEMENT "Without recourse, A. B. See" is a qualified endorsement by which the endorser does not assume the general contract of endorser specified in Section 3-414(1) of the Uniform Commercial Code, which reads as follows: "Unless the indorsement otherwise specifies (as by such words as "without recourse"), every indorser engages that upon dishonor and any necessary notice of dishonor and protest he will pay the instrument according to its tenor at the time of his indorsement to the holder or to any subsequent indorser who takes it up, even though the indorser who takes it up was not obligated to do so."
2. In the factoring of accounts receivable, discounting by vendors without recourse signifies that by agreement, the factor on approved shipments will assume the entire credit loss on the uncollected invoice if a customer, after receiving and accepting delivery, fails to pay in full because of his financial inability to pay.
See FACTOR.
3. In indirect financing of consumers by banks and finance companies, through discounting of consumer paper held by installment vendors such as automobile dealers, appliance dealers, etc., the nonrecourse plan does not require the dealer's unqualified endorsement of the customer's paper, so that the dealer has no liability once the paper is discounted by the bank or finance company. But under such nonrecourse plan, the dealer may be required to pay a nonrecourse fee on each contract, does not receive any part of the carrying charges, and may nevertheless be required to assist in repossession and collection of delinquent accounts.
See CONSUMER CREDIT, INSTALLMENT SALES.

WITTEVEEN FACILITY A supplementary source of financial aid for needy members of the INTERNATIONAL MONETARY FUND, originally recommended on October 4, 1976, by H. Johannes Witteveen, then managing director of the IMF. As of February 23, 1979, the facility was declared effective, having accumulated 7.75 billion special drawing rights as the objective for operations. The sum included at least six agreements providing for an amount not less than SDR 500 million each, including SDR 1.93 million from the Saudi Arabian Monetary Agency, SDR 1.45 million from the U.S., and SDR 1.05 million from the Deutsche Bundesbank (West Germany). Participation remained open to other lenders.

This new facility became essential upon termination in 1976 of the IMF's oil facility. The latter fund had been established in 1974 to provide additional funds (nearly SDR 7 billion over the two-year period) to assist member nations in meeting the impact of their balance of payments of sharp increases in the cost of petroleum and petroleum products.

This facility allows the fund to provide to its members in larger amounts and for longer periods financial resources supplemental to those available from quota subscriptions. Through this facility the fund borrows from members in strong balance of payments positions and lends these borrowings to other members experiencing difficulties in maintaining equilibrium in their balance of payments. The supplementary financing facility became operational in May 1979.

WOMEN'S INVESTMENTS High-grade investments in which safety of principal, regularity of income, and freedom from care are present in a high degree, i.e., defensive investments which afford steady income with least exposure to capital depreciation.

See INVESTMENT.

WOMEN'S SIGNATURES Proper registration and endorsement of stock certificates in the name of women still presents some technical considerations in certain situations.

Effective February 13, 1956, old Rule 195 of the New York Stock Exchange, which required an unmarried woman to have her marital status indicated (e.g., *Miss* Mary A. Brown), was rescinded. Registration and endorsement as simply Mary A. Brown are therefore proper.

Similarly, old Rule 196 of the New York Stock Exchange, which required widows to indicate their status (e.g., *Mrs.* Elizabeth B. Smith), was rescinded. Elizabeth B. Smith therefore is proper for both the registration and endorsement of the certificate.

Rule 208 of the New York Stock Exchange as of 1982 was still in effect with regard to married women. It reads: "A certificate in the name of a married woman shall be a delivery, except that, where applicable law limits the right of a married woman to transfer the certificate, such certificate shall be a delivery only when the assignment shall be executed jointly by husband and wife and acknowledged before a notary public or other qualified officer."

The laws of Texas, Arizona, and New Mexico still restrict the rights of married women to transfer certificates in their own names. According to Rule 208, it is proper even in those states for the stock certificate to be registered in the name of the married woman, e.g., "Amy B. See," instead of "Mrs. Amy B. See." The rule takes effect in those states, however, upon endorsement of the stock certificate by the wife in connection with sale and transfer of the certificate. This same situation applies to any foreign countries which similarly still restrict the right of married women to transfer property without their husband's joinder.

See GOOD DELIVERY.

WOOL Wool support is carried out through payments to producers. The original purpose of the wool price support program was to provide the incentive for an annual shorn wool production of up to 300 million pounds.

Payments on shorn wool are based on the percent needed to bring the average return received by all producers up to the support level. The average price received from the sale of wool becomes known early in the year following the program year for which payments are to be made. To determine individual producer's payments, this percentage is applied to the producer's net proceeds from the sale of wool.

The percentage method of payments is employed to encourage producers to improve the quality and marketing of their wool. Under this method, the producer who gets a higher market price for the wool also gets a higher incentive payment.

The law also provides for a payment on sales of unshorn lambs. (This wool is called pulled wool.) This payment is at a comparable rate to that of the shorn wool payment and is designed to encourage the normal practice of marketing lambs without shearing the wool.

WORKED OFF Denotes that prices have gradually declined, but only fractionally, on the average.

WORKING CAPITAL This term is not standardized in accounting terminology, but is usually taken to mean the net current assets, or current assets (cash, notes receivable, marketable securities and other assets of a quick and liquid nature, accounts receivable, and inventories), less the current liabilities (notes payable, other debts payable within one year, accounts payable, and current liability accruals). This excess is also referred to as free working capital or excess quick, measuring the margin of liquid assets over quick liabilities and thus the ability of a business to meet liabilities as they mature over the ensuing year. The ratio of current assets to current liabilities, however, is more indicative of such ability than the net current assets in the absolute. Net current assets are the same whether current assets are $1 million and current liabilities $500,000 or current assets are $1.5 million and current liabilities $1 million, but the current ratio is 2:1 in the first case and only 1.5:1 in the second case.

From an operating standpoint, the working capital available to a business is sometimes referred to as gross current assets, the gross in cash, cash items such as marketable securities, receivables, and working assets in inventories (raw materials in process and finished goods) which a business is turning over in its operations. From the standpoint of credit analysis, however, the net current assets are more indicative of the net funds available to a business for operations.

Working capital is useful in determining the ability of a firm to finance current operations and to meet obligations as they mature. Adequate working capital is necessary for a business to operate efficiently and effectively. Liquidity is crucial to survival and success. Short-term credit is usually obtained through trade credit, but this can be costly if discounts are not taken.

BIBLIOGRAPHY

WOELFEL, CHARLES J., and CHARLES D. MECIMORE, *The Operating Executive's Guide to Profit Planning Tools and Techniques* (Probus Publishing Co., Chicago, Ill., 1986).

WORKING CAPITAL FUND In governmental accounting, especially at the state and municipal level, a fund established to finance and to account for internal services provided for the governmental unit's own departments, such as central printing plant services, as contrasted with utility or other types of enterprise funds which provide services to the general public for fees. After such a fund is established by the receipt of the funds and acquisition of necessary assets, it is intended to be self-supporting.

WORKING CAPITAL TURNOVER In RATIO ANALYSIS, one of the "14 Important Ratios" regularly published by Dun & Bradstreet, Inc., indicative of utilization of working capital, i.e., net sales divided by average net current assets (current assets minus current liabilities). The ratio indicates the number of times the working capital has been turned over or utilized during the period.

WORKING CONTROL For accounting purposes, ownership of bare majority of a company's voting stock is required in order to consolidate the statements of the parent company and its subsidiaries thus owned. Such bare majority ownership would also assure control.

In practice, however, effective or working control may sometimes be achieved through ownership of less than a bare majority of the voting stock, either individually or by a group. This is especially possible in the case of large corporations whose stock is widely held in relatively small blocks, so that the majority of the voting stock is dispersed among many holders. Under such circumstances, a concentrated and unified minority block of shares, with the aid of proxies solicited from the scattered majority, may gain and maintain control of the corporation by gaining places on the board of directors.

See MAJORITY STOCKHOLDERS, MINORITY STOCKHOLDERS, PROXY, VOTING POWER, VOTING TRUST.

WORKING RESERVES A bank may find it necessary for operations to carry EXCESS RESERVES, as well as balances at correspondent banks, as working reserves for liquidity requirements, depending upon local conditions affecting deposit withdrawals. Working reserves include vault cash, reserve balances at the Federal Reserve bank in excess of legal reserve requirements, and balances at correspondent banks. Country banks especially are likely to carry working reserves, which represent a leakage insofar as the banking system's utilization of available excess reserves for credit expansion is concerned.

WORK IN PROCESS In a manufacturing firm which converts raw materials and components into finished goods, that part of inventories upon which such conversion has been begun but not yet completely finished as of the date of the taking of INVENTORY. Thus work in process is intermediate in nature, being neither raw materials nor finished goods, and the least liquid of these three types of manufacturing inventories. Valuation for work in process should be supported by adequate costing procedures, to accumulate the costs involved properly up to the extent of completion of the work, rather than merely estimated or guessed. Estimates or guesses may result in a grave overstatement of the total figure for inventories, which is classified as part of current assets.

WORKOUT LOANS Problem loans of banks and other lenders placed on a work-out basis. Borrowers are given such additional time and opportunity to work out their financial difficulties and repay the outstandings as the work-out program, imposed with the consent and cooperation of the borrower, permits. Such loans are fully reserved against, but if the work-out program succeeds, the recoveries from such chargeoffs and valuation reserves will be higher than the realization if legal remedy were pursued against the borrower in his present circumstances.

See EXAMINATION PROCEDURE for regulatory approach to valuation of loans.

WORLD BANK See INTERNATIONAL BANK FOR RECONSTRUCTION AND DEVELOPMENT.

WORN CURRENCY Department of the Treasury Circular No. 55, "Exchange of Paper Currency and Coin," provides that in general exchanges of the paper currency and coin of the United States and the distribution and replacement thereof will, so far as practicable, be effected through the Federal Reserve banks and their branches.

The Federal Reserve Bank of Atlanta, in its booklet "Fundamental Facts About United States Money," explains the procedures as follows.

Like any other commodity, currency wears out from handling and is sometimes accidentally damaged or destroyed. The average life of a $1 bill, for example, is about 17 or 18 months. Larger denominations usually last longer, since they do not circulate as often as the $1 bill. The Treasury asks the banks to send old, worn, torn, or soiled currency to a Federal Reserve bank to be exchanged for new.

As the Federal Reserve banks receive currency from commercial banks, they count and sort it according to fit and unfit and store the fit (reusable) currency in their vaults until it goes out again through the commercial banking system as it is needed. Currency (coin and paper money) that is unfit (not reusable) is retired. The retired, unfit currency is then canceled, verified, and destroyed. Damaged and worn coins are returned to the U.S. Assay Office for melting and making new coins.

See MUTILATED CURRENCY, PAPER MONEY.

WRAPAROUND MORTGAGE A second mortgage which conveniently expands the total amount of borrowing by the mortgagor without disturbing the original mortgage. For example, a property owner with a mortgage securing a $2 million mortgage debt on the property might obtain an additional sum of $1 million from a lender who agrees to take a wrap-around junior mortgage as security for the new total mortgage debt of $3 million on the property. The mortgagor typically makes payments on both mortgages to the wrap-around mortgagee, who in turn makes the required payments to the holder of the original senior mortgage.

BIBLIOGRAPHY

WEIMER, ARTHUR M., HOYT, HOMER, and BLOOM, GEORGE F. *Real Estate*, 7th ed., 1978.

WRITE DOWN See WRITE OFF.

WRITE OFF To reduce the book value of an asset in order to bring it into agreement with its present going, estimated, appraised, or market value. To write off, charge off, and write down are practically synonymous, except that the first two are customarily used when the entire value of the asset is charged as a loss, e.g., a bad debt fully reserved against by allowance for bad debts. The specific accounting method followed is the creation of valuation reserve against the asset, in full or to a partial extent, so that the net carrying value of the asset, after deduction of the valuation reserve, is either zero or a reduced figure. The accounting will also produce debits, which if regularly recurring in nature (e.g., bad debts expense, reflecting uncollectibility of receivables created by credit sales; or chargeoffs on loans, reflecting losses on loans extended) may be charged against current operations which generated them, in accordance with the matching principle of accounting. However, if such chargeoffs do not involve current operations, they should be charged to the accumulated allowance for possible loan losses in view of their nonoperating nature, rather than the current statement of income and expense.

See COMPTROLLER'S REGULATION, EXAMINATION PROCEDURE.

WRITER Grantor; the party that sells an option. The writer is required to carry out the terms of the option at the choice of the holder.

WRITE UP The opposite of write down, i.e., to bring the book value of an asset into agreement with the market value, appraised value, or estimated value when the latter is above the book value. The practice of writing up the value of assets is not favored as a conservative practice by accountants, as it might lead to abuse in "window dressing" surplus by crediting it with such unrealized gains. It also leads to taxation questions, especially in connection with depreciation sought to be charged on the written-up asset valuations, and valuation problems in connection with property taxation and valuation bases for rate regulatory purposes.

See COMPTROLLER'S REGULATION, EXAMINATION PROCEDURE.

X

X This term has five meanings:

1. The New York Stock Exchange's ticker symbol for the common stock of the United States Steel Corporation. Like other single-letter ticker symbols for leading stocks (see NEW YORK STOCK EXCHANGE ABBREVIATIONS), the symbol has become so identified with the stock and corporation that it is often used in lieu thereof.
2. In mathematics, the conventional notation for an unknown quantity; the abscissa in the rectangular coordinate system (the horizontal axis is the x-axis; the vertical axis is the y-axis).
3. In BOND RATINGS, the symbol for bonds considered eligible as bank investments on the basis of confirmatory ratings by the statistical services. (The Y symbol is used for issues considered ineligible for bank investment on the basis of confirmatory ratings, but not in default.)
4. A symbol customarily used as a person's mark, in the case of inability of the person to write his signature. (See MARK SIGNATURE.)
5. Regulation X of the FEDERAL RESERVE BOARD REGULATIONS.

X-DIVIDEND Without the dividend; otherwise written "ex-dividend." Stocks sell ex-dividend on the fourth business day preceding the record date fixed by the dividend declaration of the corporation or the date of the closing of transfer books. Thus a buyer buying the stock on the first ex-dividend date and thereafter until after the payment date for the subject dividend will not be entitled to the subject dividend.

This rule, which depends on the regular delivery basis (settlement and delivery five business days after the date of the transaction) for determination of the ex-dividend date, arises from the "regular way" five-day delivery rule of the New York Stock Exchange and of other securities markets. Rule 235 of the New York Stock Exchange specifically provides that transactions in stocks (except those made for cash) shall be ex-dividend or ex-rights on the fourth business day preceding the record date fixed by the corporation or the date of the closing of the books. Transactions in stocks made for cash shall be ex-dividend or ex-rights on the business day following the record date or date of closing of the transfer books. The New York Stock Exchange or other securities market concerned, however, may direct otherwise in any specific case.

See DELIVERIES.

X-INEFFICIENCY A important assumption in economic theory is that firms allocate resources and produce efficiently. Harvey Leibenstein, an economist, has developed a theory of X-inefficiency. He posits that in economic circles inefficiency is the norm arising from organizational entropy, human inertia, incomplete contracts between economic agents, and agency problems. In such a world there is persistent slack. There are many skeptics of this theory.

X-RTS Without the rights; otherwise written ex-rights. In the event of issuance of stock subscription rights to stockholders to subscribe to additional stock at a specified ratio and at a specified price customarily below prevailing market price, it is the stockholders of record date who will receive the rights on the issuance date free of charge from the corporation. The ex-rights date is the first date as of which buyers of the stock will not be entitled to receive the rights.

See RIGHT.

X-WARR Without the warrant; otherwise written ex-warrant. When senior securities (bonds, debentures, or preferred stock) are issued with stock purchase warrants attached, such senior securities will be traded with warrants. Stock purchase warrants (see STOCK PURCHASE WARRANT) are privileges, customarily on a long-term basis, to buy common stock at a specified price or prices for a specified share or shares per warrant.

Holders of the senior security with warrant attached may detach the stock purchase warrant for the purpose of sale or exercise thereof. In that event, the certificate for the senior security will now be traded x-warr and thus minus the market value prevailing for the stock purchase warrants as such.

Y

YANKEE CERTIFICATES OF DEPOSIT Foreign-domestic certificates of deposit (CDs); negotiable certificates of deposit issued in the U.S. by branch offices of major foreign banks. As of March, 1979, the New York State Banking Department indicated that there were 56 foreign banking agencies in New York City; 98 branch banks operated by 71 foreign institutions; 133 offices of representatives; 20 subsidiary trust companies; and six foreign investment companies. Most foreign banking units' activity in the U.S. has been concentrated in New York and California.

The INTERNATIONAL BANKING ACT OF 1978, enacted September 17, 1978, for the first time has made the operations of foreign banks in the U.S., through their branches, agencies, and lending companies, subject to federal law similarly required for domestic banks. The act authorized the Board of Governors of the Federal Reserve System, after consultation with state banking supervisors, to impose legal reserve requirements and interest rate limitations on branches and agencies of large foreign banks. As of early 1979, the board was in the process of preparing proposed regulations on the subject. Responsibilities for activities of foreign banks in the U.S. were also assigned in the act to the Comptroller of the Currency and the Federal Deposit Insurance Corporation, in connection with which the three agencies formed an interagency task force to implement the responsibilities.

Appeal of Yankee CDs. Now that the International Banking Act of 1978 has brought branch offices of the major foreign banks under federal regulation, there should be less reason to ignore the Yankee CDs of large strong foreign banks, with their excellent creditworthiness, market availability, and ready liquidity. Unlike Eurodollar CDs, Yankee CDs do not have sovereign risk and are not subject to foreign exchange controls of another country, as are the funds and

Bond and Stock Yields: 1970 to 1987
(Percent per year. Annual averages of monthly data, except as indicated.)

Type	1970	1975	1979	1980	1981	1982	1983	1984	1985	1986	1987
U.S. Treasury, constant maturities: [1,2]											
3-year	7.29	7.49	9.72	11.55	14.44	12.92	10.45	11.89	9.64	7.06	7.67
5-year	7.38	7.77	9.52	11.48	14.24	13.01	10.80	12.24	10.13	7.31	7.94
10-year	7.35	7.99	9.44	11.46	13.91	13.00	11.11	12.44	10.62	7.68	8.38
U.S. Govt., long-term bonds [2,3]	6.58	6.98	8.74	10.81	12.87	12.23	10.84	11.99	10.75	8.14	8.63
State and local govt. bonds, Aaa [4]	6.12	6.42	5.92	7.86	10.42	10.86	8.80	9.61	8.60	6.95	7.12
State and local govt. bonds, Baa [4]	6.75	7.62	6.73	9.02	11.76	12.46	10.17	10.38	9.58	7.75	8.17
High-graded municipal bonds (Standard & Poor's) [5]	6.51	6.89	6.39	8.51	11.23	11.57	9.47	10.15	9.18	7.38	7.73
Municipal (Bond Buyer, 20 bonds)	6.35	7.05	6.52	8.59	11.33	11.66	9.51	10.10	9.11	7.32	7.65
Corporate Aaa seasoned [4]	8.04	8.83	9.63	11.94	14.17	13.79	12.04	12.71	11.37	9.02	9.38
Corporate Baa seasoned [4]	9.11	10.61	10.69	13.67	16.04	16.11	13.55	14.19	12.72	10.39	10.58
Corporate Aaa utility bonds [6]	8.72	9.17	9.92	12.68	15.65	14.71	12.25	13.40	11.67	9.09	9.40
Corporate, by years to maturity: [7]											
5 years	8.10	7.70	9.40	12.80	13.25	13.78	9.90	10.20	10.40	7.35	6.80
10 years	8.00	8.00	9.35	12.40	13.00	13.99	10.55	11.80	11.60	8.05	7.65
20 years	7.60	8.35	9.08	12.30	13.00	14.00	11.00	12.60	12.50	8.50	8.00
30 years	7.60	8.35	9.10	12.30	13.00	14.00	11.00	12.60	12.50	8.50	8.00
Corporate (Moody's) [4]	8.51	9.57	10.12	12.75	15.06	14.94	12.78	13.49[8]	12.05	9.71	9.91
Industrials (37 bonds) [9]	8.26	9.25	9.85	12.35	14.50	14.54	12.25	13.21	11.80	9.96	9.83
Railroads (13 bonds) [10]	8.77	9.39	9.60	11.48	13.22	13.68	12.08	13.07	11.94	9.85	9.63
Public utilities (40 bonds)	8.68	9.88	10.39	13.15	15.62	15.33	13.31	14.03[8]	12.29	9.46	9.98
Stocks (Standard & Poor's): [5]											
"Preferred" (10 stocks)	7.22	8.36	9.11	10.60	12.36	12.53	11.02	11.59	10.49	8.76	8.37
Common:											
Composite (500 stocks)	3.83	4.31	5.47	5.26	5.20	5.81	4.40	4.64	4.25	3.48	3.08
Industrials (400 stocks)	3.62	3.9	5.20	4.95	4.90	5.48	4.04	4.05	3.76	3.09	2.62

[1] Yields on the more actively traded issues adjusted to constant maturities by the U.S. Treasury.
[2] Yields are based on closing bid prices quoted by at least five dealers.
[3] Averages (to maturity or call) for all outstanding bonds neither due nor callable in less than 10 years, including several very low yielding "flower" bonds.
[4] Source: Moody's Investors Service, New York, NY.
[5] Source: Standard & Poor's Corp., New York, NY, *Standard & Poor's Outlook*, weekly.
[6] Based on first trading day of each month, deferred call, new issue estimate. Source: Salomon Brothers, Inc., New York, NY, *An Analytical Record of Yields and Yield Spreads*.
[7] Source: Scudder, Stevens & Clark, New York, NY, unpublished data.
[8] The Aaa public utility average was suspended on Jan. 17, 1984 because of a lack of appropriate issues. The average corporate does not include Aaa utilities from Jan. 17 to Oct. 12. The Aaa utility average was reinstated on Oct. 12. Thirty public utility bonds were used during the period Jan. 17-Oct. 12, 1984.
[9] Covers 40 bonds for period 1970-1983 and 38 bonds for 1984-1986.
[10] Covers 23 bonds for period 1970-1981, 15 bonds for 1982, and 17 bonds for 1983.
[11] Yields based on 10 stocks, 4 yields. Issues converted to a price equivalent to $100 par and a 7 percent annual dividend before averaging.

Source: Except as noted, Board of Governors of the Federal Reserve System, *Federal Reserve Bulletin*, monthly.

YIELD

Chart 1 / Yields of Treasury Securities, December 31, 1975 (based on closing bid quotations)

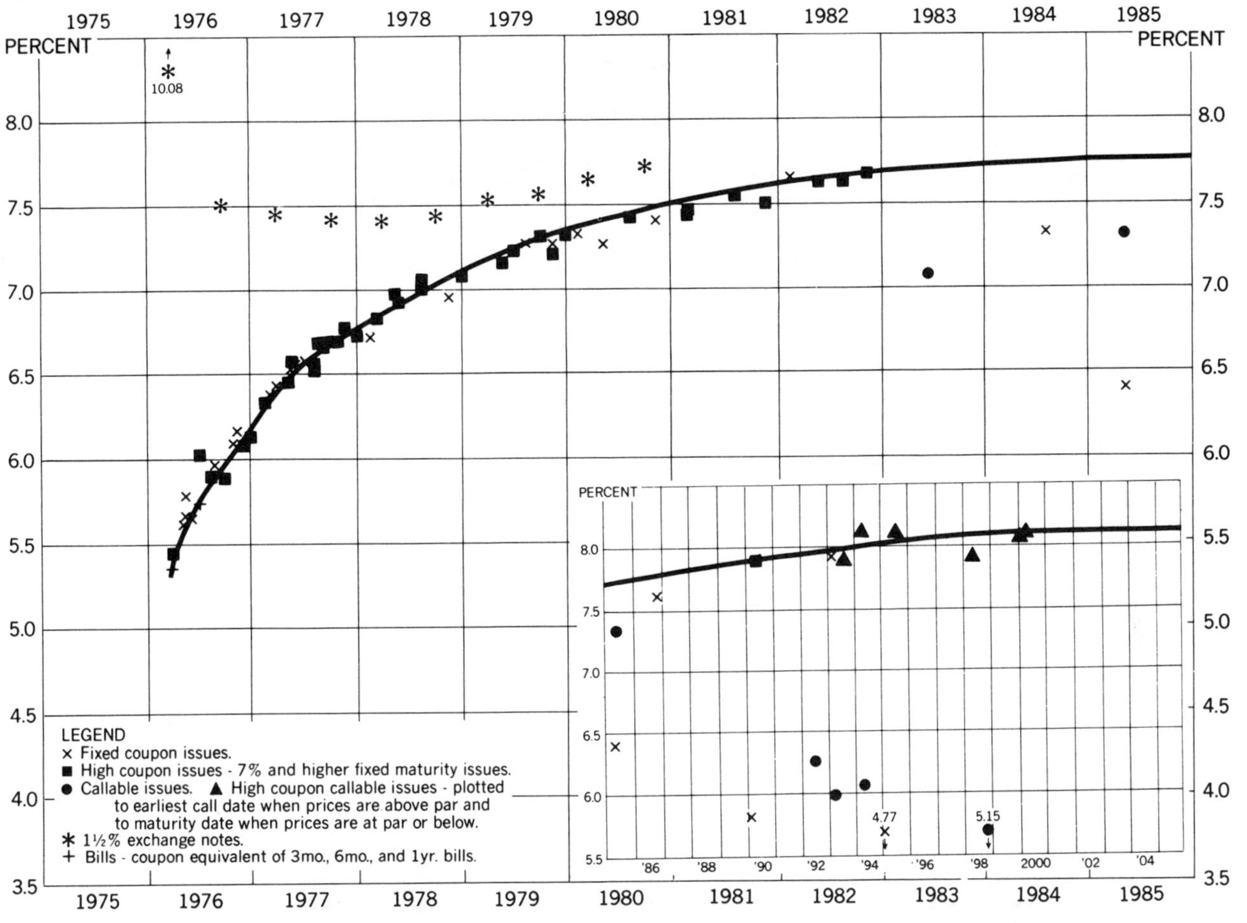

LEGEND
× Fixed coupon issues.
■ High coupon issues - 7% and higher fixed maturity issues.
● Callable issues. ▲ High coupon callable issues - plotted to earliest call date when prices are above par and to maturity date when prices are at par or below.
✱ 1½% exchange notes.
+ Bills - coupon equivalent of 3mo., 6mo., and 1yr. bills.

Note: The curve is fitted by eye. Market yields on coupon issues due in less than 3 months are excluded.

Source: Treasury Bulletin.

obligor-issuers located in the U.S. Yield spreads are reported by one dealer as having ranged in the past few years as much as 10 to 35 basis points above the yields on domestic CDs.

BIBLIOGRAPHY

VINDEKILDE, SUSANNE. "Yields on Yankee CDs, New Money Instrument, Surpass Euro, Domestic." *Money Manager*, August 21, 1978.

YIELD Investment income; investment rate of return, as distinguished from a speculative or temporary rate of return; the net income from property, but particularly applied to bonds bought as investments to be held to maturity.

The yield of a bond depends upon four variables: (1) price, (2) INTEREST rate, (3) interest period, and (4) term, i.e., remaining life of the bond to maturity. The third variable may be omitted for practical purposes, since the interest on most bonds is payable semiannually. Bonds paying interest annually are less valuable than like bonds paying interest semiannually, but this difference for all practical purposes is negligible.

A 5% bond purchased at par, regardless of its term, yields 5%. But if it is purchased at a premium, its yield to maturity is less, and if it is purchased at a discount, its yield is more, depending upon the term, because of amortization of the premium in the former case and accretion of the discount in the latter case, both on a per annum basis. The exact yield to maturity of a bond bought at a premium or discount is mathematically the internal rate of return—the discount rate which applies in equating the sum of the present values of interest payments and the principal with the present market price. This is the mathematical basis for the bond yields and values tables which are customarily referred to for convenience. (*See* BOND VALUES TABLE.) A 4% bond (interest payable semiannually) having 20 years to run and purchased at a premium of $35, i.e., $1,035, yields 3.75%, but if purchased at a discount of $33.50, i.e., $966.50, it yields 4.25%.

Bid and asked quotations on treasury notes and bills and state and municipal issues, bankers acceptances, and commercial paper are quoted on a yield basis. Prices are quoted "at a price to yield percent" since, when other factors are equal, yield is the only common denominator for comparison of market prices and investment values.

See INVESTMENT VALUE.

The terms yield and RETURN are often confused. The first is restricted in its meaning to the net income from a bond if held to maturity, whereas return denotes current income derived from either a bond or stock, without reference to maturity. In the case of stock, the variables mentioned above are not fully known. There is no term or maturity value, nor is the income certain; therefore yield cannot be computed, except by assuming a given holding period so that holding period yield (HPY) can be computed. The current return of a bond or stock is determined by dividing the purchase price into the annual cash interest or dividend. In the above

YIELD AUCTION

Chart 2 / Yields of Treasury Securities, November 28, 1980 (based on closing bid quotations)

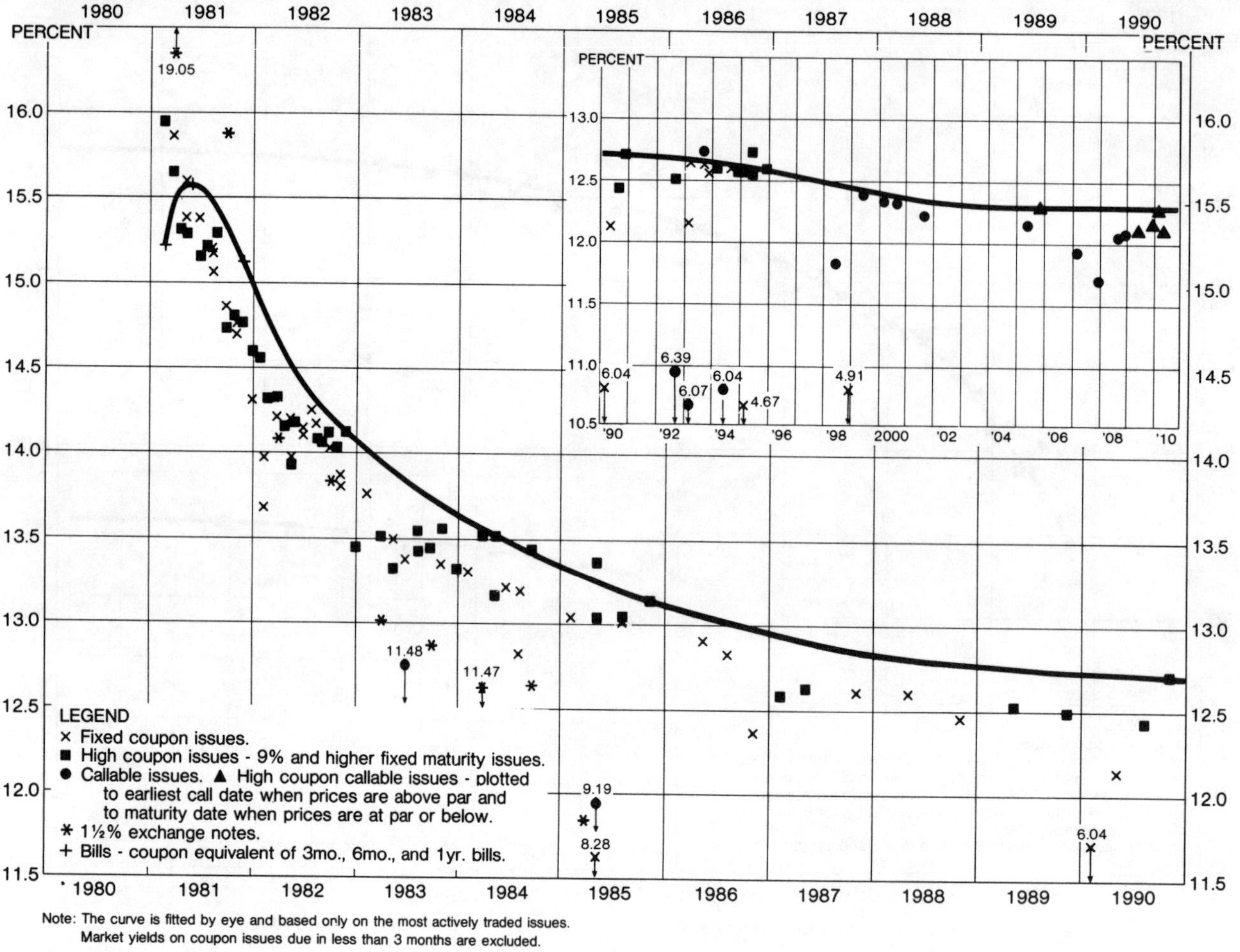

LEGEND
× Fixed coupon issues.
■ High coupon issues - 9% and higher fixed maturity issues.
● Callable issues. ▲ High coupon callable issues - plotted to earliest call date when prices are above par and to maturity date when prices are at par or below.
✱ 1½% exchange notes.
+ Bills - coupon equivalent of 3mo., 6mo., and 1yr. bills.

Note: The curve is fitted by eye and based only on the most actively traded issues. Market yields on coupon issues due in less than 3 months are excluded.

Source: Treasury Bulletin.

case, where the purchase price of the bond is $1,035 and the cash interest $40, the current return is 3.865%, whereas the yield to maturity is 3.75%. The current return of a bond bought at a premium is higher than its yield, since no deduction need be made for amortization of the premium, which is lost when the bond matures. Conversely, the current return on a bond bought at a discount is lower than its yield to maturity, since the investment value of the bond increases as it approaches maturity as the result of accretion of the discount.

The yield on optional bonds selling at a premium should be computed on the shortest possible time they may be outstanding. If the optional bonds are selling at a discount, the yield should be computed upon the longest possible time they may be outstanding.

The appended table shows bond and stock yields: 1970 to 1987. See INTEREST TABLES.

BIBLIOGRAPHY

FINANCIAL PUBLISHING CO. *Comprehensive Bond Values Table.*
WOELFEL, C.J. *Money, Time, Interest, and Yields*, 1988.

YIELD AUCTION A method of selling new issues of notes and bonds in which the maturity date of a new issue is specified prior to the auction. Investors submit tenders stating the yield to maturity they would accept on the quantity of bonds they want. Other types of auctions include subscription auctions and price auctions. In subscription auctions the issuer specifies the coupon rate, maturity, and price in advance. In a price auction, the coupon rate and maturity are specified in advance.

YIELD CURVE A smooth curve, fitted by eye through a series of points on a chart representing the different yields to maturity, as of a particular date, on securities that are identical or homogeneous in every respect except their maturities, e.g., U.S. government securities, which are all gilt-edge in quality and available in a variety of short-, intermediate-, and long-term maturities. The result is a picture of the term pattern of yields on the securities, showing variation in yields by maturities.

Plotting of the yield curve may result in an upsweeping, horizontal (flat), downsweeping, or humped shape. Appended herewith is an example of each such shape, prepared by the U.S. Treasury Department (*Treasury Bulletin*) during which pronounced changes occurred in basic demand and supply forces, investor expectations, and monetary and fiscal policies affecting the levels and relationships of yields on U.S. government securities.

1. An upsweeping shape reflects lower yields on short-term maturities than on long-term maturities. Such a pattern reflects relatively greater supply of short-term funds than long-term funds, monetary-fiscal policies favoring ease in the short-term rates, and expectations of possible future rise in yields, so that

YIELD CURVE

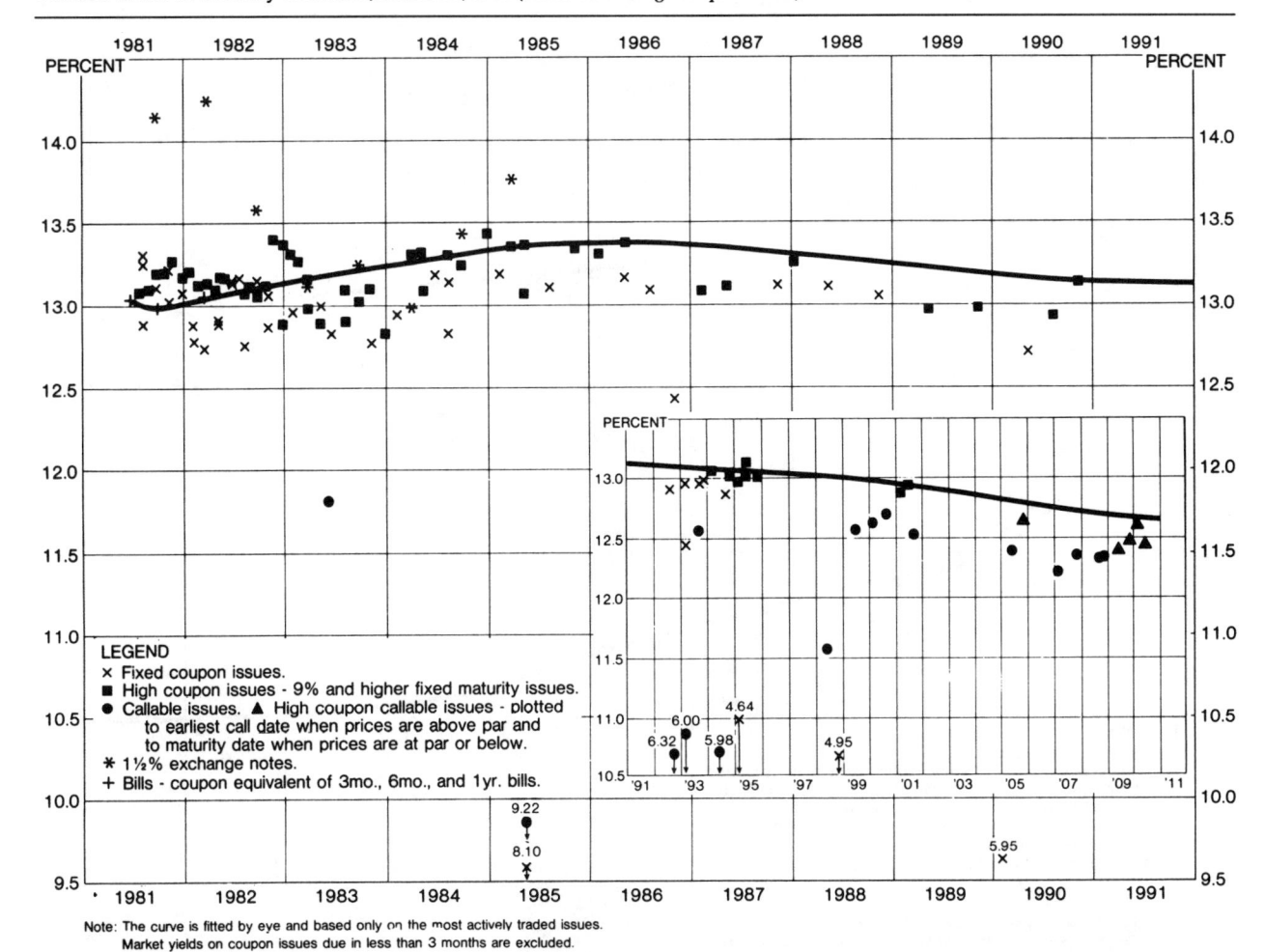

Chart 3 / Yields of Treasury Securities, March 31, 1981 (based on closing bid quotations)

LEGEND
× Fixed coupon issues.
■ High coupon issues - 9% and higher fixed maturity issues.
● Callable issues. ▲ High coupon callable issues - plotted to earliest call date when prices are above par and to maturity date when prices are at par or below.
✳ 1½% exchange notes.
+ Bills - coupon equivalent of 3mo., 6mo., and 1yr. bills.

Note: The curve is fitted by eye and based only on the most actively traded issues. Market yields on coupon issues due in less than 3 months are excluded.

Source: Treasury Bulletin.

investors favor short-term maturities over long-terms for market stability (long-term maturities would drop in prices more than the short-terms, should the rise in market yields occur) and liquidity, despite the higher prevailing yields on the long-terms.
2. A flat (horizontal) shape reflects narrowing of yield spreads among short-, intermediate-, and long-term maturities. Such a pattern reflects an approximate balancing of supply and demand forces, monetary-fiscal policies influencing short-term rates upward while nudging long-term yields downward to encourage long-term capital and mortgage activity, and expectations of an eventual decline in rates, so that investors are more willing to invest in the longer maturities (which would rise in prices more than the short-terms, should the drop in market yields occur).
3. A downsweeping shape reflects higher yields on short-term maturities than on long-terms. Such a pattern reflects very strong demand for short-term business credit coupled with a limited supply of such funds (marked, for example, by low or negative net free reserves of banks, which may be liquidating short-term securities to provide funds for business credit demand, thereby further raising short-term yields), tight monetary-fiscal policies, and investor expectations of future decline in interest rates, so that institutional investors (e.g., insurance companies, pension funds, etc.) buy long-term maturities, pushing their prices up and

yields down, for prevailing good yields and eventual capital gains (should interest rates decline in the future).
4. A humped shape of the yield curve arises, according to the expectations explanation, whenever investors expect short-term rates to rise temporarily but then to recede to lower levels. A particular example of such a yield curve prevailed as of February 28, 1979, when short-, intermediate-, and long-term yields were all at high levels.

Since the accord of March, 1951, policies of the Federal Reserve and the Treasury no longer peg short-term yields at low levels relative to long-terms, so that supply-demand forces, monetary policy, and investor expectations play a larger role in influencing a greater variety of yield curves. In more recent years, the emphasis on higher interest rates and targets of money supply by Federal Reserve monetary policy as counterinflation measures has also created more frequent changes in patterns of yield curves.

Uses of Yield Curve. Primarily, a yield curve is merely informative, giving the term structure of yields as of particular dates. But by reference to a yield curve chart, one may determine whether new issues are priced in line with prevailing yields of specific maturities; which issues are most attractively priced, among those charted, for buying or selling; which issues present profitable trading opportunities ("playing the pattern of rates," or "riding the yield curve"); and which issues present opportunities for switches (improved yield, shorter maturity, etc.). For forecasting purposes some value is

ENCYCLOPEDIA OF BANKING AND FINANCE

YIELD ON MUNICIPALS

Chart 4 / Yields of Treasury Securities, May 29, 1981 (based on closing bid quotations)

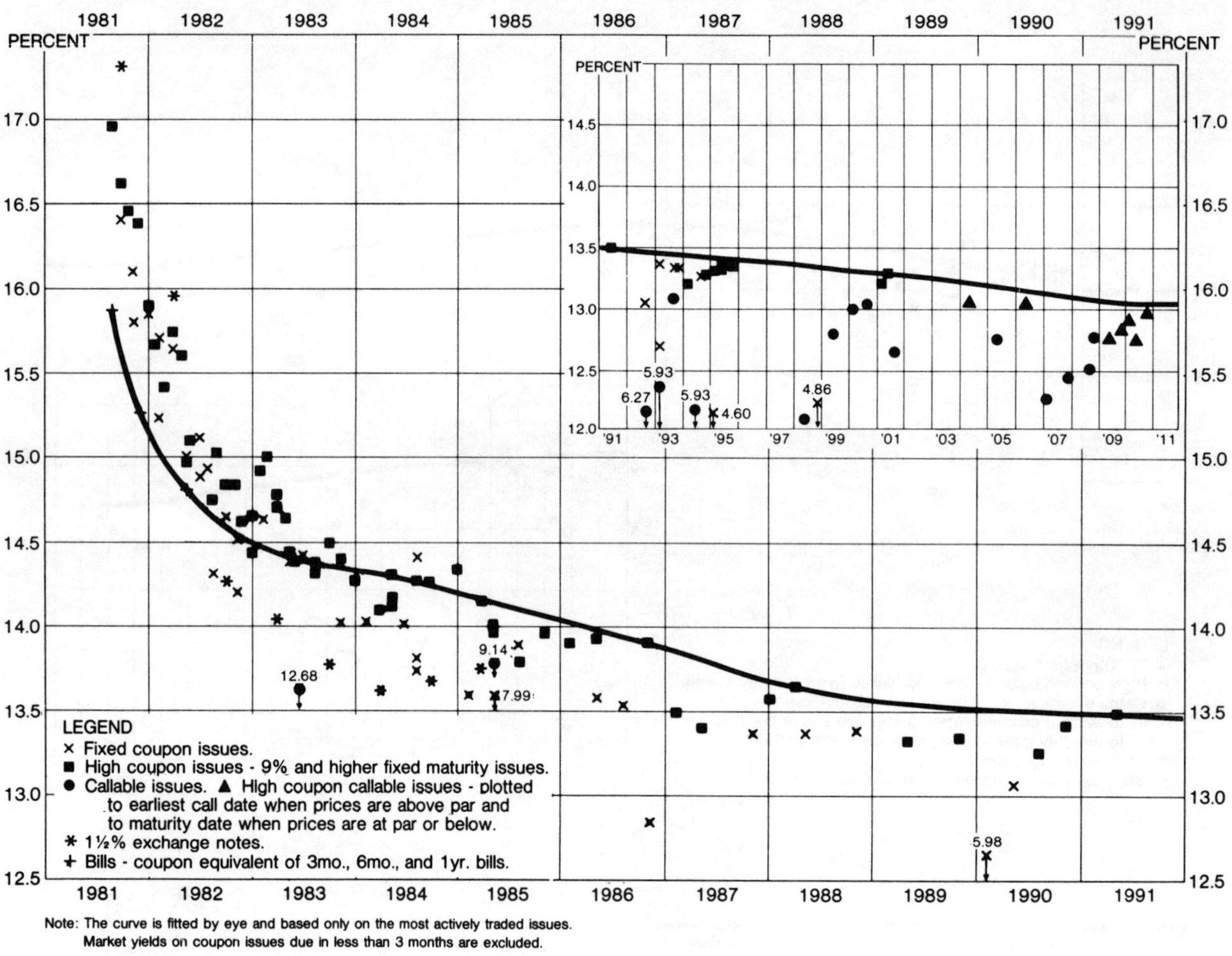

[Chart showing yields of Treasury securities from 1981 to 1991, with an inset covering 1991-2011. Legend:
× Fixed coupon issues.
■ High coupon issues - 9% and higher fixed maturity issues.
● Callable issues. ▲ High coupon callable issues - plotted to earliest call date when prices are above par and to maturity date when prices are at par or below.
✱ 1½% exchange notes.
+ Bills - coupon equivalent of 3mo., 6mo., and 1yr. bills.

Note: The curve is fitted by eye and based only on the most actively traded issues. Market yields on coupon issues due in less than 3 months are excluded.]

Source: Treasury Bulletin.

seen in the implications for future levels of yields and therefore prices implied in particular shapes of yield curves and their changes over time.

BIBLIOGRAPHY

CARR, J. L., HALPERN, P. J., and MCCOLLUM, J. S., "Correcting the Yield Curve: A Reinterpretation of the Duration Problem." *Journal of Finance,* September, 1974.

MALKIEL, B. G. "How Yield Curve Analysis Can Help Bond Portfolio Managers." *The Institutional Investor,* May, 1967.

NELSON, C. R. *The Term Structure of Interest Rates,* 1972.

YIELD ON MUNICIPALS   After the YIELD TO MATURITY is calculated on obligations of states and subdivisions of states (including municipalities), a further adjustment is necessary in order to make such tax-exempt yields comparable to the taxable yields on other issues.

Interest income from all classes of municipals, whether full faith and credit obligations, special assessments, or revenue types, is exempt from federal income taxes. Moreover, in specific states, interest income is also exempt from all present state income taxes in the case of issues of such states and their subdivisions. Issues of other states, however, would be taxable by the specific state granting tax exemption to its own domestic issues.

State and municipal securities, however, are subject to capital gains taxes. Accordingly, in the case of state and municipal issues priced in the market at discounts (below par), the net yield to maturity may be calculated (gross yield minus the capital gains tax on the accretion of the discount).

See MUNICIPALS.

YIELD TO CALL   The discount rate that equates the present value of the guaranteed cash flow (interest plus call price) if the bond is called.

YIELD TO MATURITY   Because bonds and other obligations are contractual in nature, specifying promise to pay principal at fixed future date and interest annually in the meantime, yield to maturity is the proper calculation of annual return, because it involves determination of the income elements as both the annual interest income and either accretion (appreciation per year on straight-line basis from discount cost price to full par at maturity, over remaining maturity) or amortization (depreciation per year on straight-line basis from premium cost price down to full par at maturity, over remaining maturity). In mere current return on bonds, properly used for income bonds (those whose interest payment is contingent upon earnings, and is not fixed at precise rate as fixed charge) and sometimes for bonds subject to great uncertainty of continuation of nominally fixed interest, the only income element figured is the year's annual interest projected or expected.

As an alternative to yield to maturity, it may be appropriate to calculate yield to first call date, especially in the case of U.S. government bonds, because the U.S. Treasury has been quite consistent in exercising the call feature at the first call date if the issue can be refunded at a lower interest rate.

Yield to maturity may be precisely determined mathematically, but the computation may be complex and time-consuming, and so bond yield tables, in a wide range of coupon rates, maturities, and prices, are available from publishers. These are a great convenience in determining, with a minimum of necessary interpolation, the precise yields resulting from the interplay of the above variables.

In the absence of a convenient bond yield table, the formula for approximate yield to maturity on a bond is basically the following: (1) take annual interest payment, plus accretion (discount, or aggregate dollar difference between cost price and full maturity value of the bond, divided by remaining maturity) or minus amortization (premium, or aggregate dollar difference between cost price and full maturity value of the bond, divided by remaining maturity); (2) divide by a simple average of cost price and full maturity value. Thus, if a bond is bought at 80 ($800 per $1,000 bond) pays 4% interest annually, and has 10 years' remaining maturity at the time of purchase, the approximate yield to maturity is 6.67% (interest of $40 annually, plus annual accretion of $20, divided by average principal of $900).

BIBLIOGRAPHY

FINANCIAL PUBLISHING CO. *Comprehensive Bond Values Tables.*
SCHAEFER, S. M. "The Problem with Redemption Yields." *Financial Analysts Journal*, July/August, 1977.

YOUNG BONDS The German government international 5.5% loan of 1930, originally due June 1, 1965, was popularly referred to as the Young loan, after the head of the American delegation, Owen R. Young. The issue of German reparations was laid to rest in the Lausanne Conference of 1932, but the Young bonds, including the U.S. issue and the United Kingdom portion, both as adjusted by the London Debt Agreement of 1953, are still the subject of interest. The Young loan of 1930, designed to assist the Weimar Republic in economic recovery, totaled $300 million, $98,250,000 of which was raised in the form of bonds by a public offering by a group of leading U.S. investment banking firms to U.S. investors. Pursuant to the Agreement on German External Debts, signed in London and effective September 16, 1953, provision was made for exchange of the original 1930 U.S. Young Plan bonds for the outstanding Extension 5s, with adjusted maturity date of June 1, 1980, issued amount totaling $55,468,200. These Extension 5s of 1953 have been traded on the New York Stock Exchange.

Interest and principal on the 1930 Young Plan bonds, U.S. issue, were originally obtainable at any foreign exchange market where the loan was quoted, in the respective currency at the prevailing rate of exchange. Subsequently, however, this provision was no longer observed, as it originally linked the bonds to the amount of gold that could be bought in 1930 by each of the currencies concerned. In 1952, at the insistence of the U.S. government, the U.S. dollar was substituted for gold. But instead of clearly determining that the U.S. dollar would now be the basis for repayment of interest and principal through the 1980 maturity, the 1952 agreement called for any currency recalculation to be on the "basis of the least depreciated currency," which in the German interpretation has meant devalued but not revalued currency. (The German deutschemark was revalued upwards in 1961 and 1968, and thus the German government has declined to recalculate the value of payments.)

The difference in currency valuation, for holders of dollar bonds, was reported to amount, as of 1979, to $12 million to $14 million. In the case of sterling bonds, prevailing market therefor on the London Stock Exchange as of 1979 of some £413 per £100 was considered to be about in line with the German view that the Belgian franc, pursuant to the 1952 agreement, should be considered the "least depreciated currency." But if the Swiss franc were used as the basis for repayment, each £100 bond could bring some £616 as of 1979.

In 1979 the controversy was the subject of hearings in a suit on the question brought before an international tribunal, in which a U.S. representative participated.

BIBLIOGRAPHY

BANK FOR INTERNATIONAL SETTLEMENTS. *Annual Report.*
GEDDES, JOHN. "Germany Near Solution to Pre-World War II Debts." *New York Times*, March 31, 1979, p. 28.
INTERNATIONAL CENTRE FOR SETTLEMENT OF INVESTMENT DISPUTES. *Annual Report.*
MOULTON, H. G., and PASVOLSKY, L. *War Debts and World Prosperity,* 1932.

YOUNG PLAN See YOUNG BONDS.

Z

ZEBRAs Zero-coupon bonds.
See FINANCIAL INSTRUMENTS: RECENT INNOVATIONS

ZERO-BASE BUDGETING The zero-base budgeting (ZBB) system of the federal government, originally adopted by the Carter administration in 1978, was terminated by the Reagan administration for the preparation of its first budget, that for the fiscal year 1983, on the grounds that the ZBB system had proved cumbersome in some respects and had not achieved "significant results" in holding down federal government spending.

As officially explained by the Carter administration, the ZBB system was adopted in order to accomplish four main objectives:

1. Focus the budget process on a comprehensive analysis of objectives, needs, and activities in order to make more effective use of the taxpayer's dollar.
2. Improve coordination of planning, budgeting, and evaluation.
3. Induce managers to evaluate in detail the cost-effectiveness of their operations.
4. Expand management participation in planning and budgeting at all levels of the federal government.

Zero-base budgeting requires managers to articulate objectives. In many instances it has reportedly helped to clarify agencies' functions and roles, and has increased management's opportunities to eliminate unnecessary activities and operate its programs more successfully. Zero-base budgeting also requires managers to identify and examine alternative methods of accomplishing their objectives, leading to reconsideration of the established ways of doing things.

Even more importantly, zero-base budgeting induces managers to analyze systematically the effects of various funding levels on the agency's ability to carry out its mission. It has required them to rank activities and resources in priority, from those that contribute the most toward achieving the agency's mission to those that contribute the least. These rankings indicate how program objectives can best be achieved at any given level of funding. Thus zero-base budgeting makes it easier to compare programs and identify those areas where the greatest monetary savings could be realized with the least sacrifice of program performance and service to the public.

The 1982 federal budget, which relied on the use of zero-base budgeting, termed it "a management process that provides for indepth evaluation of all proposed and existing programs and activities in conjunction with planning and budgeting."

Origins. Zero-base budgeting, although introduced into the federal sector and adopted for the federal government commencing with the fiscal year 1979, reportedly had been used by many firms in the private sector, with its origins credited to the electronics firm of Texas Instruments Inc. in 1962. After an article on the latter firm's use of ZBB appeared in the *Harvard Business Review*, its author, Peter A. Pyhrr, was retained by then Georgia Governor Carter to implement ZBB in the state of Georgia in 1971—the first governmental implementation of the system.

BIBLIOGRAPHY

EXECUTIVE OFFICE OF THE PRESIDENT, OFFICE OF MANAGEMENT AND BUDGET. *The Budget of the United States Government*, fiscal years 1979, 1980, and 1981.
HERZLINGER, R. E. "Zero-Base Budgeting in the Federal Government: A Case Study." *Sloan Management Review*, Winter, 1979.
PYHRR, PETER A. *Zero-Base Budgeting: A Practical Management Tool for Evaluating Expenses*, 1973.
TOURANGEAU, K. W. *Zero-Base Budgeting: An Operating Manual for Corporations and Governments*, 1978.

ZERO-COUPON BONDS Corporate bonds that do not pay interest periodically (semiannually) in the fashion of conventional types of bonds, but instead sell at discounts of par until their final maturity, when payment of principal at par plus all of the interest accumulated (compounded) at the rate specified at the time of original issuance of the bonds is paid in a lump sum.

This innovation in bond financing first appeared in 1981, at a time of high prevailing interest rates, and has proved to be popular under such conditions with both corporate issuers and investors. For issuing corporations, the advantages are that no cash is actually paid out until final maturity, but in the meantime the tax deductible amortization of the discount provides savings each year on income taxes. (As of 1982, the question was still unresolved as to whether the discount in full could be amortized on a straight-line basis per year or, as the Treasury maintained, the tax deduction should be based on the effective annual cost to the corporation times the discount dollar amount of principal as originally paid at issuance by the investor and accreting each year to maturity—a method which would result in lower annual amortization for the corporation than the straight-line method.)

For investors, the attraction of zero-coupon bonds is the locking in of the prevailing high interest rate at issuance of the bonds, to accumulate compounded and to be paid at final maturity along with the full principal at par. Thus a combination of high interest income (based on the specified interest rate at issuance) and the capital gain from discount price at issuance to full par at maturity would be indicated. Such has been the attraction of zero-coupon bonds that issuing corporations have been able to achieve a savings in the interest rate on such issues, fractional though it may be, as compared with prevailing market yields on conventional bonds of the same quality. For investors, zero-coupon bonds are especially suitable for tax-deferred plans, such as individual retirement accounts (IRAs), Keogh accounts, and other retirement plans. Non-IRA, etc., investors, however, would be paying taxes on the portion of the interest that accrues each year on such issues, although no cash would be received until final maturity. Also, it is pointed out that failure of the issuing corporation before the lump-sum payoff on zero-coupon bonds would imperil the success of such issues for investors.

The zero-interest idea has spread to a number of other types of issues including zero-interest insured certificates of deposit of banks; zero-coupon Eurobonds (especially active in the London market as of 1982); and non-interest-bearing receipts sold at discount evidencing claim for principal amount plus accumulated interest spaced at interim maturities for such receipts, besides the actual eventual maturity of the U.S. Treasury bonds or state or municipal obligations, notes, or unit trusts.

Noncallable Treasury issues backed by the full faith and credit of the U.S. government include:

CATS	Certificates of Accrual on Treasury Securities
TIGRs	Treasury Investment Growth Receipts
TRs	Generic Treasury Receipts
STRIPS	Separate Trading of Registered Interest and Principal of Securities

BIBLIOGRAPHY

Donoghue, W. E. "High-Risk Investments." *Executive Female*, November/December, 1988.
Foldessy, E. P., and Bettner, J. "Deduction in Danger: Tax Break Involving 'Zero-Coupon' Bonds Is Attacked by Treasury, Backed by Issuers." *Wall Street Journal*, May 19, 1982.
Narayanan, M. P., Lim, S. P. "On the Call Provision In Corporate Zero Bonds." *Journal of Financial and Quantitative Analysis*, March, 1989.
Updegrave, W. L. "Capital Gains: The Twisting Path to Appreciation." *Money*, December, 1988.
Weberman, B. "Tax-free Zeros." *Forbes*, May 29, 1989.

ZERO-COUPON CONVERTIBLE Zero-coupon bond with option to convert to common stock.

ZERO-ECONOMIC PROFIT *See* PERFECT COMPETITION.

ZERO-INTEREST DEBENTURE BONDS Deep discount bonds. Bonds sold at a discount that gives the buyer a total interest payoff at maturity. J.S. Penny sold the first publicly marketed long-term debt securities in the U.S. that do not bear interest.

ZERO-PLUS TICK *See* SHORT SALE.

ZERO-SUM A game or competition so structured that the winning player or side takes all, leaving zero for the other player or side.

BIBLIOGRAPHY

Davis, M.D. *Game Theory: A Nontechnical Introduction*, 1970.
Von Neumann, J., and Morgenstern, O. *Theory of Games and Economic Behavior*, 1947.

ZINC A bluish-white, metallic chemical element used as a protective coating for iron, as a constituent in various alloys, as an electrode in electric batteries, and in medicines as a form of salt (Webster).

The U.S. is the world's largest consumer of zinc, but is a declining producer of the metal. Zinc futures trading resumed on the COMMODITY EXCHANGE, INC. in February, 1978, but volume of trading was light. In international metals markets, London prices (London Metal Exchange, both spot and futures) are the more active.

BIBLIOGRAPHY

Reiley, R.C. "Zinc." In *1982 U.S. Industrial Outlook for 200 Industries with Projections for 1986*, U.S. Department of Commerce, 1982.

ZOLLVERIN In German, literally a CUSTOMS UNION, providing for free trade among the members of the union themselves, but for common external tariffs on trade with nonmembers. The 1834 Zollverin, originally promoted by Prussia as early as 1818, included by subsequent admissions most of the German states except Austria. Administration of the 1867 Zollverin, a tighter customs union, was subsequently taken over by the new German empire of 1871.

See COMMON MARKET, FREE TRADE AREA.

BIBLIOGRAPHY

Henderson, W.O. *The Zollverein*, 1939.
Price, A.H. *Evolution of the Zollverin*, 1949.

ZOMBIE THRIFTS Insolvent S&Ls placed under FDIC control, which continue to operate and compete with other thrifts.

ZONE-DELIVERED PRICING A pricing system whereby single- or multiple-base prices on shipments are quoted uniformly to all customers located in designated geographic zones or areas; also known as the freight-allowed system. Under this system, freight allowances may be prepaid by the shipper, allowed to customer's destination, allowed within the zone, or allowed to distribution points.

In *Fort Howard Paper Co. v. Federal Trade Commission*, 156 F.(2d) 899, the U.S. Court of Appeals held that the crepe paper industry's use of zone-delivered pricing system could not "withstand the inference of agreement" to fix prices.

See ANTITRUST LAWS.

ZONING LAWS Municipal ordinances that authorize the establishment of zoning boards and their administration of restric-tions and limitations upon uses and architectural details of buildings in particular districts (business, residential, industrial, etc.), designated in particular parts of the municipality's area, for orderly development and preservation of property values.

BIBLIOGRAPHY

Crawford, C. *Handbook of Zoning and Land Use Ordinances—With Forms.*
Ficek, E.F., Henderson, T.P., and Johnson, R.H. *Real Estate Principles and Practices*, 2nd ed., 1980.

About the Publisher

PROBUS PUBLISHING COMPANY

Probus Publishing Company fills the informational needs of today's business professional by publishing authoritative, quality books on timely and relevant topics, including:

- Investing
- Futures/Options Trading
- Banking
- Finance
- Marketing and Sales
- Manufacturing and Project Management
- Personal Finance, Real Estate, Insurance and Estate Planning
- Entrepreneurship
- Management

Probus books are available at quantity discounts when purchased for business, educational or sales promotional use. For more information, please call the Director, Corporate/Institutional Sales at 1-800-PROBUS-1, or write:

Director, Corporate/Institutional Sales
Probus Publishing Company
1925 N. Clybourn Avenue
Chicago, Illinois 60614
FAX (312) 868-6250

AAC-9160

REFERENCE
Mackay Library-Cranford
Union County College